Maine
New Hampshire
Vermont
Augusta
Montpelier
Concord
Boston
Minnesota
Lake Superior
Lake Huron
Lake Ontario
Michigan
Lake Michigan
St. Paul
Minneapolis
Wisconsin
Milwaukee
Madison
Iowa
Des Moines
Chicago
Illinois
Missouri River
Springfield
Missouri
Kansas City
St. Louis
Jefferson City
Dover
Delaware
Maryland
Baltimore
Annapolis
Richmond
Kentucky
North Carolina
Raleigh
APPALACHIAN Mts.
Nashville
Tennessee
Memphis
Mississippi River
Little Rock
Arkansas
Alabama
Columbia
South Carolina
ATLANTIC OCEAN
Atlanta
Georgia
Jackson
Montgomery
Dallas
Louisiana
Mississippi
Tallahassee
Baton Rouge
New Orleans
Houston
Florida
Miami
Gulf of Mexico
HAWAII
Kauai
Oahu
Honolulu
Molokai
Maui
Hilo
Hawaii
Kilauea
1000 km

MINJUNG'S *Essence* ENGLISH-ENGLISH KOREAN DICTIONARY

엣센스英英韓사전

民衆書林 編輯局 編

MINJUNGSEORIM

머 리 말

일찍이 엣센스 英韓·韓英辭典을 내어 많은 독자들로부터 지대한 격려와 찬사를 받아 온 저희는, 10여 년 전에 영어를 우리말로 옮기어 생각하는 인습에서 벗어나 영어를 영어로 이해하는 습관을 들여야겠다는 판단 아래 英英辭典을 기획하여 착수한 바 있었다. 그러나 그 일은 예상보다 어려움이 많아 몇 번이나 손을 놓고 재검토하는 동안 독자들로부터의 요청이 빗발쳐 왔다.

더구나 세계화를 논하는 현시점에 이르고 보니, 英英辭典의 출간이 더욱더 긴박하여, 이제는 더 이상 미룰 수 없음을 깨닫고 여러 가지 어려움을 극복하면서 총력을 기울여 이제야 겨우 햇빛을 보게 되었으며, 이 사전의 출간을 고대하던 독자들에게 만시지탄이 있음을 사과드리고자 한다.

저희가 이 사전을 기획하면서 우선 영어를 영어로 이해하기 위하여는 그 풀이가 어려워서는 안 되겠다는 생각에서 낱말을 가능한 한 쉬운 영어로 풀이하도록 노력하였다. 그러나 여기서 그친다면, 독자들에게 오히려 당혹감을 주게 될 우려도 있을 것 같아, 여기에 우리말 주석을 첨가하여 영어 주석에서 얻은 개념을 분명하게 정리하도록 함으로써, 결과적으로 '英英韓辭典'으로 귀착하기에 이르렀다.

따라서, 본사전은 본토 사전을 상고하게 될 준비 단계로 알고 이용하는 것이 좋겠다.

또한 뜻풀이만으로는 납득하기 어려운 낱말들을 위하여 삽화 약 200점을 삽입하였으므로 이해에 큰 도움이 되리라고 확신하는 바이다.

이제 간단히 본 사전의 특색을 적어 보면 다음과 같다.

1. 간명한 어의 풀이

일반적으로, 어의 풀이는 핵심이 되는 말에 수식어로 그 뜻을 한정해 나감으로써 이루어진다. 이 사전에서는 가급적 요점만을 간추려 어의 풀이를 간단하고 알기 쉽게 하는 데 심혈을 기울였다.

이를테면, 다음 세 말의 핵심은 house이며 공통되는 수식어는 small인데, 여기에 다시 수식어가 더해짐으로써 세 말의 개념 차이가 뚜렷해짐을 알 수 있다.

cottage —a small house, esp. in the country.
hut —a small, roughly-built house; a small cabin.
cabin —a small, roughly-built house, usu. of wood.

cottage는 「(시골의) 작은 집」, hut는 「(작고 허술한) 오두막」, cabin은 「(작고 허술한) 통나무집」의 뜻이다.

2. 정확한 우리말 역어

사전의 어의 풀이만으로는 모르는 말의 정확한 뜻을 파악하는 데는 한계가 있다. 외국어인 경우에는 더욱 그렇다. 따라서, 이 사전에서는 영어의 어의 뒤에 우리말 역어를 빠짐없이 실었다. 가능하면 우리말의 대응어를 보이되, 그렇지 못할 경우에는 정확한 어의를 아는 데 도움이 되도록 최선을 다하였다.

3. 말의 활용을 위한 풍부한 자료

외국어를 배울 때 가장 문제가 되는 것은 말의 뜻 이외에 그 말의 활용 방법이다. 이 사전에서는 이 점을 감안하여 풍부한 용례는 물론, 셀 수 있는 명사와 셀 수 없는 명사의 표시, 동사의 문형, 어법 및 참고 사항 등 다양한 자료를 실었다.

저희로서는 처음 시도인 바 아무래도 소루한 점이 많으리라고 염려되나, 이는 앞으로 더욱 연찬하여 보완코자 한다.

독자들의 많은 편달을 믿어 마지 않는다.

1995년 1월

민중서림 편 집 국

일 러 두 기

Ⅰ. 구 성

이 사전에서는 영어의 일반 단어, 파생어, 복합어, 접두사, 접미사, 약어, 일상 어구, 외래 어구 및 약간의 고유명사를 표제어로 엄선하여 수록하였으며, 총어휘수는 36,527어이다.

Ⅱ. 표 제 어

1. 중요어의 표시

중요어에는 다음 세 단계로 구분하여 별표로써 표제어 왼쪽에 표시하였다.

⁑ 가장 기초적인 어휘(973어)

⁎ 고등 학교 정도의 기본 어휘(1,914어)

* 대학 입시 및 대학 교양 정도의 어휘(2,722어)

2. 철 자

(1) 미식과 영식의 철자가 다를 경우에는 미식 다음에 영식을 병기하였다.

보기 : **fa·vor,** 《Brit.》 **-vour** [féivər]

(2) 같은 말의 철자가 두 가지인 것 중 발음이 같은 것은 병기하였다. 또, 발음이 달라도 배열 순서상 근접한 것은 병기하였다.

보기 : **ax, axe** [æks]

graph·ic [grǽfik], **-i·cal** [-ikəl]

(3) 철자는 같으나 그 어원이 다른 경우는 오른쪽 어깨에 작은 번호를 붙였다.

보기 : **nap**[1] [næp] *n.* Ⓒ a short, light sleep …

nap[2] [næp] *n.* Ⓤ the short hairs on the surface of cloth …

3. 분 철

(1) 분철은 중점「·」으로써 보였다. 또, 발음에 따라 분철 방법이 달라지는 경우에는 최초의 발음에 따라 분철을 보였다.

보기 : **coun·te·nance**

(2) 표제어가 어구인 경우, 독립 표제어로 수록된 단어의 분철은 생략하였다.

보기 : **carbon mon·ox·ide**

4. 배 열

(1) 모든 표제어의 배열은 ABC순으로 하되, 철자가 같은 경우에는 대문자－소문자－점 없는 것－점 있는 것－접두사－접미사의 순으로 배열하였다.

(2) 파생어 중 그 사용 빈도가 비교적 낮고 그 어의를 원말의 어의에서 쉽게 유추할 수 있는 것은 독립 표제어로 내세우지 않고 원말의 기술에 이어 ●표 뒤에 약식으로 수록하였다.

보기 : **curt** [kəːrt] *adj.* … ● **curt·ly** [-li] *adv.* **curt·ness** [-nis] *n.*

(3) 표제어가 두 단어 이상의 어구인 경우, 그 일부를 생략할 수 있는 것은 (　)로 싸고, 그 일부와 대체할 수 있는 것은 〔　〕로 쌌다.

보기 : **Davy Jones'(s) locker**

pepper castor 〔caster〕

Ⅲ. 발 음

1. 발음 기호
 (1) 발음은 국제 음성 기호(p. 9의 발음 기호표 참고)로써 표제어 바로 뒤 [ ] 안에 표기하였다.
 (2) 미식 발음과 영식 발음이 다를 때는 [미식 발음 / 영식 발음]의 순으로 하였다.
 보기 : **hot** [hɑt / hɔt]
 (3) 생략할 수 있는 발음은 이탤릭체로써 나타내었다. 다만, 생략할 수 있는 장음 기호는 ( )로 쌌다.
 보기 : **ex·empt** [igzém*p*t]
 (4) 두 가지 이상의 발음이 있을 경우에는 공통된 부분은 「-」로 표시하였다.
 보기 : **ag·glom·er·ate** [əglɑ́mərèit / -lɔ́m-]
 (5) 발음이 품사나 어의에 따라 바뀌게 될 때에는 그 품사나 어의 앞에 보였다.
 보기 : **con·cert** [kɑ́nsə(:)*r*t / kɔ́n-] ***n.*** … — [kənsə́:*r*t] ***vt.*** …
2. 악센트
 (1) 악센트는 발음 기호 바로 위에 제 1 악센트는 「ˊ」로 제 2 악센트는 「ˋ」로 표시하였다.
 보기 : **o·ri·en·ta·tion** [ɔ̀:rientéiʃən]
 (2) 발음의 악센트 위치만 나타낼 경우에는, 음절수만큼의 「—」를 나열하고 악센트 있는 음절을 「ˊ」「ˋ」로 표시하였다.
 보기 : **ad·verse** [ædvə́:*r*s, ˊ—]
 aircraft carrier [ˊ— ˋ——]

Ⅳ. 품 사

1. 품사는 발음 뒤에 약자(p. 11의 약어표 참고)로써 보였다.
2. 같은 표제어에 둘 이상의 품사가 있을 경우에는 원칙적으로 이를 분리해서 다루었으며, 품사가 바뀌는 곳에 「—」표를 썼다.
 보기 : **snore** [snɔ:*r*] *vi.* breathe noisily … — ***n.*** Ⓒ the noisy sound …
3. 관계 대명사·의문 대명사 따위와 같이 문법상 설명이 필요한 것은 어의 번호 다음에 이탤릭체로 《 》 안에 보였다.
 보기 : **where** [*h*εə*r*] *adv.* **1** 《*interrogative adverb*》 at or in what place … — *pron.* **1** 《*interrogative pronoun*》 what place … **2** 《*relative pronoun*》 the place at, in or to which …

Ⅴ. 어형 변화

다음과 같은 말의 어형 변화꼴은 품사 뒤 ( ) 안에 고딕체로 보였다.

1. 명사의 복수꼴
 (1) 불규칙 복수꼴
 (2) 어미가 「자음+y」인 말의 복수꼴
 (3) 어미가 f, o인 말의 복수꼴
 (4) 변화꼴이 두 가지인 말의 복수꼴

보기 : **work·man** [wə́:rkmən] *n.* Ⓒ (*pl.* **-men** [-mən]) …
la·dy [léidi] *n.* Ⓒ (*pl.* **-dies**) …
leaf [li:f] *n.* (*pl.* **leaves**) …
ra·di·o [réidiou] *n.* (*pl.* **-di·os**) …
pen·ny [péni] *n.* Ⓒ (**-nies** or *collectively* **pence**) …

2. 동사의 과거, 과거 분사(및 현재 분사)
(1) 불규칙 변화꼴
(2) 어미의 자음자가 겹치는 변화꼴
(3) 어미가 「자음+y」인 말의 변화꼴
(4) 미식과 영식이 다른 변화꼴
(5) 변화꼴이 두 가지인 말의 변화꼴
(6) 기타 주의해야 할 변화꼴

보기 : **draw** [drɔ:] *v.* (**drew, drawn**) …
stop [stɑp / stɔp] *v.* (**stopped, stop·ping**) …
de·fy [difái] *vt.* (**-fied, -fy·ing**) …
trav·el [trǽvəl] *v.* (**-eled, -el·ing** or 《Brit.》 **-elled, -el·ling**) …
thrive [θraiv] *vi.* (**throve** or **thrived, thrived** or **thriv·en**)…
lie[1] [lai] *vi.* (**lay, lain, ly·ing**) …
pic·nic [píknik] … — *vi.* (**-nicked, -nick·ing**) …
tie [tai] *v.* (ppr. **ty·ing**) …

3. 형용사·부사의 비교급, 최상급
(1) 불규칙 변화꼴
(2) 2음절 이상의 말로서 -er, -est의 꼴을 취하는 변화꼴
(3) 변화꼴 앞에 사용 빈도에 따라 usu., often, sometimes 등의 단서를 보였다.

보기 : **hap·py** [hǽpi] *adj.* (**-pi·er, -pi·est**) …
well [wel] *adv.* (**bet·ter, best**) …
late [leit] *adj.* (**lat·er, lat·est** or **lat·ter, last**) …
com·plete [kəmplí:t] *adj.* (often **-plet·er, -plet·est**) …

Ⅵ. 어의·역어·용례

1. 어 의
(1) 어의를 병기할 때에는 세미콜론(;)을 썼다. 또, 어의가 복잡하여 구분할 필요가 있을 때에는 품사별로 **1, 2, 3**…을, 이를 다시 세분할 때에는 ⓐ, ⓑ, ⓒ …를 썼다.

보기 : **hand·y** [hǽndi] *adj.* (**hand·i·er, hand·i·est**) **1** (of a thing) ⓐ within reach of … ⓑ easy to handle … **2** (of a person) useful; skilled with the hands …

(2) 특수 용법은 다음과 같이 어의 앞 《 》 안에 보였다.

보기 : 《*the*～》 —표제어에 the를 붙여 쓰는 경우
《*pl.*》 —표제어가 복수꼴로 쓰이는 경우
《usu. *I-*》 —보통 표제어의 첫글자를 대문자로 쓰는 경우
《in *passive*》 —표제어가 수동태로 쓰이는 경우
《used as *sing.*》 —표제어가 단수꼴로 쓰이는 경우
《as *predicative*》 —표제어가 서술적으로 쓰이는 경우

(3) 표제어와 밀접한 관계를 가진 중요한 전치사·부사 따위는 어의 앞《 》안에 이탤릭체로 보였다.

보기 : **con·ven·ient** [kənvíːnjənt] *adj.* **1** 《*to, for, doing*》 causing no trouble; handy; easy to reach or use; suitable …

(4) 타동사의 어의에는 ( ) 안에 someone, something 따위의 목적어를 보였다. 특정한 목적어를 취할 경우에는 구체적인 명사를 보였다.

보기 : **ad·vise** [ædváiz, əd-] *vt.* … **2** 《*of*》 give notice to (someone); make (someone) know; teach …

de·flate [difléit] *vt.* (P6) **1** let the air or gas out of (a balloon, tire, etc.) …

(5) 전문어와 언어 용법은 어의 앞《 》안에 보였다. 자주 쓰이는 것은 약어를 썼고(p. 11 약어표 참고), 특히 언어 용법은 이탤릭체로 보였다.

보기 : **a·baft** [əbǽft, əbɑ́ːft] *adv.* 《naut.》 toward the rear end of a ship …

flu [fluː] *n.* 《*colloq.*》 =influenza.

2. 우리말 역어

(1) 모든 영어 어의 뒤에 우리말 역어를 실었다.

(2) 이해에 도움이 되는 보조적인 말은 역어 앞 ( ) 안에 보였고, 해설 따위가 필요할 때에는 역어 뒤《 》안에 보였다.

보기 : **charge** [tʃɑːrdʒ] *vt.* (P13,14) 《*for*》 ask in payment; ask as a price; impose. (대금)을 청구하다; (세금)을 과하다…

Del·hi [déli] *n.* New Delhi. 뉴델리《인도 북부의 도시》.

(3) 동의어·반의어(상대어)·참고어를 각각 (= …), (opp. …), (cf. …)로써 역어 뒤에 보였다. 어의 중에 그 말이 포함되었을 때에는 생략하였으며, 어의가 **1**, **2**, **3**…으로 구분되어 있고 모든 어의에 해당하는 반의어는 번호 앞에 보였다. 참고어는 이탤릭체를 썼다.

보기 : **de·fend·ant** [diféndənt] *n.* Ⓒ 《law》 a person accused in a law court. 피고(opp. plaintiff, cf. *accused*) …

(4) 어법상의 문제점은 [語法] 으로, 참고 사항이나 주의 사항은 [參考] 로 다루었다.

보기 : **al·ways** [ɔ́ːlweiz, -wiz, -wəz] *adv.* **1** at all times; on all occasions. 언제나; 항상; 늘. [語法] 조동사와 be 동사 외에는 동사의 앞에 옴…

chan·cel·lor [tʃǽnsələr, tʃɑ́ːn-] *n.* … **3** 《Brit.》 the head of a university. 대학 총장(cf. 《U.S.》 *president*). [參考] Chancellor 는 명예직이며 실무는 Vice-Chancellor 가 맡음…

3. 용 례

(1) 용례는 각 품사와 어의에 따라 「¶」 뒤에 이탤릭체로 실었다.

(2) 용례와 용례 사이는 「/」로써 구분하였다.

(3) 표제어가 변화하지 않고 그대로 쓰인 경우에는 「～」로써 나타내고, 변화한 경우에는 변화꼴을 다 썼다.

(4) 뜻이 같은 용례는 「=」로써 병기하였다.

(5) 원칙적으로 모든 용례는 우리말 역어를 실었으나 자명한 것은 생략하였다.

보기 : **news** [njuːz] *n.* … **2** some new or fresh information about something. 색다른 일〔정보〕. ¶ *Is there any ～ ? =What's the ～ ?* 뭐 색다른 것 없나 / *That's quite ～ to me.* 그거 금시 초문이다 …

Ⅶ. 관 용 구

1. 관용구는 이탤릭고딕체를 써서 품사별로 일괄하여 ABC순으로 실었다.
2. 어의가 복잡한 것은 **a**), **b**), **c**)…로 구분하였다.
   보기 : ***break the ice,*** **a**) begin; start something difficult or dangerous … **b**) start being friendly …
3. 전치사를 포함한 동사구 따위에서는 목적어의 관계를 보이기 위해 다음과 같이 하였다.
   보기 : ***make against*** (=*be contrary, unfavorable, harmful to*) *something* …
4. 뜻이 같고 배열 순서상 근접한 것은 「=」를 써 병기하였다.
   보기 : ***in hopes of*** =***in the hope that*** 〔***of***〕**,** in expectation or anticipation of …
5. 용례는 어의와 우리말 역어 뒤에 표제어의 용례와 같은 형식으로 실었다.

Ⅷ. 셀 수 있는 명사와 셀 수 없는 명사

1. 셀 수 있는 명사(countable noun)에는 Ⓒ를, 셀 수 없는 명사(uncountable noun)에는 Ⓤ를 써서 명시하였다.
2. 어의에 따라 Ⓒ, Ⓤ가 다를 경우에는 각 어의 바로 앞이나 어의 번호 뒤에 보였다.
3. 한 표제어의 어의 전부 또는 대부분이 Ⓒ나 Ⓤ일 때에는 품사 뒤에 보이고, 예외적인 것은 그 해당 어의 바로 앞이나 어의 번호 뒤에 보였다.
4. Ⓒ와 Ⓤ 두 가지로 쓰일 경우에는 ⒸⓊ 또는 ⓊⒸ처럼 병기하였다. 일반적으로 앞에 있는 것이 많이 쓰이나, 경우에 따라서는 동등한 것도 있다.
   보기 : **in·sti·tu·tion** [ìnstətjúːʃən] *n.* Ⓒ **1** a society or organization for some, esp. public, purpose … **4** Ⓤ the act of establishing or beginning …

Ⅸ. 문 형

1. 문형이라고 하면 동사의 기본 5문형을 생각하게 되지만, 이 사전에서는 어의와 용법을 좀더 정확히 이해할 수 있도록 이를 30개 문형으로 세분하여 보였다(p. 10의 동사 문형표 및 p. 2032의 VERB PATTERNS 참고).
2. 동사의 문형은 어의 앞 또는 어의 번호 뒤 ( ) 안에 문형 번호(동사 문형표 왼쪽난의 P1, P2A, P2B, P3 따위)를 써서 보였다. 문형 번호를 병기할 때 「;」으로 구분한 것은 자동사와 타동사의 문형 구분이다.
3. 어의 전부 또는 대부분이 공통적으로 같은 문형을 취할 경우에는 품사 뒤 또는 어의 번호 앞에 보였다.
   보기 : **in·fil·trate** [infíltreit, ⌐–⌐] *vt., vi.* (P6,13; 1,3) **1** pass or cause (water, etc.) to pass through or into the earth, etc. … **2** (of ideas) get into people's minds …

Ⅹ. 어 원

1. 어원은 원칙적으로 표제어에 관한 기술이 끝난 뒤 [ ] 안에 보였다.

2. 어원이 동사인 경우, 라틴어와 그리스어는 1인칭 단수 현재형으로 보였고, 기타 국어는 보통의 부정사형을 썼다.
3. 영어 이외의 국어는 이탤릭체로 보인 다음 그 뜻을 영어로 보였다. 말의 일부밖에 보이지 않은 경우에는, 그 전반 또는 후반을 합쳐서 검토하고 접두어와 접미어도 염두에 두어야 한다.
4. 표제어의 어원을 직접 보이지 않고 다른 표제어의 어원을 참고토록 할 때에는 다음과 같이 나타냈다.

   보기 : [→merchant] —merchant의 어원을 보라.
   [↑] —바로 위에 있는 표제어의 어원을 보라.
   [↓] —바로 아래 있는 표제어의 어원을 보라.
5. [ ] 안에 이탤릭체로 되어 있는 것은, 그 말의 어원보다는 그 기입된 사항을 참작하라는 뜻이다.
6. [ ] 안의 >는 어의의 변천을, ?는 어원이 분명하지 않음을 나타낸다.
7. 어원이 되는 국어는 대부분 약자를 써서 나타내었다(p. 11의 약어표 참고).

XI. 기호의 특별 용법

1. ( )는 그 안의 말을 생략할 수 있음을 보이거나, 보충적인 설명, 주어·목적어 관계 따위를 보인다.

   보기 : **high-up** 항에서
   (a person) of great importance는 a person of great importance 또는 of great importance.
   ig·nite 항에서
   make (something) very hot의 something은 ignite의 목적어 관계를 나타냄.
2. 〔 〕는 그 안의 말을 앞에 있는 말과 대체할 수 있음을 보인다.

   보기 : **lac·tic** 항에서
   ~ *acid* 〔*bacteria*〕 젖산〔젖산균〕은 ~ *acid* 젖산 / ~ *bacteria* 젖산균.
3. 《 》는 전문어, 언어 용법, 우리말 역어의 부연 해설 따위를 보인다.

   보기 : **mar·gue·rite** [mɑ̀ːrgəríːt] *n.* Ⓒ 《bot.》 a kind of daisy with white flowers. 마거리트《데이지의 일종》.
   woe [wou] *n.* Ⓤ 《*poet.*》 deep grief ...
4. 《 》는 표제어의 특수 용법, 문법적 관계, 관련 전치사나 부사 따위를 보인다.

   보기 : **world** [wəːrld] *n.* Ⓒ **1** 《usu. *the* ~, used as *sing.*》 the earth; the universe ...
5. ⇨는 그 곳에 해당 사항이 있음을 보인다.

   보기 : **fly**[1] 항에서
   fly off the handle ⇨handle. 의 ⇨는 표제어 handle을 보라는 뜻.
6. ~는 표제어를 되풀이하기 위하여 썼다.

   보기 : **waiting game** 항에서
   ¶ *The government is playing a ~ with the unions that are on strike.* 의 ~는 waiting game.

발음 기호표

모 음(vowels)

단모음(simple vowels)

[i]	**it**	[it]	[ɔː]	**all**	[ɔːl]
[iː]	**eat**	[iːt]	[u]	**put**	[put]
[e]	**get**	[get]	[uː]	**food**	[fuːd]
[æ]	**cat**	[kæt]	[ʌ]	**up**	[ʌp]
[ɑ]	**box**	[bɑks / bɔks]	[ə]	**ahead**	[əhéd]
[ɑː]	**calm**	[kɑːm]	[əː]	**bird**	[bəːrd]
[ɔ]	**dog**	[dɔg]			

이중모음(diphthongs)

[ei]	**gay**	[gei]	[ɔi]	**boy**	[bɔi]
[ou]	**go**	[gou]	[iə]	**ear**	[iər]
[ai]	**sky**	[skai]	[ɛə]	**there**	[ðɛər]
[au]	**cow**	[kau]	[uə]	**tour**	[tuər]

자 음(consonants)

파열음(plosives)

[p]	**pen**	[pen]
[b]	**book**	[buk]
[t]	**tea**	[tiː]
[d]	**dog**	[dɔg]
[k]	**keep**	[kiːp]
[g]	**good**	[gud]

마찰음(fricatives)

[f]	**foot**	[fut]
[v]	**voice**	[vɔis]
[θ]	**thing**	[θiŋ]
[ð]	**then**	[ðen]
[s]	**sun**	[sʌn]
[z]	**zone**	[zoun]
[ʃ]	**ship**	[ʃip]
[ʒ]	**vision**	[víʒən]
[r]	**ring**	[riŋ]
[h]	**high**	[hai]

비 음(nasals)

[m]	**man**	[mæn]
[n]	**nine**	[nain]
[ŋ]	**king**	[kiŋ]

설측음(lateral)

[l]	**little**	[lítl]

파찰음(affricatives)

[tʃ]	**chin**	[tʃin]
[dʒ]	**bridge**	[bridʒ]

반모음(semivowels)

[j]	**yes**	[jes]
[w]	**wing**	[wiŋ]

외국어음(foreign sounds)

[ɑ̃]	**en**	[ɑ̃]
[ɔ̃]	**bon**	[bɔ̃]
[y]	**hütte**	[hýtə]
[x]	**loch**	[lɑx / lɔx]

동사 문형표(verb patterns)

Ⅰ. **S+V** (주어+동사)의 문형		
P 1	V	*Day dawns.*
P 2A	V+*adv.*	*He came in.*
P 2B	V+(for) *adv.*	*We traveled (for) six days.*
P 3	V+*prep.*+O	*The house belongs to him.*
P 4	V+Inf.	*He stopped to smoke.*
Ⅱ. **S+V+C** (주어+동사+보어)의 문형		
P 5	V+C	*This is my car. / She looks happy.*
Ⅲ. **S+V+O** (주어+동사+목적어)의 문형		
P 6	V+O	*I like sports.*
P 7	V+O+*adv.*	*He put his coat on.*
P 8	V+Inf.	*I want to see you.*
P 9	V+Gerund	*She avoided meeting him.*
P 10	V+what+Inf.	*We could not decide what to do.*
P 11	V+that Clause	*I suggested that he (should) buy a new car.*
P 12	V+what Clause	*I know what it is.*
P 13	V+O+*prep.*+O	*I congratulated him on his success.*
Ⅳ. **S+V+O+O** (주어+동사+목적어+목적어)의 문형		
P 14	V+I.O.+D.O.	*I gave him a watch.*
P 15	V+O+that Clause	*They warned us that the roads were icy.*
P 16	V+O(+what)+Inf.	*I told him what to do.*
P 17	V+O+what Clause	*I asked him what it was.*
Ⅴ. **S+V+O+C** (주어+동사+목적어+보어)의 문형		
P 18	V+O+*adj.*	*He made her happy.*
P 19	V+O+*n.*	*We call him Teddy.*
P 20	V+O+Inf.	*I told him to wait.*
P 21	V+O+(to be) C	*We think him (to be) a good teacher.*
P 22	V+O+Bare Inf.	*I saw him cross the street.*
P 23	V+O+*ppr.*	*I can smell something burning.*
P 24	V+O+*pp.*	*I heard my name called.*
Auxiliary Verbs+Verbs (조동사+동사)		
P 25	V. Aux.+Bare Inf.	*I will do it.*
P 26	V. Aux.+Inf.	*You ought to apologize.*
P 27	V. Aux.+*ppr.*	*He is reading a book.*
P28A	V. Aux.+*pp.*	*He has done it.*
P28B	V. Aux.+*pp.*	*It was done by me.*

약 어 표

Ⅰ. 품 사

adj.	adjective 형용사
adv.	adverb 부사
auxil. v.	auxiliary verb 조동사
conj.	conjunction 접속사
def. art.	definite article 정관사
indef. art.	indefinite article 부정관사
interj.	interjection 감탄사
n.	noun 명사
pref.	prefix 접두사
prep.	preposition 전치사
pron.	pronoun 대명사
rel. pron.	relative pronoun 관계대명사
suf.	suffix 접미사
v.	verb 동사
vi.	intransitive verb 자동사
vt.	transitive verb 타동사

Ⅱ. 언어 용법

abbr.	abbreviation 약어
《*arch.*》	archaic 고어
《*colloq.*》	colloquial 구어
compar.	comparative 비교급
《*contempt.*》	contemptuous 경멸적
《*dial.*》	dialect 방언
e.g.	for example 예컨대
《*emph.*》	emphatic 강조적
esp.	especially 특히
《*euphem.*》	euphemistic 완곡적
fem.	feminine 여성형
《*fig.*》	figurative 비유적
i.e.	that is 즉
Imit.	Imitative 의성어
inf.	infinitive 부정사
《*iron.*》	ironically 반어적
《*joc.*》	jocular 희어적
《*lit.*》	literal 문어
masc.	masculine 남성형
obj.	objective (case) 목적(격)
《*obs.*》	obsolete 폐어
opp.	opposite 반의어
orig.	originally 본디
p.	past 과거형
pl.	plural 복수형
《*poet.*》	poetical 시어
poss.	possessive (case) 소유(격)
pp.	past participle 과거분사
ppr.	present participle 현재분사
pres.	present 현재형
prob.	probably 대개
《*prov.*》	proverb 속담
rel.	relative 관계사
sing.	singular 단수형
《*sl.*》	slang 속어
superl.	superlative 최상급
usu.	usually 보통
《*vulg.*》	vulgar 비어

Ⅲ. 국 어

Amer-Ind.	American-Indian 아메리카 인디언어
Anglo-Ind.	Anglo-Indian 인도 영어
Arab.	Arabic 아라비아어
Aram.	Aramaic 아람어
A.S.	Anglo-Saxon 앵글로색슨어
Boh.	Bohemian 보헤미아어
Brit.	Britain, Briticism 영국(특유어)
Celt.	Celtic 켈트어
Chin.	Chinese 중국어
Corn.	Cornish 콘월어
Da.	Danish 덴마크어
Du.	Dutch 네덜란드어
E.	English 영어
F.	French 프랑스어
Flem.	Flemish 플랑드르어
G.	German 독일어
Gael.	Gaelic 게일어
Gk.	Greek 그리스어
Heb.	Hebrew 히브리어

Hind.	Hindi 힌디어	Prov.	Provençal 프로방스어
Icel.	Icelandic 아이슬란드어	Rom.	Romance 로망스어
Ir.	Irish 아일랜드어	Russ.	Russian 러시아어
It.	Italian 이탈리아어	Sc.	Scotch 스코틀랜드어
Jav.	Javanese 자바어	Scand.	Scandinavian 스칸디나비아어
L.	Latin 라틴어	Sem.	Semitic 셈어
M.E.	Middle English 중세 영어	Skr.	Sanskrit 산스크리트어
Mex.	Mexican 멕시코어	Slav.	Slavonic 슬라브어
N.	Old Norse 고대 스칸디나비아어	Sp.	Spanish 스페인어
Norw.	Norwegian 노르웨이어	Sw.	Swedish 스웨덴어
O.E.	Old English 고대 영어	Teut.	Teutonic 튜턴어
Pers.	Persian 페르시아어	Turk.	Turkish 터키어
Peruv.	Peruvian 페루어	U.S.	United States, Americanism 미국(특유어)
Pol.	Polish 폴란드어		
Portu.	Portuguese 포르투갈어		

Ⅳ. 전 문 어

《aeron.》	aeronautics 항공	《meteor.》	meteorology 기상학
《alg.》	algebra 대수학	《mil.》	military 군사
《anat.》	anatomy 해부학	《min.》	mineral 광물
《archit.》	architecture 건축	《mus.》	music 음악
《astron.》	astronomy 천문학	《myth.》	mythology 신화
《biol.》	biology 생물학	《naut.》	nautical 항해
《bot.》	botany 식물(학)	《nav.》	navy 해군
《chem.》	chemistry 화학	《opt.》	optics 광학
《comm.》	commerce 상업	《paint.》	painting 회화
《diplom.》	diplomacy 외교	《phar.》	pharmacy 약학
《dynam.》	dynamics 역학	《philos.》	philosophy 철학
《econ.》	economics 경제학	《phon.》	phonetics 음성학
《educ.》	education 교육	《photog.》	photography 사진
《electr.》	electricity 전기	《phys.》	physics 물리학
《engin.》	engineering 공학	《physiol.》	physiology 생리학
《eth.》	ethics 윤리학	《polit.》	politics 정치(학)
《fortif.》	fortification 축성(築城)	《print.》	printing 인쇄
《geog.》	geography 지리학	《psych.》	psychology 심리학
《geol.》	geology 지질학	《rhet.》	rhetoric 수사학
《geom.》	geometry 기하학	《Cath.》	Catholic 카톨릭
《gram.》	grammar 문법	《sculp.》	sculpture 조각
《gym.》	gymnastics 체조, 체육	《sociol.》	sociology 사회학
《her.》	heraldry 문장(학)(紋章(學))	《surg.》	surgery 외과
《hist.》	history 역사(학)	《teleg.》	telegraphy 전신
《log.》	logic 논리학	《theatr.》	theatrical 연극
《math.》	mathematics 수학	《theol.》	theology 신학
《mech.》	mechanics 기계	《univ.》	university 대학
《med.》	medicine 의학	《zool.》	zoology 동물(학)

a A

A

A, a [ei] *n.* Ⓒ (*pl.* **A's, As, a's, as** [eiz]) **1** the first letter of the English alphabet. 영어 알파벳의 첫째 글자. **2** the first in a series or group. (연속하는 것 중의) 첫번째(의 것). **3** the highest grade at school. (학업 성적의) 최고점; 수(秀). ¶ *straight A's* 전과목 에이[수]. **4** 《math.》 the first of known numbers or quantity. 첫째 기지수(既知數). **5** the sixth note or tone of the musical scale of C major. 가음《고정 도 창법의 '라'》. ¶ *a sonata in A major* 가 장조 소나타. **6** anything shaped like the letter A. A자 모양의 것.

do not know A from B, know nothing. 아무것도 모르다; 일자 무식이다.

from A to Z, from the beginning to the end; thoroughly. 처음부터 끝까지; 완전히; 전부.

— *adj.* **1** first in a series, group, rank, etc. 첫(번)째의; 일류의. **2** having the shape of the letter A. A자 모양[형]의. ¶ *an A tent,* A자 모양의 텐트.

A 《chem.》 argon; 《phys.》 angstrom unit.

A. American; Associate; Association; Atom(ic).

:a [ei, ə], **an** [æn, ən] *indef. art.* 《*a* before consonants, *an* before vowels and silent *h*-》 **1** one. 하나의; 한. ¶ *a book / an apple / an hour.* **2** a certain. 어떤. ¶ *It is true in a sense.* 그건 어떤 의미에서는 사실이다. **3** any; every. …라는 것은; 어느 …도. ¶ *A dog is a faithful animal.* 개는 충실한 동물이다 / *An insect has* (=*Insects have*) *six legs.* 곤충은 발이 여섯 개 있다. **4** a person called; a person like. …라는 사람; …와 같은 사람. ¶ *a Mr. Brown* 브라운 씨라는 분 / *A Mr. Smith came to see you.* 스미스 씨란 분이 당신을 찾아왔습니다 / *He is a Hercules* (=*a strong man like Hercules*). 그는 헤르쿨레스와 같은 장사이다. **5** per; each. 한 …에; 매 …에; …당(當). ¶ *once a day / ten miles an hour / He came home twice a month.* 그는 한 달에 두 번 귀가했다. **6** one and the same. 같은; 동일한. ¶ *We are of an age.* 우린 동갑이다 / *They are all of a size.* 그것들은 모두 크기가 같다 / *Birds of a feather flock together.* 같은 깃털의 새는 서로 모인다; 유유상종(類類相從). [*one*]

a. about; acre(s); adjective; afternoon; alto; ampere; *anno* (L.= year); answer; *ante* (L.=before); are[2]; adult.

a(-)[1] [ə(-)] *pref.* **1** in; on; to. '…에, …(으)로'의 뜻. ¶ *afoot / ashore /* 《*arch.*》 *abed.* **2** 《rare》 in the act of. '…(하는) 중에'의 뜻. ¶ *The house is abuilding.* 그 집은 짓는 중이다 / *go a(-)hunting.* **3** intensive. 강세. ¶ *arise.* [*on*]

a-[2] [æ-, ei-, ə-] *pref.* not; without. '비(非)…, 무(無)…'의 뜻. ¶ *apathy.* [Gk.]

-a [-ə] *suf.* **1** of feminine singular noun. 여성 단수 명사 어미. **2** of plural noun. 복수 명사 어미.

AA Alcoholics Anonymous; antiaircraft.

AAA Agricultural Adjustment Administration.

A.A.A. American Automobile Association.

A.A.A.S. American Association for the Advancement of Science.

A and M agricultural and mechanical.

A and R artists and repertory.

A.A.R. 《comm.》 against all risks. 올 리스크스 담보.

aard·wolf [áːrdwùlf] *n.* a hyenalike mammal of Africa that feeds chiefly on termites and insect larvae. 하이에나에 가까운 아프리카산 포유 동물《흰 개미나 곤충알을 먹음》. [Afr.]

Aar·on [ɛ́ərən, ǽr-] *n.* 《Bible》 a Jewish patriarch, the first Jewish high priest (Exodus iv). 아론《출애굽기 Ⅳ : 유대교(教) 최초의 제사장》.

ab [æb] *prep.* 《L.》 from. …로부터.

ab- [æb-, əb-] *pref.* 《*a*- before *m,p,* or *v* and often *abs*- before *c* or *t*》 away, from. '(…에서) 떠난, …로부터'의 뜻. [L.]

A.B. =B.A.; able-bodied seaman.

a·ba [əbáː, áːbə, ǽbə] *n.* =abaya.

ab·a·ca [æ̀bəkáː, àːbə-] *n.* Ⓤ the Manila hemp. 마닐라삼. [?]

ab·a·ci [ǽbəsài] *n.* pl. of **abacus.**

a·back [əbǽk] *adv.* to the back; backward. 뒤로; 뒤쪽으로. [a(-), *back*]

be taken aback, be surprised. 깜짝 놀라다. ¶ *I was taken ~ by the news.* 그 소식에 깜짝 놀랐다. [a(-), *back*]

ab·a·cus [ǽbəkəs] *n.* Ⓒ (*pl.* **-cus·es** or **-ci**) a frame with rows of sliding beads which are put back and forth in doing calculation. 주판; 계수기(計數器). [Gk. *abax*]

A·bad·don [əbǽdən] *n.* hell; the devil. 지옥; 나락; (지옥의) 마왕. [Heb.]

a·baft [əbǽft, əbáːft] *adv.* 《naut.》 toward the rear end of a ship. 선미(船尾)[고물] 쪽에. — *prep.* behind (in the direction of the stern). 뒤에. ¶ *~ the mast* 마스트의 뒤에서 / *the wind from ~* 순풍(順風). [a(-), *by, aft*]

ab·a·lo·ne [æ̀bəlóuni] *n.* a kind of edible

shellfish. 전복. [Sp.]

:**a·ban·don** [əbǽndən] *vt.* (P6,13) **1** give up (something) entirely. …을 버리다; 단념〔포기〕하다. ¶ ~ *all hope* 모든 희망을 버리다 / ~ *the attempt* 계획을 포기하다. **2** leave (a place) forever; forsake. …을 버리고 떠나다; 유기하다. ¶ ~ *one's home* 집을 떠나다 / ~ *one's wife and children* 처자식을 버리다 / *The crew abandoned the wrecked ship.* 승무원들은 난파선을 버리고 떠났다 / *The game had to be abandoned because of crowd trouble.* 게임은 관중의 난동 때문에 포기할 수 밖에 없었다. **3** 《*oneself to*》 yield (oneself) completely. (몸)을 내맡기다; …에 빠지다. ¶ ~ *oneself to pleasure(s)* 환락에 빠지다 / *She abandoned herself to despair.* 그녀는 절망에 빠졌다.

— *n.* Ⓤ letting oneself go; careless freedom. 멋대로 굶; 방종; 분방. [O.F. *abandoner* relinquish]

with abandon, in a wild way; very freely. 꺼리낌 없이; (제)멋대로. ¶ *sing* 〔*dance, act, speak*〕 *with* ~ 멋대로 노래하다〔춤추다, 행동하다, 말하다〕.

a·ban·doned [əbǽndənd] *adj.* **1** given up (to bad ways); forsaken. 포기된; 버림받은. ¶ *an* ~ *child* 기아(棄兒). **2** desperate; wicked; very bad; immoral. 자포 자기의; 사악한; 못된. ¶ *an* ~ *woman* 타락한〔못된〕 여자.

a·ban·don·ee [əbæ̀ndəníː] *n.* an underwriter to whom the salvage is abandoned. 피위부자(被委付者); 피유기자(被遺棄者).

a·ban·don·ment [əbǽndənmənt] *n.* Ⓤ **1** the act of abandoning; the state of being abandoned. 포기; 유기. ¶ *the* ~ *of a right* 권리의 포기. **2** lack of self-control; careless freedom. (몸을) 내맡김; 자포 자기; 분방.

a·base [əbéis] *vt.* (P6) make (someone) lower in rank, position, character, etc; make base; humble. …의 지위〔품격〕 따위를 떨어뜨리다; 비천하게 하다. ¶ *He was abased for his crimes.* 그는 범죄로 인해 품위가 떨어졌다. [ad-, L. *bassus* low]

abase oneself, lose one's good character; make oneself humble. (자신의) 품위를 떨어뜨리다; 비하〔전락〕하다.

a·base·ment [əbéismənt] *n.* Ⓤ **1** the state of being abased. 저하(低下). **2** loss of dignity and respect; humility. 영락; 비하; 낮춤.

a·bash [əbǽʃ] *vt.* (P6) 《usu. in *passive*》 make (someone) feel confused and ashamed; put to shame; embarrass. …의 낯을 붉히게 하다; 부끄럽게 하다; 당황케 하다. ¶ *be* 〔*feel*〕 ~ed 부끄러워하다; 낯을 붉히다; 당황하다 / *The girl was abashed when she saw the young man.* 처녀는 청년을 보자 당황했다. ● **a·bash·ment** [-mənt] *n.* Ⓤ [O.F. *esbahir* astonish]

a·bashed [əbǽʃt] *adj.* 《*at*》 embarrassed. 당황한.

a·bask [əbǽsk, əbɑ́ːsk] *adv.* basking. (양지에서) 햇볕을 쬐며. [a(-), *bask*]

a·bate [əbéit] *vt.* (P6) **1** make (something) less in amount or intensity; lessen; decrease. …을 감하다〔덜다〕; 누그러뜨리다. ¶ *The medicine abated his pain.* 약이 그의 고통을 덜어 주었다 / *The pain is abated.* 아픔이 누그러졌다. **2** cut down the cost or price of (something). …의 값을 내리다; 할인하다; 깎다. ¶ ~ *a tax* 세금을 감하다 / ~ *the price* 값을 깍다. **3** 《law》 destroy the cause of; put an end to. …을 없애다; …을 끝내다. ¶ ~ *a nuisance* 불법 방해를 배제하다.
— *vi.* (P1) become less in amount or intensity. 덜해〔감해〕지다; 누그러지다. ¶ *The storm abated.* 폭풍우가 가라앉았다. [ad-, L. *batuo* beat]

a·bate·ment [əbéitmənt] *n.* Ⓤ **1** the act of abating; the state of being abated. 감소; 감가; 감퇴; 완화. ¶ ~ *of debts* 빚의 감소 / *make an* ~ *of the price* 값을 깎다. **2** destroying the cause of; putting an end to 원인을 없앰; 끝을 냄. ¶ ~ *of a nuisance* 불법 방해 배제.

ab·a·tis [ǽbətiː, -tis, əbǽtiː] *n.* 《hist.》 an obstacle of felled trees. 녹채(鹿砦). [↑]

ab·at·toir [ǽbətwɑ̀ːr] *n.* 《F.》 a slaughterhouse. 도살장. [↑]

a·ba·ya [əbéijə] *n.* a sleeveless outer garment worn by Arabs. (아랍 사람의) 소매 없는 긴 겉옷. [Arab.]

ab·ba [ǽbə] *n.* =abaya.

ab·ba·cy [ǽbəsi] *n.* =Abbotcy.

Ab·bas [ǽbəs] *n.* (566-652) an uncle of Mohammed and Ancestor of Abbasid dynasty. 아바스《모하메드의 삼촌이며 아바스조(朝)의 시조》.

Ab·bas·id [əbǽsid, ǽbəsid] *n.* a member of the dynasty of Islam. 이슬람조(朝)의 한 사람.

ab·bé [æbéi, ⌐–] *n.* (a title of respect for) a French priest. 프랑스인 신부(의 존칭)(cf. *curé*). [F.]

ab·bess [ǽbis] *n.* Ⓒ the chief nun of an abbey. 수녀원장(opp. abbot). [F.]

ab·bey [ǽbi] *n.* **1** Ⓒ a building where men or women lead a religious life. 수도원; 수녀원. **2** Ⓒ a large church that is used or was once used as an abbey. 대성당. ¶ *Westminster Abbey* 웨스트민스터 대성당. **3** 《*the A-*》 =Westminster Abbey. **4** 《*collectively*》 all the men and women in an abbey. (수도원·수녀원 전체의) 수사〔수녀〕(단). [F.]

·**ab·bot** [ǽbət] *n.* Ⓒ the head man of an abbey. 수도원장(opp. abbess). [Aram. = father]

ab·bot·cy [ǽbətsi] *n.* an abbot's office. 수도원장의 직(職)〔임기〕.

ab·bre·vi·ate [əbríːvièit] *vt.* (P6) make (a word, phrase, or story) shorter; shorten. (말·이야기 따위를) 줄여서 짧게 하다; 생

략하다. ¶ *We can ~ 'foot' to 'ft.'* 'foot'를 'ft.'로 생략할 수 있다. — *adj.* relatively short. 비교적 짧은. [ab-, →brief]

*·**ab·bre·vi·a·tion** [əbrìːviéiʃən] *n.* **1** Ⓤ the act of abbreviation. 생략; 단축. **2** Ⓒ a shortened form of a word or phrase. 생략형; 약자; 약어.

ABC, A.B.C.[1] [éibìːsíː] *n.* (*pl.* **ABC's**) **1** 《usu. *pl.*》 the English alphabet. 알파벳. **2** 《often *the* ~》 something to be learned first; a basic element. 기초; 초보; 입문. ¶ *the ABC's of economics* 경제학 입문.

A.B.C.[2] Australian Broadcasting Commission; American Broadcasting Company; atomic, biological 〔bacterial〕 and chemical; Argentina, Brazil, and Chile.

ab·di·cate [ǽbdikèit] *vt., vi.* (P6;1) abandon (one's position, right, etc.); resign. (지위·권리 따위를) 포기하다; 물러나다. ¶ ~ (*from*) *the throne* 퇴위하다. ¶ *the abdicated king* 스스로 퇴위한 국왕. ● **ab·di·ca·tor** [-ər] *n.* [L. *dico* declare]

ab·di·ca·tion [æ̀bdikéiʃən] *n.* ⓊⒸ the act of abdicating; resignation. 양위; 사직; 기권.

ab·do·men [ǽbdəmən, æbdóu-] *n.* Ⓒ the part of the body below the chest. 배; 복부(cf. 《*colloq.*》 *belly*). [L.]

ab·dom·i·nal [æbdɑ́mənəl / -dɔ́m-] *adj.* of the abdomen. 배〔복부〕의. ¶ *an ~ belt* 복대(腹帶) / *~ breathing* 복식 호흡 / *an ~ operation* 개복(開腹) 수술. [↑]

ab·duce [æbdjúːs] *vt.* =abduct 2.

ab·duct [æbdʌ́kt] *vt.* (P6) **1** carry off (someone, esp. a child) by force, often for money; kidnap. (특히, 어린이)를 유괴하다. ¶ *The police think that the boy has been abducted.* 경찰은 그 아이가 유괴된 것으로 보고 있다. **2** 《physiol.》 draw from the normal position. 외전(外轉)시키다. [ab-, L. *duco* draw]

ab·duc·tion [æbdʌ́kʃən] *n.* ⓊⒸ the act of abducting. 유괴(誘拐). ¶ *the ~ of a child* 어린이 유괴.

ab·duc·tor [æbdʌ́ktər] *n.* a person who abducts. 유괴범.

Abe [eib] *n.* a nickname of Abraham. Abraham의 애칭.

a·beam [əbíːm] *adv.* 《naut.》 at a right angle to a ship's side. (배)와 직각으로; 뱃전을 마주 보고. ¶ *have the wind ~* 바로 뱃전으로 바람을 받다 / *The enemy's ship was ~ of ours.* 적함(敵艦)은 우리 배와 나란히 있었다. [a(-)]

a·be·ce·dar·i·an [èibiːsiːdɛ́əriən] *adj.* elementary. 초보의. — *n.* a pupil learning the alphabet. 초보〔초학〕자. [→ABC]

a·bed [əbéd] *adv.* 《*arch., dial.*》 in bed; on a bed. 자리〔병상(病床)〕에 (누워). ¶ *lie ~* 자리에 눕다. [a(-), *bed*]

a·beg·ging [əbégiŋ] *adj.* begging. 구걸하는. [a(-)]

A·bel [éibəl] *n.* **1** a man's name. 남자의 이름. **2** 《Bible》 the second son of Adam and Eve, killed by Cain, his elder brother. 아벨《형 카인에게 죽음》.

a·bele [əbíːl, éibəl] *n.* 《bot.》 a white poplar. 은백양. [L. *albus* white]

Ab·er·deen [æ̀bərdíːn] *n.* a city in northeastern Scotland. 스코틀랜드 동북부의 도시.

Aberdeen terrier [⌐—⌐—] *n.* a Scotch terrier. 스카치 테리어.

Ab·er·do·ni·an [æ̀bərdóuniən] *adj.* of or relating to Aberdeen. Aberdeen의.

ab·er·rance [əbérəns, ǽbər-] *n.* ⓊⒸ the state of being strayed from normal courses. 정도〔상궤(常軌)〕를 벗어남. [↓]

ab·er·rant [əbérənt, ǽbər-] *adj.* straying from normal courses. 정도〔상궤〕에서 벗어난. [L. *erro* stray]

ab·er·ra·tion [æ̀bəréiʃən] *n.* ⓊⒸ **1** the state of being abnormal; an abnormal act; temporary mental disorder. 상궤를 벗어남; 탈선; 정신 이상. ¶ *mental ~* 정신 착란. **2** 《astron.》 광행차(光行差). ¶ *the ~ of a star* 별의 광행차.

a·bet [əbét] *vt.* (**-bet·ted, -bet·ting**) (P6,13) help (someone) in a wrong way, esp. in a crime. …을 선동하다〔부추기다〕; 교사하다. ¶ ~ *a crime* 범죄를 교사하다 / ~ *someone in a crime* 아무를 부추겨 죄를 범하게 하다 / *One man did the actual stealing, but the other two abetted him.* 한 사람은 실제 도둑질을 했으나 다른 두 사람은 그를 교사했다.

aid and abet ⇨aid.

● **a·bet·ment** [-mənt] *n.* Ⓤ **a·bet·tor, -ter** [-ər] *n.* [ad-, →bait]

ab ex·tra [æb ékstrə] *adv.* 《L.》 from outside. 밖으로부터.

a·bey·ance [əbéiəns] *n.* Ⓤ the state in which something is not in use or is delayed for a short time. 중지; 중절.

fall into abeyance, be suspended for lack of use. (법령·관습 따위가) 일시 정지되다. ¶ *The law fell into ~.* 그 법률은 정지되었다.

hold (*a question*) ***in abeyance,*** leave (a question) unsettled. (문제를) 미결〔미정(未定)〕인 채로 두다.

in abeyance, not in use ; not at present in force. 일시 중지되어; 정지 중에. ¶ *The law is in ~.* 그 법률은 일시 중지되어 있다.

● **a·bey·ant** [-ənt] *adj.* [ab-, F. *beer* gape]

ab·hor [æbhɔ́ːr] *vt.* (**-horred, -hor·ring**) (P6) hate (something) very much. …을 몹시 싫어하다. ¶ *We ~ cruelty.* 우린 잔인함을 싫어한다 / *She abhors flattery.* 그녀는 아첨을 아주 싫어한다. [ab-, L. *horres* shudder at]

ab·hor·rence [æbhɔ́ːrəns, -hɑ́r-] *n.* **1** Ⓤ 《*of*》 the act of abhorring; great hatred. 혐오; 증오. ¶ *Many people show an ~ of snakes.* 많은 사람들이 뱀을 혐오한다. **2** Ⓒ a cause of great hatred. 몹시 싫어하는 것. ¶ *Flattery is my ~.* 아첨은 내가 증오하는 것

이다.

ab·hor·rent [æbhɔ́ːrənt, -hár-] *adj.* causing (someone) to feel great hatred; hateful; detestable. 몹시 싫은; 증오〔혐오〕하는; 성미에 맞지 않는.

A

·a·bide [əbáid] (**-bode** or **-bid·ed**) *vt.* (P6) **1** 《*lit.*》 wait for (something). …을 기다리다. ¶ ~ *one's time* 때가 무르익기를 기다리다 / *He will ~ my coming.* 그는 내가 오기를 기다릴거다. **2** 《usu. in *negative* or *interrogative*》 put up with (something); endure. …을 참다; …에 견디다. ¶ *I can't ~ such a rude fellow.* 그처럼 무례한 녀석은 참을〔용서할〕 수가 없다 / *She can't ~ his rudeness.* 그녀는 그의 무례함에 견딜 수가 없다. **3** face; sustain. 감수(甘受)하다. — *vi.* (P3) **1** 《*by*》 remain; act according to. (어떤 상태에) 머물다; …을 지키다〔고수하다〕; …에 따르다. **2** 《*in*》 continue. 영속(永續)하다. **3** 《*arch.*》 《*in, at, with*》 live; stay; dwell. 살다; 머물다; 거주하다. ¶ ~ *in a place* 한 곳에 살다 / *He abode there one year.* 그는 그곳에서 1년 살았다. [E. → bide]

abide by (=*remain true or faithful to*) *something.* …을 지키다. ¶ *A man must ~ by his word.* 사람은 약속을 지켜야 한다 / *You must ~ by the decision.* 너는 그 결정에 따라야 한다.

a·bid·ing [əbáidiŋ] *adj.* permanent; lasting; unchanging. 영구한; 확고한; 영속하는; 변함없는. ¶ ~ *faith* 변함없는 신념 / ~ *love* 영원한 사랑.

ab·i·gail [ǽbəgèil] *n.* a lady's maid. 귀부인의 시녀. [Heb.]

:a·bil·i·ty [əbíləti] *n.* (*pl.* **-ties**) **1** Ⓤ 《*for, in*》 power to do something; skill. 능력; 수완; 유능함. ¶ *the ~ to speak* 말하는 능력 / *a man of ~* 수완가 / *He has ~ to do the work, but he's lazy and won't do it.* 그는 능력은 있으나 게을러서 그것을 하려고 들지 않는다. **2** 《usu. *pl.*》 talents. 재능. ¶ *manifold abilities* 다방면의 재능 / *She showed ~ in music.* 그녀는 음악에 재능을 보였다. [→ able]

to the best of** one's **ability =***to** one's **best ability,*** as well as one can. 힘 닿는 한; 전력을 다하여.

ab in·i·ti·o [æb iníʃiòu] *adv.* 《L.》 from the beginning. 처음부터.

ab·i·o·gen·e·sis [èibaioudʒénəsis] *n.* Ⓤ spontaneous generation. 자연 발생. [Gk. *a* not, *bios* life, →genesis]

ab·ject [ǽbdʒekt, ─ˊ] *adj.* **1** (of condition) wretched; miserable. 비참한; 가엾은. ¶ *a man in ~ poverty* 몹시 가난한 사람. **2** (of a person) without value; mean; contemptible. 형편〔보잘 것〕 없는; 비천한; 경멸할 만한; 비열한. ¶ *an ~ timeserver* 비열한 기회주의자 / *an ~ coward* 형편없는 겁쟁이. **3** (of an action) extremely humble; involving great loss of pride. 극도로 겸허한; 비굴한. ¶ *an ~ apology* 비굴한 변명. — *n.* an abject person. 비참한 사람. ●**ab·ject·ly** [-li] *adv.* [L. *jacio* throw]

ab·jec·tion [æbdʒékʃən] *n.* Ⓤ the state of being abject. 비천; 비열.

ab·ju·ra·tion [æ̀bdʒəréiʃən] *n.* ⒸⓊ the act of abjuring; the state of being abjured. (신앙·국적 따위의) 포기. [↓]

ab·jure [æbdʒúər / əb-] *vt.* (P6) swear to give up (one's right, faith, demand, nationality, etc.); give up formally. (권리·신앙·국적 등)을 버릴 것을 맹세하다; 그만 두다. ¶ ~ *one's religion* 자신의 종교를 버리다. [L. *juro* throw]

ab·la·tive [ǽblətiv] *n., adj.* 《gram.》 (of) a case of Latin nouns denoting *from, with* or *to.* 탈격(奪格)(의). [L.]

ab·laut [áːblaut, ǽb-] *n.* Ⓤ 《gram.》 vowel changes. 모음 전환. [G.]

a·blaze [əbléiz] *adj.* 《only as *predicative*》 **1** in a blaze; on fire; burning. 불타고; 불붙고. ¶ *The house was ~ before they could call for help.* 집은 그들이 도움을 채 청하기도 전에 불길에 휩싸였다. **2** shining in bright color; flashing. 빛나고; 번쩍이고. ¶ *The room was all ~ with a hundred lights.* 방은 백 개나 되는 전등불로 휘황하게 번쩍이고 있었다. **3** very much excited. 몹시 흥분한; 격한. ¶ *His face was ~ with anger.* 그는 성이 나서 시뻘개져 있었다. [a-, →blaze]

:a·ble [éibəl] *adj.* (**a·bler, a·blest**) **1** having power to do something. …을 할 수 있는 (opp. unable). **2** skillful; clever; well done. 유능한; 솜씨 좋은; 훌륭한. ¶ *an ~ man* 〔*teacher*〕 유능한 사람〔교사〕 / *an ~ speech* 훌륭한 연설 / *He is the ablest man I know.* 그는 내가 아는 가장 유능한 사람이다.

***be able to** do,* can do. 할 수 있다. 參考 조동사 can은 미래형, 완료형이 없으므로 be able to로 대용한다. ¶ *He is ~ to speak French.* 그는 프랑스말을 할 줄 안다 / *I shall be ~ to visit you tomorrow.* 내일 찾아뵐 수 있을 겁니다 / *He has not been ~ to attend school for a week.* 그는 일 주일 동안이나 학교에 출석하지 못하고 있습니다. [L. *habeo* hold]

-a·ble [-əbəl] *suf.* **1** able to. '…할 수 있는'의 뜻. ¶ *durable.* **2** fit to; suitable for. '…에 알맞은'의 뜻. ¶ *drinkable.* **3** tending to; likely to. '…하기 쉬운'의 뜻. ¶ *changeable.* **4** having qualities of. '…질(質)의, …같은'의 뜻. ¶ *comfortable.* **5** worthy of. '…할 만한'의 뜻. ¶ *lovable.* [↑]

a·ble-bod·ied [éibəlbádid / -bɔ́d-] *adj.* strong in health. 건강〔건장〕한; 강건한. ¶ *an ~ young man* 건강〔건장〕한 젊은이. [*able,* →body]

able(-bodied) seaman [ˊ─(ˊ─) ˊ─] *n.* an experienced deck-department seaman qualified to perform routine sea duties. 숙련 유자격 갑판원〔해원·선원〕; A.B.급의 선원. 參考 A.B. 또는 AB로 생략함.

a·bloom [əblúːm] *adv., adj.* 《only as *predicative*》 in bloom. 꽃이 피어. ¶ *The garden is ~ with tulips.* 뜰엔 튤립꽃들이 피어 있다. [a(-), →bloom]

a·blush [əblʌ́ʃ] *adj.* 《only as *predicative*》 blushing. 얼굴을 붉히고. [a(-), →blush]

ab·lu·tion [əblúːʃən] *n.* UC 《usu. *pl.*》 the act of washing one's body or a part of it, esp. as a religious ceremony. (특히 종교 의식으로서의) 목욕 (재계). ¶ 《*colloq.*》 *perform one's ablutions* 몸을 씻다; 목욕하다. [ab-, L. *luo* wash]

a·bly [éibli] *adv.* in an able manner; skillfully. 훌륭[능숙]히; 교묘히; 잘. [*able*]

-a·bly [-əbli] *suf.* in an able manner. '…할 수 있게, …하게' 의 뜻. ¶ *comfortably.*

ABM antiballistic missile; Atomic Bomb Mission.

ab·ne·gate [ǽbnigèit] *vt.* (**-gat·ed, -gat·ing**) (P6) give up (one's rights, faith, etc.); renounce. 끊다; 그만두다; 포기하다; 부인하다. [L. *nego* deny]

ab·ne·ga·tion [ǽbnigéiʃən] *n.* U **1** refusal. 거절. **2** (of one's rights, etc.) abandonment. (권리 따위의) 포기. **3** self-denial. 극기(克己); 자제.

·**ab·nor·mal** [æbnɔ́ːrməl] *adj.* not normal; unusual; uncommon. 비정상[이상]의; 변태[변칙]의(opp. normal). ¶ *~ psychology* 변태 심리학 / *an ~ state of affairs* 이상 사태 / *It is ~ for a man to have six fingers on each hand.* 사람이 한 손에 여섯 손가락을 갖는다는 것은 비정상이다. ●**ab·nor·mal·ness** [-nis] *n.* [Gk. *a-* not]

ab·nor·mal·i·ty [æ̀bnɔːrmǽləti] *n.* (*pl.* **-ties**) **1** U the state of being abnormal. 비정상; 이상(異常); 변태. **2** C an abnormal thing. 이상물(物); 기형.

ab·nor·mal·ly [æbnɔ́ːrməli] *adv.* in an abnormal manner; to an abnormal extent. 비정상적으로; 병적으로.

ab·nor·mi·ty [æbnɔ́ːrməti] *n.* UC monstrosity. 비정상; 이상(異常)(한 것). [ab-, L. *norma* norm]

·**a·board** [əbɔ́ːrd] *adv., prep.* **1** on or in a ship; 《U.S.》 on or in a bus, train, airplane, etc. 배에; 선상[선내]에; 버스·기차·비행기 따위를 타고. ¶ *step ~* 올라타다 / *go* [*come*] *~ a ship* 승선(乘船)하다 / *All ~.* 여러분 모두 승선[승차]하시기 바랍니다. **2** alongside (of a ship or shore). 현측(舷側)에; 육안(陸岸) 가까이. ¶ *close ~* (…)가까이에 / *keep the land ~* 해안을 끼고 항해하다. [a(-), →board]

fall aboard (***of another ship***), strike against the side of another ship. 다른 배와 충돌하다.

·**a·bode**[1] [əbóud] *n.* C a place where a person lives. 주거; 거처; 주소. ¶ *his present ~* 그의 현재 거처 / *make* [*take up*] *one's ~* 거처를 정하고 살다. [→abide]

a·bode[2] [əbóud] *v.* p. and pp. of **abide.**

·**a·bol·ish** [əbáliʃ / əbɔ́l-] *vt.* (P6) put an end to (laws, customs, etc.). …을 폐지하다; 철폐하다. ¶ *~ slavery* 노예 제도를 폐지하다. ●**a·bol·ish·ment** [-mənt] *n.* U [L. *oleo* grow]

ab·o·li·tion [æ̀bəlíʃən] *n.* U **1** the act of abolishing. 폐지. **2** 《U.S.》 the act of abolishing slavery. 노예 제도 폐지. ●**ab·o·li·tion·ist** [-ist] *n.*

·**A-bomb** [éibàm / -bɔ̀m] *n.* C an atomic bomb. 원자 폭탄. [*atom*]

·**a·bom·i·na·ble** [əbámənəbəl / əbɔ́m-] *adj.* **1** hateful; horrible. 몹시 싫은; 지겨운; 무서운. ¶ *He showed ~ cruelty.* 그는 무서운 잔인성을 보였다. **2** 《*colloq.*》 very unpleasant; bad. 몹시 불쾌한; 나쁜. ¶ *~ weather* 지독한 날씨. [↓]

Abominable Snowman [⌐—— ⌐—], **the** *n.* a large, hairy, manlike creature reported to inhabit the Himalayas. 설인(雪人).

a·bom·i·nate [əbámənèit / əbɔ́m-] *vt.* (P6) **1** hate strongly; abhor. …을 몹시 혐오하다. **2** 《*colloq.*》 dislike strongly. 지독히 싫어하다. ¶ *I ~ bad weather.* 난 나쁜 날씨가 지독히 싫다. ●**a·bom·i·na·tor** [-ər] *n.* [→omen]

a·bom·i·na·tion [əbàmənéiʃən / əbɔ̀m-] *n.* **1** U hatred; hating very much. 혐오; 싫어함. ¶ *I hold trickery in ~.* 나는 속임수를 아주 싫어한다. **2** C anything which causes hatred; a hateful thing. 몹시 싫은[지겨운] 것.

ab·o·rig·i·nal [æ̀bərídʒənəl] *adj.* **1** existing from the earliest days; primitive. 원시 이래의. ¶ *an ~ custom of the Ainus* 아이누족(族)의 토속(土俗). **2** originally found in a certain country or region; native. 토착의. ¶ *an ~ animal* 토착 동물 / *~ inhabitants* 토착민 / *an ~ plant of India* 인도의 토착 식물. —*n.* **1** =aborigine 1. **2** 《*pl.*》 《*A-*》 =aborigine 2. [→origin]

ab·o·rig·i·ne [æ̀bərídʒəniː] *n.* **1** aboriginal inhabitants; native. 토착민; 원주민. **2** 《*pl.*》 the native plants and animals of a region. (어느 지역의) 토착 동식물군(群). [↑]

a·born·ing [əbɔ́ːrniŋ] *adv.* while being born or produced. 탄생되려고 하는; 달성되기 직전의. [a-, *born, -ing*]

a·bort [əbɔ́ːrt] *vi.* (P1) **1** come to nothing; miscarry. 무위로 끝나다; 유산[낙태]하다. **2** shrink away. 위축하다. ●**a·bort·ed** *adj.* [L. *orior* be born]

a·bor·tion [əbɔ́ːrʃən] *n.* UC **1** the birth of a baby before it has not yet grown enough to live. 유산; 낙태. ¶ *criminal ~* 낙태죄 / *have an ~* 유산하다. **2** a person born out of due season; a monstrous misshapen creature. 조산아; 기형물. **3** a failure (of a plan or an idea). (계획 따위의) 실패.

a·bor·tion·ist [əbɔ́ːrʃənist] *n.* a person who produces criminal abortions. 위법적인

A

낙태 시술자.

a·bor·tive [əbɔ́:rtiv] *adj.* **1** born before grown enough to live. 유산(流產)의; 낙태의. ¶ *an ~ birth* 유산. **2** not successful; fruitless. 실패의; 결실이 없는. ¶ *His plans proved ~.* 그의 계획은 실패였다 / *He made an ~ attempt.* 그는 헛된 시도를 했다. — *n.* a medicine producing abortion. 낙태약. [*abort, -ive*]

·a·bound [əbáund] *vi.* (P2A,3) ⟪*in, with*⟫ exist in plenty; be rich in. 많(이 있)다; …이 풍부하다. ¶ *Fish ~ in this river.* = *This river abounds in* 〔*with*〕 *fish.* 이 강에는 물고기가 많다 / *The Middle East abounds in oil.* 중동은 석유가 풍부하다. [L. *unda* wave, *abundo* overflow]

:a·bout [əbáut] *prep.* **1** concerning; of; in connection with. …에 관〔대〕해서; …에 관한. ¶ *a book ~ gardening* 원예에 관한 책 / *talk ~ business* 사업 이야기를 하다 / *What are you speaking ~?* (도대체) 무엇에 대해 이야기하고 있는 겁니까 / *He worries ~ his health.* 그는 건강을 걱정하고 있다. **2** on; by; with. …의 신변에; (…의 몸)에 지니고. ¶ *There is something elegant ~ her.* 그녀에겐 어딘가 품위가 있다 / *Have you a pencil ~ you?* 연필 가진 거 있니 / *I had lost all I had ~ me.* 나는 갖고 있던 모든 것을 잃었다. **3** near. …쯤; 약…. ¶ *~ three o'clock* 3시쯤; 약 3시. **4** somewhere near; not far from; on every side of. …주변에〔을〕; …주위에〔를〕. ¶ *Look ~ you.* 주위를 잘 살펴라 / *You will find my son somewhere ~ the house.* 내 아들은 집 근처 어디에 있을 겁니다. **5** here and there; to and fro; (all) around. …의 여기저기; …의 둘레에〔를〕. ¶ *walk ~ the streets* 거리를 돌아다니다 / *travel ~ the country* 국내 여기저기를 여행하다 / *There is a fence ~ the garden.* 뜰 둘레에 울타리가 (쳐)있다. **6** engaged in; attending to. …을 하고; …에 종사하고. ¶ *What are you ~ here?* / *He is busy ~ his packing.* 그는 짐꾸리기에 바쁘다.

***be about to** do,* be going to do; be on the point of doing. 이제 막 …하려고 하다; 막 …하려는 참이다. ¶ *She was ~ to start.* 그녀는 이제 막 떠나려던 참이었다.

What* 〔*How*〕 *about … ? What will you do about …?; What do you say about …?; What do you think about …? 어떻게 할 텐가; 뭐라고 말할 텐가; 어떻게 생각하나. ¶ *What* 〔*How*〕 *~ the weather?* 날씨가 어떤가 / *What* 〔*How*〕 *~ going there?* 거기 가는 것이 어떤가 / *What ~ having dinner together?* 저녁 식사를 함께 하는 것이 어떤가.

— *adv.* **1** around; on all sides; in every direction. …의 주위〔주변〕에; 둘레에. ¶ *She looked ~.* 그녀는 주위를 둘러보았다. **2** neary; almost. 대략; 약; 거의. ¶ *walk ~ a mile* 약 1마일을 걷다 / *~ six o'clock* 약 6시(쯤) / *He has ~ finished his work.* 그는 일을 거의 마쳤다 / *The buckets are ~ full.* 양동이가 거의 찼다 / *It is ~ time to start.* 이제 슬슬 떠날 시간이다. **3** somewhere around; nearby; somewhere near. 근처〔주변〕에; 근방에; 여기저기. ¶ *scatter the toys ~* 장난감을 여기저기 흩어 놓다 / *There was nobody ~.* 근처엔 아무도 없었다 / *Is he anywhere ~?* 부근 어디에 그 사람이 있는가. **4** in the opposite direction. 반대쪽으로; 뒤로 돌아. ¶ *turn a car ~* 차를 돌리다 / *About turn!* ⟪mil.⟫ 뒤로 돌아. **5** alternately; in succession; by turns. 번갈아; 차례로. **6** going on; in action. (소문 따위가) 퍼져; 행해지고; 움직이고. ¶ *Rumors are ~.* 소문이 퍼져 있다

about and about, alike. 비슷비슷하여.

be out and about, be able to do one's ordinary work again (after an illness). (병후에) 기운을 회복하다.

be up and about, have got up; be out of bed. (자리에서) 일어나 활동하다〔일하다〕 ¶ *He is already up and ~.* 그는 벌써 일어나 움직이고 있다.

go a long way about, make a circuit. 멀리 돌아가다.

— *vt.* (P6) put (a ship) about. (배의) 나아가는 방향을 바꾸다. [O.E. *onbūtan* on the outside of]

a·bout-face [əbáutfèis] *n.* a turning or going in the opposite direction. (방향) 전환. — [–∸∸] *vi.* (**-faced, -fac·ing**) (P1) turn or go in the opposite direction. 방향을 돌리다.

:a·bove [əbʌ́v] *prep.* **1** higher than; over; on the top of. …보다 높게; …위에(opp. below). ¶ *~ the horizon* 수평선 위에 / *the clouds ~ the mountains* 산맥 위의 구름들 / *3,000 meters ~ sea level* 해발 3천 미터 / *The sun is blazing ~ our heads.* 태양은 머리 위에서 쬐고 있다 / *The peak rises ~ the clouds.* 산봉우리가 구름 위로 치솟아 있다 / *Her voice was heard ~ the noise.* 소음 속에서 그녀의 목소리가 들렸다. **2** earlier in history than; upstream from. …보다 거슬러 올라가서; …보다 이전의; …에서 상류에. ¶ *the period ~ the 6 th century* 6세기 이전의 시대 / *There is a waterfall ~ the bridge.* 다리의 상류엔 폭포가 있다. **3** superior to; more than; better than. …보다 나은〔우수한〕; …이상으로. ¶ *~ a thousand* 1천 이상 / *~ the average* 평균 이상 / *Health is ~ wealth.* 건강은 부(富)보다 낫다 / *He is ~ all the other boys in his class.* 그는 자기 반의 누구보다도 낫다. **4** surpassing; beyond; too difficult for; ashamed of; too good for. …을 초월하여; …이 미치지 못하는; 너무 어려운; …을 부끄러이 여기고; …하기에는 너무 좋아서; 결코 …아니할. ¶ *He is ~ criticism.* 그는 비평의 여지가 없을 정도로 훌륭하다 / *This book is ~ my understanding.* 이 책은 내겐 너무 어렵다 / *You must not be ~ asking questions.* 질문하는 것을 부끄러이 여겨서는 안 된다 / *He is ~ telling a lie.* 그는 결코 거짓말을 할 사람이 아니다.

***above all* (*things*),** most importantly. 특히;

무엇보다도 먼저.

— *adv.* (opp. below) **1** in or at〔to〕a higher place; higher up; overhead. 보다 높이; 위에 (있는); 위쪽에. ¶ *clear sky* ~ 머리 위의 맑은 하늘 / *the paragraph* ~ 위의 패러그래프 / *The birds soared* ~. 새들은 하늘 높이 날았다. **2** upstairs. 위층으로. ¶ *an iron stair leading* ~ 위층으로 이어지는 철제 계단. **3** in heaven. 천상에; 하늘에. ¶ *God* ~ 하느님 / *There is God* ~. 하늘에 하느님이 계신다. **4** higher in rank or power. 상위〔상급〕에. ¶ *the courts* ~ 상급 법원. **5** upstream. (강의) 상류에. ¶ *There is good fishing* ~. 상류에서는 고기가 잘 낚인다. **6** (esp. in a book) before; earlier. (본 페이지) 위에; 처음에; 전문(前文)에. ¶ *as (is) mentioned* ~ …위〔앞〕에서 말했듯이. **7** over; in addition. 이상에. ¶ *Children of six and* ~ *should attend school.* 여섯 살 이상의 아동은 취학해야 한다.

above oneself, self-conceited. 자부〔우쭐〕하여.

above comprehension, incomprehensible. 이해할 수 없는.

from above, from heaven. 하늘로부터.

— *adj.* written above; foregoing. 상술(上述)의; 상기(上記)의. ¶ *the* ~ *explanations* 위의 설명 / *the* ~ *statement* 상기 진술 / *judging by*〔*from*〕*the* ~ *facts* 상기 사실로 판단하건대. [*on, by, up*]

a·bove·board [əbʌ́vbɔ̀ːrd] *adv.* without dishonesty; openly. 사실대로; 공명하게; 솔직하게. ¶ *He treated us* ~. 그는 우리를 공정하게 대했다.

— *adj.* 《as *predicative*》 honest; open. 공정한; 솔직한. ¶ *His dealings are all* ~. 그의 거래는 공명정대하다(opp. underhand).

open and aboveboard, 《*emph.*》 =aboveboard.

a·bove-men·tion·ed [əbʌ́vménʃənd] *adj.* mentioned before. 앞서 말한; 상기(上記)의; 전술(前述)의.

ab o·vo [æb óuvou] *adv.* 《L.》 from the beginning. 처음부터.

a·brade [əbréid] *vt., vi* (P6;1) rub off (the surface, the skin, etc.); wear away by rubbing. (표면·피부를) 까지게 하다; 벗겨지다; 닳리다; 닳다. ¶ *A glacier abrades rocks.* 빙하는 바위 표면을 깎는다. [L. *rado* scrape]

***A·bra·ham** [éibrəhæ̀m, -həm] *n.* **1** a man's name. 남자의 이름. **2** (in the Bible) the first head of the Hebrews. 아브라함《유태인의 시조》.

a·bra·sion [əbréiʒən] *n.* **1** Ⓤ the state of being abraded; the act of rubbing away. 마멸; 깎임. ¶ ~ *of a coin* 동전의 마멸 / *the* ~ *of rocks* 바위의 마멸. **2** Ⓒ an abraded place or spot. 마찰된 곳; 까진 곳; 찰과상. ¶ *This ointment will heal abrasions of the skin.* 이 연고는 찰과상을 낫게 할 것이다. [→abrade]

a·bra·sive [əbréisiv, -ziv] *adj.* rubbing away (the skin); wearing down (rocks). …을 까지게 하는; 스쳐져 벗기는; …을 닳게 하는. — *n.* Ⓒ a substance used for rubbing(e.g. sandpaper). 연마제; 연삭제(研削劑). [↑]

ab·re·ac·tion [æ̀briǽkʃən] *n.* 《psychoanal.》 the removal of a repressed emotion by reviving ideas of the event that first caused it. 해제〔해방〕 반응. [ab-]

a·breast [əbrést] *adv.* side by side. 나란히. ¶ *march three* ~ 세 명이 나란히〔3열로〕 행진하다. [a(-)]

keep abreast of (=*keep up with*) *something.* …에 뒤(떨어)지지 않도록 하다. ¶ *Keep* ~ *of the times.* 시대에 뒤떨어지지 않도록 해라.

a·bridge [əbrídʒ] *vt.* **1** (P6) make (a story, a book, etc.) shorter without changing the chief contents; shorten; condense. (이야기·책 따위)를 줄이다; 요약〔압축〕하다(opp. lengthen). ¶ ~ *a long story for school* 긴 이야기를 학교 교재용으로 요약하다. **2** (P13) 《*of*》 make less; curtail; deprive. 축소(제한)하다; 빼앗다. ¶ *The right of citizens must not be abridged without proper cause.* 정당한 이유 없이 시민의 권리를 제한해서는 안 된다. [O.F. *abreger* shorten, →abbreviate]

a·bridg·ment, -bridge- [əbrídʒmənt] *n.* **1** Ⓤ the act of abridging. 요약; 단축; 축소. ¶ ~ *of rights* 권리의 축소. **2** Ⓒ an abridged story, book, etc. 요약된 이야기, 책 따위.

a·broach [əbróutʃ] *adv., adj.* broached. (통의) 마개를 따고. [a(-), →broach]

:a·broad [əbrɔ́ːd] *adv.* **1** out of one's own country; to or in a foreign land. 해외로; 외국으로〔에〕. ¶ *go* ~ 해외로 가다 / *He lives* ~. 그는 해외에 살고 있다. **2** far and wide; broadly; in circulation; going about. 널리; 퍼져서; 자자하여; 나돌고. ¶ *scatter* ~ 널리 흩어지다 / *The news of his coming spread* ~. 그가 온다는 소식이 널리 퍼졌다 / *A report is* ~ *that the school will close.* 학교가 문을 닫으리란 풍문이 나돌고 있다. **3** 《*all* ~》 in error. 틀려서. **4** 《*arch.* in Brit.》 out of one's house. 집 밖에; 밖에 (나와). ¶ *You are* ~ *early!* 외출 한번 이르군. [a(-), →broad]

from abroad, from foreign lands. 외국으로〔해외로〕부터. ¶ *news from* ~ 해외 뉴스 / *He is just back from* ~. 그는 해외에서 막 돌아와 있다.

ab·ro·gate [ǽbrəgèit] *vt.* (P6) abolish (laws, customs, etc.); repeal; put an end to. (법률·관습 따위)를 폐지하다. ¶ ~ *a treaty* 조약을 파기하다. [L. *rogo* propose]

ab·ro·ga·tion [æ̀brəgéiʃən] *n.* Ⓤ the act of abrogating; the state of being abrogated. 폐지.

A

·ab·rupt [əbrʌ́pt] *adj.* (opp. gentle) **1** sudden; unexpected. 갑작스러운; 뜻밖의. ¶ *an ~ death* 급사 / *an ~ change in the weather* 날씨의 급변 / *He made an ~ entrance.* 그가 느닷없이 들어왔다 / *The driver made an ~ turn to avoid another car.* 운전사는 다른 차를 피하기 위해 급회전을 했다. **2** rough; impolite; rude. 거친; 무뚝뚝한; 퉁명스러운. ¶ *an ~ reply* 무뚝뚝한 대답 / *answer in an ~ manner* 퉁명스럽게 대답하다. **3** very steep. 험준한; 가파른. ¶ *an ~ slope* 가파른 비탈. **4** (of style) passing from one thought to another too suddenly. (문체 따위가) 급전하는; 비약적인. [ab-, →rupture]

·ab·rupt·ly [əbrʌ́ptli] *adv.* in an abrupt manner; suddenly; rudely. 갑자기; 무뚝뚝하게.

ab·rupt·ness [əbrʌ́ptnis] *n.* Ⓤ the state of being abrupt; rudeness. 돌연; 무뚝뚝함. ¶ *with ~* 갑자기; 무뚝뚝하게.

abs- [æbs-, əbs-] *pref.* ⇨ab-.

ab·scess [ǽbses] *n.* Ⓒ a painful part of the body, swollen with pus often resulting from an infection. 종기; 농양(膿瘍). [→cede, L. *abscessus* a going away]

ab·scis·sion [æbsíʒən, -ʃən] *n.* **1** ⟪med.⟫ the act or process of cutting off. 절단. **2** ⟪bot.⟫ the natural separation of flowers, fruit, or leaves from plants. 기관 탈리(器官脫離).

ab·scond [æbskánd / -skɔ́nd] *vi.* (P1, 2A,3) go away suddenly and hide. 자취를 감추다; 달아나다. ¶ *He stole money from the bank and absconded with it.* 그는 은행에서 돈을 훔쳐 그것을 갖고 도망쳤다. [L. *condo* hide]

:ab·sence [ǽbsəns] *n.* **1** Ⓤ the state of being away or not present. 부재; 결석; 결근(opp. presence). ¶ *~ from school* 결석. **2** Ⓒ a time when a person is away. 부재 기간. ¶ *after a long ~* 오래간만에 / *during one's ~* 부재 중에 / *return after an ~ of two years,* 2년만에 돌아오다 / *in the ~ of Mr. Smith* 스미스 씨가 없는 동안에 / *It occurred during my ~.* 그건 내가 없는 동안에 발생했다. **3** Ⓤ ⟪*of*⟫ the state of being without something; lack. 없음; 결여; 결핍. ¶ *~ of mind* 방심 / *~ of order* 무질서 / *I was struck by the total ~ of sincerity in his speech.* 나는 그의 말에서 진실성이 전혀 없음에 놀랐다 / *in the ~ of proof* 증거 불충분으로. [↓]

:ab·sent [ǽbsənt] *adj.* **1** not here; away in another place. 결석의; 부재의(opp. present). ¶ *He is ~ from class today.* 그는 오늘 결석이다 / *Three boys of the class were ~ because of illness.* 그 반의 세 학생이 병으로 안 나왔다 / *Why were you ~ from the meeting?* 너는 왜 모임에 안 나왔지. **2** not existing; lacking. …이 없는; 결여된. ¶ *Snow is ~ in some countries.* 몇몇 나라에는 눈이 내리지 않는다. **3** not paying attention. 멍(청)한 (opp. attentive). ¶ *an ~ air* 멍한 태도. — [æbsént] *vt.* (P6,13) ⟪*oneself from*⟫ stay (oneself) away; keep (oneself) away. …을 결석〔결근〕시키다. ¶ *~ oneself from class* 결석하다. [L. *abs-* away, *esse* to be]

ab·sen·tee [æ̀bsəntíː] *n.* Ⓒ **1** a person who is absent, esp. one who absents himself when he ought to be present. 부재자; 결석〔결근〕자. **2** a landowner who lives away from his estate. 부재 지주(不在地主). — *adj.* of or for a voter or voters permitted to vote by mail. 부재 투표자의.

absentee voting 〔**ballot**〕 [⊿⊿⊿ ⊿〔⊿⊿〕] *n.* voting by a person who has been permitted to vote by mail. 부재(자) 투표.

ab·sent·ly [ǽbsəntli] *adv.* in an absent manner; carelessly. 멍하니.

ab·sent-mind·ed [ǽbsəntmáindid] *adj.* paying no attention to what is happening around one; careless. 멍한; 방심한. ¶ *The ~ man put salt in his coffee and sugar on his egg.* 그 멍청한 사나이는 커피에 소금을, 달걀에 설탕을 쳤다. ● **ab·sent-mind·ed·ly** [-li] *adv.* **ab·sent-mind·ed·ness** [-nis] *n.* Ⓤ

ab·sinth(e) [ǽbsinθ] *n.* Ⓤ **1** ⟪bot.⟫ wormwood. 쓴쑥. **2** an intoxicating liqueur. 압생트. [Gk.]

:ab·so·lute [ǽbsəlùːt, ⊿⊿⊿] *adj.* **1** complete; perfect. 완전한; 절대의. ¶ *~ ignorance* 완전한 무식 / *Try to tell the ~ truth.* 완전한 진실을 말하도록 해라 / *I have ~ trust in him.* 나는 그 사람을 절대적으로 신용한다 / *You are an ~ fool.* 넌 진짜 바보다. **2** not mixed with anything else; pure. 순수한. ¶ *~ alcohol* 순수한〔무수(無水)〕 알코올. **3** not limited in any way; unconditional; uncontrolled; free. 제약 없는; 무조건의; 억제되지 않는. ¶ *an ~ ruler* 독재자 / *an ~ monarch* 전제 군주 / *the Absolute* 하느님 / *an ~ promise* 무조건의 약속. **4** certain; real; definite. 확실한; 실제의; 절대 확실한. ¶ *an ~ proof* 확실한 증거 / *an ~ fact* 절대적인 사실. **5** ⟪gram.⟫ out of grammatical relation. 문법 관계를 떠난; 독립적인. ¶ *an ~ construction* 독립 구문(e.g. *I refusing,* he left us.). ● **ab·so·lut·ism** *n.* Ⓤ. [ab-, L. *solbeo* loosen, →solve]

:ab·so·lute·ly [ǽbsəlúːtli, ⊿⊿⊿⊿] *adv.* **1** completely; thoroughly. 절대적으로; 완전히; 아주. ¶ *That's ~ ridiculous.* 그건 아주 우습다 / *It is ~ necessary to….* 그건 …에게 절대적으로 필요하다 / *not ~ impossible* 전적으로 불가능하지는 않은. **2** ⟪*colloq.*⟫ quite so; yes. 맞습니다; 그래요. 參考 특히 강조할 때엔 [ǽbsəlùːtli] 로 발음함. ¶ *You agree, I suppose? —Oh, ~.*

ab·so·lu·tion [æ̀bsəlúːʃən] *n.* Ⓤ the act of absolving; (a formal declaration of) free dom from guilt or punishment. 면죄; 사면; 사죄(赦罪)(의 선언). ¶ *The priest gave him*

～. 사제는 그에게 죄를 사면해 주었다 / *The priest pronounced the Absolution.* 사제는 사죄를 선언했다.

ab·solve [æbzálv, -sálv / -zɔ́lv] *vt.* (P6,13) **1** 《*of*》 declare (someone) free from guilt or punishment; forgive. …을 면죄하다; …에게 무죄 선언을 하다. ¶ *The priest absolved him of all his sins.* 사제는 그의 죄를 모두 사(赦)했다. **2** 《*from*》 set (someone) free from a duty or promise. (아무)의 (의무·책임을) 면제하다. [→absolute]

∗**ab·sorb** [æbsɔ́:rb, -zɔ́:rb, əb-] *vt.* (P6) **1** take in (moisture, heat, light, etc.) wholly; suck up. …을 빨아들이다; 동화하다. ¶ *Blotting paper absorbs ink.* 압지(押紙)는 잉크를 흡수한다 / *Black absorbs light.* 흑색은 빛을 흡수한다 / *The dry earth absorbs water.* 마른 땅은 물을 흡수한다. **2** cause (someone) to have a deep interest; attract (someone's attention or interest) fully; take up all the attention, time, etc. (사람)을 열중케 하다; (마음·정신·시간)을 빼앗다. ¶ *His lecture absorbs me* 〔*my interest*〕. 그의 강의는 나를 열중케 한다 / *His task absorbs him.* 그의 일이 시간을 빼앗는다. [L. ab-, *sorbeo* suck in]

be absorbed (=*be deeply interested*) ***in*** *something.* …에 열중해 있다. ¶ *He is absorbed in reading* 〔*his business*〕. 그는 독서〔사업〕에 몰두하고 있다.

ab·sorb·ent [æbsɔ́:rbənt, -zɔ́:r-, əb-] *adj.* having the quality of absorbing. 흡수성이 있는. ¶ ～ *cotton* 탈지면(脫脂綿) / ～ *powder* 흡수제. — *n.* Ⓒ anything that absorbs. 흡수제.

ab·sorb·ing [æbsɔ́:rbiŋ, -zɔ́:r, əb-] *adj.* occupying someone's attention wholly; very interesting. 열중케 하는; 매우 재미있는. ¶ *an* ～ *book* 매우 재미있는 책 / *an* ～ *tale of adventure* 매우 재미있는 모험담.

ab·sorp·tion [æbsɔ́:rpʃən, -zɔ́:rp-, əb-] *n.* Ⓤ **1** the act of absorbing. 흡수. ¶ ～ *of ink by blotting paper* 압지(押紙)에 의한 잉크의 흡수. **2** taking (food) into the body as a result of digestion. 소화 흡수. **3** giving all one's time, attention, etc. (to); having great interest (in). 열중; 열심. ¶ ～ *in one's studies* 자기 연구에의 열중 / *His* ～ *in sports prevents his progress in his studies.* 그는 스포츠에 지나치게 열중해서 학업이 진척되지 않는다.

ab·sorp·tive [æbsɔ́:rptiv, -zɔ́:rp, əb-] *adj.* having the quality of absorbing; absorbent. 흡수성의. ● **ab·sorp·tive·ness** [-nis] *n.* Ⓤ

ab·stain [æbstéin] *vi.* (P3) 《*from*》 hold (oneself) back; refrain. (의지의 힘으로 …을) 삼가다; 그만두다. ¶ ～ *from smoking* 금연하다 / ～ *from strong drink* 독한 술을 삼가다 / ～ *from all kinds of pleasure* 온갖 쾌락을 끊다. [L. abs-, *teneo* hold]

ab·stain·er [æbstéinər] *n.* Ⓒ a person who abstains, esp. from taking alcoholic drinks. 절제하는 사람; (특히) 금주가. ¶ *a total* ～ 절대 금주가.

ab·ste·mi·ous [æbstí:miəs] *adj.* not eating and drinking too much; moderate. 폭음 폭식하지 않는; 절제 있는. ¶ ～ *life* 절제 생활 / ～ *in the use of tobacco* 담배를 절제하는. [L. abs-, *temetum* strong drink]

ab·sten·tion [æbsténʃən] *n.* Ⓤ **1** the act of abstaining. 절제; 금욕. ¶ ～ *from drink* 금주. **2** Ⓒ refusal to record one's vote. (투표의) 기권. ¶ *50 votes for, 35 against, and 7 abstentions* 찬성 50표, 반대 35표, 기권 7표. [↑]

ab·ster·gent [æbstɔ́:rdʒənt] *adj.* cleansing. 씻어내는; 세척의. — *n.* Ⓒ a cleansing substance. 세척제. [L. abs-, *tergeo* wash]

ab·sti·nence [ǽbstənəns] *n.* Ⓤ the act of abstaining, esp. from eating and drinking. 절제; 금욕; 금주. ¶ *total* ～ 절대 금주 / ～ *from wine* 금주 / ～ *from smoking* 금연. [↓]

ab·sti·nent [ǽbstənənt] *adj.* moderate in eating and drinking. (음식 따위를) 자제하는; 절제하는. [→abstain]

∗**ab·stract** [æbstrǽkt, ⌐–] *adj.* **1** considered apart from any real things; only in idea; not concrete. 추상적인(opp. concrete). ¶ *an* ～ *conception* 추상적인 개념 / *an* ～ *noun* 추상 명사 / ～ *art* 추상 예술. **2** hard to understand; difficult. 이해하기 어려운; 난해한. ¶ ～ *theories about the nature of the soul* 영혼의 본질에 관한 어려운 이론. — [⌐–] *n.* Ⓒ a shortened form of the main ideas of a book or argument; a summary. 적요; 대요(大要).

in the abstract, in theory rather than in practice; theoretical(ly). 이론상(으로); 추상적으로. ¶ *He has no idea of poverty except in the* ～. 그는 가난의 맛을 추상적으로밖엔 모른다.

make an abstract (=*sum up the main points*) ***of*** *a book, argument, etc.* (책 따위)의 요점을 발췌하다.

— [–⌐] *vt.* (P6,13) **1** make an abstract of (a book, argument, etc.); summarize. (책 따위)를 발췌하다; 요약하다. ¶ ～ *a passage from a book* 한 구절을 책에서 발췌하다. **2** take away; take out. …을 제거하다; 분리하다 ¶ ～ *others' attention from one's fault* 자기의 실수를 남이 모르게 하다 / ～ *metal from ore* 광석에서 금속을 분리해내다. **3** steal. 훔치다. ¶ ～ *a man's watch from his pocket* 남자의 호주머니에서 시계를 훔치다. [L. *traho* drag]

ab·stract·ed [æbstrǽktid] *adj.* absent-minded; lost in thought. 멍한; 방심한. ¶ *with an* ～ *air* 멍한 태도로. ● **ab·stract·ed·ly** [-li] *adv.*

∗**ab·strac·tion** [æbstrǽkʃən] *n.* **1** Ⓤ the act of abstracting; the state of being abstracted. 추상; 추상 작용. **2** Ⓒ an abstract idea; a purely conceptual idea. 추상 개념; 개념적인 생각. ¶ *A line that has no width is only an* ~. 넓이가 없는 선은 단지 개념적인 생각일 뿐이다. **3** Ⓤ being lost in thought; absent-mindedness. 방심 상태. ¶ *with an air of* ~ 건성으로 / *His* ~ *was so deep that he did not eat for two days.* 멍한 상태가 아주 심해서 그는 이틀 동안이나 먹지 않았다. **4** Ⓤ taking away or out. 추출; 분리; 제거. ¶ *the* ~ *of the juice from an orange* 오렌지로부터의 주스 추출. **5** Ⓒ a work of abstract art. 추상 예술 작품. **6** Ⓤ stealing. 훔침.

ab·struse [æbstrú:s] *adj.* difficult to understand; deep in meaning. 난해한; 심원한. ¶ ~ *questions* 난해한 문제들. ● **ab·struse·ly** [-li] *adv.* **ab·struse·ness** [-nis] *n.* [L. abs-, *trudo* push]

•**ab·surd** [æbsə́:rd, -zə́:rd] *adj.* very foolish; ridiculous; unreasonable. 어이 없는; 바보 같은; 우스운; 당치 않은. ¶ *an* ~ *opinion* 어이 없는 의견 / *Don't be* ~*!* 당치 않은〔얼빠진〕 소리 마라 / *make an* ~ *statement* 〔*mistake*〕 어이 없는〔당치 않은〕 진술〔잘못〕을 하다. [ab-(intensive =very), L. *surdus* dull]

ab·surd·i·ty [æbsə́:rdəti, -zə́:r-] *n.* (*pl.* **-ties**) **1** Ⓤ the quality of being absurd; unreasonableness. 불합리; 당치 않음. **2** Ⓒ an absurd idea, act, thing, etc. 어이 없는〔바보 같은〕 생각〔행동, 일〕. ¶ *He said a number of absurdities.* 그는 바보 같은 소릴 많이 했다.

ab·surd·ly [æbsə́:rdli, -zə́:rd-] *adv.* in an absurd manner; foolishly. 불합리하게; 당치 않게; 바보같이.

•**a·bun·dance** [əbʌ́ndəns] *n.* Ⓤ 《sometimes *an* ~》 **1** an amount or quantity that is more than enough. 풍부; 많음. ¶ *an* ~ *of food* 풍성한 음식 / *a year of* ~ 풍년 / *An* ~ *of rice is produced every year.* 매년 남아돌 정도의 쌀이 생산된다. **2** wealth; riches. 부; 유복. [L. *abundo* to overflow; ab-, *undo* wave]

in abundance, in plenty. 많이; 풍부히.

live in abundance, have many things to make life pleasant and comfortable. 유복하게 살다. ¶ *They live in* ~. 그들은 풍족하게 살고 있다.

•**a·bun·dant** [əbʌ́ndənt] *adj.* plentiful; very rich in something. 많은; 풍부한. ¶ *an* ~ *harvest* 풍작 / *an* ~ *crop of rice* 쌀의 풍작 / *an* ~ *supply of food* 식량의 풍족한 공급.

be abundant (=*be rich*) ***in*** *something.* …이 풍부하다. ¶ *This country is* ~ *in natural resources.* 이 나라는 부존 자원이 풍부하다.

a·bun·dant·ly [əbʌ́ndəntli] *adv.* in a great number or amount. 많이; 풍부히.

a·bus·age [əbjú:sidʒ, -zidʒ] *n.* misuse. 오용(誤用). [↓]

•**a·buse** [əbjú:z] *vt.* (P6) **1** use (a position, privilege, etc.) for a wrong purpose; make a wrong use of (words, etc.). (권력 등)을 남용〔악용〕하다; (말 따위)를 오용하다. ¶ ~ *one's authority* 〔*power*〕 권력을 남용하다. **2** treat (someone) cruelly. …을 학대하다. ¶ ~ *a horse* 말을 학대하다. **3** use bad or violent language to (someone). (아무를) 욕하다; (아무를) 매도하다. **4** take unfair advantage of. 부당하게 …을 이용하다; …을 기회로 삼다. ¶ *You abused his kindness.* 너는 그의 친절을 악용했다. **5** find fault with. …을 흠〔탈〕잡다.

— [əbjú:s] *n.* **1** ⓊⒸ bad or wrong use. 남용; 악용; 오용. ¶ *the* ~ *of power* 권력의 남용 / ~ *of words* 말의 오용. **2** Ⓤ bad language that hurts others. 욕하는 말; 욕설. ¶ *a term of* ~ 폭언 / *A stream of* ~ *came from his lips.* 그의 입에서 욕설이 연이어 쏟아져 나왔다. **3** Ⓤ severe and cruel treatment of persons. 학대. **4** Ⓒ 《often *pl.*》 a bad or unjust custom or practice. 악습; 악폐. ¶ *the abuses of modern times* 현대의 악폐 / *the abuses of government* 정치의 악폐. ● **a·bus·er** [-zər] *n.* [L. ab-, *usus* use]

a·bu·sive [əbjú:siv] *adj.* **1** using wrong and insulting language. 입이 건; 욕지거리〔악담〕하는. ¶ *become* ~ 욕설로 나오다 / *use* ~ *language* 욕을 하다. **2** used in a wrong way. 남용되는〔적인〕. ¶ *an* ~ *exercise of power* 권력의 남용 / *He made many* ~ *remarks to me.* 그는 나에게 악담을 많이 했다.

a·but [əbʌ́t] *v.* (**a·but·ted, a·but·ting**) *vi.* (P3) 《*on, upon, against*》 be in contact at an end or edge. (토지 등이 이웃과) 경계를 접하다. ¶ *His garden abuts on the road.* 그의 뜰은 도로에 접해 있다 / *The street abuts against the railroad.* 거리는 철도에 접해 있다 / *Our house abuts on* 〔*against*〕 *the church.* 우리 집은 교회와 인접해 있다. — *vt.* border upon (something). …와 경계를 접하다. [F. *bout, butt* end]

a·but·ment [əbʌ́tmənt] *n.* **1** Ⓤ the state of being abutted. 인접; 접촉. **2** Ⓒ 《*archit.*》 that which supports an arch or a bridge. 홍예 받침대; 교대(橋臺). **3** Ⓒ a place of abutting. 접점.

〈abutment 2〉

a·bysm [əbízəm] *n.* 《*poet.*》 =abyss.

a·bys·mal [əbízməl] *adj.* very deep; bottomless. 끝 모를; 깊은; 심연(深淵)의. ¶ ~ *ignorance* 철저한 무지(無知). [↓]

a·byss [əbís] *n.* Ⓒ **1** bottomless depth. 심연(深淵). **2** anything bottomless or unlimited; something very deep. 끝 모를〔끝없는〕 것; 아주 깊은 곳. ¶ *an* ~ *of time* 영원 / *the* ~ *of despair* 절망의 구렁텅이 / *an* ~

of disgrace 더없는 창피. **3** hell. 지옥.
● **a·bys·sal** *adj.* [Gk.=bottomless]

Ab·ys·sin·i·a [æbəsíniə] *n.* 아비시니아 《Ethiopia의 옛 이름》. ● **Ab·ys·sin·i·an** [-iən] *adj., n.*

a/c account.

A·C· alternating current; Alpine Club.

a·ca·cia [əkéiʃə] *n.* Ⓒ 《bot.》 a tree with very small leaves and yellow or white flowers that grows in warm regions. 아카시아. [Gk.]

ac·a·dem·ic [ækədémik] *adj.* **1** of a school, esp. a college or university; scholarly; pedantic. 대학의; 학구적인; 현학적인. ¶ *the ~ curriculum* 대학의 교과 과정 / *an ~ degree* 학위 / *~ freedom* 학문〔학원〕의 자유. **2** 《U.S.》 of general education rather than technical or professional education. 일반 교양의. **3** of a learned society. 학계의. ¶ *~ circles* 학계. **4** having no practical effect; theoretical. 이론상의; 비실제적인. ¶ *an ~ question* 탁상 공론 / *That is merely an ~ discussion.* 그건 단지 탁상 공론에 불과하다. **5** conventional. 평범한; 형식적인. **6** of Plato's school. 플라톤 학파의. **7** sceptical. 회의적인.
— *n.* **1** a member of a university; a professional scholar. 대학생; 대학 교수; 대학인. **2** 《*pl.*》 unpractical discussions. 공리 공론. [→academy]

ac·a·dem·i·cal [ækədémikəl] *adj.* = academic. — *n.* 《*pl.*》 traditional formal clothes worn in some colleges or universities. 대학의 예복. 參考 cap and gown이라고도 함. ● **ac·a·dem·i·cal·ly** [-kəli] *adv.*

ac·a·de·mi·cian [ækədəmíʃən, əkæ̀də-] *n.* Ⓒ **1** a learned man who belongs to a society or institution for the advancement of literature, science, or art. (학술원·예술원 등의) 회원. **2** 《*A-*》 a member of the Royal Academy, the French Academy, or the American Academy of Arts and Letters. 영국 왕립 예술원, 프랑스 학술원, 미국 예술원의 회원.

***a·cad·e·my** [əkǽdəmi] *n.* Ⓒ (*pl.* **-mies**) **1** a place for higher learning. 학교; 학원; 고교 정도의 각종 학교. **2** 《U.S.》 a private secondary or high school. 사립 중·고등 학교. **3** a school for special study and instruction. 전문 학교. ¶ *an ~ of music* 음악 학교 / *a naval ~* 해군 사관 학교 / *a military ~* 육군 사관 학교 / *There are academies of medicine and painting.* 의학 학교와 미술 학교가 있다. **4** a society of learned men for the advancement of literature, science, or art. 학술원; 예술원; 학회. ¶ *the Academy =the Royal Academy (of Arts)* 왕립 미술원. (abbr. R.A.) / *the French Academy* 프랑스 학술원. [Gk. *Akadēmos* the grove where Plato taught]

a·can·thi [əkǽnθai] *n.* pl. of **acanthus.**

a·can·thus [əkǽnθəs] *n.* (*pl.* **-thus·es** or **-thi**) 《bot.》 a plant with toothed leaves. 아칸서스. [Gk.]

a cap·pel·la [à:kəpélə] *adv.* 《mus.》 without instrumental accompaniment. 반주 없이. [It. *ad* according to, *capella* church]

acc. acceptance; account; accountant; accusative.

ac·cede [æksí:d] *vi.* (P1,3) 《*to*》 **1** agree. 동의하다. ¶ *~ to a proposal* 〔*a treaty*〕 제의〔조약〕에 동의하다 / *Please ~ to my request.* 부디 내 요구에 응하시오. **2** take up a position; succeed. 취임하다; 상속하다. ¶ *~ to the throne* 왕위에 오르다 / *~ to the estate* 재산을 상속하다 / *~ to an office* 취임하다 / *Who will ~ when the king dies?* 왕이 서거하시면 누가 그 자리에 오를 것인가. **3** become a member of an organization; join. 가입〔입회〕하다; 들어가다. ¶ *He acceded to the new party.* 그는 새 당(黨)에 들어갔다. [ac-, L. *cedeo* retreat]

accel. accelerando.

ac·cel·er·an·do [æksèlərǽndou, -rɑ́:n-] *adv., adj.* 《It.》 gradually faster. 점차 빠르게〔빠른〕.

***ac·cel·er·ate** [æksélərèit] *vt.* (P6) **1** make (something) move faster; speed up. …의 속도를 빠르게 하다(opp. decelerate). **2** make (something) happen or come sooner. …을 촉진하다. ¶ *~ someone's recovery* 아무의 회복을 촉진하다 / *Death was accelerated by grief.* 슬픔으로 죽음이 촉진되었다. — *vi.* (P1) increase in speed. 빨라지다. ● **ac·cel·er·a·tive** [-tiv] *adj.* [L. *celer* swift]

ac·cel·er·a·tion [æksèləréiʃən] *n.* Ⓤ **1** the act of accelerating; the state of being accelerated. 가속(加速); 촉진. **2** 《phys.》 a change in the rate of speed of a body in motion. 가속도. ¶ *~ of gravity* 중력에 의한 가속도 / *positive* 〔*negative*〕 ~ 가(加)〔감(減)〕속도.

ac·cel·er·a·tor [æksélərèitər] *n.* Ⓒ **1** a person or thing that causes an increase in the speed of something. 가속자; 가속물〔기〕. **2** a device for increasing the speed of a motor engine. (자동차의) 가속 장치; 액셀러레이터.

:ac·cent [ǽksent / -sənt] *n.* Ⓒ **1** a special force given by the voice to one part of a word; a mark to show such a part. 악센트(부호); 강세. ¶ *In "letter", the ~ is on the first syllable.* "letter"에서 악센트는 첫 음절에 있다. **2** ⒸⓊ a special way of pronouncing. 말투; (지방) 사투리. ¶ *a broad Scotch ~* 순 스코틀랜드 말투 / *the Southern ~* 남방 사투리 / *He speaks English with a Korean ~.* 그는 한국 말투로 영어를 한다. **3** 《*pl.*》 tone of voice. 어조(語調); 가락. ¶ *She spoke in tender accents.* 그녀는 상냥한 어조로 이야기했다.
— [æksént, ⌐–] *vt.* (P6) **1** pronounce (a

A

word) with an accent. …을 힘주어 발음하다. ¶ ~ *the second syllable* 둘째 음절에 강세를 두어 말하다. **2** place special value on (something); stress; make conspicuous. …을 강조하다; 두드러지게 하다. [ad-, L. *cano* sing]

ac·cen·tu·ate [æksént∫uèit] *vt.* (P6) **1** pronounce (a word, syllable, phrase, etc.) with an accent or a stress on it. (말 따위)에 악센트를 두어 발음하다. **2** put an emphasis upon (something); distinguish (something) from others. …을 강조하다; 두드러지게 하다. ¶ ~ *certain points in a speech* 연설에서 어떤 점을 강조하다 / *Her black hair accentuated the whiteness of her skin.* 검은 머리가 그녀의 하얀 살결을 돋보이게 했다. [↑]

ac·cen·tu·a·tion [æksènt∫uéi∫ən] *n.* Ⓤ **1** the act of accentuating. 악센트를 둠. **2** emphasis. 역설; 강조.

:ac·cept [æksépt] *vt.* (P6) **1** receive gladly. …을 받다. ¶ ~ *a favor* 〔*a kindness*〕 호의를〔친절을〕 받아들이다 / ~ *a gift* 선물을 받다 / ~ *a position in a company* 회사 직책을 받아들이다 / ~ *battle* 응전(應戰)하다. **2** agree to (something). …을 승낙〔수락〕하다. ¶ ~ *a proposal* 제안에 응하다 / ~ *an appointment* 임명을 수락하다 / *Will you ~ his apology?* 그의 사죄를 받아들이겠는가 / ~ *responsibility for* …에 대한 책임을 인정하다. **3** take (something) as true. …을 용인〔인정〕하다. ¶ ~ *the excuse* 변명을 받아들이다 / ~ *the correctness of a statement* 진술이 틀림없음을 인정하다 / *His theory was widely accepted.* 그의 학설은 널리 인정되었다. **4** 《comm.》 agree to pay. (어음 지불 따위)를 인수하다. ¶ ~ *a bill of exchange* 환어음(의 지불)을 인수하다. [ad-, L. *capio* take]

ac·cept·a·bil·i·ty [æksèptəbíləti] *n.* Ⓤ the quality of being acceptable. (기분 좋게) 받아들일 수 있음; 승인.

·ac·cept·a·ble [ækséptəbəl] *adj.* **1** worth accepting; satisfactory. 받아들일〔수락할〕 수 있는. ¶ *The bargain is ~.* 흥정은 만족할 만하다. **2** agreeable; welcome. 마음에 드는; 좋은; 훌륭한. ¶ *a very ~ gift* 썩 마음에 드는 선물 / *an ~ gift to a sick person* 환자에게 좋은 선물.

·ac·cept·ance [ækséptəns] *n.* Ⓤ **1** the act of accepting; the state of being accepted. 받음; 수령; 수락(opp. refusal). ¶ ~ *of a gift* 〔*an invitation*〕 선물〔초청〕의 수락. **2** approval; assent. 승낙; 용인; 인정(opp. disapproval). ¶ ~ *of a statement* 〔*a theory, a hypothesis*〕 진술〔학설, 가설〕의 인정 / *The invention found widespread ~.* 그 발명은 널리 세상으로부터 인정받았다. **3** 《comm.》 a promise to pay. (어음 따위의) 인수. **4** an accepted bill. 인수필(畢) 어음.

ac·cep·ta·tion [æ̀kseptéi∫ən] *n.* Ⓒ the recognized meaning of a word or expression. (말의) 일반적으로 인정된 의미. ¶ *The word, in its ordinary ~, means ….* 그 말은 보통의 의미로 …을 뜻한다.

ac·cept·ed [ækséptid] *adj.* approved in general by people. 일반적으로 인정된; 공인된. ¶ *a generally ~ theory* 일반적으로 인정된 이론 / *Once it was an ~ belief that the world was flat.* 예전에는, 세상은 납작하다는 것이 공인된 믿음이었다.

ac·cep·tor [ækséptər] *n.* a person who accepts a bill of exchange. 환어음 인수인.

·ac·cess [ǽkses] *n.* **1** Ⓤ the act of coming near. 접근. ¶ *Access to the top of the mountain is difficult.* 그 산정(山頂)에 접근하기는 어렵다. **2** Ⓒ a way, chance, or right of approaching. 접근하는 방법〔기회, 권리〕. ¶ *the only ~ to the castle* 그 성에 접근할 수 있는 유일한 길. **3** Ⓒ a passage. 통로. **4** Ⓒ increase; growth. 증가; 생장. **5** Ⓒ a fit or attack of a disease; an emotional outburst. (병 따위의) 발작. ¶ *an ~ of fever* 발열(發熱) / *in an ~ of fury* 불끈 성을 내어 / *He killed his friend in an ~ of rage.* 발작적인 격노로 자기 친구를 죽였다. [ad-, L. *cedeo* retreat]

be easy* 〔*difficult*〕 *of access, be easy 〔difficult〕 to approach. 접근하기가 쉽다〔어렵다〕. ¶ *The house is easy of ~.* 그 집은 접근하기 쉽다.

gain* 〔*obtain*〕 *access to, **a**) approach to (someone). (아무)에게 접근하다. **b**) enter (a building). (건물에) 들어가다.

give access to, allow into; allow to use. 들어가게 하다; 사용하게 하다.

have access to, **a**) approach to (someone or something); get in touch with. …에(게) 접근하다; 접촉하다. ¶ *The Prime Minister has ~ to the King.* 수상은 왕을 가까이 할 수 있다 / *Has he ~ to men who could help him in his work?* 그의 작업을 도와줄 사람들을 접촉할 수 있는가. **b**) can make use of (something). …을 이용할 수 있다. ¶ *have ~ to books* 책에 접할 기회를 갖다; 책을 이용할 수 있다.

ac·ces·sa·ry [æksésəri] *adj., n.* (*pl.* **-ries**) =accessory.

ac·ces·si·bil·i·ty [æksèsəbíləti] *n.* Ⓤ the state of being easy to approach or enter. 다가갈 수 있음; 근접〔출입〕할 수 있음.

ac·ces·si·ble [æksésəbəl] *adj.* **1** easy to approach, enter, or obtain. 다가가기〔들어가기, 입수하기〕 쉬운. ¶ *A public library makes good books ~.* 공공 도서관에선 좋은 책을 대하기가 쉽다 / *He is no ~.* 그 사람은 대하기 쉽지 않다 / *The place is not ~ by land.* 그곳은 육로를 통해선 갈 수 없다. **2** 《fig.》 《to》 that can be easily influenced by something. 영향을 잘 받는; 감동되기 쉬운. ¶ *Women are more ~ to pity than men.* 여성들은 남성들보다 연민의 정이 많다 / *a man ~ to reason* 이치를 아는 사람.

ac·ces·sion [ækséʃən] *n.* Ⓤ **1** 《to》 the act of attaining to a certain condition.

(어떤 상태에) 도달; 즉위; 취임. ¶ ~ *to manhood* 성년에 이름 / *the King's* ~ *to the throne* 왕위에 오름; 즉위. **2** the act of joining; consent. 가맹; 동의. ¶ ~ *to the party* 정당에 입당 / ~ *to demand* 요구의 수락. **3** Ⓒ addition; a thing added. 증가; 증가물. ¶ *The nation grew larger by the* ~ *of new territories.* 그 나라는 몇 개의 새 영토가 늘어 더 커졌다 / *new accessions to a library* 도서관에의 신착(新着) 도서.

ac·ces·so·ry [æksésəri] *adj.* **1** additional. 부속의; 보조적인. ¶ ~ *sounds in music* 악곡의 부수적인 음. **2** 《law》 helping in a crime. 종범(從犯)의. ¶ *be made* ~ 공범으로 몰리다. —*n.* Ⓒ (*pl.* **-ries**) **1** an extra article attached to something. 부속품. ¶ *the accessories of a motorcar* 자동차의 부속품 / *toilet accessories* 화장용품류. **2** 《usu. *pl.*》 an article that is worn besides the basic clothing, such as gloves, earrings, etc. 액세서리. **3** 《law》 a person who helps in a crime. 종범; 공범. ¶ *an* ~ *to a crime* 어떤 범죄의 공범.

:ac·ci·dent [ǽksidənt] *n.* Ⓒ **1** something that happens unexpectedly; an event not expected. 우발; 우연(성); 우발 사고. **2** a harmful or unfortunate happening; a disaster. 불행한 일; 재난. ¶ *a car* ~ 자동차 사고 / *an inevitable* ~ 불가피한 사고 / *meet with an* ~ 사고를 만나다 / *He was killed in a traffic* ~. 그는 교통 사고로 죽었다. [L. *cado* fall]

by accident, by chance. 우연히(opp. on purpose, by design).

without accident, safely. 무사히.

ac·ci·den·tal [æ̀ksidéntl] *adj.* **1** happening by chance or unexpectedly. 우연의; 돌발적인; 뜻밖의(opp. voluntary). ¶ *an* ~ *death* 불의의 죽음 / ~ *homicide* 과실 치사 / *His breaking the cup was quite* ~. 그가 컵을 깬 것은 우연이었다. **2** not essential to the nature of a thing. 우유적(偶有的)인.

ac·ci·den·tal·ly [æ̀ksidéntəli] *adv.* in an accidental manner; by accident. 우연히; 뜻밖에; 생각지 않게(opp. designedly).

ac·claim [əkléim] *vt.* (P6) welcome (someone) with praise, joy, and applause along with loud shouts. …에 갈채를 보내다; 환호하다. ¶ ~ *the victor* 승자에 갈채를 보내다 / *The people acclaimed him* (*as*) *king.* 국민들은 환호하면서 그를 왕으로 모셨다. —*n.* shouts of applause. 환호; 갈채. [L. *clamo* call out, →claim]

ac·cla·ma·tion [æ̀kləméiʃən] *n.* ⓊⒸ **1** 《usu. *pl.*》 the act of acclaiming; a shout of welcome or approval. 갈채; 환호(의 소리). ¶ *hail someone with acclamation*(*s*) (아무를) 환성을 지르며 맞다. **2** an oral vote with all voters in agreement. (만장 일치로 찬성하는) 발성 투표(發聲投票). [↑]

ac·cli·mate [ǽkləmèit, əkláimit] *vt., vi.* (P6,13;1,3) accustom (someone or something) or become accustomed to a new environment, climate, etc. 새로운 환경·기후 등에 적응시키다[하다]. ¶ ~ *animals* [*plants*] *in* 짐승[식물]을 새 풍토에 적응시키다 / 《*fig.*》 ~ *oneself* 자신을 새로운 여건·환경에 순응시키다. [ad-, →climate]

ac·cli·ma·tize [əkláimətàiz] *vi., vt.* 《chiefly Brit.》 =acclimate.

ac·cliv·i·ty [əklívəti] *n.* Ⓒ (*pl.* **-ties**) a slope which goes upwards. 치받이; 오르막(opp. declivity). [ad-, L. *clivus* slope]

ac·co·lade [ǽkəlèid, ⌐⌐⌐] *n.* Ⓒ a light tap on a man's shoulder with the flat of a sword in making him a knight. 나이트작(爵) 수여(식). ¶ *receive the* ~ 나이트 작위를 받다. [ad-, L. *collum* neck]

·ac·com·mo·date [əkámədèit / əkɔ́m-] *vt.* **1** (P13) 《*to*》 make (someone or something) fit; adjust; adapt. …을 조화시키다. ¶ ~ *oneself to circumstances* 환경에 순응하다 / ~ *facts to a theory* 사실을 이론에 맞추(어 수정하)다. **2** (P13) 《*with*》 kindly give (someone) what he wants; fit out with. (아무)에게 …을 제공하다; 마련해 주다. ¶ *He will* ~ *me with the use of his car.* 그 사람은 내게 자기 차를 빌려줄 거다 / ~ *someone with money* 아무에게 돈을 융통해 주다. **3** (P6) have rooms for (persons); hold. (손)을 숙박시키다; …을 수용하다. ¶ *The hospital can* ~ *300 patients.* 이 병원은 환자 300명을 입원시킬 수 있다 / *The hotel is admirably accommodated.* 그 호텔은 시설이 괜찮다 / *Can you* ~ *a party of five for two weeks?* 일행이 다섯인데 두 주일 재워 줄 수 있겠소. **4** (P6) reconcile (disputes); settle. (분쟁)을 화해시키다; 수습[조정]하다. ¶ ~ *a dispute* / ~ *differences* 차이를 조절하다. [ad-, L. *modus* measure]

ac·com·mo·dat·ing [əkámədèitiŋ / əkɔ́m-] *adj.* kind and willing to help. 친절한; 싹싹한. ¶ *an* ~ *man* 친절한 사람 / *The man was* ~ *enough to lend me a pound.* 그 사람이 고맙게도 내게 1파운드를 빌려주더군.

ac·com·mo·da·tion [əkɑ̀mədéiʃən / əkɔ̀m-] *n.* **1** Ⓤ the act of making fit. 적응. ¶ ~ *to a new environment* 새 환경에의 적응 / *The* ~ *of our desires to a smaller income took some time.* 보다 적은 수입에 우리 욕망을 적응시키는 데에는 상당한 시간이 걸렸다. **2** Ⓒ settlement of differences. 화해; 조정. ¶ *come to an* ~ 타협이 되다; 화해하다 / *in a spirit of mutual* ~ 상호 타협의 정신으로. **3** 《*pl.*》 《U.S.》 food and lodging. 숙박. ¶ *We have no sleeping accommodations.* 저희는 숙박 시설이 없습니다 / *Can you give me accommodation*(*s*) *for tonight?* 오늘 밤 숙박할 수 있습니까. **4** Ⓒ anything that helps or is convenient. 편의; 시설. ¶ *for the* ~ *of someone* 아무의 편의를 위하여 / *This hotel has good accommodations.* 이 호텔은 숙박 시설이 좋다. **5** Ⓒ a loan. 대부금; 융자.

accommodation bill [⌐⌐⌐⌐ ⌐] *n.* a

A

bill drawn to raise money. 융통 어음.

accommodation ladder [――´― ―̀] *n.* a ladder hung over the side of a ship. 현제(舷梯); 트랩.

accommodation train [――´― ―̀] *n.* 《U.S.》 a train that stops at all or nearly all stations. 보통 열차.

ac·com·pa·ni·ment [əkʌ́mpənimənt] *n.* Ⓒ **1** something that naturally goes along with another thing. 자연히 딸리는 것; 부수물. ¶ *Disease is a frequent ~ of famine.* 질병은 흔히 기근과 함께 온다. **2** music played to support the main music. 반주. ¶ *play one's ~* 반주하다 / *sing to the ~ of a piano* 피아노 반주에 따라 노래하다. [→accompany]

ac·com·pa·nist [əkʌ́mpənist], **-ny·ist** [-niist] *n.* Ⓒ a person who plays a musical accompaniment. 반주자.

:ac·com·pa·ny [əkʌ́mpəni] *vt.* (**-nied**) **1** (P6,7) go along with (someone). …와 동반하다; …와 함께 가다. ¶ *~ a friend on a walk* 산책에 친구와 동행하다. **2** (P13) happen or exist together with (something); attend. …에 따라〔수반되어〕 일어나다〔존재하다〕; …이 따르다. ¶ *Light is accompanied by heat.* 빛에는 열이 따른다 / *The rain was accompanied by a high wind.* 비는 세찬 바람이 따랐다. **3** (P13) cause (something) to be together with other things. …이 따르게 하다; …에 덧붙이다; 곁들이다. ¶ *~ a present with a letter* 선물에 편지를 첨부하다 / *~ one's speech with gestures* 연설에 몸짓을 곁들이다 / *He accompanied his orders with blows.* 그는 명령과 동시에 주먹질이 따랐다. **4** (P6) play music in order to help (other music). …에 반주하다. ¶ *~ the violin on* 〔*at*〕 *the piano* 바이올린에 피아노 반주를 하다 / *~ a song on the piano* 노래에 피아노로 반주하다 / *The pianist accompanied the singer.* 피아니스트가 가수의 반주를 했다. [com-, L. *panis* bread, →companion]

ac·com·plice [əkámplis / əkɔ́m-] *n.* Ⓒ 《*with, in*》 a person who helps another in a wrong act. 공범자; 공모자. ¶ *an ~ in murder* 살인 공범자. [→complex]

:ac·com·plish [əkámpliʃ / əkɔ́m-] *vt.* (P6) complete successfully. (일·계획 따위)를 성취하다; 이룩하다. ¶ *~ a journey* 여행을 끝내다 / *~ one's object* 목적을 달성하다 / *Did you ~ your purpose?* 목적을 이뤘나 / *He can ~ more in a day than any other boy in his class can in two days.* 그는 제 반의 다른 아이들이 이틀 동안에 할 수 있는 것보다 하루에 더 해낼 수 있다. [ad-, →complete, L. *pleo* fill]

·ac·com·plished [əkámpliʃt / əkɔ́m-] *adj.* **1** completed; done; finished. 완성한; 끝낸. ¶ *an ~ task* 끝낸 일 / *an ~ fact* 기정 사실. **2** skillful in social arts; well-trained; practiced. (사교상의) 재예(才藝)에 뛰어난; 교양있는; 능숙한. ¶ *an ~ gentleman* 〔*lady*〕 교양있는 신사〔숙녀〕 / *an ~ dancer* 능숙한 댄서.

·ac·com·plish·ment [əkámpliʃmənt / əkɔ́m-] *n.* **1** Ⓤ achievement; completion. 완성; 성취; 실행. ¶ *The ~ of his purpose took two days.* 그의 목적을 이루는 데 이틀이 걸렸다. **2** Ⓒ a thing that has been achieved. 업적. ¶ *It was a real ~ to finish the work in two days.* 그 일을 이틀에 끝낸 것은 실로 큰 업적이었다. **3** Ⓒ 《often *pl.*》 an excellent skill or ability acquired by training. (훈련으로 얻어진) 재예(才藝); 소양. ¶ *a man of many accomplishments* 재능이 많은 사람 / *Sewing is not among her accomplishments.* 그녀는 바느질 솜씨가 없다 / *He had every ~ except that of making money.* 그는 돈버는 재주 외에는 무엇이나 할 수 있었다 / *She has many accomplishments, being able to sing, play the piano, and so on.* 그녀는 노래도 하고 피아노도 칠 줄 아는 등 많은 소양을 갖추고 있다.

ac·compt [əkáunt] *v., n.* 《*arch.*》 =account.

·ac·cord [əkɔ́:rd] *vt.* (P13,14) give; grant. …을 주다. ¶ *~ praise to someone* =*~ someone praise* 아무를 칭찬하다 / *They accorded a hearty welcome to me.* 그들은 진심으로 나를 환영해 주었다.

— *vi.* (P3) 《*with*》 agree; be in harmony with. …와 일치하다; 맞다; 조화하다. ¶ *~ with reason* 사리에 맞다 / *His account of the day accords with yours.* 그날 일에 대한 그의 설명은 당신 말과 일치한다 / *It accords with my wishes.* 그건 내 소망과 일치한다 / *That does not ~ with what you said before.* 그건 네가 전에 말한 것과 맞지 않는다.

— *n.* **1** Ⓤ the state of being in harmony or agreement. 일치; 조화. ¶ *His statement was not in ~ with the facts.* 그의 진술은 사실과 맞지 않았다. **2** Ⓒ reconciliation. 화해. **3** Ⓒ the combination of musical sounds in harmony. 화음(和音)(opp. discord). [ad-, L. *cor* heart]

be in accord (= *harmonize*) ***with*** *something.* …와 조화하다.

be of one accord, be in agreement. 일치하고 있다.

be out of accord (=*do not harmony*) ***with*** *something.* …와 조화되지 않다.

of its own accord, by itself; naturally. 자연히; 저절로.

of one's own accord, without being asked; willingly. 자발적으로; 자진해서.

with one accord, all together; in unison. 일제히.

·ac·cor·dance [əkɔ́:rdəns] *n.* Ⓒ agreement; harmony. 일치; 조화.

in accordance with, according to; in agreement with. …에 따라(서); …와 일치하여. ¶ *act in ~ with the rules* 규칙에 따라 행동하다 / *I am in ~ with him in this matter.* 나는 이 문제에 있어 그와 일치하고 있다.

ac·cor·dant [əkɔ́ːrdənt] *adj.* 《*with, to*》 in harmony; agreeing or in agreement. 일치하는; 조화돼 있는. ¶ ~ *to reason* 도리에 맞는 / ~ *to your wishes* 당신 소망에 따라.

:ac·cord·ing [əkɔ́ːrdiŋ] *adv.* in harmony. …에 따라(서).

according as, in proportion as. …에 따라(서); …에 준하여. ¶ *We have different views of a thing* ~ *as we are rich or poor.* 우리는 부자냐 가난하냐에 따라서 사물을 보는 견해가 다르다.

according to, **a**) in agreement with; in accordance with. …에 일치하여; …에 따라. ¶ *living* ~ *to one's income* 수입에 따른 생활 / ~ *to his promise* 그의 약속에 따라 / *You will be paid* ~ *to the work you do.* =*You will be paid* ~ *as you work.* 당신이 하는 일에 따라 봉급이 지급될 것이다. **b**) following what is said by; on the authority of. …에 따르면〔의하면〕. ¶ *According to the Bible, God made the world in six days.* 성경에 의하면 하느님께서는 엿새 만에 세계를 만드셨다(고 한다). [*accord*]

***ac·cord·ing·ly** [əkɔ́ːrdiŋli] *adv.* **1** in agreement with what has been said. 그에 따라(서); 적당히. ¶ *I shall arrange it* ~. 적당히 조처하지요 / *The students were given new instructions and told to act* ~. 학생들은 새로운 지시를 받고 그에 따라 행동하도록 명령받았다. **2** for this reason; therefore. 그래서; 따라서. ¶ *He was too ill to stay —* ~, *we sent him home.* 그는 병이 너무 심해서 있을 수가 없었다 — 그래서 우리는 그를 집으로 보냈다.

accordingly as, according as. …에 따라서.

ac·cor·di·on [əkɔ́ːrdiən] *n.* Ⓒ a portable musical instrument with a bellows and a keyboard. 아코디언. — *adj.* with folds like the bellows of an accordion. 아코디언 같은 주름이 있는. ¶ *a skirt with* ~ *pleats* 아코디언 같은 주름이 있는 스커트.
● **ac·cor·di·on·ist** [-ist] *n.* [→accord]

accordion pleats [–ˊ–– ˊ] *n. pl.* (in clothing) folds like the bellows of an accordion. 아코디언 플리츠〔주름〕.

ac·cost [əkɔ́(ː)st, əkást] *vt.* 《often in a bad sense》 (P6) come up and speak to (someone). (다가와서 …에게) 이야기를 걸다; 인사하다. ¶ *I was accosted by a beggar on the street.* 노상에서 거지가 말을 걸어왔다. [ad-, L. *costa* rip]

ac·couche·ment [əkuːʃmáːŋ, əkúːʃmənt] *n.* 《F.》 delivery of a child. 출산; 분만.

ac·cou·cheur [æ̀kuːʃə́ːr] *n.* 《F.》 a doctor who makes midwifery his special work. 산과의(産科醫).

ac·cou·cheuse [æ̀kuːʃə́ːz] *n.* 《F.》 a midwife. 조산사(助産師); 산파(産婆).

:ac·count [əkáunt] *n.* **1** Ⓒ counting; calculation. 계산; 셈. ¶ *cast accounts* 계산〔셈, 결산〕하다 / *He is quick at accounts.* 그는 계산이 빠르다. **2** Ⓒ a report; a story; an explanation; description. 보고(서); 설명(기사); 이야기. ¶ *newspaper accounts* 신문의 보도 / *The boy gave his father an* ~ *of the game.* 소년은 아버지에게 그 게임을 설명했다. **3** Ⓒ a record of money spent and received; a bill. 회계; 계산(서). ¶ *keep one's accounts in order* 장부에 정연히 기입하다 / *open* 〔*close*〕 *an* ~ *with a person* 아무와 거래를 트다〔그만두다〕 / *keep accounts* 기장(記帳)하다 / *Put it down to my* ~. 그건 내 셈으로 달아라. **4** Ⓒ a statement of the way in which money matters, etc. have been dealt with. (금전의) 명세(서); 계정〔청구〕서. ¶ *ask* 〔*demand*〕 *an* ~ 청구서를 요구하다 / *render an* ~ 결산 보고를 하다. **5** Ⓤ esteem; worth; value; importance. 가치; 중요성. ¶ *a matter of great* ~ 아주 중요한 일 / *a person of some* ~ 중요한 사람 / *hold something in great* ~ …을 중시하다 / *make much* 〔*little*〕 ~ *of* …을 중시〔경시〕하다. **6** Ⓤ a statement of reasons, causes and grounds; a reason. 이유. ¶ *on a different* ~ 별다른 이유로 / *on this* ~ 이 때문에. **7** Ⓤ profit; advantage; benefit. 이익. ¶ *I find no* ~ *in it.* 그것으론 이익이 안 된다; 채산이〔수지가〕 맞지 않는다. **8** Ⓒ 《*fig.*》 a quarrel; a dispute. 논쟁; 언쟁; 싸움. ¶ *settle* 〔*square*〕 *accounts with someone* 아무에게 원한을 풀다〔갚다〕. **9** 《*arch.*》 God's judgment (after death). 사후(死後)의 신(神)의 심판.

by 〔***from***〕 ***all accounts,*** according to what everyone says. 누구에게 들어봐도; 모두의 이야기로〔의견으로〕 미루어.

call 〔***bring***〕 ***to account,*** **a**) demand an explanation. 해명을 요구하다; 책임을 묻다. **b**) scold. 꾸짖다.

for someone's account =***for account of someone,*** on someone's behalf. …을 위해.

give a good account of, dispose of successfully; speak well of. …을 훌륭히 해내다; …을 칭찬하다.

go to one's account, go to face the last account (i.e. God's judgment); die. 저승으로 가다; 죽다.

lay someone's account with, be prepared for. …을 기대하다; 예기하다.

leave something out of account =take no account of.

make 〔***make no***〕 ***account of,*** think highly 〔nothing〕 of. …을 중시하다〔하지 않다〕.

of account, important. 중요한.

of much account, of much value or importance. 아주 중요한. ¶ *I don't hold him of much* ~. 나는 그를 중요시하지 않는다.

of no account, unimportant; that can be neglected. 중요하지 않은; 시시한. ¶ *That is a matter of no* ~. 그건 중요한 일이 아니다.

on account, as part-payment. (일부) 선금으로서. ¶ *pay money on* ~ 선금을 지불하다.

on account of, because of. …때문에. ¶ *The match was postponed on* ~ *of the weather.*

경기는 날씨 때문에 연기되었다.
on all accounts =***on every account,*** certainly. 아무리 보아도; 무슨 일이 있어도; 꼭.
on my account, for my sake. 나를 위해.
on no account, under no circumstances; never. 결코 …하지 않다〔아니다〕.
on one's own account, on one's own responsibility; for one's own advantage. 자기 책임으로; 자력으로; 자기 이익을 위해.
take account of, make allowance for (something); consider. …을 고려에 넣다.
take something into account, consider; give attention to something. …을 고려에 넣다. ¶ *You must take the fact into ~.* =*You must take ~ of the fact.* 그 사실을 고려해야 한다.
take no account of, do not consider; neglect; overlook. 고려하지 않다; …을 셈에 넣지 않다; 무시하다; 보지 못하고 빠뜨리다.
turn to (***good***) ***account,*** make (something) useful or helpful; get advantage or profit from (something). …을 이용하다. ¶ *He turns everything to good ~.* 그는 모든 것을 잘 이용한다.
— *vt.* (P21) hold to be; consider; estimate; judge. …을 (…라고) 생각하다; 평가하다. ¶ *I ~ myself* (*to be*) *happy.* 나는 내가 행복하다고 생각한다 / *I ~ him honest* 〔*a genius*〕. 나는 그 사람을 정직하다고〔천재라고〕 생각한다. [L. *puto* reckon]
account for, **a**) explain; make (something) plain. …을 설명하다; 밝히다. ¶ *I want you to ~ for every penny you spent.* 당신이 쓴 돈의 명세를 낱낱이 밝혀 주기를 바란다 / *How do you ~ for your absence yesterday?* 자네가 어제 결근한 것은 어떻게 설명하지 / 《*prov.*》 *There is no accounting for tastes.* 오이를 거꾸로 먹어도 제 멋 / *I cannot ~ for it.* 나는 그것을 이해〔설명〕할 수가 없다. **b**) be the reason for (something). …의 원인이다. ¶ *Poor health accounts for his failure.* 건강치 못한 것이 실패의 원인이다. **c**) answer for (a conduct or performance of duty). …에 대한 책임을 지다. ¶ *We ask you to ~ for your conduct.* 우린 당신이 한 행동에 대해 책임지기를 요구한다. **d**) speak for. …을 증명하다. **e**) 《hunting》 make an end of; kill. 잡다; 죽이다. ¶ *The terrier accounted for two of the rabbits.* 테리어는 토끼 두 마리를 잡았다.

ac·count·a·bil·i·ty [əkàuntəbíləti] *n.* Ⓒ the quality or state of being accountable. 책임; 책무(責務).

***ac·count·a·ble** [əkáuntəbəl] *adj.* **1** 《*to, for*》 responsible; answerable. 책임이 있는. ¶ *I am ~ to him for the loss.* 나는 그의 손실에 대한 책임이 있다 / *He is ~ to me for what he does.* 그는 자신이 한 행위에 대해서 나에게 해명할 책임이 있다. **2** that can be explained. 설명할 수 있는; 이상하지 않은. ¶ *Her bad temper is ~ if you remember that she has had a toothache all day.* 온종일 치통에 시달렸다는 것을 알면 그녀의 짜증이 이상할 게 없다.

ac·count·an·cy [əkáuntənsi] *n.* Ⓤ the art of keeping accounts; the profession of an accountant. 회계학; 회계직(職).

ac·count·ant [əkáuntənt] *n.* Ⓒ a person whose business is to inspect and manage business accounts. 회계원; 공인 회계사.

ac·count book [-ˊ-] *n.* a book in which accounts (usu. private) are kept. 회계부(簿); 장부.

ac·count·ing [əkáuntiŋ] *n.* Ⓒ the system of keeping business accounts and its theory. 회계(학).

ac·cou·ter, 《Brit.》 **-tre** [əkú:tər] *vt.* (P6,13) 《usu. in *passive*》 provide (someone) with special equipment and clothes, esp. for military service. …에게 어떤 특수한 복장을 차려 입게 하다; 군장(軍裝)을 시키다. ¶ *Knights were accoutred in armour.* 기사(騎士)들은 무장을 하고 있었다. [F.]

ac·cou·ter·ments, 《Brit.》 **-tre-** [əkú:tərmənts] *n.* 《usu. *pl.*》 **1** a soldier's military equipment, such as a belt, blanket, knapsack, etc. in addition to his actual clothes and weapons. (군인의) 장비; 군장(軍裝); 장구(裝具). **2** one's own clothes. 복장. [↑]

ac·cred·it [əkrédit] *vt.* **1** (P6) 《*to*》 send (an ambassador) with letters of his own government. (대사 등)에게 신임장을 주어 파견하다. ¶ *an accredited minister* 신임(信任) 공사. **2** (P13) 《*to*》 credit; attribute; consider as belonging to. (말 따위)를 …에게 돌리다; …의 것으로 생각하다. ¶ *be accredited with having said it.* 그것을 말한 것으로 간주되다 / *~ the invention of A to B,* A의 발명을 B가 했다고 하다 / *He is accredited with these words.* =*They accredited these words to him.* 그들은 그가 그 의견을 말한 것으로 간주했다. **3** (P6) believe in (someone). …을 믿다. ¶ *They have confidence in him, and anything he says will be accredited.* 그들은 그를 신임하고 있으므로 그가 말하는 것은 믿을 게다. **4** (P6) give authority to; certify. (자격이 있다고) 인정하다; 인가하다. [ad-, L. *credo* believe]

ac·cre·tion [əkrí:ʃən] *n.* **1** Ⓤ increase in size by addition from outside. (외물(外物)의 부착에 의한) 증대. ¶ *Minerals grow by ~.* 광물은 부착에 의해서 커진다. **2** Ⓒ a matter so added. 증가〔증대, 첨가〕(물). ¶ *a welcome ~ to one's income* 반가운 소득의 증대. [ad-, L. *cresco* grow]

ac·cru·al [əkrú:əl] *n.* ⓊⒸ accruing; accretion. 증가; 증대. [↑]

ac·crue [əkrú:] *vi.* (P1) **1** come as a natural result. (자연히) 더해지다; (결과로서) 생기다. ¶ *Ability to think will ~ to you from good habits of study.* 사고 능력은 좋은 학습 습관에서 생긴다. **2** come as a natural increase (esp. of money). (이자 따위가) 생기다. ¶ *interest accruing from principal* 원금에서 붙는 이자 / *Interest accrues from money left in a bank.* 이자는 은행에 맡긴 돈에서 생긴다. [↑]

acct. account.

ac·cul·tur·a·tion [əkʌ̀ltʃəréiʃən] *n.* Ⓤ the modification of culture by contact with an advanced culture. 문화 변용(變容). [ac-, *culture*]

*__ac·cu·mu·late__ [əkjú:mjəlèit] *vt.* (P6) collect; gather; amass. …을 쌓다〔모으다〕; 축적하다. ¶ ~ *wealth* 부(富)를 축적하다 / *He accumulated a large fortune by hard work.* 열심히 일해서 막대한 재산을 모았다. — *vi.* (P1) increase in amount; (of misfortune) fall. 증대하다; (불행 따위가) 쌓이다; 닥치다. ¶ *Dust accumulated on the floor.* 마룻바닥에는 먼지가 쌓여 있었다 / 《*fig.*》 *Disaster accumulated round his path.* 그의 앞길에는 재난이 겹쳐 있었다. [ad-, L. *cumulus* heap]

ac·cu·mu·la·tion [əkjù:mjəléiʃən] *n.* **1** Ⓤ the act or process of accumulating. 축적. ¶ *the* ~ *of wealth* 부의 축적. **2** Ⓒ 《often in rather a bad sense》 things accumulated; a collection; a mass. 축적물. ¶ *an* ~ *of freight* 체화물(滯貨物) / *an* ~ *of odds and ends in the attic* 고미다락의 잡동사니의 더미 / *an* ~ *of old papers* 묵은 신문지 더미.

ac·cu·mu·la·tive [əkjú:mjəlèitiv, -lət-] *adj.* tending to accumulate. 축적의; 축적적〔누적적〕인; 증대하는.

ac·cu·mu·la·tor [əkjú:mjəlèitər] *n.* Ⓒ **1** a person or thing that accumulates. 축적〔축재〕자. **2** 《mech.》 an apparatus to collect and store energy. 축력(蓄力) 장치; 축압기. **3** 《Brit.》 a storage battery. 축전지.

*__ac·cu·ra·cy__ [ǽkjərəsi] *n.* Ⓒ the state or quality of being accurate. 정확; 정밀; 엄밀. ¶ *with* ~ 정확히. [↓]

*__ac·cu·rate__ [ǽkjərit] *adj.* **1** (of a person) careful not to make errors; exact. 주의 깊은; 정확한. ¶ *He is* ~ *in all he does.* 그 사람은 자신이 하는 모든 일에 정확하다. **2** (of a statement) free from errors or mistakes; exactly true. (이야기 따위가) 정확한. ¶ ~ *statements* 정확한 진술 / *an* ~ *account of what happened* 일어난 일에 관한 정확한 설명. **3** (of a machine, instrument) working with accuracy; giving exact results. (기계 장치가) 정확한; 정밀한. ¶ ~ *machines* 정밀한 기계 / *an* ~ *watch* 정확한 시계. [ad-, L. *cura* care]

*__ac·cu·rate·ly__ [ǽkjəritli] *adv.* in an accurate manner. 정확히; 틀림없이.

ac·curs·ed [əkə́:rsid, əkə́:rst], **-curst** [əkə́:rst] *adj.* **1** cursed; under a curse. 저주받은. **2** filled with hatred. 증오할; 가증스러운. ¶ *an* ~ *deed* 증오할 행위. **3** 《*colloq.*》 troublesome; detestable. 싫은; 지겨운. [ab-, →curse]

*__ac·cu·sa·tion__ [æ̀kjuzéiʃən] *n.* **1** ⓊⒸ the act of accusing or being accused. 비난; 힐책. **2** Ⓒ a charge of doing something wrong or having broken the law. 죄목; 혐의. ¶ *The* ~ *against him was that he had stolen money from the shop.* 그의 죄목은 가게에서 돈을 훔쳤다는 것이었다. **3** Ⓒ 《law》 an indictment. 고발; 고소; 기소. ¶ *be under an* ~ 기소되어 있다 / *bring an* ~ *against someone* 아무를 고발하다. [→accuse]

ac·cu·sa·tive [əkjú:zətiv] *n., adj.* 《gram.》 (of) the objective case. 대격(對格)(의).

ac·cu·sa·to·ry [əkjú:zətɔ̀:ri / -təri] *adj.* of accusation. 비난의.

*__ac·cuse__ [əkjú:z] *vt.* (P6,13) **1** find fault with (someone); blame. …을 책(責)하다; 비난하다. ¶ *He accused me because of my mistake.* 그는 나의 과실을 비난했다. **2** charge (someone) with having broken the law. …을 고발하다; 기소하다. ¶ ~ *someone of a crime* 아무를 범죄 혐의로 고발하다 / *be accused of stealing money* 돈을 훔친 혐의로 기소되다 / ~ *falsely* 무고하다 / *Your looks* ~ *you.* 네 얼굴에 네 죄상이 드러나 있다. [ad-, L. *causa* lawsuit]

ac·cused [əkjú:zd] *n.* 《*the* ~》 the person who is charged with guilt in a court of law. 피고(opp. accuser; cf. *defendant*). ¶ *Bring forth the* ~. 피고를 데려오라.

ac·cus·er [əkjú:zər] *n.* Ⓒ **1** a person who brings a charge against others. 고발자; 원고(opp. the accused). **2** a person who blames others. 비난자.

*__ac·cus·tom__ [əkʌ́stəm] *vt.* (P13) 《*to*》 get (a person or an animal) used to or familiar with. …에 익숙해지게 하다. ¶ ~ *a dog to racing* 개를 경주에 습관들이다 / ~ *a child to sleeping alone* 어린이가 혼자 자기에 익숙해지도록 하다 / *You can* ~ *yourself to almost any kind of food.* 너는 어떤 종류의 음식에도 익숙해질 수 있다 / *She will soon* ~ *herself to the school.* 그는 곧 학교에 익숙해질 것이다. [ad-, →custom, L. *suesco* be accustomed]

be accustomed to, be〔get〕 used to; be in the habit of. 익숙해져〔습관이 되어〕 있다. ¶ *He is accustomed to staying up late.* 그는 늦게까지 안 자는 데 익숙해져 있다.

ac·cus·tomed [əkʌ́stəmd] *adj.* usual; habitual. 예의; 익숙한. ¶ *one's* ~ *way* 예의 방식 / *sit one's* ~ *seat* 늘 앉는 자리에 앉다.

AC/DC [èisi:dí:si:] *adj.* 《*sl.*》 sexually attracted to men and women. (사람이) 양성(兩性)에 대하여 성욕을 가지는; 양성의.

ace [eis] *n.* Ⓒ **1** a single spot on a card, domino, or side of a die. (카드·주사위눈의) 1; 에이스. ¶ *the* ~ *of spades* 스페이드의 1. **2** a person with great skill. (무엇에나) 제1인자; 명수. ¶ *an* ~ *at chess* 체스의 명수 / *a football* ~ 축구의 에이스. **3** a first-class fighting aviator. 하늘의 용사. ¶ *a*

flying ~ 공군의 에이스.
an ace in the hole, 《colloq.》 a man or thing helpful in an emergency. 만일의 경우에 도움이 되는 사람〔것〕.
within an ace of, escaping from something by a hair's breadth. 하마터면〔자칫〕 …하려던 참에. ¶ *He came within an* ~ *of death* 〔*of being killed*〕. 그는 하마터면 죽을 뻔했다.
— *adj.* 《colloq.》 first-class; expert. 일류의. ¶ *an* ~ *athlete* 일류의 선수. [L. *as* unity]

-a·ce·ous [-éiʃəs] *suf.* of the nature of. '…의 성질을 갖는'의 뜻. ¶ *cretaceous.* [L.]

a·cerb [əsə́:*r*b] *adj.* =acerbic.

ac·er·bate [ǽsə*r*bèit] *vt.* (**-bat·ed, -bat·ing**) (P6) embitter; exasperate. …을 시게 하다; 쓰게 하다. [→acerbity]

a·cer·bic [əsə́:*r*bik] *adj.* (of a person or manner) clever in a rather crues way. (사람 또는 태도가) 격한; 모진; 신랄한. [↓]

a·cer·bi·ty [əsə́:*r*bəti] *n.* Ⓒ **1** a sharp taste; sourness. 떫음; 심. **2** severe and bitter quality of words, manner, or temper. (언동의) 신랄함; 날카로움. [L. *acer* sharp, bitter]

ac·e·tab·u·lum [æ̀sətǽbjələm] *n.* (*pl.* **-la** [-lə]) 《anat.》 the socket in the hipbone. 비구(髀臼). [L. =vinegar cup]

ac·e·tate [ǽsətèit] *n.* Ⓤ 《chem.》 a salt of acetic acid. 아세트산염(酸塩). ¶ ~ *rayon* 아세테이트 레이온〔인견(人絹)〕. [L. *acetum* vinegar]

a·ce·tic [əsí:tik, əsét-] *adj.* having the taste of acid; of acid. 맛이 신; 초(醋)의. ¶ ~ *acid* 아세트산(酸) / ~ *anhydride* 아세트산 무수물(無水物). [↑]

a·cet·i·fy [əsétəfài, əsí:tə-] *vt.* (**-fied, -fy·ing**) (P6) turn into vinegar. …을 초(醋)가 되게 하다.

ac·e·tone [ǽsətòun] *n.* Ⓤ 《chem.》 a colorless liquid used as a solvent. 아세톤. [*acetate*]

ac·e·tous [ǽsətəs, əsí:-] *adj.* 아세트산(酸)의. [↑]

a·cet·y·lene [əsétəlì:n, -lin] *n.* Ⓤ a colorless gas with a strong odor that burns brightly with a very hot flame. 아세틸렌 (가스). [↑]

A·chae·a [əkí:ə] *n.* an ancient country in Greece. 아카이아《고대 그리스의 한 지방》.
● **A·chae·an** [-ən] *adj.* [Gk.]

***ache** [eik] *vi.* **1** (P1) have a continuous pain. 아프다; 쑤시다. ¶ *My ear aches.* 귀가 아프다 / *I am aching all over.* 전신이 쑤신다. **2** (P1) feel sympathy, pity, etc. (동정·가엾음으로) 마음이 아프다. ¶ *My heart aches.* 마음이 아프다 / *Her heart ached for the poor child.* 그 가여운 아이 때문에 그녀의 가슴이 아팠다. **3** (P4) 《colloq.》《for》 wish very much. …하고 싶어 못 견디다; 갈망하다. ¶ *She ached to be near him.* 그녀는 그 사람 곁에 있기를 갈망했다 / *I am aching to get home.* 집에 가고 싶어 몸살이 난다.
— *n.* ⒸⓊ 《often in *compounds*》 a continuous pain. 아픔. ¶ *have a headache* 두통이 있다. [E.]

Ach·er·on [ǽkərɑ̀n / -rɔ̀n] *n.* a fabled river of Hades. 삼도(三途)내. [Gk.]

:a·chieve [ətʃí:v] *vt.* (P6) **1** do successfully; accomplish. …을 이루다; 완수〔성취〕하다 (opp. fail). ¶ *We have achieved all that we expected.* 우리는 기대했던 모든 것을 성취했다. **2** gain (something) by effort. …을 거두다; 얻다. ¶ ~ *one's purpose* 〔*object*〕 목적을 이루다 / ~ *success* 성공을 거두다. [L. *ad caput venio* come to a head with]

***a·chieve·ment** [ətʃí:vmənt] *n.* **1** Ⓤ the act of achieving. 달성; 성취. **2** Ⓒ something achieved. 달성한 것; 위업; 업적; 성적. ¶ *an* ~ *test* 학력 고사 / *Flying across the Atlantic for the first time was a great* ~. 최초의 대서양 횡단 비행은 위대한 업적이었다.

A·chil·les(') tendon [əkíli:z téndən] *n.* the tendon which joins the calf muscles to the heelbone. 아킬레스건(腱). [Gk.]

ach·ro·mat·ic [æ̀krəmǽtik] *adj.* colorless. 무색의. ¶ *an* ~ *lens* 색지움 렌즈. [Gk. *a-* not]

***ac·id** [ǽsid] *n.* **1** ⓊⒸ a chemical substance with a sour taste which turns blue litmus paper red. 산(酸). **2** Ⓒ a substance with a sour taste. (맛이) 신 것. **3** 《sl.》 the drug LSD. 마약《환각제》.
— *adj.* **1** having the qualities of acid. 산(酸)의; 산성의. **2** having a sour and bitter taste. (맛이) 신. ¶ *Lemons are an* ~ *fruit.* 레몬은 맛이 신 과일이다. **3** (of manner, temper, etc.) ill-natured; sharp; unpleasant. (태도 등이) 심술궂은; 신랄한; 불쾌한. ¶ *an* ~ *reply* 신랄한 대답. [L. *acidus* sour, sharp →-ity, -ify, etc.]

a·cid·i·fy [əsídəfài] *vt.* (**-fied**) (P6) **1** make (something) sour. …을 시게 하다. **2** change (something) into an acid. …을 산성화하다. — *vi.* (P1) turn sour. 시어지다.

ac·i·dim·e·ter [æ̀sədímitə*r*] *n.* 《chem.》 an instrument measuring the strength of acids. 산정량기(酸定量器).

a·cid·i·ty [əsídəti] *n.* Ⓒ the acid quality or condition. 산미(酸味); 산성.

ac·i·do·sis [æ̀sədóusis] *n.* acid condition of blood. 산혈증(酸血症); 산중독.

acid rain [⌐–⌐] *n.* Ⓤ rain containing harmful quantities of acid as a result of industrial pollution. 산성비.

acid test [⌐– ⌐], **the** *n.* 《fig.》 the final test of the value or quality of a thing or person (from testing a metal by means of an acid to see whether it is gold or not). (시금(試金)을 위한) 아세트산 시험; (가치·품격 등의) 최종 시험.

a·cid·u·lat·ed [əsídʒəlèitid] *adj.* **1** made rather sour. 산미(酸味)를 띤. ¶ ~ *drops* 맛이 신 드롭스. **2** having a sour temper.

(기질 등이) 사근사근하지 않은; 까다로운. ¶ *an ~ old maid* 까다로운 하녀. [*acid*]

a·cid·u·lous [əsídʒələs] *adj.* **1** somewhat acid; slightly sour. 조금 신; 시큼한. **2** sharp; caustic. 날카로운; 신랄한; 통렬한.

ack-ack [ǽkæ̀k] *adj., n.* anti-aircraft (gun). 대공(對空)(의); 고사포. [*antiaircraft*]

ack em·ma [ǽk émə] *n.* **1** ante meridiem. 오전. **2** an air-mechanic. 항공 수리공(工). [A.M.]

·ac·knowl·edge [æknálidʒ, ik- / -nɔ́l-] *vt.* (P6,7,9,11,21) **1** 《*as*》 admit (something) to be true. …을 인정〔시인〕하다(opp. deny). ¶ *~ one's fault* 자기의 잘못을 인정하다 / *be acknowledged to be true* 사실이라고 인정되다 / *~ the news as false* 그 뉴스가 거짓말임을 인정하다 / *He did not ~ that he stole my watch. =He did not ~ having stolen my watch.* 그는 내 시계를 훔쳤음을 시인하지 않았다. **2** recognize the authority or claims of. (권위·주장 등)을 인정하다; 승인하다. ¶ *~ the rights of others* 남의 권리를 인정하다 / *I ~ you to be my superior.* 당신이 나의 상사라는 것을 인정합니다. **3** make known that one has received (something). (영수·도착 따위)를 알리다. ¶ *I beg to ~ your letter.* 주신 편지를 정히 받았습니다. **4** express thanks for (something). …에 대해 감사하다. ¶ *~ a letter* 편지에 대해 감사하다 / *~ gifts* 선물을 고마워하다. [ad-, →knowledge]

ac·knowl·edg·ment, 《Brit.》 **-edge·ment** [æknálidʒmənt, ik- / -nɔ́l-] *n.* **1** Ⓤ the act of acknowledging. 승인; 시인. ¶ *The man made ~ of his guilt.* 그 사나이는 자기의 죄를 시인했다. **2** Ⓒ an official document of acknowledging; a receipt. 승인장; 영수증. ¶ *A receipt is the ~ that a bill has been paid.* 영수증은 돈이 지불되었다는 증표이다. **3** ⓊⒸ an expression of thanks; something given or done for a service, favor, message, etc. 감사(의 표시). ¶ *a small ~ of kindness received* 얼마 안 되지만 고맙게 받았다는 표시.

a·clin·ic [eiklínik] *adj.* free from inclination. 무경각(無傾角)의. [Gk. *a-* not, *clinō* bend]

ac·me [ǽkmi] *n.* Ⓤ 《*the ~* 》 the top or highest point. 절정; 극치. ¶ *reach the ~ of perfection* 완벽의 극에 달하다. [Gk. *acmē* point]

ac·ne [ǽkni] *n.* a pimple. 여드름. [Gk.]

ac·o·lyte [ǽkəlàit] *n.* Ⓒ **1** a person who attends in public worship and helps a priest. (미사 때 신부를 돕는) 복사(服事). **2** an assistant. 조수. [Gk. =follower]

A·con·ca·gua [à:kɔ:ŋká:gwɑ: / æ̀kənká:gwə] *n.* a mountain in Argentina, the highest peak in the Western Hemisphere. 아콩카과 산(山). [Sp.]

ac·o·nite [ǽkənàit] *n.* **1** Ⓒ 《bot.》 a poisonous plant. 바곳. **2** Ⓤ a drug obtained from this plant. 아코니트《진정제》. [Gk.]

:a·corn [éikɔ:rn, -kərn] *n.* Ⓒ the fruit or nut of an oak tree. 도토리; 상수리. [E.]

a·cot·y·le·don [eikɑ̀təlí:dən, eikɑ̀t- / -kɔ̀t-] *n.* 《bot.》 a plant without cotyledons. 무자엽(無子葉) 식물. [Gk. *a-* not, *kotulē* cup]

a·cous·tic [əkú:stik], **-ti·cal** [-əl] *adj.* **1** of sound or the sense of hearing. 청각의. ¶ *~ nerves* 청(聽)신경 / *~ education* 음감(音感) 교육 / *Earphones are ~ aids for deaf people.* 이어폰은 귀먹은 사람들의 청각 보조 기구다. **2** of the science of sound. 음향학의. [Gk. *akouō* hear]

acoustic coupler [-⌒- ⌒-] *n.* 《tech.》 an instrument which allows computers to send and receive information through a telephone; a simple type of modem. 음향 커플러《데이터 통신에서 변복조(變復調) 장치의 하나》.

a·cous·tics [əkú:stiks] *n. pl.* **1** 《used as *sing.*》 the science of sound. 음향학. **2** the qualities of a room, hall, etc., that determine how clearly sound can be heard in it. (극장 따위의) 음향 효과. ¶ *The ~ of this room is* 〔*are*〕 *very poor.* 이 방의 음향 효과는 아주 빈약하다.

·ac·quaint [əkwéint] *vt.* (P13) **1** 《*with, of*》 tell; let know. …에게 알리다; …에게 고하다. ¶ *~ someone with the facts of the case* 아무에게 사건의 진상을 알리다 / *Did you ~ him with the fact?* 그에게 사실을 알렸는가. **2** 《*with*》 make (someone) known; make familiar; introduce. …에게 알게 하다; 숙지시키다; 소개하다. ¶ *Let me make you* (*two*) *acquainted.* 두 분을 소개합니다. [→cognizance]

acquaint** oneself **with, obtain information about. …을 알다; …에 통하다; …을 자세히 알다.

be* 〔*get, become*〕 *acquainted with, **a**) have personal knowledge of (someone). …와 아는 사이이다〔가 되다〕. ¶ *I have heard about your friend, but I am not acquainted with him.* 네 친구에 관해서는 들어서 알고는 있지만 안면은 없다. **b**) be familiar with (something). …에 정통해〔…을 훤히 알고〕 있다. ¶ *He is well acquainted with history.* 그는 역사에 밝다.

make (*someone*) ***acquainted with,*** inform of; introduce to. (아무에게) …을 알리다; (아무를) …에게 소개하다.

·ac·quaint·ance [əkwéintəns] *n.* **1** Ⓤ knowledge through experience. 알고 있음; 지식; 면식; 교제. ¶ *gain ~ with something* …을 알다 / *I have a slight* 〔*no*〕 *~ with him.* 나는 그를 좀 안다〔전혀 모른다〕. **2** Ⓒ a person whom one knows to some extent; 《*collectively*》 such persons. 아는 사람; 지인(知人). ¶ *a nodding ~* 만나면 인사할 정도의 안면 / *renew one's ~* 구교(舊交)를 돈독히 하다 / *have a wide circle of acquaintances* 교제 범위가〔안면이〕 넓다 / *He is not a* *friend of mine, but only an* ～. 그는 내 친구는 아니고 그저 아는 사이에 지나지 않는다. [↑]

make the acquaintance of** someone* = ***make** someone's **acquaintance, become friends with someone. …와 아는 사이가 되다.

strike up an acquaintance (=*become friendly*) ***with** someone.* …와 친(밀)해지다.

ac·quaint·ance·ship [əkwéintənsʃìp] *n.* Ⓤ the state of being socially acquainted. 면식; 친면.

ac·quaint·ed [əkwéintid] *adj.* **1** ⟪usu. *with*⟫ having acquaintance; having personal knowledge; informed. 안면이 있는; (정보를) 알고 있는. **2** brought into social contact; made familiar. 서로 아는; 친(숙)해진. ¶ *make oneself* ～ *with* …와 친밀해지다.

ac·qui·esce [æ̀kwiés] *vi.* (P1,3) ⟪*in*⟫ give consent silently 〔unwillingly〕; agree. 묵인하다; (제안·계획 따위에) 묵묵히〔마지못해〕 따르다. ¶ *He will never* ～. 결코 잠자코 따르지는 않을 게다 / *They have acquiesced in his resignation.* 그들은 그의 사의(辭意)를 묵낙(默諾)했다. [ad-, L. *quies* quiet]

ac·qui·es·cence [æ̀kwiésəns] *n.* Ⓤ the act of consenting or agreeing quietly. 묵낙(默諾); (마지못한) 동의.

ac·qui·es·cent [æ̀kwiésənt] *adj.* agreeing quietly. 묵묵히 따르는; 묵낙(默諾)의.

:ac·quire [əkwáiər] *vt.* (P6) **1** get (something) by effort; gain or get by oneself. …을 얻다; 배우다; (혼자 힘으로) 얻다. ¶ ～ *a knowledge of English* 영어를 습득하다 / ～ *a bad reputation* 악평을 얻다 / *He acquired a name for honesty.* 그는 정직하다는 평을 얻었다. **2** obtain (something) as one's own. …을 (제것으로서) 획득하다; 얻다; (몸에) 붙다. ¶ ～ *land by purchase* 토지를 매입하다 / ～ *wealth* 〔*a title*〕 부를〔타이틀을〕 얻다 / *an acquired taste* 몸에 익힌 취미. [ad-, L. *quaero* seek]

ac·quire·ment [əkwáiərmənt] *n.* **1** Ⓤ the act of acquiring. (학문·학술 따위의) 습득; 획득. **2** Ⓒ ⟪often *pl.*⟫ something acquired by learning or practice. (배워·훈련으로) 얻은 것; 학예; 재능. ¶ *I am proud of my son's acquirements.* 아들의 학식이 자랑스럽다 / *Her musical acquirements are remarkable for a girl of her age.* 그 나이의 소녀로서는 음악적 재능이 주목할 만하다.

ac·qui·si·tion [æ̀kwəzíʃən] *n.* **1** Ⓤ the act of gaining as one's own. (재산·학문·재능 따위의) 획득; 취득. ¶ *the* ～ *of wealth* 부(富)의 획득. **2** Ⓒ something gained or acquired. 획득〔취득〕한 것. ¶ *recent acquisitions to the library* 도서관의 신착 서적 / *The new member is a distinct* ～ *to the party.* 그 새 멤버는 그 당에 뛰어난 재목감이다. [→acquire]

ac·quis·i·tive [əkwízətiv] *adj.* **1** eager to get and keep as one's own. (지식·부 따위를) 제것으로 하려는; 탐내는; 욕심 많은. ¶ *an* ～ *person* 욕심 많은 사람 / *an* ～ *mind* 향학심; 탐욕 / *the* ～ *society* 이익 추구 사회. **2** ready to steal. 훔치려 드는. ¶ *He has rather* ～ *fingers.* 그의 손은 어지간히 도벽이 있다.

be acquisitive of, be able to acquire; be fond of acquiring. 얻을 수 있는; …을 얻고 싶어하는. ¶ *He is* ～ *of new ideas.* 그는 새로운 아이디어를 얻고 싶어한다.

● **ac·quis·i·tive·ly** [-li] *adv.* **ac·quis·i·tive·ness** [-nis] *n.* [↑]

ac·quit [əkwít] *vt.* (**-quit·ted, -quit·ting**) (P6,13) **1** ⟪*of*⟫ set (someone) free from a charge of crime or from duty. …을 무죄 방면하다; (책임 따위를 아무로부터) 면제하다. ¶ *They acquitted him of the charge.* 그들은 그를 방면했다 / *The man was acquitted of the crime.* 그 사람은 무죄 석방되었다. **2** ⟪*reflexively*⟫ behave; conduct; do one's part. 행동하다; (역할을) 수행하다. ¶ ～ *oneself well in the game* 경기에서 활약하다 / ～ *oneself very badly* 졸렬(拙劣)하게 행동하다. [L. *quies* quiet]

ac·quit·tal [əkwítəl] *n.* ⓊⒸ **1** the performance of a duty, etc. (의무 따위의) 수행. **2** ⟪law⟫ a decision freeing a person from a charge of crime. 석방; 방면(opp. conviction).

ac·quit·tance [əkwítəns] *n.* **1** Ⓤ freedom from a debt or duty. (채무·의무 따위의) 면제; 변제. **2** Ⓒ a record showing that a debt has been paid. 채무 변제 증서; 영수증.

:a·cre [éikər] *n.* Ⓒ **1** a unit of measure of land equal to 43,560 square feet. 에이커 ⟪4,046.8 평방미터⟫. **2** ⟪*pl.*⟫ lands. 토지; 땅. ¶ *broad acres* 넓은 땅. [E. =tilled land]

a·cre·age [éikəridʒ] *n.* Ⓤ the number of acres; the area of land measured in acres. 에이커 수(數); 면적. ¶ *the* ～ *under cultivation* 경작 면적 / *The* ～ *of this park is over 800.* 이 공원의 면적은 800 에이커가 넘는다.

ac·rid [ǽkrid] *adj.* **1** bitter and stinging to the mouth or nose. (맛·냄새 따위가) 쓴; 톡 쏘는. ¶ *the* ～ *smoke of gasoline* 휘발유의 독한 연기 / *Most acids have an* ～ *taste.* 대개의 산(酸)은 신맛이 있다. **2** bitter or sharp in manner, temper, or speech; caustic. (언동·성질 등이) 신랄한; 독살맞은; 심술 사나운. ¶ ～ *remarks* 신랄한 말 / *He was angry, and spoke in an extremely* ～ *way.* 그는 성이 나서 극도의 독살스런 투로 말했다. [L. *acer* keen]

Ac·ri·lan [ǽkrəlæ̀n] *n.* an acrylic fiber which is soft, strong and wrinkle resistant. 아크릴란⟪아크릴계 섬유⟫. [Trade name]

ac·ri·mo·ni·ous [æ̀krəmóuniəs] *adj.* sharp or bitter in temper, language, or manner. 신랄한; 독살스러운; 매서운. [→acrid]

ac·ri·mo·ny [ǽkrəmòuni] *n.* Ⓤ sharpness or bitterness of temper, language, or manner. (성질·언어·태도 따위의) 신랄함; 독살맞음.

ac·ro·bat [ǽkrəbæ̀t] *n.* Ⓒ a person who can do skillful and bold exercises, such as walking on a tight rope. 곡예사. [Gk. *acros* on tiptoe, *bainō* go]

ac·ro·bat·ic [æ̀krəbǽtik] *adj.* of an acrobat or like his tricks. 곡예(사)의. ¶ *an* ~ *dance* 곡예적인 춤 / ~ *feats* 곡예 / *Dancing on a rope is an* ~ *feat.* 밧줄 위에서의 춤추기는 곡예이다.

ac·ro·bat·ics [æ̀krəbǽtiks] *n. pl.* **1** 《used as *sing.*》 the art and tricks of an acrobat. 곡예(술). **2** a group of acrobatic tricks considered as a performance. (곡예에서의) 일련의 묘기. ¶ *aerial* ~ 공중 곡예.

ac·ro·bat·ism [ǽkrəbæ̀tizəm] *n.* Ⓤ acrobatic art. 곡예.

ac·ro·meg·a·ly [æ̀krəmégəli] *n.* Ⓤ 《med.》 a disease in which the tip of the limbs becomes enlarged. 말단 비대증. [Gk. *acros* at the end, *megalie* large]

ac·ro·nym [ǽkrənìm] *n.* Ⓒ a word formed from the first letters of other words. 약성어(略成語); 머리글자어(語)《e.g. UNESCO = *U*nited *N*ations *E*ducational, *S*cientific, and *C*ultural *O*rganization》. [Gk. *onoma* name]

a·crop·o·lis [əkrápəlis / -rɔ́p-] *n.* **1** Ⓒ the high, fortified part of a Greek city. (그리스 도시의) 성채(城砦). **2** 《*the A-*》 the fortified hill of Athens. (아테네의) 성채 언덕. [Gk. *acros* highest, *polis* city]

:a·cross [əkrɔ́:s, əkrás] *adv.* **1** from one side to the other; to or on the other side. 이쪽에서 저쪽까지; 지름으로; …을 건너; 가로질러. ¶ *What is the distance* ~*?* 저쪽까지의 거리는〔너비는, 지름은〕 얼마나 되나 / *The lake is 5 miles* ~. 호수는 너비가 5마일이다 / *He swam* ~ *twice.* 그는 두 번이나 헤엄쳐 건넜다. **2** so as to cross; in the form of a cross. 열십자로 어긋매껴; 교차하여. ¶ *with arms* ~ 팔짱을 끼고 / *knives laid* ~ 어긋매껴 놓은 칼들.

across from, 《U.S.》 opposite. …의 맞은편〔쪽〕에. ¶ *The store is just* ~ *from the station.* 그 가게는 정거장 바로 맞은편에 있다.

— *prep.* **1** to the other side of; from one side to the other of. 횡단하여; 가로질러; …의 저쪽으로. ¶ *walk* ~ *a street* 거리를 걸어서 건너다 / *a bridge* ~ *the river* 강을 건너질러 놓은 다리. **2** to or on the other side of; beyond. …의 저쪽〔맞은편, 건너편〕에. ¶ *He lives* ~ *the river.* 그는 강 건너에 살고 있다 / *His house is just* ~ *the street.* 그의 집은 바로 길 건너에 있다. **3** forming a cross upon. …와 어긋매껴〔교차하여〕; …와 열십자를 이루어. ¶ *He lay with his arms* ~ *his breast.* 그는 팔짱을 끼고 누웠다. [→cross, L. *crux* a cross]

across country, direct from point to point; not following the roads. (도로로 가지 않고) 들판을 횡단하여〔가로질러〕.

be across a horse's back, ride on a horse. 말을 타고 있다.

come across (= *happen to meet* or *find*) *someone or something.* …을〔와〕 우연히 만나다〔발견하다〕. ¶ *He came* ~ *an old friend.* 옛 친구를 우연히 만났다.

get across, quarrel with. …와 말다툼하다.

a·cros·tic [əkrɔ́:stik, -rás-] *n.* Ⓒ an arrangement of words in which the first, last, or certain other letters of each line, taken in order, spell a word or phrase. 이합체(離合體)의 시(詩). — *adj.* of or forming an acrostic. 이합체 시(詩)의. [Gk.]

a·cryl·ic [əkrílik] *adj.* 《chem.》 of or pertaining to an acid used in certain plastics, as lucite and plexiglass, and in paints. 아크릴 산(酸)의; 아크릴(성)의. [Gk.]

acrylic acid [-´- ´-] *n.* 《chem.》 any of a series of acids having a sharp, acrid odor, and used in plastics. 아크릴산(酸).

acrylic resin [-´- ´-] *n.* 《chem.》 a glassy thermoplastic used for cast and molded parts or as coatings and adhesives. 아크릴 수지(樹脂).

:act [ækt] *n.* Ⓒ **1** a thing done; a deed. 소행; 행위. ¶ *an* ~ *of kindness* 친절한 행위. **2** 《*the* ~》 the process of doing something. 행동(중); 현행(現行). ¶ *The robber was caught*〔*taken*〕 *in the* ~. 강도는 현장에서 잡혔다. **3** a section of a play or drama. (극·오페라 따위의) 막. ¶ *a comedy in three acts* 3막짜리 희극 / *Act II, scene iii* 제 2 막 제 3 장. **4** 《often *A-*》 a law passed by a lawmaking body. 법령; 조례. ¶ *an Act of Congress* 법령. **5** each part in a television program, variety show, etc. (텔레비전이나 쇼의) 프로그램 중의 하나. **6** 《*colloq.*》 a piece of affected or insincere conduct; pretended behavior. 짐짓 꾸민 행동; 연극; 시늉. ¶ *put on an* ~ (어떤 효과를 노리고) 연극〔시늉〕을 하다.

an act 〔***Act***〕 ***of God,*** 《law》 an accident due to natural forces which could not be controlled. 불가항력; 천재(天災).

an act of grace, **a**) something done out of kindness or of one's own free will. 관대한 행위〔조처〕. **b**) a formal pardon granted to a number of offenders. 일반 사면.

act of war, an illegal act of aggression. 불법 침입.

in the (***very***) ***act of doing,*** while one is doing. …의 현행(現行) 중에; …을 하는 현장에서. ¶ *find someone in the* (*very*) ~ *of stealing* 아무의 절도 현장을 발견하다 / *The thief was caught in the* (*very*) ~ *of taking the money.* 도둑은 돈을 훔치던 현장에서 잡혔다.

the Acts (***of the Apostles***), the fifth book of the New Testament. (신약 성서의) 사도 행

전.

— *vt.* (P6) **1** play the part of (something); perform. (극)을 상연하다; …의 역을 맡아 하다. ¶ ~ *'Romeo and Juliet'* "로미오와 줄리엣"을 상연하다 / ~ *the Queen in 'Hamlet'* "햄릿"에서 여왕역을 맡아 하다 / *She acted Nora well.* 그녀는 노라역을 잘 해냈다 / *The company acted many of Shakespeare's plays.* 그 극단은 많은 세익스피어극을 상연했다. **2** ⓐ behave like (something). …처럼 행동하다[굴다]. ¶ ~ *the fool* [*ass*] 바보같이 굴다 / *Don't* ~ *the child.* 어린애처럼 굴지 마라. ⓑ make a false show of; pretend. 짐짓 …인 체하다; …을 가장하다. ¶ ~ *a part* 어떤 역을 하다; (나쁜 뜻으로) …인 체하다. **3** play the part of in real life. (실생활에서의) 역할을 하다. ¶ ~ *one's part* 자기 역할[책임]을 하다 / ~ *one's age* 제 나이에 맞게 행동하다.

— *vi.* (P1,2A,3) **1** conduct oneself; behave; carry into effect. 행동하다; 실행하다; 굴다. ¶ ~ *wisely* [*wildly, foolishly*] 현명하게[사납게, 어리석게] 굴다 / ~ *like a lady* 귀부인같이 행동하다 / ~ *strangely* [*a sort of queer*] 이상[야릇]하게 굴다 / ~ *quickly in an emergency* 유사시에 재빨리 행동하다. **2** produce effects; work. 작용하다; (약 따위가) 듣다; (계획 등이) 잘 되어가다. **3** operate; function. (기계가) 돌다; 움직이다; 작동하다. ¶ *The machine won't* ~. 기계가 움직이지 않는다 / *The brakes failed to* ~. 브레이크가 작동하지 않았다. **4** perform on the stage as an actor. (극무대 등에서) 연기하다; 출연하다. ¶ ~ *in a play* [*film*] 극[영화]에 출연하다. **5** pretend; feign. …인 체하다; 가장하다. ¶ ~ *rich* 부자를 가장하다 / ~ *intoxicated* 취한 척하다. **6** serve as; do the work of. …로서 직무를 다하다; 대행[대리]하다. **7** be able to be acted or performed. (극이) 상연에 적합하다. ¶ *His plays don't* ~ *well.* 그의 희곡은 상연에 적합하지 않다. [L. *ago* do]

act against, violate. (법률 따위에) 저촉하다; 범하다.

act as (=*do the work of*) *someone* or *something.* …로서 그 역할[구실]을 하다. ¶ ~ *as a brake* 브레이크 노릇을 하다 / ~ *as guide* [*chairman*] 안내원[의장]을 맡아보다 / ~ *as go-between* 중매를 들다; 중개자 노릇을 하다 [語法] as 다음의 단수 보통 명사에는 흔히 관사가 붙지 않음.

act for, **a**) take someone's place. …의 대리를 보다; …을 대행하다. ¶ *He acted for his absent brother.* 그는 부재 중인 형의 대리를 보았다. **b**) do (someone) a service. …을 위해 (행)하다.

act on [***upon***]***,*** **a**) act in accordance with; follow; obey. …에 따라 행동하다; 따르다. ¶ ~ *on one's faith* [*responsibility*] 신념[책임감]에 따라 행동하다 / ~ *on someone's advice* 아무의 충고에 따라 행동하다. **b**) have an effect on; work on; influence. …에 영향을 미치다; 작용하다; …에 듣다. ¶ *Acids* ~ *on metals.* 산(酸)은 금속에 작용한다 / *The medicine acts well.* 그 약은 잘 듣는다 / *I will* ~ *on your suggestion.* 네 제안에 따르겠다.

act up, 《*colloq.*》 act in an unusual or unexpected manner; behave playfully or mischievously. 뜻밖의[부자연스런] 행동을 하다; 무례한 짓[장난]을 하다.

act up to, prove by action to be worthy of; act in accordance with; live up to. (주의·이상·약속 따위를) 지키다; 실행하다; …에 따르다; …에 따라 행동하다. ¶ ~ *up to one's reputation* [*principles*] 기대[주의]에 어긋나지 않도록 행동하다 / ~ *up to the letter of an agreement* 합의 문서 조항을 지키다.

·**act·ing** [ǽktiŋ] *adj.* **1** doing duties in place of someone else. 대리의. ¶ *an* ~ *manager* 지배인 대리 / *an* ~ *principal* 교장 대리. **2** used for the performance of a play. 연출용의. ¶ *an* ~ *copy* 극본. — *n.* Ⓤ the act or art of performing in plays or films. 연출(법); 연기. ¶ *a play suitable for* ~ 연기에 적합한 각본 / *good* ~ 좋은 연기.

ac·tin·ism [ǽktənìzəm] *n.* Ⓤ the property of radiant energy in light. 화학 방사선 작용. ● **ac·tin·ic** [æktínik] *adj.* [↓]

ac·tin·i·um [æktíniəm] *n.* Ⓤ 《chem.》 a radioactive element in pitchblend. 악티늄. [Gk. *aktis* ray]

:**ac·tion** [ǽkʃən] *n.* **1** Ⓤ the process or fact of acting. 행동; 움직임. **2** Ⓤ activity. 활동; 활발. ¶ *a man of* ~ 활동가 / *out of* ~ 활동하지 않고 / *Action of any kind is better than doing nothing.* 어떤 활동이든 아무것도 안 하는 것 보다는 낫다 / *His mind seemed incapable of* ~. 그의 마음은 활동을 못 하는 것 같았다. **3** Ⓒ an act or a thing done; conduct; behavior. 행위. ¶ *a dishonest* ~ 부정한 행위 / *a generous* [*mean*] 너그러운[야비한] 행위 / *Actions speak louder than words.* 말보다는 실천. **4** Ⓤ effect; influence. 작용; 영향; 힘. ¶ *the* ~ *of acid on iron* 철에 대한 산(酸)의 작용 / *the* ~ *of a medicine* 약의 작용 / *the* ~ *of morphine* 모르핀의 영향. **5** Ⓒ the way or manner of moving or working. 몸짓; 거동; 동작. ¶ *a clumsy* ~ 어색한 동작 / *The horse has a graceful* ~. 그 말은 동작이 우아하다. **6** Ⓤ function; mechanism. 기능; 기계장치. ¶ *the* ~ *of a typewriter* 타자기의 기능 / *the* ~ *of the heart* 심장의 기능. **7** ⒸⓊ a small battle; fight between bodies of troops. 전투; 교전. ¶ *accept* ~ 응전하다 / *break off an* ~ 전투를 중지하다 / *The soldiers are in* ~. 군인들은 전투 중이다. **8** Ⓤ series of events in a story or play. (극·이야기 줄거리 중의) 한 사건; (극·이야기의) 줄거리. **9** Ⓒ a legal process. 소송. ¶ *bring an* ~ (*against*) 소송을 제기하다; 기소하다. [L. *ago* do; *actum* to do]

a line [***mode***] ***of action,*** the form which action takes. 활동 형식[형태].

a man of action, a person who does things; a very active or practical man. 행동인; 활동가.
be put out of action, be out of order. (기계가) 움직이지 않게 되다; 고장나다.
bring into action, **a**) cause it to operate. …을 가동시키다. **b**) open a battle. 전투에 참가시키다.
in action, active; working; taking part. 활동하고 있는; 활동 중인. ¶ *put a machine in ~* 기계를 돌리다.
put 〔***set***〕 ***into action,*** put into practice. 실행에 옮기다.
take action, **a**) begin to do something; start to move, work, etc. …을 하기 시작하다; 움직이기 시작하다; 활발해지다; 행동을〔조처를〕 취하다. **b**) start a lawsuit. 소송을 제기하다.

ac·tion·a·ble [ǽkʃənəbəl] *adj.* 《law》 giving cause for an action at law. 고소〔기소〕할 수 있는. ¶ *He made statements that were ~.* 그는 고소할 수 있는 진술서를 작성했다.

action painting [⌐– ⌐–] *n.* abstract expressionism marked, esp. by the use of spontaneous techniques (as dribbling, splattering, or smearing). 행동 미술.

action station [⌐– ⌐–] *n.* an order to soldiers, sailors, etc., to take up positions ready for battle or other urgent action. 전투 배치.

ac·ti·vate [ǽktəvèit] *vt.* (P6) **1** make (something) active, esp. by chemical reaction. …을 활발화〔활성화〕하다. **2** 《phys.》 make (something) radioactive. …을 방사성으로 하다. **3** 《U.S.》 place (a military unit) in an active status. (부대를) 전시 편제하다. [↓]

:ac·tive [ǽktiv] *adj.* **1** lively in action; working or moving. 정력적인; 활동적인; 활동 중의; 분주한. ¶ *an ~ volcano* 활화산 / *a soldier on ~ service* 현역 군인. **2** energetic; having full or enough power of mind or body; busy. 활발한; 활기 있는. ¶ *an ~ market* 활기찬 시장 / *an ~ life* 활기찬 생활 / *be ~ on doing good to others* 남에게 좋은 일을 활발히 하고 있다 / *I am not so ~ as I was.* 전처럼 정력적이지 못하다. **3** actual; real; effective. 실제적인; 효과적인; 적극적인. ¶ *take an ~ interest in* 적극적인 관심을 보이다 / *I want ~ help.* 실제적인 도움을 원한다. **4** 《gram.》 showing the subject of a verb as acting. 능동태의(opp. passive). — *n.* 《gram.》 the active voice. 능동태. [*act, -ive*]

ac·tive·ly [ǽktivli] *adv.* in an active manner. 활발히; 적극적으로. ¶ *He helped ~ in the work.* 그는 적극적으로 일을 도왔다.

ac·tiv·ism [ǽktəvìzəm] *n.* Ⓤ the doctrine or practice that emphasizes energetic action. 활동〔실행〕주의.

ac·tiv·ist [ǽktəvist] *n.* Ⓒ a person taking an active part, esp. in a political movement. (정치 운동 등의) 적극적 행동주의자. ¶ *a student ~* 운동권의 학생.

:ac·tiv·i·ty [æktívəti] *n.* (*pl.* **-ties**) **1** Ⓤ the state of being active. 활동; 활력. ¶ *mental and physical ~* 정신적 및 육체적 활동. **2** Ⓤ ordinary power of mind and body. (심신의) 상태(常態). **3** 《usu. *pl.*》 things to do. (여러 가지) 활동. ¶ *student activities* (학생의) 교내 활동 / *classroom activities* 교과 활동 / *outdoor activities* 야외 활동 / *The police started activities.* 경찰은 활동을 개시했다. **4** Ⓤ liveliness. 활황(活況). ¶ *the ~ of the market* 시장의 활황.

·ac·tor [ǽktər] *n.* Ⓒ **1** a person who plays a part in a drama. (남자) 배우(opp. actress). **2** a person who takes part in some action. 행위자; 관여자. **3** 《*fig.*》 a pretender; a hypocrite. …척하는 사람; 위선자. [→act]

·ac·tress [ǽktris] *n.* Ⓒ a woman actor. 여배우(opp. actor).

:ac·tu·al [ǽktʃuəl] *adj.* **1** really existing. 현실의; 실재(實在)의(opp. imaginary). ¶ *Davy Crockett was an ~ person.* 데이비 크로켓은 실재의 인물이었다 / *Travel to the moon is not a dream but an ~ happening.* 달세계로의 여행은 꿈이 아닌 현실적인 사건인 것이다. **2** now existing; present. 현재의. ¶ *the ~ condition* 현상(現狀); 실상. [→act]

ac·tu·al·i·ty [æ̀ktʃuǽləti] *n.* (*pl.* **-ties**) **1** Ⓤ the state of being actual; reality. 현실; 사실. **2** 《usu. *pl.*》 real conditions. 실상(實狀). ¶ *in ~* 실제로.

ac·tu·al·ize [ǽktʃuəlàiz] *vt.* (P6) make actual; realize. 현실화하다.

:ac·tu·al·ly [ǽktʃuəli] *adv.* **1** at the present moment. 지금; 현재로는. **2** in fact; really. (의외지만) 정말로; 실제로. ¶ *Actually, it was only a rumor.* 실제로 그건 소문에 지나지 않았다 / *He ~ did do it.* 그는 실제로 그것을 했다. **3** as a matter of fact; to be correct. 실제에 있어; 사실상; 정확히. ¶ *Actually, he came on June 19.* 그는 사실상 6월 19일에 왔다. [→act]

ac·tu·ar·y [ǽktʃuèri / -əri] *n.* Ⓒ an expert on rates of mortality and insurance statistics. 보험 계리인(計理人). [→act]

ac·tu·ate [ǽktʃuèit] *vt.* (P6,13,20) **1** put (something) into motion or action; cause to work. (기계 따위)를 움직이다. ¶ *Our pump is actuated by a belt from an electric motor.* 우리 펌프는 전기 모터에 걸린 벨트에 의해 작동된다. **2** force (someone) to act. (자극을 주어 아무)를 …시키다. ¶ *actuated by selfish motives* 이기적인 동기에 이끌려 / *What actuated him to kill his friend?* 어떻게 해서 자기 친구를 죽이기에 이르렀나. [→act]

a·cu·i·ty [əkjú:əti] *n.* =acuteness.

a·cu·men [əkjú:mən, ǽkjə-] *n.* Ⓤ keenness of mind; quickness of insight. 예민; 통찰력. ¶ *He had the business ~ to foresee that cotton would drop in price.* 그는 솜값이

떨어지리란 것을 내다보는 상재(商才)가 있었다. [↓]

ac·u·punc·ture [ǽkjupʌ̀ŋktʃər] *n.* Ⓤ a method of treating diseases by thrusting needles into the body. 침술(鍼術). [↓]

·**a·cute** [əkjú:t] *adj.* **1** pointed; sharp at the end. 날카로운(opp. blunt). ¶ *an ~ angle* 예각 / *the ~ tip of a leaf or thorn* 잎이나 가시의 날카로운 끝. **2** (of illness) very painful; sudden and severe. (고통이) 격심한; (병 따위가) 급성인(opp. chronic). ¶ *an ~ disease* 급성병 / *Toothache often causes ~ pain.* 이앓이는 종종 격통을 일으킨다. **3** keen; sharp. (감각·지력이) 날카로운; 예민한. ¶ *an ~ observation* 날카로운 관찰 / *Dogs have an ~ sense of smell.* 개는 예민한 후각을 갖고 있다. **4** (of sounds) sharp; high. (소리가) 높은; 날카로운. ¶ *Some sounds are so ~ that we cannot hear them.* 어떤 소리들은 매우 높아서 들을 수가 없다. [ad-, L. *acus* needle]

a·cute·ly [əkjú:tli] *adv.* keenly; sharply. 날카롭게; 격렬하게.

a·cute·ness [əkjú:tnis] *n.* Ⓤ the state or quality of being acute. 날카로움; 격렬함. ¶ *the ~ of the cold* 〔*pain*〕 추위〔통증〕의 격심함.

-a·cy [-əsi] *suf.* forming nouns of quality, state, etc. 성질·상태 등의 추상 명사를 만듦. [L.]

ad[1] [æd] *n.* Ⓒ《U.S. *colloq.*》 an advertisement. 광고. ¶ *~ ballon* 애드벌룬; 광고기구(氣球) / *~ column* 광고란. [abbr.]

ad[2] [æd] *prep.* 《L.》 **1** to; toward. '…쪽으로'의 뜻. **2** up to; according to. '…에 따라서'의 뜻.

ad. adverb.

ad- [æd-, ə-, id-] *pref.* 《*ac-* before *c* or *q*, *af-* before *f*, *ag-* before *g*, *al-* before *l*, *an-* before *n*, *ap-* before *p*, *ar-* before *r*, *as-* before *s*, *at-* before *t* and *a-* before *sc*, *sp*, or *st*》 to; at; toward; change into; increase; mere intensification. '…로, …에'의 뜻. [L.]

·**A.D.** [éidí:, ǽnoudámənài, -nì: / -dɔ́m-] 《L.》 *Anno Domini* (=in the year of our Lord). 서기(西紀)(cf. *B.C.*). ¶ *in A.D. 1208,* 서기 1208 년에.

A·da [éidə] *n.* a woman's name. 여자 이름.

ad·age [ǽdidʒ] *n.* Ⓒ an old and well-known saying; a proverb. 옛 속담; 격언. ¶ *as the ~ says, "Haste makes waste."* 속담에도 "급히 먹는 밥이 목이 멘다"라고 했듯이. [L. *ad-* to, *aio* say]

a·da·gi·o [ədá:dʒou, -ʒiòu] *adv.* 《It.》《mus.》 slowly. 느리게. — *adj.* slow. 느린. — *n.* Ⓒ (*pl.* **-gi·os**) a slow part in music. 아다지오곡(曲).

·**Ad·am** [ǽdəm] *n.* 《Bible》 the first man God made in the Garden of Eden. 아담《에덴 동산에 하느님이 처음 만드셨다는 남자》(opp. Eve). [Heb. =man]

as old as Adam, very old. 태곳적부터의; 아주 오래된.

do not know *someone* ***from Adam,*** 《*colloq.*》 do not know someone at all. …을 전혀 모르다. ¶ *He greeted us every morning, but we didn't know him from ~.* 그는 아침마다 우리에게 인사했는데 전혀 모르는 사람이었다.

ad·a·mant [ǽdəmənt, -mæ̀nt] *n.* Ⓤ a thing too hard to be cut or broken. 극히 단단〔견고〕한 것. ¶ *as hard as ~* 비길 데 없이 단단한. — *adj.* very hard; not yielding. 매우 단단한; (심성·성격 따위가) 단호한; 굽히지 않는; 굳센; 부동의. ¶ *He was ~ in his refusal.* 그는 단호히 거절했다 / *I only wish he were less ~.* 그저 그가 누그러지길 바랄 뿐이다. [Gk. *a-*not, *damaō* tame]

ad·a·man·tine [æ̀dəmǽnti(:)n, -tain] *adj.* very hard; firm; not yielding. 매우 단단한; 굽히지 않는; 단호한; 완고한. ¶ *~ courage* 강용(剛勇); 불굴의 용기.

Adam's ale 〔**wine**〕 [ˊ-ˊ〔ˊ〕] *n.* water. 물.

Adam's apple [ˊ- ˋ-] *n.* a part that projects in the front of the human throat. 결후(結喉).

·**a·dapt** [ədǽpt] *vt.* (P6,13) **1** 《*for, to*》 make (someone) suitable; make fit (for). …을 적합시키다; 순응〔적응〕시키다. ¶ *~ plans to suit new conditions* 계획을 새로운 상황에 맞추다 / *She is not adapted for such work.* 그녀는 그런 일에 적응 못하고 있다. **2** 《*from, for*》 change (something) for another purpose. …을 고치다; 개작하다. ¶ *a play adapted from his novel* 그의 소설을 각색한 연극 / *The book is adapted for beginners.* 그 책은 초심자용으로 개작되어 있다 / *We can ~ the barn for use as a garage.* 우리는 헛간을 창고용으로 고칠 수 있다. **3** 《*reflexively*》《*to*》 shape one's habits etc. so as to make them suitable or agreeable to others. (습관 따위를 고쳐 환경 등에) 적응시키다. ¶ *~ oneself to one's company* 자신을 적응시켜 동료들과 어울리다 / *He adapted himself to a new job.* 그는 새로운 직업에 적응했다. [ad-, L. *aptus* fitted]

a·dapt·a·bil·i·ty [ədæ̀ptəbíləti] *n.* Ⓤ the quality of being adaptable. 적응성.

a·dapt·a·ble [ədǽptəbəl] *adj.* able to change or to be changed easily to fit different conditions. (새 환경·조건에) 적응할 수 있는; (무엇이) 고칠〔개작할〕 수 있는. ¶ *soil ~ to growth of apple trees* 사과나무 성장에 적합한 토양 / *He is a very ~ person.* 그는 아주 적응력이 좋은 사람이다.

ad·ap·ta·tion [æ̀dəptéiʃən] *n.* **1** Ⓤ the act or process of adapting; the condition of being adapted. (장소·환경에의) 적응; 순응. **2** Ⓒ something made by a process of adapting. 개작(물); 번안(물); 각색(한 것). ¶ *an ~ from an English novel* 영국 소설로부터의 번안 / *the ~ of Shakespeare's plays to the screen* 셰익스피어극의 영화로의 개작.

a·dapt·ed [ədǽptid] *adj.* 《*for*》 suitable. 적합한. ¶ *a comic book ~ for children* 어린이를 위한 만화책.

a·dapt·er, -or [ədǽptər] *n.* Ⓒ **1** a person or thing that adapts. 적응〔순응〕하는 사람〔것〕; 개작〔번안〕자. **2** 《mech.》 ⓐ a device that connects parts not designed to fit together. 다른 크기의 부품을 적합시키는 중개 기구. ⓑ a device that extends or alters the function of an apparatus. (본래 목적과는 다른 용도로 쓰기 위한) 보조 기구.

A.D.C. 1 aide-de-camp. 전속 부관. **2** Amateur Dramatic Club. (대학의) 아마추어 연극부.

:add [æd] *vt.* (P6,7,13) **1** 《*to*》 join; unite. …을 더하다〔넣다〕; 가산하다. ¶ *~ sugar to one's tea* 홍차에 설탕을 넣다 / *A bonus was added to the salary.* 봉급에 보너스가 가산되었다. **2** put (numbers) into a sum; combine (two or more numbers) so as to get a sum total. (수를) 더하다; …을 합계하다 (opp. subtract). ¶ *15 added to 35 is equal to 50.* 35 더하기 15는 50이다 / *Add 8 and 4 and you get twelve.* 8과 4를 합치면 12이다. **3** say or write further; say in addition. 덧붙여 말하다〔쓰다〕; 부언〔부기〕하다. ¶ *~ a request that…* …라는 요구를 덧붙이다 / *"And come tomorrow, please," he added.* "그리고 내일 부디 와 주게" 라고 그는 덧붙였다.
— *vi.* (P1,3) **1** 《*to*》 increase; make some addition to; make greater. 늘다; 더하다. **2** find a sum; do addition in arithmetic. 덧셈을 하다. ¶ *The little boy is learning to ~ and subtract.* 그 어린애는 덧셈과 뺄셈을 배우고 있다. [L. *addō* join]
add to, **a**) make some addition to; increase. 늘다; …을 더하다. ¶ *~ to one's cares* 걱정이 늘다 / *The lake adds to the beauty of the place.* 그 호수는 그곳의 미관을 더하고 있다 / *This knowledge only added to his fear.* 이 지식은 그의 두려움을 더해 주었을 따름이었다 / *He is adding to his weight* 〔*wealth*〕. 그는 체중이〔부(富)가〕 늘고 있다. **b**) put. …을 더하다〔넣다〕. ¶ *~ sugar to coffee* 커피에 설탕을 넣다.
add up, **a**) find the sum of. …을 합계하다. ¶ *Add up these figures.* 이 숫자들을 합계해라. **b**) 《*colloq.*》 seem reasonable; make sense. 조리〔이치〕에 닿다; 의미를 이루다.
add up to, **a**) amount to. 합계 …이 되다. **b**) mean. …을 의미하다. ¶ *What do her remarks ~ up to ?* 그녀의 말은 무엇을 의미하는가.

ad·dax [ǽdæks] *n.* Ⓒ (*pl.* **-dax·es** or **addax**) 《zool.》 a large antelope of Arabia. (아라비아산의) 큰 영양.

ad·den·da [ədéndə] *n.* pl. of **addendum.**

ad·den·dum [ədéndəm] *n.* Ⓒ (*pl.* **-da**) a thing added to something, esp. an added note. 부록; 부가물. ¶ *There are a number of addenda to this book.* 이 책에는 많은 부록이 있다. [→add]

ad·der[1] [ǽdər] *n.* Ⓒ a small poisonous snake of Europe; one of several harmless snakes of North America. 뱀의 일종《유럽산은 유독; 북아메리카산은 무독》. [E. orig. *nadder*]

add·er[2] [ǽdər] *n.* Ⓒ an adding machine. 가산기(加算器). [*add*]

ad·dict [ədíkt] *vt.* (P13) 《*reflexively*》 《*to*》 devote (oneself) to a bad habit; give oneself up to. …을 못된 버릇에 빠지게 하다. ¶ *~ oneself to gambling* 도박에 빠지다 / *He is addicted to drinking* 〔*tobacco*〕. 그는 술에 빠져 있다〔상습적으로 담배를 피운다〕. — [ǽdikt] *n.* Ⓒ a person who devotes himself to some bad habit. 탐닉자. ¶ *an ~ to drugs* 마약 중독자. [L. *dīco* say]

ad·dict·ed [ədíktid] *adj.* 《*to*》 given up to a habit. 빠져 있는. ¶ *a man ~ to opium* 아편 중독자.

ad·dic·tion [ədíkʃən] *n.* Ⓤ the state of being addicted. 탐닉; 빠짐.

Ad·dis A·ba·ba [ǽdis ǽbəbə] *n.* the capital of Ethiopia. 아디스 아바바《에티오피아의 수도》.

Ad·di·son [ǽdəsən] *n.* 애디슨. **1 Joseph** (1672-1719) an English essayist and poet. 영국의 수필가·시인. **2 Thomas** (1793-1860) an English physician. 영국의 의사. **3 Henry** (1838-1918) an American historian, writer, and teacher. 미국의 역사학자·작가·교사.

Addison's disease [´-- -´] *n.* 《med.》 a disease of the suprarenal glands. 애디슨병《부신(副腎)의 병》.

:ad·di·tion [ədíʃən] *n.* **1** Ⓤ the act of adding a thing. 부가; 가산; 증가. **2** Ⓒ something added. 부가물; 첨가물. ¶ *build an ~ to a house* 증축하다. **3** Ⓤ the process of getting a sum total by combining two or more numbers. 덧셈; 더하기. [→add]
in addition (***to***) besides; as well as. …에 더하여; …외에; …위에 또. ¶ *In ~ to automobiles, Henry Ford built many other things.* 자동차 외에도 헨리 포드는 다른 많은 것을 만들었다 / *I have other things to do in ~* (*to this*). 나는 이것 외에도 해야 할 다른 일들이 있다.

***ad·di·tion·al** [ədíʃənəl] *adj.* added; supplementary. 추가의; 부가된. ¶ *an ~ tax* 부가세 / *an ~ income* 추가 수입. ● **ad·di·tion·al·ly** [-ʃənəli] *adv.*

ad·di·tive [ǽdətiv] *n.* Ⓒ something added or to be added to a product or device. (물성(物性)의 개량·중화를 위한) 첨가〔부가〕물.

ad·dle [ǽdl] *vt.* (P6) make (something) rotten or confused. …을 썩게 하다; 혼란시키다. ¶ *an addled egg* 곯은 달걀 / *His head* 〔*brain*〕 *is addled.* 그의 머릿속은 혼란에 빠져 있다 / *become addled* 혼탁〔혼란〕해지다. — *vi.* (P1) (of eggs) go bad; become confused. (달걀이) 썩다; 혼란해지다. — *adj.* (of eggs) rotten; confused. (달걀이) 썩은; 혼란한. [E. =mud]

ad·dle·brained [ǽdlbrèind] *adj.* having confused ideas; stupid; foolish. 머리가 나쁜; 우둔한.

add-on [ǽdàn, -ɔ̀:n] *n.* Ⓒ a piece of equipment that can be connected to a computer, such as a disk-drive or a modem, that increases its usefulness. (컴퓨터 등의) 추가 기기(器機). [*add*]

:ad·dress [ədrés] *n.* **1** Ⓒ a written or spoken speech. 연설; 인사의 말. ¶ *an opening* 〔*a closing*〕 ~ 개회〔폐회〕사 / *an* ~ *of thanks* 감사의 인사말; 치사(致謝) / *read an* ~ *of welcome* 환영사를 읽다 / *give* 〔*make, deliver*〕 *an* ~ *to a number of scientists* 과학자들에게 일장 연설을 하다 / *President made a short* ~. 대통령은 짤막한 연설을 했다. **2** [《U.S.》 ǽdres] Ⓒ ⓐ a place where mail is received; a written direction on an envelope, parcel, etc., that shows where it is to be sent. (편지 따위의) 주소·성명. ¶ *the* ~ *on a postcard* 엽서에 적힌 주소·성명. ⓑ the place where a person lives. (살고 있는) 주소. ¶ *What is your* ~*?* 주소가 어디지; 어디 살지 / *tell* 〔*give*〕 *someone one's* ~ 아무에게 자기집 주소를 말하다 / *change one's* ~ 주소를 바꾸다 / *be still at the same* ~ 아직도 같은 주소에 살고 있다. **3** Ⓤ a way of speaking or behaving. (남과 이야기할 때의) 태도; 이야기투; 응대하는 태도. ¶ *a man of pleasing* ~ 응대 솜씨가 훌륭한 사람. **4** Ⓤ skilful management; ready skill; tact. (다루는) 솜씨; 수완. ¶ *He has all the* ~ *of a diplomat.* 그는 외교관으로서의 솜씨가 아주 뛰어났다 / *manage an affair with* ~ 일을 능숙하게 다루다. **5** 《usu. *pl.*》 courteous attentions to a lady; courtship. (여성에의) 구애; 구혼. ¶ *pay one's addresses to* 구애하다.

— *vt.* (P6,13) **1** make a speech to (persons); speak or write to (someone); direct (a remark or words) to. (사람들)에게 연설하다; 이야기를 걸다; …에게 (말을) 하다. ¶ ~ *a few words to someone sitting in front* 앞에 앉아 있는 아무에게 몇 마디 말을 하다 / ~ *the nation over the radio* 라디오를 통해 국민에게 호소하다 / *I was addressed by a passer-by.* 한 통행인이 내게 말을 걸었다. **2** speak or write to (someone) by using titles. (…칭호로) …을 부르다. ¶ *How do you* ~ *a mayor?* 시장을 어떻게 부르는가. **3** write on (a letter, parcel, etc.) where it is to be sent; direct. 받는 이의 주소 성명을 쓰다. ¶ ~ *a letter to someone* 아무에게 편지를 보내다 / *an envelope addressed to Mr. Smith* 수신인이 스미스씨 앞으로 된 봉투. **4** 《golf》 take an aim at (a ball) with a golf club. (골프채로) 겨냥하다. [ad-, L. *rego* put straight]

address oneself to, **a**) speak to (someone). 아무에게 이야기를 걸다. ¶ ~ *oneself to the chairman* 의장에게 발언하다. **b**) devote one's energies to (a task). …에 본격적으로 달라붙다. ¶ ~ *oneself to one's studies* 공부에 열을 올리다.

ad·dress·ee [æ̀dresí:, əd-] *n.* Ⓒ a person to whom a piece of mail is adressed. 수신인; 받는이(opp. addresser).

ad·dress·er [ədrésər] *n.* Ⓒ a person who addresses a letter, package, etc. 발신인; 발송인.

ad·duce [ədjú:s] *vt.* (P6,7) offer (something) as evidence or as an example. (증거·예증으로서) …을 제시〔인증〕하다. ¶ *Adduce your reasons.* 이유를 들어라. [ad-, L. *duco* draw]

ad·duct [ədʌ́kt] *vt.* (P6) 《physiol.》 draw to a common center. …을 내전(內轉)시키다 (opp. abduct). [↑]

ad·duc·tion [ədʌ́kʃən] *n.* Ⓤ adducing; 《physiol.》 adducting. (논거 따위의) 제시; 내전(內轉).

ad·duc·tor [ədʌ́ktər] *n.* 《physiol.》 any muscle that adducts. 내전근(內轉筋).

-ade [-eid] *suf.* **1** action of. '동작, 과정'의 뜻. ¶ *cavalcade.* **2** product of. '(행위의) 결과, 산물'의 뜻. ¶ *lemonade.*

ad·e·noids [ǽdənɔ̀idz] *n. pl.* 《med.》 a spongy growth between the upper part of the throat and the back of the nose, often diseased. 아데노이드. ● **ad·e·noi·dal** *adj.* [Gk. *adēn* gland]

ad·ept [ədépt] *adj.* 《*in*》 highly skilled. 숙련된. ¶ *be* ~ *in* 〔*at*〕 *diving* 다이빙에 숙달돼 있다. — [ǽdept] *n.* Ⓒ a person with great skill; an expert. 명수; 숙련자; 전문가. ¶ *She is an* ~ *in* 〔《*colloq.*》 at〕 *swimming.* 그녀는 수영의 명수이다 / *I am not an* ~ *in photography.* 나는 사진술의 전문가가 아니다. [L. *adipiscōr* attain]

ad·e·qua·cy [ǽdikwəsi] *n.* Ⓤ the state of being adequate. 적당; 충분. [↓]

·ad·e·quate [ǽdikwit] *adj.* 《*to, for*》 **1** sufficient; enough; as much as is needed. 충분한. ¶ ~ *intelligence* 상당한 지능 / *the means* ~ *for the purpose* 목적 달성에 충분한 수단 / *His salary is* ~ *to his needs.* 그의 봉급은 자기 필요에 충분하다. **2** having the necessary skill (for); suitable. 적당한. ¶ *a person* ~ *to the post* 그 지위에 어울리는 사람 / *He is quite* ~ *to fulfill the task.* 그는 그 과업을 완수하기에 아주 적임이다 / *This car is* ~ *to our needs.* 이 차는 우리 필요에 꼭 맞는다. [ad-, L. *aequus* equal]

ad·e·quate·ly [ǽdikwitli] *adv.* in an adequate manner. 적당히; 충분히.

·ad·here [ædhíər] *vi.* (P2A,3) 《*to*》 **1** stick. …에 끈적끈적 들러붙다. ¶ *Wax adheres to the finger.* 밀랍은 손가락에 달라붙는다. **2** be attached fast; support firmly. …을 고수하다; …에 충실하다. ¶ ~ *to one's religion* 자기 종교를 고수하다 / *I* ~ *to my original opinion.* 나는 본래의 내 의견을 고수한다 / *He adhered to the party.* 그는 당(黨)에 충실했다. ● **ad·her·er** [-ər] *n.* [ad-, L. *heareo* stick]

ad·her·ence [ædhíərəns] *n.* Ⓤ 《*to*》 the act of adhering. 부착; 고수. ¶ ~ *to one's resolution* 주의(主義)의 고수 / ~ *to a party* 당(黨)에의 충실.

ad·her·ent [ədhíərənt] *adj.* attached; sticking fast. 부착하는; 고수하는. — *n.* Ⓒ a follower; a supporter. 지지자; 신봉자. ¶ *an ~ of a political party* 정당의 지지자.

ad·he·sion [ædhí:ʒən] *n.* Ⓤ **1** the act of adhering; the state of being adhered. 부착; 점착(粘着). **2** the act of supporting or following something; faithfulness. 고수; …지지. [*adhere*]

***give in one's* adhesion,** combine. 가담〔가입〕하다; 지지를 표명하다.

ad·he·sive [ædhí:siv, -ziv] *adj.* **1** sticking. (사람이) 달라붙어 떨어지지 않는. **2** sticky. 들러붙는; 점착성의. ¶ ~ *plaster* 반창고 / ~ *tape* 접착 테이프. — *n.* Ⓤ a sticky substance. 점착물; 접착제.

ad hoc [æd hák, -hóuk] *adv., adj.* 《L.》 for this purpose; relating exclusively to the subject in question. 특별한 목적을 위해〔위한〕; 이 문제에 관해〔관한〕.

ad·i·a·bat·ic [ædiəbǽtik, èidaiə-] *adj.* 《phys.》 without transmission of heat. 단열(斷熱)의. [Gk. *a-* not, *dia* through, *baino* go]

ad·i·an·tum [ædiǽntəm] *n.* 《bot.》 a black maiden-hair. 섬공작고사리. [Gk.]

a·dieu [ədjú:] *interj.* Goodbye; Farewell. 안녕. — *n.* Ⓒ (*pl.* **a·dieus** or **a·dieux**) a farewell. 고별; 작별. [F. =to God]

***make* 〔*take*〕 *one's* adieu(s),** take one's leave; say good-bye. 작별을 고하다.

a·dieux [ədjú:z] *n.* pl. of **adieu.**

ad in·fi·ni·tum [æd ìnfənáitəm] *adv.* 《L.》 endlessly; forever. 끝없이; 한없이; 영원히.

ad in·ter·im [æd íntərim] *adv., adj.* 《L.》 in the meantime; temporarily; temporary. 중간에〔의〕; 잠정적으로〔인〕.

ad·i·pose [ǽdəpòus] *adj.* of or containing fat; fatty. 지방질의. ¶ ~ *tissue* 지방 조직. — *n.* Ⓤ animal fat. (동물성) 지방. [L. *adeps* fat]

ad·i·pos·i·ty [ædəpásəti / -pɔ́s-] *n.* Ⓤ the state of being fat; a tendency to become obese. 비만(증); 지방 과다(증).

ad·it [ǽdit] *n.* 《*to*》 a horizontal entrance. 횡갱(橫坑). [ad-, L. *eo* go]

adj. **1** adjective. **2** adjunct. **3** adjustment.

ad·ja·cent [ədʒéisənt] *adj.* 《*to*》 lying near or next to. 인접한; 부근의. ¶ *an ~ angle* 인접각 / ~ *houses* 〔*villages*〕 인접한 집들〔마을들〕 / *a house ~ to the church* 교회의 이웃집 / *The garage is ~ to our house.* 차고는 우리 집에 인접해 있다. ● **ad·ja·cen·cy** *n.* [ad-, L. *jaceo* lie]

ad·jec·ti·val [ædʒiktáivəl] *adj.* of an adjective. 형용사의. [↓]

:**ad·jec·tive** [ǽdʒiktiv] *n.* Ⓒ 《gram.》 a word used to limit or describe a noun or pronoun. 형용사. — *adj.* of an adjective. 형용사의. [ad-, L. *jacio* throw]

*****ad·join** [ədʒɔ́in] *vt.* (P6) be next to (something). …에 접하다. ¶ *Canada adjoins the United States.* 캐나다는 미국에 인접해 있다 / *His garden adjoins ours.* 그의 정원은 우리 정원과 접해 있다. — *vi.* (P1) 《*to,on*》 be in contact; be side by side. 서로〔나란히〕 접하다. ¶ *The two houses ~.* 두 집은 나란히 이웃해 있다. [ad-, →join]

ad·join·ing [ədʒɔ́iniŋ] *adj.* in contact; bordering; next. (접촉해서) 이웃의. ¶ *the ~ rooms* 옆방.

·**ad·journ** [ədʒə́:rn] *vt.* (P6) put off or stop (a meeting, etc.) until a later time. (회의 따위)를 연기하다; 휴회하다. ¶ *The president adjourned the meeting for three days.* 사장은 회의를 사흘 동안 연기했다. — *vi.* (P1) **1** come to a close. 휴회되다. ¶ ~ *without day* 무기 연기하다 / *The court adjourned till Monday.* 공판은 월요일로 연기되었다. **2** 《*colloq.*》 《*to*》 go to another place. 자리를 옮기다. ¶ *Let us ~ to the next room.* 옆방으로 자리를 옮깁시다. [L.= appoint a day]

ad·journ·ment [ədʒə́:rnmənt] *n.* **1** Ⓤ the act of adjourning; the state of being adjourned. 연기; 휴회. ¶ *decide on one week's ~* 일 주일의 연기를 결정하다. **2** Ⓒ the time during which a meeting is adjourned. 휴회〔연기〕 기간.

ad·judge [ədʒʌ́dʒ] *vt.* 《*to*》 **1** (P11,21) decide or judge by law. (아무에게) …을 선고〔판결〕하다. ¶ ~ *him to death* 그에게 사형을 선고하다 / *He was adjudged guilty.* 그는 유죄 판결을 받았다 / *He was adjudged to prison for two years.* 그에게 징역 2년이 선고되었다. **2** (P13) give (something) according to the decision, often by law. (재판·재정에 의해) …을 주다. ¶ ~ *a prize to him* 심사하여 그에게 상을 주다 / *The estate was adjudged to him.* 재산은 (재판에 의해) 그의 소유로 돌아갔다. [ad-, →judge]

ad·ju·di·cate [ədʒú:dikèit] *vt., vi.* (P6;3) 《*on, upon*》 give a judgment. 판결〔심리〕하다. ¶ ~ *a claim* 요구를 심리하다 / *Judge Smith adjudicated in the matter.* 스미스 판사가 그 사건을 재판했다. ● **ad·ju·di·ca·tive** *adj.* **ad·ju·di·ca·tor** *n.* [ad-, →judge]

ad·ju·di·ca·tion [ədʒù:dikéiʃən] *n.* **1** Ⓤ the act of adjudicating. 판결; 심리. **2** Ⓒ a decision of bankruptcy. 파산 선고.

ad·junct [ǽdʒʌŋkt] *n.* Ⓒ **1** something added to another thing, but not essential. 부속물; 종속물. ¶ *a mere ~* 단순한 부속물 / *A cushion is a useful ~ to a sofa.* 쿠션은 소파의 유용한 부속물이다. **2** 《gram.》 words or phrases that modify other words or phrases, such as adjectives and adverbs. 수식 어구. [L. *jungo* join together]

ad·ju·ra·tion [ædʒəréiʃən] *n.* ⓊⒸ the

act of adjuring; a solemn charge or prayer; a solemn command. 선서(宣誓); 간원; 엄명. [↓]

ad·jure [ədʒúər] *vt.* (P6,11,20) **1** give orders to (someone) solemnly under oath. …에게 엄명하다. **2** appeal to (someone) earnestly. (아무)에게 간원[간청]하다. ¶ *I ~ you to tell the truth.* 제발 사실을 말해다오. [L. *juro* swear]

·**ad·just** [ədʒʌ́st] *vt.* (P6,7,13) **1** 《*to*》 make (someone or something) fit. …에 맞추다. ¶ *~ a garment to the body* 옷을 몸에 맞추다 / *~ oneself to new circumstances* 새로운 환경에 적응하다. **2** put (something) in a right order or position. (기계 따위)를 조정하다; (몸차림 따위)를 매만져 다듬다. ¶ *~ the length of a coat* 코트의 기장을 조정하다 / *~ a radio dial* 라디오의 다이얼을 맞추다 / *~ a watch* 시계를 맞추다. **3** settle rightly. (…을) 조정하다; 조화시키다. ¶ *~ a difference of opinion* 의견의 차이를 조정하다 / *~ a quarrel* 언쟁을 조정하다 / *This bill is too high and must be adjusted.* 이 청구액은 너무 많아서 조정돼야겠다. [ad-, L. *juxta* near]

ad·just·a·ble [ədʒʌ́stəbl] *adj.* that can be adjusted. 조정[조절]할 수 있는.

·**ad·just·ment** [ədʒʌ́stmənt] *n.* Ⓤⓒ the act of adjusting; settlement. 맞춤; 조정; 조절. ¶ *the ~ of differences* 차이의 조절.

ad·ju·tan·cy [ǽdʒətənsi] *n.* Ⓤ 《mil.》 the office of an adjutant. 부관(副官)의 직(職). [↓]

ad·ju·tant [ǽdʒətənt] *n.* Ⓒ **1** an assistant. 조수. **2** 《mil.》 an army officer who does office work for the commanding officer. 부관(副官). **3** 《bird》 a large bird found in India and Africa. 무수리. [ad-, L. *juvo* help]

adjutant general [⌐—⌐—] *n.* 《mil.》 the adjutant of a division. 고급 부관.

ad·lib [ædlíb, ⌐—] *vt., vi.* (P6;1) (**-libbed, -lib·bing**) 《U.S. *colloq.*》 act, speak, etc. without any preparation. …을 즉석에서 하다; 즉흥적으로 말하다. [↓]

ad lib. [æd líb] *adv.* =ad libitum.

ad lib·i·tum [æd líbətəm] *adv., adj.* 《L.》 at pleasure. 임의로[의].

Adm. Admiral; Admiralty.

adm. administrator; administratrix.

ad·man [ǽdmæ̀n, -mən] *n.* an advertisement agent. 광고업자[사원]. [→advertise]

·**ad·min·is·ter** [ædmínəstər, əd-] *vt.* (P6,13) **1** manage the affairs of (a country, business, etc.); direct; conduct. …을 처리[관리, 지배]하다. ¶ *~ a company* 회사를 운영하다 / *~ a country* 나라를 다스리다 / *A housekeeper administers household affairs.* 주부는 집안 살림을 처리한다. **2** give; supply; apply. …을 주다; 베풀다; (약을) 복용시키다. ¶ *~ justice* 재판을 하다 / *~ aspirin for a headache* 두통에 아스피린을 먹이다 / *~ medicine to sick people* 환자에게 약을 주다 / *I administered him a box on the ear.* 나는 그의 뺨을 때렸다. **3** put (something) into effect. (법)을 집행하다. ¶ *~ the laws* 법률을 시행하다.

— *vi.* (P3) **1** act as manager or administrator. 관리하다. **2** 《*to*》 be helpful. 도움이 되다; 공헌하다. ¶ *~ to someone's comfort* 아무의 위안에 도움이 되다. [ad-, L. *minister* servant]

:**ad·min·is·tra·tion** [ædmìnəstréiʃən, əd-] *n.* Ⓤ **1** the act of managing a business, office, etc. 관리; 경영; 통제. ¶ *business ~* 기업 경영; 《U.S.》 경영학. **2** the management of a government. 행정; 정치. ¶ *metropolitan ~* 수도 행정. **3** 《U.S.》 《*the A-*》 the President, the members of his cabinet, and the executive departments of the government. 내각; (행)정부. ¶ *the Clinton Administration* 클린턴 행정부. **4** the application of law or medicine. (법의) 집행; 투약(投藥). ¶ *the ~ of justice* 정의를 행함; 처벌.

ad·min·is·tra·tive [ædmínəstrèitiv, -trə-, əd-] *adj.* relating to administration. 관리[경영]의; 행정의. ¶ *~ ability* 행정 수완(手腕). ●

ad·min·is·tra·tive·ly [-li] *adv.*

ad·min·is·tra·tor [ædmínəstrèitər, əd-] *n.* Ⓒ **1** a person who manages and directs public affairs. 위정자; 행정관; 장관. **2** a person who legally manages another's property. 재산 관리인.

ad·min·is·tra·tri·ces [ædminəstréitrəsi:z, əd-] *n.* pl. of **administratrix.**

ad·min·is·tra·trix [ædmìnəstréitriks, əd-] *n.* (*pl.* **-tri·ces**) a female administrator. 여자 관리자. [→administer]

***ad·mi·ra·ble** [ǽdmərəbəl] *adj.* **1** worthy of praise. 칭찬할 만한. **2** very good; excellent. 훌륭한. [→admire]

ad·mi·ra·bly [ǽdmərəbəli] *adv.* in a wonderful and excellent manner. 훌륭히; 멋지게.

***ad·mi·ral** [ǽdmərəl] *n.* Ⓒ **1** an officer of the navy who commands a fleet. 함대 사령관; 제독. **2** an officer of the highest rank of the navy. 해군 대장(cf. *general*). 參考 Adm.으로 생략함. ¶ 《U.S.》 *Fleet Admiral* = 《Brit.》 *Admiral of the Fleet* 해군 원수 / *Vice Admiral* 해군 중장. **3** the flagship of an admiral. 기함(旗艦). **4** any of the various handsome butterflies. 나비의 일종. [Arab. *amir al* ruler of]

ad·mi·ral·ty [ǽdmərəlti] *n.* (*pl.* **-ties**) **1** Ⓤ the rank or authority of an admiral. 해군 대장의 직(권). **2** 《Brit.》 《*the A-*》 the governmental department managing naval affairs. 해군성(省). **3** maritime law. 해상법. ¶ *the Court of Admiralty* = *the Admiralty Court* 해사(海事) 재판소. [↑]

***ad·mi·ra·tion** [ædməréiʃən] *n.* Ⓤ **1** a feeling of wonder, approval, and pleasure. 감탄; 칭찬. ¶ *have a great ~ for* …에

크게 감탄하다 / *excite one's ~* 칭찬의 마음이 일어나게 하다 / *I was struck with ~ for their courage.* 나는 그들의 용기에 아주 탄복했다. **2** any object of this feeling. 감탄(칭찬)의 대상. ¶ *She was the ~ of all.* 그녀는 모두에게 감탄의 대상이 되었다. [↓]

in admiration of, with admiration for. …을 기리어(찬미하여).

to admiration, in an admirable manner. 훌륭히; 멋지게. ¶ *He has solved the puzzle to ~.* 그는 어려운 문제를 멋지게 풀었다.

:ad·mire [ædmáiər, əd-] *vt.* **1** (P6) 《*for*》 regard (something) with wonder, approval, and pleasure. …에 감탄하다; …을 칭찬하다. ¶ *~ a beautiful picture* 아름다운 그림에 감탄하다 / *I admired him for his honesty.* 나는 그의 정직함을 칭찬했다 / *Visitors to Korea always ~ Mt. Sŏrak.* 한국을 찾는 사람들은 언제나 설악산에 감탄한다. **2** (P6) think highly of (someone or something); respect. …을 존경(숭배)하다. **3** (P8) 《U.S. *colloq.*》 wish; like. …을 하고 싶어하다; …을 좋아하다. [L. *ad-* at, *mirror* wonder]

***ad·mir·er** [ædmáiərər, əd-] *n.* Ⓒ **1** a person who admires. 감탄(찬미)자. ¶ *a great ~ of Ch'unwon* 춘원의 애독자. **2** a man who admires or loves a woman. 여성 찬미자; 사모하는 사람. ¶ *She has many admirers.* 그녀에게는 찬미자가 많다.

ad·mir·ing [ædmáiəriŋ, əd-] *adj.* filled with admiration. 감탄하는; 찬미의. ¶ *an ~ glance* 찬미의 눈.

ad·mir·ing·ly [ædmáiəriŋli, əd-] *adv.* with admiration. 감탄(탄복)하여.

ad·mis·si·ble [ædmísəbəl, əd-] *adj.* **1** that can be admitted. 허용될 수 있는. ¶ *The supposition is hardly ~.* 그런 추측은 거의 허용되지 않는다 / *Nobody under 12 years is ~ to this club.* 12세 미만자는 누구도 이 클럽에 들어갈 수 없다. **2** worthy of being admitted. (지위 따위)에 취임할 자격이 있는. **3** (of ideas, etc.) deserving to be held or allowed; that may be accepted as true or just. (생각 따위)가 용납될 수 있는; 인정될 수 있는. ● **ad·mis·si·bly** [-bli] *adv.* [↓]

***ad·mis·sion** [ædmíʃən, əd-] *n.* **1** Ⓤ 《*to, into*》 the right or permission to enter. (입학·입장 따위의) 허가. ¶ *grant someone ~* (아무)에게 입장을 허락하다 / *gain ~ to the society* 협회에 입회가 허가되다 / *Admission to the school is by examination only.* 학교의 입학은 시험을 통해서만 허가된다. **2** Ⓒ 《*colloq.*》 the money which must be paid to enter. 입장료. ¶ *Admission Free.* 입장 무료 / *an ~ ticket* 입장권 / *Admission to the cinema is 3,000 won.* 영화관의 입장료는 3천원이다. **3** Ⓒ a thing or person admitted. 입장이 허가된 사람(것). **4** Ⓒ 《*of*》 a statement that something is true. 승인; 고백; 자백. ¶ *He made an ~ of his guilt at last.* 그는 마침내 자기의 죄를 자백했다 / *His ~ that he was the thief solved the mystery.* 그가 훔쳤다고 자백해서 수수께끼는 풀렸다. [*admit*]

:ad·mit [ædmít, əd-] *v.* (**-mit·ted, -mit·ting**) *vt.* **1** (P6,13) 《*to, into*》 allow (someone or something) to enter; let (someone or something) in. …이 들어가는(오는) 것을 허가하다; …을 들이다. ¶ *~ a girl into* (*to*) *a school* 소녀의 입학을 허가하다 / *~ air into a room* 공기가 방에 들어오게 하다 / *This ticket admits two persons.* 이 표로 두 사람이 입장할 수 있다 / *He admitted me to his secret.* 그는 내게 비밀을 털어놓았다. **2** (P6,9,11,21) accept (something) as true or sure; acknowledge; confess. …을 인정(시인)하다. ¶ *an admitted fact* 인정된 사실 / *I ~ the mistake.* 나는 잘못을 인정한다 / *He admitted his guilt.* 그는 자기의 죄를 시인했다 / *He admits that it is true.* =*He admits it to be true.* 그는 그것이 사실임을 인정한다 / *She admits having done it herself.* 그녀는 자신이 그것을 했음을 시인한다. **3** (P6) have room or space for (someone or something). …을 수용할 수 있다. ¶ *This room admits five persons.* 이 방은 다섯 사람을 수용할 수 있다.
— *vi.* (P3) **1** 《*of*》 allow; leave room for. …의 여지가 있다. ¶ *It admits of improvement.* 향상(개선)의 여지가 있다 / *It admits of doubt.* 의문의 여지가 있다. **2** 《*to*》 ⓐ confess; state as true. 자백하다; (사실로) 인정하다. ¶ *He would not ~ to having stolen the money.* 그는 돈을 훔쳤음을 시인하려 하지 않는다. ⓑ allow entrance to; afford access to. 들어갈 수 있다; 통하다. ¶ *This gate admits to the garden.* 이 문은 정원으로 통한다. [ad-, L. *mitto* let go]

ad·mit·tance [ædmítəns, əd-] *n.* Ⓤ the act of admitting; the right or permission to enter. 입장; 입장 허가. ¶ *grant someone ~ to a meeting* 아무에게 회의에의 입장을 허가하다 / *I was refused ~.* 입장이 거절되었다 / *No ~ (except on business).* (볼일 없는 사람) 들어오지 말 것 / *Admittance only to adults.* 미성년자 사절.

ad·mit·ted·ly [ædmítidli, əd-] *adv.* by general agreement. 이의(異議) 없이; 명백히.

ad·mix [ædmíks, əd-] *vt.* (P6,13) 《*with*》 mix (things) together. …을 한데 섞다.
— *vi.* become mixed. 섞이다. [ad-, L. *misceo* mix]

ad·mix·ture [ædmíkstʃər, əd-] *n.* **1** Ⓤ the act of mixing. 섞음; 혼합. **2** Ⓒ something added by mixing. 혼합물.

ad·mon·ish [ædmániʃ, əd- / -mɔ́n-] *vt.* (P6,13,15,20) **1** give advice to (someone). (아무)에게 …하도록 타이르다(권하다). ¶ *The policeman admonished him to drive carefully.* 순경은 조심해서 차를 몰도록 그에게 타일렀다. **2** blame or scold gently. (아무)를 온건하게 꾸짖다(비난하다). ¶ *He admonished me to be more careful.* 좀더 조심하라고 나에게 주의를 주었다 / *The teacher admonished the student for his careless mistake.*

선생님은 그 학생에게 부주의로 인한 잘못을 꾸짖어 깨우쳤다. [ad-, L. *moneo* warn]

ad·mo·ni·tion [æ̀dməníʃən] *n.* Ⓤ the act of warning. 타이름; 훈계; 경고.

ad·mon·i·to·ry [ædmánitɔ̀:ri, əd- / -mɔ́nitəri] *adj.* warning. 경고하는[적인]; 타이르는.

ad nau·se·am [æd nɔ́:ziəm, -si-, -æ̀m] *adv.* 《L.》 to the point of nausea or disgust. 지겨울[신물이 날] 정도로.

a·do [ədú:] *n.* Ⓤ trouble; fuss; excitement. 곤란; 야단 법석; 소동. ¶ *make much* ~ 야단 법석을 떨다 / *much* ~ *about nothing* 헛 소동 / *with much* ~ 야단 법석을 떨고; 매우 힘들여 / *without (any) more* ~ 더 이상의 어려움 없이; 나중은 힘들이지 않고 / *She made a great* ~ *because her dress did not fit.* 그녀는 옷이 맞지 않는다고 야단 법석을 떨었다. [E. *at, do*]

a·do·be [ədóubi] *n.* Ⓤ sun-dried brick. (볕에 말린) 어도비 벽돌. — *adj.* made of sun-dried brick. 어도비 벽돌로 된. ¶ *an* ~ *house* 어도비 벽돌로 지은 집. [Sp.]

ad·o·les·cence [æ̀dəlésəns], **-cen·cy** [-sənsi] *n.* Ⓤ a period between childhood and manhood or womanhood. 청년기. [↓]

ad·o·les·cent [æ̀dəlésənt] *adj.* growing from childhood to manhood or womanhood. 청년의; 청춘기의. — *n.* Ⓒ a young person in adolescence. 청춘기의 사람. [ad-, L. *aleo* grow, →adult]

A·do·nis [ədánis, ədóu-] *n.* **1** 《Gk. myth.》 a youth loved by Venus for his beauty. 아도니스. **2** Ⓒ a beautiful youth. 미청년. **3** Ⓒ a dandy. 멋쟁이. ● **a·don·ic** [ədánik / ədɔ́n-] *adj.*

:a·dopt [ədápt / ədɔ́pt] *vt.* (P6,13) **1** choose and use (something) as one's own; take over. (생각·방법 등)을 채택[채용]하다. ¶ ~ *a new method* 새 방법을 택하다 / *words adopted from a foreign language* 외래어 / *I thought your idea a good one, so I adopted it.* 네 생각이 좋은 것으로 여겨져 그것을 택했다. **2** take another's child legally into one's family and bring up as one's own child. …을 양자로 삼다. ¶ *an adopted child* 양자 / ~ *someone as one's child* 아무를 양자로 삼다 / ~ *a child into a family* 어린애를 가족의 일원으로 하다. **3** vote to accept (a plan). …을 가결하다. [L. *opto* choose]

·a·dop·tion [ədápʃən / ədɔ́p-] *n.* ⓊⒸ the act of adopting; the state of being adopted. 채택; 선택; 양자 결연. ¶ *His* ~ *by the kind old man changed his whole life.* 그 친절한 노인이 그를 양자로 맞음으로써 그의 전생애는 바뀌었다.

a·dop·tive [ədáptiv / ədɔ́p-] *adj.* taken (related) by adoption. 양자 관계의. ¶ ~ *parents* 양(養)부모.

a·dor·a·ble [ədɔ́:rəbəl] *adj.* **1** worthy of being respected. 숭배[존경]할 만한. **2** 《*colloq.*》 very charming. 매력이 있는; 사랑스러운; 귀여운. ● **a·dor·a·bly** [-i] *adv.* [↓]

ad·o·ra·tion [æ̀dəréiʃən] *n.* Ⓤ **1** the act of worshiping. 숭배. ¶ *the* ~ *of God* 하느님 숭배. **2** deep, great love and devotion. 애모(愛慕); 동경. [*adore*]

·a·dore [ədɔ́:r] *vt.* **1** (P6) love greatly. …을 애모(愛慕)[몹시 사랑]하다. ¶ ~ *a woman* 여인을 애모하다. **2** (P6) worship. …을 숭배하다. ¶ ~ *God* 하느님을 숭배하다. **3** (P6,9) 《*colloq.*》 like very much. …을 매우 좋아하다. ¶ ~ *cakes* 케이크를 무척 좋아하다 / *He adores going to the cinema.* 그는 영화 구경 가기를 무척 좋아한다. [L. *adoro* reverence]

a·dor·er [ədɔ́:rər] *n.* Ⓒ a person who adores; an admirer. 숭배자; 애모(愛慕)자; 동경자.

a·dor·ing [ədɔ́:riŋ] *adj.* showing or expressing worship, love, etc. 숭배하는; 애모(愛慕)[동경]하는. ● **a·dor·ing·ly** [-li] *adv.*

·a·dorn [ədɔ́:rn] *vt.* (P6,13) **1** 《*with*》 make (something) beautiful. …을 장식하다[꾸미다]. ¶ ~ *oneself with jewels* 보석으로 꾸미다[치장하다]. **2** add splendor to (something). …에 광채를 더하다. ¶ ~ *one's character* 인격을 닦다 / ~ *the stage* 무대에 광채를 더하다. [ad-, L. *orno* ornament]

a·dorn·ment [ədɔ́:rnmənt] *n.* **1** Ⓤ the act of adorning; the state of being adorned. 꾸밈; 장식. **2** Ⓒ something that adorns. 장식품. ¶ *the adornments of the church* 교회의 장식물.

a·down [ədáun] *adv.* 《*arch., poet.*》 = down.

ad rem [æd rém] *adj., adv.* 《L.》 to the purpose. 요령 있는[있게]; 적절한[하게].

ad·re·nal [ədrí:nəl] *adj.* **1** near or on the kidney. 신장(腎臟) 부근의. **2** of or from the adrenal glands. 부신(副腎)의[으로부터]. — *n.* adrenal gland. 부신(副腎). [ad-, →renal, L. *resne* reins]

a·dren·al·in(e) [ədrénəlin] *n.* Ⓤ **1** hormone produced by the adrenal glands. 부신(副腎) 호르몬. **2** 《*A-*》 《trademark》 a white, crystalline drug, used to excite the heart. 아드레날린제(劑)《강장제》. [↑]

A·dri·at·ic [èidriǽtik, æ̀d-] *adj.* of the sea of this name, east of Italy. 아드리아 해의.

a·drift [ədríft] *adv., adj.* 《as *predicative*》 **1** floating without being guided; drifting. 표류하고; 물에 떠돌아다니는. ¶ *be* ~ *upon the world* 세상을 떠돌고 있다. **2** 《*fig.*》 without being guided; without moral direction. 어찌할 바를 모르고[모르는]. ¶ *a man* ~ 방황하는 사람. [a-, →drift]

go adrift, **a**) float at random. 표류하다. **b**) wander from the main subject. (이야기가 주제에서) 벗어나다; 일탈하다.

turn someone adrift, dismiss him from service; turn him out of home. …을 내쫓다. ¶ *The angry man turned his son* ~. 그 성난 사람은 자기 아들을 내쫓아 버렸다.

a·droit [ədrɔ́it] *adj.* having the ability to do

something well; skillful. 솜씨 좋은; 재주있는; 교묘한. ¶ *an ~ workman* 솜씨 있는 장색(匠色) / *He is ~ in* 〔*at*〕 *making excuses.* 그는 구실을 만드는 데 능란하다. ● **a·droit·ness** [-nis] *n.* [ad-, L. *rego* put straight]

a·droit·ly [ədrɔ́itli] *adv.* with skill and cleverness. 솜씨 좋게; 교묘하게.

ad·sci·ti·tious [æ̀dsətíʃəs] *adj.* **1** added from without. 외래(外來)의. **2** supplemental; additional. 보충적인; 부가적〔부수적〕인. [ad-, L. *scico* acknowledge]

ad·sorb [ædsɔ́ːrb, -zɔ́ːrb] *vt.* (P6) 《chem.》 gather (a gas, liquid, or dissolved substance) on a surface in a condensed layer. 흡착(吸着)하다〔시키다〕. [ad-, L. *sorbeo* suck in]

ad·sorb·ent [ædsɔ́ːrbənt, -zɔ́ːr-] *adj.* adsorbing. 흡착성(吸着性)의.

ad·sorp·tion [ædsɔ́ːrpʃən, -zɔ́ːrp-] *n.* Ⓤ adsorbing or being adsorbed. 흡착 (작용).

ad·u·late [ǽdʒəlèit] *vt.* (P6) speak too highly of (someone); praise (someone) too much. (특히 환심을 사기 위해) (아무)에게 아첨하다. ● **ad·u·la·tor** [-tər] *n.* [L. *adulor* fawn on]

ad·u·la·tion [æ̀dʒəléiʃən] *n.* Ⓤ the act of adulating; excessive praise. 아첨; 빌붙음. ● **ad·u·la·tor·y** [ǽdʒələtɔ̀ːri / -lèitəri] *adj.*

·**a·dult** [ədʌ́lt, ǽdʌlt] *adj.* full-grown; mature. 성장한; 성인〔어른〕의. ¶ *an ~ man* 성인 남자 / *~ education* 성인 교육. — *n.* Ⓒ a full-grown person or animal. 어른; 성인; 성장한 동물〔식물〕. ● **a·dult·ness** [-nis] *n.* [L. *oleo* grow]

a·dul·ter·ant [ədʌ́ltərənt] *adj.* adulterating. 섞음질의; 섞음질을 하는. — *n.* a thing of lower value mixed in with something else. 섞음질한 것; 불순물. [↓]

a·dul·ter·ate [ədʌ́ltərèit] *vt.* (P6,13) 《*with*》 make (something) poorer in quality by adding something improper. (조악품(粗惡品)을 섞어) …의 품질을 떨어뜨리다. ¶ *~ milk with water* 우유에 물을 섞다. — [-rit, -rèit] *adj.* **1** counterfeit. 가짜의. **2** adulterous. 간통의. [ad-, L. *alter* other]

a·dul·ter·a·tion [ədʌ̀ltəréiʃən] *n.* **1** Ⓤ the act of adulterating. 섞음질하기. **2** Ⓒ something adulterated. 섞음질한 것; 조악품.

a·dul·ter·er [ədʌ́ltərər] *n.* a man guilty of adultery. 간통자; 간부(姦夫).

a·dul·ter·ess [ədʌ́ltəris] *n.* a woman guilty of adultery. 간통한 여자; 간부(姦婦).

a·dul·ter·ous [ədʌ́ltərəs] *adj.* guilty of adultery. 간통의. ¶ *an ~ woman* 간통한 여자.

a·dul·ter·y [ədʌ́ltəri] *n.* ⓊⒸ (*pl.* **-ter·ies**) sexual unfaithfulness of a husband or wife. 간통.

ad·um·brate [ædʌ́mbreit, ǽdəmbrèit] *vt.* (P6) **1** show the general form of (a future event). (미래 계획 따위의) 어렴풋한 윤곽을 보이다; 윤곽을 그리다. ¶ *~ the plan* 그 계획의 개요를 말하다. **2** foreshadow; foreshow. 미리 나타내다; 예시하다. **3** overshadow. 그늘지게 하다; (부분적으로) 어둡게 하다. [L. *umbra* shade]

adv. **1** adverb; adverbial. **2** advertisement.

ad va·lo·rem [æd vəlɔ́ːrəm] *adj., adv.* 《L.》 in proportion to the value of goods. 값에 따른〔따라〕; 종가(從價)의.

:**ad·vance** [ædvǽns, -vɑ́ːns, əd-] *vi.* (P1, 2A,2B,3) **1** go 〔move〕 forward. 앞으로 나아가다〔나오다〕; 전진하다. ¶ *The troops advanced.* 군대는 전진하였다 / *We advanced three miles a day.* 우리는 하루 3 마일씩 나아갔다 / *The crowd advanced toward the station.* 군중은 정거장 쪽으로 전진했다 / *He advanced on me threateningly.* 그는 위협적인 태도로 나에게 다가왔다. **2** improve; make progress; develop. 진보〔향상〕하다; 발달하다. ¶ *~ in knowledge* 지식이 향상하다 / *He advanced in mathematics.* 그는 수학 실력이 늘었다. **3** rise in rank, price, etc. (지위·값·가치·나이 등이) 오르다; 출세〔승진〕하다. ¶ *~ in rank* 지위가 오르다 / *~ in life* 〔*in the world*〕 출세하다 / *~ in years* 나이를 먹다 / *Prices have advanced 7 percent during the year.* 물가가 연간 7 퍼센트 올랐다.

— *vt.* (P6,13,14) **1** put 〔push, move〕 (someone or something) forward. 앞으로 나아가게 하다; 내(밀어)놓다. ¶ *Please ~ the table a little.* 테이블을 앞으로 약간 내놓으시오 / *The troops were advanced.* 군대는 진군했다. **2** promote; hasten. 촉진하다; 진척시키다. ¶ *~ one's work* 일을 촉진하다 / *~ growth* 성장을 촉진하다. **3** bring forward (a suggestion, statement, claim). (제안 따위)를 제출〔제시〕하다; 내다. ¶ *The plan he advanced was a good one.* 그가 내놓은 계획은 훌륭한 것이었다 / *He advanced a large claim for damages.* 그는 많은 손해 배상 청구를 냈다. **4** raise (someone) to a higher rank or position. (아무를) 승진〔출세〕시키다. ¶ *~ someone from clerk to manager* 아무를 점원에서 지배인으로 승격시키다 / *He was advanced to the rank of General.* 그는 대장으로 승진했다. **5** raise (prices). 값을 올리다. ¶ *~ the price of milk* 우유값을 올리다 / *~ the rate of discount* 할인율을 인상하다. **6** fix an earlier date for. (날짜를) 앞당기다(opp. postpone). ¶ *Let us ~ the meeting a few days.* 회합 날짜를 며칠 앞당깁시다. **7** pay (money) before the appointed time; lend (money). 기일 전에 (돈)을 지급하다; 가불해주다; (돈)을 빌려주다. ¶ *He advanced me 10 dollars of my salary.* 그는 내 월급에서 10 달러를 가불해 주었다.

— *n.* **1** Ⓤ a forward movement. 전진; 진출. ¶ *the enemy's ~* 적의 진출 / *There were so many people that our ~ was slow.* 사람들이 무척 많아서 우리의 전진은 느렸다. **2** Ⓤ

passage (of time). (때 시간의) 진행; 지나감. ¶ *with the ~ of the evening* 밤이 이슥해짐에 따라 / *You cannot stop the ~ of old age.* 노령(老齡)의 진행은 막을 수가 없다. **3** Ⓒ progress; development; improvement. 진보; 진척; 발전; 향상. ¶ *an ~ in a task* 일의 진척 / *make an ~ in one's studies* 공부가 향상되다 / *the ~ of thought* 사상의 진보 / *There have been great advances in space travel in the last 30 years.* 지난 30 년 동안 우주 여행은 눈부신 발전을 보아왔다. **4** Ⓤ rising in rank or position. 승진. ¶ *one's ~ to the position of chief editor* 편집장으로의 승진. **5** Ⓒ a rise in price. (가격의) 상승; 오름. ¶ *an ~ in the cost of living* 생계비의 상승 / *be on the ~* 값이 오르고 있다 / *There is an ~ in wheat.* 소맥값이 상승해 있다. **6** Ⓒ payment of money before it is due; a loan. 선불(先拂); 가불; 꾸어 줌. ¶ *be given an ~ of a month's pay* 한달치 봉급의 선불을 받다 / *Please let me have an ~ of 20 dollars.* 20 달러만 가불해 주시오. **7** 《*pl.*》 offers of friendship or love. (환심을 사기 위한) 접근; 구애(求愛); (화해의) 제언(提言). ¶ *make advances to a woman* 여자에게 구애하다 / *refuse someone's advances* 아무의 제언을 거절하다.

in advance, **a**) beforehand; ahead of time. 사전에; 미리. ¶ *pay the rent in ~* 방세를 미리 내다 / *It will be necessary to get tickets well in ~.* 표는 여유있게 미리 입수해 둘 필요가 있을 게다. **b**) in front; before. 전방에; 앞에(으로). ¶ *A small force was sent on in ~.* 소부대가 전방에 파견되었다.

in advance of, **a**) ahead of time. …에 앞서. ¶ *He was thirty years in ~ of his time.* 그는 시대보다 30 년은 앞서 있었다. **b**) in front; before. …보다 앞에(으로); 전방에. ¶ *walk 2 yards in ~ of her husband* 남편보다 2 야드 앞서 걷다.

***make advances to** someone,* try to gain his friendship or good will. (환심을 사려고) …에게 접근하다; 구애(구혼)하다.

— *adj.* **1** going before. 전진하는. **2** made in advance. 예고(豫告)의. **3** having gone beyond others. (남보다) 진보한. [ad-, L. *ante* before]

advance copy [ㅡ ㅅ ㅅㅡ] *n.* a copy of a book that comes out before the official date for sending out copies. 신간 서적 견본.

·ad·vanced [ədvǽnst, -vɑ́:nst, əd-] *adj.* far ahead of others in age, ideas, progress, action, etc. (나이·사상 따위가) 진행된; 진보된. ¶ *an ~ age* 고령 / *an ~ class in French* 프랑스어 고급반 / *~ students* 상급 학생 / *an ~ idea (philosopher)* 진보적 사상(철학자) / *an ~ stage of disease* 중병 / *be ~ in years* 꽤 고령이다.

advance(d) guard [ㅡ ㅅ ㅅ] *n.* 전위(前衛)(부대).

·ad·vance·ment [ədvǽnsmənt, -vɑ́:ns-, əd-] *n.* Ⓤ the act of advancing; the state of being advanced. 전진; 진보; 승진. ¶ *the ~ of learning* 학문의 진보 / *~ in fortune* 재산의 증가 / *~ in life* 출세.

advance party [ㅡ ㅅ ㅅㅡ] *n.* a group (as of soldiers) that travels ahead of the main group. 선발대; 선견대.

:ad·van·tage [ædvǽntidʒ, -vɑ́:n-, əd-] *n.* (opp. disadvantage) **1** Ⓤ benefit; gain. 이익; 편의. ¶ *There is no ~ in doing such a thing.* 그런 일을 해도 아무런 득(得)도 안 된다. **2** Ⓒ anything that helps someone to lead over others; superiority; a better position (of or over someone). 이점(利點); 강점; 우월; 우위. ¶ *the ~ of ground* 지(地)의 이(利) / *the advantages of a good education* 좋은 교육을 받은 강점 / *I had the ~ of him.* 내가 그보다 우위에 있었다. **3** 《tennis》 the first point scored after deuce. 어드밴티지《듀스 후 1점의 득점》.

be (prove) to** someone's **advantage, be profitable or helpful to someone. 아무에게 이롭게(도움이) 되다.

gain an advantage over, do better than. …보다 잘(낫게)하다. ¶ *I gained an ~ over him.* 나는 그보다 더 잘했다.

have the (an) advantage of (over), **a**) be in a superior position or advantageous position; possess an advantage over. …보다 유리한 입장에 있다; …보다 나은 이점을 쥐고 있다. **b**) know somebody or something that he does not know. (상대가 모르는 사람·것을) 이쪽에서는 알고 있다. ¶ *I am afraid you have the ~ of me.* 실례지만 누구셨던가요.

take advantage of, **a**) make use of (something). …을 이용하다. ¶ *take ~ of an opportunity* 기회(호기)를 틈타다 / *He took full ~ of his position.* 그는 자신의 지위를 십분 이용했다. **b**) deceive (someone); impose upon, esp. unfairly by exploiting a weakness. 아무를 속이다; (…의 약점 따위)를 기화로 삼다. ¶ *He took ~ of me.* 그는 나를 속였다.

to advantage, for greater benefit or profit; to better effect. 유리하게; 돋보이도록. ¶ *appear to ~* 돋보이다 / *sell to ~* 비싸게 팔다 / *The music may be heard to ~ in the open air.* 음악은 야외에서 더 효과적으로 들릴 수 있다.

turn** something **to advantage, make the most of something; use it profitably. …을 활용하다; 이롭게 쓰다.

— *vt.* (P6) be beneficial to. 이익을 주다; 도움이 되다. [L. *ad ante* from before]

ad·van·ta·geous [ædvəntéidʒəs] *adj.* giving a benefit or help; favorable. 유리한. ¶ *an ~ position* 유리한 입장. ● **ad·van·ta·geous·ly** [-li] *adv.*

·ad·vent [ǽdvent, -vənt] *n.* Ⓤ **1** 《usu. *the ~*》 a coming; arrival. 도래(到來); 출현. ¶ *the ~ of spring* 봄이 옴. **2** 《*A-*》 the birth of Christ; the season including the four Sundays before Christmas. 그리스도의 강림; 예수 강림절. [ad-, L. *venio* come]

Ad·vent·ist [ǽdventist, ædvént-] *n.* one who maintains that the Second Advent is near at hand. 예수 재림론자.

ad·ven·ti·tious [ӕ̀dvəntíʃəs] *adj.* **1** not expected or planned; accidental; happening by chance. 기대하지 않은; 우연의. ¶ *the ~ birth of their 5th child* 뜻하지 않은 그들의 다섯 번째 아기의 출생. **2** coming from without. 외래(外來)의.

:ad·ven·ture [ædvéntʃər, əd-] *n.* **1** Ⓒ Ⓤ a bold undertaking filled with excitement and danger. 모험. ¶ *the adventures of Arctic exploration* 북극 탐험의 모험 / *Hunters often have many adventures.* 사냥꾼들은 종종 많은 모험을 하게 된다. **2** Ⓒ an exciting or unusual experience. 이상한[뜻하지 않은] 경험. ¶ *a strange ~* 기묘한 일 / *quite an ~* 정말이지 이상한 경험 / *the Adventures of Robinson Crusoe* 로빈슨 크루소의 표류 모험담 / *seek adventures* 무언가 색다른 일을 찾아다니다. **3** Ⓤ a liking for excitement and risk. 모험심. ¶ *His life was full of ~.* 그의 생애는 모험심에 가득 찬 것이었다.
— *vi.* (P1,3) do a bold thing. 모험을 하다; 위험을 무릅쓰고 감히 하다.
— *vt.* (P6) take a chance on (something). 모험을 하다; 운을 걸고 해보다. ¶ *~ one's life on the undertaking* 그 사업에 자신의 생애를 걸다. [*advent*]

ad·ven·tur·er [ædvéntʃərər, əd-] *n.* Ⓒ **1** a person who has or likes to have adventures. 모험가. **2** a person who tries to get money by questionable means. 투기꾼.

ad·ven·ture·some [ædvéntʃərsəm, əd-] *adj.* bold and daring. 모험적인; 대담한; 용감한.

ad·ven·tur·ess [ædvéntʃəris, əd-] *n.* a woman who lives a dangerous and dishonest life. 여자 모험가.

ad·ven·tur·ous [ædvéntʃərəs, əd-] *adj.* fond of adventure; bold. 모험을 좋아하는; 대담한. **2** filled with danger. 위험한. ¶ *an ~ journey* 위험한 여행.

:ad·verb [ǽdvəːrb] *n.* Ⓒ《gram.》a word which modifies a verb, adjective, or another adverb, by telling time, place, degree, etc. 부사. [ad-, →verb]

ad·ver·bi·al [ædvə́ːrbiəl] *adj.* of or used as an adverb. 부사의.

ad ver·bum [æd və́ːrbəm] *adv.*《L.》word for word. 축어적(逐語的)으로.

·ad·ver·sar·y [ǽdvərsèri / -səri] *n.* Ⓒ (*pl.* **-ries**) a person or group that opposes another; an enemy. 적대자[당]; 상대; 적. [*adverse*]

ad·ver·sa·tive [ædvə́ːrsətiv, əd-] *adj.* expressing opposition. 반대의; 반의(反意)의. ¶ *an ~ clause* 반의 접속절.

ad·verse [ædvə́ːrs, ⌐–] *adj.* **1** contrary in direction; opposed. 역(逆)의; 반대의. ¶ *an ~ current* 역류(逆流) / *~ winds* 역풍. **2** unfavorable or antagonistic; going against. 불리한; 적대하는. ¶ *~ fate* 〔*fortune*〕 불운 / *an ~ opinion* 반대 의견 / *opinions ~ criticism* 적의에 찬 비평; 비난 / *be under ~ circumstances* 역경에 처해 있다 / *The judge gave us an ~ decision.* 판사는 우리에게 불리한 판결을 내렸다 / *The situation was ~ to us.* 형세는 우리에게 불리했다. ●**ad·verse·ly** [-li] *adv.* [L. *verto* turn]

ad·ver·si·ty [ædvə́ːrsəti, əd-] *n.* Ⓤ Ⓒ (*pl.* **-ties**) misfortune; great trouble. 역경; 불운; 불행.

ad·vert [ædvə́ːrt, əd-] *vi.* (P3) **1**《*to*》turn attention; notice. 주의를 돌리다. ¶ *I didn't ~ to it.* 나는 그것에 주의를 돌리지 않았다. **2**《*to*》draw attention to in speaking or writing; refer. 언급[논급]하다. ¶ *The speaker adverted to the problem.* 연사는 그 문제에 대해 언급했다. [ad-, L. *verto* to turn]

·ad·ver·tise, -tize [ǽdvərtàiz, ⌐–⌐] *vt.* (P6) **1** make (something) generally known by means of printed matter, radio, or the like. …을 광고〔공고〕하다. ¶ *~ a house for sale* 집의 매각 광고를 하다 / *~ one's wares* 상품을 광고하다. **2**《*of*》inform. …을 알리다〔통고하다〕. — *vi.* (P1,3) **1**《*for*》put a notice in a newspaper, etc. 신문(따위)에 광고하다. ¶ *~ for a job* 구직 광고를 하다. **2** call attention to oneself. 자기 선전을 하다. ¶ *It is a pity he advertises so much.* 그가 그토록 자기 선전을 하다니 딱하다. [↑]

·ad·ver·tise·ment, -tize- [ӕ̀dvərtáizmənt, ædvə́ːrtis-, -tiz-] *n.* **1** Ⓤ the act of advertising. 광고. 參考 ad., adv., advt.로 생략함. ¶ *~ column* 광고란. **2** Ⓒ a public notice. 공고. ¶ *put an ~ in a newspaper* 신문에 광고를 내다.

ad·ver·tis·er, -tiz- [ǽdvərtàizər] *n.* Ⓒ a person who advertises. 광고자.

·ad·ver·tis·ing, -tiz- [ǽdvərtàiziŋ] *n.* Ⓤ **1** the business of advertising. 광고업. **2** advertisement. 광고. ¶ *newspaper ~* 신문 광고. — *adj.* of advertisement. 광고의. ¶ *~ agency* 광고 대행사.

:ad·vice [ædváis, əd-] *n.* **1** Ⓤ an opinion about what to do; counsel. 충고; 조언; 의견. ¶ *ask* 〔*seek*〕 *~* 조언을 청하다 / *take* 〔*follow*〕 *someone's ~* 아무의 충고에 따르다 / *act on someone's ~* 아무의 충고에 따라 행동하다 / *give someone a piece of ~* 아무에게 한마디 충고를 주다 / *take the doctor's ~* 의사의 충고에 따르다 / *Let me give you a piece* 〔*bit, word*〕 *of ~.* 한마디 충고를 하겠네. **2**《usu. *pl.*》news; information. 보고; 통지; 보도. ¶ *a letter of ~* 통지장(通知狀) / *advices from New York* 뉴욕으로부터의 정보 / *diplomatic advices* 외교상의 보고 / *Advices from China show that there will be no war.* 중국으로부터의 정보들은 전쟁이 없을 것임을 보여 주고 있다. [L. *video* see]

ad·vis·a·bil·i·ty [ædvàizəbíləti, əd-] *n.* Ⓤ the quality of being advisable. 합당함; 바람

직함; 현명.

ad·vis·a·ble [ædváizəbəl, əd-] *adj.* advised; wise. 합당한; 바람직스러운; 현명한. ¶ *It would be ~ to do so.* 그렇게 하는 것이 좋을 게다 / *It is not ~ for him to go out while he is still ill.* 그가 아직 병중인데도 외출한다는 것은 현명치 못하다. ● **ad·vis·a·bly** [-bli] *adv.*

:ad·vise [ædváiz, əd-] *vt.* (P6,9,16,17,20) **1** give advice to (someone); give an opinion of the best thing to do; recommend. 아무에게 충고[조언]하다; 권하다. ¶ *He advised me to keep my money in the bank.* 그는 돈을 은행에 넣어 두도록 나에게 충고했다 / *The doctor advised a change of air.* 의사는 전지(轉地) 요양을 권했다. **2** 《*of*》 give notice to (someone); make (someone) know; teach. (아무에게) 통지하다; 알리다. ¶ *He advised me of his arrival.* 그는 나에게 그의 도착을 알렸다 / *They were advised of the danger.* 그들은 위험을 통지받았다 / *We will ~ you when the goods arrive.* 물품이 도착하면 알려 드리겠습니다.

—*vi.* (P1) **1** give advice. 충고하다. **2** 《rare》 talk over (plans, etc.) with others. 의논[상의]하다. ¶ *I must ~ with you on the matter.* 그 문제를 자네와 상의해야겠네. [→advice]

ad·vised [ædváizd, əd-] *adj.* considered. 숙고한.

ad·vis·ed·ly [ædváizidli, əd-] *adv.* after careful thought; on purpose. 숙고한 끝에; 일부러.

ad·vise·ment [ædváizmənt, əd-] *n.* Ⓤ careful consideration. 숙고; 숙려(熟慮).

·ad·vis·er, 《U.S.》 **-vi·sor** [ædváizər, əd-] *n.* Ⓒ **1** a person who gives advice. 충고자; 조언자. **2** 《U.S.》 a teacher who advises students. 지도 교사.

ad·vi·so·ry [ædváizəri, əd-] *adj.* having authority to give advice. 충고의; 조언의; 고문[자문]의. ¶ *an ~ letter* 충고의 편지 / *an ~ committee* 자문 위원회.

ad·vo·ca·cy [ǽdvəkəsi] *n.* Ⓤ the act of speaking in favor. 변호; 옹호; 지지. [↓]

·ad·vo·cate [ǽdvəkit] *vt.* (P6,9) speak in favor of (something); defend. …을 옹호하다; 지지하다; 주창하다. ¶ *He advocates building more schools.* 그는 학교를 더 짓기를 주장한다. 語法 뒤에 that-clause를 취하지 않음. —[ǽdvəkit, -kèit] *n.* Ⓒ **1** a person who advocates. 옹호자; 주창자. ¶ *an ~ of early rising* 아침 일찍 일어나기 주창자. **2** a person who defends others in a court of law. 변호사. ● **ad·vo·ca·tion** [-kéiʃən] *n.* **ad·vo·ca·tor** [-kèitər] *n.* [ad-, L. *voco* call]

ad·y·ta [ǽditə] *n.* pl. of **adytum.**

ad·y·tum [ǽditəm] *n.* (*pl.* **-ta**) the sanctum. (교회의) 성단(聖壇); 지성소(至聖所). [Gk. *a-* not, *duō* enter]

adz, adze [ædz] *n.* Ⓒ a curved tool like an ax, used for shaping wood. 까뀌. [E.]

AEC Atomic Energy Commission.

Ae·ge·an [i(:)dʒíːən] *adj.* of the Aegean. 에게해의. —*n.* 《*the ~*》 the sea between Greece and Turkey. 에게해(海). ¶ *the ~ (Sea)* 에게해 / *the ~ Islands* 에게해 제도(諸島).

ae·ger [íːdʒər] *n.* a note certifying that a student is ill. 병 진단서. [L.=sick]

ae·gis [íːdʒis] *n.* **1** Ⓒ 《Gk. myth.》 a shield or breastplate used by Zeus or Athena. 방패; 가슴받이. **2** Ⓤ protection; support. 보호; 후원. ¶ *appear under the ~ of* (*someone*) (아무)의 보호를 받고 나타나다 / *The program was carried out under the ~ of UNESCO.* 그 계획은 유네스코 후원 아래 실행에 옮겨졌다. [Gk. *aigis*]

ae·o·li·an harp [iːóuliən hɑ́ːrp] *n.* a box-like stringed instrument that produces musical sounds when currents of air blow across it. 에올리언 하프; 풍주금(風奏琴)《바람 부는 곳에 두면 저절로 울리는》. [Gk.]

ae·on, e·on [íːən, -ɑn] *n.* a very long period of time that can be measured. (무한히) 긴 시기; 영겁(永劫). ¶ *Aeons passed before life existed on the earth.* 지구상에 생명체가 존재하기까지는 무한한 시간이 흘렀다. [Gk. *aion*]

aer·ate [ɛ́əreit, éiərèit] *vt.* (P6) **1** expose (something) to the action of the air. …을 공기[바람]에 쐬다. **2** fill (liquid) with air or gas. (액체)에 공기나 가스를 넣다. ¶ *aerated waters* 탄산수 / *aerated bread* 무효모(無酵母) 빵. [→air]

aer·a·tion [ɛəréiʃən, éiərèi-] *n.* **1** exposing to air. 공기에 쐬기. **2** filling with air or with a gas. (액체에) 공기나 가스 넣기. [→air]

aer·i·al [ɛ́əriəl, eiíər-] *adj.* **1** of like, or in the air. 공기의; 공중의. ¶ *an ~ current* 기류(氣流) / *an ~ railway* [*ropeway*] 케이블; 가공(架空) 공중 삭도 / *an ~ telegraph* 무선 전신 / *an ~ wire* 공중선 / *an ~ performance* 공중 곡예. **2** not real or solid. 가공(架空)의; 실체 없는. ¶ *~ fancies* 공상. **3** of aircraft or flight. 항공(기)에 관한. ¶ *an ~ line* [*route*] 항(공)로 / *an ~ chart* 항공도(圖) / *an ~ photograph* 항공 사진. **4** reaching high into the air. 공중 높이 치솟음. ¶ *~ spires* 하늘 높이 치솟은 뾰족탑.

—[ɛ́əriəl] *n.* Ⓒ wires or rods for sending out or receiving electric waves; an antenna. 공중선; 안테나. [→air]

aer·ie, aer·y [ɛ́əri, íəri] *n.* Ⓒ **1** a high nest of an eagle, etc. (독수리·매 등의) 높은 둥지. **2** an eagle's young. 독수리 새끼. **3** 《*fig.*》 a house or castle built on a high rock or hill. 높은 곳에 있는 집 또는 성채. [F. *aire*]

aer·i·form [ɛ́ərəfɔ̀ːrm, eiíər-] *adj.* of the form of air. 공기 모양의. [→aero-]

aer·i·fy [ɛ́ərəfài, eiíər-] *vt.* (**-fied, -fy·ing**)

(P6) convert into vapor; aerate. 기화(氣化)시키다; 공기에 쐬다. [↑]

aer·o [ɛ́ərou] *n.* 《*colloq.*》 an airplane. 비행기. [↓]

aer·o- [ɛ́ərou-] *pref.* having to do with the air. '공기, 공중, 항공'의 뜻. ¶ *aero*lite, *aero*dynamics. [Gk. *aēr* air]

aer·o·bat·ics [ɛ̀ərəbǽtiks] *n. pl.* **1** the acrobatic flight of an airplane. 곡예 비행. **2** 《used as *sing.*》 the art of doing such flights. 고등 비행술. [aero-, Gk. *baino* go]

aer·obe [ɛ́əroub] *n.* a microorganism that requires free oxygen. 호기성(好氣性) 생물(opp. anaerobe). [aero-, Gk. *bios* life] ● **aer·o·bic** [ɛəróubik] *adj.*

aer·o·do·net·ics [ɛ̀ərou*d*ənétiks] *n. pl.* 《used as *sing.*》 the science of gliding. 활공(滑空) 역학; 활공 비행술. ● **aer·o·do·net·ic** [-dənétik] *adj.* [aero-: Gk. *donein* shake]

aer·o·drome [ɛ́ərədròum] *n.* 《Brit.》 = airdrome.

aer·o·dy·nam·ics [ɛ̀əroudainǽmiks] *n. pl.* the science of the air in a state of motion. 기체(氣體)〔항공〕 역학. [aero-, Gk. *dynamis* power]

aer·o·gram, 《Brit.》 **-gramme** [ɛ́ərəgræ̀m] *n.* Ⓒ **1** a message sent by radio. 무선 전보〔전신〕. **2** a letter, parcel, or the like sent by air mail. 항공 우편〔서한〕. [aero-, →-gram]

aer·o·lite [ɛ́ərəlàit] *n.* a meteoric stone. 석질(石質) 운석(隕石). [aero-, Gk. *lithos* stone]

aer·ol·o·gy [ɛərάlədʒi / ɛərɔ́lədʒi] *n.* (*pl.* **-gies**) **1** =meteorology. **2** a branch of meteorology that deals esp. with the air. 고층 기상학《기상학의 한 부문》. [aero-, →-logy]

aer·o·me·chan·ics [ɛ̀əroumәkǽniks] *n. pl.* aerodynamics or aerostatics. 기체〔항공〕 역학. [aero-, GK. *mēchanē* machine]

aer·o·naut [ɛ́ərənɔ̀:t] *n.* an aviator. 항공사. [aero-, Gk. *nautēs* sailor]

aer·o·naut·ic(al) [ɛ̀ərənɔ́:tik(əl)] *adj.* of or having to do with aeronautics. 항공(술)의.

aer·o·nau·tics [ɛ̀ərənɔ́:tiks] *n. pl.* 《used as *sing.*》 the science of building and operating aircraft. 항공술; 항공학.

aer·o·pause [ɛ́ərəpɔ̀:z] *n.* a region beginning from 65,000 to 75,000 feet above the earth. 대기 계면(大氣界面)《지상에서 약 20-23km 사이의 대기층》. [aero-, Gk. *pausis* stopping]

:aer·o·plane [ɛ́ərəplèin] *n.* Ⓒ 《Brit.》 =airplane. [aero-, Gk. *planus* plane]

aer·o·stat·ics [ɛ̀ərəstǽtiks] *n. pl.* 《used as *sing.*》 the science of the air in a state of rest. 기체 정역학(靜力學). [aero-, Gk. *statos* sustaining]

aer·y [ɛ́əri, íəri] *n.* =aerie.

Aes·chy·lus [éskələs / í:s-] *n.* (525-456 B.C.) a Greek tragic poet. 아이스킬로스《그리스의 비극 시인》.

Ae·sop [í:səp, -sαp / -sɔp] *n.* (620 ?-560 B.C.) a Greek fable writer. 이솝《그리스의 우화 작가》. ¶ *Aesop's Fables* 이솝 이야기.

aes·thete [ésθi:t / í:s-] *n.* Ⓒ **1** a person who has a keen sensibility to beauty and art. 심미가(審美家). **2** a person who pays too much attention to art and beauty, neglecting practical matters. 탐미주의자(耽美主義者). [↓]

aes·thet·ic [esθétik / i:s-] *adj.* **1** the philosophy of beauty. 미학적인. ¶ *an* ~ *point of view* 미학적인 견지. **2** having a sense of beauty in art or nature. 심미적인. **3** artistic. 미적인. [Gk. *aisthanomai* perceive]

aes·thet·ics [esθétiks / i:s-] *n. pl.* 《used as *sing.*》 the science of beauty and good taste. 미학(美學).

ae·ther [í:θər] *n.* =ether.

ae·the·re·al, -ri·al [iθí:riəl] *adj.* =ethereal.

af- [æf-, əf-] *pref.* =ad-《f 앞에서의 ad-의 변형; affirm》.

a·far [əfά:r] *adv.* 《*poet.*》 **1** from a distance. 멀리서. **2** far off. 멀리. [a(-)]
from afar, from a distance. 멀리서.

af·fa·bil·i·ty [æ̀fəbíləti] *n.* Ⓤ the quality of being friendly and polite in speech and manner. 상냥함; 다정함; 정중함. [↓]

af·fa·ble [ǽfəbəl] *adj.* **1** easy to talk to. 접근〔가까이〕하기 쉬운. **2** friendly and polite. 다정한; 상냥한; 정중한. ¶ *He has a very* ~ *manner.* 그는 태도가 매우 상냥하다. [ad-, L. *for* speak]

:af·fair [əfɛ́ər] *n.* Ⓒ **1** an event; a happening. 사건; 일. ¶ *a strange* ~ 이상한 사건 / *a private* 〔*public*〕 ~ 사사로운〔공적인〕 일 / *His disappearance was a strange* ~. 그의 실종은 이상한 사건이었다 / *That is my* ~. 그건 내 일이다《네가 상관할 바 아니다》. **2** 《*pl.*》 business; job. (해야 할) 일; 사무. ¶ *a man of affairs* 사무에 익숙한 사람 / *a talent for affairs* 사무적 재능 / *He has many affairs to look after.* 그는 돌보아야 할 많은 일이 있다 / *Mind your own affairs.* 남의 일에 참견마라. **3** 《*colloq.*》 any matter; a thing. (막연히 일어난) 것; 일. ¶ *The journey was a very pleasant* ~. 그 여행은 매우 즐거운 것이었다 / *Her hat was a strange* ~. 그녀의 모자는 이상한 것이었다. **4** a love-affair. 연애사건; 정사(情事). [F. *a faire* to do]

:af·fect [əfékt] *vt.* (P6,8,11) **1** have an influence on (something or someone). …에 영향을 미치다; …을 해롭게 하다. ¶ *Cares* ~ *the health.* 걱정은 건강에 해롭다 / *The amount of rain affects the growth of crops.* 강우량은 농작물 성장에 영향을 준다 / *be affected by heat* 〔*cold*〕 더위〔추위〕의 영향을 받다 / ~ *someone's opinions* 아무의 견해에 영향을 미치다. **2** move the feelings of;

touch the heart of (someone). …을 감동시키다. ¶ *The stories of starving children affected him deeply.* 그 굶주린 아이들에 관한 이야기는 그를 깊이 감동시켰다. **3** ⓐ be fond of (something). …을 좋아하다. ¶ *~ a foreign style of dress* 외국 스타일의 옷을 좋아하다 / *She affects old furniture.* 그녀는 옛날 가구를 좋아한다. ⓑ make use of. …을 사용하다. ¶ *~ the Korean costume* 한복을 즐겨 입다. **4** pretend. (짐짓) …체하다; …을 가장하다. ¶ *~ ignorance* 무식한 체하다 / *~ illness* 병을 앓는 체하다 / *~ an air of kindness* 친절을 가장하다 / *He affects carelessness in dress.* 그는 옷차림에 무관심한 체한다 / *He affected to be deaf.* 그는 귀머거리인 체했다. **5** tend to assume. (사물이) …형태를 잘 취하다. ¶ *~ a peculiar shape* 특유의 형태를 취하다. **6** haunt; frequent. 자주 가다; 드나들다; 출입하다. [ad-, L. *facio* do]

af·fec·ta·tion [æ̀fektéiʃən] *n.* UC the act of pretending; a false show of manners, etc.; unnatural behavior. (짐짓) …체하기; 꾸밈; 가장. ¶ *an ~ of kindness* [*sincerity*] 친절한[성실한] 체함 / *with an ~ of wit* 재치 있는 듯이 / *without ~* 꾸밈없이; 솔직히[한].

af·fect·ed [əféktid] *adj.* **1** influenced seriously; diseased. 영향을 받은; (병 따위에) 침범된. ¶ *an ~ part of the body* 환부(患部) / *the ~ district* 피해지. **2** stirred up; moved in emotion. 감동받은. ¶ *well-affected* 탄복한 / *I was too much ~ to answer.* 너무 감동해서 대답을 못했다. **3** pretended; not natural. 짐짓 꾸민; …체하는; 부자연스러운. ¶ *an ~ girl* 짐짓 센체하는 소녀 / *an ~ way of speaking* 부자연스런 말투.

af·fect·ing [əféktiŋ] *adj.* having the power move the emotions. 감동시키는; 마음 아픈; 애처로운. ¶ *an ~ sight* 애처로운 광경 / *The man told an ~ story of suffering.* 그 남자는 가슴 아픈 재난 이야기를 했다. ● **af·fect·ing·ly** [-li] *adv.*

:af·fec·tion [əfékʃən] *n.* **1** UC friendly feeling; love; good-will. 애정; 호의(opp. dislike). ¶ *motherly ~* 모정(母情); 모성애 / *the object of ~* 사랑하는[의중의] 사람 / *have ~ for* [*toward*] *a girl* 처녀에게 애정을 품다 / *gain* [*win*] *someone's affection(s)* 아무에게 애정을 얻다 / *devote one's ~ on someone* 아무에게 애정을 바치다 / *set one's affections on* …에게 호의를 보이다. **2** C a disease. 병; 질환. ¶ *He is suffering from an ~ of the ear.* 그는 귓병을 앓고 있다. [*affect*]

·af·fec·tion·ate [əfékʃənit] *adj.* full of love and tenderness. 애정에 넘친; 사랑하는; 다정한. ¶ *an ~ mother* 자모(慈母) / *an ~ care* 다정한 배려 / *an ~ letter* [*greeting*] 애정이 담긴 편지[인사].

af·fec·tion·ate·ly [əfékʃənitli] *adv.* with love; in an affectionate manner. 애정을 담아[다하여]. ¶ *Yours ~.* =*Affectionately yours.* 친애하는 …로부터; 경구(敬具); 여불비례(餘不備禮)《편지의 맺음말》.

af·fer·ent [æ̀fərənt] *adj.* 《physiol.》 bringing to a central organ or point. (혈관·신경이) 중심부로 향하는(opp. efferent). ¶ *~ nerves* 구심(求心)신경. [L. *ferro* bear]

af·fi·ance [əfáiəns] *n.* **1** U firm faith or trust. 신뢰; 신임; 믿음. ¶ *have ~ in God* 신을 믿다. **2** C a promise of marriage. 혼약. — *vt.* (P6,13) 《usu. in *passive*》 promise (someone) to marry. …와 약혼하다. ¶ *be affianced to* …와 약혼해 있다; …의 약혼자이다 / *~ oneself to* …와 약혼하다 / *He is affianced to my sister.* 그는 내 누이와 약혼해 있다[누이의 약혼자이다]. [ad-, L. *fides* faith]

af·fi·anced [əfáiənst] *adj.* engaged to be married. 약혼한. ¶ *the ~ bride* 약혼녀.

af·fi·da·vit [æ̀fədéivit] *n.* C 《law》 a written statement made with an oath, usu. in a court of law. 선서 진술서. [L. =he has stated on faith]

af·fil·i·ate [əfílièit] *vt.* (P6,13) **1** 《*with, to*》 bring (someone or something) into close association; have (someone or something) as a member. …을 깊은 관계로 만들다; …을 회원으로 하다[가입시키다]. ¶ *~ oneself with* [*to*] *the club* 그 클럽에 가입하다 / *Our school is affiliated to* [*with*] *the University.* 우리 학교는 그 대학의 부속이다 / *All the affiliated organizations are in favor of the plan.* 모든 산하 단체들은 그 안에 찬성이다. **2** adopt (a child) as one's own. …을 양자로 삼다. **3** trace the origin and relations of. (…의) 근원을[유래를] …에 있다고 하다; …의 작(作)이라고 하다. ¶ *a sonnet affiliated to* [*on*] *Shakespeare* 세익스피어작이라는 소네트 / *~ a language* 언어의 근원을 더듬다. **4** 《law》 《*to*》 fix the paternity of. …의 아비를 확인하다. ¶ *The mother affiliated her baby to him.* 어머니는 그 유아의 아버지가 그 사람이라고 했다. [ad-, →filial]

af·fil·i·a·tion [əfìliéiʃən] *n.* UC **1** the act of joining; union. 가입; 합동. **2** 《U.S.》 a friendly relationship. 가까운[우호] 관계; 제휴. ¶ *form ~ with* …와 제휴하다 / *English has affiliations with Sanskrit.* 영어는 산스크리트어와 밀접한 관계가 있다.

af·fin·i·ty [əfínəti] *n.* CU (*pl.* **-ties**) **1** relationship by marriage. 인척 관계(cf. *consanguinity*). **2** a close relationship likeness. 밀접한 관계; 관련; 유사(성). ¶ *an ~ between the two races* 두 민족 간의 밀접한 관계 / *affinities of language and culture* 언어와 문화의 유사성 / *These two animals show a certain ~.* 이 두 동물은 어떤 유연성(類緣性)을 보여주고 있다. **3** an attraction; a liking. 마음의 끌림; 친근감; 좋아함; 취미. ¶ *have an ~ for dancing* [*children*] 춤을[어린이를] 좋아하다. **4** 《chem.》 the tendency of elements to unite. 친화력(親和力). [ad-, L. *finis* end]

·af·firm [əfə́:rm] *vt.* (P6,11) **1** declare the truth of (something). …을 단언하다; 확언하

다(opp. deny). ¶ ~ *one's loyalty* 충성을 맹세하다 / *I ~ that it is not so.* 나는 그렇지 않음을 확언한다 / *She affirmed his innocence.* 그녀는 그의 무죄를 확언했다. **2** confirm. 확인하다. —*vi.* testify in a court without an oath. 증언하다. [ad-, →firm]

af·fir·ma·tion [æfərméiʃən] *n.* UC **1** the act of affirming. 긍정; 단언하기(opp. denial, negation). **2** 《law》 a statement in court which gives evidence about something. 증언.

af·firm·a·tive [əfə́:rmətiv] *adj.* answering 'yes' to a question; positive. 긍정의(opp. negative).

—*n.* 《*the* ~》 a statement of 'yes'; the 'yes' side in an argument. 긍정의 말; 찬성측(側).

answer in the affirmative, answer 'yes'. 그렇다고 대답하다; 긍정하다. ¶ *He answerd in the* ~. 그는 긍정적으로 대답했다.

● **af·firm·a·tive·ly** [-li] *adv.*

af·fix [əfíks] *vt.* (P6,13) fix (one thing) to or on another; write down (one's signature) on a document; stick (a stamp) on a letter. …을 (꼭) 붙이다; (서명 따위)를 덧붙여 쓰다; (우표 따위)를 붙이다. ¶ ~ *a stamp to a letter* 편지에 우표를 붙이다 / ~ *a label to a parcel* 소화물에 꼬리표를 붙이다. —[ǽfiks] *n.* C 《gram.》 a prefix, suffix, or infix. 접사(接辭). [ad-, →fix]

af·flat·ed [əfléitid] *adj.* inspired. 영감(靈感)을 받은. [↓]

af·fla·tion [əfléiʃən] *n.* =afflatus.

af·fla·tus [əfléitəs] *n.* U an inspiration. 영감(靈感). [ad-, L. *flo* blow]

af·flict [əflíkt] *vt.* (P6) cause pain or grief to (someone's body or mind); make (someone) miserable; trouble greatly. (심신)을 괴롭히다; 시달리게 하다; 슬프게 하다. ¶ *be afflicted with many cares* 많은 걱정에 시달리다. [L. *fligo* dash]

af·flic·tion [əflíkʃən] *n.* **1** U pain; distress; great trouble. 고뇌; 고난; 비운(悲運). ¶ *people in* ~ 고통에 시달리는 사람들. **2** C a cause of pain, distress, or trouble; a misfortune. 고통[고뇌]의 원인; 고난; 불행.

af·flu·ence [ǽflu(:)əns, əflú:-] *n.* U rich supply; great wealth. 풍부; 부(富). ¶ *live in* ~ 풍족한 생활을 하다. [↓]

af·flu·ent [ǽflu(:)ənt, əflú:-] *adj.* **1** abundant; wealthy. 풍부[풍족]한; 유복한. ¶ *an* ~ *society* 풍요로운 사회 / *land* ~ *natural resources* 천연[부존] 자원이 풍부한 땅 / *He is very* ~. 그는 아주 유복하다. **2** flowing freely. 풍부히[도도히] 흐르는. —*n.* C a river or stream flowing into a larger one. 지류(支流); 샛강. [→fluid]

af·flux [ǽflʌks] *n.* a flowing or moving toward. (한 곳으로) 흘러드는 것; 쇄도하는 것. ¶ *an* ~ *of people* 사람의 물결. [↑]

:**af·ford** [əfɔ́:rd] *vt.* **1** (P6,8) 《usu. with *can, be able to,* or *could*》 have enough money, time, etc. for (something). …할 (시간·돈 따위의) 여유가 있다. ¶ *Can we* ~ *to buy a new car?* 우린 새 차를 살 수[여유가] 있나 / *I can't* ~ *a holiday.* 나는 휴가를 가질 여유가 없다 / *Can you* ~ *the time?* 시간을 낼 수 있겠나 / *He cannot* ~ *to waste so much time.* 그는 그렇게 많은 시간을 낭비할 수 없다. **2** (P13,14) (of things) give; yield; supply. 주다; 제공하다; (천연 자원 따위)를 산출하다. ¶ *Music affords me great pleasure.* 음악은 나에게 큰 기쁨을 준다 / *The trees* ~ *pleasant shade.* 나무들은 그늘을 제공한다 / *It affords me much satisfaction to be able to help you.* 당신을 도울 수가 있어 매우 만족스럽습니다 / *The sea affords fish.* 바다에서는 물고기가 잡힌다. [A.S. *geforthian* advance]

af·for·est [əfɔ́(:)rist, əfár-] *vt.* (P6) change (bare or cultivated land) into a forest. (헐벗은 땅이나 밭)에 나무를 심다; 조림하다 (opp. deforest). [ad-, →forest]

af·fray [əfréi] *n.* C **1** a noisy quarrel. 싸움. **2** 《law》 a fight in a public place. (공공장소에서의) 싸움; 소동. [M.E. *affrai* attack, alarm]

af·fri·cate [ǽfrikit] *n.* 《phon.》 a sound which begins with a stop and ends with a spirant. 파찰음(破擦音)《e.g. *ch* in *chin*》. [L. *frico* rub]

af·fright [əfráit] 《*arch., poet.*》 *vt.* (P6) frighten; excite with sudden fear. 놀라게 하다; 무섭게 하다. —*n.* sudden fear; fright. 공포; 경악; 협박. [→fright]

af·front [əfrʌ́nt] *vt.* (P6) **1** insult (someone) openly and on purpose. (일부러) …을 모욕하다. ¶ *He affronted her before her husband.* 그는 남편 앞에서 그 여자를 모욕했다. **2** offend the modesty or pride of. (명예·자존심 등)을 상하게 하다; 훼손하다. ¶ *The people of the village were affronted by her haughty manner.* 마을 사람들은 그녀의 오만한 태도로 자존심을 상했다. **3** meet (death) face to face. (죽음 따위)에 맞서다; 직면하다. ¶ ~ *death a hundred times* 백번이나 죽음에 직면하다.

—*n.* C an open insult. 공공연한 모욕. ¶ *put an* ~ *upon someone* (아무)를 모욕하다 / *To be called a coward is an* ~ *to a manly boy.* 겁쟁이로 불리는 것은 씩씩한 소년에겐 모욕이다. [→front]

af·fu·sion [əfjú:ʒən] *n.* 《relligion》 pouring on (of water). 관수(灌水); (세례의) 관수식(灌水式). [→fuse]

Af·ghan [ǽfgən, -gæn] *n.* C a person of Afghanistan; U the language spoken there. 아프가니스탄 사람[말]. —*adj.* of Afghanistan or its people. 아프가니스탄(사람)의.

Af·ghan·i·stan [æfgǽnəstæ̀n] *n.* a country in southwestern Asia. 아프가니스탄《수도는 Kabul》.

a·field [əfí:ld] *adv.* **1** to, on, or in the

field. 들판에〔으로〕; 전장〔전쟁터〕에. ¶ *drive cattle* ~ 소를 들로 몰고 가다. **2** to or at a distance; (far) away; away from home. 멀리 떨어져; 집〔고향〕에서 떠나. ¶ *search far* ~ 아주 멀리(까지) 찾다. **3** off the beaten path; far and wide. 상도(常道)를〔옆길로〕 벗어나; 널리. ¶ *go farther* ~ 옆길로 더 벗어나다 / *stray far* ~ *in one's reading* 널리 책을 섭렵하다. [a(-)]

a·fire [əfáiər] *adv., adj.* 《as *predicative*》 on fire. 불타고; 불타는. ¶ *a house* ~ 불타는 집 / 《*fig.*》 *with heart* ~ 마음이 불타고 / *The woods were* ~. 숲은 불타고 있었다. [a(-), →fire]

A.F.L. American Federation of Labor. 미국 노동 총연맹.

a·flame [əfléim] *adv., adj.* 《as *predicative*》 in flames; as if on fire. 불타고; (감정이) 격하여〔뜨거워져〕. ¶ *with cheeks* ~ 볼을 홍조시키고 / *be* ~ *with enthusiasm* 열의에 불타다 / *I was* ~ *with curiosity.* 나는 호기심에 불탔다 / *Her face was* ~ *with blushes.* 그녀의 얼굴은 수치심으로 불처럼 화끈거렸다 / *The fields were* ~ *with color.* 들녘은 단풍으로 불탔다. [a(-), →flame]

AFL-CIO American Federation of Labor and Congress of Industrial Organizations. 미국 노동 총연맹 산업별 회의.

a·float [əflóut] *adv., adj.* 《as *predicative*》 **1** at sea; on board a ship. 해상(海上)에; 선상(船上)에. ¶ *life* 〔*service*〕 ~ 해상 생활〔근무〕 / *On our trip round the world, we were 90 days* ~. 세계 일주 여행중에 우린 90일이나 바다에서 지냈다. **2** floating in the water or air. 물 위〔공중〕에 떠서. ¶ *One ship has sunk, the other is still* ~. 한쪽 배는 가라앉았으나 또하나의 배는 아직 떠 있다. **3** covered with water; flooded. 물을 뒤집어 쓰고; 물에 잠겨. ¶ *The kitchen was* ~ 부엌은 침수되었다 / *The main deck was* ~. 주갑판은 파도를 뒤집어썼다 / *After the rain, the whole cellar was* ~. 비가 온 뒤에 지하실은 온통 물에 잠겼다. **4** going around, as a rumor; widely current. (소문(所聞) 따위가) 떠돌아; 퍼져. ¶ *There is a story* ~ *that...* …이란 소문이 널리 퍼져 있다. **5** out of debt. 빚을 갚아〔갚고〕. [a(-), →float]

keep afloat, **a**) prevent (oneself or another) from sinking. 가라앉지 않도록 하다. **b**) 《*fig.*》 keep out of debt. 빚을 안 지다.

a·flut·ter [əflʌ́tər] *adv., adj.* 《as *predicative*》 in a flutter. 펄럭이고; 펄럭이는. ¶ *The flags were* ~ *in the breeze.* 깃발들이 미풍에 나부꼈다 / 《*fig.*》 *She was all* ~ *at the news.* 그 소식에 그녀는 몹시 흥분했다. [a(-), →flutter]

a·foot [əfút] *adv., adj.* 《as *predicative*》 **1** 《*arch., dial.*》 on foot. 걸어서. ¶ *Did you come all the way* ~. 이곳까지 내내 걸어서 왔는가. **2** about to happen; in progress; going on; on the move. 일어나고 있는; 진행 중에; 움직이고. ¶ *There is trouble* ~. 말썽이 일어나고 있다 / *He is always early* ~. 그는 언제나 일찍 일어나 있다 / *Preparations for war were* ~ *everywhere.* 각처에서 전쟁 준비가 진행 중이다 / *There is a plot* ~. 음모가 꾸며지고 있다. [a(-), →foot]

a·fore [əfɔ́ːr] *adv., prep.* 《naut.》 before; in front of. …앞에; …의 정면에. ¶ *serve* ~ *the mast* 배의 승무원으로 일하다; 배의 승무원이 되다. [a(-), →fore]

a·fore·men·tioned [əfɔ́ːrmènʃənd] *adj.* talked about above or before. 전술(前述)의; 전기의(cf. *before-mentioned*).

a·fore·said [əfɔ́ːrsèd] *adj.* said above or before. 전술(前述)의; 앞서 말한. ¶ *the* ~ *persons* 앞서 말한 사람들.

a·fore·thought [əfɔ́ːrθɔ̀ːt] *adj.* thought of beforehand; premeditated. 미리 생각한; 사전에 계획된; 고의의. ¶ *a crime* ~ 계획적 범죄.

a·fore·time [əfɔ́ːrtàim] *adv.* previously formerly. (이)전에; 본디.

a for·ti·o·ri [éi fɔ̀ːrʃiɔ́ːrai] *adv.* 《L.》 with still greater reason. 더욱 유력한 이유로.

a·foul [əfául] *adv., adj.* 《as *predicative*》 in collision; in a tangle. 충돌하여; 뒤얽혀. [a(-), →foul]

run 〔***fall***〕 ***afoul of,*** **a**) run against. …와 충돌하다; 저촉하다. ¶ *run* ~ *of the law* 법에 저촉되다 / *The students ran* ~ *of the police.* 학생들은 경찰과 충돌했다. **b**) become entangled with. …와 뒤얽히다. ¶ *The ship ran* ~ *of the floating seaweed.* 배는 떠도는 해초에 걸렸다. [a(-), →foul]

:a·fraid [əfréid] *adj.* 《as *predicative*》 **1** 《*of, that, lest, to*》 frightened; filled with fear; fearful. 두려워하여; 싫어하여; 걱정하여. ¶ *I am* ~ *of dogs* 〔*snakes*〕. 나는 개를〔뱀을〕 무서워한다 / *He was* ~ *of dying.* 그는 죽음을 두려워했다 / *Don't be* ~ *of being late.* 지각을 걱정마라 / *He is* ~ *of hurting you.* 그는 네가 다칠까봐 걱정한다 / *He is* ~ *to go through the wood.* 그는 숲속을 지나가기를 싫어한다 / *We are* ~ (*that*) *it will happen* 〔*lest it should happen*〕. 우린 그런 일이 일어나지 않을까 두렵다 / *She is* ~ *that he will die.* 그녀는 그가 죽지 않을까 두려워하고 있다. **2** 《*colloq.*》 sorry; feeling regret, unhappiness, etc. …을 유감으로 여기다; 안됐다고 생각하다. [M.E. *affrai* attack, alarm, →affray]

I'm afraid (***that***), 《*colloq.*》 I'm sorry.; I have to admit with regret. …하다고 생각하다; (유감이지만·아무래도) …라고 생각하다 (opp. I hope (that)...). ¶ *I'm* ~ *I'm late.* 아무래도 늦을 것 같다 / *I'm* ~ *I can't help you.* 안됐지만 너를 도울 수가 없다 / *I'm* ~ *it is so.* 유감이지만 그렇다(고 생각한다) / *"Will it rain ?" "I'm* ~ *so."* 비가 올까. 아무래도 그럴 것 같군요 / *"Will he succeed ?" "I'm* ~ *not."* 그 사람 성공할까. 못할 것으로 생각한다.

a·fresh [əfréʃ] *adv.* anew; again. 새로이; 다

시. ¶ *start* ~ 다시 시작하다 / *The child began to cry* ~. 그 아이는 다시 울기 시작했다. [a(-)]

:**Af·ri·ca** [ǽfrikə] *n.* the second largest continent, south of Europe. 아프리카.

Af·ri·can [ǽfrikən] *adj.* of Africa or its people. 아프리카(사람)의. — *n.* Ⓒ **1** a person of Africa. 아프리카 사람. **2** 《chiefly U.S.》 a Negro. 검둥이; 흑인.

Af·ri·kaans [æfrikɑ́:ns, -kɑ́:nz] *n.* Cape Dutch. 남아프리카 공화국 공용어의 하나. [Du. *Afrikaansch* African]

Af·ri·kan·der [æfrikǽndər] *n.* =Afrikaner.

Af·ri·ka·ner [æfrikɑ́:nər, -kǽn-] *n.* an Afrikaans-speaking white persons in South Africa. 남아프리카 태생의 백인.

aft [æft, ɑ:ft] *adv.* 《naut.》 at or toward the back part of a ship. 고물〔선미(船尾)〕에〔쪽으로〕. ¶ *right* ~ 배의 바로 뒤에. [E.]

:**af·ter** [ǽftər, ɑ́:f-] *prep.* **1** behind in place, time, or order; next to; later than; 《U.S.》 (of time) past. (장소·시간·위치·순서가) …의 뒤에; …후에; …다음에; (몇 시) 지나. ¶ ~ *school* 방과 후에 / ~ *seven o'clock* 일곱시 후에 / *ten minutes* ~ *eight*, 8시 10분 / ~ *a while* 잠시 후에 / *the day* ~ *tomorrow* 모레 / *the great dramatists* ~ *Shakespeare* 셰익스피어 이후의 대(大)극작가들 / *Shut the door* ~ *you.* 들어왔으면 문을 닫으시오 / *My name comes* ~ *yours.* 내 이름은 네 이름 다음에 나온다 / *We went to the movies* ~ *dinner.* 우리는 저녁 식사 후 영화를 보러 갔다 / *Come into the room* ~ *me.* 나를 따라 방으로 들어오시오. **2** in spite of. …에도 불구하고; …한데도. ¶ *After all my care in packing it, the clock arrived broken.* 포장에 온갖 조심을 했는데도 시계는 깨진 채 도착했다 / *After all her sufferings she is still cheerful.* 고난을 겪었음에도 그녀는 여전히 명랑하다. **3** because of; as a result of. …때문에; …이므로. ¶ *Nobody trusts her* ~ *that lie.* 그런 거짓말을 했으므로 아무도 그녀를 믿지 않는다 / *I shall not go* ~ *what has happened.* 그런 일이 있은 후이므로 나는 안 간다. **4** in search of; in pursuit of. …을 찾아; …을 뒤쫓아. ¶ *The dog ran* ~ *the rabbit.* (사냥)개는 토끼를 뒤쫓았다 / *The policeman ran* ~ *the thief.* 순경은 도둑을 뒤쫓았다 / *seek* ~ *happiness* 행복을 찾다 / *What is he* ~*?* 그는 무엇을 추구하고 있나. **5** about; concerning. …에 관하여. ¶ *ask* 〔*inquire*〕 ~ *someone* 아무의 안부를 묻다 / *look* ~ *the children* 아이들을 보살피다〔돌보다〕. **6** according to (the manner of); in imitation of; in agreement with. …을〔에〕 따라. ¶ *act* ~ *one's ideas* 자기 생각에 따라 행동하다 / *a picture* ~ *Picasso* 피카소류의 그림 / *a novel* ~ *Hemingway's style* 헤밍웨이식의 소설 / *take* ~ *one's mother* 엄마를 닮다 / *copy* ~ *a model* 본보기를 따르다 / *The boy was named* ~ *his uncle.* 그 소년은 숙부의 이름을 따라 이름지어졌다.

after a manner, not very well; rather badly. 그럭저럭; 그다지 잘.

after all, in spite of all that has been said or done. 결국; …에도 불구하고. ¶ *After all, it's not very important.* 결국 그건 그다지 중요하지 않다.

after that, then. 그리고 나서; 그 뒤에.

one after another, one by one; in succession. 잇따라서.

one after the other, by turns; alternately. 차례로; 번갈아.

— *adv.* behind; later; afterward. 뒤에; 나중에. ¶ *six days* ~ 엿새 뒤에 / *soon* ~ (그 뒤) 곧 / *look before and* ~ 앞뒤를 살피다 / *follow* ~ 뒤(를) 따르다 / *He was ill for months* ~. 그는 그뒤 몇 달 동안 앓았다.

— *conj.* later than the time at which (something happens). …한 뒤에; 나중에. ¶ *We shall start* ~ *he comes.* 우리는 그가 온 뒤에 떠난다 / *He arrived* ~ *I* (*had*) left. 그는 내가 떠난 다음에 왔다 / ~ *all is said and done* 결국.

— *adj.* **1** later in time. 뒤의. ¶ *in* ~ *days* 후일에 / *In* ~ *years I never heard from her.* 그녀는 그후 몇 해나 소식이 없었다. **2** following. 뒤따르는; 잇따라 일어나는. ¶ *The* ~ *results of the storm were terrible.* 폭풍의 여파는 가공할 만했다. [M.E. *after*]

af·ter·birth [ǽftərbə̀:rθ, ɑ́:f-] *n.* 《med.》 that which is expelled from the birth of a child. 후산(後産).

af·ter·burn·er [ǽftərbə̀:rnər, ɑ́:f-] *n.* (in jet engines) a device supplying additional fuel to the exhaust. (제트 엔진의) 연료 보급 장치.

af·ter·care [ǽftərkɛ̀ər, ɑ́:f-] *n.* Ⓤ care of patients after treatment, esp. of a mother after childbirth. 병후〔산후〕의 몸조리.

af·ter·crop [ǽftərkrɑ̀p, ɑ́:f- / -krɔ̀p] *n.* a second crop in the same year. 이모작.

af·ter·deck [ǽftərdèk, ɑ́:f-] *n.* 《naut.》 the back part of a ship's deck. 후갑판.

af·ter-din·ner [ǽftərdínər, ɑ́:f-] *adj.* following dinner. 만찬〔저녁 식사〕 후의. ¶ *an* ~ *speech* (식후의) 탁상 연설.

af·ter·ef·fect [ǽftərifèkt, ɑ́:f-] *n.* Ⓒ a result or effect that follows later. 여파; (약 따위의) 부작용. ¶ *the aftereffects of an illness* 병의 후유증.

af·ter·glow [ǽftərglòu, ɑ́:f-] *n.* Ⓒ **1** the glow in the sky after the sun has set. 저녁놀. **2** a glow after something bright has gone. 잔광(殘光).

af·ter·grass [ǽftərgræ̀s, ɑ́:f-, -grɑ̀:s] *n.* the grass that grows after the hay has been cut. 두 번째 나는 풀.

af·ter·im·age [ǽftərìmidʒ, ɑ́:ftərimidʒ] *n.* 《psych.》 an image occurring after the stimulus is withdrawn. 잔상(殘像).

af·ter·math [ǽftərmæ̀θ, ɑ́:f-] *n.* Ⓒ **1** =aftergrass. **2** an undesirable result; that which follows from a disaster, such as a flood, or fire. (흔히 재해 등에 따르는 바람직

하지 않은) 결과; 여파. ¶ *the ~ of the storm* 폭풍의 여파.

af·ter·most [ǽftərmòust, ɑ́:f- / ɑ́:ftərməst] *adj.* **1** last. 최후의. **2** 《naut.》 nearest the back part of a ship. (배의) 최후부의.

:af·ter·noon [æ̀ftərnú:n, ɑ̀:f-] *n.* Ⓒ the time between noon and evening. 오후. (cf. *morning*). ¶ *in the ~* 오후에 / *in the ~ next Monday.* 오는 월요일 오후에는. [→affer]

af·ter·thought [ǽftərθɔ̀:t, ɑ́:f-] *n.* ⓊⒸ a later thought about an action or decision; a second thought. (뒤늦은) 생각; 뒷궁리; 재고(再考).

:af·ter·ward [ǽftərwərd, ɑ́:f-], 《Brit.》 **-wards** [-wərdz] *adv.* subsequently; at a later time. 뒤〔나중〕에; 그 후. ¶ *The bud was small at first, but ~ it became a large flower.* 봉오리가 처음엔 작았으나 나중에 큰 꽃이 되었다.

ag- *pref.* ⇨ad-.

Ag. August.

Ag 《chem.》 *argentum* 《L.=silver》.

:a·gain [əgén, əgéin] *adv.* **1** once more. 다시 (한 번); 또. ¶ *try ~* 다시 해보다 / *come ~* 다시 오다 / *Once ~, please.* 다시 한번 해 보십시오 / *I won't do that ~* 그것을 다시는 하지 않겠다. **2** moreover; furthermore; besides. 더욱 더; 그 위에 (또). ¶ *Again, I must say.* 거듭 한마디 해야겠다 / *Then ~, why did he go ?* 그런데 또 그 사람은 어째서 간 거지. **3** as before; back (into a former position). 본디의 곳으로〔상태로〕; 전처럼; 먼저대로. ¶ *come home ~* 전처럼 집으로 돌아오다 / *return ~* 되돌아오다 / *get well ~* (건강이) 다시 회복되다 / *Things will be all right ~.* 일이 전처럼 잘 될게다. **4** in return or response. …에 응〔답〕하여. ¶ *answer ~* (말)대꾸하다 / *echo ~* 메아리치다. **5** on the other hand. 그런데; 다른〔또〕 한편. ¶ *It might happen, and ~ it might not.* 일이 일어날지도 모르고 또 안 일어날지도 모른다. [AS. *ongegen*]

again and again =***time and again,*** very often. 몇 번이고; 되풀이해서. ¶ *I have told you so ~ and ~.* 네게 (몇 번이나) 되풀이 말하지 않았나.

all over again, anew. 새로이.

as much 〔***many***〕 ***again,*** twice as much 〔many〕. …의 갑절만큼의 양〔수〕.

be oneself again, recover from illness. 건강을 회복하다. ¶ *He is now himself ~.* 그는 이제 건강을 되찾았다.

half as much 〔***many***〕 ***again*** (***as***), one and a half times as much 〔many〕. …의 1배 반의 〔으로〕.

now 〔***even***〕 ***and again,*** sometimes. 때때로; 이따금.

once and again ⇨once.

:a·gainst [əgénst, əgéinst] *prep.* **1** in opposition to; in an opposite direction to; toward; contrary to. …에 반대하여; …과 반대 방향으로; 거슬러; …을 향해; …에 대하여; 반대의(opp. for). ¶ *push ~ the door* 몸을 들이대고 문을 밀다 / *ride ~ the wind* 바람을 거슬러 말을 달리다 / *go ~ the stream* 〔*tide*〕 시류에 거스르다 / *~ reason* 사리에 맞지 않는 / *vote ~ him* 그에게 반대 투표하다 / *struggle ~ difficulties* 곤란과 (맞서) 싸우다 / *The dogs fought ~ the lion.* 개들은 사자와 맞서 싸웠다 / *Are you for it or ~ it ?* 그것에 찬성인가 반대인가. **2** in contact with; facing; next to. (…에) 기대어; 기대어 세워; …의 이웃〔곁〕에. ¶ *lean ~ the wall* 벽에 몸을 기대다 / *put the desk ~ the wall* 책상을 벽에 붙여 놓다 / *Rain is beating ~ the window.* 빗발이 창문을 들이치고 있다. **3** in contrast to; having as background. …에 대조를 이루어; …을 배경으로. ¶ *~ the evening sky* 저녁 하늘을 배경으로 / *The castle stood out ~ the sky.* 성은 하늘을 배경으로 우뚝 솟아 있었다 / *win by forty votes ~ twelve.* 12 대 40 의 표차로 이기다. **4** in preparation for. …에 대비하여. ¶ *Save ~ a rainy day.* 만일에 대비해서 저축을 하라 / *store up food ~ the winter* 겨울철에 대비해서 식량을 저장하다. [*again*]

against one's will, unwillingly. 마지못해.

as against, (as) compared with. …에 비해서. ¶ *twenty airplanes of theirs as ~ our three* 우리측 3대에 비해 저들의 20기나 되는 비행기.

over against, just in front of; right opposite. 바로 정면에; …와 마주보고. ¶ *over ~ the church* 교회 맞은 편에.

Ag·a·mem·non [æ̀gəmémnɑn, -nən] *n.* 《Gk. myth.》 the leader of the Greek expedition against Troy. 아가멤논《Troy 전쟁 때, 그리스군의 총대장》.

a·gam·ic [əgǽmik], **ag·a·mous** [ǽgəməs] *adj.* 《biol.》 without sexual functions. 무성(無性)(생식)의. [Gk. *a-* not, *gamos* marriage]

a·gape[1] [əgéip, əgǽp] *adv., adj.* 《as *predicative*》 with the mouth wide open in a state of wonder or surprise. (놀라서) 입을 딱 벌리고; 기가 막혀. ¶ *with mouth ~* 입을 딱 벌리고. [a(-)]

a·ga·pe[2] [ɑ:gɑ́:pei, ɑ́:gəpèi, ǽgə-] *n.* Ⓤ love of God or Christ for mankind; the spiritual love. 기독교적인 사랑. [Gk. *agapē* love]

a·gar-a·gar [ɑ́:gɑ:rɑ́:gɑ:r, æ̀gərǽgər] *n.* Ⓤ a jellylike substance produced from certain seaweeds, used to grow bacteria. 우뭇가사리; 한천(寒天)《배양기용》. [Malay]

ag·ate [ǽgit] *n.* **1** Ⓤ a kind of precious stone. 마노(瑪瑙). **2** Ⓒ 《U.S.》 a child's playing marble. 공깃돌. [Gk. *akhatēs*]

Ag·a·tha [ǽgəθə] *n.* a woman's name. 여자의 이름.

a·ga·ve [əgéivi, əgɑ́:-] *n.* 《bot.》 a genus of plants of the agave family. 용설란속(屬)의 식물. [Gk. *agavē*]

a·gaze [əgéiz] *adv.* on the gaze. 바라보고;

응시하고. [a-, →gaze]

:age[eidʒ] *n.* **1** Ⓤ Ⓒ the time of life already passed. 나이; 연령. ¶ *at the ~ of fifty,* 50세에 / *middle ~* 중년 / *trees of unknown ~* 수령(樹齡) 미상(未詳)의 나무들 / *a girl of your ~* 네 나이 또래의 소녀 / *be of tender* [*advanced*] *~* 젊은 나이[고령]이다 / *He is just my ~.* 그는 나와 동갑이다 / *My daughter is eight years of ~.* 딸은 여덟 살이다 / *What is your ~?* 몇 살인가 / *What ages are your children?* 자네 아이들은 몇 살인가 / *He looks young for his ~.* 그는 나이에 비해 젊어 뵌다. **2** the length of life. 수명. ¶ *the ~ of a horse* 말의 수명 / 《*prov.*》 *Three score and ten is the ~ of man.* 나이 70은 인간의 수명. **3** Ⓤ a particular period. 특정 연령; 성년《21세》. ¶ *over ~* 성년 이상 / *be* [*come*] *of ~* 성년에 달해 있다[이 되다] / *reach one's full ~* 성년에 달하다 / *be under ~* 미성년이다. **4** Ⓒ a generation; a period of time in history. 세대; (역사상의) 시대; 시기. ¶ *from ~ to ~* 대대(代代); 세세(世世) / *in our ~* 우리들 시대의 / *the Golden* [*Stone*] *~* 황금[석기] 시대 / *the Middle Ages* 중세 / *This is the space ~.* 지금은 우주 시대이다. **5** Ⓤ old age; the latter part of life; advanced years. 노령(老齡); 고령(opp. youth). ¶ *the wisdom of ~* 노인의 슬기 / *the infirmities of ~* 노쇠 / *provide against ~* 노후에 대비하다 / *His eyes were dim with ~.* 그의 눈은 노령으로 침침했다. **6** Ⓒ 《*colloq.*》 a long time. 장기간; 오랫동안. ¶ *ages ago* 오래 전에 / *He's been gone for ages.* 그가 떠난지 꽤 오래 되었다 / *It's an ~* [*ages*] *since I saw you last.* 꽤 오래간만이군.

of age, 21 years old or over. 성년(成年)의.

with [***from***] ***age,*** because of old age. 나이 탓으로[때문에].

— *vi.* (P1) grow old. 나이를 먹다; 늙다; 오래되다; 묵다. ¶ *His mother aged rapidly.* 그의 어머니는 빨리 늙었다.

— *vt.* (P6) make (someone) old; make (wine, cheese, etc.) mature. …을 늙게[낡게] 하다; (술 따위를) 익게 하다. ¶ *Worry and illness ~ a man.* 고생과 병은 사람을 늙게 한다 / *~ wine* 포도주를 익히다. [L. *aetas* age]

·a·ged *adj.* **1** [éidʒid] old; advanced in years. 나이먹은; 늙은; 고색창연한. ¶ *an ~ man* 노인 / *the ~* 노인들. **2** [eidʒd] of the age of. …살[세]의. ¶ *a girl ~ seven (years)* 일곱 살의 계집아이 / *She was ~ six.* 그녀는 여섯 살이었다.

age·less [éidʒlis] *adj.* never growing old; timeless. 늙지 않는; 영원히 젊은.

age·long [éidʒlɔ̀(:)ŋ, -làŋ] *adj.* lasting for a long time. 오랫동안의; 영속(永續)하는.

:a·gen·cy [éidʒənsi] *n.* (*pl.* **-cies**) **1** Ⓤ Ⓒ action; operation; power; a means. 작용; 힘; 수단. ¶ *an invisible ~* 눈에 보이지 않는 힘 / *The snow was driven into heaps by the ~ of the wind.* 눈이 바람의 작용으로 들이쳐 쌓였다. **2** Ⓒ the business of a person or firm that acts for another; an office of such a person or firm. 대리(권); 대리(취급)점. ¶ *a sole* [*general*] *~* 독점 판매점[총대리점] / *hold an ~ for...* …의 대리를[대리점을] 하다 / *secure ~* 대리권을 획득하다 / *undertake exclusive ~ for canned goods* 통조림류의 대리업을 독점 인수하다. [L. *ago* do, → agent]

through [***by***] ***the agency of...,*** by the good offices of. …의 주선[알선]으로. ¶ *Through the ~ of powerful friends he was set free.* 유력한 친구들의 주선으로 그는 석방되었다.

a·gen·da [ədʒéndə] *n. pl.* (*sing.* **-dum**) 《usu. used as *sing.*》 a program of things or a list of things to be done. 의사(議事) 일정; 회의 사항; 의제. [L. *ago* do]

a·gen·dum [ədʒéndəm] *n.* sing. of **agenda.**

:a·gent [éidʒənt] *n.* Ⓒ **1** a person or firm that acts for another; a representative; 《*colloq.*》 a traveling salesman. 대리인[점]; 주선인; 외판원. ¶ *a house ~* 가옥 소개업자 / *an estate ~* 부동산 중개업자 / *He is the European ~ for many Korean companies.* 그는 많은 한국 상사의 유럽 대리인이다. **2** a power or cause that has a certain effect. 작인(作因); 동인(動因); (어떤 변화를 일으키는) 힘. ¶ *physical ~* 물리적 작인 / *Oxygen is the ~ that causes rust.* 산소는 녹이 슬게 하는 작용제이다. **3** an active being; a person who does things. 행위자; 발동자(發動者). ¶ *I am a mere instrument, not an ~.* 나는 하라는 대로 하는 사람이지 주모자는 아니다. [L. *ago* do, →agency, agenda, action]

ag·glom·er·ate [əglɑ́mərèit / -lɔ́m-] *vi., vt.* (P1;6) gather or collect into a mass or heap. 덩어리로 뭉치(게 하)다; 밀집하다. — [-rit, -rèit] *n.* Ⓤ a mass or collection of things. 뭉친 덩어리; 집괴(集塊). — [-rit, -rèit] *adj.* gathered together into a mass. 덩어리진; 뭉쳐진; 밀집(密集)한. ¶ *~ rock* 집괴암(集塊岩). ● **ag·glom·er·a·tive** [-rèitiv, -rə- / -glɔ́mərə-] *adj.* [L. *glomus* ball]

ag·glom·er·a·tion [əglɑ̀məréiʃən / -lɔ̀m-] *n.* Ⓤ Ⓒ the act of gathering into a mass; a mass; a heap. 덩어리짐[지게 함]; 덩어리; 단괴(團塊).

ag·glu·ti·nate [əglú:tənèit] *vt.* (P6) join together (something) as with a sticky substance. …을 붙게 하다; 점착(粘着)시키다; 접합하다. — *vi.* (P1) become a sticky substance; combine. 아교 모양이 되다; 점착하다.

— [-nit, -nèit] *adj.* joined together. 접합된. [L. *gluten* glue]

ag·glu·ti·na·tion [əglù:tənéiʃən] *n.* **1** Ⓤ the act or process of agglutinating; such a condition. 접합하기; 교착(膠着)하기; 접합한 상태. **2** Ⓤ formation of a word by combination. 교착 조어법(造語法). **3** Ⓒ that which is agglutinated. 교착어(語).

ag·gran·dize [əgrǽndaiz, ǽgrəndàiz] *vt.* (P6) make (someone or a nation) greater in power, wealth, rank, etc.; make (one's opinion) appear greater; exaggerate. (권력·부(富)·지위 따위)를 증대하다; 높이다; (의견 따위)를 과장하다. ¶ *The king aggrandized the loyal knights.* 왕은 충성스러운 기사들의 권위를 높여 주었다. ● **ag·gran·dize·ment** [-mənt] *n.* [a-, →grand]

ag·gra·vate [ǽgrəvèit] *vt.* (P6) **1** make (an existing trouble) worse or more severe. …을 더욱 악화시키다. ¶ *His bad temper was aggravated by his headache.* 그의 성깔은 두통으로 인해 더욱 심해졌다. **2** 《*colloq.*》 anger; make angry. …을 성〔화〕나게 하다. ¶ *Don't ~ me!* 나를 화나게 하지 마라. [ad-, L. *gravis* heavy]

ag·gra·vat·ing [ǽgrəvèitiŋ] *adj.* making worse or more severe; 《*colloq.*》 troublesome; provoking; irritating. 더욱 나쁘게〔심하게〕 하는; 부아가 나는. ¶ *How ~!* 정말로 약올리는군.

ag·gra·va·tion [æ̀grəvéiʃən] *n.* UC **1** the act of aggravating; a thing that makes worse or more severe. 더욱 악화시킴〔시키는 것〕. **2** the state of being irritated. 부아가 남; 약오름.

ag·gre·gate [ǽgrigèit] *vt., vi.* **1** (P6) collect; unite. (한데) 모으다; 집합(集合)하다. ¶ *small particles aggregated together* 한데 집합된 미립자. **2** (P3) 《*colloq.*》 amount to. 합계 …이 되다; …에 달하다. ¶ *The money collected has aggregated one million won.* 모인 돈은 도합 백만 원에 달했다.

— [-git, -gèit] *adj.* total; formed into a mass. 합계의; 집합의.

— [-git, -gèit] *n.* 《usu. *the ~* 》 the total; a mass formed of separate things. 합계; 집합체. ¶ *the ~ of all the gifts* 선물 모두의 총계. [ag-, L. *grex* flock]

in the aggregate, as a whole; totally. 전체로서; 총계.

ag·gre·ga·tion [æ̀grigéiʃən] *n.* UC the act of aggregating; separate things collected into one whole. 집합; 집단; 집합체.

ag·gress [əgrés] *vi.* (P3) 《rare》 《*on, upon*》 begin a quarrel. 싸움을 걸다〔시작하다〕. [L. *gradior* step]

ag·gres·sion [əgréʃən] *n.* UC an attack without just cause; the act of starting a fight by entering the territory of another country; an assault. (이유 없는, 불법적) 공격; 침략; 침해. ¶ *a war of ~* 침략 전쟁.

ag·gres·sive [əgrésiv] *adj.* **1** quick to attack; offensive; quarrelsome. 침략적인; 공격의; 싸움을 좋아하는. ¶ *Which was the ~ one, John or James?* 누가 먼저 싸움을 걸었나, 존이냐 제임스냐 / *He is a very ~ man.* 그는 매우 싸우기를 좋아하는 사내다. **2** 《U.S.》 energetic; enterprising. 활동적인; 적극적인. ¶ *an ~ salesman* 적극적인 외판원.

assume 〔***take***〕 ***the aggressive,*** start a fight; take the offensive; become active before others. 공격으로 나오다; 공세를 취하다. ● **ag·gres·sive·ly** [-li] *adv.* **ag·gres·sive·ness** [-nis] *n.*

ag·gres·sor [əgrésər] *n.* C a person or country that makes the first move in a quarrel or war. 침략자〔국〕; 공격자〔국〕.

ag·grieve [əgríːv] *vt.* (P6) 《usu. in *passive*》 trouble or injure (someone) by unjust treatment. …을 괴롭히다; 학대하다; 침해〔손상〕하다. ¶ *be* 〔*feel*〕 *aggrieved* 불만을 품다; 분개하다 / *He was* 〔*felt*〕 *very much aggrieved at the insult from his friend.* 그는 친구의 모욕으로 몹시 감정이 상했다 / *He was aggrieved that he had offended Jane.* 제인을 성나게 한 것을 그는 괴로워하고 있었다. [→aggravate]

a·ghast [əgǽst, əgɑ́ːst] *adj.* 《as *predicative*》 《*at*》 struck with sudden surprise, terror, etc. 깜짝 놀라; 아연하여. ¶ *stand ~ at the sight* 〔*the news*〕 그 광경〔소식〕에 소스라치게 놀라다 / *He looked at me ~.* 그는 깜짝 놀라 나를 바라보았다. [O.E. *agastan* to terrify]

ag·ile [ǽdʒəl, ǽdʒail] *adj.* able to move quickly and easily; active. 재빠른; 경쾌〔민첩〕한; 활동적인. ¶ *be as ~ as a hare* 토끼처럼 민첩하다 / *be ~ in one's movements* 동작이 민첩하다 / *He has an ~ mind.* 그는 지력(知力)이 영민하다. [L. *ago* do, →act]

a·gil·i·ty [ədʒíləti] *n.* U the quickness or readiness of movement. 재빠름; 민첩함; 경쾌. [↑]

ag·i·o [ǽdʒiòu] *n.* (*pl.* **-os**) C a premium on money exchange. 환전의 프리미엄; 환전수수료. [It.=ease]

ag·i·o·tage [ǽdʒiətidʒ] *n.* the business of exchange. 환전업. [↑]

***ag·i·tate** [ǽdʒətèit] *vt.* (P6) **1** move or shake violently. …을 몹시 흔들다; (물결 따위)가 치게 하다. ¶ *The wind agitates the sea.* 바람이 바다를 물결치게 한다. **2** disturb; excite. (마음·사람)을 휘젓다; 동요시키다; 선동하다. ¶ *be agitated by* 〔*with*〕*…* …로 마음이 흔들리다 / *She was much agitated by the sad news.* 그녀는 그 슬픈 소식에 몹시 동요되었다. **3** excite discussion and feeling over. (여론 따위에 호소하여) 시끄럽게 논하다〔떠들어대다〕. ¶ *~ the question of…* …문제를 시끄럽게 떠들다.

— *vi.* (P3) 《*for*》 stir up the public by means of slogans, demonstrations, etc. 일반 여론이 들끓게 하다. ¶ *~ for reform* 개혁 운동을 하다 / *He agitates for a shorter working day.* 그는 작업 일수 단축 운동을 벌이고 있다. [L. *ago*, →act]

***ag·i·ta·tion** [æ̀dʒətéiʃən] *n.* **1** UC a disturbed or troubled state of the mind; excitement. (마음의) 동요; 흥분. **2** U discussion to arouse public interest. (사회적·정치적인) 선동; 운동. ¶ *anti-slavery ~* 노예 폐지 운동 / *~ for wage increase* 임금 인상 운동.

ag·i·ta·tor [ǽdʒətèitər] *n.* Ⓒ **1** a person who tries to make people dissatisfied with the present state of affairs. 선동자. **2** a machine for agitating. 교반기(攪拌機).

ag·let [ǽglit], **ai·glet** [éiglit] *n.* Ⓒ **1** a metal tag at the end of a lace. (구두끈 따위 끝의) 쇠붙이. **2** ribbons to tie dresses. 장식; 리본. **3** an aiguillette. (군복의) 장식띠. [L. *acus* needle, →acute]

a·gley [əglí:, əgléi, əglái] *adv.* askew; awry. 비스듬히; 구부러져. [Sc.]

a·glow [əglóu] *adj.* 《as *predicative*》 shining; glowing; flushed. (얼굴 따위가) 빛나고; 화끈 달아올라. ¶ *be ~ with delight* 〔*happiness*〕 기쁨〔행복〕으로 빛나다 / *Her face was ~ as she went to meet him.* 그를 만나러 갔을 때 그녀의 얼굴은 홍조를 띠고 있었다. **—** *adv.* in a glow. 불타고. [a(-), →glow]

ag·nail [ǽgnèil] *n.* the torn skin at the root of a finger-nail. 손거스러미. [E.]

Ag·nes [ǽgnis] *n.* a woman's name. 여자의 이름.

ag·no·men [ægnóumən] *n.* a nickname. 별명. [L. *gnomen* name]

ag·nos·tic [ægnástik / -nɔ́s-] *n.* Ⓒ a person who believes that a man cannot know the final nature of things, or who does not say either that God is or that God is not. 불가지론자(不可知論者).
— *adj.* of such a belief. 불가지론의. [Gk. *a-* not, *gnō* know]

:a·go [əgóu] *adj.* 《always placed after the *noun*》 past; back; gone by. 이전(에); (지금으로부터) …전(에)(cf. *before*). ¶ *two days* 〔*weeks*〕 *~* 이틀〔두 주일〕 전에 / *a few years ~* 몇 해 전에 / *He arrived an hour ~.* 그는 한 시간 전에 도착했다 / *That was a little while ~.* 그것은 조금 전(前)의 일이었다.
— *adv.* 《used after the adverb *long*》 in past time. 이전에. ¶ *It happened long ~.* 그 일은 오래 전에 일어났다 / *How long ~ was that?* 그건 얼마 전의 일이었나 / *I saw her no longer ~ than last week.* 나는 바로 지난 주에 그녀를 보았네. [E. orig. *agone* past]

a·gog [əgág / əgɔ́g] *adj.* 《as *predicative*》 excited by eagerness, expectation, etc. 흥분하여; 법석을 떨고. **—** *adv.* in a state of eagerly desiring. 열망하고; 흥분하여. ¶ *be all ~ for…* …을 열망〔갈망〕하여 / *all ~ to know* …을 알려고 열망하여 / *He was all ~ to hear the news.* 그는 소식 듣기를 열망했다. [F. *en gogues* in mirth]

ag·o·nize [ǽgənàiz] *vi.* (P1) **1** suffer greatly. 괴로워하다; 번민〔고민〕하다. **2** make a great effort. 필사의 노력을 하다. **—** *vt.* (P6) make (someone) suffer extremely. …을 몹시 괴롭히다. ¶ *~ oneself* 고민하다. [*agony*]

ag·o·niz·ing [ǽgənàiziŋ] *adj.* being in agony; suffering greatly. 괴로운; 큰 고난의; 매우 고통스러운.

·ag·o·ny [ǽgəni] *n.* ⓊⒸ (*pl.* **-nies**) **1** great pain of body or mind; great excitement. (심신의) 큰 고통; 고민; 고뇌; 극도의 격정 (따위). ¶ *in an ~ of joy* 기쁜 나머지 / *wait in an ~ of impatience* 일일 천추의 생각으로 기다리다 / *suffer an ~ of despair* 절망의 괴로움을 맛보다. **2** death struggle. 죽음의 괴로움. **3** 《*the A-*》 the last sufferings of Christ. (수난 전의) 그리스도의 고민. [Gk. *agōn* contest, →antagonist]

agony column [ˊ-- ˋ-], **the** *n.* 《*colloq.*》 the column in a newspaper in which advertisements for missing friends, requests for money, etc. appear. (찾는 사람 등의) 광고란.

ag·o·ra·pho·bi·a [æ̀gərəfóubiə] *n.* Ⓤ morbid dislike of public places. 광장(廣場) 공포증. [Gk. *agora* market, *phobos* fear]

a·gou·ti [əgú:ti] *n.* (*pl.* **-tis** or **-ties**) 《zool.》 a hare-like West Indian rodent. 아구티. [Native]

a·grar·i·an [əgrέəriən] *adj.* **1** of land, its use, or its ownership. 토지에 관한; 경작지의. ¶ *~ laws* 토지 균분법 / *~ rising* 농민 폭동. **2** for the support of the interests of farmers. 농본(農本)주의의. **—** *n.* Ⓒ a person in favor of an equal division of lands. 토지 균분(均分)론자. [L. *ager* field]

:a·gree [əgrí:] *vi.* (P1,3,4) **1** 《*to*》 consent; say 'yes'. 동의하다; 찬성하다; 승낙하다. ¶ *~ to a plan* 계획에 찬성하다 / *She agreed to go.* 그녀는 갈 것에 동의했다 / *I ~ to your proposal* 〔*offer*〕. 당신 제안에 찬성입니다. **2** 《*with*》 have the same opinion. 같은 의견이다. ¶ *I ~ with you.* 당신과 의견이 같다 / *I can't ~ with you on that point.* 그 점에 관해선 당신과 의견을 같이할 수 없습니다. **3** 《*with*》 be in harmony; correspond; match. …이 일치하다; 부합하다. ¶ *Her story agreed with his.* 그녀의 이야기는 그의 말과 일치했다 / *The two statements do not ~* (*with each other*). 두 진술은 (서로) 일치하지 않는다 / *Your story does not ~ with the facts.* 네 이야기는 사실과 부합되지 않는다. **4** 《*with*》 meet the taste; be suitable for. (취미·음식·건강·기후 따위가) 맞다. ¶ *I wonder whether the country life will ~ with her.* 시골 생활이 그녀에게 맞을는지 모르겠다 / *Smoking doesn't ~ with him.* 담배는 그의 건강에 맞지 않는다. **5** 《*with*》 get on well together; live in harmony with. …와 서로 잘 지내다; 마음이 맞다. ¶ *He and I can't ~* (*with each other*). 그와는 (서로) 잘 지낼 수가 없다. **6** 《*on*》 arrive at an understanding; come to terms. 합의하다. ¶ *~ on the terms of contract* 계약 조건에 합의하다 / *under the conditions agreed upon* 합의된 조건에서.
— *vt.* (P8,10,11) admit. …을 인정하다. ¶ *I ~ that it is too late.* 너무 늦다는 것을 인정한다 / *We agreed that we should do it.* 우리가 그것을 해야 한다는 것을 인정했다. 參考

agree that는 agree to it that...의 to it가 탈락해서 된 것으로 여겨짐. [ad-, L. *gratus* pleasing]

***agree to differ* 〔*disagree*〕,** resolve to give up quarreling though no agreement of opinions is reached. 서로의 의견 차이를 인정하지만 다투지 않기로 하다.

·a·gree·a·ble [əgríːəbəl / əgríə-] *adj.* **1** pleasant. 기분 좋은. ¶ ~ *manners* 기분 좋은 태도 / ~ *to the ears* 귀에 듣기 좋은. **2** suitable. 적합한; 맞는. ¶ *an act* ~ *to the law* 적법한 행위. **3** willing; ready to agree. 찬성하는. ¶ *Are you* ~ *to the suggestion?* 제안에 찬성인가 / 《*colloq.*》 *I am quite* ~. 바라시는 대로 하죠.

agreeable to, according to (a promise, etc.). …에 따라(서).

a·gree·a·bly [əgríːəbli / əgríə-] *adv.* **1** pleasantly; delightfully. 기분 좋게; 유쾌하게. ¶ *sing* ~ 유쾌히 노래 부르다 / *speak* ~ *to someone* 아무에게 붙임성 있게 이야기하다 / *I was* ~ *surprised.* 놀랐으나 기분은 좋았다. **2** 《*to*》 in accordance with. …에 따라(서). ¶ ~ *to my instructions* 내 지시에 따라서 / ~ *to your letter* 〔*request*〕 편지〔요청〕에 따라서.

:a·gree·ment [əgríːmənt] *n.* **1** Ⓤ Ⓒ mutual understanding; harmony of opinions or feelings. 동의; (감정·의견 따위의) 일치. ¶ *a conditional* ~ 조건부 동의 / *by mutual* ~ 쌍방의 합의로. **2** Ⓒ a contract. 협정; 계약. ¶ *make an* ~ 협정을 맺다 / *bring about an* ~ 이야기를 매듭짓다. **3** Ⓤ 《gram.》 correspondence of one word with another in gender, number, etc. (성·수·격 따위의) 일치; 호응.

arrive at* 〔*come to*〕 *an agreement, come to an understanding or make an arrangement. 합의를 보다; 협정이 성립하다.

in agreement with, in accord with; according to. …와 일치하여; …에 따라서.

a·gres·tic [əgréstik] *adj.* rural; unpolished. 시골(풍)의; 세련되지 않은. [L. *ager* field, →agriculture]

agr(ic). agricultural; agriculture.

·ag·ri·cul·tur·al [æ̀grikʌ́ltʃərəl] *adj.* of agriculture. 농업의; 농학의. ¶ *the Agricultural Age* 농경시대 / ~ *products* 농산물.

•ag·ri·cul·tur·al·ly [-rəli] *adv.* [*agriculture*]

ag·ri·cul·tur·al·ist [æ̀grikʌ́ltʃərəlist], **-tur·ist** [-tʃərist] *n.* a person concerned with agriculture; a farmer. 농업 경영자; 농부; 농학자.

:ag·ri·cul·ture [ǽgrikʌ̀ltʃər] *n.* Ⓤ the science and art of raising crops and animals on a farm. 농업; 농예(農藝); 농학. [L. *ager* field, *colo* cultivate]

ag·ro- [ǽgrou-] *pref.* field; soil; crop production. '밭, 토양, 곡물'의 뜻. [Gk. *agros* tilled land; →acre]

ag·ro·bi·ol·o·gy [æ̀groubaiɑ́lədʒi / -ɔ́lə-] *n.* the quantitative science of plant life and plant. 농업 생물학. [agro-, →biology]

a·grol·o·gy [əgrɑ́lədʒi / əgrɔ́l-] *n.* the branch of soil science dealing esp. with the production of crops. 응용 토양학. [agro-, -logy]

ag·ro·nom·ics [æ̀grənɑ́miks / -nɔ́m-] *n.* 《construed as *sing.*》 the art or science of managing land or crops. 농지 경영학. [↓]

a·gron·o·my [əgrɑ́nəmi / əgrɔ́n-] *n.* the application of scientific principles to the cultivation of land. 작물학; 농학. [agro-, →nomy]

a·ground [əgráund] *adv., adj.* 《naut.》 (of a ship) on or onto the ground. (배가) 좌초하여. ¶ *The ship goes* 〔*runs*〕 ~. 배가 좌초하다. [a:-]

a·gue [éigjuː] *n.* Ⓤ Ⓒ a malarial fever; a fit of fever; a fit of shivering. 학질; 오한(惡寒). [L. *acus* needle, →acute]

a·gu·ish [éigju(ː)iʃ] *adj.* **1** like ague; productive of agues. 학질의〔같은〕; 오한(惡寒)이 나는. **2** (of a person) subject to ague. 학질에 걸리기 쉬운. [↑]

:ah [ɑː] *interj.* a natural exclamation of sudden emotion, such as sorrow, joy, or contempt. 아아《슬픔·기쁨·경멸 따위 여러 감정을 나타냄》. [Imit.]

a.h. ampere hour.

a·ha [ɑːhɑ́ː, əhɑ́ː] *interj.* an exclamation of triumph, surprise, or contempt. 아(하); 어허; 야아; 흐응《승리·놀람·경멸을 나타냄》. ¶ *Aha, I've caught you at last!* 야아 마침내 잡았다. [Imit.]

:a·head [əhéd] *adv.* in or to the front; toward the front; forward; onward; into the future. 앞(쪽)에; 전도에; 앞〔전방〕으로; 선두에; (시간적으로) 앞서. ¶ *look* ~ 앞〔전방〕을 보다; 장래의 일을 생각하다 / ~ *of age* 〔*times*〕 시대에 앞서 / *There is a crossing* ~. 앞에 건널목이 있다 / *There is danger* ~ *on this road.* 이 길 전방에 위험이 있다 / *He was walking a little* ~. 그는 약간 앞서 걷고 있었다. [a(-), →head]

ahead of, before; in advance of. …의 앞〔전방〕에; 앞서서. ¶ *Run* ~ *of us.* 우리들 앞에서 뛰어라 / *The ship left* ~ *of time.* 배는 정시 전에 떠났다 / *She is* ~ *of her class in French.* 그녀는 반에서 프랑스어가 가장 뛰어나다.

be ahead, be in front. 앞에 있다.

get ahead, succeed, as in business. 성공하다; 출세하다.

get ahead of, exceed; surpass. …에 앞서다; …보다 낫다〔능가하다〕. ¶ *He will get* ~ *of others in English.* 그는 영어에서 다른 사람들보다 앞설 게다.

go ahead, **a**) move onward. 앞으로 나아가다. ¶ 《*colloq.*》 *Go* ~. 이야기를〔일을〕 계속하시오; 앞으로 가; 자 어서 해라; 자 먼저 (가시지요 따위). **b**) improve; make progress. 진보〔향상〕하다; 진척하다. **c**) continue. 계속하다. ¶ *Go* ~ *with the cake.* 어서 케이크를 더 먹어라 / *Go* ~ *with this work for another week.* 이 일을 한 주일만 더 계속하시오.

a·hem [əhém, mm̩m, hm] *interj.* a slight cough to attract attention, express doubt, gain time, etc. 으흠; 에헴《주의·환기 따위를 위한 헛기침》. [Imit., →hem]

a·him·sa [əhímsɑː] *n.* Ⓤ the doctrine of nonviolence or nonkilling. 비폭력; 비살생. [a-, Skr. *himsa* injury]

a·hoy [əhɔ́i] *interj.* 《naut.》 a call used by sailors for calling a ship. 어어이《딴 배를 부를 때의 소리》. ¶ *Ship ~!* 어어이 거기 있는 배. [a-]

a·hull [əhʌ́l] *adv.* 《naut.》 with sails taken in and the helm lashed alee. (폭풍우에 대비하여) 돛을 걷고 키의 손잡이를 바람 불어 가는 쪽으로 잡아. [a-]

a·i [ɑ́ːi] *n.* (*pl.* **a·is**) 《zool.》 South American threetoed sloth. 세손가락나무늘보. [Braz. Imit. of cry]

:aid [eid] *n.* **1** Ⓤ help; support; assistance. 도움; 조력; 원조. ¶ *come to someone's ~* …을 도우러 오다 / *go to someone's ~* …을 도우러〔원조하러〕 가다 / *give* 〔*render*〕 *~ to someone* …을 돕다. **2** Ⓒ something that helps; a helper; an assistant. 도움을 주는 것; 돕는 사람; 조력자; 조수. ¶ *an ~ in solving the problem* 문제를 푸는데 도움을 주는 것 / *an ~ to health* 건강을 증진시키는 것 / *He was my chief ~ in the business.* 그는 사업에서 나의 수석 보조자였다.

— *vt.* (P6,7,9,13,20,21) help; assist. …을 돕다; 거들다. ¶ *~ someone in an enterprise* 사업에서 아무를 돕다 / *~ someone to do something* 아무가 …하는 것을 돕다 / *He aided his wife in dressing.* 그는 아내가 옷 입는 것을 거들었다. — *vi.* (P1) give help or assistance. 도움이 되다. ¶ *~ in developing one's faculties* 자신의 능력을 개발시키는 데 도움이 되다. [ad-, L. *juvo* help]

aid and abet, encourage or give help (to a crime or criminal). (범행·범인)을 방조하다.

aide [eid] *n.* Ⓒ **1** =aide-de-camp. **2** a helper; an assistant. 돕는 사람; 조수; 조력자. [↓]

aide-de-camp [éiddəkǽmp, -kɑ́ːŋ] *n.* Ⓒ (*pl.* **aides-**) 《F.》 《mil.》 an army officer who aids a general. (장군을 보좌하는) 부관(副官).

aide-mé·moire [éidmeimwɑ́ːr] *n.* 《F.》 《diplom.》 각서(覺書).

AIDS [eidz] *n.* 《med.》 Acquired Immune Deficiency Syndrome; a very serious disease caused by a virus which breaks down the body's natural defences against infection. 에이즈; 후천성 면역 결핍증.

ai·grette [éigret, ⌐⌐] *n.* **1** 《bird》 any of various herons. 백로; 해오라기. **2** a tuft of the feathers used as an ornament. 장식 깃털. **3** anything like this. (깃털 장식 같은) 장식. [Teut. *heiger,* →heron]

ai·guille [eigwíːl, ⌐⌐] *n.* a sharp peak. (알프스 등의) 뾰족한 봉우리. [F.]

ai·guil·lette [èigwilét] *n.* tagged points hanging from the shoulder. (군복의) 장식 띠〔끈〕. [F.]

ail [eil] *vt.* (P6) give or cause pain or discomfort to (someone); trouble. …을 괴롭히다; 괴로움을 주다. ¶ *It ails me that ….* …라는 일로 나는 괴로움을 겪고 있다 / *What ails you?* 무슨 일이냐; 어디가 아프냐. — *vi.* (P1) be ill; feel sick. 병을 앓다. 參考 가벼운 병을 말함. ¶ *She is ailing from a cold.* 그녀는 감기에 걸려 있다 / *She has been ailing for a week.* 그녀는 1주일째 앓고 있다 / *He was ailing long before his death.* 죽기 훨씬 전부터 그는 앓고 있었다. [E.]

ai·ler·on [éilərɑ̀n / -rɔ̀n] *n.* Ⓒ 《usu. *pl.*》 the movable section of an airplane wing. (항공기의) 보조익(翼). [F.]

ail·ment [éilmənt] *n.* Ⓤ a slight disease or disorder of the body or mind; illness, esp. a mild, chronic one; sickness. (보통 가벼운 또는 만성의) 병; 불쾌. [*ail*]

:aim [eim] *vt.* (P6,13) **1** 《*at*》 point (a missile, weapon, blow, etc.) at a particular object; direct (words, acts, etc.). (총 등)을 겨누다; 겨냥하다; (빈정거리는 말 등)을 …에게 빗대다. ¶ *~ a gun at a mark* 총을 과녁에 겨냥하다 / *The remark was aimed at me.* 그 말은 나를 겨냥해서 한 것이었다. **2** try to do (something); intend. …하려고 하다; 마음 먹다; 목표 삼다. ¶ *He aims to lead the class in English.* 그는 영어에는 반에서 1등을 하려고 마음 먹고 있다.

— *vi.* (1,3,4) 《*at*》 **1** direct a missile, remark, etc.; point a weapon at an object. 겨냥하다; 겨누다; 노리다. ¶ *He aimed at the lion, but missed.* 그는 사자를 겨냥했으나 빗맞혔다. **2** direct efforts toward a particular object; intend; try. 마음 먹다; 뜻하다; 목표 삼다; …할 작정이다. ¶ *~ high* 대망을 품다 / *~ at gaining the prize* 상 타는 것을 노리다 / *~ to please another* 남의 마음에 들려고 하다 / *We ~ at success.* 우리는 성공을 목표로 한다.

— *n.* **1** Ⓤ the act of pointing a weapon, etc. 겨냥; 조준. ¶ *take good ~ at the target* 과녁에 잘 겨냥하다 / *miss one's ~* 겨냥이 빗나가다 / *His ~ was so poor that he completely missed the lion.* 겨냥 솜씨가 매우 서툴러서 그는 사자를 완전히 빗맞혔다. **2** Ⓒ something aimed at; an object; a purpose; an intention. 과녁; 목표(물); 뜻; 마음먹은 것. ¶ *a high ~ in life* 생애의 높은 목표 / *My ~ in doing this is to….* 이것을 하는 나의 목적은 …하는 것이다 / *He studied English with the ~ of going abroad.* 그는 해외에 나갈 목적으로 영어를 공부했다. [L. *aestimo,* →estimate]

aim·less [éimlis] *adj.* without aim or purpose. 목적 없는; 지향 없는. ● **aim·less·ly** [-li] *adv.* **aim·less·ness** [-nis] *n.*

aî·né [enéi] *n.* an elder son. 장남(cf. *cadet*). [F.]

·**ain't** [eint] 《*colloq.*》 =am not(cf. *an't, aren't*); 《*sl.*》 =is [are, have, has] not.

Ai·nu [áinu:] *n.* Ⓒ (*pl.* **-nus** or *collectively* **Ai·nu**) a member of a primitive race in north Japan, now becoming extinct; Ⓤ their language. 아이누 사람; 아이누어(語).

:**air** [ɛər] *n.* **1** Ⓤ the mixture of gases surrounding the earth; the atmosphere. 공기; 대기. ¶ ~ *pressure* 기압(氣壓) / *breathe fresh* [*foul*] ~ 신선한[더러운] 공기를 호흡하다 / *a breath of* ~ 산들바람. **2** Ⓤ space above the earth; the sky. 공중; 공간. ¶ *travel by* ~ 비행기 여행을 하다 / *an* ~ *force* 공군 / ~ *combat* [*fight, fighting*] 공중전 / ~ *defense* 방공(防空) / ~ *transport* [*traffic*] 공수(空輸) / *leap into the* ~ 공중으로 뛰어오르다 / *fly in the* ~ 하늘을 날다. **3** Ⓤ circulation. (소문 따위의) 퍼짐; 유포(流布). ¶ *Queer rumors are in the* ~. 묘한 소문이 떠돌고 있다. **4** 《mus.》 Ⓒ a melody; a tune. 선율; 곡조. ¶ *a sweet* ~ 아름다운 멜로디. **5** Ⓒ an outward appearance; a look; a bearing; a style; a manner. 외양; 외견; 태도. ¶ *a proud* ~ 자랑스런 태도 / *with an* ~ *of importance* 젠체하는 태도로 / *with a sad* [*cheerful*] ~ 슬픈[유쾌한] 태도로. **6** 《*pl.*》 affected manner. 짐짓 젠체하는 태도. ¶ *assume* [*put on*] *airs* 젠체하다.

(*a*) ***change of air,*** a change of [in] climate. 전지(轉地). ¶ *a change of* ~ *for the health* 전지 요양.

airs and graces, a foolish, affected way of behaving. 짐짓 젠체함[점잔부림].

beat the air, make vain efforts. 헛수고하다.

be on the air, broadcast; be broadcasted. 방송하다[되고 있다].

build castles in the air, make plans which can never be acted upon. 공중[사상] 누각을 세우다(cf. *air-castle*).

by air, by airplane. 비행기로; 항공편으로.

clear the air, 《*fig.*》 get rid of misunderstanding or ill-feeling. 의혹[이론, 긴장]을 없애다.

get the air, 《*colloq.*》 **a**) be rejected. (애인·친구 등에게) 버림받다; 딱지 맞다. **b**) be dismissed. 해고되다.

give oneself airs, put on airs. 젠체하다.

give someone the air, 《U.S. *sl.*》 **a**) dismiss someone. 아무를 해고하다. **b**) reject. (연인 등을) 차다; 버리다.

in the air, **a**) in circulation. 떠돌아; 유포되어. **b**) =up in the air.

in the open air, out of doors. 야외[집밖]에서.

live on air, live without food. 아무것도 안 먹고 살다.

off the air, 《radio》 not being broadcast. 방송되지 않고; 방송을 안 하고.

take air, become known. 널리 알려지다; 퍼지다; 유포되다.

take the air, **a**) go outdoors. 야외로 나가다; 산책 나가다. **b**) 《radio》 start broadcasting. 방송을 시작하다. **c**) 《*sl.*》 leave hurriedly. 급히 떠나다; 달아나다. **d**) (of an airplane) take off. (비행기가) 이륙하다.

take to the air, become an aviator. 비행사가 되다.

up in the air, **a**) not yet decided; vague. 미결정의. ¶ *Our plans for a vacation are still up in the* ~. 우리의 휴가 계획은 아직 확실히 정해져 있지 않다. **b**) 《*colloq.*》 angry; highly excited. 화나서; 흥분하여.

walk* [*tread*] *on air, feel very happy. 기뻐 어쩔 줄 모르다.

— *vt.* (P6) **1** expose (something) to the air; dry or purify. …을 바람에 쐬다; 바람에 말리다. **2** let air into (a room). (방안)으로 공기를 들이다. **3** 《*fig.*》 make (something) public; display. …을 공표하다; (자랑해) 보이다. ¶ ~ *costly jewels* 값비싼 보석을 자랑해 보이다 / *Don't* ~ *your troubles too often.* 자네 괴로움을 너무 떠벌리지 말게. [Gk. *aēr* lower air]

air balloon [ㄹ-ㄹ] *n.* a toy balloon. 고무풍선.

air-base [ɛ́ərbèis] *n.* a headquarters and airport for military airplanes. 공군기지. [*air,* →base]

air-blad·der [ɛ́ərblæ̀dər] *n.* a sac in most fishes and various animals and plants, filled with air. (동식물의) 기포(氣胞); 기낭(氣囊); (물고기의) 부레. [*air,* → bladder]

air·borne [ɛ́ərbɔ̀:rn] *adj.* carried by air. 공중 수송된; 공기에 의해 운반된. ¶ ~ *troops* 공정(空挺) 부대. [*air,* →borne]

air brake [ㄹㄹ] *n.* a brake operated by compressed air. 공기 제동기; 에어 브레이크.

air·brush [ɛ́ərbrʌ̀ʃ] *n.* a device for applying a fine spray (as of paint) by compressed air. 에어 브러시《압축 공기로 도료·잉크 따위를 뿜는 기구》.

air·burst [ɛ́ərbə̀:rst] *n.* the explosion of a bomb or shell in midair. (폭탄·파열탄의) 공중 폭발.

air·bus [ɛ́ərbʌ̀s] *n.* Ⓒ an extremely large airplane designed to carry a great many passengers at a time, esp. for a short distance travel. 에어버스《근거리용 대형 여객기》.

air-cas·tle [ɛ́ərkæ̀sl, -kɑ̀:sl] *n.* a castle in the air; something that is only imagined. 공중 누각; 백일몽; 몽상.

air cavalry [ㄹㄹ--] *n.* army troops equipped and trained for transportation by air. 공정[공수] 부대.

air coach [ㄹㄹ] *n.* a low-priced air passenger transport service. (근거리·싼 요금의) 보통 여객기.

air-con·di·tion [ɛ́ərkəndìʃən] *vt.* **1** furnish (a room, building, etc.) with an air-conditioning apparatus. (방·건물)에 공기 조절 장치를 비치하다. **2** treat (air) with such an apparatus. …을 공기 조절하다.

air-con·di·tioned [ɛ́ərkəndìʃənd] *adj.*

having an air conditioning system. 에어컨 장치가 돼 있는; 냉(난)방이 돼 있는.

air con·di·tion·ing [ㅅ—ㅅ——] *n.* a system to control the temperature, humidity, etc. in a building or house, esp. to cool. (온도·습도 등의) 공기 상태 조절 장치법.

air-cool [ɛ́ərkùːl] *vt.* (P6) **1** cool (an engine) by blowing air on it. (엔진을) 공랭(空冷)하다. **2** remove (heat in a room) by blowing cool air in. 냉방(冷房)하다.

·**air·craft** [ɛ́ərkræ̀ft, -krɑ̀ːft] *n.* (*pl.* **-craft**) an airplane, airship, balloon, etc. 항공기《각종 비행기·기구 따위의 총칭》. 語法 단수의 뜻으로 쓰이는 일은 비교적 드물다.

aircraft carrier [ㅅ—ㅅ——] *n.* a warship designed to carry airplanes and to serve as a landing field. 항공 모함.

air·craft·man [ɛ́ərkræ̀ftmən, -krɑ̀ːft-] *n.* (*pl.* **-men** [-mən]) 《Brit.》 a private in the Royal Air Force. 공군 이등병; 항공병.

air·drome [ɛ́ərdròum] *n.* Ⓒ 《U.S.》 an airport; an airfield. 비행장; 공항.

air·drop [ɛ́ərdrɑ̀p / -drɔ̀p] *n.* delivery of supplies from an aircraft in flight. (비행기로부터의) 공중 투하(投下).
— *vt.* (P6) (**-dropped, -drop·ping**) drop (supplies, etc.) from an aircraft. (보급품 등을) 공중투하하다.

Aire·dale [ɛ́ərdèil] *n.* a large terrier. 에어데일 종의 개《테리어의 변종》. [Place]

air·field [ɛ́ərfìːld] *n.* Ⓒ a field from which airplanes take off and on which they land. 비행장. [*air*, →field]

air·flow [ɛ́ərflòu] *n.* Ⓤ the movement of air over the surface of an aircraft in flight. (비행기가 일으키는) 기류(氣流).

air force [ㅅㅅ] *n.* a unit of military or naval forces that uses airplanes. 공군. ¶ *the United States* (*U.S.*) *Air Force* 미국 공군 / *the Royal Air Force* 영국 공군. 參考 the R.A.F.로 생략.

air gun [ㅅㅅ] *n.* a gun operated by compressed air. 공기총.

air hole [ㅅㅅ] *n.* **1** an open space in the ice on a river, pond, etc. (얼어붙은 강·연못 따위의) 얼지 않은 부분. **2** =air pocket.

air hostess [ㅅㅅ—] *n.* an air stewardess. (여객기의) 스튜어디스.

air·i·ly [ɛ́ərəli] *adv.* in an airy manner; lightly. 가볍게; 사뿐히; 쾌활하게. [*air*]

air·ing [ɛ́əriŋ] *n.* Ⓒ **1** the act of exposing to the air for drying, freshening, etc. 바람에 쬠(말림). ¶ *give something an* ~ …을 바람에 쐬어 말리다 / *I gave my fur coat a thorough* ~. 털외투를 바람에 쐬어 철저하게 말렸다. **2** a walk, drive, etc., in the open air. 외출; 산책; 드라이브. ¶ *take an* ~ 바람을 쐬다; 산책을 하다.

air·less [ɛ́ərlis] *adj.* without a breeze or fresh air; stuffy. 바람이(신선한 공기가) 없는; 통풍이 잘 안되는. ¶ *Airless rooms are very bad for the health.* 통풍이 나쁜 방은 건강에 매우 나쁘다.

air letter [ㅅㅅ—] *n.* **1** an airmail letter; an aerogram. 항공 우편. **2** a very light lettersheet for air mail. 항공우편 엽서.

air·lift [ɛ́ərlìft] *n.* Ⓒ a system for carrying persons or cargo by aircraft, esp. in an emergency; something carried by such a system. 공수(空輸); 공수 물자. — *vt.* 《*to*》 carry (something) by airlift. …을 공수하다. ¶ *We airlifted food to them.* 그들에게 식량을 공수했다.

air·line [ɛ́ərlàin] *n.* Ⓒ **1** a system for carrying persons and cargo regularly by aircraft. 항공로; 정기 항로. **2** 《*pl.* used as *sing.*》 a company that operates such a system. 항공 회사. ¶ *Korean Air Lines* 대한 항공. **3** a direct line. 일직선.

·**air·lin·er** [ɛ́ərlàinər] *n.* Ⓒ a passenger aircraft of an airlines. 정기 항공기; 여객기.

air lock [ㅅㅅ] *n.* an airtight antechamber of a submarine caisson. 기갑(氣閘).

air·mail, air-mail [ɛ́ərmèil] *n.* Ⓤ the system of sending mail by aircraft; mail carried by aircraft. 항공 우편(물). — *adj.* of airmail. 항공 우편의. ¶ *an* ~ *letter* 항공편지. — *vt.* (P6) send (a letter) by air (mail). (편지)를 항공 우편으로 보내다. ¶ *I airmailed your letter.* 네 편지를 항공 우편으로 부쳤다.

air·man [ɛ́ərmən] *n.* Ⓒ (*pl.* **-men** [-mən]) the pilot of an airplane; 《U.S. mil.》 a member of a (military) aircrew. 비행사; 항공병. 參考 항공병의 경우는 남녀 똑같이 씀. an airwoman은 여류 비행사의 뜻.

air marshal [ㅅㅅ—] *n.* an officer of the Royal Air Force ranking next below an air-chief-marshal. (영국 공군의) 공군 중장.

air mass [ㅅㅅ] *n.* 《meteor.》 a large horizontally homogeneous body of air. (기온이 같은 수평 방향의 거대한) 기단(氣團).

air-mind·ed [ɛ́ərmàindid] *adj.* interested in flying aircraft; fond of flying aircraft or of air travel. 항공에 흥미를 가진; 항공(비행기 여행)열(熱)의.

:**air·plane** [ɛ́ərplèin] *n.* Ⓒ 《U.S.》 a winged machine for flight. 비행기. 參考 영국에서는 aeroplane으로 씀.

air pocket [ㅅㅅ—] *n.* an upright current in the air that causes an airplane to make a sudden drop. 에어포켓《기류에 의해 항공기가 갑자기 밑으로 떨어지는 곳》.

:**air·port** [ɛ́ərpɔ̀ːrt] *n.* Ⓒ a place where airplanes land and take off; an airdrome. 공항; 항공기 발착소. ¶ *Kimp'o Airport* 김포 공항.

air·post [ɛ́ərpòust] *n.* =airmail.

air pump [ㅅㅅ] *n.* a machine for exhausting, compressing, or drawing in air. 공기 펌프; 배기 펌프.

air raid [ㅅㅅ] *n.* an attack by aircraft, esp. to bomb a certain area. (적기의) 공습.

air-raid [ɛ́ərèid] *adj.* for or against a

raid by aircraft. 공습의. ¶ *an ~ shelter* 방공호 / *an ~ warning*〔*alarm*〕 공습 경보.

air rifle [ˊ-ˋ-] *n.* =air gun.

air route [ˊ-ˋ] *n.* an airway. 항(공)로.

air·screw [ɛ́ərskrùː] *n.* a screw propeller of an aircraft. (항공기의) 프로펠러.

·air·ship [ɛ́ərʃìp] *n.* Ⓒ a balloon that is driven by engines in the air. 비행선. 參考 오늘날에는 일반적으로 dirigible 이라고 함.

air·sick [ɛ́ərsìk] *adj.* sick as a result of air travel. 항공병에 걸린; 비행기 멀미를 하는.

air·sick·ness [ɛ́ərsìknis] *n.* Ⓤ the state of being airsick. 비행기 멀미.

air·space [ɛ́ərspèis] *n.* Ⓤ the space lying above a nation and coming under its jurisdiction. (어느 지역 국가의) 상공; 영공(領空).

air·speed [ɛ́ərspìːd] *n.* Ⓤ the speed (as of an airplane) with relation to the air as distinguished from its speed relative to the earth. (비행기의) 대기(大氣) 속도.

air-spray [ɛ́ərsprèi] *adj.* pertaining to compressed-air spraying devices or to liquids in them. 분무기의.
● **air-sprayed** [-d] *adj.*

air·strip [ɛ́ərstrìp] *n.* Ⓒ a long runway on which planes land and from which they take off. (임시) 활주로.

air·tight [ɛ́ərtàit] *adj.* **1** so closed that no air can enter. 밀폐된; 기밀(機密)의. **2** having no weak points (open to an enemy's attack, open to criticism, etc.). 허점〔빈틈〕이 없는; 공격할 수 없는.

air-to-air [ɛ́ərtuɛ́ər, -tə-] *adj.* launched from one airplane in flight at another; involving aircraft in flight. 공대공(空對空)의.

air-to-sur·face [ɛ̀ərtəsə́ːrfis] *adj.* operating or directed from a flying aircraft to the surface of the earth. 공대지(空對地)의.

air·way [ɛ́ərwèi] *n.* Ⓒ **1** a main route for aircraft. 항공로. **2** a passage used for changing the air in a room, etc.; an air course. 통풍구(口); 환기공(孔). **3** 《*pl.*》 a name taken by companies carrying people or things by air. 항공 회사. ¶ *the Pan American Airways* 팬아메리칸 항공 회사.

air·wor·thy [ɛ́ərwə̀ːrði] *adj.* 《aeron.》 fit or safe for service in the air. 항공에 견디는〔적합한〕.

air·y [ɛ́əri] *adj.* (**air·i·er, air·i·est**) **1** in or of the air; open to the air or breezes; high up. 공기의; 공중의; 공기가 잘 통하는; 하늘 높이 치솟은. ¶ *an ~ tower* 높이 치솟은 탑 / *a large, ~ room* 크고 바람이 잘 통하는 방. **2** like air; empty; without substance; imaginary. 공기와 같은; 비현실적인; 꿈같은; 헛된. ¶ *~ dreams* 헛된 꿈 / *~ notions* 꿈같은 생각. **3** light in manner; lively; gay. 경쾌한; 명랑한. ¶ *~ songs* 명랑한 노래 / *~ laughter* 쾌활한 웃음 / *an ~ tread* 경쾌한 걸음걸이. **4** affected; unnatural. 짐짓 꾸민; 젠체하는. ● **air·i·ly** [-li] *adv.* [*air*]

·aisle [ail] *n.* Ⓒ **1** a passage between rows of seats in a church, theater, hall, etc. (교회·극장·찻간 따위의) 통로. **2** part of a church separated from the main interior area by a row of pillars. (교회의) 측랑(側廊). **3** any long or narrow passageway. 좁고 긴 통로. [L. *ala* wing]

aitch·bone [éitʃbòun] *n.* **1** the rump bone. (소의) 둔골(臀骨). **2** the cut of beef that includes this bone. (소의) 볼기살〔홍두깨〕. [L. *natis* buttock, →bone]

a·jar[1] [ədʒáːr] *adj., adv.* 《as *predicative*》 (of a gate or door) slightly open. (방문 따위가) 조금 열리어. ¶ *leave the door ~* 방문을 조금 열어두다. [A.S. *char* turn]

a·jar[2] [ədʒáːr] *adj., adv.* out of harmony. 조화되지 않고. ¶ *~ with the world* 세상과 어울리지 않아. [a(-)]

A·jax [éidʒæks] *n.* 《Gk. myth.》 a brave leader in the Trojan War. 아이아스《트로이 전쟁의 영웅》.

a·kim·bo [əkímbou] *adv., adj.* with the hands on the hips and the elbows turned outward. 두 손을 허리에 대고 팔꿈치는 옆으로 벌려〔펴고〕. ¶ *He stood with his arms ~.* 양팔을 허리에 대고 섰다. [E.]

a·kin [əkín] *adj.* 《as *predicative*》 **1** of the same kin; related. 동족의; 친척의. ¶ *She is near ~ to me.* 그녀는 나의 가까운 친척이다. **2** similar. 비슷한; 유사한. ¶ *Most girls are ~ in their love of dolls.* 대개의 소녀들은 인형을 좋아하는 것이 비슷하다 / *Pity is ~ to love.* 연민은 사랑에 가깝다. [a(-), →kin]

al- [æl-, əl-] *pref.* 《used before *l*》 =ad-.

-al [-əl] *suf.* **1** of; belonging to. '…의, …성질의'의 뜻. ¶ *comical* / *postal* / *national.* **2** forming nouns from verbs. 동사를 명사로 만듦. ¶ *trial* / *removal.*

Al 《chem.》 Aluminum.

Al·a·bam·a [æ̀ləbǽmə] *n.* a southern State of the United States. 앨라배마 주(州). 參考 Ala.로 생략. 주도(州都)는 Montgomery.

al·a·bas·ter [ǽləbæ̀stər, -bɑ̀ːs-] *n.* Ⓤ a white, glass-like mineral. 설화 석고(雪花石膏). —— *adj.* **1** made of alabaster. 설화 석고로 만든. **2** white and smooth like alabaster. (살결이) 희고 매끄러운. [Gk.]

à la carte [ɑ̀ːləkɑ́ːrt, æ̀lə-] *adv., adj.* 《F.》 by the menu. (식당에서) 메뉴에 의해〔의한〕; 주문 식단의(opp. table d'hôte). ¶ *an ~ dinner* 주문 식단〔일품〕 요리 / *eat ~* 주문식단 요리를 먹다.

a·lack [əlǽk] *interj.* 《*arch.*》 a cry of sorrow or regret; alas. (비애·유감 따위를 나타내어) 아아. [→ah, L. *lassus* weary, →alas] ***Alack-a-day!*** =***Alas and alack!*** 《*emph.*》 Alas! 아아.

a·lac·ri·ty [əlǽkrəti] *n.* Ⓤ cheerful readiness or willingness; liveliness. 시원시원함;

민첩; 활발. ¶ *do a thing with* ~ 일을 시원시원히 하다 / *accept an offer with* ~ 제의를 선뜻 수락하다 / *Although the man was very old, he still moved with* ~. 그 남자는 비록 많이 늙기는 했지만 아직도 활발히 움직였다 / *show* ~ (언행이 흐릿하지 않고) 시원시원하다. [L. *alacer* swift]

A·lad·din [əlǽdən] *n.* a youth with a magic lamp in "The Arabian Nights." 알라딘《천일 야화에서 마법 램프를 가진 소년》.

Aladdin's lamp [–⏤–] *n.* a talisman enabling the owner to gratify any wish. 마술의 램프.

à la mode [à:ləmóud, æ̀lə-], **al·a·mode** [ǽləmòud] *adj.* **1** according to the fashion; fashionable. 유행에 따라서; 최신 유행의. **2** (of dessert, pie, etc.) served with a portion of ice cream; (of beef) stewed with vegetables. 아이스크림을 곁들인; (고기를) 야채와 함께 지진. —*adv.* fashionably. 유행에 따라서. ¶ *be dressed* ~ 새 유행의 옷을 입다. —*n.* fashion. 유행. [F. =in the fashion]

Al·an [ǽlən] *n.* a man's name. 남자 이름.

:a·larm [əlá:rm] *n.* **1** Ⓒ a sound telling of danger; any device that gives such a warning. 경보(기). ¶ *a fire* ~ 화재 경보 / *give the* ~ 경보를 울리다 / *sound* 〔*ring*〕 *the* ~ 비상나팔을 불다 / *raise an* ~ 위급을 알리다. **2** Ⓤ sudden fright. 놀람; 경악. ¶ *in* ~ 깜짝 놀라 / *without* ~ 침착하게 / *take* (*the*) ~ *at something* …에 깜짝 놀라다 / *The news caused great* ~. 그 소식은 크게 놀라게 했다.
—*vt.* (P6) **1** strike (something) with sudden fear. …을 깜짝 놀라게 하다. ¶ *be alarmed at the sound* 그 소리에 깜짝 놀라다 / *I was greatly alarmed when I heard the shouting.* 그 외침을 들었을 때 나는 몹시 놀랐다. **2** give warning of danger to. 경계시키다; 위급을 알리다. ¶ *The sentry alarmed the sleeping men.* 보초는 잠들어 있는 병사들을 경계시켰다. [It. *all' arme* to arms]

alarm bell [–⏤] *n.* a bell rung to warn of approaching danger. 경종; 비상종.

alarm clock [–⏤] *n.* a clock with a bell. 자명종.

alarm gun [–⏤] *n.* a gun fired to give notice of approaching danger. 경포(警砲).

a·larm·ist [əlá:rmist] *n.* Ⓒ a person who is always warning of danger without sufficient reason. 늘 남을 놀라게 하는 사람; 기우가. —*adj.* raising or exciting alarms. 남을 놀라게 하는.

a·lar·um [əlǽrəm, -lá:r-] *n.* **1** 《*arch., poet.*》 =alarm. **2** the sound made by an alarm clock; the instrument which makes this sound. 자명종 소리; 그 장치. [*alarm*]

:a·las [əlǽs, əlá:s] *interj.* exclamation of unhappiness, pity, or grief. 아아, 슬프도다. [L. *lassus* weary]

·A·las·ka [əlǽskə] *n.* a State of the United States in northwest North America. 알래스카 주(州). 參考 Alas.로 생략.

a·late [éileit] *adj.* having wings or membranes like wings. 날개가 있는; 유시(有翅)의. [L. *āla* wing]

alb [ælb] *n.* a white linen robe with narrow sleeves worn by the priest at Mass. (성직자의) 장백의(長白衣)《미사 때 입음》. [L. *albus* white]

al·ba·core [ǽlbəkɔ̀:r] *n.* 《fish》 a large kind of tunny. 다랑어의 일종. [Arab. = young camel]

Al·ba·ni·a [ælbéiniə, -njə] *n.* a country in southeastern Europe. 알바니아. 參考 Alb.로 생략. 수도는 Tirana.

Al·ba·ni·an [ælbéiniən, -njən] *adj.* of Albania, its people, or their language. 알바니아 (사람·말)의. —*n.* Ⓒ a person of Albania; Ⓤ the language of Albania. 알바니아 사람; 알바니아어(語).

Al·ba·ny [ɔ́:lbəni] *n.* the capital of New York State. 올버니《미국 New York 주의 주도(州都)》.

al·ba·tross [ǽlbətrɔ̀(:)s, -tràs] *n.* 《bird》 a kind of petrel. 신천옹(信天翁). [→alb]

Al·bee [ɔ́:lbi:], **Edward** *n.* (1928-) an American playwright. 올비《미국의 극작가》.

al·be·it [ɔ:lbí:it] *conj.* 《*lit.*》 although; even though. …이기는 하나; 비록 …하더라도. ¶ *Albeit he has failed twice, he is not discouraged.* 비록 두 번이나 실패했지만 그는 실망하지 않고 있다. [*all be it*]

Al·bert [ǽlbərt] *n.* a man's name. 남자 이름. 參考 애칭은 Al, Bert.

al·bert (**chain**) [ǽlbərt(⏤)] *n.* a kind of watch chain. 앨버트 형의 시계줄.

al·bes·cent [ælbésənt] *adj.* growing white; whitish. 하얘지는; 희끔한. [L. *albus* white] .

al·bi·nism [ǽlbənìzəm] *n.* Ⓤ the state or quality of being albino. 색소 결핍증; (사람·동식물의) 선천성 백피(白皮)증. [↑]

al·bi·no [ælbáinou / -bí:-] *n.* (*pl.* **-nos**) a person or animal with white skin and hair and pink eyes. 선천성 색소 결핍증의 사람〔동식물〕. [↑]

Al·bi·on [ǽlbiən] *n.* 《*poet.*》 an old name for England. 영국의 아명(雅名).

:al·bum [ǽlbəm] *n.* Ⓒ a blank book for storing autographs, stamps, photographs, or the like. 사진첩; 우편 수집첩; 앨범. [L. *albus* white]

al·bu·men [ælbjú:mən] *n.* Ⓤ **1** the white of an egg. 알의 흰자위. **2** 《bot.》 a nourishing substance in a seed. 배유(胚乳). [↑]

al·bu·min [ælbjú:mən] *n.* any of various protein substances resembling white of an egg. 알부민《단백질의 일종》.

al·bu·mi·noid [ælbjú:mənɔ̀id] *adj.* like albumin. 의사(擬似) 단백질의. [↑]

al·cal·de [ælkǽldi] *n.* (*pl.* **-des**) the chief administrative and judicial officer of a Spanish or Spanish-American town.

(스페인·미국 남서부에서) 재판권을 가진 시장. [Sp.]

•**al·che·mist** [ǽlkəmist] *n.* Ⓒ a person who studied alchemy in the Middle Ages. 연금술사(鍊金術師). ¶ *The alchemists tried to turn lead into gold.* 연금술사들은 납을 금으로 바꾸려고 애썼다. [↓]

al·che·my [ǽlkəmi] *n.* Ⓤ the chemistry of the Middle Ages, the aim of which was to change the cheaper metals into gold. 연금술(鍊金術). [Arab. *al-kīmiyā*]

•**al·co·hol** [ǽlkəhɔ̀(:)l, -hɑ̀l] *n.* ⓊⒸ a colorless liquid in wine, whisky, etc.; drinks which contain alcohol. 알코올; 주정(酒精); 술. ¶ *not touch* ~ 술을 입에 대지 않다. [Arab. *al kohl*]

al·co·hol·ic [æ̀lkəhɔ́(:)lik, -hɑ́l-] *adj.* **1** of or containing alcohol. 알코올의; 알코올이 들어 있는. ¶ ~ *drinks* 알코올 음료. **2** caused by alcohol. 알코올로 인한. ¶ ~ *poisoning* 알코올 중독. — *n.* Ⓒ a person who drinks too much wine. 대주가(大酒家); 알코올 중독자.

al·co·hol·ism [ǽlkəhɔ(:)lìzəm, -hɑl-] *n.* Ⓤ a diseased condition resulting from drinking too much liquor. 알코올 중독.

Al·co·ran [æ̀lkɔːrɑ́ːn, -rǽn, -kou-] *n.* Koran.

al·cove [ǽlkouv] *n.* Ⓒ **1** a space in a room for a bed, bookcases, etc. (큰 방의) 쑥 들어가 후미진 곳. **2** a small house in the garden. (정원의) 정자. [Arab.]

〈alcove 1〉

al·de·hyde [ǽldəhàid] *n.* 《chem.》 ⓊⒸ a volatile liquid. 알데히드. [*alcohol, de, hydrogen*]

al·der [ɔ́ːldər] *n.* Ⓒ 《bot.》 a tree usu. growing in wet places. 오리나무. [E.]

al·der·man [ɔ́ːldərmən] *n.* Ⓒ (*pl.* **-men** [-mən]) **1** 《Brit.》 an officer next in rank to the mayor. 시(市)〔군(郡)〕 참사회원. **2** 《U.S.》 a member of a lawmaking body in a city. 시(市)의회 의원. [→old, man]

al·der·man·ic [ɔ̀ːldərmǽnik] *adj.* of or belonging to an alderman; characteristic of an alderman. alderman의〔같은〕; alderman에 어울리는; 호화로운. ¶ *an* ~ *feast* 호화판 연회〔잔치〕.

Al·der·ney [ɔ́ːldərni] *n.* a bull or cow bred in Alderney in the Channel Islands. 올더니 종(種)의 젖소《올더니 섬 원산》.

Al·ding·ton [ɔ́ːldiŋtən], **Richard** *n.* (1892-1962) an English poet and novelist. 올딩턴《영국의 시인·소설가》.

•**ale** [eil] *n.* Ⓤ a drink, more bitter than beer, made from hops and malt. (쌉쌀한 맛이 더한) 맥주의 일종. [E. *alu*]

a·le·a·tor·y [éiliətɔ̀ːri / -təri] *adj.* of or dependent on chance, luck, or contingency. 사행적인; 우연의; 예측할 수 없는. ¶ *an* ~ *element in life* 인생에 있어서 예측할 수 없는 요소 / *expect* ~ *profits* 우연의 이익을 기대하다. [Gk. *āleós*]

a·lee [əlíː] *adv.* 《naut.》 on or to the lee side of a ship. 바람 불어가는 쪽에〔으로〕. [a(-)]

ale·house [éilhàus] *n.* Ⓒ a house or place where ale and other drinks are sold. 비어홀; 술집. [→ale]

a·lem·bic [əlémbik] *n.* an apparatus formerly used in distilling. 증류기(蒸溜器). [Arab. *al* the, Gk. *ambix* cup]

•**a·lert** [əlɔ́ːrt] *adj.* **1** watchful; wide-awake; ready in mind and body. 경계하는; 방심 않는; 빈틈없는. ¶ *be* ~ *to make money* 돈버는 데 빈틈없다. **2** quick; brisk. 민첩한. ¶ *A sparrow is very* ~ *in its movements.* 참새는 그 동작이 매우 민첩하다. — *n.* Ⓤ **1** 《*the* ~》 the attitude of vigilance; watchfulness. 경계; 경계 태세. **2** an air-raid alarm [warning]. 공습〔경계〕 경보.

be on the alert, be wide-awake; be watchful. 방심않고 경계하다.

— *vt.* (P6,13) **1** prepare (troops, etc.) for action. 경계시키다. **2** warn of an impending raid or attack. 경보를 내다. [It. *all'erta* to the watch tower]

a·lert·ly [əlɔ́ːrtli] *adv.* in an alert manner; watchfully. 방심 않고.

a·lert·ness [əlɔ́ːrtnis] *n.* Ⓤ the state of being alert. 경계; 기민; 민첩.

A·leu·tian [əlúːʃən] *adj.* of the islands of the name. 알루샨 열도의.

Alex. Alexander.

Al·ex·an·der [æ̀ligzǽndər, -zɑ́ːn-] *n.* a man's name. 남자의 이름.

•**Alexander the Great** [--´-- -´] *n.* (356-323 B.C.) a king of Macedonia. 알렉산더 대왕.

Al·ex·an·dri·a [æ̀ligzǽndriə, -zɑ́ːn-] *n.* a seaport in the Nile delta in Egypt, founded by Alexander the Great in 323 B.C. 알렉산드리아《이집트 나일강 어귀의 항구 도시》.

Al·ex·an·drine [æ̀ligzǽndrin, -driːn, -zɑ́ːn-] *n.* 《*poet.*》 a line with six stresses. 알렉산더 격(格)(의 시)《육각 단장격(六脚短長格)》.

al·fal·fa [ælfǽlfə] *n.* Ⓒ 《bot.》 《U.S.》 a cloverlike plant of the pea family, used as food for horses and cattle. 자주개자리. [Arab.]

Al·fred [ǽlfrid, -fred] *n.* a man's name. 남

자의 이름.

al·fres·co [ælfréskou] *adv.* in the open air. 야외에(서). ¶ *We lunched* ~. 우리는 야외에서 점심을 먹었다. — *adj.* open-air. 야외(에서)의. ¶ *an* ~ *luncheon* 야외 점심. [It. =in the fresh]

al·ga [ǽlgə] *n.* sing. of **algae.**

al·gae [ǽldʒiː] *n. pl.* (*sing.* **al·ga**) a kind of water plant. 해초; 조류(藻類). [L.]

***al·ge·bra** [ǽldʒəbrə] *n.* Ⓤ a branch of mathematics. 대수학. [Arab. *al* the, *jabara* reunite]

al·ge·bra·ic [æ̀ldʒəbréiik], **-i·cal** [-ikəl] *adj.* of algebra. 대수학(상)의. ¶ *an algebraic equation* 대수 방정식 / *an algebraical solution* 대수학적 해법. ● **al·ge·bra·i·cal·ly** [-ikəli] *adv.*

Al·ger·i·a [ældʒíəriə] *n.* a country in northwest Africa. 알제리. 參考 본디 프랑스령 식민지. 수도 Algiers.

al·gol·o·gy [ælgɑ́lədʒi / -gɔ́l-] *n.* 《bot.》 a branch of botany that deals with algae. 조류학(藻類學)(cf. *alga*). [L.]

Al·gon·qui·an [ælgɑ́ŋkwiən / -gɔ́ŋ-] *n., adj.* (of) a family of North American Indian Languages. 알곤킨 어족(語族)(의). [Place]

Al·gon·quin [ælgɑ́ŋkin / -gɔ́ŋ-] *n.* an Algonquian speaking Indian (tribe). 알곤킨 어족의 사람《북아메리카 원주민의 한 부족》. [↑]

Al·ham·bra [ælhǽmbrə] *n.* 《*the* ~ 》 the palace of Moorish kings in Spain. 알함브라 궁전. [Arab. =the red (castle)]

a·li·as [éiliəs] *adv.* otherwise called. 별명은; 통칭. ¶ *Mary Brown* ~ *Dolly* 메리 브라운 별명 돌리. — *n.* Ⓒ other name; a false name. 변명(變名); 가명. ¶ *go by the* ~ *of George* 조지라는 별명으로 행세하다. [L.]

A·li Ba·ba [ɑ́:li bɑ́:bɑː, ǽli bǽbə] *n.* a poor man who became rich by the treasure of forty thieves. 알리바바《천일 야화에 나오는 인물》. [a person in Arabian Nights]

al·i·bi [ǽləbài] *n.* Ⓒ **1** 《law》 the fact of having been somewhere else when a crime was committed. 알리바이; 현장 부재 증명. ¶ *set up* 〔*prove*〕 *an* ~ 알리바이를 세우다 〔입증하다〕 / *have a cast-iron* ~ 움직일 수 없는 알리바이가 있다. **2** 《U.S. *colloq.*》 an excuse. (교활한) 변명; 구실. ¶ *What's your* ~ *for being late this time Tom ?* 톰 이번에 늦은 것에 대해선 무슨 구실을 붙일 텐가. [L. *alius ibi* elsewhere]

Al·ice [ǽlis] *n.* a woman's name. 여자의 이름.

***al·ien** [éiljən, -liən] *adj.* **1** foreign. 외국의. ¶ ~ *friends* (자국에 있는) 외국인 친구들 / *the* ~ *rule* 외국의 지배. **2** 《*from*》 different in nature (from others). (성질이) 다른. ¶ *a style* ~ *from genuine English* 진짜 영어와는 다른 문체. **3** 《*to*》 in opposition; strange to. 서로 용납되지 않는; 반(反)하는. ¶ ~ *to his thoughts* 자신의 사상에 반하는 / *Dishonesty is* ~ *to her.* 그녀에겐 부정직한 데는 전혀 없다 / *Unkindness was* ~ *to his nature.* 불친절은 그의 성격에 반하는 것이었다. — *n.* Ⓒ a foreigner. (거류) 외국인. [L. *alius* another; →alias]

al·ien·a·ble [éiljənəbəl, -liə-] *adj.* (of property) that can be separated from one ownership and transferred to another. (소유권을) 양도할 수 있는.

al·ien·ate [éiljənèit, -liə-] *vt.* (P6) **1** turn away; make (someone) unfriendly. …을 멀리하다; 불화하게 하다. ¶ ~ *A from B,* A와 B를 이간하다 / *I'm alienated from her.* 그녀와 불화하다〔사이가 틀어져 있다〕 / *His foolish acts alienated him from his friends.* 그의 어리석은 행동 때문에 친구들은 그를 멀리했다. **2** 《law》 give the ownership of (something) to another. (재산)을 양도하다; 넘겨주다. ¶ *The property of the defeated rebels was alienated.* 역도(逆徒)들의 재산은 남의 손으로 넘겨졌다.

al·ien·a·tion [èiljənéiʃən, -liə-] *n.* Ⓤ **1** the act of alienating; the state of being alienated. 멀리함; 소격(疎隔); 이간; 절교. **2** ⓊⒸ mental derangement. 정신 착란. **3** 《law》 change in the ownership of property. 양도.

al·ien·ee [èiljəníː, -liə-] *n.* 《law》 one to whom property is transferred. 양수인(讓受人).

al·ien·ist [éiljənist, -liə] *n.* a doctor who treats mad people. 정신병의(醫)(cf. *mad-doctor*).

***a·light**[1] [əláit] *vt.* (P1,2A) **1** ⓐ 《*from*》 get off or down. …에서 내리다. ¶ ~ *from a train* 〔*horse, carriage, plane*〕 열차〔말, 마차, 비행기〕에서 내리다. ⓑ finish one's journey by getting off the train, etc. (여행을 끝내고 열차 따위)에서 내리다. ¶ *He alighted at Oxford.* 그는 옥스퍼드에서 내렸다. **2** 《*on*》 (of birds, airplanes, etc.) come down and settle. (새·비행기 등이) 내려앉다; 착륙하다. ¶ *The plane alighted on the ground.* 비행기는 착륙했다 / *Some birds alighted on the tree.* 새 몇 마리가 나무에 내려 앉았다. [E.]

a·light[2] [əláit] *adj.* 《as *predicative*》 **1** lighted (up); on fire. 불을 붙여; 점화하여; (불)타고. ¶ *catch* ~ 불이 붙다; 불타다 / *set a candle* ~ 초에 불을 붙이다. **2** bright in expression. (표정이) 밝게 빛나는. ¶ *Her face was* ~ *with joy.* 그녀의 얼굴은 기쁨에 빛나고 있었다. [E.]

a·lign [əláin] *vt., vi.* (P6;1) bring (something) into a straight line; form in a line. 일렬〔한줄〕로 하다; 일렬〔한줄〕이 되다. ¶ *The students aligned themselves.* 학생들은 일렬로 섰다 / *At the sergeant's command the soldiers quickly aligned.* 중사의 지시에 따라 병사들은 잽싸게 일렬로 정렬했다. [ad-, →line]

a·lign·ment [əláinmənt] *n.* Ⓤ the act of

aligning; the state of being aligned; adjustment to a straight line. 일렬로 하기; 정렬; 일직선; 일렬. ¶ *The sights of the gun were in ~ with the target.* 총 가늠쇠는 목표에 일직선으로 조준되어 있었다.

:a·like [əláik] *adj.* 《as *predicative*》 resembling each other; similar. (서로) 비슷한; 같은. ¶ *They are very much ~.* 그들은 아주 꼭 닮았다 / *~ as two peas* 흡사한; 꼭닮은 / *He and his brother are exactly ~ in that respect.* 그와 그의 형은 그 점에서 똑같다. — *adv.* in the same way or degree; equally. 똑같이; 마찬가지로. ¶ *treat all people ~* 모든 사람을 똑같이 취급하다. [a(-)]

share and share alike, (of several persons) take part equally in the use or enjoyment of something distributed. (몇 사람이) 서로 몫을 똑같이 나누다.

al·i·ment [ǽləmənt] *n.* Ⓤ food; nutriment. 음식; 영양(자양)물. [L. *alo* nourish]

al·i·men·ta·ry [æ̀ləméntəri] *adj.* of food or nutrition. 음식의; 영양의. ¶ *the ~ canal* 소화 기관.

al·i·men·ta·tion [æ̀ləmentéiʃən] *n.* Ⓤ the act of providing nourishment; the condition of being nourished. 영양 섭취(작용); 자양; 영양.

al·i·mo·ny [ǽləmòuni / -mə-] *n.* means of living; 《esp. law》 money which is to be paid to a woman by her husband to support her after she has been separated from him by law. 생계비; (특히 이혼·별거 후에 남편이 주는) 생활비; 별거 수당. [L. *alimonia* food]

a·line [əláin] *v.* =align.

a·line·ment [əláinmənt] *n.* =alignment.

al·i·quant [ǽləkwənt] *adj.* 《math.》 not dividing evenly into another number. 딱 떨어지게 나눌 수 없는. [L.=some]

al·i·quot [ǽləkwət] *adj.* 《math.》 dividing evenly into another number. 딱 떨어지게 나눌 수 있는. — *n.* an aliquot part. 딱 떨어지게 나눠는 수. [L.=several]

:a·live [əláiv] *adj.* 《as *predicative*》 **1** living. 살아(있는)(cf. *live²*; opp. dead). ¶ *any man ~* 어떤 사람이든; 누구든 / *be buried ~* 산 채로 묻히다; 생매장되다 / *catch* 〔*capture*〕 *a fox ~* 여우를 산 채로 잡다 / *come back ~* 살아서 돌아오다 / *He is the greatest man ~.* 그는 생존하고 있는 가장 위대한 사람이다 / *Was the snake ~ or dead?* 그 뱀은 살아 있었나 죽어 있었나. **2** in force; in existence. 유효한; 소멸되지 않고. ¶ *keep a right ~* 권리를 유효하게 해두다. **3** active; lively. 활발한; 활동하여. ¶ *a man who is thoroughly ~* 아주 활동적인 사람 / *keep the fire ~* 불을 꺼지지 않게 하다 / *He is ~ and well.* 그는 씽씽하여 원기 왕성하다. **4** 《*with*》 full of people or things in motion. 활기가 넘쳐; 충만하여; 북적거려; 붐벼. ¶ *a pool ~ with fish* 고기떼로 우글거리는 웅덩이 / *a lake ~ with boats* 보트들로 붐비는 호수 / *The streets were ~ with people.* 거리는 사람들로 북적거렸다. **5** 《*to*》 taking notice of; sensitive to. 깨닫고; 알아채고; 민감하여. ¶ *~ to dangers* 위험을 깨닫고 / *He is ~ to his own interests.* 그는 자기 이익에 민감하다 / *Are you ~ to what is going on?* 무슨 일이 일어나고 있는지 깨닫고 있는가. **6** connected with a source of electricity; electrically charged. (전깃줄이) 전류가 통한; 대전(帶電)의. ¶ *The wire is ~.* 전깃줄은 전류가 통해 있다. [a-, → life]

Look alive (***there***), Hurry up! Be quick! 서둘러라; 빨리 해라.

Man alive! ⇨Sakes alive!

al·ka·li [ǽlkəlài] *n.* Ⓒ (*pl.* **-lis** or **-lies**) 《chem.》 a chemical substance that turns red litmus blue. 알칼리. [Arab., *al-qalīy*]

al·ka·li·fy [ǽlkələfài, ælkǽlə-] *vt.* (P6) 《chem.》 make into an alkali; make alkaline. 알칼리성으로 하다.

al·ka·line [ǽlkəlàin, -lin] *adj.* of or containing an alkali. 알칼리(성)의.

al·ka·lin·i·ty [æ̀lkəlínəti] *n.* Ⓤ the state or quality of being alkaline. 알칼리성(도(度)).

al·ka·lize [ǽlkəlàiz] *vt.* (P6) make alkaline. …을 알칼리화(化)하다.

al·ka·loid [ǽlkəlɔ̀id] *n.* ⓊⒸ 《chem.》 any basic, organic substance containing nitrogen. 알칼로이드《식물에 함유된 염기성 물질로 흔히 유해(有害)함》.

Al·ko·ran [æ̀lkɔːrάːn, -rǽn, -kou-] *n.* = Koran.

:all [ɔːl] *adj.* **1** 《with *sing. noun*》 ⓐ the whole of. 온(전)…; 전체(전부)의. ¶ *~ day* 〔*night*〕 온종일(밤) / *~ yesterday* 어제 하루 종일 / *~ the year* 일년 내내 / *~ one's life* 전생애 / *It rained ~ day without stopping.* 온종일 비가 쉬지 않고 내렸다 / *He spent ~ his money.* 그는 가진 돈을 몽땅 썼다 / *All the house was quiet.* 온 집안이 고요했다 / *He is ~ attention.* 그는 온 신경을 곤두세우고 있다. ⓑ only. …만. ¶ 《*prov.*》 *All work and no play makes Jack a dull boy.* 공부만 하고 놀지 않는 것은 좋지 않다. ⓒ the greatest possible; as much as possible. 최대한의; 될 수 있는 한의. ¶ *with ~ haste* 최대한 서둘러 / *in ~ kindness* 최대한의 친절로 / *run with ~ speed* 전속력으로 달리다. **2** 《with *pl. noun*》 ⓐ every one of. 모든; (하나하나) 모두. ¶ *~ the students* 모든 학생 / *All men are created equal.* 모든 사람은 평등하게 만들어졌다 / *All my friends are kind.* 내 친구들은 모두 친절하다 / *These are ~ the books I have.* 이것은 내가 가진 책의 모두이다 / *All the newspapers were full of this story.* 모든 신문들은 이 기사로 그득 채우고 있었다. ⓑ nothing but; only. …뿐인. ¶ *~ words and no thought* 말 뿐이지 사상이 없는. ⓒ full of. …로 그득한. ¶ *He was ~ smiles* 〔*ears*〕. 그는 만면에 웃음을 띠고(모든 신경을 귀에 집중시키고) 있

었다.

— *adv.* **1** entirely; completely; altogether; quite. 전적으로; 완전히; 모조리; 온통; 아주; 전(全)…. ¶ ~ *over the world* 온 세계에 / ~ *covered with mud* 온통 흙탕물을 뒤집어쓴 / ~ *alone* 홀로 / ~ *too soon* 너무나 빨리 / *His money is* ~ *gone.* 그의 돈이 몽땅 없어졌다 / *It was* ~ *his fault.* 그건 전적으로 그의 잘못이었다. **2** each. 각기; 각각. ¶ *The score was one* ~. 득점은 각기 1점씩이었다.

all alone, **a**) without company. 홀로; 혼자. ¶ *When I arrived he was* ~ *alone.* 내가 도착했을 때는 그는 혼자 있었다. **b**) without help. 혼자 힘으로; 혼자서. ¶ *Did you do that* ~ *alone?* 그걸 혼자서 했나.

all along ⇨along.

all at once, **a**) suddenly. 갑자기. ¶ *All at once someone began to laugh.* 돌연 누군가 웃기 시작했다. **b**) at the same time. 동시에; 한꺼번에. ¶ *Don't speak* ~ *at once.* 여럿이 동시에 말하지 마라.

all but, almost; nearly. 거의. ¶ *The work is* ~ *but finished.* 일이 거의 끝나 있다 / *He was* ~ *but dead.* 그는 거의 죽은 거나 마찬가지였다.

all in, **a**) 《*colloq.*》 tired out. 몹시 지친. **b**) with no restrictions; admitting of all methods. 제약 없는; 모든 수단을 인정하는. ¶ ~ *in wrestling* 자유형 레슬링.

all in all, **a**) everything. 무엇보다도〔가장〕 중요한 것. ¶ *Studying is* ~ *in* ~ *to me.* 공부는 나에게 가장 중요한 것이다. **b**) in general. 대체로. ¶ *All in all, he is a good boy.* 그는 대체로 착한 아이다. **c**) completely. 완전히. ¶ *Tell me* ~ *in all.* 나에게 모조리 말해다오.

all of, 《U.S.》 no less than. 좋이 …나 되는. ¶ *He is* ~ *of six feet.* 그는 키가 6피트나 된다.

all one (***to***), just the same thing (to). 마찬가지임; 아무래도 좋음. ¶ *It's* ~ *one to me.* 나는 아무래도 상관 없다.

all out, with every effort possible. 전력〔총력〕을 다하여. ¶ *He went* ~ *out with the new plan.* 그는 그 새 계획에 총력을 쏟았다 / *He drove* ~ *out.* 그는 전속력으로 차를 몰았다.

all over, **a**) over the whole surface of. 전면(全面)에; 온 …에; 온통. ¶ ~ *over the face* 얼굴에 온통 / *travel* ~ *over the world* 온 세계를 두루 여행하다. **b**) everywhere. 도처에; 여기저기. ¶ *Books were scattered* ~ *over.* 책들이 여기저기 흩어져 있었다. **c**) quite finished. 완전히〔아주〕 끝나. ¶ *It's* ~ *over.* 모두 끝났다 / *It's* ~ *over with him.* 그는 이제 다 틀렸다.

All right! Good! O.K. Everything is in order. I quite agree. 좋아.

all round, all around. 온통.

all the better 〔***worse***〕, so much the better 〔worse〕. 그만큼 더 좋은〔나쁜〕. ¶ *It will be* ~ *the better if you can go with us.* 함께 가주실 수 있다면 그만큼 더 좋을 테죠.

all the same, **a**) however; in spite of it. 그런대도 역시〔불구하고〕. ¶ *He was punished* ~ *the same.* 그래도 역시 그는 처벌되었다. **b**) =all one.

all told, all counted. 전부 합해서; 도합; 총계. ¶ *There were twenty of them,* ~ *told.* 전부 합해 20명이었다.

all too, 《*emph.*》 very; extremely (contrary to one's wishes). 매우; 너무나. ¶ *The vacation ended* ~ *too soon.* 휴가는 너무나 일찍 끝났다.

all up (***with***) =all over c).

all very well 〔***fine***〕, 《used to express dissatisfaction》 정말 좋긴 하지만. ¶ *That's* ~ *very well, but I can't approve it.* 매우 좋긴 하지만 찬성할 수는 없다.

— *n.* Ⓤ everything one has. (가진) 전부. ¶ *He lost his* ~. 그는 그의 모든 것을 잃었다 / *It was my little* ~. 내 얼마 안 되는 전재산이었다.

— *pron.* **1** 《used as *sing.*》 everything; the whole of anything. 모든 것; 전부. ¶ *All is over.* 모든 것이 끝났다 / *All is not gold that glitters.* 번쩍이는 모두가 금은 아니다 / *All is lost except honor.* 명예 외엔 모든 것을 잃었다 / *All that he said was true.* 그가 말한 것은 사실이었다. **2** 《used as *pl.*》 everyone. 모든 사람들. ¶ *All are happy.* 모두 행복하다 / *They are* ~ *happy.* 그들은 모두가 행복하다 / *All who have studied this question have come to the same conclusion.* 이 문제를 연구해 본 사람들은 모두 똑같은 결론에 도달했다 / *We were* ~ *surprised.* 우리들은 모두 놀랐다 / *All of them were present.* 그들은 모두 출석했다. [A.S. *eall*]

above all, before everything else; especially. 무엇보다 먼저〔우선〕; 특히.

after all, after considering everything; finally; nevertheless. 결국; 역시.

and all, including; and everything else. 그 밖의 …전부〔와 함께; 포함하여〕; …까지 모두(합쳐). ¶ *What with the snow and* ~, *we may be a little late.* 눈이다 뭐다 해서 우린 약간 늦을는지도 모른다 / *He jumped into the river, clothes and* ~. 그는 옷도 입은 채 강물 속으로 뛰어들었다.

at all, 《in *negative*(⇨not at all); *interrogative and conditional sentences*》 in any way; in the least degree. 조금도; 대체; 적어도. ¶ *Is he at* ~ *suitable for the post?* 도대체 그 사람이 그 직책에 적임인가 / *If you do it at* ~, *do it well.* 적어도 하려면 잘 해라.

be all there, 《*colloq.*》 be sane. 정신이 말짱하다; 돌지 않다. ¶ *She is not* ~ *there.* 그녀는 정신이 돌았다.

for all (***that...***), in spite of; notwithstanding. …에도 불구하고; 그래도 역시. ¶ *For* ~ *his faults, I respect him.* 결점들은 있으나 그래도 나는 그를 존경한다.

for good and all, forever. 영원히.

in all, altogether; all included. 전부 합해. ¶ *a dozen in* ~ 전부 합해 12개.

not at all, **a**) not in the least. 조금도 …아니다〔하지 않다〕. ¶ *I am not at* ~ *satisfied* *with him.* 나는 그사람에게 조금도 만족을 느끼지 못하고 있다. **b)** 《used in answer to an expression of thanks》 천만에(cf. *Don't mention it.* 《U.S.》 *You are welcome.*). ¶ *Thank you very much. —Not at* ~. 대단히 감사합니다. —천만에요.

once* (*and*) *for all, this time only and never again. (이번) 한번만; 이것을 마지막으로 한번만. ¶ *Let me say this once and for* ~. 마지막으로 한번 이것을 말씀드리겠습니다.

one and all, everyone without exception. 예외없이 모두.

***when all is said* (*and done*),** after all; finally. 결국; 최후로; 마침내.

Al·lah [ǽlə, á:lə] *n.* the name of the Supreme Being or God of Islam. (이슬람의) 알라신(神). [Arab.]

Al·lan [ǽlən] *n.* a man's name. 남자의 이름.

al·lar·gan·do [à:la:rgá:ndou] *adj., adv.* 《It.》《mus.》 gradually slower and with more power. 알라르간도; 차차 느리게〔느린〕 또 세게〔센〕. [It.]

all-a·round [ɔ́:ləráund] *adj.* able to do many things well. 무엇이나 할 수 있는; 다방면의; 만능의. ¶ *an* ~ *athlete* 만능 선수 / *an* ~ *tool* 두루 쓸 수 있는 도구. [*all, round*]

al·lay [əléi] *vt.* (P6) **1** put (fear, anger, etc.) at rest; quiet; calm. (공포·노여움 등)을 가라앉히다; 누그러뜨리다. ¶ ~ *excitement* 흥분을 진정시키다. **2** lessen (pain, etc.). (통증 따위)를 덜다; 경감〔완화〕하다. ¶ *His headache was allayed by the medicine.* 그의 두통은 약을 먹어서 가라앉았다. [a- (intensive), M.E. *leyen* lay, →lay]

al·le·ga·tion [æ̀ligéiʃən] *n.* Ⓤⓒ the act of alleging; affirmation or assertion without proof. (확증이 없음에도 사실·이유로서) 확언하기; 주장. ¶ *the* ~ *of one's rights* 자기 권리의 주장 / *The lawyer's* ~ *was proved.* 변호인의 주장은 입증되었다. [↓]

***al·lege** [əlédʒ] *vt.* (P6,11) **1** speak clearly about (something) without proof; declare. (증거도 없이) …을 강하게 주장하다. ¶ *She alleges that her watch has been stolen.* 시계를 도둑맞았다고 그녀는 주장한다 / *the alleged criminal* 범인이라고 일컬어지는 사람. **2** say (something) as an excuse. (구실로서) …을 주장하다; …의 탓이라고 하다. ¶ ~ *illness* 병 때문이라고 주장하다. [L. *exlitigo* clear at law]

al·le·giance [əlí:dʒəns] *n.* Ⓤ 《*to*》 loyalty; faithfulness. (군주·국가에 대한) 충성; 신의. ¶ *owe* ~ *to someone* …에 대한 충성의 의무를 지다 / *pledge* ~ *to someone* …에게 충성을 맹세하다 / *the* ~ *of a man to his friends* 친구에 대한 신의. [F. →liege]

al·le·gor·i·cal [æ̀ligɔ́(:)rikəl, -gár-] *adj.* of an allegory. 우의(寓意)의; 비유적인. [↓]

al·le·go·rize [ǽligəràiz] *vt., vi.* **1** (P6) treat as an allegory. …을 우화(寓話)로 하다; 비유적으로 하다. **2** (P1) use allegories. 비유를 쓰다. [*allegory*]

al·le·go·ry [ǽləgɔ̀:ri / -gəri] *n.* ⓒ (*pl.* **-ries**) a story in which a teaching is given symbolically. 우화; 비유담. [Gk. *allos* other, *agoreuō* speak]

al·le·gret·to [æ̀ligrétou] *n.* 《mus.》《It.》 a movement in music not quite as quick as allegro. 알레그레토; 좀 빠른 가락. — *adv.* rather quickly. 좀 빠르게. — *adj.* rather quick. 좀 빠른. [It.]

al·le·gro [əléigrou] *adv.* 《mus.》《It.》 in fast tempo; lively. 급속히. — *n.* a quick movement in music halfway between allegretto and presto. 알레그로; 급속조. — *adj.* quick. 급속조의; 쾌속한. [It.]

al·le·lu·ia(h) [æ̀ləlú:jə] *interj., n.* = hallelujah. [Heb.]

al·ler·gen·ic [æ̀lərdʒénik] *adj.* causing allergic sensitization. 알레르기를 일으키는. [*allergy*]

al·ler·gic [ələ́:rdʒik] *adj.* **1** of allergy; having an allergy. 알레르기의; 알레르기 체질의. ¶ *an* ~ *disease* 알레르기(성) 질환. **2** 《*colloq.*》《*to*》 having a dislike for. …을 몹시 싫어하는; 신경 과민의. ¶ *She is* ~ *to cats.* 그 여자는 고양이를 아주 싫어한다.

al·ler·gy [ǽlərdʒi] *n.* Ⓤⓒ **1** 《med.》 the state of being exceptionally sensitive to certain substances, such as food, pollen, and animals. 알레르기. **2** 《*colloq.*》《*for*》 a strong dislike. 몹시 싫어함; 반감. [Gk. *allos* other, *ergon* action]

al·le·vi·ate [əlí:vièit] *vt.* (P6) lighten (suffering); make (pain, agony, etc.) easier to endure. (심신의 고통)을 경감〔완화〕하다. ¶ *The medicine quickly alleviated her pain.* 그 약은 신속히 그녀의 통증을 덜어 주었다. [ad-, L. *levis* light]

al·le·vi·a·tion [əlì:viéiʃən] *n.* Ⓤ the act of alleviating; ⓒ something that alleviates. (심신의 고통·괴로움의) 경감; 완화; 경감시키는 것.

al·ley[1] [ǽli] *n.* ⓒ **1** a path or a walk bordered with a hedge or trees in a park or garden; a narrow back street in a city. (정원·공원 따위의) 소로(小路); 좁은 길; 뒷골목. ¶ *a blind* ~ 막다른 골목(길). **2** a long, narrow lane for bowling. (볼링) 경기대; 레인(=lane). [F. *aller* go]

al·l(e)y[2] [ǽli] *n.* a large white or colored marble. (대리석 등으로 만든) 구슬《어린이들의 marble 게임에 씀》. [→alabaster]

al·ley·way [ǽliwèi] *n.* **1** a narrow lane in a city or town. (도시 안의) 소로(小路); 좁은 길; 뒷골목. **2** a narrow passageway. 좁은 통로. [*alley*[1]]

All Fools' Day [∸∸∸] *n.* April Fools' Day (April 1). 만우절《4월 1일》.

all-fours [ɔ́:lfɔ́rz] *n. pl.* all four legs of an animal; esp. the two arms and two

legs of a man. (동물의) 네 발; (사람의) 사지; 수족. [→all, four]
be* 〔*stand*〕 *on all-fours with, be exactly equal to; be no better than. …와 똑같다; 합치〔일치〕하다. ¶ *Your reasoning is on ~ with mine.* 너의 추리는 내 것과 아주 일치한다.
go* 〔*crawl*〕 *on all-fours, go 〔crawl〕 on one's hands and knees. 기어가다. ¶ *A baby crawls on ~.* 아기가 긴다. [→all, four]

All·hal·lows [ɔ̀:lhǽlouz] *n.* All Saints' Day (Nov.1). 만성절(萬聖節)《11월 1일》. [→all, hallow]

al·li·a·ceous [æ̀liéiʃəs] *adj.* 《bot.》 of or like a garlic or leek. 파속(屬)의; 파·마늘 냄새가 나는. [L. *allium* garlic, -aceous]

***al·li·ance** [əláiəns] *n.* **1** Ⓒ a union between nations, parties, or families. (국가·당파간의) 동맹; 연합. ¶ *an ~ between A and B,* A와 B와의 동맹 / *conclude* 〔*contract*〕 *an ~* 동맹을 맺다 / *enter into* (*an*) *~ with* …와 동맹〔제휴〕하다 / *make an ~ against* …에 대항해서 동맹하다. **2** Ⓤ relationship by marriage. (결혼에 의한) 결연; 인척 관계. [→ally]

***al·lied** [əláid, ǽlaid] *adj.* **1** joined by agreement. 동맹한; 연합한. ¶ *the ~ forces* 연합군. **2** related 〔united〕 by marriage. 결연한; 인척 관계인. **3** connected by nature; similar. 유사한; 연관이 있는. ¶ *~ animals* 동류의 동물들. 參考 부가어적인 때는 보통 [ǽlaid] [→ally]

al·lies [ǽlaiz, əláiz] *n. pl.* persons or states united together. 동맹자〔국〕; 연합국; 제휴자; 동류; 인척. [↑]

al·li·ga·tor [ǽligèitər] *n.* Ⓒ 《zool.》 a large cold-blooded animal like the crocodile, living in rivers of the southern part of America or China. (미국·중국산의) 악어 《아프리카산은 crocodile》. [Sp. *el lagarto* the lizard]

all-im·por·tant [ɔ́:limpɔ́:rtənt] *adj.* very important. 매우 중요한.

all-in [ɔ́:lín] *adj.* **1** inclusive of all; unrestricted. 전부를 포함한〔통튼〕; 종합의; (레슬링의) 자유형의. **2** exhausted. 몹시 지친.

al·lit·er·ate [əlítərèit] *vi., vt.* (P1; 6) **1** (of words in a sentence or group) begin with the same consonantal sound. 두운(頭韻)을 밟다. **2** (of writers or speakers) make sentences of words beginning with the same consonantal sound. 두운을 쓰게 하다. **3** use alliteration; show alliteration. 두운을 사용하다. [↓]

al·lit·er·a·tion [əlìtəréiʃən] *n.* Ⓤ the use of the same initial sound in a group of words or line, as in 'secret snow, silent snow.' 두운법(頭韻法). [L. *ad-* to, →letter]

al·lit·er·a·tive [əlítərèitiv, -rətiv] *adj.* of alliteration. 두운(頭韻)의; 두운을 단.

al·lo·cate [ǽləkèit] *vt.* (P6,13) **1** divide (a sum of money, a share, work, etc.) for a particular purpose. …을 할당하다; 배분하다 (cf. *assign, allot*). ¶ *~ funds to new plans* 새로운 계획에 자금을 할당하다 / *~ shares to persons* 사람들에게 몫을 할당하다 / *~ persons to certain duties* 사람들에게 어떤 의무를 할당하다. **2** fix the place of (something). …의 위치를 정하다. [→locate]

al·lo·ca·tion [æ̀ləkéiʃən] *n.* ⓊⒸ the act of allocating; the state of being allocated; the share alloted. 할당〔배치〕하기; 할당된 상태; 배당액.

al·lo·cu·tion [æ̀ləkú:ʃən] *n.* a formal hortatory address. 연설; 강연; 훈시. [L.=exhort]

al·lop·a·thy [əlápəθi / əlɔ́p-] *n.* Ⓤ 《med.》 treating diseases by endeavoring to create the condition of the body contrary to that caused by the diseases. 대증(對症) 요법. [Gk. *allos* other, →pathos]

al·lot [əlát / əlɔ́t] *vt.* (P6,13,14) (**-lot·ted, -lot·ting**) give a part of (something) to each. …을 할당하다; 분배〔배당〕하다(cf. *allocate*). ¶ *~ some work to each* =*~ each some work* 각자에게 일을 할당하다 / *Tasks were allotted to everyone in the family.* 가족들 모두에게 일이 배당되었다. [ad-, →lot]

al·lot·ment [əlátmənt / əlɔ́t-] *n.* **1** Ⓤ the act of allotting; Ⓒ that which is allotted; the share or part given to each; a portion. 할당; 분배; 몫. **2** Ⓤ 《chiefly Brit.》 public land allotted for a family garden. 분할 대여 농지; 채원(菜園). **3** Ⓤ destiny. 운명.

al·lot·ro·py [əlátrəpi / əlɔ́t-] *n.* 《chem.》 variation of physical properties without change of substance. 동소(同素)(성(性)); 동질 이체성(同質異體性). [Gk. *allos* other, *tropos* manner]

al·lot·tee [əlatí: / əlɔ-] *n.* one to whom an allotment is made. 피할당자. [→allot]

all-out [ɔ́:láut] *adj.* involving all one's strength; complete. 총력을 기울인; 완전한; 철저한. ¶ *an ~ effort* 전력을 다한 노력 / *an ~ victory* 완전한 승리.

:al·low [əláu] *vt.* **1** (P6,20) permit; let; leave. …을 하게 그대로 두다; …한 채로 두다; 허락하다. ¶ *Smoking is not allowed here.* 여기서는 담배를 피워서는 안 된다 / *Allow a door to stand open.* 문을 열어 놓은 채 그대로 두어라 / *Allow me to introduce Mr. Smith to you.* 스미스씨를 소개합니다 / *She is not allowed to go on dates with boy friends.* 그녀는 남자 친구들과 데이트하러 가는 것이 허용되지 않는다 / *Children are allowed in the park.* 어린이들은 공원에 입장이 허용되고 있다 / *She refused to ~ dogs in* 〔*dogs to be brought into*〕 *the house.* 그녀는 개가 집안에 들어 오도록 하는 것을 거부했다 / *He never allowed himself to look untidy.* 그는 자신이 단정치 못하게 뵈는 것을 결코 용납치 않았다. **2** (P13,14) give; grant. …을 주다. ¶ *~ him 400,000 won a month* 그에게 매달 40만원을 주다 / *He is allowed £30 a* *month for his expense.* 그는 경비조로 매달 30 파운드를 지급받는다 / *She allowed her imagination full play.* 그녀는 마음껏 상상에 빠졌다. **3** (P6,11,21) accept as true; admit. (토론 요구 등)을 인정하다. ¶ ~ *a claim* 요구를 인정하다 / *He allowed that he was in the wrong.* = *He allowed himself to be in the wrong.* 그는 자기가 잘못이 있다는 것을 인정했다 / *We must* ~ *her to be a beauty.* 우린 그녀가 미인이라는 것을 인정해야 한다. **4** (P6,13) make cheaper by (an amount); take off; deduct. …을 할인하다; 빼다. ¶ ~ *two cents in the dollar* 1달러에 2센트를 할인하다. [ad-, L. *laudo* praise & *loco* place]

allow for, take into consideration; provide for. 고려에 넣다; (사정을) 참작하다; …에 대비하다. ¶ ~ *two pounds for waste* 허실조(虛失條)로 2파운드의 여유를 보아 두다 / ~ *an hour for dinner* 저녁 식사를 위해 한 시간을 고려에 넣다 / *She purposely made the dress larger to* ~ *for shrinking when it was washed.* 빨면 줄어들 것을 고려에 넣어 그녀는 일부러 옷을 크게 지었다 / *He failed to* ~ *for the unexpected.* 그는 예측 못 할 사태에 대비가 없었다.

allow of, permit (something) to happen or exist. …의 여지가 있다. ¶ ~ *of no excuse* 변명의 여지가 없다 / *The situation allows of no delay.* 상황은 지체할 여지가 없다. 語法 allow of 는 사람을 주어로 한 구문에는 쓸 수가 없음.

al·low·a·ble [əláuəbəl] *adj.* permissible; lawful; acceptable. 허락[허용]할 수 있는; 정당한; 승인할 수 있는. ¶ *In some parks it is* ~ *to walk on the grass.* 어떤 공원에서는 잔디 위를 걸을 수 있다.

***al·low·ance** [əláuəns] *n.* Ⓒ **1** a sum of money given weekly or monthly; a fixed share set apart. 수당금; 급여금; 일정한 할당량; 정량. ¶ *a family* ~ 가족 수당 / *retirement* ~ 퇴직금 / *She has an* ~ *of 80,000 won a month.* 그녀는 월 8만 원의 수당이 있다 / *Our* ~ *of cake is two pieces after dinner.* 저녁 식사 후 우리가 먹는 케이크의 정량은 두 조각씩이다. **2** the amount taken off from the value of goods; a discount. 할인. ¶ *That store makes an* ~ *of 20% for cash payment.* 저 가게에선 현금으로 사면 2할 깎아준다.

make allowance(s) for, take (something) into consideration. …을 고려[참작]하다. ¶ *You must make* ~ *for his youth.* 그가 나이 어림을 참작해야 한다.

al·loy [ǽlɔi, əlɔ́i] *vt.* (P6,13) **1** mix (metals); mix (a metal) with other cheaper metal. …을 합금하다; 합금하여 질을 떨어뜨리다. ¶ ~ *gold with copper* 금을 구리와 섞다. **2** make (something) worse or less valuable. …의 품질을 떨어뜨리다. ¶ *This silver, being alloyed with copper, sells at a low price.* 이 은은 구리와 합금이어서 싼 값에 팔린다. **3** impair; reduce; make less. (쾌감·즐거움 따위를) 덜하게 하다; 경감[손상]하다. ¶ ~ *pleasure with bad news* 나쁜 소식으로 모처럼의 즐거움을 경감시키다.
— [əlɔ́i] *n.* **1** ⒸⓊ a metal made by mixing two or more metals; a less valuable metal mixed with other metal. 합금; 합금용 비금속. ¶ *without* ~ 순수한; 섞음질하지 않은 / *an* ~ *of gold and* [*with*] *copper* 금과 구리의 합금. **2** Ⓤ standard or quality of gold, silver, etc. (금은의) 품위. [ad-, L. *ligo* bind]

all-pur·pose [ɔ́:lpə́:rpəs] *adj.* that can be used for any purpose. 다목적의; 널리[두루] 소용되는. [*all*, →purpose]

all-round [ɔ́:lráund] *adj.* 《Brit.》 = all-around.

All Saints' Day [ㅗㅗㅗ] *n.* November 1, celebrated in honor of all the saints. 만성절(萬聖節)《11월 1일》.

All Souls' Day [ㅗㅗㅗ] *n.* Nov. 2, a day of solemn prayer for mercy for all the souls in Purgatory. 만령절(萬靈節).

all·spice [ɔ́:lspàis] *n.* **1** Ⓒ a kind of berry of the West Indies. 올스파이스. **2** Ⓤ spice made from it. (그 열매로 만든) 향미료. [*all*, →spice]

all-star [ɔ́:lstɑ̀:r / ㅗㅗ] *adj.* drawing on, having a cast of, the best players or performers. (인기 선수·배우 등의) 스타가 전부 나오는. ¶ *an* ~ *cast* 스타 총출연. [*all*, →star]

al·lude [əlú:d] *vi.* (P3) **1** 《*to*》 speak of something indirectly. 넌지시 비추다; 언급하다. ¶ *Who(m) do you* ~ *to?* 누구 이야기를 하고 있는 건가. **2** mean; intend to say. 말하려고 하다; 가리키다. ¶ *When I say a hero, I* ~ *to my friend opposite.* 내가 영웅이라고 할 땐 맞은편의 친구를 가리키는 것이다. [ad-, L. *ludo* play]

al·lure [əlúər] *vt.* (P6,13,20) **1** 《*into, from*》 tempt (someone) to do something by promising to give something good. 유혹하다; 유인하다. ¶ ~ *someone into a party* 아무를 파티에 유인해 들이다 / ~ *someone from his duty* 아무를 유혹하여 직무를 게을리하게 하다. **2** fascinate; attract; charm. 매혹하다; 혹하게 하다. [F. →lure]

al·lure·ment [əlúərmənt] *n.* ⓊⒸ the act of alluring; temptation; fascination. 유혹(하는 것); 매혹. ¶ *the allurements of the wicked world* 악의 세계로의 유혹.

al·lur·ing [əlú(:)riŋ] *adj.* attracting; fascinating; charming. 마음을 끄는; 매혹적인; 황홀하게 하는.

al·lu·sion [əlú:ʒən] *n.* ⓊⒸ indirect speech about something. (넌지시) 비춤; 암시; 언급. [→allude]

in allusion to, mentioning indirectly; hinting at. 넌지시 …을 가리켜[암시하여]; …에 언급하여.

make an allusion to, refer to, usu. indirectly. …에 넌지시 언급하다.

al·lu·sive [əlúːsiv] *adj.* suggestive; figurative. 암시적인; 비유적인.

al·lu·vi·al [əlúviəl] *adj.* consisting of or made of clay or mud left by running water. 충적(沖積)의. ¶ ~ *epoch* 충적기(期) / ~ *soil* 충적토 / ~ *gold* 사금(砂金). [L. *luo* wash]

al·lu·vi·on [əlúːviən] *n.* **1** alluvium. 충적토(沖積土). **2** an increase of land on a shore or a river bank. 충적지(地); 모래톱. **3** a flood. 홍수.

al·lu·vi·um [əlúːviəm] *n.* (*pl.* **-vi·ums** or **-vi·a**) a deposit of sand or mud. 충적층〔토〕(沖積層〔土〕).

·al·ly[1] [əlái, ǽlai] *vt.* (**-lied**) (P6,13) **1** 《*with*》 unite (two countries, companies, persons, etc.) by treaty, marriage, etc. …을 동맹〔제휴〕시키다; (혼인 따위로) 결연을 맺다. ¶ ~ *itself* 〔*be allied*〕 *with other country* 다른 나라와 동맹을 맺다; 연합하다. **2** 《*to*》 make (something) related; belong to some kind. …을 관련시키다; …와 가까운 관계이다. ¶ *Dogs are allied to wolves.* 개는 이리와 동류(同類)이다 / *English and Dutch are nearly allied.* = *English is nearly allied to Dutch.* 영어는 네덜란드어와 가까운 관계에 있다.

— [ǽlai, əlài] *n.* Ⓒ (*pl.* **-lies**) **1** a person or nation united with another by treaty, friendship, etc.; a helper. 동맹자〔국〕; 제휴자; 협력〔조력〕자(opp. enemy, foe). ¶ *Austria was an* ~ *of Germany.* 오스트리아는 독일의 동맹국이었다. **2** a related animal. 동류(同類). [L. *ligo* bind]

ál·ly[2] [ǽli] *n.* = alley[2]

Al·ma Ma·ter, al·ma ma·ter [ǽlmə máːtər, ǽlmə méitər] *n.* the college or university in which one has been educated. 모교; 출신교. 參考 라틴말로 fostering mother의 뜻. [L. = fostering mother]

al·ma·nac [ɔ́ːlmənæ̀k] *n.* Ⓒ a calendar. 달력. [prob. Arab.]

·al·might·y [ɔːlmáiti] *adj.* **1** having all power. 전능(全能)한(cf. *omnipotent*). ¶ *Almighty God* 전능하신 하느님. **2** 《U.S. *colloq.*》 very great; huge. 엄청난; 큰. ¶ *We had an* ~ *row.* 우린 대판 싸움을 했다. — *n.* 《*the A-*》 God. 전능자; 신. — *adv.* extremely. 대단히. [*all*, →mighty]

al·mond [áːmənd, ǽlm-] *n.* Ⓒ 《bot.》 the nut or seed of a peach-like fruit; the tree itself. 편도(扁桃); 아몬드; 그 나무. [Gk.]

al·mond-eyed [áːməndàid, ǽlm-] *adj.* having long, narrow, oval-shaped eyes, as the Chinese. 아몬드 형(形)의 눈을 가진.

al·mon·er [ǽlmənər, áːm-] *n.* **1** an official in charge of the giving of alms in a monastery, a prince's house-hold, etc. (수도원·왕가 등의) 구휼품(救恤品) 분배 직원. **2** a medical social worker attached to a hospital. (병원의) 사회 사업부원. [Gk. → alms]

:al·most [ɔ́ːlmoust, ―´] *adv.* nearly; all but. 거의. ¶ *She* ~ *died.* 그녀는 거의 죽었다 / *It is* ~ *finished.* 거의 끝났다 / *Nine is* ~ *ten.* 아홉은 거의 열이다 / *He is* ~ *always out.* 그는 거의 언제나 외출하고 집에 없다. [→all, most]

·alms [ɑːmz] *n.* Ⓒ (*pl.* **alms**) money or gifts given to the poor. (가난한 사람에게) 베푸는 금품; 보시(布施); (빈민 구제의) 의연금(義捐金). ¶ *give an* ~ *to the beggar* 거지에게 보시를 주다 / *A beggar lives by* ~. 거지가 보시로 살아간다. [Gk. *éleos* mercy]

alms box [´―] *n.* a box to receive alms. 의연함(義捐函). [Gk. →box]

alms·giv·er [áːmzgìvər] *n.* a person who gives money, etc. for charity. 보시(布施)하는〔베푸는〕 사람; 자선가. [Gk. → giver]

alms·giv·ing [áːmzgìviŋ] *n.* Ⓤ the act of giving alms; charity. 자선 (행위); (보시 따위를) 베풀기; 희사(喜捨)(행위).

alms·house [áːmzhàus] *n.* Ⓒ 《Brit.》 a private poorhouse; 《U.S.》 a public poorhouse. 사립 구빈원(救貧院)〔양로원〕; 공립 구휼원(救恤院).

al·oe [ǽlou] *n.* **1** Ⓤ 《bot.》 a plant of the lily family. 알로에; 노회. **2** 《*pl.* used as *sing.*》 a drug made from aloes. 알로에즙(汁)《하제(下劑)》. [Gk.]

a·loft [əlɔ́(ː)ft, əlɑ́-] *adv.* **1** up in the air; high up; far above the earth. (하늘) 높이; 위에. **2** 《naut.》 to the top of the mast. 장두(檣頭)〔마스트 위〕에. [a(-), →loft]

go aloft, 《*colloq.*》 go to Heaven; die. 천국에 가다; 죽다.

a·lo·ha [əlóuə, ɑːlóuhɑː] *interj.* 《Hawaiian》 Hello! Good-bye! 어서 오십시오; 안녕(히 가십시오, 히 계십시오). [Hawaiian]

:a·lone [əlóun] *adj.* 《as *predicative*》 **1** quite by oneself; apart from others; solitary; single. 다만 홀로〔혼자서〕; 유일한; 고독한; 단독의. ¶ *She lives* ~ *in this house.* 그녀는 이 집에 혼자 산다 / *She likes to be* ~. 그녀는 홀로 있기를 좋아한다 / *One tree stood* ~ *on the hill.* 산 위에 나무 하나가 외로이 서 있었다 / *I am not* ~ *in this opinion.* 이 의견은 나만이 아니다. **2** 《following the *noun* or *pronoun*》 without anyone or anything else; only. (단지) …만. ¶ *He* ~ *remained.* 오직 그만이 남았다 / *I* ~ *know the story.* 나만이 그 이야기를 알고 있다 / *He* ~ *can do it.* 오로지 그사람만이 그것을 할 수 있다 / *Man shall not live by bread* ~. 사람은 빵만으로 사는 것이 아니다.

let alone, not to mention; to say nothing of. …은 말할 것도 없고; …은 고사하고. ¶ *It takes up too much time, let* ~ *the money.* 돈은 말할 것도 없고 너무 많은 시간이 걸린다 / *He did not speak to me, let* ~ *help me.* 그는 나를 돕지 않은 것은 고사하고 내게 말도 하지 않았다.

let* 〔*leave*〕** *someone or something* ***alone, do not trouble or interfere; ignore; do not touch or move. (사람·사물)을 내버려 두다; 상관하지 않고 그대로 두다. ¶ *leave her* ~ 그녀를 그대로 내버려 두다 / *Let him* ~ *to do that.* 그건 그에게 맡겨 두어라.

— *adv.* by oneself; without aid or help; solely. 혼자(서); 홀로; 혼자 힘으로; 오로지; 단지. ¶ ~ *and lonely* 혼자 쓸쓸히 / *go* 〔*travel*〕 ~ 혼자 가다〔여행하다〕 / *I can do it* ~. 나는 그것을 혼자서 할 수 있다. [= *all one*]

:along [əlɔ́ːŋ / əlɔ́ŋ] *prep.* from one end to the other end of; on or by the whole length of. …을 따라서〔끼고〕. ¶ *walk* ~ *a lake* 호수를 끼고 걷다 / *walk* ~ *the road* 길을 (따라) 걷다.

— *adv.* **1** forward; onward. 앞〔전방〕으로; 쑥쑥; 나아가; 진척되어. ¶ *run* ~ 앞으로 달리다; 달려 나가다 / *be far* ~ 많이 진척되어 있다 / *push a thing* ~ 일을 밀고 나아가다 / *Let us walk* ~. 앞으로 나아가십시다. **2** 《*by*》 by the side; near. …을 따라 (죽); 옆에; 가까이. ¶ ~ *by the hedge* 산울타리를 따라 / *Cars parked* ~ *by the stadium.* 차들이 경기장 옆에 죽 주차했다. **3** in company; with one. …와 함께〔동반하여〕; 데리고. ¶ *I took my wife* ~. 아내를 데리고 갔다 / *I'll be* ~ *in a minute.* 곧 합류하겠네. [A.S. *and lang,* → long]

all along, **a**) all the time. 처음부터 (죽). ¶ *I knew it all* ~. 난 처음부터 그것을 알고 있었다. **b**) for the whole length. 끝에서 끝까지. ¶ *The famous wall had scribbles on it all* ~. 그 유명한 벽에는 온통 낙서로 차 있었다.

along back, 《U.S. *colloq.*》 a little while ago; lately. 조금 전에; 최근에. ¶ *I've seen her* ~ *back on the street.* 나는 방금 그녀를 거리에서 보았다.

along with, together with. …와 함께; 같이. ¶ *Come* ~ *with me.* 나와 같이 가자 / *I sent the books* ~ *with other things.* 나는 그 책들을 다른 것들과 함께 보냈다.

be along, 《U.S.》 come to a place. 오다. ¶ *He will be* ~ *soon.* 그는 곧 올게다.

Get* 〔*Go*〕 *along* (*with you*)*! **a**) Get away from here! 빨리 꺼져. **b**) Don't talk such nonsense! 그런 허튼 수작하지 마라.

a·long·shore [əlɔ́ːŋʃɔ́ːr / əlɔ́ŋ-] *adv.* near or along the shore. 해변〔강변〕을 따라; 해안〔강안〕 가까이.

·a·long·side [əlɔ́ːŋsáid / əlɔ́ŋ-] *adv., prep.* at or by the side (of); side by side 〔with〕. …곁〔옆〕에; 옆으로 대어; …와 나란히. ¶ *bring a boat* ~ 배를 옆으로 대다 / *The boat was* ~ *the wharf.* 배는 부두 곁에 대어 있었다.

alongside of, by the side of; beside. …와 나란히; …의 곁에. ¶ *sit* 〔*walk*〕 ~ *of someone* 아무와 나란히 앉다〔걷다〕.

a·loof [əlúːf] *adv., adj.* 《as *predicative*》 apart; cold in manner; not interested. 떨어져(서); 냉담한; 무관심하여. ¶ *an* ~ *attitude* 냉담한 태도 / *stand* 〔*keep*〕 ~ *from something* …로부터 떨어져 있다; 초연해 있다 / 《*fig.*》 *He kept* 〔*held*〕 *himself* ~ *because he did not like them.* 그는 그들을 싫어했으므로 한데 어울리지 않았다. [→luff]

a·loof·ness [əlúːfnis] *n.* the state of being aloof. 무관심함.

:a·loud [əláud] *adv.* **1** so as to be heard; loudly. 소리를 내어; 소리높이; 큰소리로. ¶ *shout* 〔*cry*〕 ~ 큰소리로 소리치다 / *laugh* ~ 소리 높이 웃다 / *Read this passage* ~. 이 구절을 소리내어 읽어라 / *Say it* ~. *—nobody will hear you.* 크게 말하시오—아무도 당신 말이 들리지 않을 게요. **2** 《*colloq.*》 noticeably. 두드러지게. ¶ *It reeks* ~. 냄새가 물씬 풍긴다. [a-, →loud]

think aloud, talk to oneself. 혼잣말을 하다.

alp [ælp] *n.* Ⓒ **1** a high mountain. 고산(高山). **2** a green pasture-land on Swiss mountain side. 알프스의 목장. [L. *albus* white]

al·pac·a [ælpǽkə] *n.* Ⓒ 《zool.》 a South American animal like a sheep; Ⓤ its wool; the cloth made from its wool. 알파카; 그 털; 그 모직물. [Sp.]

al·pen·stock [ǽlpənstɑ̀k / -pinstɔ̀k] *n.* Ⓒ a strong stick with an iron point, used by mountain climbers. (끝에 뾰족한 물미가 달린) 등산용 지팡이; 알펜슈토크. [G. = Alps stick]

al·pha [ǽlfə] *n.* Ⓒ **1** the first letter of the Greek alphabet, A, α. 알파《그리스 문자》. ¶ *an* ~ *particle* 알파 입자 / ~ *rays* 알파선(線). **2** 《*the* ~》 the first. 처음; 시초; 최초. [Gk.]

the Alpha and Omega, **a**) the beginning and the end. 처음과 끝; 전부. **b**) the main or most necessary part. 중심적 요소; 가장 중요〔필요〕한 부분.

·al·pha·bet [ǽlfəbèt, -bit] *n.* ⓊⒸ **1** the letters of a language arranged in order. 알파벳. **2** the basic elements to be learned first. 초보. ¶ *the* ~ *of English conversation* 영어 회화의 첫걸음. [Gk.]

al·pha·bet·i·cal [æ̀lfəbétikəl] *adj.* of the alphabet; arranged in the order of the letters of a language. 알파벳의; ABC의; ABC순의. ¶ *in* ~ *order* 알파벳〔ABC〕순으로.

al·pha·bet·i·cal·ly [æ̀lfəbétikəli] *adv.* in the order of the letters of the alphabet. 알파벳 순으로.

al·pha·bet·ize [ǽlfəbitàiz] *vt.* (P6) arrange in alphabetical order. 알파벳순으로 하다.

al·pha·nu·mer·ic [æ̀lfənjuːmérik] *adj.* consisting of or utilizing letters and numerals. (컴퓨터의) 문자 숫자식의. ¶ *an* ~ *code* 문자 숫자식 코드. [→alpha, numeric]

Al·pine [ǽlpain, -pin] *adj.* **1** of the Alps. 알프스 산맥의. **2** 《*A-, a-*》 of or growing on a high mountain. 고산(高山)의. ¶ *alpine plants* 〔*flora*〕 고산 식물 / *an alpine belt* 〔*zone*〕 고산대(帶). [L. *albus* white]

Al·pin·ist [ǽlpənist] *n.* Ⓒ a person who climbs the Alps; 《*a*-》 a mountain climber. 알프스 등반가; 등산가.

Alps [ælps] *n. pl.* 《*the* ～》 a mountain range in south Europe. 알프스 산맥. [L. *albus* white]

:al·read·y [ɔːlrédi] *adv.* **1** before or by this time; even now. 이미; 벌써; 지금도. ¶ *I have ～ done it.* 난 이미 그것을 마쳤다 / *It's ～ finished.* 그건 벌써 끝났다 / *He had ～ left.* 그는 이미 떠나고 없었다 / *Let's begin at once; it's ～ late.* 곧 시작합시다, 이미 늦었지만. **2** previously; before now. 전에; 벌써. ¶ *There is no need to go, because I have seen him ～.* 나는 그 사람을 벌써 만나 보았기 때문에 갈 필요가 없다. **3** 《used in questions to show surprise》 so soon. (그렇게) 벌써 (cf. *yet*). ¶ *Is it noon ～?* (아니) 벌써 정오인가 / *Is she back ～?* 그녀가 벌써 돌아왔습니까. [→all, ready]

al·right [ɔːlráit] *adv.* =all right. 參考 잘 쓰이지만 표준 영어의 철자로서는 아직 확립돼 있지 않음.

Al·sace-Lor·raine [ǽlsæslɔːréin, ælséis-] *n.* a region in northeastern France. 알사스 로렌《프랑스 동북부의 지방》. [Place]

Al·sa·tia [ælséiʃə] *n.* a district serving as a haunt and sanctuary of criminals. 범죄자의 도피소; 소굴. [↑]

Al·sa·ti·an [ælséiʃən] *adj., n.* **1** (of) Alsace or its inhabitants. 알사스 (사람); 알사스 (사람)의. **2** a large sheep dog. 양 지키는 큰 개.

:al·so [ɔ́ːlsou] *adv.* in addition; as well; too; besides. (…도) 또(한); 역시; 똑같이 (cf. *too, as well*). ¶ *He ～ agreed with me.* 그도 나에게 동의했다 / *I ～ went.* =*I went ～.* 나도 갔다. [*all, so*]

***not only ... but*(*also*)** ⇨not; only.

al·so-ran [ɔ́ːlsouræ̀n] *n.* Ⓒ 《*colloq.*》 a horse which fails to come in among the first three in a race; a person defeated in a competition. (경마에서) 등외로 떨어진 말; (달리기·선거에) 진 선수〔사람〕; 낙선자.

alt [ælt] *n.* 《mus.》 high tone. 알토; 중고음. [L. *altus* high]

in alt, 《*fig.*》 in a haughty mood. 우쭐하여.

alt. alternate; altitude.

Al·ta·i [ǽltai, –⁻– / æltéiai] *n.* the name of a mountain range in central Asia. (중앙 아시아의) 알타이 산맥.

***al·tar** [ɔ́ːltər] *n.* Ⓒ a raised place on which sacrifices are offered to a god; a table or stand in a church, used in the communion service. 제단(祭壇); 제물단; 성찬대(聖餐臺). [L. *altus* high, →alt]

lead a woman to the altar, marry (a woman) esp. in a church. 여자와 결혼하다. ¶ *Mr. Brown led Miss Smith to the ～.* 브라운 군은 스미스 양과 결혼했다.

***al·ter** [ɔ́ːltər] *vt.* (P6,7) make (something) different; change; modify. …을 바꾸다; 고치다. ¶ *～ one's mode of life* 자기의 생활 태도를 고치다 / *～ a house* 집을 개조하다 / *If your new coat is too large, a tailor can ～ it to fit you.* 새 코트가 너무 크다면 양복장이가 당신 몸에 맞도록 고쳐 지을 수 있다. — *vi.* (P1,2A) become different, esp. for the worse. 변하다; 바뀌다; 나빠지다. ¶ *He has altered since his illness, hasn't he?* 그 사람 병을 앓고 나더니 사람이 변했군 그래. [L. *alter* other]

al·ter·a·tion [ɔ̀ːltəréiʃən] *n.* ⓊⒸ the act of altering; a change; a modification. 변경; 개조. ¶ *make an ～ on something* …을 변경〔개조〕하다 / *I want you to make some alterations my new dress.* 내 새 옷을 좀 고쳐 주기를 바랍니다.

al·ter·cate [ɔ́ːltərkèit] *vi.* (P3) 《*with*》 dispute with anger; wrangle. 격론하다; 언쟁하다. [*alter*, -ate]

al·ter·ca·tion [ɔ̀ːltərkéiʃən] *n.* ⓊⒸ an angry dispute; a quarrel. 언쟁; 말다툼; 싸움. ¶ *The boys had an ～ over the umpire's decision.* 아이들은 심판 결정에 대해 말다툼을 했다.

alter ego [⁻– ⁻–] *n.* 《L. =other I》 **1** another aspect of one's nature. 제 2의 나. **2** a very intimate friend. 절친한 친구.

***al·ter·nate** *v.* [ɔ́ːltərnèit, ǽl-] *vi.* (P1,3) take place or happen by turns; change. 번갈아〔차례로〕 일어나다; 교대가 되다. ¶ *Night and day ～ with each other.* 낮과 밤이 번갈아 온다 / *Good harvests ～ with bad.* 풍작은 흉작과 엇갈려 온다 / *Lucy and her sister ～ in doing the dishes.* 루시와 그녀의 동생은 교대로 취사를 한다 / *an alternating current* (전기의) 교류(交流).

— *vt.* (P6,13) cause (things) to happen by turns. …을 번갈아 하다; …을 교대로 하다. ¶ *～ work with pleasure* 일과 즐거움을 번갈아 하다 / *～ squares and circles* 네모와 원을 번갈아 어긋매끼다.

— [ɔ́ːltəːrnit, ǽl-] *adj.* taking place or happening by turns; every other. 교호의; 번갈아 하는; 서로 엇갈리는; 하나 걸러의. ¶ *on ～ days* 하루 걸러 / *a week of ～ rain and sunshine* 비와 갠 날이 번갈은 1주일 / *Prof. Milward lectures on English literature on ～ days.* 밀워드 교수는 영문학을 격일로 강의한다.

— [ɔ́ːltərnit, ǽl-] *n.* Ⓒ **1** 《U.S.》 a person officially named to take the place of another. 대리인. **2** a dynamo giving alternating current. 교류(交流) 발전기. [→alter]

al·ter·nate·ly [ɔ́ːltərnitli, ǽl-] *adv.* in an alternate manner; one after another; every other. 번갈아; 교대로; 하나 걸러(서).

al·ter·nat·ing [ɔ́ːltərnèitiŋ, ǽl-] *adj.* first one and then the other. 교호의; 번갈은; 어긋매낀.

alternating current [⁻–– ⁻–] *n.* 《electr.》 an electric current that changes its direction at regular intervals. 교류(交流).

al·ter·na·tion [ɔ̀:ltərnéiʃən, æ̀l-] *n.* UC the act of alternating; the state of being alternated; a change. 교호; 교대; 교체; 하나거름. ¶ *the ~ of crops* 윤작(輪作); 돌려짓기 / *the ~ of hope and despair* 번갈아 찾아드는 희망과 절망.

•**al·ter·na·tive** [ɔ:ltə́:rnətiv, æl-] *adj.* that can be chosen between two, or sometimes more, things. (둘 중의, 때로는 둘 이상 중에서) 하나를 택해야 하는; 양자 택일의. ¶ *We have no ~ course.* 달리 취할 길이 없다 / *Father offered the ~ plans of having a picnic or taking a trip on a steamer.* 아버지는 소풍을 갈 것이냐 아니면 선상(船上) 여행을 하느냐의 양자 택일의 안(案)을 내놓으셨다.
— *n.* C a choice between two things; one of two things which must be chosen. 양자(兩者)간의 선택; (또 그 중 하나를) 택해야 할 둘 중의 어느 하나. ¶ *The alternatives are death or submission.* 선택은 죽음이나 복종이냐의 둘 중 하나다 / *I have no ~.* 달리 택할 방도가 없다.

al·ter·na·tive·ly [ɔ:tə́rnətivli, æl-] *adv.* so as to choose between two; as an alternative. 선택적으로; 양자 택일적으로.

al·tho [ɔ:lðóu] *conj.* 《chiefly U.S.》 =although.

:**al·though** [ə:lðóu] *conj.* though; even if. …이긴 하지만; 비록 …하[이]기는 해도. ¶ *Although he was poor, he was always honest.* 비록 가난하긴 했지만 그는 언제나 정직했다 / *Although it rained hard, I went shopping.* 비가 몹시 왔지만 나는 쇼핑을 나갔다 / *Her voice, ~ the accent was provincial, was soft and sweet.* 비록 시골 사투리는 있었지만 그녀의 음성은 부드럽고 친절했다. [*all, though*]

al·tim·e·ter [æltímitər, ǽltəmì:tər] *n.* C an instrument for finding distance above sea level. 고도계(高度計). [L. *altus* high, →meter]

•**al·ti·tude** [ǽltətjù:d] *n.* UC **1** the height above the earth's surface or sea level. (산·천체·비행기 따위의) 높이; 해발; 표고. ¶ *What ~ did the airplane reach?* 그 비행기는 고도 얼마에 달했나 / *the ~ of a mountain* 산의 높이[고도]. **2** 《usu. *pl.*》 a high point or place. 고소(高所); 높은 곳. ¶ *In those altitudes the air is extremely thin.* 그 고도에서는 공기가 아주 희박하다. [L. *altus* high, →tude]

al·to [ǽltou] *n.* (*pl.* **-tos**) 《mus.》 U the voice between soprano and tenor; C a singer having such a voice. 알토《중고음》; 알토 가수. [It. =high]

•**al·to·geth·er** [ɔ̀:ltəgéðər, ⌐–⌐–] *adv.* **1** entirely; wholly; without exception. 아주; 완전히; 전적으로; 예외 없이. ¶ *He is ~ bad.* 그는 아주 나쁘다 / *The house was ~ destroyed by fire.* 그 집은 화재로 완전히 파괴되었다 / *His story is not ~ false.* 그의 이야긴 아주 거짓말은 아니다. 語法 부분 부정. **2** on the whole; all things considered. 대체로; 요컨대. ¶ *Altogether, the children have done very well.* 대체로 아이들은 잘했다 / *Altogether, I'm glad it's over.* 결국 다 끝나서 기쁘다. **3** all included; in all. 전부[모두]해서. ¶ *How much ~?* 전부해서 얼마죠.
taken altogether, with everything considered. 전체적으로 보아(서); 대체로. ¶ *Taken ~, there's no hope yet.* 전체적으로 보아 아직껏 희망이 없다.
— *n.* **1** 《*an ~*》 a whole. 전부. **2** 《*the ~*》 《*colloq.*》 the nude. 나체. [→all, together]

al·to-re·lie·vo [ǽltourilí:vou] *n.* (*pl.* **-vos**) high relief. 고부조(高浮彫). [L. *altus* high, →relief]

al·tru·ism [ǽltru:ìzəm] *n.* UC the principle of considering others' interests and happiness first; unselfishness. 이타심(利他心); 이타[애타]주의(opp. egoism). [It.]

al·tru·ist [ǽltru:ist] *n.* a person who thinks of the good of others rather than of his own. 이타(利他)주의자.

al·tru·is·tic [æ̀ltru:ístik] *adj.* unselfish; disinterested. 이타적(利他的)인; 사심 없는.

al·um [ǽləm] *n.* C a mineral salt used in medicine or in dyeing. 명반(明礬). [L. *alumen*]

a·lu·mi·na [əlú:mənə] *n.* (*pl.* **-nae**) the oxide of aluminum. 반토(礬土); 산화(酸化) 알루미늄.

a·lu·mi·nae [əlú:məni:] *n.* pl. of **alumina.**

al·u·min·i·um [æ̀ljumíniəm] *n.* 《esp. Brit.》 =aluminum.

a·lu·mi·num [əlú:mənəm] *n.* U 《U.S.》 a light, silver white metal. 알루미늄.

a·lum·na [əlʌ́mnə] *n.* C (*pl.* **-nae**) 《U.S.》 a woman graduate of a school, college, etc. 여자 졸업생; 여자 교우(cf. *alumnus*). [L. =fosterchild]

a·lum·nae [əlʌ́mni] *n.* pl. of **alumna.**

a·lum·ni [əlʌ́mnai] *n.* pl. of **alumnus.**

a·lum·nus [əlʌ́mnəs] *n.* C (*pl.* **-ni**) 《U.S.》 a male graduate of a school, college, etc. 남자 졸업생; 남자 교우(校友) (cf. *alumna*).

:**al·ways** [ɔ́:lweiz, -wiz, -wəz] *adv.* **1** at all times; on all occasions. 언제나; 항상; 늘. 語法 조동사와 be 동사 외에는 동사의 앞에 옴. ¶ *He ~ comes late.* 그는 언제나 늦게 온다 / *He is ~ busy.* 그는 항상 바쁘다 / *Night ~ follows day.* 밤이 새면 언제나 낮이 온다. **2** 《usu. with *progressive forms*》 again and again; repeatedly. 되풀이해서; 노상. ¶ *He is ~ grumbling.* 그는 노상 불평만 하고 있다. [*all, way*]
not always, not necessarily. 반드시 …은 아니다[…한 것은 아니다]. ¶ *The rich are not ~ happy.* 부자라고 해서 반드시 행복한 것은 아니다.

:**am** [æm, əm, m] *vi.* (P5,27,28) the first person singular present indicative of **be.**

:**A.M., a.m.** [éiém] *ante meridiem*; before noon. 오전. ¶ *at 8 a.m.* 오전 8시에 / *the 10 : 30 a.m. train* 오전 10시 30분 열차. 語法 표제·시각표 따위 외에는 흔히 소문자를 쓰며 반드시 숫자 뒤에 쓰임. [L.]

a·mah [ɑ́:mə, ǽmə] *n.* (in India, China, etc.) a nurse or maid. 유모; 하녀. [Port.]

a·main [əméin] *adv.* 《*arch., poet.*》 **1** with full force; violently. 전력으로; 맹렬히. **2** at full speed; in haste. 전속력으로; 서둘러. [Obs. *main* force]

a·mal·gam [əmǽlgəm] *n.* UC **1** any metallic mixture of mercury with some other metal(s). 아말감《주성분은 수은》. **2** a loose mixture of different substances; 《*fig.*》 a mixture. 혼합(물). [Gk.]

a·mal·gam·ate [əmǽlgəmèit] *vt.* (P6) **1** unite (a metal) with mercury. …을 수은과 섞다〔혼합하다〕. **2** join together; combine. (회사 등)을 합병〔병합〕하다. ¶ ~ *three companies into one* 세 회사를 하나로 합병하다 / *be amalgamated with something* …와 결합하다. — *vi.* (P1) **1** (of metals) combine in an amalgam. 아말감이 되다. **2** (of companies, ideas, people, etc.) unite; join 〔mix〕 together. (회사 따위가) 합병하다; (사람·사상 따위가) 융합하다. [↑]

a·mal·gam·a·tion [əmæ̀lgəméiʃən] *n.* UC the act of amalgamating; mixture; union. 아말감 만들기; 융합; 합병. ¶ *the ~ of railway companies* 철도 회사의 합병 / *an ~ of many different races* 많은 이민족의 융합.

a·man·u·en·sis [əmæ̀nju:énsis] *n.* (*pl.* **-ses** [-si:z]) **1** a person who writes down what another says; a person who copies what another has written. 필생(筆生); 사자생(寫字生). **2** a secretary. 비서 [L.=handservant]

am·a·ranth [ǽmərænθ] *n.* 《*poet.*》 an imaginary flower that never fades. (상상의) 시들지 않는 꽃. [Gk. *a-* not, *marainō* fade]

am·a·ran·thine [æ̀mərǽnθain, -θin] *adj.* 《*poet.*》 **1** never fading. 시들지 않는; 불멸의. **2** of a purple color. 자줏빛의. [↑]

am·a·ryl·lis [æ̀mərílis] *n.* C **1** 《bot.》 a plant like a lily. 아마릴리스. **2** 《*A-*》 《*poet.*》 a young girl. 소녀. [Gk.]

a·mass [əmǽs] *vt.* (P6) collect a large quantity of (something); pile up; accumulate (a fortune). …을 쌓다; 쌓아 올리다; 모으다; 부(富)를 축적하다. [ad-, →mass]

***am·a·teur** [ǽmətʃùər, -tʃər, -tər, æ̀mətə́:r] *n.* C a person who studies an art or plays a game for pleasure, not for money. 아마추어; 소인(素人); 초심자; 호사가(opp. professional). — *adj.* of or by amateurs; made or done by an amateur. 아마추어의. ¶ *an ~ musician* 아마추어 음악가. [F.]

am·a·teur·ish [æ̀mətʃúəriʃ, -tjúə-, -tə́:r-] *adj.* made or done as an amateur might do it; crude; clumsy. 아마추어 같은; 서투른. ¶ *an ~ attempt* 서투른 시도.

am·a·teur·ism [ǽmətʃuərìzəm, -tʃə-, -tjùər-, æ̀mətə́:rizəm] *n.* U amateurish practice or quality. 아마추어 기예; 취미; 비직업적 행위〔성질〕.

am·a·to·ry [ǽmətɔ̀:ri / -təri] *adj.* of love; of sexual love. 연애의; 성애(性愛)의; 연인의. [L. *amo* love]

***a·maze** [əméiz] *vt.* (P6) surprise or astonish greatly; fill (someone) with wonder. …을 깜짝 놀라게 하다. ¶ *Your knowledge amazes me.* 너의 지식에 나는 놀라움을 느끼고 있다 / *She was amazed at the news.* 그녀는 그 소식에 깜짝 놀랐다 / *We were amazed that she should want to marry such a man.* 그녀가 그런 남자와 결혼하기를 원한다는 말에 우리는 매우 놀랐다 / *I was amazed by her skill at the piano.* 나는 그녀의 피아노 솜씨에 깜짝 놀랐다. [a-, →maze]

a·mazed [əméizd] *adj.* filled with wonder; lost in astonishment. 깜짝 놀란; 아연한.

a·maz·ed·ly [əméizidli] *adv.* in wonder or astonishment. 깜짝 놀라서.

***a·maze·ment** [əméizmənt] *n.* U the state of being amazed; astonishment; great surprise. 깜짝 놀람; 경악. ¶ *She looked at me in ~.* 그녀는 깜짝 놀라서 나를 쳐다보았다 / *Your news fills me with ~.* 자네의 소식은 나를 경악시키고 있네.

to one's amazement, to one's astonishment. 놀랍게도. ¶ *To my ~, he called on me at midnight.* 놀랍게도 그는 한밤중에 나를 찾아왔다.

***a·maz·ing** [əméiziŋ] *adj.* causing great astonishment; wonderful. 깜짝 놀랄; 놀라운. ¶ *his ~ success* 그의 놀라운 성공 / *The new car goes at an ~ speed.* 그 새 차는 놀라운 속도로 달린다.

Am·a·zon [ǽməzɑ̀n, -zɔ̀n / -zən] *n.* **1** 《*the ~*》 a river in northwest South America. 아마존강. **2** 《Gk. myth.》 one of a race of warlike women. 아마존. 參考 흑해 연안에 살았다는 용맹한 여걸. **3** 《*a-*》 C a big, powerful, manly woman. 여장부; 여걸. [Gk.]

***am·bas·sa·dor** [æmbǽsədər] *n.* C **1** a government officer sent to another country to act for his own country. 대사(大使)(cf. *legation, minister*). ¶ *an ~ extraordinary (and plenipotentiary)* 특명 (전권) 대사. 參考 부를 때 Your Excellency를 씀. **2** ⓐ an official messenger. 사절(使節). ¶ *an ~ of peace* 평화의 사절. ⓑ an agent. 대리인. ¶ *act as another's ~ in a negotiation* 협상〔교섭〕에서 대리를 맡다. ● **am·bas·sa·do·ri·al** [æmbæ̀sədɔ́:riəl] *adj.* [Celt. =servant]

am·bas·sa·dress [æmbǽsədris] *n.* C **1** the wife of an ambassador. 대사 부인. **2** a woman ambassador. 여성 대사〔사절〕.

am·ber [ǽmbər] *n.* U **1** a pale yellow substance used for jewelry. 호박(琥珀). **2** the color of amber; yellow or yellowish-brown. 호박색; 황갈색; (교통 신호등의) 황색

신호. —— *adj.* yellowish in color; (made) of amber. 호박색〔황갈색〕의; 호박(제)의. [F.]

am·ber·gris [ǽmbərgrìːs, -gris] *n.* Ⓤ a grey fat produced from whales, used in making perfumes. 용연향(龍涎香)《향수 원료》. [F.]

am·bi- [ǽmbi-] *pref.* on both sides. '이면(二面), 양쪽' 의 뜻. [L.]

am·bi·dex·trous [æ̀mbidékstrəs] *adj.* able to do things equally well with either hand. 양수잡이의; 손재주가 비상한. [ambi-, →dexter]

am·bi·ent [ǽmbiənt] *adj.* surrounding. 주위〔주변〕의. ¶ *The flowers shed fragrance upon the ~ air.* 꽃들이 주변 공기에 향기를 뿜고 있다. [ambi-, L. *eo* go]

am·bi·gu·i·ty [æ̀mbigjúːəti] *n.* (*pl.* **-ties**) **1** Ⓤ doubtfulness of meaning. (뜻의) 모호함; 애매함. **2** Ⓒ a word or expression with more than one meaning. 애매한 말〔표현〕. [↓]

am·big·u·ous [æmbígjuəs] *adj.* obscure (in meaning); doubtful; uncertain. 모호한; 불분명한; 이도 저도 아닌(cf. *equivocal*). ¶ *The sentence "The policeman killed the woman with a gun" is ~.* "경찰관이 그 여인을 총으로 죽였다"는 판결은 모호하다. [ambi-, L. *ago* drive]

:am·bi·tion [æmbíʃən] *n.* ⓊⒸ the state of being ambitious; an eager desire for fame, wealth, success, position, etc.; the object of the desire itself. 야심; 야망; 대망; 야망의 대상. 語法 좋은 뜻으로나 나쁜 뜻으로도 쓰임. ¶ *Young men are full of ~.* 청년들은 야심에 차 있다 / *Her ~ is to become a doctor.* 그녀의 야망의 목표는 의사가 되는 것이다. [→ambient]

·am·bi·tious [æmbíʃəs] *adj.* **1** full of ambition; showing great ambition. 야심〔야망〕에 찬. ¶ *an ~ plan* 야심에 찬 계획. **2** 《*as predicative*》 strongly desiring; eager for. 열망〔갈망〕하고. ¶ *be ~ of wealth* 〔*power*〕 부(富)를〔권력을〕 갈망하다 / *He is very ~.* 그는 매우 야망에 차 있다 / *Boys, be ~!* 소년들이여, 야망을 품어라 / *He is ~ to succeed* 〔*of success*〕. 그는 성공을 열망하고 있다.

am·biv·a·lent [æmbívələnt] *adj.* having opposite and conflicting feelings, esp. love and hate, toward the same object. 상반되는 감정을 가진; (애증의) 반대 감정 병존(並存)의. ● **am·biv·a·lence** [-ləns] *n.* [ambi-, L. *valeo* be strong]

am·ble [ǽmbəl] *vi.* (P1,2A) 《*about, along*》 (of a person) walk at a slow pace; (of a horse) move at an easy pace by lifting both legs on the same side at once. (사람이) 천천히 걷다; (말이) 한 쪽의 두 발을 동시에 올리며 걷다(cf. *pace*). ¶ *I saw him ambling along the road.* 나는 그가 길을 천천히 걷는 것을 보았다. —— *n.* Ⓒ such an easy pace of a horse; an easy walk of a person; a stroll. (말의) 측대보(側對步); (사람의) 천천히 걷는 걸음. [L. *ambulo* walk]

am·bro·sia [æmbróuʒiə] *n.* Ⓤ **1** 《Gk.,Rom. myth.》 the food of the gods. 신찬(神饌)《불로 불사(不老不死)의 음식》(cf. *nectar*). **2** anything delicious to taste or smell. 특별히 맛있는 음식. [Gk. *a-* not, *brotos* mortal]

am·bro·sial [æmbróuʒiəl] *adj.* very delicious. 매우 맛있는.

am·bu·lance [ǽmbjuləns] *n.* Ⓒ **1** a field hospital. 야전 병원. **2** a vehicle for carrying sick or wounded persons. 부상병 운반차〔선·비행기〕; 구급차; 앰뷸런스. [→amble]

ambulance chaser [⌐-- ⌐-] *n.* 《U.S. *colloq.*》 a lawyer who incites persons to sue for damages because of accident. 피해자를 부추겨 소송을 걸게 하는 악덕 변호사.

am·bu·lant [ǽmbjulənt] *adj.* 《med.》 **1** (of a disease) shifting from one part of the body to another. (병이 체내의) 여기저기로 전이(轉移)하는. **2** (of treatment) involving exercise. (치료하여) 보행〔통원(通院)〕할 수 있는. [→amble]

am·bu·la·to·ry [ǽmbjulətɔ̀ːri / -təri] *adj.* **1** of or fitted for walking. 보행의〔하는〕; 걷기에 적합한. **2** moving from place to place. 여기저기 이동하는. **3** 《med.》 able to walk. 보행할〔걸을〕 수 있는. —— *n.* a covered place for walking. 유개(有蓋) 보도; 회랑(廻廊).

am·bus·cade [æ̀mbəskéid, ⌐-⌐] *n., vt.* =ambush.

·am·bush [ǽmbuʃ] *n.* Ⓤ the act of lying in wait to attack an enemy; Ⓒ 《*collectively*》 soldiers so hidden; a place where they are hidden. 매복; 복병; 매복 장소. ¶ *lie in ~* 매복하다 / *trap the enemy by ~* 매복했다가 적을 덫에 빠뜨리다. —— *vi., vt.* (P1;6) lie in wait; hide soldiers for a surprise attack. 매복하다; 복병을 두다; 매복하여 기습하다. ¶ *The bandits ambushed the stagecoach.* 강도들은 매복하고 있다가 역마차를 습격했다. [in-, →bush]

a·me·ba [əmíːbə] *n.* =amoeba.

a·mel·io·rate [əmíːljərèit, -liə-] *vt.* (P6) make (something) better; improve. …을 개선하다; 개량하다. ¶ *~ the workers' conditions* 근로 조건을 개선하다 / *~ plants* 식물의 품종을 개량하다. —— *vi.* (P1) become or grow better. 좋아지다(opp. deteriorate). ¶ *The situation has ameliorated.* 정세가 호전되었다. [L. *melior* better]

a·mel·io·ra·tion [əmìːljəréiʃən, -liə-] *n.* ⓊⒸ improvement. 향상; 개선; 개량. ¶ *His health shows some ~.* 그의 건강은 좀 나아졌음을 보여주고 있다.

A·men [áːmən] *n.* the sun god of ancient Egyptians. 아멘《고대 이집트의 태양신》.

a·men [éimén, áːmén] *n.* Ⓒ a word, meaning 'So be it,' used at the end of a prayer. 아멘《'그러할지어다'의 뜻》. ¶ *sing the ~* 아멘을 부르다. [Heb. =certainly]

say amen (=*agree*) ***to something.*** …에 동

의하다. ¶ *I say ~ to that.* 그것에 동의한다.

a·me·na·ble [əmíːnəbəl, əménə-] *adj.* **1** 《*to, for*》 answerable; responsive. 따라야 할; 책임이 있는. ¶ *A citizen is ~ to the laws of his country.* 국민은 국가의 법에 따라야 한다 / *You are ~ for this debt.* 이 빚을 갚을 책임이 있습니다. **2** 《*to*》 willing or ready to obey; open to advice. 쾌히 따르는; 순종하는. ¶ *He is ~ to reason.* 그는 사리를 아는 사람이다 / *He is quite ~.* 그는 아주 온순하다. [ad-, L. *mino* drive]

a·me·na·bly [əmíːnəbəli, əménə-] *adv.* in an amenable manner; in accordance (with). 복종〔순종〕하여; 고분고분; (…에) 따라서. ¶ *~ to the rules* 규범〔법칙〕에 따라서 / *be ~ disposed* 고분고분하다.

***a·mend** [əménd] *vt.* (P6) **1** change or revise (a law, bill, etc.). (의안 따위)를 고치다; 개정〔수정〕하다. ¶ *an amended bill* 수정안(案) / *~ a bill* 법안을 개정하다 / *Each time they amended the law, instead of making it better, they made it worse.* 그들은 법을 고칠 때마다 그것을 개선 대신 개악을 했다. **2** make (one's behavior, etc.) better; improve. (행동 따위)를 고치다; 개선하다. ¶ *~ one's life* 〔*ways*〕 생활 태도를 고치다. — *vi.* (P1) become better in conduct, etc. 행동이 좋아지다; 바르게 되다; 개선하다. [a-, → mend]

a·mende hon·o·ra·ble [amɑ̃ːnd ɔnɔrɑ́ːbl] *n.* 《F.》 a public apology and reparation. 공적인 사죄와 배상.

***a·mend·ment** [əméndmənt] *n.* **1** UC a change for the better; a correction. (행동·마음 등)을 고치기; 정정; 개정; 개선. **2** C a change in a law or bill. (법안 등의) 수정. ¶ *propose* 〔*move*〕 *an ~ to a law* 법률의 수정안을〔수정의 동의를〕 내다.

a·mends [əméndz] *n. pl.* 《used as *sing.*》 something to pay for harm done. 보상.

make amends for, make up for (some harm done to another). (손실·손상)에 대해서 보상하다. ¶ *You can't make ~ with money for the harm you did him.* 그에게 입힌 피해에 대해서 너는 돈으로 보상할 순 없다.

a·men·i·ty [əménəti, əmíːn-] *n.* **1** U the quality of being pleasant. (태도·기후 등의) 쾌적함; 온화함. **2** 《*the -ties*》 ⓐ something that gives comfort; agreeable features of a place, etc. 위안〔즐거움〕을 주는 것; 기분 좋음. ¶ *the amenities of home life* 〔*a warm climate*〕 가정 생활〔온화한 기후〕의 즐거움. ⓑ polite acts; pleasant ways; civilities. 예의 바름. [L. *amoenus* pleasant]

a·merce [əmə́ːrs] *vt.* (P6,13) **1** 《*in*》 fine. …에게 벌금을 과하다. **2** 《*with*》 punish. …을 벌하다. ● **a·mer·ci·a·ble** [-siəbəl, -ʃə-] *adj.* [ad-, L. *merces* reward, →mercy]

:A·mer·i·ca [əmérikə] *n.* **1** the United States of America. 미합중국. **2** North America. 북아메리카. **3** South America. 남아메리카. **4** 《often *the ~s*》 《*collectively*》 North and South America. 남북 아메리카; 미주(美洲). [Person]

:A·mer·i·can [əmérikən] *adj.* of or belonging to America, esp. the United States. 아메리카의; 미합중국의. — *n.* **1** C a person of America, esp. a citizen of the United States. 아메리카 사람; (특히) 미국 사람. **2** U American English. 미국 영어.

American cloth [–́–– ⌐] *n.* an enameled leather-like cloth. 에나멜을 입힌 광택 유포(油布)《테이블 커버 따위로 쓰임》.

A·mer·i·can·ism [əmérikənìzəm] *n.* **1** U liking for or loyalty to the United States. 미국을 좋아함; 친미주의. **2** any character, custom, or thing peculiar to the United States. 미국풍; 미국인 기질; 미국 정신. **3** UC a word or phrase which began, or is much used, in the United States. 미국 영어 어법. ¶ *'O.K.' is an ~.* 'O.K.'는 미국 영어 어법이다.

A·mer·i·can·i·za·tion [əmèrikənizéiʃən / -kənai-] *n.* U the act of Americanizing. 미국화(하기).

A·mer·i·can·i·ze [əmérikənàiz] *vt.* (P6) make (someone or something) American in character, habits, or nationality. …을 미국화하다; 미국풍〔식〕으로 하다.

am·er·i·ci·um [æ̀məríʃiəm] *n.* U 《chem.》 a radioactive metallic element. 아메리슘 《인공 방사성 원소》.

ame·thyst [ǽməθist] *n.* U a precious stone, clear purple or violet in color. 자(紫)석영; 자수정. [Gk. *a-* not, *methu* wine (believed to prevent intoxication)]

a·mi·a·bil·i·ty [èimiəbíləti] *n.* U the quality of being amiable. 애교가 있음; 온순. [↓]

a·mi·a·ble [éimiəbəl] *adj.* good-natured; friendly; kindhearted. 상냥한; 다정한; 호감을 주는; 호의적인. ¶ *an ~ gathering* 다정한 분위기의 모임. [→amicable]

a·mi·a·bly [éimiəbəli] *adv.* good-naturedly; agreeably. 상냥〔다정〕하게; 애교 있게.

am·i·ca·ble [ǽmikəbəl] *adj.* friendly; peaceful. 우호적인; 평화로운(opp. hostile). ¶ *keep ~ relations with foreign nations* 외국들과 우호 관계를 유지하다 / *settle a quarrel in an ~ way* 싸움을 평화적으로 해결하다. [L. *amicus* friend]

am·i·ca·bly [ǽmikəbəli] *adv.* in a friendly manner; peacefully. 우호적으로; 평화적으로.

am·ice [ǽmis] *n.* 《Cath.》 **1** a piece of white linen covering the shoulders of priests. (사제가 어깨에 걸치는) 개두포(蓋頭布). **2** a hood and cap of priests. 수도사의 후드모(帽). [L. *amictus* garment]

***a·mid** [əmíd] *prep.* **1** in the middle of; surrounded by; among. …의 한복판에; …중〔사이〕에. ¶ *stand ~ the crowd* 군중 속에 서다. **2** in the course of; during. 한창 …하는 중에; …동안에. ¶ *The speaker sat down ~ loud applause.* 요란한 박수 속에 연사는 앉았

다. [O.E.=in the middle]
am·ide [ǽmaid, ǽmid] *n.* 《chem.》 a compound produced by replacing hydrogen atoms of ammonia by acid radicals. 아미드. [*am*monia, *-ide*]
a·mid·ships [əmídʃips] *adv.* in or near the middle of a ship. 배의 중간에. [→amid]
a·midst [əmídst] *prep.* amid; in the middle of. …의 한가운데에. [→amid]
a·mine [əmí:n, ǽmin] *n.* 《chem.》 a compound prepared from ammonia. 아민. [*ammonia*, *-ine*]
a·mi·no acid [əmí:nou ǽsid] *n.* 《chem.》 a group of organic compounds of nitrogen forming proteins. 아미노산(酸). [*amino* =of amine]
am·i·no·ben·zo·ic [əmì:noubenzóuik] *adj.* 《chem.》 of the isomers derived from benzoic acid. 아미노 안식향산(酸). [*amino*, benzoin]
a·miss [əmís] *adv.* out of order; badly; wrongly. 탈이 나서; 좋지 않게; 잘못하여; 틀리게. ¶ *do* (*something*) ~ …을 잘못[틀리게] 하다 / *choose* [*judge*] ~ 선택[판단]을 그르치다 / *speak* ~ 잘못 말하다 / *get one's money* ~ 부당한 수단으로 돈을 입수하다 / *She thinks* ~. 그녀는 잘못 생각하고 있다 / *Nothing comes* ~ *to him.* 그는 무엇이건 할 수 있다. ***go amiss,*** go wrong. 일이 잘못되다[잘 안 되다]. ¶ *All went* ~. 만사가 실패였다.
take something amiss, be offended at something. …에 성[화]내다. ¶ *He may take it* ~ *if you point out his errors.* 잘못을 지적하면 그는 성을 낼는지도 모른다.
— *adj.* 《as *predicative*》《*with*》 wrong; out of order. 좋지 않은; 잘못되어; 틀리어; 탈이 나. ¶ *What's* ~*?* 웬일인가; 무엇이 잘못되었나 / *There's something* ~ *with him.* 그에게 무언가 탈이 있다 / *Is there anything* ~ *with your watch ?* 네 시계에 무슨 고장이라도 났는가. [a-, →miss]
not amiss, quite suitable; quite good. 아주 적합한; 썩 좋은. ¶ *This house is not* ~. 집이 아주 좋다 / *The dinner was not* ~. 저녁 식사는 아주 훌륭했다.
am·i·ty [ǽməti] *n.* Ⓤ friendly relations, esp. between nations; friendship. (특히 국가간의) 우호 관계; 친선. ¶ ~ *between nations* 국가간의 친선 / *live in* ~ *with someone* 아무와 사이좋게 지내다. [→amicable]
AMM anti-missile missile (미사일 요격용 미사일).
Am·man [ɑ́:mmɑn, ―́] *n.* the capital of Jordan. 암만.
am·me·ter [ǽmmì:tər] *n.* Ⓤ an instrument for measuring an electric current in amperes. 전류계. [→ampere, -meter]
Am·mon [ǽmən] *n.* =Amen.
am·mo·ni·a [əmóunjə, -niə] *n.* Ⓤ 《chem.》 **1** a colorless gas with a very sharp smell, used in making ice and in medicine. 암모니아. **2** a liquid containing this gas. 암모니아 용액. [Gk. *ammōniakon*]
am·mo·nite [ǽmənàit] *n.* Ⓒ a coiled, chambered shellfish which lived long ago. 암몬조개; 국석(菊石). [L. *Ammon* god with coiled horns]
am·mo·ni·um [əmóuniəm] *n.* Ⓤ 《chem.》 the radical NH_4. 암모늄기(基). ¶ ~ *chloride* [*nitrate, sulphate*] 염화[질산, 황산] 암모늄. [Gk. *ammōniakon*, →-ium]
am·mu·ni·tion [æ̀mjuníʃən] *n.* Ⓤ **1** powder, bullets, or shells to be used in war. 탄약. **2** 《*colloq.*》 any means of attack or defence. 공격[방어] 수단; 무기. ¶ *Money is our* ~. 돈이 우리의 무기이다. **3** military supplies generally; munition. 군수품. [F. *la munition*]
am·ne·si·a [æmní:ʒə] *n.* 《med.》 Ⓤ total or partial loss of memory caused by brain injury, shock, etc. 기억 상실(증). [↓]
am·nes·ty [ǽmnəsti] *n.* (*pl.* **-ties**) ⒸⓊ a general pardon, given esp. to political offenders. 특사(特赦); 일반 사면. ¶ *The Government proclaimed a general* ~. 정부는 일반 사면을 공포했다. — *vt.* (P6) (**-tied**) give an amnesty to (someone). …를 사면[특사]하다. [Gk. *a-* not, *mnē* remember]
a·moe·ba [əmí:bə] *n.* Ⓒ (*pl.* **-bas** or **-bae**) a tiny water animal that has only one cell and that constantly changes in shape as it moves. 아메바. ● **a·moe·ba-like** [-làik] *adj.* [Gk.=change]
a·moe·bae [əmí:bi:] *n.* pl. of **amoeba.**
a·mok [əmʌ́k, əmɑ́k / əmɔ́k] *adv.* =amuck.
:a·mong [əmʌ́ŋ] *prep.* **1** in the middle of; surrounded by. … 중[가운데]에; 둘러싸여; … 속을. ¶ *walk* ~ *the crowd* 군중 속을 헤치고 걷다 / *The town lies* ~ *the mountains.* 그 읍은 산에 둘러싸여 있다 / *She sat* ~ *her friends.* 그녀는 친구들에 둘러싸여 앉았다. **2** in company with. …와 함께[같이]. ¶ *live* ~ *kindly people* 다정한 사람들과 함께 살다 / *travel* ~ *a group of tourists* 일단의 여행자들과 함께 여행하다. **3** with a share for each of; within. … 간에[사이에] 각자. ¶ *Divide these* ~ *you three.* 너희들 세 사람이 이것을 나누어서 가져라 / *Decide* ~ *yourselves.* 너희들 간에 정해라. **4** in the number of; in the class or group of. … 중[가운데]에; … 중에 들어. ¶ *This is the best* ~ *the pictures of this year.* 이것이 올해 사진 작품 중 가장 우수한 것이다 / *He was* ~ *the guests.* 손님들 중에는 그 사람도 있었다 / *Among the presents there was a fine necklace.* 선물 가운데엔 훌륭한 목걸이가 있었다 / *This is counted* ~ *his best works.* 이것은 그의 최우수 작품 중에 든다. **5** shared by all or many of; by or with the whole of. … 간에; … 사이에(서). ¶ *a singer popular* ~ *the young people* 젊은 이들 사이에 인기 있는 가수 / *It's a custom* ~ *us.* 그것은 우리들 간의 관습이다. **6** each with the other; between one another;

mutually. 서로; …들끼리. ¶ *They quarreled ~ themselves.* 그들은 저희들끼리 말다툼을 했다. 語法 흔히 among은 3자 이상일 때 쓰이며 두 사람 간에는 between이 사용됨. **7** by the joint action of. …들 간에; …와 협력해서. ¶ *We will settle it ~ us.* 그건 우리들끼리 해결하겠다. [A.S. *on gemang* in the company]

·**a·mongst** [əmʌ́ŋst] *prep.* =among.

am·o·rist [ǽmərist] *n.* a person having a great many love affairs. 호색한(好色漢); 탕아. [L.]

am·o·rous [ǽmərəs] *adj.* **1** inclined to (esp. sexual) love. 호색(好色)의. ¶ *He has an ~ nature.* 그는 호색적인 기질이다. **2** showing love; loving. 요염한; 사랑하는. ¶ *She gave him an ~ look.* 그녀는 그에게 추파를 던졌다. **3** of (esp. sexual) love. 연애의; 사랑의. ¶ *~ songs* 사랑의 노래들; 연가. **4** 《*of*》 in love with; charmed by. 사랑에 빠진; …에 반한. ¶ *He is ~ of that lady.* 그는 그 여성을 사랑하고 있다. [L. *amor* love]

a·mor·phous [əmɔ́ːrfəs] *adj.* **1** formless; shapeless. 무(정)형의. **2** unorganized. 무조직의. **3** not made of crystals; not crystalline. 비결정질의. ●**a·mor·phous·ly** [-li] *adv.* [Gk. *a-* not, *morphē* form]

am·or·tize, 《Brit.》 **-tise** [ǽmərtàiz, əmɔ́ːrtaiz] *vt.* (P6) put aside money regularly for future payment of. …을 감채(減債) 기금으로 상각하다. [L. *ad mortem* to death]

:**a·mount** [əmáunt] *vi.* (P3) reach in number or amount; add up; be equal. 달하다; 같다.

amount to, **a**) add up to; come up to (a sum, quantity, etc.). 총계〔총액〕 …이 되다. ¶ *The bill amounts to 300 dollars.* 청구액은 3백 달러에 달한다. **b**) be equal to. …과 같다; …에 상당하다. ¶ *His words ~ almost to a threat.* 그의 말은 거의 협박이나 같다 / *Keeping what belongs to another amounts to stealing.* 남의 것을 갖고 있는 것은 도둑질이나 같다 / *Your answer amounts to a refusal.* 너의 대답은 거절이나 마찬가지이다 / *~ to nothing* 〔*little*〕 대단한〔대수로운〕 것이 못되다 / *It doesn't ~ to much.* 그건 대수롭지가 않다. **c**) come to be; become. …이 되다. ¶ *He is going to ~ to something in life.* 그는 생애에 대단한 인물이 될 게다.

— *n.* Ⓤ **1** 《*the ~*》 sum; total. 총계; 합계. ¶ *What is the full ~ I owe you?* 자네에게 진 빚이 얼마인가 / *the ~ of today's sales* 오늘의 매상 총계. **2** 《*the ~*》 total meaning. 요지; 결과. ¶ *This is the ~ of what she said.* 이것이 그녀가 말하고 싶었던 요지이다. **3** Ⓒ a quantity. 양(量); 액(額); 총량. ¶ *a large* 〔*small*〕 *~ of money* 거액〔소액〕의 돈 / *a great ~ of intelligence* 상당량의 정보. [ad-, L. *mons* mountain, →mount]

any amount of, large quantity. 대량. ¶ *He has any ~ of money.* 그는 큰 부자이다.

in amount, in all; in substance. 총계; 요컨대. ¶ *He paid more than 500 dollar in ~.* 총액 5백 달러 이상 지불했다.

to the amount of, as much as. (총계) …(만큼)이나; …에 달하는.

a·mour [əmúər] *n.* Ⓒ a (secret) love affair. 비밀 정사(情事); 연애 사건. [L. *amor* love]

am·pe·lop·sis [æ̀mpəlɑ́psis / -pilɔ́p-] *n.* 《bot.》 a vine creeper. 담쟁이덩굴. [Gk.]

am·per·age [æmpíːridʒ, ǽmpər-] *n.* Ⓤ 《electr.》 the strength of an electric current measured in amperes. 암페어수(數). [↓]

am·pere, -père [ǽmpiər, -ˊ] *n.* Ⓒ 《electr.》 a unit for measuring the amount of electric current flowing through a wire. 암페어. 參考 프랑스의 과학자 A.M. Ampère (1775-1836)의 이름에서.

am·per·sand [ǽmpərsæ̀nd] *n.* the sign '&'. '&'의 기호 이름. ['and *per se*(=by itself) and']

am·phi- [ǽmfi-, -fiː- / -fə-] *pref.* on both sides; around. '양(兩)…, 주위'의 뜻. [Gk.]

am·phib·i·an [æmfíbiən] *n.* Ⓒ **1** an animal or plant that can live both on land and in water. 양서(兩棲) 동물. **2** an airplane that can take off from and land on both land and water. 수륙 양용 비행기. **3** a tank or other vehicle, that can be used both on land and water. 수륙 양용 전차. — *adj.* able to live or to operate both on land and in water; amphibious. 수륙 양서(兩棲)〔양용〕의. [amphi-, Gk. *bios* life, → -ian, -ious]

am·phib·i·ous [æmfíbiəs] *adj.* **1** able to live or to operate both on land and in water. 수륙 양서〔양용〕의. ¶ *~ plants* 양서 식물 / *an ~ tank* 수륙 양용 탱크 / *an ~ airplane* 수륙 양용기(機). **2** of military operations by land, water, and air forces. 육·해·공군 공동 작전의. ¶ *an ~ attack* 육·해·공군의 합동 공격.

am·phi·the·a·ter, 《Brit.》 **-tre** [ǽmfəθìːətər / -fiθìə-] *n.* Ⓒ **1** a circular building with rows of seats around an open area. 원형 극장; 투기장(鬪技場)《주위에 계단식 관람석이 있음》. **2** anything resembling an amphitheater in shape. 원형 극장 비슷한 것. [amphi-, Gk. *thea* spectacle]

〈amphitheater 1〉

Am·phit·ry·on [æmfítriən] *n.* **1** 《Gk. myth.》 a king of Thebes and the husband of Alcmene. 암피트리온. **2** a host; an entertainer. 주인역; (대접이 좋은) 접대자. [F.]

·**am·ple** [ǽmpl] *adj.* **1** of a large size or amount; extensive. 광대한; 넓은. ¶ *an ~ room* 넓은 방. **2** quite enough; sufficient. 충분한. ¶ *There is ~ time to do the work.* 일하는 데 시간은 충분하다 / *The money is ~ for our trip.* 돈은 우리 여행에 충분하다. **3** more than enough; abundant. 풍부한(opp. scanty). ¶ *an ~ supply of food* 풍부한 식량 공급. [L. *amplus* large]

am·pli·fi·ca·tion [æ̀mpləfikéiʃən] *n.* Ⓤ **1** ⓐ the act of amplifying; the state of being amplified; expansion; enlargement. 확대; 확장; 확충. ⓑ stating in more detail. 상술(詳述); 부연. **2** 《electr.》 an increase in the strength of an electric current, voltage, or power. 증폭(增幅). [↑]

am·pli·fi·er [ǽmpləfàiər] *n.* Ⓒ **1** a person or thing that amplifies. 확대하는 사람[것]. **2** a device to increase the strength of an electric current. 증폭기; 앰프.

am·pli·fy [ǽmpləfài] *vt.* (**-fied**) (P6) **1** make (something) larger or louder; enlarge; expand. …을 크게[확대]하다; 넓히다. ¶ *~ the volume of the radio* 라디오의 볼륨을 높이다 / *~ knowledge* 지식을 넓히다. **2** explain (something) more fully; make more detailed. …을 상술(詳述)하다; 부연[전개]하다. ¶ *~ a description* 기술(記述)을 더 상세히 하다 / *~ a theory* 이론을 전개하다. **3** 《electr.》 increase the strength of (an electric current, voltage, or power). (전압·전류)를 증폭하다. — *vi.* (P3) 《*on, upon*》 write or talk in great detail. 상술(詳述)하다. ¶ *~ on one's remarks* 자기 말을 상세히 설명하다.

am·pli·tude [ǽmplitjùːd] *n.* Ⓤ the state or quality of being ample. 넓이; 크기; 충분; 풍부; 증폭. ¶ *~ of the wave* 파도의 진폭.

am·ply [ǽmpli] *adv.* **1** sufficiently; largely; fully. 충분히; 크게. ¶ *They were ~ supplied with food.* 충분한 식량이 공급되어 있었다. **2** in detail. 상세히.

am·poule, am·pule [ǽmpjuːl / -puːl] *n.* 《med.》 Ⓒ a sealed small glass tube filled with medicine. (주사액 따위의) 앰플. [L.]

am·pu·tate [ǽmpjutèit] *vt.* (P6) cut off (an arm, a leg, etc.), esp. by surgery. (수술로 수족 따위)를 절단하다. ¶ *The doctor amputated the soldier's leg.* 의사는 그 병사의 다리를 절단했다. [L. *amb-* about, *puto* prune]

am·pu·ta·tion [æ̀mpjutéiʃən] *n.* ⓊⒸ the act of amputating. (수족 따위의) 절단 (수술).

·**Am·ster·dam** [ǽmstərdæ̀m / ⌐-⌐] *n.* an important seaport and the constitutional capital of the Netherlands. 암스테르담《네덜란드의 수도》. 參考 행정상의 수도는 The Hague.

a·muck [əmʌ́k] *adv.* madly; wildly. 미친 듯이[미쳐] 날뛰어. [Malay *amog*]
run amuck, rush about madly, attacking everybody whom one meets. 미친 듯이[피에 굶주려] 날뛰다.

am·u·let [ǽmjəlit] *n.* Ⓒ a small object worn as a charm against evil or harm. 부적; 호부(護符). [L.]

·**a·muse** [əmjúːz] *vt.* (P6,13) **1** cause (someone) to feel happy; entertain. …을 즐겁게[행복하게] 하다. ¶ *~ a little boy by telling him a story* 이야기를 들려 주어 어린 아이를 즐겁게 해 주다 / *Children are amused with toys and funny pictures.* 어린이들은 장난감이나 우스운 그림을 보고 즐거워한다. **2** cause (someone) to laugh or smile. …을 웃기다; 재미나게 하다. ¶ *We were much amused at his joke.* 그의 농담에 우리는 몹시 재미있었다.
***amuse** oneself,* take delight; enjoy oneself. 재미있어 하다; 재미있게 놀다; 즐기다. ¶ *~ oneself by singing* [*with books*] 노래하며[책을 보며] 즐기다.
You amuse me. You are absurd. 웃기는군.
● **a·mus·er** [-ər] *n.* [ad-, →muse]

·**a·muse·ment** [əmjúːzmənt] *n.* **1** Ⓤ the state of being amused; delight. 즐거움; 즐김. ¶ *Her eyes shone with ~.* 그녀의 눈은 즐거움으로 빛났다. **2** Ⓒ anything which amuses; an entertainment; a pleasure. 즐겁게 하는 일; 오락. ¶ *seek amusements* 오락을 찾다 / *His chief ~ is reading novels.* 그의 으뜸가는 즐거움은 소설을 읽는 일이다.

·**a·mus·ing** [əmjúːziŋ] *adj.* **1** pleasant; entertaining. 즐거운; 재미[흥미]있는. ¶ *an ~ story* 흥미 있는 이야기. **2** causing laughter. 우스운. ¶ *an ~ motion picture* 우스운 영화. ● **a·mus·ing·ly** [-li] *adv.*

A·my [éimi] *n.* a woman's name. 여자의 이름.

:**an** [æn, ən] *indef. art.* ⇨a.

an- [æn-, ən-] *pref.* **1** not, without. '무(無)'의 뜻. [Gk.] **2** =ad-. [L.]

-an [-ən, -n] *suf.* 《forming *adj.* or *n.*》 of; of the nature of; belonging to; a person who favors; a native of. '…의, …에 속하는, …에 관계가 있는'의 뜻. ¶ *American / amphibian / republican / Italian.* [L. *-anus*]

a·na [ǽnə, ɑ́ːnə] *n.* **1** a collection of a person's sayings. 어록(語錄). **2** 《*pl.*》 a person's anecdotes. 일화집(逸話集). [L.]

an·a- [ǽnə-, ənǽ-] *pref.* up; back; anew. '상(上)…, 후(後)…, 재(再)…'의 뜻. [Gk.]

a·nab·o·lism [ənǽbəlìzəm] *n.* Ⓤ 《biol.》 the synthesis in living organisms of more complex substances from simpler ones. 동화 작용. [ana-, *meta*bolism, *cata*bolism]

a·nach·ro·nism [ənǽkrənìzəm] *n.* ⓊⒸ the state of being out of date; a person or thing out of date. 시대 착오; 시대에 뒤진 사

람〔것〕. ¶ *A belief in magic today is an* ~. 오늘날 마법에 대한 믿음은 시대 착오적인 것이다. [ana-, Gk. *khuronos* time]

a·nach·ro·nis·tic [ənæ̀krənístik] *adj.* out of date. 시대 착오의.

an·a·co·lu·thon [æ̀nəkəlú:θαn / -θɔn] *n.* (*pl.* **-tha** [-θə]) *n.* UC 《rhet.》 a sentence or words lacking grammatical sequence. 파격(破格). [Gk. *an-* not, *akolouthos* following]

an·a·con·da [æ̀nəkάndə / -kɔ́n-] *n.* C a very large snake of South America that coils around and crushes its prey. 남미산의 큰 뱀; (일반적으로) 큰 뱀. [Ceylon]

A·nac·re·on [ənǽkriən] *n.* (?563-478 B.C.) a Greek poet. 아나크레온《고대 그리스의 시인》.

a·nae·mi·a [əní:miə] *n.* =anemia.

a·nae·mic [əní:mik] *adj.* =anemic.

an·aer·obe [ǽnəròub, ænέəroub] *n.* 《biol.》 an organism that does not require air or free oxygen for maintaining life. 혐기성〔무기성〕 생물《미생물》(opp. aerobe).

an·aes·the·sia [æ̀nəsθí:ʒə, -ziə] *n.* =anesthesia.

an·aes·the·si·ol·o·gy [ænəsθì:ziάlədʒi / -ɔ́l-] *n.* =anesthesiology.

an·aes·thet·ic [æ̀nəsθétik] *adj., n.* =anesthetic.

an·aes·the·tist [ənésθətist, ænís:s-] *n.* =anesthetist.

an·aes·the·tize [ənésθətàiz, ænís:s-] *vt.* = anesthetize.

an·a·gram [ǽnəgræ̀m] *n.* C **1** a word or phrase obtained by changing the order of the letters of another word or phrase. 철자 바꾸기. 參考 보기: devil→lived; time→emit으로 하는 따위. **2** (*pl.* used as *sing.*) a game in which the players make words by changing and adding letters. 철자 바꾸기〔글자 수수께끼〕 놀이. [ana-, →gram]

a·nal [éinəl] *adj.* of the anus. 항문의. [L.]

an·a·lects [ǽnəlèkts] *n. pl.* literary extracts. 어록(語錄); 선집(選集). ¶ *the Analects of Confucius* 논어(論語). [ana-, Gk. *legō* pick]

an·al·ge·si·a [æ̀nəldʒí:ziə, -siə] *n.* 《med.》 absence of pain. 무통(無痛)(증). [Gk. *an-*, not, *algo* pain]

a·nal·o·gize [ənǽlədʒàiz] *vi., vt.* (P1;6,13) **1** use or reason by analogy. 유추(類推)하다; (…에) 유사하다. **2** explain or exhibit analogy. …을 유추해서 설명하다〔나타내다〕. [↓]

a·nal·o·gous [ənǽləgəs] *adj.* 《*to*》 having analogy; similar. 유사〔비슷〕한; 서로 닮은. ¶ *The heart is* ~ *to a pump.* 심장은 펌프와 비슷하다.

an·a·logue [ǽnəlɔ̀:g, -lɑ̀g / -lɔ̀g] *n.* something analogous. 유사물.

a·nal·o·gy [ənǽlədʒi] *n.* CU (*pl.* **-gies**) likeness; similarity. 유사; 비슷함. ¶ *bear* 〔*have*〕 *some* ~ *with* 〔*to*〕 *something* …와 유사〔비슷〕하다 / *by* ~ *with something* =*on the* ~ *of something* …로부터 유추해서 / *There is an* ~ *between the human heart and a pump.* 인간의 심장과 펌프와는 서로 같은 데가 있다. [Gk. *ana-* according to, *logos* ratio]

an·a·lyse [ǽnəlàiz] *vt.* 《chiefly Brit.》 = analyze.

a·nal·y·ses [ənǽləsì:z] *n.* pl. of **analysis**.

***a·nal·y·sis** [ənǽləsis] *n.* UC (*pl.* **-ses**) **1** the act of separating something into its parts or elements to find out what it is made of. 분해; 분석(opp. synthesis). ¶ *grammatical* ~ 문법적인 해부 / *the* ~ *of a person's character* 사람 성격의 분석 / *On* ~*, it was found out.* 필경 알아냈다. **2** 《chem.》 the separation of materials into their elements to find their kind or nature. (화학적인) 분석. ¶ *chemical* ~ 화학 분석 / *make a careful* ~ *of a poison* 독(毒)을 주의 깊게 분석하다. **3** a critical examination of an idea, a book, an event, etc. 엄밀한 검사〔검토〕. [→analyze]

in* 〔*on*〕 *the last* 〔*final*〕 *analysis, after all. 요컨대; 결국은. ¶ *In the last* ~ *the theory was proved untenable.* 결국 그 설(說)은 성립되지 않음이 입증되었다.

an·a·lyst [ǽnəlist] *n.* C **1** a person who analyzes; an analyzer. 분석〔분해〕하는 사람. ¶ *a political* ~ 정치 평론가. **2** a psychoanalyst. 정신 분석학자〔분석의(醫)〕.

an·a·lyt·ic [æ̀nəlítik], **-i·cal** [-əl] *adj.* separating a thing into its parts or elements for the purpose of study. 분석〔분해〕적인(opp. synthetic). ¶ *an* ~ *test* 분석 실험.

● **an·a·lyt·i·cal·ly** [-kəli] *adv.*

***an·a·lyze** [ǽnəlàiz] *vt.* (P6) **1** separate (something) into its parts or elements. …을 분석〔분해〕하다(opp. synthesize). ¶ ~ *a sentence* 문장을 분석하다 / ~ *water into oxygen and hydrogen* 물을 산소와 수소로 분해하다. **2** examine (something) critically. …을 (분석적으로) 검토하다. ¶ ~ *someone's statement* 아무의 진술을 검토하다 / ~ *the causes of success* 성공의 원인을 분석하다.

● **an·a·lyz·er** [-ər] *n.* [ana-, Gk. *luō* loose]

an·a·nas [ǽnənæ̀s, ənά:nəs] *n.* 《rare》 a pineapple. 파인애플. [Peruv.]

An·a·ni·as [æ̀nənáiəs] *n.* **1** 《Bible》 a person who fell dead after lying. 아나니아《하느님 앞에서 거짓말을 한 탓으로 죽은 남자》. **2** 《*colloq.*》 a liar. 거짓말쟁이. [Heb.]

an·a·paest [ǽnəpèst] *n.* =anapest.

an·a·pest [ǽnəpèst] *n.* a metrical foot consisting of three syllables. 약약강격(弱弱強格)《××⌿》. [ana-, Gk. *paiō* strike]

an·arch [ǽnɑ:rk] *n.* 《*arch.*》 =anarchist.

an·ar·chic [ænά:rkik], **-chi·cal** [-əl] *adj.* lawless; of anarchy. 무정부 (상태)의. [↓]

an·ar·chism [ǽnərkìzəm] *n.* U the doctrine that all existing governmental systems are undesirable. 무정부주의.

an·ar·chist [ǽnərkist] *n.* Ⓒ a person who believes in anarchism. 무정부주의자.

an·ar·chy [ǽnərki] *n.* Ⓤ **1** the absence of government and law. 무정부. **2** the absence of political order; lawlessness; confusion; disorder. 무질서; 혼란. [Gk. *an-* not, *arkhē* rule]

an·as·tig·mat [ənǽstigmæ̀t, æ̀nəstígmæt] *n.* 《opt.》 a lens which is free from stigmatism. 무수차(無收差) 렌즈. [→astigmatism]

a·nath·e·ma [ənǽθəmə] *n.* Ⓒ (*pl.* **-mas** or **-ma·ta**) **1** a solemn curse that excludes someone from membership in the church. 파문(破門); 저주. **2** a thing or person greatly disliked. 아주 싫은 것(자). ¶ *Alcohol is ~ to him.* 그는 술이 질색이다. **3** a thing or person damned. 저주받은 것(자). [Gk. =a thing devoted to evil]

a·nath·e·ma·ta [ənǽθəmətə] *n.* pl. of **anathema.**

a·nath·e·ma·tize [ənǽθəmətàiz] *vt., vi.* (**-tized, -tiz·ing**) (P6;1) pronounce anathemas against. …을 저주하다; 파문하다. [↑]

an·a·tom·ic [æ̀nətámik / -tɔ́m-], **-i·cal** [-əl] *adj.* **1** of anatomy. 해부(학상)의. **2** structural. 구조의. ● **an·a·tom·i·cal·ly** [-li] *adv.* [→anatomy]

a·nat·o·mist [ənǽtəmist] *n.* Ⓒ a specialist in anatomy. 해부학자.

a·nat·o·mize [ənǽtəmàiz] *vt.* (P6) **1** cut (an animal, a plant, etc.) into parts to study its structure; dissect. (동·식물체)를 해부하다. **2** analyze minutely. …을 상세히 분해(분석)하다. [↓]

a·nat·o·my [ənǽtəmi] *n.* Ⓤ **1** the study of the structure of animals and plants. 해부학. **2** the act of cutting up animals or plants to study their structures. 해부. **3** Ⓒ the structure of an animal or plant. (해부학적) 조직. ¶ *the ~ of an earthworm* 지렁이의 해부학적 구조. [ana-, Gk. *temnō* cut]

anc. ancient(ly).

-ance [-əns, -ns] *suf.* **1** state of condition. '상태·성질·정도'의 뜻. ¶ *absorptance.* **2** action. '행동'의 뜻. ¶ *continuance.* [L.]

·**an·ces·tor** [ǽnsestər, -səs-] *n.* Ⓒ a person from whom another person is descended; a forefather. 조상; 선조(opp. descendant). [→antecedent]

an·ces·tral [ænséstrəl] *adj.* **1** of ancestors; belonging to ancestors. 조상(선조)의. ¶ *~ forms of life* 생물의 원시 형태. **2** inherited from ancestors. 조상 전래의. ¶ *~ estate* 조상 전래의 재산 / *an ~ home* 조상 대대의 집.

an·ces·try [ǽnsestri, -səs-] *n.* Ⓤ 《*collectively*》 **1** all of one's ancestors. 조상; 선조. **2** the line of family descent. 가계(家系); 가문. ¶ *She was born of good ~.* 그녀는 명문 출신이다 / *He is an American of Korean ~.* 그는 한국계 미국인이다.

·**an·chor** [ǽŋkər] *n.* Ⓒ **1** a heavy iron or steel instrument used to keep a ship from moving. 닻. **2** 《*fig.*》 anything that makes someone feel safe and secure; a support. 안정을 주는 것; 의지가(힘이) 되는 것. ¶ *rely on an ~ of one's faith* 자기의 신념이라는 지주에 매달리다 / *His mother's letters were an ~ to the boy at this time.* 이번 어머니로부터의 편지는 그 아이에게 힘이 되는 것이었다. **3** a person who runs the last part of the way in a relay race. (릴레이·역전 마라톤의) 최종 주자(走者).

be 〔***lie, ride***〕 ***at anchor,*** (of a ship) be kept from moving by an anchor. 닻을 내리고(정박하고) 있다.

cast 〔***drop, slip***〕 ***anchor,*** let the anchor down. 닻을 내리다.

come to anchor, cast anchor; arrive after sailing. 닻을 내리다; 정박하다.

weigh anchor, take up the anchor; depart. 닻을 올리다; 출범하다.

— *vt.* (P6,13) **1** keep (a ship) from moving by an anchor. (배)를 정박시키다. ¶ *~ a boat in the harbor* 배를 항구에 정박시키다. **2** fix firmly; make (something) secure. …을 고정시키다. ¶ *~ a tent to the ground* 텐트를 땅에 고정시키다 / *She anchored her hopes in her son's talent for music.* 그 여자는 아들의 음악 재능에 희망을 걸었다.

— *vi.* (P3) **1** cast an anchor; lie at anchor. 닻을 내리다; 정박하다. ¶ *We anchored off the shore.* 우리는 해안에서 떨어져 닻을 내렸다. **2** be firmly fixed. 고정되다. [L. *ancora*]

An·chor·age [ǽŋkəridʒ] *n.* a seaport in South Alaska. 앵커리지.

an·chor·age [ǽŋkəridʒ] *n.* **1** Ⓤ the act of anchoring; the state of being anchored. 닻 내림; 투묘(投錨); 정박. **2** Ⓒ a place where ships are anchored. 투묘지(投錨地); 정박소. ¶ *a safe ~ in rough weather* 사나운 날씨에 안전한 정박소. **3** Ⓤ money that must be paid for anchoring a ship. 정박료. **4** Ⓒ something to depend on. 의지(되는 것).

an·cho·ret [ǽŋkərit, -rèt] *n.* =anchorite.

an·cho·rite [ǽŋkəràit] *n.* Ⓒ a person who has retired to a solitary place for religious meditation. (특히 종교를 위해 속세를 떠난) 은자(隱者). [Gk. ana-, *khōreō* retire]

an·cho·vy [ǽntʃouvi, -tʃəvi, æntʃóu-] *n.* Ⓒ (*pl.* **-vies** or *collectively* **-vy**) 《fish》 a very small fish of the herring family, found chiefly in the Mediterranean Sea. 안초비《멸치류》. 參考 소스 따위에 쓰임. [Sp.]

an·chu·sa [æŋkjúːsə, -zə, æn-] *n.* 《bot.》 a hairy stemmed plant. 지칫과의 식물《약초》. [Gk.]

an·chy·lo·sis [æ̀ŋkəlóusis] *n.* =ankylosis.

:**an·cient** [éinʃənt] *adj.* **1** of or in times long past. 고대의. ¶ *~ history* 고대사 / *the men of ~ times* 고대 사람들 / *~ civilization*

고대 문명. **2** very old. 아주 오래된; 고래(古來)의(opp. new). ¶ *an ~ tree* 고목 / *an ~ city* 고도(古都) / *in accordance with an ~ belief* 옛날부터의 신앙에 따라. **3** old-fashioned. 고풍의; 구식의(opp. modern). — *n.* Ⓒ **1** a person who lived in ancient times. 고대인. **2** 《*the ~s*》 the civilized peoples who lived long time ago, as the Greeks or Romans. 고대 문명 민족《고대 그리스·로마인 등》. ● **an·cient·ly** [-li] *adv.* [L. *ante* before]

an·cle [ǽŋkl] *n.* =ankle.

-an·cy [-ənsi, -nsi] *suf.* =-ance.

:and [ænd, ənd, nd, ən, n] *conj.* 《used to connect *words, phrases,* or *clauses*》 **1** ⓐ with; in addition to; besides; joined together. 그리고; …와; …하고; 또; 및; (…에) 더하여. ¶ *a chair ~ a table* 의자 하나와 책상 한 개 / *boys ~ girls* 소년들과 소녀들 / *man ~ wife* 부부 / *roses both white ~ red* 희고 붉은 장미꽃들 / *eat ~ drink* 먹고 마시다 / *buy ~ sell* 사고 팔다 / *You ~ she ~ I are friends.* 너와 그녀와 나는 친구이다. ⓑ added to; plus. 더하여; 더하기; 플러스. ¶ *three ~ forty,* 43 / *4 ~ 2 make(s)* 〔*are*〕 *6,* 4 더하기 2는 6이다 / *two hundred ~ sixty-three,* 263. ⓒ after that; then. 그리고(나서); 그런 다음에. ¶ *He said so ~ went out.* 그는 그렇게 말하고 나갔다. **2** 《uniting elements closely and showing as a whole》 along with; as well as. …와 함께; …임과 동시에. ¶ *bread ~ butter* [brédnbʌ́tər] 버터 바른 빵 / *a watch ~ chain* 줄이 달린 시계 / *father ~ mother* 부모 / *He is a poet ~ teacher.* 그는 시인이자 학교 선생님이다 / *There's nothing secret between you ~ me.* 너와 나 사이엔 비밀이 없다. 語法 이와 같은 합일(合一)의 관계를 나타낼 때의 동사는 단수형. **3** as a result; in consequence; then. 그러면; 만일 …하면; …하자; 그러자. ¶ *The teacher told her ~ she wept.* 선생님이 그녀에게 말하자 그녀는 울었다 / *Try it, ~ you will succeed.* 해 보아라, 그러면 성공할 게다 / *One step farther, ~ we should have fallen over the cliff.* 한 발짝만 더 나아갔다면 우린 벼랑 아래로 떨어졌을 게다. **4** 《used to emphasize addition or repetition》 then again; then once more. …이고(자꾸). ¶ *for hours ~ hours* 몇 시간이고 / *again ~ again* 몇 번이고 (되풀이해서); 재삼 재차 / *walk miles ~ miles* 몇 마일이고 한없이 걷다 / *dig a hole deeper ~ deeper* 구멍을 점점 더 깊이 파다 / *read a letter over ~ over again* 편지를 몇 번씩이나 (되풀이해서) 읽다. **5** 《expressing different examples of the same kind》 여러 가지; 각종의. ¶ *There are books ~ books.* 책에도 좋은 것과 나쁜 것 여러 가지가 있다. **6** yet; nevertheless; but; for all that. …인〔한〕데도; …함에도. ¶ *He is very poor, ~ he idles like a rich man.* 그는 몹시 가난한데도 부자처럼 편둥거린다. **7** also; what is more important. 게다가; 그것도. ¶ *He did it, ~ did it well.* 그는 그 일을 했다. 그것도 훌륭하게. **8** 《used instead of *to* after *come, go, try,* etc.》 《*colloq.*》 to; in order to. …하러〔하려고〕; …하기 위해. ¶ *Come ~ see us.* 우리를 보러 오게 / *Go ~ look at it.* 그것을 보러 가거라 / *Try ~ do better next time.* 다음 번엔 더 잘 하도록 노력해라. **9** 《placed between *two adjectives*》 《*colloq.*》 語法 2개의 형용사를 연결하여 앞의 형용사를 부사적으로 만듦. ¶ *nice ~ warm* 아주 따뜻한 / *good ~ tired* 몹시 피곤한 / *good ~ fast* 매우 빠른. [E.]

and all, including. …까지 포함하여; 그 외의 모두; …째로. ¶ *eat the fish, bone ~ all* 생선을 뼈째로 모두 먹다 / *The money had been stolen, box ~ all.* 돈은 금고째 도둑맞고 없었다.

and all that, and so forth; and the like. …따위; …등등; 기타 그와 같은 것. ¶ *Art ~ all that isn't really waste of time.* 예술이든가 그러한 것들은 결코 시간의 낭비가 아니다.

and how! of course. 그렇고말고; 정말이지.

and so, therefore; so. 그러므로; 그래서.

and so on 〔***forth***〕, and the like; et cetera. …등등; 따위.

and. andante.

an·dan·te [ændǽnti, ɑːndɑ́ːntei] *adj., adv.* 《It.》 《mus.》 moderately slow. 느린; 느리게. — *n.* Ⓒ a moderately slow movement or music. 안단테곡(曲); 완서조(緩徐調). [It.]

An·des [ǽndiːz], **the** *n. pl.* a lofty mountain range in west South America. 안데스 산맥. 參考 최고봉은 Aconcagua.

and·i·ron [ǽndàiərn] *n.* Ⓒ one of a pair of metal supports for holding firewood in a fireplace. (난로의 철제) 장작 받침. [F. *andier*]

〈andiron〉

and/or [ǽndɔ́ːr] *conj.* both or either. 및/또는; 양쪽 다 또는 어느 한쪽. 參考 상용문·공용문 따위에 쓰임. ¶ *fish ~ meat* 생선과 고기 양쪽 다 또는 어느 한쪽.

An·dor·ra [ændɔ́ːrə, -dɑ́rə] *n.* a republic between Spain and France. 안도라《프랑스·스페인 국경에 있는 공화국》.

An·drew [ǽndruː] *n.* a man's name. 남자의 이름. 參考 애칭은 Andy.

an·ec·dot·age [ǽnikdòutidʒ] *n.* **1** 《*collectively*》 anecdotes. 일화. **2** 《*joc.*》 talkative old age. 말 많은 늙은 나이. [Gk. *a-* not, *ekdidōmi* publish]

an·ec·dote [ǽnikdòut] *n.* Ⓒ a brief story, usu. amusing or instructive, told about some person or incident. 일화. ¶ *Many anecdotes are told about him.* 그에 관한 많은 일화들이 있다.

a·ne·mi·a [əníːmiə] *n.* 《med.》 Ⓤ lack of blood; an illness because of lack of blood. 빈혈(증). [Gk. *a-* not, *haima* blood]

a·ne·mic [əníːmik] *adj.* 《med.》 lacking in blood; suffering from anemia. 빈혈(증)의.

an·e·mom·e·ter [æ̀nəmάmitər / -mɔ́m-] *n.* Ⓒ an instrument for measuring the speed or pressure of the wind. 풍속계; 풍력계. [Gk. *anemos* wind, →meter]

a·nem·o·ne [ənéməni] *n.* Ⓒ **1** 《bot.》 a plant with a slender stem and white, red, or purple flowers. 아네모네. **2** 《zool.》 a sea animal with a tube-like body and many feelers or tentacles; a sea anemone. 말미잘. [Gk.=daughter of wind]

a·nent [ənént] *prep.* 《*arch.*》 about; concerning; in regard to. …에 관해서. [E.=on the level with]

an·e·roid [ǽnərɔ̀id] *n.* a barometer using no fluid. 아네로이드 기압계. [Gk. *a-* not, *nēros* wet]

an·es·the·si·a [æ̀nəsθíːʒə, -ziə] *n.* Ⓤ 《med.》 loss of the senses, esp. when caused by disease or anesthetics. 지각(知覺) 마비; 마비. [Gk. *an-* not, →*aisthētós* sensible]

an·es·the·si·ol·o·gy [æ̀nəsθìːziάlədʒi / -ɔ́l-] *n.* 《med.》 the science of administering anesthetics. 마취학.

an·es·thet·ic [æ̀nəsθétik] *n.* Ⓒ a drug or gas, such as chloroform or ether, which causes loss of sensation for a time. 마취약〔제〕. — *adj.* causing loss of sensation for a time. 마취의; 무감각의.

an·es·the·tist [ənésθətist, æníːs-] *n.* 《med.》 a person whose duty it is to give anesthetics during operations. 마취 담당자〔의사〕.

an·es·the·tize [ənésθətàiz, æníːs-] *vt.* (P6) make insensible. 감각을 잃게 하다.

an·eu·rysm [ǽnjurìzəm] *n.* 《med.》 a permanent swelling of an artery. 동맥류(動脈瘤). [ana-, Gk. *eurus* wide]

·a·new [ənjúː] *adv.* **1** over again; once more. 다시 (한 번). ¶ *write a story* ~ 이야기를 다시 쓰다 / *She wept* ~. 그녀는 또다시 울었다. **2** in a new form or manner; afresh. 새로이. ¶ *edited* ~ 새로(이) 편집된. [*of, new*]

:an·gel [éindʒəl] *n.* Ⓒ **1** a messenger of God, usu. pictured with wings. 천사. **2** a good, innocent, or lovely person. 천사 같은 사람. ¶ *an* ~ *of a child* 천사 같은 아이 / *Be an* ~ *and do it.* 착한 애니까 그걸 하는 거다. **3** a guardian spirit. 수호신. [Gk. *ángelos* messenger]

an·gel·ic [ændʒélik], **-i·cal** [-əl] *adj.* of or like an angel. 천사의; 천사 같은. ¶ *an* ~ *voice* 천사와 같은 목소리 / *the* ~ *choirs* 천사의 합창. [↑]

An·ge·lus [ǽndʒələs] *n.* Ⓒ **1** a Roman Catholic prayer said three times a day. 삼종(三鐘) 기도. **2** the bell that announces the time for this prayer; an Angelus bell. 삼종 기도를 알리는 종.

:an·ger [ǽŋgər] *n.* Ⓤ strong, hostile emotion aroused by a wrong act or remark of another person. 노여움; 성. ¶ *control* 〔*hold back*〕 *one's* ~ 노여움을 누르다 / *provoke someone's* ~ 아무의 노여움을 도발하다 / *His face turned red with* ~. 성이 나서 얼굴이 붉어졌다. — *vt.* (P6) make (someone) angry; offend. …을 성〔화〕나게 하다. ¶ *His dishonesty angered his friends.* 그의 부정직은 친구를 화나게 했다. — *vi.* become angry. 성나다. [N. *angri* distress]

an·gi·na [ændʒáinə] *n.* 《med.》 **1** any disease marked by spasmodic suffocation, as croup; an inflamatory disease of the throat. 인후통(痛). **2** =angina pectoris. [L. *angina* strangling]

angina pec·to·ris [ændʒáinə péktəris] *n.* 《med.》 a serious disease of the heart. 협심증. [L. *pectoris* breast]

:an·gle[1] [ǽŋgl] *n.* Ⓒ **1** 《geom.》 the space between two lines that meet at a point. 각도. ¶ *an acute* ~ 예각 / *an external* 〔*exterior*〕 ~ 외각 / *an internal* 〔*interior*〕 ~ 내각 / *an obtuse* ~ 둔각 / *a right* ~ 직각 / *at right angles with* …와 직각을 이루어. **2** a corner. 모〔귀〕퉁이. ¶ *in the* ~ *of a wall* 담 모퉁이에. **3** ⓐ a point of view. 관점; 견지. ¶ *find out someone's* ~ 아무의 입장을 알아내다 / *consider from various angles* 여러 각도에서 생각하다. ⓑ an aspect of an event or situation. 국면. ¶ *The situation presents a new* ~. 상황은 새로운 국면을 보이고 있다.
— *vt.* (P6) move or bend (something) in an angle. …을 어떤 각도로 움직이다〔구부리다〕.
— *vi.* (P1) move or go at an angle. 어떤 각도로 되다〔굽다〕. [L. *angulus*]

an·gle[2] [ǽŋgl] *vi.* (P1,3) 《*for*》 **1** catch fish with a hook and line. 낚시질하다. ¶ ~ *for trout* 송어를 낚다. **2** try to get by using tricks. (…을 얻으려고) 꾀어들이다; 유인하다. ¶ ~ *for praise* (농간 부려) 칭찬을 듣도록 하다. [E.]

an·gler [ǽŋglər] *n.* **1** a person who fishes with a hook and line. 낚시꾼. **2** 《fish》 a frogfish. 안강; 아귀. [*angle*[2]]

An·gles [ǽŋglz] *n. pl.* a West Germanic people that settled in Britain in the fifth century. 앵글족(族). [Teut.]

an·gle·worm [ǽŋglwə̀ːrm] *n.* a worm used as bait such as the earthworm. 낚싯밥으로 쓰이는 지렁이. [→angle[2]]

An·gli·can [ǽŋglikən] *adj.* **1** of the Church of England. 영국 국교회〔성공회〕의. **2** 《chiefly U.S.》 English. 영국 (사람)의.
— *n.* Ⓒ a member of the Church of England. 영국 국교도. [→Angles]

An·gli·cize [ǽŋgləsàiz] *vt.* (P6) make (something) English in customs, character, words, pronunciation, etc. 영국식〔풍〕으로 하다. ¶ *'Garage' is a French word which has been anglicized.* 'Garage'는 영어화한 프랑스어이다.

an·gling [ǽŋgliŋ] *n.* Ⓤ the act or art of fishing with a hook and line. 낚시질. [→angle[2]]

An·glo- [ǽŋglou-] *pref.* English. '영국의'의 뜻. [Teut.]

An·glo-A·mer·i·can [ǽŋglouəmérikən] *adj.* **1** English and American. 영미(英美)의. **2** of Anglo-Americans. 영국계 미국인의. — *n.* Ⓒ an American of English origin or birth. 영국계 미국인. [*Anglo-*]

An·glo·ma·ni·a [æ̀ŋgləméiniə, -njə] *n.* a great love of England and English ways. 영국 숭상.

An·glo·pho·bi·a [æ̀ŋgləfóubiə, -bjə] *n.* a hatred of England and English ways. 영국 혐오.

An·glo-Sax·on [ǽŋglousǽksən] *n.* **1** Ⓒ a person of the English-speaking world. 영어를 국어로 하는 사람. **2** Ⓒ a person who lived in England before the Norman Conquest. 앵글로색슨 사람. **3** Ⓒ a person of English descent. 영국계의 사람; 영국인. **4** Ⓤ the language used in Britain before the Norman Conquest; Old English. 앵글로색슨어; 고대 영어. — *adj.* **1** of the Anglo-Saxons or their language. 앵글로색슨(어)의. **2** of the English people. 영국인의.

An·go·ra [ǽŋgourə, æŋgɔ́:rə] *n.* **1** Ⓒ a cat or goat with very long, soft hair. 앙고라 고양이〔염소〕. **2** 《*a-*》 Ⓤ cloth made from the wool of an Angora goat; mohair. 앙고라 직물; 모헤어. [Place]

an·gri·ly [ǽŋgrəli] *adv.* in an angry manner. 화〔성〕내어; 노하여. [↓]

:an·gry [ǽŋgri] *adj.* (**-gri·er, -gri·est**) **1** 《*at, with, about*》 feeling or showing anger or rage. 성난; 노한; 화낸. ¶ *be ~ at the dean* 학장에게 분노를 느끼다 / *become* 〔*get, grow*〕 *~ about the snub* 냉대에 분개하다 / *He is ~ with me about it.* 그는 그 일에 대해 내게 화를 내고 있다 / *He got ~ at what I said.* 그는 내가 한 말에 노했다. **2** wild and stormy, as if angry. 험악한; 사나운. ¶ *~ words* 험악한 말 / *~ waves* 사나운 물결 / *the ~ sky* 잔뜩 찌푸린 하늘. **3** (of a cut, wound, etc.) red and painful. 아픈. ¶ *an ~ wound* 아픈 상처 / *The wound looks ~.* 상처가 아플 것 같다. [N. *angri* distress]

ang·strom unit [ǽŋstrəm jù:nit] *n.* one ten-millionth of a millimeter, a unit of measurement of the wave lengths of light. 옹스트롬 단위. [Person]

an·guish [ǽŋgwiʃ] *n.* Ⓤ great pain, grief, or suffering. 고통; 고뇌. ¶ *Fred was in ~ until the doctor set his broken leg.* 프레드는 의사가 부러진 다리를 접골시키기까지 고통스러웠다 / *~ of mind* 정신적 고뇌. [L. *angustia* tightness]

an·guished [ǽŋgwiʃt] *adj.* full of anguish. 괴로워하는; 고뇌에 찬.

an·gu·lar [ǽŋgjələr] *adj.* **1** having angles; having sharp corners. 모가 (나)있는. ¶ *an ~ piece of rock* 모가 난 돌조각. **2** lean; bony. 깡마른; 뼈만 앙상한. ¶ *Her body was very ~.* 그녀의 몸은 몹시 말라 있었다. **3** measured by all angle. 각도로 잰. ¶ *~ distance* 각거리(角距離). **4** (of someone's character) not easy to be friends with; awkward. (성격이) 모난; 가까워지기 어려운; 딱딱한; 완고한; 어색한. [→angle[1]]

an·gu·lar·i·ty [æ̀ŋgjəlǽrəti] *n.* Ⓤ the quality of having sharp corners. 모가 있음.

an·hy·dride [ænháidraid] *n.* 《chem.》 any oxide that unites with water to form acid or base. 무수물(無水物). [Gk. *an-* without, →hydrogen]

an·il [ǽnil] *n.* indigo (herb and dye). 인디고. [Arab. =dark blue]

a·nile [ǽnail, éin-] *adj.* like an old woman. 노파와 같은. [L. *anus* old woman]

an·i·line [ǽnəlin, -làin], **-lin** [-lin] *n.* Ⓤ 《chem.》 a poisonous, colorless, oily liquid, usu. obtained from nitrobenzene, used in making dyes, drugs, etc. 아닐린. — *adj.* made from aniline. 아닐린의. [Arab. *al* the, *nil* indigo]

an·i·mad·ver·sion [æ̀nəmædvə́:rʃən, -ʒən] *n.* ⓊⒸ criticism; blame. 비평; 비난. [↓]

an·i·mad·vert [æ̀nəmædvə́:rt] *vi.* 《*on*》 comment critically blame. 비평하다; 비난하다. ¶ *~ on someone's faults* 아무의 과실을 비난하다. [L. *animus* mind, →advert]

:an·i·mal [ǽnəməl] *n.* Ⓒ **1** any living thing that can feel and move about by itself, such as a man, dog, bird, fish, insect, etc. 동물. **2** any animal other than man. 인간 이외의 동물. **3** a four-legged animal. 네발 짐승. **4** a person like a brute or beast. 짐승 같은 사람. — *adj.* of animals; like an animal. 동물〔짐승〕의; 짐승 같은. ¶ *~ spirits* 활기. [L. *anima* breath]

an·i·mal·cule [æ̀nəmǽlkju:l] *n.* an animal so small that it can be seen only by means of a microscope. 극미 동물(極微動物).

an·i·mate [ǽnəmèit] *vt.* (P6) **1** give life to (someone). …을 살리다. **2** make (someone or something) lively, gay, or energetic. 활기를 불어넣다. ¶ *Laughter animated his face for a moment.* 웃음으로 잠시 그의 얼굴에 생기가 돌았다. **3** give courage to (someone); inspire; encourage. (아무를) 격려〔고무〕하다. ¶ *Love for her mother animated Alice's work.* 어머니에 대한 사랑이 앨리스의 일에 활기를 불어넣었다 / *~ someone with fresh hope* 아무를 새로운 희망으로 고무하다. **4** move (someone) to action. 행동하게 하다.
—[ǽnəmit] *adj.* **1** living; alive. 살아 있는. **2** lively; gay. 활기찬; 활발한(opp. inanimate). [L. *anima* breath]

an·i·mat·ed [ǽnəmèitid] *adj.* **1** full of life or spirit; lively. 생기〔활기〕에 찬; 활발한. ¶ *~ conversation* 〔*discussion*〕 활발한 대화〔토

론) / *an ~ face* 생기 넘치는 얼굴. **2** seeming like something alive. 살아 있는 것 같은. ¶ *an ~ doll* 살아 있는 듯한 인형.

animated cartoon [∠−−− −∠] *n.* a motion-picture made by photographing a series of drawings. 만화 영화.

an·i·ma·tion [æ̀nəméiʃən] *n.* Ⓤ **1** liveliness; spirit; life. 생기; 활기. ¶ *speech delivered with ~* 활기차게 한 연설. **2** the process of preparing an animated cartoon. 만화 영화 (제작).

an·i·mism [ǽnəmìzəm] *n.* the belief that all objects have souls. 물활론(物活論)《목석 같은 것에도 영혼이 있다고 생각하는 신앙》. [→animus]

an·i·mos·i·ty [æ̀nəmásəti / -mɔ́s-] *n.* (*pl.* **-ties**) **1** Ⓤ 《*against, toward, between*》 hatred; dislike; hostility. 원한; 증오; 적의(敵意). ¶ *animosities between classes* 계층 간의 적대감 / *a deep-seated ~ between two sisters* 두 자매 간의 뿌리 깊은 증오심 / *have ~ against* 〔*toward*〕 *someone* 아무에게 적의를 품다 / *feel ~ against* …에 원한을 느끼다. **2** Ⓒ conduct of this nature. 원한·증오·혐오 등의 행위. [↓]

an·i·mus [ǽnəməs] *n.* ill-will; active dislike; animosity. 악의(惡意); 증오; 적의. ¶ *have* (*an*) *~ against someone* 아무에게 원한을 품다〔증오를 느끼다, 적대감을 보이다〕. [L. *animus* soul]

an·i·on [ǽnaiən] *n.* a negatively charged ion. 음(陰)이온. [Gk. *an-* not, *ion* going]

an·ise [ǽnis] *n.* **1** Ⓒ 《bot.》 a plant with sweet-smelling seeds. 아니스. **2** Ⓤ the seed of this plant. 아니스 열매. [Gk. *anison*]

an·i·seed [ǽnisìːd] *n.* Ⓤ the seed of anise, used both in medicine and in flavoring. 아니스 열매. [↑]

An·ka·ra [ǽŋkərə, áːŋ-] *n.* the capital of Turkey. 앙카라《터키의 수도》.

***an·kle** [ǽŋkl] *n.* Ⓒ **1** the joint which connects the foot with the leg. 복사뼈. **2** the slender part of the leg between this joint and the calf. 발목. ¶ *The dress came down to her ankles.* 드레스는 그녀 발목까지 내려왔다. [E.]

an·klet [ǽŋklit] *n.* Ⓒ **1** a sock that reaches just above the ankle. (복사뼈까지 오는) 양말. **2** an decorative ring or chain worn around the ankle. 발목 장식. [*ankle*]

an·ky·lo·sis [æ̀ŋkəlóusis] *n.* 《med.》 the stiffening of a joint. 관절의 강직. [Gk. *ankýlos* crooked]

Ann [æn], **An·na** [ǽnə] *n.* women's names. 여자의 이름.

ann. annals; annual; annuity.

an·na [áːnə] *n.* an Indian copper coin. 아나(cf. *rupee*). [Hind.]

an·nal·ist [ǽnəlist] *n.* Ⓒ a writer of annals. 연대기(年代記) 편자. [↓]

an·nals [ǽnəlz] *n. pl.* **1** a list of events recorded year by year. 연대기(年代記). **2** historical records. 역사 기록. **3** yearly reports published by an organization. 연보(年報). [L. *annus* year]

An·nap·o·lis [ənǽpəlis] *n.* the capital of Maryland, the seat of the U.S. Naval Academy. 아나폴리스《미국 Maryland 주의 주도(州都); 미국 해군 사관 학교 소재지》.

an·neal [əníːl] *vt.* (P6) harden by heating and gradually cooling. 담금질하다. [E. = bake]

an·nex [ənéks, æn-] *vt.* (P6,13) **1** add or join (something) to a larger thing. …을 병합하다. ¶ *The U.S. annexed Texas in 1845.* 미국은 1845년에 텍사스를 병합했다. **2** 《*to*》 attach. …을 부가하다. **3** appropriate. 점유(占有)하다. —[ǽneks, -iks] *n.* Ⓒ **1** something added. 부가물. **2** an addition to a building. (호텔 등의) 별관; 분교(分校). [L. *necto* bind]

an·nex·a·tion [æ̀nekséiʃən] *n.* **1** Ⓤ the act of joining or adding something to a large thing. 병합; 부가. **2** Ⓒ something added. 부가물; 병합지.

an·nexe [ǽneks] *n.* 《Brit.》 = annex.

an·ni·hi·late [ənáiəlèit] *vt.* (P6) **1** destroy completely. …을 전멸〔근절〕시키다. ¶ *We annihilated the enemy.* 적을 전멸시켰다. **2** put an end to (something). (법령 등)을 폐지하다. [ad-, L. *nihil* nothing]

an·ni·hi·la·tion [ənàiəléiʃən] *n.* Ⓤ complete destruction. 전멸; 근절.

·**an·ni·ver·sa·ry** [æ̀nəvə́ːrsəri] *n.* Ⓒ (*pl.* **-ries**) **1** the yearly return of the date on which an event happened. 기념일. ¶ *a wedding ~* 결혼 기념일. **2** the celebration of the yearly return of such a date. 기념 축제. — *adj.* **1** returning each year; annual. 예년(例年)의. **2** of such a date. 기념일의. [L. *annus* year, *verto* turn]

An·no Dom·i·ni [ǽnou dámənài / -dɔ́m-] *adv.* since Christ was born; in the year of our Lord. (그리스도) 기원후. 參考 A.D.로 생략. 기원전은 B.C. [L.]

an·no·tate [ǽnətèit] *vt.* (P6) add explaining notes or comments to (a book, etc.). …에 주석을 달다. ¶ *a book elaborately annotated* 자세한 주석을 붙인 책. — *vi.* 《*on, upon*》 make notes or comments on a book, etc. 주석을 달다. [→note]

an·no·ta·tion [æ̀nətéiʃən] *n.* **1** Ⓤ the act of annotating. 주석(을 닮). **2** Ⓒ a note added to a text. (텍스트 등의) 주(註). [↑]

:**an·nounce** [ənáuns] *vt.* (P6,11,12) **1** make (something) known publicly; tell. …을 발표하다; 알리다. ¶ *~ a dinner* 저녁 식사를 알리다 / *The morning paper announced the death of Henry Smith.* 조간 신문은 헨리 스미스의 사망을 보도했다. **2** make known the presence or coming of (someone); say the name of (a guest). (내방·내객)을 알리다. ¶ ~ *a visitor* 손님의 내방을 알리다. **3** make known to the senses or mind; give evidence to. (마음·감각에) 알리다; 암시하다; …의 증거가 되다. ¶ *An occasional shot announced the presence of the enemy.* 이따금씩 울리는 총 소리는 적군이 있다는 것을 입증했다. [ad-, L. *nuntius* messenger]

*__an·nounce·ment__ [ənáunsmənt] *n.* **1** Ⓒ a public notice; something made known. 공표; 발표. ¶ *make an ~ of* …을 공표하다 / *I have an ~ to make.* 나는 공표해야 할 것이 있다. **2** Ⓤ the act of announcing. 고지(告知).

*__an·nounc·er__ [ənáunsər] *n.* Ⓒ **1** a person who makes announcements over the radio or television. 아나운서. **2** a person who announces. 알리는(고지(告知)하는) 사람.

*__an·noy__ [ənɔ́i] *vt.* (P6,13) **1** trouble; irritate. …을 괴롭히다; 약올리다. ¶ *be annoyed at someone's remark* 아무의 말에 약이 오르다 / ~ *someone by perpetual questioning* 질문 공세로 아무를 괴롭히다 / *I am annoyed with him for doing such a thing.* 그가 그런 짓을 해서 난처하다 / *These flies are annoying me.* 이 파리들이 나를 괴롭히고 있다 / *He was much annoyed with her.* 그는 그녀 때문에 몹시 애먹었다. **2** harm. …을 해치다. [L. *in odio* in hatred]

an·noy·ance [ənɔ́iəns] *n.* **1** Ⓤ the act of annoying. 귀찮음. **2** Ⓤ the feeling of being annoyed. 곤혹(困惑). ¶ *a look of* ~ 곤혹스런 표정. **3** Ⓒ a thing or person that annoys. 귀찮은 것(사람).

an·noy·ing [ənɔ́iiŋ] *adj.* troublesome. 귀찮은. ¶ *The flies are very* ~. 파리는 매우 귀찮다 / *an ~ child* 귀찮은 아이 / *How ~!* 정말 이지 성가시군.

:__an·nu·al__ [ǽnjuəl] *adj.* **1** in a year; for a year; during a year. 한해의; 1년간의. ¶ *Mr. White's ~ income is $ 33,000.* 화이트 씨의 연간 소득은 3만 3천 달러이다. **2** coming or occurring once a year; yearly. 1년 1회의; 해마다의. **3** (of plants) living only one year or season. (식물이) 1년생의. ¶ *an ~ plant,* 1년생 식물(cf. *perennial*). **4** taking a year to complete. 1년 걸리는. — *n.* Ⓒ **1** a plant living for one year or season. 1년생 식물. **2** a book, magazine, etc. that is published once a year. 연보(年報); 연간서(年刊書). [L. *annus* year]

an·nu·al·ly [ǽnjuəli] *adv.* yearly; each year. 1년에 한 번; 매년.

an·nu·i·tant [ənjú:ətənt] *n.* a person who receives an annuity. 연금 수령자. [↓]

an·nu·i·ty [ənjú:əti] *n.* (*pl.* **-ties**) **1** Ⓒ a sum of money paid or given each year regularly. 연금. ¶ *a life* ~ 종신 연금. **2** Ⓤ the right to receive or the duty to pay such money. 연금 수령권; 연금 지급 의무. [→annual]

an·nul [ənʌ́l] *vt.* (**-nulled, -nul·ling**) (P6) destroy the effect of (a law, etc.); do away with (something); abolish; cancel. (법률 따위)를 폐지하다; …을 소멸시키다; 무효로 하다; 취소하다. ¶ ~ *a marriage* 결혼을 무효화(취소)하다. [→null]

an·nu·lar [ǽnjələr] *adj.* shaped or formed like a ring. 환상(環狀)의. [L. *anulus* ring]

annular eclipse [´-- -´] 《astron.》 an eclipse of the sun in which a ring-shape portion of its disk is visible. 금환식(金環蝕).

an·nul·ment [ənʌ́lmənt] *n.* ⓊⒸ the act of annulling or canceling. 폐지; 취소. [→annul]

an·num [ǽnəm] *n.* 《L.》 a year. 1년; 한 해. ***per annum,*** for each year. 1년에. ¶ *10 percent interest per* ~ 연 1할의 이자.

an·nun·ci·ate [ənʌ́nsièit] *vt.* (P6,11,12) announce. 고지하다. [→announce]

an·nun·ci·a·tion [ənʌ̀nsiéiʃən] *n.* **1** making known or announcing. 고시(告示). **2** 《*the A-*》 the announcement by the angel Gabriel to the Virgin Mary that she was to be the mother of Christ. 성모 영보(聖母領報). **3** 《*the A-*》 the festival in memory of this, Lady Day (March 25). 성모 영보 축일(祝日).

an·ode [ǽnoud] *n.* Ⓒ 《electr.》 the positive pole of a battery. (전지·전해조 따위의) 양극(陽極). [→cathode]

an·o·dyne [ǽnoudàin] *n.* Ⓒ a medicine that relieves pain. 진통제. — *adj.* relieving pain. 진통의. [Gk. *a-* not, *odunē* pain]

a·noint [ənɔ́int] *vt.* (P6,19) **1** put oil or ointment on (something or someone). …에 기름을(연고를) 바르다. ¶ ~ *one's hand with cold cream* 손에 콜드 크림을 바르다. **2** pour oil on the head of (someone) in a religious ceremony. 성유(聖油)를 발라 축성(祝聖)하다. ● **a·noint·ment** [-mənt] *n.* [in-, L. *ungo* anoint]

a·nom·a·lous [ənámələs / ənɔ́m-] *adj.* away from the common rule or type; irregular; abnormal. 불규칙적인; 변칙적인. ¶ ~ *verbs* 불규칙 동사. [Gk. *a-* not, *homalos* even]

a·nom·a·ly [ənáməli / ənɔ́m-] *n.* ⒸⓊ (*pl.* **-lies**) the state of being away from the common rule or type; irregularity; a person or thing that is abnormal. 변칙; 이례적(비정상적)인 사람(것); 특이성. ¶ *A wingless bird is an* ~. 날개 없는 새는 이례적인 것이다. [↑]

*__a·non__ [ənán / ənɔ́n] *adv.* 《*arch.*》 **1** soon. 곧. **2** at once; immediately. 즉시. [*on, one*] ***ever and anon,*** every now and then; occasionally. 때때로.

anon. anonymous.

a·non·y·mous [ənánəməs / ənɔ́nə-] *adj.* **1** without the author's name listed. 작자 불명의. **2** not known by name; nameless. 무

명의; 익명(匿名)의. ¶ *an ~ author* 무명〔익명〕의 저자. ● **an·o·nym·i·ty** [æ̀nəníməti] *n.* **a·non·y·mous·ly** [-li] *adv.* [Gk. *a-* not, *onoma* name]

a·noph·e·les [ənáfəlì:z / ənɔ́f-] *n.* the kind of mosquitoes whose bite causes malaria. 말라리아 모기. [Gk. =useless]

an·o·rak [ǽnəræ̀k, á:nərà:k] *n.* a skin or cloth jacket with an attached hood. 아노락《후드 달린 상의》. [Eskimo]

:an·oth·er [ənʌ́ðər] *adj.* **1** one more. 또 하나의; 하나 더의. ¶ *~ piece of cake* 케이크 또 한 개 / *in ~ nine months* 거기다 또 9개월이 있으면 / *Have ~ cup of coffee.* 커피 한 잔 더 드시죠 / *If you fail the first time, have ~ try.* 첫번에 실패하면 또 한 번 해 보아라. **2** different; of a different kind. 다른; 딴; 별개의. ¶ *at ~ time* 다른 때에; 언젠가 / *by ~ mail* 〔*post*〕 별편(別便)으로 / *I don't like this necktie show me ~ one.* 이 넥타이는 마음에 안 드는군요, 다른 것을 보여 주세요 / *This is quite ~ matter.* 이것은 전혀 별개의 문제다 / *He came home ~ man.* 그는 마치 딴 사람처럼 되어 돌아왔다 / *One man's meat is ~ man's poison.* 갑에겐 약이 을에겐 독(毒). **3** of the same kind, degree, class, etc.; second. …와 같은; 제2의. ¶ *He may turn out to be ~ Shakespeare.* 그는 셰익스피어와 같은 극작가가 될 것이다 / *He will be ~ Newton someday.* 그는 후일 제2의 뉴턴이 될 것이다.

— *pron.* **1** one more thing or person. 또 다른 한 개〔사람〕. ¶ *Try ~.* 또 하나 잡숴 보세요 / *I've had one cup of tea, but I should like ~.* 차 한잔 했는데 한 잔 더 마시고 싶다. **2** a different one; something different. 딴 것〔사람〕; 별개의 것. ¶ *I don't like this one. Show me ~.* 이것은 좋지 않아요, 딴 것을 보여 주세요 / *To know is one thing, to practise is ~.* 안다는 것과 실행한다는 것은 별개의 문제다 / *Is it brave to die for ~?* 남을 위해 죽는 것은 용감한 일인가. **3** one just like; one like the first. …도 또한 같은 것〔그런 것〕. ¶ *He is a fool, and his brother is ~.* 그는 바보인데, 그의 아우도 같은 바보이다. [*an, other*]

like another, commonplace; ordinary. 흔한; 평범한; 보통의. ¶ *It's a skill like ~.* 그건 평범한 기술이다.

one after another, in succession. 하나 또 하나; 차례로; (하나씩) 연이어. ¶ *They disappeared one after ~.* 그들은 한 사람 한 사람씩 차례로 사라졌다.

one another, each other. 서로. ¶ *Love one ~.* 서로 사랑하라.

a·nox·i·a [ænáksiə / ænɔ́k-] *n.* 《med.》 deficiency of oxygen. 산소 결핍증. [Gk. *a-* not, oxygen]

ans. answer; answered.

:an·swer [ǽnsər, á:n-] *vt.* **1** (P6,11,13,14) reply; respond to (a question). …라고 (대)답하다; …에 회답하다. ¶ *~ my question* 내 질문에 답하다 / *~ a speech* 답사를 하다 / *~ a letter* 편지에 회답하다 / *~ a teacher* 선생님께 대답하다 / *She answered that she knew something about it.* 그녀는 그것에 대해 무언가를 알고 있다고 대답했다 / *She didn't ~ a word to us.* 그녀는 우리에게 한 마디도 대답하지 않았다. **2** (P6) act in answer for; say or do in return; give back in some way; repay. …에 응하다; (말·행동으로) 되갚다. ¶ *~ a knock* 〔*the door*〕 노크 소리에 응하여 나오다 / *~ the bell* 〔*telephone*〕 초인종 소리에 나오다〔전화를 받다〕 / *~ blows with blows* 주먹에 주먹으로 응수하다 / *The door was answered by a girl.* (노크를 하니까) 소녀가 문을 열었다. **3** speak in one's defence against; prove (something) not to be true. (비난에) 응수하다; 자기 변호하다. ¶ *~ the charge* 고소에 응수하다. **4** (P6) be enough for (something); serve; fulfill; satisfy. (목적·요건)에 맞다〔합치하다〕; 충족시키다; 소용되다. ¶ *The knife answers my purpose.* 이 나이프면 된다 / *My prayer was answered.* 나의 기원은 이루어졌다 / *The boy will ~ your desires.* 그 아이는 당신 소원에 부응할 겁니다. **5** (P6) pay for; atone for; discharge. (빚 따위)를 갚다; …의 보상을 하다. ¶ *~ a debt* 부채를 갚다 / *~ damages* 손해를 보상하다. **6** (P6) conform to; match. 합치〔부합〕하다; 조화하다. ¶ *~ a description* 기술(記述)과〔인상서와, 설명서와〕 꼭 맞다 / *Her little toque answered the note of the dress.* 그녀의 귀여운 모자는 양복과 조화되고 있었다. **7** (P6) solve. (문제 따위)를 풀다; 해답하다. ¶ *~ examination questions* 시험 문제를 풀다.

— *vi.* (P1) **1** (P1,3) 《*to*》 reply. 대답하다; 회답하다. ¶ *~ to a question* 질문에 답하다 / *~ in the affirmative* 〔*negative*〕 긍정〔부정〕의 대답을 하다 / *They called again and again, but no one answered.* 그는 몇 번이고 불렀지만 아무도 대답이 없었다 / *'Yes,' she answered calmly.* '네' 하고 그녀는 조용히 대답했다 / *To the question he answered decidedly.* 그 질문에 그는 딱 잘라 대답했다. **2** (P1) respond; act in reply to. 응하다; 응답하다; 반응을 보이다. ¶ *~ with a nod* 고개를 끄덕여 동의하다 / *I knocked at the door, but nobody answered.* 문을 두드렸으나 아무도 나오지 않았다. **3** (P1,3) 《*to*》 correspond; conform; equal; fit. (인상서 요건)에 들어맞다; 부합〔합치, 일치〕하다. ¶ *His face answered to the description.* 그의 얼굴은 인상서와 일치했다. **4** (P1,3) 《*for*》 serve the purpose; succeed. (그런대로) 쓸 수 있다; 적합하다; 성공하다. ¶ *~ for a purpose* 목적에 맞다 / *I don't believe that sort of thing ever answers.* 그런 일은 잘 되리라고 절대로 생각지 않는다 / *Our plan has not answered.* 우리의 계획은 성공하지 못했다 / *Such an excuse will not ~.* 그러한 변명은 통하지 않는다.

answer back, 《*colloq.*》 answer in a rude manner. 말대꾸〔말대답〕하다. ¶ *Well-be-*

haved children do not ~ back when scolded. 품행이 좋은 아이들은 꾸중을 들을 때 말대꾸를 하지 않는다.

answer for, a) promise; be responsible for (something). …을 약속하다; …에 책임을 지다. ¶ *I can't ~ for his honesty.* 그의 정직 여부에 대해서는 책임을 질 수 없다. b) be punished for (something). …로 벌을 받다. ¶ *You must ~ for your telling a lie.* 거짓말을 한 벌을 받아야 한다.

answer to the name of, reply to; be named. …라고 불리다; …라는 이름이다. ¶ *The boy answers to the name of John.* 그 아이는 존이라고 한다.

— *n.* Ⓒ **1** something said or written in return; a reply. 대답; 회답. ¶ *an ~ to a question* 질문에 대한 대답 / *give an ~* 대답하다 / *wait for an ~* 대답〔회답〕을 기다리다 / *He gave me a quick ~.* 그는 조속한 회답을 보내 왔다 / *I called him on the telephone, but there was no ~.* 그에게 전화를 걸었으나 아무도 받는 사람이 없었다. **2** action in return. (행위에 의한) 응답; 보복; 보답. ¶ *In ~ he fired a shot.* 응답으로 총 한 발을 쏘았다 / *The invention is a good ~ to housewives.* 그 발명은 주부들에게 반응이 좋았다. **3** the reply to a problem; a solution. 해답; 정답. ¶ *an ~ to a riddle* 수수께끼의 해답. [E. =swear against]

an·swer·a·ble [ǽnsərəbəl, ɑ́:n-] *adj.* **1** 《*to, for*》 expected to give an account; responsible. 책임져야 할; 책임 있는. ¶ *the government ~ to the people* 국민에 대해 책임이 있는 정부 / *You are ~ to me for your conduct.* 너는 (나에 대해) 자신의 행동에 책임을 져야 한다 / *Mistakes have occurred, and someone must be ~.* 잘못이 발생했는데 누군가 책임을 져야 한다. **2** that can be answered. 대답〔회답〕할 수 있는. ¶ *a question ~ by mail* 우편으로 회답할 수 있는 질문. **3** 《*to*》 ⓐ proportionate; correlative. 비례하는; 상관하는. ⓑ corresponding to; suitable to. 일치하는; 맞는; 어울리는. ¶ *The results were not ~ to our hopes.* 결과는 우리 희망과는 일치하지 않았다.

:ant [ænt] *n.* Ⓒ a small insect that lives in crowds in tunnels under the ground or in wood. 개미. ¶ *work like an ~* 개미처럼 열심히 일하다. [O.E. *æmete*]

an't [ænt, ɑ:nt, eint / ɑ:nt] 《chiefly Brit. *colloq.*》 =am not; 《*colloq.*》 =ain't

an·tag·o·nism [æntǽgənìzəm] *n.* Ⓤ dislike or opposition between two persons or groups of people; hostility; hatred. 반대; 반목; 적대; 적의. ¶ *arouse someone's ~* 아무의 적대감을 일으키다 / *be* 〔*come into*〕 *~ with* …와 반목하게 되다 / *the ~ between two persons* 〔*races*〕 두 사람〔민족〕간 반목. [→antagonize]

an·tag·o·nist [æntǽgənist] *n.* Ⓒ a person who fights or struggles with another; a rival; an opponent. 적대자; 경쟁 상대.

an·tag·o·nis·tic [æntæ̀gənístik], **-ti·cal** [-əl] *adj.* 《*to*》 opposing; hostile. 반대의; 적대하는. ● **an·tag·o·nis·ti·cal·ly** [-kəli] *adv.*

an·tag·o·nize [æntǽgənàiz] *vt.* (P6) **1** make (someone) an enemy. 적으로 만들다. **2** oppose. 반대하다. [anti-, Gk. *agōn* con test]

·ant·arc·tic [æntɑ́:rktik] *adj.* near the South Pole; of the south polar region. 남극의(opp. arctic). — *n.* 《*the A-*》 the South Pole; the region around the South Pole. 남극 (지방). [anti-, →arctic]

Ant·arc·ti·ca [æntɑ́:rktikə] *n.* the continent around the South Pole. 남극 대륙.

an·te [ǽnti] *n.* a stake put up by each poker player before drawing new cards. 판돈. — *vt.* put up (an ante); pay up. 판돈을 내다; 치르다. [L.]

an·te- [ǽnti-] *pref.* before. '…의 전의'의 뜻 (opp. post-). ¶ *anteroom* 대기실. [L.]

ant·eat·er [ǽntì:tər] *n.* Ⓒ 《zool.》 an animal with a long, slender tongue that feeds chiefly on ants. 개미핥기. [*ant*]

an·te-bel·lum [æ̀ntibéləm] *adj.* **1** before the war. 전전(戰前)의. **2** 《U.S.》 before the Civil War. 남북 전쟁 전의. [ante-, L. *bellum* war]

an·te·ced·ent [æ̀ntəsí:dənt] *adj.* 《*to*》 going before. 앞서는; 선행의. — *n.* Ⓒ **1** a person or thing that goes before. 앞서는 것〔사람〕. **2** 《*pl.*》 an ancestor; one's past life. 선조; 신원(身元); 경력. ¶ *inquire into someone's antecedents* 아무의 전력〔신원〕을 조사하다. **3** 《gram.》 a noun, pronoun, etc., that is followed by a relative pronoun or relative adverb. 선행사(先行詞). [ante-, L. *cedo* go]

an·te·cham·ber [ǽntitʃèimbər] *n.* Ⓒ a room leading into a larger room; a waiting room. 대기실. [ante-, →chamber]

an·te·date [ǽntidèit, ⌐⌐⌐] *vt.* (P6) **1** date before the true time. 실제보다도 이전의 날짜를 매기다. **2** happen before. …보다 이전에 일어나다. **3** accelerate. 가속하다. **4** anticipate. 예상하다. — *n.* a date earlier than the true date; a prior date. 사전 일부(事前日附). [ante-, →date]

an·te·di·lu·vi·an [æ̀ntidilú:viən / -vjən] *adj.* **1** of the time before the Flood. 노아의 홍수 이전의. **2** very old; oldfashioned. 태고적의; 예스러운; 고풍의. ¶ *The old woman wore an ~ bonnet and shawl.* 노부인은 고풍의 보닛과 숄을 걸치고 있었다. — *n.* Ⓒ **1** a man or animal that lived before the Flood. 노아의 홍수 이전의 사람〔동물〕. **2** 《*fig.*》 a very old person. 매우 늙은 사람; 파파 노인. [ante-, L. *luo* wash, →deluge]

an·te·lope [ǽntəlòup] *n.* Ⓒ (*pl.* **-lopes** or *collectively* **-lope**) 《zool.》 an animal like a deer which can move very quickly. 영양. [Gk.]

an·te me·rid·i·em [ǽnti mərídiəm] *adj.* before noon. 오전(의)(opp. post meridiem). 參考 a.m. 또는 A.M.으로 생략함.

[L.]
an·te·mun·dane [æntimʌ́ndein] *adj.* before the creation of the world. 개벽 전의 [ante-, *mundane*]
an·te·na·tal [æntinéitl] *adj.* before birth. 출생 전의. [ante-, *natal;* →nascent]
an·ten·na [ænténə] *n.* Ⓒ **1** (*pl.* **-nas**) wires or rods used in radio and television for receiving or sending out electric waves. 안테나. **2** (*pl.* **-nae**) a feeler on the heads of insects, lobsters, etc. 촉각; 더듬이. [L.=sail-yard]
an·ten·nae [ænténi:] *n.* pl. of **antenna.**
an·te·pe·nult [æntipí:nʌlt / ǽn-] *n.* 《phon.》 the third syllable from the end of a word. 끝에서 세 번째 음절. — *adj.* third from the end. 끝에서 세 번째의. [ante-, → penult]
an·te·ri·or [æntíəriər] *adj.* **1** fore; toward the front. 전면의. **2** 《*to*》 coming before; earlier. (시간·장소가) 앞의(opp. posterior). [L. *ante* before]
an·te·room [ǽntirù(:)m] *n.* Ⓒ a room leading into a large room; a waiting room. 대기실; 대합실. [ante-]
an·them [ǽnθəm] *n.* Ⓒ **1** a song of praise. 찬가(讚歌). ¶ *a national* ~ 국가(國歌). **2** a sacred song, usu. with words taken from the Bible; a hymn. 찬송가. [→antiphon]
an·ther [ǽnθər] *n.* Ⓒ 《bot.》 the top part of the stamen of a flower. 약(葯); 꽃밥. [Gk. *anthos* flower]
ant hill [ˊ ˋ] *n.* a pile of earth heaped up by ants in digging their tunnels to their nest. 개밋둑. [*ant*]
an·thol·o·gist [ænθálədʒist / -θɔ́l-] *n.* a person who makes an anthology. 명시선(名詩選) 편자(編者). [↓]
an·thol·o·gy [ænθálədʒi / -θɔ́l-] *n.* Ⓒ (*pl.* **-gies**) a collection of poems or prose passages by various authors. 명시선(名詩選); 명문집(名文集). [Gk. *anthos* flower, *legō* gather]
An·tho·ny [ǽntəni, -θə-] *n.* a man's name. 남자 이름. 參考 애칭은 Tony.
an·thra·ces [ǽnθrəsì:z] *n.* pl. of **anthrax.**
an·thra·cite [ǽnθrəsàit] *n.* Ⓤ hard coal that gives out great heat and little smoke or flame. 무연탄. [Gk.=coal]
an·thrax [ǽnθræks] *n.* (*pl.* **-thra·ces**) Ⓤ a disease of cattle, sheep, etc. that can spread and that usu. causes death. 탄저병(炭疽病). [↑]
an·thro·po- [ǽnθrəpou-, pə-] *pref.* having to do with man. '사람, 인류(학)'의 뜻. [Gk. *ánthrōpos* human being]
an·thro·poid [ǽnθrəpɔ̀id] *adj.* man-like; resembling man. 사람을 닮은. ¶ *the* ~ *apes* 유인원(類人猿). — *n.* Ⓒ a man-like ape, such as a chimpanzee or gorilla. 유인원. [anthropo-]
an·thro·po·log·ic [æ̀nθrəpəládʒik / -lɔ́dʒ-], **-i·cal** [-kəl] *adj.* of anthropology. 인류학(人類學)의.
an·thro·po·lo·gist [æ̀nθrəpálədʒist / -pɔ́l-] *n.* Ⓒ a person who specializes in anthropology. 인류학자.
an·thro·pol·o·gy [æ̀nθrəpálədʒi / -pɔ́l-] *n.* Ⓤ the science of the origin and development of mankind. 인류학.
an·ti [ǽnti, -tai] *n.* 《*colloq.*》 one who is opposed. 반대자. [Gk.]
an·ti- [ǽnti-, -tai-] *pref.* **1** against; opposed to. '대항, 반대'의 뜻. ¶ *anti-aircraft* 방공(防空)의 / *anti-Japan* 반일의. **2** not. '비(非)'의 뜻. ¶ *antisocial* 반사회적인. **3** preventing an effect. '항(抗)'의 뜻. ¶ *antitoxin* 항독소. 參考 모음으로 시작되는 말이나 고유명사·형용사에 붙는 경우에는 보통 하이픈을 붙임. [Gk.]
an·ti-air·craft [æntiɛ́ərkræ̀ft, -krɑ̀:ft, æntai-] *adj.* used in defense against enemy aircraft. 방공(防空)의. ¶ *an* ~ *gun* 고사포(高射砲). [anti-]
an·ti·bi·ot·ic [æ̀ntibaiátik, -tai- / æ̀ntibaiɔ́t-] *n.* Ⓒ a chemical product that kills or weakens germs, such as penicillin and streptomycin. 항생(抗生) 물질. — *adj.* able to kill or weaken germs. 항생의. [anti-, Gk. *bios* life]
an·ti·bod·y [ǽntibàdi / -bɔ̀di] *n.* Ⓒ (*pl.* **-bod·ies**) 《physiol.》 a substance in a person's blood that kills or weakens germs and other poisons. 항독소(抗毒素); 항체(抗體). [anti-]
an·tic [ǽntik] *adj.* 《*arch.*》 grotesque; strange. 기괴한; 기묘한. — *n.* 《often *pl.*》 a grotesquely ludicrous act. 기괴한(익살맞은) 짓. ¶ *laugh at someone's antics* 아무의 기괴한 짓을 보고 웃다. [L. *anticuus* ancient →antique]
antic hay, a kind of old country dance. 기묘한 옛날 시골 춤.
an·ti·christ [ǽntikràist] *n.* Ⓒ 《often *A-*》 an enemy of Christ; an opponent of Christ. 그리스도의 적; 그리스도 반대자. [anti-]
an·ti·chris·tian [æntikrístʃən, -tai- / æntikrístjən] *adj.* 《often *A-*》 of an Antichrist; opposed to Christianity. 반(反)그리스도의; 반(反)기독교의. — *n.* Ⓒ an opponent of Christianity. 기독교 반대자. [anti-]
***an·tic·i·pate** [æntísəpèit] *vt.* (P6,11) **1** ⓐ guess (something) correctly before it happens; foresee. …을 예기(예상)하다. ¶ ~ *things that may happen* 있을지도 모를 일들을 미리 예상하다. ⓑ consider in advance and satisfy. 미리 고려하여 만족시키다. ¶ ~ *someone's wishes* 아무의 바라는 바를 미리 알아차려서 하다. **2** go ahead of (another) in doing something; forestall. 상대의 움직임을 앞지르다; 선수를 치다. ¶ ~ *the*

enemy's move 적의 움직임에 선수를 치다. **3** ⓐ expect; look forward to; be sure of. 기대하다; 확신하다. ¶ ~ *a favorable decision* 바람직한 결정이 이루어지기를 기대하다 / ~ *someone's arrival with pleasure* 아무의 도착을 즐거운 마음으로 고대하다 / *I ~ being able to enjoy his company.* 그와 교제할 수 있기를 기대하고 있다. ⓑ realize and suffer from in advance. 미리 각오하다. ¶ ~ *troubles* 어려움들을 미리 각오하다. **4** see in advance and take steps to meet. 미리 예상하고 대책을 세우다. ¶ ~ *a long and heated argument* 장황하고도 열띤 토론에 대비한 대책을 세우다. **5** cause to happen earlier; accelerate. (시기를) 앞당기다. ¶ ~ *one's departure* 출발을 앞당기다. **6** take or make use of in advance. 미리 선불〔가불〕하다. ¶ ~ *one's next month's salary* 다음 달 봉급을 가불해 받다. [ante, L. *capio* take]

an·tic·i·pa·tion [æntìsəpéiʃən] *n.* Ⓤ the act of anticipating. 예기(豫期); 기대. ¶ *wait for something with ~* 기대감으로써 …을 기다리다.

in anticipation, previously. 미리; 사전에.

in anticipation of, looking forward to. …을 기대〔예기〕하고; …을 내다보고. ¶ *in ~ of an increase in salary* 승급을 예견하고.

an·ti·cli·max [æ̀ntikláimæks] *n.* 《rhet.》 a sudden and laughable loss of force, in a drama, an action, or a speech. 점강법(漸降法). ¶ *The play ended in an ~.* 그 연극은 용두 사미로 끝났다(opp. climax; cf. *bathos*). [anti-, *climax*]

an·ti·cy·clone [æ̀ntisáikloun] *n.* Ⓒ a circulation of winds moving outward from a center of high pressure; the area of high pressure. 역선풍(逆旋風); 고기압권(高氣壓圈). [anti-, →*cyclone*]

an·ti·dote [ǽntidòut] *n.* Ⓒ 《*to, for, against*》 **1** a medicine which works against a poison. 해독제(解毒劑). ¶ *Milk is an ~ for some poisons.* 우유는 일부 독물의 해독제이다 / *bane and ~* 맹독과 해독. **2** a remedy for any evil. 교정(矯正) 수단. [anti-, Gk. *didōmi* give]

an·ti·freeze [ǽntifrì:z] *n.* a substance added to a liquid to prevent it from freezing. 부동액(不凍液). [anti-, *freeze*]

an·ti·fric·tion [æ̀ntifríkʃən, -tai-] *n.* ⓊⒸ lubricant. 감마재(減摩材)(cf. *lubricant*). [anti-, →L. *frico* rub]

an·ti·his·ta·mine [æ̀ntihístəmì:n] *n.* a drug used against certain allergies. 항(抗)알레르기제(劑). [anti-]

an·ti·knock [æ̀ntinák, -tai- / æ̀ntinɔ́k] *n.* any material reducing noises. (엔진의) 내폭제(耐爆劑). [anti-]

An·til·les [æntíli:z] *n. pl.* 《*the ~*》 a chain of islands in the West Indies, including Cuba, Haiti, Jamaica and Puerto Rico. 앤틸리스 제도(諸島).

an·ti·mo·ny [ǽntəmòuni] *n.* Ⓤ 《chem.》 a silvery-white metal that is often combined with tin and lead. 안티몬. [Arab.]

an·tip·a·thy [æntípəθi] *n.* ⓊⒸ (*pl.* **-thies**) **1** 《*to, against*》 a strong dislike; a feeling against someone or something. (뿌리 깊고 본능적인) 혐오; 반감; 악감정(opp. sympathy). ¶ *racial ~* 인종적인 반감 / *have an ~ against* 〔*to*〕 *someone* 아무에게 악감을 품다 / *There was an instinctive ~ between the two.* 둘 사이엔 본능적인 혐오감이 있었다. **2** the object of such dislike. 혐오하는 것〔대상〕. ¶ *Snakes are my ~.* 뱀은 내가 싫어하는 것이다. [anti-, →pathos]

an·tip·o·des [æntípədì:z] *n. pl.* **1** places on exactly opposite sides of the earth. (지구상의) 대척지(對蹠地). **2** the direct opposite; two opposite or contrary things. 정반대(의 것). ¶ *be at the exact ~ of opinion* 의견이 정반대이다. [anti-, Gk. *pous* foot]

an·ti·pol·lu·tion [æ̀ntipəlú:ʃən, -tai-] *adj.* against pollution. 오염(汚染) 방지의. [anti-]

an·ti·quar·i·an [æ̀ntikwέəriən] *adj.* of the study of ancient things. 골동품 연구의. — *n.* Ⓒ a person who studies or collects ancient things. 골동품 연구가〔수집가〕. [↓]

an·ti·quar·y [ǽntikwèri] *n.* Ⓒ (*pl.* **-quaries**) a person who studies, collects, or sells ancient things. 골동품 연구가〔수집가〕; 골동품상. [→antique]

an·ti·quat·ed [ǽntikwèitid] *adj.* **1** old-fashioned; out-of-date. 시대에 뒤진. ¶ *be ~ in one's ideas.* 생각이 고루하다. **2** old; aged. 오래된; 낡은. ¶ ~ *furniture* 오래된 가구; 고(古)가구 / *an ~ textbook* 오래된 교과서. [↓]

an·tique [æntí:k] *adj.* **1** belonging to an age long past; ancient. 고대의. **2** old-fashioned. 구식의(opp. modern). ¶ *a dress of ~ design* 디자인이 구식인 드레스. — *n.* Ⓒ **1** something made long ago. 골동품. **2** 《*the ~*》 the antique style, usu. Greek or Roman, esp. in art. 고대 미술 양식《특히 고대 그리스·로마의》. ¶ *a lover of the ~* 고대 미술 양식 애호가. [L. *antiquus*]

an·tiq·ui·ty [æntíkwəti] *n.* (*pl.* **-ties**) **1** Ⓤ ancientness. 오래됨. **2** Ⓤ ancient times, esp. before the Middle Ages. 고대《특히 중세 이전》. ¶ *Homer and Caesar were two great men of ~.* 호머와 카이사르는 고대의 위인이었다. **3** 《usu. *pl.*》 the things of ancient times. 고대의 유물. ¶ *Greek antiquities* 그리스의 유물. [↑]

an·ti·sep·tic [æ̀ntəséptik] *adj.* having the power of killing harmful germs. 살균〔방부〕성의; 소독의. — *n.* Ⓒ a thing that kills germs. 살균〔방부〕제; 소독약. ¶ *Wash it with ~.* 그것을 살균제로 세탁해라. [anti-, Gk. *sēpō* rot]

an·ti·slav·er·y [æ̀ntisléivəri, -tai-] *n.* Ⓤ opposition to slavery. 노예(奴隸) 제도 반대. — *adj.* opposed to slavery. 노예 제도 반대

의. ¶ *an ~ movement* 노예 제도 반대 운동. [anti-]

an·ti·so·cial [æ̀ntisóuʃəl, -tai-] *adj.* **1** opposed to companionship with other people; not sociable. 비(非)사교적인. **2** opposed to social order. 반사회적인. ¶ *Crimes are ~ acts.* 범죄는 반사회적 행위이다. [anti-, L. *socius* comrade]

an·tith·e·ses [æntíθəsìːz] *n.* pl. of **antithesis.**

an·tith·e·sis [æntíθəsis] *n.* (*pl.* **-tith·e·ses**) **1** Ⓤ《*of, between*》opposition; contrast. 반대; 대조(對照). **2** Ⓤ《*of, to*》the direct opposite. 정반대. ¶ *A is the* (*very*) *~ of B in character.* A는 성격이 B의 정반대이다. **3** Ⓒ a contrast of idea, such as "Give me liberty, or give me death." 대조법. [anti-, →*thesis*]

an·ti·tox·in [æ̀ntitáksin / -tɔ́k-] *n.* Ⓒ a substance formed in the body to resist a poison or the effects of germs. 항독소(抗毒素). [anti-, →toxic]

an·ti·trust [æ̀ntitrʌ́st, -tai-] *adj.*《comm.》opposed to trusts. 반(反)트러스트의. [anti-]

ant·ler [ǽntlər] *n.* Ⓒ **1** the horn of a deer. 사슴의 뿔. **2** a branch of a deer's horn. 사슴 뿔의 가지. [L. *ante* before, *oculus* the eye]

ant·li·on [ǽntlàiən] *n.* Ⓒ an insect which, early in its life, digs a pit in which it lies in wait for ants or other insects. 개미귀신. [→ant]

an·to·nym [ǽntənim] *n.* Ⓒ a word that has the opposite meaning to another word. 반대어(opp. synonym). ¶ *'Black' is the ~ of 'white'.* 흑(黑)은 백(白)의 반대어다. [anti-, Gk. *onoma* name, →synonym]

an·tra [ǽntrə] *n.* pl. of **antrum.**

an·trum [ǽntrəm] *n.* (*pl.* **-tra**) a cavity in the body, esp. one in upper-jaw bone. (몸 특히 상악골의) 강(腔). [Gk. *antron* cave]

Ant·werp [ǽntwəːrp] *n.* a seaport in north Belgium, on the Scheldt. 앤트워프《벨기에의 항구》.

A·nu·ra [ənjúːrə] *n. pl.*《zool.》amphibians without tail. 무미류(無尾類). [Gk. *an-* without, *oura* tail]

a·nus [éinəs] *n.* Ⓒ the opening at the lower end of the body through which waste substance goes out. 항문. [L. = ring]

an·vil [ǽnvəl] *n.* Ⓒ a block of iron or steel on which a blacksmith hammers metal into shape. (대장간의) 모루. [E.]

•**anx·i·e·ty** [æŋzáiəti] *n.* Ⓤ **1** ⓐ fear of what may happen. 걱정; 우려. ¶ *be full of ~* 걱정이 많다 / *feel ~ about one's health* 〔*someone's safety*〕 자신의 건강을〔아무의 안부를〕 걱정하다 / *~ for* 〔*concerning*〕 *the future* 미래에 대한 우려. ⓑ a cause or source of such uneasy feeling; a worry. 걱정거리. ¶ *have many anxieties* 걱정거리가 많다 / *The son is her constant ~.* 아들은 그녀의 끊임없는 걱정거리다. **2**《*for, to do*》strong desire. 갈망; 열망. ¶ *~ for one's success* 성공에 대한 갈망 / *her ~ to please him* 그를 기쁘게 해 주려는 그녀의 열의. [L. *ango* cause pain]

:**anx·ious** [ǽŋkʃəs] *adj.* **1** afraid of what may happen; deeply troubled or worried. 걱정하는〔되는〕; 걱정에 싸인; 불안한. ¶ *~ about the future* 미래에 대해 불안한 / *an ~ mother* 노상 걱정이 떠나지 않는 어머니 / *be ~ over someone's safety* 아무의 안부를 걱정하다 / *spend ~ days and nights* 걱정스러운 밤낮을 보내다. **2**《*for, to do*》desiring very strongly. 열망하는. ¶ *be ~ for peace* 평화를 갈망하다. ●**anx·ious·ness** [-nis] *n.* [↑]

anx·ious·ly [ǽŋkʃəsli] *adv.* with anxiety. 걱정하여. ¶ *wait ~ for news* 마음을 졸이며 소식을 기다리다 / *look ~ at a sick baby* 앓는 아기를 걱정스러운 눈으로 보다. [↑]

:**an·y** [éni, əni] *adj.* **1** ⓐ no matter which; every. 어떤; 모든. ¶ *Any book will do.* 어떤 책이라도 좋다 / *Any boy can do it.* 어떤 소년이라도 그것을 할 수 있다 / *Any pupil knows it.* 모든 학생이 그것을 알고 있다 / *You can get this book at ~ bookshop.* 어떤 서점에서건 이 책을 구할 수 있다. ⓑ one out of many. (많은 중에서) 어떤. ¶ *Choose ~ book you like.* 어떤 책이든 네가 좋아하는 것을 골라라. **2**《in *interrogative* or *subjunctive*》some. 얼마간의; 다소의; 좀. ¶ *Have you ~ money with you?* 돈 좀 가진 거 있나 / *If you have ~ interesting book, lend it to me.* 재미있는 책 좀 있으면 빌려 다오. **3**《in *negative*》even one; even a little. 하나도; 조금도. ¶ *I haven't ~ money.* 나는 돈이 조금도 없다 / *I haven't seen ~ papers today.* 오늘은 신문을 하나도 못 읽었다. **4** enough to be noticed. 이렇다 할. ¶ *without ~ difficulty* 힘 안 들이고; 쉽게 / *I am so busy that I have hardly ~ leisure.* 나는 하도 바빠서 거의 여가란 없다.

at any rate = ***in any case,*** whatever happens. 무슨 일이 있어도; 하여튼. ¶ *I will come at ~ rate.* 무슨 일이 있어도 나는 간다 / *You may rely on me in ~ case.* 하여튼 저를 믿으셔도 좋을 겁니다.

— *pron.* **1**《usu. *pl.*》any person or persons. 누군가; 누구든; 어떤 사람들이든. ¶ *Were ~ of you absent yesterday?* 어제 누군가 결석한 사람이 있나 / *Any are free to express an opinion.* 누구든 의견을 말하는 것은 자유다. **2**《*sing.* and *pl.*》ⓐ anything or things. 무언가; 무엇〔어느 것〕이든. ¶ *Take ~ you like.* 어느 것이든 마음에 드는 것을 가져라 / *You can take these eggs if you want ~.* 원하신다면 이 달걀들을 잡수셔도 됩니다. ⓑ any part, quantity, number. 어떤 것; 얼마(의 수량). ¶ *I don't think that ~ is* 〔*are*〕 *left.* 얼마쯤이고 남아 있다고는 생각지 않는다 / *Do you want ~ of these books?* 이 책들 중 어느

것을 원하느냐.

— *adv.* **1** to some extent; somewhat. 얼마쯤; 조금은. ¶ *Is she ~ better today?* 그녀는 오늘 좀 괜찮습니까. **2** 《usu. in *interrogative* or *subjunctive*》 in some degree; at all. 조금도. ¶ *If she is ~ better, let me know.* 그녀에게 조금이라고 차도가 있으면 알려 주시오 / *He couldn't go ~ further.* 그는 조금도 앞으로 더 나아갈 수 없었다 / *Could you sleep ~ last night?* 간밤에 좀 잘 수 있었나. [→one]

:an·y·body [énibàdi, -bʌ̀di / -bɔ̀di] *pron.* any person; anyone. 누군가. ¶ *~ else's book* 누군가 다른 사람의 책 / *Anybody can do that.* 그것은 아무라도 할 수 있다 / *I didn't know ~.* 나는 아무도 알아보지 못했다 / *I haven't seen ~.* 나는 아무도 보지 못했다 / *Does ~ know?* 누가 알고 있을까.

— *n.* Ⓒ **1** an important person. 중요한 인물; 유명인. ¶ *Everybody who was ~ was there.* 다소 알려진 사람은 모두 거기 와 있었다 / *I don't think she was ~ before her marriage.* 나는 그녀가 결혼하기까진 유명인이었다고 생각지 않는다. **2** 《often *pl.*》 not important persons. 무명의 사람들. ¶ *Two or three anybodies.* 변변찮은 두세 사람. [→one]

·an·y·how [énihàu] *adv.* **1** in any way whatever; by any means. 어쨌든; 어떻게든; 어떤 방법(식)으로든. ¶ *This should be done in a few days ~.* 이것은 며칠 내로 어떻게 해서든지 끝내야 한다 / *I've tried, but I can't manage it ~.* 나는 해 보았으나 도무지 할 수가 없다. **2** in any case; at all events; whatever happens. 어쨌든; 좌우간; 무슨 일이 있어도. ¶ *Let's try it again ~.* 어쨌든 그것을 다시 한 번 해 보자. **3** carelessly. 아무렇게나. ¶ *do a thing ~* 일을 아무렇게나 하다. [→one]

all anyhow, **a**) carelessly. 아무렇게나. **b**) in any way. 어쨌든; 무슨 일이 있어도.

feel anyhow, 《*colloq.*》 feel ill. 어쩐지 컨디션이 좋지 않다.

:an·y·one [éniwʌ̀n, -wən] *pron.* any person; anybody. 누군가; 누구든. ¶ *Can ~ answer my question?* 누구든 내 질문에 대답할 수 있겠어.

:an·y·thing [éniθìŋ] *pron.* **1** anything; a thing of any kind. 아무것이나(이든); 아무것도. ¶ *Anything will do.* 아무것이나 좋다 / *You may take ~ you like.* 무엇이든 좋아하는 것을 가져도 좋다. **2** 《in *negative, interrogative,* and *conditional sentences*》 something. 무엇(인가); 아무것이나(도); …한 것. ¶ *I don't know ~ about it.* 그것에 대해선 아무것도 모른다 / *Can you think of ~ better?* 좀 더 나은 것을 생각할 수 있습니까 / *If there is ~ I can do for you, please let me know.* 당신을 위해 내가 할 수 있는 것이 있다면 알려 주시오.

anything but, far from; not in the least. …는커녕 …한; 조금도(결코) …아닌. ¶ *That little bridge is ~ but safe.* 저 작은 다리는 조금도 안전하지가 않다.

— *adv.* in any degree; at all. 조금은(도); 적어도. ¶ *Is your doll ~ like mine?* 네 인형이 조금은 내 것과 같으니 / *He is not ~ better.* 그는 조금도 낫지가 않다.

:an·y·way [éniwèi] *adv.* **1** in any manner or way. 아무리 해도; 도무지. ¶ *I cannot understand it ~.* 나에겐 그것이 도무지 이해가 안 간다. **2** by any means; in any case. 어떻게든; 어쨌든. ¶ *I'll call you up again ~.* 여하튼 다시 한 번 전화 드리죠. **3** carelessly. 아무렇게나.

:an·y·where [éni*h*wɛ̀ər] *adv.* to, in, or at any place. 어딘가로; 어디든. ¶ *~ else* 어딘가 다른 곳에 / *Did you go ~ after the party?* 파티 후에 어딘가 가셨습니까.

an·y·wise [éniwàiz] *adv.* in any way; at all. 아무리 해도; 결코.

ANZUS [ǽnzəs] *n.* Australia, New Zealand and the U.S. 앤저스. 參考 태평양 공동 방위 체제의 하나.

a/o account of. …이기 때문에.

A one, A 1 [éi wʌ́n] *adj.* 《*colloq.*》 first-rate; first-class; superior. 일류의; 최상급의. ¶ *~ tea* 최상의 차 / *an ~ musician* 일류 음악가.

a·o·rist [éiərist] *n.* 《gram.》 a tense of Greek verbs indicating simple past time. 부정(不定) 과거. [Gk. =undefined]

a·or·ta [eiɔ́ːrtə] *n.* (*pl.* **a·or·tae**) the artery that carries blood from the left side of the heart. 대동맥. [Gk. *aeirō* lift]

a·or·tae [eiɔ́ːrtiː] *n.* pl. of **aorta.**

A.P. Associated Press. (미국의) 연합 통신사.

a·pace [əpéis] *adv.* quickly; speedily. 빨리; 급히. [a(-)]

A·pach·e [əpǽtʃi] *n.* (*pl.* **-es** or **A·pach·e**) the name of an American Indian people. 아파치족. [Amer-Ind.]

a·pach·e [əpáːʃ, əpǽʃ] *n.* a dangerous thief or murderer in Paris. (파리의) 위험한 강도; 깡패; 살인자. [↓]

:a·part [əpáːrt] *adv.* **1** in or into pieces. 낱낱으로; 분해하여. **2** separated from someone or something; independently. 떨어져; 독립하여. ¶ *They live ~.* 그들은 서로 떨어져 산다. [ad-, →part]

apart from, **a**) separated from. …와 떨어져. ¶ *The house stood ~ from others.* 그 집은 다른 집들과 떨어져 있다. **b**) except for; not considering. …은 별문제로 하고; …외에는. ¶ *Apart from newspapers I read very little.* 신문 외에는 거의 읽지 않는다.

joking* [*jesting*] *apart, not trying to joke, but speaking seriously. 농담은 집어치우고.

set apart, keep for some special purpose. …을 위해 따로 떼어 두다. ¶ *He sets some money ~ for a holiday each year.* 그는 매년 휴가를 위해 얼마씩의 돈을 따로 떼어 둔다.

take something apart, break up. (기계 따위)를 분해하다. ¶ *The boy took the watch ~ to see how it worked.* 소년은 시계가 어떻게 움

직이나 보려고 분해했다.

a·part·heid [əpɑ́:rthèit, -hàit] *n.* (policy of) racial segregation. 인종 분리 (정책). [Afrikaans]

:a·part·ment [əpɑ́:rtmənt] *n.* Ⓒ a room or a few rooms to live in. (살림하는) 방; 아파트. ¶ *have* 〔*look for*〕 *a nice* ~ 좋은 아파트를 가지고 있다〔구하다〕. [It. *a parte* apart]

apartment house [-ˊ-- ˋ] *n.* 《U.S.》 a building divided into many apartments. 아파트; 공동 주택.

ap·a·thet·ic [æ̀pəθétik] *adj.* lacking in feeling or interest; unemotional; indifferent. 무감각〔무관심〕한; 냉담〔냉정〕한. [↓]

ap·a·thy [ǽpəθi] *n.* Ⓤ lack of feeling or interest; indifference. 무감각; 무관심; 냉담. ¶ *the* ~ *of the people to the election* 선거에 대한 국민의 무관심. [Gk. *a-* not-, →pathos]

ape [eip] *n.* Ⓤ **1** a large monkey without a tail, such as a chimpanzee or a gorilla. 유인원(類人猿). **2** any monkey. 원숭이. **3** a person who imitates. 흉내내는 사람. — *vt.* (P6) imitate comically; mimic. …을 흉내내다. ● **ap·er·y** [éipəri] *n.* **ap·ish** [éipiʃ] *adj.* [E.]

a·peak [əpí:k] *adv.* in a vertical position. 수직으로 되어. [ad-, →peak]

a·pe·ri·ent [əpíəriənt] *adj.* emptying the bowels. 변통(便通)이 잘 되는. — *n.* Ⓒ a medicine used to empty the bowels; a laxative. 하제(下劑). [L. *aperio* open]

a·per·i·tive [əpérətiv], **a·pér·i·tif** [ɑ:pèrití:f, əpèr-] 《F.》 an alcoholic appetizer. 식전(食前)에 마시는 술; 반주. [↑]

ap·er·ture [ǽpərtʃùər, -tʃər] *n.* Ⓒ a small opening; a hole; a gap. 구멍; 틈새. ¶ *an* ~ *for letting in light and air* 빛과 공기를 들이는 구멍. [L. *aperio* open]

a·pex [éipeks] *n.* Ⓒ (*pl.* **-es** or **a·pi·ces**) **1** the top; the peak; the summit. 정상; 꼭대기; 봉우리. ¶ *the* ~ *of a triangle* 〔*mountain*〕 삼각형의 꼭지점〔산꼭대기〕. **2** a climax. 절정. ¶ *the* ~ *of one's fortunes* 행운의 절정. [L.]

a·pha·si·a [əféiʒiə] *n.* loss of ability to use or to understand speech (as the result of brain injury). 실어증(失語症). [Gk. *a-* not, *phoneō* speak]

a·phe·li·on [æfí:liən] *n.* 《astron.》 the point of the orbit furthest from the sun. 원일점(遠日點). [Gk. *apo* from, *hēlios* sun]

a·phid [éifid, ǽf-] *n.* Ⓒ 《zool.》 a small insect that sucks the juice of plants; a plant louse. 진딧물. [made by Linnaeus]

aph·i·des [éifidi:z, ǽfi-] *n.* pl. of **aphis.**

a·phis [éifis, ǽf-] *n.* Ⓒ (*pl.* **aph·i·des**) = aphid.

aph·o·rism [ǽfərìzəm] *n.* Ⓒ a concise sentence expressing a general truth; a proverb. 격언(格言); 금언(金言). [apo-, →horizon]

aph·ro·dis·i·ac [æ̀froudíziæ̀k] *adj.* tending to produce sexual desire. 최음(催淫)의 (cf. *philter*). — *n.* substance tending to do this. 최음제(劑). [Gk.]

Aph·ro·di·te [æ̀frədáiti] *n.* 《Gk. myth.》 the goddess of love and beauty. 아프로디테. 參考 로마 신화의 비너스에 해당함. [Gk.]

a·pi·ar·y [éipièri, -əri] *n.* Ⓒ (*pl.* **-ar·ies**) a place in which bees are kept; a beehouse. 양봉장(養蜂場); 벌통. [L. *apis* bee]

a·pi·ces [ǽpəsì:z, éipə-] *n.* pl. of **apex.**

a·pi·cul·ture [éipəkʌ̀ltʃər] *n.* Ⓤ the care and management of bees for the sale of honey. 양봉(養蜂). [→apiary, culture]

a·piece [əpí:s] *adv.* to or for each one. 각각; 제각기. ¶ *He gave us fifty thousand won* ~. 그는 우리에게 각자 5만 원씩 주었다. [*a, piece*]

a·plen·ty [əplénti] *adv.* 《U.S. *colloq.*》 in plenty. 많이; 충분히; 몹시. [a-, plenty]

a·poc·a·lypse [əpɑ́kəlìps / əpɔ́k-] *n.* **1** 《*the A-*》 the last book in the New Testament. 요한 계시록(啓示錄). **2** Ⓒ a prediction of the future, esp. in early Christian history. 묵시(默示). [apo-, Gk. *kaluptō* cover]

a·poc·a·lyp·tic [əpɑ̀kəlíptik / əpɔ̀k-] *adj.* of the Apocalypse. 묵시적인; 계시록의.

A·poc·ry·pha [əpɑ́krəfə / əpɔ́kri-] *n. pl.* fourteen books included in the Roman Catholic Bible, but not accepted by Jews and Protestants. 경외서(經外書). [apo-, Gk. *kruptō* hide]

A·poc·ry·phal [əpɑ́krəfəl / əpɔ́krifəl] *adj.* **1** of the Apocrypha. 경외서(經外書)의. **2** 《*a-*》 of doubtful authority; false. (전거(典據)가) 의심스러운; 가짜인. ¶ *an* ~ *story* 전거가 의심스러운 이야기.

ap·o·gee [ǽpədʒì:] *n.* the farthest point from the earth in the orbit of a planet. 원지점(遠地點). [apo-, Gk. *gē* earth]

a·po·lit·i·cal [èipəlítikəl] *adj.* nonpolitical. 비(非)정치적인. [a-]

a·pol·li·nar·is [əpɑ̀linέəris / əpɔ̀-] *n.* a mineral water. 미네랄 워터; 광천수. [Place]

:A·pol·lo [əpɑ́lou / əpɔ́l-] *n.* (*pl.* **-los**) **1** 《Gk. and Rom. myth.》 the god of the sun, poetry, music, prophecy, and youthful manly beauty. 아폴로. **2** Ⓒ a handsome young man. 미남자. **3** 《U.S.》 a three-man spacecraft. 아폴로 우주선. [Gk.]

a·pol·o·get·ic [əpɑ̀lədʒétik / əpɔ̀l-], **-i·cal** [-ikəl] *adj.* expressing an apology or regret; excusing a fault or an error. 사죄의; 사과의. ¶ *make an* ~ *speech* 〔*gesture*〕 미안하다는 말〔몸짓〕을 하다 / *in an* ~ *manner* 〔*voice*〕 사과하는 태도〔말소리〕로. [*apology*]

a·pol·o·get·i·cal·ly [əpɑ̀lədʒétikəli / əpɔ̀l-] *adv.* in an apologetic manner; as an apology. 변명조로. [↓]

ap·o·lo·gi·a [æ̀pəlóudʒiə] *n.* a written defence of the conduct or opinion. 변명서(辨明書). [↓]

∗a·pol·o·gize [əpάlədʒàiz / əpɔ́l-] *vi.* (P1, 2A,3) 《*for*》 express regret; make an excuse. 사과하다. ¶ *"I'm sorry," she apologized.* "미안합니다"라고 그녀는 사과했다 / *You must ~ to him for your behavior.* 네 행위에 대해 그에게 사과해야 한다 / *I was apologized to.* 나는 사과를 받았다. ● **a·pol·o·giz·er** [-ər] *n.*

ap·o·logue [ǽpəlɔ̀:g, -lὰg / -lɔ̀g] *n.* a lesson; a moral fable. 교훈; 우화.

∗a·pol·o·gy [əpάlədʒi / əpɔ́l-] *n.* Ⓒ (*pl.* **-gies**) **1** an expression of regret. 사과. ¶ *make* 〔*give, offer*〕 *an ~ for something* …에 대해 사과하다 / *Make an ~ to the lady for your rudeness.* 그 여성에게 자네의 무례를 사과하게 / *Will you accept my ~?* 저의 사과를 받아들이시겠습니까. **2** a formal excuse or defense in speech or writing. 정식 변명. ¶ *a letter of ~ =a written ~* 사과장(謝過狀). **3** a poor specimen or substitute; a makeshift. 그저 명색뿐인 것. ¶ *a mere ~ for a dinner* 그저 명색만의 만찬; 몹시 초라한 저녁 식사. [Gk. *apo-* out, *legō* speak]
in apology for, apologizing for. …을 사과하여; …의 사과〔사죄〕로.

ap·o·phthegm [ǽpəθèm] *n.* =apothegm.

ap·o·plec·tic [æ̀pəpléktik] *adj.* 《med.》 **1** of apoplexy. 졸중풍(卒中風)의. **2** having or likely to have apoplexy. 졸중풍에 걸린〔걸리기 쉬운〕. ¶ *an ~ fit* 졸중풍. — *n.* Ⓒ a person who has apoplexy. 졸중풍 환자. [↓]

ap·o·plex·y [ǽpəplèksi] *n.* Ⓤ 《med.》 the sudden loss of the power to feel or move. 졸중풍(卒中風). ¶ *be seized with ~* 졸중풍에 걸리다. [apo-, Gk. *plēssō* strike]

a·pos·ta·sy [əpάstəsi / əpɔ́s-] *n.* ⓊⒸ (*pl.* **-sies**) the act of giving up one's religion, principles, political party, etc. 배교(背敎); 변절; 탈당. [apo-, Gk. *stēnai* stand]

a·pos·tate [əpάsteit, -tit / əpɔ́stit, -eit] *n.* Ⓒ a person who gives up his religion, principles, political party, etc. 배교자(背敎者); 변절자; 탈당자. — *adj.* of apostasy. 배교의; 변절한; 탈당한. [↑]

a·pos·ta·tize [əpάstətàiz / əpɔ́s-] *vi.* (P3) become an apostate. 배교(背敎)〔변절·탈당〕하다. ¶ *~ from one party to another* 한 당에서 다른 당으로 옮기다.

a pos·te·ri·o·ri [éi pɑstì:riɔ́:rai / éi pɔstèriɔ́:-] 《L.》 *adv.* from effect to cause; inductively. 귀납적으로(cf. *a priori*).

a·pos·tle [əpάsl / əpɔ́sl] *n.* **1** 《*A-*》 one of the twelve men chosen by Jesus Christ to teach the Gospel to the world. 그리스도의 12사도(使徒)의 한사람. **2** Ⓒ the first Christian missionary in any region. (어떤 지방에서의) 최초의 전도자. **3** a leader of any new belief or movement. 주창자(主唱者). ¶ *an ~ of Free Trade* 자유 무역주의의 주창자. [apo-, Gk. *stellō* send]

ap·os·tol·ic·(al) [æ̀pəstάlik(əl) / -tɔ́l-] *adj.* **1** of the Apostles. 사도의. **2** of the Pope. 교황의. [↑]

∗a·pos·tro·phe [əpάstrəfi / əpɔ́s-] *n.* Ⓒ **1** the sign (') used in writing to show: ⓐ the omissin of one or more letters, as in *I'll*(=I will); *can't*(=cannot); *'95*(=1995); ⓑ the possessive case of nouns or indefinite pronouns, as a *dog's* tail, *everybody's* duty; ⓒ the plural of letters and figures, as three *A's, 5's;* ⓓ that the sound represented in the usual spelling has not been spoken, as Good *mornin'*(=morning). 어포스트로피《ⓐ 생략; ⓑ 소유격; ⓒ 문자나 숫자의 복수; ⓓ 대화에서 발음되지 않은 문자를 나타냄》. **2** 《rhet.》 an exclamatory address. 돈호법(頓呼法). [Gk. *strepho* turn]

a·pos·tro·phize [əpάstrəfàiz / əpɔ́s-] *vt.* (P6) **1** put the sign(') to (a word). 어포스트로피를 붙이다. **2** address (a person) by an apostrophe. 돈호법(頓呼法)으로 부르다.

a·poth·e·car·y [əpάθəkèri / əpɔ́θ-] *n.* Ⓒ (*pl.* **-car·ies**) a person who is licensed to prepare and sell medicine. 약제사. [Gk. = put away]

ap·o·thegm [ǽpəθèm] *n.* a short, wise saying, a moral saying. 잠언(箴言). [apo-, Gk. *phtheggomai* cry]

a·poth·e·o·sis [əpὰθióusis / əpɔ̀θ-] *n.* (*pl.* **-ses**) **1** deification; exaltation. 신격화(神格化); 예찬. **2** giving of great glory to a person or thing. 성화(聖化). [apo-, Gk. *theos* god]

ap·pall, -pal [əpɔ́:l] *vt.* (P6) fill (someone) with horror; frighten; shock. …에게 공포감을 품게 하다; …을 흠칫 놀라게 하다. ¶ *I was appalled at the sight.* 그 광경에 깜짝 놀랐다. [ad-, L. *palleo* be pale]

ap·pall·ing [əpɔ́:liŋ] *adj.* causing horror; dreadful; shocking. 공포를 느끼게 하는; 섬뜩한. ● **ap·pall·ing·ly** [-li] *adv.*

ap·pa·nage [ǽpənidʒ] *n.* Ⓒ **1** land, property, or money set aside to support the younger children of kings or princes. (국왕이 자녀에게 주는) 영지(領地); 지급하는 돈. **2** something that goes with; a natural accompaniment; 부속물; 속성. ¶ *the appanages of wealth* 부(富)의 속성. [ad-, L. *panis* bread]

∗ap·pa·ra·tus [æ̀pəréitəs, -rǽtəs] *n.* Ⓒ (*pl.* **-tus** or **-tus·es**) **1** an equipment, instrument, etc., necessary for a special purpose. 기구(器具); 장치. ¶ *an electric ~* 전기 기구 / *an X-ray ~* 엑스(레이)선〔장치〕 / *scientific ~* 과학 장비. **2** bodily organs. (몸의) 기관(器官). ¶ *the digestive ~* 소화 기관. [ad-, L. *paro* prepare]

ap·par·el [əpǽrəl] *n.* Ⓤ **1** clothing; garments. 의복. **2** 《naut.》 things used to equip a ship, such as sails and an anchor. (배의) 장구(裝具); 선구(船具)《돛·닻 등》. — *vt.* (P6) (**-eled, -el·ing** or 《*Brit.*》 **-elled,**

-el·ling) clothe; dress. …을 입히다; 치장하다. ¶ *a queen richly appareled* 화려하게 차려입은 여왕. [ad-, L. *par* fit]

***ap·par·ent** [əpǽrənt, əpέər-] *adj.* **1** easily seen or to be seen. 눈에 보이는. ¶ ~ *to the naked eye* 육안에 보이는. **2** easily understood; evident; plain. 명백한; 분명한. ¶ *It is now quite ~ that she is greatly moved.* 그녀가 크게 감동하고 있음은 이제 아주 명백하다 / *This is a fact which is ~ to everybody.* 이건 누가 보아도 분명한 사실이다. **3** seeming to be, but not really true. 외견만[상]의; 겉보기의. ¶ *Her reluctance was only ~.* 그녀가 싫어한 것은 그저 외견적인 것에 지나지 않았다 / *His ~ honesty deceived me.* 그의 겉치레적인 정직이 나를 속였다. [ap-, L. *pareo* appear →appear]

:ap·par·ent·ly [əpǽrəntli, əpέər-] *adv.* **1** seemingly. (언뜻) 보기에는 ¶ *He is ~ a gentleman.* 그는 보기에는 신사이다 / *He is ~ about fifty years of age.* 그는 언뜻 보기에 나이 50은 된다. **2** clearly; obviously. 분명히; 명백히. ¶ *This is ~ false.* 이것은 분명히 거짓이다.

ap·pa·ri·tion [æ̀pəríʃən] *n.* **1** Ⓒ a ghost; a specter. 유령; 귀신; 도깨비. **2** Ⓒ anything strange or unexpected that comes into sight; a phantom. 갑자기 나타나는 이상한 것; 곡두; 환영(幻影).

:ap·peal [əpí:l] *vi.* (P1,2A,3) **1** 《*for, to*》 ask or request earnestly. 간청[애원]하다. ¶ ~ *for funds* 자금을 간청하다 / *The lost child appealed to the policeman for help.* 길잃은 아이는 경관에게 도움을 청했다 / *He appealed to her to let him go.* 그는 가게 해 달라고 그녀에게 간청했다. **2** 《*to*》 use something as a means; resort. (어떤 수단에) 호소하다. ¶ ~ *to arms* 무력(武力)에 호소하다 / ~ *to the public* 여론에 호소하다. **3** 《*to*》 take a law case to a higher court. 상소[항고]하다. ¶ ~ *the judgment to the Supreme Court* 대법원에 상고하다. **4** 《*to*》 move the feelings; be interesting or attractive. (사물이 사람의) 마음에 들다; 흥미를 끌다; 매력이 있다. ¶ *These pictures do not ~ to the young.* 이 그림들은 젊은이들에게 어필하지 못한다 / *This book does not ~ to me.* 이 책은 나에게 아무런 흥미도 주지 못한다 / *Her beauty appealed to the people.* 그녀의 아름다움은 사람들을 매료시켰다.

appeal to the country, 《Brit.》 break up Parliament and hold a general election. (의회를 해산하고) 총선거를 실시하다; 국민의 신임을 묻다.

— *n.* **1** Ⓒ an earnest request; an entreaty; a prayer. 간청; 애원; 기원; (무력·여론에의) 호소. ¶ *an ~ to someone for help* …에의 도움의 간청 / *make an ~ to reason* 이성에 호소하다 / *make an ~ for support* 지지를 호소하다 / *He gave me a look of ~.* 그는 호소하는 듯한 눈으로 나를 보았다. **2** ⓊⒸ a request to have a law case heard again before a higher court or judge; the right to have a law case heard again. 상소; 상고; 항고; 상소권. ¶ *a court of ~* 상고 법원 / *direct ~* 직소(直訴). **3** Ⓤ attraction; interest. 매력; (마음에의) 호소력. ¶ *sex ~* 성적 매력 / *This sort of music has much ~ for* [*to*] *them.* 그들에게는 이런 유(類)의 음악이 훨씬 매력적이다 / *He is sensitive to the ~ of natural beauty.* 그는 자연미가 풍기는 매력에 민감하다. [ad-, L. *pello* strike, move]

ap·peal·ing [əpí:liŋ] *adj.* attractive; interesting; touching. 사람의 마음을 끄는; 호소하는 듯한; 흥미 있는; 감동적인.

:ap·pear [əpíər] *vi.* (P1,2A,4,5) **1** come into sight; become clear or plain. 나타나다 (opp. disappear). ¶ *The moon appeared in the sky.* 달이 중천에 떴다 / *One by one the stars appeared.* 별들이 하나씩 나타났다 / *A stranger appeared at the door.* 현관에 웬 낯선 사람이 나타났다. **2** seem likely; seem to be; look. …처럼 보이다; …같다; …처럼 생각되다. ¶ *strange as it may ~* 이상하게 생각될는지 모르지만 / *The sky appeared almost black.* 하늘은 거의 먹물처럼 시커멨다 / *She appears* (*to be*) *rich.* 그녀는 부자인 것 같다 / *She appears to have been rich.* 그녀는 부자였던 것 같다 / *It appears from what you say that you are quite right.* 네 말을 들으니 네가 전적으로 옳은 것 같다 / *The plan appears to be a good one.* 그 계획은 좋은 것으로 생각된다. **3** come out before the public; be published. 나오다; 나다; 발간되다 ¶ ~ *in the Times* 타임스지에 나다 / *The book will ~ next month.* 그 책은 다음 달에 나올 게다 / *The magazine appears every month.* 그 잡지는 매달 나온다 / *A new movie star appeared.* 새 영화 스타가 나왔다. **4** show oneself publicly. (모습이) 나타나다; 나타내다. ¶ ~ *at a meeting* 모임에 나타나다 / ~ *before the curtain to sing* 노래하기 위해 무대 앞에 나오다. **5** act or perform publicly. (극에) 나오다; 출연[연기]하다. ¶ ~ *as Hamlet* 햄릿역을 하다 / *He appears on television.* 그는 TV에 출연한다. **6** show or present oneself formally. 출두하다. ¶ ~ *as witness* 증인으로 출두하다 / ~ *in court* 법정에 출두하다 / ~ *before a committee* 위원회에 출두하다. [ap-, L. *pareo* appear]

It appears* (*to me*) *that ..., It seems (to me) that...; I think that.... (나에게는) …라고 생각된다. ¶ *It appears to me that he is dishonest.* 그는 정직하지 못한 것 같다.

:ap·pear·ance [əpíərəns] *n.* **1** Ⓒ the act of appearing (before the public, in a law court, etc.); the publication of a book. 나타남; 출현; 출두; 발간; 출연. ¶ *The first ~ of this book.* 이 책의 첫 출간 / *make an ~ in court* [*before the judge*] 법정[판사 앞]에 출두하다 / *make one's first ~ as* …로서 첫 무대를 밟다 / *The singer made her first ~.* 그 여가수는 첫출연을 했다. **2** ⓊⒸ outward look; outward show. 외관(外觀); 외양;

겉모습; 풍채. ¶ *one's personal* ~ 풍채 / *a man of noble* ~ 훌륭한 풍채의 남자 / *judge by appearances* 겉모습으로 판단하다 / *outward* ~ 겉모습 / *put on the* ~ *of innocence* 천진한 것처럼 가장하다. **3** 《*pl.*》 outward impressions; circumstances. 형세; 상황. ¶ *By all appearances, he enjoyed himself.* 보아하니 그는 즐기고 있었다 / *Appearances are against us.* 형세는 우리에게 불리하다.

keep up* 〔*save*〕 *appearances, keep an outward show of prosperity. 체면을 세우다〔유지하다〕; 겉치레하다.

make* 〔*put in*〕 *an* 〔*one's*〕 *appearance, appear publicly; attend. 나타나다; 얼굴을 내밀다; 출두하다.

to all appearance(s), as far as one can see or judge. 보아하니.

ap·pease [əpí:z] *vt.* (P6) **1** quiet (an angry person, etc.); soothe; calm. …을 달래다. ¶ ~ *an angry person* 화난 사람을 달래다. **2** satisfy (an appetite, etc.). …을 채우다; 충족시키다. ¶ ~ *one's hunger* 〔*thirst*〕 공복을 채우다〔갈증을 풀다〕. **3** yield to the demands of (someone). …에 양보하다. [ap-, →peace]

ap·pease·ment [əpí:zmənt] *n.* Ⓤ the act of appeasing; the state of being appeased. 달램.

ap·pel·lant [əpélənt] *n.* Ⓒ 《law》 a person who appeals to a higher court. 항소인(抗訴人). — *adj.* of appeals. 항소의. [→appeal]

ap·pel·la·tion [æ̀pəléiʃən] *n.* Ⓒ a name or title by which a person or thing is known. 명칭; 칭호. ¶ *The king was called by the* ~ *of 'the Great'.* 그 임금은 '대왕'이라고 불렸다. [L. *appellàtio* name]

ap·pend [əpénd] *vt.* (P6) **1** 《*to*》 attach; add. …을 붙이다; 더하다. ¶ ~ *a label to a trunk* 트렁크에 라벨을 붙이다 / ~ *notes to a book* 책에 주석을 달다. **2** hang. …을 매달다. [ap-, L. *pendo* hang]

ap·pend·age [əpéndidʒ] *n.* Ⓒ **1** anything attached to a greater thing; an addition. 부가물(附加物). **2** any subordinate part of a body, such as an arm, a leg, or a tail. (팔·다리 따위 몸통의) 부속 기관.

ap·pen·di·ces [əpéndəsì:z] *n.* pl. of **appendix.**

ap·pen·di·ci·tis [əpèndəsáitis] *n.* Ⓤ 《med.》 a diseased condition of the human appendix. 맹장염; 충수염(蟲垂炎).

ap·pen·dix [əpéndiks] *n.* Ⓒ (*pl.* **-dix·es** or **-di·ces**) **1** anything appended; an additional part of a book to give further information. 부가물; 부록. **2** 《anat.》 a worm-like tube attached to the large intestine. 충양 돌기(蟲樣突起).

ap·per·tain [æ̀pərtéin] *vi.* (P3) 《*to*》 belong; be related or fit. 속하다; 관련되다; 어울리다. ¶ *a piece of furniture appertaining to a living room* 거실에 딸린 가구 / *the rights appertaining to the Church* 교회〔성직자〕에 속하는 특권. [ap-, L. *teneo* hold]

***ap·pe·tite** [ǽpitàit] *n.* ⒸⓊ **1** a desire for food or drink; hunger. 식욕. ¶ 《*prov.*》 *A good* ~ *is a good sauce.* 시장이 반찬 / *have a good* 〔*poor*〕 ~ 식욕이 있다〔없다〕 / *lose one's* ~ 식욕을 잃다. **2** a strong and active desire. 욕구(欲求). ¶ *an* ~ *for reading* 독서욕. [ap-, L. *peto* seek]

ap·pe·tiz·er [ǽpitàizər] *n.* Ⓒ a kind of food or drink to arouse the appetite. 식욕을 돋우는 음식.

ap·pe·tiz·ing [ǽpitàiziŋ] *adj.* **1** arousing the appetite. 식욕을 돋우는. ¶ ~ *meal* 식욕을 돋우는 음식. **2** attractive. 사람의 마음을 끄는; 구미가 동하는.

***ap·plaud** [əplɔ́:d] *vi.* (P1) show approval by clapping hands or cheering. 박수 갈채하다. — *vt.* (P6) **1** show approval of (something), esp. by clapping hands. …에 박수 갈채하다. ¶ *The audience applauded the play.* 관중은 연극에 박수 갈채를 보냈다. **2** admire; commend. …을 칭찬하다. ¶ ~ *someone for his decision* 〔*courage*〕 그의 결단〔용기〕에 대해 아무를 칭찬하다. [ap-, L. *plaudo* clap (hands), →plaudit]

***ap·plause** [əplɔ́:z] *n.* Ⓤ **1** approval, esp. shown by clapping hands. 박수 갈채. ¶ *He won general* ~ *by his scientific discoveries.* 그는 과학적 발견으로 세상의 갈채를 받았다. **2** admiration; praise. 칭찬.

:ap·ple [ǽpl] *n.* Ⓒ a round, usu. red, yellow, or green fruit; the tree that bears this fruit. 사과; 사과나무. ¶ *eat* 〔*bite*〕 *an* ~ 사과를 먹다〔깨물다〕 / *a rotten* ~ 바람직하지 않은 것. [E.]

an apple of love =***a love apple,*** a tomato. 토마토의 딴 이름.

***the apple of contention* 〔*discord*〕,** the cause of discord. 분쟁〔불화〕의 씨. 參考 Troy 전쟁의 불씨가 된 황금 사과의 고사에서.

the apple of the eye, **a**) the pupil of the eye. 눈동자. **b**) something very important. 매우 소중한 것. ¶ *love a child as the* ~ *of the eye* 눈에 넣어도 아프지 않을 만큼 어린 아이를 귀여워하다.

ap·ple-cart [ǽplkà:rt] *n.* a cart carrying apples. 사과 운반 수레.

upset the* 〔*someone's*〕 *apple-cart, ruin the plans or arrangements; cause someone's to fail. 계획〔사업〕을 망쳐놓다; 실패케 하다.

apple pie [ˊ-ˊ] *n.* a pie baked with apples and sugar under a crust. 애플 파이.

ap·ple-pie order [ǽplpai ɔ́:rdər] *n.* 《*colloq.*》 perfect or excellent order. 올바른 순서.

in apple-pie order, in perfect order. 정연하게.

ap·ple·sauce [ǽplsɔ̀:s] *n.* Ⓤ **1** apples stewed until soft. 사과 소스. **2** 《U.S. *colloq.*》 nonsense. 난센스; 객쩍은 소리.

ap·pli·ance [əpláiəns] *n.* **1** Ⓤ the act of

applying. 적용; 응용. **2** Ⓒ an article for some special purpose; an apparatus. 기구; 장치. ¶ *a medical* ~ 의료 기구. [ap-, L. *plico* fold]

ap·pli·ca·bil·i·ty [æ̀plikəbíləti] *n.* Ⓤ the quality of being applicable. 적응성.

ap·pli·ca·ble [ǽplikəbəl, əplíkə-] *adj.* that can be applied; suitable. 적용할 수 있는; 적절한. ¶ *The rule is* ~ *to this case.* 이 규칙은 이 경우에 적용할 수 있다.

ap·pli·cant [ǽplikənt] *n.* Ⓒ a person who asks for something or some position; a candidate. 지원자; 후보자. ¶ *an* ~ *for a position* 취직 지원자 / *an* ~ *for entrance* 입학 지원자.

:ap·pli·ca·tion [æ̀plikéiʃən] *n.* **1** Ⓤ the act of applying; the state of being applied. 적용; 응용. ¶ *the* ~ *of a theory to practice* 이론의 실지 적용 / *the* ~ *of the law to a case* 사건에 대한 법의 적용 / *the* ~ *of the principle to a set of facts* 일련의 사실에 대한 원칙의 적용. **2** Ⓒ a spoken or written request for a position, membership, etc. 신청; 출원(出願); 원서. ¶ *an* ~ *form* 〔*blank*〕 신청 용지 / *make an* ~ *for employment* 취직 신청을 하다. **3** Ⓤ attention; diligence; effort. 전념(專念); 근면; 노력. ¶ *show* ~ *in one's studies* 공부에 전념〔열중〕하다 / *a man of close* ~ 일에 열중〔몰두〕하는 사람. **4** Ⓤ the act of laying on; putting on. 마르기; 붙이기; 도포(塗布). ¶ *the* ~ *of paint to a house* 집에 페인트를 칠하기 / *the* ~ *of salve to a sore* 상처에 연고 바르기. [→apply]

ap·plied [əpláid] *adj.* put to or used in practical purposes. (실제에) 응용된(opp. pure). ¶ ~ *chemistry* 응용 화학.

ap·pli·qué [æ̀plikéi] *adj.* ornamented by a different material sewn on. 아플리케를 한. — *n.* Ⓤ an ornament made of a different material sewn on. 아플리케. [F.]

:ap·ply [əplái] *v.* (**-plied**) *vt.* (P6,7) **1** 《*to*》 put on; place (something) in contact; lay on. …을 가하다; 붙이다; 갖다 대다; 바르다. ¶ ~ *a match to a candle* 초에 성냥불을 켜다 / ~ *a plaster to a wound* 상처에 반창고를 붙이다 / ~ *a medicine to the skin* 피부에 약을 바르다 / ~ *paint to a house* 집에 페인트 칠을 하다 / ~ *one's eye to a telescope* 눈을 망원경에 대다 / ~ *pressure on the accelerator* 액셀러레이터를 밟다. **2** 《*to*》 use practically; put (something) into practice. …을 적용하다; 활용하다. ¶ ~ *a theory to a case* 어떤 사례에 이론을 적용하다 / ~ *force* 폭력을 쓰다. **3** use (something) for a special purpose. (특별한 목적)에 충당하다. ¶ ~ *the money for the benefit of the poor* 가난한 사람을 위해 돈을 쓰다.
— *vi.* **1** (P1,3) 《*to, for*》 ask; make a request or petition; seek. 신청하다; 지원하다; 조회하다. ¶ ~ *for a job* 일자리에 응모하다 / ~ *for information to* 〔*at*〕 *the office* 회사에 자세한 사항을 문의하다 / ~ *to a friend for aid* 친구에게 도움을 청하다 / *You can* ~ *by letter.* 서신으로 신청할 수 있습니다 / *House to let:* ~ *next door.* 셋집 있음, 옆집에 문의 바람. **2** (P1) 《*to*》 fit; be suitable; have a connection. 들어맞다; 적합하다. ¶ *My remark applies to his case.* 나의 말은 그의 사례에 들어 맞는다 / *This does not* ~ *to women.* 이것은 여성에겐 관계가 없다. [ad-, L. *plico* fold]
apply oneself 〔***one's mind***〕 ***to*** (=*concentrate on*) *something.* …에 전념하다.

:ap·point [əpɔ́int] *vt.* **1** 《*to*》 (P6,13,19) name or choose (someone) for a position; designate. …을 임명하다. ¶ *This man was appointed professor.* 이 사람은 교수로 임명되었다 / ~ *someone as an officer* 〔*to an office*〕. 아무를 임원으로 임명하다. **2** decide on (the time, date, place, etc.); fix; set. (일시·장소 등)을 정하다. ¶ ~ *the time for the meeting* 모임의 시간을 정하다 / *come at the appointed time* 정한 시간에 오다. ● **ap·point·or** [-ər] *n.* [ap-, →point]

·ap·point·ment [əpɔ́intmənt] *n.* ⒸⓊ **1** the act of appointing. 임명; 지정; 선정. ¶ *the* ~ *of someone as secretary* 아무의 비서 임명. **2** office; position. 임무; 관직. ¶ *receive a good* ~ 좋은 관직을 얻다. **3** a mutual agreement to meet; an engagement. 약속. ¶ *make an* ~ 약속하다 / *fix an* ~ *for* 〔*at*〕 *two p.m.* 오후 2시에 만날 약속을 정하다 / *keep* 〔*cancel*〕 *an* ~ 만날 약속을 지키다〔취소하다〕 / *I have an* ~ *with my dentist at two.* 2시에 치과 의사에게 갈 약속이 있다. **4** 《*pl.*》 furnishings; equipment. 설비; 장비. ¶ *All the appointments of the house were very good.* 그 집의 모든 설비물이 매우 좋았다.

ap·por·tion [əpɔ́ːrʃən] *vt.* (P13) 《*among, to*》 give a part of (something) to each; divide; distribute; allot. 분배하다. ¶ *The land was apportioned among the people.* 그 땅은 주민들 간에 분배되었다 / ~ *work to the workers* 일꾼들에게 일을 할당하다. [ap-, →portion]

ap·por·tion·ment [əpɔ́ːrʃənmənt] *n.* ⓊⒸ the act of apportioning; the state of being apportioned; distribution. 분배; 할당; (비용·손실 등의) 분담.

ap·po·site [ǽpəzit] *adj.* proper; apt; suitable. 적절한. ¶ *an* ~ *word* 적절한 말 / *an* ~ *remark to the case* 그 사례에 적절한 말. [ap-, L. *pono* put]

ap·po·si·tion [æ̀pəzíʃən] *n.* Ⓤ **1** the act of placing side by side. 나란히 놓음. **2** 《gram.》 the addition of one noun as a supplement to another. 동격(同格). ¶ *In 'This is Miss Kerry, my secretary', 'Miss Kerry' and 'my secretary' are in* ~. '이 사람은 내 비서 미스 케리입니다'에서 '미스 케리'와 '내 비서'는 동격이다.

ap·prais·al [əpréizəl] *n.* ⓊⒸ the act of

appraising; the state of being appraised; valuation. 평가; 감정. ¶ *make an ~ of someone* 아무를 평가하다. [ap-, →price]

ap·praise [əpréiz] *vt.* (P6) judge the quality, value, importance, etc. of (something); estimate. …을 평가하다. ¶ *Property is appraised for taxation* 〔*at £3,000*〕. 부동산은 과세하기 위해〔3천 파운드로〕 평가된다.

ap·pre·ci·a·ble [əpríːʃiəbl] *adj.* that can be felt or estimated. 감지(感知)할 수 있는; 평가할 수 있는. ¶ *an ~ difference between two ideas* 두 개념간의 약간의 차이. [↓]

ap·pre·ci·a·bly [əpríːʃiəbli] *adv.* to an appreciable degree; somewhat. 다소(多少). [↓]

:ap·pre·ci·ate [əpríːʃièit] *vt., vi.* **1** (P6) feel and understand the value of (something or someone); like; enjoy. (사람·사물의 진가)를 인정하다; 맛보다; 감상하다. ¶ *~ French poetry* 프랑스 시를 감상하다 / *~ good food* 좋은 음식의 맛을 음미하다 / *His great ability was fully appreciated by his friends.* 그의 위대한 능력은 친구들에게 충분히 인정되어 있었다. **2** (P6) ⓐ judge correctly; be fully aware of; understand. 바르게 평가하다; 잘 알다; 감지〔식별〕하다. ¶ *I ~ your position* 〔*difficulty*〕. 너의 입장〔어려움〕을 이해한다 / *~ small differences in sounds* 음의 작은 차이를 식별하다 / *~ the importance of what is said* 한 말의 중요성을 잘 알고 있다. ⓑ feel grateful for. 감사하다. ¶ *I greatly ~ your kindness.* 당신의 친절에 크게 감사하고 있다. **3** (P6) think highly of; value. 존중하다; 평가하다. ¶ *~ someone's ability* 아무의 능력을 평가하다 / *She was appreciated everywhere.* 그녀는 어디서나 존중되었다. **4** (P6;1,2A) raise or rise in value. 값을 올리다; 값이 오르다. ¶ *Property values appreciated yearly.* 부동산 가치는 해마다 올랐다 / *This land has been appreciated since the railway was built.* 철도가 부설된 이래 이곳 땅값이 오르고 있다. [ap-, L. *pretium* price]

·ap·pre·ci·a·tion [əprìːʃiéiʃən] *n.* Ⓤ **1** the act of appreciating. 진가를 인정함. ¶ *in ~ of something* …을 인정하여. **2** the act or ability of understanding the value. 이해. ¶ *~ of painting* 그림에 대한 이해 / *She has an ~ of art.* 그녀는 예술을 이해하고 있다. **3** gratitude; thankfulness. 감사. ¶ *in ~ of kindness received* 받은 친절에 감사하여.

ap·pre·ci·a·tive [əpríːʃətiv, -ʃièi-] *adj.* able to appreciate; feeling gratitude. 감식〔감상〕할 수 있는; 감사하는.

be appreciative of (=*be thankful for*) *something.* …에 감사하고 있다. ¶ *I am always ~ of his kindness.* 나는 언제나 그의 친절에 감사하고 있다. ●**ap·pre·ci·a·tive·ly** [-li] *adv.*

ap·pre·hend [æ̀prihénd] *vt.* **1** (P6) arrest; seize. 붙잡다. ¶ *The thief was apprehended by a policeman.* 도둑이 경관에게 붙잡혔다. **2** (P6,11) grasp the meaning of (something); understand thoroughly. (의미를) 이해하다. ¶ *I apprehended his meaning from his gestures.* 나는 그의 몸짓으로 그가 의미하는 것을 이해했다. **3** (P6) expect (something) with fear; dread. …을 걱정〔두려워〕하다. ¶ *It is apprehended that….* …할 우려가 있다. —*vi.* understand; be fearful. 이해하다; 우려하다. [ap-, L. *prehendo* grasp]

ap·pre·hen·si·ble [æ̀prihénsəbl] *adj.* that can be understood. 이해할 수 있는.

ap·pre·hen·sion [æ̀prihénʃən] *n.* Ⓤ **1** 《often *pl.*》 fear of what might happen. 우려; 불안. ¶ *entertain apprehensions* 우려를 품다 / *have ~ that one might fail* 실패를 하지나 않을까 불안해 하다 / *wait with ~* 불안하게 기다리다. **2** 《sometimes *an ~*》 the ability to understand; conception. 이해(력). ¶ *be above one's ~* 이해할 수 없다. **3** the act of arresting. 체포.

ap·pre·hen·sive [æ̀prihénsiv] *adj.* **1** fearful about something that might happen; anxious; uneasy. 불안한. ¶ *be ~ for someone's safety* 아무의 안전을 염려하다 / *be ~ of failure* 실패할까 걱정하다. **2** quick to understand; intelligent. 이해가 빠른. **3** perceptive. 지각(知覺)하는; 지각적인. ●**ap·pre·hen·sive·ly** [-li] *adv.* **ap·pre·hen·sive·ness** [-nis] *n.*

·ap·pren·tice [əpréntis] *n.* Ⓒ **1** a person who works under a skilled worker to learn a trade. 계시; 도제(徒弟). **2** a beginner; a learner. 초심자. —*vt.* (P6) put (someone) under a master to learn a trade. (아무를) 도제로 보내다. ¶ *~ one's son to a printer* 아들을 인쇄소에 도제로 보내다. [→apprehend]

be bound apprentice to, be apprenticed to. …의 도제가 되다. ¶ *He was bound ~ to a tailor.* 그는 양복점의 도제가 되었다.

ap·pren·tice·ship [əpréntisʃip] *n.* Ⓤ **1** the state of being an apprentice. 도제(의 신분). **2** the period of time for which a person works as an spprentice. 도제 연한.

ap·pressed [əprést] *adj.* pressed closely against or fitting closely to something. 밀착〔고착〕된; 꽉 붙은. [ad-, L. *primere* to press]

ap·prise, ap·prize [əpráiz] *vt.* (P6,13) inform; advise. 알리다; 충고하다. ¶ *~ someone of his danger* 아무에게 위험을 알리다. [ap-, →price]

:ap·proach [əpróutʃ] *vt.* (P6,13) **1** come or go near or nearer to (a place). (장소)에 가까이 가다; 접근하다. ¶ *~ the door* 문쪽으로 다가가다 / *An officer approached me.* 장교 한 사람이 나에게로 다가왔다. **2** 《*to*》 bring (something) near. …에 접근시키다. ¶ *~ a magnet to a piece of iron* 쇳조각에 자석을 가까이 대다. **3** come near to (something or someone) in quality, character, condition, time or amount; draw near to; come to resemble. (때·상태 따위)에 가까워지다. ¶ *It was approaching noon* 〔*the lunch hour*〕. 오정 때가〔점심 시간이〕 가까워지고 있었다 / *The work is approaching completion.* 공사는 완성에 가까워지고 있다 / *As a poet he hardly approaches Shakespeare.* 시인으로서 그는 셰익스피어에 미치지 못한다 / *This sum of money approaches the required amount.* 이 액수의 돈이면 필요액에 가깝다 / *She was approaching womanhood.* 그녀는 성숙한 여인이 되어 가고 있었다. **4** try to have personal relations with; speak to (someone). (아무)에게 접근하다; 이야기를 걸다. ¶ ~ *someone with a present* 선물을 갖고 아무에게 접근하다 / ~ *someone with a proposal* (*on a matter*) (문제에 관한) 제안을 갖고 아무에게 접근하다 / *He is easily approached.* 그는 가까이 하기 쉬운 사람이다. **5** begin to study (something). 연구에 착수하다. ¶ ~ *a problem* 문제에 착수하다.

— *vi.* (P1,3) 《*to*》 go near or nearer; come close or closer; approximate. 접근하다; 다가가다〔오다〕; 거의 …와 가깝다. ¶ *Winter* 〔*A storm*〕 *is approaching.* 겨울이〔폭풍우가〕 다가오고 있다 / *The lights* ~ *nearer.* 불빛들은 보다 더 가까이 다가온다 / *A footstep outside was approaching softly.* 밖의 발소리가 가만히 다가오고 있었다 / *No one approached.* 아무도 다가오지 않았다 / *Death approaches.* 죽음이 다가온다 / *His answer approaches to a denial.* 그의 대답은 거절이나 다름없다.

— *n.* **1** Ⓤ the act of coming near or nearer, or of going near or nearer. 접근; 가까워짐. ¶ *the* ~ *of summer* 여름이 다가옴 / *easy* 〔*difficult*〕 *of* ~ 가까이 하기 쉬운〔어려운〕 / *He waited for her* ~. 그는 그녀가 다가오기를 기다렸다. **2** Ⓒ a way of reaching a place or beginning something; access. 접근하는 길; 입구; 출입구; 연구법; 첫걸음; 입문. ¶ *an* ~ *to literature* 문학 입문 / *the* ~ *to the cave* 동굴에 이르는 길. **3** 《*pl.*》 attempts to open personal relations; advances. 교섭; 접근의 시도; 구애; 친근책; 신청. ¶ *make approaches to someone* 아무에게 구애하다 / *make one's approaches to someone* 아무와 교섭을 트다. [ap-, L. *prope* near]

ap·proach·a·ble [əpróutʃəbl] *adj.* **1** that can be approached. 접근하기 쉬운. **2** easy to talk with; friendly. 친하기 쉬운.

ap·pro·ba·tion [æ̀proubéiʃən] *n.* Ⓤ approval. 찬성; 시인; 칭찬. ¶ *a nod of* ~ 찬성의 끄덕임 / *His book gained* 〔*won*〕 *general* ~. 그의 책은 일반의 호평을 받았다. [L. *approbāre* to approve]

ap·pro·pri·a·ble [əpróupriəbl] *adj.* capable of being appropriated. 전유(專有)〔사용(私用)〕할 수 있는〔해도 좋은〕. [↓]

·ap·pro·pri·ate [əpróupriit] *adj.* 《*to, for*》 suitable; proper; peculiar. 적절한; 특유한. ¶ ~ *to the occasion* 그 경우에 맞는 / *goods* ~ *for Christmas gifts* 크리스마스 선물로 어울리는 물건.

— [əpróuprièit] *vt.* (P6,13) **1** 《*to, for*》 use (something) for a special purpose. (특별한 목적에) …을 쓰다〔유용하다〕. ¶ ~ *the money for one's new house* 새 집을 마련하는 데 돈을 유용하다. **2** take and use (something) for oneself; steal. …을 사용(私用)에 쓰다; 훔치다. ¶ ~ *public money to oneself* 공금을 도용(盜用)하다 / ~ *another person's money* 남의 돈을 도용하다. **3** set apart for some special use. (특별 용도로) 계상하다. ¶ *The money was appropriated by the government for road building.* 그 돈은 정부가 도로 건설용으로 계상하였다.

● **ap·pro·pri·ate·ly** [-itli] *adv.* **ap·pro·pri·ate·ness** [-nis] *n.* **ap·pro·pri·a·tor** [-èitər] *n.* [ap-, L. *proprius* own; →proper]

ap·pro·pri·a·tion [əpròupriéiʃən] *n.* **1** Ⓤ the act of appropriating; the state of being appropriated. 전유(專有); 유용. **2** Ⓒ money kept or used for some special purpose. 계상금; 지출금; 충당금(充當金). ¶ *An* ~ *of ten thousand dollars has been made by the city for a school.* 학교를 위해 1만달러가 시(市)에 의해 특별 계상되었다.

·ap·prov·al [əprúːvəl] *n.* Ⓤ **1** the act of approving; praise. 시인; 칭찬. ¶ *The audience showed its* ~ *by applauding.* 관중은 박수 갈채로 칭찬을 표시했다 / *The play gained* 〔*received*〕 *public* ~. 연극은 대중의 호평을 얻었다. **2** formal permission. 인가. ¶ *The committee gave its* ~ *to the plans.* 위원회는 그 계획을 승인했다 / *I hope this plan meets with the* ~ *of the council.* 나는 이 계획이 의회의 승인을 얻길 바란다.

goods on approval, goods that can be sent back if not satisfactory. 마음에 들지 않으면 반품(返品)이 가능한 물건. [↓]

:ap·prove [əprúːv] *vt.* (P6) **1** speak or think well of (someone or something). …을 좋다고 인정하다; 승인〔시인〕하다. ¶ ~ *a plan* 계획을 승인하다. **2** permit formally. …을 인가하다. ¶ *The bill was approved in parliament.* 그 의안은 의회에서 승인되었다.

— *vi.* (P3) 《*of*》 speak or think favorably. 승인〔찬성〕하다. ¶ *Mother did not* ~ *of my idea.* 어머니는 내 생각을 좋게 생각하시지 않았다 / *The new opera is generally approved of.* 신작 오페라는 일반에게 호평을 듣고 있다. [ap-, L. probo test, →prove]

ap·prov·ing [əprúːviŋ] *adj.* satisfactory. 만족하는.

ap·prov·ing·ly [əprúːviŋli] *adv.* in an approving manner; with satisfaction. 만족하여.

ap·prox·i·mate [əprάksəmit / -prɔ́k-] *adj.* fairly exact; very near; very similar. 거의 정확한; 근사(近似)한; 아주 가까운〔비슷한〕. ¶ ~ *estimate* 어림셈 / *the* ~ *number of books* 책의 어림수. — [əprάksəmèit / -rɔ́k-]

vt. (P6,13) come close to (something); approach. 접근하다. ¶ ~ *perfection* 완성에 가깝다 / ~ *a solution to a problem* 문제해결에 접근하다. — *vi.* (P3) 《*to*》 be nearly equal. (양·질 따위가) …에 가깝다. ¶ *Her description approximates to reality.* 그녀의 묘사는 진실에 가깝다 / *The crowd approximated* (*to*) *a thousand people.* 군중은 천 명에 가까웠다. [ad-, L. *proximus* next]

•**ap·prox·i·mate·ly** [əprάksəmitli / -rɔ́ks-] *adv.* in an approximate manner; very nearly; about. 대체로. ¶ *His salary is* ~ *thirty-five dollars a week.* 그의 급료는 1주일에 대체로 35달러이다 / ~ *two hours* 거의 두 시간.

ap·prox·i·ma·tion [əprὰksəméiʃən / -rɔ̀ksi-] *n.* **1** Ⓒ a fairly exact estimate. 어림셈. **2** ⓊⒸ the state of being more or less exact; a close approach. 근사(近似); 접근. ¶ *an* ~ *to perfection* 완전에 가까운 것.

ap·pur·te·nance [əpə́:rtənəns] *n.* 《usu. *pl.*》 an accessory. 부속물. ● **ap·pur·te·nant** [-nənt] *adj.* 《*to*》 belonging. …에 속한. [ap-, →pertain]

Apr. April.

a·pri·cot [éiprəkὰt, ǽp- / -kɔ̀t] *n.* **1** Ⓒ a small, soft, round, orange-colored fruit, somewhat like a peach; the tree that bears this fruit. 살구; 살구나무. **2** Ⓤ pale orange-yellow; pinkish yellow. 살구빛. [Arab. *al* the, →precocious]

⁑**A·pril** [éiprəl] *n.* the fourth month of the year. 4월. 參考 Apr.로 생략함. [L.]

April Fool's Day [⌐– ⌐ ⌐] *n.* April 1, the day when tricks and jokes are played on people (also called All Fools' Day). 만우절(萬愚節).

April weather [⌐– ⌐–] *n.* sunshine and showers coming alternately. 비가 오다 개다 하는 날씨.

a pri·o·ri [ὰ: priɔ́:ri, èi praiɔ́:rai] *adv., adj.* 《L.》 from cause to effect; from a general rule to each instance. 원인에서 결과로(의); 연역적(演繹的)으로; 연역적인. ¶ *an* ~ *argument* 연역법 / ~ *knowledge* 선험적 지식(先驗的知識)(cf. *a posteriori*).

•**a·pron** [éiprən] *n.* Ⓒ **1** a covering made of cloth, rubber, leather, etc., worn to protect clothes. 에이프런; 앞치마. **2** anything like an apron in shape or use. 에이프런 같은 것. ¶ *an* ~ *stage* (극장의) 돌출무대.

tied to one's mother's* (*wife's*) *apron strings, completely depending on one's mother (wife). 어머니(아내)에게 매인. [L.]

ap·ro·pos [æ̀prəpóu] *adv.* to the point; suitably. 적절하게. ¶ *speak* ~ 적절히 말하다.

apropos of, with reference to; concerning. …에 관(대)하여. ¶ *Apropos of the party, what are you going to wear?* 파티에 대해서 말인데 너는 무엇을 입고 갈 거니.

apropos of nothing, without any previous notice; suddenly; unconnected with the subject being talked about. 느닷없이; 불쑥. — *adj.* fitting; suitable. 적절한. ¶ ~ *words* 적절한 말 / *The remark was very* ~. 그 말은 매우 적절했다. [F.=proper]

apse [æps] *n.* Ⓒ 《archit.》 a half-round place at the east end of a church. 교회당 동쪽 끝의 반원형 천장이 있는 부분. [Gk.=vault]

ap·si·des [ǽpsədì:z / -sáidi:z] *n.* pl. of **apsis.**

ap·sis [ǽpsis] (*pl.* **ap·si·des**) *n.* 《astron.》 either of two points in an eccentric orbit, one (higher apsis) farthest from the center of attraction, the other (lower apsis) nearest to the center of attraction. 원(근)일점. [*apse*]

•**apt** [æpt] *adj.* **1** 《*to do*》 inclined likely. …의 경향이 있는; …하기 쉬운. ¶ *We are* ~ *to make mistakes.* 우리는 잘못을 저지르기 쉽다 / *Old people are* ~ *to forget.* 노인들은 잘 잊는다 / *He is* ~ *to get angry.* 그는 성을 잘 낸다 / *Good luck is* ~ *to turn out bad.* 행운은 불행으로 변하기 쉽다. **2** 《*at, in*》 quick to learn; intelligent. 이해력이 있는; 이해가 빠른 ¶ *an* ~ *pupil* 똑똑한 학생 / *She is* ~ *at music* (*in her studies*). 그녀는 음악을(공부를) 잘 한다. **3** 《*at, in*》 suitable; appropriate. 적절한; 적당한. ¶ *make an* ~ *remark* 적절한 비평을 하다 / *an* ~ *reply to the question* 질문에 대한 적절한 대답 / *He is* ~ *for this kind of job.* 그는 이런 일에 적합하다. [L. *aptus* fitted]

apt. (*pl.* **apts.**) apartment.

ap·ter·ous [ǽptərəs] *adj.* 《biol.》 without wings. (곤충·새가) 날개 없는; 무시(無翅)(무익(無翼))의. [Gk.]

ap·ti·tude [ǽptitù:d, -titjù:d] *n.* ⒸⓊ fitness; ability or quickness to learn, talent; intelligence; inclination. 적응성; 소질; 재능; 이해력; 경향. ¶ *an* ~ *test* 적성 검사 / *an* ~ *for a sailor's life* 선원 생활에 대한 적응성 / *have an* ~ *for languages* 어학에 재능이 있다. [→apt]

apt·ly [ǽptli] *adv.* in an apt manner; suitably. 적절하게.

apt·ness [ǽptnis] *n.* Ⓤ the quality of being apt; aptitude. 적응성.

a·py·ret·ic [eipairétik] *adj.* 《med.》 free from fever. 열이 없는; 무열(성)의. [a-, →pyretic]

AQ achievement quotient. 성취 지수.

aq·ua [ǽkwə] *n.* 《L.》 water. 물.

aq·ua for·tis [ǽkwə fɔ́:rtis] *n.* 《L.》 《chem.》 nitric acid. 질산.

aq·ua·lung [ǽkwəlʌ̀ŋ, ά:k-] *n.* Ⓒ a cylinder of oxygen fastened to a person's back for underwater swimming; 《*Aqua-Lung*》 trademark for such an apparatus. 애퀴렁; 이런 장비의 상표. [→aqua]

aq·ua·ma·rine [æ̀kwəmərí:n, ὰ:k-] *n.* a bluish-green beryl. 녹옥석(綠玉石). [→aqua]

a·quar·i·a [əkwέəriə] *n.* pl. of **aquarium.**

a·quar·i·um [əkwέəriəm] *n.* Ⓒ (*pl.* **-ums** or **a·quar·i·a**) **1** a tank, pond or bowl for keeping water animals and water plants. 양어지(養魚池); 양어 탱크. **2** a building used for showing collections of water animals and water plants. 수족관(水族館). [L. *aqua* water]

A·quar·i·us [əkwέəriəs] *n.* 《astron.》 the water-bearer. 물병 자리.

a·quat·ic [əkwǽtik, əkwάt-/əkwɔ́t-] *adj.* **1** living in the water. 수생(水生)의. ¶ ~ *plants* 수생 식물. **2** in or on water. 수중의; 수상(水上)의. ¶ ~ *sports* 수상 스포츠. — *n.* Ⓒ an animal or plant living in the water. 수생 동물〔식물〕. [L. *aqua* water]

aq·ua·tone [ǽkwətoun, ά:kwə-] *n.* **1** a lithographic process for printing by offset from a metal plate coated with photosensitized gelatin. 망사진(網寫眞)을 응용한 사진 평판법(平版法)의 일종. **2** a print so produced. 그 인쇄물.

aq·ue·duct [ǽkwədʌ̀kt] *n.* Ⓒ **1** a pipe or a man-made channel through which water is led from a distance. 도수관; 수로(水路). **2** a tube or passage in the body. 맥관(脈管). [↑, L. *duco* lead]

a·que·ous [éikwiəs, ǽk-] *adj.* **1** of or like water. 물의. ¶ *an* ~ *solution* 수용액. **2** produced by water. 수성(水成)의. ¶ ~ *rocks* 수성암. [L. *aqua* water, →ous]

aqueous humor [∠-- ∠-] *n.* 《anat.》 clear fluid filling the space in the eye between the cornea and the lens. (눈알의) 수양액(水樣液).

Aq·ui·la [ǽkwələ, əkwílə] *n.* 《astron.》 the Eagle, a northern constellation south of Cygnus. 독수리자리.

aq·ui·line [ǽkwəlàin] *adj.* **1** of or like an eagle. 수리의; 수리와 같은. ¶ ~ *features* 수리와 같은 용모. **2** hooked like an eagle's beak. (독수리의 부리처럼) 굽은. ¶ *an* ~ *nose* 매부리코. [L. *acquila* eagle]

a·quiv·er [əkwívər] *adj.* 《as *predicative*》 in a state of trepidation or vibrant agitation; quivering. (벌벌) 떨면서. [a-, → quiver]

Ar 《chem.》 Argon.

ar- [ær-, ər-] *pref.* =ad-. '접근, 방향, 변화, 첨가, 증가, 강조 따위'의 뜻. ¶ *arrange* / *arrear.*

-ar [-ər] *suf.* **1** pertaining to; like. '…에 속하는, …와 같은'의 뜻. ¶ *regular/singular.* **2** the person or thing pertaining to. '…에 관계하는 사람〔것〕'의 뜻. ¶ *scholar.* [L.]

Ar·ab [ǽrəb] *n.* Ⓒ **1** a person of the Arabian Peninsula or north Africa. 아라비아 사람. ¶ *a street* ~ 부랑아. **2** an Arab horse. 아라비아종의 말. — *adj.* of the Arabs; of Arabia. 아라비아 사람의. [Gk.]

ar·a·besque [æ̀rəbésk] *n.* Ⓒ a kind of fanciful Arabian design of flowers, leaves, geometrical figures, etc. 아라베스크; 당초(唐草) 무늬. [Gk.]

〈arabesque〉

A·ra·bi·a [əréibiə] *n.* a peninsula in the southwestern part of Asia. 아라비아. [Gk.]

A·ra·bi·an [əréibiən] *adj.* of Arabia; of the Arabs. 아라비아(사람)의. — *n.* **1** Ⓒ an Arab. 아라비아 사람. **2** Ⓤ the Arabic language. 아라비아 말.

Ar·a·bic [ǽrəbik] *adj.* **1** of the language of the Arabs. 아라비아 말의. **2** of the Arabs. 아라비아 사람의. **3** of Arabia. 아라비아식(式)의. ¶ ~ *architecture* 아라비아 건축. — *n.* Ⓤ the language of the Arabs. 아라비아 말.

Arabic numerals [∠-- ∠--] *n. pl.* the figures 0,1,2,3,4,5,6,7,8,9. 아라비아 숫자.

a·rab·i·nose [ərǽbinous] *n.* 《chem.》 water-soluble carbohydrate. 수용성 탄수화물. [Arab.]

ar·a·ble [ǽrəbl] *adj.* fit to be plowed or to produce crops. 경작(耕作)하기에 알맞은. ¶ ~ *land* 경작지. [L. *aro* plough]

ar·bi·ter [ά:rbitər] *n.* Ⓒ a person chosen to settle a quarrel; a judge whose decision is final. 중재인; 재결자(裁決者). [L.=a judge]

ar·bit·ra·ment [ɑ:rbítrəmənt] *n.* Ⓤ the act of deciding; Ⓒ decision by an arbiter. 재정(裁定); 재결; 심판. [↑]

ar·bi·trar·i·ly [ά:rbitrèrili/-trər-] *adv.* in an arbitrary manner; without sufficient reason. 제멋대로. [↓]

ar·bi·trar·y [ά:rbitrèri/-trəri] *adj.* **1** decided or done according to one's own wishes. 제멋대로 하는. ¶ ~ *decisions* 독단적인 결정. **2** ruled by one's own will or absolute authority. 전횡(專橫)의. ¶ ~ *rule* 전제 정치. [L. =not fixed]

ar·bi·trate [ά:rbitrèit] *vt.* (P6) settle (something) by arbitration. …을 중재에 의해서 결정하다; 조정(調停)하다. ¶ ~ *a dispute* 싸움을 조정하다. — *vi.* (P1,3) 《*in, between*》 act as an arbiter; decide. 중재하다. ¶ ~ *in a dispute* 싸움의 중재에 나서다 / ~ *between two persons* 두 사람 간의 중재를 하다. [L. =to judge]

ar·bi·tra·tion [ὰ:rbitréiʃən] *n.* ⓊⒸ settlement of a difference of opinion by the decision of a judge or an umpire. 중재(재판). ¶ *settle a matter by* ~ 문제를 중재로 해결하다 / *ask for someone's* ~ 아무의 중재를 요청하다.

submit something to arbitration, decide by arbitration. …을 중재에 부치다.

ar·bi·tra·tor [ɑ́ːrbitrèitər] *n.* Ⓒ a person who is chosen to settle a dispute. 중재자.

ar·bor [ɑ́ːrbər] *n.* Ⓒ **1** an axis of a wheel, esp. of clocks. 축(軸)《특히 시계의》. **2** a place in a garden or park made shady by trees or climbing plants. (나무·덩굴 등이 만들고 있는) 녹음(綠陰)(이 있는 곳·정자). [L. *arbor* tree]

〈arbor 2〉

Arbor day [←-←] *n.* a day set apart in many States of the United States for planting trees. 식목일(植木日).

ar·bo·re·al [ɑːrbɔ́ːriəl] *adj.* **1** of trees. 나무의. **2** living among trees. 나무에서 사는.

ar·bo·re·ous [ɑːrbɔ́ːriəs] *adj.* **1** abounding in trees; wooded. 수목이 무성한; 수목(모양)의. **2** arborescent; tree-like. 수목 같은; 수지상(樹枝狀)의. [*arbor*]

ar·bor·i·cul·ture [ɑ́ːrbərikʌ̀ltʃər] *n.* Ⓤ the cultivation of trees and shrubs. 수목 재배(법). ● **ar·bor·i·cul·tur·al** [-tʃərəl] *adj.* **ar·bor·i·cul·tur·ist** *n.* [↑]

ar·bor-vi·tae [ɑ̀ːrbərváitiː] *n.* 《bot.》 an evergreen tree. 지빵나무의 하나. [↑, L. *vita* life]

ar·bour [ɑ́ːrbər] *n.* 《Brit.》 =arbor 2.

ar·bu·tus [ɑːrbjúːtəs] *n.* 《bot.》 **1** the strawberry tree. 소귀나무. **2** a plant that has fragrant flowers. 철쭉과의 하나. [L.=bush]

·arc [ɑːrk] *n.* Ⓒ 《geom.》 a part of a circle. 호(弧). ¶ *an ~ light* 〔*lamp*〕 아크등. [L. *arcus* bow]

ar·cade [ɑːrkéid] *n.* Ⓒ **1** 《archit.》 a series of arches supported by columns. 일련의 아치기둥 복도. **2** a covered street, usu. having an arched roof and shops along the sides. 아케이드. [↑]

Ar·ca·di·a [ɑːrkéidiə] *n.* a mountain district in the southern part of ancient Greece, noted for its rural peace and simplicity. 아르카디아《옛 그리스 산 속의 이상향》. [Gk. *Arkadia*]

Ar·ca·di·an [ɑːrkéidiən] *adj.* of Arcadia; ideally rustic; simple; innocent; pastoral. 전원적인; 목가적인. [↑]

ar·cane [ɑːrkéin] *adj.* secret, mysterious. 헤아릴 수 없는; 불가해한. [L.]

:arch[1] [ɑːrtʃ] *n.* Ⓒ **1** a curved structure supporting the weight of what is above it, as in gateways, bridges, etc. 아치; 홍예. **2** anything like an arch. 아치 모양의 것. ¶ *a triumphal ~* 개선문 / *the ~ of the heavens* 하늘. — *vt.* (P6) curve (something) like an arch; form (something) in the shape of an arch. 아치 모양으로 구부리다. ¶ *A cat arches its back.* 고양이가 둥그렇게 등을 구부리다. — *vi.* (P1) become like an arch. 아치 모양이 되다. ¶ *The rainbow arches the heavens.* 무지개가 하늘에 아치를 이루고 있다. [L. *arca* chest]

arch[2] [ɑːrtʃ] *adj.* **1** chief. 주요한. ¶ *an archbishop* 대주교. 參考 주로 합성어로 쓰임. **2** pleasantly mischievous; cunning. 장난기가 있는; 교활한. ¶ *The little girl gave her mother an ~ look and ran away.* 그 어린 소녀는 제 엄마에게 장난스런 표정을 보이곤 달아났다. [Gk. *arkhō* begin, rule]

arch- [ɑːrtʃ] *pref.* chief; notable. '주요한, 대단한'의 뜻. [↑]

arch. archaic; archaism; archery; archipelago; architect(ure).

ar·chae·o·log·i·cal [ɑ̀ːrkiəlɑ́dʒikəl / -lɔ́dʒ-] *adj.* of archaeology. 고고학(상)의; 고고학적인. [↓]

ar·chae·ol·o·gist [ɑ̀ːrkiɑ́lədʒist / -ɔ́l-] *n.* Ⓒ an expert in archaeology. 고고학자.

ar·chae·ol·o·gy [ɑ̀ːrkiɑ́lədʒi / -ɔ́l-] *n.* Ⓤ the study of ancient things. 고고학. [Gk. *arkhē* beginning, -ology]

ar·chae·op·ter·yx [ɑ̀ːrkiɑ́ptəriks / -ɔ́p-] *n.* a small winged extinct animal, possibly a nonflying, feathered dinosaur. 시조새. [↑, Gk. *pteryx* wing]

Ar·chae·o·zo·ic [ɑ̀ːrkiəzóuik] *adj., n.* 《geol.》 (of) the earliest division of geological history. 시생대(의). [↑, Gk. *zōion* animal]

ar·cha·ic [ɑːrkéiik] *adj.* gone out of use or date; ancient; of ancient times. 스러진; 시대에 뒤진; 옛날의. ¶ *an ~ word* 고어. [Gk. *arkhē* beginning]

ar·cha·ism [ɑ́ːrkeiìzəm] *n.* **1** Ⓒ a word or expression no longer used. 고어. **2** Ⓤ use of what is archaic, as in art, etc. 고체(古體); 고풍.

ar·cha·ize [ɑ́ːrkeiàiz] *vt., vi.* (P6;1) make archaic; affect the archaic. 고풍으로 하다; 고풍을 흉내내다. ● **ar·cha·iz·er** *n.*

arch·an·gel [ɑ́ːrkèindʒəl] *n.* Ⓒ an angel of the highest order. 대천사. [arch-]

·arch·bish·op [ɑ̀ːrtʃbíʃəp] *n.* Ⓒ the highest of a group of bishops. 대주교. [↑]

arch·bish·op·ric [ɑ̀ːrtʃbíʃəprik] *n.* **1** a rank or office of an archbishop. 대주교의 직. **2** a church district governed by an archbishop. 대주교구

arch·dea·con [ɑ̀ːrtʃdíːkən] *n.* an official of the Episcopal Church immediately under a bishop. (영국 성공회의) 대집사(大執事). ● **arch·dea·con·ry** [-ri] *n.* **arch·dea·con·ship** [-ʃip] *n.*

arch·di·o·cese [ɑ̀ːrtʃdáiəsì(ː)s] *n.* the see of an archbishop. 대주교의 관구(管區).

arch·du·cal [ɑ́ːrtʃdúːkəl, -djúː-] *adj.* of an archduke. 대공(大公)의.

arch·duch·ess [ɑ́ːrtʃdʌ́tʃis] *n.* the wife of

an archduke; a princess of the Imperial House of Austria. 대공비(大公妃); 대공녀(大公女).

arch·duke [áːrtʃdúːk, -djúːk] *n.* Ⓒ a son of an Emperor of Austria. 대공(大公). [arch-, *duke*]

arched [ɑːrtʃt] *adj.* shaped like an arch; having an arch. 아치 모양의; 아치가 있는. [→arch[1]]

arch·en·e·my [áːrtʃénəmi] *n.* (*pl.* **-mies**) a principal enemy. 대적(大敵) ¶ *the ~ of mankind* 인류의 대적; 사탄. [arch-]

ar·che·o·log·i·cal [àːrkiəládʒikəl / -lɔ́dʒ-] *adj.* =archaeological.

ar·che·ol·o·gist [àːrkiálədʒist / -ɔ́l-] *n.* =archaeologist.

ar·che·ol·o·gy [àːrkiálədʒi / -ɔ́l-] *n.* = archaeology.

ar·che·op·ter·yx [àːrkiáptəriks / -ɔ́p-] *n.* =archaeopteryx.

ar·che·o·zo·ic [àːrkiəzóuik] *adj.* =archaeozoic.

arch·er [áːrtʃər] *n.* **1** Ⓒ a person who shoots arrows with a bow. 궁사(弓士). **2** 《astron.》 《*the A-*》 the group of stars named Sagittarius. 궁수자리. [→arc]

arch·er·y [áːrtʃəri] *n.* Ⓤ the art of shooting with bows and arrows. 궁술(弓術). [↑]

ar·che·type [áːrkitàip] *n.* Ⓒ an original model or pattern. 원형. [arch-]

arch·fiend [áːrtʃfíːnd] *n.* **1** the Satan. 마왕(魔王). [arch-]

Ar·chi·bald [áːrtʃəbɔ̀ːld, -bəld] *n.* **1** a man's name. 남자 이름. **2** 《*a-*》 an antiaircraft gun. 고사포. [arch-]

ar·chi·e·pis·co·pal [àːrkiipískəpəl] *adj.* belonging to an archbishop or his office. 대주교의. [↑]

ar·chi·man·drite [àːrkəmǽndrait] *n.* a head of a monastery or group of monasteries; abbot. 수도원장.

Ar·chi·me·des [àːrkəmíːdiːz] *n.* (287?-212 B.C.) a Greek mathematician and scientist. 아르키메데스《그리스의 수학자·과학자》.

ar·chi·pel·a·go [àːrkəpéləgòu] *n.* Ⓒ (*pl.* **-goes** or **-gos**) **1** a group of many islands in a sea. 군도(群島). **2** a sea having such a group of islands. 다도해. [arch-, Gk. *pelagos* sea]

•**ar·chi·tect** [áːrkitèkt] *n.* Ⓒ a person who plans buildings or, sometimes, ships. 건축가. ¶ *a naval ~* 조선(造船) 기사. [arch-, Gk. *tektōn* builder]

ar·chi·tec·ton·ic [àːrkətektánik / -tɔ́n-] *adj.* **1** of architecture. 건축의; 건축술의. **2** constructive. 구조적인. **3** of the systematization of knowledge. 지식 체계의. [↑]

ar·chi·tec·ton·ics [àːrkətektániks / -tɔ́n-] *n.* **1** the science of construction or structure. 건축학. **2** the science of systematizing knowledge. 지식 체계론.

ar·chi·tec·tur·al [àːrkətéktʃərəl] *adj.* of architecture. 건축의.

•**ar·chi·tec·ture** [áːrkətèktʃər] *n.* Ⓤ **1** the science or art of building. 건축학; 건축술. **2** a style or system of building. 건축 양식. **3** 《*collectively*》 buildings; structures. 건축물.

ar·chi·trave [áːrkətrèiv] *n.* 《archit.》 the main beam which rests on the top of a column. 처마도리. [arch-, L. *trabs* beam]

ar·chives [áːrkaivz] *n. pl.* **1** a place where public documents or records are kept. 공문서〔기록〕 보관소. **2** public or historical records. 고문서; 공문서(기록)류. [Gk. *arkhē* government]

ar·chi·vist [àːrkəvist] *n.* a keeper of archives. 기록 보관인.

arch-li·ar [áːrtʃlaiər] *n.* a very great liar. 큰 거짓말쟁이. [arch-]

arch·ly [áːrtʃli] *adv.* cleverly; mischievously. 장난스레. [→arch[2]]

arch·way [áːrtʃwèi] *n.* Ⓒ an entrance or passage covered with an arch. 아치로 된 입구〔통로〕. [L. *arc* bow]

arc lamp [⌐ ⌐] *n.* an arc light. 아크 등(燈). [*arc*]

arc light [⌐ ⌐] *n.* a lamp giving light by means of an electric arc. 아크 등(燈).

•**arc·tic** [áːrktik] *adj.* **1** of or near the North Pole. 북극의 (opp. antarctic). **2** very cold; frigid. 혹한(酷寒)의 — *n.* 《*the A-*》 the north polar district. 북극 (지방). [Gk. *arktos* bear]

Arctic Circle [⌐– ⌐–], **the** *n.* a line parallel to the equator at the latitude of 66° 73' North. 북극권.

Arctic Ocean [⌐– ⌐–], **the** *n.* the ocean to the north of North America, Asia and the Arctic Circle. 북극해.

Arctic Pole [⌐– ⌐], **the** *n.* the North Pole. 북극.

Arc·tu·rus [ɑːrktjúərəs] *n.* 《astron.》 a star of the first magnitude in Boötes. 아르크투루스. [→arctic]

ar·dent [áːrdənt] *adj.* **1** eager; with strong feelings. 열심인; 열렬한. ¶ *an ~ lover of music* 열렬한 음악 애호가. **2** burning; hot. 불타는 (듯한); 뜨거운. ¶ *~ desires* 불타는 욕망 / *~ love* 뜨거운 사랑 / *~ spirit* 독한 술. [L. *ardeo* burn]

ar·dent·ly [áːrdəntli] *adv.* with eagerness; eagerly. 열렬히; 열심히.

ar·dor, 《Brit.》 **-dour** [áːrdər] *n.* Ⓤ warm, strong feeling; strong love. 열정(熱情). ¶ *with ~* 열심히 / *~ for study* 연구에의 정열 / *damp someone's ~* 아무의 열의에 찬물을 끼얹다. [→ardent]

ar·du·ous [áːrdʒuəs / -dju-] *adj.* **1** very difficult; requiring much hard work. 어려운; 힘드는. ¶ *an ~ task* 어려운 임무 / *an ~ lesson* 노력을 요하는 레슨. **2** using much energy; energetic. 끈기 있는; 끈질긴.

¶ *an ~ effort* 끈질긴 노력 / *an ~ worker* 꾸준히 노력하는 사람. **3** steep; hard to climb. 험준한; 오르기 힘든. ¶ *an ~ hill* 가파른 언덕. [L. *arduus* steep]

:are[1] [ɑ:r, ər] *v., auxil. v.* (**were, been**) present plural and second person singular of **be.** [E.]

are[2] [εər, ɑ:r] *n.* Ⓒ a unit of land measure equal to 100 square meters. 아르. [↓]

:ar·e·a [έəriə] *n.* **1** ⓊⒸ the size of any surface such as land, water, or a floor. 면적. ¶ *The parking lot covers a large ~.* 주차장은 면적이 넓다. **2** Ⓒ a part of a country or district. 지역; 지방. ¶ *an industrial ~* 공업지대. **3** Ⓒ a field. 분야. ¶ *a wide ~ of scientific investigation* 과학적 연구의 넓은 분야 / *His major ~ of study is chemistry.* 그의 주된 연구 분야는 화학이다. [L.=vacant space]

·a·re·na [əri:nə] *n.* Ⓒ **1** the central place of an ancient Roman amphitheater where games or fights took place. 투기장(鬪技場). ¶ *a boxing ~* 복싱 경기장. **2** any place of public action. 활동〔활약〕 무대. ¶ *the political ~* 정계(政界) / *enter the ~ of politics* 정계에 투신하다. [L. =sand]

:aren't [ɑ:rnt] are not.

A·res [έəri:z] *n.* 《Gk. myth.》 the god of war. 전쟁의 신(=《Rom. myth.》 Mars).

ar·gent [á:rdʒənt] *n.* Ⓤ 《*poet.*》 silver. 은. — *adj.* like silver; silver-colored. 은 같은; 은색〔빛깔〕의. [L. *argentum*]

Ar·gen·ti·na [à:rdʒəntí:nə] *n.* a country in South America. 아르헨티나. 參考 수도는 Buenos Aires.

Ar·gen·tine [á:rdʒəntì:n, -tàin] *adj.* of Argentina or its people. 아르헨티나(사람)의. — *n.* Ⓒ a person of Argentina. 아르헨티나 사람.

ar·gil [á:rdʒil] *n.* potter's clay. 도토(陶土). [Gk. *argēs* white]

Ar·go [á:rgou] *n.* **1** 《Gk. myth.》 the ship in which Argonauts sailed. 아르고 선(船). **2** 《astron.》 a very large southern constellation. 아르고 자리. [Gk.]

ar·gon [á:rgɑn / -gɔn] *n.* 《chem.》 an inert gas. 아르곤. [Gk. *a-* not, *ergon* work]

ar·go·sy [á:rgəsi] *n.* Ⓒ (*pl.* **-sies**) 《hist., *poet.*》 a large merchant ship. 큰 상선(商船). [It.]

:ar·gue [á:rgju:] *vt.* **1** (P6,11) discuss (a problem, etc.); maintain (an opinion, etc.). …을 논하다; 의론하다; 주장하다. ¶ *~ one's position* 자기의 입장을 주장〔변호〕하다 / *They argued a very difficult matter.* 그들은 매우 어려운 문제를 논의했다 / *He argued that the plan was impracticable.* 그는 그 계획이 실현성이 없다고 주장했다. **2** (P13) make (someone) consent or understand by giving reasons. …을 설득하다. ¶ *~ someone out of the habit* 아무를 설득해서 그 습관을 버리게 하다 / *They argued me into staying overnight.* 나를 설득해서 하룻밤 묵게 했다 / *They argued him into joining the party.* 그들은 그를 설득해서 입당(入黨)시켰다. **3** (P6,11,21) indicate; prove; show. …을 보이다; 입증하다. ¶ *Her clothes ~ poverty.* 그녀의 옷은 가난을 드러내 보인다 / *His attitude argues him (to be) a gentleman.* 그의 태도는 그가 신사임을 입증한다 / *Her rich clothes ~ that she is wealthy.* 그녀의 값진 옷은 그녀가 부유하다는 것을 나타낸다.
— *vi.* (P1,2A,4) 《*for, against, with, about*》 discuss; dispute. 논의하다; 논쟁하다. ¶ *He argued for justice.* 그는 정의에 대한 찬성론을 폈다 / *They argued against the passage of the bill.* 그들은 의안의 통과에 반대론을 폈다 / *He argued with his father about the matter.* 그는 그 일에 관해 자기의 아버지와 논의했다. [L. =prove]

:ar·gu·ment [á:rgjəmənt] *n.* **1** ⓊⒸ a discussion; a reason for or against something. 논쟁; 논증. **2** Ⓒ a short statement of what is in a story, book, etc.; summary. (이야기나 책 따위의) 요지.

ar·gu·men·ta·tion [à:rgjəmentéiʃən] *n.* ⓊⒸ **1** the act of arguing; a discussion. 논쟁. **2** a process of reasoning. 논증; 증명.

ar·gu·men·ta·tive [à:rgjəméntətiv] *adj.* **1** fond of arguing; disputative. 논쟁을 좋아하는. ¶ *a very ~ man* 매사에 시비를 가리는 사람. **2** full of arguments. 논쟁적인.

Ar·gus [á:rgəs] *n.* 《Gk. myth.》 a giant having a hundred eyes who was killed by Hermes. 아르고스. [Gk.]

a·ri·a [á:riə, ǽər-] *n.* Ⓒ 《mus.》 a melody sung, usu. by one voice, in an opera. 아리아. [It.=air]

ar·id [ǽrid] *adj.* **1** (of soil, land) dry; not rich; barren. 건조한; 척박(瘠薄)한; 불모의. ¶ *~ soil* 메마른 땅(opp. humid). **2** dull; uninteresting. 따분한; 무미건조한. ¶ *an ~ subject* 재미 없는 주제. ● **ar·id·ly** [-li] *adv.* [L.]

a·rid·i·ty [ərídəti] *n.* Ⓤ the state of being arid; dryness; barrenness; dullness. 건조; 메마름; 불모; 무미 건조. [↑]

a·right [əráit] *adv.* rightly; correctly. 바르게. ¶ *if I remember ~* 내 기억이 틀림없다면. [a(-)]

:a·rise [əráiz] *vi.* (**a·rose, a·ris·en**) (P1,2A) 《*from, out of*》 come about; appear. 일어나다; 나타나다; 발생하다. ¶ *Difficulties arose out of the affair.* 곤란한 일들이 그 사건에서 발생했다 / *Serious results may ~ from this.* 이것으로 해서 심각한 결과들이 발생할는지도 모른다. [a-, intensive]

:a·ris·en [ərízn] *v.* pp. of **arise.**

ar·is·toc·ra·cy [æ̀rəstákrəsi / -tɔ́k-] *n.* **1** Ⓤ a government ruled by persons of the highest social class. 귀족 정치(opp. democracy). **2** Ⓒ 《*collectively*》 the nobles; the social class to which the nobles belong. 귀족; 귀족 사회〔계급〕. **3** Ⓒ a group distinguished more than most people, as because of wealth or intelligence. (재산·재능 등에서) 일류의 사람들. ¶ *the ~ of intellect* 일류의 지식인. [Gk. *aristos-* best, →-cracy]

ar·is·to·crat [ərístəkræ̀t, ǽrəs-] *n.* Ⓒ a person who belongs to the class of nobles, esp. by birth; a nobleman; a person who is attached to or who favors aristocracy. 귀족(의 한 사람); 귀족 정치주의자.

a·ris·to·crat·ic [əristəkrǽtik, æ̀rəs-] *adj.* **1** of or like an aristocrat. 귀족의〔적인〕. **2** attached to aristocracy. 귀족 정치의. **3** grand. 당당한. ●**a·ris·to·crat·i·cal·ly** [-kəli] *adv.*

Ar·is·tot·le [ǽristɑ̀tl / -tɔ̀tl] *n.* (384-322 B.C.) a Greek philosopher. 아리스토텔레스.

:a·rith·me·tic [əríθmətik] *n.* Ⓤ the science of using numbers, as by adding, subtracting, multiplying, or dividing. 산수. ¶ *mental ~* 암산 / *Reading, writing, and ~ are the basis of education.* 읽기, 쓰기, 셈하기는 교육의 기본이다. [Gk. *arithmos* number]

ar·ith·met·i·cal [æ̀riθmétikəl] *adj.* of arithmetic. 산수(상)의.

arithmetical progression [–––ˊ–– –ˊ–] *n.* a series of numbers that shows increase or decrease by a constant quantity, such as 1, 3, 5, 7, etc., or 7, 5, 3, etc. 등차 수열.

a·rith·me·ti·cian [əriθmətíʃən, æ̀riθ-] *n.* Ⓒ a person who is skilled in arithmetic. 산수에 능한 사람.

Ariz. Arizona.

Ar·i·zo·na [æ̀rəzóunə] *n.* a southwestern State of the United States. 애리조나 주(州). 參考 Ariz.로 생략함. 주도는 Phoenix.

ark [ɑːrk] *n.* **1** 《Bible.》 the ship of Noah; a ship like Noah's. 노아의 방주(方舟). 參考 노아와 그의 가족이 대홍수 때 탔던 배. **2** 《*poet., dial.*》 Ⓒ a box; a chest. 상자; 궤. [→ arch[1]]

Ark. Arkansas.

Ar·kan·sas [ɑ́ːrkənsɔ̀ː] *n.* a south central State of the United States. 아칸소 주(州). 參考 Ark.로 생략함. 주도는 Little Rock.

Ar·ling·ton [ɑ́ːrliŋtən] *n.* the largest national cemetery in the US, in Virginia. 알링턴《국립 묘지가 있는 버지니아 주 북동부의 군·시의 이름》.

:arm[1] [ɑːrm] *n.* Ⓒ **1** the part of the body of a person or monkey between the shoulder and the hand. 팔. **2** anything like an arm in shape or use. 팔 모양의 것. ¶ *the arms of a chair* 의자의 팔걸이 / *an ~ of the sea* 내포(內浦) / *the arms of the coat* 코트의 팔. **3** power; authority. 힘; 권력. ¶ *the ~ of the law* 법의 힘. [E.]

a child in arms, a child too young to walk. 아직 못 걷는 어린아이.

arm in arm, (of two persons) with arms linked. 서로 팔을 끼고. ¶ *walk ~ in ~* 팔을 끼고 걷다.

keep someone at arm's length, treat someone coldly; hold aloof from (someone). 쌀쌀〔서먹서먹〕하게 대하다; 멀리하다.

make a long arm, stretch one's arm to. 팔을 뻗다.

with one's arms folded, with folded arms. 팔짱을 끼고.

with open arms, in a warm, friendly way. 두 팔을 벌리고; 기꺼이. ¶ *receive someone with open arms* 아무를 기꺼이 맞다.

:arm[2] [ɑːrm] *n.* **1** 《usu. *pl.*》 weapons. 무기. ¶ *small arms* 소화기(小火器)《권총·소총 따위》 / *a man of arms* 무장병. **2** 《*pl.*》 deeds of war; fighting. 전투. ¶ *appeal to arms* 무력에 호소하다. **3** Ⓒ a branch or division of a country's military services. 병과(兵科). ¶ *the infantry ~* 보병과 / *the air ~* 항공병과. **4** 《*pl.*》 mark on a shield or flag as a sign of noble families. 문장(紋章).

bear arms, serve as a soldier. 군에 복무하다.

be up in arms, be protesting strongly; be in rebellion. 무기를 들고 일어나다; 반기를 들다.

coat of arms, a mark on a shield, etc. as a sign of one's family or rank. 문장(紋章).

in arms, armed; ready to fight. 무장한; 싸울 태세를 갖춘.

lay down arms, stop fighting. 무기를 버리다; 항복하다.

take up arms (***against***), rise up in arms; get ready to fight. 무기를 들다; 개전(開戰)하다.

To arms! a call to take up arms. 전투 준비!

under arms, having weapons; equipped for fighting. 전투 준비를 갖춘.

up in arms, in revolt. 반란을 일으켜.

— *vt.* (P6,13) provide (someone or something) with weapons; protect or defend; provide (someone) with what is needed. …을 무장시키다; (방호구로 몸방비)를 강화하다; (필수품)을 갖추게 하다. ¶ *~ a castle* 성의 방비를 강화하다 / *~ oneself against danger* 위험에 대비해 무장하다 / *be armed with patience* 인내심이 있다.

— *vi.* (P1) prepare for war; take weapons. 무장하다. ¶ *The soldiers armed themselves for battle.* 병사들은 전투에 대비해 무장했다 / *Since war is certain, we should ~ without delay.* 전쟁의 발발은 확실하므로 우리는 지체없이 무장을 해야 한다. [L. *arma* arms]

ar·ma·da [ɑːrmɑ́ːdə, -méi-] *n.* Ⓒ a fleet of warships. 함대. ¶ *the Invincible* 〔*Spanish*〕 *Armada* 스페인 무적 함대. [↑]

ar·ma·dil·lo [ɑ̀ːrmədílou] *n.* Ⓒ (*pl.* **-los**) 《zool.》 a small animal with a hard, armorlike covering, living chiefly in South America. 아르마딜로. [↑]

Ar·ma·ged·don [ɑ̀ːrməgédən] *n.* 《Bible》 the place of a great and final conflict between the forces of good and evil. 아마겟돈. [Heb.]

ar·ma·ment [ά:rməmənt] *n.* Ⓤ **1** 《often *pl.*》 military forces of a nation. (한 나라의) 군비(軍備). ¶ *limitation* 〔*reduction*〕 *of armaments* 군비 제한〔축소〕. **2** 《*collectively*》 all the things used for fighting. 무기. ¶ *antitorpedo* ~ 대수뢰포(對水雷砲). [L. *arma* arms]

ar·ma·ture [ά:rmətʃər, -tʃùər] *n.* Ⓒ **1** a defensive covering worn by a person for fighting; armor. 갑옷 투구. **2** a defensive, armor-like covering of an animal or a plant. (동식물의) 보호 기관. **3** 《electr.》 a piece of soft iron joining the poles of a magnet; the essential part of a dynamo. (자철(磁鐵)의) 접극자(接極子); 발전자(發電子); 전기자(電機子). [↑]

·**arm·chair** [ά:rmtʃὲər / ⌐⌐] *n.* Ⓒ a chair with side-rests for the arms. 안락 의자. [*arm*[1]]

armed [a:rmd] *adj.* provided with weapons. 무장한. ¶ ~ *forces* (육해공군을 포함한) 한 나라의 군(軍) / ~ *neutrality* 무장 중립 / *an* ~ *conflict* 무력 충돌. [*arm*[2]]

arm·ful [ά:rmfùl] *n.* Ⓒ as much as can be held in one arm or both arms. 한 아름. ¶ *an* ~ *of hay* 한 아름의 건초. [*arm*[1]]

arm·hole [ά:rmhòul] *n.* Ⓒ an opening for the arm in clothes. 진동. [↑]

ar·mi·stice [ά:rməstis] *n.* Ⓒ an agreement to stop fighting for a while. 휴전(休戰). ¶ *a separate* ~ 단독 휴전 / *an* ~ *agreement* 휴전 협정. [L. *arma* arms, *sisto* stop]

arm·let [ά:rmlit] *n.* Ⓒ **1** a band worn on the arm for ornament or identification. 완장(腕章); 팔찌. **2** a small inlet of the sea. (좁은) 후미. [*arm*[1]]

:**ar·mor,** 《Brit.》 **-mour** [ά:rmər] *n.* Ⓤ **1** a covering, usu. of metal, to protect the body from attack or in fighting. 갑옷 투구. ¶ *be* (*clad*) *in* ~ 갑옷을 입고 있다. **2** defensive metal covering or plates for tanks, warships, or motor vehicles. 장갑(裝甲). **3** any protective covering of animals or plants. (동식물의) 보호 기관. ¶ *The scales of a fish are its* ~. 물고기의 비늘은 보호 기관이다. — *vt., vi.* put armor on (someone or something). 갑옷을 입(히)다; 장갑(裝甲)하다. [→arm[2]]

ar·mored, 《Brit.》 **-moured** [ά:rmərd] *adj.* covered with armor. 갑주로 무장한; 장갑한. ¶ *an* ~ *cruiser* 장갑 순양함.

ar·mor·er, 《Brit.》 **-mour-** [ά:rmərər] *n.* Ⓒ a person who makes, repairs, or takes care of arms or armor. 무기 제조〔수선〕인; (군대의) 병기계(係).

ar·mo·ri·al [a:rmɔ́:riəl] *adj.* having to do with coats of arms. 문장(紋章)의. ¶ ~ *bearing* 문장.

armor plate [⌐-⌐] *n.* an iron or steel plate with which warships, tanks, etc. are covered. 장갑판.

ar·mor·y, 《Brit.》 **-mour-** [ά:rməri] *n.* Ⓒ (*pl.* **-mor·ies**) **1** a place where arms are kept. 무기고. **2** 《U.S.》 a place where arms are manufactured. 무기 공장; 조병창(造兵廠). [→armor]

arm·pit [ά:rmpit] *n.* Ⓒ the hollow place under the arm at the shoulder. 겨드랑이. [*arm*[1]]

arm·twist·ing [ά:rmtwìstiŋ] *n.* 《*colloq.*》 persuasion. (어떤 목적을 이루기 위한) 설득; 압력. [↑]

:**ar·my** [ά:rmi] *n.* Ⓒ (*pl.* **-mies**) **1** a large number of soldiers organized and trained to fight on land. 육군; 군대. ¶ *a standing* 〔*reserve*〕 ~ 정규〔예비〕군 / *enter* 〔*join, go into*〕 *the* ~ 입대하다 / *leave* 〔*retire from*〕 *the* ~ 제대하다 / *serve in the* ~ 군에 복무(服務)하다. **2** a body of men organized for a purpose. 단체; …군(軍). ¶ *the Blue Ribbon Army* 푸른 리본단(團)《금주 단체의 이름》 / *the Salvation Army* 구세군. **3** a very large number of anything. 대군(大群). ¶ *a great* ~ *of locusts* 메뚜기의 큰 떼 / *the* ~ *of the unemployed* 엄청난 실업자들. [L. *arma* arms]

ar·ni·ca [ά:rnikə] *n.* **1** 《bot.》 a plant of the aster family. 아르니카. **2** 《phar.》 a healing liquid from this plant. 아르니카 팅크. [L.]

Ar·nold [ά:rnəld] *n.* **1** a man's name. 남자 이름. **2** a family names. 성(姓)의 하나.

a·ro·ma [əróumə] *n.* ⓊⒸ **1** a sweet smell. 방향(芳香). **2** a characteristic quality in a work of art. (예술품의) 기품. [Gk.]

ar·o·mat·ic [æ̀rəmǽtik] *adj.* sweet-smelling. 방향(芳香)이 있는. ¶ *The cinnamon tree has an* ~ *bark.* 계수나무에는 향기 좋은 껍질이 있다. — *n.* a fragrant substance. 향료. [↑]

·**a·rose** [əróuz] *v.* p. of **arise.**

:**a·round** [əráund] *adv.* **1** on every side; all round. 사방을〔에〕; 빙 둘러. ¶ *He looked* ~ *in wonder.* 그는 놀라움으로 주위를 둘러보았다 / *The garden is fenced all* ~. 정원은 빙 둘러 담장이 쳐져 있다. **2** forming a circle. 둥글게; 원을 그리며〔이루어〕. ¶ *gather* ~ (…을 중심으로) 둥글게 모이다 / *fly* ~ *and* ~ 빙빙 맴돌며 날다. **3** here and there. 여기저기. ¶ *travel* ~ *to see the sights* 관광을 위해 여기저기 여행하다 / *"May I show you* ~ *?" "No, thank you. I'll go* ~ *myself."* "여기저기 안내해 드릴까요." "아뇨, 괜찮습니다. 혼자 돌아다녀 볼 테니까요." **4** with a rotating movement. 회전하여. ¶ *The wheels turned* ~. 차바퀴가 돌았다 / *The earth turns* ~ *on its axis.* 지구는 지축을 중심으로 회전한다. **5** by all the distance of the outside edge; in circumference. 둘레가. ¶ *The pond is 2 miles* ~. 그 연못은 둘레가 2마일이다. **6** with a return to the starting point. 한 바퀴 돌아서; (때가)

돌아서. ¶ *The season came* ~. 계절이 돌아왔다 / *when spring rolls* ~ *again* 봄이 다시 돌아오자 / *I'll see you* ~. 일간〔때가 되면〕 또 만나세. **7** not by the shortest route. 멀리 돌아서; 우회하여. ¶ *take the long way* ~ 빙 에둘러 가다 / *He goes a long way* ~. 그는 멀리 돌아서 갔다. **8** from one to another. 차례로. ¶ *pass the candy* ~ *to the boys* 소년들에게 차례로 캔디를 돌리다. **9** from beginning to end; throughout. 처음부터 끝까지. ¶ *the year* ~, 1년 내내. **10** to a certain place. (특정한) 어느 장소에. ¶ *invite him to come* ~ *for supper* 그를 저녁 식사에 초대하다 / *He came* ~ *to see me.* 그는 나를 만나러 왔다. **11** 《U.S. *colloq.*》 somewhere near. (어딘가) 가까이서; 근처에(서). ¶ *My wife is somewhere* ~. 내 아내는 근처 어딘가에 있다 / *I waited* ~ *for her.* 나는 그녀를 부근에서 기다렸다.

have been around, 《U.S. *colloq.*》 have had much worldly experience. 많은 경험을 쌓고 있다; 세상 물정에 훤하다.

— *prep.* **1** surrounding; in a circle about. …을 둘러싸고. ¶ *We sat* ~ *the fire.* 우리는 불을 둘러싸고 앉았다 / *She looked happy with her grandchildren* ~ *her.* 손자들에게 둘러싸여 있는 그녀는 행복해 보였다. **2** in all directions from. …의 둘레에. ¶ *She looked* ~ *her.* 그녀는 주위를 둘러보았다. **3** rotating about the center of. …을 중심으로 돌아. ¶ *the motion of wheels* ~ *their axis* 축을 중심으로 도는 바퀴의 운동. **4** along the outer side of. …을 따라서〔끼고〕. ¶ *go* ~ *the lake* 호수를 따라서 가다. **5** 《U.S. *colloq.*》 here and there in. …을 여기저기. ¶ *travel* ~ *the country* 그 나라의 여기저기를 여행하다. **6** near. …의 근처에서. ¶ *They were playing* ~ *the house.* 그들은 집 근처에서 놀고 있었다. **7** 《U.S. *colloq.*》 about. 대체로; 거의. ¶ ~ *here* 이 근처에 / *It's* ~ *six o'clock.* 여섯 시쯤이다 / ~ *ten dollars* 약 10달러. **8** 《U.S. *colloq.*》 reached by making a turn. …을 돌아서. ¶ *the church* ~ *the corner* 모퉁이를 돌아선 곳에 있는 교회. [a(-)]

:a·rouse [əráuz] *vt.* (P6,7) **1** awaken. …의 눈을 뜨게 하다; 깨우다. ¶ ~ *someone from sleep* 아무를 잠에서 깨우다 / *He was aroused from his thoughts by the sound.* 그 소리에 그는 생각에서 깨어났다. **2** stir (someone) to action; excite; stir up. 분발하게 하다; 부추겨 행동하게 하다; 자극하다. ¶ ~ *fear* 공포감을 일으키다 / ~ *someone to action* 아무를 행동하게 하다 / *A red rag arouses the anger of a bull.* 빨간 천은 황소를 자극해서 성나게 한다. [*a*- intensive]

ar·raign [əréin] *vt.* (P6,13) **1** call a prisoner before a court of law in order to examine him. (피고)를 법정으로 소환 심문하다. ¶ *He was arraigned on a charge of bribery.* 그는 수회(收賄) 혐의로 법정에 소환되었다. **2** find fault with (someone or something); accuse; charge. …을 비난하다. [ad-, →reason]

ar·raign·ment [əréinmənt] *n.* Ⓤ Ⓒ **1** the act of arraigning. 소환; 고소. **2** unfavorable criticism; blame. 비난.

:ar·range [əréindʒ] *vt.* (P6,11,13,16) **1** put (things) in order; adjust. …을 정리〔정돈〕하다; 다듬다. ¶ ~ *the chairs* 의자들을 정돈하다 / ~ *flowers* 꽃꽂이하다 / ~ *books on the shelf* 책을 서가에 정돈하다 / ~ *one's hair* 머리를 매만지다. **2** bring (something) to an end; settle; decide. …을 끝내다; 해결〔수습〕하다; 결정하다. ¶ ~ *a dispute* 분쟁을 조정하다 / ~ *the date of the marriage* 결혼 날짜를 정하다. **3** prepare; plan. …의 준비를 하다; 계획을 짜다; 조처하다. ¶ ~ *a meeting* 회합의 준비를 하다 / ~ *a marriage for someone* 아무의 혼사를 마련하다 / *The party was arranged for Sunday evening.* 파티는 일요일 저녁으로 잡혔다 / *It is arranged that* …. …하기로 되어 있다. **4** 《*for*》 change (something) so as to make it suitable for so new purpose; fit; adapt. …을 (…용으로) 개편〔개작〕하다; 어레인지하다. ¶ ~ *a novel for the stage* 소설을 각색하다 / *This music for the violin is also arranged for the piano.* 이 바이올린 곡은 또한 피아노곡으로도 편곡되어 있다.

— *vi.* (P3,4) **1** 《*for*》 make plans; prepare. 준비하다. ¶ *We'll* ~ *to do as you wish.* 우리는 원하시는 대로 추진할 작정입니다 / *Let's* ~ *for the trip.* 여행의 준비를 하자 / *Can you* ~ *to start early tomorrow morning?* 내일 아침 일찍 떠나도록 채비할 수 있겠나. **2** 《*with, about*》 come to an agreement. 합의를 보다; 협정하다. ¶ *We are going to* ~ *with him about it.* 우리는 그것에 대해 그와 타협하려고 한다 / *I have arranged for him to see her home.* 나는 그가 그녀의 집에 가 보도록 마련해 주었다. [F. *a*- to, *rang* rank]

:ar·range·ment [əréindʒmənt] *n.* **1** Ⓤ the act of setting or the state of being set in order. 정돈; 정리; 배열. ¶ *flower* ~ 꽃꽂이 / *the* ~ *of the furniture* 가구의 배치 / *an apt* ~ *of words* 말의 적절한 배열. **2** Ⓒ the act of setting or deciding. 합의; 결정; 협정; 타협. ¶ *countermand arrangements* 협정을 취소하다 / *make special arrangements with* …와 특약을 맺다. **3** 《usu. *pl.*》 preparations. 준비. ¶ *an* ~ *committee* 준비위원회 / *make necessary arrangements for mountaineering* 등산에 필요한 준비를 하다 / *All arrangements have been made for our trip.* 우리의 여행을 위한 모든 준비가 갖춰졌다. **4** Ⓤ the act of changing a piece of music 〔novel, etc.〕 to make it suitable for a new purpose. 편곡; 각색. ¶ *a musical* ~ *for the piano and violin* 피아노와 바이올린을 위한 편곡. **5** Ⓒ something arranged in a particular way; adaptation. (편곡·각색된) 작품.

come to 〔***arrive at***〕 ***an arrangement*** (= *reach an understanding*) ***with*** *someone.*

…와 합의에 이르다.

make an arrangement (=*arrange*) ***with*** *someone.* …와 타합(打合)하다.

ar·rant [ǽrənt] *adj.* well-known for bad deeds. 악명 높은; 지독한. ¶ *I am not such an ~ fool as to believe that.* 그것을 믿을 만큼 지독한 바보는 아니다. [E. *errant* out and out]

ar·ras [ǽrəs] *n.* **1** Ⓤ a kind of cloth with pictures on it. 애러스 직물. **2** Ⓒ a cloth hung on a wall as interior decoration. 애러스 직물의 벽걸이. [Place]

*__ar·ray__ [əréi] *vt.* (P6,13) **1** put or arrange (something) in order. …을 배열하다. **2** dress (someone) up. 차려 입다. ¶ *be arrayed like a queen* 여왕같이 차려 입다.
— *n.* **1** Ⓤ order. 대형(隊形); 배열; 대열. ¶ *be in battle ~* 전투 대형을 이루고 있다. **2** Ⓒ a large group of persons or things; display. (한 곳에 많이 모인) 진용; 전시물. ¶ *an impressive ~ of actors* 기라성같이 늘어선 배우들 / *make an ~* 죽 벌여 놓다; 정렬하다 / *The ~ of fine china attracted his attention.* 진열된 훌륭한 도자기는 그의 주의를 끌었다. **3** Ⓒ a military force; soldiers. 군대; 군인. **4** Ⓤ dress; clothes. 의상. ¶ *in bridal ~* 신부 의상을 입고 / *be in fine ~* 화려한 옷을 입고 있다. [ad-, →ready]

ar·rear [əríər] *n.* 《usu. *pl.*》 **1** money that is due, but not paid; debts. 미불〔체납〕금; 빚. ¶ *arrears of rent* 집세 체납금. **2** work that is undone. (일 따위의) 적체(積滯). [ad-, L. *retro* backwards]

in arrear(s), behind in payments, work, etc. (지급·일 따위가) 지체하여; 밀려. ¶ *I am in arrears with the rent.* 집세가 밀려 있다.

in arrear(s) of, later than. …보다 늦게 (opp. in advance of).

:**ar·rest** [ərést] *vt.* (P6) **1** stop; check. …을 저지하다; 방해하다; 막다. ¶ *~ development* 발전을 방해하다 / *~ progress* 진보를 저지하다 / *~ the flows of water* 물의 흐름을 막다 / *~ the natural growth of children* 어린이의 자연스러운 성장을 저해하다. **2** seize; capture (someone) by means of the law. 체포하다; 구속하다. ¶ *~ someone for a crime* 범죄 행위로 아무를 구속하다 / *~ someone by warrant of the judge* 판사의 영장으로 아무를 체포〔구속〕하다. **3** attract. (주의 등)을 끌다. ¶ *~ someone's attention* 아무의 주의를 끌다 / *A fine statue arrested my eyes.* 훌륭한 조상(彫像)이 나의 눈을 끌었다.
— *n.* ⓊⒸ the act of arresting; imprisonment. 체포; 구속; 구금. ¶ *effect someone's ~* 체포에 성공하다 / *The police made an ~ last night.* 경찰은 간밤에 체포했다 / *More than 30 arrests were made.* 30명 이상의 검거자가 나왔다. [ar-, L. *resto* remain]

under arrest, held by the police. 체포〔구속〕되어.

:**ar·riv·al** [əráivəl] *n.* **1** Ⓤ the act of arriving. 도착(opp. departure). ¶ *safe ~* 안착 / *belated ~* 연착(延着) / *the ~ of spring* 봄이 옴 / *an ~ platform* 도착 플랫폼. **2** Ⓒ a person or thing that arrives. 도착자; 도착물품. ¶ *a new ~* 신참자(新參者); 새로 들어온 물품〔서적〕/ *He was the first ~ here.* 그는 여기에 첫번째로 도착한 사람이었다. **3** 《*colloq.*》 a new-born child. 신생아(新生兒). [↓]

on arrival, as soon as someone arrives. 도착하는 즉시.

:**ar·rive** [əráiv] *vi.* **1** (P1,2A,3) 《*at, in*》 get or come to (some place); reach. 도착하다 (opp. depart). ¶ *~ at the station* 역에 도착하다 / *~ home* 집에 도착하다 / *~ home late for supper* 저녁 식사에 늦게 집에 도착하다 / *He arrived in London before seven.* 그는 7시 전에 런던에 도착했다 語法 도착하는 곳이 지점인 때는 at, 지역인 때에는 in이 쓰임. **2** (P3) come to a certain stage in a process. (연령·결론 따위)에 이르다. ¶ *~ at full age* 성인(成人)이 되다 / *~ at a conclusion* 〔*decision*〕 결론에 이르다. **3** (of time or opportunity) come; occur. (시기 따위가) 오다; 도래하다. ¶ *The time has arrived for you to work.* 네가 일할 때가 왔다. **4** 《*colloq.*》 gain success or fame in the world. 성공하다; 명성을 얻다. ¶ *an artist who has arrived* 성공한 예술가. [ad-, L. *ripa* shore]

ar·ro·gance [ǽrəgəns] *n.* Ⓤ the state or manner of having too great pride in oneself. 거만; 오만. [↓]

ar·ro·gant [ǽrəgənt] *adj.* very proud of oneself. 거만한. ¶ *an ~ manner* 〔*official*〕 거만한 태도〔관리〕. [ar-, L. *rogo* ask]

ar·ro·gate [ǽrəgèit] *vt.* (P6,13) **1** take (something) to oneself without right. …을 (불법으로) 제것으로 하다; 가로채다. **2** attribute without good reason. 정당한 이유 없이 …탓으로 돌리다. ¶ *~ bad motives to other people* 못된 동기를 다른 사람 탓으로 돌리다. [↑]

:**ar·row** [ǽrou] *n.* **1** Ⓒ a stick pointed at one end and used for shooting from a bow. 화살. ¶ *shoot* 〔*discharge*〕 *an ~ at* …을 겨냥하여 화살을 쏘다 / *Time flies like an ~.* 세월은 화살과 같다. **2** the sign '→'. 화살표. **3** anything shaped like an arrow. 화살 모양의 것. [E.]

ar·row·head [ǽrouhèd] *n.* Ⓒ **1** the head of an arrow. 화살촉. **2** 《bot.》 an aquatic plant that has a leaf shaped like arrowheads. 쇠귀나물속(屬)의 수초(水草).

ar·row·root [ǽrourùːt] *n.* Ⓤ 《bot.》 a tropical plant in America. 칡의 한 가지.

ar·row·y [ǽroui] *adj.* like an arrow in shape or speed; of an arrow. 화살 모양의〔같은〕.

ars [ɑːrz] *n.* 《L.》 art. 예술.

ars longa, vita brevis [ɑ́ːrz lɔ́ŋgə váitə bríːvis], Art is long, life is short. 예술은 길고 인생은

짧다.

arse [ɑːrs] *n.* 《*vulg.*》 buttocks. 엉덩이. [E.]

ar·se·nal [ɑ́ːrsənəl] *n.* Ⓒ a place where weapons are made or stored. 조병창(造兵廠); 무기고. [Arab. =workshop]

ar·se·nate [ɑ́ːrsənèit, -nit] *n.* 《chem.》 a salt of arsenic acid. 비산염(砒酸塩). [↓]

ar·se·nic [ɑ́ːrsənik] *n.* Ⓤ 《chem.》 a grayish white chemical element. 비소(砒素). [Arab. *al* the, *zernikh* golden pigment]

ar·son [ɑ́ːrsn] *n.* Ⓤ the act or crime of setting fire to buildings or goods illegally. 방화(放火); 방화죄. ● **ar·son·ist** [-ist] *n.* [L. *ardeo* burn]

ars·phen·a·mine [ɑːrsfénəmiːn] *n.* 《phar.》 a drug first known as 606. 살바르산. [→arsenic, phenyl, amine]

:art[1] [ɑːrt] *n.* **1** Ⓤ the expression or creation of what is beautiful or impressive, esp. by painting a picture. 예술; 미술. ¶ *a work of* ~ 미술 작품 / *an* ~ *critic* 미술 평론가 / ~ *and music* 미술과 음악 / *an* ~ *teacher at school* 학교의 미술 선생 / *the* ~ *of war* 전술 / *the black* ~ 마법 / *Art is long, life is short.* 예술은 길고 인생은 짧다. 參考 회화나 조각 등 이를 하나하나 가리킬 경우에, 복수가 되는 수도 있음. **2** Ⓒ 《usu. *pl.*》 literature, languages, and history studied in college or university. (대학의) 문예; 인문 과학. ¶ *a Bachelor of Arts* 문학사 / *a college of arts and sciences* 문리(文理)학부. **3** ⓊⒸ skill; some special kind of skill. (특별한) 기술; 기교. ¶ *the healing* ~ 의술 / *industrial* ~ 공예 / *the useful arts* 수예. **4** 《often *pl.*》 trick; intentional way of acting. 책략; 술책. ¶ *In spite of all her arts, I was not attracted to her.* 그녀의 온갖 술책에도 불구하고, 나는 그녀에게 끌리지 않았다. [L. *ars*]

art[2] [ɑːrt] *vi.* 《*arch., poet.*》 =are. ¶ *Thou* ~. =*You are.*

art. article; artist; artillery.

ar·te·fact [ɑ́ːrtəfæ̀kt] *n.* =artifact.

Ar·te·mis [ɑ́ːrtəmis] *n.* 《Gk. myth.》 the goddess of the hunt and the moon. 아르테미스. 參考 로마 신화의 Diana에 해당.

ar·te·ri·al [ɑːrtíəriəl] *adj.* **1** of an artery. 동맥의. ¶ ~ *blood* 동맥혈(血). **2** like an artery. 동맥 같은. ¶ *an* ~ *road* 〔*highway*〕 간선 도로. [Gk. *artēria*]

ar·te·ri·o·scle·ro·sis [ɑːrtìəriòusklərόusis] *n.* 《med.》 hardening of the walls of the arteries. 동맥 경화증. [↑]

ar·ter·y [ɑ́ːrtəri] *n.* Ⓒ **1** a tube through which blood runs from the heart to other parts of the body. 동맥(opp. vein). **2** a main road. 주요〔간선〕 도로. [↑]

ar·te·sian well [ɑːrtíːʒən wél / ɑːrtíːziən wél] *n.* a deep and narrow well filled with water. 좁고 깊이 판 우물. [Place]

art·ful [ɑ́ːrtfəl] *adj.* **1** cunning; deceitful. 교활한; 사람을 속이는. ¶ *an* ~ *trick* 교활한 속임수. **2** skillful. 교묘한. ● **art·ful·ly** [-li] *adv.* [→art[1]]

ar·thri·tis [ɑːrθráitis] *n.* Ⓒ 《med.》 inflammation of a joint. 관절염. [Gk. *arthron* joint, *itis* inflammation of]

Ar·thur [ɑ́ːrθər] *n.* a man's name. 남자의 이름.

ar·ti·choke [ɑ́ːrtitʃòuk] *n.* Ⓤ 《bot.》 a plant with thick leaves whose flowering head is eaten as a vegetable. 아티초크《국화과의 식물》. [Arab.]

:ar·ti·cle [ɑ́ːrtikl] *n.* Ⓒ **1** a piece of writing in a newspaper or magazine. (신문·잡지의) 기사(記事); 논설. ¶ 《Brit.》 *a leading* ~ =《U.S.》 *an editorial* ~ 사설(社說) / *an* ~ *on housekeeping* 가사(家事)에 관한 기사. **2** one thing written in a list. 조항. ¶ *the ninth* ~ *of the Constitution* 헌법 제 9 조. **3** thing (for sale). 물품. ¶ *domestic articles* 가정용품 / *toilet articles* 화장품 / *chief articles of export* 주요 수출품 / *buy several articles at a shop* 한 가게에서 여러 개의 물건을 사다 / *An armchair is an* ~ *of furniture.* 안락의자는 가구의 하나이다 / *What is the next* ~, *madam?* 부인, 그 밖에 또 필요하신 것은요. **4** 《gram.》 one of the words *a, an,* or *the.* 관사. ¶ *a definite* ~ 정관사 / *an indefinite* ~ 부정관사.

— *vt.* (P6,13) **1** set forth in articles (the charges against the accused). 열거하다. **2** bind by articles of agreement. 연기(年期) 계약을 맺다. ¶ *This apprentice was articled to serve seven years.* 이 도제(徒弟)는 7 년 동안 일하기로 연기 계약이 맺어져 있었다. [L. *artus* joint, limb]

ar·tic·u·late [ɑːrtíkjəlit] *adj.* **1** having distinct parts; jointed. 관절이〔마디가〕 있는. **2** (of words) spoken in distinct syllables. 발음이 또렷한. ¶ ~ *speech* 분명히 알아들을 수 있는 말 / *I was charmed with her* ~ *speech.* 그녀의 또렷한 말에 매료되었다.

— [-lèit] *vt., vi.* (P6;1) **1** unite (something) by joints; become jointed. …을 관절로 잇다; 이어지다; 결합하다. ¶ *After the injury the bones did not* ~ *as well as before.* 부상을 입은 후 뼈가 전같이 잘 이어지지 않는다. **2** speak or pronounce (a word) distinctly. 똑똑히 발음하다. ¶ *Articulate your words carefully.* 말을 똑똑히 해라. [L. *articulātus* jointed]

ar·tic·u·la·tion [ɑːrtìkjəléiʃən] *n.* **1** Ⓒ 《anat.》 a joint. 관절. **2** Ⓤ the act of connecting joints. (관절의) 접합. **3** Ⓤ the method of speaking clearly or distinctly. (말의) 똑똑한 발음. ¶ *His* ~ *is poor.* 그의 발음은 시원치 않다. 參考 A,B,C, …등 개개 문자의 발음은 pronunciation이라고 함.

ar·ti·fact, ar·te·fact [ɑ́ːrtəfæ̀kt] *n.* an artificial product. 공예품. [↓]

ar·ti·fice [ɑ́ːrtəfis] *n.* **1** Ⓤ device; skill. 고안; 기교(技巧). **2** Ⓒ a trick; craft. 술책; 계략. ¶ *by* ~ 술책을 써서. [→art[1], L. *facio* make]

ar·tif·i·cer [ɑːrtífəsər] *n.* Ⓒ a craftsman; a workman, esp. a skilled one. (뛰어난) 장색(匠色).

***ar·ti·fi·cial** [àːrtəfíʃəl] *adj.* **1** made by human skill or art; made in imitation of a natural product. 인공의; 인조의; 가짜의 (opp. natural). ¶ *~ flowers* 조화(造花) / *~ breeding* 인공 번식 / *an ~ tooth* 의치(義齒) / *an ~ foot* 의족(義足) / *~ silk* 인조견. **2** pretended; unnatural not real. 짐짓 꾸민; 부자연스러운. ¶ *an ~ smile* 억지(거짓) 웃음 / *~ manners* 허례(虛禮) / *an ~ voice* 가성(假聲).

ar·ti·fi·ci·al·i·ty [àːrtəfiʃiǽləti] *n.* (*pl.* **-ties**) **1** Ⓤ the state or quality of being artificial. 부자연스러움; 부자연스러운 상태. **2** Ⓒ something unnatural or made by human skill. 부자연스러운 것; 사람이 만든 것.

ar·ti·fi·cial·ly [àːrtəfíʃəli] *adv.* in an artificial manner; with artifice; unnaturally. 인공(인위)적으로; 부자연하게.

·**ar·til·ler·y** [ɑːrtíləri] *n.* Ⓤ **1** 《*collectively*》 large guns; cannon. 대포; 포(砲). ¶ *mobile* (*field*) *~* 야포(野砲). **2** 《*collectively*》 the part of an army in charge of the cannon. 포병. ¶ *heavy* (*light*) *~* 중(重)(경(輕)) 포병. **3** the skill or science of firing large guns. 포술(砲術). [→art[1]]

ar·til·ler·y·man [ɑːrtílərimən] *n.* Ⓒ (*pl.* **-men** [-mən]) a soldier in the artillery; a gunner. 포병.

ar·ti·san [áːrtəzən / àːrtizǽn, ⌐–⌐] *n.* Ⓒ a workman, esp. a skilled one. 장색(匠色); (특히) 숙련공. [F.]

:**art·ist** [áːrtist] *n.* Ⓒ **1** a person who practices any creative art, esp. a person who is skilled in painting. 예술가; (특히) 화가. **2** anyone who does his work with skill and good taste. 어떤 기술에 뛰어난 사람; (그 방면의) 대가; 명수. ¶ *a celebrated ~ in lacquer* 칠공예의 대가 / *This cook is a good ~.* 이 요리사는 조리 솜씨가 뛰어나다. [→art[1]]

ar·tiste [ɑːrtíːst] *n.* Ⓒ a skillful performer, esp. a singer, dancer, barber, cook, etc. 예능인; (특히) 가수·댄서·이발사·요리사 등.

***ar·tis·tic** [ɑːrtístik] *adj.* **1** of art or artists. 예술의; 예술가의. **2** (of the fine arts) done beautifully or skillfully. 예술적인; 멋있는. **3** having the ability to appreciate arts; loving fine arts. 예술을 아는; 예술을 애호하는.

ar·tis·ti·cal·ly [ɑːrtístikəli] *adv.* in an artistic manner; from an artistic standpoint. 예술적으로; 미술적으로; 예술적으로 보아.

art·ist·ry [áːrtistri] *n.* Ⓤ **1** artistic workmanship or skill. 예술가의 일(솜씨). **2** artistic effect. 예술적 효과.

art·less [áːrtlis] *adj.* **1** simple and natural. 꾸밈없는. ¶ *an ~ young girl* 꾸밈없는 (천진한) 소녀 / *Did you notice her ~ way of speaking?* 그녀의 가식 없는 이야기투를 알겠더냐. **2** lacking skill; clumsy; unskillful. 서투른. ¶ *an ~ translation* 졸렬한 번역.

Ar·y·an [ɛ́əriən] *adj.* of the Indo-European languages, such as Sanskrit, Persian and most European languages. 아리안 어족의. —*n.* **1** Ⓤ the Indo-European languages. 아리안어(語). **2** Ⓒ the people speaking any of these languages. 아리안 사람. [Skr. *arya* noble]

As 《chem.》 arsenic.

:**as** [æz, əz] *adv.* 《often used in *as... as...*》 to the same degree or extent; equally. …와 같은 정도로; …만큼. 參考 *as... as...* 에서는 앞의 as는 부사, 뒤의 as 는 접속사. ¶ *Her mother is ~ tall as she* (*is*). 그녀의 어머니는 그녀만 하다(cf. *... not so tall as ...*) / *Take ~ much as you want.* 원하는 만큼 가져라 / *Her face looked* (*~*) *white as snow.* 그녀의 얼굴은 눈같이 희게 보였다 / *I came ~ soon as I could.* 될 수 있는 대로 빨리 왔다 / *She has ~ many* (*as I have*). 그녀는 나만큼 갖고 있다 / *I can do it ~ well* (*as you can*). 나는 그것을 너만큼 잘 할 수 있다. 語法 뒤의 as 이하는 흔히 생략됨 / *I did it in three hours, but it took her ~ many days.* 나는 그걸 3 시간에 했는데 그녀는 사흘이나 걸렸다.

—*conj.* **1** 《often used in *as ... as ~, so ... as ~*》 to the same degree or extent that. …와 같이; …와 같은 정도로; …만큼. ¶ *He is as tall ~ I* (*me*). 그는 나만큼 크다 / *You are as kind ~ she* (*is*). 너는 그녀만큼 친절하다 / *It is not so easy ~ you think.* 그건 네가 생각하는 것같이 쉽지가 않다 / *Come as soon ~ possible.* 될 수 있는 대로 빨리 오너라 / *He was so kind ~ to come to see me off.* 그는 친절하게도 나를 배웅 나와 주었다. **2** in the same way or state that. …와 같이. ¶ *~ people often say* 사람들이 흔히 말하듯이 / *Do ~ you like.* 내 좋을 대로 해라 / *Do ~ you are told.* 일러준 대로 해라 / *Parks are to the city ~ lungs are to the body.* 공원과 도시의 관계는 폐와 몸의 관계와 같다. **3** during the time that; while; when. …하는 동안(사이); …때; …함에 따라서. ¶ *~ you look away* 한눈을 판 사이에 / *He entered the room ~ I was studying.* 그는 내가 공부하고 있는 동안 방에 들어왔다 / *I trembled ~ I spoke.* 나는 말하고 있는 동안 몸을 떨었다 / *As a child he lived in Seoul.* 어릴 때 그는 서울에 살았다 / *I met him ~ I was coming here.* 여기 오는 동안 그를 만났다 / *As we grow older, we come to know the limit of our ability.* 나이가 듦에 따라 우리는 능력의 한계를 알게 된다 / *Just ~ he was speaking, we felt a big earthquake.* 그가 막 이야기를 하고 있을 때 우리는 큰 지진을 느꼈다. **4** since; because. …이(하)므로; …이기(하기) 때

문에. ¶ *As she is honest, she is trusted by everyone.* 그녀는 정직하기 때문에 모든 사람에게 신뢰를 받고 있다 / *Young ~ he was, it is natural that he should have acted so foolishly.* 나이가 어렸기 때문에 그런 어리석은 행동을 한 것은 당연하다 / *As you are tired, you had better rest.* 넌 지쳤으므로 쉬는 게 좋겠다 / *He passed the examination, ~ he had studied hard.* 그는 열심히 공부했으므로 시험에 합격했다. **5** though. …이기는 하지만. ¶ *Rich ~ he is, he is not happy.* 그는 부자이지만 행복하지는 못하다 / *Pretty ~ she is, she is not clever.* 그녀는 예쁘긴 하지만 영리하지가 못하다 / *Woman ~ she was, she was brave.* 비록 여자이긴 했지만 그녀는 용감했다.
— 《used as *relative pronoun*》 **1** that; which. …(와) 같은; …하는 바의. 語法 선행사로서 such, the same, as many, as much 등이 옴. ¶ *as much money ~ I have* 내가 가지고 있는 만큼의 돈 / *such books ~ you read* 네가 읽는 책들 / *He is just such a teacher ~ we all admire.* 그분이야말로 우리 모두가 존경하는 선생님이다 / *Choose such friends ~ will benefit you.* 너에게 유익할 친구를 택해라 / *Such men ~ saw him admired him.* 그를 본 사람은 그를 칭찬했다 / *This is the same watch ~ I lost.* 이것은 내가 잃었던 것과 같은 (종류의) 시계이다 / *I have the same trouble ~ you had.* 자네가 겪었던 것과 같은 문제를 안고 있다. **2** a fact that. …하다는〔하라는〕 것. 參考 문장 전체를 받음. ¶ *He failed, ~ was expected.* 그는 예기했던 대로 실패했다 / *He appears good-natured, ~ he really is.* 그는 사람이 좋아뵈는데, 사실이 그렇다 / *He was a foreigner, ~ I knew from his accent.* 그는 외국인이었다. 말투로 알아차렸지만 / *Grandpa, ~ was usual with him, took the dog out for a walk after breakfast.* 할아버지는 여느 때와 같이 조반 후에 개를 데리고 산책을 나가셨다 / *As is the way with lonely men, he sat still for hours in the darkroom.* 고독한 사내에게 흔히 있는 일이지만, 그는 어두운 방에서 몇 시간이고 꼼짝 않고 앉아 있었다 / *As is often the case with girls of her age, she is very bashful.* 그 또래의 소녀에게 흔히 있는 일이지만 그녀는 몹시 수줍음을 탄다 / *As might have been expected, they were spoiled.* 예기되었던 대로 그들은 파멸되었다.
— *prep.* **1** in the capacity or character of. …로서. ¶ *He is famous ~ a scholar.* 그는 학자로 알려져 있다 / *He is a scientist, and ought to be treated ~ such.* 그는 과학자이니 과학자로서 대우를 받아야 한다 / *Who will act ~ go-between?* 조정역(調整役)은 누가 할 건가. **2** like. …같이. ¶ *~ dead leaves before the wind* 바람 앞의 가랑잎처럼 / *Her lips were ~ lilies.* 그녀의 입술은 백합 같았다 / *Knowledge is ~ nothing compared with doing.* 지식은 행동에 비하면 대수로운 게 아니다. [*all, so*]

as against, in comparison with. …에 비해서(의); …에 대해서(의). ¶ *The business done this year amounts to $ 500,000 ~ against $ 400,000 last year.* 금년도 사업 실적은 지난 해의 40만 달러에 비해 50만 달러에 달한다.

as ... as any, more than anyone else. 무엇〔누구〕에 못지 않은; 매우. ¶ *He is ~ rich as any in our town.* 그는 우리 읍내에서 누구에도 못지 않은 부자이다.

as for, about; concerning; in regard to; speaking of. …에 관〔대〕해서 (말하자면).

as from, on and after. (법률·계약 따위가 며칠날)부터. ¶ *The agreement starts ~ from May 31.* 조약은 5월 31일부터 발효한다.

as good as, nearly; almost ~. 거의 …나 마찬가지인. ¶ *~ good as new* 새것이나 마찬가지인.

as if, as would be the case if. 마치 …처럼. ¶ *It looks ~ if it would rain.* 마치 비가 내릴 것 같다 / *He talks ~ if he knew everything.* 그는 마치 모든 것을 다 알고 있는 듯이 말한다.

as is, in the existing condition without change. (어떤 조건·상태이건) 그대로. ¶ *We bought the table ~ is.* 그 테이블을 그대로 샀다.

as it is, in reality. 실은; 실제는. ¶ *I thought things would get better, but ~ it is they are getting worse.* 나는 일이 나아지리라 여겼으나 실제는 (그렇지가 않아) 악화 일로에 있다.

as it were, so to speak. 말하자면.

as though =as if. ¶ *He looked ~ though he had not slept.* 그는 마치 잠을 자지 못한 것처럼 보였다.

as to, **a**) about; concerning. …에 관해서〔대해서〕 (말하자면). ¶ *He said nothing ~ to when he would get there.* 그는 언제 그 곳에 도착할는지에 관해 아무 말도 안 했다. **b**) in order to. …하기 위해서.

as yet, so far; up to now. 지금까지는 (아직). ¶ *No one has come ~ yet.* 아직 아무도 안 왔다.

just as well, fortunate. 다행스러운. ¶ *It is just ~ well you did come today.* 마침 오늘 와서 다행이다.

As. **1** Asia; Asiatic. **2** Anglo-Saxon.

a.s. at sight.

as·bes·tos, as·bes·tus [æzbéstəs, æs-] *n.* Ⓤ a soft, white, mineral material which cannot be burnt, used as fireproofing. 아스베스토; 석면(石綿). [L. *asbestos;* ? E. *albestone* white stone]

:as·cend [əsénd] *vi.* (P1,2A,3) go up; rise. 올라가다; 오르다 (opp. descend). ¶ *watch an airplane ~* 비행기가 떠오르는 것을 보다 / *~ against a rushing stream* 격류를 거슬러 올라가다. — *vt.* (P6) climb; go up. (산 따위)를 올라가다. ¶ *~ a mountain / ~ stairs / ~ a lookout tower* 망루에 오르다 / *~ the throne* 왕위에 오르다. [as-, →scan]

ascend to heaven, die. 죽다.

as·cend·an·cy, -en·cy [əséndənsi] *n.* Ⓤ the quality of being ascendant; power;

domination. 우세; 지배. ¶ *obtain* 〔*gain, get*〕 ~ *over* …보다 우위에 서다 / *in the* ~ 권력을 잡고.

as·cend·ant, -ent [əséndənt] *adj.* **1** ascending. 올라가는; 상승하는. **2** superior. 우세한. — *n.* Ⓤ 《*the* ~》 **1** the fortune decided by the positions of stars at the time of birth. (출생 때의) 운세. **2** controlling power. 지배력.

as·cen·sion [əsénʃən] *n.* Ⓤ **1** the act of ascending. 오름; 상승. **2** 《*the A-*》 the bodily ascent of Jesus Christ to Heaven. 예수 승천(昇天).

as·cent [əsént] *n.* Ⓒ **1** the act of ascending or going up. 올라감. ¶ *the* ~ *of Mt. Halla* 한라산 등반 / *the* ~ *of a balloon* 기구의 상승 / *make an* ~ *of a mountain* 산에 오르다. **2** advancement in one's position, rank, etc. 승진. ¶ *achieve a spectacular* ~ *to international fame* 일약 세계적인 명성을 얻다. **3** a place or way which slopes up. 오르막길. ¶ *a gentle* 〔*rapid*〕 ~ 완만한〔가파른〕 오르막길. [→ascend]

***as·cer·tain** [æ̀sərtéin] *vt.* (P6,10,11,12, 21) find out (a fact, etc.); make sure. (사실 따위)를 확인하다. [as-, →certain]

as·cet·ic [əsétik] *adj.* giving up pleasure and comforts; self-denying. 금욕적인〔주의의〕. ¶ *lead an* ~ *life* 금욕 생활을 하다. — *n.* Ⓒ an ascetic person. 금욕주의자; 고행자. [Gk. *askeō* exercise]

as·cet·i·cism [əsétəsìzəm] *n.* Ⓒ the belief that it is better not to enjoy the pleasures of this world. 금욕주의.

as·crib·a·ble [əskráibəbəl] *adj.* that can be ascribed. …의 탓으로 돌릴 수 있는. [↓]

***as·cribe** [əskráib] *vt.* (P13) 《*to*》 give the cause, etc. of (something); believe (something or someone) to belong; attribute. (원인 따위)를 …탓으로 돌리다. ¶ *He ascribes his failure to fate.* 그는 자신의 실패를 운명 탓으로 돌리고 있다 / *The discovery of America is usually ascribed to Columbus.* 아메리카의 발견은 흔히 콜럼버스가 한 것으로 여겨지고 있다. [→scribe]

as·crip·tion [əskrípʃən] *n.* **1** Ⓤ the act of ascribing; the state of being ascribed. …탓으로 돌림. **2** Ⓒ a statement, esp. the words of praise for God at the end of a sermon. 설교 끝에 신을 찬미하는 말.

As·dic [ǽzdik] *n.* Ⓒ a kind of hydrophone. 수중 청음기(聽音器). [*A*ntisubmarine *D*etection *I*nvestigation *C*ommittee]

a·sep·tic [əséptik, ei-] *adj.* free from bacteria causing disease. 무균(無菌)의. — *n.* Ⓒ a drug which keeps off bacteria causing disease. 방부제. [Gk. *a-* not, *sēpō* rot]

a·sex·u·al [eisékʃuəl] *adj.* 《biol.》 nonsexual. 무성(無性)의. [↑, →sexual]

:**ash**[1] [æʃ] *n.* Ⓤ 《often *pl.*》 the fine grayish dust left after something has been burnt. 재. ¶ *be burnt* 〔*reduced*〕 *to ashes* 불타 없어지다; 잿더미가 되다 / *Peace to his ashes!* 영령이여 평안히 잠드소서 / *His ashes were scattered to the winds.* 그의 (화장한) 유골은 바람에 흩뿌려졌다. [E.]

lay in ashes, destroy by fire. 불태워 없애다.

turn to dust and ashes, be frustrated. 결딴나다; 못 쓰게 되다.

ash[2] [æʃ] *n.* Ⓒ 《bot.》 a tree whose wood is used for making furniture. 양물푸레나무. [E.]

:**a·shamed** [əʃéimd] *adj.* 《usu. as *predicative*》 **1** 《*of*》 feeling shame because one has done something wrong or silly. 부끄러이 여겨. ¶ *I am* ~ *of having done so.* 그런 짓을 해서 부끄럽다 / *He was* ~ *of his shabby clothes.* 그는 자신의 초라한 의복을 부끄러워했다 / *You ought to be* ~ *of yourself.* 넌 부끄러움을 알아야 할 것이다. **2** 《*to* do》 not willing to do because of shame. 부끄러워 …하고 싶지 않은〔할 수 없는〕. ¶ *He was* ~ *to tell us that he had failed.* 그는 부끄러워 자기가 실패했다는 것을 우리에게 말할 수 없었다. [*a-* intensive, →shame]

ash·en [ǽʃən] *adj.* of the color of ashes; grayish; pale. 잿빛의; 회색의; 창백한. ¶ *John turned* ~ *when he heard the report.* 존은 그 소식을 듣고 창백해졌다. [→ash[1]]

***a·shore** [əʃɔ́ːr] *adv.* to or on the shore. 물가로〔에〕. ¶ *go* 〔*come*〕 ~ (배에서) 상륙하다; 뭍에 오르다 / *run* ~ 좌초되다. [a(-)]

ash·tray [ǽʃtrèi] *n.* a dish into which smokers drop their tobacco ashes and cigarette butts, etc. 재떨이. [→ash[1]]

Ash Wednesday [ˊ ˊ–] *n.* 《Cath.》 the first day of Lent, marked by a religious ceremony using ashes to remind men of humility. 재의 수요일; 봉재 수일《사순절의 첫날. 옛날 이 날에 참회자 머리 위에 재를 뿌렸음》.

ash·y [ǽʃi] *adj.* (**ash·i·er, ash·i·est**) **1** of or like ashes; covered with ashes. 재의; 재 같은; 재투성이의. **2** pale. 창백한. [→ash[1]]

:**A·sia** [éiʒə, éiʃə] *n.* the largest continent in the world. 아시아 (대륙).

A·sian [éiʒən, -ʃən], **A·si·at·ic** [èiʒiǽtik, èiʃi-] *adj.* of Asia or its people. 아시아(사람)의. — *n.* Ⓒ a person of Asia. 아시아 사람. 參考 Asiatic 은 흔히 경멸적임.

:**a·side** [əsáid] *adv.* **1** on one side. 옆〔곁〕에서. **2** to one side. 옆〔곁〕으로. ¶ *turn* ~ 옆으로 빗나가다 / *move the chair* ~ 의자를 옆으로 치우다 / *push someone* ~ 아무를 옆으로 밀어젖히다 / *take* 〔*draw*〕 *someone* ~ (귓속말을 하기 위해) 아무를 곁으로 끌어당기다. **3** apart from. 떨어져서; 제쳐 놓고. ¶ *Joking* ~*, I mean to do it.* 농담은 제쳐 두고 난 정말 그것을 할 작정이다 / *That is* ~ *from the question.* 그것은 질문에서 벗어나 있다.

aside from, **a**) except for. …을 제외하고. ¶ *Others,* ~ *from the captain, had noticed it.*

선장 외의 다른 사람들은 그것을 보았다 / *They had no more food ~ from a few stale rolls.* 부패한 롤빵 이외엔 먹을것이 아무것도 없었다. **b**) besides; apart from. …외에; …은 제쳐놓고. ¶ *Aside from his salary, he receives money from investments.* 그는 월급 외에 투자한 것에서도 돈이 들어온다.

lay (***put, set***) ***aside,*** **a**) discard; give up. 버리다. ¶ *lay ~ bad habits* 못된 버릇을 버리다. **b**) store. 저축해 두다.

speak aside, (of actors) speak words that are not part of the dialogue, usu. to the audience. (배우가) 혼잣말하다; 방백(傍白)하다.

— *n.* 《theatr.》 words spoken aside. 방백. [a(-), →side]

as·i·nine [ǽsənàin] *adj.* **1** of or like an ass. 나귀의; 나귀와 같은. **2** silly; stupid. 어리석은. ● **as·i·nin·i·ty** [æ̀sənínəti] *n.* [→ass]

:ask [æsk, ɑːsk] *vt.* (P6,8,10,12,13,14,16,17,20) **1** 《*if, whether*》 put a question to (someone); try to get an answer to (something) by putting a question. (아무)에게 묻다; 질문하다. 語法 이 뜻으로는 뒤에 부정사(不定詞), *that-* clause는 오지 않음. ¶ *~ the way to the post office* 우체국으로 가는 길을 묻다 / *May I ~ you a question?* = *May I ~ a question of you?* 한 말씀 묻겠습니다 / *Ask him what he wants.* 그가 원하는 것을(무엇을 원하는지) 물어보아라 / *Ask him if* (*whether*) *he knows it.* 그가 그것을 알고 있는지 어떤지 물어보아라 / *I asked him where he had been.* 나는 그에게 어디 있었는지 물어 보았다 / *I asked* (*him*) *how to do it.* 나는 그에게 그것을 하는 방법을 물었다 / *A few questions were asked* (*of*) *us.* 우리에게 몇 마디 질문이 있었다. **2** request; beg. …을 의뢰하다; (요)청하다. 語法 이 뜻일 때는 뒤에 부정사(不定詞), *that-* clause 가옴. ¶ *~ someone for a favor* (*his advice*) 아무에게 부탁(조언을 청)하다 / *~ for some money* (*a cup of tea*) 돈을(홍차 한 잔을)청하다 / *~ the doctor to come* 의사에게 와 달라고 청하다 / *I ~ you to do this for me.* 나를 위해 이것 좀 해 주기를 부탁한다 / *It is too much to ~ of me.* 그것은 나에게 힘겨운 청이다 / *The boy asked his father for some money.* 그 소년은 아버지에게 돈을 달라고 했다 / *Ask him to return the book.* 그에게 책을 돌려달라고 해라 / *I asked to read the book.* = *I asked that I might be allowed to read the book.* 나는 그 책을 읽게 해 달라고 부탁했다 / *My mother asked for the curtains to be drawn.* 내 어머니는 커튼을 쳐달라고 했다. **3** 《*for*》 demand; claim; require. 요구하다; 요하다. ¶ *How much do you ~ for this hat?* 이 모자 얼마입니까 / *He asks 3,000 won for the book.* 그는 그 책을 3천 원 달라고 한다 / *The job asks much time.* 그 일에는 많은 시간이 걸린다. **4** 《*to*》 invite. 초대하다. ¶ *~ guests to a wedding* 손님을 결혼식에 초대하다 / *We asked her to the party.* 우리는 그녀를 파티에 초대했다 / *I've asked him to dinner.* 나는 그를 저녁 식사에 초대했다 / *I was asked out to dinner.* 나는 만찬에 초대되었다.

— *vi.* (P1,3) inquire; beg. 구하다; 찾다. ¶ *Ask, and it shall be given you.* 구하라, 그러면 얻을 것이다. [E.]

ask after(= *put a question about the health of*) *someone.* 안부를 묻다.

ask for, **a**) request to be given or to be told. …을 달라고(가르쳐 달라고) 하다. ¶ *~ for a pound of butter* 버터 1 파운드를 달라고 하다 / *be asked for one's name* 이름을 가르쳐 달라는 요청을 받다. **b**) try or want to see (someone). …을 만나려고 하다. ¶ *Here is a lady asking for you.* 너를 찾는 어떤 부인이 있다. **c**) 《*colloq.*》 run the risk of (something). 위험을 무릅쓰다.

ask for trouble = ***ask for it,*** take an action which will bring trouble on oneself. 곤란을 (화를) 자초하다.

ask out, invite (someone) out. …을 초대하다.

a·skance [əskǽns], **-skant** [əskǽnt] *adv.* **1** sideways; to one side. 비스듬히; 곁눈질로. **2** with suspicion or disapproval. 의심하여. ¶ *look ~ at something* 수상쩍게 보다. [?]

a·skew [əskjúː] *adv., adj.* not straight; out of order. 비스듬히(한); 비뚤어지게(진). ¶ *look ~ at something* 곁눈질로 보다 / *hang a picture ~* 그림을 비뚤어지게 걸다 / *Her hat is on ~.* 그녀는 모자를 비스듬히 쓰고 있다. [→skew]

ask·ing [ǽskiŋ, ɑ́ːsk-] *n.* an act of one who asks; a petition. 물음; 청함; 청원.

for the asking, simply by asking; for nothing. 요청이 있는 대로; 거저. ¶ *It is yours for the ~.* 달라고만 하시면 거저 드립니다. [→ask]

a·slant [əslǽnt, əslɑ́ːnt] *adv.* not straight up and down; obliquely. 비스듬하게(히).

— *prep.* slantingly across. …을 비스듬히. [→slant]

:a·sleep [əslíːp] *adj.* 《as *predicative*》 **1** in a state of sleep; sleeping. 잠들어 (있는 상태에). ¶ *fall ~* 잠들다 / *The dog is ~.* 그 개는 자고 있다(opp. awake). **2** (of the spirit) dull; inactive; (of the limbs) numb. (정신이) 잠들어; 무디어; (수족이) 마비되어. ¶ *My left hand is ~.* 내 왼손이 마비돼 있다. [a(-)]

be fast asleep, be sleeping soundly. 깊이 잠들어 있다.

ASM air-to-surface missile. 공대지(空對地) 미사일.

asp[1] [æsp] *n.* 《zool.》 a kind of small poisonous snake. 독사(毒蛇). [Gk. *aspis*]

asp[2] [æsp] *n.* 《*poet.*》 = aspen.

as·par·a·gus [əspǽrəgəs] *n.* Ⓤ 《bot.》 a vegetable whose green tender shoots are eaten for food. 아스파라거스. [Gk. *asparagos*]

·as·pect [ǽspekt] *n.* Ⓒ **1** a look; an appearance. 얼굴; 생김새; 외관. ¶ *a gentle* ~ 온화한 생김새. **2** the direction in which a house, window, etc. faces. (집 따위의) 좌향(坐向). ¶ *His house has a southern* ~. 그의 집은 남향이다. **3** a way of thinking about or looking at a problem, etc. (어떤 문제 등에 대한) 관점; 견해. ¶ *Let's consider the question from every* ~. 그 문제를 여러 가지 관점에서 고찰해 보자. **4** the side or part of a subject. 국면; 정세. ¶ *the aspects of things* 정세(情勢). [ad-, L. *specio* look]
take on* 〔*assume*〕 *a new aspect, become entirely new. 면모가 일신하다; 새로운 양상을 보이다. ¶ *The situation of war has taken on a new* ~. 전쟁의 양상이 일변했다.

as·pen [ǽspən] *n.* Ⓒ 《bot.》 a kind of poplar tree whose leaves tremble easily, even in still air. 사시나무. — *adj.* **1** of or like an aspen. 사시나무의〔같은〕. **2** trembling; quivering. 떠는. ¶ *tremble like an* ~ *leaf* 사시나무 떨 듯하다. [E. *aspe*]

as·per·i·ty [æspérəti] *n.* (*pl.* **-ties**) ⓊⒸ (of character, voice, surroundings, etc.) roughness, severity or harshness. (성격·목소리 따위의) 표독스러움; 거칠; 고생스러움. ¶ *the asperities of a very cold winter* 엄동설한의 고생스러움 / *He replied with some* ~ *in his voice.* 가시 돋친 목소리로 대답했다. [L. *asper* rough]

as·perse [əspə́:rs] *vt.* **1** (P6,13) sprinkle (water). (물)을 뿌리다; 끼얹다. **2** say cruel or false things about (someone); speak ill of (someone). (아무)를 중상(中傷)〔비난〕하다. ¶ ~ *someone's good name* 아무의 명예를 중상하다. [ad-, L. *spargo* sprinkle]

as·per·sion [əspə́:rʒən, -ʃən] *n.* ⓊⒸ the act of aspersing or speaking ill of someone. (물을) 뿌림; (남의) 욕을 함; 중상(中傷). ¶ *vehement aspersions of his honesty* 그의 성실성에 대한 지독한 중상 / *cast aspersions on* (*someone, someone's character*) 아무를 중상하다.

as·phalt [ǽsfɔ:lt / -fælt] *n.* Ⓤ hard, black material used in making roads. 아스팔트. ¶ *an* ~ *pavement* 아스팔트 포장 도로. — *vt.* pave (a road) with asphalt. (도로를) 아스팔트로 포장하다. [Gk.]

as·pho·del [ǽsfədèl] *n.* **1** 《bot.》 a plant of the lily family with spikes of white or yellow flowers. 아스포델. **2** 《Gk. myth.》 the flower of paradise blooming for ever. (시들지 않는다는) 낙원의 꽃. [Gk. → daffodil]

as·phyx·i·a [æsfíksiə] *n.* =asphyxiation.

as·phyx·i·ate [æsfíksièit] *vt.* (P6) suffocate. 질식(窒息)시키다. [Gk. *a-*, not, *sphuxis* pulse]

as·phyx·i·a·tion [æsfìksiéiʃən] *n.* Ⓤ suffocation. 질식.

as·pic[1] [ǽspik] *n.* Ⓤ a meat-jelly. 고기 젤리. [F.]

as·pic[2] [ǽspik] *n.* 《*arch.*》 =asp[1].

as·pi·dis·tra [æ̀spidístrə] *n.* 《bot.》 a plant with broad taper leaves. 엽란(葉蘭). [Gk. *aspis* shield]

as·pir·ant [ǽspərənt, əspáiər-] *n.* Ⓒ a person who aspires after a high position, honors, etc.; an ambitious person. 대망을 품은 사람; 야심가. ¶ *an* ~ *to honors* 명예를 추구하는 야심가 / *an* ~ *after* 〔*for, to*〕 …을 얻고자 하는 사람. [→aspire]

as·pi·rate [ǽspərèit] *vt.* (P6) pronounce with a breathing, or *h*-sound. 기음(氣音)〔*h* 음〕으로 발음하다. ¶ *The 'h' in 'hot' is aspirated.* 'hot'의 'h'는 기음으로 발음된다. — [ǽspərit] *adj.* pronounced with a breathing, or h-sound. 기음(氣音)으로 발음되는. — [ǽspərit] *n.* the sound of 'h'. 기음(氣音); h음.

as·pi·ra·tion [æ̀spəréiʃən] *n.* ⓊⒸ 《*after, for*》 the act of aspiring; a strong desire. 대망(大望); 열망. ¶ *have an* ~ *for* 〔*after*〕 *fame* 명성을 열망하다 / *His* ~ *to do the work has been realized.* 그 일을 하고자 한 그의 큰 뜻은 실현되었다 / *She had* ~ *to be an actress.* 그녀는 여배우가 되겠다는 야망이 있었다.

as·pire [əspáiər] *vi.* **1** (P3,4) 《*after, to, to do*》 desire eagerly or strongly. 열망하다. ¶ *He aspires to high literary honors.* 그는 문학의 세계에서 높은 명예를 얻기를 열망하고 있다 / *The whole nation aspired after independence.* 전국민이 독립을 갈망했다. **2** (P1) tower. 우뚝 솟다. [ad-, L. *spiro* breathe]

as·pi·rin [ǽspərìn] *n.* ⓊⒸ a medicine used to drive away pain. 아스피린. [↑]

·ass [æs] *n.* Ⓒ **1** 《zool.》 an animal with long ears related to the horse; a donkey. 당나귀. 參考 donkey가 일반적임. **2** a stupid person. 바보. ¶ *act like an* ~ 바보 같은 짓을 하다 / *You* ~*!* 이 바보 새끼. [E.]
make an ass of, make a fool of; make sport of. (아무)를 놀리다〔우롱하다〕.
make an ass of oneself, do something to deserve the laughter of others. (웃음거리가 될) 바보 같은 짓을 하다.

·as·sail [əséil] *vt.* (P6,13) 《*with*》 attack violently. …을 공격하다; 습격하다. ¶ ~ *someone with questions* 아무에게 질문 공세를 펴다 / *be assailed with fears* 공포의 엄습을 받다. [L. *salio* leap, jump]

as·sail·ant [əséilənt] *n.* a person who attacks; an attacker. 공격자.

as·sas·sin [əsǽsin] *n.* Ⓒ a person who murders, esp. for political purposes. 암살자; 자객. [Arab. =hashish-eater]

as·sas·si·nate [əsǽsənèit] *vt.* (P6) murder (someone) by a secret or sudden attack. …을 암살하다.

as·sas·si·na·tion [əsæ̀sənéiʃən] *n.* ⓊⒸ the act of assassinating; the state of being assassinated. 암살.

·as·sault [əsɔ́:lt] *n.* **1** Ⓒ a sudden attack. 기습(奇襲); 강습. ¶ *make an ~ on* 〔*upon*〕 *someone* 아무를 기습하다 / *take a castle by ~* 성(城)을 기습하여 빼앗다. **2** UC a violent bodily attack upon a person. 폭행. — *vt.* (P6) make an attack on (someone or something). (…)를 기습〔폭행〕하다. [as-, L. *salio* leap, →assail]

as·say [ǽsei, æséi] *vt.* (P6,8) **1** analyze (an ore) to find out the quantities of gold, silver, or other metals in it. (광석)을 시금〔분석〕하다. ¶ *~ the ore* 광석을 분석하다. **2** attempt; try; test. 시도하다; 시험하다. ¶ *~ one's strength* 자기의 힘을 시험해 보다. — *n.* U analysis of an ore. (광석의) 분석 시험. [L. *ex-* out, *ago* do, carry]

as·sem·blage [əsémblidʒ] *n.* **1** C a group of people who have come together for some purpose. 모인 일단의 사람들; 회중(會衆). **2** U the act of putting the parts of a machine, etc. together. (기계의) 조립(組立). ¶ *the ~ of the parts of the engine* 엔진 부품의 조립. [↓]

:as·sem·ble [əsémbəl] *vi.* (P1) come together in a group. 모이다; 집합하다. ¶ *~ in a playground* 운동장에 모이다. — *vt.* (P6) **1** bring (persons) together in a meeting. (…)을 모으다; 집합시키다. ¶ *~ much data* 많은 자료를 모으다 / *All the students are assembled in the hall.* 전교생이 강당에 모여 있다. **2** put (the parts of a machine) together. (기계)를 조립하다. [as-, L. *simul* together]

:as·sem·bly [əsémbli] *n.* (*pl.* **-blies**) C **1** a group of people gathered together for some purpose. 집회; 집합. ¶ *the city* 〔*municipal*〕 *~* 시의회(市議會). **2** U the act of putting or fitting the parts of a machine, etc. together. (기계의) 조립. **3** a signal on a bugle or drum for troops to assemble. (군대에서) 집합 신호 나팔〔북소리〕.

assembly line [–́–– ́–] *n.* a process of mass production by which the parts of a thing are assembled as on a conveyor belt. (공장의) 일관 작업.

as·sem·bly·man [əsémblimən] *n.* (*pl.* **-men** [-mən]) C **1** a member of a law-making body. 의원(議員). **2** 《*A-*》《U.S.》 a member of the lower house of a state law-making body. 주의회(州議會)의 하원 의원.

assembly room [–́–– ́–] *n.* **1** a room for a meeting. 회의실; 강당. **2** a factory where the parts of a machine, etc. are put together. (기계 따위의) 조립 공장.

·as·sent [əsént] *vi.* (P1,3) **1** 《*to*》 agree to (something). 동의〔찬성〕하다 (opp. dissent). ¶ *~ to a proposal* 제안에 동의하다 / *Only a few assented.* 불과 몇 사람만이 찬성했다. **2** concede; give in. 양보하다; 굴(복)하다. — *n.* U agreement. 동의. ¶ *by common ~* 전원 일치로 / *give one's ~ to someone or something* …에(게) 동의 하다. [as-, L. *sentio* think]

with one assent, unanimously. 만장 일치로.

:as·sert [əsə́ːrt] *vt.* (P6,11,21) **1** declare or insist on (something) solemnly and with certainty. …을 단언하다; …임〔함〕을 주장하다. ¶ *He asserted that he was innocent.* 그는 자신은 무죄라고 주장했다. **2** defend or support (a right, a claim, etc.). (권리·요구 따위)를 주장하다; 지지〔행사〕하다. ¶ *~ one's power* 권리를 행사하다. **3** 《*reflexively*》 defend one's rights 〔views〕; claim too much; put oneself forward. 자신의 권리를 〔의견을〕 주장하다; 너무 내세우다; 저절로 나타나다. ¶ *Virtue will ~ itself.* 덕(德)은 드러나기 마련이다. [as-, L. *sero* join]

·as·ser·tion [əsə́ːrʃən] *n.* UC the act of asserting; positive statement; declaration. 단언; 주장. ¶ *an unwarranted ~* 근거 없는 부당한 주장.

as·ser·tive [əsə́ːrtiv] *adj.* too confident in one's statements; asserting; positive. 단정적인; 자신이 강한. ¶ 《gram.》 *an ~ sentence* 서술문(敍述文).

as·sess [əsés] *vt.* (P6,13) **1** determine or fix the value of (property, income, etc.). (재산·수입 따위)를 사정(査定)하다. **2** fix the amount of (a tax, fine, damages, etc.). (세금·벌금·손해액 따위)를 정하다. ¶ *~ a tax on* 〔*upon*〕 *someone* 아무에게 과세(課稅)하다. [L. *sedeo* sit]

as·sess·ment [əsésmənt] *n.* U the act of assessing; valuation; C an amount assessed. 사정(査定); 세액 (평가).

as·ses·sor [əsésər] *n.* C **1** a person who gives advice to a judge or magistrate on technical matters. 보좌역(補佐役). **2** a person who determines the value of property, incomes, etc. for taxation. 세액 사정인(査定人).

as·set [ǽset] *n.* C something that has value; a desirable thing to have. 가치〔값어치〕 있는 것. ¶ *an ~ in negotiation* 협상시의 이점 / *be an ~ to* …에 도움이 되다 / *Good health is a great ~.* 건강은 큰 보배다. [L. *ad satis* to sufficiency]

as·sets [ǽsets] *n. pl.* valuable things; property, esp. that which may be used to pay one's debts. 자산(資産). ¶ *fixed* 〔*permanent*〕 *~* 고정 자산 / *~ and liabilities* 자산과 부채 / *cultural ~* 문화재.

as·sev·er·ate [əsévərèit] *vt.* declare solemnly; say strongly. …을 맹세하다; 단언하다. [as-, L. *severus* severe, strict]

as·sev·er·a·tion [əsèvəréiʃən] *n.* the act of asseverating; an oath. 맹세; 서언(誓言).

as·si·du·i·ty [æ̀sidjúːəti] *n.* (*pl.* **-ties**) **1** U the state of being assiduous; diligence. 근면; 면려(勉勵). ¶ *with ~* 부지런히; 근면하게. **2** 《*pl.*》 careful and eager attention. 배려. [L. *sedeo* sit]

as·sid·u·ous [əsídʒuəs] *adj.* working

steadily; eagerly attentive; diligent. 근면한 (opp. lazy). ● **as·sid·u·ous·ly** [-li] *adv.*

⁎**as·sign** [əsáin] *vt.* **1** (P13,14) 《*to*》 give a part of (something) to each; allot. …을 할당하다. ¶ ~ *homework* 숙제를 내다 / *He assigned a task to each person.* =*He assigned each person a task.* 그는 각 사람에게 임무를 할당했다 / *A large room has been assigned to us.* 우리에게 큰 방이 할당됐다. **2** (P13) fix or set a time for. (지)정하다. ¶ ~ *a day for a meeting* 회합 날을 지정하다. **3** (P13,20) 《*for, to*》 appoint. …을 선임〔지명〕하다. ¶ ~ *someone to guard duty* 아무에게 보초 근무를 명하다 / *I was assigned to watch the road.* 나는 길을 지키도록 지명되었다. **4** (P13) 《*to*》 give a cause of (something or someone); ascribe. …의 탓으로 치다. ¶ ~ *the failure to the lack of study* 실패를 연구 부족 탓으로 돌리다. **5** (P14) hand over or transfer (property, a right, etc.) legally. 양도하다. ¶ *The author assigned all rights in his book to his daughter.* 저자는 자기 저서의 권리를 딸에게 넘겨 주었다.

— *n.* Ⓒ one to whom property or right has been assigned in trust. 관재인(管財人); 양수인(讓受人). ● **as·sign·a·ble** [-əbl] *adj.* [as-, L. *signo* mark]

as·sig·na·tion [æ̀signéiʃən] *n.* **1** Ⓒ an appointment for a meeting. 회합 장소 및 일시의 지정. **2** Ⓒ a secret meeting. 밀회. **3** Ⓤ allotment. 할당. **4** Ⓤ legal transfer of property. 양도.

as·sign·ee [əsàiníː, æ̀siníː] *n.* Ⓒ an assign. 양수인(讓受人)(opp. assignor).

as·sign·ment [əsáinmənt] *n.* **1** Ⓤ the act of assigning; the state of being assigned; Ⓒ something assigned, esp. given as a piece of work to be done. 할당(된 일). **2** Ⓒ a lesson; homework. 과제; 숙제. ¶ *do an* ~ 숙제를 하다 / *Today's* ~ *in arithmetic is ten examples.* 오늘의 산수 숙제는 보기 문제 열 개이다. **3** ⓊⒸ a legal transference of property or other rights; the document by which such transference is made. (재산 따위의) 양도(讓渡); 양도 증서. **4** ⓊⒸ appointment; designation. 임명; 지정. ¶ *the* ~ *of someone to a new position* 새로운 직책에의 아무의 임명.

as·sim·i·late [əsímələ̀it] *vt.* **1** (P6,13) 《*to, with*》 cause (someone) to be like others (in customs, etc.). …를 동화(同化)시키다. **2** (P13) 《*to, with*》 compare with (something); liken. …와 비교하다; …에 비기다. ¶ ~ *one's life to a voyage* 인생을 항해에 비기다. **3** (P6) take (something) in and make it a part of oneself; digest; absorb. …을 동화하다; 소화〔흡수〕하다. ¶ *She does so much reading that she cannot* ~ *it all.* 그녀는 전부를 소화할 수 없을 만큼 많은 독서를 한다 / *China in the course of her history has assimilated many peoples.* 역사의 진전 과정에서 중국은 많은 민족을 흡수 동화했다. **4** (P6) master (knowledge); understand fully. …을 습득하다; 충분히 알다.

— *vi.* (P1,3) absorb oneself; become like others. 흡수〔동화〕되다; 같아지다. ¶ *The newcomer has assimilated quickly.* 신참자는 급속히 동화했다. [as-, L. *similus* similar]

as·sim·i·la·tion [əsìməléiʃən] *n.* Ⓤ the act of assimilating; the state of being assimilated; digestion; absorption. 동화(작용); 소화; 흡수(opp. dissimilation).

:**as·sist** [əsíst] *vt.* **1** (P6,13,20) 《*in, with*》 help. …을 돕다. ¶ *John assisted me in my work.* 존이 내 일을 도와 주었다 / *Can I* ~ *you with those parcels ?* 그 짐 좀 거들어 드릴까요. **2** (P6) further, advance. (움직여) 나아가게 하다. **3** (P6) give money to. …에게 돈을 주다. — *vi.* (P3) be present. 참석하다. ¶ ~ *at a meeting* 회합에 참석하다. [as-, L. *sisto* stand]

⁎**as·sist·ance** [əsístəns] *n.* Ⓤ the act of assisting; help. 원조; 조력. ¶ *come* 〔*go*〕 *to someone's* ~ 아무를 도우러 오다〔가다〕 / *My sister gave* ~ *to me in my homework.* 누나가 내 숙제를 도와 주었다.

⁎**as·sist·ant** [əsístənt] *n.* Ⓒ a person who assists; a helper; a co-worker. 조수; 점원. ¶ *a shop* ~ 점원. — *adj.* assisting; helping; helpful. 보좌의; 돕는. ¶ *an* ~ *professor* 조교수 / *an* ~ *manager* 부지배인.

as·siz·es [əsáiziz] *n. pl.* 《Brit.》 sessions of a special court of law held periodically in each county of England. (영국의) 순회 재판(개정기). [→assess]

Assoc. Association.

:**as·so·ci·ate** [əsóuʃièit] *vi.* (P3) **1** 《*with*》 keep company. 교제하다; 사귀다. ¶ *You must not* ~ *with dishonest people.* 정직하지 못한 사람과 사귀어서는 안 된다 / *He was forbidden to* ~ *with the boy next door.* 그는 이웃집 아이와 사귀는 것을 금지당했다. **2** 《*with*》 cooperate; work together. 제휴하다.

— *vt.* (P13) **1** 《often *reflexively*》 bring (oneself or someone) with others, usu. for a special purpose. …을 연합시키다. ¶ ~ *oneself with an enterprise* 사업에 한 몫 들다 / *We associated him with us in the attempt.* 우리는 그 계획에 그를 참가시켰다. **2** 《*with*》 connect (things) in the mind. 연상(聯想)하다. ¶ *We* ~ *the name of Einstein with the theory of relativity.* 우리는 상대성 원리하면 아인슈타인을 연상한다 / *Many people* ~ *war with death and pestilence.* 전쟁이라고 하면 죽음과 전염병을 연상하는 사람들이 많다.

— [əsóuʃiit, -èit] *n.* Ⓒ a person joined with others; a member of a group; a companion; a partner. 동료; 회원. ¶ *He has been my* ~ *for a long time.* 그는 오래 전부터의 내 동료이다.

— [əsóuʃiit, -èit] *adj.* united or joined for a

common purpose. 연합된; 동료의. ¶ *an ~ judge* 배석(陪席) 판사 / *an ~ member* 준회원. [as-, L. *socius* sharing, allied]

as·so·ci·at·ed [əsóuʃièitid] *adj.* being in association; united; joint. 연합한. ¶ *the Associated Press* 미국의 AP 통신사.

:as·so·ci·a·tion [əsòusiéiʃən, -ʃi-] *n.* **1** Ⓤ the act of associating; the state of being associated; companionship; partnership. 교제; 제휴. ¶ *~ with bad companions* 악우(惡友)와의 어울림〔사귐〕. **2** Ⓒ a group of persons acting together for some special purpose; a society. 협회. ¶ *a cooperative ~* 협동 조합 / *the Young Men's* 〔*Women's*〕 *Christian Association* 기독교 청년〔여자 청년〕회 (abbr. Y.M. 〔W.〕 C.A.). **3** Ⓤ the act of connecting ideas in the mind; Ⓒ ideas connected in the mind. 연상(聯想). ¶ *~ of ideas* 관념 연합; 연상.

in association with, in cooperation with; in connection with. …와 협동하여〔으로〕; …에〔과〕 관련하여.

association football [−−−⏊−⏊−] *n.* 《Brit.》 soccer. (아식) 축구(cf. *Rugby football*).

as·so·nance [ǽsənəns] *n.* similarity of words having the same vowel sound but different consonants. (모음이 같은) 반계음(半階音)《hat, man 따위》. [ad-, L. *sonus* sound]

as·sort [əsɔ́ːrt] *vt.* (P13) divide (things) into separate classes; classify. …을 분류하다. ¶ *These socks are assorted in size.* 이 양말은 크기대로 분류되어 있다 / *a box of assorted biscuits* 여러 종류의 비스킷이 든 상자. — *vi.* (P3) 《*with*》 match; suit. 어울리다. ¶ *The hat assorts well with his suit.* 그 모자는 그의 양복과 잘 어울린다. [→sort]

as·sort·ed [əsɔ́ːrtid] *adj.* divided into groups. 분류한.

as·sort·ment [əsɔ́ːrtmənt] *n.* ⓊⒸ the act of assorting; the state of being assorted; a set of various kinds of things. 분류; 유별(類別); 각종 배합; 구색 갖춤. ¶ *We have a complete ~ of traveling requisites.* 우리는 여행 용품이 전부 갖추어져 있다.

as·suage [əswéidʒ] *vt.* (P6) **1** lessen (pain, anger, sorrow, etc.); soften; calm. (고통·노염·슬픔 따위)를 누그러뜨리다; 완화하다; 가라앉히다. ¶ *~ one's grief* 슬픔을 가라앉히다. **2** appease; satisfy. 만족시키다; 채우다. ¶ *~ one's hunger* 배고픔을 채우다. [ad-, L. *suavis* sweet]

as·sum·a·ble [əsjúːməbl] *adj.* that can be assumed. 가정할 수 있는. [↓]

:as·sume [əsjúːm] *vt.* **1** (P6,11,21) suppose or accept (something) to be a fact; suppose or believe (someone) to be something; take for granted. 가정〔추정〕하다; (…하다고) 보다; 당연한 것으로 하다. ¶ *We assumed that the news was true.* 우리는 그 소식이 사실이라고 생각했다 / *They assumed him to be an American.* 그들은 그가 미국인일 것으로 추정했다 / *Assuming that this is true, what should I do?* 이것이 사실이라고 친다면 나는 어떻게 해야 되는가. **2** (P6) take (something) upon oneself; undertake; adopt. (책임·임무)를 떠맡다; (태도)를 취하다. ¶ *~ office* 취임하다 / *~ new duties* 새 임무를 맡다 / *~ the chair* 의장석에 앉다 / *~ a responsibility* 책임을 떠맡다 / *~ an obligation* 의무를 지다 / *~ the offensive* 공세를 취하다 / *~ a threatening attitude* 위협적인 태도를 취하다. **3** (P6,11) pretend; put on; take on. …인 체하다; …을 가장하다; (외관)을 나타내다. ¶ *~ an air of innocence* 결백한 체하다 / *~ illness* 병을 가장하다 / *~ to be ignorant* 모르는 체하다 / *He assumes to have knowledge of this fact.* 그는 이 사실에 대해 잘 아는 체한다. **4** (P6) take the form of; become like. … 모양을 취하다〔띠다〕; …같아지다. ¶ *This matter assumes a very grave character.* 이 문제는 매우 중대한 성격을 띤다. **5** (P6) take (something) as one's own. (남의 것)을 제것으로 하다; 횡령하다. [L. *sumo* take]

as·sum·ing [əsjúːmiŋ] *adj.* too bold or selfconfident; presumptuous; arrogant. 건방진; 오만한.

·as·sump·tion [əsʌ́mpʃən] *n.* ⓊⒸ **1** the act of assuming; the state of being assumed; something assumed; (a) supposition. 가정(假定). ¶ *a mere ~* 전혀 근거 없는 억측 / *Our ~ that he had stolen the ring proved incorrect.* 그가 반지를 훔쳤다는 우리들의 억측은 사실이 아닌 것으로 밝혀졌다. **2** the act of taking a position, power, etc. 취임; (권력의) 장악. ¶ *His ~ of power was welcomed by everyone.* 그의 권력 장악은 모든 사람에게 환영되었다. **3** the act of taking (something) without right. 횡령. **4** pretense; disguise. …체함; 가장; 위장. **5** 《*the A-*》 the taking up into heaven of the Virgin Mary; also, the church festival on August 15 celebrating this. 성모 몽소 승천(聖母蒙召昇天)(축일).

on the assumption (=*supposing*) ***that ….*** …라는 가정 아래.

·as·sur·ance [əʃúərəns] *n.* **1** Ⓒ the act of assuring; the state of being assured; guarantee. 보증. ¶ *a definite ~* 확실한 보증 / *He gave an ~ that the debt would be paid.* 그는 빚을 갚겠다는 보증을 했다. **2** Ⓤ certainty; sureness; confidence; self-confidence. 확신; 자신. ¶ *with ~* 확신을 가지고 / *act in the ~ of success* 성공을 확신하고 행동하다 / *She played a sonata with ~.* 그녀는 자신있게 소나타를 연주했다. **3** Ⓤ 《chiefly Brit.》 life insurance. (생명) 보험. **4** impudence; too great boldness. 뻔뻔스러움; 철면피. ¶ *He actually had the ~ to claim he had done it himself.* 그는 정말 뻔뻔스럽게도 그것을 자신이 했다고 주장했다. [↓]

:as·sure [əʃúər] *vt.* **1** (P6) bring (a certain

result) without fail. …을 약속하다; 결과를 보증하다. ¶ *Does hard work always ~ success?* 근면은 언제나 성공을 보장하는가. **2** (P13,15) 《*of*》 convince (someone) of something; say as a sure act [fact] to (someone); try to make (someone) believe. …을 확신하다; 보증하다; …에게 확신[납득]시키다. ¶ *I ~ you of his honesty.* 나는 그의 정직을 보증한다 / *I ~ you that there is no danger.* 나는 위험이 없다는 것을 보증한다 / *He assured me that his servant was trustworthy.* 그는 자기 하인이 믿을 만하다고 내게 확신시켰다 / *I wish I could be assured of its truth.* 나는 그것이 사실이기를 바란다. [as-, →sure]

as·sured [əʃúərd] *adj.* **1** certain; sure. 확실한. ¶ *an ~ income* 확실한 수입 / *an ~ position* 보장된 지위 / *the ~ life of a businessman* 사업가의 안정된 생활 / *Our victory is quite ~.* 우리의 승리는 정말 확실하다. **2** 《*of*》 feeling certain that…; confident. …임을 확신하는; 자신하는. ¶ *an ~ manner* 자신 있는 태도 / *I am ~ that he will succeed.* 나는 그가 성공하리라고 확신하고 있다.

as·sur·ed·ly [əʃúːəridli] *adv.* in an assured manner; without doubt; surely; confidently. 확실히; 단호히.

As·syr·i·a [əsíriə] *n.* an ancient country in southwest Asia. 아시리아《고대 서남 아시아의 왕국》. ● **As·syr·i·an** *adj., n.*

as·ta·tine [ǽstətìːn, -tin] *n.* 《chem.》 an unstable chemical element. 아스타틴《할로겐 원소족의 하나. 기호 At》. [Gk.]

as·ter [ǽstər] *n.* Ⓒ 《bot.》 a plant with blue, pink, or white starlike flowers. 애스터《까실쑥부쟁이속(屬)의 식물》. [Gk. *astron* star]

as·ter·isk [ǽstərisk] *n.* Ⓒ a starlike mark (*) used in printing or writing to call attention. 별표《*》. [Gk. =little star]

a·stern [əstə́ːrn] *adv.* 《naut.》 at or toward the back end of a ship. 고물로; 뒤로. ¶ *fall* [*drop*] *~* 딴 배에 앞질리다 / *Go ~!* 후진하라. [a(-), *stern*]

as·ter·oid [ǽstərɔ̀id] *n.* Ⓒ **1** 《astron.》 a small star or planet. 소행성(小行星). **2** 《zool.》 a starfish. 불가사리. ── *adj.* starlike in shape. 별 모양의. [Gk. *astron* star]

asth·ma [ǽzmə, ǽs-] *n.* Ⓤ 《med.》 a disease that makes breathing noisy and difficult. 천식(喘息). [Gk. *azō* breathe hard]

asth·mat·ic [æzmǽtik, æs-] *adj.* **1** of asthma. 천식의. **2** suffering from asthma. 천식을 앓는. ── *n.* Ⓒ a person suffering from asthma. 천식 환자. [↑]

a·stig·ma·tism [əstígmətìzəm] *n.* Ⓤ a diseased state of the eyes that causes a person to see certain parts of a thing less clearly than the rest. 난시(亂視); 난시안. [Gk. *a-* not, *stigmatos* mark]

a·stir [əstə́ːr] *adv., adj.* 《always as *predicative*》 **1** in (a state of) motion; moving; excited. 움직여; 술렁거려; 흥분해. ¶ *The town was ~ with the news.* 읍내는 그 소식으로 술렁거리고 있었다. **2** out of bed. 일어나. ¶ *be early ~* 일찍 일어나 있다. [a(-), →stir]

·as·ton·ish [əstániʃ / -tɔ́n-] *vt.* (P6) 《often in the *passive*》 surprise (someone) greatly. …을 깜짝 놀라게 하다(cf. *astound*). ¶ *The size of the elephant astonished the boy.* 코끼리의 크기는 그 소년을 깜짝 놀라게 했다 / *I was astonished at the news.* 나는 그 소식에 깜짝 놀랐다 / *I was astonished that she married such a man.* 나는 그녀가 그런 남자와 결혼한 것에 놀랐다. [L. *ex-* out, *tono* thunder]

as·ton·ish·ing [əstániʃiŋ / -tɔ́n-] *adj.* very surprising. 놀랄 만한; 놀라운. ¶ *an ~ man* 놀라운 인물 [參考] *an astonished man* 은 놀라고 있는 사람 / *The news was ~ to every country in the world.* 그 소식은 세계 각국에 놀라운 일이었다. ● **as·ton·ish·ing·ly** [-li] *adv.*

·as·ton·ish·ment [əstániʃmənt / -tɔ́n-] *n.* **1** Ⓤ the state of being astonished; great surprise. 놀람. **2** Ⓒ something astonishing. 놀라운 일.

in* [*with*] *astonishment, in surprise or amazement. 놀라서.

to one's astonishment, to one's surprise. 놀랍게도. ¶ *To my ~ he was there before us.* 놀랍게도 그는 우리에 앞서 거기에 있었다.

as·tound [əstáund] *vt.* (P6) astonish (someone) greatly; overwhelm (someone) with surprise. …을 깜짝 놀라게 하다. ¶ *I was not astonished; I was astounded.* 나는 놀란 것이 아니라 기겁을 했다. [→astonish]

as·tound·ing [əstáundiŋ] *adj.* very astonishing. 놀라운.

as·tra·khan, -chan [ǽstrəkən, -kæ̀n] *n.* Ⓤ a young lamb's skin with curled wool. 아스트라한 모피(毛皮). [參考] 러시아의 Astrakhan 지방에서 남. [Place in Russia]

as·tral [ǽstrəl] *adj.* of the stars. 별의. ¶ *~ hatch* (항공기의) 관측용 반원형창(窓). [L. *astrum* star]

a·stray [əstréi] *adj.* 《as *predicative*》 *adv.* wandering out of the right way. 길을 잃고. [→stray]

go astray, **a**) go out of the right way; lose one's way. 길을 잃다. **b**) go wrong. 타락하다.

lead** someone **astray, lead someone out of the right way. 나쁜 길에 들게 하다. ¶ *The young man was led ~ by his bad companions.* 그 젊은이는 나쁜 친구들 때문에 타락했다.

a·stride [əstráid] *adv.* with the legs apart, as in horseback riding. 두 다리를 걸치고; 걸터앉아. ¶ *ride a horse ~* 말에 걸터앉다 / *She sat ~ the horse.* 그녀는 말에 올라탔다 / *He got ~ me.* 그는 쓰러진 내 위에 올라탔다. [a(-)]

as·trin·gen·cy [əstríndʒənsi] *n.* Ⓤ the state of being astringent. 수렴성(收斂性); 엄격함. [↓]

as·trin·gent [əstríndʒənt] *adj.* **1** 《med.》 causing the skin to contract or shrink; tightening. 수렴〔수축〕성의. ¶ *an ~ liquid for the skin* 피부 수렴액(收斂液). **2** stern; severe; harsh. 모진; 엄한. —*n.* Ⓒ a substance that makes the skin contracted or shrinken. 수축〔수렴〕제(劑). [ad-, L. *stringo* bind]

as·tro·labe [ǽstrəlèib] *n.* an instrument formerly used for observing the position of the sun or stars. 천체 관측의(觀測儀). [Gk. *astron* star, *lambanō* take]

as·trol·o·ger [əstrálədʒər / -trɔ́l-] *n.* Ⓒ a person who studies the stars in order to predict the future. 점성가(占星家). [↓]

as·tro·log·i·cal [æ̀strəládʒikəl / -lɔ́dʒ-] *adj.* of astrology. 점성술의.

as·trol·o·gy [əstrálədʒi / -trɔ́l-] *n.* Ⓤ the study of the stars in order to know what will happen in the future. 점성술(占星術). [Gk. *astron* star, →-logy]

as·tro·naut [ǽstrənɔ̀:t] *n.* Ⓒ a traveler through space. 우주 비행사. [↑, L. *nautēs* sailor]

as·tro·nau·ti·cal [æ̀strənɔ́:tikəl] *adj.* of astronautics. 우주 비행의.

as·tro·nau·tics [æ̀strənɔ́:tiks] *n. pl.* 《used as *sing*》 the science and technology of space flight. 우주 비행술〔항해학〕.

as·tron·o·mer [əstránəmər / -trɔ́n-] *n.* Ⓒ a person who studies the science of the sun, stars, and planets. 천문학자. [↓]

as·tro·nom·i·cal [æ̀strənámikəl / -nɔ́m-] *adj.* **1** of astronomy. 천문학의. ¶ *an ~ observatory* 천문대. **2** (of a number or amount) enormous. (수·양 등이) 천문학적인; 거대한. ¶ *~ figures* 천문학적 숫자.

as·tron·o·my [əstránəmi / -trɔ́n-] *n.* Ⓤ the scientific study of the stars, planets, and other heavenly bodies. 천문학. [↓, Gk. *nemō* arrange]

as·tro·phys·ics [æ̀strou fíziks] *n.* astronomical physics. 천체 물리학. [Gk. *astron star,* →physics]

as·tute [əstjú:t] *adj.* very clever; shrewd; keen; cunning. 약은; 약삭빠른; 빈틈없는; 날카로운. ¶ *an ~ men of business* 빈틈없는 사업가 / *an ~ observer* 날카로운 관찰자. [L.]

as·tute·ness [əstjú:tnis] *n.* Ⓤ keenness; shrewdness. 약빠름; 기민함; 교활.

a·sun·der [əsʌ́ndər] *adv.* 《as *predicative*》 **1** into pieces; separately. 조각조각; 산산히; 뿔뿔이. ¶ *cut ~* 둘로 자르다 / *tear paper ~* 종이를 갈기갈기 찢다 / *fly ~* 뿔뿔이 날다 / *fall ~* 우르르 무너져 내리다. **2** distant from each other; (of persons) separated. (거리상으로) 떨어져; (사람이) 떨어져. ¶ *The two places lay far ~.* 그 두 곳은 멀리 떨어져 있었다. [a-, →sunder]

a·sy·lum [əsáiləm] *n.* Ⓒ **1** a place where madmen, orphans or old people are taken care of. (광인·고아 등의) 보호 시설; 수용소. ¶ *an ~ for the aged* 양로원 / *a lunatic ~* 정신 병원. **2** the protection given by one country to refugees from another country. (망명자 등에 대한) 정치적 보호. ¶ *seek political ~* 정치적 피난처를 찾다 / *grant ~ to* …에게 망명을 허용하다. [Gk. =inviolable]

At 《chem.》 astatine.

:at [æt, ət] *prep.* **1** (of a place or space) in; on; near; by. …에(서). ¶ *~ the center* 중심에 / *~ a distance* 멀리(서) / *~ the end of the line* 〔*queue*〕 열의 맨 뒤에 / *~ the bottom of the barrel* 통의 밑바닥에 / *stand ~ the door* 〔*exit*〕 현관〔출구〕에 서다 / *arrive ~ the destination* 목적지에 도착하다 / *change the trains ~ Ch'onan* 천안(天安) 역에서 갈아타다 / *Knock ~ the door.* 문을 노크해라 / *He was present ~ the meeting.* 그는 모임에 참석했다. **2** (of a place) through; by way of; from. …에서; …로부터; …을 지나서〔통해서〕. ¶ *enter ~ the front door* 정문으로 들어가다 / *get out of the house ~ the back door* 뒷문을 통해 집에서 나오다 / *look out ~ the window* 창밖을 내다보다 / *get the facts ~ their source* 사실을 소식통에서 입수하다 / *Smoke came out ~ the chimney.* 굴뚝에서 연기가 나왔다. **3** (of time) on or upon the point of; during the time of. … 때〔시〕에. ¶ *~ noon* 정오에 / *~ midnight* 한밤중에 / *~ present* 현재 / *~ six* (*o'lock*) 6시에 / *~ supper time* 저녁 식사 때 / *~ the age of 70,* 나이 70에 / *~ Christmas* 크리스마스에 / *~ the end of the month* 월말에 / *for days ~ a time* 한번에 며칠씩이나 / *arrive ~ the same moment* 동시에 도착하다. **4** engaged in; doing. …에 종사 중에〔열중하고〕; …을 하고 있는. ¶ *~ school* 학교에서 수업 중 / *~ church* 교회에서 예배 중 / *~ supper* 저녁식사 중 / *~* (*the*) *table* 식사 중 / *~ the battle* 종군하고 / *be ~ work* 〔*play*〕 일을 하고〔놀고〕 있다 / *forget one's worries ~ the piano* 피아노를 쳐서 시름을 잊다 / *What are you ~ now?* 지금 무엇을 하고 있나. **5** as to the ability in. 능력에 대해. ¶ *an expert ~ chess* 장기의 명수 / *poor ~ music* 음악을 잘 못하여 / *be slow* 〔*quick*〕 *~ learning* 이해가 더디다〔빠르다〕 / *be good ~ language* 어학을 잘하다. **6** in the state or condition of.… 상태에; …입장에; …하고. ¶ *~ gaze* 응시하고 / *~ anchor* 정박 중에 / *~ war* 전쟁 중에 / *~ odds* 불화하게 / *put the candidate ~ ease* 수험생을 마음 편하게 하다 / *The storm was ~ its worst about noon.* 폭풍우가 정오경에는 최악의 상태였다 / *They were ~ peace with Germany.* 그들은 독일과 우호 관계에 있었다 / *The driver is ~ fault.* 운전사 쪽이 나쁘다. **7** to; toward; in the direction of. …을 향하여; …을 목표로 (하여). ¶ *aim ~ a mark* 표적을 겨냥하다 / *throw a stone ~ a dog* 개에게 돌을 던지다 / *arrive ~ a conclusion* 결론에 도달하

다 / *laugh* ~ *someone* 아무를 비웃다 / *catch* ~ *a butterfly* 나비를 잡으려 하다 / *run* ~ *the enemy* 적을 향하여 내닫다 / *Look* ~ *me.* 나를 보아라 / *He came* ~ *me with a knife.* 그는 나이프를 가지고 내게 다가 왔다 / *Let's make an attempt* ~ *a solution.* 해결책을 찾을 수 있을지 해 보세. **8** because of; by reason of. …의 원인으로〔이유로〕; …하고; …을 보고〔듣고〕. ¶ ~ *my request* 나의 요청으로 / ~ *his command* 그의 명령으로 / *wonder* 〔*grieve*〕 ~ *the sight of* … 을 보고 놀라다〔슬퍼하다〕 / *faint* ~ *the sight of blood* 피를 보고 까무러치다 / *feel sick* ~ *the thought of* …을 생각만 해도 기분이 나빠지다 / *rejoice* ~ *his return to good health* 그가 건강을 회복한 것을 기뻐하다. **9** in the amount, degree, number, price, or rate of. …로; …에. ¶ ~ *6 dollars apiece* 한 개 6달러로 / ~ *a good price* 좋은 값으로 / *estimate a crowd* ~ *300,* 군중 수를 300명으로 어림하다 / *run* ~ *full speed* 전속력으로 달리다 / *be* ~ *boiling point* 비등점에 달해 있다 / *sell* ~ *a discount of 20%,* 2할 할인해서 팔다 / *walk* ~ *snail's pace* 거북이 걸음으로〔느릿느릿〕 걷다 / ~ *60 miles an hour* 시속 60 마일로 / *I bought the book* ~ *5 dollars.* 그 책을 5달러에 샀다. **10** according to; dependent on. …에 따라; …대로. ¶ ~ *will* 마음대로 / ~ *one's mercy* …이 하는 대로; …에 좌우되어 / *Come* ~ *your convenience.* 편리한 때에 오시오. [E.]

at that, moreover; nevertheless. 그래도 (역시); 그렇다 해도. ¶ *It was dear* ~ *that.* 그래도 역시 비쌌다.

at·a·vism [ǽtəvìzəm] *n.* Ⓤ **1** resemblance to a remote ancestor. 격세 유전(隔世遺傳). **2** reversion to a primitive type. 귀선 유전(歸先遺傳). [L. *atavus* ancestor]

a·tax·y [ətǽksi], **a·tax·i·a** [ətǽksiə] *n.* Ⓤ irregularity of animal functions. 운동 실조(運動失調). [GK. *a-* not, *taxis* order]

:ate [eit / et] *vt., vi.* p. of **eat.**

at·el·ier [ǽtəljèi] *n.* Ⓒ《F.》 a room where a painter or craftsman works; a workshop; a studio. 아틀리에.

a·the·ism [éiθiizəm] *n.* Ⓤ the belief that there is no God. 무신론(opp. theism). [Gk. *a-* not, *theos* god]

a·the·ist [éiθiist] *n.* Ⓒ a person who believes that there is no God. 무신론자(opp. theist).

a·the·is·tic [èiθiístik] *adj.* of atheism. 무신론의(opp. theistic).

A·the·na [əθí:nə] *n.* 《Gk. myth.》 the goddess of wisdom and the arts. 아테네 여신. 參考 로마 신화의 Minerva에 해당함. [Gk.]

A·the·ne [əθí:ni] *n.* =Athena.

A·the·ni·an [əθí:niən] *adj.* of Athens. 아테네(사람)의. — *n.* Ⓒ a person born or living in Athens. 아테네 사람.

Ath·ens [ǽθinz] *n.* the capital of Greece. 아테네.

a·thirst [əθə́:rst] *adj.* 《as *predicative*》 thirsty; wanting to drink. 갈망하여. ¶ *be* ~ *for information* 지식을 갈망하다. [a(-)]

ath·lete [ǽθli:t] *n.* Ⓒ a person who is trained for games or sports. 운동가; 운동선수. [Gk. *athlon* prize]

***ath·let·ic** [æθlétik] *adj.* of athletics; like an athlete. 운동 경기의; 운동 선수 같은. ¶ *an* ~ *meet* 〔*meeting*〕 운동회.

ath·let·ics [æθlétiks] *n. pl.* **1** exercises of physical power, speed, and skill; active games and sports. 운동 경기. **2** 《used as *sing.*》 the principles of athletic training. 체육 실기〔과목〕.

at-home [əthóum] *n.* Ⓒ informal reception at an appointed time. (비공식적인) 초대 모임. ¶ *an* ~ *day* 면회일; 집에서 손님 접대하는 날. [→at, home]

a·thwart [əθwɔ́:rt] *adv.* across from one side to another. (비스듬히) 가로질러. — *prep.* across; against. …을 가로질러; 거슬러. [a(-)]

go athwart one's purpose, cross one's purpose. 뜻대로 되지 않다.

-a·tion [-éiʃən] *suf.* forming nouns. '동작, 상태, 결과'의 뜻. ¶ *civilization* / *representation* / *combination* / *demonstration.*

:At·lan·tic [ətlǽntik] *n.* 《*the* ~》 the ocean on the east of North and South America. 대서양. — *adj.* of the Atlantic Ocean. 대서양의. ¶ 《U.S.》 *the* ~ *states* 대서양 연안의 여러 주(州). [↓]

at·las [ǽtləs] *n.* **1** Ⓒ a book of maps. 지도책. 參考 map을 모아 책으로 엮은 것. **2** 《*A-*》 《Gk. myth.》 a giant who supported the heavens on his shoulders. 아틀라스 신(神). [Gk. *atlas*]

:at·mos·phere [ǽtməsfìər] *n.* **1** Ⓤ the air surrounding the earth; the air in some place. 대기(大氣); (특정 장소의) 공기. **2** Ⓒ a general feeling. 상황; 분위기. ¶ *the political* ~ *of the country* 그 나라의 정치 상황 / *the cold* ~ *of a room* 방의 차가운 분위기 / *There was an electric* ~ *at the meeting.* 모임에서 분위기가 몹시 흥분되어 있었다. [Gk. *atmos* vapour, *sphaira* shere]

at·mos·pher·ic [æ̀tməsférik] *adj.* of atmosphere. 대기의; 대기 중의. ¶ *high* 〔*low*〕 ~ *pressure* 고기압〔저기압〕 / *The* ~ *conditions today are poor for flying.* 오늘 기상 상태는 비행에 적합지 않다.

at·mos·pher·ics [æ̀tməsfériks] *n. pl.* 《electr.》 공전(空電).

at·oll [ǽtɔ:l, ətál, ǽtoul / ǽtɔl, ətɔ́l] *n.* Ⓒ a coral island which is in the shape of a ring. 환초(環礁). [Malaya]

***at·om** [ǽtəm] *n.* **1** Ⓒ 《phys.》 the smallest element of matter. 원자. ¶ *A molecule of water is made of two atoms of hydrogen and one* ~ *of oxygen.* 물의 분자는 수소 원자

2개와 산소 원자 1개로 되어 있다. **2** a very small amount. 미소(微小)한 것. ¶ *There is not an ~ of truth in the rumor.* 그 풍문에는 진실이란 눈곱만큼도 없다. [Gk. *a-* not, *temno* cut]

·a·tom·ic [ətámik / ətɔ́m-] *adj.* **1** of atoms. 원자의. ¶ *an ~ bomb* 원자탄 / *the ~ theory* 〔*hypothesis*〕 원자론〔설〕 / *the ~ age* 원자력 시대 / *an ~ power plant* 원자력 발전소 / *~ energy* 원자력 / *the ~ number* 원자 번호 / *an ~ pile* 원자로 / *~ warfare* 원자전(戰). **2** very small; minute. 미소(微小)한.

a·tom·ics [ətámiks / ətɔ́m-] *n. pl.* 《used as *sing.*》 the branch of physics dealing with atomic energy and nuclear fission. 핵물리학; 원자학.

at·om·ize [ǽtəmàiz] *vt.* (P6) **1** separate (a matter) into atoms. 원자로 분해하다. **2** change (a liquid, etc.) into a minute spray. (액체 등을) 분무로 하여 뿜다.

at·om·iz·er [ǽtəmàizər] *n.* Ⓒ an instrument used to blow a liquid in the form of a very fine spray. 분무기(噴霧器).

at·om·y[1] [ǽtəmi] *n.* **1** an atom. 원자. **2** a tiny being. 난쟁이. [→atom]

at·om·y[2] [ǽtəmi] *n.* **1** a skeleton. 해골. **2** a very thin person. 말라깽이. [↑]

a·tone [ətóun] *vi.* (P3) 《*for*》 make repayment for a wrong or fault. 속죄하다; 보상하다. [*at, one* set at one, unite]

a·tone·ment [ətóunmənt] *n.* Ⓤ **1** the act of atoning. 속죄; 보상. **2** 《*the A-*》 the sufferings and death of Christ to atone for the sins of mankind. (예수의) 구속(救贖). [↑]

a·top [ətáp / ətɔ́p] *adv.* on or at the top. 정상(頂上)에. — *prep.* on or at the top of. …의 정상에. ¶ *~ the flagpole* 깃대 꼭대기에. [a(-)]

at·ra·bil·i·ous [æ̀trəbíljəs] *adj.* hypochondriac. 우울증(憂鬱症)의. [Gk. *atra bilis* black bile]

a·tri·a [éitriə] *n.* pl. of **atrium.**

a·tri·um [éitriəm] *n.* (*pl.* **a·tri·a, -ums**) the central court of an ancient Roman house. 안뜰; 중정(中庭). [L.]

a·tro·cious [ətróuʃəs] *adj.* very cruel; very wicked. 잔학한. ¶ *~ behavior* 잔학 행위 / *an ~ crime* 흉악 범죄. ● **a·tro·cious·ly** [-li] *adv.* [L. *atrox*]

a·troc·i·ty [ətrásəti / ətrɔ́s-] *n.* Ⓤ cruelty; brutality; Ⓒ a very cruel act. 잔학함; 잔학 행위. [↑]

at·ro·phy [ǽtrəfi] *n.* Ⓤ 《med.》 the state in which a part of the body wastes away. 위축. — *vi., vt.* (P1;6) waste away. 위축〔퇴화(退化)〕하다〔시키다〕. [Gk. *a-* not, *trephein* to nourish]

at·ro·pine [ǽtrəpìːn, -pin] *n.* 《chem.》 the poison of deadly night-shades. 아트로핀《유독 물질; 경련 완화제》. [Gk.]

:at·tach [ətǽtʃ] *vt.* **1** (P13) 《*to*》 join; fasten. …을 (붙들어)매다; 붙이다. ¶ *~ a rope to a dog* 개에 줄을 매다 / *~ a photograph to application papers with a staple* 호치키스 바늘로 원서에 사진을 붙이다 / *a strong link that attaches the individual to the whole* 개인을 전체에 붙들어 매는 강한 유대 / *Tom attached a label to the baggage.* 톰은 소화물에 꼬리표를 달았다. **2** (P13) 《*to*》 make (someone or something) belong; include. 소속시키다; 참가〔가입〕시키다. ¶ *~ her to the expedition* 그녀를 원정대에 포함시키다 / *a high school attached to a university* 대학 부속 고등 학교 / *We are attached to the San Francisco Police.* 우리는 샌프란시스코 경찰 소속의 사람이다 / *She attached herself to the party.* 그녀는 그 당에 가입했다. **3** (P6) gain over to one's side, party, etc. 자기편 따위에 끌어 넣다. **4** (P13) affix; fix. 누르다. ¶ *~ one's signature to* …에 서명 날인하다. **5** (P13) appoint. 배속하다. ¶ *~ an officer to a regiment* 장교를 연대에 배속하다. **6** (P13) bind by affection; attract. 애정의 줄로 묶다; 끌다. ¶ *I am attached to Republic of Korea.* 나는 대한 민국을 사랑한다 / *He is deeply attached to her.* 그는 그녀를 깊이 사랑하고 있다. **7** (P13) attribute; assign. (책임으로) 돌리다; (중요성·의미 따위)를 두다. ¶ *~ weight to* …에 비중을 두다 / *~ importance to* …에 중요성〔중점〕을 두다 / *The police attached the blame to the driver.* 경찰은 그 책임을 운전사의 탓으로 돌렸다. **8** (P6) seize (a person or property) according to law; arrest. 구속하다; 압류하다. ¶ *All of his salary was attached.* 그의 급료가 전액 압류되었다 / *He was attached for treason.* 그는 반역죄로 체포되었다. — *vi.* (P3) go with; belong to. 동반하다; 따르다; 속하다. ¶ *No honor attaches to this position.* 이 지위에는 아무 명예도 따르지 않는다. [F. *a-* to, *tacē* nail; to a nail]

be attached to (=*be fond of; love*) *someone.* (아무를) 좋아하다; 애착을 갖다. ¶ *She is very attached to her aunt.* 그녀는 자기 숙모를 좋아한다.

at·tach·a·ble [ətǽtʃəbəl] *adj.* that can attached. 붙일 수 있는; 압류할 수 있는.

at·ta·ché [æ̀təʃéi, ətǽʃei] *n.* Ⓒ a person who goes with an ambassador to a foreign country. 공관원(公館員); 수행원. [→attach]

attaché case [–⌐–⌐] *n.* a small, flat case for documents shaped like a suitcase. 서류 손가방.

at·tach·ment [ətǽtʃmənt] *n.* **1** Ⓤ the act of attaching; the state of being attached; Ⓒ something that is fixed. 부착; 부착〔부속〕물. **2** Ⓤ affection 애정; 애착. ¶ *~ to one's mother* 어머니에 대한 사랑.

:at·tack [ətǽk] *vt.* (P6) **1** fight against (someone or something). …을 공격하다. ¶ *~ the enemy* 적을 공격하다. **2** (of a disease, medicines, etc.) act harmfully on (a person or thing). (병 따위가) 침해하다; 덮치다; (약품 따위가) 침식〔해롭게 작용〕하다. ¶ *Influenza attacked the whole town.* 악성 감기가 온 마을에 만연했다 / *She was attacked by pneumonia.* 그녀는 폐렴에 걸렸다 / *Acids ~ metal.* 산(酸)은 금속을 부식시킨다. **3** speak or write against. (말이나 글로) 공격하다; 비난하다. ¶ *~ someone in a speech* 연설에서 아무를 공격하다. **4** begin to work energetically on (something). …에 착수하다. ¶ *~ one's dinner* 식사를 시작하다 / *He attacked a very difficult calculation.* 그는 매우 어려운 계산에 착수했다.

— *n.* **1** Ⓤⓒ the act of attacking. 공격. ¶ *Attack is the best form of defense.* 공격은 최선의 방어이다 / *make an ~ on the enemy* 적을 공격하다 / *an ~ upon someone in the press* 신문의 아무에 대한 공격. **2** ⓒ a sudden occurrence of illness; a fit. 발병(發病); 발작. ¶ *a heart ~* 심장병의 발작 / *have an ~ of a disease* 병이 발작하다 / *He is suffering from an ~ of gout.* 그는 통풍(痛風)에 걸려 고생하고 있다. [→attach]

at·tack·er [ətǽkər] *n.* ⓒ a person who attacks. 공격자.

:at·tain [ətéin] *vt.* (P6) **1** arrive at (some place); reach. …에 도달하다. ¶ *He attained the opposite bank of the river.* 그는 강의 맞은편 둑에 도달했다. **2** perform. 달성하다. ¶ *It is now impossible to ~ your ambition.* 당신의 야망을 이루기란 이제 불가능하다.

— *vi.* (P3) 《*to*》 come to reach. (도)달하다. ¶ *Wisdom is a hard thing to ~ to.* 진정한 지혜에 이르기란 어려운 것이다. [ad-, L. *tango* touch]

at·tain·a·ble [ətéinəbəl] *adj.* that can be attained. 도달할 수 있는.

at·tain·ment [ətéinmənt] *n.* Ⓤ **1** the act of attaining; achievement. 달성. **2** 《*pl.*》 skill or knowledge gained by training or study; accomplishments. 학식; 기능; 소양. ¶ *a man of great* 〔*high*〕 *attainments* 박식한 사람.

at·tar [ǽtər] *n.* Ⓤ a sweet-smelling liquid made from flowers petal. 꽃잎에서 채취한 향수. [Pers.]

:at·tempt [ətémpt] *vt.* (P6,8) **1** try; endeavor. …을 꾀하다; 시도하다. ¶ *~ a discussion* 논쟁을 시도하다 / *~ walking* 〔*to walk*〕 *six miles* 6마일을 걸어 보려고 하다/ *~* (*to climb*) *an unconquered peak* 정복되지 않은 정상의 등정을 꾀하다. **2** attack; destroy. …을 공격〔습격〕하다; 해를 주려고 하다. ¶ *~ the enemy's camp* 적의 진영을 습격하다.

attempt someone's life, try to kill someone. 아무를 죽이려고 하다.

attempt one's own life, try to kill oneself; try to commit suicide. 자살을 꾀하다.

— *n.* ⓒ **1** an effort; an endeavor; a trial. 노력; 시도(試圖); 기도. ¶ *a murderous ~* 살해의 기도. **2** an attack or assault. 공격; 습격. ¶ *an ~ upon the leader's life* 지휘관의 목숨을 노린 습격. [ad-, L. *tento* try, → tempt]

make an attempt at (=*try*) ***something.*** …을 꾀〔시도〕하다. ¶ *She made an ~ at suicide.* 그녀는 자살을 꾀했다.

make an attempt on, try to kill (someone); attack. (아무의 목숨)을 빼앗으려고 하다; …을 공격하다.

make an attempt (=*try*) ***to do.*** …하려고 하다. ¶ *He made an ~ to finish his studies.* 연구를 완성시키려고 노력했다 / *She made no ~ to hide the fact.* 그녀는 사실을 숨기려고 하지 않았다.

:at·tend [əténd] *vt.* (P6) **1** be present at (a meeting, etc). (모임 따위)에 참석〔출석〕하다. ¶ *~ school* 학교에 다니다 / *~ a lecture* 강의에 출석하다 / *~ a funeral* 장례식에 참석하다 / *Please ~ at this office at 10 a.m. on Friday morning.* 금요일 아침 10시에 이 사무실로 나와 주십시오. **2** look after or take care of (someone). …을 돌보다; 보살피다. ¶ *~ a patient* 환자를 돌보다 / *He is always attended by a nurse.* 그는 늘 간호사의 보살핌을 받고 있다. **3** accompany; follow. …을 따르다; 붙어다니다; 수행하다. ¶ *a cold attended with fever* 열을 동반한 감기 / *Great difficulties attended our plan.* 우리 계획엔 큰 어려움이 따랐다.

— *vi.* **1** (P1,3) 《*to*》 pay attention. 주의하다. ¶ *~ to a speaker* 발언자의 말을 잘〔귀담아〕 듣다 / *You must ~ to your duty as a student.* 학생으로서 네 의무에 유의해야 한다. **2** (P3) 《*on, upon*》 wait on someone; serve. 섬기다; 봉사하다. ¶ *~ upon the king* 왕을 섬기다. **3** be engaged in something. 종사하다. [L. *ad-* toward, *tendo* stretch]

·at·tend·ance [əténdəns] *n.* Ⓤ **1** the act of being present. 출석. ¶ *~ at a concert* 음악회에의 참석 / *Our English class has very good ~ today.* 오늘 영어 수업의 출석은 매우 좋다. **2** Ⓤⓒ 《*collectively*》 those who are present. 출석자. ¶ *There was a large* 〔*a small*〕 *~ at the ceremony.* 식에는 참석자가 많았다〔적었다〕 / *I came to my class and found full ~.* 교실에 나와보니 전원 출석이었다. **3** the act of serving or waiting on someone; service; care. 시중; 봉사; 돌봄. ¶ *Medical ~* 의료 봉사 / *The nurse is in ~ on him.* 그는 간호사가 돌보고 있다.

be in attendance (=*wait*) ***on someone.*** …을 시중들다; 섬기다.

·at·tend·ant [əténdənt] *adj.* **1** accompanying; following. 따라〔붙어〕 다니는; 수행하는. ¶ *war and its ~ inflation* 전쟁과 그에 따르는 인플레이션 / *Diseases are ~ on famine.* 기근에는 질병이 따른다. **2** present. 출석〔참석〕한. — *n.* ⓒ **1** a person who waits on others; a servant; a nurse; a follower. 곁따르는〔시중드는〕 사람; 사용인; 간호사; 수행원. ¶ *a medical ~ on the king* 왕의 시의(侍醫) / *an ~ on the queen* 여왕의 시종(侍從)/*The president called all his attend-*

ants together. 회장은 그의 수행원 전원을 소집했다. **2** a person who is present. 출석자.

:at·ten·tion [əténʃən] *n.* Ⓤ **1** the act of giving one's mind; careful observation. 주의; 주목. ¶ *with* 〔*in*〕 ~ 주의해서 / *be all* ~ 온신경을 집중시키고 있다 / *pay* ~ *to* …에 주의〔유의〕하다 / *attract* 〔*draw, arrest*〕 ~ 눈에 띄다; 주의를〔눈을〕 끌다 / *give* ~ *to something* …에 주의〔유의〕하다 / *call someone's* ~ *to a fact* 어떤 사실에 대해 아무의 주의를 환기시키다 / *Attention!* 차렷《구령》. **2** care; treatment. 돌봄; 치료. ¶ *medical* ~ 치료. **3** 《often *pl.*》 kindness; consideration; courtesy, esp. for women. 친절; 배려; (특히 여성에 대한) 정중함. ¶ ~ *to other's feelings* 남의 감정에 대한 배려. [→attend]

come to attention, take an erect, motionless position. 차렷 자세를 취하다.

devote** one's **attention (=*apply oneself*) ***to*** *something.* …에 전심〔몰두〕하다.

stand at attention, stand erect and motionless. 부동의 자세로 서다.

·at·ten·tive [əténtiv] *adj.* **1** paying attention; careful; observant. 주의 깊은. ¶ *be* ~ *to one's duty* 직무에 충실하다 / *be* ~ *to clothes* 복장에 마음을 쓰다 / *Be more* ~ *to your studies.* 공부에 더욱 주력해라. **2** 《*to*》 considerate; polite; courteous. 배려깊은; 동정심 있는; 정중한. ¶ *He is very* ~ *to his little sister.* 그는 누이동생에게 상냥하다.

at·ten·tive·ly [əténtivli] *adv.* with attention; carefully. 주의 깊게.

at·ten·u·ate [əténjuèit] *vi.* become thin or slender; lessen. 얇아〔약해〕지다; 줄다. — *vt.* (P6) make (something) thin or slender; weaken. …을 얇게 하다; 약하게 하다. [L. *tenuo* make thin]

·at·test [ətést] *vi., vt.* (P3;6) **1** declare the truth of (one's words); testify; certify. …의 진실임을 선서하다; 확언〔증언〕하다. ¶ ~ *the truth of a statement* 진술이 사실임을 증언하다. **2** give proof of (something); prove. 입증하다; 증거가 되다. ¶ *His ability is attested by his rapid promotion.* 그의 능력은 그의 빠른 승진으로 입증된다. [at-, L. *testis* witness]

attest to (=*be proof of*) *something.* …의 증거가 되다. ¶ *This attests to his innocence.* 이것이 그의 무죄를 증명한다.

at·tes·ta·tion [æ̀testéiʃən] *n.* ⓊⒸ the act of attesting; testimony; proof. 증명; 증거; 증언.

·at·tic [ǽtik] *n.* Ⓒ a room just under the roof of a house. 고미다락(cf. *garret*). [Gk. *Attikos*, Place]

attic salt [⸗–⸗] *n.* refined wit. 기지(機智); 세련된 익살.

·at·tire [ətáiər] *vt.* (P6,13) 《chiefly in the *passive* or *reflexively*》 dress up; put clothes on (someone). 옷을 입히다. ¶ ~ *oneself in black* 검은 옷을 입다. [→tire[2]]

·at·ti·tude [ǽtitjùːd] *n.* Ⓒ **1** the way of thinking, feeling, or acting; manner. 태도. ¶ *a serious* ~ 진지한 태도 / *a mental* ~ 심적 태도 / *his* ~ *of cold indifference to religion* 종교에 대한 그의 냉담한 태도 / *assume a wait-and-see* ~ 관망적 태도를 취하다 / *take a friendly* 〔*hostile*〕 ~ *to* 〔*toward*〕 …에 대해 우호적〔적대적〕 태도를 취하다 / *What is your* ~ *toward this question?* 이 문제에 대하여 어떤 태도를 취하렵니까. **2** a position of the body. 자세. ¶ *a threatening* ~ 위협적인 자세 / *He was sitting in a lazy* ~. 그는 나른한 자세로 앉아 있었다. [L. *apto* adjust]

strike an attitude, put on airs; pretend. (짐짓) …인 체하다.

·at·tor·ney [ətə́ːrni] *n.* Ⓒ 《law》 **1** a person who acts legally for another; an agent. 대리인. **2** a lawyer. 변호사. [at-, L. *tornos* lathe →turn]

a letter 〔***warrant***〕 ***of attorney,*** a letter indicating that a person is appointed as an agent. 위임장.

by attorney, by an agent who has a letter of attorney. (위임장을 가진) 대리인에 의하여 (opp. in person).

at·tor·ney-at-law [ətə́ːrniətlɔ́ː] *n.* Ⓒ 《*pl. attorneys-*》 a lawyer. 변호사.

attorney general [–⸗–⸗––] *n.* (*pl.* **attorneys g-** or **a- generals**) **1** the chief law officer of a country. 검찰 총장. **2** 《*A-G-*》 《U.S.》 the head of the Department of Justice, who helps his President as his chief legal advisor. 법무 장관.

:at·tract [ətrǽkt] *vt.* (P6,13) **1** draw (someone or something) toward oneself. …을 끌다. ¶ *The art exhibition attracted a crowd of visitors.* 그 미술 전람회에는 많은 관람객이 모여 들었다 / *A magnet attracts iron.* 자석은 쇠를 끌어당긴다. **2** make (someone) interested; charm. (주의·흥미 따위)를 끌다; …을 매혹하다. ¶ ~ *attention* 〔*interest*〕 주위를〔관심을〕 끌다 / ~ *censure* 비난을 초래하다 / *The actress attracted the town's people.* 그 여배우는 그 고을 주민들을 매혹시켰다. [L. *traho* draw]

·at·trac·tion [ətrǽkʃən] *n.* **1** Ⓤ the act of attracting; 《phys.》 the power that attracts. 끎; 인력(引力)(opp. repulsion). ¶ *magnetic* ~ 자기력(磁氣力). **2** Ⓒ a person or thing that attracts or charms people. (사람 눈을) 끄는 사람〔것〕; 매력. ¶ *reerect the castle as a tourist* ~ 관광객 유치를 위해 성을 재건하다 / *Susie has many attractions.* 수지는 많은 매력이 있다 / *The lions were the chief* ~ *at the circus.* 사자들은 서커스에서 가장 인기가 있었다 / *The pleasures of the senses have no longer any* ~ *for him.* 관능적 쾌락은 이제 그에겐 매력이 없다.

:at·trac·tive [ətrǽktiv] *adj.* pleasing; charming; arousing interest. (마음을) 끄는; 매력있는. ¶ *a girl with a most* ~ *smile* 가장 매력적인 미소를 지닌 처녀.

at·trac·tive·ly [ətrǽktivli] *adv.* in an attractive manner; charmingly. 눈에 띄게; 매력적으로; 흥미를 끌게.

at·trib·ut·a·ble [ətríbjutəbəl] *adj.* 《*to*》 that can be attributed. (원인 따위를) …로 돌릴 수 있는. ¶ *His failure is ~ to idleness.* 그의 실패는 게으름 탓이라고 할 수 있다. [↓]

·at·trib·ute [ətríbju:t] *vt.* (P13) 《*to*》 consider (one thing) as belonging to or caused by another. (원인·결과 따위)를 …때문인 것으로 치다; …탓으로 돌리다; (성질)을 …에 속하는 것으로 하다; …을 …의 작(作)으로 보다. ¶ *the play attributed to Shakespeare* 셰익스피어의 작으로 보는 연극 / *~ a talent to someone* 아무에게 재능이 있다고 보다 / *~ a work to a particular period* 어떤 작품을 어느 특정 시기의 것으로 보다 / *They attributed his success to good luck.* 그들은 그의 성공을 행운으로 돌렸다 / *We ~ wisdom to him.* 우리는 그에게 슬기가 있다고 생각한다 / *His death was attributed to heart failure.* 그의 사인은 심장 마비로 여겨졌다 / *The painting is attributed to Van Gogh.* 그 그림은 반 고호의 작품으로 간주되고 있다.
— [ǽtribjù:t] *n.* Ⓒ **1** a quality or an object that belongs to a special person or thing; a characteristic; a symbol. 특성; 속성; 상징. ¶ *Reason is an ~ of man.* 이성은 인간의 특성이다 / *Winged feet are the ~ of Mercury.* 날개 달린 발은 머큐리의 상징이다 / *He had many attributes of a good teacher.* 그에겐 훌륭한 선생으로서의 특성이 많았다. **2** 《gram.》 an attributive adjective. 한정 형용사. [→tribute]

at·tri·bu·tion [æ̀trəbjú:ʃən] *n.* **1** Ⓤ the act of attributing. 귀속. **2** Ⓒ a thing attributed. (부속의) 권능; 직권.

at·trib·u·tive [ətríbjətiv] *adj.* **1** expressing a quality of belonging to something. 속성을 나타내는. **2** 《gram.》 (of an adjective) used before or, sometimes, after a noun; restrictive. 한정적인 (opp. predicative).
— *n.* Ⓒ 《gram.》 an attributive adjective; a restrictive word. 한정 형용사; 한정사(限定詞).

at·tri·tion [ətríʃən] *n.* Ⓤ the act of wearing out; the state of being gradually worn out. 마찰; 마멸; 마모(摩耗). ¶ *Pebbles become smooth by ~.* 조약돌은 마찰에 의하여 매끄러워진다 / *a war of ~* 소모전(消耗戰). [at-, L. *tereo* rub, →trite]

at·tune [ətjú:n] *vt.* (P13) **1** make (the sounds of one musical instrument) agree with those of another. (악기) 가락을 다른것에 맞추다. **2** cause (one's feelings) to agree with those of another. (마음·기분 따위)를 조화시키다. ¶ *He has attuned himself to living in the quiet country.* 그는 조용한 시골 생활에 순응하게 됐다. [→tune]

Au 《chem.》 aurum. (L. =gold).

Au. Augustus.

au·burn [ɔ́:bərn] *n., adj.* (of hair, etc.) red-brown. 적갈색(의). ¶ *~ hair.* [→alb, brown]

au·cou·rant [ouku:rɑ́:ŋ] *adj.* 《F.》 acquainted with what is going on. 시세(사정)에 밝은.

auc·tion [ɔ́:kʃən] *n.* ⓊⒸ a public sale in which goods are sold to the buyer who offers the highest price. 경매. ¶ *It was sold at* (*by*) *~.* — *vt.* (P6) sell by auction. …을 경매하다. [L. *augeo* increase]
auction off, sell (goods) at auction. (물건)을 경매로 팔다. ¶ *The bookcase was auctioned off.* 책장은 경매되었다.

auc·tion·eer [ɔ̀:kʃəníər] *n.* Ⓒ a person who sells goods at auction, usu. as a business. 경매인. ¶ *come under the auctioneer's hammer* 경매에 부쳐지다. — *vt.* sell (goods) at auction. …을 경매하다.
give (***deliver, tip***) *someone* ***the auctioneer,*** 《*colloq.*》 knock a person down. 아무를 때려 눕히다.

au·da·cious [ə:déiʃəs] *adj.* very daring; impudent; shameless. 대담한; 뻔뻔스러운. ¶ *an ~ attempt* 대담한 시도 / *an ~ robbery* 뻔뻔스런 강도질. ● **au·da·cious·ly** [-li] *adv.* [L. *audeo* dare]

au·dac·i·ty [ə:dǽsəti] *n.* Ⓤ the state of being audacious; boldness; impudence. 대담함; 뻔뻔스러움. ¶ *He had the ~ to break his promise.* 그는 뻔뻔스럽게도 약속을 깨뜨렸다.

au·di·bil·i·ty [ɔ̀:dəbíləti] *n.* Ⓤ the state of being audible. 들림; 가청성(可聽性). [↓]

au·di·ble [ɔ́:dəbl] *adj.* loud enough to be heard. (똑똑히) 들리는. ¶ *barely ~* 거의 들을 수 없는 / *an ~ whisper* 들을 수 있는 속삭임. [L. *audio* hear]

:au·di·ence [ɔ́:diəns] *n.* **1** Ⓒ 《*collectively*》 ⓐ persons gathered in a place to hear a singer, a speaker, etc. or to see a play, movie, etc. 청중; 관객. ¶ *The ~ was composed of ladies.* 청중은 여성들이었다 / *Most of the ~ at the movie were* (*was*) *young men.* 영화의 관객은 대부분 청년들이었다. 語法 개개의 청중을 가리킬 때는 복수 취급. ⓑ the hearers; people who listen to a radio program or watch a television program. 청취자; 시청자. **2** ⒸⓊ a formal interview with a person of high rank. 알현(謁見); 접견; 회견. ¶ *The king granted an ~ to the famous general.* 임금은 그 유명한 장군에게 알현을 허락했다. [L. *audio* hear]
be received in audience, be admitted into a formal interview with a person of high rank. 알현(접견)이 허락되다.
give audience to =***grant an audience to,*** admit (someone) to speak to someone else. …을 접견하다; …에게 알현을 허락하다.
have audience of (=*have the chance to speak to*) *someone.* …에게 배알하다.
in open (***general***) ***audience,*** in public. 공개적으로; 공개 석상에서.

in the audience (=*in the presence*) ***of*** *someone.* …의 면전에서.

au·di·o [ɔ́:diòu] *adj.* 《radio》 **1** of a frequency which can be heard. 가청 주파(可聽周波)의. **2** of sound. 음의. [L. =hear]

au·di·o·vis·u·al aids [ɔ́:diouvíʒuəl éidz] *n. pl.* educational apparatuses designed for hearing and seeing. 시청각 교(육 기)재.

au·dit [ɔ́:dit] *n.* Ⓤ an official examination of business accounts. 회계 감사. — *vt.* (P6) **1** examine (business accounts) officially. (회계)를 감사하다. **2** 《U.S.》 attend (a college class) as a special student. 청강생으로 청강하다. [L. *audio* hear]

au·di·tion [ɔ:díʃən] *n.* Ⓤ the act or power of hearing; Ⓒ an examination to test a singer, an actor, etc. before he is hired. 청취(력); (레코드의) 시청(試聽); (가수·배우 등의)음성 테스트; 오디션. — *vt.* (P6) give (someone) an audition. 음성 테스트를〔오디션을〕 하다. [*audio*, -tion]

au·di·tor [ɔ́:ditər] *n.* Ⓒ **1** a hearer; a listener. 듣는 사람; (라디오 따위의) 청취자. **2** a person whose job is to audit business accounts. 회계 감사관.

au·di·to·ri·a [ɔ̀:ditɔ́:riə] *n.* pl. of **auditorium.**

au·di·to·ri·um [ɔ̀:ditɔ́:riəm] *n.* Ⓒ (*pl.* **-ums** or **-ri·a**) a large hall or room in which meetings are held or lectures, concerts, etc. are given. 강당; (강당·교회·극장 따위의) 청중석; 공회당. [→audit]

au·di·to·ry [ɔ́:ditɔ̀:ri, -ditòuri] *adj.* of (the sense of) hearing. 듣는; 청각의. ¶ ~ *nerves* 청신경 / ~ *education* 음감(音感) 교육 / *an* ~ *image* 청각상(像).

Au·drey [ɔ́:dri] *n.* a woman's name. 여자의 이름.

au fait [ou féi] *adj.* 《F.》 knowing all about. 잘〔환히〕 알고 있는.

put someone au fait with, tell him all the latest facts about. …을 아무에게 상세히 가르쳐 주다.

Aug. August.

au·ger [ɔ́:gər] *n.* Ⓒ **1** an instrument for making holes in wood. 큰 송곳. 參考 작은 것은 gimlet. **2** a large tool for boring into the earth. 대형 굴착기. [A.S.]

aught [ɔ:t] *pron.* 《*arch., poet.*》 anything. 어떤 것; 무언가; 무엇이든.

for aught I care, I don't care. (어떻게 되든) 아무래도 상관 없다. ¶ *You may get sick for* ~ *I care.* 네가 앓더라도 내 알 바 아니다.

for aught I know, perhaps. (잘은 모르지만) 아마. ¶ *He may be a millionaire for* ~ *I know.* 그는 아마 백만 장자일지도 모른다.

if aught there be, if any. 가령 있다 해도.

— *adv.* 《*arch.*》 at all; in any way. 조금도; 어쨌든. [E.=ever (a), *whit*]

aug·ment [ɔ:gmént] *vt., vi.* (P6;1) increase; enlarge. …을 늘리다; 증가하다. ¶ *The army was augmented by reinforcements.* 그 부대는 증원군에 의해 증강되었다. [L. *augmento* increase, →auction]

aug·men·ta·tion [ɔ̀:gmentéiʃən] *n.* **1** Ⓤ increase; addition. 증가; 부가(附加). **2** Ⓒ something increased. 증가물; 부가물.

au·gur [ɔ́:gər] *n.* Ⓒ **1** an official in ancient Rome that told the fortune from the appearance of birds. (고대 로마의) 복점관(卜占官). **2** a fortune teller. 점쟁이. — *vt.* (P6) foretell. …을 예언하다. ¶ *Cloudy skies* ~ *rain.* 구름이 낀 하늘은 비를 예고한다. — *vi.* (P2A,3) be a sign of the future. 전조(前兆)가 되다. ¶ ~ *well* 〔*bad*〕 *for* …의 길조(吉兆)〔흉조(凶兆)〕가 되다. [L.]

au·gu·ry [ɔ́:gjəri] *n.* (*pl.* **-ries**) **1** Ⓤ an art of fortunetelling. 점(占). **2** Ⓒ a prophecy; an omen. 예언; 징조.

⁑**Au·gust** [ɔ́:gəst] *n.* the eighth month of the year. 8월. 參考 Aug.로 약함. [Person]

au·gust [ɔ:gʌ́st] *adj.* majestic; causing a feeling of fear and respect. 위엄이 있는; 존엄한. [↑]

⁑**Au·gus·tan** [ɔ:gʌ́stən] *adj.* of augustus, a Roman Emperor; of the period of his reign. 아우구스투스의; 아우구스투스 (시대)의.

auld lang syne [ɔ́:ld læŋ záin, ɔ́:ld læŋ sáin] *n.* 《Sc.》 **1** the good old times. 지나간 즐거웠던 시절. **2** 《A- L- S-》 a song sung at midnight on December 3lst. 올드랭사인.

⁑**aunt** [ænt, ɑ:nt] *n.* Ⓒ a father's or mother's sister; the wife of one's uncle. 아주머니 《고모·이모·숙모》. [L. *amita*]

aunt·ie, aunt·y [ǽnti, ɑ́:nti] *n.* Ⓒ 《*child's word*》=aunt.

au·ra [ɔ́:rə] *n.* Ⓒ (*pl.* **-ras** or **-rae**) a faint smell or atmosphere lying around a thing or person like the smell round flowers. (물체에서 풍기는) 발산기(發散氣); 분위기. ¶ *An* ~ *of gentleness surrounded the new teacher.* 신임 선생님에게서 풍기는 부드러운 분위기. [Gk.=breeze]

au·rae [ɔ́:ri:] *n.* pl. of **aura.**

au·ral [ɔ́:rəl] *adj.* of the ear or hearing. 귀의; 청각의(opp. oral). [L. *auris* ear]

au·re·ate [ɔ́:riit, -èit] *adj.* golden resplendent. 황금의; 빛나는. [↓]

au·re·ole [ɔ́:riòul], **au·re·o·la** [ɔ:rí:ələ] *n.* Ⓒ a circle of bright light round the head or figure of a holy person as shown in a picture. (성상(聖像)의) 후광(後光); 광륜(光輪). [L.=golden (crown)]

au·re·o·my·cin [ɔ̀:rioumáisin] *n.* 《phar.》 a drug related to streptomycin. 오레오마이신. [L. *aureus* golden, Gk. *mykēs* fungus, →-in]

au re·voir [òu rəvwɑ́:r] *interj., n.* 《F.》 Till I see you again. 안녕.

au·ri·cle [ɔ́:rikl] *n.* Ⓒ **1** the outer part of the ear. 귓바퀴; 외이(外耳). **2** either of the two chambers of the heart that receive blood from the veins. (심장의) 심이

(心耳). [→aural]

au·ric·u·lar [ɔːríkjələr] *adj.* **1** of the ear. 귀의. **2** shaped like an ear. 귀 모양의. **3** of an auricle of the heart. 심이(心耳)의.

au·rif·er·ous [ɔːrífərəs] *adj.* producing gold. 금을 산출하는. [L. *aurum* gold, *fero* produce]

au·rist [ɔ́ːrist] *n.* an ear specialist. 이과의(耳科醫). [L. *auris* ear]

au·ro·ra [ərɔ́ːrə, ɔːrɔ́ː-] *n.* **1** 《*A-*》《Rom. myth.》 the goddess of the dawn. 오로라 《여명의 여신》. 參考 그리스 신화의 Eos에 해당함. **2** 《*the* ~》 the colored bands of light in the night sky around the North Pole. 극광(極光). [L.]

au·ro·ra aus·tra·lis [ərɔ́ːrə ɔːstréilis] *n.* the bands of light in the southern area corresponding to the aurora. 남극광(南極光). [L. *austrālis* southern]

au·rum [ɔ́ːrəm] *n.* 《L.》 gold. 금.

AUS Army of the United States.

aus·cul·ta·tion [ɔ̀ːskəltéiʃən] *n.* listening to the movement of the heart. 청진. [L. *ausculto* listen]

aus·pice [ɔ́ːspis] *n.* **1** 《usu. *pl.*》 patronage; sponsorship. 후원; 주최. **2** Ⓒ an omen; a sign of good fortune. 조짐; 전조; 길조(吉兆). ¶ *take the auspices* 길흉을 점치다 / *He took her gentle words as auspices of happiness.* 그는 그녀의 상냥한 말을 행복의 조짐으로 받아들였다. [L. *avis* bird, *specio* observe (taking omens by observing the flight of birds)]

under the auspices of, sponsored by. …의 후원으로. ¶ *be held under the auspices of the ministry of education* 교육부 주최로 개최되다.

aus·pi·cious [ɔːspíʃəs] *adj.* promising good fortune; fortunate. 상서로운; 길조(吉兆)의; 행운의(opp. inauspicious). ¶ *on this ~ day* 이와 같은 경사스러운 날에.

aus·tere [ɔːstíər] *adj.* **1** very plain and simple in appearance or living. (생활·양식 따위가) 간소한. ¶ *an ~ style of architecture* 간소한 건축 양식 / *write in an ~ style* 간결한 문체로 쓰다 / *No human language can describe the ~ beauty of that temple.* 그 절의 소박한 아름다움은 인간의 말로는 형언할 수가 없다. **2** strict in character or manner. (성격·태도의) 엄격한. ¶ *His uncle was an ~ man who never laughed or smiled.* 그의 삼촌은 결코 웃거나 미소짓는 일이 없는 엄격한 사람이었다. [Gk. *auō* dry]

aus·ter·i·ty [ɔːstériti] *n.* **1** Ⓤ strictness; severity. 엄격. **2** 《*pl.*》 severe practices; a hard life. 고행; 금욕〔내핍〕 생활. ¶ *austerities of monastery life* 수도원의 금욕 생활 / *the ~ program* 긴축 경제 계획.

aus·tral [ɔ́ːstrəl] *adj.* of the south; southern. 남쪽의. [L. *Auster* south wind]

***Aus·tral·ia** [ɔːstréiljə] *n.* **1** the continent to the southeast of Asia. 오스트레일리아 대륙. **2** the Commonwealth of Australia. 오스트레일리아 연방. 參考 수도는 Canberra. [↑]

Aus·tral·ian [ɔːstréiljən] *adj.* of Australia or its people. 오스트레일리아(사람)의. — *n.* Ⓒ a person of Australia. 오스트레일리아 사람.

***Aus·tri·a** [ɔ́ːstriə] *n.* a country in central Europe. 오스트리아. [→austral]

Aus·tri·an [ɔ́ːstriən] *adj.* of Austria or its people. 오스트리아(사람)의. — *n.* Ⓒ a person of Austria. 오스트리아 사람.

au·tar·ky [ɔ́ːtɑːrki] *n.* Ⓤ economical self-sufficiency; the state of needing no help from others. (경제의) 자급 자족. [Gk. *autos* self, *arkhē* rule]

***au·then·tic** [ɔːθéntik] *adj.* trustworthy; true; genuine. 믿을 만한; 진짜의. ¶ *an ~ report* 〔*account*〕 신뢰할 수 있는 보고〔기사〕/ *an ~ antique* 진짜 골동품 / *an ~ signature* 본인〔자필〕의 서명. [Gk. *authenticos* genuine]

au·then·ti·cate [ɔːθéntikèit] *vt.* (P6) **1** show or make (something or someone) to be true, reliable, or genuine. (사물이) 틀림없음〔진짜임〕을 증명하다. **2** prove beyond doubt the true origin of. (전거(典據)·출처를) 밝히다. ¶ ~ *a painting* 그림의 작자를 밝히다.

au·then·ti·ca·tion [ɔːθèntikéiʃən] *n.* Ⓤ the act of authenticating; the state of being authenticated. 확증.

au·then·tic·i·ty [ɔ̀ːθentísəti] *n.* Ⓤ reliability genuineness. 확실성; 진정. ¶ *the ~ of antiques* 고미술품의 출처의 확실함.

***au·thor** [ɔ́ːθər] *n.* Ⓒ **1** the writer of a book, novel, play, etc. 작가; 저작자. ¶ *I like modern authors.* 나는 현대 작가를 좋아한다. **2** a writer's publication. 저작물. ¶ *He has many authors on his shelves.* 그는 서가에 많은 작가의 작품을 소장하고 있다. **3** the first beginner of a new thing; a creator. 창시자; 장본인. ¶ *the ~ of this scheme* 이 계획의 입안자 / *Who is the ~ of this mischief?* 이 장난질의 장본인은 누구냐. [L. *augeo* increase]

the Author of our being 〔***the universe***〕, God. 조물주; 신.

au·thor·ess [ɔ́ːθəris] *n.* Ⓒ a woman author. 여류 작가.

au·thor·i·tar·i·an [əθɔ̀ːrətέəriən, əθɑ̀r-] *adj.* giving more importance to authority than to individual liberty. 권위〔독재〕주의의. — *n.* Ⓒ a person who has such a principle. 권위〔독재〕주의자. [→author]

***au·thor·i·ta·tive** [əθɔ́ːritèitiv, əθɑ́rə-/ɔ(ː)θɔ́ritətiv] *adj.* **1** having authority; commanding. 권위 있는; 명령적인. ¶ *an ~ manner* 당당한 태도 / *~ orders* 〔*permission*〕 당국의 명령〔허가〕/ *in ~ tones* 명령적인 말투로. **2** that can be trusted; reliable. 권위 있는; 믿을 만한.

au·thor·i·ta·tive·ly [əθɔ́ːritèitivli, əθɑ́rə-/

ɔ(ː)θɔ́ritə-] *adv.* commandingly. 위엄을 갖추고; 명령적으로.

:au·thor·i·ty [əθɔ́ːriti, əθár- / ɔθɔ́r-] *n.* 《*pl.* **-ties**》 **1** Ⓤ the right and power to command. 권위; 권력. ¶ *persons in* ~ 권세 있는 사람들 / *the* ~ *of a court* 법정의 권위 / *under the* ~ *of* …의 지배(支配) 밑에; …의 관할 아래 / *exercise the* ~ *over* …에 대하여 권력을 부리다[행사하다]. **2** Ⓤ permission. 허가; 권한. ¶ *by the* ~ *of* …의 권능으로; …의 허가를 얻어 / *give someone* ~ *for* 〔*to do*〕 아무에게 …의〔…할〕 권한을 주다 / *Who gave you* ~ *to come into this room ?* 누가 당신을 이 방에 들어오도록 허가했지요. **3** 《usu. *pl.*》 the group of persons who have the right and power to govern. 당국. ¶ *the school authorities* 학교 당국. **4** Ⓒ a person or book that can be relied on reading some subject. (믿을 수 있는) 권위자; 대가; 전거(典據). ¶ *He is a great* ~ *on children's diseases.* 그는 소아과의 권위자다 / *The book is the best* ~ *on the history of English literature.* 그 책은 영문학사에 관한 가장 좋은 전거이다. [→author]

au·thor·i·za·tion [ɔ̀ːθərizéiʃən] *n.* Ⓤ the act of authorizing. (권능) 수여; 인가; 허가.

·au·thor·ize [ɔ́ːθəràiz] *vt.* (P6,20) **1** give (someone) the right and power to act. …에게 권한〔권능〕을 주다. ¶ ~ *a detective to make arrests* 형사에게 체포할 권한을 주다 / *He has authorized me to act for him during his absence.* 그는 부재중에 자기를 대리하도록 나에게 권한을 주었다. **2** permit; make legal. (행동)을 인가하다; 허가하다. ¶ *a parade authorized by the police* 경찰에서 인가한 퍼레이드. **3** justify. …을 정당하다고 인정하다. ¶ *These pranks in the festival are authorized by tradition.* 축제 때의 이런 장난은 관례에 따라 인정되어 있다. [→*author*]

·au·thor·ized [ɔ́ːθəràizd] *adj.* supported by authority; given authority. 인가〔공인〕된; 권한을 부여받은. ¶ *an* ~ *textbook* 검인정 교과서 / *an* ~ *agent* 지정 대리인.

Authorized Version [ˊ-- ˊ-] *n.* 《*the* ~》 the English translation of the Bible published in 1611. 흠정(欽定) 영역(英譯) 성서. 參考 the King James Version이라고도 함.

au·thor·ship [ɔ́ːθərʃìp] *n.* Ⓤ the occupation of an author; the source or origin (of a book). 저작자임; 저술; (책의) 출처. [→author]

au·to [ɔ́ːtou] *n.* Ⓒ (*pl.* **au·tos**) 《*colloq.*》 an automobile. 자동차. [Gk. *autos* by oneself]

au·to- [ɔ́ːtou-, -tə-] *pref.* a word element meaning self. '자신의, 독자적인' 등의 뜻. ¶ *autobiography* / *autograph.* [Gk. *autos*]

Au·to·bahn [áutɔbàːn, ɔ́ːtə-] *n.* 《G.》 an expressway in Germany. (독일의) 자동차 전용 고속 도로.

au·to·bi·o·graph·i·cal [ɔ̀ːtəbàiəgrǽfikəl], **-graph·ic** [-grǽfik] *adj.* of an autobiography. 자서전(自敍傳)의. [auto-]

au·to·bi·og·ra·phy [ɔ̀ːtəbaiágrəfi / -ɔ́g-] *n.* Ⓒ a story of a person's life written by himself. 자서전(自敍傳).

au·toch·thon [ɔːtákθən / -tɔ́k-] *n.* (*pl.* **-s** or **-es** [-nìːz]) one of the original inhabitants of a country. 토착민(土着民). [auto-, Gk. *khthōn* land]

au·toch·tho·nal [ɔːtákθənəl / -tɔ́k-] *adj.* =autochthonous.

au·toch·tho·nous [ɔːtákθənəs / -tɔ́k-] *adj.* aboriginal. 토착의.

au·toc·ra·cy [ɔːtákrəsi / -tɔ́k-] *n.* (*pl.* **-ra·cies**) **1** Ⓤ government by a ruler who has absolute power; dictatorship. 독재 정치. **2** Ⓒ a government that has unlimited power. 독재 정부. [↓]

au·to·crat [ɔ́ːtəkræ̀t] *n.* Ⓒ a ruler or person who has absolute power over a group of persons. 독재자. [auto-, Gk. *kratos* might]

au·to·crat·ic [ɔ̀ːtəkrǽtik] *adj.* of or like an autocrat. 독재적인.

auto-da-fé [ɔ̀ːtoudəféi] *n.* 《Port. & Sp.= act of faith》 (*pl.* **autos-da-fé** [ɔ̀ːtouz-]) **1** the ceremony of trial and sentence by the Inquisition of a person accused of heresy. (이단자(異端者)에 대한) 종교 재판소의 선고식. **2** the burning alive of such a person. 이단자(異端者)의 화형(火刑).

au·to·gi·ro, -gy·ro [ɔ̀ːtoudʒáirou / -dʒáiərou] *n.* Ⓒ (*pl.* **-ros**) an aircraft which is an early form of helicopter. 오토자이로. [auto-, Gk. *gyros* circle]

au·to·graph [ɔ́ːtəgræ̀f, -gràːf] *n.* Ⓒ **1** a person's own handwriting. 자필(自筆). **2** a person's name written by himself. 자필 서명. — *vt.* (P6) **1** write one's signature in or on (something). …에 자필 서명하다. ¶ ~ *a book for a friend* 친구를 위해 책에 자필 서명하다. **2** write (letters, etc.) with one's own hand. (편지 따위를) 자필로 쓰다. [auto-, L. *grapho* write, →graph]

au·to·mat [ɔ́ːtəmæ̀t] *n.* Ⓒ 《U.S.》 a restaurant in which food and drink are sold by machines. 자동 판매식 식당. [*Automat* (Trademark)]

au·tom·a·ta [ɔːtámətə / -tɔ́m-] *n.* pl. of **automaton.**

au·to·mate [ɔ́ːtəmèit] *vt.* (P6) apply the principle of automation. 오토메이션〔자동〕화(化)하다. [*automation*]

·au·to·mat·ic [ɔ̀ːtəmǽtik] *adj.* **1** self-moving; acting by itself. 자동의. ¶ *an* ~ *door* 자동 문 / *an* ~ *elevator* 자동 승강기. **2** done without thought or attention; unconscious. 기계적인; 무의식적인. ¶ *Swallowing food is usually* ~. 음식을 삼키는 것은 보통 무의식적이다. — *n.* Ⓒ a machine which works by itself; a gun which works by itself. 자동 기계; 자동 소총. [auto-, Gk. *matos* thinking]

·au·to·mat·i·cal·ly [ɔ̀ːtəmǽtikəli] *adv.* in an automatic manner; by itself. 자동적으로;

기계적으로.

au·to·ma·tion [ɔ̀:təméiʃən] *n.* Ⓤ the technique, or system of doing mechanical processes by automatic means. 자동 조작; 오토메이션. [*automa*tic; oper*ation*]

au·tom·a·tism [ɔ:tάmətìzəm / -tɔ́m-] *n.* involuntary action. 자동 (작용). [Gk. → automatic]

au·tom·a·ton [ɔ:tάmətàn / -tɔ́mətən] *n.* Ⓒ (*pl.* **-tons** or **-ta** [-tə]) **1** a machine that imitates the actions of living people; a robot. 자동 기계; 로봇. **2** a person who acts like a machine, without thought of his own. 기계적으로 행동하는 사람. [↑]

:au·to·mo·bile [ɔ́:təməbì:l, ˌ—ˌ—ˊ, ɔ̀:təmóu-] *n.* Ⓒ 《chiefly U.S.》 a motorcar. 자동차. — *adj.* self-moving. 자동의. [F.]

au·ton·o·mous [ɔ:tάnəməs / -tɔ́n-] *adj.* self-governing; ruled by its own laws only. 자치의; 자율(自律)의. ●**au·ton·o·mous·ly** [-li] *adv.* [↓]

au·ton·o·my [ɔ:tάnəmi / -tɔ́n-] *n.* (*pl.* **-mies**) **1** Ⓤ (the right of) self-government. 자치(권). **2** Ⓒ a self-governing community. 자치 단체. [Gk. *nomos* law]

au·top·sy [ɔ́:tɑpsi, -təp- / -tɔp-] *n.* Ⓒ (*pl.* **-sies**) an examination of a body after death to find the cause of death. 검시(檢屍); 해부(cf. *post-mortem*). [Gk. *opsis* sight]

au·to·sug·ges·tion [ɔ̀:tousəgdʒéstʃən / -sədʒés-] *n.* 《psych.》 suggestion arising from within. 자기(自己) 암시. [auto-]

:au·tumn [ɔ́:təm] *n.* ⓊⒸ the third season of the year; the season between summer and winter. 가을(cf. 《U.S.》 *fall*). — *adj.* of autumn. 가을의. [L. *autumns*]

au·tum·nal [ɔ:tʌ́mnəl] *adj.* of autumn. 가을의. [↑]

auxil. auxiliary.

aux·il·ia·ry [ɔ:gzíljəri, -zílə-] *adj.* **1** additional. 추가의. **2** helpful. 보조의. — *n.* Ⓒ (*pl.* **-ries**) **1** a person or thing that gives aid. 조력자; 보조물. **2** 《gram.》 a word helping the function of verbs, such as *have, be, may, shall, and will.* 조동사. [L. *auxilium* help]

A.V. Authorized Version.

av. avenue; average; avoirdupois.

·a·vail [əvéil] *vi.* (P1,2A) be of use; help. 유용하다; 도움이 되다. ¶ *Such arguments will not* ～. 그런 의론은 소용없다 / *I felt that no words of condolence availed.* 어떤 위로의 말도 도움이 되지 않을 것 같았다.
— *vt.* (P13) profit. …을 이롭게 하다. ¶ *Our wealth avails us nothing.* 부(富)는 우리를 이롭게 하지 못한다 / *All our efforts availed us little in trying to effect a change.* 변화를 가져오려는 우리의 노력은 거의 효과가 없었다.
avail *oneself* (= *take advantage or make use*) **of** *something.* …을 이용하다.
— *n.* Ⓤ 《chiefly in *negative*》 use; benefit. 이익. [a-, L. *valeo* strong, be well, → valid]

a·vail·a·bil·i·ty [əvèiləbíləti] *n.* (*pl.* **-ties**) **1** Ⓤ the state of being available. 유용(성). **2** a person or thing that is available. 유용한 사람〔것〕.

:a·vail·a·ble [əvéiləbəl] *adj.* **1** ready for use; of use. 쓸모 있는; 쓸 수 있는. ¶ *There is no money* ～ *for research.* 연구에 투입할 돈이 없다 / *tickets* ～ *on day of issue only* 발행일 당일에만 유효한 표. **2** that can be obtained. 손에 넣을 수 있는.

av·a·lanche [ǽvəlæ̀ntʃ / -lɑ̀:nʃ] *n.* Ⓒ **1** a great mass of snow, ice, etc. suddenly sliding down a mountainside. 눈사태. **2** anything like an avalanche. (눈사태 같은) 쇄도. ¶ *an* ～ *of questions* 쏟아지는 질문.
— *vi.* come down like an avalanche. 밀려오다. [ad-, →vale]

avant-garde [əvɑ̀:ntgά:rd, əvæ̀nt-, æ̀vɑ:nt-, ɑ̀:vɑ:nt-] *n.* 《F.》 the group of people who create or apply new ideas and techniques in any field, esp. the arts; also such a group that is extremist, bizarre, or arty and affected. 전위파. — *adj.* of the avant-garde or artistic work that is new and experimental. 전위파의〔에 속하는〕.

av·a·rice [ǽvəris] *n.* Ⓤ too strong desire for riches. 탐욕(opp. generosity). [L. *avarus* greedy]

av·a·ri·cious [æ̀vəríʃəs] *adj.* anxious for riches; greedy. 탐욕한(opp. generous).

a·vast [əvǽst, əvά:st] *interj.* 《naut.》 stop. 그만! [Du. *houd vast* hold fast]

av·a·tar [ǽvətὰ:r, ˌ—ˊ] *n.* the appearance of a god on earth. 화신(化身). [Hind.]

avdp. avoirdupois.

AVE, Ave., ave. Avenue.

A·ve Ma·ri·a [ά:vei mərí:ə, ά:vi mərí:ə] *n.* **1** the first words of the Latin version of a prayer in the Roman Catholic Church in praise of Mary, mother of Christ. 아베마리아. **2** a recitation of this prayer. 성모송(聖母頌). [L. = Hail Mary]

a·venge [əvéndʒ] *vt.* (P6,13) punish (someone) in return for his wrong act or injury. …의 복수를 하다; 보복하다. ¶ ～ *one's father* 아버지의 원수를 갚다 / ～ *a murder* 살인의 보복을 하다 / ～ *oneself* 〔*be avenged*〕 *on someone* 아무에게 원수를 갚다; 원한을 풀다. [→vindicate, revenge]

a·ven·ger [əvéndʒər] *n.* Ⓒ a person who avenges. 복수자.

:av·e·nue [ǽvənjù:] *n.* Ⓒ **1** a wide or main street. 가로; 한길(cf. *street*). **2** a way to approach. 접근하는 수단. ¶ *Hard work is a good* ～ *to success.* 열심히 일하는 것은 성공에의 지름길이다. **3** a wide road with trees on each side. 가로수길. [L. *venio* come, →advent]

a·ver [əvə́:r] *vt.* (P6,11) assert; affirm; declare as true. …을 단언하다; 주장하다. ¶ ～ *that an event has happened* 사건이 났다

고 단언하다. ● **a·ver·ment** *n.* [ad-, →very]

:av·er·age [ǽvəridʒ] *n.* Ⓒ **1** the ordinary amount, quality, type, etc.; a common standard. 보통; 표준. ¶ *a life as happy as the* ~ 보통의 행복한 생활 / *well up to the* ~ 표준에 충분히 달하여. **2** the middle value or quantity of a set of numbers. 평균. ¶ *strike a rough* ~ 대충 평균을 내다 / *The* ~ *of 3 and 10 and 5 is 6.* 3과 10과 5의 평균은 6이다. **on an** (**the**) **average,** approximately. 평균하여. ¶ *He can read 40 pages an hour, on the* ~. 그는 1시간에 평균 40페이지 읽을 수 있다. — *adj.* **1** of an average. 평균의. ¶ *the* ~ *price* 평균가(價) / *The* ~ *temperature is higher this year than last.* 평균 기온이 올해가 작년보다 높다. **2** ordinary; usual. 보통의. ¶ *The* ~ *man is not interested in this subject.* 여느 사람들은 이 문제에 대해 흥미를 느끼지 않고 있다. — *vt.* (P6) **1** find the average of (something); have (some quantity) as an average. …의 평균을 내다; 평균하여 …이 되다. ¶ ~ *15 miles* 평균 15마일을 내다 / ~ *eight hours a day* 평균 하루 8시간이 되다. **2** divide evenly. …을 평균하다; 균분하다. — *vi.* be of an average. 평균되다; 균등하게 되다. [Du. *avarij*]

a·verse [əvə́ːrs] *adj.* unwilling; opposed. 싫어하는; 반대의. ¶ *She was not* ~ *to coming to my party.* 그녀는 내 파티에 오는 것을 반대하지 않았다 / *He is* ~ *to hard work.* 그는 열심히 일하기를 싫어한다. [→avert]

a·ver·sion [əvə́ːrʒən, -ʃən] *n.* **1** Ⓤ 《*to*》 a strong feeling of dislike. 혐오. ¶ *I have an* ~ *to such people.* 나는 그런 사람을 아주 싫어한다. **2** Ⓒ a person or thing disliked. 싫어하는 사람〔것〕. ¶ *my chief* ~.

a·vert [əvə́ːrt] *vt.* (P6,13) **1** 《*from*》 turn away. …을 돌리다. ¶ ~ *one's mind from...* …에서 마음을 돌리다 / *He averted his eyes from the horrible sight.* 그는 그 끔찍한 광경에서 눈을 돌렸다. **2** prevent; avoid. …을 피하다; 막다. ¶ ~ *a blow* / *Many highway accidents can be averted by courtesy.* 많은 고속도로 사고는 주의하면 피할 수 있다. [ad-, L. *verto* turn]

a·vi·ar·y [éivièri] *n.* Ⓒ (*pl.* **-ar·ies**) a large cage in which many birds are kept. 대형의 새장; 양금장(養禽場). [L. *avis* bird]

a·vi·ate [éivièit, ǽv-] *vi.* (P1) fly in an aircraft. 비행하다; 항공기를 조종하다. [F. → avis, L. *avis* bird]

a·vi·a·tion [èiviéiʃən, æv-] *n.* Ⓤ the act or art of flying in airplanes. 비행(술); 항공술.

a·vi·a·tor [éivièitər, ǽv-] *n.* Ⓒ a person who flies an airplane; a pilot of an airplane. 비행사; 비행기 조종사.

a·vi·a·tress, -trice [éivièitris, ǽv-] *n.* Ⓒ a woman who flies an airplane. 여류 비행사.

av·id [ǽvid] *adj.* 《*of, for*》 eager; very keen; greedy. 열망하는; 열심인; 탐욕스러운. ¶ ~ *of fame* 명성을 갈망하는 / ~ *for gold* 황금을 탐하는. [L. *avidus* greedy]

a·vid·i·ty [əvídəti] *n.* Ⓤ eagerness; greediness. 탐욕. ¶ *eat with* ~ 게걸스럽게 먹다.

a·vo·ca·do [æ̀vəkáːdou, àːvə-] *n.* (*pl.* **-s** [-z]) a pear-shaped tropical fruit. 아보카도. [Mex.]

av·o·ca·tion [æ̀voukéiʃən] *n.* Ⓒ **1** 《*colloq.*》 a vocation; a calling. 직업. **2** an occupation besides one's regular work; a hobby. 부업; 취미. [L. *avoco* call away]

:a·void [əvɔ́id] *vt.* (P6,9) **1** keep away from (something); refrain from (something). 피하다. ¶ ~ *making any promise* 약속하기를 회피하다 / *You should try to* ~ *catching cold.* 감기에 걸리지 않도록 노력해야 한다. **2** 《law》 make void. 무효로 하다; 취소하다. [ex-, F. *evuider,* →void]

a·void·a·ble [əvɔ́idəbəl] *adj.* that can be avoided. 피할 수 있는.

a·void·ance [əvɔ́idəns] *n.* Ⓤ the act of avoiding. 피함; 회피.

av·oir·du·pois [æ̀vərdəpɔ́iz] *n.* Ⓤ **1** a system of weights used in the United States and Great Britain, based on 16 ounces to the pound. (16온스를 1파운드로 정한) 형량(衡量). **2** 《*colloq.*》 one's weight; weight. 체중; 무게. [L. *habeo* have, *de* of, *pensum* weight]

a·vouch [əváutʃ] *vt.* (P6,11) **1** affirm or declare positively. …을 …라고 주장하다. **2** acknowledge; confess frankly. …을 인정하다; 고백하다. — *vi.* (P1) guarantee; affirm. 보증하다. [L. *vox* voice, →advocate]

a·vow [əváu] *vt.* (P6) declare openly. …을 공언(公言)하다; 인정하다; 고백하다; 솔직히 인정하다. ¶ ~ *one's errors* 과오를 인정하다 / ~ *oneself* (*to be*) *a patriot* 스스로 애국자라고 하다. [ad-, →vow]

a·vow·al [əváuəl] *n.* ⓊⒸ an open declaration; acknowledgment; confession. 공언(公言); 자인(自認).

a·vowed [əváud] *adj.* acknowledged; declared openly. 자인한; 공언한.

a·vow·ed·ly [əváuidli] *adv.* openly. 공공연히.

:a·wait [əwéit] *vt.* (P6) **1** wait for (someone or something); expect. …을 기다리다; 예기〔기대〕하다. ¶ *I* ~ *your reply.* 당신의 회답을 기다립니다 / *I am awaiting his decision.* 나는 그의 결정을 기다리고 있다. **2** be prepared for (someone or something). (무엇)이 …을 기다리고 있다; 준비돼 있다. ¶ *A hearty welcome awaits you.* 따뜻한 환영이 당신을 기다리고 있습니다 / *Death awaits us all.* 죽음은 우리 모두를 기다리고 있다. [F. *á* to; *guetter* wait]

:a·wake [əwéik] *v.* (**a·woke, a·waked** or **a·woke**) *vt.* (P6,13) **1** rouse (someone) from sleep; arouse; awaken. (잠에서) …를 깨우다. ¶ *The noise awoke me from my sleep.* 소란한 소리가 나를 잠에서 깨웠다. **2**

stir up; excite. …을 각성〔자각〕시키다; (기억 따위)를 불러 일으키다. ¶ ~ *a desire* 욕망에 눈뜨게 하다 / ~ *old memories* 옛 기억을 불러 일으키다 / *The affair awoke her to a sense of sin.* 그 일은 그녀에게 죄의식이 들게 했다. — *vi.* (P1,3,4) **1** stop sleeping. 눈을 뜨다; 깨다. ¶ ~ *from* 〔*out of*〕 *sleep* 잠에서 깨다 / *One morning he awoke to find himself famous.* 어느 날 아침 그가 눈을 뜨자 자신이 유명해져 있음을 알았다. **2** 《*to*》 become aware; realize. 깨닫다. ¶ *I awoke to my danger.* 일신의 위험을 깨달았다.
— *adj.* 《as *predicative*》 **1** not sleeping. 자지 않고; 깨어(opp. asleep). ¶ *lie* ~ 눈을 뜬 채 누워 있다 / *keep* (*oneself*) ~ 깨어 있다; 자지 않고 있다 / *The noise kept me awake.* 시끄러운 소음 때문에 잠을 자지 못했다 / *He was wide* ~ *all night.* 그는 밤새 통 자지 않았다. **2** watchful; alert. 방심 않는. ¶ *be* ~ *to one's interest* 자기 이익에 빈틈이 없다. [a(-)]
be awake to (=*be aware of*) *something.* …을 알고〔깨닫고〕 있다. ¶ *He was* ~ *to the danger.* 그는 위험을 알고 있었다.

:a·wak·en [əwéikən] *vt.* (P6) **1** wake up (someone). …의 눈을 뜨게 하다; 깨우다. **2** make (someone) aware. …을 깨닫게 하다. — *vi.* (P1,3,4) awake; become aware. 눈뜨다; 깨닫다. ¶ *At last he has awakened to a sense of responsibility.* 마침내 그는 책임의 중대함을 깨달았다.

a·wak·en·ing [əwéikəniŋ] *adj.* arousing. 깨어 있는. — *n.* UC the act of waking up; sudden awareness. 눈뜸; 자각. ¶ *an* ~ *of the self* 자아의 눈뜸 / *the* ~ *of children's interest in art* 어린아이들의 예술에 대한 관심의 자각 / *the* ~ *of Europe after the Dark Ages* 암흑 시대 이후의 유럽의 자각.

·a·ward [əwɔ́:rd] *vt.* (P13,14) give (something) as the result of judging or consideration. (심사하여 상품 등을) …에게 수여하다. ¶ ~ *someone an honor* 아무에게 명예를 주다 / ~ *someone a prize* 〔*reward*〕 = ~ *a prize* 〔*reward*〕 *to someone* 아무에게 상을 주다 / *be awarded a scholarship* 장학금이 수여되다 / *Damages were awarded to the injured man.* 부상자에 손해 배상이 주어졌다. — *n.* C a thing given as the result of judging or consideration; a prize. 상(賞). ¶ *Frank's dog won the highest* ~. 프랭크의 개가 최고상을 탔다. [ex-, →ward]

:a·ware [əwɛ́ər] *adj.* 《*of*》 knowing; conscious. 알고; 깨닫고. ¶ *I was too sleepy to be* ~ *how cold it was.* 너무 졸려서 얼마나 추운지 깨닫지 못했다 / *She was not* ~ *of her danger.* 그녀는 닥쳐오는 자신의 위험을 알지 못했다. ● **a·ware·ness** [-nis] *n.* [a =*ge*-intensive, →ware]

a·wash [əwɔ́:ʃ, əwɑ́ʃ / əwɔ́ʃ] *adj., adv.* 《as *predicative*》 《naut.》 scarcely above the surface of the water; just covered with water. (바위·침몰선 따위가) 수면과 거의 같은 높이로; 물결에 덮일 정도로. [a-]

:a·way [əwéi] *adv.* **1** off; from this or that place; not at home; absent; at or to a distance. 떨어져; 멀리; 부재(不在)하여; 떠나. ¶ *far* ~ 저 멀리 / *miles* ~ 몇 마일이나 떨어져 / ~ (*to the*) *west* 서쪽으로 / ~ *from the subject* 주제에서 멀리 벗어나 / *He was* ~ *from home.* 그는 집에 없었다 / *Take these books* ~. 이 책들을 치워라 / *He is* ~ *in the country.* 그는 멀리 시골에 있다 / *He is* ~ *on a journey.* 그는 여행 중에 있다. **2** aside; in another direction. 저쪽으로; 다른 쪽〔방향〕으로. ¶ *go* ~ 떠나다; 어디론가 가버리다 / *come* ~ 이리로 오다 / *turn one's eyes* ~ 눈을 딴데로 돌리다 / *turn* ~ *customers* 손님을 쫓아 보내다. **3** out of existence or notice; out of one's possession. 사라(져 없어)져; 없어져; 내주어; 사용하지 않게 되어. ¶ *burn* ~ 소실(燒失)하다 / *boil* ~ 끓어 증발돼 없어지다 / *fade* ~ 사라져 없어지다; 퇴색하다 / *die* ~ 점차 사라져 없어지다 / *wash* ~ 씻어버리다 / *give money* ~ 돈을 주어버리다 / *idle* ~ *the time of day* 시간을 헛되이 보내다 / *fool one's money* ~ 바보 같은 짓을 하여 돈을 낭비하다 / *give free catalogs* ~ 목록을 거저 주다 / *The snow melted* ~. 눈이 녹아 없어졌다. **4** continuously; without stopping; on and on; without hesitation. 끊임없이; 멈추지 않고; 부지런히; 주저없이. ¶ *work* ~ 부지런히 일하다〔공부하다〕 / *write* ~ 마구 갈겨쓰다 / *puff* ~ 담배를 뻐끔뻐끔 빨다 / *He kept hammering* ~ *at his task.* 그는 부지런히 그의 일을 계속했다 / *Fire* ~. 쏴라 / *Sing* ~. 망설이지 말고 노래해라. **5** 《U.S. *colloq.*》 far. 훨씬. ¶ *He is* ~ *behind the others in class.* 그는 학급에서 다른 애들보다 훨씬 뒤진다. [a-]
away back, 《U.S. *colloq.*》 as 〔so〕 far back as; long ago. 훨씬 전. ¶ ~ *back in 1900,* 1900년의 옛날에; 일찍이 1900년에.
away with, take away. …을 쫓아〔없애〕 버려라. ¶ *Away with him!* 그를 쫓아 버려라 / *Away with it!* 제거해 버려라; 그만둬라.
Away with you! Go away! 나가.
cannot away with, put up with. …을 참다.
far and away, beyond all doubt; very much; by far. 비할 데 없이. ¶ *This is far and* ~ *the best.* 이것이 단연 최고다.
from away, from a distance. 멀리서.
make 〔***do***〕 ***away with,*** **a**) get rid of (something). …을 없애다〔처분하다〕. **b**) kill. 죽이다.
out and away, by far. 훨씬.
right away, at once. 곧.

·awe [ɔ:] *n.* U a feeling of combined fear, respect, and wonder. 경외(敬畏); 두려움. ¶ *in* ~ *of God* 신을 두려워하여 / *keep* 〔*hold*〕 *someone in* ~ 아무를 두렵게 하다 / *We feel* ~ *when we stand near great mountains, or when we think of God's power and glory.* 우리는 태산(泰山)에 가까이 서거나, 신의 권능과 영광을 생각할 때면 두려움을 느낀다.

be struck with awe, be filled with awe. 두려움에 사로잡히다.
stand in awe of, respect and fear. 외경심을 품다.
— *vt.* (P6,13) **1** cause (someone) to feel awe; fill (someone) with awe. …에게 두려운 마음[외경심(心)]이 일게 하다. **2** influence or overcome (someone) by awe. 두려워서 따르게 하다. ¶ *~ someone into obedience* 아무를 두렵게 해 복종시키다 / *be awed into silence* 두려워서 침묵하다. [E.]

awe-in·spir·ing [ɔ́:inspàiriŋ] *adj.* arousing awe. 두려운; 장엄한.

awe·some [ɔ́:səm] *adj.* causing awe; inspiring awe. 경외감을 주는. ¶ *The explosion of an atomic bomb is an ~ sight.* 원자탄의 폭발은 경외감을 주는 광경이다.

awe-strick·en [ɔ́:strìkən] *adj.* = awe-struck.

awe-struck [ɔ́:strʌ̀k] *adj.* filled with awe. 경외(敬畏)하여; 두려워. ¶ *She was ~ by the grandeur of the mountains.* 그녀는 산의 장엄함에 두려움을 느끼고 있었다.

:aw·ful [ɔ́:fəl] *adj.* **1** dreadful; terrible. 무서운. ¶ *an ~ storm with thunder and lightning* 천둥과 번개를 동반한 무서운 폭풍. **2** 《*colloq.*》 extremely bad; very ugly. 지독한; 굉장한. — *adv.* 《*colloq.*》 very; extremely. 아주; 몹시. ●**aw·ful·ness** [-nis] *n.* [→awe]

:aw·ful·ly *adv.* **1** [ɔ́:fəli] dreadfully; terribly. 무섭게. ¶ *The earthquake was ~ destructive.* 그 지진은 무섭게 파괴적이었다. **2** [ɔ:fli] 《*colloq.*》 very; extremely. 매우; 지독히. ¶ *It's ~ cold tonight.* 오늘 밤은 지독히 춥다 / *Thanks ~.* 대단히 고맙습니다.

·a·while [əhwáil] *adv.* for a short time. 잠시. ¶ *I'll drive and you sleep ~.* 내가 운전할 테니 잠시 눈 좀 붙여라. [a(-)]

·awk·ward [ɔ́:kwərd] *adj.* **1** not skillful or graceful in movement or shape; clumsy. (사람·동작 따위가) 어색한; 데퉁스러운; 서투른. ¶ *She had large feet and her walk was ~.* 그녀는 큰 발을 가졌고 걸음걸이가 어색했다. **2** not convenient or comfortable; dangerous or difficult to deal with. 다루기 힘든[거북한, 벅찬]; 위험한. ¶ *put someone in an ~ position* 아무를 궁지에 몰아넣다 / *This is an ~ corner to turn.* 이건 돌기[꺾기] 곤란한 모퉁이다 / *This path leads to an ~ cliff.* 이 길은 위험한 벼랑에 이른다 / *It happened at an ~ time.* 그 일은 계제가 나쁜 때에 일어났다. ●**awk·ward·ly** [-li] *adv.* **awk·ward·ness** [-nis] *n.* [obs. *awk* back-handed, →ward] [E.]

awl [ɔ:l] *n.* Ⓒ a pointed instrument for making small holes in leather or wood, used esp. by shoemakers. (구둣방에서 쓰는) 송곳. [E.]

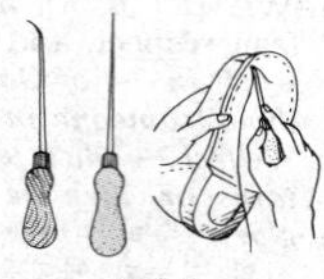
〈awl〉

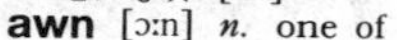

awn [ɔ:n] *n.* one of the bristly hairs on a head of barley, oats, etc. 까끄라기. [N.]

awn·ing [ɔ́:niŋ] *n.* Ⓒ a canvas roof over or in front of a door, window, etc. 차일(遮日); 차양. [F.]

·a·woke [əwóuk] *v.* p. and pp. of **awake.**

A.W.O.L. absent [absence] without leave. 무단 결석(無斷缺席).

a·wry [ərái] *adv., adj.* **1** with a turn or twist to one side. (한쪽으로) 굽어; 일그러져. ¶ *glance* [*look*] *~* 곁눈질로 보다 / *The boy pulled the tablecloth ~.* 그 아이는 테이블보를 일그러지게 당겼다. **2** away from the expected direction; wrong. 실패로; 잘못되어; 틀려. [a(-), →wry]
go awry, go wrong. 잘못되다; 실패하다. ¶ *Our plans went ~.* 계획은 실패했다.

:ax, axe [æks] *n.* Ⓒ (*pl.* **ax·es**) an instrument with a bladed head on a handle, used for cutting down trees. 도끼. [E.]
get the ax, 《*colloq.*》 **a**) be dismissed [discharged]; get the sack. 목이 잘리다; 해고되다. **b**) be rejected. (연인 등에게) 걷어채이다.
have an ax to grind, 《*colloq.*》 have a selfish motive or a special purpose for acting. 마음 속에 딴 속셈이 있다.

ax·es *n.* **1** [ǽksiz] pl. of **ax** or **axe.** **2** [ǽksi:z] pl. of **axis.**

ax·i·om [ǽksiəm] *n.* Ⓒ **1** a truth which everybody accepts as true without proof. 자명한 이치; 공리(公理). **2** an established principle; a maxim; a proverb. (일반적인) 통칙(通則); 격언. [Gk. *axios* worthy]

ax·i·o·mat·ic [æ̀ksiəmǽtik], **-i·cal** [-ikəl] *adj.* self-evident. 자명(自明)한. [↑]

ax·is [ǽksis] *n.* Ⓒ (*pl.* **ax·es** [-si:z]) **1** a straight line around which a body, such as the earth, turns. 축(軸). ¶ *the ~ of the equator* 지축(地軸) / *It turns on its own ~.* 그것은 축을 돈다. **2** a central line dividing a regular body or form symmetrically. 축선(軸線). **3** an agreement of two or more nations. 추축(樞軸). [L. = axle]

ax·le [ǽksəl] *n.* Ⓒ a pin or bar on or with which a wheel turns; a rod that joins tow wheels. 굴대; 차축(車軸). [E.]

·ay, aye[1] [ei] *adv.* 《*arch.*》 always; ever; continually. 영원히. ¶ *forever and ~* 영원히. [N. = always]

·ay, aye[2] [ai] *adv.* yes. 네; 그렇소. — *n.* an affirmative vote or voter. 찬성 (투표); 찬성 투표자. ¶ *the ayes and noes* 찬성과 반대(의 투표) / *The ayes have it.* 찬성 다수. [? ↑]

a·zal·ea [əzéiljə] *n.* Ⓒ 《bot.》 **1** a bush with many handsome flowers of various colors. 진달래. **2** the flower of this plant. 진달래꽃. [Gk. *azaleos* dry]

az·ure [ǽʒər] *adj.* sky-blue. 하늘빛[담청색(淡靑色)]의. — *n.* Ⓤ **1** sky-blue color. 하늘빛; 담청색. **2** the clear, cloudless sky. (맑게 갠) 푸른 하늘. [Arab. *al* the, Pers. *lazhward* lapis lazuli = the lapis lazuli blue]

b B

B¹, b [biː] *n.* Ⓒ (*pl.* **B's, Bs, b's, bs** [biːz]) **1** the second letter of the English alphabet. 영어 알파벳의 둘째 글자. **2** 《mus.》 the seventh note in the scale of C major. 나음(音). **3** 《alg.》 the second known quality. 제 2 의 기지수(既知數)《*b*》. **4** (in argument) the second hypothetical person. 제 2 가정자(假定者). — *adj.* second. 둘째의.

B² **1** black. 參考 연필의 흑색 농도(濃度) 표시. 경도(硬度)는 H로 표시함. **2** 《chem.》 boron. **3** 《chess》 bishop.

B. Bass; Bay.

b. base; bass; book; born; bowled.

Ba 《chem.》 barium.

B.A. Bachelor of Arts. 參考 A.B.라고도 함.

baa [bæː, bɑː / bɑː] *n.* Ⓒ a trembling cry, as of a sheep or lamb. 매《양의 울음소리》. — *vi.* (P1) (**baaed** [-d]) (of a sheep) make this sound. (양이) 매 울다. [Imit.]

Ba·al [béiəl] *n.* (*pl.* **-als** or **-al·im**) **1** the sun god of the ancient Phoenicians. 고대 페니키아 인의 태양신. **2** a false god. 사신(邪神); 우상(偶像). ¶ *bow the knee to* ~ 우상을 숭배하다. [Heb. =lord]

baa-lamb [bǽlæ̀m, bɑ́ː-] *n.* 《*child's word*》 a lamb or sheep. (새끼)양. [Imit.]

Ba·al·im [béiəlim] *n.* pl. of **Baal.**

bab·bitt [bǽbit] *n.* an alloy of tin, antimony and copper. 배빗 합금(合金). [Person]

bab·ble [bǽbəl] *vi.* (P1,2A) **1** make meaningless sounds like a baby; talk childishly or foolishly; prattle. 의미 없는 소리로 종잘거리다; 쓸데없는 말을 하다. **2** (of a brook, etc.) murmur. (시냇물 따위가) 졸졸 소리내(며 흐르)다. ¶ *a babbling brook* 졸졸 흐르는 개울. — *vt.* (P6) tell thoughtlessly; 《*out*》 make (something) known foolishly. …을 무심코 말하다; (비밀)을 누설하다. — *n.* Ⓤ **1** indistinct talk. 떠듬거리는 말. **2** idle talk. 쓸데없는 말. **3** a continuous murmuring sound. 졸졸 흐르는 소리. [Imit.]

bab·bler [bǽblər] *n.* **1** a person who babbles; a person who does much foolish talking. 말을 떠듬거리는 사람; 수다쟁이. **2** a person who tells secrets. 비밀 누설자.

·babe [beib] *n.* Ⓒ **1** 《*poet.*》 a baby. 갓난아이; 아기. **2** an inexperienced person. 물정에 어두운 사람. ¶ *He is a mere* ~ *in the ways of the world.* 그는 세상 물정에 아주 어둡다. [*baby*]

babes and sucklings, the utterly inexperienced. 풋내기들.

Ba·bel [béibəl, bǽb-] *n.* **1** 《Bible》 the tower described the Genesis 11. 바벨의 탑(塔). 參考 하늘까지 쌓아올리려 했다가 신(神)의 노여움을 사서 실패한 탑. **2** 《*b-*》 the confused state in which many languages are spoken at a time; great disorder. 언어의 혼란; 훤소; 소란. [Heb.]

ba·boon [bæbúːn / bə-] *n.* Ⓒ 《zool.》 a large, fierce monkey of Arabia and Africa with a dog-like face. 비비(狒狒). [F.]

:ba·by [béibi] *n.* (*pl.* **-bies**) Ⓒ **1** a very young child; an infant. 갓난아이; 젖먹이. ¶ *a squalling* ~ 응애응애 우는 아기 / *make a* ~ *of someone* 아무를 갓난애 취급하다. **2** a childish person. 어린애 같은 사람. ¶ *smell of the* ~ 젖비린내 나다; 어린애 같다 / *He is quite a* ~. 그는 정말 어린애 같은 사람이다. **3** 《U.S. *sl.*》 a girl or sweetheart. 아가씨; 연인. **4** 《*colloq.*》 a very young animal. 동물의 갓난 새끼.

be left holding the baby, 《*colloq.*》 be left with all the trouble, responsibility, etc., on one's hands. 성가신 역을 떠맡다.

hold [***carry***] ***the baby,*** be given a troublesome task. 귀찮은 일을 떠맡다.

— *adj.* **1** young; childish. 젊은; 어린. ¶ ~ *act* 미성년법. **2** small in size. 작은. ¶ *a* ~ *grand piano* 소형 그랜드 피아노.

— *vt.* (P6) treat as a baby. …를 갓난아이 취급하다. [child's *ba, ba*]

ba·by·hood [béibihùd] *n.* Ⓤ **1** the time or condition of being a baby. 유년(幼年) 시절; 유치(幼稚). **2** 《*collectively*》 babies. 갓난아이들; 유아들.

ba·by·ish [béibiiʃ] *adj.* childish; silly. 갓난아이 같은; 어리석은.

Bab·y·lon [bǽbələn, -lɑ̀n] *n.* **1** the capital of Babylonia. 바빌론. **2** Ⓒ any great, rich, but vicious city. 화려한 악(惡)의 대도시. [→Babel]

Bab·y·lo·ni·a [bæ̀bəlóuniə, -njə] *n.* the ancient empire in southwest Asia. 바빌로니아. 參考 서남 아시아에 있었던 고대 국가로, B.C. 2800-1000에 번영함.

Bab·y·lo·ni·an [bæ̀bəlóuniən, -njən] *adj.* **1** of or like Babylon or Babylonia. 바빌론(바빌로니아)의. **2** sinful. 악덕(惡德)의. — *n.* **1** an inhabitant of Babylonia. 바빌로니아 사람. **2** the language of Babylonia. 바빌로니아 말.

ba·by-sat [béibisæ̀t] *v.* p. or pp. of **baby-sit.**

ba·by-sit [béibisìt] *vi.* (**-sat, -sit·ting**) (P1) 《*colloq.*》 《*with*》 take care of a child while the parents are away. (집을 보며) 아이를 (돌)보다. ¶ ~ *with someone's baby* 아무

B

의 아기를 돌보다. [→baby]

ba·by-sit·ter [béibisìtər] *n.* a person who looks after children. 아이를 (돌)보는 사람.

bac·ca·lau·re·ate [bæ̀kəlɔ́:riit, -lɑ́r-] *n.* the degree of Bachelor. 학사 학위. [*bachelor*]

Bac·cha·nal [bǽkənl] *adj.* **1** of Bacchus. 바커스의. **2** riotous. 떠들썩한. — [bɑ̀:kənɑ́l, bæ̀kənǽl, bǽkənl] *n.* **1** a worshiper of Bacchus. 바커스 예찬자. **2** a reveler. 취해서 떠드는 사람. **3** 《*pl.*》 = Bacchanalia 1. [Gk.]

Bac·cha·na·li·a [bæ̀kənéiljə, -liə] *n. pl.* **1** an ancient Roman festival in honor of Bacchus. 바커스제(祭); 주신제(酒神祭). **2** 《*b-*》 noisy, drunken revelry. 떠들썩한 술잔치.

bac·cha·na·li·an [bæ̀kənéiljən] *adj.* belonging to noisy, drunken feasts. 술마시고 떠드는; 야단 법석의.

bac·chant [bǽkənt, bəkǽnt, -kɑ́:nt] *n.* a priest or worshiper of Bacchus; a drunken reveler. 바커스의 사제〔예찬자〕; 술 마시고 떠드는 사람. [Gk.]

bac·chan·te [bəkǽnti, -kɑ́:nti] *n.* a female worshiper of Bacchus; a woman fond of drunken feasting. 바커스의 여자 사제; 여자 술꾼.

Bac·chus [bǽkəs] *n.* 《Rom. myth.》 the god of wine. 바커스《술의 신》. 參考 그리스신화에서는 디오니소스(Dionysus). [Gk.]

Bach [bɑ:k, bɑ:x], **Johann Sebastian** *n.* (1685-1750) a German composer of music and organist. 바흐《독일의 작곡가》.

·**bach·e·lor** [bǽtʃələr] *n.* Ⓒ **1** a man who has not married yet. 독신 남자; 총각(cf. *spinster*). ¶ *a bachelor's baby* 사생아 / *a bachelor's wife* (총각이 꿈꾸는) 이상적인 아내. **2** a person who has taken the first degree at a college or university. 학사(學士). 參考 Bachelor of Arts = B.A. 문학사(文學士); Bachelor of Science = B.Sc. 이학사(理學士) 따위로 씀. [F.]

bach·e·lor·dom [bǽtʃələrdəm] *n.* = bachelorhood.

bachelor girl [ˊ--ˋ] *n.* a young unmarried woman who works and leads an independent life. 독신 여성.

bach·e·lor·hood [bǽtʃələrhùd] *n.* the condition of being a bachelor. 독신(獨身).

bachelor's button [ˊ--ˋ-] *n.* **1** 《bot.》 any of several kinds of flowers shaped like buttons, esp. the cornflower. 수레국화. **2** a button, as on an overall, which is attached without being sewn. 꿰매지 않고 다는 단추.

bach·e·lor·ship [bǽtʃələrʃìp] *n.* **1** bachelordom. 독신. **2** the degree of Bachelor. 학사 학위.

ba·cil·li [bəsílai] *n.* pl. of **bacillus.**

ba·cil·lus [bəsíləs] *n.* (*pl.* **-cil·li**) Ⓒ a bacterium, esp. a rod-shaped one. 바실루스; 간상균(桿狀菌)(cf. *germ*). [L. *baculus* stick]

:back [bæk] *n.* Ⓒ **1** the hinder surface of the human body; the upper surface of an animal's body. (사람·동물의) 등. ¶ *a rounded* ~ 새우등 / *a bird with brownish tint on* ~ 다갈색을 띤 등을 가진 새 / *slap someone on the* ~ 등을 찰싹 때리다 / *sit* 〔*ride*〕 *on a horse's* ~ 말을 타다 / *have* 〔*carry*〕 … *on one's* ~ …을 (짊어)지다〔지고 걷다, 업다〕 / *have one's* ~ *to someone* 아무에게 등을 돌리다 / *She has a baby on her* ~. 그녀는 아이를 업고 있다. **2** the opposite side from the front; the farthest part from a spectator. (정면에 대해서) 뒤(쪽); 안쪽; (깊숙한) 속. ¶ *the* ~ *of a house* 집 뒤 / *the* ~ *of a room* 방의 안쪽 / *the* ~ *of the head* 머리의 뒤; 후두부 / *the* ~ *of the mouth* 입속 / *with the* ~ *of one's hand* 손등으로. **3** the rear part of a thing. 배면(背面). ¶ *the* ~ *of a chair* 의자등 / *the* ~ *of a sword* 칼등 / *the* ~ *of a ship* 배의 용골(龍骨) / *the* ~ *of a hill* 산등(성이) / *on the* ~ *of the envelope* 봉투 뒤에. **4** (of football or other games) a player placed behind. (축구 따위 경기에서) 후위(後衛); 백(opp. forward). 參考 경기에 따라서 fullback, halfback, quarterback 따위로 구분함. **5** the side away from the spectator. 배경.

at the back of = ***at one's back,*** behind, esp. in support or pursuit of. …의 뒤에; …의 바로 뒤에; …을 후원〔지지〕하여; …을 추구하여. ¶ *More than half the city are at his* ~. 시민의 과반수가 그를 지지하고 있다 / *He must be at the* ~ *of this plot.* 이 음모의 배후에는 그가 있음에 틀림없다.

at the back of one's mind, forgotten for the moment. 잠깐 잊은.

back and belly, **a**) clothing and food. 의식(衣食). **b**) all over; completely. 온통; 완전히. ¶ *be surrounded* ~ *and belly by the enemy* 적군에 완전히 포위되다.

back to back, directing one's back toward another's back. 등을 맞대고. ¶ *They stood* ~ *to* ~. 그들은 등을 맞대고 서 있었다.

back to front, 《*colloq.*》 having the back where the front should be. 뒤집어서.

behind someone's back, when someone is absent; without someone's knowledge or consent. …의 등 뒤에서; 음(陰)으로; 몰래. ¶ *They laugh at her behind her* ~. 그녀가 없는 데서 그녀를 비웃는다.

be on one's back, be ill in bed; be helpless. 앓아 누워 있다; 백계(百計)를 다하다.

be on someone's back, find fault with someone. 탈〔트집〕을 잡다.

break someone's back, **a**) cause someone to fail; cause someone to become bankrupt. 아무를 실패하게 하다; 아무를 파산시키다. ¶ *His family's extravagance is breaking his* ~. 그의 가족의 낭비로 그는 파산 지경에 있다. **b**) be too hard for someone to do. …

하기가 힘에 겹다.
break the back of, **a**) finish the major or most difficult part of (a project, job, etc.). …의 가장 어려운 부분을 마치다; 고비를 넘기다. **b**) defeat the strength. …을 꺾다; 무력(無力)하게 하다.
get 〔**put**〕 *one's* **back up,** get angry. 화내다.
get 〔**put**〕 *someone's* **back up,** 《*colloq.*》 **a**) make someone angry. …를 화나게 하다. ¶ *He always puts my ~ up by making those silly jokes.* 그는 언제나 바보 같은 농담으로 나를 화나게 한다. **b**) do not obey someone. …에게 거역하다.
get off *someone's* **back,** 《*sl.*》 cease to find fault with or to disturb someone. …를 비난하는〔방해하는〕 짓을 그만두다; 트집잡기를〔괴롭히는 짓을〕 그만두다. ¶ *The fight started when they wouldn't get off my ~.* 그들이 계속 나를 비난하기 때문에 싸움이 시작되었다.
have *one's* **back to the wall,** be in a difficult or hopeless situation. 진퇴 유곡에 빠지다; 궁지에 몰리다.
have … on *one's* **back,** be burdened with …. (짐을) 짊어지다.
in back of, 《U.S. *colloq.*》 behind. …의 뒤에(서).
on the back of, **a**) on the reverse side of. …의 뒤편에. **b**) immediately following. …에 잇따라서. 語法 사건 특히 불행한 사건 등에 관해서만 씀. **c**) in addition to. …에 더하여.
put *one's* **back into,** do (something) with all one's energy. …에 전력을 쏟다. ¶ *Put your ~ into your job.* 일에 전력을 다해라.
see the back of, get rid of; drive away. 쫓아버리다. ¶ *Anybody wants to see the ~ of such a laggard as you.* 누구든 너 같은 무시근한 녀석은 내쫓고 싶을 거다.
the back of beyond, 《*colloq.*》 a very distant place. 매우 먼 곳; 벽지.
turn *one's* **back on,** turn behind; forsake; neglect. …에게 등을 돌리다; 버리다; 무시하다. ¶ *She turned her ~ in silent contempt on her mother.* 무언의 경멸로 자기 어머니를 무시했다.

— *adj.* (*superl.* **back·most**) **1** situated behind; opposite to the front. 뒤의; 안의. ¶ *a ~ door* 뒷문 / *the ~ seat of a car* 차의 뒷 좌석. **2** far from the main area; remote. 궁벽한; 외진. ¶ *a ~ country* 벽촌(僻村). **3** moving backward. 뒤로 물러나는; 후방으로의. ¶ *~ current* 역류(逆流). **4** belonging to the past. 과거의. ¶ *the ~ numbers of a magazine* (정기 간행물의) 지난 호 잡지 / *He is a ~ number.* 그는 시대에 뒤진 사람이다.
take a back seat, humble oneself. 자기를 비하(卑下)하다.

— *adv.* **1** at or to the rear. 뒤로〔에〕; 뒤쪽으로. ¶ *step ~* 뒤로 물러서다; 물러나다 / *sit ~ in a chair* 의자 깊숙이 앉다 / *move ~ in a bus* 버스 안 쪽으로 들어가다. **2** into or in an earlier, normal, true position, or condition. 본디 자리〔상태〕로; 원〔정〕위치로; …을 향하여; 되돌아가. ¶ *go ~* (되)돌아가다 / *on one's way ~* 돌아오는〔가는〕 길에 / *nurse someone ~ to health* 아무를 간호하여 본디 건강한 몸으로 되돌리다 / *He will be ~ at six.* 여섯 시면 돌아올 겁니다 / *How much to Chicago and ~?* 시카고까지 왕복 얼맙니까. **3** in return. 되돌려; 답례로. ¶ *answer ~* 회답하다 / *pay ~ a loan* 빚을 갚다 / *I hit him right ~.* 곧 그를 되쳤다. **4** to or in a retired or remote position. 속〔안〕에; 쑥 들어간 곳에; 먼 곳에. ¶ *a house standing ~ from the main street* 한길에서 (쑥) 들어간 곳에 있는 집. **5** to an earlier time. 옛날에; 이전에; 거슬러 올라가. ¶ *some years ~* 몇 해 전에 / *a while ~* 얼마 전에 / *as far ~ as 1750,* 멀리 1750년으로 거슬러 올라가 / *look ~ on one's youth* 젊었던 시절을 돌이켜보다.
back and forth, to and fro. 앞뒤로.
back from, at a distance from. …에서 멀리. ¶ *The house lies ~ from the road.* 그 집은 길에서 떨어져 있다.
back of, 《U.S.》 behind. …의 뒤에. ¶ *There is a garden ~ of the house.* 그 집 뒤에 정원이 있다.
get *one's* **own back on** *someone,* 《*colloq.*》 revenge oneself on someone. …에 보복하다.
go back from 〔***on***〕, break a promise to. …에게 식언(食言)하다; …을 배반하다.

— *vt.* **1** (P6,7) cause (someone or something) to move backward. …을 후퇴시키다. ¶ *~ a car* (*up*) 차를 후진시키다. **2** (P6,7) support; help. …을 후원하다; 뒤를 밀다; 돕다. ¶ *~ a candidate* 후보자를 지지하다 / *~ up a theory with facts* 사실을 들어 이론을 뒷받침하다 / *~ someone* (*up*) *one hundred percent* 아무를 전폭적으로 지지하다. **3** (P6) put a back to; line. (책 따위에) 등을 붙이다; 뒤를 받치다. **4** (P6,13) bet on. (돈 따위)를 걸다. ¶ *~ a horse in the race* 경마에서 어떤 말에 걸다. **5** (P6) sign on the back; endorse. …에 배서하다. ¶ *~ a bill* 어음에 배서하다. **6** (P6) get upon the back of; mount. (…의 등)에 타다. ¶ *~ a horse* 말을 타다.

— *vi.* (P1,2A,3) go backward. 뒤로 움직이다; 뒤로 물러나다. ¶ *~ up three steps* 세 발짝 뒤로 물러나다. [E.]
back and fill, 《U.S. *colloq.*》 **a**) change one's opinion or position from time to time. 의견 따위가 자주 변하다; 흔들리다. **b**) move in a zigzag way. 갈짓자로 나아가다.
back down, give up an argument, a claim, etc. 주장 따위를 철회〔포기〕하다.
back on to, have the back (usu. of a house) close against (something). (건물 따위가) …와 등을 대고 있다.
back out, withdraw or fail to keep one's promise. 약속을 취소하다〔어기다〕.
back up, **a**) support. …을 지원〔지지〕하다. **b**) move backward. 뒤로 물러서다; 후퇴하다.
back water, **a**) go backward in a rowing-boat by reversing the motion of the oars. 배를 후진시키다. **b**) withdraw. 후퇴하

다; (약속 따위를) 취소하다.

back·ache [bǽkèik] *n.* an ache or pain in the back. 등의 통증(痛症). [*back*]

back·bit [bǽkbìt] *v.* p. of **backbite.**

back·bite [bǽkbàit] *vt., vi.* (**-bit, -bit·ten**) (P6; 1) speak ill of someone who is not present. …가 없는 데서[뒤에서] 욕하다. ¶ *He backbites his friends when they are not present.* 그는 자기 친구들이 없을 때면 욕을 한다. ● **back·bit·er** [-ər] *n.*

B

back·bit·ten [bǽkbìtn] *v.* pp. of **back-bite.**

back·bone [bǽkbòun] *n.* **1** Ⓒ the main bone along the center of the back in man or other animals; the spine. 등뼈. **2** Ⓒ the most important part. 중심 세력; 주력; 중추(中樞). ¶ *the* ~ *of the attack* 공격의 주력 / *the* ~ *of the team* 팀의 주력 / *Anglo-Saxon is the* ~ *of modern English.* 앵글로색슨 말은 현대 영어의 주요소이다. **3** Ⓤ the strength of character; moral courage. 기골(氣骨); 정신력. ¶ *lack* ~ 기골이 없다 / *He has plenty of* ~. 그는 대담하다.

back·chat [bǽktʃæ̀t] *n.* 《*colloq.*》 a retort. 말대꾸; 응수.

back·door [bǽkdɔ̀:r] *n.* a rear entrance. 뒷문. — *adj.* secret. 비밀의.

back·drop [bǽkdrɑ̀p / -drɔ̀p] *n.* a curtain at the back of a stage; the background. 무대의 배경막; 배경.

back·er [bǽkər] *n.* Ⓒ a person who helps another. 후원자.

back·field [bǽkfi:ld] *n.* 《football》 **1** the players stationed behind the line of scrimmage. 후위[수비]진. **2** the positions filled by them. 후위.

back·fire [bǽkfàiər] *n.* ⓊⒸ **1** (in a gasoline engine) an explosion of gas before the right time. (가솔린 엔진의) 역화(逆火). **2** 《U.S.》 a fire which is set to stop the advance of a forest or field fire. (불길이 번지는 것을 막기 위한) 맞불. **3** an adverse reaction. 반작용. — *vi.* (P1) **1** (of gas) burst before the right time. 역화(逆火)가 일어나다. **2** start a backfire. 맞불을 놓다.

back·gam·mon [bǽkgæ̀mən, ⌐⌐–] *n.* Ⓤ a game played by two persons with a board and a dice. 서양 주사위 놀이.

·**back·ground** [bǽkgràund] *n.* **1** the distant part of a scene; the part of a picture on which the distant scene is represented. 원경(遠景). **2** the surface on or to which things are placed, attached, or drawn. 배경. ¶ *The* ~ *of this picture is very dark, isn't it?* 이 그림은 배경이 매우 어둡지, 안그래요 / *Her dress had pink flowers on a white* ~. 그녀의 드레스에는 흰 바탕에 핑크빛 꽃이 그려져 있었다. **3** the social or historical antecedents. 사회적·역사적 배경. ¶ *the* ~ *of the war* 전쟁을 일으킨 배경. **4** the past experience. 경력.

in the background, out of sight or notice. 드러나지 않고. ¶ *The shy boy kept in the* ~. 그 숫기 없는 아이는 끝내 앞에 나서지 않았다.

back·hand [bǽkhæ̀nd] *n.* Ⓒ **1** (in tennis, etc.) a stroke made from the side of the body opposite to that of the hand holding the racket. (테니스 등에서) 백핸드. **2** handwriting which slopes to the left. 왼쪽으로 기운 필적. [*back*]

back·hand·ed [bǽkhæ̀ndid] *adj.* **1** of backhand. 백핸드의; 손등의. **2** indirect. 간접의. ¶ *a* ~ *warning* 간접적인 경고. **3** unexpected. 뜻밖의. **4** awkward; clumsy. 서투른.

back·hand·er [bǽkhæ̀ndər] *n.* **1** a back-handed blow. 백핸드 스트로크; 역타(逆打). **2** an indirect attack. 간접 공격.

back·ing [bǽkiŋ] *n.* ⓊⒸ **1** something placed behind anything to support or strengthen it. 뒤를 댐[받침]. ¶ *Looking-glasses have a* ~ *of quicksilver.* 거울은 뒤에 수은을 칠했다. **2** help; support. 후원; 지지. **3** 《*collectively*》 supporters. 후원자. ¶ *He has a very strong* ~. 그에게는 강력한 후원자가 있다.

back·lash [bǽklæ̀ʃ] *n.* **1** the jarring reaction of loose or worn parts. 백래시《톱니바퀴 사이의 틈, 그로 인한 헐거움》. **2** a violent backward motion or reaction. 급격한 반동[반발]. **3** a reversal. 반전(反轉).

back·less [bǽklis] *adj.* having no back; (esp. of a dress) cut to the waist at the back. 등이 없는; (특히 여성복 따위의) 등이 많이 파진.

back·log [bǽklɔ̀(:)g, ⌐lɑ̀g] *n.* 《U.S.》 **1** something serving as a reserve. 예비. **2** a large log at the back of a hearth to keep up a fire. (오래 타게 난로 깊숙이 넣어두는) 큰 장작. **3** an accumulation, of unfulfilled business orders, unfinished work, etc. (미처리의) 주문·일 따위의 적체; 미처리분.

back number [⌐ ⌐–] *n.* an old copy of a magazine, etc.; an old-fashioned person or thing. (잡지 등의) 지난 호; 한물 지난[시대에 뒤진] 사람[것].

back·room boy [bǽkrù(:)m bɔ́i] *n.* 《often *pl.*》 《Brit. *colloq.*》 men engaged in secret research. (특히 국가 기밀의) 과학 연구원.

back·seat driver [bǽksí:t dráivər] *n.* a person with no responsibility who gives much advice. 주제넘은 사람.

back·sheesh [bǽkʃi:ʃ, –⌐] *n.* =baksheesh.

back·side [bǽksàid] *n.* the hinder parts; the rump. 둔부(臀部).

back·slid [bǽkslìd] *v.* p. and pp. of **backslide.**

back·slid·den [bǽkslìdn] *v.* pp. of **back-slide.**

back·slide [bǽkslàid] *vi.* (**-slid, -slid** or **-slid·den**) (P1) return from the good ways to the bad former ways; turn away from a religion once believed in. 악(惡)으로 되돌아

가다; 신앙을 버리다; 타락하다. ¶ *He was once active in the good cause, but he has backslidden.* 그는 한때 착하게 굴었으나 다시 나쁜 길로 빠졌다. ● **back·slid·er** [-ər] *n.* [*back*]

back·stage [bǽkstéidʒ] *adv.* in the dressing room in a theater; at or to the rear of a stage. (극장의) 분장실에서; 무대 뒤(쪽)에서 〔으로〕. —*adj.* **1** happening, placed, etc., backstage. 무대 뒤에서 일어나는〔뒤에 있는〕. **2** hidden; covert. 비밀의; 숨은.

back·stop [bǽkstɑ̀p / -stɔ̀p] *n.* **1** a fence or screen used in various games to keep the ball from going too far away. (야구장 등의) 펜스. **2** a player who stops balls in various games. (구기의) 수비 선수.

back·stroke [bǽkstròuk] *n.* Ⓒ **1** a return blow. 되받아치기. **2** (in tennis, etc.) a backhand stroke. (테니스 등의) 백핸드스트로크. **3** a stroke made by a swimmer lying on his back. 배영(背泳).

***back·ward** [bǽkwərd] *adj.* **1** directed to the back. 뒤(로)의; 뒤쪽으로의. ¶ *~ motion* 후진(後進) 운동. **2** done in a way opposite to the usual or right way. 거꾸로의; 역(逆)의. ¶ *a ~ journey* 귀로 여행 / *a ~ movement of a train* 열차의 후진(後進) / *a ~ course* 역코스 / *a ~ blessing* 저주. **3** unwilling; shy. (마음이) 내키지 않는; 수줍어하는. ¶ *a ~ lover* 수줍음을 타는 연인 / *He is ~ in asserting himself.* 그는 수줍어서 자기를 주장하지 않는다 / *Shake hands with the lady; don't be ~.* 수줍어 말고 그 여성과 악수하게. **4** behind the times; not developed. 시대에 〔발달이〕 뒤진; 보수적인; 계절에 뒤진. ¶ *a ~ child* 지진아 / *~ nations* 후진국 / *a ~ attitude* 보수적인 태도 / *a ~ state of society* 사회의 후진 상태 / *The crops are ~ this year.* 금년에는 수확이 늦다.

be backward in, be behindhand in. (준비 따위가) 지체되다.

—*adv.* **1** toward the back; toward the starting point. 뒤로; 제자리로. ¶ *fall ~* 벌렁 자빠지다 / *turn one's eyes ~* 뒤돌아보다 / *walk ~ and forward* 왔다갔다 거닐다. **2** with the back first. 뒤로 향해. ¶ *drive a car ~* 차를 후진시키다. **3** in a way opposite to the usual or right way. 거꾸로. ¶ *turn a handle ~* 핸들을 거꾸로 돌리다 / *count ~ from 100,* 100에서 거꾸로 세다. **4** toward the past. 과거로 (거슬러 올라가). ¶ *some thirty years ~* 약 30년 전에 / *look ~ over one's earlier mistakes* 옛날의 잘못을 되돌아보다. **5** from better to worse. 퇴보(退步)하여.

backward and forward, thoroughly. 완전히; 죄다.

● **back·ward·ness** [-nis] *n.*

***back·wards** [bǽkwərdz] *adv.* 《Brit.》 = backward.

back·wash [bǽkwɔ̀(ː)ʃ, ∠wɑ̀ʃ] *n.* Ⓤ water thrown back by oars; a backward current. (노를 저어 생기는) 물결; 뒷물결; 역류. [*back*]

back·wa·ter [bǽkwɔ̀ːtər, ∠wɑ̀t-] *n.* **1** ⒸⓊ water held back by a dam, etc.; calm water lying to one side of a river. 둑 따위에 부딪쳐 되밀리는 물; 배수(背水); 강 한쪽에 정체된 물. **2** Ⓒ an inactive state or condition. 침체; 정체(停滯).

back·woods [bǽkwùdz] *n. pl.* forests or wild regions far away from towns; back country. (특히 미국·캐나다의) 미개간지; 벽지(僻地).

back·woods·man [bǽkwùdzmən] *n.* Ⓒ (*pl.* **-men** [-mən]) a man who lives in the backwoods. 벽지의 주민.

back·yard [bǽkjáːrd] *n.* Ⓒ 《U.S.》 the yard at the back of a house or other building. 뒤뜰; 뒤꼍.

***Ba·con** [béikən] *n.* 베이컨. **1 Francis** (1561-1626) an English essayist, philosopher and statesman. 영국의 수필가·철학자·정치가. **2 Roger** (1214?-94) an English philosopher and scientist. 영국의 철학자·자연 과학자.

***ba·con** [béikən] *n.* Ⓤ salted and smoked pork. 베이컨. [Teut.]

bring home the bacon, 《*sl.*》 **a**) earn money sufficient to support oneself. 생활비를 벌다. **b**) succeed (in an undertaking); win. 성공하다; 승리하다.

save one's bacon, 《*colloq.*》 escape death or injury. 위해를 모면하다.

bac·te·ri·a [bæktíəriə] *n. pl.* (*sing.* **-rium**) tiny plants of one cell. 박테리아; 세균. [Gk. *bactron* stick]

bac·te·ri·al [bæktíəriəl] *adj.* of bacteria; caused by bacteria. 박테리아의; 세균에 의한.

bac·te·ri·cide [bæktíərəsàid] *n.* a substance that destroys bacteria. 살균제.

bac·te·ri·o·log·ic [bæktìəriəlɑ́dʒik / -lɔ́dʒ-], **-i·cal** [-əl] *adj.* of bacteriology. 세균학(상)의.

bac·te·ri·ol·o·gist [bæktìəriɑ́lədʒist / -ɔ́lə-] *n.* Ⓒ an expert in bacteriology. 세균학자.

bac·te·ri·ol·o·gy [bæktìəriɑ́lədʒi / -ɔ́lə-] *n.* Ⓤ the science that deals with bacteria. 세균학.

bac·ter·i·o·phage [bæktíəriəfèidʒ] *n.* 《med.》 bactericide produced within the body. 세균 분해 바이러스.

bac·te·ri·um [bæktíəriəm] *n.* sing. of **bacteria.**

:bad[1] [bæd] *adj.* (**worse, worst**) **1** not good; not right. 나쁜; 부정한; 불량한(opp. good). ¶ *a ~ boy* 불량 소년 / *a ~ man* 악인; 악당 / *a ~ life* 방종한 생활 / *~ habits* 나쁜 버릇 / *call someone ~ names* 아무를 욕하다. **2** of poor quality; worthless. 품질이 나쁜; 무가치한. ¶ *a ~ diamond* 품질이 좋지 않은 다이아몬드 / *a ~ repair job* 엉성한 수리 상태 / *~ paper* 질 나쁜 종이 / *a ~ radio tube*

결함이 있는 라디오 진공관. **3** incorrect; full of mistakes. 부정확한; 틀린 것이 많은. ¶ *a ~ guess* 부정확한 추측 / *a ~ composition* 오류투성이의 작문 / *a ~ shot* 빗나간 총알; 잘못 짚음 / *Our views proved ~*. 우리의 견해는 틀린 것으로 밝혀졌다. **4** not morally right; wicked; evil. 부도덕한; 사악(邪惡)한. ¶ *a ~ woman* 행실이 나쁜 여자 / *It is ~ to tell a lie.* 거짓말하는 것은 나쁘다. **5** rotten; spoiled. 썩은; 상한. ¶ *a ~ apple* 썩은 사과 / *a ~ tooth* 충치 / *go* 〔*turn*〕 *~* 썩다 / *This fish is ~*. 이 생선은 상했다. **6** harmful; injurious. 유해한; 좋지 않은. ¶ *be ~ to health* 건강에 나쁘다 / *a climate ~ for the health* 건강에 나쁜 기후 / *Candy is ~ for your teeth.* 캔디는 치아에 해롭다. **7** disagreeable; unpleasant. 불쾌한. ¶ *a ~ smell* 〔*taste*〕 불쾌한 냄새〔맛〕 / *sound ~* 불쾌한 소리가 나다 / *taste ~* 맛이 나쁘다 / *a ~ summer* 더위가 심한 여름 / *have a ~ time* (*of it*) 혼나다. **8** severe; serious. 지독한; (격)심한. ¶ *a ~ cold* 지독한 감기 / *a ~ accident* 중대한 사고 / *a ~ crime* 악질의 범죄 / *a ~ disease* 악성의 병; 중병 / *Is the pain very ~?* 통증이 아주 심한가. **9** ill; sick; in pain. 병이 난; 기분이 언짢은. ¶ *be taken ~* 병이 나다 / *I feel ~ today.* 오늘은 기분이 좋지 않다 / *He felt ~ from eating green apples.* 그는 설익은 사과를 먹고 속이 좋지 않았다. **10** unlucky; unfortunate. 불행한; 운이 나쁜. ¶ *a ~ year* 흉년; 불경기의 해 / *have ~ luck* 재수 없는 일을 당하다 / *He came at ~ time.* 그는 좋지 않은 시기에 왔다.

a bad lot 〔***egg, hat***〕, 《*sl.*》 a bad man or woman. 나쁜 사람; 악인.

be in a bad way, be in bad health; be almost ruined. (건강·사업·재정 따위가) 아주 나쁜 상태에 있다; 불경기다.

feel bad for 〔***about***〕, regret; be sorry for (one's mistakes). 후회하다.

go bad, rot; spoil. (음식물 따위가) 썩다; 상하다.

not bad =***not so*** 〔***half***〕 ***bad,*** 《*colloq.*》 rather good. 그리 나쁘지 않은; 어지간히 좋은. ¶ *What sort of a dinner did they give you? — Oh, not* (*so*) *~*. 그 집 만찬은 어떻던가요—괜찮았어요.

That's too bad. I'm very sorry. 그것 안 됐군. — *n.* **1** 《*the ~*》 persons of wicked character. 악인들; 못된 사람들. **2** Ⓤ 《*the ~*》 what is bad; bad quality or state. 나쁜 것; 나쁜 상태. [E.]

be ... to the bad, be on the wrong side of the account; have acquired a debt of.... 손해를 보다; 빚을 지다.

go from bad to worse, grow worse; get steadily worse. 점점 나빠지다〔악화하다〕.

go to the bad, become wicked; ruin morally. 타락하다.

in bad, 《U.S. *colloq.*》 **a**) in trouble. 곤경에. **b**) in disfavor. 미움을 받아.

bad² [bæd] *v.* p. of **bid.**

bad blood [⌐⌐] *n.* ill feeling; dislike; hatred. 악감정; 불화; 증오.

*__bade__ [bæd / bæd, beid] *v.* p. of **bid.**

BADGE Base Air Defense Ground Environment. 배지; 기지 방공 지상 경계 조직(cf. *SAGE*).

badge [bædʒ] *n.* Ⓒ a special mark or token worn as a sign of membership, authority, etc.; a symbol. 배지; 휘장(徽章); 상징. ¶ *the Red Cross ~* 적십자 배지 / *Chains are a ~ of slavery.* 쇠사슬은 노예의 상징이다. [E.]

*__badg·er__ [bǽdʒər] *n.* (*pl.* **-ers,** *collectively* **badg·er**) Ⓒ 《zool.》 a hairy animal of Europe and America which lives in holes and is active at night. 오소리. — *vt.* (P6, 13) tease; annoy; worry. …을 괴롭히다. ¶ *Stop badgering me with your foolish questions!* 그 바보 같은 질문으로 날 괴롭히지 마. [?]

bad·i·nage [bædinɑ́:ʒ, bǽdinidʒ] *n.* 《F.》 playful talk. 농담.

*__bad·ly__ [bǽdli] *adv.* (**worse, worst**) **1** ⓐ in a bad manner; in a defective or incorrect way. 나쁘게; 서투르게; 불완전〔부정확〕하게 (opp. well). ¶ *a vague ~ written letter* 애매하고 서투른 글씨로 쓴 편지 / *He behaved ~*. 그는 나쁘게 행동했다 / *He speaks English very ~*. 그는 영어를 몹시 불완전하게 한다. ⓑ unfavorably. 호의적이 아니게; 나쁘게. ¶ *think ~ of* …을 나쁘게 생각하다 / *His neighbors spoke ~ of him.* 그의 이웃들은 그를 나쁘게 말했다. **2** 《*colloq.*》 very much; to a great degree. 대단히; 매우. ¶ *I need money ~*. 나는 돈이 몹시 필요하다 / *be ~ wounded* 중상을 입다. [→bad¹]

*__bad·min·ton__ [bǽdmintən] *n.* Ⓤ a game like tennis played with a feathered cork and rackets. 배드민턴. 參考 Duke of Beaufort의 영지(領地) 이름에서 유래. [Place]

bad·ness [bǽdnis] *n.* Ⓤ the state of being bad. 나쁨; 불량; 부정.

bad-tem·pered [bǽdtèmpərd] *adj.* cross. 심술궂은. ¶ *a very ~ old man* 몹시 심술궂은 늙은이. [*bad, temper*]

Bae·de·ker [béidikər] *n.* **1** a guidebook published by Karl Baedeker. 베데커 여행 안내서. **2** a guidebook. 여행 안내서.

baf·fle [bǽfəl] *vt.* (P6) **1** bring (the efforts of someone) to nothing; perplex; puzzle. (아무의 노력 따위)를 꺾다; 곤란〔당황〕하게 하다. ¶ *~ the enemy's plan* 적의 전략의 의표를 찌르다 / *The sudden question baffled me.* 갑작스런 질문에 당황했다. **2** prevent (plans, etc.) from being carried out. (계획 따위)를 방해하다. ¶ *He succeeded in baffling all my efforts.* 그는 나의 모든 노력을 방해하는데 성공했다. — *vi.* 《*with*》 (P1,3) struggle without success. 허위적거리다; 헛애만 쓰다. ¶ *The ship baffled with a gale from the NW.* 그 배는 강한 북서풍에 시달렸다.

baffle description, be beyond description. 이루 다 말할 수 없다.

be baffled (=*fail*) ***in*** *one's attempt.* …에 실패하다; 헛수고로 끝나다.

— *n.* Ⓒ a wall or screen for checking the flow of air, water, etc. (기류(氣流)·수류(水流) 등의) 조절 장치. [? →baffy]

baf·fling [bǽfəliŋ] *adj.* difficult or impossible to understand. 난해한. ¶ *a* ~ *problem* 난해한 문제 / *a very* ~ *man* 이해할 수 없는 사람.

baf·fy [bǽfi] *n.* a short wooden golf club. 짧은 목제의 골프채. [? Scot. *baff* blow]

⁑bag [bæg] *n.* Ⓒ **1** a sack or case made of paper, cloth, leather, etc. 가방; 자루; 부대; 봉지. ¶ *a* ~ *of grain* 곡식 자루 / *put into* 〔*take out of*〕 *a* ~ 부대에 넣다〔에서 꺼내다〕. **2** a purse; a handbag. 지갑; 핸드백. ¶ *consult one's* ~ 호주머니 사정을 참작하다 / *empty one's* ~ *to the last penny* 지갑을 다 털다. **3** a suitcase; a traveling bag. 슈트케이스; 여행가방. **4** the amount a bag holds. 한 부대〔자루〕분의 양(量). ¶ *two bags of rice* 쌀 두 부대 / *five bags of coins* 동전 다섯 부대. **5** 《*colloq.*》 what is contained in a bag. 부대〔자루〕 안의 내용물. **6** all birds or animals shot by a hunter in a day. 하루에 잡은 사냥물의 양. ¶ *He made a good* 〔*bad*〕 ~. 잡은 사냥물이 많았다〔적었다〕. **7** (in baseball) a base. (야구의) 베이스; 누(壘). **8** 《*pl.*》 《Brit. *colloq.*》 trousers. 양복 바지.

a bag of bones, a very thin person or animal. 바짝 마른 사람〔동물〕.

bag and baggage, (with) all one's belongings. 소지품 전부(를 가지고); 몽땅. ¶ *They cleared out* ~ *and baggage.* 그들은 소지품 전부를 가지고 가버렸다.

get the bag, 《*colloq.*》 get the sack; be dismissed. 해고되다.

give someone the bag, dismiss; sack. …를 해고하다.

hold the bag, 《*colloq.*》 be forced to bear the entire blame, responsibility, or loss that was to have been shared. 혼자 책임을 짊어지게 되다.

in the bag, **a**) 《*colloq.*》 captured; gained; certain. 잡힌; 확실한. ¶ *My promotion is in the* ~. 나의 진급은 확실하다. **b**) drunk. 취해.

let the cat out of the bag, 《*colloq.*》 give away a secret. 비밀을 누설하다.

the whole bag of tricks, everything needed for some purpose. 온갖 수단.

— *v.* (**bagged, bag·ging**) *vt.* (P6) **1** put (something) in a bag. …을 부대〔자루〕에 넣다. **2** kill or catch (animals) in hunting. (사냥감)을 잡다. ¶ ~ *a hare* 토끼를 잡다. **3** 《*colloq.*》 ⓐ take possession of (something); steal. …을 손에 넣다; 훔치다. ⓑ help oneself to; take. 마음대로 …하다; 차지하다. ¶ *He bagged my seat.* 그는 내 자리를 차지했다 / *I've bagged some of your tobacco.* 당신 담배를 허가도 없이 실례했습니다. **4** swell (something) outward. …을 부풀게 하다.

— *vi.* (P1,2A) **1** swell outward. 부풀다. **2** hang loosely. 축 늘어지다. [O.N. *baggi*]

bag·a·telle [bæ̀gətél] *n.* **1** Ⓒ something unimportant. 하찮은 것. ¶ *a mere* ~ 그야말로 하찮은 것. **2** Ⓒ 《mus.》 a short, light composition, esp. for the piano. (피아노) 소곡(小曲). **3** Ⓤ a game played on a pin-table with nine balls and a stick. 일종의 당구. [It.]

Bag·dad, Bagh·dad [bǽgdæd, bəgdǽd] *n.* the capital of Iraq. 바그다드.

***bag·gage** [bǽgidʒ] *n.* **1** Ⓤ 《U.S.》 the trunks, bags, suitcases, etc. used for a traveler to carry with; 《mil.》 the portable things of an army, such as tents, sleeping bags, etc. 수화물(手貨物); 군용 행낭(cf. 《Brit.》 *luggage*). **2** Ⓒ a saucy or impudent girl. 뻔뻔스런 여자. [*bag*]

bag·ging [bǽgiŋ] *n.* material for making bags. 부대〔자루〕감. [→bag]

bag·gy [bǽgi] *adj.* (**-gi·er, -gi·est**) baglike; hanging loose. 자루〔부대〕 같은; 헐렁한.

bag·man [bǽgmən] *n.* (*pl.* **-men** [-mən]) 《*colloq.*》 a traveling salesman. 외판원.

bag·pipe [bǽgpàip] *n.* Ⓒ 《often *pl.*》 a Scotish musical instrument made of a windbag and pipes. 백파이프. [→bag, pipe]

bag·pi·per [bǽgpàipər] *n.* Ⓒ a person who plays the bagpipe. 백파이프 연주자.

bah [bɑː, bæ(ː)] *interj.* an exclamation to show the feeling of contempt or disgust. 흥; 체《경멸·혐오감 등을 나타내는 소리》. [F.]

Ba·ha·mas [bəhɑ́ːməz, -héi-] *n. pl.* a member of British Commonwealth in the West Indies. 바하마. 參考 수도는 Nassau.

Bai·kal [baikɑ́ːl] *n.* a lake in East Siberia. 바이칼 호(湖).

bail¹ [beil] *n.* 《law》 **1** Ⓤ freedom given to a prisoner for a certain time; money paid for getting such freedom. 보석(금). **2** Ⓒ a person or persons who pay such money for a prisoner. 보석 보증인.

go 〔***stand***〕 ***bail for,*** guarantee. …의 보석 보증인이 되다; …을 틀림없다고 보증하다.

jump bail, abscond while free on bail. 보석 중에 행방을 감추다.

out on bail, released by paying of bail. 보석 중에.

surrender to *one's* ***bail,*** appear in a due manner for trial. 보석중 법정에 출두하다.

take leg bail, 《*colloq.*》 run away. 도주하다.

— *vt.* (P6,7) 《*out*》 make (a prisoner) free by paying bail. …을 보석시키다. [L. *bajulus* porter]

bail² [beil] *n.* Ⓒ a handle of a pail, kettle, etc. 물통 따위의 손잡이. [L. *baculum* stick]

bail³ [beil] *n.* Ⓒ a pail or scoop used in dipping water out of a boat. 파래박.

— *vi., vt.* (P1,2A; 6,7) dip out water with a bail. 뱃바닥의 물을 퍼내다. [L. *baca* tub]

bail out, jump 〔drop〕 from an airplane by parachute. 낙하산으로 뛰어내리다.

bail·iff [béilif] *n.* Ⓒ **1** an assistant to a sheriff. 집행관《sheriff의 하료(下僚)》. **2** an officer of a court who guards prisoners and jurymen. 정리(廷吏). **3** 《Brit. hist.》 a governor in certain towns. 시장. **4** a land agent. 토지 관리인. [bail¹]

bairn [bɛərn] *n.* 《Sc.》 a young child; a child. 어린애. [*bear*]

B

***bait** [beit] *n.* ⒸⓊ **1** anything used to attract fish or other animals in order to catch them. 미끼. ¶ *swallow* 〔*take*〕 *the* ~ 미끼를 물다 / *fish with artificial flies as* ~ 제물 낚시질하다. **2** temptation. 유혹. ¶ *a tempting* ~ 마음을 끄는〔유혹하는〕 것. **3** food for horses. 말의 먹이(cf. *fodder*). **4** 《*arch.*》 a halt for refreshment. 짧은 휴식. ¶ *travel without a* ~ 짧은 휴식도 없이 여행하다.
— *vt.* (P6,13) **1** 《*with*》 put a bait on. …에 미끼를 달다. ¶ ~ *a hook* (*with a shrimp*) 낚시에 (새우) 미끼를 달다. **2** 《*with*》 tempt; attract. …을 꾀다; 유혹하다. ¶ ~ *someone with a show of affection* 미인계로 아무를 유혹하다. **3** feed (horses). (말 따위)를 먹여 기르다. **4** make dogs attack (an animal, such as a chained bear) for sport. (매인 곰 따위에) 개를 부추겨 공격하게 하다. **5** give trouble to (someone) by unkind or unpleasant words. …을 (불쾌한 말로) 지분거리다〔괴롭히다〕; 학대〔박해〕하다.
— *vi.* 《*arch.*》 take a rest during a journey. (여행 중에) 잠시 쉬다. [→bite]
bait the hook, allure. 미끼로 유혹하다.

baize [beiz] *n.* Ⓤ a thick and rough woolen cloth, used for curtains, table covers, etc. 설핀 모직물. [L. *badius* chestnut-colored]

:bake [beik] *vt.* (P6,18) **1** cook (bread, cake, etc.) in an oven. (빵 따위)를 굽다. ¶ *She baked the cake hard.* 그 여자는 그 케이크를 단단하게 구웠다. **2** dry and harden (bricks, china, etc.) by heat. (벽돌 따위)를 구워 굳히다. ¶ ~ *china* 도자기를 굽다. — *vi.* (P1) **1** become baked. 구워지다. ¶ *These cakes will* ~ *very quickly.* 이 케이크는 매우 빨리 구워질 것이다. **2** become brown with sunburn. 볕에 그을다. [E.]

ba·ke·lite [béikəlàit] *n.* Ⓤ 《trademark》 an artificial material used in place of bone, ivory, etc. 베이클라이트. 參考 발명자의 이름에서 옴.

***bak·er** [béikər] *n.* Ⓒ **1** a person who makes and sells bread, cakes, etc. 빵장수. **2** 《U.S.》 a portable oven. 오븐. [→bake]
a baker's dozen, thirteen. 13개.

bak·er·y [béikəri] *n.* Ⓒ (*pl.* **-er·ies**) a place where bread, cakes, etc. are made or sold; a baker's shop. 빵집.

bak·ing [béikiŋ] *n.* **1** Ⓤ the act or process of cooking in a dry heat. 오븐으로 굽기. **2** Ⓒ the quantity baked at one time. 한 번 구운 양(量). — *adj.* 《*colloq.*》 very hot. 매우 뜨거운. ¶ *a* ~ *sun* 뜨거운 태양 / ~ *hot* 타는 듯이 뜨거운.

baking powder [ˊ-- ˋ-] *n.* white powder used to make cake or biscuit larger in baking. 베이킹 파우더; 빵가루.

bak·sheesh [bǽkʃiːʃ, -ˊ] *n.* a tip. 팁; 행하. — *vt.* (P6) give a tip to. …에게 팁을 주다. [Pers. *bakhshish*]

bal·a·lai·ka [bæ̀ləláikə] *n.* a Russian musical instrument. 발랄라이카《기타 비슷한 삼각형의 악기》. [Russ.]

:bal·ance [bǽləns] *n.* **1** Ⓒ an instrument for measuring weight. 천칭; 저울. ¶ *weigh something in the* ~ 무엇을 저울에 달다. **2** Ⓒ a gear of a clock which causes it to go regularly. (시계의) 평형 기어. **3** Ⓤ the state of having the same amount on both sides. 평형; 균형. ¶ *the* ~ *of power* 세력 균형 / *keep* 〔*preserve*〕 *one's* ~ (몸·마음의) 평형을 유지하다 / *be out of* ~ 균형이 안 잡히다; 불균형이다 / *upset the* ~ 세력의 균형을 깨다. **4** ⓊⒸ a steady condition or position. 침착; 안정 (상태). ¶ *a woman of* ~ 침착한 여성 / *recover* 〔*regain*〕 *one's* ~ 마음의 평정을 되찾다 / *lose one's* ~ (몸·마음의) 안정을 잃다. **5** 《*the* ~》 sum of money not yet spent. 잔고(殘高). ¶ *the* ~ *in hand* 시재 잔액 / *one's* ~ *at the bank* =*one's bank* ~ 은행 예금 잔액 / *the* ~ *of trade* =*the trade* ~ 무역 수지. **6** Ⓤ 《*colloq.*》 the rest; the remainder. 나머지.
hold the balance, have the power to decide. 결정권을 갖다.
in the balance, not yet settled or decided. 미결로; 불안정하게. ¶ *hang in the* ~ 불안정한 상태에 있다; 아슬아슬하다 / *hold something in the* ~ 불안정한 상태로 놔두다.
off one's balance, in a position where one loses one's balance. 넘어져서; 안정〔평형〕을 잃고.
on 〔***upon***〕 ***balance,*** taking everything into account. 결국. ¶ *On* ~ *it will prove rather expensive.* 결국 그건 비싸게 치이는 꼴이 될 것이다.
strike a balance, find the difference between debit and credit. 수지를 결산하다; 청산하다. ¶ *strike a* ~ *at set seasons* 일정한 시기에 청산하다.
— *vt.* **1** (P6) measure the weight of (something). …의 무게를 달다. **2** (P6,13) bring (something) into or keep (something) in the state of balance. …의 균형을 잡다. **3** (P13) 《*with, by, against*》 make (two things) equal in weight or importance. 균형을 맞추다. **4** (P6) make the debit and credit sides (of an account) equal. 차감하다; 결산하다. ¶ ~ *one's accounts* 결산하다. **5** (P6,13) estimate the relative weight or importance of; compare. 비교 평가하다; 비교하다. ¶ ~ *all the probabilities of a situation* 사태의 온갖 가능성을 비교 검토하다.
— *vi.* **1** (P1,3) 《*with*》 be equal; come into the state of balance. 같다; 균형이 맞다. **2**

(P3) 《*between*》 waver; hesitate. 망설이다; 주저하다. [bi-, L. *lanx* scale]

balanced diet [⌐–⌐–] *n.* a diet having the correct amounts of all the kinds of foods necessary for health. 건강식(健康食).

balance sheet [⌐–⌐] *n.* a written paper to show the sum of money spent and earned by a business. 대차 대조표; 손익 계정서.

·bal·co·ny [bǽlkəni] *n.* Ⓒ (*pl.* **-nies**) a platform built out from an upper floor of a building. 발코니. [→balk]

bald [bɔːld] *adj.* **1** without hair on the head, wholly or partly. 대머리의. ¶ *a ~ man* 대머리. **2** without natural covering, as of feathers, leaves, etc. (털·잎 등이 없어) 민둥민둥한. ¶ *a ~ mountain* 민둥산. **3** not hiding; open; plain. 숨김 없는; 공개적인; 드러낸; 단조로운. ¶ *a ~ statement of the facts* 사실의 숨김 없는 진술. **4** poor; uninteresting. 시시한. ¶ *a ~ style* 시시한 문체. **5** having a white spot on the head. 머리에 흰 점이 있는. ¶ *the ~ eagle* 흰머리독수리. [?]

bal·der·dash [bɔ́ːldərdæ̀ʃ] *n.* Ⓤ nonsense. 난센스. [?]

bald·head·ed [bɔ́ːldhèdid] *adj.* having a bald head. 대머리의. [→bald]

***go for* (*at*) *something* baldheaded,** 《*colloq.*》 attack it with all one's strength, not caring about the consequences. …에 무모하게 덤비다.

bald·ly [bɔ́ːldli] *adv.* frankly; openly; without reserve. 노골적으로; 드러내놓고.

bald·ness [bɔ́ːldnis] *n.* Ⓤ **1** the state of being bald. 벗어져 있음. **2** the state or quality of being frank. 노골적임. **3** dullness. 따분함; 단조로움.

bald·pate [bɔ́ːldpèit] *n.* a baldheaded person. 대머리. [→bald]

bal·dric [bɔ́ːldrik] *n.* a belt for a sword, horn, etc., hung from one shoulder to the opposite side of the body. 어깨띠. [?]

bale¹ [beil] *n.* **1** Ⓒ a large package or bundle of goods tightly bound or wrapped for storing or shipping. 짐짝. ¶ *a ~ of cotton* 솜 짝. **2** 《*pl.*》 goods. 화물. — *vt.* (P6) make or form (something) into bales; pack. …을 짐짝으로 싸다; 포장하다. [→ball]

bale² [beil] *n.* Ⓤ 《*poet., arch.*》 misfortune; injury. 재난; 불행; 해(害). [E.]

bale·ful [béilfəl] *adj.* **1** harmful. 해로운. **2** with evil intent. 악의 있는. ¶ *a ~ look* 적의에 찬 눈. [→bale²]

Ba·li [bɑ́ːli] *n.* an island of Indonesia, east of Java. 발리 섬.

balk, baulk [bɔːk] *n.* Ⓒ **1** an obstacle; a hindrance. 방해; 장애. ¶ *a ~ to one's plan* 계획에 대한 방해 / *a ~ to traffic* 교통 방해. **2** a mistake. 실패; 실수. ¶ *make a ~* 실수를 하다. **3** 《baseball》 an unfair motion by a pitcher. (투수의) 보크.
— *vt.* (P6,13) 《*in, of*》 prevent (someone) from doing what he wishes to do; hinder. …를 방해하다. ¶ *I was balked of my purpose.* 계획이 좌절되었다.
— *vi.* **1** (P1,2A,3) stop and refuse to go; shrink; hesitate. (갑자기) 멈추어 나아가지 않다; 뒷걸음치다; 망설이다. ¶ *My horse balked.* 내 말은 멈추어 앞으로 나아가지 않았다 / *~ at making a speech* 연설하기를 망설이다. **2** (P1) 《baseball》 make a balk. (투수가) 보크하다. [E.=ridge]

Bal·kan [bɔ́ːlkən] *adj.* of the Balkan Peninsula. 발칸 반도의. ¶ *the ~ States* 발칸 제국(諸國). — *n.* 《*the ~s*》 the Balkan States. 발칸 제국.

:ball¹ [bɔːl] *n.* Ⓒ **1** ⓐ anything round. 둥근 것; 구(球); 공. ¶ *the earthly ~* 지구 / *a ~ of water* 떨어지는 물방울 / *the ~ of the eye* 눈알 / *make a handkerchief into a ~* 손수건을 둥글게 뭉치다. ⓑ a round object used in games. 공. ¶ *throw a ~* 공을 던지다 / *bat a ~* 배트로 공을 치다 / *fumble a ~* 공을 펌블하다. **2** a game played with a ball, esp. baseball. 구기(球技); 야구. **3** a bullet or cannon ball. 탄알; 포탄. **4** 《baseball》 a ball pitched outside the home plate. (스트라이크 아닌) 볼(opp. strike).

be on the ball, be alert or competent. 잽싸다; 빈틈없다; 유능하다.

carry the ball, 《*colloq.*》 **a**) assume the responsibility; bear the burden. 책임을 지다(떠맡다); 무거운 짐을 지다. **b**) take the initiative in. 솔선해서 하다.

get* (*set, start*) *the ball rolling, put into operation; start the conversation, etc. (대화·활동 따위를) 시작(개시)하다.

have the ball at* (*on*) *one's feet, have a good chance of being successful in life. 앞날이 밝다; 성공의 전망이 서다.

keep the ball rolling, keep anything going or continuing, esp. conversation. (대화 따위를) 중단되지 않게 하다; 흥미(분위기)가 깨지지 않도록 하다.

play ball, **a**) begin playing a ball game. 경기를 시작하다. **b**) 《*fig.*》 work together; cooperate. 협력하다. ¶ *union leaders suspected of playing ~ with racketeers* 공갈단원들과 한통속으로 의심받고 있는 조합 지도자들.
— *vt.* (P6,7) make (something) into a ball. …을 공 모양으로 만들다. ¶ *~ snow to make a snowman* 눈사람을 만들기 위해 눈을 둥글게 뭉치다.
— *vi.* (P1,2A) form into a ball. 공 모양이 되다. [O.N. *böl*]

ball up, confuse. 혼란시키다.

:ball² [bɔːl] *n.* Ⓒ a large, formal social party for dancing. 무도회. ¶ *give a ~* 무도회를 열다. [L. *ballo* dance]

lead* (*up*) *the ball, lead the first dance. 무도회 개시의 선도(先導)가 되다.

open the ball, **a**) lead the first dance. 무도

회 개시의 춤을 추다. **b)** 《*fig.*》 start; make a beginning with something. 개시하다.

·**bal·lad** [bǽləd] *n.* Ⓒ **1** a simple song with several verses sung to the same melody. 민요; 속요(俗謠). **2** a poem that tells a story. 민요시. [→ball²]

bal·lade [bəlɑ́:d, bæ-] *n.* a piece of romantic music, esp. for the piano. 발라드. [↑]

B

bal·last [bǽləst] *n.* Ⓤ **1** 《naut.》 heavy material carried in a ship to make it balanced. 바닥짐. **2** bags of sand carried below a balloon. (기구의) 모래 주머니. **3** small stones used for the bed of a road or railroad track. (철로·도로 등에 까는) 자갈. — *vt.* (P6) **1** place ballast in (ships, balloons, etc.). …에 바닥짐을〔모래주머니를〕 싣다. **2** put ballast on (a railroad bed). (철로·도로 등)에 자갈을 깔다. [G. *bar* bare, *last* load]

ball-bear·ing [bɔ́:lbέəriŋ] *n.* 《mech.》 a bearing in which a number of metal balls are set. 볼베어링. [*ball¹, bearing*]

bal·le·ri·na [bæ̀lərí:nə] *n.* Ⓒ (*pl.* **-nas** or **-ne**) 《It.》 a woman ballet dancer. 발레리나.

bal·le·ri·ne [bæ̀lərí:ne] *n.* pl. of **ballerina.**

bal·let [bǽlei, —́] *n.* ⒸⓊ **1** an artistic dance with a story performed to music. 발레. **2** 《*collectively*》 ballet dancers. 발레단(團). [L. *ballo* dance]

bal·let-danc·er [bǽleidæ̀nsər] *n.* a person who takes part in a ballet. 발레 댄서; 무용수.

bal·lis·tic [bəlístik] *adj.* of or connected with ballistics. 탄도(학)의. [↓]

bal·lis·tics [bəlístiks] *n. pl.* 《used as *sing.*》 the science that deals with the motion of projectiles. 탄도학(彈道學). [L.]

·**bal·loon** [bəlú:n] *n.* Ⓒ a round bag filled with some gas that is lighter than air to make it rise and float in the air. 기구(氣球); 풍선. — *vi.* (P1) **1** go up in a balloon. 기구를 타고 올라가다. **2** (of sails, etc.) swell out like a balloon. 풍선처럼 부풀다. [ball¹]

bal·loon·ist [bəlú:nist] *n.* a person who operates a balloon. 기구 조종사.

·**bal·lot** [bǽlət] *n.* **1** Ⓒ a paper used in voting. 투표 용지. ¶ *cast a* ~ 투표하다. **2** the whole number of votes cast in an election. 투표 총수. ¶ *There was a large* ~. 많은 사람들이 투표했다. **3** ⓊⒸ voting in general; Ⓤ secret voting. 투표; 무기명〔비밀〕 투표. ¶ *by single* ~ 단기 무기명 투표로 / *take a* ~ 투표로 정하다 / *elect by* ~ 투표로 선출하다. — *vi.* (P1,3) **1** 《*for, against*》 vote or decide by ballot. 투표하다; 투표로 정하다. **2** draw lots. 제비를 뽑다. [F.]

bal·lot·age [bǽlətidʒ, -tɑ̀:ʒ] *n.* the second ballot. 결선 투표. [↑]

ballot box [—́ —̀] *n.* a box into which ballots are put. 투표함(函).

ball·play·er [bɔ́:lplèiər] *n.* 《U.S.》 **1** a baseball player. 야구 선수. **2** a person who plays ball. 공놀이하는 사람. [→ball¹]

ball-point pen [bɔ́:lpɔ̀int pén] *n.* a fountain pen whose point is a small ball bearing. 볼펜.

ball·room [bɔ́:lrù(:)m] *n.* Ⓒ a large room used for dancing. 무도장(場). [L. *ballo* dance]

bal·ly·hoo [bǽlihù:] *n.* Ⓤ **1** 《U.S.》 noisy advertising. 대대적인〔요란스런〕 선전. **2** uproar. 시끌벅적함; 소란. — *vt., vi.* (P6; 1) 《U.S.》 advertise noisily. 요란하게 선전하다. [Place]

bal·ly·rag [bǽliræ̀g] *vt., vi.* (P6; 3) tease; bully. 괴롭히다. [?]

balm [bɑ:m] *n.* **1** Ⓤ a sweet-smelling oil or oily paste obtained from certain trees, used esp. as medicine for a wound. 향유. **2** ⓊⒸ anything used for relieving pain. 진통제. ¶ *It was* ~ *to his wounded spirit.* 그것은 그의 다친 마음을 진정시키는 진통제였다. **3** Ⓒ a sweet-smelling plant. 박하. [↓]

balm·y [bɑ́:mi] *adj.* (**balm·i·er, balm·i·est**) **1** sweet-smelling; fragrant. 향기로운. **2** mild; gentle. 기분 좋은; 부드러운. ¶ *a* ~ *breeze* 상쾌한 미풍. [↓]

bal·sam [bɔ́:lsəm] *n.* **1** Ⓤ balm. 향유. **2** Ⓒ a plant from which balm is taken. 향유의 원료가 되는 나무. **3** Ⓒ any of flowering plant of the touch-me-not family. 봉선화과 식물의 꽃. [L. *balsamum*]

Bal·tic Sea [bɔ́:ltik sí:], **the** *n.* a sea in North Europe. 발트 해(海).

bal·us·ter [bǽləstər] *n.* Ⓒ **1** an erect pillar or support for a railing. 난간 동자. **2** 《*pl.*》 a balustrade. 난간. [Gk. *balaustion* pomegranate flower]

bal·us·trade [bǽləstrèid, ‿‿—́] *n.* Ⓒ a row of balusters. 난간. [↑]

Bal·zac [bǽlzæk], **Honoré de** *n.* (1799-1850) a French novelist. 발자크.

·**bam·boo** [bæmbú:] *n.* ⓊⒸ (*pl.* **-boos**) 《bot.》 a tall, tree-like grass with hard, hollow, jointed stems. 대(나무). [Malay]

bam·boo·zle [bæmbú:zəl] *vt.* (P6,13) 《*colloq.*》 《*into, out of*》 hoax. …를 (감쪽같이) 속이다. ● **bam·boo·zle·ment** [-mənt] *n.* [?]

ban [bæn] *n.* Ⓒ **1** an order that something must not be done or said. 금제(禁制); 금지. ¶ *the gold* ~ 금 수출 금지. **2** a curse. 파문(破門).

under the* 〔*a*〕 *ban, prohibited. 금지된.

— *vt.* (P6) (**banned, ban·ning**) forbid; prohibit. …을 금(지)하다. ¶ *an area banning fishing* 금어구(禁漁區) / ~ *an obscene book* 외설본의 출판을 금하다 / ~ *a protest meeting* 항의 집회를 금지하다 / *Fishing is banned in this lake.* 이 호수에서는 고기잡이가 금지되어 있다. [Teut.=proclaim]

ba·nal [bənǽl, bənɑ́:l, béinl] *adj.* (of ideas,

opinions, etc.) not new; not original. 평범한; 진부한. ¶ *a ~ remark* 평범한 소견(所見). [F.]

:ba·nan·a [bənǽnə] *n.* Ⓒ 《bot.》 a tropical tree-like plant; its fruit. 바나나 (나무). [Sp.]

:band [bænd] *n.* Ⓒ **1** a group of persons doing something together. (공동의 목적으로 행동하는) 그룹; 무리; 떼. ¶ *a ~ of robbers* 〔*wild dogs*〕 도둑〔들개〕떼. **2** a group of persons playing music together. 악단; 밴드. ¶ *The ~ played several marches.* 악단은 행진곡을 몇 곡 연주했다. **3** a thin flat material for binding, fastening, etc. 끈; 띠; 밴드. ¶ *a rubber ~* 고무끈. **4** a stripe. (줄)무늬. ¶ *a ~ of color* 색(色) 줄무늬 / *a gold ~* 금줄. **5** a particular range of wavelengths in broadcasting. 주파수대(周波數帶).
— *vt.* (P6,7) **1** tie (something) with a band; put a band on or around (something). 끈으로 묶다. **2** mark with stripes on (something). …에 줄무늬를 넣다. **3** 《*together*》 cause (something or someone) to unite in a group. …을 단결시키다.
— *vi.* (P2A) unite or join in a group. 단결하다. ¶ *The people banded together to resist the common enemy.* 사람들은 공동의 적에 대항하기 위해 단결했다. [Teut.=bind]

***band·age** [bǽndidʒ] *n.* Ⓒ a strip of cloth or other material used for binding wounds. 붕대. ¶ *apply a ~ to wounds* 상처에 붕대를 하다〔감다〕. — *vt.* (P6) bind (wounds) with a bandage. …에 붕대를 감다. ¶ *~ a broken leg* 〔*a cut finger*〕 부러진 다리〔벤 손가락〕에 붕대를 감다. [Teut.= bind]

ban·dan·a, -na [bændǽnə] *n.* a large colored handkerchief, usually of silk. 큰 비단 손수건. [Hind.]

band·box [bǽndbɑ̀ks / -bɔ̀ks] *n.* Ⓒ a light box of thick and stiff paper for holding hats, collars, etc. (모자 따위를 넣는) 판지 상자. [→band]
look as if one had just come out of a bandbox, look very clean and smart. 말쑥해 보이다.

ban·deau [bændóu, ←] *n.* (*pl.* **-deaux** [-z]) a band worn round a woman's head. (여자) 머리 리본. [F.]

ban·dit [bǽndit] *n.* Ⓒ (*pl.* **-dits** or **-dit·ti**) **1** an outlaw; a highwayman; a robber. 악당; (노상) 강도. **2** a dishonest person. 무뢰한. [→ban]

ban·dit·ti [bændíti] *n.* pl. of **bandit.**

band·mas·ter [bǽndmæ̀stər, -mɑ̀ːs-] *n.* Ⓒ the leader of a musical band. 밴드마스터; 악장(樂長). [→band]

ban·do·leer, -lier [bæ̀ndəlíər] *n.* a shoulder-belt with pockets for catridges. 어깨에 메는 탄(彈)띠. [→band]

bands·man [bǽndzmən] *n.* Ⓒ (*pl.* **-men** [-mən]) a member of a musical band. 악단원. [→band]

band·stand [bǽndstæ̀nd] *n.* Ⓒ a platform, usu. with a roof, for outdoor band concerts. 야외 음악당; 주악대(奏樂臺).

band·wag·on [bǽndwæ̀gən] *n.* 《U.S.》 a decorated wagon used to carry a band of musicians in a parade. (퍼레이드의) 악대차(樂隊車).

ban·dy [bǽndi] *vt.* (**-died**) (P7,13) **1** throw, toss, or knock (a ball) to and fro. (공 따위)를 마주 던지거나 치다. **2** give and receive (words). (말)을 주고 받다.
bandy words with, quarrel. 다투다.
— *n.* the game of hockey. 하키의 한 가지.
— *adj.* bent or curved outward. 밖으로 휜. ¶ *~ legs* 안짱다리. [?]

ban·dy·leg·ged [bǽndilègid] *adj.* having bandy legs. 안짱다리의. [↑]

bane [bein] *n.* Ⓤ **1** poison. 독(毒)(cf. *ratsbane*). **2** cause of destruction, ruin, death, or any other trouble. (파멸·죽음 등의) 원인. ¶ *Disease is the ~ of life.* 질병은 목숨을 앗아가는 원인이다 / *Idleness has always been his ~.* 나태는 언제나 그의 파멸의 원인이 되어 왔다. [E.=death]

bane·ful [béinfəl] *adj.* harmful; troublesome. 유해한; 귀찮은; 말썽의. ¶ *a ~ influence* 해로운 작용.

***bang[1]** [bæŋ] *vt.* **1** (P6) strike noisily. 땅〔쾅〕하고 세게 치다. ¶ *~ a drum* 북을 쾅 치다. **2** (P13) shut (a door) noisily. (문 따위)를 쾅하고 닫다. ¶ *~ down the lid of a trunk* 트렁크 뚜껑을 탁 닫다. — *vi.* (P1, 2A,3) **1** strike noisily. 쾅 부딪치다. ¶ *~ on the door* 문을 쾅쾅 두드리다 / *~ against something* 무엇에 쾅 부딪치다. **2** make a sudden and bursting sound. 쾅〔탕, 쿵〕하고 울리다. ¶ *The guns banged all night.* 대포 소리가 밤새도록 쿵쾅 울렸다.
bang oneself against, bump oneself against. 쾅하고 부딪치다. ¶ *~ oneself against a tree* 나무에 쾅 부딪치다.
bang off, go off with a loud noise. 쾅하고 발포(發砲)하다.
bang to, shut with a loud noise. 쾅하고 닫히다.
— *n.* Ⓒ **1** a sudden or bursting sound. 쿵〔쾅〕하고 폭발하는 소리. ¶ *The gun went off with a ~.* 대포가 쾅하고 발사되었다. **2** a sharp blow. 강타. ¶ *get a ~ on the head* 머리를 강타당하다.
in a bang, in a hurry. 급히.
— *adv.* **1** with a bang. 쾅하고. **2** suddenly. 갑자기. **3** exactly; just. 정확히; 바로. ¶ *It hit him ~ in the eye.* 그것은 바로 그의 눈에 맞았다 / *The picture fell ~ on his head.* 그림이 바로 그의 머리 위로 떨어졌다. **4** completely; straight. 완전히; 곧바로. ¶ *He jumped ~ out of the window.* 그는 곧장 창밖으로 뛰어내렸다. [Scand.]
go bang, explode or shut with a bang. 쾅하고 터지다〔닫히다〕.

B

bang² [bæŋ] *n.* Ⓒ 《often *pl.*》 hair cut straight over the forehead. (이마를 덮는) 앞머리. — *vt.* (P6) cut (hair) straight across. 앞머리를 가지런히 자르다. [?]

Bang·kok [bǽŋkɑk, ─́─/bæŋkɔ́k, ─́─] *n.* the capital of Thailand. 방콕《타이의 수도(首都)》.

ban·gle [bǽŋgəl] *n.* a ring worn round the wrist, arm, or ankle. 팔찌. [Hind. *bangri*]

ban·i·an [bǽnjən] *n.* **1** an Indian trader. 인도의 상인. **2** a flannel jacket. 셔츠. **3** 《bot.》 a fig-tree of India whose branches have hanging roots that grow down to the ground and take root. 벵골 보리수. [Skr. *vanij* merchant]

***ban·ish** [bǽniʃ] *vt.* (P6,13) **1** order (someone) to go away from a place or country; exile. 추방하다; 유형(流刑)에 처하다. ¶ *He was banished* (*from*) *the country.* 그는 국외로 추방당했다 / *He was banished to Siberia.* 그는 시베리아로 유형당했다. **2** force (someone or something) to go or to be put away. (걱정·슬픔 따위)를 떨어버리다. ¶ ~ *fear* 〔*anxiety*〕 두려움〔걱정〕을 떨어 버리다. [→ban]

ban·ish·ment [bǽniʃmənt] *n.* ⓊⒸ the act of banishing; the state of being banished. 추방(追放).

ban·is·ter [bǽnəstər] *n.* **1** Ⓒ a baluster. 난간 동자. **2** 《*pl.*》 a balustrade of a staircase. 난간. [→baluster]

ban·jo [bǽndʒou] *n.* Ⓒ (*pl.* **-jos** or **-joes**) 《mus.》 a stringed musical instrument played like a guitar. 밴조. [Gk. *pandoura*]

〈banjo〉

:bank¹ [bæŋk] *n.* Ⓒ **1** a long mound or heap of earth along a river, lake, road, railway, etc. 둑. ¶ *the banks of a river* 강둑. **2** a slope. 비탈; 사면(斜面). **3** a shallow place in the sea or at the mouth of a river. 물의 얕은 곳; 여울. **4** the sloping edge of a river. 강가; 강안(江岸). ¶ *the banks of the Thames* 템스강안 / *bring a boat to the* ~ 보트를 강가에 대다. **5** a row of keys in an organ. 건반. **6** anything moundlike, as of clouds or snow. 퇴적(堆積); 더미. ¶ *a snow* ~ 눈의 퇴적 / *a* ~ *of clouds* 구름의 층.

— *vt.* **1** (P6,7) make a bank of (earth, snow, etc.); pile; heap. …을 쌓다. **2** (P7) 《*up*》 make (something) safe with a bank. 둑을 쌓아서 …을 막다. **3** (P6,7) cover (a fire) with ashes to prevent rapid burning. (불이 오래 가도록) 재를 덮다.

— *vi.* **1** (P2A) form into a bank. 둑이 되다. **2** (P1) 《aeron.》 make an airplane slope when turning. 항공기가 회전할 때 옆으로 기울다. [Teut. =bench]

:bank² [bæŋk] *n.* Ⓒ **1** an office for receiving, lending, exchanging, and issuing money. 은행. ¶ *have money in the* ~ 은행에 예금이 있다. **2** any place for keeping things safe. 저장소. ¶ *a blood* ~ 혈액 은행. **3** (in gambling) the stock of money on a table. (노름판의) 판돈.

safe as the Bank, perfectly safe. 안전하여.

— *vt.* (P6) put (money) in a bank. (돈을) 은행에 맡기다. ¶ *He banks ₩50,000 every month.* 그는 매달 5만 원을 예금한다.

— *vi.* (P1) **1** keep money in a bank 예금하다. ¶ *He banks with Commercial Bank.* 그는 상업 은행과 거래한다. **2** keep or manage a bank. 은행 영업을 하다. [↑]

bank on 〔***upon***〕, rely on. 의지하다; 믿다. ¶ *I* ~ *on you.* 나는 당신을 믿습니다 / *I am banking on the fine weather lasting till I get my hay in.* 나는 건초를 거두어들일 때까지 좋은 날씨가 계속되리라고 믿고 있다.

bank·a·ble [bǽŋkəbəl] *adj.* that can be accepted at a bank. 은행에서 (담보로) 받아들일 수 있는.

bank-bill [bǽŋkbìl] *n.* Ⓒ a note or bill issued by a bank, used as money. 은행권; 지폐.

bank·book [bǽŋkbùk] *n.* Ⓒ a book in which a bank records a person's account. 은행〔예금〕 통장(cf. *passbook*).

***bank·er** [bǽŋkər] *n.* Ⓒ **1** a person who owns or manages a bank. 은행가. 參考 행원은 a bank clerk라고 함. **2** (in gambling) the man who keeps the bank. 물주.

bank holiday [─́ ─́──] *n.* **1** 《U.S.》 a weekday on which banks are closed by law. (일요일 이외의) 은행 휴일. **2** 《Brit.》 a holiday on which banks and most shops are closed. 일반 공휴일. [↑]

bank·ing [bǽŋkiŋ] *n.* Ⓤ **1** the business of a bank or banker. 은행업. **2** the act of banking. 경사(傾斜).

bank·note [bǽŋknòut] *n.* =bankbill.

bank rate [─́ ─́] *n.* the rate of discount established by the central bank of a country. 공정 환율.

bank·rupt [bǽŋkrʌpt, -rəpt] *n.* Ⓒ 《law》 a person who is legally declared unable to pay the money he has borrowed from others and whose property is divided among them. 파산자(破産者); 지급 불능자.

— *adj.* **1** unable to pay the money one has borrowed. 파산한. ¶ *go* 〔*become*〕 ~ 파산하다. **2** lacking (some quality). 없는; 결여된. ¶ *an intellectual* ~ 지능 결여자 / *a moral* ~ 도덕 관념이 없는 사람. — *vt.* (P6) make (someone) bankrupt. …를 파산시키다. ¶ *The hard times bankrupted him.* 불경기는 그를 파산시켰다. [→bank¹, L. *rumpo* break]

bank·rupt·cy [bǽŋkrʌptsi, -rəpsi] *n.* ⓊⒸ (*pl.* **-cies**) the state of being bankrupt.

파산(破産).

·ban·ner [bǽnər] *n.* Ⓒ a flag, usu. with some design or ketters on it. 기(旗); 기치; 표지. ¶ *England's* ~ 영국기 / *the* ~ *of freedom* 자유의 깃발. —*adj.* 《U.S.》 leading; formost. 일급(일류)의; 최상의. ¶ *a* ~ *year for crops* 풍년. [Goth. *bandua* sign]

unfurl one's banner, make public one's cause, opinions, etc. 기치를 선명히 하다.

banner headline [⌐–⌐–] *n.* a prominent headline in a newspaper. 신문의 전단 표제.

ban·nock [bǽnək] *n.* Ⓒ a flat cake eaten in Scotland. 스코틀랜드식 빵. [Gael. *bannach*]

banns [bænz] *n. pl.* a notice given three times in a church that so-and-so are to be married. 교회에서의 결혼식의 공시. ¶ *have one's* ~ *called* 〔*asked*〕 교회에서 결혼식의 공시를 해달라고 하다. [→ban]

put up 〔***call***〕 ***the banns,*** give notice of a marriage 결혼을 예고하다.

·ban·quet [bǽŋkwit] *n.* Ⓒ a feast. 연회(宴會); 잔치. —*vt., vi.* **1** (P6) give a feast to. 연회를 베풀어 …을 대접하다. ¶ *give* 〔*hold*〕 *a congratulatory* ~ 축연을 베풀다. **2** (P1) enjoy a feast. 대접을 받다. [→bench]

ban·shee [bǽnʃiː, –⌐] *n.* a female spirit who, in Ireland and Scotland, is believed to cry outside a house as a warning that someone will soon die in the family. 죽음을 예고하는 요정. [Ir. =woman of fairies]

ban·tam [bǽntəm] *n.* Ⓒ a small domestic fowl. 당(唐)닭. [?]

bantam weight [⌐–⌐] *n.* a boxer who weighs 118 pounds or less. (권투의) 밴텀급 선수.

ban·ter [bǽntər] *n.* Ⓒ a good-natured, teasing talk. (악의가 없는) 농담. —*vt.* (P6) make fun of (someone) good-humoredly. …을 놀리다. —*vi.* (P1) talk jokingly. 농담을 하다. [→bandy]

bant·ling [bǽntliŋ] *n.* a child. 어린애; 꼬마. [*band*]

Ban·tu [bǽntuː] *n.* (*pl.* **Ban·tu** or **-tus**) **1** a member of a large group of African tribes living in central and South Africa. 반투족(族)의 사람. **2** any of the languages of these tribes. 반투어(語). —*adj.* of these tribes or their languages. 반투족〔반투어〕의. [Native=men]

bap·tism [bǽptizəm] *n.* ⓊⒸ the act or ceremony of baptizing. 세례(식); 침례(cf. *christening*). [→baptize]

a baptism of fire, a soldier's first battle. (병사의) 첫 출전.

the baptism of blood, martyrdom. 순교.

bap·tis·mal [bæptízməl] *adj.* of baptism. 세례의. ¶ *the* ~ *ceremony* 세례식 / *a* ~ *name* 세례명.

Bap·tist [bǽptist] *n.* **1** 《*the* ~》 John the Baptist. 세례자 요한. **2** Ⓒ 《*b-*》 a person who baptizes. 세례를 베푸는 사람. **3** Ⓒ a member of a Christian church who holds the opinion that baptism should be given only to an adult believer and by dipping his whole body under water. 침례교도.

bap·tis·tery [bǽptistəri], **-try** [-tri] *n.* a place where baptism is performed. 세례당(堂).

bap·tize [bæptáiz, ⌐–] *vt.* **1** (P6) dip (someone) into water, or put water on (someone), as a sign to wash away his sin and to admit him into the Christian church. …에게 세례〔침례〕를 베풀다; …을 기독교도로 하다. **2** (P19) give a first name to (someone). …을 명명하다. ¶ *The boy was baptized John.* 소년은 존이라 명명(命名)되었다. **3** (P6) purify; cleanse. …을 정결하게 하다. [Gk. *baptō* dip]

:bar [bɑːr] *n.* Ⓒ **1** a long, evenly shaped piece of hard material. 막대기(모양의 것). ¶ *an iron* ~ 쇠막대 / *a* ~ *of chocolate* 막대 초콜릿. **2** a fence or pole used to prevent people from passing; a barrier. 방책; 가로대; 빗장. **3** a law court; the place in a law court where a prisoner stands. 법정; 피고석. ¶ *a prisoner at the* ~ 형사 피고인 / *the* ~ *of public opinion* 여론의 심판 / *be brought to the* ~ *of judgment* 재판에 부쳐지다. **4** an obstacle; a moral obstacle. 장애(물). ¶ *a* ~ *to legislation* 입법화를 방해하는 장애물 / *Poor health is a* ~ *to success.* 좋지 않은 건강은 성공의 장애가 된다 / *a* ~ *of conscience* 양심의 가책. **5** a place or counter at which alcoholic drinks or food are served. 카운터; 술집; 식당. **6** 《*collectively*》 《*the* ~ or *the B-*》 the profession of law; the group of lawyers. 변호사의 직변호인단. **7** a sand bar. 모래톱. **8** 《mus.》 the dividing line between two bars on the musical staff. (악보의) 세로줄; 종선(縱線).

be at the Bar, work as a lawyer. 변호사로 활약하다.

be called 〔***admitted***〕 ***to the bar,*** be admitted as a barrister. 변호사 자격을 얻다.

behind bolt and bar, safely fastened up. 엄중히 구금되어〔갇히어〕.

behind the bars, in prison. 감옥에 갇혀; 옥중에서.

cross the bar, die. 죽다.

go to 〔***join***〕 ***the Bar,*** become a lawyer. 변호사가 되다.

—*vt.* (**barred, bar·ring**) **1** (P6,7) fasten (something) with bars. 빗장을〔가로대를〕 질러 잠그다. ¶ ~ *a door* 문단속을 하다 / *a hotel barred to Jews* 유태인에겐 닫혀 있는 호텔. **2** (P6,13) shut off (a road, gate, etc.) from passage. …의 통행을 차단하다; 방해하다. ¶ ~ *a road to traffic* 길을 막아 교통을 차단하다 / ~ *someone's way* 〔*path*〕 아무의 가는 길을 막다 / *They barred his entrance to the* *club.* 그들은 그가 클럽에 들어가는 것을 방해했다. **3** (P6) do not allow; prohibit. …을 금(지)하다. ¶ ~ *the use of atomic weapons* 핵무기 사용을 금하다 / *Swimming is barred there.* 그곳에서는 수영이 금지되어 있다. **4** (P6,7) 《*from*》 keep or shut (something or someone) out; prevent (someone) from getting in. …을 내쫓다; 내쫓아 들이지 않다. ¶ ~ *someone from the committee* 아무를 위원회에서 쫓아내다 / *I will ~ no honest man my house.* 정직한 사람이 집에 오는 것을 거부하지 않겠다. **5** (P6) exclude; except. 제외하다. **6** (P6,7) mark with bars. 줄을 치다; 줄무늬를 넣다. **7** (P6) 《*colloq.*》 object to; dislike. 반대하다; 싫어하다. ¶ *What I ~ is a man who talks of what he doesn't understand.* 내가 싫어하는 것은 자기가 알지도 못하는 것을 말하는 사람이다.

bar in, shut in. 가두다.

bar out, shut out. 쫓아내다.

— *prep.* except; save. …을 제외하고. ¶ ~ *one* 하나를 제외하고. [L. *barra* bar]

bar none, without exception. 예외 없이.

Ba·rab·bas [bəræ̋bəs] *n.* 《Bible》 the prisoner freed instead of Jesus. 바라바.

barb [bɑːrb] *n.* Ⓒ a sharp point projecting backward from the main point, as on an arrow, a fishhook, etc. (살촉·낚시 따위의) 미늘; 갈고리. — *vt.* (P6) furnish (something) with barbs. …에 미늘을 달다. [L. *barba* beard]

Bar·ba·ra [báːrbərə] *n.* a woman's name. 여자 이름.

bar·bar·i·an [bɑːrbέəriən] *n.* Ⓒ **1** an uncivilized person. 미개인; 야만인. **2** 《hist.》 a person who was not a Greek; a person outside of the Roman Empire; a person who was not a Christian. 그리스인 이외의 사람; 이민족; (기독교도의 입장에서 본) 이교도. **3** a foreigner. 이방인《그리스·로마 사람이 이르는》.

— *adj.* **1** of barbarians. 미개인(야만인)의. ¶ ~ *customs* 미개인의 풍속. **2** not civilized; rude. 미개한; 야만적인. [Gk. *barbaros* foreign]

bar·bar·ic [bɑːrbǽrik] *adj.* of or like barbarians; rough and rude. 미개인의(같은); 조야(粗野)한.

bar·ba·rism [báːrbərìzəm] *n.* **1** Ⓤ uncivilized condition. 미개; 야만. ¶ *fall into a state of ~* 미개한 상태에 빠지다 / *relapse into a state of ~* 미개한 상태로 되돌아가다. **2** Ⓒ a barbarous act. 야만적인 행위. **3** Ⓒ a word or expression not in accepted use. 조야(粗野)한 언행.

bar·bar·i·ty [bɑːrbǽrəti] *n.* ⓊⒸ (*pl.* **-ties**) **1** a brutal or cruel act; cruelty. 만행; 잔인(한 행위). **2** a barbaric taste, manner, etc. 조야(粗野).

bar·ba·rize [báːbəràiz] *vt., vi.* (P6; 1) make or become barbarous. 야만화하다.

bar·ba·rous [báːrbərəs] *adj.* **1** savage; uncivilized; harsh and cruel. 야만스런; 미개한; 거칠고 잔인한. ¶ ~ *peoples* 야만인 / *be given ~ treatment* 무도한 취급을 받다. **2** unrefined; crude. 야비한; 상스러운.

bar·be·cue [báːrbikjùː] *n.* **1** Ⓒ an animal roasted whole; Ⓤ meat roasted over an open fire. 통구이; 통째로 구운 고기. **2** Ⓒ 《U.S.》 an out-of-door party at which animals or meat are roasted over an open fire. 통구이가 나오는 야외 연회. **3** a device on which animals are smoked or roasted whole. 통구이틀. — *vt.* (P6) roast (an animal) whole. …을 통째로 굽다. [Haitian]

barbed [bɑːrbd] *adj.* having a barb. 미늘이 있는. ¶ *a ~ fish-hook* 낚싯바늘 / ~ *wire* 가시철사 / ~ *words* 가시돋친 말. [→barb]

bar·bel [báːrbəl] *n.* a long thin growth hanging from the mouths of some fishes. (물고기의) 촉수(觸鬚). [→barb]

bar·bell [báːrbèl] *n.* a bar with adjustable weights used in weight lifting. 바벨. [*bar+bell*]

·**bar·ber** [báːrbər] *n.* Ⓒ a person whose business is haircutting, hairdressing, and shaving. 이발사. [→barb]

— *vt.* (P6) cut the hair of. (이발사가) 이발하다.

bar·ber·ry [báːrbèri, -bəri] *n.* 《bot.》 a shrub with yellow flowers and sour berries. 매자나무속 식물. [L. *barbaris*]

barber's pole [⌐-⌐] *n.* a painted pole used by a barber as a sign. (적·백색의) 이발소 표지(간판)(기둥).

bar·bi·can [báːrbikən] *n.* a strong tower at a gateway or bridge for defending a city. 망대(望臺); 망루. [F.]

Bar·ce·lo·na [bὰːrsəlóunə] *n.* a city in Spain, on the Mediterranean. 바르셀로나.

bard [bɑːrd] *n.* Ⓒ **1** an ancient poet and singer. 음영(吟詠) 시인. **2** a poet. 시인. [Gael.]

bard·ic [báːrdik] *adj.* of a bard. (음영(吟詠)) 시인의.

:**bare** [bεər] *adj.* **1** unclothed; uncovered; naked. 알몸의; 발가벗은; 드러낸. ¶ ~ *knees* 드러낸 무릎 / *a ~ sword* (칼집에서) 뽑은 칼 / *fight with ~ hands* 맨손으로 싸우다 / *sleep on the ~ earth* 맨땅에서 자다 / *walk with ~ feet* 맨발로 걷다. **2** exposed; not hidden. 노출된. ¶ *The guilt laid ~ to the world.* 범죄가 폭로되었다. **3** without decoration; unfurnished. 장식이 없는; 설비가 안된. ¶ ~ *walls* (액자 따위) 장식이 없는 벽 / *a room ~ of furniture* 가구 없는 방. **4** small in amount; scanty. 약간의; 부족한. **5** mere. 겨우(가까스로) …인. ¶ *a ~ hundred pounds* 겨우 100 파운드 / *a ~ majority* 간신히 된 과반수 / *a ~ necessities of life* 겨우 살아갈 만큼의 필수품 / *escape with ~ life* 간신히 도망치다. **6** empty. 비어 있는; 빈. ¶ *be ~ in purse* 지갑이 비어 있다.

be bare of credit, have no reputation. 평판

이〔인기가〕 나쁘다.
have** one's **head bare, be without a hat. 모자를 쓰지 않다.
in** one's **bare skin, naked. 알몸뚱이로.
lay bare, uncover; divulge. 드러내다; 폭로하다.
— *vt.* (P6,13) 《*of*》 make (something) bare; expose; uncover; reveal. …을 알몸으로 만들다; 벗기다; 드러내다. ¶ ~ *a tree of its fruits* 나무에서 열매를 따내다 / ~ *one's head* 모자를 벗다 / ~ *one's heart* 심중을 털어놓다 / ~ *damaging new facts* 큰 타격을 입힐 새 사실을 폭로하다. [E.]

bare·back [bέərbæ̀k] *adj., adv.* on a horse without a saddle. 안장 없는 말을 탄; (말에) 안장 없이. ¶ *ride* ~ 안장 없는 말을 타다.

bare·faced [bέərfèist] *adj.* without concealment; shameless. 노골적인; 뻔뻔한. ¶ ~ *impudence* 철면피.

bare·foot [bέərfùt] *adj., adv.* with bare feet. 맨발의〔로〕. ¶ *be* 〔*go, walk*〕 ~ 맨발이다〔맨발로 가다, 맨발로 걷다〕.

bare·foot·ed [bέərfùtid] *adj.* having bare feet. 맨발의.

bare·head·ed [bέərhèdid] *adj., adv.* with the head uncovered. 모자를 쓰지 않은〔않고〕; 맨머리의〔로〕.

*__bare·ly__ [bέərli] *adv.* **1** poorly. 빈약하게. ¶ *The room furnished* ~. 방의 가구는 보잘것 없었다. **2** hardly; scarcely. 겨우; 가까스로. ¶ *He* ~ *escaped death.* 그는 간신히 죽음을 면했다 / *He has* ~ *enough money to live on.* 그는 겨우 살아갈 정도의 돈밖에 없다. **3** openly. 공공연히; 숨김없이. ¶ *He stated the unpleasant facts* ~. 그는 그 불쾌한 사실들을 숨김없이 진술했다.

bare·ness [bέərnis] *n.* Ⓤ the state of being bare; lack of covering. 알몸; 노출; 노골적임.

:**bar·gain** [bɑ́ːrgən] *n.* Ⓒ **1** an agreement in trade or business; a contract. (매매) 계약. ¶ *close* 〔*conclude, settle, strike*〕 *a* ~ 거래를 맺다 / *That's* 〔*It's*〕 *a* ~. 그것으로 결정됐다. **2** something offered or bought at a low price. 싸게 산 물건; 투매물(投賣物). ¶ *get something as a* ~ …을 싸게 사다. **3** the result of shopping. 산〔쇼핑한〕 물건. ¶ *make a good* 〔*bad*〕 ~ 유리〔불리〕한 거래를 하다; 싸게〔비싸게〕 사다.
A bargain's a bargain. We must stick to our agreement. 계약은 이행해야 한다.
drive a hard bargain, insist on terms good for oneself and hard for the other. (양보하지 않고) 유리한 조건으로 사다〔팔다〕; (값을 깎아) 흥정을 하다.
into the bargain, moreover; also. 게다가; 더욱이.
make a bargain with, come to an agreement with. …와 계약을 맺다.
make the best of a bad bargain, face bad fortune cheerfully 역경에 잘 대처하다.
— *vi.* (P1,3) 《*with*》 make an agreement; discuss the price. 계약하다; 흥정하다. [F.=haggle]
bargain away, sell at a cheap price. 싼 값에 팔다. .
bargain for, be ready for (something); expect. …을 예기하다; 기대하다.
bargain on, count or rely on (something). …을 기대하다.

bar·gain·er [bɑ́ːrgənər] *n.* a person who bargains. 파는 사람.

*__barge__ [bɑːrdʒ] *n.* Ⓒ **1** a flat-bottomed boat for carrying goods. 거룻배; 바지(선). **2** a pleasure boat. 놀잇배; 유람선. **3** 《U.S.》 a coach. 마차.
— *vt.* (P6) carry (something) by barge. …을 바지〔거룻배〕로 나르다. — *vi.* (P2,3) leap about. 뛰어다니다. [→bark[3]]
barge in, rush in rudely. 거칠게 뛰어들다.
barge into, run into. 틈입(闖入)하다.

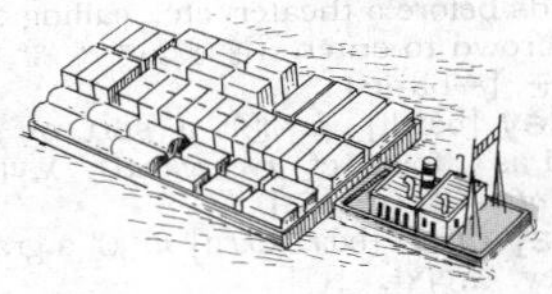

〈barge 1〉

bar·gee [bɑːrdʒíː] *n.* **1** =bargeman. **2** a rough, rude fellow. 거칠고 무례한 녀석. ¶ *a regular* ~ 불한당 같은 놈. [↑]

barge·man [bɑ́ːrdʒmən] *n.* Ⓒ (*pl.* **-men** [-mən]) a person who works on a barge. 거룻배의 사공.

bar·ite [bέərait, bǽr-] *n.* native barium sulphate. 중정석(重晶石). [↓]

bar·i·tone, 《Brit.》 **bar·y-** [bǽrətòun] *n.* 《mus.》 **1** Ⓤ a male voice between tenor and bass. 바리톤. **2** Ⓒ a singer having such a voice. 바리톤 가수(歌手). **3** Ⓒ a musical instrument having such a sound. 바리톤 악기. — *adj.* between bass and tenor. 바리톤의. ¶ *a* ~ *voice* 바리톤 음성. [Gk. *barus* heavy, *tone*]

bar·i·um [bέəriəm, bǽr-] *n.* Ⓤ 《chem.》 a soft, silver-white, metallic element. 바륨. [Gk. *barus* heavy]

:**bark**[1] [bɑːrk] *n.* Ⓤ the outer covering of trees or plants. 나무 껍질. — *vt.* (P6) **1** take the bark off (a tree). (나무 껍질)을 벗기다. **2** scrape the skin from. …의 살을 까다. ¶ *I fell down the steps and barked my shins.* 넘어져서 정강이가 까졌다. [Scand.]

:**bark**[2] [bɑːrk] *n.* Ⓒ **1** a cry made by a dog. 짖는 소리. ¶ *the* ~ *of a dog* 〔*fox*〕 개〔여우〕 짖는 소리. **2** a cry or sound like this. 짖는 듯한 소리. ¶ *the* ~ *of a gun* 요란한 총소리. — *vi.* (P1,2A,3,4) **1** cry, as a dog does. 짖다. ¶ *The dog always barks at beggars.* 그 개는 거지만 보면 짖는다 / 《*prov.*》 *A barking dog seldom bites.* 짖는 개는 물지 않는다. **2**

shout out sharply. 고함치다. ¶ *When you speak to people, don't ~ at them.* 이야기할 때는 고함을 지르지 마라. **3** 《U.S. *colloq.*》 cough loudly. 요란하게 기침하다. [E.]

bark at the moon, make futile protests. 공연히 소란을 피우다.

bark up the wrong tree, attack the wrong thing; misdirect one's energy. 허방〔잘못〕짚다.

B

bark³ [bɑːrk] *n.* Ⓒ **1** a small three-masted ship. 세대박이 돛배. **2** 《*poet.*》 a ship. 배. [L. *barca*]

〈bark³ 1〉

bar·keep·er [báːrkìːpər] *n.* Ⓒ **1** a person who runs a bar. 술집 주인. **2** a barman. 바텐더. [→bar]

bark·er [báːrkər] *n.* Ⓒ a person who stands before a theater, etc., calling out to the crowd to enter. (흥행장·가게 앞 등의) 여리꾼. [→bark²]

·**bar·ley** [báːrli] *n.* Ⓤ a sort of grain used as a food (cf. *rye, wheat*). 보리. ¶ *a field of ~* 보리밭. [E.]

bar·ley·corn [báːrlikɔ̀ːrn] *n.* Ⓒ a grain of barley. 보리알.

barm [bɑːrm] *n.* Ⓤ yeast. 효모(酵母). [E.]

bar·maid [báːrmèid] *n.* Ⓒ 《Brit.》 a girl who serves food and alcoholic drinks in a bar. (술집의) 여급(女給); 호스테스. [→bar]

bar·man [báːrmən] *n.* Ⓒ (*pl.* **-men** [-mən]) a man who serves drinks in a bar; a bartender. 바텐더(《=《U.S.》 bartender》).

Bar·me·cide [báːrməsàid] *adj.* illusory; imaginary. 가공의; 공허한. [Person in *the Arabian Nights*]

barm·y [báːrmi] *adj.* (**barm·i·er, barm·i·est**) 《*colloq.*》 light-headed; mad; foolish. 머리가 돈; 미친; 바보 같은. ¶ *go ~* 머리가 돌다. [→barm]

:**barn** [bɑːrn] *n.* Ⓒ **1** a farm building for storing hay, grain, etc., or for keeping cows, horses, etc. 헛간; 외양간. **2** 《U.S.》 a large building for streetcars, trucks, etc. 차고. [E. =barley place]

bar·na·cle [báːrnəkəl] *n.* Ⓒ a sea animal with a shell that attaches itself to rocks, logs, etc. 조개삿갓; 따개비. [F. *bernaque*]

barn-door [báːrndɔ̀ːr] *n.* **1** a large door which gives entrance to a barn. 헛간의 문. **2** a target too big to be missed. 빗나갈 리 없는 큰 과녁. ¶ *He can't hit a ~.* 사격 솜씨가 엉망이다. [→barn]

barn-storm [báːrnstɔ̀ːrm] *vi.* (P1) go about the country performing plays, giving lectures using barns. 흥행하며〔유세(遊說)하며〕 시골로 돌아다니다.

barn·yard [báːrnjɑ̀ːrd] *n.* Ⓤ a yard around or before a barn. 뒤뜰; 안뜰.

bar·o·graph [bǽrəgræ̀f, -grɑ̀ːf] *n.* an instrument that automatically records changes in air pressure. 자기(自記) 기압계. [Gk. *baros* weight, *graph*]

ba·rom·e·ter [bərámitər / -rɔ́m-] *n.* Ⓒ **1** an instrument for measuring the pressure of air. 기압계(計). **2** anything that shows changes. 지표(指標); 척도. ¶ *a ~ of public opinion* 여론의 바로미터. ● **bar·o·met·ric(al)** *adj.* [Gk. *baros* weight, *meter*]

·**bar·on** [bǽrən] *n.* Ⓒ **1** a nobleman of the lowest rank in Britain. 남작. 參考 호칭은 외국인의 경우에만 Baron..., 영국인은 Lord...라고 함. **2** 《hist.》 a nobleman who held his land under a direct grant from the king. (영지(領地)를 가진) 귀족. **3** 《U.S.》 a powerful man in business. 대(大)사업가. [L. *baro* man]

bar·on·age [bǽrənidʒ] *n.* **1** all the barons. 남작들. **2** the rank or title of a baron. 남작의 작위.

bar·on·ess [bǽrənis] *n.* Ⓒ the wife of a baron; a woman baron. 남작 부인; 여남작. 參考 호칭은 Lady..., Baroness....

bar·on·et [bǽrənit, -nèt] *n.* Ⓒ a person holding the degree of honor between baron and knight. 준(準)남작. 參考 귀족이 아니며, 호칭은 이름 앞에 Sir 를, 끝에 Bart. 라고 씀.

bar·o·ny [bǽrəni] *n.* **1** the lands of a baron. 남작령(領). **2** the rank of a baron. 남작의 작위. **3** 《Sc.》 a large manor. 대장원(大莊園).

ba·roque [bəróuk] *adj.* **1** of or like a style of art and architecture in Europe about 1550 to the late 18th century. 바로크식의. **2** fantastic; grotesque. 환상적인; 기괴한. — *n.* Ⓤ 《*the* ~》 the baroque period; the baroque style. 바로크 시대; 바로크식. [Sp. *barrucco* rough pearl]

bar·o·scope [bǽrəskòup] *n.* an instrument showing the variations in atmospheric pressure. 기압계. [→barometer]

ba·rouche [bərúːʃ] *n.* a fourwheeled carriage. 대형 사륜 마차. [bi-, L. *rota* wheel]

bar·que [bɑːrk] *n.* =bark³.

bar·rack¹ [bǽrək] *n.* Ⓒ **1** 《usu. *pl.*》 a building or a row of buildings for lodging soldiers or people. 막사; 바라크(식 건물). **2** a large plain house. 크고 엉성한 집. ¶ *a regular ~ of a place* 흡사 바라크 같은 집. [It.]

bar·rack² [bǽrək] *vt.* (P6) jeer at, esp. on a cricket field. …을 야유하다. [Austral.]

bar·ra·cu·da [bæ̀rəkúːdə] *n.* a fierce, powerful fish of the seas near the West Indies. 창꼬치류(類). [W-Ind.]

bar·rage [bərɑ́ːdʒ / bǽrɑːʒ] *n.* Ⓒ 《mil.》 a curtain of machine-gun fire to protect advancing troops or to conceal their movements. 탄막(彈幕); 일제 엄호 사격. ¶ *let loose a heavy gun ~* 중포(重砲)에 의한

탄막을 치다. [→bar]

barred [bɑːrd] *adj.* **1** having bars. 가로대가 있는. ¶ *a ~ window.* **2** marked with stripes. 줄이 있는. [→bar]

:bar·rel [bǽrəl] *n.* Ⓒ **1** a cask or container with a round, flat head and end and slightly curved sides. (중배가 부른) 통. **2** the quantity that barrel a can contain. 한 통[배럴]의 양. ¶ *a ~ of beer* [*salt, fish*] 맥주[소금, 생선] 한 통 / *five barrels of petroleum,* 5배럴의 석유. **3** the metal tube of a gun. 총신(銃身); 포신(砲身). — *vt.* (**-reled, -rel·ing,** 《Brit.》 **-relled, -rel·ling**) (P6) put or pack (something) in a barrel. …을 통에 넣다[담다]. [F. *baril*]

barrel organ [⌐–⌐–] *n.* a portable pipe organ. 휴대용 파이프 오르간《손으로 핸들을 돌려 타는》(cf. *hurdy-gurdy*).

·bar·ren [bǽrən] *adj.* **1** not producing anything; not fertile. 불모의. ¶ *~ land* 불모지. **2** (of a plant) not able to bear fruit or seed; (of an animal) unable to bear young. 열매를 맺지 못하는; 새끼를 낳지 못하는. ¶ *a ~ woman* 석녀(石女) / *a ~ flower* 암술이 없는 꽃. **3** useless; unprofitable. 무익한. ¶ *a ~ effort* 무익한 노력. **4** dull in mind; not attractive. 둔한; 매력적이지 못한. ¶ *a ~ mind* 둔한 머리(의 사람). **5** 《*of*》 lacking. …이 없는. ¶ *~ of interest* 흥미가 없는 / *a park ~ of people* 사람이 없는 공원 / *be ~ of tender feeling* 다정(多情)한 마음이 없다.

— *n.* Ⓤ 《usu. *pl.*》 a stretch of land with sandy soil and few trees. 불모의 모래땅. ● **bar·ren·ness** [-nis] *n.* [F.]

bar·rette [bərét] *n.* 《F.》 a pin with a clasp used by women for holding the hair in place. (여성용의) 머리 클립.

bar·ri·cade [bǽrəkèid, ⌐–⌐] *n.* a barrier roughly made for defense; any obstruction. 바리케이드; 장애. — *vt.* (P6) obstruct or stop up (the street, etc.) with a barricade. 바리케이드로 (길 따위)를 막다. [Sp. *barrica* cask]

·bar·ri·er [bǽriər] *n.* Ⓒ **1** a fence, wall, etc. which stands in the way to prevent passage. 방책(防柵); 방벽(防壁). **2** anything that prevents progress. 방해물; 장애; 장벽. ¶ *a ~ to success* 성공의 장애(물) / *a ~ to trade* 무역 장벽 / *a language ~* 언어 장벽. [→bar]

bar·ring [báːriŋ] *prep.* except(ing). …을 제외하고. [L. *barra* bar, →bar]

bar·ris·ter [bǽrəstər] *n.* Ⓒ 《Brit.》 a lawyer who practices in the courts; 《U.S. *colloq.*》 a lawyer. 법정 변호사; 변호사(cf. *solicitor*). [→bar]

bar·room [báːrrù(ː)m] *n.* Ⓒ a room in a ship, hotel, etc. where alcoholic drinks are served over a counter. (호텔 등의) 바. [→bar]

bar·row[1] [bǽrou] *n.* Ⓒ a flat frame with handles at each end, used for carrying things; a handcart. (들것식의) 운반대; 손수레. [Teut. →bear[1]]

bar·row[2] [bǽrou] *n.* Ⓒ an ancient mound over a grave. 고분(古墳). [E.]

Bart. Baronet.

bar·tend·er [báːrtèndər] *n.* Ⓒ 《U.S.》 a person who serves alcoholic drinks in a bar. 바텐더. [→bar]

bar·ter [báːrtər] *vi.* (P1) 《*with*》 trade by exchanging one kind of goods for other goods without money payment. 물물 교환하다. ¶ *~ with natives* 원주민과 물물 교환하다. — *vt.* (P7,13) 《*for*》 exchange. …을 교환하다. ¶ *~ eggs for cloth* 달걀을 피륙과 교환하다.

barter away, sell at too low a price. 싸게 팔아 넘기다. ¶ *~ away his pride for material gain* 물질적인 이익을 위해 자존심을 팔다.

— *n.* Ⓒ trade by bartering. 물물 교환. [F. *barat* fraud]

Bar·thol·o·mew [bɑːrθáləmjùː / -θɔ́l-] *n.* 《Bible》 Saint. one of the twelve apostles; his day is Aug. 24. 바르톨로메오.

bar·ti·zan [báːrtəzən, bàːrtəzǽn] *n.* the projecting corner at the top of a tower. 돌출한 망대(望臺). [G. *brett* board]

bar·y·tone [bǽrətòun] *n., adj.* 《Brit.》 = baritone.

bas·al [béisəl, -zəl] *adj.* forming a basis; basic; fundamental. 기초의; 기본적인. ¶ *~ characteristics* 기본적 성격 / *the ~ parts of a column* 주(柱)추 / *a ~ condition* [*argument*] 기본 조건[논거]. [→base[1]]

ba·salt [bəsɔ́ːlt, bǽsɔːlt, béi-] *n.* Ⓤ a dark, heavy rock of volcanic origin. 현무암. [L.]

bas·cule [bǽskjuːl] *n.* Ⓒ anything working like a seesaw. 시소 장치. ¶ *a ~ bridge* 도개교(跳開橋)(cf. *drawbridge*). [F. =seesaw]

base[1] [beis] *adj.* **1** morally low; mean; ignoble. 천한; 비열한(opp. noble). ¶ *To betray a friend is a ~ action.* 친구를 배신하는 것은 비열한 행위이다. **2** not pure; of inferior value. 불순한; 저질의. ¶ *~ coin* 위조 화폐. **3** (of language) not classical. (언어가) 순정(純正)하지 못한. ¶ *~ Latin* 통속 라틴어. **4** 《mus.》 bass. 베이스의. [L. *bussus* short]

:base[2] [beis] *n.* Ⓒ **1** ⓐ what a thing rests on; a bottom; a support. 기저(基底); 밑; 받침. ¶ *the ~ of a pillar* 주추 / *the ~ of a mountain* 산기슭 / *cut down a tree at the ~* 나무를 그 밑동에서 베어 넘기다. ⓑ a foundation; groundwork. 기초; 토대; 기반; 근거. ¶ *the ~ of a building* 건물의 토대 / *a candidate with a ~* (*of support*) *in the working class* 노동 계급에 지지 기반을 가진 후보 / *as a ~ of comparison* 비교의 근거로서. **2** a principle. 주의. ¶ *act on the ~ of ...* …주의에 따라 행동하다. **3** a starting point. 출발점; 기점(基點). ¶ *establish a ~ camp* 베이스 캠프를 설치하다 / *a convenient ~ from which trips and excursions radiate* 여기저

기 여행하는 기점으로서 편리한 곳. **4** a military center. 군사 기지. ¶ *a naval* 〔*an air*〕 ~ 해군〔공군〕 기지. **5** 《chem.》 a compound that reacts with an acid to form a salt. 염기(塩基). **6** the main element of a mixture. 혼합물의 주성분. ¶ *paint with a lead* ~ 납을 주성분으로 하는 안료(顔料). **7** 《gram.》 the form to which affixes are added. 기체(基體); 어근(語根). **8** 《math.》 a line on which a figure stands. 밑변(邊); 밑면. **9** a station or goal in certain games, such as baseball or hide-and-seek. (야구 따위에서) 누(壘); 베이스.

B

at the base of, at the foot of; at the bottom of. …의 기슭에; …의 밑에.

change one's base, 《*colloq.*》 retreat; decamp. 물러가다; 철수〔전진(轉進)〕하다.

off base, 《U.S. *sl.*》 **a**) completely or foolishly mistaken. 엄청나게 틀리어〔잘못되어〕. ¶ *Your idea is completely off* ~ . 네 생각은 완전히 틀렸다. **b**) unprepared. 허(의표)를 찔려. ¶ *She caught me off* ~ *with that question.* 그녀는 그 질문으로 나를 당황케 했다.

— *vt.* (P13) 《*on, upon*》 found; rest; establish. …에 기초를 두다. ¶ *a theory based on* 〔*upon*〕 *experience* 경험에 바탕을 둔 이론 / *I* ~ *my belief on this fact.* 나는 나의 생각을 이 사실에 기초를 두고 있다. [Gk. *bainō* step]

:base·ball [béisbɔ̀:l] *n.* **1** Ⓤ a game played with a bat and a ball by two teams. 야구. **2** Ⓒ the ball used in this game. 야구공. [→base²]

base·born [béisbɔ́:rn] *adj.* **1** of humble birth. 태생이 비천한. **2** illegitimate. 사생(私生)의(cf. *bastard*). [→base¹]

Bas·e·dow's disease [bɑ́:zədòuz —ˊ] *n.* exophthalmus. 바제도병(病).

base·less [béislis] *adj.* without a base; groundless 근거 없는. ¶ ~ *fears.* [→base²]

base·ly [béisli] *adv.* in a base, low manner. 천하게. [→base¹]

base·man [béismən] *n.* Ⓒ (*pl.* **-men** [-mən]) a baseball player guarding the first, second, or third base. (야구의) 베이스맨. [→base²]

base·ment [béismənt] *n.* Ⓒ the lowest story of a building, partly or wholly underground; a cellar. 지하층; 지하실. [↑]

base·ness [béisnis] *n.* Ⓤ moral meanness; inferiority in conduct or character. 비열함; 천함. [→base¹]

ba·ses [béisi:z] *n.* pl. of **basis.**

bash [bæʃ] *vt.* (P6,7,13) 《*colloq.*》 《*on*》 hit with great force. 후려갈기다. ¶ ~ *a man on the head* / ~ *one's head against a tree* 나무에 머리를 세게 부딪치다. [Imit.]

bash·ful [bǽʃfəl] *adj.* shy. 수줍어하는. ¶ *The* ~ *child was nervous with strangers.* 그 숫기없는 아이는 낯선 사람들로 인해 불안해 했다. ● **bash·ful·ly** [-i] *adv.* [→abash]

bash·ful·ness [bǽʃfəlnis] *n.* the condition of being bashful. 수줍어함.

·bas·ic [béisik] *adj.* **1** fundamental; essential. 기초의; 근본적인. ¶ ~ *data* 기초 자료 / ~ *principles* 근본 원리. **2** 《chem.》 of a base; alkaline. 염기성의. [Gk. *bainō* step]

bas·i·cal·ly [béisikəli] *adv.* **1** fundamentally; essentially. 기본적〔근본적〕으로. ¶ *probe a matter* ~ 어떤 일을 근본적으로 조사하다.

bas·il [bǽzəl, béiz-] *n.* Ⓒ 《bot.》 an aromatic herb. 박하 비슷한 식물. [Gk. *basileus* king]

ba·sil·i·ca [bəsílikə, -zíl-] *n.* Ⓒ **1** an oblong hall, used as a court or an assembly in ancient Rome. 바실리카 공회당. **2** a Christian church built in this form in the earliest or medieval period. 바실리카풍의 교회당. [↑]

bas·i·lisk [bǽsəlisk, bǽz-] *n.* **1** Ⓒ (in Greek and Roman legend) a fearful animal like a serpent. 전설상의 뱀 비슷한 괴물. 參考 안광(眼光)과 입김으로 사람을 죽였다고 함. **2** 《zool.》 a tropical American lizard. 열대 아메리카산(産) 도마뱀. [Gk.=serpent]

·ba·sin [béisən] *n.* Ⓒ **1** a round, shallow bowl. 대야. ¶ *a wash* ~ 세숫대야 / *a* ~ *of water* 한통의 물. **2** a hollow place containing water; a reservoir. 웅덩이; 저수지. **3** an area surrounded by higher lands. 분지(盆地). **4** all the land along a river. 강 유역. ¶ *a river* ~ 유역. **5** a dock with a floodgate. 선거(船渠). [L. *bachinus*]

:ba·sis [béisis] *n.* Ⓒ (*pl.* **ba·ses**) **1** a base or foundation. 기초; 원칙; 근거(지); 토대. ¶ *the* ~ *of an argument* 논거 / *a business on a commission* ~ 수수료제(制)의 일 / *furnish a satisfactory* ~ *for study* 연구에 납득할 만한 근거를 주다. **2** the chief element of a mixture. 주성분. ¶ *the* ~ *of a medicine* 약의 주성분. [Gk. *bainō* step]

bask [bæsk, bɑ:sk] *vi.* (P2A) 《*in*》 lie in pleasant warmth usu. in the sunshine; enjoy a cheerful situation. 볕을 쬐다. ¶ *You can lie on the sand and* ~ *in the sun.* 모래 위에 누워서 햇볕을 쬐도 좋다 / (*fig.*) ~ *in the smiles of Fortune* 행운을 만나다. [N.= bathe]

:bas·ket [bǽskit, bɑ́:s-] *n.* Ⓒ **1** a container made of rushes, twigs, etc. woven together. 바구니. ¶ *a shopping* ~ 장바구니. **2** the amount that a basket holds. 한 바구니의 양. ¶ *a* ~ *of eggs* 달걀 한 바구니 / *pick a* ~ *of apples* 한 바구니 가득한 사과를 따다. **3** anything like a basket. 바구니 모양의 것. **4** (in basketball) a score or goal. (농구에서) 득점; 골. [? Celt.]

:bas·ket·ball [bǽskitbɔ̀:l, bɑ́:s-] *n.* **1** Ⓤ a game played with a large ball by two teams of five persons. 농구. **2** Ⓒ a ball used in this game. 농구 공.

bas·ket·ful [bǽskitfùl, bɑ́:s-] *n.* Ⓒ **1** the quantity to fill a basket. 바구니 하나의 분량. **2** any considerable quantity. 상당한 양.

¶ *a ~ of surprises* 뜻하지 않은 많은 선물.

bas·ket·ry [bǽskitri, bɑ́:s-] *n.* **1** basket making. 바구니 제조. **2** 《*collectively*》 baskets. 바구니 세공품.

bas·ket·work [bǽskitwə̀:rk] *n.* Ⓤ wicker work. 바구니 세공.

Basque [bæsk] *n., adj.* (a member or the language) of people living in Spain. (스페인의) 바스크 사람(의). [L. *Vasco*]

bas-re·lief [bɑ̀:rili:f, bæs-, ⌐⌐] *n.* ⓊⒸ 《art》 sculpture in which the figures stand out slightly from the background. 바 릴리프; 저부조(低浮彫)《얕은 돋을새김》. [F.]

bass[1] [beis] 《mus.》 *adj.* of the lowest pitch or range. 베이스의; 저음의. ¶ *a ~ voice* 저음 / *a ~ viol* 첼로. — *n.* **1** Ⓤ the lowest male voice or part. 베이스《남성 최저음부》. **2** Ⓒ a bass singer or instrument. 베이스 가수; 저음 악기. [→base[2]]

bass[2] [bæs] *n.* Ⓒ (*pl.* **bass·es** [bǽsiz] or *collectively* **bass**) a fish found in both fresh and salt water in North America. 농어의 한 가지. [E.]

bass[3] [bæs] *n.* ⓊⒸ 《bot.》 bass-wood. 참피나무속의 식물; 그 재목. [E.]

bas·si·net [bæ̀sənét, ⌐⌐] *n.* Ⓒ a baby's basketlike cradle. 덮개 달린 요람; 유모차. [→basin]

〈bassinet〉

bas·so [bǽsou, bɑ́:s-] *n.* 《It.》 a bass; a singer with a bass voice. 저음 (가수).

bas·soon [bəsú:n, bæs-] *n.* Ⓒ 《mus.》 a deeptoned wind instrument. 바순《악기》. [→base[2]]

bast [bæst] *n.* Ⓤ the inner layer of the bark. 인피(靭皮). 參考 돗자리·밧줄 등의 재료로 쓰임. [→bass[3]]

bas·tard [bǽstərd] *n.* Ⓒ **1** a child whose parents are not legally married. 사생아. **2** anything inferior or not genuine. 잡종; 가짜; 열악품. — *adj.* **1** born of unmarried parents. 사생〔서출〕의(cf. *baseborn, illegitimate*). **2** not genuine; false. 불순한; 가짜의. ¶ *speak a ~ English* 엉터리 영어를 하다 / *~ patriotism* 불순한 애국심. **3** inferior. 저질의. **4** not standard. 비정상적인; 보통〔표준적〕이 아닌. ¶ *~ quartz* 이상(異常) 석영. [F.= packsaddle child]

baste[1] [beist] *vt.* (P6) **1** moisten with fat. 기름을 바르다. **2** hit hard. 세게 때리다. [?]

baste[2] [beist] *vt.* (P6) sew with long, loose stitches. 시침질하다. [F.]

bas·ti·na·do [bæ̀stənéidou, -nɑ́:dou] *vt.* (P6) beat upon the soles of the feet. 발바닥을 매질하다. — *n.* beating upon the soles. 발바닥 매질. [Sp. *baston* stick]

bast·ings [béistiŋz] *n. pl.* the stitches used in the first sewing of a dress. 시침. [→baste[2]]

bas·tion [bǽstʃən, -tiən] *n.* Ⓒ a projecting part of a wall of a castle. 능보(稜堡). [L. *bastio* build]

***bat**[1] [bæt] *n.* **1** Ⓒ a heavy stick or club used to hit the ball in baseball, cricket, etc. 배트. **2** Ⓒ a batsman. 타자(打者). **3** 《*colloq.*》 rate of speed. 속도.

at bat, (in baseball) taking one's turn to bat. 타순이 되어; 타석에.

go full bat, go very fast. 돌진하다.

go to bat for, **a**) intercede for. …을 위해 중재〔조정〕하다. **b**) vouch for. …을 보증하다. **c**) defend; come or go to the aid of. …을 변호하다; …을 지지〔원조〕하다.

— *v.* (**bat·ted, bat·ting**) *vt.* (P6) hit (a ball) with a bat. …을 배트로 치다.

— *vi.* (P1) use a bat. 배트를 사용하다. [L. *batuo* beat]

bat around, wander about. 돌아다니다.

bat back and forth, examine in detail. 자세히 검토하다.

:bat[2] [bæt] *n.* Ⓒ 《zool.》 a flying animal with a mouse-like body. 박쥐. [E.]

blind as a bat, completely blind. 장님이나 다름없는.

have bats in the belfry, be crazy. 미치다.

bat[3] [bæt] *vt.* (P6) blink; wink. (눈)을 깜박거리다. [?]

not bat an eyelid, **a**) not sleep at all. 한잠도 안 자다. **b**) show no surprise. 놀라지 않다; 눈하나 깜짝 않다.

batch [bætʃ] *n.* **1** Ⓒ the quantity of bread baked at one time; the quantity of anything made at one time. (빵·도자기 따위) 한번 구어낸 분량; 한 가마(분). **2** a group of persons or things taken together. 한 세트; 한 묶음; 일단; 한떼. ¶ *I have a ~ of letters to answer.* 답장을 내야 할 한 묶음의 편지가 있다 / *a ~ of workmen* 일단의 노동자. [→bake]

bate[1] [beit] *vt.* (P6) make (strength, etc.) less; make (a price) low. (힘 따위)를 줄이다; 누그러뜨리다; (값 따위)를 내리다. ¶ *~ one's demands* 요구를 누그러뜨리다 / *cannot ~ a penny* 한푼도 깎을 수 없다 / *setbacks that bated his hopes* 그의 희망을 꺾은 실패. [→abate]

with bated breath, holding one's breath in great fear, interest, etc. 숨을 죽이고. ¶ *They listened with bated breath to the sailor's story.* 그들은 숨을 죽이고 뱃사람의 이야기에 귀를 기울였다.

bate[2] [beit] *n.* 《Brit. *sl.*》 anger; temper. 노여움; 화. ¶ *be in a ~* 화내고 있다 / *get in a ~ (about anything)* (…에 대해) 노하다; 성내다. [?]

:bath [bæθ, bɑ:θ] *n.* (*pl.* **baths** [bæðz, -θs, bɑ:-]) **1** Ⓒ the act of washing or cleaning the body with water, steam, etc. 입욕; 목욕. ¶ *take* 〔*have*〕 *a ~* 목욕하다 / *a cold* 〔*hot*〕 *~* 냉수욕〔온수욕〕 / *a sun ~* 일광욕. **2** Ⓤ water for bathing. 목욕물. ¶ *Your ~ is ready.* 목욕

물이 준비되었습니다. **3** Ⓒ a tub or room for bathing. 욕조; 욕실. **4** 《chem.》 the liquid into which something is put the container holding the liquid. 침지용(浸漬用) 액체; 액반(液盤). — *vt.* (P6) 《Brit.》 give a bath to. …을 목욕시키다(cf. *bathe*). ¶ ~ *a baby* 아기를 목욕시키다. — *vi.* (P1) 《Brit.》 have a bath. 목욕하다. [E.]

B

bath-chair [bǽθtʃὲər] *n.* 《often *B-*》 《Brit.》 a three-wheeled chair for a sick or old person. (환자·노인용) 바퀴 의자.

:**bathe** [beið] *vt.* (P6) **1** give a bath to (someone); wash (a baby, wound, hand, etc.) with water or other liquid. …을 목욕시키다; 씻다. ¶ ~ *one's face* 〔*feet*〕 얼굴〔발〕을 씻다. **2** 《*in*》 dip (something) into any liquid; make (something) wet with any liquid. …을 담그다; 적시다. ¶ *be bathed in tears* 눈물에 젖다. **3** 《in *passive*》 cover (something) as water does. …을 뒤덮다. ¶ *The garden was bathed in moon-light.* 뜰에는 달빛이 가득 비치고 있었다.
— *vi.* (P1) **1** have or take a bath. 목욕하다. **2** swim; go swimming. 헤엄치다; 수영하다. ¶ ~ *in the river* 강에서 헤엄치다.
— *n.* Ⓒ 《Brit.》 the act of swimming in a river or the sea. 수영; 미역감기. ¶ *take a* ~ 미역 감다 / *go for a* ~ 헤엄치러 가다. [*bath*]

bath·er [béiðər] *n.* Ⓒ a person who takes a bathe or a bath. 미역 감는 사람; 탕치자(湯治者).

ba·thet·ic [bəθétik] *adj.* characterized by bathos. 점강법(漸降法)의. [→bathysphere]

bath·house [bǽθhàus, bɑ́:θ-] *n.* a building equipped for bathing. 목욕탕. [→bath]

bath·ing [béiðiŋ] *n.* the act of taking a bath in the sea, etc. 목욕; 입욕; 해수욕; 수영. ¶ *be fond of* ~ 수영을 좋아하다 / *The* ~ *here is rather dangerous.* 여기서 수영하는 것은 좀 위험하다. [→bath]

ba·thos [béiθɑs / -θɔs] *n.* a sudden change from very beautiful thoughts to very common or foolish ones. 점강법(漸降法); 급락(急落)(cf. *anticlimax*). [→bathysphere]

bath·robe [bǽθròub, bɑ́:θ-] *n.* Ⓒ 《U.S.》 a long, loose garment worn before and after a bath. 욕의(浴衣)(cf. 《Brit.》 *dressing gown*).

bath·room [bǽθrù(:)m, bɑ́:θ-] *n.* Ⓒ **1** a room for taking a bath. 욕실(浴室). **2** a toilet. 화장실.

bath·tub [bǽθtʌ̀b, bɑ́:θ-] *n.* Ⓒ a tub to bathe in. 욕조(浴槽).

bath·y·sphere [bǽθəsfìər] *n.* a watertight chamber with glass window, in which men can go deep down in the sea to study animal and plant life. (심해) 잠수 장치. [Gk. *bathus* deep]

bat·ik [bətí:k, bǽtik] *n.* Ⓤ **1** a method of making designs on cloth by coating with wax parts not to be dyed. 납결(臘纈)《밀랍을 이용한 염색법》. **2** cloth dyed in this way. 그렇게 염색한 피륙. [Malay]

ba·tiste [bətí:st, bæ-] *n.* Ⓤ a kind of fine thin linen or cotton cloth. 질 좋은 얇은 삼베〔무명〕. [Person]

bat·man [bǽtmən] *n.* (*pl.* **-men** [-mən]) 《Brit.》 an officer's servant. (장교의) 당번병. [Gk.]

ba·ton [bətɑ́n, bæ-, bǽtən] *n.* Ⓒ **1** a stick used by the leader of an orchestra or a band for beating time. 지휘봉. **2** a stick which is passed from one to the next runner in a relay race. (계주용) 배턴. **3** a short stick used by a policeman. 경찰봉(cf. *truncheon*). [F. *bâton*]

ba·tra·chi·an [bətréikiən] *adj.* of tailless amphibians. 양서류의. — *n.* Ⓤ amphibians. 양서류. [Gk. *batrakhos* frog]

bats [bæts] *adj.* 《*colloq.*》 mad. 머리가 돈. ¶ *He's gone* ~*!* 그는 돌아버렸어.

bats·man [bǽtsmən] *n.* Ⓒ (*pl.* **-men** [-mən]) 《Brit.》 a player at bat in baseball, cricket, etc. 타자(打者). [→bat[2]]

bat·tal·ion [bətǽljən] *n.* Ⓒ **1** 《mil.》 two or more companies of soldiers. 대대(大隊). **2** 《*pl.*》 armies; military forces; any large company. 군; 대부대; 많은 사람. ¶ *battalions of bureaucrats* 많은 관료들. **3** an organized group. 집단. [→battle]

bat·ten[1] [bǽtn] *n.* Ⓒ **1** a narrow strip of wood used in fastening two boards. 오리목. **2** a board used for flooring. 청널. — *vt.* (P6,7) fasten (two boards) with battens; strengthen. 오리목을 대다; 보강하다. [→baton]

bat·ten[2] [bǽtn] *vi.* (P1,3) grow fat. 살찌다. [N.]
batten on 〔***upon***〕, feed greedily on. …을 탐식(貪食)하다.

bat·ter[1] [bǽtər] *vt.* (P6,7) **1** ⓐ beat or strike (something) with repeated heavy blows; beat hard. 연타〔난타〕하다. ¶ ~ *someone on the head* 아무의 머리를 난타하다 / ~ *one's head against a stone wall* 돌담에 머리를 세게 부딪다. ⓑ beat (something) out of shape; crush; pound. 쳐서 찌그러뜨리다; 쳐부수다. ¶ ~ *a door open* 문을 쳐부수어 열다 / ~ *a door* 〔*a wall*〕 *down* 문〔벽〕을 쳐부수다. **2** damage (something) by hard use. …을 마구 다루어 상하게 하다. ¶ *battered type* 마멸된 활자 / *a battered hat* 오래 써 낡은 모자. **3** assail with artillery. 포격하다. **4** criticize severely. 깎아내리다. [L. *batuo* beat, →bat[1]]

bat·ter[2] [bǽtər] *n.* Ⓤ a mixture of flour, milk, and eggs, beaten together. (밀가루·우유·달걀을 섞어 이긴) 반죽. [↑]

***bat·ter**[3] [bǽtər] *n.* Ⓒ =batsman.

bat·ter·ing ram [bǽtəriŋ ræ̀m] *n.* an ancient military machine to break the walls or gates of a castle or city. 공성퇴(攻城槌). [↑]

***bat·ter·y** [bǽtəri] *n.* (*pl.* **-ter·ies**) **1** Ⓒ a

set of cells, or a single cell, producing electric current. 전지. **2** Ⓒ a set of similar articles, machines, etc. 한 벌의 기구. ¶ *a cooking ~* 요리 도구 한 벌 / *a ~ of cameras* 카메라 장비 한 벌. **3** 《mil.》 a set of big guns; a company of artillerymen. 포대(砲臺); 포열(砲列); 포대(砲隊). **4** 《baseball》 the pitcher and the catcher together. (야구에서) 배터리. **5** 《law》 the unlawful beating of another person. 구타. [F. *battre* strike, -ery]

bat·ting [bǽtiŋ] *n.* **1** hitting. 타격. **2** cotton or wool pressed into thin layer. 침구 등에 넣는 솜〔양털〕. [→bat[1]]

:bat·tle [bǽtl] *n.* Ⓒ **1** a fight between two forces (in a war); a combat. 전투; 싸움. ¶ *the ~ of Waterloo* 워털루의 전투 / *an air ~* 공중전 / *a bloody ~* 혈전(血戰) / *a close ~* 접근전 / *the field of ~* 전장(戰場) / *a ~ between two lions* 두 사자간의 싸움. **2** Ⓤ any hard struggle. 투쟁. ¶ *the ~ of life* 생존의 투쟁. **3** a war; warfare. 전쟁. ¶ *He was killed in ~.* 그는 전사했다. **4** 《*the ~*》 victory. 승리. ¶ *In life the ~ is not always to the strong.* 인생에서 승리는 반드시 강자의 것은 아니다.

do* 〔*give*〕 *battle, enter into conflict; fight. 싸우다. ¶ *do ~ with ignorance* 무지와 싸우다.

fall in battle, die in battle. 싸움에서 죽다.

gain a battle, gain victory in a battle. 싸움에서 승리하다.

half the battle, the advantage in a cause. 유리한 점.

join battle, accept the enemy's challenge. 「응전하다.

lose a battle, be defeated in a battle. 싸움에서 패하다.

— *vi.* (P3) fight; struggle; make a great effort. 싸우다; 분투하다. ¶ *~ against* 〔*with*〕 *one's enemy* 적과 싸우다 / *~ for peace* 평화를 위해 싸우다. [L. *batuo* beat]

bat·tle-ax, -axe [bǽtlæ̀ks] *n.* Ⓒ an ax used as a weapon. 전부(戰斧).

bat·tle-cruis·er [bǽtlkrùːzər] *n.* a heavy-gunned ship of higher speed and lighter armor than a battleship. 순양 전함.

bat·tle·dore [bǽtldɔ̀ːr] *n.* Ⓒ a racket used in badminton. 배드민턴 라켓.

bat·tle·field [bǽtlfìːld] *n.* Ⓒ a place on which a battle is fought. 전장(戰場).

bat·tle·ground [bǽtlgràund] *n.* Ⓒ a battlefield. 전장(戰場).

bat·tle·ment [bǽtlmənt] *n.* 《usu. *pl.*》 a castle wall with open spaces for shooting. 총안(銃眼)이 있는 흉장(胸牆).

〈battlement〉

bat·tle·plane [bǽtlplèin] *n.* Ⓒ an airplane made for combat. 전투기.

battle royal [ˊ-ˊ-] *n.* a fierce battle. 격전; 결전.

bat·tle·ship [bǽtlʃip] *n.* Ⓒ the largest and most powerful warship. 전함(cf. *battlecruiser*).

bat·ty [bǽti] *adj.* (**-ti·er, -ti·est**) 《*colloq.*》 crazy. 머리가 돈; 미친. [→bat[2]]

bau·ble [bɔ́ːbəl] *n.* Ⓒ **1** a thing which is good in appearance but valueless; a child's plaything. 겉만 번지르르한 것; 굴퉁이. **2** 《hist.》 a stick carried in old days by a jester. 어릿광대의 지팡이. [F. *babel* child's toy]

Bau·de·laire [boudəlɛ́ər], **Charles** *n.* (1821-67) a French poet, critic and moralist. 보들레르.

Bau·haus [báuhàus] *n.* a German architectural school. 바우하우스. [Gk. =house-building]

baulk [bɔːk] *n., v.* =balk.

baux·ite [bɔ́ːksait, bóuzait] *n.* Ⓤ a claylike material from which aluminum is obtained. 보크사이트. [Place]

baw·bee [bɔːbíː, ˊ-] *n.* 《Sc.》 a halfpenny. 반(半)페니. [Person]

bawd [bɔːd] *n.* a procuress; obscene talk. 여(女)포주; 음담. [?]

bawd·ry [bɔ́ːdri] *n.* Ⓤ obscenity; lewdness. 외설.

bawd·y [bɔ́ːdi] *adj., n.* obscene (talk). 외설한 (이야기)(cf. *lewd*). ¶ *a ~ house* 창녀집.

bawl [bɔːl] *vi., vt.* (P1,2A,3,4; 6,7) shout; cry out loudly. 소리〔고함〕치다; 울부짖다. ¶ *~ one's dissatisfaction* 불만을 큰소리로 소리치다 / *~ for something* 큰소리로 무언가 찾다 / *You needn't ~, I can hear quite well.* 아주 잘 들을 수 있으니 소리칠 필요는 없네 / *The pedlar bawled his goods in the street.* 행상인이 거리에서 큰소리로 자기 물건을 외쳐댔다.

bawl at, address rudely with a loud voice. …에게 큰소리로 소리치다.

bawl out, scold vociferously or vigorously. 큰소리로 호통〔야단〕치다.

— *n.* Ⓒ loud crying; noisy shouts. 외치는 소리. [L. *baulo* bark]

:bay[1] [bei] *n.* Ⓒ a part of a sea or lake extending into the shore. 만(灣); 후미. [L. *baia*]

bay[2] [bei] *n.* Ⓒ **1** a part of a wall between pillars. 기둥 사이의 벽. **2** a separate part in an airplane, esp. for carrying bombs. 비행기의 격실(隔室). **3** a place for storing hay in a barn. 헛간의 건초 저장소. **4** a space with a window in it projecting out from a wall. 창이 있는 내받이. **5** a part of the deck of a ship where the sick or wounded are placed. 환자 등을 수용하는 갑판 위의 한 구획. [F. *baer* gape]

bay[3] [bei] *n.* Ⓤ **1** the long, low cry of a dog. 개 짖는 소리. **2** a state or situation from which escape is impossible. 궁지(窮地). ¶ *be* 〔*stand*〕 *at ~* 궁지에 빠져 있

다 / *bring* 〔*drive*〕 *someone to* ~ 아무를 궁지에 빠뜨리다 / *keep an enemy at* ~ 적을 저지하다 / *turn* 〔*come*〕 *to* ~ 궁지에 몰려 덤벼들다. — *vi.* (P1,3) cry with a deep sound; bark. 짖다. — *vt.* (P6) bark at (someone or something). …을 보고 짖다. [F. *bayer* bark]

bay⁴ [bei] *n.* Ⓒ **1** a small evergreen tree; laurel tree. 월계수. **2** 《*pl.*》 a laurel ring or crown given to successful poets or victors. 월계관. **3** 《*pl.*》 honor; fame. 영예; 명성. [L. *baca* berry]

bay⁵ [bei] *n.* **1** Ⓤ color of reddish brown. 적갈색; 밤색. **2** Ⓒ a reddish brown horse. 구렁말(cf. *roan*). — *adj.* reddish brown in color. 적갈색의. [L. *badius*]

·**bay·o·net** [béiənit, -nèt] *n.* Ⓒ a dagger attached to a gun. 총검. ¶ *fix a* ~ 총검을 달다 / *fall beneath* 〔*under*〕 *a* ~ 총검에 찔려 쓰러지다. — *vt.* (P6) stab with a bayonet. 총검으로 찌르다. [Place, *Bayonne*]

bay·ou [báiu:, -ou] *n.* 《U.S.》 a marshy inlet of a lake, river, or gulf in the southern states of the United States. (미국 남부에서) 호수·늪지 등의 후미. [?]

bay rum [∠∠] *n.* a sweet-smelling toilet liquid. 베이럼《두발용 향수》. [bay⁴]

bay window [∠∠] *n.* a window projecting from the outside wall of a building. 돌출창(突出窓). [bay²]

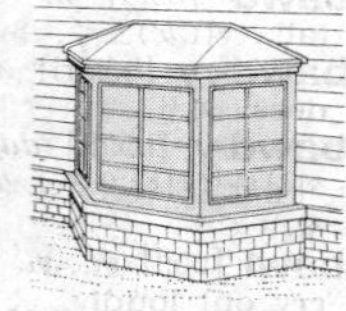
〈bay window〉

ba·zaar, -zar [bəzá:r] *n.* Ⓒ **1** a market place in Oriental countries. (동양의) 장바닥. **2** a place for the sale of various kinds of goods. 저잣거리; 시장. **3** a sale of various kinds of articles for charity or other such purpose. (자선(慈善) 등을 위한) 바자. [Pers.]

ba·zoo·ka [bəzú:kə] *n.* Ⓒ a portable rocket gun, esp. used against tanks. 바주카포(砲). [Imit.]

B.B.C. British Broadcasting Corporation.

·**B.C.** before Christ. (서력) 기원전(cf. *A.D.*).

B.D. Bachelor of Divinity.

:**be** [bi:, bi] *vi.* (pres. **am, are, is,** p. **was, were,** pp. **been**) **1** ⓐ be equal in meaning; regard or recognize as the same. …이다; 동등하다. ¶ *January is the first month.* 정월은 첫째 달이다 / *Let x* ~ *10.* x의 값이 10이라 하자 / *The first person I met was my brother.* 내가 만난 첫번째 사람은 나의 아우였다. ⓑ have as a quality or character. …의 성질을 가지다. ¶ *The leaves are green.* 잎은 푸르다. ⓒ belong to the class of. …에 속하다. ¶ *The fish is a salmon.* 그 물고기는 연어이다. **2** ⓐ exist; occupy a place or position. 존재하다; 있다; 위치를 차지하다. ¶ *I think, therefore I am.* 나는 생각한다, 그러므로 나는 존재한다 / *Once upon a time there was a knight.* 옛날 한 기사가 있었다 / *The book is on the table.* 책은 책상 위에 있다 / *Let it* ~. 그대로 놔두게. ⓑ occur; take place. 일어나다. ¶ *There was a fire last night.* 간밤에 화재가 발생했다. ⓒ amount to; cost. …에 달하다; 들다. ¶ *Twice 2 is 4.* 2의 제곱은 4가 된다 / *It is nothing to me.* 그것은 내겐 아무 것도 아니다.

be off, 《*colloq.*》 go; depart; leave somewhere. 가다; 떠나다. ¶ *We must* ~ *off early tomorrow morning.* 우리는 내일 아침 일찍 떠나야 해.

Be off **(*with you*)!** Leave here ! Get away ! (나)가; 꺼져.

— *auxil. v.* **1** 《with *pp.* of *vt.*, forming *passive*》 ¶ *He was killed.* 그는 살해되었다 / *He has been killed.* 그는 살해되고 말았다 / *The house is being built.* 그 집은 건축 중이다. **2** 《with *pp.* of some *vi.*, forming *perfect*》 ¶ *The sun is set.* 해가 졌다 / *How he is grown !* 굉장히 자랐군. **3** 《with *pres. part.*, expressing incomplete action》 ¶ *He is building a house.* 그는 집을 짓고 있다. **4** 《with *to-infinitive*, expressing duty, intention, possibility, or hypothesis》 ¶ *We are to meet at 5.* 5시에 만나기로 되어 있다 / *I am to inform you.* 당신에게 알려드립니다 / *He is to be there.* 그는 거기 있을 것이다 / *You are not to do that.* 그것을 해선 안 된다 / *Nothing was to be seen.* 아무것도 보이지 않았다 / *If I were to die…* 내가 만약 죽는다면…. [E.]

be- [bi-, bə-] *pref.* **1** all over, thoroughly. '전부에, 완전히'의 뜻. **2** make. '…으로 만들다'의 뜻. **3** call. '…라 부르다'의 뜻. **4** surround with; treat as. '…로 에워싸다, …로 취급하다'의 뜻. **5** having, ornamented with. '…을 비치하다, …로 꾸미다'의 뜻. [E., →by]

B/E bill of exchange. 환어음.

:**beach** [bi:tʃ] *n.* Ⓒ **1** a smooth shore of sand or pebbles, esp. washed over by the waves at high tide. 바닷가; 해변. **2** 《*collectively*》 the sand of the shore of a sea or a lake. 바닷가의 모래. — *vt.* (P6) run (a boat) ashore; draw up on the shore. 해안으로 얹히게 하다; 해변으로 끌어 올리다. [E.]

beach·comb·er [bítʃkòumər] *n.* **1** a large, long wave rolling in from the ocean on to the beach. 해안에 밀려 닥치는 큰 파도. **2** a poor homeless man who picks up a living somehow on the islands of the Pacific. (태평양 제도의) 부랑자.

beach·head [bí:tʃhèd] *n.* 《mil.》 the first position taken by a military force landing on an enemy shore. 상륙 거점; 교두보.

bea·con [bí:kən] *n.* Ⓒ **1** a signal fire used to guide or warn. 횃불. **2** a radio signal used for guiding airplanes or ships. 무선 표지. **3** a lighthouse. 등대. **4** a warning. 경

고. ¶ *act as a* ~ *to* …에게 경고[지표]가 되다. **5** a radar device. 전파 탐지 장치. —*vt.* (P6) give light to (something) as a signal; furnish (something) with guiding lights. …에 대해 횃불을 비추다; 표지를 설치하다. ¶ *a ship assigned to* ~ *the shoals* 여울에 표지 설치를 임무로 하는 배. —*vi.* (P1) shine brightly. 빛나다. [O.E. *beacn*, →beckon]

•**bead** [bi:d] *n.* Ⓒ **1** a small ball or piece of glass, metal, etc. with a hole through it, used in a necklace. 구슬. ¶ *the beads of a necklace* 목걸이의 구슬. **2** 《*pl.*》 a necklace of such balls; a rosary. 구슬 목걸이; 로사리오; 염주. **3** a drop of a liquid. (떨어지는) 물방울. ¶ *beads of sweat* 땀방울. **4** a bit of metal at the end of a gun to aim by. (총의) 가늠쇠.
count [***say, tell***] ***one's beads,*** say one's prayers with a rosary. 로사리오의 기도를 드리다.
draw a bead on, aim at. …을 겨냥하다.
—*vi., vt.* (P3; 6) decorate (something) with beads; form beads. 구슬로 꾸미다; 구슬이 되다. [O.E. *biddan* pray]

bead·ing [bí:diŋ] *n.* 《archit.》 a long narrow ornamental piece of wood fixed at the top of a wall. 구슬선 장식.

bea·dle [bí:dl] *n.* 《Brit.》 a certain church officer in former times. 교구(敎區)의 사환. [O.E. *beodan* bid]

bea·gle [bí:gəl] *n.* **1** a kind of small hunting-dog. 사냥개의 하나. **2** a spy. 간첩. [?]

•**beak** [bi:k] *n.* Ⓒ **1** the bill of a bird, esp. as of an eagle, a hawk, etc. (수리·매 따위의) 부리. **2** anything which looks like a bill; a hooked nose of a man. 부리 모양의 것《주전자의 귀때 따위》; 매부리코. **3** 《Brit. *sl.*》 ⓐ a judge. 재판관. ¶ *be brought before the* ~ 재판관 앞에 끌려가다. ⓑ a schoolmaster. 교장. [Celt.]

beaked [bi:kt] *adj.* having a beak; shaped like a beak. 부리가 있는; 부리같이 생긴.

beak·er [bí:kər] *n.* Ⓒ **1** a large drinking glass with a wide mouth. (부리가 있는) 큰 컵. ¶ *consume a* ~ *of gin at one gulp* 한 잔의 진을 단숨에 들이켜다. **2** a thin glass cup with a pouring lip, used in chemical experiments. (화학 실험용) 비커. [N. *bikarr*]

:**beam** [bi:m] *n.* Ⓒ **1** a long piece of wood or metal used in building. 대들보. **2** a supporting bar of wood or metal. 가로대. ¶ *the* ~ *of a balance* 저울대 / *a* ~ *and scales* 저울. **3** a ray of light. 광선. ¶ *a* ~ *of light* 한 줄기 빛. **4** a bright look or smile. 밝은 표정; 미소. ¶ *the beams of a smile* 환한 미소. **5** a set of radio signals used to guide airplanes or ships. 신호 전파; 빔. ¶ *ride the* ~ 신호 전파에 따라 비행하다.
kick the beam, prove to be far the lighter; be defeated. 훨씬 가볍다; (…에 비해) 훨씬 못하다; 완패하다.
on one's beam ends, **a**) almost capsizing; in danger. 뒤집힐 것 같아; 위험에 직면하여. **b**) without money or help. 돈이나 도움이 없이.
on the beam, **a**) (of aircraft) following the direction of a guiding radio signal. 지시 전파에 인도되어. **b**) 《*colloq.*》 on the right track. 바른 궤도에; 바르게.
—*vi.* (P1,2A) **1** shine. 빛나다. ¶ *The sun beams.* 태양이 빛난다 / *the sun beaming overhead* 머리 위에 빛나는 태양. **2** smile happily. 방긋 웃다. ¶ ~ *with joy* 기뻐서 웃다.
—*vt.* (P6) send forth (rays or radio waves). …을 방사[방송]하다. ¶ *a program beamed to children* 어린이를 위한 방송 프로 / ~ *forth rays of light* 광선을 발하다 / *This program is beamed to Europe.* 이 프로그램은 유럽으로 방송된다. [O.E. *béam* tree]
beam upon, smile happily at (something). …에 방긋 웃다.

:**bean** [bi:n] *n.* Ⓒ **1** a seed used as a vegetable. 콩. **2** any seed shaped like a bean. (콩 비슷한) 열매. ¶ *coffee-beans* 커피 열매. **3** 《*sl.*》 a coin. 돈. ¶ *I haven't a* ~. 나는 돈이 없다.
be full of beans =***have too much beans,*** 《*colloq.*》 be very active; be in high spirits. 원기 왕성하다.
give someone beans, 《*sl.*》 **a**) punish or scold him fiercely. 엄벌하다; 몹시 꾸짖다. **b**) cause much pain. 몹시 괴롭히다.
not care a bean, not care at all. 조금도 개의치 않다.
not know beans, very stupid. 숙맥이다; 큰 바보다.
old bean, 《Brit. *sl.*; a very familiar form of address》 old boy. 여보게.
spill the beans, 《*colloq.*》 tell a secret; confess all. 비밀을 누설하다; 털어 놓다.
● **bean·like** [∠laik] *adj.* [O.E. *béan*]

bean-curd [bí:nkə̀:rd] *n.* food prepared from beans. 두부.

bean·feast [bí:nfì:st] *n.* 《Brit. *colloq.*》 any merry gathering usu. including some kind of feast. 연회; 축제.

bean·stalk [bínstɔ̀:k] *n.* Ⓒ the stem of a bean plant. 콩대.

:**bear**[1] [bɛər] *v.* (**bore, borne**) *vt.* **1** (P6,7,13) carry; bring. …을 나르다; 가지고 가다. ¶ ~ *a heavy load* 무거운 짐을 나르다 / ~ *logs in* 통나무를 운반해 들이다 / ~ *gifts to one's senior* 상사에게 선물을 갖고 가다. **2** (P6,7) support; hold up; sustain. …을 버티다[지탱하다]; 지다. ¶ *a table bearing several vases* 꽃병 몇 개가 놓이어 있는 테이블 / ~ *the weight of the roof* 지붕의 무게를 지탱하다 / ~ *a heavy burden* 무거운 짐을 지다. **3** (P6,7,9,20) put up with (something); endure. …에 견디다; 참다. ¶ ~ *the sorrow* 슬픔을 참다 / *I can't* ~ *your nagging.* 네 잔소린 견딜 수가 없다 / *I can't* ~ *any more pain.* 더 이상의 고통은 참을 수가 없다 / *I can't* ~ *living alone.* 혼자 사는 것에 견딜 수가 없

다 / *I cannot ~ the sight of him* 〔~ *to see him*〕. 그 녀석 꼴도 보기 싫다. 語法 can, could를 수반하여 부정문·의문문에 쓰임. **4** (P6,9) be fit for or worthy of (something). …에 적합하다; …할 만하다. ¶ *a treatise that does not ~ translation* 번역할 가치가 없는 논문 / *This cloth will ~ washing.* 이 천은 세탁할 수 있다 / *Your opinion will ~ repeating.* 자네 의견은 되풀이해 들을 가치가 있다. **5** (P6) experience; undergo. 경험하다; 받다. ¶ ~ *pain* 고통을 당하다. **6** (P6,14) 《pp. **born** except after *have* or before *by*》 give birth to (someone); produce; yield. …을 낳다; 나다; 내다. ¶ ~ *a child* 아이를 낳다 / *She has borne him two children.* 그녀는 그와의 사이에 두 아이를 낳았다 / *This tree bears much fruit.* 이 나무는 많은 열매를 맺는다. **7** (P6,13) give; bring forward; afford; aid. 주다; 제공하다. ¶ ~ *a hand* 거들(어 주)다 / ~ *witness* 〔*testimony*〕 증언하다; 증인이 되다 / ~ *someone company* 아무와 같이 가다. **8** (P6,7) have; hold. …을 갖다; 지니다; (마음에) 품다. ¶ ~ *something in mind* 기억해두다 / ~ *someone love* 아무에게 애정을 품다 / ~ *a grudge against* …에게 원한을 품다 / *This letter bears his signature.* 이 편지에는 그의 서명이 있다. **9** be able to stand (a test); withstand. (검사 따위에) 견디다. ¶ ~ *the test* 검사에 합격하다 / *a statement that will not ~ close examination* 그다지 신빙성이 없는 진술. **10** ⓐ carry or hold (oneself or a part of the body) in a certain way. …의 자세를 취하다. ¶ ~ *one's head high* 머리를 높이 들고 있다. ⓑ 《*reflexively*》 behave; conduct. …하게 행동하다. ¶ ~ *oneself with confidence* 자신 있게 행동하다 / ~ *oneself like a soldier* 군인답게 처신하다. — *vi.* **1** (P1) be able to support. 견디다; 버틸 수 있다. ¶ *The ice will ~.* 이 얼음판은 밟아도 괜찮을 테지. **2** (P2A) be fruitful; take effect. 열매를 맺다; 성과가 있다. **3** (P3) 《*on*》 have relation. 관계가 있다. ¶ *This story does not ~ on the question.* 이 이야긴 그 문제와 관계가 없다. **4** (P1,2A) behave; conduct. 행동하다. **5** (P2A) lie; be situated. …에 위치하다. **6** (P2A) 《*on*》 lean; press. 기대다; 누르다. ¶ ~ *on a stick* 지팡이에 기대다. [O.E. *beran*]

bear a hand in, help someone in doing something. 거들다.

bear down, **a**) press down. …을 누르다. ¶ *Don't ~ down so hard.* 그렇게 세게 누르지 마라. **b**) defeat; overcome. …에 이기다; 꺾어 누르다.

bear down on 〔***upon***〕, **a**) approach. …에 접근하다. **b**) put pressure on (someone). …을 압박하다.

bear fruit, have result, usu. good. 성과를 거두다.

bear hard on 〔***upon***〕, be severe to. …을 괴롭히다.

bear in mind, do not forget; remember. 기억하다.

bear off, take away; win; endure. 가져가다; (상(賞)을) 타다; 참다.

bear on 〔***upon***〕, **a**) force upon. 향하다. **b**) have relation to (something). …와 관계가 있다.

bear out, prove (a statement, etc.) to be true. …을 증명하다.

bear up, keep one's courage; do not despair. 용기를 잃지 않다; 절망하지 않다.

bear with, suffer with patience; endure; put up with. …을 참다; 견디다. ¶ *Bear with me till I have finished my story.* 이야기가 끝날 때까지 참아라.

:bear² [bɛər] *n.* Ⓒ **1** 《zool.》 a large animal with long, hard hair and a short tail. 곰. **2** a rough or rude person. 난폭한 사람. **3** 《*the B-*》 either of two groups of stars. 곰자리. ¶ *the Great Bear* 큰곰자리 / *the Little Bear* 작은곰자리. **4** a person who waits for a fall in prices in the stock-market, so that he can buy back stock at a lower price than that at which he had sold it. 주가(株價) 하락을 기대하는 사람(cf. *bull¹*). [E.]

bear·a·ble [bɛ́ərəbəl] *adj.* endurable. 견딜 수 있는. [→bear¹]

:beard [biərd] *n.* Ⓒ **1** the hair growing on the chin of an adult man. 턱수염(cf. *mustache, whisker*). **2** the hairs on the heads of plants, like oats or wheat. 꺼끄러기. — *vt.* (P6) take by the beard; face boldy. 수염을 꺼두르다; 대담히 맞서다. [E.]

beard the lion 〔***a man***〕 ***in his den,*** go and see him and show no fear. 필사적으로 맞서다.

beard·ed [bíərdid] *adj.* having a beard. 턱수염이 난.

beard·less [bíərdlis] *adj.* **1** having no beard. 턱수염이 없는. **2** young. 어린; 풋내기의.

bear·er [bɛ́ərər] *n.* Ⓒ **1** a person or thing that carries. 운반인; 운반물. **2** a person who holds a check, or who requests the payment for a check. (수표 등의) 지참인. ¶ *This check is payable to the ~.* 이 수표는 지참인불이다. **3** a tree or plant which produces fruit or flowers. 열매를 맺는〔꽃이 피는〕 나무. ¶ *That cherry tree is a good ~.* 저 벚나무는 열매가 많이 열린다. **4** a holder of a rank or office. 재직자(在職者). [→bear¹]

·bear·ing [bɛ́əriŋ] *n.* Ⓤ **1** manner; behavior. 태도. ¶ *a man of proud ~* 태도가 거만한 사람 / *a man of dignified ~* 태도에 위엄이 있는 사람 / *his ~ toward women* 여성에 대한 그의 태도. **2** ⓊⒸ relation. (다른 것에 대한) 관계. ¶ *direct* 〔*economic*〕 ~ 직접적〔경제적〕 관계 / *That has no ~ on this accident.* 그것은 이 사고와는 관계가 없다. **3** 《usu. *pl.*》 direction; relative position. 방향; 위치. ¶ *lose one's bearings* 방향을 잃다 / *consider* *the matter in all its bearings* 그 문제를 모든 면에서 생각하다. **4** 《*pl.*》 comprehension or appreciation of one's position, environment, or situation. (자기가 처한) 위치 〔입장〕의 인식; 정세의 파악. ¶ *bring someone to his bearings* 아무에게 자기의 입장을 깨닫게 하다; 아무를 반성케 하다 / *get* 〔*take*〕 *one's bearings* 자기가 있는 위치를 확인하다; 주위의 형세를 보다. **5** Ⓒ 《usu. *pl.*》 《mech.》 a part of a machine that supports a turning shaft. (기계의) 베어링. [→bear[1]]

past 〔***beyond***〕 ***all bearing,*** more than can be suffered or allowed. 도저히 참을 수 없는. ¶ *His conduct is beyond all* ～. 그의 행동은 도저히 참을 수 없다.

bear·ish [bɛ́əriʃ] *adj.* like a bear; rough. 곰 같은; 거친. [→bear[2]]

bear·skin [bɛ́ərskìn] *n.* Ⓤ the skin or fur of a bear; Ⓒ a coat made of such skin or fur. 곰(털)가죽; 곰(털)가죽으로 만든 코트. [↑]

:beast [biːst] *n.* **1** Ⓒ any four-footed animal, esp. a large and fierce one. (네 발) 짐승; 맹수. ¶ *wild beasts* 야수. **2** 《*collectively*》 cattle. 가축(家畜). **3** Ⓒ a coarse, brutal person. 짐승같은 놈; 비인간(非人間). ¶ *You* ～*!* 개새끼. ●**beast·like** [⌐làik] *adj.* [L. *bestia*]

beast·ly [bíːstli] *adj.* (**-li·er, -li·est**) **1** like a beast; brutal; dirty. 짐승 같은; 흉악한; 더러운. ¶ ～ *appetites* 수욕(獸慾) / *a* ～ *talk* 추잡한 이야기. **2** 《Brit. *colloq.*》 unpleasant; nasty. 불쾌한; 고약한; 지독한. ¶ ～ *weather* 고약한 날씨 / *a* ～ *headache* 심한 두통(頭痛). —*adv.* 《*colloq.*》 very; unpleasantly. 몹시; 지독히; 불쾌하게. ¶ ～ *hard* 아주 단단한 / ～ *wet* 흠뻑 젖어 / ～ *drunk* 고주망태가 되어.

:beat [biːt] *v.* (**beat, beat·en** or **beat**) *vt.* **1** (P6) strike (something) again and again. …을 계속해서 치다. ¶ ～ *a drum* 계속 북을 치다 / ～ *a carpet* 양탄자를 두드려 먼지를 떨다. **2** (P6,7) punish (someone) by hitting. (벌로) …를 때리다. ¶ ～ *a truant* 게으름뱅이를 때리다 / *The boy deserves to be well beaten.* 그 아이는 흠씬 매를 맞아 마땅하다. **3** (P6,7,13) win a victory over (someone); defeat; overcome. …에 이기다; …을 타도하다. ¶ ～ *the enemy* 적에게 이기다 / ～ *the rival in the election* 선거에서 상대를 패배시키다 / ～ *him at chess* 체스에서 그를 이기다 / *I can easily* ～ *him at golf.* 골프에서 그를 손쉽게 이길 수 있다 / *That beats me.* 그건 나에게 너무 어렵다. **4** (P6) puzzle; perplex. …을 괴롭히다. **5** (P6,7,13) make (something) flat; change the shape of (metal) with a hammer. 두드려 펴다. **6** (P6) show (rhythm or time) in music by hand or stick. 박자를 맞추다. **7** (P6,7,13) stir (eggs, cream, etc.) vigorously. 휘저어 섞다. ¶ ～ (*up*) *eggs* 달걀을 휘젓다 / ～ *drugs in a mortar* 유발로 약을 갈아 섞다. **8** (P6) move (wings) up and down. (날개 따위를) 위아래로 움직이다. ¶ *The bird beats its wings.* 새가 날개친다. **9** (P6) make flat by repeated treading. 밟아 다지다. ¶ ～ *a track* 길을 밟아 다지다. —*vi.* (P1,2A,3) **1** strike again and again; throb. 계속 치다; 고동치다. ¶ *The heart beats.* 심장이 뛴다. **2** make a sound by being beaten. (두드려 맞아) 울리다. ¶ ～ *at the door* 문을 노크하다 / *The drums* ～ *loudly.* 북이 크게 울렸다.

beat about for, search for. …을 찾아다니다.

beat back, make (an enemy, a dog, etc.) retreat; defeat. …을 격퇴하다.

beat down, **a**) defeat; overcome. 패배시키다; 타도하다. **b**) make (someone) accept a lower price. 값을 깎다.

beat in, push into. 처박다.

beat into (*one's head*), teach (a subject) with difficulty. …을 머릿속에 주입시키다.

beat it, run away. (급히) 떠나다; 나가다; 달아나다.

beat off, drive. 쫓아버리다; 격퇴하다.

beat out, **a**) make (metal) flat by beating. 두들겨 …을 펴다. **b**) win a victory over (someone). …에게 이기다. **c**) make (someone) tired. …을 지치게 하다.

beat up, **a**) sail against the wind. 바람을 거슬러 항행하다. **b**) attack (an enemy) suddenly. …을 급습하다. **c**) mix (eggs, cream, etc.) by stirring. …을 휘저어 섞다. **d**) gather (persons) together. …을 모으다; 소집하다. **e**) make clear; solve. 분명히 하다; 해결하다.

—*n.* Ⓒ **1** a stroke or blow made again and again as of the heart or a drum. 침; 심장의 고동; 계속 치는 소리. ¶ *the* ～ *of the drum* 계속 치는 북소리. **2** 《mus.》 a unit of rhythm in music. 박자. ¶ *A good dancer never misses a* ～. 잘 추는 무용수는 박자를 틀리지 않는다. **3** a regular or assigned course of a policeman or a watchman. 순찰 구역. ¶ *The watchman is on his* ～. 그 경비원은 순찰중이다.

be off one's beat, be different from one's usual work. 전문 영역 밖이다.

—*adj.* tired-out. 지친. [O.E. *beatan*]

dead beat, exhausted, tired-out. 기진맥진한.

:beat·en [bíːtn] *v.* pp. of **beat.**

—*adj.* **1** whipped. 매맞은. **2** defeated; overcome; conquered. 진; 정복된. **3** shaped by beating. 두들겨 편. ¶ *This bowl is made of* ～ *silver.* 이 그릇은 은을 두드려서 만들었다. **4** hardened by footsteps; much used. 밟아 다(져)진; 많이 쓰인. ¶ *the* ～ *path* 밟아 다져진 길. **5** exhausted; worn out. 기진맥진한.

beat·er [bíːtər] *n.* Ⓒ **1** a person or thing that beats. 치는 사람; 두드리는 기구. **2** a person who makes animals or birds come out from their hiding place in hunting. (사냥의) 몰이꾼. **3** an instrument for beating eggs, cream, etc. (달걀 따위를) 휘젓는 기구.

beat generation [∠-∠-] *n.* disillusioned members of the generation following the Second World War. 비트족.

be·a·tif·ic [bìːətífik] *adj.* **1** giving blessings or happiness. 축복을 내리는. **2** blissful; happy. 행복에 넘친. [L. *beatus* blessed]

be·at·i·fy [biːǽtəfài] *vt.* (**-fied**) (P6) **1** make (someone) happy. …을 행복하게 하다. **2** 《Cath.》 declare (a dead person) to be among the blessed in heaven. …에게 시복(諡福)하다. ●**be·at·i·fi·ca·tion** [biːæ̀təfikéiʃən] *n.* [↑]

beat·ing [bíːtiŋ] *n.* UC **1** whipping, esp. as punishment. 매질. **2** a severe defeat. 패배. ¶ *give the enemy a thorough* ~ 적에게 철저한 패배를 안겨주다. **3** the act of throbbing. 고동. ¶ *the* ~ *of the heart* 심장의 고동. [→beat]

be·at·i·tude [biːǽtətjùːd] *n.* U supreme and perfect happiness; blessing. 더없는〔무상(無上)의〕 행복; 지복(至福). [→beatific]

beat·nik [bíːtnik] *n.* C 《colloq.》 a member of persons who reject conventional things and social inhibitions. 비트족(族)의 사람. [→beat]

Be·a·trice [bíːətris] *n.* a woman's name. 여자의 이름.

beau [bou] *n.* C (*pl.* **beaus** or **beaux**) **1** a man who pays much attention to the fashion of his clothes; a dandy. 멋쟁이 남자. **2** a male companion or escort for a girl or woman; a lover; a suitor. 여성의 상대역〔호위역〕인 남성; 애인. [L. *bellus* pretty]

beau·te·ous [bjúːtiəs] *adj.* 《poet.》 beautiful. 아름다운.

beau·ti·cian [bjuːtíʃən] *n.* a person who runs or works in a beauty parlor. 미용사.

:beau·ti·ful [bjúːtəfəl] *adj.* pleasant to the eye, ear, or mind; lovely; excellent. 아름다운; 예쁜; 훌륭한. ¶ *a* ~ *picture* 〔*flower, voice, woman*〕 아름다운 그림〔꽃, 목소리, 여자〕. [L. **bellus** pretty, →beau]

·beau·ti·ful·ly [bjúːtəfəli] *adv.* excellently. 훌륭하게.

beau·ti·fy [bjúːtəfài] *vt.* (**-fied**) (P6) make (something) beautiful; adorn. 아름답게 하다; 꾸미다. ¶ ~ *a garden with flowers* 꽃으로 정원을 아름답게 꾸미다. — *vi.* become beautiful. 아름답게 되다.

:beau·ty [bjúːti] *n.* (*pl.* **-ties**) **1** U a quality which pleases the mind and senses. 미(美); 아름다움. ¶ *physical* ~ 육체미 / *manly* ~ 남성미 / *her radiant* ~ 그녀의 눈부신 아름다움. **2** C something beautiful. 아름다운 것. ¶ *the beauties of nature* 자연의 미관. **3** C a beautiful girl or woman; 《*the* ~》《*collectively*》 beautiful girls or women. 미인; 미인들. ¶ *She was one of the famous beauties of the last century.* 그녀는 지난 세기의 유명한 미인들 중의 한 사람이었다. [→beau]

beauty parlor 〔**salon**〕 [∠- ∠-〔-∠〕] *n.* a place where women have their hair, skin and fingernail cared for. 미장원.

beauty sleep [∠-∠] *n.* sleep early in the night or before midnight. 초저녁잠.

beauty spot [∠-∠] *n.* **1** a small piece of black material stuck on to the face as an ornament. 멋으로 붙인 점. **2** a mole on the face. 사마귀; 점. **3** a specially beautiful place in a country. 명승지.

beaux [bouz] *n.* pl. of **beau.**

·bea·ver[1] [bíːvər] *n.* **1** C 《zool.》 a four-legged animal with soft fur and a flat tail living both in water and on land. 비버. **2** U its soft and brown fur. 비버의 모피. **3** C a high silk hat. 실크 해트. **4** U a heavy woolen cloth. 두터운 나사지(羅紗地). [O.E. *beofor*]

bea·ver[2] [bíːvər] *n.* the lower face guard of a helmet. (투구의) 턱가리개. [O.F. *bavière* bib]

be·calm [bikáːm] *vt.* **1** make (something) calm; tranquilize. …을 가라앉히다. **2** make (a ship) unable to move because of lack of wind. 바람이 자서 (돛배를) 움직일 수 없게 하다. ¶ *The ship was becalmed for ten days.* 그 배는 바람이 자서 10일간이나 움직일 수 없었다. [be-→calm]

be·calmed [bikáːmd] *adj.* (of a ship) having no wind and being unable to move. 바람이 자서 움직일 수 없게 되어. [↑]

:be·came [bikéim] *v.* p. of **become.**

:be·cause [bikɔ́ːz, -káz / -kɔ́z] *conj.* for the reason that; since; for. …라는 이유로〔원인으로〕; 왜냐하면; …때문에〔이므로〕. ¶ *He plays baseball* ~ *he likes it.* 그는 좋아하기 때문에 야구 경기를 한다 / *Why can't you come? —Because I'm busy.* 왜 올 수가 없지. —바쁘기 때문에. [*by, cause*]

because of, on account of. …때문에. ¶ *Because of the accident the train was an hour late.* 사고 때문에 열차는 한 시간 늦었다.

be·chance [bitʃǽns, -tʃáːns] *vi.* (P1,4) happen; come about. 일어나다. [be-]

beche-de-mer [bèiʃdəmέər] *n.* 《F.》 a sea-slug. 해삼.

beck[1] [bek] *n.* C a nod or other gesture, as of a call or command. 고갯짓; 손짓. [→ beckon]

be at someone's beck (***and call***), be under someone's complete control. …가 시키는 대로 하다.

have someone at one's beck, have someone under one's control. …를 턱으로〔마음대로〕 부리다.

beck[2] [bek] *n.* small stream. 시내. [N.]

·beck·on [békən] *vi., vt.* (P1;6,7,20) 《*to*》 make a signal by a motion of the head or hand. 고갯짓〔손짓〕하다; 아무에게 신호하다. ¶ *He beckoned* (*to*) *me to enter.* 그는 내게 들어오라고 손짓했다. [O.E. *biecnan*, → beacon]

be·cloud [bikláud] *vt.* (P6) darken; obscure. …을 어둡게〔흐리게〕 하다; 애매하게 하다. ¶ *His mind was beclouded.* 그의 마음은 어두워졌다. [be-, →cloud]

:be·come [bikʌ́m] *v.* (**-came, -come**) *vi.* **1** (P5) come or grow to be. …이 되다. ¶ ~ *king* 〔*rich, noted*〕 임금이〔부자가, 유명하게〕 되다. **2** (P3) 《*of*》 happen to; be the end of. …하게 되다. ¶ *What has* ~ *of him?* 그는 어떻게 되었는가 / *What will* ~ *of you if you continue such conduct?* 그런 행동을 계속한다면 어찌 되겠는가. — *vt.* (P6) be suitable to; look well on (something or someone). …에 어울리다; 걸맞다. ¶ *This hat becomes you.* 이 모자는 당신에게 어울린다. [be-, come]

be·com·ing [bikʌ́miŋ] *adj.* suitable; proper. 어울리는. ¶ *Her new hat is very* ~ *to* 〔*on*〕 *her.* 그녀의 새 모자는 그녀에게 아주 잘 어울린다 / *It is not* ~ *in a man to tell a lie.* 그것은 거짓말하는 사람에게는 어울리지 않는다.

be·com·ing·ly [bikʌ́miŋli] *adv.* suitably. 걸맞게; 어울리게.

:bed [bed] *n.* Ⓒ **1** a piece of furniture for sleeping on. 침대. ¶ *make a* ~ 잠자리를 깔다 / *stay* 〔*lie*〕 *in* ~ 잠자고 있다 / *a* ~ *of sickness* 병상(病床). **2** an animal's resting place; a litter. 동물의 잠자리; 깔짚. **3** a piece of ground for growing plants. 못자리; 화단. ¶ *an oyster* ~ 굴 양식장 / *a flower* ~ 화단. **4** a bottom or base on which a thing rests. 토대; 기초. ¶ *They set the pole in a* ~ *of concrete.* 그들은 콘크리트 바닥에 기둥을 세웠다. **5** the bottom of a river. 하상(河床); 강바닥. ¶ *the* ~ *of the sea* 해저(海底). **6** a layer of rock or earth. 암층(岩層); 지층. ¶ *a* ~ *of coal* 석탄층.

a bed of roses, an easy, pleasant position; a happy, comfortable state. 안락한 생활.

be brought to bed, give birth to a child. 출산〔분만〕하다.

bed and board, sleeping accommodations and meals; the married state. 숙박과 식사; 부부 관계; 결혼 생활. ¶ *separate from* ~ *and board* 부부가 별거하다.

be too fond of one's bed, be lazy. 게으르다.

die in one's bed, die of natural causes. 제명에 죽다.

get out of bed on the wrong side, be in a bad temper for the day. 아침부터 기분이 좋지 않다.

go to bed, lie down in order to sleep. 잠자리에 들다.

in a narrow bed, in the grave. 무덤에.

keep one's bed, be in bed from illness. 몸져 누워 있다.

lie in the bed one has made, accept the results of one's acts. 자업 자득의 보답을 받다.

make a bed, arrange the bedclothes on a bed. 잠자리를 펴다〔개다〕.

take to one's bed, go to bed because one is ill. 앓아 눕다.

— *vt.* (**bed·ded, bed·ding**) (P6,7) **1** prepare a bed for (someone). …을 위해 잠자리를 마련하다. **2** put to bed. 재우다. **3** plant (grass, etc.) in a bed. …을 화단〔못자리〕에 심다. **4** lay (things) flat or in order. 반반하게 놓다; 늘어놓다. **5** arrange in a layer. 층층이 쌓다.

— *vi.* (P1) 《*down*》 go to bed; make one's bed (on the floor, etc.) 잠자리에 들다; 잠자리를 깔다. ¶ *He bedded down on the sofa.* 소파에서 잤다. [E.]

be·dab·ble [bidǽbəl] *vt.* (P6,13) sprinkle. (물 따위)를 튀기다. [be-, →dabble]

be·daub [bidɔ́:b] *vt.* (P6,13) smear (something) with dirty or oily material; decorate (something) in a showy way. 처덕처덕 바르다; 야하게 꾸미다. [be-, →daub]

bed·bug [bédbʌ̀g] *n.* Ⓒ 《U.S.》 a small bloodsucking insect. 빈대. [→bed]

bed·cham·ber [bédtʃèimbər] *n.* Ⓒ a bedroom; a sleeping room. 침실.

bed·clothes [bédklòuz, -klòuðz] *n. pl.* the sheets, blankets, quilts, etc. used on a bed. 침구《요를 제외한》.

bed·ding [bédiŋ] *n.* Ⓤ **1** the materials for a bed. 침구. **2** the litter for cattle. (마소를 위한) 깔짚. **3** a foundation of any kind. 토대; 기초.

be·deck [bidék] *vt.* (P6) decorate; ornament; cover with. 꾸미다; …로 뒤덮이다. ¶ *a girl bedecked with flowers* 〔*jewels*〕 꽃〔보석〕으로 장식한 소녀 / *a building bedecked with flags* 깃발로 뒤덮인 건물. [be-, →deck]

be·dew [bidjú:] *vt.* (P6,13) make something wet with dew or something like dew. …을 이슬〔눈물〕로 적시다. [be-]

bed·fel·low [bédfèlou] *n.* Ⓒ **1** a wife. 아내. **2** a companion. 친구; 동료. [→bed]

be·dim [bidím] *vt.* (**-dimmed, -dim·ming**) (P6,13) 《*with*》 make (something) dark or dim. (눈·마음 따위)를 흐리게 하다. ¶ *eyes bedimmed with tears* 눈물로 흐려진 눈. [be-]

be·di·zen [bidáizən, -dízən] *vt.* (P6,13) 《*with*》 dress or decorate (something) in a showy way. …을 야하게 꾸미다. [be-]

bed·lam [bédləm] *n.* Ⓒ **1** a scene of great confusion or disorder. 혼란. **2** a hospital for mad persons; a madhouse. 정신 병원. [→Bethlehem]

bed·lam·ite [bédləmàit] *n.* Ⓒ a lunatic. 정신병자. [↑]

bed·mak·er [bédmèikər] *n.* Ⓒ a servant tending college rooms. 침실 담당 사환 《Oxford, Cambridge 대학의》. [→bed]

Bed·ou·in [béduin, bédwin] *n.* Ⓒ a wandering Arab of the desert in Arabia, Syria, or northern Africa. 베두인《아라비아·시리아·북아프리카 사막의 유목 아랍인》. [Arab. *badawin* =dweller in desert]

bed·plate [bédplèit] *n.* the base of a machine. 대좌(臺座)《기계 설치용》. [→bed]

bed·post [bédpòust] *n.* Ⓒ a supporting post of a bed. 침대의 지주〔다리〕.

be·drag·gle [bidrǽgəl] *vt.* (P6) make (a dress, etc.) weak and dirty by dragging. (옷자락 따위)를 질질 끌어서 더럽히다. [be-]

bed·rid·den [bédrìdn] *adj.* in bed for a long time because of age or sickness. 몸져 누워 있는; (오랫동안) 자리 보전하고 있는《환자 따위》. [→bed]

bed·rock [bédràk / -rɔ̀k] *n.* ⓊⒸ **1** the solid rock beneath the soil. 상암(床岩). **2** a firm foundation. 단단한 토대; 기반.

get down to bedrock, get to the real facts and truth 진상을 규명하다.

:bed·room [bédrù:m, -rùm] *n.* Ⓒ a room used for sleeping. 침실(寢室).

bed·side [bédsàid] *n.* Ⓒ 《*one's* ～》 the side of a bed. 침대 곁. ¶ *sit by a sick person's* ～ 환자의 베갯머리에 앉아 병구완하다.

bed·sore [bédsɔ̀:r] *n.* Ⓒ (of a sick person) a sore caused by lying too long in bed. (환자의) 욕창(褥瘡).

bed·spread [bédsprèd] *n.* Ⓒ a cover for a bed. 침대 커버.

bed·stead [bédstèd] *n.* Ⓒ the framework of a bed. 침대 틀〔프레임〕.

bed·time [bédtàim] *n.* Ⓤ the time to go to bed. 취침 시각. ¶ *It is past* ～. 취침 시각이 지났다 / *His regular* ～ *is nine o'clock.* 그의 일상 취침 시각은 9시이다.

:bee [bi:] *n.* Ⓒ **1** an insect with four wings and a sting that gathers honey from flowers. 꿀벌. ¶ *as busy as a* ～ 매우 바쁜 / *a queen* ～ 여왕벌 / *a working* ～ 일벌. **2** a busy worker. 일꾼. **3** 《chiefly U.S.》 a gathering for work or amusement. (일·경기 따위의) 모임; 회합. ¶ *a spelling* ～ 철자 겨루기 / *a sewing* ～ 재봉 솜씨 겨루기 모임. [E.]

have a bee in one's bonnet 〔***head, brain***〕, **a**) think of one thing only. 한 가지만을 골똘히 생각하다. **b**) have eccentric ideas; be slightly mad on a certain point. 야릇한 생각에 사로잡혀 있다; 정신이 이상하다.

swarm like bees, be crowded. 벌떼처럼 모이다; 운집하다.

beech [bi:tʃ] *n.* **1** Ⓒ 《bot.》 a tree having a smooth gray bark and bearing nuts that can be eaten. 너도밤나무. **2** Ⓤ its wood. 그 목재. [E.]

beech·en [bí:tʃən] *adj.* made of beechwood. 너도밤나무의 재목으로 만든. [↑]

bee·eat·er [bí:ì:tər] *n.* a small pretty bird which eats bees. 딱새류. [→bee]

:beef [bi:f] *n.* (*pl.* **beeves**) **1** Ⓤ meat from a cow or bull. 쇠고기. ¶ ～ *cattle* 육우(肉牛). **2** Ⓒ 《*pl.*》 adult cows or bulls raised for their meat. 육우(肉牛). ¶ *Beeves are shipped from the farm to the city.* 비육우는 사육장에서 도시에 배로 반입된다. **3** Ⓤ strength. 힘. ¶ *put too much* ～ *into a stroke* (*at tennis, billiards, etc.*) (테니스·당구 따위에서) 타구(打球)에 너무 힘을 들이다. [L. *bos* ox]

beef·eat·er [bí:fì:tər] *n.* Ⓒ **1** a person who eats beef. 쇠고기를 먹는 사람. **2** a guardsman of English royalty. 영국 왕실 근위병. **3** a guard of the Tower of London. 런던 탑의 수위.

beef·steak [bí:fstèik] *n.* ⓊⒸ a slice of beef, broiled or fried, or suitable for broiling or frying. 두껍게 저민 쇠고깃점; 비프스테이크.

beef tea [⌐⌐] *n.* a strong beef soup. 진한 고기 수프.

beef·y [bí:fi] *adj.* (**beef·i·er, beef·i·est**) **1** like beef. 쇠고기 같은. **2** strong; solid. 억센; 튼튼한. ¶ *a* ～ *young man* 억센 젊은이. ● **beef·i·ness** [-nis] *n.* [→beef]

bee·hive [bí:hàiv] *n.* Ⓒ a box made for bees in which they live. 벌통. [→bee]

bee·keep·er [bí:kì:pər] *n.* Ⓒ a person who keeps bees. 벌 치는 사람; 양봉가.

bee·line [bí:làin] *n.* Ⓒ a direct line. 일직선. ¶ *in a* ～ 일직선으로.

make 〔***take, strike***〕 ***a beeline for,*** go straight and quickly towards. …쪽으로 곧장 가다〔직행하다〕. ¶ *take* 〔*strike*〕 *a* ～ *for the door* 문쪽으로 곧장 가다 / *The children made a* ～ *for the cakes.* 아이들은 케이크 쪽으로 곧장 갔다.

Be·el·ze·bub [bi:élzəbʌ̀b, bí:lzə-] *n.* 《Bible》 the Devil. 악마. [Heb.＝fly-load]

:been [bin / bi:n, bin] *v.* pp. of **be.**

***beer** [biər] *n.* Ⓤ an alcoholic drink made from dried grain flavored with hops; Ⓒ a drink or a glass of beer. 맥주; 한 잔의 맥주. ¶ *draft* ～ 생맥주 / *ginger* ～ 진저 비어 / *a* ～ *place* 비어홀 / *be in* ～ 맥주에 취해 있다. [O.E. *beor*]

think no small beer of oneself, have a high opinion of oneself. 자부심이 강하다.

beer·y [bíəri] *adj.* of beer; a little drunk (with beer). 맥주의; (맥주에) 약간 취한.

beest·ings [bí:stiŋz] *n. pl.* the first milk from a cow. 초유(初乳). [E.]

bees·wax [bí:zwæ̀ks] *n.* Ⓤ wax produced by bees. 밀랍. [→bee]

beet [bi:t] *n.* Ⓒ 《bot.》 **1** a plant having a fleshy red or white root that is eaten. 비트《사탕무·근대 따위》. ¶ *a sugar* ～ 첨채(甜菜); 사탕무. **2** 《U.S.》 the root of such a plant. 그 뿌리. ● **beet·like** [-làik] *adj.* [E.]

***Bee·tho·ven** [béitouvən], **Ludwig van** *n.* (1770-1827) a German musical composer. 베토벤.

bee·tle[1] [bí:tl] *n.* Ⓒ **1** an insect having hard wing-cases. 투구벌레. **2** a short-sighted person. 근시(近視)인 사람. [O.E. *bitan* bite]

as blind as a beetle, almost blind. 지독한 근시의.

bee·tle[2] [bí:tl] *n.* a heavy wooden mallet. 큰 메. ― *vt.* (P6) beat with a beetle. 큰 메로 치다. [Teut. *bautan* beat]

bee·tle[3] [bí:tl] *vi.* (P1) project, overhang. 돌

출하다. ¶ *Great cliffs beetled above the narrow path.* 깎아지른 절벽이 그 협로 위로 쑥 튀어나와 있었다. — *adj.* **1** standing out; overhanging. 불쑥 나온. **2** shaggy; frowning. 털이 많은; 찌푸린 얼굴의. ¶ *a beetle-browed old man* 눈썹이 짙은 노인. [→bite]

bee·tling [bíːtliŋ] *adj.* overhanging; standing out. 툭 튀어나온; 쑥 내민. ¶ ~ *cliffs* 툭 튀어나온 절벽. [↑]

beet root [ˊ ˋ] *n.* the root of a beet plant. 첨채(甜菜)의 뿌리. [*beet*]

beet sugar [ˊ ˋ–] *n.* sugar made from white beets. 첨채당(甜菜糖)《사탕무로 만든 설탕》.

beeves [biːvz] *n.* pl. of **beef.**

B.E.F. British Expeditionary Forces.

be·fall [bifɔ́ːl] *vt., vi.* (**-fell, -fall·en**) (P6; 1) (of a bad matter) happen; happen to (someone). (좋지 않은 일이) 일어나다; 생기다. ¶ *What befell him?* 그에게 무슨 일이 생겼나 / *Evil befell the old man.* 그 노인에게 재앙이 닥쳤다. [be-]

be·fall·en [bifɔ́ːlən] *v.* pp. of **befall.**

be·fell [bifél] *v.* p. of **befall.**

be·fit [bifít] *vt.* (**-fit·ted, -fit·ting**) (P6) be suited to (something); become. …에 알맞다; 걸맞다. ¶ *Her clothes did not* ~ *the occasion.* 그의 의복은 그 행사에 걸맞지 않았다 / *It does not* ~ *you to do so.* 그런 짓을 하다니 자네답지 않네. [be-]

be·fit·ting [bifítiŋ] *adj.* suitable; becoming. 알맞은; 어울리는; 걸맞은.

be·fit·ting·ly [bifítiŋli] *adv.* suitably; properly. 알맞게; 걸맞게.

be·fog [bifág, -fɔ́(ː)g] *vt.* (**-fogged, -fog·ging**) (P6) **1** hide (something) in fog. …을 안개로 가리다. **2** make unclear; obscure; confuse. 애매[불분명]하게 하다; 어리둥절하게 하다; 곤혹시키다. ¶ *The issue was befogged with bias.* 편견으로 인해 논점이 흐려졌다. [be-]

be·fool [bifúːl] *vt.* (P6) make a fool of (someone); deceive. …을 놀리다; 속이다. ¶ *innocents befooled by confidence men* 사기꾼들에게 속아넘어간 선량한 사람들.

:be·fore [bifɔ́ːr] *adv.* (opp. after, behind) **1** (of place) ahead; in front. 앞에[을]; 전면에(서). ¶ *his garment buttoned* ~ 앞에 단추가 달린 그의 옷 / *run on* ~ 앞서서 뛰어가다 / *send a person* ~ 앞에 사람을 보내다 / ~ *and behind* 앞과 뒤에. **2** (of time) earlier; previously; already. 앞서; 전에; 이미. ¶ *three months* ~ (그때부터) 3개월 전에 / *(the) day* ~ 전날 / *as* ~ 종전대로 / *begin at noon, not* ~ 정각 정오에 시작하다 / *I have been there* ~. 전에 그 곳에 간 적이 있다 / *You were never late* ~. 넌 전엔 늦은 적이 없었다 / *I came here yesterday, but he came two days* ~. 나는 어제 왔는데 그는 나보다도 이틀 전에 왔다.

long before, a long time earlier (than that). (그보다) 오래 전에.

— *prep.* **1** in front of; ahead of. …의 앞에 (opp. behind). ¶ *a lawn* ~ *a house* 집앞의 잔디밭 / *his shadow advancing* ~ *him* 앞서 나아가는 그의 그림자 / *walk* ~ *someone* 아무의 앞에서 걸어가다 / *She stood* ~ *the door.* 그녀는 문 앞에 서 있었다 / *Put it* ~ *the mirror.* 그것을 거울 앞에 두어라. **2** earlier than. …보다 일찍; (이)전에. ¶ *the day* ~ *yesterday* 그저께 / *ten minutes* ~ *ten,* 10시 10분 전 / ~ *daylight* 해뜨기 전에 / *life* ~ *the war* 전전(戰前)의 생활 / *Come* ~ *five o'clock.* 다섯시 전에 오시오 / *They arrived* ~ *me.* 그들은 나보다 앞서 도착했다. **3** in the presence of. …의 면전에(서). ¶ *appear* ~ *an audience* 청중 앞에 모습을 나타내다 / *speak* ~ *the conference* 회의 석상에서 연설하다 / *depreciate oneself* ~ *one's betters* 어른들 앞에서 겸양하다 / *bring a question* ~ *a meeting* 회의에 문제를 제기하다 / *The question* ~ *us is a very difficult one.* 우리들 앞에 놓인 문제는 매우 어려운 문제다. **4** 《*colloq.*》 rather than. …보다는 오히려[차라리]. ¶ *die* ~ *yielding* 굴복하느니 죽음을 택하다 / *I would do anything* ~ *that.* 무엇이라도 하겠으나 그것만은 싫다. **5** in the future of; awaiting. …의 전도[장래]에; …을 기다리고. ¶ *The golden age is* ~ *us.* 우리의 전도에는 황금 시대가 기다리고 있다 / *The hardest task is* ~ *us.* 가장 곤란한 일이 우리 앞에 가로놓여 있다 / *His whole life is* ~ *him.* 그의 생애는 이제부터다 / *The Christmas holidays were* ~ *them.* 크리스마스 휴가가 그들을 기다리고 있었다. **6** higher in rank or worth; superior to; in precedence of. …보다 상위[우위]에; …에 우선하여; …보다 중요하게. ¶ *put quality* ~ *quantity* 양보다 질을 중시하다 / *put safety* ~ *everything else* 무엇보다도 안전 제일로 하다 / *We put freedom* ~ *fame.* 명성보다 자유를 중요시한다.

before long, soon. 오래지 않아; 곧.

before one's time, ahead of one's time. 태어나기 전에; 시대에 앞서.

carry all before one, be successful in everything one attempts. 하는 모든 일에 성공하다.

sail before the mast, be on a sailing ship as an ordinary seaman, not as an officer. 평선원으로 일하다.

sail before the wind, sail with the wind behind 순풍을 받고 달리다.

— *conj.* **1** earlier than. …보다 일찍; …전에. ¶ *We got home* ~ *it got dark.* 어두워지기 전에 집에 도착했다 / *He arrived* ~ *I (had) expected.* 예상보다 일찍 도착했다 / *Take it down* ~ *you forget.* 잊어버리기 전에 적어 두어라 / *I had not waited long* ~ *he came.* 그가 오기까지 오래 기다리지 않았다. **2** rather than. …하느니(차라리). ¶ *I would die* ~ *I told him.* 그에게 말하느니 죽겠다 / *He will starve* ~ *he will steal.* 그는 도둑질을 하느니 차라리 굶을게다. [be-, →fore]

before one knows where one is, in an instant; very quickly. 순식간에; 눈깜짝할 사이에.

be·fore·hand [bifɔ́ːrhæ̀nd] *adv.* ahead of time; in advance. 미리; 사전에(opp. behindhand). ¶ *get everything ready* ~ 모든 일을 미리 준비하다 / *You are rather* ~ *in your suspicions.* 자넨 지나치게 마음을 쓰네.

be·fore·men·tioned [bifɔ́ːrmènʃənd] *adj.* mentioned in an earlier part of a speeech or document. 전술〔전기〕한.

be·foul [bifául] *vt.* (P6) 《*lit.*》 make (something) dirty. …을 더럽히다. [be-]

be·friend [bifrénd] *vt.* (P6) act as a friend to (someone); aid. …편이 되다; …을 돕다. ¶ ~ *the poor* 가난한 사람들의 편이 되다. [be-]

be·fud·dle [bifʌ́dl] *vt.* (P6) make stupid with drink; confuse. 억병으로 취하게 하다; 미혹시키다. [be-]

:beg [beg] *v.* (**begged, beg·ging**) *vt.* **1** (P6, 13) 《*of, for*》 ask for (money, food, etc.) as a kindness. …을 (주기를) 빌다; 구걸하다. ¶ *I begged something to eat of him.* 그에게 먹을 것을 청했다 / *I* ~ *a favor of you.* =*I have a favor to* ~ *of you.* 부탁이 있습니다 / *May I* ~ *you some money?* 돈 좀 주시겠습니까. **2** (P6,11,20) ask earnestly; entreat; request. …을 부탁〔간청〕하다. ¶ ~ *one's life* 살려 달라고 애걸 복걸하다 / *I begged him to forgive me* 〔*to keep silent*〕. 나는 그에게 용서해 달라고 간절히 빌었다〔침묵을 지켜 달라고 부탁했다〕 / *I* ~ (*that*) *you will do the work.* 제발 그 일을 해 주십시오 / *I* ~ *you to tell the truth.* 사실을 말씀해 주십시오. — *vi.* (P1,2A,3) **1** live as a beggar. 구걸하다; 비럭질하다. ¶ ~ *on the street* 거리에서 구걸하다 / ~ *from door to door* 집집이 구걸하며 다니다. **2** 《*for*》 ask earnestly. 부탁〔간청〕하다. ¶ ~ *for mercy* 자비를 청하다 / *He begged for something to do.* 그는 어떤 일을 하게 해 달라고 간청했다. [Du.]

beg off, **a**) request or obtain release from an obligation, promise, ete. (의무·약속 따위의) 면제를 간청하다; 면제해 받다. **b**) save someone from punishment. 용서받게 해 주다.

beg the question, take for granted the very thing argued about. (논증되고 있는 미결의 문제를) 당연한 것으로 생각하다〔논거(論據)로 삼다〕; 논점을 교묘히 피하다.

go begging, not to be bought or wanted by anyone. 아무도 원하는 사람이 없다; 살 사람이 없다.

I beg leave to…, I ask permission to…. 삼가 …하는 것의 허락을 빕니다.

I beg to be excused, I wish to refuse the invitaion. 사절하고자 합니다.

I beg your pardon, **a**) I ask you to forgive me. 미안합니다. **b**) Say it once more, please. 다시 한번 말씀해 주세요.

:be·gan [bigǽn] *vt.* p. of **begin.**

be·get [bigét] *vt.* (**be·got, be·got·ten** or **be·got, be·get·ting**) (P6) **1** become the father of (a son). (아버지가) 아이를 얻다. 參考 어머니의 경우에는 bear. ¶ *He begot a son.* 그는 아들을 보았다. **2** be the cause of (something). …을 초래하다; …의 원인이 되다. ¶ *Hate begets hate and love begets love.* 미움은 미움을 낳고, 사랑은 사랑을 낳는다. ● **be·get·ter** [-ər] *n.* [be-]

:beg·gar [bégər] *n.* Ⓒ **1** a person who lives by begging. 거지. ¶ *die a* ~ (거지로) 객사하다. **2** a very poor person. 가난뱅이. — *vt.* (P6) make (someone) poor. 가난하게 하다. ¶ *His thoughtless spending will* ~ *his father.* 그의 분별 없는 낭비는 그의 아버지를 가난뱅이로 만들 것이다. [Du., → beg]

beg·gar·ly [bégərli] *adj.* **1** like a beggar; very poor. 거지 같은; 몹시 가난한; 무일푼의. **2** poor; mere; mean. 빈약한; 얼마 안되는; 야비한. ¶ *a* ~ *amount of learning* 빈약한 학문 / *He is mean over a few* ~ *won.* 불과 몇 푼 안 되는 돈에 치사하게 군다.

beg·gar·y [bégəri] *n.* Ⓤ extreme poverty. 찰가난. ¶ *be reduced to* ~ 빈털터리가 되다.

:be·gin [bigín] (**be·gan, be·gun**) *vi.* (P1,3) **1** start; commence; set in. 시작하다〔되다〕. ¶ ~ *at page 5,* 5페이지부터 시작하다 / ~ *on a piece of work* 하나의 일에 착수하다 / *School begins at nine.* 수업은 9시에 시작된다 / *The darkness began.* 어두워지기 시작했다 / *We're ready, so let's* ~. 준비가 됐으니 시작하자 / *What shall I* ~ *with?* 무엇부터 시작할까. **2** start; come into existence; arise. 일어나다; 발생하다; 근원을 발하다. ¶ *World War Ⅱ began in 1939.* 제2차 세계대전은 1939년에 일어났다 / *The river begins in the mountains.* 이 강은 저 산맥에서 발원(發源)한다 / *The custom began during the Civil War.* 이 풍습은 남북 전쟁 중에 생겼다 / *Who can tell when life began?* 생명의 기원이 언제인지 누가 알 수 있겠나. **3** start speaking. 말을 시작하다. — *vt.* **1** (P6,7,8, 9,13) start the activity of (something). …을 시작하다; …에 착수하다. ¶ ~ *one's breakfast* 아침 식사를 시작하다 / ~ *to read* 〔*reading*〕 *a new book* 새 책을 읽기 시작하다 / *It began raining.* 비가 내리기 시작했다 / *They began talking in a loud voice.* 그들은 큰 소리로 이야기하기 시작했다. **2** (P6) originate; found; be the first to do. …을 일으키다; 창시〔설립〕하다; 발명하다. ¶ ~ *a dynasty* 왕조를 수립하다 / ~ *a reform movement* 개혁 운동을 일으키다 / *Two physicists began the firm.* 두 사람의 물리학자가 회사를 설립했다. **3** (P8) 《*colloq.*》 be in no position to; not appear likely ever to. 전연 …할 것 같지 않다. ¶ *You can't* ~ *to imagine how glad I am to see you.* 자네를 만나 얼마나 반가운지 상상도 못 할 걸세. [E.]

begin at, start from. …부터 시작하다.

begin life as, start one's career or life as. …로서 인생의 첫발을 내딛다. ¶ ~ *one's life as a*

writer 작가로서 첫발을 내딛다.
begin on 〔***upon***〕, set to work at. …에 착수하다.
begin the world, start in life; enter upon one's career. 사회 생활을 시작하다; 실사회에 나가다.
begin with, take (something) first. …로〔부터〕 시작하다. ¶ *You had better ~ with this book.* 이 책부터 시작하는 것이 좋겠다 / *The ocean began with little drops of water.* 대양(大洋)도 작은 물방울로부터 시작되었다.
to begin with, in the first place. 우선 첫째로.

be·gin·ner [bigínər] *n.* Ⓒ **1** a person who is doing something for the first time. 초심자. ¶ *a beginner's dictionary* 초심자를 위한 사서 / *You skate well for a ~.* 당신은 초보자치고는 스케이트를 잘한다. **2** a person who begins anything. 창시자.

:be·gin·ning [bigíniŋ] *n.* Ⓒ (opp. end) **1** the start. 시초; 처음. ¶ *at* 〔*in*〕 *the ~ of the year* 연초에 / *from ~ to end* 처음부터 끝까지 / *from the ~* 처음부터 / *the ~ of the world* 이 세상의 시초 / *make a ~* 단서를 열다; 시작〔착수〕하다. **2** the time or place at which anything begins; the origin; the source. 시작; 발단; 기원. ¶ *the ~ of a book* 책의 첫 부분 / *the ~ and the end* 발단과 결말; 전부 / *The movement had a good ~.* 그 운동은 출발이 좋았다. **3** the first part. 초기; 당초.
the beginning of the end, the first clear sign of the final result. 마지막 결과를 예시(豫示)하는 최초의 조짐.

be·gird [bigə́:rd] *vt.* (**-girt** [-gə́:rt]) (P6) surround. 둘러싸다. ¶ *a castle begirt with a wall* 성벽으로 둘러싸인 성. [be-]

be·gone [bigɔ́(:)n, -gán] *interj., vi.* (P1) go away. 나가(다); 떠나다. ¶ *Begone!* 꺼져 / *She bade him ~.* 그녀는 그에게 나가라고 명령했다. [*be, gone*]

be·go·nia [bigóunjə, -niə] *n.* 《bot.》 a plant with brilliant foliage and waxy flowers. 베고니아. [*Begon* person]

be·got [bigát / -gɔ́t] *v.* p. and pp. of **beget.**

be·got·ten [bigátn / -gɔ́tn] *v.* pp. of **beget.**

be·grime [bigráim] *vt.* (P6) 《*with*》 make (something) dirty. …을 더럽히다. ¶ *begrimed with soot* 검댕으로 더러워진. [be-]

be·grudge [bigrʌ́dʒ] *vt.* (P13,14) **1** envy. …을 부러워하다; 질투〔시기〕하다. ¶ *~ someone his good luck* 아무의 행운을 시기하다. **2** be unwilling to give. …을 선뜻 주려 하지 않다. ¶ *He begrudges his wife money.* 아내에게 돈을 주기를 싫어한다 / *I ~ spending money for such a purpose.* 그런 목적에 돈을 쓰기는 아깝다. ● **be·grudg·ing·ly** [-iŋli] *adv.* [be-]

be·guile [bigáil] *vt.* (P6,13) **1** 《*into, of, out of*》 deceive; mislead. …을 속이다. ¶ *He beguiled me into thinking that he was my friend.* 그는 나를 속여서 내 친구인 것처럼 믿게 했다. **2** 《*with*》 entertain; amuse. …을 즐겁게 하다; 재미있게 하다. ¶ *The old sailor beguiled the boys with stories about his life at sea.* 그 늙은 뱃사람은 그의 바다 생활에 대한 이야기로 아이들을 즐겁게 했다. **3** make (time, a journey) pass quickly or pleasantly. (따분함 따위)를 달래다; 잊게 하다. ¶ *Travel is beguiled with pleasant talk.* 즐거운 이야기로 여행을 하면 지루함을 잊게 된다. [be-]

:be·gun [bigʌ́n] *v.* pp. of **begin.**

·be·half [bihǽf, -há:f] *n.* Ⓤ interest; favor. 이익. 語法 다음 성구(成句)로만 쓰임. [*by, half*]
in behalf of (=*in the interest of; for*) *someone.* …을 위해서. ¶ *I speak this in your ~.* 자네를 위해 이렇게 말하는 것일세.
on behalf of someone =***on someone's behalf,*** **a**) as a representative of someone. …을 대표〔대리〕하여. ¶ *I thank you on his ~.* 그를 대신해서 감사드립니다 / *I attended the meeting on ~ of him.* 나는 그를 대리해서 그 모임에 참석했다. **b**) in behalf of someone. …을 위해서.

·be·have [bihéiv] *vt.* (P6) 《*reflexively*》 conduct. 행동하다. ¶ *Behave yourself!* 얌전히 굴어 / *~ oneself like a man* 남자답게 행동하다. — *vi.* (P1,2A) **1** conduct. 행동하다. ¶ *~ to him in a friendly* 〔*hostile*〕 *manner* 그에게 우호적〔적대적〕으로 행동하다. **2** act well. 예절 바르게 굴다. ¶ *Did the child ~?* 그 아이는 얌전히 굴던가. [*be, have*]

·be·hav·ior [bihéivjər] *n.* Ⓤ **1** acts. 행위. **2** manners. 태도; 예절; 행실. ¶ *good ~* 착한 행실 / *His ~ showed that his feelings were hurt.* 그의 태도는 그의 감정이 상했음을 나타내고 있었다. [↑]
be on one's good behavior, take special pains to behave well. 특히 행동을 조심하다.
put someone on his good 〔***best***〕 ***behavior,*** advise him to behave well. 근신하도록 이르다.

be·hav·ior·ism [bihéivjərìzəm] *n.* 《psych.》 the doctrine that the objective acts of persons are the chief subject matter of scientific psychology. 행동주의.

be·head [bihéd] *vt.* (P6) cut off the head of (someone). …의 목을 베다. [be-]

·be·held [bihéld] *v.* p. and pp. of **behold.**

be·he·moth [bihí:məθ, bí:əmὰθ / bihí:mɔθ] *n.* 《Bible》 a huge beast like the hippopotamus. (하마 같은) 거수(巨獸)(cf. *Job.* *XL, 15.*) [Heb. *b'hemah* beast]

be·hest [bihést] *n.* Ⓒ 《*poet.*》 a command; an order. 명령. [O.E. *behǣs*]

:be·hind [biháind] *adv.* **1** in a former place; at an earlier time. 본디 장소〔시간〕에. ¶ *leave someone ~* 아무를 뒤에 남겨 두고 떠나다. **2** in or to the back. 뒤에; 뒤로. ¶ *lag ~* 꾸물거려 늦다; 낙후하다 / *look ~* 뒤를〔뒤돌아〕보다; 회고하다 / *He glanced ~.* 언뜻 뒤돌아보았다. **3** not so good as; in arrear. …만 못하여; 뒤져서; 밀리어. ¶ *be ~ in* 〔*with*〕 *one's work* 일이 더디다 / *be ~ in* 〔*with*〕 *one's rent* 집세가 밀려 있다 / *I shall not be ~ in doing so.* 나는 그렇게 하는 데 있

어 남에게 뒤지지 않는다. **4** late; slow. (시계·기간이) 늦어; 느려; 더디어. ¶ *come five minutes* ～ 5분 지각하다 / *The watch runs* ～. 이 시계는 느리다. **5** at one's back; at the back. 배후에(서); 숨어서. ¶ *There is more* ～. 아직 숨겨진 사실이 더 있다. **6** in the past. 과거에; 지나가. ¶ *My joy lies* ～. 나의 기쁨은 지난날의 것이다.

be behind with 〔***in***〕, be late with. 밀려 있다. ¶ *He is* ～ *with his work* 〔*in his payments*〕. 그는 일〔지불〕이 밀려 있다.

fall behind, not keep up; be left, as in a race. 뒤지다.

stay 〔***remain***〕 ***behind,*** stay after others have left. (남들이 떠난) 뒤에 남다.

— *prep.* **1** at the back of; hidden from view by. …의 뒤에. ¶ *a garden* ～ *a house* 집의 뒤뜰; 뒤곁 / *from* ～ *the door* 문 뒤에서 / *get* ～ *a tree* 나무 뒤에 숨다 / *He sat* ～ *me.* 그는 내 뒤에 앉았다 / *The sun has sunk* ～ *the hill.* 해가 산 너머로 졌다 / *The moon was* ～ *the clouds.* 달이 구름 속에 가려졌다. **2** later than. …보다 늦게; 뒤지어. ¶ ～ *schedule* 정각〔예정〕보다 늦게 / *The train is* ～ *its time.* 열차는 연착이다. **3** alone after someone has gone away. (아무가) 떠난〔죽은〕 뒤에. ¶ *He left five children* ～ *him.* 아이를 다섯 남기고 죽었다. **4** inferior to; less advanced. …만 못하여; …에 뒤져; 진보가 더디어. ¶ *a country far* ～ *its neighbors* 이웃 나라들보다 훨씬 뒤진 나라 / *He is* ～ *the rest of the class in mathematics.* 그는 수학에서 반의 다른 아이들보다 뒤떨어져 있다. **5** 《*fig.*》 in support of. …을 후원〔지원〕하고; 지지하고. ¶ *an argument with experience* ～ *it* 경험의 뒷받침이 있는 의론 / *He has someone* ～ *him.* 그는 뒤에서 지원하는 누군가 있다. **6** remaining after. 뒤에 남기고. ¶ *leave a good reputation* ～ *him* 죽은 뒤에 좋은 명성을 남기다 / *Someone has left an umbrella* ～ *him.* 누군가 우산을 놓아둔 채 가 버렸다. **7** in the past for. (아무에게 있어) 과거의; 지나간. ¶ *All his difficulties are now* ～ *him.* 그의 모든 고생은 이제 과거의 것이 되었다.

behind one's back, secretly; without his knowledge. 몰래; 가만히.

behind the scenes ⇨scene.

behind the times, out of date; old-fashioned (in one's idea etc.). 시대에 뒤진.

— *n.* the posterior; 《*colloq.*》 buttocks. 뒤쪽; 엉덩이. [O.E. *behindan*]

be·hind·hand [biháindhæ̀nd] *adv., adj.* late; behind in progress. 늦어; 늦은; 뒤져서; 뒤진(opp. beforehand). ¶ *be* ～ *with one's rent* 집세가 밀리다 / *Tom is* ～ *in his schoolwork.* 톰은 학업이 뒤져 있다 / *Don't wait for Helen; she is always behindhand.* 헬렌을 기다리지 마라; 그녀는 항상 늦으니까. 語法 형용사로서는 서술적 용법뿐.

:be·hold [bihóuld] *vt.* (**be·held** [-héld]) (P6) 《*lit.*》 watch; look at; take notice. …을 보다; 주목〔주시〕하다. ¶ *You have all beheld beautiful sunsets.* 당신은 아름다운 해넘이를 모두 보았다. [be-, →hold]

be·hold·en [bihóuldən] *adj.* under an obligation; indebted. 신세를〔빚을〕 진; 은혜를 입은. ¶ *I am greatly* ～ *to you for your kindness.* 신세를 졌습니다; 베푸신 친절 매우 고맙습니다.

be·hold·er [bihóuldər] *n.* an onlooker. 방관자; 구경꾼. ¶ 《*prov.*》 *Beauty is in the eye of the* ～. 제 눈에 안경이다.

be·hoof [bihú:f] *n.* Ⓤ 《*arch.*》 use; advantage. 이익. 語法 다음 성구로만 쓰임. [↓]

in 〔***for, to, on***〕 *someone's* ***behoof,*** for someone's own use or advantage. …을 위해서. ¶ *spend money for his children's* ～ 자기 아이들을 위해서 돈을 쓰다. [↓]

be·hoove [bihú:v] *vt.* (P20) be necessary for (someone). …의 의무이다. ¶ *It behooves you to ....* …함이 마땅하다 / *It behooves him to do so.* 그렇게 하는 것이 그의 의무이다. 語法 언제나 it 가 주어가 됨. [be-, →heave]

be·hove [bihóuv] *vt.* 《*chiefly* Brit.》 = behoove.

beige [beiʒ] *n.* Ⓤ **1** soft material of natural wool. 원모로 짠 모직물. **2** a very light brown color; the color of natural wool. 베이지색; 밝은 다갈색. [F.]

:be·ing [bí:iŋ] *n.* **1** Ⓤ existence; life. 존재; 인생. ¶ *the aim of our* ～ 우리 인생의 목표 / ～ *in itself* 실재 그 자체. **2** Ⓒ a living creature; a human creature. 생물; 인간. ¶ *a human* ～ 인간 / *human beings* 인류. **3** Ⓤ essential nature. 본성; 본질. [*be*]

come into being, begin to exist; be made. 생기다; 출현하다. ¶ *This world came into* ～ *long ago.* 이 세상은 오래 전에 생겨났다.

in being, in existence. 존재〔생존·현존〕하고 있는; 현존의. ¶ *the record in* ～ 현존의 기록 / *the fleet in* ～ 현유(現有) 해군력 / *A group of that sort is already in* ～. 그런 유(類)의 집단이 이미 존재하고 있다.

Bei·rut [beirú:t, ⸗⸗] *n.* the capital of Lebanon. 베이루트.

be·jew·el [bidʒú:əl] *vt.* (**-eled, -el·ing** 《Brit.》 **-elled, -el·ling**) (P6) adorn (something) with jewels. …을 보석으로 꾸미다. [be-]

be·la·bor [biléibər] *vt.* (P6) hit hard. 세게 치다. [be-, →labor]

be·lat·ed [biléitid] *adj.* **1** too late; delayed. 늦은. ¶ *a* ～ *letter* 늦게 온 편지 / ～ *efforts* 뒤늦은 노력 / *a* ～ *birthday greeting* 때 늦은 생일 축하 인사 / *make* 〔*offer*〕 *a* ～ *apology* 때 늦은 변명을 하다. **2** overtaken by darkness. 길이 저문. ¶ *the* ～ *travellers* 길이 저문 여행자들. ●**be·lat·ed·ly** [-li] *adv.* [→late]

be·lay [biléi] *vt.* (P6) 《naut.》 fasten (a rope) by winding it round a pin or cleat. 밧줄걸이에 밧줄을 감아 매다. [be-]

Belay there! 《*colloq.*》 Stop ! Enough ! 됐다, 그만 해.

belch [beltʃ] *vi., vt.* **1** (P1) throw out gas from the stomach through the mouth. 트림하다. **2** (P6,7) throw out (flame, smoke, etc.) with force. (불길·연기 따위를) 뿜어내다. ¶ *The volcano belched forth* 〔*out*〕 *fire and smoke.* 화산이 불과 연기를 내뿜었다 / *~ forth curses* 〔*insults*〕 저주〔모욕〕의 말을 내뱉다. ── *n.* Ⓤ the act of belching. 트림; 분출. [E.]

bel·dam(e) [béldəm] *n.* an ugly old woman. 추악한 못된 노파. [→belle, dame]

be·lea·guer [bilíːgər] *vt.* (P6,13) 《*lit., fig.*》 besiege. 에워싸다; 포위하다. [be-, Du. *leger* camp] 「(才士).

bel·es·prit [belesprí:] *n.* 《F.》 a wit. 재사

bel·fry [bélfri] *n.* Ⓒ (*pl.* **-fries**) a bell tower. 종탑. [Teut.]

Bel·gian [béldʒən] *adj.* of Belgium or its people. 벨기에(사람)의. ── *n.* Ⓒ a person of Belgium. 벨기에 사람.

***Bel·gium** [béldʒəm] *n.* a country in western Europe. 벨기에. 參考 수도는 Brussels.

Bel·grade [bélgreid, -grɑ:d, -græd] *n.* the capital of the Federal Republic of Yugoslavia. 베오그라드《신(新)유고 연방의》.

Be·li·al [bí:liəl, -ljəl] *n.* 《Bible》 the Devil or Satan. 마왕; 악마. [Heb. =worthlessness]

sons of Belial, the wicked. 악인들.

be·lie [bilái] *vt.* (**-lied, -ly·ing**) (P6) **1** give a false impression of (something); show to be false. …을 속이다; …이 거짓임을 나타내다. ¶ *Her cheerful speaking belied her feelings.* 그녀의 쾌활한 말씨는 감정을 속이고 있었다 / *His acts ~ his words.* 그는 언행이 일치하지 않는다. **2** fail to come up to; disappoint. …을 배반하다; 저버리다. ¶ *The result has belied our expectations.* 결과는 우리의 기대에 어긋났다. [be-]

:be·lief [bilí:f, bə-] *n.* (*pl.* **-liefs**) Ⓤ **1** something believed; a convinced opinion. 신념; 소신. ¶ *the ~ that the earth is flat* 지구는 편평하다는 신념 / *one's democratic beliefs* 민주주의의 신념 / *In spite of their statement, he remained of the same ~.* 그들의 설명에도 불구하고 그의 확신은 변하지 않았다. **2** 《*in*》 ⓐ acceptance as true or existing. 사실이라고 믿음. ¶ *~ in ghosts* 유령의 존재를 믿음. ⓑ trust. 신용; 신뢰. ¶ *a child's ~ in his parents* 부모에 대한 아이의 신뢰 / *a man worthy of ~* 충분히 믿을 만한 사람 / *I have great ~ in early rising.* 아침 일찍 일어나기의 효능을 크게 믿고 있다 / *He had a firm ~ in the boy's honesty.* 그는 그 소년의 정직성에 대해 굳은 믿음이 있었다. **3** ⓊⒸ a religious faith. 신앙; 믿음. ¶ *the Buddhist ~* 불교 신앙 / *I have no ~ in God.* 나는 신을 믿지 않는다. [→believe]

beyond belief, that cannot be believed. 믿을 수 없는.

to the best of one's belief, as far as one knows. …의 아는〔믿는〕 바로는. ¶ *To the best of my ~ there is no danger.* 내가 믿는 바로는 위험은 없다.

be·liev·a·ble [bilí:vəbəl, bə-] *adj.* that can be believed. 믿을 수 있는.

:be·lieve [bilí:v, bə-] *vt.* (P6,11,12,21) **1** accept (something or someone) as true or honest. …을 믿다. ¶ *I ~ you.* 나는 당신을 믿는다 / *I ~ what he says.* 나는 그가 말하는 것을 믿는다 / *I ~ him to be honest.* 나는 그가 정직하다고 믿는다 / *Do you ~ there is a God?* 신이 존재한다고 믿는가. **2** hold (something) as an opinion; think; suppose. …라고 생각하다. ¶ *I believe him mistaken.* 그가 잘못되었다고 생각한다 / *He is believed to be dead.* 그는 죽은 것으로 여겨지고 있다 / *Is he coming today? — I believe so* 〔*not*〕. 그가 오늘 올까 — 그러리라〔그렇지 않으리라〕 생각해. ── *vi.* (P1,2,3) **1** have firm religious faith. 신앙〔믿음〕을 가지다. **2** have a firm conviction. 확신하다; 믿다. **3** think; suppose. 생각하다. [E.]

believe in, have faith in the existence, truth, possibility, etc. of (something). …의 존재〔진실·가능성〕을 믿다. ¶ *~ in God* 〔*a religion*〕 신을〔종교를〕 믿다 / *~ in ghosts* 유령의 존재를 믿다.

be·liev·er [bilí:vər, bə-] *n.* Ⓒ a person who believes. 믿는 사람; 신앙인. ¶ *a ~ in Buddhism* 불교 신자 / *He is no longer a ~ in Christianity.* 그는 이제 기독교 신자가 아니다.

be·like [biláik] *adv.* 《*arch.*》 probably; perhaps. 아마. [be-]

be·lit·tle [bilítl] *vt.* (P6) **1** regard (something) as less important than it is; speak of (something) as unimportant. …을 가벼이〔우습게〕 보다; 얕잡아보다; 깎아내리다. ¶ *~ someone's merit* 남의 공을 과소 평가하다 / *He belittled the danger.* 그는 위험을 경시했다. **2** make (something) small. …을 작게 하다. [be-]

:bell[1] [bel] *n.* Ⓒ **1** a hollow metal cup that makes a sound when struck by a hammer. 종; 방울. ¶ *a call ~* 초인종 / *an electric ~* 전령(電鈴) / *the passing ~* 임종의 종 / *pull the ~* 줄을 당겨 벨을 울리다. **2** the sound of a bell. 종〔벨〕소리. ¶ *answer the ~* (현관 벨소리에 응해서) 내객을 맞이하다 / *We rose at the ~.* 벨소리를 듣고 일어났다. **3** a thing shaped like a bell. 종과 같이 생긴 것. ¶ a ~ glass 종 모양의 유리그릇.

(as) clear as a bell, (of sound) very clear. (소리가) 매우 맑은.

(as) sound as a bell, **a**) very sound or healthy. 매우 튼튼한; 건강한. **b**) (of a thing) in perfect condition. (무엇이) 완전한 상태에.

bear away the bell, take the prize; win. 우승하다; 성공하다.

curse by bell, book, and candle, excommunicate with all necessary solemn ceremonies (as for declaring someone to be no longer a Roman Catholic). 의식을 갖추어 파문 선고를 하다.

ring a bell, **a**) strike a response. 반응을 불

러일으키다. **b**) remind a person of. 아무에게 …을 상기시키다.

ring the bell, **a**) provide what is desired. 바라는 것을 주다. **b**) be satisfactory or successful. 뜻대로 잘 돼 가다; 성공하다.

— *vt.* (P6) put a bell on (something). …에 종〔방울〕을 달다. [E. *bhel-* cry out]

bell the cat, ⇨cat.

bell[2] [bel] *n.* a stag's cry. 수사슴의 울음소리. — *vi.* (P1) utter a cry. 울다. [E. =bark]

Bell [bel], **Alexander Graham** *n.* (1847-1922) an American scientist and the inventor of the telephone. 벨.

bell·boy [bélbɔ̀i] *n.* Ⓒ《U.S.》a man whose work is carrying baggage and doing errands at a hotel or club; a bellhop. (호텔 등의) 보이. [→bell[1]]

bell buoy [ㄹㄹ] *n.* a buoy with a bell rung by waves' motion. 방울찌.

·belle [bel] *n.* Ⓒ a beautiful woman or girl, esp. the most beautiful one in a group. (가장 아름다운) 미녀. ¶ *She was the ~ of the party.* 그녀는 파티에서 제일 가는 미인이었다. [→beau]

belles-let·tres [bellétər / -létr] *n. pl.* 《used as *sing.*》 the finer forms of literature; writings of the purely literary kind. 순수 문학. [F.]

bel·let·rist [bellétrist] *n.* a person given to the study of belles-lettres. 순수 문학자(純粹文學者). [↑]

bel·let·ris·tic [bèlitrístik] *adj.* of or belonging to belles-lettres. 순수 문학의.

bell·flow·er [bélflàuər] *n.* Ⓒ《bot.》a plant with flowers shaped like bells. 초롱꽃. [→bell[1]]

bell·hop [bélhɑ̀p, -hɔ̀p] *n.* 《U.S. *colloq.*》a boy-servant in a hotel. (호텔의) 보이. [*bell*[1], *hop*]

bel·li·cose [bélikòus] *adj.* fond of war; inclined to fight. 전쟁〔싸움〕을 좋아하는; 호전적인. ● **bel·li·cos·i·ty** [bèlikɑ́səti / -kɔ́s-] *n.* [L. *bellum* war]

bel·lig·er·ence [bəlídʒərəns], **bel·lig·er·en·cy** [-si] *n.* Ⓤ the state of being belligerent. 교전 상태. [↓]

bel·lig·er·ent [bəlídʒərənt] *adj.* **1** fond of war. 전쟁을 좋아하는. **2** being at war. 교전중인. ¶ *~ powers* 교전국. **3** of nations at war. 교전국의. — *n.* Ⓒ a nation at war. 교전국. ● **bel·lig·er·ent·ly** [-li] *adv.* [L. *bellum* war, *gero* wage]

bell metal [ㄹㄹ–] *n.* an alloy of tin and copper used to make bells. 청동(青銅); 벨메탈.

Bel·lo·na [bəlóunə] *n.* 《Rom. myth.》goddess of war. 벨로나. [L.]

·bel·low [bélou] *vi., vt.* (P1,2A; 7) **1** make a loud and deep cry, as of a bull. 큰 소리로 울다. **2** cry loudly and deeply. 크게 소리치다; 노호(怒號)하다. ¶ *a man bellowing with anger* 성이 나서 고함치는 사람. — *n.* Ⓒ the sound of bellowing. 우는〔울부짖는〕 소리. [?]

bel·lows [bélouz, -ləz] *n.* Ⓒ (*pl.* **-lows**) **1** an instrument for producing a strong blast of air. 풀무. **2** the folding part of a camera, etc. (카메라 등의) 주름상자. [→belly]

bell tent [ㄹㄹ] *n.* a tent shaped like a bell. 종 모양의 텐트. [*bell*[1]]

bell tower [ㄹㄹ–] *n.* a tower that supports or shelters a bell or bells. 종탑.

bell·weth·er [bélwèðər] *n.* Ⓒ **1** a male sheep with a bell on his neck, usu. the leader of the group. 방울을 단 길잡이 수양. **2** a leader. 지도자. [*bell*[1], *wether*]

·bel·ly [béli] *n.* Ⓒ (*pl.* **-lies**) **1** the lower front of the human body; the under part of an animal's body; the abdomen; the stomach. 사람〔동물〕의 배; 복부; 위. ¶ *lie on one's ~* 배를 깔고 엎드리다 / *hold one's ~ in* 배를 쑥 들이키다 / *have an empty* 공복이다. 語法 여성 앞에서는 보통 stomach를 씀. **2** the swelling part of anything. 불룩 나온 부분. — *vi., vt.* (P1,2A; 6) (**-lied**) swell out. 부풀다; 부풀리다. ¶ *Sails ~ out.* 돛이 부풀다 / *The sails bellied in the wind.* 돛이 바람을 받고 부풀었다. [E. =bag]

bel·ly·ache [bélièik] *n.* Ⓒ colic. 복통.

bel·ly·ful [bélifùl] *n.* Ⓒ as much as one can eat. 배 가득; 만복.

:be·long [bilɔ́(:)ŋ, -lɑ́ŋ] *vi.* (P3) **1** have a proper place; be properly placed; fit in with. (있어야 할 제자리에) 있다; 어울리다. ¶ *The book belongs on that shelf.* 그 책의 둘 곳은 저 책꽂이이다 / *The book is not where it belongs.* 그 책은 있어야 할 곳에 없다 / *The artist doesn't ~ in the uniform.* 예술가에게 군복은 어울리지 않는다. **2** 《*to*》 be the property of (someone); be a member of (something). (…의) 소유물이다; (…의) 일원이다; 속하다. ¶ *~ to a superior caste* 상류 계급에 속하다 / *This book belongs to my brother.* 이 책은 내 아우의 것이다 / *Does this cap ~ to you?* 이 모자는 네 것이냐 / *Bacteria ~ to the vegetable kingdom.* 세균은 식물계에 속한다 / *He belongs in this club.* 그는 이 클럽의 멤버이다. 語法 미국에서는 to 이외의 전치사도 씀. **3** be an inhabitant or native (of); live. …의 주민이다; 살다. ¶ *I ~ to Glasgow.* 나는 글래스고 사람이다 / *He belongs here.* 그는 이 곳 사람이다. [be-, Obs. *long* pertain]

be·long·ings [bilɔ́(:)ŋiŋz, -lɑ́ŋ-] *n. pl.* a person's property; possessions. 재산; 소유물. ¶ *personal ~* 사물(私物).

·be·lov·ed [bilʌ́vid, -lʌ́vd] *adj.* dearly loved. 사랑스러운. ¶ *He was greatly ~ by all who knew him.* 그는 그를 아는 모든 사람으로부터 매우 사랑을 받았다 / *He lost his ~ pipe* 〔*son*〕. 그는 끔찍이 아끼던 파이프를〔아들을〕 잃었다. — *n.* 《*one's ~*》 a person who is loved. 사랑하는 사람. ¶ *my ~* 여보; 당신.

[be-]

:be·low [bilóu] *adv.* (opp. above). **1** ⓐ in or to a lower place; downstairs. 아래(밑)에; 아래로; 아래층에. ¶ *in the room* ~ 아래층 방에 / *look down into the valley* ~ 눈 아래 계곡을 내려다보다. ⓑ later in a book or on a page. (책·페이지의) 아래에; 하문(下文)의. ¶ *See Section 3* ~. 아래 제 3절 참조. **2** on earth. 지상(이승)에(서). ¶ *here* ~ 여기 지상에. **3** in or to hell. 지옥에(으로). ¶ *the fiends* ~ 지옥의 귀신들. **4** in or to a lower rank or number. 하위에(로); 밑의. ¶ *in the court* ~ 하급의 법원에서.

— *prep.* (opp. above). **1** in or to a lower place than. …보다 아래에. ¶ ~ *one's eyes* 눈 아래에 / ~ *the ground* 지하에(매장되어) / ~ *(the) sea level* 해면 이하에(로) / ~ *the surface* 수면 아래에; 지중(地中)에 / *The sun has sunk* ~ *the horizon.* 해는 수평선 아래로 졌다. **2** (as in rank, amount, etc.) inferior to; less than. (계급·양 따위가) …만 못한; …보다 낮은; 보다 적은. ¶ ~ *the average income* 평균 수입 이하에 / *She is* ~ *me in the class.* 그녀는 반에서 나만 못하다. **3** not worthy of; beneath. …할 만한 값어치가 없는. ¶ *This job is* ~ *his ability.* 이 일은 그의 능력에 걸맞지 않는다 [be-, →low]

:belt [belt] *n.* Ⓒ **1** a strip of leather, cloth, etc. put around the waist; a band. 허리띠; 띠. ¶ *undo one's* ~ 띠를 풀다. **2** a district having distinctive characteristics. 지대(地帶). ¶ *a forest* ~ 산림 지대 / *a* ~ *of cotton plantations* 목화의 산지. **3** an endless band that moves by wheels. 벨트. ¶ *a* ~ *conveyer* 컨베이어 벨트.

below the belt, unfair; unfairly. 부정한; 부정하게.

tighten one's belt, be more economical. 허리띠를 졸라매다; 내핍 생활을 하다.

— *vt.* (P6,7) **1** put a belt around (something). …에 띠를 두르다. **2** fasten (something) with a belt. …을 띠로 잡아매다. ¶ ~ *on a sword* 칼을 차다. **3** thrash with a belt. 혁대로 때리다.

— *vi.* (P3) run fast. 질주하다. ¶ ~ *along the road* 도로를 질주하다. [E.]

be·ly·ing [biláiiŋ] *v.* ppr. of **belie**.

be·moan [bimóun] *vt., vi.* (P6;1) moan over (something); lament for (something). …을 슬퍼하다. ¶ ~ *one's wasted youth* 헛되이 보낸 청춘을 한탄하다. [be-]

be·muse [bimjú:z] *vt.* (P6) make stupid. …을 멍청하게 하다. ¶ *bemused with wine* 술에 취해 멍청해진. [be-, muse]

Ben [ben] *n.* a nickname of Benjamin. 벤저민의 애칭.

:bench [bentʃ] *n.* Ⓒ **1** a long seat. 벤치. **2** a judge's seat. 재판관석. ¶ *take a seat on the* ~ 재판관석에 앉다. **3** 《*collectively*》 Ⓤ judges. 재판관. ¶ *be raised* (*elevated*) *to the* ~ 판사로 승진하다 / ~ *and bar* 재판관과 변호사. **4** a law court. 법정. **5** a table at which a workman works. 작업대. [E.]

***on the bench,* a**) serving as judge in a law court. 재판관으로 있는; 심리중에. **b**) (in sports) sitting as a substitute player. 후보 선수로 있는.

:bend [bend] *v.* (**bent**) *vt.* **1** (6,7,18) force (a straight line) into a curve or an angle. …을 구부리다. ¶ ~ *the knee* 무릎을 꿇어 기도하다 / ~ *the neck* …에게 굴복하다 / *He bent the iron bar as if it had been made of rubber.* 그는 쇠막대를 마치 고무로나 된 것처럼 구부렸다. **2** 《*to*》 force (someone) to submit. …을 굴복시키다. ¶ ~ *one's will* 의지를 굽히다 / ~ *someone to one's will* 아무를 자기 의사에 따르게 하다. **3** (P13) turn (efforts, eyes, etc.) in a certain direction. …을 (어떤 방향으로) 돌리다; 기울이다. ¶ ~ *oneself to* …에 열중하다 / ~ *every effort to help one's friend* 친구를 돕기 위해 온갖 노력을 기울이다 / *He bent his mind to study.* 그는 마음을 공부하는 데 기울였다 / *He bent his steps toward home.* 그는 발길을 집으로 돌렸다. — *vi.* (P1,2A,4) **1** become curved; turn. 구부러지다. ¶ *Some woods* ~ *but do not easily break.* 어떤 나무는 구부러지지만 쉽게 꺾어지지는 않는다 / *The road bends to the left.* 길은 왼쪽으로 돌아간다. **2** stoop; crouch; bow. (몸을) 구부리다; 웅크리다; 인사하다. ¶ *The doctor bent over the sick child.* 의사는 앓는 아이 위로 몸을 굽혔다. **3** 《*to*》 submit; yield. 굴복하다. ¶ *A weak nation bends to a greater power.* 약소 국가는 강대국에 굴복한다 / *She bent to his will.* 그녀는 그의 뜻에 따랐다.

be bent (=*be determined*) ***on** something.* …에 마음이 기울다.

bend a rule, 《*colloq.*》 interpret it loosely (to suit the circumstances). (사정에 맞춰) 규칙을 적당히 해석하다.

bend before, give way. 굴복하다; 지다. ¶ *John bent before the storm of his father's anger.* 존은 아버지의 불같이 노한 기세에 지고 말았다.

bend over backward, exert oneself to the utmost; make a serious effort. 더없는 노력을 하다; 열심히 노력하다.

— *n.* **1** Ⓤ the act of bending. 굽힘; 구부림. **2** Ⓒ a curved part. 굽은 곳. [E.]

above one's bend, 《U.S.》 beyond one's powers. 힘이 미치지 못하는.

go on the* (*a*) *bend, go on the spree. (술) 마시고 떠들다.

bend·ed [béndid] *adj.* bent. 굽은.

on bended knees, kneeling. 무릎을 꿇고.

:be·neath [biní:θ, -ní:ð] *adv.* below; underneath. 아래로(에). — *prep.* **1** below; under; lower in place than. …의 아래(밑)에; (신분·지위가) 보다 낮은. ¶ *A lieutenant is* ~ *a captain.* 중위는 대위의 아래이다. **2** unworthy of. …의 가치가 없는. ¶ ~ *contempt* 경멸할 가치조차도 없는. [be-, →nether]

Ben·e·di·ci·te [bènədísəti / -dái-] *n.* **1** a song of praise to God. 찬미가. **2** 《*b-*》 an invocation for a blessing. 축복의 기도. [L. *bene* well, *dico* speak]

Ben·e·dic·tine [bènədíktin, -tain, -tiːn] *n.* **1** Ⓒ a monk or nun following the teachings of Saint Benedict. 베네딕트회의 수사(수녀). **2** [-tiːn] Ⓤ 《*b-*》 a kind of liqueur. 술의 일종. — *adj.* of Saint Benedict or the Benedictines. 성베네딕트의; 베네딕트회의.

ben·e·dic·tion [bènədíkʃən] *n.* ⓊⒸ **1** the act of asking a blessing at the end of a church service. 예배 끝의 기도(祈禱). **2** a blessing. 축복.

ben·e·fac·tion [bènəfǽkʃən, ∠-∸-] *n.* **1** Ⓤ the act of doing good. 선행(善行). **2** Ⓒ a benefit given; a gift for charity. 희사(喜捨). [→benefit]

ben·e·fac·tor [bénəfæ̀ktər, ∸-∠-] *n.* Ⓒ a person who has given money to a school, hospital, etc; a person who kindly helps. 후원자; 은인.

ben·e·fac·tress [bénəfæ̀ktris, ∸-∠-] *n.* Ⓒ a woman benefactor. 여성 후원자.

ben·e·fice [bénəfis] *n.* a church living. 성직록(聖職祿). [↓]

be·nef·i·cence [bənéfəsəns] *n.* **1** Ⓤ kindness; the act of doing good. 친절; 선행. **2** Ⓒ a kind act. 친절한 행위. **3** Ⓒ a gift. 시혜물(施惠物); 보시(布施); 선물. [→benefit]

be·nef·i·cent [bənéfəsənt] *adj.* kind; doing good. 친절한; 선행을 하는. ¶ *be* ~ *to* the *poor* 가난한 사람들에게 자비(慈悲)롭다 / *exert a* ~ *influence on* …에게 은택(恩澤)을 끼치다.

ben·e·fi·cial [bènəfíʃəl] *adj.* helpful; producing good results. 유익한. ¶ ~ *birds* 익조(益鳥) / *have a* ~ *effect on* …에 유익한 효과가 있다.

ben·e·fi·ci·ar·y [bènəfíʃièri, -fíʃəri] *n.* Ⓒ (*pl.* **-ar·ies**) **1** a person who receives benefits or profits. 이익을[은혜를] 받는 사람. **2** a person who receives money or other property under an insurance policy or a will. (보험의) 수익자; 유산 상속인. ¶ *the* ~ *in the event of the death of the insured* 피보험자 사망시에 보험금 타는 사람.

:ben·e·fit [bénəfit] *n.* Ⓒ **1** Ⓤ anything that is helpful; an advantage. 이익. ¶ *a public* ~ 공익(公益) / *Such a medicine would be of great* ~ *to the world.* 이런 약은 세상에 매우 유익할 것이다. **2** a kind act; a favor. 친절(한 행위); 은혜. ¶ *confer benefits* [*a* ~] *upon* …에 은혜를[은전을] 베풀다 / *for your special* ~ 특히 당신을 위해서. **3** money paid to a sick or an old person. 보조금. **4** a bazaar, dance, show, etc. held for charity. 자선 공연. ¶ *a* ~ *concert* 자선 음악회 / *a* ~ *game* 자선 경기. **5** Ⓒ a fine time; a fine job. 호경기; 벌이가 좋은 일.

for the benefit of, **a**) for the good of. …을 위해. **b**) for the edification of. 본때를 보이기 위해.

give someone the benefit of the doubt, assume he is innocent in a doubtful case. (증거 따위가 미심쩍을 때) '의심스러운 것만으로는 벌하지 않는다'의 원칙을 적용하다.

— *vt.* (P6) do good to (someone or something); help. …에 이익이 되다; …을 돕다. ¶ *The fresh air benefits you.* 신선한 공기는 당신에게 유익하다.

— *vi.* (P1,3) get good; receive help. 이익[도움]을 얻다. ¶ *He benefited by the inheritance.* 그는 상속으로 이익을 얻었다 / *You must* ~ *from experience.* 경험에서 도움을 얻어야 한다. [L. *bene* well, *facio* do]

Ben·e·lux [bénəlʌ̀ks] *n.* the economic union of Belgium, the Netherlands and Luxemburg. 베네룩스 (동맹).

be·nev·o·lence [bənévələns] *n.* **1** Ⓤ good will; mercy. 선의(善意); 자비심. ¶ *a man of great* ~ *of character* 매우 자비 깊은 성격의 사람(opp. malevolence). **2** Ⓒ a kind act. 선행; 자선. [↓]

be·nev·o·lent [bənévələnt] *adj.* (opp. malevolent) **1** kind. 친절한; 자혜로운. ¶ *a* ~ *rich man* 자혜로운 부자. **2** generous. 후한. [L. *bene* well, *volo* wish]

be·nev·o·lent·ly [bənévələntli] *adv.* in a benevolent manner. 자혜롭게; 후하게.

Ben·gal [beŋgɔ́ːl, ben-] *n.* a region in the northeastern part of the Indian peninsula, divided between the Indian state of West Bengal and Bangladesh. 벵골. — *adj.* of Bengal. 벵골의. ¶ *a* ~ *tiger* 벵골 호랑이.

be·night·ed [bináitid] *adj.* **1** overtaken by night; being in darkness. 갈 길이 저문; 밤이 된. ¶ *a* ~ *traveler* 갈 길이 저문 나그네. **2** not knowing right and wrong; not educated. 무지한. ¶ *a* ~ *heathen* 무지 몽매한 이교도. [be-]

be·nign [bináin] *adj.* **1** kind; gentle. 친절한; 상냥한. ¶ *a* ~ *old master* 친절한 늙은 주인. **2** favorable; mild. 좋은; 온화한. ¶ *a* ~ *climate* 온화한 기후. **3** (of diseases) not very serious. (병이) 악성이 아닌. ¶ *a* ~ *tumor* 양성(良性) 종양(opp. malignant). [L. *benignus*]

be·nig·nant [binígnənt] *adj.* **1** kind; gentle. 친절한; 자비로운. **2** useful. 유익한.

be·nig·nant·ly [binígnəntli] *adv.* **1** with kindness. 친절[상냥]하게; 자비로이. **2** in a useful manner. 유익하게.

be·nig·ni·ty [binígnəti] *n.* (*pl.* **-ties**) **1** Ⓤ the state of being kind. 친절; 자비. **2** Ⓒ a kind act; a favor. 친절한[자비로운] 행위; 은혜.

be·nign·ly [bináinli] *adv.* gently; with kindness. 친절하게.

ben·i·son [bénəzən, -sən] *n.* a blessing. 축복. [→benediction]

Ben·ja·min [béndʒəmən] *n.* a man's name. 남자의 이름.

:bent [bent] *v.* p. and pp. of **bend.** — *adj.* **1** not straight. 굽은. ¶ *He is* ~ *with age.* 그는

늙어 허리가 굽었다. **2** 《*on*》 strongly inclined; determined. 열중한; 결심한. ¶ *be ~ on buying a new car* 새 차를 사려고 벼르고 있다 / *be ~ over one's task* 일에 열중해 있다 / *He is ~ on becoming an artist.* 그는 화가가 되려고 결심하고 있다.

— *n.* 《*a ~; one's ~*》 a natural interest or ability. 경향; 성향; 좋아하기. ¶ *a ~ for poetry* 시재(詩才) / *a young man with a literary ~* 문학 청년 / *have a natural ~ for music* 태어나면서부터 음악을 좋아하다[에 소질이 있다]. [→bend]

follow** one's **bent, follow one's own tastes. 자기 취향에 따르다; 자기 소질이 있는 일을 하다.

to the top of** one's **bent, to one's heart's content. 마음껏; 실컷.

ben·to·nite [béntənàit] *n.* any of a member of valuable claylike minerals. 벤토나이트. [Place]

be·numb [binʌ́m] *vt.* 《usu. in *passive*》 (P6) **1** make (one's fingers, etc.) have no feeling or powerless. (추위 따위가) …을 무감각하게 하다. ¶ *My fingers were benumbed with cold.* 내 손가락은 추위로 곱아졌다. **2** make (the mind, will, feelings, etc.) senseless. (마음·의지·감정 따위)를 마비시키다. ¶ *~ the intellectual faculties* 지능의 기능을 마비시키다. [E.]

ben·zene [bénzi:n, –ˊ] *n.* Ⓤ a colorless liquid which is got from coal-tar and which burns easily. 벤젠《합성 수지 제조 원료》. [*benz*(oic acid), *-ene*]

ben·zine [bénzi:n, –ˊ] *n.* Ⓤ a colorless, light liquid obtained from oil. 벤진; 휘발유.

ben·zo·in [bénzouin, –ˊ–] *n.* Ⓤ a fragrant resin obtained from a certain tree of Java. 안식향(安息香); 벤조인《의약품·향수용》. [Arab. *luban jawi* frankincense]

ben·zol [bénzɑl, -zɔ(:)l] *n.* =benzene.

be·queath [bikwí:ð, -kwí:θ] *vt.* (P6,13,14) **1** give or leave (a property, etc.) by a will. (재산)을 유증(遺贈)하다. ¶ *The father bequeathed the old house to his son.* 아버지는 아들에게 오래 된 집을 유언으로 물려주었다. **2** hand down or pass on (something) to those who come after. …을 후세에 남기다; 전하다. ¶ *a sword bequeathed to the family by their forefathers* 조상 전래의 검(劍) / *The old story has been bequeathed by word of mouth.* 그 옛이야기는 구전으로 전해져 왔다. [be-, →quoth]

be·quest [bikwést] *n.* **1** Ⓒ money, property, etc. left to someone by a will. 유품; 유증물(遺贈物); 유산. ¶ *He left a ~ of ten thousand pounds to the school.* 그는 학교에 1만 파운드를 유증했다 / *A small ~ allowed her to live independently.* 작은 유산이 있어서 그녀는 남에게 의지하지 않고 살 수 있었다. **2** Ⓤ the act of bequeathing. 유증(遺贈). ¶ *a charitable ~* 자선 사업에의 유증. [↑]

be·rate [biréit] *vt.* (P6) scold sharply. 호되게 꾸짖다. [be-, *rate*]

Ber·ber [bə́:rbər] *n.* **1** one of the groups of North African tribes. 베르베르족(族). **2** the language spoken by this race. 베르베르어(語). [Arab.]

ber·ceuse [bɛərsə́:z] *n.* 《F.》 a cradle-song. 자장가.

be·reave [birí:v] *vt.* (**-reaved** or **-reft**) (P13) 《*of*》 take away; rob. …로부터 빼앗다. ¶ *His death bereft her of all her hope.* 그의 죽음은 그녀에게서 모든 희망을 앗아갔다 / *Death bereaved him of his wife.* 그는 아내를 여의었다 / *Nothing can ~ me of my memories of the past.* 아무것도 나에게서 지난날의 추억을 빼앗을 수는 없다. [be-, E.=rob. →reave]

be·reaved [birí:vd] *adj.* having lost one's husband, wife, etc. (가족 따위와) 사별(死別)한. ¶ *a war-bereaved widow* 전쟁 미망인 / *be ~ of one's wife* 아내를 잃다.

the bereaved, the person who has lost some near relation. 유족(遺族).

be·reave·ment [birí:vmənt] *n.* ⓊⒸ loss of a relative or friend by death. 사별(死別). ¶ *We sympathize with you in your ~.* 상사(喪事)에 위로 말씀드립니다.

be·reft [biréft] *v.* p. and pp. of **bereave.**

— *adj.* having lost someone; left sad and lonely by death. 잃은; 빼앗긴; 여읜. [→bereave]

be·ret [bəréi, bérei] *n.* Ⓒ a soft, flat and round woolen cap. 베레모(帽). [F.]

berg [bə:rg] *n.* Ⓒ a large mass of ice in the sea. 빙산(氷山). [Du. =hill]

Berg·son [bə́:rgsən, bɛ́ərg-], **Henri** *n.* (1859-1941) a French philosopher. 베르그송.

ber·i·ber·i [béribéri] *n.* Ⓤ 《med.》 a disease caused by a lack of vitamin B. 각기(脚氣). [Singhalese]

Ber·ing Sea [bíəriŋ sí:, bɛ́ər-] *n.* 《*the ~*》 the sea in the north Pacific between Alaska and Siberia. 베링해.

Bering Strait [ˊ–ˊ] *n.* 《*the ~*》 the narrow channel between the Bering Sea and the Arctic Ocean. 베링 해협.

ber·ke·li·um [bə:rkí:liəm, bə́:rkliəm] *n.* 《chem.》 a radioactive element. 버클륨. [Place in U.S.]

Berk·shire [bə́:rkʃiər / bɑ́:rk-] *n.* **1** a county in south England. 버크셔 주(州). **2** Ⓒ a kind of black-and-white pig. (돼지의) 버크셔종(種).

·**Ber·lin** [bə:rlín] *n.* the capital of Germany. 베를린.

Ber·mu·da [bə(:)rmjú:də] *n.* a group of British islands in the west Atlantic. 버뮤다 군도.

Bern, Berne [bə:rn] *n.* the capital of Switzerland. 베른.

Ber·nard [bə́:rnərd, bə:rnɑ́:rd] *n.* a man's name. 남자의 이름.

:**ber·ry** [béri] *n.* Ⓒ (*pl.* **-ries**) **1** a small, juicy fruit with many seeds, such as strawberries. 장과(漿果). **2** a dry seed of various plants, as of the coffee plant. (밀·커피 원두 같은) 열매; 알갱이. — *vi.* (P1) **1** gather or pick berries. 열매를 따다. ¶ *go berrying* 딸기 따러 가다. **2** form berries. 장과를 맺다. [E.]

ber·serk(·er) [bəːrsə́ːrk(ər), -zə́ːrk-, ∠—] *n.* an ancient Norse fighter. (북유럽 전설의) 광포(狂暴)한 전사(戰士). ¶ ~ *rage* (자제할 수 없는) 격렬한 노여움. [N.=bear-coat]
go berserk, become crazy. 미치다.

berth [bəːrθ] *n.* Ⓒ **1** a sleeping place on a ship, train, etc. (배·기차 등의 1인용) 침대. ¶ *book* 〔*reserve*〕 *a* ~ 침대를 예약하다. **2** a place for a ship to anchor. (배의) 투묘지(投錨地); 정박 위치. **3** a place to live in for a time. 숙소; 거처. **4** an appointment; a position; a job. 직(職); 지위; 일자리. ¶ *find a snug* ~ 편한 일자리를 찾다.
give a wide berth to, keep a safe distance from (someone or something); avoid. …에 충분한 거리를 유지하다; …을 경원하다; 피하다.
take up a berth, come to anchor. 정박하다.
— *vt.* (P6) put (a ship) in a berth; provide (someone) with a berth. (배)를 정박시키다; …에게 침대를〔침실을〕 주다.
— *vi.* (P2) have or occupy a berth. 숙박하다. [→bear[1]]

Ber·tha [bə́ːrθə] *n.* **1** a woman's name. 여자의 이름. 參考 애칭은 Bertie. **2** 《*b-*》 a woman's deep falling lace collar to a neckless dress. 여성복의 장식 깃. [Person]

ber·yl [bérəl] *n.* Ⓤ a very hard jewel stone, green or blue. 녹주석(綠柱石). [Gk.]

be·ryl·li·um [bəríliəm] *n.* 《chem.》 a rare metallic element. 베릴륨. [↑]

***be·seech** [bisíːtʃ] *vt.* (**be·sought**) (P6,13, 15, 20) 《*for*》 ask earnestly; beg. …을 간청하다; 탄원하다. ¶ ~ *someone for mercy* 〔*forgiveness*〕 아무에게 자비〔용서〕를 빌다 / ~ *that one may be allowed to leave* 떠날 수 있게 해 달라고 간청하다 / *He beseeches us to save his daughter's life.* 그는 딸의 목숨을 구해 달라고 애원한다 / *I* ~ *you to tell me the truth.* 제발이지 사실을 말씀해 주십시오. [→seek]

be·seech·ing·ly [bisíːtʃiŋli] *adv.* in a begging manner. 탄원하듯이.

be·seem [bisíːm] *vt.* (P6) 《*lit.*》 be proper for; suit; be fitting to. …에 어울리다. ¶ *It does not* ~ *you to leave your friend without help.* 친구를 돕지 않고 내버려 두는 것은 너답지 않다. [→seem]

be·set [bisét] *vt.* (**-set, -set·ting**) (P6) **1** attack (someone or something) on all sides; attack; worry. (…을) 사방에서 공격하다; 괴롭히다. ¶ *be* ~ *by many doubts* 많은 회의(懷疑)에 시달리다. **2** surround. (…을) 둘러싸다. ¶ *Dangers* ~ *her path.* 많은 위험들이 그녀의 길을 막는다 / *The story is* ~ *with contradictions.* 그 이야기는 모순투성이다. **3** 《usu. in *passive*》 set. …을 박아 넣다. ¶ *a bracelet* ~ *with jewels* 보석을 박은 팔찌. [→set]

be·set·ting [bisétiŋ] *adj.* 《usu. as *attributive*》 constantly attacking. 계속 괴롭히는. ¶ ~ *sins* 자칫 빠지기 쉬운 죄 / *a* ~ *temptation* 쉽게 빠지기 쉬운 유혹.

:be·side [bisáid] *prep.* **1** by the side of; near. …의 곁에(서); …가까이에. ¶ *a building* ~ *the gym* 체육관 가까이의 건물 / *Come and sit* ~ *me.* 이리 와서 내 옆에 앉아라 / *I want to live* ~ *the sea.* 바닷가에서 살고 싶다. **2** compared with. …와 비교해서〔하면〕. ¶ *You are quite tall* ~ *your sister.* 넌 네 누이동생과 비교하면 키가 꽤 크다. **3** away from. …을 떨어져서; …을 벗어나. ¶ ~ *the question* 문제에서 벗어나. [*by, side*]
beside oneself, out of one's mind; mad. 자신(自身)을 잊고; 제정신을 잃고. ¶ *She was* ~ *herself with excitement.* 그녀는 흥분으로 제정신이 아니었다.
beside the point 〔***mark***〕, having nothing to do with the subject being discussed. 빗나가; 벗어나; 무관계한. ¶ *Your remark is quite* ~ *the point.* 당신의 말씀은 문제의 핵심을 일탈해 있습니다 / *That question was* ~ *the mark, and need not be answered.* 질문이 문제를 벗어나 있어 대답할 필요가 없다.

:be·sides [bisáidz] *adv.* **1** also; moreover; further. 게다가; 더욱이. ¶ *I'm tired;* ~ *I'm sleepy.* 나는 피로하고 게다가 졸리다 / *Besides, I promised her we would come.* 더욱이 나는, 우리가 가겠노라고 그녀에게 약속했다. **2** otherwise; else. 그 밖에(는); 따로. — *prep.* **1** in addition to. …에 더하여. ¶ *There were six people* ~ *Tom.* 톰 말고도 여섯 사람이 있었다. **2** except; other than. …외에는; …을 제외하고. 語法 이 뜻으로 쓰이는 것은 부정문과 의문문에 한함. ¶ *He has nothing* ~ *his salary.* 그는 월급을 제외하고는 아무것도 가진 것이 없다. [↑]

be·siege [bisíːdʒ] *vt.* (P6) **1** surround or attack (a place) with armed forces. …을 포위〔공격〕하다. ¶ ~ *a city* 도시를 포위〔공격〕하다 / *the besieged* 농성군. **2** crowd. …에 몰려〔밀려〕들다. ¶ *The famous pianist was besieged by many admirers.* 그 유명한 피아니스트는 많은 팬들에게 둘러싸였다. **3** 《*with*》 trouble (someone) with requests, questions, etc. (탄원·간청·질문 따위로) …을 괴롭히다. ¶ ~ *someone with requests* 이것저것 요구하여 아무를 괴롭히다 / *The teacher was besieged with questions.* 선생은 질문 공세로 시달림을 받았다. [be-]

be·sieg·er [bisíːdʒər] *n.* Ⓒ a member of a besieging army; 《*pl.*》 a besieging army. 포위자; 포위군. 參考 '포위된 사람'은 the besieged.

be·smear [bismíər] *vt.* (P6,13) 《*lit.*》 《*with*》 cover (something) with oil, etc. …에 기름 따위를 뒤바르다. [be-]

be·smirch [bismə́ːrtʃ] *vt.* (P6) make

(something) dirty; bring shame upon (someone's honor, fame; etc.). …을 더럽히다. ¶ ~ *someone's good name* 아무의 명성을 손상시키다. [be-]

be·som [bízəm] *n.* Ⓒ a long brush for sweeping, made of thin branches. 마당비. [E.]

be·sot·ted [bisátid/-sɔ́t-] *adj.* **1** foolish; stupid; senseless. 어리석은; 의식이 없는. **2** drunk. 취한. ¶ *A ~ drunkard lay on the road.* 취객이 길에 쓰러져 있었다. [be-]

be·sought [bisɔ́:t] *v.* p. and pp. of **beseech.**

be·span·gle [bispǽŋgəl] *vt.* (P6,13) 《*with*》 make (something) beautiful with small pieces of bright metal. 번쩍번쩍 빛나는 장식으로 꾸미다. [be-]

be·spat·ter [bispǽtər] *vt.* (P6,13) **1** 《*with*》 splash; soil. …을 튀기다; …을 튀겨 더럽히다. ¶ *bespattered with mud* 흙탕을 뒤집어써 더럽혀지다. **2** speak ill of (someone). …에 욕설을 퍼붓다. [be-]

be·speak [bispí:k] *vt.* (**-spoke, -spok·en** or **-spoke**) **1** (P6) order; reserve. …을 예약하다; 주문하다. ¶ ~ *tickets for the opera* 오페라 관람권을 예약하다 / ~ *a dress* 옷을 맞추다. **2** (P6,21) give evidence of (something); show. …을 나타내다. ¶ *This bespeaks his generous nature.* 이것으로 그가 헙헙한 성격임을 알 수 있다 / *These names ~ the quality of this edition.* 이러한 이름들이 이 판(版)의 우수성을 보여 주고 있다. [be-]

be·spec·ta·cled [bispéktəkəld] *adj.* wearing glasses. 안경을 쓴. [be-]

be·spoke [bispóuk] *v.* p. and pp. of **bespeak.**

be·spok·en [bispóukən] *v.* pp. of **bespeak.**

be·sprin·kle [bispríŋkəl] *vt.* 《*poet.*》 sprinkle all over. 흩뿌리다. [be-]

Bess [bes] *n.* a nickname for Elizabeth. 엘리자베스의 애칭.

Bes·sie, Bes·sy [bési] *n.* =Bess.

:best [best] *adj.* (superl. of **good**) (opp. worst) **1** excelling all others; having the highest degree of quality. 최고의; 최상의. ¶ *the ~ book I have read for years* 요 몇 해 동안 내가 읽었던 가장 좋은 책 / *He is the ~ man for the work.* 그는 그 일에 최적임자다 / *the ~ thing to do* 해야 할 최선의 일 / *one's ~ girl* 애인 / *the ~ man* 신랑의 들러리. **2** most thorough. 가장 철저한. ¶ *the ~ liar* 철저한 거짓말쟁이 / *the ~ thrashing* 철저한 타격. **3** chief. 주요한; 으뜸의. ¶ *a ~ seller* 가장 잘 팔리는 것; 베스트 셀러.

— *n.* **1** the best thing or state. 가장 좋은 것. **2** one's highest or finest. 최고의 것; 가장 훌륭한 것. ¶ *the next* 〔*second*〕 ~ 차선.

at best, under the most favorable circumstances. 기껏; 최대한으로.

at one's* 〔*its*〕 *best, in the best state. 가장 좋은 상태에; 최호조(最好調)에.

for the best, with good intentions; for the good as the final result. 좋게 되라고; 결국은 잘 되라고.

get the best of, win in a contest ; outdo. …에 이기다.

make the best of, utilize (something) as well as one can. …을 최대한으로 이용하다.

***put* 〔*set*〕 *one's foot forward* 〔*foremost*〕,** **a**) go as quickly as possible. 될 수 있는 대로 빨리 가다; 서두르다. **b**) exert all one's efforts. 모든 노력을 하다. **c**) 《U.S.》 try to make a good impression. 될 수 있는 대로 좋은 인상을 주려고 하다.

to the best of one's ability, as well as one can. 될 수 있는 대로 잘.

to the best of one's belief, as far as one knows. …이 아는 한(에서는).

with the best, as well as anyone. 누구에게도 못지않게.

— *adv.* 《the superl. of **well**》 in the best way; most. 가장 (잘). ¶ *a hairdo that ~ suits her features* 그녀 얼굴에 가장 잘 맞는 머리형 / *He thinks he knows ~.* 그는 그가 가장 잘 알고 있다고 생각한다 / *the ~ abused book of the year* 그 해에 가장 평판이 나쁜 책 / *I love him ~.* 나는 그를 가장 사랑한다.

best of all, first of all; above all. 우선 첫째로; 다른 무엇보다(도).

You had best do, It is your best course to do. …하는 것이 가장 좋다.

— *vt.* (P6) defeat. …에 이기다. [E.]

be·stead [bistéd] *vt., vi.* (P6; 1) help; assist; serve. 돕다; …에 도움이 되다. ¶ *His threadbare coat did little to ~ him against the chill north wind.* 그의 닳아빠진 옷은 차가운 북풍을 막는 데는 거의 도움이 되지 못했다.

— *adj.* placed; situated. …한 처지에 있는. ¶ *ill ~* 괴로운 처지에 있는. [be-]

bes·tial [béstʃəl, bí:s-/béstiəl] *adj.* like a beast; cruel; very bad. 짐승 같은; 무도한; 비열한. ● **bes·tial·ly** [-li] *adv.* [→beast]

be·stir [bistə́:r] *vt.* (**be·stirred**) (P6) exert; rouse. 분발케 하다. [be-]

bestir oneself, rouse oneself to action. 분발하다.

***be·stow** [bistóu] *vt.* (P6,13) 《*on*》 **1** present (something) as a gift; give. …을 주다. ¶ *He bestowed all his books on me.* 그는 나에게 그의 책 전부를 주었다. **2** put safely; put; place. 두다. ¶ *I don't know where to ~ all my luggage.* 내 짐을 모두 어디에 두어야 할지 모르겠다. **3** 《*arch.*》 give quarters to; find room for. 묵게 하다. ¶ *Can you ~ us somewhere for the night?* 밤에 어디서건 묵게 해 주실 수 있습니까. [be-]

be·stow·al [bistóuəl] *n.* ⓊⒸ the act of giving. 증여; 수여. ¶ *the ~ of gifts* 선물 공여(供與).

be·strew [bistrú:] *vt.* (**-strewed, -strewed** or **-strewn**) (P6,13) **1** throw (things) here and there. …을 흩뿌리다. **2** 《*with*》 scatter things over (a place). …에 흩뿌리다. ¶ ~ *the room with flowers* 방에 꽃을 흩뿌리다 /

the streets bestrewn with dead leaves 마른 잎이 흩어져 쌓인 거리. [be-]

be·strewn [bistrúːn] *v.* pp. of **bestrew.**

be·strid [bistríd] *v.* p. and pp. of **bestride.**

be·strid·den [bistrídn] *v.* pp. of **bestride.**

be·stride [bistráid] *vt.* (P6) (**-strode** or **-strid, -strid·den** or **-strid**) **1** get on or sit on (something) with legs apart. …에 걸터 앉다. ¶ ~ *a horse* 말에 걸터 앉다. **2** stand astride over; step over. 넘어가다. ¶ ~ *a fence* 담을 넘어가다 / ~ *a groove* 도랑을 뛰어넘다. 參考 무지개 따위가 공중에 떠 있는 경우에도 씀. **3** 《*poet.*》 pass, extend, or reach across. 지나가다; …에 걸리다; 걸치다. [be-]

be·strode [bistróud] *v.* p. of **bestride.**

best seller [ˊ ˊ–] *n.* **1** a book, record, etc. that has the largest sale in a given period. 베스트 셀러. **2** an author of a book with a very large sale. 베스트 셀러 작가〔저자〕. [*best, seller*]

bet** [bet] *v.* (**bet** or **bet·ted, bet·ting**) *vt.* (P6,11,13,14,15) agree to give (money, etc.) to another if he guesses right. (돈 따위)를 걸다. ¶ ~ *$50 on* 〔*upon*〕 *the race* 그 레이스에 50 달러 걸다 / *I* ~ *you a dollar on his success.* 그가 성공한다는 데에 당신과 1 달러 걸겠소. ——*vi.* (P1,3) 《*on, against*》 make a bet. 내기하다. ¶ ~ *on horse races* 경마에 걸다 / *He never bets.* 그는 결코 내기를 하지 않는다 / *I'll* ~ *on* 〔*against*〕 *your winning.* 난 네가 이길〔못 이길〕 것으로 믿는다. ***I bet you =***You bet!*** Certainly; without fail. 틀림없이; 물론. ¶ *I* ~ *you he will fail.* 틀림없이 그는 실패할 거야.

——*n.* Ⓒ **1** a promise to give money, etc. to another if he guesses right. 내기. ¶ *an even* ~ 성패가 반반인 내기 / *lose* 〔*win*〕 *a* ~ 내기에 지다〔이기다〕. **2** the money or thing bet. 건 돈〔물건〕. [? E]

make a bet, lay a wage. 걸다.

be·ta [béitə / bíːtə] *n.* Ⓒ the second letter of the Greek alphabet(B, β). 베타. ¶ *a* ~ *particle* 베타 입자(粒子) / ~ *rays* 베타선(線).

be·take [bitéik] *vt.* (**-took, -tak·en**) (P6,13) 《usu. *reflexively*》 **1** cause (someone) to go. 가다. ¶ *He betook himself to the river.* 그는 강에 갔다. **2** apply oneself to (something). …에 전념하다. ¶ *Betake yourself to your studies.* 공부에 전념하라. [be-]

be·tak·en [bitéikən] *n.* pp. of **betake.**

be·ta·tron [béitətràn / bíːtətrɔ̀n] *n.* 《phys.》 a device accelerating electrons to high energy. 베타트론. [→electron]

be·tel [bíːtəl] *n.* 《bot.》 a kind of pepper plant, the leaves of which are chewed by Indians. 구장(蒟醬). [Native]

bête noire [bèit nwάːr] *n.* 《F.》 one's abomination. 몹시 싫어하는 것〔사람〕(= black beast).

Beth [beθ] *n.* a nickname for Elizabeth. 엘리자베스의 애칭.

beth·el [béθəl] *n.* **1** a hallowed spot. 움푹 들어간 곳. **2** a nonconformist chapel. 비국교도(非國敎徒)의 예배당. [Heb. =house of God]

be·think [biθíŋk] *vt.* (**-thought**) (P13,15,16, 17) 《usu. *reflexively*》 《*of, how, that*》 《*lit.*》 consider; remember. 생각하다; 생각해 내다. ¶ ~ *oneself how* 〔*of, that*〕... …은 어째서인가를 생각하다; 얼마나 …한가를 생각하다; …한 것을 생각해 내다 / ~ *oneself of family obligations* 가정적 책임을 상기하다. [be-]

Beth·le·hem [béθliəm, -lihèm] *n.* a town in Palestine; the birthplace of Jesus. 베들레헴.

be·thought [biθɔ́ːt] *v.* p. and pp. of **bethink.**

be·tide [bitáid] *vt., vi.* (P6; 1) 《*lit.*》 happen (to). 일어나다; 발생하다. ¶ *Woe* ~ *the man!* 그놈 가만 두지 않을 테다. [be-]

whatever (***may***) ***betide,*** whatever happens. 무슨 일이 있든.

be·times [bitáimz] *adv.* 《*lit.*》 **1** early. 일찍. ¶ *rise* ~ 일찍 일어나다. **2** in good time; before it is too late. 때 맞춰; 너무 늦기 전에. [→by, times]

be·to·ken [bitóukən] *vt.* (P6) be a sign of (something); show. …의 조짐이다; …을 나타내다. ¶ *Clouds* ~ *rain.* 구름은 비가 올 조짐이다. [be-]

be·ton [bétən] *n.* concrete. 콘크리트. [L.]

be·took [bitúk] *v.* p. of **betake.**

:**be·tray** [bitréi] *vt.* (P6) **1** sell (a country, etc.) to the enemy. …을 적에게 팔다; 배반하다. ¶ *He betrayed his country.* 그는 나라를 적에게 팔았다. **2** make (a secret) known; show. (비밀)을 누설하다; (무심코) 드러내다. ¶ ~ *a secret* 비밀을 누설하다 / ~ *someone's confidence* 아무의 신뢰를 배반하다 / *His words betrayed him.* 그의 말은 그의 본심을 드러냈다 / *The gate betrays its age.* 대문은 그 연조(年條)를 나타낸다. **3** deceive. …을 속이다. ¶ *He was betrayed into a snare.* 그는 속아서 덫에 걸렸다 / *He was betrayed into buying an old car.* 그는 속아서 고물차를 샀다. [→treason]

be·tray·al [bitréiəl] *n.* ⒸⓊ the act of betraying. 배반; 매국 행위. ¶ *his* ~ *of his bosom friend* 절친한 친구에 대한 배신 행위.

be·tray·er [bitréiər] *n.* Ⓒ a person who sells his country, etc. to the enemy. 매국노; 배반자.

be·troth [bitrɔ́ːθ, -tróuð] *vt.* (P6,13) 《*to*》 《usu. in *passive*》 arrange someone to marry. …를 약혼시키다. ¶ ~ *oneself to* …와 결혼의 약속을 하다 / *His daughter was betrothed to a banker.* 그의 딸은 은행가와 약혼했다. [be-]

be·troth·al [bitrɔ́ːθəl, -tróuðəl] *n.* Ⓒ a promise to marry. 약혼.

be·trothed [bitrɔ́ːθt, -tróuðd] *adj.* engaged

to be married. 약혼한. ¶ *the ~ pair* 약혼한 한 쌍. — *n.* 《*the ~, one's ~*》 a person engaged to be married. 약혼자. ¶ *my ~* 나의 약혼자 / *the ~* (한 쌍의) 약혼자(cf. *fiancé(e)*).

:bet·ter[1] [bétər] *adj.* (compar. of **good** or **well**) excelling another; having a higher degree in quality. 보다 좋은〔나은〕. ¶ *It is ~ to go away than stay.* 머무는 것보다 떠나는 것이 더 좋다 / 《*prov.*》 *Better late than never.* 늦어도 하지 않은 것보다 낫다.

be* 〔*get*〕 *better, be less unwell. 좋아지다.

one's ***better half,*** one's wife. 아내.

be better than *one's* ***word,*** do more than one has promised. 약속 이상의 일을 하다.

have seen better days, have been richer or in a better position than at present. 전에는 유복했었다; 이제 전성기는 갔다.

little* 〔*no*〕 *better than, almost the same as (someone or something not good). …와 거의 같을 만큼 나쁜; …나 마찬가지인; …에 지나지 않는. ¶ *He was no ~ than a traitor.* 그는 배반자나 다름없었다.

no better than one should be, morally inferior; of doubtful character sexually. 도덕관념이 없는; (여자가 몸가짐이) 헤픈.

the better part, the majority. 대부분.

You had better *do.* It is better for you to do. …하는 것이 좋다〔낫다〕.

— *n.* **1** 《*the ~; one's ~*》 something better. 보다 좋은〔나은〕 것. **2** Ⓒ 《usu. *pl.*》 a person of higher rank, ability, etc. 윗사람; 어른; 상사; 나은 사람. ¶ *respect for one's betters* 윗사람을 존경하다.

for better* (*or*) *for worse, in good or bad fortune. 좋든 싫든; (이제부터) 어떻게 되든. ¶ *It was time she accepted that for ~ or for worse.* 좋든 싫든 이제 그녀가 그것을 받아들일 시기였다.

get* 〔*have*〕 *the better of, win a victory over; defeat someone; get an advantage over. …에 이기다; …을 능가하다; …보다 낫다.

— *adv.* (compar. of **well**) in a more excellent manner. 더욱 좋게.

better off, richer; more comfortable. 더 잘 사는; 더욱 편한〔안락한〕.

go *someone* ***one better,*** do better (than...). (아무가 한 것보다) 한 수 위를 가다; (아무보다) 낫다.

had better, should; will be wise to. …해야 한다; …하는 것이 낫다.

know better, be not such a fool. 그런 바보는 아니다. ¶ *I know ~ than to do such a thing.* 그런 짓을 할 바보는 아니다.

think better of, change one's mind. 고쳐 생각하다.

— *vi., vt.* (P1; 6) improve; improve upon. 좋아지다; 개선하다. ¶ *~ the lot of the suburban commuter* 교외의 많은 정기 통근자의 편의를 도모하다 / *We cannot ~ his performance.* 우리는 그의 성적을 향상시킬 수 없다. [E.]

better *oneself*, get a better situation; rise in life. 출세하다.

bet·ter[2], **-tor** [bétər] *n.* Ⓒ a person who bets or makes an agreement about paying money if a certain thing happens. 내기를 하는 사람. [*bet*]

bet·ter·ment [bétərmənt] *n.* ⓊⒸ **1** improvement. 개선. **2** 《usu. *pl.*》 an improvement to the value of real property. 땅값의 오름. [→better]

bet·ting [bétiŋ] *n.* Ⓤ the act of making bets. 내기. [*bet*]

Bet·ty [béti] *n.* a nickname for Elizabeth. 엘리자베스의 애칭.

:be·tween [bitwíːn] *prep.* **1** in the time, space, or interval that separates (two points, objects, etc.). (시간·공간)의 사이에〔의〕; 중간에(서). ¶ *~ eight and nine* 여덟 시에서 아홉 시 사이에 / *~ morning and noon* 아침에서 정오 사이에 / *with a cigarette ~ one's lips* 입에 담배를 물고 / *~ the two world wars* 양차 세계 대전 사이에 / *a feeling ~ love and hate* 사랑과 증오의 중간 감정 / *Many cities lie ~ Seoul and Pusan.* 서울과 부산간에는 많은 도시가 있다. **2** in common to. (공통의) …의 사이의〔에〕. ¶ *a treaty ~ two powers* 두 나라 사이의 조약 / *a war ~ the two nations* 양국간의 전쟁 / *the opposition ~ science and religion* 과학과 종교와의 대립. **3** ⓐ in comparison of; intermediate to. (정도·선택 따위) …의 중간에〔의〕; 비교하여. ¶ *a color ~ pink and red* 핑크와 빨강의 중간색 / *lie ~ life and death* 반생반사(半生半死)의 상태로 누워 있다. ⓑ with respect to either the one or the other of (two people or things). (선택 따위) …사이에〔의〕. ¶ *choose one ~ the two* 양자 택일하다 / *There is no choice ~ the two.* 2자간에는 우열이 없다 / *You must choose ~ death and disgrace.* 죽음과 치욕 중 어느 하나를 택해야 한다. **4** by joint action or possession of. (협력·소유 따위) …의 사이에; 협력하여. ¶ *They own land ~ them.* 그들은 둘이서 토지를 공유하고 있다 / *They caught twenty fish ~ them.* 그들은 협력해서 물고기 20 마리를 잡았다. **5** from one to the other or another of. …에서 —까지. ¶ *It is about fifty miles ~ this city and that.* 이 도시에서 그 도시까지는 약 50 마일이다.

***between times* 〔*whiles*〕,** in the interval between. 사이를 두고; 때때로; 가끔.

between you and me* =*between ourselves, speaking in confidence. 은밀한〔우리끼리의〕 이야기인데.

— *adv.* between two or more points; between extremes in quantity, character, etc. 중간에; 사이에; 이도저도 아니게. [be-, →two]

betwixt and between, half-and-half. 중간에.

in between, between. …의 사이에. ¶ *There were flowers in ~ the trees.* 나무들 사이에 꽃이 있었다.

·**be·twixt** [bitwíkst] *prep., adv.* 《*arch.*》 = between.

bev·a·tron [bévətràn / -trɔ̀n] *n.* 《phys.》 a high energy cyclotron. 베바트론. [→cyclotron]

bev·el [bévəl] *n.* Ⓒ **1** a sloping edge. 사각(斜角); 경사. **2** an instrument for measuring or drawing angles. 각도자. — *vt.* (**-eled, -el·ing** or esp. 《Brit.》 **-elled, -el·ling**) (P6) give a sloping edge to (something). …을 비스듬히 베다; 비스듬하게 하다. [F.]

bevel gear [⌐–⌐] *n.* 《mech.》 either of a pair of gears with teeth cut so that the gear shafts are not parallel. 베벨기어《회전력을 평행하지 아니한 축 방향으로 전하는 우산 모양의 기어》.

bev·er·age [bévəridʒ] *n.* Ⓒ something to drink, such as tea, beer, wine, etc. 마실 것, 음료. ¶ *intoxicating beverages* 알코올 음료. [L. *bibo* drink]

bev·y [bévi] *n.* (*pl.* **bev·ies**) a small group, esp. of women or girls; a flock of birds, esp. of larks or quail. (부녀자의) 떼; (새의) 떼. ¶ *a ~ of quails* 메추라기 떼. [F.]

be·wail [biwéil] *vt., vi.* (P6; 3) mourn; weep; regret deeply. 몹시 슬퍼하다; 울다. ¶ *~ over one's misfortune* 자신의 불운을 한탄하다 / *The little girl was bewailing the loss of her doll.* 그 어린 소녀는 인형을 잃고 몹시 슬퍼하고 있었다. [be-]

·**be·ware** [biwɛ́ər] *vi., vt.* (P1,3; 6) 《*of*》 guard against (something); be careful. 조심하다. ¶ *Beware of pickpockets!* 소매치기 조심 / *Tell him to ~ of the dog.* 개를 조심하라고 그에게 이르게 / *Beware that you do not anger him.* 그를 성나게 하지 않도록 주의해라 / *We must ~ how we approach them.* 그들에게 접근하는 방법을 잘 생각해야 한다. 語法 언제나 원형(原形)으로 씀. [be-, *ware* look to]

·**be·wil·der** [biwíldər] *vt.* (P6) 《chiefly in *passive*》 confuse completely. …을 당혹케〔당황하게〕 하다. ¶ *Tom was bewildered by the examination questions.* 톰은 시험 문제에 당황했다 / *So many questions ~ me.* 그렇게 많은 질문은 나를 당황케 한다. [→wilderness]

be·wil·der·ing [biwíldəriŋ] *adj.* causing puzzlement; confusing. 당황케 하는.

be·wil·der·ing·ly [biwíldəriŋli] *adv.* in a puzzle. 당황하여; 어찌할 바를 몰라.

be·wil·der·ment [biwíldərmənt] *n.* Ⓤ the state of being confused; complete confusion. 당혹; 당황.

·**be·witch** [biwítʃ] *vt.* (P6) use a magic effect on (someone); charm; delight. …에게 마법을 걸다; …을 매혹하다. ¶ *She bewitched the boy and turned him into a frog.* 그녀는 그 소년에게 마법을 걸어 개구리로 변하게 했다 / *He felt as if bewitched by a fox.* 그는 마치 여우에게 홀린 것같이 느꼈다. [be-]

be·witch·ing [biwítʃiŋ] *adj.* delightful; charming. 황홀케 하는; 매력이 있는.

be·witch·ing·ly [biwítʃiŋli] *adv.* in a charming manner. 매혹적으로.

bey [bei] *n.* a Turkish governor. 터키의 지사(知事). [Osmanli]

:**be·yond** [bijánd / -jɔ́nd] *prep.* **1** at or to the farther side of. …저쪽〔너머〕에. ¶ *a town ~ the hill* 고개 너머 마을 / *The post office is ~ the bridge.* 우체국은 다리 건너에 있다. **2** outside the range of; out of sight or hearing of. …의 범위를 넘어. ¶ *~ control* 통제할 수 없는 / *~ possibility* 불가능하여 / *~ one's grasp* 이해할 수 없는 / *~ all hope* 아주 절망적인 / *~ compare* 비교가 안 될 만큼 (뛰어나) / *~ doubt* 의문의 여지 없이; 물론 / *~ what I can afford to buy* 나로서는 살 수 없을 정도의 / *He was ~ the help of the doctor.* 그는 의사도 손을 쓸 수 없었다. **3** more than. …이상의〔으로〕. ¶ *~ one's expectations* 기대 이상으로 / *live ~ one's means* 분수에 걸맞지 않은 생활을 하다. **4** 《usu. in *negative* or *interrogative*》 except; other than. …밖〔외〕에. ¶ *Beyond this I know nothing.* 이 밖에 나는 아무것도 모른다.

beyond endurance, unbearable. 참을 수 없는.

beyond measure, exceedingly; too much. 매우; 몹시.

It is beyond me. I cannot understand it. 이해할 수 없다.

— *adv.* **1** at or to the farther side; further on; outside. 저쪽으로〔에〕. ¶ *Beyond was a large plain.* 저쪽에는 대평원이 있었다. **2** besides. 그 밖〔외〕에. ¶ *He gave me nothing ~.* 그 밖에는 아무것도 주지 않았다.

— *n.* 《*the ~*》 life after death. 저 세상; 저승; 내세. ¶ *go to the ~* 죽다; 저승으로 가다. [be-, →yon]

the back of beyond, a very distant place; the remotest corner of the world. 아득히 먼 곳; 이 세상 끝.

bez·el [bézəl] *n.* **1** an edge of a chisel. (끌의) 날. **2** the sloping surface of a jewel; the part of a ring which holds the stone. 보석의 사면(斜面); (반지의) 거미발. [F.]

be·zoar [bíːzɔːr] *n.* a concretion found in intestines of some animals, reputed to be efficacious against poison. 짐승 체내의 결석(結石); 위석(胃石); 우황(牛黃). [Pers.]

B.F.A. Bachelor of Fine Arts.

B.F.O. British Foreign Office.

Bhu·tan [buːtáːn, -tǽn] *n.* a kingdom in the Himalayan mountains. 부탄《국명》.

Bi 《chem.》 bismuth. 비스무트.

bi- [bai] *pref.* twice; two; double. '두…, 양…, 겹…'의 뜻. ¶ *bicycle* 자전거 / *bimonthly* 한 달 걸러. [L.]

bi·an·nu·al [baiǽnjuəl] *adj.* coming twice a year. 연(年) 2회의. [L.]

bi·as [báiəs] *n.* **1** Ⓒ a slanting line. 사선(斜線). ¶ *cut a cloth on the ~* 천을 비스듬히 마르다. **2** ⒸⓊ an opinion formed before examining the facts; a prejudice. 편견;

선입관. ¶ *a racial* ~ 인종적 편견 / *an anti-communist* ~ 반공적 경향 / *have a* ~ *against* 〔*in favor of*〕 *someone* 아무에게 편견을〔호의를〕 갖고 있다 / *She is free from* ~. 그녀에게는 편견이 없다. **3** Ⓒ the weight or force that makes something lean; particular fondness. 편중; 선입관.
have* 〔*be under*〕 *a bias toward, have a liking for one side. …을 편애하다.
without bias and without favor, fairly. 공평하게.
— *adj.* slanting; sloping. 비스듬한.
— *adv.* from corner to corner. 비스듬히.
— *vt.* (P6) (**-ased, -as·ing** or 《Brit.》 **-assed, -as·sing**) influence, usu. not fairly. …을 한쪽으로 치우치게 하다; 편견을 갖게 하다. [F.]
bi·ased, bi·assed [báiəst] *adj.* **1** heavier on one side. 한 쪽으로 치우친. **2** favoring one side too much; prejudiced. 편애하는; 편견을 가진. ¶ *a* ~ *view* 편견 / *He is biased against me.* 그는 내게 편견을 갖고 있다.
bi·ath·lon [baiǽθlɑn / -lɔn] *n.* an athletic competition consisting of skiing and shooting. 바이애슬론《크로스컨트리와 사격의 복합 경기》. [Gk. bi, athlon]
bib [bib] *n.* Ⓒ **1** a cloth worn under the chin by a baby to keep his other clothing clean. 턱받이. **2** the top part of an apron. (에이프런 따위의) 가슴 부분. [L. *bibo*]
one's best bib and tucker, 《*colloq.*》 one's best clothes. 나들이옷.
bib·cock [bíbkɑ̀k / -kɔ̀k] *n.* a faucet with a bent nozzle. (주둥이가 굽은) 수도꼭지. [↑]
·**Bi·ble** [báibəl] *n.* **1** Ⓒ 《usu. *the* ~》 the sacred book of the Christian religion; the Old and New Testaments. 성서. ¶ *kiss the* ~ 성서에 입맞추다〔선서하다〕 / *on the* ~ 성서를 두고; 맹세코. **2** Ⓒ 《*b-*》 any book accepted as an authority. 권위 있는 서적. [Gk. *biblos* papyrus bark, book]
Bib·li·cal, bib- [bíblikəl] *adj.* of the Bible. 성서의. ¶ ~ *teachings* 성서의 가르침 / ~ *studies* 성서 연구 / ~ *quotation* 성서에서의 인용(구). [↑]
bib·li·og·ra·pher [bìbliɑ́grəfər / -ɔ́g-] *n.* Ⓒ a person who studies the histories of books or who describes and lists them. 서적 해제자(解題者); 서지학자(書誌學者). [↓]
bib·li·o·graph·i·cal [bìbliəgrǽfikəl] *adj.* of bibliography. 서지(書誌)의; 서지학(書誌學)적인.
bib·li·og·ra·phy [bìbliɑ́grəfi / -ɔ́g-] *n.* (*pl.* **-phies**) **1** Ⓒ a list of books about a subject or person. (어떤 주제·저자 등에 관한) 저서 목록. ¶ *a Shakespeare* ~ 세익스피어 문헌. **2** Ⓤ the study of the writers, editions, dates, etc. of books. 서지학. [→bible]
bib·lio·ma·nia [bìbliouméiniə, -njə] *n.* a craze for collecting books. 책수집광(狂); 장서광(藏書狂).
bib·li·o·phile [bíbliəfàil] *n.* Ⓒ a person who loves or collects books. 애서가(愛書家); 장서(藏書) 애호가.
bi·blot [bí:blou] *n.* a curio. 골동품.
bib·u·lous [bíbjələs] *adj.* fond of drinking alcoholic liquor. 술을 좋아하는. [L. *bibo* drink]
bi·cam·er·al [baikǽmərəl] *adj.* having two law-making assemblies, as the Congress of the United States. 양원제(兩院制)의. [bi-, L. *camera* chamber]
bi·car·bo·nate [baikɑ́:rbənit, -nèit] *n.* ⓊⒸ 《chem.》 a salt of carbonic acid, used in cooking or for medicine. 탄산수소염. ¶ *sodium* ~ 탄산수소나트륨. [bi-]
bi·cen·te·nar·y [bàisenténəri / -tí:-] *adj.* of 200 years; happening every 200 years. 200년째(마다)의. — *n.* Ⓒ (*pl.* **-nar·ies**) **1** a period of 200 years. 200년. **2** the celebration of the 200th anniversary of an event. 200년 축제. [bi-]
bi·cen·ten·ni·al [bàisenténiəl] *adj., n.* =bicentenary.
bi·ceps [báiseps] *n.* (*pl.* **biceps** or **-pses**) **1** the large muscle in the front part of the upper arm. 이두박근(二頭膊筋). **2** the muscle that bends the knee. 이두고근(二頭股筋). [bi-, L. *caput* head]
bi·ceps·es [báisepsiz] *n.* pl. of **biceps.**
bi·chlo·ride [baiklɔ́:raid] *n.* 《chem.》 a compound containing two atoms of chlorine combined with another element. 이염화물. [bi-]
bichloride of mercury, a poisonous substance. 염화제이수은; 승홍(昇汞).
bick·er [bíkər] *vi.* (P1,2A) **1** quarrel over or about small matters. 말다툼하다. ¶ ~ *over trifles* 사소한 일로 말다툼하다. **2** flow noisily. 소리내며 흐르다. **3** (of light, flame) flash. 번쩍〔번뜩〕이다. [E.]
bi·con·cave [baikɑ́nkeiv, ⌐–⌐ / -kɔ́n-] *adj.* concave on both sides. 양쪽이 오목한. [bi-]
bi·con·vex [baikɑ́nveks / -kɔ́n-] *adj.* convex on both sides. 양쪽이 볼록한.
bi·cron [báikrɑn / -krɔn] *n.* one billionth of a meter. 비크론《1 m 의 10억분의 1》. [*bi*llion, mi*cron*]
bi·cus·pid [baikʌ́spid] *n.* a double-pointed tooth. 앞어금니. — *adj.* having two points. 뾰족한 끝이 둘 있는. [→cusp]
:**bi·cy·cle** [báisikəl, -sàikəl] *n.* Ⓒ a machine with two wheels moved by turning pedals with one's feet. 자전거. 參考 구어로는 bike. — *vi.* (P1) ride a bicycle. 자전거를 타(고 가)다. ¶ ~ *to the office* 자전거로 출근하다. [bi-, →cycle]
bi·cy·cler [báisikələr, -sài-], **bi·cy·cl·ist** [báisikəlist] *n.* Ⓒ a bicycle rider. 자전거를 타는 사람.
:**bid** [bid] *v.* (**bade** or 《Brit.》 **bad, bid·den, bid·ding**) *vt.* **1** (P20,22) give an order to (someone); command. …에게 명령하다. ¶ ~ *him go* = ~ *him to go* 그에게 가라고 명령하다 / *The captain bade his men go for-*

ward. 대위는 부하들에게 전진하라고 명령했다 / *Do as I ~ you.* 시키는 대로 해라. **2** (P14) say (good-by, good morning, etc.). …에게 인사의 말을 하다. ¶ *~ someone good night* 아무에게 안녕히 주무시라고 하다 / *~ farewell to the visiting prime minister* 예방한 총리에게 작별의 인사를 하다. **3** (P13) (*p.* **bid**) 《*for*》 (at auctions, etc.) offer a price for (something). (경매 따위에서) 값을 부르다; 입찰하다. ¶ *~ a good price for the house* 그 집에 꽤 좋은 값을 부르다 / *First she bid $5 for the table; I then bid $6.* 처음에 그녀가 그 테이블에 5달러를 불렀다. 그러자 나는 6달러를 불렀다. **4** (P6) (*p.* **bid**) make (something) known to the public. …을 공표하다. **5** (P6,13) (*p.* **bid**) invite. …를 초대하다. ¶ *She was bidden to the feast.* 그녀는 잔치에 초대되었다. —*vi.* (P1,3) offer a price; make a bid. 값을 부르다. ¶ *~ against someone at auction* 경매에서 서로 값을 다투어 올리다; 경쟁 입찰하다.

bid fair to do, seem likely to do; show promise of doing. …할 가능성이 충분히 있다; …할 것 같다. ¶ *The plan bids fair to succeed.* 계획은 성공할 것 같다.

—*n.* Ⓒ **1** an offer of money; the amount offered for something. 값을 부름; 입찰가. ¶ *enter a ~ at an auction* 경매에서 값을 부르다 / *Our ~ for building the bridge was $60,000.* 교량 건설을 위한 우리의 입찰가는 6만 달러였다. **2** an attempt to get. 얻고자 하는 노력. ¶ *the world's ~ for peace* 평화를 위한 세계의 노력. [E.]

make a bid for, 《*fig.*》 attempt to get (favor, etc.). …을 얻으려고 노력하다. ¶ *make a ~ for election* 당선되려고 노력하다.

·bid·den [bídn] *v.* pp. of **bid.**

bid·der [bídər] *n.* Ⓒ a person who bids, esp. at an auction sale. 명령자; (특히) 입찰자. ¶ *the highest ~* 최고 입찰자. [*bid*]

bid·ding [bídiŋ] *n.* ⓊⒸ **1** a command. 명령; 지시. ¶ *await the ~* 지시를 기다리다 / *do someone's ~* 아무의 명령에 따르다 / *I have come at your ~.* 당신의 명령을 받고 왔습니다. **2** an invitation. 초대. **3** an offering of money for something. (경매에서) 값매기기. ¶ *a competitive ~* 경쟁 입찰.

at the bidding of (=*obedient to*) *someone.* …의 명령(분부)에 따라.

do the bidding (=*carry out the orders*) ***of*** *someone.* …의 명령대로 하다.

bide [baid] *vt.* (**bode** [boud] or **bid·ed, bided**) (P6) 《*arch., poet.*》 wait; stay; remain. 기다리다; 머물다. [E.]

bide one's time, wait till a good chance comes. 때(호기)를 기다리다.

bi·en·ni·al [baiéniəl] *adj.* **1** (of plants) lasting two years. 2년생의. **2** happening every two years. 2년마다 일어나는; 2년에 한 번의. —*n.* Ⓒ **1** a plant that lives two years. 2년생 식물(cf. *perennial*). **2** an event that happens every two years. 2년마다 일어나는 일. [bi-, L. *annus* year]

bi·en·ni·al·ly [baiéniəli] *adv.* once in two years. 2년마다.

bier [biər] *n.* Ⓒ a base for carrying a box containing a dead body. 관대(棺臺). [E.]

biff [bif] 《*sl.*》 *n.* a blow. 타격. ¶ *a ~ in the eye* 눈의 강타. —*vt.* (P6,13) strike; hit. 때리다; 치다. ¶ *He got biffed on the nose.* 그는 코를 얻어맞았다. [?]

bi·fo·cal [baifóukəl] *adj.* (of a lens) having two focuses. (렌즈가) 초점이 둘 있는; 이중 초점의. —*n.* **1** 《usu. *pl.*》 a pair of glasses having bifocal lenses. 두 초점 렌즈의 안경. **2** Ⓒ a bifocal lens. 이중 초점 렌즈. [bi-]

bi·fur·cate [báifərkèit, baifə́ːrkeit] *vt., vi.* (P6; 1) divide into two branches. 두 갈래로 가르다. [→fork]

:big [big] *adj.* (**big·ger, big·gest**) **1** large. 큰. ¶ *a ~ house* 큰 집 / *a ~ fire* 대화재 / *a ~ enterprise* 대기업 / *a ~ voice* 큰 소리 / *the ~ toe* 엄지 발가락. **2** grown-up. 성장한; 다 자란. ¶ *You're a ~ girl now. You mustn't cry.* 너는 이제 다 큰 처녀이니 울어선 안 된다. **3** 《*colloq.*》 important. 중요한. ¶ *a ~ man* 거물 / *the ~ event* 중요한 사건(행사) / *the Big Three* 3대국. **4** boastful. 자랑하는; 희떠운; 젠체하는. ¶ *a ~ talker* 허풍선이 / *~ words* 흰소리 / *looks ~* 잘난 체하다. **5** generous; noble. 너그러운; 고귀한. ¶ *a ~ nature (heart)* 너그러운 심성(마음).

big on, 《*colloq.*》 enthusiastic about. …에 열광하고.

big with (=*full of*) *something.* …로 가득찬; 임신하고. ¶ *eyes ~ with tears* 눈물어린 눈 / *~ with child* 임신하여 / *The cat is ~ with young.* 그 고양이는 새끼를 배고 있다.

too big for one's boots, 《*sl.*》 conceited. 뽐내는.

—*ad.* boastfully. 잘난 듯이. ¶ *talk ~* 허풍떨다. [E.]

big·a·my [bígəmi] *n.* Ⓤ the crime of having two wives or husbands at the same time. 중혼죄(重婚罪). [bi-, Gk. *gamos* marriage]

big bug [ˊ-ˊ] *n.* an important man. 명사(名士); 높은 사람. [*big*]

big·horn [bíghɔ̀ːrn] *n.* a wild sheep of the Rocky Mountains, having large, curved horns. (로키 산맥에 서식하는) 야생양(羊).

bight [bait] *n.* Ⓒ **1** a curve in a coastline. 해안선의 굴곡. **2** a bay. 만(灣); 후미. **3** a loop made in a rope. 밧줄의 고리. [E.]

big idea [ˊ-ˊ], **the** *n.* 《U.S. usu. *iron.*》 a plan. 계획. ¶ *What's the ~?* 엉뚱한 생각을 하는군. [*big*]

big·ness [bígnis] *n.* Ⓤ the state of being big; greatness; importance. 큼; 위대; 중대.

big noise [ˊ-ˊ] *n.* 《*colloq.*, orig. U.S.》 a person of great importance, esp. in his own opinion. (자칭) 거물; 명사; 유력자.

big·ot [bígət] *n.* Ⓒ a person who sticks blindly to his own opinion; a prejudiced person. 완고하고 우매한 사람; 고집통이. [F.]

big·ot·ed [bígətid] *adj.* sticking to one's opinion, belief, etc. without reason. 완고하고 우매한; 편협한. ¶ *He is very ~ in all matters of religion.* 그는 모든 종교 문제에는 아주 완고하다.

big·ot·ry [bígətri] *n.* (*pl.* **-ries**) ⓊⒸ the state of being bigoted; prejudice. 완고; 편벽; 편협.

big shot [⌐ ⌐] *n.* 《*sl.*》 an important person. 중요 인물; 거물.

big·wig [bígwìg] *n.* 《*colloq.*》 an important person, esp. an official. (특히 관계(官界)의) 중요 인물; 거물(cf. *big noise* 〔*shot, bug*〕). [→big]

bi·jou [bíːʒuː, ─⌐] *n.* (*pl.* **bi·joux**) 《F.》 a jewel. 보석. ── *adj.* small but perfect and very elegant. 작고 우미한. ¶ *a ~ residence* 아담한 집.

bi·joux [bíːʒuːz] *n.* pl. of **bijou.**

bike [baik] *n., v.* 《*colloq.*》=bicycle.

bi·ki·ni [bikíːni] *n.* a woman's brief two-piece bathing-suit. 비키니《노출이 심한 투피스로 된 여성 수영복》. [*Bikini,* an atoll in the Pacific Ocean]

bi·lat·er·al [bailǽtərəl] *adj.* **1** with two sides; of two sides. 양면이 있는; 양면〔양쪽의〕(cf. *unilateral*). ¶ *~ symmetry* (생물체의) 좌우 상칭(相稱). **2** concerning or made between two parties. 쌍무(雙務)의. ¶ *a ~ treaty* (두 나라간의) 상호 조약 / *a ~ contract* 쌍무 계약. [bi-]

bile [bail] *n.* Ⓤ **1** bitter, yellow, or greenish liquid produced by the liver to aid the digestion of food. 담즙(膽汁). **2** bad temper; ill humor; anger. 기분의 언짢음; 노여움. [L. *bilis*]

bilge [bildʒ] *n.* **1** the part of the bottom of a ship which is broadest. 뱃바닥. **2** the dirty water in the bottom of a ship. 뱃바닥에 괸 물. **3** the widest part of a barrel. 통의 중배. **4** 《*colloq.*》 foolish talk or writing; nonsense. 데데한 이야기〔글〕; 난센스. ¶ *Don't talk ~!* 허튼 소리 작작해. [→bulge]

bi·lin·gual [bailíŋgwəl] *adj.* **1** able to speak two languages. 두 나라 말을 하는. **2** written in two languages. 두 나라 말로 쓰인. [bi-, L. *lingua* tongue]

bil·ious [bíljəs] *adj.* **1** suffering from or caused by some trouble with the liver. 담즙(膽汁) 이상(異常)의. ¶ *a ~ patient* 담즙 과다증 환자. **2** bad-tempered. 성마른; 찌무룩한. [→bile]

bilk [bilk] *vt.* (P6) **1** avoid payment of (a bill, etc.). (돈)을 갚지 않다; 떼어먹다. ¶ *~ a taxi driver* 택시 요금을 떼먹다. **2** cheat; deceive. …을 속이다. ── *n.* **1** deception. 사기. **2** a person who avoids paying his bills. (상습적으로) 남의 돈 떼먹는 사람; 사기꾼. [→balk]

:bill[1] [bil] *n.* Ⓒ **1** a list of things for which money should be paid. 청구서; 계산서. ¶ *a ~ for…* …의 청구서 / *collect bills* 수금하다 / *pay the ~ for* …의 셈을 치르다 / *settle a ~* 셈〔계산〕을 마치다. **2** 《U.S.》 a piece of paper money. 지폐. ¶ *a ten-dollar ~* 10 달러 지폐 / *change a five-dollar ~* 5 달러 지폐를 환전하다. **3** a printed or written advertisement; a poster. 광고 전단; 포스터. **4** a plan of a law presented for discussion by a parliament. 법안; 의안(議案). ¶ *pass a ~* 법안을 통과시키다 / *reject* 〔*throw out*〕 *a ~* 법안을 부결하다. **5** a written or printed public notice. 증서; 어음. ¶ *a ~ of debt* 약속어음 / *a ~ of exchange* 환어음 / *a ~ of sale* 매도 증서 / *a ~ of lading* 선하 증권 / *a ~ of dishonor* 부도 어음 / *back a ~* 어음에 배서하다 / *draw a ~ on* …앞으로 어음을 발행하다 / *take up a ~* 어음을 인수하다.

a bill of fare, a menu. 차림표; 메뉴.

a bill of health, a list of people on a ship showing whether they are ill or well. (선원·선객의) 건강 증명서. ¶ *give someone a clean ~ of health* 아주 건강함을 보증하다.

foot the bill, 《*colloq.*》 pay the cost; settle the bill. 셈을 치르다; 비용을 부담하다. ¶ *Who's going to foot the ~?* 셈은 누가 할 건가.

── *vt.* (P6) **1** send a bill to (someone). …에게 계산서를 넘기다〔보내다〕; 계산서로 청구하다. ¶ *~ a customer every other week* 격주마다 손님 앞으로 청구서를 보내다 / *The store will ~ me.* 그 가게에서 청구서가 올 게다. **2** enter (charges) on a bill. 계산서에 …을 기입하다. ¶ *~ each month's purchases* 매달의 구입물을 기입하다. **3** announce (something) publicly. …을 광고〔발표〕하다. ¶ *~ a new shop* 새 가게를 광고하다 / *The actor was billed to appear in person.* 그 배우가 직접 나온다고 광고되었다. **4** post bills in or on (a wall, etc.). …에 포스터를 붙이다. [L. *bulla* amulet, document]

:bill[2] [bil] *n.* Ⓒ **1** a hard part of a bird's mouth; a beak. 부리. **2** anything like a bird's bill. 부리 모양의 것. ── *vi.* (P1) **1** join beaks; touch bills together. 부리를 맞대다. **2** show affection. 애무하다. [E.]

bill and coo, kiss and talk as lovers do. (남녀가) 서로 애무하다.

Bill [bil] *n.* a nickname for William. 빌.

bill·board [bílbɔ̀ːrd] *n.* Ⓒ a signboard for advertisements, notices and announcements. 게시판; 광고판. [→bill[1]]

bill broker [⌐ ⌐─] *n.* a person who deals in bills of exchange. 어음 중개인; 빌 브로커.

bil·let[1] [bílit] *n.* a thick stick of wood; a short log. 굵은 장작. [F. *bille* tree-trunk]

bil·let[2] [bílit] *n.* Ⓒ **1** a place where a soldier is lodged. (군대의) 막사. **2** an order to provide board and lodging for a soldier. (군인을 위한 민가 등에 대한) 숙소 제공 명령서. **3** 《*fig.*》 an appointment; a position.

일자리. ¶ *a good* 〔*bad*〕 ~ 좋은〔나쁜〕 일자리. — *vt.* (P6,13) assign to quarters; send for lodging. 숙소를 지정하다; …을 숙소로 보내다. [→bill¹]

bil·let-doux [bílidúː, -lei-] *n.* (*pl.* **bil·lets-doux** [-dúːz]) a love letter. 연애 편지. [F.]

bill·fold [bílfòuld] *n.* Ⓒ a folding, pocket size leather case for carrying money, paper, etc.; a wallet. 지갑. [→bill¹]

bill·hook [bílhùk] *n.* a curved knife used for cutting bushes or rough grasses. 대형의 낫; 밀낫. [→bill¹]

bil·liards [bíljərdz] *n. pl.* 《used as *pl.* and *sing.*》 a game played with a long stick and balls on a table. 당구(撞球). ¶ *play* (*at*) ~ 당구를 치다. [→billet¹]

billiard table [ˊ–ˋ–] *n.* an oblong table for playing the game of billiards. 당구대.

Bil·lings·gate [bíliŋzgèit / -git] *n.* foul, abusive language. 욕. [from fishermen in Billingsgate market]

·bil·lion [bíljən] *n.* Ⓒ **1** 《U.S.》 one thousand million. 10억. **2** 《Brit.》 one million million. 1조. [bi-, →million]

bil·lion·aire [bìljənέər, ˊ–ˋ] *n.* a person who owns a billion dollars, etc. 억만 장자 (cf. *millionaire*).

bil·low [bílou] *n.* Ⓒ a great wave of the sea. 큰 파도; 큰 놀. — *vi.* (P1,2A) rise, fall or roll like big waves. 큰 파도가 치다. ¶ *a billowing sea* 너울거리는 바다. [N.]

bil·low·y [bíloui] *adj.* rising or rolling like big waves. 파도치는.

bill·pos·ter [bílpòustər], **-stick·er** [-stìkər] *n.* one who posts or sticks bills on walls. 광고〔전단〕 붙이는 사람. [*bill*¹]

bil·ly [bíli] *n.* (*pl.* **-lies**) Ⓒ **1** 《*colloq.*》 a policeman's club. 경찰봉. **2** 《*B-*》 =Bill.

billy goat [ˊ–ˋ] *n.* 《*colloq.*》 a male goat. 수염소(cf. *nanny goat*). [→Billy]

bi·met·al·lism [baimétəlizəm] *n.* the use of both gold and silver as the basis of the money system. (화폐의 금은(金銀)) 복본위제(複本位制). [bi-, →metal]

bi·month·ly [baimʌ́nθli] *adj.* **1** happening once every two months. 두 달에 한 번의; 격월의. ¶ *a ~ event* 두 달에 한 번 있는 행사. **2** happening twice a month; semimonthly. 한 달에 두 번의. 參考 semimonthly 를 쓰는 편이 좋음. — *n.* Ⓒ (*pl.* **-lies**) a magazine published bimonthly. 격월간 간행물. — *adv.* **1** once every two months. 격월로. **2** twice a month; semimonthly. 한 달에 두 번으로. [bi-]

bin [bin] *n.* Ⓒ a box or enclosed place, usu. with a cover, for storing grain, coal, etc. (곡물·석탄 등의) 저장통; (울을 친) 저장소. [E.]

bi·na·ry [báinəri] *adj.* consisting of two; dual. 둘의; 둘로 된; 쌍〔복〕…; 2원(元)의. [L. *bini* two together]

:bind [baind] *v.* (**bound**) *vt.* **1** (P6,7,13) tie (something) with a cord, wire, etc.; hold (things) together; fasten. …을 묶다; (동여) 매다. ¶ ~ *a horse to a tree* 말을 나무에 잡아매다 / ~ *someone's legs together* 아무의 다리를 묶다. **2** (P13) deprive (someone) of his liberty; restrain. …을 속박〔구속〕하다. ¶ *bound by gratitude* 은의(恩義)에 묶여 / *He was bound hand and foot by his promise.* 그는 약속으로 인해 손발이 묶였다. **3** (P6,7,13) 《*up, about, around*》 wind; tie up; bandage. …을 (휘)감다. ¶ ~ *up a wound* 상처에 붕대를 감다 / ~ *belt about one's waist* 허리에 허리띠를 둘러매다. **4** (P8) oblige. 의무를 지우다. ¶ *I am bound to keep the contract.* 계약을 지켜야 한다. **5** (P6,7) edge with some material for protection or ornament; put a finishing edge on. …에 가선을 두르다; 휘갑치다. **6** (P6,7) fasten into the cover. 제책〔제본〕하다. ¶ *a well-bound book* 제본이 잘된 책. — *vi.* (P1) **1** hold together. 묶음이 되다; 뭉치다. **2** stick together. 달라붙다; 굳다. [E.]

be bound (=*be compelled* =*be obliged*) ***to*** *something.* …할 의무가 있다.

be bound up in, be very much interested in. …에 열중해 있다. ¶ *He is bound up in his studies.* 그는 공부에 열중해 있다.

be bound up with, be closely connected with. …와 밀접한 관계가 있다. ¶ *His illness is bound up with the pressure of his work.* 그의 병은 맡고 있는 일의 압박과 밀접한 관계가 있다.

bind oneself to do, promise or agree to do. …할 것을 약속〔맹세〕하다.

bind someone over to appear, order him to appear before a judge when called. 아무에게 법정에 출두할 것을 명하다.

bind up, tie up (something) with a bandage. …에 붕대를 감다.

bind·er [báindər] *n.* Ⓒ **1** a person who binds; a bookbinder. 묶는 사람; 제본하는 사람. **2** anything that ties or holds together. (끈 따위) 묶는〔매는〕 것. **3** a cover for holding loose sheets of paper together. (서류 따위를) 철하는 표지. **4** a machine for cutting and binding grain. 곡물을 베고 단으로 묶는 기계.

bind·er·y [báindəri] *n.* a place where books are bound. 제본소.

bind·ing [báindiŋ] *n.* Ⓒ a covering of a book. 제본; 장정(裝幀). ¶ *a leather* ~ 가죽 장정. — *adj.* **1** binding, fastening, or connecting something. 묶는; 이음의. **2** having power to hold to some agreement. 구속력이 있는. ¶ *a ~ engagement* 실행해야 할 약속 / *the ~ force of law* 법의 구속력 / *A promise given under force is not ~.* 강압하에 한 약속은 구속력이 없다 / *be ~ on someone* 아무에게 의무를 지우다.

binge [bindʒ] *n.* a spree. (법석대는) 술잔치; 혼란. ¶ *on a* ~ 마시고 떠들어. [dialect ?]

bin·na·cle [bínəkəl] *n.* 《naut.》 the box

that holds a ship's compass. 나침반 상자. [L. *habitaculum* lodge]

bi·noc·u·lar [bənákjələr, bai-/-nɔ́k-] *adj.* using both eyes; for both eyes. 두 눈의; 두 눈용(用)의. ¶ *a* ~ *telescope* 쌍안 망원경. — *n.* 《usu. *pl.*, used as *sing.*》 a field glass or opera glass for both eyes. 쌍안경. [→binary, ocular]

bi·no·mi·al [bainóumiəl] *adj.* 《math.》 having two terms. 이항(二項)의. — *n.* a binomial expression. 이항식(二項式). [bi-, L. *nomen* name]

bio- [báiou-] *pref.* having to do with life. '생명, 생물'의 뜻. ¶ *biology.* [Gk. *bios* way of life]

bi·o·chem·is·try [bàioukémәstri] *n.* Ⓤ the chemistry of living animals and plants. 생화학. [bio-, →chemistry]

bi·og·ra·pher [baiágrəfər, bi-/-ɔ́g-] *n.* Ⓒ a person who writes a biography. 전기(傳記) 작가. [↓]

bi·o·graph·i·cal [bàiougrǽfikəl] *adj.* of or about someone's life. 전기(傳記)의; 전기체(傳記體)의. ¶ *a* ~ *sketch* 약전(略傳) / *a* ~ *dictionary* 인명(人名) 사전. ●**bi·o·graph·i·cal·ly** [-ikəli] *adv.*

***bi·og·ra·phy** [baiágrəfi, bi-/-ɔ́g-] *n.* (*pl.* **-phies**) **1** Ⓒ the story of someone's life written by another. 전기(傳記). **2** Ⓤ the part of literature that consists of biographies. 전기 문학. [bio-, →graph]

bi·o·log·ic [bàiəládʒik/-lɔ́dʒ-], **-log·i·cal** [-kəl] *adj.* of plant and animal life; of biology. 생물의; 생물학의. ¶ ~ *warfare* 생물[세균]전. [↓]

bi·ol·o·gist [baiálədʒist/-ɔ́l-] *n.* Ⓒ an expert in biology. 생물학자.

***bi·ol·o·gy** [baiálədʒi/-ɔ́l-] *n.* Ⓤ the science of life or living things. 생물학. [bio-, -logy]

bi·o·met·rics [bàioumétriks] *n.* 《biol.》 the application of mathematical, statistical theory to biology. 생물 통계학. [bio-]

bi·om·e·try [baiámətri/-ɔ́m-] *n.* **1** measurement of life. 수명(壽命) 측정법. **2** = biometrics.

bi·o·phys·ics [bàioufíziks] *n.* physics of biological processes. 생물 물리학. [bio-]

bi·o·sphere [báiəsfiər] *n.* the part of the world in which life exists. 생물권(圈); 생활권. [bio-]

bi·o·tech·nol·o·gy [bàiouteknálədʒi/-nɔ́l-] *n.* the study of relationships between man and machines. 생물 공학. [bio-]

bi·par·ti·san [baipá:rtəzən] *adj.* of two political parties. 두 정당의. [bi-]

bi·par·tite [baipá:rtait] *adj.* consisting of two parts. 두 부분으로 된. [bi-]

bi·par·ty [báipà:rti] *adj.* combining two different political groups, etc. 두 정당 연합의. [bi-]

bi·ped [báiped] *n.* Ⓒ an animal having two feet, as a man or bird. (인간이나 새 같은) 두 발 동물. — *adj.* having two feet. 두 발을 가진. [→pedal]

bi·plane [báiplèin] *n.* Ⓒ an airplane having two pairs of wings, one above the other. 복엽(複葉) 비행기(cf. *monoplane*). [bi-]

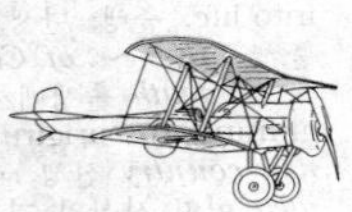
⟨biplane⟩

***birch** [bəːrtʃ] *n.* **1** Ⓒ 《bot.》 a tree with smooth bark and slender branches. 자작나무. **2** Ⓤ its wood. 자작나무 재목. **3** Ⓒ a birch stick, or a bundle of birch twigs, used for whipping; a birch rod. 자작나무 회초리. — *vt.* (P6) whip with a birch. 자작나무 회초리로 때리다. [E.]

birch·en [bə́ːrtʃən] *adj.* **1** of a birch tree. 자작나무의. **2** made of birchwood. 자작나무로 만든.

⁑**bird** [bəːrd] *n.* Ⓒ **1** a two-legged animal that has wings and feathers, and lays eggs. 새. ¶ *a* ~ *of prey* 맹금(猛禽) / *a game* ~ 엽조(獵鳥) / *a* ~ *in the nest* 보금자리에 든 새. **2** 《U.S. *sl.*》 a fellow. 녀석. ¶ *a gay* [*lively*] ~ 명랑한 녀석. **3** a young girl or child. 귀여운 아이. ¶ *a bonny* ~ 예쁜 아가씨. [E.]

a bird in the bush, what is uncertain. 불확실한 것.

a bird in the hand, what is certain. 확실한[수중에 든] 것. ¶ *A* ~ *in the hand is worth two in the bush.* 수중의 한 마리 새는 숲속의 두 마리보다 낫다.

a bird of passage, a bird which comes and goes with the seasons. 철새.

birds of a feather, people of like character. 같은 동아리. ¶ *Birds of a feather flock together.* 유유 상종.

get the bird, be hissed by an audience. 야유를 받다.

give someone the bird, hiss him. 야유하다.

kill two birds with one stone, achieve two aims at the same time. 일석 이조.

like a bird, very willingly. 흔쾌하게.

bird·cage [bə́ːrdkèidʒ] *n.* Ⓒ a cage for birds. 새장.

bird fancier [⌐⌐—] *n.* a person who knows, collects, breeds, or sells birds; a person having an interest in birds. 새장수; 애조가(愛鳥家).

bird·ie [bə́ːrdi] *n.* Ⓒ 《*child's word*》 a little bird. 작은 새.

bird·lime [bə́ːrdlàim] *n.* Ⓤ a sticky material put on branches to catch small birds. (새를 잡기 위한) 끈끈이.

bird's-eye [bə́ːrdzài] *adj.* seen from above or from a distance; general. 위에서 내려다본; 개관의. ¶ *a* ~ *view of the city* 시의 조감도 / *take a bird's-eye view of the history of ancient Rome* 고대 로마사를 개관하다.

Bir·ming·ham [bə́ːrmiŋəm] *n.* **1** a city in

England. 버밍엄《영국의 도시》. **2** [-hæ̀m] a city in central Alabama. 버밍햄《미국의 도시》.

:birth [bəːrθ] *n.* UC **1** the act of coming into life. 출생; 탄생. ¶ *the ~ of a son* 아들의 출생 / *the ~ of Christ* 예수 탄생 / *from ~ till death* 출생에서 죽을 때까지. **2** the beginning; the origin. 시작; 기원. ¶ *the ~ of a new country* 신생 국가의 탄생 / *the ~ of an idea* 어떤 사상의 기원 / *kill the cases at ~* 사건을 시초에 휘지비지(諱之祕之)하다. **3** descent; family. 태생; 집안; 가문. ¶ *by ~* 태생은; 타고난 / *from ~* 날 때부터 / *of Grecian ~* 그리스 태생의 / *a man of American ~* 미국 태생의 사람 / *a man of noble ~* 고귀한 집안의 사람. **4** a noble family or descent. 명문 집안. ¶ *a man of ~* 가문이 좋은 사람 / *a man of no ~* 가문이 좋지 않은 사람 / *a man of ~ and breeding* 집안 좋고 예의 범절이 바른 사람 / *Birth is much, but breeding is more.* 가문보다 가정 교육. **5** something produced. 신생; 갱생. [E.]

give birth to, bear; bring forth (a child, an idea, etc.); originate. …을 낳다; …의 기원이〔시초가〕되다. ¶ *She gave ~ to a daughter.* 그녀는 딸을 낳았다.

birth control [⌐–⌐] *n.* any method of preventing conception. 산아 제한.

:birth·day [bə́ːrθdèi] *n.* C the yearly return of the day on which someone was born. 생일. ¶ *celebrate one's 20th ~,* 20살 생일을 축하하다.

birth·mark [bə́ːrθmàːrk] *n.* C a mark on a person's skin at birth. 모반(母斑).

birth·place [bə́ːrθplèis] *n.* C the place or house where someone was born. 출생지; 생가.

birth rate [⌐ ⌐] *n.* the proportion of the number of births in a place during a certain period of time to the total population. 출생률.

birth·right [bə́ːrθràit] *n.* C the rights belonging to a person because he was born in a certain country or family; the rights belonging to the eldest son. 생득권(生得權); 장자 상속권. ¶ *Freedom of speech and action is an Englishman's ~.* 언론과 행동의 자유는 영국인의 생득권이다.

birth·stone [bə́ːrθstòun] *n.* a jewel related to a certain month of the year. 탄생석(誕生石)《태어난 달을 상징하는 보석》.

B.I.S. Bank for International Settlement(국제 결제 은행). British Information Services (영국 정보부).

Bis·cay [bískei, -ki] *n.* a large bay of the Atlantic between France and Spain. 비스케이만(灣).

·bis·cuit [bískit] *n.* (*pl.* **-cuits** or **-cuit**) C **1** 《U.S.》 a kind of bread baked in small, soft cakes. 과자빵. **2** 《esp. Brit.》 a flat, dry cake. 비스킷(cf. 《U.S.》 *cracker*). [L. *bis* twice, *coquo* cook]

bi·sect [baisékt] *vt.* (P6) cut or divide (something) into two (equal) parts. …을 이(등)분하다. [L. *seco* cut]

bi·sec·tion [baisékʃən] *n.* U the act of bisecting. 이등분; 양단(兩斷).

:bish·op [bíʃəp] *n.* C **1** a clergyman of high rank who administers the affairs of a church district. (개신교의) 감독; (카톨릭의) 주교. **2** one of the pieces in the game of chess. (체스의) 비숍. **3** a kind of wine. 포도주의 한 가지. [Gk. *epi-* over, *scopos* seer]

bish·op·ric [bíʃəprik] *n.* UC **1** the office or rank of a bishop. 감독·주교의 직. **2** a church district under the charge of a bishop. 감독·주교 관할 구역.

Bis·marck [bízmaːrk], **Prince Otto Eduard Leopold von** *n.* (1815-98) the first chancellor of the German Empire. 비스마르크《독일 제국의 재상》.

bis·muth [bízməθ] *n.* U 《chem.》 a hard, red-white metal used in medicine. 비스무트《금속 원소명》. [G.]

bi·son [báisən, -zən] *n.* C (*pl.* **-son**) an American buffalo; a wild oxlike animal. (미국) 들소. [Teut.]

bis·sex·tile [baisékstəl, bi-/-tail] *n.* a leap year. 윤년(閏年). — *adj.* of a leap year. 윤년의. [L. *bis* twice, *sextus* sixth]

bit¹ [bit] *n.* C **1** the part of a bridle that goes in a horse's mouth, used for controlling the horse. (말의) 재갈. **2** anything that restrains. 구속하는 것. **3** the cutting part of a tool. (연장의) 날 부분. **4** a tool for boring or drilling. 송곳.

take the bit in 〔***between***〕 ***one's teeth,*** (of a horse) get out of control. (말이) 반항하다; 말을 안 듣다.

— *vt.* (P6) (**bit·ted, bit·ting**) **1** put a bit in the mouth of (a horse). (말에) 재갈을 물리다. **2** restrain. …을 구속하다. [→bite]

:bit² [bit] *n.* C **1** a small piece; a small amount. 작은 조각; 소량; 약간; 한 입. ¶ *a ~ of chalk* 분필 토막 / *a ~ of cake* 한 조각의 케이크 / *a ~ of land* 약간의 땅 / *a ~ of one's mind* 마음의 일단 / *have a ~ of dinner* 가벼운 식사를 하다 / *Do a ~ of guessing.* 조금 생각해 봐라. **2** 《*colloq.*》 a short time. 잠시 (동안). ¶ *a ~ later* 얼마〔잠시〕 후에 / *Wait a ~.* 잠깐 기다려. **3** 《U.S. *colloq.*》 12 1/2 cents. 12센트 반. [→bite]

a bit of, rather. 조금(은); 다소(는). ¶ *He is a ~ of a poet.* 그는 조금은 시를 한다 / *I'm a ~ of tired.* 다소 피곤하다.

a good bit, a long time. 오랫동안. ¶ *He did a good ~ of waiting.* 꽤 오랫동안 기다렸다.

a nice bit of, a great deal of. 많은; 상당한 양(量)(의). ¶ *a nice ~ of money* 꽤 많은 돈.

bit by bit, little by little; gradually. 차츰; 점점; 조금씩.

come 〔***go***〕 ***to bits,*** get 〔be〕 broken. 깨지다.

do one's bit, do one's share (of the duty).

자신의 본분을 다하다.

every bit, **a)** all. 모두. **b)** in every way; perfectly. 어느 점으로〔모로〕 보나; 아주. ¶ *She is every ~ a lady.* 그녀는 어느 모로 보나 숙녀이다.

for a bit, for a little time. 잠깐; 잠시.

give someone a bit of one's mind, speak frankly; scold. 솔직히 이야기하다; 꾸짖다.

not a bit, **a)** not at all. 천만에. **b)** not in the least. 조금도 … 아니다.

:**bit**³ [bit] *v.* p. and pp. of **bite.**

bitch [bitʃ] *n.* Ⓒ **1** a female dog, wolf, or fox. (개·이리·여우 따위의) 암컷. **2** 《*sl.*》 a harlot; prostitute. 매춘부. [E.]

:**bite** [bait] *v.* (**bit, bit** or **bit·ten**) *vi.* **1** (P1,3) 《*at*》 snap with the teeth. 물다. ¶ *Barking dogs don't ~.* 짖는 개는 물지 않는다. **2** (P1) accept bait. (물고기가) 미끼를 덥석 물다. — *vt.* **1** (P6,7) cut into (something) with the teeth; cut (something) off with the teeth. 물어뜯다. **2** (P6) rot or destroy (esp. metals) by chemicals, etc. …을 부식시키다. ¶ *Acids ~ metal.* 산(酸)은 금속을 부식시킨다.

be bitten with, have a desire for something or a strong interest; be infected with. …에 물들다〔심취해 있다〕; …에 열중하다.

bite someone's head 〔***nose***〕 ***off,*** answer angrily or sharply. (남의 질문 따위에) 성이 나서 응답하다; 대들다.

bite one's lips, keep oneself with difficulty from answering back or laughing. (웃음 따위를) 꾹 (눌러) 참다.

bite off more than one can chew, attempt too great a task. 힘에 겨운 일을 꾀하다.

bite one's thumb at, **a)** challenge. 도전하다. **b)** show contempt for (someone); insult. 경멸을 보이다; 놀리다; 모욕하다.

bite the dust 〔***ground***〕***,*** **a)** fall; fall and die. 쓰러지다; 쓰러져 죽다. **b)** (esp. in a fight) be completely defeated. 일패 도지(一敗塗地)하다; 패하다.

bite the tongue, be silent. 입을 다물다.

— *n.* Ⓒ **1** the act of biting. 깨묾. ¶ *give a ~ at the bone* 뼈를 한 번 깨물다. **2** wound made by biting. 물린 상처. ¶ *a snake's ~* 뱀에 물린 상처. **3** (of a fish) the act of taking bait. (고기의) 입질. **4** a piece cut off with the teeth. 물어뜯은 조각〔한 점〕. **5** sharp pain; a cutting or stinging effect; sharpness. 격통; 얼얼함. ¶ *whisky with a ~ in it* 톡 쏘는 위스키. [E.]

bite and sup, hurried meal. 가벼운〔간단한〕 식사.

bit·er [báitər] *n.* Ⓒ **1** a person or an animal that bites; a dog. 무는 사람〔동물〕; 개. **2** a cheater. 사기꾼. ¶ *The ~ is bitten.* 사기꾼이 사기당했다. [↑]

bit·ing [báitiŋ] *adj.* **1** sharp; cutting; pungent. 에는 듯한; 날카로운; (음식 따위가) 자극성의. ¶ *a ~ wind* 〔*cold*〕 살을 에는 듯한 바람〔추위〕 / *a ~ sensation on the tongue* 혀를 톡 쏘는 느낌. **2** cutting; sneering. 신랄한; 호된. ¶ *a ~ remark* 날카로운 비평 / *a ~ caricature* 통렬하게 비꼬는 만화.

bit·ing·ly [báitiŋli] *adv.* sharply; cuttingly. 신랄하게; 예리하게.

:**bit·ten** [bítn] *v.* pp. of **bite.**

:**bit·ter** [bítər] *adj.* (usu. **-ter·er, -ter·est**) **1** tasting like black coffee. 쓴(opp. sweet). ¶ *a ~ taste* 쓴맛. **2** unpleasant to the mind. 불쾌한. **3** painful; hard to bear. 쓰라린; 격심한. ¶ *a ~ pain* 격심한 고통 / *a ~ experience* 쓰라린 경험. **4** biting; harsh; severe. 신랄한; 호된; 모진. [E.]

to the bitter end, to the last extremity. 끝까지. ¶ *fight to the ~ end* 최후까지 싸우다.

***bit·ter·ly** [bítərli] *adv.* with bitterness; with cruelty. 몹시; 비통하게; 참혹하게. ¶ *She cried ~.* 그녀는 비통하게 울었다.

bit·tern [bítə(:)rn] *n.* Ⓒ 《bird》 a small kind of bird that lives in marshes and is known for its loud cry. 알락해오라기. [F. *butor*]

***bit·ter·ness** [bítərnis] *n.* Ⓤ the state of being bitter; something that causes bitter feeling. 괴로움; 고통; 비통. [→bitter]

bit·ter·sweet [bítərswìːt] *adj.* both bitter and sweet; both painful and pleasant. 달콤씁쓸한; 고통스럽기도 하고 즐겁기도 한. — *n.* **1** sweetness and bitterness mixed. 달고 씁쓸함. **2** 《bot.》 a climbing plant with red berries. 노박덩굴. [↑]

bi·tu·men [baitjúmən, bi-] *n.* Ⓤ asphalt. 아스팔트; 역청. [L.]

bi·tu·mi·nous [baitjúmənəs, bi-] *adj.* containing bitumen. 아스팔트를 함유한. ¶ *~ coal* 역청탄《유연탄》. [L.]

bi·valve [báivælv] *n.* Ⓒ a water-animal with a shell, as oysters or clams. 쌍각류(雙殼類)《굴·대합 따위》. — *adj.* having two parts hinged together. 쌍각류 조개의; (식물의) 양판(兩瓣)의. [bi-]

biv·ou·ac [bívuæk, -vəwæk] *n.* Ⓒ a rest for the night outside, often without tents. 야영(지). — *vi.* (P1) (**-acked, -ack·ing**) pass the night without tents. (천막 없이) 야영〔노숙〕하다. [F.=by, watch]

biv·ou·acked [bívuækt, -vəwækt] *v.* p. of **bivouac.**

biv·ou·ack·ing [bívuækiŋ, -vəwækiŋ] *v.* ppr. of **bivouac.**

bi·week·ly [baiwíːkli] *adj.* **1** happening once every two weeks. 2주(週) 한 번의. **2** happening twice a week; semiweekly. 한 주(週) 두 번의. — *n.* Ⓒ a newspaper or magazine issued biweekly. 격주 출판물. — *adv.* **1** once every two weeks. 격주로. **2** twice a week; semiweekly. 한 주에 두 번. [bi-]

bi·zarre [bizáːr] *adj.* queer; grotesque; strange. 기묘한; 기괴한; 야릇한; 이상한. [F.]

Bi·zet [bizéi], **Georges** *n.* (1838-75) a French composer. 비제《프랑스의 작곡가》.
bk. bank; book.
B.L. Bachelor of Laws.
B/L, b.l. bill of lading(선하증권).
bl. bale(s); barrel(s).
blab [blæb] *vt., vi.* (P6;1) (**blabbed, blabbing**) tell (a secret); talk too much. (비밀을) 누설하다; 무심코 지껄이다; 수다떨다. ¶ *Who's been blabbing?* 누가 수다떨던가. [M.E.]
blab·ber [blǽbər] *n.* Ⓒ a person who blabs. 수다쟁이. [↑]
:black [blæk] *adj.* **1** opposite to white. 검은. ¶ *~ clouds* 먹구름 / *(as) ~ as coal* 새까만. **2** quite dark; without any light. 캄캄한; 어둠의. ¶ *a ~ night* 캄캄한 밤. **3** dark-skinned. 피부가 검은. ¶ *the ~ races* 흑인종. **4** dim; gloomy; dismal. 음울한; 우울한. **5** wicked; evil. 사악한; 흉악한. ¶ *a ~ heart* 사악한 마음 / *a ~ lie* 질 나쁜 거짓말. **6** angry; ill-tempered. 성난; 성마른. ¶ *He looks ~ at me.* 그는 성난[험악한] 얼굴로 나를 보았다. **7** dirty; soiled. 더러운; 더러워진. ¶ *Your hands are ~.* 네 손은 더럽다. **8** (of one's fortunes, fate, etc.) hopeless. (운수·운명 따위) 절망적인.
(as) black as night [soot, your hat], very dark. 캄캄한; 몹시 어두운. ¶ *The room was ~ as night.* 방은 몹시 어두웠다.
black and blue, discolored with bruises. 타박상으로 시퍼렇게 멍이 든. ¶ *The boy was beaten ~ and blue.* 소년은 멍이 들 정도로 맞았다.
black in the face, dark red from anger, effort, or choking. (노여움·노력·질식 따위로) 얼굴이 붉으락푸르락하여; 얼굴빛을 변하여.
—*n.* **1** Ⓤ black color; black paint. 검정; 흑색 도료. **2** ⓊⒸ a black speck. 검은 얼룩; 오점. **3** Ⓤ black clothes. 검은 옷. ¶ *She wears ~.* 그녀는 검은 옷을 입고 있다. **4** Ⓒ a Negro. 흑인.
be in the black, 《U.S.》 show a profit. 흑자를 보이다(opp. be in the red).
in black and white, written or printed. 쓰인; 인쇄된. ¶ *put down in ~ and white* 써 두다; 서류로 해 두다; 인쇄해 두다 / *Let me have it in ~ and white.* 그걸 내게 적어 주시오.
prove that black is white =***talk black into white,*** twist the truth by dishonest argument. 흑을 백이라고 하다.
—*vt.* (P6) make (something) black; polish (something) with blacking. …을 검게 하다; (약으로) …을 닦다. ¶ *~ boots* 구두를 닦다. —*vi.* (P1) **1** become black. 검게 되다. **2** lose consciousness. 기절하다. [M.E. *blak*; O.E. *blæc;* O.N. *blakkr*]
black out, **a**) make dark by concealing all light against air-raids. 등화 관제를 하다. **b**) lose consciousness. 의식을 잃다. ¶ *She blacked out at the sight.* 그녀는 그 광경에 기절했다.

black·a·moor [blǽkəmùər] *n.* Ⓒ **1** a Negro. 흑인. **2** a dark-skinned person. 살갗이 검은 사람. [*black*]
black art [⌐⌐] *n.* evil magic. 마술(魔術).
black·ball [blǽkbɔ̀ːl] *vt.* (P6) vote against (a candidate); shut out (someone) from a club, etc. by vote. (후보자)에 반대 투표하다; …을 배척하다. —*n.* Ⓒ a vote against (someone or something). 반대 투표.
black beetle [⌐⌐–] *n.* =cockroach.
black·ber·ry [blǽkbèri, -bəri] *n.* Ⓒ (*pl.* **-ries**) a small, black or dark-purple eatable fruit; a plant bearing this fruit. 검은딸기(나무); 나무딸기(나무).
black·bird [blǽkbə̀ːrd] *n.* Ⓒ 《bird》 any of various birds the male of which is mostly black. 지빠귀·찌르레기 무리.
:black·board [blǽkbɔ̀ːrd] *n.* Ⓒ a board for writing on with chalk or crayon. 칠판.
black cap [⌐⌐] *n.* the cap worn by a judge when ordering the death of a prisoner. (사형 선고를 할 때의) 재판관의 검은 모자.
black coffee [⌐⌐–] *n.* coffee without milk or sugar. 블랙 커피.
Black Death [⌐⌐], **the** *n.* 《med.》 a form of bubonic plague that spread over Europe in the 14th century and killed an estimated quarter of the population; pest. 페스트; 흑사병.
black di·a·mond [⌐⌐––] *n.* a dark-colored diamond; coal. 흑다이아; 석탄.
black·en [blǽkən] *vt.* **1** (P6) make (something) black. …을 검게 하다. **2** speak evil of (someone); injure. …를 헐뜯다. ¶ *~ someone's reputation* 아무의 명성을 훼손하다. —*vi.* (P1) become black. 검어지다.
black·guard [blǽgɑːrd, -gərd, blǽk-] *n.* Ⓒ a person who has no sense of honor; a rascal. 악한; 불량자. —*vt.* (P6) abuse (someone) with very bad language. …에게 욕을 하다. —*vi.* behave like a rascal. 악한처럼 행동하다.
black·guard·ly [blǽgɑːrdli, -gərd-, blǽk-] *adj.* of or like a blackguard. 악한의[같은]. —*adv.* in the manner of a rascal. 악한처럼.
black·head [blǽkhèd] *n.* a small swelling on the skin, usu. having a black top. 여드름.
black·heart·ed [blǽkhɑ́ːrtid] *adj.* evil. 「못된; 속 검은.
black·ing [blǽkiŋ] *n.* Ⓤ anything for making (shoes, boots, etc.) black and polished. 검은 구두약.
black·ish [blǽkiʃ] *adj.* black. 거무스름한.
black lead [⌐⌐] *n.* soft grey-black carbon, used in pencils. 흑연.
black·leg [blǽklèg] *n.* Ⓒ **1** 《*colloq.*》 a person who cheats; a swindler. 사기꾼; 협잡꾼. **2** 《Brit.》 a worker who works when the regular workers are on strike. 파업 비동조자(cf. *strike-breaker*).

black letter [ㅅ ㅅ–] *n.* a printing type with thick, heavy lines (also called Gothic). 고딕 활자체.

black-letter day [ㅅㅅ– ㅅ] *n.* **1** an ordinary working day. 정상 근무일. **2** an unlucky day. 불운한〔재수 없는〕 날.

black-list [blǽklist] *n.* a list of persons who are believed to be dangerous or who are to be punished. (요주의 인물의) 블랙 리스트. — *vt.* (P6) place the name of (someone) on a black-list. 블랙리스트에 올리다.

black magic [ㅅ ㅅ–] *n.* magic used for evil purposes 못된 마술.

black·mail [blǽkmèil] *n.* Ⓤ any money gained from someone by threatening to tell something bad or dishonorable about him. 갈취한 금품. — *vt.* (P6) get or try to get blackmail from (someone). (돈)을 을러 빼앗다; 갈취하다.

black·mail·er [blǽkmèilər] *n.* Ⓒ a person who blackmails. 공갈배.

black mark [ㅅ ㅅ] *n.* a mark of criticism or punishment. 검은 점; 벌점.

black market [ㅅ ㅅ–] *n.* a place where things are sold and bought at illegal prices or by illegal routes. 암시장.

black marketeer [ㅅ ㅅ–ㅅ] *n.* a person who deals on the black market. 암상인.

black·ness [blǽknis] *n.* Ⓤ **1** the state of being black; a black color; darkness. 검음; 흑색; 어두움. ¶ *the ~ of the night* 밤의 암흑. **2** wickedness. 사악; 음험.

black·out [blǽkàut] *n.* Ⓒ **1** the act of turning out or covering all the lights to protect a city, etc. against an air attack. (공습 때의) 등화 관제. **2** temporary loss of consciousness or memory. 일시적 의식 상실.

black sheep [ㅅ ㅅ] *n.* an unusual or bad member of a family or group. 말썽꾸러기; 골칫덩어리; 악한.

Black·shirt [blǽkʃə̀ːrt] *n.* a member of the Fascist party. 파시스트당원(cf. *Brownshirt*).

•**black·smith** [blǽksmìθ] *n.* Ⓒ a man who works with iron to make tools, horseshoes, etc. 대장장이.

black swan [ㅅ ㅅ] *n.* **1** strange anomaly. 드문〔귀한〕 물건〔일〕. **2** an Australian swan that is black with white wing tips and red bill. 흑고니.

black·thorn [blǽkθɔ̀ːrn] *n.* Ⓒ **1** a thorny European bush that has white flowers and dark-purple fruit. 자두나무의 일종. **2** a walking stick made from this shrub. 자두나무 지팡이.

blad·der [blǽdər] *n.* Ⓒ **1** ⟪*the* ~⟫ a soft, thin bag of skin in a human and animal body that stores waste liquid before it is passed out. 방광(膀胱). **2** ⟪*fig.*⟫ a very talkative person. 수다쟁이. [E.]

:**blade** [bleid] *n.* Ⓒ **1** the cutting part of a knife, tool, etc.; ⟪*the* ~⟫ a sword. 날; 칼; 검. **2** a leaf of grass. 풀잎. ¶ *a single ~ of grass* 풀 한 잎 / *in the ~* (이삭이 나지 않은) 잎인 때에. **3** a flat, wide part of anything, such as an oar, a paddle, etc. (노 따위의) 편편한 부분. ¶ *the shoulder ~* 견갑골(肩甲骨); 어깨뼈. **4** ⟪*colloq.*⟫ a smart or cheerful fellow. 멋쟁이; 유쾌한 사나이. ● **blade·like** [ㅅlàik] *adj.* [E.]

blain [blein] *n.* an inflamed sore. 농포(膿疱). [E.]

blam·a·ble [bléiməbl] *adj.* fit to be blamed; having a fault. 비난받을 만한; 비난해야 할. [↓]

:**blame** [bleim] *vt.* (P6,13) **1** ⟪*for*⟫ find fault with (someone or something). …을 비난하다. ¶ *He is blamed for neglect of duty.* 그는 의무를 소홀히 하여 비난받고 있다 / *I don't ~ you for doing that.* 그렇게 했다고 당신을 비난하지 않는다. **2** ⟪*on*⟫ say that a person or a thing is the cause of a certain trouble. …의 탓으로 돌리다; (과실 따위)의 책임을 …에게 지우다. ¶ *We blamed the accident on him.* 우리는 그 사고의 책임을 그에게 지웠다.

be to blame, be held responsible. 책임이 있다. ¶ *I am to ~ for it.* 그것은 내가 나쁘다 / *Who is to ~ ?* 누가 나쁜가.

— *n.* Ⓤ **1** the act of finding fault. 비난. **2** the responsibility for something wrong or bad. 책임. ¶ *bear* 〔*take*〕 *the ~ for…* …의〔에 대한〕 책임을 지다 / *lay the ~ at the door of another* 죄를 남에게 씌우다; 책임을 전가하다 / *lay* 〔*put*〕 *the ~ on someone for…* 아무에게 …의 책임을 지우다. [→blaspheme]

blame·less [bléimlis] *adj.* free from blame; doing nothing wrong; pure. 죄가 없는; 비난할 데 없는; 결백한. ¶ *He led a ~ life.* 그는 깨끗한 일생을 보냈다.

blame·wor·thy [bléimwə̀ːrði] *adj.* to be blamed. 비난받을 만한. ¶ *a ~ administration* 악정.

blanch [blæntʃ, blɑːntʃ] *vt.* (P6) **1** make (something) white. …을 표백〔희게〕하다. ¶ *~ tablecloth into white* 테이블보를 표백하여 희게 하다. **2** take the skins off. 껍질을 벗기다. ¶ *~ almonds* 아몬드의 껍질을 벗기다. — *vi.* (P1,3) turn white or pale. 희어지다; 새파래지다. ¶ *He blanched with fear.* 그는 공포로 새파랗게 질렸다. [→blank]

blanch over, make (someone) believe what is not true. …를 속이다; 겉을 꾸미다.

bland [blænd] *adj.* **1** smooth; gentle; mild. 부드러운; 온화한; 자극 없는. ¶ *~ food* 부드러운 음식 / *a ~ medicine* 먹기 좋은 약 / *a ~ manner in company* 남의 앞에서의 부드러운 태도. **2** agreeable; polite. 기분 좋은; 예의 바른. ● **bland·ness** [-nis] *n.* [L.]

blan·dish [blǽndiʃ] *vt.* (P6) flatter; coax. 아첨하다; 감언으로 구워삶다. [L. *blandus* flattering]

blan·dish·ment [blǽndiʃmənt] *n.* ⟪often *pl.*⟫ a soft and gentle word or action that flatters. 아첨; 감언.

bland·ly [blǽndli] *adv.* in a polite manner; gently. 온화하게; 부드럽게.

:blank [blæŋk] *adj.* **1** ⓐ not written or printed on. 기입하지 않은; 써[인쇄되어] 있지 않은. ¶ *a ~ sheet of paper* 백지 / *a ~ map* 백지도 / *a ~ application form* 아직 쓰지 않은 신청 용지. ⓑ empty. 빈. ¶ *a ~ cartridge* 공포(空包) / *Many ~ spaces are still left in the suburbs.* 교외에는 아직도 많은 공터가 남아 있다. **2** (of a face) without expression. 무표정한. ¶ *a ~ look* 무표정한 얼굴. **3** without effect or interest. 효과[흥미]가 없는. ¶ *a ~ existence* 공허[허망]한 생활 / *~ efforts* 헛된 노력 / *She sometimes occupied her ~ days with sewing.* 무료한 나날을 그녀는 바느질로 보낼 때가 있었다. **4** without any clear idea; having nothing in mind. 뚜렷한 생각[기억]이 없는. ¶ *My memory is ~ on the subject.* 그 건(件)에 대해서는 아무런 기억도 없다. **5** complete; thorough. 완전한. ¶ *~ despair.*
— *n.* Ⓒ a blank space in a document; an empty or vacant space; an empty surface. 공란; 여백(餘白); 빈 터. ¶ *Leave a ~ after each word.* 각 낱말 뒤에 공란을 남겨라. [Teut. orig. shining]
draw a blank, **a**) receive a useless ticket; be unsuccessful. 꽝을 뽑다; 실패하다. **b**) be completely unable to remember something. 전혀 아무 것도 기억하지 못하다.

:blan·ket [blǽŋkit] *n.* Ⓒ **1** a large, soft piece of woolen cloth. 모포; 담요. **2** anything like a blanket. 모포 같은 것. ¶ *a ~ of snow* 온통 뒤덮은 눈.
born on the wrong side of the blanket, born of unmarried parents. 사생아[서자]로 태어난.
— *vt.* (P6) **1** cover (something) with a blanket. …을 모포로 덮다. **2** cover. …을 싸다; 뒤덮다. ¶ *The snow blanketed the ground.* 눈이 온 대지를 뒤덮었다. [↑]

blank·e·ty-blank [blǽŋkitiblǽŋk] *adj., adv.* 《U.S. *colloq.*》 damned; darned. 지겨운; 터무니 없는[없이]. [*blank*]

blank·ly [blǽŋkli] *adv.* **1** in a blank manner; vacantly. 헛되이; 망연히. ¶ *She looked at me ~.* 그녀는 멍하니 나를 보고 있었다. **2** totally; fully; in every respect. 완전히; 모든 점에서. **3** flatly. 단호히. ¶ *He ~ denied ever saying such a thing.* 그는 그런 말 한 적이 없다고 잡아뗐다. [→blank]

blank·ness [blǽŋknis] *n.* Ⓤ the state of being blank or empty. 공백(의 상태); 공허; 단조.

blare [blɛər] *vt., vi.* (P7; 1) **1** make a loud sound like a trumpet. 소리 높이 울리다. ¶ *The radio blared.* 라디오 소리가 크게 울렸다. **2** cry. (큰 소리로) 외치다. ¶ *~ out the threat of the war* 전쟁이 날 우려를 소리를 높여 외치다. — *n.* ⒸⓊ **1** a loud sound. 높은 소리; 외침. **2** brightness of color. 화려한 색채. [Imit.]

blar·ney [blɑ́ːrni] *n.* Ⓤ flattering talk; too much praise. 입발림 말; 아첨의 말. — *vi., vt.* (P1; 6) flatter. 아첨하다; …에게 발림 말하다. [Place]
kiss the Blarney stone, gain a cajoling tongue. 아첨을 잘 하다.

bla·sé [blɑːzéi, ╯–] *adj.* tired of pleasure. 놀이에 지쳐. [F.]

blas·pheme [blæsfíːm, ╯–] *vi., vt.* (P1; 6) speak ill of (something sacred). …을 모독하다. ¶ *~ against God* 신을 모독하다. [Gk. *blasphēmeō*]

blas·phem·er [blæsfíːmər, ╯––] *n.* Ⓒ a person who speaks ill of God, holy things, etc. 독성자(瀆聖者); 신을 모독하는 자.

blas·phe·mous [blǽsfəməs] *adj.* speaking ill of God or holy things. 독성(瀆聖)의; 불경(不敬)스러운.

blas·phe·my [blǽsfəmi] *n.* (*pl.* **-mies**) Ⓤ contempt for God or holy things; Ⓒ a talk showing no respect for God. 독성(瀆聖); 불경스러운 말.

:blast [blæst, blɑːst] *n.* Ⓒ **1** a strong rush of wind. 일진(一陣)의 바람. ¶ *the icy blasts of winter* 겨울의 차가운 강풍. **2** a sound of a musical wind-instrument. 관악기의 소리. ¶ *sound* [*blow*] *a ~* 취주하다.
at a blast, at a blow. 단숨에.
in [***at***] ***full blast,*** vigorous(ly); fully. 세(차)게; 전력을 다하여. ¶ *turn the radio on full ~* 라디오 소리를 최대로 크게 하다 / *He was working* (*at*) *full ~ in order to complete the order before the holidays.* 휴가 전까지 주문 받은 일을 마치려고 그는 전력을 다하고 있었다.
out of blast, at rest. (활동을) 정지하고.
— *vt.* (P6) **1** blow up (something) with gunpowder. …을 폭발시키다. **2** make (a plant) dry up and die; make (someone's hope, happiness, etc.) come to nothing; ruin; wither. …을 말라죽게[시들게] 하다; 못 쓰게[헛되게] 만들다. ¶ *The hot sunshine blasted the crops.* 뜨거운 햇볕이 농작물을 말려 죽였다 / *The storm has blasted our grapes.* 폭풍우가 우리 포도(나무)를 망쳐 놓았다 / 《*fig.*》 *Our hopes were blasted.* 우리의 희망은 허망하게 되었다. [E.]
Blast it [***him, you, etc.***] ***!*** Damn it! 빌어먹을.

blast furnace [╯╯–] *n.* a furnace for melting iron by blowing hot air into it. 용광로.

bla·tant [bléitənt] *adj.* **1** noisy. 시끄러운. **2** bright and gay, but in bad taste. 야한. **3** obvious. 속 들여다뵈는; 빤한. ¶ *a ~ lie* 빤한 거짓말. [coined by Spenser]

blath·er [blǽðər] *vi.* speak foolishly. 허튼[쓸데없는] 소리를 지껄이다. — *n.* foolish talk. 허튼 소리. [O.N. *blaðr* nonsense]

:blaze[1] [bleiz] *n.* Ⓒ **1** a bright flame or fire. 불꽃. ¶ *He saw the ~ of the campfire across the beach.* 그는 해변 저쪽으로 모닥불의 불꽃을 보았다 / *in a ~* 활활 타고. **2** a sudden and violent outburst of passion. 감정의 격발. ¶ *a ~ of temper* 〔*anger*〕 노여움의 폭발 / *unleash a ~ of pent-up emotions* 눌러 참았던 감정을 폭발시키다. **3** a bright display; a strong, direct light. 번쩍임; 조사(照射). ¶ *a ~ of jewels* 보석의 번쩍임 / *the ~ of fame* 빛나는 명성.

like blazes, very vigorously. 맹렬히. ¶ *He works like blazes.* 그는 맹렬히 일한다.

What the blazes ... ? What on earth...? 도대체. ¶ *What the blazes am I to do ?* 도대체 내가 무엇을 해야 하지.

— *vi.* (P1,2A) **1** burn with a bright flame. 활활 타오르다. ¶ *A fire was blazing in the fireplace.* 불은 난로 안에서 활활 타고 있었다. **2** explode; burst. 폭발하다. **3** glow or shine like a flame. 번쩍거리다. **4** 《*with*》 burst out with strong feeling. 감정을 폭발시키다. ¶ *When I spoke of it, he blazed out at me.* 내가 그 말을 했을 때, 그는 나에게 왈칵 성을 냈다. [E. =torch]

blaze away 〔***off***〕, **a**) fire continuously with rifles, etc. …을 향해 계속해서 총을 쏘다. ¶ *~ away at a rabbit* 토끼를 향해 계속 총을 쏘다. **b**) work vigorously at. 맹렬히 일하다.

blaze up, burst into flames; show sudden anger. 확 타오르다; 격노하다.

blaze[2] [bleiz] *n.* **1** a white spot on the forehead of a horse or cow. (마소의 이마에 있는) 흰 점. **2** a mark made on a tree by cutting off some of its bark. 나무의 껍질을 벗긴 안표(眼標). — *vt.* (P6) mark by cutting off the bark of trees. 나무껍질을 벗겨 안표를 하다. [↑]

blaze[3] [bleiz] *vt.* (P7) make (news, etc.) known; spread abroad; announce. (소식 따위)를 알리다; 퍼뜨리다; 선언〔공언〕하다. [N. =blast]

blaze about 〔***abroad***〕, spread. 퍼뜨리다. ¶ *The news was soon blazed abroad.* 그 소식은 곧 널리 퍼졌다.

blaz·er [bléizər] *n.* Ⓒ a bright-colored sports jacket. 블레이저 코트. [→blaze[2]]

blaz·ing [bléiziŋ] *adj.* **1** burning. 불타(오르)는. ¶ *a ~ sun* 이글거리는 태양; 염천(炎天). **2** unusual; clear. 심한; 명백한. ¶ *a ~ lie.* **3** (of an animal's scent) very strong. (사냥감의 냄새가) 강한. ¶ *a ~ scent* (짐승이 남긴) 강한 냄새. [→blaze[1]]

bla·zon [bléizən] *vt.* **1** (P6) decorate (something) with the special mark of a family. …을 문장(紋章)으로 장식하다. **2** (P6) describe (a coat of arms). …을 그리다. **3** (P7) make known. 알리다. [F. = shield]

blazon abroad, make known widely. 널리 알리다; 공표하다.

bldg. (*pl.* **bldgs.**) building.

bleach [blíːtʃ] *vt.* (P6) make (something) white. …을 희게 하다; 표백하다. — *vi.* (P1) become white or pale. 희게 되다. — *n.* Ⓒ **1** a chemical product used in bleaching. 표백제. **2** the act of bleaching. 표백. [E. =pale]

bleach·er [blíːtʃər] *n.* **1** Ⓒ a person or thing that makes something white. 표백업자; 표백기(器); 표백제. **2** 《*pl.*》 《U.S. *colloq.*》 seats at a baseball game or other outdoor sports, usu. without a roof. 노천(露天) 관람석.

bleaching powder [ㅅ-ㅅ-] *n.* any powder used in making something white. 표백분.

bleak [bliːk] *adj.* **1** laid open to wind and cold; dreary. (버려 두어) 비바람을 그대로 맞는; 황량한; 쓸쓸한. ¶ *~ hills* 〔*house*〕 황량한 언덕〔집〕 / *this ~ world* 이 황량한 세상. **2** cold. 몹시 추운. ¶ *a ~ wind* 추운 바람. **3** without cheer; dull. 음울한. ¶ *a ~ prospect* 암담한 전망. ● **bleak·ly** [-li] *adv.* [→bleach]

blear [bliər] *adj.* dim. (눈이) 침침한. ¶ *a blear-eyed man* 눈이 침침한 사람. — *vt.* (P6) make (an eye, a surface, etc.) dim. …을 흐리게〔침침하게〕 하다. ¶ *A bad cold has made his nose run and bleared his eyes.* 악성 감기로 코에서 콧물이 흐르고 눈이 침침해졌다. [E. =pale]

blear-eyed [blíəràid] *adj.* having dim eyes. 눈이 흐린.

blear·y [blíəri] *adj.* (**blear·i·er, blear·i·est**) dim. (눈이) 침침한〔흐린〕.

bleat [bliːt] *n.* ⒸⓊ the cry made by a sheep. 양의 울음소리. — *vi.* (P1,2A) (of a sheep) cry. (양이) 울다. [E.]

bled [bled] *v.* p. and pp. of **bleed.**

***bleed** [bliːd] *v.* (**bled**) *vi.* **1** (P1,2A) lose blood. 출혈하다. ¶ *~ at the nose* 코피를 흘리다 / *~ from the mouth* 입에서 피를 흘리다 / *His knee is bleeding.* 무릎에서 피가 흐르고 있다 / *~ to death* 많은 출혈로 죽다. **2** (P1) (of a tree) lose sap 〔liquid〕. 수액(樹液)이 흘러나오다. **3** (P1,3) 《*for*》 feel pity or sorrow. 동정하다; 마음 아파하다. ¶ *My heart bleeds for you.* 당신의 일로 가슴이 아프다. **4** (P1) suffer extortion. 착취당하다. — *vt.* (P6) **1** take blood from (someone). 피를 뽑다. ¶ *~ sick people* 병자의 피를 뽑다. **2** (P6) extort money from. …에게서 돈을 착취하다. ¶ *They bled him white.* 그에게서 돈을 몽땅 빼앗았다. [→blood]

bleed·er [blíːdər] *n.* a person who bleeds profusely; esp., a hemophiliac. 출혈성의 사람; 혈우병환자(血友病患者).

bleed·ing [blíːdiŋ] *n.* Ⓤ loss of blood; a flow of blood. 출혈. — *adj.* losing blood. 출혈하는. ¶ *a ~ sore* 피가 나는 상처.

bleep [bliːp] *n.* the sound sent out by radio. (무전기의) 삐삐하는 소리. — *vi.* (P1) transmit this signal. 삐삐 신호를 보내다. [Imit.]

blem·ish [blémiʃ] *n.* Ⓒ a spot; a fault. 오점; 흠; 결점. ¶ *a ~ on the skin* 피부의 기미 / *a ~ on his record* 그의 경력에 있어서의

오점.

without blemish, perfect. 완전한.

— *vt.* (P6) **1** make (something) dirty. …을 더럽히다; …에 얼룩을 묻히다. **2** spoil the beauty or fame of (someone or something); injure. …을 훼손〔손상〕하다. ¶ ~ *one's character* 인격을 훼손하다. [F. *blème* pale]

blench [blentʃ] *vi.* (P1,3) **1** 《*from*》 jump back; draw back; shrink with fear. 껑충 물러서다; 뒷걸음치다; 움찔〔주춤〕하다. **2** 《*at*》 turn pale. 창백해지다. [→blink]

***blend** [blend] *vt.* (P6,7) 《*with*》 mix (things) together; make (something) by mixing together. …을 혼합하다; …을 섞어 만들다. ¶ ~ *paints* 그림 물감을 섞다 / ~ *coffee* 커피를 섞다 / ~ *amusement with instruction* 재미와 교훈을 섞다. — *vi.* (P1, 2A) 《*with*》 mix; become mixed. 섞이다; 혼합되다. ¶ *Oil will not ~ with water.* 기름은 물과 섞이지 않는다. — *n.* Ⓒ something made by mixing. 혼합물. ¶ *a ~ of coffee* 커피 혼합물. [Teut.]

:bless [bles] *vt.* (**blessed** [blest] or **blest**) (P6) **1** make (something) holy. …을 신성하게 하다. ¶ *God blessed the seventh day.* 신은 그 일곱번째 날을 축성(祝聖)하셨다. **2** ask God's favor for (someone or something). …을 위해 신의 가호를 빌다. ¶ *Bless this house!* 이 집에 신의 은총이 있을지어다. **3** feel grateful to (God); praise. …을 신에게 감사한다; 신을 찬양하다. ¶ *God be blessed.* 신을 찬양하라 / *We ~ the Lord.* 신에게 감사한다. **4** 《*with*》 (of God) make (someone) happy or successful. (신이) …에게 은총을 베풀다; 축복하다. ¶ *God has blessed me with riches.* 신은 나에게 부(富)의 은총을 내리셨다 / *God ~ you!* 신의 은총이 있으시기를 / *She is blessed with children.* 그녀는 자식복을 누리고 있다. **5** guard; protect. 수호하다. ¶ *Bless me from all evils!* 모든 악에서 지켜주소서. **6** 《*euphem.*》 curse; damn. …을 저주하다. [E. orig. =consecrate with blood]

bless oneself, make the sign of the cross on one's forehead and breast; be rejoiced with one's good luck. 성호〔십자〕를 긋다; 스스로를 축복하다; 기뻐하다.

Bless me! = Bless my soul! = Well, I'm blest! What a surprise!; Oh, never! 저런; 아뿔싸; 아차; 당치도 않은.

bless one's stars, be grateful for one's good fortune. 행운을 감사하다.

have not a penny to bless oneself with, be extremely poor. 몹시 가난하다.

I am blessed 〔***blest***〕 ***if,*** I am completely ignorant. 조금도〔결코〕 …않다. ¶ *I am blessed if I know.* 그런 것 알게 뭐야.

bless·ed [blésid] *adj.* **1** holy; sacred. 신성한. ¶ *the ~ saints* 거룩한 성인들 / *the ~ land* 천국. **2** happy; successful. 행복한. ¶ ~ *ignorance* 모르는 게 약 / *the Blessed Virgin* 성모 마리아 / *Blessed are the poor in spirit.* 마음이 가난한 자는 복이 있다. **3** 《*colloq.*》 giving trouble; cursed. 귀찮은; 지겨운. ¶ *I can't get this ~ window open.* 이 우라질 창문을 열 수가 없단 말야.

the whole blessed lot, 《*colloq.*》 all. 전부; 몽땅.

bless·ed·ness [blésidnis] *n.* Ⓤ happiness. 행복. ¶ *single ~* 마음 편한 독신.

:bless·ing [blésiŋ] *n.* Ⓒ **1** a prayer asking God to show His favor; the favor of God; thanks to God before or after a meal. 기도; 신의 은총; 식전〔식후〕의 감사 기도. ¶ *ask a ~* 식전〔식후〕의 기도를 하다 / *He sent us his ~.* 그는 우리에게 축복을 보냈다. **2** anything that makes happy; a thing to be thankful for. 천혜(天惠); 행복. ¶ *Health is a great ~.* 건강은 큰 복이다.

***blest** [blest] *v.* p. and pp. of **bless.** — *adj.* =blessed.

bleth·er [bléðər] *vi., n.* =blather.

***blew** [bluː] *v.* p. of **blow**[2·3].

blight [blait] *n.* **1** Ⓤ any disease that makes plants dry and lifeless. 마름병; 줄기 마름병; 잎 마름병. **2** Ⓒ an insect that causes such a disease. 줄기〔잎〕마름병을 일으키는 해충. **3** Ⓒ anything that causes ruin. 파멸의 원인. ¶ *the ~ of poverty* 가난의 원인 / *cast a ~ over* …에 어두운 그림자를 던지다. — *vt.* (P6) **1** make (a plant) dry and lifeless. …을 말라죽게〔시들게〕 하다. ¶ *The plants were all blighted.* 초목이 모두 말라 죽었다. **2** destroy; frustrate. …을 파괴하다; (희망·계획 따위)를 꺾다. ¶ ~ *oneself* 결딴나다; 파멸하다 / *Illness blighted his hopes.* 병으로 그의 꿈은 깨졌다. [N.]

:blind [blaind] *adj.* **1** without sight; unable to see. 눈이 보이지 않는. ¶ *a ~ man* 장님 / *the ~* 맹인들 / *go* 〔*become*〕 *~* 실명하다 / *He is ~ in one eye* 〔*of an eye*〕. 그는 애꾸눈이다. **2** 《*to*》 without judgment or appreciation. 판별력〔감식력〕이 없는. ¶ ~ *to the beauties of nature* 자연의 아름다움에 대해 눈뜬 장님인 / *He is ~ to his son's faults.* 자기 아들의 잘못을 모른다. **3** hard to see; difficult to follow. 알기 어려운. ¶ ~ *reasoning* 알기 어려운 이치 / *Her voice was ~ and husky.* 그녀의 목소리는 알아듣기 힘들었고 쉬어 있었다. **4** careless about results; reckless; without aim. 맹목적인; 무모한. ¶ ~ *obedience* 맹종 / ~ *forces* 분별 없는 폭력. **5** hidden. 숨겨진. ¶ *a ~ ditch* 암거(暗渠). **6** without an opening or outlet. 막다른. ¶ *a ~ alley* 막다른 골목. **7** done without seeing; by instrument alone. 보지 않고 행해진; 계기만에 의한. ¶ *a ~ flight* 맹목 비행 / ~ *landing* 맹목 착륙. **8** made without some prior knowledge. 사전지식 없이 행해진; 무계획한. ¶ *a ~ purchase* 충동 구매. **9** 《*sl.*》 very drunk. 억병으로 취한. ¶ ~ *to the world* 곤드레만드레로 취한.

blind man's holiday, the time before candles are lighted. 황혼 때.

***turn a* 〔*one's*〕 *blind eye* (*to*),** pretend not to see (something). (…을) 보고도 못 본 척하다.
— *vt.* **1** (P6) deprive (someone) of his sight. …을 눈이 멀게 하다. **2** (P6,13) make (someone) mentally blind. …의 판단력〔이성〕을 잃게 하다. ¶ *Hate blinded him.* 증오는 그의 판단을 흐리게 했다. **3** hide; conceal. …을 감추다; 숨기다.
— *n.* Ⓒ a screen for a window. 차양; 블라인드. [E.]

blind·fold [bláindfòuld] *vt.* (P6) cover (someone's eyes) with a cloth, etc. …에 눈가리개를 하다. ¶ *They blindfolded the prisoners.* 그들은 죄수들에게 눈가리개를 했다. — *adj.* **1** with the eyes covered. 눈가리개를 한. ¶ *a ~ test* 눈가리고 하는 테스트. **2** not caring about danger. 맹목적인. ¶ *~ rage* 공연한 화 / *do something ~* 무턱댄 짓을 하다. — *adv.* **1** with the eyes covered. 눈을 가리고. **2** in a blind manner. 맹목적으로. — *n.* Ⓒ a cloth or bandage put before the eyes to prevent seeing. 눈가리개 천. [↑]

blind·ly [bláindli] *adv.* recklessly; without judgment. 맹목적으로; 무모하게; 무분별하게.

blind·man's buff [bláindmæ̀nz bʌ́f] *n.* a game played by children in which one child, with his eyes covered, tries to catch the other players. (눈가리고 하는) 술래잡기.

blind·ness [bláindnis] *n.* Ⓤ the state of being blind; lack of judgment; lack of knowledge. 맹목; 무분별; 무지(無知).

***blink** [bliŋk] *vi., vt.* **1** (P1,2A; 6) open and close the eyes quickly; wink. 눈을 깜박이다. ¶ *~ one's eyes* 눈을 깜박이다 / *A tic made his eye ~ rapidly.* 안면 경련 때문에 그의 한쪽 눈은 심하게 깜작거렸다. **2** (P3) 《*at*》 glance. 흘끗 보다. **3** (P1,2A) shine with an unsteady light; turn (light) on and off quickly. 깜박이다; 명멸(明滅)하다. ¶ *A little lantern blinked in the darkness.* 작은 등이 어둠 속에서 깜박거렸다. **4** (P6) 《*fig.*》 《*at*》 refuse to know a fact; ignore. …을 못 본 체하다; 무시하다 ¶ *~ at someone's mistake* 아무의 과실을 못 본 체하다 / *~ the fact that…* …라는 사실에 눈을 감다.
— *n.* Ⓒ a glance; a moment. 흘끗 봄; 일별; 일순간. ¶ *in a ~* 순식간에. [E.]
on the blink, not working properly; in need of repair. 고장이 나; 수리할 필요가 있어. ¶ *The radio is on the ~ again.* 라디오가 또 고장이다.

blink·ers [blíŋkərz] *n. pl.* **1** colored glasses. 색안경. **2** pieces of leather fixed at the sides of a horse's eyes. 말의 눈가리개.

***bliss** [blis] *n.* Ⓤ happiness; joy. 행복; 기쁨. ¶ 《*prov.*》 *Ignorance is ~.* 모르는 것이 약. [→blithe]

bliss·ful [blísfəl] *adj.* very happy. 더없이 행복한; 기쁨에 넘친. ● **bliss·ful·ly** [-fəli] *adv.* **bliss·ful·ness** [-nis] *n.*

blis·ter [blístər] *n.* Ⓒ **1** a little, raised spot on the skin with liquid under it, caused by burns or rubbing. 물집. ¶ *My new shoes have made blisters on my heels.* 새 신을 신었더니 발꿈치에 물집이 생겼다. **2** a swelling on the surface of a plant, on metal or on painted wood. 기포(氣泡).
— *vt., vi.* (P6;1) cause a blister on (the skin); become covered with blisters. (살갗)에 물집이 생기게하다; 물집이 생기다. ¶ *The skin has blistered badly.* 살갗에 심한 물집이 생겼다. [→blaze²]

blithe [blaið] *adj.* gay; joyful; cheerful. 즐거운; 명랑한. ¶ *She seems very ~.* 그녀는 매우 즐거워 보인다. ● **blithe·ly** [⌐li] *adv.* [E. =bright]

blith·er·ing [blíðəriŋ] *adj.* foolishly talkative. 허튼〔싱거운〕 소리를 하는. [*blather*]

blithe·some [bláiðsəm] *adj.* gay; cheerful. 즐거운; 명랑한. ¶ *a ~ nature* 밝은 성격. [→blithe]

B. Litt. Bachelor of Literature.

blitz [blits] *n.* Ⓒ 《G.》 a sudden, violent attack, as by airplanes and tanks. 기습(전); 급습. — *vt.* attack (a place, an enemy, etc.) in this way. …을 급습하다.

blitz·krieg [blítskrìːg] *n.* (G. =lightning war) an intense military campaign intended to bring about a swift victory. 전격〔기습〕전.

bliz·zard [blízərd] *n.* Ⓒ a storm with a strong, cold wind and much snow. 세찬 눈보라. [Imit.]

B. LL. Bachelor of Laws.

bloat [blout] *vt.* (P6) **1** cause (something) to swell. …을 부풀리다. ¶ *his face bloated with fatigue* 피곤해서 부어오른 그의 얼굴. **2** preserve (herrings) by salting and smoking. …을 훈제(燻製)로 하다. — *vi.* (P1) swell. 부풀다. [E.]

bloat·ed [blóutid] *adj.* **1** fat and large in an unhealthy way. 부은 듯이 살찐; 비만한. ¶ *a ~ body* 뒤룩뒤룩 살찐 몸뚱이. **2** with too much pride. 거만한.

bloat·er [blóutər] *n.* Ⓒ a salted and smoked herring. 훈제(燻製) 청어.

blob [blɑb / blɔb] *n.* a drop of liquid; a small round spot. 한 방울; 작은 얼룩. [Imit.]

bloc [blɑk / blɔk] *n.* Ⓒ 《F.》 a group of nations and persons combined for a common purpose. (정치상·경제상의) 블록. ¶ *~ economy* 블록 경제 / *the Communist ~* 공산권 / *the dollar ~* 달러권(圈).
en bloc, in a lump; wholesale. 다 함께; 한꺼번에; 일괄하여.

:block [blɑk / blɔk] *n.* Ⓒ **1** a thick and solid piece of stone, wood, etc. 덩어리; 돌덩이; 블록. ¶ *a ~ of stone* (채석장에서 떠낸) 돌덩이 / *paving blocks* 포장석(鋪裝石). **2** a large piece of wood for cutting meat, fish, wood, etc. (…을 자르기 위한) 받침대〔목〕; 모탕; 도마; 단두대. ¶ *send someone to* *the* ~ 아무를 단두대로 보내다. **3** anything or any group of persons that keeps something from being done. 막히게 하는 것. ¶ *A ~ in the traffic keeps cars from moving on.* 교통의 정체로 차들이 움직이지 못하고 있다. **4** a wheel or set of wheels used for lifting heavy things. 도르래; 고패. **5** a square part of a city bounded by four streets. 거리의 1구획; 가구(街區); 블록. ¶ *He lives on my* ~. 그는 나와 같은 블록에 살고 있다 / *A factory covered the entire* ~. 공장 하나가 온 블록을 차지하고 있다. **6** the length of one side of a city square. 가구(街區) 한 변의 길이. ¶ *Walk one ~ east.* 동쪽으로 한 블록 걸어 나가시오. **7** a slow, foolish person. 바보; 멍청이. **8** a group of countries, political parties, etc. with some common policy. (공동 정책을 위한 국가·정당 등의) 블록; 단체; 연맹(cf. *bloc*). ¶ *form an economic* ~ 경제 블록을 형성하다. **9** a mold for shaping hats. 모자의 골. **10** a piece of wood or metal engraved for use in printing. 판목(版木); 금판(金版). **11** a prepared piece of building stone. 각석(角石). **12** a notice that a bill will be opposed. (법안에 대한) 반대 성명. **13** a large quantity. 대량. ¶ *a ~ of shares* 대량의 주식 / *reserve a ~ of seats (in a theater)* (극장의) 많은 좌석을 예약하다. **14** an obstacle; an obstruction. 방해(물). ¶ *His stubbornness is a ~ to all my efforts.* 그의 완고함이 내가 아무리 노력해도 방해가 된다. **15** 《usu. *pl.*》 a children's toy consisting of wooden cubes. (어린 아이의) 장난감 블록.

a chip off* 〔*of*〕 *the old block, a child who is like his father, esp. in character. 제 아버지를 (특히 성격을) 빼닮은 아이.

go to the block, have one's head cut off. 단두대로 향하다; 참수당하다.

knock someone's block off, knock someone's head off. 아무의 머리를 때리다.

— *vt.* (P6,7) **1** make (a way) unable to be passed through. (길)을 (가로)막다. ¶ *~ up a passage* 통로를 봉쇄하다 / *The streets were blocked with snow.* 거리는 눈으로 막혔다. **2** oppose. …에 반대하다. ¶ *They made every effort to ~ his election.* 그들은 그의 선출을 막기 위해서 온갖 노력을 다했다. **3** 《cricket》 stop (a ball) with a bat. 배트로 공을 막다. **4** shape. (모자꼴로) 모양을 뜨다. [Teut.]

***block in* 〔*out*〕,** sketch roughly; plan. 대충 스케치하다; (개략적인) 계획을 세우다.

block up, keep (something) shut in; obstruct. …을 막다; 봉쇄하다; 방해하다.

block·ade [blɑkéid / blɔk-] *n.* Ⓒ the act of shutting off a place by soldiers or ships to prevent passage. 봉쇄; 교통 차단. ¶ *a ~ of all the harbors of the country* 그 나라 모든 항구의 봉쇄 / *raise the* ~ 봉쇄를 풀다 / *run* 〔*break*〕 *the* ~ …의 봉쇄를 뚫다. — *vt.* (P6) put (a place, etc.) under blockade. …을 봉쇄하다. [↑]

block·age [blɑ́kidʒ / blɔ́k-] *n.* **1** the act of blocking. 봉쇄. **2** an obstruction. 방해.

block·bust·er [blɑ́kbʌ̀stər / blɔ́k-] *n.* Ⓒ a very destructive aerial bomb weighing two or more tons. 대형 고성능 폭탄.

block·head [blɑ́khèd / blɔ́k-] *n.* Ⓒ a fool; a stupid person. 멍청이; 바보.

block·house [blɑ́khàus / blɔ́k-] *n.* Ⓒ a strong military building of wood with holes for firing through. 통나무 방새(防塞)《총안(銃眼)을 갖춘 특수 구조의 감시소》.

〈blockhouse〉

block·ish [blɑ́kiʃ / blɔ́k-] *adj.* dull. 우둔한.

block letter [ˊ ˊ-] *n.* a printing type cut from wood; a style of printing type or a letter with tight curves. 목판자(字); 블록체.

bloke [blouk] *n.* 《*colloq.*》 a man; a fellow. 놈; 녀석. ¶ *an old* ~ 늙은이. [Ir.]

·blond, blonde [blɑnd / blɔnd] *adj.* having light-colored hair, blue or gray eyes, and light skin. 금발의(opp. brunette). — *n.* Ⓒ a person with such hair, eyes, and skin. 금발의 사람. [語法] blond는 남성; blonde는 여성에 쓰임. [F. *blonde*]

:blood [blʌd] *n.* Ⓤ **1** red liquid in bodies of the higher animals. 피. ¶ *a ~ bank* 혈액은행 / *~ pressure* 혈압 / *a blood-group* 혈액형 / *blood-transfusion* 수혈 / *the circulation of the* ~ 혈액의 순환. **2** passion; temperament. 격정; 기질. ¶ *a person of hot* ~ 격정가; 열혈한(熱血漢) / *excite the* ~ (아무의) 피를 끓게 하다 / *more than flesh and ~ can stand* 참을 수 없는 / *His ~ is up.* 그는 불같이 노해 있다. **3** murder; bloodshed; slaughter. 살인; 유혈; 살육. ¶ *blood-guilty* 살인죄 / *a man of* ~ 냉혈한(漢); 살인자 / *dip one's hands in* ~ 손을 피로 적시다; 죽이다 / *fight one's way to power through* ~ 유혈을 거쳐 권좌에 다가가다. **4** family; birth; descent; relationship by blood. 가문; 혈통; 핏줄; 혈연. ¶ *~ royal* 왕족 / *a prince of the* ~ 왕자 / *noble* 〔*blue*〕 ~ 고귀한 가문 출신 / *He is of good* ~. 그는 훌륭한 가문 출신이다 / *Blood is thicker than water.* 피는 물보다 진하다. **5** Ⓒ a smart young man of fashion; a rake. 멋쟁이; 난봉꾼.

flesh and blood, the human body; the ani-

mal nature. 육체; 수성(獸性).
in cold blood, on purpose; cruelly. 일부러; 잔인하게.
make** someone's **blood boil, make him very angry. …를 격노하게 하다.
make** someone's **blood run cold, fill him with terror. …를 무서워서 쭈뼛하게 하다.
squeeze [***wring***] ***blood out of a stone,*** make a pitiless person feel pity. 목석 같은 사람으로 하여금 연민을 느끼게 하다.
taste blood, **a**) (of dogs, etc.) kill and eat an animal they have hunted, thus gaining a taste for such food. 피의 맛을 알게 되다; 맛들이다. **b**) 《*fig.*》 gain a first experience of something which a person has desired. (바라던 것을) 처음 경험하다. — *vt.* (P6) **1** ⓐ give (a dog) its first taste of blood. (개 따위가) 피를 맛보게 하다. ⓑ 《*fig.*》 give (a person) a new experience. 첫경험을 하게 하다. **2** bleed. …을 출혈시키다. [A.S. *blod*]

blood·cur·dling [blʌ́dkə̀ːrdliŋ] *adj.* horrible; causing terror. 소름이 끼치는; 오싹해지는.

blood·ed [blʌ́did] *adj.* coming from good stock; of good breed. 혈통이 좋은. ¶ *a ~ horse* 혈통이 좋은 말.

blood heat [ㅅㅅ] *n.* body temperature. 체온.

blood-horse [blʌ́dhɔ̀ːrs] *n.* a thoroughbred horse. 순종 말.

blood·hound [blʌ́dhàund] *n.* Ⓒ a large, powerful dog with a keen sense of smell, used for looking for a person, etc. (후각이 예민해) 경찰견으로 쓰이는 영국산 개.

blood·i·ly [blʌ́dili] *adv.* **1** covered with blood. 피투성이가 되어. **2** in a cruel manner. 무참하게.

blood·i·ness [blʌ́dinis] *n.* **1** Ⓤ the quality of being cruel. 잔인. **2** the state of being covered with blood. 피투성이.

blood·less [blʌ́dlis] *adj.* **1** without blood; pale. 핏기 없는; 창백한. ¶ *~ lips* 창백한 입술. **2** without losing blood. 피를 흘리지 않은. ¶ *~ revolution* 무혈(無血) 혁명. **3** without energy; without spirit. 기력이 없는. **4** cold-hearted; cruel. 냉혹한; 무정한. ¶ *a ~ character* 냉혹한 성격.

blood·let·ting [blʌ́dlètiŋ] *n.* Ⓤ 《med.》 the act of opening a vein to take out blood. 사혈(瀉血).

blood poisoning [ㅅ ㅅ—] *n.* 《med.》 a diseased condition of blood, esp. through a wound, etc. 패혈증(敗血症).

blood relation [ㅅ—ㅅ—] *n.* Ⓤ relation by blood. 혈연; 혈족; 육친.

blood·shed [blʌ́dʃèd] *n.* Ⓤ **1** the flowing of blood; the killing of people. 유혈(流血); 살해. **2** a slaughter war. 살육전(殺戮戰).

blood·shot [blʌ́dʃɑ̀t / -ʃɔ̀t] *adj.* (of the eyes) red and sore; colored slightly with blood. 충혈된.

blood·stained [blʌ́dstèind] *adj.* **1** stained with blood. 피로 물든. **2** guilty of murder. 살인범의.

blood stream [ㅅㅅ] *n.* the circulating stream of blood in a body. (인체 안의) 혈류(血流).

blood·suck·er [blʌ́dsʌ̀kər] *n.* Ⓒ **1** 《zool.》 an animal that sucks blood. 흡혈 동물《거머리 따위》. **2** a person who gets money from others by power. 고혈(膏血)을 빠는 사람; 흡혈귀.

blood test [ㅅㅅ] *n.* an examination of a person's blood. 혈액 검사.

blood·thirst·y [blʌ́dθə̀ːrsti] *adj.* eager to kill others; cruel. 피에 굶주린; 잔인한. ¶ *capture a ~ criminal* 흉악범을 잡다 / *Wolves and tigers are ~ animals.* 이리와 호랑이는 잔인한 동물이다.

blood transfusion [ㅅ—ㅅ—] *n.* Ⓤ an injection of blood from one person or animal into another. 수혈(輸血).

blood type [ㅅㅅ] *n.* any one of four groups of human blood. 혈액형.

blood vessel [ㅅㅅ—] *n.* a tube in the body through which the blood flows. 혈관. ¶ *Veins and arteries are blood vessels.* 정맥과 동맥은 혈관이다.

∗blood·y [blʌ́di] *adj.* (**blood·i·er, blood·i·est**) **1** bleeding. 출혈하고 있는. ¶ *a ~ nose* 피가 나는 코. **2** stained with blood. 피투성이의. ¶ *a ~ handkerchief* 피로 물든 손수건. **3** accompanied by much killing. 살육의. ¶ *a ~ battle* 살육전. **4** eager to kill; cruel. 피에 굶주린; 살벌(殺伐)한; 잔인한. **5** 《Brit. *emph.*》 damned. 지겨운; 지독한(cf. *blessed*). ¶ *You ~ fool* [*idiot*] *!* 이 형편없는 바보새끼 / *a ~ murderer* 잔인한 살인자. — *vt.* (P6) make (something) dirty with blood. …을 피로 더럽히다. [*blood*]

blood·y-mind·ed [blʌ́dimáindid] *adj.* cruel; bloodthirsty. 흉악한; 피에 주린.

:bloom [bluːm] *n.* **1** Ⓒ a flower; a blossom; 《*collectively*》 flowers. 꽃. **2** Ⓤ the time of flowering. 개화기(開花期). ¶ *be in ~* 꽃이 피어 있다 / *come into ~* 꽃이 피기 시작하다 / *The roses are in full ~.* 장미가 만개되어 있다. **3** 《usu. *the ~*》 a time of greatest health or beauty. 전성기. ¶ *She is in the ~ of youth.* 그녀는 지금 한창 나이이다. **4** Ⓒ a bright, warm color of health and beauty. (볼에 나타나는 젊음·건강의) 윤기; 생기; 싱싱함. ¶ *take the ~ off...* …의 신선미를[아름다움을] 빼앗다 / *a girl with fresh ~ on her cheeks* 볼에 터질 듯한 젊음을 보이는 처녀. — *vi.* (P1) **1** have flowers; blossom. 꽃이 피다. ¶ *This flower blooms all the year round.* 이 꽃은 일년 내내 피어 있다 / *These roses ~ in May.* 이들 장미는 5월에 핀다. **2** be in the time of greatest health or beauty. 한창 때이다. [N.]

bloom·ers [blúːmərz] *n. pl.* loose trousers formerly worn by girls for physical training. 블루머《헐렁한 여자 운동용 바지》. 參考 창시자 Bloomer의 이름에서. [Person]

bloom·ing [blúːmiŋ] *adj.* **1** blossoming. 꽃이 핀; 한창인. ¶ *The tree is* ~. 이 나무는 꽃이 한창 피어 있다. **2** youthful; young. 청춘의. ¶ ~ *cheeks* 한창 피어나는 볼. [→bloom]

:blos·som [blɑ́səm / blɔ́s-] *n.* Ⓒ **1** a flower, esp. of a fruit tree. (과수(果樹)의) 꽃. ¶ *The blossoms are falling off the trees.* 꽃이 떨어지고 있다. **2** Ⓤ the time of flowering. 개화기. ¶ *come into* ~ 꽃이 피다 / *be in full* ~ 꽃이 한창 피어 있다(만발하다). **3** Ⓒ a youth. 청춘. — *vi.* (P1) **1** (of a tree) have blossoms. 꽃이 피다. **2** (of a person) become, usu. something good. 잘 되다. ¶ *He has blossomed into a great novelist.* 그는 훌륭한 소설가가 되었다. [E.]

***blot** [blɑt / blɔt] *v.* (**blot·ted, blot·ting**) *vt.* (P6) **1** spot (something) with ink, etc. (잉크 따위로) 더럽히다. ¶ *blotted with tears* 눈물로 얼룩진. **2** dry (ink) with soft paper. (압지 따위로) …을 빨아들이다. ¶ *Blot it before you put it in the envelope.* 그것을 봉투에 넣기 전에 압지로 누르시오. **3** bring shame or dishonor upon (someone). …의 인격·명성 등을 훼손(손상)하다. ¶ *He has blotted a fine record.* 그는 깨끗한 경력에 오점을 남겼다. — *vi.* (P1) become blotted. (잉크 따위가 종이에) 번지다.

blot one's copybook, stain one's record. 경력에 오점을 남기다.

blot out, **a**) cover up. …을 보이지 않게 하다. ¶ *The fog blotted out the view.* 안개가 시야를 가렸다. **b**) wipe out. 지우다. ¶ ~ *out unpleasant memories* 불쾌한 기억을 지워 없애다.

— *n.* Ⓒ a spot of ink; a fault; an ugly object. 잉크의 얼룩; 흠; 눈에 거슬리는 것. ¶ *a* ~ *on one's character* 인격상의 흠 / *a* ~ *on the landscape* 미관을 해치는 것. [A.S. *plott* clod]

blotch [blɑtʃ / blɔtʃ] *n.* Ⓒ **1** a large, irregular spot. 얼룩. **2** a red spot on the skin. 부스럼; 종기. — *vt.* (P6) cover (something) with blotches. …을 더럽히다. [↑]

blot·ter [blɑ́tər / blɔ́t-] *n.* Ⓒ **1** a piece of paper for drying ink. 압지(押紙). **2** a book for writing down things that happen. 메모장(帳); (거래 등의) 기록 장부. [→blot]

blotting paper [blɑ́tiŋ pèipər / blɔ́tiŋ-] *n.* a special kind of paper for drying ink. 압지(押紙).

blot·to [blɑ́tou / blɔ́t-] *adj.* 《*colloq.*》 fuddled with drink. 곤드레만드레가 된.

blouse [blaus, blauz] *n.* Ⓒ **1** a kind of shirt worn by women and children on the upper part of the body. 블라우스. **2** a French workman's loose overall, belted at the waist, for the protection of clothing during work. (셔츠 비슷한 헐거운) 작업복. [F.]

:blow[1] [blou] *n.* Ⓒ **1** a hard hit; a knock. 타격; 강타. ¶ *a* ~ *from a falling stone* 낙석에 의한 강타 / *a* ~ *from a sword* 칼의 일격 / *be at blows* 서로 치고 받고 하다; 격투하다 / *exchange blows* 주먹을 주고 받다; 싸움하다 / *He gave me a heavy* ~ *on the face.* 그는 내 얼굴을 세게 쳤다. **2** ⓐ a sudden misfortune. 뜻밖의 재난; 불행. ¶ *a* ~ *from heaven* 청천 벽력. ⓑ a shock. (불의의) 충격. ¶ *His death was a terrible* ~ *to us.* 그의 죽음은 우리에게 엄청난 충격이었다. [↓]

at one* (*a*) *blow, with one stroke; by a single action. 일격에; 단번에. ¶ *kill eight flies at one* ~ 단번에 파리 여덟 마리를 잡다.

come* (*fall*) *to blows, begin fighting. 싸움이 되다; 싸움을 시작하다.

deal* (*give, strike*) *a blow to, beat. …에 일격을 가하다; 타격을 입히다.

***strike a blow for* (*against*),** help (oppose). …에 가세(반항)하다.

without striking a blow, without any effort; quite easily. 힘 안 들이고; 수월히.

:blow[2] [blou] *v.* (**blew, blown**) *vi.* (P1,2A) **1** move as the wind does. 불다. ¶ *The wind blows.* 바람이 분다 / *It is blowing hard.* 바람이 세차게 불고 있다. 語法 wind, it의 어느 것을 주어로 해도 무방함. **2** (P1,3) ⓐ send strong air from the mouth. 입으로 불다. ¶ ~ *hard at a candle* 촛불을 입으로 세게 불다 / *He blew on his coffee.* 그는 커피를 후후 불었다. ⓑ (of a whale) send out air and water from the nose. (고래가 코에서) 물을 내뿜다. **3** (P2A) be moved or carried by the wind. 바람에 불리다. ¶ *The curtain blew in the wind.* 커튼이 바람에 흔들렸다. **4** get out of breath; gasp for breath; puff; pant. 헐떡이다; 숨차 하다. ¶ *I stopped for a moment panting and blowing.* 나는 헐떡이면서 잠시 멈추었다. **5** (P2A,3) burst with a loud noise; explode. 요란하게 터지다; 폭발하다. ¶ *The train blew up.* 열차가 폭발했다. **6** praise oneself; boast of one's skill or deeds. 자랑하다. — *vt.* **1** (P6,7) ⓐ send strong wind to (something). …을 세게 불다. ¶ *The fan was blowing a cool air.* 선풍기가 시원한 바람을 보내고 있었다. ⓑ cause to move; send flying off (out, up). …을 불어서 움직이다; (바람에) 날려 보내다. ¶ *I had my hat blown.* 바람에 모자가 날아갔다. ⓒ breathe on. 입김을 불다. ¶ ~ *one's fingers* (*to warm them*) (언 손가락을 녹이기 위해) 입김으로 손가락을 불다 / ~ *one's food* (*to cool it*) (식히기 위해) 음식을 불다 / ~ *out a candle* 훅 불어 촛불을 끄다 / ~ (*up*) *a fire* (*to make it stronger*) (불 기운을 세게 하기 위해) 불을 불다. **2** (P6) make (a wind instrument or whistle) sound. (악기 따위)를 불어서 소리를 내다. ¶ ~ *a trumpet* 트럼펫을 불다 / ~ *a whistle* 호루라기를 불다. **3** (P6) clear by driving air through. (코를) 풀다.

¶ ~ *one's nose* 코를 풀다. **4** (P6,7) force a current of air, gas, etc. into or through. (바람·가스 따위)를 불다. **5** (P6) squander. …을 낭비하다. **6** (P6) (of flies) deposit eggs on. (파리가) …에 쉬를 슬다. **7** (P7) kill (someone) by shooting. …을 쏘아 죽이다. ¶ ~ *someone's head* 〔*brains*〕 *out* 아무의 머리에 구멍을 내다. **8** (P6) make or shape by blowing. 불어서 형태를 만들다. ¶ ~ *bubbles* 불어서 거품을 만들다 / ~ *glass* 유리를 불어 부풀리다. **9** (P6) 《*sl.*》 damn; curse. …를 저주하다. **10** 《usu. in *passive*》 exhaust of breast (esp. of a horse). (말)을 헐떡이게 하다.

blow hot and cold, constantly change one's mood. 기분·마음이 변하기 쉽다; 변덕스럽다.

blow in, 《U.S. *sl.*》 go in; enter; call to see someone. …에 들어가다; 불쑥 들르다.

blow off, **a**) let out steam; let off pressure. (증기 따위를) 방출하다; 내뿜다. **b**) 《*colloq.*》 let one's emotions out; seek relief by venting one's anger. 감정을 터뜨려 긴장〔울분〕을 풀다.

blow out, **a**) extinguish by blowing. …을 불어서 끄다. **b**) fill (something) with air or gas by blowing. (바람·가스를) …에 채워 넣다. **c**) burst or break suddenly. 갑자기 터지다; 끊어지다. ¶ *A tire* 〔*fuse*〕 *blew out.* 타이어가 펑크났다〔퓨즈가 끊어졌다〕.

blow over, 《*colloq.*》 **a**) (of trouble, a quarrel, etc.) pass away. 가라앉다. **b**) be forgotten. 잊혀지다.

blow one's own trumpet, boast of oneself. 허풍 떨다; 자랑하다.

blow up, **a**) fill (something) with air or gas. …을 공기나 가스로 채우다. **b**) explode; burst. 폭발하다; 터지다. **c**) destroy (something) by an explosive. …을 폭파하다. **d**) 《*sl.*》 scold. 꾸짖다. **e**) (of a storm, etc.) arise. (폭풍 따위가) 일어나다.

— *n.* Ⓒ **1** a strong wind; a gale; a blast. 일진 강풍. **2** 《*sl.*》 a person who speaks proudly of himself. 허풍쟁이. **3** the act of speaking proudly of oneself. 허풍 떨기. [E.]

blow³ [blou] *vi.* (**blew, blown**) (P1) come into flower; be in bloom; blossom. 꽃이 피다. [E.]

blow·er [blóuər] *n.* Ⓒ **1** a person who blows. 부는 사람. ¶ *a glass* ~ 유리 부는 공원(工員). **2** a machine to send air into a building, furnace, etc. 송풍기. [*blow*²]

blow·fly [blóuflài] *n.* 쉬파리(cf. *bluebottle*). [→blow²]

:blown [bloun] *v.* pp. of **blow**²·³. — *adj.* **1** out of breath; breathless. 숨을 헐떡이는. **2** tainted by flies; dirty. 파리 투성이의; 더러운.

blow·out [blóuàut] *n.* Ⓒ **1** a burst in an automobile tire; a puncture. (타이어의) 펑크. **2** a sudden escape of air, steam, etc. (공기·김 따위의) 분출. **3** 《*sl.*》 a feast. 큰 잔치. [*blow*²]

blow·pipe [blóupàip] *n.* Ⓒ a tube for sending air or gas into a flame to make it hotter. 불 부는 관(管); 취관(吹管).

blow·torch [blóutɔ̀ːrtʃ] *n.* Ⓒ a lamp that shoots out a hot flame for melting metal. 토치램프; 용접용 버너.

blow-up [blóuʌ̀p] *n.* **1** explosion. 폭발. **2** 《*colloq.*》 outburst of anger. 격노. **3** enlargement (of a photographic print). (사진의) 확대.

blow·y [blóui] *adj.* (**blow·i·er, blow·i·est**) windy. 바람이 센.

blowz·y [bláuzi] *adj.* (**blowz·i·er, blowz·i·est**) (of a woman) coarse-looking; badly dressed; not neat; dirty-looking. 지저분한; 추레한. [Obs. *blowze* wench]

blub·ber¹ [blʌ́bər] *n.* Ⓤ the fat of whales and some other sea animals from which oil is obtained. 고래의 지방. [Imit.]

blub·ber² [blʌ́bər] *vi.* (P1) cry loudly. 큰 소리로 울다. [↑]

bludg·eon [blʌ́dʒən] *n.* Ⓒ a short, thick stick with a heavy end. 곤봉. — *vt.* (P6,7) strike (someone or something) with a bludgeon; strike; hit. …을 곤봉으로 때리다. [? F.]

:blue [bluː] *adj.* **1** colored like the clear sky or the deep sea. 푸른. **2** low-spirited; depressed; hopeless. 기운 없는; 풀죽은; 우울한; 가망 없는. ¶ *I felt* ~ *when I failed.* 실패했을 때 우울했다 / *look* ~ 우울해 보이다 / *Things look* ~. 일은 다 틀린 것 같다; 형세가 나쁘다. **3** (of women) learned. (여자가) 인텔리의.

drink till all's blue, drink till one is dead drunk. 곤드레가 될 때까지 마시다.

like blue murder, 《*colloq.*》 at top speed. 최고 속도로.

once in a blue moon, very rarely. 매우 드물게.

till all is blue, for a long time. 오랫동안.

— *n.* Ⓤ **1** blue color. 파랑. **2** blue paint or dye. 파란 (그림) 물감. **3** 《*the* ~》 the sky; the sea. 하늘; 바다. **4** Ⓒ a woman scholar. 여류 학자. **5** 《*pl.* often used as *sing.*》 low spirits. 울적함; 우울. ¶ *get the blues* 몹시 울적해 있다.

— *vt.* (P6) **1** make (something) blue. …을 푸르게 하다. **2** spend foolishly (money, etc.). (돈 따위)를 낭비하다. [Teut.]

blue·bell [blúːbèl] *n.* Ⓒ 《bot.》 a wild plant with blue, bell-shaped flowers. 야생 초롱꽃.

blue·ber·ry [blúːbèri, -bəri] *n.* 《bot.》 《U.S.》 the blue berry of a certain plant; the plant it grows on. 월귤나무의 한 가지; 그 열매.

blue·bird [blúːbə̀ːrd] *n.* Ⓒ 《bird》 a small North American songbird with a bright blue back. 지빠귓과의 파란 날개를 가진 새.

blue-black [blú:blǽk] *adj.* very dark blue. 짙은 남색의.

blue blood [ˊ ˋ] *n.* blood of a noble family. 귀족의 혈통.

blue book [ˊ ˋ] *n.* **1** 《U.S.》 a list of famous people. 명사록(名士錄). **2** a British official report with a blue cover. 청서(靑書)《영국 의회 발행 보고서》.

blue·bot·tle [blú:bὰtl / -bɔ̀tl] *n.* Ⓒ **1** a large fly with a blue body. 쉬파리 (cf. *blowfly*). **2** 《bot.》 a cornflower. 수레국화.

blue-col·lar [blú:kάlər / -kɔ́l-] *adj.* of or belonging to persons who work with their hands. 임금 노동자의; 육체 노동자의 (cf. *white-collar*).

blue devils [ˊ ˊ-] *n.* depression. 우울.

blue·eyed [blú:àid] *adj.* **1** having blue eyes. 푸른 눈의. **2** 《*colloq.*》 favorite; darling. 마음에 드는; 귀여운. ¶ *a ~ boy* 애인.

blue funk [ˊ ˊ] *n.* 《*colloq.*》 acute fear. 공포.

blue·jack·et [blú:dʒæ̀kit] *n.* Ⓒ a sailor in the navy. 수병(水兵).

blue law [ˊ ˋ] *n.* 《U.S.》 a law to control sexual morals, the drinking of alcohol, working in Sundays, etc. 엄법(嚴法)《일요일에 일이나 오락을 금함》.

blue-pen·cil [blú:pénsəl] *vt.* (**-ciled, -cil·ing** or esp. 《Brit.》 **-cilled, -cil·ling**) (P6) correct or cross out (a manuscript) with a blue pencil; edit. (원고 따위)를 청색 연필로 교정하다; 편집하다.

blue pill [ˊ ˊ] *n.* a mercurial pill. 수은제(劑).

blue·print [blú:prìnt] *n.* Ⓒ **1** a photograph made in white lines on blue paper, for building plans, etc. 청사진(靑寫眞). **2** a detailed plan; scheme. 상세한 설계도; 계획. — *vt.* (P6) make a blueprint of (something); plan. …의 청사진을 뜨다; 계획하다.

blue ribbon [ˊ ˊ-] *n.* the highest honor, given to the first-place winner in a contest; the ribbon of the Order of the Garter. 최고의 영예; 가터 훈장의 청색 리본.

blue·stock·ing [blú:stὰkiŋ / -stɔ̀k-] *n.* Ⓒ a learned woman; a woman who pretends to be learned. 여류 학자; 학자연하는 여자.

***bluff** [blʌf] *n.* **1** Ⓒ a high, steep place; a cliff. 낭떠러지; 절벽. **2** Ⓤ pretending to be very strong. 허세. **3** Ⓒ a threat that cannot be carried out. 속들여다뵈는 엄포. **4** Ⓒ one who bluffs. 허세부리는 사람. — *adj.* **1** (of a cliff) having a wide, steep front. 낭떠러지의. **2** frank and rough in manner. 솔직한; 무뚝뚝한. ¶ *His manner is rather ~.* 그의 태도는 솔직한 편이다. [Du. =baffle]

blu·ish [blú:iʃ] *adj.* somewhat blue; slightly blue. 푸른 빛이 도는. [*blue*]

blun·der [blʌ́ndər] *n.* Ⓒ a foolish and careless mistake. 실수. ¶ *commit a ~* 실수하다 / *There are many blunders in this translation.* 이 번역에는 많은 잘못이 있다. — *vi., vt.* (P1,2A,3; 7) **1** make a foolish mistake. 실수하다. ¶ *He blundered badly in answering the questions put to him.* 그는 질문에 답변하면서 큰 실수를 했다. **2** stumble. 넘어지다; 곱드러지다. **3** say (something) thoughtlessly. 무심코 입 밖에 내다. [E.]

blunder away, miss (a chance, etc.) carelessly. (기회 따위)를 부주의하게 놓치다.

blunder out, blurt out. 무심코 지껄이다.

blunder up* 〔*on*〕*, find (someone or something) by chance. …을 우연히 발견하다.

blun·der·buss [blʌ́ndərbʌ̀s] *n.* Ⓒ **1** an old short gun with a wide mouth. 나팔총. **2** a foolish person. 얼간이. [Du. *donderbus* thunder gun]

blun·der·er [blʌ́ndərər] *n.* Ⓒ a careless person. 조심성 없는 사람. [→blunder]

***blunt** [blʌnt] *adj.* **1** not having a sharp edge or point. 날〔끝〕이 무딘; 둔한(opp. sharp). ¶ *a ~ knife* 날이 무딘 칼 / *a ~ pencil* 끝이 뭉뚝한 연필. **2** frank or plain in speech or manner. 솔직한; 무뚝뚝한. ¶ *His ~ manner makes many people dislike him.* 태도가 무뚝뚝해서 많은 사람이 그를 싫어한다 / *~ of speech* 말을 솔직히 하는. **3** slow in understanding. 우둔한. — *vt.* (P6) make (something) blunt. …을 무디게 하다. ¶ *~ the edge of a knife* 칼날을 무디게 하다. — *vi.* become blunt. 무디어지다. [? E.]

blunt·ly [blʌ́ntli] *adv.* in a blunt manner; plainly. 무뚝뚝하게.

blunt·ness [blʌ́ntnis] *n.* Ⓤ the state of being blunt. 무딤; 무뚝뚝함.

blur [blə:r] *vt., vi.* (**blurred, blur·ring**) (P6; 1) **1** make (something) not clear in shape or appearance. 흐리게〔불분명하게〕하다. ¶ *Smoke blurred the landscape.* 연기 때문에 경치가 잘 보이지 않았다. **2** become dim. 흐려지다. ¶ *Mists blurred the view.* 안개로 잘 보이지 않게 되었다. **3** make (something) dirty; become dirty; stain. 더럽히다; 더러워지다. ¶ *She blurred her new dress with red ink.* 그녀는 새 드레스를 빨간 잉크로 더럽혔다.

— *n.* Ⓒ **1** the state of being not clear. 희미함; 흐림. **2** a thing not seen clearly. 또렷이 보이지 않는 것. **3** a stain; a blot. 얼룩. ¶ *a ~ on the mirror* 거울의 얼룩. [? *blear* +*blot*]

blurt [blə:rt] *vt.* (P7) 《*out*》 tell suddenly or thoughtlessly. 불쑥 말하다; 무심결에 이야기하다. ¶ *~ out a secret* 비밀을 누설하다 / *In his anger he blurted out the whole story.* 홧김에 전부 털어놓았다. [Imit.]

***blush** [blʌʃ] *n.* Ⓒ **1** the red color of the cheek or face caused by embarrassment or excitement. 붉어진 얼굴; 홍조(紅潮). ¶ *put someone to the ~* (홍분·당황 등으로) 얼굴이 붉어지게 만들다. **2** a rosy color. 장밋빛.

at* (*the*) *first blush, on first glance. 첫눈에;

얼핏 보아; 일견하여.
put** someone **to the blush, cause someone to blush. 아무를 부끄럽게 하다.
Spare my blushes. Do not praise me in my own hearing. 듣는 데서 내 칭찬을 마라.
— *vi.* (P1,3,4) 《*at, for*》 become rosy because of embarrassment or excitement; feel shame; be ashamed or embarrassed. 얼굴이 붉어지다; 부끄러워하다. ¶ ~ *up to the root of one's hair* 얼굴이 새빨개지다 / ~ *for shame* 부끄러워 빨개지다 / *I blushed to hear the story.* 나는 그 이야기를 듣고 낯이 뜨거웠다 / *I ~ to think of the things I did when I was younger.* 젊어서 한 일들을 생각하니 낯이 붉어진다. [E.]

blus·ter [blʌ́stər] *vi., vt.* (P1,2A,3; 6,7) 《*away, up, in, out*》 **1** blow noisily and violently; be windy. 바람이 세차게 휘몰아치다; 바람이 세다. ¶ *The wind blustered round the house.* 바람이 그 집을 휘몰아쳤다. **2** talk noisily and violently. 고함을 치다. ¶ *John was very excited and blustered for a while.* 존은 매우 흥분하여 한동안 고함을 질러 댔다 / *Don't ~ at me.* 나에게 소리치지 마라. **3** boast. 뽐내다. — *n.* CU **1** stormy noise. 사납게 휘몰아치는 소리. **2** noisy and violent talk. 고함; 호통. [Imit.]

blus·ter·ous [blʌ́stərəs] *adj.* **1** blowing noisily and violently; blowing like a storm. 바람이 세차게 휘몰아치는. **2** talking noisily. 고함치는; 호통치는.

B.M. Bachelor of Medicine.

bo·a [bóuə] *n.* C **1** 《zool.》 a large, long tropical American snake that is not poisonous. 보아; 왕뱀. **2** a long scarf of fur or feathers worn by a woman. 목도리. [L.]

B.O.A.C. British Overseas Airways Corporation.

boa constrictor [ㅿ– –ㅿ–] *n.* =boa.

***boar** [bɔːr] *n.* C **1** a male pig. 수퇘지. **2** a wild pig. 멧돼지. [E.]

:**board** [bɔːrd] *n.* C **1** a long, wide, thin piece of wood. 널; 판자. ¶ *a ~ fence* 널판장. **2** ⓐ a large, thick, flat piece. 반(盤); 판. ¶ *a ~ for checkers* 장기판. ⓑ a flat piece of wood used for one special purpose. (특정 목적을 위한) 평판(平板). ¶ *a cutting ~* 마름대(臺). **3** a thick, stiff paper. 판지(板紙). **4** 《*pl.*》 the stage. 무대. ¶ *go on the boards* 배우가 되다. **5** U food served; daily meals. 식사. ¶ *ten dollars a day for room and ~* 방값과 식사대로서 하루 10 달러 / *Mrs. Jones gives good ~.* 존스 부인은 좋은 식사를 제공한다. **6** a council; a committee. 회의; 위원회. ¶ *a ~ of directors* 중역회. **7** a government department. (관청의) 국; 부; 과.
above board, openly. 공명 정대하게.
board on board, side by side. (뱃전을) 나란히 하고.
board and lodging, food and houseroom. 식사도 주는 하숙.
go by the board, **a**) (of a mast) fall into the sea out of a ship. (마스트가) 쓰러져 바다로 떨어지다. **b**) fail completely; come to nothing. 완전히 실패하다.
on board, on or into a train, a ship, or an airplane. 열차(배, 비행기)를 타고.
sweep the board, **a**) take all the cards or stakes on the table. 탁상의 카드(판돈)을 몽땅 쓸어 들이다. **b**) 《*fig.*》 be very successful; win. 전승(全勝)하다.
tread* [*walk*] *the boards, be on the stage; be an actor. 무대에 서다; 배우가 되다.
— *vt.* (P6) **1** cover (something) with boards. …을 판자로 두르다. ¶ *~ up a window* 창문에 판자를 치다 / *~ over a well* 우물을 판자로 막다. **2** provide (someone) with daily meals at a fixed price. …에게 식사를 제공하다. ¶ *Do you ~ your lodgers?* 댁은 하숙인들에게 식사를 제공하십니까. **3** go on or get in (a ship, train, plane, etc.). …을 타다. ¶ *Please ~ the aircraft now.* 자 (비행기에) 탑승해 주십시오.
— *vi.* (P1,2A) get one's daily meals at a fixed price. (일정한 값에 매일의) 식사를 제공받다. ¶ *Some of them lodge at one place and ~ at another.* 그들 중엔 한 곳에 하숙하고 식사는 딴 데서 하는 사람도 있다. [Teut.=board, border]

board·er [bɔ́ːrdər] *n.* C a person who pays for meals or for room and meals at other's house, a school, etc. 하숙(기숙)인. ¶ *a ~ at the school* 기숙생. 參考 통학생은 day boy, day girl.

board·ing [bɔ́ːrdiŋ] *n.* U a structure of boards. 판자울.

boarding house [ㅿ– ㅿ] *n.* a house where persons are given meals, or room and meals, at a fixed price. 하숙집; 기숙사.

boarding school [ㅿ– ㅿ] *n.* a school where pupils are given room and meals as well as lessons. 기숙사제 학교. 參考 자택에서 통학시키는 학교는 day school.

board wages [ㅿ ㅿ–] *n. pl.* money paid for food. 식비.

board·walk [bɔ́ːrdwɔ̀ːk] *n.* C a sidewalk made of thick boards, esp. along a beach. (해변 따위의) 널을 깐 보도(步道).

:**boast** [boust] *vi., vt.* (P1,3; 6,11) 《*of*》 speak too well about oneself; be proud; be proud of having (something). 자랑하다; 떠벌리다; 자랑스럽게 여기다. ¶ *Our city boasts a fine park.* 우리 시는 훌륭한 공원을 자랑하고 있다 / *He boasts of his wealth.* 그는 자기의 재산을 자랑하고 있다.
— *n.* C **1** the act of praising oneself. 자랑. ¶ *His ~ was that he had a wonderful memory for names.* 그의 자랑은 그가 남의 이름을 잘 기억한다는 것이었다. **2** a thing to be proud of. 자랑거리. ¶ *His garden was his ~.* 그의 정원은 자랑거리였다. [E.]
make a boast (=*be proud*) ***of** something.* …을 자랑하다.

boast·er [bóustər] *n.* C a person who boasts. 자랑하는 사람; 허풍선이.

boast·ful [bóustfəl] *adj.* **1** boasting. 자랑하는. ¶ *be ~ of* …을 자랑하다. **2** fond of boasting. 자랑하기를 좋아하는. ● **boast·ful·ly** [-li] *adj.* **boast·ful·ness** [-nis] *n.*

:boat [bout] *n.* Ⓒ **1** a small open ship; a ship. 보트; 배. ¶ *a fishing ~* 어선 / *cross a river in a ~* 배를 타고 강을 건너다 / *row a ~* 배를 젓다 / *go by ~* 배로 가다. **2** a dish shaped like a boat. 배 모양의 접시.
be in the same boat, share the same danger or trouble. …와 운명을〔처지를〕 같이 하다.
burn one's boat, commit oneself irrevocably to a course. 배수(背水)의 진을 치다.
rock the boat, make matters worse for a group, at a difficult time, by expressing differences of opinion. 동요를〔파란을〕 일으키다.
take to the boats, escape in the ship's boats because the ship is sinking. (가라앉는 본선에서) 보트로 옮겨 타다.
— *vi., vt.* (P1,2A; 6) **1** go in a boat; row a boat. 배로 가다; 배를 젓다. ¶ *go boating* 배타러 가다. **2** carry (something) in a boat. …을 배로 나르다. [E.]

boat·er [bóutər] *n.* a straw hat; a person who boats. 맥고 모자; 보트를 타는 사람.

boat·house [bóuthàus] *n.* Ⓒ a house for keeping boats safely. 정고(艇庫).

boat·ing [bóutiŋ] *n.* Ⓤ the act of rowing a boat, esp. for pleasure. 보트〔뱃〕놀이.

boat·man [bóutmən] *n.* Ⓒ (*pl.* **-men** [-mən]) **1** a person who rents boats. 보트 임대업자. **2** a person who rows boats for pay. (돈 받고) 노젓는 사람; 사공.

boat race [╴╴] *n.* Ⓒ a race among rowing boats. 경조(競漕)(cf. *regatta*).

boat·swain [bóusən, bóutswèin] *n.* Ⓒ the chief of common seamen on a ship. 갑판장(長). 參考 bosun 이라고도 씀.

boat train [╴╴] *n.* a train that carries passengers to or from a steamer. (기선과 연락하는) 항만 열차.

Bob [bab / bɔb] *n.* a nickname for Robert. Robert 의 애칭.

bob[1] [bab / bɔb] *vt., vi.* (**bobbed, bob·bing**) **1** (P6; 2A) move (something) up and down with short, quick motions; move about with short, quick motions. 갑자기 위아래로 움직이다; 흔들(리)다. ¶ *~ the head* 머리를 홱 움직이다 / *A bottle was bobbing about in the river.* 병 하나가 강에 떠다니고 있었다. **2** (P1; 6) curtsey. 고개를 움직여 인사하다. ¶ *She bobbed a courtesy.* 그녀는 고개숙여 인사했다.
bob up (***again***), **a**) appear suddenly. 불쑥 나타나다. **b**) become active after a defeat. 재기(再起)하다. ¶ *~ up like a cork* 힘을 만회하다; 재기하다.
— *n.* Ⓒ a short, quick up-and-down motion; a sudden movement. 갑자기 위아래로 움직임. [E.]

bob[2] [bab / bɔb] *n.* Ⓒ **1** a short haircut for a woman or girl. 단발. **2** a weight on the end of a line. 추(錘). **3** a float for a fishing line. 낚시찌. — *vt.* (**bobbed, bob·bing**) (P6) cut (hair) short and straight. (머리)를 단발하다. ¶ *They bobbed their hair to be in style.* 그들은 유행에 맞추어 단발로 했다. [↑]

bob·ber·y [bábəri / bɔ́b-] *n.* a row, disturbance. 법석; 소동. ¶ *raise a ~* 법석을 떨다.

bob·bin [bábin / bɔ́b-] *n.* a reel or spool for holding thread, yarn, etc. 얼레; 보빈. [F.]

·bob·by [bábi / bɔ́bi] *n.* Ⓒ (*pl.* **-bies**) 《Brit. *sl.*》 a policeman. 경찰관; 순경. [Person]

bob·sled [bábslèd / bɔ́b-] *n.* Ⓒ 《U.S.》 two short sleds fastened together by a thick board, used for sliding down a snowy slope. (두대의) 연결 썰매; 봅슬레이. [→bob[1]]

bob·sleigh [bábslèi / bɔ́b-] *n.* =bobsled.

bob·stay [bábstèi / bɔ́b-] *n.* 《naut.》 a rope or chain to hold a bowsprit down. 제1 사장 지삭(斜檣支索). [→bob[1]]

bob·tail [bábtèil / bɔ́b-] *n.* Ⓒ **1** a short tail; a tail cut short. 짧은 꼬리; 짧게 자른 꼬리. **2** a horse or dog with a bobtail. 꼬리 자른 말〔개〕. — *adj.* having a bobtail. 짧은 꼬리를 한. [→bob[2]]

bob·tailed [bábtèild / bɔ́b-] *adj.* having a short tail. 짧은 꼬리를 한.

Boc·cac·ci·o [boukáːtʃiòu / bɔk-], **Giovanni** *n.* (1313-75) an Italian novelist and poet. 보카치오.

bock [bak / bɔk] *n.* a strong dark beer. 독한 흑맥주. [G.]

bode[1] [boud] *vt., vi.* (P6,13,14; 2A) be a sign of (something). …의 조짐이 되다. ¶ *The crow's cry bodes rain.* 까마귀가 우는 것은 비가 올 조짐이다 / *This bodes you no good.* 이것은 당신에게 흉조이다. [F. obs. *bode* messenger]
bode ill 〔***well***〕, be a bad 〔good〕 sign of (something). …의 흉조〔길조〕이다.

bode[2] [boud] *v.* p. of **bide.**

bod·ice [bádis / bɔ́d-] *n.* Ⓒ the close-fitting waist of a dress for women. 보디스《몸에 꼭 끼는 여성의 상의》. [→body]

〈bodice〉

bod·i·less [bádilis / bɔ́d-] *adj.* **1** without a body. 몸이〔몸체가〕 없는. **2** separated from the body. 육체에서 분리된. ¶ *a ~ spirit* 육체를 떠난 정신. [→body]

·bod·i·ly [bádəli / bɔ́d-] *adj.* having to do with the body. 몸〔육체〕의(opp. mental). ¶ *~ pain* 육체적 고통. — *adv.* **1** in person. 몸소. ¶ *Christ walked ~ among men.* 그리스도는 몸소 군중 속으로 걸어갔다. **2** all together; entirely. 전부; 몽땅; 그대로. ¶ *The building was transported ~ to another* *place.* 그 건물은 그대로 다른 곳으로 옮겨졌다.

bod·kin [bádkin / bɔ́d-] *n.* Ⓒ **1** a large, thick needle with a large eye. 돗바늘. **2** a long hairpin. 긴 머리핀. [Welsh]

:bod·y [bádi / bɔ́di] *n.* (*pl.* **bod·ies**) Ⓒ **1** ⓐ the physical structure of a man or an animal. 몸; 신체. ¶ *the human* ~ 인체 / *a healthy* ~ 건강체 / *build up one's* ~ 몸을 튼튼하게 하다. ⓑ a dead body. 사체(死體). ¶ *They buried the* ~. 그들은 시체를 묻었다. **2** the central part of a man or an animal without the head or limbs. 몸통; 동체(胴體). **3** the main or central part of anything. 본체; 주요부. ¶ *the* ~ *of a ship* 선체(船體) / *the* ~ *of a car* 차체 / *the* ~ *of an airplane* 기체(機體). **4** 《*colloq.*》 a person. 사람. ¶ *anybody / somebody* 어떤 사람 / *an honest* ~ 정직한 사람 / *a good sort of* ~ 호인. **5** a group of persons or things. 무리; 대(隊); 단체; 조직. ¶ *a learned* ~ 학회 / *the student* ~ 학생회 / *a public* ~ 공공 단체 / *A large* ~ *of children sang at the church.* 어린이 대합창대가 교회에서 노래를 불렀다. **6** a piece of matter. 물체. ¶ *a heavenly* ~ 천체 / *a solid* 〔*gaseous*〕 ~ 고체〔기체〕. **7** Ⓤ substance; thickness; strong taste. 실질; 농도; 진한맛; 감칠맛. ¶ *wine of good* ~ 감칠맛 나는 포도주. **8** a mass. 집적(集積). ¶ *A lake is a* ~ *of water.* 호수는 물의 집적체이다. **9** 《math.》 a solid. 입체. ¶ *a regular* ~ 정다면체.

in a body, all together; as a group. 다같이; 일단이 되어. ¶ *attack in a* ~ 무리를 지어 습격하다.

keep body and soul together, just manage to keep alive. 그럭저럭 살아가다.

— *vt.* (**bod·ied**) (P6) 《*forth*》 give a real shape to (something); put (an idea, etc.) into some shape which can be seen or heard. …을 구체화하다; 체현(體現)하다. [E.]

bod·y·guard [bádigɑ̀:rd / bɔ́di-] *n.* Ⓒ a man or group of men who guard an important person. 경호원; 보디가드.

B.O.E., B of E. Bank of England; Board of Education.

Boer [bɔ:r, bouər] *n.* a Dutch farmer in South Africa. 보어인(人). [Du.=peasant]

bog [bɑg, bɔ(:)g] *n.* soft, wet, spongy ground; marsh. 늪; 늪지. — *vt.* (P6) (**bogged, bog·ging**) 《usu. *passive*》 sink (something) in a bog. …을 늪〔수렁〕에 빠뜨리다. — *vi.* fall into a bog. 늪〔수렁〕에 빠지다. ¶ ~ *down* 막다른 길에 이르다. [Ir.]

be* 〔*get*〕 *bogged, sink in a bog. 늪〔수렁〕에 빠지다.

bo·gey [bóugi] *n.* Ⓒ an evil spirit; a person or a thing that causes fear. 귀신; 무서운 사람〔것〕. ¶ *Arithmetic is a* ~ *to some children.* 수학이란 어린이들에게 겁나는 과목이다. [?]

bog·gle [bágəl / bɔ́g-] *vi.* (P3) 《*at*》 hesitate. 망설이다. [→bogle]

bog·gy [bági, bɔ́:gi / bɔ́gi] *adj.* (**-gi·er, -gi·est**) soft, wet, and spongy like a bog. 수렁과 같은. ¶ *Very wet muddy ground is* ~. 몹시 질척이는 운동장이 수렁과 같다. [*bog*]

bo·gie [bóugi] *n.* =bogey.

bo·gle [bágəl / bɔ́gəl] *n.* =bogey.

bo·gus [bóugəs] *adj.* 《U.S.》 false; untrue. 가짜의. ¶ ~ *money* 가짜돈.

bo·gy [bóugi] *n.* (*pl.* **-gies**) =bogey.

Bo·he·mi·a [bouhí:miə] *n.* a region of Czech Republic; a former country in central Europe. 보헤미아 지방.

Bo·he·mi·an [bouhí:miən] *adj.* **1** of Bohemia, its people, or their language. 보헤미아(사람·말)의. **2** 《often *b-*》 free and easy. 방랑의; 방종한. — *n.* Ⓒ **1** a person of Bohemia. 보헤미아 사람. **2** Ⓤ the language of Bohemia. 보헤미아어. **3** 《often *b-*》 an artist, a writer, etc. who leads a free and easy way of life. (예술가 등) 자유 분방한 생활을 하는 사람. **4** a gypsy. 집시; 방랑자.

:boil[1] [bɔil] *vt., vi.* (P6,18; 1,2A) **1** heat (liquid) to the point of becoming gas; (of liquid) grow hot; cook (something) in water. 끓이다; 끓다; (음식 따위) 익(히)다. ¶ *boiling point* 끓는점. **2** be very angry or excited. 불끈〔흥분〕하다. ¶ *He boiled with rage.* 그는 격노했다.

boil away, **a**) continue boiling. 계속 끓다. **b**) disappear in vapor or steam; evaporate. 끓어서 김으로〔수증기로〕 증발하다.

boil down, **a**) make less in quantity by boiling. 졸이다. ¶ ~ *down the juice from sugarcane* 사탕수수의 즙을 졸이다. **b**) make shorter; condense; summarize. 줄이다; 요약하다. ¶ ~ *down an article to a few sentences* 논문을 서너 문장으로 줄이다. **c**) 《*colloq.*》 be reduced (to). …으로 요약되다.

boil over, **a**) overflow the side of a vessel while boiling. 끓어 넘치다. **b**) become very excited. 노여움을 터뜨리다.

make someone's blood boil, make someone very angry. (아무)를 불같이 노하게 하다. ¶ *His words made my blood* ~. 그의 말에 나는 울컥 화가 났다.

— *n.* Ⓒ 《often *the* ~》 the act of boiling; the state of being boiled. 비등; 끓음. [L. *bulla* bubble]

come to* 〔*go off*〕 *the boil, begin 〔stop〕 boiling. 비등을〔끓기〕 시작하다〔멈추다〕. ¶ *Water comes to the* ~ *at 100°C.* 물은 100°C에서 끓기 시작한다.

boil[2] [bɔil] *n.* 《med.》 a painful swelling on the body. 종양(腫瘍). [E.]

boil·er [bɔ́ilər] *n.* Ⓒ a large metal vessel for producing steam, keeping hot water, or boiling something. 보일러. [→boil[1]]

boil·ing [bɔ́iliŋ] *n.* **1** Ⓤ making liquids boil; cooking by boiling. 끓게 함; 요리. ¶ *Food is often cooked by* ~. 음식은 끓여 만

드는 수가 많다. **2** Ⓒ the whole of the things boiled in the same vessel. (같은 그릇에) 삶은 것. ¶ *a ~ of potatoes* 삶은 감자. — *adj.* **1** in a state of boiling. 끓(이)는. ¶ *~ water* 열탕. **2** very hot. 매우 더운. ¶ *a ~ day* 찌듯이 더운 날.

boiling point [∠-∠] *n.* the temperature at which a liquid boils. 끓는점.

bois·ter·ous [bɔ́istərəs] *adj.* **1** (of a person, etc.) noisily cheerful; rough. 활기 있고 시끄러운: 난잡한. ¶ *~ laughter* 요란한 웃음소리. **2** (of weather) violent; stormy; rough. 몹시 사나운; 거친. ¶ *a ~ wind* 〔*sea*〕 사나운 바람〔바다〕. [O.F.]

bois·ter·ous·ly [bɔ́istərəsli] *adv.* in a boisterous manner. 시끄럽게; 사납게.

⁑**bold** [bould] *adj.* **1** fearless; brave; courageous. 대담한; 용감한(opp. cowardly). ¶ *a ~ idea* 대담한 생각 / *The ~ boy challenged the giant.* 용감한 소년은 거인을 공격했다. **2** without feelings of shame; impudent. 뻔뻔스러운. ¶ *as ~ as brass* 철면피한 / *a ~ hussy* 굴러먹은 여자. **3** confident. 자신있는. **4** clear; striking; wellmarked. 뚜렷한; 두드러진. ¶ *The ~ outline of the mountain appeared ahead of us.* 그 산의 뚜렷한 윤곽이 우리 앞에 나타났다. **5** steep; abrupt. 험준한; 깎아지른 듯한. ¶ *~ cliffs* 깎아지른 절벽. [E.]

be 〔***make***〕 ***bold to,*** dare to do (something); have the courage to do (something). 감히 …하다. ¶ *I make ~ to ask you.* 감히 한마디 여쭙겠습니다.

bold·faced [bóuldfèist] *adj.* **1** impudent; impolite. 뻔뻔스러운; 무례한. **2** having thick, heavy lines. (활자가) 획이 굵은; 고딕의. ¶ *~ type* 고딕 활자.

***bold·ly** [bóuldli] *adj.* **1** in a bold manner. 대담하게. **2** clearly. 뚜렷이.

bold·ness [bóuldnis] *n.* Ⓤ the state of being bold. 대담함; 뻔뻔스러움; 뚜렷함.

bole [boul] *n.* Ⓒ the stem or trunk of a tree. 나무 줄기. [N.]

bo·le·ro [bəlέərou] *n.* Ⓒ (*pl.* **-ros**) **1** a lively Spanish dance; the music for it. 볼레로춤; 그 곡. **2** a short, loose jacket for women. (여성용의 낙낙한) 짧은 상의(上衣). [Sp.]

Bo·liv·i·a [bəlíviə] *n.* a country in west central South America. 볼리비아.

boll [boul] *n.* Ⓒ a round seedcase of cotton or flax. (아마·목화 따위의) 둥근 꼬투리. [E.]

bol·lard [bálərd / bɔ́l-] *n.* a post round which ropes holding ships are tied. 배매는 기둥; 계선주(繫船柱). [L.]

bo·lo·gna [bəlóunjə] *n.* Ⓤ a large smoked sausage made of beef, pork, etc. 대형 훈제 소시지. [Place]

Bol·she·vik [bálʃəvìk, bóul-, bɔ́(:)l-] *n.* Ⓒ (*pl.* **-viks** or **-vi·ki**) **1** a member of the Communist party of Russia. 볼셰비키의 일원. **2** an extreme radical. 과격파(派)〔주의자〕. ●**Bol·she·vism** [-vìzəm] *n.* [Russ. = of the bigger party]

Bol·she·vi·ki [bálʃəvìki:, bóul-, bɔ́(:)l-] *n.* pl. of **Bolshevik.**

bol·ster [bóulstər] *n.* Ⓒ **1** a long pillow for a bed. 침대용의 덧베개. **2** a cushion. 덧받치는 것. — *vt.* (P6,7) support. …을 받치다. [E.]

bolster up, support; keep (something) from falling. …을 지지하다; 받치다.

***bolt** [boult] *n.* Ⓒ **1** a metal pin used with a nut in fastening and holding things together. 볼트. **2** ⓐ a sliding bar for locking a door or gate. 빗장. ⓑ the sliding piece in a lock. 자물쇠청. **3** a short heavy arrow of a crossbow. 쇠뇌의 굵은 화살. **4** a flash of lightning; a thunderbolt. 번개. **5** the act of bolting. 탈주; 도망. **6** 《U.S.》 a refusal to support a candidate, platform, etc., of one's party. 자당(自黨)의 정책 거부.

do a bolt = ***make a bolt for it,*** run away quickly. 재빨리 달아나다; 탈주하다.

shoot one's bolt, make one's last effort; do all one can. 있는 힘을 다하다; 최선을 다하다. ¶ *I've shot my ~.* 내 할 일을 다했다.

— *vi., vt.* **1** (P1) escape, depart, or run away suddenly from (a place). 갑자기 달아나다〔내닫다〕. ¶ *The horse bolted.* 말이 별안간 내닫기 시작했다 / *His wife has bolted with all his money.* 아내는 그의 돈을 몽땅 가지고 달아났다. **2** (P6) swallow (food) unchewed. (음식물을 잘 씹지도 않고) 그대로 삼키다. ¶ *Don't ~ your food.* 너무 급하게 먹지 마라. **3** (P6) fasten (a door) with a bolt. (문)에 빗장을 걸다. **4** (P6) 《U.S.》 refuse to support a party platform or candidate. 자당 정책을〔후보를〕 거부하다.

bolt in 〔***out***〕, shut (someone) in〔out〕. …을 가두다〔내쫓다〕.

— *adv.* in an erect position. 곧추서; 직립하여. ¶ *~ upright* 곧추. [E.]

***bomb** [bɑm / bɔm] *n.* Ⓒ **1** a metal ball or shell filled with bursting material for causing destruction, usu. dropped from an aircraft. 폭탄. ¶ *an atomic ~* 원자 폭탄 / *a hydrogen ~* 수소 폭탄 / *Bombs are dropped from planes.* 폭탄은 비행기에서 투하된다. **2** anything made to explode like a bomb. 폭발물. — *vt., vi.* (P6;1) drop bombs on (a place, etc.). (…에) 폭탄을 투하하다; 폭격하다. ¶ *be bombed out* 폭격으로 소실되다 / *~ a city.* [Gk. *bómbos* booming]

bom·bard [bɑmbɑ́:rd / bɔm-] *vt.* (P6) **1** attack (a place, etc.) with shells from big guns. 포격하다. **2** 《*with*》 《*fig.*》 attack. …을 공격하다. ¶ *~ someone with questions* 아무에게 질문 공세를 펴다. [*bomb, -ard*]

bom·bar·dier [bɑ̀mbərdíər / bɔ̀m-] *n.* **1** 《Brit.》 a corporal in the artillery. 포병 하사관. **2** 《U.S.》 a bomb-aimer. 폭격수.

bom·bard·ment [bɑmbɑ́:dmənt / bɔm-]

n. ⒸⓊ an attack with shells or with bombs. 포격; 폭격.

bom·bast [bámbæst / bɔ́m-] *n.* Ⓤ big words or big talk with little meaning. 호언(장담); 흰소리. ¶ *A little truth is better than much* ～. 조그마한 진실이 여러 흰소리보다 낫다. [Gk. *bombȳx* silkworm]

bom·bas·tic [bɑmbǽstik / bɔm-] *adj.* using many fine words with little thought. 과장된; 야단스러운. ¶ *The politician spoke in a* ～ *way of all that he would do if elected.* 그 정치가는 자기가 당선된다면 하겠다는 공약들을 떠벌렸다.

Bom·bay [bɑmbéi / bɔm-] *n.* a seaport in western India. 봄베이.

bomb·er [bámər / bɔ́m-] *n.* Ⓒ **1** an airplane used for dropping bombs on the enemy. 폭격기. **2** a person who drops bombs. 폭격수. [→bomb]

bomb·proof [bámprùːf / bɔ́m-] *adj.* safe from bombs and shells. 방탄(防彈)의.

bomb·shell [bámʃèl / bɔ́m-] *n.* Ⓒ **1** a bomb. 폭탄. **2** something sudden and surprising. 돌발적인 놀라운 일; 돌발 사건. ¶ *drop a* ～ 폭탄 선언을 하다.

bomb·sight [bámsàit / bɔ́m-] *n.* an instrument used to aim bombs. 폭격 조준기.

bon [bɔ(ː)n, bɔ̃] *adj.* 《F.》 good. 좋은.

bo·na fi·de [bóunə fáidi, -fàid] *adj., adv.* 《L.》 sincere(ly); true(ly). 성실한〔하게〕; 진실의〔로〕. ¶ *a* ～ *offer* 성실한 제의.

bo·nan·za [bounǽnzə] *n.* Ⓒ 《U.S.》 **1** a rich mass of metal in a mine. 부광대(富鑛帶); 노다지. **2** 《*colloq.*》 anything that brings good fortune and prosperity. 성공; 히트; 행운. ¶ *in* ～ 행운을 잡아; 성공하여 / *Mr. Smith struck a* ～ *when he bought that farm, for oil has been found on it.* 스미스씨는 그 농장을 사서 뜻밖의 행운을 잡았다. 그 농장에서 석유가 발견되었기 때문이다. [Sp. =fair weather]

bon·bon [bánbɑn / bɔ́nbɔn] *n.* Ⓒ a small piece of candy. 봉봉《과자》. [F.]

:bond [bɑnd / bɔnd] *n.* Ⓒ **1** anything that joins or unites; 《*pl.*》 anything that controls someone's liberty. 유대(紐帶); 속박; 구속. ¶ *a* ～ *of friendship* 우정의 유대 / *be in bonds* 속박〔감금〕돼 있다 / *break the bonds of convention* 인습의 굴레를 깨뜨리다 / *snap one's bonds asunder* 속박을 끊다. **2** a printed paper sold by a government or company promising to pay back money. 차용〔공채〕 증서; 채권; 회사채. ¶ *a public* ～ 공채(公債) / *a treasury* ～ 국채(國債). **3** 《law》 a written agreement. 약정(서).
— *vt.* (P6) **1** bind together, as bricks, or with a bonding agent. (벽돌 따위)를 한데 잇다; 접착하다. **2** issue bonds on. 채권을 발행하다. **3** place (goods) in bond. (물품을) 보세 창고에 맡기다. [→band]

bond·age [bándidʒ / bɔ́nd-] *n.* Ⓤ **1** the condition of not being free; slavery. 노예(의 신분); 고역(苦役). ¶ *human* ～ 인간고(苦) / *the passion that held him in* ～ 그를 사로잡는 정열 / *The ancient Israelites were kept in* ～ *in Egypt.* 고대 이스라엘인들은 노예로서 이집트에 사로잡혀 있었다. **2** the condition of being under some power or influence. 속박; 굴종. [E.]

bond·ed [bándid / bɔ́nd-] *adj.* **1** secured by bonds. 담보부(擔保附)의. **2** placed in charge of a government, under a bond. 보세 창고에 유치(留置)된. ¶ *a* ～ *warehouse* 보세 창고. [→bond]

bond·hold·er [bándhòuldər / bɔ́nd-] *n.* one who owns bonds. 채권(債券) 소유자. [↑]

bond·maid [bándmèid / bɔ́nd-] *n.* = bond(s)woman. [E., →husbandman]

bond·man [bándmən / bɔ́ndz-] *n.* Ⓒ (*pl.* **-men** [-mən]) a slave. 노예. [↑]

bonds·man [bándzmən / bɔ́nd-] *n.* (*pl.* **-men** [-mən]) =bondman.

Bond Street [ˊ ˋ] *n.* a London street noted for fashionable shops. 본드스트리트《런던의 고급 상가》.

bond·wom·an [bándwùmən / bɔ́nd-], **bonds·wom·an** [bándz- / bɔ́ndz-] *n.* (*pl.* **-wom·en** [-wìmin]) a woman slave. 여자 노예. [→bondmaid]

:bone [boun] *n.* Ⓒ **1** a single part of a skeleton; Ⓤ the material of which bones consist. 뼈; 골질(骨質). ¶ *the bones of the head* 두개골. **2** 《*pl.*》 a skeleton; a body, dead or alive. 골격; 신체. ¶ *His bones were laid in Westminster.* 그의 시신은 웨스트민스터에 묻혔다. **3** a bone-like substance. 골상(骨狀) 물질. **4** a thing made of bone or ivory. 골제품(骨製品).

a bone of contention, a cause of a quarrel. 분쟁의 원인〔불씨〕.

(*as*) *dry as a bone,* very dry. 바싹 마른.

cut (*costs, etc.*) ***to the bone,*** cut down to the minimum. (비용 따위를) 최소 한도로 삭감하다.

feel in one's bones, **a**) feel sure. 확신하다. **b**) feel without reasoning. 직감하다.

have a bone to pick with *someone,* find fault with someone and want an explanation; have something to complain about to someone. …에게 불만〔할 말〕이 있다.

make no bones of 〔***about***〕, not mind doing (something); do not care about (something); feel no fear in doing. …을 마음에 두지〔마음 쓰지〕 않다; 두려워하지 않다.

spare bones, do not try one's best. 최선을 다하지 않다; 수고를 아끼다.

to the bone, completely. 완전히; 철저하게. ¶ *frozen to the* ～ 추위가 뼛속까지 스미는.
— *vt.* (P6) **1** rid (a body) of bones. …의 뼈를 발라 내다. **2** 《*colloq.*》 steal. …을 훔치다.
— *vi.* (P1,2A) 《U.S. *sl.*》 study diligently. 열심히 힘쓰다. ¶ *I must* ～ *for the exam.* 나는 시험에 대비해 열심히 공부해야 한다. [E.]

bone-dry [bóundrái] *adj.* 《*colloq.*》 very

dry or thirsty. 바싹 마른.

bone·head [bóunhèd] *n.* 《*sl.*》 a stupid person. 바보. [E.]

bon·er [bóunər] *n.* 《U.S. *sl.*》 a foolish and obvious blunder; a stupid mistake. 어처구니없는 실수; 바보짓. ¶ *make* 〔*pull*〕 *a* ~ 실수를 저지르다. [?]

bone·set·ter [bóunsètər] *n.* Ⓒ a person who sets broken bones. 접골사(接骨師). [→bone]

bon·fire [bánfàiər / bɔ́n-] *n.* Ⓒ a large fire made out of doors for burning dead leaves, rubbish, etc., or in celebration of some public event. (야외에서, 낙엽을 태우거나 축제 따위의) 모닥불. ¶ *The boys built a ~ at the picnic.* 아이들은 소풍(逍風)에서 모닥불을 피웠다. [*bone, fire*=fire for burning corpses]

make a bonfire of, burn up. 태워 버리다.

bon·ho·mie [bànəmí:, ⌐-⌐ / bɔ́nɔmi:] *n.* 《F.》 good nature; pleasantness of manner. (마음씨의) 시원시원함; 싹싹한 친절.

bo·ni·to [bəní:tou] *n.* Ⓒ (*pl.* **-tos** or **-toes,** *collectively* **-to**) 《fish》 a large salt-water food fish. 가다랑어. [Sp.]

bon·jour [bɔ̃ʒú:r] *n.* 《F.》 good day. 안녕.

bon mot [bán móu / bɔ́n-] *n.* 《F.》 (*pl.* **bons mots** [bán móu / bɔ́n-]) a clever saying. 명구(名句).

Bonn [bɑn / bɔn] *n.* the city of Federal Republic of Germany. 본《1990년까지 통일 전 서독의 수도》.

***bon·net** [bánit / bɔ́n-] *n.* Ⓒ **1** a woman's or baby's hat, usu. tied under the chin with strings of ribbons. 보닛《턱에서 매게 된 여성 모자》. **2** a cap without edge worn by men and boys in Scotland. 스코틀랜드 남성모. **3** 《Brit.》 the part of an automobile covering the engine, etc. 자동차의 보닛〔엔진 덮개〕. **4** a decoy. 미끼새. [F.]

〈bonnet 1〉

bon·ny, bon·nie [báni / bɔ́ni] *adj.* (**-ni·er, -ni·est**) **1** pretty; handsome. 아름다운; 잘생긴. **2** fine; merry; gay. 훌륭한; 즐거운; 쾌활한. **3** healthy-looking. 건강해 보이는. ¶ *What a ~ baby!* 정말이지 아기가 토실토실도 하구나. ● **bon·ni·ness** [-nis] *n.* [L. *bonus* good]

bon·soir [bɔ̃swa:r] *n.* 《F.》 good evening 〔night〕. 안녕《저녁 인사》.

bo·nus [bóunəs] *n.* Ⓒ a special money given to workers or stockholders, etc., besides their usual income. 보너스; 특별 배당금. [L. *bonus* good]

bon·y [bóuni] *adj.* (**bon·i·er, bon·i·est**) **1** of or like bone. 뼈의; 뼈 같은. ¶ *a ~ growth* 뼈의 종양. **2** full of bones. 뼈가 많은. ¶ *a very ~ fish* 가시가 많은 생선. **3** thin. 여윈. ¶ *a ~ man* 마른 사나이. [*bone*]

boo [bu:] *interj.* expressing contempt. 피이; 우우. — *n.* the sound boo. 피이〔우우〕하는 소리. — *vt.* (P6,7) hoot. …을 야유하다. ¶ *The bad actor was booed by the audience.* 그 서투른 연기자는 관중으로부터 우우하고 야유를 받았다. [Imit.]

boob [bu:b] *n.* a simpleton. 바보. [Sp.]

boo·by [bú:bi] *n.* Ⓒ (*pl.* **-bies**) a foolish, slow person; a fool. 바보; 어리보기. [Sp.]

booby prize [⌐-⌐] *n.* a prize given to a person who is last in a race or game. 꼴찌상(賞).

booby trap [⌐-⌐] *n.* **1** a practical joke, such as placing a bag of flour above a door to fall on the head of the first person to enter. 몹쓸 장난. **2** 《mil.》 a similar trap, set to explode. 부비 트랩; 위장폭탄.

boo·gie-woo·gie [bú(:)giwú(:)gi] *n.* a form of swing music. 부기우기《저(低)리듬이 반복되는 재즈 음악의 하나》.

boo·hoo [bù:hú:] *n.* (*pl.* **-hoos**) a loud crying. 엉엉 울. — *vi.* (P1) cry loudly. 엉엉 울다. [Imit.]

:book [buk] *n.* Ⓒ **1** a bundle of printed sheets of paper fastened together as a thing to be read. 책. ¶ *We read books to learn things.* 우리는 사물을 배우기 위하여 책을 읽는다. **2** literary work. 저술; 저작. **3** a main division of such a volume. (책의) 권(卷); 장(章). **4** 《*the B-*》 Bible. 성서. **5** anything fastened like a book. 책 모양으로 엮은 것; 책자. ¶ *an account ~* 회계 장부. **6** a set of tickets, checks, etc. bound together. 묶음철. ¶ *a check ~* 수표장.

bring someone to book, **a**) force someone to explain. 설명〔해명〕을 요구하다. **b**) punish someone. …을 문책하다; 벌하다.

by the book, according to the usual way. 일반적으로는; 규칙에 의해.

in someone's bad 〔***black***〕 ***books,*** out of favor with someone. 미움을 받아.

in someone's good books, in someone's favor. 아무에게 좋게 보여.

know something like a book, know something very well. …을 잘 알고 있다. ¶ *I know the park like a ~.* 나는 그 공원을 잘 알고 있다.

on the books, **a**) recorded. 기록되어. **b**) listed. 리스트에 올라; 등록되어.

suit someone's book, suit someone's plans or wishes. 아무의 형편〔뜻〕에 맞다.

take a leaf out of someone's book, follow someone's example; imitate someone. 아무의 예를 따르다; 아무의 행동을 흉내내다.

without the book, **a**) from memory. 기억으로. ¶ *speak without the* ~ 기억으로 이야기하다. **b**) without authority. 근거〔전거〕 없이. ¶ *punish without the* ~ 이유 없이 벌하다.
— *vt.* (P6) **1** record (names, data, etc.) in a book or a list. …을 기장(記帳)하다. **2** reserve. …을 예약하다. ¶ ~ *a seat* 좌석을 예약하다.
— *vi.* issue a ticket. 표를 발행하다. [M.E. *boke, book;* A.S. *boc,* pl. *bec*]
book down 〔***in***〕, write down (something) in a book. …을 적어 두다.

book·case [búkkèis] *n.* Ⓒ a cabinet or set of shelves to hold books in. 책장; 서가(書架).

book club [ㅡㅡ] *n.* **1** a group of persons who buy books to be circulated within the group. 독서 클럽. **2** a business organization that supplies certain books regularly to subscribers. 도서 판매 조직.

book·end [búkènd] *n.* 《usu. *pl.*》 a support placed at the end of a row of books to hold them upright. 북엔드; 책버팀《쓰러지지 않게 버티는》.

book·ie [búki] *n.* 《*colloq.*》 =bookmaker.

book·ing clerk [búkiŋ klə̀ːrk / -klɑ̀ːrk] *n.* **1** a person who sells tickets. 매표계원(賣票係員). **2** a person who makes seating reservations. 예약계원.

booking office [ㅡㅡ ㅡ] *n.* 《Brit.》 a place where tickets are sold. 매표소(=《U.S.》 ticket office).

book·ish [búkiʃ] *adj.* **1** fond of books. 책을 좋아하는. ¶ *a* ~ *girl* 독서 취미의 소녀. **2** knowing from books better than from real life. 탁상의; 실제에 어두운. **3** of books. 책의. **4** formal; pedantic. 딱딱한; 학자연하는. ¶ ~ *English* 딱딱한 영어 / *a* ~ *speech* 딱딱한 연설. ● **book·ish·ness** [-nis] *n.*

book·keep·er [búkkìːpər] *n.* Ⓒ a person who records business accounts. 장부계원.

book·keep·ing [búkkìːpiŋ] *n.* Ⓤ the work of recording business accounts. 부기.

book·let [búklit] *n.* Ⓒ a small book; a pamphlet. 팸플릿; 소책자.

book·lore [búklɔ̀ːr] *n.* Ⓤ book learning. 책상물림의 학문.

book·mak·er [búkmèikər] *n.* Ⓒ **1** a maker of books. (돈이 목적인) 저작자. **2** a person who makes a business of accepting bets on horse races. 마권업자(馬券業者).

book·mark [búkmɑ̀ːrk] *n.* Ⓒ anything put between the pages of a book to mark a certain place. 갈피표; 서표(書標).

book·rack [búkræ̀k] *n.* Ⓒ **1** a rack for supporting an open book. 서안(書案). **2** a rack for holding a number of books. 서가(書架).

book review [ㅡㅡ] *n.* an article written about a book, discussing its merits, faults, etc. 서평(書評).

book·sel·ler [búksèlər] *n.* Ⓒ a person whose business is selling books. 서적상(書籍商).

book·shelf [búkʃèlf] *n.* Ⓒ (*pl.* **-shelves**) a shelf, usu. part of a bookcase, for holding books. 서가(書架).

book·shelves [búkʃèlvz] *n.* pl. of **bookshelf.**

book·shop [búkʃɑ̀p / -ʃɔ̀p] *n.* 《Brit.》 = bookstore.

book·stall [búkstɔ̀ːl] *n.* Ⓒ **1** a stall at which books, usu. secondhand ones, are sold. 헌책방. **2** 《Brit.》 a stand at which newspapers are sold; a newsstand. 신문 판매대〔스탠드〕. ¶ *a* ~ *in a railway station* 역의 신문 스탠드.

book·stand [búkstæ̀nd] *n.* **1** =bookrack. **2** =bookstall.

***book·store** [búkstɔ̀ːr] *n.* Ⓒ 《U.S.》 a store where books are sold. 책방; 서점.

book·worm [búkwə̀ːrm] *n.* Ⓒ **1** a person who is always reading books. 독서광; 책벌레. **2** a small worm that makes holes in books. 반대좀.

***boom**[1] [buːm] *n.* Ⓒ **1** a deep sound, as of waves or a big gun. (대포·파도 따위의) 울리는 소리. **2** a sudden rapid increase of activity; a rise in popularity. 벼락 경기; 붐; (인기 따위의) 급상승. ¶ *a* ~ *town* 신흥 도시 / *a war* ~ 전시〔군수〕 경기.
— *vi.* (P1,2A) **1** make a deep sound. 울리다. ¶ *The big man's voice boomed out in the room.* 그 거한(巨漢)의 목소리가 방 밖으로 울려 나왔다. **2** increase suddenly in activity; grow rapidly. 갑자기 활기를 띠다; 급속히 발전하다. ¶ *Business is booming.* 사업이 갑자기 호황을 누리고 있다.
— *vt.* (P6,7) 《*out*》 speak (something) with a booming sound. …을 큰 소리로 알리다. ¶ ~ *one's friends* 〔*goods*〕 자기 친구들을〔상품을〕 알리다 / *The clocks* ~ *out the hour.* 시계가 땡땡 시간을 알린다. [Imit.]

***boom**[2] [buːm] *n.* Ⓒ **1** a long pole or beam by which a sail is stretched; the lifting arm of a derrick. 돛의 아래 활대; 데릭 기중기의 암. **2** a chain, cable, etc. that keeps logs from floating away. (강이나 항구 등의) 방재(防材). [Du.=beam]

〈boom[2] 1〉

boom·er·ang [búːməræ̀ŋ] *n.* Ⓒ a curved piece of wood used by Australian natives as a weapon which comes back when thrown. 부메랑. [Native]

***boon**[1] [buːn] *n.* Ⓒ a blessing; a great benefit; a favor. 은혜; 은전; 호의; 부탁. ¶ *ask a* ~ *of someone* 아무에게 부탁하다 /

May I ask a ~ of you ? 한 가지 부탁이 있는데요 / *The steady rain came as a ~ to the farmers.* 꾸준한 비가 하늘의 은혜처럼 농부들에게 내렸다. [Scand.]

boon[2] [bu:n] *adj.* jolly; gay; merry; close. 유쾌한; 마음 맞는. ¶ *a ~ companion* 술친구. 語法 위의 구(句)로만 쓰임. [*bon*]

boon·dog·gle [bú:ndàgəl / -dɔ̀gəl] *vi.* (P1) 《U.S. *sl.*》 do useless work. 쓸데없는 짓을 하다. — *n.* a cord of plaited leather. 가죽끈. [U.S.]

boor [buər] *n.* Ⓒ **1** a rude person with bad manners. 예절이 없는 야인(野人). **2** a peasant, esp. a Dutch or German peasant. (특히 네덜란드·독일 등의) 농부. [Du. *boer* farm worker]

boor·ish [búəriʃ] *adj.* rude; ill-mannered; clumsy. 예절이 없는; 거친.

boost [bu:st] *vt.* (P6,7) **1** lift or push (something) from below or behind. …을 (밑 또는 뒤에서) 밀다; 밀어 올리다. **2** support very earnestly. …을 후원하다. ¶ *She always boosts her home town.* 그녀는 언제나 그의 고향 마을을 후원한다. **3** raise or increase. (값 따위를) 끌어 올리다. ¶ *~ prices* 값을 올리다. — *n.* Ⓒ the act of boosting. (뒤에서) 밂; 후원; 인상; 등귀(騰貴). [U.S.]

boost·er [bú:stər] *n.* Ⓒ 《U.S. *colloq.*》 a person or a thing that boosts; an earnest supporter. (뒤에서) 밀어주는 사람; 후원(자).

:**boot**[1] [bu:t] *n.* Ⓒ **1** 《usu. *pl.*》 《U.S.》 a covering made of leather or rubber for the foot and leg; 《Brit.》 a shoe or outer foot covering reaching above the ankle. 부츠; 장화. ¶ *a pair of boots* 부츠 한 켤레 / *riding boots* 승마화(乘馬靴). **2** any protecting cover. 덮개. **3** 《*sl.*》 discharge; dismissal. 해고. **4** an automobile trunk. 차의 트렁크.

bet your boots, 《U.S.》 be certain; be quite sure. 틀림없다.

die in one's boots, die an unnatural death. 횡사하다.

get the boot, a) be kicked. 걷어채다. b) lose one's employment; be fired. 해고되다.

give someone the boot, a) kick. …을 걷어차다. b) force away. …을 해고하다.

have one's heart in one's boots, be afraid; be in low spirits with fear. 두려워하다; 흠칫거리다.

lick the boots of (=*flatter*) *someone.* …에게 아부하다.

The boot is on the other leg 〔***foot***〕. The truth is in the opposite direction. It is the other person that is to be blamed. 번지수가 다르다; 책임은 딴쪽에 있다.

— *vt.* (P6) **1** put boots on (someone). …에게 구두를 신기다. **2** kick. …을 (발로) 차다. [F.]

boot out, a) kick out. 내차다. b) 《*sl.*》 dismiss. 해고하다.

boot[2] [bu:t] *n.* advantage. 이익.

to boot, into the bargain. 게다가.

— *vt., vi.* (P6;1) profit. 도움이 되다. ¶ *It boots him little to complain.* 불평을 말하는 것은 그에게 별로 이롭지 못하다 / *What boots it to…?* …해서 무슨 소용 있나. [E.]

boot·black [bú:tblæ̀k] *n.* Ⓒ a person whose work is shining shoes and boots on the street. (거리의) 구두닦이. [*boot*[1]]

boot·ed [bú:tid] *adj.* having boots on. 구두를 신은. ¶ *~ and spurred* 장화를 신고 박차(拍車)를 달고; 승마의 채비를 하고. [*boot*[1]]

boot·ee [bú:ti:, –́] *n.* 《usu. *pl.*》 **1** a baby's soft shoe of knitted wool. (소아용의) 털실 신. **2** a woman's short boot. 여성용 단화. [*boot*[1]]

***booth** [bu:θ] *n.* Ⓒ (*pl.* **booths** [bu:ðz]) **1** a covered stall or stand at a fair or a market. (거리·시장 따위의) 매점; 노점. **2** a small, enclosed place for a special purpose. (특별한 용도의) 칸막이. ¶ *a telephone ~* 공중 전화 박스 / *a voting ~* 투표소. **3** a partly enclosed place in a café or the like, for use by a few persons. (다방 등의) 칸막이 좌석. [Scand.]

boot·lace [bú:tlèis] *n.* 《chiefly Brit.》 = shoelace.

boot·leg [bú:tlèg] *vt., vi.* 《U.S. *sl.*》 make, carry or sell (wine or other things) unlawfully. (술 따위를) 밀조〔밀매〕하다. [*boot*[1]]

boot·leg·ger [bú:tlègər] *n.* Ⓒ a person who bootlegs. 밀조〔밀매〕자; 밀수입자.

boot·less [bú:tlis] *adj.* useless. 무익한; 헛된. ¶ *a ~ effort* 헛된 노력. [*boot*[2]]

boot·mak·er [bú:tmèikər] *n.* Ⓒ a person who makes shoes. 구두장이. [*boot*[1]]

boots [bu:ts] *n.* (*pl.* **boots**) a boot-cleaner and messenger at an inn. 여관의 구두닦이 《허드렛일도 함》. [*boot*[1]]

boo·ty [bú:ti] *n.* Ⓤ **1** things taken from the enemy in time of war; goods stolen by thieves. 전리품; 노획물; 약탈물; 도난품. ¶ *The pirates got much ~.* 해적들은 많은 약탈물을 얻었다. **2** gain; profits. 획득한 것; 이득. [E.]

booze [bu:z] *n.* Ⓤ 《*colloq.*》 any alcoholic liquor or strong drink. 술.

— *vi.* (P1) drink very much. 술을 많이 마시다. [Du.]

booz·y [bú:zi] *adj.* (**booz·i·er, booz·i·est**) drunken; given to drinking. 술 취한; 모주꾼의. [↑]

bo·peep [boupí:p] *n.* Ⓤ a cry meaning "I see you" in a game played with a very young child. '아웅, 까꿍' 놀이《숨어 있다가 나타나 아이를 놀래주는 장난》. [*bo, peep*]

BOQ 《U.S.》 Bachelor Officers' Quarters.

bor. borough.

bo·rac·ic [bəræ̀sik] *adj.* =boric.

bo·rate [bóureit, bɔ́:-] *n.* Ⓤ a salt of boric acid. 붕산염(硼酸塩). — *vt.* (P6) treat with boric acid or borax. …을 붕산염으로 〔붕사로〕 처리하다. [Arab.]

bo·rax [bóurəks, bɔ́ː-] *n.* Ⓤ a white salt-like powder used for cleaning and in glass-making. 붕사(硼砂). [↑]

Bor·deaux [bɔːrdóu] *n.* Ⓤ a red or white wine made in the Bordeaux region in France. 보르도산(産) 포도주. [Place]

bor·del·lo [bɔːrdélou] *n.* a brothel. 매춘굴; 갈봇집. [O.F. *bordel*]

:bor·der [bɔ́ːrdər] *n.* Ⓒ **1** an edge. 가장자리; 끝. ¶ *a hotel on the ~ of the lake* 호반(湖畔)의 호텔. **2** a narrow strip along or around something. …을 따라 가늘고 긴 부분. **3** a line of division between two countries or states; a frontier. 경계; 국경; 변경. ¶ *a ~ town* 국경의 마을 / *over the ~* 국경을 넘어. **4** a decorative edge. 가두리〔선(縇)〕 장식. ¶ *a ~ of lace* 레이스의 선 장식 / *a garden with a ~ of pretty flowers* 둘레에 아름다운 꽃으로 가두리한 정원.
— *vt.* (P6) put a border on (something). …와 경계를 접하다; 테를 두르다. ¶ *The lawn was bordered by trees.* 잔디는 수림과 경계를 접하고 있었다.
— *vi.* (P3) 《*on, upon*》 touch; approach closely in character. 접하다; 비슷하다. ¶ *~ on the lake* 호수에 접하다 / *His actions ~ on madness.* 그의 행동은 광기에 가깝다. [→board]

bor·der·er [bɔ́ːrdərər] *n.* Ⓒ a person who lives on the border of a country. 국경 지방의 주민.

bor·der·land [bɔ́ːrdərlæ̀nd] *n.* 《*the ~*》 **1** the land on or near a frontier between two countries. 국경 지방; 경계지(地). **2** an uncertain district or space. 이도저도 아닌 영역〔어중간한 상태〕. ¶ *the ~ of consciousness* 의식의 주변; 비몽사몽.

bor·der·line [bɔ́ːrdərlàin] *n.* Ⓒ a boundary line; a dividing line. 국경〔경계〕선. — *adj.* **1** on a border or boundary. 국경선〔경계선〕상의. **2** uncertain; doubtful; between. 불명확한; 이도저도 아닌. ¶ *a ~ case* 이도저도 아닌 경우 / *If she's not a psychopath, she's a ~ case.* 그녀는 정신병자는 아닐지라도 그에 가깝다.

bore[1] [bɔːr] *vt., vi.* (P6,13; 1,3) **1** make a hole with a drill, etc. 구멍을 뚫다. ¶ *~ a plank* 판자에 구멍을 내다. **2** make (a hole, passage, tunnel, etc.) by pushing through or digging out. (구멍·통로·굴을) 뚫다. ¶ *~ a tunnel through the Alps* 알프스에 터널을 관통시키다 / *A mole has bored its way under my rose-bed.* 두더지가 나의 장미 화단 밑으로 굴을 뚫었다. **3** push forward; advance step by step. 헤치고 나아가다; 한 발짝 한 발짝 나아가다. ¶ *~ one's way through the crowd* 군중을 헤치고 나아가다.
— *n.* Ⓒ **1** a hole made by boring (송곳 따위로 뚫은) 구멍. **2** empty space inside a pipe, tube, etc. (파이프 등의) 구멍. **3** distance across the inside of a hole or a tube. 구경(口徑). ¶ *The ~ of this gun is 1 inch.* 이 총의 구경은 1인치이다. [E.]

:bore[2] [bɔːr] *vt.* (P6,13) 《*with*》 make (someone) weary by being dull or tiresome. …를 따분하게 하다. — *n.* Ⓒ a dull, tiresome person or thing. 따분한 사람〔것〕. [E.]

·bore[3] [bɔːr] *v.* p. of **bear**[1].

bore[4] [bɔːr] *n.* Ⓒ a very high sea-wave at the mouth of a river or narrow channel. 강어귀 등의 높은 파도. [Scand.]

bo·re·al [bɔ́ːriəl] *adj.* northern. 북(北)의. [Gk.]

bore·dom [bɔ́ːrdəm] *n.* **1** Ⓤ the state of being tired and not interested. 따분함; 권태. **2** Ⓒ an instance of being bored. 따분한 일. [→bore[2]]

bor·er [bɔ́ːrər] *n.* Ⓒ **1** a person who drills holes; a tool for drilling holes. 구멍을 뚫는 사람; 송곳. **2** an insect or a worm that bores into wood, fruit, etc. 나무좀. [→bore[1]]

bore·some [bɔ́ːrsəm] *adj.* dull; tiresome. 따분한; 지루한. [→bore[2]]

bo·ric [bɔ́ːrik] *adj.* boracic; of or containing boron. 붕소(硼素)의. [→boron]

boric acid [∠– ∠] *n.* a white, crystalline substance. 붕산(硼酸).

bor·ing[1] [bɔ́ːriŋ] *n.* Ⓤ the act of making or enlarging a hole. 구멍을 뚫음; 천공(穿孔). [→bore[1]]

bor·ing[2] [bɔ́ːriŋ] *adj.* tiresome; dull. 따분한. ¶ *~ people* 따분한 사람들. [→bore[2]]

·born [bɔːrn] *v.* pp. of **bear**[1]. — *adj.* **1** brought into life; brought forth. 태어난. ¶ *A baby ~ on Sunday is supposed to be lucky.* 일요일에 태어난 아기는 운수가 좋을 것으로 생각되고 있다. **2** by birth; by natural qualities. 타고난. ¶ *a ~ poet* 타고난 시인 / *a ~ fool* 선천적인 바보. [→bear]

·borne [bɔːrn] *v.* pp. of **bear**[1].

Bor·ne·o [bɔ́ːrniòu] *n.* an island in the East Indies. 보르네오.

bo·ron [bɔ́ːran / -rɔn] *n.* Ⓤ 《chem.》 a chemical element found in borax. 붕소(硼素).

bor·ough [bə́ːrou / bʌ́rə] *n.* Ⓒ **1** 《U.S.》 a combined town smaller than a city. 자치 읍면(自治邑面). **2** 《U.S.》 one of the five political divisions of New York City. 뉴욕시의 구(區). **3** 《Brit.》 a town with powers of self-government. 자치시(自治市). [E.]

:bor·row [bɔ́(ː)rou, bár-] *vt.* (P6,13) **1** 《*from*》 get (something) from another person on a promise of return. …을 빌리다; 차용하다(opp. lend). ¶ *~ money from* 〔*of*〕 …에게서 돈을 빌리다 / *John has borrowed the book from her.* 존은 그녀로부터 책을 빌렸다. **2** copy or adopt (another's thoughts, words, ideas, etc.) as one's own. …을 모방〔표절〕하다; 빌려 쓰다. ¶ *words borrowed from Eng-*

lish into Korean 영어에서 한국어에 차용한 말 / *The idea was borrowed from some foreign book.* 그 아이디어는 외국 서적에서 모방했다. — *vi.* (P1,3) 《*from*》 borrow money. 돈을 꾸다. [M.E. *borwen, borgien;* A.S. *borgian* loan]

bor·row·er [bɔ́(:)rouər, bάr-] *n.* Ⓒ a person who borrows. 차용자; 표절자.

bosh [bɑʃ / bɔʃ] *n.* Ⓤ 《*colloq.*》 nonsense; foolish talk or ideas. 허튼 소리; 터무니없는 말〔생각〕. ¶ *Don't talk* ~. 허튼 수작 작작해. [Turk. =empty]

bosk·y [bάski / bɔ́ski] *adj.* 《*poet.*》 (**bosk·i·er, bosk·i·est**) wooded; shady. 나무가 우거진; 그늘이 많은. [Rom. =bush[1]]

*__bos·om__ [bú(:)zəm] *n.* Ⓒ **1** the upper, front part of the human body; the human breast, esp. of a woman. 가슴. ¶ *press someone to one's* ~ 아무를 가슴에 꼭 껴안다 / *put a baby to the* ~ 아기에게 젖을 물리다. **2** the part of a garment covering the breast. (옷의) 가슴 부분; 품(속). ¶ *thrust a letter into one's* ~ 편지를 품속에 넣다 / *She drew a book from her* ~. 그녀는 품속에서 책을 꺼냈다. **3** the center or inmost part of (something). 한가운데; 속; 내부. ¶ *on the* ~ *of the Pacific Ocean* 태평양 한복판에(서) / *in the* ~ *of a mountain* 깊은 산속에 / *in the* ~ *of the earth* 지구의 내부에; 대지의 품속에. **4** the place where one feels deeply. 마음; 가슴속. ¶ *a friend of* ~ 마음의 벗 / *with panting* ~ 가슴을 두근거리며 / *keep something in one's* ~ 가슴속 깊이 묻어 두다. **5** the surface of a sea, lake, etc. (바다·호수 따위의) 표면. ¶ *the tranquil* ~ *of the Seine* 센 강의 잔잔한 수면.
— *adj.* close; trusted; very familiar. 친(밀)한; 속마음을 털어놓을 수 있는. ¶ *a* ~ *friend* 막역한 친구. [E.]

Bos·po·rus [bάspərəs / bɔ́s-] *n.* a strait separating Europe from Asia Minor. 보스포러스 해협.

*__boss__[1] [bɔ(:)s, bɑs] *n.* Ⓒ 《*colloq.*》 **1** a person who gives orders to workmen; a headman of any business; a foreman; a manager; a master. 우두머리; 보스; 감독자. ¶ *a political* ~ 정계의 실력자. **2** 《U.S.》 a politician who controls his party organization, usu. in a certain place. (보통 어떤 지역구 정당의) 영수(領袖); 우두머리.
— *vt., vi.* (P6;1) be the boss of (a party); give orders to (someone); control. …의 영수가 되다; 지배하다. ¶ *Who's bossing this work ?* 누가 이 일을 감독합니까 / *He is always trying to* ~ *me.* 그는 늘 나를 지배하려고 든다. [Du. *baas*]

boss[2] [bɔ(:)s, bɑs] *n.* Ⓒ a round part or ornament which stands up on a flat surface. 돌기물(突起物); 돋을새김. [Rom.]

boss·y [bɔ́(:)si, bάsi] *adj.* 《U.S. *colloq.*》 (**boss·i·er, boss·i·est**) with a character to be a boss; fond of ordering others. 보스 기질의; 명령하려 드는. [↑]

*__Bos·ton__ [bɔ́(:)stən, bάs-] *n.* a seaport and capital of Massachusetts, U.S.A. 보스턴 《Massachusetts주의 주도(州都)》.

Bos·to·ni·an [bɔ(:)stóuniən, bɑs-] *adj.* of Boston. 보스턴의. — *n.* Ⓒ a person of Boston. 보스턴 시민.

bot [bɑt / bɔt] *n.* 《insect》 a larva of a botfly. 말파리의 유충. [?]

bo·tan·ic [bətǽnik] *adj.* =botanical.

bo·tan·i·cal [bətǽnikəl] *adj.* of plants or botany. 식물(학)의. ¶ *a* ~ *garden* 식물원 / ~ *survey* 식물학상의 조사. [→botany]

bot·a·nist [bάtənist / bɔ́t-] *n.* Ⓒ a person who studies botany; a specialist in botany. 식물학자.

bot·a·nize [bάtənàiz / bɔ́t-] *vi.* (P1) **1** collect plants for study. 식물을 채집하다. **2** study plants. 식물을 연구하다. ●**bot·a·niz·er** [-ər] *n.*

*__bot·a·ny__ [bάtəni / bɔ́t-] *n.* Ⓤ the scientific study of plants; the study of plants and plant life. 식물학. [Gk. *botanē* plant]

botch [bɑtʃ / bɔtʃ] *vt.* (P6) **1** spoil (something) by poor work; do (work) badly. (일을) 망쳐 놓다. **2** mend roughly. …을 거칠게 수선하다. — *n.* Ⓒ **1** a poor piece of work; a bad job. 실패작. **2** a badly mended part. 서투르게 손질한 부분. [E.]

:**both** [bouθ] *adj.* the two; the pair of. 양쪽의. ¶ ~ (*the*) *brothers* 형제 둘 다 / *on* ~ *sides of the river* 강의 양쪽에 / *Both my parents are still living.* 나의 양친은 아직 생존해 계신다. 語法 정관사 앞에 옴.
— *pron.* the two; the one and the other. 양쪽. ¶ ~ *of them* 그들 둘 다 / *Both are dead.* 둘 다 죽고 없다 / *I saw them* ~ 〔~ *of them*〕. 두 사람 다 보았다 / *They* ~ *went.* 그들 둘 다 갔다 / *They are* ~ *true.* 그들은 둘 다 옳다. 參考 동사가 불완전 동사일 때 both는 그 뒤에 옴.
have it both ways, keep changing one's position. (의론 등에서) 양다리를 걸치다; 태도를 분명히 하지 않다.
— *conj.* 《in form of *both … and*》 together with; at once; not only … but also. …도 —도(둘 다); 모두; 동시에; …뿐 아니라 또한 (opp. neither … nor). ¶ *Both he and she are dead.* 그도 그녀도 모두 죽었다 / *It is* ~ *good and cheap.* 그것은 좋고도 값이 싸다 / *He is* ~ *a scholar and* (*a*) *poet.* 그는 학자인 동시에 시인이기도 하다. [E.]

:**both·er** [bάðər / bɔ́ð-] *vt.* (P6,7,13) 《*with*》 trouble; worry. …을 괴롭히다; 번거롭게 하다. ¶ *Don't* ~ *me with foolish questions.* 바보 같은 질문으로 나를 괴롭히지 마라 / *Don't* ~ *yourself* 〔*your head*〕 *about it.* 그것 때문에 신경쓰지 말게.
— *vi.* (P3,4) 《*about*》 trouble oneself. 걱정〔고민〕하다. ¶ *Don't* ~ *about it.* 그것 때문에 걱정말게 / *Don't* ~ *about my dinner.* 내 식사 때문에 걱정하지 마시오.

— *n.* **1** Ⓒ a cause or condition of worry or anxiety; Ⓤ trouble. 귀찮음; 말썽. ¶ *This broken zipper is a* ~. 이 망가진 지퍼가 골칫거리다 / *I find the work a great* ~. 나는 그 일이 매우 귀찮은 일임을 알 수 있다. **2** Ⓒ a person or thing that causes worry or trouble. 귀찮은 사람〔사물〕. [? Anglo-Ir. *bodder* in Swift]

both·er·some [báðərsəm / bɔ́ð-] *adj.* causing trouble; troublesome; troubling. 성가신; 귀찮은. ¶ *a* ~ *child* 귀찮은 아이.

Bots·wa·na [batswáːnə / bɔts-] *n.* a republic in southern Africa. 보츠와나《남아프리카의 공화국》.

:bot·tle [bátl / bɔ́tl] *n.* Ⓒ **1** a narrow-necked container, usu. of glass, for holding liquids. 병. ¶ *a nursing* ~ 젖병 / *the neck of a* ~ 병목 / *bring a child up on the* ~ 아이를 우유로 키우다. **2** the contents of such a container; amount that a bottle holds. 한 병 가득한 양(量). ¶ *He could drink three whole bottles of milk.* 그는 우유 세 병을 마실 수 있었다. **3** 《*the* ~》 the act or habit of drinking wine, etc.; alcoholic liquor. 음주; 술. ¶ *be too fond of the* ~ 술을 너무 좋아하다.

over a bottle, while drinking. 술을 마시면서. ¶ *Let's discuss it over a* ~. 한잔하면서 그것에 관해 토론합시다.

— *vt.* (P6) put (liquid, fruits, vegetables, etc.) into bottles. …을 병에 담다; 병조림으로 하다. ¶ ~ *milk* 병에 우유를 담다 / ~ *fruit* 과일을 병조림하다. [→butt[3]]

bottle up, **a**) keep (something) in a bottle; hold in; shut in. …을 병에 넣다. **b**) control; hide. …을 누르다; 숨기다. ¶ ~ *up one's anger* 노여움을 누르다 / *keep things bottled up* 일을 숨겨두다.

bot·tle·neck [bátlnèk / bɔ́tl-] *n.* Ⓒ **1** the neck of a bottle. 병목. **2** a narrow part of a passage or street that cannot be passed through. 좁은 통로. **3** anything that hinders progress; a check. 장애물; 애로. ¶ *a* ~ *in production* 생산의 애로. **4** a condition in which progress is stopped. 사물의 진행을 막는 상태.

:bot·tom [bátəm / bɔ́t-] *n.* Ⓒ **1** the base; the lowest part. (밑)바닥; 기부(基部). ¶ *the* ~ *of a tree* 나무 밑둥 / *the* ~ *of a house* 집의 토대 / *the* ~ *of a well* 〔*bucket*〕 우물〔버킷〕 바닥 / *the* ~ *of the hill* 산기슭 / *The berries at the* ~ *of the basket are smaller.* 바구니 바닥의 딸기는 더 작다. **2** the ground under the water. 물밑. ¶ *the* ~ *of the sea* 해저; 바닷속. **3** real nature or essential facts that exist below the surface. 마음속; 내심; 본성; (일의) 진상. ¶ *He is a good man at* ~. 그는 본성이 착한 사람이다. **4** the lowest person or thing in a class, etc. 최하층 사람〔사물〕; 말석. ¶ *He is at the* ~ *of the class.* 그는 반에서 꼴찌이다. **5** a ship, esp. a cargo ship; the outer part of a ship below the water. 배; 화물선; 선복(船腹). ¶ *foreign bottoms* 외국선. **6** 《*pl.*》 low lying land along the river. 하천의 저지(低地). **7** Ⓤ staying power; stamina. 지구력; 스태미너. ¶ *a horse with good* ~ 저력이 있는 말. **8** a seat. (의자 따위의) 앉는 자리. ¶ *This chair needs a new* ~. 이 의자는 새 좌부(座部)가 필요하다. **9** 《*colloq.*》 the buttocks. 엉덩이. **10** the farthest or inmost part. (도로·만·쑥 들어간 곳의) 안쪽; 속; 막다름. ¶ *the* ~ *of the street* 가로의 막다른 곳.

be at the bottom of (=*be the real reason for*) *something.* …의 주인(主因)이다; …에게 책임이 있다.

from 〔***to***〕 ***the bottom of one's heart,*** sincerely. 진심으로.

get to the bottom of (=*find out the real reason for*) *something.* …의 진상을 밝히다. ¶ *Let's get to the* ~ *of the matter.* 문제의 진상을 규명합시다.

go to the bottom, sink. 가라앉다.

send to the bottom, make (a ship) sink. (배를) 가라앉히다.

stand on one's own bottom, be independent. 독립하다.

touch bottom, **a**) (of a ship) run on a rock. 좌초하다. **b**) be at the lowest point. (값 따위가) 최저가〔바닥이〕 되다.

— *vt.* **1** (P6) put a bottom or seat to. …에 바닥을〔좌부(座部)를〕 대다. ¶ ~ *a chair* 의자에 좌부를 대다. **2** (P6) ⓐ find the depth of. …의 깊이를 재다. ¶ *They tried to* ~ *the river, but it was deeper than their oars.* 그들은 강의 깊이를 재 보려고 했으나 노의 길이보다도 더 깊었다. ⓑ get to the bottom of. …의 진의(眞義)를 밝히다. ¶ ~ *someone's plans* 아무의 계획의 진의를 탐색하다. **3** (P6) understand fully. …을 충분히 이해하다. **4** (P13) 《*on, upon*》 base; rest. (의론 따위)를 기인케 하다; 의거하게 하다. ¶ *His arguments were bottomed on facts.* 그의 의론은 사실에 근거를 두고 있었다. [E.; cf. G. *boden*]

bot·tom·less [bátəmlis / bɔ́t-] *adj.* without a bottom; very deep. 바닥이 없는; 헤아릴 수 없는; 매우 깊은. ¶ *the* ~ *pit* 지옥 / *a* ~ *lake in the mountains* 산 속의 몹시 깊은 호수 / ~ *stupidity* 지독한 바보 / *sunk in the* ~ *depths of the sea* 한없이 깊은 바다에 가라앉은 / *a* ~ *mystery* 완전한 수수께끼.

bou·doir [búːdwaːr] *n.* Ⓒ 《F.》 a lady's private sitting room or dressing room. 부인(婦人)의 사실(私室).

Bou·gain·vil·lae·a [bùːgənvíliə] *n.* 《bot.》 a tropical climbing plant with red flowers. 부겐빌리아. [Person]

***bough** [bau] *n.* Ⓒ one of the main branches of a tree. 큰 가지. [A.S. *boh* arm, shoulder]

:bought [bɔːt] *v.* p. and pp. of **buy.**

bouil·lon [búljan / búljɔn] *n.* Ⓤ 《F.》 a clear soup, usu. of beef. 부용《맑은 고기 수프》.

boul·der [bóuldər] *n.* Ⓒ a large piece of rock rounded or worn by water and weather. (비·바람에 깎인) 크고 둥근 돌. [E.]

boul·e·vard [bú(:)ləvà:rd] *n.* Ⓒ a broad main street, usu. having trees on each side. 넓은 가로수 길; 큰 길. [F.]

bounce [bauns] *vi.* **1** (P1,2A,3) bound like a ball. 튀다. ¶ *This ball doesn't ~ well.* 이 공은 잘 튀지 않는다 / *The ball bounced off the wall.* 공은 벽을 맞고 되튀었다 / *The ball bounced out of his gloves.* 볼은 그의 글러브에서 튀어져 나와 떨어졌다. **2** (P1,2A,3) 《*about, out of, into*》 move in a sudden or noisy rush. 거칠게〔황급히〕 움직이다. ¶ *~ into a room* 거친 기세로 방에 들어오다 / *~ out of one's bed* 침대에서 벌떡 일어나다 / *She bounced out of the room in a huff.* 그녀는 성이 나서 방을 뛰쳐나갔다. **3** 《*sl.*》 (of a check) be returned as useless. (수표가) 부도가 나서 되돌아오다.
— *vt.* **1** (P6,7) cause (something) to bounce. …을 튀게 하다; 바운드시키다. ¶ *~ a ball* 볼을 바운드시키다 / *~ a baby up and down* 아기를 가동질하다. **2** (P6,13) 《*into, out of*》 make (someone) do by force. …을 을러서 억지로 시키다. ¶ *~ someone into starting* 아무를 억지로 출발시키다 / *~ someone out of something* 아무를 을러대어 무엇을 등치다. **3** (P6,13) 《U.S. *sl.*》 eject or expel forcibly; discharge from employment. …을 내쫓다; 해고하다. ¶ *~ troublemakers out of a hall* 말썽꾼들을 회장에서 쫓아내다.
— *n.* **1** Ⓒ ⓐ a bound; a spring. 튐; 바운드. ¶ *catch a ball on the first ~* 원바운드로 볼을 잡다. ⓑ sudden spring or leap. 껑충 뜀; 벌떡 일어남. ¶ *She rose with a ~.* 그녀는 발딱 일어났다. **2** Ⓤ a boast; a lie. 허풍; 거짓말. [E.=thump]

bounc·ing [báunsiŋ] *adj.* **1** big; strong. 거대한; 강한. **2** lively; healthy. 기운찬; 건강한. ¶ *a ~ baby* 건강한 아기.

:bound[1] [baund] *v.* p. and pp. of **bind.**
— *adj.* **1** having a cover or binding. 장정(裝幀)한; 제본한. ¶ *a ~ book* 장정본(本). **2** obliged; forced; compelled. …하지 않을 수 없는. ¶ *He is ~ to go.* 그는 가지 않을 수 없다 / *I'm ~ to say so.* 그렇게 말하지 않을 수 없다. **3** certain; sure. 확실한; 반드시 …하는; 운명지워진. ¶ *It is ~ to happen.* 그것은 반드시 일어난다 / *He is ~ to fail in his examination.* 그는 틀림없이 시험에 실패한다. **4** determined; resolved. …하려고 결심하고 있는. [→bind]
be bound up in (=*be much devoted to*) *something.* …에 열중하고 있다.
be bound up in 〔***with***〕 (=*be closely connected with*) *something.* …와 밀접한 관계가 있다.

:bound[2] [baund] *vi.* (P1,2A,4) **1** jump; leap. 뛰다; 튀다. **2** leap or spring upward or onward; spring lightly along. 뛰어〔튀어〕오르다; 껑충껑충 뛰어가다. ¶ *His dog bounded to meet him.* 그의 개는 그를 맞이하기 위해 겅중겅중 뛰어갔다. **3** spring back; bounce. 되튀다. ¶ *The ball bounded from the wall* 〔*off the fence*〕. 공은 벽〔담장〕에 맞고 되튀었다.
— *n.* Ⓒ **1** a leap or spring upward or onward. 뛰어〔튀어〕오름; 도약. ¶ *a ~ forward* 약진 / *at a* 〔*single*〕 *~* 한 번〔껑충〕 뛰어; 일약 / *with one ~* 단번에; 일약. **2** a bounce. 튐; 반동. ¶ *I caught the ball on the first ~.* 나는 공을 원 바운드로 잡았다. [F. *bondir*]
by leaps and bounds, very rapidly. 급속히; 비약적으로. ¶ *advance by leaps and bounds* 비약적으로 진보하다.
on the bound, (of a ball) after the first bounce from the ground. (공이) 원 바운드를 한 다음에.

:bound[3] [baund] *n.* 《usu. *pl.*》 **1** a limit; a boundary; a limiting line. 한계; 끝; 경계(선). ¶ *within the bounds of reason* 이성의 범위 내에서 / *the farthest bounds of the earth* 대지의 끝 / *the bounds of common sense* 상식의 한계 / *break bounds* 범위를 일탈하다; 관례를 뛰어넘다. **2** the land on or near a boundary; the area within boudaries. 경계선 내〔부근〕의 영토; 경역(境域).
beyond the bounds of, beyond the power of; outside the range of. …의 범위 밖에〔인〕.
know no bounds, be boundless. 끝〔한〕이 없다.
out of bounds, not allowed to be entered. 입장이 허가되지 않는. ¶ *The park is out of bounds to students.* 그 공원은 학생의 입장이 금지되고 있다.
set 〔***put***〕 ***bounds to,*** keep within limits, set limits to. …에 한계를 두다; …을 제한하다.
within bounds, **a**) allowed to be entered. 입장이 허용되는. **b**) moderately; properly. 적당히.
— *vt.* (P6) form the boundary of (a place); limit. …에 경계를 긋다; …을 제한하다. ¶ *mountains bounding a country* 나라의 경계를 이루는 산 / *England is bounded by the sea.* 영국은 바다로 경계지워지고 있다 / *We should ~ our desires by reason.* 우리는 이성의 힘으로 욕망을 억제해야 한다. [F.]

·bound[4] [baund] *adj.* 《*for*》 going; on the way. …로 가는〔갈 예정인〕; …행(行)의. ¶ *a ship ~ for New York* 뉴욕행 배 / *a ship ~ for a voyage* 항해길에 나서려는 배 / *Where are you ~? —I am ~ for England.* 어디로 가십니까—영국으로 가려고 합니다. [N.=ready]

:bound·a·ry [báundəri] *n.* Ⓒ (*pl.* **-ries**) a limiting line; a limit; a border. 경계선; 한계; 범위. ¶ *The river is the ~ between the two countries.* 그 강은 두 나라 사이의 경계선이 된다 / *the ~ of human knowledge* 인간의 지식의 한계. [*bound*[3]]

bound·en [báundən] *adj.* required; that one must do. 하지 않으면 안 되는. ¶ *a ~ duty* 해야 할 의무. [*bound*[1]]

bound·er [báundər] *n.* 《*colloq.*》 a person with bad manners. 버릇없는 사람. [*bound*[2]]

bound·less [báundlis] *adj.* not limited; infinite; vast. 끝〔한〕없는; 광대한. ¶ *one's ~ ambition* 끝없는 야망 / *the ~ ocean* 망망대해. [→bound[3]]

boun·te·ous [báuntiəs] *adj.* **1** generous; given freely. 관대한; 활수한; 손큰. **2** plentiful; abundant. 풍부한. ¶ *a ~ harvest* 풍작. [L. *bonus* good]

boun·ti·ful [báuntifəl] *adj.* =bounteous.

boun·ty [báunti] *n.* Ⓒ **1** Ⓤ generosity. 너그러움. **2** that which is given freely; a generous gift. 아낌없이 주어진 것; 하사품(下賜品). ¶ *live on the ~ of* …의 보조를 받아 생활하다 / *This hospital is supported by the ~ of one man.* 이 병원은 한 사람의 독지로 유지되고 있다. **3** money, offered by a government, usu. as a reward. (정부로부터의) 보조금; 장려금. ¶ *the ~ on exports* 수출 보조금 / *the ~ for manufacture* 생산 장려금.

bou·quet [boukéi, bu:-] *n.* **1** Ⓒ a bunch of flowers. 꽃다발. **2** Ⓤ sweet smell; pleasant odor. 방향(芳香); 향기. [F. *boscage*]

Bour·bon [búərbən, bɔ́:r-] *n.* **1** a member of the last royal family of France. 부르봉 왕가의 사람. **2** an extreme conservative. 극단적 보수주의자. **3** 《*b-*》 a straight whisky. (물을 타지 않은) 위스키. [Person]

bour·geois [buərʒwɑ́:, ⌐—] *n.* Ⓒ (*pl.* **bour·geois**) a person of the middle class. 부르주아; 중산 계급의 사람(opp. proletarian). — *adj.* of the middle class. 부르주아의; 유산〔중산〕 계급의. [F.]

bour·geoi·sie [bùərʒwɑ:zí:] *n.* Ⓤ 《*the ~*》 the middle class. 부르주아지; 중산〔유산〕 계급. [F.]

bourn, bourne [buərn, bɔ:rn] *n.* Ⓒ a small stream; a brook. 개울; 시내. [E.]

bourse [buərs] *n.* a stock exchange in France, Germany, etc. 증권 거래소. [→purse]

bout [baut] *n.* Ⓒ **1** a test of strength or ability; a contest. 한판 승부; 경기. ¶ *a boxing ~* 권투 경기 / *have a ~ with the gloves* 권투 경기를 하다 / *play a ~ or two,* 1·2회 승부를 겨루다. **2** a period of time; a spell. 한 기간; 일시적인 기간. **3** a fit. 발작(發作). ¶ *a ~ of illness* 병의 발작. [E.]

'bout [baut] *adv., prep.* =about.

bou·tique [bu:tí:k] *n.* a small retail shop selling ladies' fashionable clothes and accessories. 양품점《유행하는 여성 의상과 장신구 등을 파는》. [F.]

bo·vine [bóuvain] *adj.* **1** of or like an ox or a cow. 소의; 소와 같은. **2** slow; stupid. 굼뜬; 느린. — *n.* Ⓒ an ox; a cow. 소(과의 동물). [L. *bos* ox]

:bow[1] [bau] *vi.* **1** (P1,2A) bend the head or body in greeting, respect, worship, or obedience. 절하다; 인사하다. ¶ *~ from the waist* 최경례를 하다; 정중하게 고개를 숙이다 / *He bowed slightly to his doctor.* 그는 의사에게 약간 고개를 숙여 인사했다. **2** (P2A,3) 《*to*》 submit; yield. 굴복하다. ¶ *~ to the inevitable* 피할 수 없는 운명에 굴복하다 / *~ before the laws of nature* 자연의 법칙 앞에 굴복하다 / *I ~ to your opinion.* 당신의 고견엔 경복(敬服)해 마지 않습니다. — *vt.* **1** (P6) express (one's feelings) by a bow. 절을 해서〔허리를 굽혀, 고개를 숙여〕 …을 표시하다. ¶ *~ one's thanks* 머리를 숙여 감사를 표시하다. **2** (P7,13) cause (someone) to submit; obey. 굴복시키다. **3** (P6,7,13) cause (something) to bend down. …을 구부리다; 굽히다. ¶ *Age had bowed his head.* 그는 노령으로 머리가 앞으로 구부정해졌다. **4** (P13) 《*in, into, out*》 lead or conduct (someone) with a bow. …에게 절을 하며 안내하다. ¶ *I was bowed into the room.* 나는 정중히 방으로 안내되었다 / *The page bowed us in.* 보이는 절을 하며 우리를 안으로 인도했다.

bow and scrape, be too eager to obey and serve. 굽실거리다.

bow down to =***bow the knee to,*** admit defeat and agree to serve. …에 무릎을 꿇다; 굴복하다.

— *n.* Ⓒ the act of bending of the head or body in greeting, respect, worship, etc. 절; 고개를 숙여서〔허리를 굽혀서〕 하는 인사. [E.]

make one's bow, **a**) show oneself publicly for the first time; make one's début. 공적으로 첫 등장하다; 데뷔하다. **b**) retire; withdraw; leave. 물러가다; 퇴장하다.

take a bow, acknowledge the applause of an audience by standing up or returning to the stage after a performance. (박수갈채에 답하여) 다시 나오다; 일어서다.

:bow[2] [bou] *n.* Ⓒ **1** a weapon for shooting arrows; anything shaped like this. 활; 활 모양의 것. **2** a slender stick with horsehairs for playing a violin, etc. (바이올린 따위의) 활. **3** a looped knot. 나비 매듭. ¶ *a ribbon tied in a ~* 나비 매듭으로 맨 리본 / *Her dress was tied at the neck with a ~.* 그녀의 옷은 목 부분에서 나비 매듭으로 매어져 있었다. **4** a curve; a bend. 만곡(彎曲). ¶ *the ~ of one's lips* 입술의 곡선.

— *vt., vi.* (P6;1) **1** bend (something) into the form of a bow. 활 모양으로 구부리다〔구부러지다〕. **2** play (a violin, etc.) with a bow. (현악기를) 활로 켜다. [E.]

draw the 〔***a***〕 ***long bow,*** talk big. 허풍을 떨다.

have two strings to one's bow, have several possibilities from which to choose. 제 2 의 방책이 있다; 만일의 경우에 대비가 되어 있다.

bow[3] [bau] *n.* Ⓒ 《usu. *pl.*》 the front part of a ship, boat, or airship. 선수; 이물 (cf. *stern*). [Scand. =bough]

bowd·ler·ize [bóudləràiz, báud-] *vt.* (P6) take out from a book those parts unfit for young readers. (젊은이에게 적당하지

않은) 불온한 문구를 삭제하다. [Person]

•**bow·el** [báuəl] *n.* Ⓒ《usu. *pl.*》 **1** a tube in the body through which food passes from the stomach; the intestines. 장(腸). **2** the inner part. 내부. ¶ *the bowels of the earth* 지구의 내부. [L. *botulus* sausage]

•**bow·er**[1] [báuər] *n.* Ⓒ《*poet.*》 **1** a shelter of tree branches or vines with leaves. 나무 그늘(진 휴식 장소). **2** a summer house; an arbor. 정자. **3** a lady's private room; a bedroom. 규방(閨房); 여성의 침실. [E.= dwelling]

bow·er[2] [báuər] *n.* the anchor carried at a ship's bow. 큰 닻. [*bow*[3]]

bow·er·y [báuəri] *adj.*《*poet.*》 like a bower; leafy; shady. 정자풍(風)의; 잎이 우거진; 나무 그늘의. [↑]

bow·ie knife [bóui nàif, bú:i-] *n.* a long hunting knife. 사냥칼. [Person]

bow·ing [bóuiŋ] *n.* the act or art of managing the bow in playing a stringed musical instrument. (현악기 연주의) 활 다루기. [→bow[2]]

:**bowl**[1] [boul] *n.* Ⓒ **1** a hollow, rounded dish. 사발; 보시기. ¶ *a rice* ~ 밥공기 / *a sugar* ~ 설탕 그릇 / *a wash-bowl* 세면기. **2** the amount that such a dish can hold. 한 사발. ¶ *He ate a* ~ *of soup.* 그는 수프 한 그릇을 먹었다. **3** a hollow, rounded part. 우묵한 부분. ¶ *The* ~ *of a pipe holds the tobacco.* 담배통에 담배를 담는다. **4** a large drinking cup. 큰 잔. **5** any bowl-shaped thing. 사발 모양의 것. **6**《U.S.》 a round open-air stadium. 원형의 노천 스타디움. [Teut.]

bowl[2] [boul] *n.* **1** Ⓒ a wooden ball used in games. (게임용의) 나무공. **2**《*pl.* used as *sing.*》 a game played with wooden balls. 나무공 굴리기.

— *vi.* (P2A) **1** play the game of bowling. 공 굴리기를 하다. **2** roll or move rapidly and smoothly. 스르르 굴러[미끄러져]가다. ¶ *Our car bowled merrily along the highway.* 우리 차는 하이웨이를 스르르 기분좋게 달렸다. — *vt.* (P6) **1** roll (a bowl) along the ground; roll (a child's hoop). 굴리다. **2** throw (the ball) in a certain way in the game of cricket. (크리켓에서 공을) 던지다. **3**《cricket》《*out*》 get a batsman out by bowling. (타자를) 아웃시키다. [L. *bulla*]

bowl down, knock down. 쓰러뜨리다.

bowl out, defeat. (상대를) 지게 하다.

bowl over, **a**) knock over. …을 쓰러뜨리다. **b**) give a great surprise to someone. …을 몹시 놀라게 하다. ¶ *I was completely bowled over by the bad news.* 나쁜 소식에 소스라치게 놀랐다.

bow·leg·ged [bóulègid] *adj.* having the legs curved outward. 안짱다리의. [*bow*[2]]

bowl·er [bóulər] *n.* Ⓒ **1** a person who bowls. 공굴리기를 하는 사람. **2**《Brit.》 a derby hat. 중산모(中山帽). [1 bowl[2], 2 Bowler *a hatter*]

bowl·ing [bóuliŋ] *n.* Ⓤ the game of bowls in which one tries to hit 10 pins down. 볼링. [→bowl[2]]

bowl·ing-green [bóuliŋgrì:n] *n.* a lawn prepared for the game of bowls. 공굴리기하는 잔디밭. [→bowl[2]]

bow·man [bóumən] *n.* Ⓒ (*pl.* **-men** [-mən]) a soldier who shoots with a bow and arrows; an archer. 궁수(弓手). [→bow[2]]

bow·shot [bóuʃɑ̀t / -ʃɔ̀t] *n.* Ⓤ the distance that a bow will shoot an arrow. 활의 사거리; 사정(射程). [→bow[2]]

bow·sprit [báusprit, bóu-] *n.* Ⓒ a long pole projecting forward from the front part of a ship. 선수 사장(船首斜檣).

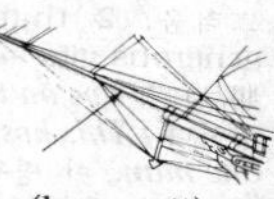
〈bowsprit〉

bow·string [bóustrìŋ] *n.* Ⓒ **1** a string of a bow[2]. 활시위; 활줄. **2** a string used for strangling offenders. 교수용(絞首用)의 줄.

bow tie [bóu tài] *n.* Ⓒ a small necktie tied in a bow at the collar. 나비 넥타이.

bow window [ˊ ˊ–] *n.* a curved bay window. 활 모양으로 내민 창.

bow·wow [báuwáu] *n.* Ⓒ **1** the bark of a dog; an imitation of this. 멍멍《개 짖는 소리》. **2** [ˊˋ]《chiefly *baby talk*》 a dog. 멍멍이. [Imit.]

the* (*big*) *bowwow style, a dogmatic tone. 독단적인 투.

:**box**[1] [bɑks / bɔks] *n.* Ⓒ **1** ⓐ a case or container of rigid material, usu. with a lid. 상자; 통. ¶ *a match* ~ 성냥갑[통] / *a money* ~ 저금통 / *a little* ~ *of a house* (보잘것 없는) 코막지만한 집. ⓑ anything which is like a box. 상자 모양의 것. **2** ⓐ the amount that a box can hold. 한 상자분(의 양). ¶ *Strawberries cost 5 hundred won a* ~. 딸기 한 상자에 5백 원 한다. ⓑ the contents of a box. 상자에 든 것[내용물]. ¶ *eat a whole* ~ *of apples* 상자의 사과를 다 먹다. **3** any enclosed space; a compartment. 칸막이가 된 곳; 칸. ¶ *a* ~ *seat* (극장의) 칸막이 좌석. **4** the driver's seat on a coach. (마차의) 마부석. **5** a present; a gift. 선물. **6** a small house or room, or a wooden shelter. 작은 건물; 초소(哨所). ¶ *a hunting* ~ 사냥막 / *a sentry* ~ 보초막 / *a police* ~ 지서. **7**《baseball》 the place where the batter stands. (야구의) 배터박스. **8** a jury-box; a witness-box. (법원의) 배심원석; 증인석.

a box and needle, a compass. 나침반.

in a* (*tight*) *box, in a fix. 어찌할 바를 몰라; 진퇴양난이 되어.

— *vt.* (P6,7) **1** put (something) into a box. …을 상자[통]에 넣다. ¶ ~ *the oranges for shipping* 선적(船積)을 위해 오렌지를 상자에 넣다. **2** keep (something or someone) within limits; confine. …을 (좁은 장소에) 처넣다; 가두다. [Gk. *puxos*]

box in, shut up (something) in a box. …을 상자 안에 넣다.
box it out, fight to the last. 최후까지 싸우다.
box off, separate with partitions. 칸막이를 하다.
box the compass, **a**) name all 32 points of the compass in their correct order. 나침의(儀)의 32 방위를 순서대로 말하다. **b**) 《*fig.*》 finish up where a person began in an argument, etc. (의론 따위가) 다시 원점으로 되돌아오다.
box up, **a**) shut up closely; confine. 꼭 가두다. ¶ *We were boxed up all night in a small room.* 우리는 밤새도록 작은 방에 간혔다. **b**) squeeze together. (비좁은 곳에) 처[밀어]넣다.

·box² [bɑks / bɔks] *n.* Ⓒ a blow with the open hand or the fist, esp. on the ear or the side of the head. 따귀 때림. ¶ *give a ~ on the ear* 따귀[귀싸대기]를 붙이다. —*vi., vt.* (P1,3; 6) **1** strike (someone) with such a blow. 손바닥[주먹]으로 치다. ¶ *~ someone's ears* 아무의 따귀를 붙이다. **2** fight with the fists as a sport. 권투하다. ¶ *He has boxed since he was 15.* 그는 열여섯 살 때부터 권투를 하고 있다. [↑]

box³ [bɑks / bɔks] *n.* **1** Ⓒ 《bot.》 a small evergreen tree or shrub. 회양목속의 나무. **2** Ⓤ its hard wood. 회양목재(材). [↑]

box·er [bɑ́ksər / bɔ́ks-] *n.* Ⓒ **1** ⓐ a person who fights with his fists in gloves as a sport. 권투 선수. ⓑ a member of a Chinese anti-foreign secret society. (중국의) 의화단원; 권비(拳匪). **2** a short-haired brown dog. 복서종의 개. [*box²*]

box·ing [bɑ́ksiŋ / bɔ́ks-] *n.* Ⓤ the sport of fighting with the fists. 권투.

Boxing Day [⌐–⌐] *n.* 《Brit.》 the first weekday after Christmas Day. 복싱 데이 《12월 26일》. 參考 고용인 등에게 선물을 함.

boxing gloves [⌐–⌐] *n. pl.* the gloves used for boxing. 권투장갑.

boxing match [⌐–⌐] *n.* a fight between two boxers. 권투 경기.

box office [⌐⌐–] *n.* the place where tickets are sold in a theater, hall, etc. (극장 등의) 매표소. [*box¹*]

box·tree [bɑ́kstrìː / bɔ́ks-] *n.* =box³.

box·wood [bɑ́kswùd / bɔ́ks-] *n.* **1** Ⓤ the hard, fine-grained wood of the box³. 회양목재. **2** Ⓒ the tree itself. 회양목. [*box³*]

:boy [bɔi] *n.* Ⓒ **1** a male child from birth to about eighteen. 소년; 남아. **2** a young servant; a page. 보이. [E.]

boy·cott [bɔ́ikɑt / -kɔt] *vt.* (P6) **1** make a promise with others to have nothing to do with (someone, a business, a nation, etc.) (서로 약속하고) …을 보이콧하다; 배척하다. **2** refuse to buy or use (good, etc.). (상품 등의) 구매·사용을 배척[거부]하다; 불매 동맹을 하다. ¶ *~ a commercial product* 상품의 구매를 거부하다. —*n.* Ⓒ the act of boycotting. 보이콧. ¶ *apply the ~* 보이콧하다. [Person]

·boy·hood [bɔ́ihud] *n.* Ⓤ **1** the time or condition of being a boy. 소년기[시절]. ¶ *in my ~* 나의 소년 시절에. **2** 《*collectively*》 boys. 소년들. [→boy]

boy·ish [bɔ́iiʃ] *adj.* **1** of a boy. 소년의. **2** like a boy. 어린애 같은. ¶ *a ~ smile* 어린애 같은 미소.

Boy Scouts [⌐⌐] *n.* a world-wide boy's organization. 보이 스카우트.

bp. baptized.

B/P bills payable; 《chem.》 boiling point.

Br 《chem.》 bromine.

Br. Britain; British.

B./R. bills receivable.

·brace [breis] *n.* Ⓒ **1** anything which supports, strengthens, or holds parts together. 받침대; 버팀대. **2** a piece of wood, metal, etc., for supporting another piece of framework. 지주(支柱). **3** (*pl.* **brace**) pair; couple. 한 쌍. ¶ *two ~ of ducks* 오리 두 쌍. **4** a handle of a drill used for holding and rotating it. (타래 송곳의) 굽은 손잡이 부분. **5** either of these signs { }, used to enclose words, figures, etc. 중괄호. **6** 《Brit.》 《*pl.*》 suspenders. 바지 멜빵.

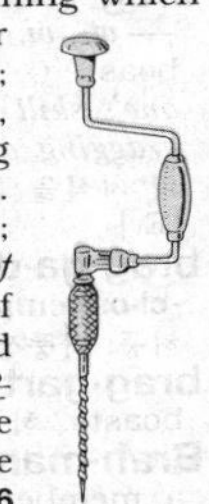
〈brace and bit〉

a brace and bit, a boring tool with a bit and a handle. 굽은 손잡이 송곳.

—*vt.* (P6,7) **1** fasten tightly. …을 단단히 죄다; 고정시키다. **2** give strength to (someone or something). …의 기운을 북돋우다. ¶ *~ oneself* 힘을 내다 / *~ oneself for a task* 힘을 내어 일에 착수하다 / *The fresh air at the seashore will ~ us.* 해변의 맑은 공기는 우리의 힘을 북돋아줄 것이다. [L. *brachium* arm]

brace·let [bréislit] *n.* Ⓒ **1** an ornamental band for the wrist or arm. 팔찌. **2** 《*colloq.*》 a handcuff. 수갑; 쇠고랑.

brac·ing [bréisiŋ] *adj.* strengthening; refreshing. 기운을 돋우는; 상쾌한(cf. *relax*). ¶ *Mountain air is ~.* 산의 공기는 상쾌하다.

brack·en [brǽkən] *n.* ⓊⒸ 《bot.》 a large fern. 고사리류. [Scand.]

brack·et [brǽkit] *n.* Ⓒ **1** ⓐ an L-shaped support for a shelf. 까치발. ⓑ a shelf supported by brackets. 까치발 버팀의 선반. **2** 《*pl.*》 either of these signs ( ) [ ], used to enclose words or figures. ( ), [ ]의 괄호. 參考 ( )는 round brackets 또는 parentheses, [ ]는 square brackets 라고 함. —*vt.* (P6,7) **1** support (a shelf) with brackets. …을 까치발로 받치다. **2** enclose (a word) within brackets. …을 괄호로 묶다. **3** mention or classify together. …을 일괄하여 분류하다; 동등하게 다루다. [L. *braccae* breeches]

brack·ish [brǽkiʃ] *adj.* **1** a little salty. 약간 짠; 소금기가 있는. ¶ *A mixture of fresh water and sea water is* ~. 민물과 바닷물을 섞으면 짭짤하다. **2** distasteful; unpleasant. 맛없는; 불쾌한. ● **brack·ish·ness** [-nis] *n.* [Scand.]

bract [brækt] *n.* 《bot.》 a small leaf at the base of a flower. 포(苞); 포엽(苞葉). [L. *bract*]

brad [bræd] *n.* a small thin nail. 곡정(曲釘). [N. =spike]

brad·awl [brǽdɔ̀:l] *n.* a small boring tool. 작은 송곳. [E.]

brae [brei] *n.* 《Sc.》 a slope; a hillside. 비탈; 산허리. [Scand.=brow]

brag [bræg] *n.* Ⓤ boasting talk. 허풍. — *vt., vi.* (**bragged, brag·ging**) (P6,11;1,3) boast. (…을) 자랑하다. ¶ ~ *of* 〔*about*〕 *one's skill* 자기의 기술을 자랑하다 / *Stop bragging about your knowledge so much!* 네 자식을 그렇게 자랑하는 것 좀 집어치워라. [E.]

brag·ga·do·ci·o [brǽgədóuʃiòu] *n.* (*pl.* **-ci·os**) empty boasting; a boasting fellow. 허풍; 허풍선이. [E.]

brag·gart [brǽgərt] *n.* Ⓒ a person who boasts. 허풍선이. [↑]

Brah·man [brɑ́:mən] *n.* Ⓒ (*pl.* **-mans**) a member of the highest caste in the Hindu social system. 브라만. [Skr.=worship]

Brah·man·ism [brɑ́:mənìzəm] *n.* Ⓤ a Hindu religious and social system. 브라만교.

Brah·min [brɑ́:min] *n.* =Brahman.

Brahms [brɑ:mz], **Johannes** *n.* (1833-97) a German composer of music. 브람스.

braid [breid] *n.* **1** Ⓤ a band of woven material used esp. for the decoration of clothing. 장식 끈. **2** Ⓒ a plait of hair. 땋은 머리. ¶ *wear one's hair in braids* 머리를 땋아 늘어뜨리다. — *vt.* (P6) **1** weave together stripes or strands of (hair, a ribbon, etc.); plait. …을 땋다; 엮다; 꼬다. ¶ ~ *one's hair* 머리를 땋다. **2** form (something) by such weaving. …을 끈으로 꼬다. **3** trim or bind (clothing) with braid. …을 꼰 끈으로 장식하다〔감다〕. [E.]

Braille, braille [breil] *n.* Ⓤ **1** the system of writing and printing for blind people by using raised dots. (맹인용) 점자법(點字法). **2** the letters themselves. 점자. 參考 고안자는 프랑스인 Louis Braille(1809-52). [Person]

:**brain** [brein] *n.* Ⓒ **1** the central nervous system within the skull. 뇌. **2** 《often *pl.*》 mind; intelligence. 두뇌; 지력(知力). ¶ *a man of brains* 두뇌 명석한 사람 / *a powerful* 〔*weak*〕 ~ 지력이 뛰어난〔약한〕 머리 / *have good brains* = *be full of brains* 머리가 좋다 / *have a lucid* ~ 명석한 두뇌를 갖고 있다.

beat one's brains, try hard to think. 머리를 짜다; 고심하다.

have (*something*) ***on the brain,*** have the mind filled with it. (어떤 일만)을 생각하다; 어떤 생각이 머리에서 떠나지 않다. ¶ *He has baseball on the* ~. 그의 머리는 온통 야구 생각뿐이다.

pick 〔***suck***〕 ***someone's brains,*** make use of his knowledge without troubling to work something out for oneself. 남의 지혜〔머리〕를 빌리다.

rack 〔***cudgel***〕 ***one's brains,*** try hard to think out or remember. 머리를 짜내다. ¶ *He racked his brains for the answer.* 그는 대답하기 위해 머리를 짰다.

turn one's brain, fascinate him. …을 열중하게〔우쭐하게〕 만들다.

— *vt.* (P6) knock out the brains of. …의 골통을 부수다. [A.S. *brægen, bregen*]

brain·fag [bréinfæ̀g] *n.* nervous exhaustion. 신경 쇠약. [*brain*]

brain·fe·ver [bréinfì:vər] *n.* 《med.》 inflammation of the brain. 뇌막염.

brain·less [bréinlis] *adj.* **1** without a brain. 지능이 모자라는. **2** stupid; foolish. 어리석은.

brain·pan [bréinpæ̀n] *n.* the upper part of the skull enclosing the brain. 두개(頭蓋).

brain·storm [bréinstɔ̀:rm] *n.* 《*colloq.*》 **1** a violent mental upset. 심한 정신 착란. **2** a sudden, brilliant idea. 갑자기 떠오르는 묘안; 인스피레이션.

brain trust [∠∠] *n.* a group of advisers to a political leader, etc. 자문 위원회.

brain·wash·ing [bréinwɑ̀ʃiŋ, -wɔ̀(:)-] *n.* Ⓤ a method for changing someone's thoughts or beliefs. 세뇌 (교육).

brain·wave [bréinwèiv] *n.* **1** 《usu. *pl.*》 a flow of an electric current of the brain. 뇌파. **2** =brainstorm.

brain·y [bréini] *adj.* (**brain·i·er; brain·i·est**) 《*colloq.*》 intelligent; clever. 머리가 좋은.

braise [breiz] *vt.* (P6) cook (meat) long and slowly in a covered pan. …을 흐물흐물하도록 삶다. [→brazier]

·**brake**[1] [breik] *n.* Ⓒ anything used for slowing or stopping the motion of a wheel or vehicle. 브레이크. ¶ *an automatic* ~ 자동 브레이크 / *put on* 〔*apply*〕 *the* ~ 브레이크를 걸다. — *vt.* (P6) slow up or stop (a car) by a brake. …에 브레이크를 걸다. ¶ ~ *a car* 차에 브레이크를 걸어 멈추다〔속력을 떨어뜨리다〕. [E.]

brake[2] [breik] *n.* Ⓒ a place covered with a thick growth of bushes; a thicket. 덤불; 숲. [→break]

brake[3] [breik] *n.* Ⓒ a large fern. 고사리류.

brake·man [bréikmən] *n.* Ⓒ (*pl.* **-men** [-mən]) a man who works brakes or helps the conductor of a railroad train. 제동수(制動手). [→brake[1]]

·**bram·ble** [brǽmbəl] *n.* Ⓒ **1** a blackberry-bush; a wild blackberry. 나무딸기; 검은딸기. **2** any rough, prickly shrub. 가시가 있는 관목. [E.]

bram·bly [brǽmbli] *adj.* **1** full of brambles. 검은딸기가 많은. **2** like brambles; prickly. 가시가 있는〔많은〕.

bran [bræn] *n.* Ⓤ the outside coat of the grains of wheat, rye, etc. 겨; 밀기울. [F.]

:branch [bræntʃ, brɑːntʃ] *n.* Ⓒ **1** a part of a tree growing out from the trunk. (나무의) 가지. ¶ *A very small ~ is called a twig.* 아주 작은 가지는 twig 라 불린다. **2** any division like a branch of a tree. 가지 모양의 분기(分岐); 분파; 지류; 지맥(支脈). ¶ *a ~ of a river* 강의 지류 / *the branches of a deer's antlers* 사슴뿔의 분지(分枝) / *a ~ road* 갈라진 길; 샛길 / *a ~ of a mountain-range* 산맥의 지맥(支脈). **3** a division; a part. 부문; (학)과. ¶ *a ~ of study* 학과 / *the various branches of learning* 학문의 여러 부문 / *the book dealing with the matter in all branches* 그 문제를 모든 면에 걸쳐 다룬 책. **4** a local office. 지부; 지점; 출장소. ¶ *a local ~* 지방 지점 / *an overseas ~* 해외 지점〔지국〕 / *open a ~* 지점을 열다.

root and branch, completely. 남김없이; 전부.

— *vi.* (P1,2A) **1** put out branches. 가지가 돋다. **2** separate into branches. 갈라지다. ¶ *~ off from the main road* 큰 길에서 갈라지다. [L. *branca* paw]

branch off, divide (something) into branches. …을 가르다.

branch out, **a**) spread branches. 가지를 뻗다. **b**) extend (business, activities, etc.). (사업·활동 따위를) 확장하다. ¶ *~ out in different directions* 여러 다른 방면으로 (활동) 영역을 넓히다.

•brand [brænd] *n.* Ⓒ **1** a certain kind, grade, or make of goods. (상표 따위로 표시되는) 품종. ¶ *the best ~ of tea* 최상급의 차 / *the Korean ~ of hippies* 한국판 히피족. **2** a trademark. 상표. ¶ *Do you like this ~ of coffee?* 이 상표의 커피를 좋아하는가. **3** a mark made by burning the skin with a hot iron. 낙인(烙印). ¶ *Cattle and horses on big ranches are marked with brands to show who owns them.* 큰 목장의 마소는 소유주를 나타내기 위해 낙인으로 표시가 되어 있다. **4** a mark of disgrace. 오명(汚名); 낙인. ¶ *the ~ of villainy* 극악 무도의 낙인.

a brand from the burning, a convert; a rescued person. 개종자; 구원받은 사람.

— *vt.* (P6,7) **1** mark (cattle) by burning the skin with a hot iron. …에 낙인을 찍다. ¶ *In former times criminals were often branded.* 예전에 죄인에게는 종종 낙인이 찍혔다 / 《*fig.*》 *The scene is branded on my memory.* 그 광경은 내 기억 속에 새겨져 있다. **2** 《as》 put a mark of disgrace on (someone). …에게 오명을 씌우다. ¶ *~ someone as a thief* 아무에게 도둑의 누명을 씌우다 / *~ him as a liar* 그에게 거짓말쟁이라는 오명을 씌우다 / *He is branded as an impostor.* 그에겐 사기꾼이라는 딱지가 붙어있다. [E.]

bran·dish [brǽndiʃ] *vt.* (P6) wave or shake (a sword, etc.) as a threat. (칼 따위)를 휘두르다. ¶ *He brandished his sword and rushed at the enemy.* 그는 칼을 휘두르며 적에게 돌진했다. [↑]

brand-new [brǽdnjúː] *adj.* very new; quite new. 아주 새로운.

bran·dy [brǽndi] *n.* Ⓤ a strong alcoholic liquor made from wine. 브랜디. ¶ *a ~* 브랜디 한 잔. [E.]

brash [bræʃ] *adj.* 《U.S. *colloq.*》 **1** hasty. 성급한. **2** impudent; saucy. 뻔뻔스러운; 건방진. [?]

Bra·sil·i·a [brɑːzíːljə] *n.* the capital of Brazil. 브라질리아.

:brass [bræs, brɑːs] *n.* Ⓤ **1** a yellow metal made by melting copper and zinc together. 놋쇠; 황동. **2** 《usu. *pl.*》 things made of brass, such as ornaments, dishes, etc. 놋제품. **3** 《usu. *the ~*》 the trumpets, horns, etc. in an orchestra. 취주〔금관〕악기. ¶ *a ~ band* 취주악대 / *the ~* (*winds*) 금관악기 / *the brasses* 금관 악기부. **4** 《*colloq.*》 money. 돈; 현금. ¶ *plenty of ~* 많은 돈. **5** 《*colloq.*》 shamelessness; impudence. 철면피. ¶ *He had the ~ to say that.* 그는 뻔뻔하게도 그걸 말했다. **6** 《U.S. *sl.*》 military officers of high rank. 고급 장교.

(*as*) *bold as brass,* very bold and confident. 뻔뻔스러운; 주제넘은.

come 〔***get***〕 ***down to brass tacks,*** 《*colloq.*》 face basic facts or tasks. 근본 문제에 당면하다.

— *adj.* made of brass. 놋쇠로 만든. ¶ *a ~ plate.* [E.]

bra·sard [brǽsɑːrd, brəsɑ́ːrd] *n.* a badge on the arm. 완장. [F.; →brace]

brass band [⌐⌐] *n.* a group of musicians playing brass wind instruments. 브라스 밴드.

bras·siere [brəzíər] *n.* Ⓒ 《F.》 a bust support worn by women. 브래지어.

brass plate [⌐⌐] *n.* a plate of brass on a door, gate, or window-ledge, with a name, trade, etc. 표찰(標札).

brass·ware [brǽswὲər, brɑ́ːs-] *n.* things made of brass. 놋제품.

brass·y [brǽsi, brɑ́ːsi] *adj.* (**brass·i·er, brass·i·est**) **1** of brass. 놋쇠의. **2** like brass. 놋쇠 같은. **3** (esp. of a woman) loud and harsh. 시끄러운; 수다스러운.

brat [bræt] *n.* Ⓒ 《*contempt.*》 a child. 애새끼. [A.S. =rag]

bra·va·do [brəvɑ́ːdou] *n.* ⓊⒸ (*pl.* **-dos** or **-does**) a great show of boldness, often without much real courage. 허세. [Sp.]

:brave [breiv] *adj.* **1** without fear; having courage. 용감한. ¶ *a ~ man* 〔*deed*〕 용감한 사람〔행위〕 / *the ~* 용감한 사람들 / *keep a ~ face* 태연한 얼굴을 하고 있다. **2** making a fine appearance; showy. (복장이) 화려한. ¶ *a ~ show* 화려한 쇼 / *a ~ new world* 멋진 신세계.

—n. Ⓒ a brave person. 용사.

—vt. (P6,7) **1** face or meet (someone or something) with courage. 용감히 맞서다. ¶ *~ misfortunes* 불행과 용감히 싸우다 / *Doctors ~ much danger.* 의사들은 감연히 많은 위험에 맞선다. **2** dare; defy. 감히 …하다; 도전하다. ¶ *He braved the king's anger.* 그는 임금의 노여움을 무릅썼다.

brave it out, disregard suspicion or blame. 의심이나 비난을 개의치 않다; 결행하다.

● **brave·ness** [ˊnis] *n.* [It. *bravo*]

***brave·ly** [bréivli] *adv.* without fear; 《*lit.*》 finely. 용감히; 훌륭하게; 화려하게.

***brav·er·y** [bréivəri] *n.* Ⓤ **1** courage; fearlessness. 용기; 용감. **2** fine appearance; showy dress. (아름다운) 치장. ¶ *Helen came to the party in all the ~ of her new dress and pink ribbons.* 헬렌은 핑크빛 리본이 달린 새 옷으로 아름답게 치장하고 파티에 참석했다.

bra·vo[1] [brάːvou, ˊˊ] *interj.* Well done !; Fine !; Excellent ! 잘했어; 브라보. **—n.** Ⓒ (*pl.* **-vos** or **-voes**) a cry of 'bravo!'. '브라보' 소리. [It.]

bra·vo[2] [brάːvou] *n.* Ⓒ (*pl.* **-vos** or **-voes**) a hired fighter or murderer. 청부 살인자; 자객(刺客). [It.]

brawl [brɔːl] *n.* Ⓒ a noisy quarrel or fight. 말다툼; 싸움. **—vi.** (P1) **1** quarrel noisily and roughly. 큰 소리로 싸우다. **2** (of streams) flow noisily. 쏴쏴 흐르다. [E.]

brawn [brɔːn] *n.* Ⓤ **1** firm, strong muscles; muscular strength. 근육; 근력(筋力). ¶ *The wrestler had brain as well as ~.* 그 레슬러는 힘도 있었고 머리도 좋았다. **2** pig's meat pickled and pressed into a pot. 절인 돼지고기. [F.]

brawn·y [brɔ́ːni] *adj.* (**brawn·i·er, brawn·i·est**) strong; muscular. 강력한; 근골(筋骨)이 억센. ● **brawn·i·ness** [-nis] *n.*

bray [brei] *n.* Ⓒ the loud, rough sound made by a donkey; noise like it. (당나귀의) 거친 울음 소리; 그 같은 소리. **—vi.** (P1) **1** make a loud, rough sound. (당나귀가) 거칠게 울다. **2** speak something in a loud, rough voice. 큰 소리로 고함치듯 말하다. [F.]

braze [breiz] *vt.* (P6) **1** solder with an alloy of brass and zinc. 땜질하다. **2** color like brass. 놋쇠빛으로 하다. [→brass]

bra·zen [bréizən] *adj.* **1** made of brass. 놋쇠로 된. ¶ *a ~ image of Buddha* 놋쇠로 만든 불상. **2** like brass in color or strength. 놋쇠 같은. **3** loud and rough. 시끄러운; 귀에 거슬리는. **4** shameless; impudent. 뻔뻔한. ¶ *a ~ lie* 뻔뻔한 거짓말 / *adopt a ~ attitude* 뻔뻔스런 태도를 취하다.

—vt. (P6,7) do shamelessly or impudently. …을 뻔뻔스럽게 하다.

brazen it out **=*brazen through,*** behave shamelessly to get rid of a bad situation; carry it off impudently. 끝까지 뻔뻔스럽게 굴다; 뻔뻔스럽게 해내다〔밀어붙이다〕.

bra·zen-faced [bréizənfèist] *adj.* openly shameless; impudent. 철면피한; 뻔뻔스러운. ¶ *a ~ hussy* 뻔뻔스러운〔굴러 먹은〕 여자.

bra·zier[1] [bréiʒər] *n.* Ⓒ a metal container to hold burning charcoal or coal. (금속제의) 화로. [→braze]

bra·zier[2] [bréiʒər] *n.* Ⓒ a person who works with brass. 놋갓장이.

Bra·zil [brəzíl] *n.* the largest country in South America. 브라질. 參考 수도는 Brasilia.

Bra·zil·ian [brəzíljən] *adj.* of Brazil or its people. 브라질(사람)의. **—n.** Ⓒ a person of Brazil. 브라질 사람.

B.R.C.S. British Red Cross Society.

breach [briːtʃ] *n.* Ⓒ **1** an opening made by breaking through; gap. 파괴된 구멍; 터진〔갈라진〕 곳. ¶ *a ~ in the wall* 벽의 갈라진 틈. **2** the act of breaking a law, promise, duty, etc.; neglect. (법·언약·의무 등의) 어김; 불이행. ¶ *For me to put it off till Saturday would be a ~ of duty.* 나에게 있어 그것을 토요일까지 미룬다는 것은 의무 태만이다 / *a ~ of promise* 파약(破約). **3** an act of breaking friendly relations; a quarrel. 절교; 불화(不和). ¶ *There has been no ~ in our relations for ten years.* 10년 동안 우리의 관계에 불화는 없었다.

stand in 〔***throw oneslef into***〕 ***the breach,*** bear the heaviest part of the attack; come forward and help in time of need or danger. 공격 선두에 서다; 난국에 대처하다.

—vt. (P6) make a breach in (something); break. …에 구멍을 뚫다; 돌파하다. ¶ *Our fierce attack breached the enemy's defences.* 우리의 치열한 공격은 적의 방어에 구멍을 뚫었다. [F. →break]

:bread [bred] *n.* Ⓤ **1** a kind of food made by baking a mixture of flour and water. 빵. **2** food; livelihood. 먹거리; 양식; 생계. ¶ *earn* 〔*make*〕 *one's ~* 생계를 세우다 / *in good* 〔*bad*〕 *~* 유복한〔어려운〕 생활을 하고 / *out of ~* 일자리를 잃어 / *Man shall not live by ~ alone.* 사람은 빵만으로 사는 것이 아니다.

a bread-and-butter letter, a letter of thanks for hospitality received. 환대에 대한 감사의 편지.

bread and butter, buttered bread slices; necessary food; 《*colloq.*》 one's living; livelihood. 버터를 바른 빵; 생계.

bread and cheese, simple food; livelihood. 간단한 식사; 생계.

bread and wine, Eucharist. 성찬(聖餐).

break bread with, **a**) share a meal with; eat with. …와 식사를 함께 하다; 같이 먹다. **b**) 《Bible》 join in the Lord's Supper. 성찬식에 참여하다.

cast 〔***throw***〕 ***one's bread upon the waters,*** do

good to others without looking for reward. 보답을 바라지 않고 은혜를 베풀다.
eat the bread of idleness 〔***affliction***〕, be idle 〔afflicted〕. 빈둥거리며〔비참하게〕 지내다.
know on which side** one's **bread is buttered, know who or what will be of most advantage to oneself; be aware of one's interests. 이해 관계에 빈틈없다; 이끗에 밝다.
take the bread out of** someone's **mouth, take away his living. 아무에게서 생계의 길을 빼앗다.
— *vt.* cover (something) with bread crumbs before cooking. …에 빵가루를 묻히다. [M.E. *breed;* A.S. *bread;* G. *brot.*]

bread·fruit [brédfrùːt] *n.* Ⓒ **1** a large, round, starchy, tropical fruit of the Pacific islands which tastes like bread when baked. 빵나무의 열매. **2** the tree bearing this fruit. 빵나무.

bread·line [brédlàin] *n.* a queue of poor people to receive food. 식량 배급을 받기 위해 줄지어 선 빈민의 열(列).

bread·stuffs [brédstʌ̀fs] *n. pl.* grain, etc. from which bread is made. 빵의 원료.

***breadth** [bredθ, bretθ] *n.* Ⓤ **1** the distance from side to side; width. 나비; 폭. ¶ *the ~ of a carpet* 양탄자의 나비. **2** (of mind, thought, etc.) largeness; broadness. (마음 따위의) 넓음; 관용. ¶ *He has ~ of mind.* 그는 마음이 넓다. [→broad]

breadth·ways [brédθwèiz, brétθ-], **breath·wise** [-wàiz] *adv.* from side to side. 옆으로.

bread·win·ner [brédwìnər] *n.* Ⓒ a person who earns a living for his family. (한 가정에서) 생계를 유지하는 사람; (집안 살림의) 대들보. [→broad]

:break [breik] *v.* (**broke, bro·ken**) *vt.* **1** (P6,7) cause (something) to come to pieces by a blow or strain; destroy; crack; smash. …을 깨뜨리다; 꺾다; 부수다; 무너뜨리다. ¶ *~ a cup* 컵을 깨뜨리다 / *~ a glass to* 〔*into*〕 *pieces* 유리잔을 산산 조각을 내다 / *~ a thread* 실을 끊어뜨리다 / *~ one's arm* 팔을 분지르다 / *~ a stick in two* 막대기를 두 동강 내다 / *I heard the rope ~.* 밧줄이 끊어지는 소리를 들었다 / *The river broke its bank.* 강물이 둑을 무너뜨렸다. **2** (P6) hurt; injure. …을 상처가 나게〔다치게〕 하다. ¶ *~ the skin* 피부에 상처를 내다. **3** (P6) put (something) out of order; make useless by rough handling, etc. …을 어지럽히다; 못 쓰게〔고장나게〕 하다. ¶ *~ a watch* 시계를 고장내다 / *~ a line* 열을 흩뜨리다 / *~ the peace* 평화를 어지럽히다. **4** (P6) fail to keep or follow; act against (a rule, law, etc.); violate; disobey. (규칙·법 따위)를 어기다; 범하다. ¶ *~ rules* 〔*a law*〕 규칙〔법〕을 어기다 / *~ one's promise* 약속을 어기다 / *~ a contract* 계약을 위반하다. **5** (P6) escape from (a place); make one's way; open (something) or enter (a place) by force. …에서 탈주하다; 비집어 열다; …에 침입하다. ¶ *~ prison* 〔*jail*〕 탈옥하다 / *be accused of attempting to ~ a house* 가택을 침입하려 한 혐의로 기소되다. **6** (P6) lessen 〔weaken〕 the force of (something); make less severe. (힘·강도 따위)를 약화시키다. ¶ *a stand of trees breaking the wind* 풍세를 약화시키는 입목(立木)들 / *Branches broke the man's fall from the window.* 나뭇가지들은 그 사나이가 창문에서 떨어지는 충격을 약화시켰다. **7** (P6) stop; put an end to (something); interrupt. …을 그만두다; 중단〔중지〕하다; 끝내다. ¶ *~ one's journey* 여행을 끝내다 / *~ someone's sleep* 아무의 잠을 깨우다 / *~ a strike in a factory* 공장의 파업을 끝내다 / *~ the habit of smoking* 흡연 습관을 버리다 / *~ one's fast* 단식을 끝내다. **8** (P6) change (a state), usu. suddenly. …을 급변시키다; (침묵·고요 등)을 깨다. ¶ *~ silence* 침묵을 깨다 / *~ the old conventions* 오랜 인습을 깨다. **9** (P6) make (a bank, company, etc.) bankrupt; ruin. …을 파산〔파멸〕시키다. ¶ *~ the bank* 은행을 파산시키다 / *Another such loss will ~ me.* 또 다른 그런 손실은 나를 파산시킬 게다 / *He was broken by the failure of his business.* 사업의 실패로 그는 파산되었다 / *I shall be broken if I play with him so often.* 그와 그렇게 자주 놀다간 파멸할 것이다. **10** (P6,13) 《*to*》 make (something) known; reveal. …을 알리다. ¶ *~ secret plans to the enemy* 적에게 비밀 계획을 알리다 / *Someone must ~ the bad news to her.* 누군가 그녀에게 그 나쁜 소식을 알려야 한다. **11** (P6,7) tame (a wild animal). (동물 따위)를 길들이다. ¶ *~ (in) a horse* 말을 길들이다 / *I never could ~ that dog.* 저 개를 전혀 길들일 수 없었다. **12** (P6) open up (the ground) with the plough; cut open (a road). (땅)을 갈다; (길)을 내다. **13** (P6) reduce in rank. 강등시키다; (지위)를 낮추다. ¶ *He was broken from sergeant to private.* 그는 하사관에서 이등병으로 강등되었다. **14** (P6) beat or better (a record); surpass. (기록)을 깨다; 갱신하다. ¶ *~ the former* 〔*all previous*〕 *records* 이전의〔전의 모든〕 기록을 깨뜨리다. **15** (P13) 《*of*》 cure (someone or oneself) of a bad habit. 나쁜 습관을 고치다. ¶ *~ a child of biting his nails* 아이가 손톱을 씹는 습관을 고치게 하다. **16** ⓐ destroy someone's health; make weak. …의 건강을 해치다; 약하게 하다. ¶ *He is broken in health.* 그는 건강이 약해져 있다. ⓑ destroy spirit or courage. (기)를 꺾다; 좌절시키다. ¶ *~ someone's heart* 아무를 낙담시키다; 큰 슬픔에 빠지게 하다. — *vi.* (P1,2A,3) **1** come into pieces by a blow or strain. 깨지다; 부서지다. ¶ *Glass breaks easily.* 유리는 잘 깨진다. **2** fall into confusion; get out of order. 혼란에 빠지다; 흐트러지다. **3** come suddenly; burst into activity. 갑자기 일어나다. ¶ *The storm broke.* 폭풍이 일었다. **4**

change suddenly. 급변하다. ¶ *His voice broke when he told the story.* 그 이야기를 할 때 그의 목소리는 갑자기 변했다. **5** dawn. 날이 새다. ¶ *The day is breaking.* 날이 샌다. **6** become weak; lose vigor. 약해지다. **7** go bankrupt. 파산하다.

break away, **a**) go away suddenly; escape. 갑자기 떠나다; 도망하다. ¶ ~ *away from home* 갑자기 집을 떠나다. **b**) start before the signal. 신호 전에 달려나가다. **c**) give up (habits, thoughts, etc.). (습관 따위)를 버리다. ¶ ~ *away from the old conventions* 낡은 인습을 버리다.

break down, **a**) knock down; destroy; smash. …을 부수다; 파괴하다. ¶ ~ *down a door* 문을 부수다. **b**) fail. 실패하다. **c**) get out of order; fail to work. 고장나다. ¶ *The car* [*engine*] *broke down.* 차가[엔진이] 고장 났다. **d**) give way under pain or emotion; lose one's control. 고통·감정에 지다; 감정을 누르지 못하다. ¶ ~ *down in grief* 슬픔을 못 이겨 울다. **e**) give way to pressure, torture, etc.; yield; submit; confess. (압력·고문 따위)에 굴하다; 자백하다. ¶ ~ *down under questioning* 문초를 받고 불다. **f**) fail in health. (건강·체력이) 약해지다; 쇠하다(cf. *breakdown*). **g**) analyze. …을 분석하다. ¶ ~ *down a problem* 문제를 분석하다.

break forth, **a**) (of a stream, etc.) spring out. (물줄기 따위)가 쏟아져 나오다; 분출하다. **b**) (of anger, etc.) burst out. (노여움 따위)가 폭발하다. ¶ *His anger broke forth.* 그는 분통을 터뜨렸다.

break free, get free by force; escape. 힘으로써 자유를 얻다; 달아나다.

break in, **a**) get ready for work or use; train or tame. …을 길들이다; 훈련하다. ¶ ~ *in a new pair of shoes* 새 구두를 길들이다 / *A new car has to be broken in.* 새 차는 길을 들여야 한다. **b**) enter (a place) by force. …에 침입하다. ¶ ~ *in a house* 가택에 침입하다. **c**) interrupt someone's talk, work, etc. 남의 일·이야기 따위를 방해하다.

break in on [***upon***]***,*** disturb abruptly; intrude upon. 방해하다; 침입하다.

break into, **a**) enter suddenly; begin suddenly; burst into. …에 갑자기 들어가다; 갑자기 시작하다. ¶ ~ *into a loud laugh* 갑자기 크게 웃다 / ~ *into a quarrel* 갑자기 말다툼을 시작하다 / *She broke into song.* 그녀는 갑자기 노래를 부르기 시작했다 / *She broke into a run to overtake him.* 그녀는 그를 따라잡기 위해 갑자기 뛰기 시작했다. **b**) enter (a place) by force. …에 무리하게 들어가다; 침입하다. **c**) interrupt. 끼어들어 방해하다. ¶ ~ *into somone's talk* 남의 이야기를 방해하다.

break loose =break free.

break** someone **of, force someone to give up (something). (아무)에게 단념시키다.

break off, **a**) separate by force. 잡아 꺾다; 떼어 내다. ¶ ~ *off a branch from a tree* 나뭇가지를 분지르다. **b**) stop or end suddenly. …을 그만두다; 끝내다. ¶ ~ *off a battle* 전투를 중지하다 / ~ *off a talk* 이야기를 중단하다. **c**) cut off (relation). (관계)를 끊다. ¶ *He broke off all relations with her.* 그는 그녀와의 모든 관계를 끊었다.

break open, open (a place) by breaking. …을 비집어 열다.

break out, **a**) escape from prison; run away. 탈옥하다; 탈주하다. ¶ *Prisoners have broken out* (*of the prison*). 죄수들이 탈옥했다. **b**) (of a fire, disease, war, etc.) begin or start suddenly. 갑자기 일어나다[시작되다]; 발생하다. ¶ *A fire broke out last night.* 간밤에 불이 났다 / *War has broken out.* 전쟁이 일어났다. **c**) exclaim. 부르짖다. ¶ *"What a fool I was !" he broke out.* "난 얼마나 바보였던가"하고 그는 외쳤다. **d**) (of a person or his body) become covered with.... (몸이) …으로 덮이다; …이 나다. ¶ ~ *out in* [*into*] *a sweat* 땀투성이가 되다 / *The child broke out with measles.* 아이는 홍역으로 몸에 발진이 돋았다.

break short, stop short. 중단하다.

break through, **a**) force a way through (a place); violate. …을 뚫고 나아가다; 돌파하다; 범하다. ¶ ~ *through the enemy's line* 적진을 돌파하다. **b**) make an appearance. 모습을 나타내다. ¶ *The sun broke through* (*the clouds*). 해가 구름 사이로 나타났다.

break up, **a**) put an end to (something); end; stop. …을 끝내다; 끝나다. **b**) scatter or be scattered; separate into parts. 흩뜨리다; (뿔뿔이) 흩어지다. ¶ *The crowd broke up.* 군중이 흩어졌다 / *The police managed to* ~ *up the angry crowd.* 경찰은 성난 군중을 무사히 해산시켰다. **c**) make or become weak in health, spirit, etc. (몸·정신을) 약하게 하다; 쇠약해지다; 좌절하다. **d**) change. 변하다. ¶ *The weather is breaking up.* 날씨가 변하고 있다.

break with, **a**) stop relations with (someone); quarrel with. …와 관계를 끊다; …와 말다툼하다. **b**) depart from. …에서 벗어나다. ¶ ~ *with tradition* 전통에서 벗어나다.

— *n.* Ⓒ **1** a gap; a broken place; an opening. 갈라진[터진] 데. ¶ *a* ~ *in the wall* 벽의 갈라진 틈. **2** a short rest; a pause in work, etc. 짧은 휴식. ¶ *work without a* ~ 휴식 없이 일하다 / *a coffee* ~ 커피 타임. **3** the beginning. 시작. ¶ *at* ~ *of day* 새벽에. **4** a sudden change. 급변. **5** (in boxing) the act of separating after a clinch. (권투의) 브레이크. **6** a fault. 결점. **7** failure. 실패. **8** 《*colloq.*》 a good chance; a piece of good luck. 좋은 기회. [E.]

break·a·ble [bréikəbəl] *adj.* easily broken. 잘 깨지는. — *n.* 《*pl.*》 breakable things. 깨지기 쉬운 것[물체].

break·age [bréikidʒ] *n.* Ⓤ **1** the act of breaking; a break. 파손. **2** things broken; damage or loss caused by breaking.

파손물; 파손으로 인한 손실.

break·down [bréikdàun] *n.* Ⓒ **1** (of a train or machine) trouble; a failure to work. 고장. ¶ *a ~ of machinery* 기계의 고장. **2** loss of health; weakness. 건강 장애; 쇠약. ¶ *a nervous ~* 신경 쇠약 / *have a ~ in health* 건강이 쇠하다. **3** a failure in business, etc. 몰락; 실패. **4** an analysis. 분석.

break·er [bréikər] *n.* Ⓒ **1** a person or thing that breaks. 깨는〔부수는〕 사람〔것〕. ¶ *a ~ of idols* 우상 파괴자. **2** a wave that breaks into foam on the shore or rocks. 부딪쳐 부서지는 파도.

:break·fast [brékfəst] *n.* ⓊⒸ the first meal of the day. 조반(朝飯). ¶ *at ~* 아침식사 때에 / *have a good ~* 훌륭한 조반을 들다. — *vi.* (P1) eat breakfast. 아침 식사를 들다. ¶ *~ on bread* 빵으로 조반을 들다. — *vt.* (P6) supply (someone) with breakfast. …에게 조반을 내다〔주다〕. [*break, fast*]

break·neck [bréiknèk] *adj.* very dangerous, esp. because it is too fast. (과속으로) 매우 위험한. ¶ *at ~ speed* 살인적인 스피드로.

break·through [bréikθrùː] *n.* Ⓒ 《mil.》 a movement or advance through and beyond an enemy's line. (적의 방어선) 돌파.

break·up [bréikʌ̀p] *n.* **1** collapse; dispersal. 붕괴; 해산. **2** a separation. (부부 등의) 절교; 절연; 별거.

break·wa·ter [bréikwɔ̀ːtər, -wɑ̀t-] *n.* Ⓒ a wall to protect a harbor against waves. 방파제(cf. *mole*³).

bream [briːm] *n.* Ⓒ (*pl.* **breams** or *collectively* **bream**) a fresh-water fish of the carp family. 잉어의 한 가지; 도미류. [Teut.]

:breast [brest] *n.* Ⓒ **1** the upper, front part of the human and animal body; the chest. 가슴; 흉부. ¶ *a pain in the ~* 가슴앓이 / *press a child to one's ~* 어린애를 꼭 껴안다 / *bare one's ~* 가슴을 드러내다. **2** the upper, front part of a coat, dress, etc. 옷의 가슴 부분. **3** the gland that gives milk. 유방; 젖가슴. ¶ *give the ~ to a baby* 아기에게 젖을 주다 / *take* 〔*suck*〕 *the ~* (아기가) 젖을 빨다. **4** heart; feelings. 가슴속; 마음. ¶ *have a troubled ~* 걱정이 있다.

make a clean breast of, confess (something) completely. …을 숨김 없이 고백하다.

— *vt.* (P6) advance against (something); face (something) with resolution. …을 무릅쓰고 나아가다; …에 맞서다. ¶ *~ the waves* 파도를 헤치고 나아가다. [E.]

breast·bone [bréstbòun] *n.* Ⓒ the thin, flat bone in the front of the chest to which the ribs are attached. 흉골(胸骨).

breast-high [brésthái] *adj.* reaching to the height of the breast. 가슴 높이의.

breast·plate [bréstplèit] *n.* Ⓒ **1** a piece of armor for the breast, used in the Middle Ages. (갑옷의) 가슴받이. **2** a garment ornamented with jewels, worn by a Jewish high priest. (유대교의 고위 성직자가 가슴에 드리우는 보석 장식의) 가슴받이.

breast·stroke [bréststròuk] *n.* Ⓤ 《*the ~*》 a kind of swimming style in which a swimmer moves both his hands from the head to the sides, at the same time moving the legs in a frog kick. 평영(平泳); 개구리 헤엄.

breast·work [bréstwə̀ːrk] *n.* Ⓒ a low, quickly-built wall for defense. 흉벽(胸壁).

:breath [breθ] *n.* **1** Ⓤ air drawn into and let out of the lungs. 숨; 호흡. **2** Ⓒ a single act of breathing. 한 호흡. ¶ *take* 〔*draw*〕 *a deep ~* 심호흡하다 / *get* 〔*recover*〕 *one's ~* 숨을 돌리다 / *give up one's ~* 숨이 끊어지다 / *lose one's ~* 숨이 차 헐떡이다. **3** Ⓒ a light, gentle wind; a slight movement in the air. 미풍. **4** Ⓤ spirit; life. 생기; 활기; 생명. ¶ *the ~ of spring* 봄기운. [E.=smell]

at a breath, with one breath. 단숨에.

below 〔***under***〕 ***one's breath,*** in a whisper; not to be heard. 작은 목소리로. ¶ *The boy protested under his ~.* 소년은 작은 목소리로 항의했다.

catch one's breath, **a**) stop breathing for a moment. 잠시 숨을 멈추다. **b**) gasp or pant. 헐떡이다; 숨이 차다.

draw a long breath, give a sign of relief. 안도의 한숨을 쉬다.

draw one's breath, breathe; live. 살아 있다.

hold 〔***keep***〕 ***one's breath,*** **a**) stop breathing. 숨을 멈추다. **b**) 《*fig.*》 be in a state of tension. 숨을 죽이다.

in a breath, at a breath; unanimously. 입을 모아; 이구 동성으로.

in the same breath, at the same time. 동시에.

not a breath of..., no... at all. …이 전혀 없는. ¶ *There is not a ~ of air.* 바람 한 점 없다.

out of breath, breathless, as from too much exercise. 숨을 헐떡이며; 숨이 차서.

save one's breath, keep quiet. 잠자코 있다.

spend 〔***waste***〕 ***one's breath,*** talk vainly. 쓸데없는 소리를 하다.

take breath, pause; rest. 잠시 쉬다; 한숨 돌리다.

take someone's breath away, surprise. 깜짝 놀라게 하다.

(***with***) ***one's last breath,*** (at) the end of life; (as) a last action. 임종에 즈음하여; 최후로.

:breathe [briːð] *vi., vt.* **1** (P1;2A) draw air into and let it out of lungs; respire. 숨쉬다. ¶ *When a man stops breathing, he dies.* 사람은 숨을 멈출 때 죽는다. **2** (P1; 6) give or take time to breathe. 쉬(게 하)다. ¶ *~ a horse* 말을 쉬게 하다. **3** (P6) speak softly; whisper. 속삭이다. ¶ *~ words of love* 사랑을 속삭이다. **4** (P6,7) give out; express. 발산하다; 나타내다. ¶ *The flower breathes perfume.* 그 꽃은 향기롭다 / *He breathed a sigh of relief.* 그는 안도의 한숨을

내쉬었다. **5** (P1,2A) be alive; live. 살아 있다. **6** (P6) put out of breath. 헐떡이게 하다. ¶ *I was so breathed that I couldn't walk.* 너무 숨이 차서 걸을 수가 없었다. [↑]

breathe again (***freely***), recover calmness; feel easy. 한숨 돌리다.

breathe a word against, grumble at. …에 불평을 하다.

breathe one's last (***breath***), die. 숨을 거두다; 죽다.

not breathe a word of, keep a secret; say nothing of. 비밀을 지키다; 아무 말도 안 하다.

breath·er [brí:ðər] *n.* Ⓒ **1** a short interval for rest. (짧은) 휴식. ¶ *take* (*have*) *a ~ after a heavy work* 격심한 일을 한 뒤 한숨 쉬다. **2** a vigorous exercise that causes heavy breathing. (숨차게 하는) 과격한 운동.

breath·ing [brí:ðiŋ] *n.* **1** Ⓤ the act of one that breathes. 호흡. **2** Ⓒ the time needed for a single breath; a moment. 순간. **3** Ⓒ a gentle breeze. 미풍.

breathing space [∸-∸] *n.* sufficient room or time to breathe easily; a pause to rest or think. 숨돌릴(생각할) 여유(틈, 공간).

breath·less* [bréθlis] *adj.* **1 out of breath. 숨찬. ¶ *I was ~ after the long run.* 나는 오래 뛰고 난 뒤에 숨이 찼다. **2** such as to cause shortness of breath; unable to breathe because of fear, interest, or excitement. 숨 막히게 하는; (공포 따위로) 숨이 막히는. ¶ *a ~ speed* 숨막히는 속도 / *with ~ interest* 숨을 죽이고 / *~ with fear* 공포로 숨막히는 / *~ listeners of the mystery story* 기괴한 이야기에 숨을 죽이고 듣는 사람들. **3** dead; lifeless. 죽은. **4** without a breeze. 바람 한 점 없는. ¶ *a ~ summer evening* 바람 한 점 없는 여름밤.

**breath·less·ly* [bréθlisli] *adv.* in a breathless manner. 숨을 헐떡이며; 숨을 죽이고.

breath-tak·ing [bréθtèikiŋ] *adj.* causing a thrill; exciting. 스릴 넘치는; 아슬아슬한. ¶ *~ horse-riding* 스릴 넘치는 말타기.

bred* [bred] *v.* p. and pp. of **breed.
— *adj.* brought up in a certain way. …하게 자란. ¶ *ill-bred* 버릇 없이 자란 / *city-bred people* 도시에서 자란 사람들.

breech [bri:tʃ] *n.* Ⓒ **1** the lower part of the back. 궁둥이. **2** the back part of a gun or cannon. 총미(銃尾); 포미(砲尾). [M.E. *breeche*]

breech·es [brítʃiz] *n. pl.* **1** short trousers reaching to the knees. 바지《승마용》. **2** 《*colloq.*》 trousers. (반)바지. [↑]

wear the breeches, rule one's husband. 남편을 휘어잡다; 내주장하다.

breed* [bri:d] *vt., vi.* (bred**) **1** (P6;1) produce (young); bear offspring. (새끼를) 낳다; 번식하다(시키다). ¶ *Mice ~ rapidly.* 생쥐들은 급속히 번식한다. **2** (P6) cause (plants or animals) to grow; raise. 기르다; 사육(재배)하다. ¶ *He breeds cattle for market.* 그는 소를 시장에 팔기 위해 기른다. **3** (P6) educate; bring up; train. 가르치다; 양육하다; 훈련하다. ¶ *He was bred to be a gentleman.* 그는 자라서 신사가 되었다. **4** (P6) be the cause of (something); bring about; result in. (바람직하지 않은 일)을 일으키다; 야기하다; 낳다. ¶ *Poverty breeds crime.* 가난은 범죄를 낳는다 / *Ignorance breeds prejudice.* 무지는 편견을 낳는다.
— *n.* Ⓒ a race or a family with the same qualities; a stock. 종속(種屬); 가계(家系); 품종. ¶ *Terriers and poodles are breeds of dogs.* 테리어와 푸들은 개의 품종이다. [E.]

breed·er [brí:dər] *n.* Ⓒ **1** a person who raises animals. 사육자. ¶ *a dog ~* 개 사육자. **2** an animal that produces young. 종축(種畜). ¶ *rapid breeders* 번식이 빠른 동물. **3** a cause; a source. 원인; 원천.

breed·ing [brí:diŋ] *n.* Ⓤ **1** the act of producing young. 번식(繁殖); 부화. ¶ *the ~ season* 번식기. **2** training; education; good manners and behavior. 양육; 훈육; 교육; 예절. ¶ *a man of ~* 교양 있는 사람 / *He lacks ~.* 그는 예절(교양)이 없다.

:breeze[1] [bri:z] *n.* Ⓒ **1** a gentle wind. 미풍. ¶ *spring breezes* 봄의 미풍 **2** 《Brit. *colloq.*》 a slight quarrel. 싸움; 말다툼. ¶ *kick up a ~* 소동을 일으키다. **3** idle talk. 허튼소리. ¶ *shoot the ~* 허풍떨다. **4** 《U.S.》 something easily done. 손쉬운 일. —*vi.* 《*colloq.*》 blow calmly. 산들바람이 불다. ¶ *It was breezing offshore.* 산들바람이 앞바다 쪽으로 불고 있었다. [Sp.]

breeze[2] [bri:z] *n.* a gadfly. 등에. [E.]

breeze[3] [bri:z] *n.* Ⓤ coal dust. 분탄(粉炭). [F. *braise*]

breez·y [brí:zi] *adj.* (**breez·i·er, breez·i·est**) **1** having a breeze; with light winds blowing. 산들바람이 부는; 바람이 잘 통하는. **2** lively; fresh; cheerful. 발랄한. ¶ *He had a ~ manner.* 그는 발랄했다 / *We enjoyed his ~ talk.* 우리는 그의 유쾌한 이야기를 즐겼다. [*breeze*[1]]

brent·goose [bréntgù:s] *n.* 《bird》 the smallest kind of wild goose. 흑기러기. [? G. *handgans*]

breth·ren* [bréðrən] *n. pl.* (*sing.* **broth·er) the members of a church or society. (같은 교회의) 신자; (같은 협회의) 회원; 동지. [E.=brothers]

Bret·on [brétən] *adj.* of Brittany, a region of northwestern France. 브리타니의. — *n.* a native of Brittany. 브리타니 사람. [→Britain]

breve [bri:v] *n.* a curved mark (˘) placed over a vowel to show that it is short. 단음 기호. [L. *brevis* short]

brev·et [brəvét, brévit] *n.* 《mil.》 a commission promoting an army officer to a higher rank without an increase in pay. 명

예 승진. ¶ *a ~ rank* 명예 계급. [↑]

bre·vi·a·ry [brí:vièri, brév-] *n.* a book of prayers to be said daily by priests of the Roman Catholic Church. 일과(日課) 기도서. [↑]

brev·i·ty [brévəti] *n.* Ⓤ **1** shortness of time. (시간 따위의) 짧음; 덧없음. ¶ *~ of human life* 인생의 덧없음. **2** briefness; conciseness. 간결. ¶ *Brevity is the soul of wit.* 간결은 기지의 요체이다. [↑]

brew [bru:] *vt., vi.* **1** (P6;1) make (beer, wine, etc.) through chemical change caused by bacteria. 양조(釀造)하다. **2** (P6; 1) make (a drink) by boiling or mixing. (섞거나 끓이거나 하여) 마실 것을 만들다; 조합하다. ¶ *~ tea* 차를 끓이다. **3** (P1) grow to ripeness. 익다. **4** (P6) plan; plot; try to bring about. …을 꾀하다; 기도(企圖)하다. ¶ *Your children are brewing some mischief.* 댁의 아이들이 짓궂은 장난을 꾀하고 있습니다. **5** (P1) impend; begin to form. (폭풍 따위가) 일어나려고 하다. — *n.* Ⓒ a drink that is brewed. 양조물. [E.]

brew·er [brú:ər] *n.* Ⓒ a person who makes beer, ale, etc. (맥주 등의) 양조업자.

brew·er·y [brú:əri] *n.* Ⓒ (*pl.* **-er·ies**) a place where beer, ale, etc., are made. (맥주 따위의) 양조장.

bri·ar [bráiər] *n.* =brier[1]; brier[2].

·bribe [braib] *n.* Ⓒ money or other gift given to someone to get his help, favor, etc., dishonestly. 뇌물(賂物). — *vt.* (P6) influence (someone) by giving a bribe. (아무)를 매수하다. ¶ *~ the official* 관리를 매수하다. ● **brib(e)·a·ble** [bráibəbəl] *adj.* **brib·er** [-ər] *n.* [F.=piece of bread]

brib·er·y [bráibəri] *n.* Ⓤ **1** the act of giving or offering as a bribe. 증회(贈賄). **2** the act of taking a bribe. 수회(收賄). ¶ *Bribery is said to be common among politicians.* 정치인들 사이에서는 증수회가 일반적으로 행해진다고들 한다.

bric-a-brac [bríkəbræ̀k] *n.* Ⓤ small things of former times having artistic value. 골동품. [F.]

:brick [brik] *n.* ⓊⒸ (*pl.* **bricks** or *collectively* **brick**) **1** a block of clay baked by sun or fire, used in building a house or paving a street. 벽돌. ¶ *build a house of red ~* 붉은 벽돌집을 짓다. **2** Ⓒ anything shaped like a brick. 벽돌 모양의 것. **3** Ⓒ 《*colloq.*》 a cheerful kindhearted person; a good fellow. 선량한 사람; 쾌남아. ¶ *He is a regular ~.* 그는 정말 믿음직한[좋은] 녀석이다.

drop a brick, do or say something careless or foolish. 실수[실언]하다.

make bricks without straw, attempt hard and unsuccessful work. 헛수고하다.

— *adj.* made of bricks. 벽돌로 된.

— *vt.* (P6,7) build or pave (something) with bricks. 벽돌로 짓다[깔다]. ● **brick·like** [⌐làik] *adj.* [F.=fragment]

brick·bat [bríkbæ̀t] *n.* a broken piece of brick, esp. one used for throwing. 벽돌 조각.

brick·lay·er [bríklèiər] *n.* Ⓒ a person whose work is building with bricks. 벽돌공.

brick·lay·ing [bríklèiiŋ] *n.* brickwork. 벽돌 쌓기[공사].

brick·work [bríkwə̀:rk] *n.* Ⓤ a thing made of bricks. 벽돌로 지은 것; 벽돌 쌓기.

brick·yard [bríkjɑ̀:rd] *n.* Ⓒ a place where bricks are made or sold. 벽돌 공장[제조장].

brid·al [bráidl] *adj.* of a bride or a wedding. 신부의; 혼인의. ¶ *a ~ veil* 신부의 면사포. — *n.* Ⓒ a wedding. 결혼식. [E.]

:bride [braid] *n.* Ⓒ a woman just married or about to be married. 신부; 새색시. [E.]

bride·cake [bráidkèik] *n.* ⒸⓊ a wedding cake. 웨딩 케이크.

·bride·groom [bráidgrù(:)m] *n.* Ⓒ a man just married or about to be married. 신랑.

brides·maid [bráidzmèid] *n.* Ⓒ a young, usu. unmarried woman attending on the bride at a wedding. (미혼의) 신부 들러리.

bride·well [bráidwel, -wəl] *n.* a jail; a house of correction. 구치소; 교도소. [Place]

:bridge[1] [bridʒ] *n.* Ⓒ **1** a structure built over a river, road, etc., that can be crossed. 다리. ¶ *a floating ~* 부교(浮橋); 배다리. **2** a platform above the deck of a ship. 선교(船橋); 함교(艦橋). **3** the upper, bony part of the nose. 콧마루; 콧등. **4** a metal clip for keeping false teeth in place. (틀니의) 브리지; 가공(架工) 의치. **5** a movable piece over which the strings of a violin, etc., are stretched. (현악기의) 기러기발.

burn one's bridges (***behind one***), cut off all chances to return; make a decision which cannot be changed. 배수진을 치다; 변경할 수 없는 결심을 하다.

— *vt.* (P6) **1** build a bridge over (something). …에 다리를 놓다. ¶ *~ the river* 강에 다리를 놓다. **2** extend over; make a passage over (something). (둘 사이)에 다리를 놓다; 이어주다. **3** overcome. 극복하다. ¶ *~ over difficulties* 난관을 이겨내다. [E.]

bridge[2] [bridʒ] *n.* Ⓤ a kind of card game. 브리지《카드놀이》.

bridge·head [brídʒhèd] *n.* Ⓒ **1** a defense covering or protecting the end of a bridge; a protected place on the enemy's side of a river. 교두보. **2** the approach to a bridge. 다리의 끝 부분.

·bri·dle [bráidl] *n.* Ⓒ **1** the head part of a horse's leather bands, by which the rider can control a horse. (말의) 굴레. ¶ *give a horse the ~* 말고삐를 늦추다. **2** anything that holds back or controls. 제어하는 것;

구속물. ¶ *put* 〔*lay*〕 *a* ~ *on one's tongue* 입을 다물다; 말을 삼가다 / *put a* ~ *on one's passions* 감정을 억제하다.
— *vt.* (P6) **1** put a bridle on (a horse). …에 굴레를 씌우다; 고삐를 달다. **2** bring (something) under control. …을 제어〔억제〕하다. ¶ *You must* ~ *your anger.* 자네는 노염을 억제해야 한다.
— *vi.* (P1,3) hold the head up high with the chin drawn back; draw up the head in anger. (경멸·분개·뽐내느라) 고개를 빳빳이 하고 얼굴을 잦히다; 머리를 쳐들고 으쓱대다.
• **bri·dler** [-dlər] *n.* [E.]

:**brief** [bri:f] *adj.* **1** (of time) short. (시간이) 짧은. ¶ *a* ~ *life* 덧없는 인생 / *a* ~ *meeting* 짧은 회합. **2** using few words; concise. 간단한; 간략한. ¶ *a* ~ *letter* 간략한 편지 / ~ *remarks* 간단한 말.
to be brief, in short. 간단히〔요약해서〕 말하면.
— *n.* Ⓒ (*pl.* **briefs**) **1** a short statement; a summary. 요점; 개요. ¶ *a* ~ *report on weather conditions* 일기 개황 / *have plenty of briefs* (변호사가) 바쁘다; 일이 많다. **2** an outline of a law case spoken by lawyers in court. 소송 사건의 개요〔요지〕서. **3** 《*pl.*》 close-fitting, legless underpants. 짧은 팬츠.
hold a brief (=*defend; support*) **for** *someone.* …을 변호〔지지〕하다. ¶ *He holds a* ~ *for me.* 그는 나를 변호한다.
in brief, in a few words; in short. 간단히; 요컨대.
make brief of, do or perform very quickly. …을 재빨리 해치우다.
— *vt.* (P6) **1** give a brief instruction to (someone). …에게 간단한 지시를 하다. **2** furnish with a brief. 요지서를 제출하다. [→breve]

brief·case [brí:fkèis] *n.* a flat case, usu. made of leather, for carrying loose papers, books, drawings, etc. 서류 가방.

***brief·ly** [brí:fli] *adv.* in brief; shortly. 간단히.

bri·er[1] [bráiər] *n.* Ⓒ 《bot.》 a thorny plant or bush of the rose family; a wild rose. 찔레나무. [E.]

bri·er[2] [bráiər] *n.* **1** ⒸⓊ 《bot.》 a white heath tree found in southern Europe, the root of which is used in making tobacco pipes. 브라이어; 히스《유럽산 석남과의 관목》. **2** Ⓒ a tobacco pipe made of this root. (그 뿌리로 만든) 브라이어 파이프. [E.]

brig [brig] *n.* Ⓒ a ship with two masts and square sails. (쌍돛대의) 범선(帆船). [*brigantine*]

bri·gade [brigéid] *n.* Ⓒ **1** a military unit smaller than a division. 여단(旅團). **2** a group of people organized for some purpose. 대(隊); 조(組). ¶ *a fire* ~ 소방대. [It. *brigare* skirmish]

brig·a·dier [brìgədíər] *n.* Ⓒ an officer who commands a brigade; a brigadier general. 여단장; 준장. [↑]

brigadier general [⌐–– ⌐––] *n.* 《U.S.》 an army officer ranking between colonel and major general. 준장(准將).

brig·and [brígənd] *n.* Ⓒ a man who lives in the forests or mountains and who robs travelers on the road; a robber. 산적; 강도. [→brigade]

brig·and·age [brígəndidʒ] *n.* Ⓤ the act of robbing by force. 강탈. [↑]

:**bright** [brait] *adj.* **1** giving much light. 빛나는; 밝은. ¶ ~ *sunlight* 빛나는 햇빛 / ~ *eyes* 반짝이는 눈 / (*as*) ~ *as a button* 〔*new pin*〕 번쩍번쩍하는. **2** very light or clear. 화창한; 활짝 갠. ¶ *a* ~ *day* 화창한 날씨 (opp. dark). **3** quick at learning; clever. 머리좋은; 영리한(opp. dull). ¶ *A* ~ *student learns quickly.* 머리좋은 학생은 빨리 배운다 / *He is the brightest boy in the class.* 그는 반에서 가장 우수한 학생이다 / *a* ~ *boy* 영리한 소년. **4** glowing; vivid. (색채가) 선명한. ¶ ~ *colors* 선명한 색채 / ~ *red* 선홍색. **5** lively; cheerful. 쾌활한; 즐거운. ¶ *a* ~ *smile* 명랑한 미소 / ~ *looks* 밝은 표정 / *Everybody was* ~ *and cheerful at the party.* 파티 석상에서 어느 누구할 것 없이 명랑하고 즐거웠다. **6** promising; favorable; splendid. 유망한; 화려한. ¶ *a* ~ *reputation* 화려한 명성 / ~ *prospects for the future* 미래에 대한 밝은 전망.
bright and early, early in the morning. 아침 일찍.
bright in the eye, slightly intoxicated. 거나하게 취해서.
look on the bright side of, take an optimistic view of. …을 낙관하다.
— *adv.* in a bright manner. 환하게. [E.]

***bright·en** [bráitn] *vt.* (P6) make (something) bright; make (someone) happy or cheerful. …을 빛나게〔밝게〕 하다; 유쾌하게〔즐겁게〕 하다. ¶ ~ *silver* 은을 번쩍이게 하다 / ~ *a room with flowers* 꽃으로 꾸며 방을 환하게 하다. — *vi.* (P1) become bright; become happy or cheerful. 밝아지다; 즐거워〔유쾌해〕지다.

***bright·ly** [bráitli] *adv.* in a bright manner. 빛나게; 환하게.

***bright·ness** [bráitnis] *n.* Ⓤ the quality of being bright. 빛남; 선명; 쾌활; 총명.

Bright's disease [bráits dizì:z] *n.* 《med.》 nephritis. 신장염(腎臟炎). [Person]

brill [bril] *n.* Ⓒ (*pl.* **brills** or *collectively* **brill**) 《fish》 a flat-fish. 넙치류. [E.]

bril·liance [bríljəns], **-lian·cy** [-si] *n.* Ⓤ **1** great brightness; glitter. 광휘; 광채; 광택. **2** splendor; magnificence. 훌륭함. **3** great ability; keen intelligence. 슬기; 재기(才氣) (발랄). ¶ *a linguist of great* ~ 재기가 넘쳐 흐르는 언어학자. [↓]

:**bril·liant** [bríljənt] *adj.* **1** shining brightly; very bright. 빛나는; 번쩍이는. ¶ ~ *sun-*

shine 빛나는 햇빛 / *a* ~ *diamond ring* 번쩍이는 다이아몬드 반지. **2** splendid; magnificent. 훌륭한. ¶ *a* ~ *discovery* 훌륭한 발견. **3** having great ability; very clever. 재기 있는; 두뇌가 날카로운. ¶ *a* ~ *idea* 멋진 아이디어 〔생각〕 / *a* ~ *scientist* 뛰어난 과학자. —*n.* Ⓒ a diamond or other gem cut so as to sparkle greatly. 브릴리언트형(型)의 다이아몬드〔보석〕. [→beryl]

bril·liant·ly [bríljəntli] *adv.* in a brilliant manner. 번쩍번쩍; 찬연히; 훌륭히.

·**brim** [brim] *n.* Ⓒ 《usu. *the* ~》 **1** the edge of a cup, bowl, etc.; a rim. (그릇의) 전; 가장자리. ¶ *I have filled my glass to the* ~. 나는 술잔을 가장자리까지 가득 채웠다. **2** the projecting edge of a hat. 모자의 챙〔양태〕 (cf. *rim*). **3** the edge bordering water. (샘·강 따위의) 물가; 둔치.

full to the brim, completely full. 가장자리까지 가득(차게).

—*v.* (**brimmed, brim·ming**) *vi.* (P1,2A) be full to the brim. 가장자리까지 가득 차다. ¶ *Her eyes brimmed with tears.* 그녀의 눈에는 눈물이 가득 고여있었다.

—*vt.* (P6,13) fill (a glass, etc.) to the brim. (컵 따위)를 전〔가장자리〕까지 가득 채우다. ¶ ~ *a glass* (*with wine*) 술잔을〔술잔에 포도주를〕 가득 채우다.

brim over with, be full of. …로 가득 차다. ¶ *He is brimming over with health and spirits.* 그는 기력이 넘쳐날 듯하다.

● **brim·less** [-lis] *adj.* [E.]

brim·ful, -full [brímfúl] *adj.* full to the brim. 전까지 가득 찬. ¶ 《*fig.*》 ~ *of humor* 〔*mischief*〕 유머〔장난기〕가 가득한.

brim·mer [brímər] *n.* a full cup. 찰랑찰랑하게 따른 컵〔잔〕.

brim·stone [brímstòun] *n.* Ⓤ a pale-yellow substance that burns with a blue flame and strong smell. 황. [*burn, stone*]

brin·dled [bríndld] *adj.* (esp. of cows, dogs, etc.) gray, tan, or brown with darker streaks and spots. 얼룩빛의; 어룽더룽한. ¶ *a* ~ *cat* 얼룩 고양이. [*brand*]

brine [brain] *n.* Ⓤ **1** very salty water. 소금물; 염수. **2** 《*the* ~》 a salt lake; the sea; the ocean. 함수호(鹹水湖); 바다. [E.]

:**bring** [briŋ] *vt.* (**brought**) **1** (P6,13,14) come with; be accompanied by (something or someone); carry. …을 데려오다; 가져오다; 날라오다. ¶ ~ *someone a book* = ~ *a book to someone* 아무에게 책을 가져다 주다 / ~ *one's friend to a party* 파티에 친구를 데리고 가다 / *Bring me the book from the room.* 방에서 책 좀 가져다 주게 / *Bring it* (*to*) *me* / *She brought a doctor with her.* 그녀는 의사를 데리고 왔다 / *I will* ~ *the photographs with me when I come* (*to your house*). 내가 갈 때 사진을 가지고 가겠다. **2** (P6,7,13,14) make (someone) come; cause to come. …을 오게 하다. ¶ *What has brought you here?* 무슨 일로 왔는가 / *Her scream brought the police.* 그녀가 외치는 소리를 듣고 경찰이 달려왔다. **3** (P6,7,13,14) persuade; lead. …하도록 하다; …하도록 이끌다. ¶ *I couldn't* ~ *myself to believe it.* 도저히 그것을 믿을 마음이 나지 않았다. **4** (P6,7,13) cause to come into a certain state or condition. (어떤 상태·동작·현상으로) 되게 하다. ¶ ~ *a matter to a close* 〔*an end*〕 일을 끝나게 하다〔끝내다〕 / ~ *a car to a stop* 차를 멈추다 / ~ *the law into effect* 법의 효력을 발생시키다 / ~ *one's temper under control* 언짢은 마음을 가라앉히다 / *be brought to disgrace* 치욕을 당하다. **5** (P7) sell for; fetch (a price). …에 팔리다. ¶ *These cars will* ~ *a good price.* 이 차들은 좋은 값에 팔릴 게다. **6** 《law》 present in a law court; start (a legal action) against (someone). 소송을 제기하다. ¶ ~ *an action for damages* 손해 배상 소송을 제기하다 / ~ *an action against the lawyer* 변호사를 상대로 소송을 제기하다. [E.]

bring about, cause (something) to happen; accomplish. …을 일으키다; …을 이루다. ¶ ~ *about a great change* 큰 변화를 일으키다 / ~ *about the desired result* 바라던 결과를 이루다.

bring along, 《U.S.》 carry with oneself. …을 가지고 가다. ¶ ~ *a gun along* 총을 갖고 가다.

bring around 〔***round***〕, **a**) make (someone) recover consciousness. …의 의식을 회복시키다. **b**) 《*to*》 persuade. …을 설득하다.

bring back, **a**) return to its owner or to the right place; put back. 되돌려 주다〔놓다〕. ¶ *Don't forget to* ~ *it back.* 그것을 잊지 말고 되돌려 주게나. **b**) call to mind; remember. …을 상기시키다. ¶ *The song brought my boyhood back to me.* 그 노래는 나에게 소년 시절을 상기시켰다.

bring** something **home to ⇨home.

bring down, **a**) cause (something) to come down. …을 떨어〔내려〕뜨리다. **b**) cause (something) to lessen; make (prices) low. …을 덜하게 하다; (값을) 내리(게 하)다. ¶ *The price was brought down to* £*5.* 가격이 5파운드로 내렸다. **c**) kill or wound. (총격·타격 등으로) 죽이다; 부상입히다. ¶ ~ *a deer down with rifle fire* 라이플 총으로 사슴을 쓰러뜨리다 / *A shot brought down a bird.* 총 한 방에 새를 잡았다.

bring down the house, carry the house. 만장의 갈채를 받다.

bring forth, **a**) give birth to; bear; produce. …을 낳다; (열매)를 맺다. ¶ ~ *forth young* 새끼를 낳다 / ~ *forth good results* 좋은 결과를 맺다. **b**) make known; disclose; show. (일반에게) 알리다; 보이다.

bring forward, **a**) present for consideration; introduce. 제안〔제시〕하다; 소개하다. ¶ ~ *forward an opinion* 의견을 제시하다 / *Who brought that evidence forward?* 누가 그 증거를 제시했는가. **b**) bring to view; show. 공개하다; 보이다. ¶ *Bring forward the prisoner.*

그 죄수를 끌어내라. **c**) advance. 앞당기다. ¶ *They decided to ~ the meeting forward from May 9 to May 3.* 그들은 회합 일자를 5월 9일에서 5월 3일로 앞당기기로 했다.
bring in, **a**) introduce. …을 들여오다. **b**) yield or produce (profits, etc.). (이익 따위를) 가져오다. ¶ *It will ~ in a lot of money.* 그것은 많은 돈을 벌게 할 것이다. **c**) declare (guilty or not guilty). (판결을) 선고하다.
bring into play, call into activity. 활동시키다.
bring into the world, give birth to. 낳다.
bring off, **a**) 《*colloq.*》 accomplish; achieve; be successful in. 이룩[성취]하다; 성공하다. **b**) rescue. 구조하다.
bring on, cause (something) to happen; lead to. …을 일으키다; 가져오다. ¶ *Overwork will ~ on a bad illness.* 과로는 좋지 않은 병을 가져온다.
bring out, **a**) make clear; show (exhibit) clearly; expose. 밝히다; 분명히 보이다; 폭로하다. ¶ *~ out the contrast of colors* 색깔의 대조를 또렷이 나타내다 / *~ out a fact* 사실을 폭로하다. **b**) bring before the public; publish. 발표하다; 출판하다. ¶ *~ out a book* 책을 출판하다. **c**) introduce (someone) to society. …을 사교계에 등장시키다.
bring over, persuade; cause (someone) to change an opinion. …을 설득하다; 아무로 하여금 생각을 바꾸게 하다. ¶ *~ other persons over to one's way of thinking* 남들로 하여금 자신의 사고 방식에 따르게 하다.
bring through, save (a sick person, etc.) (환자 등을) 구하다.
bring to, **a**) make (someone) recover consciousness. …의 의식을 회복시키다. **b**) cause (a ship) to stop. (배를) 멈추게 하다.
bring under, **a**) conquer; subdue. 굴복시키다; 진압하다. **b**) include (in a class). (…부류)에 포함시키다.
bring up, **a**) take care of (someone) in his childhood; rear; educate. (어릴 때) 보살피다; 기르다; 양육하다; 가르치다. ¶ *~ up three children* 세 아이를 기르다 / *I was brought up to be a lady.* 나는 숙녀가 되도록 교육받았다. **b**) introduce (a matter) for consideration or discussion; suggest; call attention to. (의제 따위를) 꺼내다; 제출하다; …에 대해 주의를 환기하다. ¶ *~ up a new subject* 새로운 화제를 꺼내다. **c**) begin to speak of (something). …에 언급하다. **d**) send up (food, etc.) from stomach through mouth; vomit. 게우다; 토하다. **e**) anchor (a ship); stop suddenly. (배가) 닻을 내려 멈추다; 갑자기 멈추다.

brink [briŋk] *n.* Ⓒ **1** 《usu. *the ~*》 the edge of a steep place or of land bordering water. 벼랑 따위의 끝[가장자리]; 물가. **2** a serious or dangerous situation. 위험; 위경(危境); 아슬아슬한 고비. [Scand.]
on the brink of, very near; on the point of (something). 바야흐로 …하려는 차에. ¶ *They were on the ~ of war.* 그들은 전쟁의 위험에 처해 있었다.

brin·y [bráini] *adj.* (**brin·i·er, brin·i·est**) of or like brine; salty. 소금물의; 짠. ¶ *a ~ taste* 짠 맛. — *n.* 《*sl.*》 the sea. 바다. [*brine*]

bri·quet, -quette [brikét] *n.* a block of compressed coal dust. 연탄. [*brick*]

·brisk [brisk] *adj.* **1** quick and active; lively. 활기 있는; 활발한. ¶ *a ~ walk* 힘찬 걸음. **2** sharp. (날씨가) 매운; 차끈차끈한. ¶ *cold and ~ wind* 차갑고 모진 바람. **3** (of liquors) giving off bubbles of gas. (음료가) 거품이 자꾸 이는. ¶ *~ cider* 부글부글 거품이 이는 사과술. ● **brisk·ness** [-nis] *n.* [→brusque]

bris·ket [brískət] *n.* Ⓤ **1** the meat cut from the breast of an animal. (짐승의) 가슴 고기. **2** the breast of an animal. (동물의) 가슴. [→breast]

brisk·ly [brískli] *adv.* in a brisk manner. 활발하게; 세차게.

·bris·tle [brísəl] *n.* Ⓒ one of the short, hard, rough hairs of certain animals, esp. hogs, used to make brushes. 빳빳한 털; 강모(剛毛).
— *vi.* (P1,2A) **1** raise bristles in anger or fear. 털이 곤두서다. ¶ *The cat bristled.* 고양이가 털을 곤두세웠다. **2** 《*with*》 be full. (장애·곤란 따위로) 가득하다. ¶ *The project bristled with difficulties.* 그 계획은 곤란이 많았다. **3** show temper. 성내다. **4** show many sharp points; be thickly set. 빈틈없이 들어서다; 임립(林立)하다. ¶ *The city is bristling with high chimneys.* 그 도시는 높은 굴뚝들이 임립(林立)해 있다.
— *vt.* erect (something) like bristles. (털)을 곤두세우다. [E.]

bris·tly [brísəli] *adj.* **1** rough with bristles; having bristles. 빳빳한 털의(털이 많은). ¶ *a ~ chin* 빳빳한 털이 난 턱. **2** like bristles; short and stiff. 강모 같은; 짧고 빳빳한.

Brit. British.

:Brit·ain [brítən] *n.* England, Scotland, and Wales; Great Britain. 영국; 그레이트브리튼 섬. [L. *Brittania*]

Bri·tan·ni·a [britǽnjə, -niə] *n.* **1** Britain; Great Britain. 영국. **2** the British Empire. 대영 제국. **3** a woman figure symbolizing Britain or the British Empire used in coin, etc. 브리타니아 상(像)《영국을 상징하는 여인상》.

Bri·tan·nic [britǽnik] *adj.* of Britain; British. 영국의.

:Brit·ish [brítiʃ] *adj.* of Great Britain; of the British Empire, or its people. 그레이트브리튼의; 영(英)제국의; 영국인의.
British Commonwealth of Nations, the British Empire. 대영 제국.
— *n.* 《*the ~*》 people of Great Britain or the British Empire. 영국인.

Brit·ish·er [brítiʃər] *n.* Ⓒ a person of Britain. 영국인.

Brit·on [brítn] *n.* Ⓒ **1** a person of Great Britain or the British Empire. 그레이트브리튼 사람; 영국인. **2** one of the Celtic people who lived in south Britain at the time of the Roman invasion. (고대의) 브리튼 사람.

brit·tle [brítl] *adj.* very easily broken. 부서지기[깨지기] 쉬운. ¶ *Thin glass is* ~. 얇은 유리는 깨지기 쉽다. [E.]

broach [broutʃ] *n.* Ⓒ **1** a sharp-pointed, slender rod or bar to roast meat with. 고기 굽는 꼬치. **2** a tool to make holes with. 송곳. — *vt.* (P6) **1** open (a cask or barrel of beer, etc.) by making a hole. (통 따위)에 구멍을 뚫다. **2** begin to talk about (something); speak of (something) for the first time. …을 말하기 시작하다; …말을 꺼내다. ● **broach·er** [∠ər] *n.* [Rom.=spike]

:broad [brɔːd] *adj.* (opp. narrow). **1** wide from side to side. 폭이 넓은. ¶ *a* ~ *road* 넓은 길 / *be* ~ *of chest* 가슴 폭이 넓다. **2** vast; spacious. 광대한. ¶ *a* ~ *ocean* 망망한 대양. **3** not limited; liberal. (마음이) 넓은; 너그러운. ¶ *a* ~ *mind* 관대한 마음 / ~ *views* 너그러운 견해. **4** much; large in amount. (지식 등이) 많은; 깊은. ¶ ~ *knowledge* 넓은 지식. **5** plain; clear. 명백한; 노골적인. ¶ *a* ~ *fact* 분명한 사실. **6** main; general 주요한; 일반적인; 개략의. ¶ *in a* ~ *sense* 넓은 뜻으로는 / *the* ~ *outlines* 개략적인 윤곽. **7** not delicate; rough; uneducated. 거친; 조야한; 무학의.

in broad daylight, in the daytime. 한낮에.

It's as broad as it's long. It's all the same. 결국 마찬가지다; 오십보 백보이다.

— *n.* the broad part of anything. 폭이 넓은 부분. [E.]

broad bean [∠ ∠] *n.* a large eatable flat bean. 잠두(蠶豆).

broad·brim [brɔ́ːdbrìm] *n.* Ⓒ a hat with a very wide brim, esp. worn by Quakers. (퀘이커 교도가 쓰는) 챙이 넓은 모자.

·broad·cast [brɔ́ːdkæ̀st, -kɑ̀ːst] *vt., vi.* (**-cast** or **-cast·ed**) (P6; 1) **1** send out (news, etc.) by radio or television. 방송하다. ¶ *The Prime Minister will* ~ *his message tonight.* 수상은 오늘 밤 그의 메시지를 방송한다. **2** scatter widely; spread around. 흩뿌리다; 퍼뜨리다. ¶ ~ *a secret* 비밀을 퍼뜨리다 / *The seed was* ~. 씨가 흩뿌려졌다. — *n.* ⓊⒸ **1** the act of broadcasting. 방송; 흩뿌림. **2** a thing or things broadcast; a radio program. 방송물; 방송 프로그램. — *adj.* **1** sent out by radio or television. 방송의. **2** scattered widely. 일반에게 널리 퍼진[전파된]. — *adv.* over a wide surface. 널리. [E.]

broad·cast·er [brɔ́ːdkæ̀stər, -kɑ̀ːstər] *n.* Ⓒ a person who broadcasts; an announcer. 방송자; 아나운서.

broad·cast·ing [brɔ́ːdkæ̀stiŋ, -kɑ̀ːst-] *n.* Ⓤ **1** the act of sending out speech, music, news, etc. by radio or television. 방송. **2** radio or television as a business. 방송업.

broad·cloth [brɔ́ːdklɔ̀ːθ / -klɔ̀θ] *n.* Ⓤ cloth of double width used in making shirts and dresses. (드레스·셔츠 용의) 폭이 넓은 고급 나사(羅紗).

broad·en [brɔ́ːdn] *vt., vi.* (P1; 6) make or become broad or broader. 넓게 하다; 넓어지다. ¶ ~ *one's mind* 마음을 넓게 하다 / *The river broadens* (*out*) *at this point.* 강은 이 지점에서 넓어진다.

broad-gauge [brɔ́ːdgèidʒ], **-gauged** [-gèidʒd] *adj.* **1** (of rails) having a gauge wider than the standard one. 광궤(廣軌)의. **2** broad-minded. 마음이 넓은.

broad jump [∠ ∠] *n.* a jump as long as possible. 멀리뛰기(cf. *high jump*).

broad·loom [brɔ́ːdlùːm] *adj.* woven on a wide loom in one color. 광폭직(廣幅織)의; 폭 넓게 짠. ¶ *a* ~ *carpet* 광폭직의 양탄자.

broad·ly [brɔ́ːdli] *adv.* widely; generally; about; nearly; openly. 널리; 개괄적으로; 대충; 솔직히.

broad-mind·ed [brɔ́ːdmáindid] *adj.* liberal; generous; without prejudice. 너그러운; 편견(偏見)이 없는. ● **broad·mind·ed·ness** [-nis] *n.*

broad·ness [brɔ́ːdnis] *n.* Ⓤ the quality of being broad. 넓음; 관대.

broad·sheet [brɔ́ːdʃìːt] *n.* Ⓒ a large sheet of paper printed on one side only. 한 면만 인쇄된 대판지(大版紙).

broad·side [brɔ́ːdsàid] *n.* Ⓒ **1** the whole side of a ship above the water line. 뱃전; 현측(舷側). **2** all the guns that can be fired from one side of a ship. 편현(片舷) 대포. **3** the firing of all the guns on one side of a warship at the same time. (편현 대포의) 일제 사격. **4** 《*colloq.*》 a violent attack in words, esp. in a newspaper. (욕설·비난 등의) 맹렬한 공격. **5** a large sheet of paper printed on one side only. 한 면만 인쇄된 대판지(大版紙)《광고·포스터 따위》. ¶ *Boys were giving out broadsides announcing the coming of the circus.* 소년들은 서커스단의 내연(來演)을 알리는 광고지를 나눠주고 있었다.

broad·sword [brɔ́ːdsɔ̀ːrd] *n.* Ⓒ a sword with a broad, flat blade. 날이 넓은 칼.

Broad·way [brɔ́ːdwèi] *n.* a street in New York City. (뉴욕의) 브로드웨이.

bro·cade [broukéid] *n.* Ⓤ a rich silk cloth with raised designs in gold and silver on it. (금·은실로 수놓은) 비단. [Sp.= broach]

bro·cad·ed [broukéidid] *adj.* woven into a rich cloth with a raised design. 돋을무늬로 짠.

broc·co·li [brɑ́kəli / brɔ́k-] *n.* Ⓒ 《*bot.*》 a kind of vegetable with flower heads. 브로콜리《모란채의 일종》. [It. =sprout]

bro·chure [brouʃúər, -ʃɔ́ːr] *n.* Ⓒ a small book; a pamphlet. 팸플릿. [F.]

brogue [broug] *n.* Ⓒ a heavy, strong

country shoe formerly used by Irishmen. 투박한 가죽신. [Celt.]

broil[1] [brɔil] *vt.* (P6) **1** cook, (meat, etc.) by direct heat. …을 굽다. ¶ ~ *a steak* 스테이크를 굽다. **2** make (something) very hot. …을 뜨겁게 하다. ¶ *If I stay in this room any longer, I'll be broiled alive.* 이 방안에 좀더 있다간 산 채로 구워질 게다. —*vi.* (P1) be very hot. 매우 뜨겁다. ¶ *a broiling day* 푹푹 찌는 듯한 날. —*n.* ⒸⓊ **1** the act or state of broiling. 굽는 일. **2** something broiled; broiled meat. 구운 것(고기). [? F.]

broil[2] [brɔil] *n.* Ⓒ an angry quarrel or struggle. 싸움. [F. *brouiller* mix]

broil·er[1] [brɔ́ilər] *n.* Ⓒ **1** any device for roasting. 고기 굽는 기구. **2** a young chicken for roasting. 구이용 영계. [*broil*[1]]

broil·er[2] [brɔ́ilər] *n.* a person who stirs up a quarrel; a person who is fond of fighting. 싸움을 부추기는 사람; 싸움꾼. [*broil*[2]]

:**broke** [brouk] *v.* p. of **break.** —*adj.* ⟪*colloq.*⟫ having no money; unable to pay one's debts. 무일푼의; 파산(破產)한. ¶ *He came back home* ~. 그는 빈털터리가 되어 집으로 돌아왔다. [*break*]

:**bro·ken** [bróukən] *v.* pp. of **break.** —*adj.* **1** separated into parts by a blow or by strain; crushed. 깨어진; 부서진; 꺾인. ¶ *a* ~ *cup* 깨어진 컵. **2** weakened in spirit, strength, health, etc. 약해진; 기운이 꺾인. ¶ *a* ~ *man* 실의에 빠진 사람. **3** tamed; trained. 길든. ¶ *a* ~ *elephant* 길든 코끼리 / *a well-broken horse* 잘 조련된 말. **4** uneven; rough. 울퉁불퉁한; 거친. ¶ ~ *ground* 울퉁불퉁한 땅 / ~ *water* (여울 따위의) 물결치는 수면. **5** not kept; violated. (약속 따위가) 지켜지지 않은; 어긴. ¶ *a* ~ *promise* 깨진 약속. **6** imperfectly spoken. (말이) 불완전한. ¶ ~ *English* 엉터리 영어. **7** interrupted. 중단된. ¶ ~ *sleep* 선잠. **8** shocked by grief. 비탄에 잠긴. ¶ *a* ~ *heart* 비통한 마음. **9** ruined; bankrupt. 파멸한; 파산한. ¶ *a* ~ *firm* 파산한 회사 / *the* ~ *fortunes of his family* 그의 일가(一家)의 몰락. [*break*]

bro·ken-down [bróukəndáun] *adj.* **1** broken in health; ruined. 쇠약해진. **2** unfit for use; out of order. 못 쓰게 된; (기계가) 파손된; 고장난. ¶ *a* ~ *chair* 부서진 의자.

bro·ken-heart·ed [bróukənhá:rtid] *adj.* shocked by sorrow or grief; very sad; disappointed in love. 상심한; 실연한.

bro·ken·ly [bróukənli] *adv.* with breaks, esp. of the voice. 떠듬떠듬. ¶ *speak* ~.

broken reed [⌐–⌐] *n.* an unreliable person or thing. 믿을 수 없는 사람(것).

bro·ken-wind·ed [bróukənwíndid] *adj.* (of a horse) breathing with difficulty. (말이) 헐떡거리는.

bro·ker [bróukər] *n.* Ⓒ a person who buys and sells for other people. 중개인; 브로커. [→broach]

bro·ker·age [bróukəridʒ] *n.* Ⓤ **1** the business of a broker. 중개업. **2** the money paid to a broker for his services. 구전.

bro·mide [bróumaid] *n.* Ⓒ **1** ⓊⒸ ⟪chem.⟫ a compound material of bromine. 브롬화물. ¶ ~ *paper* (사진) 인화지 / *silver* ~ 브롬화은(銀). **2** a calming medicine. 진정제. **3** a commonplace and boring person. 평범한 사람; 따분한 사람. [Gk. *brōmos* stink]

bro·mine [bróumi(:)n] *n.* Ⓤ ⟪chem.⟫ a chemical element which is dark red liquid with a strong smell. 브롬. [↑]

bron·chi [bráŋkai / brɔ́ŋ-] *n. pl.* (*sing.* **bron·chus**) ⟪anat.⟫ the two main branches of the windpipe. 기관지. [Gk.]

bron·chi·al [bráŋkiəl / brɔ́ŋ-] *adj.* of the bronchi or bronchus. 기관지의. ¶ ~ *catarrh* 기관지 카타르.

bron·chi·tis [braŋkáitis, bran- / brɔŋ-] *n.* Ⓤ a disease of the bronchi. 기관지염.

bron·cho [bráŋkou / brɔ́ŋ-] *n.* (*pl.* **-chos**) =bronco.

bron·chus [bráŋkəs / brɔ́ŋ-] *n.* sing. of **bronchi.**

bron·co [bráŋkou / brɔ́ŋ-] *n.* Ⓒ (*pl.* **-cos**) a wild-natured pony of the western United States. 브롱코⟪미국 서부산(產)의 야생마⟫. [Sp. =rough]

Bron·të [bránti / brɔ́n-] *n.* 브론테⟪영국의 세 자매 소설가⟫. **1 Charlotte** (1816-55) an English novelist. **2 Emily** (1818-48) her sister, novelist. **3 Anne** (1820-49) her sister, poet.

***bronze** [branz / brɔnz] *n.* **1** Ⓤ a brown mixture of copper and tin. 청동(靑銅). **2** Ⓒ a statue, medal, etc., made of bronze. (동상·메달 따위의) 청동 제품. **3** Ⓤ the color of bronze, reddish brown. 청동색; 적갈색. —*adj.* **1** made of bronze. 청동으로 만든. ¶ *a* ~ *statue* 동상. **2** metallic brown. 청동색의. —*vt.* (P6) make bronze in color. 청동색으로 하다. ¶ *His skin was bronzed by the sun.* 그의 피부는 볕에 타서 적갈색이 되었다. [L. *Brundusium* Brindisi town]

Bronze Age [⌐⌐], **the** *n.* a period when bronze tools, weapons, etc., were used. 청동기 시대.

brooch [broutʃ, bru:tʃ] *n.* Ⓒ an ornamental or jeweled pin worn on the clothes at the neck or breast. 브로치. [→broach]

***brood** [bru:d] *n.* Ⓒ **1** a group of young birds hatched at one time. 한 배 병아리. **2** a group; a kind. 무리; 종족; 종류.

sit on brood, think about something for a long time. (오랫 동안) 숙고하다.

—*vi.* **1** (P1) sit on eggs in order to hatch them. 알을 품다. ¶ *a brooding hen* 알을 품고 있는 암탉. **2** (P3) ⟪*on, over*⟫ think deeply. 심사 숙고하다. ¶ *She was brooding over her past.* 그녀는 지난 날을 곰곰이 생각하고 있었다. **3** hang low. (구름·어스름 따위가) 낮게 드리우다. ¶ *Dusk was brooding over* *the town.* 거리는 어둠이 찾아들고 있었다. [E. →breed]

brood·er [brú:dər] *n.* a person or thing that broods. 심사 숙고하는 사람; 병아리 보육 상자.

brood·y [brú:di] *adj.* (**brood·i·er, brood·i·est**) **1** (of a hen) wanting to sit on eggs. 알을 품고 싶어하는. **2** (of a person) moody. 뚱한; 우울한.

:brook[1] [bruk] *n.* Ⓒ a small stream. 개울. [E.]

brook[2] [bruk] *vt.* (P6,9) 《in *negative* or *interrogative*》 suffer; bear. …을 참다〔견디다〕. ¶ *I cannot ~ your interference.* 너의 간섭을 참을 수가 없다 / *We will not ~ any more of your insults.* 우리는 너의 모욕을 더이상 참지는 않을 게다 / *The affair brooks no delay.* 이 문제는 지체를 용납하지 않는다. [E.]

brook·let [brúklit] *n.* Ⓒ a little brook. 실개천; 시내. [*brook*[1]]

Brook·lyn [brúklin] *n.* a division of New York City. (뉴욕의) 브루클린.

·broom [bru(:)m] *n.* Ⓒ **1** a brush with a long handle used for sweeping. 비. ¶ 《*prov.*》 *A new ~ sweeps clean.* 새 비는 잘 쓸린다《신참자는 일을 잘 한다》. **2** a kind of plant with yellow flowers. 금작화. [E.]

broom·stick [brú(:)mstìk] *n.* Ⓒ the long handle of a broom. 빗자루. ¶ *The witch rode through the sky on a ~.* 마녀는 빗자루를 타고 공중을 날았다.

Bros., bros. brothers.

broth [brɔ(:)θ, brɑθ] *n.* ⓊⒸ water in which meat has been boiled; thin meat soup. 고깃국물; 묽은 고기 수프. [E.]

broth·el [brɔ́(:)θəl, brɑ́θ-, brɔ́(:)ð-, brɑ́ð-] *n.* Ⓒ a house of ill fame. 매춘굴. [It. = board]

:broth·er [brʌ́ðər] *n.* Ⓒ **1** one of the sons of the same parents; one of the sons of only the same mother or father. 형제; 형; 아우 (opp. sister). ¶ *an elder* 〔*older*〕 *~* 형 / *a half ~* 배다른〔아비 다른〕 형제 / *a whole ~* 부모가 같은 형제 / *a younger ~* 아우. **2** a close friend; a companion. 친구; 동료. ¶ *a ~ in arms* 전우(戰友). **3** (*pl.* **breth·ren**) a member of a church, union, etc. 같은 교회·단체의 소속원; 교우. ¶ *professional brethren* (의사·변호사 등의) 동업자. [E.]

·broth·er·hood [brʌ́ðərhùd] *n.* **1** Ⓤ the condition or quality of being a brother or brothers. 형제 사이〔관계〕. **2** Ⓒ a group of persons with common interests. 단체; 협회; 조합. **3** Ⓤ brotherliness. 우애.

broth·er-in-law [brʌ́ðərinlɔ̀:] *n.* Ⓒ (*pl.* **broth·ers-**) a brother of one's husband or wife; a sister's husband. 처남; 매부; 동서; 형부; 시숙.

Broth·er·li·ness [brʌ́ðərlinis] *n.* friendliness. 우정; 우애.

broth·er·ly [brʌ́ðərli] *adj.* of or like a brother; kind; gentle and loving. 형제의〔같은〕; 육친의; 우애 깊은. ¶ *in an ~ manner* 형제같이.

brough·am [brú:əm, bróuəm] *n.* Ⓒ a closed carriage with four wheels, drawn by one horse. 일두(一頭) 4륜 마차. [Person]

:brought [brɔ:t] *v.* p. and pp. of **bring.**

:brow [brau] *n.* Ⓒ **1** 《usu. *pl.*》 the arch of hair over each eye. 눈썹. ¶ *the heavy brows* 짙은 눈썹 / *ponder with knit brows* 눈썹을 찌푸리고 생각에 잠기다 / *knit* 〔*bend*〕 *one's brows* 눈살을 찌푸리다. **2** the front of the head above the eyes. 이마. **3** the steep slope of a hill. 절벽; 벼랑끝. [E.]

brow·beat [bráubì:t] *vt.* (**-beat, -beaten**) (P6,13) 《*into*》 make someone afraid by using rough words; frighten. …을 위협하다; 을러대다. ¶ *He ~ me into accepting.* 그는 나를 을러서 수락하게 했다.

brow·beat·en [bráubì:tn] *v.* pp. of **browbeat.**

:brown [braun] *n.* Ⓤ **1** a dark color like that of toast, coffee, etc. (다)갈색. **2** a paint having this color. (다)갈색 (그림)물감. **3** 《Brit. *sl.*》 a copper coin. 동화(銅貨); 동전.

— *adj.* **1** of this color. (다)갈색의. **2** dark-skinned; sun-tanned. 볕에 검게 탄.

do brown, 《Brit. *sl.*》 cheat. 속이다.

do it up brown, 《*colloq.*》 do thoroughly; do excellently or perfectly. 철저하게 하다; 완벽하게 하다.

in a brown study, deep in thought. 생각에 깊이 잠겨.

— *vt., vi.* (P6; 1) make (something) brown; become brown. (다)갈색으로 하다; (다)갈색이 되다.

browned off, 《Brit. *sl.*》 bored; fed up. 따분한; 물린.

● **brown·ness** [⌐nis] *n.* [E.]

brown bread [⌐⌐] *n.* bread made of unbolted flour. 흑빵.

brown coal [⌐⌐] *n.* lignite. 갈탄.

brown·ie [bráuni] *n.* Ⓒ **1** a good-natured fairy who helps secretly in household work. 브라우니 요정(妖精). **2** 《U.S.》 a flat, sweet chocolate bar containing nuts. (아몬드·땅콩이 든) 판(板)초콜릿. **3** 《*B-*》 a junior member of the Girl Scouts. 걸 스카우트의 유년 단원. [E.]

Brown·ing [bráuniŋ] *n.* **1 Robert** (1812-89) an English poet. 로버트 브라우닝. **2** 《trademark》 a type of automatic pistol or rifle. 브라우닝 총. [Person]

brown·ish [bráuniʃ] *adj.* somewhat brown. (다)갈색을 띤. [→brown]

brown paper [⌐ ⌐–] *n.* a coarse kind of paper used for parcels, etc. 하도롱지(紙).

Brown·shirt [bráunʃə̀:rt] *n.* a member of the Nazi party. 나치스 당원(cf. *Blackshirt*).

brown·stone [bráunstòun] *n.* red-brown sandstone, used as a building material. 적

갈색 사암(砂岩).

brown sugar [ㅗㅡ] *n.* sugar that is half refined. 황설탕.

browse [brauz] *vi., vt.* (P1,2A,3;6,7) **1** 《*on*》 eat grass and young leaves; feed. (동물이) 어린 잎을 먹다; (소 따위)를 놓아 먹이다. **2** read here and there in books. 책을 여기저기 읽다. —*n.* Ⓤ Ⓒ the young, soft leaves of trees. 어린 잎; 새싹. [F. *broust* bud]

Bru·in, bru·in [brú:in] *n.* Ⓒ (usu. in fairy tales) a bear. (동화 따위에 나오는) 곰; 곰 아저씨. [Du. =brown]

·**bruise** [bru:z] *n.* Ⓒ a colored place on the skin caused by a blow. 타박상; 멍. —*vt.* (P6) **1** cause a bruise. …에 타박상을 입히다. ¶ ~ *one's arm* 팔에 타박상을 입히다. **2** injure; hurt. (감정 따위)를 상하게 하다; 해치다. ¶ *His words bruised her feelings.* 그의 말이 그녀의 감정을 상하게 했다. **3** crush by beating. 때려 부수다. —*vi.* **1** (P1) become bruised. 멍들다. ¶ *A child's flesh bruises easily.* 어린아이의 살은 멍이 잘 든다. **2** (P2) 《*colloq.*》 ride recklessly. 무턱대고 타고 돌아다니다. [E.]

bruis·er [brú:zər] *n.* 《*colloq.*》 a boxer; a bully. 복서; 폭력배.

bruit [bru:t] *vt.* (P6) spread. (말 따위)를 퍼뜨리다. [F. =noise]

bru·net, -nette [bru:nét] *adj.* **1** (of skin, eyes, or hair) dark; brown. (피부·눈·머리 따위가) 검은; 갈색의. **2** (of a person) having dark or brown hair, eyes, or skin. 브루네트의. —*n.* Ⓒ a person, esp. a woman, with dark hair, eyes, and skin. 가무잡잡한 여자(opp. blonde). 參考 brunet는 남성, brunette는 여성에 씀. [F.=brown]

brunt [brʌnt] *n.* Ⓒ the main force or violence of an attack; the hardest part. (공격의) 주력; 충격; 난국(難局). ¶ *bear the* ~ *of a criticism* 비난의 화살을 정면으로 받다. [E.]

:**brush**[1] [brʌʃ] *n.* Ⓒ **1** a tool made of stiff hairs or wires fastened to a handle, used in cleaning, rubbing, painting, etc. 솔; 귀얄; 붓. ¶ *paint with a* ~ 솔로 페인트 칠을 하다. **2** an act of brushing. 솔질. ¶ *give one's hat a* ~ 모자를 솔질하다. **3** a light touch in passing. 가벼운 접촉. **4** a short, quick fight or quarrel. 작은 충돌; 승강이; 옥신각신. ¶ *a* ~ *with the enemy* 적과의 작은 충돌. **5** a fox's tail. 여우 꼬리.

—*vt.* **1** (P6,7) clean, rub, or paint (something) with a brush. …에 솔질하다; 붓으로 그리다. ¶ ~ *one's clothes* (*boots, hat, teeth, hair*) 옷(부츠,모자,이,머리)에 솔질하다. **2** (P7) 《*away, off*》 sweep or remove (the dirt) away with a brush. …(의 먼지)를 솔로 털다. **3** (P7,13) wipe (something) away. …을 닦아내다. **4** (P6) touch (something) lightly in passing. …을 가볍게 스치다. ¶ *The leaves brushed my cheek as I ran through the wood.* 내가 숲속을 달릴 때 나뭇잎이 내 뺨을 스쳤다. —*vi.* (P1,3) move lightly and quickly. 가벼이 움직이다. [F.]

brush against, touch lightly against (something) in passing. …을 가볍게 스치고 지나가다.

brush aside (***away***), **a**) put (something) aside. …을 치우다. **b**) pay little or no attention to (something or someone). …을 무시하다. ¶ ~ *opposition aside* 반대를 무시하다.

brush over, paint lightly. 가볍게 칠하다.

brush up, **a**) refresh (one's knowledge, etc.). (지식 따위)를 새롭게 하다; 복습하다. **b**) clean or polish up. 닦아 깨끗이하다.

brush[2] [brʌʃ] *n.* Ⓤ a thick growth of small trees, etc. 덤불(숲). [↑]

brush·wood [brʌ́ʃwùd] *n.* Ⓤ small trees growing thickly together. 잡목.

brusque [brʌsk / brusk] *adj.* quick and rough in manner. 무뚝뚝한. [It. =sour]

brusque·ly [brʌ́skli / brúsk-] *adj.* in a quick and rough manner. 무뚝뚝하게.

Brus·sels [brʌ́səlz] *n.* the capital of Belgium. 브뤼셀《벨기에의 수도》.

Brussels sprouts [ㅡㅡ ㅗ] *n.* a kind of cabbage having small heads along the central stick. 양배추의 하나.

bru·tal [brú:tl] *adj.* cruel; like a beast. 잔인한; 야만스런; 상스러운. ¶ ~ *treatment* 잔혹한 처사. [L. *brutus* dull]

bru·tal·i·ty [bru:tǽləti] *n.* (*pl.* **-ties**) **1** Ⓤ the state of being cruel. 잔인(함). **2** Ⓒ a very cruel act. 만행.

bru·tal·ize [brú:təlàiz] *vi.* (P1) become cruel. 잔인해지다. —*vt.* (P6) make (someone) cruel or animal-like. …을 잔인하게 하다.

bru·tal·ly [brú:təli] *adv.* in a brutal manner. 잔인하게.

·**brute** [bru:t] *n.* Ⓒ **1** an animal without power to think; a beast. 짐승. **2** a cruel person. 짐승 같은 사람. ¶ *the* ~ 수욕(獸慾); 수성(獸性) / *a* ~ *of a husband* 짐승 같은 남편. —*adj.* **1** of or like an animal; not human. 짐승과 같은. **2** cruel; without feeling. 잔인한; 무감각한. ¶ ~ *force* 폭력 / ~ *courage* 만용. [→brutal]

brut·ish [brú:tiʃ] *adj.* like a beast; cruel; rude. 짐승 같은; 잔인한; 야만적인.

B.S. Bachelor of Science; Bachelor of Surgery.

:**bub·ble** [bʌ́bəl] *n.* Ⓒ **1** a thin ball of liquid containing air or gas; an air space in a liquid. 거품; 기포. ¶ *soap bubbles* 비누 거품 / ~ *gum* 풍선 껌 / *blow bubbles* 비눗방울을 불다. **2** a plan or an idea that produces no actual results. 물거품 같은 계획.

prick the bubble, make the bubble burst; unmask the pretension. 물거품을 터뜨리다; 가면을 벗기다.

—*vi., vt.* (P1,2A;6) **1** form or produce

bubbles; make sounds like water boiling. 거품이 일다; 거품을 일으키다; 부글부글 끓다. **2** rise in bubbles; spring. (샘 따위가) 솟다. ¶ *Water bubbled out from the ground.* 물이 땅에서 솟아나왔다. [Imit.]

bubble over with laughter, give vent to laughter. 웃기 시작하다.

bu·bo [bjúːbou] *n.* Ⓒ《med.》an inflamed swelling in the groin or armpit. 가래톳. [Gk. =groin]

bu·bon·ic [bjuːbánik / -bɔ́n-] *adj.* of or attended with buboes. 가래톳의. ¶ *~ plague* 선(腺)페스트.

buc·ca·neer, -nier [bʌ̀kəníər] *n.* Ⓒ a sea robber. 해적. [Braz.]

Bu·cha·rest [bjúːkərèst] *n.* the capital of Rumania. 부쿠레슈티《루마니아의 수도》.

Buck [bʌk], **Pearl** *n.* (1892-1973) an American novelist. 펄 벅.

·**buck**[1] [bʌk] *n.* Ⓒ **1** a male deer, rabbit, etc. 수사슴; (토끼 따위의) 수컷. **2** a man who is too careful of his dress. 멋쟁이. **3** 《U.S. *sl.*》 a dollar. 1 달러. ¶ *fifty bucks of candles,* 50 달러어치의 양초 / *earn an honest ~* 정직하게 돈을 벌다. **4** a male negro. 흑인 남자. [E.]

pass the buck, 《*colloq.*》 pass something troublesome to another person; shift the responsibility (to). 성가신 것을 남에게 떠넘기다; 책임을 전가하다.

buck[2] [bʌk] *vt., vi.* (P1,2A;6,7) **1** (of a horse) jump up with all four feet off the ground. (말이) 등을 구부리고 뛰어오르다. **2** hit (something) with the head; push against (someone or something). …을 머리로 받다; …에 돌진하다. [↑]

buck off, (of a horse) throw off (a rider). (말이 기수를) 떨어뜨리다.

buck up, make (someone) more cheerful; become more cheerful. 기운을 북돋다; 힘을 내다.

:**buck·et** [bʌ́kit] *n.* Ⓒ a pail made of metal or wood. 양동이; 통. ¶ *a fire ~* 소화용 양동이 / *a ~ of water* 물통 / *a drop in the ~* 창해 일속(滄海一粟).

give the bucket, 《*colloq.*》 dismiss. 해고하다.

kick the bucket, die. 죽다.

— *vt., vi.* **1** (P6; 1) ride (a horse) mercilessly. (말을) 마구 몰다. **2** (P6) draw in buckets. …을 양동이로 긷다. **3** (P6) hurry. …을 쾌치다. **4** (P1) 《Brit.》 row a boat badly. 보트를 서투르게 젓다. [E.]

buck·et·ful [bʌ́kitfùl] *n.* Ⓒ the amount that a bucket can hold. 한 양동이. ¶ *a ~* 〔*two bucketfuls*〕 *of water* 한〔두〕 양동이의 물.

Buck·ing·ham [bʌ́kiŋəm] *n.* a county in southern England; Buckinghamshire. 버킹엄.

buck·le [bʌ́kəl] *n.* Ⓒ **1** a thing that fastens together the ends of a belt, etc. 죔쇠; 버클. **2** a metal ornament for a shoe. 구두의 장식용 죔쇠.

— *vt., vi.* (P6;1,2A) **1** fasten (things) with a buckle. 죔쇠로 죄다. **2** bend. 구부리다; 굽다. ¶ *The motorcar buckled up when it struck the lorry.* 그 자동차는 트럭을 들이받고 납작해졌다. **3** work hard. 열심히 일하다. [L. *buccula* cheek strap]

buckle (***down***) ***to a job*** =***buckle oneself to a job,*** work very hard. (일에) 전력을 쏟다.

buck·ler [bʌ́klər] *n.* Ⓒ a small, round shield; a thing that protects. (소형의) 둥근 방패; 방호물(防護物). [F. *bocle* boss]

buck·ram [bʌ́krəm] *n.* Ⓤ a rough cloth made stiff with paste. 버크럼《아교 따위를 먹여 빳빳한 천》. [F. *boquerant*]

buck·saw [bʌ́ksɔ̀ː] *n.* Ⓒ《U.S.》a saw set in a frame. 틀톱. [→buck]

〈bucksaw〉

buck·shot [bʌ́kʃàt / -ʃɔ̀t] *n.* a large size of lead shot, used for shooting deer, foxes, etc. (사슴 따위의 사냥용) 굵은 산탄(散彈).

buck·skin [bʌ́kskìn] *n.* **1** Ⓤ the skin of a deer. 사슴 가죽. **2** 《*pl.*》 short trousers made of buckskin. 사슴 가죽으로 만든 반바지.

buck·tooth [bʌ́ktúːθ] *n.* (*pl.* **buckteeth** [-tíːθ]) a projecting tooth. 덧니.

buck·wheat [bʌ́khwìːt] *n.* Ⓤ a plant producing small black grain; flour made from this grain. 메밀(가루). [*beech wheat*]

bu·col·ic [bjuːkálik / -kɔ́l-] *adj.* of country life; of shepherds. 시골풍의; 양치기의; 목가적인. ¶ *~ scenes* 전원 풍경 / *a ~ existence* 전원 생활. — *n.* Ⓒ **1** 《usu. *pl.*》 a poetry about shepherds; poets who write such poems. 목가(牧歌); 전원 시인. **2** a country person. 시골 사람. [Gk. *boukolos* herdsman]

:**bud** [bʌd] *n.* Ⓒ **1** a small, early stage of a flower, leaf, or branch. 봉오리; 싹. ¶ *a flower ~* 꽃봉오리 / *put forth buds* 싹트다. **2** any person or thing that is not fully grown. 미숙한 것; 소년; 소녀.

in bud, having buds. 싹튼. ¶ *The tree is in ~.* 그 나무는 싹트고 있다.

in the bud, at an early stage; at the very beginning. 초기에; 애당초. ¶ *a poet in the ~* 병아리 시인 / *nip in the ~* 초기에 저지하다; 미연에 방지하다 / *nip a rebellion in the ~* 반란을 조기에 진압하다.

— *v.* (**bud·ded; bud·ding**) *vi.* (P1,2A) **1** put forth buds. 싹트다. **2** begin to grow and develop. 자라기 시작하다. — *vt.* (P6) put a young bud into another tree to get a new shoot, branch, etc. …을 아접(芽椄)하다. [E.]

bud off from, separate. …에서 갈라지다〔분리하다〕.

Bu·da·pest [búːdəpèst, ⌐–⌐] *n.* the capital

of Hungary. 부다페스트《헝가리의 수도》.

·**Bud·dha** [bú:də] *n.* (563?-483? B.C.) a great religious leader of Asia, the founder of Buddhism. 부처. [Skr. *budh* awake]

·**Bud·dhism** [bú:dizəm] *n.* Ⓤ a religion started in India by Buddha in the sixth century B.C. 불교.

·**Bud·dhist** [bú:dist] *adj.* of Buddha or Buddhism. 부처의; 불교의. ¶ *a ~ temple* 절. — *n.* Ⓒ a person who believes in Buddhism. 불교 신자.

bud·ding [bʌ́diŋ] *adj.* **1** putting forth buds. 싹이 트기 시작한. **2** just beginning to show signs of future success. 가능성을 보이기 시작한; 신진의. ¶ *a ~ author* 신진 작가. [*bud*]

bud·dy [bʌ́di] *n.* Ⓒ (*pl.* **-dies**) 《U.S. *colloq.*》 a good friend. 친구. [*brother*]

budge [bʌdʒ] *vi., vt.* (P1,2B; 6) 《usu. in *negative*》 move slightly; cause (something) to move. 조금 움직이다; …을 움직이게 하다. ¶ *He won't ~ an inch.* 그는 까딱도 하지 않는다 / *The chain was so heavy that the child could not ~ it.* 그 쇠사슬은 너무 무거워 아이가 움직일 수 없었다. [F. *bouger*]

·**budg·et** [bʌ́dʒit] *n.* Ⓒ **1** a plan how to use money for a certain period in the future. 예산안. ¶ *open the ~* (의회에) 예산안을 제출하다. **2** a collection; a bundle. 한 무더기; 한 묶음. ¶ *a ~ of letters* 한 묶음의 편지. — *vi.* (P1,3) make a plan for using money. 예산을 짜다. ¶ *~ for the coming year* 새해 예산을 세우다. — *vt.* (P6) divide (something) by a plan. (자금·시간 따위)를 배분하다; 짜다. ¶ *~ one's time* 시간을 배정하다. [L. *bulga* bag]

budg·et·ar·y [bʌ́dʒitèri / -təri] *adj.* of a budget. 예산상의.

Bue·nos Ai·res [bwéinəs áiriz] *n.* the capital of Argentina. 부에노스아이레스《아르헨티나의 수도》.

buff [bʌf] *n.* Ⓤ **1** a soft, dull-yellow leather made from the skin of an ox, etc. (소·물소 따위의) 무두질한 가죽. **2** 《*colloq.*》 bare skin. 맨살. ¶ *strip to the ~* 발가벗다. **3** a dull yellow. 담황색. — *vt.* (P6) polish (something) with a buff. …을 무두질한 가죽으로 닦다. [*buffalo*]

Buf·fa·lo [bʌ́fəlòu] *n.* a city in west New York State, on Lake Erie. 버팔로《뉴욕 주 서부의 도시》.

·**buf·fa·lo** [bʌ́fəlòu] *n.* Ⓒ (*pl.* **-loes, -los** or *collectively* **-lo**) any of various wild oxen, as the water buffalo of India. 들소; 물소. [Gk. *boubalos* antelope]

buff·er[1] [bʌ́fər] *n.* Ⓒ anything that lessens the shock of a blow. 완충기. [E.]

buff·er[2] [bʌ́fər] *n.* a person or thing that polishes. 닦는 사람〔도구〕. [*buff*]

buffer state [∠-∠] *n.* a country between hostile larger ones. 완충국(緩衝國). [*buffer*[1]]

·**buf·fet**[1] [bʌ́fit] *n.* Ⓒ **1** a blow of the hand; a knock. 타격. **2** misfortune. 불운; 불행. ¶ *the buffets of fate* 불행한 운명. — *vt.* (P6,7) give a blow to (someone). …을 치다. — *vi.* (P3) struggle with or against something. (파도·역경 따위와) 싸우다. [F. *buffe* blow]

buf·fet[2] [bəféi, búfei / bʌ́fit] *n.* Ⓒ **1** a piece of furniture for holding dishes, silver, and table linen. 찬장. **2** [búfei] a counter for lunch or drinks, esp. in a station or on a train. 간이 식당. ¶ *a ~ car* 식당차 / *a ~ dinner* 뷔페식 만찬. [F.]

buf·foon [bəfú:n] *n.* Ⓒ a person who amuses people by acting in a foolish way. 어릿광대. — *vi.* (P1) play the buffoon. 어릿광대 역을 하다. [It.]

buf·foon·er·y [bəfú:nəri] *n.* ⓊⒸ (*pl.* **-eries**) tricks or jokes of a buffoon; foolish actions. 익살; 괘사.

bug [bʌg] *n.* Ⓒ **1** any insect. 곤충. ¶ *a lighting ~* 개똥벌레. **2** 《Brit.》 a small, biting insect without wings; 《U.S.》 an insect with hard front wings; a beetle. 빈대; 딱정벌레. **3** 《*colloq.*》 a germ. 병원균. **4** 《U.S. *colloq.*》 a fan. 열광자; 팬. ¶ *a shutter ~* 사진광(狂). **5** 《U.S.》 a defect. (기계의) 고장; 결함. [E.]

bug·a·boo [bʌ́gəbù:] *n.* Ⓒ (*pl.* **-boos**) an imaginary thing causing unnecessary fear. 요괴; 유령. [W. *bwg* ghost]

bug·bear [bʌ́gbɛ̀ər] *n.* =bugaboo.

bug·gy[1] [bʌ́gi] *adj.* infested with bugs. 빈대투성이의. [*bug*]

bug·gy[2] [bʌ́gi] *n.* Ⓒ (*pl.* **-gies**) a small carriage with one horse and one seat. (한 마리가 끄는) 경마차(輕馬車). 參考 영국에서는 2 바퀴, 미국에서는 4 바퀴. [→budge]

·**bu·gle** [bjú:gəl] *n.* Ⓒ a musical instrument like a small trumpet. (군대) 나팔. ¶ *blow a ~* 나팔을 불다 / *a ~ call* 소집 나팔. — *vi.* (P1) sound a bugle. 나팔을 불다. — *vt.* (P6) call (persons) with a bugle. (사람들)을 나팔로 소집하다. [L. *buculus* young bull]

bu·gler [bjú:glər] *n.* Ⓒ a person who plays the bugle. 나팔수.

:**build** [bild] *v.* (**built**) *vt.* (P6,7) **1** ⓐ make (a house, building, machine, etc.) by putting materials or parts together; construct. (집)을 짓다; 세우다; 건설하다; (기계 따위)를 조립하다. ¶ *~ a church* 〔*house*〕 교회를〔집을〕 짓다 / *~ a ship* 배를 건조하다 / *~ a bridge* 〔*railway*〕 다리〔철도〕를 놓다 / *~ a radio* 라디오를 조립하다. ⓑ make; form. …을 만들다. ¶ *~ a fire in a fireplace* 난로에 불을 때다 / *Birds ~ their nests.* 새들이 둥지를 튼다. **2** make a basis for (something); establish. …의 기초를 만들다; …을 확립하다. ¶ *~ one's theory on facts* 사실에 기초한 이론을 세우다. **3** form gradually; develop. …을 쌓아올리다; 높이다; 증진하다. ¶ *~ (up) a for-*

tune 재산을 이룩하다 / ~ (*up*) *a reputation* 명성을 높이다 / ~ *one's character* 품성을 도야하다.

— *vi.* (P1,3) **1** have a house built. 집을 짓게 하다. **2** be built. 건설되다. ¶ *The house is building.* 그 집은 건축 중이다.

build in, make as a part of the building. (집·방의) 붙박이로 만들다. ¶ *The bookcases in my room are all built in.* 내 방의 책장은 모두 붙박이장이다.

build up, **a**) make (something) step by step; form (something) by degrees. 쌓아올리다; 증진하다. **b**) make (something) strong; make (someone) healthy. …을 튼튼하게 하다. **c**) erect buildings in (a place). …에 건물을 빽빽이 짓다.

— *n.* Ⓤ **1** the shape or structure of the human body. 체격. ¶ *a man of large* ~ 큰 체격의 남자. **2** the manner in which anything is built; form; construction. 구조. [M.E. *bilde(n),* var. of *botl* dwelling]

***build·er** [bíldər] *n.* Ⓒ a person who builds; a person whose business is building. 건설〔건축〕자; 건축업자. ¶ *a master* ~ 도편수.

:**build·ing** [bíldiŋ] *n.* **1** Ⓒ anything built, such as a house, factory, barn, store, etc. 건물; 빌딩. ¶ *the Empire State Building* 엠파이어 스테이트 빌딩 / *a public* ~ 공공건물. **2** Ⓤ the art or work of making houses, etc. 건축. ¶ ~ *land* 건축 부지.

:**built** [bilt] *v.* p. and pp. of **build.**

built-in [bíltìn] *adj.* built as a part of the building. 붙박이의. ¶ *a* ~ *bookcase* 붙박이 책장.

built-up [bíltʌ́p] *adj.* (of an area) covered with houses, etc. 집〔건물〕 따위가 빽빽이 들어선.

***bulb** [bʌlb] *n.* **1** Ⓒ a round part of such plants as the onion, tulip, and lily, usu. under the ground. 구근(球根); 구경(球莖). **2** anything shaped like a bulb; an electric lamp. 공 모양의 것; 전구. — *vi.* (P1) swell into a bulb. 공 모양으로 부풀다. [Gk. *bolbos* onion]

bulb·ous [bʌ́lbəs] *adj.* **1** of the round root of certain plants. 구근(球根)의. **2** shaped like a bulb. 구근 모양의. ¶ *a* ~ *plant* 구근 식물.

Bul·gar·i·a [bʌlgɛ́əriə, bul-] *n.* a country in southeast Europe. 불가리아.

Bul·gar·i·an [bʌlgɛ́əriən, bul-] *adj.* of Bulgaria, its people, or their language. 불가리아(사람·말)의. — *n.* **1** Ⓒ a person of Bulgaria. 불가리아 사람. **2** Ⓤ the language of Bulgaria. 불가리아 말.

bulge [bʌldʒ] *n.* Ⓒ **1** a rounded part which stands out; swelling. 둥글게 내민〔부푼〕 부분; 부풂. ¶ *a* ~ *in a wall* 벽의 쑥 내민 부분. **2** 《*the* ~》 《U.S. *colloq.*》 advantage. 우세.

get 〔***have***〕 ***the bulge on*** (=*be in a better position than; defeat*) *someone.* …에게 이기다.

— *vi.* (P1,2A) 《*with*》 swell. 부풀다; 내밀다. ¶ *His pockets were bulging with apples.* 그의 호주머니가 사과로 불룩했다.

— *vt.* (P6) cause (something) to swell. …을 부풀게〔내밀게〕 하다. [↓]

bulg·er [bʌ́ldʒər] *n.* 《golf》 a club with a convex face. 타면(打面)이 불룩한 클럽. [→budget]

***bulk** [bʌlk] *n.* Ⓤ **1** large size. 크기. **2** 《*the* ~》 the greater part of. 대부분. ¶ *The* ~ *of his land is uncultivated.* 그의 땅의 대부분이 아직 개간되어 있지 않다. **3** goods or cargo not in packages, boxes, etc. 포장하지 않은 낱낱의 짐.

break bulk, unload. 짐을 풀다.

in bulk, **a**) loose; not in packages. 낱낱으로; 포장하지 않은 채로. **b**) in large quantities. 대량으로; 모개로.

— *vi.* (P1,3) **1** give the appearance of great size or importance. 크게〔중대하게〕 보이다. ¶ *The matter bulks large.* 그 문제는 중대하게 보인다. **2** grow large. 부피가 커지다. — *vt.* (P6) find out the bulk of (a cargo). (짐의) 부피를 재다. [E.=belly]

bulk up, amount to. …에 달하다.

bulk·head [bʌ́lkhèd] *n.* Ⓒ a wall inside a ship for forming watertight compartments. (배 안의) 격벽(隔壁).

bulk·y [bʌ́lki] *adj.* (**bulk·i·er, bulk·i·est**) taking up a lot of space. 부피가 큰; 방대한. ¶ *a* ~ *book* 두꺼운 책 / *a* ~ *cargo* 부피가 나가는 화물.

***bull**[1] [bul] *n.* Ⓒ **1** the male of cattle. 황소. 參考 암소는 cow, 거세한 소는 ox. **2** the male of other large animals, such as the elephant, whale, etc. (코끼리·고래 따위 큰 짐승의) 수컷. **3** 《stock》 a person who buys stocks and tries to raise their market price. (증권의) 사는 쪽(opp. bear). **4** 《U.S. *sl.*》 a policeman. 경관; 순경. [E.]

(***like***) ***a bull in a china shop,*** (like) a rough and careless person in a place where skill and care are neeeded. 닥치는 대로 부수는 난폭자(처럼); 임기 응변으로 대처하지 못 하는 사람(같이).

take the bull by the horns, attack a problem fearlessly. 용감히 난국에 맞서다.

bull[2] [bul] *n.* Ⓒ a formal writing or an official order from the Pope. 교황의 교서. [→bill[1]]

bull-calf [búlkæ̀f, -kɑ̀ːf] *n.* Ⓒ **1** a young bull. 수송아지. **2** a simpleton. 바보. [*bull*[1]]

bull·dog [búldɔ̀ːg / -dɔ̀g] *n.* Ⓒ one of an English breed of short-haired dogs. 불독. — *adj.* like that of a bulldog. 불독 같은. ¶ *a* ~ *courage* 불독 같은 용감성. [↑]

bull·doze [búldòuz] *vt.* (P6) **1** 《*colloq.*》 frighten. …을 위협하다. **2** flatten with a bulldozer. 불도저로 밀다〔고르다〕. ¶ ~ *a building site* 건축용지를 불도저로 고르다.

[*bull*[1]]

bull·doz·er [búldòuzər] *n.* Ⓒ a powerful tractor for levelling rough ground and removing obstacles. 불도저.

·**bul·let** [búlit] *n.* Ⓒ a small piece of lead, steel, etc. to be shot from a gun. 탄알; 소총탄. [O.F. *boule* ball]

·**bul·le·tin** [búlətin] *n.* Ⓒ **1** a short public announcement. 고시(告示); 게시. **2** a magazine, newspaper, or any publication appearing regularly. 공보. — *vt.* make (something) known by a bulletin. …을 고시[게시]하다. [→bull[2]]

bulletin board [⌐--⌐] *n.* a board on which notices are put up. 게시판.

bul·let·proof [búlitprù:f] *adj.* that a bullet cannot go through. 방탄(防彈)의.

bull·fight [búlfàit] *n.* Ⓒ a traditional Spanish and Latin American spectacle in which men and a bull fight in an enclosed place. 투우. [→bull[1]]

bull·fight·er [búlfàitər] *n.* Ⓒ a man who fights a bull. 투우사.

bull·finch [búlfintʃ] *n.* Ⓒ a European song bird with beautifully colored feathers and a short, rounded bill. 피리새.

bull·frog [búlfràg, -frɔ̀(:)g] *n.* Ⓒ a large frog of North America that makes a deep, loud sound. 식용개구리.

bull·head·ed [búlhédid] *adj.* stupidly stubborn; obstinate. 완고한. ●**bull·head·ed·ness** [-nis] *n.*

bul·lion [búljən] *n.* Ⓤ gold or silver in mass. 금은괴. [→boil]

bull·necked [búlnèkt] *adj.* having a short, thick neck. 목이 굵은. [→bull[1]]

bull·ock [búlək] *n.* Ⓒ **1** a young bull. 수송아지. **2** a bull from which the male sex organ has been removed. 불깐[거세한] 소. [*bull*[1]]

bull ring [⌐⌐] *n.* an enclosed place for bullfights. 투우장.

bull's-eye [búlzài] *n.* Ⓒ **1** the center of a target, or a shot hitting it. 과녁의 흑점; 정곡; 정곡을 맞힌 화살[탄알]. **2** a small, round window. 둥근 창. **3** a round, hard sweet, often of peppermint. 눈깔사탕.

bull terrier [⌐⌐--] *n.* a breed of dogs produced by crossing the bulldog and the terrier. 불테리어.

bul·ly [búli] *n.* Ⓒ (*pl.* **bul·lies**) a person who frightens, hurts or makes fun of smaller or weaker persons. 약한 자를 괴롭히는 사람; 폭한(暴漢). — *vi., vt.* (**bul·lied**) be a bully. 약한 자를 괴롭히다.

***bully** someone **into** [**out of**] doing*, force someone to do [not to do] something by frightening. 위협해서 …을 하게[못 하게] 하다.

— *adj.* 《Brit. *colloq.*》 fine; excellent. 훌륭한.

— *interj.* 《Brit. *colloq.*》 good !; well done ! 잘 했어. [*bull*[1]]

bul·rush [búlrʌʃ] *n.* Ⓒ **1** 《bot.》 a tall, thin plant that grows in water and on wet land. 큰고랭이. **2** (in the Bible) the papyrus. 파피루스. [*bull*[2]]

bul·wark [búlwərk] *n.* Ⓒ **1** a wall of earth or other material built for defense. 방벽(防壁); 보루. **2** a defense; a protection. 방어[옹호]물. ¶ *Law is the ~ of civilizatin.* 법은 문명의 보루(保壘)이다. **3** a breakwater. 방파제. **4** 《usu. *pl.*》 a ship's side above the deck. 현장(舷牆). — *vt.* (P6) provide (a place, etc.) with a bulwark or bulwarks. 방벽을 지어 굳게 지키다. [Du. *bolwerk* rampart]

〈bulwark 4〉

bum [bʌm] *n.* Ⓒ 《U.S. *sl.*》 **1** a good-for-nothing fellow. 변변치 못한 자. **2** a lazy person. 부랑자.

on the bum, on the loaf. 부랑 생활을 하여.

— *v.* (**bummed, bum·ming**) *vi.* lead an idle life. 빈둥거리며 지내다. — *vt.* borrow (something) without intention of returning. 갚을 생각도 없이 …을 빌리다; 거저 얻어 내다. [E.]

bum·ble·bee [bʌ́mblbì:] *n.* Ⓒ 《insect.》 a large hairy bee with a loud buzz. 뒝벌. [→boom[1]]

·**bump** [bʌmp] *vt.* (P6) **1** strike (some thing) heavily. …에 부딪치다; 충돌하다. ¶ *My car bumped a truck.* 내 차가 트럭을 들이받았다. **2** dismiss (someone) from a job. (아무)를 지위 등에서 몰아내다; 해고하다. — *vi.* **1** (P3) 《*against, into*》 hit or strike against something or someone. 충돌하다. ¶ *They bumped against one another.* 그들은 서로 충돌했다. **2** (P2A,3) move with a jerk. 덜거덕거리며 나아가다. ¶ *Our car bumped down the road.* 우리 차는 덜거덕거리며 길을 내려갔다.

bump into, meet by chance. 우연히 만나다.

bump off, 《U.S. *sl.*》 kill. 죽이다; 없애버리다.

— *n.* Ⓒ **1** a heavy blow or knock. 충돌. **2** a swelling caused by a blow. 타격으로 부어오른 혹. **3** unevenness on a road surface. 도로의 울퉁불퉁함. [Imit.]

bump·er [bʌ́mpər] *n.* Ⓒ **1** a metal guard for protecting the front or rear of an automobile, a truck, etc. (자동차의) 범퍼; 완충기. **2** a cup or glass filled to the brim. (찰랑찰랑하게) 가득 찬 잔. **3** 《*colloq.*》 something unusually abundant. 대풍(大豊). — *adj.* unusually abundant [large]. 대풍의; 훌륭한. ¶ *a ~ harvest* 대풍작 / *a ~ crop of cotton* 면화의 대풍작. [→bump]

bump·kin [bʌ́mpkin] *n.* Ⓒ an ungraceful person from the country. 시골뜨기.

bump·tious [bʌ́mpʃəs] *adj.* 《*joc.*》 pushing oneself forward; believing too much in one's own powers. 주제넘은.

bump·y [bʌ́mpi] *adj.* (**bump·i·er, bump·i·est**) causing bumps; uneven; rough. 덜거덕거리는; 울퉁불퉁한. ¶ *a ~ road* 울퉁불퉁한 길 / *have a ~ ride* 덜걱덜걱 흔들리며 가다.
● **bump·i·ness** [-nis] *n.*

bun [bʌn] *n.* Ⓒ a small, round, sweet roll. 롤빵. [E.]
take the bun, 《*sl.*》 be first in something; win. 첫째를 하다; 이기다(cf. *take the cake*).

bu·na [bjúːnə] *n.* 《chem.》 an artificial rubber. 합성 고무. [G.]

:bunch [bʌntʃ] *n.* Ⓒ **1** a connected group; a cluster. 송이. ¶ *a ~ of flowers* 꽃송이 / *Bananas grow in bunches.* 바나나가 송이로 자란다. **2** a group of things. 다발; 묶음. ¶ *a ~ of papers* 서류 한 묶음 / *a ~ of keys* 열쇠 다발. **3** 《*colloq.*》 a group of people. 무리. ¶ *a ~ of students* 한 무리의 학생들.
the best of the bunch, the pick of anything. 가려뽑은 것.
the bunch of fives, the fist. 주먹.
— *vt.* (P6,7) make a bunch of (something). …을 다발짓다.
— *vi.* (P1) gather together; collect into a group. 모이다; 일단(一團)이 되다. [Norw.]

bun·co [bʌ́ŋkou] *n.* swindle. 사기; 야바위. [? Sp.]

bund [bʌnd] *n.* Ⓒ (in India and the Far East) a bank along a river, etc.; an embankment. 둑; 제방. [Hind.]

***bun·dle** [bʌ́ndl] *n.* Ⓒ **1** a number of things tied or wrapped together. 단; 묶음. **2** a package. 꾸러미. ¶ *a ~ of clothes* 옷 꾸러미. **3** a group. 무리; 일단.
— *vt.* **1** (P6,7) tie or wrap (things) together. …을 꾸리다. **2** (P6) put (something) away without order. …을 아무렇게나 던지다. **3** send (persons or animals) in a hurry. …을 내몰다. — *vi.* (P1,2A) leave hurriedly. 급히 떠나다. [Du. =bind]
bundle out [***off, away***], go or send hurriedly. 부리나케 떠나다; 재촉해 쫓아내다.
bundle up, dress warmly. 따뜻하게 입다.

bung [bʌŋ] *n.* Ⓒ a stopper for the opening of a cask, etc. (통 따위의) 마개. — *vt.* (P6,7) close (something) with a stopper. …에 마개를 하다. ¶ *His eyes were bunged up.* 그의 눈두덩이 부어올랐다. [E.]

bun·ga·low [bʌ́ŋgəlòu] *n.* Ⓒ a cottage, usu. one-storied. 방갈로. [Hind.]

bun·gle [bʌ́ŋgəl] *vt., vi.* (P6;1) do or make (something) badly. 서투르게(잘못) 하다; 실수(실패)하다. ¶ *John tried to make a rabbit-house, but bungled the work.* 존은 토끼장을 지으려고 했지만 실패하고 말았다.
— *n.* Ⓒ a clumsy, unskillful performance. 실수; 실책. [Imit.]

bun·gler [bʌ́ŋgələr] *n.* Ⓒ a person who does work badly. 솜씨가 없는 사람; 일을 잘 못 하는 사람.

bun·ion [bʌ́njən] *n.* a painful swelling, esp. on the joint of the big toe. 엄지발가락 염증. [It.]

bunk[1] [bʌŋk] *n.* Ⓒ **1** a bed built against a wall like a shelf, esp. in a ship, etc. 벽에 선반처럼 만든 침상(寢床). **2** 《*colloq.*》 any bed. 침대.
do a bunk, 《*sl.*》 run away. 달아나다.
— *vi.* 《*colloq.*》 sleep in a bunk. 침상에서 자다; 입은 채 자다. ¶ *~ in the attic* 고미다락에서 자다. [Du. →bank]

bunk[2] [bʌŋk] *n.* 《U.S. *sl.*》 nonsense. 난센스. [=buncombe]

bunk·er [bʌ́ŋkər] *n.* Ⓒ **1** a place for fuel on a ship. (배 안의) 연료고(庫). ¶ *a storage ~* 저장고(통). **2** a sandy hollow or other obstruction on a golf course. (골프장의) 벙커. **3** 《mil.》 an underground shelter. 지하 엄폐호(壕). [Sc.]

bun·kum, -combe [bʌ́ŋkəm] *n.* **1** an insincere talk. 부질없는 이야기. **2** a claptrap. 인기 전술. [Place in U.S.]

***bun·ny** [bʌ́ni] *n.* Ⓒ (*pl.* **-nies**) 《*colloq.*》 **1** 《*child's word*》 a rabbit. 토끼. **2** 《U.S.》 a squirrel. 다람쥐. [E.]

Bun·sen burner [bʌ́nsən bə́ːrnər] *n.* a gas burner that produces a hot, blue flame. 분젠등(燈). [Person]

bunt [bʌnt] *vt.* (P6) **1** strike (something) with the horns, etc., as a goat does. …을 (뿔로) 받다. **2** 《baseball》 hit (a pitched ball) very gently so that the ball rolls only a short distance on the ground. …을 번트하다. ¶ *~ a curve* 커브볼을 번트하다. — *n.* Ⓒ **1** a push. 밀기. **2** 《baseball》 the act of bunting; a bunted ball. 번트(한 공). [?]

bun·ting[1] [bʌ́ntiŋ] *n.* Ⓤ **1** a thin cloth used for flags. 기(旗)를 만드는 천; 기포(旗布). **2** 《*collectively*》 flags. 기(旗) 종류; 장식기(旗). [E.]

bun·ting[2] [bʌ́ntiŋ] *n.* 《bird》 a small kind of bird. 멧새류(類). [F.]

Bun·yan [bʌ́njən], **John** *n.* (1628-88) an English preacher and religious writer. 버니언《영국의 목사·문학자》.

bu·oy [búːi, bɔi / bɔi] *n.* Ⓒ **1** a floating thing fastened to the bottom of the water with a chain to show the presence of dangerous rocks, the safe part of the channel, etc. 부표(浮標). **2** a floating ring used to save a person from drowning. 구명 부대(救命浮袋).
— *vt.* (P6,7) **1** keep (something) from sinking. …을 띄워 두다; 뜨게 하다. **2** sustain. …을 지지하다. **3** mark by means of a buoy. …을 부표로 표시하다. ¶ *~ an anchor* 닻의 위치를 부표로 표시하다. [L. *boia* chain(by which the float was anchored)]

buoy up, **a**) keep (something) from sinking. …을 띄워 두다. **b**) cause (someone) to rise. 북돋우다; 고양시키다. ¶ *buoyed up spirits* 북돋워진 기운 / *~ oneself up with hope* 희망으로 부풀다 / *an economy buoyed up by the rapid growth of industry* 산업의 급속한 성장으로 활기를 띤 경제 / *be buoyed up by hopes of recovery* 회복의 가망으로 기운이 북돋워지다.

buoy·an·cy [bɔ́iənsi, bú:jən-] *n.* Ⓤ **1** the ability to float. 부력(浮力). ¶ *Cork has more ~ than oak.* 코르크는 참나무보다 부력이 더 크다 / *The saltness of sea water increases its ~.* 바닷물의 염분은 부력을 증가시킨다. **2** the power to keep things afloat. 부양성(浮揚性)〔력〕. **3** cheerfulness; high spirits. 쾌활; 명랑.

buoy·ant [bɔ́iənt, bú:jənt] *adj.* **1** able to float; very light. 잘 뜨는; 매우 가벼운. **2** able to keep things afloat. 뜨게 하는 힘이 있는. ¶ *~ force* 부력. **3** gay; cheerful. 쾌활한. ¶ *He was walking with a ~ step.* 그는 가벼운 걸음걸이로 걷고 있었다.

bur [bə:*r*] *n.* Ⓒ **1** the rough, prickly case around the seeds of certain plants. (밤 따위의) 가시 돋친 껍데기. **2** any plant with burs. 가시 돋친 열매 껍데기가 있는 식물. **3** a person hard to shake off. 귀찮은 사람. [E.]

Bur·ber·ry [bə́:*r*bəri, -bèri] *n.* **1** Ⓒ a raincoat made by Burberry & Co., London. 바바리코트. **2** Ⓤ such cloth. 방수포(防水布). [Trademark]

:bur·den[1] [bə́:*r*dn] *n.* ⒸⓊ **1** anything that is carried; a load. 짐. ¶ *a beast of ~* 짐 나르는 동물 / *a ship* 〔*vessel*〕 *of ~* 화물선 / *carry a ~ on one's back* 짐을 져 나르다. **2** something hard to bear. 부담; 의무. ¶ *financial ~* 재정상의 부담 / *the ~ of taxation* 납세 의무 / *be a ~ to* 〔*on*〕 *society* 사회의 짐이 되다 / *bear the ~* 어려움을 견디다 / *shoulder the ~ of responsibilities* 중책을 짊어지다. **3** the weight of a ship's cargo; the carrying capacity of a ship. 적재량(cf. *tonnage*). ¶ *a ship of 150 tons ~* 적재량 150 톤의 배. — *vt.* (P6,13) 《*with*》 put a burden on (someone). …에게 큰 부담을 지우다. ¶ *~ a man with a heavy load* 사나이에게 무거운 짐을 지우다 / *~ citizens with taxation* 국민에게 세금의 부담을 지우다. [E.=bear[1]]

bur·den[2] [bə́:*r*dn] *n.* Ⓒ **1** 《usu. *the ~*》 the most important idea or message. 요지(要旨). **2** the part of a song repeated often; the refrain. (노래의) 후렴; 리프레인. [↑]

bur·den·some [bə́:*r*dnsəm] *adj.* hard to bear; troublesome; oppressive. 무거운; 귀찮은; 힘겨운. ¶ *a ~ task* 힘겨운 일.

bur·dock [bə́:*r*dɑ̀k / -dɔ̀k] *n.* Ⓒ 《bot.》 a plant with prickly burs, large leaves, and a strong smell. 우엉. [*bur*]

:bu·reau [bjúərou] *n.* Ⓒ (*pl.* **bu·reaus** or **bu·reaux**) **1** a government office. 관청; 부; 국; 과. ¶ *the weather ~* 기상국 / *the Bureau of the Mint* 조폐국. **2** 《Brit.》 a large writing table with drawers. (서랍이 달린) 사무용 책상. **3** 《U.S.》 a chest of drawers for clothing, etc. (거울 달린) 옷장. [? O.F.=cloth-covered table]

bu·reauc·ra·cy [bjuərɑ́krəsi / -rɔ́k-] *n.* ⓊⒸ (*pl.* **-cies**) **1** government by bureaus and groups of officials. 관료 정치. **2** 《*collectively*》 officials managing the government. 관료; 관리. **3** concentration of authority in administrative bureaus. 관료주의.

bu·reau·crat [bjúərəkræ̀t] *n.* Ⓒ **1** an official of a bureaucracy. 관리. **2** a formal government official who tries to center power in himself. 관료주의자.

bu·reau·crat·ic [bjùərəkrǽtik] *adj.* of a bureaucracy or a bureaucrat. 관료(정치)의; 관료적인. ¶ *be of ~ origin* 관료 출신이다 / *get ~* 관료적으로 되다.

bu·reaux [bjúərouz] *n.* pl. of **bureau.**

bu·ret(te) [bjuərét] *n.* Ⓒ 《chem.》 a graduated glass tube for measuring small amounts of liquid or gas. 뷰렛《눈금 있는 유리관》. [F.]

burg [bə:*r*g] *n.* Ⓒ 《U.S. *colloq.*》 a town. 마을. [*borough*]

bur·gee [bə́:*r*dʒi:] *n.* three-cornered pennant of yachts. 삼각기(三角旗). [F.]

bur·geon [bə́:*r*dʒən] *n.* Ⓒ a bud; a shoot. 싹. — *vt., vi.* (P6; 1) sprout. 싹트다. [F.]

bur·gess [bə́:*r*dʒis] *n.* Ⓒ a citizen. 시민; 공민. [F.]

burgh [bə:*r*g / bʌ́rə] *n.* Ⓒ a town having powers of self-government in Scotland. (스코틀랜드의) 자치시. [F.]

burgh·er [bə́:*r*gə*r*] *n.* Ⓒ a citizen of a town; a citizen. 시민.

bur·glar [bə́:*r*glə*r*] *n.* Ⓒ a thief who breaks into a building, etc. to steal. 강도; 밤도둑. [E.]

bur·glar·ize [bə́:*r*glərài*z*] *vt., vi.* (P6; 1) commit burglary. 강도질하다.

bur·gla·ry [bə́:*r*gləri] *n.* ⓊⒸ (*pl.* **-glaries**) the act of breaking into a house to steal, esp. after dark. (밤)도둑질; 주거 침입(죄). ¶ *commit* (*a*) *~* 야도죄(夜盜罪)를 범하다.

bur·gle [bə́:*r*gəl] *vt., vi.* (P6; 3) commit burglary. 침입하여 훔치다. [→burglar]

bur·go·mas·ter [bə́:*r*gəmæ̀stə*r*, -mɑ̀:s-] *n.* Ⓒ the mayor of a town in the Netherlands, Germany, etc. (네덜란드·독일 등의) 시장(市長). [Du. =town master]

bur·i·al [bériəl] *n.* ⓊⒸ the act of burying a dead body. 매장; 장례. ¶ *~ at sea* 수장(水葬). — *adj.* of burying. 매장〔장례〕의. [*bury*]

burial ground [⌐--⌐] *n.* a graveyard; a cemetery. 묘지(墓地).

burial service [⌐--⌐-] *n.* the ceremony of burying. 매장식; 장례.

bur·ied [bérid] *v.* p. and pp. of **bury.** — *adj.* laid in a grave. 매장된.

bur·lap [bə́ːrlæp] *n.* Ⓤ very rough cloth made from jute or hemp used for making sacks. (자루를 만드는) 올이 굵은 삼베[주트]. [Du.]

bur·lesque [bəːrlésk] *n.* ⒸⓊ **1** foolish imitation of a serious literary or dramatic work. 익살(극). **2** 《U.S.》 a cheap, vulgar kind of light musical comedy. 희작(戲作). — *vt.* (P6) make (something) nonsensical and laughable by imitating foolishly. 익살부리다; 패사떨다. — *adj.* comical; making people laugh. 우스운; 익살맞은. ¶ ~ *acting* 우스운 행동. [It.]

bur·ly [bə́ːrli] *adj.* (**-li·er, -li·est**) stout; strong; big. 억센; 탄탄한; 큰. ¶ *a burly-set young man* 탄탄한 몸의 젊은이. [E.]

Bur·ma [bə́ːrmə] *n.* the former name of Myanmar. 버마. 參考 미얀마의 구칭임.

Bur·mese [bəːrmíːz] *n.* (*pl.* **-mese**) **1** Ⓒ a person of Burma. 버마 사람. **2** Ⓤ the language of Burma. 버마 말. — *adj.* of Burma, its people, or their language. 버마(사람·말)의.

:burn[1] [bəːrn] *v.* (**burnt** or **burned**) *vi.* **1** (P1,2A) be on fire; blaze. 불타다; 연소(燃燒)하다. ¶ ~ *bright* 이글이글 타다 / ~ *briskly* 활활 타다 / ~ *low* 화력이 약하다 / ~ *with flame* 불꽃을 일으키며 타다 / *They set fire to a bundle of letters and watched them* ~. 그들은 편지 뭉치에 불을 붙여 그것이 타는 것을 보았다. **2** (P1) give light off; glow. 빛을 발하다; 빛나다. ¶ *A lamp is burning.* 램프 불이 빛을 발하고 있다 / *The light burned in the room.* 불빛이 방 안을 밝히었다. **3** (P1,5) be destroyed or damaged by fire, heat, or acid. 타다; 데다; 화상(火傷)을 입다. ¶ *get one's hand burnt* 손에 화상을 입다 / ~ *as a blackberry in the sun* 햇볕에 시꺼멓게 타다 / ~ *brown in the salt air* 바닷바람에 (피부가) 구릿빛으로 타다 / *Her skin burns easily in the sun.* 그녀의 피부는 볕에 잘 탄다. **4** (P1,3) feel hot; feel high body heat. 뜨겁게 느끼다. ¶ *feel one's face* ~ *with shame* 부끄러움으로 얼굴이 화끈 달아오르다 / *The patient burns with fever.* 환자의 몸이 열로 불덩이 같다. **5** (P1,3) 《*with, for*》 feel strong emotion; be eager [excited]. 세게 느끼다; 흥분하다; 열중하다. ¶ ~ *with passion* [*anger*] 불같이 노하다; 욱하다 / ~ *for utterance* 발언하고 싶어 좀이 쑤시다 / ~ *with love* (사랑으로) 애타게 그리다 / *She was burning* (*with the desire*) *to escape.* 그녀는 도망치고 싶은일념뿐이었다. **6** (P1,5) go brown with heat or light; scorch. 타다; 눋다. ¶ ~ *dry* 눌어붙다 / *I'm afraid the cakes are burning.* 케이크가 눋는 것 같구나. — *vt.* (P6,7,13) **1** cause (something) to be on fire; hurt or injure (something) by fire, heat, or acid. …을 불타게 하다; 태우다; …에게 화상을 입히다. ¶ *be burnt to the ground* 전소(全燒)되다 / ~ *one's fingers on a hot stove* 뜨거운 난로에 손가락을 데다 / *Please* ~ *those old papers.* 그 묵은 서류들을 태워 없애시오 / *The house was burned to ashes.* 집이 불타 잿더미로 되었다. **2** ⓐ damage by fire or heat; scorch. …을 태우다; 눋게 하다. ¶ ~ *a carpet* 양탄자를 태우다 / *She burned the roast again.* 그녀는 고기를 또 태웠다. ⓑ make (a hole) by fire or heat. …을 태워[눌어] 구멍이 나게 하다. ¶ ~ *a hole in one's clothing* 옷이 타서 구멍이 나다 / (《*fig.*》) *His money burns a hole in his pocket.* 그는 주머니에 돈이 붙어나지 않는다《금새 다 써 버린다》. **3** use or employ to get heat, light, or powered energy. …을 때다; 켜다; 점화하다. ¶ ~ *coal* [*wood, oil*] 석탄[장작, 기름]을 때다 / ~ *a candle* [*light*] 촛불[등불]을 켜다. **4** treat with fire; harden or finish by intense heat. …을 열처리하다; (불을 때) 굽다. ¶ ~ *bricks* 벽돌을 굽다 / ~ *wood into charcoal* 나무를 구워 숯을 만들다. **5** exhaust. …을 다 써버리다; 낭비하다. ¶ ~ *one's money* 돈을 다 소비하다. **6** 《*sl.*》 irritate. …을 약올리다. **7** give a feeling of heat. …을 톡 쏘다; 얼얼하게 하다. ¶ *The pepper burned his tongue.* 후추가 그의 혀를 얼얼하게 했다.

burn away, **a**) destroy or ruin by burning. 다 태워버리다. **b**) go on burning. 계속 타다. **c**) be exhausted through burning. 다 타서 없어지다.

burn daylight, waste time or energy. 시간·정력 따위를 낭비하다.

burn down, burn (a house, etc.) to the ground. …을 소실[전소]하다. ¶ *The house burnt down.* 집이 다 타버렸다.

burn into, **a**) (of acid) eat into. …을 부식하다. **b**) impress deeply on; make a clear impression upon. (뇌리에) 새겨지다[새기다]; 강렬하게 인상지워지다[짓다]. ¶ *The accident was burnt into his memory.* 그 사고는 그의 기억에 강하게 새겨졌다 / *The idea burned into his mind.* 그 생각이 그의 마음에서 가시지 않았다.

burn one's boats [***bridges***] (***behind one***), make retreat impossible; make it impossible to draw back from something already begun. 배수의 진을 치다; 변경할 수 없는 결심을 하다.

burn one's fingers, get into trouble, esp. by meddling in other people's affairs. (남의 일에 개입하거나 하여) 손을 데다; 혼이 나다.

burn out, **a**) burn to nothing. 끝까지 다 타 없어지다. ¶ *The candle has burned itself out.* 초가 다 타 없어졌다. **b**) drive out by fire. (짐승을) 불을 질러 쫓아내다. ¶ *We burnt the rats out of the cave.* 굴에 불을 질러 쥐를 내몰았다. **c**) 《usu. *passive*》 burn up the house or property of. 다 타서 (집과 재산)을 잃다. ¶ *They were burnt out of house and home.* 그들은 화재로 집과 가정을 잃었다. **d**) use up all one's energy through overwork. 과로로 정력을 다 써버리다.

burn up, **a**) burn completely. 다 불태워 없애다. **b**) burst into flame(s). 확 타오르다. **c**) 《*sl.*》 make or become angry. 성나(게 하)다.

have something to burn, have very much of something to spend. 주체 못 할 만큼 가지고 있다.

— *n.* Ⓒ **1** an injury or a damage caused by burning. 화상(火傷). ¶ *a* ~ *on my hand* 내 손의 화상. **2** a burned place. 불탄 자리. [E.]

burn[2] [bəːrn] *n.* 《Sc.》 a stream; a brook. 시내; 개울. [E.=bourn]

burn·er [bə́ːrnər] *n.* Ⓒ **1** the part of a lamp, furnace, etc., where the flame is produced. 불붙는 곳. **2** anything that burns. 연소기. ¶ *a gas-burner* 가스 버너. **3** a person whose work is burning something. 굽는〔때는〕 사람. ¶ *a charcoal* ~ 숯 굽는 사람.

burn·ing [bə́ːrniŋ] *adj.* **1** aflame; on fire. 불타는. ¶ *a* ~ *hotel* 불타는 호텔. **2** very hot; fiery. 뜨거운; 불 같은. ¶ ~ *sands* 열사(熱砂) / *the* ~ *heat* 뜨거운 열. **3** urgent; exciting; very important. 절박한; 긴급한; 중대한. ¶ *a* ~ *question* 다급한 문제 / *a* ~ *situation* 중대한 국면. **4** intense; passionate. 격심한; 강렬한; 열정적인. ¶ *a* ~ *thirst* 극심한 갈증 / *a* ~ *love* 열렬한 사랑 / *a* ~ *jealousy* 불타는 질투. **5** glowing; bright in color. 매우 밝은; 산뜻한; 불타는 듯한. ● **burn·ing·ly** [-li] *adv.*

bur·nish [bə́ːrniʃ] *vt.* (P6) polish (the surface of metal, etc.) by rubbing. (금속)을 닦아서 광을 내다. ¶ ~ *metal* 금속을 닦아 광을 내다. — *n.* polish. 광; 광택. ¶ *the* ~ *of brass* 놋쇠의 광. ● **bur·nish·er** [-ər] *n.* [→brown]

bur·nous, -nouse [bəːrnúːs] *n.* a kind of cloak with a hood worn by Arabs. (아랍 사람의) 두건 달린 외투. [Arab.]

:burnt [bəːrnt] *v.* p. and pp. of **burn**[1].

burr [bəːr] *n.* =bur.

·bur·row [bə́ːrou, bʌ́r-] *n.* Ⓒ **1** a hole in the ground made by a rabbit, fox, etc. for living in. (토끼·여우 따위의) 굴. ¶ *Rabbits live in burrows.* 토끼는 굴에서 산다. **2** a similar place of retreat. 은신처. — *vi., vt.* (P1,2A,3; 6) **1** make a hole or passage in the ground. 굴을 파다. **2** 《*into*》 research; investigate. 깊이 파고 들다; 탐구하다. **3** hide. 숨다. [E.]

:burst [bəːrst] *v.* (**burst**) *vi.* **1** (P1,2A,3) break open or into pieces violently and suddenly; explode; split. 터지다; 폭발〔파열〕하다. ¶ *The bomb* 〔*balloon*〕 ~. 폭탄〔풍선〕이 터졌다 / *The fireworks* ~ *while they were in the air.* 불꽃이 공중에서 터졌다 / *The trees have* ~ *into blossom.* 나무들은 꽃이 활짝 피기 시작했다. **2** (P1,3) 《generally in *ppr.*》 《*with*》 be filled to the breaking point. (터질 만큼) 충만하다. ¶ *The barn is bursting with grain.* 곳간은 곡식으로 꽉 들어차 있다 / *He was bursting with health.* 그는 건강으로 충만해 있었다. **3** (P2A,3) 《*into, upon, on*》 act or appear suddenly and violently. 갑자기 …하다. ¶ *He* ~ *into the room.* 갑자기 방 안으로 들어왔다 / *The view of the sea* ~ *suddenly upon my sight.* 갑자기 바다 경치가 눈 앞에 전개(展開)되었다.

— *vt.* (P6,7,18) cause (something) to break violently and suddenly. …을 터뜨리다; 파열(破裂)시키다.

be bursting (=*be eager*) ***to*** *do.* …하고 싶어 하다.

be bursting with (=*be full of*) *something.* …로 가득 차 있다.

burst in, **a**) open violently inward. 안으로 힘있게 열리다. **b**) interrupt. (이야기 따위)를 방해하다; 가로막다. ¶ ~ *in on* 〔*upon*〕 *a conversation* 대화에 불쑥 끼어들다. **c**) appear or come in suddenly. 갑자기 나타나다〔들어오다〕. ¶ ~ *in on* 〔*upon*〕 *someone* 아무가 있는 곳에 들이닥치다.

burst into, **a**) come into suddenly. 난입하다. **b**) begin to do something suddenly. 갑자기 …하기 시작하다. ¶ ~ *into flames* 확 타오르다 / ~ *into tears* 울기 시작하다 / ~ *into laughter* 웃음을 터뜨리다.

burst open, open violently or suddenly. 홱 열리다. ¶ *The door* ~ *open.* 문이 홱 열렸다.

burst out, **a**) exclaim; begin to speak loudly. 외치다; 큰 소리로 말하기 시작하다. ¶ ~ *out into threats* 목청을 돋우어 협박하기 시작하다. **b**) start suddenly. 갑자기 떠나다. ¶ ~ *out of a room* 갑자기 방에서 나가다. **c**) begin to do suddenly. 갑자기 …하기 시작하다. ¶ ~ *out crying* 〔*laughing*〕 느닷없이 울기〔웃기〕 시작하다.

burst up, **a**) explode. 폭발하다. **b**) (of a business, etc.) fail entirely. (사업 따위가) 완전히 망하다.

burst upon 〔***on***〕, **a**) come suddenly in sight of (someone). 갑자기 나타나다. **b**) attack suddenly. …을 급습하다.

— *n.* Ⓒ **1** the act of bursting; a split; an explosion. 파열; 폭발. ¶ *a* ~ *in a tyre* 〔*pipe*〕 타이어〔파이프〕 파열. **2** an outbreak. 돌발(突發). ¶ *a* ~ *of laughter* 돌발적인 웃음소리. **3** a sudden activity or spurt. 한바탕의 분발. [E.]

Bu·run·di [burúndi, bərʌ́ndi] *n.* a country of central Africa. 부룬디《중앙 아프리카의 나라》.

:bur·y [béri] *vt.* (**bur·ied**) **1** (P6,18) ⓐ put (a dead body) in the earth. …을 묻다; 매장하다. ¶ *be buried alive* 생매장되다 / *A dead body is usually buried.* 시체는 흔히 매장된다. ⓑ lose by death. …을 여의다; 잃다. ¶ *He has buried all his children.* 그는 자식들을 모두 여의었다. ⓒ 《*fig.*》 forget. …을 잊다. ¶ ~ *an insult* 모욕을 잊다. **2** (P6,13) hide (something) from view; cover up. …을 덮어 가리다; 파묻다. ¶ ~ *one's past* 과거를 숨기다 / ~ *oneself in the country* 시골에 묻히다 / *She buried her face in her hands.* 그녀는 두 손으로 얼굴을 가렸다. **3** (P13) 《*reflexively*》 occupy oneself completely; plunge; sink. …에 몰두하다; 빠지다. ¶ *be buried in thought* 생각에 잠기다 / *He buried himself in his work.* 그는 일에 몰두했다. [E.]

:bus [bʌs] *n.* Ⓒ a large automobile having seats or benches for passengers; an omnibus. 버스. ¶ *go by* ~ 버스로 가다 / *catch* 〔*get*〕 *a* ~ 버스를 타다.
miss the bus, lose an opportunity. 기회를 놓치다.
— *vi.* (P1) go by bus. 버스로 가다. [omnibus]

bus·by [bʌ́zbi] *n.* Ⓒ (*pl.* **-bies**) a tall fur hat worn for parades by soldiers of certain British armies. 예장용(禮裝用)의 높은 군모. [Person]

:bush [buʃ] *n.* **1** Ⓒ a low-growing plant with several branches growing from the root. 관목. ¶ *trees and bushes* 교목과 관목. **2** 《*the* ~》 wild land. 미개간지; 총림지(叢林地). ¶ *There is much* ~ *in Australia and Africa.* 오스트레일리아와 아프리카에는 미개간〔총림(叢林)〕지가 많다. [→boscage]
beat around 〔***about***〕 ***the bush,*** approach a matter in a long, slow way. 에둘러 말하다. ¶ *Do not beat about the* ~. 말을 빙빙 돌리지 마라.

***bush·el** [búʃəl] *n.* Ⓒ a measure for grain, fruit, vegetables, etc. equal to eight gallons. 부셀《약 36 리터, 약 2 말》. [→box]
hide *one's* ***light under a bushel,*** be too modest in showing one's qualities. 재능을 숨기다.

bush·ing [búʃiŋ] *n.* 《mech.》 a tube of soft metal put between two parts of a machine where they rub against each other. 부싱; 축투(軸套). [*bush*]

bush·man [búʃmən] *n.* (*pl.* **-men** [-mən]) Ⓒ **1** a woodsman, esp. a farmer, traveler, etc. in the Australian bush. (오스트레일리아의) 총림지(叢林地) 주민. **2** 《*B-*》 a member of certain tribes in South Africa. (남아프리카의) 부시맨.

bush·y [búʃi] *adj.* (**bush·i·er, bush·i·est**) **1** spreading out like a bush. 덤불이 무성한〔우거진〕. **2** covered with thick hair. 털이 많은.

***bus·i·ly** [bízəli] *adv.* in a busy manner. 바쁘게; 부지런히. [↓]

:busi·ness [bíznis] *n.* Ⓤ **1** one's work; occupation. 일; 직업. ¶ *the* ~ *of a carpenter* 목수일 / *make* ~ *of photography* 사진을 업으로 하다 / *follow the* ~ *of* …직업에 종사하다 / *What's his* ~*?* 그의 직업이 무엇인가. **2** the selling and buying of goods; trade. 장사; 매매. ¶ *He is in the cotton* ~. 그는 목화 장사를 하고 있다. **3** ⓐ a commercial or industrial enterprise. 사업; 실업; 상업. ¶ *a man of* ~ 사업가 / ~ *English* 상업 영어 / *a* ~ *school* 실업 학교. ⓑ work. 사무; 집무; 업무. ¶ ~ *hours* 영업 시간 / *a matter of* ~ 사무상의 일 / *go to* ~ 출근하다. **4** the activities of selling and buying. 상황(商況). ¶ *depression of* ~ 상황 부진; 불경기 / *Business is dull.* 거래가 저조하다. **5** Ⓒ an affair; a matter. 일; 사건. ¶ *an awkward* ~ 귀찮은 일 / *a strange* ~ 이상한 사건. **6** duty; mission. 의무; 사명; 용건. ¶ *know one's* ~ 자기의 할 일을 알고 있다 / *go to Paris on urgent* ~ 긴급한 용무로 파리에 가다. **7** 《usu. in *negative*》 what has to do with someone; right to concern. 관계 있는 일; 관여할 권리. ¶ *It's none of your* ~. 네가 알 바 아니다. [→busy]
Business is business. Business comes before personal circumstances. 장사는 장사다; 계산은 계산이다.
come 〔***get***〕 ***to business,*** start the work that is to be done. (해야 할) 일에 착수하다.
do business, carry on one's work or trade. 장사를 하다.
do *one's* ***business for*** *someone,* defeat or kill someone. 아무를 해치우다; 죽이다.
do business (=*be connected in business*) ***with*** *someone.* …와 거래하다.
enter business, begin one's work. 일을 시작하다.
Go about your business! Get away! 꺼져.
go into business, become a man of business. 실업계에 발을 내딛다.
Good business! Well done! 잘 했다.
have no business to *do,* have no right to do. …할 권리는〔자격은〕 없다.
like nobody's business, 《*sl.*》 fast or very well. 빠르게; 아주 잘; 훌륭히. ¶ *She can cook like nobody's* ~. 그녀의 요리 솜씨는 아주 훌륭하다.
make a great business of it, be embarrassed. 힘겨워〔벅차〕하다; 쩔쩔매다.
make it *one's* ***business to*** *do,* decide to do; do often as one's business. …할 것을 떠맡다; …하기를 일삼다.
mean business, be in earnest. 농담이 아니다; 진지하다.
on business, with a definite purpose. 용건으로; 사업차.
out of business, going bankrupt. 파산한.
send *someone* ***about his business,*** dismiss. 해고하다.

business card [ㅅ-ㅅ] *n.* a small card printed or engraved with a person's name and business affiliation. (업무용) 명함.

busi·ness·like [bíznislàik] *adj.* having system and method; practical. 질서 있는; 사무적인; 실제적인. ¶ *a* ~ *manner* 사무적인 태도 / *a* ~ *man* 실제적인 사람.

busi·ness·man [bíznismæ̀n] *n.* Ⓒ (*pl.* **-men** [-mèn]) a man engaged in business; a man who runs a business. 실업〔사업〕가; 경영자; 실무가; 상인.

bus·kin [bʌ́skin] *n.* Ⓒ **1** a high boot. 반장화. **2** an ancient tragic actor's boot with very thick sole. (옛 비극 배우가 신던) 편상 반장화. [Rom.]

put on the buskins, write or act a tragedy. 비극을 쓰다[연기하다].

buss [bʌs] *n.* 《*arch.*》 a kiss. 키스. — *vt., vi.* (P6; 1) kiss. 키스하다. [L. *basium*]

•**bust**[1] [bʌst] *n.* Ⓒ **1** a sculpture of a person's head, shoulders, and chest. 반신상(像); 흉상. **2** the upper, front part of the body. 흉부; 상반신. **3** a woman's bosom. (여성의) 젖가슴. [It.]

bust[2] [bʌst] *n., v.* =burst.

bus·tard [bʌ́stərd] *n.* 《bird》 a large, heavy, long-legged gamebird. 능에. [L. *avis tarda* slow bird]

bus·tle [bʌ́sl] *vi.* (P1,2A) 《*about*》 move or act noisily and in a hurry. 부산떨다. ¶ ~ *about to get the mess removed* 뒤끝을 치우느라 부산을 떨다. — *vt.* (P6,7) make (others) hurry or work hard. …을 재촉하다. ¶ *She bustled the children out of the house.* 그녀는 아이들을 다그쳐 집 밖으로 내몰았다. — *n.* Ⓤ 《sometimes *a* ~》 activity with great show of energy. 큰 소란; 법석. ¶ *in a* ~ 부산하게 / *the* ~ *of Christmas preparation* 크리스마스 준비를 위한 법석. ● **bus·tler** [-lər] *n.* [?]

⁑**bus·y** [bízi] *adj.* (**bus·i·er, bus·i·est**) **1** working; active; not free. 일하고 있는; 틈이 없는. ¶ *I'm* ~ *now.* 나는 지금 작업중이다[다른 일에 신경 쓸 틈이 없다]. **2** full of work or activity; crowded. 바쁜; 일이 많은; 혼잡한. ¶ *a* ~ *day* 바쁜 날 / *a* ~ *street* 혼잡한 거리 / *be* ~ *preparing* [*in preparation*] *for* …준비에 바쁘다 / *keep oneself* ~ *packing up to go home* 귀향을 위해 짐꾸리기 바쁘다. **3** meddlesome. 참견을 잘 하는. ¶ *an idle,* ~ *woman* 게으르고 남의 일에 참견 잘 하는 여자. **4** 《U.S.》 (of a telephone line) in use. 통화 중인. ¶ *I found the telephone* ~. 전화를 걸었더니 통화중이었다.

be busy at [*in, with*], be occupied with. …로 바쁘다.

get busy, start doing things. 일을 시작하다; 활동에 옮기다. ¶ *Then the police got* ~. 그래서 경찰은 수사 활동을 시작했다.

— *vt.* (**bus·ied**) (P6,13) 《*with, about, in, at*》 make or keep (oneself, one's hands, etc.) busy. …을 바쁘게 하다[일시키다]. ¶ *She busies herself about the house.* 그녀는 가사(家事)로 바쁘게 지낸다. [E.]

bus·y·bod·y [bízibàdi / -bɔ̀di] *n.* Ⓒ (*pl.* **-bod·ies**) a person who meddle with the affairs of others. (남의 일에) 참견하는 사람; 중뿔난 사람.

⁑**but** [bʌt, bət] *conj.* **1** ⓐ on the other hand; yet; however; still. 한편; 그러나; 하지만; …하기는 하나. ¶ *He is rich,* ~ (*he is*) *not happy.* 부자이지만 행복하지는 않다 / *You may go,* ~ *you must be home by five o'clock.* 가도 좋으나 5시까지는 집에 돌아와 있어야 한다 / *His parents were poor* ~ *cheerful.* 그의 부모는 가난했지만 명랑했다. ⓑ 《after *a negative sentence*》 on the contrary. …이[은] 아니고. ¶ *It is not a pen,* ~ *a pencil.* 그건 펜이 아니고 연필이다 / *It's not difficult,* ~ *easy.* 그건 어렵지 않고 쉽다 / *It was not my brother you saw,* ~ *my father.* 네가 본 분은 내 형이 아니라 아버지다. **2** unless; if … not. …하지 않으면; …이 아니면. ¶ *I would go abroad* ~ *that I am poor.* 내가 가난하지 않다면 외유(外遊)를 가는건데 / *She would have fallen* ~ (*that*) *I caught her.* 내가 붙들지 않았다면 그녀는 쓰러졌을 게다. **3** other than; except that. …을 제외하고; …외에는. ¶ *All are wrong* ~ *I.* 나를 제외하고 전부가 잘못돼 있다[틀렸다] / *All* ~ *he had fled.* 그 사람 외엔 모두가 달아나고 없었다 / *Nobody* ~ *she knew it.* 그녀 외에는 아무도 몰랐다. **4** 《after *negative*》 that … not. …하지 않을[…아닐] 만큼; …을 않을[못 할] 정도로. ¶ *I am not such a fool* ~ (*what*) *I understand it.* 내가 그것을 이해 못 할 만큼 바보가 아니다 / *No one is so old* ~ *that he may learn.* 아무리 나이를 먹어도 배우지 못한다는 법은 없다. **5** 《after *not doubt, deny,* etc.》 that. …이라는[하다는] 것은. ¶ *I don't doubt* ~ (*that*) *he will come.* 그가 오리라는 것을 의심치 않는다.

— *adv.* **1** only; only just. 그저(…일 따름, …밖에); 단지(…뿐, …에 지나지 않다); 오직. ¶ *He is* ~ *a child.* 그저 어린애에 불과하다 / *He has* ~ *few friends.* 그저 약간의 친구밖엔 없다 / *There is* ~ *one chance left.* 한 번의 기회밖엔 남아 있지 않다 / *He left* ~ *ten minutes ago.* 불과 10분 전에 떠났다. **2** 《*can* ~》 only; in any case; at least. 그저 …할 수밖에는; 어쨌든; 적어도. ¶ *I can* ~ *hear.* 그저 들을 따름이다 / *We could* ~ *listen to his plea.* 그의 간청을 들어줄 수밖엔 없었다.

all but, nearly; almost. 거의. ¶ *He is all* ~ *dead.* 그는 죽은 것이나 마찬가지다.

anything but, far from. 전혀 …아니다; …은 커녕.

but for, if it were not for; if it had not been for. …이 아니라면; …이 없었다면[아니었다면]. ¶ *But for you, I should have been ruined.* 당신이 아니었다면 나는 망했을 게다.

But me no buts. Don't object to me. 이의를 말하지 마라.

but then, but on the other hand. 그런데; 그 한편.

cannot but *do,* cannot help doing; must do. …하지 않을 수 없다.

cannot choose but *do,* must do. …할 수밖에 없다; …하지 않을 수 없다. ¶ *I cannot choose* ~ *laugh.* 웃지 않을 수 없었다.

do nothing but *do,* only do. (그저) …하기만 하다. ¶ *She did nothing but cry.* 그녀는 그저 울 따름이었다.

never … but, never … without. …하지 않고는 —아니하다; (—하면) 반드시 …하다. ¶ 《*prov.*》 *It never rains* ~ *it pours.* 왔다 하면

장대비다; 엎친 데 덮치기.

not but that 〔***what***〕 ***...,*** though at the same time it is true that .... …이 아니라고는 하지 않지만. ¶ *Not ~ that he believes it.* 그가 그것을 믿지 않는다고 말하는 것은 아니지만.

***not only** A **but also** B* ⇨only.

not that ... but that, not because ... but because. …때문이 아니라 —때문이다. ¶ *Not that I dislike the work, but that I have no time.* 일이 싫어서가 아니라 시간이 없기 때문이다.

nothing but, only. 그저 …뿐〔만〕. ¶ *War brings nothing ~ misery.* 전쟁은 빈곤만을 가져온다.

— *prep.* except; save. …을 빼고. ¶ *the last ~ one* 끝에서 두 번째 / *Who ~ George would do such a thing?* 조지 말고는 누가 그 짓을 했겠나.

— *pron.* 《*relative pronoun*》 who ... not; that ... not. …하지 않는. ¶ *There is no one ~ knows it.* 그것을 알지 못하는 사람은 없다. / *There is no rule ~ has exceptions.* 예외 없는 규칙은 없다. [*by, out*]

•**butch·er** [bútʃər] *n.* Ⓒ **1** a person whose business is to kill animals for food. 도살업자. **2** ⓐ a person who sells meat. 푸주한(漢). ⓑ 《*fig.*》 a cruel man; a murderer. 잔인한 사람; 살인자. **3** 《U.S.》 a seller. (열차내의) 판매원. — *vt.* (P6) **1** kill (animals) for food. …을 도살하다. **2** kill brutally. …을 학살하다(cf. *massacre*). **3** spoil (something) by poor work. (일 따위)를 망쳐 놓다. [F. =buck]

butch·er·y [bútʃəri] *n.* (*pl.* **-er·ies**) **1** Ⓤ brutal killing; cruel and needless killing. 잔인한 살생; 학살(cf. *carnage*). **2** Ⓒ a house for killing animals; a butcher's work. 도살장; 도살업. **3** Ⓒ a botch; a bungle. 실수; 서투른 솜씨. ¶ *make a ~ of* 서툰 짓을 하여 …을 망치다.

•**but·ler** [bʌ́tlər] *n.* Ⓒ **1** the chief manservant of a household who has charge of the plates and wine; a head manservant. 집사(執事). **2** a manservant in charge of the dining room. 식당 지배인. [→bottle]

butt[1] [bʌt] *n.* Ⓒ the thicker end of a tool, weapon, fishing rod, etc. (도구·무기·낚싯대 따위 등의) 굵은 쪽의 끝. [G.]

butt[2] [bʌt] *n.* Ⓒ **1** a target for shooting. (사격장의) 과녁. **2** a shooting range. 사격장. **3** a person who is laughed at or blamed by others. (조소(嘲笑)·비평 등의) 대상; 웃음가마리. ¶ *make someone the ~ of contempt* 아무를 모멸의 대상으로 하다. [F. *but* goal]

butt[3] [bʌt] *n.* Ⓒ a large barrel or cask (containing 108-140 gallons). 큰 술통. [Rom.]

butt[4] [bʌt] *vt.* (P6) strike or push (something) with the head or horns. (머리·뿔 따위로) …을 받다. — *n.* Ⓒ a push or blow with the head or horns. 박치기; 뿔로 받기. [F. *bouter*]

butte [bjuːt] *n.* 《U.S.》 a steep hill standing alone in the western parts of the United States. (미국 서부의) 고립한 가파른 언덕〔산〕. [F.]

⁑**but·ter** [bʌ́tər] *n.* Ⓤ **1** the solid yellowish fat made from cream. 버터. ¶ *spread bread with ~ =spread ~ on bread* 빵에 버터를 바르다. **2** something like butter. 버터 같은 것. ¶ *peanut ~* 땅콩 버터. **3** flattery. 아첨. ¶ *base ~* 비굴한 아첨 / *spread* 〔*lay on*〕 *the ~* 아첨하다.

look as if butter would not melt in** one's **mouth, pretend to be kind, harmless, sincere, etc. but is not really so. 위선의 탈을 쓰고 있다.

— *vt.* **1** (P6) put butter on (bread, etc.) …에 버터를 바르다. **2** 《*colloq.*》《*up*》 (P6,7) flatter. …에게 아첨하다. [Gk. *boútūron*]

know on which side** one's **bread is buttered ⇨bread.

but·ter·cup [bʌ́tərkʌ̀p] *n.* Ⓒ 《bot.》 a wild plant with bright yellow cup-shaped flowers. 미나리아재비.

•**but·ter·fly** [bʌ́tərflài] *n.* Ⓒ (*pl.* **-flies**) an insect with feelers and four wings. 나비 (cf. *moth*).

but·ter·milk [bʌ́tərmìlk] *n.* Ⓤ liquid remaining after butter has been separated from milk. 버터밀크.

but·ter·scotch [bʌ́tərskɑ̀tʃ / -skɔ̀tʃ] *n.* Ⓤ candy made from brown sugar and butter. 버터 넣은 캔디; 버터볼. — *adj.* flavored with brown sugar and butter. 버터와 흑설탕으로 맛을 낸.

but·ter·y [bʌ́təri] *adj.* **1** like butter. 버터와 같은. **2** containing butter. 버터가 든. — *n.* a storeroom for provisions. 식량 저장실. [→butter]

but·tocks [bʌ́təks] *n. pl.* the part of the body on which a person sits; a rump. 궁둥이; 둔부. [→butt[1], -ock]

⁑**but·ton** [bʌ́tn] *n.* Ⓒ **1** a small object fastened to. 단추. ¶ *fasten buttons* 단추를 끼다 / *undo* 〔*unfasten*〕 *buttons* 단추를 벗기다〔끄르다〕 / *A ~ has come off.* 단추가 떨어졌다. **2** any knob or button-shaped object to push. (벨의) 누름단추. ¶ *Press the ~, will you?* 벨을 좀 눌러 주게. **3** 《*pl.*》《Brit., *colloq.*》 a boy who serves in a hotel, club, etc., in uniform. (호텔 등의) 보이. **4** anything small or without value. 시시한〔하찮은〕 것. ¶ *not worth a ~* 매우 하찮은.

hold by the button, detain. 만류하다.

not care a button about, not care a bit about. …을 조금도 상관〔개의치〕 않다.

press the button, set something going. 일을 시작하다.

— *vt.* (P6,7) fasten with buttons. …을 단추로 잠그다. ¶ *~ (up) one's coat* 코트의 단추를 채우다 / *~ up one's mouth* 입을 다물다 / *~ up one's purse* 돈주머니 끈을 죄다.

— *vi.* (P1,3) be able to be closed; be made so as to close with buttons. 단추가 채워지다. ¶ *My collar won't* ～. 옷깃의 단추가 채워지지 않는다 / *This dress buttons down the back.* 이 옷은 등에서 단추를 채운다.
● **but·ton·less** [-lis] *adj.* [Rom. =bud]

but·ton·hole [bʌ́tnhòul] *n.* Ⓒ a hole through which a button is passed. 단춧구멍. — *vt.* **1** (P6) make buttonholes in (cloth, etc.) …에 단춧구멍을 내다. **2** (P6) hold (someone) in conversation against his will. …을 붙들고 긴 말을 늘어놓다.

but·tress [bʌ́tris] *n.* Ⓒ **1** a structure built against a wall as a support. 부벽(扶壁). **2** a support. 지지물. — *vt.* (P6) **1** make (something) strong with a buttress. …을 부벽으로 받치다. **2** support. …을 지지하다. [→butt[4]]

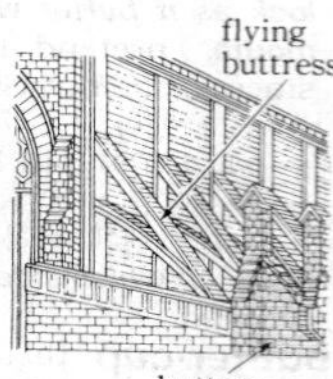

〈buttress 1〉

bux·om [bʌ́ksəm] *adj.* (of women) rounded and good to look at; healthy and cheerful. (여성이) 오동통한; 쾌활하고 건강한. ¶ *a* ～ *woman.* [→bow[1]]

:buy [bai] *vt.* (**bought**) **1** (P6,7,13,14) ⓐ get (something) in exchange for money; purchase. …을 사다. ¶ ～ *and sell for profit* 이익을 남기기 위해 사고 팔다 / ～ *something cheap* 〔*at a low price*〕 …을 싸게 사다 / ～ *something for cash* 〔*10 dollars*〕 …을 현금으로〔10 달러에〕 사다 / ～ *flowers from an old woman* 노파로부터 꽃을 사다 / *I bought her a new hat.* =*I bought a new hat for her.* 그녀에게 새 모자를 사 주었다. ⓑ (of money, etc.) serve to get (something); be the means of getting. (돈 따위가) …을 살 수 있다. ¶ *Ten dollars will* ～ *a lot of meat and beans.* 10 달러면 많은 고기와 콩을 살 수 있다 / *Money cannot* ～ *happiness.* 돈으로 행복을 살 수는 없다. **2** get (something) by means of some sacrifice. (희생·대가를 치르고) …을 얻다. ¶ ～ *fame with health* 건강을 희생하며 명성을 얻다 / ～ *favor with flattery* 아첨을 하여 환심을 사다 / *Peace was dearly bought.* 비싼 대가를 치르고 평화를 얻었다. **3** (P6,7) bribe. …을 매수(買收)하다. ¶ ～ (*over*) *a witness* 〔*public official*〕 증인〔공무원〕을 매수하다 / ～ *the jury over to a man* 배심원을 하나도 남김 없이 매수하다.

buy in, **a**) buy stock (in a company, etc.). (주식)을 사 모으다; 사들이다. **b**) 《auction》 buy (one's own goods) to prevent others from buying them too cheaply. (경매에서 팔았던 자기 물건)을 되사다.

buy off, get rid of (something) by payment; bribe. 돈을 주고 …을 모면하다; …에게 뇌물을 주다; 매수하다.

buy out, get all rights of business by paying money. 돈으로 (회사 등)의 소유권을〔권리를〕 손에 넣다; (회사 따위)를 사들이다.

buy up, buy as much of (something) as one can. …을 한껏 매점하다.

— *n.* **1** an act of buying. 매입. ¶ *make a* ～ *of wheat* 밀을 사들이다. **2** a bargain. 싸게 산 물건. ¶ *It's a good* ～ *at the price.* 그것은 그 값이면 잘 산 물건이다. [E.]

buy·a·ble [báiəbəl] *adj.* that can be bought. 살 수 있는.

·buy·er [báiər] *n.* Ⓒ a person who buys. 구매자. ¶ *a buyers' market* (수요보다 공급이 많은) 매주(買主) 시장(cf. *sellers' market*).

·buzz [bʌz] *n.* Ⓒ **1** the humming sound of a bee, etc. 윙윙〔붕붕〕거리는 소리. **2** the confused sound of many people talking quietly. 웅성거리는 소리; 술렁댐.

— *vi., vt.* (P1;6) **1** make a buzz; cause (something) to make a low, humming sound. 윙윙〔붕붕〕거리다; …을 윙윙대게 하다. **2** speak with a low, humming voice. 웅성거리다; 술렁대다. ¶ *The room buzzed with excitement.* 방 안은 흥분으로 술렁댔다. **3** spread (a rumor, gossip, etc.) secretly. (소문 따위)를 남모르게 퍼뜨리다. [Imit.]

buzz about 〔***around***〕, move about noisily. 바쁘게 돌아다니다.

buzz off, **a**) 《Brit. *colloq.*》 ring off on the telephone. 전화를 끊다. **b**) 《*colloq.*》 go away. 떠나다. ¶ *Buzz off, you nasty little child!* 꺼져, 이 성가신 꼬마녀석 같으니.

buz·zard [bʌ́zərd] *n.* Ⓒ 《bird》 a bird of the falcon family. 말똥가리. [F. *busard*]

buzz·er [bʌ́zər] *n.* Ⓒ **1** an electrical instrument that makes a buzzing sound as signal or warning. 버저. **2** a steam whistle; a siren. 고동; 기적; 사이렌. [Imit.]

B.V.(M.) Blessed Virgin (Mary).

:by [bai] *prep.* **1** near to; beside. …의 옆〔곁〕에; 곁의. ¶ *a house* ～ *the lake* 호반의 집 / *sit* ～ *the fire* 노변(爐邊)에 앉다. **2** along; at the side of. …을 따라〔따른〕; …을 끼고. ¶ *walk* ～ *the river* 강을 따라 걷다. **3** ⓐ through; cross; over; via. …을 통과하여〔지나〕; 건너; 넘어; …을 거쳐. ¶ *go* ～ *sea* 〔*land, air*〕 해로〔육로, 공로〕로 가다 / *travel* ～ *Siberia* 시베리아 경유로 여행하다. ⓑ past. 옆을 지나. ¶ *He walked* ～ *me without speaking.* 그는 말없이 내 옆을 지나쳐 갔다. **4** through the act or means of; using. …로; …에 의하여; …을 (이용하여). ¶ *catch a dog* ～ *the tail* 개의 꼬리를 붙잡다 / *He escaped* ～ *telling lies.* 그는 거짓말로 속이고 탈출했다 / *I took him* ～ *the hand.* 나는 그의 손을 잡았다 / *America was discovered* ～ *Columbus.* 아메리카는 콜럼버스에 의해 발견되었다 / *Who is this poem* ～? 이 시는 누가 썼는가. **5** to the extent of. …만큼. ¶ *short* ～ *an inch* 1인치 짧은 / *too many* ～ *one* 하나(만큼) 더 많은 / *win* ～ *a boat's length,* 1 정신(艇身)차로 이기다. **6** according to a unit of; in the measure of. …단위로. ¶ *sell* ～ *the* *pound* 파운드당 얼마로 팔다 / *He was employed ~ the month.* 그는 월급제로 고용되었다. **7** according to. …에 따라; …을 기준으로. ¶ *~ your leave* 당신의 허락으로 / *sell ~ wholesale* 도매로 팔다 / *judge someone ~ his appearance* 아무를 외양으로 판단하다. **8** concerning; in relation to; in respect of. …에 관[대]해서(는); …점에서. ¶ *a teacher ~ occupation* 직업은 교사 / *a Frenchman ~ birth* 태생은 프랑스인 / *do one's duty ~ one's parents* 부모에 대해 자식의 할 도리를 하다 / *She did well ~ her daughter.* 그녀는 딸에 대해서는 잘 해 주었다. **9** with a succession of. …씩. ¶ *~ degrees* 점차 / *piece ~ piece* 한 개씩 / *drop ~ drop* 한 방울 한 방울(씩) / *~ turns* 번갈아; 차례로 / *~ hundreds* 백 개씩. **10** at; in; during. …에는; …동안. ¶ *He worked ~ day and studied ~ night.* 그는 낮에는 일하고 밤에는 공부했다. **11** not later than. …까지는. ¶ *He will certainly come ~ three o'clock.* 그는 3시까지는 꼭 올 게다. **12** (in oaths) in the name of. …에 맹세코. ¶ *swear ~ God that ...* …을 하느님을 두고 맹세하다.

(all) by oneself, (all) alone; without help. 혼자; 홀로; 혼자 힘으로.

by far, very much. 매우; 훨씬. ¶ *too expensive ~ far* 너무나 비싼 / *~ far the best* 훨씬 좋은.

by the by(e), in passing. 이와 관련하여; 그런데(=by the way). ¶ *By the by(e), I forgot to tell you the news.* 그런데 네게 소식을 전하는 것을 잊었군.

have something by one, have something within easy reach. …을 가까이[곁에] 두다.

— *adv.* **1** near at hand. 가까이; 곁에. ¶ *Many were standing ~ at the time.* 그 때 많은 사람이 곁에 서 있었다 / *Nobody was ~ when the fire broke out.* 불이 났을 땐 아무도 부근에 없었다. **2** past. 지나서. ¶ *pass ~* 지나가다 / *go ~* (시간이) 흐르다 / *days gone ~* 옛적. **3** aside; away. 옆[곁]에. ¶ *lay something ~* 옆으로 제쳐놓다. **4** in reserve. 예비로; 따로 떼어. ¶ *lay ~ money* 돈을 따로 떼어 두다. [E.]

by and by, before long; soon. 곧; 얼마 안 있어. ¶ *You will forget him ~ and ~.* 얼마 안 있어 그를 잊게 될 것이다.

by and large, on the whole; in general. 대체로. ¶ *By and large, your plan is a good one.* 대체로 네 계획은 괜찮다.

by-and-by [báiənd́bái] *n.* 《*the* ~》 future. (가까운) 미래.

bye-bye [báibài] *interj.* 《*colloq.*》 goodby. 안녕. [E.]

by-e·lec·tion [báiilèkʃən] *n.* Ⓒ 《Brit.》 a special election to fill a vacancy. 보궐 선거.

by·gone [báigɔ̀:n, -gàn / -gɔ̀n] *adj.* past. 과거의. — *n.* Ⓒ 《*pl.*》 something in the past. 과거(지사); 지나간 일. ¶ *Let us forget bygones.* 지난 일은 잊어버리자.

by·lane [báilèin] *n.* an unfrequented lane. 샛길.

by·law [báilɔ̀:] *n.* Ⓒ **1** a law made by a local government. 조례. **2** a secondary law or rule. 내규; 세칙.

by-line [báilàin] *n.* Ⓒ 《U.S.》 a line at the beginning of a newspaper or magazine article giving the name of the writer. (신문·잡지에서) 필자명이 쓰인 행(行).

by·name [báinèim] *n.* Ⓒ a nickname. 별명.

by-pass [báipæ̀s, -pɑ̀:s] *n.* Ⓒ a side road parallel to the main road, built for fast traffic to pass by, and not through, a town. 보조 도로; 측도(側道); 우회로. — *vt.* (P6) **1** avoid (a city, etc.) by following a by-pass; go around. …을 피해서 지나가다; 우회하다. **2** get away from; avoid; escape. …을 피하다; 모면하다. ¶ *~ a question* 질문을 피하다.

by-path [báipæ̀θ, -pɑ̀:θ] *n.* Ⓒ a side path. 샛길; 옆길.

by-play [báiplèi] *n.* Ⓤ an action or speech on the stage apart from that of the main situation. 바이플레이《본 줄거리에서 벗어난 부수적인 연기·연극》.

by-prod·uct [báipràdəkt, -dʌkt / -prɔ̀d-] *n.* Ⓒ something produced while some other thing is made. 부산물(副產物).

by-road [báiròud] *n.* Ⓒ a side road. 샛길; 옆길.

By·ron [báiərən], **George Gordon** *n.* (1788-1824) an English poet. 바이런《영국의 시인》.

By·ron·ic [bairánik / -rɔ́n-] *adj.* of Byron or his poetry. 바이런(풍)의.

by·stand·er [báistæ̀ndər] *n.* Ⓒ a person who stands near or looks on but does not take part in an event and activity. 구경꾼; 방관자; 국외자.

by·street [báistrì:t] *n.* Ⓒ a side street. 뒷골목.

by·way [báiwèi] *n.* Ⓒ a side path or road. 샛길(cf. *highway*).

by·word [báiwə̀:rd] *n.* Ⓒ **1** a proverb. 격언. **2** an object of contempt. 웃음가마리. ¶ *Her idle husband was a ~ in the village.* 그녀의 게으른 남편은 마을의 웃음거리였다.

by·work [báiwə̀:rk] *n.* work done in addition to one's regular work, as in intervals of leisure. 부업(副業).

Byz·an·tine [bízəntì:n, -tàin, báizen-, bizǽntin] *adj.* of Byzantium esp. the style of architecture developed there. 비잔티움의; 비잔틴식의. — *n.* Ⓒ a person of Byzantium. 비잔틴 사람. [Gk.]

By·zan·ti·um [bizǽnʃiəm, -tiəm] *n.* the capital of the Eastern Roman Empire. 비잔티움. 參考 지금의 Istanbul.

c C

C, c [si:] *n.* Ⓒ (*pl.* **C's, Cs, c's, cs** [si:z]) **1** the third letter of the English alphabet. 영어 자모의 셋째 글자. **2**《mus.》 the first note of the musical scale of C major. 다음(音); 다조(調). **3**《alg.》 the third known quantity. 제3의 기지수. **4** the third hypothetical person or thing. 제3의 가정 인물〔가정물〕; 병(丙).

C 1《chem.》 carbon. **2** the Roman number 100. (로마 숫자의) 100.

C., c. candle; capacity; cathode; cent; center; chapter; chief; circa(= about); copper; cost; cubic.

c. centum(=100).

Ca 1《chem.》 calcium. **2**《psych.》 chronological age. 생활 연령.

Ca. Court of Appeal. 항소 법원.

C.A., c.a. chartered accountant. 공인 회계사.

c/a capital account; credit account; current account.

CAB Civil Aeronautics Board. 민간 항공국.

***cab** [kæb] *n.* Ⓒ **1** an automobile for hire; a taxi. 택시. **2** the covered part of a locomotive or truck where the engineer or driver sits. (기관차의) 기관사실; (트럭의) 운전석. **3** a carriage for hire, pulled by one horse. (말 한 필이 끄는) 역마차. — *vi.* (**cabbed**) (P1,3) go by taxi. 택시로 가다. [→cabriolet]

ca·bal [kəbǽl] *n.* Ⓒ **1** a small group of persons who work for a secret plan. 음모단(團); 비밀 결사. **2** a secret plan of such a group, esp. in politics. (특히, 정치적인) 음모. [Heb. =tradition]

cab·a·la [kǽbələ, kəbɑ́:lə] *n.* a system of esoteric theosophy. 밀교(密敎). [Heb.]

cab·al·le·ro [kæ̀bəljέərou] *n.* a Spanish gentleman; a horseman; a lady's escort. 스페인 신사; 말 탄 사람; 여성의 동반자. [Sp.]

cab·a·ret [kæ̀bəréi / ⌐–⌐] *n.*《F.》Ⓒ **1** a restaurant where entertainment of singing and dancing is given during meals. 카바레. **2** an entertainment or show given at a restaurant. 카바레의 여흥〔쇼〕.

***cab·bage** [kǽbidʒ] *n.* Ⓒ a kind of vegetable whose leaves are folded into a round head; Ⓤ these leaves cooked as a vegetable. 캐비지; 양배추; 요리한 양배추잎. 参考 중심부는 head 또는 heart. [L. *caput* head]

cab·by [kǽbi] *n.* Ⓒ (*pl.* **-bies**)《*colloq.*》 the driver of a cab. 택시 운전사; 역마차의 마부. [→cab]

⁑**cab·in** [kǽbin] *n.* Ⓒ **1** a small, roughly-built house, usu. of wood; a hut. 통나무 집; 오두막. **2** a small room, esp. in a ship or an airplane, for officers or passengers. 선실(船室); (항공기의) 객실; 승무원 방. [Celt.]

cabin boy [⌐–⌐] *n.* a boy who waits on the officers and passengers on a ship. 선실 사환.

cabin class [⌐–⌐] *n.* the class between the first and second class on a passenger ship. 캐빈급(級); 특별 2등《선박의 1등과 2등의 중간 선실》.

***cab·i·net** [kǽbənit] *n.* Ⓒ **1** a piece of furniture with shelves or drawers used to hold things, such as dishes or jewels. (접시·보석 등을 넣어 두는) 진열용 선반; 장식장. ¶ *a medicine* 〔*kitchen*〕 ~ 약장〔찬장〕. **2** 《usu. *the C-*》 a group of persons chosen by the head of a nation to advise him in government administration. 내각. ¶ *a coalition* ~ 연립 내각 / *the shadow* ~ 재야 내각(cf. *ministry*). **3**《photog.》 a particular size of a photograph, about 6 inches by 4 inches. 카비네 판(判). ¶ *a* ~ *photograph* 카비네 판 사진. **4**《*arch.*》 a small private room or office. (개인용의) 작은 방〔사실(私室)〕. [→cabin]

Cabinet council [⌐–⌐–⌐] *n.* a meeting of the Cabinet. 각의(閣議).

cab·i·net·mak·er [kǽbənitmèikər] *n.* Ⓒ a person who makes furniture and other things of wood. 소목장이.

Cabinet Minister [⌐–– ⌐––] *n.* Ⓒ a member of a Cabinet. 각료(閣僚).

cab·i·net·work [kǽbənitwə̀:rk] *n.* Ⓤ **1** beautifully made furniture and woodwork. 가구(家具). **2** the making of such furniture and woodwork. 가구 제작; 소목일.

***ca·ble** [kéibəl] *n.* Ⓒ **1** a strong, thick rope, usu. made of twisted wires. 닻줄; 굵은 밧줄(cf. *cord*). **2** a protected bundle of wires under the ocean used for sending messages by electric telegraph. 해저 케이블. **3** a message sent by ocean cable. 해저 전신〔전보〕. ¶ *send a* ~ 해외로 타전(打電)하다. — *vt., vi.* (P6;1) send (a message) by ocean cable. (통신을) 해저 전신으로 보내다. ¶ ~ *information* 정보를 해저 전신으로 보내다. [L. *caplum* halter]

cable car [⌐–⌐] *n.* a car pulled by a moving cable. 케이블 카.

ca·ble·gram [kéibəlgræ̀m] *n.* Ⓒ a message sent by ocean cable. 해저 전신.

cab·man [kǽbmən] *n.* Ⓒ (*pl.* **-men** [-mən]) a man who drives a cab. 택시 운전사; 역마차 마부. [→cabriolet]

ca·boo·dle [kəbúːdl] *n.* 《*colloq.*》 the lot; group. 일단의 사람〔물건〕; 무리. ***the whole caboodle,*** 《*sl.*》 (of things or persons) all the lot. 모두; 전부.

ca·boose [kəbúːs] *n.* Ⓒ **1** 《U.S.》 the last, small car on a freight train, used chiefly by the trainmen. (화물 열차 맨 뒤의) 승무원 칸. **2** a kitchen on the deck of a ship. (기선 갑판 위의) 요리실. [Du.]

cab·ri·o·let [kæ̀briəléi] *n.* **1** a light, hooded one-horse carriage. (말 한 필이 끄는) 접포장 2륜 마차. **2** an automobile somewhat like a coupé, with a folding top. (접포장의) 쿠페형 자동차. [→caper]

cab·stand [kǽbstæ̀nd] *n.* a place where taxis are allowed to wait for hire. 택시 주차장〔승차장〕. [→cab]

ca'can·ny [kɔːkǽni, kə-] *n.* 《Sc.》 Ⓤ the policy of limiting output. 태업(怠業). [Sc. *ca* call, →canny]

ca·ca·o [kəkáːou, -kéi-] *n.* Ⓒ (*pl.* **-ca·os**) seeds of a tropical tree from which cocoa and chocolate are made; the tree itself. 카카오 열매〔나무〕. [Mex.]

cach·a·lot [kǽʃəlɑ̀t, -lòu / -lɔ̀t] *n.* = sperm-whale.

cache [kæʃ] *n.* Ⓒ **1** a hiding place for food or anything useful. (식량 등을) 숨겨 두는 곳. **2** a hidden store of food or anything useful. 저장물; 은닉 식량〔물자〕. —*vt.* (P6) put (something) in a cache; hide. …을 숨겨 두다; 감추다. ¶ ~ *food* 식량을 숨겨 두다. [co-, L. *ago* bring]

ca·chet [kæʃéi, ⌐—] *n.* 《F.》 **1** a private seal or stamp. 봉인(封印). **2** a distinguishing mark or sign to prove genuineness, excellence, or superiority. (다른 것과 구분이 되는) 표시; (증명이 되는) 특징. **3** 《med.》 a hollow wafer for enclosing a medicine. 교갑; 캡슐; 오블라트.

ca·chex·y [kəkéksi] *n.* a bad state of bodily health. 건강 불량 상태. [Gk. *kakos* bad, *hexis* condition]

cach·in·nate [kǽkənèit] *vi.* (P1) laugh loudly. 큰소리로 웃다. [L.]

cach·in·na·tion [kæ̀kənéiʃən] *n.* loud laughter. 큰 웃음(소리).

cack·le [kǽkl] *vi.* (P1) **1** (of a hen) make a shrill, broken noise after laying an egg. (암탉이 알을 낳고) 꼬꼬댁거리다. **2** laugh or talk noisily. 시끄럽게 웃다〔지껄이다〕. —*n.* **1** ⓊⒸ the noise made by a hen when it has laid an egg. 꼬꼬댁거리는 소리. **2** Ⓒ laughter. 시끄러운 웃음(소리). **3** Ⓤ noisy chatter; idle talk. 재잘거림; 수다. [Imit.]

ca·co·de·mon [kæ̀kədíːmən] *n.* **1** an evil spirit. 악령. **2** a malignant person. 악인(惡人). [Gk. *kakos* bad, *demon*]

ca·coph·o·nous [kækáfənəs / -kɔ́f-] *adj.* harsh and discordant. (소리가) 귀에 거슬리는; 불협화음의. [Gk.]

ca·coph·o·ny [kækáfəni / -kɔ́f-] *n.* a harsh, discordant sound. 불협화음. [Gk.]

cac·ti [kǽktai] *n.* pl. of **cactus.**

cac·tus [kǽktəs] *n.* Ⓒ (*pl.* **-tus·es** or **-ti**) 《bot.》 a tropical plant without leaves, whose thick stems are covered with prickles. 선인장. [Gk.]

cad [kæd] *n.* Ⓒ a fellow whose behavior is bad, esp. toward women. (특히 여성에게) 상스러운〔야비한〕 남자. [→cadet]

ca·das·tral [kədǽstrəl] *adj.* of taxable land. 지적(地籍)의; 토지 대장의. [L. *capus* head]

ca·da·ver [kədǽvər, -déi-] *n.* a dead human body; a corpse. 시체; 송장. [L. *cadaver* corpse]

ca·dav·er·ous [kədǽvərəs] *adj.* **1** like a dead body. 시체 같은. **2** deadly pale. 창백한; 사색(死色)의. ¶ *He had a ~ face.* 얼굴이 창백했다.

cad·die [kǽdi] *n.* Ⓒ a person who attends a golf player, carrying golf clubs, finding lost balls, etc. (골프의) 캐디. [→cadet]

cad·dish [kǽdiʃ] *adj.* like a cad; ill-mannered. (태도·말씨가) 상스러운; 야비한.

cad·dy[1] [kǽdi] *n.* Ⓒ (*pl.* **-dies**) a small box or a can, often used to hold tea. (작은) 차통(茶筒)(cf. *canister*). [Malay]

cad·dy[2] [kǽdi] *n.* (*pl.* **-dies**) =caddie.

ca·dence [kéidəns] *n.* ⓊⒸ **1** rhythm. 운율(韻律). **2** the rise and fall of the voice; intonation. 억양. **3** 《mus.》 a series of chords that shows the end of a melody. (악장의) 종지(법). [L. *cado* fall]

ca·det [kədét] *n.* Ⓒ **1** a student in training for service as an officer in a naval or military college. (육·해군) 사관 학교 생도. ¶ ~ *corps* 학생 군사 훈련단 / *an air-force* ~ 공군 사관 후보생. **2** a younger son or brother. (장남 이외의) 아들; 막내 동생. [L. *capus* head]

cadge [kædʒ] *vi., vt.* (P1;6) 《*colloq.*》 **1** get (money etc.) by begging from others; beg. 구걸하다; 조르다; 얻다. ¶ *He is always cadging.* 그는 늘 조르기만 한다 / *May I ~ a cigarette?* 담배 한 개비 주시겠습니까. **2** peddle. 행상하다. ● **cadg·er** [-ər] *n.* [E.]

ca·di [káːdi, kéi-] *n.* a Muhammadan judge. (이슬람국의) 판사. [Arab.]

Ca·di·lac [kǽdilæ̀k] *n.* **1** **Antoine de la Mothe** (1658-1730) the founder of Detroit. 디트로이트의 창건자. **2** a name of a deluxe car. 고급 승용차의 이름; 캐딜락. [Trademark]

cad·mi·um [kǽdmiəm] *n.* Ⓤ 《min.》 a soft, silverwhite metal like tin. 카드뮴. [Gk.]

Cad·mus [kǽdməs] *n.* 《myth.》 the founder

of Thebes. 테베의 건설자.

ca·dre [kǽdri, kɑ́:drei] *n.* 《F.》 **1** a framework. 뼈대. **2** 《mil.》 officers on the staff of a regiment. (연대의) 기간(基幹) 요원. [F. = square]

ca·du·ce·i [kədjú:siài] *n.* pl. of **caduceus.**

ca·du·ce·us [kədjú:siəs, -ʃəs] *n.* Ⓒ (*pl.* **-ce·i**) a stick with two snakes twined around it and a pair of wings on top, often used as a symbol of the medical profession. Mercury의 지팡이《두 마리의 뱀이 감겨 있고 꼭대기에 두 날개가 있으며, 흔히 의학의 휘장으로 쓰임》. [Gk.]

ca·du·cous [kədjú:kəs] *adj.* 《bot.》 unenduring. 조락성(早落性)의. [→cadence]

cae·ca [sí:kə] *n.* pl. of **caecum.**

cae·cum [sí:kəm] *n.* (*pl.* **-ca**) =cecum.

·**Cae·sar** [sí:zər] *n.* **1 Gaius Julius** (100?-44 B.C.) a Roman general and statesman. 카이사르《로마의 장군·정치가》. **2** the title of the Roman emperors from Augustus to Hadrian. 로마 황제《칭호》. **3** Ⓒ an emperor. 황제. **4** Ⓒ a dictator; a tyrant. 전제 군주; 폭군. [Name]

Cae·sar·e·an, -i·an [sizέəriən] *adj.* of Julius Caesar or the Caesars. 카이사르의; 황제의.

Caesarean operation〔section〕 [-⌐–– ––⌐–〔⌐–〕] *n.* an operation by which a baby is delivered from the uterus by cutting through the walls of the abdomen and uterus. 제왕 절개(帝王切開).

cae·su·ra [siʒúrə, -zúrə, -zjú-] *n.* a pause or break in a line of poetry. (시의) 행중(行中)의 휴지(休止)《예를 들면 *To be or not to be —that is the question.*》. [L. *caedo* cut]

ca·fé [kæféi, kə-] *n.* **1** Ⓒ (in England) a place where non-alcoholic drinks and light meals are sold; a coffee-house or tea-shop. 간이 식당; 다방. **2** (in Europe) a restaurant of any kind. 식당. **3** Ⓤ coffee. 커피. [F.]

café au lait [kǽfei ou léi] *n.* coffee with milk. 밀크 (넣은) 커피.

café chantant [kǽfei ʃɑ̃́:ntɑ̃:ŋ] *n.* a coffee-house with music, etc. 카바레.

café noir [kǽfei nwɑ́:r] *n.* black coffee. 블랙 커피.

caf·e·te·ri·a [kæ̀fitíəriə] *n.* Ⓒ a lunch room or a restaurant where people serve themselves. 카페테리아《셀프서비스의 식당》. [Sp. =coffee shop]

caf·feine, -fein [kæfí:n, kǽfi:in] *n.* Ⓤ a bitter compound found in coffee beans and tea leaves, used as a stimulating drug. 카페인《흥분제》. [→coffee]

caf·tan [kǽftən, kɑ:ftɑ́:n] *n.* an eastern long-sleeved, girdled garment. 띠 달린 긴 소매 옷. [Turk.]

:**cage** [keidʒ] *n.* Ⓒ **1** a boxlike structure or enclosure with wires or bars for keeping birds and wild animals. 새장; 우리. ¶ *a bird in a* ~ 조롱 속의 새. **2** a thing shaped like a cage; esp. one used to take miners up and down the shaft of a mine. 새장 같은 것; (특히 수갱(竪坑)의) 승강기. ¶ *the* ~ *of an elevator* 엘리베이터의 칸. **3** a prison. 감옥; 옥사. — *vt.* (P6,7) put or keep (something) in a cage. …을 새장〔우리〕 안에 넣다. ¶ *a caged bird* 새장에 갇힌 새 / ~ *someone up in a small room* 아무를 작은 방 안에 가두다. [→cave]

ca·gey [kéidʒi] *adj.* 《colloq.》 **1** cautious; secretive. 조심스러운; 신중한; 숨기는. ¶ *a* ~ *reply* 신중한 대답. **2** 《U.S.》 cunning. 교활한. [→cage, -y]

cai·man [kéimən, keimǽn] *n.* 《zool.》 an alligator. 악어의 일종. [Sp.]

Cain [kein] *n.* **1** 《Bible》 the eldest son of Adam and Eve, who killed his brother Abel. 카인《아우 Abel을 죽임》. **2** Ⓒ a murderer. 살인자.

cairn [kεərn] *n.* Ⓒ a heap of stones used as a memorial, tomb, or landmark. 돌무덤; 길잡이; 도표(道標). [Gael.]

Cai·ro [káiərou] *n.* the capital of Egypt. 카이로《이집트의 수도》.

cais·son [kéisən, -sɑn / -sɔn] *n.* Ⓒ **1** a box or chest for explosives, such as shells and bombs. 탄약통. **2** a wagon to carry shells, bombs, etc. 탄약차. **3** 《engin.》 a watertight chamber in which men can work under water. 케송; 잠함(潛函). [F., →case²]

caisson disease [⌐– –⌐] *n.* a disease of workers in compressed air, as in caissons, etc. 케송〔잠함〕병(病).

cai·tiff [kéitif] 《*arch., poet.*》 *n.* a mean, evil person; a coward. 비열〔비겁〕한 사람; 겁쟁이. — *adj.* mean; cowardly. 비겁한. [→captive]

ca·jole [kədʒóul] *vt.* (P6,13) **1** persuade (someone) to do something with pleasant words. …을 감언으로 속이다. ¶ ~ *someone into going* 아무를 구슬러서 가게 하다 / ~ *someone out of money* = ~ *money out of someone* 아무를 속여서 돈을 옭아내다 / *He cajoled her into doing what he wanted.* 그녀를 부추겨서 그가 원하는 것을 하게 했다. **2** deceive. 속이다. ● **ca·jole·ment** [-mənt] *n.* [F.]

ca·jol·er·y [kədʒóuləri] *n.* persuasion by flattery, etc. 감언으로 속임.

:**cake** [keik] *n.* **1** ⓊⒸ a sweet baked food made with flour, sugar, eggs, etc. 케이크. ¶ *a sponge* ~ 카스텔라 / 《*prov.*》 *You cannot eat your* ~ *and have it, too.* 먹은 과자는 남지 않는다; 동시에 양쪽 다 좋을 수는 없다. **2** Ⓒ a pancake; a griddlecake. 팬케이크. **3** Ⓒ a small and flat mass shaped and pressed. 덩어리; 한 개. ¶ *a* ~ *of soap* 비누 한 개 / *a* ~ *of ice* 얼음 한 덩이.

a piece of cake, 《*sl.*》 something very

pleasant and easy. 쉬운〔유쾌한〕 일; 누워 떡 먹기.
cakes and ale, merry-making; pleasures of life. 즐거움; 인생의 쾌락.
go off like hot cakes, sell amazingly well. 날개 돋친 듯이 팔리다.
take the cake, 《*sl.*》 win the prize; excel. 수상(受賞)하다; 뛰어나다.
— *vt., vi.* (P6;1) cause (something) to harden; become hard. …을 굳히다; 굳어지다. ¶ *His shoes were caked with mud.* 신발은 진흙 덩이였다 / *caked blood* 말라붙은 피. [Scand.]

cake eater [ˊ–ˋ–] *n.* a party-going person. 놈팡이; 한량.
Cal. California.
cal·a·bash [kǽləbæ̀ʃ] *n.* **1** 《bot.》 a gourd. 호리병박. **2** the dried shell of the fruit of the calabash, used as a bottle, bowl, pipe, etc. (술병·주발 등으로 쓰이는) 말린 호리병박. [Pers. =melon]
ca·lam·i·tous [kəlǽmitəs] *adj.* disastrous. 재난이 많은; 비참한; 불행한. ¶ *a ~ event* 불행한 사건 / *a ~ defeat* 참패. [↓]
•**ca·lam·i·ty** [kəlǽməti] *n.* UC (*pl.* **-ties**) a great misfortune; sudden disaster; misery. 비운; 재난; 불행. ¶ *the ~ of war* 전화(戰禍). [L.]
ca·lash [kəlǽʃ] *n.* **1** a light, low carriage that usu. has a folding top. (흔히 접포장 있는) 경(輕)마차. **2** a folding top. 접포장. **3** a kind of silk hood or bonnet worn by women in the 18th century. (18세기의) 여성용 비단 후드〔보닛〕. [F. *calèch* wheel]
cal·car·e·ous [kælkέəriəs] *adj.* **1** of or containing lime or limestone. 석회(질)의; 석회질을 함유한. **2** of or containing calcium. 칼슘의; 칼슘을 함유한. [→calx]
cal·ces [kǽlsi:z] *n.* pl. of **calx.**
cal·cif·er·ous [kælsífərəs] *adj.* containing or producing lime. 석회를〔탄산칼슘을〕 함유한〔내는〕. [↓]
cal·ci·fy [kǽlsəfài] *v.* (**-fied**) *vi.* (P1) become hard by the deposit of lime. 석회질이 되다; 경화(硬化)하다. — *vt.* (P6) change (something) into lime. …을 석회질로 만들다; 경화시키다. [→calcium]
cal·ci·mine [kǽlsəmain, -min] *n.* U a white or colored liquid used on ceilings and walls. 칼시민《백색〔착색〕 수성 도료(塗料)》. [↓]
cal·cine [kǽlsain, -sin] *vt., vi.* (P6;1) **1** change to lime by burning. 구워서 석회로 만들다〔되다〕. **2** burn to ashes or powder. 태워 재〔가루〕로 만들다. ¶ *calcined bones* 타서 재가 된 뼈. [↓]
cal·ci·um [kǽlsiəm] *n.* U 《chem.》 a soft, silvery-white chemical element. 칼슘. [L. *calx*=lime]
cal·cu·la·ble [kǽlkjələbəl] *adj.* **1** that can be measured. 계산할 수 있는. **2** reliable; dependable. 신뢰할〔믿을〕 수 있는.
•**cal·cu·late** [kǽlkjəlèit] *vi., vt.* **1** (P6,10, 11,12) ⓐ find out by mathematical methods; reckon; compute. …을 계산하다; 산출하다. ¶ *~ the cost of a journey* 여행 비용을 계산하다 / *~ the lunar eclipse* 월식(月蝕)의 일시(日時)를 산정하다 / *~ the velocity of light* 광(光) 속도를 계산하다 / *be calculated at one million dollars* 100만 달러로 산정되다. ⓑ judge or determine by reasoning; estimate. (추리·상식에 의해) …을 추정하다; 평가〔어림〕하다. **2** (P3) 《*on, upon*》 rely; depend; count. 기대하다; 기대를 걸다. ¶ *You cannot ~ upon his help.* 그의 도움을 기대할 수는 없다. **3** (P7) 《usu. in *passive*》 《*for*》 intend; plan; fit, or arrange for a special purpose. …을 계획〔의도〕하다; 꾀하다; 셈에 넣다; 적합시키다. ¶ *a calculated lie* 〔*insult*〕 의도적인 거짓말〔모욕〕 / *a calculated crime* 계획적인 범죄 / *His remarks was calculated to inspire confidence.* 그의 말은 신뢰심을 일으키기를 계산에 넣은 것이었다. **4** (P6, 11,12) 《U.S. *colloq.*》 think; suppose; believe. …라고 생각하다. ¶ *I ~ it will clear up before noon.* 정오까지는 갤 것으로 생각한다. [→calculus]
be calculated for, be fitted to (something); be suitable for (something). …에 적합하다. ¶ *These laws are not calculated for modern conditions.* 이 법들은 현대 상황에 적합치 않다.

cal·cu·lat·ed [kǽlkjəlèitid] *adj.* **1** arranged beforehand; designed. 계획적인; 고의적인. ¶ *a ~ threat* 계획적인 협박. **2** likely; suitable. …할 것 같은; 적합한.
cal·cu·lat·ing [kǽlkjəlèitiŋ] *adj.* shrewd; careful. 빈틈 없는; 조심스러운. ¶ *a ~ politician* 빈틈 없는 정치가.
calculating machine [ˊ––– –ˋ] *n.* a machine that calculates mechanically. 자동 계산기.
•**cal·cu·la·tion** [kæ̀lkjəléiʃən] *n.* **1** U the act of calculating. 계산; 셈. ¶ *make a rapid ~* 빠르게 계산하다. **2** U careful thinking or planning. 신중; 숙고; 신중한 계획. ¶ *done with* 〔*without*〕 *~* 신중하게〔아무렇게나〕 한 / *after much ~* 여러 가지로 생각한 끝에. **3** C a result found by calculating. 계산(의 결과).
cal·cu·la·tive [kǽlkjəlèitiv / -lətiv] *adj.* **1** of calculation. 계산의. **2** tending to be calculating; shrewd. 타산적인; 빈틈없는.
cal·cu·la·tor [kǽlkjəlèitər] *n.* C a person or machine that calculates. 계산자; 계산기.
cal·cu·li [kǽlkjəlài] *n.* pl. of **calculus.**
cal·cu·lus [kǽlkjələs] *n.* (*pl.* **-li** or **-lus·es**) **1** U a way of calculation in higher mathematics. 계산법. ¶ *differential* 〔*integral*〕 *~* 미〔적〕분학. **2** C 《med.》 a stony mass that has formed in the body. 결석(結石). [L. = abacus-ball]
Cal·cut·ta [kælkʌ́tə] *n.* a seaport in East India. 캘커타.
cal·de·ra [kældí:rə, kɔ:l-] *n.* 《geog.》 a

C

large crater formed by the collapse of the central part of a volcano. 칼데라《화산 중심부가 내려앉아 생긴 원형 분지》. [Sp.]

cal·dron, caul- [kɔ́:ldrən] *n.* Ⓒ a large kettle or boiler. 큰 솥〔냄비〕. [L. *calidus* warm]

Cald·well [kɔ́:ldwel, -wəl], **Erskine** *n.* (1903-87) an American novelist. 콜드웰《미국의 소설가》.

Cal·e·do·ni·a [kæ̀lidóuniə] *n.* 《*poet., arch.*》 Scotland. 스코틀랜드. [L.]

Cal·e·do·ni·an [kæ̀lidóuniən] *n.* Ⓒ 《*poet.*》 a person of ancient Scotland. 옛 스코틀랜드 사람.

ca·lem·bour [kæ̀ləmbúər / kæ̀lɑ:m-] *n.* 《F.》 a pun. 결말; 익살.

:**cal·en·dar** [kǽləndər] *n.* Ⓒ **1** a list of the months, weeks and the days printed year by year. 달력. ¶ *a ~ month* 역월(曆月). **2** a method by which the beginning, length, and divisions of the year are fixed. 역법(曆法). ¶ *the lunar* 〔*solar*〕 *~* 태음〔태양〕력. **3** a list; a record; a catalog; a table exhibiting a given year's arrangement. 표; 일람; 목록; 일정표; 연중 행사 일람. ¶ *put a bill on the ~* 의안을 일정에 올리다. — *vt.* (P6) enter in the list. …을 표에 (써)넣다. [→calends]

cal·en·der [kǽləndər] *n.* Ⓒ a roller-machine in which cloth, paper, etc. is pressed and smoothed. 캘린더《종이·피륙 따위를 눌러 윤을 내는 기계》. — *vt.* (P6) put (something) through a calender. …을 캘린더에 걸다. [→cylinder]

cal·ends [kǽləndz] *n. pl.* the first day of the month in the old Roman calendar. (고대 로마력(曆)의) 초하룻날. [L.]

·**calf**[1] [kæf, kɑ:f] *n.* (*pl.* **calves**) **1** Ⓒ the young of a cow or of some other animals. 송아지; (코끼리·고래·사슴 따위의) 새끼. **2** Ⓤ leather with a smooth finish, made from the skin of a calf. 무두질한 송아지 가죽. ¶ *a book bound in ~* 송아지 가죽 장정의 책 / *~ shoes* 송아지 가죽 구두. **3** Ⓒ a foolish young man. 어리석은 젊은이. [E.]
kill the fatted calf, make a feast to celebrate (something) or welcome (someone). …의 축전을 베풀다; …을 환대하다. 参考 성서(聖書) Luke 15:27.

calf[2] [kæf, kɑ:f] *n.* Ⓒ (*pl.* **calves**) the thick part of the back of the leg between the knee and the foot. 장딴지; 종아리. [Scand.]

calf love [ㅅㅅ] *n.* childish love affair. 풋사랑.

calf·skin [kǽfskìn, kɑ́:f-] *n.* Ⓤ **1** the skin of a calf. 송아지 가죽. **2** leather with a smooth finish, made from the skin of a calf. 무두질한 송아지 가죽.

Cal·i·ban [kǽlibən] *n.* a degraded bestial man. (셰익스피어 작품 속의) 반인반수(半獸)의 사람. [Shakespearian person]

cal·i·ber, 《Brit.》 **-bre** [kǽləbər] *n.* **1** Ⓒ ⓐ the inside diameter of the bore of a gun, tube, etc. (총포 따위의) 구경. ¶ *a pipe of three-inch ~* 안지름 3인치의 파이프. ⓑ the diameter of a bullet. (탄알 따위의) 직경. **2** Ⓤ 《*fig.*》 ability or character. 능력; 재간; 역량. ¶ *a man of excellent ~* 뛰어난 기량의 사람 / *a mathematician of high ~* 뛰어난 역량의 수학자. [Arab.=mould]

cal·i·brate [kǽləbrèit] *vt.* (P6) **1** measure the caliber. …의 구경(口徑)을 재다. **2** determine, check, or adjust the graduations of (a measuring instrument). (계기의) 눈금을 정〔조사·조절〕하다. [↑]

cal·i·co [kǽlikòu] *n.* ⓊⒸ (*pl.* **-coes** or **-cos**) **1** 《U.S.》 a cotton cloth usu. printed on one side. 사라사. **2** 《Brit.》 a plain white cloth, used for bed sheets. 캘리코; 옥양목. ¶ 《*fig.*》 *a ~ cat* 〔*fish*〕 캘리코 같은 반점이 있는 고양이〔물고기〕. [Place in India]

calico ball [ㅅ-ㅅ] *n.* a ball at which only cotton dresses are worn. 무명옷만 입는 무도회.

Calif. California.

ca·lif [kéilif, kǽlif] *n.* =caliph.

cal·if·ate [kǽləfèit, -fit, kéilə-] *n.* =caliphate.

·**Cal·i·for·ni·a** [kæ̀ləfɔ́:rnjə, -niə] *n.* a western state of the United States, on the Pacific coast. 캘리포니아. 参考 Calif. 로 생략함. 주도(州都)는 Sacramento.

Cal·i·for·ni·an [kæ̀ləfɔ́:rniən] *adj.* of California. 캘리포니아의. — *n.* Ⓒ a person of California. 캘리포니아 사람.

cal·i·for·nium [kæ̀ləfɔ́:rniəm] *n.* 《chem.》 a radioactive element. 캘리포르늄.

cal·i·pers, cal·li- [kǽləpərz] *n. pl.* Ⓒ a tool with two legs resembling a draftsman's compass, used to obtain inside and outside measurements. 캘리퍼스; 양각 측경기(兩脚測徑器). ¶ *outside* 〔*inside*〕 *~* 외경(外徑)〔내경(內徑)〕 캘리퍼스. — *vt.* (P6) measure with calipers. calipers로 재다. [Arab. *qalib* →caliber]

outside calipers
inside calipers
〈calipers〉

ca·liph [kéilif, kǽl-] *n.* Ⓒ the head of an Islamic state; the title given to him. 칼리프《이슬람국의 왕》. 参考 calif, khalif 라고도 씀. [Arab.=successor]

cal·iph·ate [kǽləfèit, -fit, kéilə-] *n.* the rank, reign, or territory of a caliph. caliph의 지위〔직, 통치, 영토〕.

cal·is·then·ics, cal·lis- [kæ̀ləsθéniks] *n. pl.* **1** 《used as *sing.*》 the practice or art of developing a strong and graceful body. 미용 체조법. **2** 《used as *pl.*》 exercises of this. 미용 체조. [Gk. *kallos* beauty, *thedos* strength]

calk[1], **caulk** [kɔ:k] *vt.* (P6) fill or close a seam, joint, etc. to keep water, air, etc.

from leaking; make (a ship) watertight. (틈새 따위)를 메워 새는 것을 막다. ¶ ~ *boats with tar* 타르로 배의 틈새를 막다 / ~ *the joints of a pipe* 파이프의 이음매를 막다. [L. *calco* tread]

calk[2] [kɔ:k], **calk·in** [kɔ́:kin] *n.* one of the projecting parts of a horse-shoe or boot to prevent from slipping. (편자·구두의) 뾰족징. [L. *calx* heel]

:call [kɔ:l] *vt.* **1** (P6,7) cry out (something) in a loud voice. (큰 소리로) …을 부르다. ¶ *'Alice !' she called loudly.* '앨리스'하고 그녀는 큰 소리로 불렀다 / *I heard my mother calling me.* 어머니가 나를 부르는 것을 들었다 / *He called her name to see if she was home.* 그는 그녀가 집에 있는지의 여부를 알기 위해 이름을 불렀다 / *She called to me when I passed her gate.* 그녀의 문 앞을 지날 때 그녀는 나를 불렀다 / *He called, but there was no answer.* 그는 불러 보았지만 아무 대답도 없었다. **2** (P6) read over (something) in a loud voice. (큰 소리로) …을 읽다〔부르다〕. ¶ *The teacher called the roll of the class.* 선생님은 출석을 불렀다. **3** (P6,7) cry out to (someone) in order to make him come; ask (someone) to come or to pay attention by sending a message or signal or by telephoning. …을 불러 오게 하다; 오라고 청하다; …의 주의를 불러일으키다. ¶ ~ *a doctor* 의사를 부르다 / ~ *a witness* 증인을 소환하다 / ~ *someone to the door* 아무를 현관으로 부르다 / ~ *one's children home* 아이들을 집으로 불러들이다 / *Call a taxi for me.* 택시 좀 불러 주시오. **4** (P6) command; request. …을 명(령)하다; 요구하다. ¶ ~ *a halt* 정지를 명하다. **5** (P6) gather persons to hold (a meeting); summon; convoke. …을 소집하다. ¶ ~ *an emergency meeting* 긴급 회의를 소집하다. **6** (P6) rouse (someone) from sleep. …을 잠에서 깨우다. ¶ *Call me (up) at seven tomorrow morning.* 내일 아침 7시에 깨워 주시오. **7** ⓐ (P19) give a name to; name. …라고 부르다; 이름짓다; 칭하다. ¶ *a place called Wicklow* 위크로라고 부르는 곳 / ~ *one's child John* 아이 이름을 존이라고 부르다 / *Miss Kelly — or may I* ~ *you Mary ?* 켈리양 — 달리 메리라고 불러도 되나요 / *Michael is called Mike for short.* 마이클은 줄여서 마이크라고 부른다 / *What do you* ~ *this in English ?* 이걸 영어로는 뭐라고 하나요 / *All called the party a success.* 모두가 파티는 성공적이라고 했다. ⓑ (P19,21) consider; look on; assume to be. …라고 생각하다; …로 보다; 여기다. ¶ *I* ~ *this a very good house.* 나는 이 집이 아주 좋다고 생각한다 / *Do you* ~ *three dollars a salary ?* 자넨 3달러도 월급이라고 보나 / *I* ~ *myself a doctor.* 나는 자신을 의사라고 생각한다. **8** (P6) 《U.S.》 telephone to (someone). …에게 전화를 걸다. ¶ *He called me this morning.* 그는 오늘 아침 내게 전화를 했다 / *Call me when you arrive.* 도착하시면 전화 주십시오. **9** cause to come; bring to a certain state or condition. (어떤 상태로) 나타나게 하다; 가져오다. ¶ ~ *into being*〔*existence*〕 출현시키다; 낳다 / ~ *the past events to mind* 과거의 일을 상기하다. **10** (P6,13) 《U.S.》 (of sports) stop; suspend. 중지하다. ¶ *The game was called because of rain.* 경기는 비 때문에 중지되었다.

— *vi.* **1** (P1,2A,3) 《*to*》 speak loudly, as to attract attention. 큰 소리로 말하다; 부르다; 소리치다; 외치다. ¶ *She called to the children.* 그녀는 큰 소리로 아이들을 불렀다 / *He called to his friends for help.* 그는 친구들에게 사람 살리라고 외쳤다. **2** (P1,2,3,4) go to someone's house, office, etc. for a short visit or on business. …에 잠깐 들르다; 방문하다. ¶ ~ *on someone* 아무를 찾다〔방문하다〕 / ~ *at someone's office* 아무의 회사에 들르다 / *He calls for an hour every Sunday.* 그는 일요일마다 한 시간 정도 들렀다 간다 / *I am sorry I was out when you called.* 들러 주셨는데 출타 중이어서 미안합니다. **3** (P1,3,4) telephone. 전화를 걸다. ¶ *He promised to* ~ *at noon.* 정오 때 전화하겠다고 약속했다 / *May I ask who is calling, please ?* (상대에게) 실례지만 누구신지요.

call after, a) call loudly to from behind. …을 뒤에서 부르다. **b**) name after. …을 따서 —라고 부르다. ¶ *He was called John after his uncle.* 그는 삼촌의 이름을 따서 존이라고 불렸다.

call at, visit (some place) for a short time. …에 잠깐 방문하다〔들르다〕.

call away, 《usu. *passive*》 **a**) cause (someone) to leave or go; summon. (딴 곳으로) 가게 하다; 떠나게 하다; 불러내다. ¶ *The doctor was called away to an accident.* 의사는 사고 현장으로 불려 갔다. **b**) divert (one's mind). (마음)을 딴 데로 돌리다; 흩뜨리다.

call back, **a**) bring back; summon; recall. 되돌아오게 하다; 되부르다; 소환하다. ¶ *He called back the messenger.* 그는 심부름꾼을 되불렀다. **b**) speak in answer loudly. 큰 소리로 대답하다. ¶ *"We'll come in a minute," she called back.* "곧 돌아오겠어요."하고 그녀는 크게 대답했다. **c**) 《U.S.》 telephone again or in return. (전화를 받은 쪽에서) 나중에 전화를 다시 걸다; 전화로 회답하다. ¶ *Call me back later.* 나중에 다시 전화를 하게. **d**) withdraw (one's words, opinion, etc.); retract. …을 철회〔취소〕하다. ¶ ~ *back an accusation* 고소를 취하하다.

call down, **a**) cause to come down; pray for; invoke. (축복·천벌 등이 내리기)를 빌다; 기원하다. ¶ ~ *down the wrath of God* 하느님의 노여움이 내리도록 빌다 / ~ *down a blessing upon someone* 아무에게 은총이 있기를 기원하다. **b**) 《U.S. *colloq.*》 scold sharply; rebuke. …을 몹시 꾸짖다; 비난하다.

call for, **a**) ask for; demand. …을 요청〔요구〕하다. ¶ ~ *for help* 도움을 요청하다. **b**) need; require. …을 필요로 하다; 요하다.

¶ *The case calls for immediate action.* 사태는 즉각적인 행동을 필요로 한다. **c**) go to pick up (someone or something). …을 데리러〔가지러〕 가다〔오다〕. ¶ *Call for me on your way.* 가는 길에 나를 데리러 와주게.

call forth, come to appear; draw out; bring into action. …을 불러일으키다; 끄집어내다; 환기시키다. ¶ *April showers ~ forth May flowers.* 4월달 소나기는 5월의 꽃을 피운다 / *The difficult situation called forth all his hidden abilities.* 어려운 상황은 그의 온갖 잠재 능력을 유발케 했다 / *His strange behavior called forth various rumors.* 그의 이상한 행동은 여러 가지 소문을 낳았다.

C

call heaven to witness, swear by God. 하느님께 맹세하다.

call in, **a**) demand the payment or return of; withdraw from circulation; collect. …을 지불할〔갚을〕 것을 요구하다; 회수하다. ¶ ~ *in debts* 빚을 회수하다 / ~ *in gold certificates* 금(金) 증권을 회수하다. **b**) ask to come; ask for the help of. 초대하다; (도움을 청해 사람)을 부르다; 원조를 청하다. ¶ ~ *in a doctor* 〔*the police*〕 의사를〔경찰을〕 부르다 / ~ *in professional advice* 직업상의 조언을 구하다.

call in question, doubt; dispute. 이의(異議)를 제기하다.

call into being, bring into being. 생기게〔낳게〕 하다.

call** someone **names, abuse. …을 욕하다.

call off, **a**) cancel; withdraw. 취소하다; 중지하다. ¶ ~ *off a meeting* 〔*one's engagement*〕 회의를〔약혼을〕 취소하다. **b**) make go away. 불러서 가게 하다; 데려가다. ¶ *Call off your dog at once.* 이 개를 좀 즉시 데려가게. **c**) divert. (마음)을 흩어지게 하다.

call on 〔***upon***〕, **a**) visit (someone) for a short time. …을 잠깐 방문하다; 들르다. **b**) require; appeal to; implore. 요구〔청〕하다; 호소하다; 간청하다. ¶ ~ *on someone for help* 〔*a speech*〕 아무에게 도움〔연설〕을 요청하다.

call out, **a**) speak in a loud voice; shout. 큰 소리로 부르다; 소리치다. ¶ ~ *out a list of names alphabetically* 명부를 알파벳 순으로 크게 부르다. **b**) protest; challenge to duel. 이의(異議)를 말하다; 결투에 도전하다. **c**) summon (persons) into service or action; bring out; elicit. …을 불러내다; 이끌어 내다.

call over, read out a list of names. 이름을 부르다; 점호하다.

call to order, **a**) command to obey a rule of order. 정숙(靜肅)을 명하다. **b**) summon to begin. 개시를 선포하다. ¶ ~ *a meeting to order* 개회를 선포하다.

call up, **a**) rouse from bed. 잠자리에서 일어나다. ¶ *The doctor called up three times last night.* 간밤에 의사는 세 번이나 자다 일어났다. **b**) order to join the armed forces; summon (troops) for action. (군대)에 소집하다. **c**) cause to remember (something); recollect. (마음)에 불러일으키다; 생각나게 하다. ¶ ~ *up memories of the past* 지난 기억을 불러일으키다. **d**) ring up on the telephone. 전화(로 연락)하다. ¶ *I'll ~ you up (on the telephone).* 전화하겠네.

—*n.* **1** ⓐ the voice calling; a cry or shout. 부르는〔외치는〕 소리; 부르짖음. ¶ *a ~ for help* 사람 살리라고 외치는 소리. ⓑ the special cry or sound of a bird or animal; a signal of a bugle, bell, etc. (새·짐승의) 울음소리; (나팔·종의) 신호 소리. **2** a ring on the telephone; a talk over the telephone. 전화의 벨 소리; 통화. ¶ *receive* 〔*answer, take*〕 *a* (*telephone*) ~ 전화를 받다 / *have a* (*phone*) ~ 전화가 걸려 오다 / *answer no phone* ~ 전화를 받지 않다 / *make a long-distance* ~ 장거리 전화를 하다. **3** reading out a list of names; a roll-call. 출석 부르기; 점호. **4** duty or work regarded as appointed by God; vocation; an inward conviction on one's duty. 소명(召命); 천직(天職); 사명(감). ¶ *I got the ~ to lead people.* 국민을 이끌라는 소명을 받았다. **5** an order to come; an invitation. 부름; 초청; 초대. ¶ *a ~ to a dinner* 만찬에의 초대 / *accept* 〔*decline*〕 *a ~ to a professorial chair* 교수로의 초빙을 받다〔사절하다〕. **6** a short visit. 짧은 방문; 들름. ¶ *make* 〔*pay*〕 *a ~ on someone* 〔*at a house*〕 아무에게〔집에〕 들르다 / *The ship made a short ~ at Pusan.* 배는 부산에 잠시 기항했다. **7** 《usu. in *negative* or *interrogative*》 a need or necessity; a reason. 필요; (…할) 이유. ¶ *There is* 〔*You have*〕 *no ~ to be afraid.* 두려워할 필요가 없다. **8** Ⓤ Ⓒ ⓐ a demand or claim. 요구; 수요. ¶ *a ~ of nature* 생리적 욕구 / *a ~ for medicine* 약의 수요 / *The task makes a great ~ on our money* 〔*time*〕. 그 일에는 엄청난 돈〔시간〕이 요구된다. ⓑ a demand for payment. 청구. **9** Ⓤ a strong attraction; charm. 매력. ¶ *the ~ of the sea* 바다의 매력. [O.N. *kalla* to name, call]

at 〔***on***〕 ***call,*** (of money) that should be paid any time requested; (of a doctor, etc.) available for serve at any time. 청구하는 대로 지불되는; 아무때고 이용할 수 있는. ¶ *money* 〔*deposit*〕 *on ~* 요구불 돈〔예금〕 / *The doctor was on ~ all night.* 의사는 밤새 대기하고 있었다.

make 〔***pay***〕 ***a call,*** stop at a place; visit. …에 방문하다; 들르다.

within call, not far away; close at hand. 가까이에; 부르면 들리는 곳에. ¶ *Please stay within ~.* 부르면 들리는 곳에 계시오.

call bell [⌐⌐] *n.* a bell used to call others. 초인종.

call box [⌐⌐] *n.* 《Brit.》 a booth with a public telephone. 공중 전화실.

call boy [⌐⌐] *n.* Ⓒ **1** a bellboy in a hotel, on a ship, etc. (호텔·여객선 등의) 사환; 보이. **2** a boy who calls actors when it is time for them to go on the stage. (극장의) 호출계.

call·er [kɔ́:lər] *n.* Ⓒ **1** a person who makes a short visit; a visitor. 방문자. **2** a person who calls. 부르는 사람. **3** a person who calls out names, etc., in a loud voice. 욕지거리하는 사람.

cal·lig·ra·phy [kəlígrəfi] *n.* Ⓤ **1** handwriting; penmanship. 필적; 서예. **2** beautiful handwriting. 달필(達筆). [Gk. *kallos* beauty, →graph]

call·ing [kɔ́:liŋ] *n.* Ⓒ **1** an occupation; a business; a profession; a trade. 직업; 생업. ¶ *He is a tailor by* ~. 그는 양복장이가 직업이다. **2** an invitation; summons. 초대; 소집. **3** a strong impulse. 강한 충동(욕구). [*call*]

calling card [⌐–⌐] *n.* a small card with a person's name, occupation, address, etc. on it, used in business and on visits; a visiting card. (방문용) 명함(cf. *business card*).

cal·li·pers [kǽləpərz] *n. pl.* =calipers.

cal·lis·then·ics [kæ̀ləsθéniks] *n. pl.* = calisthenics.

call loan [⌐⌐] *n.* a loan that must be paid back when demanded. 콜론; (은행간의) 단기 대출금.

call money [⌐⌐–] *n.* money borrowed that must be paid back when requested. 콜머니《요구불 단기 차입금》.

call number [⌐⌐–] *n.* a number used for books in a library. (도서관의 도서) 신청 번호.

cal·los·i·ty [kəlɑ́səti / -lɔ́s-] *n.* (*pl.* **-ties**) **1** Ⓒ a thick, hardened part of the skin; a callus. (피부 따위의) 못. **2** Ⓤ lack of feeling; hardness of heart. 무감각; 무정; 냉담. [L. *callus* hardskin]

cal·lous [kǽləs] *adj.* **1** (of the skin) hard; hardened. (피부가) 굳어 딱딱한. ¶ ~ *skin* 못이 박힌 피부. **2** (of the mind) unfeeling; not sensitive. 무정(냉담)한(opp. sensitive). ¶ *a* ~ *liar* 태연히 거짓말하는 사람 / *His behavior on that occasion was extremely* ~. 그 때 그의 처사는 정말 인정머리 없었다. [↑]

cal·low [kǽlou] *adj.* (**-er, -est**) **1** young and without experience. 풋내기의. ¶ *He was only a* ~ *youth.* 그는 풋내기에 불과했다. **2** (of birds) without feathers for flying. (새가) 깃털이 나지 않은. **3** not fully grown. 아직 덜 자란. ¶ ~ *young* 미(未)성년. [L. *calvus* bald]

call-up [kɔ́:lʌ̀p] *n.* an order to serve in the armed forces; conscription. 소집; 징병. ¶ *the age of* ~ 징집 연령.

cal·lus [kǽləs] *n.* Ⓒ (*pl.* **-lus·es**) **1** a hard, thickened part of the skin. (피부의) 못. **2** (of plants) a substance growing over a wounded or cut surface of a stem. (식물의) 유합(癒合) 조직; 가피(假皮). [L. =hardened skin]

:calm [kɑ:m] *adj.* **1** not stormy or windy; quiet. 잔잔한; 고요한. ¶ *a* ~ *sea* 잔잔한 바다. **2** peaceful; (of a person) not excited. 평온한; 침착한. ¶ *a* ~ *voice* 침착한 목소리 / *Do be* ~, *don't get excited.* 침착해라, 흥분하지 말고.

— *n.* **1** Ⓤ 《usu. *a* ~》 absence of motion or wind; quietness; stillness. 고요; 잔잔함. ¶ *a* ~ *before the storm* 폭풍 전의 고요. **2** Ⓤ absence of excitement; peacefulness. (마음의) 평온; 냉정.

— *vi.* (P1,2A) 《*down*》 become calm. 고요(잠잠)해지다; 가라앉다.

— *vt.* (P6,7) make (something) calm. …을 고요(조용)하게 하다; 가라앉히다. ¶ ~ *oneself* 마음을 가라앉히다 / ~ *one's passions* 격정을 진정시키다 / *We tried to* ~ *down the angry man.* 우린 그 성난 사람을 진정시키려 했다. [Gk. *kauma* heat]

·calm·ly [kɑ́:mli] *adv.* in a calm manner; quietly; coolly. 조용(고요)하게; 침착(냉정)하게.

calm·ness [kɑ́:mnis] *n.* Ⓤ the state of being calm. 고요; 침착.

cal·o·mel [kǽləməl, -mèl] *n.* Ⓤ 《med.》 a white, tasteless, crystalline powder used in medicine. 감홍(甘汞)《하제(下劑)》. [Gk. *kalos* fair, *melas* black]

ca·lor·ic [kəlɔ́:rik, -lɑ́r- / -lɔ́r-] *n.* Ⓤ heat. 열. — *adj.* of heat or calorie. 열의; 칼로리의. [↓]

·cal·o·rie, -ry [kǽləri] *n.* Ⓒ (*pl.* **-ries**) **1** 《phys.》 a unit of heat. 칼로리《열량 단위》. **2** a unit of the energy supplied by food. 식품의 열량 단위. ¶ *An ounce of sugar will produce about a hundred calories.* 설탕 1 온스는 약 100 칼로리를 낸다. [L. *calor* heat]

cal·o·rif·ic [kæ̀ləríf ik] *adj.* belonging to or generating heat. 열을 내는.

cal·o·rim·e·ter [kæ̀lərímitər] *n.* Ⓒ an instrument for measuring quantities of heat or calories. 열량계(計).

cal·o·rim·e·try [kæ̀lərímitri] *n.* measurement of heat. 열량 측정.

cal·u·met [kǽljəmèt] *n.* Ⓒ a pipe with a long stem, smoked by the American Indians in ceremonies. 긴 담뱃대. [L. *calamus* reed]

smoke the calumet together, make peace. 화해하다.

ca·lum·ni·ate [kəlʌ́mnièit] *vt.* (P6) say untrue things about (someone); slander. …을 중상하다; 비방하다. ¶ *He began to* ~ *his former friends.* 그는 옛 친구들을 비방하기 시작했다. ●**ca·lum·ni·a·tor** [-ər] *n.* [L. *calvi* deceive]

ca·l·um·ni·ous [kəlʌ́mniəs] *adj.* of calumny; containing calumny. 중상의; 비방하는. ¶ *say* ~ *things about one's neighbors* 이웃을 헐뜯어 말하다.

cal·um·ny [kǽləmni] *n.* ⓊⒸ (*pl.* **-nies**) a false statement made to hurt someone's reputation; slander. 중상; 비방; 무고.

Cal·va·ry [kǽlvəri] *n.* **1** the place near Jerusalem where Jesus died on the cross. 갈보리《예수가 십자가에 못 박힌 땅》. **2** (C-) a representation of the Crucifixion. 예수 십자가상(像). [L.=skull]

calve [kæv, kɑ:v] *vi.* (P1) give birth to a calf. 송아지를 낳다. ¶ *The cow calved yesterday.* — *vt.* (P6) set loose apart. …을 떼어놓다; 분리하다. [*calf*]

calves [kævz, kɑ:vz] *n.* pl. of **calf**[1,2].

Cal·vin [kǽlvin], **John** *n.* (1509-64) a French leader of the Protestant Reformation in Switzerland. 칼뱅《프랑스의 종교 개혁자》.

Cal·vin·ism [kǽlvinìzəm] *n.* Ⓤ the religious teachings of John Calvin. 칼뱅교(敎)[주의].

Cal·vin·ist [kǽlvinist] *n.* a follower of Calvinism. 칼뱅교도.

calx [kælks] *n.* (*pl.* **cal·ces** or **calx·es**) Ⓒ slack formed by melting metals. 금속회(金屬灰); 광회(鑛灰). [L. *calcis* lime]

ca·ly·ces [kǽləsì:z, kéilə-] *n.* pl. of **calyx.**

ca·lyp·so [kəlípsou] *n.* 《mus.》 Ⓒ (*pl.* **-sos**) a topical, often improvised, song originated in the West Indies. 칼립소.

ca·lyx [kéiliks, kǽl-] *n.* (*pl.* **-ly·ces** or **-lyx·es**) 《bot.》 outer covering of a flower. 꽃받침. [Gk. *kalux* husk]

Cam., Camb. Cambridge.

cam [kæm] *n.* Ⓒ 《mech.》 a projecting part of a wheel or shaft that changes a circular motion into an up-and-down or back-and-forth motion. 캠《회전 운동을 상하 또는 전후 운동으로 바꾸는 장치》. [→comb]

ca·ma·ra·de·rie [kæ̀mərǽdəri, -rɑ́:d-, kɑ̀:mərɑ́:d-] *n.* Ⓒ 《F.》 friendship and good feeling among comrades. 동지애(同志愛). [→comrade]

cam·ber [kǽmbər] *n.* ⒸⓊ **1** a slight arch, as of a road or piece of timber. (노면·목재 따위가 약간) 휘어 오름. **2** the slight arch of the wing of an airplane. (항공기 날개의) 만곡(도). — *vi.* (P1,2A) have a camber. 위로 휘다. — *vt.* (P6) give (something) a camber. …을 위로 휘게 하다. [L. *camero* vault →camera]

cam·bi·um [kǽmbiəm] *n.* 《bot.》 the soft tissue between the bark and wood. 형성층(形成層). [L.=change]

Cam·bo·di·a [kæmbóudiə] *n.* country in the southern Indochinese Peninsula. 캄보디아. 參考 수도는 Phnom Penh.

Cam·bria [kǽmbriə] *n.* 《*poet.*》 the old name of Wales. 웨일스의 옛 이름.

Cam·bri·an [kǽmbriən] 《geol.》 *adj.* **1** having to do with an early geological period or group of rocks. 캄브리아기(紀)[계(系)]의. **2** of or belonging to Wales. 웨일스의. — *n.* **1** 《*the* ～》 an early geological period or group of rocks. 캄브리아기층(紀層). **2** Ⓒ a native or inhabitant of Wales; a Welshman. 웨일스 사람. [Place in Wales]

cam·bric [kéimbrik] *n.* Ⓤ fine, thin, white linen or cotton cloth. 흰 삼베의 일종. [Place in France]

·**Cam·bridge** [kéimbridʒ] *n.* **1** a city in eastern England. 케임브리지. **2** the university located there. 케임브리지 대학. **3** a city in Massachusetts. 케임브리지《미국 매사추세츠 주의 도시》. 參考 Havard 대학 소재지.

:**came** [keim] *v.* p. of **come.**

·**cam·el** [kǽməl] *n.* Ⓒ a long-necked animal with one or two humps on its back, used for riding and for carrying goods in the desert. 낙타. [Arab. *jamala* carry]

cam·el·eer [kæ̀məlíər] *n.* Ⓒ a camel driver. 낙타 모는 사람.

ca·mel·li·a [kəmí:ljə] *n.* Ⓒ 《bot.》 a shrub with shiny evergreen leaves and white or red roselike flowers; the flower of this shrub. 동백나무; 동백꽃. [Person]

cam·e·lo·pard [kəméləpɑ̀:rd] *n.* 《*arch.*》 a giraffe. 기린. [*camel, pard*]

Cam·em·bert (cheese) [kǽməmbɛ̀ər (tʃí:z)] *n.* Ⓤ a soft, rich, strong-smelling but delicately flavored cheese produced in France. 카멈베어 치즈《냄새가 진하며 연하고 맛이 좋음》. [Place in France]

cam·e·o [kǽmiòu] *n.* Ⓒ (*pl.* **-os**) a precious stone or shell having two layers and with a figure carved in one layer. 카메오《돋을새김을 한 보석이나 조가비》. [It.]

:**cam·er·a** [kǽmərə] *n.* Ⓒ **1** a machine for taking photographs or motion pictures. 사진기; 카메라. ¶ *load a* ～ 카메라에 필름을 넣다 / *snap the* ～ *at someone* 아무에게 사진기를 대고 찰깍 찍다. **2** a machine that changes images into electrical impulses for television broadcasting. 텔레비전 카메라. [L.=vault]

in camera, 《law》 in the judge's private room; privately. 방청 금지로. ¶ *The case was heard in* ～. 사건은 비공개리에 심리되었다.

cam·er·a·man [kǽmərəmæ̀n] *n.* Ⓒ (*pl.* **-men** [-mèn]) a person who operates a camera. 사진 기사; 카메라맨.

camera ob·scu·ra [kǽmərə ɑbskjúərə / kǽmərə ɔbskjúərə] *n.* a tracing apparatus. 어둠 상자; 암실.

Cam·e·roon, -roun [kæ̀mərú:n] *n.* 《geol.》 a republic in western Africa. 카메룬.

cam·i·knick·ers [kǽminìkərz] *n. pl.* camisole and knickers combined. (아래위가 붙은) 여자 속옷. [↓]

cam·i·sole [kǽmisòul] *n.* a woman's loose linen jacket worn under her dress. 캐미솔. [Sp. →chemise]

cam·let [kǽmlit] *n.* Ⓤ light cloth for cloaks. 캠릿; 낙타 모직물. [F. →camel]

cam·o·mile [kǽməmàil] *n.* 《bot.》 an aromatic plant. 카밀레. [Gk. *khamaimēlon* earth-apple]

cam·ou·flage [kǽmuflɑ̀:ʒ, kǽmə-] *n.* ⓊⒸ

1 《mil.》 the art of giving things a false appearance to deceive others. 위장; 미채(迷彩); 카무플라주. **2** disguise; concealment. 가장; 기만; 속임수. — *vt.* (P6) disguise; deceive. …을 속이다; 위장하다. ¶ ~ *a gun* 포에 미채를 씌워 위장하다. [F. *camouflet* smoke-puff]

:camp [kæmp] *n.* Ⓒ **1** a group of tents, huts, etc. where people live for a short time. 야영용의 천막이나 오두막의 무리. **2** a place where a camp is put up. 야영지. **3** 《*collectively*》 a group of people living in a camp. 야영하는 사람들. **4** 《*collectively*》 a group of people who agree on a subject or work together. 동지(同志). ¶ *be in the same* ~ 동지이다. — *vt., vi.* (P6;1,2A) make a camp; live or stay in a camp. 캠프를 치다; 야영하다. ¶ ~ *out in the woods for the summer* 여름 동안 숲에서 야영하다 / *go camping* 캠프하러 가다; 캠핑가다. ¶ *The hunters camped near the river.* 사냥꾼들은 하천 부근에 천막을 쳤다. [L. *campus* field]

:cam·paign [kæmpéin] *n.* Ⓒ **1** military operations with a particular purpose. (군사) 작전. ¶ *the Waterloo* ~ 워털루의 싸움. **2** organized action for a particular purpose. (조직적인) 운동. ¶ *a political* ~ 정치 운동 / *A* ~ *was begun to raise funds for a hospital.* 병원 설립의 기금 모집을 위한 운동이 시작되었다 / *a* ~ *against mosquitoes* 모기 퇴치 운동. — *vi.* (P1) take part in or go on a campaign. 작전[운동]에 참가하다. [→camp]

cam·paign·er [kæmpéinər] *n.* Ⓒ a person who takes part in a campaign. 종군자; 캠페인 참가자. ¶ *an old* ~ 노련한 사람; 베테랑.

cam·pa·ni·le [kæ̀mpəníːli] *n.* (*pl.* **-les, -li**) a bell-tower, esp. in Italy. 종루(鐘樓). [L. *campana* bell]

cam·pa·ni·li [kæ̀mpəníːliː] *n.* pl. of **campanile.**

cam·pan·u·la [kæmpǽnjələ] *n.* 《bot.》 any of various plants with bell-shaped flowers. 초롱꽃(속(屬)의 식물).

camp bed [ㅅㅅ] *n.* a small portable bed made to fold up flat. 캠프용 접침대.

camp chair [ㅅㅅ] *n.* a light folding chair. (캠프용)접의자.

camp·er [kǽmpər] *n.* Ⓒ a person who camps. 야영자.

camp·fire [kǽmpfàiər] *n.* Ⓒ **1** a fire in a camp used for warmth or cooking. 캠프파이어. **2** a social gathering around such a fire. (campfire 를 둘러싼) 모임; 친목회.

cam·phor [kǽmfər] *n.* Ⓒ a white substance with a strong odor obtained from the camphor tree and used in medicine, mothballs, etc. 장뇌(樟腦). ¶ *a* ~ *tree* 녹나무 / *a* ~ *ball* 장뇌알(방충약). [Malay *kapur* chalk]

cam·phor·ate [kǽmfərèit] *vt.* (P6) treat with camphor. …에 장뇌를 넣다[로 처리하다].

cam·phor·a·ted [kǽmfərèitid] *adj.* containing camphor. 장뇌가 든. ¶ ~ *oil* 장뇌유(油).

cam·pi·on [kǽmpiən] *n.* 《bot.》 kinds of flowering plants. 석죽과의 식물.

camp-meet·ing [kǽmpmìːtiŋ] *n.* 《U.S.》 a religious meeting, usu. lasting for several days, held in a large tent or in the open air. (종교적) 야외 집회. [→camp]

cam·po·ree [kæ̀mpəríː] *n.* an assembly of Boy Scouts. 보이스카우트 집회(cf. *jamboree*). [→camp, (jamb)oree]

cam·pus [kǽmpəs] *n.* Ⓒ 《U.S.》 the grounds of a school, college, or university. 캠퍼스; 교정(校庭); 학교 구내(構內). [L.= field]

:can[1] [kæn, kən] *auxil. v.* (**could**) **1** 《in *infinitive,* p. & pp. supplied by *be able to*》 be able to; know how to. …할 수 있다; …할 줄 알다. ¶ *I* [*He*] ~ *swim.* 나[그]는 헤엄칠 줄 안다 / *She* ~ *not play the piano.* 그녀는 피아노를 못 친다 / *Can you speak English?* 영어를 할 줄 아나요. **2** 《*colloq.*》 have the right to. …할 권리가 있다. ¶ *You can't attend the meeting.* 당신은 회의에 참석할 권리가 없다. **3** 《usu. in *interrogative*》 be possible. (대체) …일까(cf. *must*). ¶ *Can it be true?* 사실일까 / *Who* ~ *he be?* (도대체) 그가 누구일까. **4** 《usu. in *negative*》 have no possibility. …할[일] 리가 없다(opp. must be true). ¶ *The news* ~ *not be true.* 그 소식은 사실일 리가 없다 / *I* ~ *not have said so.* 내가 그렇게 말했을 리가 없다. **5** may; have permission to; be allowed to. …해도 좋다. 參考 미국 구어에서는 May I ...? 대신 Can I ...? 을 쓰는 일이 많음. ¶ *You* ~ *go now.* 이제 가도 좋다 / *Anyone* ~ *cross the street here.* 누구든 여기 길을 건너도 된다 / *Can I speak to you a moment?* 잠깐 당신과 얘기 좀 해도 괜찮겠습니까. **6** want to; feel inclined to. …하고 싶다. ¶ *You may leave whenever you* ~. 가고 싶을 땐 언제고 가도 좋다. [O.E. *cunnan* know]

***cannot but** do* ⇨but.

cannot do* (*it*) *too well, impossible (for one) to do (it) too well. 아무리 잘 해도 지나치지 않다.

***cannot help** doing*, must do. …하지 않을 수 없다.

:can[2] [kæn] *n.* Ⓒ **1** a metal container. 깡통. ¶ *a milk* ~ 우유(깡)통 / *an oil* ~ 기름통 / *a* ~ *of fruit* 과일 통조림 한 통. **2** contents of a can. 통조림 식품[내용물]. — *vt.* (**canned, can·ning**) (P6) **1** put (food) into a can to preserve it. …을 통조림으로 하다. ¶ *canned fruit* 통조림한 과일. **2** 《U.S. *colloq.*》 dismiss. …을 해고하다. [O.E. *canne*]

Ca·naan [kéinən] *n.* 《Bible》 the region that God promised to the Israelites. 가나안 땅. 參考 지금의 팔레스타인 지방. [Gk. & Heb.]

·Can·a·da [kǽnədə] *n.* a country in North America. 캐나다. 參考 수도는 Ottawa.

Ca·na·di·an [kənéidiən] *adj.* of Canada or its people. 캐나다의; 캐나다 사람의. — *n.* Ⓒ a person of Canada. 캐나다 사람.

ca·naille [kənéil, -náil] *n.* 《F.》 the rabble; the masses. 하층 사회[계급]; 대중; 오합지졸.

:ca·nal [kənǽl] *n.* Ⓒ **1** a man-made waterway for ships or for irrigation. 운하. ¶ *the Suez Canal* 수에즈 운하 / *the Canal Zone* 파나마 운하 지대. **2** a tube-like passage in an animal body or a plant for carrying food, liquid, air, etc. (동식물 체내의) 도관(導管). ¶ *the alimentary* ~ 소화관(消化管). [L.=pipe]

ca·nal·ize [kənǽlaiz, kǽnəlàiz] *vt.* (P6) provide with canals; convert (a river) into a canal. …을 운하화하다; (강)을 운하로 만들다.

ca·na·pé [kǽnəpi, -pèi] *n.* 《F.》 a cracker or small square slice of toasted bread spread with cheese, meat, etc. 카나페《전채(前菜)의 일종》.

ca·nard [kənɑ́ːrd] *n.* 《F.》 Ⓒ a false rumor. 허위 보도; 헛소문.

:ca·nar·y [kənέəri] *n.* (*pl.* **-nar·ies**) **1** Ⓒ 《bird》 a small yellow songbird. 카나리아. **2** Ⓤ light yellow. 선황색(鮮黃色). **3** Ⓤ a wine much drunk in England in the 16th and 17th centuries. 포도주의 일종. [Place]

Canary Islands [-ˊ- ˊ-] *n.* a group of islands in the Atlantic. 카나리아 제도.

Ca·nav·e·ral [kənǽvərəl] *n.* a cape on the east coast of a peninsula, Florida, former name of Cape Kennedy. 캐나베랄《미국 플로리다 동부 해안의 곶》.

Can·ber·ra [kǽnbərə] *n.* the capital of Australia. 캔버라.

canc. canceled; cancellation.

can·can [kǽnkæ̀n] *n.* 《F.》 an indecent dance. 캉캉춤.

can·cel [kǽnsəl] *vt.* (**-celed, -cel·ing** or 《Brit.》 **-celled, -cel·ling**) (P6) **1** cross out; mark (something) so as to make it void. …을 지우다; …에 소인(消印)을 찍다. ¶ ~ *a stamp* 우표에 소인을 찍다 / *a canceled stamp* 소인 찍힌 우표. **2** take back; withdraw; do away with. …을 취소하다. ¶ ~ *an appointment* 약속을 취소하다 / *He canceled his order for the books.* 책주문을 취소했다 / *This will* ~ *your debt to me.* 이로써 내게 대한 빚은 없어진다 / *Permission was canceled.* 허가는 취소되었다.

— *n.* Ⓒ **1** the act of canceling. 말소; 취소; 해약. **2** something canceled. 취소[말소, 철회]된 것. [L. *cancellus* =crossed bars]

can·cel·la·tion [kæ̀nsəléiʃən] *n.* ⓊⒸ **1** the act of canceling; the state of being canceled. 취소; 해약. **2** Ⓒ the mark showing that something has been canceled. 소인(消印).

can·cer [kǽnsər] *n.* **1** ⓊⒸ 《med.》 a growth in the body of a person or an animal that is very harmful to life. 암(癌). ¶ *lung* ~ 폐암 / *gastric* ~ 위암 / *I am with* [*I have*] ~. 암에 걸려 있다. **2** Ⓒ anything bad or harmful that destroys by growing. 해악(害惡). **3** 《*C-*》 《astron.》 one of the signs of the Zodiac. 게자리. [L.=crab]

can·cer·ous [kǽnsərəs] *adj.* of, like, or having cancer. 암의; 암 같은; 암에 걸린. ¶ *an attempt to stop the* ~ *growth* 암의 성장을 저지할 시도.

can·de·la·bra [kæ̀ndilɑ́ːbrə] *n.* pl. of **candelabrum.**

can·de·la·brum [kæ̀ndilɑ́ːbrəm] *n.* Ⓒ (*pl.* **-bra** or **-brums**) a candlestick with ornamental branches. 장식 가지 촛대. [→candle]

can·des·cent [kændésənt] *adj.* glowing with heat. 백열(白熱)의(cf. *incandescent*). ●**can·des·cence** *n.* [L. *candeo* be white, →incandesce]

can·did [kǽndid] *adj.* frank; sincere, outspoken. 솔직[정직]한; 기탄없는. ¶ *a* ~ *opinion* [*friend*] 솔직한 의견[친구]. [L. = white]

***to be quite* [*perfectly*] *candid* (*with you*),** to speak quite openly; hiding nothing. 솔직히[까놓고] 말하면.

can·di·da·cy [kǽndidəsi] *n.* Ⓤ 《U.S.》 the fact or state of being a candidate. 입후보; 출마. ¶ *Three boys spoke in favor of John's* ~ *for president of the club.* 세 소년이 클럽 회장으로 존 후보를 지지하는 발언을 했다. [↓]

·can·di·date [kǽndədèit, -dit] *n.* Ⓒ 《*for*》 a person who seeks or takes part in a contest for a prize or position. 후보[지원]자. ¶ *a* ~ *for President* 대통령 입후보자 / *a* ~ *for admission* [*examination*] 입회[수험] 지망자 / *There is only one* ~ *for mayor of the city.* 시장 입후보자는 단 한 사람뿐이다. [L. *candidatus* white-robed]

can·di·da·ture [kǽndidətʃùər, -tʃər] *n.* 《Brit.》=candidacy.

candid camera [ˊ- ˊ--] *n.* a small camera for taking photographs of people often without their knowledge. 소형 스냅 사진기.

can·did·ly [kǽndidli] *adv.* in a candid manner; frankly. 솔직하게.

can·did·ness [kǽndidnis] *n.* the state of being candid. 솔직함.

can·died [kǽndid] *adj.* **1** turned into sugar. 당화(糖化)한. ¶ *candied honey* 말라서 굳어진 꿀. **2** cooked or preserved in sugar. 설탕절임한. ¶ ~ *fruits* 설탕절임의 과일. **3** 《*arch.*》 made sweet or agreeable; flattering. 달콤한; 알랑대는. ¶ ~ *words* 감언. [→candy]

:can·dle [kǽndl] *n.* Ⓒ **1** a stick of tallow or wax with a wick through its center that is burned to give light. (양)초. ¶ *burn candles to see by* 주위를 보려고 촛불을 켜다. **2** a unit of luminous intensity. 촉광(燭光). **3** anything shaped like a candle. 양초 모양의 것. [L. *candeo* shine]

burn the candle at both ends, stay up late and get up early; use up one's strength and resources rapidly; work too hard. 늦도록 일하고 일찍 일어나다; 지나친 활동으로 체력에 부담을 주다; 무리를 하다.

cannot* 〔*be not fit to*〕 *hold a candle to, be greatly inferior to. …와는 비교도 안 되다; …의 발밑에도 못 미치다.

not worth the candle, not worth doing. 애쓸 가치가 없다.

can·dle·light [kǽndllàit] *n.* Ⓤ **1** the light of a candle. 촛불. **2** dusk; twilight. 황혼; 땅거미.

by candlelight, in the evening; after daylight has gone. 저녁에; 황혼에.

Can·dle·mas [kǽndlməs, -mæ̀s] *n.* February 2, a church festival in honor of the purification of the Virgin Mary. 성촉절(聖燭節).

candle power [ㅿ- ㅿ-] *n.* a unit of luminous intensity. 촉광(燭光).

can·dle·stick [kǽndlstìk] *n.* Ⓒ a holder for a candle. 촛대.

can·dle·wick [kǽndlwìk] *n.* Ⓒ the wick of a candle. 초의 심지.

can·dor, 《Brit.》 **-dour** [kǽndər] *n.* being candid, honest and fair. 솔직; 담박(淡泊); 공정(公正). ¶ *consider an issue with* ~ 문제를 공정히 생각하다. [L. *candor* whiteness → candid]

:can·dy [kǽndi] *n.* ⓊⒸ (*pl.* **-dies**) **1** 《U.S.》 something to eat made chiefly of sugar combined with fruits, nuts, etc. 캔디 (cf. 《Brit.》 *sweets*). **2** Ⓤ 《Brit.》 sugar candy. 사탕. **3** Ⓒ one piece of such a sweet. 캔디〔사탕〕 한 개. — *vt.* (P6) (**-died**) cook (food) in sugar syrup; coat or preserve (food) with sugar. …을 설탕에 조리다; 설탕을 입히다. — *vi.* (P1) turn into sugar. 설탕이 되다. [Arab.]

can·dy·tuft [kǽnditʌ̀ft] *n.* 《bot.》 any of a genus of garden plants of the crucifer family, with clusters of white, pink, or purplish flowers. 이베리스꽃.

·cane [kein] *n.* Ⓒ **1** the slender, long, and flexible stem of certain plants, such as bamboo, rattan, and blackberry. (대나무·등나무 따위의) 줄기. **2** a walking stick. 지팡이. **3** a stick used for beating. 매; 회초리. — *vt.* (P6) **1** beat (someone or something) with a cane. …을 매질하다. **2** make or furnish (chairs, etc.) with cane. …을 등나무로 만들다. [Gk. *kanna* reed]

cane sugar [ㅿ ㅿ-] *n.* sugar obtained from sugar cane. 사탕수수 설탕.

ca·nine [kéinain, kǽn-] *adj.* **1** of or like a dog. 개의; 개 같은. **2** of the dog family. 개속(屬)의. — *n.* Ⓒ a canine tooth. 송곳니. [L. *canis* dog]

canine tooth [ㅿ-ㅿ] *n.* one of the four sharp-pointed teeth of a man or an animal. 송곳니.

Ca·nis [kéinis] *n.* 《zool.》 the canine genus. 개속(屬).

can·is·ter [kǽnistər] *n.* Ⓒ **1** a box or can for tea, coffee, tobacco, etc. (차 따위를 넣어두는) (양철)통(cf. *caddy*[1]). **2** a case filled with bullets. 산탄통(霰彈筒). [Gk. *kanastron* basket]

can·ker [kǽŋkər] *n.* Ⓒ **1** 《med.》 a sore, esp. in the mouth. 구강 궤양(口腔潰瘍); 옹(癰). **2** a disease of plants that causes them to decay slowly. (수목의) 암종병(癌腫病). **3** 《*fig.*》 Ⓤ anything causing decay or rot. 해독; 해악. ¶ *the cankers that eat the heart of a democracy* 민주주의의 핵심을 좀먹는 폐해. — *vt., vi.* (P6;1) **1** infect or be infected with canker. 구강 궤양에 걸리(게 하)다; 옹이 나(게 하)다. **2** decay; rot. 썩(게 하)다. [→cancer]

can·ker·ous [kǽŋkərəs] *adj.* of or like a canker; causing a canker. canker의 〔같은〕; canker를 일으키는.

can·ker·worm [kǽŋkərwə̀ːrm] *n.* Ⓒ 《insect》 a caterpillar that feeds on the leaves of plants. 자벌레.

can·na [kǽnə] *n.* Ⓒ 《bot.》 a tropical plant with large, pointed leaves and large red, pink, or yellow flowers; the flower of this plant. 칸나; 그 꽃. [→cane]

·canned [kænd] *adj.* **1** put or preserved in a can. 통조림한. ¶ ~ *food* 통조림 식품. **2** 《*colloq.*》 recorded. 녹음한. [↓]

can·ner [kǽnər] *n.* 《U.S.》 one who cans food. 통조림 제조업자. [→can[2]]

can·ner·y [kǽnəri] *n.* Ⓒ 《U.S.》 (*pl.* **-ner·ies**) a factory where foods are canned. 통조림 공장. [↑]

can·ni·bal [kǽnəbəl] *n.* Ⓒ **1** a human being who eats human flesh. 사람 고기 먹는 사람; 식인종. ¶ *a* ~ *race* 식인종 / *He was eaten by cannibals.* 그는 식인종에게 잡아먹혔다. **2** any animal that eats its own kind. (동류를) 서로 잡아먹는 동물. — *adj.* of or like cannibals. 식인의; 식인종 같은; 서로 잡아먹는. [Carib.]

can·ni·bal·ism [kǽnəbəlìzəm] *n.* Ⓤ **1** the act or habit of eating one's own kind. 식인(食人); 서로 잡아먹기. **2** 《*fig.*》 barbarous cruelty. 잔인(행위); 만행.

can·ni·bal·is·tic [kæ̀nəbəlístik] *adj.* of or like cannibals. cannibal의〔같은〕.

can·ni·bal·ize [kǽnəbəlàiz] *vt.* (P6) remove serviceable parts from a machine for use in another. (다른 기계·차량의 수리를 위해) 쓸 수 있는 부품을 떼어내다. ¶ ~ *a wrecked car for tyres* 파손된 차의 타이어를 떼어내다.

can·ni·kin [kǽnəkin] *n.* Ⓒ a small can; a small cup. 작은 (양철)통; 컵. [→can[2]]

can·ni·ly [kǽnili] *adv.* cautiously; prudently. 조심스럽게; 신중하게. [→canny]

·**can·non**[1] [kǽnən] *n.* Ⓒ (*pl.* **-nons** or *collectively* **-non**) a large old-fashioned heavy gun. 대포《지금은 보통 gun》. [It. *cannone* great tube →cane]

can·non[2] [kǽnən] *n.* 《billiard》 hitting two balls successively. 캐넌《두 표적공에 연속해 맞는 일》. [Sp.]

can·non·ade [kæ̀nənéid] *n.* Ⓒ a continuous firing of cannons; an attack with cannons; the noise made by this. 포격; 포성. —— *vt., vi.* (P6;1) bombard. 포격하다. [→cannon[1]]

can·non·ball [kǽnənbɔ̀:l] *n.* Ⓒ a heavy, large ball of iron or other metal, formerly fired from cannons. (옛날의 둥근) 포탄《지금은 보통 shell》.

can·non-fod·der [kǽnənfɔ̀dər] *n.* soldiers considered as materials to be consumed in war. 대포의 밥《전쟁 소모품으로서의 병졸》.

·**can·not** [kǽnɑt, -∸, kənɑ́t / kǽnɔt, kənɔ́t] =can not.

can·ny [kǽni] *adj.* (**-ni·er, -ni·est**) **1** shrewd; cautious. 교활한; 빈틈 없는. ¶ *a ~ businessman* 빈틈 없는 사업가. **2** careful in spending. 검소한; 검약하는; 알뜰한. [→can[1]]

:**can·oe** [kənú:] *n.* Ⓒ a light, narrow boat moved with paddles. 카누.
paddle one's own canoe, 《*colloq.*》 get along without another's help. 제 일은 제가 하다; 독립 자활하다.
—— *vi., vt.* (P1;6) travel or carry in or by a canoe. 카누로 가다[나르다]. [Haytian *canoa*]

·**can·on**[1] [kǽnən] *n.* Ⓒ **1** a law or rule of a church. 교회 법규; 종규(宗規); 계율. **2** a principle or rule by which things are judged. 판단의 기준. ¶ *according to the cannons of good taste* 훌륭한 감식(鑑識) 규준에 따라. **3** 《*the C-*》 the list of books of the Bible accepted by the church. 정전(正典). ¶ *the Books of the Canon* 정경서(正經書). **4** a list of saints. 성인록(聖人錄). **5** a member of a body of clergymen living according to a certain rule. 성직자 평의원회 회원. [Gk. *kanōn* rule]

can·on[2] [kǽnən] *n.* =canyon.

canon law [∸-∸] *n.* ecclesiastical law. 교회법.

ca·non·i·cal [kənɑ́nəkəl / -nɔ́n-] *adj.* **1** according to the church law. 교회법에 따른. **2** belonging to the canon of the Bible. 정전(正典)으로 인정된. ¶ *the Canonical books of the Bible* 정경서(正經書). **3** authorized; accepted. 규범적인; 정전(正典)의. —— *n.* 《*pl.*》 the clothes that a clergyman must wear at a church service. 제의(祭衣). [→canon[1]]

can·on·ize [kǽnənàiz] *vt.* (P6) **1** declare (a dead person) to be a saint; add (a dead person's name) to the list of saints. (죽은 사람)을 시성(諡聖)하다; 성인으로 추앙하다. ¶ *Joan of Arc was canonized in 1920.* 잔 다르크는 1920년에 시성되었다. **2** recognize (some book) as canonical. …을 정전(正典)으로 인정하다. **3** glorify. …을 상찬(賞讃)[찬미]하다. [↑]

ca·noo·dle [kənú:dl] *vi., vt.* (P1;6) 《*U.S. sl.*》 fondle. 껴안다; 애무하다. [?]

can-opener [kǽnòupənər] *n.* a device for opening cans. 깡통따개. [→can[2]]

can·o·py [kǽnəpi] *n.* Ⓒ (*pl.* **-pies**) **1** a cloth covering fixed above a bed, throne, entrance, etc. 닫집. **2** 《*fig.*》 any overhanging covering. (닫집 모양의) 가리개. ¶ *a ~ of leaves* 지붕처럼 내리덮인 나뭇잎들. **3** the sky. 하늘; 창공. ¶ *the ~ of (the) heaven(s)* 창공. —— *vt.* (P6) (**-pied**) cover (something or someone) with a canopy. …을 canopy로 덮다. [Gk.=mosquito net]

ca·no·rous [kənɔ́:rəs] *adj.* melodious; resonant. 음악적인; 공명하는. [L. *canōrus* tuneful]

·**canst** [kænst, kənst] *auxil. v.* 《*arch.*》 = can. 參考 주어가 thou일 때.

Cant. Canterbury; Canticles.

cant[1] [kænt] *n.* Ⓤ **1** an insincere statement expressive of goodness or piety. 빈말; 위선적인 말. **2** the peculiar language of a special group. 은어; 변말. ¶ *the ~ of thieves* 도둑들의 변말 / *college ~* 대학(가)의 은어.
—— *vi.* (P1) talk in cant. 변말을 쓰다; 빈말[위선적인 말을]하다. [→chant]

cant[2] [kænt] *n.* **1** a sloping or slanting surface; a slope; a slant. 사면(斜面); 비탈. ¶ *the ~ of a roof* 지붕의 물매. **2** a corner. 모퉁이; 구석. —— *vt., vi.* (P6;1) slant; slope. 기울(이)다. ¶ *The carriage canted and upset.* 차가 기우뚱하더니 뒤집혔다. [Rom.=edge]

:**can't** [kænt / kɑ:nt] 《*colloq.*》 =cannot.

Can·tab, -ta·brig·i·an [kǽntæb], [kæ̀ntəbrídʒiən] *n.* a member of Cambridge University. Cambrige 대학인[사람]《재학생, 졸업생, 관계자》.

can·ta·bi·le [kɑ:ntɑ́:bilèi / -bilè] 《*It. mus.*》 *adj., adv.* songlike; in an easy and flowing manner. 노래와 같은[같이]; 부드럽고 매끄러운[매끄럽게]. —— *n.* a cantabile style, passage, or piece. 칸타빌레 양식[조(調), 곡]. [It.]

can·ta·loup, -loupe [kǽntəlòup / -lù:p] *n.* Ⓒ a sort of melon with sweet and juicy flesh. 멜론의 일종. [Place]

can·tan·ker·ous [kəntǽŋkərəs, kæn-] *adj.* ill-natured; quarrelsome. 심통사나운; 툭하면 싸우는. [? ME.]

can·ta·ta [kəntɑ́:tə] *n.* Ⓒ 《*It. mus.*》 a musical composition telling a story. 칸타타. [L. *cano* sing]

can·teen [kæntí:n] *n.* Ⓒ **1** a small container used for carrying water or other drinks. 수통. **2** 《Brit.》 a small store in a factory, office, or camp where food, drinks, tobacco, etc. are sold. 구내 매점; 주보. [It. *cantina* cellar]

can·ter [kǽntər] *n.* Ⓒ a slow gallop. (말의) 느린 구보(cf. *trot, walk*). ¶ *The horse came at a* ～. 말이 느린 구보로 달려왔다.
win at* 〔*in*〕 *a canter, win easily. 쉽게 이기다; 낙승하다.
— *vi.* (P1,2A) go at a canter. 느린 구보로 가다. ¶ ～ *along the road* 길을 천천히 달리다.
— *vt.* (P6) make (a horse) go at a canter. (말)을 느린 구보로 가게 하다. ¶ ～ *a horse* 말을 캔터로 가게 하다. [from pilgrim's pace to the place]

Can·ter·bur·y [kǽntərbèri, -bəri] *n.* **1** a city in southeast England. 캔터베리시(市). 參考 영국 국교 총본산 소재지. **2** 《c-》 a stand for portfolios, music, etc. 악보대(樂譜臺). [↑]

can·thar·i·des [kænθǽrədìːz] *n. pl.* 《med.》 a preparation made from the Spanish fly used as diuretic, etc. 칸다리스《이뇨제(利尿劑)》. [Gk. *kantharis*]

can·ti·cle [kǽntikəl] *n.* Ⓒ a song whose words are taken from the Bible, used in church services. (성구(聖句)에 곡을 단) 성가(聖歌). [→cantata]
the Canticles, 《Bible》 the Song of Solomon. 솔로몬의 아가(雅歌).

can·ti·le·ver [kǽntəlèvər, -lìvər] *n.* 《archit.》 a large bracket. 캔틸레버; 외팔보. ¶ *a* ～ *bridge* 캔틸레버식 다리. [Sp. =raising-dog]

can·tle [kǽntl] *n.* **1** a slice cut off. 얇은 조각; 박편. **2** the hind bow of a saddle. 안미(鞍尾); 안장 뒷가지. [→cant[2]]

can·to [kǽntou] *n.* Ⓒ (*pl.* **-tos**) one of the main divisions of a long poem. (장편시의) 편(篇). ¶ *A* ～ *of a poem is like a chapter of a story.* 시의 편은 소설의 장(章)과 같다. [L. *cano* sing, →cantata]

can·ton [kǽntn, -tɑn / kǽntɔn, -⌐] *n.* Ⓒ a small political division of a country, esp. of Switzerland. (스위스 연방 따위의) 주(州). — *vt.* (P6) **1** divide into cantons. …을 주〔군·시〕로 가르다. **2** [kæntɑ́n, -tóun / kəntúːn, kæn-] put in quarters. …을 숙영(宿營)시키다. [→cant[2]]

can·ton·ment [kæntóunmənt, -tɑ́n- / -túːn-] *n.* 《usu. *pl.*》 a place where soldiers live for a short time. (군대의) 숙영지(宿營地).

cant phrase [⌐⌐] *n.* temporary catchwords. 유행어; 통용어.

Ca·nuck [kənʌ́k] *n., adj.* 《*sl.*》 French Canadian; 《U.S.》 Canadian. 프랑스계 캐나다인(의); 캐나다인(의).

Ca·nute [kənjúːt] *n.* (994-1035) a king of England. 카뉴트왕.

·can·vas [kǽnvəs] *n.* **1** Ⓤ rough, thick, and strong cloth made of cotton, hemp, etc. used for tents, sails, tennis shoes, etc. 즈크; 범포(帆布). **2** ⒸⓊ a material on which to paint in oil; Ⓒ an oil painting. (유화용의) 화포(畫布); 캔버스; 유화(油畫). **3** Ⓒ something made of canvas, as a tent or sail. 즈크 제품《천막, 돛 따위》.
under canvas, **a**) (of troops) in tents. 텐트를 치고; 야영 중에. ¶ *sleep under* ～ 텐트에서 자다. **b**) (of ships) with sails spread. 돛을 펴고. ¶ *sail under full* ～ 온 돛을 올리고 항행하다.
— *adj.* made of canvas. 즈크로 만든. [↓]

can·vass [kǽnvəs] *vt., vi.* **1** (P6,13) examine or look over (something) thoroughly; discuss (something) in detail. …을 정밀 검사〔검토〕하다; 자세히 논구(論究)〔토의〕하다. ¶ *British opinion as canvassed by the broadcasting corporation.* 그 방송국이 조사한 영국의 여론 / *His policy is much canvassed.* 그의 정책〔방침〕은 충분히 검토돼 있다. **2** (P1,2;13) 《*for*》 go through (places) or among (people) asking for votes, opinions, orders, etc. 부탁하며〔주문 받으러〕 다니다; 선거 운동을 하다. ¶ ～ *a district for votes* 득표를 위해 지역구를 돌다 / *Mary canvassed the village for scriptions to the weekly paper.* 메리는 주간지(紙) 구독 신청을 받기 위해 마을을 돌아다녔다.
— *n.* Ⓒ the act of canvassing. 조사; 면밀한 검사; 투표〔주문〕의 권유; 선거 운동. [Gk. *kannabis* hemp, toss in sheet]

can·yon [kǽnjən] *n.* Ⓒ a deep, long valley between high cliffs, usu. along a stream; a gorge. 계곡; 협곡. [Sp. =cane, tube]

can·zo·net [kæ̀nzənét] *n.* a light song. 소가곡(小歌曲); 칸초네타.

caou·tchouc [kautʃúːk, káutʃuk] *n., adj.* (of) rubber. 고무(로 만든). [Carib.]

:cap [kæp] *n.* Ⓒ **1** a covering for the head, usu. without a brim. (테없는) 모자(cf. *hat*). ¶ *a hunting* ～ 사냥 모자 / *a utility* ～ 작업모 / *a nurse's* ～ 간호사 모자 / *a fool's* ～ 광대 모자. **2** a special head-dress showing rank, occupation, etc. 제모(制帽). **3** anything like a cap in use or shape. 모자 모양의 것. ¶ *the* ～ *of a mushroom =a mushroom* ～ 버섯의 갓 / *a* ～ *on a bottle* 병마개 / *the knee-cap* 슬개골. **4** the highest part; the top. 정상. ¶ *the* ～ *of fools* 큰 바보. **5** =percussion cap. **6** =toe-cap.
a feather in one's cap, ⇨feather.
cap and bells, the sign of a jester. 방울 달린 모자《어릿광대의 표시》.
cap and gown, **a**) the dress of a teacher. 교사복. **b**) =academical.
cap in hand, 《*fig.*》 humbly. 겸손하게; 공손히.
cap of liberty, a conical cap worn by a freed Roman slave, now as Republican symbol. (옛날 해방된 노예가 쓴) 깔때기 모

자 ; 리버티 캡《오늘날엔 공화당의 상징》.

cap of maintenance, a cap worn as symbol of official dignity. 관모(官帽).

If the cap fits, wear it. If the remark suits your case, apply it to yourself. 남의 말이 네게 맞거든 너 자신의 경우로 생각해라.

***set one's cap at* 〔*for*〕,** (of a woman) try to get (a man) as an admirer, lover, or husband; try to attract the attention of (a man). (여자가) 남자의 마음을 끌려고 하다. — *v.* (**capped, cap·ping**) *vt.* (P6) **1** put a cap on (someone); cover the top of (something). …에게 모자를 씌우다; …의 정상을〔꼭대기를〕 덮다. ¶ ~ *a bottle* 병에 마개를 하다 / *Snow has capped the mountain.* 눈이 산꼭대기를 덮었다. **2** complete. …을 끝내다; 마무리하다. **3** do or say something better than (what somebody else has done or said). 동등 또는 그 이상의 것을 하다; …을 능가하다. ¶ ~ *a story* 〔*joke*〕 좀더 재미있는 이야기를〔농담을〕 하다. — *vi.* (P1) raise one's cap to someone. (아무에게) 모자를 벗어 인사하다; 경의를 표하다. [Rom. = cloak]

cap an anecdote, tell a better anecdote. 한층 더 재미 있는 이야기를 하다.

cap the climax, 《U.S.》 **a**) be or do better than expected. 기대 이상이다〔이상의 것을 하다〕. **b**) go to the extreme limit. 극한을 넘다; 극단에 흐르다.

to cap* (*it*) *all, lastly and best or worst of all; in the end. 마침내는; 필경; 게다가.

CAP Civil Air Patrol.

cap. capacity; capital; capitalize; captain; capital letter.

ca·pa·bil·i·ty [kèipəbíləti] *n.* Ⓤ **1** ability; the power of doing something. 재능; 능력. **2** 《*pl.*》 undeveloped abilities, qualities, etc. that can be developed. 잠재 능력; 가능성; 소질. [↓]

:ca·pa·ble [kéipəbəl] *adj.* **1** skillful; able; having ability. 숙련된; 능력 있는; 유능한. ¶ *a* ~ *instructor* 유능한 교사. **2** 《*for*》 (of a person) qualified for. …할 자격이 있는; 적합한.

capable of, **a**) having the necessary ability or qualities or inclination for doing something. …할 능력이 있는; …할 수 있는; 능히 …까지도 할. ¶ *a man* ~ *of hard work* 힘든 일을 할 수 있는 사람 / *a man* ~ *of murder* 능히 살인까지도 할 사람 / *a man* ~ *of judging art* 예술을 평가할 수 있는 사람 / *be* ~ *of tears* 인간미를 지니고 있다 / *This room is* ~ *of holding six persons.* 이 방은 6명을 수용할 수 있다 / *He is* ~ *of such an act* 〔*of doing such a thing*〕. 그는 능히 그런 짓도 서슴지 않을 위인이다. **b**) (of a thing, situation, circumstances) patient of. 견디는; 감내할. ¶ *a situation* ~ *of improvement* 개선의 여지가 있는 상황. [L. *capio* hold]

ca·pa·bly [kéipəbli] *adv.* with ability; in a capable manner. 잘; 훌륭하게.

ca·pa·cious [kəpéiʃəs] *adj.* **1** that can hold much; spacious. 용적이 큰; 너른. ¶ *a* ~ *room* 널찍한 방 / *a* ~ *mouth* 큰 입. **2** broad; ready to receive much. (마음이) 너그러운; 도량이 넓은. ¶ *a* ~ *mind* 너그러운 마음. [L. *capio* hold]

ca·pac·i·tate [kəpǽsətèit] *vt.* (P6,13,20) enable; make (someone) capable. …에게 할 수 있게 하다; (…할) 능력〔자격〕을 주다. ¶ ~ *someone for* 〔*to do*〕 *his task* 아무에게 일을 할 수 있게 해주다 / *a person capacitated to vote* 선거권이 주어진 사람. [L.]

:ca·pac·i·ty [kəpǽsəti] *n.* (*pl.* **-ties**) **1** Ⓤ 《often *a* ~ 》 the power or ability of receiving and holding. 수용 능력; 용적; 용량. ¶ *be filled* 〔*crowded*〕 *to* ~ 만원이다 / *be crowded beyond* ~ 초만원이다 / *breathing* 〔*vital*〕 ~ 폐활량 / *The hall has a* ~ *of 500.* 홀은 5백명이 들어간다 / *This box has a* ~ *of 2 cubic meters.* 이 상자는 용적이 2입방 미터다. **2** Ⓤ 《sometimes *a* ~ 》 ability; power. 능력; 역량. ¶ *a man of great* ~ 대단한 능력의 사람 / *the* ~ *for knowing the future* 미래를 알 수 있는 능력. **3** Ⓒ a position; a relation; a character. 지위; 자격. ¶ *in one's* ~ *as a judge* 재판관의 자격으로 / *He went in a private* ~. 그는 개인 자격으로 들어갔다. [→capacious]

filled to capacity, quite full. 꽉 들어찬; 만원의.

in the capacity of, acting as. (으)로서; …의 자격으로 ¶ *I have come in the* ~ *of a legal adviser.* 나는 법률 고문 자격으로 왔다.

capacity house [–⌐–– ⌐] *n.* a packed house. 대만원의 회장〔극장〕.

cap-a-pie [kæ̀pəpíː] *adv.* 《F.》 from head to foot; completely. 전신(全身)에; 완전히. ¶ ~ *armed* 완전 무장한. [F.=head to foot]

ca·par·i·son [kəpǽrisən] *n.* Ⓒ 《often *pl.*》 **1** an ornamental cloth for a horse. 장식 마의(馬衣)〔마구〕. **2** gay or rich dress. 미복(美服); 호화로운 의상. — *vt.* (P6) put a caparison on (a horse); dress (someone) richly. …에 마의를 입히다; …에게 화려한 옷을 입히다. [Sp. *caparazón* akin to *capa*, →cape[1]]

cape[1] [keip] *n.* Ⓒ an outer sleeveless garment worn loosely over the shoulders. 케이프《어깨에 걸치는 소매없는 망토》. [Sp.]

:cape[2] [keip] *n.* **1** Ⓒ a point of land going out into the sea. 곶; 갑(岬). **2** 《*the C-*》 the Cape of Good Hope. 희망봉(喜望峰) 《남아프리카 남단》. [L. *caput* head]

Cape Ken·ne·dy [kèip kénədi] *n.* the base camp for experiments on rockets in Florida, U.S.A. 케이프 케네디《유명한 미국의 로켓 발사 기지》.

ca·per [kéipər] *vi.* (P1,2A) **1** jump about playfully. (깡충깡충) 뛰어다니다. **2** 《*fig.*》 act in a foolish way. 까불다. — *n.* Ⓒ **1** a playful jump. (깡충깡충) 뛰어다님. **2** 《of-

ten *pl.*) (*fig.*) a wild, foolish action; a silly trick. 까불; 경박한 행동; 얕은 꾀. ¶ *I am tired of all his capers.* 그의 얕은 수작엔 이제 신물이 난다. [L. *caper* goat →capriole]
cut a caper [**capers**], **a**) jump about playfully. (깡충깡충) 뛰(어다니)다; 까불다. **b**) (*fig.*) play foolish tricks. 얕은 꾀를 쓰다.

ca·pers [kéipərz] *n. pl.* flower buds used in making a sauce. 풍조목속(風鳥木屬)의 꽃망울(소스 등의 조미제로 쓰임). [Gk. *kapparis*]

cap·ful [kǽpfùl] *n.* the amount that will fill a cap. 모자 하나 가득한 양. ¶ *a ~ of beans* 모자 하나 가득한 양의 콩. [→cap]

cap·il·lar·i·ty [kæ̀pəlǽrəti] *n.* Ⓤ (phys.) the state of being capillary; the power of exerting capillary attraction or repulsion. 모상(毛狀); 털 모양; 모세관 현상. [↓]

cap·il·lar·y [kǽpəlèri / kəpíləri] *n.* Ⓒ (*pl.* **-lar·ies**) a hairlike tube with a very slender opening. 모세관. — *adj.* **1** like hair; very thin. 털모양의; 매우 가느다란. **2** of or in capillary tubes. 모세관의. ¶ *a ~ tube* 모세관 / *~ attraction* 모관(毛管)인력(引力). [L. *capillus* hair]

:**cap·i·tal**[1] [kǽpitl] *n.* Ⓒ **1** a city or a town where the government of a country or State is placed. 수도; 서울. ¶ *London is the ~ of England.* 런던은 영국의 수도이다 / *Each State of the United States has a ~.* 미합중국은 주(洲)마다 수도가 있다. **2** a large letter of the alphabet like A, B, C and D. 대문자(大文字). **3** Ⓤ (often *a ~*) the amount of money or wealth that is used in carrying on a business; the capitalist class. 자본; 자본가 계급. ¶ *fixed ~* 고정 자본 / *circulating* [*floating*] *~* 유동 자본 / *The company has a ~ of 80,000,000 won.* 그 회사는 자본금이 8천만원이다 / *Capital and Labor* 노사(勞使) / *~ goods* 자본재(資本財)(opp. consumer(s') goods).
make capital (=*take advantage*) (**out**) **of** *something.* …을 이용하다.
— *adj.* **1** of capital. 수도의; 자본의. ¶ *a ~ city* 수도 / *~ stock* 주식 자본금. **2** very important; main; chief; principal. 매우 중요한; 주요한; 주된. ¶ *a ~ ship* 주력함(艦) / *the ~ points in a discussion* 토론의 요점. **3** very good; excellent. 우수한; 뛰어난; 훌륭한. ¶ *He's ~ fellow.* 그는 멋진 친구다 / *What a ~ speech* [*idea, plan*]*!* 정말이지 훌륭한 연설 [생각, 계획]이다 / *We had ~ fun at the party.* 우리들은 파티에서 아주 즐거웠다. **4** punishable by death. 죽어 마땅한; 사형에 처해야 할. ¶ *a ~ crime* 사죄(死罪); 죽을 죄. **5** at the head; leading. 수위의. ¶ *a ~ letter* 머리글자; 대문자. [L. *caput* head]
Capital! Very good! 잘한다; 좋았어.

cap·i·tal[2] [kǽpitl] *n.* Ⓒ (archit.) the ornamental top part of a column. (기둥의) 대접받침. [↑]

capital fund [ˊ–– ˊ] *n.* money or property owned or used in business by a person, corporation, etc.; capital. 자본금.

cap·i·tal·ism [kǽpitəlìzəm] *n.* Ⓤ an economic system based on the owners of capital. 자본주의.

cap·i·tal·ist [kǽpitəlist] *n.* Ⓒ **1** a person who owns much wealth used in business. 자본가; 전주(錢主). **2** a person who believes in capitalism. 자본주의자.

cap·i·tal·is·tic [kæ̀pitəlístik] *adj.* of capitalism or capitalists. 자본주의의; 자본가의.

cap·i·tal·i·za·tion [kæ̀pitəlizéiʃən] *n.* Ⓤ **1** the act of capitalizing. 자본화(化). **2** the sum resulting from a process of capitalizing. 자본 총액. **3** the capital stock of a business. 주식 자본.

cap·i·tal·ize [kǽpitəlàiz] *vt.* (P6) **1** write or print (words) with a capital letter. …을 대문자로 쓰다[인쇄하다]. ¶ *Names of towns are capitalized.* 도시 이름들은 대문자로 쓰인다. **2** turn (money) into capital; use (money) as capital. …을 자본화하다. **3** calculate the present value of (an income). (수입 등)을 현가(現價) 계산하다. **4** (U.S.) take advantage of (something). …을 이용하다. ¶ *~ on a rival's mistake* 경쟁자의 잘못을 이용하다.

capital stock [ˊ–– ˊ] *n.* the total stock issued by a corporation, used in carrying on a business. 주식 자본; 회사 발행 주식 총수.

cap·i·tate [kǽpətèit] *adj.* (bot.) forming like a head or dense cluster. 두상화서(頭狀花序)의. [→capital[1]]

cap·i·ta·tion [kæ̀pətéiʃən] *n.* Ⓒ a tax or fee of the same amount for every person. 인두세(人頭稅); 머릿수 할당.

•**Cap·i·tol** [kǽpitl] *n.* **1** (*the ~*) (U.S.) the building in which the U.S. Congress meets, located in Washington, D.C. (미국의) 국회 의사당. **2** Ⓒ (U.S.) (often *c-*) the building in which a state's law-making body meets. 주(州)의회 의사당. **3** (*the ~*) (hist.) the ancient temple of Jupiter in Rome. (옛 로마의) 주피터 신전. [*capital*[1]]

ca·pit·u·lar [kəpítʃələr] *adj., n.* (a member) of a chapter. 성직자회(會)의 (회원). [L. *capitulum* chapter]

ca·pit·u·late [kəpítʃəlèit] *vi.* (P1) surrender on certain conditions. 조건부 항복을 하다. [L. *caput* head]

ca·pit·u·la·tion [kəpìtʃəléiʃən] *n.* **1** ⓊⒸ the act of capitulating. 조건부 항복. **2** (*pl.*) agreement; condition. (항복의) 문서; 조건. [↑]

ca·pon [kéipən, -pɑn] *n.* a castrated cock, esp. when prepared for the table. 거세한 수탉(특히 식용의). [L. *capo* cut]

ca·pot [kəpɑ́t, -póu / -pɔ́t] *n., vi.* (P1) win(ning) all tricks (by one player). (카드놀이에서) 전승(全勝)(하다). [F.]

ca·pote [kəpóut] *n.* **1** 《U.S.》 a long cloak with a hood. 두건 달린 긴 외투. **2** a close-fitting bonnet with strings. 턱끈 있는 보닛. [→cape]

ca·pric·cio [kəprí:tʃiòu] *n.* (*pl.* **-s**) 《It.》 **1** = caprice. **2** a lively piece of music played in a free, irregular style. 기상곡(奇想曲); 카프리치오. [L. *cap* head, *riccio* hedgehog]

ca·price [kəprí:s] *n.* UC a sudden change of mind or behavior without reason; whim. 변덕. ¶ *Her refusal to go to the party is a mere* ~. 파티에 안 가겠다는 그녀의 말은 그저 변덕에 불과하다. [↓]

C

ca·pri·cious [kəpríʃəs] *adj.* guided by caprice; changeable. 변덕맞은. ¶ *His wife is very* ~. 그의 아내는 몹시 변덕스럽다.

Cap·ri·corn [kǽprikɔ̀:rn] *n.* 《astron.》 Goat in the zodiac. 염소자리; 마갈궁(磨羯宮). ¶ *the Tropic of*~ 남회귀선. [L. *caper* he- goat, *cornu* horn]

cap·ri·ole [kǽpriòul] *n., vi.* (P1) (do) high leaps and kicks. 도약(하다). [↑]

cap·si·cum [kǽpsikəm] *n.* 《bot.》 a tropical herb. 고추. [L. *capsa* box]

cap·size [kǽpsaiz, ⌐⌐] *vi., vt.* (P1;6) turn upside down; upset. 전복하다〔시키다〕. ¶ *The boat capsized, and three children were drowned.* 보트가 뒤집혀 세 아이가 익사했다. [Sp. *capuzar* sink by the head]

cap·stan [kǽpstən] *n.* C **1** a machine used for lifting or pulling heavy objects, around which men walk pushing levers. (닻 따위를) 감아올리는 기구. **2** a small pulley used to control the speed of the tape in a tape-recorder. (테이프 리코더의) 캡스턴. [L. *capio* hold]

cap·stone [kǽpstòun] *n.* the top stone of a wall or other structure. 갓돌; 관석(冠石). [→cap, stone]

cap·sule [kǽpsəl / -sju:l] *n.* C **1** a small soluble case for a dose of medicine. (약을 싸는) 캡슐. **2** 《bot.》 a small case containing dry seeds. 꼬투리; 삭과(蒴果). **3** a cap for a bottle. (유리병의) 마개. **4** the part of a rocket holding instruments or persons. (우주 로켓의) 캡슐. **5** 《physiol.》 a membranous envelope. 피막(被膜). **6** 《chem.》 a shallow saucer. (증발용) 작은 접시. [L. *capsa* box]

Capt. Captain.

:cap·tain [kǽptin] *n.* C **1** a leader; a chief. 지도〔지휘〕자; 장(長); 수령. ¶ *Julius Caesar was a great* ~. 카이사르는 위대한 영도자였다 / 《*fig.*》 *a* ~ *of industry* 대기업주(主). **2** an army officer ranking below a major and above a lieutenant. 육군 대위. **3** a navy officer ranking below an admiral and above a commander. 해군 대령. **4** the commander of a ship. 선장. — *vt.* (P6) lead (a team) as the captain; command. …을 지휘하다; 통솔하다. ¶ *He captained the team.* 그는 팀을 이끌었다. [L. *caput* head, →capital]

cap·tain·ship [kǽptinʃìp] *n.* U **1** the position of a captain. captain의 직〔자리〕. **2** leadership. 통솔자의 자격; 통솔력.

cap·tion [kǽpʃən] *n.* C **1** a title or heading used to explain a picture, photograph, etc. (그림·사진 따위의) 표제; 설명문; (영화의) 자막. **2** seizing; arrest. 체포. — *vt.* (P6) put a caption on (something). …에 표제를 붙이다. [↓]

cap·tious [kǽpʃəs] *adj.* ready to find fault. 탈〔트집〕잡는; 헐뜯는. ¶ ~ *criticism* 헐뜯기 위한 비평. [L. *capio* seize]

cap·ti·vate [kǽptəvèit] *vt.* (P6) **1** take hold of (something) by beauty or interest; charm; fascinate; enchant. …을 매혹하다〔사로잡다〕. ¶ *He was captivated by the poem.* 그는 그 시에 매혹되었다 / *Her beauty captivated many people.* 그녀의 아름다움은 많은 사람을 매혹했다. **2** hold as a prisoner. …을 붙잡다. ● **cap·ti·va·tor** [-ər] *n.* [→captive]

cap·ti·vat·ing [kǽptəvèitiŋ] *adj.* charming; fascinating. 매혹적인; 사로잡는.

cap·ti·va·tion [kæ̀ptəvéiʃən] *n.* U the act of captivating; the state of being captivated; charm. 매혹; 매료; 뇌쇄.

·cap·tive [kǽptiv] *n.* C a prisoner; a person who is captivated. 포로; 사로잡힌〔매혹된〕 사람. ¶ *He was taken* ~. 그는 사로잡혔다 / *The general returned from the campaign with two thousand captives.* 장군은 싸움에서 2천명의 포로를 데리고 돌아왔다. — *adj.* taken or kept as a prisoner. 포로의; 사로잡힌. [L. *capio* seize]

captive balloon [⌐-⌐] *n.* C a balloon which is fixed by a rope from the ground. 계류 기구(氣球).

cap·tiv·i·ty [kæptívəti] *n.* U the condition of being held as a prisoner; the state of being in prison. 사로잡힘; 감금. ¶ *in* ~ 사로잡혀 / *He was held in* ~. 그는 사로잡힌 몸이 되었다. [→captive]

cap·tor [kǽptər] *n.* C a person who holds a prisoner. (붙)잡는 사람; 체포하는 사람. ¶ *captors and captured* 잡는 자와 잡힌 자. [↑]

:cap·ture [kǽptʃər] *vt.* (P6) take (someone) as a prisoner; seize or catch. …을 사로잡다; 붙잡다; 획득하다. ¶ ~ *a thief* 도둑을 잡다 / ~ *attention* 주의를 끌다 / *He captured a prize.* 그는 상을 획득했다. — *n.* **1** C a captured person or thing. 잡힌 사람; 포로; 노획물. **2** U the act of capturing or seizing. 획득; 노획; 공략. [↑]

Cap·u·chin [kǽpjutʃin] *n.* a Franciscan friar. 프란체스코파(派)의 탁발승. [It.=cowl]

:car [ka:r] *n.* C **1** a vehicle or carriage that moves on wheels. 차; 수레. **2** an automobile; a motorcar. 자동차. 參考 미국에서는 승용차는 automobile, auto, motorcar보다는 흔히 car라고 말함. ¶ *I came in my* ~. 내 차를 타고 왔다. **3** a railroad vehicle that carries things or passengers. (열차의) 객차; 화차. ¶ *a passenger* ~ 〔《Brit.》 *carriage*〕 객차 / *a freight* ~ 화차. **4** a vehicle that runs on rails; a streetcar; a carriage. 열차; 전차. **5** a part of an elevator, a balloon, etc, for things or passengers. (승강기의) 칸; (기구 따위의) 곤돌라. **6** 《*poet.*》 a chariot. (옛날의) 전차(戰車). [L. *curro* run]

Car, C.A.R. Civil Air Regulations (민간 항공 규칙).

Car. Charles.

car. carat.

Ca·ra·cas [kərɑ́:kəs, -rǽ-] *n.* the capital of Venezuela. 카라카스《베네수엘라의 수도》.

car·a·cole [kǽrəkòul] *n.* a horse's half-turn. 반선회(半旋回). [Sp.]

ca·rafe [kərǽf, -rɑ́:f] *n.* Ⓒ a glass water bottle to be used at the table. (식탁용) 유리 물병. [F.]

car·a·mel [kǽrəməl, -mèl] *n.* **1** Ⓤ burnt sugar used for coloring or flavoring food. (착색·조미용의) 바짝 조린 설탕액. **2** Ⓒ a small piece of candy made of burnt sugar. 캐러멜. [Sp. *caramelo*]

car·a·pace [kǽrəpèis] *n.* the shell on the back of a tortoise or crab. (거북·게·새우 따위의) 등딱지. [Sp.]

car·at [kǽrət] *n.* Ⓒ **1** a unit of weight for jewels, equal to 1/5 gram. 캐럿. **2** a unit to measure the amount of pure gold. 순금 단위; 금위(金位). ¶ *24* ~ *gold* 24금; 순금. [Gk. *keration*]

car·a·van [kǽrəvæ̀n] *n.* Ⓒ **1** a group of persons traveling together across a desert or a dangerous land. (사막 따위의) 대상(隊商); 캐러반. **2** ⓐ a large, covered wagon used by people in traveling. (곡마단·집시 등의) 큰 포장 마차. ⓑ a house on wheels; a trailer; a van. 이동 주택; 트레일러. [Pers. *kārwān*]

car·a·van·sa·ry [kæ̀rəvǽnsəri] *n.* Ⓒ (*pl.* **-ries**) **1** a kind of inn, usu. with a large courtyard, where caravans rest in. 대상(隊商) 숙박소《흔히 넓은 안뜰이 있음》. **2** a large inn. 큰 여관. [↑]

car·a·van·se·rai [kæ̀rəvǽnsərài] *n.* = caravansary.

car·a·vel [kǽrəvèl] *n.* a light ship. 경쾌한 돛배. [It.]

car·a·way [kǽrəwèi] *n.* 《bot.》 a plant whose seeds are used in cooking. 캐러웨이 《회향풀의 하나》. [Arab.]

car·bide [kɑ́:rbaid, -bid] *n.* Ⓤ 《chem.》 a compound of carbon. 카바이드; 탄화물. [→carbon, -ide]

car·bine [kɑ́:rbin, -bain] *n.* Ⓒ a short rifle or musket, used esp. by horsemen. 카빈총; (옛날의) 기병총. [F. *carabine*]

carbo- [kɑ́:rbou-, -bə-], **carb-** [kɑ:rb-] *pref.* carbon. '탄소'의 뜻.

car·bo·hy·drate [kɑ̀:rbouháidreit] *n.* ⓊⒸ 《chem.》 a substance made of carbon, hydrogen, and oxygen. 탄수화물; 함수탄소. [L. *carbo* charcoal]

car·bo·lat·ed [kɑ́:rbəlèitid] *adj.* containing carbolic acid. 석탄산을 함유한.

car·bol·ic [kɑ:rbɑ́lik / -bɔ́l-] *adj.* of an acid derived from coal or coal tar. 석탄산의.

carbolic acid [-ˊ- ˊ-] *n.* phenol. 석탄산.

car·bo·lize [kɑ́:rbəlàiz] *vt.* (P6) treat (something) with carbolic acid. …을 석탄산으로 처리하다.

·car·bon [kɑ́:rbən] *n.* **1** Ⓤ a very common nonmetallic element. 탄소. **2** Ⓒ a carbon rod used in arc lamps, etc. (아크등의) 탄소봉(棒). **3** ⓊⒸ a piece of carbon paper; Ⓒ a copy made with carbon paper. 카본지(紙); 복사물; 사본. [L. *carbo* charcoal]

car·bo·na·ceous [kɑ̀:rbənéiʃəs] *adj.* of carbon. 탄소의.

car·bon·ate [kɑ́:rbənèit, -nit] *n.* ⓊⒸ salt of carbonic acid. 탄산염(炭酸塩). — [kɑ́:rbənèit] *vt.* (P6) **1** change (something) into carbonate. …을 탄산염으로 바꾸다. **2** charge (water, etc.) with carbon dioxide. …을 탄산가스로 채우다〔포화시키다〕.

carbon di·ox·ide [kɑ́:rbən daiɑ́ksaid, -sid / -ɔ́ksaid] *n.* a heavy, colorless gas with no smell. 탄산가스; 이산화탄소.

car·bon·ic [kɑ:rbɑ́nik / -bɔ́n] *adj.* made from carbon. 탄소의.

carbonic acid [-ˊ- ˊ-] *n.* a weak acid which is made when carbon dioxide is dissolved in water. 탄산.

carbonic acid gas [-ˊ- ˊ- ˋ] *n.* a gas which is made when carbonic acid is dissolved. 탄산가스.

car·bon·if·er·ous [kɑ̀:rbənífərəs] *adj.* producing or containing carbon or coal. 석탄을 산출〔함유〕하는. ¶ *the Carboniferous period* 석탄기(石炭紀); 석탄층.

car·bon·ize [kɑ́:rbənàiz] *vt.* (P6) **1** turn into carbon. …을 탄화(炭化)하다. **2** coat or combine with carbon. …에 탄소를 바르다; 탄화시키다. [→carbon]

carbon mon·ox·ide [kɑ́:rbənmɑnɑ́ksaid, -mən- / -mɔnɔ́k-] *n.* a very poisonous gas with no color and smell, formed when carbon burns without enough air. 일산화 탄소.

car·bon-pa·per [kɑ́:rbənpèipər] *n.* carbon-coated paper used for taking copies. 카본지(紙).

car·bo·run·dum [kɑ̀:rbərʌ́ndəm] *n.* an extremely hard compound of carbon and silicon, used for grinding, polishing, etc. 탄화규소(硅素)《연마용 금강사(金剛砂)》. [L. *carbo* charcoal]

car·boy [kɑ́:rbɔi] *n.* a very large, glass bottle, usu. enclosed in basket-work or in a wooden box or crate to keep it from being broken. 카보이《파손을 막기 위해 바구니〔나무

상자]에 넣은 큰 유리병》. [Pers. *qarāba* large flagon]

car·bun·cle [ká:rbʌŋkəl] *n.* Ⓒ **1** 《med.》 a painful swelling under the skin. 옹(癰); 뾰루지. **2** ⓊⒸ a smooth, deep-red jewel. 홍옥(紅玉). [L. *carbo* charcoal]

car·bu·ret [ká:rbəreit, -bjərèt] *vt.* (**-ret·ed, -ret·ing** or esp. 《Brit.》 **-ret·ted, -ret·ting**) (P6) combine (something) with carbon. …을 탄소와 화합시키다; …에 탄소를 혼입(混入)하다. [→carbo-, -uret]

car·bu·re·tor, -ret·er, 《Brit.》 **-ret·tor** [ká:rbərèitər, -bjə-, -re-] *n.* a machine for mixing air with gas. 기화기(氣化器); 카뷰레터. ¶ *The engine of a motorcar is supplied with a mixture of gasoline and air by the* ~. 자동차 엔진에는 휘발유와 공기의 혼합물이 카뷰레터에 의해 공급된다. [↑]

car·ca·net [ká:rkənèt] *n.* 《*arch.*》 an ornamented chain for the neck. 목걸이. [O.H.G. =throat]

car·case [ká:rkəs] *n.* =carcass.

car·cass [ká:rkəs] *n.* Ⓒ **1** the dead body of an animal. (짐승의) 시체(cf. *corpse*). **2** 《*contempt.*》 the human body alive or dead. 인체(人體). **3** the framework. 뼈대. [F.]

to save one's carcass, for fear of death. 목숨이 아까워서.

:card[1] [ka:rd] *n.* Ⓒ **1** a rectangular piece of stiff paper. (직사각형의) 판지(板紙); 카드; 표; 권(券). ¶ *a visiting* [《U.S.》 *calling*] ~ 명함 / *a* ~ *of admission* 입장권 / *leave one's* ~ *on someone* 아무에게 명함을 남겨 놓고 오다. **2** one of a pack of cards used in playing games. 카드놀이 패. ¶ *cut* [*shuffle*] *the cards* 카드를 치다[섞다] / *deal* (*out*) *the cards* 카드를 도르다. **3** 《*pl.*》 a game or games played with cards. 카드놀이. ¶ *play* (*at*) *cards* 카드놀이를 하다 / *be at cards* 카드놀이를 하고 있다. **4** a program; a table of rules, records, etc. 프로그램; 규칙서; 기록표 (따위). **5** 《*colloq.*》 a peculiar fellow. 괴짜; 녀석. **6** one's trick or plan. (목적 달성을 위한) 수단; 방책. ¶ *play one's last* ~ 최후 수단을 쓰다. [Gk. *khartēs* papyrus-leaf]

castle [***house***] ***of cards,*** an unsafe plan. 불안전한 계획; 사상의 누각.

have one's [***a***] ***card up one's sleeve,*** have a secret plan in reserve. 비책이 있다.

in [***on***] ***the cards,*** likely to happen; probable. 있을 것 같은; 일어날 것 같은. ¶ *A reorganization is in the cards.* 개편 (작업)이 있을 것 같다.

play one's best cards, show one's reserved skill. 비장의 카드를[방책을] 쓰다.

play one's cards, execute one's plans. 계획을 실행하다. ¶ *play one's cards badly* [*well*] 일의 처리가 서투르다[능숙하다].

put one's cards on the table =***show one's cards,*** make one's plans, intentions, etc. known. 손속을 보이다; 계획을[의도를] 드러내 보이다.

speak by the card, speak clearly or precisely. 명확히[정확히] 말하다.

the (***proper***) ***card,*** the correct thing. 적절한 것.

throw up one's cards, give up one's plan. 계획을 포기하다.

card[2] [ka:rd] *n.* Ⓒ a wire brush. 쇠솔. —*vt.* (P6) clean or comb (wool) with a card. (털 따위)를 빗질하다; …에 보풀을 일으키다. [L. *carduus* thistle]

car·da·mom [ká:rdəməm], **-mum** [-məm] *n.* 《bot.》 a seed with a strong taste. 생강과의 식물(의 열매)《약용 또는 향료》. [Gk.]

card·board [ká:rdbɔ̀:rd] *n.* Ⓤ a thick, stiff paper used in making cards or boxes. 판지; 마분지. [→card[1], board]

card-car·ry·ing [ká:rdkæ̀riiŋ] *adj.* being a fully paid-up member, esp. of the Communist party. 회원증[당원증]을 가진; 정식으로 소속하는. ¶ *a* ~ *Communist* 정식 공산당원.

car·di·ac [ká:rdiæ̀k] *adj.* **1** of the heart; of a heart disease. 심장의; 심장병의. ¶ ~ *asthma* 심장(성) 천식 / ~ *failure* 심(기능)부전(不全). **2** of the upper part of the stomach. (위의) 분문(噴門)의. —*n.* Ⓒ **1** medicine to stimulate the heart or the stomach. 강심[건위]제. **2** a person suffering from a heart disease. 심장병 환자. [Gk. *kardia* heart]

car·di·gan [ká:rdigən] *n.* Ⓒ a knitted woolen sweater. 카디건 스웨터. [Person]

car·di·nal [ká:rdənl] *adj.* **1** chief; fundamental; of first importance. 주요한; 기본적인; 극히 중요한. ¶ ~ *principles* 기본 원리 / *the* ~ *points* (*of the compass*) 방위 기점(方位基點) / *a matter of* ~ *significance* 극히 중요한 문제. **2** bright-red. 진홍[주홍]색의.

—*n.* **1** Ⓤ a bright-red color. 진홍[주홍]색. **2** Ⓒ 《Cath.》 a high member of the Roman Catholic Church, appointed by the Pope. 추기경. ¶ *Cardinals wear red robes and red hats.* 추기경들은 붉은 법의(法衣)에 붉은 모자를 쓴다. **3** Ⓒ an American song bird with a bright-red color. 홍관조(紅冠鳥). 參考 딴이름으로는 cardinal bird. **4** 《usu. *pl.*》 =cardinal numbers. **5** a woman's short hooded cloak. 후드 달린 여성용 짧은 외투. [L. *cardo* hinge]

cardinal number [´-- ´-] *n.* the numbers one, two, three, etc. 기수(基數) (opp. ordinal number).

card index [´-] *n.* an alphabetically arranged list written on cards. 카드식 색인.

car·di·o·graph [ká:rdiəgræ̀f, -grà:f] *n.* an instrument that records the strength and nature of movements of the heart. 심전계(心電計). [Gk. *kardia* heart]

card·sharp·er [ká:rdʃà:rpər] *n.* a professional cheater at card games. (전문적인) 카드놀이 사기꾼〔타짜꾼〕. [→card¹]

:care [kεər] *n.* **1** ⓊⒸ ⓐ anxious feeling; trouble; concern. 근심; 걱정. ¶ *drown one's cares in drink* 술로 시름을 달래다 / *Care has aged him.* 걱정으로 그는 늙었다 / *I wish I could be free from* ~. 걱정이 없었으면 싶다. ⓑ 《often *pl.*》 cause of sorrow and anxiety. 걱정거리. ¶ *worldly cares* 속세의 걱정거리 / *He is without a* ~ *in the world.* 세상에 걱정할 것이 없다. **2** Ⓤ watchful keeping; charge; responsibility; protection. 감독; 보관; 돌봄; 책임; 보호. ¶ *leave valuable things in someoen's* ~ 귀중품을 아무의 보관에 맡기다 / *take a motherly* ~ *of a war orphan* 전쟁 고아를 엄마처럼 돌보다 / *The children are in* 〔*under*〕 *the* ~ *of a nurse.* 아이들은 보모가 돌보고 있다. **3** ⓊⒸ attention; caution. 주의; 조심. ¶ *want of* ~ 부주의 / *have a* ~ 조심하다 / *write an essay with great* ~ 신중하게 논문을 쓰다 / *Take* ~ *not to break the glass.* 이 컵을 깨뜨리지 않도록 해라. **4** Ⓤ pains. 노고; 수고. **5** Ⓒ something that requires care or attention; an object of anxiety. 마음을 써야〔주의해야〕 할 것; 걱정의 대상.

be free from cares, be better-off. 걱정거리가 조금도 없다.

bestow 〔***give***〕 ***great care upon,*** apply oneself closely to. …에 고심하다.

care of, in charge of. …씨 댁〔방(方)〕; …전교(轉交)《c/o, c.o.로 생략함》. ¶ *A* ~ *of B,* B씨 방 A씨 귀하.

have a care =***take care,*** be careful. …을 조심하다. ¶ *Take* ~ (*that*) *you don't hurt yourself.* 다치지 않도록 조심해라.

in care of 《Brit.》=care of.

take care of, **a**) look after; watch over (a baby, a patient, etc.). …을 돌보다〔보살피다〕. ¶ *take* ~ *of one's children* 아이들을 보살피다 / *take* ~ *of oneself* 자기 몸을 돌보다. **b**) be careful about (something). …에 조심하다. **c**) 《*colloq.*》 deal with; attend to (something). …을 처리하다; …에 종사하다.

under the care of, be protected by. …의 보호 아래.

with care, carefully. 조심해서.

— *vi., vt.* **1** (P1,2A,3,4;11,12) 《usu. in *negative*》 《*for, about*》 feel anxiety, sorrow, or interest. 걱정하다; 관심을 가지다. ¶ *not* ~ *about* …에 무관심하다; …을 상관 않다 / *He doesn't* ~ *what I say.* 그는 내 말에 상관치 않는다 / *He seemed not to* ~ *about anything.* 그는 무엇에나 관심이 없는 것 같았다 / *I don't* ~ (*about*) *what they say about me.* 그들이 나에 관해 무어라 하든 상관없다 / *We don't* ~ *if it rains.* 비가 오더라도 상관없다. **2** 《usu. in *negative* or *interrogative*》 (P3;8) ⓐ 《*for*》 feel a strong liking for; like. 좋아하다. ¶ *I do not* ~ *for him very much.* 그를 그다지 좋아하지 않는다 / *She really does* ~ *for desserts.* 그녀는 디저트를 무척 좋아한다. ⓑ wish; be willing; be inclined 〔disposed〕. …하고 싶다. ¶ *I don't* ~ *to answer.* 대답하고 싶지 않다 / *Would you* ~ *to read this book?* 이 책 읽고 싶지 않은가 / *I don't* ~ *to dance now.* 지금 춤추고 싶지 않다. **3** (P3) look after; take charge of; provide for. 돌보다; 보살피다. ¶ *Will you* ~ *for the children while I am away.* 내가 없는 동안 아이들 좀 돌봐 주지 않겠나. [O.E. *caru* sorrow]

care about, **a**) 《usu. in *negative* or *interrogative*》 feel anxiety; be worried about (something). …을 걱정하다. ¶ *I don't* ~ *about the matter.* 나는 그 일을 걱정 않는다. **b**) be interested in (something). …에 관심을 가지다. ¶ *He cares about music.* 그는 음악에 관심이 있다.

care for, **a**) look after; watch over (a baby, a patient, etc.); protect. …을 돌보다. **b**) 《in *negative* or *interrogative*》 want; like; love. …을 좋아하다; 하고 싶어하다. ¶ *Would you* ~ *for a walk?* 산보 안 하겠나 / *She does not* ~ *for him.* 그녀는 그를 싫어한다.

for all I care, **a**) probably. 어쩌면; 혹시. **b**) it matters little me whether. 조금도 상관없다; 내 알 바 아니다.

CARE [kεər] *n.* Cooperative for American Remittances to Europe, Inc. 케어《미국 원조 물자 발송 협회》. ¶ ~ *good* 케어〔구호〕 물자.

ca·reen [kəríːn] *vi.* (P1) lean to one side; tilt. 기울어지다; 기울다. — *vt.* (P6) cause (a ship) to lean to one side for repair or cleaning. (수리·청소를 위해 배)를 기울이다. ¶ *A great wind careened the boat.* 거센 바람으로 배는 한쪽으로 쏠렸다. [L. *carina* keel]

·ca·reer [kəríər] *n.* Ⓒ **1** a general course of action or development through life. 생애; 경력. ¶ *Lincoln's* ~ *as a statesman* 정치가로서의 링컨의 생애 / *abandon one's stage* ~ 무대생활을 그만두다 / *follow a business* ~ 사업가로서의 생애를 보내다 / *Young people should read much of the careers of great men.* 젊은이들은 위인전을 많이 읽어야 한다. **2** a way of earning a living; a profession for part or the whole of one's life. (일생의) 직업. ¶ *pursue a journalistic* ~ 신문기자를 평생의 직업으로 하다 / *He is going to take up education for his* ~. 그는 교육을 직업으로 가지려고 한다. **3** one's progress through life; development. 출세; 성공; 발전. ¶ *advance one's* ~ 출세하다. **4** Ⓤ speed; full speed. 속력; 전속력.

in full career, at full speed. 전속력으로. ¶ *His car was in full* ~. 그의 차는 전속력으로 달리고 있었다.

make a career, rise in the world; be successful. 출세〔성공〕하다.

— *vi.* (P2A,3) 《*about, along, through, over*》 run along wildly; dash. 질주하다.

— *adj.* 《U.S.》 professional. 직업적인.

¶ *a ~ woman* 〔*girl*〕《U.S. *colloq.*》 직업 여성 / *a ~ diplomat* 직업 외교관. [L. *curro* run]

ca·reer·ist [kəríːərist] *n.* intent on personal advancement. 출세주의자.

care·free [kɛ́ərfrìː] *adj.* without worry; gay. 태평한; 즐거운. [→care]

⁑**care·ful** [kɛ́ərfəl] *adj.* **1** 《*about*》 thinking much about what one says or does; watchful; cautious. 신중한; 조심스러운. ¶ *a ~ person* 조심스러운 사람 / *Be ~ not to go too far.* 너무 멀리 가지 않도록 조심해라 / *Be ~ what you eat.* 음식에 주의해라 / *Be ~ of your health.* 건강에 유의하시오 / *He is very ~ with his work.* 그는 하는 일에 아주 신중하다. **2** done with enough thought or care; exact; thorough. 꼼꼼한; 정확한; 철저한. ¶ *a ~ study* 면밀한 연구 / *a ~ piece of work* 공들인 작품 / *The doctor gave us a ~ examination.* 의사는 우리들을 자세하게 진찰했다. [→care, -ful]

be careful (= *take good care*) ***of*** *something.* 소중히 하다; 주의하다. ¶ *be ~ of money* 돈을 소중히 하다 / *be ~ of another's feelings* 남의 감정에 신경을 쓰다.

⁑**care·ful·ly** [kɛ́ərfəli] *adv.* with care. 주의깊게; 조심스럽게. ¶ *Hold it very ~, please.* 그걸 잘 (붙)잡으세요.

care·ful·ness [kɛ́ərfəlnis] *n.* Ⓤ the state of being careful. 주의 깊음; 신중(함).

*__care·less__ [kɛ́ərlis] *adj.* **1** not thinking much about what one says or does; not careful or cautious. 부주의한. ¶ *Don't be ~ in crossing the street.* 도로를 무턱대고 건너서는 안 된다 / *How ~ you are to say such a thing to him!* 그에게 그런 말을 하다니 정말이지 멍청하기도 하군 / *She is ~ of her clothes.* 그녀는 옷에 신경을 안 쓴다. **2** done without enough thought or care; not exact in doing work; thoughtless. 경솔한; 정확하지 않은; 되는 대로의. ¶ *a ~ mistake* 경솔한 잘못 / *~ work* 날림일 / *He is a ~ reader.* 그는 책을 되는 대로 읽는 사람이다. **3** not troubling; meeting without complaining. 개의치 않는; 상관 않는. ¶ *be ~ of the rights of others* 남의 권리를 개의치 않다 / *be ~ about one's dress* 복장에는 돈단무심(頓斷無心)이다 / *be ~ in morals* 몸가짐이 나쁘다. **4** without worry; happy; light-hearted. 근심 걱정이 없는; 태평한. ¶ *a ~ life* 태평한 생활. [→care, -less]

be careless about (= *be indifferent to*) *something.* …에 상관치 않다.

be careless (= *be regardless*) ***of*** *something.* …에 무관심하다. ¶ *Those people were ~ of discomfort.* 그 사람들은 부자유엔 무관심하다.

care·less·ly [kɛ́ərlisli] *adv.* without care; in a careless manner. 부주의하게; 되는 대로. ¶ *He did it ~.* 적당히 해버렸다.

care·less·ness [kɛ́ərlisnis] *n.* Ⓤ the state of being careless. 부주의; 경솔.

*__ca·ress__ [kərés] *n.* Ⓒ a touch or stroke showing love; an embrace; a kiss. 애무; 포옹; 키스. — *vt.* (P6) touch or stroke (someone) with love; embrace; kiss. …을 애무〔포옹〕하다. [L. *carus* dear]

ca·ress·ing [kərésiŋ] *adj.* showing love. 애무하는; 쓰다듬는.

ca·ress·ing·ly [kərésiŋli] *adv.* in a caressing manner. 애무하여.

car·et [kǽrət] *n.* Ⓒ a mark (∧) in writing or printing to show where something should be put in. 탈자(脫字) 기호《∧》. [L. = lacks]

care·tak·er [kɛ́ərtèikər] *n.* Ⓒ **1** a person who remains in charge of an empty building, church, etc. 수위; 경비. **2** 《U.S.》 a person who has charge of a building and keeps it clean, warm, etc. 빌딩 관리인. [→care]

care·worn [kɛ́ərwɔ̀ːrn] *adj.* tired; worn by care; weary. 걱정에 지친; 피곤한. ¶ *a ~ face* 걱정에 찌든 얼굴.

car·fare [kɑ́ːrfɛ̀ər] *n.* Ⓒ money paid for riding on a bus, train, etc. 찻삯; 버스 요금. [→car]

*__car·go__ [kɑ́ːrgou] *n.* ⓊⒸ (*pl.* **-goes** or **-gos**) goods carried on a ship. 뱃짐; 화물; 선하(船荷). ¶ *an inward* 〔*outward*〕 *~* 수입〔수출〕 화물 / *load a ~* 화물을 싣다 / *unload* 〔*discharge*〕 *a ~* 뱃짐을 부리다. [Sp. = load]

car·go-boat [kɑ́ːrgoubòut] *n.* Ⓒ a ship to carry cargo. 화물선.

Car·ib·be·an [kæ̀rəbíːən, kəríbiən] *n.* 《*the ~*》 the sea bounded by Central America, the West Indies, and South America. 카리브 해. — *adj.* **1** of this sea. 카리브해의. **2** of the Caribs, a tribe of Indians living in the southern West Indies or in northeastern South America. 카리브인(人)의.

Caribbean Sea [––´– ´], **the** *n.* = the Caribbean.

car·i·bou [kǽrəbùː] *n.* (*pl.* **-bous** or *collectively* **-bou**) 《zool.》 an American reindeer. 순록(馴鹿). [Native]

car·i·ca·ture [kǽrikətʃùər, -tʃər] *n.* **1** Ⓒ a funny picture drawn or description made in an exaggerated way. 풍자화〔문〕; 만화. **2** Ⓤ the art of making such pictures or descriptions. 풍자〔만화〕화(化). — *vt.* (P6) make a caricature of (something). …을 풍자하다; 만화화(化)하다(cf. *cartoon*). ¶ *He caricatured many famous politicians.* 많은 유명 정치인들을 풍자적으로 그렸다. [It. →car]

car·i·ca·tur·ist [kǽrikətʃùərist, -tʃər-] *n.* Ⓒ a person who makes caricatures by profession. 풍자화가; 만화가.

car·ies [kɛ́əriìːz] *n.* Ⓤ 《med.》 decay of teeth or bones. 카리에스. ¶ *~ of a tooth* 충치. [L.]

car·il·lon [kǽrəlɑ̀n, -lən / kəríljən] *n.* Ⓒ **1** a

set of bells for playing melodies. 편종(編鐘); 카리용. **2** a melody played on such bells. 카리용 곡. [F., →quadrille]

car·i·ole [kǽriòul] *n.* =carriole.

cark·ing [kά:rkiŋ] *adj.* 《only in the phrase below》 worrying; burdensome. 괴롭히는; 성가신. ¶ ～ *care(s)* 걱정; 심로(心勞). [→cargo]

Car·lism [kά:rlizəm] *n.* the principles of Carlists. 카를로스주의. ●**Car·list** [-list] *n.* a supporter of Don Carlos in Spain. 카를로스 당원.

car·load [kά:rlòud] *n.* Ⓤ goods carried by a car; the minimum weight of goods that a car can hold or carry. 한 화차분의 화물; 화차의 최저 적재량. [*car*]

Car·lyle [ka:rlάil], **Thomas** *n.* (1795-1881) an English philosopher, historian, and essayist. 칼라일《영국의 사상가·역사가·평론가》.

car·man [kά:rmən] *n.* Ⓒ (*pl.* **-men** [-mən]) **1** a person who drives a cart. 짐마차 마부. **2** a motorman; a conductor of a streetcar. 운전 기사; 전차 승무원《운전사 또는 차장》. [*car*]

Car·mel·ite [kά:rməlàit] *n.* a white friar. 카르멜파(派) 수도사. [Place]

Car·mi·chael [kά:rmaikəl], **Stokely** *n.* (1941-) an American civil rights leader. 카마이클《미국 민권 운동 지도자》.

car·min·a·tive [ka:rmínətiv, kά:rmənèi-] *n., adj.* (a drug) capable of curing flatulence (장내(腸內)의) 가스를 내보내는; 구풍제(驅風劑). [L.]

car·mine [kά:rmin, -main] *n.* Ⓤ a deep red color. 카민; 양홍(洋紅); 연지(臙脂). — *adj.* deep red; purplish-red. 양홍색의; 연짓빛의. [→crimson]

car·nage [kά:rnidʒ] *n.* Ⓤ the act of killing a great many people; slaughter. 살육; 대량 학살(cf. *massacre, butchery*). [L. *caro* flesh]

car·nal [kά:rnl] *adj.* **1** of the body; sensual. 육체의; 육욕의. ¶ ～ *desires* 육욕. **2** worldly. 속세의; 세속의. [↑]

car·na·tion [ka:rnéiʃən] *n.* **1** Ⓒ 《bot.》 a flower of a red, white, or pink color and with a sweet smell. 카네이션. **2** Ⓤ a rosy pink or deep red color. 담홍(淡紅)색; 살색. — *adj.* rosy-pink; deep-red. 담홍〔심홍〕색의; 살색의. [↑]

Car·ne·gie [kά:rnəgi, ka:rnéigi], **Andrew** *n.* (1835-1919) an American industrialist. 카네기《미국의 사업가》.

car·nel·ian [ka:rní:ljən] *n.* 《min.》 =cornelian. 홍옥수(紅玉髓).

car·ni·val [kά:rnəvəl] *n.* Ⓒ **1** 《often without *an article*》 Ⓤ a time of feasting and merrymaking during the week before Lent. (카톨릭의) 사육제(謝肉祭)《사순절(四旬節) 직전의 1주일간의 축제》. ¶ *in a ～ mood* 들뜬 기분으로; 들떠서. **2** a traveling show with merry-go-round, etc. 순회 흥행; 이동쇼. **3** feasting and merrymaking. 야단법석; (들떠) 법석떨기. [L. *carnem levare* to put away meat]

car·ni·vore [kά:rnəvɔ̀:r] *n.* Ⓒ an animal that eats flesh. 육식 동물.

car·niv·o·rous [ka:rnívərəs] *adj.* flesh-eating. 육식의(cf. *herbivorous*). ¶ ～ *animals* 〔*plants*〕 육식 동물〔식충 식물〕. [L. *caro* flesh, *voro* devour]

car·ol [kǽrəl] *n.* Ⓒ a song of joy; a joyful religious song; a hymn. 캐럴; 기쁨의 노래; 찬(송)가(cf. *noel*). ¶ *Christmas carols* 크리스마스 캐럴. — *vt.* (P6) (**-oled, -ol·ing** or 《Brit.》 **-olled, -ol·ling**) sing joyously; celebrate with carols. …을 기뻐하여 노래하다. [F.]

Car·o·li·na [kæ̀rəláinə] *n.* either North Carolina or South Carolina, States in the south of the United States. 남〔북〕캐롤라이나.

Car·o·line [kǽrəlàin, -lin] *n.* a woman's name. 캐럴라인《여자 이름》.

car·om [kǽrəm] *n.* =cannon[2].

ca·rot·id [kərάtid / -rɔ́t-] *n., adj.* (of) one of the two great arteries of the neck. 경동맥(頸動脈)(의). [Gk.]

ca·rous·al [kəráuzəl] *n.* Ⓒ a noisy drinking party. 떠들썩한 술잔치; 주연(酒宴). [↓]

ca·rouse [kəráuz] *n.* Ⓒ a noisy drinking party or feast. 주연(酒宴); 술잔치. — *vi.* (P1) drink heavily; drink merrily at a feast. 진탕 마시다; 마시고 떠들다. [G. *gar aus* (drink) right out]

car·ou·sel [kèrusél, -zél] *n.* =carrousel.

carp[1] [ka:rp] *vi.* (P1,3) 《*at*》 find fault; complain about a trifle. 탈〔흠〕잡다; 말꼬리를 잡다. ¶ *carping criticism* 흠잡기 위한 비평 / ～ *at minor errors* 사소한 과실에도 탈을 잡다 / *He is always carping at my faults.* 늘 나의 결점을 잡고는 잔소리를 한다. ●**carp·er** [-ər] *n.* [Scand. =brag]

carp[2] [ka:rp] *n.* Ⓒ (*pl.* **carps** or esp. *collectively* **carp**) 《fish》 a fresh-water fish living in a lake or pond. 잉어. [F.]

car·pal [kά:rpəl] *adj.* of the carpus. 완골(腕骨)〔손목뼈〕의. [→carpus]

car·pel [kά:rpəl] *n.* **1** 《bot.》 a single pistil. 암꽃술. **2** a single member of a compound pistil. 합생(合生) 암꽃술. [Gk. *karpos* fruit]

***car·pen·ter** [kά:rpəntər] *n.* Ⓒ a person whose work is to make a thing or building of wood. 목수. ¶ *a carpenter's shop* 목수의 일터; 목공소. — *vt., vi.* (P6;1) do such work. 목수일하다. [L. *carpentum* wagon]

car·pen·try [kά:rpəntri] *n.* Ⓤ **1** the work of a carpenter. 목수일〔직업〕. ¶ *learn* ～ 목수일을 배우다. **2** a thing or building made by a carpenter. 목공품.

***car·pet** [kά:rpit] *n.* Ⓒ a thick cloth used for covering floors and stairs; something like this. 카펫; 양탄자; 이와 같은 것. ¶ *a ~ of flowers* 양탄자를 편 듯이 만발한 꽃 / *lay* 〔*put down*〕 *a ~* 양탄자를 깔다.

on the carpet, a) 《of a question, etc.》 under discussion or consideration. 심의 중에; 고려 중에. **b)** 《*colloq.*》 (of a person) being scolded. 질책을 받고; 소환되어.

— *vt.* (P6) **1** cover (something) with a carpet. …에 양탄자를〔융단을〕 깔다. ¶ *~ the stairs* 〔*a room*〕 계단에〔방에〕 양탄자를 깔다 / *The field was carpeted with dandelions.* 들은 온통 민들레로 덮여 있었다. **2** 《chiefly Brit. *colloq.*》 call (someone) into the room in order to blame or scold him. (견책하기 위하여) …을 방으로 불러들이다. [L. *carpo* pluck]

car·pet·bag [kɑ́ːrpitbæ̀g] *n.* Ⓒ a traveling bag made of carpet. 융단제(製) 여행 가방.

car·pet·bag·ger [kɑ́ːrpitbæ̀gər] *n.* 《U.S.》 a person from the Northern states who went to the South after the Civil War to take advantage of the confused political and social conditions (so called because he traveled to the South with all of his property in a carpetbag). 뜨내기 정상배 《남북 전쟁 후 전재산을 carpetbag에 챙기고 한탕하려 남부로 내려온 북부인》.

carpet bombing [´-- ´-] *n.* dropping bombs so as to cover an area as if by a carpet. 융단 폭격.

car·pi [kɑ́ːrpai] *n.* pl. of **carpus.**

carp·ing [kɑ́ːrpiŋ] *adj.* faultfinding; captious. 흠〔트집〕잡는. [→carp[1]]

car·port [kɑ́ːrpɔ̀ːrt] *n.* Ⓒ 《U.S.》 a roof projecting from the side of building and serving to make a garage. 간이 차고《건물 옆으로 내민 지붕 밑의》. [→car]

car·pus [kɑ́ːrpəs] *n.* (*pl.* **-pi**) 《anat.》 the wrist. 손목. [L.]

car·rel [kǽrəl] *n.* a small recess in a library for private study. (도서관 서고 안의) 개인 열람석. [E.]

:**car·riage** [kǽridʒ] *n.* **1** Ⓒ a vehicle with wheels, usu. pulled by horses and used to carry people. 마차. ¶ *a ~ and pair* 쌍두 마차 / *a baby ~* 유모차 / *keep a ~* 자가용 마차를 소유하다. **2** Ⓒ 《Brit.》 a part of a train in which passengers sit; a railway coach. (철도의) 객차(cf. 《U.S.》 *car*). ¶ *a first* 〔*second*〕*-class ~,* 1〔2〕등 찻간 / *a sleeping ~* 침대차. **3** Ⓤ the act or cost of carrying. (여객·화물의) 수송; 운임. ¶ *~ free* 운임 무료 / *~ paid* 운임 선불 / *~ forward* 운임 수취인 지급 / *the expenses of ~* 운반비; 운임 / *the ~ on the goods* 화물의 운임 / *the ~ of goods by sea* 〔*rail*〕 화물의 해상〔철도〕 수송 / *charge ~ by bulk* 〔*weight*〕 부피〔무게〕로 운임을 받다. **4** 《usu. *a ~*》 bearing; manner. 몸가짐; 태도. ¶ *a conceited ~* 짐짓 점잔 빼는 태도 / *a wifely ~* 주부 같은 태도 / *She has a graceful ~.* 그녀는 몸가짐이 우아하다. **5** Ⓤ management; handling. (사업 따위의) 처리; 경영; 관리. **6** Ⓒ a movable frame work on which a gun is mounted. 포가(砲架). **7** Ⓒ a sliding part of a machine, as in a typewriter. (타자기 따위의) 활동부(滑動部). [→carry]

carriage drive [´-- ´] *n.* a road from a gate to a main, large building. (현관으로 통하는) 차도.

car·riage·way [kǽridʒwèi] *n.* the part of a road for vehicles. 자동차 도로; 차도.

·**car·ri·er** [kǽriər] *n.* Ⓒ **1** a person or thing that carries something. 나르는 사람〔것〕. **2** 《U.S.》 a person who carries or delivers mail. 우편 집배(集配)원(cf. chiefly 《Brit.》 *postman*). **3** 《med.》 a person or thing that gives a disease to others. 보균자〔물〕. ¶ *a ~ of typhoid bacillus* 장티푸스균 보균자 / *Water and milk are often carriers of disease germs.* 물과 우유는 때로 병원균을 함유한다. **4** the part of a bicycle for carrying luggage. (자전거의) 짐받이. **5** =carrier pigeon. [→carry]

carrier pigeon [´-- ´-] *n.* a pigeon used to carry messages; a homing pigeon. 전서구(傳書鳩).

car·ri·ole [kǽriòul] *n.* **1** a small carriage drawn by one horse. 말 한 필이 끄는 소형 마차. **2** a covered cart. 유개(有蓋) 짐마차. [→carry]

car·ri·on [kǽriən] *n.* Ⓤ dead or decaying flesh. 썩은 고기. — *adj.* **1** of or like carrion. 썩은 고기의〔같은〕. **2** feeding on carrion. 썩은 고기를 먹는. [→carnage]

carrion crow [´-- ´] *n.* a common European crow. (유럽산) 까마귀의 일종.

Car·ros·sa [kɑːrɔ́sə], **Hans** *n.* (1878-1956) a German poet and novelist. 카로사《의사로서 시와 소설을 발표했음》.

car·rot [kǽrət] *n.* Ⓒ **1** a vegetable whose long orange-red root is eaten. 당근. **2** 《*pl.*》 《*colloq.*》 a red-haired person. 머리털이 붉은 사람. [Gk. *karōton*]

car·rot·y [kǽrəti] *adj.* **1** like a carrot in color. 당근 빛깔의. **2** having red hair. 붉은 머리털의.

car·rou·sel [kæ̀rusél, -zél] *n.* Ⓒ a merry-go-round. 회전 목마. [It.]

:**car·ry** [kǽri] *v.* (**-ried**) *vt.* **1** (P6,7,13) take from one place to another; convey; transport. …을 나르다; 운반하다; 전하다. ¶ *~ a stone back to its place* 돌을 제자리에 갖다 놓다 / *~ food to one's mouth* 음식을 입에 가져가다 / *~ a thing on one's shoulder* 물건을 어깨에 져 나르다 / *~ a baby* 〔*a thing*〕 *on one's back* 아기를 등에 업고 가다〔물건을 등에 져 나르다〕 / *He carried the news* 〔*message*〕 *to her.* 그녀에게 소식을〔메시지를〕 전했다 / *Railroads ~ coals from the mines to your town.* 철도가 석탄을 광산에서 도시로 나른다 / *The wind carries sounds.* 바람은 소리를 전달한다. **2** (P6) possess; wear. …을 가지고〔지니고〕 있다. ¶ *~ a watch* 시계를 갖고 있다 / *~ a* *stick in one's hand* 지팡이를 짚고 다니다 / ~ *arms* 〔*a rifle*〕 무기를〔총을〕 휴대하다 / ~ *sorrow in one's heart* 가슴 속에 슬픔을 지니고 있다 / *Do you always ~ an umbrella?* 늘 우산을 갖고 다니나. **3** (P6) bear the weight of (something); support; hold up. (…의 무게 따위)를 떠받치다; 지탱하다. ¶ *Those columns ~ the roof.* 그 기둥들이 지붕을 받치고 있다. **4** (P7,13) hold (one's body and head) in a certain way. (몸·머리)를 어떤 자세로 유지하다. ¶ ~ *one's head on one side* 머리를 한쪽으로 갸웃하다 / ~ *one's head high* 머리를 곧추 들다. **5** (P7) 《*reflexively*》 conduct (oneself); behave. 처신하다; 행동하다. ¶ ~ *oneself well* 훌륭히 처신하다 / ~ *oneself with assurance* 자신을 갖고 행동하다 / *He carries himself like a soldier.* 그는 군인같이 행동한다. **6** (P6,13) have as its proper quality; involve necessarily; bring as a result. (속성·결과로서) 가지(고 있)다; 수반하다; 가져오다; 내포하다. ¶ ~ *weight* 무게가〔영향력이〕 있다 / *a grandiloquence that carries no conviction* 자신 없는 장담 / *Power carries responsibility with it.* 권력에는 책임이 따른다 / *The word carries a peculiar sense.* 이 말은 특별한 의미를 내포하고 있다 / *Passion carried him to destruction.* 격정은 그를 파멸로 이끌었다. **7** (P6,13) influence by mental or emotional appeal. …을 감동시키다; 마음을 사로잡다. ¶ *The actor carried his audience with him.* 그 배우는 관객을 감동시켰다 / *He carried his audience with his eloquence.* 그는 웅변으로써 청중을 사로잡았다. **8** (P7,13) make longer in a certain direction or to some point; extend or prolong in space, time, or degree. …을 연장〔확대〕하다; 진척시키다. ¶ ~ *the road into the mountains* 도로를 산속까지 연장하다 / ~ *a plan into effect* 〔*practice*〕 계획을 실행에 옮기다 / *The war was carried into Asia.* 전쟁은 아시아로 확대되었다. **9** (P6) overcome; win; win the support of. 이기다; 쟁취하다; 지지를 얻다. ¶ ~ *an election* 선거에 이기다 / ~ *one's point* 주장을 관철하다 / ~ *the enemy's position* 적진을 점령하다 / *The bill was carried unanimously.* 법안은 만장일치로 통과되었다. **10** (P6) influence greatly. …에 영향을 주다. **11** (P6) keep on hand for sale. (가게에 물건을) 들여놓고 있다; 가지고 있다. ¶ *The store carries a full line of canned goods.* 그 가게는 통조림이라면 무엇이나 갖추고 있다.

—*vi.* (P1) **1** act as bearer. 나르는 일을 하다. **2** (P2A,2B) have the power to reach; cover the distance. (소리·탄알 등이) 미치다. ¶ *His voice will ~ to the back of the room.* 그의 목소리는 방 뒤쪽까지 들릴 것이다 / *Our guns would not ~ as far as the enemy ship.* 우리의 포는 적함에까지 미치지 못했다 / *The sound of guns carried many miles.* 포 소리가 여러 마일까지 들렸다.

carry all 〔**everything**〕 **before** *one,* be very successful; sweep away everything in one's way. 대성공을 거두다; 파죽지세로 나아가다.

carry a tune, sing accurately or on key. 정확히〔정확한 가락으로〕 노래하다.

carry away, **a**) 《usu. in *passive*》 cause (someone) to lose self-control. (흥분 따위로) 자제력을 잃게 하다; 열중케 하다. ¶ *be carried away by one's feelings* 자제력을 잃다 / *He was carried away by her beauty.* 그녀의 아름다움에 넋을 잃었다. **b**) take (something) to another place. …을 가져가〔휩쓸어 가〕 버리다. **c**) 《naut.》 (a rope or mast) break off. 부러〔꺾어〕지다; 끊어지다.

carry (*someone*) **back,** cause someone to recollect. (아무에게) 회상시키다.

carry *one's* **bat,** be not out. 아웃이 안 되다.

carry conviction, be convincing. 설득력이 있다.

carry forward, **a**) make progress with (something). (사업 따위)를 진행시키다; …을 추진하다. **b**) take (figures) to the top of the next page. (부기에서) 이월하다.

carry off, **a**) win (a prize, honor, etc.). (상·명예 등을) 얻다; 타다. ¶ ~ *off the first prize,* 1등상을 타다. **b**) deal with (something) successfully. 잘 해내다. ¶ ~ *off the interview* 면접을 잘 치르다. **c**) cause the death of (someone). (병 따위가) 목숨을 빼앗다; 죽이다. ¶ *Many were carried off by cholera.* 많은 사람이 콜레라로 죽었다.

carry on, **a**) keep on; keep going; continue. …을 계속하다. ¶ ~ *on the struggle* 싸움을 계속하다 / ~ *on a conversation* 〔*the work*〕 대화를〔일을〕 계속하다 / ~ *on under difficult conditions* 어려운 조건 밑에 속행하다. **b**) do; manage; conduct. 하다; 경영〔처리〕하다. ¶ ~ *on business* 사업을 하다 / ~ *on many improvements* 많은 개선을 하다. **c**) 《*colloq.*》 behave in an excited or foolish manner; speak angrily and at length. 추태를 부리다; 성난 소리로 떠들어대다. ¶ ~ *on shamefully* 부끄러운 행동을 하다 / *Don't ~ on so!* 그렇게 떠들어대지 마라.

carry out, put (something) into operation; execute; accomplish; perform. …을 실행〔실시〕하다; 성취〔달성〕하다. ¶ ~ *out a plan* 계획을 실행하다 / ~ *out orders* 명령을 이행하다.

carry over, **a**) hold something until a later time. …을 미루다; 연기하다. **b**) =carry forward.

carry the day, win; be completely successful. 승리를 거두다; 대성공을 거두다. ¶ *The Republicans carried the day.* 공화당이 압승했다.

carry the war into the enemy's camp, bring counter charges. 반격으로 나오다.

carry through, **a**) finish; complete; accomplish. 완수하다; 완성하다. ¶ ~ *an undertaking through* 맡은 일을 완수하다 / *In spite of a long struggle we succeeded in car-*

rying most of our plans through. 오랜 싸움에도 불구하고 대부분의 우리 계획을 완수하는데 성공했다. **b**) support or help through a difficult situation. (위기 따위)를 벗어나게 하다. ¶ *His courage will ~ him through all difficulties.* 그는 용기가 있어 모든 난관을 뚫고 나아갈 수 있을 것이다.

carry something too far, make something go beyond the limits of good tastes, sense, etc. 도를 지나치다; 극단에 흐르게 하다. ¶ *You carried the joke too far.* 너는 농담이 지나쳤다.

— *n.* Ⓒ the distance that something goes; range. 무엇이 미치는 거리; 사정(射程). [→car]

car·ry·all [kǽriɔ̀ːl] *n.* Ⓒ **1** =carriole. **2** a traveling bag. 여행 가방. **3** a passenger automobile. 여객 버스.

car·ry·ing [kǽriiŋ] *adj.* taking a person or thing from one place to another. 운송[운반]의.

car·ry-o·ver [kǽriòuvər] *n.* **1** Ⓒ a part left over for future use. 훗날을 위해 남긴 것. **2** Ⓤ 《bookkeeping》 the sum moved to the next page, column, or book. 이월액(移越額).

car·sick [kɑ́ːrsìk] *adj.* sick because of a car's motion. 차멀미가 난. ¶ *get ~* 차멀미하다.

Car·son City [kɑ́ːrsnsíti] *n.* the capital of Nevada. 카슨 시《미국 네바다 주의 주도》.

:cart [kɑːrt] *n.* Ⓒ **1** a vehicle with two wheels pulled by a horse and used for carrying heavy goods. (2륜) 짐마차(cf. *wagon*). ¶ *a ~ horse* 짐마차 말; 복마(卜馬). **2** a light wagon for delivery. 경장(輕裝) 마차. **3** a small vehicle on wheels, moved by hand. 손수레.

be in the cart, 《*sl.*》 be in bad case. 곤란한 입장[처지]에 있다.

put* [*set*] *the cart before the horse, do or place things in the wrong order. 거꾸로 하다; 본말을 전도하다.

— *vt.* (P6,7) carry (something) in a cart. …을 짐마차로 나르다. ¶ *~ away rubbish* 쓰레기를 마차에 실어 나르다 / *Cart the hay to the farm.* 이 건초를 농장으로 실어 날라라.

— *vi.* (P1) drive a cart. 짐마차를 몰다. [Scand.]

cart about, carry about with one (탐탁지 않은 것)을 가지고 다니다. ¶ *He always carts a lot of useless things about with him.* 늘 쓸데없는 것을 잔뜩 가지고 다닌다.

cart·age [kɑ́ːrtidʒ] *n.* Ⓤ (the cost of) carrying in a cart. 짐마차 운송(삯).

carte blanche [kɑ́ːrt blɑ́ːntʃ] *n.* 《F.》 **1** a blank sheet given to a person on which to write his own opinion. 백지 위임장. 參考 본디 프랑스 말인데 글자 뜻은 '백지'. **2** freedom to use one's own judgment. 자유 재량권. ¶ *give someone ~* 아무에게 자유 재량권을 주다.

carte-de-vi·site [kɑ́ːrtdəviːzíːt] *n.* 《F.》 (*pl.* **cartes-**) (a photograph on) a small card. 명함(판 사진).

car·tel [kɑːrtél] *n.* Ⓒ **1** a large group of business companies formed to control prices, etc. 기업 연합; 카르텔(cf. *trust*). **2** a written agreement relating to exchange of prisoners. 포로 교환 조약서. **3** a letter of challenge. (결투의) 도전장. [→card[1]]

Cart·er [kɑ́ːrtər], **Jimmy** *n.* (1924-). the 39th President of the United States of America. 카터《미국의 제39대 대통령》.

car·ter [kɑ́ːrtər] *n.* Ⓒ a person whose work is driving a cart. 짐마차꾼. [→cart]

Car·te·si·an [kɑːrtíːʒən] *adj.* of Descartes. 데카르트(파)의. [Person]

Car·thage [kɑ́ːrθidʒ] *n.* an ancient city in northern Africa. 카르타고.

Car·tha·gin·i·an [kɑ̀ːrθədʒíniən] *adj.* of or connected with Carthage. 카르타고의. — *n.* a native of Carthage. 카르타고 사람. [L.]

cart horse [⊿ ⊿] *n.* a big, strong horse fit for drawing heavy loads. 짐마차 말.

car·ti·lage [kɑ́ːrtilidʒ] *n.* Ⓒ 《anat.》 a firm, elastic substance at the ends of bones. 연골(軟骨) (조직). [L.]

car·ti·lag·i·nous [kɑ̀ːrtilǽdʒənəs] *adj.* of or like cartilage. 연골(질(質))의.

cart·load [kɑ́ːrtlòud] *n.* Ⓒ **1** the amount that a cart can carry. 한 마차의 적재량. **2** 《*colloq.*》 an indefinitely large amount. 대량. ¶ *collected by the ~* 대량으로 수집된. [→cart]

car·tog·ra·phy [kɑːrtɑ́grəfi / -tɔ́g-] *n.* the art of making maps. 지도 제작법. [→card[1], graph]

car·to·man·cy [kɑ́ːrtəmæ̀nsi] *n.* Ⓤ divination by cards. 카드점(占). [→card[1], L. *mantis* seer]

car·ton [kɑ́ːrtən] *n.* Ⓒ a box made of strong cardboard. (두꺼운) 판지 상자. [It. *cartone* pasteboard]

car·toon [kɑːrtúːn] *n.* Ⓒ **1** a comic sketch or drawing for the purpose of making a person laugh or think (esp. about political events). (정계 등의) 풍자 만화. **2** a sketch made in preparation for a big picture. 실물 크기의 밑그림. **3** a strip cartoon. 연속 만화. **4** an animated cartoon. 동화(動畫); 만화 영화. — *vt.* (P6) draw a cartoon of (something). …을 만화화(化)하다. — *vi.* (P1,3) draw a cartoon. 만화를 그리다. [↑]

car·toon·ist [kɑːrtúːnist] *n.* Ⓒ a person who draws cartoons. 만화가.

car·touche [kɑːrtúːʃ] *n.* 《archit.》 a scroll-like design. 소용돌이 장식. [↓]

car·tridge [kɑ́ːrtridʒ] *n.* Ⓒ **1** a small, round case for holding gunpowder. 탄약통. ¶ *a ~ case* 탄피; 약협(藥莢) / *a ball ~* 실탄. **2** a roll of camera film. 필름통. [It. *cartoc-*

cis roll of paper]

cart·wheel [ká:*r*thwì:l] *n.* Ⓒ **1** a wheel of a cart. (짐마차의) 바퀴. **2** a sideways somersault. 옆재주넘기. [→cart]

cart·wright [ká:*r*tràit] *n.* Ⓒ a person who makes carts. 수레 목수.

car·un·cle [kǽrʌŋkl, kənʌ́ŋkl] *n.* 《anat.》 a fleshy lump. 볏; 육부(肉阜). [→carnage]

***carve** [kɑ:*r*v] *vt.* (P6,7,13) **1** cut (stone or wood). (돌·나무)를 파다; 새기다. ¶ ~ *one's name on a tree* 나무에 자기 이름을 새기다. **2** make (figures) by cutting. …을 조각하다. ¶ ~ *a statue out of stone* 돌로 조상(彫像)을 조각하다. **3** cut (something) into pieces or slices. (식탁에서 고기 따위)를 자르다; 썰다. ¶ ~ *the meat at the table.* **4** 《*fig.*》 make or get as if by cutting; shape; secure. (혼자 힘으로) 개척하다; 길을 만들다. ¶ ~ *one's way to fortune* 성공에의 길을 열다.
— *vi.* (P1,3) **1** carve figures. 새기다; 조각하다. **2** cut meat. 고기를 썰다. ¶ *Shall I* ~ *you another slice of chicken ?* 닭고기 한 점 더 썰어 드릴까요. [E.]

carved [kɑ:*r*vd] *adj.* decorated by cutting. 조각된.

car·vel [ká:*r*vəl] *n.* =caravel.

carv·er [ká:*r*və*r*] *n.* Ⓒ **1** a person who carves. 조각자(사(師)). **2** a knife used for cutting up meat. 고기 써는 칼.

carv·ing [ká:*r*viŋ] *n.* **1** Ⓒ a work produced by cutting. 조각품(물). ¶ *a wood* ~ 목각(木刻) / *a stone carving* 석각(石刻) / *carvings in ivory* 상아 조각. **2** Ⓤ the act or art of one that carves. 조각; 조각술.

carv·ing-knife [ká:*r*viŋnàif] *n.* a big knife for meat-carving. 고기 써는 큰 칼.

car·y·at·id [kæ̀riǽtid] *n.* Ⓒ 《archit.》 a female figure as a pillar. 여상주(女像柱). [Gk.]

Cas·a·blan·ca [kæ̀səblǽŋkə, kɑ̀:səblɑ́:ŋkə] *n.* a city and major port of Morocco. 카사블랑카.

Cas·a·no·va [kæ̀zənóuvə, -sə-] *n.* a romantic or promiscuous man; a libertine. 엽색가(獵色家); 카사노바. [It.]

cas·cade [kæskéid] *n.* Ⓒ a small waterfall. (작은) 폭포(cf. *cataract*). — *vi.* fall in the form of a small waterfall. 작은 폭포가 되어 떨어지다. [L. *cado* fall]

cas·car·a [kæskɛ́ərə] *n.* Ⓤ a laxative. 완하제(緩下劑). [Sp.]

:case[1] [keis] *n.* Ⓒ **1** something that has happened; an instance; an occurence; an example. 사건; 일; 사례; 실례. ¶ *a* ~ *in point* 적절한 예 / *a* ~ *of love at first sight* 첫눈에 반한 실례 / *as is often the* ~ *with many children* 많은 아이들에게 흔히 있는 일이지만(일인데) / *This is a* ~ *of poor judgment.* 이것은 판단력을 그르친 한 예다. **2** a special condition of affairs; a situation. 사정; 경우. ¶ *in that* ~ 그렇다면; 그 경우에는 / *in either* ~ 어떤 경우든; 어떻든 / *as the* ~ *may be* 경우 여하로; 사정에 따라 / *The man told of the sad* ~ *of starving children in India.* 그 사람은 굶주리는 인도 어린이들의 비참한 사정을 이야기했다. **3** 《*the* ~ 》 the actual state of things. 사실; 진상. ¶ *This is not the* ~. 그것은 사실이 아니다 / *Is it the* ~ *that you have sold your house ?* — *Yes, it is the* ~. 자네 집을 팔았다는 게 정말인가 — 그렇다네, 사실이야. **4** a question or problem of moral conduct. (도덕적인) 문제. ¶ *a* ~ *of conscience* 양심의 문제 / *a* ~ *of murder* 살인사건. **5** ⓐ 《law》 a matter for a law court to decide; a suit. 소송 (사건). ¶ *a civil* (*criminal*) ~ 민사(형사) 사건 / *a leading* ~ 판례(判例) / *win the* ~ 소송에 이기다 / *lose the* ~ 패소(敗訴)하다. ⓑ facts, arguments, etc. used in favor of one party, esp. in a law court. (특히 법정에서 한쪽 당사자에게 유리한) 일련의 사실; 주장; 진술. ¶ *the* ~ *for the defendant* 피고에게 유리한 주장(진술) / *plead* (*put, state, make out*) *one's* ~ 자기의 주장을 말하다 / *have a good* ~ (소송에 이길만한) 충분한 이유가 있다. **6** ⓐ a person who has a disease or injury. 환자. 參考 case 는 병에 중점을 두며, patient 는 환자 그 자체를 가리킴. ¶ *a serious* ~ 중환자 / *emergency cases* 응급 환자 / *The worst cases are sent to hospital.* 심한 환자들은 병원으로 보내어진다. ⓑ an example of a disease or injury. 병례(病例); 병증(病症). ¶ *a* ~ *of measles* 홍역. **7** 《gram.》 (changes in) the form of a word showing its relationship with other words in a sentence. 격(格). ¶ *'Me' is the object* ~ *of 'I'.* Me 는 I 의 목적격이다. **8** 《U.S. *colloq.*》 a strange person. 기인(奇人); 괴짜. [L. *cado* fall]

as the case stands, as matters are now. 현 상태로는.

be in good case, be well off. 잘 지내다.

in any case, anyhow; under any circumstances; no matter what happens. 사정은 어떻든; 어쨌든. ¶ *In any* ~ *, there won't be any necessity for you to come along.* 글쎄 어쨌건 네가 따라올 필요는 없다.

in case, lest; if it should happen that... …면 안되므로; 만약 …의 경우에는. ¶ *in* ~ *it rains* 만일 비가 오면.

in case of, in the event of. …의 경우에는; …한 때에는. ¶ *in* ~ *of fire* 불이 났을 때에는 / *in* ~ *of my absence* 내가 없을 경우에는.

in nine cases out of ten, 십중 팔구.

in no case, by no means; never. 무슨 일이 있어도(결코) …않다(아니다). ¶ *He should in no* ~ *be allowed to get up until he has completely recovered from his illness.* 병이 완전히 나을 때까지는 결코 일어나서는 안 된다.

in this (**that**) **case,** if this (that) happens; if this (that) is true; in these (those) circumstances. 이런(그런) 경우에는.

make out someone's case, prove that

someone is right. …의 옳음을 입증하다.
put the case that …, suppose… …라고 가정하다.
such being the case, because of the circumstances; as these things are true. 사정〔사실〕이 이러하므로. ¶ *Such being the ~, I can't go.* 사정이 이러하므로 갈 수가 없다.

:case² [keis] *n.* Ⓒ **1** a box; a chest. 상자; 갑; 궤. ¶ *a jewel ~* 보석함 / *a packing ~* 짐꾸리는 상자. **2** a sheath; an outer covering. (칼)집; 겉싸개; 커버. ¶ *a watch with a silver ~* 은딱지의 (손목)시계 / *a pillowcase* 베갯잇 / *Put the knife back in its ~.* 칼을 칼집에 도로 넣어라. **3** a glass box for exhibiting goods; a showcase. 유리 진열장(欌). **4** a framework; a surrounding frame. (창문·문짝 등의) 틀. ¶ *a window ~* 창틀. **5** the amount that a case can hold. 한 상자의 양. ¶ *There are dozen bottles to a ~.* 한 상자엔 병 12개다.
— *vt.* (P6,7) put (something) in a case; enclose. …을 상자에 넣다; …을 싸다. ¶ *~ up goods* 물건을 상자에 넣다. [L. *capsa* box; *capio* contain]

case·hard·en [kéishὰ:rdn] *vt.* (P6) **1** harden the surface of. …의 표면을 담금질하다〔경화시키다〕. **2** make unfeeling. 무신경하게 만들다.

case·hard·ened [⌐hὰ:rdnd] *adj.* **1** 《metal.》 made hard by heat treatment. 담금질한; 열처리한. **2** insensible; impudent. 무신경한; 뻔뻔한.

ca·se·in [kéisi:n, -si:in] *n.* Ⓤ 《chem.》 the solid part of milk, of which cheese is made. 카세인; 건락소(乾酪素). [L. *caseus* cheese]

case·mate [kéismèit] *n.* a bombproof chamber in a fort. (요새의) 포대(砲臺). [It.]

case·ment [kéismənt] *n.* Ⓒ a window which opens outwards or inwards. 여닫이창. [It.]

casement cloth [⌐-⌐] *n.* cotton cloth for curtains. 커튼감.

·cash [kæʃ] *n.* Ⓤ **1** money, esp. money on hand; coins and bills. 현금; 소지금. ¶ *~ in* 〔*on*〕 *hand* 수중의 현금 / *pay* (*in*) *~* 현금으로 지급하다 / *convert* 〔*turn*〕 *a check into ~* 수표를 현금으로 바꾸다 / *be hard up for ~* 돈에 궁하다. **2** money, or an equivalent, such as a check. (지급할) 현금; 수표. ¶ *be short of ~* 돈이 부족하다; 지급하기 어렵다. **3** 《colloq.》 money in any form; wealth. 돈; 부(富).
be in cash, have money. 현금이 있다.
be out of cash, have no money. 현금이 떨어져 없다.
cash down, immediate payment in cash. 맞돈; 즉시 현금 지급.
cash on delivery, payment in cash when goods are delivered. 상환급; 현금 지급(abbr. C.O.D., c.o.d.).
— *vt.* (P6,13) turn (something) into cash. (수표·어음 따위)를 현금으로 바꾸다. ¶ *~ a check / Where can I get this cashed?* 이걸 어디서 현금으로 바꿀 수 있습니까. [case²]
cash in, turn (something) into cash. …을 현금으로 바꾸다.
cash in on, 《colloq.》 **a**) make a profit from (something). …에서 이익을 얻다. **b**) turn (something) to one's advantage. …을 이용하다.

cash-and-car·ry [kǽʃənkǽri] *adj.* of no credit and no delivery service. 무배달 현금 판매의.

cash·book [kǽʃbùk] *n.* Ⓒ a book to record the sum of money received and paid out. 현금 출납부.

cash·ew [kǽʃu:, kəʃú:] *n.* Ⓒ 《bot.》 a tropical American tree and its nut. 캐슈《열대 아메리카의 옻나뭇과(科) 식물》; 그 열매. [Braz.]

cash·ier¹ [kæʃíər, kə-] *n.* Ⓒ a person in a bank or restaurant who receives and pays out money. 현금 출납계원; 회계원. [→cash]

cash·ier² [kæʃíər] *vt.* (P6) dismiss (an officer) suddenly from service. 파면시키다; 징계 면직하다. [L. *quatio* shake]

cash·mere [kǽʃmiər, kǽʒ-] *n.* **1** fine, soft wool from Kashmir and Tibet goats. 캐시미어 모직. ¶ *a ~ shawl* 캐시미어숄. **2** a fine, soft woollen cloth. 곱고 보드라운 모직. [Place in India]

cash register [⌐ ⌐--] *n.* a cash box to indicate the amount of a sale. 금전 등록기.

cas·ing [kéisiŋ] *n.* **1** Ⓒ a case or covering; Ⓤ enclosing material. 상자; 싸개; 덮개; 포장재. **2** Ⓒ a framework, as of a window or door. (창·문짝 따위의) 틀. [→case²]

ca·si·no [kəsí:nou] *n.* (*pl.* **-nos**) **1** Ⓒ a public building or room for shows, dancing, gambling, etc. 카지노. **2** Ⓤ a game played for money. 카드놀이의 하나. [L. *casa* cottage]

cask [kæsk, kɑ:sk] *n.* Ⓒ **1** ⓐ a barrel to hold liquids. 통. ¶ *an empty ~* 빈 통. ⓑ the barrel and its contents. 통 속에 든 것. ¶ *a ~ of beer* 맥주 담은 통. **2** the amount that a cask can hold. 한 통의 양. [Sp.]

cas·ket [kǽskit, kɑ́:s-] *n.* Ⓒ **1** a small box to hold jewels, letters, etc. (귀중품 등을 넣는) 작은 상자. **2** 《U.S.》 a coffin. 관(棺). [Sp. *casco*]

Cas·pi·an [kǽspiən] *adj.* of the Caspian Sea. 카스피해의.

Caspian Sea [⌐-- ⌐], **the** *n.* an inland sea in Asia. 카스피해.

casque [kæsk] *n.* 《*arch., poet.*》 a helmet. 투구. [Sp.]

Cas·san·dra [kəsǽndrə] *n.* 《Gk. myth.》 a prophetess of Troy; a woman who warns in vain of coming evil. 카산드라《Troy의 왕녀로 흉사의 예언가》. [Homeric person]

cas·sa·va [kəsɑ́:və] *n.* Ⓒ 《bot.》 an West-Indian plant. 카사바 나무. [Hayti]

cas·se·role [kǽsəròul] *n.* Ⓒ a covered baking-dish, usu. of earthenware or glass, in which food can be cooked and then served at table. 카세롤《뚜껑 있는 찜냄비》. [F.]

en casserole [ɑ:ŋ-], served in this way. 카세롤로 차려낸. ¶ *meat en* ~ 카세롤에 찐 고기.

·cas·sette [kæsét, kə-] *n.* Ⓒ a container for a role of film or magnetic tape (for use with a ~ taperecorder). 카세트. [F.]

cas·sia [kǽʃə, kǽsiə] *n.* **1** Ⓤ an inferior kind of cinnamon. 카시아 계피(桂皮). **2** Ⓤ the bark of certain tropical trees, used to derive cassia. 카시아를 내는 열대수(樹)의 껍질. **3** Ⓒ a tree with such bark. 그 나무. [Heb.]

Cas·si·o·pei·a [kæ̀siəpí:ə] *n.* 《astron.》 a northern constellation. 카시오페이아 자리. [Gk.]

cas·sock [kǽsək] *n.* Ⓒ a long garment, usu. black, worn by a clergyman. (검은) 성직자복. [F.]

cas·so·war·y [kǽsəwὲəri] *n.* 《bird》 a large bird related to an ostrich. 화식조(火食鳥). [Malay]

:cast [kæst, kɑ:st] *v.* (**cast**) *vt.* **1** (P6,7,13) throw; throw up or down; throw off or away. …을 던지다; 버리다. ¶ ~ *a stone at a dog* 개한테 돌을 던지다 / 《*fig.*》 ~ *the blame on someone* 아무에게 비난을 퍼붓다. **2** (P6,7) put off; shed. (허물·옷 따위)를 벗다; (털·열매·잎 따위)를 떨어뜨리다. ¶ ~ *hair* 머리털이 빠지다 / ~ (*off*) *one's clothes* 옷을 벗어던지다 / *The snake* ~ *its skin.* 뱀이 허물을 벗었다. **3** (P6) let (something) fall or drop; throw out. …을 내리다; 드리우다; 내던지다. ¶ ~ *a net* 투망하다 / ~ *an anchor* 닻을 내리다 / *The angler* ~ *his line.* 낚시꾼은 낚싯줄을 던졌다. **4** (7,13) direct; turn (something) in a certain direction. (눈·눈길 따위)를 …쪽으로 돌리다; 향하다. ¶ ~ *one's eyes up to* …을 쳐다보다 / ~ *a look* 〔*glance*〕 *at* …에 눈길을 던지다; …을 보다. **5** (P6,13) cause (light, shadow, etc.) to fall on something or in a certain direction. (빛을) 발하다; (그림자)를 던지다〔드리우다〕. ¶ ~ *a shadow on the ground* 땅에 그림자를 드리우다 / ~ *a soft light* 약한 빛을 발하다 / *The deed* ~ *glory upon his name.* 그 행위가 그의 이름을 높였다. **6** (P6,13) form (something) by pouring hot liquid metal into a mold and letting it harden. …을 부어 만들다; 주조하다. ¶ ~ *a bell in bronze* 청동으로 종을 주조하다. **7** (P6) draw by chance. (제비)를 뽑다; (주사위)를 던지다. ¶ ~ *a lots or dice* 제비를 뽑거나 주사위를 던져 결정하다. **8** (P6,13) deposit or give. (표)를 넣다; 던지다. ¶ ~ *a vote for* 〔*against*〕 …에 찬성〔반대〕 투표를 하다. **9** (P13) assign a part to (an actor); assign an actor to (a part). 배역하다. ¶ ~ *an actor for a certain part* 어떤 역에 어떤 남우(男優)를 배역하다. **10** (P6,7) ⓐ calculate; add. …을 계산하다; 더하다. ¶ ~ *accounts* 계산하다. ⓑ calculate the value of. …을 평가하다. **11** dismiss; reject. …을 해고하다; 거부하다; 폐기하다. **12** (of an animal) bring forth (young) prematurely. (새끼)를 조산(早産)하다. **13** 《naut.》 veer; turn. (닻줄)을 풀어내다; (방향)을 돌리다. **14** (P6) vomit. …을 토하다; 게우다. ¶ ~ *one's dinner* 먹은 음식을 토하다. **15** 《law》 defeat. …을 패소(敗訴)케 하다. ¶ *be* ~ *in* 〔*for*〕 *damages* 손해 배상을 선고받다. — *vi.* (P1) **1** throw; throw a line or a fly in fishing. 던지다; (제물) 낚시를 던져 넣다. **2** be formed in a mold. 주조되다. **3** calculate. 계산하다. **4** forecast. 예상〔예측〕하다.

cast about, **a**) search; try to find (something). …을 찾다; …을 찾으려고 애쓰다. ¶ ~ *about for means of escape* 도망갈 방법을 찾다. **b**) make plans. 궁리하다; 계획〔획책〕하다.

cast ashore, throw up on the shore. 해안〔강기슭〕으로 밀어올리다.

cast aside, throw away; discard. …을 버리다. ¶ *Let us* ~ *aside minor details.* 사소한 세부 사항은 제쳐놓자.

cast a spell on, bewitch. …에 마법을 걸다; 홀리다.

cast a stone at, reprobate the conduct of. …의 행동을 비난하다.

cast away, **a**) throw away; abandon. (내)버리다. ¶ *Let us* ~ *away all prejudices.* 모든 편견을 버리자. **b**) spend (money) foolishly. …을 낭비하다. **c**) wreck (a ship). …(배 따위)를 난파〔파선〕시키다.

cast back, **a**) recollect; recall. …을 회상하다. **b**) revert to. (전(前)으로) 되돌아가다. ¶ ~ *back to barbarism* 야만 상태로 되돌아가다.

cast down, **a**) throw down; overthrow; upset; lower. …을 내리던지다; 뒤엎다; (시선·품위·지위 등)을 떨어뜨리다. **b**) 《*fig.*》 make (someone) discourage. …을 낙담시키다; 기운을 죽이다(cf. *downcast*). ¶ *The bad news greatly* ~ *me down.* 그 나쁜 소식은 나를 크게 낙심케 했다.

cast in one's lot with, share fortunes of. …와 운명을 함께 하다.

cast something in someone's teeth ⇨tooth.

cast into prison, imprison. …을 교도소에 넣다; 투옥하다.

cast loose, detach. …을 떼어놓다; 풀다. ¶ ~ *a boat loose* (매어놓은) 배를 풀어놓다.

cast off, **a**) put off (clothes, etc.); let go or let loose. (옷)을 벗다; (매어놓은 배)를 풀어놓다. **b**) throw away; abandon; 《*fig.*》 free oneself from. 버리다; 그만두다; 끊다. ¶ ~ *off a vicious habit* 못된 버릇을 버리다.

cast out, 《often *passive*》 drive out or away; dispel. …을 몰아내다; 내쫓다.

cast up, **a**) add up; calculate. 합산하다; 계산하다. ¶ ~ *up a column of figures* 세로난의 수를 합산하다. **b**) vomit. 토하다; 게우다. ¶ ~ *up one's food* 먹을 것을 토하다. **c**) cast a shore. 해안〔강기슭〕으로 밀어올리다. **d**) turn up; appear. 모습을 나타내다; 나타나다. — *n.* Ⓒ **1** the act of casting; something that is thrown off. 던짐; 던진〔벗은〕것. ¶ *with one ~ of an eye* 흘끗 보고 / *A snake's ~ is the skin it has cast off.* 뱀의 허물은 벗어 버린 껍질이다. **2** fortune. 운. ¶ *the last ~* 마지막 기회 / *try another ~* 다시 한번 해보다 / *succeed at the first ~* 한번에 성공하다. **3** a thing formed by molding or pressing. 거푸집에 부어 만든 것; 주물. **4** a mold into which metal is poured or soft material pressed. 주형(鑄型); 거푸집. **5** appearance; style; inclination. 외관; 형(型); 경향. ¶ *a ~ of mind* 기질 / *things of this ~* 이러한 유형의 것들 / *a ~ to insomnia* 불면증의 경향 / *His features have a melancholy ~.* 우울한 기색이 있다. **6** calculation. 계산; 산출. ¶ *make a ~ of profits and losses* 손익 계산을 하다. **7** (of the eyes) a slight squint. 사팔눈; 사시(斜視). ¶ *have a ~ in one's eye* 사팔뜨기이다. **8** a slight tinge of some color. …기가 도는 색조. ¶ *a ~ of blue* 푸른 기. **9** the set of actors in a play. 배역; 배역진. ¶ *an all-star ~* 스타 총출연. [Scand. *kasta*]

cas·ta·nets [kæ̀stənéts] *n. pl.* a pair of instruments of hard wood or ivory used to beat time to music. 캐스터네츠. [→chestnut]

cast·a·way [kǽstəwèi, ká:st-] *adj.* **1** thrown away; of no value. 버림받은; 무가치한. **2** shipwrecked. 난파〔파선〕한. — *n.* Ⓒ **1** a person or thing thrown away; an outcast. 버림받은 사람〔물건〕. ¶ *castaways from God* 하느님에게 버림받은 사람들. **2** a shipwrecked person. 난선자(難船者); 표류자. [*cast*]

caste [kæst, kɑ:st] *n.* **1** Ⓒ a Hindu social class. 카스트. **2** Ⓒ an exclusive social group. (배타적) 계층; 집단. **3** Ⓤ social position. 사회적 지위. [Sp.=lineage]

lose caste, lose social position or rank. 사회적 지위를 잃다; 영락하다.

cas·tel·lat·ed [kǽstəlèitid] *adj.* built like a castle; having many castles. 성처럼 지은; 성이 많은. [→castle]

cast·er [kǽstər, ká:stər] *n.* Ⓒ **1** a person or thing that casts. 던지는 사람〔물건〕. **2** a small wheel for supporting and moving furniture. (가구 따위의) 다리 바퀴. **3** a bottle on the table for serving salt, vinegar, or other seasoning. (식탁용) 양념병. **4** a stand for such bottles. 양념병 받침. 參考 ②, ③, ④는 castor 라고도 씀. [*cast*]

cas·ti·gate [kǽstəgèit] *vt.* (P6) **1** punish. …을 벌주다; 징계하다. ¶ *be castigated for one's mischief* 못된 장난 때문에 벌받다. **2** criticize severely. …을 혹평하다. ¶ *He was castigated by the newspapers.* 신문에서 호되게 얻어맞았다. [L. *castigo*]

cas·ti·ga·tion [kæ̀stəgéiʃən] *n.* ⓊⒸ **1** punishment. 처벌; 징계. **2** severe criticism. 혹평.

Cas·tile [kæstí:l] *n.* a region in northern and central Spain. (스페인 중북부의) 카스티야 지방《옛날의 왕국》. [Sp.]

Castile soap [ㅡ ㅡ́] *n.* a pure hard soap made from olive-oil and sodium hydroxide. 카스티야 비누.

Cas·til·ian [kæstíljən] *adj.* of or belonging to Castile. 카스티야의〔에 속하는〕. — *n.* **1** Ⓒ a native of Castile. 카스티야 사람. **2** Ⓤ Castilian Spanish. 카스티야어. ¶ *~ is now the standard form of the Spanish language.* 카스티야어가 지금은 스페인어의 표준형이다.

cast·ing [kǽstiŋ, ká:st-] *n.* Ⓤ **1** throwing; the act of casting. 던짐; 투척. **2** Ⓒ a thing formed by pouring a liquid into a mold to harden. 주조물. ¶ *an iron ~ for a stove* 난로 제조용 거푸집. **3** Ⓒ a part; a role. 배역. [*cast*]

casting vote [ㅡ́ ㅡ ㅡ́] *n.* the deciding vote of the chairman when the votes are equally divided. 결정 투표; 캐스팅 보트.

cast iron [ㅡ́ ㅡ́ ㅡ] *n.* a soft and strong mixture of iron, carbon, and other elements. 주철(鑄鐵)(cf. *wrought iron*).

cast-iron [kǽstáiərn / ká:st-] *adj.* **1** made of cast iron. 주철제(鑄鐵製)의. **2** inflexible; stern. 불굴의; 엄격한. ¶ *~ rules* 철칙(鐵則).

:cas·tle [kǽsl, ká:sl] *n.* Ⓒ **1** a large house of old times strengthened against attack. 성(城); 성채. ¶ *go to see an old ~* 옛 성을 구경가다 / 《*prov.*》 *An Englishman's home is his ~.* 영국인의 집은 그의 성이다《남의 침입을 허용치 않는다》. **2** a large and stately mansion. 으리으리한 저택. **3** 《chess》 a piece in chess, shaped like a castle tower; rook. (체스의) 성장(城將). [L. *castrum* fort]

a castle in the air [***in Spain***]***,*** something imagined but not likely to be realized. 공중누각.

cast·off [kǽstɔ̀:f, ká:st- / -ɔ̀f] *adj.* thrown away. 버림받은. — *n.* a person or thing that has been cast off. 버림받은 사람〔것〕.

cas·tor[1] [kǽstər, ká:stər] *n.* =caster (②, ③, ④).

cas·tor[2] [kǽstər, ká:stər] *n.* Ⓒ **1** a beaver. 비버; 해리(海狸). **2** a hat made of beaver fur. 비버털 모자. **3** Ⓤ an oily substance with a strong smell produced by beavers. 해리향(香). [Gk.]

cas·tor oil [ㅡ ㅡ́ ㅡ́] *n.* Ⓤ a purgative vegetable oil. 아주까리〔피마자〕기름. [?]

castor sugar [ㅡ́ ㅡ ㅡ̀ ㅡ] *n.* 《Brit.》 very finely powdered sugar. 가루 백설탕.

cas·trate [kǽstreit] *vt.* (P6) **1** remove the male sexual glands from (an animal). …을

거세하다. ¶ *A capon is a castrated cock.* capon 은 거세된 수탉이다. **2** omit; deprive (something) of its most important part. 골자〔알맹이〕를 빼다. ¶ ~ *a bill* 법안에서 알맹이를 빼다 / *a castrated literary work* (삭제에 의해) 김빠진 문학 작품. ● **cas·tra·tion** [kæstréiʃən] *n.* [L.]

Cas·tro [kǽstrou], **Fidel** *n.* (1927-) a Cuban revolutionary and prime minister since 1959. 카스트로《쿠바의 혁명가·정치가》.

***cas·u·al** [kǽʒuəl] *adj.* **1** happening by chance; unexpected. 우연의; 뜻밖의. ¶ *a ~ meeting* 기우(奇遇) / *a ~ visit* 뜻밖의 방문. **2** without serious intention. 무심코의; 아무 생각 없이 하는; 생각나는 대로의. ¶ *a ~ remark* 무심코 한 말 / *make a few ~ conversations* 두서너 마디 문뜩 생각난 것을 말하다 / *give a ~ glance* 훌끗 보다. **3** irregular; occasional. 부정기의; 임시의; 불시의; 이따금의. ¶ *~ expenses* 임시 지출 / *a ~ hand* 임시 고용자 / *~ labor* 임시적인 일 / *a ~ laborer* 뜨내기 인부; 자유 노동자. **4** careless; not concerned or interested. 무심한; 무관심한; 태평스런; 태연한. ¶ *a ~ air* 무관심한 태도. **5** (of clothes) designed for wearing at home; informal. 집에서 입는; 평상복의; 약식의. ¶ *~ attire* 평상복 / *in ~ wear* 평상복으로 / *the ~ atmosphere in the classroom* 교실 안에서의 딱딱하지 않은 분위기.

—*n.* Ⓒ **1** a casual laborer. 임시 인부; 자유 노동자. **2** a vagrant. 부랑자. [L. *cado* fall]

cas·u·al·ly [kǽʒuəli] *adv.* accidentally; occasionally; carelessly. 우연히; 이따금; 무심코.

cas·u·al·ty [kǽʒuəlti] *n.* Ⓒ **1** an accident; an unfortunate accident. 사고; 재해; 재난. ¶ *~ insurance* 상해 보험 / *have* 〔*meet with*〕 *a ~* 재난을 당하다. **2** 《*pl.*》《mil.》 soldiers wounded or killed in a battle. (병력의) 사상자(수). ¶ *heavy casualties* 많은 사상자 / *a list of casualties* =*a ~ list* 사상자 명단. **3** a person hurt or killed in an accident. (사고로 인한) 사상자. ¶ *a traffic ~*.

cas·u·ist [kǽʒuist] *n.* Ⓒ **1** a person who studies and decides questions of conscience. 결의론자(決疑論者). **2** a person who reasons and argues cleverly but falsely. 궤변가. ● **cas·u·is·tic** [kæ̀ʒuístik] *adj.* [L. *casus* case]

ca·sus bel·li [kéisəs bélai, ká:səs béli:] *n.* 《L.》 a cause of war. 개전(開戰)의 이유. [→case[1]]

:cat [kæt] *n.* Ⓒ **1** a small, fur-covered animal often kept as a pet, to catch mice, etc.; any animal of the cat family, such as a lion or a tiger. 고양이; 고양잇과의 동물. ¶ *a tom ~* 수고양이 / *a tabby ~* = *a she-cat* 암고양이 / *A ~ mews* 〔*miaows*〕. 고양이가 야옹거리다 / *climb like a ~* 고양이처럼 기어오르다 / *have as many lives as a ~* 목숨이 질기다. **2** an ill-natured woman; a malicious woman. 심술궂고 고약한 여자. ¶ *a regular old ~* 지독한 악녀(惡女). **3** 《bot.》 a catmint; a catnip. 개박하.

A cat has nine lives. 《*prov.*》 A cat is much more likely to escape death than are most animals. 고양이는 목숨이 아홉개다《여간해서는 죽지 않는다》.

A cat may look at a king. 《*prov.*》 Even the humblest have some privileges in the presence of the great. 아무리 비천한 사람이라도 그 나름의 권리는 있다.

bell the cat, take the danger of a common enterprise on oneself. 공동 사업의 위험을 혼자 떠맡다.

enough to make a cat laugh, very funny. 매우 우스꽝스러운; 우습기 짝이 없는.

fight like Kilkenny cats, fight till both are killed. 쌍방이 다 죽을 때까지 싸우다.

lead a cat and dog life, be always quarreling. 견원지간(犬猿之間)이다; 앙숙이다.

let the cat out of the bag, tell a secret. 비밀을 누설하다.

like a cat on a hot bricks 〔***tin roof***〕, 《Brit.》 very nervous or anxious. 불안해서 침착을 잃고; 안절부절 못 해.

rain cats and dogs, rain very heavily. 비가 억수로 퍼붓다.

see how the cat jumps, refuse to do anything until one sees how events develop. 형세를 관망하다.

see 〔***watch***〕 ***which way the cat will jump*** = see how the cat jumps.

turn the cat in the pan, change sides. 변절하다; 배반하다.

wait for the cat to jump =see how the cat jumps.

—*vt.* (**catted**) (P6) **1** 《*colloq.*》 vomit. 토하다. **2** hoist. 내걸다. **3** flog. 매질하다. [G. *katze*]

cata- [kǽtə-], **cath-** [kæθ-], **cat-** [kæt-] *pref.* down-, mis-, against, throughly, along. '하(下), 오(誤), 반(反), 전(全), 측(側)'의 뜻. [Gk.]

cat·a·bol·ism [kətǽbəlìzəm] *n.* Ⓤ the metabolic change of complex compounds into simpler ones. 이화(異化) 작용. [Gk. *cata-*, *bállein* to throw, →metabolism]

cat·a·clysm [kǽtəklìzəm] *n.* Ⓒ **1** a great flood of water. 대홍수. **2** 《geol.》 an earthquake, or any sudden and violent physical change in the earth. 지진; (지각의) 대변동. **3** a sudden overturning of society, or the political system. (사회·정치의) 격변. ¶ *The First World War was a ~ for all Europe.* 제1차 세계 대전은 전유럽에 있어 일대 변혁이었다. [Gk. *cata* mis-, *khraomai* use]

cat·a·comb [kǽtəkòum] *n.* 《usu. *pl.*》 an underground place for graves or tombs. 지하 납골당(納骨堂). [L. *cata* at, *tumbas* tomb]

cat·a·falque [kǽtəfæ̀lk] *n.* an ornamental table on which a coffin is put. 영구대(靈柩臺). [Rom.]

Cat·a·lan [kǽtələn, -læ̀n] *adj.* of Catalonia. 카탈로니아의. —*n.* the language or a native of Catalonia. 카탈로니아어(語)〔사람〕.

cat·a·lec·tic [kæ̀təléktik] *adj.* a syllable short. 한 음절이 부족한. [Gk. *cata-, lēgō* cease]

cat·a·lep·sy [kǽtəlèpsi], **cat·a·lep·sis** [kæ̀təlépsis] *n.* 《med.》 an illness in which the whole body appears to be dead. 전신 경직증(硬直症). ● **cat·a·lep·tic** [kæ̀təléptik] *adj.* [Gk. *cata-* down-, *lambanō* seize]

•**cat·a·log** [kǽtəlɔ̀:g, -lɑ̀g / -lɔ̀g] *n.* Ⓒ **1** a list of things to be shown or for sale. 카탈로그; 목록. ¶ *a ~ of names* 〔*books*〕 인명〔도서〕 목록 / *send a ~* 카탈로그를 보내다 / *priced catalogs of articles for sale* 상품 가격 목록. **2** 《U.S.》 a book or pamphlet of a college or university listing rules, courses to be given, etc. (대학의) 요람(要覽)(cf. 《Brit.》 *calendar*).
—*vt.* (P6) make a catalog of (something); enter (something) in a catalog. …의 목록을 만들다; …을 목록에 싣다. ¶ *~ books* 〔*wines*〕 도서〔포도주〕 목록을 만들다 / *This book has not yet been cataloged.* 이 책은 아직 카탈로그에 올라 있지 않다. [Gk. *cata-, legō* hoose]

cat·a·logue [kǽtəlɔ̀:g, -lɑ̀g / -lɔ̀g] *n., vt.* =catalog.

Cat·a·lo·ni·a [kæ̀təlóuniə, -njə] *n.* an old province of Spain. 카탈로니아《스페인의 옛 주》.

ca·tal·pa [kətǽlpə] *n.* 《bot.》 a tree with heart-shaped leaves, bell-shaped flowers, and long bean-like pods. 개오동나무. [W. Ind.]

ca·tal·y·ses [kətǽləsì:z] *n.* pl. of **catalysis.**

ca·tal·y·sis [kətǽləsis] *n.* (*pl.* **-ses**) 《chem.》 acceleration of a reaction. 접촉 반응; 촉매 작용. [Gk. *lūo* loosen]

cat·a·lyst [kǽtəlist] *n.* Ⓒ 《chem.》 a substance producing catalysis. 촉매. [↑]

cat·a·ma·ran [kæ̀təmərǽn] *n.* **1** a raft of yoked logs. 뗏목. **2** a cross-grained woman. 앙알거리는 여자. [Tamil.]

〈catapult 1〉

cat·a·pult [kǽtəpʌ̀lt] *n.* Ⓒ **1** an ancient military engine for throwing stones, spears, etc. 쇠뇌; 투석기. **2** a device for launching an airplane from the deck of a ship. 캐터펄트《항모의 비행기 사출(射出) 장치》. **3** 《Brit.》 a slingshot. (장난감) 새총.
—*vt., vi.* (P6;1) shoot (a stone, an airplane, etc.) with a catapult. (…을) 캐터펄트로 쏘다. [Gk. *pullo* hurl]

cat·a·ract [kǽtərǽkt] *n.* Ⓒ **1** a great waterfall. 폭포(cf. *cascade*). **2** a violent rush or fall of water or rain; a deluge. 분류(奔流); 억수; 홍수. ¶ *cataracts of rain* 호우; 큰비 / *the cataracts of the Nile* 나일강의 범람. **3** 《med.》 a disease of the eye which makes a person partly or entirely blind. 백내장. [Gk. *cata-, arassō* dash]

ca·tarrh [kətɑ́:r] *n.* Ⓤ **1** a diseased condition of the throat or back of nose, as in a cold. 카타르《점막의 염증》. **2** 《Brit. *colloq.*》 a cold. (기침이 나는) 감기. [Gk. *cata-, rheō* flow]

ca·tas·tro·phe [kətǽstrəfi] *n.* Ⓒ **1** a sudden and widespread disaster. (갑작스러운) 큰 재난. ¶ *an awful* 〔*a terrible*〕 *~* 무서운 참사 / *A big earthquake or flood is a ~; so is a big fire.* 큰 지진이나 홍수는 재난이다. 대화재도 마찬가지다. **2** 《theatr.》 an unhappy ending; a subversive event. (비극 등의) 대단원; 비극적 결말; 파국. **3** 《geol.》 a sudden violent change in nature. 대이변(大異變)(=cataclysm). [Gk. *cata-, strephō* turn]

cat·a·stroph·ic [kæ̀təstrɑ́fik / -strɔ́f-] *adj.* disastrous; calamitous. 비참한; 재난의; 비극적인.

cat·boat [kǽtbòut] *n.* a small sailing-boat with one mast placed far forward. 외대박이 작은 돛배. [*cat*]

cat-bur·glar [kǽtbə̀:rglər] *n.* a thief who enters a house by climbing, e.g. through a window upstairs. (위층 창문 등으로 침입하는) 밤도둑.

cat·call [kǽtkɔ̀:l] *n.* Ⓒ a cry like that of a cat, used to express disapproval at a theater, a meeting, etc. (회합 등에서 고양이 울음 소리를 흉내낸) 야유.

⁝**catch** [kætʃ] *v.* (**caught** [kɔ:t]) *vt.* **1** (P6, 13) take and hold; capture. …을 (붙)잡다; 붙들다(opp. lose). ¶ *~ a thief* 도둑을 잡다 / *~ a rat in a trap* 덫으로 쥐를 잡다 / *~ a lion alive* 사자를 사로잡다 / *~ someone by the arm* 〔*sleeve*〕 아무의 팔을〔소매를〕 잡다 / *A rabbit was caught in a snare.* 토끼가 덫에 치였다. **2** (P6) get hold of (something moving, flying, etc.); receive and hold. (움직이는 것)을 잡다; 받다. ¶ *~ a ball* 볼을 잡다〔받다〕 / *~ dripping water in a basin* 떨어지는 물을 물동이에 받다. **3** (P6,7,13) grasp with the senses or mind; see; hear; understand. …을 알아채다; 알아듣다; 이해하다. ¶ *~ the meaning* 뜻을 이해하다 / *~ some-*

one's words 아무의 말을 알아듣다 / *~ sight of* …을 발견하다 / *I cannot ~ what you say.* 댁의 말씀을 알 수가 없습니다. **4** (P6) be in time for 〔to take〕; come to or catch up with. (열차·배 따위)에 시간을 대어 타다; …을 따라잡다. ¶ *~ the 8:00 limited express,* 8시발 특급을 타다 / *I caught him before he had gone far.* 그가 멀리 가기 전에 따라붙었다 / *I wanted to ~ the train, but missed it by five minutes.* 열차를 타려고 했으나 5분 늦어 놓쳐 버렸다. **5** (P6) become infected with (a disease); form (habits); contract; incur. (병)에 걸리다; 감염하다; (습관)에 물들다; (바람직하지 않은 일 등)을 당하다; 초래하다. ¶ *~ (a) cold* 감기에 걸리다 / *catch (the) measles* 홍역에 걸리다 / *~ hatred* 〔*danger*〕 증오를〔위험을〕 초래하다 / *~ his manner* 그의 태도에 물들다. **6** (P6) take; get; receive and reflect. (불)이 붙다; …을 받아 되쏘다. ¶ *~ fire* 불이 붙다 / *A window caught the sunset.* 창문이 저녁 햇살을 비쳤다 / *Tin roofs ~ the heat of the sun.* 양철 지붕은 태양열을 받는다. **7** (P7) put out (a batsman) by catching the ball. 볼을 잡아 (타자)를 아웃시키다. **8** (P6) attract (the attention); arrest. (주의·사람 눈)을 끌다. ¶ *~ someone's* 〔*the*〕 *eye* 아무의 눈을 끌다 / *She caught his fancy.* 그녀는 그의 마음에 들었다 / *His speech caught our attention.* 그의 연설은 우리의 주목을 끌었다. **9** (P6,7,13,23) come upon suddenly; find (someone) in some action; discover; surprise. …을 불시에 덮치다; (…하는 것)을 발견하다〔잡다〕. ¶ *be caught in a shower* 소나기를 만나다 / *I caught him (in the act of) stealing.* 그가 훔치는 현장을 목격하였다 / *He was caught (in the act of) stealing.* 그는 훔치다가 들켰다 / *They were caught kissing each other.* 그들은 키스하는 장면을 들켰다 / *The enemy caught us unawares.* 적은 우리를 기습했다. **10** (P6,13) strike suddenly; hit. …을 때리다; 치다. ¶ *He caught her on the cheek.* 그는 그녀의 뺨을 후려 갈겼다 / *He caught a stone on the forehead.* 그의 이마에 돌이 맞았다 / *The wind catches a sail.* 바람이 돛을 때린다. **11** (P6) take and hold (someone's arm, sleeve, etc.). (아무의 팔·소매 등)을 붙잡다. ¶ *He caught my sleeve and pulled it.* 그는 내 소매를 잡고 당겼다 / *I caught her hands in mine.* 그녀의 손을 내 손 안에 쥐었다. **12** (P6) stop; check; restrain. 멈추다; 억제하다. ¶ *He caught himself in time to keep from opening his mouth.* 그는 말이 나오려는 것을 꾹 참았다. **13** (P6,13) ⓐ grasp and hold; grip, hook, or entangle. (못·옷 따위가) …에 걸리다; 얽히다. ¶ *A nail caught her skirts.* 못이 그녀 치맛자락에 걸렸다 / *Her hair was caught in a bush.* 그녀의 머리카락이 덤불에 얽혔다. ⓑ allow to be caught or gripped. (사람이 틈·못 따위에) …을 끼이게〔걸리게〕 하다; 걸리다. ¶ *~ one's finger in a door* 손가락이 문틈에 끼이다 / *~ one's feet in the ropes* 밧줄에 발이 걸리다 / *He caught his coat on a hook.* 그는 옷이 갈고리에 걸렸다. — *vi.* (P1,3) **1** 《*at*》 try to seize suddenly or rudely. 잡으려고 하다. **2** become entangled or hooked; be seized and held. 얽히다; 걸리다. ¶ *The kite caught in a tree.* 연이 나무에 걸렸다 / *The lock won't ~.* 자물쇠가 채워지지〔잠기지〕 않는다 / *Her stocking caught on a nail.* 그녀의 스타킹이 못에 걸렸다. **3** take fire; burn. 불이 붙다. ¶ *The match won't ~.* 성냥이 켜지지 않는다. **4** be communicated, as a disease or enthusiasm. (병 따위가) 유행하다; 퍼지다. **5** 《baseball》 play as a catcher. 캐처〔포수〕 노릇을 하다.

catch a glimpse of, see (something) for a short time. …을 흘긋〔얼핏〕 보다.

catch as catch can, act without any plan or order. 닥치는 대로 붙잡다; 무계획적으로 달려들다.

catch at, try to take hold of; reach for; grasp at; seize eagerly or desperately. 붙잡으려고 하다 ; 달려들다. ¶ *~ at an opportunity* 기회를 잡으려고 발바투 덤비다 / 《*prov.*》 *A drowning man will ~ at a straw.* 물에 빠진 자는 지푸라기라도 붙잡으려 한다.

catch** one's **breath, stop breathing for a moment from surprise, fear, shock, etc. (놀람·두려움·충격 등으로) 잠시 숨을 멈추다〔죽이다〕. ¶ *She caught her breath in surprise.* 그녀는 놀라서 숨을 죽였다.

catch hold of, **a**) grasp. 잡다. **b**) turn to account. 이용하다.

catch it, 《*colloq.*》 receive a scolding; get punished. 야단맞다; 혼나다.

Catch me! No fear of my doing that. 내가 그런 짓을 할까 보냐.

catch off, get to sleep. 잠들다.

catch on, **a**) 《*colloq.*》 become popular or fashionable. 유행하다; 인기를 얻다. ¶ *The song caught on.* 그 노래가 유행되었다. **b**) understand; grasp the point of (something). 이해하다; 알다. ¶ *~ on to the meaning* 뜻을 이해하다 / *I tried to make him ~ on.* 그를 이해시키려고 했다.

catch out, **a**) 《cricket, baseball》 put (a batsman) out by catching the ball straight from his bat. (타자를) 캐치아웃시키다. **b**) find (someone) in some action, usu. wrongdoing. (부정 따위를) 간파하다. ¶ *I have caught him out in several lies.* 나는 그가 몇 가지 거짓말을 하는 것을 알았다.

catch up, **a**) pick up or seize suddenly and quickly; snatch. 느닷없이 집어〔들어〕올리다; 잡아채다. ¶ *~ up one's skirts in a hand* 한 손으로 치맛자락을 걷어 올리다. **b**) 《*with*》 come up to; overtake. 따라붙다. ¶ *~ someone up in walking* 보행에서 아무를 따라잡다 / *She ran and caught up with him.* 그녀는 달려가서 그를 따라붙었다. **c**) check (a speech, etc.) by an interruption; point out an error, etc. to (someone). (이야기 따위를) 방해하다; (아무에게) 잘못〔거

짓 등]을 지적하다. **d**) 《usu. in *passive*》 become involved or entangled. 말려[끌려]들다. ¶ *~ up someone in an evil scheme* 아무를 음모에 끌어들이다 / *be caught up by flattery* 아첨에 말려들다 / *He was caught up by the life of the city.* 그는 도시 생활에 빠져들었다 / *His clothing was caught up in the machine.* 그의 옷이 기계에 말려 들어갔다.
— *n.* Ⓒ **1** the act of catching. 잡음; 붙듦. ¶ *make a good ~ with one hand* 한 손으로 잘 잡다[받다]. **2** what is caught, as a quantity of fish. 포획량; 어획고. ¶ *make a good ~ of fish* 어획량이 많다 / *The fisherman brought home a large ~.* 어부는 많이 잡아 가지고 돌아왔다. **3** 《*colloq.*》 a person or thing that is worth getting. 붙들 만한 가치 있는 사람[것]; 좋은 결혼 상대; 횡재물. ¶ *a matrimonial ~* 결혼 상대로서 안성맞춤인 사람 / *It's not much of a ~.* 그건 대수로운 게 못 된다 / *Most of the girls think Tommy is quite a ~.* 대부분의 처녀들은 토미를 훌륭한 결혼 상대감으로 여기고 있다. **4** something intended to trick; a cunning question. 올가미; 함정; 책략. ¶ *This question has a ~ in it.* 이 문제에는 함정이 있다. **5** 《mus.》 a song for a number of voices starting one after another. 윤창(輪唱). **6** a game of throwing and catching a ball. 공받기 놀이; 캐치볼. ¶ *play ~* 캐치볼을 하다. **7** something that catches or fastens; a fastening. 움직이지 못하게 하는[잠그는] 것; 걸쇠; 고리; 멈추개. ¶ *the ~ of a window* 창문의 잠그개 / *fix the ~ on the wicket* 쪽문에 문고리를 달다. **8** sudden stoppage of the breath or voice. (숨·음성의) 일시적 멈춤; 막힘; 끊김. [L. *capio* take]

by catches, now and then. 때때로; 이따금.
no catch, 《*colloq.*》 a bad bargain. 비싸게[속아] 산 물건.

catch·er [kǽtʃər] *n.* Ⓒ **1** a person or thing that catches. 잡는 사람[물건]. **2** 《baseball》 the player behind the batter and home base to catch the pitched ball. 포수; 캐처(cf. *pitcher*[2]).

catch·ing [kǽtʃiŋ] *adj.* **1** liable to spread from one to another. 전염성의. ¶ *a ~ disease* 전염병 / *This illness is very ~.* 이 병은 전염이 매우 빠르다. **2** attractive. 매혹적인; 매력적인. ¶ *a ~ personality* 매력적인 인품 / *She sang with a very ~ air.* 그녀는 아주 매력적으로 노래했다.

catch·pen·ny [kǽtʃpèni] *adj.* of no real value. 겉만 번드레한; 싸구려의. — *n.* Ⓒ a worthless thing made only to sell. 겉만 번드레한 싸구려 물건.

catch·up [kǽtʃəp, kétʃ-] *n.* =ketchup.

catch·word [kǽtʃwə̀ːrd] *n.* Ⓒ **1** a slogan. 슬로건; 표어. **2** a word printed at the top of a page in a dictionary. (사전 따위의) 난외 표제어. **3** an actor's cue. 상대 배우가 다음 대사를 잇도록 넘겨 보내는 말.

catch·y [kǽtʃi] *adj.* (**catch·i·er, catch·i·est**) **1** attractive; easily remembered. 매력적인; (재미 있어) 외기 쉬운. ¶ *a ~ tune* 외우기 쉬운 곡. **2** tricky; puzzling; deceptive. 걸려들기 쉬운; 함정이 있는. ¶ *a ~ question in an examination* 함정이 있는 시험 문제.

cate [keit] *n.* 《usu. *pl.*》 《*arch.*》 dainty. 미미(美味); 진미(珍味). [L.]

cat·e·chise [kǽtəkàiz] *vt.* =catechize.

cat·e·chism [kǽtəkìzəm] *n.* Ⓒ **1** an elementary book used for teaching Christian doctrine. 교리 문답서. **2** a set of questions and answers about a subject, esp. religion. (교리) 문답집. **3** ⓊⒸ a series of questions. 일련의 질문. [Gk. *cata-* thoroughly, *ēkheō* sound]

put** someone **through a [*his*] ***catechism,*** question someone closely. 엄중히 추궁하다.

cat·e·chize [kǽtəkàiz] *vt.* (P6) **1** instruct by questions and answers. (교리)를 문답식으로 가르치다. **2** question searchingly or excessively. …을 심문하다; 따지다.

cat·e·gor·i·cal [kæ̀təgɔ́ːrikəl, -gɑ́r- / -gɔ́r-] *adj.* **1** of or in a category. 범주의; 범주에 속하는. **2** absolute; positive and definite. 절대적인; 명백한; 정언적인. ¶ *a ~ denial of an accusation* 죄상(罪狀)의 전면적 부인 / *reply in a ~ manner* 단호한 태도로 대답하다.
● **cat·e·gor·i·cal·ly** [-i] *adv.* [↓]

cat·e·go·ry [kǽtigɔ̀ːri / -gəri] *n.* Ⓒ (*pl.* **-ries**) **1** 《log.》 any of the basic concepts into which all knowledge can be classified. 범주. **2** a class; a division. 종류; 부류. ¶ *of a different* [*the same*] *~* 다른[같은] 부류의 / *These are classified under* [*into*] *two categories.* 이것들은 두 부류로 분류된다. [Gk. *agoreuō* speak]

ca·te·na [kətíːnə] *n.* (*pl.* **-nae**) connected series. 연속. [L. =chain]

ca·te·nae [kətíːniː] *n.* pl. of **catena.**

ca·te·nar·y [kǽtənèri / kətíːnəri] *n.* (*pl.* **-naries**) 《math.》 a curve formed by a chain hanging from two fixed points. 현수선(懸垂線).

cat·e·nate [kǽtənèit] *vt.* (P6) connect in a series. 연쇄(連鎖)하다.

ca·ter [kéitər] *vi.* (P3) **1** 《*for*》 provide food, supplies, etc. 음식 따위를 제공하다. ¶ *the catering trade* 식당업. **2** 《*for, to*》 provide means of pleasure; satisfy a need or taste. 즐겁게 하다; 요구를[취향을] 만족시키다. ¶ *~ to* [*for*] *artistic taste* 예술적인 취향을 충족시키다. [→cate]

cat·er·an [kéitərən] *n.* a Scottish highland robber. 약탈자; 산적(山賊). [Gael.]

ca·ter·er [kéitərər] *n.* Ⓒ a person who caters. 요리[음식] 제공자. [*cater*]

·**cat·er·pil·lar** [kǽtərpìlər] *n.* Ⓒ **1** a worm with many legs which later changes into a butterfly or moth. 모충(毛蟲). **2** a kind of tractor. 무한궤도차. [L. *catta* cat, *pilus* hair]

cat·er·waul [kǽtərwɔ̀ːl] *vi.* (P1) cry

like a cat in mating season. (교미기의 고양이처럼) 울다; 울부짖다. —*n.* Ⓒ such a cry. 그런 울음 소리. [*cat*]

cat-eyed [kǽtàid] *adj.* able to see in the dark. 어둠 속에서도 볼 수 있는. [*cat*]

cat·fish [kǽtfìʃ] *n.* Ⓒ (*pl.* **-fish** or **-fish·es**) a scaleless fish having some fancied resemblance to a cat. 메기의 일종.

cat·gut [kǽtgʌ̀t] *n.* Ⓤ a strong string, used for musical instruments, etc. 장선(腸線).

ca·thar·ses [kəθɑ́ːrsiːz] *n.* pl. of **catharsis.**

ca·thar·sis [kəθɑ́ːrsis] *n.* (*pl.* **-ses**) ⓊⒸ **1** 《med.》 purging. 세정(洗淨); 배변(排便). **2** the purification of the emotions through art, esp. tragedy. (감정의) 배설; 배출; 카타르시스. [Gk. *katharos* clean, pure]

ca·thar·tic [kəθɑ́ːrtik] *n.* Ⓒ a strong medicine used for emptying out the bowels. 하제(下劑). —*adj.* emptying out the bowels; purgative. 하제의; 통변(通便)의.

Ca·thay [kæθéi, kə-] *n.* 《*poet., arch.*》 China. 중국. [L.]

:ca·the·dral [kəθíːdrəl] *n.* Ⓒ a large or important church presided over by a bishop. (bishop이 있는) 대성당. ¶ *a ~ town* 대성당이 있는 마을. [cata-, Gk. *hedra* seat]

Cath·e·rine [kǽθərin] *n.* a woman's name. 여자 이름. [→catharsis]

Catherine wheel [⌐-- ⌐] *n.* a rotating fire-work, 윤전(輪轉) 불꽃.

turn Catherine wheels, turn lateral somersault. 옆재주넘기를 하다.

cath·e·ter [kǽθitər] *n.* a slender metal or rubber tube to be inserted into a duct of the body. 카테터; 도뇨관(導尿管). [Gk. *kathetḗr* to send or let down]

cath·ode [kǽθoud] *n.* the negative pole. 음극(陰極)(opp. anode). [cata-, Gk. *hodos* way]

cathode ray [⌐- ⌐] *n.* the invisible stream of electrons from the cathode. 음극선.

:Cath·o·lic [kǽθəlik] *adj.* **1** of the Christian church led by the Pope; Roman Catholic. (교황이 이끄는) 기독교회의; 로마 카톨릭의. **2** of the orthodox Christian churches, different from Reformed or Protestant churches. 구교의. —*n.* Ⓒ a member of a Catholic church. 카톨릭교도; 구교도. [Gk. *holos* whole]

:cath·o·lic [kǽθəlik] *adj.* **1** including all; of interest or use to all people; general; universal. 모든 것을 포함한; (관심이나 용도가) 모두에게 관계 있는; 일반적인; 보편적인. ¶ *a ~ problem* 보편적인 문제. **2** broad in interests, sympathies, etc.; broad-minded. (관심·동정 따위가) 광범위한; 마음이 넓은. ¶ *be ~ in one's tastes* 취미가 다양하다.

Ca·thol·i·cism [kəθɑ́ləsìzəm / -θɔ́l-] *n.* Ⓤ the faith, doctrine, and system of the Roman Catholic Church. 카톨릭교의 신앙·교리·조직.

cath·o·lic·i·ty [kæ̀θəlísəti] *n.* Ⓤ the quality of being universal; the quality of having a wide mind. 보편성; 포용성; 마음의 넓음.

「Catherine 의 애칭.

Cath·y [kǽθi] *n.* a nickname for Catherine.

cat·i·on [kǽtàiən] *n.* positive ion. 양(陽)이온(opp. anion). [Gk. =going down]

cat·kin [kǽtkin] *n.* Ⓒ a kind of hanging flower, as of the willow. (버드나무 따위의) 유제(葇荑) 꽃차례.

cat·like [kǽtlàik] *adj.* like a cat; secret. 고양이 같은; 은밀한. [*cat*]

cat·mint [kǽtmìnt] *n.* 《bot.》 a fragrant plant related to mint. 개박하.

cat-nap [kǽtnæ̀p] *n.* a short, light sleep. 얕은 잠.

cat·nip [kǽtnìp] *n.* 《U.S.》 =catmint.

cat-o'-nine-tails [kæ̀tənáintèilz] *n.* Ⓒ (*pl.* **-tails**) a whip with nine tied cords fastened to a handle. 아홉 가닥으로 된 채찍; 구승편(九繩鞭). [*cat*]

cat's cradle [⌐ ⌐-] *n.* a framework made of string held between the fingers. 실뜨기.

Cats·kill Moun·tains [kǽtskil máuntənz] *n. pl.* a mountain range in southeastern New York. 캐츠킬 산맥《뉴욕 주 남동부의》.

cat's-meat [kǽtsmìːt] *n.* Ⓤ meat for a cat; poor meat. 고양이 먹이; 맛없는 고기. [*cat*]

cat's-paw, cats·paw [kǽtspɔ̀ː] *n.* Ⓒ a person used as a tool by another. 앞잡이; 끄나풀. ¶ *act as someone's ~* 아무의 앞잡이 노릇을 하다.

make a cat's-paw of, use (someone) as a tool. …을 앞잡이로 부리다.

cat·sup [kǽtsəp, kétʃəp] *n.* Ⓤ catchup; ketchup. 케첩. [*ketchup*]

:cat·tle [kǽtl] *n.* 《*collectively,* used as *pl.*》 **1** cows; bulls; oxen. 소; 축우(畜牛). ¶ *a herd of ~* 한 떼의 소 / *five head of ~* 소 다섯 마리 / *beef* 〔*dairy*〕 *~* 육우〔젖소〕/ *pasture ~* 소에게 풀을 뜯어 먹게 하다 / *rear ~* 소를 기르다. **2** domestic animals. 가축. **3** 《*contempt.*》 worthless people. 하찮은 인간들. [→capital]

cat·tle·man [kǽtlmən, kǽtlmæ̀n] *n.* (*pl.* **-men** [-mən]) a man who raises or takes care of cattle. 목축업자; 소치는 사람.

cat·ty [kǽti] *adj.* (**-ti·er, -ti·est**) **1** sly; cunning. 교활한; 음험한. **2** like a cat. 고양이 같은. [*cat*]

cat·walk [kǽtwɔ̀ːk] *n.* a narrow pathway on the sides of a bridge. (다리 양쪽의) 좁은 통로. [*cat*]

Cau·ca·sian [kɔːkéiʒən, -ʃən / -zjən] *adj.* **1** of the Caucasus or its inhabitants. 코카서스 지방〔사람〕의. **2** of the white race. 백인의. —*n.* Ⓒ **1** a native of the Caucasus. 코카서스 사람. **2** a white person. 백인. [Place]

Cau·ca·sus [kɔ́:kəsəs] *n.* a mountain range in southwestern Asia. 코카서스 산맥.

cau·cus [kɔ́:kəs] *n.* Ⓒ **1** a small body of leaders of a political party. 정당 간부. **2** 《U.S.》 a meeting of leaders of a political party. (정당의) 간부 회의. — *vi.* hold a caucus. 간부회를 열다. [U.S.]

cau·dal [kɔ́:dəl] *adj.* of or near the tail; like a tail. 꼬리(부근)의; 꼬리 같은. ¶ *a ~ fin* 꼬리지느러미. [L.]

:caught [kɔ:t] *v.* p. and pp. of **catch.**

caul [kɔ:l] *n.* 《anat.》 the membrane enveloping the fetus. (태아의 머리를 싸는) 대망막(大網膜). [F.]

caul·dron [kɔ́:ldrən] *n.* =caldron.

cau·li·flow·er [kɔ́:ləflàuər] *n.* ⒸⓊ a kind of cabbage having a head with large white flowers, used as a vegetable. 꽃양배추. [L. *caulis* stem]

caulk [kɔ:k] *vt.* =calk.

caus·al [kɔ́:zəl] *adj.* **1** of a cause; being a cause. 원인의; 원인이 되는. ¶ *a ~ force* 원인이 되는 힘. **2** expressing a cause or reason. 원인을[이유를] 나타내는. **3** having to do with cause and effect. 인과 관계의. ¶ *~ relation* 인과 관계. ●**caus·al·ly** [-i] *adv.* [L. *causa*]

cau·sal·i·ty [kɔ:zǽləti] *n.* Ⓤ the relation of cause and effect 인과 관계. ¶ *the law of ~* 인과율(律).

cau·sa·tion [kɔ:zéiʃən] *n.* Ⓤ **1** the relation of cause and effect. 인과 관계. **2** a cause. 원인. **3** producing an effect. 결과를 낳음.

caus·a·tive [kɔ́:zətiv] *adj.* **1** 《*of*》 acting as a cause; productive. 원인이 되는. ¶ *a ~ agency* 작인(作因) / *an event ~ of war* 전쟁을 일으키는 사건. **2** 《gram.》 expressing a cause. 사역(使役)의.

:cause [kɔ:z] *n.* **1** ⓊⒸ a person, thing, or event that makes a thing happen; that which produces an effect or result. 원인 (opp. effect). ¶ *the ~ of the fire* 화인(火因) / *~ and effect* 원인과 결과 / *the causes of war* 전쟁의 원인 / *What is the ~ of his death?* 그가 죽은 원인은 무엇인가. **2** Ⓤ reason; motive. 이유; 동기. ¶ *be dismissed for ~* 정당한 이유가 있어 면직되다 / *complain without ~* 이유 없이 불평하다 / *accuse someone without* (*just*) *~* (정당한) 이유 없이 아무를 비난하다 / *There is no ~ for anxiety.* 걱정할 필요가 없다 / *She had good ~ to do so.* 그녀가 그렇게 한 데에는 충분한 이유가 있었다. **3** Ⓒ an object for which a group of people start a movement or campaign. (사람·집단이 그것을 위해 헌신하는) 이상; 목적; 주의. ¶ *the Socialist ~* 사회주의의 신조 / *the ~ of better housing* 보다 나은 주택을 지향하는 목표 / *in the ~ of justice* 정의를 위하여 / *fight for the ~ of world peace* 세계 평화를 위해 싸우다 / *work in the ~ of science* 과학의 발전을 위해 일하다. **4** Ⓒ 《law》 a case to be decided by the court; a suit. 소송 (사건). **5** Ⓤ the side (in a struggle). …측; …쪽.

in a good cause, in order to do good. 좋은 일을 하기 위해.

make common cause with, work with (someone) for the same object; support. (동일 목적을 위해) …와 제휴하다; …와 일치 협력하다.

— *vt.* (P6,13,14,20) **1** be the cause of; bring about. …의 원인이 되다; …을 가져오다. ¶ *~ someone trouble* 아무에게 폐를 끼치다 / *~ great excitement* 굉장한 흥분을 가져오다 / *The fire caused much damage.* 화재는 큰 손해를 가져왔다 / *A fever caused her death.* 고열(高熱)이 그녀의 사인(死因)이었다. **2** get (someone or something) to do; compel to do. …하게 하다; …시키다. ¶ *The thought caused him to tremble.* 그 생각은 그를 오싹하게 했다 / *What caused the tire to puncture* [*go flat*]? 타이어가 무엇 때문에 펑크 났나 / *He caused a new house to be built.* 그는 새 집을 짓게 했다. [L. *causa*]

cause cé·lè·bre [kɔ́:z səlébrə] *n.* 《F.》 an exciting lawsuit. 유명한 재판 사건.

cause·less [kɔ́:zlis] *adj.* **1** having no apparent cause. 뚜렷한 이유 없는. **2** without proper reason. 까닭 없는. ¶ *~ anger* 까닭 없는 분노. **3** happening by chance. 우연의. [*cause*]

cau·se·rie [kòuzəríː] *n.* 《F.》 **1** an informal talk or discussion. 잡담; 한담. **2** a short written article. 짧은 글[수필]; 소품(小品). [L. *causa*]

cause·way [kɔ́:zwèi] *n.* Ⓒ **1** a raised road or path over wet ground, or shallow water, etc. (습지(濕地)나 얕은 물 등에 흙을 돋우어 만든) 두렁길; 둑길. **2** a paved road. 포장 도로. — *vt.* (P6) provide with a causeway. 둑길[두렁길]을 만들다. [→caulk]

cau·sey [kɔ́:zi] *n.* =causeway.

caus·tic [kɔ́:stik] *adj.* **1** having the power of burning or destroying flesh by chemical action. 부식성(腐蝕性)의. ¶ *~ soda* 가성소다. **2** 《*fig.*》 sharp; bitter; cutting. 신랄한; 통렬한. ¶ *a ~ tongue* 독설 / *a ~ remark* 신랄한 말. — *n.* Ⓒ a caustic substance. 부식제. ¶ *common ~* 가성(苛性) 칼리 / *lunar ~* 질산은(銀). [Gk. *kaustikós* capable of burning]

cau·ter·i·za·tion [kɔ̀:tərizéiʃən] *n.* = cautery.

cau·ter·ize [kɔ́:təràiz] *vt.* (P6) burn (a wound, etc.) with a hot iron or needle, or with a caustic substance. (불에 달군 바늘·부식제 따위로 상처)를 지지다; 뜸을 뜨다; 소작(燒灼)하다. ¶ *Doctors ~ snake bites to prevent the poison from spreading.* 의사들은 독이 퍼지는 것을 막기 위해 뱀에 물린 데를 소작한다. [Gk. *kautēriázein* to sear with a hot iron]

cau·ter·y [kɔ́:təri] *n.* **1** Ⓤ cauterizing. 소작(燒灼)하기; 뜸질. **2** Ⓒ a hot iron for surgical searing. 소작 인두. [Gk. *kaiō* burn]

***cau·tion** [kɔ́:ʃən] *n.* **1** Ⓤ care taken to avoid danger or error; careful attention. 주의; 조심. ¶ *take ~ against accidents* 사고가 나지 않도록 조심하다 / *for caution's sake* 경고〔주의〕를 주기 위해; 좀더 확실히 하기 위하여 / *use* 〔*exercise*〕 *~ in acting* 〔*speaking*〕 행동〔말〕에 조심하다. **2** Ⓒ a warning against danger, harm, etc. 경고. ¶ *a word of ~* 경고의 말 / *give someone a ~* 아무에게 경고를 주다 / *inflict a punishment as a ~ to others* 다른 사람들에게 본때를 보이기 위해 벌을 과하다. **3** Ⓒ 《*colloq.*》 an ugly person; a staggering sight. 못생긴 사람; 깜짝 놀랄 사람〔것〕; 주의 인물.
by way of caution, as a warning. 경고로서.
with caution, carefully. 조심하여; 신중히.
— *vt.* (P6,13,15,20) 《*against, not to do*》 give a caution to (someone); warn; advise. …을 조심시키다; 경고하다. ¶ *~ someone against* 아무에게 …을 조심하라고 하다〔…하지 않도록 경고하다〕 / *~ children not to wake the baby up* 아이들에게 아기를 깨우지 말도록 주의를 주다 / *He cautioned me not to be late again.* 그는 내게 다시 늦지 말도록 경고했다. [L. *caveo* take heed]

cau·tion·ar·y [kɔ́:ʃənèri / -əri] *adj.* warning; urging caution. 경고〔경계〕의; 주의〔조심〕하는. ¶ *~ words* 경고의 말.

***cau·tious** [kɔ́:ʃəs] *adj.* very careful; afraid of making mistakes. 신중한; 조심스러운; 소심한(opp. careless). ¶ *a ~ driver* 조심성 있는 운전사 / *in a ~ manner* 조심스럽게; 신중하게 / *be ~ in one's movements* 행동에 조심스럽다 / *be ~ of one's tongue* 말을 삼가다 / *be ~ not to do* …하지 않도록 조심하다.
● **cau·tious·ness** [-nis] *n.*

***cau·tious·ly** [kɔ́:ʃəsli] *adv.* very carefully. 조심스럽게; 신중히.

cav·al·cade [kæ̀vəlkéid] *n.* Ⓒ **1** a long line of moving people riding on horses or in carriages. 기마〔마차〕 행렬. **2** a line of people or things. 행렬; 행진. [L. *caballus* horse]

cav·a·lier [kæ̀vəlíər] *n.* Ⓒ **1** 《hist.》 a knight; a soldier on a horse. 기사; 기마 무사. **2** a brave and polite gentleman; an escort for a lady. 예의 바른 신사; 여성을 호위하는 사람. — *adj.* **1** very proud; haughty; full of contempt. 오만한. ¶ *a ~ refusal* 무례한 거절. **2** free and easy; careless. 스스럼없는; 소탈한. [↑]

***cav·al·ry** [kǽvəlri] *n.* Ⓒ (*pl.* **-ries**) **1** 《*collectively,* usu. used as *pl.*》 soldiers on horses. 기병대. **2** a branch of the armed forces equipped with horses or, now, armed motor vehicles. 기갑 부대(cf. *infantry*). [↑]

cav·al·ry·man [kǽvəlrimən] *n.* Ⓒ (*pl.* **-men** [-mən]) a member of a force of soldiers on horses. 기병(騎兵).

:cave [keiv] *n.* Ⓒ a large hole under the ground or in a cliff. 굴; 동굴. — *vt., vi.* (P6;2) 《*in*》 《*colloq.*》 **1** hollow out. 파다; 후벼〔도려〕내다. **2** (cause to) fall in or sink down; collapse. 내려앉(게 하)다; 무너지(게 하)다. **3** (cause to) yield or give in. 굴복하(게 하)다; 손들(게 하)다. [L. *cavus* hollow]
cave in, fall in; collapse; smash in. 내려앉다; 함몰하다; 무너지다; 굴하다. ¶ *The ground* 〔*roof*〕 *suddenly caved in.* 땅〔지붕〕이 갑자기 내려앉았다.

cave dweller [⌐ ⌐—] *n.* **1** a cave man. 혈거인(穴居人). **2** 《*colloq.*》 one that lives in a city apartment building. 도시 아파트 거주자.

cave man [⌐ ⌐] *n.* **1** a human being who lived in a cave before history began. (유사 이전의) 혈거인. **2** 《*colloq.*》 a rude 〔rough, violent〕 man. 난폭한 사람.

***cav·ern** [kǽvərn] *n.* Ⓒ a large cave. 굴; 동굴. [→cave]

cav·ern·ous [kǽvərnəs] *adj.* **1** like a large cave; hollow; deep. 동굴 같은; 우묵한. ¶ *~ cheeks* 푹 꺼진 볼〔뺨〕. **2** full of caverns or holes. 굴이 많은; 구멍투성이의.

cav·i·ar, -are [kǽviɑ̀:r, ⌐—⌐] *n.* Ⓤ the salted eggs of sturgeon or a large fish. 캐비아《철갑상어 따위의 알젓》. [It.]
caviar to the general, something too good or delicate to be appreciated by common peopel. 보통 사람은 그 가치를 알아보지 못하는 일품(逸品)《돼지에 진주》. [It.]

cav·il [kǽvəl] *vi.* (P1,3) (**-iled, -il·ing** or 《Brit.》 **-illed, -il·ling**) 《*at, about*》 find fault unnecessarily; blame. 흠〔트집〕잡다; 비난하다. ¶ *~ at the terms of a contract* 계약 조건에 트집을 잡다 / *~ at someone's fault* 아무의 잘못을 트집잡다 / *~ about everything* 무엇에나 흠을 잡다. — *n.* Ⓒ a small objection. 하찮은 이의(異議); 흠잡기. [L.]

***cav·i·ty** [kǽvəti] *n.* Ⓒ (*pl.* **-ties**) a hole; a hollow place. 구멍; 강(腔); 우묵한 곳. ¶ *a ~ in a tooth* 충치 구멍 / *the mouth* 〔*oral*〕 *~* 구강 / *the abdominal ~* 복강. [→cave]

ca·vort [kəvɔ́:rt] *vi.* (P1) 《U.S. *colloq.*》 (usu. of a horse) jump around. (말이) 날뛰다; 껑충거리다. ¶ *~ for joy* 좋아 날뛰다. [U.S.]

ca·vy [kéivi] *n.* 《zool.》 any of a family of short-tailed South American rodents, as the guinea pig. 기니피그; 모르모트《남아메리카산》.

caw [kɔ:] *n.* Ⓒ the cry of a crow. 까마귀 우는 소리; 까악까악. — *vi.* (P1) make this cry or similar sound. 까악까악거리다. [Imit.]

cay·enne [kaién, keién] *n.* Ⓤ very hot-tasting red powder made from a pepperplant. 고춧가루 (=cayenne pepper). [Braz.]

cc, cc., c.c. cubic centimeter(s). (입방 센

티미터).

cc. chapters.

c.c. carbon copy; cashier's check; city council; county clerk.

•**cease** [si:s] *vi.* (P1,3) 《*from*》 come to an end; stop. 그치다; 끝나다. ¶ ~ *from strife* 싸움을 그치다 / *The rain has ceased.* 비가 그쳤다. — *vt.* (P6,8,9) put an end to (one's action); leave off. …을 끝내다; 그만두다; 중지하다. ¶ ~ *work* 〔*talking*〕 일을〔이야기를〕 그만두다 / ~ *searching* 〔*to search*〕 찾기를 그만두다 / ~ *payment* 지불을 정지하다 / *Cease fire!* 사격 중지 / *They ceased to be boys long ago.* 그들은 벌써부터 어린애가 아니었다. — *n.* end; stopping. 끝; 종지(終止). ¶ *without* ~ 끊임없이. [L. *cesso*]

cease·fire [sí:sfáiər] *n.* Ⓒ a stop of fighting for a time. 휴전. ¶ *a* ~ *agreement* 휴전 협정.

:**cease·less** [sí:slis] *adj.* never ending; going on without a stop. 끊임없는. ¶ *a* ~ *stream of talk* 〔*cars*〕 그칠 줄 모르는 이야기〔차량의 물결〕.

cease·less·ly [sí:slisli] *adv.* endlessly; constantly; without stopping. 끊임없이.

ce·ca [sí:kə] *n.* pl. of **cecum.**

Cec·il [sí:səl, sésəl] *n.* a man's name. 남자 이름.

ce·cum [sí:kəm] *n.* (*pl.* **-ca**) 《anat.》 the blind gut. 맹장(盲腸). ● **ce·cal** [sí:kəl] *adj.* [L. *caecus* blind]

CED Committee for Economic Development.

•**ce·dar** [sí:dər] *n.* **1** Ⓒ a cone-bearng tree. 히말라야 삼목. **2** Ⓤ the wood of this tree. 그 재목. [Gk.]

cede [si:d] *vt.* (P6,13) **1** 《*to*》 give up; yield; hand over to another. (권리·영토 따위)를 양도〔할양〕하다 (opp. keep). ¶ *a province ceded by one country to another* 다른 나라에 할양된 지방. **2** give way to force; surrender. …에 양보〔허용〕하다. ¶ ~ *a point in debate* 토론에서 어떤 점을 양보하다. [L. cedo retreat]

ce·dil·la [sidílə] *n.* Ⓒ a mark (Ç) placed under *c* as a sign that it is sounded as [s]. ç처럼 c자 아래에 붙는 부호《[s]로 발음됨을 나타냄》. [Gk.]

cee [si:] *n.* C. c자. [C]

Cee spring [⌒⌒] C-shaped spring. C자형 용수철.

ceil [si:l] *vt.* (P6) put a ceiling in; provide with a ceiling. …에 천장판(板)을 대다. [L. *caelum* sky]

:**ceil·ing** [sí:liŋ] *n.* Ⓒ **1** the inside top roof of a room, opposite to the floor. 천장(판). **2** 《U.S.》 a top limit set for prices, wages, etc. (가격·임금 등의) 최고 한도; 상한(上限). ¶ *set* 〔*put*〕 *a* ~ *on* …의 최고 한계를 정하다. **3** 《aeron.》 the highest place to which an airplane or airship can rise under certain conditions. 상승 한도. [↑]

cel·an·dine [séləndàin] *n.* Ⓒ 《bot.》 a kind of yellow spring field flower. 애기똥풀. [Gk.=swallow flower]

Cel·a·nese [sélənì:z, ⌒⌒⌒] *n.* an acetate rayon material. 아세테이트《상표명》. [*cellulose, acetate, -(n)ese*]

Cel·e·bes [séləbì:z, səlí:biz] *n.* an island of Indonesia, in the Malay Archipelago. 셀레베스 섬《말레이 제도에 있는 섬》.

cel·e·brant [séləbrənt] *n.* the priest who celebrates. 의식을 행하는 성직자. [↓]

:**cel·e·brate** [séləbrèit] *vt., vi.* (P6;1) **1** perform a religious ceremony. (종교적) 의식·제전을 행하다. ¶ ~ *Christmas* 성탄절 행사를 하다 / *The priest celebrates Mass.* 신부가 미사를 집전하다. **2** perform a ceremony in honor of (an occasion, event, etc.); commemorate; rejoice. (식을 올려 특정의 날·일)을 축하하다. ¶ ~ *a victory* 승리를 축하하다 / ~ *a wedding* 〔*birthday*〕 결혼〔생일〕을 축하하다. **3** praise and honor in public. 찬양하다; 기리다. ¶ ~ *a brave soldier in a song* 노래로 용사를 기리다. **4** 《*colloq.*》 have a merry time. 즐겁게 놀다; 들떠 법석을 떨다. [L. *celeber* frequented]

•**cel·e·brat·ed** [séləbrèitid] *adj.* 《*for*》 famous; well-known. 유명한; 세상에 알려진. ¶ *a* ~ *painter* 이름난 화가 / *a scientist* ~ *for his discovery* 그 발견으로 유명해진 과학자.

•**cel·e·bra·tion** [sèləbréiʃən] *n.* ⒸⓊ the act of showing that an event or time is important. 축하(회); 축전(祝典). ¶ *hold a* ~ 축하회를 열다.

in celebration of, in honor of (an event). …을 축하〔기념〕하여.

cel·e·bra·tor [séləbrèitər] *n.* one who celebrates. 축하하는 사람.

ce·leb·ri·ty [səlébrəti] *n.* (*pl.* **-ties**) **1** Ⓤ the state of being talked about or praised; fame. 명성. ¶ *an actor of* ~ 고명한〔명성이 자자한〕 배우 / *works of worldwide* ~ 세계적으로 알려진 명작 / *gain* 〔*attain*〕 ~ 유명해지다 / *jump into* ~ 일약 유명해지다. **2** Ⓒ a famous person. 저명 인사; 유명인.

ce·ler·i·ty [səlérəti] *n.* Ⓤ the quality of being quick; speed. 민첩; 신속. ¶ *act with* ~ 날쌔게 행동하다. [L. *celer* swift]

cel·er·y [séləri] *n.* Ⓤ 《bot.》 a vegetable, used raw for salads. 셀러리. [Gk. *selinon* parsley]

ce·les·tial [səléstʃəl] *adj.* **1** of the heavens; of the sky. 하늘의; 천국의 (opp. terrestrial). ¶ *a* ~ *body* 천체 / ~ *abodes* 천상계(天上界). **2** of or coming from heaven; very beautiful. 거룩한; 이 세상의 것이라고는할 수 없을 만큼 아름다운. ¶ *a* ~ *music* 이 세상 것이라고 여겨지지 않을 만큼 아름다운 음악; 천상의 음악. **3** like the color of the sky. 하늘빛의. ¶ ~ *blue* 하늘색. **4** 《*C-*》 of the former Chinese Empire. 옛 중국의. — *n.* **1** an inhabitant of Heaven. 천인(天人). **2** 《*C-*》 a Chinese. 중국인. ● **ce·les·tial·ly** [-i] *adv.* [L. *caelum* sky]

Celestial Empire [–´– ´–], **the** *n.* China. 중국.
cel·i·ba·cy [séləbəsi] *n.* Ⓤ the unmarried state. 독신 (생활). [L. *caelebs* unmarried]
cel·i·bate [séləbit, -bèit] *n.* a person who does not get married. 독신자. — *adj.* unmarried. 독신의. [↑]
:cell [sel] *n.* Ⓒ **1** a small room in a large building, such as a prison, etc.; a small hut. (수도원의) 독실(獨室); (교도소의) 독방; 암자의 방. ¶ *put someone in a* ~ 아무를 독방에 넣다. **2** a very small hollow, as of a nest of a bee. (벌집 따위의) 구멍. **3** 《electr.》 a box containing materials for producing electricity. 전지(電池). **4** 《biol.》 a very small unit of living things. 세포. ¶ ~ *nucleus* 세포핵(核) / *a reproduction* ~ 생식세포 / *the cells of the brain* 뇌(腦)세포. **5** a small political group. (정당 조직의) 세포. ¶ *a local* ~ *of the Communist party* 공산당의 지역 세포. [L. *cella* small room]
:cel·lar [sélər] *n.* Ⓒ **1** a room under the ground of a building. 지하 저장실; 지하실. ¶ *a coal-cellar* 지하 저탄실 / *keep canned food in the* ~ 통조림 식품을 지하실에 저장하다. **2** a room for storing wines; a stock of wines. 포도주 저장실; 저장된 포도주. ¶ *keep a good* ~ 많은 포도주를 저장하고 있다. — *vt.* (P6) store in a cellar. …을 지하실에 저장하다. [↑]
cel·lar·age [séləridʒ] *n.* cellar accommodation. 지하(저장)실; 땅광.
cel·lar·et [sèlərét] *n.* a cupboard for wine bottle. 포도주병〔술병〕 선반.
cel·list, 'cel·list [tʃélist] *n.* Ⓒ a person who plays the cello. 첼로 연주자. [*cello, -ist*]
cel·lo, 'cel·lo [tʃélou] *n.* Ⓒ (*pl.* **-los**) a musical instrument like a violin, but larger and deeper in tone. 첼로. 參考 violoncello 의 준말. [*violoncello*]
cel·lo·phane [séləfèin] *n.* Ⓤ a clear, paper-like material, used to wrap food, tobacco, etc. 셀로판(지). ¶ *wrapped in* ~ 접근하기 어려운; 도도한. [Gk. *phainō* show]
cel·lu·lar [séljələr] *adj.* of or like a cell. 세포(모양)의. ¶ *a* ~ *phone* 〔*telephone*〕 (셀 방식) 무선 전화(기). [→cell]
cel·lule [sélju:l] *n.* Ⓒ a very small cell. 작은 세포. [↑]
cel·lu·loid [séljəlɔ̀id] *n.* Ⓤ a material which looks like glass, but that can be bent and that burns easily. 셀룰로이드. [→cell, -oid]
cel·lu·lose [séljəlòus] *n.* Ⓤ the substance forming the chief part of all plants and trees. 셀룰로오스; 섬유소(素). [↑]
Cel·si·us [sélsiəs, -ʃəs] *n.* centigrade. 섭씨. [Person]
Celt [selt, kelt] *n.* a member of peoples including the Irish, Welsh, Highland Scots, etc. 켈트인(人). [L. *Celta*]
Celt·ic [séltik, kél-] *adj.* of the Celts or their languages. 켈트인〔어(語)〕의. — *n.* **1** the group of languages spoken by the Celts. 켈트어. **2** a person speaking the Celtic language. 켈트인.
·ce·ment [simént] *n.* Ⓤ **1** a gray powder used for joining bricks, making concrete, etc. 시멘트. **2** anything used to bind or unite things together. 접합〔접착〕제. **3** something which holds firm. (우정·애정을) 이어주는 것; 유대. — *vt., vi.* (P6;1) **1** join with cement. 시멘트로 접합하다〔를 바르다〕. **2** 《*fig.*》 unite closely; make solid. 결합하다; (우정·애정 따위를) 굳히다. ¶ ~ *a friendship* 우정을 공고히 하다. [L. *caedo* cut (stone-chips)]
·cem·e·ter·y [sémətèri / -tri] *n.* Ⓒ (*pl.* **-ter·ies**) a place for burying the dead that is not next to a church. (교회에 부속되지 않은) 묘지; 공동 묘지(cf. *churchyard*). ¶ *He sleeps* 〔*is buried*〕 *in the* ~. 그는 묘지에 잠들어〔묻혀〕 있다. [Gk. *koimaō* put to sleep]
cen. central; century.
cen·o·bite [sí:nəbàit, sénə-] *n.* a member of a religious convent. 수도사; 수사(修士). [L.]
cen·o·taph [sénətæ̀f, -tɑ̀:f] *n.* Ⓒ **1** a monument built in memory of a dead person whose body is buried somewhere else. 기념 묘비. **2** 《*the C-*》 the monument in Whitehall, London, in honor of those who fell in the World Wars. (런던의) 무명 전사의 묘. [Gk. *kenos* empty, *taphos* tomb]
Ce·no·zo·ic [sì:nəzóuik, sènə-] *adj.* of the latest era of geologic time. 신생대(新生代)의. [Gk.]
cense [sens] *vt.* (P6) perfume with incense. …에 향을 피우다. [→incense]
cen·ser [sénsər] *n.* Ⓒ a hanging pot in which sweet-smelling powder is burned. 향로(香爐)《끈으로 매닮》. [↑]
cen·sor [sénsər] *n.* Ⓒ **1** a person who examines books, news reports, movies, etc. to remove or prohibit anything considered unsuitable. (출판물·영화 등의) 검열관. ¶ *a film* ~ 영화 검열관 / *pass the* ~ 검열을 통과하다. **2** a Roman officer who controlled the manners or morals of citizens. (옛 로마의) 검찰관. **3** a person who tells others how they ought to behave. 풍기 단속자. **4** an official in some English universities and colleges. (영국 대학의) 학(생)감. **5** a person who finds fault. 남의 흠을 〔탈을〕 잘 잡는 사람. — *vt.* (P6) examine (letters, books, etc.) …을 검열하다.
● **cen·so·ri·al** [sensɔ́:riəl] *adj.* [L. *censeo* rate]
cen·so·ri·ous [sensɔ́:riəs] *adj.* severely critical; fond of finding fault. 비평적인; 몹시 까다로운; 탈〔흠〕잡기 좋아하는.

cen·sor·ship [sénsərʃip] *n.* Ⓤ **1** the act or system of censoring. 검열(제도). ¶ *pass the* ~ 검열을 통과하다. **2** the work or position of a censor. 검열관의 직무〔지위〕.

cen·sur·a·ble [sénʃərəbəl] *adj.* deserving censure; to be blamed. 비난해야 할; 비난을 면할 길 없는. [↓]

cen·sure [sénʃər] *n.* ⓊⒸ an expression of disapproval; blame; severe judgment. 불신임; 비난; 혹평. ¶ *a vote of* ~ 불신임 투표〔결의〕/ *deserve* ~ 비난받아 마땅하다 / *receive public* ~ 일반의 비난을 받다.
— *vt.* (P6,13) 《*for*》 blame; find fault with. …을 비난〔비판〕하다; …의 흠〔탈〕을 잡다; …을 혹평하다. ¶ *His conduct was severely censured.* 그의 행동은 호되게 비난받았다. [L. *cēnsūra* judgment]

cen·sus [sénsəs] *n.* Ⓒ an official count of the population of a country, etc. 국세(國勢)〔인구〕 조사. ¶ *take a* ~ *of unemployment* 실업 조사를 하다 / *make a* ~ *of the population* 인구 조사를 하다. [L. *censeo* rate]

:cent [sent] *n.* **1** Ⓒ the unit of money equal to $^1/_{100}$ of a dollar, in the United States, Canada, etc.; a coin of this value. 센트; 1센트 동전. ¶ *pay six dollars and fifty cents for books* 책값으로 6달러 50센트를 지불하다. **2** Ⓤ a hundred. (단위로서의) 100. [L. *centum* 100]
cent per cent, 100 per cent. 100 퍼센트.
per cent, in every hundred. 100에 대하여; 퍼센트(%).

cent. centigrade; centimeter; central; century.

cen·taur [séntɔːr] *n.* Ⓒ **1** 《Gk. myth.》 an animal having the head, breast, and arms of man, and the body and legs of a horse. 켄타우로스《반인 반마(半人半馬)의 괴물》. **2** a perfect horseman. 명기수(名騎手). [Gk.]

cen·te·nar·i·an [sèntənέəriən] *n.* Ⓒ a person who is at least 100 years old. 백 살(이상)의 사람. — *adj.* of 100 years. 백 살의. [↓]

cen·te·nar·y [séntənèri, senténəri / sentíːnəri] *n.* Ⓒ (*pl.* **-nar·ies**) **1** a period of 100 years; a century. 백년(간); 1세기. **2** a 100th return of a certain date. 백주년 기념제. — *adj.* of a centenary. 백년(째)의; 백주년 기념제의. [L. *centeni* set of 100]

cen·ten·ni·al [senténiəl] *adj.* **1** of 100 years. 백년의. **2** of the 100th return of a certain date. 백년제(祭)〔째〕의. — *n.* Ⓒ a 100th return of a certain date. 백주년 기념제. [↑]

:cen·ter, 《Brit.》 **-tre** [séntər] *n.* Ⓒ **1** 《usu. *the* ~》 ⓐ 《geom.》 the middle point; the point equally distant from all points on a circle or sphere. 중점; 중심. ¶ *the* ~ *of a circle* 〔*sphere*〕 원〔구(球)〕의 중심. ⓑ the middle point, part, or place of anything. …의 중앙; 가운데. ¶ *the* ~ *of the city* 시(市)의 한복판 / 《phys.》 *the* ~ *of gravity* 중심(重心) / *sit in the* ~ *of the room* 방 한가운데에 앉다. **2** an important point, object, or place about which things gather or to which they come. 중심지; 주요부; 중심〔종합〕 시설. ¶ *a* ~ *of trade* 무역의 중심(지) / *a* ~ *of government* 정부의 중심지 / *an amusement* ~ 오락가(街) / *a tourist* ~ 행락지; 관광지 / *a medical* 〔*shopping*〕 ~ 의료〔쇼핑〕 센터. **3** a person, thing, or group in the middle. 중간의 사람〔것; 그룹〕. ⓐ 《sports》 a player who takes the middle position in various games. (축구·농구 등의) 센터. ⓑ 《mil.》 a body of soldiers placed in the middle of a battle line. (군대의) 중앙 부대; 본대(本隊). ⓒ 《*the C-*》 《polit.》 the party between the right and the left. 중간〔중도〕파. **4** a person or thing that attracts attention and interest. (인기·흥미를 끄는) 사람〔것〕; 핵심; 중심 인물. ¶ *the* ~ *of attraction* 인기의 대상 / *He is the* ~ *of the plot.* 그는 음모의 중심 인물이다.
— *vt.* (P6,13) **1** place (something) in or on a center. …을 중심〔중앙〕에 두다. ¶ *She centered the clock on the desk.* 그녀는 탁상시계를 탁자 한가운데에 놓았다. **2** collect (things) to or around a center. …을 중심에 모으다; 집중시키다. ¶ ~ *one's affections on* 〔*in*〕 *someone* 아무에게 애정을 쏟다 / ~ *one's hopes on him* 그에게 희망을 걸다 / *All eyes were centered on her.* 모든 시선이 그녀에게 쏠렸다.
— *vi.* (P3) 《*on, around, in*》 be in or at the center; gather or come, as toward a center. 중심에 있다〔모이다〕; 집중되다. ¶ *The interest centers on* 〔*around*〕 *this question.* 관심은 이 문제에 쏠려 있다 / *Our thoughts* ~ *upon one idea.* 우리들의 생각은 하나의 개념에 집중된다 / *The story centers on his adventure.* 이야기는 그의 모험을 중심으로 전개된다. [Gk. *kéntron* point, center of a circle]

cen·ter·piece [séntərpìːs] *n.* Ⓒ a beautiful piece of silver, glass, lace, etc. put in the center of a table. 식탁 중앙의 장식물; 센터피스.

cen·tes·i·mal [sentésəməl] *adj.* reckoned by hundreds. 백진(百進)법의. [→cent]

cen·ti- [séntə-] *pref.* a word element meaning 100 or a 100th part. '100, $^1/_{100}$'의 뜻. [L. *centum* hundred]

cen·ti·are [séntiὲər, -àːr] *n.* Ⓒ one square meter. 1 평방미터.

cen·ti·grade [séntəgrèid] *adj.* **1** divided into 100 degrees. 100분도(分度)의 (cf. *Fahrenheit*). ¶ *the* ~ *thermometer* 100분도〔섭씨〕 온도계. **2** of a centigrade thermometer. 섭씨의. 參考 C., c., cent. 로 생략함. [→cent(i)-]

cen·ti·gram, 《Brit.》 **-gramme** [séntəgræ̀m] *n.* Ⓒ a 100th part of a gram. 센티그

램; 1/100 그램. 參考 cg. 로 생략함.

cen·ti·li·ter, 《Brit.》 **-tre** [séntəlìːtər] *n.* 1/100 of a liter. 1/100 리터.

cen·time [sɑ́ːntiːm] *n.* 《F.》 the unit of money equal to 1/100 of a franc in France, Belgium, etc. 상팀《1/100 프랑》.

cen·ti·me·ter, 《Brit.》 **-tre** [séntəmìːtər] *n.* Ⓒ a 100th part of a meter. 센티미터. 參考 cm, cm.으로 생략함.

cen·ti·pede [séntəpìːd] *n.* Ⓒ 《zool.》 a small animal like a worm, with many pairs of legs. 지네. [→cent, pedal]

cen·to [séntou] *n.* (*pl.* **-tos**) a literary work pieced together from the works of several authors. 그러모은 시문(詩文); 남의 작품에서 따모은 저작. [L.]

:cen·tral [séntrəl] *adj.* **1** of the center. 중심의; 중앙의. ¶ *the* ~ *office* 본부; 본국 / *the Central Post Office* 중앙 우체국 / *a* ~ *point* 〔*district*〕 중심점〔지구〕 / *the* ~ *block of the city* 그 도시의 중심 가구(街區) / *Our district is very* ~. 우리 지역은 바로 중앙이다. **2** principal; chief; leading. 주요한. ¶ *the* ~ *figure in a drama* 극의 중심 인물 / *the* ~ *thought* 중심 사상. — *n.* Ⓒ 《often *C-*》 《U.S.》 a telephone exchange. 전화(교환)국. ¶ *get* ~ 교환국을 불러내다. ● **cen·tral·i·ty** [sentrǽləti] *n.* [→center]

Central America [⌐— —⌐—] *n.* the part of North America between Mexico and South America. 중앙 아메리카.

central heating [⌐— ⌐—] *n.* a system used for heating all parts of a building by carrying hot steam, water, or air from a central place. 중앙 난방식.

cen·tral·ism [séntrəlìzəm] *n.* Ⓤ a system of bringing power or authority under the central government. 중앙 집권제〔주의〕.

cen·tral·i·za·tion [sèntrəlizéiʃən] *n.* Ⓤ **1** the act of bringing things to a center. 집중. **2** the act of bringing power or authority to the central government. 중앙 집권화.

cen·tral·ize [séntrəlàiz] *vt.* (P6) **1** bring (things) to a center; gather together. …을 집중시키다. **2** bring (things) under one control. …을 중앙 집권으로 하다. ¶ ~ *a government* 정부를 중앙 집권화하다.

cen·tral·ized [séntrəlàizd] *adj.* brought to a center or under one control. 집중〔중앙 집권〕의.

cen·tral·ly [séntrəli] *adv.* at or near the center. 중심에; 중앙에.

:cen·tre [séntər] *n., v.* 《Brit.》 =center.

cen·tre·piece [séntərpìːs] *n.* 《Brit.》 = centerpiece.

cen·tric [séntrik], **-tri·cal** [-əl] *adj.* central. 중심〔중앙〕의.

cen·tric·i·ty [sentrísəti] *n.* Ⓤ relation to the center. 중심성; 중심에 있음.

cen·trif·u·gal [sentrífjəgəl] *adj.* **1** having a tendency away from the center. 중심에서 떨어지려는; 원심성의. ¶ ~ *force* 원심력. **2** making use of this force. 원심력을 이용한〔에 의한〕(opp. centripetal). ¶ *a* ~ *pump* 원심 펌프. ● **cen·trif·u·gal·ly** [-gəli] *adv.* [L. *centrum* center, *fugio* flee]

cen·tri·fuge [séntrəfjùːdʒ] *n.* a machine for separating particles by means of centrifugal force, as cream from milk. 원심 분리기(遠心分離機).

cen·trip·e·tal [sentrípətl] *adj.* **1** having a tendency to the center. 중심으로 향하는; 구심성의. ¶ ~ *force* 구심력. **2** making use of force. 구심력을 이용한〔에 의한〕(opp. centrifugal). [L. *centrum* center, *peto* seek]

cen·tu·ple [séntəpəl, -tjuː-] *adj.* 100 times as much or as many. 100 배나 되는〔큰〕; 100 배의. — *vt.* (P6) make 100 times as much or as many. 100 배하다. [→cent(i)-, -ple]

cen·tu·ri·on [sentjúəriən] *n.* 《hist.》 an officer commanding a unit of 100 men in the Roman army. (옛 로마 군대의) 백인대장(百人隊長). [→cent]

:cen·tu·ry [séntʃuri] *n.* Ⓒ (*pl.* **-ries**) **1** 100 years. 100 년. ¶ *for a* ~ 백년 동안 / *This book is three centuries old.* 이 책은 3 백년 된 것이다. **2** one of the unit of 100 years before or after the birth of Christ. 1 세기. ¶ *the* 20 *th* ~ 20 세기 / *a quarter of a* ~ 사반세기(四半世紀)《25 년》. **3** a group of 100 men or 100 things. (단위로서의 사람·물건의) 100. [↑]

ce·phal·ic [səfǽlik] *adj.* **1** of the head. 머리의; 두부(頭部)의. **2** near, on, or in the head. 머리쪽에 있는. [Gk. *Kephalē* head]

ce·ram·ic [sərǽmik] *adj.* of products made from clay, like pottery; of the art of making such products. 도자기의; 제도술(製陶術)의. 參考 keramic 으로도 씀. ¶ ~ *art* 도예 / *the* ~ *industry* 요업(窯業). [Gk.]

ce·ram·ics [sərǽmiks] *n. pl.* **1** 《used as *sing.*》 the art of making pottery, etc. 제도술(製陶術); 요업. **2** 《used as *pl.*》 articles made of clay, pottery, etc. 요업제품; 도자기.

Cer·ber·us [sə́ːrbərəs] *n.* **1** 《Gk. myth.》 a dog with three heads which guarded the entrance to Hades. 케르베로스《지옥의 문지기 개》. **2** a harsh watchful guard. 무서운 문지기. [Gk.]

cere [siər] *n.* 《zool.》 a wax-like membrane. 납막(蠟膜). [L. *cera* wax]

***ce·re·al** [síəriəl] *n.* 《usu. *pl.*》 **1** a grain used for food, such as rice, wheat and corn. (쌀·밀·옥수수 따위의) 곡물; 곡류. **2** any plant that produces a grain used for human food. 곡식 식물. **3** Ⓤ 《U.S.》 food made from grain, esp. a breakfast food. 곡물식(穀物食)《아침 식사용 oatmeal, cornflakes 따위》. — *adj.* of or having to do with grain or the plants producing it. 곡물의; 곡식 식물의. [L. *Ceres* corn-godess]

cer·e·bel·la [sèrəbélə] *n.* pl. of **cerebellum.**

cer·e·bel·lum [sèrəbéləm] *n.* Ⓒ (*pl.* **-lums** or **-la**) 《anat.》 the small back part of the brain. 소뇌(小腦). [L.]

cer·e·bra [sérəbrə] *n.* pl. of **cerebrum.**

cer·e·bral [sérəbrəl, sərí:-] *adj.* 《anat.》 of the brain. (대)뇌의. ¶ ~ *anemia* 뇌빈혈 / ~ *hemorrhage* 뇌출혈. [L.]

cer·e·brum [sérəbrəm, sərí:-] *n.* Ⓒ (*pl.* **-brums** or **-bra**) 《anat.》 the upper, front, and largest part of the brain. 대뇌(大腦). [L.]

cere·ment [síərmənt] *n.* 《usu. *pl.*》 the clothes in which a dead body is wrapped for burial. 수의(壽衣). [→cere]

cer·e·mo·ni·al [sèrəmóuniəl] *adj.* **1** of ceremony. 의식(儀式)의. ¶ *a* ~ *occasion* 축제 / ~ *usage* 의식상의 관례. **2** formal; used in a ceremony. 정식의; 공식의. ¶ *a* ~ *visit* 공식 방문. — *n.* Ⓒ **1** a system or rules of ceremony. 의식 (절차). **2** a formality, esp. of etiquette; the observance of ceremony. 의례(儀禮); 예식. [↓]

cer·e·mo·ni·al·ly [sèrəmóuniəli] *adv.* in a ceremonial manner. 의례적으로; 예법상; 형식적으로.

cer·e·mo·ni·ous [sèrəmóuniəs] *adj.* full of ceremony; formally polite; stiff. 의식에 치우친; 격식을 차린; 딱딱한; 딱딱할 정도로 예의바른. ¶ *a* ~ *welcome* 의례적인 환영 / *a* ~ *person* 〔*manner*〕 딱딱한 사람〔태도〕.

***cer·e·mo·ny** [sérəmòuni / -mə-] *n.* (*pl.* **-nies**) **1** Ⓒ 《often *pl.*》 the solemn show that goes with a religious or important public event. 의식; 식. ¶ *a wedding* 〔*marriage*〕 ~ 결혼식 / *a funeral* ~ 장례식 / *with all ceremonies* 자못 엄숙히 / *perform the graduation* ~ 졸업식을 거행하다. **2** Ⓤ very polite conduct; manners. 예의(바른 행동); 예절. ¶ *He thanked me with much* ~. 그는 매우 정중하게 나에게 감사했다 / *I am treating you as a friend and without* ~. 난 자네를 허물없는 친구로 대하고 있는 걸세. **3** Ⓤ an empty formality. 형식 차린 행위; 허례. [L. *caerimonia*]

a master of ceremonies, a person who sees that a program is carried through in an orderly way. 사회자. 參考 이 뜻으로는 흔히 M.C. [émsí:] 로 생략함.

stand on 〔***upon***〕 ***ceremony,*** be very formal; be too polite. 너무 형식에 집착하다; 딱딱하다; 체면치레하다.

Cer·es [síəri:z] *n.* 《Rom. myth.》 the ancient Roman goddess of agriculture. 케레스《곡물의 여신(=Gk. myth. Demeter)》. [→cereal]

cer·iph [sérif] *n.* =serif.

ce·rise [sərí:s, -rí:z] *adj.* of a cherry-red color. 담홍색의. — *n.* Ⓤ cherry-red; a light, clear red. 담〔선〕홍색. [F. =cherry]

cer·i·um [síəriəm] *n.* 《chem.》 세륨. [Gk.]

cert [sə:rt] *n.* 《*colloq.*》 확실한 것〔결과〕. ¶ *a dead* ~ 매우 확실한 일〔것〕. [↓]

:cer·tain [sə́:rtən] *adj.* **1** beyond doubt or question; (of the future) true. 의심의 여지 없는; 확실한; 틀림없는. ¶ *a* ~ *fact* 틀림없는 사실 / *There is no* ~ *cure for this disease.* 이 병에는 확실한 치료법이 없다 / *One thing is* ~; *someone is to be blamed for this.* 한 가지 일만은 분명하다; 즉 누군가 이에 대한 책임을 져야 한다는 것이다. **2** 《as *predicative*》 not doubtful; sure. 확신하고 있는. ¶ ~ *evidence* 확증 / *be* ~ *of victory* 승리를 확신하다 / *I am* ~ *he will come.* 그가 꼭 올것으로 확신한다(=He is ~ to come.) / *I feel* ~ (*that*) *she is alive.* 그녀는 꼭 살아 있을 것 같다 / *Does he know? — I am* ~ *of it.* 그가 알고 있나 — 그렇다고 확신한다. **3** sure to come or to happen. 반드시 …하게 되어 있는; 반드시 …하는; 피할 수 없는. ¶ *Death is* ~ (*to come*). 죽음은 피할 수 없다 / *He is* ~ *to be there.* 그는 반드시 거기 있다〔온다〕. **4** 《as *attributive*》 ⓐ fixed; agreed on. 일정한; 정해진. ¶ *on a* ~ *day* 일정한 날에 / *for a* ~ *amount* 일정한 양〔액〕으로. ⓑ known but not mentioned; some. 어떤; 아무의. 語法 확실히 말하고 싶지 않을 때 쓰임. ¶ *a* ~ *person* 어떤 사람 / *a* ~ *Mr. Brown* 브라운씨인가 하는 분 / *a lady of a* ~ *age* 상당한 연배의 숙녀 / *A* ~ *person said it.* 아무개가 그렇게 말했다 / *Certain plants will not grow in this country.* 어떤 식물은 이 나라에서 자라지 않는다. ⓒ some; not much. 상당한; 다소의; 약간의. ¶ *to a* ~ *extent* 어느 정도 / *for a* ~ *time* 잠시 동안 / *have a* ~ *hesitation* 다소 망설이다 / *There is a* ~ *charm about him.* 그에게 다소 매력이 있다. [L. *certus*]

be certain of, be convinced of. …을 확신하고 있다. ¶ *He is* ~ *of the correctness of his view.* 그는 자기 견해(見解)가 옳다고 확신하고 있다.

be certain that, be convinced that. …이라는〔하다는〕 것을 확신하고 있다.

be not certain whether 〔***if***〕***,*** be not sure if. …인지 아닌지 확실치 않다. ¶ *I am not* ~ *whether I can do it.* 내가 할 수 있을지 없을지 모르겠다.

for certain, without any doubt; surely. 의심할 여지 없이; 확실히. ¶ *I don't know for* ~ *if he's coming or not.* 그가 올지 안 올지 확실히는 모른다.

make certain of 〔***that***〕***,*** make sure of 〔that〕; ascertain. …을 확인하다. ¶ *I looked inside to make* ~ (*that*) *she was asleep.* 그녀가 자는지 확인하기 위해 안을 들여다보았다.

:cer·tain·ly [sə́:rtənli] *adv.* **1** surely; without fail; without doubt. 확실히; 반드시; 틀림없이. ¶ *He will* ~ *come.* 그는 꼭 온다. **2** (in answer to questions) yes, of course. (대답으로서) 그렇고말고; 물론이죠; 좋습니다. ¶ *May I take it? — Certainly.* 가져도 되나요 — 물론이죠 / *Will you lend me your glasses? — Certainly not.* 안경 좀 빌려 주겠나 — 어림없는 소리 / *It is* ~ *the case, but....* 과연 그렇긴 하지만 그러나….

*__cer·tain·ty__ [sə́ːrtənti] *n.* (*pl.* **-ties**) **1** Ⓤ the state of being sure. 확실(성). ¶ *objective* ~ 객관적 확실성 / *This at least may be said with* ~. 적어도 이것만은 장담할 수 있다. **2** Ⓒ something that is sure to occur. 확실한 〔필연적인〕 일〔것〕. ¶ *bet on a* ~ 확실하다고 보고 돈을 걸다 / *His success was a* ~ *from the first.* 그의 성공은 처음부터 보장된 것이었다 / *Death and taxes are certainties.* 죽음과 세금은 피할 수 없다.

for 〔to〕 a certainty, surely; without doubt. 확실히; 꼭; 의심의 여지 없이. ¶ *I know this for a* ~. 이것은 확실히 알고 있다.

with certainty, certainly. 확실히; 분명히. ¶ *I cannot say with* ~ *whether he is still alive.* 그가 아직 살아 있는지 아닌지 확실히는 모른다. 「확실히.

cer·tes [sə́ːrtiz] *adv.* 《*arch.*》 certainly.

*__cer·tif·i·cate__ [sərtífəkit] *n.* Ⓒ a written or printed statement that declares something to be a fact. 증명서; 면〔허〕장. ¶ *a birth* 〔*health*〕 ~ 출생〔건강〕 증명서 / *a teacher's* ~ 교원 자격증 / *a death* ~ 사망 증명서. —— [-kèit] *vt.* (P6) give a certificate to. …에게 증명서〔면허〕를 주다. [→certain]

cer·ti·fi·ca·tion [sə̀ːrtəfəkéiʃən] *n.* **1** Ⓤ the act of declaring the truth of something by a written statement. 증명서 교부. **2** Ⓤ the state of being confirmed; assurance. 보증; 확인. **3** Ⓒ a formal notice. 증명(서); 검정.

cer·ti·fy [sə́ːrtəfài] *vt.* (P6,7,11,13,18) declare (something) true or correct, usu. in writing; approve the quality or value of (something). …을 증명하다; 인증〔보증〕하다. ¶ *certified milk* 보증 우유 / ~ *a check* (은행이) 수표의 지급을 보증하다 / ~ *someone as a naval officer* 아무가 해군 장교임을 증명하다 / *His report was certified* (*as*) *correct.* 그의 보고는 정확한 것으로 증명되었다 / ~ *the cause of someone's death* 아무의 사인(死因)을 증명하다 / ~ *a document with an official seal* 공인(公印)을 눌러 문서를 보증하다 / *This is to* ~ *that....* 본증(本證)은 …이 틀림없음을 증명함 / *The doctor certified that Nancy had been vaccinated.* 의사는 낸시가 예방 접종을 마쳤음을 증명했다.
—— *vi.* (P1,3) 《*to, for*》 give assurance. 보증하다; 증인이 되다. ¶ ~ *to someone's character* 아무의 인격을 보증하다. [→certain]

cer·ti·tude [sə́ːrtətjùːd] *n.* Ⓤ the state of being sure; confidence. 확실(성); 확신.

ce·ru·le·an [sərúːliən] *adj.* of a deep clear blue; sky-blue. 하늘색의. [L.]

Cer·van·tes [sərvǽntiːz], **Miguel de** *n.* (1547-1616) the Spanish author who wrote Don Quixote. 세르반테스.

cer·vi·cal [sə́ːrvikəl] *adj.* 《anat.》 of the neck. 목의; 경부(頸部)의. [L.]

cer·vi·ces [səːrváisiːz, sə́ːrvəsìːz] *n.* pl. of **cervix.**

cer·vix [sə́ːrviks] *n.* (*pl.* **-vix·es** or **-vi·ces**) 《anat.》 the neck, esp. the back of the neck. 목; (특히) 목덜미. [L.]

ces·sa·tion [seséiʃən] *n.* **1** ⓊⒸ a stop; a pause. 중지; 중단; 휴지; 정지. ¶ ~ *of hostilities* 〔*arms*〕 휴전; 정전 / ~ *from work* 휴업 / *a* ~ *of production* 생산 중지 / ~ *of friendship* 절교 / *read without* ~ 쉬지 않고 읽다. **2** Ⓒ that which is given up. 중지된 것. [→cease]

ces·sion [séʃən] *n.* ⓊⒸ the act of giving up land, rights, etc. to another. (영토의) 할양(割讓); (권리·재산의) 양도. ¶ *the* ~ *of territory* 영토의 할양 / *the* ~ *of rights* 권리의 양도. [→cede]

cess·pool [séspùːl] *n.* Ⓒ **1** a pool or hollow for holding the dirty water which flows out of a house. 시궁창; 분뇨 구덩이. **2** any dirty place. 불결한 곳. ¶ *a* ~ *of iniquity* 악의 소굴. [It. *cesso* privy]

cet. par. *ceteris paribus* (L.=other things being equal).

Cey·lon [silɑ́n / -lɔ́n] *n.* =Sri Lanka

cf. [síːéf, kənpɛ́ər, kənfə́ːr] compare; confer. 참조; 참고. [L. *confer* compare]

Ce·zan·ne [sizǽn], **Paul** *n.* (1839-1906) a French painter. 세잔《프랑스의 화가》.

c.f.m., cfm cubic foot a minute. 분당(分當) …입방 피트.

c.g.s., cgs. centimeter-gram-second (system).

Ch., ch. **1** (*pl.* **Chs., chs.**) chapter. 장(章). **2** chief. **3** church.

c.h. customhouse.

chafe [tʃeif] *vt., vi.* **1** (P6;3) rub (the skin, etc.) to make it warm. (살갗 따위를) 비벼 따뜻하게 하다. ¶ ~ *cold hands* 비벼서 언 손을 녹이다. **2** (P13;3) wear or be worn away by rubbing. (마찰로 …을) 닳게 하다; 닳다; 무지러지다. ¶ *The rope has* 〔*is*〕 *chafed against the rock.* 밧줄이 바위에 쓸려 닳았다. **3** (P6;1) make or become painful by rubbing. 쓸려 아프(게 하)다. ¶ *The stiff collar chafed his neck.* 빳빳한 깃에 쓸려 목이 얼얼했다. **4** (P6) make (someone) angry; irritate. …을 성나게 하다; 속타게 하다; 약올리다. ¶ *The dripping of the faucet chafed her nerves.* 수도 꼭지의 물 떨어지는 소리가 그녀의 신경을 건드렸다. **5** (P1,3) 《*at, under*》 become angry; be irritated. 성나다; 속타다; 약오르다. ¶ ~ *at the delay of the train* 열차가 늦어 속이 타다 / ~ *under restraint* 마음대로 못해 안달하다 / *He chafed under her teasing.* 그녀가 놀려 그는 약이 올랐다. **6** (P3) 《*against*》 (of a beast, a river, etc.) rub itself. (짐승이) 몸을 비비다; (강물이 기슭에) 부딪치다. ¶ *The cat chafed against the wall.* 그 고양이는 벽에 몸을 비벼댔다 / *The river chafes against the rocks.* 강물이 바위에 세차게 부딪쳐 흐른다.
—— *n.* **1** Ⓒ a chafed place on the skin. 쓸려 까진 데; 찰과상. **2** Ⓤ irritation. 속탐; 약오름. [L. *calefacio* make warm]

in a chafe, in the state of nervous irritation. 애가 타서; 약이 올라; 안달하여.

chaff[1] [tʃæf / tʃɑːf] *n.* Ⓤ **1** the outer coverings of grains, usu. separated from the seed. 왕겨. **2** hay or straw cut fine for cattle. 여물. **3** any worthless matter; rubbish. 시시한 것; 잡동사니; 쓰레기. ¶ ~ *and dust* 폐물. [E.]

chaff[2] [tʃæf / tʃɑːf] *vt.* (P6,13) 《*about*》 make fun of (someone) in a good-humored way; jest; tease. (악의 없이) …을 놀리다; 농을 하다. ¶ *a chaffing friendship* 서로 스스럼없이 농지거리하는 사이 / *The boys chaffed the old man.* 아이들은 그 늙은이를 놀려댔다. — *n.* Ⓤ good-natured joking or teasing; banter. (악의 없는) 농담; 놀림. ¶ *be caught with* ~ 쉽게 속아 넘어가다. [E.]

chaf·fer [tʃǽfər] *vi.* (P1,3) bargain; haggle; argue about a price. 흥정하다. ¶ ~ *over a price* 값을 흥정하다. — *vt.* (P6) trade or deal in. …을 거래하다. — *n.* Ⓒ bargain. 흥정. [E.]

chaf·finch [tʃǽfintʃ] *n.* Ⓒ a European songbird. 되새. [→chaff[1]]

chaf·ing-dish [tʃéifiŋdìʃ] *n.* a pan with a lamp under it for cooking or heating food at the table. (자체 가열기가 붙은) 식탁용 냄비. [→chafe]

cha·grin [ʃəgrín / ʃǽgrin] *n.* Ⓤ a feeling of disappointment; regret. 분함; 실망; 유감. ¶ *to one's* ~ 분하게도; 유감스럽게도 / *with* ~ 실망하여 / *Much to his* ~*, John did not get a prize.* 분하게도 존은 입상을 못 했다. — *vt.* (P6,13) 《usu. in *passive*》 cause (someone) to feel chagrin. …을 분하게 하다. ¶ *be* 〔*feel*〕 *chagrined at* 〔*by*〕 *something* …을 분하게 여기다. [F.]

:**chain** [tʃein] *n.* Ⓒ **1** a series of links or rings joined together. 사슬. ¶ *an endless* ~ (자전거 등의) 체인 / *a watch and* ~ 줄이 달린 시계 / *a silver* ~ *to a watch* 회중 시계의 은사슬 줄 / *keep a dog on a* ~ 개를 사슬에 매어 두다. **2** 《usu. *pl.*》 bonds; imprisonment. 속박; 구속; 굴레; 감금. ¶ *a man in chains* 투옥된 사람 / *live one's life in chains* 구속된 굴종의 생활을 보내다. **3** a series of connected things or events. 연속(된 것); 연쇄. ¶ *a* ~ *of islands* 열도(列島) / *a* ~ *of events* 일련의 사건 / *a* ~ *of ideas* 잇따라 떠오르는 생각 / *a* ~ *of mountains* 연산(連山); 산맥. **4** a measuring instrument like a chain. 측정쇄(鎖).

be in chains, be bound; be not free. 구속돼 있다; 잡혀 있다.

— *vt.* (P6,7,13) fasten (something) with a chain; restrain; make a slave of. …을 사슬에 매(놓)다; 속박〔구속〕하다; 얽매이게 하다. ¶ ~ (*up*) *a dog to a post* 개를 사슬로 말뚝에 매 놓다 / ~ *a prisoner to the wall* 죄인을 사슬로 벽에 묶어 놓다 / *He is chained to his work* 〔*the desk*〕. 일에 얽매여 있다. [L. *catena*]

chain bridge [´ ´] *n.* a suspension bridge. 사슬 적교(吊橋).

chain mail [´ ´] *n.* a kind of armor made of metal rings linked together. 미늘 갑옷.

chain reaction [´ ´–] *n.* 《chem., phys.》 a chemical change resulting in products which themselves cause more changes, and then these changes are similarly repeated again and again. 연쇄 반응.

chain smoker [´ ´–] *n.* a person who smokes continually. 줄담배 피우는 사람; 골초.

chain stitch [´ ´] *n.* a kind of ornamental sewing. 사슬뜨기; 사슬수(繡).

chain store [´ ´] *n.* 《U.S.》 a number of stores in different places all owned and managed by the same company. 연쇄점 (=《Brit.》 multiple shop).

:**chair** [tʃɛər] *n.* Ⓒ **1** a single seat with a back. 의자. ¶ *take a* ~ 착석하다 / *sit* (*down*) *in a* ~ (팔걸이 있는) 의자에 앉다 / *sit on a* ~ (팔걸이 없는) 의자에 앉다 / *arise* 〔*get up*〕 *from one's* ~ 의자에서 일어서다 / *pull one's* ~ *up to the table* 의자를 탁자에 당기다. **2** 《*the* ~》 ⓐ a seat from which a professor delivers his lectures; an official office or position, esp. of a professor. (대학의) 강좌; (특히 대학 교수의) 지위. ¶ *He holds the Chair of History* 그는 역사 교수다. ⓑ (the seat of) a chairman. 의장(직). ¶ *appeal to the* ~ 의장에게 (채결)을 요청하다 / *call someone to the* ~ 아무를 의장으로 선출〔지명〕하다 / *leave the* ~ 의장석을 떠나다; 폐회하다 / *take the* ~ 의장석에 앉다; 개회하다. **3** 《U.S.》 a chairlike machine for killing certain criminals; an electric chair. (사형용의) 전기 의자 ¶ *send* 〔go〕 *to the* ~ 사형에 처하다〔처해지다〕 / *get the* ~ 사형이 되다.

— *vt.* (P6) **1** put (someone) into a chair; seat. …을 의자에 앉히다. **2** put (someone) in a position of authority. …을 (권위 있는) 지위에 앉히다. **3** preside over as chairman. 의장직을 맡다; 사회를 맡다. **4** 《Brit.》 place (a person) in a chair etc. and carry him aloft in honor of his success or victory. (성공·승리한 사람)을 의자에 앉혀 높이 쳐들어 축하하다. [→cathedral]

:**chair·man** [tʃɛ́ərmən] *n.* Ⓒ (*pl.* **-men** [-mən]) a person who controls a meeting; a master of ceremonies; a person at the head of a committee. 의장; 사회자; 위원장.

chair·man·ship [tʃɛ́ərmənʃip] *n.* Ⓤ the office or position of a chairman. chairman 의 직〔신분·지위·자격〕.

chair·wom·an [tʃɛ́ərwùmən] *n.* Ⓒ (*pl.* **-wom·en** [-wìmin]) a woman chairman. 여성 의장.

chaise [ʃeiz] *n.* Ⓒ a light open carriage, usu. with a hood. (4륜 또는 2륜의) 여행용

경마차. [→chair]

chaise-longue [ʃéizlɔ́ŋ] *n.* Ⓒ (*pl.* **-longues**) a long, couch-like chair on which one can sit and stretch out one's legs. (다리를 뻗을 수 있는) 긴 의자.

Chal·de·a [kældí(ː)ə] *n.* an ancient region in the southwestern Asia. 칼데아《서남 아시아의 옛 지역》. [Sem.]

Chal·de·an [kældí(ː)ən], **-dee** [-díː] *adj.* of Chaldea. 칼데아의. — *n.* Ⓒ a person of Chaldea; Ⓤ the language of Chaldea. 칼데아 사람〔언어〕. [Sem.]

chal·dron [tʃɔ́ːldrən] *n.* a measure for coal. 석탄 등의 건량 단위(=36 bushels). [→cauldron]

chal·et [ʃæléi, ⌐–] *n.* Ⓒ **1** a Swiss summer hut. 샬레《스위스 산 속의 양치기 오두막》. **2** a cottage or house built in this style. 샬레풍의 집〔별장〕. **3** a street lavatory. 공중 변소. [F.-Swiss]

chal·ice [tʃǽlis] *n.* Ⓒ **1** 《poet.》 a drinking-cup. 술잔. **2** a cup used in church services. 성작(聖爵). **3** a flower shaped like a cup. 잔 모양의 꽃. [L. *calix*]

:chalk [tʃɔːk] *n.* **1** Ⓤ a soft, white, natural stone. 백악(白堊). **2** Ⓒ a stick of this or of a like substance used for writing or drawing. 백묵; 분필. ¶ *a piece of* ~ 백묵 하나 / *write in red* ~ 붉은 분필로 쓰다. **3** Ⓒ a mark made with chalk. 백묵으로 그은 표지.

(as) different as chalk from cheese =**(as) like as chalk and cheese.** 《Brit.》 quite different; utterly unlike. (외양이 비슷하면서도) 아주 딴판인; 본질적으로 다른. ¶ *These two plants are as like as chalk and cheese.* 이 두 식물은 본질적으로 다르다.

by a long chalk =**by (long) chalks,** 《*colloq.*》 by far; by a great deal. 훨씬; 단연. ¶ *be better by a long* ~ 훨씬 좋다 / *win by a long* ~ 압승하다.

not by a long chalk, 《Brit. *colloq.*》 not at all. 조금도 …않다.

— *vt.* (P7) mark, draw, or write (something) with chalk; rub or whiten (something) with chalk. …을 백묵으로 표시하다〔그리다, 쓰다〕; …에 분필칠을 하다. [L, *calx* lime]

chalk out, plan; mark out. …을 설계하다; 계획하다.

chalk up, a) record; score. (득점 등)을 기록하다; 득점하다. **b**) 《*to*》 ascribe to. …의 탓으로 돌리다.

chalk·y [tʃɔ́ːki] *adj.* (**chalk·i·er, chalk·i·est**) **1** of chalk. 백악질의. **2** like chalk; white as chalk. 백악 같은; 백악처럼 흰.

***chal·lenge** [tʃǽlindʒ] *n.* Ⓒ **1** a call to fight, play a game, etc. to see which is better in strength, skill, etc. 도전(장). ¶ *give a* ~ 도전하다 / *accept* 〔*take up*〕 *a* ~ 도전에 응하다. **2** a demand to answer and explain. 답변〔설명〕의 요구. **3** a guard's cry, "Who goes there ?" (보초 등의) 수하(誰何). ¶ *give the* ~ 수하하다 / *hear a* ~ *in the jungle at night* 밤에 정글에서 수하 소리를 듣다. **4** 《law》 a formal objection made to a person's serving on a jury. (배심원에 대한) 기피; 거부.

— *vt.* (P6,13,20) **1** 《*to*》 offer to fight or contest with (someone). …에게 결투를 신청하다; …에 도전하다. ¶ *He challenged us to another race.* 또 다른 레이스를 갖자고 도전해 왔다. **2** call on (someone, etc.) to answer and explain; question; doubt. …에게 답변〔설명〕을 요구하다; …을 의심하다. ¶ ~ *the wisdom of a procedure* 어떤 조치가 현명했었는지를 의심하다. **3** stop (someone) and question what he is doing or where he is going. …을 수하(誰何)하다. ¶ *"Who goes there ?" the guard challenged me.* "누구냐"하며 보초가 나에게 수하했다. **4** demand (attention, etc.); claim (something) as due. (주의 따위)를 요구하다; 당연한 것으로서 요구하다. ¶ ~ *someone's attention* 아무의 주의를 요구하다 / *I* ~ *you to point out where I am mistaken.* 나의 잘못된 곳을 지적할 것을 요구한다. **5** 《law》 object to (a jury, vote). (배심원)을 기피하다; (투표)를 거부하다. **6** accuse. …을 힐난〔비난〕하다. [→calumny]

chal·leng·er [tʃǽlindʒər] *n.* Ⓒ a person who challenges. 도전자; 수하자(誰何者).

:cham·ber [tʃéimbər] *n.* Ⓒ **1** ⓐ a room in a house, esp. a bedroom. 방; 침실. ¶ *retire to one's* ~ 자기 방으로 물러가다. ⓑ = chamber pot. **2** 《*pl.*》 ⓐ 《Brit.》 a set of rooms in a building arranged for a person to live in, or for offices. (빌딩의) 죽 이어진 방; 사무실. ⓑ the office of a judge or lawyer. (법원의) 판사실; 변호사실. **3** ⓐ a hall for the meeting of persons, esp. who make laws; a group of persons who make laws. 회의장; 의사당; 의회. ¶ *the Upper Chamber* 상원(= 《Brit.》 the House of Lords; 《U.S.》 the Senate) / *the Lower Chamber* 하원(= 《Brit.》 the House of Commons; 《U.S.》 the House of Representatives) / *The United States Congress is made up of two chambers.* 미국 의회는 상하 양원으로 되어 있다. ⓑ a group of people organized for some business purpose. 사업을 위한 조직체. ¶ *the Chamber of Commerce* 상공 회의소. **4** a walled or enclosed space in the body of an animal or plant; a cavity. (동식물 체내의) 방; 소실(小室); 구멍. ¶ *a* ~ *of the heart* 심실(心室). **5** the part of a gun or pistol that holds the charge or cartridge. (총포의) 약실(藥室). [→camera]

Cham·ber·lain [tʃéimbərlin], **Arthur Neville** *n.* (1869-1940) a British primeminister. 체임벌린《영국 수상》.

cham·ber·lain [tʃéimbərlin] *n.* Ⓒ **1** a palace official; the manager of a great nobleman's house, lands, etc. 시종(侍

從); 가령(家令). ¶ *the Lord Chamberlain* 시종장(長). **2** a treasurer. 출납 계원.

cham·ber·maid [tʃéimbərmèid] *n.* Ⓒ a maid who takes care of bedrooms in a hotel or an inn. (호텔 따위의) 객실 담당 여종업원. [*chamber*]

chamber music [⌐–⌐–] *n.* music played in a room or a small concert hall, usu. for a trio, quartet, etc. 실내악.

chamber pot [⌐– ⌐] *n.* a pot for urine used in a bedroom. 실내 변기; 요강.

cham·bray [ʃǽmbrei] *n.* Ⓤ a variety of gingham. 샴브레이직(織)《깅엄의 일종》. [Place]

cha·me·le·on [kəmíːliən, -ljən] *n.* Ⓒ **1** 《zool.》 a small animal that changes the color of its skin according to its background. 카멜레온. **2** a person of changeable character or habits. 변덕쟁이; 무절조한 사람. [Gk. =earth-lion]

cham·ois [ʃǽmi / ʃǽmwɑː] *n.* **1** Ⓒ (*pl.* **-ois**) 《zool.》 a small, goatlike antelope animal living in the high mountains of Europe and southwestern Asia. 섀미《유럽 및 서남 아시아 산(産) 영양의 일종》. **2** [usu. ʃǽmi] Ⓤ soft leather made from the skin of chamois, sheep, deer, etc. 섀미 가죽《영양 따위의 무두질한 가죽》. 參考 chammy로도 씀. [F.]

champ[1] [tʃæmp] *vi., vt.* (P1,2A,3,4; 6) **1** (of horses) bite (food) noisily or impatiently. 어적어적 소리내어 씹다〔물다〕. ¶ *The horses were champing (their food).* **2** grind one's teeth with impatience. (속이 타서) 이를 갈다. ¶ ~ *at the bit* (말이) 재갈을 씹다; (사람이) 안달하다 / *The train was late and the passengers were champing to get home.* 열차가 연착되어 승객들은 집에 갈 일에 속이 탔다. [Imit.]

champ[2] [tʃæmp] *n.* 《U.S. *colloq.*》 =champion.

cham·pagne [ʃæmpéin] *n.* Ⓤ a high-priced white wine, first made in Champagne, France. 샴페인. [→camp]

cham·paign [ʃæmpéin] *n.* Ⓒ a level, open country; a plain. 들판; 평야. [↑]

cham·pi·gnon [ʃæmpínjən] *n.* 《bot.》 a kind of mushroom. 식용 버섯의 하나. [↑]

:**cham·pi·on** [tʃǽmpiən] *n.* Ⓒ **1** a person who defends or fights for another or for some good cause; a supporter. (타인·주의 따위를 위해 싸우는) 전사(戰士); 옹호자. ¶ *a* ~ *of liberty* 자유의 투사 / *a* ~ *for justice* 정의를 위해 싸우는 사람 / *a* ~ *of the poor* 가난한 자의 옹호자. **2** ⓐ the best of all the players at a certain game. (경기의) 우승자; 선수권자; 챔피언. ¶ *the defending* ~ 선수권 방어자. ⓑ an animal, or thing that takes the first place in a sport or contest. 최고상을 탄 동물〔물건〕. ¶ *the* ~ *of a cattle show* 가축 품평회에서 1등상을 탄 가축.

— *adj.* **1** having won the first place in a sport or contest. (경기·품평회에서) 우승한; 선수권을 딴. ¶ *the* ~ *team* 우승 팀 / *a* ~ *rose* 최우수상을 탄 장미. **2** 《*colloq.*》 first-class; very good. 일류의; 뛰어난; 더없는.

— *vt.* (P6) fight for; defend; support. …을 위해 싸우다; 옹호〔지지〕하다. ¶ ~ *someone* 〔*the cause of human rights*〕 아무를〔인권 운동을〕 옹호하다. [→camp]

cham·pi·on·ship [tʃǽmpiənʃip] *n.* **1** Ⓒ the state of being a champion. 선수권. ¶ *win a* ~ 선수권을 따다 / *hold the ping-pong* ~ *of the world* 세계 탁구 선수권을 보유하다 / *lose a* ~ 선수권을 잃다. **2** Ⓒ a series of matches to decide the champion. 결승전; 선수권 대회. ¶ *the tennis championships for 1995,* 1995년도 테니스 선수권 대회. **3** Ⓤ the defense of a person or cause. 옹호; 투쟁. ¶ ~ *of the underdog* 약자의 옹호 / *his* ~ *of the cause of peace* 그의 평화주의를 위한 투쟁.

:**chance** [tʃæns, tʃɑːns] *n.* **1** Ⓤ the cause of events for no known reason; fortune; luck; fate. 우연(한 일); 운. ¶ *a game of* ~ 우연에 의해 승패가 결정되는 게임 / *Chance governs all.* 우연이 만사를 지배한다 / *Chance led to our finding of the diamondmine.* 우연한 일로 우리는 다이아몬드 광산을 발견하게 되었다 / *Leave it to* ~. 운에 맡기자. **2** Ⓒ opportunity. 기회; 호기. ¶ *a capital* ~ 절호의 기회 / *a* ~ *to make some money* 돈을 벌 기회 / *the* ~ *of a lifetime* 일생에 다시 없는 기회 / *miss one's only* ~ 유일한 기회를 놓치다 / *wait for a (good)* ~ (좋은) 기회를 기다리다 / *Is there any* ~ *of my seeing you ?* 언제고 만나 뵐 기회가 있을까요. **3** ⓊⒸ possibility; probability. 가능〔가망〕성; 성산; 승산. ¶ *an even* ~ 반반의 가능성 / *a good* ~ *of success* 충분히 성공할 가능성 / *nine chances out of ten* 십중 팔구 / *have a slender* ~ *of success* 성공은 어려울 것 같다 / *There is not the least* ~. 전혀 가망〔성산〕이 없다 / *The chances are against snow in May.* 5월에 눈이 올 가능성은 없다. **4** Ⓒ a risk; a gamble. 모험; 도박. ¶ *take the* ~ *(of)* (…을) 운에 맡기고 해 보다 / *run a* ~ *of failure* 실패할 위험이 있(지만 해 보)다.

by any chance, by any possibility. 만일; 혹시. ¶ *Do you by any* ~ *know his address ?* 혹시 그의 주소를 알고 있나.

by chance =***by some chance,*** by accident; unintentionally. 우연히. ¶ *We met by* ~. 우리는 우연히 만났다.

leave to chance, trust to chance. 운에 맡기다.

on the chance of 〔***that…***〕, hoping for the possibility of 〔that〕.... 은근히 …을 기대〔예기〕하고; …일지도 모르므로.

on the off chance, in the very slight hope. 만일을 기대하고; 운을 내맡기고.

stand a good chance, have a good expectation. 가망이 (충분히) 있다. ¶ *You stand a good* ~ *of being elected.* 네가 당선될 공산이

크다.
***take* 〔*stand*〕 *one's* chance,** trust to luck; let things go as they may. 운에 맡기고 해 보다; 되어 가는 형편에 맡기다.
— *adj.* happening by chance; not expected; accidental. 우연의; 뜻밖의. ¶ *a* ~ *meeting* 뜻밖의 만남.
— *vi.* (P3,4) **1** do or experience something by accident. 우연히 하다. ¶ *I chaned to meet him.* 나는 우연히 그를 만났다. **2** 《after *it*》 come about by accident. 뜻하지 않게 일어나다〔…한 일이 생기다〕; 뜻밖에 하다. ¶ *It chanced that our arrivals coincided.* 뜻하지 않게 우리의 도착이 일치했다. — *vt.* (P6) 《*colloq.*》 take a risk of; venture to do (something). (모험적으로) …을 해 보다. ¶ ~ *one's luck* 운을 시험하다 / *Let's* ~ *it.* 운을 하늘에 맡기고 해 보자. [→ case[1]]
chance *one's* arm, take a chance of success; though failure is possible; take a risk. (실패할 위험은 있으나) 모험적으로 해 보다.
chance on 〔*upon*〕, meet or find (someone or something) by chance; come across. 우연히 만나다〔발견하다〕.

chan·cel [tʃǽnsəl, tʃɑ́ːn-] *n.* Ⓒ the space about the altar of a church for the clergy and the choir. (교회당 안의) 성상(聖像) 안치소; 성단소(聖壇所). [→cancel]

chan·cel·lor [tʃǽnsələr, tʃɑ́ːn-] *n.* Ⓒ **1** 《Brit.》 the official chiefly entrusted with the king's business. 대신; 장관. ¶ *Chancellor of the Exchequer* 재무장관 / *Lord Chancellor* 대법관. **2** 《U.S.》 a chief judge of a court of chancery. 형평법(衡平法) 재판소장. **3** 《Brit.》 the head of a university. 대학 총장(cf. 《U.S.》 *president*). 參考 Chancellor는 명예직으로 실무는 Vice-Chancellor가 맡음. ¶ *the Chancellor of London University* 런던 대학 총장. **4** the prime minister in Germany. (독일 등의) 수상. **5** the chief secretary. 일등 서기관. [↑]

chan·cer·y [tʃǽnsəri, tʃɑ́ːn-] *n.* Ⓒ (*pl.* **-cer·ies**) **1** 《Brit.》 《*the C-*》 a high court of law. 대법관청. **2** 《U.S.》 a court of equity. 형평법(衡平法) 재판소. **3** an office where public records are kept. 공문서 보관소. [↑]

chan·de·lier [ʃændəlíər] *n.* Ⓒ a branched support for lights suspended from a ceiling. 샹들리에. [→candle]

chan·dler [tʃǽndlər, tʃɑ́ːn-] *n.* Ⓒ **1** a maker or seller of candles. 양초 제조〔판매〕 업자. **2** a merchant selling candles, soap, oil, etc. (양초·비누·기름 따위를 파는) 잡화상; 상인. ¶ *a ship's* ~ 선구상(船具商) / *a corn* ~ 곡물상(商). [↑]

:change [tʃeindʒ] *vt.* **1** (P6,13) make (something) different in form, appearance, or nature. (모양·성질·내용 등을) 바꾸다; 변경하다. ¶ ~ *one's opinion* 〔*character*〕 의견〔성격〕을 바꾸다 / ~ *water into steam* 물을 수증기로 바꾸다 / ~ *the subject of conversation* 화제를 바꾸다 / ~ *one's mind* 〔*plan*〕 마음〔계획〕을 바꾸다 / *Failure changed his mind.* 실패로 그의 마음이 바뀌었다 / *The witch changed herself into a lion.* 마법사는 사자로 둔갑했다. **2** (P6,13) take another in place of; give in return (for another); exchange. …을 교환하다; 바꾸다. ¶ ~ *places with someone* 아무와 자리를 바꾸다 / ~ *letters with a friend* 친구와 편지를 주고받다 / ~ *seats with each other* 서로 자리를 바꾸다 / *Will you* ~ *this for that ?* 이것과 그것을 바꾸지 않겠나. **3** (P6,13,14) give or get smaller money of a sum equal to (larger money); give or get another money equal value to (one money). 잔돈으로 바꾸다; 환전하다. ¶ ~ *a bank-note for* 〔*into*〕 *coins* 지폐를 주화(鑄貨)로 바꾸다 / ~ *dollars into francs* 달러를 프랑으로 바꾸다 / *Can you* ~ *me a dollar bill ?* 1 달러 지폐를 잔돈으로 바꿔 줄 수 있나. **4** (P6,13) take off (one kind of clothing) to put on another. (옷을) 갈아 입다. ¶ ~ *everyday wear for dress* 평상복을 정장으로 갈아 입다 / ~ *soiled clothes for clean ones* 더러워진 옷을 깨끗한 것으로 갈아 입다. **5** (P6) leave (a train, etc.) in order to get on another. (차 따위를) 갈아 타다. ¶ ~ *trains* 열차를 갈아타다. — *vi.* (P1,3) **1** become different. 변하다; 달라지다. ¶ ~ *for the better* 〔*worse*〕 호전〔악화〕되다 / *His voice changed.* 그의 목소리가 변성되었다 / *Water changes to steam.* 물은 증기로 변한다 / *Colors* ~ *if they are exposed to the sun.* 빛깔은 햇볕에 노출되면 변한다 / *Summer changed to autumn.* 여름은 가고 가을이 되었다. **2** make a change or an exchange. 교환하다; 교체하다. **3** get off one train, bus, etc. and get on another. 갈아타다. ¶ ~ *at Taejŏn* 대전에서 갈아 타다 / ~ *into another train* 열차를 갈아 타다 / *Change here for Kwangju.* 광주행 손님은 여기서 갈아 타십시오 / *All* ~ *here, please !* 모두 여기서 갈아 타시기 바랍니다. **4** 《*into, out of*》 put on other clothes. 옷을 갈아 입다. ¶ *She changed into a dinner dress.* 그녀는 정찬용(正餐用) 드레스로 갈아 입었다.
change about, be inconstant. 변절하다.
change front, **a**) face a different way. (공격) 방향을 바꾸다. **b**) alter one's attitude. 태도를 바꾸다.
change hands, pass from one owner to another. 다른 손으로 넘어가다; 임자가 바뀌다.
change over, make a complete change. 일변시키다〔하다〕; 전환시키다〔하다〕.
— *n.* **1** Ⓒ the act or fact of changing; an alternation. 변화; 변경; 변혁. ¶ *a* ~ *of heart* 변심; 전향 / *a* ~ *for the worse* 개악 / *the* ~ *from flower to fruit* 꽃에서 열매로의 변화 / *the* ~ *of seasons* 〔*weather*〕 계절〔날씨〕의 변화 / *a hasty* ~ *in one's plan* 계획의 조급한 변경 / *make a* ~ *for the better* 나아지다 / *undergo a* ~ 일변하다 / *I have noticed a great* ~ *in him.* 그에게서 큰 변화를 알아챘다.

2 Ⓒ anything or any person taking the place of another; substitution. 교체(인, 물); 대용(품); 교환; 교대. ¶ *a ~ of one thing for another* 어떤 물건의 다른 물건과의 교환. 3 Ⓒ a fresh set of clothing. 갈아 입을 옷. ¶ *three changes of garments* 갈아 입을 옷 세 벌. 4 Ⓤ the money returned to a buyer as the difference between the price and the amount he has paid; smaller units of money. 거스름돈; 잔돈. ¶ *I have no ~ about me.* 가진 잔돈이 없다. 5 Ⓒ a rest or holiday taken in another circumstances. 전지(轉地)(요양). ¶ *go to the country for a ~ (of air)* 전지 요양을 위해 시골로 가다. 6 Ⓒ《C-》 the place where merchants meet. 거래소. [L. *cambio* barter]

change of life, the cessation of the menses. (여성의) 폐경기; 갱년기.

for a change, for variation. 기분 전환을 위해.

ring the changes, repeat the same thing in different ways. 이 수법 저 수단을 다 써서 하다; 수법을 달리해서 하다.

take the* 〔*one's*〕 *change out of, requite. …에게 대갚음하다; 보복하다.

the Book of Changes, one of the five Chinese Classics. 역경(易經).

change·a·bil·i·ty [tʃèindʒəbíləti] *n.* Ⓤ the state of being changeable. 변하기 쉬운 성질; 가변성(可變性).

·**change·a·ble** [tʃéindʒəbəl] *adj.* 1 that can be changed; likely to change or vary; fickle. 변하기 쉬운; 가변성(可變性)의; 변덕스러운. ¶ *April weather is ~.* 4월달 날씨는 변덕스럽다 / *Do not trust her love — she is ~.* 그 여자 사랑이란 믿지 말게—변덕스러운 여자니까. 2 changing color when seen from a different direction. 방향에 따라 빛깔이 다르게 보이는.

change·ful [tʃéindʒfəl] *adj.* variable; full of change. 변하기 쉬운; 변화가 많은; 불안정한. ¶ *stand watching the ~ sea* 무시로 변하는 바다를 서서 지켜 보다. ●**change·ful·ly** [-fəli] *adv.*

change·less [tʃéindʒlis] *adj.* 1 not changing; not likely to change; constant. 변화 없는; 일정한. 2 monotonous. 단조로운.

change·ling [tʃéindʒliŋ] *n.* a child left by fairies in place of one carried off by them (often applied to a small, ugly child or animal). 요정이 바꿔친 아이《흔히 작고 못생긴 아이나 동물을 이렇게 부름》.

:**chan·nel**[1] [tʃǽnl] *n.* Ⓒ 1 a passage for water; the bed of a river; a narrow stretch of sea. 수로; 물길; 강바닥; 해협. ¶ *a ~ in a river* 강바닥 / *The (English) Channel lies between the North Sea and the Atlantic.* 영국 해협은 북해와 대서양 사이에 있다. 2《*fig.*》 the means by which something may be carried; a course; a route. 경로; 루트; 수단. ¶ *channels of trade* 무역 루트 / *through the proper* 〔*secret*〕 *channels* 정당한〔비밀〕 경로를 거쳐 / *I got this information through official channels.* 이 정보를 공식 소식통으로부터 입수했다. 3 a range of wave frequencies used by a radio or television station. (라디오·TV의) 주파수대(帶); 채널. 4 a hollow line cut into something. (문지방 등의) 홈. — *vt.* (P6) (**-neled, -nel·ing** or 《Brit.》 **-nelled, -nel·ling**) form a channel in; cut out as a channel; convey through a channel. …에 수로를 열다; …에 홈을 파다; …을 수로를 통해 나르다. [→canal]

chan·nel[2] [tʃǽnl] *n.* 《naut.》 a projecting prank to broaden the base for shrouds with. 현측계류판(舷側繫留板). [*chain-wall*]

chan·son [ʃǽnsən / ʃɑːŋsɔ́ːŋ] *n.* 《F.》 a song. 노래; 샹송.

·**chant** [tʃænt, tʃɑːnt] *n.* Ⓒ 1 a slow song, esp. used in a church service; prayer. 노래; (기도문의) 영창(詠唱); 성가《특히 Plain Chant, Gregorian Chant》. 2 a dull way of talking. 단조로운 말투. — *vi., vt.* (P1;6) 1 sing; sing as to a chant; praise in song. 노래하다; 노래로 찬미하다. 2 say or tell over and over again. (단조로운 말투로) 이야기하다; 되풀이하다. ¶ *~ someone's praises* 아무의 칭찬을 되풀이하다. [L. *cano* sing]

chan·tey [ʃǽnti, tʃǽn-] *n.* =chanty.

chan·ti·cleer [tʃǽntəklìər] *n.* a name for the cock. 수탉. [↑]

chan·try [tʃǽntri, tʃɑ́ːn-] *n.* Ⓒ (*pl.* **-tries**) 1 an endowment for singing of masses. (미사의) 연보; 헌금. 2 a chapel of a church, used for the less important services. 소(小)〔부속〕 예배당. [↑]

chant·y [ʃǽnti, tʃǽn-] *n.* Ⓒ (*pl.* **chant·ies**) a song sung by sailors to keep time as they pull ropes or do other work. (일할 때 장단을 맞추는) 뱃노래. ¶ *a sea ~* 뱃노래. [↑]

cha·os [kéiɑs / -ɔs] *n.* Ⓤ 1 the state of being infinite or formless before the world began. (천지 창조 전의) 혼돈(混沌). 2 the state of being completely confused or in disorder. 혼란(상태); 무질서(opp. cosmos). ¶ *economical ~* 경제의 혼란 / *The city was thrown into ~.* 도시는 대혼란에 빠져들었다. [Gk.]

cha·ot·ic [keiɑ́tik / -ɔ́t-] *adj.* in a state of chaos; completely disordered; very confused. 혼돈된; 무질서한(opp. cosmic). ¶ *a ~ mind* 혼란된 정신 / *John's room was a ~ mess of clothes, books, and toys.* 존의 방은 옷가지, 책, 장난감 들이 어지러이 널려 있었다.

*__chap__[1] [tʃæp] *n.* Ⓒ 《*colloq.*》 a fellow; a man or boy. 사내; 녀석; 놈. ¶ *a nice* 〔*good*〕 *~* 좋은 녀석 / *Hello, old ~!* 여보게 친구. [→chapman]

*__chap__[2] [tʃæp] *n.* 《usu. *pl.*》 a crack in the skin caused by frost. etc. (추위 따위로) 살갗이 튼 데. — *vi., vt.* (P1;6) (**chapped, chap·ping**) (of the skin) crack; make or become rough. (살갗이) 트(게 하)다; 거칠어지(게 하)다. ¶ *My hands are terribly chapped.* 손이 몹시 텄다 / *The skin often chaps in cold weather.* 피부는 흔히 추운 날씨엔 거칠어진다. [M.Du. *kappen* to cut]

chap³ [tʃæp] *n.* **1** 《*pl.*》 jaws; cheeks. 턱; 뺨. **2** the lower jaw. 아래턱. [E.]

chap. chapel; chaplain; chapter.

chap·a·ra·jos, -re·jos [tʃæpəréious / tʃɑ̀:pəréihous] *n. pl.* 《U.S.》 =chaps. [Mex.]

·chapel [tʃǽpəl] *n.* Ⓒ **1** a small place of worship in a cathedral. (교회에 딸린) 소(小)예배당(cf. *chaplain*). **2** a place of worship in a school, palace, prison, etc. (학교·왕궁·교도소 따위의) 예배당〔실〕. **3** a service held in a chapel. (chapel 에서의) 예배(식). ¶ *go to* ~ 예배 보러 가다 / *miss* 〔*lose*〕 *a* ~ 예배에 참석지 않다. **4** 《Brit.》 a church not belonging to the Church of England or the Roman Catholic Church. (비국교도의) 교회. **5** a printing-shop. 인쇄소. [L. *cappa* cloak]

chap·er·on, -one [ʃǽpəròun] *n.* Ⓒ a married or older woman who watches over a young unmarried woman on public occasions. (사교계에 나가는 아가씨)의 곁따르는 보호녀(女); 샤프롱. — *vt.* (P6) act as a chaperon to (a girl). (아가씨에) 곁따르다; …의 샤프롱 노릇을 하다. [→cap]

chap·e·ron·age [ʃǽpəròunidʒ] *n.* Ⓤ a chaperon's care. 샤프롱 노릇.

chap·fall·en [tʃǽpfɔ̀:lən] *adj.* in low spirits; sad and hopeless. 풀〔기〕죽은; 의기 소침한.

chap·lain [tʃǽplin] *n.* Ⓒ a clergyman or priest who performs religious services in the army or navy, a school, a private house, prison, etc. 교목(校牧); 군목(軍牧); (교도소의) 교회사(敎誨師). [→chapel]

chap·lain·cy [tʃǽplinsi] *n.* Ⓒ a chaplain's office. chaplain 의 집무실〔직분〕.

chap·let [tʃǽplit] *n.* Ⓒ a ring of flowers, leaves, etc. worn on the head; a string of beads. (머리에 쓰는) 화관(花冠); 묵주(默珠). [→cap]

Chap·lin [tʃǽplin], **Charles Spencer** (Charlie Chaplin) *n.* (1889-1977) a film actor and producer. 채플린《영화 배우·감독》.

Chap·man [tʃǽpmən], **George** *n.* (1559-1634) an English poet. 채프먼《영국의 시인》.

chap·man [tʃǽpmən] *n.* Ⓒ (*pl.* **-men** [-mən]) 《Brit.》 a person who buys or sells at the door; a pedler. 행상인; 도붓장수. [→cheap]

chap·py [tʃǽpi] *adj.* cracked. 피부가 몹시 튼. [*chap¹*]

chaps [tʃæps] *n. pl.* 《U.S.》 strong leather trousers without a back. 가죽 바지. [Mex. *chaparajos*]

:chap·ter [tʃǽptər] *n.* Ⓒ **1** a main division of a book. (책의) 장(章). 參考 chap., ch. 또는 c.로 생략함. ¶ *the first* ~ = ~ *one* 제1장. **2** ⓐ an important part or section of anything. (역사·인생 등의) 한 시기; 한 장(章). ¶ *begin a new* ~ *in one's life* 인생의 새 장을 시작하다 / *The atomic bomb opened a new* ~ *in history.* 원폭은 역사의 새로운 장을 열었다. ⓑ a succession (of. events). (사건의) 연속. ¶ *a* ~ *of accidents* 사고의 연속. **3** a branch of a society or organization. (노조·정당 따위의) 지부; 분회. ¶ *the Inch'ŏn* ~ *of the Democratic Party* 민주당 인천 지구당. **4** a meeting of clergymen. 성직자 집회〔총회〕. ¶ *the chapter-house* 성직자 집회소. [→capital]

chapter and verse, exact authority for a statement. 정확한 출처〔전거(典據)〕.

to* 〔*till*〕 *the end of the chapter, 《*fig.*》 forever; to the very last. 영구히; 최후까지.

char¹ [tʃɑ:r] *vt., vi.* (P6;1) (**charred, charring**) change (wood) into charcoal; burn slightly or partly. 숯을 굽다; 새까맣게 타다〔태우다〕; 눋(게 하)다. [→charcoal]

char² [tʃɑ:r] *n.* 《fish》 a fish of trout kind. 곤들매기류(類). [Gael.]

char³ [tʃɑ:r] *n., v.* 《Brit.》 =chare.

char-à-banc [ʃǽrəbæŋk] *n.* 《Brit.》 a long vehicle for holidaymakers. 대형 관광 버스. [F.]

:char·ac·ter [kǽriktər] *n.* Ⓒ **1** ⓊⒸ qualities that make any person or thing different from others; any distinctive mark; moral and mental nature. 성격; 특성; 특징; 품성. ¶ *the national* ~ 국민성 / *the American* ~ 미국인의 특성〔기질〕/ *a man of* ~ 인격 있는 사람 / *good* 〔*bad*〕 ~ 좋은〔나쁜〕 성격 / *a girl without any significant* ~ 이렇다 할 특징이 없는 여자 아이 / *build* 〔*form, develop*〕 *one's* ~ 품성을 기르다 / *These trees are of a peculiar* ~. 이들 나무에는 특이한 성질이 있다 / *We like his* ~. 우리는 그의 성격을 좋아한다 / *What is the* ~ *of the plan you suggest?* 자네가 말하는 계획의 다른 점은 무엇인가. **2** ⓐ a person of some particular nature; a well-known person. 특이한 성질의 사람〔인물〕; 명사. ¶ *a public* ~ 공인(公人) / *a weak* ~ 의지 박약한 사람 / *a well-known* ~ 저명인사; 명사 / *an interesting* 〔*agreeable*〕 ~ 흥미있는〔유쾌한〕 인물 / *He is a* ~ *in this district.* 그는 이 지역의 유지다. ⓑ 《*colloq.*》 a person, esp. who does something unusual. 별난 사람; 괴짜. ¶ *He is quite a* ~. 그 사람 정말이지 괴짜다. **3** Ⓤ position; status; capacity. 지위; 자격. ¶ *in his* ~ *as ambassador* 대사의 자격으로 / *act in the* ~ *of guardian* 후견인의 자격으로 행동하다. **4** a person in a play or novel. (극·소설의) 인물. ¶ *the characters in the novel* 그 소설의 등장인물. **5** reputation. 명성; 평판. ¶ *get a good* ~ 좋은 평판을 얻다 / *gain a* ~ *for*... …로 명성을 날리다 / *lower one's* ~ 평판을 떨어뜨리다 / *lose* 〔*regain*〕 *one's* ~ 명성을 잃다〔회복하다〕 / *blacken someone's* ~ 아무의 명성에 먹칠을 하다 / *bear a good* ~ *among* *one's friends* 친구 사이에 평이 좋다. **6** a letter given by a former employer to an employee to aid in obtaining a job; a recommendation. (전 고용주의) 인물 추천장. ¶ *give someone a good* ~ 아무에게 좋은 추천장을 써 주다 / *engage a servant without a* ~ 인물 추천장 없이 하인을 채용하다. **7** a figure; a sign; a letter. 기호; 문자. ¶ *a Chinese* ~ 한자(漢字) / *a Korean syllabic* ~ 한글. [Gk. *kharattō* engrave]

in character, as expected; right; suitable. 걸맞아; 어울려; 적합하여.

out of character, not as expected; not right; not suitable. 어울리지 않아; 부적당하여.

character actor [ˊ-ˋ-- ˊ-] *n.* an actor in roles of eccentric individuality. 성격 배우.

:char·ac·ter·is·tic [kæ̀riktərístik] *adj.* different from others; special; typical. 특유의; 독특한. ¶ *Korea's* ~ *arts* 한국 특유의 미술 / *the* ~ *smell of bananas* 바나나 특유의 냄새 / *Sympathy is the feeling* ~ *of mankind.* 동정은 인류 특유의 감정이다. — *n.* Ⓒ **1** a special mark or quality. 특징; 특성; 특질. ¶ *individual characteristics* 개성 / *An elephant's trunk is its most noticeable* ~. 코끼리의 코는 그 가장 두드러진 특징이다. **2** an integral part. 지표.

char·ac·ter·is·ti·cal·ly [kæ̀riktərístikəli] *adv.* in a characteristic way; specially. 특징[특성]을 나타내도록; 특색[특징]으로서.

char·ac·ter·i·za·tion [kæ̀riktərizéiʃən] *n.* Ⓤ **1** the act of characterizing. 특징[특성]을 나타냄. **2** the description of characteristics. 성격 묘사. ¶ *Charles Dickens is famous for* ~. 찰스 디킨스는 성격 묘사로 유명하다.

·char·ac·ter·ize [kǽriktəràiz] *vt.* (P6) **1** show or describe the special qualities or features of (someone or something). …의 특색을 나타내다; 특성을 묘사하다. ¶ *He characterized her in a few well-chosen words.* 그는 그녀의 인품을 몇 마디 적절한 말로 나타냈다. **2** distinguish; mark out. 특징지우다. ¶ *Quick decision characterizes him.* 신속한 결정이 그의 특징이다 / *His style is characterized by simplicity.* 간결함이 그의 문체의 특징이다.

cha·rade [ʃəréid / -rɑ́:d] *n.* a game of guessing a word in which each syllable or part is shown in pantomime or dumb show. 말 알아맞히기《몸짓으로 나타낸 각 음절이나 마디로 어떤 말을 알아맞히는 놀이》. [F.]

char·coal [tʃɑ́:rkòul] *n.* Ⓤ wood burnt black, used as fuel. 숯; 목탄. ¶ *activated* ~ 활성탄(炭). [*char*]

charcoal burner [ˊ- ˋ-] *n.* **1** a person who makes charcoal. 숯 굽는 사람. **2** a kind of stove in which charcoal is burned. 숯풍로.

chare [tʃɛər] *n.* 《Brit.》 **1** Ⓒ a woman hired to do housework or cleaning. 가정부; 파출[잡역]부; 세탁부. **2** 《usu. *pl.*》 a part-time job, esp. of housework or cleaning. (가정의 시간제) 잡일. — *vi.* work at cleaning house by the day or hour. (일당·시간제로) 세탁소에서 일하다. — *vt.* do (a part-time jobs, housework, etc.). (잡일)을 하다. [E. =burn]

:charge [tʃɑ:rdʒ] *vt.* **1** (P13,14) 《*for*》 ask in payment; ask as a price; impose. (대금)을 청구하다; (세금)을 과하다. ¶ ~ *a dollar a lesson* 레슨 1회당 1달러를 받다 / ~ *a tax on an income* 세금을 과하다 / *That store charges $5 for gloves.* 저 가게에서는 장갑 한 켤레에 5달러 한다 / *How much do you* ~ *for a room?* 방값은 얼마나 받나요. **2** (P13) 《usu. *in passive*》 give (someone) a task as a duty; burden. (일·임무)를 지우다; 과하다; 맡기다. ¶ *be charged with a task* 임무가 맡겨지다 / *be charged with heavy responsibilities* 중책이 짊어지워지다 / *He was charged with an important mission.* 그에게 중요한 사명이 맡겨졌다. **3** (P6,13) 《*with*》 blame; accuse. …을 비난하다; 고발하다. ¶ ~ *someone as a agitator* 아무를 선동자로 비난하다 / ~ *someone with murder* 아무를 살인죄로 고발하다 / *They charged him with theft.* 그는 절도죄로 고발되었다 / *This man is charged with stealing a gun.* 이 사람은 총기를 훔친 죄로 고발돼 있다. **4** (P6,13) ⓐ put into; fill; load. …에 (채워) 넣다; (탄알을) 장전하다. ¶ ~ *a camera* 카메라에 필름을 넣다 / ~ *a pen* 만년필에 잉크를 넣다 / ~ *a gun with bullets* 총에 탄알을 장전하다. ⓑ store electricity in (a battery) …에 충전하다. ¶ ~ *a storage battery* 축전지에 충전하다. ⓒ 《*fig.*》 fill; excite. (감정으로) 그득 채우다; 넘치게 하다. ¶ *Her voice was charged with emotion.* 그녀의 음성은 감동에 차 있었다. **5** (P13) load; burden. (마음·머릿속을 부담·고민 따위로) 괴롭히다; 짓누르다. ¶ *a heart charged with cares* 근심 걱정으로 무거운 마음 / *His mind was charged with weighty matters.* 그의 마음은 여러 중요한 문제들로 고민하고 있었다. **6** (P20) command; order; instruct; request. …에게 명령[지시]하다; 요구하다. ¶ *He charged her to be careful.* 그는 그녀에게 조심할 것을 당부했다 / *The sentinels were charged to remain at their posts.* 보초들은 각자 자기 위치를 지키라는 지시를 받았다 / *He charged me not to forget what he said.* 그는 자기가 한 말을 명심하라고 했다. **7** (P6,13) put down as a debt; hold liable for payment. 차변(借邊)에 기입(記入)하다; …의 셈[부담]으로 하다. ¶ *Charge it to me* [*my account*]. 내 앞으로 달아 놓으시오. **8** (P6) rush at; attack. 돌진[공격]하다; 돌격[습격]하다. ¶ *The soldiers charged the enemy.* 병사들은 적군을 향해 돌진했다.

— *vi.* (P1,2A,3) **1** demand a price. 값[요금]을 요구하다. ¶ *He charges too much for his service.* 그는 서비스 대가를 너무 많이 요구한다 / *We* ~ *by the hour when we rent our* boats. 보트 임대료는 시간당 얼마로 받습니다. **2** 《*on, at*》 make an attack; rush. 공격〔돌진〕하다. ¶ ~ *into a house* 집으로 뛰어들다 / *The children charged at the tall boy.* 어린이들은 키 큰 소년에게 대들었다.

charge off, take away (some amount of money) as a loss. 결손으로서 공제하다.

charge off to, regard as the result of (something). …의 탓으로 돌리다.

charge** oneself **with (=*hold oneself responsible for*) *something.* …의 책임을 떠맡다.

— *n.* **1** Ⓒ《often *pl.*》 the payment asked; the price demanded; the expenses; tax. 요금; 값; 비용; 세금. ¶ *the* ~ *for board* 식비(食費) / *the* ~ *for a room* 방값 / *the* ~ *for trouble* 수고비 / *at a reasonable* ~ 합당한 값으로 / *His charges are too high.* 그의 청구액이 너무 많다 / *No* ~ *for admission.* 입장 무료. **2** Ⓤ load; burden. (무거운) 짐. **3** Ⓒ a work as a duty; Ⓤ responsibility. (의무로서의) 일; 임무; 책임. ¶ *a* ~ *laid upon him* 그에게 과해진 임무 / *lay the mistake to his* ~ 잘못을 그의 책임〔탓〕으로 돌리다. **4** ⓐ Ⓤ care; management; trust. 돌봄; 보호; 감독; 관리; 운영; 위탁. ¶ *a doctor* 〔*an officer*〕 *in* ~ 담당 의사〔직원〕 / *in* ~ *of a shop* 〔*a party*〕 가게를〔당을〕 운영하는 / *The nurse is in* ~ *of the children.* 아이 보는 여자가 애들을 돌보고 있다. ⓑ Ⓒ a person or thing placed in one's care or management. 맡겨진 사람〔것〕; 위임받은 것; 수탁물. ¶ *young charges* 맡겨진〔맡아 돌보는〕 아이들. **5** Ⓒ accusation. 비난; 고발. ¶ *make a* ~ *of carelessness against* 부주의하다 하여 …을 비난하다 / *make a false* ~ *against* …에 대해 무고하다; …에게 트집을 잡다 / *bring a* ~ *of murder against him* 그를 살인죄로 고발하다. **6** Ⓤ an order or direction. 명령; 지시. ¶ *the* ~ *of a judge to a jury* 배심원에 대한 판사의 지시. **7** an amount of electricity in an object. 충전(량). **8** Ⓒ an attack. 공격. ¶ *a fierce* ~ 맹렬한 공격. [→car]

free of charge, without fee. 무료로.

give** someone **in charge, **a**) entrust. …을 위탁하다〔맡기다〕. **b**) give someone up to the police. (경찰에) 넘기다.

have charge of, =take charge of. ¶ *Who has* ~ *of the children?* 이 아이들은 누가 돌보는가.

in full charge, impetuously. 맹렬하게; 쏜살같이 달려.

return to the charge, begin again. 다시 하다.

take charge of (=*be responsible for*) *something.* …을 떠맡다; 담당하다. ¶ *take* ~ *of a class* 학급 담임을 맡다 / *take* ~ *of the money* 돈 관리를 하다.

charge·a·ble [tʃáːrdʒəbəl] *adj.* that may or should be charged. (죄·세금·부담·비용 등이) 지워져야 할. ¶ *The expense is* ~ *on him.* 비용은 그가 내야 한다 / *He is* ~ *with theft.* 그는 절도로 고발해야 한다.

char·gé d'af·faires [ʃaːrʒéi dəféər, ⌐– –⌐] *n.* (*pl.* **char·gés d-**) 《F.》 a deputy ambassador. 대리 대사〔공사〕.

charg·er [tʃáːrdʒər] *n.* Ⓒ **1** an army officer's horse. 군마(軍馬). **2** a large flat dish. 큰 접시. [*charge*]

·**char·i·ot** [tʃǽriət] *n.* Ⓒ 《hist.》 a cart with two wheels, drawn by horses and used in ancient times for fighting, racing, etc. (옛 로마·그리스의) 2륜 마차의 전차(戰車). [→car]

char·i·ot·eer [tʃæ̀riətíər] *n.* Ⓒ a person who drives a chariot. chariot를 모는 전사(戰士).

cha·ris·ma [kərízmə] *n.* (*pl.* **-mata**) *n.* a divinely conferred gift or power; a special quality of leadership. 카리스마; 비범한 능력. [Gk.]

cha·ris·ma·ta [kərízmətə] *n.* pl. of **charisma.**

char·i·ta·ble [tʃǽrətəbəl] *adj.* **1** merciful; generous; kindly. 자비로운; 관대한. ¶ *a very* ~ *person* 〔*nature*〕 매우 자비심 많은 사람〔성품〕 / *He is very* ~ *in his opinions of others.* 그는 다른 사람에 대한 평가에 무척 너그럽다. **2** having to do with charity. 자선의. ¶ *a* ~ *institution* 〔*organization*〕 자선 시설〔단체〕 / ~ *enterprises* 〔*works*〕 자선 사업. ● **char·i·ta·bly** [-i] *adv.* [L. *carus* dear]

:**char·i·ty** [tʃǽrəti] *n.* **1** Ⓤ ⓐ mercy; Christian love. 자비; 자애; (기독교적인) 사랑. ¶ *in* 〔*out of*〕 ~ *with* …을 가엾이 여겨 / *help someone out of* ~ 인정심에서 아무를 돕다 / *live on the unwilling* ~ *of one's relations* 친척들의 마지못한 의리에 매달려 생활하다. ⓑ kindness in judging people's faults. 관용. **2** Ⓤ a gift to the poor; the help given to the poor. 구호물〔금〕; 시여물; 자선(행위). ¶ ~ *for the poor and weak* 가난한 자와 병약자들을 위한 구호물 / *beg* 〔*ask for*〕 ~ 자선을〔시여를〕 청하다. **3** 《usu. *pl.*》 a society for helping the sick and the poor. 자선 시설〔사업〕. ¶ *A free hospital is a noble* ~. 시료원(施療院)은 숭고한 자선 시설이다. [↑]

char·la·tan [ʃáːrlətən] *n.* Ⓒ a person who pretends to have more knowledge or more wonderful cures than he really has. 허풍선이; 협잡꾼; 아는 체하는 사람; 돌팔이 의사(cf. *quack*²). [It. =patterer]

Char·le·magne [ʃáːrləmèin] *n.* (742-814) the emperor of the Holy Roman Empire. 샤를마뉴《신성 로마 제국의 황제》.

Charles [tʃaːrlz] *n.* a man's name. 남자 이름.

Charles's Wain [tʃáːrlziz wéin], 《Brit. astron.》 *n.* the Big Dipper. 북두 칠성.

Char·lotte [ʃáːrlət] *n.* a woman's name. 여자 이름.

:**charm** [tʃaːrm] *n.* **1** ⓊⒸ a power to attract or please; magic power. 매력; 마력. ¶ *physical* ~ 육체적 매력 / *possess* ~ *of manner* 몸가짐에 사람을 끄는 매력이 있다 / *be under a* ~ 마력에 걸려 있다. **2** 《usu. *pl.*》 a quality that attracts; appeal; beauty.

(여자의) 아름다움; 미모; 매력. ¶ *succumb to feminine charms* 여자의 아름다움에 압도되다 / *fall a victim to her charms* 여자의 미색에 혹하다 / *She has lost her charms.* 그녀의 미모는 이제 한물 갔다. **3** Ⓒ a word or words having magical power. 주문(呪文). ¶ *chant a* ~ 주문을 외다. **4** Ⓒ anything supposed to have magic power or to bring good luck. 부적(符籍). ¶ *a* ~ *against bad luck* 재난을 피하는 부적 / *wear a* ~ *to ward off diseases* 병 예방을 위해 부적을 몸에 지니고 있다.

like 〔***to***〕 ***a charm,*** as if by magic; wonderfully. 마법에라도 걸린 듯이; 놀랍게. ¶ *This medicine acts*〔*works*〕 *like a* ~. 이 약은 신기하게 잘 듣는다.

— *vt.* (P6,7) **1** attract; fascinate. …을 매혹하다; 황홀케 하다. ¶ *be charmed with the music* 음악에 도취되다 / *He was charmed by the girl's smiles.* 그는 처녀의 미소에 매혹되었다. **2** give pleasure to (someone). …을 기쁘게 하다. ¶ *I am charmed to meet you.* 뵙게 되어 반갑습니다. **3** influence (something) as by magic power; protect (something) as by a spell; use magic on (something). 마력으로 …하게 하다; …에 마법을 걸다; …을 마법으로 보호하다. ¶ ~ *someone asleep* 마법으로 아무를 잠들게 하다 / ~ *a secret out of someone* 아무에게 마법을 걸어 비밀을 캐내다 / ~ *away one's cares* 마력으로 걱정을 없애다. — *vi.* (P1) be attractive. 매력이 있다; 마음을 빼앗다. ¶ *Goodness often charms more than mere beauty.* 선(善)은 종종 단순한 미(美)보다 더 매력이 있다. [L. *carmen* song]

bear a charmed life, be invulnerable. 불사신이다.

charm·er [tʃáːrmər] *n.* Ⓒ **1** a person who charms. 마술사. ¶ *a snake* ~ 뱀을 길들여 부리는 사람. **2** a very attractive girl or woman. 미녀(美女).

:charm·ing [tʃáːrmiŋ] *adj.* full of charm; attractive; delightful. 매력있는; 아름다운; 즐거운. ¶ *a* ~ *girl* 매혹적인 처녀 / *Her manner is very* ~. 그녀의 몸가짐이 아주 매력적이다. ● **charm·ing·ly** [-li] *adv.*

char·nel house [tʃáːrnl hàus] *n.* a place where the bodies or the bones of the dead are laid. 납골당(納骨堂); 묘소. [→carnage]

Char·on [kέərən] *n.* 《Gk. myth.》 the boatman who took the spirits of the dead across the river in the lower world. 삼도(三途)내의 나루지기(cf. *Styx*). [Gk.]

***chart** [tʃaːrt] *n.* Ⓒ **1** a sailor's map of the sea. 해도(海圖); 수로도(水路圖). **2** a sheet giving information by means of curves, lines, etc.; a rough map; a list; a table. 백지도(白地圖); 도(圖); 도표(圖表). ¶ *a weather* ~ 일기도 / *a temperature* ~ 온도〔체온〕표 / *a* ~ *of price changes* 물가 변동표. — *vt.* (P6) draw a chart of (something); show (something) on a chart. …의 해도〔도표〕를 만들다; …을 그림으로〔표로〕 나타내다. ¶ ~ *unknown seas* 알려지지 않은 해역의 해도를 만들다. ● **chart·less** [-lis] *adj.* [→card[1]]

***char·ter** [tʃáːrtər] *n.* Ⓒ **1** a formal paper of rights, permission to do something, etc. given by a ruler or government. (통치자·정부가 주는) 특허장; 면허장. **2** a formal paper defining the right to organize a new organization, chapter, branch, etc. (목적·강령의) 선언(서); 헌장(憲章). ¶ *the Great Charter* 《Brit. hist.》 대헌장 / *the Charter of the United Nations* 유엔 헌장. — *vt.* (P6) **1** grant a charter or special right to. …에게 특허를〔특권을〕 주다; 면허하다. **2** hire (a ship, airplane, etc.). (선박·비행기 따위)를 전세 내다. ¶ ~ *a ship* 용선(傭船)하다. [→card[2]]

char·tered [tʃáːrtərd] *adj.* **1** given or allowed by a chart 〔charter〕. 특허를 받은; 공인의. ¶ 《Brit.》 *a* ~ *accountant* 공인 회계사. **2** hired. 전세낸.

Char·ter-house [tʃáːrtərhàus] *n.* an almshouse in London. 런던 양로원.

charter party [ˊ-- ˋ-] *n.* an indenture between a shipowner and a merchant. 용선(傭船) 계약(서).

Chart·ism [tʃáːrtizəm] *n.* 《Brit. hist.》 working class movement to achieve the political reform in the 19th century England. 차티스트〔인민 헌장〕 운동《노동자 계급에 의한 정치 개혁 목적의 운동》. [*Chart*]

char·wom·an [tʃáːrwùmən] *n.* Ⓒ (*pl.* **-wom·en** [-wìmin]) a woman hired by the day or hour for doing odd jobs in a house or public building. (일당·시간제로 일하는) 파출부. [→chare]

char·y [tʃέəri] *adj.* (**char·i·er, char·i·est**) 《*of*》 **1** careful; cautious. 조심스러운; 주의깊은; 세심한. ¶ *be* ~ *of one's fame* 자기 평판에 신경을 쓰다 / *be* ~ *of catching cold* 감기에 걸리지 않도록 조심하다. **2** shy. 부끄럼을 타는; 수줍어하는. ¶ *a* ~ *girl* 내향적인 소녀 / *be* ~ *of strangers* 낯선 사람 만나기를 수줍어하다. **3** unwilling to give; stingy. 인색한; 아끼는. ¶ *be* ~ *of speech* 말수가 적다 / *He is* ~ *of his praise.* 그는 칭찬에 인색하다. **4** fastidious; choosy. 까다로운; 가리는. [E.→care]

:chase[1] [tʃeis] *vt.* (P6,7,13) **1** run after (someone or something) to catch or kill; pursue. …을 (뒤)쫓다; 추적하다. ¶ ~ *a criminal* 범죄자를 추적하다 / ~ *a fox* 여우를 뒤쫓다 / ~ *the enemy's ship* 적함을 추격하다. **2** drive away. …을 몰(아내)다; 쫓아내다. ¶ ~ *someone off* 아무를 쫓아내다 / ~ *cats out of the garden* 고양이를 뜰 밖으로 몰아내다 / *He chased all fear from the mind.* 그는 모든 공포심을 떨쳐버렸다. — *vi.* follow in pursuit. 뒤쫓다; 추적하다. ¶ ~ *after a thief* 도둑의 뒤를 쫓다.

chase down, examine closely to find out

the fact. 사실을 알아내기 위해 면밀히 조사하다.

— *n.* Ⓒ **1** an earnest pursuit. 추적; 추격; 추구. ¶ *a ~ after a murderer* 살인자의 추적 / *the ~ of pleasure* 쾌락의 추구 / *in ~ of* …을 뒤쫓아; …을 추적[추구]하여. **2** 《usu. *the ~*》 ⓐ hunting as a sport; a district where this sport is pursued. 사냥; 사냥터. ¶ *lovers of the ~* 사냥 애호가. ⓑ 《*collectively*》 hunters. 사냥꾼들. ⓒ a hunted animal. 엽수(獵獸); 사냥감. ¶ *The ~ escaped.* 사냥감을 놓쳤다. **3** a ship running away from another. 쫓기는 배. [→catch]

give chase to, run after (someone); chase. …을 뒤쫓다; 추적[추격]하다. ¶ *give ~ to the enemy* 적을 추격하다.

chase[2] [tʃeis] *vt.* (P6) ornament (metal or other hard material) by engraving or embossing. (금속 따위)에 돋을새김하다; (무늬)를 양각하다. [→case[2]]

chas·er [tʃéisər] *n.* Ⓒ **1** a person or thing that chases; a hunter; a pursuer. 뒤쫓는 사람[것]; 사냥꾼; 추격[추적, 추구]자. **2** 《mil.》 a small, fast airplane or ship used to pursue the enemy. 추격기(機); 추격함(艦). **3** a gun on a ship, used during pursuit of or by another ship. (함정의) 추격포(砲). **4** 《*colloq.*》 cold water or beer taken after raw spirits. 독한 술 뒤에 마시는 찬 물이나 맥주. [→chase[1]]

chasm [kǽzəm] *n.* Ⓒ **1** a deep opening in the earth; gap. (지면 따위의) 깊게 갈라진 틈; 간극(間隙). ¶ *~ in the wall* 벽의 균열. **2** a wide difference of feelings or opinions, etc. between people or groups. (감정·의견 따위의) 큰 차이; 간격. ¶ *bridge over a ~* 간격을 메우다 / *The ~ between the two countries grew wider and wider, and at last resulted in war.* 양국 간의 감정의 골은 점점 깊어져 마침내 전쟁에까지 이르렀다. [Gk. = gape]

chas·sis [ʃǽsi:] *n.* Ⓒ (*pl.* **chas·sis** [-z]) **1** the frame, wheels or machinery that supports the body of an automobile, airplane, etc. (자동차의) 차대(車臺); (비행기의) 기대(機臺); 각부(脚部). **2** the framework in which the parts of a radio or television set are mounted. (라디오·TV의) 섀시《세트를 조립하는 대》; 밑판. [F.<L. *capsa* box]

chaste [tʃeist] *adj.* **1** morally pure; sexually pure; virtuous. 순결한; 정숙한(opp. immoral). **2** modest. (언동이) 조신(操身)스러운; 점잖은. **3** (of style, ornament, etc.) pure in taste; simple. (문체·장식 따위가) 차분한; 간소한. ● **chaste·ly** [-li] *adv.* [L. *castus* pure]

chas·ten [tʃéisən] *vt.* (P6,13) **1** punish (someone) in order to correct; train (someone) by pain or trials. (고치려고) …를 징계하다; …을 단련시키다. ¶ *a spirit chastened by adversity*[*suffering*] 역경[고난]에 의해 단련된 정신 / *~ a son with a rod* 회초리로 아들을 징계하다. **2** bring (something) under control; subdue. …을 누르다; 억제하다; 누그러뜨리다. ¶ *~ one's passions* 격정을 억누르다. **3** refine; purify. …을 세련되게 [품위 있게] 하다. ● **chas·ten·er** [-ər] *n.* [L. *castigo* castigate]

chas·tise [tʃæstáiz] *vt.* (P6) **1** correct (a child, etc.) with a rod. (아이 등)을 회초리로 징계하다. **2** punish. …을 벌하다. ¶ *~ someone for his fault* 과실을 범한 사람을 처벌하다. [→chasten, -ize]

chas·tise·ment [tʃæstáizmənt, tʃǽstiz-] *n.* ⓊⒸ punishment; beating. 징벌; 징계; 매질.

chas·ti·ty [tʃǽstəti] *n.* Ⓤ **1** purity; virtue; virginity. 순결; 동정(童貞); 처녀성. ¶ *keep one's ~* 순결을 지키다. **2** simplicity of taste, style, etc. (취미·문체 등의) 고아(高雅); 간결; 간소. [→chaste, -ity]

chas·u·ble [tʃǽzjəbəl, tʃǽs-] *n.* a sleeveless mantle of a celebrant. 사제(司祭)의 소매 없는 망토; 제의(祭衣). [L. *casa* cottage]

·**chat** [tʃæt] *n.* Ⓒ **1** an easy and familiar conversation; gossip. 무간(無間)한 이야기; 세상 이야기; 잡담. ¶ *have a ~ with a friend* 친구와 잡담하다 / *I called on him for a ~.* 잡담이나 나누려고 그를 찾았다. **2** idle or foolish talk; chatter. 쓸데없는 이야기; 수다. ¶ *Let me have none of your ~.* 시시한 이야기 좀 집어치우게. — *vi.* (P1,2A,3) (**chatted, chat·ting**) talk in an easy and friendly way. 잡담[한담]하다. ¶ *~ over tea* [*cigarettes*] 차를 마시면서[담배를 피우면서] 잡담하다 / *~ with friends* 친구들과 잡담하다. [→chatter]

châ·teau [ʃætóu] *n.* Ⓒ (*pl.* **-s, -teaux**) a French castle or country mansion. (프랑스의) 성; 대저택. [→castle]

châ·teaux [ʃætóuz] *n.* pl. of **château.**

chât·e·laine [ʃǽtəlèin] *n.* **1** the mistress of a château or a large country house. 성주(城主)의 아내; 여(女)성주; 시골 대저택의 여주인. **2** a chain worn at a woman's waist to which keys, purse, etc. are fastened. (여인의) 장식 띠사슬《열쇠·패물 따위를 늘어뜨림》. [↑]

chat·tel [tʃǽtl] *n.* Ⓒ 《usu. *pl.*》 a movable possession; a piece of personal property besides houses or land. 동산; 가재(家財). ¶ *goods and chattels* 가재 도구. [→cattle]

*****chat·ter** [tʃǽtər] *vi.* (P1,2A,3) **1** (of a person) talk fast, constantly and foolishly. (시시한 소리를) 빠르게 지껄이다; 재잘거리다. ¶ *~ with a friend* 친구와 지껄이다 / *~ like a flock of magpies* 까치떼처럼 시끄럽게 지껄여대다. **2** (of birds, monkeys, etc.) make short, quick sounds. (새·원숭이 따위가) 짹짹[깍깍]거리다. ¶ *The monkey chattered in anger.* 원숭이는 성이 나서 깍깍거렸다. **3** (of teeth, parts of a machine, etc.) make a noise by hitting each other.

(추워서 이가) 딱딱 맞부딪치다; (기계 따위가) 덜컥(달각)거리다. ¶ *His teeth chattered with cold.* 그는 추워서 이가 딱딱 마쳤다. — *n.* Ⓒ Ⓤ **1** idle, rapid talk. 재잘거림; (쓸데없는) 수다. ¶ *I don't want to have idle* ~. 쓸데없는 수다를 떨고 싶지는 않다. **2** quick, short sounds. (새의) 지저귐; (원숭이 따위의) 꺅꺅거림; 달각(덜컥)거리는 소리. [Imit.]

chat·ter·box [tʃǽtərbɑ̀ks / -bɔ̀ks] *n.* Ⓒ a person who chatters a great deal. 수다쟁이. [↑]

chat·ter·er [tʃǽtərər] *n.* Ⓒ a person who chatters. 수다떠는 사람.

Chat·ter·ton [tʃǽtərtn], **Thomas** *n.* (1752-70) an English poet. 채터톤《영국의 시인》.

chat·ty [tʃǽti] *adj.* (**-ti·er, -ti·est**) fond of chatting; talkative. 잡담을(이야기를) 좋아하는. [*chatter*]

Chau·cer [tʃɔ́:sər], **Geoffrey** *n.* (1340?-1400) an English poet. 초서《영국의 시인》.

chaud-froid [ʃóufrwɑ́:] *n.* a dish of filleted poultry served cold in jelly or sauce. 쇼프루아《젤리나 소스를 쳐 차게 내놓는 새고기 요리》. [F.]

chauf·feur [ʃóufər, ʃoufə́:r] *n.* Ⓒ a person whose work is to drive another's automobile. (남의 차) 운전사. [→chafe]

chauf·feuse [ʃoufə́:z] *n.* a female chauffeur. (남의 차) 여자 운전사. [↑]

chau·tau·qua [ʃətɔ́:kwə] *n.* 《U.S.》 a meeting for educational purposes and entertainment by lectures, concerts, etc. 문화 강습회. [Place]

chau·vin·ism [ʃóuvənìzəm] *n.* Ⓤ unreasoning devotion to one's country; warlike patriotism. 맹목적(호전적) 애국주의; 국수주의. [Person, a soldier of Napoleon]

chau·vin·ist [ʃóuvənist] *n.* Ⓒ an unreasoning patriot; a warlike person. 맹목적(호전적) 애국주의자. — *adj.* =chauvinistic.

chau·vin·is·tic [ʃòuvənístik] *adj.* of chauvinism or chauvinists. 맹목적 애국주의(자)의.

Ch. E. Chemical Engineer (화학 기사).

:cheap [tʃi:p] *adj.* **1** low in price; not expensive. (값이) 싼; 비싸지 않은(opp. expensive; dear). ¶ ~ *and nasty* 값싸고 질이 나쁜 / *a* ~ *edition* 염가판 / *be (as)* ~ *as dirt* 무척 싸다 / *Fuel isn't* ~. 연료값이 비싸다. **2** worth more than its cost. 싸고도 좋은. ¶ *be* ~ *for a thousand won* 천 원이면 싸다 / *It's* ~ *at $20.* 20 달러면 싼 편이다. **3** asking low prices. 싸게 파는. ¶ *a* ~ *dealer* (*shop*) 싸게 파는 상인(가게). **4** of poor quality; worthless; easily obtained; common. 저질(싸구려)의; 시시한; 손쉽게 얻을 수 있는; 흔해 빠진. ¶ *a* ~ *novel* 싸구려 소설 / *a* ~ *victory* 낙승 / *make oneself (too)* ~ (자신을) 값싸게 굴다 / *Talk is* ~. 말하는 것엔 밑천이 안 든다. **5** 《colloq.》 out of sorts. 풀이 죽은; 기운 없는.

dirt cheap =***cheap as dirt,*** extremely cheap. 터무니없이 싼.

feel cheap, 《sl.》 **a**) feel ill. 기분이 좋지 않다. **b**) feel inferior and ashamed. 열등감을 느끼다; 주눅이 들다.

hold** someone or something **cheap, put little value on someone or something; despise. …을 얕보다. ¶ *He holds life* ~. 그는 목숨을 우습게 여긴다.

on the cheap, 《colloq.》 cheaply. 싸게; 경제적으로. ¶ *I got it on the* ~. 그것을 싸게 샀다.

— *adv.* at a low price; cheaply. 싸게. ¶ *get* (*sell*) *something* ~ …을 싸게 사다(팔다). [E.=price]

cheap·en [tʃí:pən] *vt.* (P6) **1** make (something) cheap or cheaper. …을 싸게 하다. **2** make to look small; bring into contempt; belittle. …을 경시하다; 얕보다; 우습게 보다. ¶ ~ *someone* 아무를 깔보다 / ~ *oneself* 치신없이 굴다. — *vi.* become cheap. 싸지다.

cheap Jack [´ ´] *n.* a travelling hawker. 행상인.

cheap·ly [tʃí:pli] *adv.* at a low price; in a cheap manner. 싼 값에; 쉽게.

cheap·ness [tʃí:pnis] *n.* Ⓤ the state of being cheap. 값쌈.

***cheat** [tʃi:t] *vt.* (P6,7,13) **1** 《*out of, into*》 deceive; deprive (someone) of something by trickery. …을 속이다; 속여 빼앗다. ¶ ~ *someone on the price...* 아무에게 가격을 속이다 / ~ *someone into the belief that...* 아무를 속여 …라고 믿게 하다 / ~ *someone into marrying* 아무를 속여 결혼하게 하다 / *He cheated his customers in business.* 그는 장사에서 손님을 속였다 / *He cheated me out of my money.* 그는 나에게서 돈을 사취했다. **2** escape by skill. …을 용케 면하다. ¶ ~ *the gallows* 교수형을 모면하다. **3** while away; beguile. (슬픔·지루함 등)을 달래다; (시간)을 그럭저럭 보내다. ¶ ~ *one's sorrow* (*the tedium*) 슬픔(따분함)을 달래다 / ~ *dull hours by reading* 독서로 따분한 시간을 보내다.

— *vi.* (P1) act dishonestly. 속임수를 쓰다; 부정한 짓을 하다. ¶ ~ *at cards* 카드 놀이에서 속이다 / ~ *in* (*on*) *an examination* 시험에서 커닝을 하다.

— *n.* Ⓒ a person who deceives another; a cheater; a dishonest trick. 속이는 사람; 사기꾼; 속임수. ¶ *He is a* ~. 그는 사기꾼이다. [M.E.; L. *cado* fall]

:check [tʃek] *n.* Ⓒ **1** a sudden stop; a restraint or control. 정지; 저지; 억제; 방해. ¶ *a journey without a* ~ 순조로운 여행 / *come to a* ~ 갑자기 정지하다 / *give a* ~ *to* … 을 저지하다 / *keep a* ~ *on* …을 억제하다 / *meet with a* ~ 저지당하다 / *The plan met with a* ~. 계획은 저지당했다. **2** any person or thing that controls or holds back action. 저지(억제)하는 사람(것, 수단). **3** ⓐ a test by comparison; an examination or investigation. (대조) 검사; 점검; 조사; 체크. ¶ *a periodical* ~ 정기 검사 / *give a doc-*

ument a quick ~ 서류를 급히 조사하다 / *make a complete* ~ *of a list* 리스트를 빈틈없이 체크하다 / *make a* ~ *on someone* 아무에 관한 조사를 하다. ⓑ 《U.S.》 a mark showing that something has been examined or compared. 대조표〔인(印)〕; 검인(檢印). **4** 《U.S.》 a written order for money, drawn upon a bank. 수표(cf. 《Brit.》 *cheque*). ¶ *a* ~ *for $200,* 200 달러 수표 / *draw a* ~ 수표를 발행하다. **5** a ticket or piece of metal given to show the owner of an article. 물표; 교환표. ¶ *a baggage* ~ (맡긴) 수화물의 물표 / *a* ~ *for a coat* 외투의 물표. **6** a pattern made of squares; a single one of these squares. 격자〔체크〕 무늬. **7** 《chess》 the state in which the king is in danger; a word meaning that the opponent's king is in this state. 장군(!).
hand in one's check, 《U.S. *fig.*》 **a**) die. 죽다. **b**) give up; surrender. 포기하다.
keep 〔***hold***〕 ***in check,*** control; restrain. (억)누르다; 억제하다.
— *vt.* (P6,7) **1** ⓐ stop the motion or progress of; stop suddenly. (움직임)을 갑자기 멈추다; 저지하다. ¶ ~ *one's step* 갑자기 발걸음을 멈추다 / ~ *a horse with reins* 고삐를 당겨 말을 급히 멈추다 / ~ *a person who is running* 달리는 사람을 막다 / ~ *the progress of a boat* 배를 멈추다. ⓑ hold back; control; restrain. (억)누르다; 억제하다; 참다. ¶ ~ *one's impulse* 〔*anger*〕 충동〔노염〕을 억제하다 / ~ *the rise in wages and prices* 임금과 물가의 상승을 억제하다 / *He started to say something, but checked himself.* 그는 무엇인가 말을 꺼냈으나 입을 다물어 버렸다. **2** examine (something) to prove it true or correct, as by comparison; investigate. (대조 따위로) …을 확인〔체크〕하다; 조사하다. ¶ ~ *a copy with the original* 사본을 원본과 대조하다 / ~ *someone's statement* 아무의 진술서를 확인하다 / ~ *over* 〔*through*〕 *a document* 〔*the evidence*〕 서류〔증거〕를 철저히 조사하다 / ~ *the time on the clock* 시계로 시간을 확인하다. **3** 《U.S.》 leave (one's possession) for short safekeeping. (물표를 받고) …을 잠시 맡기다. ¶ ~ *one's umbrella at the entrance* 우산을 현관에 맡겨두다. **4** 《U.S.》 get a ticket, a piece of wood, metal, etc. that shows one's right to receive (something). …의 물표를 받다. **5** 《often *off*》 mark with a check (✓). 대조〔점검〕 표시를 하다; …를 체크하다. ¶ ~ *off the telephone numbers one by one* 전화 번호를 하나하나 체크하다. — *vi.* (P1,2A,3) **1** make a stop. (갑자기) 멈추다; 멈춰 서다. **2** 《U.S.》 change a check for cash. 수표를 발행하다. [Arab. *shah* king(in chess); Arab. *mata* is dead]
check at, be angered by. …에 노하다.
check in, **a**) register one's name as a guest at a hotel. (호텔에 도착하여) 숙박 절차를 밟다; 체크인하다. ¶ ~ *in at a hotel* 호텔에 투숙하다 / *He telephoned soon after he checked in.* 호텔에 투숙하자 그는 곧 전화했다. **b**) die. 죽다.
check something off, mark something as having been examined or done. 대조필〔검사필〕의 표(✓)를 하다.
check out, **a**) pay one's bill and leave, as from a hotel. 숙박료를 치르고 호텔을 떠나다. ¶ ~ *out of a motel* 숙박비를 물고 모텔을 떠나다. **b**) die. 죽다.
check up on 〔***upon***〕***,*** test; compare to prove (something) correct; investigate. …을 조사〔대조〕하다. ¶ *We have to* ~ *up on her.* 그 여자에 대해 알아봐야겠다.
check (***up***) ***with,*** fulfill requirement of. …와 부합〔일치〕하다.

check·book [tʃékbùk] *n.* Ⓒ 《U.S.》 a book containing blank checks on a bank. 수표장(帳)(cf. 《Brit.》 *chequebook*).

checked [tʃekt] *adj.* with a checker pattern. 바둑〔체크〕 무늬의.

check·er [tʃékər] *vt.* (P6) **1** mark (something) with small squares of different colors; mark (something) with light and shade. …을 바둑판 무늬로 하다; 얼룩덜룩하게 하다; 명암이 엇갈리게 하다. ¶ *be checkered with sunlight and shade* 햇빛〔볕〕과 그늘로 얼룩덜룩해지다 / *The cook wore a blue and white checkered apron.* 요리사는 청백의 체크 무늬 앞치마를 걸치고 있었다. **2** mark by changes. 변화를〔다양성을〕 주다. ¶ *a checkered career* 파란 만장의 생애.
— *n.* Ⓒ **1** a pattern with squares of different colors. 바둑판 무늬. **2** one of the flat, round pieces used in the game of checkers. 체커〔서양 장기〕의 말. **3** 《U.S.》 《*pl.* used as *sing.*》 a game played on a checkerboard. 체커; 서양 장기(cf. 《Brit.》 *draughts*). 參考 체스판 위에서 12 개의 말을 써서 하는 게임. [*check*]

check·er·board [tʃékərbɔ̀ːrd] *n.* Ⓒ a board divided into 32 red squares and 32 black squares, on which the games of checkers and chess are played. 체커판. 參考 붉고 검은 64개의 바둑 무늬가 있는 판으로서 체커나 체스 게임에 쓰임.

check·ered [tʃékərd] *adj.* **1** of a checker pattern; checked. 바둑판 무늬의; 얼룩덜룩한. **2** various; with many ups and downs. 다양한; 변화 많은.

check·list [tʃéklìst] *n.* Ⓒ a list of things to be checked off. 대조표; 조사표.

check·mate [tʃékmèit] *vt.* (P6) **1** 《chess》 put (an opponent's king) in a position from which escape is impossible. (체스에서) 외통수로 몰다. **2** cause to fail; defeat completely. …을 실패케 하다; 완패시키다. ¶ ~ *a plan* 계획을 좌절시키다. — *n.* Ⓒ **1** 《chess》 the act of putting the opponent's king in check, thus ending the game. 외통수. **2** a complete defeat. 완전한 패배.

check·off [tʃékɔ̀ːf, -àf] *n.* 《U.S.》 a system of collecting union dues through wage deductions. 급료에서의 조합비 공제 제도.

check·room [tʃékrù(:)m] *n.* Ⓒ a room where coats, hats, etc. may be left until called for later. 휴대품 보관소.

check-up [tʃékʌ̀p] *n.* Ⓒ 《U.S.》 a careful examination; a physical examination. 점검; 검사; 건강 진단. ¶ *a medical* ~ 건강 진단 / *They gave the motor a* ~. 모터를 점검했다.

Ched·dar [tʃédər] *n.* a kind of hard cheese. 체더 치즈. [Place]

chee-chee [tʃíːtʃìː] *n.* 《*contempt.*》 a Eurasian; an effeminate thing. 유럽·아시아 혼혈인; 나약한 것. [Hind.]

:**cheek** [tʃiːk] *n.* **1** Ⓒ 《usu. *pl.*》 either side of the face below the eye. 볼; 뺨. ¶ *rosy cheeks* 볼그레한 뺨. 語法 eyes, ears와 마찬가지로 보통 복수로 쓰임. **2** 《*pl.*》 something suggesting the human cheek in shape or position. (기계·도구 따위의) 측면(側面)《양 볼에 해당된다는 뜻에서》. **3** Ⓤ 《*colloq.*》 impudence; rudeness. 뻔뻔스러움; 건방짐. ¶ *give someone* ~ 아무에게 건방진〔뻔뻔스런〕 소리를 하다 / *What* ~*!* 정말 뻔뻔스럽기도 하군 / *None of your* ~*!* 건방진 소리 하지 마. [E.]

cheek by jowl (=*close together; intimate*) ***with*** *someone*. …와 바짝 붙어; 친하게.

have the cheek *to do,* have the rudeness to do; dare to do. 뻔뻔스럽게도 …을 하다.

to *one's* ***own cheek,*** alone. 혼자서; 멋대로.

tongue in cheek, insincerely. 불성실〔무성의〕하게.

cheek·bone [tʃíːkbòun] *n.* Ⓒ either of the bones just below the eye. 광대뼈.

cheek·y [tʃíːki] *adj.* (**cheek·i·er, cheek·i·est**) 《*colloq.*》 rude. 건방진; 뻔뻔스러운. ¶ *a* ~ *boy* 건방진 아이. ● **cheek·i·ly** [-li] *adv.* **cheek·i·ness** [-nis] *n.*

cheep [tʃiːp] *vi.* (P1) make a short, weak, shrill sound like a young bird, etc.; chirp; peep. (병아리 따위가) 삐약삐약 울다; (어린 새끼새가) 짹짹거리다. —*vt.* utter with a cheeping sound. 째지는 소리로 말하다. —*n.* Ⓒ a short, weak, shrill sound like that of a young bird, etc.; chirp; peep. 삐약거리는〔짹짹 우는〕 소리. [Imit.]

cheep·er [tʃíːpər] *n.* a young partridge. 새끼 자고《메추라기의 일종》.

:**cheer** [tʃiər] *n.* **1** Ⓤ good spirits; joy; gladness; gaiety. 좋은 기분; 기쁨; 명랑; 생기. ¶ *make* ~ 명랑〔유쾌〕하게 하다; 들떠 떠들다 / *give* ~ *to a dreary life* 쓸쓸한 생활에 활기를 주다. **2** ⓊⒸ encouragement; something that promotes cheerfulness. 격려; 북돋우어 주는 것. ¶ *He spoke words of* ~. 격려의 말을 했다. **3** 《chiefly *pl.*》 a shout of joy, applause, or encouragement. 박수 갈채; 환호; 성원. ¶ *amid deafening cheers* 귀청이 찢어질 것 같은 갈채 속에 / *give a* ~ 갈채하다 / *raise a* ~ 환호성을 올리다. **4** Ⓤ the state of mind 〔feeling〕; spirits. 기분. ¶ *He is of good* ~. 그는 기분이 좋다 / *What* ~*?* 《*colloq.*》 기분이 어떤가. **5** Ⓤ good food or drink; entertainment. (맛있는) 음식; 성찬. ¶ *make good* ~ 즐겁게 진수 성찬을 먹다.

give three cheers, cry or shout 'Hurrah !' three times. 만세 삼창을 하다. 參考 Hip, hip, hurrah를 세 번 되풀이함. ¶ *We gave three cheers for the boys who won the baseball game.* 야구 경기에 이긴 아이들에게 우리는 만세 삼창을 했다.

with good cheer, cheerfully; willingly. 쾌히; 기꺼이. ¶ *He set off for his trip with good* ~. 그는 기쁜 마음으로 여행을 떠났다.

—*vt., vi.* **1** (P6,7;2A) 《often *up*》 make or become happier; comfort or be comforted. 기쁘게 하다〔되다〕; (기운)을 북돋우다; 북돋아지다. ¶ *I tried to* ~ *him* (*up*). 그를 고무하려고 애썼다 / *He* (*was*) *cheered up at the news.* 그 소식에 그는 기운이 났다 / *Cheer up!* 기운을 내라 / *Your visit cheered up the sick man.* 자네의 방문으로 환자는 기운이 났네. **2** (P6;1) show praise and approval by loud shouts; applaud. …에 박수 갈채하다; 환호하다. ¶ *The speaker was cheered.* 연사는 박수 갈채를 받았다 / *The audience stood up and cheered as the king entered.* 왕이 입장하자 관중들은 일어서서 환호했다. **3** (P6,7) 《often *on*》 urge on with shouts; encourage. 성원하다; 응원하다. ¶ *We cheered our team* (*on*) *to victory.* 우리 팀이 이기도록 응원했다. [L. *cara* face]

:**cheer·ful** [tʃíərfəl] *adj.* **1** in good spirits; joyful; gay; merry. (사람·표정 따위가) 활기찬; 기쁜; 쾌활〔명랑〕한; 좋은 기분의. ¶ *a* ~ *face* 기쁜 표정의 얼굴 / *a* ~ *old man* 명랑한 노인. **2** filled with cheer; bright and pleasant. (방·환경이) 밝고 즐거운; 유쾌한. ¶ *a* ~ *room* 쾌적한 방. **3** willing; eager. 기꺼이〔자진해서〕 …하는; 진심으로의. ¶ *a* ~ *helper* 기꺼이 도와주는 사람 / *a* ~ *worker* 자진해서 일하는 사람 / *a* ~ *giver* 희사자(喜捨者).

·**cheer·ful·ly** [tʃíərfəli] *adv.* in a cheerful manner. 활기 있게; 기분 좋게.

cheer·ful·ness [tʃíərfəlnis] *n.* Ⓤ **1** the state of being cheerful. 기분 좋음; 쾌활; 기쁨. **2** good spirits. 활기; 원기. **3** willingness. 기꺼이〔자진해서〕 하기.

cheer·i·ly [tʃíərili] *adv.* in a cheery manner. 쾌활하게; 기분좋게.

cheer·io [tʃìərióu] *interj.* 《chiefly Brit. *colloq.*》 **1** goodby! good luck! 안녕(히 가십쇼〔계십쇼〕). **2** 《in drinking》 To your health! 건강을 위해 축배를.

cheer·less [tʃíərlis] *adj.* without cheer; gloomy; dreary. 즐거움이 없는; 쓸쓸한; 음울한. ¶ *a* ~ *room* 음침한 방 / *a* ~ *day* 음울한 날 / *The future looks pretty* ~. 앞날은 꽤 암담해 보인다.

cheer·y [tʃíəri] *adj.* (**cheer·i·er, cheer·i-**

est) full of cheer; merry; pleasant; gay; lively. 명랑한; 즐거운; 활기찬.

:cheese [tʃi:z] *n.* **1** Ⓤ a kind of solid food made from milk. 치즈. ¶ *green* ~ 생(生)치즈 / *bread and* ~ 치즈와 빵; 조식(粗食) / *Say* ~*!* (사진 찍을 때) 웃으세요. **2** Ⓒ a mass of this cheese pressed into a shape. 일정한 모양으로 굳힌 치즈. **3** Ⓤ a kind of curtsey. 여성 인사의 한 가지《허리와 무릎을 굽힘》. **4** Ⓤ 《*colloq.*》 the correct thing. 안성맞춤(의 것).
— *vt.* (P6) stop. 멈추다; 그만두다. ¶ *Cheese it!* 그만 둬라. ●**cheese·like** [∠làik] *adj.* [L. *caseus*]

cheese cake [∠∠] *n.* **1** a pie made of cheese, eggs, etc. 치즈 케이크. **2** 《U.S. *colloq.*》 photographs which emphasized physical charm. 누드 사진.

cheese-cloth [tʃí:zklɔ̀:θ, -klɑ̀θ] *n.* Ⓤ thin, loosely woven cotton cloth. 성기게 짠 무명.

cheese·par·ing [tʃí:zpɛ̀əriŋ] *adj.* very careful of money; economical; miserly. 인색한; 쩨쩨한. ¶ *He has* ~ *habits.* 쩨쩨하게 구는 버릇이 있다. — *n.* 《*pl.*》 saving made by miserliness. 푼푼이[지독히 아껴] 모은 돈.

chees·y [tʃí:zi] *adj.* (**chees·i·er, chees·i·est**) **1** like cheese. 치즈 같은. **2** stylish. 멋진; 화려한. **3** of poor quality. 저질의; 저속한. ¶ *a* ~ *party* 저속[빈약]한 파티.

chee·tah [tʃí:tə] *n.* Ⓒ 《zool.》 a flesh-eating animal like a leopard. 치타. [Hind.]

chef [ʃef] *n.* Ⓒ 《F.》 a head cook in a hotel, etc. 수석 요리사; 주방장.

Che·khov [tʃékɔ:f / -ɔf], **Anton** *n.* (1860-1904) a Russian playwright and novelist. 체호프《러시아의 극작가·소설가》.

chem. chemical; chemist; chemistry.

∗chem·i·cal [kémikəl] *adj.* of chemistry; produced by or used in chemistry. 화학의; 화학 작용의[에 의한]. ¶ *a* ~ *agent* 화학적 작인(作因) / *a* ~ *combination* 화합(化合) / ~ *engineering* [*fiber*] 화학 공업[섬유] / ~ *energy* 화학 에너지 / ~ *change* 화학적 변화 / ~ *warfare* 화학전 / ~ *products* [*weapons*] 화학 제품[무기] / *a* ~ *formula* 화학식(式).
— *n.* 《usu. *pl.*》 a substance produced by or used in a chemical process. 화학 약품[제품]. [→chemist]

chem·ical·ly [kémikəli] *adv.* according to chemistry; by chemical means. 화학적으로.

che·mise [ʃəmí:z] *n.* Ⓒ a woman's loose, shirtlike undergarment. 슈미즈. [F.<L. *camisia* shirt]

∗chem·ist [kémist] *n.* Ⓒ **1** a expert or student in chemistry. 화학자. **2** 《Brit.》 a druggist. 약제사; 약종상. [→alchemy. Gk. →therapy; *ourgia* the working of]

∗chem·is·try [kémistri] *n.* ⓊⒸ (*pl.* **-tries** [-tri:z]) the science that deals with or examines the nature of elements or simple substances. 화학. ¶ *applied* [*practical*] ~ 응용 화학 / *organic* [*inorganic*] ~ 유기[무기] 화학.

chem·o·ther·a·py [kèmouθérəpi, kì:-] *n.* the treatment of disease by means of chemicals. 화학 요법. [→chemist]

chem·ur·gy [kémə:rdʒi] *n.* a branch of chermistry dealing with the use of organic raw materials. 농산 화학(農產化學).

:cheque [tʃek] *n.* 《Brit.》 =check.

cheque·book [tʃékbùk] *n.* 《Brit.》 = checkbook.

cheq·uer [tʃékər] *vt., n.* 《Brit.》 =checker.

cheq·uered [tʃékərd] *adj.* 《Brit.》 = checkered.

∗cher·ish [tʃériʃ] *vt.* (P6) **1** love; treat (someone) with affection; care for (someone) tenderly or kindly. …을 사랑[귀여워]하다; 소중히 하다. ¶ ~ *one's native land* 조국을 사랑하다 / *A mother cherishes her baby.* 엄마는 아기를 귀여워한다. **2** keep (something) in mind; entertain; cling to. …을 잊지 않고 있다; 마음에 품다[간직하다]. ¶ *one's long cherished desire* 숙원(宿願) / ~ *the memory of a happy life* 행복했던 생활을 늘 그리워하다 / ~ *a grudge against someone* 아무에게 원한을 품다 / ~ *no resentment* 원한을 품지 않다. [→charity]

che·root [ʃərú:t] *n.* a cigar with both ends open. 양 끝을 자른 엽궐련. [Tamil]

∗cher·ry [tʃéri] *n.* (*pl.* **-ries** [-ri:z]) **1** Ⓒ a small, round, bright red fruit with a stone in the center; the tree that it grows on. 체리; 버찌; 벚나무. ¶ ~ *blossoms* 벚꽃. **2** Ⓤ the wood of this tree. 벚나무재(材). **3** Ⓤ a bright red. 앵두빛.
make [***take***] ***two bites at a cherry,*** boggle; make great ado about nothing. 꾸물거리다; 하찮은 일에 안달하다.
— *adj.* **1** made of cherry wood. 벚나무재(材)의. **2** bright-red. 앵두빛의. ¶ ~ *lips* 앵두빛 입술. [Gk.]

cherry stone [∠- ∠] *n.* Ⓒ **1** the stone of a cherry. 체리[버찌]씨. **2** a kind of shellfish; a clam. 대합조개.

cher·ub [tʃérəb] *n.* Ⓒ (*pl.* **cher·u·bim**) **1** an angel of the second class. 지품천신(智品天神); 케루빔. 參考 아홉 천사 중 둘째이며 지식을 관장하는 천사. **2** a picture or statue of a child with wings or the head of such a child. 케루빔의 그림·상(像)《날개 달린 아이》. **3** (*pl.* **-s**) a sweet, innocent, good child; a child with a round, innocent face. 천사 같은 아이; 통통하고 귀여운 아이. [Heb.]

che·ru·bic [tʃərú:bik] *adj.* **1** of or like a cherub. 케루빔의[같은]. **2** lovely and innocent; round-faced. 귀엽고 순진한; 통통한 얼굴의. ¶ ~ *face* 토실토실하고 귀여운 얼굴.

cher·u·bim [tʃérəbim] *n.* pl. of **cherub.**

Chesh·ire [tʃéʃər] *n.* a place in England. 체셔《영국 잉글랜드 서북부의 주》.
grin like a Cheshire cat, smile very widely

all the time. 히죽거리다.

•**chess** [tʃes] *n.* Ⓤ a game played by two persons on a chessboard. 체스; 서양 장기. 參考 장기판 위에서 32개의 말을 씀. [→check]

chess·board [tʃésbɔ̀:rd] *n.* Ⓒ a board divided into 32 red squares and 32 black squares, used in playing chess. 체스판.

chess·man [tʃésmæ̀n, -mən] *n.* (*pl.* **-men** [-mèn]) Ⓒ one of the pieces used in the game of chess. (체스의) 말.

:**chest** [tʃest] *n.* Ⓒ **1** the upper front part of the body between the neck and the stomach. 가슴; 폐. ¶ *a cold in the* ~ 기침 감기 / *have a weak* ~ 가슴이 나쁘다《폐병이다》/ *throw out one's* ~ 가슴을 펴다. **2** a large box with a lid. (뚜껑 달린) 큰 상자[궤]; 통. ¶ *a carpenter's* ~ 목수의 연장통 / *a jewelry* ~ 보석함 / *a medicine* ~ 약상자. **3** a sealed container for gas, steam, etc. (가스·액체 등을 넣는) 밀폐 용기. **4** the place where money is kept; treasury; a (public) fund. 금고; 기금. ¶ *the community* ~ 공동 모금. [Gk. *kistē*]

a chest of drawers, a case fitted with sliding drawers. (서랍 달린) 장롱; 옷장(cf. 《U.S.》 *bureau*).

get (*something*) ***off one's chest,*** 《*colloq.*》 relieve oneself of (some annoyance, trouble, etc.) by talking about it. (고민 따위를) 털어놓아 후련해지다.

ches·ter·field [tʃéstərfì:ld] *n.* **1** a deep, soft sofa with two upright ends for two or three persons. (2·3인용의) 소파. **2** a single-breasted overcoat with the buttons hidden. 체스터필드《단추가 보이지 않게 한 싱글 외투》. [Person]

•**chest·nut** [tʃésnʌ̀t, -nət] *n.* **1** Ⓒ a kind of eatable nut; the tree it grows on. 밤; 밤나무. **2** Ⓤ the wood of this tree; the color of a chestnut; a reddish-brown color. 밤나무재(材); 밤색; 고동색. **3** Ⓒ a reddish-brown horse. 구렁말.

pull someone's chestnuts out of the fire, be pressed into rescuing someone from difficulty, etc. 불속의 밤을 줍다《남을 구하려다 자신이 위험에 빠지다; 남의 앞잡이가 되다》.

— *adj.* reddish-brown. 밤색의; 밤색털의. ¶ *a* ~ *horse* 구렁말의. [Gk. *kastanea* nut]

che·tah [tʃí:tə] *n.* =cheetah.

che·val-glass [ʃəvǽlglæ̀s, -glɑ̀:s] *n.* a large looking-glass showing the whole body and hung on upright supports so that it can be adjusted to any angle. 체경. [↓]

chev·a·lier *n.* [ʃèvəlíər] **1** 《*arch.*》 a knight. 기사. **2** a member of the Legion d'Honneur. 훈작사(勳爵士). [→cavalier]

chev·i·ot [tʃéviət, tʃí:v-] *n.* Ⓤ **1** a rough woollen cloth. 투박한 모직물; 체비오트. **2** a cotton cloth looking like this. 체비오트 비슷한 면직물. [Place]

chev·ron [ʃévrən] *n.* Ⓒ **1** a V-shaped design worn on the sleeves of a police or military uniform, etc. 갈매기표 수장(袖章). 參考 '∧; ∨'형으로 군인복·경관복 소매에 붙임. 《Brit.》 에서는 근무연한; 《U.S.》 에서는 계급을 나타냄. **2** a V-shaped design used in coats of arms, architecture, etc. ∨자 모양의 의장(意匠)[장식]. [L. *caper* goat]

*•***chew** [tʃu:] *vt.* (P6,7) crush or grind (something) with the teeth. …을 씹다[씹어으깨다]. ¶ *You must always* ~ *your food carefully.* 음식은 항상 잘 씹어 먹어야 한다. — *vi.* (P1,3) **1** think very much; consider; ponder. …을 숙고하다[되새기다]. ¶ *He is chewing* (*up*) *on* [*over*] *it.* 그 일에 관해 곰곰 되새겨 보고 있다. **2** bite repeatedly with the teeth. (짓)씹다; 저작(咀嚼)하다.

bite off more than one can chew, undertake something which is beyond one's capacity or power. 힘에 부치는 일을 하려고 하다.

chew out, scold harshly. 호되게 꾸짖다; 야단[호통]치다.

chew the cud, ⇨cud.

chew the fat [***rag***], 《*sl.*》 **a**) grumble; complain. 투덜대다; 불평하다. **b**) chat. 잡담하다; 노닥거리다.

— *n.* Ⓒ the act of chewing; a piece (of food, etc.) to be chewed. (짓)씹기; 저작(咀嚼); 씹는[씹힌] 것. [E.]

chew·ing-gum [tʃú:iŋgʌ̀m] *n.* a gum prepared for chewing, usu. sweetened and flavored. 껌.

Chey·enne [ʃaién, -ǽn] *n.* **1** a tribe of Algonquian-speaking North American Indians; a member of this tribe; the language of it. 샤이엔족(族)(의 사람·말)《북아메리카 인디언의 하나》. **2** the capital of Wyoming. 샤이엔《Wyoming주의 주도(州都)》.

Chiang Kai-shek [tʃǽŋ kaiʃék] *n.* (1887-1970) the Chinese General and head of the national government. 장개석.

chi·a·ro·scu·ro [kiɑ̀:rəskjú:rou] *n.* 《It.》 the treatment of light and shade in a picture. 키아로스쿠로; 명암법(明暗法). [It.=clear-obscure]

chic [ʃi(:)k] *n.* Ⓤ 《F.》 (esp. of women or their clothes) a smart, elegance of style and manner. 멋; 우아; 독특한 스타일. — *adj.* (**chicqu·er, chiqu·est**) stylish; in good taste. 멋있는; 세련된.

*•***Chi·ca·go** [ʃiká:gou, -kɔ́:-] *n.* a large city of the United States, in the state of Illinois. 시카고《Illinoise주 Michigan호(湖)에 면한 미국 제2의 대도시》.

chi·cane [ʃikéin] *vi., vt.* (P1;6,13) 《*into, out of*》 deceive. 속이다. — *n.* =chicanery. [Pers.=polostick]

chi·can·er·y [ʃikéinəri] *n.* ⓊⒸ (*pl.* **-er·ies** [-əri:z]) trickery; unfair practice; false arguments. 속임수; 책략; 궤변. ¶ *use* ~ 속임수를 쓰다.

chick [tʃik] *n.* Ⓒ (contr. from **chicken**) **1** a baby chicken; a young bird. 병아리; 새끼 새. **2** a child; a young girl. 어린애; 소녀. [E.]

chick·a·bid·dy [tʃíkəbìdi] *n.* a chick; a child. 병아리; 착한 아이.

:chick·en [tʃíkin] *n.* Ⓒ **1** ⓐ a young hen or rooster. 병아리; 영계. ⓑ 《U.S.》 a hen or rooster of any age. (일반적으로) 닭. ¶ 《*prov.*》 *Don't count your chickens before they are hatched.* 너구리 굴보고 피물(皮物) 돈 내어쓴다. **2** any young bird. 새끼 새. **3** Ⓤ the flesh of a chicken. (특히 영계) 닭고기; 치킨. **4** 《U.S. *colloq.*》 a young person or girl. 풋내기; 어린애; 계집아이. ¶ *She's no* (*longer a*) ~. 그 여자는 (이젠) 계집아이가 아니다. **5** 《*sl.*》 a coward. 겁쟁이. ¶ *Don't be such a* ~*!* 용기를 좀 내라. — *adj.* young; small; of or like a chicken; cowardly. 어린(애의); 작은; 닭의[같은]; 겁 많은. [E.]

chick·en-feed [tʃíkinfì:d] *n.* a food for poultry. 닭모이.

chick·en-heart·ed [tʃíkinhɑ́:rtid] *adj.* lacking courage; timid. 겁이 많은; 소심한.

chick·en·pox [tʃíkinpɑ̀ks / -pɔ̀ks] *n.* 《med.》 mild, feverish disease. 수두(水痘); 작은 마마.

chick·weed [tʃíkwì:d] *n.* Ⓒ 《bot.》 a common, white-flowering weed. 별꽃.

chic·o·ry [tʃíkəri] *n.* Ⓤ **1** 《bot.》 a plant whose leaves are used for salad. 치코리. **2** its root used instead of coffee. 그 뿌리《커피 대용》. [Gk.]

chid [tʃid] *v.* p. and pp. of **chide.**

chid·den [tʃídn] *v.* pp. of **chide.**

chide [tʃaid] *vi., vt.* (**chid** or 《U.S.》 **chid·ed, chid·den** or **chid** or 《U.S.》 **chid·ed**) 《*for*》 blame; scold; find fault; cry impatiently. …을 책(망)하다; 꾸짖다; 잔소리하다; (소리치며) 사납게 날뛰다. ¶ *Our teacher chided a boy for coming late.* 선생님은 지각했다고 한 아이를 꾸짖었다. [E.]

:chief [tʃi:f] *n.* Ⓒ (*pl.* **chiefs**) a leader of a group, organization, department, etc.; a commander; the head of a tribe. (조직·집단의) 장(長); 우두머리; 추장. ¶ *a* ~ *judge* [*justice*] 부장 판사; 재판장 / 《U.S.》 *a* ~ *of police* 경찰서장 (=《Brit.》 chief constable) / *the* ~ *of staff* 참모장.

in chief, **a**) chiefly; especially; most of all. 주로; 특히. ¶ *with this object in* ~ 주로 이 목적으로. **b**) supreme; highest in rank. 최고(위)의. ¶ *a commander-in-chief* 《army》 총사령관; 《nav.》 사령관.

— *adj.* **1** highest in rank; at the head. 최고(위)의; 장(長)[우두머리]의. ¶ *the* ~ *priest* 사제장; 주교. **2** most important; main. 중요한; 주요한. ¶ *the* ~ *object* 주목적; 주안(主眼) / *the* ~ *point* 주요점; 중점 / *his* ~ *merit* 그의 주된 장점 / *the* ~ *rivers of France* 프랑스의 주요 하천 / *the* ~ *thought in one's mind* 마음속의 주된 생각. ● **chief·less** [tʃí:flis] *adj.* 우두머리[지휘자]가 없는. [→ capital]

:chief·ly [tʃí:fli] *adv.* **1** mainly; mostly. 주로; 대체로. **2** most of all; first of all. 우선 첫째로; 맨 먼저.

chief·tain [tʃí:ftən] *n.* Ⓒ **1** the leader of a tribe or a clan. 추장; 족장(族長). **2** a leader; the head of a group. 지도자; 우두머리; 수령; 대장(隊長).

chief·tain·cy [tʃí:ftənsi] *n.* ⓊⒸ (*pl.* **-cies**) the position or rank of a chieftain. chieftain의 지위[직분].

chiff-chaff [tʃíftʃæ̀f] *n.* 《bird》 a small warbler. 솔새 무리 명금의 일종. [Imit.]

chif·fon [ʃifɑ́n, ⌐⌐ / ʃífɔn] *n.* 《F》 **1** Ⓤ a very soft, thin silk or rayon cloth. 시퐁; 비단 모슬린. **2** 《usu. *pl.*》 laces, ribbons, etc. 레이스; 리본. [F. *chiffe* rag]

chif·fo·nier [ʃìfəníər] *n.* Ⓒ **1** 《U.S.》 a high, narrow bureau or chest of drawers, sometimes with a mirror. (높직하고 거울이 달린) 서양 옷장. **2** 《Brit.》 a low movable cupboard with a top that can be used as a side table at meals. (이동식의 낮은) 찬장《식탁을 겸함》.

chil·blain [tʃílblèin] *n.* 《usu. *pl.*》 a red swelling on the hands or feet caused by cold. 동상(凍傷). ● **chil·blained** [-blèind] *adj.* [→chill, A.S. *blegen* sore]

:child [tʃaild] *n.* (*pl.* **chil·dren**) Ⓒ **1** a boy or girl; a baby; an infant; a son or daughter. 아이; 아기; 유아(幼兒); 아들; 딸. ¶ *as a* ~ 어렸을 때에 / *bring up one's* ~ 아이를 키우다 / *Don't be a* ~. 철부지짓 좀 그만둬라 / *I have known him from a* ~. 나는 그가 어렸을 때부터 알고 있다 / 《*prov.*》 *The* ~ *is father of* [*to*] *the man.* 세 살 적 버릇 여든까지 간다. **2** a descendant. 자손. ¶ *a* ~ *of Abraham* 아브라함의 자손; 유대인. **3** a person regarded as the product of a particular place, time, etc. (특정의 장소·시대 따위에서 자란) 사람. ¶ *a* ~ *of the age* 시대의 총아 / *a* ~ *of the Revolution* 혁명아 / *a* ~ *of nature* 자연아(兒); 천진한 사람. **4** a person like a child; a foolish person. 어린애 같은 [유치한] 사람. ¶ *a mere* ~ *in the ways of the world* 세상 물정에 어두운 사람. **5** product; result. 소산(所產); 결과. ¶ *fancy's children* 상상의 산물 / *a* ~ *of one's imagination* 상상이 낳은 것 / *Abstract art is a* ~ *of the 20th century.* 추상 예술은 20세기의 소산이다. **6** one closely associated with a school of thought, etc. 제자; 숭배자. [E.]

with child, having a baby in the body. 임신하고.

child·bear·ing [tʃáildbɛ̀əriŋ] *n.* Ⓤ the act or process of giving birth to children. 출산; 분만. ¶ *be past* ~ (연령적으로) 이제 아이를 낳지 못하다.

child·bed [tʃáildbèd] *n.* ⓊⒸ the state of a

woman giving birth to a child. 산욕(産褥). ¶ *lie in* ~ 산욕 중이다 / *die in* ~ 해산 중에 죽다.

child·birth [tʃáilbə̀ːrθ] *n.* Ⓤ the act of giving birth to a child; the birth rate. 출산; 분만; 출산율. ¶ *a difficult* ~ 난산.

:child·hood [tʃáildhùd] *n.* Ⓤ **1** the state of being a child. 어림; 유소(幼少)(cf. *manhood*). **2** the time during which a person is a child. 어릴 때; 유년 시대. ¶ *in one's* ~ 어릴 적에 / *from early* ~ 매우 어렸을 때부터 / *be in one's second* ~ 망령이 들다.

***child·ish** [tʃáildiʃ] *adj.* **1** of or like a child. 어린애의(다운). ¶ ~ *simplicity* 어린애 같은 순진함. **2** not proper for a grown person; weak; silly; foolish. 어린애 같은; 무력한; 유치한; 어리석은. ¶ *a* ~ *idea* 유치한 생각 / *a* ~ *attempt* 어리석은 시도.

child·ish·ly [tʃáildiʃli] *adv.* in the state of being a child or acting like a child; sillily. 어린애같이(답게); 유치하게.

child·ish·ness [tʃáildiʃnis] *n.* Ⓤ the state of being childish. 어린애 같음(다움).

child·less [tʃáildlis] *adj.* having no child. 아이가 없는. ¶ *die* ~ 아이가 없이 죽다.

child·like [tʃáildlàik] *adj.* like a child; fit for a child; innocent; frank; simple. 어린애 같은; 어린아이에 적합한; 천진한; 솔직(단순)한. ● **child·like·ness** [-nis] *n.*

:chil·dren [tʃíldrən] *n.* pl. of **child.**

child's play [ㅅㅅ] *n.* something very easy to do. 손쉬운 일. ¶ *That is mere* ~ *for him.* 그건 그에게는 식은죽 먹기다.

Chil·e [tʃíli] *n.* a country in southwestern South America. 칠레. 參考 수도는 Santiago.

chile, chil·li [tʃíli] *n.* =chili.

Chil·e·an [tʃíliən] *adj.* of or connected with Chile or its people. 칠레 (사람)의(에 관한). — *n.* a native of Chile. 칠레 사람.

Chile saltpeter [ㅅ—ㅅ—] *n.* sodium nitrate. 칠레 초석(硝石).

:chil·i [tʃíli] *n.* (*pl.* **chil·ies**) **1** Ⓒ a hot-tasting red pepper; the tropical American plant that bears this pepper. (열대 아메리카산) 고추의 일종; 그 나무. **2** Ⓤ a dish made of beans and this pepper. 콩과 chili 고추로 만든 요리. [Mex.]

:chill [tʃil] *n.* Ⓒ **1** unpleasant coldness. 냉기; 한기(寒氣). ¶ *a* ~ *in the air* 공기의 차가움 / *the* ~ *of early dawn* 새벽녘의 냉기. **2** a sudden bodily coldness with shivering. 오한(惡寒). ¶ *fevers and chills* 열과 오한 / *chills and fever* 학질 / *have* (*feel*) *a* ~ 추워서 오싹거리다 / *catch* (*take*) *a* ~ 몸이 으스스하다; 한기를 느끼다. **3** unfriendliness; coolness in manner. 냉담; 차가움. **4** a sudden fear; discouragement. 축기(縮氣); 풀죽음; 의기 저상(沮喪). ¶ *He cast a* ~ *over our joy.* 우리들 즐거움에 찬물을 끼얹었다.

take the chill off, warm (liquids, etc.) slightly. (물·술 등)을 약간 데우다; 거냉하다.

— *adj.* **1** unpleasantly cold. 차가운; 으스스한. ¶ *a* ~ *wind* 차가운 바람. **2** unfriendly; cold in manner. (태도가) 차가운; 냉담한. ¶ *a* ~ *reception* 냉랭한 접대. **3** in low spirits; discouraging. 우울(음울)한; 싫은; 실망시키는. ¶ ~ *prospects* 어두운 전망.

— *vt.* (P6,7) **1** make (something) cool; cause (someone) to become cool. …을 차게(냉동, 냉각)하다; 춥게 하다. ¶ ~ *the air* 공기를 차게 하다 / ~ *beer* 맥주를 차게 하다 / *chilled meat* 냉동육 / *I am chilled to the bone.* 뼛속까지 얼었다. **2** depress; discourage; dispirit. 우울하게(실망케) 하다; (기 따위를) 꺾다. ¶ *Don't* ~ *his enthusiasm.* 그의 열의를 꺾지 마라. **3** 《metal.》 harden (a metal) by sudden cooling. (쇠를) 냉경(冷硬)하다.

— *vi.* (P1) become cool; feel cool. 차가워지다; 추워서 떨다. ● **chill·ness** [-nis] *n.* [E.]

***chill·y** [tʃíli] *adj.* (**chill·i·er, chill·i·est**) **1** uncomfortably cool; rather cold. (공기가) 차가운; 으스스 추운. ¶ *a* ~ *room* 냉기가 도는 방 / *The weather is* ~. 날씨가 차다. **2** cold in manner; unfriendly. (태도가) 차가운; 쌀쌀(냉담)한. ¶ *a* ~ *manner* 차가운 태도.

***chime** [tʃaim] *n.* **1** Ⓒ 《often *pl.*》 ⓐ a set of bells or something imitating this in a church tower. (음계를 맞춘) 한 벌의 종; 차임; 교회탑의 이와 비슷한 것. ⓑ the bells in a striking clock. 타종 시계의 종. ⓒ a musical instrument consisting of a set of metal pipes tuned to the musical scale and played by a hammer. (파이프로 구성된) 편종(編鐘); 차임 악기. ⓓ the music made by a set of tuned bells. 차임악(樂); 그 소리. ¶ *listen to the chimes* 차임 소리를 듣다. **2** Ⓤ harmony; agreement. 조화; 일치. ¶ *keep* ~ *with someone* …와 가락을 맞추다.

fall into chime with, be harmonious with (something or someone). …와 조화가 되다; 일치하다.

in chime, in harmony; 《*fig.*》 in agreement. 조화하여; 일치하여.

— *vt.* (P6) **1** ring or strike a bell or a set of bells. 종(차임)을 울리다. **2** tell the hour by chimes. (시각)을 종을 쳐서 알리다. ¶ *The clock chimed five.* 시계가 다섯시를 쳤다. — *vi.* (P1,2A) **1** ring out musically. 맑은 소리가 나다. **2** 《*with*》 harmonize; agree. 가락을 맞추다; 일치하다. ¶ ~ *with one's mood* 기분과 일치하다. [→cymbal]

chime in, **a**) break into or join in conversation. 맞장구를 치다; 이야기에 끼어들다. **b**) 《*with*》 harmonize: agree fully. 조화하다; 일치하다. ¶ *His plan chimmed in with me.* 그의 계획은 내것과 들어맞았다.

chi·me·ra, -mae- [kimíːrə, kai-] *n.* Ⓒ **1** 《Gk. myth.》 a fire-breathing monster. 키메라. 參考 사자머리, 양의 몸통, 용의 꼬리를 가진 불을 뿜어내는 괴물. **2** a terrible imaginary creature. (무서운 상상의) 괴물. **3** a wild dream; an idle fancy. 망상; 공상.

[Gk. *chimaera*]

chi·mer·i·cal [kimérikəl, kai-] *adj.* imaginary; nonsensical; widly fanciful; impossible. 공상의; 터무니없는; 황당 무계한. [↑]

:chim·ney [tʃímni] *n.* Ⓒ **1** an upright structure for carrying smoke from a fireplace, a furnace, etc. 굴뚝. ¶ *smoke like a* ~ 굴뚝같이 연기를 뿜어대다《담배를 몹시 피우다》. **2** a glass tube around a lamp flame. (램프의) 등피. **3** a crack or opening in a rock, mountain, etc. (등산에서) 침니. 參考 산·암벽이 세로로 갈라진 틈. 이 틈 사이를 타고 오름. [L. *caminus* oven]

chimney corner [ㄹ- ㄹ-] *n.* the corner or side of a fireplace. 난롯가; 노변(爐邊).

chimney piece [ㄹ- ㄹ] *n.* a mantelshelf; a mantelpiece. 벽난로의 선반〔앞 장식〕.

chimney pot [ㄹ- ㄹ] *n.* a pipe of earthenware or metal fitted to the top of a chimney. 굴뚝머리의 통풍관(管).

chimney stack [ㄹ- ㄹ] *n.* **1** a number of pipes embodied in one chimney. 한 굴뚝 위의 여러 굴뚝. 參考 그 하나하나가 chimney pot. **2** the part of a chimney rising above a roof. 옥상에 나온 굴뚝.

chimney sweep [ㄹ- ㄹ] *n.* a person whose work is to clean out chimneys. 굴뚝 청소부.

chim·pan·zee [tʃìmpænzíː/-pǽn-] *n.* Ⓒ a dark brown manlike African monkey. 침팬지. [Native]

***chin** [tʃin] *n.* Ⓒ the part of the face below the mouth. 턱. ¶ *push out one's* ~ (반항적으로) 턱을 내밀다 / *up to the* ~ 턱까지 (물에 잠겨); 깊숙이 빠져. — *v.* (**chinned, chin·ning**) *vt.* 《*reflexively*》 pull (oneself) up by the hands until one's chin is on a level with a horizontal bar. 턱걸이(운동)하다. — *vi.* talk too much; chatter. 너무 지껄이다; 수다 떨다. [E.]

:Chi·na [tʃáinə] *n.* a large country in East Asia. 중국. ¶ ~ *clay* 고령토 / *the People's Republic of* ~ 중화 인민 공화국 / *the Republic of* ~ 중화 민국. [Place.]

chi·na [tʃáinə] *n.* Ⓤ 《*collectively*》 **1** a fine, white object made of clay baked by a special process. 자기(瓷器); 도기(陶器). **2** dishes, vases, etc. made of china. (일반적으로) 도자기; 사기 (그릇). ¶ *a* ~ *cup* 사기잔 / *a piece of* ~ 도자기 한 개. [↑]

Chi·na·man [tʃáinəmən] *n.* Ⓒ (*pl.* **-men** [-mən]) a person of China; a Chinese. 중국인. 語法 Chinese에 비해 좀 경멸적인 말.

chi·na·ware [tʃáinəwὲər] *n.* Ⓤ dishes, vases, etc. made of china. 도자기; 사기.

chin·chil·la [tʃintʃílə] *n.* **1** Ⓒ 《zool.》 a South American animal like a squirrel. 친칠라. **2** Ⓤ its fur. 그 모피. [Sp.]

chine [tʃain] *n.* Ⓒ **1** the backbone; spine; (of meat) a cut of an animal's backbone with the meat still on it. 등뼈; 등뼈에 붙어 있는 고기. **2** a ridge. 산등성이; 능선. **3** a deep ravine. 협곡(峽谷). [E.]

Chi·nee [tʃainíː] *n.* 《*colloq.*》 Chinaman. 중국인. [*China*]

:Chi·nese [tʃainíːz, -níːs] *n.* (*pl.* **-nese**) **1** Ⓒ a person of China. 중국인. ¶ *the* ~ 중국 국민(전체). **2** Ⓤ the language of China. 중국어. — *adj.* of China, its people, or their language. 중국(인·어)의. ¶ ~ *ink* 먹 / ~ *characters* 한자 / *the* ~ *classics* 중국 고전; 한문 / *the* ~ *Wall* 만리 장성. [*China*]

Chinese lantern [ㄹ- ㄹ-] *n.* a paper lantern. 종이 초롱.

Chinese puzzle [ㄹ- ㄹ-] *n.* a very complicated puzzle; anything very complicated. 아주 복잡한 수수께끼; 난문(難問).

Chink [tʃiŋk] *n.* Ⓒ 《*colloq.*》 Chinaman. 중국인. [*China*]

chink[1] [tʃiŋk] *n.* Ⓒ a narrow opening; a crack. 갈라진 틈. ¶ *a* ~ *in a wall* 벽에 금간 곳 / *The chinks in the hut let in wind and snow.* 오두막의 틈새로 눈과 바람이 들이쳐다. — *vt.* (P6,7) 《*up*》 fill up the chinks in (something). …의 갈라진 틈새를 메우다. ¶ *The cracks in the log wall were chinked with plaster.* 통나무 벽의 틈새는 회반죽으로 메워졌다. [E. =a fissure]

chink[2] [tʃiŋk] *n.* Ⓒ **1** a sharp ringing sound as of coins or glasses struck lightly. (쇠붙이·동전 등의) 짤랑짤랑 소리; 쨍강〔땡그랑〕 소리. ¶ *the* ~ *of ice in a glass* 술잔 속의 얼음의 딸그락 소리. **2** 《*colloq.*》 money. 돈. — *vt.* (P6,7) cause (something) to jingle. …을 짤랑〔쨍그랑, 딸그락〕거리게 하다. ¶ *They chinked their glasses* (*in drinking a toast*). (축배를 들며) 술잔을 쨍하고 부딪쳤다. — *vi.* jingle. 짤랑짤랑〔쨍그랑〕 소리가 나다. [Imit.]

chintz [tʃints] *n.* Ⓤ a cotton cloth printed in various colored patterns. 사라사 무명. [Skr.]

***chip** [tʃip] *n.* Ⓒ **1** a small piece of wood, stone, or china split off a bigger piece. (나무) 지저깨비; 돌조각; 사금파리. **2** a gap left when a small piece is cut or broken off from something. (깨지거나 자르거나 떼어낸) 자국; 깨진 데. ¶ *a* ~ *in the edge of a cup* 잔 가장자리의 이가 빠진 데 / *This glass has a* ~. 이 술잔은 금이 가 있다. **3** 《usu. *pl.*》 a small, thin piece of food or candy. (음식·과자 따위의) 얇은 조각. ¶ *potato chips* 감자 칩〔튀김〕. **4** 《*pl.*》 wood or straw, etc. in thin strips for weaving into hats or baskets. (모자·바구니를 엮어 만드는) 나무오리; 밀짚. **5** a minute square of a thin semiconducting material. 반도체의 칩. **6** 《*pl.*》 《*colloq.*》 a ship's carpenter. 배목수. **7** 《golf》 a short stroke used in approaching the green. 단타(短打).

a chip off the old block, a child that is very much like either of its parents. 부모를 빼쏜 아이.

dry as a chip, very dry. 무미 건조한.

have a chip on one's shoulder, 《*colloq.*》 have an inclination to quarrel. 잘 싸우는 성질이 있다; 도전적이다.

with a chip on one's shoulder, ready to fight. 시비조로; 도전적으로.

— *v.* (**chipped, chip·ping**) *vt.* (P6,13) **1** cut or break off a small part of (something). …을 잘라〔깎아, 떼어〕내다; 찢다; 깨뜨리다. ¶ ~ *wood* 나무를 깎다 / ~ *the piece from* 〔*off*〕 *a rock* 바위에서 조각을 떼어 내다 / ~ *the edge of a teacup* 찻잔 가장자리의 이가 빠지다. **2** chop or cut (as with an ax); shape (something) by cutting. (도끼 따위로) …을 빼개다〔자르다〕; …의 모양을 깎아 만들다. ¶ ~ *a figure out of wood* 나무를 깎아 상(像)을 만들다. — *vi.* (P1,3) be easily broken off. (사기가) 쉽게 깨지다; 이가 빠지다. [E.]

chip at, find fault with (someone or something) severely; strike at. …을 혹평하다; 대들다.

chip in, 《*colloq.*》 **a**) intervene suddenly in conversation, discussion, fight. (이야기·싸움에) 불쑥 끼어들다. **b**) contribute (money, help, etc.). (돈 따위)를 기부하다; 원조하다. **c**) join with others in an enterprise. (사업 따위)에 참여하다; 동업하다.

chip·munk [tʃípmʌŋk] *n.* Ⓒ a small, striped squirrel living in North America. (북아메리카산의) 얼룩다람쥐. [Amer- Ind.]

Chip·pen·dale [tʃípəndèil] *adj., n.* (furniture) of an elegant style. 고급의 (가구)《영국 가구사의 이름에서》. [Person]

chip·per [tʃípər] *adj.* 《U.S. *colloq.*》 lively; cheerful. 생기 있는; 명랑한. [*chirrup*]

chip·py [tʃípi] *adj.* (**-pi·er, -pi·est**) **1** dry; uninteresting. 무미 건조한. **2** 《*colloq.*》 parched after drunkenness. 속이 쓰린《과음으로》. **3** irritable. 성마른; 속태우는. [→chip]

chirk [tʃəːrk] *adj.* 《U.S. *colloq.*》 cheerful. 쾌활한. — *vi.* (P1) be or become cheerful. 기운이 나다; 쾌활해지다. [E.]

chi·rog·ra·phy [kairágrəfi / -rɔ́g-] *n.* handwriting; calligraphy. 필적(筆跡); 서예. [↓]

chi·ro·man·cy [káirəmæ̀nsi] *n.* Ⓤ palmistry. 수상술(手相術); 손금보기. [Gk. *kheir* hand, *-mancy* divination]

chi·ro·man·cer [káirəmæ̀nsər] *n.* a person who practices chiromancy. 수상쟁이; 손금쟁이. [↑]

chi·ro·prac·tic [kàirəprǽktik] *n.* **1** the method of curing diseases by manipulating the spinal column. 지압 요법(指壓療法). **2** =chiropractor. — *adj.* having to do with the treatment of diseases by manipulating the spine. 지압 요법의〔을 쓰는〕. [Gk. *kheir* hand, →practice]

chi·ro·prac·tor [káirəprǽktər] *n.* Ⓒ one who treats disease by manipulating the spine. 지압사(指壓師). [↑]

***chirp** [tʃəːrp] *vi.* (P1) **1** make a short, sharp sound such as certain birds or insects do. (새·벌레 따위처럼) 짹짹〔찍찍〕 울다. ¶ *Crickets* ~. 귀뚜라미가 귀뚤귀뚤 운다. **2** speak in a shrill, cheerful voice. 새된 소리로 말하다. — *vt.* (P6,7) utter (something) in a short, sharp tone. 새된〔날카로운〕 소리로 …을 말하다. ¶ ~ *a song* 새된 소리로 노래하다. — *n.* Ⓒ a short, sharp sound. 새된 소리; 짹짹〔찍찍〕 소리. ¶ *The sparrow gave two or three chirps.* 참새는 두세 번 짹짹 울었다. [Imit.]

chirr [tʃəːr] *vi.* (P1) trill like a grasshopper. (여치·귀뚜라미 따위가) 울다. — *n.* Ⓒ the sound of chirring. 찌르르찌르르〔귀뚤귀뚤〕 우는 소리. [↑]

chir·rup [tʃírəp, tʃə́ːrəp] *vi.* **1** chirp repeatedly. 찍찍〔짹짹〕거리다; 지저귀다. **2** make such sounds. 그런 소리를 내다. — *n.* Ⓒ the sound or the act of chirruping. 짹짹〔찍찍〕거림; 지저귐. [↑]

chis·el [tʃízl] *n.* Ⓒ a tool with a sharp edge for cutting or shaping wood, stone, or metal. 끌; 정. ¶ *a woodworking* 〔*carpenter's*〕 ~ 목공〔목수〕용 끌 / *a stone cutter's* ~ 석수(石手)용 정.

— *vt.* (P6,13) (**-eled, -el·ing** or 《Brit.》 **-elled, -el·ling**) **1** cut or sharpen (something) with such a tool. …을 끌로 파다〔깎다〕; 정으로 쪼다. ¶ *chiseled features* 이목구비가 반듯한 얼굴 / ~ *a statue out of marble* 대리석상(像)을 쪼아 만들다. **2** 《*colloq.*》 《*out of*》 cheat; get (something) by cheating. …을 속이다; 속여 옭아 내다. ¶ ~ *customers* 손님을 속이다 / ~ *someone out of his money* 아무를 속여 돈을 옭아 내다. **3** give finish to. …을 끝내다; 마무리하다. [L. *caedo* cut]

chit[1] [tʃit] *n.* Ⓒ a child; a young, small, slender girl. 어린애; (건방진) 계집애. 語法 경멸적으로 쓰일 때가 많음. [→kitten]

chit[2] [tʃit] *n.* Ⓒ a sprout from a rout or seed. 눈; 싹. [E.]

chit[3] [tʃit] *n.* Ⓒ a short letter or note; a note of a small sum of money owed for drink, etc. 짧은 편지〔메모〕; 쪽지; 전표. ¶ *sign a* ~ 전표에 서명하다. [→chat]

chit-chat [tʃíttʃæ̀t] *n.* Ⓤ **1** friendly, informal talk. 잡담; 한담. **2** idle talk about other people; gossip. 남에 대한 소문 이야기; 수다. [↑]

chiv·al·ric [ʃivǽlrik / ʃívəl-] *adj.* **1** = chivalrous.

chiv·al·rous [ʃívəlrəs] *adj.* **1** having to do with chivalry; having the qualities of an ideal knight; brave; polite; honorable. 기사(도)의; 기사적인; 용감한; 예의바른; 의협적인. **2** of the age of chivalry. 중세 기사 시대의. [→cavalier]

chiv·al·rous·ly [ʃívəlrəsli] *adv.* in the qualities of being chivalrous. 기사 답게; 의협적(義俠的)으로.

chiv·al·ry [ʃívəlri] *n.* U **1** the ideal quality of a knight. 기사도 (정신). **2** the systems of knighthood in the Middle Ages. (중세의) 기사 제도. **3** 《*collectively*》 a group of knights. 기사들〔단〕. **4** inclination to defend the weaker. 의협(義俠).

chive [tʃaiv] *n.* 《bot.》 a plant like a leek or an onion. 골파《조미료》. [L.]

chlor·al [klɔ́:rəl] *n.* U 《chem.》 a liquid with a strong smell and bitter taste. 클로랄. [Gk. *khlōros* green]

chlo·rate [klɔ́:reit, -rit] *n.* C 《chem.》 salt of chloric acid. 염소산염. ¶ *potassium* ~ 염소산 칼륨 / *sodium* ~ 염소산 나트륨.

chlo·ric [klɔ́:rik] *adj.* 《chem.》 of or containing chlorine. 염소의; 염소를 함유하는. ¶ ~ *acid* 염소산.

chlo·ride [klɔ́:raid, -rid] *n.* UC 《chem.》 a compound of chlorine. 염화물. ¶ ~ *of lime* 클로르 석회; 표백제.

chlo·rine [klɔ́:rin] *n.* U 《chem.》 a greenish-yellow, poisonous, gaseous chemical element with an unpleasant smell. 염소. ¶ ~ *dioxide* 이산화 염소.

chlo·ro·form [klɔ́:rəfɔ̀:rm] *n.* 《chem.》 U a colorless liquid with a rather sweet smell. 클로로포름《마취약》. — *vt.* (P6) **1** make (someone) unconscious or dead with chloroform. …을 클로로포름으로 마취시키다〔죽이다〕. ¶ *The man chloroformed the sick cat.* 그 사람은 병든 고양이를 클로로포름으로 죽였다. **2** steep in chloroform. (헝겊 등)을 클로로포름에 적시다. [↑, →formic]

chlo·ro·my·ce·tin [klɔ̀:roumaisí:tn] *n.* U an antibiotic drug. 클로로마이세틴. [Gk. *mukes* fungus]

chlo·ro·phyll, -phyl [klɔ́:rəfil] *n.* U the green coloring matter of plants. 엽록소. [Gk. *phullon* leaf]

chlo·ro·sis [klɔ:róusis] *n.* 《med.》 greensickness. 위황병(萎黃病). [Gk. *khlōros* green, *osis* condition]

chock [tʃɑk / tʃɔk] *n.* C a wooden block used to prevent things from rolling. (구르는 것을 막는) 굄목; 쐐기. ¶ *put a* ~ *under the wheel of a cart* 수레바퀴 밑에 굄목을 괴다. — *vt.* (P6,7) make fast with chocks. 괴목을 괴(어 움직이지 않게 하)다. [→choke]

chock up, wedge tightly; encumber. 쐐기로 단단히 고정시키다; 빽빽이 처넣다.

***choc·o·late** [tʃɔ́:kəlit, tʃɑ́k- / tʃɔ́k-] *n.* U **1** ⓐ a piece of candy made of chocolate. 초콜릿. ¶ *a bar of* ~ 판초콜릿 하나 / ~ *in powder* 분말 초콜릿. ⓑ a drink made of chocolate. 초콜릿 음료. **2** a dark-brown color. 초콜릿빛; 암갈색. **3** a sweet made from chocolate. 초콜릿 과자. — *adj.* made of chocolate; dark-brown. 초콜릿으로 만든〔이 든〕; 초콜릿빛의. [Mex.]

:**choice** [tʃɔis] *n.* **1** C selection; the act of choosing. 선택. ¶ *the way of my own* ~ 내가 선택한 길 / *make a good* 〔*bad*〕 ~ 잘〔잘못〕 고르다 / *give first* ~ *to* …을 맨 먼저 택하다〔고르다〕 / *You may take your* ~. 좋은 대로 골라잡으시오. **2** UC an opportunity or possibility of choosing; power to choose. 선택의 기회; 선택권; 선택력. ¶ *offer someone a* ~ 아무에게 선택의 기회를 주다 / *You don't have much* ~ *now.* 이제 이것저것 가릴 여지가 없다. **3** C a thing or person that is chosen. 선택된〔고른〕 것〔사람〕. ¶ *This book is my* ~. 이 책은 내가 택한 것이다 / *What is your* ~*?* 어느 것으로 하시겠습니까. **4** C a collection to choose from. (선택할 수 있는) 여러 가지의 것; 이것저것. ¶ *a* ~ *of hats* 다양한 구색의 모자 / *There is a wide* 〔*poor*〕 ~ *of articles.* 골라잡을 물건이 많다〔적다〕.

a great choice of, a great variety to choose from. …의 여러 가지로 갖춰진 물건들.

at one's (***own***) ***choice,*** as one likes. 좋아하는 대로; 마음대로.

by 〔***for***〕 ***choice,*** **a**) of one's free will; willingly. 좋아서; 자유 의사로. ¶ *I do not live here by* ~. 좋아서 여기 살고 있는 건 아니다. **b**) if one must choose. 만약 골라야 한다면.

have one's choice, can choose. 선택할 수 있다; 선택하다.

have no choice, be indifferent. 특히 어느 것이 좋다는 건 아니다; 어느 것이든 상관없다.

have no choice but to do, cannot help doing; must do. …하지 않을 수 없다; …할 수밖에 없다. ¶ *I had no* ~ *but to do what I was asked.* 하라는 대로 할 수밖에 없었다.

make (***one's***) ***choice of,*** choose. …을 고르다; 선택하다; 골라잡다.

of choice, of fine quality. 뽑아 낸; 뛰어난; 상등품의.

without choice, promiscuously. 닥치는 대로.

— *adj.* **1** excellent; carefully selected; specially good; of fine quality. 훌륭한; 정선된; 상등〔최우량〕의. ¶ *the choicest wines* 특급 포도주. **2** 《*of*》 fastidious. 가리는; 까다로운. ¶ *He is* ~ *of his food.* 그는 식성이 까다롭다. [Teut.→choose]

***choir** [kwáiər] *n.* C **1** a group of singers, usu. in a church. (교회의) 성가대; 합창대. **2** the part of a church in which the choir sings. 성가대석(席). **3** any group of singers who meet to perform vocal music. (일반적으로) 합창단. **4** the group of birds singing. 지저귀는 새떼. — *vi., vt.* (P1;6) 《*poet.*》 sing in chorus. (새·천사 등이) 합창하다. [→chorus]

choir-school [kwáiərskù:l] *n.* a school maintained by a church, etc. for choirboys and other pupils. (교회 부속의) 성가대 (양성) 학교.

***choke** [tʃouk] *vt.* (P6,7) **1** stop the breathing of (someone). …을 질식시키다. ¶ ~ *someone into unconsciousness* 목을 졸라 기절시키다 / ~ *someone to death* = ~ *the life out of someone* 아무를 질식사시키다. **2** 《*up*》 fill up or block; prevent or stop up the passage through (something) by filling. …을 막(히게 하)다. ¶ *The chimney was choked with soot.* 굴뚝은 검댕으로 막혔다 / *The river is becoming choked (up) with sand.* 강바닥은 모래가 쌓여 막혀 가고 있다 / *The roads into Seoul were so choked up with traffic that even the fire engine couldn't get through.* 서울로의 진입로는 엄청난 차량에 막혀 소방차조차도 통과할 수 없었다. **3** stop the growth of (a plant); put out by cutting off air. (식물의) 생육을 멈추게 하다; (공기를 차단하여 불)을 끄다. ¶～ *a fire* 불을 끄다. **4** 《*down, back*》 control; hold; prevent. …을 (억)누르다; 억제하다. ¶ *He choked down his anger.* 그는 노여움을 억제했다 / *She choked back her tears.* 그녀는 눈물을 참았다 / *Sobs choked her utterance.* 그녀는 흐느껴 울며 말을 못 했다.

— *vi.* (P1) **1** be unable to breathe. 숨이 막히다. **2** be filled up. 막히다.

choke off, **a**) kill (someone) by choking. …을 목졸라 죽이다. ¶～ *someone off to death* 아무를 목졸라 죽이다. **b**) persuade (someone) not to do. …을 못 하게 하다; 말리다. **c**) get rid of (something); put away. …을 없애다; 제거하다.

— *n.* **1** Ⓤ the act or sound of choking. 숨막힘; 질식; 흐느낌 (소리). **2** Ⓒ a valve in an automobile engine, to control the intake of air. (자동차 엔진의) 공기 흡입 조절판(瓣). [E.]

choke·damp [tʃóukdæ̀mp] *n.* Ⓤ a heavy gas which causes difficulty in breathing. 질식 가스. 參考 탄갱 속이나 깊은 우물 따위에 괴는 이산화탄소.

cho·ky [tʃóuki] *n.* 《Brit. *colloq.*》 a prison. 감옥; 교도소.

chol·er [kálər / kɔ́l-] *n.* Ⓤ 《*arch.*》 **1** one of the four humors; yellow bile. 담즙(膽汁). **2** anger. 화; 분노; 불뚱이. [↓]

chol·er·a [kálərə / kɔ́l-] *n.* Ⓤ an infectious and deadly Asiatic disease. 콜레라. ¶ *Asiatic* 〔*epidemic, malignant*〕 ～ 진성 콜레라 / *European* 〔*summer*〕 ～ 비전염성 콜레라 / *suspected* ～ 의사(擬似) 콜레라. [Gk.]

chol·er·ic [kálərik / kɔ́l-] *adj.* easily angry. 툭하면 성내는〔불끈거리는〕. [↑]

cho·les·ter·ol [kəléstəròul, -rɔ̀:l / -rɔ̀l] *n.* Ⓤ white waxy substance found in human tissues. 콜레스테롤《지방 조직에 함유된 성분》. [Gk.]

:choose [tʃu:z] *v.* (**chose, cho·sen**) *vt.* (P6,7,8,13,14,19,20) **1** select (something) as most desirable. …을 고르다; 선택하다. ¶～ *one between the two* 양자(兩者) 택일하다 / ～ *one among* 〔*out of*〕 *many things* 많은 것 중에서 하나를 고르다 / ～ *death before dishonor* 굴욕보다는 죽음을 택하다 / ～ *between duty and pleasure* 의무와 쾌락 중 하나를 택하다 / *You may* ～ *the largest apple in the dish.* 접시에서 가장 큰 사과를 집어도 좋다 / *There is nothing* 〔*not much*〕 *to* ～ *between them.* 그들 사이에는 이렇다 할 우열의 차이는 없다. **2** elect. …을 선출하다; 뽑다. ¶～ *someone by vote* 〔*election*〕 투표〔선거〕로 아무를 뽑다 / *They chose him chairman.* 그들은 그를 의장으로 선출했다. **3** prefer, decide, or think fit to do something. (…하는 쪽)을 택하다; 바라다; (…하기로) 정하다. ¶ *He chose to accept her offer.* 그는 그녀의 제의를 받아들이기로 했다. **4** 《*colloq.*》 want; desire. …을 원하다; 바라다. ¶ *do what one chooses* 하고 싶은 일을 하다 / *Take whichever* 〔*anything*〕 *you* ～. 어느 쪽이든 좋아하는 것을 가지시오 / *She didn't* ～ *to go.* 그녀는 가고 싶어하지 않았다. — *vi.* (P1,2A,3) **1** make a choice. 선택하다. ¶～ *between one thing and another* 둘 중 어느 것을 고르다. **2** make a decision; be inclined. 결정하다; 바라다. ¶ *You may stay here if you* ～. 좋으시다면 여기 머무르셔도 괜찮습니다. [E.]

as you choose, as you like. 좋을 대로; 마음대로.

cannot choose but, must; have to. …할 수밖에 없다; …하지 않을 수 없다. ¶ *They could not* ～ *but obey.* 그들은 복종할 수밖에 없었다.

choose A before B, prefer A to B. B 보다는 A를 택하다.

choos·y, -ey [tʃú:zi] *adj.* (**choos·i·er, choos·i·est**) 《*colloq.*》 difficult to please; very careful or fussy in choosing. (사람이) 까다로운; 가리는. [E.]

:chop[1] [tʃap / tʃɔp] *v.* (**chopped, chop·ping**) *vt.* (P6,7) **1** cut or make (something) by strokes with an ax. (도끼 따위로) …을 자르다; 베다. ¶～ *twigs with an ax* 도끼로 나뭇가지를 자르다 / ～ *logs* 통나무를 빼개다. **2** cut (something) into small pieces. …을 잘게 썰다; 저미다. ¶～ *up an onion* 양파를 잘게 썰다. — *vi.* (P2A,3) make cutting strokes as with an ax. 자르다; 찍다; 저미다. ¶～ *at a tree* 나무를 자르다.

chop about 〔***round***〕, (esp. of the wind) change direction suddenly. (특히 풍향이) 갑자기 바뀌다.

chop and change, keep changing one's plans, opinions, or occupation (방침·의견·직업 따위를) 끊임없이 바꾸다.

chop at, strike at. 치고 덤비다.

chop back, suddenly go back. 갑자기 되돌아오다〔가다〕.

chop down, remove or cause to fall by chopping; fell. 베어 넘기다. ¶～ *a tree down* 나무를 베어 넘기다.

chop in, chip in. 말참견하다.

chop logic 〔***words***〕, exchange opinions by talking or discussing with someone. …와 논쟁하다; 궤변을 농하다.

chop off, separate one thing from another by chopping. 잘라 내다. ¶～ *a branch off* 나뭇가지를 잘라 내다.

chop through, make (one's way) by cutting trees down. 나무를 베어 내면서 나아가

다. ¶ ~ *a path through a forest* 숲을 뚫어 길을 내다.

chop up, **a**) cut (something) into small pieces. 잘게 썰다; 저미다. ¶ ~ *up meat* 〔*cabbage*〕 고기〔양배추〕를 저미다. **b**) crop up. 나타나다; 노출하다.

— *n.* **1** Ⓒ a short, cutting blow; the act of chopping. 일격; 절단. **2** Ⓒ a slice of meat (as of lamb, pork, etc.). 고깃점; 육편(肉片). ¶ *a pork* ~ 돼지고기 한 토막 / *I'll have a couple of chops for my dinner.* 저녁으로 고기 두어 점 먹겠다. **3** Ⓤ a sudden motion of waves. 갑자기 일렁이는 물결. [E. →chap[2]]

get the chop, 《*sl.*》 be dismissed from work. 해고되다. ¶ *He got the* ~ *for being late.* 지각으로 인해 해고당했다.

chop[2] [tʃɑp / tʃɔp] *n.* Ⓒ 《usu. *pl.*》 the jaws; the chin. 턱. [↑]

lick one's chops, 《*colloq.*》 await with pleasure; anticipate. 즐거움으로 기다리다; 고대하다.

chop[3] [tʃɑp / tʃɔp] *n.* **1** (in India & China) an official stamp; a seal; a permit. 관인(官印); 도장; 허가증. **2** a class; rate; quality. 등급; 품질. [Hind.=stamp]

chop·house [tʃɑ́phàus / tʃɔ́p-] *n.* Ⓒ a restaurant dealing chiefly with slices of meat, etc. (주로 육류를 파는) 간이 음식점. [*chop*[1]]

Cho·pin [ʃóupæn / ʃɔ́pæn], **François** *n.* (1814-49) a Polish composer. 쇼팽.

chop·per [tʃɑ́pər / tʃɔ́p-] *n.* Ⓒ **1** a person who chops. 자르는〔베는〕 사람. **2** a tool or machine for chopping. 자르는 기구《도끼 따위》. [*chop*[1]]

chop·py [tʃɑ́pi / tʃɔ́pi] *adj.* (**-pi·er, -pi·est**) **1** with sharp, sudden movements. 급격히 움직이는. **2** (of a lake, etc.) moving in short, rough waves. (수면 따위가) 물결이 이는; 거친. ¶ *a* ~ *sea* 거친 바다. **3** full of cracks. (피부 따위가) 많이 튼; 터진 데투성이의. **4** (of the wind, etc.) changing suddenly. (풍향이) 갑자기 바뀌는; 변하기 쉬운. [→chop[1]]

chop·stick [tʃɑ́pstìk / tʃɔ́p-] *n.* Ⓒ 《usu. *pl.*》 a small stick used in pairs to carry food to the mouth. 젓가락. [Chin. *chop* nimble, stick]

chop su·ey [tʃɑ́p súːi / tʃɔ́p -] *n.* Ⓤ meat cooked together with vegetables. 잡채《중화요리》. [Chin.]

cho·ral [kɔ́ːrəl] *adj.* of a choir or chorus; sung by a choir or chorus. 합창(대)의; 합창으로 노래되는. ¶ ~ *singing* 합창 / *a* ~ *service* 합창 예배. — *n.* Ⓒ a hymn tune. 성가; 찬송가. ● **cho·ral·ist** [-rəlist] *n.* a choral singer. 성가 대원; 합창 단원. [→chorus]

chord[1] [kɔːrd] *n.* Ⓒ 《mus.》 a combination of several musical notes sounded together in harmony. 화음(和音). [↓]

chord[2] [kɔːrd] *n.* Ⓒ **1** 《math.》 a straight line joining any two points on a circle. 현(弦). **2** 《anat.》 a chordlike structure in an animal body. 건(腱); 심줄. ¶ *the vocal chord(s)* 성대(聲帶) / *the spinal* ~ 척수(脊髓). **3** a string of a musical instrument. (악기의) 줄; 현. **4** Ⓤ feeling; emotion. 감정; 마음. ¶ *touch* 〔*strike*〕 *the right* ~ 심금(心琴)을 울리다. [Gk. *khordē*]

chore [tʃɔːr] *n.* Ⓒ **1** ⓐ a small or odd job. 잡(雜)일. ⓑ 《*pl.*》 household tasks. 집안일. ¶ *My chores include sweeping the floors.* 마루 청소도 내가 맡은 일이다. **2** a hard or disagreeable task. 힘든〔싫은〕 일. [→chare]

cho·re·og·ra·phy [kɔ̀ːriɑ́grəfi / kɔ̀ːriɔ́g-], 《Brit.》 **cho·reg-** [kərég-] *n.* the planning of dance steps and movements of a ballet. (무용·발레의) 안무. [Gk. *khoreia* dance]

chor·ic [kɔ́ːrik, kɑ́r- / kɔ́r-] *adj.* of Greek chorus. (그리스) 합창곡의. [→chorus]

chor·is·ter [kɔ́ːristər, kɑ́r- / kɔ́r-] *n.* Ⓒ **1** a singer in a choir. (교회의) 합창자; 성가대원. **2** a leader of a choir. 합창대 지휘자. [→chorus]

chor·tle [tʃɔ́ːrtl] *vi.* (P1) laugh loudly and joyously. (기쁜 듯이) 소리내어 웃다. ¶ ~ *in one's joy* 즐거워 껄껄 웃다. — *n.* Ⓒ a joyous laugh. 소리내어 웃음. [→portmanteau]

***cho·rus** [kɔ́ːrəs] *n.* Ⓒ **1** a group of singers who sing together; a piece of song or musical composition sung by many singers together. 합창대; 합창(곡). ¶ *mixed* ~ 혼성 합창 / *join in a* ~ 합창에 참여하다. **2** the repeated part of a song; a refrain. 후렴. **3** a number of voices speaking at once. 일제히 하는〔외치는〕 말이나 소리. ¶ *in* ~ 이구 동성으로; 일제히 / *a* ~ *of noes* 이구 동성의 반대 / *with a* ~ *of approval* 일동의 찬성으로. **4** a group of singers and dancers. (뮤지컬 쇼 따위에서) 무용수와 가수의 집단. — *vt., vi.* sing or speak all together. 일제히〔이구 동성으로〕 말하다; 합창하다. [Gk. *khoros*]

cho·rus-girl [kɔ́ːrəsgə̀ːrl] *n.* Ⓒ a young woman who sings and dances in a musical play. 가무단의 여성 가수〔무용수〕.

***chose** [tʃouz] *v.* p. of **choose.**

***cho·sen** [tʃóuzn] *v.* pp. of **choose.** — *adj.* selected 뽑힌; 선택〔정선〕된. ¶ *the* ~ *people* 〔*race*〕 신의 선민(選民)《유대인의 자칭》.

chouse [tʃaus] *vt., n.* (P6,13) 《*colloq.*》 swindle. 사기(하다); 협잡(하다). [Turk.]

chow [tʃau] *n.* **1** a kind of Chinese dog, with a thick coat of brown or black hair and a black tongue. (중국산) 개의 일종《혀는 검고 갈색 또는 검은 털이 밀생함》. **2** Ⓤ 《*sl.*》 food of any kind. 음식물. [?]

chow·der [tʃáudər] *n.* Ⓤ a thick souplike food which usu. contains fish, shellfish, and various vegetables. 해물잡탕의 하나《생선·조개 및 각종 채소가 듦》. [F. = pot]

:Christ [kraist] *n.* a title given to Jesus, the founder of the Christian religion; the Savior. 그리스도; 예수; 구세주. — *interj.* an interjection of surprise, indignation, etc. 저런; 제기랄. [Gk. *khristos* anointed, *pholos* bearing]

chris·ten [krísn] *vt.* **1** (P6) take (someone) into a Christian church by baptism; baptize. …에게 세례를 베풀다. **2** (P19) give a first name to (a baby) at baptism. 세례를 주고 이름을 붙이다. ¶ *He was christened John after his grandfather.* 세례를 받고 할아버지 이름을 따라 존이라고 명명되었다. **3** (P19) give a name to (a ship, a bell, etc.); often at a formal ceremony. (흔히 의식을 치르고 선박·종 따위)에 이름을 붙이다. **4** 《U.S. *colloq.*》 use for the first time, esp. with ceremony. (의식을 치르고) 처음으로 사용하다. [↑]

Chris·ten·dom [krísndəm] *n.* Ⓤ **1** 《*collectively*》 all Christians. 전(全)기독교도. **2** the Christian world. 기독교계(界); 전기독교국(國). **3** Christianity. 기독교(신앙).

chris·ten·ing [krísniŋ] *n.* ⒸⓊ the act or ceremony at which a baby is christened; baptism. 세례; 세례식; 명명식. ¶ *Several christenings took place today.* 오늘 몇 차례의 세례식이 있었다.

:Chris·tian [krístʃən] *adj.* **1** of Christ; believing in Christ. 그리스도의; 기독교를 믿는. ¶ *a ~ name* 세례명 / *the ~ church* 기독교회 / *the ~ Era* 서력 기원 / *a ~ faith* 기독교신앙 / *~ countries* 기독교 국가. **2** showing the good qualities taught by Christ. 기독교적인. 參考 사랑·겸양·친절을 나타냄. ¶ *a truly ~ act* 진정한 기독교인다운 행동. **3** of Christianity or Christians. 기독교(도)의. — *n.* Ⓒ **1** a believer in Christ; a member of the religion founded by Jesus Christ. 기독교인. **2** 《*colloq.*》 a good and honorable person; civilized person. 점잖은[훌륭한] 사람; 문명인.

Chris·ti·an·i·ty [krìstʃiǽnəti] *n.* Ⓤ the religion taught by Christ; the Christian religion; Christian beliefs, faith, spirit, etc. 기독교; 기독교 신앙; 기독교적 정신.

Chris·tian·ize [krístʃənàiz] *vt.* (P6) make (someone) Christian or like a Christian; convert (someone) to Christianity. …을 기독교인으로 만들다; 기독교로 개종시키다.

Christian Science [⌐– ⌐–] *n.* a religious sect that believes in the idea of healing disease by mental treatment. 크리스천 사이언스《신앙 요법으로 병을 고친다고 믿는 기독교의 한 파》.

Christ·like [kráistlàik] *adj.* like Jesus Christ, esp. in qualities or spirit. 그리스도 같은; 그리스도의 정신을 나타내는.

:Christ·mas [krísməs] *n.* Ⓤ the celebration held on December 25th in honor of the birth of Christ. 크리스마스; 성탄절. ¶ *have a jolly ~* 즐거운 성탄절을 지내다. [→Christ]

Christmas box [⌐– ⌐] *n.* 《Brit.》 a present given at Christmas to the postman, delivery boys, etc. in return for their services. 크리스마스 선물《우편 집배원·배달 소년 등에게 줌》.

Christmas card [⌐– ⌐] *n.* a card for mailing at Christmas to express good wishes. 크리스마스 카드. 參考 send a Christmas card 라고 함.

Christmas carol [⌐– ⌐–] *n.* a Christmas song. 크리스마스 송가(頌歌).

Christmas Eve [⌐–⌐] *n.* the evening before Christmas Day. 크리스마스 전야《12월 24일》.

Christ·mas·tide [krísməstàid], **Christ·mas-time** [-tàim] *n.* Ⓤ the season of Christmas; the period before and after Christmas. 크리스마스 계절.

Christmas tree [⌐–⌐] *n.* an evergreen tree decorated with candles or small electric lights at Christmas time. 크리스마스 트리.

Chris·to·pher [krístəfər] *n.* a man's name. 남자 이름. [→Christ]

chro·mat·ic [kroumǽtik] *adj.* **1** of color or colors. 색(채)의; 착색의. ¶ *a ~ sensation* 색채 감각 / *~ printing* 색채 인쇄. **2** 《mus.》 progressing by half tones. 반음(계)의. ¶ *the ~ scale* 반음계. [Gk. *khrōma* color]

chro·mat·ics [kroumǽtiks] *n. pl.* 《used as *sing.*》 the science of color. 색학(色學); 색채론.

chro·ma·tin [króumətin] *n.* Ⓤ 《biol.》 a tissue that can be stained. 염색질(質).

chro·ma·tism [króumətìzəm] *n.* Ⓤ **1** natural coloring. 자연 채색. **2** chromatic aberration. 색수차(色收差).

chrome [kroum] *n.* Ⓤ **1** =chromium. **2** chrome yellow. 크롬옐로; 황연(黃鉛). [Gk. *khrōma* color]

chrome steel [⌐⌐] *n.* a very strong, hard, steel that contains chromium. 크롬강(鋼).

chro·mi·um [króumiəm] *n.* Ⓤ 《chem.》 a shiny, hard, rust-resistering metallic element. 크롬; 크로뮴.

chro·mo·lith·o·graph [kròumoulíθougræ̀f, -grɑ̀:f] *n.* a picture lithographed in color. 착색 석판쇄(石版刷). [→chrome]

chro·mo·some [króuməsòum] *n.* 《biol.》 any of the microscopic filaments composed of chromatin. 염색체.

chro·mo·sphere [króuməsfìər] *n.* 《astron.》 a scarlet layer of gas around the sun. (태양 주위의) 채층(彩層).

Chron. Chronicles.

chron·ic [kránik / krɔ́n-] *adj.* **1** (of a disease) lasting for a long time; long-continued. (병이) 만성의; 오래 끄는(opp. acute). ¶ *a ~ case* 만성병 환자 / *a ~ disease* 만성질환. **2** continuing for a long time; constant; habitual. 장기에 걸친; 끊임없는; 습관

적〔상습적〕인. ¶ *a ~ smoker* 담배 중독자; 골초 / *a ~ liar* 상습적인 거짓말쟁이. **3** 《Brit. *vulg.*》 very bad; severe. 아주 나쁜; 지독한. ¶ *The food was absolutely ~!* 그 음식은 아주 형편없었다. [Gk. *khronos* time]

chron·i·cal·ly [kránikəli / krɔ́n-] *adv.* in a manner of being; chronic. 만성적으로; 오래 끌어.

*****chron·i·cle** [kránikl / krɔ́n-] *n.* Ⓒ a record of events in the order in which they happened. 연대기(記); 편년사(編年史); 기록; 역사. ¶ *a ~ of the war* 전기(戰記) / *the Chronicles* (성서의) 역대기(歷代記) / *enter in a ~* 역사에 이름을 남기다. — *vt.* (P6) record (something) in a chronicle; write or tell the history or story of (something). …을 연대기에 싣다; 기록에 남기다.

chron·i·cler [krániklər / krɔ́n-] *n.* Ⓒ a writer of a chronicle; a recorder of events; a historian. 연대기 작가; 기록자; 편사가(編史家).

chron·o·log·i·cal [krɑ̀nəlɑ́dʒikəl / krɔ̀nəlɔ́dʒ-] *adj.* arranged in the order of occurrence. 연대순(順)의; 연대의; 연대적인. ¶ *a ~ table of the world history* 세계사(史) 연표(年表) / *Put the dates in ~ order.* 날짜를 연대순으로 하시오. ● **chron·o·log·i·cal·ly** [-kəli] *adv.* [*chronic*]

chro·nol·o·gy [krənɑ́lidʒi / -nɔ́l-] *n.* (*pl.* **-gies**) **1** Ⓤ the science dealing with events and arranging their dates in proper order. 연대학(年代學). **2** Ⓒ a table or list of events arranged in their proper order of occurrence; the arrangement of events in their proper order of occurrence. 연(대)표; 연대기(記).

chro·nom·e·ter [krənɑ́mitər / -nɔ́m-] *n.* Ⓒ an instrument like a clock or watch for measuring time very exactly (esp. on ships). 크로노미터; (일반적으로) 정밀 계시기(計時器).

chrys·al·i·des [krisǽlədìːz] *n.* pl. of **chrysalis.**

chrys·a·lis [krísəlis] *n.* Ⓒ (*pl.* **chrys·a·lis·es** or **chrys·al·i·des**) **1** the inactive form of an insect when it is in a case; a pupa. 번데기; (특히, 나비류의) 고치. **2** anything in such a stage; an undeveloped stage. 준비〔과도〕기; 미발달의 상태. [Gk. *khrusos* gold]

chry·san·the·mum [krisǽnθəməm] *n.* Ⓒ a plant of the aster family which blooms late in the autumn. 국화. 參考 미국 구어에서는 그냥 mum이라고 함. [Gk. = gold flower]

chrys·o·lite [krísəlàit] *n.* a green precious stone. 귀감람석(貴橄欖石). [Gk. *khrusos* gold, *lithos* stone]

chub [tʃʌb] *n.* (*pl.* **chubs** or **chub**) a river fish of the carp family. 황어속(黃魚屬)의 물고기. [E.]

chub·by [tʃʌ́bi] *adj.* (**-bi·er, -bi·est**) round and plump; rather fat. 토실토실 살찐; 똥똥한. ¶ *a ~ face* 〔*child*〕 통통한 얼굴〔아이〕. ● **chub·bi·ness** [-nis] *n.* [N.]

chuck[1] [tʃʌk] *vt.* (P6,7) **1** pat or tap lovingly esp. under the chin. …을 가볍게 치다〔두드리다〕. ¶ *~ someone under the chin* 아무의 턱 밑을 토닥거리다. **2** throw; toss. 핵 던지다; 버리다. ¶ *~ a ball* 공을 던지다 / *~ the letter into the wastebasket* 편지를 휴지통에 던져 넣다 / *Chuck me the suitcase.* 그 가방 좀 던져 주게 / *Chuck it away.* 그것을 버려라. **3** 《*colloq.*》 throw away; dismiss; give up. …을 포기하다; 버리다; 해고하다. ¶ *~ one's friend* 친구를 버리다〔못 본 체 돌보지 않다〕 / *I'm going to ~ it.* 난 그 일을 포기하련다 / *He's chucked his plans.* 그는 계획을 중지했다.

chuck away, a) throw away. 내던지다; 내버리다. b) lose or waste (time, money, etc.). (시간·돈 따위)를 허비하다; 놓치다.

chuck it! 《*sl.*》 Stop doing that! 그만 해; 닥쳐. ¶ *Chuck it or I'll hit you.* 닥쳐라, 안 그러면 패 주겠다.

chuck out, a) throw out of a room, theater, etc. with force. …을 내쫓다. ¶ *~ someone out of the room* 아무를 방에서 쫓아내다. b) throw out a bill or motion. (법안·동의를) 부결하다.

chuck up, give up; abandon (one's job, etc.) in disgust. …을 내던지다; 포기하다. ¶ *~ up one's job* 일자리를 내던지다.

— *n.* Ⓒ **1** a light pat or tap (under the chin). (턱 밑을) 가볍게 치기. **2** a toss; a throw. (내)던지기; 버리기. [?]

get the chuck, 《*sl.*》 be dismissed. 해고당하다

give someone the chuck, 《*sl.*》 dismiss him suddenly. 아무를 갑자기 해고하다.

chuck[2] [tʃʌk] *n.* **1** Ⓒ a device for holding a tool or a piece of wood or metal in a lathe or drill. (선반 따위의) 척; 물림쇠. **2** Ⓤ the part or cut of beef between the neck and the shoulder. (쇠고기에서) 목에서 어깨의 고기. [*chock*]

chuck·er-out [tʃʌ́kəráut] *n.* (*pl.* **chuck·ers-out**) 《Brit.》 a man employed to throw out troublesome persons from a public-house or meeting. (행패꾼 등을 내쫓는) 장내 경비원. [→chuck[1]]

*****chuck·le** [tʃʌ́kl] *vt.* (P1,2A) **1** laugh quietly to oneself. 가만히〔킥킥〕 웃다; 낄낄거리다. ¶ *He chuckled to himself over the funny cartoon.* 우스운 만화를 보고 혼자 킬킬댔다. **2** 《*fig.*》 feel satisfaction. 만족해하다. ¶ *He must be chuckling at his success.* 자신의 성공에 만족해하고 있음에 틀림없다. — *n.* Ⓒ a chuckling sound; a hen's call. 낄낄거리는 소리; (암탉의 병아리 부르는) 꼬꼬하는 소리. ● **chuck·ler** [-lər] *n.* [Imit.]

chuck·le-head [tʃʌ́klhed] *n.* a dolt. 바보. ● **chuck·le-head·ed** [-id] *adj.*

chug [tʃʌg] *n.* Ⓒ the short, loud, explosive sound made by an engine. (발동기 따위의)

통퉁〔폭폭, 칙칙〕하는 소리. — *vi.* (**chugged, chug·ging**) (P2A) make short, loud, explosive sounds; move while making such sounds. 위와 같은 소리를 내다〔내면서 가다〕. [Imit.]

chuk·ker [tʃʌ́kər] *n.* a period of play in a polo match. (폴로 경기의) 한 회(回).

chum [tʃʌm] *n.* Ⓒ 《*colloq.*》 **1** an intimate, dear friend (esp. among boys). 친한 친구; 짝궁. ¶ *boyhood chums* 어렸을 때의 친한 친구 / *get*〔*make*〕 *chums with* …와 친해지다; 친구가 되다. **2** a roommate. 한 방 동료〔친구〕. — *vi.* (**chummed, chum·ming**) (P2A,3) **1** be intimate friends with someone. …와 친한 사이이다; 친하게 지내다. ¶ ~ *up*〔*in*〕 *with someone* …와 사이좋게〔친하게〕 지내다. **2** 《*with, together*》 room together. …와 방을 같이 쓰다. ¶ *He chummed with his friend.* 친구와 한방을 썼다 / *They chummed together.* 그들은 한방을 썼다. [*chamber*]

chum·mer·y [tʃʌ́məri] *n.* chums. 친구들.

chum·my [tʃʌ́mi] *adj.* (**-mi·er, -mi·est**) 《*colloq.*》 very friendly; intimate. 아주 친한; 친밀한. ¶ *be* ~ *with* …와 친(밀)하다.
● **chum·mi·ly** [-li] *adv.*

chump [tʃʌmp] *n.* Ⓒ **1** 《*colloq.*》 a foolish or silly person. 바보; 얼간이. **2** a short, thick piece of wood〔meat〕. 뭉뚝한 나무토막; 고깃덩이. **3** 《*sl.*》 the head. 대가리. [? *chop*+*lump*]

chunk [tʃʌŋk] *n.* Ⓒ **1** a short, thick piece or lump, as of wood, meat, or cheese. (나무·고기·치즈 따위의) 큰 덩어리〔토막〕. ¶ *a* ~ *of bread* 큰 빵 덩어리 / *a* ~ *of meat* 두껍게 벤 고깃덩이. **2** 《U.S.》 a stocky person or animal. 똥똥한〔땅딸막한〕 사람; 모착한 동물. ¶ *a fine* ~ *of man* 크고 단단한 몸집의 남자. ● **chunk·y** [-i] *adj.* [→ chock]

:church [tʃəːrtʃ] *n.* **1** Ⓒ a building in which Christians meet to worship God. 교회(당); 성당. 參考 흔히 기독교의 교회를 말하나 영국에서는 국교(國教)의 교회당만을 가리킬 때가 있음. **2** Ⓤ 《without *an article*》 public worship; religious service in a church. 예배. 參考 이 뜻일 때는 보통 관사가 안 붙음. ¶ *attend*〔*go to*〕 ~ *regularly* 거르지 않고 예배보러 다니다 / *Church begins at 10 o'clock.* 예배는 열 시에 시작한다 / *They are at*〔*in*〕 ~. 그들은 예배를 보고 있다. 參考 They are in the church. 는 "그들은 교회당에 있다"의 뜻. **3** 《*the C-, collectively*》 (전체) 기독교인. **4** Ⓒ a group of people with the same religious beliefs. (조직체로서의) 교회; 교파. ¶ *the Greek Church* 그리스 정교회(= Eastern Church) / *the Church of England* 영국 국교; 성공회(=the Anglican Church) / *the Church of Rome* 로마 카톨릭 교회. **5** Ⓤ 《*the C-*》 the clergy as a profession. 성직(聖職).
as poor as a church mouse, very poor. 매우 가난한; 찰가난의.
enter〔*go into*〕 *the Church,* become a priest. 성직자가 되다.
— *vt.* (P6) bring or conduct (someone) to church, esp. for special services; perform a church service of thanksgiving for (a woman after childbirth). (순산 따위 특별 예배에) …을 교회에 안내하다; (순산한 산모를) 위해 감사 예배를 드리다. ¶ *The mother was churched.* 어머니를 위해 감사 예배가 있었다.
— *adj.* of or having to do with the Church. 교회의. ¶ ~ *music* 교회 음악 / ~ *architecture* 교회 건축 [Gk. *kurios* lord]

church·go·er [tʃə́ːrtʃgòuər] *n.* Ⓒ a person who goes to church regularly. (빠지는 일 없이) 교회에 다니는 사람.

church·go·ing [tʃə́ːrtʃgòuiŋ] *n.* Ⓤ church attendance esp. when habitual. 교회에 다니기. — *adj.* attending church regularly. 교회에 빠지지 않고 다니는.

Church·ill [tʃə́ːrtʃil], **Sir Winston** *n.* (1874-1965) a Prime Minister of the United Kingdom. 처칠《영국의 수상》.

church·man [tʃə́ːrtʃmən] *n.* Ⓒ (*pl.* **-men** [-mən]) **1** a clergyman; a priest. 목사; 성직자. **2** 《Brit.》 《sometimes *C-*》 a member of the Church of England. 영국 국교도(國教徒).

church·ward·en [tʃə́ːrtʃwɔ̀ːrdn] *n.* Ⓒ **1** a church officer, not a priest, whose duties are chiefly concerned with the management of church business, property, finances, etc. (평신도의) 교회 관리 위원. 參考 영국 교회·미국 성공회에서 parish(교구)를 대표하여 교회를 관리하는 사람. **2** 《Brit. *colloq.*》 a long clay tobacco pipe. (도제(陶製)의) 긴 담뱃대.

church·wom·an [tʃə́ːrtʃwùmən] *n.* (*pl.* **-wom·en** [-wìmin]) a female member of a church, esp. of the Established Church in England. (특히, 영국 국교의) 여신도.

church·yard [tʃə́ːrtʃjɑ̀ːrd] *n.* Ⓒ a yard or graveyard very near a church; a cemetery. 교회의 경내(境內)(에 있는 묘지).

churl [tʃəːrl] *n.* a rude, bad-mannered person; a peasant. 막되고 예절 없는 사람; 농사꾼. [E. =man]

churl·ish [tʃə́ːrliʃ] *adj.* rude; ill-bred; mean. 야비한; 막된; 예절 없는; 인색한.

churn [tʃəːrn] *n.* **1** Ⓒ a wooden tub or machine in which milk or cream is made into butter. (버터 만드는) 교유기(攪乳器). **2** Ⓒ 《Brit.》 a large milk can. 대형 우유통. **3** Ⓤ the act of stirring violently. 세게 휘젓기. — *vt.* (P6,7,13) **1** stir or shake (cream or milk) in a churn. 교유기로 (크림이나 우유)를 휘젓다. **2** make (butter) in a churn. 크림을 휘저어 (버터)를 만들다. **3** 《*fig.*》 shake or stir (water, etc.) violently. (물 따

위)를 세차게 휘젓다〔요동시키다〕. ¶ *The wind churned the waters to foam.* 바람으로 물이 요동쳐 거품이 일었다. —*vi.* (P1) **1** work a churn. 교유기를 쓰다. **2** move as if churned. 세차게 요동치다. ¶ *The water churns around* 〔*among*〕 *the rocks.* 물이 바위들 사이를 소용돌이치고 있다. [E.]

chute [ʃuːt] *n.* Ⓒ **1** an inclined passage, tube, etc. for conveying things from a higher to a lower level. 슈트; 활강 투하로(滑降投下路); 투하 장치. ¶ *a letter* 〔*coal*〕 ~ 편지〔석탄〕투하 장치. **2** water passage by which water falls to a lower level. 홈통. **3** rapids in a river; waterfall. 급류; 폭포. **4** a long, narrow ledge; a steep slope. 활주 사면(斜面); 급한 비탈. **5** 《*colloq.*》 a parachute. 낙하산. [L. *cado* fall]

chut·ney [tʃʌ́tni] *n.* a sauce or relish of East Indian origin. 처트니《동인도의 맛이신 조미료》. [Hind.]

chyme [kaim] *n.* Ⓤ 《physiol.》 a pulpy, semi-liquid mass into which food is changed by the action of the stomach. 유미즙(乳糜汁). [Gk. *kheō* pour]

CIA Central Intelligence Agency.

ci·ca·da [sikéidə, -kɑ́ːdə] *n.* Ⓒ (*pl.* **-das** or **-dae**) a large insect with four transparent wings. 매미. 參考 미국에서는 locust라고도 함. [L.]

ci·ca·dae [sikéidiː / -kɑ́ː-] *n.* pl. of **cicada.**

ci·ca·la [sikɑ́ːlə] *n.* =cicada.

cic·a·trice [síkətris], **cic·a·trix** [-trìks] *n.* (*pl.* **-tri·ces**) **1** a scar of healed wound. 상처 자국; 흉터; 상흔(傷痕). **2** 《bot.》 a scar left by a fallen leaf. 엽흔(葉痕). [L.]

cic·a·tri·ces [sìkətráisiːz] *n.* pl. of **cicatrice.**

cic·e·ly [sísəli] *n.* 《bot.》 a kind of flowering plant. 미나릿과의 식물. [Gk. *seselis*]

Cic·e·ro [sísəròu] *n.* (106-43 B.C.) a Roman statesman, orator and writer. 키케로.

cic·e·ro·ne [sìsəróuni, tʃitʃə-] *n.* Ⓒ (*pl.* **-nes** or **-ni**) a guide for sightseers who explains the history or interesting places, etc. 관광 안내인. ¶ *do the* ~ 관광 안내를 하다. [It.]

cic·e·ro·ni [sìsəróuniː] *n.* pl. of **cicerone.**

Cic·e·ro·ni·an [sìsəróuniən] *adj.* eloquent as Cicero. 키케로 같은 웅변의.

ci·der [sáidər] *n.* Ⓤ **1** apple juice. 사과즙. **2** 《Brit.》 a light wine; an alcoholic drink made from apples. 사과술. ¶ *hard* ~ 발효시킨 사과술 / *soft* ~ 비(非)발효의 사과술. [Heb. =strong drink, F. *Cidre*]

cider press [∠-∠] *n.* a machine that presses the juice out of apples. 사과 착즙기(搾汁器).

ci·ga·la [sigɑ́ːlə] *n.* =cicada.

C.I.F., c.i.f. 《comm.》 cost, insurance & freight (운임·보험료 포함 가격 (조건)).

***ci·gar** [sigɑ́ːr] *n.* Ⓒ a small roll of tobacco leaves for smoking. 시거; 여송연. [Sp.]

***cig·a·rette** [sìgərét, ∠-∠] *n.* Ⓒ a thin roll of finely cut tobacco wrapped in a thin sheet of paper for smoking. 궐련; 담배. ¶ *a packet of cigarettes* 담배 한 갑 / *a* ~ *butt* 담배 꽁초 / *light a* ~ 담배에 불을 붙이다 / *smoke a* ~ 담배를 피우다. [↑]

cig·a·rette-case [sigərétkèis] *n.* a case for carrying cigarettes. 담뱃갑.

cil·i·a [síliə] *n. pl.* (*sing.* **cil·i·um**) **1** the eyelashes. 속눈썹. **2** fine hairs on leaves, wings, or insects and certain very tiny animals. 섬모(纖毛); 솜털. ●**cil·i·a·ry** [síləri / -əri] *adj.* **cil·i·at·ed** *adj.* [L.]

cil·i·um [síliəm] *n.* sing. of **cilia.**

Cim·mer·i·an [simíəriən] *adj.* having to do with a people said to live in unending darkness; very dark and gloomy. (영원한 어둠의 나라에 살았다는) 키메르족(族)의; 암흑의; 어두운. ¶ ~ *darkness* 칠흑 같은 어둠. [Homeric person]

cinch [sintʃ] *n.* 《U.S.》 **1** a band round a horse's belly. (말의) 뱃대끈. **2** 《*sl.*》 a certainty; a sure or easy thing. 확실한 일; 쉬운 일. ¶ *It is* ~ *that...* …하다는 것은 확실하다. —*vt.* (P6) put on with a cinch; bind firmly. 뱃대끈을 매다; 단단히 매다; 단단히 쥐다. [Sp.=saddlegirth]

cin·cho·na [siŋkóunə, sin-] *n.* **1** Ⓒ 《bot.》 a tropical tree of South America, the East Indies, India, and Java, valuable for its bark. 기나수(幾那樹). 參考 원산지는 남아메리카. **2** Ⓤ its bitter bark. 기나피(皮). 參考 키니네를 만듦. [Person]

Cin·cin·nat·i [sìnsənǽti] *n.* an industrial city of south-western Ohio, on the Ohio River. 신시내티《Ohio 주 남서부의 도시》.

cinc·ture [síŋktʃər] *n.* **1** Ⓒ a belt or girdle. 띠; 끈. **2** Ⓤ enclosure. 둘러싼 경계; 울. ¶ *an island in the* ~ *of the sea* 사방이 바다로 둘러싸인 섬. —*vt.* (P6) put a belt round; encircle. 띠를 두르다; 둘러싸다. [L. *cingo* gird]

cin·der [síndər] *n.* **1** Ⓤ 《often *pl.*》 a small piece of coal, etc. partly burned and no longer flaming. 타다 남은 것; 뜬숯. ¶ *be burnt to cinders* 까맣게 타다〔눋다〕 / *The cook has burnt the meat to a* ~. 요리사는 고기를 새까맣게 태웠다. **2** 《*pl.*》 ashes. 재. ¶ *volcanic cinders* 화산재. [E.=slag]

Cin·der·el·la [sìndərélə] *n.* **1** a pretty girl in a fairy tale. (동화의) 신데렐라. **2** Ⓒ a beautiful girl who is oppressed in poor surroundings. (불우한 처지에 있는) 숨은 미인. [↑]

Cinderella dance [--∠- ∠] *n.* a small dancing-party which ends at midnight. 한밤중에 끝나는 무도회.

cin·der-path 〔**-track**〕 [síndərpæ̀θ, -pɑ̀ːθ 〔-træ̀k〕] *n.* a footpath or running track laid with small cinders. (석탄재를 깔아 굳힌) 경주로.

cin·e·cam·e·ra [sínəkæ̀mərə] *n.* Ⓒ a

camera used for taking motion pictures. 영화 촬영기. [↓]

cin·e·film [sínəfilm] *n.* a film used in cinecameras. (영화 촬영용) 필름.

:**cin·e·ma** [sínəmə] *n.* Ⓒ《chiefly Brit.》**1** a motion picture; a motion-picture theater. (한 편의) 영화; 영화관(=《U.S.》movie). ¶ *go to the* 〔*a*〕 ～ 영화 보러 가다. **2** 《*the* ～, *collectively*》 motion pictures; the business or art of motion pictures. 영화; 영화 사업〔예술〕. [Gk. *kínēma* motion]

Cin·e·ma·scope [sínəməskòup] *n.* 《trademark》 a process of moving picture reproduction that achieves a realistic three-dimention effect. 시네마스코프.

cin·e·mat·o·graph [sìnəmǽtəgræ̀f, -grɑ̀:f] *n.* Ⓒ **1** 《Brit.》 a motion-picture projector. 영사기(映寫機). **2** a camera for taking motion pictures. 영화 촬영기. 參考 kinematograph라고도 함. [→cinema]

cin·e·ma·tog·ra·phy [sìnəmətágrəfi-/-tɔ́g-] *n.* the art of making motion pictures. 영화 촬영 기술.

cin·e-pro·jec·tor [sínəprədʒèktər] *n.* a machine which projects a motion picture upon a screen. 영사기.

Cin·er·am·a [sìnərɑ́:mə, -rǽmə] *n.* 《trademark》 a motion picture medium that uses a camera with three lenses and a large curved screen and a system by which sound is reproduced from the direction of its original source. 시네라마.

cin·e·rar·ia [sìnərέəriə] *n.* 《bot.》 kinds of flowering plant. 시네라리아《국화과의 일종》. [L. *cinis* ashes]

cin·er·a·ry [sínərèri/-rəri] *adj.* of ashes. 재의; 유골을 담는. [↑]

Cin·ga·lese [sìŋgəlí:z] *adj., n.* =Singhalese.

cin·na·bar [sínəbɑ̀:r] *n.* **1** a reddish mineral that is the chief source of mercury. 진사(辰砂). **2** artificial mercuric sulfide, used as a red pigment. 황화 수은(黃化水銀)《적색 안료》. **3** bright red. 주홍(朱紅). [Gk.]

cin·na·mon [sínəmən] *n.* **1** Ⓒ an East Indian tree; Ⓤ the bark of this tree. 육계(肉桂)나무; 계피(桂皮). **2** Ⓤ the yellowish-brown spice made from the inner bark of this tree. 계피가루《향미료》. **3** Ⓤ a light, rather red brown. 육곗빛; 황갈색. — *adj.* having the color of cinnamon. 황갈색의. [Heb.]

cinque, cinq [siŋk] *n.* five. 다섯; 5. [L. *quinque* 5]

Cinq Ports [∠ ∠], **the** *n.* Dover, Sandwich, Hastings, Romney and Hythe. 다섯 항구《영국 남동 연안에 있는 다섯 항구로서, 중세 영국의 연안 경비에 공헌한 특별항》.

cinque·foil [síŋkfɔ̀il] *n.* **1** 《bot.》 a plant having small, yellow flowers and leaves that are divided into five leaflets. 양지꽃속(屬)의 식물. **2** 《archit.》 an ornament in architecture, made of five connected semicircles or part circles. 매화 무늬 (장식). [L. =five leaves]

ci·pher [sáifər] *n.* Ⓒ **1** zero; 0. (숫자의) 영(零); 제로. **2** any Arabic numeral. 아라비아 숫자. **3** a person or thing of no importance. 하찮은 사람〔것〕; 무가치한 것. ¶ *He is little more than a* ～. 그 녀석은 거의 쓸모없는 존재이다. **4** a code; a method of secret writing. 암호; 암호로 쓰기. ¶ *a* ～ *telegram* 암호 전보 / *He sent me a telegram in* ～. 그는 내게 암호 전문을 보내 왔다. **5** Ⓤ a key explaining secret writing or a code. 암호 해독법. ¶ *a* ～ *code* 〔*telegram*〕 암호표(表)〔전보〕. **6** interlaced initials; a monogram. (이름 머리글자를) 짜 맞춘 문자; 모노그램.
— *vt.* (P6,7) **1** 《*out*》 ⓐ work out by arithmetic; calculate. …을 계산하다. ¶ ～ *out a sum* 합계를 내다. ⓑ think out. 생각해 내다; 안출하다. ¶ ～ *out a plan* 계획을 생각해 내다. **2** express (something) in secret writing. …을 암호로 쓰다(opp. decipher).
— *vi.* (P1) **1** do arithmetic. 계산을 하다. ¶ *Nancy can read, write, and* ～. 낸시는 읽기, 쓰기와 셈을 할 줄 안다. **2** use a secret code. 암호문을 사용하다. [Arab.]

cir·ca [sə́:rkə] *prep., adv.* 《L.》 about. 대략; 약; …경(頃). 參考 c., ca., circ.로 약함. ¶ ～ *1980-90*, 1980년 무렵에서 1990년경에 걸쳐 / *c. 700 B.C.* 기원전 약 700년경. [L.]

Cir·ce [sə́:rsi] *n.* **1** 《Gk. myth.》 a female magician. 키르케. 參考 Homer의 작(作) Odyssey에서, 남자를 돼지로 만든 마녀. **2** Ⓒ a very charming woman. 요부(妖婦)(형의 미녀). [Homeric person]

:**cir·cle** [sə́:rkl] *n.* Ⓒ **1** a plane figure of perfectly round. (평면적인) 원. ¶ *draw a* ～ 원을 그리다. **2** something round like a circle; a ring. 원형의〔둥근〕 것; 고리. ¶ *stand* 〔*sit*〕 *in a* ～ 빙 둘러 서다〔앉다〕 / *dance in a* ～ 원무(圓舞)를 추다 / *make a complete* ～ *around* …을 완전히 한 바퀴 돌다. **3** Ⓤ a series ending at the starting point. 순환; 일주. ¶ *the* ～ *of the seasons* 사계절의 순환 / *the vicious* ～ *of high wages and inflation* 고임금과 인플레이션의 악순환 / *argue in a* ～ 순환 논법으로 논하다. **4** a section of seats in a theater. (극장 2·3 층의) 원형 관람석. ¶ *the dress* ～ (2층 전면의) 특석 / *the upper* ～ (관람료가 싼) 일반석. **5** a society of persons having the same interests. 동료; 사회; …계(界). ¶ *educational* 〔*business*〕 *circles* 교육〔실업〕계 / *the upper circles* 상류 사회 / *in literary circles* 문단에. **6** a sphere of influence or interest; what has come within a person's knowledge. 영향〔세력〕 범위; 영역. ¶ *a large* ～ *of acquaintances* 넓은 교제 범위 / *a wide* ～ *of ideas* 넓은 사고(思考) 영역. **7** 《astron.》 the path in which a heavenly body moves about another. (천체의) 궤도.

come full circle, (esp. of ideas) end at the starting point. (특히, 사고(思考)가) 원점으로 되돌아오다; 일주하다.
have a large circle of friends, have large social connections. 교제 범위가 넓다.
square the circle, attempt the impossible. 불가능한 것을 시도하다.
— *vt.* (P6) **1** enclose (something) with a circle; surround. …을 둘러[에워]싸다. ¶ *The boys circled the Christmas tree.* 아이들은 크리스마스 트리를 빙 둘러쌌다. **2** move in a circle around (a place). …둘레를 돌다; 선회하다. ¶ *The moon circles the earth.* 달은 지구 둘레를 돈다.
— *vi.* (P1,2A) move in a circle. 돌다; 회전하다. ¶ ~ *round* (술잔이) 돌다; 선회하다 / *The hawk circled about its prey.* 매는 먹이 주변을 맴돌았다. [→circus]

cir·clet [sə́ːrklit] *n.* Ⓒ **1** a small circle. 작은 원; 동그라미; 소환(小環). **2** a round ornament for the head, neck, arm, or finger. (금·보석 따위의) 둥근 장식 고리; 머리[목]에 끼우는 고리; 반지; 팔찌. [↑]

circs [səːrks] *n. pl.* 《*colloq.*》 circumstances. 환경; 상황; 처지.

***cir·cuit** [sə́ːrkit] *n.* Ⓒ **1** Ⓤ the boundary line around an area; the area so bounded. 주위; 범위. ¶ *the* ~ *of the earth* 지구의 주위. **2** the act of going around; a round trip; a detour. 주행(周行); 순회[회유](여행); 일주; 우회(로). ¶ *make a long* ~ 멀리 우회하다 / *the* ~ *of the earth around the sun* 지구의 태양 둘레 주행 / *make a* ~ *in order to avoid her* 그녀를 피하기 위해 에둘러 가다. **3** a way or district over which a person or group regularly travels at certain times for the purpose of holding court or performing certain duties. (목사·재판관 등의) 순회; 순회 교구; 순회 재판(구); 순회 변호사회; (외판원의) 순회 구역. ¶ *a salesman's* ~ 외판원의 순회 구역 / *on the* ~ 순회 중인 / *ride the* ~ 말 타고 순시하다 / *make a* ~ *of* …을 한 바퀴 돌다 / *A country postman has a long* ~. 시골의 집배원은 먼 구역을 돈다. **4** 《electr.》 the path of an electric current. (전류의) 회로. ¶ *a short* ~ 단락(短絡) / *a closed* [*an integrated*] ~ 폐쇄[집적] 회로 / *a leak in an electric* ~ 누전(漏電). **5** a number of theaters etc. under one control. (극장 따위의) 흥행 계열; 체인. [L. *circuitus* going round]

circuit court [⌐–⌐] *n.* a Federal court whose judges hold court regularly at certain places in a district. 순회 재판소. 參考 1911년에 폐지.

cir·cu·i·tous [səːrkjúːitəs] *adj.* roundabout; indirect; circumlocutory. (멀리) 돌아가는; 간접적인; 에두르는. ¶ *a* ~ *route* (멀리) 도는 길 / *a* ~ *argument* 우회적인 논법 / *a* ~ *mode of reasoning* 간접적인 추리법 / *take a* ~ *route to downtown to avoid busy roads* 시내로 들어가는 번잡한 길을 피해 우회로를 택하다. ● **cir·cu·i·tous·ly** *adv.* **cir·cu·i·tous·ness** *n.*

***cir·cu·lar** [sə́ːrkjələr] *adj.* **1** round. 둥근; 원형의. ¶ *a* ~ *tower* 둥근 탑. **2** ⓐ going around a circle; revolving; moving or occurring in a cycle or round. 빙빙 도는; 회전[일주]하는; 순환하는. ¶ *the* ~ *succession of the seasons* 사철의 변이(變移) / *a* ~ *trip* 회유(回遊) 여행. ⓑ moving in a circle; forming a circle. 순환 운동을 하는; 순환적인; 환상(環狀)의. ¶ *the* ~ *rotation of the earth* 지구의 자전 / *a* ~ *railroad* (철도의) 순환선. **3** sent to each of many persons. 회람의; 많은 사람에게 돌리는. ¶ *a* ~ *letter* 회람장 / *a* (*bank's*) ~ *letter of credit* 순회(巡廻) 신용장. **4** roundabout; indirect. 빙 에두르는; 간접적인. ¶ *a* ~ *expression* 완곡한 표현 / *a* ~ *argument* 우회 논법.
— *n.* Ⓒ a letter, notice, or advertisement sent to each of many persons. 회람(장); 광고 쪽지. ¶ *a patent liver pill* ~ 특허 간장약 안내문. ● **cir·cu·lar·ly** [-li] *adv.* [circum, L. *eo* go]

cir·cu·lar·ize [sə́ːrkjuləràiz] *vt.* (P6) send letters or circulars to, for information or advertising. …에 회람[안내장, 광고문]을 돌리다.

cir·cu·late [sə́ːrkjəlèit] *vi.* (P1,2A,3) **1** go around; pass from one person or place to another; move round in a course. 돌다; 순회하다; 순환하다. ¶ *Blood circulates in the body.* 피는 몸 속을 돈다 / *He circulated among his guests.* 그는 손님들 사이를 누비며 돌아다녔다. **2** be handed from person to person; be sold. (신문 등이) 배포되다; 판매되다. ¶ *This magazine circulates widely.* 이 잡지는 널리 보급되어 있다. **3** go from one person or place to another. 유포되다; 유통되다. ¶ *Money circulates quickly in times of inflation.* 돈은 인플레이션 시대에는 빨리 유통된다 / *Wild rumors were circulating about her.* 그녀에 관한 터무니없는 소문이 나돌고 있었다 / *The story circulated through the village.* 그 이야기는 온 마을에 퍼졌다.
— *vt.* (P6) cause (something) to move around from one person or place to another; place (something) in circulation. …을 돌리다; 퍼뜨리다; 배포하다; 회람하다; 유통시키다. ¶ ~ *the wine* 포도주 잔을 돌리다 / ~ *a rumor* 소문을 퍼뜨리다. [→circus]

cir·cu·lat·ing library [sə́ːrkjəlèitiŋ láibrèri, -brəri / -brəri] *n.* a library from which books are borrowed or lent. 순회[이동] 도서관.

***cir·cu·la·tion** [səːrkjəléiʃən] *n.* Ⓤ **1** the act of circulating; the movement of the blood. 돎; (공기·물 따위의) 유통; 혈액의 순환. ¶ ~ *of the air* 공기의 유통 / ~ *of the blood* 혈액 순환 / *have a good* [*bad*] ~ 혈행(血行)이 좋다[나쁘다] / *An electric fan keeps the air in* ~. 선풍기는 공기를 계속 순환케 한다. **2** (of papers, books, etc.) the state of being circulated. (신문·책 따위의) 배포; 보급. ¶ *a magazine with national* ~ 전국적으로 팔리고 있는 잡지 / *The book is not longer in* ~. 그 책은 이제 절판되었다. **3** Ⓤⓒ the number of copies of a newspaper, etc. that are sent out or sold in a given time. 발행 부수; 팔림새. ¶ *have a large* 〔*limited*〕 ~ 발행 부수가 많다〔제한되어 있다〕/ *The paper has a* ~ *of 300,000.* 그 신문은 발행 부수가 30만이다. **4** the passage of something, such as money or news, from one person or place to another. (화폐의) 유통; (소문 따위의) 유포. ¶ *the* ~ *of money* 통화의 유통 / *the* ~ *of a rumor* 소문의 유포 / *put ... in* ~. …을 유통〔유포〕시키다 / *Many forged notes are in* ~. 많은 위조 지폐가 나돌고 있다.

cir·cu·la·to·ry [sə́ːrkjələtɔ̀ːri / ⌐—léitəri] *adj.* of or having to do with circulation. 순환의; 순환성의. ¶ *the* ~ *system of the human body* 인체의 순환계.

cir·cum- [sə́ːrkəm] *pref.* **1** round about; on all sides. '(…의) 주위에' '여러 방향으로'의 뜻. **2** in a circle; around. '원형을 이루어', '둘레에'의 뜻. [L.]

cir·cum·am·bi·ent [sə̀ːrkəmǽmbiənt] *adj.* surrounding; encompassing. 둘러싼; 에워싸고 있는; 주위의. ¶ *the* ~ *air.* [circum-, →ambient]

cir·cum·cise [sə́ːrkəmsàiz] *vt.* (P6) **1** cut off the foreskin of, esp. in the religious rite of the Jews, etc. …에게서 포피(包皮)를 잘라내다; 할례(割禮)를 행하다. **2** purify. (마음을) 깨끗이 하다. [circum-, L. *caedo* cut]

cir·cum·ci·sion [sə̀ːrkəmsíʒən] *n.* Ⓤⓒ the act or ceremony of circumcising. 할례(割禮).

cir·cum·fer·ence [sərkʌ́mfərəns] *n.* Ⓤⓒ the line that bounds a circle; the distance around. 원주; 주변; 주위; 둘레선. ¶ *the* ~ *of one's chest* 가슴 둘레 / *The ratio of the* ~ *of any circle to its diameter is constant.* 직경에 대한 원주의 비(比)는 불변이다. [circum-, L. *fero* carry]

cir·cum·fer·en·tial [sərkʌ̀mfərénʃəl] *adj.* **1** of, at, or near the circumference. 원주의; 주위의. **2** circuitous; indirect. 에두르는; 간접적인; 완곡한.

cir·cum·flex [sə́ːrkəmflèks] *n.* a mark over a letter used to indicate a variant pronunciation. 곡절(曲折) 악센트 기호(ˆ;⌒;˜) [circum-, L. *flecto* bend]

cir·cum·flu·ent [sərkʌ́mfluənt] *adj.* flowing round; surrounding. 주변을 흐르는; 둘러싸고 있는. ¶ *two* ~ *rivers* 주변을 흐르는 두 개의 강. [circum-, →fluent]

cir·cum·fuse [sə̀ːrkəmfjúːz] *vt.* (P13) **1** pour or spread round. 둘레에 붓다〔쏟다〕; 흩뿌리다. **2** surround. 에워싸다. **3** 《*with, in*》 bathe. 끼얹다; 쬐다. [circum-, L. *fundo* pour]

cir·cum·gy·ra·tion [sə̀ːrkəmdʒairéiʃən] *n.* Ⓤⓒ 《*joc.*》 rotation; revolution. 회전; 선회. [circum-, →gyrate]

cir·cum·lo·cu·tion [sə̀ːrkəmloukjúːʃən] *n.* Ⓤⓒ a roundabout or indirect expression. 우회〔완곡한〕 표현; 핑계. [circum-, L. *loquor* speak]

cir·cum·loc·u·to·ry [sə̀ːrkəmlɑ́kjətɔ̀ːri / -lɔ́kjətəri] *adj.* characterized by circumlocution. 빙빙 돌려 말하는; 에두른.

cir·cum·nav·i·gate [sə̀ːrkəmnǽvəgèit] *vt.* (P6) sail completely around (the earth, etc.). …을 주항(周航)하다; 배로 일주하다. ¶ *Magellan was the first man to* ~ *the globe.* 마젤란은 배로 지구를 일주한 최초의 사람이었다. ● **cir·cum·nav·i·ga·tor** [-tər] *n.* [circum-, →navigate]

cir·cum·nav·i·ga·tion [sə̀ːrkəmnæ̀vəgéiʃən] *n.* Ⓤ the act of sailing around the earth, etc. (세계) 주항(周航); 일주 항해.

cir·cum·scribe [sə̀ːrkəmskráib, ⌐—⌐] *vt.* (P6) **1** draw a line around (something); encircle; encompass. …의 둘레에 선을 긋다; 둘레를 에워싸다. **2** limit; keep (something) within bounds; show clearly; restrict. …을 제한〔한정〕하다; 속박하다. ¶ ~ *the powers of a king* 왕의 권력을 제한하다 / ~ *the area of a science* 학문의 영역을 한정하다. **3** 《geom.》 draw (a figure) round another figure. 외접(外接)시키다(cf. *inscribe*). [circum-, →scribe]

cir·cum·scrip·tion [sə̀ːrkəmskrípʃən] *n.* **1** the act of circumscribing; the state of being circumscribed. 에워쌈〔싸임〕. **2** a boundary; an outline. 한계선; 경계; 윤곽. **3** a limitation or restriction. 한계; 제한. **4** a circumscribed space. 구역; 영역; 범위. **5** an inscription around a coin, medal, etc. (화폐·메달 따위 가장자리의) 명각(銘刻).

cir·cum·spect [sə́ːrkəmspèkt] *adj.* careful; cautious; prudent. 조심스러운; 신중한. ¶ *a very* ~ *young man* 신중한〔빈틈없는〕 청년. ● **cir·cum·spect·ly** [-li] *adv.* [circum-, L. *specio* see]

cir·cum·spec·tion [sə̀ːrkəmspékʃən] *n.* Ⓤ care; caution; prudence. 주의; 신중.

:cir·cum·stance [sə́ːrkəmstæ̀ns / -stəns] *n.* **1** 《usu. *pl.*》 all the conditions of an act or event; environment. 사정. ¶ *without considering all the circumstances* 모든 사정을 고려치 않고 / *as far as circumstances permit* 사정이 허락하는 한 / *Do you know all the circumstances of the case?* 자넨 사건의 온갖 사정을 알고 있나 / *It depends on circumstances.* 사정 여하에 달려 있다. **2** 《*pl.*》 ⓐ the facts or events which surround and influence something. 주위의 사정; 환경; 처지. ¶ *through force of circumstances* 주변 사정으로 어쩔 수 없이. ⓑ financial condition. 경제 사정. ¶ *persons in easy circumstances* 아무 부족도 없이 지내는 사람들 / *a family in reduced* 〔*bad*〕 *circumstances* 생활에 어려움을 겪고 있는

가정. **3** Ⓒ an event; a happening; a fact. (있던) 일; 사건. ¶ *omit no important ~ in a report* 보고에서 중요치 않은 일은 생략하다 / *It was a lucky ~ that she found her money.* 그녀가 돈을 찾은 것은 운좋은 일이었다. **4** Ⓤ full detail. 자세한 내용. ¶ *He told of his adventure with great ~.* 아주 자세히 자기의 모험담을 이야기했다. **5** Ⓤ ceremonious accompaniment or display. 의식[형식]을 차림; 어마어마함. ¶ *without ~* 형식을 차리지 않고; 가볍게 / *with great pomp and ~* 아주 어마어마하게.

be not a circumstance to, 《U.S. *colloq.*》 be insignificant by comparison with. …와는 비교가 안 되다.

under* [*in*] *no circumstances, never; by no means. 결코[어떤 일이 있어도] …않다.

under* [*in*] *the circumstances, such being the case; because of the conditions. 사정이 이러하므로; 그러한 사정이므로.

with circumstances, in detail. 상세히.

— *vt.* 《in *passive*》 place (someone) in certain circumstances. …을 어떤 사정[상황, 환경]에 두다. ¶ *circumstanced as we are* [*were*] 그러한 사정이므로[이었으므로] / *be awkwardly circumstanced* 거북한 입장에 놓이다. [circum-, L. *sto* stand]

cir·cum·stan·tial [sə̀ːrkəmstǽnʃəl] *adj.* **1** depending on circumstances. (증거 따위가) 상황에 달린. ¶ *~ evidence* 정황 증거 (opp. direct evidence). **2** happening; not important. 우연적인; 부수적인; 중요치 않은. ¶ *of ~ importance* 제2차적으로 중요한. **3** full of details; detailed; minute. 자세한; 상세한. ¶ *a ~ story* 자세한 이야기.

● **cir·cum·stan·tial·ly** [-li] *adv.*

cir·cum·stan·ti·ate [sə̀ːrkəmstǽnʃièit] *vt.* (P6) support by a statement of relevant details. (상세히) 실증하다.

cir·cum·vent [sə̀ːrkəmvént] *vt.* (P6) **1** go around (something). …을 돌다[일주하다]. ¶ *~ the lake* 호수를 한 바퀴 돌다. **2** catch (someone) in a trap; defeat or block (someone's plan, etc.) by better trickery; outwit. (계략에) 빠뜨리다; 덫에 걸리게 하다; (계획 따위를) 저지[방해]하다; 의표를 찌르다. ¶ *~ evil designs* 못된 의도를 꺾다. [L. *venio* come]

cir·cum·ven·tion [sə̀ːrkəmvénʃən] *n.* Ⓤ the act of circumventing; the state of being circumvented. 속여 넘김; 계략에 빠뜨림[빠짐]; 우회.

***cir·cus** [sə́ːrkəs] *n.* Ⓒ **1** a traveling show of acrobats, clowns, horses, wild animals, etc.; a building or large tent for such a performance. 곡예; 곡마단; 서커스; 그 공연장. **2** in ancient Rome, a round or level space with rows of seats around it, used for chariot races, games, etc. (고대 로마의) 경기장. **3** 《Brit.》 a circular open place where many streets meet. (가로(街路)가 한데 모이는) 원형 광장. 參考 방사상의 많은 가로가 한 곳으로 모임. ¶ *Piccadilly Circus* (런던의) 피카딜리 광장. [L.=ring]

cirque [səːrk] *n.* 《*poet.*》 **1** a circular space. 원형의 장소. **2** a natural amphitheater. 천연의 원형 극장. [↑]

cir·rho·sis [siróusis] *n.* the excessive formation of connective tissues. (간장(肝臟) 따위 장기(臟器)의) 경변(증)(硬變(症)). [Gk. *kirrhos* tawny]

cir·ri [sírai] *n.* pl. of **cirrus.**

cir·ri·ped [sírəpèd] *n.* kinds of crustacean with slender appendage. 만각류(蔓脚類)의 동물. [L.=curl]

cir·rus [sírəs] *n.* Ⓒ (*pl.* **-ri**) **1** 《meteor.》 a thin, narrow, white cloud very high in the air. 새털구름. **2** 《bot.》 a tendril. 덩굴손. **3** 《zool.》 a filament or slender appendage. 촉모(觸毛). [L.=curl]

cis·sy [sísi] *n.* an effeminate man. 계집애 같은 남자; 나약한 사내. [*sister*]

Cis·ter·cian [sistə́ːrʃən, -ʃiən] *adj.* of a monastic order. 시토 수도회의. — *n.* Cistercian monk or nun. 시토 수도회의 수사[수녀]. [Place]

cis·tern [sístərn] *n.* Ⓒ a tank for holding water. 물탱크; 수조(水槽). [→chest]

cit. citation; cited; citizen.

cit·a·del [sítədl] *n.* Ⓒ **1** a fortress on a high place to protect a city; a strongly defended place. (시가지를 내려다보는 위치의) 성채; (일반적으로) 견고한 요새. **2** a safe place; a shelter. 안전한 곳; 피난처. [→city]

ci·ta·tion [saitéiʃən] *n.* **1** ⓊⒸ a direct quotation or reference. 인용; 인용구(句). ¶ *This book contains many citations from old writers.* 이 책은 옛 작가들로부터 많은 부분이 인용돼 있다. **2** Ⓒ a statement honoring a soldier, etc. for bravery in war. 감사장; 표창(장). ¶ *Presidential ~* 대통령 표창. **3** ⒸⓊ an official order to someone to appear before a law court. 소환(장); 법원 출두 명령. [↓]

***cite** [sait] *vt.* (P6) **1** quote (a passage from a book, article, etc.) …을 인용하다. ¶ *~ a passage* [*book*] 문장[책]을 인용하다 / *He cited lines from the Bible.* 그는 성경에서 몇 구절을 인용했다. **2** bring forward or tell (facts, etc.) as proof or as an example. 예로 들다; 예증(例證)[예시(例示)]하다; …에 언급하다. ¶ *~ an instance from one's own experience* 자신의 경험에서 예를 들다 / *to ~ an instance* [*example*] 일례를 들면 / *Can you ~ another case at all like this one?* 대체 이와 같은 또다른 경우를 예시(例示)할 수 있느냐. **3** 《U.S.》 praise (a soldier, etc.) for bravery in war. …을 표창하다; 특기하다. ¶ *The brave soldier was cited in official reports.* 그 용감한 병사는 공식 보고서에 특기되었다. **4** officially call (someone) to appear before a law court. (법정에) 소환하다; 출두를 명하다. ¶ *~ someone for contempt*

아무를 법정 모욕죄로 소환하다. [L. *cieo* set in motion]

cith·ern [síθərn], **cit·tern** [sítəːrn] *n.* an old musical instrument somewhat like a guitar. 시턴《기타 비슷한 현악기》. [Gk. *kithara*]

cit·ied [sítid] *adj.* formed into [like] a city. 도시화된; 도시 같은. [→city]

:cit·i·zen [sítəzən] *n.* Ⓒ **1** a member of a state or nation. (한 나라의) 국민; 공민 (opp. alien). ¶ *Not a few foreigners have become citizens of Korea.* 적지 않은 외국인이 한국 국민이 되었다. **2** an inhabitant of a city or town; a townsman. (특히 시민권을 가진) 시민. ¶ *the citizens of Seoul* 서울 시민. **3** a civilian as different from a soldier, a policeman, etc. (군인·경관 등에 대해) 일반인; 민간인; 문민(文民). [→city]
a citizen of the world, a cosmopolitan. 세계인; 국제인.

cit·i·zen·ry [sítəzənri, -sən-] *n.* Ⓤ 《*collectively*》 citizens as a group. (일반) 시민; 서민.

cit·i·zen·ship [sítəzənʃìp] *n.* Ⓤ **1** the condition of being a citizen. 시민[공민]임. **2** the duties, rights, etc. of a citizen. 시민의 의무·권리 (따위).

cit·rate [sítreit, sáit-] *n.* 《chem.》 salt of citric acid. 구연산염; 시트르산 나트륨. [↓]

cit·ric [sítrik] *adj.* 《chem.》 of the citron or lemon; belonging to or derived from lemons or fruits of the same genus. 구연산의; 시트르산의. ¶ ~ *acid* 시트르산. [↓]

cit·ron [sítrən] *n.* Ⓒ **1** a fruit like a lemon, but larger and not so sour; a small tree bearing this fruit. 구연(枸櫞)(나무)《감귤류(類)》. **2** Ⓤ the rind of citron. 구연피(皮). [L. *citrus*]

cit·ro·nel·la [sìtrənélə] *n.* a fragrant oil used for keeping insects away. 시트로넬라유(油)《방향성 구충제》. [*citron*]

cit·rous [sítrəs] *adj.* of such fruits as lemons and oranges. 감귤류의. [↑]

cit·rus [sítrəs] *n.* Ⓒ any tree bearing lemons, oranges, or similar fruit. 감귤류의 식물. — *adj.* =citrous. [↑]

:cit·y [síti] *n.* Ⓒ (*pl.* **cit·ies**) **1** a large or an important town. 시(市); 도시. ¶ *the capital* ~ 수도 / *provincial cities* 지방 도시 / *a really modern* ~ 참된 근대적인 도시 / *a* ~ *council* 시의회 / *go to the* ~ 도시로 가다 / *the City of David* 다윗의 도시《Jerusalem 또는 Bethlehem》/ *the City of God* (=the Celestial City) 천국 / *the City of* (*the*) *Seven Hills* 일곱 언덕의 도시《로마》/ *the Eternal City* 영원의 도시《로마》. **2** 《U.S.》 a legal body holding a charter from the state in which it is located and serving as a unit of local government. 주(州)정부의 허가에 의한 자치체; 시. **3** 《Canada》 a municipality of the highest rank. 최고의 자치체; 시. **4** 《Brit.》 a chartered town, which is or has been the seat of a bishop. 칙허장(勅許狀)에 의한 시; 주교가 있는 지역. **5** 《*the* ~》 (all) the people living in a city. 도시의 주민. **6** 《*the C-*》 the business and financial district of London. 시티《런던의 상업·금융의 중심지》. [L. *civis* citizen]

cit·y-bred [sítibrèd] *adj.* born and raised in a city. 도시에서 태어나고 자란.

cit·y·bust·er [sítibʌ̀stər] *n.* 《*colloq.*》 an atomic or hydrogen bomb. 원자 폭탄; 수소 폭탄.

city hall [´-´] *n.* 《U.S.》 the headquarters of the officials, etc. of a city government. 시청사(市廳舍).

city manager [´-´--] *n.* 《U.S.》 a person appointed by a city council or similar body to act as manager of the city. 시정(市政) 관리자《시의회에 의해 임명됨》.

cit·y-state [sítistéit] *n.* an independent state consisting of a city and the territories depending on it (e.g. ancient Athens). (고대 아테네 같은) 도시 국가.

cit·y·ward(s) [sítiwərd(z)] *adv., adj.* to, toward, or in the direction of the city. 도시로[의].

civ. civil; civilian.

civ·et [sívit] *n.* **1** 《zool.》 a small, spotted animal having a strong, musk-like perfume. 사향(麝香)고양이. **2** perfume got from the civet. 사향. [Arab.]

civ·ic [sívik] *adj.* of a city, citizens, or citizenship. 시(市)의; 시민의; 공민의. ¶ ~ *rights* [*duties*] 시민의 권리[의무] / ~ *pride* 시민의 자랑 / ~ *problems* 도시 문제. [→city]

civic crown [´-´] *n.* an oak garland given to an ancient Roman who saved another's life in battle. 시민의 영관(榮冠)《전우의 생명을 구한 자에게 주어진 떡갈나무 잎의 관(冠)》.

civ·ics [síviks] *n. pl.* 《used as *sing.*》 the science or study of the duties, rights, and privileges of citizens. 공민학(學); 시정학(市政學); (학과로서의) 공민과(科). [→city]

civ·ies [síviz] *n. pl.* civilian clothes. 평복(平服).

:civ·il [sívəl] *adj.* **1** ⓐ of a citizen or citizens. 시민의; 공민의. ¶ ~ *rights* 공민권 / ~ *life* [*society*] 시민 생활[사회] / ~ *liberty* 시민으로서의 자유 / ~ *disobedience* 시민적 불복종[보이콧] / *Every citizen has* ~ *rights and* ~ *duties.* 모든 시민은 공민으로서의 권리와 의무를 지닌다. ⓑ having to do with the state. 국가의; 국내의. ¶ ~ *affairs* 국내 문제; (외국군 점령하의) 민정 / ~ *war* 내란; 내전. **2** not connected with the church or the military. (군인·성직자에 대하여) 일반인[민간인]의; 문민[문관]의. ¶ ~ *aviation* 민간 항공 / *a* ~ *servant* 공무원; 문관 / ~ *defence* 민간 방위 / *the civil service* 행정 사무 / *leave the army and enter* [*return*] *to* ~ *life* 군에서 퇴역하여 시민 생활로 돌아가다. **3** polite; courteous; civilized. 정중한; 예의바른; 문명

의. ¶ *keep a ~ tongue in one's head* 말을 삼가다〔조심하다〕/ *Her mother is ~ to everyone she meets.* 그녀 어머니는 만나는 모든 이에게 예를 다한다 / *I must say something ~ to him.* 의례적으로라도 그에게 무언가 말을 해야만 한다. **4** 《law》 relating to legal proceedings in connection with private, not public, rights. 민사(民事)의(opp. criminal). ¶ *the ~ law* 민법 / *Civil Law* 로마법. [→city]

civil engineer [ˊ– ––ˊ] *n.* a person who designs public works, as roads, bridges, dams, harbors, or supervises their construction or maintenance. 토목 기사.

civil engineering [ˊ– ––ˊ–] *n.* the work or profession of a civil engineer. 토목 공학.

ci·vil·ian [sivíljən] *n.* Ⓒ **1** a person who is neither a soldier nor a sailor. 일반 시민; 민간인; 문관. **2** one studying the civil law. 민법학자. — *adj.* of civilians; not military or naval. 일반인의; 민간의; 문관의.

ci·vil·i·ty [sivíləti] *n.* (*pl.* **-ties**) **1** Ⓤ politeness; good manners. 예의(바름); 정중. ¶ *do ~* 예절을 다하다 / *He treated the man with ~.* 그는 그 사나이를 정중히 대했다. **2** (*pl.*) a civil act or speech. 예의바른〔정중한〕언동. ¶ *exchange civilities* 인사를 주고 받다.

:civ·i·li·za·tion [sìvəlizéiʃən] *n.* **1** Ⓤ the act of civilizing; the state of being civilized; improvement in culture. 문명화; 교화(敎化); 개화. **2** Ⓤ the civilized condition; Ⓒ the special culture of a people or a period. 문명; 문화(opp. barbarism). ¶ *high ~* 고도의 문명 / *modern ~* 근대 문명 / *the development of ~* 문명의 발달 / *beyond the bounds of ~* 문명이 미치지 않는 곳에. **3** 《*collectively*》 the nations and peoples which are in a high stage of social development. 문명 사회〔국가〕; 문명인. ¶ *The village is hundreds of miles away from ~.* 마을은 문명 사회로부터 몇 백 마일이나 떨어져 있다. [→city]

***civ·i·lize** [sívəlàiz] *vt.* (P6) **1** bring (someone) out of a primitive way of life; instruct (someone) in culture, science, and art; educate. …을 문명화하다; 교화(敎化)〔계발〕하다. ¶ *~ away* 교화하여 (야만적인 풍습)을 없애다 / *Those facilities are intended to ~ the wild tribes of Africa.* 그 시설들은 아프리카 야만족들의 교화를 목적으로 하고 있다. **2** make (someone) better in culture and good manners. …을 세련되게 하다; 고상하게 하다. ● **civ·i·liz·er** [-ər] *n.*

civ·i·lized [sívəlàizd] *adj.* **1** advanced in social organization, art, and science; of civilized nations or persons. 교화〔개화〕된; 문명화된; 교양있는(opp. barbarous). ¶ *~ life* 문화 생활 / *~ countries* 문명화된 여러 나라. **2** courteous; refined. 예의바른; 세련된.

civil list [ˊ– ˊ] *n.* 《Brit.》 the provision of money by Parliament for the king and his household. 왕실비(王室費).

civ·il·ly [sívəli] *adv.* **1** politely; courteously. 정중하게; 예의바르게. **2** by the civil law. 민(사)법에 따라서; 민법상.

civil marriage [ˊ– ˊ–] *n.* a marriage not begun with a religious ceremony but still recognized by law. (종교 의식에 의하지 않는) 민법상 결혼; 신고 결혼.

civil service [ˊ– ˊ–] *n.* **1** the departments of administration of a government concerned with public service that are not military, naval, legislative, or judicial. 문관 근무; 행정 사무. **2** 《*collectively*》 the body of persons working in those branches. 문관; 공무원.

civil war [ˊ– ˊ] *n.* **1** war between two groups of citizens of one nation. 내전(內戰); 내란. **2** 《*the C- W-*》 ⓐ 《U.S.》 the war between the Northern and Southern States of the United States (1861-65). (미국의) 남북 전쟁. ⓑ 《Brit.》 the war between the English Parliament and the Royalists (1642-46; 1648-52). (영국의) Charles 1세와 국회와의 전쟁.

ck. cask, check; cook.

Cl 《chem.》 chlorine.

cl. centiliter; class; clause; clergyman; cloth.

clack [klæk] *vi., vt.* (P1;6) make a short, sharp sound; talk. 짤깍 소리를 내다; 지껄이다.

— *n.* Ⓒ a short, sharp sound; a clatter; a chatter. 짤깍 소리; 지껄이는 소리; 수다. ¶ *the ~ of a typewriter* 타자기의 타닥 소리. [Imit.]

***clad** [klæd] *v.* 《*arch.*》 p. and pp. of **clothe.** — *adj.* having clothes on; dressed; dressed in a particular manner. 옷을 입은; (몸에) 걸친; 덮인. ¶ *iron-clad vessels* 철갑선 / *be ~ in rags* 누더기를 걸치고 있다 / *He was up and fully ~ by 5 o'clock.* 그는 아침에 일어나서 5시까지는 옷을 모두 입고 있었다. [→clothe]

:claim [kleim] *vt.* **1** (P6,8,11) ask for (something) on the ground of right; ask or insist on (something) as one's own. (당연한 권리로서) …을 요구하다; 주장하다. ¶ *~ a reward* 보수를 요구하다 / *~ an estate inheritance* 상속권에 의해 재산을 요구하다 / *~ the right to the patent* 〔*to speak*〕 특허의〔말할〕 권리를 주장하다 / *He claimed the money found.* 그는 발견된 돈이 자기 것이라고 주장했다 / *Does anyone ~ this book?* 이 책의 임자는 없습니까. **2** (P6,8,11) tell (something) as a fact. (사실로서) …을 주장하다; 단언하다. ¶ *He claimed to have reached there.* =*He claimed that he had reached there.* 그는 거기에 갔었음을 주장했다. **3** (P6) (of a thing) deserve; call for; require. (사물이) …할 만하다; …을 요(구)하다. ¶ *The problem claims our attention.* 본문제는 주목할 만하다 / *The care of the baby claims half my time.* 아기를 돌보는 데

내 시간의 절반을 빼앗긴다. **4** (P6,8,11) demand the recognition of. …의 승인을 요구하다. ¶ ~ *championship* 선수권(의 승인)을 요구하다 / ~ *to have won the victory* 승리했음을 주장하다.
— *vi.* (P1,3) insist on a right; make a claim for damages. (권리를) 주장하다; (손해배상을) 청구하다. ¶ *Unless he pays up I shall ~ against him.* 돈을 갚지않는 한 그에게 손해 배상을 청구할 것이다.
— *n.* Ⓒ **1** 《*for, to*》 a demand for something as one's own. (정당한) 요구; 청구. ¶ *meet the ~* 요구를 충족시키다 / *make a ~ for damages* 손해 배상을 요구하다 / *Nobody made a ~ to this suitcase.* 이 가방의 임자는 나타나지 않았다. **2** 《*to, on, upon*》 right to ask for something. 요구할 권리; 청구권. ¶ *a legal ~ on an estate* 재산에 대한 법률상의 청구권 / *He has no ~ to the property.* 그는 재산을 요구할 권리가 없다. **3** anything that is claimed, esp. a piece of public land claimed and marked out by a miner, settler, etc. 청구물; 불하 청구지(地). ¶ *jump someone's ~* 아무가 선취한 토지를〔채굴권을〕 가로채다. [L. *clamo* call out]
lay claim to, declare that one should have (something). …에 대한 권리를〔소유권을〕 주장하다; 자격이 있음을 주장하다.
put in a claim for, say that (something) is or should be one's own. …에 대한 권리〔요구〕를 제기하다.

claim·a·ble [kléiməbəl] *adj.* capable of claiming. 청구할 수 있는.

claim·ant [kléimənt] *n.* Ⓒ a person who makes a claim. 청구자; 신청자; 원고(原告). ¶ *a ~ for throne* 왕위 청구자.

clair·voy·ance [klɛərvɔ́iəns] *n.* Ⓤ **1** the supposed power of knowing about things not seen by other persons. 투시력; 천리안. **2** unusual insight. 예리한 통찰력. [↓]

clair·voy·ant [klɛərvɔ́iənt] *adj.* **1** having the power of seeing things not seen by other persons. 투시력의; 투시력이 있는; 천리안의. **2** unusually keen. 통찰력이 있는.
— *n.* Ⓒ a clairvoyant person. 천리안이 있는 사람; 통찰자. [→clear, view]

clam [klæm] *n.* Ⓒ (*pl.* **clams** or *collectively* **clam**) **1** 《zool.》 a shellfish which can be eaten, like an oyster. 대합. **2** 《U.S. *colloq.*》 a silent, retiring person. 말이 없는 사람. [E.]
shut up like a clam, be silent in an unpleasant way. 뚱하니 입을 다물다.

clam·bake [klǽmbèik] *n.* a picnic at the seashore at which clams and other seafood are baked on hot stones under a covering of seaweed. 달군 돌에 대합을 구워 먹는 바닷가 소풍.

clam·ber [klǽmbər] *vi.* (P1,2A,3) 《*up*》 climb with effort or difficulty. 힘들여 기어오르다〔내려가다〕. ¶ ~ *up a rocky slope* 바위로 된 비탈을 기어오르다 / ~ *to one's feet* 겨우 일어서다 / ~ *out of the mire* 수렁에서 빠져 나오다; 곤경을 벗어나다. — *n.* Ⓒ an awkward or difficult climb. 기어오름; 등반. [E.]

clam·mi·ly [klǽmili] *adv.* in a clammy manner. 끈끈하게; 축축하게.

clam·my [klǽmi] *adj.* (**-mi·er, -mi·est**) covered with something cold and wet. 끈끈한; 축축한; 냉습한. ¶ *hands ~ with sweat* 땀으로 축축한 손. [E.]

·**clam·or,** 《Brit.》 **-our** [klǽmər] *n.* ⓊⒸ loud noise or shouting, esp. of a crowd; a noisy demand. (군중 등의) 크게〔시끄럽게〕 떠드는 소리; 아우성; 소란.
— *vt., vi.* (P6,7,11,13; 1,2A,3) ask or request noisily. 시끄럽게 요구하다; 떠들어대(어 …하게 하)다. ¶ ~ *for admission* 시끄럽게 입장을 요구하다 / ~ *against* 〔*for*〕 *the proposal* 제안에 대해 시끄럽게 반대〔찬성〕하다 / ~ *for higher wages* 시끄럽게 임금 인상을 요구하다. [→claim]
clamor down, trouble (a speaker) completely by speaking in loud voices. (연사를) 야유하여 연설을 못 하게 하다.
clamor** someone **into, force someone to do (something) by making loud demands. 시끄럽게 요구하여 …로 하여금 —하게 하다.
clamor** someone **out of, force someone to stop (something) by making loud demands. 시끄럽게 떠들어 …로 하여금 —을 그만두게 하다. ¶ *The newspapers clamored him out of office.* 신문이 떠들어대어 그를 실각시켰다.

clam·or·ous [klǽmərəs] *adj.* noisy; making noisy complaints. 시끄러운; 성가신; 성가시게 불평하는. ¶ *be ~ for something* …을 시끄럽게 요구하다.

clamp [klæmp] *n.* Ⓒ a brace, band, or other device for fastening things together or supporting them. 멈춤〔고정〕쇠; 죔쇠. — *vt.* (P6,7) fasten (something) with a clamp. 죔쇠〔꺾쇠〕로 죄다; 고정시키다. [E.]

〈clamp〉

clamp down (***on***), put down (something) by force; exert pressure upon (weak people). 탄압하다; 단속하다; 압박하다.

clan [klæn] *n.* Ⓒ **1** a group of people in the Scottish Highlands supposed to have come from a common ancestor. (특히 스코틀랜드 고지인의) 씨족; 일족; 일문. **2** a group of people united together by some common interest; a party; a set. 도당; 일당; 동지; 파벌. ● **clan·like** [-làik] *adj.* [Gael.; →plant]

clan·des·tine [klændéstin] *adj.* secret. 비밀〔내밀〕의. 語法 흔히 나쁜 의미로 쓰임. ¶ *a ~ meeting* 비밀 회합. [L.]

clang [klæŋ] *n.* Ⓒ a loud, ringing sound,

as when metal strikes on other metal. 쨍그렁〔땡그렁, 꽝꽝〕 소리《금속성의 큰 반향음》. — *vt., vi.* (P6; 1) make or cause to make a clang. 쨍그렁〔꽝꽝〕 소리를 내다〔소리가 나다〕. [L.]

clan·gor, 《Brit.》 **-gour** [klǽŋgər] *n.* Ⓒ a continued clanging. 쨍그렁쨍그렁〔꽝꽝〕 (소리); 땡그렁거림. ● **clan·gor·ous** [klǽŋgərəs] *adj.* [↑]

clank [klæŋk] *n.* Ⓒ a sharp, harsh metallic sound. 쨍그렁〔짤깍, 짤랑, 땡그랑〕 소리. ¶ *the ~ of a heavy chains* 무거운 쇠사슬의 짤랑거리는 소리. — *vi., vt.* (P1;6) make a sharp, harsh sound; cause (something) to clank. 쨍그렁〔짤깍, 짤랑〕 소리가 나다〔소리를 내다〕. [Imit.]

clan·nish [klǽniʃ] *adj.* **1** of or related to a clan. 씨족(氏族)〔일족〕의; 일문의. **2** closely united together; having a narrow view of strangers; cliquish. 당파심〔파벌심〕이 강한; 편협한; 배타적인. ● **clan·nish·ness** [-nis] *n.* [→clan]

clan·ship [klǽnʃip] *n.* **1** a clannish feeling; a party feeling. 당파〔파벌〕 근성; 동족 의식. **2** unity; clannism. 단결; 족벌(族閥).

clans·man [klǽnzmən] *n.* Ⓒ (*pl.* **-men** [-mən]) a member of a clan. 같은 씨족의 일원; 일족〔일문〕인 사람.

***clap** [klæp] *n.* Ⓒ **1** a sudden noise, such as the sound of hands struck together; a sharp blow; a slap. 박수 소리; 탁; 철썩(때리기); 날카로운 일격. ¶ *at a* 〔*one*〕 *~* 일격에 / *He gave me a ~ on the shoulder.* 그가 내 어깨를 탁 쳤다. **2** a sharp, explosive loud noise, as of thunder. 우르르; 꽝; 쿵《파열음·천둥소리 따위》.

— *vi., vt.* (**clapped, clap·ping**) (P1,2B;6,13) **1** strike together loudly or lightly; (of birds) move (wings) up and down. 찰싹〔탁, 가볍게〕 치다; (새가) 홰치다. ¶ *~ someone on the back* 아무의 등을 톡톡 치다《친한 사이의 인사》. **2** strike hands to praise (someone). 박수 갈채하다. ¶ *The audience clapped the violinist.* 청중들은 그 바이올린 연주자에게 박수를 보냈다. **3** strike or move with a sudden sharp noise. 세차게 부딪(치)다; 탁〔탕〕 때리다. ¶ *~ a book on the table* 책으로 테이블을 탁 치다 / *~ one's head on the ceiling* 머리를 천장에 꽝 부딪치다. **4** put or place quickly or with force. (재빨리·힘차게) 놓다; 갖다 대다; 올려놓다; 처넣다. ¶ *~ a hat on one's head* 머리에 모자를 핵 쓰다 / *~ a cigaret into one's mouth* 잽싸게 담배를 입에 물다. [E.]

clap eyes on, 《*colloq.*》 《esp. *negative*》 catch sight of (someone); see. …을 목격하다; 보다. ¶ *I have never clapped eyes on such a big car.* 나는 이렇게 큰 차를 본 적이 없다.

clap hold of, take hold of. …을 붙잡다.

clap someone in 〔***into***〕 ***prison*** 〔***jail***〕, put (someone) in prison. …을 감옥에 처넣다.

clap up, **a**) (of business) do business with (someone) hastily. (거래 따위를) 서둘러 끝내다. **b**) put (someone) in prison. …을 투옥하다.

clap·board [klǽpbərd, -bɔ̀ːrd] *n.* Ⓒ **1** a long, thin, overlapping board used in covering the outer walls of a wooden house; a weatherboard. 미늘판자벽. **2** a piece of oak board, used for making barrels. 통 만드는 떡갈나무 판자. — *vt.* (P6) cover (a house) with clapboards. (집)에 미늘벽 판자를 치다.

clap·per [klǽpər] *n.* Ⓒ **1** a person or thing that claps. 치는 사람〔것〕; 박수 치는 사람. **2** the tongue of a bell. (종·방울의) 추. **3** any device for making noise. 소리 내는 기구; 딱딱이.

clap·per·claw [klǽpərklɔ̀ː] *vt., vi.* (P6;1) hit and scratch. 때리고 할퀴다.

clap·trap [klǽptræ̀p] *n.* Ⓤ empty language or insincere words used to win public attention. 즉석의 인기를 끌기 위한 말; 인기를 노린 수단. — *adj.* showy and insincere. 인기를 노린.

claque [klæk] *n.* 《F.》 **1** a group of persons hired to applaud in a theater or at a public meeting. (고용·동원된) 박수부대. **2** a group of selfish followers. (사리(私利)를 위해 모여드는) 아첨배들.

Clar·a [klέərə, klǽrə] *n.* a woman's name. 여자 이름.

Clare [klεər] *n.* a man's name or a woman's name; a nickname for Clara, Clarence, Clarice, Clarissa의 애칭.

clar·ence [klǽrəns] *n.* a closed four-wheeled carriage. 4륜마차. [Place]

clar·en·don [klǽrəndən] *n.* a thick-faced type. 클래런던 활자. [Place]

clar·et [klǽrit] *n.* Ⓤ **1** red wine of Bordeaux. (보르도 산의) 적(赤)포도주. **2** rich red color. 적포도주 빛깔. [→clarify]

clar·i·fi·ca·tion [klæ̀rəfikéiʃən] *n.* Ⓤ the act of clarifying; the state of being clarified; an explanation. 맑게 함; 정화(淨化); 설명; 해명. [↓]

clar·i·fy [klǽrəfài] *vt., vi.* (**-fied**) (P6; 1) make or become clear, pure, or easily seen through. 깨끗이〔맑게〕 하다; 분명히 하다; 맑아지다; 투명해지다. ¶ *clarified butter* 정제(精製) 버터 / *~ an issue* 논쟁점을 분명히 하다 / *He clarified the difficult problem by giving a full explanation.* 그는 자세한 설명에 의해 그 어려운 문제를 밝혔다. [→clear]

clar·i·net [klæ̀rənét, klǽrinət] *n.* Ⓒ 《mus.》 a wooden wind musical instrument played by covering and uncovering holes and moving keys. 클라리넷《목관악기의 하나》. [→clear]

clar·i·net·tist [klæ̀rənétist, klǽrinət-] *n.* a player of clarinet. 클라리넷 주자(奏者).

clar·i·on [klǽriən] *n.* **1** Ⓒ a trumpet with clear, sharp tones formerly used in war. 클라리온《음색이 맑은 나팔》. **2** Ⓤ 《chiefly *poet.*》 the sound made by this trumpet. 클라리온 소리; 명쾌한 울림. — *adj.* 《chiefly *lit.*》 clear and loud. 명쾌한 음색의. [↑]

clar·i·o·net [klæ̀riənét] *n.* =clarinet.

clar·i·ty [klǽrəti] *n.* Ⓤ clearness. 청징(淸澄); 명료; 명랑; 투명. [→clarinet]

***clash** [klæʃ] *n.* Ⓒ **1** a loud, broken sound like that of striking weapons or of bells rung together. 꽝[쨍그렁] (소리); 짤랑짤랑 (소리). ¶ *the ~ of arms* 무기의 쨍그렁 소리 / *The automobiles collided with a terrible ~.* 차끼리 무서운 소리를 내며 충돌했다. **2** a disagreement; a conflict; (of opinions) a quarrel; discord. 충돌; 격돌; 불일치; 대립. ¶ *a ~ of opinions* [*views*] 의견[견해]의 충돌 / *the border clashes* 국경 분쟁 / *avoid a ~ with* …와의 충돌을 피하다.

— *vi.* (P1,2A,3) **1** strike together with a clash. 꽝[쨍그렁] 소리가 나다. **2** come together with force; strike together suddenly. (힘과 힘이) 부딪치다; (야단스런 소리를 내며) 충돌하다. ¶ *~ into someone* 아무와 부딪치다 / *They clashed with the enemy.* 그들은 적과 충돌했다. **3** 《*with*》 (of an event) occur at the same time and so interfere with. (일 따위가) …와 겹치다; 저촉되다. ¶ *Your lecture tomorrow clashes with mine.* 내일의 선생 강의는 내 강의와 겹칩니다. **4** (of opinions, temper, etc.) disagree; be opposed; conflict. (의견·이해·감정 따위가) 충돌하다; 일치하지 않다; 상반되다. ¶ *~ with one's interests* 자기 이해와 상반되다 / *The two statesmen clashed in debate.* 두 정치가는 토론에서 의견이 상반되었다.

— *vt.* (P6,7) cause to clash; strike together noisily. 꽝[쨍그렁]하고 부딪치게 하다; 부딪쳐 요란한 소리를 내다. ¶ *In her haste, she clashed the saucepan against the stove.* 서두르는 통에 그녀는 스튜냄비를 풍로에 탕 부딪쳤다. [Imit.]

***clasp** [klæsp, klɑːsp] *n.* Ⓒ **1** a thing to fasten two parts together, such as a buckle or brooch. 혹; 멈춤[고정]쇠; 죔쇠. ¶ *a ~ for paper money* 지폐 다발 물리개 / *fasten a ~* 멈춤쇠를 잠그다. **2** a firm hold; a grasp; an embrace. 꽉 잡음[쥠]; 포옹. ¶ *~ someone round the neck* 아무의 목을 부둥켜 안다 / *She held her child in a loving ~.* 그녀는 아이를 사랑스러운 듯이 꼭 껴안았다 / *I could not escape from the ~ of her arms.* 껴안은 그녀 팔에서 헤어날 수가 없었다.

— *vi., vt.* **1** (P1; 6,13) fasten (something) with a clasp. (멈춤쇠로) 고정시키다; 죄다. ¶ *~ a bracelet round one's wrist* 손목에 팔찌를 끼다. **2** hold closely; grasp; embrace. 단단히 쥐다[잡다]; 안다; 달라붙다. ¶ *~ hands* 양손을 꼭 쥐다 / *~ a baby to one's bosom* 아기를 가슴에 꼭 껴안다 / *~ someone round the neck* 아무의 목을 부둥켜 안다. **3** (P6,13) shake hands. 악수하다. [E.]

clasp-knife [klǽspnàif, klɑ́ːsp-] *n.* a large folding knife. 대형의 접이칼.

:class [klæs, klɑːs] *n.* Ⓒ **1** 《often *pl.*》 a social rank. (사회의) 계급; 계층 (cf. *the masses*). ¶ *the upper* [*middle, lower*] *classes* 상류[중류; 하층] 계급 / *the working ~* 노동자 계급 / *the intellectual ~* 지식 계급. **2** a group of students under one teacher or studying together; a classroom. 학급 (학생들); 반; 교실. ¶ *a ~ of beginners* 초급반 / *He is at the top* [*bottom*] *of his ~.* 그는 반에서 첫째[꼴찌]이다. **3** a meeting or time of such a group for study. 수업(시간); 강의. ¶ *social studies ~* 사회과의 수업 / *between classes* 쉬는 시간에 / *be in ~* 수업 중이다 / *attend a ~* 강의에 나가다 / *take classes in cookery* 요리의 수업을[강의를] 받다. **4** 《U.S.》 《*collectively*》 a group of students in the same year in a school or college and graduating together. (대학의) 동기 졸업생. ¶ *the ~ of 1994,* 1994년도 졸업 동기생. **5** 《Brit.》 the grading of candidates after examination. 우등 시험 합격 등급; 우등 졸업 학위. ¶ *take a ~ at Cambridge* 케임브리지 대학에서 우등을 하다. **6** a level according to quality, value, or rank. 등급. ¶ *a first ~ hotel* 일류 호텔 / *a journal of high ~* 일류 신문 / *first* [*second*] *~ railway carriages* (철도의) 1등[2등] 찻간. **7** kind; sort; division. 종류; 부류. ¶ *a good ~ of man* 좋은 부류에 드는 사람 / *a ~ of historical novels* 역사 소설류. **8** Ⓤ 《*colloq.*》 high quality; excellence. 고급; 상등; 우수. ¶ *a dress with ~* 고급 옷 / *be no ~* 축에 들지 못하다; 아주 뒤떨어지다.

be in a class by itself [*oneself*], 《U.S.》 be far better than others. 단연 우수하다.

be not in the same class with, 《U.S.》 cannot be compared with (others). 비교가 안 되다.

— *vt.* (P6) put (things or persons) into groups; arrange (things or persons) according to characteristics; classify. …을 분류하다; … 부류에 넣다.

— *vi.* (P2A) be placed or ranked, as in a class. (부류·등급 따위에) 속하다. ¶ *those who ~ as Christians* 기독교 신자인 사람들. [L. *classis* summons, assembly]

class-con·scious [klǽskɑ́nʃəs, klɑ́ːs- / klɑ́ːskɔ́n-] *adj.* aware of one's social rank. 계급 의식의[이 있는].

class·fel·low [klǽsfèlou, klɑ́ːs-] *n.* =classmate.

***clas·sic** [klǽsik] *adj.* **1** of the first class; very good. 제1급의; 최고의; 일류의; 뛰어난. ¶ *~ taste* 최고급 취미 / *a ~ author* 일류 저자 / *a ~ authority on* …의 최고 권위. **2** of or like the art or culture of ancient Greece or Rome. 옛 그리스·로마(풍)의; 고전적인. **3** cited as a model; serving as a standard, or guide. 모범적인; 전형적인; 표준적인.

— *n.* Ⓒ **1** a work of literature or art which has been generally recognized to be of the first rank. 고전 작품; 명작. ¶ *"Hamlet" is a ~.* 햄릿은 명작이다. **2** a writer or an artist whose works have been so regarded. 문호(文豪); 대예술가. ¶ *Milton is a* ～. 밀턴은 대문호이다. **3** 《*the* ～*s*》 ⓐ classical studies. 고전의 연구. ⓑ the literature of ancient Greece and Rome. 고전 문학. [→class, -ic]

·clas·si·cal [klǽsikəl] *adj.* **1** first-class, esp. in literature or art. 일류의; 궤범적인. **2** of the classics. 고전의; 고전파의. ¶ ～ *music* 〔*art*〕 고전 음악〔예술〕/ ～ *studies* 고전 연구 / ～ *literature* 고전 문학. **3** standard; traditional. 표준적인; 전통적인; 정통의. **4** of ancient Greek or Roman art or culture. 그리스·로마(풍)의. ¶ *the* ～ *period* 고전 시대《그리스·로마기(期)》. ● **clas·si·cal·ly** [-li] *adv.*

clas·si·cal·i·ty [klæ̀səkǽləti] *n.* the quality of being classic. 고전적 특질; 고아(古雅).

clas·si·cism [klǽsəsìzəm], **clas·si·cal·ism** [klǽsikəlìzəm] *n.* Ⓤ **1** rules of classic literature and art. 고전주의. **2** the following of the classic style. 고전어풍〔어형〕. **3** classical learning or scholarship. 고전 지식.

clas·si·cist [klǽsəsist], **clas·si·cal·ist** [klǽsikəlist] *n.* **1** a follower of the principles of classicism in literature and art. (문학·예술의) 고전주의자. **2** a person who is an authority on ancient Greece and Rome. 고전의 권위(자); 고전학자. **3** a person who urges the study of Greek and Latin. 고전 연구의 창도자.

clas·si·fi·ca·tion [klæ̀səfikéiʃən] *n.* Ⓤ the act of classifying. 분류(법); 등분; 급별(級別); 유별. ● **clas·si·fi·ca·to·ry** [klǽsifikeitɔ̀:ri / -təri] *adj.* [*classify*]

clas·si·fied [klǽsəfàid] *adj.* **1** arranged according to classes or groups. 분류〔유별〕된. ¶ *a* ～ *list* 분류표 / *a* ～ *ad* (항목별) (3행) 광고《구인·구직 광고》. **2** 《U.S.》 kept secret except to certain people. 기밀 취급의; 군사 기밀의.

·clas·si·fy [klǽsəfài] *vt.* (**-fied**) (P6,7,13) group (books, etc.) according to classes; arrange (things or persons) in classes. …을 분류〔유별〕하다; 등급으로 가르다. ¶ ～ *women into three types* 여성을 세 유형으로 분류하다 / ～ *many kinds of peoples by skin color* 여러 민족을 피부 색깔로 분류하다. ● **class·si·fi·a·ble** [-əbəl] *adj.* **clas·si·fi·er** [-ər] *n.* [*class*]

:class·mate [klǽsmèit, klɑ́:s-] *n.* Ⓒ a member of the same class in school. 급우; 동급생; 동창생. [*class*]

:class·room [klǽsrù(:)m, klɑ́:s-] *n.* Ⓒ a room in a school where classes meet. 교실.

class-war [klǽswɔ̀:r, klɑ́:s-], **class-war·fare** [klǽswɔ̀:rfɛ̀ər, klɑ́:s-] *n.* the struggle or strife between one social class and another. 계급 투쟁.

class·y [klǽsi, klɑ́:si] *adj.* (**class·i·er, class·i·est**) superior, excellent. 우수한; 고급의. [→class, -y]

·clat·ter [klǽtər] *n.* Ⓒ 《usu. *sing.*》 **1** a loud noise like that of plates struck together. 덜거덕덜거덕〔딸그락딸그락〕하는 소리. **2** noisy, confused talk and laughter. 시끄러운 담소 소리. — *vi., vt.* (P1,2A;6) **1** make a confused noise. 덜거덕덜거덕〔딸그락딸그락〕 소리가 나다〔소리를 내(며 움직이)다〕; 짤깍짤깍〔재깍재깍〕 소리 나다〔내다〕. **2** talk noisily. 시끄럽게 지껄이다. [E.]

clatter about, walk about in a quick, noisy way. 바삐 소란을 피우며 돌아다니다.

·clause [klɔ:z] *n.* Ⓒ **1** 《gram.》 a part of a sentence having a subject and predicate of its own. 절(節). ¶ *a principal* 〔*subordinate*〕 ～ 주절〔종속절〕. **2** a single item in a law or contract, or any other written agreement. (법률·조약의) 개조(個條); 조항. ¶ *a penal* ～ 벌칙 / *a saving* ～ 단서(但書). [→close²]

claus·tral [klɔ́:strəl] *adj.* **1** of monastery or nunnery. 수도원의. **2** secluded. 은둔의. [→cloister]

clau·stro·pho·bi·a [klɔ̀:strəfóubiə] *n.* Ⓤ morbid dread of closed places. 폐소(閉所) 공포증. [L.]

clave [kleiv] *v.* p. of **cleave**².

clav·i·chord [klǽvəkɔ̀:rd] *n.* an ancient keyboard instrument, predecessor of piano. 클라비코드《피아노의 전신》. [↓]

clav·i·cle [klǽvəkəl] *n.* 《anat.》 collarbone. 쇄골(鎖骨). [L. *clavis* key]

cla·vic·u·lar [kləvíkjələr] *adj.* 《anat.》 of clavicle. 쇄골(鎖骨)의. [↑]

clav·ier¹ [klǽviər] *n.* **1** a keyboard. 건반. **2** a dummy keyboard. (연습용) 무음(無音) 건반. [L. *clāvis* key]

clav·ier² [kləvíər] *n.* any stringed keyboard instrument. (일반적으로) 건반 악기《협의로는 오르간을 제외함》.

·claw [klɔ:] *n.* Ⓒ **1** a sharp, pointed nail on a bird's or animal's foot. (새·짐승의) 발톱. ¶ *a cat's claws* 고양이의 발톱 / 《*fig.*》 *in someone's* ～ 아무의 마수에 걸려. **2** anything like a claw. (새·짐승의) 발톱 비슷한 것. ¶ *crab claws* 게의 집게발 / *The part of a hammer used for pulling nails is the* ～. 장도리의 못뽑이에 쓰이는 부분은 노루발이다. **3** a grappling iron. (적선(敵船) 따위를 걸어잡는) 갈고랑쇠.

cut someone's claws, reduce someone's power for mischief. …의 위해력(危害力)을 빼앗다; …을 무력하게 하다.

— *vt.* (P6) **1** scratch or tear (something) with claws or hands; snatch at (something). …을 발톱〔손〕으로 찢다〔북 긁다, 할퀴다〕; 와락 낚아채다. ¶ *The kitten was clawing the door.* 새끼고양이가 문을 박박 긁고 있었다. **2** gather (money, etc.) eagerly. (돈 따위)를 긁어 모으다. [E.]

claw hold of, seize eagerly with claws or hands. 발톱이나 손으로 꽉 붙잡다.

claw off, 《naut.》 beat to the windward

from the shore. 뱃머리를 바람 불어오는 쪽으로 돌리다.

claw-hammer [klɔ́ːhæ̀mər] *n.* a hammer having a head with its rear bent and divided for pulling out nails. 장도리.

:clay [klei] *n.* Ⓤ **1** a stiff, sticky kind of earth, used for making bricks, dishes, and vases. 점토; 찰흙. **2** earth. 흙. ¶ *die and turn to* ~ 죽어 흙이 되다. **3** 《Bible》 the human body. 인체; 육체.
moisten* 〔*wet*〕 *one's clay, 《*joc.*》 drink. 술을 마시다; 한잔하다.
— *adj.* human. 인간의. [E.]

clay·ey [kléii] *adj.* (**clay·i·er, clay·i·est**) **1** of or containing clay; clay-like. 점토가〔찰흙〕이 많은; 점토질의; 찰흙 같은. **2** covered with clay. 점토를 바른. [↑]

clay-pi·geon [kléipídʒən] *n.* a clay disk thrown into air as a target for shooting. 클레이피전《사격의 표적으로 공중에 날리는 흙원반》.

:clean [kliːn] *adj.* **1** ⓐ not dirty; neat. 깨끗한; 청결한(opp. dirty, foul). ¶ *a* ~ *room* 깨끗한 방 / (*as*) ~ *as a new pin* 아주 깨끗한 / *keep oneself* ~ 몸을 청결히 해두다 / *Keep your hands* ~. 손을 늘 깨끗이 해두어라. ⓑ without impure matter. 이물질이 섞이지 않은; 섞음질하지 않은; 순수한. ¶ ~ *water* 담수; 단물 / ~ *gold* 순금. **2** 《*fig.*》 pure; innocent. (정신적·도덕적으로) 깨끗한; 결백한. ¶ *lead a* ~ *life* 청렴한 생활을 하다 / *The saint had a* ~ *heart.* 성자(聖者)는 마음이 순결했다. **3** well-proportioned 〔-shaped〕; symmetrical. 균형이 잡힌; 모양이 좋은. ¶ *a* ~ *figure* 균형 잡힌 자태. **4** having no rough edges; smooth. 울퉁불퉁하지 않은; 매끈한. ¶ *A sharp knife makes a* ~ *cut.* 예리한 칼은 매끈하게 벤다. **5** perfect; complete. 완전한; 철저한. ¶ *a* ~ *break with tradition* 전통과의 완전한 단절 / *lose a* ~ *hundred dollars* 백 달러를 몽땅 잃다. **6** skillful; clever; nice. 솜씨 좋은; 멋진; 훌륭한. ¶ *a* ~ *shot* 깨끗한 슛 / *a* ~ *serve in tennis* 테니스의 멋진 서브. **7** ⓐ (of paper, etc.) not written on; fair. 아무 것도 써 있지 않은; 백지의. ¶ *a* ~ *page* 백면 페이지 / *He has a* ~ *record.* 그는 전력이 깨끗하다. ⓑ just washed; not yet used; fresh. 갓 세탁한; 신품의; 새. ¶ *put on a* ~ *collar* 새 칼라를 달다 / *put* ~ *sheets on the bed* 침대에 새 홑이불을 씌우다. **8** 《Bible》 (of certain animals) fit for food. (짐승이) 먹어도 괜찮은; 부정하지 않은. ¶ *Jews must only eat meat from* ~ *animals.* 유태인들은 금기되지 않은 짐승의 고기를 먹어야만 한다.
clean fish, fish not at or soon after spawning. (산란기에 있지 않은) 식용어(食用魚).
have clean hands, be innocent of wrongdoing. 나쁜 일에 관계치 않다; 결백하다.
keep the hands clean =have clean hands.
make a clean breast of, tell (one's secret) to another frankly. …을 모조리 털어놓다. ¶ *His guilty conscience forced him to make a* ~ *breast of everything.* 그는 죄책감 때문에 모든 것을 털어놓지 않을 수 없었다.
make a clean sweep of, take away (something) completely; win completely. …을 일소(一掃)하다.
— *adv.* **1** in a clean manner; cleanly. 깨끗이. **2** completely; entirely. 완전히; 아주 (cf. *clear*). ¶ ~ *mad* 〔*wrong*〕 아주 미친〔나쁜〕 / *I* ~ *forgot to ask.* 묻는 것을 깨끗이 잊고 있었다 / *The boy jumped* ~ *over the fence.* 소년은 거뜬히 담을 뛰어 넘었다. **3** exactly. 바로. ¶ *I was hit* ~ *in the eye.* 정통으로 눈을 맞았다.
come clean, 《*sl.*》 confess everything; tell the truth. 모든 것을 자백하다; 사실을 말하다.
— *vt.* (P6,7) make (something) clean; purify. …을 깨끗이 하다. ¶ ~ *one's hands* 손을 깨끗이 닦다 / ~ *shoes* 구두를 닦다 / *Washing cleans clothes.* 빨래는 옷을 깨끗이 한다.
— *vi.* (P1,2A) perform the act of cleaning. 깨끗해지다.
clean down, **a**) brush, sweep or wipe dirt from (walls, etc.). (벽 따위)를 깨끗이 쓸어 내리다; 닦아 없애다. **b**) brush down (a horse). (말)을 씻어주다.
clean house, wipe out corruption, inefficiency. (조직 내의) 부패를 일소하다; 비능률을 없애다; (기강을) 숙정하다.
clean out, **a**) empty (something) in order to clean it. (정돈·청소를 위해) 비우다. **b**) remove dirt and dust from inside; get rid of. (내부의 먼지·오물 따위를) 쓸어내다; 없애다. ¶ ~ *out the rubbish* 쓰레기를 청소해 내다. **c**) 《*colloq.*》 use up; take up all one's money. 다 써버리다; 무일푼이 되게 하다. ¶ *His betting losses have cleaned him out.* 도박에 잃음으로써 그는 무일푼이 되었다. **d**) steal everything from (a place). …에서 몽땅 털다.
clean up, **a**) remove dirt and rubbish from (a room, etc.); 《*fig.*》 put in order. …을 청소하다; 잘 정돈〔정리〕하다(cf. *clear up*). **b**) finish a piece of work. …을 마치다; 끝내다. **c**) 《U.S. *colloq.*》 make large profits. 큰 돈을 벌다. **d**) free (a place) of an evil state of affairs. (좋지 않은 요소들을) 제거하다; 일소하다.
— *n.* 《*a* ~》 an act of cleaning. 청소. ¶ *Give your room a good* ~. 방을 잘 청소해라. [E.]

clean-cut [klíːnkʌ́t] *adj.* **1** sharply outlined or defined. 윤곽이 뚜렷한. **2** well-shaped; well-formed. 모양이 좋은; 잘 생긴. ¶ *a face with* ~*, almost sharp features* 이목구비가 번듯하여 날카로운 느낌을 주는 얼굴. **3** 《*fig.*》 clear; distinct. 명확한; 명백한. **4** good; innocent. 선량한; 천진한.

clean·er [klíːnər] *n.* Ⓒ **1** a person who cleans (offices, rooms, etc.). (빌딩·사무

실 등의) 청소부. **2** the owner or worker of a dry-cleaning establishment. 세탁집 주인〔종업원〕. **3** ⓐ any instrument for cleaning. 청소기. ⓑ a vacuum cleaner. 진공 청소기. **4** a substance that removes dirts, stains, etc. 세제(洗劑).

clean-limbed [klí:nlímd] *adj.* having well-formed limbs. 팔다리가 미끈한〔날씬한〕.

clean·li·ness [klénlinis] *n.* Ⓤ the state or habit of being clean; cleanness; habitual cleanness. 청결; 결벽(潔癖).

•**clean·ly**[1] [klénli] *adj.* (**-li·er, -li·est**) clean; habitually clean. 깨끗한; 깨끗함을 좋아하는; 결벽(潔癖)의.

clean·ly[2] [klí:nli] *adv.* in a clean manner. 깨끗이; 결벽하게. ¶ *live* ~ 깨끗이 살다 / *The knife cut* ~ *through the meat.* 칼은 고기를 깨끗이 베었다.

clean·ness [klí:nnis] *n.* Ⓤ the state or quality of being clean. 깨끗함; 청결; 결백. ¶ *the* ~ *of the rooms* 방들의 청결 상태.

cleanse [klenz] *vt.* (P6) **1** make (something) clean. …을 깨끗이〔청결히〕 하다. ¶ ~ *one's hands* 〔*body*〕 손〔몸〕을 깨끗이 하다. **2** purify (something). …을 씻어 깨끗이 하다; 정화하다. ¶ ~ *a wound* 상처를 씻다 / ~ *sin from the soul* 영혼에서 죄를 씻어 깨끗이 하다. ● **cleans·er** [-ər] *n.* [E.]

clean-shav·en [klí:nʃéivən] *adj.* with the mustache and beard shaved off. 깨끗이 수염을 깎은.

clean·up [klí:nʌ̀p] *n.* Ⓒ **1** the act of cleaning up. 정화(운동); 청소; 일소. **2** 《*colloq.*》 money made; profit. 번 돈; 막대한 이윤.

:clear [kliər] *adj.* **1** ⓐ that can easily be seen through. 맑은; 투명한. ¶ *the* ~ *waters of the lake* 호수의 맑은 물 / *This wine is not* ~. 이 포도주는 맑지가 않다. ⓑ not cloudy; bright. (날씨 따위가) 맑게 갠; 밝은; 산뜻한(opp. cloudy, dark). ¶ *the* ~ *sky* 맑은 하늘 / *a* ~ *yellow* 샛노랑 / *a* ~ *blue* 밝은 파랑 / *a* ~ *complexion* 밝은 얼굴 빛 / *A* ~ *sky is free from clouds.* 맑게 갠 하늘엔 구름이 없다 / *Healthy children have* ~ *skins.* 건강한 아이들은 피부가 깨끗하다. **2** ⓐ that can be easily seen, heard. (소리 따위가) 맑고 깨끗한; (윤곽 따위가) 뚜렷한; 명확한. ¶ *a* ~ *voice* 맑은 목소리 / *a* ~ *outline* 뚜렷한 윤곽 / *a* ~ *photograph* 선명한 사진 / *the* ~ *note of a bell* 맑은 방울 소리. ⓑ easy to understand; distinct. 알기 쉬운; 명쾌한; 또렷한. ¶ ~, *concise answers* 간결하고 명쾌한 답 / *a* ~ *statement* 〔*explanation*〕 명쾌한 진술〔설명〕 / *He never makes things* ~. 그는 사정을 명백하게 하는 일이 없다 / *The meaning is* ~. 의미는 뚜렷하다. **3** without doubt; certain. 분명한; 명백〔명확〕한. ¶ *a* ~ *case of misbehavior* 분명한 비행(非行) 사례 / *It is* ~ *(that) you have been deceived.* 자네가 이제껏 속아왔음은 명백하다 / *I am quite* ~ *what I ought to do.* 내가 무엇을 해야 할 지 아주 분명하다. **4** easy or safe to pass along; open. 장애물이 없는; 탁 트인. ¶ *a* ~ *space* 빈 터 / *a* ~ *view* 〔*road*〕 탁 트인 전망〔길〕 / *The road is* ~ *now.* 도로에는 지금 교통이〔왕래가〕 없다. **5** not confused. 명석한. ¶ *a* ~ *head* 명석한 두뇌. **6** entire; full; net. 완전한; 꼬박; 에누리없는; 알속의. ¶ *a* ~ *month* 온 한 달 / *three* ~ *days* 꼬박 사흘 동안 / *a* ~ *$1,500,* 세금을 공제한 실 수령액 천 5 백 달러.

(***as***) ***clear as day,*** clear as the light of day. 극히 명료한; 명약 관화한.

clear of, without; free from. (의무·빚 따위에서) 해방된; …이 없는. ¶ ~ *of doubt* 〔*worry*〕. 빚〔걱정〕이 없는 / *The road is now* ~ *of snow.* 도로에는 이제 눈이 없다.

keep clear of, keep at a safe distance from; avoid. …에 일정 거리를 유지하다; …을 피하다. ¶ *keep one's dress* ~ *of the mud* 옷에 진흙을 묻히지 않다.

see one's way clear, 《*fig.*》 have no difficulty. (앞길에) 어려움이 없다.

The coast is clear., there is no difficulty; there is nothing to be afraid of. 어려움이 없다; 두려워할 것은 아무것도 없다.

— *adv.* **1** completely; quite. 완전히(cf. clean). ¶ *climb* ~ *to the top* 정상까지 완전히 오르다 / *cut a piece* ~ *off* 한 조각을 완전히 베어내다 / *run* ~ *off the road* 완전히 도로를 벗어나 달리다. **2** clearly. 분명〔명확〕히; 또렷이. ¶ *Speak loud and* ~. 큰소리로 똑똑하게 말해라. **3** apart; without contact. 떨어져; 접촉하지 않고. ¶ *stand* ~ *of* …에서 떨어져 있다 / *They sat perfectly* ~ *of each other.* 그들은 서로 완전히 떨어져 앉았다.

— *vt.* **1** (P6,7) make (something) clear. …을 명확히 하다; …을 깨끗이〔맑게〕 하다. ¶ ~ *muddy water* 흙탕물을 맑게 하다. **2** (P6,13) make (someone or something) free from blame, dishonor, guilt, etc.; prove (someone) to be innocent. (명예 따위가) 손상 받지 않게 하다; …의 결백을 증명하다; (오명을) 씻다. ¶ ~ *one's honor* 명예를 회복하다 / *She was cleared from the charge.* 그녀의 결백이 입증(立證)되었다. **3** (P6,7,13) make (something) free from doubt. …의 의혹을 풀다. ¶ *That clears it all up.* 이로써 의혹이 풀렸다. **4** (P6,7,13) get rid of (obstacles); take away. …을 제거하다; 치우다. ¶ ~ *the pavement of snow* 포도의 눈을 치우다 / ~ (*dishes from*) *the table* 식탁(의 접시)을 치우다. **5** (P6) pass by or jump over (something) without touching. (장애물 따위에 스치지 않고) 빠져나가다〔뛰어넘다〕. ¶ ~ *a fence* 울타리를 뛰어넘다 / *My car just cleared the other car.* 내 차는 다른 차를 건드리지 않고 간신히 빠져 나왔다. **6** (P6) gain (a given amount) as a net profit or earnings. …의 순익을 올리다; 벌다. ¶ ~ *one's expenses* 지출비만큼 벌다 / ~ *$2,000 in a transaction* 거래에서 2천 달러의 수익을

올리다. **7** (P6) disentangle. 엉클어진 것을 풀다. **8** (P6) 《comm.》 get rid of stock by selling at a reduced price; sell off. (재고품 정리를 위해) 떨이로 팔다. **9** (P6,13) 《naut.》 free (a ship or cargo) by paying harbor dues. (배·화물의) 출항[입항] 절차를 끝내다; 통관하다. **10** (P6) settle (a debt). (빚을) 청산하다. **11** (P6) 《comm.》 pass (a check) through a clearing-house. (수표·어음 등을) 어음 교환소에서 교환하다.

— *vi.* **1** (P1,2A) become clear; become bright. 맑아지다; 분명해지다; (구름·안개가) 걷히다; 개다. ¶ *wait for the rain to* ~ 비가 개기를 기다리다 / *The sky is clearing.* 하늘이 개고 있다 / *The situation slowly began to* ~. 상황이 점차 분명해지기 시작했다. **2** (P1,2A) 《naut.》 comply with customs and harbor requirements in leaving or entering a port. (배가) 출항[입항]의 필요 절차를 밟다. **3** (P2A) 《*sl.*》 《*out, off*》 go away; leave. 떠나다. [L. *clarus*]

clear away, **a**) take away (obstacles, etc.). …을 (걷어) 치우다. ¶ ~ *away all the table* 테이블 위의 물건들을 치우다. **b**) get rid of. …을 제거하다; 없애다. ¶ ~ *away doubts* 의혹을 떨어버리다. **c**) (of mist, fog, etc.) vanish. (안개 따위가) 걷히다. ¶ *The clouds have cleared away.* 구름이 걷히었다.

clear off, **a**) complete; finish. 마치다; 끝내다. ¶ ~ *off the work.* **b**) drive out. 몰아내다; 내쫓다. ¶ ~ *bad workmen off the premises* 못된 공원(工員)들을 구내에서 쫓아내다. **c**) (of rain, clouds, etc.) ⇨clear away c). **d**) 《*colloq.*》 get out; go quickly away. 나가다; 급히 떠나다[퇴거하다].

clear out, **a**) take away dirt, etc. from. 깨끗이 치(우)다; 없애다. ¶ ~ *out a drain* 도랑을 치다. **b**) 《*colloq.*》 use up one's money. 돈을 다 써 버리다(cf. *clean out*). ¶ *That loss has cleared me out completely.* 그 손실은 나를 완전히 빈털터리로 만들었다. **c**) 《*colloq.*》 go away; leave. 떠나다. ¶ *We must* ~ *out of this room at once.* 우리는 곧 이 방에서 떠나야 한다.

clear up, **a**) get in order; make (a room etc.) tidy; finish. 깨끗이 정돈[정리]하다; 끝내다(cf. *clean up*). ¶ ~ *up the unfinished work* 못 끝낸 일을 마무리하다. **b**) solve; explain. 해결하다; 설명하다. ¶ ~ *up a question* [*doubt*] 의문[의혹]을 풀다. **c**) (of weather) become fine. 날씨가 좋아지다; 개다. ¶ *The weather* [*It*] *has cleared up.* 날씨가 들었다.

clear·ance [klíərəns] *n.* **1** UC the act of making clear. 치움; 철거; 제거; 정리; 청소. ¶ *a* ~ *sale* (재고품 정리) 염가 판매 / *the* ~ *of slums* 달동네의 철거 / *make* ~ *of something* …을 일소하다 / *make a* ~ *of* (*one's old clothes, etc.*) (헌 옷가지 등)을 처분하다. **2** CU an official certificate that a ship has been cleared at the Custom House. (배의) 출항[입항] 절차[허가]; 통관 절차. **3** U cutting down trees to open up land. (개간을 위한) 산림 벌채. **4** U the act of exchanging checks and other commercial documents between different banks. (은행간의) 어음 교환. **5** UC 《mech.》 the space between a moving object and fixed one. 틈새; 여유 공간; 공극(空隙). **6** permit to leave government employment. 관리의 퇴직 허가 [사표 수리]. **7** net profit. 순익(純益). [→clear]

clear-cut [klíərkʌ́t] *adj.* **1** with clear, sharp outlines. (얼굴 따위) 윤곽이 뚜렷한. **2** clear; distinct. 분명[명확]한; 명쾌한.

clear·head·ed [klíərhédid] *adj.* having a clear understanding; sharp-witted. 머리가 명석한; 명민한.

clear·ing [klíəriŋ] *n.* **1** C an open space of land in a forest which has been cleared for cultivation. (산림의) 개척(지). **2** U the act of exchanging checks, etc. between different banks. 어음 교환.

clearing house [←-←] *n.* a place where banks exchange checks, etc. with one another. 어음 교환소; 증권 청산소.

:clear·ly [klíərli] *adv.* **1** in a clear manner; undoubtedly. 분명[명확]히; 의심할 나위 없이; 똑똑히. ¶ *see* ~ 똑똑히 보다 / *speak* ~ 분명하게 말하다 / *state one's case* ~ 자신의 경우를 명확히 진술하다. **2** brightly. 밝게; 맑게. ¶ *The sun shone* ~. 태양이 밝게 빛났다 / *The river runs* ~. 강물이 맑게 흐르고 있다.

clear·ness [klíərnis] *n.* U **1** the state or quality of being clear. 명료; 선명; 맑음. **2** plainness; brightness. 분명함; 명백. **3** freedom from obstacles. 무장애(無障碍).

clear·sight·ed [klíərsáitid] *adj.* **1** that can see clearly; having good eye-sight. 눈이 잘 보이는[좋은]. **2** that can understand well. 명민[明敏]한; 총명한.

cleat [kli:t] *n.* C **1** a strip of wood or iron fixed to something for support or sure footing. 고정[버팀, 보강] 쐐기; 미끄럼막이. **2** 《naut.》 a piece of wood or metal having one or two projecting horns on which ropes can be fastened. 지삭전(支索栓); 밧줄걸이. [E.]

cleav·age [klí:vidʒ] *n.* CU **1** the act of cleaving; the state of being cleft; split. 쪼음; 쪼어짐; 분할; 분열; 벽개(劈開). **2** 《biol.》 the division of an egg into smaller parts. 난할(卵割); 열개(裂開). **3** a split, division, separation between persons, or in their opinions, etc. (사람·의견 따위의) 분열; 의견의 상위(相違). ¶ *a* ~ *in the village* 마을의 분열 / *a* ~ *regard to policy* 정책에 관한 의견의 분열. [→cleave[1]]

cleave[1] [kli:v] *vt., vi.* (**clove** or **cleft, cloven** or **cleft**) (P6,7,18; 1,2) **1** split; divide. 쪼개(지)다; 쪼(어지)다. ¶ ~ *open* 쪼어[쪼개] 벌리다 / ~ *a block of wood in two* 큰 나무토막를 둘로 빠개다 / ~ *an apple in two with knife* 칼로 사과를 두 쪽으로 쪼개다 /

Wood cleaves along the grain. 나무는 결을 따라 쪼개진다. **2** cut one's way through. 밀(어 헤치)고 나아가다; 돌진하다. ¶ ~ *one's way through* 길을 헤치고 나아가다. [E.]

in a cleft stick, in a fix. 진퇴 양난에 빠져.

show the cloven hoof, betray oneself; throw off the mask. 본성을 드러내다.

● **cleav·a·ble** [-əbəl] *adj.* [E.]

cleave² [kli:v] *vi.* (P2,3) (《*arch.*》 **clave** or **cleaved, cleaved**) 《*to*》 cling; hold fast; be faithful to (someone). 착 달라붙다; 점착하다; 집착하다; 충실하다. ¶ ~ *to one's principle in spite of persecution* 박해에도 불구하고 자기 주의를 고수하다. [E.]

cleav·er [klí:vər] *n.* Ⓒ **1** a person or thing that cleaves. 쪼개는 사람[것]; 찢는 사람[것]. **2** a tool used by a butcher for chopping meat or bone. (푸주에서 고기를 토막 내는) 큰 식칼. [→cleave¹]

cleav·ers [klí:vərz] *n.* 《bot.》 a goose grass. 갈퀴덩굴속(屬)의 식물. [L. *clivre*]

cleek [kli:k] *n.* in iron-headed golf-club. 아이언 골프채. [E.]

clef [klef] *n.* Ⓒ 《mus.》 a symbol placed on a staff to indicate the pitch of the notes. 음자리표. ¶ *C* ~ 다음자리표《가온음자리표》/ *F* ~ 바음자리표《낮은음자리표》/ *G* ~ 사음자리표 《높은음자리표》. [L. *clavis* key]

cleft¹ [kleft] *adj.* split; separated; divided. 쪼개진; 갈라진; 분열된. ¶ *in a ~ stick* 진퇴유곡에 처해 / ~ *palate* 구개(口蓋) 파열. —*n.* Ⓒ a space or opening made by splitting. 갈라진 틈[데]; 열편(裂片). ¶ *There is a ~ in the rock here.* 여기 있는 바위에 균열이 있다. [Teut. →cleave¹]

cleft² [kleft] *v.* p. and pp. of **cleave**¹.

cleg [kleg] *n.* 《insect》 a large gray fly. 등에; 말등에. [Scand.]

clem [klem] *vi., vt.* (P1; 6) starve. 굶주리(게 하)다. [E.]

clem·a·tis [klémətis] *n.* 《bot.》 a plant which grows up walls etc., and has purple or white flowers. 참으아리속(屬)의 식물. [Gk.]

Cle·men·ceau [klèmənsóu], **Georges** *n.* (1841-1929) a French statesman. 클레망소《프랑스의 정치가》.

clem·en·cy [klémənsi] *n.* Ⓤ **1** mercy; mildness of temper; gentleness. 자비; 관대(한 조치); 관용; 온후. ¶ *decide with* ~ 관대한 결정을 하다 / *The judge showed ~ toward the young prisoner.* 판사는 젊은 죄수에게 관대함을 보였다. **2** (of the weather) mildness. (기후의) 온화; 온난. ¶ *The ~ of the weather allowed them to live outdoors.* 따뜻한 날씨가 그들이 야외에서 생활할 수 있게 했다. [L.]

clem·ent [klémənt] *adj.* **1** merciful; gentle. 자비 깊은; 온후[온건]한; 관대한. **2** (of the weather) mild and pleasant; calm. (기후가) 온화한; 온난한. [L.]

clench [klentʃ] *vt.* (P6) **1** ⓐ press (something) firmly together; close (the fist, fingers, etc.) tightly; seize firmly. …을 단단히 죄다; (주먹·손가락 따위)를 꽉 쥐다; 단단히 (붙)잡다. ¶ *a clenched fist* 불끈 쥔 주먹 / ~ *one's teeth* 이를 악물다 / *He clenched my arm.* 그는 내 팔을 꽉 붙들었다. ⓑ 《*fig.*》 make a firm determination. 굳은 결심을 하다. **2** clinch (a nail, etc.). (박은 못 따위의) 끝을 때려 구부리다. **3** conclude (an argument, etc.) definitely. (의론 따위)에 결말을 내다.

—*vi.* (P1) (of hands, teeth, etc.) close tightly. (손 따위가) 꽉 쥐어지다[움켜지다]; (이가) 악물리다.

—*n.* Ⓒ **1** a firm grasp. 단단히 쥠[잡음]; 이를 악묾. **2** 《boxing》 a clinch. 클린치. [E.]

clench·er [kléntʃər] *n.* =clincher.

Cle·o·pa·tra [klì:əpǽtrə, -pá:trə] *n.* (69-30 B.C.) a queen of Egypt. 클레오파트라《이집트의 여왕》.

cle·re·sto·ry [klíərstɔ̀:ri, -stòuri] (*pl.* **-ries** [-ri:z]) *n.* 《archit.》 the upper section of a large church with windows above the aisles. (교회당의) 고창층(高窓層). [→clear, story²]

***cler·gy** [klə́:rdʒi] *n.* Ⓤ 《*the* ~》《*collectively.*, used as *pl.*》 the body or group of men who have been selected by God for religious work, such as ministers, pastors, and priests. 사목자(司牧者); 목사; 성직(자). [Gk. *klēros* inheritance]

***cler·gy·man** [klə́:rdʒimən] *n.* Ⓒ (*pl.* **-men** [-mən]) *n.* a member of the clergy. 목사; 성직자.

cler·ic [klérik] *n.* Ⓒ a clergyman. 성직자; 목사. —*adj.* of a clergyman; clerical. 목사의; 성직의. [→clergy]

cler·i·cal [klérikəl] *adj.* **1** of a clerk. 서기의; 사무원의. ¶ *a ~ error* (사소한) 오기(誤記) / *a ~ job* 사무직 / *the ~ staff* 사무원 / *A big bank employs many persons for ~ work.* 큰 은행은 사무를 위해 많은 행원을 고용한다. **2** of a clergyman. 성직의; 목사의. ¶ ~ *garments* 성직자 복(服). —*n.* **1** Ⓒ a clergyman. 성직자; 목사. **2** 《*pl.*》 clothing worn by clergymen. 성직복.

cler·i·cal·ism [klérikəlìzəm] *n.* clerical principles. 교권주의. ● **cler·i·cal·ist** [-ist] *n.*

cler·i·cal·ize [klérikəlàiz] *vt.* (P6) **1** try to extend the power of church. 교권을 확장시키려 하다. **2** ordain. 성직에 취임시키다.

:clerk [klə:rk / kla:rk] *n.* Ⓒ **1** an assistant in business; a salesman or saleswoman. (상점의) 점원; 판매원. **2** a person who is employed in keeping records or accounts, copying letters, etc. in an office. 사무원. **3** an official who keeps records in a law court, a legislature, etc. 서기. —*vi.* (P1) work as a clerk. 점원[서기] 노릇을 하다. [→cleric]

clerk in holy orders, a clergyman of the

Church of England. 영국 국교회의 목사. ***clerk of St. Nicholas,*** a highwayman. 노상강도.

:clev·er [klévər] *adj.* **1** quick to learn or understand; quick-witted; intelligent. 영리한; 똑똑한; 재기(才氣)〔재치〕 있는. ¶ *a ~ boy* 똑똑한 아이 / *a ~ story* 재치 있는 이야기 / *He is the cleverest boy in the class.* 그는 반에서 가장 머리 좋은 아이이다 / *It is ~ of you to solve the problem.* 그 문제를 풀 수 있다니 매우 영리하구나 **2** skillful. 솜씨좋은; 교묘한. ¶ *a ~ carpenter* 솜씨 야무진 목수 / *a ~ piece of work* 정교한 작품 / *be ~ at* 〔*in*〕 … 을 잘하다; …에 능하다 / *be ~ with the pen* 글씨를 잘 쓰다 / *make a ~ play* 교묘한 플레이를 하다 / *She is ~ at cooking.* 그녀는 요리를 잘한다. ● **clev·er·ly** [-li] *adv.* **clev·er·ness** [-nis] *n.* [E.]

clev·is [klévəs] *n.* a U-shaped piece of metal with a bolt through the ends. (양끝을 나사나 볼트로 죈) U-자형 죔쇠. [?]

clew [kluː] *n.* Ⓒ **1** anything that helps in solving a mystery or problem. (해결의) 단서; 실마리. 參考 흔히 clue로 씀. **2** a ball of thread or yarn. 실꾸리; 실몽당이. **3** 《naut.》 a lower corner of a square sail; a metal loop fastened at a corner of a sail; cords for a hammock. 돛귀; 돛귀의 고리; 해먹을 달아매는 줄. — *vt.* (P6,7) **1** 《*up*》 wind (thread) into a ball. (실을) 둥글게 감다. **2** 《*up, down*》 raise or lower a sail by a clew. (돛을) 활대에 끌어올리다〔끌어내리다〕. — *vi.* 《*up*》 finish off a piece of work. 일을 다 끝내다. [E.]

cli·ché [kli(ː)ʃéi] *n.* 《F.》 an expression or idea that has become stale from too much use. 진부한 문구. ¶ *run into a ~* 상투어(語)가 되다. [F. =stereotype block]

***click** [klik] *n.* Ⓒ a light, sharp sound. 짤깍하는 소리. — *vi., vt.* (P1; 6,7) **1** make or cause (something) to make a light, sharp sound. 짤깍소리가 나다〔소리를 내다〕. ¶ *~ one's tongue* 혀를 쩍〔쯧〕하다 / *The door clicked shut.* 문이 철컥 닫혔다 / *~ one's heels together* 구두 뒤꿈치를 찔꺽 맞추다《차렷자세·경례를 위해》. **2** 《*sl.*》 have luck; secure one's object; get on immediate friendly terms with a person of the opposite sex. 행운을 안다; 목적물을 얻다; 이성과 곧 친한 사이가 되다. [Imit.]

***cli·ent** [kláiənt] *n.* Ⓒ **1** a person who appeals to a lawyer for advice. 소송〔변호〕 의뢰인. ¶ *That lawyer has many clients.* 저 변호사는 의뢰인이 많다. **2** a customer of a tradesman. 단골; 고객. [L. *cluo* obey]

cli·en·tele [klàiəntél, klìːɑːntéil] *n.* Ⓒ 《*collectively*》 **1** clients; customers. 소송〔변호〕 의뢰인들; 고객들. **2** personal followers. 추종자들; 부하들; 졸개들.

:cliff [klif] *n.* Ⓒ a very high and steep slope of rock. 단애; 벼랑; (특히 해안의) 절벽. [E.]

cliffs·man [klífsmən] *n.* (*pl.* **-men** [-mən]) a rock-climber. 암벽 등반의 명수.

cli·mac·ter·ic [klaimǽktərik, klàimæktérik] *adj.* **1** constituting a turning point. 변환기〔전환기〕(期)의. **2** of a period of decrease of reproductive activity in men and women. 갱년기의. — *n.* **1** ⓐ an important turning point. 변환기; 전환기. ⓑ a period in life when important changes take place in the human body. 액년(厄年). ¶ *grand ~* 대액년《63세》. **2** =menopause. [→climax]

:cli·mate [kláimit] *n.* Ⓒ **1** the state of heat and cold, wetness and dryness, wind and calm in a certain place. (어느 지방의) 기후; 풍토(cf. *weather*). ¶ *a mild ~* 온난한 기후 / *a frigid* 〔*torrid*〕 *~* 한대〔열대〕성 기후. **2** a region in respect of its weather conditions. (기후상으로 본) 지방; 지역; 지대. ¶ *I want to go south to a warmer ~.* 남쪽의 보다 따뜻한 지역으로 가고 싶다. **3** 《*fig.*》 the general trend or attitude of a community or period. (어떤 사회·시대의) 풍조; 경향; 풍토. ¶ *the ~ of opinion* 여론의 경향 / *the political ~* 정치 풍토〔정세〕. [Gk. *klinō* slope]

cli·mat·ic [klaimǽtik] *adj.* of or having to do with climate. 기후(상)의; 풍토의. ¶ *~ conditions* 기후 조건.

cli·ma·tol·o·gy [klàimətálədʒi / -tɔ́l-] *n.* a branch of meteorology that deals with climate. 기후학(學); 풍토학.

cli·max [kláimæks] *n.* Ⓒ **1** the highest point, as of excitement or interest. 정점(頂點); 절정; 최고조. ¶ *the ~ of a play* 극의 클라이맥스 / *be at the ~ of one's fame* 명성의 절정에 있다 / *come to a ~* 정점에 달하다. **2** 《rhet.》 the arrangement of ideas or expressions in an ascending scale. (점차 문세(文勢)를 높여 나가는) 점층법(漸層法)(opp. anticlimax). — *vt., vi.* (P6;1) bring or come to a climax. 최고조에 달하(게 하)다. [Gk. =ladder]

:climb [klaim] *vt., vi.* **1** (P6,7;1,2A) ⓐ go up step by step; mount; ascend. (한 발짝 한 발짝씩) 오르다; 올라가다; 등반하다. ¶ *~ (up) a hill* 언덕을 오르다 / *~ a mountain to its top* 꼭대기를 향해 산을 오르다 / *~ to the top of a mountain* 산의 정상에 오르다 / *~ stone steps* 돌계단을 오르다. ⓑ go up or down by holding; ascend or descend with hands and feet. 붙잡고 오르다〔내리다〕; (손발을 써서) 기어오르다〔내리다〕. ¶ *~ (up) a tree* 〔*ladder*〕 나무〔사다리〕에 기어오르다 / *~ up* 〔*down*〕 *a branch* 나뭇가지에 기어오르다〔를 기어내리다〕 / *~ down from a truck* 트럭에서 기어내리다 / *~ over a fence* 울타리를 넘어가다. **2** (P6; 2A,3) rise by steps or by effort; work one's way up. 출세〔승진〕하다; 높아지다. ¶ *~ in reputation* 명성이 높아지다 / *~ to power* 권력에 오르다 / *~ the path of* *fame* 영달의 길을 오르다 / ~ *to the head of the class* 반 수석의 자리에 오르다. **3** (P7; 2A) (of plants) creep up a tree, wall, etc. by means of tendrils. (덩굴손으로) 감겨붙어오르다; 기어오르다. ¶ *climbing plants* 덩굴성 식물 / *The ivy climbed to the roof.* 담쟁이덩굴이 지붕에까지 기어올랐다. **4** (P1; 6) rise in the sky. (하늘에) 떠오르다; 뜨다. ¶ *The sun climbs higher and higher.* 해가 점점 높이 뜬다 / *The moon climbs the heavens.* 달이 중천에 떠오른다. **5** (P1) slope upward. 비탈진 언덕길〔오르막〕이 되다. ¶ *The road began to* ~. 길은 오르막이 되기 시작했다.

climb down, a) get down from (a tree, etc.) (나무 따위에서) 내려오다. **b**) abandon one's position. 자리〔지위〕에서 물러나다. **c**) admit that one is mistaken or wrong; withdraw from one's former opinion or position. 자신의 잘못을 인정하다; (종전의 주장·입장 따위를) 철회하다; 항복하다.

— *n.* Ⓒ **1** the act of going up; an ascent or rise 오름; 등반; 상승. ¶ *a stiff* 〔*an arduous*〕 ~ *up a mountain* (산의) 어려운〔힘드는〕 등반 / *be on the upward* ~ 상승 경향에 있다 / *Their* ~ *took three hours.* 그들의 등반은 3시간 걸렸다. **2** a thing or place to be climbed; a slope. 올라가야 할 것〔곳〕; 비탈; 오르막. ¶ *an easy* 〔*a steep*〕 ~ 완만한〔가파른〕 비탈. [E.]

climb·er [kláimər] *n.* Ⓒ **1** a person or thing that climbs. 기어오르는 자〔것〕; 등반자; 등산가. **2** 《*colloq.*》 a person who is always trying to rise in society. (출세를 열망하는) 야심가. **3** a climbing plant. 덩굴성 식물. [E.]

clime [klaim] *n.* Ⓒ 《*poet.*》 a country; a district; a climate. 지방; 지역; 기후; 풍토. ¶ *seek some happier* ~ 보다 좋은 신천지를 찾다. [→climate]

clinch [klintʃ] *vt.* (P6) **1** fasten (a driven nail) by beating down the point. (못의 한 끝을) 쳐서 구부려 붙박다. **2** fix (something) firmly. …을 고정시키다. ¶ ~ *two boards together* 두 널빤지를 못을 박아 고정시키다. **3** 《*fig.*》 settle (an argument, bargain, etc.) finally. (의론·흥정 따위에) 결말〔매듭〕을 짓다; 결정하다. ¶ ~ *an argument* 토론을 매듭짓다 / *the moment to* ~ *the victory* 승리를 결정지을 순간. — *vi.* (P1) 《boxing》 hold one another tightly. 클린치 하다.

— *n.* Ⓒ **1** the act of clinching. (때려박아) 못 끝을 구부려 고정시키기. **2** 《boxing》 a tight hold. 클린치. [E.]

clinch·er [klíntʃər] *n.* Ⓒ **1** a person or thing that clinches. 못을 때려 굽혀 붙박는 사람; 때려 굽히는 붙박이 기구. **2** 《*colloq.*》 something decisive, as in an argument. (반론의 여지없는) 결정적인 의론; 결정적인 요인.

***cling** [kliŋ] *vi.* (**clung** [klʌŋ]) (P1,2A,3) 《*to*》 **1** fix onto something closely; stick fast; adhere. 들러붙다; 매달려 떨어지지 않다; 집착하다. ¶ ~ *together* 들러붙어 떨어지지 않다 / ~ *to the last hope* 마지막 희망을 버리지 않다 / *Wet clothes* ~ *to the body.* 젖은 옷은 몸에 달라 붙는다 / *He clings to old-fashioned ideas.* 낡은 사고를 버리지 못한다 / *The child clung to its mother.* 아이는 엄마에 매달려 떨어지지 않았다. **2** keep close to; remain near. 곁을 떠나지〔떨어지지〕 않다. **3** grasp; embrace. 꽉 쥐다; 껴안다. [E.]

cling·ing [klíŋiŋ] *adj.* that clings; adhering closely. 달라붙는; 밀착하는; 꼭 끼는. ¶ ~ *clothes* 〔*garments*〕 몸에 착 붙는 옷.

clin·ic [klínik] *n.* Ⓒ **1** a place for medical treatment. 진료소. **2** the act of teaching medical students by treating patients in their presence. 임상 강의. ¶ *a speech* ~ 언어 교정 교실. **3** a place for practical teaching and treatment. 임상 교실. [Gk. *klinē* bed]

clin·i·cal [klínikəl] *adj.* **1** of or having to do with a clinic. 임상(강의)의. ¶ ~ *instruction* 〔*lecture*〕 임상 강의. **2** used in a sickroom. 병상(病床)의. ¶ *a* ~ *thermometer* 검온기; 체온계. **3** cold; appearing more interest in the scientific than personal details of a case. 냉정한; 객관적인; 있는 그대로의.

clink[1] [kliŋk] *n.* Ⓒ a light, sharp, ringing sound. 쨍; 짤랑; 땔랑 (소리). ¶ *the* ~ *of coins* 동전의 짤랑 소리. — *vi., vt.* (P1; 6) make or cause to make a clink. 쨍〔짤랑〕하고 소리나다〔하는 소리를 내다〕. ¶ ~ *glasses* 쨍하고 술잔을 부딪치다《축배를 들 때》/ ~ *one's money in one's pocket* 호주머니의 돈을 짤랑거리다. [Imit.]

clink[2] [kliŋk] *n.* 《*sl.*》 a prison. 교도소; 감옥. ¶ *be in* ~ 수감〔투옥〕되어 있다 / *go to* ~ 감옥에 가다. [↑]

clink·er [klíŋkər] *n.* **1** Ⓒ a hard Dutch brick. (도로 포장용) 단단한 벽돌. **2** ⓊⒸ a mass of slag. 용재(鎔滓)덩이. **3** Ⓒ 《*sl.*》 a failure. 실패작; 불량품. ¶ *In spite of our efforts, the play was a real* ~. 우리의 노력에도 불구하고 연극은 형편없는 실패작이었다. **4** Ⓒ 《Brit. *colloq.*》 first-class specimen. 일류의 것〔사람〕.

clink·ing [klíŋkiŋ] *adj.* 《*colloq.*》 excellent. 일류의; 매우 좋은.

cli·nom·e·ter [klainámitər / -nɔ́m-] *n.* an instrument for measuring the angle of an incline. 경사계(傾斜計); 클리노미터. [Gk. *klíein* slope]

Cli·o [kláiou] *n.* 《Gk. myth.》 the muse of history. 클레이오《사시(史詩) 및 역사의 신》. [Gk. *kleiō* celebrate]

***clip**[1] [klip] *vi., vt.* (**clipped, clip·ping**) (P6, 7,18; 1) **1** cut short or cut off (hair, grass, twigs, etc.) with shears or scissors. (머리털, 잔디 등을) 가위로 깎다〔자르다〕; 치다. ¶ ~ *the wool of a sheep* 양의 털을 깎다. **2** cut articles or pictures from a newspaper, magazine, etc. (신문·잡지 따위에서)

기사를〔그림을〕 오려내다. ¶ ～ *an article off* 〔*from*〕 *the paper* 신문에서 기사를 오려내다. **3** 《*colloq.*》 move rapidly. 빠르게 움직이다; 질주하다. **4** 《*colloq.*》 hit (someone) sharply. 한 대 먹이다; 후려 갈기다. ¶ *get clipped by someone* 아무에게 한방 먹다 / *He clipped her on the face.* 그는 그녀의 얼굴을 세게 때렸다. **5** drop parts of (words) in hurried speech. (연설에서) 말을 줄여 빨리 끝내다. **6** cut the edge of (coin). (주화(鑄貨)의) 가장자리를 깎아내다.

clip someone's wing* = *clip the wings of, make (someone) weak. …을 무력하게 만들다.

— *n.* **1** Ⓤ the act of clipping; Ⓒ something clipped off. 깎기; 깎아〔잘라〕낸 것. **2** ⓊⒸ the amount of wool that is cut off in one season. (한 철에) 깎아내는 양털의 양(量). **3** Ⓒ a rapid motion. 잽싼 동작. **4** Ⓒ 《*colloq.*》 a quick, sharp blow. 강타(強打). [E.]

·**clip**² [klip] *vt.* (P6,7) (**clipped, clip·ping**) grasp or hold (something) tight. (클립으로) …을 단단히 끼우다〔물리다〕. ¶ ～ *papers together* 서류를 클립으로 한데 철하다. — *n.* Ⓒ a thing used for holding (things) together. 클립; 집게; 끼우개. ¶ *a paper* ～ 종이 끼우개. [E.]

clip·per [klípər] *n.* Ⓒ **1** a person who cuts hair, grass, etc. 잘라내는〔깎는〕 사람. **2** 《often *pl.*》 a tool for cutting or shearing. 잘라내는〔깎는〕 기구; 큰 가위. ¶ *hair-clippers* 바리캉《이발 기계》 / *nail-clippers* 손톱깎이. **3** a sailing ship built for great speed. 쾌속(범)선. **4** a large, fast airplane. 대형 여객기《옛날의 프로펠러식》. **5** a fast horse. 쾌속마(馬); 준마.

clip·ping [klípiŋ] *n.* Ⓒ 《usu. *pl.*》 **1** an article or picture cut out of a newspaper, magazine, etc. (신문·잡지에서) 오려낸 것 《기사·사진 따위》. **2** that which is clipped off. (가위로) 잘라 낸 것. [→clip¹]

clique [kli:k, klik] *n.* Ⓒ a small, closely-united group of people. 도당(徒黨); 파벌(派閥). ¶ *an academic* ～ 학벌(學閥). [F.]

cli·quish [klí:kiʃ] *adj.* like a clique; inclined to form a clique. 파당적인; 파벌로 분열하기 쉬운.

cli·to·ris [klítəris, klái-] *n.* 《anat.》 the small, sensitive, erectile organ of the vulva. 음핵(陰核). [Gk. *kleio*]

:**cloak** [klouk] *n.* Ⓒ **1** a loose outside dress. (팔없는) 외투; 망토. **2** anything that covers or hides (something); a disguise. 덮어가리는〔숨기는〕 것; 위장; 가면; 구실.

under a cloak of (*snow*), covered by (*snow*). (눈)에 덮이어.

under the cloak of, **a**) under the mask of (something). …의 가면을 쓰고; …을 빙자하여; …의 미명(美名) 아래. **b**) taking advantage of (something). …을 틈타. ¶ *attack the enemy under the* ～ *of darkness* 어둠을 틈타 적을 공격하다.

— *vt.* (P6) **1** cover (someone) with a cloak. …을 망토로 덮다; …에게 망토〔외투〕를 입히다. **2** hide. …을 덮어가리다〔감추다〕; 숨기다. ¶ *He cloaked his sorrow with gay talk.* 그는 명랑한 이야기로 슬픔을 감췄다 / *Fog cloaked the tower.* 그 탑은 안개에 가려져 있었다. [L. *cloca* bell]

cloak·room [klóukrù(:)m] *n.* Ⓒ **1** a room where coats, hats, etc. may be left for a time, as in a theater or hotel. (극장·호텔 등의) 외투·휴대품 보관소. **2** an office where passengers' luggage and parcels are taken care of. (역의) 수화물 일시 보관소. ¶ *He left his suitcase in the* ～ *of the station.* 그는 가방을 정거장의 일시 보관소에 맡겼다. **3** 《Brit.》 a toilet. 화장실.

clob·ber [klábər / klɔ́b-] *vt.* 《*sl.*》 **1** hit with force; strike heavily. 세게 때리다. **2** defeat decisively. 완패시키다. **3** denounce or criticize vigorously. 맹렬히 비난하다; 혹평하다. [?]

cloche [klouʃ] *n.* a woman's bell-shaped hat. 종 모양의 여성모(帽). [F.=bell]

:**clock**¹ [klak / klɔk] *n.* Ⓒ an instrument for measuring and showing time. 시계《괘종시계·탁상 시계 따위》(cf. *watch*). ¶ *set a* ～ *by the radio* 시계를 라디오에 맞추다 / *tell the* ～ 시간을 재다〔기록하다〕 / *work against the* ～ 정한 시간에 맞추려고 일을 서두르다.

around 〔***round***〕 ***the clock,*** day and night; during all 24 hours; without stopping; constantly. 24시간 계속하여; 쉬지 않고; 늘.

like a clock, as exactly as a clock. 시계처럼 정확히.

put 〔***set, turn***〕 ***the clock back,*** **a**) move the hand of the clock back. 시계바늘을 되돌리다; 시계를 늦추다. **b**) 《*fig.*》 take reactionary measures. 진보를 방해하다; 시대에 역행하다. **c**) go back to an earlier state of affairs. 옛 시대〔상태〕로 돌아가다.

— *vt.* (P6,7) measure or record the time of. 시간을 재다〔기록하다〕. ¶ ～ *a race* (스톱워치로) 시간을 재다.

— *vi.* (P1) 《*in, out*》 (of workmen, etc.) record one's entry or exit by means of an automatic clock. (타임리코더로) 출퇴근 시간을 기록하다. [M.E. *clok* clock with bells]

clock² [klak / klɔk] *n.* a long, narrow design on the outside of a sock or stocking. 양말의 자수 장식. [↑]

clock·wise [klákwàiz / klɔ́k-] *adj., adv.* moving in the direction of the hands of a clock. 시계바늘처럼 우로〔오른쪽으로〕 도는; 오른쪽으로 돌아서(opp. counter-clockwise).

clock·work [klákwə̀:rk / klɔ́k-] *n.* Ⓤ the mechanism of a clock. 시계〔태엽〕 장치. ¶ *a* ～ *bomb* 시한 폭탄 / *like* ～ 시계처럼 정확히 / (*as*) *regular* 〔*regularly*〕 *as* ～ 매우 규칙적인〔으로〕.

clod [klɑd / klɔd] *n.* **1** Ⓒ ⓐ a lump of earth or clay; soil. 흙덩이; 흙; 토양. ⓑ 《*poet.*》 a man's dead body. 유체(遺體); 시체. **2** Ⓒ a silly person; a fool. 바보; 멍텅구리. [→clot]

clod·hop·per [klɑ́dhɑ̀pər / klɔ́dhɔ̀pər] *n.* **1** a rough fellow from the country. 시골 무지렁이; 농부. **2** a stupid, awkward fellow. 메부수수한 사람. **3** 《*pl.*》 large, heavy shoes. 크고 무거운 신발.

clog [klɑg / klɔg] *vt., vi.* (**clogged, clog·ging**) (P6; 1) **1** choke up (something); become choked up. …을 막(히게 하)다; 메우다; 막히다. ¶ ~ *a drain* 배수구를 막히게 하다 / *The pipe is clogged with frozen snow.* 파이프가 얼어붙은 눈으로 막혀 있다 / *This pipe is so small that it clogs very easily.* 파이프가 너무 작아서 아주 잘 막힌다. **2** hinder; prevent; stop. …을 방해하다. ¶ ~ *one's movements* 운동을 방해하다. **3** ⓐ cause difficulty in working. 일의 기능을 둔화시키다. ¶ *Sawdust clogs the teeth of the saw.* 톱밥이 묻어 톱니가 잘 켜지지 않는다. ⓑ make heavy. 무겁게 하다. ¶ *boots clogged with mud* 진흙이 묻어 무거워진 장화.
— *n.* Ⓒ **1** a thing that prevents. 방해(물); 장애물. ¶ *a* ~ *on the progress of science* 과학 발전에 장애가 되는 것. **2** a block of wood used to tie a leg of an animal to prevent its movement. (동물의 다리에 매는 묵직한) 나무토막《행동을 방해하기 위한》. **3** a shoe, usu. with a wooden sole. 나막신. [Sw.]

clog·dance [klɑ́gdæ̀ns, -dɑ̀ːns / klɔ́g-] *n.* a dance by beating the floor with clogs. (마루를 구르며 박자를 맞추는) 나막신춤.

clog·gy [klɑ́gi / klɔ́gi] *adj.* apt to clog; sticky. 막히기 쉬운; 들러붙는.

clois·ter [klɔ́istər] *n.* Ⓒ **1** a passageway along the wall of a building, esp. a church, with an open arcade. 회랑(回廊). **2** a place in which a special religious life is lived; a nunnery; a monastery. 수도원; 수녀원. **3** a quiet, retired place. 은둔처.
— *vt.* (P6) keep (someone) in a monastery or convent; shut away in a quiet place. …을 수도원〔수녀원〕에 가두다; 세상에서 격리시키다. [→close[1]]

clois·tered [klɔ́istərd] *adj.* having a cloister walk; retired from the world. 회랑(回廊)이 있는; 세상을 등진. ¶ *a* ~ *life* 세상을 등진 생활; 은둔 생활.

clois·tral [klɔ́istrəl] *adj.* of a cloister. 수도원의; 은둔한.

clo·nus [klóunəs] *n.* 《med.》 a series of muscular contractions. 간대성(間代性)〔간헐성〕 경련. [Gk.]

:close[1] [klouz] *vt.* (P6,7) **1** shut; make fast. …을 닫다; 다물다; (눈을) 감다. ¶ ~ *a door* 문을 닫다 / ~ *a book* 책을 덮다 / ~ *shutters* 〔*blinds*〕 셔터〔블라인드〕를 내리다 / ~ *an umbrella* 우산을 접다 / ~ *one's mouth* 〔*eyes*〕 입을 다물다〔눈을 감다〕 / ~ *the door to someone* 문을 닫고 아무를 들이지 않다 / ~ *one's eyes to* …에 일부러 눈을 감(고 못 본 체하)다; …을 일부러 무시하다. **2** fill (an opening); stop up; prevent (passage). (구멍·틈)을 막다〔메우다〕; (…로의) 통로를 막다; 폐쇄하다. ¶ ~ *a border to tourists* 여행자에게 국경 통과를 금지하다 / *The street was closed to traffic during the parade.* 행진이 있는 동안 가로는 통행이 폐쇄되었다. **3** stop work, business, etc. (사무·영업 따위)를 끝내다; 쉬다; 휴업〔폐점〕하다. ¶ ~ *a store for the night* 밤에는 가게를 닫다 / ~ *one's business on Sundays* 일요일에는 가게를 쉬다 / ~ *business at 5 p.m.* 오후 다섯 시 폐점 / *Closed today.* 오늘 휴업《게시》 / *When does the shop* ~? 가게는 언제 닫습니까. **4** bring (something) to an end. …을 끝내다; 마감하다. ¶ ~ *one's speech* 〔*debate*〕 연설〔토론〕을 끝내다 / ~ *the books* 결산하다 / ~ *one's military career* 군인 생활을 끝내다 / ~ *the subscription list* 기부의 접수를 마감하다. **5** bring (things) together; join; unite. …을 잇다; 결합하다; (열을) 죄다. **6** arrange the final details of. (상품·거래 따위)를 최종적으로 매듭짓다. ¶ ~ *a sale on a car* 자동차의 상담을 타결짓다. — *vi.* (P1,2A,3) **1** become shut 〔closed〕. (문 따위가) 닫히다; 막히다. ¶ *The window won't* ~ *tight.* 창문이 꼭 닫히지 않는다 / *The shop closes at five.* 가게는 다섯 시에 닫는다. **2** come to an end. 끝나다. ¶ *The service closed with a hymn.* 예배는 찬송가로 끝났다 / *The speech abruptly closed.* 연설이 갑자기 끝났다. **3** ⓐ come near; approach. (바짝) 접근하다. ¶ *They closed on the heels of the runner.* 그들은 주자(走者)의 바로 뒤를 바짝 따라붙었다. ⓑ come together; join. 붙다; (눈이) 감기다; 다물어지다; 오므라지다. ¶ *Her lips closed firmly.* 입술이 꽉 다물어져 있었다. ⓒ 《often *with*》 rush to attack, capture, etc. 맞붙어 싸우다; 접근전을 하다. ¶ ~ *with the enemy* 적과 접전하다.

close about 〔(***a***)***round***〕, surround; encircle. 둘러〔에워〕싸다. ¶ *Darkness closed me around.* 내 주위는 어둠에 감싸였다.

close a deal (***with***), settle a business agreement. 상담을 매듭짓다; 계약을 맺다.

close down, **a**) bring to an end the work of. 사업〔영업〕을 그만두다; 중지하다; 걷어치우다; 폐업〔폐쇄〕하다. ¶ ~ *down a shop* 가게를 걷어치우다 / ~ *down an air base because of budget cuts* 예산 삭감 때문에 공군 기지를 폐쇄하다. **b**) stop; suppress. …을 금지〔억압〕하다. ¶ *The law closed down on gambling.* 법은 도박을 금했다. **c**) (of a radio or television station) stop broadcasting for the night. 방송을 종료하다.

close in, **a**) draw nearer and surround. 육박하다; 날이 저물다; 밤이 다가오다. ¶ *The enemy is closing in* (*on us*). 적군이 다가오고 있다 / *The night has closed in.* 밤이 다가왔다.

b) grow shorter. 해가 점점 짧아지다. ¶ *The days are closing in.* 낮이 점점 짧아지고 있다. **c**) shut in. 가두다. **d**) enclose; surround. 에워[둘러]싸다. ¶ *The garden is closed in by walls.* 정원은 담으로 둘러싸여 있다.

close out, 《U.S.》 sell (all goods), usu. by a bargain sale. (재고품을) 염가로 판매하다.

close up, **a**) come nearer together (esp. of persons in a line). (열 따위가) 좁혀지다; 밀집 대형으로 되다. **b**) (of a wound) unite; heal up. (상처가) 아물다. **c**) shut or stop up entirely. 꼭 막아버리다; 폐쇄하다. ¶ *The old well has been closed up.* 그 오래된 우물은 지금 폐쇄되어 있다.

close with, **a**) come nearer in order to attack (someone). …에 접근[육박]하다. **b**) accept (an offer, etc.); settle an agreement with; make a bargain with. …을 수락하다; 계약을 맺다; 상담을 매듭짓다. ¶ *I am willing to ~ with your terms.* 당신의 조건들을 기꺼이 수락합니다. **c**) grapple with. …와 맞붙어 싸우다.

—*n.* Ⓒ **1** a conclusion; an end. 종결; 끝; 종말; 결말. ¶ *at the ~ of a year* 연말에 / *the ~ of a meeting* [*war*] 회의[전쟁]의 종결 / *bring* (*something*) *to a ~* …을 끝내다[끝맺다] / *The winter drew to a ~.* 겨울도 종말이 다가왔다. **2** a struggle. 맞붙어 싸움; 격투; 접전. **3** an enclosed place. 둘러싸인 곳; 경내; 구내. [L. *claudo* shut]

:close² [klous] *adj.* **1** fast shut. 꼭 닫은[닫힌]; 밀폐한(opp. open). ¶ *a ~ box* 꼭 닫힌 상자. **2** confined; strictly guarded. 감금된; 경비가 엄중한. ¶ *a ~ prison* 감시가 엄중한 감옥 / *under ~ observation* 엄중한 감시하에. **3** 《*to*》 (of space, time, etc.) near. (공간적·시간적으로) 가까운; 접근한. ¶ *a ~ view* 가까이서 본 조망 / *in ~ contact* 밀접히 접촉하여 / *keep ~ to the wall* 담에 바싹 접근해 있다 / *She came* [*stepped*] *~ to him.* 그녀는 그에게로 다가왔다 / *The two houses were ~ to each other.* 두 집은 서로 가까이 있었다. **4** intimately associated; very friendly. 친(밀)한. ¶ *a ~ friend* 아주 절친한 친구. **5** ⓐ not widely separated; crowded. 밀집한. ¶ *a ~ thicket* 빽빽이 우거진 숲; 밀림 / *a troop in ~ formation* 밀집 대형의 군대 / *march in ~ order* 밀집 대형으로 행군하다. ⓑ tightly made; dense; compact. 발이 고운; 촘촘한. ¶ *a ~ texture* 발이 고운 직물. **6** careful; strict. 면밀한; 정밀한; 엄밀한. ¶ *a ~ attention to detail* 세부에 걸친 면밀한 주의 / *keep a ~ watch on* …을 주의깊게 감시하다 / *make a ~ study* 면밀히 연구하다 / *read with ~ attention* 주의깊게 읽다. **7** nearly even or equal in ability, power, etc.; without much difference. 백중한; 호각의. ¶ *a ~ combat* [*fight*] 접전 / *a ~ game* 호각의 경기. **8** not liberal (in money); stingy. 인색한. ¶ *live ~* 알뜰히 살다 / *be ~ with one's money* 돈에 인색하다. **9** lacking space; narrow. 비좁은; 옹색한. ¶ *~ quarters* 비좁은 곳. **10** lacking fresh air; stifling; oppressive. 환기가 나쁜; 답답한. ¶ *a hot, ~ room* 후텁지근하고 답답한 방 / *~ weather* 답답한 날씨. **11** limited by law. 금렵(禁獵)의; 금어(禁漁)의. ¶ *a closed season on deer* 사슴 금렵기(期). **12** near in kind or relationship. (종류·관계에 있어) 가까운. ¶ *a ~ relative* 가까운 친척; 근친 / *a ~ flower to a lily* 백합에 가까운 꽃 / *a state ~ to hysteria* 히스테리에 가까운 상태 / *There is a ~ resemblance between them.* 둘 사이엔 크게 닮은 데가 있다. **13** shut away from observation; hidden; secluded. (가만히) 숨은; 숨겨진; 내밀의. ¶ *a ~ design* 음모 / *keep a matter ~* 일을 숨겨 두다 / *keep oneself ~* 숨어 있다. **14** concealing one's thoughts or feelings; cautious; reserved. (생각·감정을) 숨기는; 신중한. **15** 《*colloq.*》 (of money) difficult to get; scarce. (돈에) 궁핍한; (금융이) 핍박 상태에 있는. **16** (of hair, lawn, etc.) cut short. (두발·잔디를) 짧게 깎은; (수염을) 깨끗이 민.

keep [***lie***] ***close,*** hide oneself. 숨어 있다.

keep something close, keep something secret. …을 비밀로 하다.

press someone close, treat someone severely. …을 호되게 대하다.

—*adv.* closely. 접근하여; 밀접히; 짧게; 꼭 맞아. [↑]

close at hand, near by. (시간적·공간적으로) 가까운; 절박[박두(迫頭)]한.

close by, quite near. 바로 가까이[근처에].

close on [***upon***]***,*** about; almost. 거의; 대략 …가까이. ¶ *~ on fifty years ago* 약 50 년 전에 / *be ~ upon 10 o'clock* 대략 열 시 가까이 되다.

keep close, lie close; hide oneself; hide. 숨다; 숨기다.

close call [´ ´] *n.* 《*colloq.*》 a narrow escape. 아슬아슬한 탈출; 위기 일발.

close-cropped [klóuskrápt / -krɔ́pt] *adj.* (of hair) cut very short. (두발을) 짧게 깎은.

close-cut [klóuskʌ́t] *adj.* =close-cropped.

closed circuit [´ ⌣´] *n.* **1** 《electr.》 an electric current without any break in continuity. 폐회로(閉回路)(cf. *open circuit*). **2** a television service restricted to viewers. 유선(有線) 텔레비전 방식.

closed shop [´ ´] *n.* a shop that employs trade union members only. 노조원(勞組員)만을 채용하는 사업장[공장](opp. open shop).

close-fit·ting [klóusfítiŋ] *adj.* fitting tightly to the body. (몸에) 꼭 맞는.

close-grained [klóusgréind] *adj.* having a grain which is fine and close, such as mahogany. (마호가니 목재 처럼) 결이 촘촘한; 나뭇결이 고운.

close-hauled [klóushɔ́:ld] *adj.* 《naut.》 having sails set windward for sailing. (바람을 옆으로 받도록) 돛을 눕혀 편.

:close·ly [klóusli] *adv.* in a close manner; tightly; intently. 접근하여; 바싹 조여; 꽉; 친밀히; (몸에) 꼭 맞아; 주의깊게. ¶ *watch (something)* ~ …을 주의깊게 지켜보다 / ~ *packed* 꽉 들어찬 / *Her coat fits* ~. 그녀 코트가 몸에 꼭 맞는다.

close·ness [klóusnis] *n.* **1** the state of being close. 가까움; 접근; 치밀. **2** narrowness. 비좁음. **3** lack of fresh air. 환기가 나쁨; 답답함. **4** nearness. 친밀함. ¶ *the* ~ *of our friendship* 우리들 우정의 친밀함. **5** stinginess. 인색함.

close quarters [´- ´--] *n. pl.* **1** close contact with the enemy. 접(근)전; 백병전. ¶ *come to* ~ 접전이 되다. **2** a place or position with little space. 비좁은 장소; 옹색한 곳.

***clos·et** [klάzit / klɔ́z-] *n.* Ⓒ **1** a small, private room. 작은 방; 사실(私室). **2** 《U.S.》 a cupboard for storing clothes, china, linen, etc. 반침; 벽장. ¶ *a clothes* ~ 의상실; (붙박이) 옷장. **3** a toilet; a water closet. 변소; 화장실.
— *vt.* shut up (someone) in a private room for a secret talk. (밀담을 위해) …을 사실(私室)에 가두다. 語法 흔히 재귀적으로 또는 과거 분사로 쓰임. [L. *claudo* shut]
be closeted with, have a secret talk with (someone). …와 밀담하다. ¶ *He was closeted with the American ambassador.* 그는 미국 대사와 밀담을 했다.

close-up [klóusʌ̀p] *n.* Ⓒ **1** 《photo.》 a picture taken at very close range. 클로즈업; 근접 촬영; 대사(大寫). **2** a close view. 아주 가까운 광경. [↑]

clo·sure [klóuʒər] *n.* Ⓒ **1** the act of closing; the state of being closed; anything that closes. 폐쇄(상태); 폐지; 마감; 닫는〔잠그는〕 것. **2** ⓐ an end; a conclusion. 끝; 종지(終止); 종결. ⓑ (in Parliament) the closing of a debate by vote. (의회에서) 토의 종결. — *vt.* (P6) apply closure to; end by closure. …을 종결시키다. [↑]

clot [klαt / klɔt] *n.* Ⓒ a half-solid lump. 엉겨붙은 덩어리; 응괴(凝塊). ¶ *a blood* ~ 엉긴 핏덩어리. — *vi., vt.* (**clot·ted, clot·ting**) (P1;6) form or cause (liquid) to form into clots. 엉겨붙(게 하)다; 응결하다〔시키다〕. ¶ *Blood clots when it is exposed to air.* 피는 공기에 노출되면 엉겨붙는다. [E.]

:cloth [klɔ(:)θ, klαθ] *n.* (*pl.* **cloths** [klɔðz, klɔθs] 參考 복수형 발음 [-ðz]는 pieces of cloth, [-θs]는 kinds of cloth의 뜻으로 흔히 씀) **1** Ⓤ a material made by weaving wool, cotton, silk, etc. 천; 직물; 옷감. ¶ *cotton* ~ 무명천. **2** Ⓒ a piece of this material for some special purpose; a tablecloth, etc. 특수 용도의 천《제단보 따위》; 테이블보; 걸레 따위. ¶ *lay the* ~ 테이블보를 깔다. **3** Ⓒ customary clothing. (직업을 나타내는) 제복. **4** 《*the* ~》 the profession, esp. of clergymen. 성직(聖職). ¶ *men* 〔*gentlemen*〕 *of the* ~ 목사; 성직자 / *pay the respect due to the* ~ 성직자에게 합당한 경의를 표하다 / *renounce the* ~ 성직을 버리다. [E.]
cut one's coat according to one's cloth, live within one's means. 분수에 맞는 생활을 하다.
remove 〔***draw***〕 ***the cloth,*** clear away the table things. (식사 후에) 식탁을 치우다.

:clothe [klouð] *vt.* (**clothed** or 《*arch., lit.*》 **clad**) (P6,13) **1** 《usu. replaced by *dress*》 put clothes on (someone); give (someone) clothes; dress. …에게 옷을 입히다; 의복을 공급하다. ¶ *a girl clad in a bathing suit* 수영복을 입은 소녀 / ~ *one's wife and family* 처와 가족에게 옷을 마련해주다 / *He clothed himself in his Sunday best.* 그는 나들이옷을 입었다 / *She was clothed in wool.* 그녀는 모직(毛織) 옷을 입고 있었다. **2** 《*fig.*》 cover as if with clothes; express. (옷을 입힌 듯) …을 덮다; 표현하다. ¶ *a garden clothed with pine trees* 온통 소나무가 우거져 있는 정원 / ~ *one's face with smiles* 만면에 웃음을 띄우다 / *The trees are clothed in green leaves.* 나무들은 푸른 잎으로 뒤덮여 있다 / *We* ~ *our thoughts in suitable words.* 우리는 적절한 말로 우리의 생각을 나타낸다. **3** give power to (someone); give (power, etc.) to someone. (특히 권력)을 …에게 부여하다. ¶ *clothed with authority* 권위가 부여된 / ~ *someone with authority* 아무에게 권위를 주다. [E.]

:clothes [klouðz] *n. pl.* **1** coverings for the body. 옷; 의복. ¶ *a* ~ *tree* (기둥 모양의) 코트·모자걸이 / *a suit of* ~ 옷 한 벌 / *in one's best* 〔*everyday*〕 ~ 외출복〔평상복〕을 입고 / *put on* 〔*take off*〕 *one's* ~ 옷을 입다〔벗다〕 / 《*prov.*》 *Fine* ~ *make the man.* 옷이 날개. **2** bedclothes. 침구(寢具); 이부자리. [E.]

clothes bag [´- ´] *n.* a bag for holding and carrying clothes to be washed. 세탁물 주머니.

clothes basket [´- ´--] *n.* a basket for holding and carrying the laundry. 빨랫광주리; 세탁물 광주리.

clothes·brush [klóuðzbrʌ̀ʃ] *n.* Ⓒ a brush for freeing clothes from dust or mud. 양복솔; 옷솔.

clothes horse [´- ´] *n.* a frame on which to hang clothes for drying or airing. 빨래 너는 틀.

clothes·line [klóuðzlàin] *n.* Ⓒ a rope or wire on which to hang clothes for drying or airing. 빨랫줄.

clothes peg [´- ´] *n.* 《Brit.》 =clothespin.

clothes·pin [klóuðzpìn] *n.* Ⓒ 《U.S.》 a small clip for fastening clothes on a line. 빨래 물리개〔무집게〕.

clothes·press [klóuðzprès] *n.* Ⓒ a chest, closet, etc. for storing clothes. 옷장.

cloth·ier [klóuðjər, -ðiər] *n.* Ⓒ a seller or maker of clothing; a dealer in cloth.

나사상(羅紗商); 옷(감)장수; 피복상; 직물 제조상〔판매상〕; 피륙상.

:cloth·ing [klóuðiŋ] *n.* Ⓤ 《*collectively*》 **1** clothes. 의류(衣類); 의복. ¶ *an article* 〔*a piece*〕 *of* ~ 옷가지 1점. **2** covering. 덮개.

clot·ted [klátid / klɔ́t-] *adj.* thickened; coagulated. 엉겨 굳은; 응고한. [E.]

clot·ty [kláti / klɔ́ti] *adj.* full of clots; tending to clot. 덩어리가 많은; 덩어리지기 쉬운. [E.]

clo·ture [klóutʃər] *n.* 《U.S.》 Ⓒ a way of ending a discussion in Congress. (의회에서의) 토의 종결. 參考 closure 라고도 하며 미국 의회 용어. [F.]

:cloud [klaud] *n.* Ⓤ **1** ⓊⒸ ⓐ a white or gray mass of water vapor floating in the sky. 구름. ¶ *a sea of* ~ 운해(雲海) / *mountains covered with clouds* 구름에 싸인 산들 / *The sun is sometimes hidden by clouds.* 해는 때로는 구름에 가려진다. ⓑ 《*pl.*》 the sky. 하늘. **2** a mass of smoke, sand, dust, etc. 자욱이 피어오르는 연기〔모래; 티끌; 먼지 따위〕. ¶ *a* ~ *of dust* 자욱한 먼지. **3** a great multitude; a cloud-like mass. 구름떼(같은 무리); 대군(大群). ¶ *a* ~ *of flies* 새까만 파리떼 / *a* ~ *of locusts obscuring the sun* 햇빛을 가릴 정도의 엄청난 메뚜기떼 / *a* ~ *of arrows* 어지러이 날아가는 무수한 화살. **4** 《*fig.*》 anything which darkens or causes fear. 어둡게〔우려하게〕 하는 것. ¶ *under the* ~ *of night* 야음을 틈타 / *a* ~ *on someone's happiness* 아무의 행복에 드리운 그늘 / *have a* ~ *on one's brow* 어두운 얼굴을 하고 있다 / *He is under a* ~. 그는 혐의를〔의심을〕 받고 있다 / *The clouds of war hang over the Middle East.* 중동 지역에 전운(戰雲)이 감돈다. **5** a streak or spot, as in marble. (대리석·보석 따위의) 흐림; 흠집. ¶ *take a* ~ *off the glass* 거울의 흐림을 닦아 없애다.

be under a cloud, be at a disadvantage; be under suspicion; be in trouble. 노여움을 사고 있다; 의혹을〔혐의를〕 받고 있다; 곤혹스러워 하고 있다.

in the clouds, **a**) far up in the sky. 하늘 높이. **b**) absent-minded; given to day-dreaming. 멍청히; 공상에 빠져. **c**) fanciful; imaginary. 가공의; 비실제적인.

— *vt.* (P6) **1** cover (something) with, or as with, clouds; dim; darken. …을 흐리게〔어둡게〕 하다. **2** make (something) gloomy; darken (something) with trouble. …에 어두운 그림자를 던지다; …을 괴롭히다. ¶ ~ *one's happiness* 행복에 어두운 그림자를 던지다. — *vi.* (P1,2A) be overcast with, or as with, clouds. 흐려지다; 어두워지다. ¶ *The sky has clouded* (*over*). 하늘이 (잔뜩) 흐려졌다. [E. =clod]

cloud·burst [kláudbə̀ːrst] *n.* a sudden, violent rainfall. (갑자기 퍼붓는) 억수; 호우.

cloud-capped [kláudkæ̀pt] *adj.* having clouds around the top. 구름 위로 치솟은.

cloud-cas·tle [kláudkæ̀sl] *n.* a castle in the air. 몽상; 공상; 백일몽.

cloud-drift [kláuddrìft] *n.* clouds in motion. 뜬〔열〕구름.

cloud·i·ness [kláudinis] *n.* Ⓤ the state of being cloudy. 흐림; 어두움.

cloud-kiss·ing [kláudkìsiŋ] *adj.* sky-high. 하늘을 찌르는. ¶ *a* ~ *mountain* 구름 위에 솟은 산.

cloud·land [kláudlæ̀nd] *n.* a realm of fantasy. 공상의 세계; 꿈나라.

cloud·less [kláudlis] *adj.* clear; bright; without clouds. 맑은; 갠; 구름없는.

cloud·scape [kláudskèip] *n.* a picture of clouds. 구름이 있는 풍경; 운경(雲景)(화(畫)).

cloud-seed·ing [kláudsìːdiŋ] *n.* scattering particles of chemicals in clouds so as to increase or produce rain. 인공 강우법(降雨法).

·cloud·y [kláudi] *adj.* (**cloud·i·er, cloud·i·est**) **1** covered with clouds. 흐린; 구름으로 뒤덮인. ¶ ~ *weather* 흐린 날씨. **2** of or like clouds. 구름의; 구름 같은. **3** not clear; dark; dim. 흐릿한; 맑지 않은; 어렴풋한. ¶ *a* ~ *picture* 희미한 사진 / *a* ~ *liquid* 탁한 액체 / ~ *ideas* 애매 모호한 생각. **4** spotted. 반점〔얼룩〕이 있는. ¶ ~ *marble* 얼룩이 있는 대리석. **5** gloomy; troubled. 우울한; 찌무룩한. ¶ ~ *looks* 어두운 얼굴 / *one's* ~ *mood* 우울한 기분.

clout [klaut] *n.* Ⓒ **1** 《*colloq.*》 a blow; a rap. (특히 손으로) 때림; 강타. ¶ *a* ~ *on the head* 머리의 강타 / *give someone a* ~ 아무를 세게 때리다. **2** 《archery》 a target made of white cloth; a shot that hits this. (흰천으로 만든) 과녁; 적중. ¶ *in the* ~ 맞히어. **3** 《*arch.*》 a patch; a piece of cloth for cleaning a desk, the floor, etc. (깁는) 천조각; 걸레. — *vt.* (P6) **1** patch or mend roughly (esp. of boots and shoes). (구두·신 따위)를 조각을 대어 깁다. **2** 《*colloq.*》 blow; rap. …을 탁 때리다. [E.]

clove[1] [klouv] *n.* Ⓒ **1** the dried flower bulbs of a tropical tree, used as a strong-smelling spice. (짙은 향료로 쓰이는) 정향(丁香). **2** the tree which produces cloves. 정향나무. [L. *clavus* nail]

clove[2] [klouv] *n.* Ⓒ a small, divided section of a compound bulb, as in a lily. (백합 등의 어미뿌리의) 작은 인경(鱗莖). [→ cleave[1]]

clove[3] [klouv] *v.* p. of **cleave.**

clove·hitch [klóuvhìtʃ] *n.* 《naut.》 a form of hitch for fastening a rope around a bar. (밧줄의) 감아매기《결삭법(結索法)의 하나》.

clov·en [klóuvən] *adj.* split; divided. 갈라진; 째진. ¶ *Cows have* ~ *hoofs.* 암소의 발굽은 갈라져 있다.

show the cloven hoof, betray oneself; throw off the mask. 본색을 드러내다.

clo·ven-foot·ed [klóuvənfútid], **-hoofed**

[-hú:ft] *adj.* **1** having cloven feet. 발굽이 갈라진. **2** like a devil. 악마와 같은.

*__clo·ver__ [klóuvər] *n.* Ⓒ a low-growing plant of the same family as the pea; any similar plant. 클로버; 토끼풀. [E.]
live* 〔*be*〕 *in clover, live in luxury and ease. 호화롭게 살다; 아무 부자유도 없이 살다.

clo·ver·leaf [klóuvərlì:f] *n.* (*pl.* **-leaves**) a system of road construction in which one highway crosses another on a higher level. 입체 교차로.

clown [klaun] *n.* Ⓒ **1** a man whose business is to amuse others by jokes and foolish behavior, as in a circus. 어릿광대. ¶ *play the* ~ 익살떨다. **2** an impolite person; a silly person. 뒤틈바리.
— *vi.* (P1) act like a clown; act silly. 어릿광대짓을 하다; 괘사 떨다. [→clod]

clown·ish [kláuniʃ] *adj.* **1** of or like a clown. 어릿광대의〔같은〕. **2** impolite; ill-mannered; rough. 버릇없는; 막된.

cloy [klɔi] *vt.* (P6) 《*with*》 make (someone) weary by too much of something. 넌더리나게 하다; 물리게 하다. ¶ *be cloyed with pleasure* 쾌락에 물리다 / ~ *by the sweets* 단것에 물리다. [E.]

:**club** [klʌb] *n.* Ⓒ **1** a heavy stick of wood. 곤봉. **2** a stick or bat used for hitting a ball in certain games. 타구봉(棒). ¶ *golf clubs* 골프채. **3** a group of people joined together for a certain purpose; a clubhouse. 클럽; 동호회; 클럽 회관. ¶ *a social* 〔*tennis*〕 ~ 사교〔테니스〕 클럽 / *an Alpine* ~ 산악회. **4** ⓐ a playing card with one or more black marks shaped like clover leaves on it. (카드놀이의) 클럽. ⓑ 《*pl.*》 the suit formed by these cards. 클럽의 패 (전부). ¶ *the king of clubs* 클럽의 킹.
— *vt.* (**clubbed, club·bing**) **1** (P6,7) beat or hit (something) with a club. …을 곤봉으로〔몽둥이로〕 때리다. ¶ ~ *a dog to death* 개를 때려 죽이다 / ~ *with a rifle* 소총으로 때리다. **2** (P6) use as a club. 곤봉 대용으로 쓰다. ¶ ~ *a rifle* 소총을 거꾸로 쥐고 몽둥이로 쓰다. **3** combine (people or things) for some common purpose. …을 한데 모으다; 결속〔단결〕시키다. ¶ ~ *persons together* 사람들을 한데 모으다. — *vi.* (P2A) 《*with*》 join together for a certain purpose. 클럽을 조직하다; 합동〔결속〕하다. [E.]

club·foot [klʌ́bfùt] *n.* Ⓒ (*pl.* **-feet**) an unnaturally formed foot from birth. 내반족(內反足).

club·foot·ed [klʌ́bfùtid] *adj.* having a clubfoot. 내반족(內反足)의.

club·haul [klʌ́bhɔ̀:l] *vt.* (P6) 《naut.》 tack by anchoring and cutting the cable. 바람 불어가는 쪽의 닻을 내려 방향을 바꾸다.

club·house [klʌ́bhàus] *n.* Ⓒ a building used by a club. 클럽 회관.

club·law [klʌ́blɔ̀:] *n.* the reign of force. 폭력; 폭력 지배.

cluck [klʌk] *n.* Ⓒ a cry made by a hen in calling her chickens. (암탉의 병아리 부르는) 꼬꼬 소리. — *vi.* (P1) make a cluck-like cry. (암탉이) 꼬꼬거리다. [Imit.]

clue [klu:] *n.* Ⓒ something that helps to solve a mystery, a problem, etc. 단서; 실마리. ¶ *get* 〔*find*〕 *a* ~ *to a question* 문제 해결에의 실마리를 얻다〔찾다〕 / *I have no* ~ *to it.* 그 단서는 전연 없다 / *The murderer left one* ~ — *a fingerprint.* 살인범은 한 가지 단서 즉 지문을 남겼다. [E.]

clump [klʌmp] *n.* Ⓒ **1** a group of trees, shrubs, etc. that grow closely together. 빽빽이 들어선 나무 따위; 숲. ¶ *a* ~ *of bamboos* 대숲. **2** a lump, as of earth. (흙 따위의) 덩어리. ¶ *a* ~ *of earth* 흙덩어리. **3** a sound of heavy footsteps. 무거운 발소리.
— *vt.* plant (trees, etc.) in clusters. (나무 따위)를 군생(群生)시키다. — *vi.* (P1) tramp heavily. 무거운 걸음으로 걷다. ¶ *The lame man clumped away.* [E.]

clum·sy [klʌ́mzi] *adj.* (**-si·er, -si·est**) **1** not skillful; lacking grace; awkward. (솜씨가) 야무지지 못한; 서투른; 어색한. ¶ *be* ~ *with one's hands* 손끝이 야무지지 못하다 / *be* ~ *at a task* 일이 서투르다 / *be* ~ *in one's movements* 동작이 어색하다. **2** not well-shaped or well-made; not elegant. 볼품없는. ¶ *a* ~ *tool* 투박한 연장. ● **clum·si·ly** [-li] *adv.* **clum·si·ness** [-nis] *n.* [E.→clem]

clung [klʌŋ] *v.* p. and pp. of **cling.**

*__clus·ter__ [klʌ́stər] *n.* Ⓒ **1** a number of things of the same kind growing or gathered together. (과실·꽃 따위의) 덩어리; 송이. ¶ *a* ~ *of grapes* 포도 한 송이. **2** a group of persons and things. (사람·물건의) 집단; 떼. ¶ *bees in a* ~ 벌떼 / *a* ~ *of spectators* 일단의 구경꾼들 / *in a* ~ = *in clusters* 떼지어.
— *vi.* (P2A,3) form a cluster or clusters. 덩어리〔송이〕를 이루다; 주렁주렁 열리다; 군생(群生)하다; 떼를 이루다; 모이다. ¶ *The girls clustered around the old man.* 소녀들은 그 노인 주위에 모여들었다. — *vt.* (P6) gather (things or persons) into a cluster or clusters. …을 떼짓게 하다. ¶ *Most of foreign embassies are clustered in this area.* 대개의 외국 대사관은 이 지역에 몰려 있다. [E.]

*__clutch__ [klʌtʃ] *n.* ⓊⒸ **1** a firm hold; a tight grasp. 꽉 잡음〔쥠〕. ¶ *make a* ~ *at* …을 움켜잡으려고 하다. **2** 《usu. *pl.*》 control; power; cruel grasp. 수중; 지배력; 독수(毒手); 마수. ¶ *be in the clutches of the police* 경찰에 잡혀 있다 / *beyond the clutches of circumstance* 주위의 영향에 좌우되지 않고. **3** a device in a machine for connecting or disconnecting the working parts; a grasping claw, hand, etc. (기계의) 연축기(連軸器); 클러치. **4** a brood of chickens. 한배의 병아리.
fall* 〔*get*〕 *in* (*to*) *the clutches of, get into (someone's) power. …의 수중〔손아귀〕에

떨어지다. ¶ *The soldier fell into the clutches of the enemy.* 병사는 적군에 사로잡혔다.

get out of the clutches of, get out of (someone's) power. …의 손아귀[독수(毒手)]에서 벗어나다. ¶ *get out of a moneylender's clutches* 대금업자의 마수를 헤어나다.

— *vt.* (P6) hold [grasp] tightly. 꽉 잡다[쥐다]; 움켜잡다. ¶ ~ *hold of* …을 움켜잡다 / *She clutched her handbag to her breast.* 그녀는 핸드백을 가슴에 꼭 껴안고 있었다.

— *vi.* (P1,3) 《*at*》 catch eagerly; snatch. 잡으려 들다; 덤벼[달려]들다. ¶ 《*prov.*》 *A drowning man will ~ at a straw.* 물에 빠진 사람은 지푸라기라도 잡는다. [E. = claw; N. = hatch]

clut·ter [klʌ́tər] *n.* Ⓤ a disorder; confused noises. 난잡; 혼란 (상태); 소동. ¶ *be in a ~* (실내 따위가) 어지럽게 흩어져 있다. — *vt.* (P6,7) make (a room) dirty by distributing things in a disorderly manner. …을 어지러이 흩뜨려 놓다. ¶ *His study was cluttered (up) with books and papers.* 그의 서재에는 책과 신문들이 흩어져 있었다. — *vi.* (P1,3) make a confused noise. 시끄러운 소리를 내다. ¶ ~ *along* 시끄럽게 뛰다. [→clot]

cm, cm. centimeter; centimeters.

Co 《chem.》 cobalt.

Co. [kou, kʌ́mpəni] *n.* Company. 회사. ¶ *Jones & Co.* 존스 회사.

co. county.

c.o., c/o 1 (in) care of. …씨 전교(轉交); …방(方). **2** carried over. 이월(移越).

co- [kou-] *pref.* with, together, joint; equally. '함께, 공동으로, 똑같이'의 뜻. ¶ *cooperate / coauthors.* [L.]

***coach** [koutʃ] *n.* Ⓒ **1** an old form of four-wheeled carriage with seats inside and often on top also; a state carriage. 대형 4륜 마차《흔히 네 필의 말이 끎》; (국왕·국빈용) 공식 마차. ¶ *a ~ and four* 사두(四頭) 대형 마차 / *a mourning ~* 장례 마차 / *a stagecoach* 역마차. **2** a passenger car of a railroad train; a railway carriage. (열차의) 객차. **3** an automobile like a sedan. 세단형 자동차. **4** a bus. 대형 버스. **5** a trainer of sports teams, etc.; a private teacher. (운동의) 코치; 지도원; 가정 교사; 개인 교사. ¶ *a baseball ~* 야구 코치.

— *vt.* (P6,13) **1** train or teach; prepare (students) for an examination. 코치하다; 훈련하다; (가정 교사가) 수험 지도를 하다. **2** transport by coach. coach 로 나르다.

— *vi.* (P1) **1** make ready for a special test; act as a coach. (가정 교사의 지도를 받아) 수험 준비를 하다; (경기의) 코치를 하다. ¶ ~ *for a living* 생활 지도를 하다. **2** ride in a coach. coach 를 타다; 마차로 여행하다. [Place]

coach·man [kóutʃmən] *n.* Ⓒ (*pl.* **-men** [-mən]) **1** a driver of a coach. 마부. **2** a kind of fish hook. 제물낚시.

co·ad·ju·tor [kouǽdʒətər, kòuədʒúːtər] *n.* Ⓒ **1** an assistant; a helper. 조수; 보좌인. **2** an assistant of a bishop. 보좌 신부; 사교보(司敎補). [→adjutant]

co·ag·u·late [kouǽgjəlèit] *vt.* (P6) cause (a liquid, etc.) to become a thickened mass. …을 엉겨붙게 하다; 응고시키다. ¶ *Vinegar coagulates milk.* 식초는 우유를 응고시킨다. — *vi.* (P1) (of a liquid) become a thickened mass. 엉기다; 응고하다. ● **co·ag·u·la·tor** [-tər] *n.* [L. *ago* bring]

co·ag·u·la·tion [kouæ̀gjəléiʃən] *n.* ⓊⒸ the act of coagulating; the state of being coagulated; a coagulated mass. 응고; 응고물; 엉긴 덩어리. ¶ *If ~ did not take place after a wound, the wounded person might bleed to death.* 부상 뒤에 응고 작용이 없다면 부상자는 출혈로 죽을 게다.

:**coal** [koul] *n.* **1** ⓐ Ⓤ black mineral material that burns; Ⓒ a piece of this. 석탄. ¶ *hard ~* 무연탄 / *soft ~* 역청탄 / *small ~* 분탄(粉炭) / *a red-hot ~* 시뻘겋게 이글거리는 석탄 / *put coals [coal] on the fire* (난롯)불에 석탄을 지피다. ⓑ 《*pl.*》 heap of coal ready for use. (아무 때고 때기 위한) 석탄 더미. ¶ *lay in coals* 석탄을 저장하다. **2** Ⓤ charcoal. 숯; 목탄.

as black as (a) coal, very black. 새까만.

blow the coals, stir up one's anger. 노여움[싸움]을 부채질하다.

call [haul, rake, drag, take] someone over the coals for, scold or blame someone for (something). …을 호되게 꾸짖다[비난하다].

carry coals to Newcastle, do something unnecessary. 쓸데없는 짓을 하다. 參考 Newcastle은 석탄 산지.

heap [cast] coals of fire on someone's head, return good for evil. 악을 선으로 갚다.

— *vt.* (P6) supply with coal. 석탄을 공급하다. — *vi.* (P1) take in coal. 석탄을 싣다[실어들이다]. ¶ *The ship coaled at Gibraltar.* 배는 지브롤터에서 석탄을 실었다. [E. *col;* Gk. *kohle* charcoal]

coal-black [kóulblæ̀k] *adj.* very black. 새까만; 시커먼. ¶ ~ *hair* 새까만 머리.

coal-cel·lar [kóulsèlər] *n.* a small usu. underground room where coal is stored. 지하 석탄고.

coal·er [kóulər] *n.* Ⓒ **1** a ship, a railroad, etc. that carries or supplies coal. 석탄선(船); 석탄 수송 철도. **2** a worker or merchant who supplies coal. 석탄 신는 사람; 석탄상(商).

co·a·lesce [kòuəlés] *vi.* (P1) **1** grow or come together. 유착(癒着)하다. **2** unite into one body, mass, party, etc.; combine. 일체가 되다; 합동[연합]하다. [L. *alo* nourish]

co·a·les·cence [kòuəlésns] *n.* Ⓤ **1** the act of growing or coming together. 유착(癒着). **2** union; combination. 합체(合體); 합동; 연합. ● **co·a·les·cent** [-snt] *adj.*

coal-field [kóulfì:ld] *n.* a district where beds of coal are found. 탄전. [→coal]

coal-gas [kóulgæ̀s] *n.* mixed gases extracted from coal; gas given off by burning coal. 석탄 가스.

coal-heav·er [kóulhì:vər] *n.* a man employed in moving coal. 석탄을 싣고 부리는 인부; 석탄 운반인.

coaling station [⌐–⌐–] *n.* a place where ships, trains, etc. can obtain supplies of coal. (기선에의) 급탄항(給炭港); (기관차의) 급탄소(所).

co·a·li·tion [kòuəlíʃən] *n.* **1** Ⓤ the act of joining together. 연합; 연립; 합동. **2** Ⓒ a group of statesmen, etc. cooperating for some special purpose for a short time. (정치인 등의 일시적) 결합; 결탁; 제휴. ¶ *a ~ cabinet* 〔*ministry*〕 연립 내각. [→coalesce]

coal-mas·ter [kóulmæ̀stər, -mɑ̀:stər] *n.* an owner of coal mine. 탄광주(主). [→coal]

coal-mine [kóulmàin] *n.* a mine or pit from which coal is obtained. 탄광. ● **coal-min·er** [-màinər] *n.*

coal-oil [kóulɔ̀il] *n.* 《U.S.》 **1** kerosene. 등유(燈油). **2** petroleum. 석유.

coal-pit [kóulpìt] *n.* a pit where coal is dug. 탄갱(炭坑).

coal-scut·tle [kóulskʌ̀tl] *n.* a box or bucket for holding and carrying coal for use in a room. (실내용) 석탄통.

coal-tar [kóultɑ̀:r] *n.* a black, sticky liquid material left after gas is made from coal. 콜타르.

coal-tit [kóultìt] *n.* 《bird》 a dark species of titmouse. 진박새.

coal·y [kóuli] *adj.* of or like coal. 석탄의; 석탄 같은.

coam·ing [kóumiŋ] *n.* 《naut.》 a raised border round a ship's hatches. (갑판 승강구 등의) 테두리판《물이 듦을 막음》. [?Du.=comb]

·**coarse** [kɔ:rs] *adj.* **1** not fine or small; not finely woven; rough. 발〔결〕이 곱지 않은; (알맹이가) 굵은; 거친(opp. fine). ¶ *~ cloth* 〔*weave*〕 발이 곱지 않은 천〔직물〕 / *~ sand* 굵은 모래 / *~ skin* 거친 피부. **2** rough; common; inferior; poor. 조잡한; 조악한; 열등한. ¶ *~ food* 거친 음식; 조식(粗食) / *~ clothes* 조의(粗衣) / *~ imitations* 조악한 모조품 / *~ grass* 잡초. **3** not delicate; not refined; not polite. (언동 따위가) 조야한; 세련되지 않은; 상스러운; 저속한. ¶ *a ~ taste* 세련되지 않은 취미 / *a ~ joke* 상스러운 농담 / *a man of ~ character* 성격이 거친 사나이 / *be ~ in manner* 〔*speech*〕 태도가〔말이〕 거칠다. [→course =ordinary]

coarse-grained [kɔ́:rsgréind] *adj.* having a coarse texture; not refined. 올〔결〕이 거친; 조잡한; 상스러운.

coarse·ly [kɔ́:rsli] *adv.* in a coarse manner. 거칠게; 조잡하게; 상스럽게.

coars·en [kɔ́:rsən] *vt., vi.* (P6; 1) make or become coarse. 조잡하게 하다; 조잡해지다; 거칠게 하다; 거칠어지다.

coarse·ness [kɔ́:rsnis] *n.* Ⓤ the quality or state of being coarse. 거칠음; 조잡; 저질.

:**coast** [koust] *n.* **1** Ⓒ the land along the edge of the sea; the seashore; the coastal region. 해안; 연안; 연안 지방. ¶ *on the ~* 연안 (지방)에(서) / *off the west ~ of an island* 섬의 서해 난바다에 / *sail along* 〔*by*〕 *the ~* 해안을 따라 항해하다. **2** 《*the C-*》 《U.S.》 the region along the Pacific Ocean. 태평양 연안 지방. **3** Ⓒ 《U.S.》 a slope on which a slide is taken; a slide or ride down a hill without the use of power. 썰매 타는 비탈; (썰매 따위의) 활강(滑降).

The coast is clear. There is nothing or no one in the way. (연안 경비가 없다는 말에서) 위험〔장애물〕은 사라졌다.

— *vi., vt.* **1** (P1; 6) sail〔go〕 along or near the coast; sail from port to port. 연안을 항해하다; 항구에서 항구로 항해하다. **2** (P1,2A) 《U.S.》 ride or slide down a hill without using effort or power. (썰매로) 활강하다; (자전거 따위가) 페달을 밟지 않고 내려가다. [L. *costa* side]

coast·al [kóustəl] *adj.* of, at, near, or along a coast. 연안〔연해〕의; 해안을 따른.

coast·er [kóustər] *n.* Ⓒ **1** a ship trading along a coast. 연안 무역선. **2** 《U.S.》 a sled or wagon to coast on. (비탈용) 썰매. **3** an amusement railway, such as a roller coaster. (오락용) 코스터. **4** a small tray or mat placed under a bottle, pitcher or drinking glass. (병·컵 따위의) 받침 접시; 밑받침.

coast·er-brake [kóustərbrèik] *n.* a clutch-brake of a bicycle enabling a rider to check his speed by back pressure on the pedals. 코스터브레이크.

coast guard [⌐⌐] *n.* **1** 《*C- G-*》 《U.S.》 a group of men working to save lives and prevent secret importing or exporting along the coast. 연안 경비대. 參考 평시에는 재무부, 전시에는 해군부의 직할로 들어감. **2** 《Brit.》 an officer on police duty along the coast; a group of such officers. 연안〔해안〕 경비대(원).

coast·guard·man [kóustgɑ̀:rdmən], **-guards-** [-gɑ̀:rdz-] *n.* Ⓒ (*pl.* **-men** [-mən]) a member of the coast guard. 연안 경비대원.

coast·ing [kóustiŋ] *adj.* going along the coast. 연안〔해안〕 항해의.

coast·land [kóustlæ̀nd] *n.* Ⓒ the region or land along a coast. 연안〔해안〕 지대.

coast·line [kóustlàin] *n.* Ⓒ the line or shape of a coast. 해안선.

coast·wise [kóustwàiz] *adv., adj.* along the coast. 연안에〔의〕; 해안을 따라; 근해의 (opp. overseas).

:**coat** [kout] *n.* Ⓒ **1** a piece of outer clothing

with sleeves; an overcoat. 웃옷; 상의; 외투. ¶ *a ~ and skirt* 여성용 슈트〔외출복〕/ *a ~ for formal wear* 정장에 어울리는 코트. **2** a natural outer covering of an animal or plant; skin; fur. (동식물의) 외피(外被); 막; 모피. ¶ *a ~ of bark on a tree* 나무의 수피(樹被) / *the coats of an onion* 양파의 껍질. **3** an outer layer of anything, as of paint or plaster. (페인트 따위의) 칠; 도장(塗裝); 켜; 층(層). ¶ *a ~ of dust* 보얗게 쌓인 먼지 / *give a door two coats of paint* 문에 페인트를 두 번 칠하다.

***cut** one's **coat according to** one's **cloth**,* live within one's income. 분수에 맞게 살다.

***find** 〔**pick**〕 **a hole** 〔**holes**〕 **in** someone's **coat**,* find a fault 〔faults〕 with someone. …의 흠〔탈〕을 잡다.

***take off** one's **coat**,* 《fig.》 prepare to fight; set about (a task) with energy. 싸울 채비를 갖추다; (일)에 본격적으로 대들다〔착수하다〕. ¶ *take off one's ~ to the work.*

***turn** 〔**change**〕 one's **coat**,* change one's ways or causes, esp. in politics. 변절하다.

***wear the king's** 〔**queen's**〕 **coat**,* 《Brit.》 be a soldier. 군복을 입다; 군인이 되다.

— *vt.* (P6,13) **1** cover or provide (something) with a coat. …에 웃옷을〔외피를〕 입히다. ¶ *The pill is coated with sugar.* 그 알약엔 당의가 입혀져 있다 / *The boy's tongue was coated white.* 그 아이의 혀에는 백태(白苔)가 끼어 있었다. **2** cover (something) with a layer of anything. (…에) …을 바르다〔칠하다〕. ¶ *~ the wall with paint* 벽에 페인트를 칠하다. [L. *cotta*]

coat·ee [koutíː] *n.* a short-tailed coat. 짧은 웃옷; 쇼트코트.

coat·ing [kóutiŋ] *n.* **1** Ⓒ Ⓤ a thin layer or covering. (얇게) 바름; 입힘. **2** Ⓤ material for making coats. 코트용(用) 옷감.

coat of arms [kóutəváːrmz] *n.* (*pl.* **coats of a-**) **1** a picture or design showing symbols of a family's history on a shield, used esp. by knights, noble families, etc. (방패꼴의) 문장(紋章). **2** a light garment decorated with such designs, and worn over armor. (갑옷 위에 덧입는) 문장 박힌 겉옷.

coat of mail [ˊ-ˊ] *n.* (*pl.* **coats of m-**) a piece of outer clothing made of metal rings or plates, worn by soldiers. 쇠미늘 갑옷.

co·au·thor [kouɔ́ːθər] *n.* a joint author. 공저자(共著者). [co-]

coax [kouks] *vt., vi.* (P6,7,13,20; 1) **1** 《*out, into*》 persuade by means of soft words. 달콤한 말로 …하게 하다. ¶ *~ a child out* 아이를 달래서 밖으로 데리고 나오다 / *~ a child to take* 〔*into taking*〕 *his medicine* 아이를 잘 달래서 약을 먹이다 / *I coaxed a smile from the baby.* 아기를 얼러서 웃게 했다. **2** get (something) by soft words. …을 감언으로 손에 넣다. ¶ *He coaxed the secret from her.* 그는 그녀를 구슬러 비밀(祕密)을 알아냈다.

● **coax·er** [-ər] *n.* [E. *cokes* a fool]

cob [kab / kɔb] *n.* Ⓒ **1** 《U.S.》 the center part of an ear of corn. 옥수수속. **2** a strong, short-legged horse for riding. 다리가 짧고 튼튼한 승용마(馬). **3** a male swan. 백조의 수컷. **4** 《*pl.*》 《chiefly Brit.》 a small mass or lump, as of coal. (석탄 따위의) 둥근 덩이. [E.]

co·balt [kóubɔːlt] *n.* Ⓤ **1** a hard, silver-white, metallic chemical element. 코발트. **2** a dark-blue. 코발트 그림물감; 감청색. [G.]

cobalt bomb [ˊ-ˊ] *n.* a hydrogen bomb incased in a shell of cobalt. 코발트 폭탄.

cob·ble[1] [kábəl / kɔ́bəl] *vt.* (P6) mend (shoes, etc.); patch; put (something) together unskillfully or roughly. (구두 등)을 고치다; …을 엉성한 솜씨로 깁다. [→ cobbler]

cob·ble[2] [kábəl / kɔ́bəl] *n.* Ⓒ **1** ⓐ 《usu. *pl.*》 a stone worn round and smooth by water. 조약돌; 자갈. ⓑ coals of cobble size. 둥근 석탄. **2** a pebble pavement. 자갈을 깐 길. — *vt.* pave (road, etc.) with cobblestones. (길 따위)에 자갈을 깔다. [E. *cob* lump]

cob·bler [káblər / kɔ́blər] *n.* Ⓒ **1** a mender of shoes. 구두 수리공; 신기료 장수. **2** an unskillful workman. 서투른 장색(匠色). **3** 《U.S.》 a fruit pie with a thick top crust. (껍질이 두껍고 파삭파삭한) 과일 파이. **4** an iced drink made of wine, fruit juice, sugar, etc. 청량 음료의 하나. [*cobelere*]

cob·ble·stone [káblstòun / kɔ́bl-] *n.* Ⓒ a rounded stone, formerly often used in paving. 조약돌; 자갈.

Cob·den·ism [kábdənìzəm / kɔ́b-] *n.* a policy based on Free Trade. 자유 무역주의. [Person]

co·bel·lig·er·ent [kòubəlídʒərənt] *n.* a nation that helps another nation carry on a war. 참전국. [co-]

COBOL, Co·bol [kóubɔːl] *n.* 《computer》 a programming language for a computer. 코볼; 사무용 공통프로그래밍 언어. [*Com*mon *B*usiness *O*riented *L*anguage]

co·bra [kóubrə] *n.* Ⓒ 《zool.》 a very poisonous snake of India and Africa. 코브라. [Port.]

cob·web [kábwèb / kɔ́b-] *n.* Ⓒ **1** a spider's web or a single thread of this. 거미집(의 줄). **2** anything like a spider's web. (거미줄같이) 얇고 섬세한 것. **3** 《*pl.*》 confusion; a lack of order. 헝클어짐; 혼란. ¶ *blow away the cobwebs from one's brain* (산책 따위로) 머릿속을 깨끗이 하다; 기분을 전환하다. [M.E. *coppe* spider]

cob·webbed [kábwèbd / kɔ́b-] *adj.* covered or filled with cobwebs. 거미줄을 친; 거미줄 투성이의.

coc·a [kóukə] *n.* 《bot.》 a Bolivian shrub; its dried leaves. 코카; 코카잎. [Peruv.]

Co·ca-Co·la [kóukəkóulə] *n.* 《trademark》 a kind of refreshing drink. 코카콜라.

co·caine, -cain [koukéin, ´–] *n.* Ⓤ a strong drug used to deaden pain. 코카인 《마취제》. [Peruv.]

co·cain·ism [koukéinizəm] *n.* a morbid state resulting from excessive use of cocaine. 코카인 중독증.

co·cain·ize, 《chiefly Brit.》 **-ise** [kou-kéinaiz] *vt.* (P6) treat with cocaine. 코카인으로 마비시키다.

coc·ci [káksai / kɔ́k-] *n.* pl. of **coccus.**

coc·cus [kákəs / kɔ́kəs] *n.* (*pl.* **coc·ci**) a bacterium shaped like a sphere. 구균(球菌). [Gk. *kokkos* berry]

coc·cy·ges [káksidʒìːz, kɔ́k-] *n.* pl. of **coccyx.**

coc·cyx [káksiks / kɔ́k-] *n.* (*pl.* **-cy·ges**) 《anat.》 the bone ending the spinal column. 미골(尾骨). [Gk. =cuckoo]

co·chin [kóutʃin, kátʃin] *n.* 《bird》 a breed of fowl. 코친(종(種)의 닭). [Place]

coch·i·neal [kátʃəniːl, ´–´, kóutʃə-] *n.* Ⓤ **1** a red coloring dye obtained from certain insects. 양홍(洋紅). **2** the insect itself. 연지벌레. [L. *coccum* scarlet]

:cock[1] [kak / kɔk] *n.* Ⓒ **1** ⓐ a male chicken. 수탉(opp. hen). ⓑ 《in *compounds*》 a male bird. 새의 수컷. ¶ *a peacock* 공작새 《수컷》 / *a cocksparrow* 수참새. **2** a tap for regulating the flow of water in a pipe. 수도꼭지. ¶ *at* 〔*on*〕 *full* ~ 꼭지를 다 틀어 / *turn on* 〔*off*〕 *a* ~ 꼭지를 틀다〔잠그다〕. **3** a hammer of a gun. (총의) 공이치기. ¶ *at full* ~ 공이치기를 완전히 당겨; 준비를 완전히 갖추고 / *at half* ~ 공이치기를 반쯤 당겨; 준비를 다 갖추지 못하고. **4** a weather vane in the shape of a cock. (수탉 모양의) 바람개비; 풍향계. **5** a leader; a chief; a headman. 두목; 수령; 보스. ¶ *the* ~ *of the school* 학교의 전체 수석 학생; 골목 대장. **6** 《*vulg.*》 a pennis. 음경(陰莖).

live like fighting cocks, live on the best possible food; live in a very rich manner. 미식(美食)하며 호화롭게 살다.

Old cock ! 《familiar and affectionate form of address》 old boy〔man〕. 여 자네; 여보게.

the cock of the loft 〔***walk, dunghill, roost***〕, the leading man in a small group; the most important person in a place. 두목; 유력자.

the cock that won't fight, the plan etc. that will not succeed. 잘 되지 않을 계획 (따위).

— *vt., vi.* (P6,7; 1,2A) **1** set (the hammer of a gun) to fire. (쏘기 위해 총의) 공이치기를 당기다. ¶ ~ *a pistol* 피스톨의 공이치기를 당기다《발사 준비를 하다》. **2** ⓐ turn up the brim of (a hat). (모자 챙)을 위로 젖히다. ⓑ raise (the ears, the tail, etc.) stiffly. (귀를) 쫑긋 세우다; (귀가) 쫑긋 서다; (꼬리 따위를) 빳빳이 위로 세우다〔서다〕. ¶ *The dog cocked its ears at the sound.* 개는 그 소리에 귀를 쫑긋 세웠다. ⓒ turn (the eyes, etc.) upward or sideward to showing attention, etc. (눈을) 치뜨다; 옆으로 돌리다; 턱을 치켜 올리다; 눈짓하다. ¶ ~ *one's eye at someone* 아무에게 눈짓하다 / ~ *one's nose* 코를 치켜들고 사람을 업신여기다. [E.]

knock into a cocked hat, ruin. 파멸시키다.

cock[2] [kak / kɔk] *n.* a small pile of hay shaped like a cone. 원뿔꼴의 건초 더미. — *vt.* (P6) pile (hay) in cocks. …을 원뿔 모양으로 쌓다. [E.]

cock·ade [kakéid / kɔk-] *n.* Ⓒ a knot of ribbon or a similar thing worn on the hat as a badge. 꽃 모양의 모표(帽標). [F.]

cock-a-doo·dle-doo [kákədùːdldúː / kɔ́k-] *n.* Ⓒ **1** the sound made by a cock. 꼬끼오《수탉 울음소리》. **2** a cock. 꼬꼬; 수탉《아기 말》.

cock-a-hoop [kàkəhúːp / kɔ̀k-] *adj.* in a state of exultation. 우쭐한; 의기양양한. [*cock*[1]]

cock-and-bull story [kákənbúl stɔ̀ːri / kɔ́k-] *n.* a foolish and unbelievable story; an unreal and impossible story that no one can believe. (아무도 믿을 수 없는) 허황된 이야기. [*cock*[1]]

cock·a·too [kàkətúː / kɔ̀k-] *n.* 《bird》 a parrot with a large crest. 앵무새의 일종. [Malay]

cock·a·trice [kákətris / kɔ́k-] *n.* a monster whose look was supposed to cause death, usu. represented as part cock and part snake. (전설상의) 괴사(怪蛇)《몸의 일부는 수탉, 일부는 뱀의 모양을 하고 있다 함》(cf. *basilisk*). [L. *calco* tread]

cock-boat [kákbòut / kɔ́k-] *n.* a small boat tied to a ship. 모선(母船)에 딸린 작은 배《모선과 부두와의 연락용》. [*cock*[1]]

cock·chaf·er [káktʃèifər / kɔ́k-] *n.* a large, winged beetle. 풍뎅이의 일종. [Sc.]

cock·crow [kákkròu / kɔ́k-] *n.* Ⓤ the time when cocks begin to crow; early morning. 첫닭이 울 때; 첫새벽. [→cock[1]]

cock·er [kákər / kɔ́k-] *n.* a breed of spaniel. 코커스파니엘《스파니엘 개의 일종》.

cock·er·el [kákərəl / kɔ́k-] *n.* Ⓒ a young cock, not more than one year old. (한 살 미만의) 수탉. [→cock[1]]

cock·eyed [kákàid / kɔ́k-] *adj.* **1** looking sideways; cross-eyed. 사팔뜨기의; 사시(斜視)의. **2** 《*sl.*》 twisted to one side; slanted; crooked. 한쪽으로 기운; 비뚤어진. ¶ *The pictures are hung all* ~. 그림들이 모두 비뚤게 걸려 있다. **3** stupid; absurd; crazy. 어리석은; 당치 않은; 미친. ¶ *a* ~ *war* 바보 같은 전쟁.

cock·fight [kákfàit / kɔ́k-] *n.* a fight between gamecocks. 투계(鬪鷄); 닭싸움.

cock·horse [kákhɔ̀ːrs / kɔ́k-] *n.* Ⓒ **1** a rocking horse. (어린이용의) 흔들목마(木馬). **2** a stick with a horse's head, used as a child's plaything. (어린이 놀이용) 말《말머리의 나무막대·대말 따위》.

cock·le[1] [kákəl/kɔ́kəl] *n.* Ⓒ **1** an edible shellfish; its shell. 새조개(의 조가비). **2** a small, light, shallow boat. (바닥이 얕은) 가볍고 작은 배. **3** a wrinkle. 주름(살). ¶ *a ~ in fabric* 직물의 주름. **4** 《*pl.*》 the bottom. (마음의) 깊은 속. ¶ *warm the cockles of someone's heart* 아무의 마음을 훈훈하게 하다; 아무를 기쁘게 하다. — *vi., vt.* (P1; 6) tend to curl up; wrinkle. 잘 구겨지다; 주름지(게 하)다. ¶ *This paper cockles easily.* 이 종이는 쉽게 구겨진다. [E.]

cock·le[2] [kákəl/kɔ́kəl] *n.* 《bot.》 a kind of weed growing in grainfields. 선옹초《잡초의 일종》. [E.]

cock·ney [kákni/kɔ́k-] *n.* (*pl.* **-neys**) *n.* Ⓒ **1** a person born in London; a Londoner. 런던 토박이; 런던내기. **2** a dialect of London. 런던 사투리(영어). — *adj.* of Londoners; of London. 런던 토박이의; 런던의. ¶ *the Londoner with a ~ accent* 런던 말투를 쓰는 런던 사람. [E. *cock's egg*]

cock·pit [kákpìt/kɔ́k-] *n.* Ⓒ **1** an enclosed place for fights between cocks. 투계장(鬪鷄場). **2** the scene of a great war. 전란의 터; 싸움터. **3** (in an airplane) the small place where the pilot sits. (비행기의) 조종실. **4** a room for lower officers in an old warship, used in battle for the wounded. (예전 군함의) 준사관실《맨밑 갑판의 후부에 있으며, 전시에는 부상병 수용실로 사용했음》. [*cock*[1]]

cock·roach [kákròutʃ/kɔ́k-] *n.* Ⓒ a large, black, dirty insect often found in kitchens. 바퀴. [Sp.]

cocks·comb [kákskòum/kɔ́ks-] *n.* **1** the comb of a cock. (수탉의) 볏(cf. *coxcomb*). **2** 《bot.》 a garden-flower somewhat like the comb of a cock. 맨드라미. **3** a pointed cap worn by a clown. (어릿광대가 쓰는) 뾰족모자. [*cock, comb*]

cock·sure [kákʃúər/kɔ́k-] *adj.* **1** very sure; completely certain. 틀림없는; 절대 확실한; 확신하는. ¶ *I am ~ of* (*about*) *his success.* 그의 성공을 확신한다. **2** 《*to do*》 be sure to do (something). 꼭 …하는. ¶ *She is ~ to come.* 그녀는 꼭 온다. [*cock*[1]]

cock·swain [káksən, -swèin/kɔ́k-] *n.* =coxswain.

cock·tail [káktèil/kɔ́k-] *n.* Ⓒ **1** a mixed alcoholic drink. 칵테일; 혼합주(酒). ¶ *a ~ party* 칵테일 파티. **2** 《U.S.》 a mixture of foods served in a glass at the beginning of a meal; an appetizer. 전채(前菜) 요리《토마토 소스를 친 게살 따위》. [*cock*[1]; ? F. *coquetel*]

cock·y [káki/kɔ́ki] *adj.* (**cock·i·er, cock·i·est**) 《*colloq.*》 sure of oneself in a rude and bold way; very proud; conceited; arrogant. 자부심이 강한; 우쭐하는; 건방진; 젠체하는. [*cock*[1]]

co·co [kóukou] *n.* Ⓒ (*pl.* **co·cos**) 《bot.》 a tropical palm tree; its fruit or seed. 야자나무; 그 열매(씨). [Port. *coco* grimace]

co·coa [kóukou] *n.* Ⓤ **1** brown powder made from crushed cacao seeds. 코코아. **2** a drink made of this powder. 코코아 음료. **3** a dull brown color; a yellowish-brown color. 코코아빛(색); 황갈색; 다갈색. [→ cacao]

co·co·nut, co·coa- [kóukənʌ̀t] *n.* Ⓒ the large, round, brown, edible nut of the coco palm. 야자 열매; 코코넛. [→coco]

co·coon [kəkúːn] *n.* Ⓒ a silky covering spun by a silkworm, etc. to live in while in the pupa stage. (누에) 고치. [F. *coque* shell]

cod [kad/kɔd] *n.* Ⓒ (*pl.* **cods** or *collectively* **cod**) 《fish》 a large edible fish with white flesh; a codfish. 대구. [→codfish]

C.O.D., c.o.d. **1** 《Brit.》 cash on delivery; 《U.S.》 collect on delivery. 대금 상환 인도; 현금 상환불(拂). **2** Concise Oxford Dictionary.

co·da [kóudə] *n.* Ⓒ 《mus.》 a final passage which brings a piece of music to a formal close. 코다; 결미(結尾); (악장의) 종결 부분. [It.]

cod·dle [kádl/kɔ́dl] *vt.* (P6,7) **1** 《*up*》 treat (a child, etc.) tenderly. (아이 등)을 어하다; 응석받이로 기르다; 너무 소중히 다루다. ¶ *~ oneself* 몸을 지나치게 아끼다; 건강에 신경을 너무 쓰다 / *~ children when they are sick* 아이들이 병나면 응석을 받아주다. **2** cock (boil) (something) slowly. 뭉근불로 …을 익히다(끓이다). [? L. *caldus* warm]

·**code** [koud] *n.* Ⓒ **1** a group of laws arranged in an orderly manner. 법전. ¶ *the civil* (*criminal*) *~* 민(형)법전 / *the Code Napoleon* 나폴레옹 법전 / *the ~ of civil* (*criminal*) *procedure* 민사(형사) 소송법. **2** a set of rules or principles of conduct generally accepted by society or by a group of people. (어떤 사회의) 규칙; 관례. ¶ *the social ~* 사회의 관례 / *the moral ~* 도덕률 / *the medical ~* 의사의 윤리 / *the ~ of censor* 검열 규정 / *You must live up to the ~ of the school.* 학교 규칙에 어긋나지 않도록 생활해야 한다. **3** a system of signs; a set of signals showing letters, etc. used in sending messages by telegraph; a system of secret writing. 신호 (체계); 부호; 약호; 암호. ¶ *a ~ telegram* (*message*) 암호 전보 / *the International Code* 국제 전신 약호 / *the Morse ~* 모스 전신 부호 / *a telegraphic ~* 전신 암호 / *break the enemy's ~* 적의 암호를 풀다.
— *vt.* (P6) **1** put (a message, etc.) into a code. …을 암호로 하다. ¶ *coded signals* 암호 통신 / *have the message coded* 통신문을 암호화하다. **2** codify. …을 법전화하다. [→ codex]

co·deine [kóudiːn] *n.* a drug obtained

from opium. 코데인《아편에서 뽑은 알칼로이드; 진정제》. [Gk. *hodeia* poppy head]

co·dex [kóudeks] *n.* (*pl.* **co·di·ces**) an ancient book written by hand. 고사본(古寫本). [L. *cōdex* writing tablet, book, etc.]

cod·fish [kádfiʃ/kɔ́d-] *n.* Ⓒ (*pl.* **-fish·es** or *collectively* **-fish**) a cod or its flesh. 대구; 그 살. [E. *cod* bag]

codg·er [kádʒər/kɔ́dʒər] *n.* 《*colloq.*》 a queer or odd man. 괴짜. [→cadger]

co·di·ces [kóudisi:z] *n.* pl. of **codex**.

cod·i·cil [kádəsil/kɔ́d-] *n.* 《law》 something added to a will. 유언 보완서. [→codex]

cod·i·fi·ca·tion [kàdəfikéiʃən, kòu-] *n.* Ⓤ the act of codifying; the state of being codified. 법전 편찬; 성문화(成文化). [↓]

cod·i·fy [kádəfài, kóu-] *vt.* (P6) (**-fied**) arrange (laws, etc.) according to a system. (법률 따위)를 법전으로 편찬하다; 법전화하다. ¶ *Napoleon had the French laws codified.* 나폴레옹은 프랑스 법률을 법전화(法典化)했다. ● **cod·i·fi·er** [-ər] *n.* [→code]

cod·ling[1] [kádliŋ/kɔ́d-] *n.* a young codfish. 대구의 새끼. [→cod[1]]

cod·ling[2] [kádliŋ/kɔ́d-], **-lin** [-lin] *n.* a kind of cooking apple. 요리용 사과. ¶ *the codlin(g) moth* 나방의 일종《유충은 과수를 해침》. [M.E. *querdling*]

cod-liv·er oil [kádlivər ɔ́il/kɔ́d-] *n.* the oil got from the liver of cod, used as a medicine. (대구의) 간유(肝油). 参考 비타민 A 와 D 가 많음. [→codfish]

co·ed, co-ed [kóuéd] *n.* Ⓒ 《U.S. *colloq.*》 a girl student at a coeducational school or college. 남녀 공학 학교의 여학생. [co-]

co·ed·u·ca·tion [kòuedʒukéiʃən] *n.* Ⓤ the education of boys and girls at the same school or college. 남녀 공학. [co-]

co·ed·u·ca·tion·al [kòuedʒukéiʃənəl] *adj.* educating both boys and girls together at the same school or college. 남녀 공학의.

co·ef·fi·cient [kòuəfíʃənt] *n.* Ⓒ **1** 《math., phys.》 a number or algebraic symbol placed before and multiplying another quantity. 계수(係數). ¶ *the ~ of expansion of steel* 철강의 팽창계수 / *a differential ~* 미분계수. **2** a joint agent. 공동 작인(作因). — *adj.* cooperating. 공동 작용의. [co-]

coe·no·bite [sí:nəbàit, sénə-] *n.* a monk. 수도 단원; 수도 수사(修士). ● **coe·no·bit·i·cal** [sì:nəbítikəl, sènə-] *adj.* **coe·no·bit·ism** [-izəm] *n.* [Gk. *koinos bios* common life]

co·e·qual [kouí:kwəl] *adj.*, *n.* (an) equal. 동등한 (사람). [co-]

co·erce [kouə́:rs] *vt.* (P6,13,20) **1** hold back or put down (someone) by force, esp. by legal authority. (법률 등의 힘으로) …을 억누르다[구속하다]. ¶ *~ voters with a high hand* 고압 수단으로 유권자에게 압력을 넣다 / *~ someone into silence* 아무를 위압하여 침묵시키다. **2** compel; force. …을 강제하다. ¶ *~ obedience* 복종을 강요하다 / *~ someone into drinking* [*to drink*] 아무를 억지로 술마시게 하다. ● **co·er·cer** [-sər] *n.* [L. *arceo* shut up]

co·er·ci·ble [kouə́:rsəbəl] *adj.* that can be coerced. 강제[억압]할 수 있는.

co·er·cion [kouə́:rʃən] *n.* Ⓤ **1** the act of coercing; the state of being coerced; the act of preventing by force. 강제; 강요; 억압. ¶ *under ~* 강제되어. **2** government by force. 탄압 정치; 압정(壓政).

co·er·cive [kouə́:rsiv] *adj.* compelling; having the power to force. 강제적인; 고압적인. ¶ *~ government* 압정 / *~ manners* 고압적인 태도.

co·es·sen·tial [kòuisénʃəl] *adj.* of the same substance. 동질(同質)의; 동체의. ¶ *be ~ with God* 신과 일체이다. [co-]

co·e·ter·nal [kòuitə́:rnəl] *adj.* alike eternal. 영원히 공존하는. [co-]

co·e·val [kouí:vəl] *adj.* of or belonging to the same age or period; present. 동시대의; 동시기의; 당대의. — *n.* Ⓒ a person or thing of about the same age or period. 동시대의 사람[것]. ● **co·e·val·ly** [-vəli] *adv.* [L. *aevum* age]

co·ex·ist [kòuigzíst] *vi.* (P1,3) exist together, at the same time or in the same place. 동시[같은 곳]에 존재하다; 공존하다. [co-]

co·ex·ist·ence [kòuigzístəns] *n.* Ⓤ existence together; existence at the same time or in the same place. 공존(共存). ¶ *peaceful ~* 평화 공존 / *the policy of ~* (평화) 공존 정책.

co·ex·ist·ent [kòuigzístənt] *adj.* existing at the same time or in the same place. 공존의; 병존의; 동시대의.

co·ex·tend [kòuiksténd] *vi.*, *vt.* (P1;6) extend equally or to the same limits. 같은 넓이로 퍼지(게 하)다. ● **co·ex·ten·sive** [kòuiksténsiv] *adj.*

:cof·fee [kɔ́:fi, káfi/kɔ́fi] *n.* **1** Ⓤ a dark-brown drink made from the roasted and ground seeds of the tropical tree or shrub; Ⓒ the shrub or tree itself; 《*collectively*》 the seeds. 커피; 그 나무; 그 열매. ¶ *a cup of ~* 커피 한 잔 / *black ~* 블랙 커피《우유나 크림, 설탕을 섞지 않은 것》/ *~ and milk* 우유를 섞은 커피 / *strong* [*weak*] *~* 진한[묽은] 커피. **2** Ⓤ dark brown. 암갈색; 커피빛. [Arab.]

coffee bean [⌐–⌐] *n.* a seed of the coffee plant. 커피콩.

coffee break [⌐–⌐] *n.* 《U.S.》 a short rest from work when coffee is usu. drunk. 차 마시는 시간; 휴식 (시간).

coffee cup [⌐–⌐] *n.* a cup used to drink coffee. 커피 잔.

cof·fee·house [kɔ́:fihàus, káf-/kɔ́f-] *n.* a

place where coffee and other light refreshments are sold. 커피점《커피와 함께 가벼운 청량 음료를 팖》.

coffee mill [ㅅ- ㅅ] *n.* a machine for grinding coffee beans. 커피 콩을 가는 기구.

coffee pot [ㅅ- ㅅ] *n.* a container, usu. with a lid, in which coffee is made or served. 커피 (끓이는) 주전자.

coffee room [ㅅ- ㅅ] *n.* =coffee shop.

coffee shop [ㅅ- ㅅ] *n.* a shop or restaurant where coffee, light refreshments, and usu. meals are served. (간단한 식당을 겸한) 다실; 다방.

cof·fer [kɔ́ːfər, káf-] *n.* Ⓒ **1** a large, strong box, chest or trunk, esp. for keeping money or valuable articles. (귀중품을 넣어 두는) 함(函); 궤. **2** 《*pl.*》 a place for keeping money; a treasury; funds. 금고; 국고; 자금; 기금. ¶ *the state coffers* 국고. [Gk. *kophinos* basket]

·cof·fin [kɔ́ːfin, káf-] *n.* Ⓒ a box or case into which a dead person is placed for burial. 관(棺).

a nail in* 〔*into*〕 *someone's coffin, something bad which will bring someone's ruin nearer. 목숨을 줄이는〔파멸을 재촉하는〕 원인이 되는 것. ¶ *drive* 〔*put*〕 *a nail in* 〔*into*〕 *one's* ~ 파멸〔죽음〕을 재촉하다.

in one's coffin, dead and buried. 죽어 매장되어.

— *vt.* (P6) put (a dead person) into a coffin; shut up (books, etc.) tightly. …을 입관(入棺)하다; (서책 따위)를 사장(死藏)하다; 닫아〔잠가〕 두다. [↑]

cog [kag / kɔg] *n.* Ⓒ one of a number of teeth on the edge of a wheel which enables it to move with another wheel. (톱니바퀴의) 톱니. [E.]

a cog in the machine, an unimportant person or branch of a firm in a very large business or organization. (대조직 속에서 톱니바퀴의 톱니처럼) 작은 역할을 하는 사람〔존재〕.

slip a cog, make a mistake. (생각지 않은) 실책을〔실수를〕 하다; 실패하다; 잘못하다.

co·gen·cy [kóudʒənsi] *n.* the state of being cogent; power to convince. 설득력 (있음); 타당함. [↓]

co·gent [kóudʒənt] *adj.* (of a reason, argument, etc.) having a powerful appeal to the mind; compelling. 설득력 있는; 강제력 있는. ¶ ~ *reasoning* 설득력 있는 이론. [co-, L. *ágo* drive, do]

cog·i·tate [kádʒətèit / kɔ́dʒ-] *vi.* reflect; consider; think seriously. 깊이 생각하다; (심사)숙고하다. ¶ ~ *upon* 〔*over*〕 *something* …을 숙고하다; 궁리하다. — *vt.* think over or about (something); plan. …을 숙고하다; 궁리하다; 계획하다. ¶ ~ *a scheme* 계획을 짜다. [co-, →act]

cog·i·ta·tion [kàdʒətéiʃən / kɔ̀dʒ-] *n.* Ⓤ **1** deep thought; meditation. 숙고; 심사(深思). **2** 《often *pl.*》 a design or plan. 고안; 계획.

cog·i·ta·tive [kádʒətèitiv / kɔ́dʒətə-] *adj.* meditative. 숙고〔명상〕하는.

co·gnac [kóunjæk, kán-] *n.* Ⓤ a kind of French brandy. 코냑. 參考 프랑스 Cognac 지방 특산. [Place]

cog·nate [kágneit / kɔ́g-] *adj.* **1** having the same origin; coming from a common origin. 기원(起源)이 같은; 같은 어족의. ¶ ~ *language* 동족 언어 / *English 'eat' is* ~ *with* 〔*to*〕 *German 'essen'*. 영어의 'eat'는 독어의 'essen'과 어원이 같다. **2** having the same ancestor. 조상이 같은; 동족의. **3** having the same quality or nature; closely related. 동계(同系)〔동종(同種)〕의; 동질(同質)의; 관계가 밀접한. ¶ *astronomy and the* ~ *sciences* 천문학 및 동계의 여러 과학.

— *n.* Ⓒ **1** a person related to another by a common ancestor. 친족; 친척. **2** a thing or word having a common origin with another. 기원이 같은 것; 어원이 같은 말. [co-, L. *gnatus* born]

cognate object [ㅅ- ㅅ-] *n.* 《gram.》 an object having a common original form with the verb. 동족 목적어《die a death 의 *a death,* dream a dream의 *a dream,* live a happy life의 *a life* 따위》.

cog·ni·tion [kagníʃən / kɔg-] *n.* ⓊⒸ the act of knowing; awareness; anything that is known. 인식(력); (인식 작용의 결과인) 지식; 인식된 것. [co-, L. *gnosco* learn]

cog·ni·za·ble [kágnəzəbl, kagnái- / kɔ́g-] *adj.* knowable; within the sphere. 인식〔인지〕할 수 있는; (법원의) 관할 내에 있는. [↓]

cog·ni·zance, -sance [kágnəzəns / kɔ́g-] *n.* Ⓤ **1** the fact of being aware; knowledge or sense; notice; the scope of knowledge, etc. (보거나 하여) 앎; 지각(知覺); 인지; 인식 (범위). ¶ *come to someone's* ~ 아무에게 알려지다 / *be beyond one's* ~ 인식 범위 밖에 있다. **2** a legal hearing. 심리(審理). **3** the right to hold a legal hearing. 재판 관할권. ¶ *within the* ~ *of* …의 심리의 관할 내에서. **4** Ⓒ a badge; the distinguishing crest. 문장(紋章); 기장(記章); 배지. [co-, L. *gnosco* apprehend]

have cognizance of, recognize; know. …을 알(고 있)다.

take cognizance of, notice; recognize (something) officially. …을 인지하다; 알아채다; 인정하다.

cog·ni·zant, -sant [kágnəzənt / kɔ́g-] *adj.* having cognizance of something; aware. (어떤 일을) 인식하고; 알고.

be cognizant of, know. …을 알고〔인지하고〕 있다. ¶ *He was* ~ *of the difficulty.* 그는 그 어려움을 알고 있었다.

cog·no·men [kagnóumən / kɔgnóumen] *n.* Ⓒ (*pl.* **-no·mens** or **-nom·i·na**) a family name; a surname; a nickname. 성(姓);

별명. [co-, →nomen]

cog·nom·i·na [kɑgnɑ́mənə / -nɔ́m-] *n.* pl. of **cognomen.**

cog·wheel [kɑ́ghwìːl / kɔ́g-] *n.* Ⓒ a wheel with teeth on the rim; a gear wheel. 톱니바퀴. [M.E. →cog, wheel]

co·hab·it [kouhǽbit] *vi.* (P1,3) 《*with*》 **1** live together as husband and wife do, generally used of persons not married. (결혼하지 않은 남녀가) 동거 생활하다. **2** live together. 함께 살다. [co-]

co·heir [kouέər] *n.* a joint heir. (법정) 공동 상속인. [co-]

co·here [kouhíər] *vi.* (P1) **1** stick together. 들러붙다; 밀착[결합]하다. ¶ *Brick and mortar* ~. 벽돌과 모르타르는 붙는다. **2** (of reasoning, etc.) be connected logically. (논리 따위가) 일관되다; 조리가 있다. [co-, L. *haereo* stick]

co·her·ence [kouhíərəns], **-cy** [-si] *n.* Ⓤ **1** the act of cohering. 밀착(성). **2** consistency; logical connection. (논리 따위의) 일관성; 조리.

co·her·ent [kouhíərənt] *adj.* **1** able to stick together. 밀착성의; 밀착하는. **2** logically clear and well connected. 조리 있는; 시종 일관된. ¶ *a* ~ *argument* 조리 있는 의론.

co·her·er [kouhíərər] *n.* 《wireless》 a radio-detector. 코히러《검파기(檢波器)의 일종》.

co·he·sion [kouhíːʒən] *n.* ⓊⒸ **1** the act of sticking together; a habit of sticking together. 점착(粘着)(력); 결합(력); 단결. ¶ *the* ~ *of free nations* 자유주의 국가들의 단결 / *There is* ~ *in clay but not in gravel.* 찰흙에는 점착력이 있지만 자갈에는 없다. **2** 《phys.》 the force by which the particles of a substance are bound together. (분자 따위의) 응집력; 결합력.

co·he·sive [kouhíːsiv] *adj.* sticking together; apt to stick together. 점착성 있는; 결합력[밀착력]이 있는. ¶ *a* ~ *agent* 점착제. ● **co·he·sive·ly** [-li] *adv.* **co·he·sive·ness** [-nis] *n.*

co·hort [kóuhɔːrt] *n.* Ⓒ **1** (in ancient Rome) a body of soldiers of from 300 to 600 men. (고대 로마의) 보병대(隊)《300-600명으로 구성됨》. **2** 《often *pl.*》 a group of soldiers; a group; a band. 군대; 군단; 그룹; 대(隊); 단(團). ¶ *a* ~ *of admirers* 일단의 숭배자들. [L.]

coif·feur [kwɑːfə́ːr] *n.* 《F.》 a hairdresser. 이발사.

coif·fure [kwɑːfjúər] *n.* 《F.》 a way of dressing or arranging the hair. 이발의 양식; 머리형.

***coil** [kɔil] *vt., vi.* (P6,7,13;2A,3) wind (a rope, etc.) around into circles; form coils. 둘둘 말(리)다; 칭칭 감(기)다; 서리다. ¶ ~ *a rope* 밧줄을 감다 / *The vine coiled around the tree.* 덩굴은 나무를 칭칭 감고 있었다 / *The snake coiled itself up.* 뱀은 몸을 서렸다.

— *n.* Ⓒ **1** anything wound in a circle. 둘둘 만[감은] 것; 사리. ¶ *a* ~ *of rope* 밧줄 한 사리 / *a snake in a* ~ 몸을 서린 뱀 / *wind a rope in a* ~ 밧줄을 서리다. **2** one of the circles of a spiral. 나삿니의 한 바퀴. **3** a spiral of wire or pipe for conducting electricity, hot water, or the like. 코일; 감긴 선; (난방기 따위의) 나사관(管). [→collect]

:coin [kɔin] *n.* **1** Ⓒ a piece of metal used as money; 《*collectively*》 metal money. 화폐; 통화; 경화(硬貨); 주화(鑄貨)(opp. paper money, notes). ¶ *a current* ~ 통화 / *a copper* [*silver*] ~ 동[은]화 / *a false* ~ 가짜돈; 《*fig.*》 가짜. **2** Ⓤ 《*colloq.*》 the money. 돈; 금전. ¶ *have plenty of* ~ 돈이 많다.

pay someone (***back***) ***in his own coin,*** treat someone as he has treated you. 똑같이 보복하다; 대갚음하다.

— *vt.* (P6) **1** make (metal) into coins; make (coins) by shaping pieces of metal. (화폐)를 주조하다; (금속)을 화폐화하다. **2** invent or make up (a new word, etc.). (새 말 따위)를 만들어내다. ¶ ~ *a new word* 신어(新語)를 만들다 / ~ *a new expression* 새로운 표현을 생각해 내다. [L. *cuneus* wedge; F. =the die to stamp money]

coin money, 《*colloq.*》 make large profits; grow rich. 큰 돈을 벌다; 재산이 쌓이다. ¶ *He is coining money in his new business.* 그는 새 사업으로 돈을 많이 벌고 있다.

coin·age [kɔ́inidʒ] *n.* **1** Ⓤ the act of making coins; a system of money. 화폐 주조; 화폐 제도. **2** 《*collectively*》 coin used in a country. 화폐; 통화. **3** Ⓤ the act of making or inventing, esp. words; Ⓒ the new word itself. 만들어 냄; 발명(품); 신어; 신조어(新造語). ¶ *the* ~ *of fancy* [*the brain*] 공상[두뇌]의 산물 / *a word of his* ~ 그의 신조어.

co·in·cide [kòuinsáid] *vi.* (P1,2A,3) **1** ⓐ (of two events) happen at the same time. (두 일이) 동시에 일어나다. ¶ *Our vacations coincided this year.* 올해에는 우리 휴가 시기가 같았다. ⓑ (of two things) occupy the same place; be the same shape and cover the same area. (위치가) 동일 공간을 차지하다; (외형이) 동일하다. ¶ *The centers of concentric circles* ~. 동심원(同心圓)의 중심은 일치한다 / *The unlucky boy's birthday coincided with Christmas.* 불행히도 그 소년의 생일은 크리스마스와 겹쳤다. **2** 《*with*》 agree with; correspond exactly to. (의견 따위가) 일치하다; 부합하다. ¶ *Our opinions* ~ (*with each other*). 우리들의 의견은 일치돼 있다 / *This story coincides with the facts.* 이 이야기는 사실과 부합한다. [co-, →incidence]

co·in·ci·dence [kouínsədəns] *n.* **1** Ⓤ the act or state of coinciding. 동시 발생; 동시 공존. **2** Ⓒ an unusual occurrence of events, ideas, etc. at the same time by mere chance; Ⓤ agreement by chance. 동시에 일어난 사건; 우연의 일치. ¶ *by a curious ~* 기이한 운명〔인연〕으로 / *by the wildest ~* 극히 우연한 일치로.

co·in·ci·dent [kouínsədənt] *adj.* 《*with*》 happening at the same time in exact agreement. 동시에 일어난; 일치〔합치〕된; 부합한. ¶ *be ~ with something* …와 일치하다 / *What has happened is ~ with my hopes.* 발생한 사태는 내가 희망하는 일과 일치한다.

co·in·ci·den·tal [kouìnsədéntl] *adj.* characterized by coincidence. 부합하는; 일치를 보이는. ● **co·in·ci·den·tal·ly** [-i] *adv.*

coin·er [kɔ́inər] *n.* Ⓒ a maker of coins, esp. one who makes false coins; an inventor, esp. of new words. 화폐 주조자; 가짜 돈 만드는 사람; (새 말) 조어자(造語者). [→coin]

coir [kɔiər] *n.* fiber made from the husk of the coconut, used for ropes, mats, etc. 코이어《야자 껍질에서 뽑은 섬유》. [Malay]

coke [kouk] *n.* **1** Ⓤ gray lumps of fuel made by heating soft coal in a closed apparatus. 코크스; 해탄(骸炭). **2** 《*sl.*》 cocaine. 코카인. **3** 《*C-*》 《trademark, U.S. *colloq.*》 Coca-Cola. 코카콜라. ── *vt., vi.* change (coal) into coke. …을 코크스로 만들다; 코크스가 되다. [E. =core]

co·ker·nut [kóukərnʌ̀t] *n.* =coconut.

col [kɑl / kɔl] *n.* Ⓒ a gap between peaks in a mountain range used as a pass. 고개; 재; 협로(峽路); (산맥간의) 저지(低地). [→collar]

Col. [kɑl / kɔl] **1** Colonel. **2** Colorado.

col·an·der [kʌ́ləndər, kɑ́l-] *n.* a metal pot with holes in it, used to drain water from boiled vegetables, etc. (삶은 야채 따위의) 물을 받는〔빼는〕 그릇. [L. *colo* strain]

:cold [kould] *adj.* **1** of a low temperature; very cool; chilly. 추운; 차가운(opp. hot). ¶ *~ water* 냉수 / *~ meat* 냉육 / *~ weather* 추운 날씨 / *a ~ day* 추운 날 / *a ~ war* 냉전 / *a ~ bath* 냉수욕 / *(as) ~ as ice* 〔*marble*〕 얼음〔대리석〕처럼 차가운 / *It is ~.* (날씨가) 춥다 / *I feel ~.* 오한이 난다. **2** showing no feeling or passion. 냉정한; 차가운. ¶ *a ~ heart* 매정함; 비정(非情) / *~ reason* 냉철한 이성. **3** feeling no warmth; indifferent; not friendly. 냉담한; 쌀쌀한. ¶ *a ~ reply* 쌀쌀한 대답 / *a ~ reception* 차가운 접대 / *He grew ~ toward me.* 내게 대한 태도가 냉랭해졌다. **4** discouraging. 실망시키는; 낙담케 하는; 우울한. ¶ *~ news* 낙담시키는 소식 / *the ~ atmosphere of a hospital waiting room* 병원 대기실의 우울한 분위기. **5** not fresh. 진부한; 시시한. ¶ *a ~ jest* 진부한 익살. **6** (of scent in hunting) faint. (사냥에서 짐승 냄새가) 희미한. ¶ *a ~ scent* (짐승이 남긴) 희미한 냄새(cf. *blazing scent*). **7** (of colors) suggesting cold. (색조가) 차가운; 찬 느낌의. ¶ *Gray and blue are ~ colors.* 회색과 청색은 한색(寒色)이다.

give* 〔*turn*〕 *someone the cold shoulder on, treat someone in an unfriendly way. …을 냉대하다.

have* 〔*get*〕 *someone cold, have someone at one's mercy. …을 마음대로 하다; 꼼소리 못하게 하다.

have cold feet, 《*colloq.*》 be afraid; be cowed. 두려워하다; 겁내다.

in cold blood, in one's normal state. 냉혹하게; 아무렇지도 않게; 예사로. ¶ *kill a man in ~ blood* 사람을 예사로 죽이다.

leave someone cold, fail to interest him. 아무의 흥미를 끌지 못하다.

make someone's blood run cold, frighten someone greatly. 아무를 오싹〔쭈뼛〕하게 하다.

throw cold water on, discourage 〔dampen〕 another's enthusiasm for. (남의 계획 따위)에 찬물을 끼얹다; …에 탈을 잡다.

── *n.* **1** Ⓤ a low temperature; chilliness. 추위; 차가움; 한랭(opp. heat). ¶ *The ~ was terrible.* 추위가 매서웠다 / *Warm clothes protect us against the ~ of winter.* 따뜻한 옷은 우리를 추위에서 막아준다. **2** Ⓤ temperature below the freezing point. 어는 점 이하; 영하. ¶ *ten degrees of ~* 영하 10도. **3** Ⓒ an illness marked by a sore throat, a running nose, coughing, a headache, etc. 감기. ¶ *a ~ in the head* 〔*nose*〕 코감기 / *a ~ on the chest* 〔*lungs*〕 기침 감기 / *have a ~* 감기에 걸려 있다 / *catch* 〔*take*〕 *(a) ~* 감기에 걸리다. [E.]

cold without, 《*colloq.*》 cold unsweetened spirit and water. (설탕은 타지 않고) 물만 탄 브랜디.

(left) out in the cold, neglected; shunned; avoided. 무시〔묵살〕되어; 따돌림을 당하여. ¶ *When the new director came, Edward found himself out in the ~.* 새 감독이 왔을 때 에드워드는 자신이 무시당하고 있음을 알았다 / *He left me out in the ~.* 그는 나를 따돌렸다.

cold-blood·ed [kóuldblʌ́did] *adj.* **1** having a body temperature the same as that of the surroundings. 냉혈의(opp. warm-blooded). ¶ *Fish and reptile are ~ animals.* 물고기와 파충류는 냉혈〔찬피〕 동물이다. **2** cruel; without pity. 냉혹한; 잔인한; 비정(非情)의. ¶ *a ~ murder* 냉혹(冷酷)한 살인. ● **cold-blood·ed·ly** [-li] *adv.*

cold cream [스스] *n.* a creamy substance used for softening and cleansing the skin. 콜드 크림.

cold-heart·ed [kóuldhɑ́:rtid] *adj.* without feeling, sympathy or love. 냉담〔냉혹〕한; 무정한. [E.]

·cold·ly [kóuldli] *adv.* in a cold manner. 냉정히; 차갑게. ¶ *consider ~* 냉정히 생각하다 / *The wind blows ~.* 바람이 차갑게 분다 / *He treated me ~.* 그는 나를 차갑게 대했

다. [cold]

cold meat [ˊ ˊ] *n.* ⟪*sl.*⟫ a dead body. 시체; 사체.

cold·ness [kóuldnis] *n.* Ⓤ the state of being cold. 추위; 차가움; 냉담. ¶ *with* ~ 차갑게; 냉담하게 / *the* ~ *of the weather* 날씨의 추움 / *He greeted me with great* ~. 그는 나를 아주 차갑게 맞이했다.

cold pig [ˊ ˊ] *n.* ⟪*sl.*⟫ the cold water thrown on a person to wake him. 잠을 깨우기 위해 끼얹는 찬물.

cold storage [ˊ ˊ–] *n.* a refrigerator. 냉장고.

cold war [ˊ ˊ] *n.* a sharp conflict in diplomacy, economics, etc. between states regarded as possibly leading to real war. 냉전⟪무력에 의하지 않고 외교 선전에 의한 신경전⟫.

cold wave [ˊ ˋ] *n.* **1** the fall of temperature traveling over a large area. 한파(寒波). **2** a kind of permanent hair. 퍼머넌트 웨이브의 일종.

cole [koul] *n.* a general name for plants of the cabbage family. 양배추속(屬) 식물의 총칭. [L. *caulis*]

Cole·ridge [kóulridʒ], **Samuel Taylor** *n.* (1772-1834) an English poet and essayist. 콜리지⟪영국의 시인·수필가⟫.

col·ic [kálik / kɔ́l-] *n.* Ⓤ severe pains in the stomach and bowels. 복통; 산통(疝痛). ● **col·ick·y** [-i] *adj.* [Gk. *kolon*]

col·i·se·um [kɑ̀lisíːəm / kɔ̀l-] *n.* Ⓒ **1** a large building or stadium for sports, contests, etc. 대경기장; 대체육관. **2** ⟪*C-*⟫ = Colosseum. [L.]

co·li·tis [kəláitis, kou-] *n.* Ⓤ ⟪med.⟫ inflamation of the lining of the colon. 대장염; 결장염. ¶ *acute* ~ 급성 결장염. [*colon*]

coll. colleague; collection; college; collegiate; colloquial.

col·lab·o·rate [kəlǽbərèit] *vi.* (P1,2A,3) **1** work together with someone, as on a literary work. 공동으로 일하다; 합작하다. ¶ ~ *with someone in a work* [*in doing a work*] 아무와 협력하여 어떤 일을 하다 / *We collaborated on the novel.* 우리는 공동으로 소설을 썼다. **2** work with, or willingly help, an enemy of one's country. (적국을) 돕다; (적에게) 협력하다. [co-, →labor]

col·lab·o·ra·tion [kəlæ̀bəréiʃən] *n.* Ⓤ the act of collaborating. 협력; 공동; 합작; 제휴. ¶ *in* ~ *with* …와 협력[협조, 제휴]하여 / *with* ~ *from* [*of*] …의 협력을 얻어.

col·lab·o·ra·tion·ist [kəlæ̀bəréiʃənist] *n.* a person who collaborates with an enemy of his country. 적과의 협력자.

col·lab·o·ra·tor [kəlǽbərèitər] *n.* Ⓒ a person who collaborates. 협력자; 공저자; 공동 제작자[연구자].

col·lage [kəlɑ́ːʒ] *n.* a picture made by an unusual combination of bits of paper, photograph, etc. 콜라주⟪신문 오려낸 것·종잇조각·사진 조각 따위를 한 화면에 짜넣어 예술 효과를 내는 화법의 하나⟫. [F. =gluing]

col·laps·a·ble [kəlǽpsəbəl] *adj.* =collapsible.

***col·lapse** [kəlǽps] *vi.* (P1,2A,3) **1** fall down or in. 무너지다; 붕괴하다. ¶ ~ *under the weight of* …의 무게에 눌려 무너지다[찌부러지다] / *The little chair collapsed when my uncle sat down on it.* 작은 의자는 숙부가 앉자 찌부러졌다 / *The building collapsed.* 건물이 붕괴했다. **2** fold together. (겪여) 접히다. ¶ *This table collapses.* 이 테이블은 접을 수 있다. **3** (of a plan, hope, etc.) fail utterly; come to ruin. (계획·희망 따위가) 꺾이다; 좌절[실패]하다; 깨지다. ¶ *The scheme collapsed.* 계획이 좌절되었다 / *Our hope has collapsed.* 희망이 깨졌다. **4** lose strength or courage; break down physically. 갑자기 힘을[용기를] 잃다; 체력이 떨어지다; 쇠약해지다. ¶ *His health collapsed.* 그의 건강이 쇠했다.

— *vt.* (P6) cause (something) to fail or fall in; fold. …을 꺾(이게 하)다; 좌절[실패]시키다; (의자 따위를) 접다. ¶ ~ *a counter movement* 반대 운동을 좌절시키다 / *He collapsed the table easily.* 그는 테이블을 간단히 접었다.

— *n.* Ⓒ the act of collapsing. 붕괴; 도괴(倒壞); 좌절; 몰락; 쇠약. ¶ *the* ~ *of a roof* 지붕의 붕괴 / *the* ~ *of the Roman Empire* 로마제국의 몰락 / *the* ~ *of plans* [*hopes*] 계획[희망]의 좌절 / *the* ~ *of a Bank* 은행의 파산 / *Five people were killed by the* ~ *of the building.* 그 건물이 무너져서 다섯 사람이 죽었다. [L. *labor* slip, decay]

col·laps·i·ble [kəlǽpsəbəl] *adj.* that can be folded up. (보트·의자 따위가) 접을 수 있는; 접이식의. ¶ ~ *boat* 접이식 보트.

:col·lar [kɑ́lər / kɔ́lər] *n.* Ⓒ **1** the part of a shirt, dress or coat fitting around the neck. 칼라; 깃. ¶ *a turned-down* ~ 꺾어젖힌 깃 / *hold* [*seize, take*] *someone by the* ~ 아무의 멱살을[목덜미를] 잡다. **2** a divided piece of linen, lace, etc. worn around the neck. (계급·훈장의) 경식(頸飾). **3** a band of leather, etc. for the neck of a dog, a horse, etc. (개 따위의) 목걸이; (말 따위) 목받이띠; 경대(頸帶). ¶ *a dog's* ~ 개 목걸이. **4** a metal ring used to join two pipes or rods. 이음고리; 칼라.

against the collar, in the face of difficulty. 곤란과 싸워.

in collar, ⟪*colloq.*⟫ attending to one's business. 취업하여; 일을 하고.

out of collar, out of work. 실직하여.

slip (***the***) ***collar,*** escape from restraint. 속박[어려움]에서 벗어나다.

wear [***take***] ***the collar,*** ⟪*colloq.*⟫ obey another's orders. 남의 명령에 따르다.

— *vt.* (P6) **1** put a collar on. 깃을[칼라를] 달다; (개 따위에) 목걸이를 달다. **2** ⓐ catch (someone) by the collar. …의 멱살을[목덜미를] 잡다. ¶ *The policeman collared the thief.* 경찰은 도둑의 목덜미를 잡았다. ⓑ take without permission. 훔치다. ¶ *He collared all my money.* 내 돈을 몽땅 훔쳤다. ●**col·lar·less** [-lis] *adj.* [L. *collum* neck]

col·lar·bone [kɑ́lərbòun / kɔ́lər-] *n.* Ⓒ a bone connecting the shoulder blade and the breastbone. 쇄골(鎖骨)(=clavicle).

collat. collateral(ly).

col·late [kəléit, kou-, kɑ́leit] *vt.* (P6,13) **1** 《*with*》 compare (two or more pieces of writing) to see whether there are any differences. (주로 책을 다른 책)과 맞쇠다[대조하다]. **2** 《*to*》 appoint to a benefice. 성직에 임명하다. ●**col·la·tor** [-ər] *n.* [com-, L. *fero* carry]

col·lat·er·al [kəlǽtərəl / kɔl-] *adj.* **1** side by side; parallel. 평행한; 나란한. **2** attendant or secondary; indirect; additional. 부수적인; 이차적인; 간접의; 부(副)의. ¶ ~ *evidence* 간접 증거; 방증 / *a* ~ *circumstances* 부대 상황. **3** coming from a common ancestor but in a different line. 방계(傍系)의. ¶ *Cousins are* ~ *relatives.* 사촌은 방계 친척이다. **4** 《comm.》 secured by collateral. 담보로 보증된. ¶ *a* ~ *loan* 담보부 대부. —*n.* **1** Ⓤ 《sometimes *a* ~》 a secondary security for a loan. 담보물. **2** Ⓒ a collateral relative. 방계친(榜系親). [com-]

col·la·tion [kəléiʃən, kou-, kɑl-] *n.* **1** Ⓒ a light meal. 가벼운 식사. **2** Ⓤ ⓐ the act of collating. 성직 임명. ⓑ a careful comparison. 맞쇰; 대조. [→collate]

col·league [kɑ́liːg / kɔ́l-] *n.* Ⓒ an associate in an office or in a profession; a fellow worker. (관청·회사·학교 등의) 동료; 동업자. ¶ *work as someone's* ~ 아무의 동료로서 일하다. [co-, L. *lego* choose, gather]

:col·lect [kəlékt] *vt.* (P6,7) **1** gather (something) together; gather (stamps, etc.) as a hobby; gather (people). …을 모으다; 수집하다; 집합시키다. ¶ ~ *students in a hall* 강당에 학생을 집합시키다 / ~ *data* 자료를 모으다. **2** call for and receive pay for (debts, taxes, bills, etc.). …을 거두다; 징수[수금]하다. ¶ ~ *bills* 부금을 거두다 / ~ *taxes* 세금을 징수하다. **3** gather together (one's thoughts, etc.); recover control of (oneself). (생각)을 집중[정리]하다; (마음)을 가라앉히다. ¶ ~ *one's thoughts* 생각을 가다듬다 / ~ *one's courage* 용기를 내다 / ~ *a horse* 말을 잘 다루다 / ~ *oneself* 마음을 가라앉히다. —*vi.* (P1,2A,3) **1** gather or come together. 쌓이다. ¶ *Dust and rubbish soon* ~. 먼지와 쓰레기는 금방 쌓인다. **2** meet or assemble. 모이다. ¶ *A crowd collects.* 군중이 모여든다. **3** collect payments, etc. 수금하다. ¶ ~ *for 'Life'* 라이프지(誌)의 수금을 하다. —*adj., adv.* to be paid for by the receiver 요금 수신자 부담의[으로]. ¶ *a* ~ *call* 요금 수신자 부담 전화. [col-, L. *lego* gather]

col·lect·ed [kəléktid] *adj.* gathered together; calm and self-possessed; cool; quiet. 모은; 모인; 침착한; 냉정한. ¶ *a* ~ *manner* 침착한 태도 / *the money* ~ *to build an orphanage* 고아원 건립을 위해 모인 돈. ●**col·lect·ed·ly** [-li] *adv.*

:col·lec·tion [kəlékʃən] *n.* **1** ⓐ ⓊⒸ the act of collecting; an example of this. 모음; 수집; 채집; 집합. ¶ *a stamp* ~ 우표수집 / *make a* ~ *of old coins* 고전(古錢)을 수집하다. ⓑ Ⓒ a group of things collected and preserved. 모은 것; 수집품; 소장품. ¶ *have a large* ~ *of books* 많은 책을 소장하고 있다 / *Our school has a fine* ~ *of pictures.* 우리 학교에는 훌륭한 그림들이 소장되어 있다. **2** ⓊⒸ money gathered from people; the act of taking in due; the amount received. 기부금; 모금; (세금 따위의) 징수; 수금(액). ¶ *make* [*start*] *a* ~ 모금을 하다[시작하다] / *take up a* ~ *in aid of hospitals* 병원 원조의 기부금을 모집하다. **3** Ⓒ a mass; a heap. (먼지·쓰레기 따위의) 더미; 퇴적. ¶ *There is a* ~ *of dust in an unused room.* 사용하지 않는 방에 먼지가 수북히 쌓여 있다. **4** 《*pl.*》 《Brit.》 the college terminal examination. 대학의 학기말 시험.

col·lec·tive [kəléktiv] *adj.* **1** of a group; having to do with a group. 집단의; 공동의. ¶ *a* ~ *agreement* 단체 협약 / ~ *ownership* 공동 소유(권) / ~ *emigration* 집단 이민 / *the* ~ *leadership* 집단 지도제 / *the* ~ *economy of a village* 촌락의 공동 경제. **2** formed by collecting; forming a collection or whole. 모은; 모인; 축적된; 총체의; 전체를 이루는. ¶ *a* ~ *effort* 전체의 힘; 총력 / *a* ~ *edition of Shakespeare's works* 셰익스피어 전집 / *the* ~ *knowledge of all ages* 태곳적부터 축적된 인지(人智) / *the* ~ *wishes of the people* 국민 전체의 희망[총의]. **3** 《gram.》 singular in form, but plural in meaning. 집합적인. —*n.* Ⓒ **1** 《gram.》 a collective noun. 집합명사. **2** any collective enterprise. 집단으로서 공동으로 하는 사업.

collective bargaining [-ˊ-- ˊ---] *n.* talk between organized workers and their employers in order to reach an agreement on wages, hours, and working conditions. (노사 간의) 단체 교섭.

collective farm [-ˊ-- ˊ] *n.* a farm formed by a group and under collective management. 집단 농장.

col·lec·tive·ly [kəléktivli] *adv.* in a collective manner; in a collective sense. 집합적으로; 총체로서.

collective noun [-ˊ-- ˊ] *n.* 《gram.》 one noun used to describe a group of things. 집합 명사 《family, class, crew 따위》.

collective security [-ˊ-- -ˊ--] *n.* a system or policy of international peace in which all the nations taking part agree to take action against a nation that attacks any one of them. (국제간의) 집

단 안전 보장.

col·lec·tiv·ism [kəléktəvìzəm] *n.* Ⓤ the collective ownership of land and means of production as a social gospel. 집산(集產) 주의. ● **col·lec·tiv·ist** [-ist] *n., adj.* **col·lec·tiv·is·tic** [kəlèktəvístik] *adj.*

col·lec·tor [kəléktər] *n.* Ⓒ a person who collects; a person whose business is to collect money due. 수집가; 채집가; 수금자; 수세리(收稅吏). ¶ *a book* ~ 책 수집가 / *an art* ~ 미술품 수집가 / *a tax* ~ 세금 징수인 / *a* ~ *for a company* 회사의 수금 사원 / *a ticket* ~ (역의) 집찰 계원.

⁑**col·lege** [kálidʒ / kɔ́l-] *n.* Ⓒ **1** 《Brit.》 a part of a university. (종합 대학의 일부인) 학료(學寮). 參考 옥스퍼드·케임브리지 대학의 자치체. **2** 《U.S.》 an educational institution above the high school that gives degrees; a university; the academic department of a university for general study. 대학《졸업과 함께 bachelor 학위가 수여됨》; (university 내의) (교양) 학부. ¶ *a* ~ *student* 대학생 / *attend* ~ 대학에 다니다 / *be in* ~ 대학 재학 중이다. **3** a school of higher learning for study in the liberal arts or in professional studies. 단과 대학; 특수 전문 학교. ¶ *a medical* ~ 의과 대학 / *a* ~ *of medicine* 약학 대학. **4** the building and grounds used by a college. (전문 학교·대학의) 건물과 운동장. **5** a body of persons having certain common rights or duties. (일정한 권한·자격·의무를 가진) 단체; 협회; 학회. ¶ *the College of Physicians* 의사회. **6** 《*colloq.*》 a prison. 감옥; 교도소. [→colleague]

col·le·gi·an [kəlí:dʒiən] *n.* Ⓒ a college student; a member of a college. 대학생; 단체〔협회〕의 일원.

col·le·gi·ate [kəlí:dʒit, -dʒiit] *adj.* of or like a college; connected with a college; of or characteristic of college students. college 의; college 조직의; 대학생의; 대학생 같은 〔특유의〕. ¶ *a* ~ *life* 대학 생활.

col·lide [kəláid] *vi.* (P1,3) **1** rush against; run into; hit or strike violently together. 부딪치다; 충돌하다. ¶ ~ *against a wall* 벽에 부딪치다 / *The two motorcars collided.* 두 자동차가 충돌했다. **2** disagree strongly; be in conflict. (의견·이해 따위가) 일치하지 않다; 상충되다. ¶ *He collided with me over politics.* 그는 정치에 관해서 나와 의견이 상충되었다. [col-, L. *laedo* hurt]

col·lie [káli / kɔ́li] *n.* Ⓒ a Scottish sheep dog with a hairy coat. 콜리견(犬). [said to be *coaly*]

col·lier [káljər / kɔ́l-] *n.* Ⓒ a coal miner; a ship for carrying coal. 탄갱부; 석탄선(船). [→coal]

col·lier·y [káljəri / kɔ́l-] *n.* Ⓒ (*pl.* **-lier·ies**) a coal mine and the buildings connected with it. 탄갱(炭坑); 채탄소《건물 기타 모든 설비를 포함함》.

Col·lins [kálinz / kɔ́l-] *n.* 콜린스. **1 Wilkie** (1824-89) an English novelist. 영국의 소설가. **2 William** (1721-59) an English poet. 영국의 시인.

·**col·li·sion** [kəlíʒən] *n.* ⓊⒸ the act of colliding or meeting violently; a clash of interests, ideas, etc. 충돌; 격돌; (의견·이해 따위의) 상충. ¶ *the* ~ *of two airplanes* 두 비행기의 충돌 / *a sanguinary* ~ *between* …간의 유혈 충돌 / *be in* ~ *with* (의견·이해 따위가) 상충〔상반〕돼 있다 / *Nine people were killed in the motorcar* ~. 자동차 충돌로 9명이 사망하였다. [→collide]

come into collision (=*collide* or *conflict*) ***with something.*** …와 충돌하다. ¶ *The two trains came into* ~. 열차와 열차가 충돌했다.

in collision with, smashing into. …와 충돌하여.

col·lo·cate [káləkèit / kɔ́l-] *vt.* set or place together; arrange in proper order. 함께 두다; 정리하다; (일정한 순서로) 배열〔배치〕하다. ¶ ~ *books on a shelf* 책을 서가에 가지런히 정리해 두다. [Gk. *collōco* place together]

col·lo·ca·tion [kàləkéiʃən / kɔ̀l-] *n.* Ⓤ **1** the act of arranging or placing together. 배치; 배열. **2** the arrangement, esp. of words in a sentence. 낱말의 배열; 연어(連語) (관계).

col·lo·cu·tor [kəlákjətər, káləkjù:tər] *n.* one's partner in colloquy. 대화의 상대; 말상대. [→colloquy]

col·lo·di·on [kəlóudiən] *n.* 《chem.》 a solution of gun-cotton. 콜로디온액(液). [Gk. *kolla* glue]

col·logue [kəlóug] *vi.* (P1,2) 《*colloq.*》 talk privately; plot mischief. 밀담(密談)하다; 음모를 꾸미다. [F.]

col·loid [kálɔid / kɔ́l-] *adj.* 《chem.》 gluey; in non-crystalline solid state. 콜로이드(모양)의. —*n.* a colloid substance. 콜로이드; 교질(膠質). [→collodion]

col·loi·dal [kəlɔ́idl] *adj.* being, containing, or like a colloid. 교질(膠質)의; 콜로이드성의.

col·lop [káləp / kɔ́l-] *n.* **1** a slice of meat. 얇은 육편(肉片). **2** 《rare》 a fold of flesh or skin on the body. 피부의 주름. [E.]

col·lo·qui·a [kəlóukwiə] *n.* pl. of **colloquium.**

col·lo·qui·al [kəlóukwiəl] *adj.* used in common conversation, not usu. used in formal or literary style. 구어(체)의; 대화의; 회화의(opp. literary). ¶ ~ *language* 구어(口語) / ~ *style* 구어체. ● **col·lo·qui·al·ly** [-i] *adv.* [co-, L. *loquor* speak]

col·lo·qui·al·ism [kəlóukwiəlìzəm] *n.* ⓊⒸ a colloquial word or expression; a colloquial quality, style or usage. 구어적 어구(語句)〔표현〕; 구어체; 구어 어법.

col·lo·qui·um [kəlóukwiəm] *n.* Ⓒ (*pl.* **-qui·ums** or **-qui·a**) **1** an informal meeting for discussion. 회담을〔협의를; 그룹 토의

를] 위한 비공식 모임. **2** an academic seminar on some broad field of study. (연구 분야의) 학술 세미나.

col·lo·quy [kɑ́ləkwi / kɔ́l-] *n.* UC (*pl.* **-quies**) a talk or conversation, esp. a formal conversation. 대담; 대화; 자유 토의; 회담. ¶ *hold ~ with* …와 대담하다 / *be in ~* 회의중이다.

col·lo·type [kɑ́loutàip / kɔ́l-] *n.* a gelatine photographic plate. 콜로타이프판(版) 《젤라틴을 판면(版面)으로 하는 사진 인쇄판》. [→collodion, type]

col·lude [kəlúːd] *vi.* (P1) conspire. 공모하다. [co-, L. *ludo* play]

col·lu·sion [kəlúːʒən] *n.* UC secret agreement for an unlawful or evil purpose. 공모; 결탁. ● **col·lu·sive** [-siv] *adj.*

col·ly·wob·bles [kɑ́liwɑ̀blz / kɔ́liwɔ̀blz] *n. pl.* 《*colloq.*》 rumbling in the intestines. 복통(腹痛). [Imit.]

col·o·cynth [kɑ́ləsinθ / kɔ́l-] *n.* 《bot.》 a gourd plant; a purgative of colocynth. 콜로신스《박과의 식물》; 그 열매로 만든 하제(下劑). [Gk.]

co·logne [kəlóun] *n.* U a perfumed toilet water. 화장수《Cologne 원산》.

Co·lom·bi·a [kəlʌ́mbiə] *n.* a country in the northwest part of South America. 콜롬비아《남아메리카 서북부의 나라》. 參考 수도는 Bogota. ● **Co·lom·bi·an** [-n] *adj., n.*

***co·lon**[1] [kóulən] *n.* C a punctuation mark (:) used to introduce quotations, examples, etc. (구두점의) 콜론《:》. [Gk. *kōlon* limb]

co·lon[2] [kóulən] *n.* C 《anat.》 the lower part of the large intestine. 결장(結腸). [Gk. *kōlon*]

***colo·nel** [kə́ːrnəl] *n.* C **1** the rank below that of a brigadier general in the army. 육군 대령. **2** the officer who commands a regiment of soldiers. 연대장. [It.]

***co·lo·ni·al** [kəlóuniəl] *adj.* **1** of a colony or colonies. 식민(지)의; 식민지풍의. ¶ *the ~ administration* 식민지 통치 / *~ idiom* 식민지풍의 말씨. **2** 《often *C-*》 of the thirteen British colonies that became the United States. (후일 미합중국이 된) 영령(英領) 식민지의. —*n.* C a person of a colony. 식민지의 주민. [L. *colo* till]

co·lo·ni·al·ism [kəlóuniəlizəm] *n.* U the policy of a nation seeking to extend or retain its authority over other people or territories. 식민(화) 정책.

***col·o·nist** [kɑ́lənist / kɔ́l-] *n.* C **1** a person who lives in a colony. 식민지의 주민. **2** a person who takes part in founding a colony. 식민지 개척자[건설자].

col·o·ni·za·tion [kɑ̀lənizéiʃən] *n.* U the act of founding and developing a colony or colonies or sending settlers to a colony. 식민지 건설[개척]; 식민지화. ¶ *These countries took part in the ~ of Africa.* 이 나라들은 아프리카 식민지 건설에 참여했다.

col·o·nize [kɑ́lənàiz / kɔ́l-] *vt.* (P6) establish a colony in (a place); send colonists to and settle in (a place). …을 식민지로 만들다; …에 식민지를 건설[개척]하다; (이민)을 식민지로 보내다. ¶ *England colonized Australia.* 영국은 오스트레일리아를 식민지로 만들었다. —*vi.* (P1) establish in a colony; settle in a colony. 식민하다; 식민지에 이주하다. ¶ *go out to Australia to ~* 식민을 위해 오스트레일리아로 가다.

col·on·nade [kɑ̀lənéid / kɔ̀l-] *n.* C **1** a row of columns regularly spaced along the side or sides of a building. 주랑(柱廊); 열주(列柱). **2** a (double) row of trees. (2열로) 늘어선 가로수. [→column]

〈colonnade 1〉

:col·o·ny [kɑ́ləni / kɔ́l-] *n.* C (*pl.* **-nies**) **1** 《*collectively*》 a group of people who leave their native country and settle in another land, but remain subject to the mother country. (본국에 종속된) 식민단(團); 이민단. ¶ *send out a ~ to Canada* 캐나다로 이민단을 보내다. **2** a place or area settled in this way; any distant territory belonging to a nation. 식민지; 멀리 떨어진 영토. ¶ *Great Britain and her colonies* 대영제국과 그 식민지 / *establish* [*settle, found*] *~* 식민지를 건설하다. **3** a group of people living together and closely connected by race, occupation, or the like; a place settled or occupied by any such group. (나라 또는 도시내의) 외인 거류 민단; 거류지; 조계; (같은 직종인 등의) 집단 (거주지); …촌. ¶ *the American ~ in Paris* 파리 시의 미국인 거주지 / *an artist's ~* 예술인촌. **4** 《*the Colonies*》 the thirteen British Colonies that became the first states of the United States. 독립 전쟁 후 최초로 독립한 13주(州). **5** a group of animals, plants, insects, etc. living or growing together. (동·식물의) 군생(群生); 군락(群落). ¶ *a ~ of plants* 식물의 군락 / *We found a ~ of ants under the tree.* 나무 밑에서 개미의 집단을 발견했다. [L. *colo* till]

col·o·phon [kɑ́ləfɑ̀n / kɔ́ləfən, -fɔ̀n] *n.* C words or inscription placed at the end of a book. (책의) 간기(刊記). [Gk. =summit]

co·loph·o·ny [kɑ́ləfòuni, kəlɑ́fəni / kəlɔ́fə-] *n.* U a kind of dark resin. 송진; 수지(樹脂). [Place]

:col·or, 《Brit.》 **-our** [kʌ́lər] *n.* U **1** UC ⓐ yellow, red, blue, and combinations of these; hue; tint. 빛(깔); 색; 색채. ¶ *a ~ between yellow and red* 빨강과 노랑의 간색 / *be bright in ~* 색이 선명하다. ⓑ a color produced by pigments through the skill of an artist. 채색; 착색. ¶ *a movie in ~* 컬러

〔천연색〕 영화 / *a picture in* ~ 채색화. **2** 《usu. *pl.*》 paint. 그림물감; 안료. ¶ *lay on the colors* 색칠을 하다. **3** 《*sometimes a* ~》 the color of the face; complexion. 안색. ¶ *have a fine* ~ 안색이 좋다 / *have very little* ~ 혈색이 아주 나쁘다 / *regain* ~ 혈색을 되찾다. **4** the skin color of any people or race that is not white; negro. 피부빛; 흑인. ¶ *a person of* ~ 유색인. **5** 《*pl.*》 an outward appearance. 외관; 모양. ¶ *an old idea in a new* ~ 새로움을 가장한 낡은 생각 / *His story has some* ~ *of truth about it.* 그것에 관한 그의 이야기엔 표면적으론 어느 정도 진실성이 있다. **6** red color in the cheeks. 얼굴을 붉힘; 홍조. ¶ *Color rushed up her face.* 그녀는 얼굴을 확 붉혔다. **7** 《usu. *pl.*》 a flag of a nation; a flag of a military unit. 국기; 군기(軍旗). ¶ *the King's* 〔*Queen's*〕 *color(s)* 영국 국기 / *the regimental colors* 연대기(旗) / *hoist* 〔*lower*〕 *the colors* 국기를 게양〔하강〕하다 / *salute the colors* 국기〔군기〕에 대해 경례하다. **8** (esp. in a literary work) liveliness; vividness; atmosphere. (문학 작품 따위의) 생채(生菜); 생생함; 맛. ¶ *His Russian memories came in brilliant* ~. 그의 러시아에서의 기억이 생생히 떠올랐다. **9** a special quality. 특질. ¶ *a novel with local* ~ 지방색이 넘치는 소설.

change color, (of a face) grow paler or redder than usual. 안색이 변하다〔빨개지다, 파래지다〕.

come off with flying colors, make a great success of something. 대성공을 거두다.

gain color, come to look well. 혈색이 좋아지다.

get *one's* colors, be included in an athletic team. (운동 팀의) 선수가 되다.

give a false color to, twist (a statement, act, etc.); give a wrong description of. (진술·행위 따위)의 진상을 왜곡하다〔왜곡하여 전하다〕.

give 〔**lend**〕 **color** (=*give an appearance of probability*) **to** *something.* …을 그럴싸하게 꾸미다.

in *one's* true colors, a) in one's true character. 본성을 드러내어. **b**) as one really is. 있는 그대로. ¶ *see things in their true colors* 사물의 진상을 보다.

join the colors, join the army. 입대하다.

lay on the colors too thickly, 《*fig.*》 describe in exaggerated terms. 너무 과장해서 말하다; 대서 특필하다.

lose color, turn pale. 창백해지다.

lower *one's* colors, give up one's demand. 요구를 철회하다; 공손하게 나오다.

nail *one's* colors to the mast, show a strong determination not to change one's opinion or decision; refuse to yield. 끝까지 의지를 굽히지 않다; 끝까지 저항하다.

off color, looking a little ill; not feeling well; unwell. (평소보다) 얼굴 빛이 나쁜; 몸이 좋지 않은.

paint in bright 〔**dark**〕 **colors,** 《*fig.*》 describe favorably 〔unfavorably〕. 좋게〔나쁘게〕 말하다; 좋은〔나쁜〕 면만 들다.

put false colors upon, falsify. 속이다.

sail under false colors, a) (of a ship) raise the flag of a country other than her own. (배가) 남의 나라 깃발로〔국적을 속이고〕 항행하다. **b**) (of a person) pretend to be other than one really is. 위선적 행위를〔생활을〕 하다; 정체를 속이며 살아가다.

serve with the colors, serve in the army. 병역에 복무하다; 군인이다.

show *one's* true colors, show oneself as one really is; declare one's opinions and plans. 본성을 드러내다; 의견〔생각〕을 밝히다; 본심을 토로하다.

stick to *one's* colors, refuse to change one's party, opinions, etc. 자기의 주의를〔주장을〕 고수하다; 절개를 지키다.

strike *one's* colors, yield. 항복하다.

take *one's* color from *someone*, imitate someone. …의 주의·주장을 받아들이다; …을 흉내내다; …에 물들다.

under color of, on the pretense of. …을 구실로〔빙자하여〕.

with flying colors, triumphantly. 대성공을 거두어; 의기 양양하게.

— *vt.* **1** (P6,18) give color to (something). …에 착색〔채색〕하다. **2** (P6) express wrongly; misrepresent; exaggerate. …을 거짓 표현하다; 왜곡하다; 과장하다. ¶ ~ *the description* 윤색하여 묘사하다 / *facts colored by his prejudices* 편견으로 왜곡된 사실.

— *vi.* **1** (P1,2) blush. 얼굴을 붉히다. **2** (P1) (of fruits, grain) ripen and become colored. (과일·곡식 따위가) 익어서 물들다. [L. *color*]

Col·o·rad·o [kɑ̀lərǽdou, -rɑ́ː- / kɔ̀lərɑ́ː-] *n.* a western State of the United States. 콜로라도《미국 서부의 주》. 參考 Colo.로 생략함. 주도(州都)는 Denver.

col·or·a·ble, 《Brit.》 **-our-** [kʌ́lərəbəl] *adj.* **1** that can be colored. 착색〔채색〕할 수 있는. **2** specious; plausible; counterfeit. 정말 같은; 그럴 듯한; 거짓〔가짜〕의. ¶ *a* ~ *opinion* 그럴 듯한 의견 / ~ *sorrow* 가장된 슬픔 / *a* ~ *imitation* 위조품. [→color]

col·or·a·tion, 《Brit.》 **-our-** [kʌ̀ləréiʃən] *n.* Ⓤ the act of coloring; the arrangement of colors, as in an animal or plant. 착색(법); 채색(법); 배색; (생물의) 천연색. ¶ *warning* ~ 경계색 / *protective* ~ 보호색.

col·o·ra·tu·ra [kɑ̀lərətjúərə, kʌ̀l- / kɔ̀l-] *n.* 《mus.》 Ⓤ an ornamental passage in music; Ⓒ a soprano who sings such passages. 콜로라투라《화려한 기교적 장식》; 콜로라투라 가수.

col·or-blind, 《Brit.》 **-our-** [kʌ́lərblàind] *adj.* unable to recognize or see certain colors. 색맹의.

color blindness [´-`-] *n.* the condition of being unable to distinguish colors.

색맹.

col·or·cast [kʌ́lərkæ̀st, -kɑ̀ːst] *n.* Ⓒ a television broadcast in color. 컬러 텔레비전 방송. — *vt.* (P6) broadcast (a television program) in color. (프로그램)을 컬러 텔레비전 방송을 하다.

∗**col·ored,** 《Brit.》 **-oured** [kʌ́lərd] *adj.* **1** having color. 착색된; 색채가 있는. ¶ ~ *shirts* 무색 셔츠 / ~ *glass* 착색 유리 / ~ *spectacles* 색안경 / ~ *pencils* 색연필. **2** belonging to a race other than the white race, esp. the Negro race. 유색(인종)의; (특히) 흑인의. ¶ *a ~ man* 유색인; 흑인 / *a ~ race* 유색 인종; 흑인종 / *a ~ school* 흑인 학교. **3** a little influenced by emotion, prejudice, etc. (감정·편견 등에) 영향받은; 왜곡된; 색안경을 쓴. ¶ *a ~ view* 편견 / *overcome one's ~ beliefs* 편견으로 일그러진 생각을 극복하다.

col·or·ful, 《Brit.》 **-our-** [kʌ́lərfəl] *adj.* rich in color; interesting; exciting the imagination; vivid. 색채가 풍부한; 다채로운; 화려한; 생생한; 선명한.

col·or·ing, 《Brit.》 **-our-** [kʌ́ləriŋ] *n.* Ⓤ **1** the way in which color is used by an artist. 착색(법); 채색. ¶ *the ~ of a picture* 그림의 채색 / *give ~ to* …에 채색을 하다. **2** ⓊⒸ a substance used to give color to something, such as a pigment, a dye, etc. 염료; 안료; (그림)물감. ¶ ~ *matter* 착색제; 색소. **3** a false appearance or look. 겉치레; 외양; 가장(假裝). ¶ *lies under the ~ of truth* 그럴 듯이 진실을 가장한 거짓말. **4** the color of a person's face. 안색. ¶ *healthy* ~ 건강색.

col·or·ist, 《Brit.》 **-our-** [kʌ́lərist] *n.* Ⓒ a person using colors; an artist skillful in using colors. 착색자; 채색자; 채색에 뛰어난 화가.

col·or·less, 《Brit.》 **-our-** [kʌ́lərlis] *adj.* **1** without color. 색이 없는. ¶ ~ *liquids* 무색의 액체. **2** pale; pallid; dull. 창백한; (날씨가) 흐린. ¶ *a ~ sallow complexion* 혈색이 좋지 않은 창백한 안색 / *a ~ sky* 찌푸린 하늘. **3** 《*fig.*》 without interest or character. 재미없는; 특색 없는. ¶ *a ~ person* 〔*speech*〕 따분한 사람〔연설〕. **4** 《*fig.*》 unbiased; neutral; indifferent. 공평한; 중립의. ¶ *a ~ opinion* 공평한 의견.

color scheme [ˊ-ˋ] *n.* a pattern, or combination of colors to produce a harmonious effect. (실내 장식·정원 따위의) 색채의 배합 설계.

co·los·sal [kəlɑ́səl / -lɔ́sl] *adj.* huge; very large; splendid; incredible. 거대한; 훌륭한; 어마어마한; 엄청난. ¶ ~ *dramas* 방대한 희곡 / *a man of ~ stature* 거대한 사나이 / *a ~ sum* 막대한 금액 / *a ~ lier* 엄청난 거짓말쟁이 / *have a ~ row* 대소동을 일으키다. [→ colossus]

Col·os·se·um [kɑ̀ləsíːəm / kɔ̀lə-] *n.* a large open-air theater built in Rome about 80 A.D. and used for games, fights, etc. 콜로세움《고대 로마의 거대한 원형 극장》. [↓]

co·los·si [kəlɑ́sai / -lɔ́s-] *n.* pl. of **colossus.**

co·los·sus [kəlɑ́səs / -lɔ́s-] *n.* Ⓒ (*pl.* **-los·si** or **-los·sus·es**) a very large statue; any huge person or object; a very great man. 거상(巨像); 거인; 거대한 물건; 위인. ¶ *such a ~ as Napoleon* 나폴레옹 같은 위인. [Gk. *kolossós* a gigantic statue]

The Colossus of Rhodes [roudz], a figure of Apollo at Rhodes, made about 280 B.C. and known as one of the seven wonders of the world. 로도스의 콜로서스《에게 해의 섬 Rhodes에 세워졌다는 Apollo 의 청동상》.

⁝**col·our** [kʌ́lər] *n., v.* 《Brit.》 =color.

col·our·a·ble [kʌ́lərəbəl] *adj.* 《Brit.》 =colorable.

col·oured [kʌ́lərd] *adj.* 《Brit.》 =colored.

col·our·ful [kʌ́ləfəl] *adj.* 《Brit.》 =colorful.

col·our·ing [kʌ́ləriŋ] *n.* 《Brit.》 =coloring.

col·our·less [kʌ́lərlis] *adj.* 《Brit.》 =colorless.

col·por·teur [kɑ́lpɔ̀ːrtər / kɔ́l-] *n.* (*pl.* **-s**) a person who is employed by a religious society to travel and distribute Bibles. 성서〔종교 서적〕 보급원. [F. =hawker]

∗**colt** [koult] *n.* Ⓒ **1** a young horse, donkey or zebra. 망아지《말·당나귀·얼룩말의》. **2** a young, inexperienced person. 풋내기; 미숙자. **3** 《*C-*》 a kind of revolver, invented by Samuel Colt. 콜트식 자동 권총. [E.]

colts·foot [kóultsfùt] *n.* Ⓒ (*pl.* **-foots**) 《bot.》 a large leaved weed. 머위. [↑]

∗**Co·lum·bi·a** [kəlʌ́mbiə] *n.* 《poet.》 the United States. 미국.

col·um·bine [kɑ́ləmbàin / kɔ́l-] *n.* Ⓒ **1** 《bot.》 a garden plant with showy flowers; the flowers of this plant. 매발톱꽃. **2** 《*C-*》 the mistress of Harlequin. 어릿광대의 아내역(役). — *adj.* of a dove; dovelike. 비둘기의; 비둘기 같은. [L. *columba* dove]

∗**Co·lum·bus** [kəlʌ́mbəs], **Christopher** *n.* (1446?-1506) an Italian who discovered America in 1492. 콜럼버스《이탈리아의 아메리카 대륙 발견자》.

⁝**col·umn** [kɑ́ləm / kɔ́l-] *n.* Ⓒ **1** a slender, upright structure; a large round post in a building. 원주(圓柱); 기둥. **2** anything shaped like a column. 기둥 모양의 것. ¶ *a ~ of water* 물기둥 / *columns of smoke* 연기 기둥 / *a ~ of mercury* 수은주 / *a thick ~ of orange fire* 오렌지색의 큰 불기둥 / *the ~ of the nose* 콧마루. **3** a narrow division of a newspaper often used for a special subject. (신문 따위의) 난(欄); 단(段); (신문·잡지의) 특별 기고란. ¶ *a contributor's ~* 투서란 / *the 'wants' ~* 구인·구직란 / *in the columns of this paper* 본란에서; 본지상(本紙上)에서 / *There are three columns on this page.* 이 페이지는 3단조(組)이다. **4** 《mil.》 a line of soldiers or ships placed one behind another. (군인·군함의) 종대(縱隊);

종렬. [L.]

col·um·nist [káləmnist / kɔ́l-] *n.* Ⓒ a person who regularly writes a special column in a newspaper. (신문 시평(時評) 따위의 정기적인) 특별란 기고가.

com- [kəm-, kɔm-] *pref.* with; together; completely. '함께, 전혀, 전부'의 뜻. [L. *cum* with]

co·ma [kóumə] *n.* Ⓒ a deep, unconscious sleep caused by disease, injury, etc. 혼수(昏睡). ¶ *fall* 〔*lapse*〕 *into a* ~ 혼수 상태에 빠지다 / *come out of the* ~ 혼수 상태에서 깨어나다. [Gk. *cōma* deep sleep]

com·a·tose [kóumətòus, kám-] *adj.* in a coma. 혼수 상태의; 인사 불성의. [↑]

***comb** [koum] *n.* Ⓒ **1** a narrow, short piece of metal, bone, etc. with teeth, used to arrange or clean the hair. 빗. ¶ *pass* 〔*run*〕 *a* ~ *through one's hair* 머리를 빗다. **2** anything shaped or used like a comb, esp. an instrument for combing wool. 빗 모양의 것; 소모기(梳毛機). **3** the crest of a bird. (닭 따위의) 볏(=cockscomb). **4** the top of a wave. 물마루. **5** a honeycomb. 벌집; 봉와(蜂窩).

cut the comb of, lower the pride of; make ashamed. 거만한 콧대를 꺾다; 욕박지르다; 창피를 주다.

— *vt.* (P6,7) **1** arrange or set (the hair) with a comb; clean (wool, flax, etc.) with a comb. (머리)를 빗다; (양털·아마(亞麻) 따위)를 빗질하다. **2** search (something) thoroughly. …을 샅샅이 찾다〔수색하다〕. ¶ *We combed the city to find our lost dog.* 잃은 개를 찾기 위해 온 시를 샅샅이 뒤졌다. — *vi.* (P1, 3) (of waves) roll over or break at the top. 놀치다; (파도가) 물결을 일으키며 치솟다; 물마루져 흩어지다. [E.]

comb out, get rid of by combing; select carefully; search thoroughly. 제거하다; 가려내다; 샅샅이 수색하다; 이 잡듯 하다.

***com·bat** [kəmbǽt, kámbæt, kʌ́m-] *vt., vi.* (**-bat·ed, -bat·ing** or 《Brit.》 **-bat·ted, -bat·ting**) (P6; 1,3) 《*with, against, for*》 fight; battle; struggle. (…와) 싸우다; 격투하다; 항쟁하다. ¶ ~ *for a cause* 주의(主義)를 위해 싸우다 / ~ *a disease* 병마와 싸우다 / ~ *an opinion* 의견과 싸우다 / ~ *against temptation* 유혹과 싸우다 / ~ *against overwhelming odds* 압도적인 대적과 싸우다 / ~ *with someone for one's right* 자기의 권리를 위해 아무와 싸우다.

— [kámbæt, kʌ́m-] *n.* Ⓒ a struggle; a battle; a fight. 싸움; 투쟁; 격투; 전투. ¶ *a mortal* ~ 목숨을 건 싸움 / *a* ~ *with difficulties* 곤란과의 싸움 / *a single* ~ 결투; 일대일의 싸움. [com-, L. *batuo* beat]

com·bat·ant [kəmbǽtənt, kámbət-, kʌ́m-] *n.* Ⓒ a person who fights. 투쟁자; 투사; 전투원. ¶ *The two combatants fought each other with might and main.* 두 사람은 서로 사력을 다해 싸웠다. — *adj.* fighting. 싸우는. ¶ *a* ~ *spirit* 투지.

com·bat·ive [kəmbǽtiv, kámbətiv, kʌ́m-] *adj.* ready to fight; fond of fighting. 전투적〔호전적〕인; 싸움을 좋아하는.

combe, coomb [ku:m] *n.* Ⓒ 《Brit.》 a narrow valley. 작은 골짜기. [O.E.]

comb·er [kóumər] *n.* Ⓒ **1** a person that combs. (목화·양털·아마(亞麻) 따위를) 빗질하는 사람. **2** a wave that rolls over at the top. 밀려오는 파도. [*comb*]

:com·bi·na·tion [kàmbənéiʃən / kɔ̀m-] *n.* ⓊⒸ **1** the act or process of joining together. 결합; 합동. ¶ *make a good* ~ 좋은 결합이 되다. **2** one whole made by combining two or more different things. 결합물〔체〕. ¶ *a* ~ *of ideas* 관념들의 결합. **3** 《*pl.*》 a piece of underwear joining upper and lower garments in one piece. 콤비네이션《위아래 하나로 이어진 속옷》. **4** a group of persons or parties joined together for some common purpose. 일당; 연합〔단결〕(체); 조합. ¶ *form a strong* ~ 강력한 연합체를 만들다 / *enter into a* ~ *with* …와 연합〔제휴〕하다 / *show a good* ~ 좋은 팀워크를 발휘하다. **5** ⓐ the series of numbers or letters to which a dial on a lock is turned to open it. (자물쇠를 열기 위한) 맞춤숫자〔문자〕. ¶ *a* ~ *lock* 맞춤숫자식 자물쇠. ⓑ 《*pl.*》 《math.》 any of the different sets into which a number of letters may be grouped. (수학의) 조합. **6** 《chem.》 the union of materials to form a chemical compound. 화합(化合). [↓]

in combination with, joining with (someone). …와 공동으로.

:com·bine [kəmbáin] *vt.* (P6,7,13) **1** 《*with*》 join together; join so as to form one; unite. …을 결합하여 하나로 하다; …을 겸하다. ¶ ~ *efforts* 노력을 결집하다 / ~ *several fields to form a park* 공원을 조성키 위해 몇 개의 밭을 합치다 / ~ *the office of mayor with that of company president* 시장직과 회사 사장직을 겸하다. **2** 《chem.》 unite (different substances) into a compound. …을 화합(化合)시키다. ¶ *The acid and alkali are combined into a salt.* 산과 알칼리는 화합해서 염(塩)이 된다.

— *vi.* (P1,2A,3,4) unite; mix. 결합〔화합〕하다; 연합〔합동〕하다. ¶ *Two parties will* ~ *to defeat a third.* 두 당은 제3당을 패배시키기 위해 연합할 것이다 / *Oil and water will not* ~. 물과 기름은 섞이지 않는다.

— [kámbain / kɔ́m-] *n.* Ⓒ **1** 《U.S. *colloq.*》 a group of people, corporations, etc. (정치상·사업상의 이익 따위를 위한) 합동; 연합(체); 결합. **2** 《U.S.》 a machine for harvesting. 콤바인; 복식(複式) 수확기《수확과 탈곡을 동시에 하는 농업 기계》. [L. *bini* pair, two by two]

com·bus·ti·ble [kəmbʌ́stəbəl] *adj.* **1** apt to catch fire or burn; easily burned. 가연성(可燃性)의; 인화하기 쉬운. ¶ *Celluloid is* *highly* ~. 셀룰로이드는 가연성이 매우 높다. **2** easily excited. 격하기〔흥분하기〕 쉬운. ¶ *a* ~ *temper* 흥분 잘 하는 기질. —*n.* 《usu. *pl.*》 materials which are easily set on fire. 가연성 물질. [L. *comburo* burn]

com·bus·tion [kəmbʌ́stʃən] *n.* Ⓤ **1** the act or process of burning. 연소. ¶ *complete* ~ 완전 연소 / *spontaneous* ~ 자연 발화. **2** oxidation. (유기체의) 산화(酸化).

Comdr. Commander.

Comdt. Commandant.

:come [kʌm] *v.* (**came, come**) *vi.* **1** ⓐ (P1,2,3,4) move towards the speaker; move from 'there' to 'here'. 오다. ¶ ~ *for someone* 아무를 맞으러 오다 / *They will* ~ *soon.* 그들은 곧 올 게다 / *Come here* (*close to me*). 이리 (가까이) 오너라 / *I was waiting till you came.* 네가 올 때까지 기다리고 있었다 / *You must* ~ *and see us sometime.* = *You must* ~ *to see us sometime.* 언젠가 놀러 오게나. 參考 구어에서는 come and see를 쓰는 것이 보통임. ⓑ (P1,2) move to or towards the speaker or the person addressed to. (말하는 이가 상대방에게(로)) 가다. ¶ *I will* ~ *to you.* 자네에게로 가겠네 / *I am coming now.* 곧 갑니다. ⓒ (P1,2) go with the speaker. (말하는 이와) 함께 가다; 따라가다. ¶ *Will you* ~ *with me to Kwangju?* 광주에 나와 함께 가지 않으려나 / *Are you coming my way?* 나와 같은 방향으로 가십니까. **2** (of time) ⓐ (P2,3) draw near; arrive in due course. (때·철·순서가) 다가오다; 돌아오다; (…때가) 되다. ¶ *generations to* ~ 오는 세대 / *Evening is coming.* 밤이 다가오고 있다 / *The time has* ~ *to say good-bye.* 작별할 때가 왔다 / *Spring comes next to winter.* 봄은 겨울 다음에 온다. ⓑ 《used as *subjunctive present*》 when (the time) comes. …이(오)면. ¶ *She will be twenty years old* ~ *April.* 그녀는 오는 4월이면 스무살이 된다 / *She is getting married* ~ *the spring.* 봄이면 그녀는 결혼한다. **3** (P2,3) become seen, heard, etc.; appear. 보이다; 들리다; 나타나다. ¶ *Flowers and fruits* ~ *each year.* 꽃과 과일은 해마다 나타난다 / *The light comes and goes.* 빛이 보였다 사라졌다 한다 / *A smile came to her lips.* 그녀 입가에 미소가 떠올랐다 / *There came the sound of knocking at the door.* 문에서 노크하는 소리가 들려왔다. **4** (P1) arrive; reach. 오다; 도착하다. ¶ *Has he* ~ *yet?* 그 사람 벌써 와 있습니까 / *Nobody has* ~ *yet.* 아직 아무도 도착해 있지 않다. **5** (P2A,3) happen; take place. 일어나다; 생기다. ¶ *Misfortune comes to all.* 불행은 모든 사람에게 닥친다 / *I'm ready for whatever comes.* 무슨 일이 있든 각오가 돼 있다 / *How does it* ~ *that you didn't know of it?* 자네가 그 일을 몰랐다니 어찌 된 건가 / *How comes it that you were there?* 자네가 거기 있다니 어찌된 셈인가. **6** (P1,5) arrive at completion; be produced; be offered. (물건이) 되어 나오다; 생산〔공급〕되다; 시장에 나오다. ¶ *The butter came very quickly today.* 오늘은 버터가 무척 빨리 되었다 / *The book comes hardbound.* 그 책은 견고한 표지본(本)으로 발매된다. **7** (P1,3) occur to the mind; be called to mind. (생각 따위가) 떠오르다. ¶ *A thought came to him.* 그에게 생각이 떠올랐다 / *The inspiration never came.* 도무지 영감이 떠오르지 않았다 / *The solution of the problem has just* ~ *to me.* 문제의 해결책이 문뜩 떠올랐다. **8** (P3) 《*of, from*》 result from; be caused by. (…의 결과로서) 생기다; (…으로) 말미암다. ¶ *Diseases often* ~ *from intemperance.* 질병은 흔히 무절제의 결과로 생긴다 / *This comes from* 〔*of*〕 *carelessness.* 이는 부주의로 말미암아 생긴다 / *No good comes of dishonesty.* 부정직해서는 아무 좋은 일도 생기지 않는다. **9** (P3) 《*from, of*》 ⓐ proceed from (a source); be derived from. (…로부터) 나오다; 비롯되다. ¶ *His money comes from his wife.* 그의 돈은 아내한테서 나온다 / *The word came from Greek.* 그 말은 그리스어(語)에서 나왔다 / *Nothing good can* ~ *of that.* 그것에서는 아무 좋은 결과도 나올 수 없다. ⓑ be descended from; spring from. (…의) 출신이다; 자손이다. ¶ *He comes from* 〔*of*〕 *a good family.* 그는 좋은 가문의 출신이다. ⓒ be a native of; be born in. (…의) 태생이다. ¶ *I* ~ *from Chejudo.* 나는 제주도 태생이다 / *Where do you* ~ *from?* 당신은 고향이 어디십니까. 參考 Where did 〔have〕 you come from? "어디서 오셨습니까"와 구별할 것. **10** (P2,3) ⓐ 《*to*》 reach; extend; amount. (…에) 이르다; 달하다. ¶ ~ *to a large sum* 거액에 달하다 / *Our debts* ~ *to $500.* 우리의 빚은 500 달러에 달한다 / *The dress does not* ~ *to her knees.* 드레스가 그녀 무릎에 미치지 않는다. ⓑ mean as much as; be equal to; become. …와 (결국) 같은 뜻이 되다; …와 같다; …이 되다. ¶ *What you say comes to this.* 자네의 말은 결국 이런 뜻이 된다. **11** ⓐ (P2,5) 《with *adj.* or *pp.*》 become; turn out to be. …이 되다. ¶ *His dream came true.* 그의 꿈은 실현되었다 / *It'll* ~ *easy soon.* 곧 쉬워질 게다 / *His shoes came untied.* 구두끈이 풀어졌다. ⓑ (P4) be brought to do; get to do. (사람이) …하게 되다. ¶ ~ *to know someone better* 아무를 더 잘 알게 되다 / *How did you* ~ *to do that?* 대체 어떻게 자네가 그런 짓을 하게 되었나 / *They came to love each other.* 두 사람은 서로 사랑하게 되었다 / *He has* ~ *to see that he has lost all his fortune.* 그는 자신의 재산을 몽땅 날렸다는 사실을 깨닫게 되었다 / *He came to be known as a great poet.* 그는 위대한 시인으로 알려지게 되었다. **12** (P3) 《*in, into*》 be brought to (a certain state or condition); pass or enter into. (어떤 상태·조건에) 이르다; 달하다; …로 들어가다; …하게 되다. ¶ ~ *into popular use* 널리 사용하게 되다 / ~ *to an agreement* 합의에 이르다 / ~ *to a conclusion* 결론에 달하다 / ~ *to grief* 슬픔을 당하게 되

다 / *The bus came to halt*〔*stop*〕. 버스는 정지하게 되었다. **13** 《in *imperative*》 Look!; See here! 자; 이봐. ¶ *Come, show it to me!* 이봐 그것 좀 보여다오 / *Now ~, be patient.* 자 참아라. — *vt.* 《*colloq.*》 play the part of (someone); behave. …인 것처럼 행동하다; …연하다; …체하다. ¶ ~ *the grande dame* 귀부인같이 굴다 / *Don't ~ the moralist over me!* 내게 도덕군자처럼 굴지 마라. [E.]

come about, happen; occur. 일어나다; 발생하다. ¶ *How did it ~ about?* 그게 어떻게 일어났나.

come across, **a**) cross. …을 횡단하다. ¶ ~ *across the sea* 바다를 횡단하다. **b**) meet or find unexpectedly; happen to meet with. …을 뜻밖에 만나다; 우연히 발견하다. ¶ ~ *across an old friend* 뜻밖에 옛 친구를 만나다 / ~ *across a rare book* 우연히 희귀본(本)을 발견하다. **c**) 《U.S. *colloq.*》 pay one's debt; do one's duty; confess. 빚을 갚다; 의무를 이행하다; 자백하다. **d**) be effective and well received. (말 따위가) 효과적이다; 이해하기 쉽다. ¶ *Your speech came across very well.* 자네 연설은 매우 이해하기 쉬웠네.

come across the mind, occur or suggest itself to one. (생각 따위가) 문뜩 마음 속에 스치다〔떠오르다〕.

come after, **a**) follow; succeed to; take the place of. …의 뒤를 따르다; 뒤에 오다; 뒤를 잇다. ¶ *Spring comes after winter.* 봄은 겨울 뒤에 온다 / *Who came after Lincoln?* 누가 링컨의 뒤를 이었나. **b**) make efforts to gain; seek. …을 찾다.

come along, **a**) take one's way along (a street, etc.). (길 따위)를 지나다; 가다. **b**) accompany; go with. …와 함께 가다. ¶ *Come along* (*with me*). 같이 가자. **c**) come near; approach; appear. 다가오다; 접근하다; 나타나다. ¶ *I saw a bus coming along.* 버스가 오는것을 보았다 / *wait for a friend to ~ along* 친구가 나타나기를 기다리다. **d**) get along. 잘 해나가다; (잘) 지내다. **e**) 《in *imperative*》 Make haste! 자 빨리; 서둘러라. ¶ *Come along! Quick!* 서둘러라 어서.

come and go, pass to and fro; be constantly changing. 왔다갔다하다; 오가다; 세월따라 변해가다.

come apart, break into pieces without the need of force. 힘없이 조각조각 떨어져 나가다; 깨지다; 무너지다. ¶ *My shirt has ~ apart at the seams.* 셔츠는 솔기 부분이 터졌다.

come around, **a**) arrive at; come in the regular course of rotation. 오다; 돌아오다. **b**) recover consciousness; revive; come to life. 의식을 되찾다; 소생〔재생〕하다. ¶ *It was a long time before he came around.* 오랜 시간 뒤에 의식이 돌아왔다. **c**) change one's opinion, esp. to agree with another's. (동조하기 위해) 자신의 의견을〔결의를〕 바꾸다. ¶ *He came around to our point of view.* 그는 우리 견해에 동조했다. **d**) visit informally. (예고 없이) 불쑥 들르다. **e**) hoodwink; persuade. 눈을 속이다; 설득하다.

come at, **a**) arrive at; attain. …에 도착하다; …에 (도)달하다; …을 손에 넣다. ¶ ~ *at a true understanding* 참된 이해에 이르다. **b**) rush at; make an attack. …에 덤벼들다; 달려들다; …을 공격하다. ¶ *He came at me like a bull.* 그는 황소처럼 내게 덤벼들었다.

come away, **a**) leave. 떠나(가)다. **b**) get unfastened or separated; become loose; fall off. 풀어지다; 헐거워지다; 떨어〔벗겨〕지다; 빠지다.

come back, **a**) return. (되)돌아오다. ¶ ~ *back home* 집에 돌아오다 / ~ *back to power* 권좌에 되돌아오다. **b**) return to one's memory. (기억이) 되살아나다; 생각이 나다. ¶ *The memory kept coming back to me.* 기억이 계속 되살아나고 있었다. **c**) 《*sl.*》 talk back; retort. 말대답하다; 되쏘아붙이다.

come before, **a**) come to the attention of (an authority, etc.). …에 부쳐지다; 심의〔상정〕되다. ¶ ~ *before a meeting* 회의에 상정되다. **b**) have advantage over; be superior to. …의 우위〔상위〕에 서다; …보다 낫다.

come between, divide or separate (two things or persons); estrange. (둘 사이)를 갈라〔떼어〕놓다; …사이를 이간하다. ¶ *Love of money came between the sisters.* 금전욕(慾)이 자매 사이를 갈라놓았다 / *He tried to ~ between us*〔*you and me*〕. 그는 우리 〔너와 나〕 사이를 이간하려고 했다.

come by, **a**) get; acquire. …을 손에 넣다; 얻다. ¶ *How did you ~ by the money?* 자넨 어떻게 그 돈을 입수했나 / *These are hard things to ~ by nowadays.* 이것들은 요즘 입수하기 어려운것들이다. **b**) pass by; approach. (근처를) 지나가다; 다가오다. ¶ *A car came by and picked us up.* 차 하나가 다가와서 우리를 태워 주었다. **c**) drop in. 들르다.

come clean, 《*colloq.*》 confess. 모두 말해 버리다; 자백하다.

come down, **a**) move to a lower position. 내려오다; 내리다. **b**) lose one's social position, wealth. (지위·재산 따위를) 잃다. ¶ ~ *down in the world* 영락하다 / ~ *down in one's fortunes* 재산을 잃다. **c**) be handed down; descend. 전해지다; 전해 내려오다. ¶ *The custom has ~ down to us from the past.* 그 풍습은 과거부터 전해져왔다. **d**) 《*colloq.*》 pay; give money. 돈을 내다〔주다〕. ¶ ~ *down handsome*(*ly*) 돈을 후하게 주다.

come down on 〔**upon**〕, 《*colloq.*》 **a**) criticize strongly; blame; scold; punish. …을 호되게 비평하다; 비난하다; 벌하다. ¶ ~ *down on someone like a ton* 〔*thousand*〕 *of bricks* 아무를 맹렬히 비난하다. **b**) voice one's opposition to. …에 반대하다. **c**) demand (money, etc.) from. …에게 (돈 따위)를 요구하다.

come down with, **a**) 《*colloq.*》 pay money. 돈을 내다〔지불하다〕. ¶ ~ *down with some money to the society* 그 단체에 얼마의 돈을 기부하다. **b**) 《U.S. *colloq.*》 become ill with. 병에 걸리다; 병이 나다. ¶ ~ *down with* *influenza* 독감에 걸리다.

come easy 〔***natural***〕 ***to,*** be easy for (someone) to do or learn. (…에게) 배우기〔하기〕 쉽다; 노력을 요하지 않다.

come forth, appear; be published. 나오다; 출판〔공표〕되다.

come forward, **a**) approach; present oneself. 앞으로 나오다〔나서다〕. **b**) stand as a candidate; offer to do. 지원하다; 후보자로 나서다.

come home, **a**) return to one's house. 귀가하다. **b**) touch one's feelings. 가슴에 와닿다; 심금을 울리다.

come in, **a**) enter. 들어오다〔가다〕. ¶ ~ *in at the door* 문으로 들어오다 / *Ask her to* ~ *in.* 그녀에게 들어오라고 하시오 / *Come in, Jane!* 제인 들어 와. **b**) arrive or be received. 도착하다; (수입이) 들어오다. ¶ *What time does the train* ~ *in?* 열차가 몇 시에 도착하나요 / *A little money is coming in.* 돈이 좀 들어온다. **c**) (of a period of time) begin; (of the tide) rise. (계절 따위가) 시작되다; 밀물이 들어오다. ¶ *The Christmas season came in with unwelcome heavy snowstorms.* 크리스마스 시즌이 달갑지 않은 폭설로 시작되었다. **d**) come into use or fashion. 쓰이게〔유행하게〕 되다. ¶ *Short skirts came in.* 짧은스커트가 유행되기 시작했다. **e**) begin to be seasonable. 제 철이 되다. ¶ *At what time does the apple crop* ~ *in?* 사과의 성숙기는 언제쯤입니까. **f**) be among the winners. (…등으로 결승점에) 들어오다. ¶ *The horse came in third* (*in a race*). (경마에서) 그 말은 셋째로 들어왔다. **g**) come into power. 정권을 잡다. **h**) take one's part; perform one's function. …의 역할〔기능〕을 다하다.

come in for, 《*colloq.*》 receive; get a share of (money); bring (something unwelcome) upon oneself. (몫)을 받다; (달갑지 않은 일)을 가져오다; 당하다. ¶ ~ *in for blame* 비난을 받다 / *She came in for a fortune when her mother died.* 어머니가 돌아가자 그녀는 재산의 자기 몫을 받았다.

come in handy 〔***useful***〕***,*** be useful some time or other; serve a purpose. 쓸모가 있다; 소용되다; 편리하다. ¶ *The tool will* ~ *in very handy.* 그 도구는 갖고 있으면 편리할 것이다.

come into, **a**) enter (some place). …에 들어가다. ¶ ~ *into a room* 〔*house*〕 방에〔집으로〕 들어가다. **b**) enter into (some state); enter upon (power or office). …상태가 되다; (권력 따위의 자리)에 앉다. ¶ ~ *into the world* (세상에) 태어나다 / ~ *into existence* 태어나다; 나타나다; 성립되다 / ~ *into power* 권력을 장악하다 / ~ *into force* 효력을 발하다 / *Tears came into her eyes.* 그녀 눈에 눈물이 어렸다. **c**) inherit; get; acquire. …을 상속하다; …을 얻다. ¶ ~ *into a great deal of money* 막대한 돈을 입수하다. **d**) agree to join, support, etc. …에 참가〔참여〕하다; …을 지지하다. ¶ ~ *into a plan* 계획에 참여하다.

come into one's own, receive fair and proper recognition; get the place or position due to one. 당연한 것으로 인정받게 되다; 당연한 지위를 얻다.

come it a bit (***too***) ***strong,*** go beyond the truth of something; say or do more than is necessary. 사실 이상으로 과장되다; 좀 지나치게 (말)하다. ¶ *It would be coming it a bit too strong if I said I hated my sister, but it's true I dislike her.* 내 누이를 미워한다면 좀 지나치지만, 내가 그녀를 싫어한다는 건 사실이다.

come near doing, almost do; nearly do. 하마터면〔까딱하면〕 …할 뻔하다.

come of, **a**) come from (a good family, etc.). …의 출신〔태생〕이다. **b**) result from (something). …(결과)로서 생기다; …의 결과다. ¶ *I don't know if any good will* ~ *of your actions.* 네 행동에서 어떤 좋은 결과가 있을지 모르겠다. **c**) happen to or become of (someone). (아무)에게 일어나다; (아무)가 어떤 상태로 되다. ¶ ~ *of age* 성년이 되다.

come off, **a**) be taken away. 떨어지다; 빠지다; 벗겨지다; 풀리다. ¶ *The handle has* ~ *off.* 손잡이가 떨어졌다 / *The paint is coming off.* 칠이 벗겨져 떨어지고 있다. **b**) take place; happen. 일어나다; 행해지다. ¶ *The meeting came off.* 회의가 열렸다. **c**) 《*colloq.*》 reach the end (with success, etc.); prove 〔turn out〕 to be. 결과가 …하게 되다; …로 끝나다. ¶ ~ *off well* 잘 되다; 성공하다 / ~ *off badly* 실패로 끝나다 / ~ *off victorious* 〔*a victor*〕 승리자가 되다 / ~ *off with honors* 우등으로 나오다 / ~ *off with flying colors* 승리를 거두다; 훌륭히 성공하다.

come on, **a**) make progress; develop; become better. (잘) 진행〔진전〕되다; 좋아지다. ¶ *He is coming on well in his studies.* 그의 공부가 향상되고 있다. **b**) (of night, winter, bad weather) draw near; begin; come; approach. 다가오다; 시작되다. ¶ *A storm is coming on.* 폭풍우가 다가오고 있다. **c**) attack. 공격하다; 덮치다. ¶ *The enemy came on.* 적이 공격해 왔다. **d**) meet or find by chance; come across. 우연히 만나다; 뜻밖에 발견하다. **e**) appear on the stage. (무대에) 등장하다. **f**) 《in *imperative*》 《*colloq.*》 hurry up; get started; please. 자 빨리; 자 어서. ¶ *Come on, get out!* 자 어서 꺼져.

come out, **a**) appear; become evident. 나타나다; 명백해지다. ¶ *The sun comes out.* 해가 나타난다. **b**) be published; become public; be made known. 출판되다; 일반에게 퍼지다; 알려지다. ¶ *A book* 〔*new fashion*〕 *comes out.* 새 책이 나온다〔새로운 유행이 퍼지고 있다〕 / *The affair will* ~ *out in the newspapers.* 그 일은 신문에 날 것이다 / *The secret came out.* 비밀이 드러났다. **c**) make one's first appearance in society or on the stage. (사교계·무대에) 첫 등장하다. **d**) end up 〔result〕 in a certain way; prove 〔turn out〕 to be. …한 결과로 되다; …로 판명되다. ¶ ~ *out first* 일등〔수석〕이 되다 / ~ *out true* 〔*false*〕 사실로〔거

짓으로) 판명되다 / *It will ~ out as I expected.* 기대했던 대로의 결과가 나올 것이다. **e**) go on strike. 파업[동맹 휴학]을 하다. **f**) be taken out; disappear. 지워[없어]지다; 빠지다. ¶ *These dirty spots won't ~ out.* 이 얼룩들이 도무지 빠지지 않는다. **g**) (of a flower) come into full bloom; come out the bud. (꽃이) 피다; (나무가) 잎을 내다. ¶ *The buds are coming out.* 싹이 돋아나고 있다.

come out against, declare one's opposition to (someone or something). …에 반대[반항]하다

come out for, support (someone), esp. in an election. (특히 선거 등에서) …을 지지하다.

Come out of that! 《*colloq.*》 Clear out! 게 비켜라; 그만둬라.

come out with, **a**) say (something) openly; make known. …을 공표[발표]하다; 알리다. **b**) tell without thought; reveal; confess. (무심코) 지껄이다; 입 밖에 내다; 말하다. ¶ *He came out with the whole story.* 그는 모든 사실을 토설(吐說)했다. **c**) offer (something) to the public or for sale. …을 세상에 내놓다; 시장에 내놓다. **d**) take out; bring out. 꺼내다. ¶ *He searched his pocket and came out with a handful of coins.* 그는 호주머니를 뒤져 한 줌의 주화(鑄貨)를 끄집어 내었다.

come over, **a**) come from a distance. (멀리서) 오다. **b**) happen to; affect; seize. 일어나다; (감정·병 따위가) 덮치다. ¶ *What has ~ over you?* 너 웬 일로 기운이 없는 거냐 / *A strange feeling came over me.* 묘한 기분이 엄습해 왔다. **c**) make a short informal visit. 잠시 들르다. **d**) change sides or opinions. (주의·의견 따위가) 이쪽으로 돌아서다; 변절하다.

come round =come around.

come through, **a**) be successful. 성공하다. **b**) overcome (a danger, etc.) successfully. (위기 따위)를 이겨[버텨]내다; 헤어나다. **c**) 《*sl.*》 pay. 지불하다.

come to, **a**) return to consciousness. 의식을 회복하다. **b**) amount to; reach. (금액·총계가) …에 달하다; …이 되다; …(하기)에 이르다. ¶ ~ *to a conclusion* 결론에 이르다 / ~ *to an agreement* 합의[협약]에 이르다.

come to pass, happen; occur. 일어나다; 발생하다.

come to pieces, break. 부서지다. ¶ *It came to pieces in my hands.* 손 안에서 부서졌다.

come to the point, touch the most important point of the matter. 요점에 언급되다.

come true, prove to be correct; be realized. 사실이 되다; 실현되다.

come under, **a**) be included under; belong to. …의 부류[항목]에 들다; …으로 분류되다. ¶ *Under what class does this grass ~?* 이 풀은 어떤 강(綱)에 드는가. **b**) be under (an influence, authority, etc.). (영향 따위)를 받다; …의 관할에 들어가다.

come up, **a**) come near; approach. 다가가다[오다]; 접근하다. ¶ *A stranger came up (to me).* 어떤 낯선 사람이 (나에게) 다가왔다 / *The storm is coming up.* 폭풍우가 다가오고 있다. **b**) be put forward for discussion; be mentioned. 화제에 오르다; 언급되다; 상정(上程)되다. ¶ *The question will ~ up at the next meeting.* 그 문제는 다음 회의에 상정될 예정이다. **c**) rise above the ground; spring. 움터 나오다; 싹트다. ¶ *The grass will ~ up again in the spring.* 풀은 봄에 다시 싹이 튼다.

come up against, meet (usu. a difficulty or opposition). (어려움·반대 따위)를 만나다; …에 부딪치다.

come upon, **a**) meet (someone) or find (something) by chance. …을 우연히 만나다; 뜻하지 않게 발견하다. **b**) attack; assail. …을 덮치다; 공격하다. **c**) ask (someone for). …에게 —을 요구하다. **d**) fall to. …의 책임이 되다.

come up to, **a**) reach; extend to. …에 이르다; 달하다. ¶ ~ *up to the knee* 무릎까지 오다[닿다]. **b**) come near to; approach. …에 다가가다[오다]; 접근하다. **c**) be equal to. …에 필적하다; …에 미치다. ¶ *My work doesn't ~ up to yours.* 내 작품은 당신 것의 수준에는 못 미칩니다.

come up with, **a**) overtake; catch up. …을 따라잡다. **b**) present or propose (a suggestion, etc.). …을 제안하다; 제출하다.

come what may, in spite of whatever may happen. 어떤[무슨] 일이 있든.

How come? 《*colloq.*》 Why? 어째서.

come-and-go [kʌ́məndgóu] *n.* coming and going; traffic. 왕래; 내왕.

come-at-a·ble [kʌmǽtəbəl] *adj.* 《*colloq.*》 easy to reach; readily obtained or acquired. 접근[가까이]하기 쉬운; 손에 넣기 쉬운. ¶ *a ~ man* 가까이 하기 쉬운 사람 / *a ~ place* 접근하기 쉬운 곳.

come·back [kʌ́mbæ̀k] *n.* Ⓒ **1** 《*colloq.*》 a return to a former position, power, etc. (전직·권력 따위에의) 복귀; 컴백. ¶ *make* [*stage*] *a ~* 복귀[재기]하다. **2** 《*sl.*》 a clever answer; a retort. 교묘한 대답; 말대꾸. **3** 《*colloq.*》 a cause for complain. 불평의 씨. [E.]

COMECON [kámikən / kɔ́m-] *n.* Council for Mutual Economic Assistance. 코메콘《구소련 중심의 동유럽 경제 상호 원조 회의》.

co·me·di·an [kəmíːdiən] *n.* Ⓒ **1** an actor who plays in comedies; a professional entertainer who tells jokes, sings comic songs, etc. 희극 배우; 코미디언. ¶ *a low ~* 저속한 코미디언. **2** a writer of comedy. 희극 작가. [→comedy]

co·me·di·enne [kəmìːdién, -mèid-] *n.* Ⓒ 《F.》 an actress of comedies. 희극 여배우; 여자 코미디언.

come·di·et·ta [kəmìːdiétə] *n.* 《It.》 a short comedy. 단막물(物) 희극.

come·down [kʌ́mdàun] *n.* Ⓒ 《*colloq.*》 a

change for the worse; a cause of embarrassment. 영락(零落); 몰락; 곤혹(困惑)의 원인. [→come]

*****com·e·dy** [kámədi / kɔ́m-] *n.* (*pl.* **-dies**) **1** ⒸⓊ a play, movie, or show of a light and humorous character and with a happy ending. 희극; 코미디(opp. tragedy). ¶ *a low* ~ 저속한 희극 / *a musical* ~ 희가극. **2** Ⓒ any amusing event in daily life. (실생활에서의) 희극적인 사건〔장면〕. ¶ *a* ~ *of misunderstandings* 오해에서 생기는 희극. [→comic, ode]

come·li·ness [kʌ́mlinis] *n.* Ⓤ **1** beauty of personal appearance. 용모가 단정함; 예쁨. **2** fitness; suitableness; propriety. 적합; 적당. [E.]

come·ly [kʌ́mli] *adj.* (**-li·er, -li·est**) **1** having a pleasant appearance; graceful; charming. 용모가 단정한; 아름다운. ¶ *a* ~ *maiden* 예쁜 처녀. **2** 《*arch.*》 suitable; proper. 적당한. [E.]

com·er [kʌ́mər] *n.* Ⓒ **1** a person who comes. 오는 사람. ¶ *the first* ~ 선착자 / *a chance* ~ 어쩌다 불쑥 오는 사람 / *a self-invited* ~ 불청객 / *a new* ~ *to pictures* 영화계의 신인. **2** 《U.S. *colloq.*》 a person who is likely to succeed in the future. (장래가) 유망한 사람. [→come]

co·mes·ti·ble [kəméstəbəl] *adj.* 《*rare*》 fit to be eaten. 먹을 수 있는. ¶ ~ *seaweed* 식용 해초. — *n.* 《usu. *pl.*》 things to eat, food. 식(료)품; 음식. [com-, →edible]

·**com·et** [kámit / kɔ́m-] *n.* Ⓒ a bright heavenly body with a tail of light. 혜성(彗星); 살별; 꼬리별. [Gk. *kome* hair]

com·et·a·ry [kámitèri / kɔ́mitəri] *adj.* of or like a comet. 혜성의〔같은〕.

com·fit [kʌ́mfit] *n.* Ⓒ a sweetmeat; a kind of candy usu. with a fruit or nut center. (호두 따위를 넣은) 사탕. [→confection]

:**com·fort** [kʌ́mfərt] *vt.* (P6) **1** ease the grief or sorrow of (someone); encourage. …을 위로하다; 격려하다. ¶ ~ *oneself with the thought that*… …하다고 생각하고 스스로 위안하다 / ~ *those who were crippled in the war* 전쟁에서 불구가 된 사람들을 위로하다. **2** make (someone) free from physical pain. (육체적 고통)을 덜어 주다. ¶ ~ *one's aching feet in hot water* 아픈 발을 따뜻한 물에 담가 고통을 가라앉히다.

— *n.* **1** Ⓤ anything that gives cheer, hope, etc.; consolation. 위안; 위로. ¶ *a cold* ~ 기쁘지 않은 위로 / *take* ~ *from*… …로 스스로의 위안을 받다 / *He could not give* ~ *to her.* 그는 그녀에게 위로를 줄 수 없었다 / *The old man took* ~ *in reading.* 노인은 독서로 스스로를 달랬다 / *That news brings great* ~ *to me* 〔*brings me great* ~〕. 그 소식은 내게 크나큰 위안을 가져다 준다. **2** Ⓒ a person or thing that comforts someone. 위안을 주는 사람〔것〕. ¶ *a* ~ *bag* 위문대(袋) / *She was a great* ~ *to her parents.* 그녀는 부모에게 큰 위안거리였다. **3** Ⓤ relief from pain, discomfort, etc. (고통·근심 없는) 안락한 상태; 편안; 쾌적. ¶ *live in* ~ 안락하게 살다 / *He loves* ~. 그는 안락함을 좋아한다. **4** 《*pl.*》 things that make life rich. 생활을 풍족히 하는 것. ¶ *the comforts of home life* 가정 생활을 즐겁게 해주는 것. **5** Ⓒ 《U.S.》 a quilted bedcover. 이불(=comforter 2). [L. *com*-Intensive, *fortis* strong =make strong]

:**com·fort·a·ble** [kʌ́mfərtəbəl] *adj.* **1** providing comfort. 기분 좋은; 쾌적한. ¶ *a* ~ *room* 쾌적한 방 / *feel* ~ 기분이 좋다 / *We had a* ~ *journey.* 즐거운 여행을 하였다. **2** free from pain, etc.; at ease. 안락한; 편(안)한. ¶ *make oneself* ~ 편안히 하다 / *I am* 〔*feel*〕 *quite* ~. 아주 편안하다. **3** quite sufficient for one's needs. 충분한. ¶ *a* ~ *income* 충분한 수입(收入). — *n.* Ⓒ 《U.S.》 a quilted bedcover. 이불. ● **com·fort·a·ble·ness** [-nis] *n.*

·**com·fort·a·bly** [kʌ́mfətəbəli] *adv.* in a comfortable manner. 마음 편히; 기분 좋게. ¶ *The key fits the lock quite* ~. 열쇠가 자물쇠에 아주 잘 들어맞는다 / *The drawer goes in and out* ~. 서랍이 잘 여닫힌다.

com·fort·er [kʌ́mfərtər] *n.* Ⓒ **1** a person or thing that comforts (someone). 위로〔위안〕하는 사람; 위안을 주는 것. ¶ *a Job's* ~ 위로한답시고 도리어 상대에게 괴로움을 주는 사람. **2** 《U.S.》 a padded or quilted bed-covering. (두툼한 깃털) 이불(=comfortable). **3** a long woolen scarf. 긴 털목도리. **4** 《Brit.》 a dummy teat for a baby to suck. 고무 젖꼭지(=《U.S.》 pacifier). **5** 《*the C-*》 the Holy Spirit. 성령(聖靈).

com·fort·less [kʌ́mfərtlis] *adj.* **1** giving no comfort to the mind. (마음에) 위안을 주지 않는. ¶ ~ *words* 위안이 되지 않는 말들. **2** without the comforts of life. 위안(물)이 없는; 쓸쓸한. ¶ *a* ~ *room* 쓸쓸한 방. **3** not comforted; miserable. 위안을 받지 못한; 비참한. ¶ *a* ~ *man.*

com·fy [kʌ́mfi] *adj.* (**-fi·er, -fi·est**) 《*colloq.*》 =comfortable.

com·ic [kámik / kɔ́m-] *adj.* **1** of or like a comedy. 희극의; 희극 같은(opp. tragic). ¶ *a* ~ *actor* 희극 배우 / ~ *writers* 〔*dramatists*〕 희극 작가. **2** funny; humorous. 우스운; 익살스러운. ¶ *a* ~ *book* 만화책 / *a* ~ *strip* (신문 등) 연재 만화. — *n.* 《*colloq.*》 Ⓒ **1** a comic actor. 희극 배우. **2** Ⓤ the comic side of art, life, etc. (미술·인생 따위의) 희극적 측면〔요소〕. **3** Ⓒ 《*pl.*》 《*colloq.*》 comic strips. 연재 만화. [Gk. *kōmos* revel]

com·i·cal [kámikəl / kɔ́m-] *adj.* funny; amusing; odd. 우스운; 재미있는; 익살스러운. ¶ *He was really a* ~ *sight.* 그는 정말이지 우스꽝스러운 몰골이었다. ● **com·i·cal·ly** [-i] *adv.*

Com·in·form [kámínfɔ̀ːrm / kɔ́m-] *n.* Communist Information Bureau. 공산당

정보국; 코민포름. [→Com(*munist*), Inform(*ation Bureau*)]

:com·ing [kʌ́miŋ] *n.* ⒸⓊ the act of approaching; arrival. 접근; 옴; 도래(到來). ¶ *flowers that herald the ~ of spring* 봄이 왔음을 전하는 꽃들. — *adj.* **1** approaching; next. 오는; 다음의. ¶ *the ~ year* 오는 해; 내년. **2** promising. 앞길이 유망한. ¶ *a ~ actor* 유망한 신인 배우. [→come]

Com·in·tern [kámintə̀:rn / kɔ́m-] *n.* Communist International. 국제 공산당; 코민테른. [→Com(*munist*), Intern(*ational*)]

com·i·ty [káməti / kɔ́m-] *n.* Ⓤ politeness. 예양(禮讓); 예절. ¶ *the ~ of nations* 〔*states*〕 (상대국을 존중하는) 국제간의 예양. [L. *comis* courteous]

***com·ma** [kámə / kɔ́mə] *n.* Ⓒ a punctuation mark(,). 콤마. [Gk. *koptō* cut]

:com·mand [kəmǽnd, -má:nd] *vt.* **1** (P6, 11,20) order; bid; direct. …에게 명(령)하다; 지시하다. ¶ *~ silence* 정숙을 명하다 / *The master commanded me to go there.* 주인은 나더러 그 곳에 가라고 지시했다 / *I commanded that he (should) do it.* =*I commanded him to do it.* 그에게 그것을 하도록 명령했다. **2** (P6) be in control of; control or direct (something) authoritatively; be master of. …을 지배〔지휘〕하다. ¶ *~ the air*〔*sea*〕 제공권〔제해권〕을 장악하다 / *~ an action* 전투를 지휘하다 / *A general commands an army.* 장군은 군대를 지휘한다. **3** (P6) keep control of (one's feelings, etc.); restrain. …을 억제하다; 제어하다. ¶ *~ oneself*〔*one's temper*〕 자제하다. **4** (P6) have (something) at one's disposal or use. …을 마음대로 (사용)하다. ¶ *~ a tremendous amount of money* 거액의 돈을 마음대로 주무르다 / *~ the French language* 프랑스어를 구사하다. **5** (P6) demand to be given (something) as one's due; deserve and get. (당연한 것으로) …을 강요하다; 마땅히 받을 만하다. ¶ *~ respect* (당연한) 존경을 받다 / *Such sufferings ~ our sympathy.* 이러한 수난은 우리의 동정을 받을 만하다. **6** (P6) control by position; overlook (=look over) from a height. 요지를 차지하다; (높은 곳에서) 내려다보다. ¶ *a hill commanding the port* 항구가 내려다보이는 산 / *The hotel commands a fine view of the bay.* 호텔에서 아름다운 만이 내려다보인다. **7** (P6) bring; fetch. 가져오다; (어떤 값에) 팔리다. ¶ *~ a good price* 좋은 값에 팔리다. — *vi.* (P1) **1** be in authority. 지휘권을 가지다; 명령하다. ¶ *Who commands here?* 이곳 지휘관은 누군가. **2** look down on some place from a higher position. 내려다〔굽어〕보다; 내다보다.

Yours to command, (at the end of a letter) Yours obediently. 여불비례(餘不備禮).

— *n.* **1** Ⓒ an order; a commandment. 명령; 지휘; 지시. ¶ *issue a ~* 명령을 내리다 / *Who is the officer in ~?* 지휘관은 누군가 / *He gave the ~ to fire.* 그는 사격 명령을 내렸다. **2** Ⓤ 《sometimes *a ~*》 the right to command; control; ruling power. 지휘권; 지배력; 구사력; 제어(력). ¶ *~ of one's passions* 감정을 누르는 힘; 자제력 / *exercise ~ over the troops* 군대의 지휘권을 행사하다 / *She has an excellent ~ of English.* 그녀는 영어를 훌륭히 구사한다. **3** ⓊⒸ wide view; extent of vision; outlook. 내다봄; 전망(展望). **4** Ⓒ the troops or district under a commander. 예하(隷下) 부대 또는 관구(管區). [→mandate]

at (someone's) command, (of a thing) ready to be used at will. 마음대로 쓸 수 있는. ¶ *all the power and money at my ~* 내 마음대로 할 수 있는 모든 권력과 돈.

at the command of, ready to receive orders from; ready to obey. …의 명(령)에 따라.

have a good command of, have skill in (something). …을 마음대로 구사할 수 있다. ¶ *have a good ~ of words* 말주변이 좋다.

in command of, in charge or control of. …을 지휘하고. ¶ *The general is in ~ of the army.* 그 장군은 군을 지휘하고 있다.

take command of, begin to act as the commander of (an army, etc.). …을 지휘하다.

under (the) command of, commanded by. …의 지휘 밑에.

com·man·dant [káməndæ̀nt, -dà:nt / kɔ̀məndǽnt, -dá:nt] *n.* Ⓒ a commanding officer. 지휘관. ¶ *the ~ of a naval base* 해군 기지 사령관.

com·man·deer [kàməndíər / kɔ̀m-] *vt.* (P6) **1** take (private property such as horses and food) for military or other public use. …을 징발하다. ¶ *All horses were commandeered by the army.* 말은 모두 군에 징발당했다. **2** force (men) into military service. …을 군에 징집하다. **3** 《*colloq.*》 take (something) by force. …을 강제로 빼앗다.

:com·mand·er [kəmǽndər, -má:nd-] *n.* Ⓒ **1** a person who commands. 지휘자; 지도자. **2** an officer commanding an army. 지휘관; 사령관. **3** 《U.S. nav.》 an officer ranking just below a captain. 해군 중령.

commander in chief [⌐—⌐] *n.* Ⓒ (*pl.* **commanders in c-**) **1** ⓐ 《army》 an officer commanding all the armed forces of a nation. (육군의) 최고 지휘관〔사령관〕. ⓑ 《nav.》 the head of all warships of a station. (해군의) 사령관. **2** 《*C-*》《U.S.》 the President of the United States. (전군의 지휘관으로서의) 미국 대통령.

com·mand·ing [kəmǽndiŋ, -má:nd-] *adj.* **1** having the power to command. 지휘하는. **2** authoritative. 위엄〔권위〕 있는; 당당한. ¶ *a man of ~ appearance* 당당한 풍채의 사람. **3** having a wide view. 시계가〔전망이〕

트인. ¶ *a ~ bluff* 전망이 좋은 절벽.

*__com·mand·ment__ [kəmǽndmənt, -máːnd-] *n.* Ⓒ an order; a law; a command. 명령; 법; 계율. ¶ *"Thou shalt (=You shall) not kill" is one of the Ten Commandments.* '살인하지 말지어다'는 모세 십계명의 하나이다.

com·man·do [kəmǽndou, -máːn-] *n.* (*pl.* **-es** [-z]) **1** a specially trained military unit used for surprise, destructive raids. 특별 기습 부대; 특공대. **2** 《U.S.》 a member of such a unit. 특공 대원. [*command*]

comme il faut [kɔ̀m iːl fóu] *adj.* 《F.》 as it ought to be; proper. 적절한; 바른.

com·mem·o·rate [kəmémərèit] *vt.* (P6) **1** preserve the memory of (something). …을 후세에 전하다; 기념하다. ¶ *a new stamp commemorating lunar landing* 달 착륙을 기념하는 새 우표 / *The monument commemorates their victory.* 그 비석은 그들의 승리를 기념하고 있다. **2** give honor to the memory of (something); celebrate. (식·행사 따위로) …을 기념하다; 축하하다. ¶ *Lincoln commemorated the soldiers killed in the battle in his address.* 링컨은 연설에서 전사자들을 추도했다. ● **com·mem·o·ra·tive** [-rèitiv, -rə-] *adj.* [com-, →memory]

com·mem·o·ra·tion [kəmèməréiʃən] *n.* **1** Ⓤ the act of commemorating; celebration. 기념(하기); 축하. ¶ *deserve ~* 기념할 만하다. **2** Ⓒ a service in memory of some person or event. 기념식〔제〕.

in commemoration of, for the memory of; in the honor of. …을 기념하여. ¶ *in ~ of the foundation of our school* 우리 학교 설립을 기념하여.

*__com·mence__ [kəméns] *vi., vt.* (P1,3;6,8,9) 《*doing*》 begin; start. 시작되다; …을 시작〔개시〕하다. 語法 보통, commence 뒤에서는 부정사를 사용치 않음. ¶ *~ a meal* 식사를 시작하다 / *~ negotiating* 협상을 개시하다 / *~ the study of law* = *~ studying law* 법률 공부를 시작하다 / *~ on a research* 조사에 나서다 / *~ with easy modern English* 쉬운 현대 영어부터 시작하다. [com-, L. *ineo* enter]

com·mence·ment [kəménsmənt] *n.* ⓊⒸ **1** a beginning; a start. 시작; 개시; 처음. ¶ *He was there at the ~ of hostilities.* 개전(開戰) 당시 그는 거기 있었다. **2** 《*the ~*》 the ceremony or day of graduation in universities, etc. 졸업식(날). ¶ *hold the ~* 졸업식을 거행하다.

*__com·mend__ [kəménd] *vt.* (P6,13) **1** 《*for, to*》 praise; speak highly of (someone). …을 칭찬하다; …을 추천하다. ¶ *~ a soldier for bravery* 군인의 용감함을 칭찬하다 / *be highly commended* 격찬을 받다 / *~ someone to the notice of another* 아무를 다른 사람에게 소개하다 / *~ an applicant for employment* 취직 희망자를 추천하다. **2** 《*reflexively*》 make a good impression on; attract. 좋은 인상을 주다; 마음에 들다. ¶ *The proposal does not ~ itself to me.* 그 제안은 마음에 들지 않는다. **3** 《*to*》 give (someone or something) into the care of. …에게 맡기다. ¶ *~ one's soul to God* 영혼을 하느님에게 맡기다; 안심하고 죽다 / *I commended my child to her care.* 내 아이를 그녀에게 맡겼다. [com-, L. *do* give]

com·mend·a·ble [kəméndəbəl] *adj.* worthy of praise. 칭찬할 만한.

com·men·da·tion [kɑ̀məndéiʃən / kɔ̀m-] *n.* Ⓤ **1** praise; approval; favorable mention. 칭찬; 추천; 추거(推擧). ¶ *terms of high ~* 칭찬의 말 / *earn ~ (for a job well done)* (훌륭히 일을 해내) 칭찬을 받다. **2** the act of entrusting. (보호의) 위탁; 맡김.

com·men·da·to·ry [kəméndətɔ̀ːri / -təri] *adj.* approving; mentioning favorably. 칭찬하는; 추천하는.

com·men·su·ra·ble [kəménʃərəbəl] *adj.* **1** measurable by the same standard. (…와) 같은 단위로 잴 수 있는. **2** 《math.》 (of numbers) divisible without remainder by the same quantity. 같은 수로 나눌 수 있는; 약분할 수 있는. ● **com·men·su·ra·bil·i·ty** [kəmènʃərəbíləti] *n.* ⓊⒸ [↓]

com·men·su·rate [kəménʃərit] *adj.* **1** 《*to, with*》 in the proper portion. …와〔에〕 비례하는; 걸맞은; 균형잡힌; 적절한. ¶ *The salary should be ~ with the responsibility attaching to the post.* 봉급은 직위에 따르는 책임에 걸맞아야 한다. **2** having the same measure or size. 같은 양〔부피〕의. [com-, → measure]

:__com·ment__ [kɑ́ment / kɔ́m-] *n.* ⒸⓊ **1** a short statement or remark; criticism; opinion. 논평; 비평; 의견; 소견. ¶ *without further ~* 그 이상 말이 없이 / *make relevant comments based on a wide knowledge* 넓은 지식에 기초를 둔 적절한 비평을 하다 / *No ~.* 아무것도 할 말이 없습니다 / *He made some useful comments on my work.* 그는 나의 작품에 관해서 몇 마디 유익한 논평을 했다. **2** an explanatory or critical note supplied to a text. 주석; 해설.

— *vi.* (P1,3) 《*on, upon*》 make a comment or comments. 비평〔논평〕하다; 주석을 붙이다; 해설하다. ¶ *~ on someone's conduct* 아무의 행동에 대해 이러쿵저러쿵하다 / *~ on the original* 원전에 주석을 달다 / *~ on the day's happenings* 그 날의 사건에 대해서 논평하다. [L. *comminiscor* contrive]

com·men·tar·y [kɑ́məntèri / kɔ́məntəri] *n.* Ⓒ (*pl.* **-tar·ies**) **1** a series of comments or explanations. 주석; 해설. ¶ *a ~ on the Bible* 성서 주석. **2** an essay or treatise helping to making clear. 주석서; 해설서. **3** a criticism. 비평; 논평.

com·men·ta·tor [kɑ́məntèitər / kɔ́m-] *n.* Ⓒ **1** a person who makes commentaries. 주석자. **2** a person who discusses news, etc., as on the radio, etc. 실황 방송(해설)자; 시사(時事) 해설자. ¶ *a news ~*

뉴스 해설자.

:com·merce [kámərs / kɔ́m-] *n.* Ⓤ **1** the act of buying and selling on a large scale, esp. between different countries; business. 상업; (특히)통상; 무역. ¶ *Chamber of Commerce* 상공 회의소 / *foreign* 〔*international*〕 ~ 외국〔국제〕 무역 / *domestic* 〔*internal*〕 ~ 국내 교역 / *promote* ~ 교역을 촉진하다. **2** social relations. (사교적인) 교섭; 교제. ¶ *have no* ~ *with others* 다른 사람과의 교제가 전혀 없다. [L. *merx* merchandise]

:com·mer·cial [kəmə́:rʃəl] *adj.* **1** connected with commerce. 상업(상)의; 무역〔통상〕의. ¶ ~ *art* 상업 미술 / ~ *correspondence* 상업 통신(문) / *a* ~ *transaction* 상거래 / *a* ~ *treaty* 통상 조약 / *a* ~ *traveler* 순회 외판원. **2** engaged in commerce. 상업에 종사하는; 장사하는. **3** made for sale. 판매용의; 영리적인. ¶ *a* ~ *corporation* 영리 회사. **4** 《U.S.》 supported by an advertiser. 광고·선전용의. — *n.* Ⓒ **1** 《U.S.》 a short announcement or visible presentation as an advertisement on the radio, T.V., etc. (라디오·TV 등의) 선전〔광고〕 방송; 커머셜. **2** 《Brit.》 a traveling salesman. 순회 외판원.

com·mer·cial·ism [kəmə́:rʃəlìzəm] *n.* Ⓤ **1** methods and spirit of commerce; too much emphasis on profit, success, or immediate results. 상업〔영리〕주의; 상혼(商魂). **2** business custom or expressions. 상(商)관습; 상용어(語).

com·mer·cial·ize [kəmə́:rʃəlàiz] *vt.* (P6) **1** make (something) commerical. …을 상업화〔영리화〕하다. **2** offer (something) for sale; make available as a commodity. …을 팔기 위해 내놓다; 상품화하다. ¶ *He intends to* ~ *his invention.* 그는 자신의 발명을 상품화할 작정이다.

com·mer·cial·ly [kəmə́:rʃəli] *adv.* from the point of view of business; in a businesslike way. 상업적〔영리적〕으로; 통상상(通商上).

Com·mie [kámi / kɔ́mi] *n.* 《*colloq.*》 a Communist. 공산당원.

com·mi·nate [kámənèit / kɔ́m-] *vt.* (P6, 13) menace; curse. …을 으르다; 저주하다. [com-, →menace]

com·min·gle [kəmíŋgl] *vt., vi.* (P6; 1) 《*with*》 mix together. …을 섞다〔혼합하다〕; 섞이다. [→mingle]

com·mi·nute [kámənjù:t / kɔ́m-] *vt.* (P6) reduce to minute particles. …을 부수다; 분쇄하다. ● **com·mi·nu·tion** [kàmənjú:ʃən / kɔ̀m-] *n.* [→minute]

com·mis·er·ate [kəmízərèit] *vt.* (P6) feel or show sorrow for (something). …을 가엾게〔딱하게〕 여기다; 동정하다. ¶ ~ *someone for his poverty* 아무의 가난에 동정하다 / ~ *another's misfortune* 남의 불행을 가엾이 여기다. — *vi.* (P3) 《*with*》 sympathize. 동정하다. ¶ ~ *with a boy on his grief* 소년의 슬픔에 동정하다. [→miser]

com·mis·er·a·tion [kəmìzəréiʃən] *n.* Ⓤ pity; sympathy. 연민; 동정.

com·mis·sar [kámәsà:r / kɔ̀m-] *n.* Ⓒ the head of a governmental department in the U.S.S.R. until 1946. (구(舊)소련의) 인민(人民) 위원. 參考 지금은 공식(公式)적으로는 minister. [→commissary]

com·mis·sar·i·at [kàməsɛ́əriət / kɔ̀m-] *n.* Ⓒ **1** 《hist.》 any of the major governmental divisions of the U.S.S.R. until 1946. (구(舊)소련의) 인민 위원회. 參考 지금은 공식적으로는 ministry. **2** a department of an army that provides food, etc. 병참부. **3** the supply itself. 양식의 공급.

com·mis·sar·y [káməsèri / kɔ́məsəri] *n.* Ⓒ (*pl.* **-sar·ies**) **1** a store that sells food, etc., esp. in an army. (군대 따위의) 매점. **2** an officer of the commissariat. 병참 장교〔부원〕. **3** someone who acts for someone or a certain group; a representative. 대리자; 대표자. **4** a person in charge of a special state department in the U.S.S.R. until 1946. (구(舊)소련의) 인민 위원(=commissar). [→commit]

:com·mis·sion [kəmíʃən] *n.* **1** Ⓒ the act of entrusting; authority. 위임; 위탁; (위탁받은) 직권. ¶ ~ *sale* 위탁 판매 / *the* ~ *of authority to someone* 아무에게 권한을 위임하기 / *on* ~ 위탁을 받고 / *go beyond one's* ~ 월권 행위를 하다 / *have a* ~ *of all powers* 전권을 위임받고 있다. **2** Ⓒ a written order giving certain duties and powers, esp. in the armed forces. (장교·치안 판사의) 임명서; 사령(辭令). ¶ *be on the* ~ 치안 판사직에 있다 / *My brother has just received his* ~ *as lieutenant in the army.* 형님은 막 육군 중위로 임관되었다. **3** Ⓒ 《*collectively*》 a group of people chosen to do things. 위원(회). ¶ *a secret* ~ 비밀 위원회 / *the* ~ *of inquiry* 조사 위원회. **4** Ⓒ small business done by a person as a favor to another, such as delivering a message, buying some article, etc. 부탁(할〔받은〕 일); 위임(받은 일); 위촉된 일. ¶ *I have one or two commissions for you if you are going into town.* 읍내로 들어간다면 한두 가지 부탁할 일이 있네. **5** Ⓤ the act of doing or performing some action, esp. a bad one. (범죄·과실 따위를) 저지름; 수행. ¶ *sins of* ~ 저지른 죄 / *be charged with the* ~ *of a crime* 범죄를 저지른 혐의로 고소되다. **6** ⓐ Ⓤ agency. (업무의) 대리. ⓑ Ⓒ a payment based on a percentage of money from sales. (판매 실적에 따른) 구전; 수당; 커미션. ¶ *Many salesmen receive, in addition to their salaries, a* ~ *of 10 percent on all sales made.* 많은 외판원은 월급 외에 자신의 총판매액에 대한 10프로의 수당을 더 받는다.

get* 〔*lose*〕 *one's commission, become 〔cease to be〕 an officer. 임관〔면관〕되다.

in commission, **a**) in service. 현역의. **b**) in use; in operating order. 사용되고; 곧 쓰일

수 있는 상태로. ¶ *get a broken bicycle in ~ again* 고장난 자전거를 다시 탈 수 있게 하다. **c**) having delegated authority. 임무를 띤.

on commission, as an agent for another. 위탁을 받고. ¶ *sell on ~* 위탁 판매하다.

out of commission, **a**) not in service. 퇴역하여. ¶ *go out of ~* 퇴역하다 / *place ship out of ~* 군함을 퇴역시키다. **b**) not in use; not in working order. 사용되지 않게 되어; 고장이 나서.

— *vt.* (P6,19,20) **1** give a commission to (someone). …에게 직권을 주다. **2** 《*to do*》 give (someone) a right or power. (권한 따위)를 주다〔위임하다〕. **3** put (a warship) into service; appoint. …을 취역시키다; 장교로 임명하다. ¶ *a commissioned officer* 장교 / *a commissioned warship* 취역 전함(戰艦). [L. *mitto* send]

com·mis·sion·aire [kəmìʃənέər] *n.* Ⓒ 《Brit.》 a doorkeeper usu. a retired old soldier in uniform at a hotel, a department store, etc.; a messenger, etc. 제복 입은 문지기《백화점·호텔 등의》.

com·mis·sioned [kəmíʃənd] *adj.* possessing or given a commission. 임명된.

·**com·mis·sion·er** [kəmíʃənər] *n.* Ⓒ **1** a member of a commission. 위원. **2** a government official in charge of a department or district. (행정) 장관; 판무관(辦務官). ¶ *High Commissioner* 고등 판무관 / *the police ~* 《U.S.》 (시의) 경찰부장; 《Brit.》 (런던의) 시경국장.

:**com·mit** [kəmít] *vt.* (**-mit·ted, -mit·ting**) **1** (P6,13) give (something or someone) in trust to someone or something else. …을 위임〔위탁〕하다; 맡기다. ¶ *~ the sale of goods to an agent* 상품 판매를 대리점에 위탁하다 / *She committed her baby to the girl's care.* 그녀는 아기를 소녀에게 맡겼다. **2** (P6) perform or do (something wrong). (죄·잘못)을 저지르다. ¶ *~ suicide* 자살하다 / *~ murder* 〔*an error*〕 살인〔잘못〕을 저지르다. **3** (P13) consign. 넘기다; 보내다; 수용하다. ¶ *~ a thief to prison* 도둑을 감옥에 보내다 / *~ a juvenile delinquent to a reformatory* 비행 소년을 감화원에 수용하다 / *~ someone to hospital* 아무를 병원에 입원시키다. **4** (P6,7) 《usu. *reflexively*》 express one's opinion as an assurance; bind oneself. …에게 언질을 주다; 약속하다; 속박하다. ¶ *~ oneself to a promise* 확약(確約)하다 / *~ oneself to do* 〔*doing*〕 …할 약속을 하다 / *I have committed myself now and cannot draw back.* 이제 약속을 했으므로 철회할 수는 없다 / *Do not ~ yourself.* 언질을 주지 마라. **5** (P13) refer (a bill, etc.) for consideration. (법안 따위)를 심의에 부치다〔돌리다〕. **6** give (oneself) wholeheartedly; undertake (something) sincerely. …에 전적으로 따르다; 경도(傾倒)하다; 전심〔전념〕하다. ¶ *~ oneself to a teacher's advice* 선생님 조언에 전적으로 따르다 / *~ oneself to reading a book* 독서에 전념하다. [L. *mitto* send]

commit the body to the earth 〔***the flames***〕, bury 〔burn〕 the body. (사체)를 매장〔화장〕하다.

commit oneself to, bind oneself by speeches or actions to. …에게 언질을 주다.

commit something to memory, learn something by heart; memorize. …을 암기하다; 외다. ¶ *~ an address to memory* 주소를 외다.

commit something to paper 〔***writing***〕, write something down. …을 적어 두다.

com·mit·ment [kəmítmənt] *n.* **1** Ⓤ the act of entrusting, performing, or committing. 위탁; 수행; 범행. ¶ *on a ~ basis* 위탁 판매로; 위탁의 조건으로. **2** ⓊⒸ the act of sending someone to prison or to an asylum; the state of being sent to prison. 감옥·수용소에 보냄; 투옥; 구류; 수감. **3** Ⓒ an order sending a person to prison. 수감〔수용(收容)〕 명령. **4** Ⓒ a pledge or promise. 언질; 약속; 공약. ¶ *He is under a ~ to finish the task by March 1.* 그는 3월 1일까지 일을 마친다는 약속에 묶여 있다.

com·mit·ed [kəmítid] *adj.* devoted; biased. 헌신적인; 편견을 가진.

com·mit·tal [kəmítl] *n.* = commitment.

:**com·mit·tee** [kəmíti] *n.* Ⓒ **1** a group of people appointed or elected to do certain things. 위원회. 語法 구성원을 중심으로 할 때는 복수 취급. ¶ 《Brit.》 *the Committee of Supply* 예산 위원회 / *a standing* 〔*steering, joint*〕 *~* 상임〔운영, 합동〕 위원회 / *~ of ways and means* (하원의) 재정〔세입〕 위원회 / *be in ~* 위원회를 열고 있다 / *be* 〔*sit*〕 *on the ~* 위원회의 일원이다 / *go into ~* 위원회에 참석하다 / *call a meeting of the ~* 위원회를 소집하다. **2** a person to whom the charge of a lunatic is committed. (심신 장애자의) 후견인. [→commit]

com·mit·tee·man [kəmítimən, -mæ̀n] *n.* Ⓒ (*pl.* **-men** [-mən, -mèn]) a member of a committee. 위원.

com·mix [kəmíks, kɑm- / kɔm-] *vt., vi.* (P6,13; 1,3) 《*arch.*》 《*with*》 mix. 한데 섞(이)다. [com-]

com·mode [kəmóud] *n.* Ⓒ **1** a chest of drawers; a cabinet. (서랍이 달린) 작은 장롱; 소형 캐비닛. **2** a washstand. 세면대. **3** a piece of bedroom furniture to hold a chamber pot. 침실용 변기(가 달린 의자). [→commodore]

com·mo·di·ous [kəmóudiəs] *adj.* **1** vast; roomy; spacious. (집·방이) 넓은. ¶ *a ~ apartment* 널찍한 아파트. **2** convenient; handy. 편리한; 간편한. ● **com·mo·di·ous·ly** [-li] *adv.*

·**com·mod·i·ty** [kəmɑ́dəti / -mɔ́d-] *n.* Ⓒ (*pl.* **-ties**) 《often *pl.*》 **1** anything that is bought and sold. 상품; 물자; 일용품. ¶ *~ prices* 물가 / *staple commodities* 주요 상품 / *The prices of commodities are rising daily.* 물가가 매일같이 오르고 있다. **2** any useful thing. 유용한 것.

com·mo·dore [kámədɔ̀ːr / kɔ́m-] *n.* Ⓒ **1** ⓐ 《U.S. nav.》 an officer in command, ranking above a captain. (해군의) 준장. ⓑ 《Brit. nav.》 an officer in the navy higher than a captain and in command of a squadron. (해군의) 전대(戰隊) 지휘관; 준장. **2** a title of honor given to the head of a yacht club. 요트 클럽의 회장. [L. *modus* measure]

:com·mon [kámən / kɔ́m-] *adj.* **1** belonging to the community; public. 공공의; 공적인; 공중의. ¶ *a ~ nuisance* 치안 방해 / *~ welfare* 공공의 복지 / *the ~ good* 공익(公益) / *a ~ water supply system* 공공 급수 시설. **2** of all; general. 일반의; 잘 알려진. ¶ *a matter of ~ knowledge* 주지(周知)의 일; 상식화되어 있는 일 / *a ~ belief* 〔*superstition*〕 널리 믿어지고 있는 신앙〔미신〕. **3** belonging equally to two or more persons or things. 공통의; 공동의. ¶ *a ~ defense* 공동 방위 / *a ~ kitchen* 공동 주방 / *the ~ property* 공동 재산 / *a ~ factor* 공통 인수 / *~ interests* 공동〔공통의〕 이해(利害) / *a ~ language or history* 공통의 언어와 역사 / *by ~ consent* 만장 일치로; 일반에게 인정되어 / *be ~ to all* 모두에게 공통이다 / *make ~ cause with* …와 공동 전선을 펴다 / *find a ~ ground for beginning negotiations* 협상을 시작하기 위해 (대립된 의견의) 공통점을 찾다. **4** usual; ordinary; regular. 보통의; 평범한; 흔히 있는(opp. rare). ¶ *a ~ event* 〔*sight*〕 흔히 있는 일〔풍경〕 / *a ~ mistake* 흔히 있는 잘못 / *a ~ insect* 〔*flower*〕 흔한 곤충〔꽃〕 / *a ~ cold* 보통 감기 / *the ~ people* 보통 사람들; 서민. **5** not excellent or well-known in tone or quality; not polite; low. (질적으로) 보통의; 저속한; 저질의; 상스런; 거친. ¶ *a ~ make* 보통 제품 / *~ manners* 상스러운 태도 / *a man with a ~ French accent* 상스러운 프랑스어 말투의 남자 / *a woman with ~ clothes* 싸구려 옷을 입은 여인 / *not a jewel but a ~ piece of glass* 보석 아닌 보통의 유릿조각. **6** 《math.》 belonging equally to several quantities. 공통의; 공약의; 맞줄임의. ¶ *a ~ denominator* 공통 분모 / *a ~ root* 공통근(根). **7** 《gram.》 (of a noun) that can be used for any of a group or a class; (of gender) that is either masculine or feminine. 보통(명사)의; 중성의. ¶ *a ~ noun* 보통 명사.

common or garden, very usual and well-known; very familiar. 극히 평범한; 흔히 있는. ¶ *a ~ or garden experience* 아주 평범한 경험.

— *n.* **1** 《*the ~*, or *the ~s*》 a tract of land considered as the property of the public, such as a park in a city. (공원 등지와 같은) 공유지(公〔共〕有地). ¶ *Boston Common* 보스턴 광장. **2** Ⓤ 《law》 a profit or right of one person in the land of another. 공유권(共有權); 공동 수익권. ¶ *~ of pasture* 공동 방목권(放牧權). [L. *communis*]

in common (***with***), held or enjoyed equally; shared by all of a group. 공통으로; …와 똑같이. ¶ *have something in ~* 공통점이 있다.

out of (***the***) ***common,*** unusual; uncommon. 비범한; 이상한; 드문. ¶ *something out of the ~* 진품(珍品).

com·mon·al·ty [kámənəlti / kɔ́m-] *n.* Ⓒ (*pl.* **-ties**) 《usu. *the ~*》 **1** the common people. 보통 사람들; 일반 대중; 서민. **2** the people as a group. 단체.

common carrier [⌐– ⌐–] *n.* a forwarding agent. 운송 업자.

com·mon·er [kámənər / kɔ́m-] *n.* Ⓒ **1** one of the common people. 보통 사람; 일반인. **2** 《Brit.》 a member of the House of Commons. (영국의) 하원 의원. **3** 《Brit.》 a student who pays all his own expenses. 자비(自費) 학생. **4** a person who has a joint right in land. 토지 공유권 소유자.

common law [⌐– ⌐] *n.* the unwritten law, esp. of England, based on custom or court decision. 불문율(律); 관습법(opp. statute law).

***com·mon·ly** [kámənli / kɔ́m-] *adv.* **1** usually; generally. 일반적으로; 보통. ¶ *Boys ~ enjoy sports.* 남자애들은 일반적으로 스포츠를 즐긴다. **2** in an ordinary degree or amount. 보통 정도로; 여느 …와 같이. ¶ *a ~ successful man* 세상 여느 사람들처럼 성공한 사나이.

com·mon·ness [kámənnis / kɔ́m-] *n.* the state of being common. 평범(함).

***com·mon·place** [kámənplèis / kɔ́m-] *adj.* **1** ordinary; usual. 보통의; 평범한; 흔히 있는. ¶ *a ~ idea* 평범한 생각. **2** not new or original. 진부한. ¶ *a ~ remark* 진부한 말.
— *n.* Ⓒ **1** a common or everyday thing. 일상의〔평범한〕 일. ¶ *the ~ of life* 일상적인 일; 항다반사. **2** an ordinary thing 〔remark〕; an uninteresting saying. 진부한 일〔것, 말〕. ¶ *a polite ~* 정중하나 진부한 말.

commonplace book [⌐––⌐] *n.* a book in which noteworthy quotations, poems, comments, etc. are written. 메모 수첩; 비망록.

common pleas [⌐– ⌐] *n.* civil procedure. 민사 소송.

com·mons [kámənz / kɔ́m-] *n. pl.* **1** the common people. 평민; 서민. **2** allowance of food. 정량의 식사; 음식. ¶ *be on short ~* 음식이 충분치 않다. **3** 《*the C-*》 the House of Commons; the members of the House of Commons. (영국의) 하원; 하원 의원.

common saying [⌐– ⌐–] *n.* a proverb. 격언; 속담.

common sense [⌐–⌐] *n.* good sense in everyday matters; practical judgment. 상식; 양식(良識).

common table [⌐– ⌐–] *n.* a table at which all dine. 공동 식탁.

common time [⌐–⌐] *n.* 《mus.》 two or four beats. 2 박자 또는 4 박자.

com·mon·weal [kámənwìːl / kɔ́m-] *n.* Ⓤ the public happiness; the public good. 복리; 공익.

com·mon·wealth [kámənwèlθ / kɔ́m-] *n.* Ⓒ **1** the group of people who make up a nation; the state. 국민; 국가. ¶ *for the good of the* ~ 국가를 위해서. **2** a republic. 공화국. ¶ *France and the United States are commonwealths.* 프랑스와 미국은 공화국이다. **3** 《*C-*》 a group of nations and their dependencies. 연방. ¶ *the Commonwealth of Nations* 영연방 (= *the British Commonwealth*) / *the Commonwealth of Australia* 오스트레일리아 연방. **4** Ⓤ 《*the C-*》 《hist.》 the government in England under Cromwell. (크롬웰이 편) 영국 공화 정치 《1649-1660》. **5** any State of the United States. (미국의) 주(州). **6** a group of persons, etc. (공통의 목적·이익으로 맺어진) 단체.

com·mo·tion [kəmóuʃən] *n.* ⓊⒸ **1** violent movement; disorder. 격동; 동요. ¶ *be in* ~ 몹시 흔들리고 있다 / *cause a tremendous* ~ *in the literary world* 문학계에 세찬 동요를 일으키다. **2** confusion; noisy moving about; disturbance; insurrection. 동란; 격변(激變); 폭동. ¶ *three years of* ~ 3년에 걸친 동란 / *cause* 〔*produce*〕 *a* ~ 폭동을 일으키다. **3** excitement. 흥분. ¶ ~ *of the nerves* 신경의 흥분. [com-]

com·mu·nal [kəmjúːnəl, kámjə- / kɔ́m-] *adj.* of a community; public; common. 공동 사회의; 자치 단체의; 공동의. ¶ ~ *life* 사회 생활 / ~ *ownership* 공유(共有)(권) / *a* ~ *toilet* 공중 변소. [→common]

com·mune[1] [kəmjúːn] *vi.* (P2,3) **1** 《*with*》 talk in a very friendly manner; have spiritual contact. 서로 친밀〔다정〕하게 이야기하다; 정신적으로 사귀다. ¶ ~ *with oneself* 깊이 생각하다 / ~ *with nature* 자연과 사귀다. **2** receive Holy Communion. 성찬(聖餐)을 받다. —[kámjuːn / kɔ́m-] *n.* Ⓤ friendly talk. 간담(懇談); 교제. [↑]

com·mune[2] [kámjuːn / kɔ́m-] *n.* Ⓒ **1** the smallest division for local government in France, Belgium, etc. (프랑스 등의) 최소 자치구(區). **2** 《*the C-*》 a revolutionary group that governed Paris from 1792 to 1794; the Paris Commune. 파리 코뮌《1792-94년까지 프랑스 혁명 때 파리 시정(市政)을 장악한 혁명 단체》. [↑]

com·mu·ni·ca·ble [kəmjúːnikəbəl] *adj.* that can be communicated; that can be spread from person to person. 전(달)할 수 있는; 전파될 수 있는. ¶ *a* ~ *disease* 전염병 / *Thought is* ~ *chiefly by words.* 생각은 주로 말로써 전달된다. [↓]

·**com·mu·ni·cate** [kəmjúːnəkèit] *vt.* (P6,13) **1** give (opinions, etc.) to another; transmit. (의견·지식·정보(情報)·열 따위)를 전(달)하다. ¶ ~ *ideas* 생각을 전하다 / ~ *one's happiness to someone* 자신의 행복함을 아무에게 알리다. **2** infect. (병)을 감염(感染)시키다. ¶ *The prisoners communicated the disease to others.* 그 죄수는 다른 죄수들에게 병을 옮겼다.

— *vi.* **1** 《*with*》 ⓐ (P1,3) give or exchange messages by talking, writing, etc.; correspond. 통신〔교신〕하다; 서신을 주고받다; 연락하다. ¶ ~ (*with someone*) *by telegram* (아무와) 전보로 통신하다. ⓑ (P3) hold social intercourse with. …와 교제하다; 사귀다. ¶ ~ *with one's friends* 친구들과 사귀다. **2** (P3) 《*with*》 be connected. (길·방 따위가) 통하다; 연결되다. ¶ ~ *with the next room by a door* 옆방과 문으로 통하다 / *The dining-room communicates with the kitchen.* 식당은 주방과 통해 있다. **3** (P3) be infected; be transmitted. 감염되다; 전해지다. [L. *communis* common]

:**com·mu·ni·ca·tion** [kəmjùːnəkéiʃən] *n.* **1** Ⓤ the act of communicating. 통신; 교신; (의사의) 전달. ¶ *be in* ~ *with someone* 아무와 서신 연락을 하고 있다 / *maintain* ~ *with* …와 연락을 유지하다 / *Communication with deaf people is difficult.* 귀머거리들과의 의사 전달은 어렵다 / *All* ~ *was broken off by the storm.* 폭풍우로 모든 통신이 끊겼다. **2** Ⓒ information given in this way. 전언; 소식; 편지; 전보. ¶ *receive a* ~ *from someone* 아무에게서 편지를 받다 / *send a personal* ~ *to* …에게 친서를 보내다. **3** ⒸⓊ means of communicating; a passage. 교통(연락); 교통 기관. ¶ *a means of* ~ 교통 기관 / *There is no* ~ *between the two places.* 두 지역간에는 교통편이 없다. **4** 《*pl.*》 a system of communicating by telephone, radio, etc. 통신 기관〔시설〕.

com·mu·ni·ca·tive [kəmjúːnəkèitiv, -kətiv] *adj.* ready to communicate; talkative. (마음을) 터놓은; 통신의; 수다스러운.

com·mun·ion [kəmjúːnjən] *n.* Ⓤ **1** the act or state of sharing. 공유(共有)(상태). **2** exchange of thoughts and feelings; spiritual relation; friendly talk. 사상·감정의 교류; 영적 교감(靈的交感); 간담(懇談). ¶ *the* ~ *of heart with heart* 이심 전심 / *in the* ~ *with nature* 자연을 마음의 벗으로 삼아 / *hold* ~ *with oneself* 깊이 내성(內省)하다. **3** close relations between two or more persons. 교제; 친교; 친밀. **4** Ⓒ a group of people who have the same religious beliefs. (공통의 종교를 믿는) 신앙〔종교〕 단체. ¶ *be of the same* (*religious*) ~ 같은 종교 단체에 속하다. **5** 《Rom. Cath.》 《*C-*》 the act of sharing in or celebrating the Lord's Supper. 성찬식(聖餐式); 성체 배령(聖體拜領). ¶ *Communion Service* 성찬식 / *receive* 〔*partake of*〕 *Communion* 성찬에 참여하다; 성체를 배령(拜領)하다. [→communicate]

com·mu·ni·qué [kəmjúːnikèi, ---´] *n.* 《F.》 Ⓒ an official statement or announcement. 코뮈니케; 공식 발표; 성명서. ¶ *a joint* ~ 공동 성명. [↑]

***com·mu·nism** [kámjənìzəm / kɔ́m-] *n.* Ⓤ 《often *C-*》 a theory or system of social change directed toward the ideal of a classless society, developed by Karl Marx. 공산주의. ¶ *primitive* ~ 원시 공산 체제. [F. *communisme,* →common]

***com·mu·nist** [kámjənist / kɔ́m-] *n.* Ⓒ **1** a person who believes in and supports communism. 공산주의자. **2** 《*C-*》 a member of the Communist Party. 공산당원. — *adj.* communistic. 공산주의(자)의. ¶ *the* ~ *party* 공산당.

com·mu·nis·tic [kàmjənístik / kɔ̀m-] *adj.* of or like communists or communism. 공산주의(자)의; 공산주의적인.

:com·mu·ni·ty [kəmjú:nəti] *n.* **1** Ⓒ ⓐ a group of people with common cultural or other conditions and living in the same place. (지역적) 공동 사회; 지역 공동체. ¶ *a village* ~ 부락 공동체. ⓑ a social, religious, occupational, or other group sharing common characteristics or interests. (공통의 특징·이해 관계를 갖는) 특수 사회; …계(界). ¶ *the artists'* ~ 예술가 사회 / *the* ~ *of scholars* 학계 / *the Korean* ~ *in L.A.* L.A.의 한국인 사회. **2** 《*the* ~》 the people of any district or town; the public; society. 어느 지역〔도시〕 사람들; 공중(公衆); (일반)사회. ¶ *gain the approval of the* ~ 지역민의 승인을 얻다. **3** Ⓤ the act of sharing; the state of being the same. 공유(共有); (사상·이해 관계의) 공통; 유사; 일치. ¶ *the* ~ *of interests* 이해(利害)의 일치 / ~ *of property* 재산의 공유. [→common]

community center [–⌐–– ⌐–] *n.* a building where the people of a community meet for recreation, social purposes, etc. (미국·캐나다의) 공민 회관.

com·mut·a·ble [kəmjú:təbəl] *adj.* capable of being commuted. 교환〔대체(代替)〕 가능한. [↓]

com·mu·tate [kámjətèit / kɔ́m-] *vi.* (P1) commute. 정기권(定期券)으로 통근하다. — *vt.* (P6) 《electr.》 reverse the direction of an electric current. 전류의 방향을 바꾸다; 정류(整流)하다. [↓]

com·mu·ta·tion [kàmjətéiʃən / kɔ̀m-] *n.* Ⓤ **1** substitution; exchange. 대체(代替); 교환. **2** Ⓒ a reduction of a punishment or a penalty. 감형(減刑). ¶ *The prisoner obtained a* ~ *of the death sentence to life imprisonment.* 죄수는 사형에서 종신 징역으로 감형을 받았다. **3** 《U.S.》 regular travel over some distance between home and a work place by train or car. (집에서 직장으로의) 통근. [→commute]

commutation ticket [––⌐– ⌐–] *n.* 《U.S.》 a season ticket. 정기 승차권; 회수권.

com·mu·ta·tor [kámjətèitər / kɔ́m-] *n.* Ⓒ 《electr.》 a device for reversing the direction of an electric current. 전류 전환기; 정류기(整流器).

com·mute [kəmjú:t] *vt.* **1** (P6,13) exchange; substitute. …을 교환〔대체〕하다; 바꾸다. **2** (P6,13) change (one kind of payment) for another. (지불 방법 따위)를 대체(對替)하다. **3** (P6,13) make (a punishment, etc.) less severe. …을 감형(減刑)하다. ¶ ~ *the death penalty to imprisonment for life* 사형에서 종신형으로 감형하다. — *vi.* (P3) 《U.S.》 travel regularly or daily back and forth from one's home to one's office. (정기권·회수권으로) 교외에서 통근하다. [com-, L. *mūtāre* to change entirely]

com·mut·er [kəmjú:tər] *n.* Ⓒ 《U.S.》 a person who travels back and forth from his home, usu. in the suburbs, to his work place, usu. in the city; a person who uses a commutation ticket. (교외로부터의) 통근자; 정기〔회수〕권 사용자.

***com·pact**[1] [kəmpǽkt, kámpækt] *adj.* **1** closely or firmly connected; packed tightly together. 꽉 짜인; 빽빽이 찬; 촘촘한. **2** (of style) condensed; short. (문체가) 압축(壓縮)된; 간결한. ¶ *a* ~ *expression* 간결한 표현. — *vt.* (P6) **1** pack (things) tightly together. …을 꽉 채워 넣다. **2** condense. …을 압축시키다; 간결히 하다. — [kámpækt / kɔ́m-] *n.* Ⓒ a small case carried by ladies containing face powder and often rouge. (휴대용) 분갑(粉匣); 콤팩트.
● **com·pact·ly** [-li] *adv.* **com·pact·ness** [-nis] *n.* [L. *pango* fix]

com·pact[2] [kámpækt / kɔ́m-] *n.* ⒸⓊ an agreement; a contract. (정식의) 동의; 협약; 계약. ¶ *a* ~ *between parties* 쌍방의 동의 / *a three-nation* ~ 3국 협정. [L. *paciscor* make bargain]

:com·pan·ion[1] [kəmpǽnjən] *n.* Ⓒ **1** ⓐ a person who keeps company with someone; a person who travels with another or others; a comrade. 친구; 상대; 동반자; 길동무; 동료. ¶ *a* ~ *at* 〔*in*〕 *arms* 전우 / *a* ~ *in robbery* 강도의 공범 / *a* ~ *for life* 일생의 반려 / *a* ~ *of one's misery* 슬픔을 같이할 친구 / *make a* ~ *of solitude* 고독을 벗으로 삼다. ⓑ a person who happens to be in another's company. 우연히 함께 된 사람. ¶ *My* ~ *in the railway carriage was a total stranger to me.* 열차에서 동석(同席)하게 된 사람은 전혀 모르는 사람이었다. **2** one of a pair or set. (짝을 이루는 것의) 한쪽. ¶ *a* ~ *volume* 자매편(篇) / *Where is the* ~ *to this stocking?* 이 양말의 한 짝은 어디 있나. **3** a friendly, cheerful person. 유쾌한 사람. ¶ *a first-rate* 〔*poor*〕 ~ 매우 유쾌한〔시시한〕 상대. — *vt.* (P6) **1** act as a companion to. …의 상대 노릇을 하다. **2** accompany. …을 동행하다. ● **com·pan·ion·less** [-lis] *adj.* [com-, L. *panis* bread]

com·pan·ion[2] [kəmpǽnjən] *n.* Ⓒ 《naut.》 **1** a hood over the top of a companionway. 뒷갑판 천창(天窓). **2** a companionway. 선실 승강구 (계단). [↑]

com·pan·ion·a·ble [kəmpǽnjənəbəl] *adj.* pleasant to be with; sociable; agreeable. 친하기 쉬운; 남에게 호감을 주는; 붙임성 있는.

com·pan·ion·ate [kəmpǽnjənit] *adj.* in the manner of companions. 친구의(같은); 동반자의; 우호적인. ¶ ~ *marriage* 우애 결혼.

companion ladder [–ˊ–– ˋ–] *n.* 《naut.》 a ladder leading to the officer's cabin. (선내의) 승강구 사다리(계단).

*__com·pan·ion·ship__ [kəmpǽnjənʃìp] *n.* Ⓤ agreeable association; fellowship; company. 사귐; 교제; 친교; 우호. ¶ *enjoy the ~ of* …와 친하게 사귀다 / *be in ~ with someone* 아무와 교제하고 있다.

com·pan·ion·way [kəmpǽnjənwèi] *n.* Ⓒ 《naut.》 the stairway or staircase leading from the deck of a ship to a cabin. 선실(船室) 승강구 (계단).

:**com·pa·ny** [kʌ́mpəni] *n.* Ⓒ (*pl.* **-nies**) **1** a group of people. 사람들; 일단; 일행. ¶ *a ~ of soldiers* 일단의 군인 / *a large ~ of mathematicians* 많은 수학자의 일행 / *A great ~ came to the fair.* 엄청나게 많은 사람이 박람회에 왔다. **2** Ⓤ a number of invited guests. 초청객; 손님들. ¶ *We shall have ~ for dinner tomorrow.* 내일 저녁 식사에 초청객들이 있다. **3** Ⓤ 《*collectively*》 a friend; a person who goes with others; a companion or companions. 친구; 동행자; 반려; 동료. ¶ *He is good ~.* 그는 대하기가 유쾌한 친구다 / *A man is known by his ~.* 사람(됨)은 그 친구를 보면 알 수 있다. **4** Ⓤ companionship; society. 사귐; 교제; 동석(同席); 동반(同伴). ¶ *for ~* 교제상; 사교를 위해 / *in ~ with* …와 함께 / *bear* (*keep*) *someone ~* 아무의 상대를 해 주다; 아무와 동행(아무를 동반)하다 / *be fond of ~* 교제를 좋아하다 / *keep ~ with* …와 교제하다 / *enjoy someone's ~* 아무와의 동석을 즐기다 / *be in ~ with* …와 사귀고 있다 / *give someone one's ~* …와 사귀다 / *I don't seek the ~ of him.* 그와의 교제를 원치 않는다. **5** a business firm. 회사; 상사. ¶ *a joint-stock ~* 주식 회사 / *a publishing ~* 출판 회사 / *John Smith and Company* 존 스미스 상사. 參考 John Smith & Co.로 생략. **6** the part of an army commanded by a captain. 중대. ¶ *a ~ commander* 중대장. **7** a party of actors playing together. 배우의 일단. ¶ *a theatrical ~* 극단. **8** the whole crew of a ship. (배의) 전(全)승무원. [→companion¹]

be good* (*bad*) *company, be entertaining (dull). 재미있다(시시하다).

err in good company, err with persons of repute. 높은 분들도 같은 실수를 하다(그러니까 크게 염려할 것 없다).

fall into company with, travel together with. …와 길동무가 되다.

get one's company, be promoted to the rank of captain. 대위로 승진하다.

get into bad company, mix with bad friends. 못된 친구들과 어울리다.

keep company with, be friends with. …와 친밀해지다.

keep good* (*bad*) *company, associate with good (bad) friends. 좋은(나쁜) 친구와 사귀다.

part company with, part from; cease association or friendship. …와 갈라지다; 교제를 끊다.

company manners [ˊ–– ˋ–] *n.* decency. 남 앞에서의 예절.

company union [ˊ––– ˋ–] *n.* 《U.S.》 a union of workers dominated by the employers. 어용 노조.

com·pa·ra·ble [kámpərəbəl / kɔ́m-] *adj.* **1** 《*with*》 that can be compared. 비교할 수 있는. ¶ *be ~ with* …와 비교할 수 있다 / *This is not at all ~ with that.* 이것은 그것과는 전혀 비교가 안 된다. **2** 《*to*》 worthy of comparison. 필적하는; 견줄 수 있는. ¶ *No other boy in our class is ~ to him.* 반에서 그에게 필적할 만한 아이는 없다. [→compare]

·**com·par·a·tive** [kəmpǽrətiv] *adj.* **1** of comparison. 비교의. ¶ *the ~ faculty* 비교 능력. **2** based on or involving comparison. (연구 방법 등이) 비교에 의(거)한. ¶ *~ literature* 비교문학 / *the ~ studies of languages* 언어의 비교 연구 / *by the ~ method* 비교연구법에 의해서. **3** measured by comparison with something else; moderate. 비교적인; 상대적인; 꽤. ¶ *live in ~ comfort* 꽤 안락한 생활을 하다 / *read with ~ ease* 비교적 쉽게 책을 읽다. **4** 《gram.》 showing the comparative degree. 비교급의. ¶ *the ~ degree* 비교급(cf. *positive, superlative*).

— *n.* Ⓒ 《*the ~*》 《gram.》 a form of an adjective or adverb used in comparisons, such as 'longer' or 'sooner'; the comparative degree. 비교급.

·**com·par·a·tive·ly** [kəmpǽrətivli] *adv.* in a comparative manner; relatively. 비교적(으로). ¶ *Snakes are ~ rare in England.* 뱀은 영국에서는 비교적 드물다 / *He is ~ rich.* 그는 비교적 부유하다.

:**com·pare** [kəmpέər] *vt.* **1** (P6,13) 《*with*》 examine in order to find out likeness and unlikeness. …을 비교하다. ¶ *~ a translation with the original* 번역문을 원문과 비교하다 / *She compared several samples of silk for a dress.* 그녀는 드레스용의 비단 견본을 몇 개 비교해 보았다 / *as compared with China* 중국과 비교하면. **2** (P13) 《*to*》 describe (one thing) as being similar to another thing. …에 비기다; 비유하다. ¶ *Life is sometimes compared to a voyage.* 인생은 때로 항해에 비유된다. **3** (P6) 《gram.》 give the positive, comparative, and superlative degrees of (an adjective or adverb). (형용사·부사의) 비교 변화를 보이다; 비교급·최상급을 만들다. — *vi.* (P1,3) 《usu. *negative* or *interrogative*》 be worthy of comparison. 필적하다; 견줄(비견할) 만하다. ¶ *Dekker's plays cannot ~ with Shakespeare's.* 데커의

극(劇)은 셰익스피어의 극에는 견줄 수가 없다 / *Can Milton ~ with Shakespeare?* 밀턴은 셰익스피어에 비견될 수 있을까.

compare notes, exchange ideas. 의견을 교환하다.

not to be compared with, very different from (something). …와 비교가 안 되는; 훨씬 못한. ¶ *His drama is not to be compared with Shakespeare.* 그의 극은 셰익스피어의 극과 비교가 안 된다.

— *n.* Ⓤ comparison. 비교. [com-, L. *par* equal]

beyond* 〔*past, without*〕 *compare, very excellent; incomparably; unequaled. 비길 데 없이. ¶ *She is lovely beyond* 〔*past, without*〕 *~.* =*Her loveliness is beyond* 〔*past, without*〕 *~.* 그녀는 비길 데 없이 아름답다.

·com·par·i·son [kəmpǽrisən] *n.* ⓊⒸ **1** the act of comparing. 비교. ¶ *a ~ between town and country life* 도시와 시골 생활의 비교 / *in ~* 비교적; 꽤; 뜻밖에 / *institute* 〔*establish, make*〕 *a ~ between A and B,* A와 B를 비교하다 / *make a favorable ~ with* …와 비교하여 뛰어나다 / *There is no ~ between the two.* 양자는 도저히 비교가 되지 않는다. **2** likeness. 유사(類似). ¶ *the points of ~* 유사점. **3** a statement that one thing is like another in some way; likening. 비유. ¶ *the ~ of life to voyage* 인생을 항해에 비유하기 / *'Hair white as snow' is a common ~.* '눈처럼 새하얀 머리'란 말은 일상적인 비유이다. **4** a possibility of comparison. 비교될〔견줄〕 수 있음. ¶ *There is no ~ between them.* 그것들은 비교가 되지 않는다. **5** 《gram.》 the change in an adjective or adverb to give degrees. 비교 변화. [↑]

bear comparison with, equal. …에 필적하다; 비견되다.

beyond comparison, incomparable; incomparably. 비길〔견줄〕 데 없는〔없이〕.

by comparison, when compared together. 비하면; 비교해 보면.

in comparison with, compared with; as compared to. …에 비하여; …와 비교하면.

without* 〔*out of* (*all*)〕 *comparison, =beyond comparison.

com·part·ment [kəmpɑ́:rtmənt] *n.* Ⓒ **1** a part separated from the whole; a division; a section. 구획된 부분; 칸. ¶ *a watertight ~* (배의) 방수(防水) 구획실 / *be* 〔*live*〕 *in a watertight ~* 다른 사람〔것〕과 완전히 격리〔고립〕돼 있다 / *The pencil-box has several compartments for holding different things.* 필통에는 각각 다른 물건을 넣기 위해 몇 개의 칸막이가 있다. **2** ⓐ《U.S. railroads》 a private bedroom. (열차 따위의 개인용) 침실. ⓑ《Brit.》 a division of a carriage. (칸막이 한) 차실(車室). [com-]

:com·pass [kʌ́mpəs] *n.* **1** Ⓒ an instrument for showing direction by means of a magnetic needle. 나침반. ¶ *a ~ needle* 자침(磁針). **2** Ⓤ the boundary of an area; range; extent. 경계; 한계; 범위. ¶ *within a limited ~* 한정된 범위 내에서 / *beyond the ~ of imagination* 상상의 한계를 넘어서. **3** Ⓤ 《mus.》 the extent of a voice or of a musical instrument. 음역(音域). **4** the distance around any space; circuit. 주위; 둘레. **5** 《usu. *pl.*》 an instrument for drawing circles. 컴퍼스. ¶ *a pair of compasses* 컴퍼스 한 개.

beyond one's compass, beyond one's powers. …의 힘이 미치지 않는.

fetch* 〔*go*〕 *a compass, go a long way about. 멀리 돌아가다.

within compass, within due limits; within moderate bounds. 적당히; 조심스럽게. ¶ *keep one's desires within ~* 욕망을 적당히 누르다.

within one's compass, within one's powers. 힘이 미치는.

— *vt.* (P6) **1** surround. …을 둘러싸다. ¶ *an island compassed by the sea* 바다에 둘러싸인 섬. **2** accomplish. …을 달성〔성취〕하다. ¶ *~ one's object* 목적을 이루다. **3** plot; contrive; plan. …을 꾀하다; 꾸미다; 계획하다. ¶ *~ the death of the king* 국왕 시해를 꾀하다. **4** grasp (something) with the mind; understand. …을 이해하다. [com-, →pace]

com·pas·sion [kəmpǽʃən] *n.* Ⓤ 《*on, for*》 sorrow and pity for the sufferings of others; sympathy. 연민; 동정. [com-, →passion]

***have* 〔*take*〕 *compassion on* 〔*upon*〕,** pity and help. …을 깊이 동정하다.

com·pas·sion·ate [kəmpǽʃənit] *adj.* feeling or showing compassion; merciful. 동정심이 많은; 인정 많은. ¶ *a ~ person* 인정 많은 사람 / *a ~ letter* 동정심에 찬 편지 / *He is ~ to the poor.* 그는 가난한 사람들에게 동정심이 많다.

com·pat·i·bil·i·ty [kəmpæ̀təbíləti] *n.* Ⓤ the state of being compatible. 양립(성); 적합(성). [↓]

com·pat·i·ble [kəmpǽtəbəl] *adj.* 《*with*》 able to live together in harmony; capable of both being true. 양립〔화합〕할 수 있는; 적합한; 모순 없는. ¶ *a ~ partner* 사이 좋게 지낼 수 있는 상대 / *His action is ~ with his character.* 그의 행동은 자신의 성격과 어울린다 / *These two statements are not ~ (with each other).* 이 두 진술은 (서로) 모순된다. [com-, L. *patior* suffer]

com·pat·i·bly [kəmpǽtəbəli] *adv.* in a compatible manner; with compatibility. 양립할 수 있게; 적합하게.

com·pa·tri·ot [kəmpéitriət / -pǽt-] *n.* Ⓒ a fellow countryman or countrywoman. 동국인; 동포. — *adj.* of the same country. 같은 나라의. [com-]

com·peer [kəmpíər, kʌ́mpiər / kɔ́m-] *n.* Ⓒ **1** an equal. 동등한〔대등한〕 사람. **2** a companion. 동료; 동지(cf. *peer*). [com-, L. *par* equal]

:com·pel [kəmpél] *vt.* (**-pelled, -pel·ling**) **1**

(P6,20) force. (아무)를 강제하여 …하게 하다; 강제로 …시키다. ¶ ~ *someone to sign a paper* 억지로 서류에 서명시키다 / *be compelled to leave* 부득이 떠나게 되다 / *I was compelled by illness to spend several days in bed.* 병으로 며칠간 병석에서 지내야 했다. **2** (P6) get (something) by force; enforce. …을 강요하다. ¶ ~ *obedience* 〔*silence*〕 *from her* 그녀에게 복종〔침묵〕을 강요하다 / ~ *tears of sympathy from someone* 아무에게 동정의 눈물을 자아내게 하다. **3** (P6) cause to yield. …을 굴복시키다. ¶ ~ *someone to one's will* 아무를 자기 뜻에 따르게 하다. [com-, L. *pello* drive]

com·pen·di·a [kəmpéndiə] *n.* pl. of **compendium.**

com·pen·di·ous [kəmpéndiəs] *adj.* concise. 간결한. [↓]

com·pen·di·um [kəmpéndiəm] *n.* Ⓒ (*pl.* **-di·ums** or **-di·a**) **1** a concise treatise. 개론(概論); 개설. ¶ *a ~ of modern medicine* 현대 의학 개론. **2** an outline. 대요(大要); 요약. [→pendant]

com·pen·sate [kámpənsèit / kɔ́m-] *vt.* (P6,13) pay (someone) for his loss or service. …을 보상하다; 메우다. ¶ ~ *a worker injured on his job* 작업 중 부상한 근로자에게 보상을 하다 / *We will ~ you for any damage done to your house while we are in it.* 당신 집에 입주해 있는 동안 집에 끼치는 어떠한 손해에 대해서도 보상하겠습니다.

— *vi.* (P3) 《*for, to, with*》 **1** make up for somehing. 보상하다; 메우다. ¶ ~ *to someone with money* 아무에게 돈으로 보상하다 / *Nothing can ~ for the loss of a mother.* 어머니를 잃은 것에 대해서는 아무 것으로도 메울 수가 없다. **2** 《mech.》 correct aberration. 보정(補正)하다. [com-, L. *pendeo* hang]

***com·pen·sa·tion** [kàmpənséiʃən / kɔ̀m-] *n.* ⓊⒸ **1** the act of compensating; the state of being compensated. 보상; 메움. ¶ *Tom gave me a new knife as ~ for the one of mine he had lost.* 톰은 내게 자신이 잃어버린 내 칼 대신 새 칼로 보상했다. **2** anything, esp. money, that makes up for a loss. 보상품〔금〕; 대상(代償). ¶ *pay someone $2,500 as ~ for the loss of his car* 아무에게 잃어버린 차에 대한 보상금으로 2천 5백 달러를 지급하다. **3** 《U.S.》 salary; pay. 봉급. ¶ *He said that equal ~ should be given to men and women for equal work.* 그는 같은 일을 하면 남자나 여자나 똑같은 임금을 준다고 했다. **4** 《mech.》 compensating. 보정(補正).

make compensation for, compensate for. …을 보상하다; 메우다.

com·pen·sa·to·ry [kəmpénsətɔ̀:ri / -təri] *adj.* serving to compensate. 보상의; 보상이 되는.

***com·pete** [kəmpí:t] *vi.* (P1,3) **1** 《*against, with, for*》 ⓐ try to win. 겨루다; 경쟁하다. ¶ ~ *against other countries in trade* 무역에서 다른 나라와 겨루다 / ~ *with a rival firm* 라이벌 회사와 경쟁하다. ⓑ rival; vie with another in a quality. 대항하다; 필적하다; 어깨를 겨루다. ¶ *No painting can ~ with this here.* 여기서는 이 그림과 겨룰 만한 것이 없다. **2** 《*in*》 take part (in a contest). (경기)에 참가하다. ¶ *Do you intend to ~ in the swimming race?* 경영(競泳)에 참가할 작정인가. [com-, L. *peto* seek]

com·pe·tence [kámpətəns / kɔ́m-], **-ten·cy** [-tənsi] *n.* **1** Ⓤ 《*for*》 the state of being competent; ability. 자격; 능력; 적임. ¶ *one's ~ for a duty* 임무 수행 능력 / *I doubt his ~ for such a post.* 나는 그러한 지위에 대한 그의 적임 여부가 의심스럽다. **2** 《usu. *a* ~》 a sufficient fortune. 상당한 자산〔자력〕. ¶ *enjoy* 〔*have*〕 *a modest ~* 약간의 재산을 갖고 있다 / *lay up ~* 상당한 자산을 모으다. **3** Ⓤ 《law》 legal authority. 권능; 권한. ¶ *exceed* 〔*go beyond*〕 *one's ~* 월권 행위를 하다. [L. =being fit]

***com·pe·tent** [kámpətənt / kɔ́m-] *adj.* **1** able; fitted; well qualified. 유능한; 적임의; 능력〔자격〕이 있는. ¶ *a ~ teacher* 유능한 교사 / *a man ~ for the post* 그 지위의 적임자. **2** sufficient. 충분한; 만족한. ¶ *have a ~ knowledge of a subject* 주제에 관한 충분한 지식이 있다. **3** 《law》 having the necessary power of right to do an act. 권능〔권한〕이 있는. ¶ *the ~ authorities* 당해(當該) 관청.

● **com·pe·tent·ly** [-li] *adv.* [↑]

:com·pe·ti·tion [kàmpətíʃən / kɔ̀m-] *n.* **1** Ⓤ the act of competing; the state of being a rival. 경쟁; 대항. ¶ *a sense of ~* 경쟁의식 / *in ~ with others* 다른 사람들과 경쟁하여 / *lose in ~ with* …와의 경쟁에서 지다. **2** Ⓒ a contest. 경기; 경기 대회. ¶ *the Olympic ~* 올림픽 경기 / *a boxing* 〔*swimming*〕 *~* 권투〔수영〕 경기. [→compete]

be* 〔*stand*〕 *in competition with* (*someone*) *for, compete with (someone) for. …을 얻으려고 (아무)와 경쟁하다.

put* (*someone*) *in* 〔*into*〕 *competition with, make someone compete with. (아무)를 …와 경쟁시키다.

com·pet·i·tive [kəmpétətiv] *adj.* of competition. 경쟁의; 겨루는. ¶ ~ *sports* 〔*games*〕 경기 / ~ *spirit* 경쟁심 / *a ~ examination for the job of clerk* 사무직의 경쟁 시험.

● **com·pet·i·tive·ly** [-li] *adv.*

com·pet·i·tor [kəmpétətər] *n.* Ⓒ a person or team that competes; a rival. 경쟁자〔팀〕; 경쟁 상대. ¶ *competitors in business* 사업 경쟁 상대.

com·pi·la·tion [kàmpəléiʃən / kɔ̀m-] *n.* **1** Ⓤ the act of compiling. 편집; 편찬. **2** Ⓒ anything compiled. 편집된 것; 편찬서. [↓]

com·pile [kəmpáil] *vt.* (P6,13) collect facts, stories, etc. in one (book); make (a book) from various materials. …을 편집〔편찬〕하다. ¶ ~ *a dictionary* 사전을 편찬하다. [com-, L. *pilo* rob]

com·pil·er [kəmpáilər] *n.* Ⓒ a person

who compiles. 편찬자; 편집자. [↑]

com·pla·cence [kəmpléisəns], **-cen·cy** [-sənsi] *n.* Ⓤ a feeling of safety; self-satisfaction. 안심(감); 만족감; 자기 만족. [↓]

com·pla·cent [kəmpléisənt] *adj.* pleased with oneself; only self-satisfied. 흡족해 하는; 만족한; 자기 만족의. ¶ *a ~ smile* 흡족해 하는 미소. ● **com·pla·cent·ly** [-li] *adv.* [com-, L. *placeo* please]

:com·plain [kəmpléin] *vi., vt.* (P1,3; 11) **1** 《*of, about*》 express discontent with something. 불평을 하다. ¶ *~ of ill treatment* 대우가 나쁘다고 불평하다 / *~ to the manager about the service* 지배인에게 서비스가 나쁘다고 불평하다 / *He is always complaining.* 그는 늘 불평만 하고 있다 / *He complains that the room is dirty.* 그는 방이 더럽다고 불평한다. **2** 《*of, about*》 tell of one's pains. (고통)을 호소하다. ¶ *~ of indigestion* 〔*a stomachache*〕 소화 불량〔복통〕을 호소하다 / *~ about a pain in one's back* 등이 아프다고 호소하다. **3** ⓐ find fault. 흠〔탈〕잡다. ⓑ make a report (about something wrong); accuse. (정식으로) 신고하다; 고소하다. ¶ *You should ~ to the police about the public nuisance.* 공해를 경찰에 알려야 한다. **4** 《*poet.*》 emit mournful sound. 구슬픈 소리를 내다; 신음하다. [L. *plango* beat breast]

com·plain·ant [kəmpléinənt] *n.* Ⓒ **1** a person who complains. 불평하는 사람. **2** 《law》 a person who charges another in a court. 고소인; 원고.

***com·plaint** [kəmpléint] *n.* **1** ⓐ ⓊⒸ an expression of discontent. 불평; 불만. ¶ *the ~ of the people against the government* 정부에 대한 국민의 불만 / *make a ~ against someone* 아무에 대해 불평을 하다 / *have no ~ to make* (*about*) (…에 대해) 아무 불평도 없다 / *He is full of complaints about the food.* 그는 음식에 대해 불평이 많다. ⓑ Ⓒ a cause of discontent. 불평의 씨〔원인〕. **2** Ⓒ sickness. 병. ¶ *a chronic ~* 만성병 / *a constitutional ~* 지병(持病) / *have* 〔*suffer from*〕 *a ~ in the chest* 가슴에 병이 있다. **3** Ⓒ 《law》 a formal charge. 고소. ¶ *make* 〔*lodge*〕 *a ~ against someone* 아무를 고소하다.

com·plai·sance [kəmpléisəns, -zəns, kámpləzæ̀ns] *n.* Ⓤ readiness to please or to oblige; courtesy. 남을 기쁘게〔만족하게〕 하기; 친절; 공손; 순종. [→complacent]

com·plai·sant [kəmpléisənt, -zənt, -kámpləzæ̀nt] *adj.* yielding to the wishes of others; eager to please; polite; compliant. 남을 만족하게〔기쁘게〕 하려는; 친절한; 붙임성 있는; 공손한; 순종하는. ¶ *very ~ smiles* 매우 상냥한 미소. ● **com·plai·sant·ly** [-li] *adv.*

***com·ple·ment** [kámpləmənt / kɔ́m-] *n.* Ⓒ **1** anything that makes an imperfect thing complete. (보완하여) 완전하게 하는 것. **2** a number required to be filled or made complete; the full number; 《nav.》 all the officers and men necessary for a ship. 보족수(량); 전수(全數); 전량; 정원. **3** 《gram.》 words that complete a predicate. 보어. **4** 《math.》 the quantity needed to make an angle equal to 90°. 여각(餘角).

— [-mènt] *vt.* (P6,13) make (something) perfect; complete. …을 보완하다; 완전하게 하다. [com-, L. *pleo* fill]

com·ple·men·tal [kàmpləméntl / kɔ̀m-] *adj.* =complementary.

com·ple·men·ta·ry [kàmpləméntəri / kɔ̀m-] *adj.* completing. 보완의; 보충의. ¶ *~ colors* 보색 / *a ~ angle* 여각 / *be ~ to one another* 상호 보완하다.

:com·plete [kəmplí:t] *adj.* (often **-plet·er, -plet·est**) **1** lacking nothing; whole; entire. 완비한; 전부 갖춰진. ¶ *a ~ set of Hemingway's novels* 헤밍웨이의 소설 전집. **2** finished; ended. 완성〔완결〕된; 끝난. ¶ *My work is now ~.* 나의 일은 이제 끝났다. **3** perfect in quality. 완벽한; 더할 나위 없는. ¶ *a ~ gentleman* 나무랄 데 없는 신사. **4** perfect; absolute. 완전한; 전혀〔아주〕 …한. ¶ *a ~ victory* 완승 / *a ~ success* 완전한 성공 / *a ~ stranger* 전혀 모르는 사람 / *a ~ ass* 지독한 바보.

— *vt.* (P6) **1** make (something) whole or perfect. …을 완전히 하다; 채우다. ¶ *One more volume will ~ the set.* 한 권만 더 있으면 전집을 채우게 된다 / *The good news completes my happiness.* 그 좋은 소식이 내 행복감을 채워준다. **2** finish. …을 완성하다; 끝내다. ¶ *~ a piece of work* 한 작품을 완성하다 / *The building is now completed.* 건물이 이제 완공되었다. [com-, L. *plēre* to fill]

:com·plete·ly [kəmplí:tli] *adv.* entirely; thoroughly. 완전히; 아주. ¶ *The house was ~ rebuilt.* 집이 완전히 재건되었다 / *The experiment* 〔*operation*〕 *was ~ successful.* 실험〔수술〕은 아주 성공적이었다.

com·plete·ness [kəmplí:tnis] *n.* Ⓤ the state of being complete. 완전함.

com·ple·tion [kəmplí:ʃən] *n.* Ⓤ the act of completing; the state of being completed; fulfillment. 완성(된 상태); 완료; 성취; 달성. ¶ *the ~ of a plan* 계획의 완성 / *bring something to ~* …을 완성하다〔끝내다〕.

***com·plex** [kəmpléks, kámpleks / kɔ́m-] *adj.* **1** made up of many parts. 복합의; 합성〔혼성〕의. ¶ *a ~ sentence* 복문(複文) / *a ~ highway system* 입체 고속 도로 방식. **2** hard to understand or deal with; complicated; not simple. 복잡한. ¶ *a ~ problem* 〔*machine*〕 복잡한 문제〔기계〕 / *His political ideas were too ~ to get support from ordinary people.* 그의 정치적 견해는 너무 복잡해서 일반 사람들의 지지를 못 받았다.

— [kámpleks / kɔ́m-] *n.* Ⓒ **1** a complex whole. 복합체; 합성물. ¶ *a ~ of buildings* 복합 건물 / *a housing ~* 주택 단지. **2** ⓐ a system of ideas that causes abnormal behavior. 관념 복합; 콤플렉스. ⓑ《colloq.》 a strong prejudice; an irrational dislike or fear; an obsession. 강한 편견; 지나친 혐오〔공포〕; 강박 관념. ¶ *He has a ~ against foreigners.* 외국인에 대해 심한 편견을 갖고 있다. [L. *plecto* plait, interweave]

·com·plex·ion [kəmplékʃən] *n.* Ⓒ **1** the natural color and appearance of the skin, esp. of the face. 피부빛깔; 안색. ¶ *a woman with* 〔*of*〕 *a fair ~* 살갗이 흰 여자 / *have a fine ~* 안색이 좋다. **2** general appearance. 형세; 상황. ¶ *put a different* 〔*another*〕 *~ on* …의 국면〔상황〕을 바꾸다 / *The ~ of the war was changed by two great victories.* 두 번의 큰 승리로 전쟁의 국면이 바뀌었다. ● **com·plex·ion·al** [-əl] *adj.*

com·plex·i·ty [kəmpléksəti] *n.* (*pl.* **-ties**) **1** Ⓤ the state of being complex. 복잡(성). ¶ *The ~ of the problem puzzled him.* 문제의 복잡성은 그를 당황케 했다. **2** Ⓒ something complex. 복잡한 것.

com·pli·ance [kəmpláiəns] *n.* Ⓤ **1** the act of complying. 승낙. **2** a tendency to obey others; submission. 순종; 복종. [*comply*]

in compliance with, yielding to; according to. …에 응하여〔따라〕. ¶ *in ~ with the demands* 요구에 응하여.

com·pli·ant [kəmpláiənt] *adj.* complying; yielding. …에 응하는; 따르는; 순종하는.

com·pli·ca·cy [kɑ́mpləkəsi, kɔ́mpli-] *n.* Ⓤ **1** the quality or state of being complicated. 복잡; 착잡. **2** something that is complicated. 복잡한 것. [↓]

·com·pli·cate [kɑ́mplikèit / kɔ́m-] *vt.* (P6) **1** make (something) complex or difficult to understand; mix up. …을 복잡하게 만들다; 뒤섞다. ¶ *~ matters* 일을 복잡하게 만들다 / *His policy was complicated with his private interest.* 그의 정책은 사적인 이익과 뒤얽혀 있었다. **2** 《med.》 make worse by the addition of another trouble. (딴 병의 병발(倂發)로) 더욱 악화시키다. ¶ *a headache complicated by eye trouble* 눈병으로 인해 더욱 악화된 두통. [L. *plico* fold]

com·pli·cat·ed [kɑ́mplikèitid / kɔ́m-] *adj.* made up of many parts; complex; not simple. 복잡한. ¶ *a ~ machine* 〔*problem*〕 복잡한 기계〔문제〕 / *a ~ puzzle* 복잡한 수수께끼 / *a ~ person* 이해하기 어려운 사람.

com·pli·ca·tion [kɑ̀mplikéiʃən / kɔ̀m-] *n.* **1** ⓊⒸ a complex state of affairs hard to understand or settle. 복잡(한 상태). **2** Ⓒ anything that complicates; anything that increases difficulty or confusion. 복잡하게 하는 것; 혼란〔분규〕의 불씨. **3** 《med.》 a fresh element, symptom, or a disease that arises during the course of an illness, and make it difficult. (딴 병의) 병발(倂發); 합병증.

com·plic·i·ty [kəmplísəti] *n.* Ⓤ partnership in crime. 공모(共謀); 공범. ¶ *He was accused of ~ in the crime.* 그는 범죄의 공범 혐의로 기소되었다. [→complicate]

·com·pli·ment [kɑ́mpləmənt / kɔ́m-] *n.* **1** Ⓒ something good said about someone; something said in praise of; flattery. 찬사; 치렛말; 발림말; 공치사; (말·행위로 나타내는) 경의. ¶ *in ~ to* …에게 경의를 표하여 / *pay* 〔*make*〕 *someone a high ~* 아무에게 높은 찬사를 보내다 / *I did him the ~ of inviting him.* 경의를 표하여 그를 초대했다 / *I take it as a ~ to be asked to speak.* 연설을 요청받은 것을 저의 영광으로 여기는 바입니다 / *a doubtful* 〔*left-handed*〕 *~* 비아냥조의〔속검은〕 찬사. **2** 《*pl.*》 polite, formal greetings. (정중한) 인사; 안부의 인사(말). ¶ *the compliments of the season* 시후(時候)의 인사; (크리스마스·새해 따위의) 축하의 인사 / *Give her my compliments.* 그녀에게 안부 전해 주시오 / *With the compliments of the author* 저자 근정(著者謹呈). ── [-mènt] *vt.* (P6,13) **1** 《*on*》 pay a compliment to (someone). …에게 찬사를 말하다; 치렛말을 하다. ¶ *~ a child on his good behavior* 아이의 예절 바름을 칭찬하다. **2** 《*on*》 congratulate. …에게 축하의 말을 하다. ¶ *~ him on the birth of a son* 그에게 득남(得男)한 것을 축하하다. [→complement]

compliment** someone **into, persuade someone by flattery. (아무)에게 아첨의 말을 하여 …하게 하다.

***compliment** someone **on** (his courage),* applaud someone of (his courage). (아무의 용기)를 칭찬〔찬양〕하다.

com·pli·men·ta·ry [kɑ̀mpləméntəri / kɔ̀m-] *adj.* **1** expressing admiration, praise, respect, etc. 칭찬의; 경의를 표하는; 인사의. ¶ *a ~ address* 축사 / *a ~ remark* 찬사; 칭찬의 말. **2** flattering. 아첨〔치렛말〕을 잘 하는. **3** given free, as a token of respect. 무료의; 우대의. ¶ *a ~ ticket to the play* 연극 초대권.

·com·ply [kəmplái] *vi.* (P1,3) (**-plied**) **1** 《*with*》 act in accordance to (a request or a command). (요구·명령에) 따르다; 응하다. ¶ *~ with someone's request* 아무의 요구에 응하다 / *~ with the rules* 규칙에 따르다. **2** yield; give way. 굴(복)하다. ¶ *Threats, commands, entreaties were useless: he would not ~.* 협박도, 명령도, 탄원도 아무 소용 없었다. 그는 굴복하려 들지 않았다. [com-, L. *pleo* fill]

com·po·nent [kəmpóunənt] *adj.* necessary to make up a whole; composing. 성분의; 구성하는. ── *n.* Ⓒ a component part. 성분. ¶ *the various ~ of a medicine* 의약의 여러 가지 성분. [com-, L. *pono* put]

com·port [kəmpɔ́ːrt] *vt.* (P6) 《*reflexively*》 conduct or behave (oneself). …하게 행동하다. ¶ *The judge must ~ himself blamelessly.* 판사는 깨끗〔결백〕하게 처신해야 한다. ── *vi.* (P3) 《*with*》 suit; agree. 일치하다; 어울리다.

¶ *His behavior does not* ~ *with ranks.* 그의 행동은 신분에 어울리지 않는다. [com-, L. *porto* carry]

com·port·ment [kəmpɔ́ːrtmənt] *n.* UC behavior. 행동; 태도.

:com·pose [kəmpóuz] *vt.* (P6) **1** 《*of*》 make (something) by putting its parts together; make up; constitute. …을 구성하다. ¶ *Water is composed of hydrogen and oxygen.* 물은 수소와 산소로 돼 있다 / *Our party was composed of three grown-ups and four children.* 우리 일행은 어른 셋과 아이들 넷으로 구성돼 있었다. **2** create (a poem, a picture, etc.). …을 창작하다. ¶ ~ *a novel* 소설을 쓰다 / ~ *a sonata* 소나타를 작곡하다. **3** calm; settle (a quarrel, etc.); adjust. (논쟁·쟁의 따위)를 조정하다; 진정시키다. ¶ ~ *a dispute* 쟁의(爭議)를 조정하다 / ~ *one's difficulties* 난국을 타개하다. **4** make (oneself) calm. …을 가라앉히다. ¶ ~ *one's mind* 마음을 가라앉히다 / ~ *oneself to read* 마음을 진정시키고 읽다 / *He tried to* ~ *himself before the examination.* 시험 전에 그는 침착하려고 애썼다. **5** 《print.》 set up (types). (활자)를 짜다; 식자[조판]하다. **6** lay out (a dead body). (시신을) 안치하다. [com-, →pose]

be composed (=*be made up*) ***of things.*** …로 되어 있다.

compose** one's **features, calm oneself. 마음을 가라앉히다.

compose** one's **thoughts for action, get oneself ready to act. 단단히 마음 먹고 활동을 시작하다.

com·posed [kəmpóuzd] *adj.* calm in mind; free from anxiety. 침착한; (마음이) 평온한, 근심 없는. ¶ *a* ~ *face* 침착한 얼굴. ●**com·pos·ed·ly** [-idli] *adv.*

com·pos·er [kəmpóuzər] *n.* C **1** a person who composes. 구성자; 조정자. **2** a person who writes music. 작곡가. **3** an author. (소설·시 따위의) 작자; 작가. [↓]

com·pos·ite [kəmpázit, kɑm- / kɔ́mpɔzit] *adj.* made up of various separate parts; compound. 합성의; 혼성[혼합]의. ¶ *a* ~ *phenomenon* 복합 현상 / *a* ~ *drawing* 합성화(畫) / *the Composite order,* 《archit.》 (이오니아식과 코린트식의) 혼합 양식. ― *n.* C **1** a compound. 혼합[합성]물. **2** 《bot.》 a composite plant. 국화과 식물. [L. *com-,* with, *poser* place, meaning influenced by L. *pono* put]

***com·po·si·tion** [kàmpəzíʃən / kɔ̀m-] *n.* **1** UC the act of composing or putting together. 구성; 합성; 창작. ¶ *the* ~ *of short stories* 단편 소설의 창작 / *He spent five years in the* ~ *of his first novel.* 그는 첫 소설의 구상에 5년을 소비했다. **2** C something composed, such as a piece of music, writing, etc.; a work of art. (하나의) 작문; 작곡; 예술 작품. ¶ *The boys were told to write a English* ~. 학생 아이들은 영작문을 짓도록 지시받았다. **3** C a mixture of substances. 혼합물; 합성물. ¶ *a* ~ *of rubber and cork* 고무와 코르크의 합성물. **4** UC the parts of which anything is made up; what is in it. 성분; 성질; 구성물. ¶ *The* ~ *of this candy includes sugar, chocolate, and milk.* 이 캔디의 성분에는 설탕, 초콜릿 및 우유가 포함돼 있다. **5** C constitution of mind. 기질. ¶ *There is no meanness in his* ~. 그의 성품에는 야비한 데란 전혀 없다. **6** C 《print.》 the setting-up of type. 식자(植字). **7** C agreement; a settlement. 화해; 타협. [→ composite, -tion]

com·pos·i·tor [kəmpázitər / -pɔ́z-] *n.* C a typesetter. 식자공(工); 식자기(機).

com·pos men·tis [kàmpəs méntis / kɔ́m-] *a.* 《law》 sane. 정신이 멀쩡한[건전한]. [L. =having power over one's mind]

com·post [kámpoust / kɔ́m-] *n.* C **1** a mixture of various decayed things used for fertilizing land. 혼합 비료; 두엄. **2** a compound. 혼합물. ― *vt.* (P6) treat with compost. 두엄을[퇴비를] 주다. [→pose]

com·po·sure [kəmpóuʒər] *n.* U a peaceful state of mind; calmness. (마음의) 평정; 침착(opp. agitation). ¶ *keep one's* ~ *in a crisis* 위기에서 침착을 잃지 않다. [*compose*]

com·pote [kámpout / kɔ́m-] *n.* **1** UC stewed fruit, usu. served as a dessert. 시럽찜[설탕절이] 과일. **2** C a dish with a base and stem for fruit, nuts, candy, etc. (과일 따위를 담는) 굽 달린 접시. [F.]

***com·pound**[1] [kəmpáund, kámpaund / kɔ́mpaund] *vt.* (P6) **1** make (something) by combining parts or elements; mix; combine. …을 혼합[합성]하다; 짜맞춰 만들다. ¶ ~ *drugs to form a new medicine* 약제를 조합하여 신약을 만들다 / ~ *a new plan from parts of several former plans* 전에 나왔던 몇 개의 안을 절충해서 새로운 계획을 세우다. **2** settle (a quarrel, a debt, etc.) by mutual agreement. …을 매듭[타협]을 짓다; 해결하다; 사화(私和)하다. ― *vi.* (P1,3) agree; compromise. 타협[화해]하다.

compound a felony, forbear prosecution on private motives. (기소를 보류하고) 중죄를 합의하다; 사태를 악화시키다.

compound with, come to terms with. …와 타협하다; 사화로 끝내다.

― [kámpaund, ―́ / kɔ́m-] *adj.* made up of two or more parts or elements. 합성의; 혼합의(opp. simple). ¶ *a* ~ *leaf* 겹잎; 복엽(複葉) / *a* ~ *eye* 겹눈 / *a* ~ *sentence* 중문(重文) / ~ *interest* 복리.

― [kámpaund / kɔ́m-] *n.* C **1** a substance formed by chemical combination of two or more elements. 화합물. ¶ *Water is a* ~ *of hydrogen and oxygen.* 물은 수소와 산소의 화합물이다. **2** something made by mixing substances or combining parts; a mixture. 혼합물; 합성물. ¶ *Air is a* ~ *of several gases.* 공기는 몇가지 기체의 혼합물이다. **3** a compound word. 복합어; 합성어. [L.

pono put]

com·pound² [kámpaund / kɔ́m-] *n.* 《in the East》 the enclosed space in which foreigners' houses stand. (울타리를 두른) 외국인 거주 지역; 구내. [Malay]

com·preg·nate [kəmprégneit] *vt.* impregnate veneer with liquid and bond in layer under pressure. (여러 겹의 베니어판을) 가압(加壓) 접착시켜 합판을 성형하다《수지 용액을 침윤시켜 압착·가열함》. ¶ *compregnated wood* 고압(성형)합판; 강화목. [*Compress, impregnate*]

*__com·pre·hend__ [kàmprihénd / kɔ̀m-] *vt.* (P6) **1** grasp the meaning of (something); understand. …을 이해〔파악〕하다. ¶ ~ *a question* 〔*meaning*〕 문제〔의미〕를 이해하다. **2** take in; contain. …을 포함〔내포〕하다; 의미하다. ¶ *Europe comprehends many nations.* 유럽에는 많은 나라가 있다. [L. *prehendo* take]

com·pre·hen·si·bil·i·ty [kàmprihénsəbíləti / kɔ̀m-] *n.* Ⓤ the state of being comprehensible. 알기 쉬움.

com·pre·hen·si·ble [kàmprihénsəbəl / kɔ̀m-] *adj.* that can be understood; understandable. 이해할 수 있는.

com·pre·hen·sion [kàmprihénʃən / kɔ̀m-] *n.* Ⓤ **1** the act of comprehending; the ability to understand; mental grasp. 이해; 파악; 이해력. ¶ *His* ~ *of physics is amazing for a young student.* 그의 물리학에 대한 이해는 어린 학생으로서는 아주 놀랍다. **2** the act of taking in or including; inclusive power. 포함; 포용(력).

***be above* 〔*beyond*〕 *one's* comprehension,** be hard to understand. 이해할 수 없다. ¶ *plays which are above the* ~ *of plain people* 보통 사람들에게는 이해할 수 없는 연극.

past comprehension, incomprehensive. 불가해(不可解)한.

com·pre·hen·sive [kàmprihénsiv / kɔ̀m-] *adj.* **1** of wide scope; including much. 범위가 넓은; 포괄적인. ¶ *a* ~ *term* 의미가 넓은 말 / *a* ~ *grasp* 포괄적인 파악 / *He has a* ~ *knowledge of science.* 그는 광범한 과학 지식을 가지고 있다. **2** able to understand. 이해력 있는. ¶ *the* ~ *faculty* 이해력.

com·pre·hen·sive·ly [kàmprihénsivli / kɔ̀m-] *adv.* in a comprehensive manner; with a wide scope. 포괄적으로; 알기 쉽게.

com·press [kəmprés] *vt.* (P6,13) press (things) tightly together; make (something) smaller by pressing; condense. …을 압축하다; …으로 간추리다〔요약하다〕. ¶ *compressed air* 압축 공기 / ~ *one's lips* 입술을 꽉 다물다 / ~ *a report to essentials* 보고를 요점만으로 간추리다 / ~ *cotton into bales* 솜을 고리에 눌러 넣다. — [kámpres / kɔ́m-] *n.* Ⓒ a wet pad applied to some part of the body to give pressure, moisture, cold, or heat. 압박 붕대; 습포(濕布). [com-]

com·press·i·ble [kəmprésəbəl] *adj.* that can be compressed. 압축할 수 있는.

com·pres·sion [kəmpréʃən] *n.* Ⓤ **1** the act of compressing; the state of being compressed. 압축. **2** summary. 요약.

com·pres·sor [kəmprésər] *n.* Ⓒ **1** a person or thing that compresses. 압축하는 사람〔것〕. **2** 《surg.》 an instrument for compressing a part of the body. 압박기(器). **3** a machine for increasing the pressure of air, gas, etc. (공기·가스 따위의) 압착〔압축〕기계; 컴프레서. ¶ *an air* ~ 공기 압축기.

*__com·prise, -prize__ [kəmpráiz] *vt.* (P6) contain; consist of (something). …을 포함하다; …로 되어 있다. ¶ *This book comprises five chapters.* 이 책은 5장(章)으로 되어 있다. [F. *compris* pp. of *comprendre* comprehend]

be comprised in, be among the parts, within the scope of. …에 포함되다.

*__com·pro·mise__ [kámprəmàiz / kɔ́m-] *n.* **1** ⓊⒸ an agreement on something made by giving up a part of the wishes of both sides; the result of such an agreement. 타협; 절충. ¶ *make* 〔*arrange*〕 *a* ~ *with* …와 타협하다 / *reach a* ~ 타협이 성립되다. **2** Ⓒ anything existing between two different things. 중간물; 타협〔절충〕안.

— *vt.* (P6) **1** make a compromise about (something). …을 타협해서 해결〔처리〕하다; 화해하다. ¶ ~ *a dispute* 분쟁을 타협으로 해결하다 / ~ *a lawsuit* 소송을 사화(私和)하다. **2** put (something) in danger or under suspicion. (평판·신용 따위)를 위태롭게 하다; 의심스럽게 하다. ¶ ~ *one's credit* 신용을 떨어뜨리다 / *Such conduct will* ~ *your reputation.* 이런 행동은 자네의 평판을 의심스럽게 할 걸세.

— *vi.* (P1,3) **1** 《*with*》 make a compromise; give way. 타협〔화해〕하다. **2** make a shameful concession. 치욕적인 양보를 하다; 굴종하다. ¶ *I would rather die than* ~. 굴복하느니 차라리 죽겠다. [L. →promise]

be compromised by, be involved in trouble. …에게 누를 끼치게 되다.

compromise oneself, disgrace oneself. 평판을 떨어뜨리다; 체면을 손상하다.

comp·trol·ler [kəntróulər] *n.* = controller 1.

com·pul·sion [kəmpʌ́lʃən] *n.* Ⓤ the act of compelling; the state of being compelled. 강제; 강요. [→compel]

by compulsion, by force. 강제적으로. ¶ *John will take his medicine only by* ~. 존은 강제적이어야만 약을 먹는다.

under* 〔*on, upon*〕 *compulsion, because one is compelled. 강제되어. ¶ *An agreement signed under* ~ *is not legal.* 강요에 의해 서명한 협약은 무효이다.

com·pul·sive [kəmpʌ́lsiv] *adj.* forcible; that cannot be resisted. 강제적인. ● **com·pul·sive·ly** [-li] *adv.*

com·pul·so·ry [kəmpʌ́lsəri] *adj.* that which must be done; compelled; needed.

강제적인; 의무적인; 필수의(opp. voluntary). ¶ ~ *education* 의무 교육 / ~ *examinations* 필수 시험 / ~ *execution* 강제 집행 / 《Brit.》 *a ~ subject* 필수 과목(=《U.S.》 required subject) / ~ *measures to control rioting* 폭동을 규제하는 강제 수단.

com·punc·tion [kəmpʌ́ŋkʃən] *n.* Ⓤ **1** the pain of the conscience; a sense of guilt; regret. 양심의 가책; 후회. ¶ ~ *for former sins* 전에 저지른 죄에 대한 회한의 정 / *I felt some ~ at having kept her waiting.* 그녀를 기다리게 했던 것에 대해 다소의 가책감을 느꼈다. **2** hesitation. 망설임; 주저. ¶ *tell a lie without ~* 태연히 거짓말을 하다. [L. *pungo* prick]

without* (*the slightest*) *compunction, making no scruple. (아무) 거리낌없이; (매우) 천연스럽게. ¶ *He ate all the pie without the slightest ~.* 조금도 망설임이 없이 파이를 몽땅 먹어치웠다.

com·pu·ta·tion [kàmpjutéiʃən / kɔ̀m-] *n.* Ⓤ **1** calculation. 계산; 산정(算定). **2** the amount computed. 산출액; 계수. [↓]

com·pute [kəmpjúːt] *vt., vi.* (P6,13; 1) reckon; count; make a calculation. 계산하다; 산정(算定)하다. ● **com·put·a·ble** [-əbəl] *adj.* [L. *puto* reckon]

com·put·er [kəmpjúːtər] *n.* Ⓒ **1** a person or thing that computes. 계산자(者); 계산기. **2** an electronic calculator. 전(자 계)산기; 컴퓨터.

com·pu·ter·ize [kəmpjúːtəràiz] *vt.* (P6) furnish with a computer system. 컴퓨터로 처리(관리)하다; 컴퓨터로 자동화하다.

***com·rade** [kámræd, -rid / kɔ́m-] *n.* Ⓒ **1** a dear companion or friend. 동료; 동지; 벗. **2** a fellow member of a group, a political party, etc. 같은 조합(당파의) 사람. ¶ *comrades at arms* 전우(戰友). [→chamber]

com·rade·ship [kámrædʃìp, -rid- / kɔ́m-] *n.* Ⓤ **1** the state of being a comrade. 동지임. **2** the relation of comrades. 동료 관계; 우정.

COMSAT, Com·sat [kámsæt / kɔ́m-] *n.* an artificial satellite used for relaying radio waves. 콤샛; 통신 위성. [*Com*munication *Sat*ellite]

Comte [kɔːnt], **Auguste** *n.* (1798-1857) a French philosopher. 콩트《프랑스의 철학자》.

Com·tism [kámtizəm / kɔ́ːn-] *n.* the philosophy of Comte, positive philosophy. (콩트의) 실증 철학. [Person]

con[1] [kan / kɔn] *adv.* against. 반대하여(하고)(opp. pro[1]).

pro and con, for and against. 찬부(贊否) 양론의. ¶ *argue a matter pro and ~* 찬부 양론으로 문제를 논하다.

— *n.* Ⓒ an argument against something. 반대론(論). [→contra]

the pros and cons, arguments for and against. 찬부 양론. ¶ *weigh the pros and cons of a question* 문제의 찬부 양론을 고려하다.

con[2] [kan / kɔn] *vt.* (**conned, con·ning**) (P6,7) 《*over*》 study; learn by heart. …을 배우다; …을 외다(암기하다). [→can]

con[3] [kan / kɔn] *n.* Ⓒ something (as a ruse) used deceptively to gain another's confidence. 사기; 신용 사기; 횡령. ¶ *a ~ man* 사기꾼 / *a ~ game* 신용 사기.

— *vt.* (P6) swindle; trick. 사기하다; 사취(詐取)하다. [*con*fidence]

con[4] [kan / kɔn] *prep.* 《mus.》 with. …을 가지고; …하게. ¶ ~ *brio* 힘차게; 발랄하게 / ~ *fuoco* 정열을 가지고. [It.]

con. concerto; conclusion; connection; consul.

con-[1] [kan / kɔn] *pref.* ⇨contra-.

con-[2] [kən, kan / kən, kɔn] *pref.* ⇨com-.

con·cat·e·na·tion [kankæ̀tənéiʃən / kɔn-] *n.* ⓊⒸ connection as of chainlinks; string or series of ideas or events, etc. 연결; 연속. [→catena]

con·cave [kankéiv, ⌐– / kɔn-] *adj.* curved inside. 오목한; 오목면(面)의; 요면(凹面)의(opp. convex). ¶ *a ~ lens* 오목 렌즈. — [⌐–] *n.* Ⓒ a concave surface or thing. 오목면(형); 요면체; 오목한 곳. [com-, L. *cavus* hollow]

:con·ceal [kənsíːl] *vt.* (P6) **1** hide; cover; keep from sight. …을 숨기다(감추다). ¶ ~ *oneself* 몸을 숨기다; 잠복하다 / ~ *one's emotions* 감정을 드러내지 않다. **2** keep (a matter) secret. …을 비밀로 하다. ¶ ~ *the truth* 사실을 숨기다 / ~ *one's real self* 자신의 참모습을 보이지 않다. [L. *celo* hide]

con·ceal·ment [kənsíːlmənt] *n.* **1** Ⓤ the act of concealing; the state of being concealed. 숨김; 숨음; 감춤. ¶ *the ~ of crime* 범죄의 은닉 / *remain in ~* 숨어 있다. **2** Ⓒ a place for hiding. 숨을(숨길) 곳; 은닉 장소.

***con·cede** [kənsíːd] *vt.* (P6,11,13,14) **1** 《*in*》 admit (something) to be true; yield. …을 인정하다; …을 양보하다. ¶ ~ *a point in argument* 의론에서 한 발짝 양보하다 / ~ *that lying is wrong* 거짓말하는 것은 나쁘다는 것을 인정하다 / *He refused to ~ an inch.* 한치도 양보하기를 거부했다. **2** 《*to*》 give (a right, a privilege, etc.). (권리 따위)를 주다; 허가하다. ¶ *He conceded us to walk through his land.* 그는 우리들에게 자기 땅을 걸어서 통과하기를 허락했다. [*cede*]

***con·ceit** [kənsíːt] *n.* **1** Ⓤ too much pride in one's own ability, appearance, etc. 자부(심); (자신의) 과대 평가. ¶ *be full of ~* 자부심이 강하다 / *take the ~ out of someone* 아무의 오만한 코를 납작하게 하다. **2** Ⓒ a very fanciful idea. 생각; (기발한) 착상. [→conceive]

be out of conceit with, be no longer pleased with. …이 시틋해지다; …에게 정나미가 떨어지다. ¶ *be out of ~ with one's former self* 이전의 자기 자신이 정말 미워지다.

in one's own conceit, in one's own judgment. 자기 판단으로는; 제딴에는. ¶ *He is* *wise in his own* ~. 그는 제딴엔 자신이 현명한 줄 안다.

con·ceit·ed [kənsíːtid] *adj.* having high conceit about one's own ability, appearance, etc. 자부심이 강한; 우쭐한. ¶ *be ~ of one's own talents* 자신의 재능에 대해 자부심이 강하다.

well-conceited, 《*about*》 well planned. 착상이 재미있는.

con·ceiv·a·ble [kənsíːvəbəl] *adj.* imaginable; imagined as possible. 상상할 수 있는; 있을 법한. ¶ *every ~ methode* 생각할 수 있는 온갖 방법 / *the only ~ escape* 생각할 수 있는 유일한 도피구. [*conceive*]

con·ceiv·a·bly [kənsíːvəbəli] *adv.* possibly. 아마; 필시.

*__con·ceive__ [kənsíːv] *vt.* **1** (P6,11,12,21) ⓐ form (an idea, a purpose, etc.) in the mind. …을 마음에 품다. ¶ ~ *a hatred* 〔*an idea*〕 적의를〔어떤 생각을〕 품다. ⓑ imagine; think up; think out. …을 상상하다; 생각해 내다. ¶ *a badly conceived plan* 착상이 좋지 않은 계획 / *Can you ~ life without electricity?* 전기 없는 생활을 상상할 수 있습니까. ⓒ understand. 이해하다. ¶ *I cannot ~ what he means.* 그의 말을 이해할 수 없다. **2** (P6) become pregnant with (young). 아이〔새끼〕를 배다. ¶ ~ *a child* 임신하다.
— *vi.* (P1,3) **1** 《*of*》 imagine; suppose. 상상하다; 생각하다. ¶ ~ *of someone as a genius* 아무를 천재로 여기다. **2** become pregnant. 임신하다. [L. *capio* take]

*__con·cen·trate__ [kánsəntrèit / kɔ́n-] *vt.* **1** (P6,13) give all one's attention to (something); fix (one's mind) on something. …에 집중하다; …을 일점(一點)에 모으다. ¶ ~ *rays of light into a focus* 광선을 한 초점에 모으다 / ~ *one's attention* 〔*efforts*〕 *on a problem* 문제에 주의를〔노력을〕 집중하다. **2** (P6) make (something) stronger; increase the strength of (something). …을 강화하다; …을 농축〔응축〕하다. ¶ ~ *a solution by evaporation* 용액을 증발시켜 농축하다. **3** (P6) 《mine》 make pure; dress. 선광(選鑛)하다; 불순물을 제거하다.
— *vi.* (P1,3) **1** 《*in, on,* etc.》 come to a center. (한 곳에) 집중하다. **2** 《*on, upon*》 fix one's efforts and attention on (a single point); do one's best. (능력·노력 따위)를 집중하다; 전념하다; 전력을 쏟다. ¶ ~ *on solving a problem* 문제 해결에 전력을 기울이다 / ~ *on a book* 독서에 열중하다. [→centre]

con·cen·trat·ed [kánsəntrèitid / kɔ́n-] *adj.* **1** gathered together closely in a center. 집중된; 밀집한. ¶ *a ~ attack on* …에의 집중 공격 / *the ~ masses in the slums* 빈민가(街)에 밀집해 사는 대중. **2** made denser or stronger. 농축된; 농후한. ¶ ~ *feed* 농축 사료.

*__con·cen·tra·tion__ [kànsəntréiʃən / kɔ̀n-] *n.* Ⓤ **1** the act of concentrating; the state of being concentrated. 집중 (상태). ¶ ~ *of population* 인구 집중. **2** close attention to one thing. (정신·주의 따위의) 집중; 전념. ¶ *He has great power of ~.* 그는 대단한 집중력이 있다. **3** thickness; density. 농도. ¶ *high ~ of salt* 소금의 높은 농도.

concentration camp [--´-´] *n.* a camp for prisoners of war, political enemies, etc. (포로 등의) 집단〔강제〕 수용소.

con·cen·tric [kənséntrik] *adj.* having a common center. 같은 중심의; 동심(同心)의(opp. eccentric). ¶ ~ *circles* 동심원(圓).
● **con·cen·tri·cal·ly** [-kəli] *adv.*

con·cept [kánsept / kɔ́n-] *n.* Ⓒ a general idea. 개념. [↓]

:**con·cep·tion** [kənsépʃən] *n.* **1** Ⓤ the act of conceiving; the state of being conceived. 개념 작용. **2** Ⓤ the creation of a new life in the mother's body. 임신; 잉태. **3** Ⓒ a notion; an idea; a concept. 관념; 개념; 생각. ¶ *a clear* 〔*vague*〕 ~ 뚜렷한〔막연한〕 개념 / *a splendid ~* 훌륭한 생각 / *the ~ of the universe* 우주라는 개념 / *I have no ~ (of) what it is like.* 그것이 어떤 것인지 전연 생각이 잡히지 않는다. **4** Ⓒ a design; a plan. 착상; 구상; 계획. ¶ *a grand ~* 웅대한 구상. [→conceive]

con·cep·tion·al [kənsépʃənəl] *adj.* of mental conceptions. 개념의; 개념에 관한.

con·cep·tu·al [kənséptʃuəl] *adj.* =conceptional.

:**con·cern** [kənsə́ːrn] *vt.* **1** (P6) relate to; have to do with (someone or something). …와 관계가 있다. ¶ *The water shortage concerns all.* 물 부족은 모두에게 관계되는 문제다 / *This letter concerns nobody but me.* 이 편지는 나 외엔 아무와도 관계가 없다. **2** 《usu. in *passive*》 make (someone) anxious; trouble. …을 걱정〔우려〕하게 하다; 마음 졸이게 하다. ¶ *with a concerned air* 초조〔불안〕한 태도로 / *be concerned to hear the news* 〔*at the news*〕 그 소식을 듣고 걱정하다 / *Don't let my illness ~ you.* 제 병은 걱정하지 마십시오.

as concerns, regarding; about; as to. …에 관해서는.

as* 〔*so*〕 *far as someone be concerned, to the extent that someone is connected with the matter. …에 관한 한. ¶ *as far as I am concerned* 나에 관한 한.

***be concerned about* 〔*for, over*〕** (=*be anxious* 〔*worried*〕 *about*) *something.* …을 걱정하다.

***be concerned with* 〔*in*〕** (=*have relation to*) *something.* …와 관계를 가지다; …에 관계가 있다.

***concern oneself about* 〔*with*〕,** a) be worried 〔anxious〕 about (someone or something). …을 걱정하다. b) take an interest in (someone or something). …에 관계하다; 관심이 있다.

— *n.* Ⓒ **1** relation; connection; interest. 관계; 이해 관계. ¶ *have no ~ with* …와는

관계가 없다. **2** anything that concerns or relates to one; something which is a part of one's business. 관계되는 일; 관심사; 문제. ¶ *a matter of great* ~ 중요한 관심사 / *It's no* ~ *of mine.* 내 알 바 아니다. **3** Ⓤ anxiety; uneasiness. 걱정; 불안. ¶ *a* ~ *for his safety* 그의 안전에 대한 불안 / *with deep* ~ 매우 우려하여 / *be full of* ~ 매우 걱정하다. **4** 《often *pl.*》 affairs. 일; 사정. ¶ *everyday concerns* 일상의 일 / *private concerns of a family* 집안의 사사로운 일 / *manage one's own concerns* 제 일을 제가 처리하다 / *Mind your own concerns.* 쓸데없는 참견은 마라《네 일에나 정신을 쏟아라》. **5** Ⓤ importance. 중요성. ¶ *a matter of some* ~ 다소 중요한 일 / *a matter of the utmost* ~ 극히 중대한 사건. **6** Ⓒ an enterprise; a business. 사업; 기업(企業); 업무; 회사. ¶ *a flourishing* ~ 번성하는 사업〔회사〕/ *a going* ~ 영업 중인 회사; 순조롭게 진행 중인 사업. [L. *cerno* regard]

feel concern about 〔*over, for*〕 (=*be anxious about*) *something.* …을 걱정하다. ¶ *feel* ~ *for* 〔*about*〕 *one's future* 장래를 걱정하다.

have a concern in, have an interest in. …에 관계가 있다. ¶ *have a* ~ *in a business* 사업에 관계하고 있다.

of concern, of importance. 중요한.

con·cerned [kənsə́ːrnd] *adj.* **1** 《*in, with*》 interested. 관계(하고) 있는; 당해(當該). ¶ *the authorities* ~ 관계 당국 / *the partner* ~ 이해 관계자; 당사자 / *all* ~ 관계자 전원. **2** 《usu. *about, at*》 troubled 〔anxious〕 about. 걱정하는; 염려하는. ¶ *a* ~ *look* 걱정스러운 얼굴 / *with a* ~ *air* 걱정스러운 태도로 / *I was much* ~ *about her.* 그녀에 관해 염려를 많이 했다.

con·cern·ed·ly [kənsə́ːrnidli] *adv.* in a concerned manner; anxiously. 걱정〔염려〕스럽게.

:con·cern·ing [kənsə́ːrniŋ] *prep.* about; as to. …에 관하여. ¶ ~ *the matter* 그 사건에 관하여.

con·cern·ment [kənsə́ːrnmənt] *n.* Ⓤ **1** importance. 중요(성); 중대. ¶ *a matter of special* ~ 특별히 중요한 일 / *a matter of* ~ *to all voters* 모든 투표자에게 중요한 일. **2** anxiety. 걱정; 우려. **3** interest. 관계.

·con·cert [kánsə(ː)rt / kɔ́n-] *n.* **1** Ⓤ a mutual agreement; accord. 협정; 협약; 일치. ¶ *do by* ~ 합의해서 하다 / *in* ~ *with*… 와 협력〔공동·제휴〕하여. **2** Ⓒ a musical entertainment. 음악회; 연주회; 콘서트. ¶ *attend a* ~ 음악회에 참석하다 / *give a* ~ 연주회를 열다〔개최하다〕/ *give a* ~ *on the guitar* 기타 독주회를 열다.

in concert, together. 일제히; 이구 동성으로; 협력하여. ¶ *We decided to act in* ~ *over this matter.* 우리는 이 문제에 대해 함께 대처하기로 결정했다.

—[kənsə́ːrt] *vt.* (P6) plan or make (something) together with others; act in harmony with (someone or something). …을 공동으로 고안〔계획〕하다; …와 협조하다. [It.]

con·cert·ed [kənsə́ːrtid] *adj.* **1** agreed beforehand. 합의한; 협정된. ¶ *a* ~ *plan of operations* 예정된 작전. **2** combind. 협동〔협력〕에 의한. ¶ *take* ~ *action* 공동 일치의 행동을 취하다 / *The ants made a* ~ *attack upon the injured wasp.* 개미들은 부상한 말벌에 대해 공동 공격을 가했다. **3** arranged for several musical instruments or voices. 합주용〔합창용〕으로 편곡된.

con·cer·ti·na [kànsərtíːnə / kɔ̀n-] *n.* Ⓒ a musical instrument like an accordion. 콘서티나《아코디언 비슷한 6각형 악기》. [It.]

con·cert·mas·ter [kánsə(ː)rtmæ̀stər / kɔ́nsərtmɑ̀ːs-] *n.* Ⓒ 《U.S.》 a leader of an orchestra, usu. the leading violinist. 수석 주자(奏者).

con·cer·to [kəntʃértou] *n.* Ⓒ (*pl.* **-tos**) a kind of musical composition for an orchestra. 협주곡; 콘체르토. ¶ *a piano* ~ 피아노 협주곡.

con·ces·sion [kənséʃən] *n.* **1** ⓊⒸ the act of giving way, allowing or yielding. 양보; 양여(讓與). ¶ *his* ~ *to her* 그녀에 대한 그의 양보 / *make a* ~ …에게 양보하다 / *make mutual concessions* 서로 양보하다 / *make* 〔*grant*〕 *a major* ~ *to* …에게 대폭 양보를 하다. **2** Ⓒ ⓐ anything conceded or yielded. 양보〔양여〕된 것; 양보 사항. ⓑ a right given by a government; a special right; a privilege. 특허; 이권; 특권. ¶ *an oil* ~ 석유 채굴권 / *obtain political* ~ 정치상의 특권을 얻다. **3** Ⓒ a piece of territory of which the occupation and use is granted. 조차지(租借地). [*concede*; →cede]

con·ces·sive [kənsésiv] *adj.* apt to give way; granting. 양보하는; 양보적인. ¶ 《gram.》 *a* ~ *clause* 양보절(節).

conch [kaŋk, kantʃ / kɔŋk, kɔntʃ] *n.* (*pl.* **-s** [kaŋks / kɔŋks], **con·ches** [kántʃiz / kɔ́n-]) **1** a long spiral shell, sometimes blown like a horn. 소라. **2** 《Gk. myth.》 Triton's shell trumpet. Triton의 소라. **3** 《archit.》 a doomed roof of semicircular apse. 반월형 지붕. **4** 《anat.》 the external ear. 외이(外耳). [Gk. *kogkhē* mussel]

con·chol·o·gy [kaŋkálədʒi / kɔŋkɔ́l-] *n.* the study of shells or shellfish. 패류학(貝類學). [↑]

con·ci·erge [kànsiέərʒ / kɔ̀n-] *n.* 《F.》 doorkeeper; janitor. 문지기; 수위; (공동주택의) 관리인.

con·cil·i·ate [kənsílièit] *vt.* (P6) **1** calm the anger of (someone); pacify; win over. …을 달래다; 유화(宥和)하다; 회유(懷柔)하다. ¶ ~ *the child with a present* 아이를 선물로써 달래다 / ~ *an enemy* 적을 회유하다. **2** gain the friendship, good will, etc. of (someone). 아무의 (호의·존경 따위)를 얻다. [→council]

con·cil·i·a·tion [kənsìliéiʃən] *n.* Ⓤ the act of conciliating; the state of being conciliated. 유화(宥和); 회유(懷柔); 조정; 화해. ¶ *a ~ court* 조정 재판소 / *labor trouble ~* 노동 쟁의 조정.

con·cil·i·a·to·ry [kənsíliətɔ̀:ri / -təri] *adj.* apt to conciliate someone or settle a quarrel. 달래는; 유화하는; 회유적인; 조정의. ¶ *a ~ manner* 유화적인 태도 / *~ comments* 조정을 꾀하는 의견.

con·cise [kənsáis] *adj.* short but full of meaning. 간결한; 간명한. ¶ *a quick and ~ explanation* 짧고도 간결한 설명 / *with a ~ style* 간결한 문체로. ● **con·cise·ness** [-nis] *n.* [L. *caedo* cut]

con·ci·sion [kənsíʒən] *n.* conciseness. 간결(성).

con·clave [kánkleiv, káŋ- / kɔ́n-, kɔ́ŋ-] *n.* Ⓒ **1** a private meeting of the cardinals for the election of a pope; a room in which such a meeting is held. (추기경에 의한) 교황 선거 회의(실). **2** a private or secret meeting. 비밀 회의. ¶ *sit in ~* 비밀 회의에 참석하다. [L. *clavis* key]

:con·clude [kənklú:d] *vt.* **1** (P6,13) bring (something) to an end; close; finish. …을 끝내다; 종결하다. ¶ *~ a speech* 연설을 끝내다 / *~ a party with a song* 노래로 파티를 끝내다 / *Concluded.* (연재 기사의 끝에 붙여) (이번 회) 완결 / *To be concluded.* (다음 회) 완결. **2** (P6) settle finally. …을 맺다〔체결하다〕; 매듭짓다. ¶ *~ a bargain* 흥정을 매듭짓다 / *~ a peace treaty* 평화 조약을 체결하다 / *~ an agreement with* …와 협정〔계약〕을 맺다. **3** (P11) reach an idea of (something) by thinking; arrive at an opinion by reasoning. …을 추단(推斷)〔판단〕하다. ¶ *From this I ~ that….* 이 사실로 미루어 …라고 판단한다 / *From what you say I ~ that he is innocent.* 말씀으로 미루어보면 그는 무죄로군요 / *We concluded that his life was in danger.* 우리는 그의 목숨이 위험에 처해 있다고 판단했다.

— *vi.* (P1,3) **1** end one's speech. 이야기를 끝내다. ¶ *~ by saying that….* = *~ with the remark that….* …라는 말로 이야기를 끝내다. **2** come to an end. 끝나다. ¶ *The meeting concluded early.* 회의는 일찍 끝났다 / *The report concludes as follows.* 보고는 다음과 같이 끝나고 있다. [→close]

:con·clu·sion [kənklú:ʒən] *n.* Ⓒ **1** a final result. 종결; 종말; 결말. ¶ *an effective ~ of the war* 전쟁의 효과적인 종결 / *at the ~ of the contest* 경기의 종말에 / *bring to a ~* 끝내다; 종결시키다. **2** a final opinion reached by reasoning. 결론. ¶ *form conclusions from experience* 경험으로 미루어 판단을 내리다 / *jump to* 〔*at*〕 *a ~* 결론을 서두르다; 속단(速斷)하다 / *draw conclusions* 결론을 끄집어 내다〔내리다〕. **3** an arrangement; final settlement or agreement. 체결; 타결. ¶ *the ~ of a peace treaty* 평화 조약의 체결.

come to the conclusion that…. reach the final opinion that…. …라는 결론에 도달하다.

try conclusions with, take part in a trial of skill with. …와 자웅을 겨루다.

con·clu·sive [kənklú:siv] *adj.* decisive; final. 결정적인; 최후적인; 확실한. ¶ *~ evidence* 결정적인 증거; 확증 / *a ~ argument* 반론의 여지 없는 의론.

con·clu·sive·ly [kənklú:sivli] *adv.* decisively; finally. 결정적으로; 최종적으로.

con·coct [kankákt, kən- / kənkɔ́kt] *vt.* (P6) **1** prepare (something) by mixing various things together. …을 섞어 만들다. ¶ *~ a meal from leftovers* 먹다 남은 것으로 식사를 만들다. **2** 《*fig.*》 make up; undertake. (이야기 따위)를 만들어〔꾸며〕내다; 조작하다; 계획하다. ¶ *~ a plan* 계획을 세우다 / *~ an excuse* 구실을 만들다 / *~ an alibi* 알리바이를 조작하다 / *~ a story* 이야기를 꾸며내다. [com-, L. *coquo* cook]

con·coc·tion [kankákʃən, kən- / kənkɔ́k-] *n.* **1** ⓐ Ⓤ the act of concocting. 혼합; 조합(調合). ⓑ Ⓒ thing prepared by mixing. 혼합물; 만들어낸〔조작된〕 것; 날조. ¶ *meat concoctions* 고기가 든 요리 / *His story was a ~.* 그의 이야기는 조작된 것이었다. **2** Ⓒ a plan. 계획.

con·com·i·tance [kankámətəns, kən- / kənkɔ́m-] *n.* Ⓤ coexistence, especially of body and blood of Christ in each of the eucharistic elements. 부수(附隨); 수반(隨伴); 병존《특히 성체(聖體)에 그리스도의 살과 피와의 병존》. [↓]

con·com·i·tant [kankámətənt, kən- / kənkɔ́m-] *adj.* attendant; accompanying. 수반하는; 따르는; 공존의. ¶ *a ~ pleasure* 수반되는 즐거움 / *an event and its ~ circumstances* 사건과 이에 부수되는 사정 / *~ with* …에 수반〔부수〕하여 / *be ~ to something.* …에 수반하다. — *n.* Ⓒ a thing which accompanies. 부수물; 공존(성). [L. *comes* companion]

con·cord [káŋkɔ:rd, káŋ- / kɔ́ŋ-, kɔ́n-] *n.* Ⓤ **1** agreement; harmony. 일치; 조화; 화합 (opp. discord). ¶ *in ~ with* …와 일치하여 / *live in ~* 사이좋게 지내다. **2** 《mus.》 a harmonious combination of melodies. 협화음. **3** 《gram.》 agreement between words (in person, number, gender, and case). 일치; 호응. [→cordial]

con·cord·ance [kankɔ́:rdəns, kən- / kən-] *n.* **1** Ⓤ agreement; harmony. 일치; 조화; 화합. ¶ *in ~ with* …와 일치하여; …에 따라. **2** Ⓒ a dictionary or list of words used in a certain book or by a certain author. 용어 색인. ¶ *a ~ to Shakespeare* 셰익스피어 용어 색인.

con·cord·ant [kankɔ́:rdənt, kən- / kən-] *adj.* agreeing; harmonious. 일치하는; 조화된. ¶ *results ~ with the experimental data* 실험에서 얻은 자료와 일치하는 결과.

con·cor·dat [kankɔ́:rdæt / kən-] *n.* Ⓒ

an agreement; a contract. 협정; 협약.

con·course [kánkɔːrs, káŋ- / kɔ́ŋ-, kɔ́n-] *n.* Ⓒ **1** the act or state of meeting or coming together. 집합; 합류. ¶ *the ~ of particles* 분자의 집합 / *the ~ of two rivers* 두 강의 합류(점). **2** a crowd. 군집; 군중. ¶ *a large ~ of people* 대(大)군중. **3** 《U.S.》 a central hall in a railroad station; a central place in a park. (역사(驛舍)의) 중앙홀; (공원의) 중앙 광장. **4** a driveway; boulevard. 차도(車道); 큰 길. [com-]

***con·crete** [kánkrit, káŋ-, kankríːt / kɔ́n-] *adj.* **1** actual; having a real existence; real. 현실〔실제〕의; 구체적인. ¶ *a ~ fact* 구체적인 사실 / *~ ideas* 현실적〔실제적〕적인 생각 / *put the question in the more ~ form* 좀 더 구체적으로 질문하다. **2** solid; made of concrete. 단단한; 고체(固體)의; 콘크리트로 만든. ¶ *a ~ pavement* 콘크리트 포장 도로. **3** 《gram.》 expressing a real thing, not a quality, state, or action. 구상적(具象的)인. ¶ *a ~ noun* 구상〔구체〕 명사.
— *n.* **1** Ⓒ a concrete substance. 구체물; 고형체. ¶ *in the ~* 실제적〔구체적〕으로. **2** Ⓤ a stonelike material made of cement, sand, gravel, etc. 콘크리트. ¶ *reinforced ~* 철근 콘크리트.
— *vi., vt.* (P1; 6) **1** [kankríːt, kən-] harden. 굳어〔단단해〕지다; 굳게〔단단하게〕 하다. **2** cover (something) with concrete. …을 콘크리트로 덮다. ¶ *~ a pavement* (도로를) 콘크리트로 포장하다. [L. *cresco* grow]

con·cre·tion [kankríːʃən, kaŋ-, kən-] *n.* **1** Ⓤ the act of forming into a solid mass. 응고(凝固); 응결. **2** Ⓒ a hardened mass. 응고물.

con·cu·bine [káŋkjəbàin, kán- / kɔ́ŋ-, kɔ́n-] *n.* a woman who cohabits with a man without marriage. 내연의 처; 첩. ¶ *keep a ~* 첩을 두다. ● **con·cu·bi·nage** [kankjúːbənidʒ / kɔn-] *n.* [L. *cubo* lie]

con·cu·pis·cence [kankjúːpisəns, kəŋ- / kɔŋ-, kɔn-] *n.* **1** sexual appetite. 정욕; 성욕. **2** 《Bible》 desire for worldly things. 탐욕. ● **con·cu·pis·cent** [-pisənt] *adj.* [L. *cupio* desire]

con·cur [kənkə́ːr] *vi.* (**-curred, -cur·ring**) **1** (P1,2,3) agree; be in harmony. 동의하다; 일치하다. ¶ *~ with someone's proposal* 아무의 제안에 동의하다 / *All will ~ in this opinion.* 이 의견에 모두가 동의할 게다. **2** (P3,5) happen at the same time; come together; work together. 동시에 일어나다; 협력〔협동〕하다. ¶ *Right and victory do not always ~.* 정의와 승리가 늘 함께 있는 것은 아니다 / *Everything concurred to make him happy.* 여러 사정이 서로 잘 어우러져 그의 행복을 가져왔다. **3** (P1,2,3) meet in one point. (선 따위가) 한 점에서 만나다. [L. *curro* run]

con·cur·rence [kənkə́ːrəns, -kʌ́r-] *n.* Ⓤ **1** 《*in*》 an agreement; the act of working together; the act of coming together. 동의; 협동; 공점(共點). ¶ *the ~ of many lines* 많은 선분의 공점 / *his ~ in my views* 내 견해에 대한 그의 동의 / *have the full ~ of the members* 회원 일치의 찬동을 얻다. **2** 《sometimes *a ~*》 the state of happening at the same time. 동시 발생. [↑]

con·cur·rent [kənkə́ːrənt, -kʌ́rənt] *adj.* **1** harmonious; working together; meeting at a single point. 일치의; 협력의; 한 점에서 만나는. **2** happening at the same time. 동시 발생의. ¶ *~ attacks by land, sea, and air* 육해공에 의한 동시 공격. — *n.* a concurrent thing or event. 동시 발생물〔발생 사건〕.

con·cur·rent·ly [kənkə́ːrəntli, -kʌ́rəntli] *adv.* **1** unitedly. 함께. **2** 《*with*》 at the same time. …와 동시에.

con·cus·sion [kənkʌ́ʃən] *n.* ⓊⒸ **1** a sudden and violent shaking; shock. 격동(激動); 충격. **2** a (brain) injury caused by a blow. 진탕(震蕩). ¶ *a ~ of the brain* 뇌진탕. [L. *quatio* shake]

:con·demn [kəndém] *vt.* **1** (P6) 《*for*》 blame; disapprove of. …을 비난하다; 책하다. ¶ *~ someone's cruelty* 〔*someone for his cruelty*〕 아무의 잔인함을 비난하다. **2** (P6,13) pronounce guilty of crime. 형을 선고하다. ¶ *~ someone to imprisonment* 아무에게 징역형을 선고하다 / *~ someone to be hanged* 아무에게 교수형을 선고하다. **3** (P6,13) 《*for, of*》 declare (someone) to be guilty. …을 유죄로 판정하다. ¶ *be condemned of treason* 반역죄로 판정되다 / *The prisoner was tried and condemned.* 피의자는 재판에 회부되어 유죄 판결을 받았다. **4** (P6) doom. …하게 운명지우다. ¶ *be condemned to a life of suffering* 고통의 생활을 보내도록 운명지워지다. **5** (P6) declare (something) to be unfit for use; pronounce forfeited. …이 부적합하다고〔사용할 수 없다고〕 판정하다; 몰수를 선언하다. ¶ *He condemned the meat as unfit for human consumption.* 그는 그 고기가 식용에 부적합하다고 선언했다. **6** (P6) declare (something) to be taken for public use. …을 (공공용으로) 접수〔수용〕하다. [L. *damno*]
be condemned to (***death***), be sentenced to (death). (사형) 선고를 받다.

con·dem·na·tion [kàndemnéiʃən / kɔ̀n-] *n.* **1** ⓊⒸ the act of condemning; the state of being condemned. 비난; 유죄의 선고; 부적합의 판정; 접수; 수용. ¶ *a ~ against* …에 대한 비난 / *the ~ of a prisoner by a judge* 피의자에 대한 판사의 유죄 선고 / *the ~ of an unsafe bridge* 불안전한 다리라는 판정 / *She merits every ~.* 그녀는 모든 비난을 받아 마땅하다. **2** Ⓒ a cause of being condemned. 비난〔선고〕의 이유〔근거〕.

con·den·sa·tion [kàndenséiʃən / kɔ̀n-] *n.* ⓊⒸ **1** the act of condensing; the state of being condensed. 응축(凝縮); 압축; 응결. ¶ *the ~ of milk by removing most of the* *water from it* 대부분의 물기를 제거하는 우유의 응축. **2** something condensed or made short. 응축물; 농축물; 요약〔간약〕체. ¶ *a ~ of a novel* 소설의 요약. [com-]

·con·dense [kəndéns] *vt., vi.* **1** ⓐ (P6,13; 1,3) make (something) dense; become dense. (…을) 응축〔압축〕하다. ¶ *condensed milk* 연유(煉乳). ⓑ gather (things) to one point; concentrate. (광선)을 한 점에 모으다. ¶ *a condensing lens* 집광(集光)렌즈. **2** (P6,13; 1,3) 《chem., phys.》 《*into*》 reduce from a gas or a vapor to a liquid. 응결하다; 액화하다. ¶ *If steam touches cold surfaces, it condenses* 〔*is condensed into water*〕. 증기가 찬 표면에 닿으면 결로(結露)한다〔물방울이 된다〕. **3** (P6,13) shorten. …을 단축〔요약〕하다. ¶ *A long story may be condensed into a few sentences.* 긴 설화는 몇 개의 문장으로 요약될 수 있다. [com-]

con·dens·er [kəndénsər] *n.* Ⓒ **1** a device for holding a charge of electricity. 축전기; 콘덴서. **2** a device for changing gas into liquid. 응축기(凝縮器). **3** 《opt.》 a lens for gathering light to one point. 집광(集光) 렌즈.

con·de·scend [kàndisénd / kɔ̀n-] *vi.* **1** (P1,4) stoop from a high (social) position to show kindness to inferior. (아랫사람에게) 겸손하게 굴다; 스스로를 낮추다; 으스대지 않고 …해주다. ¶ *He never condescends to speak to me.* 거만해서 그는 내게 말을 거는 일이 없다. **2** (P3) lower oneself by low conduct. (저열한 행동으로) 자신을 낮추다〔타락시키다〕. ¶ *~ to accept bribes* 절의(節義)를 굽혀 뇌물을 받다 / *~ to trickery* 영락하여 사기를 치다. **3** act patronizingly. (우월감을 의식하면서) 짐짓 겸손〔친절〕하게 굴다; (우월한 신분에서) 짐짓 저자세를 취하다; 생색내는 행동을 하다. [com-]

con·de·scend·ing [kàndiséndiŋ / kɔ̀n-] *adj.* having a manner which condescends. (아랫사람에게) 겸손한. ¶ *in a ~ manner* 겸손한 태도로.

con·de·scen·sion [kàndisénʃən / kɔ̀n-] *n.* Ⓤ the act of condescending; patronizing behavior. (아랫사람에게) 겸손함; 생색내려는 태도.

con·dign [kəndáin] *adj.* (of punishment) deserved; fit; proper. (형벌 따위가) 마땅〔타당〕한; 적당한. ¶ *~ punishment* 적절한 처벌 / *~ vengeances* 당연한 복수. [L. *dignus* worthy]

con·di·ment [kándəmənt / kɔ́n-] *n.* ⓊⒸ something that gives flavor to food. 조미료; 양념. [L. *condio* pickle]

:con·di·tion [kəndíʃən] *n.* **1** ⓊⒸ the state in which a person or thing exists. 상태; 현상(現狀). ¶ *the ~ of one's health* (자신의) 건강 상태 / *a couple in marital ~* 결혼한 남녀 / *living conditions of the poor* 빈민의 생활 상태 / *be in* 〔*out of*〕 *~* 몸 컨디션이 좋다〔나쁘다〕 / *be in grave ~* 중태이다 / *The house was in a very dirty ~.* 집이 아주 불결한 상태에 있었다 / *The ~ of my health prevents me from working.* 건강 때문에 일을 하지 못한다. **2** 《*pl.*》 circumstances. 사정; 상황. ¶ *financial conditions* 금융〔재정〕 사정 / *favorable conditions for business* 사업에 유리한 상황 / *Under these* (*existing*) *conditions I cannot attend.* 이러한 상황하에서는 참석할 수 없다. **3** Ⓒ 《often *pl.*》 something needed before something else is possible; a very important factor. (필요) 조건; 요인(要因). ¶ *conditions of acceptance* 수락(受諾)의 선행 조건 / *impose conditions* = *make a ~* 조건을 붙이다 / *make it a ~ that....* …을 조건으로 하다. **4** Ⓒ the social position. (사회적) 신분; 지위. ¶ *people of humble ~* 신분이 비천한 사람들 / *in a lowly ~* 비천한 신분의. **5** Ⓒ the stipulation; restriction. (계약 따위의) 조항; 제약(制約).

***be in* (*good*) 〔*out of*〕 *condition*,** **a**) be in good 〔poor〕 health; be physically prepared 〔unprepared〕. 건강이 좋다〔나쁘다〕. **b**) (of food) fit 〔unfit〕 to eat. 먹기에 적합〔부적합〕하다.

***be in no condition to do*,** be unfitted to do. …하기에 적합하지 않다.

***change one's condition*,** marry. 결혼하다.

***on condition* (*that*),** if only; provided (that).... 만일 …하면〔이면〕. ¶ *I will do it on ~ that you help me.* 자네가 나를 도와 준다면 하겠네.

— *vt.* (P6,8,11,13) **1** put into a certain state or condition; determine. …을 어떤 상태로 하다; 한정하다. ¶ *the circumstances which ~ our lives* 우리 생활을 제한하는 사정 / *Supply is conditioned by demand.* 공급은 수요에 따라 제약된다. **2** bring into a desired state or condition; make fit (esp. dogs, horses, etc.). …을 바라는 상태로 하다; 조절하다; 길들이다. ¶ *soldiers conditioned to jungle warfare* 정글전(戰)에 익숙하도록 훈련된 병사 / *~ a horse for a race* 경마에 나갈 수 있도록 말을 길들이다. **3** 《psych.》 cause (a dog, etc.) to respond in a certain manner to a certain stimulus. …에 조건 반사를 일으키게 하다. ¶ *~ a dog to bark at the sound of a bell* 벨 소리를 들으면 개가 짖도록 만들다. [L. *dico* say]

con·di·tion·al [kəndíʃənəl] *adj.* **1** dependent on a certain condition; not perfect; not certain. 조건이 붙은; 잠정의; …나름의. ¶ *~ acceptance* 조건부 수락 / *a ~ sale* 조건부 판매 / *My stay is ~ on your plans.* 나의 체재 여부는 자네 계획 여하에 달려 있네. **2** 《gram.》 expressing or containing a condition. 조건〔가정〕을 나타내는. ¶ *a ~ clause* 조건절.

con·di·tion·al·ly [kəndíʃənəli] *adv.* under or with a condition or conditions. 조건부로.

con·di·tioned [kəndíʃənd] *adj.* subject to a condition. … 상태에 있는; 조건부〔제한부〕의.

con·do·la·to·ry [kəndóulətɔ̀:ri / -təri] *adj.* expressing sorrow for another. 슬픔을〔애도를〕 나타내는; 조위(弔慰)의. ¶ *a ~ address* 조사(弔辭) / *a ~ letter* 문상하는 편지. [↓]

con·dole [kəndóul] *vi.* (P3) 《*with*》 express one's sympathy or sorrow for another. 문상(問喪)하다; 애도의 뜻을 나타내다. ¶ *I condoled with him on the loss of his wife.* 상배(喪配)한 그에게 조의를 표했다. [L. *doleo* grieve]

con·do·lence [kəndóuləns] *n.* Ⓤ 《often *pl.*》 a message expressing sorrow or sympathy. 문상(問喪); 애도. ¶ *present one's condolences* 애도의 뜻을 나타내다.
express one's condolences to, condole. …에게 애도의 말을 하다; 문상하다.

con·do·min·i·um [kàndəmíniəm / kɔ̀n-] *n.* **1** ⓊⒸ a joint control of a state by two or more other states. 공동 지배〔통치〕. **2** Ⓒ 《U.S.》 individual ownership of a unit in a multiunit structure (as an apartment building); also a unit so owned. 분양 아파트; 그 한 집. [→dominate]

con·done [kəndóun] *vt.* (P6) **1** pardon; excuse; overlook. (죄)를 용서하다; 눈감아주다. ¶ *~ someone's faults* 아무의 잘못을 용서해주다. **2** (of actions) atone for (an offence). (행위가 죄를) 속죄(贖罪)하다.
● **con·don·a·tion** [kàndounéiʃən / kɔ̀n-] *n.* [→donate]

con·dor [kándər, -dɔ:r / kɔ́ndɔ:r] *n.* Ⓒ 《bird》 a very large bird with a bald head and neck. 콘도르《남미산(產)의 독수리》. [Peruv.]

con·dot·tie·re [kɔ̀:ndətjέərei, -ri:] *n.* 《It.》 (*pl.* **-ri**) the captain of mercenaries. 용병대장(傭兵隊長).

con·dot·tie·ri [kɔ́:ndətjέəri] *n.* pl. of **condottiere.**

con·duce [kəndjú:s] *vi.* (P3,4) 《*to, towards*》 lead (to a good result); contribute. (바람직한 결과에) 이르다; …의 도움이 되다; 이바지하다. ¶ *Exercise conduces to health.* 운동은 건강에 도움이 된다 / *Wealth does not always ~ to happiness.* 부(富)가 반드시 행복에 이르게 하지는 않는다. [L. *duco* lead]

con·du·cive [kəndjú:siv] *adj.* 《*to*》 helpful to; favorable to. …에 이바지하는; 도움이 되는. ¶ *Fresh air is ~ to health.* 신선한 공기는 건강에 도움을 준다.

:**con·duct** [kándʌkt / kɔ́n-] *n.* Ⓤ **1** behavior; deportment. 행위; 태도. ¶ *good* 〔*right*〕 *~* 좋은〔올바른〕 행위 / *He's quite above such ~.* 그는 결코 그런 짓을 할 사람이 아니다. **2** management; direction; control. 경영; 관리; 처리; 통제. ¶ *the ~ of a business* 〔*war*〕 사업〔전쟁〕의 수행. **3** leading; guidance. 지도; 안내. ¶ *under the ~ of someone* 아무의 지도 밑에.
— [kəndʌ́kt] *vt.* **1** (P6,7,13) lead; guide; escort. …을 인도〔안내〕하다; 호송하다. ¶ *~ someone to the door* 아무를 현관까지 안내하다 / *He conducted the visitors around the museum.* 그는 방문객을 박물관에 안내하며 돌아다녔다 / *Conduct me to your teacher.* 네 선생님한테 안내해라. **2** (P6) direct; manage; carry on. …을 지도하다; 관리〔경영〕하다. ¶ *~ a business* 〔*meeting*〕 사업을〔집회를〕 운영하다 / *~ a marriage* 결혼의 주례를 보다. **3** (P7) 《*reflexively*》 behave. 행동〔처신〕하다. ¶ *The nurse conducts herself obsequiously.* 그 간호사는 아첨하듯이 행동한다 / *He conducts himself without any reserve whatever.* 그는 도무지 거리낌없이 행동한다. **4** (P6) pass on; convey; carry. …을 보내다; 전달〔전도(傳導)〕하다; 운반하다. ¶ *~ water through a pipe* 파이프를 통해 물을 보내다 / *Metal conducts electricity.* 쇠붙이는 전기를 전도한다.
— *vi.* (P1) **1** serve as a conductor or leader. 지휘자〔지도자〕 노릇을 하다. **2** direct; lead; guide. 지도하다; 안내하다. [→conduce]

·**con·duc·tion** [kəndʌ́kʃən] *n.* Ⓤ the act of carrying water through a pipe; the act of passing on heat or electricity. (관(管)으로) 끌어들임; 유도(작용); (열·전기 따위의) 전도(傳導). ¶ *the ~ of electricity along a wire* 전선을 통한 전기의 전도.

con·duc·tive [kəndʌ́ktiv] *adj.* having the power of conducting. 전도성(傳導性)의; 전도력(傳導力)이 있는. ¶ *~ power* 전도력.

con·duc·tiv·i·ty [kàndʌktívəti / kɔ̀n-] *n.* Ⓤ the power of passing on heat or electricity. 전도성〔력〕(傳導性〔力〕).

·**con·duc·tor** [kəndʌ́ktər] *n.* Ⓒ **1** a guide; a leader; a manager. 안내자; 지도자; 경영〔관리〕자. **2** a person in charge of a streetcar or bus. (전차·버스의) 차장; 《U.S.》 a person in charge of a railroad train. (열차의) 차장(cf. 《Brit.》 *guard*). **3** a director of an orchestra or a chorus. (오케스트라·합창단의) 지휘자. **4** a substance which passes on electricity, heat, or water; a lightning rod. 전도체(傳導體); 피뢰침.

con·duit [kándjuit, -dit / kɔ́n-] *n.* Ⓒ a pipe for carrying water; a tube or subway for electric wires. 도관(導管); 수도(관); 도랑; 전선 도관. [→conduct]

cone [koun] *n.* Ⓒ **1** a solid body with a flat, round bottom and a pointed top; anything shaped like this. 원뿔〔원추〕(형); 원뿔꼴의 것. ¶ *an ice cream ~* (원뿔 모양의) 아이스크림콘. **2** a seed case of the pine, cedar, and certain other evergreen trees. (솔방울 같은) 구과(毬果). [Gk.]

Con·el·rad [kánəlræ̀d / kɔ́n-] *n.* 《U.S.》 a system of controlling radio wave over broadcasting. 방송 전파 관리(放送電波管理). [*Con*trol of *El*ectromagnetic *Rad*iation]

co·ney [kóuni] *n.* =cony.

Co·ney Is·land [kóuni áilənd] *n.* an island in New York, famous for its beach and amusement park. 뉴욕 Long Island에 있는 해안 유원지.

con·fab·u·late [kənfǽbjəlèit] *vi.* (P1,2,3) 《rare》《*with*》 chat or talk together in an easy way. (…와) 담소(談笑)하다. 參考 구어에서는 confab형으로도 쓰임. [→fable]

con·fab·u·la·tion [kənfæ̀bjəléiʃən] *n.* UC **1** the act of confabulating. 담소(談笑); 간담(懇談). **2** 《med.》 the replacement of a gap in memory by a falsification. 작화(作話)(증(症)).

con·fec·tion [kənfékʃən] *n.* C **1** ⓐ U the act or process of mixing. 섞음; 혼합; 조제. ⓑ C the thing mixed. 섞은 것; 섞어 만든 것. **2** a piece of candy; a sweetmeat. 과자; 당과(糖菓). **3** a sweetened pill or drug. 당제(糖劑). [→fact]

con·fec·tion·er [kənfékʃənər] *n.* C a person who makes or sells confections. 제과(製菓) 판매인; 과자상(商).

con·fec·tion·er·y [kənfékʃənèri / -nəri] *n.* (*pl.* **-er·ies**) **1** U 《*collectively*》 all kinds of candy, ice cream, etc. 과자류; 당과(糖菓). **2** C a candy store. 과자점(店).

con·fed·er·a·cy [kənfédərəsi] *n.* C (*pl.* **-cies**) **1** the act of forming a union. 연합; 동맹. **2** a union of states or nations. 연합국; 동맹국. **3** 《U.S. hist.》《*the* (*Southern*) *C-*》 남부 연방(=the Confederate States of America). [↓]

·**con·fed·er·ate** [kənfédərit] *adj.* **1** joined together or allied. 동맹을 맺은; 연합의. **2** 《U.S. hist.》《*C-*》 of the Confederacy. 남부 연방의. ¶ *the Confederate Army* 남(부 연방)군 / *the Confederate States* (*of America*) 남부 연방《남북 전쟁 때 미합중국에서 떨어져 나간 남부 11개 주의 연방》.
— *n.* C **1** a person or state joined or allied with another. 동맹자(국). **2** a partner in crime. 공모(공범)자. ¶ *The thief and his confederates escaped to another city.* 그 도둑과 공범들은 다른 시로 도주했다. **3** 《U.S. hist.》《*C-*》 a person who fought for, or was faithful to, the Confederate States. 남부 연방 지지자.
— [-dərèit] *vi., vt.* (P1,3; 6,7,13) join together; ally. 동맹(연합)하(게 하)다. ¶ ~ *oneself with another* …와 동맹(공모)하다. [L. *foedus* league]

con·fed·er·a·tion [kənfèdəréiʃən] *n.* C **1** countries or nations joined together by agreement. 연합(동맹)국; 연방. **2** a league; an alliance. 연합; 연맹; 동맹.

·**con·fer** [kənfə́ːr] *vt., vi.* (**-ferred, -fer·ring**) **1** (P6,13) 《*on, upon*》 give. …을 주다; 수여하다. ¶ ~ *a gift* (*an honor*) *on someone* 아무에게 선물을(명예를) 주다. **2** (P1,2,3) 《*with*》 talk over together. …와 협의하다. ¶ ~ *with someone about* (*on*) *something* 어떤 일에 관해서 아무와 상의하다. **3** (P6) 《in *imperative*》 compare. 비교하다. 參考 cf.로 생략함. [L. *fero* bring]

:**con·fer·ence** [kánfərəns / kɔ́n-] *n.* **1** U the act of consulting together; consultation. 협의; 상의(相議). **2** C a meeting for discussion or for making public announcements, esp. to newspaper reporters. 회의; 회견. ¶ *a summit* ~ 정상(수뇌) 회의 / *attend a* ~ 회의에 참석하다 / *be in* ~ *with* … …와 회의 중이다 / *call a* ~ 회의를 소집하다 / *hold a press* ~ 기자 회견을 하다.
have a conference with, consult with. …와 협의하다.

con·fer·ment [kənfə́ːrmənt] *n.* U the act of conferring. (학위 따위의) 수여.

:**con·fess** [kənfés] *vt., vi.* **1** (P6,8,9,11,21; 1,3) tell of (one's faults, crimes, etc.); admit; acknowledge. …을 고백(자백)하다; 인정(자인)하다. ¶ ~ *one's crime* 범죄를 자백하다 / *He confessed that he had done wrong.* 그는 나쁜 짓을 했음을 인정했다 / *The prisoner refused to* ~. 피고는 자백을 거부했다 / *She confessed herself* (*to be*) *guilty.* 그녀는 유죄를 인정했다 / *I* ~ *I was surprised to hear it.* 솔직히 말해 나는 그 말을 듣고 놀랐다. **2** (P6,13; 1,3) ⓐ acknowledge one's belief or faith in (God, etc.). (신앙)을 고백하다; (충성)을 표명하다. ¶ ~ *allegiance to one's country* 국가에의 충성을 표명하다. ⓑ tell of (one's sins), esp. to a priest; (of a priest) hear the confession of (someone). (사제·신에게) 죄를 고백하다; 고해하다; (사제가) …의 고백을(고해를) 듣다. ¶ ~ *one's sins to God* 신에게 자신의 죄를 고백하다 / *The priest confessed a murderer.* 사제는 살인범의 고해를 들었다. **3** (P6) 《*arch.*》 manifest; attest. (사정 따위가) …함(임)을 보이다; 입증하다. [L. *fateor* confess]
confess to *something* or *doing,* acknowledge; admit. …을 인정하다.

con·fess·ed·ly [kənfésidli] *adj.* admittedly; avowedly. 본인 스스로도 인정하듯이; 명백히.

·**con·fes·sion** [kənféʃən] *n.* UC **1** the act of confessing. 자백; 고백; 자인. ¶ *make* (*a*) ~ *to someone* 아무에게 자백하다 / *make a frank* ~ *of one's crime* 자신의 범죄를 솔직히 털어놓다 / *get* ~ *out of suspects* 용의자들로부터 자백을 얻어내다. **2** a thing confessed. 고백(한 것); 고해. ¶ *hear confessions* (사제가) 고해를 듣다. **3** a (written) profession of belief. (신앙의) 고백(서). ¶ *a* ~ *of faith* 신앙의 고백.

con·fes·sion·al [kənféʃənəl] *n.* C a small room where a priest hears confessions. 고해실(室). — *adj.* of a confession. 고해의; 고백의.

con·fes·sor [kənfésər] *n.* C **1** a person who confesses; a priest who hears confessions. 고백(자백)자; 고해자(告解者); 고해를 듣는 사제. **2** a saint who is not a martyr. 증성자(證聖者)《순교는 안 했으나 박해에 굴하지 않은 남자 성인》.

con·fet·ti [kənféti(ː)] *n. pl.* 《used as *sing.*》

bits of colored paper, used as missiles in the carnival, at weddings, etc. 색종이 조각. [It.]

con·fi·dant [kὰnfidǽnt, ∸−∸ / kɔ̀n-, ∸−∸] *n.* Ⓒ《F.》a person entrusted with knowledge of one's private affairs. (믿고 모든 비밀을 털어놓을 수 있는) 친구; 심복. [→confide]

con·fi·dante [kὰnfidǽnt, ∸−∸ / kɔ̀n-, ∸−∸] *n.* Ⓒ《F.》a close woman friend. 가까운 여자 친구. [↑]

∗**con·fide** [kənfáid] *vi.* (P3)《*in*》**1** have trust or faith in. 믿다; 신뢰(신임)하다. ¶ *~ in someone* 아무를 신뢰하다 / *He confided in his own ability.* 그는 자신의 능력을 믿었다. **2** tell secrets, private affairs, etc. (아무를 믿고) 내밀한 일을 털어놓다; 개인의 사적인 일을 이야기하다. ¶ *I want to ~ in you.* 네게 비밀을 털어놓고 싶다.
— *vt.* (P13)《*to*》**1** tell as a secret. (비밀이 지켜질 것을 믿고) 털어놓다. ¶ *~ one's troubles to a friend* 친구에게 고민을 털어놓다. **2** entrust; hand over. …을 맡기다; 위탁하다. ¶ *~ a task to someone's charge* 일을 아무의 책임에 맡기다 / *I ~ my property to your care.* 내 재산을 자네의 관리에 맡기네. [L. *fido* trust]

:**con·fi·dence** [kɑ́nfidəns / kɔ́n-] *n.* **1** Ⓤ《*in*》trust; firm belief. 신용; 신뢰. ¶ *have ~ in the future* 장래에 희망을 걸고 있다 / *win someone's ~* 아무의 신뢰를(신임을) 얻다 / *betray someone's ~* 아무의 신뢰를 배반하다 / *enjoy the fullest ~ of one's master* 주인의 전폭적인 신뢰를 받고 있다 / *I place every ~ in his honesty.* 그의 정직성에 전폭적인 신뢰를 둔다. **2** Ⓤ ⓐ firm self-reliance; belief in oneself. 자신; 확신. ¶ *be full of ~ =have a lot of ~* 자신에 차 있다 / *acquire (lose) ~* 자신을 얻다(잃다) / *lack ~ in one's ability* 자기 능력에 자신이 없다. ⓑ boldness; rudeness. 대담; 뻔뻔스러움. ¶ *have the ~ to do…* 대담(뻔뻔)하게도 …하다. **3** Ⓒ something told as a secret. 털어놓는 이야기; 비밀. ¶ *listen to someone's ~* 아무의 내밀한 이야기를 듣다. [↑]
give confidence to =have (place, repose) confidence in, credit. …을 신용하다.
in (strict) confidence, in secret. (극히) 비밀히; 내밀히.
make confidence to (*someone*) ***=take*** (*someone*) ***into one's confidence,*** allow to know his secrets. (아무)에게 비밀을 털어놓다.

confidence game (trick) [∸−−∸(∸)] *n.* any fraud in which the swindler takes advantage of the victim's confidence. 신용 사기.

confidence man [∸−−∸] *n.*《U.S.》a swindler. 사기꾼.

∗**con·fi·dent** [kɑ́nfidənt / kɔ́n-] *adj.* **1**《*of*》firmly believing; assured; sure. 확신하(고 있)는; 굳게 믿는. ¶ *I am ~ of success.* 나는 성공을 확신한다 / *I feel ~ that everything will go well.* 만사가 다 잘 되리라고 확신한다. **2** self-reliant. 자신있는. ¶ *a ~ manner (smile)* 자신에 찬 태도(웃음). **3** bold; impolite. 대담한; 건방진; 무례한. [→confide]

∗**con·fi·den·tial** [kὰnfidénʃəl / kɔ̀n-] *adj.* **1** treated with confidence; trustworthy. 믿음직한; 신임(신뢰)할 수 있는. ¶ *a ~ servant* 신임이 두터운 하인. **2** secret. 내밀한; 비밀의. ¶ *a ~ talk* 내밀한 이야기 / *~ documents* 비밀문서 / *a ~ letter* 친전서(親展書) / *a ~ agent* 밀정(密偵). **3** showing trust. 내밀한 일을 털어 놓는; 무간한; 친밀한. ¶ *become ~ with a stranger* 남과 무간해지다.

con·fi·den·tial·ly [kὰnfidénʃəli / kɔ̀n-] *adv.* in a confidential manner. 은밀하게; 털어놓고; 친밀하게.

con·fi·dent·ly [kɑ́nfidəntli / kɔ́n-] *adv.* in a confident or self-assured manner; with confidence or self-assurance. 확신하여.

con·fid·ing [kənfáidiŋ] *adj.* trusting. 남을 (잘) 믿는; 신뢰하는. ¶ *a ~ nature* 남을 잘 믿는 성질.

con·fig·u·ra·tion [kənfìgəréiʃən] *n.* Ⓒ the relative positions of the parts of a thing; the arrangement of parts; the external form or shape. (부분·요소의) 배치; 배열; 외형. ¶ *the ~ of the country* 그 지방의 지세 / *electron ~* 전자 배치. [→figure]

:**con·fine** [kɑ́nfain / kɔ́n-] *n.*《usu. *pl.*》a border (line); a boundary; a limit. 경계(선); 국경; 한계. ¶ *within the confines of* …의 한계 내에 / *on the confines of night and day* 밤과 낮의 경계에 / *on the confines of ruin* 파멸에 직면하여 / *extend the confines of knowledge* 지식을 넓히다.
— [kənfáin] *vt.* (P13)《*to*》**1** keep (something) within limits; restrict. …을 한정(제한)하다. ¶ *His remarks are confined to the subject.* 그의 발언은 그 문제에 국한되어 있다 / *His business is now confined to a single branch.* 그의 사업은 이제 단 한 지점에만 국한돼 있다 / *He did not ~ himself to visiting Paris.* 파리를 방문하는 데 그치지 않았다. **2** (P6,13)《*within, in, to*》keep (someone) within doors; shut up; imprison. …을 가두다; 감금하다. ¶ *be confined to one's room* 방에 틀어박혀 있다 / *The thief is confined in prison.* 그 도둑은 교도소에 수감돼 있다. **3**《usu. in *passive*》keep (oneself) in bed at childbirth. 해산으로 자리에 눕다; 산욕부(産褥婦)로 자리에 들다. [→finis]
be confined to barracks, be kept indoors. 외출이 금지되다.

con·fined [kənfáind] *adj.* **1** limited; narrow. (장소가) 제한된; 좁은. ¶ *a very ~ space* 매우 좁은 장소. **2** withdrawn from society before giving birth to a child. 산욕에 있는; 분만의. ¶ *be ~ of a baby* 아기를 분만하다 / *She expects to be ~ in May.* 그녀는 5월이 해산할 달이다 / *She is about to be ~.* 그녀는 해산이 가깝다.

con·fine·ment [kənfáinmənt] *n.* **1** Ⓤ

the act of confining; the state of being confined. 가둠; 감금; 제한; 속박; 틀어박힘. ¶ *be placed in* ~ 감금 상태에 놓이다 / *be kept in solitary* ~ 독방에 감금되다 / *feel the* ~ *of an office* 직위의 속박을 느끼다. **2** UC childbirth. 해산; 분만. ¶ *a difficult* ~ 난산 / *approach one's* ~ 해산이 임박하다.

·con·firm [kənfə́:rm] *vt.* **1** (P6) make (something) certain. …을 확실히 하다; 확증하다. ¶ ~ *a rumor* 소문이 사실임을 확인하다 / *be confirmed by experience* 경험으로 확증하다 / *The letter from her confirmed what you had told us before.* 그녀의 편지는 네가 전에 말했던 것이 사실임을 입증했다. **2** (P6,13) make (something) strong; strengthen; fortify. (결심 따위)를 굳히다; 더 강하게[견고히] 하다. ¶ ~ *someone in his belief* 아무의 신념을 더욱 견고히 하다 / *He was confirmed in his decision.* 그의 결심이 더욱 굳어졌다 / *His advice confirmed my decision to go abroad.* 그의 조언으로 나는 해외 여행의 결심을 굳혔다. **3** (P6) give a formal agreement to (something, esp. a treaty). (조약)을 비준하다; 승인하다. ¶ *The treaty was confirmed by the king.* 조약은 국왕에 의해 비준되었다 / ~ *an appointment* 임명을 승인하다. **4** (P6) admit to full membership in the Christian Church by a special rite. …에게 견진 성사(堅振聖事)를 베풀다. [L. *firmus;* →firm[1]]

con·fir·ma·tion [kɑ̀nfərméiʃən / kɔ̀n-] *n.* UC **1** the act of confirming; the state of being confirmed. 확정; 확인; 비준; 확증. ¶ *the* ~ *of one's statements* 자기 진술의 확인 / *The report lacks* ~. 그 보도는 확인돼 있지 않다. **2** 《usu. *C-*》 a rite or ceremony by which a person is admitted after baptism to full membership in the Christian Church. 안수례(按手禮); 견진 성사(堅振聖事).

con·firmed [kənfə́:rmd] *adj.* **1** definitely or clearly proved or established; formally recognized. 확정된; 비준된. **2** habitual; constant. 상습적인; 만성의. ¶ *a* ~ *drunkard* 모주꾼 / *a* ~ *invalid* 고질 환자.

con·fir·mee [kɑ̀nfə:rmí: / kɔ̀n-] *n.* a person to whom confirmation is administered. 확인된 사람; 견진 성사를 받은 사람.

con·fis·cate [kɑ́nfiskèit, kənfís- / kɔ́n-] *vt.* (P6,13) seize or take (someone's property) for public use by authority. …을 몰수[압수, 징발]하다. ¶ ~ *smuggled goods* 밀수품을 몰수하다 / *The police confiscated the liquor.* 경찰은 술을 압수했다. [→fiscal]

con·fis·ca·tion [kɑ̀nfiskéiʃən / kɔ̀n-] *n.* UC the act of confiscating; the state of being confiscated. 몰수; 압수; 징발. ¶ *the* ~ *of wealth* 재산의 몰수.

con·fis·ca·tor [kɑ́nfiskèitər / kɔ́n-] *n.* one who confiscates. 몰수[압수]하는 사람.

con·fis·ca·to·ry [kənfískətɔ̀:ri / -təri] *adj.* of confiscation. 몰수의.

con·fla·gra·tion [kɑ̀nfləgréiʃən / kɔ̀n-] *n.* C **1** a great fire. 큰 불; 대화재. **2** a great outbreak of war. 대전의 발발. [→flagrant]

:con·flict [kɑ́nflikt / kɔ́n-] *n.* C **1** a struggle; a fight. 투쟁; 싸움; 분쟁. ¶ *a* ~ *of arms* 전쟁 / *a bloody* ~ 피투성이의 싸움 / *man's* ~ *with nature* 인간의 자연과의 싸움. **2** a quarrel. 말다툼; 언쟁; 논쟁. ¶ *a wordy* ~ 언쟁 / *conflicts between church and state* 교회와 국가 간의 논쟁. **3** a sharp disagreement; a collision. (의견·감정·이해 따위의) 충돌; 대립. ¶ *a domestic* ~ 가정의 불화 / *a* ~ *of ideas* 사상의 대립 / *a* ~ *between duty and love* 의무와 사랑 간의 갈등 / *in* ~ *with another opinion* 남의 의견과 충돌하여.
— [kənflíkt] *vi.* (P1,3) **1** 《*with*》 fight. 싸우다. **2** 《*with*》 be in contradiction. 충돌[대립]하다; 모순[상반]되다. ¶ *conflicting accounts* [*opinions*] 상반되는 설명[의견] / *Our interests conflicted with theirs.* 우리의 이해 관계는 그들의 것과 대립했다. ● **con·flic·tion** [kənflíkʃən] *n.* [L. *fligo* strike]

con·flu·ence [kɑ́nfluəns / kɔ́n-] *n.* C **1** the place where two rivers meet; the state of this. (강의) 합류(점). ¶ *The city stands at the* ~ *of two rivers.* 그 시(市)는 두 강이 합류하는 곳에 있다. **2** a throng; a crowd. 군집(群集); 군중. [com-]

con·flu·ent [kɑ́nfluənt / kɔ́n-] *adj.* (esp. of rivers and streams) flowing or running together. (강 따위가) 합류하는. — *n.* C a river flowing into another. 합류하는 강; 지류(支流).

con·flux [kɑ́nflʌks / kɔ́n-] *n.* =confluence.

con·form [kənfɔ́:rm] *vt.* (P13) make (something) equal or very similar to another; adapt. …을 (규준에) 맞추다; 순응[일치]시키다. ¶ ~ *one's taste to her husband* 남편의 취미에 맞추다 / ~ *oneself to the social orders* 사회의 질서에 따르다 / *He conformed his manners to those of his associates.* 그는 자신의 예법을 동료들의 예법에 순응시켰다.
— *vi.* (P1,3) 《*to*》 **1** ⓐ be in harmony with what is required. 일치하다. ¶ ~ *to the wishes of others* 타인의 요망에 따르다. ⓑ be shaped according to the form of. …의 모양에 맞추다. ¶ *A coat must* ~ *to the figure of the wearer.* 코트는 입을 사람의 모양에 맞춰야 한다. **2** act according to the law, custom, etc. (규칙·습관에) 따르다. ¶ ~ *to directions* 지시에 따르다 / *You must* ~ *to the rules of the school.* 너는 교칙(校則)에 따라야 한다. [com-]

con·form·a·ble [kənfɔ́:rməbəl] *adj.* 《*to, with*》 similar; adapted; obedient. 비슷한; 일치[합치]한; 적합한; 순종하는. ¶ *a* ~ *disposition* 순종하는 기질 / ~ *to social conventions* 사회 관습에 합치되는 / *Man is* ~ *to reason.* 인간은 이성에 순종한다.

con·form·ance [kənfɔ́:rməns] *n.* =conformity.

con·for·ma·tion [kɑ̀nfɔ:rméiʃən / kɔ̀n-] *n.* **1** C the act of conforming; the state of being conformed; structure. 일치; 형상; 구조. **2** Ⓤ adaptation. 적합. [com-]

con·form·ism [kənfɔ́:rmizəm] *n.* readiness to conform to established authority. 준봉(遵奉)〔순응〕주의; 순응적 태도.

con·form·ist [kənfɔ́:rmist] *n.* Ⓒ **1** 《usu. *contempt.*》 a person who conforms. (집단·사회 관행 따위에) 따르는 사람; 준봉〔순응〕자. **2** 《*C-*》 a member of the Church of England. 영국 국교도.

con·form·i·ty [kənfɔ́:rməti] *n.* Ⓤ **1** likeness; agreement. 유사(類似); 일치; 적합. ¶ ~ *with one's idea* 자신의 생각과의 일치 / ~ *to fashion* 유행에 맞춤 /~ *between physical and mental states* 심신(心身) 상태의 조화. **2** action in agreement with what is usu. accepted, expected by custom, etc. 복종; 순종; 준봉(遵奉).

in conformity with, in accordance with. …에 따라(서). ¶ *in* ~ *with your orders* 당신의 명령〔분부〕에 따라.

·con·found [kənfáund, kan- / kɔn-] *vt.* **1** (P6,13) confuse; mix up (things); mistake (one person or one thing) for another. …을 (—과) 혼동하다. ¶ *truth confounded with error* 잘못과 혼동된 진실 / *I always* ~ *him with his brother.* 나는 언제나 그를 그의 형과 혼동한다 / *Never* ~ *right and wrong.* 옳고 그른 것을 혼동하지 마라. **2** (P6) astonish; throw into perplexity. 당혹〔당황〕케 하다; 혼란에 빠뜨리다. ¶ *He was confounded at the sight of the busy street.* 그는 번화한 거리를 보고 당황했다. **3** (P6) defeat (plans, hopes, etc.). (계획·희망 따위)를 무너뜨리다; 꺾다. **4** 《*colloq.*》《used to express *anger, disappointment,* etc.》 damn. 제기랄; 염병할. ¶ *Confound it* 〔*you*〕*!* 젠장; 우라질. [L. *fundo* pour]

con·found·ed [kənfáundid, kan- / kɔn-] *adj.* **1** confused. 당황한; 혼란한. **2** 《*colloq.*》 damned; hateful. 지겨운; 지긋지긋한. ¶ *a* ~ *fool* 지독한 바보 / *a* ~ *heat* 지겨운 더위.

con·fra·ter·ni·ty [kànfrətə́:rnəti / kɔ̀n-] *n.* Ⓒ (*pl.* **-ties**) **1** a brotherhood. 결사(結社). **2** a group of men formed for some purpose, esp. religious or professional. (특히 종교·직업상의) 단체; 조합. [→fraternal]

con·frère [kánfrɛər / kɔ́n-] *n.* 《F.》 a fellow-member of a society; a fellow worker; a colleague. 조합원; 동료. [↑]

·con·front [kənfrʌ́nt] *vt.* **1** (P6) stand in front of (someone); face boldly. …와 마주보게 하다; …에 맞서다. ¶ ~ *danger* 〔*death*〕 위험〔죽음〕에 맞서다. **2** (P6,13) 《*with*》 bring face to face. …을 대면〔대결〕시키다; (증거)를 들이대다. ¶ ~ *a man with his accuser* 사나이를 고발자와 대면시키다 / ~ *a man with evidence of guilt* 사나이에게 죄증을 들이대다. **3** (P6) stand opposite to (something). …의 바로 맞은편〔정면〕에 있다. [com-]

be confronted with 〔***by***〕 (=*face*) *something.* …에 직면하다. ¶ *I am confronted with many difficulties.* 나는 많은 어려움에 직면해 있다.

Con·fu·cian [kənfjú:ʃən] *adj., n.* (a follower) of Confucius. 공자의; 유교의; 유자(儒者). [↓]

Con·fu·cius [kənfjú:ʃəs] *n.* a Chinese philosopher. 공자(孔子). [Person]

Con·fu·cian·ism [kənfjú:ʃənìzəm] *n.* Ⓤ the system of the moral teachings of Confucius and his followers. 공자의 가르침; 유교.

·con·fuse [kənfjú:z] *vt.* **1** (P6) mix up (things) in the mind; throw (ideas, etc.) into disorder. …을 혼란시키다. ¶ *The shock confused me completely.* 그 충격은 나를 완전히 혼란에 빠뜨렸다. **2** (P6) puzzle. …을 당황〔당혹〕케 하다. ¶ *be* 〔*become, get*〕 *confused* 당황하다 / *feel confused* 곤혹하다. **3** mistake (one thing) for another. …을 (—과) 혼동하다. ¶ ~ *liberty with license* 자유와 방종을 혼동하다 / ~ *the means with the end* 수단과 목적을 혼동하다 / *You are confusing two quite different things.* 자넨 전혀 다른 두 개의 것을 혼동하고 있네. [L. *fundo* pour]

con·fused [kənfjú:zd] *adj.* **1** thrown into disorder. 혼란에 빠진. ¶ *a* ~ *account* 〔*statement*〕 혼란하여 지리멸렬한 설명〔진술〕/ *His mind became* ~. 그의 정신은 혼란에 빠졌다. **2** perflexed; disconcerted. 곤혹스런; 당황한. ¶ *look* ~ 곤혹스러워 보이다.

con·fus·ed·ly [kənfjú:zidli] *adv.* in a confused manner. 난잡하게; 당황하여.

con·fus·ing [kənfjú:ziŋ] *adj.* that confuses, puzzles, disorders, etc. 혼란시키는; 당황케 하는.

:con·fu·sion [kənfjú:ʒən] *n.* Ⓤ **1** the act of confusing. 혼란시킴; 당황케 함. ¶ ~ *of ideas* 사상의 혼란. **2** the state of being confused; embarrassment; disorder. 혼란(상태); 당황; 당혹; 난잡. ¶ *be thrown into* ~ 혼란에 빠지다 / *throw them into* ~ 그들을 혼란에 빠뜨리다 / *leave one's affairs in* ~ 자기 일을 혼란 상태로 두다 / *in the* ~ *of the moment* 혼란을 틈타 / *The army retreated in* ~. 군대는 혼란에 빠져 후퇴했다. **3** the act of mistaking one thing for another; failure to distinguish between things. 혼동; 구별이 안됨. ¶ *Words like 'believe' and 'receive' are a cause of* ~ *in spelling.* 'believe'와 'receive' 같은 말들은 쓰기에 혼동을 일으키는 원인이 된다.

con·fu·ta·tion [kànfjutéiʃən / kɔ̀n-] *n.* Ⓤ the act of confuting; something that confutes. 논파(論破); 논박. [↓]

con·fute [kənfjú:t] *vt.* (P6) prove (something) to be false; disprove; prove (someone) to be wrong. …을 논박하다; 허위〔잘못〕임을 입증하다; 반증하다. ¶ ~ *one's opponent* 논적(論敵)을 육박지르다. [→futile]

con·gé [kánʒei / kɔ́:n-] *n.* 《F.》 **1** a sudden dismissal. 면직(免職); 해고. ¶ *give someone* *his* ～ 아무를 면직하다 / *get one's* ～ 면직〔해고〕되다. **2** =congee.

con·geal [kəndʒíːl] *vt.* (P6) freeze; make (one's blood) stiff because of horror. …을 얼리다; 오싹하게 하다. ¶ *Ice is congealed water.* 얼음은 언 물이다 / *My very blood was congealed at the sight of the scene.* 그 광경을 보고 온몸의 피가 얼어붙었다. — *vi.* (P1) freeze; stiffen; become hard because of cold. 얼다; 응결하다; 응고하다. [L. *gelo* freeze]

con·gee [kándʒiː / kɔ́n-] *n.* 《*arch.*》 a formal bow; a greeting, esp. on departure. 작별 인사. ¶ *make one's congees* 작별 인사를 하다. [F.]

con·ge·la·tion [kàndʒəléiʃən / kɔ̀n-] *n.* the process or result of congealing. 동결(凍結); 응결; 응고. [→congeal]

con·ge·ner [kándʒənər / kɔ́n-] *n.* a thing of the same kind. 동종〔동류〕의 것. [com-, L. *gigno* beget; →genus]

con·gen·ial [kəndʒíːnjəl] *adj.* **1** having the same tastes and interests; getting on well together. 마음에 맞는; 같은 성질〔취미〕의. ¶ ～ *friends.* **2** 《often *to*》 agreeable to; suitable for; fit. 마음〔취미〕에 맞는; 적합한; 쾌적한. ¶ *a climate* ～ *to health* 건강에 적합한 기후 / *a task* ～ *to one's personality* 개성에 맞는 일. [com-]

con·gen·i·tal [kəndʒénətl] *adj.* (of diseases, defects, etc.) existing from one's birth; inherited; by nature. (병·결점 따위가) 타고난; 선천적인. ¶ *a* ～ *defect*〔*disease*〕 선천적 결함〔질병〕 / *a* ～ *idiot* 타고난 백치. [com-]

con·ger [káŋgər / kɔ́ŋ-] *n.* Ⓒ 《fish》 a large sea eel. 붕장어. [Gk.]

con·gest [kəndʒést] *vt.* **1** (P6) fill (something) too full; pack densely; 《usu. in *passive*》 overcrowd. …을 너무 처넣다; …을 붐비게 하다〔혼잡하게 하다〕. ¶ *The street are congested.* 거리가 북적이고 있다 / *The traffic congested the street.* 사람 왕래로 거리가 붐볐다. **2** (P6) cause too much blood to gather in (one part of the body). …을 충혈〔울혈〕되게 하다. ¶ *The doctor said that my lungs were congested.* 의사는 내 폐에 울혈이 있다고 말했다. — *vi.* become congested; become too full of blood. 막히다; 충혈되다. ¶ *His throat congested with phlegm.* 그의 목에 가래가 찼다. [L. *gero* bring]

con·gest·ed [kəndʒéstid] *adj.* **1** (of places, street, people) too much; overcrowded. 지나치게 붐비는; 혼잡한. ¶ ～ *traffic* 혼잡한 교통. **2** containing too much blood. 충혈돼 있는.

con·ges·tion [kəndʒéstʃən] *n.* Ⓤ **1** the state of being congested. 혼잡; 밀집. ¶ *traffic* ～ 교통 혼잡. **2** too much blood in one part of the body. 충혈; 울혈. ¶ ～ *of the brain* 뇌충혈.

con·glom·er·ate [kənglámərèit / -glɔ́m-] *vi.* (P1) gather into a rounded mass. 둥글게 굳다〔모이다〕. — *vt.* (P6) gather (things) into a rounded mass. …을 둥글게 하다; 응집체로 하다; 덩어리지게 하다. — [kənglámərət / -glɔ́m-] *adj.* **1** gathered in a rounded mass. (모여서) 둥그렇게 굳은; 집괴상(集塊狀)의. **2** (of rock) made up of many materials gathered from various sources. 역암질(礫岩質)의. — [-glámərət / -glɔ́m-] *n.* Ⓒ **1** a mass made up of separate substances. 집합체; 집괴(集塊). **2** rock made up of small stones. 역암(礫岩). [L. *glomus* ball]

con·glom·er·a·tion [kənglàməréiʃən / -glɔ̀m-] *n.* **1** Ⓤ the act of conglomerating; the state of being conglomerated. 응집(凝集); 집성(集成). **2** Ⓒ a mixed-up mass of various things; a cluster. 집합(체); 집괴(集塊).

Con·go [káŋgou / kɔ́ŋ-] *n.* a river or country in West Africa. 콩고강(江); 콩고 공화국.

Congo snake〔**eel**〕 [∸-∸〔∸〕] *n.* an eellike amphibian with very small, weak legs. 일종의 양서(兩棲)동물.

con·gou [káŋguː / kɔ́ŋ-] *n.* a black China tea. 중국산 홍차의 일종. [Chin.]

***con·grat·u·late** [kəngrǽtʃəlèit] *vt.* (P6, 13,15) 《*on, upon*》 express one's joy at the happiness or good fortune of another. …을 축하하다; 경하(慶賀)하다. ¶ *I* ～ *you on your success*〔*marriage*〕. 성공〔결혼〕을 축하합니다 / *I congratulated my friend on her birthday.* 친구인 그녀의 생일을 축하했다. [con-, L. *gratus*]

***congratulate** oneself **on**〔**upon**〕(=be proud of; be pleased with) something.* …을 기뻐하다; 우쭐해하다.

·**con·grat·u·la·tion** [kəngrætʃəléiʃən] *n.* **1** Ⓤ the act of congratulating. 축하. ¶ *a matter of* ～ 축하할 일; 경사(慶事) / *in* ～ *of* …을 축하하여. **2** Ⓒ 《usu. *pl.*》 an expression of pleasure at another's happiness or good fortune. 축하의 말; 축사. ¶ *Congratulations!* 축하합니다 / *offer one's congratulations* 축하의 말을 하다.

con·grat·u·la·to·ry [kəngrǽtʃələtɔ̀ːri / -əri] *adj.* expressing congratulations. 축하의; 경하(慶賀)의. ¶ *a* ～ *speech* 축하의 말; 축사.

con·gre·gate [káŋgrigèit / kɔ́ŋ-] *vi.* (P1) gather; come together in a great number. (특히 대집단으로) 모이다; 집합하다. ¶ *The people congregated in the theater.* 사람들은 극장에 모였다. — *vt.* (P6) gather. …을 모으다; 소집하다; 집합시키다. [L. *grex* flock]

con·gre·ga·tion [kàŋgrigéiʃən / kɔ̀ŋ-] *n.* Ⓒ **1** Ⓤ the act of congregating; the state of being congregated. 집합. **2** a gathering of people; an assembly. 회합; 집회. **3** 《*collectively*》 a group of people attending a church service. (교회의) 회중(會衆). 參考 음악회·강연회 따위의 청중은 audience.

con·gre·ga·tion·al [kàŋgrigéiʃənəl / kɔ̀ŋ-] *adj.* **1** of a congregation. 집합〔집회〕의; 회중(會衆)의. ¶ ~ *singing* 합창. **2** 《*C*-》 of or belonging to congregationalism. 조합 교회제(制)의.

Con·gre·ga·tion·al·ism [kàŋgrigéiʃənəlìzəm / kɔ̀ŋ-] *n.* the faith and form of organization of a Protestant denomination in which each church is independent and self-governing. 조합 교회주의.

:**con·gress** [káŋgris / kɔ́ŋgris] *n.* **1** Ⓒ ⓐ a coming together of people; a meeting. 집합; 집회. ⓑ a meeting of representatives for discussion. (대표자의) 회의; 대회. ¶ *a medical* ~ 의학자 회의 / *the Social Democratic party's* ~ 사회 민주당 대회. **2** 《usu. *C*-》 the national lawmaking body, as of the United States. (미국 등의) 의회; 국회(cf. *diet²*, *parliament*). ¶ *be in Congress* 의회 개원 중이다 / *speak in Congress* 의회에서 연설하다. [L. *gradior* walk]

con·gres·sion·al [kəngréʃənəl, kəŋ- / kɔŋ-] *adj.* **1** of a congress. 회의〔집회〕의; 대회의; 평의원회(會)의. **2** 《usu. *C*-》 of the Congress of the United States. 미국 의회의.

con·gress·man [káŋgrismən / kɔ́ŋ-] *n.* Ⓒ (*pl.* **-men** [-mən]) 《often *C*-》 **1** a member of Congress. 국회 의원. **2** a member of the House of Representatives of the United States. (미국의) 하원 의원(cf. *senator*).

con·gru·ence [káŋgruəns, kəngrúːəns / kɔ́ŋ-], **-en·cy** [-ənsi] *n.* Ⓤ agreement; harmony. 일치; 적합; 조화. [↓]

con·gru·ent [káŋgruənt, kəngrúː- / kɔ́ŋ-] *adj.* **1** agreeing; suitable; fit. 일치하는; 적합한. ¶ *Your plan is ~ with our aims.* 너의 계획은 우리의 목표와 합치한다. **2** 《geom.》 of the same shape and size. 합동의. ¶ ~ *triangles* 합동 삼각형. [L. *congruo* agree]

con·gru·i·ty [kəngrúːiti, kəŋ- / kɔŋ-] *n.* **1** agreement; harmony. 일치; 적합(성); 조화. ¶ *the ~ of thought and action* 사고와 행동의 일치. **2** 《geom.》 the exact coincidence of lines, angles, figures, etc. 합동. **3** a point or instance of agreement. 일치점.

con·gru·ous [káŋgruəs / kɔ́ŋ-] *adj.* 《*to, with*》 agreeing; suitable; fitting; proper. 일치되는; 맞는; 적절한. ¶ *work ~ to his character* 그의 성격에 맞는 일.

con·ic [kánik / kɔ́n-], **-i·cal** [-ikəl] *adj.* of a cone; shaped like a cone. 원뿔의; 원뿔 모양의. ¶ ~ *sections* 원뿔 곡선. ● **con·i·cal·ly** [-kəli] *adv.* [→cone]

co·ni·fer [kóunəfər, kánə- / kɔ́n-] *n.* Ⓒ a tree such as the pine and cypress, most of which are evergreen and bear cones. 침엽수; 구과(毬果)식물. [↑]

co·nif·er·ous [kounífərəs] *adj.* bearing cones. 구과(毬果)를 맺는.

conj. conjugation; conjunction; conjunctive.

con·jec·tur·al [kəndʒéktʃərəl] *adj.* **1** doubtful; having doubt. 추측의; 억측적인. ¶ *His opinion was merely ~.* 그의 의견은 순전히 추측이었다. **2** inclined to make conjectures. 추측을 좋아하는. [↓]

con·jec·ture [kəndʒéktʃər] *n.* Ⓒ a guess; the act of guessing. 추측; 억측. ¶ *form* 〔*make*〕 *a ~ upon* …에 추측을 하다 / *give a plausible ~* 그럴 듯한 추측을 하다 / *hazard a ~* 짐작으로 말하다. — *vt., vi.* (P6,11; 1) guess; make a guess. 추측하다; 억측하다. [L. *jacio* throw]

con·join [kəndʒɔ́in] *vi., vt.* (P1,3; 6) join together; become joined; unite; combine. 결합하다〔시키다〕; 연접하다. ● **con·join·er** [-ər] *n.* [com-]

con·joint [kəndʒɔ́int, kan- / kɔndʒɔ́int] *adj.* joined together; united; combined; associated. 결합한; 공동〔합동〕의; 연합의.

con·joint·ly [kəndʒɔ́intli, kan- / kɔn-] *adv.* joined together; in combination. 공동으로; 합동으로. ¶ *Two clubs gave a party ~.* 두 클럽은 합동으로 파티를 열었다.

con·ju·gal [kándʒəgəl / kɔ́n-] *adj.* **1** married; of marriage. 결혼의; 혼인(상)의. **2** of husband and wife. 부부의. ¶ ~ *affection* 부부애 / ~ *boredom* 부부간의 권태. ● **con·ju·gal·ly** [-i] *adv.* [L. *jungo*]

con·ju·gate [kándʒəgèit / kɔ́n-] *vt.* (P6) 《gram.》 give the forms of (a verb) in regard to number, tense, etc. (동사)를 활용〔변화〕시키다. — *vi.* join together; unite. 결합〔접합〕하다. — [kándʒəgit, -gèit / kɔ́n-] *adj.* **1** joined together, esp. in a pair; united. 결합〔접합〕한; (한) 쌍〔짝〕으로 된. **2** (of words) derived from the same root. (낱말이) 같은 뿌리의; 동원(同源)의. ¶ *a ~ word* 동근어(同根語). [L. *jugum* yoke]

con·ju·ga·tion [kàndʒəgéiʃən / kɔ̀n-] *n.* **1** ⓊⒸ 《gram.》 the systematic arrangement of verb forms. 동사의 활용; 어형 변화 (cf. *declension, inflection*). ¶ *regular* 〔*irregular*〕 ~ 규칙〔불규칙〕 활용. **2** ⓊⒸ the act of conjugating; the state of being conjugated; connection. 결합; 연결. **3** Ⓤ the union of two cells of the same type. 세포의 접합.

***con·junc·tion** [kəndʒʌ́ŋkʃən] *n.* **1** Ⓤ the state of being joined together; union; combination. 결합; 연결(상태); 공동. **2** Ⓒ 《gram.》 a word that connects words, phrases, clauses, or sentences, such as *and, or* and *but*. 접속사. [→join]

in conjunction with, together with. …와 함께; 연속하여.

con·junc·ti·va [kàndʒʌŋktáivə / kɔ̀n-] *n.* (*pl.* **-vas, -vae**) 《anat.》 the mucous membrane lining the inner surface of the eyelids. (눈알의) 결막(結膜).

con·junc·ti·vae [kàndʒʌŋktáiviː] *n.* pl. of **conjunctiva.**

con·junc·tive [kəndʒʌ́ŋktiv] *adj.* **1** joining

together; connecting. 결합[연결]하는; 접속하는. ¶ ~ *tissue* 결합 조직. **2** joint; joined; united. 공동의; 합동의. **3** 《gram.》 words, phrases, or clauses connecting in both meaning and construction. (말 따위가) 접속 작용이 있는; 접속의. ¶ *a ~ adverb* 접속 부사.

con·junc·ti·vi·tis [kəndʒʌ̀ŋktəváitis] *n.* 《med.》 inflammation of the conjunctiva. 결막염(炎).

con·junc·ture [kəndʒʌ́ŋktʃər] *n.* Ⓒ a combination of events or circumstances. (여러 가지 사정의) 결합; 국면; 때; 위기. ¶ *at* [*in*] *this ~* 이 (위급한) 때에; 이런 중대 시(時)에.

con·jur·a·tion [kɑ̀ndʒəréiʃən / kɔ̀n-] *n.* **1** a solemn appeal; invocation. 서원(誓願); 기원; 주문으로 불러냄. **2** the practice of magic. 마법; 마력. ¶ *The boy was changed to a toad by ~.* 소년은 마술에 의해 두꺼비로 둔갑되었다. **3** a magical spell. 주문(呪文); 진언(眞言). [↓]

con·jure [kɑ́ndʒər, kʌ́n-] *vt.* **1** (P6,7,13) force (a spirit, etc.) to appear by using magic; cause (something) to appear esp. by moving the hand. (악령 따위)를 마법[주문]으로 불러내다; 요술로 나오게 하다. ¶ *~ up a devil* 주문을 외어 악마를 불러내다 / *~ a pigeon out of an empty hat* 요술로 빈 모자에서 비둘기가 나오게 하다. **2** [kəndʒúər] (P15,20) make a serious appeal to (someone); beg (someone) earnestly. …을 서원(誓願)[기원]하다; 간원하다. ¶ *I ~ you to grant my request.* 제 요구를 들어주시기를 간원합니다 / *I ~ you not to betray me.* 저를 배반하지 말도록 간원합니다. —*vi.* (P1,3) practice magic; perform a trick; call upon a devil by means of a spell. 마법을 쓰다; 요술을 부리다; (주문으로) 마귀를 불러내다. [L. *juro* swear]

a name to conjure with, a name of vast influence. 유력한 이름.

conjure out, produce by jugglery. 요술로 나오게 하다.

conjure up, **a**) cause to appear by magic or as if by magic. 마술로[마술에 의한 것처럼] 나타나게 하다. **b**) cause to appear in the mind. 마음에 떠오르게 하다. ¶ *~ up visions of the past* 지난 날의 광경이 떠오르다.

con·jur·er, -or [kɑ́ndʒərər, kəndʒúərər, kʌndʒər-] *n.* Ⓒ **1** a magician. 마법사. ¶ *He was so clever a speaker that he seemed a veritable ~.* 말솜씨가 아주 교묘한 연사였으므로 그는 진짜 마술사처럼 보였다. **2** a person who performs tricks; a juggler. 요술사.

con·jur·ing [kɑ́ndʒəriŋ, kʌ́n-] *adj., n.* performing with quick, deceiving movements of the hands. 요술(을 부리는). ¶ *a ~ trick* 요술.

conk [kɑŋk / kɔŋk] *vt.* (P1,2A) 《*out*》 《*colloq.*》 break down. 부서지다; 고장나다. [?]

Conn. Connecticut.

:con·nect [kənékt] *vt.* **1** (P6,13) 《*to, with*》 join (one thing) to another; unite; link. …을 잇다; 연결하다. ¶ *~ the cities by a railroad* 도시를 철도로 연결하다 / *please ~ me with New York.* 뉴욕에 연결해 주십시오 / *A bus line connects the two cities.* 버스 노선이 두 시를 이어주고 있다 / *Let's ~ this wire to that one.* 이 철사를 그 철사와 연결하자. **2** 《usu. *passive* or *reflexively*》 join in some business or by a personal relationship. …와 관계하다; 친척[인척] 관계가 있다. ¶ *~ oneself with a group of like-minded persons* 뜻을 같이 하는 사람들과 관계를 가지다 / *He is connected with the Johnsons by marriage.* 그는 혼인에 의해서 존슨 집안과 인척 관계가 된다. **3** (P13) think of (one thing) with another; associate in the mind. …을 결부시켜 생각하다; 연상하다. ¶ *~ A with B in one's mind,* A를 b와 연결시켜 생각하다 / *~ his success with his diligence* 그의 성공은 근면함에 있는 것이라고 생각하다.

—*vi.* (P1,2,3) **1** (of trains, etc.) run so that passengers can change from one to another without delay. (갈아 탈 수 있도록 열차·버스가) 연결[연락, 접속]되다. ¶ *This train connects with another at Taejŏn.* 이 열차는 대전에서 다른 열차와 연결된다. **2** be united or joined. 이어지다. ¶ *The two ends of the pipe ~ with the collar.* 파이프의 두 끝은 링으로 이어진다. [L. *necto* bind]

con·nect·ed [kənéktid] *adj.* **1** joined; united; coherent. 앞뒤가 맞는; 동당는; 일관된. ¶ *a ~ account* 앞뒤가 맞는 설명. **2** related or associated with others. 관련된; 관계가 있는; 연고가 있는. ¶ *~ thoughts* 관련 사상 / *be distantly ~ with* …와 먼 친척이다; …와 먼 관계가 있다. **3** 《*with*》 participating in; involved in. 관여한; 연루된. ¶ *He was ~ with the crime.* 그는 범죄에 연루되었다.

con·nect·er, -tor [kənéktər] *n.* a person or thing that connects. 결합하는 사람[것]; 연결자[물].

Con·nect·i·cut [kənétikət] *n.* a northeastern State of the United States. 코네티컷 주(州). 參考 Conn.으로 생략함. 주도(州都)는 Hartford.

:con·nec·tion [kənékʃən] *n.* **1** ⒸⓊ the act of connecting; the condition of being connected; union; link. 결합; 연결; 접속; 연락. ¶ *the ~ of trains* 객차의 연결. **2** Ⓒ something that joins other things together; a point where two things are connected. 접속하는 것; 연결 기구; 연결점(點). **3** Ⓤ relation; relationship; communication. 관계; 교제. ¶ *form useful connections* 유익한 관계[교제]를 맺다 / *cut* [*break off*] *the ~ with* …와(의) 관계를 끊다 / *I have no ~ with the company.* 그 회사와는 관계가 없다. **4** Ⓒ a relative, esp. by marriage. 친척; 인척. ¶ *She is my intimate* [*remote*] *~.* 그녀는 나의 가까운[먼] 친척이 된다. **5** Ⓤ the meeting of trains, buses, etc. that enables passengers to change vehicles within a short time. (다른 교통편과의 연결을 위한) 탈것의 접속〔연락〕(편). ¶ *There is a bus ~ with this train.* 이 열차는 (갈아 탈) 버스와 연결되어 있다. **6** Ⓒ ⓐ a group of people. 단체; 종파. ⓑ a group of customers. 단골(들); 고객. ¶ *a firm with a good ~* 좋은 단골이 있는 회사. [→connect]

in connection with, in regard to. …와〔에〕 관련하여.

in this connection, about this matter. 이 점에 관련하여.

run in connection, arrive and start making connections. (갈아 탈) 교통편에 연락이 닿다.

con·nec·tive [kənéktiv] *adj.* joining; serving to connect. 접속의; 결합의. ¶ *~ tissue* 결합 조직. —*n.* Ⓒ **1** a thing that connects. 연결물. **2** 《gram.》 a word used to connect words, phrases, and clauses. 연결사(詞).

con·nex·ion [kənékʃən] *n.* 《Brit.》 =connection.

con·ning tower [kániŋ tàuər / kɔ́niŋ-] *n.* a small tower on the deck of a warship or a submarine, from which the ship is guided and observations are made. (군함의) 사령탑; (잠수함의) 전망탑.

con·niv·ance [kənáivəns] *n.* Ⓤ the act of conniving. 모른 체하기; 묵인. ¶ *~ at someone's wrongdoing* 아무의 비행의 묵인 / *his ~ in the conspiracy* 그 음모에 대한 그의 묵과(默過). [↓]

con·nive [kənáiv] *vi.* (P3) **1** 《*at*》 shut one's eyes to something wrong; pretend to be unaware of something. (나쁜 짓 따위를) 보고도 못 본 체하다; 눈감다; 묵인하다. ¶ *~ at the violation of the rule* 규칙 위반을 묵인하다. **2** 《*with*》 act together secretly. 공모하다; (적측과) 음모를 꾀하다. [L. *conniveo* wink]

con·nois·seur [kànəsə́ːr, -súər / kɔ̀n-] *n.* Ⓒ an expert; a fault-finding judge. 감식가; 감정가; (그 방면의) 권위. ¶ *a ~ of fine arts* 미술품 감식가. [L. *gnosco* apprehend]

con·no·ta·tion [kànoutéiʃən / kɔ̀n-] *n.* ⓊⒸ **1** the act of connoting; that which is connoted; an implication. 함축; 언외(言外)의 의미. ¶ *'Politician' has different connotations from 'statesman'.* 'politician'은 'statesman'과는 다른 함축성이 있다. **2** 《log.》 the whole set of qualities or meanings of a term. 내포(內包). [↓]

con·note [kənóut] *vt.* (P6) suggest (something) in addition to the simple meaning; imply; 《*colloq.*》 mean. (언외(言外)의 다른 뜻)을 암시하다; 함축하다; 의미하다. ¶ *A holiday connotes enjoyment.* 휴일하면 즐김을 함축한다. [com-]

con·nu·bi·al [kənjúːbiəl] *adj.* of marriage; married. 혼인의; 결혼 생활의; 부부의 (cf. *conjugal*). ¶ *~ rites* 혼인의 의식 / *~ love* 부부애(愛) / *in ~ harmony* 부부가 화목〔화합〕하여. [L. *nubo* become wife]

:**con·quer** [káŋkər / kɔ́ŋ-] *vt.* (P6) **1** win the victory over (the enemy, etc.) in war. …와 싸워 이기다. **2** overcome (something) by force; gain; defeat. …을 정복하다; 획득하다; …에 이기다. ¶ *~ bad habits* 악습을 타파하다 / *~ passions* 격정을 누르다 / *~ Mt. Everest* 에베레스트 산을 정복하다 / *~ the difficulties* 어려움을 이겨내다. —*vi.* (P1) be victorious; gain a victory. 승리를 얻다. [L. *quaero* seek]

***con·quer·or** [káŋkərər / kɔ́ŋ-] *n.* **1** Ⓒ a person who conquers; a victor. 정복자; 승자. ¶ *play the ~* 결승전을 하다. **2** 《*the C-*》 《Brit. hist.》 William I, of Normandy, who conquered England in 1066. 노르망디 공(公) 윌리엄 1세.

***con·quest** [káŋkwest / kɔ́ŋ-] *n.* **1** Ⓤ the act of conquering; victory; subjugation. 정복. ¶ *the ~ of a foreign land* 외국 영토의 정복 / *complete the ~ of a country* 어떤 나라를 완전히 정복하다. **2** Ⓒ anything conquered. 정복된 것; 획득한 것〔땅, 사람〕. ¶ *the conquests of Napoleon* 나폴레옹이 정복한 땅. **3** Ⓤ the act of gaining the affections of someone. (호의·애정 따위의) 획득. **4** Ⓒ 《*colloq.*》 a person whose love or favor has been won. 애정에 끌린〔휘어든〕 이성(異性).

make a conquest of, **a**) conquer. …을 정복하다. **b**) win the love of (someone). …의 애정을 얻다.

Con·rad [kánræd / kɔ́n-], **Joseph** *n.* (1857-1924) a Polish-born English novelist. 폴란드 태생의 영국 소설가.

con·san·guin·e·ous [kànsæŋgwíniəs / kɔ̀n-] *adj.* having the same blood; belonging to the same family. 같은 혈족의; 혈연(血緣)의; 동족의. [→sanguine]

con·san·guin·i·ty [kànsæŋgwínəti / kɔ̀n-] *n.* Ⓤ relationship by blood or birth; kinship. 혈족; 혈연; 동족. ¶ *They are united by ties of ~.* 그들은 혈연이라는 유대로 결속돼 있다. [↑]

:**con·science** [kánʃəns / kɔ́n-] *n.* ⓊⒸ the sense of right and wrong; a moral judgment or sense. 양심; 선악의 관념; 도의심. ¶ *a merchant with little ~* 비양심적인 상인 / *pangs of ~* 양심의 가책 / *have a good* 〔*clear*〕 *~* 양심에 거리끼는〔부끄러운〕 점이 없다 / *have a bad* 〔*guilty*〕 *~* 마음에 거리끼는 데가 있다. [L. *scio* know]

for conscience(') sake, to satisfy one's conscience. 양심 때문에; 양심에 걸려; 제발.

have (*something*) ***on one's conscience,*** feel guilty or bad about some misdeed. … 일로 양심에 가책〔죄책〕을 느끼다.

have the conscience to *do,* be shameless enough to do; be so bold as to do. 뻔뻔하게도 …하다. ¶ *have the ~ to ask for money* 뻔뻔하게도 돈을 요구하다.

***in* (*all*) *conscience,* a**) surely; certainly. 확실히; 참으로. **b**) in all reason and fairness. 도리상; 공정하게. ¶ *I cannot, in ~, do such a thing.* 도리상 그런 짓은 할 수 없다.
make something a matter* (*question*) *of conscience, have scruples about doing something. …을 양심의 문제로 하다; 양심적으로 처리하다.
upon one's conscience, 《used as an oath》 surely; certainly. 양심에 걸고; 확실히; 꼭.

conscience clause [ˊ-ˋ] *n.* 《law》 a clause in a law relieving a person from performing acts because of their religious scruples. 양심 조항.

conscience money [ˊ- ˋ-] *n.* money paid because one now feels one ought to pay it. 양심에 의한〔자발적인〕 납금; 속죄의 헌금.

con·science-strick·en [kάnʃənsstrìkən / kɔ́n-] *adj.* suffering from a feeling of having done something wrong. 양심에 가책을 느끼는; 양심에 찔리는.

con·sci·en·tious [kὰnʃiénʃəs / kɔ̀n-] *adj.* **1** (of a person) careful to act according to conscience. 양심적인; 주의 깊은. ¶ *a ~ judge* 양심적인 재판관. **2** (of an action) done carefully and honestly. 성실한. ¶ *a ~ piece of work* 성실한 작품.

conscientious objector [--ˊ- --ˊ-] *n.* a person who does not take an active part in warfare because he believes that fighting is sinful. 양심적 참전 거부자《종교·주의상 전쟁에 반대하는 사람》.

con·scion·a·ble [kάnʃənəbəl / kɔ́n-] *adj.* 《*obs.*》 according to conscience; just. 양심에 따르는; 양심적인; 바른. [→conscience]

:con·scious [kάnʃəs / kɔ́n-] *adj.* **1** aware of something; knowing. …을 의식하고 있는; 알고〔깨닫고〕 있는(opp. unconscious). ¶ *be ~ of one's own fault* 자기의 결점을 알고 있다 / *Man is a ~ being.* 인간은 의식이 있는 존재이다 / *She was not ~ of his presence in the room.* 그녀는 그가 방 안에 있음을 의식하지 못했다 / *Are you not ~ of a strong smell of gas?* 자넨 강한 가스 냄새를 느끼지 못하는가 / *He was ~ that his strength was failing.* 그는 체력이 쇠퇴하고 있음을 깨달았다. **2** able to feel; sensible; sane. 지각(知覺)이 있는; 정신이 멀쩡한. ¶ *become ~* 의식을 회복하다; 제 정신이 들다 / *He was ~ to the last.* 그는 최후까지 의식이 말짱했다. **3** known to oneself; felt by oneself. (자기 행위 따위를 스스로) 알고 있는; 자각하고 있는. ¶ *~ guilt* 알면서 저지르는 죄 / *a ~ liar* 거짓말인 줄 자각하면서 하는 사람. **4** deliberate; intentional; intended. 의도〔의식〕적인; 고의적인. ¶ *a ~ insult* 의도적인 모욕 / *He made a ~ effort to please.* 그는 마음에 들게 하려고 의식적인 노력을 했다. **5** self-conscious; shy. 자의식이 강한; 남의 앞을 의식하는. ¶ *with a ~ air* 남의 앞을 의식하여; 수줍은 태도로. [↑]
with conscious superiority, feeling one's own superiority. 우월감을 가지고.

con·scious·ly [kάnʃəsli / kɔ́n-] *adv.* in a conscious manner; intentionally. 의식적으로; 자각하고.

·con·scious·ness [kάnʃəsnis / kɔ́n-] *n.* Ⓤ **1** 《sometimes *a ~*》 the state of being conscious; awareness. 의식; 자각. ¶ *a stream of ~* 의식의 흐름 / *lose ~* 의식을 잃다 / *regain* (*recover*) *~* 의식을 되찾다. **2** all one's ideas and feelings. 지각(知覺).

con·script [kənskrípt] *vt.* (P6) force (someone) by law to serve in the army or navy; draft; take (someone) for government service. …를 징집〔징용〕하다. — [kάnskript / kɔ́n-] *adj.* conscripted; drafted. 징집된. — *n.* Ⓒ a conscripted soldier or sailor. 징집병(兵). [→scribe]

con·scrip·tion [kənskrípʃən] *n.* Ⓤ **1** the system by which a person is forced to serve in the army or navy ; draft. 징병(제도). ¶ *the privilege of exemption from ~* 병역〔징집〕 면제의 특전 / *evade ~* 징병〔병역〕을 기피하다. **2** the act or system of forcing contributions of money, labor, etc. to the government, esp. during wartime. (전시중 돈·노동력 따위의) 강제 징발; 징용.

con·se·crate [kάnsikrèit / kɔ́n-] *vt.* (P6,13) **1** set (something) apart as sacred; make (something) holy or sacred. …을 신성하게 하다; 성별(聖別)하다. **2** devote (something) to a special purpose. (특수한 목적에) …을 바치다; 봉납(奉納)하다. ¶ *~ a church* 헌당(獻堂)하다 / *a life consecrated to science* 과학에 바친 일생 / *~ one's life to a cause* 어떤 주의를 위해 일생을 바치다 / *He consecrated himself to helping the poor.* 그는 가난한 사람들을 돕는 데 헌신했다. [→sacred]

con·se·cra·tion [kὰnsikréiʃən / kɔ̀n-] *n.* Ⓤ **1** the act of consecrating; the condition of having been consecrated. 성별(聖別); 봉납; 봉헌(奉獻). **2** devotion. 바침; 헌신(獻身). ¶ *the ~ of one's life to study* 일생을 연구에 바침. **3** the ceremony of placing someone in a holy office, esp. that of a bishop. 성직 수임(聖職授任)(식). ¶ *the ~ of a new bishop* 새 주교의 서품식.

con·sec·u·tive [kənsékjətiv] *adj.* **1** following continuously. 연속하는; 계속된. ¶ *six ~ numbers* 연속된 6개의 수 / *for five ~ years* 내리 5년 동안 / *win three ~ victories* 세 번 연승하다. **2** made up of parts that follow each other in regular order. 앞뒤 맥락이 닿는; 시종 일관된. ¶ *~ thinking* 앞뒤 일관성 있는 사고. ● **con·sec·u·tive·ly** [-li] *adv.* [→sequence]

con·sen·sus [kənsénsəs] *n.* Ⓒ a general agreement of opinion, feeling, etc. (의견·감정 따위의) 일치; 합의. ¶ *the ~ of opinion* 다수 의견; 여론 / *arrive at a ~* 의견의 일치를 보다. [→sense]

:con·sent [kənsént] *vi.* (P1,2A,3,4) 《*to*》

agree to opinions, etc.; permit. (의견에) 동의하다; 승낙〔허락〕하다(opp. disapprove). ¶ *the consenting party* 찬성측 / *~ to a suggestion* 〔*proposal*〕 제의〔제안〕에 동의하다 / *She consented to marry him.* 그녀는 그와 결혼할 것에 동의했다 / *Her father would not ~ to her marrying him.* 그녀 아버지는 딸이 그와 결혼하는 것을 허락하려 하지 않았다 / *He consented that an envoy should be sent.* 그는 사자(使者)를 보내는 것에 찬동했다.
— *n.* Ⓤ agreement; permission. 동의; 승낙; 허가. ¶ *with one ~* 만장일치로 / *do something without ~* 승낙없이 무엇을 하다 / *We have mother's ~ to go swimming.* 수영 가는 데 어머니의 허락(許諾)을 얻었다. [→sense]

by common 〔***general, universal***〕 ***consent,*** with the agreement of all; unanimously. 만장일치로.

the age of consent, the age at which the law recognizes one's right to marry, etc. 승낙 연령《결혼이 법적으로 승인되는 나이》.

:con·se·quence [kάnsikwèns / kɔ́nsikwəns] *n.* **1** Ⓒ a result; an effect. (필연의) 결과; 영향. ¶ *as a ~ of drinking* 음주의 결과로서 / *The ~ was that he lost his position.* 그 결과 그는 지위를 잃게 되었다. **2** Ⓤ importance; value. (영향·사회적인) 중요성; 중대함. ¶ *a matter of great ~* 극히 중대한 문제 / *a matter of no ~* 아주 하찮은 일〔문제〕/ *a man of ~* (사회적으로) 중요한 지위에 있는 사람; 저명한 사람. **3** Ⓒ a logical result. (논리적) 귀결; 결론. ¶ *as a logical ~* 논리적인 귀결로서. [com-]

in consequence, as a result; therefore; hence. 그 결과로서; 그 때문에.

in consequence of, as a result of; on account of. …의 결과; …때문에.

take the consequences, accept 〔be responsible for〕 what happens because of one's own action. (자신의 행위 따위의) 결과를 감수하다; 결과에 책임을 지다.

con·se·quent [kάnsikwènt / kɔ́nsikwənt] *adj.* **1** 《*on, upon, to*》 following as an effect or result. 결과로 발생하는. ¶ *the confusion ~ upon the conflagration* 대(大)화재의 결과 일어나는 혼란 / *a rise in production and a ~ fall in price* 생산의 상승과 이에 따른 물가의 하락. **2** logically consistent. (논리상) 일관된.
— *n.* Ⓒ a result; an effect. 결과.

con·se·quen·tial [kὰnsikwénʃəl / kɔ̀n-] *adj.* **1** following as a result. 결과로서 발생하는〔따르는〕; 필연의; 간접의. ¶ *~ damages* 간접적 손해 / *the coal mine gas explosion and the ~ loss of many lives* 탄갱의 가스 폭발과 그에 따른 많은 인명의 손실. **2** self-important. 젠체〔난체〕하는. ¶ *have ~ manners* 난체하는 태도가 있다. **3** logically connected; coherent. (논리적으로) 앞뒤 맥락이 닿은; 시종 일관된. ¶ *His talk is not very ~.* 그의 이야기는 그다지 논리적이지 못하다.

***con·se·quent·ly** [kάnsikwèntli / kɔ́n-] *adv.* as a result; therefore. 그 결과(로서); 그러므로; 따라서. ¶ *He is ill and ~ cannot attend the meeting.* 그는 병이 나서 회의에 참석할 수 없다.

con·serv·an·cy [kənsə́ːrvənsi] *n.* **1** conservation of natural resources. 천연 자원의 보호〔관리〕. **2** 《Brit.》 a commission controlling a port, river, forest, etc. (항만·하천·산림 등의) 관리 위원회. [↓]

con·ser·va·tion [kὰnsəːrvéiʃən / kɔ̀n-] *n.* Ⓤ the prevention of waste, loss or damage with regard to forests, rivers, etc., esp. those under official protection and care; protection from loss or from being used up. (산림·하천 따위의) 보호; 보존(opp. dissipation). ¶ *~ of wildlife* 야생 조수의 보호 / *~ of a historic spot* 사적(史蹟)의 보존 / *The ~ of forests is very important.* 산림 보호는 매우 중요하다. [L. *servo* keep]

conservation of energy, 《phys.》 the principle that the total amount of energy in the universe does not vary. 에너지의 불멸〔보존〕설.

con·serv·a·tism [kənsə́ːrvətìzəm] *n.* Ⓤ opposition to change; the principles of a conservative party. 보수주의〔기질〕; 보수당의 주의〔강령〕.

***con·serv·a·tive** [kənsə́ːrvətiv] *adj.* **1** opposed to change; preserving. 보수적인; 보수〔전통〕주의의; 보존성의〔하는〕(cf. *liberal, progressive*). ¶ *~ policy* 보수 정책 / *be ~ of historic sites* 사적(史蹟)을 보존하다 / *be ~ in one's habits* 습관을 좀처럼 바꾸지 않다. **2** 《often *C-*》 of the major political party in Great Britain or Canada. (영국·캐나다의) 보수당의. ¶ *the Conservative Party* 보수당. **3** 《*colloq.*》 moderate; careful; cautious. 온건한; 중용의; 조심스러운; 줄잡은. ¶ *~ estimates* 줄잡은 어림.
— *n.* Ⓒ **1** a conservative person. 보수적인 사람; 보수주의자. **2** 《often *C-*》 a member of the Conservative Party in Great Britain or Canada. (영국·캐나다의) 보수당원. **3** any substance that will prevent decay or harm. 방부제. ●**con·serv·a·tive·ly** [-li] *adv.* [→conserve, -ative]

con·ser·va·toire [kənsə̀ːrvətwάːr, ─ ─ ́] *n.* 《F.》 Ⓒ a public school for teaching music and the arts. (특히 프랑스의) 공립 예술 학교; 음악 학교.

con·ser·va·to·ry [kənsə́ːrvətɔ̀ːri / -təri] *n.* Ⓒ (*pl.* **-ries**) **1** a greenhouse or room covered with glass, for growing and showing flowers, plants, etc. 온실; 그린하우스. **2** 《U. S.》 a school of music. 음악 학교 (= conservatoire). — *adj.* preservative. 보존하는〔할 수 있는〕.

con·serve [kənsə́ːrv] *vt.* **1** keep (something) from change, loss or decay; keep (something) unchanged. (부패·손상·변질하지 않도록) …을 보존〔유지〕하다. ¶ *~ one's health* 건강을 유지하다 / *~ money for fu-*

ture use 장래 쓸 것에 대비해서 돈을 챙겨두다. **2** keep (fruit) with sugar. …을 설탕조림으로 해두다. ── [kánsəːrv, kənsə́ːrv / kɔ́nsəːrv] *n.* 《usu. *pl.*》 fruit preserved in sugar; jam. 사탕조림의 과일; 잼. [L. *servo* keep]

:con·sider [kənsídər] *vt.* **1** (P6,9,10,11,12) ⓐ think about (something) in order to understand it; think over. …을 고려하다; 숙고하다. ¶ ~ *his suggestion* 그의 제안을 잘 생각해 보다 / ~ *a problem before coming to a decision* 결정하기에 앞서 문제를 숙고하다 / ~ *a matter from different standpoints* 문제를 여러 다른 견지에서 생각해 보다. ⓑ allow for (something); take (someone) into account. …을 참작하다; 고려에 넣다. ¶ ~ *the feeling of others* 남의 마음을 헤아리다 / ~ *the poor and helpless* 가난하고 의지할 데 없는 사람들을 고려에 넣다 / *His health is good if you* ~ *his age.* 그의 나이를 고려한다면 그의 건강은 좋은 편이다. **2** (P7,11,21) think (someone) to be something; regard as. …을 (—하다고) 생각하다; …라고 보다. ¶ ~ *exercise a waste of energy* 운동을 정력의 낭비로 보다 / ~ *someone (to be) worthy of confidence* 아무를 신용할 만한 사람으로 생각하다 / *I* ~ *that he has been badly treated.* 나는 그가 구박을 받아왔다고 생각한다 / *I* ~ *Shakespeare the greatest dramatist.* 나는 셰익스피어를 최대의 극작가라고 생각한다. 語法 consider Shakespeare as... 와 같이 as를 씀은 잘못. [L. *considero*]

all things considered, taking everything into account. 모든 것을 고려에 넣으면[고려하여].

:con·sid·er·a·ble [kənsídərəbəl] *adj.* **1** worth thinking about; important. 고려할 만한; 중요한. ¶ *The matter is* ~. 이 문제는 고려해 봄직하다. **2** not a little; much. 상당한; 꽤 …한. ¶ *a* ~ *distance* 상당한 거리 / *a* ~ *sum of money* 상당한 금액 / *not completely but to a* ~ *extent* 완전히까지는 아니더라도 어지간한 정도까지 / *She gets a* ~ *income.* 그녀는 상당한 수입이 있다.

·con·sid·er·a·bly [kənsídərəbli] *adv.* a good deal; much. 상당히; 꽤 (많이). ¶ *He is* ~ *taller than Jim.* 그는 짐보다 키가 상당히 더 크다.

con·sid·er·ate [kənsídərit] *adj.* thoughtful of others and their feelings; careful. (남의 처지·기분을) 헤아려 주는; 이해[배려] 깊은; 사려 있는. ¶ *be* ~ *of* [*to*] *other people* 남을 헤아려[배려해] 주다 / *It is very* ~ *of her to have said so.* 그렇게 말을 했다니 그녀는 매우 인정이 많구나. ● **con·sid·er·ate·ly** [-li] *adv.*

:con·sid·er·a·tion [kənsìdəréiʃən] *n.* **1** Ⓤ the act of thinking in order to understand; careful thought. 고려; 고찰; 숙고. ¶ *after due* ~ 충분히 생각하고 나서 / *I will give your project full* ~. 자네의 계획을 잘 생각해 보겠네. **2** Ⓒ something thought of as a reason; a fact to be taken into account. 고려해야 할 일[사항]; 요건. ¶ *the first* ~ 첫째 요건 / *The most important* ~ *in this case is time.* 이 경우에 가장 중요한 것은 시간이다. **3** Ⓒ money or payment; a reward. 보수; 대가. ¶ *a* ~ *paid for the work* 그 일에 대해 지급되는 보수 / *without* ~ 무보수로. **4** Ⓤ thoughtful care for someone or of something. 헤아림; 동정심; 배려. ¶ *show* ~ *for someone* 아무에 대한 배려를 보이다 / *You have no* ~ *for my feelings.* 내 감정에 대한 헤아림이 없다. **5** Ⓤ importance. 중요함; 중대성. ¶ *It is of no* ~ *at all.* 그건 조금도 중요치 않다.

for a consideration, for a reward. 보수를 위해; 보수를 주면. ¶ *He did it for a* ~. 그는 보수를 바라고 그것을 했다 / *He will do anything for a* ~. 그는 돈이 생기는 일이라면 어떤 짓도 할 것이다.

in consideration of, **a**) taking into account; on account of. …을 고려하여; …한 이유로; …때문에. **b**) in return for. …의 보수[대가]로.

leave** something **out of consideration, make light of or neglect something. …을 도외시하다; 무시하다.

on [***under***] ***no consideration,*** not for any reason; in no case; never. 어떤 일이 있어도 [결코] …않다. ¶ *On no* ~ *could I agree.* 결코 찬성할 수 없다.

out of consideration for, taking into account; out of regard for. …을 고려해서.

take into consideration, take into account; consider; make allowance for. …을 고려에 넣다; 참작하다.

under consideration, being thought about; being discussed. 고려 중에. ¶ *a proposal under* ~ 고려 중인 제안 / *The plan is under* ~. 그 안(案)은 심의 중에 있다.

·con·sid·er·ing [kənsídəriŋ] *prep.* taking into account; in view of something. …을 고려하면; …에 비해서는. ¶ *Considering her age, she has done well.* 그녀는 나이에 비해서 잘 해냈다. ── *adv.* taking everything into account. 그런대로; 비교적. ¶ *That's not so bad,* ~. 그건 모든 점을 감안하면 그다지 나쁘지 않다.

con·sign [kənsáin] *vt.* **1** (P13) 《often *to*》 hand over; deliver. …을 넘겨[건네]주다. ¶ ~ *a body to the flames* [*watery grave*] 사체를 화장[수장]하다 / ~ *a fortress to the enemy* 요새를 적에게 내어주다 / *The man was consigned to jail.* 사나이는 교도소에 넘겨졌다. **2** (P13) put (someone or something) into another's care; entrust. …을 맡기다; 위탁하다. ¶ ~ *one's soul to God* 영혼을 하느님에게 맡기다; 죽다 / ~ *a child to a nurse* 아이를 보모에게 맡기다 / ~ *money to* [*in*] *a bank* 돈을 은행에 예금하다 / *She consigned her baby to her sister's care.* 그녀는 아기를 언니에게 맡겼다. **3** (P6,13) 《comm.》 send; deliver. (상품 따위를) 보내다; 발송[탁송]하다. ¶ ~ *goods by ship* 물건을 배로 보내다. [com-]

con·sign·ee [kὰnsainíː / kɔ̀n-] *n.* Ⓒ a person to whom goods are consigned. (판매품의) 수탁자(受託者); 하수인(荷受人) (opp. consignor).

con·sign·ment [kənsáinmənt] *n.* 《comm.》 **1** Ⓤ the act of consigning; the state of being consigned. 위탁 (판매); 탁송(託送). **2** Ⓒ goods sent to a trader for selling. 적송품(積送品); 위탁 판매품; 위탁 화물.

con·sign·or, -er [kənsáinər] *n.* Ⓒ a person who consigns goods to another. (판매품의) 위탁자; 적송인(積送人); 하주 (opp. consignee).

:con·sist [kənsíst] *vi.* (P3) **1** 《*of*》 be made up of; be formed. …으로 (구성)되다. ¶ *Water consists of hydrogen and oxygen.* 물은 수소와 산소로 돼 있다 / *The committee consists of seven members.* 위원회는 7명으로 구성돼 있다. **2** 《*in*》 be contained; lie in. (…에) 있다. ¶ *Happiness consists in contentment.* 행복은 만족하는 데에 있다. **3** 《*with*》 agree; be in harmony; be compatible. …와 일치〔조화〕하다; 양립하다. ¶ *Health consists with temperance only.* 건강은 절제와만 양립한다 / *Such deceit does not ~ with your reputation for honesty.* 그러한 사기는 정직하다는 자네 이름에 어울리지 않는 것일세. [L. *sisto* stop]

con·sist·ence [kənsístəns], **-en·cy** [-ənsi] *n.* Ⓤ **1** the state of firmness; stiffness. 견실함; 단단함. **2** harmony; agreement; accordance. 일치; 조화; 모순이 없음. ¶ *consistency of colors throughout the house* 집 전체의 색깔의 조화. **3** the degree of firmness, stiffness, thickness, or density. 견고도; 강도; 농도; 밀도. ¶ *the consistency of a liquid* 액체의 농도 / *Train-oil has much greater consistence than petrol.* 고래 기름은 석유보다 밀도가 훨씬 높다. **4** the quality of being consistent; keeping to the same principles. 일관성; 언행 일치; 절조(節操).

·con·sist·ent [kənsístənt] *adj.* 《*with*》 **1** continuing without change; agreeing with the same rules, etc. 변함없는; 양립하는. ¶ *opinions ~ with each other* 서로 모순되지 않는 의견 / *This is ~ with your principles.* 이건 네 주의와 양립한다. **2** in agreement; in accord with something. 일치하는; 일관된 (opp. contradictory). ¶ *This is not ~ with what you said yesterday.* 이것은 자네가 어제 말한 것과 일치되지 않는다 / *He is not ~ in his action.* 그는 행동에 일관성이 없다.

con·sist·ent·ly [kənsístəntli] *adv.* in a consistent manner. 시종 일관되게; 모순 없이; 견실하게.

con·sis·tor·y [kənsístəri] *n.* a court of church officials to decide church matters. 종교〔추기경〕 회의. ¶ *The Pope held a ~ of cardinals.* 교황은 추기경 회의를 열었다.

con·so·la·tion [kὰnsəléiʃən / kɔ̀n-] *n.* **1** Ⓤ comfort. 위안; 위로. ¶ *find ~ in religion* 종교에서 위안을 찾다 / *I tried to give him ~.* 나는 그를 위로하려고 애썼다. **2** Ⓒ a person or thing that consoles. 위안이 되는 것〔사람〕. [→solace]

con·sol·a·to·ry [kənsálətɔ̀ːri / -sɔ́lətəri] *adj.* comforting; consoling. 위로의; 위문의. ¶ *a ~ letter* 위문 편지.

·con·sole[1] [kənsóul] *vt.* (P6,13) comfort; cheer up. …을 위로〔위안〕하다; 위문하다. ¶ *~ one's friend in his sorrow* 슬픔에 젖은 친구를 위로하다 / *~ oneself by thinking…* …라 생각하고 자위하다. [→solace]

con·sole[2] [kánsoul / kɔ́n-] *n.* Ⓒ **1** the part of a pipe organ at which the organist sits, containing the keyboard, stops, and pedals. (파이프 오르간의) 연주대. **2** a radio or television cabinet. (라디오·TV 따위의) 캐비닛. **3** 《archit.》 a heavy, ornamental bracket. (건물의 소용돌이 꼴) 장식 까치발. **4** a table to be placed 〔designed to fit〕 against a wall. (까치발로) 벽에 고정시킨 테이블. [F.]

con·sol·i·date [kənsálədèit / -sɔ́l-] *vt.* (P6) **1** make (something) firm or strong; strengthen. …을 공고히 하다; 강화하다. ¶ *~ one's leadership* 지도력을 강화하다 / *~ one's position in society* 사회적 지위를 공고히 하다. **2** 《*into*》 unite; combine. (회사 따위)를 합병하다; 하나로 정리 통합하다. ¶ *~ colleges into a university* 단과 대학을 종합 대학으로 통합하다. **3** make (something) solid. …을 단단히 하다. — *vi.* (P1) **1** become solid or strong. 단단해지다; 강해지다. **2** unite; combine. 통합〔합병〕되다. [→solid]

con·sol·i·da·tion [kənsὰlədéiʃən / -sɔ̀l-] *n.* Ⓤ the act of consolidating; the state of being consolidated; combination. 강화(強化); 합병; 통합. ¶ *~ of public loans* 공채(公債)의 통합 / *~ of principles and beliefs* 주의 및 신념의 강화.

con·sols [kánsalz, kənsálz / kɔ́nsɔlz] *n. pl.* 《Brit.》 the different debts of the British government made into one single debt at the same rate of interest in 1751. 콘솔 공채(公債)《각종 공채를 정리해 만든 영구 공채》. [→consolidate]

con·som·mé [kὰnsəméi / kənsɔ́mei] *n.* Ⓤ 《F.》 a clear, strong soup made by boiling meat, and sometimes vegetables, in water. 콩소메《맑은 수프》.

con·so·nance [kánsənəns / kɔ́n-] *n.* Ⓤ **1** harmony; agreement; accordance. 조화; 일치. ¶ *in ~ with* …와 일치〔조화, 공명〕하여 / *act in ~ with custom* 습관대로 행동하다. **2** harmony of sounds; concordant. 음의 조화; 협화음(opp. dissonance). [↓]

·con·so·nant [kánsənənt / kɔ́n-] *n.* Ⓒ **1** a letter of the alphabet other than a, e, i, o, u. 자음 글자(cf. *vowel*). **2** a sound that such a letter represents. 자음. ¶ *a syllabic ~* 음절 주음적(主音的) 자음. — *adj.* **1** harmonious; in accordance to or with something. 조화하는; 일치하는. ¶ *behavior*

～ *with his character* 그의 성격에 어울리는 행동. **2** agreeing in sound. 협화음의. ● **con·so·nant·ly** [-li] *adv.* [L. *sono* sound]

con·sort [kánsɔ:rt / kɔ́n-] *n.* Ⓒ **1** a husband or wife, esp. of a king, queen or ruler. 배우자《특히 국왕·여왕의》. ¶ *the queen-consort* 왕비 / *the prince-consort* (군주로서의) 여왕의 부군. **2** a partner. 상대; 동아리; 동료. **3** a ship sailing with another. 요함(僚艦); 요선(僚船). — [kənsɔ́:rt] *vi.* (P2,3) **1** 《*with*》 associate with someone; go well. 사귀다; (한데) 어울리다. ¶ *He consorts with bad companions.* 그는 못된 친구들과 어울린다. **2** agree; accord. 일치하다; 조화하다. [com-, L. *sors* lot]

con·sor·ti·a [kənsɔ́:rʃiə] *n.* pl. of **consortium.**

con·sor·ti·um [kənsɔ́:rʃiəm, -tiəm] *n.* (*pl.* **-ti·a**) an agreement among bankers of several nations to give financial aid to another nation. (특히 개발 도상국에 대한) 국제 차관단. [L.]

con·spec·tus [kənspéktəs] *n.* Ⓒ a general view of a subject; an outline of a subject. 개관(概觀); 개요. [L. *specio* see]

·**con·spic·u·ous** [kənspíkjuəs] *adj.* **1** easily seen; clearly visible. 눈에 띄는; 뚜렷한; 분명한(opp. obscure). ¶ *a ～ place* 사람 눈에 띄는 장소 / *a ～ road sign* 눈에 띄는 도로 표지 / *several ～ errors* 몇 개의 분명한 잘못. **2** attracting attention; worthy of notice; remarkable. 남의 눈을 끄는; 두드러진; 현저한; 저명한. ¶ *a ～ statesman* 저명한 정치가 / *stand* 〔*look*〕 ～ 눈에 잘 띄다 / *cut a ～ figure* 이채를 띠다. [↑]

be conspicuous by** one's* 〔*its*〕 ***absence, call attention by not being where someone or something is expected. 없음으로써 도리어 주목을 끌다.

make** oneself **conspicuous, behave in a way that attracts attention. 일부러 눈에 띄게 행동하다.

con·spic·u·ous·ly [kənspíkjuəsli] *adv.* in a conspicuous manner; remarkably. 두드러지게; 현저하게; 빼어〔뛰어〕나게.

·**con·spir·a·cy** [kənspírəsi] *n.* (*pl.* **-cies**) **1** Ⓤ the act of conspiring. 공모(함); 음모를 꾀함. ¶ *in ～* 공모하여 / *be in one ～ to do* 일단이 되어 …하다; 서로 미리 짠 듯이 …하다. **2** Ⓒ a plot. 음모; 모의. ¶ *the ～ to murder the king* 국왕 시해(弑害)의 음모 / *form a ～ against someone's life* 아무의 살해를 모의하다. [→spirit]

conspiracy of silence [-ˊ-- - ˊ-] *n.* an agreement not to discuss something, esp. publicly; a determination to keep secret what ought to be made known. 묵살〔묵인〕하자는 약조〔결탁〕.

con·spir·a·tor [kənspírətər] *n.* Ⓒ a person who conspires; a plotter. 공모자; 음모자.

con·spir·a·to·ri·al [kənspìrətɔ́:riəl] *adj.* of, related to, or concerning a conspiracy. 공모의; 음모의.

con·spire [kənspáiər] *vi.* (P1,2,3,4) **1** 《*against, with*》 form or take part in an unlawful plot. 음모를 꾸미다; 공모하다; 작당하다. ¶ ～ *against someone's life* 아무의 암살을 꾀하다 / ～ *against the throne* 왕위 찬탈 음모를 꾸미다 / ～ *with someone* 아무와 공모하다. **2** (of events) act or work together toward one result; combine. (동일 목적을 위해) 같이 일〔행동〕하다; 협력하다. ¶ *Events seemed to be conspiring to bring about his ruin.* 겹치는 사건들은 그의 파멸을 가져오려는 것 같았다 / *All things conspired for a happy day.* 만사가 잘 되어 행복한 날을 맞이했다. — *vt.* (P6) plot. (못된 짓·범죄 따위)를 꾀하다; 꾸미다. ● **con·spir·er** [-spáiərər] *n.* [→spirit]

con·sta·ble [kánstəbəl / kʌ́n-] *n.* Ⓒ **1** a policeman. 경관; 순경. ¶ 《Brit.》 *the chief ～* 경찰서장. **2** a keeper of a royal fortress or castle. (옛날 성채나 성의) 관리 장관. 參考 const., Const., cons., Cons.로 생략함. [L. *comes stabuli* count of the stable]

outrun the constable, get into debt. 빚을 지다.

con·stab·u·lar·y [kənstǽbjəlèri / -ləri] *n.* Ⓒ (*pl.* **-lar·ies**) an organized body of policemen; state police. 경찰대(隊); 국가 경찰. ¶ *the local ～* 지방 경찰대. — *adj.* having to do with the police. 경찰(대)의; 경찰력의. ¶ *the ～ force* 경찰력.

con·stan·cy [kánstənsi / kɔ́n-] *n.* Ⓤ **1** the state or quality of being always the same; unchangeableness. 불변(성); 항구성. ¶ *have no ～ in love* 애정이 변하기 쉽다; 바람기가 있다. **2** faithfulness; honesty; firmness. 성실; 충실; 견고. [↓]

:**con·stant** [kánstənt / kɔ́n-] *adj.* **1** always the same; unchanging. 일정 불변의; 항구의(opp. variable). ¶ *The conditions in scientific experiments ought to be ～.* 과학 실험에서 조건은 늘 일정해야 한다. **2** ceaseless; continuous. 끊임없이 계속되는; 부단한. ¶ *a ～ anxiety* 끊임없는 걱정 / *～ danger* 끊임없는 위험 / *～ give-and-take* 언제나 공정한 주고받음. **3** faithful; loyal; firm. 성실〔충실〕한; (지조가) 굳은(opp. false). ¶ *a ～ wife* 정숙한 아내 / *He is ～ in friendship.* 그는 우정에 변함이 없다. **4** (of the mind, purpose) firm; determined. 마음이 흔들리지 않는; 확고한.

— *n.* Ⓒ 《math., phys.》 a number or quality that does not change. 정수(定數); 불변수; 정량(定量). [L. *sto* stand]

Con·stan·ti·no·ple [kɑ̀nstæntinóupəl / kɔ̀n-] *n.* old name (A.D. 330-1930) of Istanbul. 콘스탄티노플《Istanbul의 구칭》.

:**con·stant·ly** [kánstəntli / kɔ́n-] *adv.* **1** always; without change. 항상; 변함없이. **2** without stopping; continuously. 끊임없이. ¶ *A living language changes ～.* 산 언어

는 끊임없이 변화한다. **3** frequently. 자주; 빈번히. ¶ *I am ~ being asked to recommend books on Korean literature.* 나는 자주 한국 문학에 관한 책을 추천해 달라는 요청을 받고 있다. [→constant]

con·stel·la·tion [kɑ̀nstəléiʃən / kɔ̀n-] *n.* Ⓒ **1** 《astron.》 a group of stars, usu. with a name. 별자리; 성좌(星座). **2** a brilliant gathering. 기라성 같은 사람들의 일단〔모임〕. [L. *stella* star]

con·ster·na·tion [kɑ̀nstərnéiʃən / kɔ̀n-] *n.* Ⓤ dismay; surprise and fear. 깜짝 놀람; 경악. ¶ *in* 〔*with*〕 *~* 깜짝 놀라 / *to one's ~* 몹시 놀랍게도. [L. *sterno* lay flat]

con·sti·pate [kɑ́nstəpèit / kɔ́n-] *vt.* (P6) cause constipation in. 변비에 걸리게 하다. ¶ *be constipated* 변비에 걸리다. [L. *stipo* press]

con·sti·pa·tion [kɑ̀nstəpéiʃən / kɔ̀n-] *n.* Ⓤ a condition of the bowels when it is difficult to void waste matter. 변비. [↑]

con·stit·u·en·cy [kənstítʃuənsi] *n.* Ⓒ (*pl.* **-cies**) **1** 《*collectively*》 all the voters in a district. (의원 선거구의) 유권자들; 선거민. **2** an electoral district. 선거구. **3** 《*collectively*》 a group of supporters, customers, etc. 지지자들; 고객층; 구독자층. ¶ *The paper has a large ~.* 그 신문은 많은 구독자를 가지고 있다. [↓]

con·stit·u·ent [kənstítʃuənt] *adj.* **1** making up a whole; that composes. 구성하는; 성분을 이루는. ¶ *the ~ parts of an engine* 엔진의 구성 부품. **2** having a right to vote. 선거〔투표〕권이 있는. **3** having power to make or change a constitution. 헌법 제정〔개정〕권이 있는. ¶ *a ~ assembly* 헌법 제정〔개정〕 회의. — *n.* Ⓒ **1** a necessary part; a component; an element. 구성물; 성분; 요소. ¶ *Sugar is the main ~ of candy.* 설탕은 캔디의 주요 성분이다. **2** a member of a constituency; a voter. 선거인; 투표자. ¶ *my constituents* 나의 선거구민. [↓]

***con·sti·tute** [kɑ́nstətjùːt / kɔ́n-] *vt.* **1** (P6) make up (something); form; compose. …을 구성하다; 형성하다. ¶ *mortar constituted of lime and sand* 석회와 모래로 된 모르타르 / *Seven days ~ a week.* 7일이 한 주일을 이룬다 / *The parts ~ the whole.* 부분이 전체를 구성한다. **2** (P6,19) appoint; elect. …를 (…으로) 선정〔선임〕하다; 임명하다. ¶ *be constituted representative of* …의 대표자로 선정되다 / *They constituted him manager.* 그들은 그를 지배인으로 임명했다. **3** (P6) set up; establish. …을 제정하다; 설립하다. ¶ *~ an acting committee* 임시 위원회를 설치하다. [L. *statuo* set up]

***constitute oneself* (*a judge*),** become (a judge) for oneself. 스스로 (심판관)이 되다; 심판역을 자청하다.

the constituted authorities, the officials. 관헌(官憲).

:**con·sti·tu·tion** [kɑ̀nstətjúːʃən / kɔ̀n-] *n.* **1** Ⓒ a systematic description of the fundamental laws and principles of a government. 헌법. ¶ *a written* 〔*an unwritten*〕 *~* 성문〔불문〕 헌법 / *establish a ~* 헌법을 제정하다. **2** Ⓒ ⓐ the physical structure and condition of a human body. 체격; 체질. ¶ *by ~* 타고난 체질로서; 체질상 / *have a ~ like iron* =*have an iron ~* 무쇠처럼 단단한 체격을 갖고 있다 / *have a good* 〔*poor*〕 *~* 체질이 건전〔빈약, 허약〕하다. ⓑ characteristics. 소질; 성질; 성향. ¶ *a nervous ~* 신경질. **3** Ⓤ the way in which a thing is composed; nature; make-up. 구성; 구조; 조직; 본질. ¶ *the physical ~ of the moon* 달의 물리적 구조. **4** Ⓤ establishment; appointment. 설립; 임명. **5** the way in which a country or society is organized; a system of government. 국가·사회의 조직 형태; 정체. ¶ *a republican ~* 공화 정체. **6** 《hist.》 an ordinance; a decree. 법령(法令). **7** 《*the C-*》 the constitution of the United States. 미합중국 헌법.

***con·sti·tu·tion·al** [kɑ̀nstətjúːʃənəl / kɔ̀n-] *adj.* **1** of or caused by one's constitution. 타고난; 체질의. ¶ *a ~ disease* 체질성 질환 / *a ~ peculiarity* 체질적 특징; 이상 체질. **2** of or according to the constitution of a nation, a state or a group. 헌법의; 입헌적. ¶ *a ~ amendment* 헌법 개정 / *~ government* 입헌 정체〔정치〕 / *a ~ monarchy* 입헌 군주국. **3** good for one's health. 몸〔건강〕에 좋은. ¶ *a ~ walk* 건강에 좋은 산책. — *n.* Ⓒ a walk or other exercise taken for one's health. 건강을 위한 산책〔운동〕. ¶ *He takes a ~ every morning.* 그는 매일 아침 건강을 위한 운동을 한다.

con·sti·tu·tion·al·ism [kɑ̀nstətjúːʃənəlìzəm / kɔ̀n-] *n.* Ⓤ constitutional government; constitutional rules. 입헌제; 입헌주의.

con·sti·tu·tion·al·ist [kɑ̀nstətjúːʃənəlist / kɔ̀n-] *n.* Ⓒ **1** a supporter of constitutional rules. 입헌주의자(者); 호헌론자(護憲論者). **2** a person who makes a special study of constitutions. 헌법 학자.

con·sti·tu·tion·al·i·ty [kɑ̀nstətjùːʃənǽləti / kɔ̀n-] *n.* being in accordance with the constitution of a state. 입헌적임; 합헌성; 합법성.

con·sti·tu·tion·al·ize [kɑ̀nstətjúːʃənəlàiz / kɔ̀n-] *vt., vi.* (P6; 1) **1** make constitutional. 입헌적으로〔입헌 제도로〕 하다. **2** take a constitutional. 건강을 위한 운동을 하다.

con·sti·tu·tion·al·ly [kɑ̀nstətjúːʃənəli / kɔ̀n-] *adv.* **1** in or by physical structure; by nature. 소질상; 체격적으로; 성격상. ¶ *He is ~ frail.* 그는 체질상 약하다. **2** according to a constitution of a nation, etc. 헌법적으로 보아; 헌법상.

con·strain [kənstréin] *vt.* (P6,20) **1** force or compel. (아무)에게 강제하다; 억지로 …시키다. ¶ *He constrained me to go.* 그는 나를 역

지로 가게 했다 / *His conscience constrained him to admit the mistake.* 양심의 가책으로 그는 잘못을 인정했다. **2** 《usu. in *passive*》 be forced to do (something). 어쩔 수 없이 … 하다. ¶ *be constrained to agree* 할 수 없이 찬성하다 / *I feel constrained to go.* 나는 가야만 할 것같은 마음이 든다. **3** confine forcibly; imprison. 속박하다; 구속하다. [L. *stringo* tie]

be constrained to, be forced to. 부득이 〔하는 수 없이〕 …하다.

constrain oneself, control oneself. 자제(自制)하다.

con·strained [kənstréind] *adj.* **1** forced; compelled. 강제적인; 강제된. ¶ ~ *confession* 강요된 자백. **2** uneasy; stiff; unnatural. 불안한; 거북한; 어색한; 부자연스런. ¶ *a* ~ *smile* 억지 웃음 / *a* ~ *manner* 어색한 태도.

con·strain·ed·ly [kənstréinidli] *adv.* in a constrained manner. 강제적으로; 거북하게; 부자연스럽게.

con·straint [kənstréint] *n.* Ⓤ **1** the act of compelling; the state of being compelled; force. 강제; 속박; 구속. ¶ *by* ~ 무리하게; 억지로 / *under* 〔*in*〕 ~ 강제되어; 어쩔 수 없이 / *smile with* ~ 억지웃음을 웃다. **2** the act of controlling or the state of being controlled one's natural feelings. (감정의) 억제; 거북함; 어려워함; 조심스러움. ¶ *with* ~ 스스러워; 어려워서 / *feel* ~ 어려워하다.

con·strict [kənstríkt] *vt.* (P6) pull (things) together; contract; press together. …을 죄다; 긴축하다; 압축하다; 수축시키다. ¶ *a constricted outlook* 좁은 전망 / ~ *the throat* 목을 죄다 / ~ *a vein* 혈관을 수축시키다 / *be constricted in the middle* 한가운데가 잘록해지다. [→constrain]

con·stric·tion [kənstríkʃən] *n.* **1** Ⓤ the act of pulling together; contraction; compression. 긴축; 압축. **2** Ⓤ the feeling of tightness. 죄어드는 느낌; (꼭 끼이는) 거북함. **3** Ⓒ a constricted part. 압축된〔잘록한〕 부분.

con·stric·tive [kənstríktiv] *adj.* tending to constrict. 죄는; 수축하는; 수축성의; 긴축적인.

con·stric·tor [kənstríktər] *n.* Ⓒ **1** something that constricts. 긴축시키는 것; 압축기. **2** 《anat.》 a muscle that constricts a part of the body. 괄약근(括約筋). **3** a snake that kills by coiling around its prey. (먹이를 칭칭 감아 죽이는) 뱀.

:con·struct [kənstrʌ́kt] *vt.* (P6) **1** build; make; put or fit (things) together. …을 건조〔건설〕하다; 만들다; 짓다; 세우다(opp. destroy). ¶ ~ *a house* 집을 짓다 / ~ *a bridge* 다리를 놓다 / *be constructed of* …로 되어 있다. **2** draw (something) so as to fulfil given conditions. …을 작도(作圖)하다. ¶ ~ *a triangle* 삼각형을 그리다. **3** arrange or form (something) in one's mind; plan out. …을 꾸미다; 안출(案出)하다; (글·이론 따위)를 구성하다. ¶ ~ *a theory* 이론을 세우다 / ~ *the plot of a novel* 소설의 줄거리를 구상하다. [L. *struo* pile]

:con·struc·tion [kənstrʌ́kʃən] *n.* **1** Ⓤ the act of building or constructing. 건설; 건조(建造). ¶ *be under* 〔*in course of*〕 ~ 공사 중이다. **2** Ⓤ the way in which a thing is constructed. 구조(법). ¶ *a building of solid and ingenious* ~ 튼튼하고도 교묘한 구조의 건물. **3** Ⓒ something constructed; a building. 건(조)물; 구축〔영조〕물. ¶ *a beautiful* ~ 아름다운 건조물. **4** Ⓒ a meaning; an explanation. 해석. ¶ *put a wrong* ~ *on* 〔*upon*〕 …을 오해하다 / *She puts a bad* ~ *upon everything I say or do.* 그녀는 나의 언행(言行) 모두를 나쁜 뜻으로 해석한다. **5** Ⓒ 《gram.》 the arrangement, connection, or relation of words in a sentence. 구문(構文). ¶ *an absolute principal* ~ 독립 분사 구문.

put a false construction on, garble. …을 곡해하다; 곱새기다.

put a good construction upon, take it in a favorable sense. …을 선의로 해석하다.

con·struc·tion·al [kənstrʌ́kʃənəl] *adj.* of construction; structural. 건설상의; 구조상의.

con·struc·tive [kənstrʌ́ktiv] *adj.* **1** helping to construct; building up; helpful. 건설적인 (opp. destructive). ¶ *a* ~ *suggestion* 건설적인 제안 / ~ *criticism* 건설적인 비평. **2** of construction; structural. 구조(상)의; 구조적인. ¶ *a* ~ *defect* 구조상의 결점. **3** not directly expressed; suggested. 해석에 의한; 추정의〔추정에 의한〕. ¶ ~ *permission* (허가된 것으로 추정된) 추정상의 허가. ● **con·struc·tive·ly** [-li] *adv.*

con·struc·tor [kənstrʌ́ktər] *n.* Ⓒ a person who constructs; a builder. 건설자; 건조자; 건설 청부업자.

con·strue [kənstrú:] *vt.* **1** (P6,13) 《*as*》 explain the meaning of (actions, etc.); expound; interpret. (언동 따위)를 해석하다. ¶ *His speech was construed as an attack on the government.* 그의 연설은 정부에 대한 공격으로 받아들여졌다. **2** (P6) translate. …을 번역하다. **3** (P6) 《gram.》 show the grammatical construction and meaning. …을 문법적으로 분석하다. **4** 《gram.》 combine (words) grammatically. (말)을 문법적으로 짜맞추다. —*vi.* (P1) be capable of being analyzed. (문법적으로) 분석되다; 해석되다. ¶ *This sentence does not* ~. 이 문장은 문법적으로 분석할 수 없다. [→construct]

con·sub·stan·tial [kànsəbstǽnʃəl / kɔ̀n-] *adj.* of one substance. 동질(同質)의; 동체(同體)의. [com-]

con·sue·tude [kánswitjù:d / kɔ́n-] *n.* custom; habit; social usage. 관습; 관행. [F.]

con·sul [kánsəl / kɔ́n-] *n.* Ⓒ **1** a government officer who lives in a foreign city to help his country's people and their business. 영사. ¶ *an acting ~* 대리 영사 / *a ~ general* 총영사. **2** 《Rom. hist.》 either of the two highest officials of the ancient Roman Republic. (옛 로마의) 집정관. [L.]

con·su·lar [kánsələr / kɔ́nsjul-] *adj.* of a consul. 영사의; 집정관의. ¶ *be in the ~ service* 영사로 근무하다.

con·su·late [kánsəlit / kɔ́nsju-] *n.* **1** Ⓤ a consul's position. 영사직(職). **2** Ⓒ an official residence or office of a consul. 영사관.

con·sul·ship [kánsəlʃip / kɔ́n-] *n.* Ⓤ **1** a consul's position. 영사직(職). **2** a consul's term of office. 영사의 임기.

·**con·sult** [kənsʌ́lt] *vt.* (P6) **1** seek information or advice from (someone). …에게 의견을 묻다; 진찰을 받다. ¶ *~ a doctor* 의사의 진찰을 받다 / *~ a specialist* 전문가의 의견을 청하다 / *You can ~ persons, dictionaries, or maps to find out what you wish to know.* 알고자 하는 바를 알아내기 위해 남들과 상의하거나 사전을 찾거나 지도를 볼 수 있다. **2** consider; have regard to. …을 고려하다; 염두에 두다; 참작하다. ¶ *~ one's own convenience* 자기의 형편만 생각하다 / *~ someone's pleasure* 아무의 형편(의향)을 묻다. **3** refer to. …을 조사(참고)하다; 보다. ¶ *~ a dictionary* 사전을 보다 / *~ a note* 주(註)를 참고로 하다 / *Consult your watch.* 네 시계를 봐라. — *vi.* (P3) 《*with, about*》 exchange ideas with someone; take counsel. 서로 이야기하다; 상의(협의)하다. ¶ *~ with someone about the matter* 그 일을 아무와 상의하다 / *We consulted as to what should be done.* 우리는 어떻게 해야 할지 협의했다. [L. *consulto*]

consult with one's pillow, take a night for reflection. 하룻밤 천천히 생각하다.

con·sult·ant [kənsʌ́ltənt] *n.* Ⓒ **1** a person who consults another. 의논(협의) 상대. **2** an expert who gives professional or technical advice (as a consulting physician). 고문; 컨설턴트; 자문 의사.

con·sul·ta·tion [kànsəltéiʃən / kɔ̀n-] *n.* **1** Ⓤ the act of consulting. 상담; 협의; 진찰. ¶ *call someone into ~* 아무를 불러 상담하다 / *be in ~* 현재 상담(협의)중이다. **2** Ⓒ a meeting for consulting. (전문가의) 회의; 심의(협의)회.

con·sul·ta·tive [kənsʌ́ltətiv] *adj.* having to do with consultation. 상담(협의)의; 자문의.

con·sult·ing [kənsʌ́ltiŋ] *adj.* **1** that consults. 상담하는; 진찰의. **2** employed in giving professional advice. 상담역의; 고문(자문)의. ¶ *a ~ lawyer (engineer)* 고문 변호사(기사) / *a ~ room* 진찰실.

consulting physician [–´– –´–] *n.* a doctor who is called in by colleagues or applied to by patients for advice in special cases. 자문(입회) 의사《왕진·투약하지 않는》.

·**con·sume** [kənsú:m] *vt.* (P6) **1** use up (something) completely; waste away. …을 다 써버리다; 소비(소모)하다; 낭비하다. ¶ *~ much of his time in studying* 공부에 대부분의 시간을 소비하다 / *~ a roll of film* 필름 한 통을 다 쓰다. **2** eat or drink up. …을 다 먹어(마셔) 없애다. ¶ *~ several kegs of beer* 맥주 몇 통을 다 마셔버리다. **3** destroy; burn up. …을 다 태워 없애다. ¶ *The flames consumed the whole building.* 불길로 건물은 전소(全燒)됐다. **4** 《usu. in *passive*》 get deeply into a person's mind. (아무의) 마음속에 파고 들다; 몰두케 하다. ¶ *be consumed with envy* 질투로 속을 태우다 / *He is consumed with zeal for dancing.* 그는 댄스 열기에 빠져 있다 / *He was consumed with rage.* 그는 불같이 노했다. — *vi.* (P2A, 2B) 《*away*》 spend; waste away; become weak. 소비(소모)되다; 다하다; 여위다; 쇠약해지다. ¶ *~ away with grief* 슬픔으로 초췌해지다. [L. *sumo* take]

be consumed by a fire, be reduced to ashes. 잿더미가 되다.

·**con·sum·er** [kənsú:mər] *n.* Ⓒ a person who consumes. 소비(수요)자(opp. producer). ¶ *the consumer's price* 소비자 가격.

consumer(s') goods [–´– ´] *n.* 《econ.》 goods, such as food and clothing, which are consumed by use. 소비재(財)(opp. capital goods, producer(s') goods).

con·sum·mate [kánsəmèit / kɔ́n-] *vt.* (P6) complete; finish; make (something) perfect, especially marriage by sexual intercourse. …을 완성하다; 완료하다; 신방에 들어 (결혼을) 완성하다. ¶ *~ a marriage* 신랑 신부가 잠자리에 들다. — [kənsʌ́mət] *adj.* complete; perfect. 완전한; 더없는. ¶ *~ virtue* 완전 무결한 덕 / *a ~ master of the violin* 바이올린 최고의 명수 / *a ~ ass* 더없는 바보 / *The pilot showed ~ skill.* 비행기 조종사는 기술의 극치를 보였다. [L. *summus* highest]

con·sum·ma·tion [kànsəméiʃən / kɔ̀n-] *n.* Ⓤ **1** the act of consummating; the state of being consummated; completion, especially of marriage. 완성; 성취; 결혼의 완성. ¶ *the ~ of marriage.* **2** an ultimate end or goal. 완결; 종결. ¶ *the ~ of the world* 세상의 종말.

·**con·sump·tion** [kənsʌ́mpʃən] *n.* Ⓤ **1** the act of consuming; the state of being consumed; use. 소비; 소모; 멸실(滅失)(opp. production). ¶ *~ duty (tax)* 소비세 / *have a tendency to ~* 소비벽(癖)이 있다. **2** the amount used up. 소비액(량). ¶ *have a high ~ of* …의 소비량(액)이 많다 / *The ~ of coal in that factory is six tons a day.* 그 공장에서의 석탄 소비량은 하루 6톤이다. **3** a disease of the lungs; tuberculosis. 소모성 질환; 폐결핵. ¶ *catch ~* 폐병에 걸리다. [→ consume]

con·sump·tive [kənsʌ́mptiv] *adj.* **1** apt to consume; wasteful; destructive. 소비의; 소모성의; 파괴적인. ¶ *~ fires* 모든 것을 소진

(燒盡)시키는 화재 / *a ~ war* 소모전. **2** having or likely to have tuberculosis of the lungs. 폐병질의; 폐결핵성의. ¶ *a ~ patient* 폐결핵성 환자. — *n.* Ⓒ a person who has tuberculosis of the lungs. 폐결핵 환자. ● **con·sump·tive·ly** [-li] *adv.* [↑]

:con·tact [kántækt / kɔ́n-] *n.* **1** Ⓤ the act of touching; touch. 접촉. ¶ *a point of ~* 접(촉)점 / *be in* 〔*out of*〕 *~ with someone* 아무와 접촉하고 있(지 않)다; 아무와 가까이 하고 있(지 않)다 / *bring A into ~ with B,* A를 B에 접촉시키다 / *break ~* 접촉을 끊다. **2** Ⓒ 《U.S.》 close association; connection; communication. 친밀한 접촉; 교제; 연락. ¶ *a man of many contacts* 교제가 넓은 사람 / *establish one's ~ with* …와 접촉하다〔연락을 갖다〕 / *be brought into ~ with other minds* 다른 사람들과 접촉하게 되다 / *A club is a good place to make good contacts.* 클럽은 친교를 맺기에 좋은 곳이다. **3** 《electr.》 Ⓒ connection between two conductors of electricity. 접촉; 혼선. ¶ *make* 〔*break*〕 *~* 전류를 통하다〔끊다〕. **4** Ⓒ 《med.》 a person likely to carry contagion through contact with an infected person. 보균 용의자.

come into contact with, **a**) touch. …와 접(촉)하다. **b**) come across. …와 만나다. ¶ *He came into ~ with many interesting people in his travels.* 그는 여행 중 재미있는 사람들을 많이 만났다.

— *adj.* 《aeron.》 within sight of the ground. 눈으로 보는; 목시(目視) 비행의. ¶ *~ flight* 〔*flying*〕 시각 비행《비행사가 지상을 항상 볼 수 있는 비행》.

— [kántækt, kəntǽkt / kɔ́ntækt] *vt., vi.* (P6,13; 1,3) 《Brit.》 《*colloq.*》 get in touch with (someone). 접촉시키다〔하다〕; 교제시키다〔하다〕. [L. *tango* touch]

contact lens [∠-∠] *n.* a thin plastic or glass lens resting directly on the eyeball to correct defects in vision. 콘택트 렌즈.

con·ta·gion [kəntéidʒən] *n.* **1** Ⓤ the spreading of disease to others by contact. (접촉) 전염; 감염. ¶ *spread by ~* 접촉 전염으로 퍼지다(cf. *infection*). **2** Ⓒ a disease spread in this way. 접촉 전염병. **3** ⒸⓊ an evil influence; a moral rottenness. 악영향; 악풍; 타락. [→contact]

con·ta·gious [kəntéidʒəs] *adj.* **1** spreading by contact. (접촉) 전염의. ¶ *a ~ disease* 접촉 전염병 / *the ~ ward* 전염 병동 / *Scarlet fever is ~.* 성홍열은 전염된다. **2** 《*fig.*》 easily spreading from one person to another. 퍼지기 쉬운; 옮기〔전염하기〕 쉬운. ¶ *Laughter* 〔*Yawning*〕 *is ~.* 웃음〔하품〕은 잘 옮는다. [↑]

:con·tain [kəntéin] *vt.* (P6) **1** ⓐ have or hold (something) within itself; have (something) as a part. …을 넣다; (속에) 포함하다; 함유하다. ¶ *The box contains thirty apples.* 상자에 사과 30개가 들어있다 / *This beverage does not ~ alcohol.* 이 음료엔 알코올이 함유돼 있지 않다 / *This newspaper contains an account of the accident.* 이 신문에 그 사고의 기사가 실려 있다. ⓑ be capable of holding. 넣을〔들어갈〕 수 있다; (얼마가) 들어가다 ¶ *The bottle contains two ounces of liquid.* 이 병엔 2온스의 물이 들어간다 / *This room won't ~ all of them.* 이 방엔 모두가 다 들어갈 수 없다. **2** be equal to (something). …와 같다. ¶ *A pound contains 16 ounces.* 1파운드는 16온스와 같다. **3** keep (oneself or one's feelings) under control; hold back; prevent. (자신·감정)을 억제하다〔누르다〕; 참다. ¶ *~ oneself* 자제하다 / *I could not ~ myself for joy.* 기뻐 견딜 수가 없었다 / *She could hardly ~ herself when the boy kicked her dog.* 그 아이가 그녀의 개를 걷어차는 것을 보고 그녀는 참을 수가 없었다. **4** 《math.》 be divisible by (a figure). (수가) 우수리없이 나뉘어 떨어지다. ¶ *Ten contains five.* 10은 5로 나뉜다. **5** 《geom.》 enclose (a figure or angle). (변이 각을) 끼고 있다; (도형을) 둘러싸다. [L. *teneo* hold]

con·tain·er [kəntéinər] *n.* Ⓒ anything for containing something, such as a box or a can. 그릇; 용기(容器). ¶ *an ice-cream in a paper ~* 종이 용기에 담은 아이스크림.

con·tain·ment [kəntéinmənt] *n.* Ⓤ the act of containing; the policy of restricting the influence of hostile nation. 억제; 속박; 봉쇄 (정책). ¶ *~ policy* 봉쇄 정책.

con·tam·i·nate [kəntǽmənèit] *vt.* (P6) **1** make (something) bad or dirty by contact, etc. (접촉 따위로) …을 더럽히다; 불결〔불순〕하게 하다; 오염하다(cf. *decontaminate*). ¶ *~ a well with sewage* 하수로 우물을 오염시키다 / *Flies ~ food.* 파리는 음식을 오염시킨다. **2** have a bad effect on (someone). …를 악에 물들게 하다. ¶ *~ someone's morals by evil example* 못된 모범을 보여 아무의 도덕심을 오염시키다. ● **con·tam·i·na·tor** [-ər] *n.* [→contact]

con·tam·i·na·tion [kəntæ̀mənéiʃən] *n.* **1** Ⓤ the act of contaminating; the state of being contaminated. 오염(시킴); 불결. **2** Ⓒ a thing that contaminates. 오염〔타락〕시키는 것; 해독을 끼치는 것. **3** a process of combining two words into one form. 혼성(混成); 혼성어. 參考 예를 들면 motel = *mo*tor+*hotel*; smog=*sm*oke+*fog* 따위.

conte [kɔ̃:*nt*] *n.* 《F.》 a short story (of adventure). 콩트; 단편(短篇) 소설.

con·temn [kəntém] *vt.* 《*lit.*》 (P6) have no respect for (someone); look down on; despise; scorn. …을 경멸〔모멸〕하다; 깔보다. [L. *temno* despise]

·con·tem·plate [kántəmplèit, kɔ́ntem-] *vt.* (P6,8,9) **1** look at (something) for a long time; study carefully. …을 숙시(熟視)하다; 눈여겨보다; 면밀히 관찰하다. ¶ *~ the stars* 별을 관찰하다. **2** examine in the mind; think deeply of; meditate; consider. 깊이 생각하다; 명상하다; 숙고하다. ¶ *~ a* *problem* 문제를 숙고하다. **3** look forward to (something); expect. …을 기대〔예상〕하다. ¶ *I don't ~ any opposition from him.* 그의 반대는 예상하지 않는다. **4** have (something) in mind; intend. …을 의도하다; …하려고 생각하다. ¶ *I ~ giving up my work here next year.* 내년엔 여기 일을 그만 둘 작정이다. [→temple]

con·tem·pla·tion [kàntəmpléiʃən / kɔ̀n-tem-] *n.* Ⓤ **1** the act of contemplating. 응시(凝視); 숙시(熟視). ¶ *the ~ of mountain scenery* 산 경치를 눈여겨 봄 / *He buried himself in the ~ of his treasure.* 넋을 잃고 자신의 보물을 바라보고 있었다. **2** deep thought. 깊은 생각; 침사(沈思); 명상; 숙고. ¶ *religious ~* 종교적인 묵상(默想) / *lost* 〔*sunk*〕 *in ~* 명상에 잠기어. **3** expectation. 기대; 예상. **4** intention. 의도; 기도; 계획. ¶ *an enterprise under ~* 계획 중인 사업 / *have something in ~* 어떤 일을 계획하고 있다.

con·tem·pla·tive [kəntémplətiv, kɑ́ntəmplèitiv / kɔ́ntemplèi-] *adj.* thoughtful; deep in thought. 명상의; 깊이 생각하는. ¶ *be ~ of* …을 숙고〔응시〕하고 있다.

con·tem·po·ra·ne·ous [kəntèmpəréiniəs] *adj.* existing or happening at the same time; at the same period, usu. in the past. 동시 존재〔발생〕의; 동시대의. ¶ *The opening of the Panama Canal was ~ with World War I.* 파나마 운하의 개통은 1차 대전과 동시기에 있었다. [↓]

·con·tem·po·rar·y [kəntémpərèri / -pərəri] *adj.* **1** of or belonging to the present time; of the day. 현대의; 당대의. ¶ *~ literature* 현대 문학 / *a lecture on the ~ novel* 현대 소설에 대한 강연. **2** of the same age or date; living or happening at the same time; belonging to the same period of time. …와 동시대〔같은 시기〕의; 같은 시기에 있은〔일어난, 속하는〕.

— *n.* Ⓒ (*pl.* **-rar·ies**) **1** a person who belongs to the same period of time. 동시대〔동시기〕의 사람. ¶ *our contemporaries* 당대〔현대〕의 사람들 / *Darwin and Lincoln were contemporaries.* 다윈과 링컨은 동시대의 사람이었다 / *his contemporaries at college* 그의 대학 동기생. **2** a person, a newspaper, etc. of the same age or date. 같은 나이〔연배〕의 사람; 동시대 발행의 다른 신문. ¶ *our ~* 동업지(紙). [com-, →temporary]

·con·tempt [kəntémpt] *n.* ⓊⒸ **1** the act of despising; the state of being despised; scorn; disregard. 멸시; 경멸; 모욕; 치욕. ¶ *in ~ of a rule* 규칙을 무시하고 / *have* 〔*feel*〕 *a ~ for…* …을 경멸하다 / *show ~* 경멸을 나타내다 / *have an air of ~* 경멸하는 태도를 취하다 / *We feel ~ for a coward.* 우리는 비겁한 자를 경멸한다 / *He deserved the ~ of all men.* 그는 모두에게 경멸당할 만했다 / *He went into the cave in ~ of danger.* 그는 위험을 무시하고 동굴로 들어갔다 / *Familiarity breeds ~.* 친할수록 예의를 지켜라. **2** 《law》 open disobedience to the order of a court. 법정 모욕죄. ¶ *~ of court.* [→contemn]

bring someone into contempt, put shame or dishonor upon someone. …에게 치욕을 주다〔가져다 주다〕. ¶ *His foolish conduct will bring him into ~.* 바보스런 행동은 그에게 치욕을 안겨 줄 것이다.

fall into contempt, be abashed. 창피를〔모멸을〕 당하다.

have 〔***hold***〕 ***someone in contempt,*** look down on someone; despise someone. …을 경멸〔멸시〕하다.

con·tempt·i·ble [kəntémptəbəl] *adj.* deserving contempt or scorn. 경멸할 (만한); 비열한. ¶ *~ conduct* 경멸할 행동 / *a ~ man* 비열한 사람.

con·temp·tu·ous [kəntémptʃuəs] *adj.* showing or expressing contempt; scornful. (사람·태도가) 경멸을 나타내는; 모욕하는; 깔보는. ¶ *a ~ way of speaking* 사뭇 경멸하는 말투. ● **con·temp·tu·ous·ly** [-li] *adv.* **con·temp·tu·ous·ness** [-nis] *n.*

·con·tend [kəntend] *vi.* **1** (P3) 《*against, with, for*》 fight; struggle; take part in a contest. 다투다; 싸우다; 겨루다. ¶ *~ with someone for first prize* 아무와 1등상을 다투다 / *~ with the enemy for control of the port* 항구의 지배권을 둘러싸고 적과 싸우다 / *~ with* 〔*against*〕 *difficulties* 어려움과 싸우다 / *Our troops contended with the enemy for the hill.* 아군은 그 고지를 차지하기 위해 적과 싸웠다. **2** (P1,3) 《*with*》 argue; dispute; discuss. 논쟁〔시비〕하다; 격론을 주고 받다. ¶ *He is fond of contending about everything.* 그는 모든 일에 논쟁을 좋아한다.

— *vt.* (P11) maintain; assert. …을 강하게 주장하다. ¶ *I ~ that he is not guilty.* 나는 그가 무죄임을 주장한다. [com-, L. *tendo* stretch]

have much to contend with, have many difficulties to strive with. 이겨내야 할 많은 어려움이 있다.

:con·tent[1] [kɑ́ntent / kɔ́n-] *n.* **1** Ⓒ 《*usu. pl.*》 ⓐ what is contained in something. 내용물; 속에 든 것. ¶ *the contents of a bag* 〔*bottle*〕 가방〔병〕 속의 내용물. ⓑ what is written in a book. (책 따위의) 내용; 기사; 차례. ¶ *the contents of a book* 책의 내용 / *a table of contents* 목차(目次). **2** Ⓤ the facts and ideas stated; the real meaning. 취지; 요지; 의미; 내용. ¶ *the ~ of a speech* 연설의 취지 / *a book with little ~* 내용이 빈약한 책 / *a clever play that lacks ~* 훌륭하나 내용이 없는 연극. **3** ⒸⓊ the power of containing; capacity; the amount contained; volume. 수용력; 용적; 용량(容量); 함유량. 參考 단수형은 일반적으로 추상적인 뜻에, 복수형은 구체적인 의미에 쓰임. ¶ *the dust ~ of air* 공기 속의 먼지 함유량. [→contain]

:con·tent[2] [kəntént] *vt.* **1** (P6,13) satisfy; please. …에게 만족을 주다; …을 만족시키다. ¶ *Nothing will ever ~ them.* 아무것도 그들을

만족시키지 못할 게다 / *Will it ~ you if I let you have some candy tomorrow?* 내일 캔디 좀 준다면 너는 만족하겠느냐. **2** 《*reflexively*》 ⓐ be satisfied. 만족하다. ¶ *~ oneself with dry bread* 마른 빵에 만족하다. ⓑ do nothing more than. …하기만 하다; …로 만족하다. ¶ *~ oneself with looking on* 구경하는 것만으로 만족하다.

— *adj.* 《usu. not placed before *n.*》 satisfied; pleased; willing; ready. 만족해 있는; 기뻐하는. ¶ *He was never ~ with his success.* 그는 자기의 성공에 결코 만족해하지 않았다 / *He is ~ with what he has.* 그는 (얼마 안 되지만) 그가 갖고 있는 것에 만족하고 있다.

— *n.* Ⓤ contentment; satisfaction. 만족(감). ¶ *in (perfect) ~* (아주) 만족하게 / *live in peace and ~* 평화롭고 풍족하게 지내다. [↑]

to one's heart's content, *as much as one wants.* 마음껏; 실컷.

·con·tent·ed [kənténtid] *adj.* satisfied with things as they are; pleased; willing. 만족하고 있는. ¶ *a ~ look* 만족한 표정 / *with a ~ mind* 만족스런 마음으로 / *lead a ~ life* 만족한 생활을 보내다 / *be ~ with one's lot* 자기의 운명을 감수하고 있다 / *~ with a low salary* 박한 봉급에 만족하다 / *be ~ to do something* …하는 것에 만족하다. ● **con·tent·ed·ness** [-nis] *n.*

con·tent·ed·ly [kənténtidli] *adv.* in a contented manner. 만족하여.

con·ten·tion [kənténʃən] *n.* **1** Ⓤ argument; dispute; quarrel. 논쟁; 논전; 논의. ¶ *a bone of ~* 분쟁(불화)의 불씨; 쟁점(爭點). **2** Ⓒ a statement or point that a person has made or insisted on. 주장; 논점(論點). ¶ *His ~ was that the price was too high.* 그의 논점은 가격이 너무 비싸다는 것이었다 / *My ~ turned out to be correct.* 나의 주장이 옳다는 것이 판명되었다. [→contend]

con·ten·tious [kənténʃəs] *adj.* **1** fond of quarreling; apt to argue; quarrelsome. 논쟁(싸움)을 좋아하는; 투쟁적인. ¶ *a man of ~ temper* 논쟁을 좋아하는 사람. **2** causing disagreement. 논의를(논쟁을) 일으키는; 논쟁에 말려들게 하는. ¶ *~ issues* 논쟁을 일으키는 문제.

con·tent·ment [kənténtmənt] *n.* Ⓤ satisfaction; the state of being pleased. 만족; 안심; 흐뭇함. [*content*[2]]

con·ter·mi·nous [kəntə́ːrmənəs / kɔn-] *adj.* **1** 《*with, to*》 having a common boundary; meeting at their ends. 경계선을 함께 하고 있는; 접해 있는. **2** coextensive. 동일 연장의. [→term]

:con·test [kántest / kɔ́n-] *n.* Ⓒ **1** a fight or struggle. 싸움; 투쟁; 항쟁. ¶ *man's ~ with nature* 인간의 자연과의 싸움. **2** an argument; a discussion. 논쟁; 논의; 논점(論點). **3** a competition. (입상을 위한) 경쟁; 경연; 경기. ¶ *a speech* (*an oratorical*) *~* 변론(웅변) 대회 / *a beauty ~* 미인 선발 대회 / *be in a ~ for* …을 목표로 경쟁하다 / *win* (*lose*) *a ~* 경기에 이기다(지다). — [kəntést] *vt.* **1** (P6) fight for; struggle for (something). …와 싸우다; 투쟁하다; 다투다. ¶ *~ a victory with someone* 아무와 승리를 다투다. **2** (P6,11) argue against; dispute about (something); call in a question. (…에 대항하여) 논쟁하다; (…에 관하여) 격론을 주고 받다. ¶ *~ a controversial question* 논의의 대상인 문제로 논전을 벌이다. **3** (P6) try to win. …을 겨루다; 경쟁(경기)하다. ¶ *~ a prize* 상(賞)을 겨루다 / *~ an election* 선거에서 겨루다.

— *vi.* (P3) 《*with, against, for*》 fight; compete; take part in a contest. 싸우다; 경쟁하다; 논쟁하다. ¶ *~ with* (*against*) *an opponent in an argument* 의론에서 반대자와 논전을 하다 / *~ for the cup* 우승컵을 다투다. [L. *testis* witness]

con·test·ant [kəntéstənt] *n.* Ⓒ a person who takes part in a contest; a person who runs in an election, plays in a game, etc. 다투는(겨루는) 사람; 경쟁자; (선거 따위에서) 경쟁 상대.

con·tes·ta·tion [kàntestéiʃən / kɔ̀n-] *n.* Ⓤ controversy; assertion. 논쟁; 논의; 주장. ¶ *in ~* 논쟁 중의.

con·text [kántekst / kɔ́n-] *n.* ⒸⓊ the parts just before and after a word, a sentence, etc. that fix its meaning. (문장의 뜻을 명확히 하는) 앞뒤 관계; 문맥. ¶ *in this ~* 이와 관련하여; 이같은 맥락에서 / *It is often impossible to tell the meaning of a word apart from its ~.* 단어 하나의 뜻을 문맥에서 떼어놓고는 알기 불가능할 때가 종종 있다. [com-]

con·tex·tu·al [kəntékstʃuəl] *adj.* related to the context. 문맥상의; 앞뒤 관계로 본. ¶ *the ~ meaning* 문맥상으로 본 의미.

con·tex·ture [kəntékstʃər] *n.* Ⓒ **1** act, mode, of weaving together. 직물의 짜임새. **2** structure. 구조; 구성. **3** fabric. 직물; 직조물. **4** mode of literary composition. 문(文)의 짜임.

con·ti·gu·i·ty [kàntəgjúː(ː)iti / kɔ̀n-] *n.* Ⓤ **1** contact. 접촉. **2** nearness. 근접; 인접. **3** a continuous mass; an unbroken stretch. 연속. [→contact]

con·tig·u·ous [kəntígjuəs] *adj.* **1** in actual contact; touching. 접촉(인접)해 있는; 상접(相接)하는. ¶ *two ~ properties* 두 개의 인접한 땅 / *a ~ lot to a road* 도로에 접해 있는 땅. **2** joining; near. 접근한; 근접한. [↑]

con·ti·nence [kántənəns / kɔ́n-] *n.* Ⓤ control of one's own desires; moderation; purity. 자제; 절제; 금욕; 정절. ¶ *~ in speech* 말의 자제. [L. *teneo* hold]

:con·ti·nent[1] [kántənənt / kɔ́n-] *n.* Ⓒ **1** a continuous land; a mainland. 본토; 육지. **2** one of the six great masses of land, North America, South America, Europe, Africa, Asia, and Australia. 대륙. **3** 《*the C-*》 the mainland of Europe. (영국과 구별하

여) 유럽 본토. ¶ *spend one's holidays on the Continent* 휴가를 유럽 본토에서 보내다. [↑]

con·ti·nent² [kántənənt / kɔ́n-] *adj.* self-controlled; temperate; chaste. (욕망을) 자제하는; 절제 있는; 정절을 지키는. [↑]

·**con·ti·nen·tal** [kàntənéntl / kɔ̀n-] *adj.* **1** of or belonging to a continent; like that of a continent. 대륙의; 대륙적인〔성의〕(opp. insular). ¶ *a ~ climate* 대륙성 기후. **2** 《usu. *C-*》 of the mainland of Europe. 유럽 대륙의. **3** 《usu. *C-*》 of the American colonies at the time of the American Revolution. (미국 독립전쟁 당시의) 식민지의. — *n.* Ⓒ 《usu. *C-*》 a person living on the Continent; a European. 유럽 대륙의 사람; 유럽인.

con·ti·nen·tal·ize [kàntənéntəlàiz / kɔ̀n-] *vt.* (P6) assimilate to continental usage. 대륙 관습에 동화시키다; (특히) 유럽화시키다.

con·tin·gen·cy [kəntíndʒənsi] *n.* (*pl.* **-cies**) **1** Ⓤ uncertainty of occurrence. 우연성. **2** Ⓤ chance. 우발. **3** Ⓒ an uncertain event. 우발 사건. ¶ *a remote* 〔*future*〕 *~* 먼 장래에 일어날지도 모르는 일 / *You must be ready for any ~.* 어떤 돌발사에도 대비해 두어야 한다. **4** Ⓤ incidental expenses. 임시비(費). [↓]

con·tin·gent [kəntíndʒənt] *adj.* **1** 《*on, upon*》 conditional; depending on something else. …을 조건으로 하는; …여하에 달린. ¶ *a fee ~ on* 〔*upon*〕 *cure* 〔*success*〕 나으면 〔성공하면〕 주기로 한 사례금 / *Whether she will come or not is ~ on the weather.* 그녀가 올지 안 올지는 날씨 여하에 달렸다. **2** likely, but not certain to happen; possible; uncertain. 있을 수 있는; 불확실한. ¶ *Such risks are ~ to the trade.* 그 같은 위험은 그 사업에 흔히 있을 수 있는 일이다. **3** happening by chance; accidental; unexpected. 우연의; 우발적인; 뜻하지 않은. ¶ *a ~ fund* 긴급 준비금 / *a ~ event* 우발 사건 / *~ occurrences that cannot be foreseen* 예측할 수 없는 우발사. — *n.* Ⓒ **1** a contingency. 부수(付隨) 사건. **2** a body of people that is part of a large group. 분견대(分遣隊). **3** an accidental or unexpected event. 우발사(事); 뜻하지 않은 사건. **4** that which falls to one's share. 나눔몫; 분담액. [L. *tango* touch]

con·tin·u·a [kəntínjuə] *n.* pl. of **continuum.**

·**con·tin·u·al** [kəntínjuəl] *adj.* **1** going on without stopping; endless. 끊임없는; 잇따라 일어나는; 연속적인. ¶ *the ~ flow of the river* 강물의 끊임없는 흐름 / *in ~ worry* 끊임없이 걱정하여. **2** repeated many times; very frequent. 자주 일어나는; 빈번한. ¶ *~ attacks of toothache* 빈번한 이앓이. [*continue*]

·**con·tin·u·al·ly** [kəntínjuəli] *adv.* without stopping; again and again. 끊임없이; 빈번히; 자꾸. ¶ *He's ~ whining about something.* 그는 언제나 무엇엔가 푸념을 하고 있다.

con·tin·u·ance [kəntínjuəns] *n.* **1** 《*sing.* only》 the act of going on all the time; the period of time during which a thing lasts. 연속; 계속; 잇따름; 계속 기간. ¶ *a ~ of bad weather* 잇따른 악천후 / *a ~ of war* 전쟁의 계속 / *of long ~* 오래 계속되는 / *during one's ~ in office* 재직 중. **2** Ⓤ 《sometimes *a ~*》 ⓐ remaining in the same condition. (같은 상태의) 지속. ¶ *a ~ of famine* 기근의 지속; 계속되는 기근 / *a ~ of* 〔*in*〕 *happiness* 행복의 지속. ⓑ remaining in the same place; staying. (같은 장소에) 머물러 있음; 존속. ¶ *in ~ one's old home* 옛 집에 머무름. **3** Ⓤ 《law》 postponement. (소송 절차의) 연기.

con·tin·u·a·tion [kəntìnjuéiʃən] *n.* **1** Ⓤ the act or fact of continuing; the state of being continued; continuance. 계속; 지속; 존속(存續). ¶ *the senseless ~ of the nuclear arms race* 분별없는 핵(核)군비 경쟁의 계속 / *the ~ of the monarchy in the direct line* 직계 계승에 의한 왕국의 존속 / *The further ~ of misrule must be prevented.* 이 이상의 비정(秕政)의 계속은 저지되어야 한다. **2** Ⓤ carrying on, or beginning again after being interrupted. (휴식·중단 후의) 재개; 계속; 속행. ¶ *the ~ of the work after a break* 휴식 후의 작업의 속행 / *request the ~ of a loan* 차관(借款)의 계속을 요청하다 / *Continuation of my work after the Christmas holidays was difficult at first.* 크리스마스 후 일을 다시 시작하기가 처음에는 어려웠다. **3** Ⓒ ⓐ anything by which a thing is continued; an added part. 계속(된 것); 연장; 속편(續篇). ¶ *The ~ of this story will be found on page 25.* 이 이야기는 25페이지에 계속됩니다. ⓑ something added to another thing. 이어댄〔늘인〕 것; 증축. ¶ *build a ~ to a room* 방의 증축을 하다. **4** Ⓒ ⓐ gaiters continuous with knee-breeches. 반바지에 이어진 각반. ⓑ 《*colloq.*》 trousers. 바지. [→continue]

continuation school [—–—⌐— —⌐] *n.* a school giving instruction to persons who have finished their regular schooling and are usu. in employment. (근로 청소년을 위한) 정시제(定時制) 중·고등 학교.

con·ti·nu·a·tive [kəntínjuèitiv, -njuətiv] *adj.* in the process of continuation. 연속의; 연속〔계속〕적인.

:**con·tin·ue** [kəntínju:] *vt.* **1** (P6,7,8,9) keep on with; go on; carry forward. …을 계속하다; 속행하다. ¶ *~ an action* 행동을 계속하다 / *~ to talk* 이야기를 계속하다 / *We can't ~ living this way.* 우리는 이런 생활을 계속해 나갈 수는 없다. **2** (P6) take up again; begin again. …을 다시 시작〔계속〕하다. ¶ *The story will be continued next month.* 이야기는 다음달에 계속됩니다 / *To be continued.* 이하 계속. **3** (P6) cause (something) to last or remain. 계속〔존속〕시키다; 계속 머무르게 하다. ¶ *~ an old servant in office* 늙은 하인을 계속 그 직에 머무르게 하다.

— *vi.* **1** (P2A,2B,3,4) ⓐ last; endure. 계속〔존속〕되다. ¶ *The desert continues for miles.* 사

막은 몇 마일이나 이어져 있다 / *The rain continued all day.* 비는 하루 종일 계속되었다. ⓑ 《*in*》 remain. (…에) 머무르다; …채로 있다. ¶ ~ *in power* 권좌에 계속 앉아 있다 / ~ *single* 독신인 채로 있다 / *She still continues in weak health.* 그녀는 변함없이 건강이 좋지 않다. **2** (P1,2A,2B) keep on. …상태를 계속하다. ¶ *He continues idle.* 그는 여전히 게으르다. **3** (P1) start again; go on again after a pause. (휴식·중단 후에) 재개하다; 속행하다. ¶ *The story will ~ next month.* 이야기는 내달에 계속된다. [L. *teneo* hold]

con·ti·nu·i·ty [kὰntənjúːəti / kɔ̀n-] *n.* (*pl.* **-ties**) Ⓤ **1** the state of being continuous. 계속(성). **2** smooth succession. 연속. **3** Ⓒ 《cinema》 an arrangement of a motion picture; a scenario. 콘티(script); (영화의) 촬영 대본. **4** 《Radio》 the remarks made between the parts of a radio program. 방송 프로의 연결 아나운스. [↑]

con·tin·u·a [kəntínjuə] *n.* pl. of **continuum.**

·**con·tin·u·ous** [kəntínjuəs] *adj.* without a stop or break; unbroken; extended. 끊임없는; 계속되는; 연속적인. ¶ ~ *labor* 내리 계속하는 일 / *a ~ series of blasts* 일련의 폭발 / ~ *line of cars* 꼬리를 무는 차량의 행렬 / *show ~ development* 계속적인 발전을 보이다.

con·tin·u·ous·ly [kəntínjuəsli] *adj.* in a continuous manner. 잇따라; 계속해서. ¶ *The noise went on ~.* 소음이 잇따라 계속되었다.

con·tin·u·um [kəntínjuəm] *n.* ⓊⒸ (*pl.* **-tin·u·a**) continuous quantity; series. 연속(체).

con·tort [kəntɔ́ːrt] *vt.* (P6,13) twist or bend (something) out of its natural shape. …을 뒤틀다〔일그러뜨리다〕; 비틀다. ¶ ~ *one's limbs* 손발을 뒤틀다 / *a face contorted with pain* 고통으로 일그러진 얼굴. [L. *torqueo* twist]

con·tor·tion [kəntɔ́ːrʃən] *n.* **1** Ⓤ the act of contorting. 뒤틂; 뒤틀림; 일그러짐. ¶ *make ~ of the face* 얼굴을 찡그리다. **2** Ⓒ a contorted condition. 뒤틀려〔일그러져〕 있음.

con·tour [kɑ́ntuər / kɔ́n-] *n.* Ⓒ **1** an outline of a figure, a thing, etc. 외형; 윤곽(선). ¶ *the ~ of mountains* 산의 윤곽 / *The ~ of the west coast of Korea is very irregular.* 한국의 서해안선은 매우 불규칙하다. **2** =contour line. — *vt.* (P6) **1** mark (something) with contour lines; make or form the outline of (something). …에 등고선(等高線)을 표시하다; …의 윤곽을 그리다〔나타내다〕. **2** build (a road, etc.) around the contour of a hill. 산허리 둘레에 (길)을 내다. — *adj.* showing the outlines of mountains, etc.; of a contour line. 외형의; 등고선의. [→turn]

contour line [⌐-⌐] *n.* a line drawn on a map through points all at the same height above sea level. (지도의) 등고선.

contr. contract(ed); contraction.

con·tra- [kɑ́ntrə- / kɔ́n-] *pref.* **1** against; opposite. '대응, 반대, 역(逆)'의 뜻. **2** 《mus.》 the pitch of the octave below. '보통의 저음(bass)보다 1 옥타브 낮은'의 뜻. [L.]

con·tra·band [kɑ́ntrəbæ̀nd / kɔ́n-] *adj.* against the law; stopped by the law or a rule. 위법〔불법〕의; 금제(禁制)의. ¶ ~ *trade* 밀수 / ~ *goods* 금제품 / *The sale of stolen goods is ~ in this country.* 장물의 판매는 이 나라에서 위법이다. — *n* Ⓤ **1** goods imported or exported unlawfully. 수출입 금제품. ¶ ~ *of war* (무기·탄약 따위의) 전시 금제품 / *absolute* 〔*unconditional*〕 ~ 절대 금제품 / *conditional* ~ 조건부 금제품. **2** unlawful trade of such goods. 밀수품의 불법 거래; 금지 무역. [→ban]

con·tra·bass [kɑ́ntrəbèis / kɔ́n-] *n.* Ⓒ 《mus.》 the lowest bass voice or instrument; a double bass. 콘트라베이스; 최저음(악기). [contra-]

con·tra·cep·tion [kὰntrəsépʃən / kɔ̀n-] *n.* Ⓤ prevention of conception; birth control. 피임(법); 산아 조절. [→conceive]

con·tra·cep·tive [kὰntrəséptiv / kɔ̀n-] *adj.* of or used for contraception. 피임의; 피임을 위한. — *n.* a device or drug for contraception. 피임구(具); 피임제(劑).

:**con·tract**[1] [kɑ́ntrækt / kɔ́n-] *n.* Ⓒ **1** an agreement; a business agreement; a promise. 계약; 약속. ¶ *an oral* 〔*a verbal*〕 ~ 구두 계약 / *a temporary* ~ 임시 계약 / *the parties to a* ~ 계약 당사자 / *on a three-year* ~ 3년 계약으로 / *make* 〔*enter into*〕 *a* ~ *with someone* = *put someone under* ~ 아무와 계약하다. **2** a written agreement enforced by law. 계약서. ¶ *draw up a* ~ 계약서를 작성하다. **3** the work carried out under a contract. 청부; 도급. ¶ *by* ~ 청부로 / *give a* ~ *to* …에게 도급을 주다. **4** a formal agreement of marriage or betrothal. (정식의) 혼약.

— [kəntrǽkt] *vt.* (P6,8,9,13) **1** [《U.S.》 kɑ́ntrækt] make a legal agreement of (something); undertake by contract. …와 계약〔약정〕하다; 청부하다. ¶ ~ *building a house* 집의 건축을 청부맡다 / ~ *an alliance with a country* 어떤 나라와 동맹을 맺다. **2** enter into (relations); form (a friendship, a habit, etc.). (친교 따위)를 맺다; (악습 따위)에 물들다. ¶ ~ *friendship with someone* 아무와 친교를 맺다. **3** 《usu. in *passive*》 betroth. 혼약하다. ¶ *be contracted to someone* 아무와 약혼하였다.

— *vi.* (P4) 《*with, for, to*》 make a contract. 계약을 맺다. ¶ ~ *to build a bridge for $ 50,000,* 5만 달러에 다리를 가설키로 계약하다. [↓]

con·tract[2] [kəntrǽkt] *vt.* **1** (P6) draw up; tighten. (근육 따위)를 수축〔긴장〕시키다. ¶ ~ *a muscle* 근육을 수축시키다. **2** (P6) draw together. 찌푸리다; 찡그리다. ¶ ~ *one's eyebrows* 〔*forehead*〕 눈살〔이맛살〕을 찌푸리다. **3** (P6,13) ⓐ make (something)

smaller or shorter. 줄이다. ⓑ shorten (a word, etc.) by omitting of the letters or sounds. (글자나 음을 생략하여) 말 따위를 단축하다. **4** (P6) become infected with (a disease); take; catch; get. (병)에 걸리다; (악습 따위에) 물들다. ¶ ~ *a disease* / ~ *a habit* 버릇이 붙다. **5** (P6) incur; become liable for. (의무·빚 따위)를 지게 하다; 초래하다. ¶ ~ *a debt* 부채가 생기게 하다.
— *vi.* (P1,2) draw together; become smaller, shorter, tighter, or narrower. 수축하다; 줄(어 들)다; 짧아지다; 단축되다; 좁아지다. ¶ *Wood contracts as it dries.* 나무는 건조에 따라 수축한다. [com-, →tract]

con·tract·ed [kəntrǽktid] *adj.* **1** shortened; made smaller. 수축된; 단축된. **2** narrow-minded. (마음·사상·견해 등이) 좁은; 편협한. ¶ *a ~ view of minority rights* 소수자의 권리에 대한 편협한 견해. **3** acquired. 계약한.

con·trac·tile [kəntrǽktil] *adj.* that can contract or be contracted; producing contraction. 수축할 수 있는; 수축성의(이 있는). ● **con·trac·til·i·ty** [kὰntræktíləti / kɔ̀n-] *n.*

con·trac·tion [kəntrǽkʃən] *n.* **1** Ⓤ the act of contracting; the state of being contracted. 수축; 단축. ¶ *The ~ of mercury by cold makes it go down in the thermometer.* 추위로 인한 수은의 수축은 온도계에서 그것을 내려가게 한다. **2** Ⓒ something contracted; a shortened form. 간약(簡約)(축약(縮約))(어·형). ¶ *'Can't' is a ~ for 'cannot'.* 'can't'는 'cannot'의 간약형이다. **3** Ⓤ the act of forming a bad habit; getting a disease, accumulating a debt, etc. (악습에) 물듦; (병에) 걸림; (빚을) 짐.

con·trac·tive [kəntrǽktiv] *adj.* tending to contraction. 수축되기 쉬운; 수축성의.

con·trac·tor [kəntrǽktər] *n.* Ⓒ **1** [kάntræktər] a businessman who agrees to do things for others, esp. in building houses, etc. 계약자; 도급(청부)인. ¶ *a general ~* 도급업자. **2** 《anat.》 a muscle that serves to contract. 수축근(筋).

con·trac·tu·al [kəntrǽktʃuəl] *adj.* of a contract. 계약(상)의.

con·tra·dict [kὰntrədíkt / kɔ̀n-] *vt.* (P6) **1** deny; say the opposite of (what someone has said). …을 부정(부인)하다; (남의 말)에 대해 반박(반대)하다. ¶ ~ *a report* 소문을 부정하다 / ~ *someone's statement* 아무의 말을 반박하다 / *He is always contradicting me.* 그는 항상 내게 반대만 한다. **2** be opposed or contrary to; disagree with (something). (진술 따위가) …와 모순하다; 상반되다. ¶ *No truth contradicts another truth.* 진리는 서로 모순되지 않는다 / *The two accounts ~ each other.* 두 이야기는 서로 모순된다. [→diction]

con·tra·dic·tion [kὰntrədíkʃən / kɔ̀n-] *n.* ⓊⒸ **1** the act of contradicting; denial. 반박; 반대; 부정. ¶ *a ~ of rumor* 소문의 부정. **2** contrary conditions; repugnancy; logical inconsistency; disagreement. 모순; 배치; 자가 당착.
in contradiction to, to the contrary. …에 반(反)하여; …을 반박하여.

con·tra·dic·to·ry [kὰntrədíktəri / kɔ̀n-] *adj.* **1** contradicting; in disagreement. 반박하는; 반대의. **2** inclined to contradict. 모순(상반)하는; 반박적인. ¶ ~ *statements* 모순된 진술. — *n.* (*pl.* **-ries**) a thing which is logically opposed to another. 모순되는 것(말); 정반대(의 것). ¶ *These two things are contradictories.* 이 두 물건은 정반대이다.

con·tra·dis·tinc·tion [kὰntrədistíŋkʃən / kɔ̀n-] *n.* Ⓤ distinction by contrast. 대비(對比); 대조적 차이. ¶ *in ~ to* (*from, with*) …와 대조적으로 구별하여 / *soul in ~ to body* 육체와 대조적으로 구별되는 것으로서의 영혼. [contra-]

con·tra·dis·tin·guish [kὰntrədistíŋgwiʃ / kɔ̀n-] *vt.* (P13) distinguish by contrasting. 대조(비교)하여 구별하다; 대비하다.

con·trail [kάntreil / kɔ́n-] *n.* Ⓒ a cloud-like trail left by a plane flying at a high altitude. 비행기 구름. [→trail]

con·tral·ti [kəntrǽlti:] *n.* pl. of **contralto.**

con·tral·to [kəntrǽltou] *n.* (*pl.* **-tral·tos** or **-tral·ti**) **1** Ⓤ the lowest woman's voice. 여성 최저음; 콘트랄토. **2** Ⓒ a person of a musical group who sings this part. 콘트랄토 가수. — *adj.* of or for a contralto. 콘트랄토(음역)의. [contra-]

con·tra·po·si·tion [kὰntrəpəzíʃən / kɔ̀n-] *n.* ⓊⒸ **1** antithesis; contrast. 대치; 대립. **2** 《log.》 a mode of conversion; conversion by negation. 환질 환위법(換質換位法); 대우(對偶). [contra-]

con·trap·tion [kəntrǽpʃən] *n.* Ⓒ 《*colloq.*》 a contrivance; a newfangled device. 신안(新案); 기묘한 장치(기계). [? *contrive, deception*]

con·tra·pun·tal [kὰntrəpʌ́ntl / kɔ̀n-] *adj.* 《mus.》 having to do with counterpoint. 대위법의. [L. *pungo* prick]

con·tra·punt·ist [kὰntrəpʌ́ntist / kɔ̀n-] *n.* Ⓒ one who writes counterpoint. 대위법 작(곡)가.

con·tra·ri·e·ty [kὰntrəráiəti / kɔ̀n-] *n.* (*pl.* **-ties**) **1** Ⓤ the state or quality of being contrary. 반대; 불일치; 모순. **2** Ⓒ something contrary. 상반하는 것; 모순점. [contra-]

con·tra·ri·ly [kάntrerəli / kɔ́n-] *adv.* 《*colloq.*》 **1** in a contrary manner. 반대로; 거꾸로. **2** [usu. kəntrέərəli] perversely. 빙퉁그러져; 심술궂게.

con·tra·ri·wise [kάntreriwàiz / kɔ́n-] *adv.* in the opposite way or direction; on the contrary. 반대로; 거꾸로; 이에 반하여.

:con·tra·ry [kάntreri / kɔ́n-] *adj.* **1** opposed; opposite (in nature or tendency). (성질·성격이) 반대의; …에 반하는. ¶ *be ~ to fact* (*one's wishes*) 사실(소망)에 반하다 / *hold a ~ opinion* 반대의 의견을 갖다 / *My sister's* *taste in dress is just* ~ *to my own.* 언니의 옷 취미는 나와 정반대다. **2** opposite in direction; unfavorable. (방향·위치가) 반대의; 역(逆)의; (형편·상태가) 좋지 않은; 불리한. ¶ ~ *weather* 나쁜 날씨 / *a* ~ *wind* 역풍 / *in* ~ *direction* 반대 방향으로. **3** [kəntrέəri] 《*colloq.*》 always saying or doing the opposite; stubborn; perverse. (언행이) 항상 엇가는; 제멋대로 구는; 옹고집의; 심술궂은. ¶ *a* ~ *child.*

— *n.* Ⓒ(*pl.* **-ries**) **1** 《*the* ~ ; *sing.* only》 the fact or quality that is the opposite of something els; the exact opposite; contradiction. (정)반대; 모순. ¶ *prove the* ~ *of a statement* 진술의 반대를 입증하다; 반증을 들다 / *He is neither tall nor the* ~. 그는 키가 크지도 않지만 그 반대도 아니다 / *Cold is the* ~ *of hot.* '차다'는 '덥다'의 반대다. **2** 《usu. *pl.*》 one of two opposing things. 두 상반(相反)하는 것의 한쪽; 대립되는 것.

by contraries, **a**) by way of opposition. 반대로. **b**) contrary to expectation. 예상과는 반대로.

on the contrary, far from it; in opposite to what has previously been said. 그렇기는커녕; 이에 반(反)하여. ¶ *You think me idle, but on the* ~ *I am very busy.* 자넨 내가 게으르다고 생각하지만 그 반대로 나는 매우 분주하다네.

to the contrary, to the opposite effect; in the opposite sense. 그와 반대로(의); 그렇지 않다는. ¶ *evidence to the* ~ 그 역(逆)의 증거 / *unless I hear to the* ~ 그렇지 않다는 말이 없으면; 반대되는 보도가 없으면 / *I will come if I do not write to the* ~. 가지 않겠다는 편지가 없는 한 나는 간다.

— *adv.* in a contrary manner. 반대로(되게). ¶ *act* ~ *to your advice* 네 충고에 반대되게 행동하다 / ~ *to what I feared* 두려워했던 것과는 반대로. [contra-]

contrary to one's expectation, to one's surprise; unexpectedly. 뜻밖에도; 예상과 반대로. ¶ *Contrary to my expectation, all went well.* 예상과는 반대로 만사가 잘 되었다.

:con·trast [kάntræst / kɔ́ntrɑːst] *n.* **1** Ⓤ a striking difference between things or persons compared. 두드러진 차이; 대조; 대비. ¶ *stand in* ~ 대조를 이루다 / *This book shows the* ~ *between life now and life a hundred years ago.* 이 책은 오늘날의 생활과 백년 전의 생활 간의 두드러진 차이를 보여 주고 있다. **2** Ⓒ anything that shows difference from another thing. 대조적으로 다른 것; 대조가 되는 것. ¶ *be a* ~ *to* …을 대조적으로 돋보이게 하다 / *form* 〔*present*〕 *a striking* 〔*strange*〕 ~ *to* …에 대해 두드러진(묘한) 대조를 이루다 / *His school record was a decided* ~ *to* 〔*was in decided* ~ *with*〕 *his brother's.* 학교 성적이 그의 형의 것과는 뚜렷한 대조를 이루고 있었다 / *His white hair is in sharp* ~ *to* 〔*with*〕 *his dark skin.* 그의 백발은 검은 피부와 두드러진 대조를 이루고 있다.

in contrast with 〔*to*〕, as compared with. …와 대조를 이루어.

— [kəntrǽst, kάn-] *vt.* (P6,13)《*with*》 compare (things) so that the differences are made clear; set off by contrast. …을 대조하다; 돋보이게 하다. ¶ *Contrast these imported goods with the domestic products.* 이 수입품들을 국산품과 대비해 보라.

— *vi.* (P2,3) 《*with*》 show a difference when compared. (…와) 좋은 대조를 보이다; 대조적이다. ¶ *His actions* ~ *badly with his promises.* 그의 행동과 약속과는 크게 다르다 / *The black and the gold* ~ *prettily in that design.* 그 디자인에서 흑색과 금빛이 아름답게 대조를 보이고 있다. [L. *sto* stand]

con·tras·tive [kəntrǽstiv] *adj.* forming a contrast. 대조〔대비〕적인. ¶ *a* ~ *grammar* 대조 문법 / ~ *linguistics* 대조 언어학.

con·tra·vene [kὰntrəvíːn / kɔ̀n-] *vt.* (P6) **1** disagree with (something); oppose; contradict; attack (a statement, principle, etc.); defeat. …에 반대〔반박〕하다; 모순하다; 논파하다. ¶ ~ *a statement* 성명서를 반박하다. **2** go against (a custom, a law, etc.); violate; break. (법·규정)을 어기다; 위반하다. ¶ ~ *a law* 〔*rule*〕 법〔규정〕을 어기다. **3** (of things) conflict with. 충돌하다; 저촉하다. [L. *venio* come]

cor·tra·ven·tion [kὰntrəvénʃən / kɔ̀n-] *n.* ⓊⒸ the act of contravening; opposition; conflict; violation. 반대; 반박; 모순; 위반; 위배. ¶ *act in* ~ *of a law* 법률에 위반되는 행위를 하다.

con·tre·temps [kάntrətὰːŋ / kɔ́n-] *n.* Ⓒ (*pl.* **temps** [-z]) 《F.》 an unexpected and unfortunate event. 뜻하지 않은 사고〔사건〕.

:con·trib·ute [kəntríbjuːt] *vt.* (P6,13) **1** ⓐ give with others (money or help) for a common purpose; furnish; make a contribution. (돈·도움 따위)를 주다; 기부〔기여〕하다; 제공하다. ¶ ~ *food for the sufferers* 이재민에게 음식을 제공하다 / ~ *money to relieving the poor* 빈민 구제에 돈을 기부하다 / ~ *time and energy to the work* 그 일에 시간과 정력을 바치다. ⓑ give or furnish (knowledge, ideas, etc.). (지식·아이디어 따위)를 주다; 제공하다. ¶ ~ *suggestions* 암시를 주다 / ~ *new information* 〔*ideas*〕 새로운 정보〔아이디어〕를 제공하다. **2** write (something) for (a newspaper, magazine, etc.). …을 기고(寄稿)하다. ¶ ~ *articles to a newspaper* 신문에 기사를 기고하다.

— *vi.* (P1,3) 《*to*》 **1** give to (a common fund, etc.); assist; help. (…에) 기부하다; 기여〔공헌〕하다; 조력하다. ¶ ~ *to an orphan asylum* 고아원에 기부하다. **2** write something for. …에 기고하다. **3** help to bring about. 일조(一助)가〔한 원인이〕 되다. ¶ *Drink contributed to his ruin.* 음주가 그의 파멸에 한 원인이 되었다. [→tribute]

·con·tri·bu·tion [kὰntrəbjúːʃən / kɔ̀n-] *n.* **1** ⓐ Ⓤ the act of contributing. 기부; 기여; 기증. ⓑ Ⓒ something contributed. 기부금;

기증물. ¶ *collect contributions* 기부금을 모으다. **2** Ⓒ an article written for a newspaper or magazine. 기고(寄稿) (기사). **3** Ⓒ a tax. 세(稅); 부과금.

lay under contribution, compel the payment of contributions from. 강제로 기부하게 하다.

make a contribution to 〔***towards***〕, **a**) do much towards. …에 공헌하다. **b**) make a donation to. …에 기부하다.

con·trib·u·tor [kəntríbjətər] *n.* Ⓒ **1** a person who contributes. 기부자; 기여〔공헌〕자. **2** a person who writes articles for a newspaper or magazine. 기고가(寄稿家); 투고자. ¶ *a regular ~ to the 'Times'* 타임스지의 정기 기고자.

con·trib·u·to·ry [kəntríbjətɔ̀ːri / -təri-] *adj.* **1** contributing; helping to bring about. 공헌〔기여〕하는; …에 이바지하는; 일조(一助)가 〔한 원인이〕 되는. ¶ *The drought was a ~ cause of the fire.* 가뭄이 그 화재의 요인이었다. **2** of or having to do with contributions. contribution 의〔에 관한〕.

con·trite [kəntráit, kɑ́ntrait / kɔ́ntrait] *adj.* **1** very sorry for having done wrong. 죄를 뉘우치는; 회한(悔恨)의. ¶ *a ~ heart* 죄를 뉘우치는 마음 / *shed ~ tears* 회한의 눈물을 흘리다. **2** showing deep regret and sorrow. 회한의 정을 나타내는. ● **con·trite·ly** [-li] *adv.* [com-, L. *tero* rub]

con·tri·tion [kəntríʃən] *n.* Ⓤ **1** deep sorrow for sin; penitence. 회오(悔悟); 회한(悔恨). **2** deep regret (for sins, etc.). 깊은 후회; 통회(痛悔).

con·triv·ance [kəntráivəns] *n.* **1** Ⓒ a thing invented; a plan or scheme; a mechanical device. 고안물(考案物); (기계) 장치; 계획; 계략. **2** Ⓤ the act or manner of contriving. 고안; 안출(案出); 발명(의 재능). ¶ *by his ~* 그의 고안으로. [↓]

***con·trive** [kəntráiv] *vt.* **1** (P6) invent; devise; design. …을 고안〔안출〕하다; 발명하다; 궁리해 내다. ¶ *~ a new kind of engine* 신형 엔진을 고안하다 / *~ an excuse* 구실을 생각해 내다 / *They contrived a way to escape.* 그들은 도망갈 방도를 궁리했다. **2** (P6) plan; scheme; plot. …을 기도〔도모〕하다; 꾀하다. ¶ *~ someone's murder* 아무의 살해를 기도하다. **3** (P8) manage. …을 그럭저럭 잘 처리하다〔해내다〕. ¶ *I will ~ to get there by three.* 어떻게든지 3 시까지는 거기로 가겠다 / *He contrived to gain their votes.* 그럭저럭 그들의 표를 그러모았다.

— *vi* (P1,4) **1** invent; plan; plot. 고안〔궁리〕하다; 기도하다; 꾀하다. **2** manage well. 잘 처리하다. **3** manage household affairs. 살림을 꾸려나가다. ¶ *cut and ~* 적은 수입으로 요령있게 꾸려나가다. [L. *turbo* stir up]

con·triv·er [kəntráivər] *n.* Ⓒ a maker of plans, inventions, etc. 계략가; 고안〔안출〕자. ¶ *He is a good ~.* 그는 훌륭한 고안자이다.

:con·trol [kəntróul] *n.* **1** Ⓤ power or authority to direct and govern. 지배(력); 지휘; 감독; 통제. ¶ *~ of lights* 등화 관제 / *be under the direct ~ of* …의 직접 감독 밑에 있다; …직할이다 / *be in full ~ of* …을 완전히 장악〔관리〕하고 있다 / *gain ~ of* …을 지배〔통제〕하다. **2** Ⓤ restraint; holding back; keeping down. 억제; 제어. ¶ *get out of ~ =lose ~ of* …을 억누르지 못하게 되다 / *lose ~ one's temper* 화를 누르지 못하다 / *lose ~ of the car* 차의 제동이 안 듣다 / *He has no ~ of* 〔*over*〕 *himself.* 자제력이 없다. **3** Ⓒ means of holding back; check. 통제〔억제〕 수단. **4** Ⓒ 《usu. *pl.*》 a device or apparatus for regulating and guiding a machine. (기계의) 조종〔통제, 제어〕 장치. ¶ *He sat at the controls of the plane.* 비행기의 조종 장치 앞에 앉았다. **5** Ⓒ a standard of comparison for the testing truth or correctness. (실험 결과의) 조사(照査) 표준; 대조부(簿). ¶ *a ~ experiment* 대조 실험.

be beyond 〔***out of***〕 ***one's control,*** that cannot be held back. 제어할〔누를〕 수가 없다; 힘에 벅차다.

be in control of (*=have authority over*) *something.* …을 관리하고 있다.

bring 〔***get, keep***〕 ***under control,*** control. …을 억제하다〔억누르다〕; 제어〔진압〕하다. ¶ *He brought his temper under ~.* 그는 분노를 억제했다.

have no control over, get out of control. …을 억누를 수가 없다.

under the control of (*=under the supervision of*) *someone.* …의 관리하에.

without control, freely. 제멋대로. ¶ *He behaved without ~.* 그는 제멋대로 굴었다.

— *vt.* (**-trolled, -trol·ling**) (P6) **1** have power over (something); direct; command. …을 관리하다; 지배〔지휘〕하다. ¶ *A captain controls his ship.* 선장은 그의 배를 지휘한다. **2** hold back; keep down; restrain. …을 억제하다; 제어하다. ¶ *~ oneself* 자제하다 / *~ one's anger* 〔*emotions*〕 노여움〔감정〕을 누르다. **3** adjust (something) so that it works well; regulate. …을 조절〔통제〕하다; 규제하다. ¶ *~ prices and wages* 물가와 임금을 규제하다. **4** test or check by comparison with a recognized standard. (…을) 조사(照査)하다. ¶ *~ a text* 원본을 조사하다. [counter², → roll]

con·trol·la·ble [kəntróuləbəl] *adj.* that can be controlled. 제어할 수 있는; 조종할 수 있는.

con·trol·ler [kəntróulər] *n.* Ⓒ **1** an officer who examines expenditures or accounts; a comptroller. 회계 감사관(官). **2** a person who controls or directs. 통제〔관리〕자; 지배자. **3** a device for regulating the speed of a machine. 제어기.

con·tro·ver·sial [kɑ̀ntrəvə́ːrʃəl / kɔ̀n-] *adj.* **1** of controversy; debatable; disputed. 논쟁의; 쟁론(爭論)의 대상인. ¶ *a ~ matter*

〔*question*〕 논쟁의 대상인 문제. **2** (of a person) fond of controversy. 논쟁을〔논의를〕 좋아하는. ● **con·tro·ver·sial·ly** [-li] *adv.* [contra-, L. *verto* turn]

con·tro·ver·sial·ist [kàntrəvə́:rʃəlist / kɔ̀n-] *n.* Ⓒ a person who takes part in a controversy. 논쟁자; 논객(論客).

•**con·tro·ver·sy** [kántrəvə̀:rsi / kɔ́n-] *n.* ⓊⒸ (*pl.* **-sies**) **1** an argument; a discussion. 논쟁; 이론. ¶ *a heated* 〔*hot*〕 ~ *with someone* 아무와의 열띤 논쟁 / *a* ~ *over freedom of speech* 언론 자유에 관한 논쟁 / *arouse* 〔*create*〕 ~ 논쟁을 일으키다. **2** quarrel; debate. 언쟁; 말다툼.

be beyond controversy, be no longer a subject of discussion. 논쟁〔의론〕의 여지가 없다; 물론이다.

con·tro·vert [kántrəvə̀:rt / kɔ́n-] *vt.* (P6) **1** deny; oppose. …을 부정하다; 논박〔반론, 반대〕하다. **2** dispute about(something); discuss; talk about (a question). …을 논쟁하다; 토론하다.

con·tu·ma·cious [kàntjuméiʃəs / kɔ̀n-] *adj.* resisting authority; not willing to obey. 복종하지 않는; 완고한. [↓]

con·tu·ma·cy [kántjuməsi / kɔ́n-] *n.* ⓊⒸ (*pl.* **-cies**) going against authority; the state of being contumacious. 순종치 않음; 반항; 완고. [L. *tumeo*]

con·tu·me·ly [kəntjú:məli, kántjumə̀:li / kɔ́n-] *n.* (*pl.* **-lies**) **1** Ⓤ the state of being proud, not polite, and rude. 오만; 무례. ¶ *The nobles treated the peasants with* ~. 귀족들은 농민들을 오만하게 대했다. **2** Ⓒ severe criticism of someone; bad language or behavior to someone; an insult. 모욕(적인 말·행위).

con·tuse [kəntjú:z] *vt.* (P6) injure by blow without breaking the skin, bruise. …에 타박상을 입히다. ¶ *a contused wound* 타박상. [L. *tundo* thump]

con·tu·sion [kəntjú:ʒən] *n.* Ⓒ 《med.》 a bruise. 좌상(挫傷); 타박상.

co·nun·drum [kənʌ́ndrəm] *n.* Ⓒ **1** a puzzle. (신소리와 같은) 수수께끼. **2** a hard problem. 난문(제). [university L. slang]

con·ur·ba·tion [kànə:rbéiʃən / kɔ̀n-] *n.* Ⓒ an extensive urban area formed by the expansion of several cities or towns. 집합 도시; 광역 도시권《위성 도시들의 팽창으로 인한》. [L. *urban*]

con·va·lesce [kànvəlés / kɔ̀n-] *vi.* (P1) get better; grow stronger after illness. 건강을 회복하다; 차도를 보이다. ¶ *The patient is convalescing slowly.* 환자는 점차 회복되고 있다. [→valid]

con·va·les·cence [kànvəlésns / kɔ̀n-] *n.* Ⓤ a gradual recovery of health and strength after illness. 차도; (건강) 회복기; 예후(豫後). ¶ *He is now in a state of* ~. 그는 현재 회복 단계에 있다.

con·va·les·cent [kànvəlésnt / kɔ̀n-] *adj.* getting better; growing stronger after illness. 회복기의; 차도가 있는. — *n.* Ⓒ a person who is getting well. (병)회복기에 있는 사람. ¶ *a* ~ *patient* 회복기의 환자 / *a* ~ *hospital* (회복기 환자의) 요양소.

con·vec·tion [kənvékʃən] *n.* Ⓤ **1** the act of conveying. 전달. **2** 《phys.》 the transfer of heat from one place to another by means of currents of heated liquid or gas. (열의) 대류(對流); 환류(環流). [L. *convectio* carry together]

con·vene [kənví:n] *vi.* (P1) come together; assemble; gather. 모이다; 집합하다. ¶ *The committee convenes once a week.* 위원회는 주(週)에 한 번 모인다. — *vt.* (P6) call together; send for (someone). …을 소집하다; 모으다; 소환하다. ¶ ~ *a meeting* 회의를 소집하다. [L. *venio* come]

•**con·ven·ience** [kənví:njəns] *n.* **1** Ⓤ the quality of being convenient; comfort; Ⓒ advantage. 편리; 편익; 유리한 형편. ¶ *for convenience' sake* 편의상 / *for the* ~ *of* …의 편의를 위하여 / *It is a great* ~ *to live near a bus stop.* 버스 정류장 근처에 산다는 것은 매우 편리하다 / *He rented the house because of the* ~ *of it's location.* 편리한 위치 때문에 그 집에 세들었다. **2** Ⓒ anything handy or easy to use. 편리한 것; 편리한 설비. ¶ *camping conveniences* 캠핑 용구 / *a hotel with modern conveniences* 현대 시설을 갖춘 호텔 / *a house full of conveniences of every sort* 온갖 설비가 갖춰진 집 / *Electric light is a great* ~. 전깃불은 대단한 (문명의) 이기(利器)이다. **3** Ⓒ 《Brit.》 a water-closet; a privy. (수세식) 화장실; 변소. [↑]

a marriage of convenience, a marriage not for love, but for material advantage. (물질을 노린) 정략 결혼.

at one's earliest convenience, as soon as it suits one. 형편 닿는 대로 빨리. ¶ *Please send me an answer at your earliest* ~. 되도록이면 속히 회답을 주시오.

at one's (***own***) ***convenience,*** so as to suit oneself as to time, place, or other conditions. 형편〔사정〕에 유리하게.

***make a convenience of** someone,* use someone's willing service unreasonably; abuse his good nature. …을 멋대로 이용하다; …의 사람 좋음을 역이용하다.

suit 〔***await***〕 *someone's* ***convenience,*** consult his wishes as to manner, time, place, etc. 아무의 형편에 맞추다; 형편이 나아지기를 기다리다.

•**con·ven·ient** [kənví:njənt] *adj.* **1** 《*to, for, doing*》 causing no trouble; handy; easy to reach or use; suitable. 편리한; 쓰기 쉬운; 알맞은(opp. inconvenient). ¶ *a* ~ *tool* 편리한 도구 / *a place* ~ *for bathing* 미역감기에 알맞은 곳 / *live in a* ~ *house* 편리한 집에 살다 / *meet at a* ~ *place* 편리한 장소에서 만나다 / *if it is* ~ *for* 〔*to*〕 *you* (그렇게 하는 것이) 형편에 좋으시다면 / *I will come when* (*it is*)

~ *to you.* 형편 닿으실 때 찾아뵙겠습니다. **2** 《*colloq.*》 near. 가까운. ¶ *Our house is ~ to the station.* 우리 집은 역에서 가깝다.

con·ven·ient·ly [kənvíːnjəntli] *adv.* in a convenient manner. 편리하게.

·con·vent [kánvənt / kɔ́n-] *n.* Ⓒ **1** a society of women who have given themselves to a religious life; a nunnery. 수녀단. **2** a building for such a society. 수녀원(cf. *monastery*). ¶ *go into a ~* 수녀가 되다. [→convene]

con·ven·ti·cle [kənvéntikl] *n.* Ⓒ **1** formerly, a secret religious meeting of Protestants who had separated from the Church of England. (비(非)국교도의) 비밀집회. **2** 《*contempt.*》 a small building used for religious services by Nonconformists. (비국교도의) 집회소; 교회당. [↑]

:con·ven·tion [kənvénʃən] *n.* **1** Ⓒ a large meeting for some special purpose; a gathering; an assembly; a conference. 집회; 협의회; 회의; 대회. ¶ *the annual ~* 연차(年次) 대회 / *the party ~* 당(黨)대회 / *meet in ~* 대회를 열다. **2** Ⓒ 《*collectively*》 representatives to a meeting or assembly. 대표자. **3** Ⓒ an agreement between parties or nations; a treaty. 조약; 협약. **4** ⓊⒸ general consent; custom; a custom approved by general agreement; tradition. 관습; 인습; 전통. ¶ *conventions of daily life* 일상 생활의 관례 / *observe ~* 관습을 지키다 / *break* 〔*follow*〕 *established conventions* 예전부터의 인습을 깨뜨리다〔에 따르다〕/ *abandon the formal conventions of the past* 과거의 형식적 관습을 버리다. [↑]

·con·ven·tion·al [kənvénʃənəl] *adj.* **1** (of a person, etc.) depending on conventions; behaving according to convention. 인습적인. ¶ *He has a ~ mind.* 그는 인습적인 정신을 갖고 있다. **2** customary; formal; commonplace; not new or orignal. 관례의; 관습〔형식〕적인; 틀에 박힌; 평범〔진부〕한. ¶ *a ~ greeting* 상투적인 인사 / *~ phrases* 틀에 박힌 말 / *make ~ remarks* 형식적인 말을 하다 / *lead a ~ life* 평범한 생활을 하다. **3** (of art, etc.) following custom rather than nature; following the standards of a certain school; not natural or original. 전통을 따르는; 기존 양식에 바탕을 둔. **4** 《law》 based on consent or agreement. 협정의; 협약에 의한. ¶ *the ~ tariff* 협정 세율. **5** 《mil.》 not atomic. 핵(核)이 아닌. ¶ *~ weapons* 재래식 무기.

con·ven·tion·al·ism [kənvénʃənəlìzəm] *n.* **1** Ⓤ adherence to conventions. 인습〔전통〕주의; 관습 존중. **2** Ⓒ a conventional expression, idea, attitude, etc. 관례적인 표현〔생각, 태도〕; 틀에 박힌 것.

con·ven·tion·al·i·ty [kənvènʃənǽləti] *n.* (*pl.* **-ties**) **1** Ⓤ conventional quality. 인습성. **2** Ⓒ 《*the -ties*》 conventional customs or rules. 관례; 습속. **3** Ⓤ adherence to conventions. 관습 고수; 관례 존중.

con·ven·tion·al·ly [kənvénʃənəli] *adv.* in a conventional or usual manner. 인습적으로; 평범하게.

con·verge [kənvə́ːrdʒ] *vi.* (P1,2) **1** meet at a point; come together. (한 점에) 모이다; 만나다(opp. diverge). ¶ *rays which ~ into a focus* 한 초점에 모이는 빛. **2** 《*fig.*》 (of ideas, actions) be directed toward a single point or toward the same purpose or result. (공통의 목적·결과에) 집중하다. ¶ *All the interest of the town converged upon the election.* 온 마을 사람들의 관심은 선거에 집중되었다. — *vt.* (P6,7) cause (something) to converge. …을 모으다. [→verge]

con·ver·gence [kənvə́ːrdʒəns] *n.* **1** Ⓤ the act, process, or fact of converging. 한 점에 모임; 폭주(輻輳); 수렴(收斂); 귀일(歸一)(opp. divergence). **2** Ⓒ the point at which things converge. 집합점.

con·ver·gent [kənvə́ːrdʒənt] *adj.* converging. 한 점에 모이는; 수렴하는.

con·vers·a·ble [kənvə́ːrsəbəl] *adj.* fond of or pleasant in conversation. 이야기하기 좋아하는; 말 붙이기 쉬운. [→converse[1]]

con·ver·sance [kənvə́ːrsəns] *n.* Ⓤ familiarity, acquaintance. 정통(精通); 능통.

con·ver·sant [kənvə́ːrsənt, kánvər- / kɔ́nvər-] *adj.* 《*with,in*》 familiar with; having a knowledge of. …에 환한; …에 정통한; 친교가 있는. ¶ *~ with a subject* 주제에 훤한 / *~ with a person* 아무와 친교가 있는 / *be ~ in two languages* 2개 국어에 정통하다.

:con·ver·sa·tion [kànvərséiʃən / kɔ̀n-] *n.* **1** Ⓒ a familiar talk. 이야기. ¶ *a topic of ~* 화제 / *have a long ~* 오랫동안 이야기하다 / *address one's ~ to* …에게 이야기를 걸다. **2** Ⓤ talking. 서로 이야기함; 대화. ¶ *I saw him in ~ with my father.* 그가 우리 아버지와 대화하고 있는 것을 보았다. **3** Ⓤ familiar association. 친교. **4** Ⓤ 《*arch.*》 a behavior or manner of life. 풍속; 세태. ¶ *a ~ piece* 풍속화. [→converse[1]]

enter into conversation with, begin to talk with. …와 이야기하기 시작하다.

hold 〔***have***〕 ***a conversation with,*** converse with. …와 이야기하다.

con·ver·sa·tion·al [kànvərséiʃənəl / kɔ̀n-] *adj.* **1** of conversation. 대화의; 이야기의. ¶ *a book written in ~ style* 대화체로 쓰인 책 / *a ~ tone of voice* 대화조의 목소리. **2** fond of conversation. 이야기하기를 좋아하는. **3** good at conversation. 말을 잘하는.

con·ver·sa·tion·al·ist [kànvərséiʃənəlist / kɔ̀n-] *n.* Ⓒ a person who likes or who is good at conversation. 이야기를 좋아하는 사람; 이야기를 잘하는 사람.

·con·verse[1] [kənvə́ːrs] *vi.* (P1,3) talk familiarly together; chat. 환담〔대담〕하다; 이야기하다. ¶ *~ with someone on a subject* 어떤 화제로 아무와 이야기하다 / *~ in English* 영어로 대화하다. — [kánvəːrs / kɔ́n-] *n.* 《*arch., poet.*》 Ⓤ **1** conversation. 이야기; 대화. **2** familiar social intercourse. 교제; 사교. [L. *verto* turn]

·**con·verse**[2] [kənvə́ːrs, kɑ́nvəːrs / kɔ́n-] *adj.* opposite; contrary. 역(逆)의; 반대의. — [kɑ́nvəːrs / kɔ́n-] *n.* 《often *the*～》 something that is opposite or contrary; the reverse. 정반대의 것; 역. ¶ *Converses are not always true.* 역(逆)이 꼭 참은 아니다. [↑]

con·verse·ly [kənvə́ːrsli, kɑ́nvəːrs- / kɔ́n-vəːrsli] *adv.* contrarily; on the contrary. 역으로; 반대로. ¶ *Gray is lighter than black;* ～, *black is darker than gray.* 회색은 흑색보다 밝다. 거꾸로 흑색은 회색보다 어둡다.

con·ver·sion [kənvə́ːrʒən, -ʃən] *n.* Ⓤ **1** the act of converting. 전환; 변화. ¶ *the ～ of a solid into a liquid* 고체의 액체화. **2** change from one religion, etc. to another. 개종; 전향; 개심. ¶ *the ～ of the heathen* 이교도의 개종. **3** exchange. 환산. ¶ *a ～ table* 환산표. **4** 《law》 the unlawful appropriation of another's property. 횡령. ¶ ～ *of public money to one's own use* 공금 횡령. [↓]

·**con·vert** [kənvə́ːrt] *vt.* (P6,13) **1** 《*into*》 ⓐ change; turn; transform. …을 바꾸다; 변질〔변형〕시키다; 개조하다. ¶ ～ *water into steam* 물을 증기로 바꾸다 / ～ *grain into flour* 곡물을 가루로 만들다 / ～ *the sittingroom into a bedroom* 거실을 침실로 개조하다 / *We converted defeat into victory.* 우리는 패배를 승리로 바꾸어 놓았다. ⓑ exchange (something) for another thing that is equal in value. …을 (같은 가치의 것으로) 바꾸다; 환산하다. ¶ ～ *goods into money* 상품을 돈으로 바꾸다 / ～ *bank notes into gold* 은행권을 금으로 바꾸다. **2** 《*to*》 cause (someone) to change opinions or beliefs. …을 개종〔전향〕시키다; (마음·의견 따위)를 바꾸게 하다. ¶ ～ *the Moslems to Christianity* 이슬람교도를 기독교로 개종시키다 / ～ *a heathen to belief in God* 이교도로 하여금 하느님의 존재를 믿게 만들다. **3** cause (someone) to change from unbelief to faith. …을 귀의(歸依)시키다; 믿음이 생기게 하다. **4** 《law》 appropriate and use another's or public property unlawfully. …을횡령하다.

— *vi.* change one's opinions or beliefs. 개심하다; 전향하다.

— [kɑ́nvəːrt / kɔ́n-] *n.* Ⓒ a person who has been converted. 개종자; 개심자. ¶ *a ～ to Christianity* 기독교로 개종한 사람. [L. *verto* turn]

con·vert·er, -tor [kənvə́ːrtər] *n.* Ⓒ **1** a person or thing that converts. 전환시키는 사람〔것〕. **2** 《electr.》 an apparatus that changes the form of electric current. 변환기; 변류기. **3** a furnace for changing pig iron into steel. 전환로(轉換爐).

con·vert·i·ble [kənvə́ːrtəbəl] *adj.* **1** that can be converted or changed. 바꿀 수 있는; 전환〔환산〕할 수 있는. ¶ *a ～ note* 태환권(兌換券) / ～ *paper currency* 태환 지폐 / *Wood is ～ into paper.* 나무는 종이로 바꿀 수 있다 / *Heat is ～ into electricity.* 열은 전기로 전환할 수 있다. **2** (of an automobile) having a top that can be folded down. (자동차가) 접는 포장 지붕의. — *n.* Ⓒ a car with a folding top. 접는 포장 지붕의 자동차. ● **con·vert·i·bly** [-bli] *adj.* [→convert]

con·vex [kɑnvéks, kən- / kɔn-] *adj.* having a surface that curves out. 볼록한; 철면(凸面)의(opp. concave). ¶ *a ～ lens* 볼록렌즈. [L. *veho* bring]

con·vex·i·ty [kənvéksəti / kɔn-] *n.* Ⓤ the state of being convex. 볼록꼴〔면〕.

·**con·vey** [kənvéi] *vt.* (P6,13) 《*to*》 **1** take (something) from one place to another; carry. …을 나르다; 운반〔수송〕하다. ¶ ～ *goods by express* 지급편으로 화물을 보내다 / *A bus conveys passengers from the train to the boat.* 버스가 승객을 열차에서 배 있는 데로 태워 나른다. **2** pass on; conduct; transmit. (소리·열 따위)를 전달하다; 전도하다. ¶ *Air conveys sound.* 공기는 소리를 전달한다. **3** give (ideas, etc.) to another; make known; communicate. (사상·의미 따위)를 전하다; 알리다. ¶ *This poem conveys (to us) that he loved nature deeply.* 이 시는 (우리에게) 그가 자연을 깊이 사랑했다는 것을 알게 해 준다 / *words that ～ nothing to me* 내가 전혀 알 수 없는 말 / ～ *an expression of grief to someone* 아무에게 애도의 뜻을 전하다 / *Do my words ～ any meaning to you?* 내 말뜻을 알아듣겠나. **4** 《law》 transfer (property) from one person to another by a formal written paper. (정식의 증서로 재산)을 양도하다. ¶ *Mr. Wilkinson conveyed his farm to his son last year.* 윌킨슨씨는 작년에 농장을 아들에게 정식으로 넘겨주었다. [L. *veho* bring]

con·vey·a·ble [kənvéiəbəl] *adj.* that can be conveyed. 운반〔전달, 양도〕할 수 있는.

con·vey·ance [kənvéiəns] *n.* **1** Ⓤ the act of carrying; transportation. 수송; 운수; 전송(傳送). **2** Ⓒ a thing that conveys something; a vehicle. 운수 기관; 탈것《열차·선박·차량 등》. ¶ *I want a ～ to take me to the hotel.* 호텔까지 타고 갈 차가 필요하다. **3** Ⓤ communication. 전달. **4** ⓊⒸ 《law》 ⓐ a transfer of property from one person to another. (재산의) 양도; 이전. ⓑ the document by which a thing is transferred. 재산 양도〔이전〕 증서.

con·vey·er, -vey·or [kənvéiər] *n.* Ⓒ **1** a person or thing that conveys goods. 운송자〔하는 것〕. **2** a mechanical device that conveys goods. 반송대(搬送帶); 컨베이어.

·**con·vict** [kənvíkt] *vt.* (P6,13) 《*of*》 **1** prove or declare (someone) to be guilty. …의 유죄를 증명〔선고〕하다. ¶ *a convicted prisoner* 기결수 / *be convicted of theft* 절도에 관해 유죄로 인정되다 / ～ *someone of a murder* 아무를 살인에 대한 유죄로 확정하다. **2** 《*fig.*》 《usu. in *passive*》 prove to someone that he is wrong; impress with a sense of guilt. …에게 죄를 깨닫게 하다; (양심 따위의) 가책을 받게

하다. ¶ *be convicted of sin* 죄를 자각하고 있다 / *be convicted by one's conscience* 자기 양심의 가책을 받다.
— [kánvikt / kɔ́n-] *n.* Ⓒ a person convicted by a court; a person serving a prison sentence for some crime. 유죄가 선고된 사람; 죄수. ¶ *an ex-convict* 전과자 / *a ~ prison* 교도소. [→convince]

·con·vic·tion [kənvíkʃən] *n.* ⒸⓊ **1** the act of proving or declaring guilty. 유죄 선고; 유죄 판결. ¶ *a summary ~* 즉결 판결 / *The ~ of the prisoner was expected.* 죄수에 대한 유죄 판결이 예상되었다. **2** a firm belief; an assurance. 신념; 확신. ¶ *confirm the ~ that...* …라는 확신을 굳히다 / *He is a man of strong convictions.* 그는 강한 신념의 사나이다. **3** awakened consciousness of sin. 죄의 자각; 회오(悔悟). ¶ *the ~ of sin* 죄의 자각.
be open to conviction, be amenable to reason. 사리에 따르다; 설득을 받아들이다.
carry conviction, have a power to convince someone. 설득력이 있다.
in the* (*full*) *conviction, firmly convinced that.... …라고 (충분히) 확신하고.

:con·vince [kənvíns] *vt.* (P6,13,15) 《*of*》 make (someone) certain; cause (someone) to believe; make (someone) realize. …을 확신시키다; …에게 (죄·잘못 따위)를 깨닫게 하다; 설득하다; 납득시키다. ¶ *~ someone of his errors* 아무에게 잘못을 깨닫게 하다 / *~ oneself of* …을 확신하다 / *I am convinced of his innocence.* 그의 무죄를 확신하고 있다 / *He convinced himself that it was the best way.* 그는 그것이 최선의 방법임을 확신했다. [L. *vinco* conquer]

con·vinc·ing [kənvínsiŋ] *adj.* that convinces; persuading by proofs. 납득시키는; 설득력 있는. ¶ *a ~ proof* 유력한 증거 / *in a ~ manner* 납득할 수 있게.

con·vinc·ing·ly [kənvínsiŋli] *adv.* in a convincing or persuading manner. 납득할 수 있게; 설득력 있게.

con·viv·i·al [kənvíviəl] *adj.* **1** gay; cheerful. 유쾌한; 즐거운. ¶ *~ atmosphere* 즐거운(우호적인) 분위기. **2** fond of feasts; of a feast or an official dinner. 잔치를 좋아하는; 연회의. [L. *vivo* live]

con·viv·i·al·i·ty [kənvìviǽləti] *n.* Ⓤ fondness for feasts. 연회를 좋아함.

con·vo·ca·tion [kànvəkéiʃən / kɔ̀n-] *n.* **1** Ⓤ the act of calling together a meeting. (회의·의회의) 소집. ¶ *the ~ of Parliament* 의회의 소집. **2** Ⓒ a meeting. (소집된) 집회. **3** Ⓤ 《Brit.》 《usu. *C-*》 the law-making assembly of the Church of England. (영국국교의) 성직자 회의. **4** Ⓒ 《Brit.》 the law-making assembly of graduates of Oxford and Durham Universities. (Oxford, Durham 대학의) 평의회. ● **con·vo·ca·tion·al** [-ʃənəl] *adj.* [↓]

con·voke [kənvóuk] *vt.* (P6) call together; summon (a parliament, etc.) to assemble. (회의·의회)를 소집하다(opp. dissolve). ¶ *Parliament was convoked in April.* 의회가 4월에 소집되었다. ● **con·vok·er** [-ər] *n.* [com-, →vocation]

con·vo·lute [kánvəlù:t / kɔ́n-] *adj.* (of flowers, leaves, shells, etc.) rolled or wound up. 회선(回旋)하는. [↓]

con·vo·lut·ed [kánvəlù:tid / kɔ̀n-] *adj.* 《zool.》 twisted (e.g. a ram's horn). 휘어져 말린.

con·vo·lu·tion [kànvəlú:ʃən / kɔ̀n-] *n.* Ⓒ **1** a coil; a twist; something which has folds. 소용돌이 (상태); 회선(回旋); 뒤틂. ¶ *the convolutions of a snake* 뱀의 똬리 틂. **2** 《anat.》 one of the convex folds on the surface of the brain. 뇌회(腦回). [→voluble]

con·vol·vu·li [kənválvjəlai / -vɔ́l-] *n.* pl. of **convolvulus.**

con·vol·vu·lus [kənválvjələs / -vɔ́l-] *n.* (*pl.* **-li** or **-es**) 《bot.》 a bindweed. 메(꽃).

con·voy [kánvɔi, kənvɔ́i / kɔ́n-] *vt.* (P6) (of a warship) go with a ship, etc. to protect it; escort. (군함 따위가) …을 호송하다; 호위하며 가다. ¶ *A destroyer convoyed the merchant ships.* 구축함 한 척이 상선들을 호위했다. — [kánvɔi / kɔ́n-] *n.* **1** Ⓤ escort; protection. 호송; 호위. ¶ *under ~ of* …에 호위되어. **2** Ⓒ a group of warships, soldiers, etc. led or guarded by an escort. 호송되는 수송함단. **3** Ⓒ a ship, etc. that acts as an escort. 호송선. [→convey]

con·vulse [kənvʌ́ls] *vt.* (P6) **1** shake violently. 진동시키다. **2** 《usu. in *passive*》 disturb or agitate violently; cause unrest. (정치적·사회적으로) 격동시키다; 뒤흔들다. ¶ *Spain was convulsed with civil strife.* 스페인은 내란으로 뒤흔들렸다. **3** throw into convulsions from pain, disease. (고통 따위로) …에 경련을 일으키다; …을 뒤틀다. ¶ *be convulsed with pain* 고통으로 몸부림치다 / *His face was convulsed with grief.* 그의 얼굴이 슬픔으로 일그러졌다. **4** cause to laugh uproaringly. 포복절도하게 하다. ¶ *be convulsed with laughter* 자지러지게 웃다 / *The speaker convulsed the audience with his funny stories.* 연사는 우스운 이야기로 청중을 자지러지게 웃겼다. [L. *vello* pull]

con·vul·sion [kənvʌ́lʃən] *n.* Ⓒ **1** 《usu. *pl.*》 the irregular shaking of the limbs or whole body caused by illness. 경련; 쥐. ¶ *be seized with convulsions* 경련이 일어나다 / *The baby fell into a fit of convulsions.* 아기는 경기를 일으켰다. **2** a fit of laughter. 포복절도. ¶ *The funny story threw us into convulsions.* 그 우스운 이야기는 우리를 자지러지게 웃겼다. **3** a violent disturbance. (정치·사회적인) 격동; 동란; 동요. ¶ *times of political convulsions* 정치적 격동의 시대 / *Spain's internal convulsions* 스페인의 내란.

con·vul·sive [kənvʌ́lsiv] *adj.* of convulsion; having or producing convulsions. 경련(성)의; 발작적인. ¶ *~ laughter* 발작적인

웃음. ● **con·vul·sive·ly** [-li] *adv.*

co·ny, co·ney [kóuni] *n.* Ⓒ (*pl.* **-nies** or **-neys**) a rabbit fur. (한 마리분의) 토끼 모피. [L. *cuniculus*]

coo [ku:] *n.* Ⓒ a soft sound made by doves or pigeons. 구구《비둘기 울음소리》. — *v.* (**cooed, coo·ing**) *vi.* (P1) make a soft, murmuring sound. 구구하다; (남녀가) 사랑을 속삭이다. — *vt.* (P6) murmur softly; say (something) in a soft, loving manner. …을 속삭이듯 달콤한 말로 이야기하다. ● **coo·er** [ˊ-ər] *n.* [Imit.]

bill and coo, make love by soft words and caresses. 애무하며 달콤한 사랑을 속삭이다.

Cook [kuk], **James** *n.* (1728-79) an English navigator, and explorer. 쿡《영국의 항해가·탐험가》.

:cook [kuk] *vt.* **1** (P6,13,14) prepare (food, etc.) by boiling, baking, etc. …을 요리하다. ¶ ~ *the dinner* 저녁 식사를 만들다 / *The meat is not properly cooked.* 고기가 알맞게 익지 않았다. **2** (P6,7) 《*colloq.*》 《*up*》 make up; invent; prepare falsely. 조작[날조]하다; 속이다. ¶ ~ *reports* 보고를 허위로 꾸미다 / ~ *the books* 장부를 속이다 / ~ *up a story* [*an alibi*] 이야기[알리바이]를 조작하다. **3** (P6) 《*colloq.*》 tamper with. 만지작거리다; 주무르다. **4** (P6) exhaust. 몹시 지치게 하다. — *vi.* (P1) **1** be cooked. 요리되다; 익다. ¶ *This meat cooks well.* 이 고기는 잘 익는다. **2** prepare food by heating; work as a cook. 취사를 하다. ¶ *We use coal, gas, oil, and electricity for cooking.* 우리는 취사용으로 석탄, 가스, 기름 및 전기를 사용한다.

cook accounts, make accounts of money look correct although they are untrue. 장부끝을 속이다.

cook someone's goose, spoil someone's plans [enthusiasm]; ruin his chances or hopes. 아무의 계획을[열의를] 꺾다; 기회를[희망을] 없애다.

— *n.* Ⓒ a person whose work is cooking. 숙수; 요리사. ¶ *a man* ~ 남자 요리사. [L. *coquus*]

Too many cooks spoil the broth. 《*prov.*》 One in charge is enough. 사공이 많으면 배가 산으로 간다.

cook·book [kúkbùk] *n.* Ⓒ 《U.S.》 a book telling how to cook various kinds of foods. 요리책(=《Brit.》 cookery book).

cook·er [kúkər] *n.* **1** Ⓒ an instrument, esp. a stove, for cooking food. 취사용구[기구]. ¶ *a gas* ~ 가스 레인지. **2** Ⓤ kinds of fruit, etc. in relating to how well they can be cooked. 요리용 과일. **3** one who cooks (accounts) or concocts. 속이는 사람. [↑]

cook·er·y [kúkəri] *n.* (*pl.* **-er·ies**) **1** Ⓤ the art or practice of cooking. 요리법[술]. ¶ *a* ~ *book* 요리책 / *an inn noted for fine* ~ 훌륭한 요리로 유명한 여관. **2** Ⓒ a place or the tools for cooking. 요리하는 곳; 조리실; 요리 기구.

cook·ie, cook·y [kúki] *n.* Ⓒ 《U.S.》 a small, flat, sweet cake. 쿠키(cf. 《Brit.》 *biscuit*).

:cool [ku:l] *adj.* **1** moderately cold; cold to a pleasant degree; neither warm nor very cold. 시원한; 서늘한; 찬(opp. warm). ¶ *a* ~ *chamber* 냉장실 / *a* ~ *day* 서늘한 날 / *a* ~ *dress* 시원한 옷 / *keep something in a* ~ *place* …을 서늘한 곳에 간수해 두다 / *It is getting* ~. (날씨가) 서늘해지고 있다 / *The tea is* ~ *enough to drink.* 차가 마시기 좋게 식어 있다 / *Don't touch the iron till it has got* ~. 쇠는 식을 때까지 손을 대지 마라. **2** (of a person or behavior) calm; not excited. 냉정한; 침착한. ¶ *a* ~ *head* 냉정한 머리 / *keep* ~ 침착을 유지하다 / *remain* ~ 당황하지 않다 / *be* ~ *in the face of danger* 위험에 직면하여 침착을 잃지 않다 / *take a* ~ *look at* …을 냉정하게 보다 / *Keep* ~*!* (흥분하지 말고) 냉정해라. **3** lacking in eagerness or interest; not friendly; indifferent. 열의 없는; 냉담한; 쌀쌀한. ¶ *a* ~ *greeting* 겉치레의 인사 / *He gave me a* ~ *reception.* 그는 나를 차갑게 맞이했다. **4** 《*colloq.*》 calmly impudent. 뻔뻔한. ¶ *a* ~ *lie* 낯두꺼운 거짓말 / *He is a* ~ *customer* [*fish, hand*]. =*He has a* ~ *cheek.* 그는 지독히 뻔뻔스런 녀석이다. **5** 《*colloq.*》 (of a sum, amount, or distance) without exaggeration. 에누리 없는; 알속의; 딱. ¶ *a* ~ *twenty miles* 딱 20 마일 / *He lost a* ~ *thousand dollars.* 그는 거금 천 달러나 잃었다. **6** bluish, greenish, or graysh. 청색[녹색, 회색]이 섞인; 찬색(色)의. **7** (of scent in hunting) faint; weak. (사냥에서 짐승 냄새가) 희미한; 약한.

(***as***) ***cool as a cucumber*** ⇨cucumber.

— *n.* Ⓤ **1** 《usu. *the* ~》 something cool; a cool place or time. 냉기; 서늘한 곳[때]. ¶ *in the* ~ *of the morning* 아침 서늘한 때에 / *keep food in the* ~ 음식을 서늘한 곳에 두다. **2** 《*sl.*》 calm temper. 냉정; 침착. ¶ *recover one's* ~ 냉정을 되찾다.

— *vt., vi* (P6; 1,2A) make or become cool. 식(히)다; 서늘하게[차게] 하다; 서늘해지다; 가라앉다. ¶ ~ *oneself* 시원한 바람을 쐬다; 납량하다 / *The rain has cooled the air.* 비가 공기를 식혔다 / *That will* ~ *your enthusiasm.* 그것은 네 열의에 찬물을 끼얹을 게다 / *His anger hasn't cooled yet.* 그의 노여움은 아직도 가라앉지 않았다. [E.]

cool one's coppers ⇨ copper.

cool down [***off***], become or get cool; become calm. 차지다; 식다; 냉정[침착]해지다.

cool one's heels, be kept waiting. 오래 기다리게 되다.

Keep your breath to cool your porridge. Don't waste your words. 쓸데없는 말을 하지 마라.

cool·er [kú:lər] *n.* Ⓒ **1** a vessel which cools foods or drinks or keeps them cool. 냉각 용기; 냉장기(器). **2** anything that makes cool, such as a cold drink. 청량 음료. **3** an air-conditioner. 냉방 장치; 에어컨. **4** 《*sl.*》 a prison; a jail. 교도소; 감옥.

cool-head·ed [kú:lhédid] *adj.* calm. 침착한; 냉정한. ¶ *be ~ in the presence of danger* 위험에 직면하여 당황하지 않다.

coo·lie, coo·ly [kú:li] *n.* Ⓒ an unskilled workman or a laborer who does hard work for little pay in China, India, etc. (중국·인도 등의) 막노동자; 쿨리. [Hind.]

cool·ly [kú:*l*li] *adv.* in a cool way; calmly; in a friendly manner. 냉정히; 침착히; 유들유들하게. [*cool*]

cool·ness [kú:lnis] *n.* Ⓤ the state of being cool. 서늘[시원]함; 냉정; 유들유들함.

·**coon** [ku:n] *n.* Ⓒ 《U.S.》 **1** 《*colloq.*》 a raccoon. 너구리의 일종. **2** 《*sl.*》 a Negro. 흑인. ¶ *a ~ song* 흑인의 노래 / *a gone ~* 구제할 길 없는 사람; 절망적인 상황[사태]. [→racoon]

coop [ku(:)p] *n.* Ⓒ a small cage or box for chickens or small animals. 닭장; 닭의어리; 우리. — *vt.* (P6,7) **1** keep or put (something) in a coop. …을 닭장[우리]에 넣다. **2** 《*up, in*》 keep (someone or an animal) in a very small space. …을 가두다. ¶ *They were cooped up in a small room.* 그들은 작은 방안에 갇혔다. [→cupola]

co-op [kóuɑ̀p, ⌐⌐ / kóuɔ̀p] *n.* Ⓒ 《*colloq.*》 a cooperative store, society, etc. 협동[소비] 조합(의 매점).

co-op. co-operative.

coop·er [kú(:)pə*r*] *n.* Ⓒ **1** a man who makes or mends barrels, tubs, etc. 통메장이. **2** a drink of stout and porter mixed. 혼합 맥주. [→coop]

·**co·op·er·ate, co-op·er·ate** [kouɑ́pərèit / -ɔ́p-] *vi.* (P1,3,4) **1** work or act together for a common purpose. 협력[협동]하다. ¶ *~ with a friend in doing the work* 친구와 협력하여 일을 하다. **2** (of a thing) combine in producing an effect. (사정 따위가) 서로 작용하여 (…한) 결과를 낳다. [co-]

:**co·op·er·a·tion, co-op·er·a·tion** [kouɑ̀pəréiʃən / -ɔ̀p-] *n.* **1** Ⓤ the act of cooperating. 협력; 협동. **2** Ⓒ an association of people who share in both profits and losses. 협동 조합. ¶ *a consumers'* [*producers'*] *~* 소비자[생산자] 조합.

co·op·er·a·tive, co-op·er·a·tive [kouɑ́pərèitiv, -ərətiv / -ɔ́pərətiv] *adj.* of cooperation; willing to work together with others. 조합의; 협동의; 협력적인. ¶ *a ~ society* 협동 조합 / *a ~ shop* [*store*] 협동 조합 매장. — *n.* a cooperative society. 협동 조합. ¶ *a farmers' ~* 농업 협동 조합.

co·op·er·a·tor, co-op·er·a·tor [kouɑ́pərèitə*r* / -ɔ́p-] *n.* Ⓒ **1** a person who cooperates. 협력자; 협동자. **2** a member of cooperative society. 협동 조합원.

co·opt, co-opt [kouɑ́pt / -ɔ́pt] *vt.* (P6) add (someone) to a committee or some other group by election of those who are already members. (현재의 회원·위원들이) …을 새 회원[위원]으로 선출하다. ●**co·op·ta·tion** [kòuɑptéiʃən / -ɔp-] *n.* **co·op·ta·tive** [kouɑ́ptətiv / -ɔ́p-] *adj.* [→optative]

co·or·di·nate, co-or·di·nate [kouɔ́:*r*dənit, -nèit] *adj.* **1** of equal importance; on the same level. 동격의; 대등한. ¶ *be ~ with* …와 동등하다[동격이다]. **2** 《gram.》 joining words, phrases, or clauses of equal grammatical importance. 등위의 (cf. *subordinate*). ¶ *a ~ clause* 등위절 / *a ~ conjunction* 등위접속사《and, but, for, or 따위》.
— *n.* Ⓒ **1** a coordinate person or thing. 동등한 사람[것]. **2** 《usu. *pl.*》 《math.》 a system of magnitudes used to fix position of point, line, plane. 좌표.
— [kouɔ́:*r*dənèit] *vt.* (P6) **1** cause (persons or things) to work together for a common purpose; bring (parts) into a proper relation; harmonize. …을 통합[조정]하다; (한 계통의 각 부문)을 조화시키다. ¶ *~ the departments of a business* 일의 각 부문을 조화시키다. **2** make (things) equal in importance. …을 대등[동등]하게 하다. [→order]

co·or·di·na·tion, co-or·di·na·tion [kouɔ̀:*r*dənéiʃən] *n.* Ⓤ **1** the act of coordinating. 동등(하게 함); 조정. **2** the state or relation of being coordinated. 동격; 대등 관계. **3** the harmonious functioning of mus cles in the execution of a complex task. (여러 근육 운동의) 협동.

coot [ku:t] *n.* **1** 《bird》 a waterbird like a duck with a white spot on its head. 큰물닭; 검둥오리(=bald coot). ¶ *(as) bald as a ~* (큰물닭처럼) 이마가 벗어진. **2** 《*colloq.*》 a fool. 바보; 얼간이. [E.]

cop [kɑp / kɔp] *n.* Ⓒ 《*colloq.*》 a policeman. 경찰관. — *vt.* (**copped, cop·ping**) (P6) **1** steal. …을 훔치다. **2** catch; arrest. 붙잡다; 체포하다. [Obs. *cap* seize]

cop it, catch it; receive punishment. 벌을 받다.

co·part·ner [koupɑ́:*r*tnə*r*] *n.* Ⓒ a partner; an associate. (기업의) 협동자; 동료. [co-]

co·part·ner·ship [koupɑ́:*r*tnə*r*ʃìp] *n.* Ⓤ partnership. 협동; 협동 조합(원의 신분·권리). [co-]

·**cope**[1] [koup] *vi.* (P3) 《*with*》 struggle; deal successfully. (대등·유리한 상태에서) 대항하다; (문제·난국 따위를) 잘 처리[대처]하다. ¶ *~ with the crowds* 군중과 대항해 싸우다 / *~ with a situation* 정세에 대처하다 / *~ with the fear of death* 죽음의 공포에 맞서다 / *He was unable to ~ with his difficulties.* 그는 어려움에 대처할 수 없었다. [→coup]

cope[2] [koup] *n.* **1** a long cape worn by priests at special times. 코프《성직자가 특별한 행사 때 걸치는 망토 모양의 옷》. **2** something which covers like a cope; the sky. (코프처럼) 덮은 것; 하늘. ¶ *the ~ of heaven* 하늘 / *under the ~ of night* 밤의 장막을 틈타. **3** =coping. — *vt.* cover (someone) with a cope. …에게 코프를 입히다. [→cap]

co·peck [kóupek] *n.* =kopeck.

Co·pen·ha·gen [kòupənhéigən, -há-] *n.* the capital of Denmark. 코펜하겐《덴마크의 수도》.

Co·per·ni·can [koupə́:rnikən] *adj.* according to the theory of Copernicus. 코페르니쿠스 설(說)의.

Copernican theory [-ˊ-- ˋ--] *n.* the theory that the earth and the planets move round the sun. 태양 중심설; 지동설.

Co·per·ni·cus [koupə́:rnikəs], **Nicolaus** *n.* (1473-1543) a Polish astronomer. 코페르니쿠스《폴란드의 천문학자》.

cope·stone [kóupstòun] *n.* =coping-stone.

cop·i·er [kápiər / kɔ́p-] *n.* Ⓒ **1** a person who copies; a copyist. 사자(寫字)〔필경〕하는 사람; 등사인. **2** an imitator. 모방자. [→copy]

co·pi·lot [kóupàilət] *n.* the assistant or second pilot of an aircraft. (비행기의) 부조종사. [co-]

cop·ing [kóupiŋ] *n.* the sloping top of a wall of brick or stone serving to drain off the rain. 갓돌. [→cope²]

coping saw [ˊ- ˋ] *n.* a narrow saw in a U-shaped frame, used to cut curves. 실톱.

cop·ing-stone [kóupiŋstòun] *n.* Ⓒ **1** one of the stones of a coping. 갓돌(= copestone). **2** 《*fig.*》 the completing act in a piece of work; a finishing stroke. 최후 마무리. [→cope²]

co·pi·ous [kóupiəs] *adj.* abundant; plentiful. 풍부한; 많은. ¶ *a ~ harvest* 풍작 / *a ~ supply of coal* 석탄의 풍부한 공급 / *~ information* 많은 정보 / *have a very ~ vocabulary* 풍부한 어휘를 알고 있다. ● **co·pi·ous·ly** [-li] *adv.* [L. *copia* plenty]

:cop·per[1] [kápər / kɔ́p-] *n.* **1** Ⓤ a red-brown metal. 구리; 동(銅). **2** Ⓒ a thing made of copper. 구리제품. **3** Ⓒ a copper coin, such as the U.S. cent. 동화(銅貨); 동전《영국의 penny, 미국의 cent 따위》. ¶ *toss* 〔*cast*〕 *a ~ to a beggar* 거지에게 동전을 던져주다.

***cool** one's* **coppers,** 《*colloq.*》 cool one's throat by drinking water. 술깨기 위해 물을 마시다.

— *vt.* (P6) put a coat of copper on (something). …에 동을〔구리를〕 입히다.

— *adj.* **1** of copper; made of copper. 동의; 동제의. ¶ *a ~ coin* 〔*piece*〕 동전. **2** copper-colored. 구릿빛의. [*Cyprus*]

cop·per[2] [kápər / kɔ́p-] *n.* 《*sl.*》 a policeman. 경찰관(=cop). [*cop*]

cop·per·as [kápərəs / kɔ́p-] *n.* 《chem.》 녹반(綠礬). [→copper¹]

cop·per·head [kápərhèd / kɔ́p-] *n.* a poisonous North American snake which has a copper-colored head, and grows to be about three feet long. 미국살무사. [→copper¹]

cop·per·plate [kápərplèit / kɔ́p-] *n.* **1** ⓊⒸ 《print.》 a flat plate of copper on which pictures, designs, etc. are cut. (인쇄용) 동판(銅版). **2** Ⓒ a print made from such a plate. 동판 인쇄물. **3** Ⓒ copperplate printing. 동판쇄(刷). ¶ *write like ~* (동판처럼) 깨끗이 쓰다. **4** Ⓤ a fine, elegant style of handwriting. 가늘고 예쁜 필기체. — *adj.* like an impression from a copperplate; very neat. 동판쇄와 같은; 깨끗한.

cop·per·smith [kápərsmìθ / kɔ́p-] *n.* Ⓒ a man who works in copper. 구리 세공인.

cop·per·y [kápəri / kɔ́p-] *adj.* containing copper; like copper. 동을〔구리를〕 함유한; 구리와 같은.

cop·pice [kápis / kɔ́p-] *n.* Ⓒ a wood of small trees, bushes, shrubs, etc. 잡목숲. [→coup]

cop·ra [káprə / kɔ́p-] *n.* Ⓤ the dried meat of the coconut, which yields coconut oil. 코프라《야자의 과육을 말린 것》. [Port.]

copse [kaps / kɔps] *n.* Ⓒ =coppice.

Copt [kapt / kɔpt] *n.* a native Egyptian. 콥트 사람《이집트 원주민》. [Arab.]

Cop·tic [káptik / kɔ́p-] *adj.* of or by the Copts. 콥트 사람〔어(語)〕의. — *n.* the former language of the Copts. 콥트어.

cop·u·la [kápjələ / kɔ́p-] *n.* 《gram.》 the word that connects the subject and the predicate, generally *be* as in "He is a boy." 연결사. [L.]

cop·u·late [kápjəleit / kɔ́p-] *vi.* (P1) unite sexually. 교접〔교미〕하다. [↑]

cop·u·la·tion [kàpjəléiʃən / kɔ̀p-] *n.* sexual union. 성교; 교미.

cop·u·la·tive [kápjəlèitiv, -lə- / kɔ́p-] *adj.* **1** serving to connect. 연결하는. **2** 《gram.》 connecting predicate with subject; implying combination and not alternative choice. 계사(繫辭)의; 연결어적인. **3** of sexual union. 교접의; 교미의. — *n.* a copulative particle. 연결 접속사; 계사.

:cop·y [kápi / kɔ́pi] *n.* Ⓒ (*pl.* **cop·ies**) **1** a thing made like another; an imitation; a reproduction. 베낌; 사본; 모사(模寫); 모방; (그림 따위의) 복사. ¶ *a fair* 〔*clean*〕 *~* 청서 / *a rough ~* 초고 / *a ~ from Raphael* 라파엘의 모사 / *keep a ~ of* …의 사본을 떠두다 / *take a ~ of* …을 복사하다 / *I made a ~ of the letter.* 편지의 사본을 만들었다. **2** one of a number of books, magazines, newspapers, etc. made at the same printing. (동시 인쇄된 책·잡지·신문 등의) 한 부(部). ¶ *two copies of 'Life'* 라이프지(誌) 2부 / *a ~ of the first edition* 초판본(本) / *returned copies* 반품본〔잡지〕 / *a ~ in choice binding* 미장본(美裝本). **3** something set or used as a model or pattern. 본. ¶ *paint* 〔*write*〕 *from a ~* 본을 보고 그리다〔쓰다〕. **4** Ⓤ typed or written material ready to be printed. (인쇄) 원고. ¶ *follow ~* (활자를) 원고대로 짜

다 / *Printers demand* ~ *at once.* 인쇄소들은 원고를 즉시 요구한다. **5** a transcript of manorial court-roll. 초본; 등본.
— *v.* (**cop·ied**) *vt.* (P6,13) **1** make a copy of (something). …을 베끼다; 모사하다; 복사하다. ¶ ~ *a document* 서류를 베끼다 / ~ *out a picture* 그림을 모사하다 / *Copy this page.* 이 페이지를 베껴라. **2** imitate (someone) in manner, behavior, speech, etc.; take (someone) as a model and example. …을 본뜨다; 모방하다. ¶ ~ *someone's voice* 아무의 목소리를 흉내내다 / *He tries to* ~ *me.* 그는 나를 본뜨려고 애쓰고 있다 / *We should* ~ *his good points.* 그의 좋은 점을 보고 배워야 한다.
— *vi* (P1,3) make a copy; imitate. 베끼다; 모사하다; 모방하다. ¶ ~ *from* (*the*) *life* 사생하다 / ~ *after Raphael* 라파엘을 모사하다 / ~ *into a notebook* 노트에 베끼다 / *He often copies during examinations.* 그는 시험 중에 흔히 커닝을 한다. [→copious]

cop·y·book [kápibùk / kɔ́p-] *n.* Ⓒ a book containing models of handwriting for learners to copy. 습자본.
blot one's copybook, 《Brit. *colloq.*》 spoil one's record. 자기 이력에 오점을 남길 잘못을 저지르다; 경솔한 짓을 하다.

copybook maxims [**morality**] [´–– ´– [–´–––]] *n.* one of commonplace kind, like the sentences in a copybook. 진부한 격언[교훈].

cop·y·hold [kápihòuld / kɔ́p-] *n.* Ⓤ land-tenure resting on custom of a manor and with copy of its court-roll as title. 등본 보유권(에 의해 소유하는 부동산).
— *adj.* held by this tenure. 등본 보유권에 의해 소유된.

cop·y·hold·er [kápihòuldər / kɔ́p-] *n.* a person holding land by copyhold. 등본 소유권자.

cop·y·ist [kápiist / kɔ́p-] *n.* Ⓒ **1** a person who makes copies, esp. of old documents. 필생(筆生); 필경인. **2** an imitator. 모방자.

cop·y·right [kápiràit / kɔ́p-] *n.* Ⓤ the right of one person or body to publish and sell a literary or artistic work for a limited time. 저작권; 판권. ¶ *own the* ~ *on a book* 책의 판권을 소유하다 / *infringe the* ~ 저작권을 침해하다. — *adj.* protected by a copyright. 저작권[판권]이 있는. — *vt.* (P6) protect (a book, etc.) by a copyright. …의 판권을 취득하다; …을 판권으로 보호하다. ¶ ~ *a book* 책의 판권을 취득하다 / *Literary works are usually copyrighted.* 문학 작품은 보통 판권으로 보호된다.

cop·y·writ·er [kápiràitər / kɔ́p-] *n.* Ⓒ a writer of copy, esp. for advertisements. 광고 문안 작성자; 카피라이터.

co·quet [koukét] *vi.* (**-quet·ted, quet·ting**) 《*with*》 (P1,3) **1** try to attract the attention of others (usu. of the opposite set) with a pretense of fondness; flirt. 남(특히 남자)의 마음을 끌려고 하다; 교태를 짓다; 꼬리치다. ¶ *a nymphomaniac who coquets with every fellow she sees* 남자만 보면 교태를 보이는 색정광. **2** 《*fig.*》 act or treat something jokingly; trifle. 장난삼아 손을 대다; 농락하다; 만지작거리다. ¶ ~ *with politics* 심심풀이로 정치에 손을 대다. [↓]

co·quet·ry [kóukitri, –´–] *n.* ⓊⒸ (*pl.* **-ries**) the act of coquetting; the state of being coquettish. 교태; 요염함; 가지고 놂. [→cock]

co·quette [koukét] *n.* Ⓒ a woman who tries to attract men's attention or admiration to please her vanity; a flirt. 교태부리는 여자; 바람둥이 여자; 요부. [↑]

co·quet·tish [koukétiʃ] *adj.* of or like a coquette; showing coquetry. 요염한; 교태가 있는. ¶ *The woman gave him a* ~ *smile.* 여인은 그에게 요염한 웃음을 보냈다.

cor·a·cle [kɔ́:rəkl, kár- / kɔ́r-] *n.* Ⓒ a small fishing boat made of animal skin or oilcloth covering a wooden frame. (고리로 결은 뼈대에 짐승 가죽을 입힌) 작은 배. [Welsh.]

***cor·al** [kɔ́:rəl, kár- / kɔ́r-] *n.* **1** Ⓤ a hard substance made out of the skeletons of certain sea animals. 산호. **2** Ⓒ a sea animal whose skeleton forms coral. 산호충. **3** Ⓒ a piece of coral used in jewelry; a toy made of coral. 산호 세공물. **4** Ⓤ the color of red coral; deep pink. 산호빛. — *adj.* **1** of or made of coral. 산호(제)의. **2** deep pink. 산호빛의. ¶ ~ *lips* 붉은 입술. [Gk.]

coral island [´– ´–] *n.* an island formed of coral. 산호섬.

cor·al·line [kɔ́:rəlàin, kár- / kɔ́r-] *adj.* of or like coral. 산호의; 산호 같은.

coral reef [´–`] *n.* 산호초.

cor·bel [kɔ́:rbəl] *n.* Ⓒ 《archit.》 stone or timber projection from a wall to support something. (무게 따위를 받치는) 벽의 돌출부; (벽에 달아 붙인) 받침대. — *vt., vi.* (**-(l)ed**) furnish with corbels; support by corbels. corbel을 대어 받치다. [L. *corvus* raven]

:cord [kɔ:rd] *n.* **1** Ⓤ a thin rope or thick string; Ⓒ a piece of this. 굵은 끈; 노끈; 가는 밧줄. **2** Ⓒ 《anat.》 a part in an animal body resembling a cord. 삭상(索狀) 조직; 인대(靭帶). ¶ *the spinal* ~ 척수(脊髓) / *the vocal cords* 성대(聲帶). **3** ⒸⓊ 《electr.》 a long, narrow device for conveying an electric current. 코드. **4** Ⓤ ribbed fabric; corduroy. 골지게 짠 천; 코르덴. **5** 《*pl.*》 corduroy trousers. 코르덴 바지. **6** Ⓤ 《often *pl.*》 any force or influence acting as a tie or bond. 굴레; 구속; 속박. ¶ *the cords of love* 사랑의 굴레 / *the cords of discipline* 규율의 구속[속박]. **7** Ⓒ a measure for cutting wood. 코드척(尺) 평수《장작 부피의 단위로; 128 cubic feet》.
— *vt.* (P6,7) 《*up*》 fasten or connect (some-

thing) with a cord. …을 끈으로 동여매다(잇다). ¶ ~ (*up*) *a box* 상자를 끈으로 동이다(묶다). [Gk. *khordē* gut]

cord·age [kɔ́ːrdidʒ] *n.* Ⓤ **1** a collection of cords or ropes, e.g. those on a sailing ship. 끈; (밧)줄; (특히) 배의 삭구(索具). **2** the amount of wood as measured in cords. (목재·장작 따위를) 코드척(尺)으로 잰 부피; 그 평수.

Cor·de·li·a [kɔːrdíːljə] *n.* a feminine personal name. 여자 이름.

***cor·dial** [kɔ́ːrdʒəl / -diəl] *adj.* **1** hearty; friendly. 충심으로부터의; 따뜻한; 진심어린. ¶ *a ~ welcome* (*reception*) 따뜻한 환영(환대) / *a ~ handshake* 진심어린 다정한 악수 / *be ~ to anybody* 누구에게나 친절하다. **2** encouraging the heart; reviving. 기력을 북돋우는; 강심성의. ¶ *a ~ drink* 강장 음료. — *n.* Ⓒ a stimulating medicine, drink. 강심(강장)제; 흥분제. [L. *cor* heart]

cor·dial·i·ty [kɔ̀ːrdʒiǽləti, kɔːrdʒǽl- / -diǽl-] *n.* **1** Ⓤ friendliness; sincerity. 친절; 진심; 온정. ¶ *He greeted us with ~.* 그는 진심으로 우리를 환영했다. **2** Ⓒ a cordial act or remark. 진심이 넘치는 언동; 친절한 말(행위). ¶ *exchange of cordialities* 다정한 인사의 교환.

cor·dial·ly [kɔ́ːrdʒəli] *adv.* in a cordial manner; heartily; sincerely. 마음으로부터; 진심으로.

cor·dil·le·ra [kɔ̀ːrdəljɛ́ərə, kɔːrdílərə] *n.* Ⓒ 《Sp.》 a long, narrow mountain range, esp. in South and Central America. 연산(連山); 산계(山系); 대륙의 주요 산맥《특히 라틴 아메리카의》.

cord·ite [kɔ́ːrdait] *n.* Ⓤ a smokeless explosive. 무연(無煙) 화약. [*cord*]

cor·don [kɔ́ːrdn] *n.* Ⓒ **1** a line or circle of policemen, soldiers, ships, etc. enclosing or guarding a place. 비상(경계)선; 초병선. ¶ *draw* (*place, throw*) *a ~* 비상선을 펴다 / *pass a ~ of police* 경찰의 비상망을 뚫다 / *a sanitary ~* (전염병 구역의) 방역선 / *A ~ of policemen was drawn around the hotel.* 호텔 주위에 경찰의 비상선이 쳐졌다. **2** a cord worn as an ornament or as a mark of honor. 수장(綬章); 장식 리본. ¶ *the blue ~* 청(靑)수장 / *the grand ~* 대수장. **3** a course of stone projecting from the surface of a wall. (벽면의 중간 또는 기부에 수평으로 설치된) 돌출 석층(石層).
— *vt.* (P7) surround with a line of soldiers, policemen, etc. (군인·경찰이 줄지어) 에워싸다; …에 비상선을 (둘러) 치다. [F., → cord]

cor·du·roy [kɔ́ːrdərɔ̀i, ⌐–⌐] *n.* **1** Ⓤ thick cotton cloth with raised lines on its surface. 코르덴. **2** 《*pl.*》 trousers made of corduroy. 코르덴 바지. — *adj.* **1** made of corduroy. 코르덴제의. **2** 《U.S.》 made of logs laid across low wet land. (습한 땅에 길 따위를) 통나무를 놓아 만든. ¶ *a ~ road* 통나무길. [F. *cord de roi* cord of the king]

CORE [kɔːr] 《U.S.》 Congress of Racial Equality. 인종 평등 회의.

core [kɔːr] *n.* Ⓒ **1** ⓐ the central part of a thing. …의 심(心); 중심부. ¶ *the ~ of rock* 암심(岩心) / *the ~ of a pencil* 연필의 심. ⓑ the hard, central part of fruits. 과일의 속; 핵(核). ¶ *This pear is rotten at the ~.* 이 배는 속까지 썩어 있다. **2** 《*fig.*》 the central and most important part. 중심; 핵심; 정수. ¶ *the ~ of a dispute* 논의의 핵심. **3** 《electr.》 a bar of soft iron in an induction coil. (유도 코일의) 철심(鐵心). **4** an internal mold. 주물(鑄物)의 심형(心型); 코어《공간을 내기 위한》. ***to the core,*** thoroughly. 속속들이; 철두철미. ¶ *rotten to the ~* 속속들이 썩은 / *He is American to the ~.* 그는 철두철미한 미국인이다.
— *vt.* (P6,7) remove the core from (an apple, etc.). …의 심(속)을 빼다. ¶ ~ *an apple* 사과 속을 빼내다. [L. *cor* heart]

Co·re·a [kɔríːə] *n.* =Korea.

core curriculum [⌐ –⌐––] *n.* the curriculum of a course of education in which all the subjects are based on a certain theme. 코어 커리큘럼《사회생활에 중점을 두어 핵심적으로 편성하는 교과 과정》.

co·re·li·gion·ist [kòurilídʒənist] *n.* Ⓒ a person having the same religion as another. 같은 종교를 믿는 사람. [co-]

cor·er [kɔ́ːrər] *n.* Ⓒ a device for removing cores from fruit. (과일의) 심 빼내는 기구. [*core*]

co·re·spond·ent [kòurispɑ́ndənt / -pɔ́nd-] *n.* Ⓒ 《law》 a person proceeded against together with the respondent in divorce suit. 이혼 소송의 공동 피고. [co-]

Co·rin·thi·an [kərínθiən] *adj.* **1** of Corinth. (고대 그리스의 도시) 코린트의. **2** 《archit.》 of the classical orders of Greek architecture. 코린트식의. — *n.* **1** Ⓒ a native of Corinth. 코린트 사람. **2** 《*pl.*》 《Bible》 either of two books of the New Testament consisting of two letters written by Saint Paul to the Christians in Corinth. 고린도서(書). [Gk.]

***cork** [kɔːrk] *n.* **1** Ⓤ the bark of a kind of oak. 코르크(나무의 껍질). **2** Ⓒ a cork oak. 코르크 나무. **3** Ⓒ a piece of cork used as a stopper for a bottle, etc. 코르크 마개. ¶ *the ~ of a bottle* 코르크 병마개. — *adj.* made of cork. 코르크제(製)의. ¶ *a ~ sole* (구두의) 코르크 창 / *a ~ carpet* 코르크제 깔개. — *vt.* (P6,7) **1** stop (a bottle, etc.) with a cork; put (a cork) in a bottle. …에 코르크마개를 하다. **2** 《*up*》 hold back; check. 억제하다; 저지하다. ¶ ~ *up one's feelings* 감정을 억누르다. **3** blacken (the face, etc.) with burnt cork. (얼굴 따위)를 태운 코르크로 검게 칠하다. ¶ ~ *one's eyebrows* 코르크로 눈썹을 그리다. [L. *quercus* oak]

cork·screw [kɔ́ːrkskrùː] *n.* Ⓒ a tool for

removing corks from bottles. (병의) 코르크 따개. — *adj.* shaped like a corkscrew; spiral. 나사모양의. ¶ *a ~ staircase* 나선 계단 / *a ~ path* 꾸불꾸불한 길. — *vt., vi.* (P6; 1) move or advance in a spiral or zigzag course. 나사 모양으로 움직이다[나아가다].

cork·y [kɔ́:rki] *adj.* (**cork·i·er, cork·i·est**) **1** of or containing cork. 코르크의; 코르크를 포함한. **2** like cork. 코르크 같은. **3** 《*colloq.*》 lively; frivolous; skittish. 활발한; 경박한; 변덕스러운.

corm [kɔ:rm] *n.* Ⓒ 《bot.》 a bulb like underground stem of plants such as the crocus. 구경(球莖). [Gk.]

cor·mo·rant [kɔ́:rmərənt] *n.* Ⓒ **1** a large, long-necked sea bird, used in catching fish. 가마우지. **2** 《*fig.*》 a person who always desires more food or more things. 욕심쟁이. [L. *corvus marinus* sea raven]

:corn[1] [kɔ:rn] *n.* **1** Ⓒ a single seed of a grain such as wheat, barley or rye. (곡식의) 낟알. **2** Ⓤ 《U.S.》 a tall plant that bears large grains on ears; Indian corn. 옥수수. **3** Ⓤ 《Brit.》 wheat; 《Scot.》 oats. 밀; 귀리. ¶ *a field of ~* 밀[귀리, 옥수수]밭. **4** Ⓤ 《*collectively*》 grain in general. 곡류. ¶ *gather* [*reap*] ~ 곡식을 거두어들이다. **5** Ⓤ a plant that produces such seeds. 곡초(穀草). ¶ *cut* [*mow*] *the ~* 곡초를 베어들이다.

corn in Egypt, a good harvest. 풍요(豐饒).

eat one's corn in the blade, live in luxury in anticipation of earnings. 수입을 내다보고 사치 생활을 하다.

— *vt.* (P6) **1** keep or preserve (meat, etc.) with salt in the form of grains. (고기 따위를) 소금에 절여 보존하다. **2** sow land with corn. 곡식 낟알을 뿌리다. — *vi.* (P1) (of wheat, barley, etc.) form grain. 여물다. [E.]

corn[2] [kɔ:rn] *n.* Ⓒ a hardened part of the skin, esp. on the toes. 티눈. ¶ *Shoes that do not fit properly often cause corns on the toes.* 잘 맞지 않는 신발은 종종 발가락에 티눈이 생기게 한다. [L. *cornu* horn]

tread on someone's corns, hurt someone's feelings. 아무의 감정을 해치다.

corn bread [⌐⌐] *n.* 《U.S.》 bread made of corn meal. 옥수수빵.

corn chandler [⌐⌐–] *n.* 《Brit.》 a merchant dealing in grain. 곡물상(商).

corn·cob [kɔ́:rnkɑ̀b / -kɔ̀b] *n.* Ⓒ the long wood-like core of an ear of maize, used for a tobacco-pipe. 옥수수의 속대. ¶ *a ~ pipe* 옥수수 속대로 만든 곰방대. [→corn[1]]

cor·ne·a [kɔ́:rniə] *n.* Ⓤ 《anat.》 horny transparent structure in front of the eyeball. (눈의) 각막. [→corn[2]]

corned [kɔ:rnd] *adj.* preserved or kept with salt. 소금에 절인. ¶ ~ *beef* 콘비프. [→corn[1]]

cor·nel [kɔ́:rnəl] *n.* Ⓒ 《bot.》 kinds of trees, especially Cornelian cherry. 산딸나무속(屬)의 관목류. [L. *cornus*]

cor·ne·lian [kɔ:rní:ljən] *n.* Ⓒ a red stone used in jewelry. 홍옥수(紅玉髓)(=carnelian). [↑]

:cor·ner [kɔ́:rnər] *n.* Ⓒ **1** ⓐ the point or angle where two lines or surfaces meet. 모서리; 모[귀]퉁이. ¶ *the corners of a table* 테이블 모서리. ⓑ the place where two streets meet. 길모퉁이. ¶ *a drugstore at* [*in*] *the ~ of the street* 길모퉁이의 약국 / *turn a ~* 길모퉁이를 돌다. **2** the enclosed angle formed by meeting walls of a room, sides of a box, etc. 구석. ¶ *a chair in the ~ of the room* 방 한구석에 있는 의자 / *stand* [*put*] *a child in the ~ of a room* (*as a punishment*) (벌로) 아이를 방구석에 세워두다. **3** a distant or hidden place; an out of the way place. 멀리 떨어진 곳; 외진[궁벽한] 곳. ¶ *remote corners* 궁벽한 시골. **4** a secret place; a region. 눈에 띄지 않는 곳; 지역. ¶ *The money was hidden in odd corners all over the house.* 돈은 온 집안 구석구석 눈에 안 띄는 곳에 숨겨져 있었다. **5** an awkward position from which escape is difficult. 궁지; 난처한 입장. ¶ *in a tight ~* 궁지에 빠져 / *I was put* [*driven*] *into a ~.* 나는 궁지에 몰렸다. **6** a piece to protect a corner. 코너《보호하기 위해 귀퉁이에 대는 것》. **7** 《comm.》 the purchase of a large amount of some stock or article to raise its price. (값을 올리기 위한) 대량 매점; 사재기. ¶ *a ~ in wheat* 밀의 사재기. **8** 《soccer》 =corner-kick.

(a)round the corner, near at hand; not far off. 바로 가까이; 가까운 곳에.

be in a tight corner, be in a difficult or threatening position from which escape is difficult. 궁지에 빠져 있다.

cut corners, **a**) take a shorter way. 지름길로 가다. **b**) reduce the money, time or labor required. 절약하다.

do in a corner, do in secret. 비밀로[몰래] 하다.

drive someone into a corner, 《*fig.*》 put someone into a difficult position. 아무를 궁지에 몰아넣다.

establish [***make***] ***a corner in,*** buy up. …을 매점(買占)하다.

keep a corner, keep a room. 약간의 장소를 남겨두다.

turn the corner, **a**) pass round the corner into another street. 길모퉁이를 돌다. **b**) 《*fig.*》 pass a crisis safely (in illness, etc.). (병 따위의) 고비를 넘기다.

— *vt.* (P6) **1** supply (something) with a corner. …에 모서리를 내다. **2** drive or put (someone or something) into a corner. …을 구석으로 보내다; 구석에 두다. **3** force (someone) into an awkward or difficult position. …을 궁지에 몰아넣다. **4** 《comm.》 buy up (some stock or article) to raise its

price. …을 매점(買占)하다.
— *vi.* (P3) **1** 《comm.》 buy up; form a corner. 매점을 하다. ¶ ~ *in cotton* 솜을 사재다. **2** (of a car) tarn a corner. (길)모퉁이를 돌다.
— *adj.* at or on a corner. 모퉁이(구석)의. ¶ *a ~ store* 모퉁이 가게. [→corn²]

cor·ner-kick [kɔ́:rnərkìk] *n.* 《soccer》 a free kick from the corner of the field. 코너킥.

cor·ner·stone [kɔ́:rnərstòun] *n.* Ⓒ **1** the stone at the corner of a building foundation. (건물의) 초석; 귓돌. **2** the most important or basic thing; a foundation. 중요한 것; 기본적인 것; 기초; 토대. ¶ *lay a ~ in the foundation of physical chemistry* 물리 화학의 기초를 쌓다.

cor·ner·wise [kɔ́:rnərwàiz], **cor·ner·ways** [-wèiz] *adv.* **1** with the corner in front; forming a corner. 모서리를 앞으로 하여; 모서리를 이루어. **2** from one corner to the opposite corner. 대각선으로.

cor·net [kɔ:rnét, kɔ́:rnit] *n.* Ⓒ **1** a musical brass instrument like a trumpet. 코넷《악기》. **2** a cone-shaped piece of paper for candy, etc; 《Brit.》 a cone-shaped wafer for containing ice cream. 원뿔 모양의 종이 봉투; (아이스크림용) 원뿔꼴 웨이퍼. [→corn²]

cor·net·ist [kɔ:rnétist, kɔ́:rnit-] *n.* Ⓒ a cornet-player. 코넷 주자(奏者).

corn·field [kɔ́:rnfì:ld] *n.* Ⓒ a field in which corn is grown. 옥수수(밀)밭. [*corn*¹]

corn·flakes [kɔ́:rnflèiks] *n. pl.* a breakfast food consisting of small toasted flakes made from corn and eaten with milk and sugar. 콘플레이크스.

corn flour [∠∠] *n.* 《U.S.》 flour made from corn; 《Brit.》 flour made from grain. 옥수수 가루; 곡물 가루.

corn·flow·er [kɔ́:rnflàuər] *n.* Ⓒ 《bot.》 a name of various plants growing among corn. 수레국화; 선옹초(류).

cor·nice [kɔ́:rnis] *n.* Ⓒ **1** 《archit.》 an ornamental molding placed along the top of a wall, a pillar, etc. 배내기; 외벽 윗부분에 두른 수평 쇠시리 장식. **2** projecting snow at the edge of a precipice. 벼랑 끝에 처마 모양으로 얼어붙은 눈덩이. [It.]

〈cornice 1〉

Cor·nish [kɔ́:rniʃ] *adj.* of or belonging to Cornwall. (영국) 콘월 지방의. — *n.* Ⓤ the Cornwall language (extinct since 18th c.). (18세기 이후 사라진) 콘월 말. [Celt.]

Corn Laws [∠∠] *n. pl.* 《Brit. hist.》 a series of laws for regulating trade in corn, effective until 1846. 곡물법(穀物法).

corn meal [∠∠] *n.* Ⓤ **1** 《U.S.》 meal made from corn. 맷돌에 탄 옥수수. **2** 《Sc.》 oatmeal. 오트밀.

cor·no·pe·an [kɔ:rnóupiən, kɔ̀:rnəpí:ən] *n.* =cornet.

corn rent [∠∠] *n.* a rent paid in, or varying with the price of, corn. (밀로 내는, 또는 시세 변동에 따라 달라지는) 소작료.

corn·starch [kɔ́:rnstà:rtʃ] *n.* Ⓤ 《U.S.》 a kind of flour made from corn and used in cookery. 콘스타치《옥수수의 녹말》. [→corn¹]

cor·nu·co·pi·a [kɔ̀:rnjukóupiə] *n.* **1** 《myth.》 the horn of the goat Amalthea, which gave milk to Zeus. (제우스에게 젖을 주었다는) 아말테아의 양뿔. **2** a horn-shaped container or ornament. (원)뿔 모양의 그릇(장식). **3** the horn of plenty represented with fruits, flowers, and corn flowing from it. 풍요의 뿔《원하는 대로 온갖 음식·과일 따위가 나왔다고 함》. **4** 《*fig.*》 a plentiful supply or store. 풍부한 공급(여축). **5** a symbol of plenty; abundance. 풍부의 상징; 풍요. [→corn², copious]

Corn·wall [kɔ́:rnwɔ:l] *n.* a county in southwestern England. 잉글랜드 남서부의 주(州). [Celt.]

corn·y [kɔ́:rni] *adj.* **1** of or abundant in corn. 곡류의; 곡류가 풍부한. **2** 《*sl.*》 old-fashioned; weakly sentimental. 낡은; 구식의; 진부한. ¶ ~ *jokes* 진부한 농담. [*corn*¹]

co·rol·la [kərálə / -rɔ́lə] *n.* Ⓒ 《bot.》 the petals of a flower. 화관; 꽃부리. [↓]

cor·ol·lar·y [kɔ́:rəlèri, kár- / kərɔ́ləri] *n.* Ⓒ (*pl.* **-la·ries**) **1** 《math.》 a statement which may be taken for granted when another has been proved. 계(系)《정리(定理)에서 추측할 수 있는 명제》. **2** a natural result. 자연의 귀결(결과). [↓]

co·ro·na [kəróunə] *n.* Ⓒ (*pl.* **-nas** or **-nae**) **1** a crown; something shaped like a crown. 관(冠); 관 모양의 것. **2** ⓐ a ring of light seen around the sun or the moon. 광환(光環); 광륜(光輪)(cf. *halo*). ⓑ 《astron.》 a bright ring seen around the sun during a total eclipse. (개기(皆旣)일식 때의) 광관(光冠); 코로나. [L. *corona* crown]

co·ro·nae [kəróuni:] *n.* pl. of **corona.**

cor·o·nal [kɔ́:rənəl, kár- / kɔ́r-] *n.* Ⓒ **1** a circular ornament (of gold, gems, etc.) for the head. (머리에 쓰는) 장식 고리; 보관(寶冠). **2** a garland (of flowers, etc.) for the head. 화관(花冠). — [kəróunəl, kɔ́:rə-, kárə- / kɔ́rə-] *adj.* **1** 《astron.》 of or belonging to a corona. 광환(光環)의; 코로나의. **2** of the crown of the head. 왕관의; 화관의. [→corona]

cor·o·na·ry [kɔ́:rənèri, kár- / kɔ́rənəri] *adj.* of or resembling a crown. 관(冠)의; 관과 같은.

coronary thrombosis [∠—— ∠—] *n.* 《med.》 thrombosis of the heart, involving a coronary artery. 심장 관상 동맥 혈색(血塞).

cor·o·na·tion [kɔ̀:rənéiʃən, kàr- / kɔ̀r-] *n.*

Ⓒ the act or ceremony of crowning a king, a queen, or another ruler. 대관식(戴冠式).

cor·o·ner [kɔ́:rənər, kár- / kɔ́r-] *n.* Ⓒ a local official whose duty is to investigate any unnatural death. 검시관(檢屍官). ¶ *coroner's inquest* 검시. ● **cor·o·ner·ship** [-ʃip] *n.*

cor·o·net [kɔ́:rənit, kár- / kɔ́r-] *n.* Ⓒ **1** a small crown worn by princes or nobles. (귀족의) 보관(寶冠); 소관(小冠). **2** an ornamental band worn around the head. (여성용의) 작은 관 모양의 머리 장식. **3** 《*poet.*》 a garland for the head. 화관(花冠). [L. *corona* crown]

Co·rot [kɔróu], **Jean Baptiste Camille** *n.* (1796-1875) a French painter. 코로《프랑스의 화가》.

Corp. Corporal; Corporation.

cor·po·ra [kɔ́:rpərə] *n.* pl. of **corpus.**

cor·po·ral[1] [kɔ́:rpərəl] *n.* Ⓒ a soldier in the army below a sergeant. 상(등)병. [It. *caporale*]

cor·po·ral[2] [kɔ́:rpərəl] *adj.* **1** of the body; bodily. 인체(人體)의; 신체상의(cf. *corporeal*). ¶ ~ *punishment* 체벌. **2** personal. 개인의. ¶ ~ *possession* 사유물(私有物). [L. *corpus* body]

cor·po·ral·i·ty [kɔ̀:rpərǽləti] *n.* **1** body. 육체. **2** 《*pl.*》 bodily matters, wants, etc. 육체상의 일〔욕망〕.

cor·po·rate [kɔ́:rpərit] *adj.* **1** forming a corporation. 법인 조직의. ¶ ~ *property* 법인 재산 / *a body* ~ =*a* ~ *body* 법인 단체. **2** of or related to a corporation. 공동의; 단체의〔에 관계있는〕. ¶ ~ *responsibility* 공동 책임. **3** united; combined; as a group. 일체가 된; 합체한; 단결한. [L. *corpus* body]

:cor·po·ra·tion [kɔ̀:rpəréiʃən] *n.* Ⓒ **1** a group of people permitted by law to act for purposes of business. (사단) 법인. **2** ⓐ any group of persons united in one body. (일반적으로) 단체; 조합. ⓑ the body of persons who have charge of the public business of a city or town. 자치체. **3** 《U.S.》 a limited liability company or a joint-stock company. 유한(有限)〔주식〕회사. **4** 《*colloq.*》 a large and prominent abdomen. 올챙이배.

cor·po·re·al [kɔ:rpɔ́:riəl] *adj.* **1** bodily; physical. 신체〔육체〕상의 (opp. spiritual) (cf. *corporal*[2]). **2** material; physical; tangible. 물질의〔적인〕; 유체(有體)의. ¶ ~ *capital* 유형(有形) 자본 / ~ *property* 유체 재산. ● **cor·po·re·al·i·ty** [kɔ:rpɔ̀:riǽləti] *n.* **cor·po·re·i·ty** [kɔ̀:rpərí:əti] *n.* [L. *corpus* body]

·corps [kɔ:r] *n.* Ⓒ (*pl.* **corps** [kɔ:rz]) **1** a part of an army consisting of two or more divisions. 군단; 병단. ¶ *an army* ~ 군단. **2** a specialized branch of the armed forces. 대(隊); 반(班). ¶ *the Marine Corps* 해병대 / *the Signal Corps* 통신대 / *the Medical Corps* 의료반. **3** a group of people united in some special work. (일반적인) 단체; 단(團). ¶ *the diplomatic* ~ 외교단 / *an editorial* ~ 기자단 / *a* ~ *de ballet* [də bǽlei] 발레단 / *a* ~ *of 300 demonstrators,* 3백명의 데모대. [↓]

corpse [kɔ:rps] *n.* Ⓒ (usu. of a human being) a dead human body. (인간의) 시체; 사체(cf. *carcase*). [L. *corpus* body.]

cor·pu·lence [kɔ́:rpjələns], **-len·cy** [-si] *n.* Ⓤ largeness or stoutness of body; fatness. 비만; 비대. [↓]

cor·pu·lent [kɔ́:rpjələnt] *adj.* (of a human being) stout; fat; fleshy. 비만한; 살찐; 뚱뚱한.

cor·pus [kɔ́:rpəs] *n.* (*pl.* **-po·ra**) Ⓒ **1** a part of a bodily organ; a body. 기관(器官); 몸. **2** a collection of writings or laws, esp. the whole collection of a particular period etc. 집성(集成); 전집. ¶ *the* ~ *of Latin poetry* 라틴시(詩)전집. [L. *corpus* body]

Cor·pus Chris·ti [kɔ́:rpəs kristi] *n.* feast of the body of Christ on Thursday after Trinity Sunday. 성체 축일(聖體祝日).

cor·pus·cle [kɔ́:rpəsəl, -pʌsəl], **cor·pus·cule** [kɔ:rpʌ́skju:l] *n.* Ⓒ **1** a very small particle. 미립자. **2** one of the cells which float in the blood. 혈구; 피톨. ¶ *red* 〔*white*〕 *corpuscles* 적〔백〕혈구. **3** 《phys.》 an electron. 전자. [→corpus]

cor·pus de·lic·ti [kɔ́:rpəs dilíktai] *n.* essence of any particular breach of law. 범죄 사실; 범죄의 기초적 요소.

cor·pus ju·ris [kɔ́:rpəs dʒúəris] *n.* the law as the sum of laws. 법전(法典).

cor·ral [kərǽl / kɔrá:l] *n.* Ⓒ **1** a circular fence to hold horses, cattle, etc.; a pen. 가축을 가두는 우리. **2** a defensive enclosure surrounded by wagons. 야영자가 둥글게 둘러친 수레들. — *vt.* (**-ralled**) (P6) **1** drive or put (animals) into a corral. (마소)를 우리 안으로 몰아넣다. **2** form such a circle with (wagons). (수레)로 둥글게 진을 치다. [L. *curro* run]

:cor·rect [kərékt] *adj.* **1** in accordance with facts; true; right. 옳은; 진실의; 정확한. ¶ *a* ~ *answer* 정답 / *the* ~ *time* 정확한 시간 / *a* ~ *statement* 틀림없는 진술 / ~ *pronunciation* 정확한 발음 / *His prediction proved* ~. 그의 예언이 정확했음이 판명되었다. **2** agreeing with a good standard of taste; proper; suitable. 표준에 맞는; 적당한; 적절한. ¶ ~ *manners* 바른 예절 / *She wore the* ~ *dress for a wedding.* 그녀는 예식용 정장을 입었다.

the correct thing, something suitable to the circumstances, what is expected. 바로 그것〔일〕; 의당 그래야 할 일.

— *vt.* (P6,13) **1** make (something) right; point out the errors of (something). …을 정정하다; 바로잡다; 고치다. ¶ ~ *errors* 〔*mistakes*〕 잘못을 고치다 / ~ *proofs* 교정하다 / ~ *one's watch* 시계를 맞추다 / *The teacher corrected my composition.* 선생님은 내 작문을 고

쳐주셨다. **2** punish (someone) in order to correct a bad action. …을 벌하다. ¶ ~ *a boy for disobedience* 말을 안 듣는다고 아이를 벌주다. **3** cure; neutralize. (병)을 고치다; 치료[중화]하다. ¶ ~ *acidity in the stomach* 위산 과다를 치료하다. **4** adjust. …을 보정(補正)[조정]하다. ¶ ~ *the parallax* 시차(視差)를 보정하다. [co-, L. *rego* rule]

stand corrected, accept correction. 정정을 받아들이다. ¶ *I stand corrected.* 정정을 받아들입니다.

·cor·rec·tion [kərékʃən] *n.* UC **1** the act of correcting. 고침; 정정; 수정; 조정. ¶ *the ~ of a composition* 작문의 첨삭 정정. **2** a thing that is put in place of a mistake. 정정한 것; 정정 자구(字句); 정정한 곳. ¶ *This exercise is full of corrections.* 이 연습 문제는 고친 곳 투성이다. **3** punishment. 벌; 징계; 교정(矯正). ¶ *subject a student to ~* 학생을 징계하다.

a house of correction, a reformatory; a prison. 소년원; 교도소.

speak under correction, speak with consciousness that what one says may not be accurate. 틀린 점이 있으면 정정 받도록 하고 이야기하다.

cor·rect·i·tude [kərékt**ə**tjù:d] *n.* U the quality of being correct in conduct. 품행 방정; 단정; 적정.

cor·rec·tive [kəréktiv] *adj.* tending to correct. 고치는; 교정하는; 바로잡는. ¶ ~ *exercises* 교정 체조 / ~ *punishment* 교정적 체벌 / *I have to take ~ measures.* 교정책을 강구해야만 한다. — *n.* C something serving to correct. 교정하는 것[수단, 대책]; 중화물.

cor·rect·ly [kəréktli] *adv.* in a correct way. 바르게; 정확히. ¶ *behave* [*speak*] ~.

cor·rect·ness [kəréktnis] *n.* U the quality or state of being correct. 바름; 정확(함); (행동의) 방정; 단정.

cor·re·late [kɔ́:rəlèit, kɑ́r- / kɔ́r-] *vt.* (P6,13) 《*with*》 bring (something) into a common relation with another thing. …을 서로 관련시키다. ¶ ~ *the findings of geography with those of history* 지리학상의 발견을 역사의 그것과 관련시키다 / *We may ~ crime with poverty.* 범죄를 빈곤과 관련시킬 수 있다. — *vi.* (P1,3) 《*to, with*》 have the same relation with a second thing toward a third thing. 서로 관련하다; 상관 관계에 있다. ¶ *Crime and poverty often ~ (to* [*with*] *each other).* 범죄와 빈곤은 흔히 상호 관계가 있다. — *n.* C either of two closely related things. 상호관계에 있는 것(의 한쪽). — *adj.* closely related. 서로 관련이 있는; 상관 관계에 있는. [com-]

cor·re·la·tion [kɔ̀:rəléiʃən, kɑ̀r- / kɔ̀r-] *n.* U the same relation between two or more things toward something else. 상호관계; 상관관계. ¶ *the ~ between climate and crops* 기후와 수확간의 상관관계.

cor·rel·a·tive [kərélətiv] *adj.* **1** having correlation. 상호[상관] 관계에 있는. **2** 《gram.》 regularly used in pairs. 서로 호응해서 사용되는; 상관적인. ¶ ~ *conjunctions* 상관 접속사. — *n.* C 《gram.》 a correlative word. 상관어(語). ¶ *Pairs of words like 'not only ...but also', 'man and wife', are called correlatives.* 'not only ...but also', 'man and wife' 처럼 짝을 이룬 말들을 상관어라고 한다.

·cor·re·spond [kɔ̀:rəspɑ́nd, kɑ̀r- / kɔ̀rəspɔ́nd] *vi.* (P1,3) **1** 《*to, with*》 agree in amount, position, etc.; come up to; fit. 일치[합치]하다; 부합하다; 어울리다. ¶ *His promises do not ~ with his actions.* 그의 약속과 행동이 일치하지 않는다 / *The reality does not always ~ with one's expectations.* 현실은 반드시 기대와 일치하지는 않는다 / *His house corresponds to his wealth.* 집이 그의 부(富)에 어울린다. **2** 《*to*》 be equal to; be like or similar. (…에) 상당하다; …와 같다. ¶ *The broad lines on the map ~ to roads.* 지도의 굵은 줄은 도로에 상당한다 / *The U.S. Congress corresponds to the British Parliament.* 미국의 Congress는 영국의 Parliament에 해당하는 것이다. **3** 《*with*》 communicate by letters. 서신 왕래를 하다. ¶ *I ~ with her regularly.* 그녀와 정기적으로 서신 왕래를 하고 있다. [→respond]

·cor·re·spond·ence [kɔ̀:rəspɑ́ndəns, kɑ̀r- / kɔ̀rəspɔ́nd-] *n.* U **1** agreement; harmony. 일치; 부합; 조화. ¶ *Your account of the accident has little ~ with the story John told.* 사고에 대한 너의 설명은 존의 이야기와는 거의 일치하지 않는다. **2** similarity. 상당; 해당; 유사. **3** 《*with*》 communication by exchanging letters with each other. 서신왕래. ¶ *be in regular ~ with someone* 아무와 정기적으로 서신을 주고 받다 / *I have been in ~ with him.* 그와 서신왕래를 해왔다 / *They kept up ~ during the summer.* 그들은 여름 동안 편지를 주고받았다. **4** 《*collectively*》 letters. 편지.

correspondence course [–––´– ˊ] *n.* a series of lessons given by a correspondence school on a subject. 통신 교육 과정.

correspondence school [–––´– ˊ] *n.* a school that gives lessons by mail. 통신 교육 학교.

:cor·re·spond·ent [kɔ̀:rəspɑ́ndənt, kɑ̀r- / kɔ̀rəspɔ́nd-] *n.* C **1** a person who exchanges letters with someone. 서신 교환[왕래]자. ¶ *My pen pal is a good ~.* **2** a person hired by a news agency, etc. to gather and send news from a distant place. 특파원; 통신원[기자]. ¶ *a London ~* 런던 통신원 / *a war ~* 종군 기자 / *a foreign ~ for the New York Times* 뉴욕타임스 해외 통신원 / *as a special ~ of the Times* 타임스지(紙)의 특파원으로서. **3** 《comm.》 a person or company having regular business relations with another, usu. in a distant city. (상사 등의) 원격지 거래 담당원; 지방 주재원[대리점]. — *adj.* in agreement. 일치하는; 상응[대응]하는; 상당하는. ¶ *be ~ to* …와 일치[유사]하

다; …에 대응하다. [→respond]

cor·re·spond·ing [kɔ̀:rəspándiŋ, kɑ̀r- / kɔ̀rəspɔ́nd-] *adj.* **1** 《*to*》 agreeing; equivalent. (…에) 상당하는; 일치하는; 유사한. ¶ *the ~ period of last year* 작년의 같은 시기. **2** accompanying (…에) 수반하는; 따르는. ¶ *rights and ~ duties* 권리와 그에 따르는 의무. **3** communicating by letters. 통신하는 〔의〕; 서신을 주고받는. ¶ *a ~ clerk* (회사의) 통신담당원. ● **cor·re·spond·ing·ly** [-li] *adv.*

·**cor·ri·dor** [kɔ́:ridər, kár-, -dɔ̀:r / kɔ́ridɔ̀:r] *n.* Ⓒ **1** ⓐ a passageway; a long hallway. 복도. ¶ *I went through the ~.* 복도를 따라서 갔다. ⓑ a narrow passage from end to end of a railway coach. (열차의) 객차의 복도. **2** 《polit. geog.》 a narrow strip of land with foreign territory on either side. 회랑 지대(回廊 地帶). ¶ *the Danzig* [dǽntsig] *Corridor* 단치히 회랑. [→corral]

cor·ri·gen·da [kɔ̀:ridʒéndə, kɑ̀r- / kɔ̀r-] *n.* pl. of **corrigendum**.

cor·ri·gen·dum [kɔ̀:ridʒéndəm, kɑ̀r- / kɔ̀r-] *n.* Ⓒ (*pl.* **-da**) **1** an error to be corrected in a manuscript, printing, etc. (정정해야 할) 잘못; 오식. **2** 《*pl.*》 a list of corrections of errors in a book. 정오표(正誤俵). [↓]

cor·ri·gi·ble [kɔ́:ridʒəbəl, kár- / kɔ́r-] *adj.* **1** that can be corrected. 고칠〔교정할〕 수 있는. ¶ *He is a ~ criminal.* 그는 갱생할 가망이 있는 죄인이다. **2** willing to be reformed. 순순히 고치는. [→correct]

cor·rob·o·rant [kərábərənt / -rɔ́b-] *adj.* **1** corroborating; confirming. 확증하는; 확증적인. **2** invigorating. 강하게 하는; 기운을 북돋는. ¶ *a ~ medicine* 강장제. [↓]

cor·rob·o·rate [kərábərèit / -rɔ́b-] *vt.* confirm; strengthen. …을 확증(確證)하다; 강화하다. ¶ *~ one's authority* 권위를 강화하다 / *~ a rumor* 〔*report*〕 풍설이〔보도가〕 사실임을 확증하다. [L. *robur* strength]

cor·rob·o·ra·tion [kərɑ̀bəréiʃən / -rɔ̀b-] *n.* Ⓤ **1** the act of corroborating. 확실히 함; 강화; 확증. **2** anything that corroborates or confirms. 확증하는 것〔사실〕.

cor·rob·o·ra·tive [kərábərèitiv, -rət- / -rɔ́bə-] *adj.* corroborating; confirming. 확인의; 확증적인.

cor·rob·o·ra·tor [kərábərèitər / -rɔ́b-] *n.* Ⓒ a person or thing that corroborates or confirms. 확증인(人)〔물〕.

cor·rode [kəróud] *vt.* (P6) **1** eat away gradually by chemical action; eat into the surface of (something); rust. …을 침식〔부식〕하다. ¶ *Rust and acids ~ iron.* 녹과 산(酸)은 쇠를 부식시킨다. **2** 《*fig.*》 weaken or destroy (spirit, strength or force); consume; impair. (마음·성격 따위)를 좀먹다; 나쁘게 만들다. ¶ *Jealousy corroded her character.* 질투로 인해 그녀의 성격은 나쁘게 변했다. — *vi.* (P1) become corroded; wear away. 부식하다; 좀먹히다. ¶ *Iron corrodes quickly.* 쇠는 급속히 부식한다. [L. *rodo* gnaw]

cor·ro·sion [kəróuʒən] *n.* Ⓤ **1** the act of corroding; the state of being corroded; gradual decay. 부식 (작용·상태); (마음을) 좀먹어듦. ¶ *a ~ inhibitor* 부식 방지제. **2** a product of corroding. 부식에 의해 생기는 물질《녹 따위》. [↑]

cor·ro·sive [kəróusiv] *adj.* having the power to corrode; eating away. 부식성의. ¶ *Some acids are ~ to the skin.* 어떤 산(酸)은 피부를 부식시킨다. — *n.* Ⓒ anything that causes corrosion. 부식제(劑).

cor·ru·gate [kɔ́:rəgèit, kár- / kɔ́rə-] *vt.* (P6) shape (something) into wavelike folds. …을 물결 모양으로 하다; …에 물결 모양의 주름을 잡다. ¶ *~ the brows* 〔*forehead*〕 눈살〔이맛살〕을 찌푸리다. — *vi.* (P1) become corrugated. 물결 모양이 되다; 주름이 지다. [L. *ruga* wrinkle]

cor·ru·gat·ed [kɔ́:rəgèitid, kár- / kɔ́rə-] *adj.* formed into folds; wrinkled. 물결 모양의; 주름진. ¶ *~ iron* 〔*paper*〕 골함석〔골판지〕.

cor·ru·ga·tion [kɔ̀:rəgéiʃən, kɑ̀r- / kɔ̀rə-] *n.* ⓊⒸ **1** the act of corrugating; the state of being corrugated. 물결 모양으로〔골지게〕 하기〔되기〕; 주름이 잡힘. **2** a fold; a wrinkle; a furrow. 물결 모양의〔골이 진〕 것; 주름; 홈.

·**cor·rupt** [kərʌ́pt] *adj.* **1** rotten; changed from a sound condition to an unsound one. 부패한; 오염된. ¶ *~ meat* 부패한 고기 / *~ teeth* 충치 / *a ~ smell* 썩은 냄새 / *a ~ river with waste from factories* 공장에서의 폐기물로 오염된 강. **2** evil; wicked; taking bribes; dishonest. 타락한; 악덕의; 뇌물이 통하는; 부정(직)한. ¶ *a ~ society* 타락한 사회 / *~ practices* 부정 행위 / *a ~ judge* 독직판사. **3** (of words) different from standard usage. 사투리의; 전와(轉訛)된. **4** (of writings, text, etc.) made inferior by errors; not genuine or complete. 개악된; 원형이 훼손된. — *vt.* (P6) **1** cause (someone) to be dishonest or wicked. …을 타락시키다; (도덕적으로)부패시키다. ¶ *~ youth* 젊은이를 타락시키다. **2** offer money to cause (someone) to do what is wrong. …을 뇌물로 매수하다. ¶ *~ an official* / *~ voters* 투표자를 매수하다. **3** make (something) impure; decay. …을 부패시키다. **4** make (a text, etc.) worse by changing it. (원문에 손을 대어) 개악하다. ¶ *a text corrupted by a careless copyist* 부주의한 필경자에 의해 개악된 원문. **5** cause (a form or meaning) to differ from standard usage. (언어)를 전와(轉訛)시키다. — *vi.* (P1) become corrupt or rotten. 부패하다; 타락하다. [L. *rumpo* break]

cor·rupt·i·ble [kərʌ́ptəbəl] *adj.* that can be corrupted. 부패〔타락〕하기 쉬운; 매수할 수 있는. ● **cor·rupt·i·bil·i·ty** [kərʌ̀ptəbíləti] *n.*

cor·rup·tion [kərʌ́pʃən] *n.* Ⓤ **1** the act of decaying; rottenness. 부패; 썩음. ¶ *the ~ of the body* 육신의 부패 / *the political ~* 정계의 부패. **2** lack of moral principle. 타락. **3** the act of offering money, etc. to do what is wrong; bribery; dishonesty. 증수회; 독직; 부정. ¶ *a case of* ~ 수회 사건. **4** the act of making something impure. 불순화; 오염. **5** the act of changing for the worse; the state of being changed for the worse. (원작의) 개악. **6** the act of causing the form or meaning of a word to differ from standard usage. (언어의) 전와(轉訛). ¶ *the ~ of a language* 언어의 전와.

cor·rup·tive [kərʌ́ptiv] *adj.* tending to corrupt. 부패성의; 타락시키는; 퇴폐적인.

cor·sage [kɔːrsɑ́ːʒ] *n.* Ⓒ the waist of a woman's dress. 코르사주. [L. *corpus* body]

cor·sair [kɔ́ːrsɛər] *n.* Ⓒ **1** a pirate. 해적. **2** a pirate ship. 해적선(船). **3** =privateer. [L. *curro* run]

corse [kɔːrs] *n.* 《*poet.*》=corpse.

corse·let [kɔ́ːrslit] *n.* a coat of armor protecting the body. 흉갑(胸甲). [↓]

cor·set [kɔ́ːrsit] *n.* Ⓒ 《often *pl.*》 a close-fitting kind of underclothes worn by women to give shape to the waist and hips. 코르셋. [→corsage]

Cor·si·ca [kɔ́ːrsikə] *n.* a French island in the Mediterranean. 코르시카 (섬). ● **Cor·si·can** [-sikən] *adj.*

cor·tege, -tège [kɔːrtéiʒ] *n.* Ⓒ 《F.》 《*collectively*》 **1** a line or group of persons walking along in a ceremonial way; a ceremonial march. 의식 행렬. **2** a group of followers, attendants, etc. 한떼의 수행자들.

Cor·tes [kɔ́ːrtez / -tes] *n. pl.* the Parliament of Spain or Portugal. 코르테스《스페인 또는 포르투갈의 의회》. [→court]

cor·tex [kɔ́ːrteks] *n.* Ⓒ (*pl.* **-ti·ces**) **1** 《bot.》 the skin on the outside of a tree; the bark. 피층(皮層); 수피(樹皮). **2** 《anat.》 the outer layer of some organs, esp. outer gray matter of the brain. 외피(外皮); (특히 뇌의 회백질의) 외층(外層). [L. =bark]

cor·ti·cal [kɔ́ːrtikəl] *adj.* of or connected with a cortex. 외피(外皮)의; 피질(皮質)의; 피층(皮層)의. [↑]

cor·ti·ces [kɔ́ːrtəsìːz] *n.* pl. of **cortex.**

cor·ti·sone [kɔ́ːrtəsòun, -zòun] *n.* a hormone derived from adrenal gland. 코르티손《부신 피질 호르몬의 일종》. [↑]

co·run·dum [kərʌ́ndəm] *n.* Ⓤ a crystallized mineral allied to sapphire and ruby used as polishing powder. 강옥석(鋼玉石); 금강사(砂). [Tamil.]

cor·us·cate [kɔ́ːrəskèit, kɑ́r- / kɔ́r-] *vi.* (of stars, jewels, etc.) sparkle; flash; shine. 번쩍이다. ¶ *a coruscating star* 반짝이는 별 / 《*fig.*》 *coruscating wit* 번뜩이는 재치. [L.]

cor·us·ca·tion [kɔ̀ːrəskéiʃən, kɑ̀r- / kɔ̀r-] *n.* a sudden flash or spark of light, wit, etc. 번쩍임; (재치 따위의) 번뜩임.

cor·vée [kɔːrvéi] *n.* 《F.》 **1** (in feudal times) unpaid, forced labor performed by peasants on roads, etc. (봉건(封建) 시대의) 강제 노역(勞役); 부역(賦役). **2** a hard, unwillingly performed duty. (의무로서 부과되는) 고된 봉사 노역; 근로 봉사. [com-, L. *rogo* demand]

cor·vette [kɔːrvét] *n.* **1** 《*arch.*》 a flush-decked warship with one tier of guns. 평(平)갑판 일단 포장(一段砲裝)의 군함. **2** a small fast naval escort-vessel. 소형의 쾌속 경장(輕裝)의 호위함(艦). [L. *corbis* basket]

cor·ymb [kɔ́ːrimb, kɑ́r / kɔ́r-] *n.* 《bot.》 a species of inflorescence; raceme in which lower flower-stalks are proportionally longer. 산방화서(繖房花序). ● **co·rym·bose** [kərímbous] *adj.* [Gk.]

cor·y·phée [kɔ̀ːriféi, kɑ̀r- / kɔ́rifèi] *n.* 《F.》 the leading dancer in a ballet. 소군무(小群舞)에서 리드하는 발레 댄서.

cos. cosine.

C.O.S., cos cash on shipment.

cosec. cosecant.

cos [kɑs / kɔs] *n.* Ⓒ 《bot.》 a crisp long-leaved lettuce. 상추의 일종. [Place]

cosh [kɑʃ / kɔʃ] 《chiefly Brit. *sl.*》 *n.* a short thick stick used as a weapon; an attack with a cosh. 곤봉 (공격). — *vt.* strike with a cosh. 곤봉으로 때리다. [Romany =stick]

co·sig·na·to·ry [kousígnətɔ̀ːri / -təri] *adj.*, *n.* (a person) signing jointly with others. 연서(連署)의; 공동 서명자. [co-]

co·sine [kousáin] *n.* Ⓤ 《math.》 the sine of the complement of an angle. 코사인; 여현(餘弦). [L. *cosinus* sine of the complement]

cos·met·ic [kɑzmétik / kɔz-] *n.* Ⓒ things used for beautifying the skin, the lips, etc. such as powder, lipstick, and face cream. 화장품. — *adj.* beautifying the skin, the hair, the nails, etc. 화장용의; 미용의. ¶ ~ *salves* 화장용 연고. [→cosmos]

cos·me·ti·cian [kɑ̀zmətíʃən / kɔ̀z-] *n.* a person whose occupation is making, selling, or applying cosmetics. 화장품 제조〔판매〕업자; 미용사.

cos·mic [kɑ́zmik / kɔ́z-] *adj.* **1** of or belonging to the cosmos or the whole universe. 우주의. ¶ ~ *laws* 우주의 법칙 / ~ *dust* 우주진(塵) / ~ *philosophy* 우주 진화론 / ~ *fog* 〔*clouds*〕 성운(星雲) / ~ *rays* 우주선. **2** orderly. (질서) 정연한(opp. chaotic). **3** universal; vast. (시간적·공간적으로) 무한한; 광대 무변한. [→cosmos]

cos·mog·o·ny [kɑzmɑ́gəni / kɔzmɔ́g-] *n.* **1** the origin of the universe. 우주의 기원(起源). **2** a theory of the origin of the universe. 우주 개벽론. [→cosmos]

cos·mog·ra·phy [kɑzmɑ́grəfi / kɔzmɔ́g-] *n.* description or mapping of universe or earth. 우주 형상지(形狀誌); 우주 구조론. ● **cos·mog·ra·pher** [-fər] *n.*

cos·mol·o·gy [kɑzmɑ́lədʒi / kɔzmɔ́l-] *n.* theory of the nature of the universe. 우주론(論). ● **cos·mo·log·i·cal** [kɑ̀zmoulɑ́dʒikəl /

kɔ̀zmouládʒ-] *n., adj.* **cos·mol·o·gist** [kazmálədʒist / kɔzmɔ́l-] *n.*

cos·mo·naut [kázmənɔ̀:t / kɔ́z-] *n.* an astronaut. 우주 비행사.

cos·mo·poli·tan [kàzməpálətən / kɔ̀zməpɔ́l-] *adj.* **1** belonging to all parts of the world; widely spread. 전세계에 걸친; 세계(국제)적인. ¶ *a ~ city* 국제 도시. **2** feeling at home all over the world; free from national or local prejudices. 세계를 내집으로 삼는; 한 나라(지방)의 편견을 초월한. ¶ *a ~ outlook* 세계적인 시야(견해) / *~ ideals* 세계주의적인 이상 / *~ traits* (*indifference*) 코스모폴리탄적인 특성(무관심). — *n.* Ⓒ a cosmopolitan person; a person who feels at home in all parts of the world. 세계인; 세계주의자. [↓]

cos·mop·o·lite [kazmápəlàit / kɔzmɔ́p-] *n.* a citizen of the world. 세계주의자; 세계인. — *adj.* free from national prejudices. 국가적 편견(偏見)이 없는. ● **cos·mo·pol·i·tism** [-tìzəm] *n.*

·cos·mos [kázməs / kɔ́zmɔs] *n.* (*pl.* **-mos·es**) **1** Ⓤ the universe considered as an orderly, harmonious system. (질서 정연한 체계로서의) 우주(opp. chaos). **2** Ⓤ a complete and harmonious system. (관념·사상 등의) 체계; 질서; 조화. **3** Ⓒ 《bot.》 a tall garden plant of the aster family that blooms in autumn. 코스모스. [Gk. =world, order, adornment]

cos·mo·tron [kázmətràn / kɔ́zmətrɔ̀n] *n.* 《phys.》 an atomic accelerator. 코스모트론 《가속기(加速器)의 일종》. [*cosmos*+*electron*]

Cos·sack [kásæk, -sək / kɔ́sæk] *n.* a member of a Turkish people subject to Russia and famous as light cavalry. 코사크인(人). [Turk.]

cos·set [kásit / kɔ́s-] *vt.* (P6,7) treat as a pet or very tenderly. 어하다; 몹시 귀여워하다. ¶ *~ a sick child* 앓는 아이를 떠받들다. — *n.* a pet lamb. 어미 없이 키운 새끼양. [E.]

:cost [kɔ:st / kɔst] *vt.,vi.* (**cost**) (P6,7,14;2B) 語法 본디 cost는 자동사이므로 수동형으로 할 수 없음. **1** require as the price; need. (비용·대가 등이) 들다; (시간 등이) 걸리다; …을 요하다. ¶ *The house ~ him £4,000.* 그 집을 사는데 4천 파운드 들었다 / *What does it ~?* 값이 얼마인가 / *How much does it ~ to build such a house?* 이런 집을 짓는데 얼마나 드나 / *That attempt ~ much time and effort.* 그 시도에는 많은 시간과 노력을 요했다 / *His education ~ him nothing.* 그는 돈 한 푼 들이지 않고 교육을 받았다. **2** cause a loss. …을 희생으로 하다; 대가로 치르다; …을 잃게 하다. ¶ *a victory that ~ 50,000 lives* 5만 명의 생명을 대가로 치르고 얻은 승리 / *It may ~ your life* (*fortune, health*). 그걸로 인해 자넨 생명(재산, 건강)을 잃을지도 모른다 / *The work ~ me many a sleepless night.* 그 사업 때문에 나는 며칠 밤이나 잠을 못 잤다. **3** 《comm.》 calculate the cost of producing an article. 생산비를 어림하다.

***cost** someone **dear**(**ly**),* **a**) involve someone in much loss or expenditure. …에게 막대한 손실을 끼치다(비용이 들게 하다). **b**) make someone have a terrible experience. …을 혼나게 하다.

cost what it may, by all means; at any price. 무슨 일이 있어도; 꼭.

— *n.* **1** ⓊⒸ the price paid in return for a thing; expense; charge. 값; 원가; 비용. ¶ *the ~ of living* 생계비 / *the ~ of production* 생산비; 제조원가 / *prime* (*first*) *~* 구입원가 / *at my ~* 내 비용으로 / *at a reduced ~* 할인 가격으로 / *sell at* (*below*) *~* 원가(이하)로 팔다 / *bring back the ~* 밑천을 뽑다 / *What was the ~ of your hat?* 자네 모자 얼마 줬나. **2** 《*pl.*》 the expenses of a lawsuit. 소송 비용. **3** Ⓒ a sacrifice or loss of time, money, labor, health, etc. (시간·돈·노력·건강 따위의) 희생; 손실; 고통. ¶ *the ~ in manpower* 인력의 손실 / *at someone's ~* 아무를 희생시켜; 아무에게 손해를 끼치고 / *at a heavy* (*great*) *~* 큰 손해를 보고; 큰 희생을 치르고. [co-, L. *sto* stand; →constant]

at all costs, however much it may cost. 어떤 비용이 들어도; 어떤 희생을 치르더라도 (=at any cost). ¶ *We have to obtain our rights at all costs.* 무슨 일이 있어도 우리의 권리를 획득해야 한다. 「꼭; 기어코.

at any cost, by all means. 무슨 일이 있어도;

at the cost of, at the loss; at the expense of. …을 희생으로 하여. ¶ *He saved the child at the ~ of his own life.* 그는 자기 목숨을 버리고 그 아이를 구했다.

cost free=free of cost.

count the cost, consider all the circumstances beforehand. 사전에 모든 사정을 고려하다.

free of cost, free of charge. 무료로; 거저.

to one's cost, to one's loss, injury or disadvantage. 피해(손해)를 보고; 쓰라린 경험을 하고. ¶ *He found to his ~ that motoring is dangerous.* 그는 혼이 나고서야 차 운전이 위험하다는 것을 알았다.

cos·tal [kástl / kɔ́stl] *adj.* 《anat.》 of the ribs. 늑골의. [L. *costa* rib]

Cos·ta Ri·ca [kástə rí:kə, kɔ́:s- / kɔ́s-] *n.* a republic in Central America. 코스타리카.

cos·ter [kástər / kɔ́s-] *n.* 《colloq.》 =costermonger.

cos·ter·mon·ger [kástərmʌ̀ŋgər / kɔ́stər-] *n.* Ⓒ 《esp. Brit.》 a person who sells fruit, vegetables, fish, etc. from a handcart or stand in the street. (과일·생선 따위를 파는) 거리의 도붓장수; 행상인. [*costard* apple]

cos·tive [kástiv / kɔ́s-] *adj.* **1** (of the bowls) difficult to empty. 변비의(로 고생하는). **2** niggardly; jejune. 인색한; 빈약한. **3** 《*fig.*》 slow in expressing one's thoughts and feelings, etc.; excessively reserved in manner. (의견 발표 등이) 굼뜬; 느린; 입이 무거운. [co-, L. *stipo* press]

cost·li·ness [kɔ́stlinis] *n.* Ⓤ great cost; the state of being costly. 고가(高價). [→cost]

:cost·ly [kɔ́ːstli / kɔ́st-] *adj.* (**-li·er, -li·est**) of great value; valuable; expensive. 고가(高價)의; 귀중한; 비용이 많이 드는.

·cos·tume [kástjuːm / kɔ́s-] Ⓒ **1** ⓐ complete set of clothes, esp. of a woman. (특히 여성의 위아래) 갖춤 의상; 복장. ¶ *Korean girls look better in their national* ~. 한국 여성은 한복이 더 잘 어울린다. ⓑ clothes generally. (일반적으로) 의상; 옷. ¶ *Her* ~ *was simple but expensive.* 그녀의 의상은 단순했으나 비쌌다. **2** clothes for a special purpose. (특수 목적의) 의복; 옷. ¶ *a riding* [*dancing*] ~ 승마[댄싱]복 / *a hunting* ~ 사냥복 / *a* ~ *ball* 가장 무도회. **3** Ⓤ clothes of a certain place or period of time. (어떤 지방·시대의) 의상. ¶ *Highland* ~ 스코틀랜드 고지 의상 / *Victorian* ~ 빅토리아조(朝)의 의상.
— [-⌐] *vt.* (P6) provide a costume for (someone); dress. …에게 의상을 입히다. [→custom]

costume piece [⌐-⌐] *n.* a play in which actors wear historical costume. 역사극《시대 의상을 입고 연기하는》.

cos·tum·er [kástjuːmər, -⌐- / kɔ́s-, -⌐-], **cos·tum·i·er** [-iər] *n.* a person who makes or deals in costumes. 옷 만드는[파는] 사람.

co·sy [kóuzi] *adj.* (**-si·er, -si·est**) =cozy.

·cot[1] [kat / kɔt] *n.* Ⓒ **1** a narrow, portable bed, sometimes made of canvas stretched on a frame. (즈크를 댄) 간이 침대. **2** 《Brit.》 a child's crib. 소아용 침대. [Hind.]

:cot[2] [kat / kɔt] *n.* Ⓒ **1** 《*poet.*》 a cottage. 초라한 집; 오두막. **2** a small place of shelter for birds, sheep, etc. (가축·새의) 우리. [E.]

cot. cotangent.

cote [kout] *n.* Ⓒ a shelter or shed for small animals, birds, etc. (가축·새의) 우리. ¶ *a dovecote* 비둘기장. [E.]

co·ten·ant [kouténənt] *n.* a tenant sharing the same property with another or others. 공동 차지(借地)[차가(借家)]인. [co-, →tenant]

Côte d'I·voire [kòut divwáːr] *n.* =the Ivory Coast. [F.]

co·te·rie [kóutəri] *n.* Ⓒ a group of persons who are joined together by common interests and who often meet socially. (취미·목적을 함께 하는) 동아리; 동인(同人); 그룹. [F.]

co·til·lion [koutíljən] *n.* Ⓒ a lively dance for four couples. 코티용《8인이 추는 춤》. [F.]

:cot·tage [kátidʒ / kɔ́t-] *n.* Ⓒ **1** a small house, esp. in the country. 작은 집; (조그만) 시골집. ¶ *from the modest* ~ *to the most splendid mansion* 조그만 주택에서 훌륭한 저택에 이르기까지. **2** 《U.S.》 a house at a summer resort. (휴양지 등에 있는 여름철) 별장. [→cot[2]]
love in cottage, marriage on a small income; a poor but happy married life. 가난하지만 살뜰한 사람의 보금자리.

cottage cheese [⌐-⌐] *n.* a soft cheese made of curd. 코티지 치즈《매우 연하고 순한 풍미의 치즈》.

cottage loaf [⌐-⌐] *n.* a loaf of bread made of two round parts, one stuck on top of the other. 대소 2개의 생빵을 포개어 구운 둥근 빵.

cottage piano [⌐- ⌐-] *n.* a small upright piano. 작은 수형(竪型) 피아노.

cot·tag·er [kátidʒər / kɔ́t-] *n.* Ⓒ a person who lives in a cottage. 시골집[오두막]에 사는 사람. [→cot[2]]

cot·tar, cot·ter[1] [kátər / kɔ́t-] *n.* a cottager, esp. a Scottish peasant who works for a farmer and lives in a cottage on the farm. (스코틀랜드의) 소작인. [↑]

cot·ter[2] [kátər / kɔ́t-] *n.* 《mech.》 a wedge or bolt to hold parts of machinery together. 코터; 쐐기전(栓). [Du. *keutel* cotter]

:cot·ton [kátn / kɔ́tn] *n.* Ⓤ **1** soft, white fibers attached to the seeds of a certain plant. 솜; 목화. ¶ *raw* ~ 원면(原綿). **2** the plant that produces these fibers. 목화(나무). **3** thread made of cotton fibers. 면사(綿絲); 실. ¶ *a needle and* ~ 무명실을 꿴 바늘. **4** cloth made of cotton thread. 면포(綿布); 무명.
— *adj.* made of cotton. 면제(綿製)의; 무명의. ¶ ~ *cloth* 무명.
— *vi.* (P1,2A,3) 《*to, with*》 become friendly with; be favorably impressed (by an idea, etc.). …와 사이좋게 지내다; 친해지다; 찬성[동조]하다. ¶ *I don't* ~ *to him at all.* 그를 좋아하지 않는다. [Arab.]
cotton on to, 《*colloq.*》 take a liking to ; understand. …이 좋아지다 ; 이해하다.
cotton up to, 《*arch.*》 become friends with. …와 친해지다.

cotton cake [⌐-⌐] *n.* cattle food made by pressing out oil from cottonseeds. 면화씨 깻묵《사료용》.

cot·ton-gin [kátndʒìn / kɔ́tn-] *n.* 《U.S.》 a machine for separating the fibers of cotton from the seeds. 조면기(繰綿機).

cot·ton·oc·ra·cy [kàtənákrəsi / kɔ̀tənɔ́k-] *n.* the cotton planting interest. 면업자(綿業者); 면업계(綿業界).

cot·ton-plant [kátnplæ̀nt / kɔ́tn-] *n.* the plant which bears cotton. 목화나무.

cot·ton·seed [kátnsìːd / kɔ́tn-] *n.* the seed of the cotton-plant. 목화씨; 면실(綿實). ¶ ~ *oil* 면실유(綿實油).

cot·ton·tail [kátntèil / kɔ́tn-] *n.* a common American rabbit with a short white tail. 야생 토끼의 일종《미국산》.

cot·ton·wood [kátnwùd / kɔ́tn-] *n.* 《bot.》 a kind of American poplar. 사시나무의 일종《미국산》.

cot·ton·wool [kátnwúl / kɔ́tn-] *n.* Ⓤ

raw cotton. 원면(原綿).

cot·ton·y [kátni / kɔ́t-] *adj.* of or like cotton. 솜의; 솜 같은.

cot·y·le·don [kàtəlí:dən / kɔ̀t-] *n.* 《bot.》 the first leaf growing from a seed. 떡잎; 자엽(子葉). [Gk. *kotulē* cup]

:couch [kautʃ] *n.* Ⓒ **1** a thing on which a person lies to sleep or to rest. 누워 잘 수 있는 긴 의자; 낮은 소파. **2** a place to sleep or rest. 침소; 잠자리; 쉬는 곳; 보금자리; 굴. ¶ *retire to one's* ~ 잠자리에 들다 / *The lion got up from its grassy* ~ 사자는 그의 풀밭 잠자리에서 일어섰다.

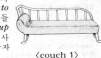

〈couch 1〉

— *vt.* **1** (P6,13) 《usu. in *passive*》 lay (oneself) down. (몸)을 눕히다. ¶ *be couched upon the ground* 땅 위에 눕다. **2** (P6,13) put (an idea, etc.) into words; state. 말로 나타내다 〔표현하다〕. ¶ *a refusal couched in very polite terms* 매우 정중한 말로 넌지시 비추는 거절. **3** (P6) put in a position ready to attack. 공격 자세를 취하다. ¶ ~ *a spear* 창을 꼬느다.
— *vi.* (P1,3) **1** lie down on a couch; repose. 침상〔소파〕에 눕다; 휴식을 취하다. **2** lie in hiding in order to attack later. (덤벼들려고) 몸을 도사리다. [→collocate]

couch·ant [káutʃənt] *adj.* 《her.》 lying down with the head up. (사자가) 머리를 쳐든 자세로 웅크린. ¶ *a lion* ~. [↑]

cou·gar [kú:gər] *n.* Ⓒ (*pl.* **-gars** or *collectively* **-gar**) 《zool.》 a large, brownish-yellow American wildcat; a puma. 퓨마. [S-Amer.]

·cough [kɔ:f, kɑf / kɔf] *vi., vt.* (P1; 6,7) force air with noise from the lungs in order to clear the throat. 기침을 하다. ¶ ~ *oneself hoarse* 기침으로 목이 쉬게 하다.

cough down, (of audiences) silence (a speaker) by coughs. (청중이) 기침을 하여 (연설자를) 침묵시키다〔방해하다〕.

cough out, get rid of (phlegm, etc.) by means of coughing. 기침을 하여 (가래 따위를) 뱉어내다.

cough up, **a**) force out (something) by coughing. 기침을 하여 …을 내뱉다. ¶ ~ *up a fishbone* 기침을 하여 생선 가시를 뱉어내다. **b**) 《U.S. *colloq.*》 make (a secret, etc.) known carelessly; pay up (something) unwillingly. 무심결에 지껄이다; 마지 못해 지불하다. **c**) give; hand over. 건네〔넘겨〕 주다.
— *n.* Ⓒ **1** the act or repeated acts of coughing. 기침. **2** a disease marked by coughing. 기침을 하는 병. ¶ *have a bad* ~ 기침을 몹시 하는 병에 걸린다. [Imit.]

churchyard cough, a very severe cough. 극심한 기침; 다 죽어가는 맥없는 기침.

cough drop [⌐⌐] *n.* a tablet taken to alleviate a cough. 진해정(鎮咳錠).

:could [kəd, kud] *auxil. v.* p. of **can¹**. **1** 《expressing capacity, permission》 ⓐ 《a single action; only *negative* or *interrogative*》 ¶ *My homework was so difficult that I* ~ *not do it.* 숙제가 하도 어려워서 할 수가 없었다. ⓑ 《continuous or habitual past action》 ¶ *When I was young, I* ~ *run fast.* 젊었을 때 나는 빨리 달릴 수 있었다. ⓒ 《in *indirect speech*》 ¶ *He said* (*that*) *he* ~ *run a mile.* 그는 1마일을 뛸 수 있다고 했다. **2** 《in unfulfilled conditions》 ¶ *If I* ~ *go, I would be glad.* 갈 수 있다면 좋을 텐데 / *He* ~ *have passed the examination if he had studied hard.* 열심히 공부했더라면 시험에 합격할 수 있었을 텐데. **3** 《expressing a polite request in the *present*》 ¶ *When you go out,* ~ *you post this letter?* 외출하실 때 이 편지 좀 부쳐 주시겠습니까. [*can*]

:could·n't [kúdnt] =could not.

·couldst [kudst] *auxil. v.* 《*arch., poet.*》 = could. 語法 주어 thou에 쓰임.

cou·lee [kú:li] *n.* **1** 《U.S.》 a deep ravine or gulch, usually dry in summer. 깊은 골짜기 〔협곡〕. **2** a stream of lava. 용암류(熔岩流). [F. *couler* to flow]

cou·lomb [kú:lɑm / -lɔm] *n.* 《electr.》 the practical unit of quantity measuring electricity. 쿨롱《전기량의 실용 단위》. [Person]

:coun·cil [káunsəl] *n.* Ⓒ a meeting or a group of elected persons for making plans or carrying out some special business. 회의; 협의〔심의〕회; 평의회. ¶ *a cabinet* ~ 각의(閣議) / *a family* ~ 가족 회의 / *a* ~ *of war* 군사 회의 / *a city* ~ 시의회 / *in* ~ 회의 중에〔인〕; 자문 기관에 자문을 얻어 / *hold* 〔*give into*〕 *a* ~ 회의를 열다; 협의하다 / *call someone to* ~ 아무를 회의에 소집하다. [L. *concilium*]

the Council of Economic Advisers, 《U.S.》 a board which advises the President on economic matters. (대통령의) 경제 자문 위원회.

council house [⌐⌐] *n.* **1** the house in which a council meeting is held; a town hall. 의사당. **2** 《Brit.》 a low-rent house or an apartment built for low-income families by the local government. (저소득 가정을 위한) 공영 주택.

coun·cil·man [káunsəlmən] *n.* Ⓒ (*pl.* **-men** [-mən]) a member of the council of a city or town. (시(市)·읍(邑) 등 지방 의회의) 의원(議員).

coun·cil·or, -cil·lor [káunsələr] *n.* Ⓒ a member of a council. 고문관; 평의원; 참사관; (시·읍 따위의) 의원(議員).

:coun·sel [káunsəl] *n.* Ⓤ **1** the act of exchanging opinions. 의견(意見) 교환; 협의; 상담. ¶ *hold* ~ (*with*) (…와) 협의(協議)하다 / *take* ~ *with oneself* 스스로 잘 생각해 보다. **2** advice; guidance. 충고; 조언. ¶ *give good* ~ 좋은 조언을 말해주다〔의견을 말하다〕 / *ask* ~ *for someone* 아무의 조언을 구하다. **3** Ⓒ (*pl.* **-sel**) a person or a group of persons that gives advice about matters of law; a lawyer who speaks in a law court. 변호사; 변호인단; 법률 고문.

a counsel of perfection, a) a good plan which can hardly be carried out. 실행할 수 있을 것 같지도 않은 이상안(案). b) 《*the counsels of perfection*》 the evangelical counsels of poverty, chastity and obedience, observed in religious life. (청빈·정숙·순종의) 복음적 권고.

keep one's own counsel, say nothing about one's ideas and plans; keep silent. 생각을 밝히지 않다; 비밀을 지키다.

take counsel (= *exchange ideas or opinions; consult*) ***with** someone.* …와 상담하다.

— *v.* (**-seled, -sel·ing** or 《Brit.》 **-selled, -sel·ling**) *vt.* (P6,20) give advice to (someone); speak favorably of (someone). …에게 충고(조언)하다; 권하다. ¶ *I counseled her to be careful.* 그녀에게 주의하도록 충고했다 / *I ~ you to go at once.* 나는 네가 곧 갈 것을 충고한다 / *I ~ instant action.* 즉각적인 행동을 권한다. — *vi.* consult together. 상의(상담)하다. [L. *consilium*]

coun·se·lor, 《Brit.》 **-sel·lor** [káunsələr] *n.* Ⓒ **1** a person who gives advice; an adviser. 권고자; 상담역; 카운슬러. **2** 《U.S.》 a lawyer. 변호사; 법률 고문.

:count¹ [kaunt] *vt.* **1** (P6) find the number or total of (something); add up; calculate. …을 세다; 계산(합계)하다. ¶ ~ *my money* 돈을 세다 / ~ *twenty* 스물을 세다 / ~ *cars passing the police station* 경찰서를 통과하는 차의 총계를 내다 / *Don't forget to ~ your change.* 거스름돈을 세는 것을 잊지 마라. **2** (P6,7) take account of (something); take into account; include. …을 수(셈)에 넣다. ¶ *There are ten of us, counting the children.* 아이들까지 넣어 우리는 열 명이다 / *Did you ~ the broken one?* 부서진 것까지 숫자에 넣었니 / *I no longer ~ him among my friends.* 나는 이제 그를 내 친구로 치지 않고 있다. **3** (P7,11,18,19,21) consider; think. …라고 생각하다; …로 보다. ¶ ~ *one's life of no importance* 목숨을 초개(草芥)같이 보다 / *I ~ myself lucky.* 나는 자신이 운이 좋다고 생각한다 / *I ~ it folly to do so.* 그렇게 하는 것은 어리석다고 생각한다 / *I ~ myself fortunate in being here.* 내가 여기 있는 것은 운이 좋다 / *I ~ that he will come.* 나는 그가 오리라고 생각한다. — *vi.* (P1,2A,2B,3) **1** say numbers in orders. (수를) 세다. ¶ ~ *from 1 to 50.* 1에서 50까지 세다 / *He can't ~ yet.* 아직 셀 줄 모른다. **2** be of value; have an influence. 가치가 있다; 중요하다. ¶ *Every vote counts.* 매(每)한 표가 중요하다 / *Everything we do counts.* 우리들의 하는 일 하나하나가 중요하다 / *He doesn't ~.* 그는 하찮은 사람이다 / *Honesty does not seem to ~ these days.* 요즘에는 정직이 무가치한 것 같다. **3** be included in counting or thinking. 셈(숫자)에 들어가다. ¶ *You ~ among my best friends.* 자넨 내 가장 친한 친구 축에 든다. **4** 《mus.》 keep time by counting or beating. 박자를 맞추다.

be counted for (***as***), be considered as being (dead). …로 간주되다. ¶ *be counted as lost* 행방 불명된 것으로 간주되다.

be counted on one's fingers, be not many, be few. 많지 않다.

count down, count backward from some number to zero. (로켓 발사 때와 같이) 초읽기를 하다.

count for little (***nothing***), be of no importance. 중요치 않다.

count for much, be of much value or importance. 중요하다.

count in, include. …을 셈(숫자)에 넣다. ¶ *Don't ~ me in.* 나는 수에 넣지 마라.

count kin with, 《Sc.》 be a blood-relation with. …와 혈족(血族)이다.

count off, 《mil.》 sort out. 번호를 불러 반(班)으로 가르다; 반별로 하다.

count on (***upon***), depend or rely on. …에 의지하다; …을 믿다(기대하다). ¶ ~ *on someone for help* 아무에게 도움을 기대하다 / *I thought I could ~ on him, but he turned out to be an enemy.* 그에게 기댈 수 있으리라 생각했지만 그는 적으로 판명되었다.

count out, a) say the numbers in order up to. 수를 세다. b) count taking from a stock. 세어 꺼내다. c) omit; exclude. (수에서) 빼다; 제외하다. ¶ *Please ~ me out.* 나를 제외시켜 다오. d) defeat by counting ballots wrongly. 유효표를 불법으로 잘못 세어 낙선시키다. e) 《boxing》 declare beaten a fighter who fails to rise within a given number of seconds (usu. ten) after being knocked down. (10까지 세어 쓰러진 선수의) 패배를 선언하다. f) 《Brit.》 break off for lack of a quorum. (의회에서) 정족수 미달을 이유로 유회(流會)를 선언하다. ¶ ~ *out the House* (정족수 미달로) 의회를 유회하다.

— *n.* ⓊⒸ **1** the act of adding up or finding out how many. 셈; 계산. ¶ *by* ~ 세어(계산해) 보니 / *leave out of* ~ …을 셈(계산)에 넣지 않다 / *The ~ showed that 6,132 people had abstained from voting.* 계산 숫자는 6,132명이 투표를 기권했음을 보여주었다. **2** 《*arch.*》 the total number; the sum total. 합계; 총계. ¶ *his ~ of years* 그의 나이. **3** regard; notice; account. 고려; 주의; 평가. ¶ *take ~ of* …을 중시하다. **4** 《law》 each charge in a formal accusation. (기소장의) 소인(訴因); 항목. [L. *computo* reckon]

keep count of, be aware how many there have been. …의 수를 기억하고 있다; …을 계속 세어 나가다.

lose count of, fail to know how many there have been. …을 셀 수 없게 되다; …의 수를 잊다.

on all counts, in every respect. 모든 점에서.

out of count, too many to count; numberless. 너무 많아 셀 수 없는; 무수한.

set no count on, make nothing of. …을 수에 넣지 않다.
take count of, find out the whole number of; count. …을 세다.
take* (*make*) *no count of, take no notice of. …을 중요시하지 않다.

·**count²** [kaunt] *n.* Ⓒ a nobleman on the Continent, equal in rank to an English earl. (영국 이외의) 백작. [L. *comes* companion]

·**count·a·ble** [káuntəbəl] *adj.* that can be counted. 셀 수 있는(opp. uncountable). [→count¹]

count·down [káuntdàun] *n.* ⒸⓊ the act of counting backward from some number to zero (e.g. 9, 8, 7, ... 1, 0) when giving a signal for starting something. (로켓 발사 때 등의) 초(秒)읽기.

·**coun·te·nance** [káuntənəns] *n.* **1** ⓊⒸ the appearance or look of the face. 얼굴의 표정. ¶ *a sad ~* 슬픈 표정 / *put on a serious ~* 진지한 표정을 짓다. **2** ⓊⒸ face; features. 얼굴; 용모; 안색. ¶ *an expressive ~* 표정이 풍부한 얼굴 / *a pleasing ~* 호감을 주는 얼굴 / *change one's ~* 얼굴 빛이 변하다. **3** Ⓤ approval; moral support; encouragement. 찬성; 정신적 지지; 격려. ¶ *find no ~ in* …에게 지지를 못 얻다 / *have the ~ of* …의 원조를 얻다 / *Father gave ~ to my plan.* 아버지는 내 계획을 지지하셨다. **4** Ⓤ calmness; peace of mind. 침착; 냉정; 평정. ¶ *with a good ~* 침착하게 / *give oneself ~* 마음을 가라앉히다.
in the light of someone's countenance, supported by. …의 원조에 의해서.
keep one's countenance, **a**) show no feeling; control one's expression. 표정을 나타내지 않다; 태연히 있다. **b**) keep from smiling or laughing. 웃지 않고 있다; 새침 떨고 있다.
keep someone in countenance, **a**) help someone from being ashamed. 아무의 낯을 세워주다. ¶ *I will take another glass of wine to keep you in ~.* 자네 체면을 생각해서 포도주 한잔 더하겠네. **b**) encourage. 격려하다; 북돋다.
lose countenance, get excited; show one's feeling. 평정(침착)을 잃다; 감정을 나타내다.
put someone out of countenance, make someone uneasy, angry, perplexed, or ashamed. …을 당황케 하다; 면목을 잃게 하다.
— *vt.* (P6) **1** 《*in*》 encourage; support. …을 격려하다; 원조(지지)하다. ¶ *He countenanced our plan.* 그는 우리 계획을 지지했다. **2** allow (something) against one's own feeling; permit. …을 용납하다; 참다. ¶ *I don't ~ violence in any situation.* 어떤 경우든 폭력을 용납하지 않는다. [→contain]

·**count·er¹** [káuntər] *n.* Ⓒ **1** a thing used for counting. 계산기. **2** a person who counts. 계산하는 사람. **3** an imitation coin used in games for keeping score. (게임 득점 계산용) 산(算)가지《모조 화폐》. **4** 《esp. U.S.》 a long table in a store, a bank, a restaurant, etc. at which goods are sold and money is handed. (가게·은행 따위의) 카운터; 판매대. [*count¹*]
sit* (*serve*) *behind a counter, work as a salesclerk in a store. 점원 일을 보다. [→count¹]

coun·ter² [káuntər] *adv.* 《now chiefly in a moral sense》 in the opposite direction; opposed; contrary; against. 반대방향으로; 역으로. ¶ *~ to one's inclinations* 성향과는 반대로 / *go ~ to the current of the world* 세계의 대세에 역행하다.
run counter to, be contrary to. …에 반(反)하다. ¶ *His actions run ~ to the rules.* 그의 행동은 규칙에 위배된다.
— *adj.* opposite; contrary. 반대의; 역의. ¶ *the ~ direction* (*side*) 반대 방향(쪽).
— *vt., vi.* (P6;3) **1** go or act counter to; oppose. 반대하다. ¶ *He countered my plan with one of his own.* 그는 자기의 제안을 내놓아 내 안(案)에 반대했다. **2** 《boxing》 give a blow in return for that of an opponent. 되받아치다.
— *n.* Ⓒ **1** that which is opposite or contrary to something else. 반대(물). **2** 《boxing》 a blow given in return for that of an opponent. 맞받아침; 카운터 블로. [L. *contrā* against, opposite]

coun·ter- [káuntər-] *pref.* opposite; fighting against; corresponding. '반(反)', 역(逆), 대응'의 뜻. [↑]

coun·ter·act [kàuntərǽkt] *vt.* (P6) **1** act against (something); hinder. …에 반대로 작용하다; …을 방해하다; 반작용하다. ¶ *~ someone's influence* 아무의 세력을 꺾다. **2** weaken the effects of (something); neutralize. …의 효력을 약화시키다; 중화하다. ¶ *~ the effects of a poison* …의 독 기운을 중화시키다. [counter-]

coun·ter·ac·tion [kàuntərǽkʃən] *n.* ⓊⒸ one action in opposition to another action; prevention. 반대 행동; (약의) 중화; (계획의) 방해.

coun·ter·at·tack [káuntərətæ̀k] *n.* Ⓒ an attack made in return for an enemy's attack. 반격; 역습. — [kàuntərətǽk] *vt., vi.* (P6; 1) attack in return. 반격하다; 역습하다.

coun·ter·at·trac·tion [kàuntərətrǽkʃən] *n.* a thing that draws one away from what was attracting him. 다른 것에 마음을 끄는 것; 반대 인력(引力).

coun·ter·bal·ance [káuntərbæ̀ləns] *n.* Ⓒ **1** a weight balancing another. 평형추(錘); 균형. **2** an influence, a power, etc. balancing another. 균형을 유지하는 힘; 평형력; 대항 세력. — [kàuntərbǽləns] *vt.* (P6) act as a counterbalance to (something). …을 균형(평형) 잡히게 하다; (…의 부족)을 메우다.

coun·ter·check [káuntərtʃèk] *n.* Ⓒ **1** a check that restrains or opposes; an obstacle. 대항적 방지(수단); 억제. **2** a check controlling another check. (확실히 하기 위한) 재(再)대조.

coun·ter·claim [káuntərklèim] *n.* an opposing claim. 반대 요구; 반소(反訴). ―[kàuntərkléim]. *vi.* (P3) 《*for, against*》 bring a counterclaim (for an amount, against a person). 반소(反訴)하다.

coun·ter·clock·wise [kàuntərklákwàiz / -klɔ́k-] *adv., adj.* in the direction opposite to the normal direction of the hands of a clock. 시계 바늘과 반대 방향으로(방향의); 왼쪽으로 도는(돌게)(opp. clockwise).

coun·ter·deed [káuntərdì:d] *n.* 《law》 a secret contract. 반대(비밀) 증서.

coun·ter·es·pi·o·nage [kàuntəréspiənidʒ, -nà:ʒ] *n.* espionage directed toward thwarting an enemy espionage. 대(對)간첩 활동.

coun·ter·feit [káuntərfit] *vt.* (P6) **1** copy or imitate (something) in order to deceive; forge. …을 위조(모조)하다; 모뜨다. ¶ ~ *ten-dollar bills* 10달러 지폐를 위조하다 / ~ *someone's voice* 아무의 목소리를 흉내내다. **2** pretend. (감정)을 속이다; …한(인) 체하다; …을 가장하다. ¶ ~ *sorrow* 슬픈 체하다 / ~ *death* 죽은 체하다. ― *n.* Ⓒ a copy or an imitation made to deceive. 가짜; 모조(위조)품; 모사(模寫). ― *adj.* **1** not real; sham. 가짜의; 모조의. **2** pretended. …을 가장한. [counter-, L. *facio* make]

coun·ter·foil [káuntərfɔ̀il] *n.* Ⓒ 《chiefly Brit.》 a part of a check, a money order, etc. which is kept as a record. 부본(副本)《어음·수표 등을 떼어 주고 남겨두는 쪽지》 (cf. *stub*). [counter-]

coun·ter·ir·ri·tant [kàuntərírətənt] *n.* 《med.》 a substance for stimulating one part to relieve a pain or inflammation in another part of the body. 반대(유도(誘導)) 자극약. [counter-]

coun·ter·mand [kàuntərmǽnd, -má:nd] *vt.* (P6) **1** (of an order, a command, etc.) withdraw; cancel. (명령·주문 따위)를 철회(취소)하다. **2** recall. …을 되불러오다. ―[káuntərmæ̀nd / -mà:nd] *n.* the act of countermanding; an order cancelling an earlier order. 취소 명령. [counter-, →mandate.]

coun·ter·march [káuntərmà:rtʃ] *n.* Ⓒ a march in the opposite direction. 배면(역(逆)) 행진; 배진(背進); 반대 행진; 역전(逆轉). ―[kàuntərmá:rtʃ] *vi., vt.* march back. 역행진하다(시키다); 배진하다(시키다). [counter-]

coun·ter·mark [káuntərmà:rk] *n.* an additional mark. 부가 각인(刻印); 부인(副印).

coun·ter·mine [káuntərmàin] *n.* **1** 《army》 a mine made to meet and destroy an enemy mine. 항적 갱도(抗敵坑道). **2** 《nav.》 a mine sunk to explode the enemy's mines. (적의 기뢰를 사전에 폭파하는) 역(逆)기뢰. ―[kàuntərmáin] *vt., vi.* (P6; 1) make a countermine (against an enemy mine). 적의 기뢰(갱도)를 폭파하다; 역기뢰를 부설하다. [counter-,→mine²]

coun·ter·of·fen·sive [kàuntərəfénsiv] *n.* an attack on a large scale undertaken by a defending force to seize the initiative from the attacking enemy force. 반격(反擊). [counter-]

coun·ter·pane [káuntərpèin] *n.* Ⓒ a coverlet for a bed; a bedspread. 침대의 (장식적) 이불. [L. *culcita puncta* stitched quilt]

coun·ter·part [káuntərpà:rt] *n.* Ⓒ **1** a copy; a duplicate. 사본(寫本); 부본; 정부(正副) 두 통 중의 한 통. **2** a person or thing closely resembling another. 아주 비슷한 사람. ¶ *She is her mother's* ~. 그녀는 엄마를 빼쏘았다. **3** one of two parts that makes something complete when added to the other. (짝을 이루는 것의) 한쪽(짝); 상대물(인). [counter-]

coun·ter·plot [káuntərplɑ̀t / -plɔ̀t] *vt., vi.* (**-plot·ted, -plot·ting**) (P6;1) plot to defeat another plot. (상대의) 계획의 의표를 찌르다. ― *n.* Ⓒ a plot to defeat another plot. 대항책.

coun·ter·point [káuntərpɔ̀int] *n.* 《mus.》 **1** Ⓒ a melody added to another as an accompaniment. 대위 선율(對位旋律). **2** Ⓤ the art of combining melodies. 대위법(對位法).

coun·ter·poise [káuntərpɔ̀iz] *n.* **1** Ⓒ a weight balancing another weight; a counterbalancing weight. 저울추. **2** Ⓤ any equal and opposing power or force. 평형력; 균형 세력. **3** Ⓤ the condition of being in balance. 균형(상태); 안정. ¶ *be in* ~ 평형을 유지하고 있다. ― *vt.* (P6) act as a counterpoise to (something); bring (something) into balance. …와(을) 균형을 맞추다; 균형을 유지하게 하다.

coun·ter·rev·o·lu·tion [kàuntərrèvəlú:ʃən] *n.* Ⓒ a revolution against a government itself recently established by a revolution. 반혁명.

coun·ter·sign [káuntərsàin] *n.* Ⓒ **1** a secret word given to a sentry when one is asked who and what one is; a password. (보초의 수하(誰何)에 답하는) 암호. ¶ *give the* ~ 암호를 대다. **2** a secret sign given by one member of a group on receiving the sign from another. (어떤 신호에 대한) 응답의 신호. **3** signature added to another signature to confirm it. 부서(副署). ― *vt.* (P6) sign (a document) already signed by someone else; confirm. 부서하다; 확인하다.

coun·ter·sink [káuntərsìŋk, ⌐-⌐] *vt.* (**-sunk**) (P6) **1** widen (a hole) for the head of a screw or bolt so that it may be level with the surface of the wood, etc. (나사·볼트 대가리를 쳐 박기 위해) 구멍 언저리를 넓히다. **2** sink (the head of a screw or bolt) into such a hole. (나사·볼트 대가리를) 구멍에 박아 묻다. — *n.* a hole countersunk. 위의 구멍.

coun·ter·sunk [káuntərsʌ̀ŋk] *v.* p. & pp. of **countersink.**

coun·ter·vail [kàuntərvéil] *vt.* (P6) **1** act against (another action, etc.) with equal power, effect, etc. …을 필적하게 하다; …을 상쇄하다. ¶ *countervailing duties* 상계(相計) 관세. **2** pay for (something). …을 보상하다. — *vi.* (P3) be equal to an opposing force. 필적하다; 균형을 이루다. [counter-, →valid]

coun·ter·work [káuntərwə̀:rk] *vt.* (P6) work in opposition to; try to frustrate. …에 반대로 작용하다; (계획 따위)를 좌절시키다. [counter-]

count·ess [káuntis] *n.* Ⓒ **1** 《Brit.》 the wife or widow of an earl or a count. 백작 부인. **2** a lady having the rank equal to that of an earl or a count. 백작과 동등한 지위에 있는 부인. [→count²]

count·ing house [káuntiŋ hàus] *n.* 《Brit.》 a building, room, or office in which accounts are kept and business is done. 회계 사무소; 회계과(실). [*count*¹]

***count·less** [káuntlis] *adj.* too many to count; innumerable. 셀 수 없는; 무수한. ¶ *the ~ stars* 무수한 별. [↑]

coun·tri·fied [kʌ́ntrifàid] *adj.* **1** looking or acting like a person from a rural area. 시골뜨기 같은. **2** countrylike; rustic; rural. 시골 같은; 촌스러운 데가 있는. ¶ *When one lives too long in the country, one gets ~.* 시골에 너무 오래 살면 사람은 촌스러워진다. [↓]

:coun·try [kʌ́ntri] *n.* Ⓒ (*pl.* **-tries**) **1** the land of one nation; nation. 국토; 국가. ¶ *a small ~* 작은 나라 / *an agricultural ~* 농업국 / *the countries of Europe* 유럽의 나라들 / *the wine of the ~* 국산 포도주 / *all over the ~* 전국에. **2** 《*sing.* only, often without *an article*》 a piece of land; a region; a district. 지역; 지방. ¶ (*a*) *mountainous ~* 산악 지방 / *good ~ for sheep* 양치기에 알맞은 지역 / *unfamiliar ~* 낯선 지방 / *miles of densely wooded ~* 수마일에 걸친 밀림 지대. **3** 《*the ~*》 open land without many houses; a rural district. 시골; 전원 지방(cf. *town, suburbs*). ¶ *live in the ~* 시골에 살다 / *leave the ~ and move into the town* 시골을 떠나 도회지로 이사가다. **4** one's home country; one's fatherland. 고향; 고국; 조국. ¶ *love of one's ~* 향토(조국)애 / *leave the ~* 고국을 떠나다 / *die* (*fight*) *for one's ~* 조국을 위해 죽다(싸우다). **5** 《*the ~*》 the people of a nation. 국민. ¶ *All the ~ is opposed to war.* 온 국민이 전쟁에 반대하고 있다.

go* (*appeal*) *to the country, 《Brit.》 hold a general election. (의회를 해산하여) 국민의 총의(總意)를 묻다; 총선거를 하다.

put* (*throw*) *oneself upon the country, demand a trial by jury. 배심 재판을 요구하다.

— *adj.* **1** of a country. 나라의; 국가의. **2** of the country, as opposed to the town. 시골의; 지방의. ¶ *~ life* 전원(田園)(시골) 생활. [L. *contrā* opposite]

country club [ㅗ-ㅗ] *n.* 《orig. U.S.》 a club or clubhouse in the suburbs for social activities, outdoor sports, esp. golf. 컨트리 클럽《테니스·골프 따위의 설비를 갖춘 교외 클럽으로 사교 활동의 장소가 됨》.

country cousin [ㅗ- ㅗ-] *n.* a rural person not used to city life and confused or excited by it. 도시에 갓 올라온 시골 사람.

coun·try·folk [kʌ́ntrifòuk] *n.* 《*collectively,* used as *pl.*》 people living in rural areas; people who come from the same country. 시골 사람들; 동향 사람.

***country house** [ㅗ- ㅗ] *n.* a home in the country. (귀족·부호 등의) 시골 저택; 별장.

***coun·try·man** [kʌ́ntrimən] *n.* Ⓒ (*pl.* **-men** [-mən]) **1** a man of one's own country. 동국인(同國人); 동포; 동향 사람. **2** a man living in a rural area. 시골 사람.

coun·try·peo·ple [kʌ́ntripì:pl] *n.* =countryfolk.

coun·try·seat [kʌ́ntrisì:t] *n.* Ⓒ a country mansion or estate, esp. a fine one. 시골의 대(大)저택.

coun·try·side [kʌ́ntrisàid] *n.* **1** Ⓤ 《usu. *the ~*》 a rural area; a certain part of the country. 시골; (전원) 지방. **2** 《*collectively*》 the people living in a rural area. 지방의 주민; 시골 사람들.

coun·try·wom·an [kʌ́ntriwùmən] *n.* Ⓒ (*pl.* **-wom·en** [-wìmin]) **1** a woman of one's own country. 동향(同鄕)의 여자. **2** a woman living in a rural area. 시골 여자.

:coun·ty [káunti] *n.* Ⓒ (*pl.* **-ties**) **1** 《U.S.》 one part of a State forming a political unit. 군(郡)《State 다음의 행정 구획》. **2** 《Brit.》 one part of England forming a political unit. 주(州)《shire에 해당》. **3** the inhabitants of a county. 군(郡)의 주민; 주민(州民). **4** 《Brit.》 《*the C-*》 county families. 주(州)(지방)의 명문. [→count²]

coup [ku:] *n.* Ⓒ (*pl.* **coups** [ku:z]) 《F.》 a sudden, brilliant stroke; a master stroke. 멋진 일격; 대성공(히트). ¶ *make* (*pull off*) *a great ~* 대성공을 거두다; 대히트를 치다.

coup de grâce [ku: də grɑ́:s] *n.* 《F.》 **1** a death blow, esp. one delivered mercifully to end suffering. 자비의 일격《죽어가는 사람·동물의 고통을 덜어주기 위한》. **2** 《*fig.*》 any finishing or decisive stroke. 결정(치명)타.

coup de main [ku: də mɛ̃] *n.* 《F.》 an unexpected or surprise attack. 기습.

coup d'état [kù: deitɑ́: / kú:-] *n.* 《F.》 《polit.》 a sudden change in the political affairs of a country, brought about by unconstitutional methods. 쿠데타; (비합법·폭력적인) 정변(政變).

coup de theâtre [kú: də teiɑ́:trə] *n.* 《F.》 a theatrical hit; 《*fig.*》 a showy trick.

즉석의 인기 끌기(끄는 행위); 극적인 트릭(급전환); 연극 같은 짓.

cou·pé [ku:péi] *n.* Ⓒ 《F.》 **1** [《U.S.》 ku:p] a closed, two-door automobile, with the seat for the driver outside. 쿠페형 자동차. **2** a four-wheeled closed carriage with one seat for two persons and an outside seat for the driver. 쿠페형 4륜 마차. **3** the end compartment in a train having seats on one side only. (열차 후미의) 한쪽에만 좌석이 있는 칸; 쿠페.

:cou·ple [kʌ́pl] *n.* Ⓒ **1** a pair; two of the same class or kind. 한 쌍; (같은 종류의) 두 개(사람). **2** a pair of people, closely associated esp. a man and his wife, partners in a dance, etc. 밀접한 관계의 두 사람; (특히) 남녀 한 쌍; 부부. ¶ *a married* (*wedded*) ~ 부부 / *a well-matched* ~ 잘 어울리는 부부 / *a good old* ~ 화목한 노부부 / *a young* (*newly wedded*) ~ 젊은(신혼) 부부 / *a* ~ *of rogues,* 2인조의 악당 / *a* ~ *of players,* 2인 1조의 경기자.

a couple of, a) two. 둘의; 두 개(사람)의. ¶ *a* ~ *of apples* 사과 두 개 / *a* ~ *of dollars,* 2 달러 / *a* ~ *of persons* 두 사람. b) a few. 두서넛의; 몇 개(사람, 날)의. ¶ *I spent a* ~ *of days in the country.* 2, 3일간 시골에서 보냈다.

go* (*hunt, run*) *in couples, go, etc. in pairs, i.e. making groups of two. 늘 둘이 함께 다니다; 협력(제휴)하다.

in couples, in pairs; two together. 둘이; 쌍으로.

— *vt.* (P6,7,13) **1** ⓐ join (things) together; link; connect. (두 개의 것)을 한데 잇다; 연결(관련)시키다. ¶ ~ *the freight cars* 화물차를 연결하다 / ~ *acts with words* 언행을 일치시키다. ⓑ associate (things or ideas) together in the mind. …을 연상하다; 결부시켜 생각하다. ¶ ~ *the name of Oxford with the idea of learning* 옥스퍼드라고 하면 학문을 연상하다. **2** unite or join (two persons in marriage); mate (two animals) together. (두 사람을) 결혼시키다; (암수를) 교미(交尾)시키다.

— *vi.* (P1) **1** marry. 결혼하다. **2** (of animals) mate. 교미하다. **3** come together; unite. 연결되다; 협력하다; 결합하다. [→copula]

cóu·plet [kʌ́plit] *n.* two lines of poetry of the same length, united by rhyme. 대구(對句); 2행 연구(連句)(《e.g.》 *Those who in quarrels interpose / Must often wipe a bloody nose*). [→copula]

cou·pling [kʌ́pliŋ] *n.* **1** ⓊⒸ the act of joining together. 연결. **2** Ⓒ a device for joining parts of machinery. 연결 장치. **3** Ⓒ a link used to connect two railroad cars. (차량의) 연결기(器). [↑]

cou·pon [kjúːpɑn / -pɔn] *n.* Ⓒ **1** a ticket showing that one has a right to receive goods or services. 쿠폰(권); 이권(利券). **2** a printed statement of the interest due on a bond which can be cut off the bond and presented for payment. (공채·채권 따위의 이자 지불) 이표(利票). **3** a part of a printed advertisement to be cut off for use as a form of application. (떼어 쓰게 된) 표·광고 등의 한 쪽. **4** 《Brit. *colloq.*》 a party leader's recognition of a parliamentary candidate as deserving election. (당수가 주는) 입후보 공천(공인). [→coup]

:cour·age [kə́ːridʒ, kʌ́r-] *n.* Ⓤ the quality of being brave; the mental power of facing danger, difficulty, etc. without fear. 용기. ¶ *a man of* ~ 용기 있는 사람 / *lose* ~ 용기를 잃다 / *have the* ~ *of one's convictions* (남의 비판에 개의치 않고) 자기 신념에 따라 행동하다. [→cordial]

take* (*pluck up, muster up, screw up*) *courage, stir oneself to brave feelings. 용기를 내다.

take one's courage in both hands, gather enough courage to do something that needs a lot; venture boldly. 과감히(눈 딱 감고) 해보다.

cou·ra·geous [kəréidʒəs] *adj.* full of courage; brave; fearless. 용감한; 대담한. ●**cou·ra·geous·ly** [-li] *adv.*

cour·i·er [kúriər, kə́ːri-] *n.* Ⓒ **1** a messenger sent in haste, esp. by horse. 급사(急使); 파발꾼. **2** a person hired by a group of travelers to take care of hotel reservations, tickets, etc. for them. (단체 여행의) 안내원. **3** a title given to general newspapers. (신문 명칭에 붙여) … 신문(신보). ¶ *the Liverpool Courier* 리버풀 신문. [L. *curro* run]

:course [kɔːrs] *n.* Ⓒ **1** ⓊⒸ 《often *the* ~》 a continuous forward movement; an onward movement; progress; development. 전진; 진행; 경과. ¶ *the* ~ *of events* 사건의 추이 / *the* ~ *of a disease* 병의 경과 / *the* ~ *of life* 인생 행로; (사람의) 일생 / *keep on the* ~ 진행(전진)을 계속하다. **2** 《*the* ~ or *one's* ~》 a route; a way; the direction to advance. 진로; 진행의 방향. ¶ *the* ~ *of a river* 강의 진로 / *change the ship's* ~ 배의 진로를 바꾸다. **3** a manner of action or behavior. (행동의) 방침; 방향. ¶ *the best* ~ *to take* 최선의 방책 / *hold* (*change*) *one's* ~ 자신의 방침을 계속하다(바꾸다) / *take a safe* ~ 안전한 길을 취하다 / *adopt a middle* ~ 중도를 택하다. **4** a series of studies or lessons. 과정(課程); 학과; 단위. ¶ *a* ~ *of study* 학습 과정 / *the postgraduate* ~ 대학원 과정 / *the literary* (*science*) ~ 문과(이과) / *complete one's high school* ~ 고교의 과정을 수료하다. **5** a part of a meal served at one time. (식사의) 일품; 코스. ¶ *a dinner of six courses,* 6품 요리의 식사. **6** a piece of land marked out for a sport. (경기 따위의) 코스. ¶ *a race* ~ (경마의) 트랙 / *a golf* ~ 골프 코스. **7** a row of bricks or stones on the same level, along a surface of a building. (쌓은 벽돌·석축 따위

의) 수평층(層).

(as) a matter of course, as a natural thing; naturally. 당연한 일로서.

by course of, following a custom. 관례(慣例)에 따라.

course of events, the developments. 사태의 진전.

course of things, the situation. 사태(事態).

in course of, in process of. …중에.

in due course, at the proper time or season; in the natural order; without too much delay. 마침 좋은〔알맞은〕 때에; 일이 순조롭게 진행되어〔되면〕; 마침내. ¶ *in due ~ of time* 때가 오면; 마침내는 / *We shall know the results of the examination in due ~.* 때가 되면 시험 결과를 알게 될 게다.

in the course of, during. …중(中)에; …(이 경과하는) 동안에. ¶ *in the ~ of this month* 〔*year*〕 이달 중〔연내〕에.

in the course of nature = **in the ordinary course of things,** normally; as part of the normal or expected result of events. 보통 같으면; 자연히; (일이 순조로우면) 머지않아.

of course, a) as one might expect; naturally. (추세로서) 당연히. **b**) certainly; without doubt. 물론.

run 〔**take**〕 **its** 〔**their, etc.**〕 **course,** develop in a normal way; go on to the usual end. (사태·세월·병 따위가) 자연스럽게 경과해가다〔되어가다〕; 당연한 추이를 거치다; 되어가는 대로 놔두다. ¶ *It's best to let this kind of sickness run its ~.* 이런 병은 그냥 진행되어가는 대로 놔두는 것이 가장 좋다 / *Thirty years have run their ~.* 30년이라는 세월이 경과했다.

shape *one's* **course,** steer one's course. 진로를 정하다.

stay the course, be able to continue to the end of the race, the struggle, etc.; not give up half-way. 끝〔최후〕까지 계속하다; 중도에서 포기하지 않다.

take *one's* **(own) course,** have one's own way; do as one wishes. 마음〔뜻〕대로 하다.

take to evil course, take to fast living. 방탕을〔난봉을 부리기〕 시작하다.

— *vt.* (P6) **1** hunt or run after (animals) with hounds; chase. (사냥개를 부리어 사냥감)을 뒤쫓다; 사냥하다. **2** cause (a horse, etc.) to run; urge (a horse, etc.) to speed. (말 따위)를 달리게 하다. **3** run through or over (fields, etc.). …을 가로지르다; 뛰어다니다.

— *vi.* (P1,3) **1** move quickly; (of liquids) run. 빨리 달리다; 흐르다. **2** hunt or run after animals with hounds. (사냥개로) 사냥을 하다. [L *curro* run]

cours·er [kɔ́:sər] *n.* Ⓒ 《*poet.*》 a swift horse. 준마(駿馬). [↑]

:court [kɔ:rt] *n.* Ⓒ **1** a space partly or wholly enclosed by walls or buildings. (담이나 건물에 둘러싸인) 안뜰; 공터. **2** a space set off for a game. (테니스 따위의) 코트. ¶ *a tennis ~ / a grass ~* 잔디 코트. **3** a short street, esp. one partly enclosed by poor houses; a blind alley. (초라한 집들의) 골목길; 뒷골목; 막다른 골목. **4** a large mansion. (대)저택. **5** 《often *C-*》 a place for a king, queen, or other ruler; a royal palace. 궁정; 왕궁; 궁중. ¶ *the ~ of King Solomon* 솔로몬왕의 궁정 / *go to ~* 입궐하다 / *be presented at ~* (신임 대사〔공사〕 등이) 왕을 알현하다. **6** 《*collectively*》 the royal family and its followers living in the palace. 왕족; 조신(朝臣)들. ¶ *the queen and her ~* 여왕과 그 조신들. **7** a sovereign and his advisers as a ruling body or power. 군주와 조신들; 조정(朝廷). **8** a state gathering or reception held by a sovereign. 왕이 주재하는 정식 회의; 어전〔궁중〕 회의; 알현. ¶ *hold (a) ~* 어전 회의를 열다. **9** ⓐ a place where justice is administered. 재판소; 법정. ¶ *the supreme ~* 대법원 / *a ~ of justice* 〔*law*〕 재판소; 법정 / *a criminal* 〔*civil*〕 *~* 형사〔민사〕 법정 / *contempt of ~* 법정 모욕 / *hold a ~* 재판을 열다; 개정(開廷)하다 / *go to ~* 소송을 일으키다 / *end in ~* 결국 소송 사건이 되다 / *The prisoner was brought to ~ for trial.* 죄인은 재판을 받기 위하여 출정(出廷)했다. ⓑ 《*collectively*》 a judge or judges in a law court. 재판관; 판사. ¶ *a decision of the ~* 판결 / *The ~ found him guilty.* 판사는 그를 유죄로 판결했다. **10** Ⓤ the act of getting someone's favor or love. 알랑거림; 아첨; 구애(求愛). ¶ *pay* 〔*make*〕 *(one's) ~ to a pretty woman* 아름다운 여인에게 구애하다 / *pay one's ~ to a king* 임금에게 아첨하다.

appear in court, present oneself at the court. 출정(出廷)하다.

court of appeal, the high court. 고등 법원.

Court of St. James, the court of the monarch of Great Britain. 영국 궁정.

out of court, a) without a court trial. 법정 밖에서. ¶ *settle a case out of ~* 사건을 사화(私和)로 해결하다. **b**) 《*fig.*》 not entitled to a hearing in a law court. 법정에서 기각되는; 고려할〔일고의〕 가치도 없는. ¶ *laugh something out of ~* …을 일소에 부치다.

put *oneself* **out of court,** 《*fig.*》 behave or speak in such a way that one is not considered to a hearing. 남이 거들떠보지도 않을 짓〔말〕을 하다.

— *vt.* (P6) **1** try to get the favor or love of (someone); please. …의 비위를 맞추다; …에게 구애〔구혼〕하다. **2** try to get (something); seek. …을 얻으려고 하다; 구하다. ¶ *~ popularity* 인기를 얻으려고 하다 / *~ the shade* 나뭇그늘을 찾다. **3** behave in such a way as to invite or provoke. …을 초래하다; 가져오다. ¶ *~ danger* 위험을 초래하다 / *Such folly courts disaster.* 그런 어리석은 짓은 화를 가져온다. [L.]

court card [⌐⌐] *n.* (in playing cards) the king, the queen, or the jack. (카드놀이

에서) 그림이 있는 패(=face-card).

·**cour·te·ous** [kə́ːrtiəs / kɔ́ːr-] *adj.* polite; civil; thoughtful of others. 예의바른; 정중한; 친절한. ¶ *a* ~ *manner* 정중한 태도 / *be* ~ *to guests* 손님에게 예의바르다. ● **cour·te·ous·ness** [-nis] *n.* [→court]

cour·te·ous·ly [kə́ːrtiəsli / kɔ́ːr-] *adv.* in a courteous manner. 예의바르게; 정중하게; 친절하게.

cour·te·san, -zan [kɔ́ːrtəzən / kə́ːr-] *n.* a woman who sells herself for money; prostitute. 창부(娼婦).

·**cour·te·sy** [kə́ːrtəsi] *n.* (*pl.* **-sies**) **1** ⓊⒸ the quality of being courteous; politeness. 예의(바름); 정중. **2** Ⓒ a kind act; an example of polite behavior. 친절한 행동; 예의바른 동작. ¶ *a visit of* ~ 의례적인 방문 / *return the* ~ 답례하다. **3** ⓊⒸ kindness; favor. 친절; 호의. ¶ *by* (*the*) ~ *of someone* 아무의 호의로. [→court]

court·house [kɔ́ːrthàus] *n.* Ⓒ (*pl.* **-hous·es** [-hàuziz]) **1** a building in which law courts are held. 법원. **2** 《U.S.》 a building used for the government of a county. 군청(郡廳).

cour·ti·er [kɔ́ːrtiər] *n.* Ⓒ **1** (in former times) a noble who often present at the court of a king, etc.; a court attendant. 조신(朝臣). **2** a person who seeks the favor of another by flattering him. 아첨꾼; 환심 사려는 사람. [*court*]

court·li·ness [kɔ́ːrtlinis] *n.* Ⓤ politeness; elegance. 정중; 우아.

court·ly [kɔ́ːrtli] *adj.* (**-li·er, -li·est**) polite; elegant. 정중한; 우아한; 품위 있는.

court-mar·tial [kɔ́ːrtmáːrʃəl] *n.* Ⓒ (*pl.* **courts-**) a court consisting of army or navy officers for the trial of offenses against military or naval laws; a trial by such a court. 군사 법원; (군사 법원에 의한) 재판. — *vt.* (P6) try (someone) in a court-martial. …을 군사 법원에 부치다〔회부하다〕. ¶ *He was court-martialed and dismissed from the army.* 군사 법원에 회부되어 예편당했다. [*court*]

court·plas·ter [kɔ́ːrtplæ̀stər, -plàːstər] *n.* a sticking plaster. 반창고.

court·room [kɔ́ːrtrù(ː)m] *n.* Ⓒ a room where a law court is held. 법정(法廷).

court·ship [kɔ́ːrtʃìp] *n.* Ⓤ the wooing of a woman; the period during which wooing lasts. (여자에의) 구혼; 구애; 그 기간.

·**court·yard** [kɔ́ːrtjàːrd] *n.* Ⓒ a space surrounded by walls or large buildings on all or most sides. (성·여관 따위 대건축물의) 안뜰.

⁑**cous·in** [kʌ́zn] *n.* Ⓒ **1** a child of one's uncle or aunt. 사촌. 參考 first cousin, full cousin, cousin-german이라고도 함. ¶ *a second* ~ 재종; 6촌 형제〔자매〕/ ~ *once removed* 당질(녀). **2** a distant relative. 먼 친척; 일가. **3** a term of address used by a sovereign when he speaks to another sovereign or to a high-ranking nobleman. 경(卿)《국왕이 타국의 왕 등에 쓰는 호칭》. ● **cous·in·ly** [-li] *adj.* [com-, L. *soror* sister]

call cousins with, recognize kinship with. …의 사촌〔친척〕이라고 하다.

cous·in·hood [kʌ́znhùd], **-ship** [-ʃip] *n.* Ⓤ 《*collectively*》 being cousins. 사촌들; 일가 친척.

cou·tu·ri·er [kuːtúəriè i] *n.* 《F.》 a man who makes women's clothing. 여성복의 남자 양재사.

cove[1] [kouv] *n.* Ⓒ **1** a small bay; an inlet on the shore. 작은 후미〔내포〕; 작은 만(灣). **2** a concave arch, esp. of a ceiling or an inner roof. (천장·지붕 안쪽의) 활 모양으로 굽어져 올라간 곳. [E.]

cove[2] [kouv] *n.* Ⓒ 《*sl.*》 a fellow. 놈; 녀석. ¶ *a queer* ~ 이상한 녀석. [Gypsy *covo* that man]

cov·e·nant [kʌ́vənənt] *n.* **1** a solemn agreement between two or more persons or groups. 맹약; 서약(誓約); 계약. ¶ *keep* 〔*break*〕 ~ *with* …와의 약속을 지키다〔어기다〕. **2** 《law》 ⓐ a sealed contract; a contract under seal. 계약서. ⓑ a particular clause in a contract in which an undertaking is given. 계약 조항. **3** 《Bible》 the promise of God to the Israelites under Moses. (신(神)이 이스라엘 백성들에게 한) 계약; 약속. ***the land of the covenant,*** Canaan (in Palestine). 약속의 땅《가나안》.

— *vi.* (P1,3) make a covenant. 계약〔서약〕하다. ¶ ~ *with someone for*… …을 위하여 아무와 계약하다. — *vt.* (P6,8,11,13) promise by covenant. 계약에 의해 약속하다. ¶ *I covenanted to pay £ 50 a year to help rebuild the college.* 대학 재건의 지원으로 연 50 파운드를 내기로 서약했다. [→convene]

Cov·en·try [kʌ́vəntri, kʌ́v- / kɔ́v-] *n.* a city in central England. 커번트리《잉글랜드 중부의 도시》.

send someone to Coventry, refuse to speak to or associate with him. 아무를 따돌리다.

⁑**cov·er** [kʌ́vər] *vt.* (P6,7,13) **1** ⓐ place something on, over, or in front of, so as to hide or protect. (감추거나 보호를 위해) …을 덮다; 씌우다; 가리다. ¶ ~ *a chair with leather* 의자에 가죽을 씌우다 / ~ *floors with carpets* 마룻바닥에 양탄자를 깔다 / ~ *a wall with paper* 〔*paint*〕 벽에 종이〔페인트〕를 바르다. ⓑ provide with a cover or covering; cover with a lid, clothing, etc. 덮개로 덮다; 뚜껑을 하다. ¶ ~ *a sleeping child with one's coat* 잠자는 아이를 자기의 웃옷으로 덮어주다 / ~ *one's shoulders with a shawl* 어깨에 숄을 걸치다 / ~ *a kettle with a lid* 솥에 뚜껑을 덮다. **2** ⓐ hide by covering; keep (something) from view. 덮어 가리다; 안 보이게 하다. ¶ ~ *one's face in shame* (*with one's* *hands*) 부끄러워 얼굴을 (두 손으로) 가리다 / *A thick cloud covered the sun.* 두꺼운 구름이 해를 가렸다 / *The paint covered the nail holes.* 페인트 칠이 못구멍을 덮어 안 보이게 했다. ⓑ hide; conceal; keep secret. (감정·행위 따위)를 덮어 감추다; 숨기다. ¶ ~ *one's confusion with laughter* 당황스러움을 웃음으로 얼버무리다 / ~ *one's shame* 〔*mistake*〕 수치를〔잘못을〕 덮어 감추다 / ~ *one's tracks* 〔*trail*〕 종적을 감추다; 자기 의도를〔계획을〕 숨기다. **3** spread or scatter over thickly; be crowded with; be full of. 온통 뿌리다〔바르다〕; 뒤덮다. ¶ *a face covered with freckles* 〔*wounds*〕 주근깨〔상처〕투성이의 얼굴 / ~ *bread with butter* 빵에 버터를 바르다 / *be covered with dust* 온통 먼지로 뒤덮이다 / *be covered with flies* 파리 떼로 뒤덮이다 / *His clothes were covered with mud.* 그의 옷은 흙탕물로 뒤발하고 있었다. **4** keep from harm or danger; protect; shelter. …을 방어〔보호〕하다; 엄호하다. ¶ ~ *the retreat of friendly troops* 우군의 퇴각을 엄호하다 / ~ *people by social security* 사람들을 사회 보장에 의해서 보호하다 / *He covered his wife from a madman's attack.* 미친 사내의 공격에서 아내를 보호했다. **5** be sufficient to meet (an expense, loss, etc.); suffice to defray; offset. (비용·손실 따위)를 메우기에 충분하다; (비용·지출)을 메우다; 상쇄하다. ¶ ~ *the loss with insurance* 손실을 보험으로 메우다 / *My salary fully covers all expenses.* 내 월급은 모든 지출을 충당하기에 충분하다 / *The price barely covers the cost.* 그 가격은 겨우 원가밖에 안 된다. **6** extend over; include; deal with. (범위가) …에 걸치다〔미치다〕; 포함〔망라〕하다; …을 다루다. ¶ *His studies* ~ *a wide field.* 그의 학문은〔연구는〕 넓은 범위에 걸쳐 있다 / *This clause covers all possible cases.* 이 조항은 온갖 경우에 적용된다 / *The city covers ten square miles.* 시역(市域)은 10 평방마일에 달한다 / *The word covers various meanings.* 이 말은 여러가지 의미를 포함하고 있다. **7** 《*oneself with*》 bring upon oneself; acquire. (명예·치욕 따위)를 가져오다; (한몸에) 안다〔받다〕. ¶ ~ *oneself with glory* 〔*dishonor*〕 영광을〔불명예를〕 한몸에 안다〔누리다〕. **8** pass or travel over (a route); go (a certain distance). (어떤 길·거리를) 가다; 통과하다. ¶ ~ *200 miles a day* 하루 2백 마일을 가다 / ~ *the entire distance on foot* 전 노정을 걸어서 가다. **9** report (for a newspaper, magazine, etc.). 보도하다; 취재하다. ¶ *I want our best reporters sent to* ~ *the Gulf War.* 걸프전(戰) 취재를 위하여 가장 우수한 기자들을 보내주기 바란다. **10** keep a gun aimed at (someone). …에게 총을 겨누다. ¶ ~ *someone with a pistol* 아무에게 권총을 겨누다. **11** (in cricket, baseball etc.) stand behind (a fielder) to stop a ball in case he misses it. (야수가 볼을 놓치는 경우에 대비하여) 뒤를 받치다. **12** (of certain animals) copulate with. (동물의 암수가) 교미하다; 붙다.

cover in, **a**) fill in (a hole) with something. (구멍을) …으로 막다〔메우다〕. ¶ ~ *in a grave* 무덤에 흙을 덮다. **b**) complete covering of. …의 지붕을 이다.
cover over, cover completely. 완전히 덮다; 덮어막다. ¶ ~ *over a hole in the roof* 지붕의 구멍을 막다.
cover up, **a**) cover thoroughly. 폭 싸다; 감싸다. ¶ ~ *up a child in bed* 침대에 있는 아이를 감싸주다. **b**) hide; conceal; keep secret. 숨기다; 비밀로 해두다. ¶ ~ *up stolen goods* 장물을 감추다 / ~ *up a fact* 사실을 숨기다 / ~ *up one's ignorance* 자신의 무지를 감추다.
cover oneself with, win glory, etc. (영예 따위)를 안다; 한몸에 받다.

— *n.* **1** Ⓒ ⓐ anything that protects or hides by covering. 덮개; 커버. ¶ *a* ~ *for a chair* 의자 씌우개 / *lay* 〔*take off*〕 *a* ~ 덮개를 씌우다〔걷어치우다〕. ⓑ a lid. 뚜껑. ¶ *a* ~ *for a pot* 항아리 뚜껑. ⓒ a case to keep something from dust, etc. (먼지 따위를 막는) 씌움 상자. ¶ *a glass* ~ (인형 따위의) 유리 상자. ⓓ an outer wrapping for a letter. (편지)봉투; 겉봉. ¶ *under the same* ~ 동봉하여 / *send a letter under another* 〔*separate*〕 ~ 편지를 별봉으로 보내다. ⓔ the outer part of a book or magazine; the front and back part of the binding. (책의) 표지; 장정. ¶ *a book in paper covers* 종이 표지의 책. **2** Ⓒ a set of table-utensils (e.g. knives, forks, glasses) laid out for one person at a meal. (식탁 위의) 1인분 식기(食器). ¶ *a dinner* ~ *of ten covers,* 10 인분의 식사 / *lay covers for twenty* (*persons*), 20 인분의 식사를 마련하다. **3** Ⓤ protection; shelter. 보호〔차폐〕(물); 엄호. ¶ *under* ~ *of an umbrella* 우산을 쓰고 / *under* ~ *of darkness* 〔*night*〕 야음을 틈타 / *We were under* ~ *during the storm.* 폭풍우가 치는 동안 우리는 대피해 있었다 / *The soldiers had no* ~ *from the enemy guns.* 병사들은 적의 포화를 피할 엄폐물이 없었다. **4** Ⓤ false show; disguise; pretence. 가장; 구실; 핑계. ¶ *under* ~ *of friendship* 우정이라는 미명하에; 우정을 가장하여. **5** 《comm.》 money deposited against possible loss through a fall in prices. (손해를 대비한) 담보물; 보증금. **6** =covert. [→covert]

break cover, (of an animal) come out suddenly from a hiding place. 은신처에서 뛰어나오다.
from cover to cover, (of a book) from beginning to end. 처음부터 끝까지. ¶ *He read the book from* ~ *to cover.* 책을 처음부터 끝까지 다 읽었다.
take cover, seek shelter or safety. 숨다; 피신〔피난〕하다. ¶ *When it started raining, we took* ~ *under a tree.* 비가 내리자 우리는 나무 밑으로 피신했다.
under cover, **a**) sheltered from the weather; under the roof. 비바람을 피하여; 지붕 밑에. **b**) disguised. 변장〔가장〕하여.

c) secretly. 가만히; 비밀히.
under* (*the*) *cover of, a) with ostensible show of; under the pretext of. …을 가장하여; …을 빙자하여. b) under favor of. …을 틈타.
under cover to, in outer envelope and addressed to. …앞으로의 편지에 동봉하여.

cov·er·age [kʌ́vəridʒ] *n.* UC **1** 《insurance》 the extent to which something is insured. (보험의) 보상 범위. **2** the amount of time and space given by television, a newspaper, etc., to a particular news or subject. (T.V. 등의) 시청권; 미치는 범위; (신문 등의) 보도 범위·시간. **3** 《fin.》 the value of funds held to back up or meet liabilities. 정화(正貨) 준비금.

cover charge [ˊ-ˋ] *n.* 《U.S.》 a charge made by a restaurant or nightclub in addition to the charge for food and drink; a restaurant's extra charge for a floor show. (레스토랑·나이트 클럽에서 식대 이외로) 추가 청구되는 서비스료.

cov·ered [kʌ́vərd] *adj.* **1** having a cover; covering. 덮개가[지붕이] 있는; 덮인. **2** wearing one's hat or cap. 모자를 쓴.

cover girl [ˊ-ˋ] *n.* a girl whose picture appears on the cover of a magazine. 잡지 표지의 모델 여성; 커버걸.

cov·er·ing [kʌ́vəriŋ] *n.* C anything that covers. 덮개; 뚜껑; 외피.

covering letter [ˊ--ˋ-] *n.* a letter sent along with another document. 동봉한 서신[설명서].

covering party [ˊ-- ˋ-] *n.* a party that protects. 엄호대(隊).

cov·er·let [kʌ́vərlit] *n.* C **1** an outside covering for a bed. 이불. **2** a covering. 덮개. [*cover,* L. *lectus* bed]

cov·ert [kʌ́vərt, kóu-] *adj.* **1** secret; hidden; sheltered; disguised. 비밀의; 숨은; 암암리의; 눈에 띄지 않는(opp. overt). ¶ *a ~ threat* 은밀한 협박 / *He threw ~ glances at the girl.* 그는 여자를 슬쩍 훔쳐 보았다. **2** 《law》 protected by a husband. 남편의 보호를 받는; 유부(有夫)의. ¶ *a feme ~* 기혼 여성; 유부녀. — *n.* C **1** a shelter; a protected place. 은신처; 잠복처. **2** a small, thickly wooded area in which animals hide. (짐승들이 숨는) 숲; 덤불. **3** a part of the feathers of a bird. (새의) 우비깃.
break covert, (of game, etc.) come out from a covert. (사냥감 따위가) 은신처에서 뛰쳐나오다.
draw a covert, search it for game or a fox. 사냥감을 숨은 곳에서 몰아내다.
●**cov·ert·ly** [-li] *adv.* [com-, L. *operio* close]

cov·ert·coat [kʌ́vərtkòut] *n.* a light overcoat. 커벗코트《가볍고 짧은 외투》.

cov·er·ture [kʌ́vərtʃər] *n.* **1** 《*arch.*》 a cover or covering. 덮개; 외피. **2** 《law》 the status of a married woman. 유부녀의 신분. [↑]

cov·et [kʌ́vit] *vt.* (P6) desire (something that belongs to another) eagerly. (남의 것)을 탐하다. ¶ *He coveted John's new hat.* 그는 존의 새 모자를 탐냈다. [L. *cupio* long for]

·**cov·et·ous** [kʌ́vitəs] *adj.* very eager to get or to own something that belongs to another. (남의 것을) 탐내는; 탐욕스러운. ¶ *~ of honors* 명예를 탐내는. ●**cov·et·ous·ly** [-li] *adv.* **cov·et·ous·ness** [-nis] *n.*

cov·ey [kʌ́vi] *n.* C **1** a brood or a small flock of game birds, such as of partridges or quails. (자고·메추라기 등, 아직 어미새와 함께 있는) 엽조의 무리; 떼. **2** 《*joc.*》 a group of persons. (사람의) 떼; 일행. ¶ *a ~ of schoolgirls* 한 무리의 여학생. [L. *cubo* lie]

:**cow**[1] [kau] *n.* C **1** a full-grown female domestic animal that gives milk. 암소; (특히) 젖소(cf. *ox*). **2** a female of various other animals, such as the elephant and the whale. (코끼리·고래 따위의) 암컷(cf. *bull*[1]). [E.]
cow with the iron tail, a pump as used in adulterating milk. 우유에 물을 타 묽게 하기 위한 펌프.
till the cows come home, for a long time; forever. 오랫동안; 언제까지나. ¶ *Though you may call till the cows come home, the dog will not pay any attention to you.* 아무리 오랫동안 불러봐야 그 개는 들은 체도 않을 게다.

cow[2] [kau] *vt.* (P6) make (someone) afraid; frighten with threat. …을 으르다; 겁주다; 협박[위협]하다. ¶ *a cowed look* 겁먹은 얼굴 / *be cowed* 겁내다. [↓]

:**cow·ard** [káuərd] *n.* C a person who lacks courage; a person who is shamefully timid. 겁쟁이; 비겁한 사람. ¶ *play the ~* 비겁한 짓을 하다 / *Don't be a ~!* 겁낼 것 없다. — *adj.* lacking courage; timid. 겁 많은; 비겁한; 소심한. [L. *cauda* tail]

cow·ard·ice [káuərdis] *n.* U lack of courage; shameful fear. 겁; 소심; 비겁.

cow·ard·li·ness [káuərdlinis] *n.* =cowardice.

cow·ard·ly [káuərdli] *adj.* **1** (of persons or animals) not brave; lacking courage. 비겁한; 겁쟁이의; 소심한. **2** (of words, actions, etc.) like a coward; mean. (말·행동이) 겁쟁이 같은; 비겁[비열]한. ¶ *a ~ lie* [*behavior*] 비열한 거짓말[짓].

cow·boy [káubɔ̀i] *n.* C 《U.S.》 a man who looks after cattle usu. on horseback. 목동; 카우보이. [→cow[1]]

cow·catch·er [káukæ̀tʃər] *n.* C 《U.S.》 a metal frame on the front of a locomotive, a streetcar, etc. to clear obstacles from the track. (기관차의) 배장기(排

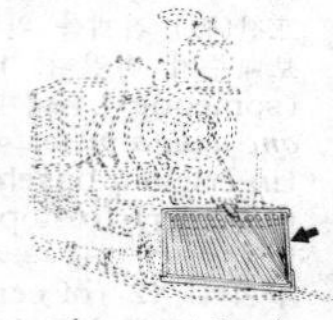
<cowcatcher>

障器); (전차의) 구조망(網). [→*cow*[1]]

cow·er [káuər] *vi.* (P1) bend one's body from cold, fear or shame. (추위나 공포·부끄럼으로) 몸이 움츠러들다; 외축(畏縮)하다. ¶ ~ *before a lion* 사자 앞에서 움츠러들다 / *sit cowering over a fire* 난로 앞에 몸을 쭈그리고 앉다 / *The whipped dog cowered under the table.* 매 맞은 개는 테이블 밑에 움츠리고 있었다. [E.]

cow hand [ˊ ˊ] *n.* 《U.S.》 =cowboy.

cow·herd [káuhə̀:rd] *n.* Ⓒ a person who looks after cows. 소 치는 사람. [*cow*[1]]

cow·hide [káuhàid] *n.* **1** Ⓤ the skin of a cow; leather made from it. 소의 생가죽; 그 무두질한 가죽. **2** Ⓒ 《U.S.》 a strong leather whip. 쇠가죽의 채찍. — *vt.* whip (someone or something) with a cowhide. …을 쇠가죽 채찍으로 때리다. [*cow*[1]]

cowl [kaul] *n.* Ⓒ **1** a monk's hood, usu. attached to a gown; a hooded garment. (수사(修士)의) 가운에 붙은 후드; 후드가 달린 수사복(服). **2** anything shaped like a cowl. 후드 모양의 것. **3** ⓐ a hoodlike cover for the top of a chimney. 굴뚝 끝의 통풍갓. ⓑ a metal cover, e.g. for an engine; cowling. 엔진 후드. [L. *cucullus* hood]

Cow·ley [káuli], **Abraham** *n.* (1618-67) an English poet. 카울리《영국의 시인》.

cowl·ing [káuliŋ] *n.* Ⓒ a metal covering over the engine of an airplane. (항공기의) 카울링《엔진의 덮개》. [*cowl*]

co·work·er [kóuwə̀:rkər, ˊˊ–] *n.* Ⓒ a person who works with another. 협력자. [co-]

cow·pea [káupì:] *n.* 《bot.》 a plant with very long pods. 광저기《소의 사료》. [*cow*[1]]

Cow·per [kú:pər, káu-], **William** *n.* (1731-1800) an English poet. 쿠퍼《영국의 시인》.

cow·pox [káupàks / -pɔ̀ks] *n.* Ⓤ 《med.》 a disease of cows causing small spots containing pus on the breasts. 우두(牛痘). [*cow*[1]]

cow·rie, cow·ry [káuri] *n.* Ⓒ a small shell used as a coin in parts of Asia and Africa. 자패(紫貝); 그 조가비. [Hind.]

cow·slip [káuslip] *n.* Ⓒ 《bot.》 **1** a wild plant with yellow flowers; an English primrose. 프리뮬러《앵초의 일종; 초여름 목초지에 꽃이 피는 야생 화초》. **2** 《U.S.》 the marsh marigold. 눈동이나물의 일종. [E. =cowdung]

cox [kaks / kɔks] *n.* Ⓒ 《*colloq.*》 a coxswain. (배의) 키잡이. — *vt., vi.* (P6; 1) act as coxswain (of). (…의) 키잡이가 되다. [→coxswain]

cox·comb [kákskòum / kɔ́ks-] *n.* Ⓒ **1** an empty-headed dandy; a silly man. (머리에 든 것이 없는) 멋쟁이; 바보. **2** a cockscomb. (닭의 볏 같은) 어릿광대 모자. [*cock's comb*]

cox·swain [káksən, -swèin / kɔ́k-] *n.* Ⓒ a person who controls the course of a boat. (배의) 키잡이; 정장(艇長). 參考 cox 로 생략. [*cockboat, swain*]

coy [kɔi] *adj.* **1** (esp. of a girl) shy; modest; bashful. 수줍음을 잘 타는; 암띤. ¶ *be ~ of* …을 수줍어(부끄러워)하다. **2** seeming to be modest in order to attract. (짐짓) 수줍은 체하는; 얌전을 가장하는. [→quiet]

coy·ly [kɔ́ili] *adv.* in a coy manner. 부끄러워(수줍어)하여.

coy·o·te [káiout, kaióuti / kɔ́iout, kɔióuti] *n.* Ⓒ (*pl.* **-tes** or *collectively* **-te**) 《zool.》 a small wolf on the plains of western North America. 코요테《북 아메리카 서부 초원의 승냥이》. [Mex.]

coz·en [kʌ́zn] *vt., vi.* (P6,13; 3) 《*arch.*》 cheat; deceive. (…을) 기만하다; 속이다. [F. *cousiner*]

co·zy [kóuzi] *adj.* (**-zi·er, -zi·est**) warm and comfortable; snug. (아담하고 포근하여) 기분(살기) 좋은; 쾌적한. ¶ *a ~ town* 쾌적한 도시. — *n.* Ⓒ (*pl.* **co·zies**) a cloth cover or cap for a teapot, used to keep the contents hot. 보온 커버. 參考 cosy 로도 씀. [Norw.]

cp. compare.

Cr 《chem.》 chromium.

cr. credit; creditor.

·crab[1] [kræb] *n.* Ⓒ **1** 《zool.》 a water creature with a hard outer cover and ten legs, well-known for walking sideways. 게. **2** a machine for lifting heavy weights. 자아틀; 윈치. **3** 《*the C-*》 《astron.》 a constellation; Cancer. 게자리. **4** 《*colloq.*》 a disadvantage; a failure. 불리; 실패. **5** 《insect.》 a crab-louse. 사면발이.

catch a crab, 《rowing》 lose the balance of a boat by thrusting one's oar too deeply into the water. 노를 너무 물속 깊이 넣고 저어 배가 균형을 잃다.

— *vi.* (**crabbed, crab·bing**) (P1) catch or hunt for crabs. 게를 잡다. [E.]

crab[2] [kræb] *n.* Ⓒ **1** an ill-natured person. 심술궂은(찌무룩한) 사람; 꾀까다로운 사람. **2** =crab apple. — *vt.* (**crabbed, crab·bing**) (P6) **1** 《*colloq.*》 speak ill of; find fault with. …을 나쁘게 말하다; 탈(트집)을 잡다. **2** 《*colloq.*》 spoil. 못쓰게 하다; 결딴내다. **3** object to; try to prevent (an action). 반대(방해)하다. ¶ *He crabbed my act.* 그는 내 행동에 반대했다. [E.]

crab apple [ˊ ˊ–] *n.* a small, wild, sour apple. 야생 사과의 일종.

crab·bed [krǽbid] *adj.* **1** (of a person, speech, etc.) ill-natured; easily showing anger; cross. 심술궂은; 성마른; 꾀까다로운. **2** (of handwriting, style, etc.) hard to understand; hard to read. (필체·문체 따위가) 난해한; 판독하기 어려운. [E.]

:crack [kræk] *vi.* (P1,2A) **1** ⓐ break or split suddenly. 우지끈(탁·뚝) 소리를 내며 깨지다; 부러지다; 끊어지다. ¶ *The rope cracked under pressure.* 밧줄은 압력을 받아 뚝 끊어졌다 / *The branch cracked under the weight of* *snow.* 나뭇가지가 눈의 무게로 우지끈 부러졌다. ⓑ (of a rifle or whip) make a sudden, sharp noise. 갑자기 날카로운 소리를 내다; 탕[철석] 소리가 나다. ¶ *The whip cracked.* 채찍이 철썩하고 소리를 냈다 / *A rifle cracked somewhere.* 어디선가 탕하고 총소리가 났다. **2** (of a brittle substance, glass, ice, etc.) open into fissures; spring apart. 금이 가다; 갈라지다. **3** ⓐ (of the voice) become harsh suddenly. (목소리가) 쉬다. ⓑ (of male voices) become lower in pitch, esp. when a boy becomes physically mature. (남자 아이가) 변성(變聲)하다. — *vt.* **1** (P6,7) cause to make a sudden, sharp noise. …을 (찰싹, 탕, 쨍그랑 따위의) 날카로운 소리를 내게 하다. ¶ ~ *a pistol* 권총을 탕 쏘다 / ~ *a whip* 채찍질을 하여 소리내다. **2** (P6,7) cause a narrow split, esp. in a brittle substance such as glass, china, etc.; break without separating into parts. (유리·사기 따위)를 금이 가게 하다; 갈라지게 하다. ¶ ~ *the cup across the bottom* 컵 바닥에 금이 가게 하다. **3** (P6) break by continuous pressure. …을 짓눌러 깨뜨리다[부수다, 으스러뜨리다]. ¶ ~ *a walnut* 호두를 까다. **4** (P6,7) break by a sudden sharp blow. (쳐서) 빼개다; 깨뜨리다. ¶ ~ *a skull* 두개골을 빼개다. **5** 《chiefly in *passive*》 break or crush mentally; cause to be mentally ill. …을 (정신이) 돌게 하다; 미치게 하다. ¶ *He is cracked.* 그는 정신이 돌았다. **6** (P6) tell (a joke). (농담)을 하다. ¶ ~ *a joke* 농담을 하다.

crack a bottle, open a bottle and drink the contents. 병을 따고 속엣것을 마시다. ¶ ~ *five bottles of wine* 포도주 다섯 병을 따 마시다.

crack a crib, 《*sl.*》 break into a house. 집에 침입하다.

crack down (***on***), 《*colloq.*》 take severe measures against. (…에) 단호한 조처를 취하다; (…을) 엄중히 단속하다. ¶ ~ *down on drunken driving* 음주 운전을 엄중히 단속하다.

crack on, **a**) 《*colloq.*》 crowd on (the sails). (돛)을 전부 펴다. **b**) put on steam. 기운을 내다.

crack up, **a**) praise highly. …을 높이 칭찬하다. **b**) show signs of wear, old age, decay (of persons, health, etc.); lose strength. (육체적·정신적으로) 약해지다; 건강이 망가지다. **c**) (of an airplane) suffer damage. (비행기가) 결딴나다.

— *n.* Ⓒ **1** a sudden sharp or loud sound. (불시의) 날카로운 소리. ¶ *the ~ of thunder* 천둥 소리 / *the ~ of a rifle* 탕하는 총소리. **2** a line between parts without a complete separation; a split; a narrow opening. 갈라진 틈; 금; 균열. 參考 흔히 부사적으로 쓰임. ¶ *a ~ in the ground* [*in wood*] 땅[나무]의 균열 / *There is a ~ in this cup.* 이 컵에는 금이 간 데가 있다 / *Open the window a ~.* 문을 조금 열어라. **3** a sudden, sharp blow. 강타; 일격. ¶ *hit someone a ~ on the head* …의 머리를 쥐어박다. **4** a mental or physical defect. (정신적·육체적인) 결함; 정신 이상. **5** a peculiar sound or tone of the voice. 목쉼; 변성.

in a crack, in a moment. 순식간에.

the crack of day, daybreak. 새벽.

the crack of doom, the sound which will announce the end of the world; the Day of Judgment. 최후의 심판의 날(을 알리는 천둥소리).

— *adj.* 《*colloq.*》 first-class. 일류의.

— *adv.* sharply. 날카롭게. ¶ *hit him ~ in the eye* 그의 눈을 철썩 때리다. [E.]

crack·brained [krǽkbrèind] *adj.* crazy; mad; foolish. 광기의; 미친; 어리석은. [E.]

crack·down [krǽkdàun] *n.* punitive action taken to stop an unlawful or disapproved activity. (불법 행위에 대한) 단호한 조처; 엄중한 단속. [E.]

cracked [krækt] *adj.* **1** having a crack or cracks; split; broken. 금이 간; 갈라진; 깨진. ¶ *a ~ bell* 금이 간 종 / *a ~ reputation* 금이 간[손상된] 평판. **2** (of the voice) broken; having harsh notes. (목소리가) 변한; 쉰. ¶ *a ~ voice* 쉰 목소리. **3** 《*colloq.*》 rather mad; crazy. 정신이 돈; 미친. ¶ *He's slightly ~.* 그는 머리가 약간 돌았다. [E.]

·crack·er [krǽkər] *n.* Ⓒ **1** a thin, hard, and dry biscuit. 크래커《얇고 파삭파삭한 비스킷》. **2** a small firework which bursts with a sharp noise. 폭죽(爆竹). **3** an ornamented pipe of paper which contains a small gift and breaks with a sharp noise when the two ends are pulled apart. 크래커 봉봉《끈을 잡아당기면 폭음을 내면서 과자·장난감 따위가 튀어나오게 된 종이 통》. **4** 《*pl.*》 an instrument that cracks nuts. 호두 까는 기구. **5** 《U.S. *sl.*》 a low-class inhabitant of the southern U.S. 미국 남부 지방의 빈민(貧民). [E.]

crack·ers [krǽkərz] *adj.* 《*predicative*》 《Brit. *sl.*》 mad; out of one's mind. 머리가 돈; 미친. ¶ *drive someone ~* 아무를 미치게 하다 / *He's gone crackers!* 그는 돌았다. [E.]

·crack·le [krǽkəl] *vi.* (P1) make a series of short, sharp sounds. 탁탁 튀는[우지끈, 우지직, 으드득] 소리를 내다. ¶ *a fire crackling on the hearth* 난로에서 탁탁 소리를 내며 타고 있는 불. — *n.* Ⓤ **1** the sound of crackling. 탁탁[우지직, 우지끈] 소리. **2** a surface or glaze of fine, irregular cracks on some kinds of china, glass, etc. (도자기 따위 표면의) 금. [E.]

crack·ling [krǽkliŋ] *n.* ⒸⓊ **1** the hard, dry, and brown skin of roasted pork. 바싹 구운 돼지고기의 바삭바삭한 겉살. **2** a series of small, sharp, crackling sounds. 탁탁[우지직, 우지끈] 소리. [E.]

crack-up [krǽkʌ̀p] *n.* Ⓤ 《U.S.》 **1** (of cars or airplanes) crash. (차 따위의) 충돌; (비행기의) 추락. **2** a mental or physical collapse. (정신적·육체적인) 파탄; 쇠약. [E.]

cracks·man [krǽksmən] *n.* (*pl.* **-men** [-mən]) a burglar. 도둑. [E.]

crack·y [krǽki] *adj.* liable to crack. 깨지기 쉬운. [E.]

-cra·cy [-krəsi] *suf.* rule, government. '지배, 정치'의 뜻. ¶ *aristocracy / democracy.* [Gk. *kratos* power]

***cra·dle** [kréidl] *n.* Ⓒ **1** a baby's little bed which can be gently swung or rolled. 요람. ¶ *rock a* ~ 요람을 흔들다. **2** the place in which anything begins its growth; the place of origin. 발상지; 기원(起源). ¶ *the* ~ *of European civilization* 유럽 문명의 발상지. **3** 《*the* ~》 the period of early childhood. 유년기; 요람 시대. ¶ *from the* ~ *to the grave* 요람에서 무덤까지; 한평생. **4** a frame attached to a scythe for harvesting grain. 낫의 덧살《낫에 덧대는 틀》. **5** a frame for supporting a ship in dry dock. (조선소의) 선가(船架). **6** a box on rockers to wash gold from the earth. (금광의) 선광기(選鑛器). **7** a frame to keep the bedclothes from pressing upon a wounded limb. (상처에 이불이 닿지 않게 하기 위한) 침구 버팀틀.

from the cradle, from early childhood. 어린 시절부터.

in the cradle, in one's early days. 어렸을 때에.

the cradle of the deep, the sea. 바다.

— *vt.* (P6) **1** 《chiefly *poet.*》 place or rock (a baby) to sleep in a cradle; lull to rest as in a cradle. …을 요람에 넣어 잠재우다[흔들다]; 흔들어 어르다. ¶ ~ *a baby to sleep* 아기를 흔들어 재우다 / ~ *a child in* [*on*] *one's arms* 어린애를 안고 흔들어 어르다. **2** guard or train (someone) in early life. …을 어릴 때 보호[훈련]하다. ¶ *be cradled in luxury* 호사스럽게 자라다. **3** support (a ship, etc.) in a cradle. (배 따위)를 선가(船架)에 올리다. **4** wash auriferous earth in a cradle. 선광(選鑛)하다. [E.]

***craft** [kræft, krɑːft] *n.* **1** Ⓤ skill, esp. in making things by hand. 기교; 기능; 솜씨. **2** Ⓒ ⓐ art or work requiring special skill. (손으로 하는) 특수한 기술; 수예(手藝); 수공업. ¶ *the* ~ *of a mason* 석공의 기술 / *art*(*s*) *and craft*(*s*) 미술 공예 / *learn a* ~ 기술을 배우다. ⓑ a trade or employment requiring skilled work. 손기술을 요하는 직업. **3** Ⓒ the association of persons engaged in any trade; a labor union; a guild; the members of a skilled trade. 동업 조합. ¶ *compose a* ~ 동업 조합을 만들다. **4** Ⓤ cunning; skill in deceiving others. 교활; 간지(奸智); 술책. ¶ *an imposter full of* ~ 간지에 뛰어난 사기꾼 / *By* ~ *he got all their money from them.* 그는 못된 술책으로 그들의 돈을 몽땅 빼앗았다. **5** (*pl.* **craft**) boats, ships or aircraft. 배; 항공기. ¶ *The harbor was full of all kinds of craft.* 항구에는 온갖 종류의 선박들로 꽉 차 있었다. [E.; G. *Kraft* strength]

craft·i·ness [krǽftinis, krɑ́ːft-] *n.* Ⓤ the state of being crafty; cunning. 교활; 교묘.

crafts·man [krǽftsmən, krɑ́ːfts-] *n.* Ⓒ (*pl.* **-men** [-mən]) **1** a skilled workman. 장색; 명장(名匠). **2** an artist. 예술가.

crafts·man·ship [krǽftsmənʃip, krɑ́ːfts-] *n.* Ⓤ the skill, art, or work of a craftsman. (장색(匠色)의) 기교; 기능; 기량.

craft·y [krǽfti, krɑ́ːf-] *adj.* (**craft·i·er, craft·i·est**) skillful in deceiving others; tricky. 교활한; 노회한. ¶ *a* ~ *fox* 교활한 여우.

crag [kræg] *n.* Ⓒ a steep, rugged rock or cliff; a projecting rock. 깎아지른 듯한 바위; 단애(斷崖). [E.]

crag·gy [krǽgi] *adj.* (**-gi·er, -gi·est**) with many rocks; rugged; rough. 바위가 많은; 울퉁불퉁한.

cram [kræm] *v.* (**crammed, cram·ming**) *vt.* (P6,7,13) **1** 《*with, into*》 force into; fill or pack tightly; stuff. 억지로 처넣다; 잔뜩 채워 넣다. ¶ ~ *one's clothes into the trunk* 옷을 트렁크 속에 처넣다 / ~ *people into a bus* 사람들을 버스 안에 꽉 채워 넣다 / ~ *one's mouth with food* 입에 음식을 잔뜩 처넣다 / ~ *oneself with food* 음식을 잔뜩 먹다. **2** ⓐ 《*fig.*》 crowd, stuff (the mind with facts, information), esp. for an examination. (수험을 위해) …을 주입식으로 공부시키다. ¶ ~ *a pupil for the entrance exam* 입학 시험을 위해 학생을 주입식으로 공부시키다. ⓑ 《often *up*》 learn (a subject) hastily for an examination. (시험을 위해) …을 벼락치기로 공부하다. ¶ ~ (*up*) *math for the examination* 벼락치기로 수학의 시험 공부를 하다. **3** feed (poultry) by packing food down their throat, in order to fatten them for the table. (살찌우기 위해 가금(家禽)에게 먹이를) 잔뜩 먹이다.

— *vi.* (P1) **1** pack food into one's mouth; eat too much. 잔뜩[게걸스레] 먹다; 과식하다. **2** 《*fig.*》 fill the mind hastily with knowledge, esp. for an examination. 벼락치기식 공부를 하다. [E.]

cram·mer [krǽmər] *n.* Ⓒ 《Brit.》 **1** a special teacher who crams students for examinations. (수험 준비를 위해) 주입식으로 가르치는 교사. **2** a student who crams for an examinaiton. (시험을 위해) 벼락치기로 공부하는 학생(cf. *grind*).

cramp[1] [kræmp] *n.* **1** Ⓒ a metal bar bent at both ends, used for holding together blocks of stone, timbers, etc. 꺾쇠. **2** a clamp. 죔쇠. **3** something that restricts or confines. 속박하는 것. — *vt.* (P6) **1** fasten or hold (something) together with a cramp. …을 꺾쇠로 죄다. **2** ⓐ keep (something) from having free action. (행동 따위)를 속박하다. ⓑ 《*fig.*》 shut into a small space; limit. 가두다; 제한하다. ¶ *His work was cramped by the time-limit.* 그의 일은 시간 제한 때문에 제약을 받았다. [F. *crampe* hook]

cramp[2] [kræmp] *n.* Ⓤ **1** a sudden, sharp pain in the muscles, making movement impossible. 경련; 쥐. ¶ ~ *in the calf* 장딴지〔다리〕의 쥐 / *be seized with ~ while swimming* 수영 중에 다리에 쥐가 나다 / *I've got* (*the*) *cramps.* 경련이 일어났다. **2** 《*pl.*》《U.S.》 very sharp pains in the abdomen. 격심한 복통; 진통. —*vt.* (P6) cause (something) to have a cramp. …에 일으키게 하다.

cramped [kræmpt] *adj.* **1** (of hand writing) badly shaped; difficult to read. (글씨가) 판독하기 어려운. **2** convulsed. 경련을 일으킨.

cram·pon [krǽmpən] *n.* 《usu. *pl.*》 an iron plate with spikes, worn on the shoe for walking on ice, etc. 아이젠; 동철(冬鐵). [→cramp[1]]

cran·ber·ry [krǽnbèri / -bəri] *n.* Ⓒ (*pl.* **-ries**) 《bot.》 a firm, sour, red berry; the shrub on which these berries grow. 덩굴월귤(의 열매); 그 관목. [G.]

***crane** [krein] *n.* Ⓒ **1** a machine for lifting and moving heavy weights. 기중기; 크레인. **2** an iron arm used for suspending pots or kettles over a fire. (불 위에 냄비 따위를 거는) 자재(自在) 갈고리. **3** a large bird with very long legs and a long neck. 두루미; 학(鶴). —*vt.* (P6,7) **1** raise (things) by a crane. …을 기중기로 들어올리다〔옮기다〕. **2** stretch (the neck) to see better. (잘 보려고 목)을 길게 빼다〔늘이다〕. ¶ ~ *one's neck to get a better view* 좀더 잘 보려고 목을 길게 빼다. —*vi.* (P1,4) stretch out one's neck. 목을 길게 빼다. ¶ ~ *back to look at someone* 아무를 보려고 고개를 뒤로 한껏 돌리다. [E.]

crane fly [⌐⌐] *n.* 《insect》 daddy-long-legs. 꾸정모기.

cra·ni·a [kréiniə] *n.* pl. of **cranium.**

cra·ni·al [kréiniəl, -njəl] *adj.* of the skull. 두개(頭蓋)의; 두개골의. [Gk.]

cra·ni·om·e·try [krèiniámitri / -5m-] *n.* the art of measuring skulls. 두개(頭蓋) 측정학. [↑]

cra·ni·um [kréiniəm] *n.* Ⓒ (*pl.* **-ni·ums** or **-ni·a**) the skull; the part of the skull enclosing the brain. 두개(頭蓋); 두개골. [Gk.]

crank [kræŋk] *n.* Ⓒ **1** 《mech.》 a part or handle that is turned to work a machine. 크랭크(축). **2** a sudden change of speech or thought; a strange idea or act. 변덕; 묘한 생각; 기상(奇想). **3** 《U.S. *colloq.*》 a person with odd ideas or one fixed idea. 기인(奇人); 괴짜. **4** 《*colloq.*》 an ill-tempered person. 심술궂은 사람; 꾀까다로운 사람.
—*vt.* (P6,7) **1** 《mech.》 work or move (a motor) with a crank. …을 크랭크로 회전시키다. ¶ ~ (*up*) *an engine* 크랭크로 엔진을 회전시키다. **2** bend (something) into the shape of a crank. …을 크랭크 모양으로 굽히다.
—*vi.* (P1) turn a crank. 크랭크를 돌리다.
—*adj.* loose; uneasy. 헐거워 흔들거리는; 불안정한. [E.]

crank·y [krǽŋki] *adj.* (**crank·i·er, crank·i·est**) **1** cross; easily showing anger; ill-natured. 심술궂은; 성마른; 꾀까다로운. **2** 《*colloq.*》 (of a person) strange; not common. 이상한; 야릇한. **3** (of machinery, building, etc.) apt to turn over; loose; not strong. 불안정한; 헐거운; 흔들거리는. [E.]

cran·nied [krǽnid] *adj.* full of small openings or cracks. (갈라진) 틈이 많은; 금이 간. [↓]

cran·ny [krǽni] *n.* Ⓒ (*pl.* **-nies**) a small, narrow opening in a rock, a wall, etc.; a crack. (벽 따위의) 갈라진 틈; 금; 균열. [F.]

crape [kreip] *n.* **1** Ⓤ crepe. 크레이프《오글쪼글한 비단》. **2** Ⓒ piece of black cloth worn or displayed as a sign of sorrow at the death of someone. 검은 상장(喪章). [→crêpe]

crap·u·lent [krǽpjələnt] *adj.* feeling ill after drinking too much. 과음으로 불쾌한; 숙취의. [Gk.]

:crash[1] [kræʃ] *n.* Ⓒ **1** a sudden, loud noise; a falling, hitting, or breaking with force and a loud noise. 갑자기 나는 요란한 소리; 광〔쨍, 우르르, 와르르, 우지끈〕하는 소리. ¶ *the sudden ~ of dishes* 갑자기 접시가 쨍하고 깨짐 / *a ~ of applause* 우레 같은 박수 / *the ~ of thunder* 〔*artillery*〕 우르르(쾅)하는 천둥 소리〔포성〕 / *The wall fell with a ~.* 담이 와르르 무너졌다. **2** 《*fig.*》 sudden ruin; serious failure in business. 갑작스런 파멸; (사업의) 실패; 붕괴. ¶ *a ~ on the Stock Exchange* (증권) 장세(場勢)의 폭락. **3** ⓐ (of an airplane) a fall to the earth; a bad landing. (비행기의) 추락; 불시착. ¶ *He was killed in a plane ~.* 그는 비행기의 추락으로 죽었다. ⓑ (of cars, etc.) a violent collision. (차 따위의) 충돌; 격돌. ¶ *a train* 〔*car*〕 ~ 열차〔자동차〕 충돌.
—*vi.* **1** (P1,2A,3) make a sudden, loud noise; fall, hit, or break with force and a loud noise. (갑자기) 요란한 소리를 내다; 광〔와르르〕 부딪치다〔무너지다, 깨지다〕. ¶ ~ *against* 〔*into*〕 *a train* 열차에 충돌하다 / *The door crashed open.* 쾅하고 문이 열렸다 / *The dishes crashed to the floor.* 접시가 바닥에 떨어져 쨍그렁하고 깨졌다. **2** (P1,2A) 《*fig.*》 be suddenly ruined; fail in business. 돌연히 파멸〔실패〕하다; 붕괴하다. ¶ *The firm crashed.* 회사는 망했다. **3** (P1,2A,3) (of an aircraft) fall or land suddenly out of control. 추락하다; 불시착하다.
—*vt.* (P6) **1** break (something) to pieces noisily; smash. 요란한 소리와 함께 부수다. ¶ ~ *a glass against a wall* 술잔을 벽에 내던져 쨍그렁 깨뜨리다. **2** damage or destroy (an airplane) in landing. (비행기)를 손상하다; 추락〔불시착〕시키다.
crash down, run, slide or descend rapidly with much noise. 와르르 요란한 소리를 내며

무너져 내리다. ¶ *The avalanche crashed down the mountainside.* 사태가 나서 산허리가 무너져 내렸다.

crash down on, oppress. 탄압하다.

crash into, run into; dash against. 부딪다; 충돌하다. ¶ *The car crashed into a gate.* 차가 대문을 들이받았다.

● **crash·er** [-ər] *n.* [Imit.]

crash² [kræʃ] *n.* a coarse cotton or linen cloth used for towels, clothing, etc. (타월·하복용 따위의) 거친 천(아마포). [?→crass]

crash-dive [krǽʃdàiv] *n.* a sudden dive by a submarine, esp. to avoid attack. (공격을 피하기 위한) 급속 잠항(潛航). — *vi.* (P1) dive in this way. 급속 잠항하다. [→crash¹]

crash helmet [∠∠] *n.* a protective helmet worn by motorcyclists, racing drivers, etc. (머리 보호를 위한) 안전 헬멧《오토바이 운전자·자동차 레이스 선수 등이 씀》.

crash-land [krǽʃlǽnd] *vi.* (P1) (of an aircraft) land hurriedly in an emergency, often with damage to the aircraft. (비행기가 기체 손상을 각오하고) 비상 착륙하다. — *vt.* (P6) land (an aircraft) in this way. (비행기 등)을 비상 착륙시키다.

crass [kræs] *adj.* **1** dull; foolish. 어리석은; 둔감한. **2** utter; complete. 심한; 지독한. ¶ ~ *ignorance* (*stupidity*) 지독한 무지(우둔). [L. *crassus* coarse]

crate [kreit] *n.* Ⓒ a large frame, box, basket, etc. used for packing or carrying various articles. 크레이트《과일·가구 따위의 포장 운반용 나무틀·궤짝·바구니 따위》. — *vt.* (P6) put in a crate. 크레이트에 넣다. [L. *cratis* hurdle]

cra·ter [kréitər] *n.* Ⓒ **1** an opening of a volcanic mountain that sends out fire and smoke. (화산의) 분화구. ¶ *Hot melted rock flows from the ~ of the volcano.* 뜨거운 용암(熔岩)이 화산 분화구에서 흘러나오고 있다. **2** 《mil.》 a hole in the ground caused by an explosion. (폭탄 따위의 폭발로 생긴) 큰 구덩이. [Gk. =mixing bowl]

cra·vat [krəvǽt] *n.* Ⓒ **1** 《*arch.*》《comm.》 a necktie. 넥타이. **2** a cloth worn around the neck; a scarf. 목 장식 스카프. [*Croat*]

•**crave** [kreiv] *vt.* (P6,8) **1** have a strong desire for (something). …을 열망(갈망)하다. ¶ ~ *water* 물을 갈망하다 / ~ *affection* 애정을 갈망하다 / *He craves to become a pop music star.* 그는 유행가 인기 가수가 되기를 갈망하고 있다. **2** ask for (something) in an earnest manner; beg. …에게 간청하다. ¶ ~ *someone's pardon* (*mercy*) 아무의 용서(자비)를 빌다. — *vi.* (P3) 《*for*》 have a great desire for. 갈망(열망)하다. ¶ *I am simply craving for a drink.* 술이 몹시 마시고 싶다. [E.]

cra·ven [kréivən] *adj.* cowardly. 겁 많은; 소심한. — *n.* Ⓒ a person who is not brave; a coward. 소심한 사람; 겁쟁이. [L. *crepo* rattle]

cry craven, give in; surrender. 항복하다.

crav·ing [kréiviŋ] *n.* Ⓒ a strong desire. 갈망; 열망. ¶ *have a ~ for fame* 명성을 갈망하다. [→crave]

craw·fish [krɔ́:fiʃ] *n.* Ⓒ (*pl.* **-fish·es** or *collectively* **-fish**) a fresh-water creature with a shell and ten legs resembling a lobster; a crayfish. 가재. — *vi.* 《U.S. *colloq.*》 go back. 뒷걸음질하다; 꽁무니 빼다. [O.F. *crevice* crab]

:**crawl** [krɔ:l] *vi.* (P1,2A,3) **1** move the body slowly along the ground; creep. 기다; 기어다니다. ¶ ~ *on hands and knees* (*on all fours*) 엎드려 네 발로 기다 / ~ *on the belly* 배를 깔고 나아가다; 포복 전진하다. **2** move or do something very slowly or carefully. 느릿느릿(조심조심) 움직이다; (일이) 조금씩 진척되다. ¶ ~ *along an icy road in a car* 차를 몰고 빙판길을 거북이걸음으로 나아가다 / *The work crawled.* 일은 천천히 진척되었다. **3** 《*fig.*》 abase oneself before another. 비굴하게 굴다. ¶ *When I complained he crawled with abject apologies.* 내가 불평을 하자 그는 굽실거리며 사과했다. **4** be alive with crawling things. (벌레 따위가) 득실거리다. ¶ *The floor was crawling with spiders.* 바닥에는 거미들이 득실거렸다. **5** feel creepy. (벌레가 기는 것처럼) 스멀(근질)거리다; 오싹하다. ¶ *My flesh crawled at the thought* (*sight*). 생각(보기)만 해도 몸이 오싹했다. **6** move in secret. 가만히(은밀히) 움직이다.

— *n.* Ⓒ **1** a slow movement along the ground. 김; 천천히 나아감; 서행(徐行). ¶ *go for a ~* 어슬렁어슬렁 산책을 나가다. **2** 《usu. *the ~*》 a way of swimming with the head kept low in the water. 크롤 (수영법). [E.]

go at a crawl, walk, drive etc. very slowly. 천천히 걷다(몰다).

crawl·er [krɔ́:lər] *n.* Ⓒ **1** a person or an animal that crawls; a louse. 기어다니는 사람(동물); 이. **2** 《often *pl.*》 a garment for a baby to wear while creeping about on the floor. (아기가) 엉금엉금 길 때 입는 옷. **3** 《Brit.》 a cab moving slowly in search of passengers. 손님을 찾아다니는 택시. [E.]

crawl·y [krɔ́:li] *adj.* (**crawl·i·er, crawl·i·est**) 《*colloq.*》 feeling as if things are crawling over one's skin. (벌레가 기듯) 스멀거리는; 근질거리는. [E.]

cray·fish [kréifiʃ] *n.* Ⓒ (*pl.* **-fish·es** or *collectively* **-fish**) =crawfish.

cray·on [kréiən, -an / -ɔn] *n.* Ⓒ **1** a stick of soft, colored chalk, used for drawing or writing. 크레용. ¶ *a picture drawn in* (*with a*) ~ 크레용(으로 그린) 그림. **2** a drawing made with crayons. 크레용화(畫). — *vt.* (P6) draw (something) with crayons. …을 크레용으로 그리다; …의 밑그림을 (크레용으로) 그리다. [L. *creta* chalk]

craze [kreiz] *n.* Ⓒ **1** an eager but short-lived interest in doing something. (일시적인) 열광; 열중. ¶ *a ~ for stamp-col-*

lection 우표 수집열 / *have a* ~ *for skiing* 스키에 열중하다. **2** a popular fashion. 대유행. ¶ *This computer game is the latest* ~ *in Korea.* 이 컴퓨터 게임이 최근 한국에서 대유행이다. **3** a crack. (도자기 표면의) 갈라진 금. — *vt.* (P6) **1** 《usu. in *passive*》 make (someone) mad. …을 미치게 하다; 열광시키다. ¶ *be crazed by drink* 술에 취해 미치광이처럼 되다. **2** produce a cracked effect in the glaze of (pottery, etc.). (도자기에 바른 유약에) 잔금이 생기게 굽다.
— *vi.* (P1) become mad; be finely cracked. 미치다; 잔금이 가다.
● **cra·zi·ly** [kréizili] *adv.* **cra·zi·ness** [kréizinis] *n.* [Sw.]

:cra·zy [kréizi] *adj.* (**-zi·er, -zi·est**) **1** ⓐ having a deranged mind; mad. 정신 이상의; 미친. ¶ *drive someone* ~ 아무를 미치게 하다 / *This noise is driving me* ~. 이 시끄러운 소리가 나를 미치게 만든다. ⓑ 《*colloq.*》 foolish. 바보 같은; 미련한. ¶ *a* ~ *idea* 터무니없는 생각. **2** 《*colloq.*》 excited; unreasonably eager. (열)광적인; 열중한. ¶ *be* ~ *about baseball* 야구에 미치다. **3** (of a structure) not strong or sound; shaky; weak. (건축·배 따위가) 튼튼치 못한; 금이 간; 흔들흔들한; 약한. ¶ *a* ~ *old building* 무너질 것 같은 낡은 건물. **4** (of a pavement, quilt, etc.) made of irregular pieces fitted together without pattern. (한데 맞춘) 모양이 일정치 않은; 고르지 않은. ¶ *a* ~ *pavement* (돌 포장이) 울퉁불퉁한 포도. [*craze*]

CRB Central Reserve Banks.

creak [kri:k] *vi., vt.* (P1; 6) make, or cause (something) to make a sharp, high sound. 삐걱거리(게 하)다. ¶ *Hinges* ~ *when they need oiling.* 경첩은 기름이 마르면 삐걱거린다. — *n.* Ⓒ a sharp, high cry or noise. 삐걱(거리는) 소리. ¶ *When I sat down in the chair it gave a loud* ~. 의자에 앉자 요란하게 삐걱 소리가 났다. [Imit.]

creak·y [krí:ki] *adj.* (**creak·i·er, creak·i·est**) apt to make a sharp, high sound. 삐걱거리는.

:cream [kri:m] *n.* Ⓤ **1** the rich, yellow, oily part of milk that comes to the top. 크림; 유피(乳皮); 유지. **2** dessert or food made of cream or like cream. 크림이 든 식품. ¶ *vanilla* ~ 바닐라 아이스크림 / ~ *of tomato soup* 크림이 든 토마토 수프. **3** a soft fat used as a medicine for the skin. (화장용·약용) 크림. ¶ *cold* (*vanishing*) ~ 콜드(배니싱) 크림. **4** a light yellow color. 담황색; 크림빛. **5** 《*fig.*》 《*the* ~》 the best part. 가장 좋은 부분; 정수. ¶ *the* ~ *of the story* 이야기의 압권 / *the* ~ *of the lecture* 강연의 클라이맥스.
cream of lime, milk of lime. 석회유(乳).
cream of tartar, purified tartar. 주석영(酒石英); 타르타르산 칼륨.
get the cream of, take the essence of. …의 정수를 뽑다.
— *vt.* (P6) **1** add cream to (tea or coffee). …에 크림을 넣다(치다). **2** take the cream from milk; take the best part from (something). (우유)에서 크림을 떠내다; 정수(精粹)를 뽑아내다. **3** ⓐ make into a mixture like cream. 크림 모양으로 하다. ¶ ~ *butter and sugar together for a cake* 케이크를 만들기 위해 버터와 설탕을 섞어 크림 상태로 하다. ⓑ cook or serve with cream or a cream sauce. 크림으로(크림 소스로) 조리하다. ¶ *creamed chicken* 크림 소스를 친 닭고기.
— *vi.* (P1) **1** (of milk) form into cream. 크림이 되다(생기다). **2** (of other liquids) form into a thick layer like cream on the top; foam. (액체에) 더껑이가 생기다; 거품이 일다.
— *adj.* **1** containing cream or milk; like cream. 크림을 함유한; 크림 같은. **2** light yellow. 크림빛의; 담황색의. [Gk. *khriō* anoint]

cream cheese [´ ´] *n.* soft and rich cheese made from cream and unskimmed milk. 크림 치즈.

cream·er [krí:mər] *n.* Ⓒ a small pitcher for holding cream. 크림 그릇; 크리머.

cream·er·y [krí:məri] *n.* Ⓒ (*pl.* **-er·ies**) **1** a place where cream, butter, and cheese are made. 크림·버터·치즈의 제조소. **2** a store where cream, milk, and butter are sold. 크림·우유·버터의 판매점.

cream·y [krí:mi] *adj.* (**cream·i·er, cream·i·est**) **1** like, of, or full of cream. 크림(모양)의; 크림이 많은(많이 든). **2** cream-colored. 크림(담황)색의.

crease [kri:s] *n.* Ⓒ **1** a line or mark made by folding cloth, paper, etc.; a fold. 접어서 생긴 주름. ¶ *the* ~ *in trousers* 바지의 주름. **2** a mark on the ground in cricket to show the position of the batsman or the bowler. 타자(打者)의 정위치 지시선《크리켓에서》. — *vt.* (P6) make a crease or creases in (something). …에 금(주름)을 내다. ¶ ~ *one's trousers.* — *vi.* (P1) become creased; fall into creases. 금이 나다; 주름잡히다. [→crest]

:cre·ate [kri:éit] *vt.* **1** (P6) ⓐ produce from nothing. …을 창조하다. ¶ *God created heaven and earth.* 하느님은 천지를 창조하셨다. ⓑ bring about; cause to exist. …을 가져오다; 낳다. ¶ *New forms of life are created by the forces of evolution.* 진화의 힘으로 새로운 삶의 형태를 낳게 되었다. **2** (P6) produce (something new) in thought or imagination. …을 만들어 내다; 창작(창안)하다. ¶ *protagonists created in his novels* 그의 소설에서 만들어진 주인공들 / ~ *an epic* (*a drama*) 서사시를(희곡을) 창작하다 / ~ *a system of philosophy* 철학 체계를 만들어 내다. **3** (of an actor) be the first to represent (a role in a play, or the like). (배우가 어떤 역)의 새로운 형(型)을 만들어 내다. ¶ ~ *a new Hamlet* 햄릿역의 새로운 형을 만들어 내다. **4** (P6) make; produce. …을 만들다; 창시하다. ¶ ~ *an army* 창군(創

軍)하다 / ~ *an empire* 제국을 일으키다. **5** (P6) bring into existence by law. …을 신설하다; 설정하다. **6** (P6,19) give a new status or rank to a person; appoint. (새로운 신분·작위·직위)를 주다; 임명하다. ¶ ~ *a man a peer* 아무를 귀족의 반열에 들게 하다 / ~ *someone a new administrative post* 아무를 새로운 관리직에 임명하다. **7** (P6) give rise to; cause; produce. 일으키다; 원인이 되다. ¶ ~ *a sensation* 〔*a revolution*〕 센세이션〔혁명〕을 일으키다 / ~ *a feeling of surprise* 놀라운 감정을 일으키다. [L. *creo* bring into being; grow]

•**cre·a·tion** [kriːéiʃən] *n.* **1** Ⓤ ⓐ the act of creating; the state of being created. 창조. ⓑ 《often *the C-*》 the act of creating of the world by God. (신에 의한) 천지 창조. **2** Ⓤ all that God created. 창조물; 천지 만물; 삼라 만상. ¶ *the Lord of Creation* 만물의 영장; 인간 / *the whole* ~ 만물. **3** ⓐ Ⓤ the act of producing a new work of thought or imagination. (사고·상상에 의한) 창작. ¶ *the* ~ *of great poetry* 위대한 시의 창작. ⓑ Ⓒ a thing produced by intelligence or skill, usu. an important or original one. 창작물; 예술 작품. ¶ *the creations of a poetic genius* 천재 시인의 창작 작품 / *a great* ~ *of art* 위대한 예술 작품. **4** ⓐ Ⓤ the act of making an office, rank, etc. by law. (제도·신분·직위 등의) 신설; 작위 수여(爵位授與); 임명. ¶ *the* ~ *of a special committee* 특별 위원회의 창설 / *a baron of recent* ~ 최근 새로 작위를 받은 남작. ⓑ Ⓒ the rank, etc. thus created. (그렇게 신설된) 지위; 작위. **5** ⓐ Ⓤ the act of making or producing some new material thing. 창시; 창설. ¶ *the* ~ *of an empire* 제국의 창시 / *the* ~ *of a new city* 새 도시의 탄생. ⓑ Ⓒ the production of a new design in clothes. (창의성이 풍부한) 신형의 옷〔모자〕. ¶ *the newest Paris creations* 최신의 파리 의상. **6** Ⓤ production by the work of natural or social forces. 발생; 일어남. ¶ *the* ~ *of new species* 새로운 종(種)의 발생 / *the* ~ *of social unrest* 사회 불안의 발생.

creation myth [-´-- ´] *n.* a story accounting for the origin of the world by creation. 천지창조의 신화.

cre·a·tive [kriːéitiv] *adj.* having the power to create; original. 창조〔독창〕적인; 창작의. ¶ ~ *power* 창조력 / ~ *talent* 창조적 재능 / *have a* ~ *mind* 독창적인 머리가 있다. ●

cre·a·tive·ly [-li] *adv.*

cre·a·tiv·i·ty [krìːeitívəti] *n.* Ⓤ the state of being creative; ability to create. 창조; 창조〔독창〕력.

cre·a·tor [kriːéitər] *n.* **1** Ⓒ a person who creates (something). 창조〔창안〕자; 창설〔창작〕자. **2** 《*the C-*》 God. 조물주.

:**crea·ture** [kríːtʃər] *n.* Ⓒ **1** anything created. 창조물. **2** a living thing; a person; an animal. 생명이 있는 것; 생물; 인간; 동물. ¶ *a good* 〔*kindly*〕 ~ 친절한 사람 / *a lovely* ~ 여자 / *a fellow* ~ 동포 / *dumb creatures* 말없는 동물 / *a* ~ *from outer space* 우주에서 온 생물 / *Poor* ~*!* 가엾게도. **3** a person who is a tool of another. 앞잡이; 예속자; 수하; 노예. ¶ *a* ~ *of circumstances* 환경의 노예 / *one of the king's creatures* 국왕의 측근 중 한 사람 / *He was her* ~. 그는 그녀의 말대로 하는 사람이었다. [L. *creātūra* a thing created]

crèche [kreiʃ] *n.* 《Brit.》 a public day nursery for infants while their mothers are at work. 탁아소. [F.]

cre·dence [kríːdəns] *n.* **1** Ⓤ the act of believing; belief. 믿음; 신용; 신임. ¶ *a letter of* ~ 신임장 / *find* ~ *with* …에게 신용을 얻다 / *give* ~ *to a rumor* 떠도는 소문을 믿다 / *refuse* ~ *to* 〔*withhold* ~ *from*〕 *miracle* 기적을 믿으려 하지 않다. **2** Ⓒ a small table in a church by the side of the altar on which the bread and wine are placed ready for the Eucharist. (교회에서 성찬식 때의) 제구대(臺)(=credence table). [L. *credo* believe]

cre·den·tials [kridénʃəlz] *n. pl.* letters of introduction. (대사·공사의) 신임장. ¶ *The new ambassador presented his* ~ *at court.* 신임 대사는 신임장을 왕에게 봉정했다.

cred·i·bil·i·ty [krèdəbíləti] *n.* Ⓤ the fact or quality of being believable. 신용할 수 있음; 신빙〔확실〕성. ¶ *an account lacking in* ~ 믿을 수 없는 이야기.

cred·i·ble [krédəbəl] *adj.* that can be trusted; worthy of trust; that can be believed. 신용〔신뢰〕할 수 있는; 믿을 수 있는. ¶ *a* ~ *statement* 믿을 수 있는 진술 / *a* ~ *witness* 믿을 만한 증인 / *It seems hardly* ~ *that Ned has made a large fortune.* 네드가 한밑천 잡았다는 이야기는 믿을 수 없을 것 같다.

:**cred·it** [krédit] *n.* **1** Ⓤ trust; belief. 신용; 신빙성. ¶ *a witness of* ~ 믿을 수 있는 증인 / *deserve no* ~ 믿을〔신용할〕 수 없다 / *put* 〔*place*〕 ~ *in a report* 풍문을 믿다. **2** ⓐ Ⓤ good name; honor; praise. 명성; 명예; 칭찬. ¶ *give someone* ~ *for what he has done* 그가 한 일에 대해 칭찬하다 / *Edison has the* ~ *of his discoveries.* 에디슨은 자신의 발명으로 명성을 누리고 있다 / *It is to his* ~ *that he saved a drowning child.* 물에 빠진 아이를 구출하여 그는 칭찬을 받았다. ⓑ Ⓒ a person or thing that adds honor. 명예가 되는 것; 자랑(거리). ¶ *be a* ~ *to one's family* 가문의 명예가〔자랑이〕 되다 / *He is a* ~ *to his school.* 그는 학교의 자랑이다. **3** ⓊⒸ 《comm.》 ⓐ a loan. 융자; 대출. ¶ *a long* 〔*short*〕 *term* ~ 장기〔단기〕 신용 대부. ⓑ trust in a person's, a company's or a state's promise to pay. (거래에서) 신용. ¶ *a letter of* ~ 신용장 / *a* ~ *bureau* 흥신소 / *a* ~ *condition* 신용 상태 / *a* ~ *union* 신용 조합 / *buy on* ~ 외상으로 사다 / *cut off* ~ 외상 판매를 끊다 / *give* 〔*allow, grant*〕 ~ 신용 대출하다; 외상으로 주다 / *No* ~ *is given at this shop.* 당점(當店)에서 외상은 사절합니다 / *My* ~ *is good at his shop.* 그의 가게에서 나의 신용도는 높다 /

His ~ is gone. 그의 신용은 떨어졌다. **4** Ⓤ Ⓒ the amount of someone's money kept in a bank, etc. 예금액. **5** Ⓒ 《bookkeeping》 an entry of money paid on account. 대변(貸邊)(opp. debit). **6** official acceptance and recording of the work of student in a particular course of study. 학점 인정.

be a credit to, do honor to. …의 명예가 되다.

be to** someone's **credit, bring honor to someone. 아무의 명예가 되다.

do credit to** someone =**do** someone **credit, bring honor or a good reputation to someone. …의 명예가 되다.

gain** [**lose**] **credit, be (not) trusted. 신용을 얻다[잃다].

get credit for, be reputed to be. …의 평판을 얻다.

give** [**allow**] **credit, permit customers to buy goods on credit. 외상을 주다.

give** someone **credit for, a) lend someone. 빌려주다. b) attribute to someone. …을 …의 공으로 돌리다. c) expect someone to have [to be]. …을 가진 것으로 기대하다. ¶ *I gave him ~ for being a sensible man.* 그가 분별 있는 사람일 것으로 기대했다.

give credit to, believe; trust. …을 믿다; 신용하다. ¶ *give ~ to a statement* 진술을 믿다.

have credit at, have deposit in. …에 예금이 있다.

have credit of =get credit for.

have credit with, be trusted by. …의 신용을 얻다.

on credit, promising to pay later. 외상으로. ¶ *sell on ~* 외상으로 팔다.

reflect credit on, give honor or reputation to; do honor to. …의 명예가 되다.

— *vt.* (P6,13) **1** believe; accept (something) as true. …을 믿다; 신용하다. ¶ *I can ~ all that you are telling me.* 자네가 말하는 것은 모두 믿을 수 있네. **2** 《*with*》 give (someone) the credit of possessing some quality or doing something. (어떤 성질·감정)을 갖고 있다고 믿다; 생각하다; …을 한다고 믿다. ¶ *~ him with honesty* 그를 정직하다고 여기다 / *You would hardly ~ him with having acted so foolishly.* 그가 그런 어리석은 짓을 했다고는 믿지 않으실 테죠 / *He is credited with having much imagination.* 그는 상상력이 풍부한 사람으로 여겨지고 있다. **3** extend credit to. …에게 신용 대부하다. **4** 《bookkeeping》 enter on the credit side of an account. 대변(貸邊)에 기입하다. [→credence]

cred·it·a·ble [kréditəbəl] *adj.* bringing credit, honor, reputation, or respect. 신용할 수 있는; 명예가 되는; 칭찬할 만한; 훌륭한. ¶ *a ~ deed* 훌륭한 행위 / *a very ~ piece of work* 매우 훌륭한 작품.

cred·it·a·bly [kréditəbli] *adv.* in a creditable manner. 훌륭히.

***cred·i·tor** [kréditər] *n.* **1** a person to whom money or goods are owed. 채권자. (opp. debtor). **2** 《bookkeeping》 the credit side of an account. 대변(貸邊)(opp. debtor). 參考 Cr.로 생략함.

cre·do [kríːdou] *n.* (*pl.* **-dos**) Ⓒ = creed.

cre·du·li·ty [kridjúːləti] *n.* Ⓤ willingness to believe statements too easily. 쉽게 믿음; 경신(輕信)(opp. incredulity). ¶ *with ~* 가볍게 믿고. [→creed]

cred·u·lous [krédʒələs] *adj.* too ready to believe things without sufficient grounds. 쉽게 믿는; 곧 곧이듣는. ¶ *He was so ~ that anybody could deceive him.* 그는 쉽게 믿는 성질이었으므로 아무라도 속일 수가 있었다.

***creed** [kriːd] *n.* Ⓒ **1** a brief statement of the main points of Christian belief. (종교의) 신조. **2** any statement of faith, rules, opinions, etc. (일반적인) 신념; 주의; 강령. ¶ *one's political ~* 정치적인 신념 / *a scientist's ~* 과학자의 신조. **3** 《*the C-*》 the Apostles' Creed. 사도 신경(使徒信經). [L. *credo* believe]

***creek** [kriːk] *n.* Ⓒ **1** 《esp. U.S.》 a small stream, larger than a brook. (brook보다 큰) 시내; 크리크; 수로. **2** 《esp. Brit》 a narrow bay. 작은 만; 후미. [E.]

creel [kriːl] *n.* Ⓒ **1** a basket for carrying fish. 종다래끼《물고기를 담는 것》. **2** a basket like trap for catching fish, etc. 통발. [E.]

:creep [kriːp] *vi.* (**crept** [krept]) (P1,2A,2B,3) **1** move along close to the ground like a baby; crawl. (네 발로) 기다. ¶ *~ under the fence* 울타리 밑을 기다 / *~ along the ground* 땅위를 기다 / *A baby learns to ~ before it learns to walk.* 아기는 걸음마를 배우기 전에 기는 것을 배운다. **2** move slowly or secretly. 살금살금 (발소리를 죽이고) 걷다. ¶ *The cat crept silently toward the birds.* 고양이는 살금살금 새들에게 다가갔다. **3** (of a plant) grow along the ground, a wall, or other surface. (식물이) 널리 뻗어 퍼지다. ¶ *Ivy creeps over wall.* 담쟁이덩굴이 벽면을 뒤덮어 뻗어 있다. **4** move slowly and unsteadly like a sick or old person. (병자·노인처럼) 비슬비슬 걷다. **5** (of time, age, feeling, etc.) come on or appear gradually without being noticed. 어느덧 다가오다; 엄습하다. ¶ *Old age crept upon him.* 노년이 어느 틈엔가 그에게 다가왔다 / *A loneliness crept over me.* 일말의 고독감이 스며 왔다 / *A feeling of drowsiness crept over her.* 졸음이 그녀를 엄습해 왔다. **6** 《*fig.*》 behave timidly or servilely; fawn. 흠칫흠칫 (비굴하게) 행동하다; 은근히 환심을 사다. **7** feel as if something were creeping over the skin; have a sensation of fear. 오싹[섬뜩]하다; 소름이 끼치다. ¶ *The ghost story made my flesh ~.* 유령 이야기는 나의 몸을 오싹하게 했다.

creep into** (=win) someone's **favor, …의 환심을 사다.

***creep on** [**upon**],* come on gradually. 서서히 다가오다.

make** someone **creep all over, freeze someone with fright. …을 오싹하게 하다.

—*n.* Ⓒ **1** the act of creeping. 김; 포복. **2** 《*pl.*》《*colloq.*》 a nervous sensation as if insects were creeping on the skin. 오싹함. **3** ⓐ 《geol.》 a gradual movement of loose material. (지층 등의) 점동(漸動). ⓑ 《mine》 a slow rising of the floor of a gallery. (갱도 비닥의) 불룩한 곳. **4** an opening in a hedge, etc. for animals to pass through. (울타리 밑 등의) 개구멍. [E.]

creep·er [kríːpər] *n.* Ⓒ **1** a person or thing that creeps. 기는 사람; (벌레·새 따위의) 기는 것. ¶ *the tree* ~ 딱따구리. **2** any plant that grows along the ground or over walls. 덩굴풀. **3** 《*pl.*》 a baby's garment combining waist and pants. (아기의) 길 때 입는 옷; 내리닫이. **4** 《*pl.*》 spikes or nails fitted to boots for climbing or walking on ice. (미끄럼 방지용) 구두 스파이크.

creep·ing [kríːpiŋ] *adj.* **1** (of an insect, etc.) crawling. 기어다니는. ¶ ~ *things* 기어다니는 벌레들. **2** (of a plant) tending to run along the ground. 뻗어서 퍼지는. ¶ ~ *plants.* **3** slow; feeble. 느린; 약한. ¶ *a* ~ *gait* 느린 걸음걸이. **4** trying to get the favor of others. 은근히 환심을 사려드는.

creep·y [kríːpi] *adj.* (**creep·i·er, creep·i·est**) **1** creeping. 기는. **2** having or causing a sensation as if insects were creeping on the skin. 오싹하는.

creep·y-crawl·y [kríːpikrɔ́ːli] *adj.* = creepy. [E.]

creese [kriːs] *n.* a Malay dagger with a wavy blade. (날이) 물결 모양의 단검. [Native]

cre·mate [kríːmeit, krìméit] *vt.* (P6) **1** burn a dead body to ashes. (사체)를 화장하다. **2** burn. …을 태워 버리다; 소각하다. [L. *cremo* burn]

cre·ma·tion [kriméiʃən] *n.* Ⓤ Ⓒ the act of cremating. 화장.

cre·ma·to·ri·a [krìːmətɔ́ːriə, krèm-] *n.* pl. of **crematorium.**

cre·ma·to·ri·um [krìːmətɔ́ːriəm, krèmə-] *n.* Ⓒ (*pl.* **-ri·ums** or **-ri·a**) **1** a building where dead human bodies are burnt to ashes. 화장장(터). **2** a refuse destructor. 쓰레기 소각장. [↓]

cre·ma·to·ry [kríːmətɔ̀ːri, krémə- / krémətəri] *n.* Ⓒ (*pl.* **-ries**) **1** a furnace for burning dead bodies. 화장로(爐). **2** a building that has a furnace for burning dead bodies; a crematorium. 화장터. —*adj.* of cremation. 화장의. [→cremate]

crème de la crème [krém də laː krém] *n.* 《F.》 the very pick. 가장 좋은 것; 추려낸 것; 정수(精粹).

crème de menthe [krèm də máːnt] *n.* 《F.》 green liqueur flavored with peppermint. 박하가 든 녹색 리큐어주(酒).

Cre·ole [kríːoul] *n.* **1** a person of pure European descent born in the West Indies or Mauritius or the South American states. 크레올 사람. **2** 《*c-*》 a person half Negro and half European. 흑백 혼혈인. —*adj.* of or having to do with the Creoles. 크레올의; 크레올 특유의. [Sp]

cre·o·sote [kríː(ː)əsòut] *n.* Ⓤ **1** an oily liquid with a strong smell, obtained from wood tar and used to keep wood from decaying or as a medicine. 크레오소트. ¶ *Wood is dipped in* ~ *to keep it from rotting.* 나무는 부패를 막기 위해 크레오소트에 담근다. **2** a similar substance obtained got from coal tar. 석탄산(酸). [Psuedo- Gk. = meat-saver]

crepe, crêpe [kreip] *n.* 《F.》 Ⓤ a thin silk, cotton, rayon, or woolen cloth with many small folds in the surface. 크레이프.

crêpe de Chine [krèip də ʃíːn] *n.* 《F.》 a soft, rather thin silk crêpe, used for women's blouses, etc. 프랑스 크레이프; 크레이프 드신《표면이 오글오글한 비단》.

crêpe paper [kréip pèipər] *n.* 《F.》 thin paper with a crinkled texture, used for decorations. 크레이프 페이퍼《장식용의 쪼글쪼글한 종이》.

crep·i·tate [krépətèit] *vi.* (P1) make sharp, repeated crackling sounds; crackle; rattle. 계속해서 딱딱 소리가 나다. [L. *crepo* creak]

***crept** [krept] *v.* p. and pp. of **creep.**

cre·pus·cu·lar [kripʌ́skjələr] *adj.* **1** of twilight; dim. 황혼의; 어스레한. **2** 《zool.》 appearing or flying by twilight. 어스레한 때에 활동하는. ¶ ~ *insects.* [L.]

cres., cresc. crescendo.

cre·scen·do [kriʃéndou] *adj., adv.* 《mus.》 《It.》 slowly increasing in loudness or in power of tone. 점점 센[세게]; 크레센도로. 參考 기호는 <. —*n.* Ⓒ (*pl.* **-dos**) a gradual increase in loudness, etc. 크레센도; 점강음(漸強音). [↓]

cres·cent [krésənt] *n.* Ⓒ **1** the shape of the moon in its first or last quarter. 초승달. **2** ⓐ anything shaped like this; the national symbol of Turkey. 초승달 모양의 것; 터키의 기장(旗章). ¶ *the Cross and the Crescent* 기독교와 이슬람교. ⓑ 《Brit.》 a row of houses built in more or less such a shape. 초승달 모양으로 늘어선 집들. —*adj.* **1** shaped like a crescent. 초승달 모양의. ¶ *the Crescent City,* New Orleans 시(市)의 딴이름. **2** 《*poet.*》 growing; increasing. (달이) 점차 커지는. [L. *cresco* grow]

cre·sol [kríːsoul, -sɔːl] *n.* a colorless substance used as disinfectant. 크레졸《소독제》. [*creosote*]

cress [kres] *n.* 《bot.》 Ⓤ a plant whose leaves have a peppery taste. 양갓냉이; 후추풀. [E.]

cres·set [krésit] *n.* an iron vessel for burning oil. (화톳불 태우는) 쇠그릇. [→grease]

Cres·si·da [krésidə] *n.* 《Gk. myth.》 a Trojan lady who first loved Troilus but later forsook him for Diomede. 크레시다 《Troilus 를 배반한 Troy 의 여인》.

·**crest** [krest] *n.* Ⓒ **1** a bunch of feathers or hair, a thick red piece, etc. on the head of a bird or an animal. (새 따위의) 관모(冠毛); 볏; (동물의) 갈기. **2** ⓐ a decoration, feathers, etc. on the top of a helmet. (투구 위의) 깃장식. ⓑ 《*poet.*》 a helmet. 투구. **3** a decoration at the top of a family badge. (문장(紋章)의) 꼭대기 장식. ¶ *a family* ~ 가문(家紋). **4** the top part; the top of a hill, a wave, etc.; a peak. (무엇의) 꼭대기; 산정(山頂); 물마루. ¶ *a mountain* ~. **5** the arched neck of a horse and the mane upon it. (말의) 목덜미와 갈기.
on the crest of wave, 《*fig.*》 at the highest, most favorable point of one's fortunes. 득의(得意)의 절정에; 전성기에.
— *vt.* **1** (P6,13) 《*with*》 furnish with a crest; crown; top. …의 꼭대기에 장식을 달다; (산) 꼭대기를 이루다. ¶ *a wave crested with foam* 물마루에 흰 거품을 쓴 파도 / *Wood* ~ *the hill.* 수림들이 산의 꼭대기를 이루고 있다. **2** (P6) mount to the top of. …의 정상에 이르다. ¶ ~ *a hill.*
— *vi.* (P1) rise into or form a crest. 강이 최고 수위에 달하다; 물마루를 이루다. [L. *crista*]

crest·ed [kréstid] *adj.* having a crest. 관모(冠毛)가[볏이] 있는; 꼭대기 장식이 있는.

crest·fall·en [kréstfɔ̀:lən] *adj.* with a bowed head; in low spirits; discouraged. 고개를 숙인; 풀이[기가] 죽은; 실망한. ¶ *be* ~ *over one's failure* 실패에 의기 소침해 있다.

cre·ta·ceous [kritéiʃəs] *adj.* of or like chalk; containing chalk. 백악(白堊)(질)의; 백악을 함유한. [→crayon]

Cre·tan [krí:tn] *adj.* of or belonging to the island of Crete or its natives. Crete 섬(사람)의. — *n.* a native of Crete. Crete 섬 사람. [↓]

Crete [kri:t] *n.* a Greek island in eastern Mediterranean. 크레타 섬. [Gk.]

cre·tic [krí:tik] *n.* 《*poet.*》 a metrical foot consisting of one short syllable between two long ones. (시(詩)에서의) 장단장격(長短長格)《—∪—》. [↑]

cret·in [krí:tn / krétin] *n.* a person afflicted with cretinism. 크레틴병 환자《기형의 백치와 같은 사람》. ● **cret·in·ous** [krí:tnəs / krétinəs] *adj.* [*Christian* > *human being* > *cretinism*]

cret·in·ism [krí:tnìzəm / krétin-] *n.* a combination of deformity and idiocy. 크레틴병《기형·소인증·백치를 그 특징으로 함》.

cre·tonne [kritán, krí:tan / kretɔ́n, krétɔn] *n.* Ⓤ a strong, cotton cloth used for curtains and furniture covers. 크레톤 사라사. [F.]

cre·vasse [krivǽs] *n.* Ⓒ **1** a deep crack in a great mass of ice on a mountain. 크레바스. **2** 《U.S.》 a break in the bank of a river, etc. (둑 따위의) 터진 데. [L. *crepo* creak]

crev·ice [krévis] *n.* Ⓒ a narrow opening or crack. (바위 따위의)틈; 갈라진 데. [↑]

:**crew** [kru:] *n.* Ⓒ 《*collectively*》 **1** all the members belonging to one ship or aircraft, rowing a boat, etc. (함선·비행기 등의) 승무원《고급 선원도 포함》; (대학 따위의) 조정(漕艇)팀; 조정부원. ¶ *the passengers and* ~ 승객과 승무원 / *a flight* ~ 비행기의 탑승원《전원》/ *the officers and* ~ 고급 하급 선원 전부; 전승무원. **2** all the men, except the officers, belonging to one ship or aircraft. (배·비행기의 일반) 선원; 승무원. **3** a group of persons engaged in same work. 같은 일에 종사하는 사람; 업무원. ¶ *the* ~ *of a train* 열차 승무원《전원》/ *a repairing* ~ *on the railway* 철도 보선반. **4** 《usu. *contempt.*》 a group of people in general; a crowd; a gang. 동아리; 패거리; 집단. ¶ *The boys on that street are a rough* ~. 그 거리의 아이들은 난폭한 패거리들이다. [→crescent]

crib [krib] *n.* Ⓒ **1** a small bed with enclosed sides for a baby. (소아용의) 가두리가 있는 작은 침대. **2** a barred manger for feeding horses and cows; a stall for cattle. 구유; 여물시렁; 외양간. **3** a box, a bin, or a building for storing grain, salt, etc. (곡물·소금 따위의 저장)통; 칸막이 곳간. **4** ⓐ a heavy framework of logs or woods used in building. (건축용) 통나무 엮음. ⓑ a framework of timbers supporting mine-shaft. (갱도를 버티는) 동바리. **5** a hut or small house; a small room. (초라한) 작은 집; 작은 방. **6** a wicker basket. 고리 바구니. **7** 《*colloq.*》 the act of using another's words or ideas as one's own; a translation or key to help a student, sometimes in violation of rules. 표절; 도용; 자습서; (대역으로 된) 직역 참고서《학생이 커닝에 쓰는》.
— *v.* (**cribbed, crib·bing**) *vt.* **1** (P6) shut up (something) in a small space. (좁은 곳에)…을 가두다. **2** (P6) 《*colloq.*》 steal and use (another's ideas) as one's own. …을 도용(盜用)하다. **3** furnish (a stall, stable, etc.) with a crib or cribs. (축사 따위)에 구유를 비치하다.
— *vi.* (P1) 《*colloq.*》 use a crib, as in a test; copy from another and pretend the work is one's own. 남의 것을 베껴 쓰다; 커닝하다. [E.]

crib·bage [kríbidʒ] *n.* Ⓤ a game played by two, three, or four people with playing cards. 카드놀이의 일종. [↑]

crick [krik] *n.* Ⓒ a sudden painful stiffness of the muscles of the neck, the back, etc. (목·등 따위의) 근육 경련; 강직(強直). [→wrick]

crick·et[1] [kríkit] *n.* Ⓒ **1** a small insect which makes a loud, high sound. 귀뚜라미. ¶ *be as merry* [*lively*] *as a* ~ 매우 명랑하다. **2** 《U.S.》 =cicada. [F.]

·**crick·et**[2] [kríkit] *n.* Ⓤ **1** a British outdoor game played by two teams of eleven players each with ball, bats, and two sets of three straight sticks placed in the ground. 크리켓. **2** 《*colloq.*》 fair play; sportsmanship. 공명 정대; 페어플레이; 신사적 행위. ¶ *play* ~ 공명 정대하게 행동하다. ***That's not quite cricket.*** 《*colloq.*》 That is unfair or unsportsmanlike. 그건 불공정하다 〔비신사적이다〕. —*vi.* (P1) play cricket. 크리켓을 하다. [F.]

crick·et[3] [kríkit] *n.* a small foot-stool. (낮은 목제의) 발판. [A.S. *cricc* crutch]

cri·er [kráiər] *n.* Ⓒ **1** (esp. of a young child, etc.) a person who cries. 외치는 사람; 울보. **2** ⓐ a person who shouts out announcements of goods for sale. 외치며 파는 상인(商人). ⓑ an official who shouts out public announcements. 고지(告知) 사항을 알리며 다니는 사람. **3** an official who shouts out public announcements in a court of law. (공판정의) 정리(廷吏); 호출리(呼出吏). [*cry*]

:**crime** [kraim] *n.* Ⓒ Ⓤ **1** an act that is against the law; a serious sin which can be punished by law. 범죄(cf. *sin, vice*). ¶ *a capital* ~ 죽을 죄; 사죄(死罪) / *commit a* ~ 죄를 저지르다 / *To steal is a* ~. 훔치는 것은 범죄이다. **2** any evil or bad act; sinful conduct. (일반적으로) 죄악; 못된 짓; 악행. ¶ *He is steeped in* ~. 그는 악(惡)에 젖어 있다 / *It's a* ~ *to overfeed a dog like that.* 개를 그같이 너무 먹이는 것은 죄악이다. **3** 《*fig.*》 a foolish, useless action. 어리석은 행위. [L. *crimen*]

Cri·me·a [kraimíːə, kri-] *n.* a peninsula in Ukraine. 크림《흑해 북안, 우크라이나 공화국의 한 주 및 반도》. ● **Cri·me·an** [-ən] *adj.*

:**crim·i·nal** [krímənl] *n.* Ⓒ a person guilty of a crime. (형사상의) 죄인; 범죄자(cf. *culprit*). ¶ *a habitual* ~ 상습범. —*adj.* **1** guilty of a crime; can be punished by law. 죄를 범한; 범죄를 구성하는. ¶ *a* ~ *attempt* 범죄 미수 / *a* ~ *act* 범죄 행위 / *a* ~ *person* 범인 / ~ *conversation* 〔*connection*〕 간통. **2** of crime or the punishment of crime. 범죄의; 형사상의. ¶ *a* ~ *action* 형사소송 / *a* ~ *court* 형사 법원 / *a* ~ *offense* 형사범 / *the* ~ *law* 형법 / *the code of* ~ *procedure* 형사 소송법. **3** 《*colloq.*》 senseless; foolish. 어리석은. [→crime]

criminal assault [´-- -´] *n.* an attack by physical force liable to criminal prosecution. 폭행죄.

criminal contempt [´-- -´] *n.* an act against the dignity or authority of a court. 법정 모욕죄.

crim·i·nal·i·ty [krìmənǽləti] *n.* (*pl.* **-ties**) **1** Ⓤ the quality or state of being criminal; guilt. 범죄성; 유죄. **2** Ⓒ a criminal act. 범죄 행위.

crim·i·nate [krímənèit] *vt., vi.* (P6; 1) **1** charge with a crime; accuse. 죄를 짊어지우다; 고발하다. **2** incriminate; censure. 유죄라고 하다; 비난하다. **3** prove (oneself, etc.) guilty of a crime. 자신에게 불리한 것을 증언하다. ● **crim·i·na·tion** [krìmənéiʃən] *n.* **crim·i·na·tor** [krímənèitər] *n.* [→crime]

crim·i·na·tive [krímənèitiv / -nə-] *adj.* involving crimination; accusatory. 죄를 지우는; 비난조의; 비난하는.

crim·i·nol·o·gy [krìmənάlədʒi / -nɔ́l-] *n.* Ⓤ the study of crime and criminals. 범죄학; 형사학.

crim·i·nous [krímənəs] *adj.* 《*arch.*》 criminal. 죄를 범한. 參考 다음 구로만 쓰임. ¶ *a* ~ *clerk* 파계 성직자.

crimp[1] [krimp] *vt.* (P6) **1** press (paper or cloth) into small regular folds; make (hair, etc.) wavy. …에 주름을 잡다; (머리)를 곱슬곱슬하게 하다. ¶ ~ *one's hair* 머리를 지지다. **2** slash the flesh of (fresh-caught fish). (어육)에 진집을 내다. —*n.* **1** Ⓤ the act of crimping. 지짐; 주름 잡음. **2** Ⓒ something crimped; a fold; a wave. 주름(살); 접은 금; 곱슬곱슬한 모양. **3** 《*pl.*》 waved or curled hair. 지진〔고수〕 머리. ***put a crimp in,*** 《*colloq.*》 hinder; interfere with. …을 방해하다. ● **crimp·er** [-ər] *n.* [E.]

crimp[2] [krimp] *n.* an agent procuring men for service as sailors or soldiers either by decoying or by force. (감언·설득·협박해서 선원·군인 등으로 팔아먹는) 유괴〔납치〕 알선업자. —*vt.* (P6) enlist (soldiers, sailors) by such means. …을 유괴〔납치〕하다. [?]

crimp·y [krímpi] *adj.* (**crimp·i·er, crimp·i·est**) curly. 물결 모양의; 곱슬곱슬한. [→crimp[1]]

*__crim·son__ [krímzn] *n.* Ⓤ a deep red color. 심홍색(深紅色). —*adj.* deep red. 심홍색의. ¶ *a* ~ *rose* 새빨간 장미. —*vt.* (P6) color (something) deep red. …을 심홍색으로 〔새빨갛게〕 하다. ¶ *The sunset crimsons the lake.* 저녁 노을이 호수를 붉게 물들인다. —*vi.* (P1) turn deep red in color; blush. 심홍색으로 되다; 새빨개지다. [Arab.]

cringe [krindʒ] *vi.* (P1) **1** bend low or go down on the knees, esp. in fear or shame. (두려움·부끄럼으로) 움츠러지다. **2** behave towards another person in a very humble way in order to get favor or attention. (남에게) 비굴하게 굴다; 아첨하다. —*n.* Ⓒ the act of cringing. 움츠림; 위축(蝟縮); 외축(畏縮); 아첨. ● **cring·er** [-ər] *n.* [E.]

cring·ing [kríndʒiŋ] *adj.* servile. 움츠린; 비굴한.

crin·kle [kríŋkl] *vi., vt.* (P1; 6) **1** form or move with many small folds or waves. 주름지(게 하)다; 물결치(게 하)다. ¶ *crinkled paper* 구겨진 종이 / *Paper crinkles when it is crushed.* 종이는 뭉개면 구겨진다. **2** make slight, sharp sounds. 버스럭 소리를 내다.

—*n.* Ⓒ **1** a small fold on the surface of material; a twist. 주름; 굴곡. **2** a crinkling sound. 바스락 소리. [E.]

crin·kly [kríŋkli] *adj.* (**-kli·er, -kli·est**) full of crinkles; wrinkled; wavy. 주름이 많이 진; 오그라진; 물결 모양의.

crin·o·line [krínəli:n] *n.* **1** Ⓤ a hard, rough cloth used as a lining. 크리놀린《안감용의 질기고 거친 천》. **2** Ⓒ a petticoat of crinoline worn by a woman under a skirt to support it on all sides. 크리놀린으로 만든 페티코트《여자의 스커트 받침 속치마》. **3** Ⓒ a hoop skirt. 버팀테로 받쳐 부풀린 스커트. **4** Ⓒ a framework of timber and wire used as a protection against torpedoes on warship. (군함의) 어뢰 방어망(網). [L. *crinis* hair]

***crip·ple** [krípl] *n.* Ⓒ a person whose legs, arms, or body cannot be moved well; a lame person. 불구자; 지체 부자유자. ¶ *war cripples* 상이 군인 / *a mental* 〔*sexual*〕 ~ 정신적〔성적〕 불구자 / *After the war the streets were full of cripples.* 전후(戰後) 거리에는 불구자투성이었다.

—*vt.* (P6) **1** make a cripple of (someone). …을 불구가 되게 하다. ¶ *be crippled with rheumatism* 류머티즘으로 다리를 절게 되다 / *have a crippled foot* 다리를 절다 / *He was crippled in World War II.* 그는 제2차 세계 대전에서 불구가 되었다. **2** 《*fig.*》 damage; make (someone or something) unable to act properly; weaken. …을 손상하다; …할 수 없게〔활동력을 잃게〕 하다; 약화시키다. ¶ ~ *someone's activities* 아무의 활동을 약화시키다 / *The country was crippled by the strike.* 나라는 파업으로 마비되었다. [E.]

cris [kri:s] *n.* =creese.

cri·ses [kráisi:z] *n.* pl. of **crisis**.

***cri·sis** [kráisis] *n.* Ⓒ (*pl.* **-ses**) **1** a turning point for better or worse in an illness. (병의) 고비. ¶ *The sick man passed the* ~. 환자는 고비를 넘겼다. **2** a time of great danger and difficulty in politics, money affairs, history, etc.; a very serious moment in any course of action; emergency. (정치·사회·경제상의) 중대 시국; 위기; 공황. ¶ *a food* ~ 식량 위기 / *a financial* ~ 금융 공황 / *bring... to a* ~ …을 위기에 이르게 하다 / *Things came to a* ~ *about a week ago.* 1주일쯤 전에 사태는 중대한 국면을 맞이하게 되었다. [Gk. *krino* judge]

***crisp** [krisp] *adj.* **1** hard but easily breakable. 파삭파삭한. ¶ ~ *toast* 〔*biscuits*〕 파삭파삭한 토스트〔비스킷〕. **2** (of air) fresh; sharp and clear. 상쾌한; 신선한. ¶ ~ *air* 상쾌한 공기 / ~ *weather* 상쾌한 날씨 / ~ *autumn breezes* 시원한 가을 바람. **3** (of manners, speech, etc.) active; lively; sharp; decided. (태도·말이) 힘찬; 시원시원한; 발랄〔명쾌〕한; 단호한. ¶ *a* ~ *manner* 시원스런 태도 / *a* ~ *reply* 단호한 대답. **4** (of hair, etc.) curly and wavy. (머리 따위가) 곱슬곱슬한. ¶ ~ *hair* 곱슬곱슬한 머리.

—*vi., vt.* (P1; 6) make or become crisp. (머리 따위를) 곱슬곱슬하게 하다; 주름이 지(게 하)다; 잔물결이 일(게 하)다; 파삭파삭하게 하다〔되다〕. [L. *crispo* curl]

crisp·y [kríspi] *adj.* (**crisp·i·er, crisp·i·est**) = crisp.

criss·cross [krískrɔ̀:s / -krɔ̀s] *n.* Ⓒ a mark or pattern made of crossed lines. 열십자; 열십자 표지. ¶ *a* ~ *of streets* 십자로.

—*adj.* made or marked with crossed lines; crossed; crossing. 열십자의; 교차하는〔된〕. —*adv.* in different cross directions; in the form of a cross; at cross-purposes. 열십자로; 교차하여; 어긋나; 엇갈려. ¶ *Everything went* ~. 모든 일이 어긋났다. —*vt.* (P6) mark or cover (something) with crossing lines. …을 열십자로 교차시키다; 교차선을 긋다. —*vi.* (P1) cross. 교차하다. [=Christ's Cross]

cri·te·ri·a [kraitíəriə] *n.* pl. of **criterion**.

cri·te·ri·on [kraitíəriən] *n.* Ⓒ (*pl.* **-ri·a** or **-ri·ons**) a standard by which to determine the correctness of a judgment. (판단·비판의) 표준; 기준. ¶ *a* ~ *for the examination* 심사의 기준 / *resort* 〔*appeal*〕 *to a* ~ 기준에 의존하다 / *A person's appetite is a good* ~ *of his health.* 사람의 식욕은 그의 건강을 판단하는 좋은 기준이 된다. [→crisis]

***crit·ic** [krítik] *n.* Ⓒ **1** a person who judges, esp. one who judges works of art. (문예·미술의) 비평가; 평론가. ¶ *a literary* ~ 문학〔문예〕 평론가. **2** a person who points out others' faults or who judges severely. 비판자; 흠〔탈〕잡는 사람. [→crisis]

***crit·i·cal** [krítikəl] *adj.* **1** inclined to find fault or judge unfavorably. 흠〔탈〕잡기 좋아하는; 혹평적인; 까다로운. ¶ *a* ~ *disposition* 흠잡기 좋아하는 성질. **2** concerned with, busy with or skilled in criticism. 비평의; 평론의. ¶ ~ *essays* 평론. **3** near a turning point or crisis; crucial. 위기의; 중대한; 결정적인. ¶ *a* ~ *moment* 위기 / ~ *problems* 중대한 문제 / ~ *evidence* 결정적 증거. **4** very dangerous; causing anxiety. 매우 위험한; 위독한. ¶ *a* ~ *wound* 치명상 / *The patient is in a* ~ *condition.* 환자는 중태이다.

critical age [⌐–⌐], **the** *n.* menopause. 갱년기.

critical angle [⌐–⌐–] *n.* the least angle of incidence. 임계각(臨界角).

crit·i·cal·ly [krítikəli] *adv.* in a critical manner; with criticism. 비판적으로.

critical philosophy [⌐–––⌐––] *n.* philosophy of Kant. (칸트의) 비판 철학.

critical temperature [⌐––⌐–––] *n.* a point of temperature above which a gas can not be reduced to a liquid. 임계(臨界) 온도.

***crit·i·cism** [krítisìzəm] *n.* ⒸⓊ **1** the act or art of judging good points and faults, esp. of works of art or literature; an opinion, spoken or written, on what is good or bad about works of art; a critical opinion. 비평; (특히 문예 따위의) 비평법〔술〕; 평론; 강평. ¶ *make a ~ of* …의 비평을 하다. **2** the act of pointing out faults; blame. 흠잡기; 비난; 비판. ¶ *suffer harsh ~ from* …에게서 호된 비평〔혹평〕을 받다.

·crit·i·cize, ⦅chiefly Brit.⦆ **-cise** [krítisàiz] *vt.* (P6,13) **1** judge or speak of as a critic. …을 비평하다; 비판하다. ¶ *~ a plan as unworkable* 안(案)을 실행 불가능한 것으로 평하다 / *~ a report favorably* 보고서를 호의적으로 비평하다 / *Will you please ~ my work ?* 내 작품 좀 비평해 주시겠습니까 / *He criticized three novels in one review.* 그는 3편의 소설을 한 편의 비평 기사에서 논했다. **2** find fault with (others); blame. …의 흠을 잡다; 비난〔혹평〕하다. ¶ *He likes to ~ people's conduct.* 그는 사람들의 행동을 흠잡기 좋아한다.

cri·tique [kritíːk] *n.* **1** Ⓒ an article or essay criticizing a work of art; a review. (문예·미술 작품 따위의) 평론. **2** Ⓤ the art of criticism. 비평법. [→critic]

croak [krouk] *n.* Ⓒ a deep, rough sound, made by a frog, a crow, etc. (개구리·까마귀 따위의) 울음소리. — *vi.* (P1) **1** make a deep, rough sound. 깍깍〔개굴개굴〕 울다. **2** predict misfortune; take a gloomy view of things; complain. 불길한 소리를 하다; 비관적으로 말하다; 투덜거리다. **3** ⦅*sl.*⦆ die. 죽다. — *vt.* (P6,7) say (something) in a deep, rough voice. …을 음침한〔쉰〕 소리로 말하다. [Imit.]

croak·er [króukər] *n.* **1** one who croaks. 깍깍〔개굴개굴〕 우는 것⦅까마귀·개구리 따위⦆; 목쉰 소리로 말하는 사람. **2** a prophet of evil. 불길한 일을 예언하는 사람.

Cro·at [króuæt, -ət] *n.* a native or inhabitant of Croatia. 크로아티아 사람. ● **Cro·a·ti·a** [krouéiʃiə] *n.* **Cro·a·ti·an** [krouéiʃiən] *adj.* [Slav.]

cro·chet [krouʃéi / ⌐–, -ʃi] *vi., vt.* (P1;6) knit (sweaters, lace, etc.) with a single long needle having a hook at one end. (스웨터·레이스 따위를) 코바늘로 뜨다. — *n.* Ⓤ knitting done in this way. 코바늘 뜨개질. [F. *croche* hook]

cro·ci [króusai, -kai] *n.* pl. of **crocus.**

crock[1] [krɑk / krɔk] *n.* Ⓒ **1** a pot or jar made of baked clay. (도기(陶器)의) 항아리; 단지. **2** a broken piece of earthenware. 사금파리. [E.]

crock[2] [krɑk / krɔk] *n.* ⦅*colloq.*⦆ an old broken-down horse; an old worn-out person, car, etc. 늙어 쓸모없게 된 말; 낡아 못 쓰게 된 것⦅차·배 따위⦆; 늙은이. — *vi.* (P1,2A) ⦅*up*⦆ become a crock. 못 쓰게〔쓸모없게〕 되다. — *vt.* (P6) ⦅usu. in *passive*⦆ disable. …을 쓸모없게 하다. [E.]

crock·er·y [krɑ́kəri / krɔ́k-] *n.* Ⓤ ⦅*collectively*⦆ dishes, jars, etc. made of baked clay; earthenware. 도자기; 사기; 도기(陶器). [→crock[1]]

crock·et [krɑ́kit / krɔ́k-] *n.* ⦅archit.⦆ one of the curled leaves or similar ornaments up the sides of a pinnacle, etc. 당초(唐草)무늬. [→crochet]

croc·o·dile [krɑ́kədàil / krɔ́k-] *n.* Ⓒ **1** a large water animal with a long head and long, sharp teeth. 악어(cf. *alligator*). **2** ⦅Brit. *colloq.*⦆ a group of schoolgirls out for a walk. 여학생들의 긴 행렬. [Gk.]

shed crocodile tears, pretend to be sorry. 거짓 눈물을 흘리다.

croc·o·dil·i·an [krɑ̀kədíliən / krɔ̀k-] *adj.* of or like a crocodile. 악어의〔같은〕; 위선의.

cro·cus [króukəs] *n.* (*pl.* **-cus·es** or **cro·ci**) ⦅bot.⦆ a dwarf bulbous plant with yellow or purple flowers. 크로커스⦅붓꽃과에 속하는 다년초, 구근류⦆. [Gk.]

Croe·sus [kríːsəs] *n.* **1** the last king of Lydia noted for his great wealth. 크리서스⦅기원전 Lydia의 마지막 왕, 엄청난 부(富)로 유명⦆. **2** a very rich man. 큰 부호. ¶ *Croesus' wealth* 거만(巨萬)의 부 / *(as) rich as ~* (크리서스 정도로) 큰 부자인.

croft [krɔːft / krɔft] *n.* Ⓒ ⦅Brit.⦆ **1** a small field near a house. (집 부근의) 작은 밭; 텃밭. **2** a very small rented farm. 소작지. [E.]

croft·er [krɔ́ːftər / krɔ́ft-] *n.* ⦅Brit.⦆ a person who rents or works a croft. 소작인; 소농(小農).

Cro-Mag·non [kroumǽgnən, -mǽnjən] *adj., n.* (of) a prehistoric race of men. 크로마뇽 사람(의) ⦅구석기 시대 사람⦆. [Place in France]

crom·lech [krɑ́mlek / krɔ́m-] *n.* a prehistoric structure consisting of large flat stone laid horizontally on upright ones. 크롬렉⦅환상 열석(環狀列席), 선돌⦆. [W.]

Crom·well [krɑ́mwel / krɔ́mwəl], **Oliver** *n.* (1599-1658) Lord Protector of England. 크롬웰⦅영국의 정치가, 호민관(護民官)⦆.

crone [kroun] *n.* Ⓒ an ugly old woman. 쭈글쭈글한 할멈. [L. *caro* flesh]

Cro·nus [króunəs] *n.* ⦅Gk. myth.⦆ one of the Titans, overthrown by his son, Zeus. 크로노스⦅아들 제우스에게 왕위에서 쫓겨남⦆ (=⦅Rom. myth.⦆ Saturn). [Gk.]

cro·ny [króuni] *n.* Ⓒ (*pl.* **-nies**) a very familiar friend. 친우; 옛친구. [Gk. *chronios* contemporary]

crook [kruk] *vi., vt.* (P1; 6) bend or curve. 구부러지다; 구부리다. ¶ *~ one's arm* 〔*finger*〕 팔〔손가락〕을 굽히다.
— *n.* Ⓒ **1** a hook; a bend; a curve. 굽은 것; 갈고리; 굴곡; 만곡. ¶ *There is a ~ in the stream round the cliff.* 절벽을 감싸고 냇물이 굽이져 있다. **2** a hooked, curved, or bent part of something. 구부러진〔갈고리 모양의〕 부분; 만곡부. **3** a shepherd's stick with a bent or curved end. (양치기의) 손잡이가 구부러진 지팡이. **4** ⦅*colloq.*⦆ a dishonest

person; a thief. 부정직한 사람; 사기꾼; 도둑. [E.]
by hook or by crook, by all means. 기어코; 어떻게 하든.
crook in one's lot, a misfortune. 불행.
have a crook in one's back, be crook-backed. 등이 굽어 있다.
on the crook, 《*sl.*》 dishonestly. 부정직하게.

crook·back [krúkbæ̀k] *n.* Ⓒ a person with a crooked, rounded back. 곱사등이.

·crook·ed [krúkid] *adj.* **1** bent; curved; twisted; not straight. 구부러진; 뒤틀그러진(opp. straight). **2** 《*fig.*》 not upright in conduct; not honest; wicked. (사람이나 행동이) 부정직한. ¶ ~ *dealing*〔*profits*〕 부정거래〔이득〕. **3** (of the body or limbs) badly formed. 기형의.

Crookes [kruks], **Sir William** *n.* (1832-1919) an English physicist. 크룩스《영국의 물리학자》.

Crookes tube [⌐ ⌐] *n.* 《phys.》 a vacuum tube in which gases are rarefied to high degree. 크룩스(진공)관(管).

croon [kru:n] *vi., vt.* (P1,3; 6) sing or hum in a low voice; sing in a low voice with exaggerated emotion. 작은 소리로 노래 부르다; 흥얼거리다; 감상적으로 가만히 노래하다. ¶ ~ *a lullaby* 작은 소리로 자장가를 부르다 / ~ *to a baby* 아기에게 낮은 소리로 노래를 불러 주다 / ~ *to oneself* 작은 소리로 혼자 흥얼거리다 / *The mother crooned her baby to sleep.* 엄마는 작은 소리로 노래를 불러 아기를 재웠다. — *n.* Ⓒ a low, gentle singing, humming or murmuring. 저음의 노랫소리. [E.]

croon·er [krú:nər] *n.* a soft singer of sentimental songs. 감상적인 노래를 부드럽게 부르는 가수.

:crop [krap / krɔp] *n.* Ⓒ **1** 《*the* ~*s*》 the food plants produced in one year; a harvest of any food plant. (그 해·계절의) 전(全) 작물; 농작물; 작황; 수확(량). ¶ *the rice* ~ 미(米)작황 / *an abundant*〔*good*〕 ~ 풍작 / *a bad* ~ 흉작 / *an average* ~ 평년작 / *The crops are promising.* 작황이 좋다 / *What are the crops like around here?* 이 주변에서는 어떤 작물이 됩니까. **2** a group of persons or collection of things all arising at the same time. (동시에 나는 또는 모이는 사람·사물의) 떼; 무리; 다수; 속출. ¶ *a* ~ *of lambs* 한 떼의 어린 양 / *a* ~ *of spots on the face* 얼굴에 많이 난 종기 / *a* ~ *of lies* 잇달은 거짓말 / *this year's* ~ *of students* 올해 졸업한 다수의 학생들 / *suffer from a* ~ *of troubles* 속출하는 분쟁에 시달리다. **3** a short hair cut. (머리를) 바싹 깎기; 몽구리. **4** the first stomach of a bird. (새의) 멀떠구니. **5** ⓐ a riding whip with a short handle and a flat loof of leather. (가죽 고리가 달린) 짧은 승마채찍. ⓑ the handle of a whip. 채찍의 손잡이. **6** the entire tanned hide of an animal. (동물의) 한 마리 통째로 무두질한 가죽.
in*〔*under*〕 *crop, in plant cultivation. 농사를 지어.
out of crop, out of cultivation. 농사를 짓지 않고.
— *v.* (**cropped, crop·ping**) *vt.* **1** (P6,18) cut or bite off the top of; graze. (풀·줄기의 끝)을 베다; 뜯어먹다. **2** (P6,13) 《*with*》 sow; plant. …에 씨를 뿌리다; (작물)을 심다. ¶ ~ *a field with barley* 밭에 보리를 심다. **3** (P6,18) cut short. 바싹 깎다〔자르다〕. ¶ ~ *the hair* 머리를 바싹 깎다 / ~ *the tail of a dog* 개의 꼬리를 바싹 자르다. **4** (P6) gather; reap. …을 모으다; 거두어들이다. — *vi.* (P1,2A) bear or produces a crop or crops. (농작물이) 나다; 되다. [E.]
crop out, 《geol.》 (of a seam, rock, etc.) come to the surface; appear at the surface. (표면에) 나타나다; 노출하다(cf. *outcrop*).
crop up, 《*fig.*》 come or appear unexpectedly. 뜻하지 않게〔갑자기〕 나타나다. ¶ *An old friend cropped up yesterday.* 옛친구가 어제 홀연히 나타났다 / *Difficulties are always cropping up.* 어려움은 항상 발생하고 있다.

crop-eared [krápìərd / krɔ́p-] *adj.* **1** having the ears cropped. 귀를 벤《가축》. **2** (of Puritans) with the hair cut so short that the ears show. (귀가 드러나도록) 머리를 짧게 깎은.

crop·per [krápər / krɔ́p-] *n.* Ⓒ **1** a person or thing that crops. (농작물 따위를) 베는 사람〔기계〕; 재배자. **2** a plant that produces a crop. (수확이 있는) 농작물. ¶ *a good*〔*poor*〕 ~ 잘〔안〕 되는 농작물. **3** 《*colloq.*》 a heavy fall. 털썩 떨어짐. **4** 《*colloq.*》 a failure; a defeat. 실패; 추락. [E.]
come a cropper, 《*colloq.*》 **a**) fall heavily. 털썩 떨어지다; 곤두박질치다. **b**) 《*fig.*》 fail badly; meet with great misfortune. 큰 실패를 하다; 불행을 당하다.

cro·quet [kroukéi / króukei, -ki] *n.* Ⓤ a lawn game played by knocking wooden balls through small ∩-shaped wire arches with hammer-like sticks. 크로케《나무 망치로 목제 공을 치는 야외 공놀이》. [F. *croche* hook]

cro·quette [kroukét] *n.* Ⓒ a small ball of chopped meat, potatoes, etc. cooked in fat. 크로켓《양요리의 하나》. [F.]

cro·sier, -zier [króuʒər] *n.* Ⓒ a bishop's hooked stick, serving as a sign of his position; 《*fig.*》 the office of a bishop. (bishop이나 abbot의) 목장(牧杖); 홀장(笏杖); 사교장(司敎杖); 주교(主敎)의 직(職). [L. *croccus* hook]

:cross [krɔ:s / krɔs] *n.* Ⓒ **1** a stick or post with a bar across it, on which criminals were put to death. 십자가. ¶ *the penalty of the* ~ 책형(磔刑) / *die on the* ~ 십자가에 못박혀 죽다. **2** ⓐ 《*the C-*》 the Cross upon which Christ died. (예수가 못박힌) 십자가. ⓑ any model or picture of this as a religious symbol. (종교적 상징인) 십자가상(像)〔그림〕. ⓒ the Christian religion. 기독교. ¶ *the Cross and the Crescent* 기독교와 이슬람교. **3** a mark made by drawing one line across another; anything like a cross in shape. 열십자 표시〔기호〕; 열십자 모양의 것. ¶ *the Southern Cross* 남십자성(星) / *make the sign of the* ~ 성호(聖號)를 긋다. **4** trial; suffering; trouble. 시련; 수난; 고난. ¶ *bear*〔*take up*〕 *one's* ~ 고난을 견디다; 십자가를 지다 / *No* ~*, no crown.* 고난 없이 영관(榮冠)은 없다. **5** a staff with a cross at the head of it, borne before an archbishop as a sign of his office. (대주교의) 십자장(杖). **6** a monument in the form of a cross, esp. in the center of a town, etc. (시장·묘비 따위를 표시하는) 십자표; 십자탑〔비〕. ¶ *a boundary* ~ 경계표. **7** ⓐ a mixing of varieties or breeds of plants or animals. 이종 교배(異種交配). ⓑ a plant or animal as the product of such a mixture; a hybrid. 교배종; 잡종. ⓒ a mixture between different races. 혼혈; 튀기. ¶ *a* ~ *between a Malay and a Chinese* 말레이 사람과 중국 사람과의 혼혈아. **8** an ornament, badge, or medal shaped like a cross. 십자장식; 십자 기장〔훈장〕. ¶ *a Victoria Cross* 빅토리아 훈장.

cross and pile, odd and even; a luck. 거죽과 뒤; 운(運).

on the cross, **a**) not at right angles. 비스듬히. **b**) unfairly or dishonestly. 부정(직)하게.

—*adj.* **1** crossing. (열십자로) 교차한; 가로지른. ¶ *a* ~ *street* 교차로. **2** bad-tempered; out of humor. 성난; 성마른; 찌무룩한. ¶ *get* ~ 성나다 / *Why are you so* ~ *with me?* 내게 왜 그다지 화를 내고 있나. **3** contrary; opposite. 반대의. ¶ *a result* ~ *to the purpose* 목적에 반대되는 결과. **4** unfavorable. 불리한; 역(逆)의. ¶ ~ *luck*〔*fortune*〕 불운. **5** reciprocal. 교호의; 상호의. **6** (of blood or race) mixed. 혼혈의; 잡종의.

(***as***) ***cross as two sticks,*** 《*colloq.*》 complaining; very irritable. 성을 잘 내는; (성미가) 몹시 까다로운; 찌무룩한.

cross voting, voting against one's own party. 자당(自黨)에의 반대 투표.

run cross to, be contrary to. …에 반(反)하다.

—*vt.* **1** (P6) lay or place (something) over or across. …을 교차시키다. ¶ ~ *one's knife and fork* 나이프와 포크를 교차시켜 놓다 / ~ *one's arms* 팔짱을 끼다. **2** (P6) make the sign of the cross by moving the hand upon or over (one's body). …에 성호(聖號)〔십자〕를 긋다. ¶ ~ *one's heart* 가슴에 성호를 긋다《진실을 맹세한다는 표시로》 / ~ *oneself*〔*one's breast*〕 성호를 긋다. **3** (P6) go from one side to another of (something); go or walk across (something). …을 횡단하다; 가로지르다. ¶ ~ *a road* 도로를 횡단하다 / ~ *over a bridge* 다리를 건너다 / ~ *to the other side of a street* 길을 횡단하여 건너편으로 가다. **4** (P6,7) draw a line or lines across. …에 횡선(橫線)을 긋다. **5** (P6) (of traveling persons or letters in the post) meet and pass. …와 엇갈리다. ¶ *Your letter crossed mine.* 네 편지는 내 것과 엇갈렸다 / *We crossed* (*each other*) *on the road.* 우리는 노상에서 서로 엇갈렸다. **6** (P6,13) oppose; hinder; prevent. …을 반대하다; 방해하다. ¶ ~ *his plan* 그의 계획을 방해하다 / ~ *someone's will* 아무의 의사를 거역하다. **7** (P6) occur to (the mind); come over. (마음)에 떠오르다; 스치다. ¶ *A nice idea crossed his mind.* 멋진 안(案)이 그의 마음에 떠올랐다 / *A shadow crossed her face.* 그녀 얼굴에 어두운 그림자가 스쳤다. **8** (P6,13) mix breeds of (plants or animals). (동식물)을 교배하다. **9** 《*up*》 《*sl.*》 cheat; deceive; betray. …을 속이다; 배반하다. **10** (P6,7) 《often *off, out*》 cancel or strike out by marking with a cross or a line or lines; remove; erase. …을 열십자 기호로〔줄을 그어〕 지우다. ¶ ~ *off someone's name* 아무의 이름을 지우다 / ~ *a wrong word out* 틀린 말을 지우다. —*vi.* **1** (P1, 2A) go across. 가로지르다. **2** (P1,2A) pass, move or extend from side to side. (한쪽에서 다른 쪽으로) 건너다. **3** (P1) meet and pass. 엇갈리다. **4** (P1) breed together. 교배하다; 잡종이 되다. [L. *crux*]

be crossed in, be disappointed at. …에 실망〔낙심〕하다. ¶ *He has been crossed in love.* 그는 실연했다.

cross a check, draw two lines across a check it so that it can be paid through the bank. 수표에 횡선을 긋다.

cross a horse, mount a horse. 말에 올라타다.

cross one's legs, sit cross-legged. 책상다리를 하다; 가부좌 틀다.

cross swords with someone, **a**) fight. …와 싸우다. **b**) argue with someone. …와 논전하다.

cross the cudgels, submit. 항복〔굴복〕하다.

cross the palm of, pay money to; offer a bribe to. …에게 돈을 쥐어주다; 뇌물을 주다.

cross the path of someone, **a**) meet someone unexpectedly. 뜻밖에 …와 만나다. **b**) oppose someone's plan, wishes, etc. (…의 계획 따위)를 방해하다.

cross one's t's and dot one's i's, be careful and exact in speech and conduct. 언행에 조심하다.

cross·bar [krɔ́ːsbɑ̀ːr / krɔ́s-] *n.* Ⓒ **1** a bar, line, or stripe fixed across others. 빗장; 가로대. **2** a bar of wood fixed between goal posts, as in football and soccer. (축구·럭비의 골문이나 높이뛰기의) 가로대; 크로스바. [*cross*]

cross·beam [krɔ́ːsbìːm / krɔ́s-] *n.* 《*archit.*》 a large beam placed across two upright beams or from wall to wall. 대들보.

[*cross*]

cross·bench [krɔ́:sbèntʃ / krɔ́s-] *n.* a bench in the British Parliament, on which neutral or independent members sit. (영국 의회의) 무소속 의원석(席).

cross·bones [krɔ́:sbòunz / krɔ́s-] *n. pl.* two large bones placed crosswise, usu. below a skull. (해골 밑의) 교차시킨 두 개의 뼈.

cross·bow [krɔ́:sbòu / krɔ́s-] *n.* Ⓒ an old-time weapon for shooting stones and short arrows. 석궁(石弓)《중세의 격발식 활》.

<crossbow>

cross·bred [krɔ́:sbrèd / krɔ́s-] *v.* p. and pp. of **crossbreed.** — *adj.* of a mixed breed or race. 교배종의; 잡종의.

cross·breed [krɔ́:sbrì:d / krɔ́s-] *vi., vt.* (**-bred, -breed·ing**) breed by mixing kinds or races. 이종(異種) 교배하다. — *n.* Ⓒ a person, an animal, or a plant that came from parents of different races or kinds. 교배종(種); 잡종; 혼혈인.

cross-bun [krɔ́:sbʌ̀n / krɔ́s-] *n.* a bun marked with a cross, eaten on Good Friday; hot cross bun. 열십자가 찍힌 빵.

cross-coun·try [krɔ́:skʌ́ntri / krɔ́skʌ́n-] *adj.* **1** across open country or fields instead of along or over a road. 들녘·숲 따위를 횡단하는; 크로스컨트리의. ¶ *a* ~ *race* 크로스컨트리 경기. **2** from one end of the country to the other. 국토의 끝에서 끝까지의; 전국을 횡단하는. ¶ *a* ~ *flight* 전국 횡단 비행.

cross·cut [krɔ́:skʌ̀t / krɔ́s-] *adj.* made for cutting across the grain of wood. 가로켜는; 옆으로 베는. ¶ *a* ~ *saw* 동가리톱. — *n.* a cut or way across. 가로켜기; 횡단로; 지름길. — *vt.* cut or go across. …을 가로켜다; 횡단하다; 가로지르다.

cross-ex·am·i·na·tion [krɔ́:sigzæ̀mənéiʃən / krɔ́s-] *n.* ⓊⒸ **1** 《law》 the act of cross-examining; the state of being cross-examined. 반대 심문. **2** a severe, close questioning. 엄중한 힐문(詰問); 심한 추궁.

cross-ex·am·ine [krɔ́:sigzǽmin / krɔ́s-] *vt.* (P6) **1** 《law》 question (a witness who has already been questioned by the opposing side) closely to test the truth of his evidence. …에게 반대 심문을 하다. ¶ *A lawyer cross-examines the witnesses of the opposing side to test the truth of their evidence.* 변호인은 증언의 진실성 여부를 가리기 위해 상대방 증인들에게 반대 심문을 한다. **2** question closely. …을 호되게 힐문하다. ¶ *I don't see why you should have to* ~ *me like this.* 자네 왜 이렇게 나를 추궁해야 하는지 모르겠네. ● **cross-ex·am·in·er** [-ər] *n.* [*cross*]

cross-eyed [krɔ́:sàid / krɔ́s-] *adj.* having one or both eyes turned toward the nose. 사시(斜視)의; 모들뜨기의. [*cross*]

cross-fer·ti·li·za·tion [krɔ́:sfə̀:rtəlizéiʃən / krɔ́s-] *n.* 《bot.》 fertilization of one flower by pollen from another. 이화 수정(異花受精); 딴꽃정받이.

cross-fer·ti·lize [krɔ́:sfə́:rtəlàiz / krɔ́s-] *vt.* (P6,13) cause the cross-fertilization of. …을 이화 수정〔딴꽃정받이〕시키다.

cross-fire [krɔ́:sfàiər / krɔ́s-] *n.* **1** 《mil.》 lines of fire from two or more positions, crossing one another. 십자 포화(砲火). **2** a rapid exchange of words, speech, etc. (말·의견 따위의) 활발한 교환. ¶ *a* ~ *of question and answer* 질의 응답의 활발한 주고받기.

cross-grained [krɔ́:sgréind / krɔ́s-] *adj.* **1** (of a board) having an irregular grain. (목재가) 나뭇결이 불규칙한. **2** 《*fig.*》 (of a person) hard to manage; bad-tempered; ill-natured. (사람이) 꾀까다로운; 심술 궂은; 빙퉁그러진.

cross·ing [krɔ́:siŋ / krɔ́s-] *n.* **1** ⓊⒸ the act of going across; a trip across a large body of water, such as a sea or a lake; a sea passage. 횡단; 도항(渡航); 해로(海路). ¶ *have a good* 〔*rough*〕 ~ 도항할 때 바다가 잔잔하다〔거칠다〕. **2** Ⓒ a place where streets, railways, rivers, etc. cross each other; a place provided for going across a street or railroad tracks. 교차점; 네거리; 횡단 보도; 건널목. ¶ *a railroad* ~ 철도 건널목 / *Always cross the road at the* ~. 길은 항상 횡단 보도에서 건너라. **3** Ⓤ the act of making a cross (over one's body). 성호(聖號) 긋기. **4** ⓊⒸ the act of mixing breeds. 이종(異種) 교배. [*cross*]

cross-leg·ged [krɔ́:slégid / krɔ́s-] *adj.* having one leg over the other when a person sits. 책상다리를 한; 가부좌를 튼.

cross·ly [krɔ́:sli / krɔ́s-] *adv.* in a cross or angry manner. 심술궂게; 성이 나서.

cross·ness [krɔ́:snis / krɔ́s-] *n.* Ⓤ bad temper; the state of being cross. 찌무룩함; 심술이 나 있음; 성남.

cross·patch [krɔ́:spæ̀tʃ / krɔ́s-] *n.* 《*colloq.*》 a cross, bad-tempered person. 꾀까다로운 사람.

cross-pol·li·nate [krɔ́:spɑ́lənèit / krɔ́spɔ́l-] *vt.* (P6,13) cause cross-fertilization in. 딴꽃가루받이를 하게 하다.

cross-pur·pose [krɔ́:spə́:rpəs / krɔ́s-] *n.* Ⓒ an opposing purpose. 반대의 목적〔의향〕. ***be at cross-purposes,*** **a**) misunderstand each other's purpose; act so as to prevent each other's success. 서로 (의도를) 오해하다; 서로 상대의 성공을 방해 하다. **b**) act under a misunderstanding. 오해하여 서로 엇갈린 행동을 하다.

cross-ques·tion [krɔ́:skwéstʃən / krɔ́s-] *vt.* (P6) 《law》 question closely or strictly;

cross-examine. (상대의 증인)을 반대 심문하다; 엄중히 힐문하다. — *n.* Ⓒ a question asked by means of cross-examination. 반대 심문. [*cross*]

cross reference [ˊ-ˊ--] *n.* a reference from one part of a book, an index, etc. to another part. (책 중의) 다른 항 참조; 앞뒤 참조.

cross·road [krɔ́:sròud / krɔ́s-] *n.* Ⓒ **1** a road that crosses a main road; a road that runs from one main road to another. 교차 도로; (두 개의 주(主)도로를 잇는) 기로(岐路). **2** 《usu. *pl.*, used as *sing.*》 a place where two or more roads meet. 교차점; 십자로; 네거리.

be* 〔*stand*〕 *at the* 〔*a*〕 *crossroads, 《*fig.*》 be at a time when a person must decide what to do. 기로에 서다; 중대한 결정을 내려야 할 시점에 직면하다.

cross section [ˊ-ˊ-] *n.* **1** the act of cutting anything across. 가로 벰. **2** a section cut in this way. 횡단면. ¶ *cut a ~ of a tree trunk and count the rings* 나무의 줄기를 횡단면으로 잘라 나이테를 세다. **3** a model selection; a sample showing all characteristic parts, relationships, etc. 대표적 단면(표본, 실례). ¶ *a ~ of college life* 대학 생활의 한 단면.

cross-stitch [krɔ́:sstìtʃ] *n.* **1** one stitch crossed over another, forming an X. X형의 십자뜨기. **2** embroidery made with this stitch. 십자뜨기의 수(繡). — *vt., vi.* (P6; 1) embroider or sew with this stitch. 십자뜨기하다. [*cross*]

cross·trees [krɔ́:strì:z / krɔ́s-] *n. pl.* 《naut.》 two horizontal pieces of timber fixed to the top of the lower mast to support the upper mast. 돛대 위의 가로장.

cross vot·ing [krɔ́:s vòutiŋ / krɔ́s-] *n.* voting againtst one's own party. 자기 당에 대한 반대 투표.

cross·way [krɔ́:swèi / krɔ́s-] *n.* =crossroad.

cross·ways [krɔ́:swèiz / krɔ́s-] *adv.* = crosswise.

cross·wise [krɔ́:swàiz / krɔ́s-] *adv.* **1** across. 비스듬하게; 가로로. **2** in the form of a cross. 열십자(꼴)로. **3** opposite to what is required; wrongly. 역(逆)으로; 반대로. ¶ *Things are going ~.* 사태는 역행하고 있다.

cross·word puzzle [krɔ́:swə:rd pʌ̀zl / krɔ́s-] *n.* a puzzle with a set of squares to be filled in with letters. 십자말 풀이; 크로스워드 퍼즐.

crotch [kratʃ / krɔtʃ] *n.* Ⓒ the point of separation of branches or legs; a fork. (나무의) 아귀; 가랑이; 샅; (포크처럼) 끝이 갈라진 것. [F.]

crotch·et [krátʃit / krɔ́tʃ-] *n.* Ⓒ **1** a small hook or hooklike part. 갈고리(모양의 부분). **2** an odd notion or fancy. 묘한 생각; 기상(奇想); 변덕. ¶ *The old man had many crotches.* 노인은 변덕이 심했다. **3** 《Brit. mus.》 a quarter note in music. 4분음표(=《U.S.》 quarter-note). [→crochet]

crotch·et·y [krátʃiti / krɔ́tʃ-] *adj.* full of whims; easily irritated. 변덕스러운; 별난 생각을 가진; 꾀까다로운. ¶ *a ~ old man* 꾀까다로운 노인.

cro·ton [króutən] *n.* 《bot.》 a tropical plant which has medicinal properties. 파두 《열대 식물》. [Gk.]

croton oil [ˊ-ˊ] *n.* a powerful purgative oil. 파두 기름《강력 완하제》.

***crouch** [krautʃ] *vi.* (P1,2A,4) 《*down*》 bend low or close to the ground. (몸을) 웅크리다; 움츠리다. ¶ *~ at someone's feet* 아무의 발 밑에 쭈그리다 / *~ over the fire* 몸을 구부려 불을 쬐다 / *The tiger crouched in the grass.* 호랑이는 풀 속에 몸을 웅크렸다. — *n.* Ⓒ the act of crouching. 웅크림; 움츠림. [E.]

croup[1] [kru:p] *n.* Ⓤ 《med.》 a children's disease marked by a heavy cough. 크루프; 위막성 후두염(僞膜性喉頭炎). [Imit.]

croup[2]**, croupe** [kru:p] *n.* the rump of a horse, etc. (말 따위의) 엉덩이. [F. →crop]

crou·pi·er [krú:piər] *n.* a man who takes in and pays out the money at a game played for money. (노름판에서) 돈을 내거나 챙기는 사람. [↑]

crou·ton, croû- [krú:tan, -ˊ / -tɔn] *n.* 《F.》 a small piece of toasted or fried bread, often served in soup. 크루톤《굽거나 버터에 튀긴 빵 조각》.

crow[1] [krou] *vi.* (P1,3) **1** (**crowd** or esp. 《Brit.》 **crew, crowd**) (of a cock) make a loud cry. (수탉이) 울다; 홰를 쳐 새벽을 알리다. ¶ *Every cock crows at the dawn of day.* 모든 수탉은 첫새벽에 운다. **2** (of a baby) make a happy sound. (아기가) 기뻐서 소리치다. ¶ *As the father entered the room, the child crowed and held out its arms.* 아빠가 방안에 들어오자 아기는 소리치며 팔을 내밀었다. **3** 《*fig.*》 (of persons) feel or express delight at victory over another. (사람이) 환성을 올리다; 미칠 듯이 기뻐하다.

crow over, boast about; triumph over. 자랑하다; 환성을 올리다; 의기양양해 하다. ¶ *~ over one's success* 성공을 자랑하다.

— *n.* Ⓒ **1** a loud cry made by a cock. 수탉의 울음 소리. **2** a happy sound made by a baby. 아기의 기뻐서 내는 소리. [E.]

***crow**[2] [krou] *n.* Ⓒ **1** a large black bird which cries "Caw! Caw!". 까마귀. ¶ *(as) black as a ~* 새까만 / *a white ~* 진기한 것. **2** a crowbar. 쇠지렛대. [E.]

as the crow flies, in a straight line. 일직선으로; 곧장.

eat crow, 《U.S. *colloq.*》 be forced to accept or do something disagreeable and dishonorable. (하기 싫은 일을) 할 수 없이 하게 되다; 굴욕을 참다.

have a crow to pluck* 〔*pick, pull*〕 *with some-

one, have an unpleasant matter to discuss and settle with someone. …와 시비를 가리거나 해결해야 할 일이 있다; …에게 할 말이 있다.

crow·bar [króubɑ̀ːr] *n.* Ⓒ a strong iron or steel bar, used for lifting heavy things. 쇠지렛대. [↑]

:crowd [kraud] *n.* Ⓒ **1** a large number of people or things gathered closely together. 군중; 붐빔. ¶ *large crowds in the streets* 거리의 인파 / *in crowds* 떼지어 / *gather in crowds* 떼지어 모이다. **2** 《*the* ~》 people in general; the common people or the masses. 민중; 대중. ¶ *The ~ needs leadership.* 대중은 리더십이 필요하다 / *far from the madding ~* 광란의 속세를 멀리 떠나서. **3** 《*colloq.*》 a special group of people; a company; a set. 패거리; 동아리; 일단. ¶ *a jolly ~* 유쾌한 패거리 / *Tom and his ~ went to the movies.* 톰과 그의 패거리들은 영화 구경을 갔다. **4** a large number of things collected or pressed together. 다수(의 것); 많은 것. ¶ *a ~ of books* 많은 책 / *a ~ of papers and books on the desk* 산더미 같은 책상 위의 서류와 책 / *attract a large* [*great*] *~ of people* 많은 사람을 끌다 / *have a ~ of things to do* 할 일이 많다.

follow [***go with***] ***the crowd,*** do (something) as most people do. 대중의 행동에 따르다.

might pass in a crowd, be ordinary. 보통이다.

— *vi.* (P2A,3,4) **1** gather in large numbers; press together. 떼지어 모이다; 붐비다. ¶ *The main street is crowded with shops.* 중심가에는 점포들이 즐비하게 늘어서 있다 / *We crowded around her to offer our congratulation.* 축하의 말을 하기 위해 그녀 주위에 몰려들었다. **2** press forward; advance by pushing. 밀치며 나아가다. ¶ *~ into a room* 많은 사람이 방으로 밀치며 들어가다 / *They crowded in for seats.* 그들은 자리를 잡으려고 밀치며 들어왔다. **3** come to mind thick and fast; rush into the mind. (마음에) 문뜩 떠오르다. ¶ *Ideas* [*Memories*] *~ upon me* [*my mind*]. 내게 문뜩 생각[기억]이 떠올랐다. — *vt.* (P6,7,13) **1** press (people or things) closely together; fill to excess; pack. (사람·물건)을 처[쑤셔]넣다; 넘칠 정도로[잔뜩] 채우다. ¶ *~ clothes into a suitcase* 가방에 옷을 처넣다 / *~ a room with furniture* 방을 가구로 채우다 / *Students crowded the lecture hall.* 학생들은 강의실을 꽉 메웠다. **2** push; press; shove. …으로 밀어 보내다; 밀다. ¶ *~ someone off the pavement* 아무를 밀어 포도 밖으로 몰아내다 / *He was crowded into a ditch.* 그는 밀려 도랑에 빠졌다 / *I crowded him, step by step, to the wall.* 한발짝 한발짝 그를 벽쪽으로 밀고 갔다. **3** 《*colloq.*》 put (someone) under pressure; press urgently. (성가시게) 조르다; 강요하다. [E.]

be crowded with, be congested with. …으로 혼잡하다; 붐비다.

crowd (***on***) ***sail,*** 《naut.》 raise more sails to make a ship go faster. (속력을 내기 위해) 돛을 한껏 펴다.

·crowd·ed [kráudid] *adj.* **1** filled with a crowd; packed; close together; too close together. 붐비는; 만원의; 꽉 찬. ¶ *~ streets* 붐비는 거리 / *~ bookshelves* 책들이 꽉 들어찬 서가(書架) / *a room ~ with furniture* 가구들이 들어차 있는 방 / *~ passengers on a bus* 만원 버스의 승객 / *The carriage was ~.* 찻간은 만원이었다. **2** (of periods of time) packed with action, experience, etc. 사건이 많은; 경험이 풍부한; 경험·사건들로 찬. ¶ *a ~ life* 파란만장한 생애 / *a ~ day* 바쁜 하루.

:crown [kraun] *n.* Ⓒ **1** ⓐ a head-covering of a king or queen. 왕관. ⓑ Ⓤ 《*the ~* or *the C-*》 the power and authority of a king, a queen, etc.; a king or queen. 왕위; 왕권; 통치(권); 군주; (여)왕. ¶ *succeed to the ~* 왕위를 계승하다 / *abdicate the ~* 퇴위하다 / *an officer of the ~* (국왕이 임명하는) 관리 / *the demise of the ~* (왕의) 붕어(崩御). **2** ⓐ a wreath for the head, esp. as a sign of victory. (승리의) 화관(花冠); 영관. ¶ *The winner received a laurel ~.* 우승자는 월계관을 받았다. ⓑ 《*fig.*》 a reward. 영예; (더없는) 광영. ¶ *the martyr's ~* 순교자가 받는 광영. **3** ⓐ the top or highest part. 정상; 꼭대기. ¶ *from ~ to toe* 머리끝에서 발끝까지 / *the ~ of a hat* [*mountain*] 모자[산] 꼭대기 / *the ~ of the head* 머리끝. ⓑ the head. 머리. ¶ *break a man's ~* 사나이의 골통을 부수다. **4** the highest state or quality of anything. 절정; 극치; 최후를 장식하는 것. ¶ *the ~ of life* 생애 최고 / *the ~ of the year,* 1년 중에서의 수확기. **5** the exposed part of a tooth; an artificial substitute for the crown of a tooth. (인공)치관(齒冠)(opp. root). **6** a former British silver coin worth five shillings. 크라운 화폐《5실링 은화》. **7** a size of paper, 15" × 20". 크라운 《인쇄 용지 크기의 단위》. **8** 《archit.》 the highest part of an arch. 관정(冠頂).

— *vt.* (P6,13,19) **1** put a crown on; enthrone. …에게 왕관을 씌우다; …을 왕위에 앉히다. ¶ *~ someone king* 아무를 왕위에 오르게 하다. **2** give honor to (someone); reward. …에게 영예를 주다; (영예 따위로) 보답하다. ¶ *~ someone with glory* 아무에게 영광을 안겨주다. **3** occupy the top of (something); be at the top of. … 의 꼭대기에 있다; 머리에 이다. ¶ *a tower crowned with a spire* 꼭대기에 뾰족탑이 있는 탑 / *A palace crowns the hill.* 언덕 위에 궁전이 있다. **4** make (something) perfect or complete; add the finishing touch to (something). …의 유종의 미를 장식하다; 최후의 마무리를 하다. ¶ *The Nobel prize crowned his career as a scientist.* 노벨상이 과학자로서의 그의 생애 마지막을 장식했다. **5** cover (a tooth) with

gold or other material as a protection. 치관(齒冠)을 씌우다.
be crowned with, bring; result in. …을 가져오다. ¶ *His efforts have been crowned with success.* 그의 노력은 성공을 가져왔다.
crowned heads, kings or queens. 왕들과 여왕들.
to crown all, in the end; lastly and best of all; worst of all. 마침내는; 끝에 가서는; 게다가; 그 위에 더.
— *adj.* **1** of a crown. 왕(관)의. **2** belonging to a crown. 왕실 직할의. ¶ *Crown Colony* 직할 식민지. **3** of the first class. 최상급의. [L. *corona*]

crown glass [ㅅ ㅅ] *n.* thick glass used for windows. 크라운 글라스《두꺼운 창유리》.

crown·ing [kráuniŋ] *adj.* culminating; highest. 더없는; 무상의; 최고의. ¶ *his ~ joy* 그의 더없는 기쁨 / *the ~ glory* 무상의 영예. [→crown]

crown land [ㅅ ㅅ] *n.* 《Brit.》 land that belongs to the Crown. 왕실 소유지.

crown prince [ㅅ ㅅ] *n.* the heir to a king. 황태자.

crown princess [ㅅ ㅅ–] *n.* the wife of a crown prince. 황태자비(妃).

crow's-feet [króuzfiːt] *n.* pl. of **crow's-foot.**

crow's-foot [króuzfùt] *n.* Ⓒ (*pl.* **-feet**) 《usu. *pl.*》 lines at the outside corner of the eye. 눈초리의 주름. [*crow*]

crow's-nest [króuznèst] *n.* Ⓒ a small, enclosed platform near or at the top of a mast, used for looking out over the sea. (돛대 위의) 망대. [*crow*]

cro·zier [króuʒər] *n.* =crosier.

cru·ces [krúːsiːz] *n.* pl. of **crux.**

cru·cial [krúːʃəl] *adj.* **1** very important; critical; decisive. 극히 중대한; 위기의; 결정적인. ¶ *a ~ decision* 최종〔중대〕 결정 / *a ~ test* 〔*experiment*〕 극히 중대한 실험. **2** severe; very hard; difficult. 호된; 괴로운; 어려운. ¶ *a ~ period* 〔*question*〕 곤란한 시기〔문제〕. **3** 《surg.》 shaped like a cross. 십자형(十字形)의. ¶ *a ~ incision* 십자 절개(切開).
●**cru·cial·ly** [-i] *adv.* [L. *crux* cross]

cru·ci·ble [krúːsəbl] *n.* Ⓒ **1** a pot for melting things that require very great heat. 도가니. ¶ *~ steel* 도가니강(鋼) 《도가니에서 용제(熔製)한 질 좋은 강철》. **2** 《*fig.*》 a severe test or trial. 호된 시련. [↑]
in the crucible, undergoing a severe trial. 호된 시련을 겪고.

cru·cif·er·ous [kruːsífərəs] *adj.* 《bot.》 with four equal petals arranged crosswise. 십자형 화관(花冠)을 가진; 겨잣과(科)의. [↓]

cru·ci·fix [krúːsəfiks] *n.* Ⓒ **1** a model of Christ on the cross. 십자가에 못 박힌 예수상(像). **2** a cross used as a Christian symbol. 십자가. [→crucial, *figo* fix]

cru·ci·fix·ion [krùːsəfíkʃən] *n.* **1** Ⓤ the act of putting someone to death on a cross. (십자가에 의한) 책형(磔刑). **2** Ⓒ 《*the C-*》 the death of Christ on the cross; a picture or statue representing this scene. 그리스도의 십자가에서의 죽음; 그것을 나타낸 그림〔상(像)〕. **3** 《*fig.*》 great suffering. 큰 고난.

cru·ci·form [krúːsəfɔ̀ːrm] *adj.* shaped like a cross. 십자형의. ¶ *a ~ church* 십자형의 성당. [↑]

cru·ci·fy [krúːsəfài] *vt.* (**-fied, -fy·ing**) **1** put (someone) to death by fastening him to a cross. (아무)를 십자가에 못박다; 책형에 처하다. **2** treat severely; cause severe pain to (someone). …을 몹시 괴롭히다; 학대〔박해〕하다. **3** subdue (passion, etc.). 억제하다; 누르다. [*crucifix*]

***crude** [kruːd] *adj.* **1** in a natural or raw state; not refined. (가공하지 않은) 천연 그대로의; 생(生)…의(opp. cultivated, refined). ¶ *~ oil* 원유(原油) / *~ materials* 원료 / *~ flesh* 날고기 / *~ rubber* 생고무 / *~ sugar* 조당(粗糖). **2** ⓐ not mature; unripe. (과일 따위가) 미숙한; 덜 익은. ⓑ badly arranged; not thought out. (생각·의견 따위가) 유치한; 미숙한. ¶ *a ~ opinion* 미숙한 의견 / *~ theories* 유치한 이론. **3** ⓐ rough; coarse; bare. 교양 없는; 거친; 노골적인. ¶ *a ~ person* 상스런 사람 / *~ behavior* 무례한 태도 / *a ~ fact* 있는 그대로의 사실. ⓑ (of speech or work) not well finished; lacking grace, taste, or refinement. 미완성의; 불완전한; 세련되지 않은. ¶ *a ~ summary* 불완전한 요약 / *~ speech* 어색한 연설〔말투〕. **4** (of colors) too bright or highly colored. (색이) 야한.
●**crude·ly** [-li] *adv.* [L. *crudus*]

cru·di·ty [krúːdəti] *n.* (*pl.* **-ties**) **1** Ⓤ the quality or state of being crude; unripeness; roughness; lack of finish. 생짜임; 미숙; 생경; 조잡. **2** Ⓒ a rude or rough action; a crude thing. 거친〔교양 없는〕 언동; 미숙한 것; 미완성품. [↑]

:**cru·el** [krúːəl] *adj.* (**-el·er, -el·est** or 《Brit.》 **-el·ler, -el·lest**) **1** fond of causing pain to others; not caring about the pain and suffering of others. (사람·행위가) 잔혹〔잔인〕한; 무자비한; 무정한. ¶ *a ~ master* 매몰찬 주인 / *~ acts* 잔인한 행위. **2** showing the results of cruelty; causing suffering; painful. 무참〔비참〕한; 끔찍한; 몹시 고통스러운; 지독한. ¶ *a ~ wound* 지독한 부상 / *a ~ sight* 끔찍한 광경 / *a ~ blow* 몹시 아픈 일격 / *a ~ remark* 심한 말 / *a ~ war* 참혹한 전쟁. — *adv.* 《*colloq.*》 very; extremely. 몹시; 무척. ¶ *be ~ hot* 몹시 덥다. [→crude]

cru·el·ly [krúːəli] *adv.* in cruel manner. 참혹〔잔혹〕하게; 끔찍하게.

***cru·el·ty** [krúː(ː)əlti] *n.* (*pl.* **-ties**) **1** Ⓤ the quality of being cruel; the tendency to give pain to others; taking pleasure in hurting others. 잔혹; 잔인; 무자비. ¶ *the ~ of man* 인간의 잔인성 / *a man of ~* 잔인한 사람 / *the ~ of fate* 운명의 냉혹함. **2** Ⓒ 《*pl.*》 a cruel act. 잔혹한 행위. ¶ *commit cru-*

elties 잔혹한 짓을 하다 / *He died by the ~ of his enemies.* 그는 적의 잔학 행위로 죽었다.

cru·et [krú:ət] *n.* Ⓒ **1** a small glass bottle for holding mustard, oil. etc. (식탁에서 쓰는 겨자·기름 따위를 담는) 유리병. ¶ *Pass the cruets, please.* 양념병 좀 집어 주시오. **2** =cruet-stand. [F.]

cru·et-stand [krú:ətstæ̀nd] *n.* Ⓒ a small stand for holding cruets. 양념병대(臺).

cruise [kru:z] *vi.* (P1,2A,3) **1** travel by ship with no definite end of one's journey in mind; sail about touching at a series of ports instead of going directly to one port only; make a similar trip on or over land. 순항(巡航)하다; (이렇다 할 목적(지) 없이) 돌아다니다; 만유(漫遊)하다. ¶ *~ along the shore* 연안을 순항하다 / *~ on the Pacific* 태평양을 순항하다. **2** move or drive about slowly, looking for customers or for something remarkable. (손님·주의를 끄는 것을) 찾아다니다. ¶ *a cruising taxi* 손님을 찾아 돌아다니는 택시. **3** (of cars, aircraft) travel at the most efficient speed. 적당한 속도로 주행〔비행〕하다.
— *vt.* (P6) sail about (a place) with no special destination. …을 순항하다.
— *n.* Ⓒ a trip made by a ship or an airplane that is cruising. 순항; 항해; 만유(漫遊). [→cross]

cruis·er [krú:zər] *n.* Ⓒ **1** a warship with less armor and more speed than a battleship. 순양함. ¶ *an armored* 〔*a belted*〕 *~* 장갑 순양함. **2** a motorboat, an airplane, a taxi, etc. that cruise. 순항정(巡航艇); 순행 비행기; 손님 찾아 돌아다니는 택시. **3** a police car connected with head quarters by radio; a patrol car. (경찰의) 순찰차. **4** a timber estimator. (산림의) 입목(立木) 견적인(見積人).

crul·ler [krʌ́lər] *n.* a light sweet cake. 도넛. [G.]

•**crumb** [krʌm] *n.* **1** 《usu. *pl.*》 a small piece, esp. of bread, broken or rubbed off. 빵 부스러기. ¶ *crumbs from the table* 식탁에서 떨어진 빵 부스러기. **2** Ⓤ the soft, inner part of bread. 빵의 말랑말랑한 속(cf. *crust*). **3** Ⓒ a little bit; a scrap. 약간; 조금; 소량. ¶ *a ~ of hope* 〔*comfort*〕 약간의 희망〔위안〕 / *mere crumbs of knowledge* 극히 미미한 지식.
to a crumb, minutely; strictly. 세부에 이르기까지; 자세히; 정확히.
— *vt.* (P6) **1** break into crumbs. …을 부스러뜨리다. **2** cover (fish, etc.) with crumbs, for frying or baking. …에 빵가루를 묻히다. [E.]

•**crum·ble** [krʌ́mbl] *vt.* (P6,7) 《*up*》 break (something) into small pieces. …을 부수다; 가루로 하다. — *vi.* (P1,2A) 《*away*》 fall to pieces; become ruined; decay. 부서지다; 무너지다; 멸망하다; 없어지다. ¶ *crumbling walls* 무너지는 벽 / *The great empires of the past have crumbled and fallen.* 과거의 대제국들은 멸망해 없어졌다. / *My dearest hopes have crumbled to nothing.* 내 소중한 희망들이 사라졌다. [E.]

crum·bly [krʌ́mbli] *adj.* (**-bli·er, -bli·est**) tending to crumble; easily crumbled. 부서지기 쉬운. ● **crum·bli·ness** [-nis] *n.*

crump [krʌmp] *vi.* (P6) hit hard. 강타하다.
— *n.* **1** a hard hit. 강타. **2** a heavy fall. 털썩 쓰러짐. **3** 《mil. *sl.*》 an exploding shell. 폭렬탄(爆裂彈). [Imit.]

crum·pet [krʌ́mpit] *n.* Ⓒ **1** 《esp. Brit》 a thin, unsweetened cake eaten after it has been heated and buttered. 크럼펫《버터를 발라 살짝 구운 핫케이크》. **2** 《*sl.*》 the head. 머리. **3** 《*sl.*》 sex appeal. 성적 매력. [↓]

crum·ple [krʌ́mpl] *vt.* (P6,7) **1** press or crush (something) into irregular folds; wrinkle. …을 구기다; 꾸깃거려 쭈글쭈글하게 하다. ¶ *~ one's clothes* 옷을 구기다 / *~ a letter into a ball* 편지를 꾸깃거려 뭉치다. **2** cause to collapse. 찌부러뜨리다; 무너뜨리다.
— *vi.* (P1,2A) **1** become bent into many folds. 구겨지다; 쭈글쭈글해지다. ¶ *This cloth crumples very easily.* 이 천은 아주 쉽게 구겨진다. **2** give way. 무너지다; 붕괴되다. [Obs. *crump* crooked]
crumple up, **a**) roll up and press in the hand, esp. of a dry material such as paper. …을 구기다; 꾸깃거리다. **b**) 《*fig.*》 reduce to helplessness; overcome. 압도하다. ¶ *~ up an opponent* 상대를 압도하다. **c**) break or yield completely and suddenly. 부서지다; 무너지다. ¶ *The wall is crumpled* (*up*). 담이 붕괴되었다 / *He crumpled up under the blows he received.* 주먹 몇 대를 얻어맞고 그는 쓰러졌다.

crunch [krʌntʃ] *vi., vt.* (P1; 6) **1** chew noisily. 우두둑〔아짝〕 깨물다; 씹(히)다. ¶ *~ a carrot* 당근을 우두둑 씹다. **2** crush or grind noisily; make such a sound when walked on. 우둑우둑 바수다; 사박사박 소리를 내며 걷다〔밟다〕. ¶ *The gravel crunched under the wheels of the car.* 자갈이 차바퀴 밑에서 바지직 소리를 냈다 / *He crunched his way through the snow to the school.* 그는 눈길을 서벅서벅 밟으며 학교에 갔다. [Imit.]

crup·per [krʌ́pər] *n.* **1** a leather band attached to the back of a harness and passing under the horse's tail. (말의) 껑거리끈. **2** the part of a horse's back between the saddle and the root of the tail. 말의 궁둥이. [→croup[2]]

•**cru·sade** [kru:séid] *n.* Ⓒ **1** 《often *C-*》 any of the wars fought by Christians to win back their Holy City, Jerusalem. 십자군 원정. **2** a war begun by the Church in the name of religion. 성전(聖戰). **3** any campaign for improvement or reform. 개혁 운동; 박멸 운동. ¶ *a ~ against polio* 소아 마비 박멸 운동 / *a ~ against illitaracy* 문맹 퇴치 운

동. —*vi.* (P1,3) go on or take part in a crusade. 십자군〔개혁 운동〕에 참가하다. [→cross]

cru·sad·er [kru:séidər] *n.* Ⓒ a person who takes part in a crusade. 십자군의 전사(戰士).

cruse [kru:z, kru:s] *n.* 《*arch.*》 a jug, pot or cup for holding water, oil, honey, etc. 물병; 단지. [E.]

:crush [krʌʃ] *vt.* **1** (P6,7,13) ⓐ press together and break (something) with force; break (something) into small pieces. …을 눌러서 뭉개다; 부수다. ¶ ~ *quartz* 석영(石英)을 부수어 가루〔분말(粉末)〕로 만들다 / ~ *a beetle with the foot* 딱정벌레를 밟아 뭉개다 / *be crushed to death* 깔려 죽다 / *The bicycle was crushed by a heavy wagon.* 자전거가 무거운 짐수레에 눌려 찌부러졌다. ⓑ press (something) out of shape; force the liquid out of. …을 찌그러뜨리다; 짜다. ¶ ~ *a hat* 모자를 눌러 찌그러뜨리다 / *be crushed flat* 납작하게 찌그러지다 / ~ *grapes for wine* 포도주를 만들기 위해 포도를 으깨다. **2** (P6,7) bruise; crumple. 구기다. ¶ ~ *up a letter* 편지를 구기다. **3** (P6) 《*fig.*》 conquer; put down (a rebellion, opposition, etc.); defeat utterly; destroy (a military force, hopes; etc.). (반란 따위)를 평정〔진압〕하다; (군대)를 궤멸시키다; (희망 따위)를 꺾다. ¶ ~ (*down*) *a revolt* 반란을 진압하다 / ~ *someone's hopes* 아무의 희망을 꺾다. —*vi.* **1** (P1) be or become crushed. 찌부러〔찌그러〕지다; 구겨지다. ¶ *Silk crushes very easily.* 비단은 아주 잘 구겨진다. **2** (P3) (of a crowd of persons) press; come crowding (into). 우르르 몰려들다. ¶ ~ *into a small room* 좁은 방으로 우르르 몰려 들어가다 / *The people crushed through the gates.* 사람들이 문으로 쇄도했다.

crush down **a**) press down by weight. 눌러 찌부러뜨리다. **b**) break into small pieces. 부수다; 분쇄하다. **c**) put down. (억)누르다. ¶ ~ *down opposition* 반대를 억누르다.

crush out, **a**) conquer; put down (a rebellion, etc.). 박멸하다; 평정〔진압〕하다. **b**) extract by pressing or squeezing. (기름 따위)를 짜다. **c**) burst out. 뚫고 나오다.

crush up, **a**) make into powder. 부수어 가루로 만들다. **b**) press into a ball in the hand. 구겨서 뭉치다. ¶ ~ *up a piece of paper* 종이를 구겨 뭉치다.

—*n.* **1** Ⓤ the act of crushing. 찌부러뜨림; 분쇄; 압도; 궤멸; 진압. **2** Ⓒ ⓐ a dense crowd. 쇄도; 붐빔. ¶ *There was such a* ~ *on the train that I could hardly breath.* 열차가 어찌나 붐비던지 숨을 못 쉴 지경이었다. ⓑ 《*colloq.*》 a crowded social gathering. 군중. **3** Ⓤ a drink made of the juice of crushed fruit. 과즙; 스쿼시. ¶ *orange* ~ 오렌지스쿼시. ● **crush·er** [-ər] *n.* [F.]

crush·ing [krʌ́ʃiŋ] *adj.* overcoming; final; having the power to decide. 압도적인; 결정적인. ¶ *a* ~ *blow* 결정타 / *a* ~ *defeat* 궤멸.

·crust [krʌst] *n.* ⓊⒸ **1** the hard, outside part of bread; a piece of hard, dry bread. 빵 껍질(opp. crumb); 딱딱한 빵의 한 조각. **2** the outside covering of a pie. 파이의 겉껍데기. **3** any hard outside covering. (물건의) 딱딱한 외피(外皮). ¶ *a* ~ *of snow* / *a thin* ~ *of ice on the aeroplane's wing* 비행기 날개에 덮인 엷은 얼음. **4** the solid outside part of the earth. 지각(地殼).

earn one's crust, earn one's living. 생활비를 벌다; 생계를 세우다.

—*vt., vi.* (P6; 1,2A) **1** cover (something), or become covered, with a crust. 외피로 덮(이)다; 외피가 생기다. **2** form into a crust. 딱지가 되다〔앉다〕. [L. *crusta* shell]

Crus·ta·ce·a [krʌstéiʃiə] *n.* 《zool.》 a large class of animals with hard shells. 갑각류(甲殼類). [↑]

crus·ta·ce·an [krʌstéiʃən] *adj.* of the Crustacea. 갑각(甲殼)(류)의. —*n.* Ⓒ an animal of this class (commonly called *shellfish*). 갑각류 동물.

crust·ed [krʌ́stid] *adj.* **1** having a crust. 외피(外皮)가〔외각(外殼)이〕 있는. **2** (of wine) having deposited a crust in the bottle. (포도주가 오래되어) 병에 술버캐가 앉은. **3** ancient; old; venerable. 오래된; 묵은; 고색 창연한.

crust·y [krʌ́sti] *adj.* (**crust·i·er, crust·i·est**) **1** having a crust; like a crust; hard. 겉껍질〔외각〕이 있는; 껍데기 같은; 단단〔딱딱〕한. ¶ ~ *bread* 굳어 딱딱한 빵. **2** 《*fig.*》 (of a person) ill-natured; impolite or rough in manner. (성미가) 괴까다로운; 성 잘 내는; 조포(粗暴)한; 거친. ¶ *a* ~ *old soldier* 완미(頑迷)한 노병 / *a* ~ *remark* 막된〔거친〕 말.

crutch [krʌtʃ] *n.* Ⓒ **1** 《often *a pair of crutches*》 a stick or support to help a lame person in walking. (장애인의) 목발. ¶ *on crutches* 목발을 짚고. **2** anything like a crutch in shape or use. (모양·용도가) 목발 같은 것; 버팀. **3** 《*fig.*》 support; help. 의지되는 것; 도움. ¶ *He is the* ~ *of his old father.* 그는 늙은 아버지가 의지하는 아들이다. **4** 《Brit.》 a forked support for an oar of a rowboat. (보트의) 크러치; 노받이. [E.]

crutched [krʌtʃt] *adj.* **1** supported on crutches. 목발에 의지한. **2** [krʌ́tʃid] wearing a cross. 십자가를 단〔걸어 놓은〕.

crux [krʌks] *n.* Ⓒ (*pl.* **crux·es** or **cru·ces**) **1** the most important point. 가장 중요한〔근본적인, 결정적인〕 점. **2** a difficult point to explain; a hard question. 난점; 난문제. **3** a cross. 십자가. **4** 《*the C-*》 the Southern Cross. 남십자성. [L.=cross]

:cry [krai] *v.* (**cried**) *vt., vi.* (P6,7,11,13,14, 18; 1,2A,3) **1** speak in a loud voice; shout; call out. 부르짖다; 외치다; 소리쳐 부르다. ¶ ~ *in anger* 〔*surprise*〕 성이 나서〔놀라서〕 소리치다 / ~ *for* 〔*with*〕 *joy* 기뻐서 외치다 / ~ *with pain* 아파 소리를 지르다 / *'No!'*

he cried. '안 돼!' 하고 그는 외쳤다. **2** ⓐ weep; sob; shed tears (sometimes silently); mourn. (소리내어) 울다; 눈물을 흘리다; 한탄하다. ¶ ~ *over one's misfortune* 불운을 한탄하다 / *The toy broke and she began to* ~. 장난감이 망가지자 그녀는 울기 시작했다. ⓑ bring to a certain state by weeping. 울어서 …상태로 하다. ¶ ~ *oneself blind* 눈이 퉁퉁 붓도록 울다 / ~ *oneself to sleep* (어린 아이 등이) 울다가 잠들다. **3** announce (something) for sale; make (somthing) known by calling out. …을 외치며 팔다; …을 큰 소리로 알리다. ¶ ~ *one's wares* 〔*goods*〕 *for sale* 상품을 소리쳐 팔다 / ~ *the news all over the town* 그 소식을 온 마을에 소리쳐 알리다. **4** 《*lit.*》 beg or plead for; implore. …을 요구하다; 탄원〔애원〕하다. ¶ ~ *quarter* (포로 따위가) 살려 달라고 애걸하다 / ~ (*someone*) *mercy* 〔*pardon*〕 (아무에게) 자비〔용서〕를 빌다.

cry against, denounce. …을 비난하다.

cry back to, **a**) turn back to. …에 되돌아가다. **b**) revert to. …에 격세 유전을 하다.

cry down, **a**) speak of (something) as unimportant or less valuable; decry; make little of; disparage. …을 나쁘게 말하다; 깎아내리다; 경시(輕視)하다. ¶ ~ *down a new theory* 새 이론을 내리깎다. **b**) silence or put down by cries. 야유를 퍼부어 말을 못하게 하다. ¶ *The audience cried him down.* 청중은 그에게 야유를 퍼부어 강연을 계속 못하게 했다.

cry one's eyes out, **a**) weep very bitterly. 몹시 울다. **b**) have one's eyes swollen with tears. 눈이 퉁퉁 붓도록 울다.

cry for, **a**) demand loudly; need greatly. …을 소리 높이 요구하다; 크게 필요로 하다. ¶ ~ *for a raise in wage* 봉급 인상을 목청 높이 요구하다. **b**) want to get (something) earnestly. …을 갈망하다. ¶ ~ *for the moon* 얻을 수 없는 것을 갖고 싶어하다; 없는 것을 떼쓰다.

cry for company, cry in sympathy or imitation. 같이 울어주다; 덩달아 울다.

cry halves, demand a share. 절반의 몫을 요구하다.

cry one's heart out, weep bitterly. 하염 없이 울다.

cry off, refuse to carry out (a promise or undertaking); break off; decline after having made a commitment. (…을) 거절〔취소〕하다; (…에서) 손을 떼다. ¶ *He tried to* ~ *off at the last moment, but we held him to his promise.* 그는 마지막 순간에 발을 빼려고 했으나 우리는 그의 약속에 책임을 지라고 했다.

cry out, **a**) exclaim; speak loudly; shout. 큰 소리로 말하다; 소리치다; 외치다. **b**) 《*against*》 protest; warn. 소리 높이 항의하다; 경고〔충고〕하다. ¶ ~ *out against war* 전쟁 반대를 소리 높이 외치다.

cry shame upon, denounce; disparage. …을 비난하다; 매도하다.

cry stinking fish, depreciate one's own wares. 자기 물건을 깎아내리다〔헐뜯다〕.

cry to, call upon for help. …에게 도움을 청하다; 울며 매달리다. ¶ ~ *to God* 신의 가호를 청하다 / ~ *to someone for help* 도와달라고 아무에게 울며 매달리다.

cry up, praise highly. 크게 칭찬하다. ¶ ~ *up a new book* 신간서를 칭찬하다.

cry wolf, raise a false alarm. 거짓 경고를 말하다.

— *n.* Ⓒ (*pl.* **cries**) **1** a loud or passionate voice; a shout; a call. 외치는 소리; 울음 소리. ¶ *a* ~ *for help* 살려달라고 외치는 소리 / *give* 〔*utter, raise*〕 *a* ~ *of triumph* 승리의 환성을 지르다. **2** the act of weeping. 큰 소리로 욺. ¶ *I want to have a good* ~. 실컷 울고 싶다. **3** an advertisement by calling. 외쳐대며 파는 소리. **4** a public voice; a rumor. 여론; 소문. ¶ *a* ~ *for reform* 〔*against a measure*〕 개혁 요구 〔법안 반대〕의 여론. **5** an appeal; an entreaty. 탄원; 애원. ¶ *be deaf to someone's cries* 아무의 탄원에 귀를 기울이지 않다. **6** a political or party phrase; a slogan. 표어; 슬로건. **7** a battle cry. 함성. **8** a pack of hounds; a party. 한 떼의 사냥개; 한 떼. [L. *quirito* cry]

a hue and cry, **a**) pursuit. 추적. **b**) an expression of public anger. 여론의 노호(怒號).

all cry and no wool, much effort with little result; much ado about nothing. 헛수고; 헛소동; 태산 명동 서일필.

follow in the cry, follow the lead. 부화 뇌동(附和雷同)하다.

in full cry, **a**) (of dogs) going after a hunted animal and making much noise; in hot pursuit. (사냥개가) 맹렬히 추격하여. ¶ *The pack followed in full* ~. 사냥개들은 쏜살같이 뒤따라 갔다. **b**) in full force; all together. 전원이 달라 붙어; 일제히.

much cry and little wool = all cry and no wool.

out of cry, faraway off; out of hearing; beyond one's reach. 멀리; 들리지 않는 곳에; 손이 미치지 않는 곳에.

within cry (of), near enough to hear. (…에서) 부르면 들리는 곳에; 가까이.

cry·ba·by [kráibèibi] *n.* Ⓒ (*pl.* **-bies**) a person who cries easily for very little reason. 울보; 우지.

cry·ing [kráiiŋ] *adj.* **1** that cries; weeping. 우는; 울부짖는; 외치는. **2** calling for attention; urgent; very bad. 긴급한; 심한; 지독한. ¶ *a* ~ *need* 〔*want*〕 긴급한 일; 급무 / *a* ~ *evil* 심한 폐해 / *The state of roads is a* ~ *shame.* 도로 상태는 말이 아니다.

crypt [kript] *n.* Ⓒ **1** a room under the main floor of a church, frequently used for graves. (교회당의) 지하실. **2** 《anat.》 a secreting cavity. 선와(腺窩). [Gk. *kruptō* hide]

cryp·tic [kríptik], **-ti·cal** [-tikəl] *adj.* **1**

hidden; secret. 숨은; 비밀의. ¶ *a ~ writing* 비밀 문서. **2** mysterious. 신비한; 불가해한. ¶ *a ~ message* 〔*remark*〕 수수께끼 같은 전언(傳言)〔말〕. **3** 《zool.》 apt to conceal; suitable for concealing. 몸을 숨기기에 적합한. ¶ *~ color*〔*coloring*〕 은폐〔보호〕색. ● **cryp·ti·cal·ly** [-kəli] *adv.*

cryp·to·gam [kríptougæ̀m] *n.* any of the flowerless and seedless plants like mosses. 민꽃〔은화〕 식물. [→crypt]

cryp·to·gram [kríptougræ̀m] *n.* secret writing. 암호문(文).

cryp·to·graph [kríptougræ̀f, -grɑ̀:f] *n.* **1** = cryptogram. **2** a system of secret writing. 암호 서기법(書記法).

cryp·to·me·ri·a [krìptəmíəriə] *n.* 《bot.》 a genus of Japanese evergreen trees of pine family. 삼나무.

***crys·tal** [krístl] *n.* **1** Ⓤ a hard mineral (quartz) that is clear like glass. 수정; 석영. ¶ *(as) clear as ~* 수정처럼 투명한〔맑은〕. **2** Ⓒ a piece of crystal shaped into an ornament. 수정 제품. ¶ *a necklace of crystals* 수정 목걸이. **3** Ⓤ glass of a very superior clearness, used for making table articles; glassware made of this glass. 크리스털 유리; 크리스털 유리로 만든 식기류. ¶ *silver and ~* 은 식기와 유리 식기. **4** Ⓒ 《U.S.》 a glass cover over a watch dial. 시계 유리. **5** Ⓒ 《chem.》 a solid body formed of angles and flat surfaces. 결정(체). ¶ *crystals of snow* 눈의 결정. **6** Ⓒ 《wireless》 a piece of quartz used in a radio. (라디오의) 검파용(檢波用) 광석. ¶ *a ~ detector* 광석 검파기 / *a ~ set* 광석 라디오. **7** Ⓒ a ball of crystal used by fortune-tellers to foresee future events. (점치는 데 쓰는) 수정 구슬.

— *adj.* **1** made of crystal. 수정제(製)의. **2** like crystal; clear as crystal. 수정 같은; 수정 같이 투명한. ¶ *a ~ lake* 수정 같이 맑은 호수 / *~ glass* 무색 투명한 유리. [Gk.]

crystal gàzing [ㄴ-ㄴ-] *n.* the method of foreseeing future events by looking into a crystal ball. 수정(水晶)점.

crys·tal·line [krístəlin, -təlàin] *adj.* **1** consisting of or like crystal. 수정으로 되어 있는; 수정 같은. ¶ *the ~ lens* (눈알의) 수정체. **2** very clear; transparent; of or of the nature of a crystal or crystals. 투명한; 결정성의.

crys·tal·li·za·tion [krìstəlizéiʃən] *n.* **1** Ⓤ the act or process of crystallizing. 결정화(結晶化). **2** Ⓒ a crystallized form. 결정(체).

crys·tal·lize, 《Brit.》 **-lise** [krístəlàiz] *vt.* (P6) **1** form (something) into crystals. …을 결정(結晶)시키다. ¶ *crystallized sugar* 얼음 사탕. **2** give a definite form to (a plan, an idea, etc.). (계획·사상 따위)를 구체화시키다. **3** coat (fruits, etc.) with sugar. …을 설탕절임으로 하다. ¶ *crystallized fruits* 설탕절임한 과일.

— *vi.* (P1,3) **1** form into crystals. 결정하다. ¶ *Honey crystallizes if kept too long.* 꿀은 너무 오래 저장하면 결정한다. **2** 《fig.》 《into》 form into a definite shape. 구체화하다; 뚜렷한 형태를 갖추다. ¶ *Her vague idea crystallized into a definite plan.* 그녀의 막연한 생각이 뚜렷한 계획으로 되었다 / *His plans crystallized into action.* 그의 계획은 행동으로 구체화되었다.

Cu 《chem.》 cuprum (L. =copper).

cu. cubic.

cub [kʌb] *n.* Ⓒ **1** a young fox, bear, lion, tiger, etc. (여우·곰·사자·호랑이 따위의) 새끼. ¶ *a lion ~.* **2** a rough or awkward boy. 버릇 없는 사내아이; 선머슴. ¶ *a ~ reporter* 햇병아리 기자 / *an unlicked ~* 버릇 없는 아이〔젊은이〕. — *vi., vt.* (P1; 6) bring forth. 새끼를 낳다. [E. *cubbe* young fox]

Cu·ba [kjú:bə] *n.* a republic on the largest island in the West Indies. 쿠바. 參考 수도는 Havana.

Cu·ban [kjú:bən] *adj.* of Cuba or its people. 쿠바의; 쿠바 사람의. — *n.* Ⓒ a person of Cuba. 쿠바 사람.

cub·by [kʌ́bi] *n.* =cubbyhole.

cub·by·hole [kʌ́bihòul] *n.* a very small room; a snug place. 아주 작은 방; 아늑한 곳. ¶ *She works in a little ~ at the end of corridor.* 그녀는 복도 끝의 작은 방에서 일하고 있다. [E.]

***cube** [kju:b] *n.* **1** Ⓒ a solid figure with six equal, square faces. 입방체; 정육면체. **2** Ⓒ anything like a cube; a block of stone for paving. 입방체의 것; 포장(鋪裝) 블록〔벽돌〕. ¶ *a ~ sugar* 각사탕 / *an ice ~* (냉장고에서 만든) 각빙. **3** Ⓤ 《math.》 the product that results when a number is multiplied by itself twice; the 3rd power. 3제곱; 입방. ¶ *The ~ of 3 is 27.* 3의 세 제곱은 27이다 / *The ~ root of 27 is 3.* 27의 입방근(根)은 3이다.

— *vt.* (P6) **1** make or form (something) into the shape of a cube. …을 입방체로 하다. **2** find the cube of (a number). 3제곱하다. ¶ *2 cubed is 8.* 2의 3제곱은 8이다 / *If you ~ 10, the result is 1,000.* 10을 3제곱하면 1,000이 된다. **3** pave with cubes. …에 포장 블록〔벽돌〕을 깔다. **4** cut (vegetables) into cubes. (무 따위)를 주사위 모양으로 썰다〔자르다〕. [Gk.]

cu·bic [kjú:bik] *adj.* **1** shaped like a cube. 입방체의. **2** having length, breadth and height. 입방의; 3제곱의. ¶ *the ~ content* 용적; 부피 / *a ~ foot,* 1입방 피트 / *a ~ equation,* 3차 방정식. [↑]

cu·bi·cal [kjú:bikəl] *adj.* =cubic.

cu·bi·cle [kjú:bikl] *n.* Ⓒ a very small room esp. a bedroom, in a dormitory. (칸막이가 된) 작은 침실. [L. *cubo* lie]

cub·ism [kjú:bizəm] *n.* Ⓤ 《art》 a school of modern art in which objects are shown as cubes and other geometrical forms. 입체파(派). [→cube]

cub·ist [kjú:bist] *n.* Ⓒ an artist who practises cubism. 입체파의 예술가.

cu·bit [kjú:bit] *n.* Ⓒ an ancient measure of length, about 18 to 22 inches, originally the length from the elbow to the tip of the middle finger. 큐빗; 완척(腕尺)《고대의 척도》. [→cube]

cuck·old [kʌ́kəld] *n.* a husband of an unfaithful wife. 오쟁이진 남편; 부정한 여자의 남편. — *vt.* (P6) make a cuckold of. (남편)을 속여 서방질하다. ● **cuck·old·ry** [kʌ́kəldri] *n.* [↓]

·**cuck·oo** [kú(:)ku:] *n.* Ⓒ (*pl.* **cuck·oos**) **1** a bird whose call sounds like its name. 뻐꾸기. **2** a cry of this bird. 뻐꾸기의 울음소리. **3** 《*sl.*》 a fool. 바보; 얼뜨기. — *adj.* 《*sl.*》 crazy; silly. 미친; 어리석은. [Imit.]

cuckoo clock [ㅗ-ㅗ] *n.* a clock which marks the hour by the call and the movement of a toy cuckoo. 뻐꾹 시계.

cuck·oo·flow·er [kú(:)ku:flàuər] *n.* 《bot.》 a meadow plant. 황새냉이.

cuck·oo·pint [kú(:)ku:pìnt] *n.* 《bot.》 a wild arum. 천남성.

cu·cum·ber [kjú:kəmbər] *n.* Ⓒ 《bot.》 a vegetable that has a long green fruit, eaten in salads and as pickles. 오이. [L. *cucumis*]

(**as**) ***cool as a cucumber,*** very cool; calm; not excited. 극히 냉정한.

cud [kʌd] *n.* Ⓤ food which some animals, like cows, bring back into the mouth from the first stomach and chew slowly again. (반추동물의) 새김질거리. [E.]

chew the cud, **a**) bring back from the stomach and chew a second time. 새김질[반추]하다. **b**) 《*fig.*》 think over and over again; reflect. 곰곰 생각하다; 되씹어보다; 반성하다.

cud·dle [kʌ́dl] *vt.* (P6) hold closely and tenderly; embrace lovingly. …을 꼭 껴안다. ¶ ~ *a baby* 아기를 꼭 껴안다. — *vi.* (P2A) lie close and comfortable; lie curled. 꼭 붙어 자다; 서로 부둥켜 안다; 웅크리고 자다.

***cuddle up* [*together*],** lie closely and comfortably together. 꼭 붙어 자다[눕다]. ¶ *Two kittens cuddled together on a sofa.* 두 새끼 고양이는 소파 위에 꼭 붙어 자고 있었다.

— *n.* Ⓤ an act of cuddling; a hug. 껴안음; 포옹. ¶ *have a bit of* ~ 서로 꼭 껴안다. [M.E. *cuthen* make familiar]

cud·dle·some [kʌ́dlsəm] *adj.* suitable for cuddling; tempting to cuddle; lovable. 꼭 껴안고 싶은; 귀여운.

cud·dly [kʌ́dli] *adj.* =cuddlesome.

cud·dy [kʌ́di] *n.* Ⓒ (*pl.* **-dies**) a donkey; a stupid person. 당나귀; 바보.

cudg·el [kʌ́dʒəl] *n.* Ⓒ a short, heavy stick used as a weapon; a club. 곤봉; 몽둥이. ¶ ~ *play* 봉술(棒術) 시합.

take up the cudgels for, strongly defend. …을 감연히 변호하다.

— *vt.* (P6) beat (something or someone) with a cudgel. …을 곤봉으로[몽둥이로] 때리다. ¶ *They cudgeled the dogs to death.* 그들은 개를 몽둥이로 때려 죽였다. [E.]

cudgel one's brains, 《*fig.*》 force oneself to think hard. 머리를 짜다; 골똘히 생각하다. ¶ *We cudgeled our brains to remember the lost address.* 잊은 주소를 기억해 내려고 우리는 머리를 짰다.

cud·weed [kʌ́dwì:d] *n.* 《bot.》 a woolly herb. 떡쑥속(屬)의 식물. [E.]

cue[1] [kju:] *n.* Ⓒ **1** a hint; a suggestion. 암시; 힌트; 지시; 실마리. ¶ *give someone his* [*the*] ~ 아무에게 암시[힌트]를 주다 / *take one's* ~ *from someone* 아무에게서 힌트를 얻다. **2** the last words of an actor serving as a sign to the next actor to speak, act or enter. 큐《대사의 마지막 말. 다음 배우의 등장·연기의 신호가 됨》; 계기. **3** the part that an actor is to play. 역할. **4** 《*arch.*》 a mood; a frame of mind. 기분. ¶ *be in good* ~ 기분이 좋다. [*Q* of L. *Quando* when]

cue[2] [kju:] *n.* Ⓒ **1** a long stick used for striking the ball in billiards. (당구의) 큐. **2** a queue. 변발(辮髮). [L *cauda* tail]

stand in cue, queue up. 줄을 서다[짓다].

·**cuff**[1] [kʌf] *n.* Ⓒ **1** a wristband of shirts, coats, etc. 커프스; 소맷부리. **2** 《U.S.》 a fold around the bottom of a trouser leg. (접어젖힌 바지의) 아랫단(=《Brit.》 turn-up). [M.E. =hand-covering]

cuff[2] [kʌf] *vt.* (P6,13) strike (esp. on the head or face) with the open hand. 손바닥으로 때리다. ¶ ~ *a boy on the head* 손바닥으로 아이의 머리를 때리다. — *n.* a blow, esp. on the head, given with the open hand. (특히 머리를) 손바닥으로 때리기. ¶ *be at cuffs with* …와 주먹다짐하다. [Sw. *kuffa* strike]

cuffs and kicks, assaults. 폭행.

cuff link [ㅗ ㅗ] *n.* one of a pair of linked buttons for fastening a shirt cuff. 커프스 단추.

cu. in. cubic inch.

cui·rass [kwirǽs] *n.* a piece of armor covering the breast and back. (가슴 부위를 보호하는) 갑옷, 흉갑(胸甲). [L. *corium* leather]

cui·ras·sier [kwìrəsíər] *n.* a horse-soldier wearing a cuirass. 갑기병(甲騎兵).

cui·sine [kwizí:n] *n.* 《F.》 **1** ⓊⒸ the manner or style of cooking; the food prepared, as at a restaurant. 요리법; 요리. **2** Ⓒ the kitchen or the cooking department. 주방; 조리장. [→cook]

cul-de-sac [kʌ́ldəsæ̀k, kúl-] *n.* 《F.》 Ⓒ **1** a street or lane open at only one end; a blind alley. 막다른 골목(길). **2** 《*fig.*》 a situation from which there is no escape; a trap. (피할 길 없는) 궁지. [F. =bottom of a bag]

cu·li·nar·y [kʌ́lənèri, kjú:- / -nəri] *adj.* of cooking or the kitchen. 요리의; 주방(용)의. ¶ *the ~ art* 요리법 / *~ vegetables* 야채류; 푸성귀. [L. *culina* kitchen]

cull [kʌl] *vt.* (P6) pick out (flowers, etc.); choose and gather; make selections out of (something). (꽃)을 따다; 골라[뽑아] 모으다; 가려내다; 발췌하다. ¶ *extracts culled from American writers* 미국 작가로부터의 발췌 / *~ the choicest lines from poems* 시에서 가장 잘 된 시구(詩句)를 발췌하다. —*n.* Ⓒ 《usu. *pl.*》 **1** something picked out as being poor or worthless. (좋지 않은 것으로) 가려낸 것. **2** 《*sl.*》 a dupe. 바보; 얼간이. [→collect]

cul·len·der [kʌ́ləndər] *n.* =colander.

culm [kʌlm] *n.* Ⓤ **1** coal dust. 분탄(粉炭). **2** hard coal of poor quality. 저질 무연탄. [E.]

cul·mi·nate [kʌ́lmənèit] *vi.* (P1,3) **1** 《*in*》 reach the highest point or degree; reach a climax; result. 극점[절정]에 달하다; 전성을 극하다; 결국 …이 되다. ¶ *Her jealousy culminated in murder.* 그녀의 질투는 마침내 살인으로 끝났다 / *Animal life culminates in man.* 동물은 최고도로 발달하여 인간이 된다 / *a series of minor clashes culminating in full-scale war* 전면전으로 치닫는 일련의 국지적 충돌. **2** (of the sun, etc.) reach the meridian. 남중(南中)하다. [L. *culmen* top]

cul·mi·na·tion [kʌ̀lmənéiʃən] *n.* **1** Ⓒ the highest point or position reached; the climax. 최고점[조]; 절정; 정상; 극점. **2** Ⓤ the reaching of the highest point. 전성; 극치. ¶ *The discovery was the ~ of his life's work.* 그 발견은 그의 필생의 사업에서의 극치였다.

cu·lottes [kju:láts / -lɔ́ts] *n. pl.* 《F.》 women's trousers cut to resemble skirts. 퀼로트; 치마바지.

cul·pa·ble [kʌ́lpəbl] *adj.* deserving blame; guilty. 비난받아 마땅한; 유죄의. ¶ *The policeman was dismissed for ~ neglect of duty.* 경찰관은 직무 태만죄로 파면되었다. [L. *culpo* blame]

cul·pa·bly [kʌ́lpəbli] *adv.* in a culpable manner. 발칙하게(도); 무도하게.

cul·prit [kʌ́lprit] *n.* Ⓒ **1** a guilty person; an offender. 죄인; 범인. **2** a person who is accused of a crime; a prisoner in court. 범죄 혐의자; 피고인. [→culpable]

cult [kʌlt] *n.* Ⓒ **1** a system of religious worship. (종교적) 의식; 제식(祭式). **2** great admiration or devotion for a person, or thing, esp. for only a short time; worship; craze; a fashion. 숭배; (일시적인) 열광; …열(熱); 유행. ¶ *a ~ of Napoleon* 나폴레옹 예찬 / *an idolatrous ~* 우상 숭배 / *the ~ of baseball* 야구열. **3** 《*collectively*》 a group of persons showing such admiration. 숭배[예찬]자의 무리[집단]. ¶ *the ~ of Keats* 키츠 예찬자들. [L. *colo* cultivate]

:cul·ti·vate [kʌ́ltəvèit] *vt.* (P6) **1** prepare and work on (land, etc.) for growing crops; 《U.S.》 loosen the soil around (growing plants). …을 갈다; 경작하다; (재배중인 작물 주위)를 사이갈이하다. ¶ *~ the soil* 땅을 갈다. **2** help (plants, etc.) grow by giving labor and care. (초목)을 재배하다; 양식하다. **3** ⓐ improve; develop (one's ability, etc.) by education or training. (교육·훈련으로 재능 따위)를 기르다; 교화하다; 함양[도야]하다. ¶ *~ one's mind* 정신을 도야하다 / *~ a moral conscience* 도덕적 양심을 기르다 / *~ a knowledge of music* 음악에 대한 지식을 기르다. ⓑ devote oneself to (something). …에 몰두[전념]하다. ¶ *~ a hobby* 취미에 몰두하다. **4** seek the acquaintance or friendship of (someone). …와의 면식을[교제, 친교를] 구하다. ¶ *~ someone's acquaintance [friendship]* 아무와의 교제를 구하다 / *~ the society of someone* 아무와 친해지고 싶어하다. [L. *colo*]

cul·ti·va·ted [kʌ́ltəvèitid] *adj.* **1** prepared for growing crops. 경작[개간]된(opp. native). ¶ *~ land* 경지(耕地). **2** grown with human care; not wild. 재배된(opp. wild). **3** 《*fig.*》 educated; cultured; refined. 교양 있는; 세련된. ¶ *~ taste* 세련된 취미 / *a ~ man* / *a ~ audience* 교양 있는 청중.

•cul·ti·va·tion [kʌ̀ltəvéiʃən] *n.* Ⓤ **1** the process or art of cultivating the soil and its products. 경작; 재배; 양식; 경작 상태. ¶ *the ~ of oysters* 굴 양식 / *bring waste land under ~* 황무지를 개간하다. **2** 《*fig.*》 improvement of the mind; development of the body. 함양; 수양; 도야; 수련. **3** 《*fig.*》 culture; refinement. 교양; 세련.

cul·ti·va·tor [kʌ́ltəvèitər] *n.* Ⓒ **1** a person or thing that cultivates. 경작자; 경작하는 것; 재배자; 양식자. **2** a tool or machine used to loosen the soil and dig up weeds around growing plants. 경운기.

•cul·tur·al [kʌ́ltʃərəl] *adj.* of culture. 배양의; 교양의; 문화의. ¶ *a ~ film* 문화 영화 / *Literature, art, and, music are ~ studies.* 문학, 미술 및 음악은 교양 과목이다. [culture]

cultural anthropology [ˊ---ˋ--ˊ--] *n.* the scientific study of primitive peoples through their languages, behaviors, etc. 문화인류학 (cf. *physical anthropology*).

cultural lag [ˊ--- ˊ] *n.* slowness in development in respect to another part. 문화적 지체[후진].

•cul·ture [kʌ́ltʃər] *n.* **1** Ⓤ the development of the mind or body by education, training, etc. 수양; 교화(敎化); 훈련. ¶ *the ~ of mind and body* 심신의 수양. **2** Ⓤ the result of the careful training of the mind, training in manners, etc.; refinement. 교양; 세련. ¶ *a man of ~* 교양 있는 사람. **3** ⓊⒸ the sum total of the ways of living built up by a race of people; the state of cultivation among a group of

people. 문화. ¶ *Greek* ~ 그리스 문화. **4** Ⓤ the cultivation of land. (땅의) 경작. **5** ⓊⒸ ⓐ the rearing of plants. 재배. ¶ *the* ~ *of cotton* 면화 재배. ⓑ the proper care given to the production of bees, fish, silk, or germs. 양식(養殖)《양봉, 양어, 세균 배양 등》. ¶ *the* ~ *of silk* 양잠.
— *vt.* (P6) cultivate. …을 재배하다; 배양하다. [L. *colo* cultivate]

culture complex [∠-∠-] *n.* a group of culture traits. 문화 복합체.

cul·tured [kʌ́ltʃərd] *adj.* **1** having or showing culture; educated; refined. 교양 있는; 문화가 있는; 세련된. ¶ *a* ~ *state* 문화 국가 / *a* ~ *person* 교양 있는 사람. **2** produced or grown under artificial conditions. 배양된; 양식된. ¶ ~ *pearls* 양식 진주 / ~ *bacteria* 배양된 균.

culture hero [∠-∠-] *n.* a mythical figure being considered to have furnished a people with the means of existence, as Prometheus who stole fire from the gods. (신화상의) 문화.

cul·vert [kʌ́lvərt] *n.* Ⓒ a small channel or passage for water crossing under a road or railroad. (철도·도로 따위 밑의) 암거(暗渠); 지하 수로. [Person]

cum [kʌm] *prep.* 《L.》 with. …이 붙은, 딸린. ¶ *one's garage-cum-workshop* 작업장이 딸린 차고(車庫).

Cumb. Cumberland.

cum·ber [kʌ́mbər] *vt.* (P13) burden; trouble; hinder; make it impossible for (someone or something) to come in or go out; block up. …을 곤란케 하다; 괴롭히다; 방해하다; 막다. ¶ ~ *oneself with* …로 고생하다; 애먹다 / *The man's heavy boots cumbered him in walking.* 사나이의 무거운 장화가 걷는 데 거치적거렸다 / *She was cumbered with household cares.* 그녀는 살림살이가 힘에 겨웠다. — *n.* Ⓒ hindrance. 방해. [→cumulus]

cum·ber·land [kʌ́mbərlənd] *n.* a former county of northwestern England, now part of Cumbria county. 잉글랜드 북서부의 옛 주(州).

cum·ber·some [kʌ́mbərsəm] *adj.* difficult to deal with or move; burdensome; troublesome; badly made. 다루기 힘든; 성가신; 볼품 없는. ¶ *Old-time armor was* ~. 옛 갑주는 볼품이 없었다 / 《*fig.*》 *the firm's* ~ *salary system* 회사의 골치 아픈 봉급 체계. [*cumber*]

cum·brous [kʌ́mbrəs] *adj.* =cumbersome.

cum dividend [∠∠--] *adv., adj.* with dividend. 배당부(配當附)로[의]. 参考 cum div. 로 생략함.

cum·in, cum·min [kʌ́min] *n.* 《bot.》 a plant with aromatic seeds. 커민《미나리과의 식물》. [Gk.]

cum lau·de [kʌm lɔ́ːdi, -láudə] *adv., adj.* 《L.》 with praise or honors. 우등으로[의].

cum·mer·bund [kʌ́mərbʌ̀nd] *n.* a waist sash. 넓은 허리 띠. [Hind.]

cum·quat [kʌ́mkwɑt / -kwɔt] *n.* 《bot.》 a small orange-like fruit. 금귤(의 열매). [Chin.]

cu·mu·late [kjúːmjəlit, -lèit] *v.* 《rare》 =accumulate.

cu·mu·la·tive [kjúːmjəlèitiv, -lət-] *adj.* growing by successive additions; heaped up; gathered together. 축적한; 누진(累進)하는; 점증적인. ¶ ~ *evidence* [*proof*] 중복 증거[입증] / *the* ~ *effect of more evidence* 보다 많은 증거에 의한 누적(累積) 효과 / ~ *voting* 누적 투표. [L. *cumulus* heap]

cu·mu·li [kjúːmjəlai] *n.* pl. of **cumulus.**

cu·mu·lus [kjúːmjələs] *n.* Ⓒ (*pl.* **cu·mu·li**) **1** a heap; a mound. 퇴적; 누적(累積). **2** ⓊⒸ a cloud with a flat base and rounded masses often piled up like a mountain. 뭉게구름; 적운(積雲). [→cumulative]

cu·ne·i·form [kjúːniəfɔ̀ːrm, kjuːníːə-] *adj.* shaped like an arrowhead, as the characters in the writing of the ancient Persians, the Babylonians, etc; wedge-shaped. (문자가) 쐐기 모양의. ¶ ~ *characters* 설형(楔形) 문자. — *n.* Ⓒ such a written character. 설형 문자. ¶ *a text written in* ~ 설형 문자로 쓰인 원문. [L. *cuneus* wedge]

cun·ni·lin·gus [kʌ̀nilíŋgəs] *n.* oral stimulation of clitoris or vulva. (입술·혀에 의한) 여성 성기의 자극. [L.]

:cun·ning [kʌ́niŋ] *adj.* **1** clever in deceiving; crafty; sly. 교활한; 간사한. ¶ *a* ~ *villain* 간사한 악당 / (*as*) ~ *as a fox* 여우처럼 교활한. **2** 《*arch.*》 skillful; clever in doing. 교묘한; 솜씨 좋은. ¶ *a* ~ *toy* 교묘한 장난감 / *With* ~ *hand he shaped the little pieces.* 그는 교묘한 솜씨로 작은 물건들을 만들었다. **3** 《U.S. *colloq.*》 pretty and lovable; attractive. 귀여운; 매력적인. ¶ *What a* ~ *baby!* 정말 귀여운 아기야. — *n.* Ⓤ **1** cleverness at deceiving. 교활함. ¶ *Some animals have a great deal of* ~. 어떤 동물들은 잔꾀가 많다. **2** 《*arch.*》 skill; dexterity. 숙련; 솜씨 좋음; 교묘함. ¶ *My hand has lost its* ~. 나의 손은 숙련도를 잃었다. [→can[1]]

cun·ning·ly [kʌ́niŋli] *adv.* in a cunning manner; cleverly; artfully. 교활하게; 교묘히.

cunt [kʌnt] *n.* 《*vulg.*》 the vulva; a woman regarded as a sexual object. (여성의) 외음부; (성적인 대상으로서의) 여자. [G.]

:cup [kʌp] *n.* Ⓒ **1** a small drinking vessel with a handle. (커피·홍차용의) 찻잔; 술잔; 컵. ¶ *a coffee* ~ 커피 잔 / *a* ~ *and saucer* 접시에 받친 찻잔. **2** as much as a cup holds; a cupful. 한 잔[컵] 그득(한 양). ¶ *a* ~ *of tea* (홍)차 한 잔 / *three cups of flour* 밀가루 3컵 / *half a* ~ *of milk* 반 잔(분)의 밀크 / *drink* [*take*] *two cups of coffee* 커피 두 잔을 마시다 / *add one* ~ *of sugar to* …에 설탕을 한 컵 넣다. **3** a large silver or gold vessel given to the winner in games. 상배(賞杯); 우승배[컵]. ¶ *win the* ~ 우승하다. **4** an object shaped like a cup. 잔 모양의 것. ⓐ a hollow in the ground; a valley with hills around it. (지면의) 우묵한 곳; (산으로 둘러 싸인) 계곡; 골짜기. ⓑ 《bot.》 the calyx of a flower. 꽃받침. ⓒ the woody outer case of an acorn. 깍정이; 각두(殼斗). ⓓ 《anat.》 the socket of certain bones. 배상와(杯狀窩). **5** 《*the* ~ or *pl.*》 wine; drinking. 포도주; 술; 음주. ¶ *talk over one's cups* 술을 마시며 이야기하다 / *be fond of the* ~ 술을 좋아하다. **6** 《*fig.*》 fate; that which we must receive or suffer. 운명; (인생의) 경험; 체험. ¶ *drink a bitter* ~ 고배를 들다; 쓰디 쓴 경험을 하다 / *drain* 〔*drink*〕 *the* ~ *of life to the bottom* 〔*the dregs*〕 인생의 쓴맛 단맛을 다 맛보다 / *drain* 〔*drink up*〕 *the* ~ *of humiliation* 지독한 굴욕을 당하다 / *His* ~ *of happiness* 〔*misery*〕 *was full.* 그의 행복〔비참함〕은 그 극에 달했다. **7** 《religion》 (성체 성사의) 성배(聖杯); 성찬배(聖餐杯).

a cup too low, depressed; gloomy. 우울하여.

One's cup is full. One is exceedingly happy or sad. 행복〔슬픔〕의 절정에 있다.

in one's cups, drunk. 얼근히 취해.

the cups that cheer but not inebriate, cups of tea. (홍)차의 별칭.

— *vt.* (**cupped, cup·ping**) (P6) **1** form (something) in the shape of a cup. …을 찻종 모양으로 하다. ¶ ~ *one's hands to catch a ball* 공을 잡으려고 손을 우묵하게 하다. **2** take or put (something) in a cup. …을 찻종〔컵〕으로 받다〔뜨다〕. ¶ ~ *water from a stream* 시내에서 찻종〔컵〕으로 물을 떠내다. **3** 《med.》 extract blood from by means of a cupping glass. (환자에게) 흡각을 대어 피를 뽑다. [→cupola]

cup·bear·er [kʌ́pbὲərər] *n.* a person who fills and hands round the cups. (귀족 연회 등에서) 술잔을 따라 돌리는 사람.

***cup·board** [kʌ́bərd] *n.* Ⓒ a piece of furniture with shelves used for storing dishes, food, etc. 찬장.

cry cupboard, cry that one is hungry; cry for food. 배고프다고 소리치다.

cupboard love [ˊ-ˊ] *n.* a show of love in order to get sweets or food. 타산적인 애정.

***cup·ful** [kʌ́pfùl] *n.* Ⓒ as much as a cup can hold; (in cooking) half a pint. 찻종〔컵〕 하나 그득(한 양); (요리에서) 1파인트의 반.

Cu·pid [kjúːpid] *n.* **1** 《Rom. myth.》 the god of love, the son of Venus. 큐피드《사랑의 신》(Gk. myth. *Eros*). **2** Ⓒ 《*c-*》 a picture or statue of a winged baby, used as a symbol of love; a representation of Cupid. 큐피드의 그림〔상(像)〕《날개 달린 아기로서 사랑의 상징》; 사랑의 사자. [L. *cupio* long for]

cu·pid·i·ty [kjuːpídəti] *n.* Ⓤ eager desire, esp. for wealth; greed. 탐욕; 강한 욕심. [↑]

cu·po·la [kjúːpələ] *n.* Ⓒ **1** a small dome on a building; a small tower built on top of a roof or building. 둥근 지붕〔천장〕; 돔. **2** a furnace for melting iron. 용광로(鎔鑛爐). **3** 《naut.》 a dome-shaped revolving turret. 선회 포탑(砲塔). [L. *cupa* cask]

cup·ping [kʌ́piŋ] *n.* 《med.》 the former process of drawing blood to the surface of the skin by creating a vaccum at that point. 흡각법(吸角法). [→cup]

cu·pre·ous [kjúːpriəs] *adj.* of or like copper. 구리〔동(銅)〕의; 구리 같은. [→copper]

cu·pric [kjúːprik] *adj.* containing copper. 구리를〔동(銅)을〕 함유하는. ¶ ~ *oxide* 산화 제2구리. [↑]

cu·prous [kjúːprəs] *adj.* 《chem.》 containing copper as a univalent element. 제1구리의. ¶ ~ *oxide* 산화 제1구리. [↑]

cu·prum [kjúːprəm] *n.* 《chem.》 copper. 구리; 동(銅). [↑]

cur [kəːr] *n.* Ⓒ **1** a worthless dog; a dog of mixed breed. 들개; 똥개. **2** 《*fig.*》 a mean, worthless person. 천한 인간; 쌍놈. [E.]

cur·a·ble [kjúərəbəl] *adj.* that can be cured. 치료할〔고칠〕 수 있는. ¶ *With proper care and medicine tuberculosis is a* ~ *disease.* 결핵은 적당한 주의와 약으로 치료될 수 있는 병이다.

● **cur·a·bil·i·ty** [kjùərəbíləti] *n.* **cur·a·ble·ness** [-nis] *n.* [→cure]

cu·ra·çao, -çoa [kjùərəsáu, -sóu] *n.* a sweet liqueur flavored with the peel of bitter oranges. 큐라소《오렌지 껍질로 쌉쌀한 맛을 낸 리큐어》. [Place]

cu·ra·cy [kjúərəsi] *n.* Ⓤ the position or office of a curate. 목사보(補)의 직〔지위〕. [→curate]

cu·ras·sow [kjúərəsōu] *n.* a bird like a turkey. 봉관조(鳳冠鳥). [Place]

cu·rate [kjúərit] *n.* Ⓒ 《esp. Brit.》 a clergyman who helps a pastor, a rector, or a vicar. 목사보(補); 부목사. [L. *cura* care]

cur·a·tive [kjúərətiv] *adj.* having the power to cure. 치료의; 치료하는 힘이 있는. ¶ *a* ~ *medicine* 치료약. — *n.* Ⓒ a medicine or any form of treatment that cures. 치료약; 치료법.

cu·ra·tor [kjuəréitər] *n.* Ⓒ a person in charge of a museum, a library, etc. (박물관·도서관 따위의) 관리자; 관장(館長).

● **cu·ra·to·ri·al** [kjùrətɔ́ːriəl] *adj.*

***curb** [kəːrb] *n.* Ⓒ **1** a chain or strap under a horse's mouth, used to control the horse. 재갈 사슬; 고삐. **2** 《*fig.*》 anything that holds back; a check; a restraint. 구속; 억제. ¶ *put a* ~ *on* 〔*upon*〕 *one's desires* 욕망을 억누르다 / *put a* ~ *to violence* 폭력을 막다. **3** a line of raised stones, concrete, or wood separating a sidewalk from the street. (가로의) 연석(緣石)(cf. 《Brit.》 *kerb*).

— *vt.* (P6) **1** hold (a horse) in or back by the curb. (말)에 재갈 사슬을 물리다. **2** 《*fig.*》 check; control. …을 억제하다; 구속하다.

¶ ~ *one's excitement* 흥분을 누르다 / ~ *the king's power* 왕권을 제한하다 / ~ *extremist political activity among students* 학생 간의 과격파에 의한 정치 활동을 억제하다. [→curve]

curb·stone [kə́ːrbstòun] *n.* Ⓒ a stone or the stones forming a curb. (보도(步道)의) 연석(緣石).

curd [kəːrd] *n.* ⓊⒸ 《often *pl.*》 the thick, soft part of milk of which cheese is made. 응유(凝乳). [↓]

cur·dle [kə́ːrdl] *vt.* (P6) **1** change (something) into curd; cause (something) to thicken. …을 엉기게 하다; 응결시키다. ¶ *Acid curdles milk.* 산(酸)은 우유를 엉기게 한다. **2** 《*fig.*》 cause (the blood) to curdle through fright, etc. (공포심으로) 피가 얼어붙게 하다 (cf. *bloodcurdling*). ¶ *Terror curdled my blood.* 나는 공포로 피가 얼어붙었다. —*vi.* (P1) turn to curd; grow thick. 엉겨붙다; 응유(凝乳)로 되다. ¶ *The milk has curdled.* 우유가 엉겼다 / *The sight made my blood* ~. 나는 그 광경을 보고 피가 얼어붙는 것 같았다. [E.]

:cure [kjuər] *vt.* (P6,13) **1** 《*of*》 bring (someone) back to health; take away (a disease). …을 치료하다; 고치다. ¶ ~ *a cold* 감기를 치료하다 / ~ *a patient of a disease* 환자의 병을 고치다 / *be cured of a disease* 병이 낫다 / *This medicine cures headaches quickly.* 이 약은 두통이 빨리 낫는다. **2** 《*of*》 get rid of (something bad). …을 교정하다; 없애다. ¶ ~ *drunkenness* 과음증을 고치다 / ~ *mental worry* 정신적 고뇌를 없애다 / ~ *a man of bad habits* 남자의 못된 버릇을 고치다. **3** preserve (meat, fish, etc.) by salting, drying, or smoking. (훈제·건조하거나 소금에 절여 육류)를 보존하다. ¶ ~ *bacon* [*fish*] 베이컨을[물고기를] 훈제로 하다. —*vi.* (P1) **1** become well. (병이) 낫다. **2** be preserved by salting, etc. (소금 절임·훈제·건조 등으로) 보존하다.

be cured of, get rid of. …이 낫다.

cure oneself of, get rid of (something) by oneself. …을 스스로 고치다.

—*n.* Ⓒ **1** that which recovers health or does away with an evil; a medicine; a method of curing anything. 의료; 치료약[법]; 구제법. ¶ *a rest* ~ 안정 요법 / *a* ~ *for laziness* 게으름의 교정법 / *Aspirin is a certain* ~ *for a headache.* 아스피린은 두통에 확실한 치료약이다. **2** the act of curing; the state of being cured. 치료; 치유; 회복. ¶ *undergo a* ~ 치료를 받다 / *be past* [*beyond*] ~ 치료할 도리가 없다; 회복의 가망이 없다 / *I cannot promise a* ~. 치유된다고 약속할 수 없습니다. **3** the method of preserving meat, etc. by salting, etc. (육류·어류의) 보존(법). **4** religious care; the priestly office. (영혼의) 구제; 목사직(職). ¶ *the* ~ *of souls* 영혼의 구제.

● **cure·less** [-lis] *adj.* [L. *cura* care]

cu·ré [kjúərei, -⊿] *n.* 《F.》 a parish priest in France. 교구(教區) 목사(cf. *abbé*). [↑]

cure-all [kjúərɔ̀ːl] *n.* Ⓒ a medicine or any form of treatment supposed to cure all diseases. 만능약; 만병 통치약.

cu·rette [kjurét] *n.* 《med.》 a scraping instrument. 퀴레트《소파 수술에 쓰이는 날카로운 숟가락 모양의 기구》. [→cure]

cur·few [kə́ːrfjuː] *n.* Ⓒ **1** a signal, esp. by a bell, at a certain time in the evening; the time set for this; the bell itself. 만종(晩鐘)(의 시각). **2** (under martial law) the ringing of a bell at a fixed hour in the evening as a signal for people to leave the streets. 통행금지 저녁종(소리). [→cover, focus]

Cu·rie [kjúəri, kjuríː] *n.* **1** French physicists and chemists, who discovered radium in 1898. Marie C. (1867-1934), and her husband Pierre C. (1859-1906). 퀴리《프랑스의 물리·화학자 부처; 라듐을 발견》. **2** 《*c-*》 《phys.》 the unit of radioactivity. 퀴리《방사능 세기의 단위》.

cu·ri·o [kjúəriòu] *n.* Ⓒ (*pl.* **-os**) a thing which is valued because it is rare, unusual, or odd. 골동품; 진기한 물건. [↓]

:cu·ri·os·i·ty [kjùəriásəti / -ɔ́sə-] *n.* (*pl.* **-ties**) **1** Ⓤ an eager desire to know or learn 호기심. ¶ *out of* [*from*] ~ 호기심에서 / *in open* ~ 노골적인 호기심을 드러내어 / *satisfy* ~ 호기심을 만족시키다 / *This book excites the reader's* ~. 이 책은 독자의 호기심을 일으킨다. **2** Ⓒ a strange, rare, or novel object; a curio. 진기한[신기한] 것; 골동품. ¶ *a collection of curiosities* 골동품 수집 / *a* ~ *shop* 골동품점. [↓]

:cu·ri·ous [kjúəriəs] *adj.* **1** ⓐ eager to know or learn. (사물을) 깊이 알고 싶어하는; 호기심이 많은. ¶ *a* ~ *student* 지식욕이 왕성한 학생 / *be* ~ *to know the result* 결과를 알고 싶어하고 있다 / *I am* ~ *to know if…* …인지 어떤지를 알고 싶다. ⓑ (in a bad sense) inquisitive. (나쁜 의미로) 남의 일에 꼬치꼬치 캐고 싶어하는. ¶ ~ *neighbors* (남의 일에 지나친) 호기심을 보이는 이웃들 / *hide things from* ~ *eyes* 호기심에 찬 눈을 피하여 물건을 감추다 / *He is too* ~ *about other people's business.* 그는 남의 일에 지나친 흥미를 갖고 있다. **2** ⓐ strange; hard to explain; unusual. 이상한; 기묘한. ¶ *a* ~ *sight* [*sound, story*] 이상한 광경 [소리, 이야기] / *It's a* (*very*) ~ *thing that…* …하다니 (매우) 묘한 일이다. ⓑ 《*colloq.*》 (of a person) very odd; peculiar. (사람이) 이상한; 야릇한; 우스운. ¶ *a* ~ *sort of person* 괴짜 / *a curious-looking man* 괴상하게 생긴 사나이. **3** ⓐ (of mental activities) very careful. 면밀한. ¶ ~ *research* [*inquiry*] 면밀한 조사. ⓑ (of things) showing the result of care and attention; elaborate. 공들인; 정교한. ¶ *a* ~ *design* 정교한 디자인. [→cure]

curious to say, strange to say; it is odd, but…. 기묘하게도….

·cu·ri·ous·ly [kjúəriəsli] *adv.* in a curious manner. 이상한 듯이; 기묘하게.

cu·ri·um [kjúəriəm] *n.* ⟪chem.⟫ an element produced by bombardment of plutonium and uranium by helium ions. 퀴륨 ⟪방사성 원소⟫. [*Curie*]

:curl [kəːrl] *vt.* (P6,7) make (hair, etc.) into waves or rings; twist or roll into rings. (머리)를 곱슬곱슬하게 하다; 물결〔소용돌이〕치게 하다; 비틀어 구부리다; 꼬다. ¶ *Mother curled Nancy's hair.* 엄마는 낸시의 머리를 컬했다 / *It curled the waves.* 물결이 일었다. —*vi.* (P1,2A,3) become curved; roll into curls; take a spiral shape. 꼬부라지다; 오그라들다; 물결〔소용돌이〕치다. ¶ *The smoke from the camp fire curled upwards.* 모닥불 연기가 소용돌이쳐 올랐다 / *Does her hair ~ naturally?* 그녀의 머리는 타고난 고수머리인가.

curl one's lip, sneer scornfully. 비웃다; 경멸하여 입을 비쭉하다. ¶ *He curled his lips in scorn.* 경멸하여 입을 비쭉했다.

curl *oneself* **up,** curdle. (잔뜩 오그리고) 새우잠을 자다.

curl up, a) sit or lie down cozily. 편히 앉다; 눕다. ¶ *~ up with a good book* 좋은 책을 손에 들고 편히 앉다. **b**) roll (something) up by bending edges; roll up. 말아올리다; 오므라들다; 오그리고 (새우잠) 자다. ¶ *The frost made the young leaves ~ (up).* 서리는 어린 잎을 오그라들게 했다 / *The hedgehog curled up as I came near.* 가까이 다가가자 고슴도치는 몸을 곱송그렸다. **c**) suffer a severe shock; (cause to) collapse. 심한 충격을 입다; 무너지(게 하)다; 쓰러지(게 하)다. ¶ *The blow completely curled him up.* 그 일격으로 그는 완전히 뻗었다.

—*n.* **1** Ⓒ ⓐ a curled lock of hair. 곱슬곱슬한 머리 타래. ⓑ ⟪*pl.*⟫ curly hair; hair in general. 고수머리; 머리털. **2** Ⓒ anything curled or bent into a curve. (대팻밥처럼) 말린 것; 소용돌이 모양의 것. ¶ *a ~ of smoke* 〔*a wave*〕 연기〔물결〕의 소용돌이 / *a ~ of the lips* 냉소. **3** Ⓤ the state of being curled; the act of curling. 말린〔컬을 한, 물결치는, 소용돌이치는, 뒤틀린〕 상태; 맒. ¶ *keep one's hair in ~* 머리를 컬을 해두다. [E.]

cur·lew [kə́ːrluː] *n.* Ⓒ (*pl.* **-lews** or *collectively* **-lew**) a bird with long legs and a long curved bill. 마도요. [F.]

curl·ing [kə́ːrliŋ] *n.* Ⓤ a Scottish game played by sliding large, smooth stones over ice towards a mark. 컬링⟪스코틀랜드의 빙상 투석 게임⟫. —*adj.* that curls; used for curling. 말기 쉬운; 컬용(用)의. [E.]

curling iron [⌐-⌐-] *n.* an iron used for curling or waving hair. 헤어 아이론.

•curl·y [kə́ːrli] *adj.* (**curl·i·er, curl·i·est**) **1** curling; wavy; tending to curl. 곱슬머리의; 오그라든; 컬한. **2** having curls. 소용돌이 모양의. [E.]

cur·mudg·eon [kərmʌ́dʒən] *n.* Ⓒ a bad-tempered person; a person who does not easily part with his money. 심술궂은 사람; 구두쇠. [? F. *coeur méchant* evil heart]

cur·rant [kə́ːrənt, kʌ́r-] *n.* Ⓒ **1** a small, dried, seedless raisin, used in cakes, etc.(씨 없는) 알이 잔 건포도. **2** ⟪bot.⟫ a small, sour, edible berry that grows in bunches. 까치밥나무. [*Corinth,* Place in Greece]

•cur·ren·cy [kə́ːrənsi / kʌ́r-] *n.* (*pl.* **-cies**) **1** ⒸⓊ money in use. 통화(通貨). ¶ *gold ~* 금화 / *paper ~* 지폐 / *metallic ~* 경화(硬貨). **2** Ⓤ a continual passing from one person to another; circulation. 유통; 유포. ¶ *a belief that has wide ~* 널리 행해지고 있는 신앙 / *give ~ to a rumor* 소문을 퍼뜨리다 / *These slang words have an extensive ~ in Korea.* 이 속어들은 한국에서는 널리 사용되고 있다. **3** Ⓤ general use; common acceptance; current value or estimation. 통용; 일반적인 수용〔인정〕; 시세; 성가(聲價). ¶ *the words in common ~* 일반적으로 통용되고 있는 말 / *I estimate his intellect at his own ~.* 그의 지능은 그가 말하는 대로라고 여긴다. [↓]

gain 〔**obtain**〕 **currency,** circulate; become widely discussed. 일반에게 널리 퍼지다.

:cur·rent [kə́ːrənt / kʌ́r-] *n.* Ⓒ **1** a flow; a stream. 유동; 흐름. ¶ *a strong ~ in the river* 강물의 세찬 흐름 / *a swift ~* 급류 / *the upper air ~* 상층 기류 / *The swimmer was caught in a ~ and carried out to sea.* 수영자는 물줄기에 휩쓸려 바다로 떠내려 갔다. **2** the flow of electricity along a wire, etc. 전류. ¶ *an electric ~* 전류 / *an alternating* 〔*direct*〕 *~* 교〔직〕류. **3** (of events, opinions) a general tendency, course, or movement. 경과; 추세; 풍조; 동향; 경향. ¶ *the ~ of thought* 사조 / *the troublesome ~ of life* 고생 많은 인생 행로 / *the ~ of public opinion* 여론의 대세 / *swim with* 〔*against*〕 *the ~* 대세에 따르다〔거스르다〕.

—*adj.* **1** ⓐ (of time) now passing. 지금의. ¶ *the ~ week* 금주 / *the ~ month* 이 달 / *the 10th ~* 이 달 10일 / *~ topics* 오늘의 화제; 시사 문제. ⓑ present; of the present time; latest. 현재의; 최근의. ¶ *buy shares at the ~ market price* 현재의 시장가격으로 주식을 사다 / *the ~ issue number of a magazine* 잡지의 최근호. **2** ⓐ passing or handed on from person to person; prevalent; in general use. 유통〔유포〕되고 있는; 널리 행해지는; 널리 사용〔통용〕되는. ¶ *a ~ coin* 통화 / *~ money* 유통 통화 / *a rumor that is ~* 유포되고 있는〔떠도는〕 소문 / *~ English* 일상 영어 / *the ~ practice* 일반의 습관. ⓑ ⟪*fig.*⟫ commonly accepted. 일반적으로 받아들여지는〔인정되는〕. [L. *curro* run]

go 〔**pass, run**〕 **current,** circulate; become widely accepted. 통용〔유통〕하다; 세상에서 인정받다.

current account [⌐-⌐] *n.* ⟪econ.⟫ an account from which money can be drawn for present use. 당좌 예금〔계정〕.

cur·rent·ly [kə́ːrəntli / kʌ́r-] *adv.* **1** at present; now. 현재는; 지금(은). ¶ *a film*

〔movie〕 ~ *showing in town* 지금 시중에서 상영 중인 영화. **2** generally; commonly. 일반적으로; 널리.

cur·ric·u·la [kəríkjələ] *n.* pl. of **curriculum.**

cur·ric·u·lar [kəríkjələr] *adj.* of a curriculum. 교과 과정의. [↓]

cur·ric·u·lum [kəríkjələm] *n.* Ⓒ (*pl.* **-lums** or **-la**) a course of study in a school, a college, etc. (학교의) 학과 과정. [→current]

curriculum vi·tae [kəríkjələm váiti:] *n.* (*pl.* **cur·ric·u·la v-**) an outline of one's educational career, experience, etc. used in applying for a position; a personal history. 이력서.

cur·ri·er [kə́:riər, kʌ́r-] *n.* Ⓒ a person who curries leather after it has been tanned. 가죽 다듬는 사람; 피혁 제조공. [→curry[1]]

cur·rish [kə́:riʃ, kʌ́r-] *adj.* of a worthless dog; like a cur; mean; ill-bred. 들개의〔같은〕; 비열한; 막된; 버릇〔본데〕 없는. [→cur]

cur·ry[1] [kə́:ri, kʌ́ri] *vt.* (**-ried**) (P6) **1** rub down or clean (a horse, etc.) with a brush or comb. (말의 털 따위)를 빗질〔솔질〕하다. **2** prepare (tanned leather) by wetting, beating, etc. (무두질한 가죽)을 다듬다. [→com-, ready]

curry favor with, try to get (someone's) favor by flattering him. …의 비위를 맞추다; 환심을 사다.

cur·ry[2] [kə́:ri, kʌ́ri] *n.* (*pl.* **-ries**) **1** Ⓤ a peppery sauce or powder containing seeds, vegetables, etc. and flavored with various spices, used in cooking. 카레(가루). **2** ⓊⒸ a dish of meat, rice, etc. flavored with curry. 카레 요리. ¶ ~ *and rice* 카레라이스. 語法 and로 이어졌지만 단수 취급. — *vt.* (P6) prepare or flavor (food) with curry. (음식)을 카레로 조미하다. [Tamil]

cur·ry·comb [kə́:rikòum / kʌ́ri-] *n.* a comb with metal teeth, held by a handle, used for cleaning a horse's hair and skin. 말빗《말의 털·피부를 깨끗이 빗질하는 도구》. [→curry[1]]

curry powder [ㅗ-ㅗ-] *n.* a powdered mixture of turmeric and various strong spices. 카레 가루. [→curry[2]]

:curse [kə:rs] *v.* (**cursed** or **curst**) *vt.* (P6,13) **1** ask God to punish or hurt (someone or something); wish to harm. …을 저주하다; (…에게 재앙이 있으라고) 방자하다. ¶ *He cursed his enemy solemnly.* 그는 엄숙하게 자신의 적을 저주했다. **2** 《usu. in *passive*》 cause great evil to (someone); torment. …에게 빌미붙다; …을 괴롭히다; 화를 입히다. ¶ *cursed with blindness* 장님이 되는 화를 입은 / *He was cursed with bad habits.* (무슨 업보인지) 그는 못된 습관이 붙어버렸다. **3** swear at (someone). …을 매도하다; 욕지거리하다. — *vi.* (P1,3) swear; use bad language. 저주하다; 매도하다; 불경한 말을 하다. ¶ ~ *and swear* 갖은 욕설을 하다 / ~ *at someone* 아무에게 욕지거리하다.

— *n.* Ⓒ **1** a prayer that harm or injury may come to someone; a word or words used in such a prayer. 저주(의 말); 방자. ¶ 《*prov.*》 *Curses, like chickens, come home to roost.* 남잡이가 제잡이. **2** the evil or harm that comes as if in answer to a curse; a thing that causes evil or harm. 앙얼; 재앙; 재난의 원인이 되는 것. ¶ *call down a ~ upon someone* 아무를 저주하다 / *Curse upon him.* 그 자식 뒈져버려라 / *Drink is a ~ to many.* 술은 많은 사람에게 파멸의 원인이다. **3** something that is cursed. 저주받은 것. [E.]

do not care 〔***give***〕 ***a curse for*** (=*be indifferent to*) *something.* …을 조금도 상관〔개의〕치 않다; 아무래도 관계 없다.

not worth a curse, useless; worthless. 전혀 가치 없는.

the curse of drink, the disastrous effects of drink. 음주의 큰 피해.

under a curse, cursed. 저주를 받고.

curs·ed [kə́:rsid, kə:rst] *adj.* **1** under a curse; damned. 저주받은. **2** deserving a curse; evil; hateful. 저주받아야 할; 지겨운. **3** 《Brit. *colloq.*》 perverse. 비뚤어진; 빙퉁그러진. ¶ *a ~ boy* 빙퉁그러진 아이. **4** 《*arch.*》 《usu. *curst*》 ill-tempered. 심술궂은; 꾀까다로운. ● **curs·ed·ly** [-li] *adv.*

cur·sive [kə́:rsiv] *adj.* (of handwriting) with the letters joined together. (필적이) 필기〔초서〕체의; 갈겨 쓴. ¶ ~ *hand* 〔*script*〕 행서; 초서. — *n.* ⓊⒸ a letter made to join other letters. 초서. ¶ *write in ~* 필기〔초서〕체로 쓰다. ● **cur·sive·ly** [-li] *adv.* [→current]

cur·so·ri·ly [kə́:rsərili] *adv.* hastily; in a cursory manner. 황급히; 총총히; 조잡하게. [↓]

cur·so·ry [kə́:rsəri] *adj.* hasty; quick and careless; without paying attention to details. 급한; 날림〔대충〕의; 소략(疏略)한. ¶ ~ *reading* 대충 읽음 / *give a ~ glance at a list* 표를 대충 훑어보다. [→current]

curst [kə:rst] *adj.* = cursed. — *v.* p. and pp. of **curse.**

curt [kə:rt] *adj.* short; rudely brief; abrupt. 짧은; 간략한; 무뚝뚝한; 쌀쌀한. ¶ *a ~ answer* 매정한 대답 / *a ~ refusal* 푸접없는 거절 / *a ~ way of talking* 무뚝뚝한 이야기투. ● **curt·ly** [-li] *adv.* **curt·ness** [-nis] *n.* [L. *curtus* short; *-tail* corrupt. of obs. *a. curtal*]

cur·tail [kə:rtéil] *vt.* (P6) cut (something) short; reduce; shorten. …을 줄이다; 생략〔요약〕하다; …에서 일부를 떼어내다; 삭감〔절감〕하다. ¶ ~ *a speech* 연설을 짧게 하다 / ~ *expenditure* 지출을 줄이다 / *have one's pay curtailed* 감봉당하다 / *He wants to ~ my pay.* 그는 내 임금을 깎고 싶어한다. [↑]

cur·tail·ment [kə:rtéilmənt] *n.* Ⓤ the act or result of curtailing. 줄임; 삭감; 절감; 단축.

:cur·tain [kə́ːrtən] *n.* Ⓒ **1** a covering for a window, a cupboard, etc. 커튼. ¶ *draw the curtains* 커튼을 치다. **2** a large piece of cloth or a hanging screen let down or pulled across between the stage and the audience in a theater. (무대의) 막(幕). ¶ *draw the* ~ 막을 올리다〔내리다〕/ *The* ~ *rises* 〔*falls*〕. 막이 오르다〔내리다〕; 이야기가 시작되다〔끝나다〕. **3** a thing that covers, hides, or divides. 차단하는〔가로막는〕 것. ¶ *a* ~ *of smoke* 연막(煙幕) / *a* ~ *of fire* 탄막(彈幕) / *The stars are behind a* ~ *of clouds.* 온통 구름에 가려져 별은 보이지 않는다.

behind the curtain, in secret; secretly; in concealment. 가만히; 몰래; (배후에) 숨어서.

draw the curtain on 〔***over***〕, **a**) bring to a close. …을 끝내다. ¶ *draw the* ~ *on a long career of public service* 오랜 공직 생활에 종지부를 찍다. **b**) keep secret; conceal. …을 비밀로 해두다; 숨기다.

lift the curtain on, **a**) reveal something hidden; disclose. …을 밝히다; 알리다 ; 공표하다. **b**) start; commence. …을 시작하다.

— *vt.* (P6,7) **1** hang or provide (something) with curtains; decorate (something) with curtains. …에 막〔커튼〕을 치다. ¶ ~ *a window* 창문에 커튼을 치다. **2** cover; hide. …을 가리다; 숨기다. [L. *cortina*]

curtain off, separate or shut off (a room, etc.) by a curtain or curtains. …을 커튼으로 막다〔가리다〕.

curtain call [⌐– ⌐] *n.* a call to return to the stage. (연기자를) 무대로 다시 불러내기.

curtain lecture [⌐– ⌐–] *n.* a wife's lecture to her husband in bed. 베갯머리 송사.

curtain raiser [⌐– ⌐–] *n.* a short play given before the main play in a theater. 개막〔서막〕극.

curt·sey [kə́ːrtsi] *n., vi.* =curtsy.

curt·sy [kə́ːrtsi] *n.* Ⓒ (*pl.* **-sies**) a bow of respect or greeting by women, made by bending the knees and inclining the head and shoulders slightly. (여성이 무릎과 상체를 굽히는) 인사; 절. ¶ *drop* 〔*make*〕 *a* ~ (여성이) 무릎을 굽혀 인사〔절〕하다.

make one's curtsy to the queen, (of a woman) be presented at court. (여성이 궁중에서) 여왕을 배알하다.

— *vi.* (P1,3) (**-sied**) make a curtsy. (여성이 무릎을 굽혀) 절〔인사〕하다. [*courtesy*]

cur·va·ture [kə́ːrvətʃər] *n.* Ⓤ the act of bending; the state of being bent; something curved or bent. 굽음; 구부림; 굴곡; 만곡(부). ¶ ~ *of the spine* 척추의 이상 만곡(彎曲). [↓]

***curve** [kəːrv] *n.* Ⓒ **1** a line that has no straight part; a rounded bend. 곡선. ¶ *a hyperbolic* ~ 쌍곡선. **2** a thing that has the shape of a curve; a bend. 굴곡; 휘어짐; 커브. ¶ *a* ~ *in the road* 도로의 굴곡〔커브〕. **3** (in baseball) a ball thrown so as to curve just before it reaches the batter. (야구에서) 커브(볼); 곡구(曲球). ¶ *break* 〔*spin*〕 *a* ~ 커브를 던지다.

— *vt.* (P6,7) cause (something) to bend or turn from a straight line. …을 구부러지게 하다; 만곡시키다. ¶ *a curved line* 곡선; 만곡선. — *vi.* (P1,2A) bend; turn. 구부러지다; 만곡하다. ¶ *The road curves round* (*to the left*). 길이 (왼쪽으로) 구부러져 있다.

— *adj.* curved. 구부러진; 굽은. [L. *curvus* curved]

cur·vet [kə́ːrvit] *n.* a movement of a horse raising both forelegs and leaping forward from the hind legs. (승마에서) 등약(騰躍). — *vi., vt.* (**-vet·(t)ed**) (P1;6) (of a horse) leap in this way; (of a rider) make a horse do this. (말이) 등약하다; (말을) 등약시키다. [↑]

cur·vi·lin·e·ar [kə̀ːrvilíniər], **-lin·e·al** [-líniəl] *adj.* 《archit.》 consisting of or enclosed, by curved lines. 곡선으로 된〔둘러싸인〕. [↑]

***cush·ion** [kúʃən] *n.* Ⓒ **1** a soft bag filled with feathers, air, etc. to sit, kneel, or lie on. 쿠션; 방석. **2** any soft thing which makes a shock or noise less. 쿠션 모양의 것; 완충물. **3** the soft, rubber, inner side of a billiard table. (당구대의) 쿠션.

— *vt.* (P6) **1** provide or furnish (something or someone) with cushions. …에 쿠션을 대다〔마련하다〕. **2** protect (something or someone) with cushions; suppress quietly. …을 쿠션으로 보호하다; 가만히 누르다. [L. *coxa* hip]

cush·y [kúʃi] *adj.* (**cush·i·er, cush·i·est**) 《*sl.*》 easy; comfortable; profitable. 쉬운; 편한; 편하게 돈 버는. ¶ *a* ~ *job* 돈벌이가 좋은 직업. [Hind. *khush* pleasant]

cusp [kʌsp] *n.* Ⓒ **1** a pointed end; a point made by the meeting of two curved lines, e.g. like the horns of a crescent moon. 뾰족한 끝; 첨단; 두 곡선이 만나는 뾰족한 점《특히 초승달의 뾰족한 끝》. **2** a pointed part of the crown of a tooth or a leaf. (이·잎 따위의) 뾰족한 끝. [L.=spear-head]

cus·pi·date, -dat·ed [kʌ́spədèit], [-id] *adj.* having a sharp, pointed end, esp. of leaves. (특히 잎 따위가) 뾰족한 끝을 가진. [↑]

cus·pi·dor [kʌ́spədɔ̀ːr] *n.* Ⓒ 《U.S.》 a bowl to spit into. 타구(唾具). [L.]

cuss [kʌs] *n.* **1** 《U.S. *sl.*》 a curse word; an oath. 저주(의 말); 독설; 욕. **2** a fellow. 녀석; 사나이. ¶ *a strange but likable* ~ 괴짜지만 좋은 녀석. — *vt., vi.* (P6; 1) 《*sl.*》 curse. 저주하다; 욕하다. [→curse]

cus·tard [kʌ́stərd] *n.* ⒸⓊ a yellow food made of eggs, sugar, milk, etc. boiled or baked. 커스터드《우유·설탕·달걀 따위를 섞어 만든 크림 비슷한 과자》. [→crust]

cus·to·di·al [kʌstóudiəl] *adj.* of the custody. 보관의; 보호 관리의. [↓]

cus·to·di·an [kʌstóudiən] *n.* Ⓒ a person in charge of something; a person who takes care of a public building; a janitor. 관리인; 보관자; 수위.

cus·to·dy [kʌ́stədi] *n.* Ⓤ **1** the act of keeping or guarding; the state of being guarded or watched; care; charge. 보호; 후견; 보관; 관리. ¶ *in the ~ of her father* 그녀 아버지의 보호 감독 아래 / *have the ~ of* …을 보관〔관리, 보호〕하고 있다; 보호 의무가 있다. **2** imprisonment 구금; 감금. [L. *custos* guard]

in custody, in the care of the police; in prison. 구금되어; 수감되어.

take into custody, arrest (someone) and put him under guard. (아무)를 구속하다.

:cus·tom [kʌ́stəm] *n.* **1** ⒸⓊ any usual action or habit. 습관. ¶ *as is one's ~* 늘 하는 대로; 여느 때와 같이 / *I make it a ~ to do so.* =*It is my ~ to do so.* 나는 늘 그렇게 하기로 하고 있다; 그렇게 하는 것이 습관이다 / *It was his ~ to go for a walk before breakfast.* 식전에 산책을 하는 것이 그의 습관이었다 / *Custom is a second nature.* 습관은 제2의 천성이다. **2** ⒸⓊ a habit done for so long that it has almost the force of law. 관례; 관습. ¶ *the ~ of trade* 상(商)관습 / *the ~ of society* 사회의 관행(慣行) / *follow the ~ of merchants* 상관행(商慣行)에 따르다. **3** Ⓤ ⓐ support given to a business by its customers. (가게에 대한 손님의) 애고(愛顧); 애호. ¶ *draw ~ to one's store* 가게의 단골을 만들다 / *give one's ~ to* …에 애고를 베풀다; …의 단골 손님이 되다 / *withdraw one's ~ from a shop* 사지〔팔아주지〕 않기로 하다. ⓑ 《*collectively*》 the customers or patrons of a shop or trader. 고객(顧客); 단골. ¶ *The shop has plenty of ~.* 그 가게는 단골 손님이 많다. **4** ⓐ 《*pl.*》 taxes or duties paid to the government on goods brought in from foreign countries. 관세(關稅) (cf. *excise*[1]). ⓑ 《*the C-s*》 the department of the government that gathers these taxes. 세관.
— *adj.* 《U.S.》 made to order; made esp. for each customer, etc. 주문의; 맞춤의; 주문품만 취급하는. ¶ *~ clothes* 맞춤옷 / *a ~ tailor* 맞춤 전문의 양복점. [con-; L. *suesco* be wont]

cus·tom·ar·i·ly [kʌ̀stəmérəli / -məri-] *adv.* in a customary manner; usually. 습관적으로; 관례상; 일반적으로; 흔히.

·cus·tom·ar·y [kʌ́stəmèri / -məri] *adj.* according to custom; usual; established by custom. 습관적인; 통례의; 관례적인. ¶ *one's ~ exercise* 늘 하는 운동.

cus·tom-built [kʌ́stəmbìlt] *adj.* built to order, e.g. of a car body; not readymade. (자동차 따위) 개인의 주문에 따라 만든; 주문제(製)의.

:cus·tom·er [kʌ́stəmər] *n.* Ⓒ **1** a person who buys regularly from the same store. 고객; 단골. **2** 《*colloq.*》 a person; a fellow; a person one has to deal with. (상대해야 할) 너석; 사람. ¶ *a tough ~* 만만치 않은 상대 / *a queer ~* 이상한 녀석.

custom house [⌐-⌐] *n.* a government building or office where taxes on imported, or sometimes on exported goods, are collected and where travelers' luggage is examined. 세관(稅關).

cus·tom-made [kʌ́stəmméid] *adj.* 《U.S.》 made to order; made esp. for each customer, etc. 맞춤의; 주문품의.

customs duties [⌐-⌐-] *n.* taxes imposed by a government on imported and occasionally exported goods. 관세.

customs union [⌐-⌐-] *n.* a union of several nations with an agreement in common for customs duties. 관세 동맹.

:cut [kʌt] *v.* (**cut, cut·ting**) *vt.* **1** (P6,7,13, 14,18) ⓐ make an opening or wound in with a sharp-edged tool. (날붙이 따위로) 베다; 상처를 내다. ¶ *~ one's fingers with a knife* 나이프에 손가락을 베다 / *~ one's own throat* 자기 목을 찌르다; 자멸을 초래하다 / *~ oneself* (잘못하여) 날붙이로 상처를 입다. ⓑ divide with a sharp-edged tool; sever; separate. …을 잘라〔베어〕 가르다; 절단하다; 분리하다. ¶ *~ a rope* 〔*wire*〕 밧줄을〔철사를〕 끊다 / *~ a sheet of paper in three* 종이를 셋으로 자르다 / *~ a cake in two* 〔*into pieces*〕 케이크를 둘로〔여러 조각으로〕 자르다 / *Please ~ me a slice of bread.* 빵 한 조각만 잘라 주시오. ⓒ take off by cutting; remove. (본체에서) 잘라 내다. ¶ *~ flowers* 칼로 잘라 꽃을 따다. ⓓ cause to fall by cutting; chop down; fell. (도끼·톱 따위로) 벌채하다; 자르다. ¶ *~ (down) timber* 〔*trees*〕 나무를 자르다; 벌채하다. **2** (P6,13) ⓐ shape or prepare (a hard substance, etc.) by cutting, carving, chiselling. (단단한 것)을 자르고〔깍고 다듬어〕…모양을 만들다; 조각하다. ¶ *~ a jewel* 〔*diamond*〕 보석을〔다이아몬드를〕 깍다 / *~ a stone in various forms* 돌을 여러 형태로 깎아〔잘라, 다듬어〕 내다 / *~ a figure in wood* 나무에 상(像)을 새기다 / *~ one's name on a tree* 나무에 이름을 새기다. ⓑ make by cutting, breaking, chiselling. 파다; 뚫다. ¶ *~ a trench* 참호를 파다 / *~ a road through a hill* 산을 깎고 뚫어 길을 내다. **3** (P6) cut with a sickle, scythe, etc.; mow; reap or harvest. (낫 따위로) 베다; 깎다; (곡물을) 거두어들이다. ¶ *~ grass* 〔*hay*〕 풀을〔건초를〕 베다 / *~ the crops* 곡물을 베어 들이다. **4** (P6,18) ⓐ make short by clipping, pruning, etc.; trim. …을 짧게 깎다; (가위로) 자르다. ¶ *~ one's nails* 손톱을 깍다 / *have one's hair ~ at the barber* 이발소에서 머리를 깎다. ⓑ make short by omitting; shorten; abridge. 짧게 하다; 줄이다; 생략하다. ¶ *~ one's speech* 〔*visit*〕 연설〔방문〕을 단축하다 / *~ a newspaper article* 신문 기사를 줄이다 / *to ~ a long story short* 줄여서 말하면; 요컨대. **5** (P6,7) 《*colloq.*》 reduce in amount, price, etc.; lower; lessen. (양 따위)를 줄이다; (값)을 내리다; 삭감하다; 낮추다. ¶ ~

prices 값을 내리다 / ～ *expenses* 지출을 줄이다 / ～ *down the TV sound* 텔레비전 소리를 줄이다. **6** (P6,7,13) cause sharp pain to; affect deeply; hurt the feeling of. …에게 사무치는 고통을 주다; 깊은 상처를 주다; 감정을 몹시 해치다. ¶ *The icy wind* ～ *me to the bone.* 차가운 바람이 뼛속까지 스며들었다 / *His words* ～ *me to the heart*〔*quick*〕. 그의 말은 내 가슴속 아픈 데를 찔렀다 / *He said nothing; he was* ～ *to the heart.* 그는 말 한마디 안 했다. 몹시 감정을 다친 것이었다. **7** (P6) pretend not to see or know (someone); ignore. …을 모르는 체하다; 몽따다. ¶ ～ *someone dead* 아무를 전혀 모르는 체하다 / ～ *someone in the street* 거리에서 만나고도 모르는 체하다. **8** (P6) 《*colloq.*》 stay away from (without permission); be not present at. …을 (무단) 결석하다; (수업)을 빼먹다. ¶ ～ *a lecture*〔*class*〕 강의를〔수업을〕 빼먹다 / ～ *a meeting* 모임에 참석지 않다. **9** (P6) (of a line, road, etc.) cross; intersect. 교차하다. ¶ *A line cuts another at right angles.* 하나의 선이 다른 선과 직각으로 교차한다. **10** (P6,13) make (something) loose; dissolve; dilute. …을 용해하다; 묽게 하다. ¶ ～ *wine* 포도주를 묽게 하다 / ～ *tar with gasoline* 타르를 가솔린으로 녹이다. **11** (P6) shape, prepare, or make (a garment) by cutting cloth; fashion. (옷 따위)를 마르다; 재단하다. ¶ ～ *a pair of trousers* 바지를 마르다. **12** (P6) strike sharply. (채찍 따위로) 세게 치다. ¶ ～ *a horse with a switch* 채찍으로 말을 세게 치다 / ～ *someone across the face* 아무의 따귀를 치다. **13** (P6) give a spinning motion to a ball in cricket or tennis. (공에 스핀을 먹여) 깎아치다. ¶ ～ *a ball.* **14** (P7, 18) carry out (a brisk movement); perform. (두드러진 동작·태도·모습)을 보이다. ¶ ～ *a fine figure* 두드러지다; 이채를 발하다 / ～ *a poor figure* 초라해 보이다. **15** (P6) divide (a deck of cards) by removing cards from the top. (카드놀이에서 패)를 떼다. **16** (P6) castrate. …을 거세하다; 불까다. ¶ *This horse ought to be* ～. 이 말은 거세해야 한다. **17** grow or acquire (teeth). (이)가 나게〔자라게〕 하다. ¶ ～ *a tooth* 이가 나다 / ～ *one's eyeteeth*〔*wisdom teeth*〕 어른이 되다; 철이 들다.

— *vi.* **1** (P1,2A,3) do cutting; work as a cutter. 베다; 날이 들다. ¶ *This knife doesn't* ～ *well.* 이 칼은 잘 들지 않는다. **2** (P1,2A) take cutting; be cut. 베어지다. ¶ *The wood cuts easily.* 그 나무는 잘 베어진다. **3** (P1,2A) hurt by or as by sharp piercing strokes. (살을 에는 듯이) 아프다; 아리다; 사무치다. ¶ ～ *at the enemy* 적에게 강한 일격을 가하다 / *The lash* ～ *like a knife.* 채찍은 날붙이처럼 아팠다 / *The wind* ～ *through his thin clothes.* 바람이 얇은 옷을 통해 스며들어 살을 에는 듯하였다 / *The remark* ～ *deep.* 그 말은 통렬히 사무쳤다. **4** (P1) run away quickly; leave hastily. 급히 달아나다; 급히 떠나다. ¶ *I must* ～. 난 달아나야 한다 / *Cut!* 빨리 떠나라. **5** 《*sl.*》 go by a shorter route. 질러가다; 지름길로 가다. **6** 《sports》 hit a ball so that it is hit away and sometimes also made to spin. 볼을 커트하다; 깎아치다. **7** (P3) pass or go through; cross. 빠져 나가다; 통과하다. ¶ ～ *through the water* 물결을 헤치고 나아가다 / *He* ～ *through the crowd.* 군중 속을 헤치고 빠져나갔다.

cut (=*run*) ***about*** *some place,* 뛰어다니다.

cut across, take a short course by going straight across (some place). (가로)질러가다; 지름길로 가다. ¶ ～ *across the field* 들판을 가로질러 지나가다.

cut after (=*hurry after; pursue*) *something* or *someone,* 급히 뒤쫓다; 쫓아가다.

cut and come again, 《*colloq.*》 take or eat plenty; take a helping freely. 몇 번이고 얼마든지 실컷 먹다.

cut and run, get away quickly; make off. 급히 달아나다; 급히 떠나다.

cut at, **a**) aim a stroke at; strike at. …에게 치고 덤비다; 덤벼들어 치다. ¶ *He* ～ *at me with his sword.* 그는 검으로 나를 내리쳤다. **b**) tend to destroy. 깨다. ¶ *That cuts at all my hopes.* 그 일로 나의 모든 희망이 깨졌다.

cut away, **a**) take (something) off by cutting. 잘라버리다; 떼어내다. ¶ ～ *away dead branches from a tree* 나무에서 삭정이를 잘라내다. **b**) 《*sl.*》 run away; escape. 달아나다.

cut back, **a**) make (something) shorter by cutting off the end; shorten. (끝을 잘라) 짧게 하다; (나뭇가지 따위)를 자르다. ¶ ～ *back the shoots of a tree* 나무의 어린 가지를 짧게 치다. **b**) reduce; curtail. …을 줄이다; 깎다. ¶ ～ *back production* 생산을 줄이다. **c**) return suddenly to earlier events. (영화 등에서) 먼저 이야기로〔사건으로〕 되돌아가다.

cut both ways, have contrary effect; do harm as well as good. 상반되는 두 가지 효과가 있다; 좋은 면도 있고 나쁜 면도 있다.

cut *one's* ***coat according to*** *one's* ***cloth*** ⇨ coat.

cut corners, **a**) take a shorter course. 지름길을 취하다. **b**) reduce cost, labor, etc.; economize. 비용과 노동력 따위를 줄이다; 절약하다.

cut down, **a**) cause (a tree, etc.) to fall by cutting it. …을 베어넘기다. ¶ ～ *down a tree.* **b**) kill or injure (someone) by striking him with a sword, etc. 아무를 칼 따위로 베어〔쳐〕 죽이다〔상처를 입히다〕. **c**) (of a disease) deprive (someone) of life or health. (병이) …을 쓰러뜨리다. ¶ *He was* ～ *down by a disease.* 그는 병으로 쓰러졌다. **d**) make (something) shorter 〔less, smaller〕; lessen. …을 줄이다; 깎다; 삭감〔절하, 인하〕하다; 내리다. ¶ ～ *down the price* 값을 내리다 / ～ *down one's expenses* 지출을 줄이다. **e**) destroy; disable. …을 파괴하다; 무력하게

하다.

cut in, **a**) move in suddenly; interrupt. 갑자기 끼어들다; 가로막다. ¶ *He ~ in* 〔*into*〕 *our conversation abruptly.* 불쑥 우리들 이야기에 끼어들었다. **b**) (of a car) overtake and get in front of another; outrun. (자동차가) 앞질러 남의 차 앞에 끼어들다; 추월하다. **c**) 《*colloq.*》 change suddenly one's dancing partner. (댄스 중인 사람에게 다가가서) 춤 상대를 바꾸다.

cut into, **a**) interpose. 주제넘게 말 참견하다 〔끼어들다〕. **b**) eat into; make an inroad upon. 파고들다; (밑천·자본 등)을 잠식하다. ¶ *~ into one's capitals* 자본을 잠식하다 / *The rope with which his hands were tied ~ into the flesh.* 양손을 묶은 포승줄이 살에 파고들었다.

cut it fine, 《*colloq.*》 leave very little time to spare; leave a very small margin of time, money, etc. to do what is needed. (돈·시간 따위)를 얼마 남기지 않다.

cut it out, 《*colloq.*》 stop doing. (…하는 것)을 그만두다.

cut it too fat, carry it too far. 도를 지나치다.

cut loose, **a**) set free; separate; release. (묶인 것)을 풀다; 놓아 주다; 해제〔해방〕하다. ¶ *~ a boat loose from a ship* 배에 매인 보트를 풀다 / *~ loose someone from prison* 죄수를 석방하다. **b**) act or speak without restraint; behave wildly. 자유로이 행동〔말〕하다; 멋대로 굴다.

cut one's losses, stop taking part in a failing business, firm, etc. before one loses too much money. (시원치 않은 사업 따위에서 손을 떼어) 손실을 줄이다.

cut off, **a**) separate from other parts; take off. …을 절단하다; 떼어〔잘라〕내다. **b**) bring (something) to an end. …을 끝내다; 그치다. ¶ *~ off debate* 토론을 끝내다. **c**) stop the supply of. (공급)을 끊다; 중단하다. ¶ *~ off (the supply of) gas* 〔*water, electricity*〕 가스〔수돗물, 전기〕 공급을 끊다 / *~ off food* 〔*money*〕 식량〔돈〕의 공급을 중단하다. **d**) prevent (sight, conversation, etc.); hinder; intercept. …을 가로막다; 차단하다; 방해하다. ¶ *be ~ off from communication* 통신이 차단되다 / *be ~ off in a talk on the telephone* 전화 통화 중 끊기다 / *~ oneself off from the world* 세상과의 관계를 끊다 / *A thick fog ~ off our view.* 짙은 안개로 앞이 안 보였다. **e**) kill; destroy. …을 죽이다; (병·부상 따위가) 목숨을 빼앗다. ¶ *He was ~ off in early youth.* 그는 요절했다.

cut off with a shilling, leave little or nothing to (someone) at one's death; disinherit. (죽을 때) …에게 유산을 조금만 남겨 주다; 유산을 한 푼도 남겨 주지 않다; 폐적(廢嫡)하다.

cut on, hurry; move on speedily. 서두르다; 급히 나아가다.

cut out, **a**) take off (something) by cutting around it. …을 잘라〔베어〕내다. ¶ *She ~ the advertisement out of the newspaper so that she would remember it.* 그녀는 기억해 두기 위해 신문에서 광고를 오려냈다. **b**) make or shape by cutting. (옷감)을 마르다; 재단하다. ¶ *~ out a dress* 옷을 마르다. **c**) stop; finish. …을 그만두다; 끊다; 끝내다. ¶ *Cut it out!* (그런 일) 그만둬; (입) 닥쳐 / *I must ~ out smoking and strong drinks.* 나는 담배와 독한 술을 끊어야 한다 / *Let's ~ out the talking and get back to work!* 이야기를 그만하고 일로 돌아갑시다. **d**) (of a motor) stop suddenly. 갑자기 멈추다. ¶ *Everytime I got my car started the engine ~ out after a few minutes.* 내 차에 시동을 걸 때마다 늘 몇 분 후면 엔진이 멎는다. **e**) (esp. of a car) move sharply to one side. (차가) 급히 한 편으로 비키다. **f**) leave hastily. 급히 떠나다. **g**) take the place of (a rival); oust and replace; outdo. (…자리에) 대신 들어앉다; …을 앞지르다. ¶ *~ out another in getting an appointment* 남을 앞질러 임명을 받다. **h**) prepare; arrange. 준비〔마련〕하다; 예정하다.

cut** something **short, make something shorter. …을 짧게 하다; 줄이다.

cut one's stick, run away. 달아나다.

cut under, undersell. …보다 싸게 팔다.

cut up, **a**) cut small; cut into pieces. 잘게 썰다〔자르다〕; (잘게) 토막치다. ¶ *~ up wood* 나무를 잘게 토막내다 / *~ up meat* 고기를 잘게 썰다. **b**) act noisily; misbehave. 예절 없이 행동하다. **c**) criticize severely. 혹평하다; 호되게 까다. ¶ *~ up a book* 책을 혹평하다. **d**) 《usu. *passive*》 give severe pain to; cause grief to; distress. (정신적으로) 고통을 주다; 마음 아프게〔슬프게〕 하다; 괴롭히다. ¶ *His son's death ~ him up badly.* 아들의 죽음은 그를 몹시 슬프게 했다 / *Don't be so ~ up about it.* 그 일로 그리 마음 아파하지 말게. **e**) be cut up. 재단되다. ¶ *This cloth will ~ up into several suits.* 이 옷감은 몇 벌의 옷으로 재단된다.

cut up rough 〔***nasty***〕, 《*colloq.*》 become ill-tempered; get angry. 시무룩해지다; 성나다.

cut up well, 《*colloq.*》 die rich. 유복한 가운데 죽다.

—*n.* Ⓒ **1** the act of cutting; a sharp stroke or blow. 벰; 자름; (채찍·칼 따위의) 일격. ¶ *make a ~ with a sword* 검으로 내리치다 / *He gave her a ~ on the head.* 그녀 머리에 일격을 가했다. **2** a mark, scratch, or wound made by cutting; a notch. 베인 자국〔상처〕; 새긴 금. ¶ *a ~ in the finger* 손가락의 벤 상처 / *a skin ~ = a ~ on the skin* 피부의 베인 상처. **3** ⓐ a passage or canal made by cutting or digging; a railway cutting. 깎아 뚫거나 파서 만든 길; 수로; 산을 뚫어 만든 철도. ⓑ a course or route straight across or through. 곧장 빠지는 길; 횡단로. ¶ *a ~ through the woods* 숲을 통과하는 길. **4** a slice or piece cut off. 베어낸 조각. ¶ *a ~ of a pie* 베어낸 파이 한 조각. **5** ⓐ the style or fashion in which something is cut. (옷의 디자인을 특징지우는) 재단(법); 스

타일; (머리의) 깎은 형(型). ¶ *the ~ of a dress* 의복의 재단 / *the ~ of one's hair* 깎은 머리형(型) / *a garment of the latest ~* 최신 스타일의 옷. ⓑ general style or appearance. 외형; 유형; 종류; 겉모습. ¶ *a woman of old-fashioned ~* 구식의 여성 /《*colloq.*》*the ~ of one's jib* 〔*rig*〕 외양; 풍채; 인품 / *We need a man of his ~ in this firm.* 이 회사에서는 그와 같은 유형의 사나이가 필요하다. **6** a reduction in amount, price, etc. (경비의) 삭감; 절감; 깎아내림; (값의) 할인. ¶ *a ~ in expenses* 지출의 절감 / *a 5 percent ~ in income taxes* 소득세의 5퍼센트 삭감. **7** the omission of a part; a part omitted. (일부를) 잘라냄; (부분적) 삭제; 삭제 부분; 생략. ¶ *The editor made many cuts in my article.* 편집부장은 내 기사를 많이 삭제했다. **8** a remark, etc. that hurts someone's feelings. 남의 감정을 해치는 말〔행위〕. ¶ *a ~ at someone* 아무를 (겨냥해) 빗댄 말 / *That was a cruel ~.* 그것은 매정한 처사였다. **9** ⓐ a plate or block engraved for printing. (인쇄용의) 금속판; 목판. ⓑ the impression or picture made from this. (위에 의한) 쇄(刷); 판화; 삽화. **10** a refusal to recognize or greet someone on meeting. (사람을) 고의로 피함; 짐짓 모른 체함. **11** 《U.S.》 a snack. 가벼운 식사.

a cut above 〔***below***〕, a degree above 〔below〕. …보다 한 수 위〔아래〕. ¶ *be a ~ above one's neighbors* 이웃보다 신분이 한층 높다.

draw cuts, draw lots. 제비를 뽑다.

— *adj.* **1** divided or severed. 자른; 잘라〔베어〕낸; 잘게 썬. ¶ *~ tobacco* 살담배 / *~ flowers* (장식용으로) 잘라 낸 꽃(opp. growing flowers). **2** wounded by being opened. (칼 따위에) 베인. ¶ *a ~ finger* (칼에) 베인 손가락. **3** shaped or fashioned by cutting. (특정 모양으로) 깎아 다듬은; 재단한. ¶ *a ~ diamond* 깎아 다듬은 다이아몬드 / *~ sugar* 각설탕. **4** castrated; gelded. 거세(去勢)한. **5** reduced in amount, price, etc. (수량 따위를) 줄인; 삭감한; (값을) 깎은; 할인한. ¶ *sell at ~ prices* 할인 가격으로 팔다. [E.]

be cut up, be sad. 슬프다.

cut and dry 〔***dried***〕, **a**) prepared or arranged beforehand. 사전에 준비된. **b**) lifeless; dull; boring. 무미건조한; 신선미가 없는.

cut and thrust, **a**) a sword play with the edge as well as the point. 치거나 찌르거나 하는 검술 경기. **b**) a lively interchange. 활발한 응수.

cut and try, experimental. 실험적인.

cut out for, fitted for; capable of. …에 적합한; …할 수 있는.

cu·ta·ne·ous [kju:téiniəs] *adj.* of or having to do with the skin. 피부의; 피부에 관한. [L. *cutis* skin]

cut·a·way [kʌ́təwèi] *adj.* (of a coat) having a part cut away from the waist in front. (상의의) 앞자락을 뒤쪽으로 어슷하게 재단한. — *n.* Ⓒ a cutaway coat, worn by men for formal daytime occasions. 모닝 코트. [*cut*]

cut·back [kʌ́tbæ̀k] *n.* Ⓒ **1** 《cinema》 a return in the course of a motion picture, etc. to earlier events. (앞서의 사건·이야기로) 되돌아감. **2** a reduction in output. 감소; 축소; 삭감. ¶ *a ~ in orders* 주문의 감소 / *a ~ in production* 생산의 축소. [*cut*]

cute [kju:t] *adj.* 《*colloq.*》 **1** 《U.S.》 pleasingly pretty; charming; attractive. 귀여운; 매력있는. ¶ *a ~ cocker spaniel* 귀여운 코커 스파니엘 개 / *What a ~ baby!* 정말이지 귀여운 아기다. **2** clever; shrewd; sharp. 약삭빠른; 빈틈 없는. [*acute*]

cu·ti·cle [kjú:tikl] *n.* Ⓒ the outer layer of skin, esp. that around the base of fingernails or toenails. 외피(外皮); 표피(表皮); (손톱·발톱 끝의) 각피(角皮); 큐티클라층(層). [L. *cutis,* →cutacious]

cu·tie [kjú:ti] *n.* a charming, cute girl. 귀여운 여자 아이. [→cute]

cut·lass, -las [kʌ́tləs] *n.* Ⓒ a short, heavy, rather curved sword with a wide blade, esp. used by seaman. 단검(短劍)《몸체가 휘고 나비가 넓은 칼》. [L. *culter*]

cut·ler [kʌ́tlər] *n.* Ⓒ a person who makes, sells, or mends knives, scissors, and other cutting tools. 날붙이 만드는〔파는, 고치는〕 사람. [↑]

cut·ler·y [kʌ́tləri] *n.* Ⓤ **1** 《*collectively*》 knives, scissors, and other cutting tools. 날붙이. **2** knives, forks, spoons, etc. used in cutting or serving food. (나이프·포크 등 식탁용) 철물. **3** the business of a cutler. 날붙이 제조〔판매, 수선〕업.

cut·let [kʌ́tlit] *n.* Ⓒ **1** a slice of meat for frying. 얇게 저민〔썬〕 고깃점. **2** a flat, fried piece of meat or fish. 커틀릿. [→coast]

cut·off [kʌ́tɔ̀:f, ∠ɑ̀f / ∠ɔ̀f] *n.* Ⓒ **1** 《U.S.》 a short cut. 지름길. ¶ *the ~ to Suwon* 수원으로 가는 지름길. **2** a mechanism that cuts off flow, as of steam or water. (흐름을 막는 기계의) 차단 장치. [→cut]

cut·out [kʌ́tàut] *n.* Ⓒ **1** ⓐ a figure cut out of something else such as a picture, a shape, or a design on paper or cardboard. 도려낸 것〔그림〕. ⓑ a shape or design to be cut out. 도려내는 그림·도형. **2** a switch or device for breaking an electric current. 개폐기(開閉器); 안전기(器). **3** a device for disconnecting an engine from its muffler. (내연 기관의) 배기판(瓣). [→cut]

cut·purse [kʌ́tpə̀:rs] *n.* 《*arch.*》 =pickpocket.

cut·ter [kʌ́tər] *n.* Ⓒ **1** a person who cuts. 자르는 사람; 재단자. ¶ *a tailor's ~* 재단사. **2** a tool or machine for cutting. 자르는〔베는〕 것; 절단기; 재단기. ¶ *a meat ~* 고기 써는 기계 / *a grass ~* 풀 베는〔잔디 깎는〕 기계 / *a paper ~* 종이 재단기. **3** a small boat used by warships for carrying passengers and supplies to and from the shore. 군함용의 소정(小艇); 커터. **4** ⓐ a kind of a small sailboat with one mast. 외대박이 돛배의 일종. ⓑ 《U.S.》 a small, fast boat used by the Coast Guard. (연안 경비대의) 감시선(船). **5** a small, light, sleigh, usu. pulled by one horse. (말이 끄는) 작은 썰매. [→cut]

cut·throat [kʌ́tθròut] *n.* Ⓒ a murderer. 살인자. — *adj.* **1** murderous; cruel; destructive; severe. 살인의; 잔혹한; 파괴적인; 격렬한; 가혹한. ¶ *a ~ competition* 격심한 경쟁. **2** (of razors) open; unprotected by any safety device. (면도기가) 안전 장치가 없는. [→cut]

cut·ting [kʌ́tiŋ] *n.* Ⓒ **1** Ⓤ the act of cutting. 자름; 절단; 벌채. **2** something cut off. 잘라낸 것[조각]. **3** a small shoot or branch cut from a plant in an attempt to grow a new plant. (꺾꽂이용의) 자른 가지; 삽목. **4** 《Brit.》 a short piece cut out from a newspaper or magazine to be preserved. (신문·잡지 등에서) 오려낸 것(=《U.S.》 clipping). ¶ *a newspaper[press] ~*. **5** a passage or tunnel cut through high ground for a road, a railway, etc. (산 따위를) 깎아 뚫어서 낸 길[철로]. ¶ *a railway ~*. — *adj.* **1** that cuts; sharp. (날이) 잘 드는; 예리한. ¶ *a ~ blade* 예리한 날 / *a ~ edge of a knife* 서슬이 퍼런 나이프의 날. **2** ⓐ causing pain like that of cutting. 살을 에는 듯한; 몹시 추운. ¶ *a ~ wind* (살을 에는 듯한) 매서운 바람. ⓑ 《*fig.*》 hurting the feelings; sarcastic. 감정을 해치는; (뼈에) 사무치는; 통렬한; 비꼬는. ¶ *a ~ remarks* 신랄히 비꼬는 말 / *a ~ glance* 날카롭게 쏘아보는 눈초리. ● **cut·ting·ly** [-li] *adv.* [→cut]

cut·tle·fish [kʌ́tlfìʃ] *n.* Ⓒ (*pl.* **-fish·es** or *collectively* **-fish**) a seacreature which sends out a black, inky liquid when attacked. 오징어. ¶ *~ tactics* (구축함 따위의) 연막 전술. [E.]

cut·up [kʌ́tʌ̀p] *n.* 《U.S. *colloq.*》 one who shows off or play tricks. 젠체하는[과시하는] 사람; (못된) 장난을 치는 사람. [→cut]

cut·wa·ter [kʌ́twɔ̀:tər, -wɑ̀t-] *n.* the front part of a ship's prow. 이물의 물결 헤치는 부분.

cut·worm [kʌ́twə̀:rm] *n.* a caterpillar that cuts off the stalks of young plants near or below the ground. 뿌리 잘라먹는 벌레《몇몇 나방 종류의 유충》.

cwt. hundredweight(=《Brit.》 112 pounds, 《U.S.》 100 pounds).

-cy [-si] *suf.* used to form abstract nouns. 성질·신분 따위를 나타내는 추상명사를 만듦. ¶ *captaincy / bankruptcy.*

cy·an·ic [saiǽnik] *adj.* 《chem.》 of or containing cyanogen. 시안의; 시안을 함유한.

cyanic acid [-ˊ-ˊ ˊ-] *n.* 《chem.》 a colorless, poisonous liquid. 시안산(酸); 청산.

cy·an·o·gen [saiǽnədʒin] *n.* 《chem.》 a colorless, poisonous, imflammable gas. 시안. [Gk. *kuanos* a blue mineral]

cy·a·no·sis [sàiənóusis] *n.* Ⓤ 《med.》 blueness or lividness of the skin caused by lack of oxygen in the blood. 치아노제; 청색증(青色症). [↑]

Cyb·e·le [síbəli:] *n.* 《Gk. myth.》 the goddess of nature. 대지의 여신.

cy·ber·net·ics [sàibərnétiks] *n.* 《U.S.》 the study of complex calculating machines in comparison with the human nervous system in order to understand better the functioning of the human brain. 사이버네틱스; 인공 두뇌학(人工頭腦學). [Gk. *kybernetes* helmsman]

***cy·cle** [sáikl] *n.* Ⓒ **1** a period of time, or a series of events or actions, that repeats itself regularly and in the same order. 주기(週期); 순환(기); 반복. ¶ *the ~ of the seasons* 계절의 순환 / *a business[vicious] ~* 경기의[악] 순환 / *a ~ of events* 사건의 반복 / *in a thirty-year ~* 30년 주기로. **2** a complete set or series; a group of poems, stories, legends, etc. about a great event or hero. (집성된) 한 조(組); 전권(全卷); 일군의 이야기[시가, 전설, 극]. ¶ *the Trojan ~* 트로이 사시 대계(史詩大系). **3** a great length of time; an age. 긴 세월; 한 시대. **4** 《*colloq.*》 a bicycle; a motorcycle; a tricycle. 자전거; 오토바이; 삼륜차. **5** 《phys., electr.》 a unit of measurement of the frequency of an electric current. 주파; 사이클. — *vi.* (P1) **1** ride or travel by bicycle, etc. 자전거[오토바이]를 타다. **2** pass through a cycle; move in a cycle. 순환하다. [Gk. *kuklos* circle]

cy·clic [sáiklik, sík-], **-cli·cal** [-klikəl] *adj.* **1** of a cycle; moving or happening in cycles. 순환의; 주기적인. ¶ *10 ~ years,* 10년 주기 / *~ phenomena* 주기적 현상. **2** of a cycle of poems. 시가군(詩歌群)의.

cy·cling [sáikliŋ] *n.* Ⓤ the act or sport of riding or traveling by bicycle, etc. 사이클링; 자전거[오토바이] 타기.

cy·clist [sáiklist] *n.* Ⓒ a person who rides or travels by bicycle, etc. 자전거[오토바이] 타는 사람.

cy·cloid [sáiklɔid] *adj.* like a circle 원형의; 환상(環狀)의. — *n.* 《geom.》 a curve traced by a point on the circumference of a circle rolling on a straight line. 사이클로이드.

cy·clom·e·ter [saiklɑ́mitər / -klɔ́-] *n.* an instrument that measures the distance that a wheel travels by recording its revolutions. 주행(走行) 거리계(計). [→cycle]

cy·clone [sáikloun] *n.* Ⓒ **1** a wind blowing roundly and around esp. in a storm. 선풍; 구풍(颶風). **2** a storm moving around its center. 열대성 저기압. [→cycle]

Cy·clo·pe·an [sàikləpí:ən] *adj.* **1** of or like a Cyclops. 외눈의 거인 Cyclops의[같은]. **2** 《often *c-*》 huge; immense. 거대한.

cy·clo·pe·di·a, -pae- [sàikloupí:diə] *n.*

Ⓒ a book giving classified information on all branches of knowledge; an encyclopedia. 백과 사전.

Cy·clo·pes [saiklóupi:z] *n.* pl. of **Cyclops**.

Cy·clops [sáiklɑps / -klɔps] *n.* (*pl.* **Cy·clop·ses** or **Cy·clo·pes**) **1** 《Gk. myth.》 a one-eyed giant. 키클로프스《외눈의 거인》. **2** 《*c*-》 a one-eyed person. 애꾸. [→cycle]

cy·clo·style [sáikləstàil] *n.* a duplicating apparatus. 등사기. [↑]

cy·clo·tron [sáiklətràn / -trɔ̀n] *n.* Ⓒ 《phys.》 an atom smasher. 사이클로트론《원자핵 가속 장치》. [↑, *electron*]

cy·der [sáidər] *n.*《Brit.》 =cider.

cyg·net [sígnit] *n.* Ⓒ a young swan. 고니〔백조〕의 새끼. [L. *cygnus* swan]

•**cyl·in·der** [sílindər] *n.* Ⓒ **1** a solid or empty body, long and round, with its two ends equal and parallel. 원통; 원주; 원통형의 것. **2** a round empty box in which a piston works. 실린더; 기통(氣筒). [Gk. *kulindō* roll]

cy·lin·dri·cal [silíndrikəl] *adj.* of a cylinder; shaped like a cylinder. 원통형의; 원주(모양)의. ¶ *Candles and water pipes are usually* ~. 양초와 수도 파이프는 보통 원통형이다.

cym·bal [símbəl] *n.* 《usu. *pl.*》 《mus.》 one of a pair of brass plates which produce a ringing sound when clashed together. 심벌즈《타악기》. [Gk.]

cyme [saim] *n.* 《bot.》 an inflorescence. 취산화서(聚繖花序). [Gk. *kuma* wave]

Cym·ric [kímrik, sím-] *adj.* of Wales; Welsh. 웨일스 사람〔말〕의. [W.]

cyn·ic [sínik] *n.* Ⓒ **1** a person who does not believe in the goodness of human nature; an ill-natured person. (남의 성실을 믿지 않는) 냉소가(家); 비꼬는 사람. **2** 《*C*-》 a member of a group of ancient Greek philosophers who taught that the most important element of virtue is self-control. 견유학파(犬儒學派)의 사람.
— *adj.* **1** cynical. 냉소적인. **2** 《*C*-》 of the Cynics or their doctrines. 견유학파의. [Gk. *kuon* dog]

cyn·i·cal [sínikəl] *adj.* doubting the honesty and goodness of human nature; like a cynic. 냉소적인; 비아냥거리는. ¶ *be* ~ *of someone's efforts* 아무의 노력에 냉소적이다 / *a* ~ *smile* 빈정거리는 웃음. ● **cyn·i·cal·ly** [-kəli] *adv.* **cyn·i·cal·ness** [-nis] *n.*

cyn·i·cism [sínəsìzəm] *n.* Ⓤ **1** the quality of being cynical; a cynical opinion. 비꼼; 냉소벽(癖). **2** 《*C*-》 the doctrines or practice of the Cynics. 견유(犬儒)주의. **3** a cynical remark. 냉소적인〔비아냥거리는〕 말.

cyn·o·sure [sáinəʃùər, sínə-] *n.* **1** 《astron.》 《*the C*-》 the Little Bear. 작은곰자리; 북극성. **2** a center of attraction. 주목의 대상. ¶ *the* ~ *of all eyes* 중인(衆人) 주시(注視)의 대상. [↑, Gk. *oura* tail]

Cyn·thi·a [sínθiə] *n.* **1** 《Gk. myth.》 Diana. 달의 여신 Diana의 딴이름. **2** 《*poet.*》 the moon. 달.

cy·pher [sáifər] *n., v.* =cipher.

cy·press [sáipris] *n.* **1** Ⓒ an evergreen tree of the pine family, having dark leaves; Ⓤ the wood of this tree. 삼나무의 일종; 이 나무의 재목. **2** Ⓒ 《*poet.*》 this tree, or a branch of it, used as a symbol of mourning. 이 나무 또는 나뭇가지《애도의 상징으로 쓰임》. [Gk. *kuparissos*]

Cy·pri·an [síprian] *adj.* of Cyprus; wanton. 키프로스의; 음란한. — *n.* a native of Cyprus. 키프로스 사람.

Cy·prus [sáiprəs] *n.* an island republic in the Mediterranean. 키프로스《지중해의 섬·공화국》.

cyst [sist] *n.* **1** a small bag-like growth in the body containing diseased matter. 낭종(囊腫). **2** a hollow in the body. 포(胞). **3** 《biol.》 an animal cell containing embryos, etc. 포낭(胞囊). [↓]

cyst·ic [sístik] *adj.* of the urinary bladder. 방광의. [Gk. *kustis* sac]

cys·to·scope [sístəskòup] *n.* an instrument for cystic examination. 방광경(膀胱鏡). [↑]

cy·tol·o·gy [saitάlədʒi / -tɔ́l-] *n.* the study of the cells. 세포학(細胞學). [Gk. *kutos* vessel]

czar [zɑ:r] *n.* 《often *C*-》 **1** the title of the former emperors of Russia. 차르; 옛 러시아 황제. ¶ *Czar Peter the Great* 표트르 대제(大帝). **2** Ⓒ an emperor; an autocrat. 황제; 전제 군주. [*Caesar*]

cza·ri·na [zɑ:rí:nə] *n.* the title of the former empresses of Russia; the wife of a czar. (옛 러시아의) 황후; 차르의 아내. [↑]

czar·ism [zά:rizəm] *n.* autocracy; dictatorship. 전제〔독재〕 정치.

cza·rit·za [zɑ:rítsə] *n.* =czarina.

Czech [tʃek] *n.* **1** Ⓒ a native or inhabitant of Czech Republic. 체크 사람. **2** Ⓤ the West slavic language of the Czechs. 체크말. — *adj.* of the Czechs, their language or their culture. 체크의; 체크어〔문화〕의. [Native]

Czech·o·slo·vak, -Slo·vak [tʃékəslóuvɑ:k, -væk] *adj.* of Czechoslovakia, its people. 체코슬로바키아(사람)의. — *n.* Ⓒ a Czech or Slovak living in Czechoslovakia. 체크 또는 슬로바키아 사람. [Czech, Slovak]

Czech·o·slo·va·kia, -Slo·va·kia [tʃèkəsləvά:kiə, -vǽk-] *n.* a former country in central Europe, in 1993 it was divided into Czech Republic and Slovakia. 체코슬로바키아.

Czech Republic [ˊ–ˊ–] *n.* a country in central Europe; formerly the western constitutent republic of Czechoslovakia. 체코 공화국.

d D

D, d [di:] *n.* Ⓒ (*pl.* **D's, Ds, d's, ds**) **1** the fourth letter of the English alphabet. 영어 알파벳의 넷째 글자. **2** 《mus.》 the second note or tone of the musical scale of C major. 라조(調); 라음(音). **3** the Roman number for 500. (로마 숫자의) 500. ¶ *XD*, 490 / *MDLI*, 1551.

D. December; Democrat(ic); Dutch.

d. date; degree; died; denarius (L.=penny); denarii (L.=pence); dollar; dose.

d- =damn.

'd 《*colloq.*》 a shortened form of *had* and *would*, chiefly after *I, we, you, he, she, they*. ¶ *I'd, we'd*.

dab[1] [dæb] *vi., vt.* (**dabbed, dab·bing**) (P3;6,7,13) **1** touch or tap lightly. 가볍게 대다[누르다]; 가볍게 두드리다. ¶ ~ *paper with a brush* = ~ *a brush against paper* 종이에 붓을 대다 / ~ (*at*) *one's face with a powder puff* 분첩으로 얼굴을 토닥거리다 / ~ *one's eyes with a handkerchief* 두 눈을 손수건으로 가볍게 누르다. **2** pat or brush a material with a series of light strokes. 계속해 바르다. ¶ ~ *butter on the bread* 빵에 버터를 바르다 / *He dabbed the salve on his burned finger.* 덴 손가락에 고약을 처덕처덕 발랐다. —*n.* Ⓒ **1** a quick, light blow or touch. 가볍게 두드림; 경타(輕打). ¶ *give one's face a* ~ *with the puff* 얼굴을 분첩으로 토닥대다 / *She gave me a* ~ *with her umbrella.* 그녀는 우산으로 나를 톡톡 건드렸다. **2** ⓐ a smear; a little bit. 한번 바름; 소량; 조금. ¶ *a* ~ *of butter* 소량의 버터 / *put a* ~ *of lipstick on one's mouth* 입술에 립스틱을 바르다. ⓑ a small soft mass. (촉촉하고 말랑한 것의) 작은 덩어리. ¶ *a* ~ *of mustard* 겨자의 작은 덩어리. [E.]

dab[2] [dæb] *n* 《Brit. *colloq.*》 a skillful person; expert. 잘하는 사람; 명수; 능수. ¶ *a* ~ (*hand*) *at tennis* 테니스의 명수. [? corrupt. of adapt]

dab[3] [dæb] *n.* 《fish》 a small flat-fish. 작은 가자미류(類). [→dab[1]]

dab·ber [dǽbər] *n.* a person who dabs. (가볍게) 두드리는 사람; 바르는[칠하는] 사람.

dab·ble [dǽbəl] *vt., vi.* (P6;1,3) **1** dip (hands, feet, etc.) in and out of water or mud; splash. (손·발 따위)를 물[흙탕] 속에 잠그다; (물)을 튀기다; 첨벙이다. **2** 《*in, at*》 do (something) as an amateur; work a little. (취미로) 손을 대다; 좀 하다. ¶ ~ *at gardening* 원예에 손을 대다 / ~ *in literature* 문학을 좀 해 보다 / *He dabbled in politics.* 정치에 손 좀 대 보았다. [Du.]

da ca·po [dɑ: kɑ́:pou] *adv.* 《It.》 《mus.》 from the beginning. 처음부터 다시 (되풀이해서)《연주의 지시어》.

dace [deis] *n.* Ⓒ (*pl.* **dac·es** or *collectively* **dace**) 《fish》 any small, silvery river fish. 황어. [→dart]

dachs·hund [dɑ́:kshùnt, dǽkshùnd, dǽʃhùnd] *n.* Ⓒ a German dog with a long body and very short legs. 닥스훈트《짧은 다리에 몸이 긴 독일산의 개》. [G.=badger-hound]

da·coit [dəkɔ́it] *n.* a member of a gang of robbers (in India or Myanmar). (인도·미얀마의) 강도단의 일원. [Hind.]

dac·tyl [dǽktil] *n.* Ⓒ 《prosody》 a foot of three syllables, one long followed by two short in quantitative meter, or one stressed followed by two unstressed in accentual meter. (운(韻)의) 강약약격(強弱弱格)《´××》; (운(韻)의) 장단단격(長短短格) 《–∪∪》. [Gk.=finger]

dac·tyl·ic [dæktílik] *adj.* composed of dactyls. 강약약격(強弱弱格)[장단단격(長短短格)]으로 된. ¶ ~ *verse* 장단단격의 시.

dac·ty·lol·ogy [dæ̀ktəlɑ́lədʒi / -lɔ́l-] *n.* the use of the fingers and hands to convey ideas, as in the manual alphabet used by the deaf. (농아의) 수화(법); 지화술(指話術). [Imit.]

:dad [dæd] *n.* Ⓒ 《*colloq.*》 father. 아빠.

Da·da·ism [dɑ́:dɑ:ìzəm, dɑ́:də-] *n.* a movement in art characterized by fantastic, formless expression of subconscious matters. 다다이즘《허무적 예술의 한 파》. ● **Da·da·ist** [-ist] *n.* [Person]

dad·die [dǽdi] *n.* =daddy.

***dad·dy** [dǽdi] *n.* (*pl.* **-dies**) =dad.

dad·dy-long·legs [dǽdilɔ́:ŋlègz / -lɔ́ŋ-] *n. pl.* 《used as *sing.* and *pl.*》 **1** a harmless insect with very long legs; a crane fly. 꾸정모기. **2** 《U.S.》 a spiderlike creature usu. with very long legs. 장님거미. [Imit.]

da·do [déidou] *n.* (*pl.* **-does, -dos**) 《archit.》 the lower part of a roomwall wainscoted or colored. 징두리판벽《벽면의 하부》. [→die]

dae·dal [dí:dl] *adj.* 《*poet.*》 of mysterious complexity or skill. 교묘한. [↓]

Daed·a·lus [dédələs / dí:-] *n.* 《Gk. myth.》 a great creator and inventor who devised the labyrinth in Crete and the wings of Icarus. 다이달로스《Crete 섬의 미로(迷路) 및 비행 날개를 만든 명장(名匠)》. [Gk.]

dae·mon [dí:mən] *n.* =demon.

***daf·fo·dil** [dǽfədìl] *n.* 《bot.》 **1** Ⓒ kinds of pale-yellow narcissus. 나팔수선화. **2** the color of a daffodil; pale-yellow. 담황색. [→asphodel]

daf·fy [dǽfi] *adj.* (**-fi·er, -fi·est**) foolish; crazy. 바보 같은; 미친. [↓]

daft [dæft, dɑːft] *adj.* foolish; crazy; mad. 어리석은; 머리가 돈; 미친. ¶ *go* ~ 미치다; 발광하다. [E.=mild]

daft·ly [dǽftli / dɑ́ːft-] *adv.* foolishly; madly. 어리석게; 미치어; 미친 듯이.

dag·ger [dǽgər] *n.* Ⓒ **1** a short, pointed double-edged sword or knife, used as a weapon. (양날의) 단검. **2** 《print.》 a mark (†) of reference used in printing. (참조용의) 칼표(†). ¶ *a double* ~ 이중 칼표(‡). [E.]

at daggers drawn, about to fight. 곧 싸울 것 같이; 일촉 즉발의 상태에. ¶ *be at daggers drawn with each other* 서로 노려보며 곧 싸움을 시작할 상태에 있다.

look daggers at, look at (someone) with anger or hatred. …을 무서운 눈초리로 노려보다.

speak daggers to, speak to (someone) so as to wound. …에게 독설을 퍼붓다; …을 매도하다.

da·go [déigou] *n.* (*pl.* **-gos, -goes**) 《*contempt.*》 a dark-skinned person from the south of Europe. 스페인〔이탈리아〕계의 사람. [Sp.]

Da·gon [déigɑn / -gɔn] *n.* the national god of the Philistines, half man and half fish. 반인반어체(半人半魚體)의 신. [Heb.]

da·guerre·o·type [dəgέərətàip, -riə-] *n.* an early (type of) photograph. 은판(銀板) 사진(술). [*Daguerre*, Person]

dahl·ia [dǽljə, dɑ́ːl- / déil-] *n.* 《bot.》 Ⓒ a garden plant with bright-colored flowers. 달리아. 參考 스웨덴의 식물학자 A. Dahl 의 이름에서. [Person]

:dai·ly [déili] *adj.* happening or done every day (often except Sunday). 매일의; 일상의; (흔히 일요일 외의) 매일의. ¶ ~ *life* 일상 생활 / *a thing of* ~ *occurrence* 매일 있는 일; 일상사 / *gain one's* ~ *bread* 생계비를 벌다. —*n.* Ⓒ (*pl.* **-lies**) **1** a newspaper published every day. 일간 신문. **2** 《Brit. *colloq.*》 a non-resident maidservant. 드난살이하는 가정부; 파출부. ¶ *We have a* ~. 드난 가정부를 쓰고 있다. —*adv.* every day; day by day. 날마다; 나날이. ¶ *walk* ~ *in the park* 매일 공원을 산책하다 / *It happens* ~. 날마다 발생한다. [*day*]

dain·ti·ly [déintili] *adv.* in a dainty manner; delicately; gracefully. 고상하게; 우아하게; 맛있게; (음식을) 까다롭게 가리어. ¶ *fare* ~ 미식(美食)하다 / *She was very* ~ *dressed.* 그녀는 매우 우아하게 차려 입고 있었다. [→dainty]

dain·ti·ness [déintinis] *n.* Ⓤ the state of being dainty; delicacy. 우아; 맛좋음; 퍽 까다로움; 결벽(潔癖).

·dain·ty [déinti] *adj.* (**-ti·er, -ti·est**) **1** delicate and elegant in appearance. 우아한; 섬세한. ¶ *a* ~ *young girl* 우아한 처녀. **2** having refined or particular tastes. (취미가) 고상한; (특히 음식에) 까다로운; 가리는. ¶ *She is* ~ *about her eating* 〔*food*〕. 그녀는 음식에 까다롭다. **3** delicious. 맛있는. ¶ *a* ~ *dish* 맛있는 요리. —*n.* Ⓒ (*pl.* **-ties**) an especially nice piece of food; something delicious. 맛있는 음식; 진미(珍味). [→dignity]

·dair·y [dέəri] *n.* Ⓒ (*pl.* **-ies**) **1** a place where milk and cream are kept and made into butter or cheese. 착유장(搾乳場); 낙농장. **2** a shop or company selling milk, butter, cheese, etc. 유제품(乳製品) 판매점〔회사〕; 우유점(店). **3** the business of making such products. 유제품 제조업; 낙농업. [E.]

dairy cattle [ㅿ-ㅿ-] *n.* cows raised to produce milk. 젖소.

dairy farm [ㅿ-ㅿ] *n.* a farm where milk and cream are produced and butter and cheese made. 낙농장.

dair·y·ing [dέəriiŋ] *n.* the business of a dairy. 낙농업의 일; 낙농업.

dair·y·maid [dέərimèid] *n.* Ⓒ a woman employed in a dairy. 낙농장에서 일하는 여자; 젖 짜는 여자.

dair·y·man [dέərimən] *n.* Ⓒ (*pl.* **-men** [-mən]) a man employed in a dairy; the owner or manager of a dairy; a dealer in milk, cream, butter, and eggs. 낙농장에서 일하는 남자; 낙농장 경영자; 낙농품·달걀을 파는 사람.

da·is [déiis] *n.* Ⓒ a raised platform in a large room or hall to hold a speaker's desk, throne, or the like. (방·홀 따위의) 단(壇); (강당의) 연단; 교단(敎壇). [→disk]

:dai·sy [déizi] *n.* Ⓒ (*pl.* **-sies**) **1** 《bot.》 a very common small flower, yellow in the center and white around it. 데이지(꽃). **2** 《*sl.*》 something fine or notable. 일품(逸品); 훌륭한 것. [*day's eye*]

daisy chain [ㅿ-ㅿ] *n.* a string of daisies linked to form a chain. 데이지 화환.

Dak. Dakota.

Da·kar [dɑːkɑ́ːr] *n.* a seaport in and the capital of Senegal. 세네갈의 수도〔항구〕.

Da·ko·ta [dəkóutə] *n.* a former territory in the United States, divided into the states of North Dakota and South Dakota. 다코타.

dal., dal decaliter.

·dale [deil] *n.* Ⓒ 《*poet., dial.*》 a small valley. (작은) 골짜기. ¶ *over hill and* ~ 산을 넘고 골짜기를 건너. [E.]

dales·man [déilzmən] *n.* (*pl.* **-men** [-mən]) a person who lives in a valley (esp. in the North of England). (특히 영국 잉글랜드 북부 지방의) 골짜기에 사는 사람.

Dal·las [dǽləs] *n.* a city in Texas where President Kennedy was assasinated. 댈러스《미국 Texas 주의 도시. 케네디 대통령이 암

살된 곳》.

dal·li·ance [dǽliəns] *n.* Ⓤ a lovemaking; flirtation; sensuality. 연애 유희; 농탕침; 불장난; 호색. [F]

dal·ly [dǽli] *v.* (**-lied**) *vi.* (P1,3) **1** 《with》 act in a playful manner; toy; play. 농락하다; 희롱〔새롱〕거리다; 농탕치다. ¶ ~ *with a lover* 애인과 새롱거리다 / ~ *with temptation* 유혹의 손을 뻗치다. **2** idle; waste time; hesitate. 빈둥빈둥 보내다; (시간을) 허비하다; 머무적〔꾸물〕거리다. ¶ *He dallied over his work.* 일을 가지고 꾸물거렸다. **3** hesitate to accept, etc. 받아들이기를 망설이다. ¶ ~ *with an offer* 제의를 받아들이기를 망설이다. — *vt.* (P6,7) waste (time). (시간을) 낭비하다. ¶ ~ *a way precious time* 귀중한 시간을 헛되이 보내다. [F]

Dal·ma·tian [dælméiʃiən] *adj.* of Dalmatia, a part of Croatia. 달마티아의. — *n.* a kind of spotted dog. 달마티아 개《지키는 개》. [Place]

D

•**dam**[1] [dæm] *n.* Ⓒ **1** a wall or bank built to keep back water. 댐; 방죽; 둑. ¶ *The* ~ *has burst.* 방죽이 터졌다. **2** the water held back a dam. 댐에 가둔 물; 댐 저수(貯水). — *vt.* (**dam·med, dam·ming**) (P6,7) **1** hold back (water, etc.) with a dam. (댐으로) …을 막다. ¶ ~ (*up*) *a stream* 댐으로 강물을 막다. **2** 《*fig.*》 keep back or block up with anything; control. …을 누르다. ¶ ~ *up one's feelings* 감정을 (억)누르다 / ~ *up inflation* 인플레이션을 막다 / ~ *back one's tears* 눈물을 억제하다. [E.]

dam[2] [dæm] *n.* a mother animal. (네발 짐승의) 어미; 어이. [→dame]

:**dam·age** [dǽmidʒ] *n.* **1** Ⓤ 《*from, to*》 harm, hurt or injury; loss. 손상; 손해. ¶ *flood* ~ 수해 / *do* ~ *to something* …에(게) 손해를 주다 / *sustain great a* ~ 큰 손해를 입다 / *The typhoon caused much (a great deal of)* ~ *to the crops.* 태풍은 농작물에 막대한 손해를 끼쳤다 / *He is always doing* ~. 그는 항상 무엇을 만졌다 하면 일을 저지른다. **2** 《*pl.*》 《law》 money or amount claimed or allowed by a court in return for harm or injury. 손해 배상(금). ¶ *claim damages* 손해 배상금을 요구하다 / *The tramcar company paid him damages.* 전차 회사는 그에게 손해 배상을 했다. **3** 《*colloq.*》 cost; expense. 비용; 대가(代價). ¶ *What's the* ~ ? 돈이 얼마나 드나 / *I'll stand the* ~. 비용은 내가 부담하겠다.
— *vt.* (P6) harm; hurt; injure; destroy. …에게 손해를 끼치다; 손상시키다. ¶ ~ *someone's reputation* 아무의 명성을 손상시키다 / *I damaged my shoes in baseball practice.* 야구 연습에서 구두를 망가뜨렸다.
•**dam·age·a·ble** [-əbəl] *adj.* [L. *damnum*]

dam·ag·ing admission [dǽmidʒiŋ ædmíʃən] *n.* an admission that weakens one's case. 불이익을 가져오는 승인.

Da·mas·cus [dəmǽskəs] *n.* the capital of Syria. 다마스쿠스.

dam·ask [dǽməsk] *n.* Ⓤ **1** a species of beautiful silk or linen material with figures and designs. 단자(緞子); 능직(綾織)(천). **2** a tough fine steel made in Damascus, the capital of Syria. 다마스크강(鋼)(=damask steel). **3** deep pink color; rose-color. 장밋빛; 분홍빛. — *adj.* **1** made of damask. 단자의; 능직의. **2** rose-colored. 장밋빛의. — *vt.* (P6) **1** weave or adorn with elaborate design, as damask cloth. 다마스크풍의 무늬를 넣어 짜다. **2** suffuse with damask color. (뺨을) 붉히다. [*Damascus*]

•**dame** [deim] *n.* Ⓒ **1** 《*arch.*》 a noble lady; the mistress of a house. 귀부인; 부인(夫人). **2** 《*D-*》 《Brit.》 ⓐ a title of honor, often given to a knight's or baronet's wife. knight 또는 baronet 부인의 정식 존칭. ⓑ recently the title of a woman who has personally received an order of knighthood. 나이트 훈위(勳位)를 받은 여성에 대한 존칭. ¶ *Dame Ellen Terry* 엘렌 테리 여사. **3** an old woman. 노부인. **4** 《*arch., joc.*》 a woman esp. a married woman. 여성; (특히) 기혼여성. ¶ *date a good-looking* ~ 미인과 데이트하다. **5** The keeper of Eton boarding house. (Eton 기숙사의) 사감(舍監). [L. *donima* mistress]

dame school [ㅅㅅ] *n.* a small private school kept by an old woman. 노부인이 경영하는 초등 학교.

•**damn** [dæm] *vt.* (P6) **1** (of God) send (someone) to everlasting punishment. (신이 아무를) 영원히 지옥에 떨어뜨리다. ¶ *I'll be damned if*.... 죽어도 …하지 않겠다. **2** declare or judge (something) as bad or a failure. …을 나쁘다고 (판정)하다; 깎아내리다. **3** cause (someone) to fail; ruin. …을 결딴내다; 파탄시키다. **4** express anger, dislike, etc. by using bad language. …을 저주하다; …의 욕을 하다. ¶ *Damn it!* 젠장; 염병할 / *Damn the rain!* 빌어먹을 놈의 비 / *Damn you!* 이놈의 자식 / *The priest damned the murderer.* 사제는 살인자를 저주했다. — *vi.* (P1) say 'damn'; swear. 저주하다; 독설하다. ¶ *Oh,* ~*!* 에이 지겨워.
damn with faint praise, praise so coolly as to suggest disapproval. 내키지 않는〔냉담한〕 칭찬을 해서 실제로는 깎아내리다.
— *n.* Ⓒ **1** a cry of anger or dislike; a curse. 매도; 저주. **2** 《in nonassertive》 something of little value; a bit. (부정 구문에서) 조금도.
do not care* 〔*give*〕 *a damn, 《*colloq.*》 don't care at all. 조금도 상관〔개의〕하지 않다; 조금도 관심이 없다. ¶ *I don't care* 〔*give*〕 *a* ~ *what he does.* 그가 무엇을 하든 상관 않는다.
not worth a damn, worthless. 아무 가치도 없다. ¶ *His promise isn't worth a* ~. 그의 약속은 아무 가치도 없다.
— *adj., adv.* damned. 증오할; 지긋지긋한〔해

게). [L. *damno*]

dam·na·ble [dǽmnəbəl] *adj.* **1** deserving or causing to be damned; hateful. 비난해야 할; 증오할 만한; 지긋지긋한. ¶ *a ~ lie* 증오해 마땅한 거짓말. **2** 《*colloq.*》 very bad. 몹시 나쁜; 형편없는. ¶ *The dinner was ~.* 저녁 식사는 형편없었다. ● **dam·na·bly** [-bli] *adv.*

dam·na·tion [dæmnéiʃən] *n.* Ⓤ **1** the act of damning; the state of being damned; ruin. 지옥에 떨어짐(떨어뜨림); 파멸. **2** eternal punishment after death. (사후의) 영원한 벌. **3** 《as an expression of anger, annoyance, disappointment, etc.》 curse. 저주(의 말); 매도. ¶ *Damnation!* 빌어먹을; 염병할; 제기랄.

damned [dæmd] *adj.* **1** condemned as bad. 저주받은. **2** sent to eternal punishment. 지옥에 떨어진.

the damned, the souls in hell. 지옥에 떨어진 영혼들.

— *adv.* 《*colloq.*》 very. 매우; 몹시.

dam·ni·fi·ca·tion [dæ̀mnəfəkéiʃən] *n.* 《law》 damage. 손상(損傷) (행위); 침해(侵害) (행위). [↓]

dam·ni·fy [dǽmnəfài] *vt.* (P6) 《law》 cause injury to. 손상을 주다; 침해하다. [L. *damnum* harm]

Dam·o·cles [dǽməklìːz] *n.* a flatterer to whom Dionysius demonstrated the danger of the ruler's life by seating him below a sword hanging by a hair. 다모클레스 《Syracuse 의 독재왕 Dionysius 의 아첨꾼 신하》. [Person]

sword of Damocles, any impending danger. 다모클레스 (머리 위)의 검(劍)《행복한 속에서도 항상 신변에 닥치는 위험》.

Da·mon and Pyth·i·as [déimən *ənd* píθiəs] *n.* a pair of devoted friends. 둘도 없는 친구. [Rom. legend]

***damp** [dæmp] *adj.* **1** slightly wet. 약간 젖은; 습기 있는; 축축한. ¶ *~ weather* 우중충한 날씨 / *My shirt was still ~ this morning.* 오늘 아침 내 셔츠는 아직도 축축했다. **2** 《*fig.*》 unenthusiastic; dejected; depressed. 열의를 잃은; 기가 꺾인; 풀이 죽은.

— *n.* **1** Ⓤ a damp condition; wetness. 축축함; 습기. **2** 《*a ~*》 depression of spirits. 낙담; 의기 소침. **3** 《usu. *pl.*》 any harmful gas in a mine. (광산 안의) 유독 메탄 가스(= firedamp).

cast (***strike***) ***a damp over*** (***into***), cause (someone) loss of joy or hope; depress. …의 기운을 떨어뜨리다(꺾다); …에 어두운 그림자를 던지다; …의 흥을 깨다.

— *vt.* (P6) **1** make (something) slightly wet. …을 적시다; 축이다. ¶ *The rain has damped your coat.* 비가 자네 코트를 적셨네. **2** make (someone's feelings) less strong or bright. (기·열의 따위)를 꺾다. ¶ *~ someone's spirits* (*ardor*) 아무의 기운을(열의를) 꺾다. **3** check; put out. (행동 따위)를 저지하다. [E.]

damp down, make (a fire) slower in burning; make (sound) less loud. (불)을 약하게 하다; 사위지 않게 묻다; (소리)를 약화시키다.

damp off, (of a plant shoots, etc.) wither and die. (새싹 따위가) 시들어 죽다.

damp·en [dǽmpən] *vt.* (P6) **1** make damp. 적시다. **2** 《chiefly U.S.》 = damp. ¶ *The bad news dampened our spirits.* 나쁜 소식이 우리를 의기 소침케 했다.

damp·er [dǽmpər] *n.* Ⓒ **1** a person or thing that damps, dulls, or checks. 적시는 사람(것); 흥을 깨는 사람(것). **2** a metal plate to control the current of air to a fire in a stove or furnace. (난로 따위의) 바람문; 공기 조절판. **3** 《mus.》 a device for checking vibration, esp. of piano strings. (피아노의) 단음(斷音) 장치.

cast (***put***) ***a damper on,*** cause (something) to be less merry. …의 흥을 깨다. ¶ *cast a ~ on a party* 파티의 흥을 깨다 / *The news put a ~ on our fun.* 그 소식이 우리의 즐거운 무드를 깼다.

damp·ish [dǽmpiʃ] *adj.* slightly damp. 약간 젖은; 좀 축축한.

damp·ly [dǽmpli] *adv.* in a damp way or state. 습하게; 축축히.

damp·ness [dǽmpnis] *n.* Ⓤ the quality or state of being damp. 젖음; 축축함; 습기.

***dam·sel** [dǽmzəl] *n.* Ⓒ 《*arch., poet.*》 a girl; a maiden. 여자; 처녀; 아가씨. [→dame]

***dam·son** [dǽmzən] *n.* Ⓒ a small, dark, blue plum; the tree bearing it. 서양 자두(나무). [→damask]

Dan. **1** Daniel. **2** Danish.

⁑**dance** [dæns, dɑːns] *vi.* (P1,2A) **1** move the body, esp. the feet, in rhythm, ordinarily to music. 춤추다; 댄스하다. ¶ *~ in the hall* (*at the ball*) 홀에서(무도회에서) 춤추다 / *~ to music* 음악에 맞춰 춤추다 / *~ with someone* 아무와 춤추다. **2** move lightly and gaily about. 껑충껑충 뛰다; 뛰어 돌아다니다. ¶ *~ for* (*with*) *joy* 기뻐 껑충껑충 뛰다 / *~ with rage* 성이 나서 펄쩍펄쩍 뛰다. **3** (of light, inanimate objects) move up and down. (가벼운 것·무생물이) 상하로 움직이다; 흔들리다; 춤추다. ¶ *The boat danced on the waves.* 배는 물결에 까불었다 / *The leaves are dancing in the wind.* 나뭇잎들이 바람에 흔들리고 있다. — *vt.* (P6,7) **1** perform or take part in (a dance). (춤을) 추다. ¶ *~ a waltz* 왈츠를 추다. **2** cause (someone) to dance; give a dancing motion to. …을 춤추게 하다; 아래위로 흔들다(까부르다). ¶ *~ a child on one's knee* 무릎위에서 어린애를 까불다. **3** bring to a particular state or condition by dancing. 춤을 추어 …하게 하다. ¶ *She danced him weary.* 그녀는 그를 춤추어 지치게 했다.

dance attendance on (***upon***) *someone,* wait on (someone) often and attentively; be excessively polite and obedient to (someone). (…을 따라다니며) 비위를 맞추다; 알찐거리다.

***dance away* [*off*],** lose by dancing. 춤추어서 없애다. ¶ ~ *away one's worry* 춤을 추어 근심을 잊다.

***dance on* [*upon*] *air* [*a rope, nothing*],** be hanged. 교수형을 받다.

dance to another tune, change one's opinion, attitude, or behavior. 의견(태도, 행동)을 바꾸다.

***dance to someone's tune* [*pipe*],** 《*fig.*》 do his bidding. 남의 장단에 춤추다; 시키는 대로 하다.

— *n.* Ⓒ **1** ⓐ a rhythmic movement of the feet or body, ordinarily to music; the art of dancing. 춤; 댄스; 무용. ¶ *lead the* ~ 춤을 리드하다. ⓑ one round of dancing. 춤 한판. ¶ *May I have* (*the pleasure of*) *the next* ~ ? 다음 춤의 상대를 해 드리게 해 주시겠습니까. **2** a particular kind of dance; a piece of music for dancing. 춤의 한 종류; 춤곡(曲). ¶ *a social* ~ 사교춤. **3** a dancing party. 댄스 파티. ¶ *give a* ~ 무도회를 개최하다. [F.]

lead someone a pretty dance, give someone a lot of trouble; make someone follow here and there. (귀찮은 또는 불필요한 일을 강요하여) 아무를 곤혹시키다; 이리저리 끌고 다니다.

lead the dance, take the initiative. 솔선하다.

dance band [⊿⊿] *n.* a band which performs for dances. 댄스 음악의 밴드.

dance hall [⊿⊿] *n.* a public hall or room in which dances are held. 댄스 홀.

danc·er [dǽnsər, dáːns-] *n.* Ⓒ **1** a person who dances. 춤추는 사람; 무희; 댄서. **2** a person who makes his living by dancing. (직업) 댄서; 무용가.

danc·ing [dǽnsiŋ, dáːns-] *n.* Ⓤ the art or act of dancing. 춤; 무용(법). [F.]

dancing girl [⊿— ⊿] *n.* a girl who dances for pay. (직업) 댄서; 무희(舞姬).

dancing master [⊿— ⊿—] *n.* a teacher of dancing. 춤 교사.

dan·de·li·on [dǽndəlàiən] *n.* Ⓒ 《bot.》 a common weed with small, yellow flowers. 민들레. [F. *dent de lion* lion's tooth]

dan·der [dǽndər] *n.* 《*one's* ~ 》《*colloq.*》 anger; temper. 성; 분노; 울화통. [? Sc.]

get one's* [*someone's*] *dander up, lose one's [someone's] temper; get angry; make him angry. 불뚱거리(게 하)다; 성나(게 하)다.

Dan·die Din·mont [dǽndi dinmɑnt / -mɔnt] *n.* a breed of terrier. 테리어의 일종. [Person]

dan·dle [dǽndl] *vt.* (P6,7) **1** move (a baby, etc.) up and down on one's knees or in one's arms. (어린애 등을) 안거나 무릎 따위에서 까불어 어르다. **2** pet; pamper. 귀여워하다; 어하다. [It.=trifle]

dan·druff [dǽndrəf] *n.* Ⓤ small pieces of dead skin found in the hair. (머리의) 비듬(=dandriff). ¶ *My head* [*hair*] *is full of* ~. 내 머리는 비듬투성이다. [?]

dan·dy [dǽndi] *n.* Ⓒ (*pl.* **-dies**) a man who pays great attention to his dress and looks. 멋쟁이. — *adj.* (**-di·er, -di·est**) **1** of a dandy; very carefully dressed. 멋내는; 멋쟁이의. **2** 《U.S. *colloq.*》 fine; good; splendid. 훌륭한; 멋진. [Sc.]

Dane [dein] *n.* Ⓒ a person of Denmark. 덴마크 사람. [Teut.]

:dan·ger [déindʒər] *n.* (opp. safety) **1** Ⓤ the state in which there may be harm or loss of life. 위험; 위난(危難). ¶ *the* ~ *from fire* 화재의 위험 / *run the* ~ *of* …의 위험에 노출시키다 / *run into* ~ 위험에 빠지다 / *His life is in* ~. 목숨이 위독하다 / *A soldier at the front faces* ~ *every day.* 일선의 군인은 매일 위험에 직면하게 된다. **2** Ⓒ a thing or a person that may cause harm or death. 위험(인)물; 장애; 위협. ¶ *a* ~ *to peace* 평화에 대한 위협. **3** Ⓤ the position of a signal giving warning of danger. 위험 경계 표시. [→dominate]

at danger, in the position giving a signal of danger. 위험 신호가 되어. ¶ *The signal is at* ~. 위험 신호가 나와 있다; 적신호(위험 신호)이다.

in danger of, likely to incur danger of. …할 위험이 있는. ¶ *She is in* ~ *of losing her life.* 그녀는 생명이 위독하다.

make danger of, regard as dangerous. …을 위험시하다.

out of danger, free from danger. 위험을 벗어나.

:dan·ger·ous [déindʒərəs] *adj.* not safe; full of risks; likely to do harm. 위험한 (opp. safe). ¶ *a* ~ *illness* 위독한 병 / ~ *occupations* 위험한 직업 / *a* ~ *river to cross* 건너기 위험한 강 / *a* ~ *man* 위험 인물 / *look* ~ 무서운 얼굴을 하고 있다 / *The river is* ~ *to swim in.* 저 강은 헤엄치기에는 위험하다.
●**dan·ger·ous·ness** [-nis] *n.*

dan·ger·ous·ly [déindʒərəsli] *adv.* in a dangerous manner. 위험하게.

danger signal [⊿— ⊿—] *n.* a sign of danger to be avoided. 위험 신호; 적신호.

dan·gle [dǽŋgəl] *vi.* **1** hang or swing loosely. (흔들흔들) 매달리다; 늘어지다. ¶ ~ *from the ceiling* 천장에 달려 있다 / *The eye-glass is dangling from the ribbon.* 안경이 리본에 매달려 있다. **2** (P3) 《*after*》 hang about; follow. 붙어(따라) 다니다; 뒤를 쫓아다니다. ¶ ~ *after a woman* 여자 뒤꽁무니를 쫓아다니다.

— *vt.* **1** (P6,13) hold (something) so that it swings and hangs loosely; cause (something) to dangle. (흔들흔들) 늘어뜨리다. ¶ ~ *a toy before a child* 아이 앞에 장난감을 늘어뜨리다. **2** (P6) 《*fig.*》 display an attraction; tempt with. (마음이 동하게) 눈앞에 얼씬거려 보여 주다; …로 유혹하다. ¶ ~

bright prospects before someone 아무 앞에 밝은 전도를 보여 주다. [E.]

Dan·iel [dǽnjəl] *n.* **1** a man's name. 남자 이름. 參考 약칭은 Dan. **2** 《Bible》 one of the great Hebrew prophets. 헤브라이의 대(大) 예언자. **3** a book in the Old Testament of the Bible. 다니엘서(書). **4** 《*fig.*》 Ⓒ a wise and honest judge. 명재판관.

Dan·ish [déiniʃ] *adj.* of Denmark, the Danes or their language. 덴마크의; 덴마크 사람〔말〕의. — *n.* Ⓤ the language of the Danes. 덴마크 말〔어〕. [E.]

dank [dæŋk] *adj.* wet and cold; unpleasantly damp. 축축한; 친친한; 구중중한. [E.]

Dan·te [dǽnti], **Alighieri** *n.* (1265-1321) a famous Italian poet. 단테《'신곡(神曲)'을 쓴 이탈리아의 시인》.

Dan·tesque [dæntésk] *adj.* after the manner of Dante. 단테풍의; 단테 작품과 같은.

Dan·ube [dǽnju:b], **the** *n.* the river flowing through central Europe to the Black Sea. 다뉴브 강《중부 유럽을 흘러 흑해로 들어감》. ●**Dan·u·bi·an** [dænjú:biən] *adj.*

dap [dæp] *vi., vt.* (**dapped, dap·ping**) (P1;6) **1** fish by letting the bait fall on the water. (수면에) 미끼를 던져 낚다. **2** bounce. (돌멩이 따위가) 튀(게 하)다; 튀어 스치다. — *n.* bouncing. 튐. [E.]

Daph·ne [dǽfni] *n.* **1** 《Gk. myth.》 a nymph who escaped from Apollo by becoming a laurel. 다프네《Apollo에게 쫓겨 월계수가 된 요정》. **2** Ⓒ 《*d-*》 《*bot.*》 ⓐ a kind of shrub with sweet-smelling flowers. 팥꽃나무 과의 관목. ⓑ a laurel. 월계수. [Gk.]

dap·per [dǽpər] *adj.* **1** neat; dressed with care. 말쑥한. **2** (of a person) small and active. 몸집이 작고 재빠른; 날렵한. ●**dap·per·ly** [-li] *adv.* [E.]

dap·ple [dǽpəl] *n.* Ⓒ **1** a spot or dot. 반점; 얼룩. **2** an animal marked with spots. 털이 얼룩얼룩한 동물. — *adj.* spotted. 얼룩진. ¶ *a ~ horse* 얼룩말. — *vt., vi.* mark (something) with spots; become marked with spots. …을 얼룩지게 하다〔되다〕. [N.]

dap·pled [dǽpəld] *adj.* spotted. 얼룩진; 반점이 있는. ¶ *a ~ horse* 얼룩말.

dap·ple-gray, -grey [dǽpəlgréi] *adj., n.* (a horse) of gray with darker spots. 회색 돈점박이의 (말). [N.]

DAR 《U.S.》 Daughters of the American Revolution. 독립 전쟁 유족 부인 애국단.

dar·bies [dɑ́:rbiz] *n. pl.* 《*colloq.*》 handcuffs. 수갑. [?]

Dar·by and Joan [dɑ́:rbi ən dʒóun] *n.* a devoted old married couple. 금실 좋은 노부부. [from an old song]

:dare [dɛər] *auxil. v.* (p. **dared** or 《*arch.*》 **durst**) (P25) have enough courage or boldness for some act; be fearless; venture. 감히 …하다; 대담하게도〔뻔뻔스럽게도〕 …할 용기가 있다. 語法 아래 타동사 1과 같은 뜻이지만, 부정문·의문문에서는 조동사로도 쓰임. 다만, 오늘날에는 일반 동사로서 사용되는 경향이 있음. ¶ *He daren't do it.* 그에겐 그것을 할 용기가 없다 / *Dare he do it?* 그에게 그것을 할 용기가 있을까? / *I daren't speak about it.* 나는 감히 그 일에 관해 이야기를 못 하고 있다 / *They dared not look me in the face.* 그들은 감히 내 얼굴을 정면으로 보지 못했다 / *How ~ you say such a thing?* 감히 그런 말을 할 수 있다니.

I dare say, I suppose; probably. 아마(도) …일〔할〕 것이다. ¶ *I ~ say he will arrive tonight.* 아마 그는 오늘 밤 올 것이다.

— *vt.* **1** (**dared** or 《*arch.*》 **durst, dared**) (P8) be bold, impudent, or brave enough to do. 감히 …하다; 대담하게도〔뻔뻔스럽게도〕 …하다. ¶ *He doesn't ~ to jump the fence.* 그는 담을 뛰어 넘을 용기가 없다 / *She does not ~ to tell him.* 그녀는 그에게 말할 용기가 없다 / *He dares to insult me.* 그가 감히 나를 모욕한다 / *I have never dared to speak to him.* 감히 그에게 이야기를 해 본 적이 없다. **2** (P6) have the courage to face. …에 용감히 맞서다. ¶ *~ any danger* 어떠한 위험도 무릅쓰다 / *~ someone's anger* 아무의 노여움도 아랑곳하지 않다. **3** (P20) challenge; defy. …에 도전하다. ¶ *~ a man to fight* 덤빌 테면 덤벼보라고 하다 / *I ~ you to jump.* 뛰어오를 수 있으면 뛰어 보아라 / *The other boys dared him to dive from the bridge.* 다른 아이들은 다리에서 뛰어내려 보라고 그를 부추겼다.

— *n.* Ⓒ an act of daring; challenge. 감히 함; 도전. ¶ *give a ~* 도전하다 / *take a ~* 도전에 응하다. [E.]

dare·dev·il [dɛ́ərdèvəl] *n.* Ⓒ a reckless person. 무모한 사람. — *adj.* reckless; bold. 무모한; 목숨 아까운 줄 모르는. ¶ *a ~ driver* 무모한 운전사. [E.]

dar·ing [dɛ́əriŋ] *n.* Ⓤ courage to take risks; bravery. 대담 무쌍; 용감. — *adj.* courageous; fearless. 용감한; 대담(무쌍)한; 두려움을 모르는. ¶ *a ~ raid* 대담 무쌍한 습격 / *show great ~ (in doing something)* (무엇을 하는 데) 과감함을 보이다. ●**dar·ing·ly** [-li] *adv.* [E.]

Da·ri·us [dəráiəs] *n.* (558?-486 B.C.) a king of Persia. 다리우스《페르시아의 왕》.

:dark [dɑ:rk] *adj.* **1** without light; with little light. 어두운; 캄캄한; 암흑의(opp. light). ¶ *a ~ room* 어두운 방 / *a ~ night* 캄캄한 밤 / *It is getting* 〔*growing,* 《rare》 *becoming*〕 *~.* (점점) 어두워지고 있다. **2** ⓐ (of hair, skin, or face) black or deep brown. (머리·피부 등이) 검은; 가무잡잡한. ¶ *~ eyes* 까만 눈 / *~ hair* 〔*skin*〕 검은 머리〔피부〕 / *~ complexion* 가무잡잡한 얼굴빛. ⓑ (of color) near black. (색이) 거무스름한; 어두운; 짙은. ¶ *~ blue* 암청〔감청〕색 / *~ red* 암적색 / *~ window shades* 짙은 빛깔의 창문 커튼. **3** not easily understood; secret; hidden; obscure. 알기 어려운; 비밀의; 숨겨진; 불명

(不明)의. ¶ *a ~ secret* 아무도 모르는 비밀 / *The meaning is still ~.* 그 의미는 아직도 불명하다 / *He kept his plan ~.* 그는 그의 계획을 비밀로 해 두었다. **4** evil; wicked. 사악한; 흉악한; 속 검은. ¶ *a ~ plot* 음모 / *a ~ deeds* 〔*thoughts*〕 엉큼한 행동〔생각〕 / *by ~ means* 사악한 수단으로. **5** gloomy; dismal; sad; cheerless. 우울한; 음울한; 어두운. ¶ *a ~ expression* 우울한〔찌무룩한〕 표정 / *a ~ prospect* 어두운 전망 / *~ days* 비운〔실의〕의 시대; 불길한 나날 / *look on the ~ side of things* 사물의 어두운 면을 보다; 사물을 비관적으로 보다. **6** unenlightened. 지성〔교양〕이 없는; 무지 몽매한; 미개한. ¶ *~ souls* 무지 몽매한 사람들 / *live in the darkest ignorance* 아주 깜깜한 무식쟁이로 살다.

keep dark, keep it a secret; remain in hiding. 비밀로 해 두다; 숨어 있다.

— *n.* **1** Ⓤ the state of being dark; the absence of light. 어둠; 암흑. ¶ *I can't see well in the ~.* 어둠 속에서는 잘 보이지 않는다. **2** Ⓤ night; nightfall. 밤; 해질녘. ¶ *at ~* 저녁때〔저물녘〕에 / *before ~* 어둡기 전에 / *after ~* 날이 저문 후에 / *with the fall of ~* 어둠의 장막이 깔리자. **3** ⓊⒸ a dark color or shade; a dark place. 어두운 색〔부분〕; 어두운 곳. ¶ *the lights and darks of a picture* 그림의 명암. **4** Ⓤ ignorance; secrecy. 무지; 비밀. ¶ *I am in the ~ about the plan.* 나는 그 계획에 관해 모른다 / *Why do you keep me in the ~?* 어째서 나에겐 알리지 않는가. [E.]

Dark Ages [´ ´], **the** *n.* the Middle Ages, esp. the early part, from the 6th century onward. (중세의) 암흑 시대.

Dark Continent [´ ´‐‐], **the** *n.* Africa. 아프리카.

·**dark·en** [dá:rkən] *vt.* (P6) **1** make (something) dark or darker. …을 어둡게 〔검게〕 하다. ¶ *~ the color* 색을 칙칙하게 하다 / *~ a room (by drawing the blinds, etc.)* (블라인드 따위를 내려) 방을 어둡게 하다. **2** cast a shadow over (something); fill (something) with gloom. (기분 따위를) 음울하게 하다; 애매하게 하다. — *vi.* (P1) become dark or darker. 어두워〔검어〕지다. ¶ *The sky darkened.* 하늘이 컴컴해졌다 / *The theater darkened and the play began.* 극장이 어두워지고 연극이 시작되었다. [→dark]

darken counsel, confuse the issue. 더욱더 혼란시키다.

darken** someone's **door 〔***doorway***〕***,*** enter someone's house; visit. …을 찾다; 방문하다. ¶ *Don't ~ my door(s) again.* 우리 집을 다시 찾아오지 마시오.

dark·ey [dá:rki] *n.* 《*colloq.*》 a Negro. 흑인; 검둥이.

dark horse [´ ´] *n.* a race horse that little is known about; an unexpected competitor. (경마에서) 실력이 아직 알려지지 않은 말; 예상 밖의 실력을 가진 경쟁자; 다크호스.

dark·ie [dá:rki] *n.* =darkey.

dark·ish [dá:rkiʃ] *adj.* somewhat dark. 좀 어두운; 어두컴컴한; 거무스름한.

dark lantern [´ ´‐] *n.* a lantern whose light can be hidden by a cover or dark glass. (차광(遮光) 장치가 있는) 각등(角燈).

dark·ling [dá:rkliŋ] *adv.* 《chiefly *poet.*》 in the dark. 어둠 속에. ¶ *sit ~* 어둠 속에 앉다. — *adj.* growing dark. 어두워지는. ¶ *the ~ wood* 어두워져 가는 숲. [E.]

dark·ly [dá:rkli] *adv.* **1** in a dark manner. 어둡게; 검게. **2** gloomily; malignantly. 음울〔음침〕하게; 악의를 품고; 위협하듯. ¶ *He looked at me ~.* 험악한 표정으로 나를 보았다. **3** not clearly; obscurely; secretly. 불분명〔희미〕하게; 어렴풋이; 막연하게; 비밀히. ¶ *answer ~* 분명치 않게 대답하다 / *an idea held ~ in one's mind* 마음 속에 막연히 품고 있는 생각.

:**dark·ness** [dá:rknis] *n.* Ⓤ **1** the state of being dark. 어둠; 암흑. ¶ *in the ~* 어둠 속에서 / *the Prince of ~* 마왕(魔王). **2** blindness; the absence of knowledge. 맹목(盲目); 암우(暗愚); 무지(無知). ¶ *walk in ~* 맹목적인 행동을 하다. **3** obscurity; secrecy. 불명료; 애매; 비밀.

deeds of darkness, iniquity. 나쁜 짓; 악행.

dark·room [dá:rkrù(:)m] *n.* Ⓒ 《photog.》 a darkened room used when developing film, etc. 암실.

dark·some [dá:rksəm] *adj.* 《*poet.*》 **1** dark; darkish. 어두운; 어둠침침한. **2** gloomy. 음울한. ¶ *the ~ time of sorrow* 슬픔으로 음울한 때.

dark·y [dá:rki] *n.* =darkey.

:**dar·ling** [dá:rliŋ] *n.* Ⓒ **1** a much loved person; a favorite; a pet. 사랑스러운 사람; 귀여운 것. ¶ *My ~!* 여보 / *the ~ of all hearts* 만인의 사랑을 받는 사람 / *the ~ of fortune* 운명〔행운〕의 총아. **2** a charming, lovable person. 아름다운〔예쁜〕 사람. ¶ *a perfect ~* 정말이지 예쁜 사람. — *adj.* **1** very dear; tenderly loved. 귀여운; 사랑스러운. ¶ *my ~ child* 우리 귀여운 아이. **2** much longed-for; much desired. 동경의; 간절히 바라는. ¶ *My ~ hope was to see him before he died.* 나의 간절한 소망은 그가 죽기 전에 만나 보는 것이었다. [→dear]

·**darn**[1] [dɑ:rn] *vt., vi.* (P6;1) mend or repair (clothes, etc.) by weaving thread back and forth with a needle. (뚫어진 구멍·해진 데)를 꿰매다; 깁다. ¶ *~ a stocking* 양말을 깁다. — *n.* Ⓒ a place thus mended; the act of darning. 꿰맨 데; 꿰매어 깁기; 감치기. [? F.]

darn[2] [dɑ:rn] *vt., vi., n.* 《*colloq.*》 (P6;1) a milder form of 'damn'. 'damn'의 부드러운 표현. ¶ *Darn it!* 염병할; 젠장할. [*damn*]

dar·nel [dá:rnl] *n.* 《bot.》 a weed growing in corn. 독보리. [E.]

darn·ing [dá:rniŋ] *n.* the act of repairing a hole by means of a darn; the articles that have been darned or are to be darned. 꿰매어 기움; 꿰맴질; 기운〔꿰맨〕 것. ¶ *I have a lot of ~ to do.* 꿰맬 것들이 많다. [→darn[1]]

darning needle [ㅡ ㅡ] *n.* a long, large-eyed needle used in darning. 꿰매는 바늘.

:dart [dɑːrt] *n.* Ⓒ **1** a small pointed missile used as a weapon or in game. (화살 같은) 표창; 던지는 살. **2** 《*pl.* used as *sing.*》 a game in which small darts are tossed at a target. 표창 던지기《과녁을 맞히는 실내 게임》. **3** a sudden, swift movement. 급속한 동작; 돌진. ¶ *make a ~ for*〔*on*〕 …을 향하여 쏜살같이 돌진하다 / *make a sudden ~ across* …을 쏜살같이 빠져 나가다. **4** an insect's stinger. (곤충의) 침. **5** a sharp look, word, etc. 험악한 표정〔말〕 따위.

〈dart 1〉

— *vi.* (P2A,3) move forward suddenly and swiftly. (쏜살같이) 달려가다; 돌진하다. ¶ *~ away*〔*off*〕 홱 달려가 버리다 / *~ through the air* 공중을 쏜살같이 날아가다 / *~ at an opponent* 상대를 향해 돌진하다 / *~ into a room* 방안으로 뛰어들다.

— *vt.* (P6,7,13) send out (something) suddenly and swiftly; shoot out. …을 홱 던지다; 쏘다; (시선)을 던지다. ¶ *~ an angry look at someone* 아무에게 성난 시선을 던지다 / *The sun darts its beams.* 태양은 빛을 발한다 / *The savages darted spears at the lion.* 야만인들은 사자를 향해 창을 던졌다. [F.]

dart·er [dɑ́ːrtər] *n.* Ⓒ **1** a person or thing that darts or moves suddenly. 표창(鏢槍)을 던지는 사람; 돌진하는 사람〔것〕. **2** a small fresh-water fish that swims very quickly. 시어(矢魚)《화살처럼 날래게 움직이는 미국산 작은 담수어의 하나》.

Dar·win [dɑ́ːrwin], **Charles** *n.* (1809-82) an English naturalist. 다윈《영국의 박물학자》.

Dar·win·i·an [dɑːrwíniən] *adj.* of Darwin or his doctrines. 다윈의; 다윈설(說)의. — *n.* a follower of Darwin. 다윈 신봉자; 진화론자.

Dar·win·ism [dɑ́ːrwinìzəm] *n.* the theory of evolution. 진화론(論).

Dar·win·ist [dɑ́ːrwinist] *n.* = Darwinian.

:dash [dæʃ] *vt.* **1** (P6,7,13) throw or strike violently; smash; shatter. …을 (세게) 내던지다; 내던져 부수다; 깨뜨리다. ¶ *~ someone to the ground* 아무를 땅에 메어치다 / *~ a cup to pieces on the floor* 술잔을 바닥에 동댕이쳐 산산 조각으로 깨뜨리다 / *He dashed the box to bits against the wall.* 상자를 벽에 던져 산산이 부수었다. **2** (P13) splash; sprinkle. (물 따위)를 끼얹다; 튀기다; (뿌리듯) 바르다. ¶ *~ water on*〔*in*〕 *someone's face* 아무의 얼굴에 물을 끼얹다 / *He was dashed with mud.* 그는 흙탕물을 뒤집어썼다. **3** (P6,7) 《*fig.*》 cast down; depress; ruin; destroy. …을 낙담〔실망〕시키다; (기운·희망 따위)를 꺾다; 분쇄하다. ¶ *Don't ~ his high spirits.* 그의 의기를 꺾지 마라 / *My hopes were dashed.* 나의 희망은 꺾이고 말았다. **4** (P13) 《*with*》 mix (something) with another substance; tinge. …에 가미하다; 섞다; 섞음질하다. ¶ *~ wine with water* 포도주에 물을 타다 / *coffee dashed with a little brandy* 약간의 브랜디를 탄 커피. **5** (P7) 《*off*》 do quickly and roughly. …을 단숨에 해치우다; 급히 하다. ¶ *~ off a letter* 편지를 단숨에 써 내려가다. — *vi.* **1** (P2A,3) rush; move with violence. 돌진하다. ¶ *~ out of the room* 방에서 뛰어나가다 / *~ up to the door* 문 쪽으로 달려가다 / *They dashed for the bus.* 그들은 버스를 향해 돌진했다 / *At the cry of 'fire' the audience dashed out.* '불이야' 소리에 청중들은 밖으로 뛰어나갔다 / *I dashed back to my house.* 나는 급히 집으로 돌아왔다. **2** (P3) 《*against*》 strike violently. 세게 부딪치다; 충돌하다. ¶ *The huge waves dashed against the cliff.* 거대한 물결이 벼랑에 부딪쳤다.

dash against 〔***upon***〕, collide with. …와 부딪치다; 충돌하다.

dash off, **a**) leave; hurry away. 급히 떠나다. ¶ *He dashed off to London.* 그는 런던으로 급히 떠났다. **b**) write, make, sketch, etc. hastily. 급히 쓰다〔만들다, 그리다〕.

— *n.* Ⓒ **1** ⓐ a sudden and violent movement; a rush. 맹렬한 움직임; 돌진. ¶ *make a ~ for the goal* 〔*at the enemy*〕 결승점〔적〕을 향해 돌진〔돌격〕하다. ⓑ 《U.S.》 a short race run at top speed. 단거리 경주(=《Brit.》 sprint). ¶ *win the 100-meter ~,* 100미터 경주에서 1착하다. **2** a splash; a smash; a blow. (물이) 세차게 부딪침〔부딪치는 소리〕; 충돌; 타격. ¶ *a ~ of rain* 쏴하고 쏟아지는 비〔빗소리〕 / *the ~ of the waves on the beach* 해변에 밀어닥쳐 부딪치는 소리 / *We heard the ~ of the rain on the windows.* 빗발이 창문을 때리는 소리가 들렸다. **3** something that depresses or discourages. (기운·희망 따위를) 꺾는 것; 장애. ¶ *a ~ to his hopes* 희망을 좌절시키는 것. **4** a small amount. 소량(의 주입·첨가·혼합). ¶ *whisky with a ~ of water* 물을 약간 탄 위스키 / *a yellow with a ~ of green* 약간의 녹색을 띤 황색. **5** Ⓤ energy; spirit. 기운; 기력; 활기. ¶ *He has both skill and ~.* 기능도 뛰어나고 기력도 충분하다. **6** the mark(—); a long signal in the Morse code(—). 대시 기호; 모스 기호의 장(長)부호 (cf. *dot*(·)). **7** Ⓤ display; showy appearance. 허세. [E.]

at a dash, quickly and without rest. 단숨에.

cut a dash, make a brilliant show; be showy. 이채를 발하다; (남을 의식하여) 허세를 부리다; 자기를 과시하다. ¶ *cut a ~ with fine clothes* 화려한 옷으로 허세를 부리다.

dash·board [dǽʃbɔ̀ːrd] *n.* Ⓒ **1** an instrument board in front of the driver in an automobile, airplane, etc. (자동차·비행기 조종석 앞의) 계기판(計器板). **2** a protecting shield at the front or side of a wagon, boat, etc. to keep off mud. (마차의) 흙받기; (배의) 파도막이판.

dash·er [dǽʃər] *n.* Ⓒ **1** a person or thing that dashes. 돌진하는 사람(것). **2** a device for stirring cream. (크림) 교반기(攪拌器).

dash·ing [dǽʃiŋ] *adj.* **1** bold; lively. 대담한; 기운찬; 활발한. ¶ *a ~ hero* 용감한 영웅. **2** making much show; gay. 허세부리는; 화려한; 야한. ¶ *a ~ costume* 야한 옷.

dash·y [dǽʃi] *adj.* (**-i·er; -i·est**) =dashing.

das·tard [dǽstərd] *n.* Ⓒ a mean fellow without courage. 비겁자; 겁쟁이. — *adj.* mean; cowardly. 비열한; 비겁한. [E.]

D

das·tard·ly [dǽstərdli] *adj.* mean; cowardly. 비열한; 비겁한. ¶ *a ~ act* 비겁한 행동.

da·ta [déitə, dɑ́:-, dǽtə] *n. pl.* (*sing.* **da·tum**) facts and figures from which conclusions can be drawn; information. 논거(論據); 자료; 통계; 데이터. 語法 단수형 datum은 보통 쓰이지 않음. ¶ *the scientific ~ on which the solution depends* 해결책이 달려있는 과학적인 자료 / *gather ~ on* …에 관한 자료를 모으다 / *He was collected the ~ for his report.* 그는 논문을 쓰기 위한 자료를 수집했다. [L. *do* give]

:date[1] [deit] *n.* Ⓒ **1** the time shown by the day, month, and year. 날짜; 연월일; 정한 날짜; 기일. ¶ *the ~ on a letter* 편지에 써 넣은 날짜 / *the ~ of birth* 생년월일 / *What's the ~ today?* 오늘이 며칠인가요. **2** ⓊⒸ a period of time. 시절; 시대; 연대. ¶ *at an early ~* 초기에 / *art of an early ~* 초기의 미술 / *At that ~ there were no airplanes.* 그 시절에는 비행기가 없었다. **3** 《U.S. *colloq.*》 ⓐ an appointment to meet at a certain time. (시간을 정한) 면회 약속; (특히 이성과) 만날 약속; 데이트. ¶ *make* 〔*have*〕 *a ~ with a girl* 여자와 데이트 (약속을) 하다 / *break* 〔*cut*〕 *the ~* 만날 약속을 깨다. ⓑ the person with whom an appointment is made. 데이트의 상대. ¶ *My ~ today was Nancy.* 오늘 나의 데이트 상대는 낸시였다.

down to date, to this day. 현재까지.

out of date, not in current use; old-fashioned. 시대에 뒤(떨어)진; 구식의; 스러진.

to date, so far; until now; yet. 이제〔지금〕까지; 아직.

up to date, **a**) to the present time. 오늘(날)까지; 지금까지(의). ¶ *Up to ~ we have no news of him.* 지금까지 그의 소식이 없다. **b**) in fashion; modern. 최신식의; 현대적인. ¶ *All the equipment was up to ~.* 모든 장비가 최신식이었다.

— *vt.* (P6) **1** mark (something) with the date. …에 날짜를 쓰다〔적다〕. ¶ *a letter dated the 30th of September,* 9월 30일자의 편지 / *Please ~ the check as of today.* 수표를 오늘 날짜로 해 주시오. **2** find out or decide the date of (something). …의 시기〔연대〕를 알아내다〔추정하다〕. ¶ *It is not possible to ~ this document.* 이 문서의 연대를 추정하는 것은 불가능하다. **3** 《U.S. *colloq.*》 make a promise with (someone) to have a date. (이성과) 만날 약속을 하다; 데이트하다. ¶ *I'll ~ Jane for the dance.* 제인과 댄스 약속을 해야겠다.

— *vi.* (P3) **1** ⓐ be dated; have the date. (편지 따위에) 날짜나 발신지가 표시되어 있다. ⓑ 《*from,* back *to*》 go back to; have origin in a particular time in the past. (연대가 …로) 거슬러 올라가다; (과거의 특정 시기에) 속하다; (…시대에) 시작되다. ¶ *Oxford dates back to 1167.* 옥스퍼드 대학의 창립 연대는 1167년으로 거슬러 올라간다 / *This custom dates from before the war.* 이 관습은 전전(戰前)에 시작된 것이다 / *His family dates back to the (Norman) Conquest.* 그의 가문은 노르만 정복 시대로 거슬러 올라간다. **2** be old-fashioned. 시대에 뒤떨어지게 되다; 구식〔고풍〕이 되다. ¶ *Most fashions soon ~.* 대개의 유행은 곧 스러져 구식이 된다. **3** 《U.S. *colloq.*》 have a date. 이성과 만날 약속을 하다; 데이트하다. [L. *do* give]

date[2] [deit] *n.* Ⓒ the small sweet fruit of a kind of palm tree; a tall tree bearing this fruit. 대추야자(의 열매). [→dactyl]

dat·ed [déitid] *adj.* **1** marked with a date; showing a date on it. 날짜가 있는〔찍힌〕. **2** old-fashioned; out-of-date. 시대에 뒤떨어진; 구식의. [→date[1]]

date·less [déitlis] *adj.* **1** without a date. 날짜가 없는. **2** endless. 무한한; 영원한. ¶ *the ~ night of death* 죽음이라는 영원한 밤. **3** of permanent interest. 언제나 흥미 있는.

date line [⌐⌐] *n.* a line on the earth, mostly along the 180° meridian, where each calendar day first begins. 날짜 변경선 《동경 또는 서경 180도의 자오선》.

da·tive [déitiv] *adj.* 《gram.》 showing the indirect object of a verb. 여격(與格)의. ¶ *the ~ case* 여격; 간접 목적격. — *n.* Ⓒ the dative case; a word in this case. 여격; 여격어(語). [L. *do* give]

da·tum [déitəm, dɑ́:-, dǽ-] *n.* sing. of **data.**

daub [dɔ:b] *vt.* **1** (P6,7,13) coat or cover (a wall, etc.) with mud, clay, etc. …에 (회반죽·진흙·칠 따위)를 (처)바르다; (매대기치듯) 문지르다. ¶ *~ a canvass with paint* 화포(畫布)에 그림 물감을 처바르다 / *~ plaster on a brick wall* 벽돌담에 회반죽을 바르다. **2** (P6,7) paint badly. …을 서투르게 그리다. ¶ *He doesn't paint; he only daubs.* 그는 그림을 그리는 것이 아니라 그리는 흉내만 낼 뿐이다. **3** (P6,13) soil; make dirty. (묻혀) 더럽히다. ¶ *Nancy has daubed her skirt with mud.* 낸시는 치마에 흙탕물을 묻혀 더럽혔다. — *vi.* paint crude or cheap pictures. 서투른〔싸구려〕 그림을 그리다.

—*n.* **1** ⓐ Ⓒ anything daubed on. 바른〔칠한〕 것. ⓑ Ⓤ the act of daubing. 바름; 칠하기. **2** Ⓒ a picture poorly painted. 서투른 그림. [de-, L. *albus* white]

daub·er [dɔ́:bər] *n.* **1** a person or thing that daubs. 미장이; 바르는〔칠하는〕 도구. **2** an unskillful painter. 서투른 화가.

:daugh·ter [dɔ́:tər] *n.* Ⓒ **1** a female child. 딸(opp. son). **2** a female descendant. 여자 자손. ¶ *a ~ of Eve* 여성 / *a ~ of Abraham* 유태인 여자. **3** a woman who is the spiritual product of. (…이 낳은) 여성. **4** a thing regarded as a female descendant. 딸에 비유되는 것; 소산(所産). ¶ *a ~ of the Revolution* 혁명의 소산. [E.]

daugh·ter-in-law [dɔ́:tərinlɔ̀:] *n.* Ⓒ (*pl.* **daugh·ters-**) a son's wife. 며느리.

daugh·ter·ly [dɔ́:tərli] *adj.* like or befitting a daughter. 딸로서의; 딸다운〔같은〕.

daunt [dɔ:nt] *vt.* (P6) frighten; make (someone) less courageous. …을 주춤〔움찔〕하게 하다; …의 기를 꺾다. ¶ *~ one's adversaries* 적을 위압하다 / *He was daunted by the difficulty of the task.* 그는 일이 어려워 기가 꺾이었다. [L. *domo* tame]

nothing daunted, not at all frightened or discouraged. 조금도 굴하지 않고.

daunt·less [dɔ́:ntlis] *adj.* brave; fearless. 용감한; 움쭉도 않는; 불굴의. ¶ *a ~ hero* 두려움을 모르는 영웅 / *~ courage* 불굴의 용기.

dau·phin [dɔ́:fin] *n.* 《hist.》 the title of the eldest son of the King of France, from 1349 to 1830. 프랑스 황태자의 칭호. [Place]

dau·phin·ess [dɔ́:finis] *n.* 《hist.》 a dauphin's wife. (프랑스의) 황태자비(妃).

dav·en·port [dǽvənpɔ̀:rt] *n.* Ⓒ **1** 《U.S.》 a large sofa, often one that can be changed into a bed. (침대 겸용의) 소파. **2** 《Brit.》 a small writing desk. (접는 뚜껑식의) 작은 책상. [Person]

Da·vid [déivid] *n.* **1** a man's name. 남자 이름. **2** 《Bible》 the second king of Israel. 다윗《이스라엘의 왕》.

Da·vid and Jon·a·than [déivid ənd dʒɑ́nəθən] *n.* a pair of devoted friends. 막역한 친구.

dav·it [dǽvit, déivit] *n.* Ⓒ one of a pair of curved bars on a ship's side for holding or lowering small boats. (보트를 달아 오르내리는) 쇠기둥. [*David*]

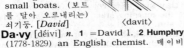

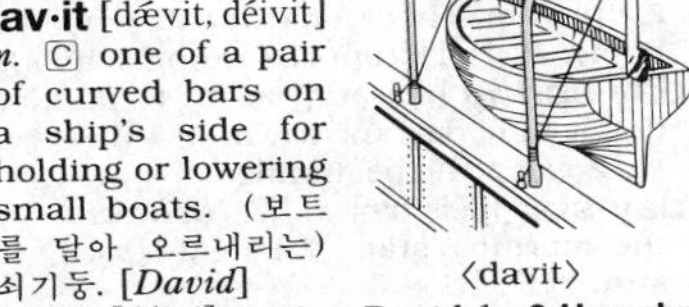
〈davit〉

Da·vy [déivi] *n.* **1** =David 1. **2 Humphry** (1778-1829) an English chemist. 데이비《영국의 화학자》.

Davy Jones [∠-∠] *n.* the spirit of the sea, who has a large box into which he puts everything that sinks. 해마(海魔).

Davy Jones'(s) locker [∠-∠∠-] *n.* the bottom of the sea, esp. as the grave of persons drowned at sea. (특히 바다에서 죽는 모든 사람의 무덤으로서의) 해저(海底); 바다밑. ¶ *go to ~* 바다에 빠져 죽다.

Davy lamp [∠-∠] *n.* a miner's safety-lamp. 갱내(坑內) 안전등(燈).

daw [dɔ:] *n.* Ⓒ 《bird》 a kind of crow found in Europe. (유럽산) 갈가마귀. [E.]

daw·dle [dɔ́:dl] *vt., vi.* (P7;1,3) waste (time); idle; move slowly. 빈둥거리다; 시간을 허송하다; 꾸물거리다. ¶ *~ over work* 일을 가지고 꾸물거리다 / *be dawdling all day long* 하루 종일 빈둥거리다 / *I could see him dawdling along the road.* 그가 길을 어슬렁거리며 걷는 것을 볼 수 있었다 / *~ away one's time* 빈둥빈둥 시간을 보내다. [Imit.]

:dawn [dɔ:n] *n.* Ⓤ **1** the break of day; the first light in the east; daybreak. 새벽; 동틀녘; 먼동; 여명. ¶ *work from ~ till dusk* 첫새벽부터 땅거미질 때까지 일하다 / *Dawn breaks.* 날이 샌다 / *I got up at ~.* 나는 첫새벽에 일어났다. **2** the beginning. 시작; 발단; 초기. ¶ *the ~ of civilization* 문명의 시작 / *since the ~ of history* 역사가 시작된 이래.

—*vi.* (P1,3) **1** begin to grow light in the morning. 밤〔날〕이 새다; 동이 트다. ¶ *The day dawned.* 밤이 새었다 參考 "밤이 새다"를 "Night dawns." 라고는 하지않음. **2** 《*fig.*》 begin to appear; develop. 나타나기〔보이기〕 시작하다; (서서히) 발달하기 시작하다. ¶ *dawning consciousness* 나타나기 시작한 의식 / *a dawning mustache* 나기 시작한 콧수염 / *With Pasteur, a new era dawned in medicine.* 파스퇴르에 의해 의학에 새로운 시대가 열리기 시작했다. [E.]

dawn on 〔***upon***〕, begin to be clear to the mind of (someone). 이해되기 시작하다; (일이) 점점 분명해지다. ¶ *The meaning suddenly dawned on him.* 돌연 그는 그 뜻을 알게 되었다 / *It began to ~ on him that....* 그는 …하다는 것을 알게 되었다.

:day [dei] *n.* **1** Ⓤ the period of light between sunrise and sunset; daylight. 낮; 주간(晝間)(opp. night). ¶ *by ~* 낮에는 / *before ~* 날이 새기 전에 / *at the break of the ~* 새벽에. **2** Ⓒ the 24 hours of day and night. 날; 하루; 일주야. ¶ *every ~* 날마다; 매일 / *every other ~ =every second ~* 하루걸러; 격일로 / *the other ~ =a few days ago* 일전(에); 며칠 전 / *We pay our clerks seven dollars a ~.* 우리는 판매원에게 하루 7 달러 지급한다. **3** ⒸⓊ a particular day on which some special event has taken, or will take, place. 특정한 날. ¶ *a pay ~* 급료날 / *the first ~ of the week* 일요일 / *Christmas Day* 성탄절. **4** 《*the ~*》 a contest, victory. 승부; 승리. ¶ *win* 〔*carry*〕 *the ~* 승부에 이기다 / *lose the ~* 승부에 지다 / *The ~ is ours.* 승리는 우리의 것이다. **5** 《often *pl.*》 period of time; epoch. (특정한) 시기; 시대. ¶ *the* *days of Queen Elizabeth* 엘리자베스 여왕 시대 / *the present* ~ 현대 / *the men of the* ~ 시대의 (중요한) 인물들 / *in* (*the*) *days of old* 옛날에 / *in this* ~ 오늘날; 요즈음 / (*in*) *these days* 요즈음; 최근 / (*in*) *those days* 그 때; 당시 / *in days to come* 장래에 (있어서). **6** 《*one's* ~》 one's lifetime; a good period of one's lifetime. (아무의) 일생; 활동〔전성〕시대. ¶ *end one's days* 생애를 마치다; 죽다 / *He was a great singer in* 〔*on*〕 *his* ~. 그는 젊었을 때에 굉장한 가수였다. [E.]

all day long, as long as the sun is up. 하루〔온〕종일.

(as) clear as day, clear as the light of day. 낮과 같이 밝은; 대낮같이 분명한.

as the day is long =all day long.

by day, during the daytime. 낮에는.

call it a day, consider that one has done a day's work. (하루의 일을) 끝내다.

day about, on every other day. 하루 걸러.

day after day = ***day by day*** = ***day in, day out,*** every day. 날마다; 매일; 나날이.

days of grace, extra days allowed beyond the fixed day for paying a bill. (어음 따위의) 지급 유예 기간.

from day to day =day after day.

have one's day, be prosperous. 번성하다; 한창 좋다. ¶ *She has had her day.* 그녀에게도 좋은 때는 있었다.

in a day, in a short time. 하루에; 하루 아침에.

in broad day, in daylight. 백주에; 대낮에.

in days gone by, in old days. 옛날〔예전〕에.

keep one's day, 《*arch.*》 be punctual. 기일을 지키다.

know the time of day, 《*arch.*》 be wide-awake. 잘 알고 있다.

of the day, of those days; of today. 당시의; 현대의; 오늘날의.

one day, **a**) =some day. ¶ *One day I will pay you.* 언젠가 후일 돈을 지급하겠네. **b**) on a certain day in the past. (과거) 어느 날.

one of these (***fine***) ***days,*** before long. 머지않아; 근일중에.

some day, at some future time. 머지않아; 언젠가.

the day after tomorrow, (on) the day that will come after tomorrow. 모레.

the day before yesterday, the day that had gone by before yesterday. 그저께.

this day week 〔***month, year***〕, on the same day of next or last week 〔month, year〕. 내주〔내달, 내년〕의 오늘; 지난 주〔달, 해〕의 오늘.

to a day, exactly. (하루도 틀리지 않고) 정확히. ¶ *three years ago to a day* 정확히 3년 전(에).

to this day, till now. 지금까지.

without day, indefinitely. 무기한으로.

day·book [déibùk] *n.* Ⓒ **1** 《book-keeping》 a book in which each day's accounts are kept. (부기의) 일기장. **2** a diary. 일기.

day boy [⌐⌐] *n.* 《Brit.》 a student at a boy's boarding school who lives at home. (기숙생에 대하여) 남자 통학생(cf. *boarder*).

day·break [déibrèik] *n.* Ⓤ the earliest light of day; dawn. 새벽; 동틀녘.

day coach [⌐⌐] *n.* 《U.S.》 an ordinary railroad passenger car. 보통 객차《침대차 등과 구별하여》.

day·dream [déidrì:m] *n.* Ⓒ a dreamy thought about pleasant things; an idle fancy. 백일몽; 공상. ¶ *be in a* ~ 몽상에 빠져 있다. —*vi.* (P1) think dreamily about pleasant things. 공상에 빠지다; 몽상하다. ¶ *Instead of working he just daydreams.* 그는 일은 하지 않고 공상에만 빠져 있다.

day girl [⌐⌐] *n.* 《Brit.》 a girl who attends school daily, while living at home. 여자 통학생.

day laborer [⌐ ⌐--] *n.* an unskilled worker paid by the day. 날품팔이꾼.

·day·light [déilàit] *n.* Ⓤ **1** light of day. 햇빛; 일광. **2** openness. 공공연함; 주지(周知); 공표. **3** daytime. 낮; 주간. ¶ *in broad* ~ 백주에; 대낮에. **4** daybreak; dawn. 새벽; 동틀녘. ¶ *before* ~ 날이 새기 전에 / *from* ~ *to dark* 새벽부터 어두울 때까지 / *He arose at* ~. 그는 날샐녘에 일어났다.

let daylight into, stab or shoot. …을 찌르다; 쏘다.

see daylight, 《*colloq.*》 **a**) understand. 이해하다; 분명해지다. **b**) approach the end of a hard job. (난문제 따위의) 끝이 보이다; 해결이 가까워지다〔에 이르다〕.

day·light-sav·ing time [déilaitsèiviŋ tàim] *n.* the time that is one hour faster than the standard time. 서머 타임; 일광 절약 시간.

day·long [déilɔ̀(:)ŋ, -lɑ̀ŋ] *adj., adv.* through the whole day. 온종일(의).

day nursery [⌐ ⌐--] *n.* **1** 《U.S.》 a nursery for taking care of small children during the day, esp. when their mothers are at work. 보육원; 탁아소(=《Brit.》 crèche). **2** a room (in a home) where children play, have their meals, etc. (아이들을 위한 가정의) 놀이방; 식사실.

day school [⌐⌐] *n.* **1** a school held in the daytime. 주간 학교(opp. night school). **2** a private school for students who live at home. 통학 학교(opp. boarding school).

day·spring [déispriŋ] *n.* Ⓤ **1** 《*poet.*》 the first light of day; the dawn. 동틀녘; 먼동; 새벽. **2** 《*fig.*》 the beginning. 시작.

day·star [déistɑ̀:r] *n.* Ⓒ 《usu. *the* ~》 **1** the morning star. 샛별. **2** 《*poet.*》 the sun. 태양.

day ticket [⌐ ⌐-] *n.* a return ticket which is available both ways on one day only. 당일만 통용되는 왕복 열차표.

·day·time [déitàim] *n.* Ⓤ 《*the* ~》 the time when it is day. 주간; 낮. ¶ *Owls sleep in the*

~. 올빼미는 낮에 잔다.

***daze** [deiz] *vt.* (P6) cause (someone) to feel stupid; make (someone) unable to think clearly; blind (someone) for a moment with a very bright light. …을 망연케〔멍하게〕 하다; (빛 따위가) 눈부시게 하다. ¶ *He was dazed by a blow on the head.* 머리를 한 대 맞고 그는 아찔해졌다. ― *n.* Ⓒ a dazed condition. 멍한 상태; 망연 자실. ¶ *be in a* ~ 멍해 있다. [E.]

***daz·zle** [dǽzl] *vt.* (P6) make (someone or the eyes) unable to see well with a sudden bright light; cause (someone) great admiration by a brilliant performance. (아무)를 눈이 부시게 하다; 경탄케 하다. ¶ *Coming from the dark house, he was dazzled by the sudden sunlight.* 어두컴컴한 집에서 나오자 그는 갑작스런 햇빛에 눈이 부셨다 / *His eyes were dazzled with the light.* 불빛에 그는 눈이 부셨다 / *The headlight of the car dazzled me* 〔*my eyes*〕. 차의 헤드라이트 빛이 나를〔내 눈을〕 부시게 했다.
― *vi.* (P1) **1** be blinded by light; excite admiration by a brilliant performance. 눈이 부시다; 경탄하다. **2** shine or reflect brilliantly. 번쩍이다. ¶ *polished germs dazzling in the sunlight* 햇빛을 받아 번쩍이는 닦은 보석.
― *n.* ⓊⒸ **1** the act of dazzling; a dazzled condition. 눈부심; 현혹. **2** a dazzling brightness. 눈부시게 밝음. ¶ *the* ~ *of powerful electric light* 고촉광 전등불의 눈부시게 밝음. [E.]

db decibel(s).

d.b.a. doing business as 〔at〕.

D.C. **1** District of Columbia. 컬럼비아 특별구. **2** 《electr.》 direct current. 직류(cf. *A.C.*).

DCB 《U.S.》 Defence Commission Board.

D.C.L. Doctor of Civil Law.

D.C.M. 《Brit.》 Distinguished Conduct Medal. 수훈장(殊勳章).

D/D demand draft. 요구불 환어음(=sight draft).

D.D. Doctor of Divinity. 신학 박사.

d.d., d/d **1** delivered. 인도(引渡)의; 배달비 포함의. **2** days after date; days' 〔day's〕 date. 날짜 후 …일.

D-day [díːdèi] *n.* **1** 《mil.》 a day on which a military or other carefully planned operation is to be started. 디데이《행동〔공격〕 개시 예정일》. **2** 《hist.》 the day (June 6, 1944) on which the Allied forces invaded France during World War II. 디데이《제2차 대전 때 연합군에 의한 북부 프랑스 공격 개시일》. [D =day]

DDT [diːdìːtíː] (the symbol for) a kind of odorless and very powerful insect killer. 디디티《강력 살충제》. [*d*ichloro-*d*iphenyl-*t*richloroethane]

de[1] [diː] *prep.* 《L.》 from; out of; concerning. '…의, …에서, …에 관한'의 뜻.

de[2] [də] *prep.* 《F.》 from, belonging to. '…에서, …에 속한'의 뜻.

de- [di-, də-, diː-] *pref.* **1** down-. '저하, 감소'의 뜻. **2** off-. '분리, 제거'의 뜻. **3** completely. '완전히'의 뜻. **4** un-. '비(非)…, 반대'의 뜻. [L.]

dea·con [díːkən] *n.* **1** (in the Anglican and Roman Churches) a member of the clergy below a priest in rank. 부제(副祭). **2** (in the Presbyterian Church) a layman appointed to attend to the affairs of the church. (교회의) 집사. ― *vt.*(P6) 《U.S.》 **1** read out at a time. (한 구절 한 구절씩) 소리 높이 낭독하다. **2** falsify. 속이다. [Gk. = servant]

dea·con·ess [díːkənis] *n.* a woman appointed or elected to serve as an assistant in a church. 여부제(女副祭).

:dead [ded] *adj.* **1** ⓐ no longer living; without life. 죽은; 생명이 없는(opp. living, alive). ¶ *a* ~ *body* 사체(死體) / *be* ~ *and gone* 죽고 없다 / *shoot someone* ~ 아무를 쏘아 죽이다 / *He is* ~. 그는 죽었다. ⓑ having no organic life. 유기체의 생명이 없는. ¶ ~ *matter* 무기물. **2** 《*fig.*》 looking like death, insensible; without feeling. 죽은 것 같은; 무감각한. ¶ *a* ~ *sleep* 깊은 잠 / ~ *fingers* 마비된 손가락 / *be* ~ *to reason* 사리를 말해도 통하지 않다 / *He is* ~ *to pity.* 그는 연민의 정을 모른다. **3** without power, movement, spirit, etc. 생기〔활력〕 없는; 움직이지 않는. ¶ ~ *water* 흐르지 않는 물 / *a* ~ *market* 침체 상태의 시장 / *a* ~ *party* 활기 없는 파티 / *the* ~ *hours* (*of the night*) 한밤중. **4** no longer in use. 사용〔통용〕되지 않는; 스러진. ¶ *a* ~ *language* 사어(死語) / *a* ~ *law* 사문화된 법률. **5** out of play; not in the game. (경기 따위에서) 플레이가 일시 중단된. ¶ *a* ~ *ball* 시합 정지구(球). **6** worn out; tired out. 몹시 지친; 녹초가 된. ¶ *He felt* ~ *from 8 hours' walking.* 그는 8시간이나 걸어서 몹시 지쳤다. **7** complete; absolute; entire. 완전한; 절대적인; 아주 …한. ¶ *a* ~ *loss* 전손(全損) / *a* ~ *silence* 깊은 침묵 / *in* ~ *earnest* 아주 진지하게. **8** quite certain; sure; exact. 아주 정확한; 확실한. ¶ *a* ~ *shot with a rifle* 라이플 사격의 명수. **9** sudden. 갑작스러운; 돌연한.

(*as*) ***dead as mutton*** 〔***a doornail***〕, quite dead. 완전히 죽어; 스러져.

come to a dead stop, stop completely. 갑자기 멈추다. ¶ *The horses came to a* ~ *stop.* 말들이 갑자기 딱 멈춰 섰다.

dead and gone, dead. 죽은.

dead from the neck up, very stupid. 매우 어리석은.

dead to the world, very deeply asleep or unconscious. 깊은 잠에 빠져; 의식을 잃고.

― *adv.* **1** absolutely; completely. 아주; 절대로; 완전히. ¶ ~ *tired* 몹시 지친 / ~ *drunk* 몹시 취한 / *be* ~ *right* 절대로 옳다. **2** directly. (곧)바로; 직접. ¶ ~ *ahead* 바로 앞

에 / *run* ~ *away* 쏜살같이 달아나다.
— *n.* **1** ⓐ 《*the* ~ 》 a person who has died. 사자(死者). ⓑ 《*collectively*》 those who have died. 죽은 사람들. ¶ *the living and the* ~ 산 자(者)와 죽은 자들. **2** Ⓤ the time when it is darkest or coldest. 가장 캄캄한 때; 가장 추울 무렵. ¶ *in* 〔*at*〕 *the* ~ *of night* 한밤중에 / *in the* ~ *of winter* 한창 추운 겨울에. [E.]

dead-a·live [dédəláiv] *adj.* dull; spiritless. 활기 없는; 불경기의.

dead beat [´ ´] *adj.* 《*colloq.*》 utterly exhausted. 몹시 지친.

dead·beat[1] [dédbí:t] *adj.* 《mech.》 beating without recoil. (탈진기(脫進機)의 앵클과 톱니가 접촉할 때) 톱니의 퇴각이 일어나지 않는.

dead·beat[2] [dédbì:t] *n.* **1** Ⓒ 《U.S. *colloq.*》 a worthless fellow; a lazy person. 보잘것 없는 사람; 게으름뱅이. **2** 《*contempt.*》 a beatnik. 비트족.

dead-born [dédbɔ̀:rn] *adj.* stillborn. 사산(死産)의.

dead center [´ ´–] *n.* 《mech.》 either of two positions of the crank which exerts no effective power. 사점(死點).

dead dog [´ ´] *n.* a useless thing. 무용지물.

dead-drunk [déddrʌ́ŋk] *adj.* completely drunk. 곤드레만드레 취한.

dead·en [dédn] *vt.* (P6) weaken (one's vigor, etc.); make (something) less strong. (활기·감정 따위)를 죽이다; 약화시키다. ¶ ~ *sound* 소리를 죽이다 / ~ *the senses* 무감각하게 하다 / ~ *one's pain* 고통을 완화시키다 / ~ *the force of a ball* 볼의 속도를 죽이다. — *vi.* (P1) become dead; lose vigor. 죽다; 힘이 약화되다.

dead end [´ ´] *n.* **1** a street, passage, etc., closed at one end. 막다른 길〔골목〕. **2** a job or situation without any hope of getting better. 더 나아질 가망이 없는 자리〔일〕; 막다른 골; 궁지.

dead-end [dédénd] *adj.* blind. 막다른 골의.

dead·fall [dédfɔ̀:l] *n.* a trap for large game. (사냥용) 함정.

dead·head [dédhèd] *n.* Ⓒ 《*colloq.*》 **1** a person who uses a free ticket for admission to a show or passage on a train. (우대권 따위를 소지한) 무임 승객; 무료 입장자. **2** a person who does not contribute to the activity of a business or organization. (회사·조직체 등에의) 공헌이 없는 사람; 무능자.

dead heat [´ ´] *n.* a race in which two runners come in level with each other and both win. 동시 도착《달리기에서 두 사람 이상이 결승점에 동시에 들어오기》.

dead·house [dédhàus] *n.* a place where bodies are kept. (병원 등의) 영안실; 시체 임시 안치장.

dead letter [´ ´–] *n.* **1** a letter that cannot be delivered because it is wrongly addressed, etc. 배달 불능 우편물. **2** a law, rule, etc., which is no longer observed. (법률·규칙 따위의) 사문(死文).

dead·light [dédlàit] *n.* a strong shutter for a cabin-window. 선창(船窓) 뚜껑; 현창(舷窓).

dead·line [dédlàin] *n.* Ⓒ **1** the time limit for finishing something, such as payment or writing stories for magazines, etc. (지급 따위의) 최종 기한; (신문·잡지 원고의) 마감 시간. ¶ *The* ~ *for payment is the end of this month.* 최종 지급 기한은 이 달 말이다. **2** a boundary which must not be crossed. 넘지 말아야 할 선(線); 사선(死線).

dead·lock [dédlɑ̀k / -lɔ̀k] *n.* Ⓒ a condition in which no one will give way; a standstill. (협상 따위의) 정돈(상태); 정체. ¶ *bring a* ~ *to an end* = *break a* ~ 고착 상태를 타개하다 / *come to* 〔*reach*〕 *a* ~ 교착〔정돈〕 상태에 이르다 / *be at a* ~ 교착 상태에 있다. — *vt.* (P6) bring (a meeting, etc.) to a deadlock. (회의 따위)를 정체시키다; 교착 상태에 빠뜨리다. — *vi.* (P1) come to a deadlock. 정체〔교착〕되다.

***dead·ly** [dédli] *adj.* (**-li·er, -li·est**) **1** ⓐ causing death; fatal; deathly. 치명적인; 목숨에 관계되는. ¶ *a* ~ *poison* 맹독 / *a* ~ *wound* 치명상 / *a* ~ *blow* 치명타. ⓑ untill death; implacable. 살려 둘 수 없는; 앙심 품은. ¶ *a* ~ *enemy* 불구대천의 원수. **2** deathlike. 송장 같은. ¶ *a* ~ *paleness* 송장같이 핼쑥함. **3** extreme. 극단의; 지독한. ¶ *a* ~ *dullness* 지독히 따분함 / *a* ~ *satire* 지독한 빈정거림 / *in* ~ *haste* 몹시 서둘러.

dead march [´ ´] *n.* a funeral music. 장송곡.

dead·ness [dédnis] *n.* being dead. 죽음; 「죽은 상태.

dead·pan [dédpæ̀n] *adj.* 《U.S. *colloq.*》 expressionless. 무표정한. ¶ *a* ~ *face* 무표정한 얼굴. — [dédpǽn] *n.* such a face. 무표정한 얼굴.

dead point [´ ´] *n.* =dead center.

dead reckoning [´ ´––] *n.* 《naut.》 a way of estimating the position of a ship by means of the compass, etc., rather than by the sun or stars. 추측 항법.

dead shot [´ ´] *n.* a person who never misses in shooting. (백발 백중의) 명사수.

dead weight [´ ´] *n.* **1** a thing that has the heaviness and awkwardness of a lifeless body. 중하(重荷); 중량품(重量品). **2** an oppressive burden or difficulty. 무거운 짐〔부담〕.

dead wind [´ ´] *n.* 《naut.》 a contrary wind. 맞바람; 역풍.

dead·wood [dédwùd] *n.* Ⓤ **1** dead branches or trees. (말라) 죽은 가지〔나무〕. **2** 《orig. U.S.》 useless people or things. 무용의 인원; 쓸모 없는 것.

***deaf** [def] *adj.* **1** unable to hear. 귀머거리의; 귀먹은. ¶ *a* ~ *man* 귀먹은 남자 / *the* ~

귀머거리들 / *be ~ in one ear* 〔*of an ear*〕 한쪽 귀가 안 들리다. **2** not willing to listen; unwilling to give attention to something. 들으려 하지 않는; 귀를 기울이지 않는.

(*as*) *deaf as a post* 〔*an adder*〕, quite deaf. 귀가 아주 절벽인.

be deaf and dumb, not able to hear and speak. 농아이다.

be deaf (=*not willing to listen*) ***to*** *something.* …을 들으려 하지 않다; 귀를 기울이지 않다. ¶ *be ~ to all advice* 온갖 충고를 들으려 하지 않다 / *He was ~ to all pleas for mercy.* 자비를 베풀어 달라는 온갖 탄원에 그는 귀를 기울이지 않았다.

fall on deaf ears, not be heard or not needed. (상대가) 들어 주지 않다.

turn a deaf ear (=*not willing to listen*) ***to*** *something.* …에 전혀 귀를 기울이지 않다.

● **deaf·ly** [-li] *adv.* [E.]

deaf-aid [défèid] *n.* an electric device to assist hearing. 보청기(補聽器).

deaf-and-dumb [défəndʌ́m] *adj.* unable to hear and speak. 귀머거리에다 벙어리인; 농아의. ¶ *the ~ alphabet* (농아자용) 지화(指話) 문자.

deaf·en [défən] *vt.* (P6) make (someone) deaf; make (someone's hearing) impossible due to noise. …을 귀머거리로 만들다; 귀가 먹먹하게 하다; (소음 때문에) 들을 수 없게 하다. ¶ *The medicine deafened her for life.* 그 약으로 그녀는 한평생 귀머거리가 되었다 / *The noise deafens me.* 그 소음 때문에 들을 수 없다.

deaf·en·ing [défəniŋ] *adj.* tending to cause deafness; very loud. 귀가 먹먹해지는; 귀청이 찢어질 것 같은. ¶ *a ~ noise* 〔*applause*〕 귀청이 찢어질 것 같은 소리〔박수 소리〕.

deaf-mute [défmjù:t, ⌐⌐] *n.* Ⓒ a person who is deaf and dumb. 농아자.

deaf·ness [défnis] *n.* Ⓤ the state of being deaf; the state of giving no attention to someone or something. 귀가 들리지 않음; 귀를 기울이지 않음.

:deal[1] [di:l] *v.* (**dealt** [delt]) *vi.* (P3) **1** 《*with*》 be concerned; be related. 관계하다; 사귀다; 상종하다. **2** 《*with, toward*》 behave toward; act. (남에 대해서) 행동하다; 굴다. ¶ *He deals fairly with all people.* 그는 모든 사람에게 공명 정대하게 대한다. **3** 《*in, with*》 carry on business; buy and sell. 장사하다; 거래〔매매〕하다. ¶ *~ with a firm* 회사와 거래하다. **4** give out the cards among several players. (카드놀이에서) 패를 도르다. ¶ *It is your turn to ~.* 네가 도를 차례다.

— *vt.* (P6,7,13,14) **1** give out (something) to each; distribute. …을 도르다; 분배하다. ¶ *Deal the cards.* 카드를 돌라라 / *~ out five hands of six cards each* 다섯 사람에게 카드를 6장씩 도르다 / *The food must be dealt out fairly.* 양식은 공평하게 분배되어야 한다. **2** give. (타격 따위)를 가하다; 주다. ¶ *~ him a blow* = *~ a blow at him* 그에게 일격을 가하다.

deal (=*buy goods*) ***at,*** *a certain store.* …에서 구입하다; 대놓고 사다. ¶ *I ~ at the neighborhood market.* 나는 근처 시장에서 물건을 산다.

deal in, **a**) be concerned in (something); have to do with (something). …에 종사〔관계〕하다. ¶ *~ in politics* 정치에 관계하다. **b**) buy and sell; trade. …을 거래하다; 매매하다; 취급하다. ¶ *He deals in oil.* 그는 석유를 취급하고 있다.

deal with, **a**) keep company with; associate with. …와 사귀다; 상종하다. ¶ *He is hard to ~ with.* 그는 사귀기가 힘들다 / *I refuse to ~ with him.* 그와는 사귀지〔상종치〕 않는다. **b**) manage or control; settle. …을 처리하다; 조치〔조처〕하다. ¶ *~ with a difficult problem* 난문제를 처리하다 / *~ harshly with the rebels* 반란자들을 엄하게 조치하다 / *The sick man was difficult to manage, but the nurse dealt with him all right.* 환자를 취급하기 어려웠으나 간호사는 그를 잘 조처했다. **c**) treat; argue; discuss. …을 다루다; 논구(論究)하다. ¶ *a book dealing with economics* 경제학을 다루고 있는 책. **d**) act or behave oneself toward others. …을 대(우)하다. ¶ *~ fairly with everyone* 모든 사람에게 공평히 대하다. **e**) do business with (someone, a firm, a store, etc.). …와 거래하다. ¶ *We refuse to ~ with that firm any longer.* 저 회사와는 이제 거래를 하지 않는다.

— *n.* Ⓒ **1** a business arrangement; a bargain; treatment. 거래; 흥정; 처리; 취급; 대우. ¶ *a fair* 〔《*colloq.*》 *square*〕 *~* 공정한 대우 / *a raw ~* 불공정한 대우 / *make* 〔*conduct*〕 *a ~* 거래를 하다 / *enter into a ~ with him* 그와 거래하다. **2** a policy; a plan. 정책; 계획. ¶ *the New Deal* 뉴딜 정책. **3** the distribution of cards; a player's turn to deal. 카드패 도르기; 도르는 차례. ¶ *Whose ~ is it? —My ~!* 누가 도를 차렌가 —내 차례다. **4** 《only in certain phrases》 quantity; amount. 양(量); 액(額). [E.]

a good 〔***great***〕 ***deal,*** **a**) a large amount. 다량; 많은 액수. ¶ *a great ~ of money* 많은 액수의 돈 / *I have a good ~* 〔《*colloq.*》 *a ~* 〕 *to do.* 할 일이 많다. **b**) to a great extent or degree; much. 매우; 꽤; 많이. ¶ *a good ~ better* 훨씬 나은 / *He drinks a good ~.* 그는 술을 많이 마신다 / *Do you read much? —Yes, I read a good ~.* 많이 읽는가 —응, 많이 읽어.

do a deal with *someone,* come to terms with someone; make a compromise with someone. …와 타협하다.

deal[2] [di:l] *n.* Ⓤ a board of pine or fir wood; pine or fir wood. 송판; 전나무판; 소나무〔전나무〕 목재. [E.]

·deal·er [dí:lər] *n.* Ⓤ **1** a man who trades. 상인. **2** 《*the ~*》 《cards》 the player whose turn it is to give out the cards. 카드 도르는 사람.

·deal·ing [dí:liŋ] *n.* Ⓤ **1** one's behavior toward others. (타인에 대한) 행동; 행위. ¶ *honest* ~ 정직한 행동 / *fair* ~ 공정한 행위 / *double* ~ 표리 있는 행동. **2** 《usu. *pl.*》 business relation; friendly relations. 거래; 장사; 관계; 교제. ¶ *commercial dealings* 상거래 / *have dealings with* …와 관계〔거래〕가 있다.

:dealt [delt] *v.* p. and pp. of **deal.**

***dean** [di:n] *n.* Ⓒ **1** the head officer in charge of a cathedral or church. (대성당의) 수석 사제(司祭); (영국 국교의) 지방 부감독. **2** 《chiefly U.S.》 the head of a department of a university; a fellow in charge of student discipline. (대학의) 학장; 학생감(監). ¶ *the* ~ *of a faculty* 학장. **3** a very famous, older man. 고참자; 장로. [L. *decanus*]

dean·er·y [dí:nəri] *n.* **1** Ⓒ the house of a dean. dean의 저택. **2** Ⓤ the office of a dean. dean의 직(職). **3** Ⓒ the jurisdiction of a dean. dean의 관할구. [↑]

:dear [diər] *adj.* **1** much loved; beloved. 친애하는; 사랑하는; 귀여운. ¶ *my* ~ *mother* 사랑하는 나의 어머니 / *this* ~ *land* 이 사랑하는 땅 / *a* ~ *friend of mine* 친애하는 나의 친구 / *a* ~ *little thing* 귀여운 아이〔아기〕 / *hold someone* ~ 아무를 귀엽게 여기다. **2** much valued; precious; earnest. 소중한; 귀중한; 절실한. ¶ *my dearest wish* 나의 절실한 소원 / *one's* ~ *possessions* 소중한 소지품 / *I hold life* ~. 나는 목숨을 소중하게 여긴다. **3** ⓐ costing much money; high priced. (값이) 비싼; 고가의(opp. cheap). ¶ *$10 is very* ~ *for a pipe.* 담배 파이프 하나에 10달러는 너무 비싸다 / *Apples are* ~ *this year.* 사과가 올해에는 비싸다. ⓑ asking high prices. 비싼 값을 요구하는. ¶ *a* ~ *shop* 비싸게 파는 가게.

— *n.* Ⓒ a loved one; one's sweetheart; one's darling. 사랑하는〔귀여운〕 사람; 애인; 연인. 參考 흔히 '여보, 당신'처럼 부를 때에도 씀. ¶ *a shepherd and his* ~ 양지기 목동과 그의 연인 / *What dears they are!* 정말이지 귀여운 애들이군 / *Come along, my* ~. (어서) 와요, 여보.

— *adv.* **1** at a high price or cost. 비싸게; 비싼 값에(opp. cheap). ¶ *sell* 〔*buy*〕 ~ 비싸게 팔다〔사다〕 / 《*fig.*》 *pay* ~ *for one's experience* 경험의 대가를 비싸게 치르다. **2** 《*poet.*》 = dearly 1.

— *interj.* an expression of distress, surprise, pity, etc. 아이고; 저런; 어머(나). ¶ *Dear me!* 저런; 아이고. [E.]

dear·ie [díəri] *n.* =deary.

dear·ly [díərli] *adv.* **1** with deep love; affectionately. (깊은) 애정으로써. ¶ *love someone* ~ 아무를 깊은 애정으로 사랑하다. **2** 《*fig.*》 at a high price; expensively. 비싼 값으로; 비싸게. ¶ *The peace was* ~ *won.* 평화는 값비싼 희생을 치르고 얻어졌다.

dear·ness [díərnis] *n.* Ⓤ **1** high price; constliness. 값비싼; 고가. **2** affection; fondness. 애정.

dearth [də:rθ] *n.* Ⓤ 《sometimes *a* ~》 **1** lack; too small a supply. 부족; 결핍. ¶ *a* ~ *of food* 식량 부족 / *a* ~ *of information* 정보 부족. **2** lack of food; famine. 기근. ¶ ~ *of water* 물 기근 / *in time of* ~ 기근 때에. [E.]

dear·y, dear·ie [díəri] *n.* Ⓒ (*pl.* **dear·ies**) 《*colloq.*》 a dear one; a loved one. 귀여운 사람; 사랑하는 사람. 參考 부를 때 쓰며 흔히 여성 용어. [E.]

:death [deθ] *n.* **1** ⓊⒸ the act of dying; the state of being dead. 죽음; 사망. ¶ *a violent* ~ 변사(變死); 비명 횡사 / *a field of* ~ 전장(戰場) / *die a natural* ~ 자연사(死)하다; 천수(天壽)를 다하다 / *in the hour of* ~ 임종에 / *meet one's* ~ 죽다 / *be burnt* 〔*frozen, starved*〕 *to* ~ 불타〔얼어, 굶어〕 죽다 / *drink oneself to* ~ 과음으로 죽다 / *lie still in* ~ 죽어 조용히 누워 있다. **2** 《*D-*》 the god of death. 사신(死神). 參考 해골이 낫을 든 모습으로 나타냄. **3** 《*fig.*》 《*the* ~》 destruction; end. 절멸; 파멸; 소멸. ¶ *the* ~ *of one's hopes* 희망의 소멸. **4** 《*the* ~, *one's* ~》 a cause of death. 죽음의 원인; 사인(死因). ¶ *He will be the* ~ *of his father.* 그이 때문에 아버지는 죽을 게다 / *Drinking was the* ~ *of him.* 그는 술로 목숨을 빼앗겼다. **5** the manner of dying. 죽음의 양상. ¶ *die a hero's* ~ 영웅다운 죽음을 하다 / *die a dog's* ~ 비참한 죽음을 하다; 개죽음을 하다. [E.]

(as) still as death, perfectly still. 쥐죽은 듯 고요한.

as sure as death, surely. 틀림없이; 확실히.

at death's door, almost dead; in danger of dying. 죽음에 직면하여; 빈사 상태에.

be as pale as death, be deadly pale. (송장처럼) 창백하다.

be in at the death, see the fox killed in a hunting or some enterprise completed. (여우 사냥에서) 여우의 죽음을 지켜 보다; (사건의) 전말을 끝까지 보다.

be the death of, cause to die. …의 사인(死因)이 되다.

put *someone* ***to death,*** kill. …을 죽이다; 처형하다.

to death, **a**) completely. 아주. **b**) to an extreme degree; very much. 극도로; 몹시.

to the death, until one is killed. 최후까지; 죽을 때까지. ¶ *He fought to the* ~. 그는 최후까지 싸웠다.

worse than death, extremely bad. 죽기보다도 나쁜〔쓰라린〕; 아주 지독한.

death·bed [déθbèd] *n.* Ⓒ **1** a bed on which a person dies. 죽음의 자리. ¶ *be on one's* ~ 죽어 가고 있다; 죽음에 임하다. **2** the last hours of someone's life. 임종. ¶ *a* ~ *confession* 〔*will*〕 임종시의 참회〔유언〕.

death·blow [déθblòu] *n.* Ⓒ a blow that kills; a thing that destroys. 치명적 타격. ¶ *deal a* ~ 치명타를 가하다 / *the* ~ *to one's hopes* 희망을 꺾어 버리는 것.

death duty [⌐ ⌐] *n.* 《Brit.》 《often *pl.*》 a tax on a dead man's wealth paid by his heir to the government. 상속세.

death·less [déθlis] *adj.* living forever; never dying; immortal; eternal. 불사(不死)의; 불멸의. ¶ ~ *honor* 불후의 명성.

death·like [déθlàik] *adj.* like that of death; as in death. 죽음〔송장〕과 같은. ¶ *a ~ silence* 죽음 같은 고요.

death·ly [déθli] *adj.* like death or a dead person; deadly. 죽음〔죽은 사람〕 같은; 치명적인. ¶ *a ~ dullness* 지독하게 따분함 / *~ wounds* 치명상(傷) / *a ~ poison* 맹독 / *a ~ weapon* 흉기. — *adv.* **1** as if dead. 죽음〔죽은 것〕같이. ¶ *be ~ pale* 송장같이 창백하다. **2** very; utterly. 몹시; 아주. ¶ *~ afraid* 몹시 두려워하고 / *be ~ ill* 병세가 아주 심하다.

death mask [⌐⌐] *n.* a clay, wax, or plaster cast of a person's face taken after his death. 데스마스크; 사면(死面).

death rate [⌐⌐] *n.* the proportion of deaths to the population. 사망률.

death rattle [⌐⌐-] *n.* the sound heard in the throat of a dying person. 임종 때의 가래 끓는 소리.

death roll [⌐⌐] *n.* a list of the dead. 사망자 명부.

death's-head [déθshèd] *n.* Ⓒ a human skull symbolizing death. 해골《죽음의 상징》.

death·trap [déθtræ̀p] *n.* a building or situation which conceals unseen danger. 죽음의 함정《위험한 건물·상황》.

death warrant [⌐⌐-] *n.* a warrant for the execution(=carrying out) of a death sentence. 사형 집행 영장.

death·watch [déθwɑ̀tʃ / -wɔ̀tʃ] *n.* **1** a vigil kept beside a dying or dead person. 임종을 지켜 봄; (초상집에서의) 밤샘. **2** 《U.S.》 a guard for a person about to be put to death. 사형수 감시인.

de·ba·cle [deibɑ́:kl, -bǽkl] *n.* Ⓒ 《F.》 **1** sudden ruin. 갑작스런 붕괴; 와해. **2** the breaking up of ice in a river. (강의 얼음이) 깨짐.

de·bar [dibɑ́:r] *vt.* (**-barred, -bar·ring**) (P13) 《*from*》 shut out; exclude; prevent from enjoying. …을 내쫓아 들이지 않다; 제외하다; 방해〔저지〕하다; 금하다. ¶ *~ someone from voting* 〔*entering a room*〕 아무가 투표하는〔방에 들어오는〕 것을 금하다. [→bar]

de·bark [dibɑ́:rk] *vt.* (P6) put (goods, people, etc.) on shore from a ship. …을 상륙〔양륙〕시키다(=disembark). ¶ *~ troops* 군대를 상륙시키다. — *vi.*(P1) go on shore from a ship; disembark. 상륙하다; 양륙하다. [→bark[3]]

de·base [dibéis] *vt.* (P6) make (something) lower in value, character, quality, etc.; lessen the value of (something). (인품·가치 따위)를 떨어뜨리다; (품질 따위)를 저하시키다. ¶ *~ oneself* 〔*one's character*〕 *by evil action* 못된 행동을 하여 품성을 떨어뜨리다. [→base[1]]

de·base·ment [dibéismənt] *n.* Ⓤ the act of debasing; the state of being debased. (품질·가치 따위의) 저하; (품성의) 저하; 타락.

de·bat·a·ble [dibéitəbəl] *adj.* that can be debated; open to dispute or question; questionable. 논쟁의 불씨가 되는〔여지가 있는〕; 이론(異論)이 있는; 의심스러운. ¶ *~ land* 계쟁지(係爭地) / *be willing to discuss ~ issues* 논쟁의 여지가 있는 문제를 자발적으로 토의하다. [↓]

:de·bate [dibéit] *vt., vi.* (P6,10;1) **1** talk about some question; discuss thoroughly; argue. 논의〔토의, 논쟁〕하다. ¶ *~ a question* 〔*point*〕 문제를 토의하다 / *~ on a subject of life* 인생 문제에 대해 논하다 / *They debated all night.* 그들은 밤새도록 논의했다. **2** think about; consider. 숙고하다; 고려하다. ¶ *~ a matter in one's mind* 문제를 마음 속으로 곰곰 생각하다.

— *n.* **1** ⓊⒸ discussion of reasons for and against a subject, etc. 토론; 토의; 논쟁. **2** Ⓒ a public meeting in which a question is talked over by two parties. 토론회; (의회의) 토론회. ¶ *a TV ~*, TV 토론회. [→battle]

debate with oneself, consider deeply. 깊이 생각하다. ¶ *~ with oneself before deciding to do something* 무엇을 하기로 결정하기 전에 숙고하다.

de·bat·er [dibéitər] *n.* Ⓒ a person who debates. 토론자; 토의자.

de·bauch [dibɔ́:tʃ] *vt.* (P6) 《usu. in pp.》 lead (someone) astray; cause (someone) to be immoral; seduce. …을 타락시키다; 유혹하다. ¶ *~ oneself by intemperance* 폭음으로 신세를 망치다 / *He led a debauched life.* 그는 방탕한 생활을 했다. — *n.* Ⓒ the act of taking part in sensual pleasures, etc.; immoral behavior. 방탕; 난봉; 도락; 폭음; 타락. ¶ *a wild ~* 지독한 방탕. [F.]

de·bauch·er·y [dibɔ́:tʃəri] *n.* Ⓤ the act of indulging excessively in sensual pleasures; seduction from duty, virtue, or morality. 방탕; 난봉; (악(惡)의 길로의) 유혹. ¶ *live a life of ~* 방탕한 생활을 하다.

de·ben·ture [dibéntʃər] *n.* Ⓒ a written promise of a government or of a business company to pay a debt. 사채권(社債券); 채권. [L. *debentur* are owed]

de·bil·i·tate [dibílətèit] *vt.* (P6) make (someone) weak; weaken. …을 (쇠)약하게 하다. ¶ *a body debilitated by disease* 병으로 쇠약해진 몸. [L. *debilis* weak]

de·bil·i·ty [dibíləti] *n.* Ⓤ weakness usu. of the body. (특히 몸의) 허약; 쇠약. ¶ *nervous ~* 신경 쇠약. [↑]

deb·it [débit] *n.* Ⓒ 《book-keeping》 a statement of debt in an account book. 차변(借邊)(기입)(opp. credit). ¶ *a ~ slip* 지급 전표. — *vt.* (P13) enter (a sum of money) as a debt. (금액)을 차변에 기입하다. ¶ *~ Mr. A* 〔*Mr. A's account*〕 *with $700,*

D

700 달러를 A씨 계정 차변에 기입하다. [→debt]

deb·o·nair, -naire [dèbənέər] *adj.* **1** gay; cheerful; light-hearted. 유쾌한; 명랑[쾌활]한. ¶ *speak in a gay and* ~ 쾌활하고 발랄하게 이야기하다. **2** courteous; affable. 정중한; 예의바른; 상냥한. [F.]

Deb·o·rah [débərə] *n.* 《Bible》 prophetess of Israel. 데보라《이스라엘의 여자 예언자》.

de·bouch [dibú:ʃ, -báutʃ] *vi.* **1** (of rivers and streams) flow out (at the mouth). (강물·시냇물이 물목에서) 넓은 곳으로 흘러 나오다. ¶ *A stream debouches into a larger river, and this into the sea.* 시냇물은 강으로 흘러가고 이것은 다시 바다로 흘러든다. **2** (of men, an army, etc.) come out from a small space. (사람·군대가) 좁은 곳에서 나오다; 진출하다. [L. *bucca* mouth]

D

de·bris, dé·bris [dəbrí:, débri:] *n.* Ⓤ **1** broken, useless remains caused by destruction. (파괴된 것의) 파편(더미); 부스러기. **2** 《geol.》 a heap of broken pieces of rock, etc. at the bottom of a mountain or cliff. (산기슭이나 벼랑 밑의) 암설(岩屑) 더미. [F.]

:debt [det] *n.* **1** ⓊⒸ a sum of money that has to be paid. 빚; 부채. ¶ *a national* ~ 국채(國債) / *a* ~ *of five dollars,* 5달러의 빚 / *a bad* ~ 떼어먹힌 빚; 대손금(貸損金) / *my* ~ *to him* 그에게 진 빚 / *pay one's debts* 빚을 갚다 / *pay off a* ~ 빚을 다 갚다 / *give security for a* ~ 차용금에 저당을 잡히다. **2** Ⓒ obligation. 의리; 은의(恩義). ¶ *owe a* ~ *of gratitude to someone* 아무에게 은의를 입고[신세를 지고] 있다. [L. *debeo* owe]

a debt of honor, a gambling debt. 노름빚《명예를 걸고 꼭 갚아야 할 빚이라는 뜻에서》.

be in someone's debt =***be in debt to*** *someone,* owe. …에게 빚을[신세를] 지고 있다.

be out of debt, have no debts; owing no money. 빚이 없다.

get out of debt, pay one's debts. 빚을 갚다.

keep out of debt, live a life without debt. 빚 안 지고 살다.

pay one's debt of [***to***] ***nature,*** die. 죽다.

run into debt, get into debt. 빚을 지다.

debt·or [détər] *n.* (opp. creditor) Ⓒ **1** a person who owes something to another. 빚진 사람; 채무자. ¶ *a* ~ *nation* 채무국(國) / *The* ~ *ran away to escape his creditors.* 채무자는 빚쟁이들을 피해 달아났다. **2** 《book-keeping》 the left or debit side of an account. 차변(借邊)(abbr. Dr(.)).

de·bunk [dibʌ́ŋk] *vt.* (P6) 《U.S. *colloq.*》 remove (nonsense, false sentiment or claims). (거짓·잘못 따위의) 정체를 폭로하다; 가면을 벗기다. [*bunk*[2]]

de·but, dé·but [deibjú:, di-, déibju:] *n.* 《F.》 Ⓒ **1** the first time to take one's place in society. (사교계에의 정식) 첫 데뷔. **2** (of an actor) the first time to be seen on the stage. (배우 등의) 첫무대; 첫출연. ¶ *make one's public* ~ 첫무대를 밟다; 사교계에 처음으로 발을 내딛다.

de·bu·tante, dé·bu·tante [débjutɑ:nt, -bjə-] *n.* 《F.》 Ⓒ a young woman making her debut in society. (사교계에) 데뷔하는 여자.

Dec. December.

dec(a)- [dèk(ə)-] *pref.* a word element meaning *ten.* '10 배'의 뜻. [Gk.]

·dec·ade [dékeid / dəkéid] *n.* Ⓒ **1** ten years. 10년간. ¶ *in the sixth* ~ (=*the 50's*) *of the present century* 금세기 50년대에 / *for the last few decades* 지난 2, 30년 동안. **2** a group of ten. 10개 한 벌[조]. [Gk.]

dec·a·dence [dékədəns, dikéidns] *n.* Ⓤ the state of being decadent; decay. 쇠퇴; 타락. ¶ *the* ~ *of morals* 도의의 퇴폐 / *The* ~ *of the empire can be attributed to internal troubles.* 제국의 쇠망은 내분(內紛) 탓으로 돌릴 수 있다. [→decay]

dec·a·dent [dékədənt, dikéidənt] *adj.* falling off in moral quality; growing worse. 쇠퇴해 가는; 퇴폐[타락]적인. ¶ *a* ~ *civilization* 퇴폐적인 문명. —*n.* Ⓒ a decadent person, esp. a decadent artist or writer. 퇴폐자; (특히) 데카당파의 예술가[작가]. [↑]

dec·a·gon [dékəgàn / dékəgən] *n.* Ⓒ 《geom.》 a ten-sided plane figure. 10변형; 10각형. [dec(a)-]

de·cag·o·nal [dikǽgənəl] *adj.* of a decagon; having ten sides. 10변형의; 10각형의. [dec(a)-]

dec·a·gram, 《Brit.》 **-gramme** [dékəgræ̀m] *n.* a weight of ten grams. 데카그램《무게의 단위: 10*g*》. [dec(a)-]

dec·a·he·dra [dèkəhí:drə] *n.* pl. of **decahedron.**

dec·a·he·dron [dèkəhí:drən] *n.* Ⓒ (*pl.* **-drons,** or **-dra**) a solid figure having ten surfaces. 10면체. [deca-, Gr. *hedra* face]

dec·a·li·ter, 《Brit.》 **-tre** [dékəlì:tər] *n.* Ⓒ a measure of capacity, ten liter. 데카리터《용량 단위: 10 *l*》. [dec(a)-]

Dec·a·logue, -log [dékəlɔ̀g, -làg], **the** *n.* the Ten Commandments in the Bible. (모세의) 십계명. [→logos]

dec·a·me·ter, 《Brit.》 **-me·tre** [dékəmì:tər] *n.* Ⓒ a measure of length equal to 10 meters. 데카미터《길이의 단위: 10*m*》. [dec(a)-]

de·camp [dikǽmp] *vi.* (P1) **1** depart from a camp; pack up and leave a camping-ground. (캠프를 걷어치우고) 야영지를 떠나다. **2** run away; go away quickly and secretly. 달아나다; 재빨리[몰래] 떠나다. ¶ *The treasurer decamped with the funds.* 회계원은 기금을 갖고 도망했다. ●**de·camp·ment** [-mənt] *n.* [de-, *camp*]

de·cant [dikǽnt] *vt.* (P6) pour (liquor) gently from one vessel to another, without disturbing the sediment. (포도주 따위의) 웃물을 앙금이 일지 않도록 가만히 따르다; (하

나의 그릇에서 딴 그릇에) 옮겨 따르다. [→cant²]

de·can·ter [dikǽntər] *n.* Ⓒ **1** an ornamental glass wine-bottle. (마개 달린) 식탁용 유리 포도주병. **2** 《chem.》 a bottle used to decant. 경사기(傾瀉器). [↑]

〈decanter 1〉

de·cap·i·tate [dikǽpətèit] *vt.* (P6) **1** cut off the head of (someone). …의 목을 자르다. **2** 《U.S. *colloq.*》 dismiss from a job. …을 해고하다. [→capital]

de·cap·i·ta·tion [dikæ̀pətéiʃən] *n.* the act or process of decapitating. 참수(斬首).

de·cath·lon [dikǽθlɑn / -lɔn] *n.* an athletic contest consisting of ten different track or field events. 십종 경기(cf. *pentathlon*). [deca-, Gk. *athlon* contest]

:de·cay [dikéi] *vi.* (P1) **1** go bad; rot. 썩다; 부패[부식]하다. ¶ *vegetation that was decaying* 썩어 가던 야채 / *When trees get old they begin to ~ inside.* 나무는 늙으면 내부에서 썩기 시작한다 / *This tooth has begun to ~.* 이 이빨은 썩기 시작했다. **2** grow less in power, wealth, strength, or beauty; become feeble; decline. 쇠약해지다; 쇠퇴[타락]하다; 기울어져 가다. ¶ *The power of the Roman Empire was decaying at the time of Nero.* 로마 제국의 세력은 네로 때 쇠퇴해 가고 있었다.
— *vt.* (P6) make (something) bad or feeble. …을 부패시키다; 쇠퇴시키다. ¶ *a decayed tooth* 썩은 이; 충치.
— *n.* Ⓤ **1** ⓐ the process of rotting; the state of being rotten. 썩음; 부패. ¶ *tooth ~* 충치. ⓑ a decayed part. 썩은 부분. ¶ *I cut out the ~ and ate the rest of the apple.* 썩은 부분을 잘라 내고 사과의 나머지를 다 먹었다. **2** the gradual loss of power, strength, wealth, beauty, etc. 쇠퇴; 쇠망; 감퇴; 퇴폐. ¶ *the ~ of a family* [*state*] 가문[국가]의 쇠퇴 / *the ~ of woman's beauty* 여자의 아름다움의 쇠퇴 / *go to* [*fall into*] *~* 쇠하다; 썩다. [L. *cado* fall]

de·cease [disíːs] *n.* Ⓤ 《chiefly in law》 death. 죽음. — *vi.* (P1) die. 죽다. [L. *cedo* go]

de·ceased [disíːst] *adj.* dead. 죽은; (지금은) 죽고 없는; 돌아간; 고(故)…(cf. *defunct*). ¶ *the ~* 죽은 사람; 고인(故人) / *one's ~ father* 돌아간 아버지 / *the family of the ~* 유족.

de·ce·dent [disíːdənt] *n.* 《U.S. law》 the dead person. 사자(死者); 고인(故人). [→decease]

de·ceit [disíːt] *n.* ⓊⒸ **1** the act of deceiving or lying. 속임; 사기; 기만; 거짓; 허위. ¶ *The merchant used ~ in his business dealings.* 상인은 거래에서 속임수를 썼다. **2** a dishonest trick; a lie spoken or acted. (속이기 위한) 흉계; 계략; 술책; 거짓말. **3** the quality in a person that makes him deceive others. 기만성; 거짓말하는 근성; 불성실. [→deceive]

de·ceit·ful [disíːtfəl] *adj.* ready or willing to deceive; deceptive. 남을 속이는; 거짓[허위]의; 사기적인. ● **de·ceit·ful·ly** [-fəli] *adv.*

:de·ceive [disíːv] *vt.* (P6,13) **1** make (someone) believe what is not true; delude. …을 속이다; 미혹시키다. ¶ *be deceived by appearance* 외관에 속다 / *~ someone into going* 아무를 속여 가게 하다 / *~ someone into a belief* [*into believing*] *that…* 아무를 속여 …이라고 믿게 만들다 / *The bad boy deceived his teacher.* 그 못된 아이는 자기 선생님을 속였다 / *His eyes deceived him.* 그는 잘못 보았다. **2** disappoint. 기대에 어긋나게 하다; 실망시키다. ¶ *You must not ~ him.* 그를 실망시켜서는 안 된다. — *vi.* use or practice deceit. 속이다; 사기를 하다. ¶ *words meant to ~* 속이려는 말. [L. *capio* take]
deceive oneself, **a**) persuade oneself of what is false. 자신을 속이다. **b**) be under a delusion. 잘못 생각하다.

de·ceiv·er [disíːvər] *n.* Ⓒ a person who deceives. 속이는 사람; 사기꾼.

de·cel·er·ate [diːsélərèit] *vt., vi.* (P6;1) cause (something) to go more slowly; slow down. 속도를 늦추다[떨어뜨리다]; 감속하다(opp. accelerate). [→accelerate]

:De·cem·ber [disémbər] *n.* the twelfth and last month of the year. 12월. 參考 Dec.로 약함. [L. *decem* 10, the ancient-Roman first month being March]

de·cen·cy [díːsnsi] *n.* **1** Ⓤ the quality of being decent; propriety of behavior; what is becoming. 예의바름; 점잖음; 신분에 어울림; 온당함; 체면. ¶ *offences against public ~* 풍속 파괴 / *a breach of ~* 무례 / *for decency's sake* 체면상. **2** 《*the decencies*》 requirements of respectable behavior in society. 여느 사람과 같은 생활·활동에 필요한 것; 항산(恒産); 예절. **3** something decent or proper. 고상한[점잖은] 것; 온당한 것. **4** 《*colloq.*》 kindness of nature; kindness in manner. 친절; 관대. [*decent*]

de·cen·ni·al [disénial] *adj.* **1** consisting of ten years. 10년(간)의. **2** occurring every ten years. 10년마다 일어나는. ¶ *a ~ census,* 10년마다의 인구 조사. — *n.* a tenth anniversary. 10년 기념일; 10년제. [dec(a)-]

:de·cent [díːsnt] *adj.* **1** (of manner, language, etc.) modest; fit and proper; right. (태도·말 따위가) 예절에 맞는; 점잖은; 온당한; 조신한. ¶ *be ~ in conduct* 행동이 점잖다 / *It is not ~ to chatter in class.* 수업중에 잡담하는 것은 온당치 못하다. **2** (of dress, etc.) good enough; fitting; suitable; becoming. (옷 따위가) 보기 싫지 않은; 적절한; 어울리는. ¶ *go to church in ~ clothes* 점잖은 복장으로 교회에 가다. **3** respectable; worthy. 훌륭한; 상당한 신분의. ¶ *a ~ house* 훌륭한 집 / *She comes of a ~ family.* 그녀는 상당

D

한 가문의 출신이다. **4** 《*colloq.*》 ⓐ 《often with pretty, quite, etc.》 not wonderful and not very bad; satisfactory; fair. 꽤 좋은; 그리 나쁘지 않은; 괜찮은; 상당한. ¶ *a pretty ~ house* 꽤 좋은 집 / *get quite ~ marks* 괜찮은 점수를 받다. ⓑ kind; generous. 친절한; 관대한. ¶ *That's very ~ of you.* 그렇게 해 주시다니 친절도 하십니다. [L. *decet* beseems]

de·cent·ly [díːsntli] *adv.* **1** in a decent manner. 점잖게; 꽤. ¶ *be ~ dressed* 점잖게 차려 입고 있다. **2** 《*colloq.*》 generously; kindly. 관대하게; 친절히.

de·cen·tral·i·za·tion [diːsèntrəlizéiʃən] *n.* Ⓤ the state of being decentralized. 분산; 집중 배제; 지방 분권. [↓]

de·cen·tral·ize [diːséntrəlàiz] *vt.* (P6) distribute (something) among more groups, places, local governments, etc. (행정권·권력·조직 따위)를 분산시키다; 지방 분권으로 하다. ¶ *~ the national government* 나라의 행정권을 지방으로 분산시키다. [de-]

de·cep·tion [disépʃən] *n.* **1** ⓊⒸ the act of deceiving; the condition of being deceived. 사기; 속임(수). ¶ *practice ~ on someone* 아무를 속이다 / *There is no ~ in what he does.* 그가 하는 일에 속임수는 없다. **2** Ⓒ a trick; a sham. 술책; 가짜. [→deceive]

de·cep·tive [diséptiv] *adj.* deceiving; giving a false impression; misleading. (사람을) 속이는; 미혹시키는; 그르치는; 믿을 수 없는. ¶ *give food a ~ appearance of freshness* 식품을 신선하게 보이게 하다 / *Appearances are often ~.* 외관은 흔히 믿을 게 못 된다. ● **de·cep·tive·ly** [-li] *adj.* **de·cep·tive·ness** [-nis] *n.*

deci- [dési-] *pref.* a word element meaning *one tenth.* '10분의 1'의 뜻. [L.]

dec·i·bel [désəbèl] *n.* 《phys.》 a unit used to express the loudness of sounds. 데시벨(abbr.db).

:de·cide [disáid] *vt.* (P6,8,10,11,12,20) **1** settle or fix by judging; resolve; determine. 결정하다; 결심하다; 해결하다. ¶ *~ a question* 〔*a point in doubt*〕 문제를〔문제점을〕 해결하다 / *~ what to do* 〔*how to do it*〕 무엇을〔어떻게〕 해야 할지 결정하다. **2** bring (something) to an end; cause (someone) to reach a decision. …을 끝내다; 종결시키다; 결심케 하다. ¶ *~ a battle by sending in fresh troop* 새 군대를 보내어 전쟁을 끝내다 / *The fact decided him to act.* 그 사실은 그로 하여금 행동하기로 결심케 했다. **3** 《law》 give judgment in (a case); pass judgment (for or against someone). 재정(裁定)을 내리다; 판결하다. ¶ *The judge decided the case against the plaintiff.* 판사는 사건을 원고에게 불리하게 판결했다 / *The case was decided in our favor.* 사건은 우리에게 유리하게 판결이 났다. —*vi.* (P1,3) make up one's mind; reach a decision; resolve; settle. 결정하다; 결의하다; 해결하다. ¶ *~ between A and B,* A와 B 중 어느 쪽으로 정하다. [L. *caedo* cut]

decide on 〔***upon***〕, choose; select; resolve to take. …으로 선정〔결정〕하다. ¶ *Finally she decided on the yellow dress instead of the green one.* 결국 그녀는 녹색 드레스 대신 노란색 드레스로 결정했다 / *I've decided on buying* 〔*to buy*〕 *a new car.* 나는 새 차를 사기로 했다.

:de·cid·ed [disáidid] *adj.* **1** clear; definite. 명백한; 분명한; 의심의 여지 없는. ¶ *a ~ difference* 뚜렷한 차이 / *a ~ victory* 결정적인 승리 / *a man of ~ opinions* 의견이 분명한 사람 / *~ smell of gas* 분명한 가스 냄새. **2** firm; determined; not hesitating. 확고한; 단호한; 흔들림이 없는. ¶ *a ~ character* 확고한 성격 / *give a ~ answer* 단호한 대답을 하다.

de·cid·de·ly [disáididli] *adv.* in a decided manner; clearly and undoubtedly. 명백히; 단호하게; 의심의 여지 없이; 확실히. ¶ *~ better* 단연 나은 / *answer* 〔*speak*〕 *~* 단호히 대답〔말〕하다.

de·cid·u·ous [disídʒuəs] *adj.* (of trees) losing leaves every fall; falling off at a certain time. 낙엽성의; 탈락성의 (opp. evergreen). ¶ *~ teeth* 젖니 / *~ antlers of deer* 탈락성의 사슴뿔 / *Oaks and elms are ~ trees.* 참나무와 느릅나무는 낙엽수이다. [→decay]

dec·i·gram, 《Brit.》 **-gramme** [désigræ̀m] *n.* Ⓒ a weight equal to one-tenth of a gram. 데시그램《1/10 그램》. [↓]

dec·i·li·ter, 《Brit.》 **-tre** [désilìːtər] *n.* Ⓒ a measure of volume equal to one-tenth of a liter. 데시리터《1/10 리터》. [deci-]

dec·i·mal [désəməl / -si-] *adj.* 《math.》 based upon ten or tenths; progressing by tens. 10진법의; 소수의. ¶ *the ~ system,* 10진법 / *a ~ point* 소수점 / *a ~ fraction* 소수(小數) / *~ coinage,* 10진 화폐제. —*n.* Ⓒ figures at the right of a decimal point. 소수. ¶ *a recurring* 〔*circulating, repeating*〕 *~* 순환 소수. ● **dec·i·mal·ly** [-li] *adv.* [L. *decem* ten]

dec·i·mate [désəmèit] *vt.* (P6) **1** destroy one tenth of; kill every tenth man (esp. in ancient Rome), as a punishment for a large body of troops, etc. 열 명에 한 명을 골라 죽이다. **2** kill large numbers of. (유행병이) 많은 …을 죽이다. ¶ *The plague decimated the population.* 흑사병으로 많은 사람이 죽었다. [deci-]

dec·i·me·ter, 《Brit.》 **-tre** [désəmìːtər] *n.* Ⓒ a measure of length equal to one-tenth of a meter. 데시미터《1/10 미터》. [↑]

de·ci·pher [disáifər] *vt.* (P6) **1** change (something in cipher) into ordinary language or writing. (암호문)을 번역하다. **2** discover the meaning of (difficult or secret writing, etc.). …을 판독〔해독〕하다.

¶ ～ *an old manuscript* 고문서를 판독하다 / ～ *a secret message* 비밀 통신문을 해독하다. ● **de·ci·pher·ment** [-mənt] *n.* [de-]

:**de·ci·sion** [disíʒən] *n.* UC **1** ⓐ the act of making up one's mind; deciding; settlement; the opinion or judgment reached. 결정; 해결; 판정. ¶ *the* ～ *of the matter* 문제의 해결 / *a* ～ *by majority vote* 다수결 / *give* 〔*make*〕 *a* ～ 결정하다. ⓑ a judgment on point of law, given by a judge when sitting officially in a court of law. (법정에서의) 판결. ¶ *a* ～ *about a case* 사건의 판결 / *give a* ～ *for* 〔*against*〕 …에게 유리한〔불리한〕 판결을 내리다. **2** the quality of being able to come to a decision; being decided; firmness. 결단(력); 과단(성); 확고 부동. ¶ *a man of* ～ 과단성 있는 사람 / *lack* ～ 결단력이 없다. [→decide]

arrive at* 〔*come to*〕 *a decision, decide. 결정하다.

with decision, decisively. 단호하게. ¶ *He spoke with* ～. 그는 단호히 말했다.

de·ci·sive [disáisiv] *adj.* **1** having the quality of decision; showing decision; decided. 결정적인. ¶ ～ *ballots* 결승 투표 / *a* ～ *battle* 결전 / *a* ～ *victory* 결정적인 승리 / *play a* ～ *role* 결정적인 역할을 하다. **2** definite; beyond doubt. 명확한; 분명한. ¶ ～ *evidence* 확증. **3** having or showing decision. 단호한; 결단성〔과단성〕 있는. ¶ *a* ～ *character* 과단성 있는 성격 / *give a* ～ *answer* 단호히 대답하다. ● **de·ci·sive·ness** [-nis] *n.* [↑]

de·ci·sive·ly [disáisivli] *adv.* in a decisive manner; decidedly. 결정적으로; 단연. ¶ *The evidence of this witness weighed* ～. 이 증인의 증언은 단연 중시되었다.

:**deck** [dek] *n.* C **1** ⓐ the floor or platform of a ship. 갑판. ¶ *the upper* 〔*main, middle, lower*〕 ～ *of a ship* (배의) 상〔주, 중, 하〕갑판. ⓑ a floor of a bus. 버스 안의 바닥. **2** 《chiefly U.S.》 a pack of playing cards. 카드 패의 한 벌.

clear the decks, get ready for action. (행동) 준비를 하다; 태세를 취하다.

on deck, **a**) on the upper deck. 상갑판에 나와. ¶ *get on* ～ 갑판에 나오다. **b**) ready for duty; on hand. 준비를 갖추고; 다음 차례를 기다리고.

— *vt.* (P6,7,13) **1** 《*out*》 cover; dress; adorn. …을 아름답게 치장하다; 꾸미다. ¶ ～ *a room with flowers* 꽃으로 방을 꾸미다 / ～ *oneself out with jewels* 보석으로 몸을 치장하다. **2** provide (a ship, etc.) with a deck. 갑판을 깔다. [Du. =cover]

deck chair [⌐⌐] *n.* a portable folding-chair with a canvas back. (휴대용) 갑판 의자; 접의자.

deck·er [dékər] *n.* C **1** a person who decks. 장식자. **2** a ship or omnibus possessing decks. …층의 갑판이 있는 배; …층의 버스. ¶ *a two-decker,* 2층함(艦).

deck·le-edge [dékəlèdʒ] *n.* the rough edge of hand-made paper (before trimming). (손으로 뜬 종이의) 도련하지 않은 가장자리. [→deck]

de·claim [dikléim] *vi.* (P1,3) speak like an orator, as though addressing an audience; make a formal speech. 열변을 토하다; 연설하다. ¶ *He likes to* ～ *before large audiences.* 그는 많은 청중 앞에서 연설하기를 좋아한다. — *vt.* (P6) repeat (verses, etc.) loudly, as though to an audience. …을 큰 소리로 낭독하다. [→claim]

declaim* (=*protest*) *against someone* or *something. …을 격렬히 비난하다; 항의하다.

dec·la·ma·tion [dèkləméiʃən] *n.* UC the act of declaiming; a loud and emotional talk. (도도한) 연설; 열변; 웅변(술); 낭독(법). [↑]

de·clam·a·to·ry [diklǽmətɔ̀:ri / -təri] *adj.* of declaiming; loud and emotional. 웅변술의; 연설조의; 열변적인; 낭독풍의. [↑]

***dec·la·ra·tion** [dèkləréiʃən] *n.* UC the act of declaring; a formal announcement. 공표; 선언; 포고; 진술; 고백. ¶ *a* ～ *of war* 선전 포고 / *make a* ～ 포고〔선언〕하다.

The Declaration of Independence, the statement made by the British colonies in North America, on July 4th, 1776. (미국의) 독립 선언《1776년 7월 4일》. [*declare*]

de·clar·a·tive [diklǽrətiv] *adj.* making a statement; explanatory. 선언〔포고〕하는; 단정적인; 진술적〔서술적〕인. ¶ *a* ～ *sentence* 서술문.

:**de·clare** [diklɛ́ər] *vt.* **1** (P6,13) make(something) known to the public; announce publicly and officially; proclaim. …을 공표하다; 선언〔선포〕하다; 포고하다. ¶ ～ *war against* 〔*upon*〕 …에 대해 선전 포고를 하다 / ～ *a state of emergency* 비상 사태를 선포하다 / ～ *the result*(*s*) *of an election* 선거 결과를 공표하다 / ～ *one's position in a controversy* 논쟁에서 자기 입장을 표명하다. **2** (P6,11,21) say strongly; affirm. …을 단언하다; 주장하다. ¶ *I* ～ *his story to be false.* 그의 이야기가 거짓임을 단언한다 / *He declared me a liar.* 그는 나를 거짓말쟁이라고 주장했다 / *The boy declared that he had not done it.* 그 아이는 제가 그 일을 하지 않았노라고 주장했다. **3** (P6) make a formal statement (to customs officials) about (dutiable goods, or the like). (세관에 과세품)을 신고하다. ¶ *Have you anything to* ～ ? 과세품을 갖고 계신가요.

— *vi.* (P3) **1** make a declaration; state firmly. 선언하다; 단언하다. ¶ *Well, I* ～ *!* 난처하군; 이거 놀랍군; 설마. **2** ⓐ 《*for*》 make a declaration in favor of. (찬성의 입장·의견을) 표명하다. ¶ *He declared for the plan.* 그 계획에 찬성의 뜻을 표했다. ⓑ 《*against*》 make a declaration not in favor of. (반대의 입장·의견을) 표명하다. ¶ *He declared against the proposal.* 그 제안에 반대 의사를 표명했다. [L.

de- intens., *clarus* clear]
declare oneself, show what one really is or thinks; announce oneself to be. 신분을 밝히다; 소신을 말하다. ¶ ~ *oneself king* 자신이 왕임을 밝히다.
declare off, break a bargain or engagement. 해약(解約)을〔취소를〕 선언하다.

de·clas·si·fy [di:klǽsəfài] *vt.* (P6,7,13) 《U.S.》 remove from a classified or secret list. (정보·서류 따위)를 비밀분류에서 해제하다. [→classify]

de·clen·sion [diklénʃən] *n.* UC **1** the act of declining; falling away. 경사; 내리받이; 쇠퇴; 타락; 거절. ¶ *his ~ from* 〔*of*〕 *virtue* 그의 도덕의 퇴폐. **2.** 《gram.》 the act of giving the different forms of a noun, a pronoun, or an adjective (e.g. who, whose, whom) according to its case. 어미 변화; 격변화《명사·대명사·형용사의》. 參考 동사의 변화는 conjugation. [→decline]

dec·li·na·tion [dèklənéiʃən] *n.* UC **1** the act of bending or sloping downward. (밑으로의) 경사; 하강(下降); 쇠퇴. **2** 《phys.》 a deviation of the needle of a compass east or west from true north. (나침반의) 편차(偏差). **3** 《U.S.》 ⓐ a polite refusal. 정중한 사절. ⓑ deterioration. 타락. [↓]

:de·cline [dikláin] *vt.* **1** (P6,8,9) refuse (something) politely. …을 정중히 거절〔거부〕하다; 사절〔사양〕하다(opp. accept). ¶ ~ *an offer* 〔*invitation*〕 제의를〔초청을〕 사절하다 / *He declined the offer with thanks.* 그는 감사하지만이라고 하면서 그 제의를 거절했다. **2** (P6) 《gram.》 give the different forms of a noun, pronoun, or adjective. …을 (격)변화시키다(cf. *conjugate*).
— *vi.* (P1) **1** slope downward. 아래로 경사지다〔향하다〕; 내리막이 되다. ¶ *The road declines sharply.* 길은 가파르게 내리막이 되어 있다 / *The hill declines to lake.* 산은 호수까지 경사져 있다. **2** ⓐ draw to an end. 끝이 가까워지다; (해가) 기울다; 저물다. ¶ *Day was declining and the shadows fell.* 해가 기울면서 그림자를 드리웠다. ⓑ grow less in strength and power; grow worse. (힘·세(勢) 따위가) 약해지다; 쇠퇴〔쇠미, 감퇴〕하다; (인격·가치 따위가) 떨어지다; 영락하다. ¶ *one's declining fortune* 쇠운(衰運) / *one's declining years* 늘그막; 만년 / *The fever has declined.* 열이 떨어졌다 / *The birthrate has been declining for some years.* 출생률이 몇 해 동안 계속 떨어지고 있다 / *The statesman has declined to a miserable state.* 그 정치가는 비참한 상태로 영락했다.
— *n.* C **1** ⓐ a falling to a lower level. 떨어짐; 하락; (해가) 기욺; 저묾. ¶ *the ~ of the sun to the horizon* 해가 지평선으로 기욺 / *a ~ in prices* 물가의 하락. ⓑ a gradual falling away; losing strength; growing worse. (점진적인) 약화; 쇠퇴; 쇠미; 저하; 감퇴. ¶ *a mental ~* 지능 감퇴 / *the ~ and fall of the Roman Empire* 로마제국의 쇠망 / *a ~ in religious interest* 종교적 관심의 저하. **2** the last part of anything. 최후의 부분; 종국. ¶ *the ~ of one's life* 늘그막; 만년 / *with the ~ of the day* 해가 짐에 따라. [L. *declino*]
fall into a decline, lose strength; esp. suffer from consumption. 쇠약해지다; (특히) 폐결핵을 앓다.
on the decline, declining. 내리막에.

de·cliv·i·ty [diklíviti] *n.* C a downward slope. 내리받이 경사(면); 내리막(cf. *acclivity*). [L. *clivus* slope]

de·clutch [dì:klʌ́tʃ] *vi.* (P1) disconnect the clutch of a motorcar so that the engine continues running but the car stands still. (자동차의) 클러치를 풀다. [de-]

de·coct [di:kákt / -kɔ́kt] *vt.* (P6) boil down; extract the essence, flavor, etc. of by boiling. 달이다; 끓여 우리다. [→cook]

de·coc·tion [di:kákʃən / di:kɔ́k-] *n.* a liquid got by boiling something for a long time in water. 달여낸 것; 달여 우려낸 것.

de·code [di:kóud] *vt.* (P6) find the meaning of (secret writing, etc.) by the use of key words; translate from a code. (암호 따위)를 풀다; 해독하다; 보통문으로 번역하다. ● **de·co·der** [-ər] *n.* [de-]

dé·col·le·té [deikὰlətéi / -kɔ̀lə-] *adj.* 《F.》 wearing a low-necked dress; (of a dress) having a low neck. 데콜테《깃·목 부분을 깊이 판 옷》를 입은; (의상이) 어깨와 목이 드러난. ¶ *All the women at the dance party were ~.* 댄스파티에 나온 모든 여성이 데콜테를 입고 있었다.

de·col·or, 《Brit.》 **-our** [di:kʌ́lər] *vt.* (P6) take away the color from; bleach. 색을 빼다; 탈색하다; 표백〔마전〕하다. [de-]

de·com·pose [dì:kəmpóuz] *vt., vi.* **1** (P6,13;1) separate (something) into basic parts; analyse. (성분·원소로) 분해〔환원〕하다; 분석하다. ¶ ~ *water into hydrogen and oxygen* 물을 수소와 산소로 분해하다. **2** (P6;1) become bad; rot. 썩(이)다; 부패하다. ¶ *Fallen leaves gradually ~.* 낙엽은 서서히 썩는다 / *The dead body had decomposed beyond recognition.* 사체는 알아볼 수 없을 정도로 부패해 있었다. [→compose]

de·com·po·si·tion [dì:kampəzíʃən] *n.* U the act of decomposing; the state of being decomposed. 분해; 부패.

de·con·tam·i·nate [dì:kəntǽmənèit] *vt.* (P6) make safe by removing poisons, radioactive agents, or other dangerous materials. 오염을 제거하다〔없애다〕; 정화(淨化)하다(cf. *contaminate*). ¶ ~ *a sickroom* 병실을 소독하다. [de-]

de·con·trol [dì:kəntróul] *vt.* (P6) (**-trolled**) free from control, esp. from government control. 통제를 풀다. ¶ ~ *prices.* [de-]

dé·cor, de·cor [deikɔ́:r] *n.* 《F.》 **1** a style or mode of decoration. 장식 양식. **2** 《theatr.》 scenery. 무대 장치.

·**dec·o·rate** [dékərèit] *vt.* (P6,13) **1** make (something) beautiful. …을 장식하다[꾸미다]. ¶ ~ *walls with murals* 벽을 벽화로 장식하다 / ~ *a town for a royal visit* 국왕의 방문에 대비, 시(市)를 단장하다 / *We decorated the room with flowers.* 방을 꽃으로 꾸몄다. **2** give a medal to (someone) as an honor. …에게 훈장을 수여하다. ¶ ~ *someone with the Order of the Garter* 아무에게 가터 훈장을 수여하다. [L. *decus* beauty]

·**dec·o·ra·tion** [dèkəréiʃən] *n.* **1** Ⓤ the act of decorating; Ⓒ a thing used to decorate; an ornament. 장식. ¶ *interior* ~ 실내 장식 / ~ *display* (가게의) 장식 진열. **2** Ⓒ a medal. 훈장; 메달. ¶ *confer a* ~ *on* [*grant a* ~ *to*] *someone* 아무에게 훈장을 수여하다.

Decoration Day [--´- ´] *n.* 《U.S.》 Memorial Day. 전몰 장병 기념일; 현충일《5월 30일》.

dec·o·ra·tive [dékərèitiv, -rə-] *adj.* decorating; ornamental. 장식의; 장식적인. ¶ ~ *art* / ~ *illumination* 전식(電飾).

·**dec·o·ra·tor** [dékərèitər] *n.* Ⓒ a person who decorates, esp. a person who papers or paints a house. 장식(업)자. ¶ *an interior* ~ 실내 장식가.

dec·o·rous [dékərəs] *adj.* (of behavior, dress, etc.) showing good taste; well-behaved. 고상한; 품위있는; 점잖은; 예의바른. ¶ *a* ~ *appearance* 점잖은[단정한] 외관. ● **dec·o·rous·ly** [-li] *adv.* [→decent]

de·co·rum [dikɔ́:rəm] *n.* Ⓤ **1** the act of acting in a way suitable in good society; good and decent behavior. (태도·행동·말따위가) 예의에 맞음; 점잖음; 단정. ¶ *behave with* ~ 예의 바르게 행동하다. **2** 《often *pl.*》 etiquette. 에티켓; 예절; 예법. ¶ *Nancy was taught to observe all the little decorums.* 낸시는 세세한 모든 에티켓을 지키도록 교육 받았다. [↑]

de·coy [dikɔ́i] *n.* Ⓒ **1** an artificial or real bird used to bring other birds into the range of guns; a person used to lead (someone) into a trap. (꾀어들이기 위한) 미끼(새); (위험·덫 따위로) 유인하는 사람. ¶ *a police* ~ 위장 잠입 형사. **2** a netted pond into which wild ducks may be led. (오리사냥을 위한) 유인용(誘引用) 못. — *vt.* (P6,7,13) lead (someone, bird, animal, etc.) into danger with a decoy. (위험한 곳으로) …을 꾀어들이다; 유인하다. [*de* Du. article?, →cage]

·**de·crease** [dikrí:s] *vi., vt.* (P1;6) become less; cause (something) to grow less. (서서히) 줄(이)다; 감소[감퇴]하다; 감소시키다. ¶ *On high mountains the snow does not* ~ *till midsummer.* 높은 산악 지대에서는 한여름이 되기까지는 적설이 줄지 않는다 / *The members of our club have decreased in number.* 우리 클럽의 회원수가 줄어들었다. —[dí:kris, dikrí:s] *n.* Ⓤ the act of decreasing; the condition of being decreased; Ⓒ the amount by which something decreases. 감소; 감퇴; 점감(漸減); 감소량(opp. increase). ¶ *the* ~ *in sales* 판매량의 감소 / *a* ~ *in population* 인구의 감소 / *a* ~ *in the number of crimes* 범죄 숫자의 감소. [→crescent]

on the decrease, gradually decreasing. 점차 감소하고; 감소 일로에.

de·creas·ing·ly [dikrí:siŋli] *adv.* in a manner showing gradual decrease. 점감적(漸減的)으로.

·**de·cree** [dikrí:] *n.* Ⓒ **1** an order given out by a ruler or government and having the force of law. 법령; 포고. ¶ *issue a* ~ 법령을 발하다 / *obey the decrees passed by the government* 정부에서 통과된 법령을 지키다. **2** a judgment of a court of law. (법정의) 판결; 명령. ¶ *the final* ~ 최종 판결. **3** ⓐ 《theol.》 the fixed and eternal purpose of God. 미리 정해진 신의 영원한 의도. ¶ *a divine* ~ 신려(神慮). ⓑ 《*fig.*》 anything fixed and unchangeable. 정해진 불변의 것. ¶ *a* ~ *of the fate* 예정된 운명. — *vt., vi.* (P6,11;1) issue a decree; command by a decree. 법령을 발하다; 포고하다. [L. *cerno* sift]

decree nisi [-´ ´-] *n.* a decree, esp. of divorce, that will become absolute at a later date. 이혼 가판결《일정 기간 안에 이의 제기가 없으면 확정 판결이 됨》.

de·crep·it [dikrépit] *adj.* **1** weakened by old age; old and having no power. 노쇠(老衰)한; 늙어 약한. ¶ *a* ~ *man* 노쇠한 사람. **2** (of things) worn out by age or long use. 오래 써 낡은; 노후한. [L. *crepo* creak]

de·crep·i·tude [dikrépitjù:d] *n.* Ⓤ the state of being decrepit; weakness, usu. from old age. 노쇠[노후]한 상태. [↑]

decresc. decrescendo.

de·cre·scen·do [dì:kriʃéndou] *n.* (*pl.* **-dos**) 《It., mus.》 (opp. crescendo) a gradual decrease in the volume of tone; a passage played in this manner. 데크레셴도《점점 여림. 또 여린 악절(abbr. dec.)》. — *adj., adv.* gradually reducing force or loudness. 점점 여린[여리게]. [→decrease]

de·cre·tal [dikrí:təl] *n.* a papal decree. (로마) 교황의 교령(敎令)[교서]. — *adj.* pertaining to, of the nature of, or containing a decree or decrees. 법령의; 법령의 성격을 지닌. [→decree]

de·cry [dikrái] *vt.* (**-cried**) (P6) **1** say bad things about (something); denounce (something) openly. …을 공공연히 비난하다; 내리깎다. ¶ ~ *modern dancing* 현대무용을 깎아내리다. **2** make little of. …을 얕보다; 경시하다. ¶ *The ignorant may* ~ *the value of education.* 무식한 사람은 교육의 가치를 경시할지도 모른다. ● **de·cri·er** [-ər] *n.* [→cry]

·**ded·i·cate** [dédikèit] *vt.* (P6,13) 《*to*》 **1** set apart (something) for some holy purpose; give (something) to God. …을 바

치다; 봉납(奉納)하다. ¶ ~ *a new church building* 신축된 교회당을 헌당하다. **2** give up to a special purpose; devote (one's life) to something sacred. (사람·목적을 위해 생애·시간 따위)를 바치다; 헌신[전념]하다. ¶ ~ *one's life to work* 일에 생애를 바치다 / ~ *one's time* 〔*oneself*〕 *to business* 사업에 전념하다. **3** address (a book) to someone for expressing thanks. …을 헌정(獻呈)하다. ¶ *Dedicated to….* …에게 이 책을 드림《권두에 씀》. [L. *dē-* to, *dico* proclaim, declare]

ded·i·ca·tion [dèdikéiʃən] *n.* **1** Ⓤ the act of dedicating. 바침; 봉납; 헌신(獻身); 전념. ¶ *the ~ of a new church* 신축 교회당의 헌당식(獻堂式). **2** Ⓒ the words dedicating a book or other work to a friend, etc. (책 따위에 쓰는) 헌사(獻辭).

ded·i·ca·tor [dédikèitər] *n.* Ⓒ a person who dedicates. 봉납자; 헌정자.

ded·i·ca·to·ry [dédikətɔ̀:ri, -touri] *adj.* serving as a dedication. 봉납〔헌납〕의; 헌정(獻呈)의.

de·duce [didjú:s] *vt.* (P6,11,13) 《*from*》 reach (a conclusion) as a result of considering a general rule or principle. 연역(演繹)하다; 추론(推論)하다(opp. induce). [↓]

de·duct [didʌ́kt] *vt.* 《*from*》 take away (an amount, etc.). …을 빼다; 공제하다. ¶ ~ *5% from the profits for commission* 이익에서 구전으로 5프로를 떼다 / ~ *income tax from salary* 급료에서 소득세를 공제하다. [L. *duco* draw]

de·duc·tion [didʌ́kʃən] *n.* **1** Ⓤ the act of taking away. 공제; 뺌. ¶ *a compulsory ~ from the wages of the man in debt* 빚진 사람의 임금에서의 강제적 공제. **2** Ⓒ the amount deducted. 공제액. ¶ *After deductions there was not much left.* 공제액을 땐 뒤엔 얼마 남지 않았다. **3** Ⓒ a conclusion reached by considering a general rule or principle. 추론; 연역(opp. induction). **4** Ⓒ a thing deduced; a conclusion. 추론된 것; (추론의) 결과.

de·duc·tive [didʌ́ktiv] *adj.* of, using, or reasoning by deduction. 연역의〔적인〕; 추론적인(opp. inductive). ¶ ~ *argument* 연역적 논법 / ~ *reasoning* 연역적 추리 / *the ~ method* 연역법. ● **de·duc·tive·ly** [-li] *adv.*

:deed [di:d] *n.* Ⓒ **1** a thing done; an act; an action. 행위; 행동. ¶ *a bad ~* 악행 / *good* 〔*evil*〕 *deeds* 착한〔못된〕 행위 / *kind deeds* 친절한 행위 / *commit a wicked* 〔*foul*〕 ~ 비행을 저지르다 / *Deeds, not words, are needed.* 말이 아니라 행동이 요구된다 / *Deeds are better than words when people are in trouble.* 사람이 곤경에 처해 있을 때에는 말보다 행동이 낫다. **2** actual fact; reality. 사실. ¶ *in ~ not in name* 명목상이 아닌 실제로 / *in ~ as well as in name* 명실공히. **3** a written, printed, or signed document, containing some contract. (날인)증서. ¶ *a title ~* 부동산 권리 증서 / *a trust ~* 담보를 위한 신탁 증서.

in* (*very*) *deed, really; indeed; actually. 실로; 참으로; 정말로.

— *vt.* transfer (something) by a written or printed document. (증서로써) …을 양도하다. [→do]

·deem [di:m] *vt.* (P8,11,21) 《*lit.*》 think; believe; suppose; consider. 생각하다; 믿다; …로 간주하다. ¶ *I ~ him highly.* 나는 그를 존경한다 / *I deemed it my duty to do so.* 그렇게 하는 것이 내 의무라고 생각했다 / *He deemed it wise to do so.* 그는 그렇게 하는 것이 현명할 것으로 믿었다 / *I ~ that this will never be proved.* 이것은 결코 증명될 수 없으리라고 생각한다. [E.]

:deep [di:p] *adj.* **1** going far down, back, or inward. 깊은; (안으로) 깊숙한(opp. shallow). ¶ ~ *snow* 깊은 적설(積雪) / *a ~ well* 깊은 우물 / *a ~ cave* 깊숙한 동굴 / *a ~ shelf* 깊숙한 선반 / *a ~ wound* 깊은 상처 / ~ *water* 깊은 물 / *The ocean is ~ here.* 바다는 이곳이 깊다. **2** having a certain depth. 깊이…의. ¶ *a well ten meters ~* 깊이 10미터의 우물 / *in the knee-deep water* 무릎까지 닿는 물 속에. **3** profound; hard to understand; beyond the grasp of the ordinary mind. 심원한; 이해하기〔헤아리기〕 어려운. ¶ *a ~ book* 난해한 책 / *a ~ insight* 깊은 통찰력 / *a ~ problem* 어려운 문제 / *a ~ truth* 심원한 진리 / *a ~ mystery* 〔*secret*〕 헤아릴 수 없는 신비〔비밀〕. **4** intense; great in degree; extreme. 강렬한; 강도(強度)의; 극도의; (밤·계절·잠 따위가) 깊은. ¶ ~ *sleep* 깊은 잠 / ~ *sorrow* 깊은 슬픔 / *a ~ night* 깊은〔으슥한〕 밤; 심야 / ~ *in the autumn* 가을도 깊어 / *in ~ summer* 한여름에. **5** strongly felt; heartfelt. 진정으로의; 마음으로부터의. ¶ *a ~ gratitude* 진심으로의 감사 / ~ *affections* 깊은 애정. **6** strong; heavy. 심한. ¶ *a ~ drinker* 술고래. **7** 《usu. *in*》 having the mind occupied with; giving one's whole mind to; profoundly absorbed in. (…에) 몰두해 있는; 열중해 있는. ¶ ~ *in study* 연구에 몰두해 있는 / *be ~ in thought* 깊은 생각에 잠겨 있다 / *He was ~ in talk* 〔*a book*〕. 그는 이야기〔책〕에 열중해 있었다. **8** ⓐ remote. 멀리 떨어진; 외진; 깊숙한 곳에 위치한. ¶ *a house ~ in the valley* 골짜기 깊숙히 있는 집 / ~ *in the mountains* 〔*country*〕 궁벽한 산속〔시골〕에. ⓑ placed or found far from the surface or from the outside edge. (표면 또는 외변(外邊)에서) 깊숙히 먼 곳에 위치한〔있는〕. ¶ *Gold is found ~ in the ground.* 금은 땅 속 깊은 곳에 있다 / *Tigers are found ~ in the jungle.* 호랑이는 깊은 정글 속에 있다. **9** immersed or submerged in or heavily covered with. 표면 밑에 묻힌; 매몰된. ¶ *a road ~ in mud* 진창길 / *roads ~ in snow* 눈에 파묻힌 도로. **10** (of colors) dark and rich. (색이) 진한; 짙은. ¶ *a ~ red* 진홍색 / *a ~ carnation* 짙은 색깔의 카네이션. **11** (of sounds) low in pitch. ((목)소리가) 굵고

찌렁찌렁한; 낮은; 저음의. ¶ *in a ~ voice* 낮은 목소리로. **12** profoundly cunning or artful. 몹시 교활한; 속이 검은; 빈틈없는. ¶ 《*colloq.*》 *He's a ~ one.* 그는 아주 교활한 녀석이다.

(be) in deep water(s), 《*fig.*》 (be) in difficulties [trouble]. 어려운 처지에 빠져(있다); 곤경에 처해(있다).

go (in) off the deep end, 《*sl.*》 lose one's temper suddenly or violently. 자제심을 잃다; 욱하다.

— *n.* 《*the ~*》 **1** a deep place on land or in the sea, a river, etc. (육지의) 깊숙한 곳; 내륙; (바다·강 따위의) 깊은 곳; 심연(深淵). **2** 《*poet.*》 the sea; the ocean. 바다; 대해(大海). ¶ *the great [mighty] ~* 망망 대해; 창해(滄海). **3** the most intense part. (밤·계절 따위) 한창 …인 때. ¶ *in the ~ of night* 한밤중에 / *in the ~ of winter* 한겨울에.

— *adv.* **1** deeply; far down; to or at a great depth. 깊이; 깊숙한 곳에; 꽤 아래쪽에[으로]. ¶ *dig ~ for water [to find water]* 물을 찾기 위해 깊이 파내려가다 / *sink ~* 깊이 가라앉다 / *be buried ~* 깊이 묻히다 / *They talked ~ into the night.* 그들은 밤이 이슥해지도록 이야기했다 / 《*prov.*》 *Still waters run ~.* 빈수레가 요란하다. **2** 《*fig.*》 very much. 매우 많이. ¶ *drink ~* 과음(過飮)하다 / *breathe ~* 심호흡하다. [E.]

deep·drawn [dí:pdrɔ́:n] *adj.* deeply drawn. (한숨 따위)를 깊이 쉰.

***deep·en** [dí:pn] *vt.* (P6) make (something) deeper. 깊게[짙게] 하다. ¶ *~ a well* 우물을 더 깊게 하다 / *~ one's knowledge* 지식을 함양하다 / *~ a color* 색깔을 짙게 하다 / *~ one's impression* 인상을 깊게 하다. — *vi.* (P1) become deeper. (더욱) 깊어[짙어]지다. ¶ *The water deepened at every step.* 강은 걸음을 뗄 때마다 깊어졌다 / *His anxiety deepened.* 그의 걱정이 깊어졌다. [deep]

deep·felt [dí:pfélt] *adj.* strongly felt. 깊이 느낀.

deep·freeze [dí:pfrí:z] *vt.* (**-froze; -frozen**) freeze (food) quickly at a low temperature. (식품을) 급속히 냉동하다.

deep·laid [dí:pléid] *adj.* secretly and carefully planned. 몰래 꾸민; 교묘히 계획된. ¶ *a ~ plot* 교묘히 꾸며진 음모.

deep·ly [dí:pli] *adv.* **1** to a considerable depth. (꽤) 깊이. ¶ *dig ~* 깊이 파다. **2** strongly; to a great degree; thoroughly. 강(렬)하게; 깊이; 매우; 철저하게. ¶ *a ~ moving play* 깊이 감동시키는 연극 / *feel [regret] ~* 깊이 느끼다[뉘우치다] / *be ~ versed in* …에 정통하다 / *respect someone ~* 아무를 깊이 존경하다 / *I am ~ grateful to you.* 깊이 감사드리고 있습니다 / *He is ~ in debt.* 빚을 많이 지고 있다.

deep·ness [dí:pnis] *n.* Ⓤ the quality of being deep; depth. 깊음; 깊이; 심원(深遠).

deep·root·ed [dí:prú:tid] *adj.* having deep roots; firmly fixed. 깊이 뿌리박은; 뿌리 깊은. ¶ *a ~ dislike for snakes* 뱀에 대한 뿌리 깊은 혐오 / *a ~ habit* 뿌리박힌 습관.

deep·sea [dí:psí:] *adj.* 《as *attributive*》 of or in the deeper parts of the sea. 심해(深海)(에서)의; 원양(에서)의. ¶ *~ fishery* 원양어업.

deep·seat·ed [dí:psí:tid] *adj.* **1** (of diseases, feelings, etc.) firmly established; firmly fixed. 뿌리 깊은; 깊이 뿌리박은. ¶ *a ~ disease* 고질병 / *a ~ tradition* 뿌리 깊은 전통. **2** far below the surface. 심층(深層)의. [E.]

deep-set [dí:psét] *adj.* set deeply; firmly fixed. 깊이 팬; 움푹 들어간; 뿌리박힌. ¶ *~ eyes* 움펑눈.

:deer [diər] *n.* Ⓒ (*pl.* **deer**) a swift, graceful animal, the male of which has horns. 사슴. ¶ *a herd of ~* 사슴떼 / *a deer-hunter* 사슴 사냥꾼 / *go deer-hunting* 사슴 사냥하러 가다. [E.]

run as deer, run fast. 질주하다.

small deer, insignificant persons or things. 시시한 사람[것]들.

deer·skin [díərskìn] *n.* ⓊⒸ the leather made from the skin of a deer. 사슴 가죽; 녹비.

deer·stalk·er [díərstɔ̀:kər] *n.* **1** a hunter who stalks deer to shoot them. 사슴 사냥꾼. **2** a cloth cap with a peak in front and behind (as worn by Sherlock Holmes). 앞뒤에 챙이 있는 사냥모(帽).

de·es·ca·late [di:éskəlèit] *vi., vt.* (P1;6) decrease in intensity or magnitude. (격렬도·크기)를 줄이다[가 줄다]; (규모)를 축소시키다[가 축소되다]; (긴장)을 완화하다[이 완화되다](cf. *escalate*). [de-]

def. defective; defendant; defense; deferred; definite; definition.

de·face [diféis] *vt.* (P6) **1** spoil the appearance of (something) by marking or damaging the surface. (손상하거나 파손하거나 하여) 외양을 보기 흉하게 하다. ¶ *~ a wall by scribbling on it* 벽에 낙서를 하여 더럽히다. **2** make illegible. (판독 못 하게) 표면을 마멸시키다. ¶ *~ an inscription* 비문(碑文)을 마손시키다. [→face]

de·face·ment [diféismənt] *n.* **1** Ⓤ the act of defacing; the state of being defaced. 파손; 오손(汚損). **2** Ⓒ a thing that defaces. 손상시키는 것.

de fac·to [di: fǽktou, dei-] *adv., adj.* 《L.》 in fact, whether legal or not. 사실상(의)(cf. *de jure*). ¶ *a ~ government* 사실상의 정부 / *Although his title was prime minister, he was ~ president of the country.* 비록 직함은 수상이었지만 그는 사실상의 대통령이었다. [=from the fact]

de·fal·cate [difǽlkeit, -fɔ́:l-] *vi.* (P1) 《rare》 use other people's money for one's own purposes. (공금)을 유용하다; 횡령[착복]하다 (cf. *embezzle*). [L. *falx* scythe]

de·fal·ca·tion [dì:fælkéiʃən, -fɔ:l-] *n.* **1**

Ⓤ the act of stealing or misusing the money that is entrusted to one. 부정 유용(流用); 배임 횡령. **2** Ⓒ an amount of money stolen or misused. 부정 유용액. ¶ *His defalcations amounted to thousands of dollars.* 그의 유용액은 수천 달러에 달했다.

def·a·ma·tion [dèfəméiʃən] *n.* Ⓤ harm that is given to one's reputation. 명예 훼손; 중상. ¶ *sue the newspaper for ~ of character* 명예 훼손으로 그 신문을 고소하다. [↓]

de·fam·a·to·ry [difǽmətɔ̀:ri / -təri] *adj.* intending to harm someone's reputation. 명예 훼손의; 중상적인. ¶ *a ~ statement* 중상적인 성명.

de·fame [diféim] *vt.* (P6) harm the reputation of (someone); speak ill of (someone). …의 명예를 손상시키다; …을 중상하다. ¶ *His article defamed the well-known artist.* 그의 기사는 그 유명한 예술가를 중상했다. ● **de·fam·er** [-ər] *n.* [→fame]

de·fault [difɔ́:lt] *n.* Ⓤ **1** failure to do a duty; failure to pay a debt; failure to appear in a court of law. (의무·채무 따위의) 불이행; 태만; (법정에의) 궐석. ¶ *judgment by ~* 궐석 재판 / *lose a chance by ~* 태만으로 기회를 잃다 / *win a game by ~* (상대의) 불참으로 경기를 이기다; 부전승(기권승)하다. **2** absence; lack. 결여; 결핍; 부족. ¶ *owing to ~ of water* 물 부족 때문에.

in default of, in the absence of; for want of (a thing required). …이 없을 때에는; …이 없어서. ¶ *He was silent in ~ of any excuse.* 변명의 여지가 없어서 그는 잠자코 있었다.

make default, 《law》 be absent; fail to appear in a court of law. (출정해야 할 경우에) 궐석하다.

— *vi., vt.* (P1;6) **1** fail to do a duty; fail to pay a debt. (의무)를 태만히 하다; (채무)를 갚지 않다. **2** fail to appear in a court of law. 재판에 궐석하다; 출정(出廷)하지 않다. ● **de·fault·er** [-ər] *n.* [→fail]

:de·feat [difí:t] *vt.* (P6) **1** overcome; win a victory over (someone). (…)을 지게 하다; 이기다; 패배시키다. ¶ *~ the enemy in a battle* 전투에서 적을 무찌르다 / *~ A school at* (*in*) *basketball* 농구에서 A교를 패배시키다 / *He has been defeated in the recent election.* 그는 이번 선거에서 패했다. **2** make (something) useless; bring to nothing. …을 꺾다; 좌절시키다; 무로 되게 하다. ¶ *~ one's plan* 계획을 망치다 / *Our hopes were defeated.* 우리의 희망은 꺾였다.

defeat one's own object (***purpose, end***), cause oneself to fail to do what one is trying to do. 실패하다; 목적을 이루지 못하다.

— *n.* **1** ⓐ Ⓤ the act of defeating. 패배시킴; 격파. ¶ *one's ~ of the enemy* 적군의 격파. ⓑ ⓊⒸ the state or an instance of being defeated. 패배(opp. victory). ¶ *one's ~ in the election* 선거에서의 패배 / *Our team has never suffered* (*from*) *~.* 우리 팀은 이제까지 져 본 일이 없다. **2** making useless, destruction. 못쓰게 함; 좌절. ¶ *the ~ of one's hopes* (*plans*) 희망(계획)의 좌절. [→fact]

de·feat·ism [difí:tìzəm] *n.* Ⓤ the state or action of a defeatist. 패배주의(적 행동).

de·feat·ist [difí:tist] *n.* Ⓒ a person who admits the inevitable defeat of his country, party, etc. 패배주의자.

def·e·cate [défikèit] *vt., vi.* (P6;1) clear of impurities, refine; void excrement. 불순물을 제거하다; 깨끗이 하다; 배변(排便)하다. [L. *faex* dregs]

·de·fect [difékt] *n.* Ⓒ the lack of something necessary to completeness; a fault; an imperfection. 결함; 결여; 결점; 약점; 불완전. ¶ *a ~ in one's character* 성격의 결함 / *a physical ~* 육체적 결함 / *a ~ in a machine* 기계의 결함 / *What defects can you find in this system ?* 이 제도에 어떤 결함이 있다고 생각하십니까.

in defect, wanting. 결여되어.

— *vi.* (P1,2A) desert a cause. (주의·당 따위를) 버리다; 변절하다. [L. *deficio* fail]

de·fec·tion [difékʃən] *n.* **1** Ⓤ the act of abandoning one's loyalty, duty, religion, etc.; Ⓒ an instance of this. (충성·의무·종교 따위를) 버림; 변절; 탈당; 탈퇴; 배신; 배교(背教). ¶ *~ from a party* 탈당. **2** Ⓒ lack; loss. 결핍; 상실.

de·fec·tive [diféktiv] *adj.* **1** having a fault; not perfect. 결함이 있는; 불완전한 (opp. perfect). ¶ *a ~ machine* (*engine*) 결함이 있는 기계(엔진) / *a ~ hearing* 난청(難聽) / *a ~ memory* 불완전한 기억. **2** ⓐ lacking; wanting. (…이) 결여된; 없는. ¶ *~ in courage* 용기가 없는. ⓑ 《gram.》 lacking one or more of the usual forms of conjugation. (동사가) 활용(변화)하는 부분이 없는. ¶ *~ verbs* 결여 동사. **3** below average in intelligence. 지능이 정상 이하의. ¶ *a ~ child* 지능이 낮은 아이. — *n.* a person who is below normal, mentally or bodily. (정신적·육체적으로) 정상 이하인 사람; 결함있는 사람. ● **de·fec·tive·ly** [-li] *adv.*

:de·fence [diféns] *n.* 《Brit.》 =defense.

de·fence·less [difénslis] *adj.* 《Brit.》 = defenseless.

:de·fend [difénd] *vt.* (P6,9,13) **1** protect; guard (someone or something). …을 막다; 지키다; 방어하다. ¶ *~ a castle* (*one's country*) *against the enemy* 적의 공격으로부터 성을 (나라를) 지키다 / *~ a child from danger* 위험으로부터 어린이를 지키다 / *~ oneself with a stick* 지팡이로 자신을 방어하다. **2** act, speak, or write favor of (someone or something). …을 변호하다; 변명하다; 옹호(지지)하다. ¶ *~ a case* 사건을 변호하다 / *He made a speech defending his ideas.* 그는 자신의 생각을 옹호하는 연설을 했다 / *The newspapers defended the governor's action.* 신문들은 지사의 행동을 옹호했다 / *I believe to have defended myself well.* 충분히 나의 입장을

변명했다고 믿는다. [L. *fendo* push, strike]

de·fend·ant [difénd*ə*nt] *n.* Ⓒ《law》 a person accused in a law court. 피고(opp. plaintiff, cf. *accused*). ¶ *This ~ is accused of theft.* 이 피고인은 절도혐의로 기소돼 있다. — *adj.* of a defendant. 피고(측)의.

de·fend·er [difénd*ər*] *n.* Ⓒ a person who defends; a protector. 방어자; 옹호자; 변호자. ¶ *the Defender of the Faith* 신교(信敎)의 옹호자《영국왕》.

:de·fense, 《Brit.》 **-fence** [diféns] *n.* Ⓤ **1** ⓐ the act of defending. 방어; 방위; 수비(opp. attack, offense). ¶ *legal ~* 정당 방위 / *national ~* 국방 / *offensive ~* 공세 방어 / *make no ~ against an attack* 공격에 대한 방어를 하지 않다 / *put up a good ~* 훌륭히 방어하다 / *put oneself in the state of ~* 방어 자세를 취하다. ⓑ an argument in support of something; justification. 옹호론. **2** Ⓒ something that defends; a thing used to guard against attack. 방어물; 방어시설〔수단〕. ¶ *a line of ~* 방어선 / *the defenses (of a town)* 방비 / *A wall around a city was a ~ against enemies.* 시 둘레의 성곽은 적의 공격에 대비한 방어시설이었다. **3** the act of defending in boxing or fencing; Ⓒ the group defending a goal in a game. (권투·펜싱의) 수비; 방어; 수비측의 팀. **4** ⓊⒸ an action, speech, etc. in favor of something. 변호; 옹호; 변명. ¶ *make a ~* 변호를 하다. **5** 《law》 ⓐ the denial or pleading of the defendant to the charge against him. 피고의 답변; 항변. ⓑ 《*collectively*》 a defendant and his legal counsel. 피고측(opp. prosecution). [→defend]

in defense of, in order to defend. …을 지키기 위하여; …을 변호하여. ¶ *fight in ~ of one's country* 나라를 지키기 위해 싸우다.

de·fense·less, 《Brit.》 **-fence-** [difénslis] *adj.* having no defense. 방비가 없는. ¶ *a ~ city* 무방비 도시 / *A baby is quite ~.* 아기는 아주 무방비 상태이다.

de·fen·si·ble [difénsəb*ə*l] *adj.* that can be defended or justified. 방어할 수 있는; 변호〔옹호〕할 수 있는. ¶ *The general decided that the place was not ~.* 장군은 그 곳을 방어할 수 없다고 판단했다 / *His conduct is quite ~.* 그의 행동은 전적으로 변명될 수 있다.

de·fen·sive [difénsiv] *adj.* ready to defend; for defense; of defense. 방어의; 방어를 위한; 방어용의(opp. offensive). ¶ *~ warfare* 방위전(戰) / *a ~ attitude* 방어〔수비〕 태세 / *take ~ measures* 방어 조치를 취하다. — *n.* 《*the ~*》 the position, attitude, etc. of defense. 방어; 수비; 수세; 변호. ¶ *assume the ~* 수세를 취하다 / *be* 〔*act*〕 *on the ~* 수세에 서다 / *play the ~ in a game* 경기에서 수비를 하다 / *be on the ~ about one's mistakes* 실책의 변명을 하다.

de·fer¹ [difə́:*r*] *vt., vi.* (**-ferred, -fer·ring**) (P6;1) put off; postpone; delay. 연기하다; 미루다; 늦추다. ¶ *~ action* 〔*payment*〕 행동〔지불〕을 연기하다 / *We deferred our departure till the next day.* 우리의 출발을 이튿날로 연기했다 / *You have deferred too long.* 너무 지체했다. [L. *differo*]

de·fer² [difə́:*r*] *vi.* (**-ferred, -fer·ring**) (P3) 《chiefly *to*》 yield to (someone, another's opinion, etc.); yield with courtesy. (남의 판단·의견 따위에) 따르다; 양보하다. ¶ *~ to one's parent's opinions* 부모 의견에 따르다 / *We all ~ to him in these matters.* 우리는 모두 이런 일에 있어서는 그의 의견에 따른다. [L. *defero* offer]

def·er·ence [déf*ə*r*ə*ns] *n.* Ⓤ the act of obeying the judgment or opinion of another; great respect. 따름; 복종; 존경. ¶ *blind ~* 맹종 / *undue ~ to authorities* 권위자에의 부당한 맹종 / *treat someone with ~* 아무를 정중히 대접하다 / *show* 〔*pay*〕 *~ to someone* 아무에게 경의를 표하다 / *out of ~ to public opinion* 여론을 중시하여. [→defer²]

in deference to, showing respect for. …을 존중하여; …에 따라. ¶ *in ~ to someone's wishes* 아무의 희망에 따라.

with all due deference to you, a formula used when expressing a difference of opinion. 지당하신 말씀입니다만《상대와 다른 의견을 말할 때》. [↑]

def·er·en·tial [dèf*ə*rénʃ*ə*l] *adj.* showing deference; very respectful. 경의를 표하는; 정중〔공손〕한. ● **def·er·en·tial·ly** [-ʃ*ə*li] *adv.*

de·fer·ment [difə́:*r*m*ə*nt] *n.* Ⓤ the act of putting off; postponing. 연기; 유예. [→defer¹]

·de·fi·ance [difáiəns] *n.* Ⓤ **1** open resistance; refusal to recognize or obey authority. (권위·손윗사람에 대한) 공공연한 저항; 반항; 공공연한 무시; 멸시. ¶ *~ of danger* 위험의 무시 / *make an open show of ~* 공공연히 반항하다 / *be at open ~ with* … 에게 공공연히 반항하고 있다. **2** a call to fight; challenge. 도전. [*defy*]

bid defiance to, act without regard for; challenge. …을 무시하다; …에 도전〔반항〕하다.

in defiance of, without regard for; in spite of. …을 무시하고; …에도 불구하고.

set at defiance =bid defiance to.

de·fi·ant [difáiənt] *adj.* showing no respect; openly disobedient. 반항적인; 도전적인. ¶ *The boy said, 'I won't', in a ~ manner.* '싫어'하고 아이는 반항적인 태도로 말했다. ● **de·fi·ant·ly** [-li] *adv.* [↑]

·de·fi·cien·cy [difíʃ*ə*nsi] *n.* (*pl.* **-cies**) **1** ⓊⒸ lack or absence of something needed. 부족; 결핍; 결함. ¶ *~ disease* 비타민 결핍(증) / *moral ~* 도덕적 결함 / *remedy a ~* 결함을 고치다. **2** Ⓒ the sum or amount by which something falls short. 부족분〔량, 액〕. ¶ *a ~ $500,* 5백 달러의 결손. [→defect]

·de·fi·cient [difíʃ*ə*nt] *adj.* not sufficient in

quantity; lacking; incomplete; defective. 부족한; 결여된; 결함 있는; 불완전한. ¶ ~ *in faith* 〔*understanding*〕 믿음이〔이해가〕 부족한 / *be* ~ *in common sense* 상식이 부족하다 / *be mentally* ~ 정신 박약이다. ● **de·fi·cient·ly** [-li] *adv.* [↑]

def·i·cit [défəsit] *n.* Ⓒ the amount by which a sum of money falls short. 부족액; 결손; 적자(opp. surplus). ¶ *We have a great* ~ *this year.* 올해에는 적자폭이 크다. [→defect]

deficit spending [ˊ--ˋ-] *n.* the spending of money obtained by borrowing. 지출 초과.

de·file[1] [difáil] *vt.* (P6) make (something) dirty; destroy the purity of (something). …을 더럽히다〔오염하다〕; 불결하게 하다; …의 신성을 모독하다. ¶ ~ *a river* 강을 오염시키다 / ~ *a sanctuary with blood* 성역을 피로 더럽히다 / *clothes defiled with dirt* 흙이 묻어 더러워진 옷. ● **de·file·ment** [-mənt] *n.* [A.S. *ful* foul]

de·file[2] [difáil, dí:fail] *vi.* (P1) march in a line. 열을 지어 나아가다; 종대로 행진하다. —*n.* Ⓒ a narrow way, passage, etc. 좁은 길. [→file[1]]

de·fin·a·ble [difáinəbəl] *adj.* that can be defined. 정의할〔한정 지을〕 수 있는. [↓]

·**de·fine** [difáin] *vt.* (P6) **1** ⓐ make clear the meaning of (a word). …의 뜻을 분명히 하다; 정의를 내리다. ¶ *A dictionary defines words and phrases.* 사전은 낱말과 구(句)의 뜻을 명확히 정의한다. ⓑ make (something) clear 〔distinct〕; explain the nature of. …을 분명히 하다; (성질·본질 따위)를 설명하다. ¶ *ill-defined duties* (목적 따위가) 분명하지 않은 임무 / ~ *one's meaning* 〔*position*〕 진의를〔입장을〕 분명히 하다 / ~ *one's responsibility* 자기의 책임을 명확히 하다 / ~ *judicial functions* 재판관의 직능을 명시하다. **2** make or settle the limits of (something); show clearly the outlines of (something). …의 한계〔범위〕를 정하다; …의 윤곽을 또렷이 보이다. ¶ ~ *a boundary* 경계를 정하다 / *a well-defined footprint* 윤곽이 뚜렷한 발자국. [→finis]

:**def·i·nite** [défənit] *adj.* **1** having exact, well-marked limits; fixed. 명확히 한정된; 확정된; 일정한. ¶ *a* ~ *quantity* 일정량(量). **2** having a clear, exact meaning; precise. 확실한; 명확한; 정확한(opp. indefinite). ¶ *a* ~ *reason* 명확한 이유 / *to be* ~ 분명히 말하면 / *I want a* ~ *answer, yes or no.* 나는 예스냐 노냐의 분명한 대답을 듣고 싶다. **3** 《gram.》 limiting; limited; restricting. 한정적인. ¶ *the* ~ *article* 정관사. [↑]

·**def·i·nite·ly** [défənitli] *adv.* **1** clearly; in a definite manner. 분명히; 확정〔한정〕적으로. ¶ *refuse* ~ 딱 거절하다 / *He answered* ~ *that he would not go.* 그는 가지 않겠다고 확실히 대답했다. **2** 《*colloq.*》 certainly. 물론.

def·i·ni·tion [dèfəníʃən] *n.* **1** Ⓤ ⓐ the act of making clear the meaning of a word. 명확히 확정〔한정〕함. ⓑ Ⓒ a statement that makes clear the meaning of a word. 정의(定義); 어의(語義). ¶ *give a* ~ *of the word* 그 낱말의 정의를 내리다. **2** Ⓤ clearness of outline; degree of distinctness. (윤곽·경계 따위의) 또렷함; 명확함. ¶ *give the colors* ~ 색채를 또렷이 하다.

de·fin·i·tive [difínətiv] *adj.* **1** decisive; conclusive; final. 결정적인; 최종적인. ¶ *a* ~ *answer* 결정적인 대답 / *a* ~ *sentence* 최종 판결 / *a* ~ *edition* 결정판(版). **2** limiting; defining. 한정적인; 명확히 하는. ¶ *clarify with a* ~ *statement* 분명히 말하여 오해가 없도록 하다. —*n.* Ⓒ a word that defines a noun. 한정사(限定辭). ● **de·fin·i·tive·ly** [-li] *adv.* **de·fin·i·tive·ness** [-nis] *n.*

de·flate [difléit] *vt.* (P6) **1** let the air or gas out of (a balloon, tire, etc.). (기구·타이어 따위)에서 공기〔가스〕를 빼다. **2** 《econ.》 reduce the prices of; reduce the amount of (money) in circulation. (물가 수준)을 끌어내리다; (통화)를 수축시키다(opp. inflate). [→flatulent]

de·fla·tion [difléiʃən] *n.* Ⓤ **1** the act of deflating. 공기〔가스〕 빼기. **2** a reduction in the amount of available money in circulation, causing prices to go down. 디플레이션; 통화 수축(opp. inflation).

de·flect [diflékt] *vi.* (P1,3) bend or turn aside; deviate. (본래 진로에서) 벗어나다〔비끼다〕; 쏠리다. ¶ ~ *a little to the left* 조금 왼쪽으로 쏠리다. —*vt.* (P6,13) change the direction of (something). …의 방향을 벗어나게〔비끼게〕 하다; 굴절시키다. ¶ ~ *rays of light* 광선을 굴절시키다 / ~ *someone from the right course of action* 아무를 정도(正道)에서 벗어나게 하다. [→flexible]

de·flec·tion, 《Brit.》 **-flex·ion** [diflékʃən] *n.* ⓊⒸ the act of bending or turning aside. (방향·진로에서) 벗어남; 빗나감; 휨; 쏠림. ¶ *the* ~ *of the course of a bullet* 탄알코스의 빗나감.

de·flec·tive [difléktiv] *adj.* causing deflection; tending to turn aside. deflection을 일으키는; (옆으로) 빗나가는.

de·flex·ion [diflékʃən] *n.* 《Brit.》=deflection.

de·flo·ra·tion [dèfləréiʃən, dì:flɔ:-] *n.* the act of deflowering. 꽃을 꺾음〔지게 함〕; 처녀성을 빼앗음; 처녀 능욕. [↓]

de·flow·er [difláuər] *vt.* (P6) **1** strip (a tree) of flower 꽃을 꺾다〔따다〕; 꽃이 지게 하다. **2** 《*fig.*》 spoil; damage. 망가뜨리다; 손상시키다. **3** deprive (a woman) of her virginity. …의 처녀성을 빼앗다; (처녀)를 능욕하다. [→flower]

De·foe [difóu], **Daniel** *n.* (1659?-1731) an English author. 디포《영국의 소설가》.

de·for·est [di:fɔ́:rist, -fár- / -fɔ́r-] *vt.* (P6) cut trees off from (land). 산림을 벌채하다; 수목(樹木)을 베내다; 산림을 개척하다. ● **de·for·est·a·tion** [di:fɔ̀:ristéiʃən, -fàr- /

-fɔ̀r-] *n.* [de-]

de·form [difɔ́:rm] *vt.* (P6) **1** spoil the form or shape of (something). …의 모양을 망치다[손상하다]. ¶ *Tight shoes will ~ your feet.* 꼭 끼는 구두는 발 모양을 못쓰게 한다. **2** make (something) ugly. …을 보기 흉하게 하다. ¶ *Pain deformed his face.* 고통으로 그의 얼굴은 일그러졌다. ●**de·form·er** [-ər] *n.* [→form]

de·for·ma·tion [dì:fɔ:rméiʃən] *n.* **1** Ⓤ the act of deforming something. 변형시킴; 흉하게 함. **2** Ⓤ the state of being deformed. 기형; 불구.

de·formed [difɔ́:rmd] *adj.* **1** badly shaped. 모양이 손상된; 기형[불구]의. ¶ *give birth to a terrible ~ baby.* 지독한 기형아를 낳다. **2** ugly. 추한.

de·form·i·ty [difɔ́:rməti] *n.* (*pl.* **-ties**) **1** Ⓤ the state of being badly shaped. 모양이 손상돼 있음; 기형; 불구; 결함. **2** Ⓒ a badly shaped person or thing. 불구자; 기형물. **3** Ⓤ ugliness. 추(악)함. ¶ *the ~ of our nature* 우리 본성의 추악함.

de·fraud [difrɔ́:d] *vt.* (P6,13) take away money, rights, etc. from (someone) by deception. (돈·권리 따위)를 사취(詐取)하다. ¶ *They defrauded him of his money.* = *He was defrauded of his money.* 그는 돈을 사취당했다 / *I have been defrauded* (*out*) *of ₩5,000,000.* 5백만 원을 사취당했다. ●**de·fraud·er** [-ər] *n.* [→fraud]

de·fray [difréi] *vt.* (P6) pay (expenses) bear the cost of. (비용·경비)를 부담하다; 지불하다. ¶ *The expenses of national parks are defrayed by the government.* 국립공원의 경비는 정부가 부담한다. ●**de·fraud·al** [-əl], **de·fraud·ment** [-mənt] *n.* Ⓤ [F.]

deft [deft] *adj.* skillful or expert, esp. with fingers. 솜씨가 좋은; 능숙한. ¶ *a ~ mechanic* 능숙한 직공 / *a ~ potter* 솜씨 좋은 도공(陶工). [→daft]

deft·ly [déftli] *adv.* in a skillful manner. 솜씨 있게; 능숙하게.

deft·ness [déftnis] *n.* Ⓤ the quality of being deft; skillfulness. 솜씨(좋음); 능숙(함).

de·funct [difʌ́ŋkt] *adj.* dead; no longer existing. 죽은; 현존치 않는; 폐지[소멸]된. ¶ *a ~ law* 폐기된 법 / *a ~ organization* 없어진 단체 / *a ~ practice* 지금은 행해지지 않는 관습. —*n.* 《*the ~* 》 a dead person. 고인(故人). ¶ *the survivors of the ~* 고인의 유족 / *The ~ left no will.* 고인은 유언을 남기지 않았다. [de-, L. *fungor* perform]

·**de·fy** [difái] *vt.* (**-fied, -fy·ing**) (P6,13,20) **1** (of a person) show no fear of or no respect for; be in open disobedience to. …에 공공연히 반항하다[무시하다]. ¶ *~ one's parents* 부모에게 반항하다 / *~ the law* 법을 무시하다. **2** (of a thing) offer great difficulties to; resist; withstand. …을 거부하다; 거스르다; 불가능하게 하다. ¶ *~ every criticism* 비평의 여지가 없다 / *The door defies all attempts to open it.* 그 문은 아무리 해도 열리지 않는다 / *The problem defies solution.* 그 문제는 도무지 해결이 안 된다. **3** show the will to fight against (someone). …에 도전하다. ¶ *I ~ you to do this work.* 이 일을 할 수 있으면 해봐라. [de-, L. *fides* faith]

defy* (*all*) *description, can never be described. (이루 다) 형용할 수 없다. ¶ *The beauty of the scenery defies description.* 그 경치의 아름다움은 필설로 형용할 수가 없다.

defy comparison, be incomparable. …에게 비길[견줄, 필적할] 것이[사람이] 없다.

deg. degree(s).

de·gas [di:gǽs] *vt.* (P6) remove poisonous gases from. 가스나 독성을 처리 (제거)하다. [de-]

de Gaulle [də goul], **charles** *n.* (1890-1970) a French stateman and general. 드골《프랑스의 정치가·장군》.

de·gauss [di:gáus] *vt.* neutralize the magnetism of. 소자(消磁)하다. [de-]

de·gen·er·a·cy [didʒénərəsi] *n.* Ⓤ the state of being degenerate. 퇴화; 쇠퇴; 타락; 퇴폐. [↓]

de·gen·er·ate [didʒénərèit] *vi.* (P1,3) **1** 《*into*》 grow worse in quality. (육체적·정신적·도덕적으로) 나빠지다; 타락[퇴폐]하다. ¶ *John's school-work has degenerated this year.* 올해 들어 존의 학교 성적이 떨어졌다. **2** 《biol.》 sink to a lower type or state. 퇴화하다. —[didʒénərit] *adj.* showing a slow loss of good qualities; having become worse. 저하(低下)한; 퇴보[퇴화, 타락, 퇴폐]한. ¶ *~ times* 퇴폐한 시대. —[didʒénərit] *n.* Ⓒ a person having an evil character. 타락자. [L. *genus* race]

de·gen·er·a·tion [didʒènəréiʃən] *n.* Ⓤ the act of degenerating; the state of being degenerated. 타락; 퇴보; 퇴화; 쇠퇴.

de·glu·ti·tion [dì:glu:tíʃən] *n.* Ⓤ swallowing. 삼킴; 연하(嚥下). [L.]

deg·ra·da·tion [dègrədéiʃən] *n.* Ⓤ the act of degrading; the state of being degraded. (위계의) 떨어짐; 하락; 좌천; 파면; 저하; 악화; 타락; 쇠퇴. [↓]

de·grade [digréid] *vt.* (P6,13) **1** 《*from, to*》 put(someone) in a lower rank, esp. as punishment. (벌로서) 지위를 떨어뜨리다[박탈하다]; 면직[파면]하다. ¶ *be degraded from public office* 공직에서 파면당하다. **2** make (someone) worse; debase. (품성 등)을 떨어뜨리다; 비천하게 하다; 타락시키다. ¶ *You ~ yourself when you cheat at examinations.* 시험에서 부정을 하면 스스로의 품위를 떨어뜨리는 것이 된다. ●**de·grad·er** [-ər] *n.* [L. *gradus* step]

:**de·gree** [digrí:] *n.* **1** Ⓒ the relative amount or extent; a step or stage reached. 정도; 단계. ¶ *a high ~ of mastery* 고도의 숙달 / *a question* (*a matter*) *of ~* 정도의 문제 / *to a high ~* 고도로 / *differ in ~* 정

도의 차이가 있다 / *to such a* ~ *that* …일[할] 정도로 / *To what* ~ *will he cooperate?* 그는 어느 정도까지 협력할 것인가. **2** Ⓤ position; rank. 지위; 신분; 위계; 계급. ¶ *a man of high* [*low*] ~ 신분이 높은[낮은] 사람 / *a lady of* (*the*) *highest* ~ 최상층의 부인. **3** Ⓒ (in universities) a rank of title given to a student. 학위. ¶ *a doctor's* ~ 박사 학위 / *the* ~ *of M.A.* 문학 석사 학위 / *take one's* ~ (*at the university*) (대학에서) 학위를 따다 / *give a* ~ 학위를 수여하다. **4** Ⓒ a unit for measuring temperature, angles, etc. (온도·각도 따위의) 도(度). ¶ *40 degrees of latitude* [*longitude*] 위도[경도] 40도 / *water at 10 degrees centigrade* 섭씨 10도의 물. **5** Ⓤ nearness to a common ancestor. 친등(親等); 촌수. ¶ *degrees of consanguinity* 친등 / *a cousin in the second* ~, 6촌; 재종. **6** Ⓒ 《gram.》 a grade of comparison of adjectives and adverbs. (형용사·부사의) 비교를 나타내는 급(級). ¶ *the positive* [*comparative, superlative*] ~ 원급[비교급, 최상급]. [de-, →grade]

a degree, a little. 조금; 약간. ¶ *a* ~ *better* 약간 더 나은 / *a* ~ *warmer* 좀 더 따뜻한.

by degrees, slowly; gradually; little by little. 점차; 조금씩.

degree of frost, degree below zero. 빙점하(氷點下); 영하. ¶ *We had five degrees of frost last night.* 간밤은 영하 5도였다.

in a degree, somewhat; to some extent. 조금은; 어느 정도.

in a great degree, greatly. 크게; 매우.

in due degree, moderately. 적당히; 적절히.

in full degree, too much. 충분히.

in its degree, according to one's station in life. 분수에 따라서.

in some degree, to a certain extent. 어느 정도는; 얼마쯤; 다소.

not in the slightest [***least***] ***degree,*** not at all. 조금도 …아니다[않다].

to a degree, **a**) to a great extent. 꽤; 매우. **b**) somewhat; rather. 좀; 조금은.

to the last degree, extremely. 극도로.

de·hy·drate [di:háidreit] *vt.* (P6) take water or wetness from (something). …을 탈수(脫水)하다; 말리다. [de-, →hydrate]

de·ic·er [di:áisər] *n.* a device for the prevention of the formation of ice. (비행기 따위의) 방빙(防氷) 장치. [de-]

de·i·fi·ca·tion [dì:əfikéiʃən] *n.* Ⓤ the act of deifying; the state of being deified. 신(神)으로 모심[모셔짐]; 신격화. [↓]

de·i·fy [dí:əfài] *vt.* (**-fied, -fy·ing**) (P6) worship (someone) as a god. …을 신처럼 받들다; 신으로 모시다; 신격화하다. ¶ *Some people* ~ *wealth.* 어떤 사람들은 부(富)를 신처럼 숭상한다. [L. *deus* god]

deign [dein] *vi.* (P4) **1** condescend; be gracious enough. (황송하게도) …하시다[해 주시다]. ¶ *The king deigned to grant an audience.* 황송하옵게도 국왕께서는 알현을 허락하셨다. **2** lower oneself. (스스로를 굽히어) …하다. ¶ *He would not* ~ *to discuss the matter with us.* 그분께서는 우리와 그 문제를 의논하시려 하지 않았다 / *I do not* ~ *to reply to so rude a question.* 그런 무례한 질문에 대답할 수는 없다. — *vt.* (P6) condescend to give (an answer, etc.) (대답 따위)를 주시다. [→dignity]

de·ism [dí:izəm] *n.* Ⓤ 《philos.》 a belief in a God based on science and reason. 이신론(理神論); 자연신론(自然神論)(cf. *theism*). [L. *deus* god, →deify]

de·ist [dí:ist] *n.* a believer in deism. 이신론자(理神論者).

de·i·ty [dí:əti] *n.* (*pl.* **-ties**) **1** Ⓒ a god; a goddess. 신(神); 여신. ¶ *the Deity* 천제(天帝); 유일신. **2** Ⓤ divine nature; the state of being a god. 신성(神性); 신의 신분; 신격(神格). [→deify]

de·ject [didʒékt] *vt.* (P6) make (someone) sad or unhappy. …을 슬프게 하다; 의기소침케 하다(cf. *depress*). [de-, L. *jacio* throw]

de·ject·ed [didʒéktid] *adj.* in low spirits; depressed; sad. 의기소침한; 슬픈; 낙담한. ¶ *I felt very* ~ *all day.* 온종일 의기소침했다.

● **de·ject·ed·ly** [-li] *adv.* **de·ject·ed·ness** [-nis] *n.*

de·jec·tion [didʒékʃən] *n.* Ⓤ lowness of spirits; sadness. 의기소침; 낙담; 슬픔.

de·jeu·ner [déiʒənèi] *n.* 《F.》 breakfast, as on the Continent, taken about midday. 늦은 조반; 오찬.

de ju·re [di: ʒúəri] *adv., adj.* 《L.》 by right; of right. 권리에 의해[의한]; 권리상; 정당한(cf. *de facto*).

Del. Delaware.

del. delegate; *delineavit*(L.=he [she] drew it).

Del·a·ware [déləwɛ̀ər] *n.* an eastern State of the United States. 델라웨어주(州). 參考 Del.로 생략함. 주도(州都)는 Dover.

·**de·lay** [diléi] *vt.* (P6) **1** put off (something) till a later time; postpone. …을 연기하다. ¶ ~ *a party* 파티를 연기하다 / *We delayed the trip for a week.* 여행을 1주일 연기했다. **2** make (something) late. …을 지체시키다; 늦어지게 하다(opp. hasten). ¶ *Never* ~ *things.* 일을 늦추지 마라 / *The train was delayed three hours by heavy snow.* 열차는 폭설로 3시간이나 연착했다 / *The work delayed me at the office.* 일 때문에 회사에서 늦었다. — *vi.* (P1) act slowly; be late; stop for a while. 느릿느릿 행동하다; 꾸물대다; 늦어지다. ¶ *He delayed and the chance was lost.* 꾸물거리다가 기회를 놓쳤다.

— *n.* ⒸⓊ the act of delaying; a case fact of being delayed. 지연; 지체; 유예. ¶ *a long* ~ 오랜 지체 / *avoid* ~ 늦어지지 않도록 하다 / *Permit no* ~ *in doing what is good.* 좋은 일은 서둘러라. [→defer[1]]

without (***any***) ***delay,*** at once; immediately.

지체 없이; 즉각.

de·lec·ta·ble [diléktəbəl] *adj.* very pleasant; delightful. 매우 즐거운; 기쁜; 유쾌한. [↓]

de·lec·ta·tion [dì:lekteiʃən] *n.* Ⓤ pleasure; delight. 즐거움; 기쁨; 유쾌. ¶ *The old man performed many tricks for the ~ of the children.* 노인은 아이들을 즐겁게 하기 위해 많은 요술을 부렸다. [L.]

del·e·ga·cy [déligəsi] *n.* Ⓒ (*pl.* **-cies**) a group of delegates. 대표단. [↓]

***del·e·gate** [déligit, -gèit] *n.* Ⓒ a person given power to act for others. 대표자; 대리자(cf. *deputy*). —[déləgèit] *vt.* (P6,13,20) **1** appoint or send (someone) as a delegate. …을 대표자[대리]로 임명[파견]하다. ¶ *~ someone to negotiate for the loan* 아무를 차관 교섭의 대표로 임명하다 / *They delegated him to attend the meeting.* 그들은 그를 그 회합에 대표자로 파견했다. **2** 《*to*》 give over (one's power or authority) to another. (권한·임무 따위를) 위임하다; 위촉하다. ¶ *~ authority to a representative* 대표에게 권한을 위임하다. [→legacy]

del·e·ga·tion [dèligéiʃən] *n.* **1** Ⓤ the act of delegating; the state of being delegated. 대표 임명[파견]. **2** Ⓒ a group of delegates or representatives. 대표단.

de·lete [dilí:t] *vt.* (P6) cross out or omit (something written or printed.) (쓰인 것·인쇄된 것)을 삭제하다; 말소하다. ¶ *~ a word* [*letter*] 낱말[글자] 하나를 지우다 / *His name was deleted from the list.* 그의 이름은 명부에서 말소되었다. [L. *deleo*]

del·e·te·ri·ous [dèlətíəriəs] *adj.* harmful. 유해한. ¶ *~ gases* 유독 가스 / *Too much drinking has a ~ effect upon the body.* 과음은 몸에 해로운 영향을 끼친다. [Gk.]

de·le·tion [dilí:ʃən] *n.* ⓊⒸ the act of deleting; the state of being deleted. 삭제(됨); 말소(됨). [→delete]

delf [delf], **delft** [delft] *n.* a kind of glazed earthenware, usu. decorated in blue, made at, or imitating that made at, Delft in Holland. 델프트 도기(陶器)《흰 바탕에 청색의 불투명한 유약을 입힌 것》. [Place in Holland]

Del·hi [déli] *n.* New Delhi. 뉴델리《인도 북부의 도시》.

***de·lib·er·ate** [dilíbərèit] *vt., vi.* (P6,10, 12;1,3) 《*on, over, about*》 think over carefully; discuss. 숙고(熟考)하다; 토의하다. ¶ *~ a proposal* 제의를 숙고하다 / *~ what to do* 무엇을 해야 할지 숙고하다 / *~ over the question of raising taxes* 증세 문제를 토의하다. —[dilíbərit] *adj.* **1** carefully thought out beforehand; done on purpose. 신중히 고려[숙고]한; 미리 계산된; 고의의. ¶ *a ~ lie* 계획적인 거짓말 / *~ murder* 모살(謀殺) / *a ~ judgment* 숙고한 끝의 판단. **2** slow and careful in action, movements, speech, etc. 신중한; 사려 깊은. ¶ *a ~ decision* 신중한 결정 / *a man of ~ nature* 사려 깊은 성질의 사람. **3** slow; not hurried. 침착한; 서두르지 않는. ¶ *walk with a ~ step* 침착한 걸음으로 천천히 걷다. [de-, L. *libro* weigh]

***de·lib·er·ate·ly** [dilíbəritli] *adv.* carefully; intentionally; slowly. 신중히; 고의로; 천천히. ¶ *walk ~* 천천히 걷다 / *He ~ made trouble for me.* 그는 내게 일부러 말썽을 일으켰다.

de·lib·er·a·tion [dilìbəréiʃən] *n.* **1** Ⓤ the act of deliberating; careful thought. 숙고. ¶ *After long ~ , he decided not to go.* 긴 숙고 끝에 그는 가지 않기로 결정했다. **2** ⓊⒸ discussion. 토의; 심의. ¶ *the deliberations of Congress* 미국 의회의 심의 / *~ upon a matter* 어떤 문제의 토의. **3** carefulness; slowness. 신중(함); 침착. ¶ *speak with ~* 신중히 말하다.

de·lib·er·a·tive [dilíbərèitiv, -rit-] *adj.* **1** related to deliberation or discussion. 심의에 관련된. ¶ *a ~ assembly* [*body*] 심의회[기관]. **2** slow and careful; thoughtful. 신중한; 생각이 깊은. ● **de·lib·er·a·tive·ly** [-li] *adv.*

del·i·ca·cy [délikəsi] *n.* Ⓤ (*pl.* **-cies**) **1** delicate quality or nature; fineness. 섬세(함); 우미(優美); 우아; 고상함. ¶ *the ~ of a flower* 꽃의 아름다운 모습 / *the ~ of silks* 비단의 섬세함. **2** sensitiveness. (지각·감정 따위의) 섬세함; 민감함. ¶ *~ of hearing* 청각의 예민함 / *the ~ of her taste in music* 그녀의 음악적 취미의 예민함. **3** need of care or tact. (취급상의) 신중함; 미묘함; (기계 따위의) 정교함. ¶ *a situation of extreme ~* 매우 미묘한 상황. **4** 《sometimes *a ~* 》 consideration for the feelings of others. (남의 감정에 대한) 세심한 마음씀; 배려; 동정. ¶ *a man of extreme ~* 무척 배려 깊은 사람. **5** the quality of being easily made ill; weakness. 연약함; 허약. ¶ *~ of health* 허약한 건강 / *a ~ of constitution* 약한 체질 / *The child's ~ has always worried his parents.* 아이의 몸이 약해서 부모는 늘 걱정해 왔다. **6** Ⓒ esp. nice food. 미식(美食); 진수; 진미. ¶ *all the delicacies of the season* 계절의 온갖 진미. [→delicate]

feel a delicacy about, feel constraint about. …을 어려워하다; 스스러워하다.

:del·i·cate [délikit] *adj.* **1** pleasing to the taste; mild; dainty. (맛·향기 따위가) 감미로운; 풍미 있는; 맛좋은. ¶ *~ foods* 맛있는 음식 / *~ fragrance* 감미로운 향기. **2** soft; tender; gentle. 부드러운; 차분한. ¶ *a ~ shade of pink* 부드러운 색조의 핑크. **3** finely sensitive; fine or precise in action; exquisite. 민감한; 예민한; 정교[정밀]한. ¶ *a ~ sense of smell* [*touch*] 예민한 후각[촉각] / *a ~ ear for music* 음악에 민감한 귀 / *a ~ machine* 정교한 기계. **4** difficult to handle; requiring great care or skill. 다루기 힘든; 세심한 주의를 요하는; 솜씨를 필요로 하는. ¶ *a ~ situation* [*question*] 미묘한 국면[문제] / *a ~ task* [*mission*] 어려운 일[사명]. **5** difficult to perceive or describe because of fineness;

subtle. (감지할 수 없을 정도로) 미미한; 미묘한. ¶ ~ *differences* 미묘한 차이. **6** easily torn, broken, or made ill; frail; feeble; fragile. 깨지기[부서지기, 찢어지기, 손상되기] 쉬운; 허약한; 무른. ¶ *a* ~ *vase* 깨지기 쉬운 꽃병 / ~ *skin* 약한 피부 / *a* ~ *child* 허약한 아이. **7** mindful of or sensitive to the feelings of others; considerate. (남의 감정에 대해) 마음을 쓰는; 세심한 배려를 하는. ¶ ~ *attention* 세심한 배려 / *a* ~ *refusal* (상대의 마음을 다치지 않도록 신경을 쓴) 정중한 사절. ● **del·i·cate·ly** [-li] *adv.* [L. *deliciae* delight]

del·i·ca·tes·sen [dèlikətésn] *n. pl.* 《chiefly U.S.》 **1** Ⓒ 《used as *sing.*》 a store that sells ready-to-eat foods. 인스턴트식품 판매점. **2** Ⓤ 《*collectively*》 cooked meats, smoked fish, cheese, salads, etc. (위 가게에서 파는) 인스턴트 식품류. [G.]

·**de·li·cious** [dilíʃəs] *adj.* **1** very pleasing to taste or smell. 맛·향기가 매우 좋은. ¶ *a* ~ *dinner* 맛있는 저녁 식사 / *a* ~ *smell* 향기로운 냄새 / ~ *to taste* 맛있는. **2** very delightful; agreeable. 매우 재미있는[즐거운]; 기분 좋은; 유쾌한. ¶ *a* ~ *story* [*book*] 재미있는 이야기[책] / ~ *air* 상쾌한 공기. — *n.* 《*D-*》 Ⓒ a kind of red apple with a fine flavor. 딜리셔스《빨간 사과의 한 품종》. ● **de·li·cious·ness** [-nis] *n.* [→delicate]

de·li·cious·ly [dilíʃəsli] *adv.* in a delicious manner. 맛[풍미]있게; 향기 좋게; 기분 좋게; 재미있게.

:**de·light** [diláit] *n.* **1** Ⓤ great pleasure; joy. 큰 기쁨; 환희. ¶ *give* ~ *to* …을 기쁘게 하다. **2** Ⓒ something that gives great pleasure; a cause of great pleasure. 큰 기쁨[즐거움]을 주는 것; 즐거운 것. ¶ *Dancing is her* ~. 춤은 그녀의 즐거움이다.

take delight in (=*amuse oneself with*) *something.* …을 즐기다. ¶ *take* ~ *in music* 음악을 즐기다.

to one's delight, to one's joy. 기쁘게도.

with delight, joyfully. 기꺼이; 기쁘게.

— *vt.* (P6) please greatly. …을 크게 기쁘게[즐겁게] 하다. ¶ ~ *the ear* [*eye, heart*] 귀를[눈을, 마음을] 즐겁게 하다 / *I am delighted to see you.* 만나뵈어 기쁩니다 / *I shall be delighted to go with you.* 기꺼이 동반하겠습니다. — *vi.* (P3) 《*in*》 have great pleasure. 크게 기뻐하다. ¶ ~ *in books* 책을 매우 좋아하다 / *Children* ~ *in toys.* 아이들은 장난감을 무척 좋아합니다. [→delicate]

be delighted at [***with***], be pleased with (something). …을 기뻐하다. ¶ *He was delighted at the news.* 그 소식을 듣고 기뻐했다.

de·light·ed [diláitid] *adj.* joyful; glad. 기쁜; 즐거워하는. ● **de·light·ed·ly** [-li] *adv.*

:**de·light·ful** [diláitfəl] *adj.* **1** (of a thing) giving joy; very pleasing. 기쁨을 주는; 무척 즐거운. ¶ ~ *books* 기쁨을 주는 책 / ~ *holidays* 매우 즐거운 휴가. **2** (of a person) charming; winning. 반하게 하는; 애교 있는. 參考 I am delightful. 이라고는 하지 않음. ¶ *a* ~ *young lady* 애교 있는 젊은 여성 / *make oneself* ~ *to* …에게 애교를 부리다. ● **de·light·ful·ly** [-fəli] *adv.*

de·lim·it [dilímit] *vt.* (P6) mark or define the boundaries of (something). …의 경계[한계]를 정하다. [→limit]

de·lim·i·tate [dilímitèit] *vt.* 《rare》 =delimit.

de·lim·i·ta·tion [dilìmitéiʃən] *n.* **1** Ⓤ the act of delimiting. 경계 확정; 한계 설정. **2** Ⓒ a boundary. 한계; 경계.

de·lin·e·ate [dilínièit] *vt.* (P6) trace or draw the outline of (something); describe in words. …의 윤곽을 그리다; 말로 묘사하다; 기술하다. ● **de·lin·e·a·tor** [-ər] *n.* [→line]

de·lin·e·a·tion [dilìniéiʃən] *n.* ⓊⒸ the act of delineating; description; a sketch. 묘사; 기술(記述); 약도(略圖).

de·lin·quen·cy [dilíŋkwənsi] *n.* (*pl.* **-cies**) **1** Ⓤ the neglect of a duty; the habit of behaving unlawfully. (의무·직무의) 불이행; 태만; 비행 습관. **2** Ⓒ a misdeed; an offense. 비행; 범죄. [L. *linquo* leave]

de·lin·quent [dilíŋkwənt] *adj.* **1** neglecting a duty; behaving unlawfully. 의무를 태만히 하는; 의무 불이행의; 비행의. **2** guilty of an offense. 죄를 저지른; 유죄의. — *n.* Ⓒ a delinquent person; an offender. 태만자; 비행[범법]자.

del·i·quesce [dèlikwés] *vi.* (P1) **1** 《chem.》 become liquid by absorbing moisture from the air. 조해(潮解)하다. **2** melt away. 녹다; 용해하다. [de-, →liquid]

del·i·ques·cent [dèlikwésnt] *adj.* 《chem.》 becoming liquid by absorbing moisture from the air. 조해성(潮解性)의.

de·lir·i·a [dilíriə] *n.* pl. of **delirium.**

de·lir·i·ous [dilíriəs] *adj.* **1** (of a person) out of one's senses; wandering in mind and saying meaningless things. 제정신을 잃은; 헛소리하는; 정신 착란에 빠진. ¶ *be* ~ *from fever* 고열(高熱)로 헛소리하다. **2** (of speech, etc.) wildly excited. 몹시 흥분한. [de-, L. *lira* furrow; *tremo* tremble]

de·lir·i·um [dilíriəm] *n.* (*pl.* **-lir·i·ums** or **-lir·i·a**) **1** Ⓤ a temporary disorder of the mind caused by illness. 일시적 정신 착란(상태). **2** Ⓒ the state of being wildly excited. 맹렬한 흥분. [↑]

delirium tre·mens [dilíriəm trí:mənz] *n.* 《med.》 delirium caused by excessive drinking. 진전섬망(震顫譫妄).

:**de·liv·er** [dilívər] *vt.* (P6,7,13) **1** take (something or someone) to a certain person or place; distribute; convey. …을 배달하다; (전언 따위)를 전하다. ¶ ~ *a message* 메시지를 전하다 / *Postmen* ~ *letters from door to door.* 우편 집배원은 편지를 집집이 배달한다. **2** give forth in words, utter;

speak formally. (연설 따위)를 하다; (의견 따위)를 말하다; (판결 따위)를 내리다. ¶ ~ *a speech* 〔*an address*〕 연설을 하다 / ~ *a verdict* 평결을 내리다 / ~ *orders to* …에게 명령을 내리다. **3** strike or aim (a blow, etc.); launch; pitch. (공격·타격 따위)를 가하다; 던지다. ¶ ~ *a blow to the nose* 코빼기에 일격을 가하다 / ~ *a fast ball* 속구를 던지다. **4** bring and hand to another; give up; hand over; transfer. 건네〔넘겨〕주다. ¶ ~ *a bond* 증서를 넘겨주다 / ~ *someone to the police* 아무를 경찰에 넘기다. **5** save from (danger, suffering, death, etc.); set free; rescue. (위험·죽음 따위에서) …을 구해내다; 자유롭게 하다; 해방하다. ¶ ~ *someone from death* …을 죽음에서 살려내다 / ~ *the prisoners from the enemy* 적군으로부터 포로를 구출하다 / *be delivered from bondage* 속박에서 해방되다. **6** help (a woman) in giving birth to a child; 《in. *passive*》 give birth to (a child). 분만을 돕다; 분만시키다; 낳게 하다. ¶ *The doctor delivered the child.* 의사는 아이를 분만시켰다. **7** give forth; emit. …을 내다; 분출(噴出)하다. ¶ *This well delivers much water.* 이 우물은 많은 물을 분출한다. [de-, L. *liber* free; →liberate]

be delivered of, give birth to. …을 낳다. ¶ *She was delivered of a child.* 그녀는 아이를 낳았다.

deliver oneself of, give out, express, utter(one's opinion, etc.). (의견 따위)를 말하다; 공표하다.

deliver the goods, a) hand over the goods; fulfill one's promise. 화물을 인도하다; 약속을 이행하다. b) 《U.S.》 act up to one's expectation. 기대했던 결과를 가져오다; 기대에 부응하다.

deliver oneself to (*the police*), give oneself up to. (경찰)에 자수하다.

de·liv·er·ance [dilívərəns] *n.* **1** Ⓤ the act of setting free; rescue; the state of being set free. 구출; 구조; 해방; 석방. ¶ *one's ~ from prison* 교도소에서의 석방 / ~ *from the bondage of sin* 죄의 구속으로부터의 해방. **2** Ⓒ the formal pronouncement of an opinion. (의견의) 공표; 공표된 의견.

de·liv·er·er [dilívərər] *n.* Ⓒ a person who delivers. 구조자; 배달인; 넘겨주는 사람.

·de·liv·er·y [dilívəri] *n.* (*pl.* **-er·ies**) **1** Ⓤ the act of carrying letters, goods, etc. to someone or destination. (편지·물건 따위의) 배달; 송부(送付); …편. ¶ *special* ~ 속달(편) / *free* ~ 무료 배달 / *by the first* ~ 제1편으로. **2** Ⓒ a periodical taking of letters, goods, etc. to a designated person or place. 정기적인 배달편. ¶ *How many mail deliveries are there in this town every day?* 이 읍내에서는 매일 몇 번의 우편 배달이 있습니까. **3** ⓊⒸ the act of handing over. 넘겨〔건네〕줌; 인도(引渡); 교부. ¶ *the ~ of the ransom* 몸값의 교부 / *pay the charge on* ~ 현물 인도 때 대금을 지급하다. **4** Ⓒ 《usu. *sing.*》 manner of speaking. 이야기 솜씨. ¶ *a good* 〔*poor*〕 ~ 훌륭한〔서투른〕 말솜씨 / *Our teacher's ~ of the speech was excellent.* 우리 선생님의 말솜씨는 뛰어났다. **5** Ⓒ the act of giving birth to a child. 출산(出産); 분만. ¶ *an easy* 〔*a difficult*〕 ~ 순〔난〕산 / *artificial* 〔*painless*〕 ~ 인공〔무통(無痛)〕 분만. **6** Ⓒ 《cricket, etc.》 delivering. 투구(投球). ¶ *the ~ of a ball by the bowler* 투수의 투구.

dell [del] *n.* Ⓒ a small valley, usu. with trees on both sides. (보통 양쪽 벼랑이 수목으로 덮인) 작은 골짜기. [E.]

Del·lin·ger [délindʒər], **John Howard** *n.* (1886-1962) an American radio engineer. 델린저《미국의 전기학자》.

Dellinger phenomenon [ㅗ--ㅗ--] *n.* an obstacle to wireless communication caused by a magnetic storm. 델린저 현상《단파 통신이 자기(磁氣)폭풍으로 방해받는 현상》.

de·louse [di:láus] *vt.* remove lice from. …에서 이를 없애다. [de-]

Del·phi [délfai] *n.* an ancient town in Greece. 델피. [Place]

Del·phi·an [délfiən] *adj.* =Delphic.

Del·phic [délfik] *adj.* **1** of the temple and oracle of Apollo at Delphi. 아폴로 신전(神殿)〔신탁〕의. **2** with double meaning; obscure. 수수께끼 같은; 모호한.

del·ta [déltə] *n.* Ⓒ **1** the fourth letter of the Greek alphabet(Δ or δ). 델타《그리스어 알파벳의 넷째 글자》. **2** a delta-shaped(Δ) piece of land at the mouth of a river between two or more branches. (강어귀의) 삼각주. ¶ *the Nile Delta* 나일강 하구의 삼각주. [Gk. Δ]

del·toid [déltɔid] *adj.* delta-shaped. (그리스 알파벳의) 델타 글자(Δ) 모양의. ¶ *a ~ muscle* 삼각근(筋). [↑]

de·lude [dilú:d] *vt.* (P6,13) deceive; mislead. …을 속이다; 미혹시키다. [L. *ludo* mock]

delude oneself, be led into a false idea or opinion. 망상〔환상〕에 사로잡히다; 잘못 생각하다.

del·uge [délju:dʒ] *n.* Ⓒ **1** ⓐ a great flood. 대홍수. ⓑ 《*the D-*》 《Bible》 the great flood in the days of Noah. 노아의 홍수. **2** a heavy fall of rain; a heavy rush of water, fire, tears, words, etc. 큰비; 쏟아져 나오는 것《물·눈물·말 따위》. ¶ *After me* 〔*us*〕 *the ~.* 나중이야 어찌되건 내 알 바 아니다. **3** anything that comes like a flood. 밀려드는〔들이닥치는〕 것; 쇄도. ¶ *a ~ of orders* 〔*visitors*〕 주문〔방문객〕의 쇄도 / *a ~ of questions* 쏟아지는 질문.

— *vt.* (P6,13) **1** flood; overflow. 침수시키다; 범람시키다. ¶ *The fields were deluged with rain.* 논밭이 비로 침수되었다. **2** come down on or cover (something or someone) like a flood. (홍수처럼) 쏟아지다; 밀어닥치다; 쇄도하다. ¶ ~ *someone with invita-*

tions 아무에게 초청장이 밀려들다 / *He was deluged with questions.* 그에게 질문이 쏟아졌다. [→dilute]

de·lu·sion [dilúːʒən] *n.* **1** Ⓤ the act of deluding; the state of being deluded. 미혹; 속임; 기만. **2** Ⓒ a false notion or belief. 망상; 잘못된 생각〔신념〕. ¶ *a ~ of persecution* 피해망상 / *fall into a ~* 망상에 빠지다 / *The mad boy had a ~ that he was a king.* 그 미친 소년은 자신이 왕이라는 망상을 갖고 있었다. [→delude]

a snare and a delusion, a snare. 덫.

under a delusion, mistaken. 잘못 생각하고.

de·lu·sive [dilúːsiv] *adj.* misleading; deceptive. (사람을) 그르치는; 미혹시키는; 속이는; 거짓의. [↑]

de luxe, de·luxe [də lúks, -lʌ́ks] *adj.* 《F.》 of exceptionally fine quality; luxurious. 특히 좋은; 호화〔사치〕스러운. ¶ *a ~ hotel* (특급) 호화 호텔 / *a ~ edition* 호화판(版).

delve [delv] *vi., vt.* (P1,3;6) **1** 《*arch.*》 dig. 파다. ¶ *~ the ground* 땅을 파다. **2** 《*fig.*》 look deeply; do research. 철저히 조사〔탐구〕하다. ¶ *~ into the past* 〔*the secrets of nature*〕 과거를〔자연의 비밀을〕 철저하게 파헤치다 / *~ into a crime* 범죄를 규명하다 / *~ in a library for information* 도서관에서 자료를 찾다. [E.]

Dem. Democrat; Democratic.

de·mag·net·ize [diːmǽgnətàiz] *vt.* (P6) deprive of magnetism. 자기(磁氣)를 없애다. [de-]

dem·a·gog, -gogue [déməgɔ̀ːg, -gàg / -gɔ̀g] *n.* Ⓒ a political leader who stirs up the people by speeches that appeal to the feelings instead of the reason. 민중 선동자; 선동 연설가〔정치가〕. [Gk.]

dem·a·gog·ic [dèməgádʒik, -gɑg- / -gɔ́g-], **-i·cal** [-əl] *adj.* of or like a demagog. 선동의; 선동적인.

dem·a·gogu·er·y [déməgɔ̀ːgəri, -gàg- / -gɔg-] *n.* 《U.S.》 methods or principles of a demagogue. 선동 (행위); 악선전.

dem·a·go·gy [déməgòudʒi, -gɔ̀ːgi, -gàgi / -gɔ̀gi, -gɔ̀dʒi] *n.* **1** =demagoguery. **2** character of a demagogue. 선동가적인 성격.

:de·mand [dimǽnd, -máːnd] *vt.* **1** (P6,8, 11,13,20) 《*of, from*》 ask for (something). …을 요구〔청구〕하다; 강요하다; 힐문하다. ¶ *~ an immediate answer* 즉각적인 대답을 요구하다 / *~ surrender* 항복을 강요하다 / *~ an answer of* 〔*from*〕 *someone* 아무의 대답을 요구하다 / *~ payment of the debt* 빚을 갚기를 요구하다 / *He demanded to be told the truth.* 그는 사실을 들려주기를 요구했다 / *She demanded to know where I lived.* 그녀는 내가 사는 곳을 알고 싶다고 했다 / *He demanded that I (should) tell him all about the accident.* 그는 나에게 사고에 관해 모든 것을 이야기해 줄 것을 요구했다. **2** (P6) 《*fig.*》 (of things) need; require. (사물이) …을 요하다; 필요로 하다. ¶ *This task demands great patience* 〔*special knowledge*〕. 이 일은 많은 인내를〔특별한 지식을〕 필요로 한다.

— *n.* **1** Ⓒ a request as by right or authority; requirement; need; claim. (권리로서의) 요구; 청구; 필요로 하는〔요구되는〕 것. ¶ *a ~ for payment* 지급 요구 / *satisfy a ~* 요구를 충족시키다 / *make a ~ for money* (*on someone*) (아무에게) 돈을 요구하다 / *We have many demands on our time.* 여러가지로 시간을 빼앗기는 일이 많다《해야 할 일이 많다》 / *I have a ~ to make of him.* 그에게 요구하고 싶은 것이 있다. **2** 《econ.》 ⓊⒸ desire to have or get; call. (상품 따위에 대한) 수요; 판로. ¶ *~ and supply* 수요와 공급 / *There is a great ~ for computers.* 컴퓨터에 대한 수요가 많다. [→mandate]

be in demand, be sought after. 수요가 있다. ¶ *Fresh flowers are now in great ~.* 싱싱한 꽃은 지금 수요가 많다.

on demand, upon request for payment. 청구하는 대로. ¶ *The bill is payable on ~.* 그 어음은 일람출급이다.

de·mar·cate [díːmɑːrkèit] *vt.* (P6) mark and fix the boundary of (lands, etc.); separate. (지역 따위의) 경계를 정하다; 분리하다. [→mark[1]]

de·mar·ca·tion [dìːmɑːrkéiʃən] *n.* ⓊⒸ the act of demarcating; separation. 경계〔한계〕를 정함; 경계〔한계〕 확정; 분리; 구획. ¶ *a line of ~* 경계선.

de·mean[1] [dimíːn] *vt.* (P6) 《usu. *reflexively*》 make (someone or something) mean or lower in value, quality, dignity, character, etc. …의 품위를 떨어뜨리다. ¶ *She demeaned herself by begging for food.* 그녀는 음식을 구걸할 정도로 영락했다. [de-, →mean[2]]

de·mean[2] [dimíːn] *vt.* (P6,7) 《*reflexively*》 《*arch.*》 behave, conduct (oneself). 행동하다. ¶ *~ oneself well* 훌륭히 행동하다 / *Demean yourselves like men.* 남자답게 굴어라. [de-, →minatory]

de·mean·or, 《Brit.》 **-our** [dimíːnər] *n.* Ⓤ behavior; conduct. 행동; 태도. ¶ *a quiet ~* 조용한 행동. [↑]

de·ment·ed [diméntid] *adj.* out of one's mind; mad. 정신이 돈; 미친. ¶ *like one ~* 미치광이처럼 / *be* 〔*become*〕 *~* 미치다; 발광하다. [↓]

de·men·ti [deimáːntiː] *n.* 《F.》 《diplom.》 an official denial. (당국의) 공식 부인(否認). [de-, →mental]

de·men·tia [diménʃiə] *n.* 《med.》 madness. 치매(癡呆). ¶ *precocious ~* =*~ praecox* [príːkɑks / -kɔks] 《L.》 조발성 치매증(早發性癡呆症). [L. *dēmentem* out of one's mind]

de·mer·it [diːmérit] *n.* Ⓒ **1** a defect; a fault. 결점; 단점. ¶ *merits and demerits* 장점과 단점; 득실; 공죄(功罪). **2** 《U.S.》 a mark against a pupil's record for poor work or bad behavior. (성적 불량·나쁜 행실

에 대한) 벌점(=demerit mark). [→merit]

de·mesne [diméin, -mí:n] *n.* **1** Ⓤ 《law》 possession of land as one's own; land not let to others but held as one's own. 토지의 소유; 빌려주지 않고 갖고 있는 사유지. **2** Ⓒ a domain; a realm. 영지; 범위; 영역. [→domain]

De·me·ter [dimí:tər] *n.* 《Gk. myth.》 the goddess of agriculture. 농업의 여신(女神). 參考 로마 신화의 Ceres에 해당.

dem·i- [demi-] *pref.* half; in part. '반(半)…, 부분적 …'의 뜻(cf. *semi-*). [L. *dimidium* half]

dem·i·god [démigàd / -gɔ̀d] *n.* Ⓒ a god that is partly divine, partly human. 반신반인(半神半人). [→god]

dem·i·john [démidʒàn / -dʒɔ̀n] *n.* Ⓒ a large bottle enclosed in wicker. 채롱에 든 큰 병. [F.]

de·mil·i·ta·rize [dí:milətəràiz] *vt.* (P6) free from military control or occupation. 비무장〔비군사〕화하다. [de-]

dem·i·monde [démimànd / -mɔ́nd] *n.* 《F.》 《*the* ～》 a class of women whose reputation and morals are doubtful. 그늘 속 여인들의 사회; 윤락녀〔창녀〕의 세계. [demi-, F. *monde* society]

dem·i·rep [démirèp] *n.* one of the demimonde. 화류계 여자; 몸파는 여자. [demi-, *rep*utation]

de·mise [dimáiz] *n.* Ⓒ **1** the giving up, transferring to another, of land, money, etc. at death. 재산권의 이전〔양도〕. **2** death. 사망; 사거(死去). — *vt.* (P6,13,14) give up or transfer (land, money, etc.) at death. (죽을 때 재산권)을 이양〔양도〕하다; 유증하다. ¶ ～ *the Crown* 양위(讓位)하다. [→dismiss]

de·mist [dimíst] *vt.* (P6) clear mist from. (창문이나 유리 따위)에서 흐린 것을 닦아 없애다. [*mist*]

de·mit [dimít] *vt.* (P6) (**-mit·ted**) resign (an office). 사직(辭職)하다. [L. *mitto* send]

dem·i·tasse [démitæ̀s, -tà:s] *n.* a small cup of coffee. 작은 커피잔. [F. *tasse* cup]

de·mo·bi·lize [di:móubəlàiz] *vt.* (P6) 《mil.》 **1** set (someone) free from military service. …을 복원〔제대〕시키다. **2** break up or dismiss (forces, etc.). (군대의) 동원을 풀다; 해대(解隊)하다. [de-]

***de·moc·ra·cy** [dimákrəsi / -mɔ́k-] *n.* (*pl.* **-cies**) **1** Ⓤ government either directly by the people or through elected persons. 민주주의; 민주 정치. ¶ *direct* 〔*representative*〕 ～ 직접〔대의(代議)〕 민주제(制) / *Democracy is the government of the people, by the people, and for the people.* 민주주의란 국민의, 국민에 의한, 국민을 위한 정치이다. **2** Ⓒ a country having such a government. 민주주의 국가. **3** 《*the* ～》 the lower classes; the common people. 평민 계급; 서민; 민중. **4** 《*D-*》 《U.S.》 the Democratic Party. (미합중국의) 민주당. **5** Ⓤ treating other people as one's equals. (인간을 동등하게 대하는) 평등〔평민〕주의; 민주주의. ¶ *The old gentleman's* ～ *charmed everybody.* 그 노신사의 평민주의는 모든 사람을 매료시켰다. [Gk. *dēmos* the people]

***dem·o·crat** [déməkræ̀t] *n.* Ⓒ **1** a person who believes or supports democracy. 민주주의(신봉·옹호)자. **2** 《*D-*》 《U.S.》 a member of the Democratic Party. (미 합중국의) 민주당원(cf. *Republican*). **3** a person who holds or acts on the belief that all people are his equals. (인간의 평등을 주장하는) 평등〔평민〕주의자; 민주주의자. [↑]

:dem·o·crat·ic [dèməkrǽtik] *adj.* **1** of democracy; based on democracy. 민주주의의; 민주적인. ¶ ～ *government* 민주 정치. **2** 《*D-*》 《U.S.》 of the Democratic Party. 민주당의. **3** treating all classes of people as one's equals. (모든 사람을 자신과 동등하게 대하는) 평등〔평민〕주의의; 평민적인. ¶ ～ *tastes* 평민적인 취미 / *a man* ～ *of speech and bearing* 이야기투나 태도가 평민적인 사람.

de·moc·ra·tize [dimákrətàiz / -mɔ́k-] *vt., vi.* (P6;1) make or become democratic. 민주화(化)하다; 민주주의화하다. ●**de·moc·ra·ti·za·tion** [dimàkrətizéiʃən / -mɔ̀krətai-] *n.*

de·mo·de [dèimɔ:déi] *adj.* 《F.》 out of fashion. 유행〔시대〕에 뒤진; 구식의.

De·mo·gor·gon [dì:məgɔ́:rgən] *n.* a demon of the underworld. 마왕(魔王). [*demon, Gorgon*]

de·mog·ra·phy [dimágrəfi / di:mɔ́g-] *n.* Ⓤ the study of statistics of births, deaths, etc. (출생·사망 등의) 인구 통계학. [Gk. *dēmos*, -graphy]

de·mol·ish [dimáliʃ / -mɔ́l-] *vt.* (P6) **1** pull down (an old building, etc.); destroy; make an end of. (낡은 건물 따위)를 헐다; 부수다; 파괴하다; 끝내다; 그만두다. ¶ ～ *an argument* 논의를 끝내다. **2** 《*colloq.*》 eat up; finish. 다 먹어치우다. ¶ ～ *three eggs for breakfast* 아침 식사로 달걀 3개를 먹다. [L. *de-* down, *moles* mass, construction]

dem·o·li·tion [dèməlíʃən] *n.* Ⓤ destruction. 파괴; 헒; 철거; 분쇄. [↑]

de·mon [dí:mən] *n.* Ⓒ **1** an evil spirit; a devil. 악령(惡靈); 악마; 귀신. ¶ *malevolent* ～ 악귀. **2** 《Gk. myth.》 a spirit ranking between gods and men. 다이몬《신(神)과 인간의 중간에 위치하는 2차적인 신》. **3** a very cruel and wicked person. 극악무도한〔악마 같은〕 사람. ¶ *a regular* ～ 순 악마 같은 사람 / *a* ～ *of jealousy* 질투의 화신. **4** a person who has great energy or skill. (초인적) 정력가; (일의) 귀재; 명인. ¶ *a* ～ *at golf* 골프의 명수 / *He is a* ～ *for work.* 그는 일하는 데 귀신이다. [Gk. *daimōn* spirit]

a little demon, a naughty child. 선머슴; 장난꾸러기.

de·mo·ni·ac [dimóuniæ̀k] *adj.* **1** of a

demon; like a demon; devilish. 악마의; 악마 같은; 악마적인. ¶ *a ~ laughter* 악마 같은 웃음. **2** possessed by a demon. 악마에 들린(씌인). — *n.* Ⓒ a person supposed to be possessed by an evil spirit. 악마(귀신) 들린 사람. [↑]

de·mo·ni·a·cal [dìːmənáiəkəl] *adj.* = demoniac.

de·mon·ic [dimάnik / -mɔ́n-] *adj.* of the nature of genius. 천재적인.

de·mon·ol·o·gy [dìːmənάlədʒi / -ɔ́l-] *n.* the study of demons. 악마 연구; 귀신학(學). [→demon]

dem·on·stra·ble [démənstrəbəl] *adj.* that can be proved or shown clearly by giving examples. 논증(증명)할 수 있는. [↓]

·**dem·on·strate** [démənstrèit] *vt.* (P6,11) **1** show or prove (something) clearly by giving proof or examples. …을 증명(입증·논증)하다. ¶ *Magellan demonstrated that the earth is round.* 마젤란은 지구가 둥글다는 것을 증명했다. **2** explain (something) by experiment. (실험·실례로써) …을 설명하다; (상품의) 실물(實物) 선전을 하다. ¶ *~ a new washing machine* 신형 세탁기의 실물을 선전하다 / *~ the force of gravity by dropping an object* 물체를 낙하시켜 중력(重力)의 작용을 설명하다. **3** show (one's feelings) openly. (감정)을 솔직하게 드러내다(나타내다). ¶ *~ one's anger by slamming a door* 문을 쾅 닫아 노여움을 나타내다.
— *vi.* (P1,3) **1** show, advertise, or make publicly known. 선전하다. **2** make a show of public feeling by a parade, meeting, etc. 시위하다; 데모하다. ¶ *The crowd demonstrated before the Japanese Embassy.* 군중은 일본 대사관 앞에서 시위를 했다. **3** 《mil.》 make a show of force or readiness to fight, etc. 시위행동을 하다; 양동작전을 하다. [L. *monstro* show]

·**dem·on·stra·tion** [dèmənstréiʃən] *n.* ⓊⒸ **1** a clear proof. 논증; 입증; 실증; 증거; 증명. **2** an explanation with the use of experiments. 실험; 설명; 가르침; 실연. **3** an open show of one's feelings. (감정의) 표명; 표출. ¶ *give a ~ of love* 애정을 드러내다. **4** a show of public feeling by a parade, meeting, etc. 시위(示威); 데모. ¶ *a student ~* 학생 데모. **5** 《mil.》 a show of force planned to cause fear or to show preparedness for war. 시위행동; 양동(작전).

de·mon·stra·tive [dimάnstrətiv / -mɔ́n-] *adj.* **1** showing clearly. 분명히 나타내는; 명시적인. **2** 《gram.》 pointing out. 지시하는. ¶ *a ~ adjective* (*pronoun*) 지시형용사(대명사). **3** ⓐ (of a person, character, etc.) expressing one's feelings freely and openly. 감정을 노골적으로 드러내는; 표현적인; 표정이 강한. ¶ *a ~ person* (*behavior*) 노골적인 사람(태도). ⓑ (of feelings, etc.) expressed freely and openly. 분명히 드러낸(표출된). — *n.* Ⓒ 《gram.》 a word that points out. 지시사(指示詞)《this, that 따위》. ● **de·mon·stra·tive·ly** [-li] *adv.*

dem·on·stra·tor [démənstrèitər] *n.* Ⓒ **1** a person who demonstrates. 증명자; 입증(논증)자. **2** a person who takes part in a demonstration. 시위(데모) 참가자. **3** a person who teaches and shows something by demonstration. (영국 대학의) 실물(실험)교수; (사용법 따위)를 실연하는 사람; 실물 선전자. ¶ *a ~ in anatomy* 해부학의 실제 수업의 조수.

de·mor·al·i·za·tion [dimɔ̀ːrəlizéiʃən, -mὰr- / -mɔ̀r-] *n.* Ⓤ the act of demoralizing; the state of being demoralized. 풍속 괴란; 도덕 퇴폐; 타락; 사기 저상. [↓]

de·mor·al·ize [dimɔ́ːrəlàiz, -mάr- / -mɔ́r-] *vt.* (P6) **1** ruin the morals or character of (someone or something); corrupt. …의 도덕을 퇴폐시키다; 풍기(風紀)를 어지럽히다. ¶ *Drinking and gambling often ~ people.* 음주와 도박은 사람들의 마음을 타락시킨다. **2** weaken or spoil the spirit, courage of (someone). …의 사기를 저상시키다; 용기를 꺾다. ¶ *The Iraqian Army was demoralized by its defeat.* 이라크군은 패배로 사기가 떨어졌다. [→moral]

de·mos [díːmɑs / -mɔs] *n.* Ⓤ (often in a bad sense) the common people; lower classes. 대중; 민중; 평민. [Gk. *dēmos* the common people]

De·mos·the·nes [dimάsθənìːz / -mɔ́s-] *n.* (384? – 322 B.C.) the most famous orator and statesman of ancient Greece. 데모스테네스《고대 그리스의 웅변가·정치가》.

De·mos·then·ic [dimɑsθénik, dèm-] *adj.* eloquent; fervid. 웅변인; 열렬한.

de·mote [dimóut] *vt.* 《orig. U.S.》 reduce to a lower class. 계급을(지위를) 낮추다; 강등(降等)시키다(opp. promote). [de-, pro*mote*]

de·mot·ic [dimάtik / -mɔ́t-] *adj.* **1** belonging to the people; popular. 민중(대중)의; 인민의. **2** of or belonging to a simplified system of ancient Egyptian writing. (고대 이집트 문자가 간략화된) 민용(民用)문자의(cf. *hieratic*).

de·mo·tion [dimóuʃən] *n.* ⓊⒸ lowering in rank. 강등(降等); 강직(降職); 격하. [de-]

de·mount [diːmáunt] *vt.* (P6) **1** take from its mounting. (대포 따위를 달아 놓은 곳에서) 떼어내다. **2** take apart; disassemble. 해체하다; 분해하다. [de-]

de·mul·cent [dimʌ́lsənt] *adj.* soothing; mollifying. (약제 따위가) 통증을 가라앉히는; 진통의; 완화시키는. — *n.* 《med.》 a preparation for soothing. (점막 염증에 의한 통증의) 완화제; 진통약. [de-]

de·mur [dimə́ːr] *vi.* (**-murred, -mur·ring**) (P1,3) 《*at, to*》 give a reason against something; raise objections to. (…에) 반대하다; 이의(異議)를 말하다. ¶ *~ to a suggestion* 제안에 이의를 말하다 / *He demurs at* *working on Sunday.* 그는 일요일 근무에 반대한다. — *n.* Ⓤ objecting; objection. 이의를 말하기; 반대; 불복(不服). ¶ *No* ~. 이의 없음 / *He made no* ~ *about accepting it.* 그는 그것을 받아들이는 데 이의가 없었다. [L. *mora* delay]

without demur, without objection. 이의 없이.

de·mure [dimjúər] *adj.* (**-mur·er, -mur·est**) **1** modest; quiet and serious in manner. 내향적이고 조신한; 조용하고 진지한. **2** assuming the air of being serious or modest. 짐짓 진지하고 조신한 체하는; 새침떠는. ¶ *the* ~ *smile of a flirt* 바람난 여자의 얌전한 체하는 미소. ● **de·mure·ly** [-li] *adv.* **de·mure·ness** [-nis] *n.* [→mature]

de·mur·rage [dimə́:ridʒ, -mʌ́r-] *n.* Ⓤ **1** the detention of a vessel, freight car, etc. beyond the time agreed upon. 체선(滯船); 초과 정박; 체화차(滯貨車). **2** money paid for this. 체선료(滯船料); 화차(貨車) 유치료(留置料). [→demur]

de·mur·rer [dimə́:rər, -mʌ́rər] Ⓒ 《law》 **1** a pleading setting up that the truth is insufficient. 방소(妨訴) 항변; 이의 신청〔제기〕. **2** a person who demurs. 항변자; 반대자; 이의 신청자. [→demur]

put in a demurrer, demur. 이의를 신청〔제기〕하다.

***den** [den] *n.* Ⓒ **1** a place where a wild animal lives. 야수의 굴. ¶ *a bear's* ~ 곰의 굴. **2** a place where thieves live. 도둑의 소굴. ¶ *a robber's* ~ 강도의 소굴. **3** a small, dirty room. 작고 누추한 방. **4** 《*colloq.*》 a quite, private room for reading and work. 아늑한 사실(私室)《독서·작업용》; 서재. ¶ *He's in his* ~ *studying.* 그는 사실에서 공부하고 있다. [E.]

den·a·ry [dénəri, dí:-] *adj.* 《math.》 of ten; increasing by tens. 십(十)의; 십진(十進)의. [L. *decem* ten]

de·nat·u·ral·ize [di:nǽtʃərəlàiz] *vt.* (P6) deprive of true nature; make unnatural. 본성을 바꾸다; 특질을 빼앗다; 부자연스럽게 하다. [↓]

de·na·ture [di:néitʃər] *vt.* (P6) **1** change the nature of. 특질을 빼앗다; 본성을 바꾸다. **2** make (alcohol, food, etc.) unfit for eating or drinking (without destroying its usefulness for other purposes). (다른 용도로서의 성질은 보존한 채) 먹기에 부적합하게 변성시키다. ¶ *denatured alcohol* 변성 주정(變性酒精). [de-]

den·drol·o·gy [dendrálədʒi / -drɔ̀l-] *n.* the study of trees. 수목학(樹木學). [Gk. *déndron* tree]

den·gue [déŋgi, -gei] *n.* Ⓤ 《med.》 an infectious fever characterized by severe pains and rash. 뎅기열(熱). [Sp.]

de·ni·a·ble [dináiəbəl] *adj.* that can be denied. 부인〔부정〕할 수 있는; 거절할 수 있는. [*deny*]

de·ni·al [dináiəl] *n.* ⓊⒸ **1** a statement that something is not true. 부정(否定)(opp. affirmation). ¶ *a* ~ *of the truth of a statement* 진술의 사실에 대한 부정 / *I have not a word in* ~. 부정할 말도 없다. **2** refusing to acknowledge; refusing a request. 부인(否認); 거절(opp. admittance). ¶ *the* ~ *of a request for help* 원조 요청에 대한 거절 / *give a flat* ~ 딱 잘라 거절하다 / *His* ~ *of our request seemed very impolite.* 우리 요청을 그가 거부한 것은 몹시 무례하게 생각되었다. **3** getting along without things that one wants. 극기; 자제. ¶ ~ *of oneself* 극기. [*deny*]

give a denial to, refuse. …을 부정하다; …을 거절하다.

make a denial of =give a denial to.

take no denial, do not accept a refusal. 싫단 말을 못하게 하다.

de·ni·er[1] [dináiər] *n.* one who denies. 부인자(否認者). [↑]

de·nier[2] [diníər] *n.* a unit of weight used to indicate the fineness of silk, etc. 데니어《견사 등의 굵기를 측정하는데 쓰는 단위》. [F. =denary]

den·im [dénim] *n.* Ⓤ heavy, coarse cotton cloth. 투박한 면포(綿布); 데님. [F. *serge de Nimes* serge of Nimes]

den·i·zen [dénəzən] *n.* Ⓒ **1** 《*poet.*》 an inhabitant. 거주자; 주민. ¶ *Birds are denizens of the forest.* 새는 숲의 주민이다. **2** a foreigner who is given certain rights. 거류외인(外人); 귀화인(歸化人). **3** a foreign word, plant, or animal that has been naturalized. 외래어; 외래 동〔식〕물. [L. *dē intus* from within]

Den·mark [dénma:rk] *n.* a small country in northern Europe. 덴마크. 參考 수도는 Copenhagen.

denom. denomination.

de·nom·i·nate [dinámənèit / -nɔ́m-] *vt.* (P6,19) give a name to (someone); name (someone) as something. …에게 이름을 붙이다; 명명하다; …을 …라고 부르다. [→nominal]

***de·nom·i·na·tion** [dinàmənéiʃən / -nɔ̀m-] *n.* **1** ⓊⒸ the act of naming; a name, esp. for a class of things. 명명; 이름; 명칭; 호칭. **2** Ⓒ a group of people or things under one name. (한 이름으로 유별된 것·사람의) 종류; 종목; 부류. ¶ *plants falling under different denominations* 여러 가지 명칭으로 구분되는 각종 식물. **3** Ⓒ a religious group or sect. 종파; 교파. ¶ *the Methodist* ~ 메소디스트파 / *all sects and denominations* 온갖 종파 / *What* ~ *do you belong to?* 당신은 무슨 종파입니까. **4** Ⓒ a class of units (of money, weights, numbers, etc.). (화폐·도량형·수치 등의) 단위 명칭. ¶ *money of small denominations* 소액의 화폐 / *reduce feet and inches to one* 〔*the same*〕 ~ 피트와 인치를 같은 단위로 하다.

de·nom·i·na·tion·al [dinɑ̀mənéiʃənəl / -nɔ̀m-] *adj.* having to do with a denomination or class. 명칭[명목]상의; 종파의; 분파적인.

de·nom·i·na·tor [dinɑ́mənèitər / -nɔ́m-] *n.* Ⓒ 《math.》 the number below the line in a fraction. 분모. 參考 분자는 numerator.

de·no·ta·tion [dìːnoutéiʃən] *n.* **1** Ⓤ the act of denoting. 표시(함); 호칭(함); 명칭. **2** Ⓤ the meaning or exact force of a word. (말의) 의미. **3** Ⓒ 《log.》 the class of objects to which a term may be applied. 외연(外延). [↓]

·de·note [dinóut] *vt.* (P6,11) be the sign of (something); indicate; mean. …의 표시[기호]이다; …을 나타내다; 의미하다(opp. connote). ¶ *A red flag denotes danger.* 붉은 기(旗)는 위험을 표시한다 / *Wide-open eyes ~ fear.* 크게 뜬 눈은 공포를 나타낸다 / *His spelling denotes ignorance* [*that he is ignorant*]. 그의 글씨는 무식함을 나타내고 있다 / *The word 'stool' denotes a small chair without a back.* 'stool'이란 등받이가 없는 작은 의자를 의미한다 / *A fever denotes sickness.* 열이 있다는 것은 병을 의미한다. [→ note]

de·noue·ment [deinúːmaːŋ] *n.* 《F.》 **1** the untying of a knot. 해결; 결말; 종국. **2** 《*fig.*》 the end of a play, story, etc. where everything is made clear. (연극·소설 따위의) 마지막 장면; 대단원.

de·nounce [dináuns] *vt.* (P6,7) **1** ⓐ speak openly against (something). …을 공공연히 비난[공격]하다. ¶ *~ someone as a traitor* 아무를 배반자라고 비난하다 / *He was denounced as a coward.* 그는 비겁자라고 공격당했다. ⓑ accuse; give information against. …을 고발하다. ¶ *~ someone to the police as a murderer* 아무를 살인자라고 경찰에 고발하다. **2** give notice of the termination of (a treaty, etc.). (조약 따위의) 종결을[폐기를] 통고하다. ●**de·nounc·er** [-ər] *n.* [de-, L. *nuntius* messenger]

de·nounce·ment [dináunsmənt] *n.* = denunciation.

·dense [dens] *adj.* **1** closely packed together; thick; crowded. 빽빽한[촘촘한]; 짙은; 밀집한; 붐비는(opp. sparse). ¶ *a ~ fog* 짙은 안개 / *a ~ forest* 밀림 / *a ~ crowd* 붐비는 군중 / *~ population* 조밀 인구 / *~ texture* 올이 촘촘한 직물 / *The traffic was ~.* 교통이 붐비고 있었다. **2** 《*fig.*》 slow of understanding; stupid; dull. 머리가 둔한; 우둔한. ¶ *a ~ head* / *Dense students are a great nuisance to a teacher.* 머리 나쁜 학생들은 선생에게 큰 골칫거리이다. ●**dense·ly** [-li] *adv.* [L.]

den·si·ty [dénsəti] *n.* (*pl.* **-ties**) **1** Ⓤ the state of being dense. 짙음; 빽빽함; 촘촘함; 밀집 상태. ¶ *the ~ of a forest* 숲의 울창한 상태 / *The ~ of the fog prevented us from seeing more than a little way ahead.* 짙은 안개로 인해 우리는 앞을 조금밖에는 볼 수가 없었다. **2** ⓊⒸ 《phys.》 the quantity of matter in a unit of volume. 밀도; 농도. ¶ *The ~ of lead is greater than that of wood.* 납의 밀도는 나무의 밀도보다 높다. **3** 《*fig.*》 stupidity. 우둔.

dent. dentist; dentistry.

dent [dent] *n.* Ⓒ a hollow made by a blow or by pressure. 움푹 팬 곳; 쑥 들어간 곳(cf. *dint*). ¶ *Your desk shows the dents of many years' use.* 네 책상은 여러 해 사용한 흔적을 보여 주고 있다.

make a dent, **a**) make a first step towards success in. 초보적 진보를 보이다; 초보적 단계를 통과하다. **b**) cause to take heed; make an impression. 주의하게 하다; 인상지우다.

— *vt.* (P6) make a dent or dents in (something). …을 움푹 패게 하다; 자국을 내다.

— *vi.* (P1) become dented; get dented. 움푹 패다; 쑥 들어가다. [→dint]

den·tal [déntl] *adj.* of or for the teeth or a dentist's work. 이의; 치아(齒牙)의; 치과의. ¶ *a ~ office* 치과 의원 / *~ sounds* 치음(齒音) / *a ~ surgeon* 치과의(醫) / *~ surgery* 구강 외과 / *a ~ caries* 충치. — *n.* 《phon.》 Ⓒ a dental sound. 치음(齒音)(《't, d, θ, ð' 따위》). [L. *dens* tooth]

den·tate [dénteit] *adj.* 《bot., zool.》 having toothlike projection; toothed. 이빨 모양의 돌기가 있는; 이가 있는.

den·ti·frice [déntəfris] *n.* Ⓤ paste or powder for cleaning the teeth. 치마분(齒磨粉); 치약. [→dental]

den·tin [déntin], **-tine** [déntiːn] *n.* the hard, bony material that forms the main part of a tooth. (치아의) 상아질(象牙質). [→dental]

den·tist [déntist] *n.* Ⓒ a doctor whose work is to take care of the teeth. 치과 의사.

den·tist·ry [déntistri] *n.* Ⓤ the art or occupation of a dentist. 치과 의술(업); 치과학.

den·ti·tion [dentíʃən] *n.* teething; characteristic arrangement of teeth. 치생(齒生); 잇바디; 치열.

den·ture [déntʃər] *n.* a set of artificial teeth. 한 벌의 의치(義齒); 틀니 한 벌.

de·nude [dinjúːd] *vt.* (P6,13) 《*of*》 **1** make (someone) bare; strip (something) of covering. …을 발가벗기다; …에게서(옷·외피물 따위)를 벗기다. ¶ *a hill denuded of trees* 나무가 하나도 없게 된 민둥산 / *~ someone of clothing* …의 옷을 벗겨 알몸으로 하다 / *Most trees are denuded of their leaves in winter.* 대개의 나무는 겨울에 잎이 떨어져 나목(裸木)이 된다. **2** deprive of. (특질·재산·희망 따위)를 빼앗다; 박탈하다. ¶ *be denuded of hope* 희망이 없어지다 / *be denuded of all one's money* 돈을 전부 빼앗기다 / *~ someone of his political rights* 아무에게서 정치상의 권리를 박탈하다. [→nude]

de·nun·ci·ate [dinʌ́nsièit, -ʃi-] *vt.* (P6,7) =

denounce.

de·nun·ci·a·tion [dinʌ̀nsiéiʃən, -ʃi-] *n.* UC the act of denouncing or accusing; an instance of this. (공공연한) 비난; 고발; 조약의 종결〔폐기〕 통고. ¶ *a teacher's ~ of lying* 거짓말에 대한 선생님의 비난. [→denounce]

:de·ny [dinái] *vt.* (**-nied**) **1** (P6,21) say that something is not true; declare (a statement, etc.) to be false. …을 부정하다 (opp. affirm). ¶ *~ an accusation* 비난받을 일은 한 적이 없다고 하다 / *~ the truth of what he said* 그가 한 말은 거짓말이라고 하다 / *We cannot ~ the fact.* 그 사실은 부정할 수 없다 / *He denied having said so.* 그는 그렇게 말하지 않았다고 했다 / *I ~ that his statement is true.* 그의 진술이 진실임을 부정한다. **2** (P6,11,13,14) ⓐ refuse to acknowledge. …을 부인하다; 인정치 않다; 관계가 없다고〔모른다고〕 하다(opp. admit). ¶ *~ one's faith* 〔*country*〕 신앙을〔나라를〕 부인하다 / *~ one's signature* 자신의 서명이 아니라고 하다 / *~ someone's gods.* 아무가 믿는 신을 부인하다. ⓑ refuse; refuse to give. …을 거부하다; 거절하다. ¶ *~ oneself the pleasure of….* …의 쾌락을 절제〔자제〕하다 / *Can you ~ my request?* 자네 내 요구를 거부할 수 있는가 / *He denied his son nothing.* 그는 아들에게 무엇이든 안 된다고 못 했다. [de-, →negation]

de·o·dar [díːədɑ̀ːr] *n.* 《bot.》 a large Himalayan cedar. 히말라야 삼나무. [Hind.]

de·o·dor·ant [diːòudərənt] *n.* a liquid, powder, or cream which destroys bad smells on the body. 탈취제(脫臭劑); 방취제. — *adj.* having the power of deodorizing. 탈취의; 방취 효과가 있는. [→odor]

de·o·dor·i·za·tion [diːòudərizéiʃən] *n.* U the act of deodorizing. 방취(防臭); 탈취.

de·o·dor·ize [diːóudəràiz] *vt.* (P6) remove bad smells from. 냄새를 없애다; 탈취하다. ¶ *~ a lavatory* 변소의 냄새를 없애다. [de-, →odor, -ize]

de·o·dor·iz·er [diːóudəràizər] *n.* =deodorant.

De·o vo·len·te [déiou voulénti, díː-] *adv.* if God wills. 신이 허락하신다면; 사정이 허락하면(abbr. D.V.). [L. =God willing]

de·ox·y·ri·bo·nu·cle·ic acid [diːɑ́ksəràibounjuːklíːik ⌐] *n.* a polymeric chromosomal constituent of living cell nuclei. 디옥시리보 핵산(核酸)(abbr. DNA). [*ribose*]

dep. departs.

:de·part [dipɑ́ːrt] *vi.* (P1,3) 《*for, from.*》 **1** set out; leave; start. 떠나다; 출발하다(opp. arrive). ¶ *~ from one's home* 집〔고향〕을 떠나다 / *It is time to ~.* 출발 시간이다 / *Departs 18:30.* 18시 30분 발 / *This train departs at 3 p.m. from Seoul Station.* 이 열차는 오후 3시에 서울역을 출발한다. **2** 《*from*》 turn aside; deviate; change. (상궤·관습 따위에서) 벗어나다; 반하다; 다르다. ¶ *~ from one's usual way of working* 여느 때의 일하는 식에서 벗어나다 / *~ from the truth* 진실에서 벗어나다 / *~ from one's word* 〔*promise*〕 약속과 다르다; 약속에 어긋나다. **3** 《*arch.*》 die. 죽다. ¶ *Poor old Jones has departed at last.* 가엾은 존스 노인은 마침내 죽었다. [→part]

depart (***from***) ***this life,*** die. 죽다.

de·part·ed [dipɑ́ːrtid] *adj.* **1** dead. 죽은. **2** gone; past. 지나간; 과거의. — *n.* 《*the* ~ ; *sing., pl.* in use》 the dead; the deceased. (특정의) 고인(故人); 죽은 사람〔자〕.

:de·part·ment [dipɑ́ːrtmənt] *n.* C **1** a separate part of a business, government, university, etc.; a division. (회사·관청·대학 따위의) 부분; 부(部); 국(局); 과(課·科). ¶ *the accounting ~* 회계과 / *the fire ~* 《U.S.》 소방국 / *the ~ of economics* 경제학과 / *the men's clothing ~* (백화점의) 신사용 의복부. **2** a field of knowledge or activity. (학문 따위의) 부문; 분야. ¶ *a ~ of learning.* **3** (in France) an administrative district of local government. (프랑스의) 현(縣). [*depart*]

de·part·men·tal [dipaːrtméntl / dìːpaːrt-] *adj.* of a department. 각 부(문)의.

department store [-⌐- ⌐] *n.* 《orig. U.S.》 a big store that sells many kinds of articles arranged in separate departments. 백화점. 參考 영국에서는 (big) stores라고 함.

·de·par·ture [dipɑ́ːrtʃər] *n.* CU **1** the act or fact of leaving. 출발; 발차(發車)(opp. arrival). ¶ *the board showing arrivals and departures of buses.* 버스의 발착을 알리는 게시판 / *one's ~ from home* 고향을 등짐 / *She wept on his ~.* 그의 떠남에 즈음하여 그녀는 울었다. **2** a turning aside; a change. (표준·상궤 따위에서의) 변경; 일탈(逸脫). ¶ *a ~ from ancient ways* 구습을 버림 / *a bold ~ from accepted teaching methods* 일반적으로 인정돼 있는 교수법에서 벗어남. **3** U 《*arch.*》 death. 죽음; 사망. [*depart, -ure*]

a new departure, a new course of action or thought; a change of method. 새 방침; 신기축(新機軸).

on one's departure, when one starts. 떠날 때에.

take one's departure, start; go away. 떠나다; 출발하다.

:de·pend [dipénd] *vi.* (P3,1) **1** 《usu. *on* 〔*upon*〕》 ⇨depend on 〔upon〕. **2** 《*from*》 《*arch.*》 hang down from. 늘어지다; 매달리다. ¶ *The lamp depends from a hook.* 램프가 걸쇠에 매달려 있다. [→pendant]

depend on 〔***upon***〕, **a**) trust and count on …을 믿다; 신뢰〔신용〕하다. ¶ *I ~ on your word.* 자네 말을 믿네 / *We can ~ on him.* 우린 그를 신뢰할 수 있다. **b**) rely on (someone or something) as a source of help or supply. …을 의지〔의존〕하다; 기대다. ¶ *a pitch that depends more on skill than on speed* 스피드보다 기술에 의지하는 투구(投球) / *~ on what can earn* (벌어들이는) 소득에 의존하다 / *~ on someone for food and* *clothing* 아무에게 의식(衣食)을 의지하다 / *They are men to be depended upon.* 그들은 의존할 수 있는 사람들이다 / *I ~ on you for support.* 나는 당신 지원에 의존하고 있다. **c**) be influenced or determined by something else. (…에) 달리다〔의하다〕; …에 좌우되다; …여하에 달리다. ¶ *Our trip depends upon the weather.* 우리의 여행은 날씨에 달렸다 / *Victory depends on strength and courage.* 승리는 병력과 사기 여하에 의한다 / *Health depends on good food, fresh air and enough sleep.* 건강은 좋은 음식과 신선한 공기 및 충분한 잠 여하에 달려 있다 / *Whether you pass the exam depends on how hard you work.* 시험에의 합격 여부는 얼마나 공부를 열심히 하느냐에 달려 있다. 語法 구어에서는 how 따위 앞의 전치사가 생략됨.

depend upon** someone **for, get ... from him. 아무에게서 …을 얻다.

depend upon it, 《used at the beginning or end of a sentence》 You can be quite certain. 틀림없이; 반드시. ¶ *The war will ruin the country, ~ upon it.* 틀림없이 전쟁은 나라를 멸망시킬거다 / *Depend upon it, he won't come tonight.* 확실히 그는 오늘밤 안 올 걸세.

It (all) depends. =That depends.

That depends. 《*colloq.*》 it is impossible to say with certainty until certain other facts are known. 그건 경우〔사정〕에 달렸다; 일률적으로 말할 수 없다.

de·pend·a·ble [dipéndəbl] *adj.* reliable; trustworthy. 의지〔신뢰〕할 수 있는; 믿을 수 있는. ¶ *~ news* 믿을 수 있는 뉴스 / *a ~ workman* 믿을 수 있는 일꾼.

de·pend·ant [dipéndənt] *n.* Ⓒ a person who gets help or support from another. (원조·생활 따위를) 남에게 의존하는 사람; 하인; 부하; 기식자(寄食者); 부양 가족.

•**de·pend·ence** [dipéndəns] *n.* Ⓤ **1** the state of being a dependant. (생활 따위의)의존; 의지; 종속(상태)(opp. independence). ¶ *live in ~ on another* 남에게 붙어 살다 / *He refused to live in ~ on his uncle.* 숙부에게 의존해 살기를 거부했다. **2** trust; confidence. 믿음; 신뢰. ¶ *have ~ on someone* 아무를 신뢰하다 / *Do not put* 〔*place*〕 *your ~ in him, for he sometimes deceives us.* 그를 믿지 말게, 가끔 우리를 속이니까. **3** the fact of being controlled by something else. (다른 것에 의해) 좌우됨; 의존 관계. ¶ *the ~ of an effect upon a cause* 결과의 원인에 대한 의존 관계.

de·pend·en·cy [dipéndənsi] *n.* Ⓒ (*pl.* **-cies**) **1** depending on another person or thing for support. 종속(從屬). **2** a country controlled by another country. 속국(屬國); 속령(屬領).

•**de·pend·ent** [dipéndənt] *adj.* **1** 《*on, upon*》 getting help or support from another. (원조·생활 따위를 남 또는 다른 것에) 의존하고 있는; 신세지고 있는(opp. independent). ¶ *He is ~ on his uncle.* 그는 숙부에 얹혀 살고 있다 / *She is ~ on my earnings.* 그녀는 내 수입에 의존하고 있다. **2** 《*on, upon*》 depending on; controlled by something else. …(여하에) 달린; …에 좌우되는. ¶ *A farmer's success is ~ on having the right kind of weather for his crops.* 농사꾼의 성패는 농작물에 대한 좋은 날씨 여하에 좌우된다 / *Strength is ~ on health.* 체력은 건강 여하에 달려 있다. **3** 《gram.》 subordinate. 종속의. ¶ *a ~ clause* 종속절.
— *n.* =dependant.

de·pict [dipíkt] *vt.* (P6,7) show (something) with a picture; describe (something) in words. …을 그림으로 나타내다; 말로 서술〔묘사〕하다. ¶ *~ a scene* 〔*battle*〕 풍경〔전투 장면〕을 그리다 / *a novel depicting Korean customs* 한국의 풍속을 묘사한 소설. ● **de·pict·er** [-ər] *n.* [→pictorial]

de·pic·tion [dipíkʃən] *n.* ⓊⒸ the act of depicting; the state of being depicted. 묘사; 서술.

de·pil·a·to·ry [dipílətɔ̀:ri / -təri] *n.* Ⓒ a liquid or cream used for removing superfluous hair from the body. 탈모제(脫毛劑). [L.]

de·plane [di:pléin] *vi.* (P1) descend from an airplane. 비행기에서 내리다. [de-, *airplane*]

de·plete [diplí:t] *vt.* (P6) **1** empty; use up; exhaust, as of energy, fund, etc.; make less. …을 비우다; …을 다 써 버리다〔고갈시키다〕; 줄게 하다. ¶ *a depleted bottle* 빈 병 / *~ one's strength* 체력을 다 소모하다 / *~ one's resources* 백계(百計)가 다하다. **2** bleed. 방혈(放血)〔사혈(瀉血)〕하다. [L. *dēpleo* empty out]

de·ple·tion [diplí:ʃən] *n.* Ⓤ the act of depleting; the state of being depleted. 소모; 고갈.

de·plor·a·ble [diplɔ́:rəbl] *adj.* 《*to*》 to be deplored; lamentable; regrettable. 슬픈; 통탄〔한탄〕스러운; 유감스러운. ¶ *a ~ accident* 통탄스러운 사고 / *~ behavior* 통탄스러운 행동. [*deplore*]

de·plor·a·bly [diplɔ́:rəbli] *adv.* in a deplorable manner. 통탄스럽게; 유감스럽게.

de·plore [diplɔ́:r] *vt.* (P6) **1** be very sorry about (something); grieve over (something); lament; regret. …을 슬퍼하다; 통탄〔한탄〕하다; 유감으로 여기다. ¶ *~ the present state of morality* 도덕의 현상(現狀)을 한탄하다 / *~ a quarrel between nations* 국가간의 분쟁을 유감으로 여기다. **2** feel remorse for. …을 깊이 뉘우치다. ¶ *~ one's past sins* 지난날의 죄를 뉘우치다. [de-, L. *ploro* wail]

de·ploy [diplɔ́i] *vt., vi.* (P6;1) 《mil.》 spread out (an army) in line; open out. (군대)를 전개하다. ● **de·ploy·ment** [-mənt] *n.* Ⓤ [→display]

de·po·lar·ize [di:póulərài z] *vt.* (P6) 《electr.》 remove polarization of. 감극(減極)〔소극〕하

다. [de-]

de·pone [dipóun] *vt.* testify under oath. 선서 뒤에 증언〔공술〕하다. [↓]

de·po·nent [dipóunənt] *n.* 《law》 one who gives evidence. (특히 선서한) 증인; 공술자. [de-, L. *pono* put]

de·pop·u·late [di:pápjəlèit / -pɔ́p-] *vt.* (P6) destroy or decrease the population of (a country, etc.) (파괴·추방 따위로) 인구를 감소시키다; 주민을 절멸시키다. ¶ *The plague depopulated the cities of Italy.* 흑사병이 이탈리아 도시의 인구를 감소시켰다. [→people]

de·pop·u·la·tion [di:pàpjəléiʃən / -pɔ̀p-] *n.* Ⓤ the act of depopulating; the state of being depopulated. 주민 절멸; 인구 감소.

de·port [dipɔ́:rt] *vt.* **1** (P6) 《*from*》 force (someone) to leave the country; banish. (국외로) 추방하다; 퇴거시키다. ¶ ~ *dangerous aliens* 위험한 외국인을 국외 추방하다. **2** (P7) 《*reflexively*》 behave (oneself) in a particular manner. 행동〔처신〕하다. ¶ ~ *oneself well* 〔*ill*〕 예절 있게〔없게〕 행동하다 / ~ *oneself like a gentleman* 신사처럼 굴다. [L. *porto* carry]

de·por·ta·tion [dì:pɔ:rtéiʃən] *n.* Ⓤ the act of deporting; the state of being deported. 국외 추방; 유형(流刑). ¶ *a* ~ *order* 퇴거 명령 / *He was sentenced to* ~. 국외 추방이 선고되었다.

de·port·ment [dipɔ́:rtmənt] *n.* Ⓤ a manner of behaving; behavior; conduct. 행동; 태도. ¶ *a model of good* ~ 훌륭한 행동의 모범.

de·pose [dipóuz] *vt.* **1** (P6) put (someone) out of a high office; remove (someone) from a throne. …을 면직하다; 폐하다; 퇴위시키다. ¶ ~ *someone from office* 아무를 면직하다 / ~ *a king* 왕을 퇴위시키다. **2** (P11) 《law》 declare under oath. 선서하고 증언〔공술〕하다. ¶ *He deposed that he had seen the prisoner on that day.* 그는 그 날 피고를 만났음을 증언했다. — *vi.* (P3) 《*to*》 give evidence. 선서 증언하다. ¶ ~ *to a fact* 어떤 사실을 선서 증언하다. [→pose]

·de·pos·it [dipázit / -pɔ́z-] *vt.* (P6,13) **1** put (something) down; set down; place. …을 놓다〔두다〕. ¶ ~ *a book on the desk* 책을 책상에 놓다. **2** leave (something) lying; leave behind. …을 퇴적시키다; 침전시키다. ¶ *soil deposited by a stream* 유수(流水)에 의해 퇴적된 흙 / *The flood deposited a lot of mud and sand on the streets of the city.* 홍수는 진흙과 모래 따위를 시내 도로에 퇴적시켰다. **3** put (something) in a place for safekeeping. …을 맡기다. ¶ ~ *money in a bank* 은행에 예금하다 / ~ *valuables with someone* 아무에게 귀중품을 맡기다. **4** give (a sum of money) in advance as part payment. 선금〔보증금, 착수금〕을 지급하다. ¶ *If you will* ~ *₩20,000, we will hold the overcoat for you.* 선금 2만 원을 맡기시면 외투를 팔지 않고 두겠습니다. **5** (of birds, insects, fish, etc.) lay. (알)을 낳다. ¶ ~ *eggs in the ground* 마당에 알을 낳다.
— *n.* Ⓒ **1** something left lying. 퇴적물; 침전물(cf. *sediment*). ¶ *a* ~ *of soil* 진흙의 퇴적 / *the* ~ *at the bottom of a wine-bottle* 포도주병 바닥의 침전물. **2** ⓐ money put in a bank; part of a payment made in advance. 은행 예금; 선금; 보증금. ¶ *place money on* ~ 은행에 예금하다. ⓑ something put in a certain place for safekeeping. (안전을 위한) 보관물; 기탁물. **3** 《geol.》 a mass of some mineral in rocks or in the ground. 광상(鑛床); 매장물. [→deponent; L. *pono* put]

on deposit, in a bank. 예금하고. ¶ *have money on* ~ *in a bank* 은행에 예금해 있다.

place on deposit, deposit. 맡기다.

de·pos·i·ta·ry [dipázitèri / -pɔ́zitəri] *n.* **1** a person who receives a deposit. 보관인; 피(被)기탁인. **2** =depository.

dep·o·si·tion [dèpəzíʃən] *n.* **1** Ⓤ the act of putting someone out of office; removal from a throne. 면직; 파면; 폐위(廢位). **2** 《law》 ⓊⒸ a declaration or statement made under oath. 선서(宣誓) 증언; 공술서(書). **3** Ⓤ the act of depositing. 맡김; 기탁; 예치; 퇴적(작용); 침전(작용). ¶ *the* ~ *of sediment in a liquid* 액체 속의 앙금의 침전 / *the* ~ *of money in a bank* 돈의 은행 예치. **4** Ⓒ something that is deposited; a deposit. 맡겨진 것; 퇴적〔침전〕물; 예금.

de·pos·i·tor [dipázitər / -pɔ́z-] *n.* Ⓒ a person who deposits money in a bank etc. (은행)예금자; 공탁자.

de·pos·i·to·ry [dipázitɔ̀:ri / -pɔ́zitəri] *n.* Ⓒ (*pl.* **-ries**) a place where a thing is put for safekeeping; a storehouse. 보관소; 수탁소; 저장소; 창고(cf. *repository*). ¶ *This library is a* ~ *of information.* 이 도서관은 지식의 광이다.

de·pot [dí:pou, dép- / dép-] *n.* Ⓒ **1** 《U.S.》 a railroad station; a bus station. (철도) 정거장; 역; 버스 정류장. **2** a house for storing something. 저장소. **3** 《mil.》 a place where military supplies are stored, and where new soldiers are trained. 물자 집적소; 신병 보충 부대. [→deposit]

depot ship [∠-∠] *n.* a tender. 모함(母艦).

de·prave [dipréiv] *vt.* (P6) make (something) bad; corrupt the morals of. …을 악화시키다; 부패〔타락〕시키다. ¶ ~ *someone's character* 아무의 성격을 타락시키다. [L. *pravus* crooked]

de·praved [dipréivd] *adj.* immoral; wicked; corrupt. 타락한; 부패한.

de·prav·i·ty [diprǽvəti] *n.* (*pl.* **-ties**) Ⓤ vice; corruption. 사악(邪惡); 부패; 타락; Ⓒ a corrupt or wicked act. 못된 행위; 악행.

dep·re·cate [déprikèit] *vt.* (P6) protest or speak against (something); disapprove. …에 항의〔반대〕하다; …을 비난하다. ¶ *I* ~ *his rudeness.* 나는 그의 무례함에 항의한다 / *Peace-*

lovers ~ *war.* 평화 애호자들은 전쟁에 반대한다. [→pray]

dep·re·ca·tion [dèprikéiʃən] *n.* UC the act of deprecating; a protest made against something. 항의; 비난; 반대.

dep·re·ca·to·ry [déprikətɔ̀:ri / -təri] *adj.* deprecating; protesting. 비난하는; 항의〔반대〕의.

be deprecatory of, deprecate. 비난〔항의〕하다.

de·pre·ci·ate [diprí:ʃièit] *vt.* (P6) **1** make (something) less in value. …의 가치를 저하시키다. **2** say or think of (something) that it has little value. …을 얕보다; 경시하다. ¶ ~ *another's work* 남의 일을 얕보다 / ~ *the value of swimming* 수영의 진가를 경시하다 / *Don't* ~ *yourself.* 스스로를 비하(卑下)하지 마라. —*vi.* (P1) become less in value or price. 가치가〔가격이〕 떨어지다 (opp. appreciate). ¶ *The value of a company's property depreciates year by year.* 회사의 자산 가치가 해마다 떨어진다. [de-, →price]

de·pre·ci·a·tion [diprì:ʃiéiʃən] *n.* UC **1** the act of depreciating. 가치 하락; 저하; 감가(減價)(opp. appreciation). ¶ *the* ~ *of the dollar* 달러화(貨)의 평가 절하. **2** the act of speaking slightingly of someone. 경멸; 멸시; 경시.

de·pre·ci·a·tive [diprí:ʃièitiv] *adj.* =depreciatory.

de·pre·ci·a·to·ry [diprí:ʃiətɔ̀:ri / -təri] *adj.* tending to lessen the value of (something); slighting. 하락 경향의; 가치 저락의; 경멸적인; 얕보는. ¶ ~ *remarks* 남을 얕보는 말. [→depreciate]

dep·re·date [déprədèit] *vt.* (P6) plunder. 약탈하다; 강탈하다. [→prey]

dep·re·da·tion [dèprədéiʃən] *n.* UC **1** plundering; robbery. 약탈; 강탈. **2** 《*pl.*》 the act of robbing; ravages. 약탈 행위; 참해(慘害). ¶ *the depredations of the invaders* 침략자의 약탈 행위.

dep·re·da·tor [déprədèitər] *n.* a person who plunders. 약탈자.

de·press [diprés] *vt.* (P6) **1** press down; make lower. 누르다; 낮추다. ¶ ~ *the keys of a piano* 피아노 건반을 누르다 / ~ *the muzzle of a gun* 총구를 낮추다. **2** make the activity or power of (something) less; weaken. …을 약하게 하다; 약화〔둔화〕시키다. ¶ *Trade is depressed.* 장사가 부진하다 / *Some medicines* ~ *the action of the heart.* 어떤 약은 심장 기능을 약화시킨다. **3** make (someone) sad or gloomy; make (someone) low in spirits. …을 슬프게〔우울하게〕 하다; 낙담시키다; 의기소침하게 하다. ¶ *Rainy weather always depresses me.* 비오는 날씨는 항상 나를 우울하게 한다 / *The boy is depressed by the death of his bird.* 소년은 그의 새가 죽어서 슬퍼하고 있다. [→press]

de·pres·sant [diprésənt] *adj.* that depresses. 누르는; 우울하게 하는; 낙담시키는; 의기소침케 하는. —*n.* a sedative. 진정제; 억제제(劑). [↑]

de·pressed [diprést] *adj.* **1** sad; gloomy; discouraged. 슬픈; 우울한; 의기 소침한. ¶ *I feel* ~. 나는 기분이 우울하다. **2** with a low volume of business activity. 불경기의; 불황〔부진〕의.

de·press·ing [diprésiŋ] *adj.* tending to depress; gloomy. 의기 소침케 하는; 우울한; 답답한. ● **de·press·ing·ly** [-li] *adv.*

·**de·pres·sion** [dipréʃən] *n.* **1** U the act of pressing down. (내리)누름; 내림; 강하; 저하(低下). **2** U sadness; low spirits; melancholy. 의기 소침; 낙담; 우울. ¶ *nervous* ~ 신경 쇠약 / *in a state of deep* ~ 몹시 의기 소침하여 / *suffer from* ~ 우울증에 시달리다. **3** C the reduction of business activity; a bad state of trade. 불경기; 불황. ¶ *a business* ~ 불경기. **4** C a low place; a hollow. 우묵 들어간 곳; 구렁; (주위보다) 낮은 저지(低地). **5** C a lowering of the atmospheric pressure. 저기압.

dep·ri·va·tion [dèprəvéiʃən] *n.* UC **1** the act of depriving; the state of being deprived. 박탈; 면직; 파면. **2** loss. 상실; 손실. [↓]

·**de·prive** [dipráiv] *vt.* (P13) take something away from (someone) by force; dispossess. …을 박탈하다; …에게서 (무엇)을 빼앗다. ¶ ~ *a king of his power* 왕의 권력을 빼앗다 / ~ *a man of his books* 〔*hope, life*〕 그의 책〔희망, 생명〕을 빼앗다 / ~ *someone of his reason* 아무의 이성을 잃게 하다 / *He was deprived of his sight by the traffic accident.* 그는 교통사고로 실명했다. [→private]

de pro·fun·dis [di: prəfʌ́ndis] 《L.》 *adv.* out of the depths of sorrow. (비탄·절망의) 구렁텅이에서. —*n.* 《*a* ~》 any cry of sorrow or despair. 절망〔고뇌〕의 절규.

dept. department; deputy.

:**depth** [depθ] *n.* U **1** the quality of being deep; deepness. 깊음; 심원(深遠). **2** UC the distance from top to bottom. 깊이; 심도(深度). ¶ *a foot in* ~ 깊이 1피트 / *the* ~ *of a hole* 〔*lake*〕 구멍〔호수〕의 깊이. **3** UC the distance from front to back. 안(쪽으로의) 길이. ¶ *the* ~ *of a house* 집의 안 길이. **4** C a deep place. 깊은 곳. **5** 《usu. *pl.*》 C the deepest part; a chasm. 최심처(最深處); 깊이 갈라진 데〔구렁텅이〕; 바다. ¶ *the depths of a forest* 숲속 깊은 곳 / *in the* ~ *of the country* 나라의 오지(奧地)에 / *in the depths of one's heart* 가슴 속 깊이 / *in the depth(s) of despair* 절망의 구렁텅이에. **6** the most central part; middle. 중심부; 한가운데; 한창 …일 때. ¶ *in the* ~ *of winter* 한겨울에. **7** deepness of thought; profoundness; intensity. 심원; 심오; 심각함. ¶ *a book of no great* ~ 이렇다 할 깊이가 없는 책 / *show* ~ *of knowledge* 지식의 깊이를 나타내다. **8** lowness of pitch; intensity of color, etc. (음의) 저조(低調); (색깔 따위의) 농도; 강도. ¶ *the* ~ *of color* 색깔의 농도. **9** 《*poet.*》

《usu. *pl.*》 deep waters; the sea. 깊은 물; 바다. [→deep]

***beyond* [*out of*] *one's depth*,** a) in water too deep for one. 키를 넘는 깊은 곳에. b) 《*fig.*》 trying to study something that is too difficult. 이해할 수 없는; 능력이 미치지 못하는.

***from the depth of the mind*,** sincerely. 충심으로.

***in depth*,** completely. 철저히.

depth bomb [ㅅㅅ] *n.* =depth charge.

depth charge [ㅅㅅ] *n.* a bomb dropped from a ship or airplane into the sea and arranged to explode at a certain depth to destroy enemy submarines. (잠수함 폭파용) 수중 폭뢰(爆雷).

dep·u·ta·tion [dèpjətéiʃən] *n.* **1** Ⓤ the act of deputing. 대리 (행위); 대리 위임. **2** Ⓒ a group of persons given the power to act for others. 대리인; 대표단. ¶ *send a ~ to a conference* 회의에 대표단을 파견하다. [↓]

de·pute [dipjú:t] *vt.* (P13,20) **1** appoint (another) to do something for oneself or to act in one's place. …을 (자신의) 대리로 명하다. ¶ *The teacher deputed Ted to take charge of the class while he was away.* 선생님은 자기가 없는 동안 테드를 학급 담임 대리로 임명했다. **2** give (one's work, etc.) to another. (일 따위의 대행)을 위임하다. [→putative]

dep·u·tize [dépjətàiz] *vi.* (P1,3) 《*for*》 act for someone. 대리를 보다. — *vt.* (P6) 《chiefly U.S.》 appoint (someone) as a deputy; appoint (another) to act in one's place. …을 대리로 임명(위임)하다.

•**dep·u·ty** [dépjəti] *n.* Ⓒ (*pl.* **-ties**) **1** a person appointed to act for another. 대리; 대표(cf. *delegate*). ¶ *A policeman is a ~ of the law.* 경찰관은 법의 대리자이다 / *by ~* 대리로. **2** 《*D-*》 an elected person in a parliament, esp. in France. (프랑스 따위의) 국회의원. ¶ *a member of the Chamber of Deputies* (본디 프랑스의) 하원 의원. — *adj.* acting as a deputy. 대리의; 부(副)…. ¶ *the First Deputy Premier* (소련의) 제1 부수상 / *a Deputy Mayor* 부시장 / *a Deputy Speaker* (의회의) 부의장.

De Quincey [di kwínsi:], **Thomas** *n.* (1785-1859) an English essayist. 디퀸시 《영국의 수필가》.

der., deriv. derivation; derivative; derive(d).

de·rail [diréil] *vt.* (P6) 《usu. in *passive*》 make (a train, etc.) go off the rails. …을 탈선시키다. ¶ *be* [*get*] *derailed* 탈선하다 / *The train was derailed.* 열차가 탈선했다. — *vi.* run off the rails. 탈선하다. [→rail]

de·rail·ment [diréilmənt] *n.* ⓊⒸ the act of derailing; the state of being derailed. 탈선.

de·range [diréindʒ] *vt.* (P6) **1** throw (someone) into confusion; put out of order; disturb. …을 혼란(교란)시키다. ¶ *~ the life of the public* 대중의 생활을 혼란시키다. **2** upset the mental balance of; make (someone) mad; disorder. …을 미치게 하다; 뒤틀어지게 하다. ¶ *be* [*become*] *deranged* 미치다; 발광하다 / *~ the plan* 계획을 틀어지게 하다 / *She is deranged with worry.* 그녀는 걱정으로 제정신이 아니다. [de-]

de·range·ment [diréindʒmənt] *n.* Ⓤ disorder; disturbance; insanity. 무질서; 교란; 혼란; (정신의) 착란.

Der·by[1] [dɔ́:rbi / dɑ́:rbi] *n.* a city in central England. 더비《잉글랜드 중부의 도시》.

Der·by[2] [dɔ́:rbi / dɑ́rbi] *n.* Ⓒ (*pl.* **-bies**) **1** 《*the ~*》 a famous annual horse race, at Epsom in England. 더비 경마《매년 영국 Epsom에서 거행됨》. **2** any horse race of similar importance. (그 밖의) 대(大)경마.

der·by [dɔ́:rbi / dɑ́:rbi] *n.* Ⓒ (*pl.* **-bies**) 《chiefly U.S.》 a stiff felt hat with a round top and narrow brim. 중산 모자 (cf. 《Brit.》 *bowler*). 參考 Derby 경마에서 쓰는 데서. [Place]

der·e·lict [dérəlikt] *adj.* **1** abandoned; left; deserted. 버림받은; 버려진; 유기된. ¶ *a ~ child* 기아(棄兒) / *a ~ ship* 유기된 배. **2** 《U.S.》 failing in one's duty; neglecting. 직무 태만의; 무책임한. ¶ *be ~ in one's duty* 의무를 게을리하다. — *n.* Ⓒ **1** something abandoned, esp. a ship abandoned at sea. 유기물; 유기된 배. **2** a worthless person. (사회에서) 버림받은 사람; 낙오자. **3** 《U.S.》 a person who neglects his duty. 직무 태만자. [→relic]

der·e·lic·tion [dèrilíkʃən] *n.* ⓊⒸ **1** neglect of duty. 직무(의무) 태만. ¶ *a ~ of duty* 직무 태만. **2** the act of abandoning; the state of being deserted. 포기; 유기.

de·req·ui·si·tion [dirèkwəzíʃən] *vt.* release (a house, hotel, etc.) from requisitioning. (…의) 접수를 해제하다. [→requisition]

de·ride [diráid] *vt.* (P6) make fun of (someone); laugh at (someone); jeer. …을 우롱하다; 조소하다; 비웃다. ● **de·rid·ing·ly** [-iŋli] *adv.* [→ridicule]

de·ri·sion [diríʒən] *n.* **1** Ⓤ the act of deriding; the state of being derided; ridicule; contempt. 조소; 비웃음; 우롱. ¶ *be in ~* 비웃음을 받고 있다 / *have* [*hold*] *someone in ~* 아무를 비웃다(놀리다) / *They brought him into ~.* 그들은 그를 조소의 대상으로 삼았다. **2** Ⓒ an object of derision. 웃음거리; 조소의 대상. ¶ *an object of ~.* [↑]

de·ri·sive [diráisiv] *adj.* **1** expressing derision. 조소적인; 비웃음의. ¶ *~ laughter* 비웃는 웃음. **2** deserving derision. 비웃을 만한. ¶ *a ~ attempt* 비웃을 만한 시도.

de·ri·sive·ly [diráisivli] *adv.* in a derisive manner. 비웃듯이; 조소하여.

de·ri·so·ry [diráisəri] *adj.* =derisive.

de·riv·a·ble [diráivəbəl] *adj.* that can be

derived. (이)끌어낼 수 있는; 유도(誘導)할 수 있는. ¶ *pleasure ~ from home life* 가정 생활에서 얻을 수 있는 기쁨. [↓]

der·i·va·tion [dèrəvéiʃən] *n.* **1** Ⓤ the act of deriving; the state of being derived. (이)끌어내기; 유도(誘導). **2** Ⓤ the source; the origin. 유래; 기원. **3** ⒸⓊ the origin and development of a word. (낱말의) 어원(語源); 파생. [→derive]

de·riv·a·tive [dirívətiv] *adj.* gotten from something else; not original. 파생의; 유도된; 유래하는. —*n.* Ⓒ **1** something derived. 파생물. **2** a word derived from another. 파생어. ¶ *Many English words are derivatives of Latin words.* 많은 영어 낱말은 라틴말의 파생어들이다 / *'Derivative' is a ~ of 'derive'.* *'Derivative'*는 *'derive'*의 파생어이다. ● **de·riv·a·tive·ly** [-li] *adv.*

:de·rive [diráiv] *vt.* (P13) **1** 《*from*》 get; draw; receive. …을 얻다; 끌어내다. ¶ *~ much pleasure from books* 책에서 많은 기쁨을 얻다. **2** trace (a word, etc.) from its origin. …의 유래를 더듬다; 어원을 보여주다. ¶ *~ a word from its base* 어간(語幹)을 더듬어 한 낱말의 파생 경과를 밝히다 / *~ one's family from the Conqueror* 가계가 정복왕 윌리엄으로부터 유래되었음을 알다. **3** get knowledge of (something) by reasoning; deduce; infer. …을 추론(推論)하다; 연역(演繹)하다. **4** draw (one chemical compound) from another. …을 유도(誘導)하다.
—*vi.* (P3) 《*from*》 come; originate; spring. …에서 나오다; 유래하다. ¶ *a word derived from Greek* 그리스어에서 나온 말. ● **de·riv·a·ble** [-əbəl] *adj.* [L. *rivus* stream]

der·ma·tol·o·gy [də̀ːrmətálədʒi / -tɔ́l-] *n.* the specical study of the skin, its diseases, etc. 피부병학. [Gk.]

der·ni·er [də́ːrniər] *adj.* 《F.》 the last; the latest. 최후의; 최신의; 최근의.

dernier cri [də́ːrniər kriː] *n.* 《F.》 the lastest thing. 최신 유행품.

dernier res·sort [də́ːrniər rəsɔ́ːr] *n.* the last resort. 최후의 수단. [F.]

der·o·gate [dérougèit] *vi.* (P3) 《*from*》 **1** take away fame, etc.; detract. (명성·권위 따위가) 떨어지다; 감소하다; 없애다. ¶ *~ from one's authority* 권위를 손상하다. **2** become worse. 타락하다. [de-, →rogation]

der·o·ga·tion [dèrougéiʃən] *n.* Ⓤ **1** the act of lessening power, reputation, etc. (권력·명성 따위의) 손상; 저하; 하락. **2** the state of becoming worse. 타락.

de·rog·a·to·ry [dirágətɔ̀ːri / -rɔ́gətəri] *adj.* tending to lessen the value of; detracting from. (권위·명성·품위 따위를) 감손〔하락〕시키는; (가치·품위(品位)를) 떨어뜨리는; 손상하는. ¶ *His conduct is ~ to his dignity.* 그의 행동은 그의 위엄을 손상시킨다. ● **de·rog·a·to·ri·ly** [-li] *adv.*

der·rick [dérik] *n.* Ⓒ **1** a large machine for lifting and moving heavy objects; a crane. (특히 선박용) 데릭 기중기. **2** a framework like a tower, over an oil well, etc., to support drilling machinery. 유정탑(油井塔). [Person]

der·rin·ger [dérindʒər] *n.* a pistol of large caliber. 데린저 권총《휴대용의 총열이 짧고 구경이 큼》. [Person]

der·vish [də́ːrviʃ] *n.* Ⓒ a Mohammedan monk. 이슬람의 탁발 수도사. [Person]

a dancing* 〔*whirling*〕 *dervish, a dervish who dances and spins about. 춤추며 빙빙 도는 의식을 하는 이슬람 수도사.

a howling dervish, a dervish who sings and shouts loudly. 노래하며 요란하게 소리치는 의식을 행하는 이슬람 수도사.

desc. descendant.

des·cant [diskǽnt] *vi.* (P1,3) **1** 《*on, upon*》 talk at great length about something. …을 길게〔자세히〕 이야기하다; 논평〔상론〕하다. ¶ *~ on the wonders of nature* 자연의 경이에 관하여 여러가지로 이야기하다. **2** sing. 노래부르다. —[déskænt] *n.* Ⓒ a melody or song; a melody to be played or sung with another melody. 가곡(歌曲); 노래; 반주 선율. [→chant]

:de·scend [disénd] *vi.* **1** (P1,2A,3) ⓐ come or go down. 내려오다〔가다〕(opp. ascend). ¶ *~ from the hill-top* 산정(山頂)에서 내려오다 / *~ into a cellar* 지하실로 내려가다. ⓑ slope downwards. (아래로) 경사지다; 내리받이가 되다. ¶ *The road descended steeply.* 길은 가파르게 내리받이가 되었다 / *The hill descends by a gradual slope to the plain.* 산은 완만한 경사를 이루며 평지로 이어진다. **2** (P2A,3) ⓐ (of property, qualities, rights) be handed down from parent to child; be inherited. 전해지다; 상속되다; 유전하다. ¶ *~ from father to son* 부전자전이다 / *Land descends to the eldest son.* 토지는 장남에게 상속된다. ⓑ come down from earlier times. 전래하다. ¶ *The custom descended from the ancient Greeks.* 이 풍습은 고대 그리스 때부터 전해 내려왔다. **3** (P3) 《*to*》 ⓐ lower oneself to; come down to; stoop. 타락하다; …까지 하게 되다. ¶ *~ to telling lies* 거짓말까지 하게 되다 / *They were surprised that he descended to cheating.* 그가 사기를 하기까지 타락한 것에 그들은 놀랐다. ⓑ pass on to; go from generalities to particulars, as in a discussion. (총론에서 각론으로) 들어가다〔옮아가다〕; 언급되다. ¶ *~ to details* 세부(細部)로 들어가다. **4** (P3) 《*on, upon*》 ⓐ make a sudden attack on. (갑자기) 덮치다〔공격하다〕; 급습하다. ⓑ 《*fig.*》 visit suddenly and unexpectedly. 불시에 방문하다. —*vt.* (P6) come down (a hill, etc.); go down. (산 따위에서) 내려오다; 내려가다(opp. ascend). ¶ *~ the hill* 〔*stairs*〕 산을〔계단을〕 내려오다. [de-, L. *scando* climb]

be descended from, have (someone) as one's ancestor. …의 자손이다. ¶ *Are men descended from apes?* 인간은 원숭이의 자손인

가.
descend on (***upon***), make a sudden attack or visit. 갑자기 …을 덮치다(공격하다); 느닷없이 방문하다. ¶ ~ *upon enemy soldiers* 적병을 급습하다 / *The wolves descended on the sheep and killed them.* 이리들은 양떼를 급습하여 죽였다 / ~ *on someone uninvited* 불청객이 아무를 불시에 방문하다 / *His anger descended on my head.* 그의 노염이 나에게 폭발했다.

·de·scend·ant [diséndənt] *n.* Ⓒ a person descended from a certain family, group, etc. 자손; 후예(opp. ancestor). ¶ *the descendants of King David* 다윗왕의 자손들 / *a remote* (*direct*) ~ *of* …의 먼(직계) 자손 / *They were the descendants of Normans.* 그들은 노르만의 후예였다. —*adj.* descending; coming down. 내려오는; 강하하는.

·de·scent [disént] *n.* **1** ⓊⒸ the act of coming down or going down. 내려옴(감); 하강(opp. ascent). ¶ *the* ~ *on skis* 스키에 의한 활강 / *the* ~ *of a balloon* 기구의 하강 / *a* ~ *with a parachute* 낙하산 하강. **2** Ⓒ a down slope. 내리받이. ¶ *a steep* ~ 가파른 내리받이 / *The land slopes to the sea by a gradual* ~. 국토는 완만한 경사를 이루며 바다로 이어진다. **3** Ⓤ the state or fact of being handed down from parent to child. 상속; 세습; 유전. ¶ *the* ~ *of property from father to son* 아버지로부터 아들에의 재산상속. **4** Ⓤ a family line. 가계; 가문; 혈통. ¶ *by* ~ 가계는; 태생은 / *a man of high* ~ 명문출신. **5** Ⓒ a sudden attack. 급습; 습격. ¶ *a* ~ *upon a village* 마을에 대한 습격 / *make a* ~ *on the coast* 해안을 급습하다. [*descend*]

de·scrib·a·ble [diskráibəbəl] *adj.* that can be described. 묘사(기술)할 수 있는. [↓]

:de·scribe [diskráib] *vt.* (P6,7,12,13) **1** tell or write about (something or someone); picture (something) in words. (특징 따위)를 말하다; 기술(묘사)하다; …을 —라고 부르다(평하다). ¶ ~ *a man* (*scene*) 인물(장면)을 묘사하다 / ~ *what one saw* 자기가 본 것을 말하다(묘사하다) / *I can't* ~ *it as pleasant.* 그것이 유쾌하다고는 말할 수 없다 / *He describes himself as a poet.* 그는 스스로를 시인이라 칭하고 있다. **2** 《geom.》 mark out; draw; trace. (도형)을 그리다; 작도하다. ¶ ~ *a circle* 원을 그리다. [→scribe]

:de·scrip·tion [diskrípʃən] *n.* **1** ⓊⒸ ⓐ the act of describing. 기술; 서술; 묘사. ¶ *The scenery was beautiful beyond* ~. 경치는 형언할 수 없을 정도로 아름다웠다. ⓑ a report or an account of the characteristics, chief qualities. (특질·주된 성질 따위의) 설명(서); 인상서. ¶ *a man answering to that* ~ 그 인상서에 들어맞는 사람 / *Give me a* ~ *of the thief.* 도둑의 인상을 설명해 주시오. **2** Ⓒ a kind; a sort; a class. 종류; (상품의) 품목; 등급. ¶ *motorcars of every* ~ 온갖 종류의 자동차 / *a man of that* ~ 그런 부류의 사람 / *a speech of the poorest* ~ 형편 없는 연설.

de·scrip·tive [diskríptiv] *adj.* describing; given to or skillful at describing. 기술적(서술적, 설명적)인; 묘사의; 기사(체)의. ¶ *a* ~ *style* 기술체 / *a* ~ *adjective* 서술 형용사 / *This novel is well* ~ *of the characters.* 이 소설은 성격을 잘 묘사하고 있다. ● **de·scrip·tive·ly** [-li] *adv.* **de·scrip·tive·ness** [-nis] *n.*

de·scry [diskrái] *vt.* (**-scried, -scry·ing**) (P6) catch sight of (something) in the distance; see at a distance. 멀리 …을 보다. ¶ *The shipwrecked sailors descried a sail on the horizon.* 난파된 선원들은 아득한 수평선상의 범선을 보았다. [dis-, →cry; old sense *make public*]

des·e·crate [désikrèit] *vt.* (P6) treat (a holy thing) without respect. …의 신성(神聖)을 더럽히다; …을 모독하다(opp. consecrate). ¶ ~ *a temple to false worship* 신전(神殿)을 사신(邪神) 숭배를 위해 쓰다. [→sacred]

des·e·cra·tion [dèsikréiʃən] *n.* Ⓤ the act of desecrating. 신성 모독.

de·seg·re·gate [di:ségrigèit] *vt.* (P6) abolish racial segregation. 인종 차별을 폐지(철폐)하다. ¶ ~ *all schools* 모든 학교의 인종차별을 철폐하다. [de-]

:des·ert[1] [dézərt] *n.* Ⓒ a dry and sandy region, usu. without trees or water; a wilderness. 사막; 황무지. ¶ *the Desert of Gobi* 고비 사막 / *the ship of the* ~ 사막의 배 《낙타》. —*adj.* **1** like a desert; having no plants. 사막과 같은; 불모의. **2** not inhabited or cultivated; wild. 사람이 살지 않는; 쓸쓸한. ¶ *a* ~ *island* 무인도. [→desert[2]]

:de·sert[2] [dizə́:rt] *vt.* (P6) leave; abandon; give up. 버리(고 돌보지 않)다; 못 본 체하다; 방치하다; 포기하다(cf. *forsake*). ¶ ~ *one's post* (*ship*) 지위(배)를 버리다 / ~ *one's family* 처자식을 못 본 체하다 / *The streets were deserted.* 거리에는 인기척이 없었다 / *His courage deserted him.* 용기가 스러졌다. —*vi.* (P1,3) 《*from*》 leave military service without permission; run away from duty. 군무(의무·직무)를 버리다; 도망(탈주)하다. ¶ ~ *to the enemy* 적군에 투항하다 / *A soldier who deserts is punished.* 탈영범은 처벌된다. [de-, L. *sero* join]

de·sert[3] [dizə́:rt] *n.* **1** Ⓤ the fact of deserving reward or punishment. 마땅히 상(벌)을 받을 만함. **2** Ⓒ 《usu. *pl.*》 suitable reward or punishment. 마땅히 받아야 할 상(벌). ¶ *get* (*obtain, meet with*) *one's deserts* 당연한 보답(상벌)을 받다 / *They punished the thief according to his deserts.* 그들은 그 죄질에 따라 그 도둑을 처벌했다. **3** Ⓒ one's valuable deed; a merit. 공적; 훈공; 미점(美點). ¶ *His* ~ *is small.* 그의 장점은 적다. [→deserve]

de·sert·ed [dizə́:rtid] *adj.* **1** abandoned; forsaken. 버림받은; 포기된. ¶ *the miserable lot of* ~ *wives and children* 버림받은 처

자식들의 비참한 운명. **2** without any person living in it. 사람이 살지 않는. ¶ *a ~ village* 사람이 없는 마을; 폐촌. [→desert²]

de·sert·er [dizə́ːrtər] *n.* Ⓒ **1** a person who abandons. (가족·의무 등을) 버린 사람; 유기자(遺棄者). **2** a person who runs away from duty without permission, such as a soldier, etc. 탈영병; 도망자. [↑]

de·ser·tion [dizə́ːrʃən] *n.* ⓊⒸ the act of deserting; the state or fact of being deserted; the act or crime running away from duty without permission. 유기; 탈영; 도망; 탈당. [↑]

:de·serve [dizə́ːrv] *vt.* (P6,8) have a right to (do something); be worthy of (something); earn. …을 받을[할] 만하다; …할 값어치가 있다. ¶ *~ attention* 주목할 만하다 / *~ to be punished* 마땅히 처벌을 받을 만하다 / *He deserves his promotion.* 그는 승진되어 마땅하다. —*vi.* (P3) be worthy. 보답을 받을 만하다. ¶ *He deserves well of his country.* 그는 자기 나라에서 우대받아 마땅한 공적이 있다. ●**de·serv·er** [-ər] *n.* [→serf]

de·serv·ed·ly [dizə́ːrvidli] *adv.* according to what is deserved; justly; properly. 공죄에 따라서; 당연히; 정당히; 적당히. ¶ *be ~ praised* [*punished*] 정당하게 칭찬을 받다[처벌되다].

de·serv·ing [dizə́ːrviŋ] *adj.* worthy of; worth helping. …할 만한; …할 자격이 있는. ¶ *the ~ poor* 보호 대상이 되는 영세민들 / *He is ~ of trust.* 그는 신용할 만하다. ● **de·serv·ing·ly** [-li] *adv.*

des·ha·bille [dèzəbíːl,-bíl] *n.* 《F.》 =dishabille.

des·ic·cate [désikèit] *vt.* (P6) dry (something) thoroughly. …을 건물(乾物)로 하다; 건조시키다. ¶ *desiccated milk* 분유. —*vi.* (P1) become completely dry. 바싹 마르다; 건조하다. ●**des·ic·ca·tive** [-kèitiv] *adj.* [L. *siccus* dry]

des·ic·ca·tion [dèsikéiʃən] *n.* Ⓤ the act of desiccating; the state of being desiccated. 건조(작용); 탈수; 고갈.

des·ic·ca·tor [désikèitər] *n.* a desiccating apparatus. 건조기(장치).

de·sid·er·a·ta [disìdəréitə] *n.* pl. of **desideratum.**

de·sid·er·ate [disídərèit,-zíd-] *vt.* (P6) 《*lit.*》 feel lack of, and desire to supply; recognize as missing, but necessary. 원하다; 바라다. [L. *de* from, *sidus* star]

de·sid·er·a·tive [disídərèitiv, -rə-] *adj.* 《gram.》 expressing desire. 원망(願望)을 나타내는.

de·sid·er·a·tum [disìdəréitəm] *n.* (*pl.* **-ta**) something desired or needed. 바라는 것; 원하는 것. ¶ *A good Korean dictionary is a great ~.* 훌륭한 국어 사전은 몹시 바라는 것이다.

:de·sign [dizáin] *vt.* **1** (P6) draw up a plan for; sketch a pattern or outline for (something). …을 계획[기획·입안]하다; 설계하다; 디자인하다. ¶ *~ a policy* 정책을 세우다 / *~ a house* [*a bridge, an engine*] 집을[다리를, 엔진을] 설계하다 / *~ a dress* 옷을 디자인하다. **2** (P6,8,9,11) have in mind to do; mean to do. …할 뜻을 품다; …을 의도하다. ¶ *Did you ~ this result?* 이런 결과를 의도하였느냐. **3** (P7,13,20) intend (a person or thing) for a particular purpose. …을 (어떤 목적을 위해) …하려고 하다; …할 예정[작정]이다. ¶ *~ a room as a bedroom* 방 하나를 침실로 하려고 하다 / *~ one's son for* [*to be*] *a soldier* 아들을 군인으로 만들려고 하다 / *The room was designed to be* [*as*] *my study.* 그 방은 내 서재로 꾸며진 것이었다 / *She designed to be a teacher.* 그녀는 교사가 되려고 했다.

—*vi.* (P1) make drawings, sketches, or plans; plan and fashion the form of an object; be a designer. 계획[입안]하다; 설계[도안]하다; 디자이너로 일하다. ¶ *He designs for our dress department.* 그는 우리 의상부의 디자이너로 일한다.

—*n.* **1** Ⓒ a pattern; a draft; a sketch; an outline. 도안; 무늬; 설계(도); 의장(意匠). ¶ *a ~ of flowers* 꽃 도안 / *a ~ for a building* 건축 설계. **2** Ⓤ ⓐ plan; idea; artistic invention. 디자인; 착상; 구상. ¶ *This picture is poor in ~.* 이 그림은 구도가 엉성하다. ⓑ a suitable arrangement of the parts, etc., for beauty or use, of any constructed work. 구조. ¶ *a machine of excellent ~* 구조가 잘 짜인 기계. **3** Ⓒ a purpose; an aim; a plan. 목적; 의도; 계획. ¶ *carry out one's designs* 계획을 실행하다 / *It was done by ~ and not by accident.* 그건 우연이 아니라 고의로[의도적으로] 한 것이었다. **4** 《*pl.*》 evil intention; plot. (…에 대한) 위해(危害)의 의도; 음모. ¶ *They have designs upon* [*against*] *her life.* 그들은 그녀에게 살의를 품고 있다; 그들은 그녀의 목숨을 노리고 있다. [→sign]

des·ig·nate [dézignèit] *vt.* **1** (P6) make out or point out (something) clearly; show. …을 분명히 가리키다[나타내다]; 지적[지시]하다. ¶ *~ faults* 결점을 지적하다 / *~ the boundaries of a country* 나라의 국경을 명시하다 / *Will you ~ the flowers you wish?* 원하시는 꽃을 지시해 주시겠습니까. **2** (P7,19) give a name to (someone); name. …을 ―라고 부르다; 칭하다. ¶ *~ someone as a despot* 아무를 폭군이라 부르다. **3** (P6,7,20) 《*as, to, for*》 select (someone) for duty, etc.; appoint. …으로 지명하다; 임명하다. ¶ *~ someone for the post of manager* 아무를 지배인으로 임명[지명]하다.

—[dézignèit, -nit] *adj.* appointed; selected. 지명을 받은; 임명된; 뽑힌. 參考 흔히 명사 뒤에 옴. ¶ *an ambassador ~* 임명되었으나 아직 취임치 않은 대사 / *a bishop ~* 지명된 (미취임의) 주교. [de-, L. *signum* sign]

des·ig·na·tion [dèzignéiʃən] *n.* **1** Ⓤ the act of designating; clear indication. 지시;

지정; 명시. **2** Ⓤ the act of naming; the state of being named. 지명; 임명. ¶ *The ~ of Smith as president pleased the students.* 스미스씨의 총장 임명은 학생들을 기쁘게 했다. **3** Ⓒ a descriptive title; a name. 존칭; 칭호; 명칭.

de·signed [dizáind] *adj.* planned; intended. 계획(의도)적인; 고의의. [→design]

de·sign·ed·ly [dizáinidli] *adv.* by design; on purpose; intentionally. 계획(의도)적으로; 고의로; 일부러(opp. accidentally).

de·sign·er [dizáinər] *n.* Ⓒ **1** a person who designs. 설계자; 고안(입안)자; 도안가; 디자이너. **2** a plotter; a person who schemes. 계획자; 음모자.

de·sign·ing [dizáiniŋ] *adj.* scheming; plotting; artful. 흉계가 있는; 음모적인; 음흉한. ¶ *a ~ woman* 음흉한 여자. —*n.* Ⓤ the art of making plans, patterns, etc. 설계; 의장(意匠) 도안.

·**de·sir·a·bil·i·ty** [dizàiərəbíləti] *n.* Ⓤ the state or quality of being desirable. 바람직함. [→desire]

·**de·sir·a·ble** [dizáiərəbəl] *adj.* **1** worth wishing for; to be desired. 바람직한; 멋진. **2** pleasant; satisfying; good. 마음에 쏙 드는; 손에 넣고 싶은; 좋은; 탐나는. ¶ *a very ~ property for sale* 무척 탐나는 매물 부동산. ●**de·sir·a·bly** [-bli] *adv.* **de·sir·a·ble·ness** [-nis] *n.*

:**de·sire** [dizáiər] *vt.* (P6,8,11,20) **1** wish for (something); wish earnestly for (something); want. …을 원하다(바라다); 열망하다. ¶ *~ a woman for one's wife* 어떤 여자를 아내로 맞기를 원하다 / *leave much* (*nothing*) *to be desired* 유감스러운 점이 많다(없다) / *He desires that you should come back.* 그는 자네가 꼭 돌아오기를 원하고 있네. **2** express a wish or ask for (someone or something); request. …해주기를 —에게 요구하다. ¶ *I ~ you to go at once.* 곧 가 주기를 요망하네 / *The king desired the presence of his ministers.* 왕은 대신들의 참석을 명했다.

—*n.* **1** ⓊⒸ 《*for, of, to do*》 a wish; a strong wish (longing). 바람; 욕망; 욕구. ¶ *a strong ~ for fame* 명성에 대한 강한 욕구 / *have a ~ for a glass of beer* 맥주 한 잔 하고 싶다 / *satisfy one's ~* 욕망을 충족시키다 / *accomplish one's ~* 소망을 성취하다 / *have a ~ to do* …을 하고 싶다 / *Most people have a ~ to collect things.* 대부분의 사람들은 수집욕(收集欲)이 있다 / *I have no ~ for money.* 돈 따위는 원치 않는다. **2** Ⓒ 《usu. in *sing.*》 a request. 희망; 요구. ¶ *at the ~ of the manager* 지배인의 요구대로(희망에 따라) / *In accordance with your desire(s), I am sending you….* 요구하시는 바에 따라 …을 부쳐드리는 바입니다. **3** Ⓒ a thing desired. 원하는(바라는) 것. ¶ *get one's ~* 바라는 것을 손에 넣다. [*desiderate*]

de·sir·ous [dizáiərəs] *adj.* having or showing desire; desiring; eager. 원하고 (바라고) 있는; …하고 싶어하는. ¶ *be ~ to succeed* =*be ~ of success* 성공하고 싶어하다 / *be ~ to go abroad* 해외로 나가고 싶어하다 / *I am ~ to know further details.* 더 상세한 것을 알고 싶습니다 / *He is ~ of getting a good job.* =*He is ~ to get a good job.* 그는 좋은 일자리를 얻고 싶어한다.

de·sist [dizíst] *vi.* (P1,3) 《*from*》 cease; stop. 그만두다; 그치다; 단념하다. ¶ *~ from talking* 수다를 그치다 / *It's no good, so you had better ~.* 좋지 않으므로 그만두는 것이 좋겠다. [L. *sisto* stop]

:**desk** [desk] *n.* Ⓒ a piece of furniture with a flat or sloping top for reading, writing, or drawing. 책상. ¶ *be* (*sit*) *at the* (*one's*) *~* 책상에 앉아 책을 읽고(글을 쓰고, 사무를 보고) 있다. [→disk]

·**des·o·late** [désəlit] *adj.* **1** ⓐ (of a house, home, etc.) not lived in; neglected. 사람이 살지 않는; 황폐한. ¶ *a ~ house* 사람이 살지 않는 집. ⓑ (of a land, etc.) without people in it; deserted; barren; wretched. 주민이 없는; 황량한; 버림받은; 비참한. ¶ *The land is ~ of all vegetation.* 그 땅은 식물 하나 없이 황량하다. **2** (of a person, etc.) left alone; solitary; lonely; unhappy. 고독한; 쓸쓸한; 외로운; 불행한. ¶ *a ~ life* 고독한 생활 / *comfort a ~ heart* 쓸쓸한 마음을 달래다 / *She looked ~.* 그녀는 불행해 보였다.

—[désəlèit] *vt.* (P6) make (a land, etc.) desolate; make (someone) sad or lonely. …을 황폐시키다; …을 살지 않게 하다; …을 쓸쓸하게(외롭게) 만들다. ¶ *An earthquake desolated the city.* 지진이 그 도시를 황폐케 했다 / *We are desolated to hear that you are going away.* 네가 떠난다는 얘기를 들으니 섭섭하다. ●**des·o·late·ness** [désəlitnis] *n.* [→solitary]

des·o·late·ly [désəlitli] *adv.* lonely; sadly. 쓸쓸하게; 황량하게.

·**des·o·la·tion** [dèsəléiʃən] *n.* **1** Ⓤ the act of desolating. 황폐. **2** Ⓒ a desolate place. 쓸쓸한(황량한) 곳. **3** Ⓤ sadness; loneliness. 쓸쓸함; 외로움.

:**de·spair** [dispέər] *n.* **1** Ⓤ loss of hope; hopelessness. 절망; 자포자기. ¶ *a feeling of ~* 절망감 / *be driven to ~* 절망에 몰리다 / *yield* (*give way*) *to ~* 절망에 빠지다 / *in ~* 절망하여 / *out of ~* =*in the depths of ~* 절망한 나머지 / *Despair took hold of him.* 그는 절망감에 사로잡혔다. **2** Ⓒ a person or thing that causes despair. 절망시키는 사람(것). ¶ *He is my ~.* 그에게는 두 손 들었다.

—*vi.* (P1,3) 《*of*》 lose hope; be in despair. 희망을 잃다; 절망하다; 단념하다. ¶ *~ of humanity* 인류(인간성)에 절망하다 / *We despaired of his life.* =*His life was despaired of.* 그의 목숨을 구할 가망은 없었다 / *They despaired of saving the child's life.* 그들은 그 아이의 생명을 구할 희망을 포기했다. [L. *spero* hope]

de·spair·ing [dispέəriŋ] *adj.* feeling or showing despair; hopeless. 자포자기의; 절망의. ¶ *a ~ look* 절망한 표정. ● **de·spair·ing·ness** [-nis] *n.*

de·spair·ing·ly [dispέəriŋli] *adv.* in the state of having lost all hope; hopelessly. 자포자기가 되어; 절망적으로.

·**des·patch** [dispǽtʃ] *v., n.* =dispatch.

des·per·a·do [dèspəréidou, -rά:-] *n.* Ⓒ (*pl.* **-does** or **-dos**) a bold, reckless criminal; a person ready for any desperate and criminal deed. 무모한 무법자; 목숨 아까운 줄 모르는 흉한(凶漢). [↓]

:**des·per·ate** [déspərit] *adj.* **1** reckless because hope is gone; ready to run any risk. 자포자기의. ¶ *~ remedy* 비상 수단 / *a ~ character* 무뢰한(無賴漢). **2** showing recklessness caused by despair; violent. 기를 쓰는; 필사적인; 난폭한. ¶ *a ~ struggle* 필사적인 싸움 / *He is making ~ efforts to improve it.* 그것을 개선하기 위해 필사적인 노력을 하고 있다. **3** with little improvement; hopeless; beyond hope; extremely dangerous or serious. (회복·개선의) 가망이 없는; 절망적인; 위험한. ¶ *a ~ illness* (나을 가망이 없는) 중병 / *a ~ fool* 지독한 바보 / *a ~ state of affairs* 절망적인 사태. ● **des·per·ate·ness** [-nis] *n.* [→despair]

·**des·per·ate·ly** [déspəritli] *adv.* in the state of being desperate; extremely. 절망적으로; 자포자기하여; 무모하게; 필사적으로; 극단적으로.

des·per·a·tion [dèspəréiʃən] *n.* Ⓤ the state of being desperate; willingness to run any risk. 무모; 필사; 자포자기. ¶ *drive someone to ~* 아무를 자포자기하게 만들다 / *be driven to ~* 필사적이 되다; 자포자기가 되다 / *in ~* 필사적으로; 자포자기가 되어.

des·pi·ca·ble [déspikəbəl, dispík-] *adj.* to be looked down on; contemptible. 비열한; 경멸할 만한. ¶ *It is ~ to leave a poor cat behind to die.* 가엾은 고양이를 죽게 내버려 두는 것은 비열한 짓이다. [→despise]

des·pi·ca·bly [déspikəbəli, dispík-] *adv.* in a despicable manner. 비열하게.

·**de·spise** [dispáiz] *vt.* (P6) look down on (someone) as worthless; feel contempt for (someone); scorn. …을 업신여기다; …을 경멸[멸시]하다(opp. admire). ¶ *An honest man despises those who lie.* 정직한 사람은 거짓말쟁이를 경멸한다. [de-, L. *specio* look at]

·**de·spite** [dispáit] *prep.* in spite of. …에도 불구하고. ¶ *go sailing ~ the storm* 폭풍우를 아랑곳 않고 출범하다 / *He went for a walk ~ the rain.* 비가 오는데도 그는 산책을 나갔다 / *Despite our efforts we failed.* 우리는 노력했음에도 불구하고 실패했다 / *He listened ~ himself to her.* 그는 듣지 않겠다고 생각하면서도 그녀의 말에 귀를 기울였다.
— *n.* 《*arch.*》 Ⓤ **1** malice; hatred; spite. 악의(惡意); 증오; 원한(怨恨). **2** scorn; contempt; insult. 경멸; 모욕; 무례. **3** the doing of harm; injury. 위해; 상해. [↑]
(*in*) ***despite of,*** in spite of; in defiance of. …에도 불구하고; …을 무시하고.
in one's own despite, 《*arch.*》 unwillingly. 본의 아니게; 마지못해.

de·spite·ful [dispáitfəl] *adj.* 《*arch.*》 = spiteful.

de·spoil [dispɔ́il] *vt.* (P6,13) 《*of*》 steal (something) by force; rob; strip. …을 약탈[강탈, 탈취]하다; 빼앗다. ¶ *~ a ship* 배를 강탈하다 / *~ someone of his goods* 아무에게서 그의 물건을 빼앗다. [→spoil]

de·spoil·ment [dispɔ́ilmənt] *n.* Ⓤ the act of robbing. 약탈; 강탈.

de·spond [dispάnd / -spɔ́nd] *vi.* (P1) lose hope. 실망[낙담]하다. ¶ *Continued poverty caused him to ~.* 끊임 없는 가난은 그를 실망케 하였다. — *n.* =despondence. ● **de·spond·ing·ly** [-iŋli] *adv.* [→spouse]

de·spond·ence [dispάndəns / -pɔ́nd-], **-en·cy** [-ənsi] *n.* Ⓤ loss of courage or hope; discouragement; melancholy. 낙심; 낙담; 의기 소침.

de·spond·ent [dispάndənt / -spɔ́nd-] *adj.* 《*over*》 showing or feeling despondency; discouraged. 낙담한; 실의에 빠진; 기운 없는.

des·pot [déspət, -pαt / -pɔt] *n.* Ⓒ a ruler who uses his power unjustly or cruelly; a tyrant. 전제[독재] 군주; 폭군(暴君). [Gk. *despotēs* master]

des·pot·ic [dispάtik / despɔ́t-] *adj.* of a despot or tyrant; cruel; unjust. 전제적[독재적]인; 포학[횡포]한.

des·pot·ism [déspətìzəm] *n.* **1** Ⓤ the rule of a despot; tyranny. 전제[독재] (정치); 폭정. **2** Ⓒ a country or government ruled by a despot. 전제 군주국; 독재 정부.

·**des·sert** [dizə́:rt] *n.* ⓊⒸ a course served at the end of a meal. 디저트《양식에서 식사 끝에 나오는 과일·과자·아이스크림 따위》. ¶ *serve ~* 디저트를 내놓다. [dis-, →serve]

des·sert·spoon [dizə́:rtspù:n] *n.* Ⓒ a spoon for dessert. 디저트용 숟갈.

de·sta·lin·i·za·tion [di:stὰ:linizéiʃən] *n.* removal of the influence of Stalin. 비(非)스탈린화(化). [de-]

·**des·ti·na·tion** [dèstənéiʃən] *n.* Ⓒ **1** the place to which a person is going or a thing is being sent. 목적[행선]지; 도착지. ¶ *My ~ is Rome.* 나의 목적지는 로마이다 / *What is the ~ of that letter?* 그 편지는 누구 앞으로 된 것입니까. **2** an intention; a purpose; one's ultimate end. 의도; 목표; 용도; 최종 목적. [↓]

·**des·tine** [déstin] *vt.* 《usu. in *passive*》 **1** (P13,20) 《*for*》 set (something) apart for a particular purpose or use; intend; design. (특정 목적·용도를 위해) 따로 떼어두다; 예정해 두다. ¶ *fruits destined for some rich man's table* 부자의 식탁용으로 예정된 과일들 / *~ a room for the reception of a noble per-*

son 귀한 분의 환대를 위해 방 하나를 할당하다 / *His father destined him for a political career.* 아버지는 그를 정치가로 만들기로 정하였다. **2** (P11,13,20) cause by fate; predetermine (신의 뜻으로) 미리 정하다; 운명지우다. ¶ *Fate destined that he shall die.* 운명은 그가 죽도록 정해졌다 / *be destined to be a queen* 여왕이 되기로 되어 있다 / *We are destined never to meet again.* 우리는 다시 만나지 못할 운명이다. [L.]

(be) destined for, a) intended to go to (a place). …행(行)(이다). ¶ *a plane destined for New York* 뉴욕행(行)의 비행기. **b)** intended for (something). …으로 될 운명이다. ¶ *He was destined for the church.* 성직자가 될 운명이었다.

·des·ti·ny [déstəni] *n.* (*pl.* **-nies**) **1** UC a person's lot or fate. 운명; 숙명; 운. ¶ *a* 〔*the*〕 *man of* ~ 운명을 지배하는 사람 / *work out one's own* ~ 자력으로 운명을 개척하다 / *It was his* ~ *to die happy.* 행복하게 죽는 것은 그의 운명이었다. **2** U 《*D-*》 the goddess of destiny; Providence. 운명의 여신; 하늘의 뜻. **3** 《*the Destinies*》 the three Fates. 운명의 3여신(女神).

des·ti·tute [déstitjù:t] *adj.* **1** in a state of poverty; deprived of one's means of support. 가난〔빈궁〕한; 빈곤의; 생계 수단을 잃은. ¶ *a* ~ *family* 극빈 가정 / *be left* ~ 곤궁에 빠져 있다 / *the* ~ 가난한 사람들. **2** 《*of*》 having no; devoid; lacking. …이 없는; …이 결핍되어 있는. ¶ *people* ~ *of common sense* 〔*experience*〕 상식〔경험〕이 없는 사람들. [→state]

des·ti·tu·tion [dèstətjú:ʃən] *n.* U the state of being destitute; lack; extreme poverty. 극빈; 빈곤; 결핍. ¶ *live in complete* ~ 극빈 생활을 하다.

:de·stroy [distrɔ́i] *vt.* (P6) **1** break (something) to pieces; make (something) useless; ruin; spoil. …을 파괴하다〔허물다〕; …을 못쓰게 만들다; 망치다(opp. construct). ¶ ~ *a building* 〔*town*〕 건물을〔도시를〕 파괴하다 / ~ *the beauty of the place* 그 장소의 미(美)를 망치다. **2** bring to nothing. 헛되게〔없어지게〕 하다; 망치다. ¶ ~ *someone's hopes* 아무의 희망을 망치다. **3** put an end to (something); kill. …을 구제(驅除)하다; 박멸하다; 죽이다. ¶ ~ *vermin* 해충을 박멸하다 / ~ *someone* 아무를 죽이다 / ~ *oneself* 자살하다. **4** make (something) powerless; nullify; invalidate. …을 무효로 하다; 파기하다. ¶ ~ *a document* 문서를 파기하다. [L. *strus* build]

·de·stroy·er [distrɔ́iər] *n.* C **1** a person or thing that destroys. 파괴하는 것〔사람〕; 파괴자; 박멸자. **2** a small, fast, powerful warship with guns, torpedoes, etc. 구축함.

de·struct·i·ble [distrʌ́ktəbəl] *adj.* that can be destroyed; liable to destruction. 파괴할 수 있는; 파괴되기 쉬운. [↓]

:de·struc·tion [distrʌ́kʃən] *n.* U the act of destroying; the state of being destroyed; that which causes ruin. 파괴; (문서의) 파기(죄); 구제; 멸망; 파멸(의 원인)(opp. construction). ¶ *The storm left* ~ *behind it.* 폭풍우가 지나간 뒤에 파괴의 자국을 남겼다 / *Overconfidence was his* ~. 과신(過信)이 그의 파멸의 원인이었다. [→destroy]

·de·struc·tive [distrʌ́ktiv] *adj.* **1** causing destruction; harmful. 파괴적인; 유해한(opp. constructive). ¶ *a* ~ *power* 파괴력 / *a* ~ *windstorm* 파괴력이 큰 폭풍 / *a* ~ *animal* 유해한 동물 / *be* ~ *of* 〔*to*〕 *health* 건강에 해롭다 / *be* ~ *to morals* 풍기를 해치다. **2** aiming at destruction; given to destroying. 파괴주의적인; 파괴를 좋아하는. ¶ ~ *criticism* 마구 깎아내리는 비평. ● **de·struc·tive·ly** [-li] *adv.*

des·ue·tude [déswitjù:d] *n.* U the state of being no longer used; disuse. 폐지(상태); 폐절(廢絕). ¶ *fall into* ~ 폐절되다; 스러지다 / *The custom is in* ~. 그 풍속은 사라져서 없다. [L. *suesco* become used]

des·ul·to·ry [désəltɔ̀:ri / -təri] *adj.* jumping from one thing to another; disconnected; without aim or method; random. 변덕스러운; 종작 없는; 만연〔산만〕한; 일관성 없는; 목적 없는; 닥치는 대로의. ¶ *a* ~ *conversation* 산만한 대화 / *A* ~ *reading of many books is often a waste of time.* 많은 책을 마구잡이로 읽는 것은 흔히 시간의 낭비가 된다. ● **des·ul·to·ri·ly** [-li] *adv.* [→salient]

de·tach [ditǽtʃ] *vt.* (P6,13) **1** 《*from*》 loosen and remove; unfasten; separate; disconnect. …을 떼다; 분리하다(opp. attach). ¶ ~ *one's watch from its chain* 시계줄에서 시계를 떼다 / ~ *a sheet from a looseleaf notebook* 루스리프식 노트에서 한 장을 떼어내다. **2** 《mil.》 send away (someone) on a special mission. (특수 임무로) 파견〔분견〕하다. [→tack]

de·tach·a·ble [ditǽtʃəbəl] *adj.* that can be detached. 뗄〔분리할〕 수 있는; 파견〔분견〕할 수 있는. ¶ *a notebook with* ~ *leaves* 책장을 떼었다 끼웠다 할 수 있는 노트.

de·tached [ditǽtʃt] *adj.* **1** separate from others; disconnected; isolated. 분리된; 떨어진; 떼어낸; 분견된; 고립된. ¶ *a* ~ *house* 독립 가옥; 단독 주택 / *a* ~ *train* 떼어낸 차량 / *a* ~ *palace* 별궁(別宮) / *a* ~ *force* 분견대. **2** not moved by others or by one's own interests, etc.; fair. 사심〔편견〕 없는; 공평한; 초연한. ¶ *a* ~ *judgment* 공평한 판단 / *take a* ~ *view of things* 사물을 공평히 보다.

de·tach·ment [ditǽtʃmənt] **1** U the act of detaching; separation. 분리(함); 뗌. ¶ ~ *of a key from a key-ring* 열쇠 고리에서 열쇠를 떼어냄. **2** C 《mil.》 a unit of troops or ships sent on some special duty. (부대·함선 따위의) 분견(分遣); 파견대. **3** U the act of standing apart; aloofness. 고립; 초연(함); 초탈; 무관심. ¶ *with an air of* ~ 초연한 태도로; 초연히 / ~ *from the turmoil of the* *outside world* 시끄러운 외부 세계에 대한 무관심.

:de·tail [dí:teil, ditéil] *n.* Ⓒ **1** a small unimportant part; a tiny item. (중요치 않은) 말초적〔사소한〕 부분; 세부(細部); 세목. 《usu. *pl.*》 particulars. 상세; 자세한 점. ¶ *a mere* ~ (아무래도 좋은) 시시한 / *a matter of* ~ 자잘한〔사소한〕 일 / *omit some details* 몇몇 세세한 점을 생략하다 / *give the full details of a thing* 일의 자초지종을 말〔기술〕하다 / *I cannot tell you any details.* 자세한 것은 아무것도 말할 수 없다. **2** Ⓤ (in art, architecture, etc.) a small decoration or accessory in a building, picture, machine, etc. (건축·미술 따위의) 세부 장식; 상세도(圖); 세부(묘사). **3** Ⓒ 《mil.》 a small group chosen for or sent on some special duty. 분견대(分遣隊); 선발대.

enter* 〔*go*〕 *into details, give all the details; be particular and thorough. 자세히 말하다; 상술(詳述)하다.

in detail, item by item; thoroughly; with particulars. 상세히; 한 항목 한 항목. ¶ *in surprisingly full* ~ 놀라울 정도로 자세히 / *I had no time to explain it in* ~. 자세히 설명할 시간이 없었다.

— *vt.* **1** (P6) tell (something) fully; give a minute report on (something). …을 자세히 말〔기술〕하다; 상술(詳述)하다. ¶ ~ *a story* 자세히 이야기하다. **2** (P6,7,13) 《mil.》 《*for, on, to*》 choose (someone) for or send on a special mission. (특별 임무에) 임명하다; …을 파견하다. ¶ *The captain detailed ten men to guard the station.* 대위는 철도역을 지키기 위해 10 명의 부하를 파견했다. [→tally]

de·tailed [dí:teild / ditéild] *adj.* having many details; described minutely. 상세한; 세목에 걸친. ¶ *a* ~ *account* 자세한 설명 / *give* ~ *explanations of* …을 상세히 설명하다.

de·tain [ditéin] *vt.* (P6,13) **1** keep (someone) from going; delay. …을 붙들다; 만류하다; 기다리게 하다; 지체시키다. ¶ *be detained by business* 일 때문에 지체되다. **2** 《law》 confine; keep under arrest. …을 감금〔구류, 억류〕하다. ¶ ~ *a suspect for further examination* 더 심문하기 위해 용의자를 구금하다. **3** keep; withhold (things). 보류하다. ¶ ~ *a worker's wages* 노동자의 임금 지급을 보류하다. [→tenable]

***de·tect** [ditékt] *vt.* (P6,13) **1** find out; discover. …을 발견하다. ¶ ~ *someone in the act of stealing* 아무가 훔치는 현장을 발견하다 / *Can you* ~ *any defects in his composition?* 그의 작문에서 잘못을 발견할 수 있는가. **2** discover the existence of (something). (…존재)를 탐지〔간파〕하다; 알아내다. ¶ ~ *the odor of gas* 가스 냄새를 맡다 / ~ *a spy* 간첩임을 알아채다 / ~ *a sound in the distance* 먼 곳의 소리를 감지하다 / ~ *a student in a falsehood* 학생의 거짓말을 알아채다. [L. *tego* cover]

de·tec·tion [diték∫ən] *n.* Ⓤ **1** the act of detecting; discovery. 발견; 탐지; 간파; 발각. ¶ *the* ~ *of crime* 범죄의 발각 / *chance* ~ *of smuggling* 밀수의 우연한 발견. **2** 《electr.》 changing of an alternating current into a direct current; demodulation. 정류(整流); 검파(檢波).

***de·tec·tive** [ditéktiv] *n.* Ⓒ a person whose work is to find information secretly or to discover who commited a crime. 탐정; 형사. ¶ *a private* ~ 사립〔비밀〕 탐정 / *put a* ~ *on someone* 아무에게 탐정을 붙이다. — *adj.* of or for detection. 탐정〔형사〕의; 탐정〔검출〕을 위한; 탐지용의. ¶ *a* ~ *story* 탐정〔추리〕 소설 / *various* ~ *devices* 각종의 탐지〔검출〕 장치.

de·tec·tor [ditéktər] *n.* Ⓒ **1** a person or thing that detects. 발견〔간파〕자; 발견〔탐지, 검출〕기. **2** 《electr.》 a device, usu. a vacuum tube or crystal in a radio, which changes an alternating current into a direct current; a rectifier. 정류기(整流器); 검파기.

de·tente [deitá:nt] *n.* 《F.》 ⓊⒸ a relaxing. (국제 관계의) 긴장 완화; 데탕트.

de·ten·tion [ditén∫ən] *n.* Ⓤ **1** the act of detaining; the state of being detained; delay. 억지; 억류; 지체. **2** ⓐ keeping in after school hours as a punishment. (벌로) 방과 후에 학교에 남음. ⓑ the act of keeping someone in confinement. 구류; 유치; 구금; 감금. ¶ *be under* ~ 구류중에 있다 / *a* ~ *camp* 임시 수용소 / *a* ~ *hospital* 격리 병원 / *a house of* ~ 유치장. [→detain]

de·ter [ditə́:r] *vt.* (**-terred, -ter·ring**) (P6,13) 《*from*》 cause to hesitate; prevent (someone) by discouraging; keep back; hinder; check. 망설이게 하다; 그만두게 하다; 단념케 하다. ¶ *The extreme cold deterred us from going out.* 지독히 추워서 외출할 생각을 그만두었다 / *Nothing could* ~ *him from attempting to reach the unconquered peak.* 그 미정복의 산봉우리에 오르려는 그의 시도는 아무 것도 막을 수가 없었다. [L.]

de·terge [ditə́:rdʒ] *vt.* (P6) wipe or wash away; cleanse. …을 씻어〔닦아〕내다; 깨끗이 하다; 정화〔세정(洗淨)〕하다. [L.]

de·ter·gent [ditə́:rdʒənt] *adj.* cleansing. 깨끗이 하는; 정화〔세정〕하는. — *n.* cleanser. 세제(洗劑). ¶ *synthetic detergents* 합성 세제. [↑]

de·te·ri·o·rate [ditíəriərèit] *vi.* (P1) become worse; lessen in value. (질·가치가) 나빠지다; 악화하다; 저하하다. ¶ *The weather had deteriorated during the night.* 날씨가 밤사이에 악화되었다. — *vt.* (P6) make (something or someone) worse. …을 나쁘게 하다; 악화시키다; 저하시키다. ¶ ~ *one's health* 건강을 해치다 / ~ *relations with other countries* 타국과의 관계를 악화시키다. [L.]

de·te·ri·o·ra·tion [ditìəriəréi∫ən] *n.* Ⓤ the act of deteriorating; the state of being deteriorated. 악화; 저하; 타락.

de·ter·mi·nant [ditə́:rmənənt] *n.* Ⓒ a thing that determines. 결정하는 것; 결정 요소. — *adj.* determining. 결정하는. ¶ *a ~ factor* 결정 요인. [→determine]

de·ter·mi·nate [ditə́:rmənit] *adj.* **1** limited; fixed; definite. 한정된, 확정된; 명확한. ¶ *assume a ~ shape* 명확한 형태를 취하다. **2** determined; resolute. 결정적인; 단호한. ¶ *a ~ reply* 확답.

·**de·ter·mi·na·tion** [ditə̀:rmənéiʃən] *n.* Ⓤ **1** the act of determining, deciding, or settling beforehand; the state of being determined; resolution. 결정; 확인; 해결. **2** a fixed purpose; a firm intention. 결심; 결의; 결단력. ¶ *come to a ~* 결심이 서다 / *His ~ to carry out the plan was not weakened by the difficulties he met with.* 계획을 실행하려는 그의 단호한 결심은 부닥친 어려움으로 약화되지는 않았다. **3** 《phys.》 the act of finding out the exact amount; calculation. (정확한 양·비율 따위의) 측정(법). ¶ *the ~ of the amount of iron in ore* 광석의 철 함량(含量) 측정. **4** 《law》 a decision. 재결(裁決); 판결.

de·ter·mi·na·tive [ditə́:rmənèitiv,-nətiv] *adj.* determining; defining. 결정력이 있는; 한정적인. — *n.* Ⓒ a thing that determines. 결정〔한정〕하는 것.

:**de·ter·mine** [ditə́:rmin] *vt.* (P6,8,10,11, 12,13,20) **1** resolve; decide. …을 결심시키다; 결정케 하다. ¶ *I determined to go.* 가기로 결정했다 / *The news determined me to act at once.* 그 소식을 듣고 즉각 행동으로 옮길 결심이 섰다 / *He is determined to explain the matter to them.* 그는 그들에게 그 문제를 설명할 결심이 돼 있다. **2** find out exactly; fix the position of (something); ascertain. 정확히 정하다; …의 위치를 정하다; 확정하다. **3** fix or settle beforehand. …을 예정하다; 결정하다. ¶ *They determined the date for our party.* 그들은 우리의 파티 날짜를 결정했다. **4** be the cause of in deciding the form, quality, etc. of. (원인이 되어) 결정하다. ¶ *The size of a boot is determined by the foot.* 구두의 크기는 발에 의해 결정된다 / *The lives of most men are determined by their environment.* 대부분의 사람의 일생은 환경에 의해 결정된다. **5** 《law》 end; terminate. (분쟁 따위를) 끝내다; 종결하다; 판결하다. **6** 《log.》 limit (a notion); define. …을 한정〔규정〕하다. **7** 《*arch.*》 fix the extent of; mark out. 측정하다.
— *vi.* (P3) 《*on, upon*》 **1** make up one's mind. 결정하다; 결심하다. ¶ *~ up* 〔*upon*〕 *a course of action* 행동방침을 결정하다 / *I determined on going.* 갈 것을 결심했다. **2** 《law》 come to an end; close. (효력 따위가) 종결하다; 소멸하다. ¶ *The contract determines on the 20th of next month.* 계약은 내월 20일이면 효력이 소멸된다. [→terminus]

·**de·ter·mined** [ditə́:rmind] *adj.* with one's mind firmly made up; resolved; firm; resolute; decided. 굳게 결심한; 단호한; 결연한; 결정한. ¶ *in a ~ manner* 결연히 / *I am determined not to ask you.* 네게 묻지 않기로 굳게 결심하고 있다 / *He faced me with a ~ look.* 그는 결연한 표정으로 나를 직시했다.

de·ter·min·ism [ditə́:rminìzəm] *n.* 《philos.》 the doctrine that man's actions are determined by various conditions independent of his will. 결정론(決定論).

de·ter·rent [ditə́:rənt, -tér-] *adj.* tending to deter; restraining. 방해하는; 억지〔저지〕하는. ¶ *~ punishment* 못 하게 하는 처벌. — *n.* Ⓒ a thing that deters. 억지〔저지〕물; 못 하게 하는 것. ¶ *a nuclear ~* 전쟁 억지력으로서의 핵무기 / *Capital punishment is a ~ to murder.* 사형은 살인을 억지하는 역할을 한다. [→terrible]

de·test [ditést] *vt.* (P6) dislike very much; hate deeply. …을 몹시 싫어하다; 증오〔혐오〕하다. ¶ *~ evil* 악을 미워하다 / *He detests cats.* 그는 고양이를 싫어한다 / *He was detested by all.* 모두가 그를 싫어했다. [de-, →testify]

de·test·a·ble [ditéstəbəl] *adj.* deserving to be detested; hateful. 증오할; 가증스러운.
● **de·test·a·ble·ness** [-nis] *n.*

de·tes·ta·tion [dì:testéiʃən] *n.* **1** Ⓤ very strong dislike; hatred. 몹시 싫어함; 증오; 혐오. ¶ *be in ~* 몹시 미움을 받고 있다 / *He had a strong ~ of lying.* 그는 거짓말하는 것을 몹시 싫어했다. **2** Ⓒ a detested person or thing; an object or hatred. 미움받는 사람〔것〕; 증오〔혐오〕의 대상. ¶ *Snakes are her ~.* 뱀은 그녀의 혐오의 대상이다.
have 〔***hold***〕 ***something in detestation,*** dislike strongly. …을 몹시 싫어하다.
regard with detestation, detest. 증오하다.

de·throne [diθróun] *vt.* (P6,13) 《*from*》 remove (someone) from a throne; 《*fig.*》 depose (someone) from an important position, or from the place he holds in popular estimation. (임금)을 퇴위〔폐위〕시키다; …을 (중요한 지위에서) 면직시키다; 물러나게 하다. [→throne]

de·throne·ment [diθróunmənt] *n.* Ⓤ the act of dethroning; the state or fact of being dethroned. 폐위.

det·o·nate [détənèit] *vt.* (P6) cause (something) to explode with a loud noise. (요란한 소리와 함께) …을 폭발시키다. — *vi.* (P1) explode with a sudden loud noise. (큰소리를 내며) 폭발하다. ¶ *A powder magazine detonated.* 화약고가 폭발했다. [L. *tono* thunder]

det·o·na·tion [dètənéiʃən] *n.* ⓊⒸ the act of detonating; the state of being detonated; a loud noise. 폭발(작용); 폭음.

det·o·na·tor [détənèitər] *n.* Ⓒ a detonating fuse or powder. 기폭(起爆) 장치〔약〕; 뇌관(雷管).

de·tour, dé- [dí:tuər, ditúər] *n.* Ⓒ 《F.》 a

road that is used when the regular or direct road cannot be traveled; a turning aside from the direct road; a roundabout way. 우회(로). ¶ *make a ~* 우회(迂廻)하다. — *vi.* use a detour. — *vt.* (P6) **1** cause (someone or something) to make a detour. …을 우회시키다; 돌아가게 하다. **2** avoid. …을 피하다. ¶ *We detoured the hill.* 우리는 언덕을 피해 갔다. [→turn]

de·tract [ditrǽkt] *vt.* (P6,13) ⟪*from*⟫ **1** take away a part from the merit, credit, reputation of (a person); make less the usefulness or advantage of (a thing). (가치·명성·효용성·이점)을 감소시키다; 떨어뜨리다. ¶ *~ charm from the landscape* 경관의 매력을 떨어뜨리다. **2** speak ill of. …을 욕하다. — *vi.* (P3) ⟪*from*⟫ make something less in value. (가치가) 떨어지다; 감소되다. ¶ *~ from the beauty of a picture* 그림의 아름다움을 손상하다 / *That does not ~ from his merit.* 그것으로 그의 가치가 떨어지지는 않는다. [L. *traho* drag]

de·trac·tion [ditrǽkʃən] *n.* Ⓤ **1** the act of detracting. 감손(減損). **2** the act of speaking ill of another. 욕; 중상; 비난; 비방; 훼손.

de·trac·tor [ditrǽktər] *n.* Ⓒ a person who detracts or speaks ill of another. (명예) 훼손자; 욕하는 사람; 중상자.

de·train [diːtréin] *vi.* (P1) (of troops, etc.) get off a train. 열차에서 내리다; 하차하다. — *vt.* (P6) set down (troops, etc.) from a train. (열차에서) 내리게 하다; 하차시키다. [→train]

det·ri·ment [détrəmənt] *n.* Ⓤ damage; loss; injury; harm. 손해; 손실; 손상; 상해. ¶ *without ~ to someone's character* …의 성격을 손상시킴이 없이 / *He always overeats to the ~ of his health.* 그는 늘 과식을 하여 건강을 해치고 있다. [L. *tero* rub]

det·ri·men·tal [dètrəméntl] *adj.* damaging; injurious; harmful. 손해가 되는; 유해한. ¶ *reports ~ to a reputation* 명성을 손상시키는 보고 / *Lack of sleep is ~ to one's health.* 수면 부족은 건강에 해롭다. ● **det·ri·men·tal·ly** [-i] *adv.*

de·tri·tus [ditráitəs] *n.* Ⓒ ⟪geol.⟫ a mass of fragments worn away from rocks, etc. 암설(岩屑); 쇄암(碎岩). [↑]

***De·troit** [ditrɔ́it] *n.* a city in southeastern Michigan. 디트로이트⟪미국 Michigan 주 남동부의 도시⟫.

de trop [də tróu] *adj.* ⟪F.⟫ ⟪not placed before *n.*⟫ too many; not wanted; unwelcome; in the way. 너무 많은; 불필요한; 방해되는. ¶ *It was warm and an overcoat was ~.* 날씨가 따뜻해서 외투가 필요 없었다.

deuce[1] [djuːs] *n.* Ⓒ **1** a card or the side of a die having two spots. (카드패·주사위의) 2점. ¶ *the ~ of hearts* 하트의 2. **2** ⟪tennis⟫ a tie score of 40-40. 듀스. [L. *duo* two]

deuce[2] [djuːs] *n.* ⟪*the ~*⟫ ⟪*colloq.*⟫ bad luck; devil. 불운; 재난; 악마. ¶ *the ~ and all* 모조리; 일체; 무엇 하나 변변한 것이 (없다) / *The ~ it is!* (이거) 놀랍군; (그렇다니) 괘씸하군 / *The ~!* 염병할; 젠장 / *The ~ take it!* 빌어먹을; 아뿔싸 / *What* [*Who*] *the ~ is that?* 도대체 그건 뭐[누구]야 / *Where in the ~ is she?* 대체 그 여자는 어디 있는 건가. [↑, *two at dice* =the lowest]

Deuce knows! God knows! 아무도 모른다.

go to the deuce, **a**) be ruined; degenerate. 파멸하다; 타락하다. **b**) ⟪*imperative*⟫ be off. 꺼져라.

like the deuce, vehemently; vigorously. 맹렬히; 무서운 기세로.

play the deuce (***with***), cause great trouble (to); spoil. 큰 재난이 되다; 망치다. ¶ *The weather played the ~ with our plans.* 날씨가 우리 계획을 망쳤다.

(***the***) ***deuce a bit,*** not at all. 조금도 …아니다[않다].

the deuce a man, no one. 단 한 사람도 (…않다).

the deuce of a, ⟪meaningless words used to give force to a saying⟫ very many; very much. 많은; 엄청난. ¶ *I have the ~ of a lot work to do.* 실로 많은 일이 있다.

the deuce to pay, trouble to be expected. 예기되는 좋지 않은 결과; 뒤탈. ¶ *There will be the ~ to pay.* 뒤탈이 두렵다.

deuc·ed [djúːsid / djuːst] *adj., adv.* ⟪chiefly Brit. *colloq.*⟫ like the devil; confounded(ly); extreme(ly). 지긋지긋한[하게]; 엄청난[나게]; 지독한[히]. [→deuce[2]]

de·us ex ma·chi·na [díːəs eks mǽkinə] *n.* ⟪L.⟫ the power that comes in the nick of time. 절박한 때 초자연적 개입으로 해결하는 신의 힘.

Deu·ter·on·o·my [djùːtərɑ́nəmi / -rɔ́n-] *n.* ⟪Bible⟫ the fifth book of the Old Testament. 신명기(申命記)⟪구약성서 중의 하나⟫.

de·val·u·ate [diːvǽljuèit] *vt.* (P6) **1** lessen the value of (something). …의 가치를 낮추다[떨어뜨리다]. **2** ⟪econ.⟫ lower the exchange value of (a currency). (통화의) 평가를 절하하다. ¶ *~ the dollar.* [de-, → value]

de·val·u·a·tion [dìːvæljuéiʃən] *n.* Ⓤ the act of devaluating; the state of being devaluated. (가치·지위·신분의) 저하; 평가 절하.

dev·as·tate [dévəstèit] *vt.* (P6) lay waste; destroy. …을 황폐시키다; 파괴시키다. ¶ *a town devastated by war* 전쟁으로 황폐된 도시. [→vast]

dev·as·tat·ing [dévəstèitiŋ] *adj.* **1** causing devastation. 황폐시키는; 파괴적인. **2** ⟪*colloq.*⟫ very bad; ironic. 신랄한; 통렬한.

dev·as·ta·tion [dèvəstéiʃən] *n.* ⓊⒸ destruction; desolation. 파괴; 황폐.

:de·vel·op [divéləp] *vt.* **1** (P6,13) cause to grow; make (something) larger or better; strengthen. …을 발육시키다; 발달[발전, 신장]시키다. 강하게 하다. ¶ *~ one's health* 건

강을 증진하다 / ~ *one's muscles* 근육을 발달시키다 / ~ *one's business* 사업을 발전시키다 / ~ *one's faculties* 능력을 개발하다 / ~ *natural resources* 천연 자원을 개발하다 / ~ *the mind* 정신을 도야하다 / ~ *a mine* 광산을 개발하다. **2** (P6) work out (something) in greater detail; explain (treat) more fully. (의론·사색 따위)를 상세히 설명하다 (밝히다); 전개하다. ¶ ~ *a theory* 이론을 전개하다 / *I will ~ these answers in turn.* 순서를 따라 답(答)을 전개해 나가도록 하지요. **3** (P6) 《photog.》 treat (a film) with chemicals to bring out a picture. …을 현상(現像)하다. ¶ ~ *a film* (*plate*) 필름(원판)을 현상하다.

— *vi.* (P1,2A,3) grow up; become larger, better, or more complete. 발육하다; 발전(발달)하다; 전개되다; 발육(발전)해서 …이 되다. ¶ *Blossoms ~ from buds.* 봉오리에서 꽃이 된다 / *Seeds ~ into plants.* 씨가 자라서 식물이 된다 / *The story gradually developed in his mind.* 이야기의 줄거리가 점차 그의 머릿속에 전개돼 왔다. [F.]

de·vel·op·er [divéləpər] *n.* Ⓒ **1** a person or thing that develops. 개발자; 개발하는 것. **2** 《photog.》 a chemical used to make a picture visible on a film, plate, print, etc. 현상액(약).

developing country [–⌐–––⌐–] *n.* a not fully industrialized country. 발전 도상국.

:de·vel·op·ment [divéləpmənt] *n.* **1** Ⓤ the act of developing; growth; evolution. 발육; 성장; 발달; 발전; 진전. ¶ *achieve a remarkable ~* 눈부신 발달을 이루다 / *watch the ~ of the situation* 사태의 진전을 지켜보다. **2** ⓊⒸ a stage of advancement; an outcome; a result. 개발; 발달(발전)의 단계; (발전·발달의) 결과; 소산. ¶ *the latest medical developments* 최근의 의학의 진보 / *modern developments in aviation* 현대에 있어서의 항공술 발달의 소산. **3** Ⓤ 《photog.》 the act of developing a picture. (사진의) 현상(現像).

de·vi·ate [dí:vièit] *vi.* (P3) 《*from*》 turn aside from something. 벗어나다; 빗나가다; 일탈하다. ¶ ~ *to the left* 왼쪽으로 벗어나다 / ~ *from the norm* (*right way*) 상궤를 (바른 길에서) 벗어나다 / ~ *from the truth* (*the rules of grammar*) 진실(문법 규칙)에서 벗어나다. — *vt.* (P6) cause to turn aside. (옆으로) 벗어(비켜)나게 하다; 일탈시키다.

● **de·vi·a·tor** [-ər] *n.* [→via]

de·vi·a·tion [dì:viéiʃən] *n.* ⓊⒸ the act of deviating; the act of turning aside. 벗어남; 빗나감; 일탈; 쏠림; 편차. ¶ *standard ~* 표준편차 / *a ~ from the rules* 규칙에서 벗어남.

● **dev·i·a·tor** [dí:vièitər] *n.*

de·vi·a·tion·ism [dì:viéiʃənìzəm] *n.* Ⓤ a deviationist's doctrine. 당(黨) 노선으로부터의 일탈.

de·vi·a·tion·ist [dì:viéiʃənist] *n.* Ⓒ a person who deviates; a person who deviates from the principles of a political party, esp. from Communism. 일탈자; 당, 특히 공산당 노선으로부터의 일탈자.

:de·vice [diváis] *n.* Ⓒ **1** a plan; a design; a scheme. 계획; 안(案); 고안. ¶ *through a legal ~* 합법적 수단으로 / *hit upon a simple ~* 간단한 계획을 생각해 내다. **2** 《often *pl.*》 a trick. 책략; 계책; 간계. ¶ *the devices of the devil* 악마의 간계 / *By some ~ the thief got the boy to let him into the house.* 그 아이를 간계로 속여 도둑은 집 안으로 들어가는 데 성공했다. **3** a mechanical invention for a special purpose; a machine; an apparatus. 발명품; 고안물; (기계적) 장치. ¶ *a safety ~* 안전 장치 / *an electronic ~* 전산 장치 / *a ~ for catching flies* 파리 잡는 장치. **4** an ornamental picture or design; words used for this purpose. 도안; 의장(意匠); 제명(題銘). **5** a trade mark. 상표. [→devise]

leave someone to his own devices, let someone do as he wishes; give him no help. (조언도 원조도 주지 않고) 아무가 제멋(마음)대로 하게 내버려 두다.

:dev·il [dévl] *n.* Ⓒ **1** a wicked spirit; a demon; 《*the D-*》 Satan. 악마; 악귀; 마왕(魔王). ¶ 《*prov.*》 *Talk of the ~, and he is sure to appear.* 호랑이도 제 말하면 온다. **2** a wicked or cruel person. (악마와 같은) 극악인; 음흉한 사람; 잔혹한 사람. ¶ *a hideous ~* 머리끝이 쭈뼛해지는 놈 / *A boy is no ~, whatever boys may be.* 아이라는 것은 어떤 아이든 결코 악인이 아니다. **3** ⓐ an unfortunate or pitiful person. 불행(불운)한 사람; 가엾은(비참한) 사람. ¶ *a poor ~* 불쌍한 녀석. ⓑ a person who is esp. clever, active, etc. 영리한 사람; 활기찬 사람; 민완가. ¶ *a clever ~* 영리한 녀석 / *a ~ of a fellow* 활기찬(위세 좋은) 사나이; 굉장한 녀석. **4** a person who holds a subordinate(=less important) position in business. 조수; 보조원; (어린) 견습공. ¶ *a printer's ~* 인쇄소의 말단 견습공. **5** 《*the ~*》 《*colloq.*》 《used in exclamations, expressing *disgust, anger, hatred, surprise,* etc.》 the deuce. 빌어먹을; 도대체. ¶ *The ~ he did!* 그가 그 짓을 했다고 《있을 수 없다》 / *What* (*Who, Where, How, Why*) *the ~ …?* 도대체 무엇이 (누가, 어디서, 어떻게, 왜) … / *What the ~ is he doing?* 도대체 그 녀석 무엇을 하고 있는거야.

a (***the***) ***devil of a ...,*** hellish; damned; extremely. 싫은; 지겨운; 지독한; 귀찮은; 엄청나게. ¶ *a ~ of a noise* 몹시 성가실 정도의 소음 / *a ~ of a lot of money* 엄청난 대금 / *He is a ~ of a boy.* 정말이지 지겨운 아이다 / *I had a ~ of time trying to solve the problem last night.* 간밤엔 문제를 풀고자 지겨운 시간을 보냈다.

between the devil and the deep (***blue***) ***sea,*** having two choices, both of which are bad; in a very difficult position. 진퇴유곡에 빠져.

devil a bit, at all 결코〔조금도〕 …아니다〔않다〕.
devil a one, not one at all. 하나도 (…않다〔없다〕).
devil's darning-needle, a dragonfly. 잠자리.
Devil take it! Hang it! 제기랄; 염병할.
give the devil his due, be fair even to a bad or disliked person. (미운 녀석에 대해서도) 공평히 대해 주다; 좋은 점은 인정해 주다.
go to the devil, **a**) be ruined. 완전히 실패하다; 파멸하다. **b**) become depraved. 타락하다. **c**) 《as *imperative*》 Be off! Go to hell! 뒈져라.
like the devil, with great energy, etc. 맹렬히; 필사적으로. ¶ *He worked like the* ~. 그는 맹렬히 일했다.
paint the devil blacker than he is, exaggerate one's sinful deeds. …을 과장해서 나쁘게 말하다.
play the devil with, 《*colloq.*》 do much harm to (something); ruin; upset. …을 철저히 파괴하다; 엉망으로 만들다.
raise the devil, 《*colloq.*》 **a**) make a great disturbance. 대소동을 일으키다. **b**) make an emphatic protest; take drastic measures. 강경하게 항의하다; 강경 수단을 취하다.
the devil among the tailors, **a**) a free fight. 큰 싸움. **b**) a kind of firework. 불꽃놀이의 일종.
the devil and all, everything bad. 무엇이든 모조리; 좋은 것 나쁜 것 할 것 없이 몽땅; 무엇 하나 변변한 것이 (없다).
the devil to pay, much trouble ahead. 앞길의 어려움〔고난〕; 기다리고 있는 재난.
— *v.* (**-iled, -il·ing** or 《Brit.》 **-illed, -il·ling**) *vt.* (P6) cook (food) with strong and hot condiments. (음식)을 맵게 조리하다. ¶ *deviled chicken* 맵게 한 닭고기. — *vi.* (P3) do subordinate work for another. (인쇄소·변호사 등의) 조수를〔보조역을〕 하다. ¶ ~ *for a barrister* 법정 변호사의 보조를 하다. [Gk. *diabolos* planderer]

dev·il·fish [dévlfìʃ] *n.* Ⓒ (*pl.* **-fish·es** or *collectively* **-fish**) **1** a giant ray. 쥐가오리. **2** an octopus. 낙지.

dev·il·ish [dévliʃ] *adj.* **1** like a devil; very cruel. 악마 같은; 극악한. **2** 《*colloq.*》 extreme. 심한; 극도의. — *adv.* 《*colloq.*》 excessively; extremely. 몹시; 극단으로. ¶ ~ *cold* 지독히 추운.

dev·il-may-care [dévlmeikέər] *adj.* careless; reckless. 저돌적인; 무모한; 돈단 무심(頓斷無心)의; 무책임한.

dev·il·ment [dévlmənt] *n.* **1** a devilish action; devilish behavior. 악마적인 소행; 악행. **2** mischief. 못된 장난.

dev·il·ry [dévlri] *n.* ⓊⒸ **1** devilish art. 요술; 마법. **2** cruel behavior; extreme wickedness. 악행; 극악 무도(한 짓). **3** devils in general. 악마.

de·vi·ous [díːviəs] *adj.* **1** winding; round-about; indirect. 꾸불꾸불한; 멀리 돌아가는; 에도는. ¶ *take a* ~ *course* 우회로를 취하다. **2** (of thought, conduct, etc.) straying from the proper course; not straightforward; dishonest. 정도를 벗어난; 솔직〔정직〕하지 못한. ¶ *a man of* ~ *nature* 정직하지 못한 사람 / *He got his wealth by* ~ *means.* 부정한 수단으로 재산을 얻었다.
●**de·vi·ous·ness** [-nis] *n.* [→via]

*__de·vise__ [diváiz] *vt.* (P6) **1** think out; plan; invent. …을 고안〔안출〕하다; 발명하다. ¶ ~ *an engine* 엔진을 고안하다 / ~ *a plan of attack* 공격 계획을 마련하다 / ~ *a means of escape* 도망 방법을 안출하다. **2** 《law》 give or leave (something) by a will. (부동산 따위)를 유증(遺贈)하다. — *n.* 《law》 **1** Ⓤ a gift or real property left by a will. 유증(遺贈). **2** Ⓒ a will or part of a will doing this. 유언서 (조항). [→divide]

de·vi·see [diváizíː, dèvəzíː] *n.* a person to whom property is given by a will. 수증자(受贈者).

de·vis·er [diváizər] *n.* one who devises. 고안자; 안출자.

de·vi·sor [diváizər] *n.* 《law》 a person by whom property is given a will. (특히 부동산의) 유증자(遺贈者).

de·vi·tal·ize [diːváitəlàiz] *vt.* (P6) **1** take the life of (something); kill. …을 죽이다. **2** make (someone) less vital. …에게서 활력을 빼앗다; 무기력하게 하다; 약화시키다. [*vital*]

de·vo·cal·ize [diːvóukəlàiz] *vt.* (P6) utter without vibrating the vocal cords. (유성음을) 무성음화하다. [de-, →vocal]

de·void [divɔ́id] *adj.* 《*of*》 lacking; completely without. …이 없는; …이 결여된. ¶ *be* ~ *of courage* 용기가 없다 / *He is* ~ *of taste.* 그는 취미가 없다 / *He is* ~ *of common sense.* 그는 상식이 없다. 語法 명사 앞에는 쓰이지 않음. [→void]

de·voir [dévwɑːr] *n.* 《F.》 《*arch.*》 **1** duty; service. 의무; 본분; 책무. ¶ *do one's* ~ 본분을 다하다. **2** 《*pl.*》 acts of respect; polite attentions. 공손한〔예의 바른〕 행위; 경의의 표현. ¶ *pay* 〔*show*〕 *one's devoirs to a person* (예방하여) 아무에게 경의를 표하다. [→debt]

dev·o·lu·tion [dèvəlúːʃən / dìːv-] *n.* ⓊⒸ the act of devolving. (단계적) 이행(移行); 변화; 이양(移讓); 양도; 상속. [↓]

de·volve [diválv / -vɔ́lv] *vt.* (P13) 《*on, upon, to*》 (of functions, duties, etc.) transfer. …을 맡기다〔위임하다〕; 이양(移讓)하다. ¶ ~ *a duty upon a representative* 임무를 대표자에게 위임하다 / ~ *work upon* 〔*on*〕 *an assistant* 일을 조수에게 맡기다. — *vi.* (P3) 《*on, upon*》 be passed to someone else; be handed down. 이전(移轉)되다; 돌아가다; 귀속하다; 상속〔계승〕되다. ¶ *It devolved upon me to....* 내가 …하기로 되었다 / *After his death the work devolved upon me.* 그가 죽은 후에 그 일은 내가 맡게 되었다. [→voluble]

:de·vote [divóut] *vt.* (P13) 《*to*》 give (oneself) completely to something or someone. …을 바치다; 전념[몰두]시키다; 집중하다. ¶ *~ oneself to art* 예술에 몰두하다 / *~ much time to study* 연구에 많은 시간을 바치다 / *~ one's life to working among the poor* 가난한 사람들 속에서 일하는 것에 일생을 바치다 / *be deeply devoted to each other* 서로 깊이 사랑하고 있다. [→vow]

de·vot·ed [divóutid] *adj.* loyal; faithful; very loving; deeply attached to someone. 헌신적인; 충실한; 몹시 사랑하는. ¶ *a ~ wife* 헌신적인 아내 / *She seems very ~.* 그녀는 남편과 아이들에게 매우 헌신적인 것 같다 / *She is ~ to her children.* 그녀는 자식들을 끔찍이 사랑한다.

de·vot·ed·ly [divóutidli] *adv.* in a devoted manner; loyally; faithfully. 헌신적으로; 충실히; 애정 깊이.

dev·o·tee [dèvoutíː] *n.* Ⓒ **1** a person deeply devoted to something; an enthusiastic fan or supporter. 열중하는 사람; 심취자; 애호자; 팬. ¶ *a ~ to pursuit* 일에 열심인 사람 / *a ~ of* [*to*] *Napoleon* 나폴레옹 심취자. **2** a person deeply devoted to religion. (광신적인) 종교 신자. ¶ *a ~ of religion.*

de·vo·tion [divóuʃən] *n.* Ⓤ **1** deep, strong love; loyalty; faithfulness. 깊은 애정; 헌신; 충실. ¶ *the ~ of a mother to her child* 아이에게 끌리는 강한 어머니의 애정 / *one's ~ to the cause of justice* 정의 수호를 위한 헌신. **2** the act of devoting; the state of being devoted. 애착; 열중; 열심; 전념. ¶ *~ to one's study* 연구에의 몰두 / *one's ~ to tennis* 테니스에 대한 애착. **3** religious worship. 신앙. **4** 《*pl.*》 religious observances; prayers. 기도; 예배.

de·vo·tion·al [divóuʃənəl] *adj.* characterized by devotion; having to do with worship. 신앙심이 두터운; 경건한; 예배의; 기도의. ¶ *a ~ life* 신앙 생활. ● **de·vo·tion·al·ly** [-li] *adv.*

:de·vour [diváuər] *vt.* (P6) **1** eat (something) greedily or hungrily. 게걸스럽게 먹다; 걸신들린 듯이 먹다. ¶ *The lion devoured its prey.* 사자는 잡은 먹이를 게걸스럽게 먹었다 / *The hungry boy devoured everything on his plate.* 굶주린 소년은 접시의 모든 음식을 걸신들린 듯이 먹어 치웠다. **2** (of fire, etc.) lay waste; destroy; swallow up. (불이) 다 태워 버리다; 황폐시키다; 파괴[파멸]시키다; 삼키다. ¶ *Fire devoured the old museum.* 불이 오래 된 박물관을 다 태워 버렸다. **3** 《*fig.*》 take in (something) greedily with the eyes or ears. 탐하듯이 보다; 넋을 잃고 듣다. ¶ *~ new book* 신간서(書)를 탐하듯이 읽다 / *His eyes devoured the scene.* 그의 눈이 빨려들 듯이 그 광경을 보고 있었다. **4** (of strong emotion) absorb (something) wholly; move deeply. (호기심·걱정 따위가) 주의를 빼앗다; 압도하다; 열중하다. ¶ *devoured by anxiety* 걱정에 휩싸인 / *be devoured with curiosity* 호기심에 사로잡히다. [→voracious]

de·vour·ing·ly [diváuəriŋli] *adv.* as if devouring; with great longing. 탐하듯이; 넋을 잃고. ¶ *gaze ~ at a picture* 그림을 넋을 잃고 보다.

de·vout [diváut] *adj.* **1** very religious; pious. 신앙심(心)이 깊은; 경건한. ¶ *a ~ Catholic* 신앙심이 깊은 카톨릭 교도 / *~ prayer* 경건한 기도. **2** earnest; sincere; hearty. 열심인; 진지한; 성실한; 진심으로의. ¶ *a ~ admirer* 열심인 숭배자 / *my ~ wishes for your happiness* 당신의 행복을 비는 나의 진정한 바람. [→devote]

de·vout·ly [diváutli] *adv.* in a devout manner. 신심 깊게; 경건하게; 진지[성실]하게; 열심히; 진심으로. ¶ *I ~ hope….* …하시기를 진심으로 바랍니다.

:dew [djuː] *n.* ⓊⒸ **1** the moisture from the air that condenses and appears in small drops on cool surfaces during the night. 이슬. ¶ *the morning ~* 아침 이슬. **2** any moisture in small drops. 물방울. ¶ *the ~ of sweat* [*tears*] 땀[눈물]방울 / *the ~ of one's labor* 노동의 땀방울. **3** 《*poet.*》 anything regarded as refreshing like dew. 상쾌함[한 것]. ¶ *the ~ of youth* 청춘의 싱그러움 / *the golden ~ of sleep* 상쾌한 숙면. — *vt., vi.* (P6;2A) wet with dew; fall as dew. …을 이슬로 적시다; 이슬처럼 내리다. ¶ *dewed with blood* 피로 젖은 / *It will ~ tonight.* 오늘밤 이슬이 내릴 게다. [E.]

dew·ber·ry [djúːbèri] *n.* 《bot.》 a kind of blackberry. 나무딸기의 일종.

dew·drop [djúːdràp / -drɔ̀p] *n.* Ⓒ a small drop of dew. 이슬 (방울).

dew·fall [djúːfɔ̀ːl] *n.* **1** ⓊⒸ the formation of dew. 이슬이 맺힘; 결로(結露). **2** Ⓤ the time at which dew begins to form. 이슬이 내릴 시각; 저녁때.

dew·lap [djúːlæ̀p] *n.* the fold of loose skin under the throat of cattle. (소 따위의) 목정.

dew point [ˊ ˋ] *n.* 《phys.》 the temperature of the air at which dew begins to form. (습도의) 이슬점.

·dew·y [djúːi] *adj.* (**dew·i·er, dew·i·est**) **1** covered with dew; wet with dew. 이슬로 덮인; 이슬에 젖은. ¶ *~ grass* 이슬에 젖은 풀 / *on a ~ morning* 이슬이 내린 아침에. **2** ⓐ like dew; refreshing. 이슬 같은; 상쾌한; 신선한. ¶ *~ tears* 이슬 같은 눈물 / *a ~ maiden* 이슬처럼 청순한 아가씨 / *a ~ sleep* 상쾌한 잠. ⓑ 《*poet.*》 looking as if wet with dew; wet with tears. 이슬에 젖은 것 같은; 눈물에 젖은. ¶ *~ eyes* 촉촉이 젖은 눈. [E.]

dex·ter·i·ty [dekstérəti] *n.* Ⓤ **1** skill, esp. in handling something; cleverness. (손끝·몸놀림 따위의) 기민함; 재치; 민첩; 빈틈없음. ¶ *manual ~* 손끝의 야무짐 / *the ~ at sword and pistol* 검과 권총을 다루는 솜씨의

민첩함. **2** the habitual use of the right hand in preference to the left. 오른손잡이. [↓]

with dexterity, dexterously; skillfully. 야무지게; 교묘하게. ¶ *He handled the airplane with great* ~. 그는 아주 교묘히 비행기를 조종했다.

dex·ter·ous [dékstərəs] *adj.* **1** skillful in using one's hands. 솜씨가 좋은; 교묘한. ¶ *a* ~ *use of tools* 도구의 능숙한 사용 / *be* ~ *at driving a car* 자동차 운전을 잘한다 / *A typist must be* ~. 타자수는 솜씨가 능숙해야 한다. **2** having skill with the mind; clever. 재기(才氣) 넘치는; 기민한; 빈틈없는. ¶ *A manager should be* ~ *in handling men.* 지배인은 사람 다루는 데 빈틈이 없어야 한다. **3** using the right hand in preference to the left. 오른손을 잘 쓰는. [L. =right]

dex·ter·ous·ly [dékstərəsli] *adv.* **1** skillfully. 솜씨 있게; 능숙[교묘]하게. **2** cleverly. 빈틈없이; 민첩하게.

dex·tral [dékstrəl] *adj.* right; right-handed. 오른쪽의; 오른손잡이의.

dex·trose [dékstrous] *n.* 《chem.》 a sugar less sweet than cane sugar. 우선당(右旋糖); 포도당.

dex·trous [dékstrəs] *adj.* =dexterous.

dex·trous·ly [dékstrəsli] *adv.* =dexterously.

DF, D/F direction finder. 방향 탐지기.

dhar·ma [dá:rmə, dɔ́:r-] *n.* the essential quality of the cosmos; the ultimate law. (우주·성격 따위의) 본체; 본성; 법(法); 덕(德). [Sans.]

dho·ti [dóuti] *n.* a Hindoo loincloth. 도티《힌두 남자의 허리천》. [Hind.]

dhow [dau] *n.* any of various types of two- or three-masted sailing vessels, used by Arabs on the coasts of Africa, Arabia, and India. 다우 범선(帆船)《아랍인이 아프리카·아라비아·인도 연해를 항해하는 두 대 또는 세 대박이 돛배》. [Arab.]

di- [dai-] *pref.* **1** two. [Gk. *dis* twice] **2** through; across. **3** =dis-.

di·a- [dáiə-] *pref.* =di- 2. [Gk. *dia* through]

di·a·be·tes [dàiəbí:tis, -ti:z] *n.* Ⓤ 《med.》 a disease in which there is an excessive amount of sugar in the urine. 당뇨병. [Gk. *baino* go]

di·a·bet·ic [dàiəbétik] *adj.* of or having to do with diabetes. 당뇨병의[에 걸린]. — *n.* Ⓒ a person suffering from diabetes. 당뇨병 환자. [↑]

di·a·bol·ic [dàiəbálik / -bɔ́l-], **-i·cal** [-ikəl] *adj.* like the devil; devilish; very cruel. 악마 같은; 극악무도한; 잔혹한. ¶ *a* ~ *plot* 극악무도한 책략[음모]. [→devil] 「무도.

diabolical cruelty, extreme wickedness. 극악

di·a·bol·i·cal·ly [dàiəbálikəli / -bɔ́l-] *adv.* in a diabolical manner; devilishly; cruelly. 악마같이; 극악무도하게; 잔혹하게.

di·ab·o·lism [daiǽbəlìzəm] *n.* **1** the worship of the devil or of demons. 악마 숭배; 악마주의. **2** qualities, a nature, or action, like that of the devil. 마성(魔性); 악마 같은 짓. [→devil]

di·ab·o·lo [di:ǽbəlòu] *n.* a kind of top sent up in the air from a string attached to two sticks; a game played with it. 디아볼로; 공중 팽이《손에 든 두 개의 막대 사이에 켕긴 실 위에서 돌리는 팽이; 그 놀이》.

di·a·chron·ic [dàiəkránik / -krɔ́n-] *adj.* 《ling.》 of the diachronic linguistics. 통시적(通時的)인. [*dia-, chronic*]

diachronic linguistics, historical linguistics. 통시 언어학.

di·ac·o·nal [daiǽkənəl] *adj.* belonging to a deacon. 부제(副祭)[집사]의. [→deacon]

di·a·crit·ic [dàiəkrítik] *n.* a diacritical mark. 발음 구별 기호; 분음(分音) 표시 기호. — *adj.* =diacritical. [↓]

di·a·crit·i·cal [dàiəkrítikəl] *adj.* used to distinguish. 구분에 사용[도움]되는; 판별적인. ¶ ~ *marks* (문자상(文字上)의) 발음[구분] 표시 기호《(˘)(ˆ)(´)(¨)(umlaut) 따위》 / ~ *elements in culture* 문화의 판별적 요소. [→crisis]

di·a·dem [dáiədèm] *n.* **1** Ⓒ a crown; a headband of cloth. 왕관; 환상(環狀)의 머리띠. **2** Ⓤ 《*fig.*》 royal power. 왕위; 왕권. [Gk. *deō* bind]

di·a·demed [dáiədèmd] *adj.* wearing a diadem; crowned. 왕관을 쓴; 왕권을 부여한.

di·aer·e·sis [daiérəsis] *n.* (*pl.* **-ses** [-si:z]) a mark, generally two dots, placed on the second of two consecutive vowels, to show that it forms a separate syllable from the first. 음절(音節)의 분음(分音) 기호 (e.g. coöperate). [Gk. separation]

di·ag·nose [dáiəgnòus, ⌐-⌐] *vt.* (P6,7) 《*as*》 find out the nature of (something) by an examination. …을 진단하다. ¶ *The doctor diagnosed her illness as diabetes mellitus.* 의사는 그녀의 병을 진성 당뇨병으로 진단했다. 參考 항상 병을 목적어로 하며, diagnose he as…로 함은 잘못임. [→gnome]

di·ag·no·ses [dàiəgnóusi:z] *n.* pl. of **diagnosis.**

di·ag·no·sis [dàiəgnóusis] *n.* ⒸⓊ (*pl.* **-ses**) 《med.》 the act of diagnosing. 진단; 진찰. ¶ *make a* ~ *on* [*upon*] *the case of* …환자의 진찰을 하다 / *form a correct* ~ *on* [*upon*] *a disease* 병에 관해 정확한 진단을 내리다 / *mistake in* ~ 오진(誤診)하다. [↑]

di·ag·nos·tic [dàiəgnástik / -nɔ́s-] *adj.* of or used in a diagnosis. 진찰의; 진단의[에 도움이 되는]. — *n.* **1** a symptom. 증후; 징후. **2** 《*pl.*》 the art of diagnosing. 진단학; 진단술.

di·ag·nos·ti·cian [dàiəgnastíʃən / -nɔs-] *n.* an expert at diagnosis. 진단 전문의(醫); 진단의 명의.

di·ag·o·nal [daiǽgənəl] *n.* Ⓒ a straight

line cutting across in a slanting direction. 대각선. — *adj.* **1** taking the direction of a diagonal. 대각선의. ¶ *a ~ line* 대각선. **2** ⓐ going from corner to corner; oblique. 비스듬한. ¶ *a ship sailing on a ~ course* 비스듬한 항로로 항해하는 배. ⓑ crossed by oblique lines. 사선(斜線)이 있는; 사능직(斜綾織)의. ¶ *~ cloth* 능직. [Gk. *gōnia* angle]

di·ag·o·nal·ly [daiǽgənəli] *adv.* in a diagonal direction. 대각선으로; 비스듬히.

di·a·gram [dáiəgræ̀m] *n.* Ⓒ a drawing or sketch showing the important parts of something. 도형(圖形); 도표; 도식; 설계도; 약도. ¶ *a ~ of an engine* 엔진의 설계도 / *He drew a ~ to show me how to get to the post office.* 그는 우체국으로 가는 길을 내게 가르쳐 주기 위해 약도(略圖)를 그렸다. — *vt.* (**-gramed, -gram·ing** or 《Brit.》 **-grammed, -gram·ming**) (P6) make a diagram of (something); show (something) by a diagram. …을 도해하다; 도표를 만들다; 도시하다. [→grammar]

di·a·gram·mat·ic [dàiəgrəmǽtik] *adj.* of or like a diagram; in outline only. 도형의; 도표〔도식·도면〕의; 선도(線圖)의.

di·a·gram·ma·tize [dàiəgrǽmətàiz] *vt.* (P6) make a diagram of. 도형으로 하다; 도표로 만들다.

di·al [dáiəl] *n.* Ⓒ **1** a clocklike face on which an indicator shows the amount of something. (계기류의) 지침면(指針面); 문자반; 눈금판. ¶ *the ~ on a gas meter* 가스 계량기의 계기판. **2** a plate, disk, etc., on a radio or television set for locating stations; such a plate on an automatic telephone with numbers, letters, etc. (라디오·TV·자동식 전화의) 다이얼; 숫자판. **3** a sundial. 해시계. — *vt.* (**-aled, -al·ing** or 《Brit.》 **-alled, -al·ling**) (P6) **1** tune in (a radio station, program, etc.) by using a radio dial. (라디오·TV를) …에 다이얼을 맞추다. **2** call (someone) by means of a telephone dial. (다이얼을 돌려) …에게 전화를 걸다. ¶ *~ the fire station* 전화로 소방서를 부르다 / *~ 02 for long distance to Seoul* 서울로의 장거리 전화를 위해 다이얼 02를 돌리다. [L. *dies* day]

dial. dialect, dialectal.

di·a·lect [dáiəlèkt] *n.* ⒸⓊ **1** a form of speech used in a fairly definite region of a country. 방언; 사투리. ¶ *Scottish ~* 스코틀랜드 방언 / *the various dialects spoken in North Korea* 북한에서 사용되는 여러 사투리. **2** words or pronunciations of certain professions or classes of people. (어떤 직업·계층의) 통용어; 전용어(專用語); 변말. ¶ *a literary ~* 문학 용어 / *the sporting* 〔*lawyer's*〕 *~* 스포츠〔법률〕 용어 / *the Negro ~* 흑인 특유의 통용어. [Gk. *legō* speak]

di·a·lec·tal [dàiəléktl] *adj.* of a dialect. 방언의; 통용어의.

di·a·lec·tic [dàiəléktik], **-ti·cal** [-tikəl] *n.* Ⓒ 《philos.》 **1** the art or practice of logical discussion to find out the truth of a theory or opinion. 변증법. **2** 《often *pl.*》 a discussion of the logical truth of an opinion or theory. 논리 토론; 논증. — *adj.* **1** of logical discussion. 변증(법)적인. **2** =dialectal. [Gk. *dia-* between, *legō* speak]

di·a·lec·ti·cian [dàiəlektíʃən] *n.* a person skilled in dialectics. 변증가; 변증법론자.

·di·a·logue, 《U.S.》 **-log** [dáiəlɔ̀ːg, -lɑ̀g / -lɔ̀g] *n.* **1** Ⓒ ⓐ a conversation or talk. 회화; 대화; 대담. ⓑ an exchange of ideas and opinions. 의견의 교환; 토론. ¶ *carry on a ~ upon the university reform* 대학 개혁에 관해서 토론〔논의〕하다. **2** Ⓒ a written work in the form of a conversation. 대화체 작품. **3** ⓊⒸ a conversation in a play, story, etc. (극·소설 따위의) 대화; 대화의 부분. ¶ *The ~ in this novel is poor.* 이 소설 속의 대화 부분은 엉성하다. [→dialect]

di·al·y·ses [daiǽləsìːz] *n.* pl. of **dialysis.**

di·al·y·sis [daiǽləsis] *n.* (*pl.* **-ses**) 《chem.》 the separating of solutions by means of their unequal diffusion through moist membranes. 투석(透析). [Gk. *diálusis* separation]

di·a·mag·net·ic [dàiəmægnétik] *adj.* 《phys.》 being repelled by both poles of a magnet and hence tending to lie at right angles to the poles. 반자성(反磁性)적인; 역(逆)자기의. [→dia, magnetic]

·di·am·e·ter [daiǽmitər] *n.* ⒸⓊ a straight line passing through the center of a circle; the length of such a line. 직경; 지름. ¶ *the ~ of a tree trunk* 나무 줄기의 지름 / *5 feet in ~* 직경 5피트. [→meter]

di·am·e·tral [daiǽmətrəl] *adj.* of a diameter. 직경의; 지름의.

di·a·met·ric [dàiəmétrik], **-ri·cal** [-əl] *adj.* **1** of or along a diameter. 직경〔지름〕의. **2** exactly opposite. 정반대의.

di·a·met·ri·cal·ly [dàiəmétrikəli] *adv.* **1** in a diametric direction. 직경의 방향으로. **2** directly opposite. 정반대로. **3** entirely. 완전히; 아주. ¶ *~ opposed views* 정반대의 견해 / *He is ~ opposed* 〔*opposite*〕 *to your opinion.* 그는 너의 의견과 정반대이다.

:di·a·mond [dáiəmənd] *n.* Ⓒ **1** a brilliant precious stone formed in crystals of nearly pure carbon, of great value and hardness. 다이아몬드; 금강석(金剛石). ¶ *a ~ field* 다이아몬드 산지 / *a ~ of the first water* 최상급의 다이아몬드; 일류의 인물. **2** a figure shaped like this. 다이아몬드형(形); 마름모꼴(◇). **3** a playing card with this figure; 《*pl.*》 the suit of playing cards with this figure. (카드의) 다이아; 다이아몬드 패 한 조(組). **4** 《baseball》 the infield; the whole playing field. (야구의) 내야(內野); 야구장. **5** a tool with a diamond tip for cutting glass. 유리칼. [→adamant]

diamond cut diamond, two well-matched persons disputing or struggling against each other. (교활함 따위에 있어서) 서로 상대에 못지 않은 맞수; 여우와 너구리의 서로 속이기.

diamond in the rough, **a**) an uncut diamond. 미가공(未加工)의 다듬지 않은 다이아몬드. **b**) 《*fig.*》 a person who is worthy, though having poor manners. 거칠지만 갈고 다듬으면 빛날 사람; 훌륭한 인격이지만 교양·세련됨이 없는 사람.

diamond anniversary [⌐-- --⌐--] *n.* the sixtieth [seventy-fifth] celebration of an event. 제 60[75] 회 기념제.

Diamond Jubilee [⌐-- --⌐], **the** *n.* a sixtieth anniversary. 60주년 기념(식).

Diamond state [⌐--⌐], **the** *n.* Delaware. (미국) 델라웨어 주(州).

diamond wedding [⌐-- ⌐-] *n.* the sixtieth or seventy-fifth anniversary of a wedding. 다이아몬드 혼식(婚式)《결혼 60돌 또는 75돌의 축하 잔치》.

Di·an·a [daiǽnə] *n.* **1** 《Rom. myth.》 the Roman goddess of the hunt and of the moon, worshipped esp. as the protectress of women. 다이아나《달과 사냥의 여신》. 參考 Artemis 참조. **2** Ⓒ a huntress; a lady who hunts. 여자 사냥꾼; 사냥하는 여성. [L.=moon-goddess]

di·an·thus [daiǽnθəs] *n.* 《bot.》 a plant of the genus which includes carnations and pinks. (카네이션을 포함한) 패랭이꽃속(屬)의 식물. [Gk.]

di·a·pa·son [dàiəpéizən, -sən] *n.* Ⓒ 《mus.》 **1** a harmony. 화음. **2** a harmony of many parts. 전(全)협화음. **3** the whole range of a voice or instrument. 전음역(全音域). **4** a fixed standard of musical pitch. 표준 기음(基音). **5** either of two principal stops in an organ. 다이아페이슨 음전(音栓). [Gk.=through all (notes)]

di·a·per [dáiəpər] *n.* **1** Ⓒ 《U.S.》 a small cloth used as a sanitary towel for babies. 기저귀. **2** Ⓤ a pattern of small repeated geometric figures. 마름모꼴 무늬. **3** a white cotton or linen cloth with such a pattern. 마름모꼴 무늬의 린네르[천].

〈diaper 2〉

— *vt.* (P6) **1** put a diaper on. 기저귀를 채우다. **2** ornament (something) with a diaper pattern. …을 마름모꼴 무늬로 장식하다. [dia-, Gk. *aspros* white]

di·aph·a·nous [daiǽfənəs] *adj.* (of cloth, etc.) so fine that it can be seen through; transparent. (천 따위가 얇아서) 속이 내비치는; 투명한. ¶ *a* ~ *fabric* 내비치는 천 / ~ *air* 맑고 상쾌한 공기 / *The water of this lake is highly* ~. 이 호숫물은 매우 맑다. [→phantasm]

di·a·pho·re·sis [dàiəfəríːsis] *n.* 《med.》 copious perspiration, esp. when produced artificially. 발한(發汗); (특히) 인위적인 발한. [Gk. =sweat]

di·a·phragm [dáiəfræ̀m] *n.* Ⓒ **1** 《anat.》 a wall of muscle between the chest and the abdomen. 횡격막(橫隔膜). **2** a partition. 보강 격벽(隔壁); 칸막이판. **3** a vibrating disk in a telephone. (전화기의) 진동판. **4** a device to control the amount of light entering a camera, microscope, etc. (카메라·현미경 등의) 조리개. ● **di·a·phrag·mat·ic** [dàiəfrægmǽtik] *adj.* [Gk. *phrassō* bar]

di·ar·chy [dáiɑːrki] *n.* ⓊⒸ government by two joint rulers. 양두(兩頭) 정치. [di-, →arch]

di·a·rist [dáiərist] *n.* Ⓒ a person who keeps a diary. 일기를 쓰는 사람. [→diary]

di·ar·rhe·a, 《Brit.》 **-rhoe·a** [dàiəríːə] *n.* Ⓤ 《med.》 too frequent and too loose movements of the bowels. 설사. ¶ *have* ~ 설사를 하다. [Gk. *rheō* flow]

:di·a·ry [dáiəri] *n.* Ⓒ (*pl.* **-ries**) a daily record of what one has done or thought about, or of the events during the day; a book for keeping this record. 일기; 일지; 일기장. ¶ *keep a* ~ 일기를 쓰다 / *write down in a* ~ 일기장에 적다. [L. *dies* day]

Di·as·po·ra [daiǽspərə] *n.* **1** the dispersion (=scattering) of the Jews after the Babylonian captivity. 바빌론 유수(幽囚) 후에, 유태 민족이 이산된 일. **2** Jews living outside Palestine. 팔레스타인 이외의 지역에 이산되어 사는 유태인들.

di·a·stase [dáiəstèis] *n.* Ⓤ an organic chemical substance that changes a white, tasteless food substance into sugar. 디아스타아제; 전분 (녹말) 당화 효소(糖化酵素). [Gk. *diastasis* separation]

di·as·to·le [daiǽstəlìː(ː)] *n.* the rhythmical expansion of the cavities of the heart. 심장 확장; 심이완(心弛緩). [Gk. *stellō* send]

di·as·tro·phism [daiǽstrəfìzəm] *n.* 《geol.》 any of the processes through which the earth's crust is deformed. 지각(地殼) 변동. ● **di·a·stroph·ic** [dàiəstrάfik / -strɔ́f-] *adj.* [Gk. *diastrophé* dislocation]

di·a·ther·my [dáiəθə̀ːrmi] *n.* 《med.》 a method of treating diseases by heating the tissues beneath the skin with an electric current. 전기 투열(透熱) 요법《고주파 이용의 온열 요법》. [Gk. *thermoē* heat]

di·ath·e·ses [daiǽθəsìːz] *n.* pl. of **diathesis.**

di·ath·e·sis [daiǽθəsis] *n.* (*pl.* **-ses**) 《med.》 constitutional predisposition. 특이체질; (신체의 병적) 소질. [→thesis]

di·a·tom [dáiətəm] *n.* 《bot.》 a minute one-cell waterplant. 규조류(硅藻類). [→tome]

di·a·ton·ic [dàiətάnik / -tɔ́n-] *adj.* 《mus.》 involving only the tones, intervals or harmonies of a major or minor scale without chromatic alteration. 온음계적인. ¶ *the ~ scale* 온음계. [→tone]

di·a·tribe [dáiətràib] *n.* Ⓒ Ⓤ a bitter and violent attack in words against something or someone. 격렬한 비난; 혹평; 비방. [Gk.=discourse]

dib·ber [díbər] *n.* =dibble.

dib·ble [díbəl] *n.* Ⓒ a small curved, pointed tool for making holes in the ground. (지면에 구멍을 파서 씨나 모종을 심는) 구멍 파는 기구. — *vt.* (P6) plant with a dibble. (구멍을 파서) 식물을 심다. ¶ *~ in potatoes.* [→dab]

dibs [dibz] *n. pl.* 《*colloq.*》 money in small amounts. (소액의) 돈. [?]

dice [dais] *n. pl.* (pl. of **die**²) **1** small cubes with each side marked with from one to six spots. 주사위. ¶ *play at ~* 주사위놀이를 하다; 도박을 하다. **2** a game played with dice. 주사위로 하는 게임; 노름. — *vi.* (P1) play dice. 주사위놀이를 하다; 주사위로 도박을 하다. — *vt.* (P6) **1** cut (something) into small cubes. …을 작은 주사위 모양으로 썰다. ¶ *~ carrots* 당근을 작은 주사위 모양으로 썰다. **2** lose (something) by gambling with dice. 주사위놀이로[노름으로] (돈 따위)를 잃다. ¶ *~ away one's fortune* 노름으로 재산을 날리다. [→die²]

dice·box [dáisbɑ̀ks / -bɔ̀ks] *n.* Ⓒ a box from which dice are thrown. (주사위를 넣어 흔들어 던지는) 주사위통.

di·chot·o·my [daikɑ́təmi / -kɔ́t-] *n.* Ⓤ **1** 《log.》 the act of dividing into two parts. 2분; 양분; 2분법. **2** 《bot.》 branching repeatedly into two parts. 두 갈래 분지(分枝); 대생(對生). [Gk. *dikha* apart, →tome]

dick [dik] *n.* **1** 《*D-*》 a nickname for Richard. Richard의 애칭. **2** 《*sl.*》 a detective. 형사; 탐정. ¶ *a plain-clothes ~* 사복 형사.

***take one's* dick,** swear. 맹세하다. ¶ *I'll take my ~ she is wrong.* 절대로[맹세코] 그녀가 잘못이다.

***up to* dick,** 《*colloq.*》 knowing; excellent. 빈틈없는; 훌륭한.

Dick·ens [díkinz], **Charles** *n.* (1812-70) an English novelist. 디킨스《영국의 소설가》.

dick·ens [díkinz] *n.* Ⓒ **1** devil. 악마. **2** 《*the ~* 》 exclamation expressing surprise. (놀라움·증오 따위를 나타내어) 어렵쇼; 쳇; 빌어먹을. **3** 《*the ~* 》 often used as a mild curse. (도)대체. ¶ *What the ~ is it?* 도대체 뭐야. [*Dick*]

dick·er [díkər] *vi.* (P1) 《U.S.》 **1** trade by barter or on a small scale. 물물 교환하다; 소액 거래를 하다. **2** talk about the price of an article, trying to make it less; bargain. (값을 깎으려고) 흥정하다; 에누리하다. — *n.* Ⓒ **1** the number or quantity ten. 십(十); 10개. **2** a small bargain. 소액 흥정[거래]. [L.]

dick·y¹, **dick·ey** [díki] *n.* **1** 《child's word》 =**dick(e)y-bird,** a small bird. 작은 새. **2** 《Brit. *colloq.*》 a third small seat at the back of a two-seater motorcar. (2인승 자동차의) 뒤쪽 임시 좌석(=dick(e)y-seat). **3** 《*colloq.*》 a false shirt-front. (뗄 수 있는) 와이셔츠의 가슴판. [*Dick*]

dick·y² [díki] *adj.* 《*sl.*》 not in good health; not steady; liable to fail. (몸이) 약한; 흔들흔들[비실비실]하는; 불확실한. [↑]

dict. dictator; dictionary.

dic·ta [díktə] *n.* pl. of **dictum.**

Dic·ta·graph [díktəgræ̀f, -grɑ̀:f] *n.* =Dictograph.

Dic·ta·phone [díktəfòun] *n.* 《trade mark》 a machine which records spoken words and produces them again afterward to be typed or written down. 딕터폰《속기용 구술 녹음기》. [↓]

***dic·tate** *v.* [díkteit, -ˊ] *vt.* (P6,13) **1** 《*to*》 say or read (something) aloud to be written down by another person. …을 받아쓰게 하다; 구술하다. ¶ *~ a letter to someone* 아무에게 편지를 받아쓰게 하다 / *~ a passage to be taken down* 한 구절을 구술하여 받아쓰게 하다. **2** command with authority; give orders for. (권위로써) 명령하다; 지시하다. ¶ *~ peace terms to the vanquished enemy* 패적(敗敵)에게 화평 조건을 지시[명령]하다.

— *vi.* (P1,3) **1** say or read something aloud to be taken down. 구술하여 받아쓰게 하다. ¶ *~ to a class* 반 학생들에게 받아쓰기를 시키다 / *~ to a clerk* 서기에게 받아쓰게 하다 / *~ to one's typist* 타자수에게 받아 찍게 하다. **2** give orders; direct. 명령하다; 지시하다. ¶ *I refuse to be dictated to.* 남에게서 지시받는 것은 사절이다.

— [díkteit] *n.* Ⓒ 《often *pl.*》 an order by an authoritative person; a command. 명령; 지시. ¶ *the dictates of the teacher* 선생님의 지시 / *the dictates of reasons* 이성이 명하는 바 / *follow the dictates of one's conscience* [*reason*] 양심[이성]이 명하는 바에 따르다. [L. *dico* say, speak]

***dic·ta·tion** [diktéiʃən] *n.* Ⓤ **1** the act of dictating 받아쓰기; 구술. Ⓒ the words to be taken down. 받아쓰게 한[구술한] 것. ¶ *give ~ to the class* 반 학생들에게 받아쓰기를 시키다 / *The girl took the ~ and typed it out later.* 그 아가씨는 구술을 받아쓰고 나서 뒤에 그것을 타자했다. **2** the act of giving orders ~ ; something commanded. 명령; 지시. ¶ *I did it at my father's ~.* 아버지 지시에 의해서 했다.

dic·ta·tor [díkteitər, -ˊ-] *n.* Ⓒ **1** a ruler with absolute power and authority. 독재 집정관; 독재[전제]자. **2** a person who dictates. 받아쓰게 하는 사람; 구술자.

dic·ta·to·ri·al [dìktətɔ́:riəl] *adj.* **1** of or like a dictator. 독재자의; 독재적인. **2** behaving like a dictator; imperious. 명령적인; 싫단 말을 못하게 하는; 우격으로 밀어붙이는. ¶ *The* *members of the party disliked the ~ manner of their leader.* 대원들은 그들 대장의 횡포한 태도를 싫어했다.

dic·ta·tor·ship [díkteitərʃìp, -⌐-⌐] *n.* Ⓤ **1** the position or rank of a dictator; the period that a dictator's rule lasts. 집정관직(職)[임기]. **2** absolute authority. 독재권; 절대권; 전제.

dic·tion [díkʃən] *n.* Ⓤ the way of expressing ideas in words; the style of speaking or writing; the choice of words. 표현; 말; 어법; 용어(의 선택). ¶ *poetic* ~ 시어(詩語) / *good* ~ 적절한 표현. [↓]

:dic·tion·ar·y [díkʃənèri / -ʃənəri] *n.* Ⓒ (*pl.* **-ar·ies**) a book containing the words of a language, usu. arranged alphabetically, with explanations of their meanings. 사서(辭書); 사전. ¶ *consult an English-Korean* ~ 영한 사전을 찾다 / *turn up a* ~ 사전의 책장을 넘기다. [L. *dico* speak]

Dic·to·graph [díktəgræ̀f, -grɑ̀ːf] *n.* 《trade mark》 an apparatus for (secretly) listening to or recording conversations in another room. 딕터그래프《별실에서의 대화를 엿듣거나 녹음하는 장치》. [↑]

dic·tum [díktəm] *n.* Ⓒ (*pl.* **-tums** or **-ta**) **1** a saying; a maxim; a proverb. 격언; 금언; 속담. **2** an authoritative opinion; a formal assertion. (권위 있는) 의견; 주장; 단언. [↑]

:did [did] *v.* p. of **do.**

di·dac·tic [daidǽktik], **-ti·cal** [-tikəl] *adj.* intended to be instructive. 교훈적인; 교사인 체하는. ¶ *a* ~ *story* 교훈적인 이야기 / *in a* ~ *manner* 교사와 같은 태도로 / *She is too* ~ *toward her younger brother.* 그녀는 남동생에게 지나치게 설교적이다. [Gk. *didaskō* teach]

did·dle [dídl] *vt.* 《*sl.*》 cheat. 속이다; 협잡질하다. ¶ ~ *someone out of his money* 아무를 속여 돈을 빼앗다.

:did·n't [dídnt] =did not.

didst [didst] *v.* 《*arch.*》 =did. 語法 주어는 thou.

:die[1] [dai] (*ppr.* **dy·ing**) *vi.* **1** (P1,2A,5) ⓐ come to the end of life; stop living; become dead. 죽다. ¶ ~ *by violence* 비명에 죽다 / ~ *fighting* 싸우다 죽다 / ~ *in battle* 전사(戰死)하다 / ~ *for one's country* [*faith, principle*] 나라[신념, 주의]를 위해 죽다 / ~ *happy* [*young*] 행복한 가운데[젊어서] 죽다 / ~ *a rich man* [*beggar*] 부자[거지]가 되어 죽다 / *I wish to live and* ~ *here.* 나는 여기서 살다가 죽고 싶다 / *My mother died in 1988.* 어머니는 1988년에 돌아가셨다. ⓑ 《*of, from, with*》 meet death by reason of. …이 원인으로 죽다. ¶ ~ *from an accident* [*a wound, carelessness, the effect of too much drinking*] 사고로[부상으로, 부주의로, 과음한 탓에] 죽다 / ~ *of* (*an*) *illness* [*cold, heat, grief, old age*] 병으로[추위로, 더위로, 슬픔 때문에, 노령으로] 죽다 / *nearly* ~ *of laughing* 죽을 듯이 웃어 자지러지다 / ~ *with joy* [*shame*] 지나친 기쁨으로[치욕을 못 견뎌] 죽다. 語法 die of는 병, 부상, 노령, 낙담 따위가 사인일 때 가장 일반적인 표현이며 die from의 대용이 될 때도 있음. Ⓒ 《~ *a death*》 die. (…으로) 죽다. ¶ ~ *a natural death* 늙어서 죽다 / ~ *a violent death* 비명에 죽다; 변사(變死)하다 / ~ *the death of a hero* 영웅같이 죽다. **2** (P1,2A) 《Bible》 suffer the agony of death 죽음의 고통을 겪다. **3** (P1,3) cease to exist; come to an end. 소멸하다; 없어지다; 끝나다. ¶ *The smile died on her lips.* 그녀 입가의 미소가 사라졌다 / *The secret died with him.* 그 비밀은 그의 죽음과 함께 소멸했다《죽을 때까지 굳게 비밀을 지켰다》 / *Superstitions* ~ *slowly.* 미신은 좀처럼 없어지지 않는 법이다 / *Reading his letter, her hopes died within her.* 그의 편지를 읽고 그녀의 희망은 사라졌다 / *The day died into night.* 낮이 끝나고[해가 지고] 밤이 되었다. **4** (P2A,3) 《often *away, down*》 lose force or strength; become fainter or weaker; fade away; pass over. 힘을 잃다; 약해지다; 희미해지다; 끝나다. ¶ *The wind* [*noise*] *died gradually.* 바람[소음]은 점차 약해졌다 / *The trouble died down.* 분쟁이 가라앉았다 / *The laughter died away.* 웃음이 가시었다. **5** (P3) 《*to*》 become indifferent or not sensible to. 무관심[무감각]해지다. ¶ ~ *to worldly affairs* 세상일에 무관심해지다 / ~ *to sin* (도덕적인) 죄를 짓고도 태연해하다. **6** (P3,4) 《*colloq.*》 《usu. in *participle*》 《*for*》 wish very much; be very desirous. …을 하고 싶어 못 견디다; 몹시 바라다; 열망[갈망]하다. ¶ *I am just dying to meet him.* 그 사람을 몹시 만나 보고 싶다 / *I am dying for a glass of beer.* 맥주 한 잔 하고 싶어 못 견디겠다. [E.]

die a dog's death, die a miserable death. 비참한 죽음을 하다, 비참한 최후를 마치다.

die away, (of wind, sound) gradually become weaker until ceasing. (바람·소리 따위가) 점차 약해지다; 사라지다; 조용해지다.

die back [***down***]***,*** (of a plant) wither to the roots. (식물이) 가지 끝으로부터 뿌리로 서서히 말라죽다; 점차 말라죽어 뿌리만 남다.

die by one's own hand, kill oneself. 스스로 목숨을 끊다; 자살하다.

die down, become less strong or violent; become calm; subside. 약해지다; 조용해지다; 진정하다.

die game, fight bravely to the last. 최후까지 용감히 싸우다; 분전하다; 죽다.

die hard **a**) resist obstinately to the end; struggle until death. 끝까지 버티다; 마지막까지 싸우다; 사투(死鬪)하다. **b**) (of old beliefs, customs, etc.) take a long time to disappear; remain long. 오래도록 없어지지 않다[남다]. ¶ *Old prejudices* [*superstitions*] ~ *hard.* 오래 된 편견[미신]은 좀처럼 없어지지 않는다.

die in one's bed, die a natural death. 노령[노환]으로 죽다.

die in one's boots, die by violence; be hanged. 비명 횡사하다; 변사하다; 교수(絞首)되다.
die in harness, die while still at work. 일하다가[직무에 종사 중] 죽다; 순직하다.
die in the last ditch, fight to the very end. 끝까지 싸우다 쓰러지다; 힘이 다할 때까지 버티다.
die off, die one after another until all are dead; be extinguished; disappear. 차례로 죽다; 사멸하다; 사라지다.
die out, become extinct; come to a complete end. 없어지다; 사멸하다. ¶ *The custom died out.* 그 풍습은 사라졌다.
Never say die!, Never give up hope!, Keep up your courage! 약한 소리 하지 마라; 용기를 잃지 마라.

:die² [dai] *n.* Ⓒ **1** a small cube marked with figures from one to six. 주사위. ¶ *as level* [*straight, true*] *as a die* 주사위처럼 반듯한[정직한, 성실한] / *The ~ is cast.* 주사위는 던져졌다《운명은 이미 정해졌다》. **2** 《mech.》 any tool or apparatus used for molding, shaping, cutting, or stamping something. (주조(鑄造)용) 거푸집; 주형(鑄型); (화폐·메달 따위의 각인(刻印)용) 틀; 형(型); 다이스; (금속·플라스틱을 일정한 형태로 찍어 내는) 본; 형판(型板). — *vt.* (P6) stamp or shape with a die. 다이스로 형(型)을 뽑다[찍어내다, 자르다]. [L. *do* give]

die·hard [dáihà:rd] *adj.* resisting to the last. 마지막까지 버티는; 완강히 저항하는. ¶ *a ~ segregationist* 완고한 인종 차별주의자. — *n.* Ⓒ a person who resists vigorously to the last. 최후까지 저항하는 사람; 완고한 보수주의자. [*die¹*]

di·e·lec·tric [dàiiléktrik] *n.* a nonconductor of electricity. 불량 도체(不良導體). [die-]

di·er·e·sis =diaeresis.

Die·sel [dí:zəl] *n.* **1** **Rudolf** (1858-1913) a German engineer who invented the Diesel engine. 디젤《디젤 엔진을 발명한 독일의 공학자》. **2** Ⓒ a Diesel (or diesel) engine. 디젤 기관. [Person]

·di·et¹ [dáiət] *n.* Ⓒ **1** what a person or animal usu. eats and drinks; daily fare. 음식(물). **2** a special selection of food for health, usu. to reduce one's weight. (건강, 체중 감량을 위한) 규정식; 식이(食餌); 다이어트. ¶ *a ~ low in sugar* 당분이 적은 식사 / *a special ~ prescribed by the doctor* 의사 지시에 따른 특별 식사 / *be on a ~* 다이어트를 하고 있는 중이다 / *put a patient on a special ~* 환자에게 규정식을 취하게 하다. — *vt., vi.* (P6;1) 《oneself *on*》 (have someone or oneself) take special food and drink. 규정식을 먹(게 하)다. ¶ *The doctor dieted her on vegetables.* 의사는 그녀에게 채식을 하도록 식사를 제한했다. [Gk. *diaita* way of life]

·di·et² [dáiət] *n.* **1** Ⓒ a formal assembly. 정식 회의. **2** 《often *D-*》 the national parliamentary assembly, as in Japan, Denmark, Sweden, etc. (일본·덴마크·스웨덴 등의) 의회; 국회. 參考 미국에서는 Congress, 영국에서는 Parliament라고 함. ¶ *The Diet is now sitting.* 국회는 현재 개회 중이다. [L. *diēs* day]

di·e·tar·y [dáiətèri / -təri] *adj.* having to do with diet. 음식[식사]의; 식이(食餌)[규정식]의. ¶ *a ~ cure* 식이 요법. — *n.* (*pl.* **-tar·ies**) **1** Ⓤ allowance of daily food in a hospital, prison, etc. (병원·교도소 따위의) (식사의) 규정량. ¶ *the prison ~* 교도소의 급식량. **2** ⓊⒸ a system of diet; rules for regulating food. 규정식; 식사 규정. [→diet¹]

di·e·tet·ic [dàiətétik], **-i·cal** [-ikəl] *adj.* of diet. 식사의; 식이 요법의. [↑]

di·e·tet·ics [dàiətétiks] *n. pl.* 《used as *sing.*》 the study of the amount and kinds of food needed for health. (응용) 영양학.

di·e·ti·cian [dàiətíʃən] *n.* =dietitian.

di·e·ti·tian [dàiətíʃən] *n.* Ⓒ an expert in dietetics. 영양학자; 영양사.

dif- *pref.* ⇨dis-.

diff. difference; different.

:dif·fer [dífər] *vi.* (P1,2A,3) **1** 《*from, in*》 be different; be unlike. 다르다. ¶ *Tastes ~.* 취미(趣味)가 다르다 / *French grammar differs from English grammar in many points.* 프랑스어(語) 문법은 영어 문법과 여러 가지 점에서 다르다 / *Men ~ in habits and appearance.* 사람은 습관과 외양이 다르다. **2** 《often *with, from*》 be of another opinion; disagree with; quarrel with. 의견이 다르다; 생각이[의견이] 맞지 않다; 말다툼하다(opp. agree). ¶ *I beg to ~ (from you).* 실례지만 동의할 수 없습니다 / *I ~ with you on that matter.* 그 문제에 대해선 자네와 의견이 다르네. [L. *fero* carry]
agree to differ, give up trying to persuade each other. 서로 의견이 다름은 어쩔 수 없다고 인정하다. ¶ *Let us agree to ~.* 우리는 각자 의견의 차이를 인정합시다.

:dif·fer·ence [dífərəns] *n.* ⒸⓊ **1** the state of being unlike. 다름; 상이(相異); 차이. ¶ *a ~ in quality* [*appearance*] 성질[생김새]의 다름 / *wide differences of opinion* 큰 의견의 차이. **2** the way or point in which people or things are different; distinction. 상이점; 차이점; 특성; 차별. ¶ *the ~ between Tom and John* 톰과 존의 차이(差異)점 / *There are some minor differences between the two models.* 두 모델 사이엔 약간의 차이점이 몇 개 있다. **3** the condition of having a different opinion; disagreement; quarrel. 의견의 불일치; 불화; 말다툼 (opp. agreement). ¶ *a ~ with one's boss* 고용주와의 불화 / *They have had differences and won't speak to each other.* 그들은 사이가 틀어져 서로 말도 안 한다. **4** 《math.》 the amount by which one quantity is greater or less than another; the remainder left when one quantity is subtracted from another. 차(差); 차액. ¶ *100 won ~ in price* 값으로 백원의 차 / *a ~ of an inch,* 1 인치의 차 / *The ~ between 4 and 7 is 3.* 4와 7의 차는 3이다. [↑]

make a difference, a) 《usu. in *negative*》 give different treatment. 차별하다. ¶ *make no ~ between them* 양자간에 차별〔구별〕을 두지 않다. b) matter; be important; have an effect. 관계되다; 중요하다; 영향을 미치다. ¶ *It makes a ~ to us.* 우리에게 있어서는 관계가 있다 / *One false step will make a great ~.* 한 발 헛디디면 큰 일이 될 게다.

pay the difference, pay the excess of demand. 차액을 지불하다.

split the difference, a) compromise; meet halfway. 절충하다; 타협하다. b) divide the remainder equally. 나머지를 등분하다.

What's the difference? 《colloq.》 What does it matter? 그게 어쨌다는 건가.

:dif·fer·ent [dífərənt] *adj.* (opp. same) **1** 《*from, to, than*》 not alike; not like; not the same; separate. 다른; 딴; 별개의. ¶ *~ people with the same name* 동명 이인 / *things of ~ kinds* 다른 종류의 것들 / *~ in many ways* 여러 점에서 다른 / *at ~ times* 다른 때에 / *Their tastes are quite ~.* 그들의 취미는 아주 다르다 / *Your ideas are ~ from* 〔《U.S.》 *than*〕 *mine.* 네 생각은 내 생각과 다르다. **2** various; unusual. 여러(가지의); 이상한; 색다른. ¶ *a ~ sort of poet* 색다른 시인 / *Different people saw her.* 여러 사람이 그녀를 보았다 / *She has a very ~ way of dressing.* 그녀는 퍽 색다르게 옷을 입고 있다.

dif·fer·en·tial [dìfərénʃəl] *adj.* **1** of a difference; having, showing, or depending on a difference; distinctive. 차별적인; 특정한; 특이한. ¶ *a ~ tariff* 차별 관세 / *~ wages* 차별 임금 / *a ~ character* 특이한 성격 / *~ diagnosis* 감별 진단. **2** 《mech.》 making use of the differences of two or more motions. 차동(差動)의. —*n.* **1** Ⓤ the amount of difference in pay. 차(差); 차별적 요금. **2** Ⓒ 《mech.》 a differential gear. 차동(差動) 톱니바퀴(장치). [→differ]

dif·fer·en·ti·ate [dìfərénʃièit] *vt.* (P6,13) **1** 《*from, between*》 make a difference between (things or persons); find out the difference between (things). …을 구별짓다; 식별하다; 분간하다. ¶ *~ A from B,* A와 B를 구별하다 / *I cannot ~ between the two.* 나는 그 둘을 식별할 수가 없다. **2** 《math.》 form the differential. 미분(微分)하다. —*vi.* (P1,2A,3) become different. 달라지다; 구별이 생기다; 분화하다. ¶ *One genus of plants often differentiates into many species.* 한 속(屬)의 식물은 흔히 여러 종(種)으로 분화한다.

dif·fer·en·ti·a·tion [dìfərènʃiéiʃən] *n.* Ⓤ the act of differentiating; the process of becoming differentiated; the state of being differentiated. 구별; 판별; 식별; 차별; 분화(分化). ¶ *the ~ of labor* 노동의 분화.

dif·fer·ent·ly [dífərəntli] *adv.* in a different manner. 다르게. ¶ *~ from* 〔*to, than*〕 …와는 달리〔달라〕.

dif·fi·cile [dìfisí:l] *adj.* 《F.》 hard to get on with. 상대하기 어려운; 까다로운.

:dif·fi·cult [dífikʌ̀lt, -kəlt] *adj.* (opp. easy) **1** hard to do or understand; not easy. …하기 어려운; 알기 힘든; 곤란한. ¶ *a ~ question* 〔*book*〕 어려운 문제〔책〕 / *be ~ of access* 접근하기 어렵다 / *be ~ to answer* 대답하기 어렵다 / *English grammar is ~ for foreigners.* 영문법은 외국인에겐 어렵다 / *The food is ~ to digest.* 이 음식은 소화하기가 어렵다 / *It is ~ for me* 〔*I find it ~*〕 *to stop smoking.* 나는 담배 끊기가 어렵다. **2** hard to deal with; stubborn. 까다로운; 다루기 힘든. ¶ *a ~ situation* 어려운 상황 / *He is a ~ person to deal with.* 그는 다루기 까다로운 사람이다. [dif-, →facile]

:dif·fi·cul·ty [dífikʌ̀lti, -kəlti] *n.* ⓊⒸ (*pl.* **-ties**) **1** the state or condition of being difficult. 어려움; 곤란. ¶ *a task of ~* 곤란한 일 / *the ~ of a task* 일의 어려움 / *without ~* 쉽게; 어렵지 않게 / *walk with ~* 간신히〔힘들여〕 걷다. **2** something that is difficult; an obstacle. 어려운 일; 난사(難事); 곤란(한 일); 장애; 지장; 이의(異議). ¶ *a task presenting many difficulties* 많은 어려움이 생기는 일 / *face* 〔*overcome*〕 *every ~* 온갖 어려움에 직면하다〔을 극복하다〕 / *be under a ~* 역경에 있다 / *find no ~ in doing something* 어렵지 않게 …하다 / *put difficulties in the way* 훼방하다. **3** 《usu. *pl.*》 financial troubles. 궁경; 재정 곤란. ¶ *tide over difficulties* 궁지를 벗어나다.

be in difficulties, lack money; have financial troubles. 돈에 궁해 있다.

make 〔***raise***〕 ***difficulties,*** object to someone or something. 이의〔반대〕를 제기하다; 불만을 만들다.

dif·fi·dence [dífidəns] *n.* Ⓤ the state of being diffident; lack of self-confidence; shyness. 겁냄; 자신없음; 주눅듦; 수줍음. ¶ *with nervous ~* 머뭇〔쭈뼛〕거리며. [↓]

dif·fi·dent [dífidənt] *adj.* lacking in self-confidence; shy. 자신 없는; 수줍은; 겁많은. [dif-, →fidelity]

dif·fi·dent·ly [dífidəntli] *adv.* in a diffident manner. 자신 없는 듯이; 사양하며; 수줍어하며.

dif·fract [difrǽkt] *vt.* (P6) break up (a ray of light, sound waves, etc.) into separate parts. (빛·음파 따위를) 분산시키다; 회절(回折)시키다. [→fraction]

dif·frac·tion [difrǽkʃən] *n.* Ⓤ 《phys.》 the act of breaking up sound waves, electricity, etc. around obstacles. (전파·음파 따위의) 회절(回折).

dif·fuse [difjú:z] *vt.* (P6) spread out; scatter widely. 방산(放散)〔발산〕시키다; 퍼뜨리다; 보급시키다. ¶ *~ light* 〔*heat*〕 빛〔열〕을 방산하다 / *~ a rumor* 소문을 퍼뜨리다 / ~

learning〔*knowledge*〕 학문〔지식〕을 보급시키다 / ~ *certain doctrines and principles* 어떤 주의·주장을 퍼뜨리다. —*vi.* (P1) mix together by spreading into one another. 흩어지다; 퍼지다; 보급되다; 유포되다. — [difjú:s] *adj.* **1** widely spread; scattered. 흩어진; 널리 퍼진; 확산된. **2** wordy; not concise. (표현 등이) 군말이 많은; 산만한. ¶ *a ~ writer* (표현이) 산만한 작가. ● **dif·fuse·ness** [-fjú:snis] *n.* [→fuse[1]]

dif·fuse·ly [difjú:sli] *adv.* in a diffuse manner. 널리 (보급하여); 장황하게; 산만하게.

dif·fu·sion [difjú:ʒən] *n.* Ⓤ **1** the act of diffusing; the state of being diffused. 방산(放散); 발산; 보급; 유포. ¶ *The invention of printing helped the ~ of learning.* 인쇄술의 발명은 지식의 보급을 도왔다. **2** wordiness. 군말이 많음. **3** 《phys.》 mixing together by spreading into one another. 확산; (빛의) 산란(散亂). ¶ *the ~ of gases* 가스의 확산.

dif·fu·sive [difjú:siv] *adj.* **1** having a tendency to diffuse; showing diffusion. 퍼지기 쉬운; 보급되기 쉬운; 확산성의〔적인〕. **2** wordy. (표현이) 산만한; 용만한.

:dig [dig] *v.* (**dug** or 《*arch.*》 **digged, dig·ging**) *vt.* **1** (P6,7) break up or loosen (earth, sand, etc.), as with a spade. (땅·흙 따위)를 파다; 파헤치다. ¶ ~ *the ground* 땅을 파다 / ~ *a field up* 밭을 파일구다. **2** (P6,7) make (a hole) in the ground. (구멍 따위)를 파다〔뚫다〕. ¶ ~ *a hole*〔*well*〕 구멍〔우물〕을 파다 / ~ *a tunnel through the hill* 산을 뚫어 터널을 내다. **3** (P6,7) 《*up*》 get (something) by digging. …을 파〔캐〕내다. **4** (P6,7,13) 《*fig.*》 《often *out*》 search for; search in; examine carefully. …을 찾다; 조사해〔캐〕내다. **5** (P13) 《*colloq.*》 poke; thrust. …을 쿡 찌르다; 찔러 넣다. ¶ ~ *a horse with spurs* 말에 박차를 가하다 / ~ *someone in the ribs* (손가락 또는 팔꿈치로) 아무의 옆구리를 쿡 찌르다. —*vi.* (P1,2,3) **1** 《*into, through*》 break up, turn over, or remove (earth, sand, etc.) as with a spade. 흙〔땅〕을 파다. ¶ ~ *deep* 깊이 파다 / ~ *for gold* 금을 찾아 땅을 파다 / ~ *in the vegetable garden* 채마밭을 파헤치다. **2** make one's way as by removing or turning over material. 파나아가다; 뚫다. ¶ ~ *under the mountain* 산 밑을 파나아가다 / ~ *through the hill* 산을 뚫어 굴을 내다. **3** 《*at, into, for*》 《U.S. *colloq.*》 search; study hard. 면밀히 조사〔탐구, 연구〕하다; 열심히 공부하다. ¶ ~ *through the files* 서류철 더미를 면밀히 조사하다 / ~ *for information* 정보를 얻어내려고 하다 / *He is digging at mathematics.* 그는 수학 공부를 열심히 하고 있다.

dig at, speak to (someone) in an unpleasant way. …에게 불쾌감을 주는 투로 이야기하다.

dig one's heels in, refuse to do something. …하기를 거부하다.

dig in, **a**) dig trenches for protection. 참호를 파 몸을 숨기다(=dig oneself in). **b**) work hard. 맹렬히 공부〔일〕하다. **c**) make certain of (one's) position; get (oneself) firmly settled. 확고히 자리잡(히게 하)다. **d**) help oneself to food and start eating. (마음대로) 걸신들린 듯 먹기 시작하다. **e**) mix (something) into the soil by digging. (비료 따위를) 땅을 파서 섞어 넣다.

dig into, **a**) start eating (something). …을 게걸스레 먹기 시작하다; 덤벼들어 먹다. **b**) examine thoroughly. …을 깊이 조사하다; 깊이 파고들다. **c**) push〔thrust〕 (something) into. …을 찔러 박다. ¶ ~ *a fork into meat* 포크를 고기에 꽂다 / ~ *one's fingers into the mud* 손가락을 진흙 속에 찔러 넣다.

dig out, **a**) find or discover (something) by an effort or search. …을 찾아내다〔발견하다〕; 탐구하다. ¶ ~ *out the fact from a book* 책에서 사실을 탐구하다. **b**) make a careful inquiry. 조사해내다; 캐내다. ¶ ~ *out a secret* 비밀을 캐내다 / ~ *the truth out* (*of him*) (그에게서) 진상을 알아내다. **c**) get out by digging; free from being buried. (묻힌 것을) 파내다; 발굴하다. ¶ ~ *treasure out of the ruins* 폐허에서 보물을 발굴하다. **d**) 《U.S.》 (esp. of animals) move quickly. (동물 따위가) 잽싸게 달아나다.

dig over, reconsider. (문제 따위를) 재고하다.

dig up, **a**) break up earth by digging; remove (something) from the ground by digging. (땅·흙을) 파헤치다; …을 파내다. ¶ ~ *up potatoes* 감자를 캐다. **b**) find out; examine; expose. 발견하다; 손에 넣다; 조사해〔밝혀〕내다. ¶ ~ *up an oldcoin in the garden* 마당에서 고전(古錢) 하나를 발견하다.

—*n.* Ⓒ **1** the act of digging; a thrust or poke; a remark against someone. (한 번) 팜〔파기〕; (손가락으로) 쿡 찌르기; 빗대는〔비꼬는〕 말. ¶ *give him a ~ in the ribs* 그의 옆구리를 손으로 쿡 찌르다 / 《*at*》 *That's a ~ at me.* 그것은 나에 대한 빈정거림이다. **2** a diligent student. (공부를) 지독히 파는 학생. **3** 《*pl.*》 lodgings. 하숙. [F. *diguer*]

·di·gest [didʒést, dai-] *vt.* (P6) **1** change (food) into a state in which the body can absorb it. …을 소화하다. ¶ *foods difficult to ~* 소화시키기 어려운 음식. **2** think (something) over; understand and absorb mentally. …을 숙고하다; 이해하여 제것으로 하다. ¶ ~ *a mass of facts* 많은 사실을 이해하다 / ~ *a book* 책에서 지식을 얻다. **3** arrange (something) according to some system. (계통적으로) 정리하다; 분류하다. ¶ ~ *the laws* 법률을 체계화하다. **4** 《chem.》 dissolve. …을 침지(浸漬)〔숙성(熟成)〕하다. **5** put up with; endure. 참다; 견디다. ¶ ~ *an insult* 모욕을 참다 / *That conduct is more than I can ~.* 그 행동은 더는 참을 수 없는 것이다.

—*vi.* (P1) be digested; digest food. 소화되다; 음식을 소화하다. ¶ *Fruit digests easily.* 과일은 소화가 잘 된다.

— [dáidʒest] *n.* Ⓒ **1** a summary or outline of what is in a longer book or article. (책·기사 따위의) 간추림; 요약; 개요. **2** a magazine containing books or articles. (책·기사의) 간추린 잡지. **3** a summary or systematic collection of laws or court decision. (법령·판례를 조직적으로 요약·유별한) 법규 유찬(類纂). [di-, L. *gero* carry]

di·gest·i·ble [didʒéstəbəl, dai-] *adj.* that can be digested. 소화하기 쉬운; 요약하기 쉬운.

di·ges·tion [didʒéstʃən, dai-] *n.* ⓊⒸ **1** the act of digesting; the condition of being digested. 소화 (작용). **2** the power of digesting. 소화력; 동화 흡수; 숙성(熟成). ¶ *have a good* 〔*weak*〕 ~ 위가 좋다〔약하다〕.

di·ges·tive [didʒéstiv, dai-] *adj.* of, for, or helping digestion; having the power to digest. 소화의; 소화를 촉진하는; 소화력이 있는. ¶ ~ *trouble* 소화 기능의 탈 / *a* ~ *organ* 소화관(管) / *a* ~ *pill* 소화약. — *n.* Ⓒ something that aids digestion. 소화제〔약〕.

dig·ger [dígər] *n.* Ⓒ **1** a person that digs. 파〔캐〕내는 사람; 갱부. ¶ *a gold-digger* 채금 갱부. **2** any tool or machine for digging. 채굴〔굴착〕 기구〔기계〕. [*dig*]

dig·gings [díginz] *n. pl.* **1** a place where people dig for gold. (금의) 채굴지; 채광지. **2** 《Brit. *colloq.*》 lodgings. 하숙(= digs). ¶ *look for* ~ 하숙을 찾다. [*dig*]

dight [dait] *vt.* (**dight** or **dight·ed**) 《*arch.*》 《usu. in *pp.*》 prepare; clothe; adorn. 갖추다; 장비하다; 옷치장하다; 장식하다. [→dictate]

dig·it [dídʒit] *n.* Ⓒ **1** a finger or toe. 손가락; 발가락. **2** any of the figures from 0 to 9. (아라비아 숫자의) 0에서 9까지. [L. =finger, toe]

dig·it·al [dídʒitl] *adj.* of or like a digit. 손가락의; 계수〔디지털〕형의. ¶ *a* ~ *computer* 디지털〔수치형〕 계산기. — *n.* a finger; a key struck by the finger, as of a piano. 손가락; (건반 악기의) 키〔건반〕.

dig·i·tal·is [dìdʒitǽlis, -téi-] *n.* **1** Ⓤ a medicine made from foxglove and used for stimulating the heart. 강심제의 일종 《디기탈리스로 만듦》. **2** Ⓒ 《bot.》 a kind of plant; foxglove. 디기탈리스. [L.]

dig·ni·fied [dígnəfàid] *adj.* having and showing dignity; majestic; noble. 위엄 있는; 당당한; 고귀한. ¶ ~ *conduct* 위엄 있는 행동. ● **dig·ni·fi·ed·ly** [-li] *adv.* [↓]

dig·ni·fy [dígnəfài] *vt.* (**-fied**) (P6,13) **1** give dignity to (someone or something); make (someone or something) noble or worthy. …에 위엄을 주다; …을 고귀하게 하다; …을 가치있게 하다. ¶ *The cottage was dignified by the great trees around it.* 오두막은 주변의 거목들로 해서 운치를 더했다. **2** give a high-sounding name to (someone or something). …에 어마어마한 이름을 붙이다. ¶ ~ *cowardice with the name of prudence* 겁 많음을 신중함이라고 하며 젠체하다 / ~ *one's few books by the name of a library* 몇 안 되는 책을 장서라는 어마어마한 이름을 붙이다. [L. *dignus* worthy]

dig·ni·tar·y [dígnətèri / -təri] *n.* Ⓒ (*pl.* **-tar·ies**) a person holding a position of honor, esp. in a church. 고위층의 사람; 고관; 고위 성직자. [↑]

dig·ni·ty [dígnəti] *n.* (*pl.* **-ties**) **1** Ⓤ ⓐ the quality of character that wins the respect and high opinion of others; a calm and grand manner. 위엄; 당당함. ¶ *walk with* ~ 당당한 태도로 걷다 / *impair one's* ~ 위엄을 손상하다. ⓑ noble quality; being noble. 고귀함; 고결; 숭고함. ¶ *the* ~ *of labor* 노동의 고귀〔신성〕함. **2** Ⓒ a high rank, office, or title. 고위(高位); 고관. ¶ *a* ~ *in the government* 정부의 고위직(職) / *the* ~ *of the presidency* 대통령이라는 높은 지위. **3** Ⓒ a person of high rank, office, or title. 고위층 인사; 고관; 고위 성직자. [↑]

be beneath one's dignity, be unsuitable for one to do; degrade. 위엄을 손상시키다; 품위를 떨어뜨리다.

stand* 〔*be*〕 *upon one's dignity, assume an air of importance; refuse to do what one considers to be undignified. 젠체하다; 도도하게 굴다.

with dignity, with an air of importance; solemnly. 무게〔위엄〕 있게; 엄숙히.

di·graph [dáigræf, -grɑːf] *n.* Ⓒ two letters to represent a single sound, such as sh, ea, etc. 이중자(二重字) 《두 글자로 한 음을 이루는 sh, ea 따위》. [di-, →grammar]

di·gress [daigrés, di-] *vi.* (P1,3) 《*from, into*》 turn away from the main subject in talking or writing. (주제에서) 옆길로 벗어나다; 탈선하다. [di-, →grade]

di·gres·sion [daigréʃən, di-] *n.* ⓊⒸ the act of getting away from the main subject in talking or writing. 본제를 벗어남; 여담; 탈선.

di·gres·sive [daigrésiv, di-] *adj.* being digressed; digressing. 본제를 벗어난; 지엽에 걸친; 탈선하기 쉬운. ● **di·gres·sive·ness** [-nis] *n.*

digs [digz] *n. pl.* 《chiefly Brit. *colloq.*》 = diggings 2.

di·he·dral [daihíːdrəl] *adj.* **1** having two plane surfaces. 두 평면을 가진. **2** formed by two plane surfaces. 두 평면으로 이루어진. **3** making a dihedral angle. 2면각을 이루는. — *n.* the figure formed by two intersecting plane surfaces. 2면각. [di-]

dike, dyke [daik] *n.* Ⓒ **1** ⓐ a bank of earth built as a defense against flooding. 방축; 둑; 제방. ⓑ 《Brit.》 a low wall of turf enclosing or dividing lands. 땅을 가르거나 둘러싸기 위해 쌓은 낮은 흙담. **2** a ditch. 도랑. — *vt.* (P6) **1** provide or protect (something) with dikes. …에 둑을 쌓다. **2** drain with a ditch. …에 도랑을〔해자를〕 파 두르다. [E. =ditch]

di·lap·i·dat·ed [dilǽpədèitid] *adj.* falling to pieces; ruined; shabby. 무너진; 황폐한; 초라한. ¶ *a ~ cabin in the woods* 숲 속에 쓰러져가는 작은 집. [di-, →lapidary]

di·lap·i·da·tion [dilæ̀pədéiʃən] *n.* Ⓤ the state of being dilapidated; ruin. 황폐; 파손; 붕괴.

dil·a·ta·tion [dìlətéiʃən, dàilə-] *n.* Ⓤ the act of dilating; the state of being dilated. 팽창 (상태); 확장. [↓]

di·late [dailéit, di-] *vi.* (P1,3) **1** become larger or wider. 넓어〔퍼〕지다; 부풀다; 팽창하다. ¶ *The pupil of the eye dilates when it grows dark.* 눈동자는 어두워지면 커진다. **2** 《*on, upon*》 speak or write in detail. 부연(敷衍)하다; 상설(詳說)하다.
— *vt.* (P6) make (something) larger or wider; enlarge. …을 넓히다; 크게 하다. ¶ *~ the eyes* 눈을 크게 뜨다 / *~ the lungs with air* 공기로 폐를 팽창시키다. [di-, →latitude]
dilate on 〔***upon***〕, speak or write a lot about. 장황하게 늘어놓다.

di·lat·ed [dailéitid, di-] *adj.* widened; expanded. 넓어진; 퍼진; 커진; 확장〔팽창〕된.

di·la·tion [dailéiʃən, di-] *n.* Ⓤ the act of dilating; the state of being dilated; enlargement. 팽창; 확대; 확장(=dilatation).

di·la·tor [dailéitər, di-] *n.* that which dilates. 팽창〔확장〕시키는 사람〔것〕. [*dilate*]

dil·a·to·ry [dílətɔ̀:ri / -təri] *adj.* given to delay; not prompt; causing delay. 완만한; 지지한; 꾸물대는. ¶ *a ~ person* 느린 사람. [→defer[1]]

di·lem·ma [dilémə] *n.* Ⓒ **1** any situation requiring a choice; a difficult situation. 딜레마; 진퇴 양난; 궁지. ¶ *be in a ~* 궁지에 빠져 있다 / *put someone in(to) a ~* 아무를 궁지에 빠뜨리다 / *The ~ is whether to lower the price or to accept fewer sales.* 값을 내릴 것이냐 매상의 감소를 감수해야 할 것인가 궁지에 몰려 있다. **2** 《log.》 an argument forcing an opponent to choose between equally unfavorable alternatives. 양도 논법. [di-, Gk. *lambanō* take]
be on the horns of the dilemma, be faced with a choice between equally unfavorable alternatives. 진퇴 양난에 빠지다.

dil·et·tan·te [dìlətá:nt, -tǽnti] *n.* Ⓒ (*pl.* **-tes** or **-ti**) **1** a lover of the fine arts. 예술 애호가. **2** a person who follows an art or science only for amusement. 호사가; 아마추어 동호자. — *adj.* not thorough. 아마추어의; 어설픈; 수박 겉핥기의. [→delight]

dil·et·tan·ti [dilətá:nti:] *n.* pl. of **dilettante.**

dil·et·tant·ism [dìlətǽntizəm] *n.* **1** a mere dabbling in art and literature. 아마추어풍; (아마추어) 예술〔문학〕 취미. **2** a superficial knowledge of a subject. 피상적인 〔수박 겉핥기식의〕 지식.

·dil·i·gence[1] [dílədʒəns] *n.* Ⓤ the state of being diligent; hard work; careful effort; industry. 부지런함; 근면; 정려(精勵); 노력; 열심. ¶ *with ~* 부지런히; 열심히. [di-, L. *lego* choose]

dil·i·gence[2] [díləʒɑ̀:ns, -dʒəns] *n.* 《F.》 Ⓒ a public stagecoach formerly used in France. (프랑스의 옛날) 승합 마차; 역마차.

·dil·i·gent [dílədʒənt] *adj.* hard-working; industrious; attentive to one's duties; careful and steady. 근면한; 부지런한; 애쓴; 공들인(opp. idle). [→diligence]

dil·i·gent·ly [dílədʒəntli] *adv.* in a diligent manner. 부지런히; 힘써서; 애써; 공들여.

dil·ly·dal·ly [dílidæ̀li] *vi.* (**-lied**) 《*colloq.*》 waste time; act in an indecisive manner; loiter. 꾸물대다; 결심을 못하고 우물쭈물하다; 빈둥거리다. [Imit.]

di·lute [dilú:t, dai-] *vt.* (P6,13) **1** 《*with*》 make (a liquid) weaker or thinner by adding water or some other liquid. (액체를 물 따위를 타서) 묽게〔엷게〕하다. ¶ *~ whisky with water* 위스키에 물을 타서 묽게 하다. **2** weaken or lessen. …을 약하게 하다; 엷게 하다. — *adj.* weakened or thinned by the addition of water, etc. 물을 탄; 묽은; 약해진; 퇴색한. [di-, L. *luo* wash]

di·lu·tion [dilú:ʃən, dai-] *n.* **1** Ⓤ the act of diluting; the state of being diluted. 물탐; 희석(도). **2** Ⓒ something diluted. 희석물; 희석액. [↑]

di·lu·vi·a [dilú:viə, dai-] *n.* pl. of **diluvium.**

di·lu·vi·al [dilú:viəl, dai-] *adj.* **1** 《geol.》 of deluvium. 홍적층의. ¶ *~ deposits* 홍적층. **2** of a flood, esp. that of Noah. 홍수의; (특히) 노아의 대홍수의. [→dilute]

di·lu·vi·um [dilú:viəm, dai-] *n.* (*pl.* **-vi·a** or **-ums**) 《geol.》 diluvial deposits. 홍적층(洪積層). [↑]

:dim [dim] *adj.* (**dim·mer, dim·mest**) **1** not bright; not clear; shadowy; dark. 어스레한; 칙칙한; 어두운. ¶ *the ~ light of evening* 초저녁의 어스레한 (햇)빛. **2** not clearly seen, heard, or understood; vague. 어슴푸레한; 아련한; 몽롱한. ¶ *a ~ figure in the shadow* 그늘 속의 희미한 그림자 / *a ~ idea* 막연한 생각 / *The memory of it has grown ~.* 그 기억이 희미해졌다. **3** not seeing. (눈이) 침침한; 흐린. ¶ *grow ~* 침침해지다 / *Her eyes were ~ with tears.* 그녀 눈에 눈물이 어렸다 / *His eyesight is getting ~.* 그의 시력은 점점 희미해지고 있다. **4** stupid; dull. 바보의; 둔한.
take a dim view of, regard with disfavor. …을 비관적으로 보다; 회의적으로 보다.
— *v.* (**dimmed, dim·ming**) *vi.* (P1) become dim; fade. 어둠침침해지다; 희미해지다.
— *vt.* (P6) make dim. 어둠침침〔어두컴컴〕해지다. ¶ *The sun's light was dimmed by the thick trees.* 햇빛은 굵은 나무들에 가려져 어둠침침했다. [E.]

dim. diminuendo; diminutive.

dime [daim] *n.* **1** a silver coin of the

United States and Canada, equal to 10 cents. (미국·캐나다의) 10센트 은화《1/10달러》. **2** something cheap and of poor quality. (질 나쁜) 싸구려 물건. ¶ *a ~ novel* 싸구려 소설 / *a ~ store* 싸구려 상점. [→decimal]

di·men·sion [dimén∫ən, dai-] *n.* Ⓒ **1** any measurement of length, breadth, or thickness. (길이·나비·두께 따위의) 치수. ¶ *of one ~* 선의; 길이의 / *of two dimensions* 평면의; 길이와 나비의 / *of three dimensions* 입체의. **2** 《usu. *pl.*》 size; extent. 크기; 범위. ¶ *in dimensions* 크기는 / *of great* 〔*vast*〕 *dimensions* 몹시 큰; 거대한 / *a house of considerable dimensions* 상당히 큰 집. **3** 《phys., math.》 a literal factor. 차원; 차(次). [di-, →measure]

di·men·sion·al [dimén∫ənəl] *adj.* of dimension or dimensions; capable of being measured. 치수의; 치수로 잴 수 있는. ¶ *a three-dimensional picture* 입체 영화.

dim·e·ter [dímitər] *n.* 《*poet.*》 a verse containing two measures. 2보격(步格)(의 시). [di-]

·di·min·ish [dəmíni∫] *vt.* (P6) **1** make (something) smaller in size, amount, number, etc.; lessen; reduce; decrease. (크기·양 따위)를 줄이다; 축소하다; 작게 하다. ¶ *~ the risk of war* 전쟁의 위험을 감소시키다. **2** make less in importance; weaken. 중요성을 감소시키다; 약하게 하다. ¶ *The power of wealth was diminished.* 부(富)의 힘이 감소되었다. —*vi.* (P1,3) become smaller or less. 작아〔적어〕지다; 감소〔축소〕하다; 줄다. ¶ *~ in speed* 속도가 줄다. [di-, →minute]

di·min·u·en·do [dimìnjuéndou] *n.* Ⓒ (*pl.* **-dos**) 《It. mus.》 **1** a gradual lessening of loudness. 점차 약주음(弱奏音)(abbr. dim.); the sign(>) indicating this. 위를 나타내는 기호(>). **2** a passage to be played or sung with a diminuendo. 디미누엔도 악절(樂節). —*adj., adv.* 《mus.》 with a diminuendo. 점차 약한〔약하게〕. [↓]

dim·i·nu·tion [dìmənjú:∫ən] *n.* ⓊⒸ the act of diminishing; the state of being diminished; the condition of lessening in quantity, quality, etc.; decrease. 감소; 축소; 삭감; 저감(低減). ¶ *My resources show a considerable ~.* 나의 자력(資力)이 상당한 감소를 보이고 있다. [di-, →minute]

di·min·u·tive [dimínjətiv] *adj.* **1** very small; tiny. 아주 작은; 조그만. ¶ *a ~ child* 조그만 아이. **2** 《gram.》 expressing smallness. 지소(指小)의. ¶ *Such words as 'booklet' and 'lambkin' have ~ endings.* 'booklet'와 'lambkin' 같은 말들은 지소어미(指小語尾)를 갖고 있다. —*n.* Ⓒ **1** a small person or thing. 작은 사람〔것〕. **2** 《gram.》 a word formed from another by the addition of a suffix expressing smallness. 지소사(指小詞). 參考 duck*ling*, stream*let*의 -ling, -let 따위. [↑]

dim·ly [dímli] *adv.* in a dim manner. 어슴푸레〔희미〕하게; 어둠침침하게. [*dim*]

dim·ness [dímnis] *n.* Ⓤ the state of being dim. 어슴푸레함; 희미함; 어두컴컴함.

dim·out [dímàut] *n.* a lessening or partial concealment of light at night, esp. to protect a city, etc. against aerial attack. 등화관제. [*dim*]

dim·ple [dímpəl] *n.* Ⓒ **1** a small natural hollow in the cheek or chin. 보조개. **2** any small, hollow place; a ripple. 움푹 들어간 데; 잔물결. —*vt.* (P6) make dimples in (something). …에 보조개를 만들다; 잔물결을 일으키다. ¶ *The wind dimples the surface of the lake.* 바람은 호수면에 잔물결을 일으킨다. —*vi.* (P1) show or form dimples. 보조개가 생기다; 잔물결이 일다. ¶ *~ with laughter* 웃음으로 보조개가 생기다 / *The girl dimples whenever she smiles.* 그 소녀는 웃을 때면 보조개가 생긴다. ● **dim·ply** [-pli] *adj.* [G. *dümpel* deep hole in water]

dim·wit [dímwìt] *n.* 《*sl.*》 a stupid or mentally slow person. 바보; 우둔한 사람. ● **dim-wit·ted** [-wítid] *adj.* [E.]

din [din] *n.* Ⓤ 《sometimes *a ~*》 a loud, confused noise. 시끄러운 소리; 소음; 떠들썩함. ¶ *in the ~ of* …의 소음 속에서 / *There was a ~ of voices in the market.* 장바닥엔 사람들 소리로 와글대고 있었다.
—*vt.* (**dinned, din·ning**) (P13) strike (something) with a din; say over and over; repeat noisily. …을 시끄럽게 울려퍼뜨리다; 되풀이해 시끄럽게 말하다. ¶ *~ an idea into someone's ears* 아무에게 어떤 생각을 귀가 아프도록 들려주다. —*vi.* (P2A) make a din. 시끄럽게 울리다. [E.]

:dine [dain] *vi.* (P1,2A,3) eat dinner. 정찬(正餐)을 들다; 식사를 하다. ¶ *~ late* 늦게 식사하다. —*vt.* (P6) **1** give a dinner to or for (someone). (…를) 정찬〔저녁 식사〕에 초대하다; 저녁 식사를 대접하다. **2** (of a room, table, etc.) be large enough for dining. (방·식탁 따위가) …사람이 식사할 만큼 넓다. ¶ *This table will ~ 6 persons.* 이 식탁에서 여섯 사람이 먹을 수 있다. [F.]
dine out, eat dinner away from home. 밖에서 식사하다; 외식하다.

din·er [dáinər] *n.* Ⓒ **1** a person who dines. 식사하는 사람. **2** a railroad dining-car. (열차의) 식당차. [↑]

ding [diŋ] *vt., vi.* (P6;1) make the sound of a bell. 종을〔종이〕 땡땡 울리다; (벨을) 따르르 울리다; (벨이) 따르르 울리다. —*n.* this sound. 그 종〔벨〕소리. [Imit.]

ding·dong [díŋdɔ̀(:)ŋ, -dàŋ] *n.* Ⓤ the sound made by a bell; any similar sound; the continuous ringing of a bell. (종의) 땡땡 소리; (벨의) 따르르 울리는 소리. —*adj.* evenly matched. 팽팽한; 쫓고 쫓기는. ¶ *a ~ battle* 팽팽한 접전 / *a ~ struggle between the two teams* 두 팀 사이의 엎치락뒤치락의 싸움. [Imit.]

din·gey [díŋgi] *n.* (*pl.* **-geys**) =dinghy.

din·ghy [díŋgi] *n.* (*pl.* **-ghies**) a small boat carried on a ship; a small pleasure boat. 함재 소정(艦載小艇); (오락용의) 작은 보트. [Hind.]

din·gi·ly [díndʒili] *adv.* in a dingy manner. 거무스름하게 되어; 더러워져. [↓]

din·gi·ness [díndʒinis] *n.* Ⓤ the condition of being dingy. 거무스름함; 검댕색; 초라함. [*dingy*]

din·gle [díŋgəl] *n.* a small, deep valley. 깊은 소계곡. [E.]

din·go [díŋgou] *n.* (*pl.* **-goes**) an Australian wild dog. 들개의 일종《오스트레일리아산》. [Native]

din·gy [díndʒi] *adj.* (**-gi·er, -gi·est**) dirty-looking; dull. 더러운; 거무스레한; 추레한. [? *dung, -y*]

din·ing [dáiniŋ] *n.* having meals. 식사. [*dine*]

dining car [∠-∠] *n.* a railroad car in which meals are served. (열차의) 식당차.

dining room [∠-∠] *n.* a room in which people eat their meals. 식당《가정·호텔의 정식 식사의》.

dining table [∠-∠] *n.* a table on which meals are served. 식탁.

dink [diŋk] *vt.* (P6) deck. 꾸미다; 장식하다. [↓]

dink·y [díŋki] *adj.* (**dink·i·er, dink·i·est**) 《*colloq.*》 **1** 《Brit.》 pretty; neat. 말쑥한. **2** 《U.S.》 small; unimportant; trifling. 작은; 소형의; 그리 중요하지 않은; 하찮은. [Scot.]

:din·ner [dínər] *n.* **1** ⓊⒸ the main meal of the day, usu. taken in the evening or at midday. 정찬(正餐). **2** Ⓒ a formal meal in honor of someone or on some special occasion. 성찬(盛饌); (공식의) 오찬[만찬]회. ¶ *a bridal* ~ 결혼 피로연 / *ask someone to* ~ 아무를 식사에 초대하다. [→dine]

at dinner, at table. 식사 중에

dinner without grace, sexual intercourse before marriage. 혼전 성교.

give a dinner in honor of, hold a dinner party in honor of. …을 위해 만찬회를 열다.

dinner jacket [∠-∠-] *n.* a tuxedo jacket. 약식 야회복.

dinner party [∠-∠-] *n.* an evening party to which guests are invited for dinner. 만찬회(晚餐會).

dinner service [∠-∠-] *n.* a special set of plates; dishes used at dinner. 정찬용 식기류 한 벌.

dinner set [∠-∠] *n.* =dinner service.

di·no·saur [dáinəsɔ̀ːr] *n.* Ⓒ any of a group of very large reptiles that lived a long time ago. (중생대의) 공룡. [Gk. *deinos* dire, *thēr* beast]

dint [dint] *n.* Ⓒ **1** a violent stroke. 일격; 타격. **2** a mark or slight hollow in a hard surface made by a blow or pressure; a dent. (치거나 누르거나 하여 생긴) 맞은 자국; 우묵한 곳. **3** Ⓤ force or power. 힘.

by dint of, by means of something. …에 의해서[…힘으로]; …덕분으로. ¶ *He succeeded by* ~ *of hard work.* 그는 정진한 덕분에 성공했다.
— *vt.* make a dent in (something). …이 쑥 들어가게 하다. [E.]

di·oc·e·san [daiásəsən / -ɔ́s-] *adj.* of or concerning a diocese. 교구(敎區)의. ¶ ~ *business* 교구의 일. — *n.* a bishop in charge of a diocese. 교구를 관할하는 주교[사교]. [↓]

di·o·cese [dáiəsis, -sìːs] *n.* Ⓒ the district under a bishop's authority. bishop의 감독 관구; 주교 관구. [di-, Gk. *oikeō* inhabit]

Di·og·e·nes [daiádʒəniːz / -ɔ́dʒ-] *n.* (412?-323 B.C.) a Greek Cynic philosopher. 디오게네스《그리스 키니코스학파의 철학자》.

Di·o·ny·sus [dàiənáisəs] *n.* 《Gk. myth.》 the god of wine. 디오니소스《주신(酒神)》. 參考 로마 신화의 Bacchus 에 해당.

di·o·ram·a [dàiərǽmə, -rάːmə] *n.* a partly translucent picture, made realistic by various lights and viewed through an opening; a building where these are exhibited. 디오라마; 투시화(透視畫); 디오라마관(館). [dia-, Gk. *horaō* see]

di·ox·ide [daiáksaid, -sid / -ɔ́ksaid] *n.* 《chem.》 an oxide with two atoms of oxygen in the molecule. 이산화물. [di-]

:dip [dip] *v.* (**dipped, dip·ping**) *vt.* **1** (P6,13) put (something) into a liquid for a moment, as to wet or to color it. …을 살짝 액체에 담그다[적시다]; …에 담가 물들이다. ¶ ~ *one's fingers in water* 손가락을 물에 담그다 / ~ *a pen into the ink* 펜촉을 잉크 속에 잠그다 / ~ *the bread in the wine* 빵을 포도주에 살짝 적시다 / ~ *one's hands in blood* 손을 피로 적시다; 살인을 하다. **2** (P6,13) ⓐ wash or clean (something) by putting in a liquid. …을 액체에 담가 씻다[빨다]. ⓑ wash in disinfecting preparation. 소독하다. ¶ ~ *sheep* 양을 소독액에 담그다. **3** (P6,7,13) put (one's hand, a spoon, etc.) into something to take something else out; get or take out (something) by scooping up with a container, the hand, etc. …을 떠내기 위해 (손·스푼 따위)를 넣다; 손·그릇으로 퍼[떠]내다. ¶ ~ *up water from a well* 우물에서 물을 푸다 / ~ *water out of a boat* 보트에서 물을 퍼내다. **4** (P6) lower and quickly raise (a flag, etc.) again. 내렸다 곧 들어 올리다. ¶ ~ *one's headlights* (눈이 부시지 않게) 헤드라이트를 낮추다 / ~ *a flag* 기를 잠깐 내렸다 다시 올리다. — *vi.* **1** (P1,2A,3) plunge into water or other liquid and emerge quickly. 잠깐 잠기다; 잠겼다 나오다. ¶ *The boat dipped into the waves.* 배는 파도를 타고 자맥질했다. **2** (P1,2A,3) 《geol.》 sink; descend gradually; incline or slope downward. 침하(沈下)하다; 서서히 경사지다; 밑으로 기울다. ¶ *The road dips.* 도로가 내리받이이다 / *The sun dipped below the hori-*

zon. 해가 지평선 밑으로 기울었다. **3** (P1) read random passages of a book; study superficially. (책 따위를) 대충 읽다; (…에) 조금 손을 대보다.

dip candles, make candles by dipping wicks into melted wax. 녹인 밀랍에 심을 박아 초를 만들다.

dip deep into the future, think over one's future deeply. 장래를 깊이 생각하다.

dip one's hand into one's purse, spend money freely. 돈을 마음대로 쓰다.

dip into, **a**) take out a small portion of. 조금 꺼내다. **b**) study cursorily; study. 조금 손을 대보다; 연구하다.

— *n.* **1** Ⓒ the act of dipping of any kind, esp. of plunging into water. 담그기; 잠그기; 적시기. **2** Ⓤ a liquid in which something is dipped for cleaning, dyeing, etc. 침액(浸液). ¶ *sheep-dip* 세양액(洗羊液). **3** Ⓒ an act of sinking down; a short downward slope; a slight hollow. 침하(沈下); 경사; 우묵한 데. ¶ *a ~ in the stock-market prices* 주가(株價)의 일시적 하락 / *a ~ in the road* 도로의 침하. **4** Ⓒ a candle made by dipping. 양초. [E.]

have a dip (*in*), bathe (in). 목욕하다. ¶ *have a ~ in the sea* 해수욕을 한차례 하다.

the dip of the compass, the angle made by the needle with the horizon. 자침의 복각(伏角).

diph·the·ri·a [difθíəriə, dip-] *n.* Ⓤ 《med.》 a dangerous, quickly spreading disease of the throat. 디프테리아. [Gk. *diphthera* hide]

diph·thong [dífθɔ(:)ŋ, díp-] *n.* Ⓒ **1** a combination of two vowel sounds pronounced in one syllable. 이중 모음(《'ai, ɔi, ei' 따위》). **2** two vowel letters joined together. 이중 모음자(《'æ, œ' 따위》). [di-, Gk. *phthoggos* voice]

dipl. diplomatic.

di·plo·ma [diplóumə] *n.* Ⓒ (*pl.* **-mas** or **-ma·ta**) **1** a certificate given to a student by a school, college, or university. (대학 따위의) 졸업 증서; 면(허)장. ¶ *get one's* [*a*] *~* 면장을 따다; 졸업하다. **2** any official document showing honors, privileges, etc. 공문서; 특허장. [Gk. *diplous* double]

di·plo·ma·cy [diplóuməsi] *n.* Ⓤ **1** the management of relations between nations. 외교. **2** tactful skill in handling others; tact. 외교 수완. ¶ *use ~* 외교적 수완을 발휘하다.

dip·lo·mat [dípləmæ̀t] *n.* Ⓒ **1** a representative of a government whose work is to look after the interests of his own nation in a foreign country. 외교관. **2** a tactful person. 외교가; 외교적 수완이 뛰어난 사람. [→diploma]

di·plo·ma·ta [diplóumətə] *n.* pl. of **diploma.**

dip·lo·mat·ic [dìpləmǽtik] *adj.* of diplomacy; tactful and skillful in dealing with people. 외교의; 외교 수완이 있는; 사람을 잘 다루는. ¶ *the ~ service* 대[공]사관원; 외교관 근무 / *~ corps* 외교단 / *a ~ answer* 빈틈없는 답변 / *settle by ~ means* 외교적 방법으로 해결하다.

dip·lo·mat·i·cal·ly [dìpləmǽtikəli] *adv.* in a diplomatic manner; according to the rules of diplomacy. 외교적으로; 외교상.

dip·lo·mat·ics [dìpləmǽtiks] *n. pl.* 《used as *sing.*》 the study of ancient official documents. 고문서학(古文書學).

di·plo·ma·tist [diplóumətist] *n.* Ⓒ a diplomat. 외교관; 외교가.

dip·per [dípər] *n.* Ⓒ **1** a person or a thing that dips; a cup with a long handle used to dip water. 푸는[뜨는] 사람[것]; 국자. **2** 《*the D-*》 either of two groups of stars in the northern sky in the shape of a dipper. 북두 칠성; 소북두성. ¶ *the Big Dipper* 북두칠성 / *the Little Dipper* 소북두성. [→dip]

dip·so·ma·ni·a [dìpsouméiniə] *n.* an irresistible desire for strong drink. 음주광(飮酒狂)[벽]; 알코올 중독. [Gk. *dipsa* thirst]

dip·so·ma·ni·ac [dìpsouméiniæ̀k] *n.* a person who has dipsomania. 알코올 중독자.

dire [daiər] *adj.* (**dir·er, dir·est**) horrible; terrible; dreadful. 무서운; 비참한; 심한. ¶ *a ~ calamity* 무서운 재난 / *a ~ heat* 격심한 더위 / *the ~ news of the explosion* 끔찍한 폭발 소식 / *He is in ~ need of help.* 그는 도움의 손길을 애타게 필요로 하고 있다. [L.]

:di·rect [dirékt, dai-] *vt.* **1** (P6) manage; control; guide. …을 관리하다; 지휘한다; 이끌다. ¶ *~ a company* 회사를 이끌다 / *~ the building of a house* 집의 건축을 지휘하다 / *Policemen ~ traffic.* 순경이 교통 정리를 하다. **2** (P6,11,20) order; command. 명령하다; 지시하다. ¶ *The captain directed his men to retreat.* 대장은 부하들에게 후퇴하도록 명령했다 / *He directed that you should start at once.* 너는 곧 떠나라는 그의 명령이었다. **3** (P13) aim at (something); turn (one's attention, efforts, etc.) to something. …을 겨냥하다; 돌리다. ¶ *~ one's attention to* …에 주의를 돌리다 / *~ radio waves around the globe* 지구 도처에 전파를 보내다. **4** (P6,7,13) tell or show the way; lead; guide. 길을 가리키다; 안내하다. ¶ *~ someone to a chair* 아무를 좌석으로 안내하다 / *Can you ~ me to the station?* 역으로 가는 길을 가르쳐 주시겠습니까. **5** (P13) address (a letter, an envelope, etc.) to someone or place; make (remarks) to. (편지 따위)를 …앞으로 보내다; …을 향해 말하다. ¶ *~ a parcel to* 소포를 …앞으로 보내다 / *a letter directed to him* 그 사람 앞으로의 편지 / *~ one's remarks to* …을 향해 말을 하다.

— *adj.* **1** straight. 곧바른; 일직선의. ¶ *a ~ road* 똑바른 길 / *Our house is in a ~ line with the school.* 우리집은 학교와 일직선상에 있다. **2** frank; clear. 솔직한; 분명한 ¶ *a ~ answer* [*question*] 솔직한 대답[질문]. **3** with

nothing or no one between; immediate. 직접의. ¶ *a ~ influence* 직접 영향 / *a ~ hit* 직격탄 / *make ~ contacts with him* 그와 직접 접촉하다. **4** without stopping. 직통의. ¶ *a ~ train* 직통 열차. **5** in an unbroken line. 직계의. ¶ *He is a ~ descendant of Lord Lytton.* 그는 리튼경의 직계 후손이다.
— *adv.* straight; without stopping on the way; without making a detour. 직접; 곧장. ¶ *go ~ to the West* 곧장 서부 지방으로 가다 / *The train goes there ~.* 열차는 곧장 거기로 간다. [di-, L. *rego* put straight]

direct current [–´ ´–] *n.* 《electr.》 an electric current which flows in one direction. 직류. 參考 D.C.로 생략함.

:di·rec·tion [dirékʃən, dai-] *n.* **1** Ⓤ instruction; guidance. 지휘; 지도; 감독. ¶ *work under the ~ of Mr. P,* P씨의 지휘하에 일을 하다 / *Our school is under the ~ of a good principal.* 우리 학교는 훌륭한 교장 지도하에 있다. **2** Ⓒ 《usu. *pl.*》 telling what to do, how to do, where to go, etc.; an order; a command. 지시; 명령. ¶ *under his directions* 그의 명령하에 / *follow his directions* 그의 지시에 따르다 / *give directions to* …에게 지시하다 / *full directions* 설명서; 사용법. **3** Ⓒ 《usu. *pl.*》 the address on a letter or parcel. (편지·소포 따위의) 받는 이의 주소 성명. **4** ⒸⓊ the way a person or thing faces. 방향. ¶ *a sense of ~* 방향 감각 / *from all directions* 모든 방향으로부터 / *in every* 〔*all*〕 *directions* 사방 팔방에 / *go in the right* 〔*opposite*〕 *~* 오른〔반대〕쪽으로 가다.

di·rec·tive [diréktiv, dai-] *adj.* giving orders; directing. 지시적인; 지휘하는. — *n.* an order or instruction. 지시; 지령; 훈령.

:di·rect·ly [diréktli, dai-] *adv.* **1** in a direct manner; straight. 곧장; 똑바로; 직접. ¶ *look ~ at someone* 아무를 똑바로 보다 / *This road leads ~ to the lake.* 이 길은 곧장 호수로 통한다. **2** (of place) ⓐ immediately; closely. 바로; 바짝. ¶ *The truck was parked ~ behind my car.* 트럭이 내 차 바로 뒤에 주차되어 있었다. ⓑ exactly; precisely. 바로; 정확히. ¶ *~ opposite the station* 정거장 바로 반대쪽에. **3** (of time) at once; right away; immediately. (…와) 동시에; 바로; 즉시. ¶ *Go there ~.* 지금 즉시 거기로 가거라.
— *conj.* as soon as…. …하자마자. ¶ *He gets up ~ the bell rings.* 그는 종이 울리자마자 일어난다.

di·rect·ness [diréktnis, dai-] *n.* Ⓤ the state of being direct. 직접; 똑바름; 솔직함.

:di·rec·tor [diréktər, dai-] *n.* Ⓒ **1** a manager; a leader; a person who directs the production of a play, film, dancing, or television. (이끄는) 책임자; 지도〔지휘〕자; (영화 따위의) 감독; (극의) 연출가. **2** a member of a board chosen to carry on the affairs of a company or society. (회사·단체의) 이사; 중역. ¶ *a board of directors* 이사회 / *a personnel ~* 인사부장 / *a managing ~* 전무 이사. [→direct]

di·rec·to·rate [diréktərət, dai-] *n.* Ⓒ **1** the office of a director. 감독〔이사〕의 직(職)〔권능〕. **2** a group of directors. 중역〔이사〕회; 간부회. [↑]

di·rec·tor·ship [diréktərʃìp, dai-] *n.* Ⓤ the position or term of office of a director. 이사(理事) 따위의 직〔임기〕.

di·rec·to·ry [diréktəri, dai-] *n.* Ⓒ (*pl.* **-ries**) **1** a book of names and addresses. 주소〔성명〕록; 인명부. ¶ *a telephone ~* 전화 번호부 / *a business ~* 상공 인명록. **2** a book of rules or directions. 규칙서. — *adj.* directing; leading; instructing. 지휘의; 지시적〔지도적〕인; 관리의.

direct speech 〔**narration, discourse**〕 [–´ ´〔–´–, ´–〕] *n.* 《gram.》 reported speech using the words actually spoken. 직접 화법《e.g. *He said, "I am ill."* cf. *He said that he was ill.*》.

direct tax [–´ ´] *n.* tax demanded directly of the actual persons who must pay it, as a polltax, income tax, etc. 직접세.

dire·ful [dáiərfəl] *adj.* dreadful; awful; terrible. 무서운; 끔찍한. ¶ *a ~ misfortune* 끔찍한 불행. [→dire]

dirge [dəːrdʒ] *n.* Ⓒ a song of grief or sorrow; a lament. 애가(哀歌); 비가(悲歌); 만가(輓歌). [L. *dirige* lead thou]

dir·i·gi·ble [díridʒəbəl, dirídʒə-] *n.* Ⓒ an airship. 비행선. — *adj.* that can be controlled. 조종할 수 있는. ¶ *a ~ balloon* 비행선. [→direct]

dirk [dəːrk] *n.* Ⓒ a dagger. 단검(短劍); 비수. — *vt.* wound (someone) with a dirk. (…를) 단검으로 찌르다. [Teut.]

·dirt [dəːrt] *n.* Ⓤ **1** unclean matter of any kind, dust, etc. which soils skin, clothing, houses, or furniture; wet mud. 오물; 때; 먼지; 쓰레기; (진)흙. ¶ *roll in the ~* 쓰레기 속에 뒹굴다 / *My hands are covered with ~.* 내 손은 먼지 투성이다. **2** 《esp. U.S.》 loose earth or soil. 푸석푸석한 흙〔땅〕. ¶ 《U.S.》 *a ~ road* 포장되지 않은 길. **3** the state of being unclean. 불결 (상태). ¶ *live in a state of ~* 불결하게 살다. **4** anything valueless. 무가치한 것; 비천한〔하찮은〕 것. ¶ (*as*) *cheap as ~* 거저나 마찬가지로 싼 / *treat someone like ~* 아무를 하찮게 대하다. **5** scandalous gossip. (특히 악의에 찬) 소문. [E.]

do someone dirt, 《U.S.》 play a dirty trick on someone. …에게 비열한 짓을 하다.

eat dirt, put up with an insult. 굴욕〔비난〕을 참다.

throw* 〔*fling*〕 *dirt at, abuse; talk scandal about. …을 매도하다; 욕을 하다.

dirt·cheap [dəːrttʃíːp] *adj.* 《*colloq.*》 very cheap. 무척 싼; 똥값의. ¶ *This house is ~.* 이 집은 무척 싸다.

dirt farmer [´ ´–] *n.* a plowman. 농사꾼.

dirt·i·ly [də́:rtili] *adv.* in a dirty manner. 더럽게; 불결하게; 상스럽게.

dirt·i·ness [də́:rtinis] *n.* U the state of being dirty. 불결; 음란함.

dirt track [⌐ㅗ] *n.* a path of rolled earth used for racing. 석탄재를 깐 경주로(路).

:**dirt·y** [də́:rti] *adj.* (**dirt·i·er, dirt·i·est**) **1** soiled with dirt; unclean. 흙으로 더러워진; 더러운; 불결한. ¶ *a ~ face* 더러운 얼굴 / *a ~ road* 더러운 길. **2** unclean in color; grayish. 색이 맑지 않은; 칙칙한. ¶ *a ~ red* 검붉은 색. **3** 《*fig.*》 not clean in speech, action, or thought; crude. 상스러운; 비열한; 경멸할. ¶ *~ conduct* 〔*flattery*〕 비열한 행동〔아첨〕/ *~ money* 부정한 돈 / *do one's ~ work for someone* 아무의 뒤치다꺼리를 하다. **4** rough; stormy. (날씨가) 거친; 찌푸린. ¶ *~ weather* 사나운 날씨.

do the dirty, play a shabby trick. 더러운〔비열한〕 짓을 하다.

— *vt., vi.* (**dirt·ied**) make (something or someone) dirty; become dirty; put (someone) to shame. …을 더럽히다; 더러워지다; …을 욕보이다. ¶ *White cloth dirties easily.* 흰 천은 쉬이 더러워진다. [→dirt]

dis- [dis-] *pref.* **1** opposition. '부정'의 뜻. ¶ *disagree.* **2** reverse. '반대'의 뜻. ¶ *discourage.* **3** apart; away. '분리, 제거'의 뜻. ¶ *dismiss.* [L.]

dis·a·bil·i·ty [dìsəbíləti] *n.* U lack of physical or mental ability. 무력; 무능; 불구; 무자격. ¶ *be excused because of mental ~* 정신상의 결함 때문에 용서받다. [dis-]

dis·a·ble [diséibəl] *vt.* (P6,13) **1** 《*from, for*》 make (something or someone) unable or unfit; make (something or someone) useless; cripple. …을 쓸모〔소용〕 없게 하다; 무력하게 하다; 불구로 하다. ¶ *a disabled soldier* 상이 군인 / *His old age disabled him from working.* 그는 노령 때문에 일을 할 수가 없었다. **2** disqualify legally. 법률적으로 무자격으로 하다. [dis-]

dis·a·ble·ment [diséibəlmənt] *n.* U **1** the act of disabling. 무(능)력; 무자격. **2** disability. 불구.

dis·a·buse [dìsəbjú:z] *vt.* (P6,13) 《*of*》 free (someone) from wrong ideas or mistakes. …의 잘못〔어리석음〕을 깨우치다; 오해를 풀다. ¶ *Education should ~ people of superstition.* 교육은 사람들을 미신에서 깨어나게 해야 한다. [dis-]

dis·ad·van·tage [dìsədvǽntidʒ, -vɑ́:n-] *n.* **1** C something that prevents success; an unfavorable situation. 불리한 입장〔상태, 조건〕. ¶ *be at a ~* 불리한 입장에 서다 / *put someone at a ~* 아무를 불리한 입장에 서게 하다 / *He sold goods at a ~.* 그는 손해를 보고〔불리한 입장에서〕 상품을 팔았다 / *It is no ~ to be small.* 작다는 것은 불리하지 않다. **2** U loss; injury. 불이익; 손(損); 손상. [dis-]

be taken at a disadvantage, be taken by surprise. 기습을 당하다.

dis·ad·van·ta·geous [disæ̀dvəntéidʒəs, dìsæd-] *adj.* unfavorable to success; inconvenient. 불리한; 형편상 나쁜.

dis·af·fect·ed [dìsəféktid] *adj.* unfriendly; discontented. 불만을 품은; 정나미 떨어진. [→ affect]

dis·af·fec·tion [dìsəfékʃən] *n.* U lack of affection or good will; discontent. (인심의) 이반(離叛); 불만; 불평. ¶ *Lack of food caused ~ against the government.* 식량 부족이 정부에 대한 불만의 원인이 되었다.

dis·a·gree [dìsəgrí:] *vi.* (P1,3) **1** 《*with, in*》 fail to agree; be different. 일치하지 않다; 다르다. ¶ *Your story disagrees with his.* 자네 이야기는 그의 이야기와 다르다. **2** 《*with*》 have different opinions; quarrel; talk angrily. 의견이 다르다; 말다툼하다. ¶ *She disagrees with her mother-in-law.* 그녀는 시어머니와 의견이 맞지 않는다 / *Whenever we meet, we ~.* 우리는 만나기만 하면 언제나 다툰다. **3** 《*with*》 have bad effects upon the health of; cause physical pain or discomfort; not suit with. (체질에) 맞지 않다; 고통을 주다. ¶ *Hot weather disagrees with me.* 더운 기후는 내 몸에 맞지 않는다. [dis-]

dis·a·gree·a·ble [dìsəgrí:əbəl] *adj.* **1** unpleasant; offensive. 불쾌한; 싫은. ¶ *a ~ experience* 불쾌한 경험 / *make a ~ impression on* …에게 불쾌한 인상을 주다 / *Advice sometimes sounds ~.* 충고는 때로 불쾌감을 준다. **2** unpleasant in manner; bad-tempered. (성질 따위가) 못된; 비뚤어진; 괴까다로운. ¶ *He is a ~ man.* 그는 사귀기 어려운 사람이다.

dis·a·gree·a·bly [dìsəgrí:əbli] *adv.* in a disagreeable manner. 불쾌하게; 괴까다롭게.

dis·a·gree·ment [dìsəgrí:mənt] *n.* **1** U difference of opinion; lack of agreement. 일치하지 않음; (의견 따위의) 불일치. **2** C an argument; a quarrel. 쟁론; 말다툼; 불화. ¶ *have a ~ with one's wife* 아내와 말다툼하다.

dis·al·low [dìsəláu] *vt.* (P6) refuse to permit (something); reject. (요구 따위)를 허락〔인가〕하지 않다; 거부하다; 기각하다. ¶ *~ a proposal* 제안을 물리치다 / *They disallowed our request for a new trial.* 그들은 우리의 새로운 재판의 요구를 기각했다. [dis-]

:**dis·ap·pear** [dìsəpíər] *vi.* (P1,3) go out of sight; be no longer seen; become lost. 보이지 않게 되다; 사라지다; 없어지다(opp. appear). ¶ *The sun disappeared behind a cloud.* 해가 구름에 가려져서 보이지 않았다 / *When spring comes, the snow disappears.* 봄이 오면 눈이 스러진다 / *Dinosaurs disappeared from the earth millions of years ago.* 공룡은 수백만년 전에 지구에서 사라졌다 / *The money disappeared mysteriously from the safe.* 이상하게도 그 돈이 금고에서 사라졌다. [dis-]

dis·ap·pear·ance [dìsəpíərəns] *n.* UC

the act of disappearing; the state of having disappeared. 사라짐; 소실; 실종; 행방 불명(opp. appearance).

:**dis·ap·point** [dìsəpɔ́int] *vt.* (P6) **1** cause (someone) sorrow by failing to satisfy his expectation, desire, hope, etc. …을 실망시키다; …의 기대에 어긋나다. ¶ *be disappointed in someone* 〔*something*〕 아무〔무엇〕에 실망하다 / *The result disappointed me.* 결과는 나를 실망시켰다 / *We were disappointed at the news.* 우리는 그 소식에 실망했다 / *I was disappointed in my new teacher.* 나는 신임 교사에 실망했다 / *They were disappointed that she did not come.* 그들은 그녀가 오지 않은 것에 실망했다. **2** 《*arch.*》 break one's promise to (someone). …와의 약속을 깨뜨리다. **3** upset (one's hopes, plan, etc.). (희망·계획 따위)를 뒤엎다; 꺾다. ¶ *be disappointed of one's dream* 꿈이 깨지다. [dis-]

be disappointed of, fail to get what one has desired. …의 기대가 빗나가다. ¶ *He was disappointed of the first prize.* 그는 1등상의 기대가 어그러졌다.

dis·ap·point·ed [dìsəpɔ́intid] *adj.* sad at not seeing one's hopes, etc. come true. (희망·기대가 꺾여) 실망한.

dis·ap·point·ing [dìsəpɔ́intiŋ] *adj.* causing disappointment. 실망시키는; 기대에 반(反)하는.

***dis·ap·point·ment** [dìsəpɔ́intmənt] *n.* **1** Ⓤ the state of being disappointed; the act of disappointing. 실망(상태); 실망함〔시킴〕. ¶ *to one's ~* 실망스럽게도 / *have a severe ~* 몹시 실망하고 있다. **2** Ⓒ a person or thing that disappoints. 실망시키는 사람〔것〕; 기대에 어긋나는 사람〔것〕. ¶ *The play was a ~.* 그 연극은 기대에 어긋나는 것이었다.

dis·ap·pro·ba·tion [disæ̀proubéiʃən] *n.* =disapproval.

dis·ap·prov·al [dìsəprúːvəl] *n.* Ⓤ the act of disapproving; failure to approve. 불찬성; 동의 않음. [dis-]

dis·ap·prove [dìsəprúːv] *vt., vi.* (P6;1,3) **1** 《*of*》 have or express an unfavorable opinion of (something); think (something) wrong. (의견·행위 따위를) 좋지 않다고 생각하다; 불가하다고 하다; 찬성하지 않다. ¶ *~ someone's action* 아무의 행동을 나쁘게 생각하다 / *I wholly ~ of his attitude.* 그의 태도에는 전혀 찬성하지 않는다. **2** refuse to approve; reject. (안(案)을) 인가하지 않다; 부인〔기각〕하다. ¶ *The court disapproved the verdict.* 법정은 배심원의 평결을 인가하지 않았다. [dis-]

dis·ap·prov·ing·ly [dìsəprúːviŋli] *adv.* in a disapproving manner; showing disapproval. 불찬성의 뜻을 나타내어; 비난하여. ¶ *He looked at me ~.* 그는 나를 비난하듯 바라 보았다.

dis·arm [disάːrm] *vt.* (P6,13) **1** 《*of*》 take weapons from (someone). …의 무기를 빼앗다; 무장을 해제하다. ¶ *~ prisoners* 포로의 무장을 해제하다. **2** get rid of ill-feeling or suspicion in (someone); make (someone) friendly. …의 노여움〔의혹〕을 없애다; 누그러지게 하다. ¶ *Religion disarms death of its terror.* 종교는 죽음의 공포를 없앤다. — *vi.* (P1) abandon or reduce the quantity of military equipment. 군비를 철폐하다; 군비를 축소하다. [→arm²]

dis·ar·ma·ment [disάːrməmənt, diz-] *n.* Ⓤ the act of disarming; the reduction of armed forces. 무장 해제; 군비 축소. ¶ *a ~ conference* 군축 회의.

dis·ar·range [dìsəréindʒ] *vt.* (P6) break up the proper arrangement of (something); disorder. …를 어지럽히다; 혼란〔교란〕시키다. ¶ *~ someone's plan* 〔*hair*〕 아무의 계획을 교란시키다〔두발을 흩뜨리다〕 / *The wind disarranged the papers on the desk.* 바람이 책상 위의 서류를 흐트러뜨렸다. [dis-]

dis·ar·range·ment [dìsəréindʒmənt] *n.* Ⓤ the act of disarranging; the state of being disarranged; disorder. 어수선함; 혼란(상태); 난맥.

dis·ar·ray [dìsəréi] *vt.* (P6) **1** throw into disorder; disturb. …을 어지럽히다; 혼란시키다. **2** 《*arch.*》 remove the clothes of; undress. …의 옷을 벗기다; 벌거벗기다. — *n.* a state of disorder; confusion. 무질서; 난잡; 혼란. ¶ *a room in total ~* 극도로 어지러운 방 / *a ~ of huddled houses* 다닥다닥 밀집해 늘어선 집들. [dis-]

dis·as·sem·ble [dìsəsémbəl] *vt.* (P6) take apart. …을 해체하다; 분해하다. [dis-]

***dis·as·ter** [dizǽstər, -άːs-] *n.* ⒸⓊ a sudden event which causes great unhappiness, such as a big fire, an earthquake, or a flood. 천재; 재난; 대참사; 불행. ¶ *victims of a railroad ~* 대(大)철도 참사의 희생자 / *This temple has had many disasters since 1700.* 이 사찰은 1700년 이래 많은 재난을 겪어 왔다. [Gk. *astron* star]

dis·as·trous [dizǽstrəs, -άːs-] *adj.* causing great loss or injury; very unhappy. 재해의; 비참한; 손해가 큰; 불행한. ¶ *a ~ war* 파멸을 가져오는 전쟁 / *~ results* 비참한 결과.

dis·as·trous·ly [dizǽstrəsli, -άːs-] *adv.* in a disastrous manner. 비참하게.

dis·a·vow [dìsəváu] *vt.* (P6) deny; refuse. …을 부인하다; 거부하다. ¶ *The king disavowed the statement bearing his signature.* 국왕은 자신이 서명한 그 성명을 부인했다. [dis-]

dis·a·vow·al [dìsəváuəl] *n.* ⓊⒸ the act of disavowing; refusal to approve; denial. 부인(否認); 거절; 거부.

dis·band [disbǽnd] *vt., vi.* (P6;1) **1** discharge (someone) or retire from military service. …을 제대시키다〔하다〕; 해대(解隊)하다. **2** break up (an organization, etc.).

(…을) 해산하다. ¶ *The groups refused to* ~. 그 그룹들은 해산하기를 거부했다 / *The guerrillas disbanded after the war.* 유격대는 전쟁 후에 해산했다. ● **dis·band·ment** *n.* [dis-]

dis·bar [disbɑ́:*r*] *vt.* (**-barred, -bar·ring**) (P6) deprive (a lawyer) of the right to appear in court as a lawyer or to practice law. …을 법조계에서 추방〔제명〕하다; …의 법정(法廷) 변호사 자격을 박탈하다. [dis-]

dis·bar·ment [disbɑ́:*r*mənt] *n.* Ⓤ the act of disbarring; the state of being disbarred. 변호사 자격 박탈; 법조계 제명.

dis·be·lief [dìsbilí:f] *n.* Ⓤ the act of disbelieving; denial of belief; unbelief. 믿지〔신용하지〕 않음; 불신; 의혹; 불신앙. [dis-]

dis·be·lieve [dìsbilí:v] *vi., vt.* (P1,3;6) fail to believe; doubt; distrust. 믿지〔신용하지〕 않다; 신앙하지 않다; 의심하다. ¶ ~ *a story* 이야기를 믿지 않다 / ~ *a witness* 증인을 믿지 않다.

disbelieve in, distrust. …을 믿지 않다; 신앙하지 않다. ¶ ~ *in a religion* 종교를 믿지 않다 / ~ *in someone* 〔*in what he says*〕 아무를 〔그가 하는 말을〕 믿지 않다.

dis·bur·den [disbə́:*r*dn] *vt.* (P6,13) **1** take away a burden from (something); unload; get rid of a burden. …에서 무거운 짐〔부담〕을 내리다; 한시름 놓(게 하)다. ¶ ~ *one's mind* 마음의 무거운 짐을 내리다 / *They disburdened me of my grief.* 그들은 나의 슬픔을 덜어주었다. **2** express (thought). (생각)을 말하다; 털어놓다. ¶ *The boy disburdened his mind to his mother.* 그 아이는 제 생각을 엄마에게 말했다. [dis-]

dis·burse [disbə́:*r*s] *vt., vi.* (P6;1) pay money. 지불하다. [→bourse]

dis·burse·ment [disbə́:*r*smənt] *n.* **1** Ⓤ the act of disbursing; payment. 지불; 지급. **2** Ⓒ the money that is so paid. 지불금; 지급금.

disc [disk] *n.* =disk.

dis·card [diskɑ́:*r*d] *vt.* (P6) throw away (something useless); give up; dismiss. (소용없는 것으로서) …을 버리다; 포기하다; 폐기하다. ¶ ~ *old clothes* 헌 옷을 버리다 / ~ *ways of doing things* …을 하는 식을 버리다. — [⌐—] *n.* **1** Ⓤ abandonment. 버림; 포기. **2** Ⓒ something or someone discarded. 버림받은 것〔사람〕. ¶ *throw into the* ~ 버리다. [dis-]

put into the discard, discard. 폐기하다. ¶ *You may put the old book into the* ~ *now.* 헌 책은 이제 폐기해도 좋다.

dis·cern [disə́:*r*n, -zə́:*r*n] *vt.* (P6,13) **1** see or understand clearly; recognize. …을 분명히 보다; 뚜렷이 인식〔이해〕하다. ¶ ~ *a distant object* 멀리 있는 물체를 보다 / *They discerned a sail on the horizon.* 그들은 수평선상의 범선을 보았다. **2** distinguish with the mind. …을 분간〔식별〕하다. ¶ ~ *good and evil* = ~ *good from evil* 선악을 식별하다. — *vi.* (P1,3) see a difference. 식별하다; 구별하다. ¶ ~ *between right and wrong* 옳고 그름을 식별하다. [dis-, L. *cerno* sift]

dis·cern·i·ble [disə́:*r*nəbəl, -zə́:*r*n-] *adj.* that can be seen clearly; distinguishable. 식별〔분간〕할 수 있는.

dis·cern·ing [disə́:*r*niŋ, -zə́:*r*n-] *adj.* able to see and judge; having sound common sense. 식별〔통찰〕력 있는; 명민한.

dis·cern·ment [disə́:*r*nmənt, -zə́:*r*n-] *n.* Ⓤ the power of discerning. 식별력; 통찰력; 안식(眼識).

:dis·charge [distʃɑ́:*r*dʒ] *vt.* (P6,13) **1** take off (a load) from a ship; unload. …(짐)을 내리다; (배)에서 짐을 풀다. ¶ ~ *a cargo* 뱃짐을 풀다 / ~ *a ship of her cargo* 배에서 짐을 부리다. **2** shoot; fire off. …을 발사〔발포〕하다; 쏘다. ¶ ~ *a gun* 총을 쏘다 / ~ *a shot from a gun* 총 한 방을 쏘다. **3** send out; give out; emit. …을 방출하다; 배출하다; 토하다. ¶ ~ *smoke* 연기를 내뿜다 / *The wound is still discharging pus.* 상처에서는 아직도 고름이 나온다. **4** set (someone) free; release. …을 풀어주다; 방면〔석방〕하다. ¶ ~ *a prisoner* 죄수를 석방하다 / ~ *a patient from* (*the*) *hospital* 환자를 퇴원시키다 / *be discharged from the army* 육군에서 제대하다. **5** send (someone) away from his employment; dismiss; fire. …을 해고〔해임〕하다; 면직하다. ¶ ~ *a housemaid for misconduct* 행실이 나빠 가정부를 해고하다. **6** do; perform. (직무·역할 따위)를 수행하다; 이행하다. ¶ ~ *one's commission* 임무를 수행하다 / ~ *one's official duties* 공무를 집행하다. — *vi.* (P1,3) get rid of a burden; (of water, color, etc.) pour forth; run; (of a gun) fire. 짐을 내리다〔부리다〕; 흘러나오다; 번지다; 발사하다. ¶ *The river discharges into Kyŏnggi Bay.* 강은 경기만으로 흘러든다. — *n.* **1** ⓊⒸ the act of discharging. 짐부리기; 발사; 발포; 방출; 유출; 제대; 해임; 해직; 해방; 면제; 지불〔의무〕의 수행〔이행〕. ¶ *a* ~ *of shots* 총탄의 발사 / *a port of* ~ 짐부리는 항구 / *the* ~ *of prisoners* 죄수의 석방 / *the* ~ *of water* 물의 유출 / ~ *from service* 제대 / *The* ~ *of this cargo will not take long.* 이 뱃짐을 부리는 것은 오래 걸리지 않는다. **2** Ⓒ a flow of electricity. 방전(放電). ¶ *a* ~ *of electricity from the clouds* 구름의 방전. **3** Ⓒ a writing that shows someone's release. 제대증; 해임장. [dis-]

dis·ci [dískai] *n.* pl. of **discus.**

dis·ci·ple [disáipəl] *n.* Ⓒ **1** a student; a follower. 제자; 문하생; 신봉자. **2** a follower of Jesus, esp. one of the twelve apostles. 예수의 12사도의 한 사람. [L. *disco* learn]

dis·ci·pli·nar·i·an [dìsəplənέəriən] *n.* Ⓒ a person who supports strict discipline. (엄격한) 훈련자; 규율을 강제하는 사람. [↑]

dis·ci·pli·nar·y [dísəplənèri / -nəri] *adj.* **1** of or for discipline. 훈련의; 규율상의. **2** intended to punish the violation of order or discipline. 징계의; 징계적인. ¶ ~ *pun-*

ishment 〔*action*〕 징계 처분.

·**dis·ci·pline** [dísəplin] *n.* Ⓤ **1** training. 훈련; 단련. ¶ *mental* ~ 정신 훈련 / *courage without* ~ 만용(蠻勇) / *military* ~ 군사 훈련; 군기 / *the* ~ *of adversity* 역경의 시련. **2** orderly conduct among school children, soldiers, etc. 수양; 규율. ¶ *When the fire broke out, the pupils showed good* ~. 화재가 났을 때 학생들은 훌륭한 규율을 보여주었다. **3** punishment. 징계; 처벌. ¶ *impose hard* ~ 호된 징계를 가하다 / *A little* ~ *would do him much good.* 약간의 징계는 그에게 매우 유익할거다. **4** Ⓒ a branch of knowledge. 학문(분야); 학과. ¶ *ecology as a separate* ~ 독립된 학문 분야로서의 생태학. — *vt.* (P6) **1** train; instruct; educate. …을 훈련하다; 가르치다. **2** punish. …을 벌하다; 징계하다. ¶ ~ *a rude boy for his bad behavior* 못된 행동 때문에 버릇없는 아이를 징계하다. [L. *disco* learn]

dis·claim [diskléim] *vt.* (P6,11,13) **1** disapprove; deny. (권위·관계 따위)를 부인하다; 거부하다. ¶ ~ *all participation* 일절 관여하지 않다 / *They* ~ *the authority of Jesus Christ.* 그들은 예수 그리스도의 권위를 부인한다. **2** reject as not belonging to oneself; disown. (…에 대한) 권리를 포기하다; 권한을 거부하다; 기권하다. ¶ *He disclaimed ownership of the dog.* 그는 개의 소유권을 포기했다. [dis-]

·**dis·close** [disklóuz] *vt.* (P6) show; make (something) known. …을 나타내다〔드러내다〕; 폭로하다; 밝히다; 발표하다. ¶ ~ *one's plan* 계획을 밝히다 / ~ *a secret* 비밀을 폭로하다. [dis-]

dis·clo·sure [disklóuʒər] *n.* **1** Ⓤ the act of disclosing; the state of being disclosed. 발표; 적발; 폭로; 발각. **2** Ⓒ a thing which is disclosed. 표면화한〔드러난〕 것; 폭로〔발각〕된 것.

make a disclosure of, disclose or tell of (something). …을 폭로하다.

dis·co [dískou] *n.* (*pl.* **-cos**) **1** a kind of popular dance music with elements of soul music, a strong Latin American beat, and simple and repetitious lyrics, usu. accompanied by pulsating lights, etc. 디스코 음악《춤곡》. **2** discothèque. 디스코테크. [→discothèque]

dis·col·or, 《Brit.》 **-our** [diskʌ́lər] *vt.* (P6) change the color of (something). …을 변색시키다. ¶ *Acids* ~ *clothing.* 산(酸)은 의류를 변색시킨다. — *vi.* (P1) change in color; lose freshness; fade. 변색하다; 퇴색하다; 바래다. [dis-]

dis·col·or·a·tion, 《Brit.》 **-our-** [diskʌ̀ləréiʃən] *n.* **1** Ⓤ the act of discoloring; the state of being discolored. 변색; 퇴색. **2** Ⓒ a discolored mark; a stain. 변색된 부분; 얼룩.

dis·com·fit [diskʌ́mfit] *vt.* (P6) **1** defeat (the enemy) completely. …을 완패(完敗)〔패주〕시키다; 무찌르다. **2** overthrow; upset. (계획·희망 등)을 뒤엎다; 꺾다; 의표를 찌르다. **3** make (someone) uneasy or confused; embarrass. 곤혹스럽게 하다; 당황하게 하다. ¶ *be discomfited by a question* 질문을 받고 당황해 하다. [→confection]

dis·com·fi·ture [diskʌ́mfitʃər] *n.* Ⓤ the act of discomfiting; the state of being discomfited; a complete defeat; failure of plans or hopes; confusion. 완패; 패배; 좌절; 실패; 당황.

dis·com·fort [diskʌ́mfərt] *n.* **1** Ⓤ lack of comfort or pleasantness; uneasiness. 불쾌; 불안. ¶ *at personal* ~ 불편을 참고 / *without* ~ 불편 없이. **2** Ⓒ anything causing discomfort. 불쾌하게 하는 것. ¶ *neglect minor discomforts* 사소한 불편은 무시하다. [dis-]

dis·com·mode [dìskəmóud] *vt.* (P6) cause inconvenience to; annoy; trouble. …을 불편하게 하다; 괴롭히다. [dis-]

dis·com·pose [dìskəmpóuz] *vt.* (P6) disturb the peace and quietness of (someone); make (someone) anxious. …의 침착〔평온〕을 잃게 하다; 불안하게 하다; 마음을 동요시키다. [dis-, →compose]

dis·com·po·sure [dìskəmpóuʒər] *n.* Ⓤ the act of discomposing; the state of being discomposed; agitation; anxiety; uneasiness. 혼란; 마음의 동요; 불안.

dis·con·cert [dìskənsə́ːrt] *vt.* (P6) **1** disturb; embarrass; confuse. …을 당황〔당혹〕하게 하다; 침착을 잃게 하다. ¶ *Nancy was disconcerted to find that she had left her book at home.* 낸시는 책을 집에 두고 온 것을 알고 당황했다. **2** throw (a plan, etc.) into confusion; upset. (계획)을 뒤엎다; 혼란시키다. ¶ *The late arrival of the speaker disconcerted our plans for the evening.* 연사가 늦게 와서 우리의 밤 행사 계획은 뒤죽박죽이 되었다. [dis-]

dis·con·cert·ed [dìskənsə́ːrtid] *adj.* disturbed; confused. 마음이 동요된; 침착을 잃은; 당혹한.

dis·con·cert·ment [dìskənsə́ːrtmənt] *n.* Ⓤ the act of disconcerting; the state of being disconcerted; embarrassment; confusion. 당혹; 당황; 혼란.

dis·con·nect [dìskənékt] *vt.* (P6,13) separate; cut off (a telephone, etc.). …을 떼다; 분리하다; 끊다. ¶ ~ *a locomotive from a train* 열차에서 기관차를 떼다 / ~ *oneself from a bad companion* 못된 친구와 손을 끊다 / ~ *a machine* 기계를 떼어 분해하다. [dis-]

dis·con·nect·ed [dìskənéktid] *adj.* **1** separated. 연락이 끊긴; 따로따로 떨어진. **2** unrelated; unreasonable; not logical. 앞뒤가 맞지 않는; 동닿지 않는; 지리 멸렬한. ¶ *a* ~ *argument* 앞뒤가 맞지 않는 의론.

dis·con·nect·ed·ly [dìskənéktidli] *adv.* in a disconnected manner. 앞뒤가 맞지 않

게; 지리 멸렬하게. ¶ *speak* 〔*think*〕 ~ 동닿지 않게 말하다〔생각하다〕.

dis·con·nect·ed·ness [dìskənéktidnis] *n*. the quality of being disconnected. 연락〔접속〕이 끊김; 분리; (앞뒤) 동닿지 않음; 지리 멸렬.

dis·con·nec·tion, 《Brit.》 **-nex·ion** [dìskənékʃən] *n*. Ⓤ the act of disconnecting; the state of being disconnected. 분리; 절단; 지리 멸렬.

dis·con·so·late [diskánsəlit / -kɔ́n-] *adj*. comfortless; hopeless; sad; gloomy; melancholy. 마음을 풀 길 없는; 슬픈; 처량한; 쓸쓸한. [→solace]

***dis·con·tent** [dìskəntént] *n*. Ⓤ dissatisfaction; uneasiness; Ⓒ a cause of this. 불평; 불만; 불평〔불만〕거리; 불만의 원인. —*vt*. (P6,13) 《usu. in *passive*》 make discontented or dissatisfied. …을 불만스럽게 하다. ¶ *be discontented with one's lot* 자신의 운을 불만스럽게 여기다 / *She was discontented with the result.* 그녀는 그 결과에 불만이었다. [dis-, →content]

·**dis·con·tent·ed** [dìskənténtid] *adj*. dissatisfied; unhappy. 불평을 품고 있는; 불만의. ¶ *He had a ~ look.* 그는 불만스러운 표정이었다 / *I am ~ with my position.* 나는 내 지위에 불만이다.

dis·con·tent·ment [dìskənténtmənt] *n*. Ⓤ discontent; dissatisfaction. 불평; 불만.

dis·con·tin·u·ance [dìskəntínjuəns] *n*. Ⓤ the act of discontinuing; the state of being discontinued; stoppage; interruption. 중단 (상태); 중절 (상태); 중지. [↓]

dis·con·tin·u·a·tion [dìskəntìnjuéiʃən] *n*. =discontinuance.

dis·con·tin·ue [dìskəntínju:] *vt*. (P6,9) put an end to (something); stop. …을 그만두다; 중지〔정지〕하다. ¶ ~ *a business* 〔*one's visits*〕 사업〔방문〕을 그만두다 / ~ *one's doing something* …하는 것을 중지하다. —*vi*. (P1) come to an end; cease. 끝나다; 그치다; 중지되다. ¶ *The publication of this magazine will ~.* 이 잡지는 폐간이 될거다. [dis-, →continue]

dis·con·ti·nu·i·ty [dìskantənjú:əti / -kɔn-] *n*. ⓊⒸ the state, or quality of being discontinuous; interruption. 불연속; 단절; 중절. ¶ *a ~ of ideas* 사고의 무일관성.

dis·con·tin·u·ous [dìskəntínju:əs] *adj*. not continuous; interrupted. 중절된; 끊긴; 중단된.

dis·co·phile [dískəfàil] *n*. a collector of phonograph records. (특수한) 레코드 수집〔연구〕가. [disco-, →phile]

dis·cord [dískɔ:rd] *n*. **1** Ⓤ difference of opinion; disagreement; strife. 의견의 상위(相違); 불일치; 불화. ¶ *domestic ~* 가정 불화. **2** ⓊⒸ 《mus.》 lack of harmony. 불협화음(opp. harmony).

be in discord with, do not agree or be not in harmony with (someone or something). …와 불화하다; 조화되지 않다.

—[dískɔ:rd, –́] *vi*. (P3) fail to agree; be out of harmony; be at variance. 일치하지 않다; 의견이 맞지 않다; 불화하다. [L. *cor* heart]

dis·cord·ance [diskɔ́:rdəns], **-an·cy** [-ənsi] *n*. Ⓤ **1** (of feelings, etc.) disagreement. 부조화; 불일치; 불화. **2** 《mus.》 lack of harmony. 불협화음; 소음.

dis·cord·ant [diskɔ́:rdənt] *adj*. **1** not harmonious; harsh. 조화되지 않는; 귀에 거슬리는; 가락이 안 맞는. ¶ *a ~ sound* 귀에 거슬리는 소리. **2** disagreeing; incongruous; being at variance. 일치하지 않는; 사이가 나쁜. ¶ *Many ~ opinions were expressed.* 각기 다른 많은 의견들이 개진되었다.

dis·cord·ant·ly [diskɔ́:rdəntli] *adv*. in a discordant manner. 조화되지 않게; 귀에 거슬리게.

dis·co·thèque [dískətèk] *n*. 《F.》 a nightclub for dancing to recorded music, etc. 디스코테크《디스크를 틀어 놓고 춤을 추게 하는 나이트클럽》. [*disk;* Gk. *theca* collection]

dis·count [dískaunt, –́] *vt*. (P6) **1** take away (a certain amount) from a price; reduce a price by a certain percentage. …을 할인하다. ¶ ~ *all the electric fans for sale* 매출중인 모든 선풍기의 값을 할인하다. **2** 《*fig.*》 take (a story, etc.) at less than face value. …을 에누리해서 듣다〔생각하다〕. ¶ *You must ~ what he tells you.* 그가 말하는 것은 에누리해서 들어야 한다. **3** lessen the value of; put a lower value on. …의 가치·효과를 덜다; 감소시키다. ¶ ~ *one's gains by subsequent losses.* 나중의 손실로 번 것을 감소시키다. **4** sell or buy (a bill, etc.) at a reduction of a certain percentage. (어음 따위를) 할인해서 사다〔팔다〕.

—[–́] *n*. ⒸⓊ **1** a reduction from an original price. 할인. ¶ *bank* 〔*banker's*〕 ~ 은행 할인 / *cash* ~ 현금 할인 / *allow* 〔*make*〕 *a 10 percent ~,* 10프로 할인을 하다 / *At some shops you get a ~ if you pay cash.* 어떤 가게에서는 현금을 지불하면 할인받을 수 있다. **2** 《comm.》 the rate of interest charged for discounting a bill. (어음 따위의) 할인율. ¶ *give 5% ~ for cash* 현금불(拂)은 5프로 할인한다. **3** 《*fig.*》 an allowance for exaggeration. (과장된 또는 편향된 이야기의) 참작; 에누리(하여 듣기). ¶ *accept a story with some ~* 이야기를 어느 정도 에누리해서 받아들이다. [→count[1]]

at a discount, **a**) below face value. 액면 이하로; 할인하여(opp. at a premium). **b**) not in demand; less esteemed than formerly; easy to obtain. 판로가 없어; 불필요하여; 평판이 나빠; 경시〔괄시〕되어. ¶ *These goods are at a ~ at present.* 이 상품은 현재 팔리지를 않는다.

give 〔***allow***〕 ***a discount on,*** make the price of (something) lower. …을 할인하다.

dis·coun·te·nance [diskáuntənəns] *vt.* (P6) **1** discourage; disapprove. (용기 따위)를 꺾다; …에 반대하다. **2** put (someone) to shame; embarrass. …을 창피를 주다; 당황하게 하다. [dis-]

***dis·cour·age** [diskə́:ridʒ, -kʌ́r-] *vt.* (P6,13) **1** make (someone) lose courage; disappoint. …의 용기를[희망을, 자신을] 잃게 하다; …을 실망[낙심]시키다(opp. encourage). ¶ *be discouraged at the news* 소식을 듣고 낙심하다 / *Repeated failure discourages anyone.* 거듭된 실패를 하다보면 누구나 용기가 꺾인다. **2** 《*from*》 persuade (someone) not to do; try to prevent. …을 단념하게 하다; …을 못하게 막다. ¶ ~ *him from going out* 그의 외출을 단념시키다 / *They discouraged me from taking that step.* 그들은 내가 그 조치를 취하지 못하게 했다. **3** put difficulties in the way of. …을 방해하다. ¶ ~ *all our attempts* 우리의 모든 시도를 방해하다. [dis-, →courage]

dis·cour·age·ment [diskə́:ridʒmənt, -kʌ́r-] *n.* **1** Ⓤ the act of discouraging; the state of being discouraged; disappointment. 낙담; 의기 저상. **2** Ⓒ something that discourages. 낙담하게 하는 것; 실망시키는 것.

dis·cour·ag·ing [diskə́:ridʒiŋ, -kʌ́r-] *adj.* apt to discourage; depressing. 낙심시키는; 기운을 꺾는. ¶ ~ *prospects* 비관적인 전망.

***dis·course** [dískɔ:rs, −ˊ] *n.* Ⓒ **1** a lecture; a speech. 강연; 연설; 설교. ¶ *make a stirring* ~ 감동적인 강연을 하다. **2** 《*arch.*》 a talk; a conversation. 이야기; 담화; 대화. **3** a written study on a subject; a treatise. 논문. **4** 《gram.》 narration. 화법. —[−ˊ] *vi.* (P3) give a lecture; talk or write formally and at some length; converse. 강연하다; 이야기하다; 논하다. ¶ ~ *on* [*about, of*] *politics* 정치에 관해 이야기를 하다 / ~ *upon Korean literature* 한국 문학을 논하다. [→discursive]

dis·cour·te·ous [diskə́:rtiəs] *adj.* impolite; rude. 무례한; 예절 없는. [dis-]

dis·cour·te·sy [diskə́:rtəsi] *n.* (*pl.* **-sies**) **1** Ⓤ impoliteness; bad manners. 실례; 무례. **2** Ⓒ an impolite act or opinion. 무례한 행동; 실례되는 언동. [↑]

:dis·cov·er [diskʌ́vər] *vt.* (P6,11,12,21) **1** find or find out (something) for the first time. …을 발견하다. ¶ ~ *electricity* [*a new star*] 전기를[새 별을] 발견하다 / ~ *America* 아메리카 대륙을 발견하다 / *Radium was discovered by Pierre and Marie Curie.* 라듐은 피에르와 마리 퀴리에 의해 발견되었다. **2** be aware of (something); realize; learn. …을 깨닫다; …을 알다. ¶ ~ *the facts* 사실을 깨닫다 / ~ *someone to be a liar* 아무가 거짓말쟁이임을 알다 / *I discovered him to be dishonest.* =*I discovered that he was dishonest.* 그가 부정직함을 알았다 / *They are discovering what has happened.* 그들은 무슨 일이 일어났는지 깨닫고 있다. **3** 《*arch.*》 make known; show; reveal. …을 알리다; 보이다; 밝히다. ¶ ~ *a secret to others* 비밀을 남에게 알리다. [dis-]

dis·cov·er·er [diskʌ́vərər] *n.* Ⓒ a person who discovers. 발견자; 창안자.

***dis·cov·er·y** [diskʌ́vəri] *n.* (*pl.* **-er·ies**) **1** Ⓤ the act of discovering or finding. 발견. ¶ *make a new* ~ 새 발견을 하다 / *an epochmaking* ~ *of science* 과학상의 획기적 발견 / *make many discoveries about the heavenly bodies* 천체에 관해 많은 발견을 하다. **2** Ⓒ a thing that is discovered. 발견된 것; 발견물.

dis·cred·it [diskrédit] *vt.* (P6) **1** throw doubt on; destroy belief in (a person, a story told, something thought to be true, etc.); damage the reputation of. …을 의심하다; …의 신용을 손상시키다; 신용[명성·평판]을 떨어뜨리다. ¶ *His behavior has discredited him hopelessly with the public.* 그의 행동은 그에 대한 세상의 신용을 형편 없이 떨어뜨렸다. **2** refuse credit to; refuse to believe. …을 믿지[신용하지] 않다. ¶ *He discredited all that was said.* 그는 들은 말 모두를 믿지 않았다.

—*n.* **1** Ⓤ disbelief; doubt. 신용하지[믿지] 않음; 의혹. **2** Ⓤ loss of respect; disgrace; dishonor. 신용 실추; 불면목; 치욕; 불명예. **3** Ⓒ 《usu. *a* ~》 a person or thing causing such loss. 불면목[불명예]의 씨[원인]. ¶ *a thing to one's* ~ 불명예가 되는 것 / *a* ~ *to our family* 집안의 수치 / *bring someone into* ~ 아무의 이름을 더럽히다 / *fall into* ~ 평판이 나빠지다 / *bring* ~ *on oneself* 불신용[불면목, 악평]을 초래하다. [dis-]

dis·cred·it·a·ble [diskréditəbəl] *adj.* disgraceful; dishonorable; shameful. 신용을 손상시키는; 불명예의; 부끄러운.

dis·creet [diskrí:t] *adj.* 《*in*》 careful; prudent. (언동 따위가) 조심스러운; 분별 있는; 사려 깊은. [→discern]

dis·creet·ly [diskrí:tli] *adv.* in a discreet manner; carefully. 신중히; 사려깊게.

dis·cre·pan·cy [diskrépənsi] *n.* (*pl.* **-cies**) **1** Ⓤ difference; disagreement; inconsistency. 차(差); 차이; 불일치; 모순. ¶ ~ *between two reports* 두 개 보고서의 상위(相違) / ~ *in ability* 능력의 차이. **2** Ⓒ an example of disagreement. 차[상위, 차이]가 있는 문제; 차이[상위]점. ¶ *There were a number of discrepancies in the two reports of the accident.* 사고에 대한 두 보고서에는 많은 차이점이 있었다. [L. *crepo* sound]

dis·crep·ant [diskrépənt] *adj.* different; disagreeing. 상위(相違)하는; 일치하지 않는; 모순된. [↑]

dis·crete [diskrí:t] *adj.* **1** separate; discontinuous. 별개의; 분리된; 불연속의. ¶ *six* ~ *parts,* 6개의 별개의 부분. **2** made up of different parts. 별개의 부분으로 된. ● **dis·crete·ly** [-li] *adv.* [→discern]

dis·cre·tion [diskréʃən] *n.* Ⓤ **1** freedom of judgment or choice. 판단(선택)의 자유; 자유 재량; 결정권. ¶ *at* ~ 자기 판단으로; 임의로; 무조건 / *use one's own* ~ 자기 자신의 결정권을 행사하다 / *It is within* (*in*) *your* ~ *to do it.* 그것을 하는 것은 너의 재량에 속한다. **2** the quality of being discreet; carefulness; prudence. 사려; 분별; 신중(함). ¶ *act with* ~ 신중히 행동하다 / *show* ~ *in carrying it out* 그 실시에 신중함을 보이다; 신중히 실시하다 / 《*prov.*》 *Discretion is the better part of valor.* 군자는 위험한 것을 피한다. [dis-, ↑]

at the discretion of someone*=*at someone's discretion, in accordance with his judgment; as he wishes. …의 판단(재량)으로; …마음대로.

leave to someone's discretion, leave to his judgment. …의 재량(판단)에 맡기다.

surrender at discretion, surrender unconditionally. 무조건 항복을 하다.

the age* (*years*) *of discretion, the age at which a person is capable of choosing his own course of action. 분별 연령《영·미에서는 14세》.

dis·cre·tion·ar·y [diskréʃənèri / -əri] *adj.* left to individual judgment or choice; voluntary. 임의의; 자유 재량(선택)의; 일임된 (opp. compulsory). ¶ *a* ~ *order* 시세에 따르는 주문 / *a* ~ *principle* 독단주의 / ~ *powers to act* 행동의 자유 재량권.

dis·crim·i·nate [diskrímənèit] *vt., vi.* (P6,13;3) **1** 《*between, from*》 observe the difference; see clearly. 구별(분간)하다; 식별하다. ¶ ~ *A from B,* A를 B와 구별하다 / *It is difficult to* ~ *between good books and poor ones.* 좋은 책과 무가치한 책을 구별하기는 어렵다. **2** make a difference in treatment; show partiality or prejudice. …을 차별(대우)하다; 편벽되게 굴다.

***discriminate in favor of* (*against*),** treat (someone) well (badly). …을 우대(優待) (냉대)하다. ¶ ~ *in favor of someone* 아무를 편애하다 / ~ *against someone* 아무를 냉대하다 / *The law does not* ~ *against any person.* 법률은 누구에게나 차별을 두지 않는다. — *adj.* marked by discrimination; clear; distinct. 식별력이 있는; 명확한. [dis-, L. *cerno* shift]

dis·crim·i·nat·ing [diskrímənèitiŋ] *adj.* **1** able to discriminate; seeing a difference clearly. 식별력이 있는; 명확히 분간(구별)하는. ¶ *a* ~ *eye* 감식안(鑑識眼); 비평안(眼). **2** treating something differently. 차별적인. ¶ ~ *tariff* 차별 세율.

dis·crim·i·na·tion [diskrìmənéiʃən] *n.* Ⓤ **1** the act of discriminating; distinction. 구별; 식별; 차별. ¶ ~ *between right and wrong* 정사(正邪)의 구별 / *bombing without* ~ 무차별 폭격. **2** the ability to observe a difference; judgment. 식별(판별)력. **3** the act of making a difference in treatment. 차별(대우). ¶ *racial* ~ 인종 차별 / *show* ~ *against foreigners* 외국인을 차별하다.

dis·crim·i·na·tive [diskrímənèitiv, -nətiv] *adj.* **1** (of persons) discriminating. (사람이) 식별력이 있는; 차이를 분간하는. **2** (of things) serving to distinguish; characteristic. (사물이) 구별을 나타내는 데 도움이 되는; 특이한; 특수한.

dis·crim·i·na·to·ry [diskrímənətɔ̀ːri / -təri] *adj.* =discriminative.

dis·cur·sive [diskə́ːrsiv] *adj.* **1** moving about from one topic to another; wandering. (이야기가) 두서 없는; 산만한; 만연한. ¶ *a* ~ *talk* 종잡을 수 없는 이야기. **2** proceeding by argument. 논증적인. [L. *curro* run]

dis·cus [dískəs] *n.* (*pl.* **-cus·es** or **dis·ci**) Ⓒ a heavy, round plate of stone or metal, thrown for distance as a test of strength and skill. 원반(圓盤); 투원반. ¶ *the* ~ *throw* 투원반. [→disk]

:dis·cuss [diskʌ́s] *vt.* (P6,10,12) **1** talk over (something) together; argue; debate; examine. …을 논의하다; 토론(토의)하다; 검토하다. ¶ ~ *a subject* (*question*) (*with someone*) (아무와) 주제(문제)를 토의하다 / ~ *the proposed law on taxes* 조세 법안을 심의하다 / *We discussed what to do next.* 다음엔 무엇을 해야 할지 논의했다. 參考 discuss는 타동사이므로 전치사를 사용하지 않음. discuss about a problem은 잘못임. **2** 《*joc.*》 eat or drink with enjoyment. …을 음미하며 먹다(마시다). ¶ ~ *a bottle of wine* 포도주 한 병을 맛있게 비우다. [L. *quatio* shake]

:dis·cus·sion [diskʌ́ʃən] *n.* ⓊⒸ the act of discussing; argument; debate. 논의; 변론; 토론; 토의. ¶ *a lively* (*hot*) ~ 활발한(열띤) 토론 / *a question under* ~ 심의 중의 문제 / *have a* ~ *on* (*about*) *the question* 그 문제에 관해 토론하다 / *keep the matter in* ~ 그 문제의 토의를 계속하다.

dis·dain [disdéin] *vt.* (P6,8,9) **1** look down on (someone or something); scorn. …을 경멸하다; 모멸하다. ¶ ~ *flatterers* 아첨배를 경멸하다 / ~ *a man for his snobbishness* 아무의 속물 근성을 경멸하다. **2** be too proud to do (something). (…하는 것)을 떳떳이 여기지 않다; (마음에 두거나 …할) 가치가 없다고 생각하다. ¶ ~ *to notice* (*noticing*) *an insult* 모욕을 아예 무시하다 / *He disdained asking for help.* 도움을 청하는 것을 떳떳하지 않게 여겼다. — *n.* Ⓤ an attitude or feeling of scorn. 경멸; 모멸. ¶ *treat someone with* ~ 아무를 경멸적으로 대하다. [→dignity]

dis·dain·ful [disdéinfəl] *adj.* expressing scorn or contempt; proud. 경멸적인; 거드름 피우는. ¶ *a* ~ *look* 경멸적인 표정 / *be* ~ *of someone* 아무를 경멸하다.

:dis·ease [dizíːz] *n.* ⓊⒸ **1** illness; sickness. 병. ¶ *a serious* ~ 중병 / *a family* ~ 유전병 / *an acute* (*a chronic*) ~ 급성(만성) 질

환 / *a contagious* 〔*an infectious*〕 ~ 전염병 / *catch* 〔*take, suffer from*〕 *a* ~ 병에 걸리다 / *be cured of a* ~ 병이 낫다. **2** an abnormal condition of a plant. (식물 따위의) 병변(病變). **3** a bad condition of the mind, public affairs, etc. (정신·사회 따위의) 불건전한 상태; 병폐. ¶ *Poverty is a social* ~. 빈곤은 사회적 병폐이다. [dis-]

dis·eased [dizí:zd] *adj.* sick; unhealthy; abnormal; morbid. 병에 걸린; 병적인; 불건전한. ¶ *a* ~ *part* 병에 걸린 부분 / *a* ~ *mind* 병든 마음 / *a* ~ *society* 불건전한〔병든〕 사회.

dis·em·bark [dìsembá:rk] *vt.* (P6) take (something) away from a ship to the land; unload. …을 양륙(揚陸)시키다; 상륙시키다. ¶ ~ *an army* (배에서) 군대를 상륙시키다. — *vi.* (P1,3) leave a ship for the land; land. 상륙하다; 하선(下船)하다. [dis-]

dis·em·bar·ka·tion [dìsembɑ:rkéiʃən] *n.* Ⓤ the act of landing or unloading. 상륙; 양륙(揚陸).

dis·em·bar·rass [dìsembǽrəs] *vt.* free from embarrassment, entanglement. (부담·곤혹·걱정으로부터) 해방하다; (복잡한 상태에서) 풀어 주다. [dis-]

dis·em·bod·y [dìsembádi, -im-/-bɔ́di] *vt.* (**-bod·ied**) make (a spirit, etc.) free from the body. (영혼 따위)를 육체에서 분리시키다. ¶ *a disembodied spirit* 육체를 떠난 영혼. [dis-]

dis·em·bogue [dìsembóug] *vi., vt.* (P1, 3; 6,13) (of a river, etc.) pour forth; issue. (강물이 강어귀에서) 쏟아져들다; 흘러들다. ¶ *a river that disembogues into the ocean* 바다로 흘러드는 강. [Sp.]

dis·em·bow·el [dìsembáuəl] *vt.* (**-eled, -el·ing** or 《Brit.》 **-elled, -el·ling**) (P6) take out the bowels of (an animal, etc.). …의 창자를 빼내다; 배를 가르다. ● **dis·em·bow·el·ment** [-mənt] *n.* [dis-]

dis·em·broil [dìsembrɔ́il] *vt.* (P6,13) free from a confused or entangled state or situation. 얽히고 설킨 상태를 풀다; 분규 상태를 풀다. [dis-]

dis·en·chant [dìsentʃǽnt, -tʃɑ́:nt] *vt.* (P6,13) set (something) free from the power of magic or illusion. 마법을 풀다; 환상을 깨뜨리다. ¶ *be disenchanted* 미혹에서 깨어나다 / *He will be disenchanted with her.* 그는 그녀에게 환멸을 느낄 것이다. ● **dis·en·chant·ment** [-mənt] *n.* [dis-]

dis·en·cum·ber [dìsenkʌ́mbər] *vt.* (P6,13) free from (a trouble or burden); disburden. (무거운 짐)을 내리다〔제거하다〕; 귀찮은 것을 없애다. [dis-]

dis·en·gage [dìsengéidʒ] *vt.* (P6,13) **1** set (someone) free from an engagement, duty, etc. …을 (약속·일)에서 해방하다. ¶ ~ *oneself from one's promise* 약속을 취소하다. **2** unfasten; loosen. …을 풀다; 떼다. ¶ *She disengaged her hand from his.* 잡힌 손을 그의 손에서 뺐다. [dis-]

dis·en·gaged [dìsengéidʒd] *adj.* **1** having no appointments; not busy. 약속이 없는; 한가로운. ¶ *The teacher is* ~ *now, so he says he will see you.* 선생님은 지금 선약이 없으셔서 너를 만나 보겠다고 하신다. **2** unoccupied; empty. (장소 따위가) 비어 있는.

dis·en·gage·ment [dìsengéidʒmənt] *n.* Ⓤ the act or process of disengaging; freedom from duty. 해방; 자유.

dis·en·tan·gle [dìsentǽŋgl] *vt.* (P6,13) make (something) free from what is confused; untwist; 《*fig.*》 set in order and make clear. 엉킨 것을 풀다; (분규 따위에서) 해방하다. ¶ ~ *a complicated knot* 복잡한 매듭을 풀다 / ~ *truth from error* 잘못을 바로잡아 진실을 밝히다 / ~ *oneself from political affairs* 정치와 절연하다. [dis-]

dis·en·tan·gle·ment [dìsentǽŋglmənt] *n.* Ⓤ the act or process of disentangling; the state of being disentangled. (엉킨 것을) 풂; 해방.

dis·en·thral [dìsenθrɔ́:l] *vt.* (P6) free from bondage. (속박·굴레에서) 해방하다; 자유롭게 하다. [dis-]

dis·e·qui·lib·ri·um [disì:kwəlíbriəm] *n.* Ⓤ loss or lack of equilibrium. 불균형; 불안정. [dis-]

dis·es·tab·lish [dìsistǽbliʃ] *vt.* (P6) **1** upset an established state of (something); remove (someone) from an established position. (기성 제도 등을) 폐지〔타파〕하다; …의 관직을 잃게 하다. **2** deprive (a church) of the official support of the State. (교회의) 국교제(國敎制)를 폐하다. [dis-]

dis·es·tab·lish·ment [dìsistǽbliʃmənt] *n.* Ⓤ the act of disestablishing; the state of being disestablished. 면관; 해직; 폐지. ¶ *the* ~ *of the Church* (교회의) 국교제(國敎制) 폐지.

dis·es·teem [dìsestí:m] *vt.* (P6) scorn; pay little attention to (someone). …을 경멸〔경시〕하다. — *n.* Ⓤ scorn; dislike; disfavor. 경멸; 경시; 혐오; 반감. [dis-]

dis·fa·vor, 《Brit.》 **-vour** [disféivər] *n.* Ⓤ **1** dislike; displeasure. 미움; 혐오; 불쾌. ¶ *regard someone with* ~ 아무를 좋지 않게 보다 / *incur the* ~ *of* …의 미움을 사다; 눈밖에 나다 / *look upon a plan with* ~ 계획에 호의를 보이지 않다. **2** a state in which a person is unpopular. 인기〔인망〕 없음. ¶ *be in* ~ *with someone* 아무에게 인기가 없다 / *fall* 〔*come*〕 *into* ~ 인기가 떨어지다; 인기를 잃다. — *vt.* (P6) treat unkindly; dislike. …을 냉대하다; 싫어하다. [dis-]

dis·fig·ure [disfígjər / -fígər] *vt.* (P6,13) spoil the appearance, shape, or value of (something). …의 외관〔모양〕을 망치다; …을 보기싫게 하다; …의 가치를 손상하다. ¶ ~ *the countryside with advertising signs* 광고 간판들이 근교의 경관을 해치다. [dis-]

dis·fig·ured [disfígjərd / -fígərd] *adj.* with a

spoiled appearance or shape. 모양〔외관〕이 손상된.

dis·fig·ure·ment [disfígjərmənt / -fígər-] *n.* **1** Ⓤ the act of disfiguring; the state of being disfigured. 외관〔모양〕을 손상함; 모양이 손상된 상태. **2** Ⓒ something that disfigures; a deformity or blemish. 외관〔모양〕을 손상하는 것; 상처; 오점.

dis·for·est [disfɔ́:rist, -fár- / -fɔ́r-] *vt.* clear the forest from. …의 산림을 벌채〔개척〕하다 (=disafforest). [dis-]

dis·fran·chise [disfrǽntʃaiz] *vt.* (P6) **1** take away a right of citizenship, esp. the right to vote, from (someone). …에게서 공민〔선거〕권을 빼앗다. ¶ *a disfranchised person* 공민권을 박탈당한 사람. **2** take away from (someone) a right, privilege, or power. …에게서 권리를〔특권을〕 빼앗다. [dis-]

dis·gorge [disgɔ́:rdʒ] *vt.* (P6,13) **1** throw out (something) from the throat. …을 토해 내다. **2** pour forth. 힘차게 배출하다〔쏟아내다〕; 흐르게 하다. ¶ *That river disgorges itself* 〔*its water*〕 *into the Pacific Ocean.* 강은 태평양으로 흘러든다. **3** 《*fig.*》 give up (unjust gains) unwillingly. (부정 소득 따위)를 마지못해 돌려 주다; 게우다. — *vi.* (P1,3) (of a river) pour forth. 흐르다. ¶ ~ *into a lake* 호수로 흘러들다. [dis-]

∗**dis·grace** [disgréis] *n.* **1** Ⓤ dishonor; shame. 불명예; 치욕; 오명. ¶ *the* ~ *of criminals* 죄인의 몸이라는 불명예 / *bring* ~ *on* 〔*upon*〕 *one's family* 집안의 명예를 더럽히다. **2** Ⓒ a cause of disgrace. 명예를 더럽히는 것; 치욕이 되는 것〔행위〕. ¶ *a national* ~ 국치(國恥) / *He is a* ~ *to our family.* 그 녀석은 우리 가문의 수치이다 / *The affair is a* ~ *to him.* 그 일은 그에게 치욕이 된다. **3** Ⓤ loss of favor or good name. (윗사람의) 노여움; 역정; 불인기; 불신. ¶ *fall into* ~ *with* … 의 미움을 사다; 눈밖에 나다 / *He is now in* ~. 그는 총애를 잃고 있다.

— *vt.* (P6) **1** bring a bad name to (someone or something). …을 욕보이다; 명예를 더럽히다. ¶ ~ *oneself* 창피를 당하다; 면목을 잃다 / ~ *one's family* 가문의 명예를 더럽히다 / *Don't* ~ *the school name.* 학교의 명예를 더럽히지 마라. **2** remove (someone) from a position. …의 지위를 빼앗다; 실각시키다. [dis-]

dis·grace·ful [disgréisfəl] *adj.* shameful; dishonorable. 부끄러운; 불명예의. ¶ ~ *conduct* 부끄러운 행동. ● **dis·grace·ful·ly** [-fəli] *adv.*

dis·grun·tled [disgrʌ́ntld] *adj.* discontented; displeased. 불만인; 기분이 언짢은. [→grunt]

∗**dis·guise** [disgáiz] *vt.* (P6,7,13) 《*as, from*》 **1** hide the real appearance of (someone). 변장하다; 가장〔위장〕하다. ¶ ~ *oneself* 〔*be disguised*〕 *as a policeman* 순경으로 가장하다 / *They disguised him as a woman.* 그를 여자로 변장시켰다. **2** hide the true nature of (something); hide the real state of. …의 본성을〔정체를〕 숨기다; 속이다. ¶ ~ *one's intentions* 〔*feelings*〕 의도를〔감정을〕 숨기다 / ~ *one's voice* 가성(假聲)을 내다 / ~ *one's age* 나이를 속이다 / ~ *one's anger beneath a serene look* 잔잔한 얼굴로 노여움을 감추다 / *cannot* ~ *the fact that…* …라는 사실은 감출 수 없다.

— *n.* ⓊⒸ **1** a change of appearance. 변장. ¶ *a prince* 〔*detective*〕 *in* ~ 변장한 왕자〔형사〕 / *attend a party in* ~ 변장하고 파티에 참석하다. **2** false show; pretense. 가장; 위장. ¶ *without* ~ 숨김없이; 솔직히 / *His anger was all* ~. 그의 노여움은 모두 거짓이었다 / *His seeming friendliness was mere a* ~. 그의 겉으로의 친절은 가장된 것에 불과했다. [dis-]

a blessing in disguise, good fortune which at first seems to be a misfortune. 처음에는 불행처럼 보이는 축복.

throw off one's disguise, reveal one's real intentions. 정체〔본심〕를 드러내다.

∗**dis·gust** [disgʌ́st] *n.* Ⓤ very strong and sickening dislike. 혐오; (음식이) 역겨움; 싫음. ¶ *have a* ~ *for snakes* 뱀을 싫어하다 / *The smell of the rotten fish filled her with* ~. 썩은 생선 냄새에 그녀는 비위가 몹시 상했다. — *vt.* (P6) cause strong dislike in (someone); sicken. 싫어지게 하다; 넌더리나게 하다. ¶ *be disgusted at* 〔*by, with*〕 *her chatter* 그녀 수다에 질리다 / *His rudeness disgusted everybody.* 그의 무례함은 모두를 불쾌하게 했다. [L. *gustus* taste]

dis·gust·ed [disgʌ́stid] *adj.* being sick and tired. 넌더리〔진절머리〕가 난; 싫증이 난; 시틋해진. ¶ *a* ~ *look* 정떨어진 얼굴. ● **dis·gust·ed·ly** [-li] *adv.*

dis·gust·ful [disgʌ́stfəl] *adj.* causing disgust; disagreeable. 불쾌한; 정나미 떨어진; 정말이지 싫은.

∗**dis·gust·ing** [disgʌ́stiŋ] *adj.* causing to feel disgust; very disagreeable. 구역질나는; 불쾌한; 몹시 싫은. ¶ *Your behavior last night was* ~. 간밤 너의 행동은 아주 불쾌했다.

dis·gust·ing·ly [disgʌ́stiŋli] *adv.* in a disgusting manner. 구역질〔진저리〕나게; 불쾌하게.

:**dish** [diʃ] *n.* Ⓒ **1** a plate, bowl, etc. used for serving food. 접시. ¶ *a meat* ~ 고기 접시. **2** the food served in a dish. 접시에 담긴 음식〔요리〕. ¶ *a plain* 〔*rich*〕 ~ 담백한〔기름진〕 요리 / *made dishes* 배합〔모듬〕 요리 / *a standing* ~ 틀에 박힌 요리 / *three dishes of beans* 세 접시의 콩. **3** a dish-shaped thing. 접시 모양의 것. ¶ *an evaporating* ~ 증발 접시.

— *vt.* **1** (P6,7) 《usu. *up*》 ⓐ serve (food) in a dish. …을 접시에 담다; 접시에 담아 요리를 내놓다. ¶ ~ *up the dinner* 저녁 식사를 제공하다. ⓑ 《*fig.*》 present to someone's attention. (이야기를) 적절히 안배하다; …의 관

심을 끌도록 꾸미다. ¶ *He dished up the story in a humorous way.* 그 이야기를 재미있고 우습게 꾸몄다. Ⓒ 《usu. *out*》 serve from the communal dish on to individual plates. (음식을 큰 그릇에서 퍼서) 나누다; 분배하다. **2** shape (something) like a dish. …을 접시 모양으로 하다. **3** (P6) 《*colloq.*》 upset; ruin; spoil. (계획 따위)를 뒤엎다; 망치다; 꺾다. ¶ ~ *one's plans* 계획을 잡치다. [→disk]

dis·ha·bille [dìsəbíːl] *n.* Ⓤ informal dress; everyday clothes. 실내복; 약복(略服); 평상복. ¶ *She was in* ~. 그녀는 실내복을 입고 있었다. [F.]

dis·har·mo·ni·ous [dìshɑːrmóuniəs] *adj.* lacking harmony. 부조화의; 불일치의; 불협화의. [↓]

dis·har·mo·ny [dishɑ́ːrməni] *n.* ⓊⒸ (*pl.* **-nies**) the state of having no harmony; disagreement. 부조화; 불협화음. [dis-]

dish·cloth [díʃklɔ̀(ː)θ, -klɑ̀θ] *n.* Ⓒ a cloth used for washing dishes; a dish-towel. (접시 닦는) 행주. [→dish]

dis·heart·en [dishɑ́ːrtn] *vt.* (P6) discourage; disappoint. 기운(용기, 희망)을 잃게 하다; 낙담시키다. ¶ *The news of his failure disheartened us.* 그의 실패 소식은 우리를 낙담시켰다. ● **dis·heart·en·ment** *n.* [dis-, *heart*]

di·shev·eled, 《Brit.》 **-elled** [diʃévəld] *adj.* (of clothes or hair) not arranged; untidy. 흐트러진; 단정(칠칠)치 못한. ¶ ~ *hair* (*clothes*) 흐트러진 머리(옷). [→capillary]

:**dis·hon·est** [disɑ́nist / -ɔ́nist] *adj.* **1** (of a person) not honest; not trustworthy; faithless. (사람이) 부정직한; 불성실한; 믿을(신용할) 수 없는. ¶ *a* ~ *person* 부정직한 인간 / *It was* ~ *of the boy to pretend that the penknife was his own.* 아이가 그 주머니칼이 제것인 척한 것은 정직하지 못했다. **2** (of action, words, etc.) intended to deceive others, etc. (행위·수단·말 따위가) 부정한; 거짓의; 속임수의. ¶ *a* ~ *trick* 부정한 술수; 속임수 / ~ *gains* 부정 이득 / *a* ~ *advertisement* 사기 광고. **3** (of work) not carefully done; careless; done so as to deceive. (일이) (겉)날림의; 되는 대로의; 눈속임의. **4** (of thought) not considering difficult facts; avoiding undesired conclusions. (사고가) 어려움을 고려치 않는; 바람직하지 않은 결론을 회피하는. [dis-, *honest*]

·**dis·hon·est·ly** [disɑ́nistli / -ɔ́nist-] *adv.* in a dishonest manner. 부정직하게; 불성실하게.

dis·hon·es·ty [disɑ́nisti / -ɔ́nisti] *n.* (*pl.* **-ties**) **1** Ⓤ lack of honesty. 부정직; 불성실. **2** Ⓒ a dishonest act; a lie. 부정행위; 거짓; 사기.

·**dis·hon·or,** 《Brit.》 **-our** [disɑ́nər / -ɔ́nər] *n.* **1** Ⓤ loss of honor; disgrace; shame. 명예 실추; 불명예; 치욕; 창피. ¶ *an act of* ~ 명예스럽지 못한 행위 / *bring* ~ *on one's family* 가문의 수치를 가져오다. **2** Ⓒ a cause of dishonor. 불명예가 되는 것(사람); 치욕이 되는 것. ¶ *He is a* ~ *to his family.* 그는 가문의 수치이다. **3** Ⓤ lack of respect; insult. 모욕; 무례(한 언동). ¶ *do someone* ~ 아무를 모욕하다 / *I offered him no* ~. 그에게 무례를 범치 않았다. **4** Ⓤ failure to pay a check. (어음 따위의) 부도; 지불(인수) 거절. ¶ *a notice of* ~ 부도 통지.

— *vt.* (P6) **1** bring shame to (someone); disgrace. …의 명예를(이름을) 더럽히다; 창피를 주다; 욕보이다; 모욕하다. ¶ ~ *oneself* 불명예를 초래하다. **2** 《comm.》 refuse to pay (a check). (어음·수표)의 지급을(인수를) 거절하다; 부도로 하다. ¶ *a dishonored bill* 부도 어음 / ~ *a bill* 어음을 부도내다. **3** rape; seduce. (여자의) 정조를 더럽히다; 욕보이다; 폭행하다; 유혹하다. **4** refuse to perform. (약속)을 이행치 않다; 무효로 하다. ¶ ~ *one's promise* 언약을 파기하다. [dis-]

dis·hon·or·a·ble, 《Brit.》 **-our·a·ble** [disɑ́nərəbəl / -ɔ́nə-] *adj.* shameful; disgraceful; having no honor. 부끄러운; 창피한; 수치스러운; 명예롭지 못한. ● **dis·hon·or·a·bly** [-bəli] *adv.*

dis·il·lu·sion [dìsilúːʒən] *n.* Ⓤ the state of being free from illusion; disenchantment. 환상(미혹(迷惑))에서 깨어남; 각성; 환멸. — *vt.* (P6) make (someone) free from a mistaken belief; disenchant. …를 미혹(몽상·잘못)에서 깨어나게 하다; …에 환멸을 느끼게 하다. ¶ *be* (*become*) *disillusioned* 환멸을 느끼다. [dis-]

dis·il·lu·sion·ment [dìsilúːʒənmənt] *n.* Ⓤ the state of being disillusioned. 환멸감(感).

dis·in·cen·tive [dìsinséntiv] *n.* 《*to*》 a practice, system, etc. that discourages actions or effort. 행동을 억제하는 것; 의욕을 꺾는 것. [dis-]

dis·in·cli·na·tion [dìsinklinéiʃən] *n.* Ⓒ Ⓤ 《usu. *a* ~ or *one's* ~》 a dislike; the state of being unwilling. 시틋함; 내키지 않음. ¶ *have a* ~ *for work* 일할 마음이 나지 않다 / *have a* ~ *to do something* …을 할 마음이 내키지 않다. [↓]

dis·in·cline [dìsinkláin] *vt.* (P6,13,20) 《usu. in *passive*》 make (someone) unwilling to do something. …에 싫증이 나게 하다; 마음이 내키지 않게 하다. ¶ *I am disinclined to accept it* (*do the work*). 그것을 받아들일(일을 할) 마음이 안 난다. — *vi.* (P1) 《rare》 be unwilling. 마음이 내키지 않(게 되)다. [dis-]

dis·in·fect [dìsinfékt] *vt.* (P6) destroy the harmful bacteria of (something). …을 살균(소독)하다. ¶ *the disinfecting power* 살균력 / ~ *oneself and one's clothes* 자신과 옷을 소독하다. [dis-]

dis·in·fect·ant [dìsinféktənt] *n.* Ⓒ a thing used for disinfecting. 소독(살균)제. ¶ *Carbolic acid is a* ~. 석탄산은 소독제이다. — *adj.* disinfecting. 소독의; 소독(살균) 효과

가 있는.

dis·in·fec·tion [dìsinfékʃən] *n.* Ⓤ the act of disinfecting. 소독; 살균.

dis·in·fla·tion [dìsinfléiʃən] *n.* 《econ.》 counteracting inflation. 디스인플레이션《인플레이션의 완화》. [dis-]

dis·in·gen·u·ous [dìsindʒénjuːəs] *adj.* dishonest; unfair; insincere. 부정직한; 솔직하지 않은; 불성실한. ¶ *a ~ remark* 음험한 말. [dis-]

dis·in·her·it [dìsinhérit] *vt.* (P6) take away the right as a heir from (someone). …에게서 상속권을 빼앗다; …을 의절〔폐적(廢嫡)〕하다. ¶ *The son was disinherited by his father.* 아들은 아버지에 의해 폐적되었다. [dis-]

dis·in·her·i·tance [dìsinhéritəns] *n.* Ⓤ the act of disinheriting; the state of being disinherited. 상속권 박탈; 폐적(廢嫡); 의절.

dis·in·te·grate [disíntigrèit] *vt., vi.* (P6;1) break up (into pieces); disunite; destroy the unity of. 붕괴시키다〔하다〕; 분해시키다〔하다〕. ¶ *~ society* 사회를 붕괴시키다 / *Frost disintegrates rock.* 서리는 암석을 붕괴시킨다 / *The papers had disintegrated into a pile of dust.* 서류는 삭아서 한 무더기 먼지로 분해돼 있었다. [dis-]

dis·in·te·gra·tion [disìntigréiʃən] *n.* Ⓤ the process of disintegrating. 분해; 붕괴; 분열. ¶ *the ~ of an empire* 제국의 붕괴 / *the ~ of personality* 인격의 분열.

dis·in·ter [dìsintə́ːr] *vt.* (**-terred, -ter·ring**) **1** dig up or remove from a grave, etc. (매장된 곳에서) 꺼내다; 파내다; 발굴하다. **2** 《*fig.*》 dig up (what is hidden); bring to light. (잊혀진 것·묻혀진 것)을 세상에 드러내다; 햇빛을 보게 하다. ¶ *~ an old quarrel* 해묵은 말다툼을 다시 들춰 내다. ● **dis·in·ter·ment** [-mənt] *n.* [dis-]

dis·in·ter·est [disíntərist, -rèst-] *n.* Ⓤ lack of interest; indifference. 무관심; 냉담. [dis-]

dis·in·ter·est·ed [disíntəristid, -rèst-] *adj.* **1** fair; just; unselfish. 공평 무사한; 사심〔사욕〕 없는. ¶ *a ~ decision* 공평 무사한 결정 / *a ~ zeal for public service* 사회를 위해 봉사하겠다는 사심없는 열의. **2** 《U.S. *colloq.*》 not interested; indifferent. 흥미〔관심〕 없는; 냉담한.

dis·in·ter·est·ed·ness [disíntəristidnis, -rèst-] *n.* Ⓤ freedom from selfish motives. 공평무사; 사심 없음.

dis·jec·ta mem·bra [disdʒéktə mémbrə] *n. pl.* 《L.》 《*of*》 the scattered fragments. 흩어진 단편(斷片) 조각. [L.]

dis·join [disdʒɔ́in] *vt., vi.* (P6,13;1) divide; separate. 분리시키다〔하다〕; 떼다; 떨어지다. [dis-]

dis·joint [disdʒɔ́int] *vt., vi.* (P6;1) **1** put out of place; separate. (관절을) 삐(게 하)다; 탈구시키다〔하다〕; 해체하다. ¶ *He disjointed a chicken for cooking.* 요리를 위해 닭을 토막냈다. **2** 《*fig.*》 put out of order; destroy the unity, coherence, or connection of. 혼란시키다; 지리 멸렬하게 하다. [dis-]

dis·joint·ed [disdʒɔ́intid] *adj.* **1** separated; broken up; out of joint. (뿔뿔이) 해체된; 관절을 삔; 탈구(脫臼)한. ¶ *a ~ wrist* 삔 팔목. **2** deprived of order; lacking logical connection or coherence. 혼란한; 조리가 서지 않는; 지리 멸렬한. ¶ *a ~ discourse* 지리 멸렬한 담화.

dis·junc·tion [disdʒʌ́ŋkʃən] *n.* ⓊⒸ separation; disconnection. 뗌; 떨어짐; 분리; 분열. [dis-, *junction*]

dis·junc·tive [disdʒʌ́ŋktiv] *adj.* causing separation. 분리하는. ¶ *a ~ proposition* 《log.》 선언 명제(選言命題) / *a ~ conjunction* 《gram.》 이접(離接)〔선택〕 접속사《e.g. (*either…*) *or; but*》.

disk, disc [disk] *n.* Ⓒ **1** a thin, flat, round thing. 평원반(平圓盤); 원반. **2** a flat and round surface. 평원반의 표면. ¶ *the moon's ~* 달의 표면 / *the ~ of a watch* 손목 시계의 표면. **3** 《*sl.*》 a phonograph record. (축음기의) 음반; 판. [Gk. *diskos*]

dis·kette [diskét] *n.* 《computer》 =floppy disk.

disk harrow [⌐-⌐] *n.* a harrow with disks instead of teeth. 원반형 써레《트랙터용 농기구》.

disk jockey [⌐⌐-] *n.* 《U.S. *colloq.*》 an announcer who carries on a radio program of recorded music. 디스크 자키.

·**dis·like** [disláik] *n.* Ⓒ 《usu. *a ~*》 a feeling of not liking; distaste; antipathy. 싫음; 혐오; 반감. ¶ *have a ~ of* 〔*for*〕 *snakes* 뱀을 싫어하다 / *She has a strong ~ for* 〔*of*〕 *insects.* 그녀는 곤충을 몹시 싫어한다 / *He took a ~ to us.* 그는 우리를 싫어했다 / *I can't overcome my ~ for him.* 그에 대한 반감을 불식할 수가 없다. —*vt.* (P6,9) have a feeling against (someone or something); hate. …을 싫어〔미워〕하다. ¶ *I ~ rats.* 쥐를 싫어한다 / *I ~ traveling by plane.* 비행기 여행을 싫어한다. [dis-]

dis·lo·cate [díslouкèit, ⌐-⌐] *vt.* (P6) **1** put out of place; 《med.》 put (bones) out of joint. 위치를 바꾸다; …을 탈구(脫臼)시키다. ¶ *have* 〔*get*〕 *one's knee dislocated* 무릎뼈가 퉁겨지다. **2** put out of order; disarrange; disturb. (상태·순서·위치 따위)를 뒤죽박죽이 되게 하다; 혼란시키다. ¶ *~ traffic* 교통을 혼란시키다. [dis-]

dis·lo·ca·tion [dìsloukéiʃən] *n.* ⓊⒸ the act of dislocating; the state of being dislocated. 탈구(脫臼); 혼란; 사태.

dis·lodge [dislɑ́dʒ / -lɔ́dʒ] *vt.* (P6,13) **1** remove (a person or thing) from his or its normal or regular position. (특정한 장소에서) 제거하다; 치우다; 없애다. ¶ *~ a stone from a building* 건물에서 돌을 치우다. **2** drive away from a position of hiding or defence. (은신처·진지·지위 등에서) 몰아〔쫓

아)내다; 격퇴하다. ¶ ~ *the enemy from a hill* 적을 고지로부터 물리치다. ● **dis·lodg(e)·ment** [-mənt] *n.* [dis-]

dis·loy·al [dislɔ́iəl] *adj.* unfaithful; false; dishonest. 불충의; 신의가 없는; 불성실한. ¶ *a ~ wife* 부정한 아내 / *be ~ to one's family* 가족에 불충실하다 / *be ~ to one's country* 조국에의 충성심이 없다. ● **dis·loy·al·ly** [-i] *adv.* [dis-, *loyal*]

dis·loy·al·ty [dislɔ́iəlti] *n.* (*pl.* **-ties**) **1** Ⓤ the state of being disloyal. 불충; 신의 없음; 불성실. **2** Ⓒ a disloyal act. 불충한[신의 없는] 행위. ¶ *He was killed for ~ to his country.* 그는 조국을 배반한 혐의로 처형되었다.

*__dis·mal__ [dízməl] *adj.* **1** gloomy; dark. 음울[음침]한; 어두운. ¶ ~ *weather* 음울한 날씨 / ~ *prospects* 어두운 전망 / *a ~ story* 음울한 이야기 / *Rain made the day ~.* 비가 와서 그 날을 음울하게 했다. **2** unhappy; depressed; not cheerful. 비참한; 슬픈; 쓸쓸한. ¶ *Bad fortune makes a person ~.* 악운(惡運)이 사람을 비참하게 한다. [L. *dies mali* ill days]

dis·mal·ly [dízməli] *adv.* in a dismal manner. 무섭게; 음울[음산]하게; 비참하게.

dismal science [ㅡㅡ], **the** *n.* 《*arch.*》 political economy. 경제학.

dis·man·tle [dismǽntl] *vt.* (P6,13) 《*of*》 **1** take away all the sails, furniture, accessories, etc. from (a ship, house, etc.). (가구·장비 따위)를 …에서 제거하다. ¶ ~ *a ship* 배의 의장(艤裝)을 풀다 / ~ *a fortress* 요새의 방비를 철거하다 / ~ *a house of its roof* 집에서 지붕을 떼어 없애다. **2** take apart; take (a machine) to pieces. …을 떼어내다; 분해하다; 해체하다. ¶ ~ *an engine* 엔진을 해체하다. [dis-]

dis·mast [dismǽːst, -mάːst] *vt.* (P6) destroy or break off the mast or masts of. (강풍 따위가 배에서) 돛대를 앗아가다; 돛대를 부러뜨리다. ¶ *The ship was dismasted in the storm.* 배는 폭풍으로 돛대가 꺾였다. [dis-]

*__dis·may__ [disméi] *n.* Ⓤ fright; discouragement. 놀람; 용기의 상실; 완전한 의기 소침. ¶ *exclaim in ~* 깜짝 놀라 소리치다 / *to one's ~* 깜짝 놀란 것은; 실망스럽게도 / *be struck with ~ at the news* 그 소식을 듣고 몹시 당황하다. —*vt.* (P6) terrify; dishearten. …을 깜짝 놀라게 하다; 낙담시키다. ¶ *I was dismayed at the news.* 나는 그 소식에 실망했다. [?]

dis·mem·ber [dismémbər] *vt.* (P6) **1** cut away the limbs of (a dead body). (사체의) 수족을 끊다[절단하다]. ¶ ~ *a human body.* **2** separate (a nation) into two or more parts; divide. (나라)를 분할하다. ¶ ~ *a kingdom* 왕국을 분할하다 / *The war dismembered the country.* 전쟁으로 그 나라는 분할되었다. [dis-]

dis·mem·ber·ment [dismémbərmənt] *n.* Ⓤ the act of dismembering; the state of being dismembered. 수족의 절단; 해체; 분할.

*__dis·miss__ [dismís] *vt.* (P6,13) **1** ⓐ send away; allow to go. …을 보내다; 가게 하다. ¶ *after school was dismissed* 방과 후 / *The teacher dismissed the pupils at ten o'clock because of the storm.* 선생님은 폭풍우 때문에 10시에 아이들을 보냈다. ⓑ permit all persons in (a meeting, etc.) to go away. (회합 따위)를 해산시키다. ¶ ~ *the assembly* 집회를 해산하다 / *Dismissed!* 해산《구령》. **2** send (someone) away from an office; discharge. …을 해고[면직]하다. ¶ ~ *an officer from his position* 관리를 해임하다 / *He was dismissed (from) the service.* 그는 해고되었다. **3** put away from one's mind; stop thinking about (something). (생각 따위)를 염두에서 떠나게 하다; 잊어버리다. ¶ ~ *an anxiety from one's thoughts* 걱정을 잊어버리다 / ~ *one's fear* 공포심을 버리다 / *He dismissed all thoughts of revenge.* 그는 복수하려는 생각을 모두 버렸다. **4** 《law》 not accept (a claim) in a court. (소송)을 기각하다. ● **dis·miss·i·ble** [-əbəl] *adj.* [→mission]

dis·miss·al [dismísəl] *n.* Ⓤ the act of dismissing; the state of being dismissed; discharge; release. 해산; 퇴거; 해고; 방면.

dis·mount [dismáunt] *vi.* (P1,3) get off (a horse, etc.). (말·자전거·열차 따위에서) 내리다. —*vt.* (P6,13) **1** throw or take away (someone or something) from a horse, etc. …을 (말·자전거 따위에서) 떨어뜨리다; 내리다. **2** take away (something) from its mounting. …을 (대(臺)·틀 따위에서) 떼다. ¶ ~ *a picture* 그림을 액자에서 떼다 / ~ *a gun from its carriage* 대포를 포차에서 떼다. [dis-]

Dis·ney [dízni], **Walt Elias** *n.* (1901-66) an American cartoonist and motion picture producer. 디즈니《미국의 동화(動畫)·영화 제작자》.

dis·o·be·di·ence [dìsəbíːdiəns] *n.* Ⓤ the act of disobeying; refusal to obey orders. 순종치 않음; 불복종; 반항; 위반. ¶ ~ *to the law* 법률 위반. [dis-]

dis·o·be·di·ent [dìsəbíːdiənt] *adj.* refusing to obey orders. 복종[순종]치 않는; 반항적인. ¶ *a ~ son* 반항적인 아들 / ~ *to one's parents* 부모의 말을 듣지 않는.

*__dis·o·bey__ [dìsəbéi] *vt., vi.* (P6;1) refuse or fail to obey (orders, rules, etc.). (…에) 따르지 않다; 반항하다; 어기다. ¶ ~ *one's parents* 부모에게 따르지 않다 / ~ *the orders of one's father* 아버지 명령을 어기다. [dis-]

dis·o·blige [dìsəbláidʒ] *vt.* (P6) **1** refuse to oblige (someone). …에게 불친절하게 하다. **2** disregard the wishes of (someone); offend; give inconvenience to (someone). …의 뜻에 어긋나다; 희망을 어기다; …에게 폐를 끼치다. [dis-]

dis·o·blig·ing [dìsəbláidʒiŋ] *adj.* unkind; unhelpful. 불친절한; 무뚝뚝한; 폐가 되는. ¶ *She is ~ to me.* 그녀는 나에게 불친절하다.

*__dis·or·der__ [disɔ́:rdər] *n.* **1** Ⓤ lack of order; disarrangement; confusion. 무질서; 난잡; 난맥. ¶ *The room was in ~.* 방은 어수선했다. **2** Ⓤ abnormal political confusion. (사회적·정치적인) 불안; 혼란; 소동. ¶ *fall into ~* 혼란에 빠지다 / *At that time Korea was in a state of great ~.* 그 당시 한국은 큰 혼란 상태에 있었다. **3** ⒸⓊ an abnormal state of the body or mind; an illness. (몸의) 이상; (가벼운) 병. ¶ *nervous disorders* 신경 장애 / *a ~ of the stomach* 위장 장애.
— *vt.* (P6) **1** break the order of (something); confuse; disturb. …의 질서를 어지럽히다; …을 난잡하게 하다; 혼란시키다. ¶ *a disordered room* 난잡한 방. **2** put out of health; upset the health of (the body or mind). …을 병이 나게 하다; (몸·정신)에 이상을 일으키다. ¶ *~ one's health* 건강에 이상을 일으키다. [dis-]

dis·or·dered [disɔ́:rdərd] *adj.* in confusion; out of order; ill. 질서 없는; 어지러운; 혼란한; 상태가 좋지 않은; 병난. ¶ *a ~ mind* 정신 착란 / *~ digestion* 소화 이상(異常).

dis·or·der·ly [disɔ́:rdərli] *adj.* **1** out of order; confused. 무질서한; 난잡한. ¶ *a ~ conduct* 풍기 문란한 행위 / *a ~ room* 난잡한 방. **2** causing disorder; lawless; unruly. 질서를 어지럽히는; 무법의; 어거하기 힘든. ¶ *He was arrested for ~ conduct.* 그는 풍기 문란 행위로 구속되었다.

disorderly house [-ˊ--ˋ] *n.* a bawdy, gaming, or betting house. 창녀집; 도박판을 벌이는 집.

dis·or·gan·i·za·tion [disɔ̀:rgənizéiʃən] *n.* Ⓤ the act of disorganizing; disunion; disarrangement. (조직체의) 해체; 붕괴; 분열; 혼란. [dis-]

dis·or·gan·ize [disɔ́:rgənàiz] *vt.* (P6) break up the order or system of (something); confuse. …의 조직을[질서를] 파괴하다; …을 와해시키다; 혼란에 빠뜨리다. ¶ *~ a labor union* 노조를 와해시키다.

dis·o·ri·ent [disɔ́:riənt, -ènt] *vt.* (P6) confuse; esp. cause to lose one's sense of direction, place, or time. …을 혼란시키다; …에게 방향[위치, 시간] 감각을 잃게 하다. ¶ *The strange streets disoriented him.* 생소한 거리여서 그는 길을 잃었다. ● **dis·o·ri·en·ta·tion** [disɔ̀:riəntéiʃən] *n.* [dis-, →orient]

dis·own [disóun] *vt.* (P6) refuse to admit (someone or something) as one's own. (소유권·의무·관계 따위)를 부인하다; 자기 것으로 인정치 않다; 관계를 끊다. ¶ *He disowned his son.* 그는 자기 아들과 의절했다. [dis-, →own]

dis·par·age [dispǽridʒ] *vt.* (P6) speak ill of (someone); say that something or someone is valueless; belittle. …을 나쁘게 말하다; 내리깎다; 하찮게 보다; 경시(輕視)하다. [dis-, →par[1]]

dis·par·age·ment [dispǽridʒmənt] *n.* **1** Ⓤ the act of disparaging. 비난; 비방; 경멸. ¶ *I am not saying that in ~ of him.* 그를 깎아 내려고 그렇게 말하는 것은 아니다. **2** Ⓒ something that causes loss of reputation. 치욕거리; 비난거리; 불명예; 오명(汚名). ¶ *Poverty is no ~ to greatness.* 가난은 위대함에 흠이 되지는 않는다.

dis·pa·rate [díspərit, dispǽr-] *adj.* essentially different; unable to be compared; unlike. 본질적으로 다른; 비교할 수 없는; 같지 않은. ¶ *~ concepts* 본질적으로 다른 개념. [L. *paro* set]

dis·par·i·ty [dispǽrəti] *n.* ⓊⒸ (*pl.* **-ties**) inequality; unlikeness. 같지 않음; 부동(不同); 부등(不等); 상위(相違). ¶ *~ of years* 나이의 차이 / *a ~ in rank* 신분의 차이 / *~ in their reports* 그들의 보고의 불일치. [↑]

dis·park [dispɑ́:rk] *vt.* (P6) convert (a park land) to other uses. (개인의 정원 따위를) 개방하다; 다른 용도로 돌리다. [dis-]

dis·part [dispɑ́:rt] *vt., vi* (P6;1) separate; divide into parts. 분리하다[되다]; 분할하다. [dis-]

dis·pas·sion·ate [dispǽʃənit] *adj.* free from passion; calm; fair. 감정에 동요되지 않는; 냉정한; 공평한. ¶ *a ~ judge* 공평 무사한 재판관. [dis-, →passion]

*__dis·patch, des-__ [dispǽtʃ] *vt.* (P6,13) **1** send out (something) with speed or at once; send (someone) off carrying a very important message. …을 급히 보내다; 급송(急送)하다; 급파하다. ¶ *~ a messenger* 사자를 급파하다 / *~ a letter* [*parcel*] 편지[소포]를 급송하다 / *~ someone on an errand* 아무를 급히 심부름 보내다. **2** ⓐ finish (a job) quickly. (일)을 신속히 끝내다[처리하다]. ¶ *~ (one's) business* 업무를 신속히 처리하다. ⓑ 《*colloq.*》 eat up (a meal). (식사)를 먹어치우다. ¶ *~ one's dinner* 저녁 식사를 깨끗이 비우다. **3** kill; finish off. …을 처치하다; 저승으로 보내다; 죽이다. ¶ *~ a prisoner* [*deer*] 죄수를[사슴을] 죽이다.
— *n.* **1** Ⓤ the act of dispatching; the state of being dispatched. 발송; 급송; 급파. ¶ *the date of the ~ of the parcel* 소포 발송의 날짜 / *demand for the ~ of an embassy* 사절단의 급파를 요청하다. **2** Ⓒ something dispatched; a very important message or report; an official message. 급송[급파]된 것; 지급편(至急便)[속달]; 특보; 공문서. ¶ *by ~* 속달로. **3** Ⓤ quickness of action; promptness. 재빠른 처리; 신속. ¶ *do something with ~* …을 신속히 처리하다 / *The matter requires ~.* 그 일은 신속한 처리를 요한다. **4** ⓊⒸ the act of killing. 살해; 사형 집행. ¶ *the ~ of the spies* 간첩의 처형 / *the happy ~* 할복. [L. *pango* fasten]

dispatch box [-ˊ ˋ] *n.* a box for carrying dispatch and other document. 공문서함(函).

dispatch rider [–ˊ ˋ–] *n.* 《mil.》 a motorcyclist or horseman carrying military messages. 전령사(傳令使).

dis·pel [dispél] *vt.* (**-pelled, -pel·ling**) (P6) drive (doubt, fears, etc.) away; cause to disappear. (의혹·걱정 따위)를 몰아내다; 없애다; 일소하다. ¶ ~ *fears* 공포감을 없애다 / *His words dispelled my doubts.* 그의 말로 나의 의혹이 풀렸다. [dis-, →pulse]

dis·pen·sa·ble [dispénsəbəl] *adj.* that can be done without; not important; needless; unnecessary. 없어도 되는; 중요하지 않은; 필요하지 않은(opp. indispensable). [→dispense]

dis·pen·sa·ry [dispénsəri] *n.* Ⓒ (*pl.* **-ries**) **1** a place in a hospital, school, etc., where medicines are prepared and handed out. (병원·학교 등의) 약국. **2** an institution where medicines and medical treatment are given free or for a small fee. 시료소(施療所); 보건소. [→dispense]

dis·pen·sa·tion [dìspənséiʃən, -pen-] *n.* **1** Ⓤ the act of dispensing or giving out; distribution. 나눠 줌; 분배. ¶ *the ~ of food* 식량의 분배. **2** Ⓒ a thing which is given out or distributed. 분여물(分與物); 분배품. **3** Ⓤ a rule; management. 통치; 관리. ¶ *under the old ~* 오랜 통치(제도) 아래. **4** Ⓒ something that is ordered by Providence. (하늘의) 배려; 섭리. ¶ *The flood was a ~ of Providence.* 홍수는 하느님의 섭리였다. **5** Ⓒ 《theol.》 any religious system. 율법. ¶ *the new Christian ~* 그리스도에 의한 새로운 율법. **6** ⓊⒸ 《Catholic》 official permission to disregard a rule. 관면(寬免)(장).

dis·pen·sa·to·ry [dispénsətɔ̀ːri / -təri] *n.* (*pl.* **-ries**) **1** a pharmacist's manual. 의약품〔약처방〕 해설서; 조제 입문서. **2** =dispensary.

dis·pense [dispéns] *vt.* (P6) **1** give out to each; distribute. …을 나누어 주다; 분배하다. ¶ ~ *food and clothing to the war-sufferers* 전쟁 피해자에게 식량과 옷가지를 분배하다. **2** carry out; apply; administer. (법률 따위)를 시행하다; 실시하다. ¶ ~ *justice* 법을 시행하다. **3** make up (a new medicine) by mixing several kinds. (처방에 의해 약을) 조제하다. ¶ ~ *a prescription* 처방약을 조제하다. — *vi.* (P1,3) dispense medicines. 조제하다. ¶ *He practices medicine here, but does not ~.* 그는 이 곳에서 약국을 하고 있으나, 조제는 하지 않는다. [dis-, L. *pendo* weigh]

dispense with, **a**) make (something) unnecessary; allow the lack of. …을 불필요하게 하다; (…의 수고)를 덜다. ¶ *Machinery dispenses with much labor.* 기계는 크게 노력을 덜어 준다 / *This new office machine will ~ with the need for a secretary.* 이 새 사무기기는 비서가 필요 없게 할 게다. **b**) do without. …없이 때우다. ¶ ~ *with someone's services* 아무의 도움 없이 해 나가다; 아무를 해고하다 / *I cannot ~ with this dictionary.* 이 사전 없이는 해 나갈 수가 없다. **c**) grant exemption from. (법의 적용, 약속의 이행 따위)를 면제하다. ¶ ~ *with a penal statute* 형벌 법규의 적용을 면제하다.

dis·pens·er [dispénsər] *n.* a person who dispenses or gives out; esp. a person who dispenses medicines. 나누어 주는 사람; 분배자; 약제사.

dis·peo·ple [dispíːpəl] *vt.* (P6) depopulate. 주민이 없어지게 하다; 주민을 감소시키다. [dis-]

dis·per·sal [dispə́ːrsəl] *n.* Ⓤ the act of dispersing; the state of being dispersed. 살포; 소산(消散); 해산; 분산; 소개(疎開). ¶ *the ~ of population* 인구의 분산 / *the ~ of a crowd* 군중의 해산. [↓]

dis·perse [dispə́ːrs] *vt.* (P6) **1** scatter (something) in all directions; drive away; dispel (clouds, fog, etc.); cause to disappear. …을 뿔뿔이 흩뜨리다; (사방으로) 흩뜨려 쫓아 버리다; (구름·안개 따위)를 소산(消散)시키다; 스러지게 하다. ¶ ~ *a crowd* 군중을 해산시키다 / *After school the children dispersed to their homes.* 방과 후 아이들은 뿔뿔이 흩어져 집으로 갔다 / *The wind has dispersed the clouds.* 바람에 구름이 흩어졌다. **2** 《opt.》 separate (light) into its colored rays. (빛)을 분광시키다. **3** place in more or less widely separated positions; spread widely. …을 분산시키다; 퍼뜨리다. ¶ ~ *knowledge* 지식을 전파하다 / ~ *troops along a bank* 둑을 끼고 군대를 분산시키다.
— *vi.* (P1) scatter; break up; spread in all directions. 흩어지다; 해산하다; 소산〔소실〕하다. ¶ *The meeting dispersed.* 집회는 해산하였다 / *The class dispersed as soon as the bell rang.* 학급 아이들은 종소리가 나자마자 뿔뿔이 흩어졌다. [di-, →sparse]

dis·per·sion [dispə́ːrʒən, -ʃən] *n.* Ⓤ **1** the act of dispersing; the state of being dispersed. 분산; 이산(離散); 산란(散亂); 살포; 해산; 소산(消散). ¶ *the ~ of an assembly* 집회의 해산. **2** 《opt.》 the breaking up of light into its color rays by a prism. 빛의 분산; 분광. **3** 《*the D-*》 the scattering of the jews in various countries outside Palestine after they were sent out of Babylon. 디아스포라《바빌론 유수(幽囚) 후의 유태인의 이산(離散)》(=Diaspora).

dis·pir·it [dispírit] *vt.* (P6) discourage; disappoint. …의 기운을〔열의를〕 잃게 하다; 의기를 꺾다; …을 낙담시키다. [dis-]

dis·pir·it·ed [dispíritid] *adj.* sad and without hope. 풀죽은; 의기 소침한.

dis·place [displéis] *vt.* (P6) **1** remove (something) from its place; shift. …을 바꾸어 놓다; 이동하다. ¶ *a displaced person* (특히, 전쟁 중의) 피난민. **2** remove (someone) from a position; discharge. …을 해직〔면직〕하다; 파면하다. ¶ ~ *an officer from a regiment* 장교를 연대에서 파면하다. **3** take the place of; replace. …의 대신 들어서다; …을

대신하다. ¶ *The streetcar was displaced by the bus.* 전차가 버스로 대체되었다. [dis-]

dis·place·ment [displéismənt] *n.* Ⓤ **1** the act of displacing; the state of being displaced. 대체(代替); 전치(轉置); 해직; 면직. ¶ *Laziness may bring about ~ from office.* 게으름은 파면을 가져올 수 있다. **2** the weight of the volume of water. 배수량. ¶ *a ship of 10,000 tons ~* (배수 톤수) 1만 톤의 배.

displacement tonnage [–⌐– ⌐–] *n.* tons of displacement. 배수 톤(수).

:dis·play [displéi] *vt.* (P6) **1** spread (goods) before people; show; exhibit; hoist. …을 늘어놓다; 보이다; 전시〔전람·진열〕하다; 자랑해 보이다; 내걸다. ¶ *~ goods* 상품을 진열하다 / *~ the national flag* 국기를 내걸다 / *~ a sign* 간판을 내걸다 / *~ a new car* 새 차를 과시하다 / *The peacock displayed its feathers.* 공작은 깃털을 과시했다. **2** show (one's feelings, ability, etc.); make known. (감정·능력 따위)를 나타내다; 드러내다; 발휘하다. ¶ *~ bravery* 용감함을 보이다 / *~ no fear* 공포를 드러내지 않다. **3** open out (newspapers, etc.); unfold. (신문 따위)를 펼치다; 펴다. ¶ *~ a sail* 돛을 올리다.
— *n.* ⒸⓊ **1** an exhibition; a show. 진열; 전시; 쇼; 발휘. ¶ *a ~ of fireworks* 불꽃놀이 / *the fine vases on ~* 진열돼 있는 꽃병 / *be on ~ at* …에 전시돼 있다. **2** the act of showing one's knowledge, wealth, etc.; showing off. (지식·부(富) 따위의) 자랑해 보임; 과시; 발휘. ¶ *without ~* 꾸밈 없이 / *make a great ~ of learning* 학식을 몹시 자랑하다 / *make a ~ of one's skill* 기술을 과시하다 / *be too fond of ~* 자랑하기를 너무 좋아하다 / *out of ~* 자랑삼아; 이것 보라는 듯이. **3** 《print.》 an arrangement of printing type to attract attention. 의장(意匠) 조판《특정의 어구·활자 따위의 배열·선택을 눈에 띄게 하기》. [L. *plico* fold]

dis·please [displí:z] *vt.* (P6) make (someone) angry or annoyed; dissatisfy. …을 불쾌하게〔골나게〕 하다. ¶ *be displeased at someone's remark* 아무의 말이 귀에 거슬리다〔마음에 안 들다〕 / *She is displeased with me.* 그녀는 내게 불만을 품고 있다 / *The results of the examination ~ me.* 시험 결과가 마음에 안 든다. [dis-]

dis·pleas·ing [displí:ziŋ] *adj.* (usu. of a thing) not pleasing to someone; disagreeable. 불쾌한; 마땅찮은; 싫은; 화나는. ¶ *That is ~ to me.* 그것은 내겐 불쾌하다.

dis·pleas·ure [displéʒər] *n.* Ⓤ 《sometimes *a* ~》 the state of being displeased; dissatisfaction; anger; annoyance; pain. 기분을 상함; 불만; 노여움. ¶ *incur the ~ of someone* 아무의 노여움을 사다 / *show ~* 불만을 나타내다 / *take (a) ~ in* …을 불쾌하게 여기다; …에 노하다.

dis·plume [displú:m] *vt.* (P6) 《*colloq.*》 **1** strip of feather. …의 깃털을 쥐어뜯다. **2** strip of honors. …의 명예〔위계〕를 박탈하다. [dis-]

dis·port [dispɔ́:rt] *vt., vi.* (P6;1) 《usu. *reflexively*》 play; amuse (oneself). 놀다; 즐겁게 놀다. ¶ *~ oneself to one's heart's content* 실컷 즐기다 / *We disported ourselves on the beach.* 우리는 해변에서 유쾌히 놀았다. [L. *porto* carry]

dis·pos·a·ble [dispóuzəbəl] *adj.* **1** that can be disposed of. (간단히) 처분할 수 있는; 사용 후 버릴 수 있는. ¶ *~ syringes* 1회용 주사기. **2** available for use at any time. (아무 때고) 마음대로 사용할 수 있는; 이용 가능한. [↓]

dis·po·sal [dispóuzəl] *n.* Ⓤ **1** the act of disposing. 정리; 처리; 처분. ¶ *the ~ of business affairs* 사무의 처리 / *speedy ~ of legal actions* 소송의 신속한 처리 / *His ~ of the difficulty pleased everybody.* 그의 난관을 처리하는 솜씨는 모든 사람을 만족시켰다. **2** the act of giving away or getting rid of something; transfer; sale. (증여·제거 등에 의한) 처분; 양도; 매각. ¶ *the ~ of an old house* 낡은 집의 매각 / *the ~ of rubbish* 쓰레기의 처분. **3** the act of placing in a certain order or position; arrangement. 배치; 배열. ¶ *the ~ of the troops* 군대의 배치. **4** the power or right to use or manage; control. 자유 사용권; 처분권; 지배권.
at* 〔*in*〕 *one's disposal, at one's service. 마음대로; 자유로. ¶ *I have all the money at my ~.* 이 돈은 모두 내 마음대로 할 수 있다.

:dis·pose [dispóuz] *vt.* **1** (P6) put in a certain order or position; arrange. …을 배열하다; 배치하다. ¶ *~ troops* 군대를 배치하다. **2** (P6) deal with or settle or regulate (affairs). …을 처리〔조처〕하다; 결말짓다. ¶ *God disposes all things according to His will.* 하느님은 그의 의지에 따라 만물을 조처한다. **3** (P13,20) 《*for*》 make (someone) willing or ready; incline. …에게 —하고 싶은 마음이 들게 하다; 자칫 —하게 하다. ¶ *His advice disposed me to read it.* 그의 권고로 그것이 읽고 싶어졌다. [→pose]
dispose of, **a**) put (something) away; get rid of (something). …을 치우다; 처치〔정리〕하다. ¶ *~ of rubbish* 쓰레기를 치우다. **b**) give away (something); transfer; sell. …을 처분하다; 매도〔매각〕하다. **c**) 《*colloq.*》 eat or drink. 먹어 치우다; 마시다.
dispose of oneself, map out one's future course. 앞으로의 처신을 정하다.

dis·posed [dispóuzd] *adj.* inclined; liable; tending. …할 마음이 있는; 경향이 있는; …하기 쉬운. ¶ *be ~ to help someone* 아무를 돕는 경향이 있다 / *be ~ to think so* 그렇게 생각하기 쉽다 / *I am not ~ to agree.* 동의할 마음이 나지 않는다 / *Are you ~ for a walk?* 산책할 마음이 있나.
be well disposed, **a**) be good-natured. 마음씨가 곱다. **b**) 《usu. with *toward*》 be friendly. 호의적이다. ¶ *She is well ~ toward him.* 그녀는 그에게 호의적이다.

***dis·po·si·tion** [dìspəzíʃən] *n.* Ⓒ 《usu. *sing., a* ~》 **1** a natural tendency; a nature; a personal character. 성질; 기질; 성향; 성벽. ¶ *a mild* ~ 유순한 기질 / *a cheerful* [*selfish, cruel, changeable*] ~ 유쾌한[이기적인, 잔인한, 변덕스러운] 성질 / *Mary was of a kind* ~. 메리는 천성이 친절했다. **2** a tendency. 경향; 의향. ¶ *a* ~ *to quarrel* 말다툼 잘 하는 경향 / *a* ~ *toward worldly pleasures* 세속적인 쾌락을 추구하는 경향 / *show a* ~ *to put it off* 그것을 연기하려는 의향을 보이다. **3** the act or way of placing or putting in order; arrangement. 배치; 배열. ¶ *the* ~ *of troops* 군대의 배치 / *the* ~ *of furniture* 가구의 배치 / *make one's* ~ 만반의 준비를 갖추다. **4** the act of giving away or getting rid of something; transfer; sale. 처치; 처분; 양여; 매각. ¶ *the* ~ *of one's estate* 부동산의 양도 / *the* ~ *of goods* 상품의 처분. **5** the power or right to arrange or manage; control. 자유 처분[사용, 재량]권. [→dispose]
at one's disposition, as one likes. 마음[뜻]대로; 자유로.

dis·pos·sess [dìspəzés] *vt.* (P6,13) **1** 《*of*》 take away a house, etc. from (someone); remove property from. (아무에게서 집 따위)를 빼앗다; 소유권을 빼앗다. ¶ ~ *the king of his crown* 왕위를 빼앗다 / 《*fig.*》 *He is dispossessed of his senses.* 그는 분별을 잃고 있다. **2** turn (someone) out of a place. …을 몰아내다; 쫓아내다. [dis-]

dis·pos·ses·sion [dìspəzéʃən] *n.* Ⓤ the act of dispossessing; the state of being dispossessed. 쫓아냄; 강탈; 탈취.

dis·praise [dispréiz] *vt.* (P6) find fault with; blame. …을 비난하다; 나쁘게 말하다; 내리깎다. —*n.* Ⓤ blame; criticism. 비난; 비방; 나쁘게 말하기. ¶ *speak in* ~ *of someone* 아무를 비난하다. [dis-]

dis·proof [disprúːf] *n.* **1** Ⓤ the act of disproving; refutation. 반증; 반박; 논박. **2** Ⓒ a piece of evidence or fact that disproves. 반증물. [dis-]

dis·pro·por·tion [dìsprəpɔ́ːrʃən] *n.* Ⓤ the state of being out of proportion; a lack of proportion; inequality. 불균형. —*vt.* (P6) make disproportionate. …을 불균형이 되게 하다. [dis-]

dis·pro·por·tion·ate [dìsprəpɔ́ːrʃənit] *adj.* not in proportion; out of balance. 불균형의. ¶ *The windows are* ~ *to the height of this house.* 그 창문은 이 집의 높이와 균형이 맞지 않는다.

dis·prove [disprúːv] *vt.* (P6) prove (something or someone) to be false. …의 그릇됨을 입증하다; 반증을 들다. ¶ ~ *a statement* 진술이 허위임을 증명하다. [dis-]

dis·pu·ta·ble [dispjúːtəbəl] *adj.* not yet decided; questionable. 의론[논쟁]의 여지가 있는; 의심스러운; 불확실한(opp. indisputable). ¶ ~ *opinions* 의심스러운 의견. [→dispute]

dis·pu·tant [dispjúːtənt] *adj.* disputing. 토론[논쟁]하고 있는. —*n.* Ⓒ a person who disputes; a person who takes part in a dispute. 논쟁자; 토론자.

dis·pu·ta·tion [dìspjutéiʃən] *n.* ⓊⒸ the act of disputing; argument; discussion. 논쟁; 의론; 토론.

dis·pu·ta·tious [dìspjutéiʃəs] *adj.* fond of arguing; apt to dispute. 의론을 좋아하는; 논쟁적인. ¶ *a* ~ *person* 의론을 좋아하는 사람.

:dis·pute [dispjúːt] *vi.* (P1,3) 《*about, with, against*》 debate; argue. 논쟁[언쟁]하다; 토론하다. ¶ ~ *with* [*against*] *someone over* [*on, about*] 아무와 …에 관해서 논쟁하다.
—*vt.* (P6,10,12,13) **1** argue; debate; discuss. …을 논의하다; 토의[토론]하다. ¶ ~ *how to do* …하는 방법에 대해 토의하다 / ~ *a question* [*the rights and wrongs of...*] 문제를 […의 옳고 그름을] 논의하다. **2** question the truth of (something); oppose. …의 진위(眞僞)를 문제삼다; 이의를[의문을] 제기하다; …을 반대하다. ¶ ~ *a proposal* 제안에 반대하다 / ~ *a will* 유언의 정당성에 이의를 제기하다. **3** contend for (something); resist. …을 다투다; 겨루다; …에 저항[반항]하다. ¶ ~ *every inch of ground* 한 치의 땅도 내어 주지 않으려고 싸우다 / ~ *the enemy's advance* 적군의 진격을 저지하다 / ~ *the victory* [*a prize*] *with someone* 아무와 승리를[상금을] 다투다.
—*n.* ⓊⒸ the act of disputing; argument; quarrel. 토론; 토의; 논쟁; 말다툼. ¶ *a labor* ~ 노동 쟁의 / *They had a bitter* ~ *about money.* 그들은 돈 문제로 격렬한 말다툼을 했다 / *A* ~ *arose between the two leaders.* 두 지도자 간에 논쟁이 벌어졌다. [L. *puto* reckon]
beyond [***without, past***] ***dispute,*** not needing discussion; not doubtful. 의론[의문]의 여지(도) 없이; 명백히.
in [***under***] ***dispute,*** in course of dispute; still being disputed. 논쟁 중의[에]; 미해결의[에]. ¶ *a point in* ~ 쟁점.

dis·qual·i·fi·ca·tion [diskwɑ̀ləfikéiʃən / -kwɔ̀l-] *n.* **1** Ⓤ the act of disqualifying; the state of being disqualified. 자격 박탈; 무자격; 실격. **2** Ⓒ a cause that disqualifies something. 실격 이유; 결격 사항. [↓]

dis·qual·i·fy [diskwɑ́ləfài / -kwɔ́l-] *vt.* (**-fied**) (P6,13) **1** 《*for*》 make (someone) unable to do something. …의 자격을 빼앗다. ¶ *a disqualified person* 결격자 / *Age disqualified him for the job.* 노령 때문에 그는 그 일을 할 수 없었다. **2** take a right or privilege away from (someone) legally. …의 (법률상) 권리를 빼앗다; …을 무능력하게 하다. ¶ *be disqualified from competing in a race* 레이스의 출장 자격을 빼앗기다 / *I am disqualified by my weak heart from serving in the army.* 나는 심장병 때문에 군복무를 할 수

가 없다. [dis-]

dis·qui·et [diskwáiət] *vt.* (P6) make (someone) anxious or uneasy. …을 불안하게 하다; 걱정하게(마음 졸이게) 하다. ¶ ~ *oneself* 마음 졸이다 / *My heart is disquieted.* 마음이 불안하다 / *The news disquieted Tom's mother.* 그 소식은 톰의 어머니를 불안하게 했다. —— *n.* Ⓤ anxiety; uneasiness. 불안; 걱정; 근심; 동요. [dis-]

dis·qui·e·tude [diskwáiətjùːd] *n.* Ⓤ anxiety; uneasiness; trouble. 불안(한 상태); 걱정; 불온.

dis·qui·si·tion [dìskwəzíʃən] *n.* Ⓒ a long, formal speech or writing on some subject; a discourse; a treatise. 논문; 논설; 논고(論考). [→quaere]

dis·re·gard [dìsrigáːrd] *vt.* (P6) pay no attention to (someone or something); treat (someone) without proper respect; ignore. …에 주의를 하지 않다; …을 무시(경시)하다; 고려치 않다. ¶ ~ *a sign* 신호를 무시하다 / *Don't ~ the footnotes.* 각주(脚注)를 무시하지 마라. —— *n.* Ⓤ 《sometimes *a* ~》 lack of attention or respect; indifference. 무시; 무(관)심; 등한히 함. ¶ ~ *of traffic rules* 교통 법규의 무시 / ~ *for other's feelings* 남의 감정에 대한 무관심 / *have a ~ for money* 돈에 무관심하다. [dis-]

dis·rel·ish [disréliʃ] *vt.* (P6) dislike. …을 싫어하다; 혐오하다. ¶ ~ *certain kinds of food* 어떤 유(類)의 음식을 싫어하다 / ~ *advice* 충고를 싫어하다. —— *n.* ⓊⒸ dislike. 싫어함; 혐오. ¶ *have a ~ for raw fish* 날물고기를 싫어하다. [dis-]

dis·re·pair [dìsripéər] *n.* Ⓤ the condition of needing repairs; ruin. 파손(상태); 황폐. ¶ *be in* ~ (수리가 불가능할 정도로) 파손돼 있다. [dis-]

dis·rep·u·ta·ble [disrépjətəbəl] *adj.* unpopular; disgraceful; shameful. 평판이 나쁜; 부끄러운. [↓]

dis·re·pute [dìsripjúːt] *n.* Ⓤ lack of repute; bad reputation; dishonor; disfavor. 평판이 나쁨; 악평; 불명예. ¶ *be in* ~ 평판이 나쁘다 / *fall into general* ~ 세간의 평판이 나빠지다. [dis-, →reputation]

dis·re·spect [dìsrispékt] *n.* Ⓤ lack of respect; rudeness; impoliteness. 존경이(경의가) 없음; 무례; 실례; 불경. ¶ *one's ~ to one's teacher* 선생님에 대한 무례 / *show ~ for one's seniors* 윗사람에 대해 실례되는 태도를 취하다. —— *vt.* (P6) 《*colloq.*》 regard with no respect; treat rudely. 경의를 표하지 않다; 무례하게 대하다; 경멸하다. [dis-]

dis·re·spect·ful [dìsrispéktfəl] *adj.* showing lack of respect; rude; discourteous; impolite. 경의를 표하지 않는; 실례인; 무례한. ¶ *a ~ manner* (*remark*) 무례한 태도(말).

dis·robe [disróub] *vi., vt.* (P1;6) take off the clothes (of oneself or someone else); undress. 옷을 벗(기)다; 벌거벗(기)다. ¶ ~ *oneself* 옷을 벗다. [dis-]

dis·root [disrúːt, -rút] *vt.* (P6) uproot; dislodge. 뿌리째 없애다; (고정된 위치에서) 없애다; 제거하다. [dis-]

dis·rupt [disrʌ́pt] *vt., vi.* (P6;1) break up; tear apart; split up; throw into confusion. 분리(분열, 분단)시키다(하다); 잡아 떼다; 와해(붕괴)시키다(하다); 혼란에 빠뜨리다. ¶ ~ *a government* 정부를 와해시키다. [→rupture]

dis·rup·tion [disrʌ́pʃən] *n.* **1** Ⓤ the act of disrupting; the state of being disrupted. (국가·제도 따위의) 분열; 와해; 붕괴. ¶ *the ~ of the state* 나라의 파멸. **2** 《*the D-*》 a split in Church of Scotland in 1848. 스코틀랜드 교회 분열.

dis·rup·tive [disrʌ́ptiv] *adj.* causing or likely to cause disruption. 분열(파괴)적인; 붕괴를(파멸을) 가져오는.

dis·sat·is·fac·tion [dissæ̀tisfǽkʃən] *n.* Ⓤ the state of not being satisfied; discontent; Ⓒ something that causes dissatisfaction. 불만의 씨(원인). ¶ ~ *with the present world* 현 세상에 대한 불만 / *express ~ at* (*with*) *something* …에 불만을 표시하다. [dis-]

dis·sat·is·fac·to·ry [dissæ̀tisfǽktəri] *adj.* 《chiefly U.S.》 =unsatisfactory.

dis·sat·is·fied [dissǽtisfàid] *v.* pp. of **dissatisfy.** —— *adj.* not satisfied; discontented; displeased. 만족하지 않는; 불만인; 불쾌한. ¶ *a ~ look* 불만스런 표정 / ~ *elements* 불평분자 / *I am most ~ with your work.* 자네의 일에 아주 불만일세.

dis·sat·is·fy [dissǽtisfài] *vt.* (**-fied**) (P6) fail to satisfy (someone); discontent; displease. …을 만족시키지 않다; 불만스럽게(불평을 품게) 하다; 불쾌하게 하다. ¶ *I am dissatisfied with* (*at*) *my position.* 나는 내 지위에 불만이다. [dis-]

dis·sect [disékt, dai-] *vt.* (P6) **1** cut (something) in pieces. …을 잘게 자르다(절단하다). **2** separate (a dead body, animals, plants, etc.) to examine; anatomize. …을 해부하다. ¶ *a dissecting knife* (*room*) 해부도(실) / ~ *a human body* 인체를 해부하다. **3** 《*fig.*》 criticize, or examine (something) in detail; analyze minutely. …을 상세히 비평(조사)하다; 분석하다. ¶ ~ *a problem* 문제를 검토하다 / ~ *someone's state of mind* 아무의 정신 상태를 분석하다. ● **dis·sec·tor** [-séktər] *n.* [→section]

dis·sec·tion [disékʃən, dai-] *n.* Ⓤ **1** the act of dissecting; analysis 절개; Ⓒ something that has been dissected. 해부(한 것). ¶ *a ~ of a head and neck* 머리와 목의 해부 모형. **2** a detailed examination. 면밀한 조사; 분석적인 조사.

dis·sem·ble [disémbəl] *vt.* (P6) **1** hide (one's feeling, intentions, etc.). (감정·의도 따위)를 감추다; 속이다. ¶ ~ *one's anger by smiling* (*with a smile*) 웃음으로 노여움을 숨기다. **2** put on the appearance of. …을 가장

하다; …체하다. ¶ ~ *madness* 미친 체하다 / ~ *innocence* 시치미를 떼다. **3** 《*obs.*》 pretend not to see or notice; ignore. 못 본 체하다; 무시하다. —*vi.* (P1) hide one's feelings, intention, etc.; give a false impression; pretend not to notice. 감정·의도 따위를 숨기다; 모르는〔못 본〕 체하다; 시치미 떼다; …을 속이다. [→similar]

dis·sem·i·nate [disémənèit] *vt.* (P6) scatter; spread; propagate. …을 (흩)뿌리다; 살포하다; (교의 따위)를 전파하다; 퍼뜨리다; 보급〔선전〕하다. ¶ ~ *ideas* 사상을 전파하다 / ~ *Christianity among the villages* 마을에 기독교를 전파하다. [→semen]

dis·sem·i·na·tion [disèmənéiʃən] *n.* Ⓤ the act of disseminating; the state of being disseminated; wide distribution (of ideas or doctrines). 파종; 살포; (사상·교의 따위의) 전파; 유포.

dis·sen·sion [disénʃən] *n.* Ⓤ disagreement in opinion; difference 의견의 상위(相違); 불화; 알력. Ⓒ a quarrel. 싸움; 말다툼. ¶ *family* ~ 가정 불화 / *internal* ~ 내분(內紛). [↓]

dis·sent [disént] *vi.* (P1,3) **1** 《*from*》 disagree in opinion. 의견을 달리하다; 이의(異議)를 제기하다(opp. consent). ¶ ~ *from the prevailing opinion* 일반의 견해에 따르지 않다 / *They dissented from each other.* 그들은 서로 의견을 달리했다. **2** 《Brit.》 reject the rules and beliefs of present churches. 국교(國敎)에 반대하다; (국교회의) 교의에 따르지 않다.

—*n.* Ⓤ **1** disagreement or difference in opinion. 의견의 상위(相違); 이의(異議). ¶ *express strong* ~ 강한 이의를 제기하다. **2** 《Brit.》 separation from the Church of England. 국교회로부터의 분리; 국교 반대; 《*collectively*》 nonconformity. 비(非)국교도. [→sense]

dis·sent·er [diséntər] *n.* Ⓒ **1** a person who is different in opinion. 반대자; 이의자(異議者). **2** 《often *D-*》 a nonconformist. 영국 국교 반대자.

dis·sen·tient [disénʃiənt] *adj.* disagreeing in opinion; objecting. 의견을 달리하는; 이의를 말하는; 반대하는. ¶ *without a* ~ *voice* 이의〔반대〕 없이. —*n.* Ⓒ a person who disagrees. 반대자; 불찬성자; 이의를 말하는 사람. ¶ *The bill was passed with only one* ~. 법안은 반대 1표만으로 통과됐다.

dis·ser·ta·tion [dìsərtéiʃən] *n.* Ⓒ a treatise or thesis, esp. one required for a university degree. 논설; (형식을 갖춘) 논술; 논문(cf. *thesis*). ¶ *a doctoral* ~ 학위 청구 논문. [→series]

dis·serv·ice [dissə́ːrvis] *n.* Ⓤ 《often *a* ~》 an ill treatment; a harmful action. 구박; 학대; 불친절; 해(害). ¶ *do someone a* ~ 아무에게 모질게 굴다. [dis-]

dis·sev·er [disévər] *vt., vi.* (P6;1) cut apart; separate; disunite. …을 떼다; 분리〔분할〕하다. [dis-]

dis·si·dent [dísədənt] *adj.* disagreeing. (의견·태도·성격 따위를) 달리하는; 이론(異論)을 가진. —*n.* Ⓒ a person who disagrees. 의견을 달리하는 사람; 반대자. [dis-, L. *sedeo* sit]

dis·sim·i·lar [dissímələr] *adj.* not similar; different. 같지 않은; 다른; 부동(不同)의. ¶ ~ *tastes* (서로) 다른 취미 / ~ *to each other* 서로 같지 않은. [dis-, →similar]

dis·sim·i·lar·i·ty [dissìməlǽrəti] *n.* (*pl.* **-ties**) Ⓤ the state of dissimilar; difference 같지 않음; 상위(相違); 부동; Ⓒ a point of difference. 상위점.

dis·sim·u·late [disímjəlèit] *vt., vi.* (P6;1) hide (one's feelings, intention, etc.) by pretense; pretend. (감정·의도 따위를) 거짓 속이다; 짐짓 시치미떼다. [→similar]

dis·sim·u·la·tion [disìmjəléiʃən] *n.* Ⓤ the act of dissimulating; pretense; hypocrisy; disguise. (감정을) 감춤; 시치미 뗌; 은폐; 위선; 가장.

dis·si·pate [dísəpèit] *vt.* (P6) **1** scatter (something) in all directions. (사방으로) 흩뜨리다. ¶ *The wind dissipated the fog.* 바람으로 안개가 걷혔다. **2** drive (something) completely away. …을 몰아내다; 해소시키다; 풀다. ¶ ~ *sorrows* 〔*anxiety*〕 슬픔〔걱정〕을 해소시키다 / ~ *the enemy forces* 적군을 물리치다 / ~ *a suspicion* 혐의를 풀다. **3** waste (time, money, strength, etc.) in various foolish ways. …을 낭비〔허비〕하다. ¶ ~ *one's fortune* 〔*time*〕 재산〔시간〕을 낭비하다 / ~ *someone's energies* 아무의 정력을 허비케 하다.
—*vi.* (P1) **1** vanish; disappear. 흩어지다; 사라지다. ¶ *The clouds have dissipated before the wind.* 구름이 바람 앞에 흩어져 없어졌다. **2** lead a wasteful life. 방탕한 생활을 하다; 난봉부리다. ¶ *He is always dissipating and idling.* 그는 늘 방탕하고 빈둥거리는 생활을 하고 있다. [L.]

dis·si·pat·ed [dísəpèitid] *adj.* **1** scattered. 흩어진; 분산한. **2** indulging in pleasure to excess; wasted. 방탕한; 낭비적인. ¶ *lead a* ~ *life* 방탕한 생활을 하다.

dis·si·pa·tion [dìsəpéiʃən] *n.* **1** Ⓤ the act of dissipating; dispersion. 흩어짐; 분산; 소실(消失). ¶ *the* ~ *of clouds* 구름의 흩어져 없어짐 / *the* ~ *of doubts* 〔*sorrows*〕 의혹〔슬픔〕의 해소 / *the* ~ *of fog* 안개의 걷힘. **2** Ⓒ a pastime; an amusement. 기분 전환; 오락. **3** Ⓤ excessive indulgence in pleasure. 방탕; 난봉. **4** Ⓤ wasteful spending. 낭비; 허비. ¶ *the* ~ *of one's time* 〔*money*〕 시간〔돈〕의 낭비.

dis·so·ci·ate [disóuʃièit] *vt.* (P6,13) **1** ⓐ break the connection with (someone); disunite. …을 분리하다; 떼어 놓다. ¶ *dissociated personality* 분열 인격 / ~ *the two ideas* 2개의 관념을 분리하다 / *It is difficult to* ~ *the man from his office.* 그 사람과 직위를 따로 떼어 생각하기는 어렵다. ⓑ 《*reflexively*》 say that one has nothing to do with a person or thing. …와의 관계를 끊다; 관계가 없다고 하다. ¶ ~ *oneself from (someone)* 아무와의 관계를 끊다 / ~ *oneself from what has been said* 그러한 말과는 관계가 없다고 부인하다. **2** 《chem.》 separate. …을 해리(解離)하다. ● **dis·so·ci·a·tive** [-ʃièitiv, -ʃiə-] *adj.* [→sociable]

dis·so·ci·a·tion [disòusiéiʃən] *n.* the act of dissociating; the state of being dissociated. 분리(작용·상태); 분열; 해리(解離).

dis·sol·u·bil·i·ty [disɑ̀ljəbíləti / -sɔ̀l-] *n.* Ⓤ the quality of being dissoluble; solubility. 용해(분해)성. [↓]

dis·sol·u·ble [disɑ́ljəbəl / -sɔ́l-] *adj.* that can be divided into parts; dissolvable. 가용성(可溶性)의; 분해할 수 있는. [→dissolve]

dis·so·lute [dísəlùːt] *adj.* loose in behavior and morals; immoral; dissipated. 행실이 나쁜; 방탕(방종)한.

dis·so·lu·tion [dìsəlúːʃən] *n.* ⓊⒸ **1** the act of breaking up; decomposition. 분해(작용); 해체; 분리. **2** an ending; finish. 해소; 해산. ¶ *the ~ of the National Assembly* 국회의 해산 / *the ~ of the partnership* 제휴의 해소. **3** destruction; ruin. 괴멸. **4** death. 죽음.

dis·solv·a·ble [dizɑ́lvəbəl / -zɔ́lv-] *adj.* that can be dissolved. 분해(용해)할 수 있는.

:dis·solve [dizɑ́lv / -zɔ́lv] *vt.* (P6) **1** make (something) liquid; melt. …을 녹이다; 용해하다. ¶ ~ *salt in water* 소금을 물에 녹이다 / ~ *sugar into syrup* 설탕을 녹여 시럽으로 만들다 / 《*fig.*》 *be dissolved in tears* 목놓아 울다; 울음을 터뜨리다 / *The sun dissolves the snow.* 햇빛은 눈을 녹인다. **2** put an end to (a marriage, partnership, etc.); break up; dismiss. …을 해소시키다; 해산하다. ¶ ~ *a bond* 계약을 해소하다 / ~ *a marriage* 혼인을 무효로 하다 / ~ *a meeting (parliament)* 집회(국회)를 해산하다. **3** clear up (something); solve; explain. …을 해결하다(풀다); 설명하다. ¶ ~ *doubts* 의문점을 설명하다.

— *vi.* (P1) **1** become liquid; melt away. 녹다; 용해하다. ¶ *Sugar dissolves in water.* 설탕은 물에 녹는다. **2** disunite; break up. 해소하다; 해산하다; 붕괴하다. ¶ *The assembly dissolved.* 집회(集會)는 해산되었다. **3** ⓐ fade away; become faint; vanish. 점차 스러져 없어지다; 희미해지다. ¶ *The vision seemed to ~ before our eyes.* 그 광경은 점차 우리의 눈앞에서 사라지는 것 같았다. ⓑ become emotionally weakened. 감정적으로 약해지다. ¶ ~ *in grief* 슬픔(비탄)에 젖다.

— *n.* Ⓤ (Motion pictures, Television) the gradual disappearing or appearing of figures in a scene; a fade-out; a fade-in. (영화·텔레비전의) 용암(溶暗); 용명(溶明). [L. *solvo* loosen]

dissolving views [-ˊ-- ˊ] *n.* lantern pictures of which one fades as another appears on the screen. 환등화(幻燈畫).

dis·sol·vent [dizɑ́lvənt / -zɔ́l-] *n., adj.* (a substance) that causes another to dissolve. 용해력(溶解力)이 있는; 용제(溶劑) (=solvent). [→dissolve]

dis·so·nance [dísənəns] *n.* **1** Ⓤ disagreement; disharmony. 불화; 불일치; 부조화. **2** ⓊⒸ 《mus.》 a disharmonious sound; a lack of harmony. 불협화음(opp. consonance). [dis-, →sound]

dis·so·nant [dísənənt] *adj.* **1** unpleasant to the ear; harsh. 귀에 거슬리는; 불협화(음)의. ¶ ~ *sounds* 귀에 거슬리는 소리. **2** disharmonious; disagreeing. 부조화의; 불일치의; 불화의.

dis·suade [diswéid] *vt.* (P6,13) 《*from*》 advise (someone) not to do something wrong. …에게 —하는 것을 단념시키다(opp. persuade). ¶ ~ *someone from going alone to a dangerous zone* 아무를 설득해 위험 지대에 혼자 가는 것을 막다 / *He was easily dissuaded from the attempt.* 그는 쉽게 설득당하여 그 시도를 포기하였다. [→suasion]

dis·sua·sion [diswéiʒən] *n.* Ⓤ the act of dissuading; advice. 마음을 돌리게 함; 간(諫)하여 말림.

dis·sua·sive [diswéisiv] *adj.* tending to dissuade; intended to dissuade. 단념케 하는; 제지하는.

dis·syl·lab·ic [dìsilǽbik] *adj.* = disyllabic.

dis·syl·la·ble [disíləbəl, díssì-] *n.* = disyllable.

dist. distance; distinguish(ed); distilled; distinct.

dis·taff [dístæf, -tɑːf] *n.* Ⓒ **1** a stick to hold wool, etc. for spinning into thread. 실톳대《실 잣는 데 씀》; 실 감는 막대; (물레의) 가락. **2** 《*the* ~》 woman's work. 여성의 일; 물레질. **3** 《*the* ~》 the female sex. 여성. [E.]

the distaff side, the female members of a family. 모계(母系)(opp. spear side).

:dis·tance [dístəns] *n.* Ⓒ **1** ⒸⓊ the space between one and another. 거리; 간격. ¶ *the ~ between Korea and China* 한국과 중국 간의 거리 / *at a ~ of ten miles,* 10마일 떨어져(거리에) / *within hearing ~* 지호지간에 / *What is the ~ from here to the station?* 여기서 정거장까지의 거리는 얼마나 됩니까. **2** the place far away. 먼 곳. ¶ *at some ~ from here* 여기서 좀 떨어진 곳에(좀 멀리) / *a good (great) ~ off* 꽤 먼 곳 / *live at a ~* 좀 떨어져서 살다 / *The plane flew away into the ~.* 비행기는 멀리 날아가 버렸다 / *We saw a light in the ~.* 멀리 불빛을 보았다 / *It's quite a ~ from here.* 여기서 상당히 멀다. **3** space of time; interval. (시간의) 경과; 동안; 기간; 간격. ¶ *a ~ of three years* 3년의 간격 / *the ~ between birth and death* 태어나서 죽을 때까지의 동안 / *It is impossible to judge at this ~ of time.* 이제 와서(이렇게 시간이 지

난 지금에 와서] 판단을 내리기란 불가능하다. **4** coldness of manner; lack of friendship. 서먹서먹함; 냉랭함. **5** a marked difference. 뚜렷한 차이; 동떨어짐. ¶ *the ~ between the art of the Romans and that of the Greeks* 로마 미술과 그리스 미술 간의 뚜렷한 차이.

in the distance, far away. 멀리. ¶ *Hills are blue in the ~.* 산들이 멀리 푸른 모습을 보이고 있다.

keep** someone **at a distance, treat him coldly. …를 냉랭[서먹서먹]하게 대하다; 가까이하지 않다.

keep** one's **distance, not go too near; not be too friendly or familiar. 가까이하지 않다; 스스러워하다.

— *vt.* (P6) **1** leave far behind in a race; surpass. (레이스에서 상대를) 떼어 놓다; 앞지르다. **2** place or hold at some distance; make seem far off. 멀리(떼어) 두다; 멀리 있는 것처럼 보이게 하다. [dis-, →state]

:dis·tant [dístənt] *adj.* **1** far away in time or space. (시간적·공간적으로) 먼; (멀리) 떨어진. ¶ *a ~ hill* 먼 산 / *a ~ view* 원경(遠景) / *a ~ signal* 원거리 신호기 / *The city is ten miles ~ from Paris.* 그 도시는 파리에서 10 마일 떨어져 있다. **2** far off in relationship, likeness, etc. (관계·유사점 따위가) 먼. ¶ *a ~ likeness* 약간의 유사 / *a ~ relative* 먼 친척. **3** not friendly; cool in manner; reserved. 서먹서먹한; 냉담한; 격의 있는. ¶ *a ~ air* 냉담한 태도 / *treat someone with a ~ politeness* 아무에게 남남처럼 대하다 / *Her manner was ~.* =*She was ~ in manner.* 그녀의 태도는 냉랭했다. [↑]

dis·taste [distéist] *n.* Ⓤ 《often *a ~*》 dislike. 싫음. ¶ *have a ~ for hard work* 고된 일을 싫어하다. [dis-, →taste]

dis·taste·ful [distéistfəl] *adj.* tasteless; poor; unpleasant; disagreeable. 맛 없는; 싫은; 불쾌한. ¶ *a ~ task* 싫은 일 / *Work is ~ to him.* 그는 일을 싫어한다.

dis·tem·per[1] [distémpər] *n.* Ⓤ **1** an easily-spread disease, chiefly of young dogs. 디스템퍼《강아지의 열병》. **2** 《*arch.*》 a disorder in the body or the mind; disease. (정신·육체의) 이상; 병. **3** 《*fig.*》 social disorder or confusion. 사회적 불안; 혼란.

— *vt.* (P6) disorder; confuse. (몸)의 상태를 어지럽히다. ¶ *a distempered mind* 어지러운 마음 / *a distempered illusion* 병적 환상. [dis-]

dis·tem·per[2] [distémpər] *n.* **1** Ⓤ paint made by using eggs or glue instead of oil. 디스템퍼《기름 대신 물에 노른자위 또는 아교를 갠 그림물감》. **2** Ⓒ a tempera paint. 템페라 그림. — *vt.* (P6) paint (something) in distemper. 디스템퍼로 그리다. [dis-]

dis·tend [disténd] *vt., vi.* (P6;1) swell; enlarge; expand. 부풀(리)다; 넓히다; 넓어지다. ● **dis·ten·si·ble** [-ténsəbəl] *adj.* [L. *tendo* stretch]

dis·ten·sion, -tion [distén∫ən] *n.* Ⓤ the act of distending; the state of being distended; enlargement; expansion. 확대; 팽창; 확장. ¶ *the ~ of the lungs* 폐의 팽창.

dis·tich [dístik] *n.* 《prosody》 a group of two lines of verse; a couplet. 대련(對聯); 대구(對句). [Gk.]

dis·till, 《Brit.》 **-til** [distíl] *vt.* **1** (P6) heat (a liquid) until it is changed to steam. (액체)를 증류하다. **2** (P6,13) get (something) by the process of distillation. 증류하여 …을 만들다. ¶ *~ fresh water from sea water* 바닷물을 증류하여 담수를(단물을) 얻다. **3** (P6) 《*fig.*》 extract the essence of (something). …의 정수(精粹)를 뽑아내다; 발췌하다; 순화(純化)하다. **4** (P6) give out in drops (똑똑) 떨어뜨리다; 듣게 하다. ¶ *Clouds ~ rain.* 구름은 비를 뿌린다.

— *vi.* (P1) **1** fall in drops; drip. 똑똑 떨어지다; 듣다. **2** practice distillation; purify; refine. 증류하다; 순화하다. [di-, L. *stillo* drip]

dis·til·la·tion [dìstəléi∫ən] *n.* **1** Ⓤ the act of distilling. 증류. ¶ *dry ~* 건류(乾溜). **2** Ⓒ a thing distilled. 증류물[액].

dis·tilled [distíld] *adj.* produced by distilling. 증류한; 증류해서 얻은. ¶ *~ water* 증류수.

dis·till·er [distílər] *n.* Ⓒ **1** a person or an apparatus that distills. 증류자; 증류기. **2** a person or company that makes alcoholic liquors, esp. whisky. 양조자; 양조 회사.

dis·till·er·y [distíləri] *n.* (*pl.* **-er·ies**) Ⓒ a place where distillation is carried on. 증류소; 양조장.

:dis·tinct [distíŋkt] *adj.* **1** not exactly the same; separate. 별개의; 다른. ¶ *keep two things ~* 양자를 구별하다 / *White bears are ~ from pandas.* 흰곰은 판다와는 다르다 / *His private and public lives are ~.* 그의 사생활과 공적 생활은 분명히 구별돼 있다. **2** different in nature or quality. (성질이) 다른. ¶ *Iron is ~ from gold.* 쇠와 금은 다르다. **3** clear; plain. 명백[분명]한; 명료한. ¶ *~ pronunciation* 분명한 발음. **4** definite; unmistakable. 명확한; 틀림없는. ● **dis·tinct·ness** [-nis] *n.* [L. *distinguo* distinguish]

:dis·tinc·tion [distíŋk∫ən] *n.* **1** Ⓤ the act of making a distinct separation; division. 구별; 차별. ¶ *without ~* 차별없이 / *~ of birth* 태생[가문]의 차 / *make no ~ between A and B,* A와 B와의 구별을 하지 않다. **2** Ⓒ a difference; a point of difference. 상위(相違); 차이(점). ¶ *make a ~ without a difference* 차별없는[불필요한] 구별을 하다 / *I can see no ~ between the two.* 둘 사이의 차이점을 발견할 수 없다. **3** Ⓒ a characteristic difference. 특이성; 특질. ¶ *There was no ~ in his appearances.* 그의 풍채에는 이렇다 할 특성이

없었다. **4** Ⓤⓒ honor; fame. 영예; 명성. ¶ *rise to* ~ 명성을 얻다; 유명해지다 / *gain* ~ *as a scholar* 학자로서 명성을 얻다. **5** the quality of being superior or excellent. 발군; 탁월(성). ¶ *a man* 〔*singer*〕 *of* ~ 비범한 사람〔가수〕.

dis·tinc·tive [distíŋktiv] *adj.* marking a difference; remarkable; special. 구별을 나타내는; 두드러진; 특유의; 독특한. ¶ *the* ~ *stripes of the zebra* 얼룩말 특유의 줄무늬.

·dis·tinct·ly [distíŋktli] *adv.* in a distinct manner; clearly; precisely. 분명히; 뚜렷이; 명확히. ¶ *speak* ~ 분명히 말하다.

dis·tin·gué [distǽŋgei] *adj.* 《F.》 **1** suggestive of social position. 상류의 사람다운. **2** distinct; clear. 분명한; 뚜렷한.

·dis·tin·guish [distíŋgwiʃ] *vt.* **1** (P13) 《*from*》 see or show the difference between (two things). …을 구별하다. ¶ ~ *different makes of cars* 차종을 구별하다 / ~ *right from wrong* 정사(正邪)를 구별하다 / *They are so alike that I can hardly* ~ *one from the other.* 그들은 너무 비슷하여 구별할 수가 없다. **2** (P6,13) admit or perceive clearly. …을 식별〔분간〕하다; 감지하다. ¶ ~ *someone at a distance* 먼데 사람을 식별하다 / ~ *good from evil* 선과 악을 식별하다 / ~ *her from her sister* 그녀와 그녀 언니를 분간하다. **3** (P6,13) ⓐ be a mark, sign, or quality of; characterize. 두드러지게 하다; 특징지우다. ¶ *A trunk distinguishes the elephant.* 코가 코끼리를 특징짓는다. ⓑ 《usu. *reflexively*》 make (someone) famous; show one's excellence; give oneself honor. 유명〔현저〕하게 하다. ¶ *a man distinguished for courage* 용감하기로 유명한 사람 / ~ *oneself in battle* 무훈을 세우다 / ~ *oneself by scholarship* 학문으로 이름을 드러내다. **4** separate (persons or things) into groups according to kind; classify. …을 분류하다. ¶ ~ *sounds into high and low* 음을 높낮이에 따라 가르다.

— *vi.* (P1,3) 《often *between, among*》 see or show the difference. 구별하다. ¶ ~ *between right and wrong* 정(正)과 사(邪)를 구별하다. [→distinct]

dis·tin·guish·a·ble [distíŋgwiʃəbəl] *adj.* that can be distinguished. 구별〔식별〕할 수 있는.

·dis·tin·guished [distíŋgwiʃt] *adj.* **1** famous; wellknown; admirable. 유명〔저명〕한; 두드러진. ¶ *a* ~ *family* 명문(名門) / *a* ~ *writer* 유명한 작가. **2** having the appearance of a great person; having dignity in conduct or appearance. 기품 있는; 위엄 있는; 고귀〔고상〕한. ¶ *a* ~ *manner* 점잖은 태도 / ~ *services* 수훈(殊勳).

dis·tort [distɔ́:rt] *vt.* (P6) **1** change the natural shape of (something); twist. …을 일그러뜨리다; 뒤틀다. ¶ ~ *one's face* 얼굴을 찡그리다 / *His face was distorted with* 〔*by*〕 *fury.* 그의 얼굴은 격노로 일그러졌다. **2** change the truth or original meaning of (something); give a false impression or account of. (사실)을 왜곡하다; (뜻을) 곡해하다; 잘못 전하다. ¶ ~ *the facts* 사실을 왜곡하다 / ~ *the news to make it sensational* 센세이션을 일으키기 위해 사실을 왜곡한 뉴스를 전하다. [→torment]

dis·tor·tion [distɔ́:rʃən] *n.* **1** Ⓤ the act of distorting; the state of being distorted. 일그러짐; 뒤틀림; 억지; 왜곡. ¶ *the* ~ *of the face* 얼굴의 일그러짐 / *his* ~ *of my statement* 내 말에 대한 그의 곡해〔왜곡〕. **2** ⓒ anything distorted. 일그러진 것; 왜곡된 것. ¶ *This statement is a* ~ *of the truth.* 이 진술은 사실을 왜곡한 것이다.

dis·tract [distrǽkt] *vt.* (P6,13) **1** 《usu. *from*》 turn (the mind, attention, etc.) in a different direction; divert. (마음·주의 따위)를 흩뜨리다; 다른 데로 돌리다. ¶ *Reading distracts the mind from grief.* 독서는 슬픔을 잊게 해 준다 / *I cannot work if my attention is being distracted.* 주의가 딴 데로 흩뜨려져 있으면 일을 할 수가 없다. **2** disturb; confuse. …을 곤혹시키다; 혼란시키다. ¶ *The noise distracts me.* 그 소음이 내 마음을 산만하게 한다 / *Her mind was distracted by grief.* 그녀 마음은 슬픔으로 어지러워져 있었다. **3** drive (someone) mad. (아무를) 미치게 하다. [L. *traho* draw]

dis·tract·ed [distrǽktid] *adj.* (of the mind) confused; troubled; insane. 혼란된; 미친. ¶ *drive someone* ~ 아무를 미치게 하다.

dis·trac·tion [distrǽkʃən] *n.* **1** Ⓤ the act of distracting; the state of being distracted. 마음이 흩뜨러짐; 마음의 혼란; 미침. ¶ *drive to* ~ 미치게 하다 / *love to* ~ 미칠 듯이 사랑하다. **2** ⓒ anything that distracts. 마음을 흩뜨리는〔산란케 하는〕 것. ¶ *Television is a* ~ *when you are trying to read.* 텔레비전은 독서하려고 할 때 마음을 흩뜨리는 것이다. **3** ⓒ a diversion; an amusement. 기분 전환; 오락. ¶ *We need some distractions after work.* 일한 후에는 기분 전환이 필요하다.

dis·train [distréin] *vt., vi.* (P6,13;1,3) 《*upon, from*》 《law》 seize and hold (someone's property) for debt. 압류하다. ¶ ~ *property from someone* 아무의 재산을 압류하다 / ~ *upon someone's goods for rent* 임대료를 받기 위해 아무의 재산을 압류하다. [di-, →strain[1]]

dis·traught [distrɔ́:t] *adj.* **1** in a state of confusion; mentally confused. 곤혹스런. **2** driven mad; crazed. 미친. [→distract]

:dis·tress [distrés] *n.* **1** Ⓤ great mental pain or sorrow; anxiety. 큰 고뇌〔슬픔〕; 심통(心痛); 근심. ¶ *suffer* ~ 비탄에 젖다 / *feel acute* ~ *at* …에 심한 고통을 느끼다. **2** ⓒ a cause of distress. 고뇌〔고통〕의 원인; 걱정거리. ¶ *He is a great* ~ *to his father.* 그는 아버지에게 큰 골칫거리다. **3** Ⓤ a dangerous condition; danger; difficulty; trouble. 위난; 어려움; 곤경; 곤궁; 빈고(貧苦); 조난. ¶ *a ship in* ~ 조난선 / *a signal of* ~ =*a* ~ *signal* 조난 신호 / *be in deep* 〔*bitter*〕 ~ 심한 어려움에

처해 있다 / *relieve ~ among the poor* 빈민들의 어려움을 덜어 주다 / *The ship is in ~.* 배가 파선할 위험에 있다. **4** Ⓤ the state of being tired out; physical fatigue. 지침; 피로. ¶ *The runner showed signs of ~.* 주자(走者)는 지친 기색을 보였다.
— *vt.* (P6,13) **1** trouble; embarrass. …을 괴롭히다; 슬프게〔걱정케〕 하다. ¶ *~ oneself* 괴로워하다; 고뇌하다 / *be distressed at* 〔*to hear*〕 *the news* 그 소식에〔을 듣고〕 비관하다 / *be distressed with debts* 빚에 쪼들려 있다 / *Her child's illness distressed her.* 아이의 병이 그녀를 슬프게 하였다. **2** wear out with too great effort; cause bodily pain. 지치다; 육체적 고통을 주다. ¶ *The hard climb has distressed my heart.* 힘겨운 등반으로 심장에 부담을 주었다. [→distraint]

dis·tress·ful [distrésfəl] *adj.* **1** causing distress; painful. 고통스러운; 고난이 많은. **2** unhappy; miserable. 불행한; 비참한.

:dis·trib·ute [distríbju:t] *vt.* (P6,13) **1** give (things) to each; hand out. …을 분배하다; 배급하다. ¶ *~ pamphlets to the audience* 청중에게 팸플릿을 배포하다 / *~ papers among the pupils* 학생들에게 시험지를 도르다. **2** spread out; scatter. 분포시키다; 살포하다; 뿌리다. ¶ *a widely-distributed animal* 널리 분포된 동물. **3** divide (things) into groups; classify. …을 구분하다; 분류하다. ¶ *~ books according to subject* 책을 주제에 따라 분류하다 / *The plants are distributed into 20 classes.* 그 식물은 20종으로 분류된다. **4** 《*log.*》 use (a term) in its full extention so that it includes every individual of the class. (개념을) 확충하다; 주연(周延)하다. [dis-,→tribute]

·dis·tri·bu·tion [dìstrəbjú:ʃən] *n.* Ⓤ the act or manner of distributing; Ⓒ an instance of this. 분배; 배급(품); 배포; 분포(상태). ¶ *the ~ of wealth* 부(富)의 배분 / *the equal ~ of property* 재산의 균등한 분배 / *This animal has a wide ~.* 이 동물은 널리 분포해 있다.

dis·trib·u·tive [distríbjutiv] *adj.* **1** of distribution. 배급의; 분배의. **2** of each member of a group. 개별적인. — *n.* Ⓒ a distributive word. 배분사(配分詞)〔형용사〕. 參考 each, every, either 따위.

dis·trib·u·tor [distríbjətər] *n.* Ⓒ a person, thing, or company that distributes. 분배자; 배급자; 분배기(器).

:dis·trict [dístrikt] *n.* Ⓒ **1** any region; a part of a country; an area. (일국 내의) 지방; 지역; 지구. ¶ *an agricultural* 〔*a wooded*〕 *~* 농업〔산림〕 지대 / *a residential* 〔*residence*〕 *~* 주택 지구 / *a shopping ~* 상점가 / *the Lake District* (영국 잉글랜드 북부의) 호수 지방. **2** a part of a country, state, or city, marked off for a special purpose. 행정구; 관할구. ¶ *a police ~* 경찰서 관할구 / *a school ~* 학구(學區) / *an election ~* 선거구.
— *vt.* (P6) divide up into districts. 지구〔관구〕로 나누다. [di-, →strict]

district attorney [⌐–⌐–] *n.* 《U.S.》 the prosecuting officer of a judicial district. 지방 검사.

District Railway [⌐–⌐–] *n.* the railway serving parts of London and suburbs. 런던 교외 철도.

district visitor [⌐–⌐––] *n.* a person working under a parson in one of the sections of a parish. 교구(教區) 목사 보좌.

·dis·trust [distrʌ́st] *vt.* (P6) disbelieve; doubt; suspect. …을 믿지〔신용치〕 않다; 의심하다. — *n.* Ⓤ 《sometimes *a ~*》 disbelief; lack of trust; doubt; suspicion. 불신(임); 의혹. ¶ *an atmosphere of ~ and suspicion* 불신과 의혹에 찬 분위기 / *have a ~ of someone* 아무를 불신하는 마음을 품다. [dis-]

dis·trust·ful [distrʌ́stfəl] *adj.* not trusting; doubtful; suspicious. 신용치 않는; 좀처럼 믿지 않는; 의심 많은.

:dis·turb [distə́:rb] *vt.* (P6) **1** break the calm condition of (something); stir up. …을 교란하다; 혼란시키다; 어지럽히다; 휘젓다. ¶ *~ the peace* 평화를〔치안을〕 어지럽히다 / *~ the smooth surface of a lake* 잔잔한 호수면을 휘젓다. **2** make (someone) uneasy or anxious; bother; trouble. …을 불안하게 하다; 괴롭히다. ¶ *be disturbed by strange behavior* 이상한 행동에 당황하다 / *His unhealthy paleness disturbs me.* 그의 병적인 창백함은 나를 불안하게 만든다. **3** interrupt; interfere with. 방해하다. ¶ *~ someone in his sleep* 〔*study*〕 아무의 잠을〔공부를〕 방해하다 / *~ a sleeping baby* 잠자는 아기를 깨게 하다 / *~ someone's plans* 아무의 계획을 방해하다 / *I'm sorry to ~ you.* 방해해서 죄송합니다. **4** change the usual position or natural condition of; put (something) out of order. (위치·순서 따위가) 뒤죽박죽이 되게 하다; 어지럽히다. ¶ *~ the order of the house* 집안을 어지럽히다. [→turbid]

·dis·turb·ance [distə́:rbəns] *n.* **1** Ⓤ the act of disturbing; the state of being disturbed. 어지럽힘; 교란; 방해; 불안. **2** Ⓒ a thing that disturbs something. 어지럽히는 것.

dis·turbed [distə́:rbd] *adj.* showing symptoms of mental or emotional illness. 신경증의 증세를 보이는.

di·sul·fide, 《Brit.》 **-phide** [daisʌ́lfaid] *n.* 《chem.》 a chemical compound containing two sulfur atoms. 이황화물. [di-]

dis·un·ion [disjú:njən] *n.* Ⓤ **1** separation. 분리; 분열. **2** disagreement; discord. 불화(不和); 내분(內紛); 불통일; 불일치. [dis-, →unite]

dis·u·nite [dìsju:náit] *vt., vi.* (P6;1) **1** separate; disjoin. 분리〔분열〕시키다; 분리〔분열〕하다. **2** make (things or persons) disagree. 불화하게 하다; 반목시키다. [dis-]

dis·use [disjú:z] *vt.* (P6) 《chiefly in *passive*》 cease to use; use no longer. …의

사용을 그만두다; (더 이상) 사용하지 않다. ¶ *a disused word* 폐어 / *a disused meaning* 안쓰게 된 의미. —[disjú:s] *n.* Ⓤ disusage; abandonment. 쓰이지 않음; 폐기. ¶ *The machine has rusted from* ~. 기계는 사용하지 않아 녹이 슬었다. [dis-]

fall into disuse, go out of use. 쓰이지 않게 되다.

di·syl·lab·ic, dis·syl·lab·ic [dàisilǽbik, dìsi-] *adj.* having two syllables. 2음절의.

di·syl·la·ble, dis·syl·la·ble [dáisiləbəl, disíl-] *n.* Ⓒ a word of two syllables. 2음절어. [di-, →syllable]

·**ditch** [ditʃ] *n.* Ⓒ a long, narrow channel dug in the earth; a channel; a gutter. 도랑; 배수구; (관개용) 수로; 해자. ¶ *dig a* ~ *beside the road* 길 옆에 도랑을 파다.

be driven to the last ditch, be in a difficult situation; be cornered. 궁지에 몰리다.

die in a ditch, die on the road; die poor. 노상에서 죽다; 불쌍하게 죽다.

die in the last ditch, defend one's position to the last. 끝까지 지키다가 죽다.

— *vt.* (P6) **1** dig ditches in or around. …에 도랑을 파다; 해자를 두르다. **2** ⓐ throw (a car, etc.) into a ditch. (자동차 따위를) 도랑에 빠뜨리다[처박다]. ¶ *The drunken driver ditched the car.* 음주 운전자는 차를 도랑에 빠뜨렸다. ⓑ 《U.S.》 throw (a train, etc.) off the track; derail. (열차 따위)를 탈선시키다. ⓒ make a forced landing in the sea. (비행기)를 바다에 불시착시키다. ¶ *be* [*get*] *ditched* 해상에 불시착하다. **3** leave in the lurch. 내버려 못 본 체하다; 버리다. **4** 《*sl.*》 get rid of. 없애다; 처분하다.

— *vi.* (P1) **1** make or repair a ditch. 도랑을 만들다[보수하다]. **2** run into a ditch. 탈선하다. [E.]

hedging and ditching, repair the hedging and ditching. 산울타리나 도랑의 보수.

ditch·wa·ter [dítʃwɔ̀:tər, -wɑ̀t-] *n.* stagnant water collected in a ditch. 도랑에 괸 물; 괸 오수(汚水).

(*as*) ***dull as ditchwater,*** very dull and boring. 몹시 침체된[따분한].

dit·to [dítou] *n.* Ⓒ (*pl.* **-tos**) the same. 위와 같음; 동상(同上); 동전(同前). 參考 d°, do. 로 생략. ¶ *say* ~ *to someone* 아무와 같은 의견이라고 말하다. — *adv.* as before. 앞과 마찬가지로. [L. *dico* say]

dit·ty [díti] *n.* Ⓒ (*pl.* **-ties**) a short, simple song. 소가곡(小歌曲); 소곡. [→ditto]

di·u·ret·ic [dàijuərétik] *adj.* of a drug acting to increase the flow of urine. 배뇨 촉진의; 이뇨(利尿)의. — *n.* Ⓤ a diuretic agent. 이뇨제(劑). [dia-, →urine]

di·ur·nal [daiə́:rnəl] *adj.* **1** daily. 하루의; 날마다의. ¶ ~ *work* 하루의 일. **2** belonging to the daytime. 낮의; 주간의(opp. nocturnal). ¶ ~ *heat* 낮의 더위. **3** ⓐ 《bot.》 opening in the daytime and closing at night. 낮에 피(고 밤에 오므라드)는. ⓑ 《zool.》 active mainly in the daytime. 주간 활동성의. **4** 《astron.》 performed in twenty-four hours. 24 시간의. ¶ *the earth's* ~ *revolution* 지구의 일주(日周) 운동. [L. *diēs* day]

div. divided; dividend; division; divisor; divorced.

di·va [dí:və] *n.* (*pl.* **-vas** or **-ve**) =prima donna.

di·va·lent [daivéilənt] *adj.* 《chem.》 having a valence of two. 이가(二價)의. [di-, L. *valent* value]

di·van [daivǽn, di-] *n.* Ⓒ **1** a long, low sofa with cushions, usu. against a wall. (벽 옆에 놓이는) 쿠션 달린 긴 소파. **2** ⓐ a court or a council of state in Turkey and other Oriental countries. (중동 여러 나라의) 법정; 국정 회의. ⓑ the room in which such councils are held. (국정) 회의실. **3** a smoking room or coffee-room. 흡연실; 다실(茶室). [Pers.]

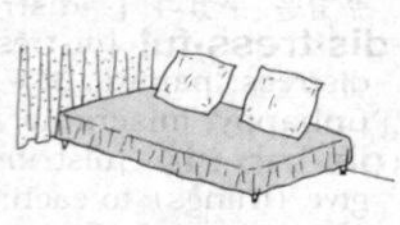
〈divan 1〉

·**dive**[1] [daiv] *vi.* (**dived** or 《U.S.》 **dove**) (P1,2A,3) **1** go down head first into water; go into water suddenly. (머리부터) 물 속에 뛰어들다; 급히 잠수하다. ¶ ~ *in the water* 물 속에 잠수하다 / ~ *for pearls* 진주 채취를 위해 잠수하다 / *He dived into the sea.* 그는 바다로 뛰어 들었다 / *The submarine dived.* 잠수함이 잠수했다. **2** rush suddenly into something; go out of sight suddenly. 갑자기 뛰어들다; 갑자기 모습을 감추다; 잠입하다. ¶ ~ *into a doorway* 현관으로 뛰어들다 / ~ *down an alley* 골목으로 뛰어들다 / ~ *into the bushes* 덤불 속으로 잠입하다. **3** thrust one's hand suddenly into a pocket, bag, etc. (주머니 따위에) 손을 찔러 넣다; 뒤져 더듬다. ¶ ~ *into a purse* 지갑 속에 손을 넣다 / *He dived into his pocket and brought out a coin.* 호주머니에 손을 찔러 넣어 동전 한닢을 꺼냈다. **4** go down in the air at a steep angle; nose-dive. 급강하하다; 곤두박이치다. ¶ *The airplane dived out of the clouds.* 비행기는 구름을 뚫고 급강하했다. **5** 《*fig.*》 enter into a subject. 몰두하다. ¶ ~ *into one's work* 일에 몰두하다 / ~ *into economics* [*politics*] 경제학[정치]에 몰두하다.

— *n.* Ⓒ **1** an act of diving. 뛰어듦; 잠수; 급강하. ¶ *a fancy* ~ (수영의) 다이빙. **2** 《orig. 《U.S.》 *colloq.*》 a cheap drinking-place, esp. one in a basement. 싸구려 술집. ¶ *an opium* ~ 아편굴. [E.]

take a dive into, be absorbed in. …에 몰두하다.

take a dive off, jump into the water from. …에서 (물 속으로) 뛰어들다.

dive[2] [dí:vei] *n.* pl. of **diva.**

dive-bomb [dáivbɑ̀m / -bɔ̀m] *vt., vi.* (of an aircraft) drop bombs over a target while diving steeply down towards it. 급강하 폭격을 하다. [E.]

dive bomber [´-ˋ-] *n.* Ⓒ an aircraft designed to drop bombs over a target while in a steep dive. 급강하 폭격기.

div·er [dáivər] *n.* Ⓒ **1** a person or thing that dives. 뛰어드는 사람[것]; 잠수하는 사람[것]. **2** a person whose job is diving. 잠수부. **3** a diving bird, as the grebe or loon. 무자맥질하는 새《농병아리 따위》. [E.]

di·verge [divə́ːrdʒ, dai-] *vi.* (P1,3) **1** (of roads, etc.) go in different directions from the same point; branch off. (길 따위가) 갈라지다; 분기(分岐)하다(cf. *converge*). ¶ *~ from the main road* 본길에서 갈라지다. **2** (of opinions, etc.) differ; become different. (의견 따위가) 다르다; 갈라지다; (모양 등이) 달라지다. [di-, →verge]

di·ver·gence [divə́ːrdʒəns, dai-], **-gen·cy** [-si] *n.* ⓊⒸ the act of diverging; the state of being diverged; separation; difference. 갈라짐; 분기(分岐); 분출(分出); 다름; 상위(相違).

di·ver·gent [divə́ːrdʒənt, dai-] *adj.* separating; different. 갈라지는; 분출(分出)[분기(分岐)]하는; 다른; 구구한.

di·vers [dáivəːrz] *adj.* various; several; different. 여러 (가지의); 몇 개의; 잡다한; 다른. [di-, →versatile]

di·verse [divə́ːrs, dai-, dáivəːrs] *adj.* **1** unlike in character; different. 다양한; 다른. **2** various. 여러 가지의. ● **di·verse·ly** [-li] *adv.*

di·ver·si·fi·ca·tion [divə̀ːrsəfikéiʃən, dai-] *n.* ⓊⒸ the act of diversifying; the state of being diversified; variation; change. 다양(하게 하기); 다양[다각]화; 변화.

di·ver·si·fy [divə́ːrsəfài, dai-] *vt.* (**-fied**) (P6) give variety to (something); vary; change. …에 변화를 주다; …을 변화시키다; 다양하게 하다. ¶ *be diversified* 다양화되다; 변화가 풍부하다 / *This company has diversified its production.* 이 회사는 생산을 다양화시켰다. [di-, →versatile]

di·ver·sion [divə́ːrʒən, -ʃən, dai-] *n.* **1** Ⓤ the act of turning aside. 딴데로 돌림; (주의의) 전환. ¶ *the ~ of a river* 강의 흐름을 딴데로 돌리기 / *the ~ of the mind from one's study* 마음을 공부에서 딴 데로 돌림. **2** Ⓒ 《Brit.》 an alternative route when a road is closed to traffic. (길이 폐쇄됐을 때의) 우회도로; 돌아가는 길. **3** Ⓒ a recreation; an amusement. 기분 전환; 오락. ¶ *Golf is a popular ~.* 골프는 대중적 오락이다.

di·ver·si·ty [divə́ːrsəti, dai-] *n.* ⓊⒸ (*pl.* **-ties**) remarkable difference; unlikeness; variety. 상위(相違); 부동(不同); 다양(성). ¶ *a ~ of methods* 여러 가지 방법 / *The ~ of food on the table made it hard for him to choose.* 식탁 위엔 음식이 다양해서 골라 먹기가 어려웠다.

di·vert [divə́ːrt, dai-] *vt.* (P6,13) **1** turn (someone or something) aside. …을 딴 데로 돌리다; 전환하다. ¶ *~ one's attention* 주의를 딴 데로 돌리다 / *~ someone from his cares* 마음을 딴 데로 돌리어 근심을 잊게 하다 / *~ the course of a stream* = *~ a stream from its course* 흐름의 진로를 바꾸다 / *be diverted into a side issue* 지엽적인 문제에 이르다. **2** please; amuse. 기분을 풀다[전환하다]; 즐겁게 하다. ¶ *~ oneself by dancing* 춤을 추어 기분을 풀다. [di-, L. *verto* turn]

di·vert·ing [divə́ːrtiŋ, dai-] *adj.* amusing; entertaining. 재미나는; 즐거운. ¶ *a ~ game* 재미있는 게임.

di·ver·tisse·ment [divə́ːrtismənt] *n.* 《F.》 a short ballet, etc. between the acts of a play. 디베르티스망《막간에 삽입되는 짧은 발레 따위》.

di·vest [divést, dai-] *vt.* (P13) 《usu. *of*》 take something away from (someone); strip. …을 떼다; 빼앗다; 박탈하다; 벗기다. ¶ *be divested of something* …을 잃다 / *~ oneself of something* …을 벗다; 버리다; 포기하다 / *~ someone of his office* [*rank*] 아무의 지위를 빼앗다 / *I was divested of my coat.* 나의 상의를 빼앗겼다 / *The wind divested the trees of their leaves.* 바람으로 잎이 떨어져 나무들이 벌거숭이가 되었다. ● **di·vest·ment** [-mənt] *n.* Ⓤ [di-,→vest]

:di·vide [diváid] *vt.* (P6,7,13) 《*among, between, into, from, with, up*》 **1** ⓐ split up; separate (something) into parts. …을 나누다; 쪼개다; 분리하다.¶ *~ an apple into two* 사과를 둘로 쪼개다 / *~ the students into four groups* 학생을 4개 그룹으로 나누다 / *The school year is divided into three terms.* 학년도는 3학기로 나뉜다. ⓑ classify. 유별(類別)[종별]하다; 분류하다. ¶ *~ temples into various types according to their peculiarities* 사찰을 그 특색에 따라 여러 유형으로 분류하다. ⓒ part; cut off. 경계를 짓다; 분계(分界)하다. ¶ *a river dividing the two towns* 두 시의 경계를 이루는 강. ⓓ set apart. 분리하다; 격리하다. ¶ *~ the sheep from the goats* 양들을 염소들과 분리하다 / *~ the sick from the rest* 환자를 다른 사람들로부터 격리하다. **2** separate into parts and distribute; share. …을 분배하다; 나누다. ¶ *~ the profits with a friend* 이익을 친구와 나누다 / *~ something between two persons* [*among several persons*] …을 두사람[몇 사람]이 나누다 / 《*fig.*》 *~ one's time between work and play* 시간을 일과 노는 시간으로 나누다. **3** differ from (something) in feeling, opinion, etc.; disagree. (감정·의견 따위)를 분열시키다. ¶ *Our opinions were divided on the point.* 우리 의견은 그 점에서 분열됐다. **4** 《math.》 see how many times one number contains another. (수)를 나누다. ¶ *Divide 8 by 2, and you get 4.* = *8 divided by 2 is* [*equals, gives*] *4.* 8 나누기 2는 4이다 / *7 divides 42.* 42는 7로 나눠어 떨어진다.

— *vi.* (P1) **1** become separate; branch off; part. 나뉘다; 갈라지다; 의견이 분열하다. ¶ *The stream divides there.* 흐름은 그곳에서 갈라진다. **2** separate into groups in voting

on a question. (두 파로 갈라져) 찬반의 투표를 하다. **3** 《math.》 separate into equal parts. 나눗셈을 하다; 나머지 없이 나뉘다. ¶ *49 divides by 7.* 49는 7로 나뉜다.
divide against itself, yield internal troubles. 내분(內紛)이 생기다.
divide up, part. 분할하다.
— *n.* Ⓒ **1** a division; distribution. 분할; 분배. **2** something that divides, esp. a watershed or ridge. 분수령〔계〕. [L.]

divided skirt [⌐⌐– ⌐] *n.* loose trousers resembling a skirt. 치마 바지.

div·i·dend [dívidènd] *n.* Ⓒ **1** 《math.》 a number to be divided by a divisor. 피제수(被除數)(opp. divisor). **2** a sum of money to be divided among stockholders; one shareholder's portion of this money. 배당금; 배당. ¶ *declare a* ~ 배당 지분을 발표하다. [*devide*]

di·vid·ers [diváidərz] *n. pl.* Ⓒ a pair of small compasses used for dividing lines. (분할) 컴퍼스. 語法 a pair of dividers로 쓰임.

div·i·na·tion [dìvənéiʃən] *n.* **1** Ⓤ the act of foretelling the future. 점(占); 역(易). **2** Ⓒ a skillful guess; a prediction. 예지(豫知); 예언; 예측. [L.]

:di·vine [diváin] *adj.* **1** of God; Godlike. 신〔하느님〕의; 신같은. ¶ ~ *judgment* 신의 심판 / *the* ~ *Being* 〔*Father*〕 신. **2** given by God. 하느님〔하늘〕이 준; 신수(神授)의. ¶ *the* ~ *right of kings* 왕권 신수(설) / *a* ~ *call* 하느님의 부르심; 천명 / *a* ~ *punishment* 천벌. **3** for or to God; religious; holy. 신에게 바친; 종교적인; 신성한. ¶ *a* ~ *service* 예배식. **4** very excellent. 아주 훌륭한〔멋진〕; 비범한. ¶ *What* ~ *weather!* 참 좋은 날씨다.
— *n.* Ⓒ a priest; a scholar of Christianity. 목사; 신학자.
— *vt., vi.* (P6,12;1) tell something about the future; find out (something) by inspiration; guess. 점치다; 꿰뚫어보다; 예지〔예언〕하다. [L.]

di·vine·ly [diváinli] *adv.* in a divine manner; by the influence of God; excellently. 신처럼; 신의 힘으로; 절묘하게.

di·vin·er [diváinər] *n.* Ⓒ a magician; a fortuneteller; a predictor; a guesser. 점치는 사람; 점쟁이; 예언자; 예측자.

div·ing bell [dáiviŋ bèl] *n.* a steel room shaped like a bell, in which men can work under water. 잠수종(潛水鐘). [*dive*]

diving board [⌐–⌐] *n.* a springboard. (수영의) 다이빙대(臺). [*dive*]

div·in·ing rod [diváiniŋ ràd / -rɔ̀d] *n.* a stick used for divining the presence of water. (지하의 물을 찾는) 점지팡이. [↑]

di·vin·i·ty [divínəti] *n.* (*pl.* **-ties**) **1** Ⓒ ⓐ a divine being. 신. ⓑ 《*the D-*》 God, the Lord. (기독교의) 신; 하느님. **2** Ⓤ a divine quality; godhood. 신성(神性). **3** Ⓤ the study of Christianity. 신의 연구; 신학. ¶ *a doctor of* ~ 신학 박사. [L. *divinitas*]

divinity school [⌐⌐–– ⌐] *n.* a theological school. 신학교.

di·vis·i·ble [divízəbəl] *adj.* **1** that can be divided. 나눌〔분할할〕 수 있는. **2** 《math.》 that can be divided without leaving a remainder. (나머지없이) 나누어 떨어지는.
● **di·vis·i·bil·i·ty** [divìzəbíləti] *n.* [↓]

:di·vi·sion [divíʒən] *n.* **1** ⒸⓊ the act of dividing; the state of being divided; separation into parts. 나눔; 분할; 분리; 구분. **2** ⒸⓊ the act of sharing; distribution. 분배. ¶ *(the)* ~ *of labor* 분업. **3** ⒸⓊ 《math.》 the process of dividing one number by another. 나눗셈(opp. multiplication). **4** Ⓒ something that divides; a boundary; a separating wall. 칸막이; 격벽(隔壁); 경계선. **5** Ⓒ a part; a department; a section. (분할된) 부분; 한 구획. **6** Ⓒ ⓐ 《mil.》 a part of an army under one commander. 사단. ⓑ 《nav.》 a group of four warvessels. (함선 4척으로 편성된) 전대(戰隊); 분대(分隊). **7** ⒸⓊ a difference of opinion, thought, or feeling; disagreement. (의견·감정 따위의 불일치로 인한) 분열; 불화. ¶ *the present* ~ *in our society* 우리 사회에 현존하는 대립. [→divide]

di·vi·sion·al [divíʒənəl] *adj.* that divides; of a division. 구분하는; 분할상의; 일부의; 나눗셈의; 사단의. ¶ *a* ~ *commander* 사단장.

di·vi·sor [diváizər] *n.* Ⓒ 《math.》 the number or quantity by which another number or quantity is divided. 제수(除數)(opp. dividend). ¶ *a common* ~ 공약수(公約數).

·di·vorce [divɔ́:rs] *n.* **1** ⒸⓊ the legal or formal ending of a marriage. 이혼. ¶ *get* 〔*obtain*〕 *a* ~ *(from someone)* (아무와) 이혼하다. **2** Ⓒ a complete separation. (완전한) 분리. ¶ *a* ~ *between thought and action* 사상과 행동의 분리.
— *vt.* (P6,13) **1** put an end to a marriage of (someone) legally or formally. …을 이혼시키다. ¶ *The judge divorced the couple.* 판사는 부부를 이혼시켰다. **2** get rid of (a husband or wife) by a divorce. (남편 또는 아내)와 이혼하다. ¶ ~ *one's husband* = *be divorced from one's husband* = ~ *oneself from one's husband* 남편과 이혼하다. **3** 《*fig.*》 《*from*》 separate. …을 분리하다. ¶ ~ *one's conduct from one's principles* 자기 행동을 주의와 분리시키다 / *His talk is divorced from reason.* 그의 이야기는 사리와 동떨어져 있다 / *He divorced himself from reality.* 그는 현실에서 도피했다. [di-, →versatile]

di·vor·cé [divɔ:rséi, ––⌐] *n.* 《F.》 a divorced person. 이혼(당)한 사람.

di·vor·cée, -cee [divɔ:rséi, -sí:, ––⌐] *n.* 《F.》 a divorced woman. 이혼(당)한 여자.

di·vulge [divʌ́ldʒ / dai-] *vt.* (P6) make (something) known; tell; reveal. …을 누설

하다; 입밖에 내다; 폭로하다. ¶ ~ *a secret plan to the enemy* 적에게 비밀 계획을 알리다 / ~ *the source of one's information* 정보의 출처를 밝히다. ●**di·vulge·ment** [-mənt] *n.* **di·vul·gence** [-dʒəns] *n.* [di-, →vulgar]

diz·zi·ness [dízinis] *n.* the state of being dizzy. 현기증. [↓]

diz·zy [dízi] *adj.* (**-zi·er, -zi·est**) **1** feeling as if everything were turning around; not steady; likely to make dizzy. 현기증 나는; 아찔한. ¶ *a* ~ *height* 아찔한 높이 / *get* 〔*feel*〕 ~ 현기증이 나다 / *He became* ~ *from the heat and fainted.* 그는 더위로 현기증이 나 까무러쳤다. **2** confused; bewildered. 혼란한; 당혹한. —*vt.* (**-zied**) (P6) make (someone) dizzy. 현기증이 나게 하다. ●**diz·zi·ly** [-li] *adv.* [E.]

Dja·kar·ta, Ja- [dʒəkɑ́ːrtə] *n.* the capital of Indonesia. 자카르타《인도네시아의 수도》.

D/L demand loan.

dl, dl. deciliter.

D.Lit., D.Litt. *Doctor Lit(t)erarum* (L.= Doctor of Literature or Letters).

dlr. dealer.

dm, dm. decimeter.

D.M. Doctor of Medicine.

D.Mus. Doctor of Music.

DMZ Demilitarized Zone.

DN 《U.S.》 Department of the Navy. 국방부 해군부.

d—n damn.

DNA deoxyribonucleic acid.

D.N.B. Dictionary of National Biography. 영국 인명 사전.

:do [duː, du, də] *v.* (**did, done**) *vt.* **1** (P6) ⓐ perform; fulfil; carry out. …을 하다; 수행하다. ¶ ~ *one's work* 〔*duty*〕 일을〔의무를〕 수행하다 / ~ *a good deed* 선행을 하다 / ~ *the talking* 〔*shopping*〕 이야기를〔쇼핑을〕 하다 / *Do your best.* 최선을 다해라 / *I have nothing to* ~. 할 일이 아무 것도 없다 / *What can I* ~ *for you?* (점원이 손님에게) 무엇을 도와 드릴까요. ⓑ have as one's regular work or occupation. (직업으로서) …일을 하다. ¶ ~ *a hauling job* 짐 운반하는 일을 하다 / *What do you* ~*?* 직업이 무엇입니까. **2** (P6,9) finish; complete. 끝내다; 마치다. 語法 흔히, be done, have done의 형태로 쓰임. ¶ *I have already done it.* 이미 그것을 마쳤다 / *His work is done.* 그의 일은 다 끝났다 / *I have done reading.* 독서를 끝냈다 / *Have done crying!* 그만 울어라 / *What is done cannot be undone.* 끝난 일을 되돌릴 수는 없다. **3** (P6,13,14) bring about; cause; give. …을 가져오다; 생기게 하다; 주다. ¶ ~ *justice to* …을 공평하게 평가하다〔다루다〕 / ~ *someone honor* 아무에게 명예를 주다 / *Bad books* ~ (*us*) *great harm.* 나쁜 책은 (우리에게) 큰 해를 끼친다 / *Will you* ~ *me a favor?* 부탁이 하나 있는데요. **4** (P6) produce; create. 만들(어 내)다; 제작하다. ¶ ~ *a movie* 영화를 제작하다 / *He does lovely oil portraits.* 멋진 유화 초상화를 그린다. **5** adapt; translate. …을 각색(脚色)하다; 번역하다; 바꾸다. ¶ ~ *Shakespeare into Korean* 셰익스피어 작품을 한국어로 번역하다 / ~ *a poem into prose* 시를 산문으로 바꾸다 / *Walt Disney did the book into a movie.* 월트 디즈니는 그 책을 영화화했다. **6** (P6) deal with; put (something) in order; arrange. …을 처리하다; 가지런히 (정돈)하다. ¶ ~ *the flowers* 꽃꽂이를 하다 / ~ *one's face* 화장하다 / ~ *the bedroom* 침실을 치우다 / ~ *the dishes* 접시를 닦다 / ~ *one's teeth* 이를 닦다 / ~ *one's hair* 머리를 다듬다. **7** (P6) work; study; solve. …에 종사하다; 공부하다; 해결하다. ¶ ~ *engineering at university* 대학에서 공학을 공부하다 / ~ *the problem* 문제를 풀다 / *He spent several hours a day doing French.* 매일 프랑스어 공부에 몇 시간씩 소비했다. **8** (P6) serve; suit; meet the needs of. 도움이 되다; 충분하다. ¶ *Will this* ~ *you?* 이것이면 되겠습니까 / *Fifty dollars will* ~ *me.* 50 달러면 충분합니다. **9** (P6) act (a play, etc.); play the part of (something). …역(役)을 하다. ¶ ~ *Hamlet* 햄릿역을 하다 / *She did the hostess admirably.* 그녀는 여주인 역할을 훌륭히 했다. **10** (P6,7) exhaust; tire; wear out. 지치게 하다. ¶ *That last set of tennis did me.* 테니스의 마지막 세트에서 지쳤다 / *I'm done—I can walk no farther.* 녹초가 됐다—더는 못 걷겠다. **11** (P6) 《*colloq.*》 visit; travel as a sightseer. …을 방문하다; 여행하다; 구경〔관광〕하다. ¶ ~ *the sights* 명소를 관광하다 / ~ *Korea in twenty days,* 20일간 한국 관광을 하다 / *Have you done the Tower* (*of London*) *yet?* 런던 탑을 벌써 구경하셨나요. **12** (P6) travel (a certain distance); travel at the rate of (a certain speed); cover. (어떤 거리)를 가다; …속도로 나아가다. ¶ *He did thirty miles a day on foot.* 그는 하루 30마일을 걸었다 / *He was doing 80 when they arrested him.* 잡힐 때 그는 시속 80마일로 운전하고 있었다. **13** (P6,7) 《usu. in *pp.*》 cook; prepare. (요리)를 만들다〔하다〕. ¶ *I will* ~ *the salad.* 샐러드를 만들겠다 / *I like my meat well-done.* 내 고기를 잘 구웠으면 싶다. **14** (P6,7) 《Brit. *sl.*》 entertain; treat. …을 대접〔접대〕하다; 대우하다. ¶ ~ *someone handsomely* 아무를 융숭하게 대접하다 / *They* ~ *you very well at that restaurant.* 저 식당에서는 아주 좋은 음식이 나온다 / *He does himself fairly well.* 그는 꽤 안락한 생활을 하고 있다. **15** (P6,7) 《*colloq.*》 《*out of*》 cheat; deceive. 속이다. ¶ ~ *someone in the eye* 아무를 속이다 / *He did her out of her money.* 그는 그녀를 속여 돈을 빼앗았다 / *I am afraid you have been done.* 너는 속았다고 생각한다 / *He did me over that bargain.* 그는 흥정에서 나를 속였다 / *I will never get done.* 결코 속지 않겠다. **16** 《*sl.*》 undergo (a term of imprisonment). (형(刑)을) 살다; 복역하다. ¶ ~ *five years for forgery* 위조죄로 5년 징역을 살다 / *The bank robbers did ten years.* 은행 강도들은 징역 10년을 복역했다. —*vi.*

(P1,2A,3) **1** behave; act; work. 행(동)하다; 하다; 일을 하다. ¶ *Don't talk. Only* ~ . 말을 말고 실행만 해라 / *Let us be up and doing.* 적극 나서서 잘해 봅시다. **2** 《*with;* used in *pp.*》 finish; be finished. 끝내다; 마치다. ¶ *I have done with him.* 그와는 손을 끊었다 / *Have done.* 그만두어라. **3** get along; live. 지내다; 해나가다; 살아가다. ¶ *How do you* ~ *?* 안녕하십니까《첫대면 인사》/ *Mother and child are doing well.* 모자는 잘 지내고 있다 / *My son is doing very well at school.* 아들은 학교에서 잘 해나가고 있다. **4** grow well. (환자가) 좋아지다. ¶ *The patient will* ~ *now.* 환자는 이제 좋아질 것이다. **5** be suitable; be good enough; serve the purpose. (어떤 목적에) 적합하다; 도움이 되다; 좋다. ¶ *Any chair will* ~ . 어떤 의자든 괜찮다 / *Any time after five will* ~ . 5시 후면 언제든지 좋다 / *This won't* ~ . 이것으론 안 된다.

do away with, **a**) put an end to; get rid of (something); abolish. …을 끝내다; …을 없애다; 폐지하다. ¶ ~ *away with mice* 쥐를 없애다. **b**) kill. 죽이다. ¶ ~ *away with oneself* 자살하다.

do by, deal with (something); treat. …을 다루다; 대(우)하다. ¶ *I was feeling hard done by.* 심한 처사를 당하고 있는 듯한 마음이 들었다 / *He does well by his friends.* 그는 친구들을 잘 대해 준다.

do for, **a**) 《*colloq.*》《chiefly in *pp.*》 ruin; destroy; kill. 파멸시키다; 망가뜨리다; (신발 따위를) 닳게 하다; 죽이다. ¶ *I am done for.* 이제 글렀네 / *That was the shot that did for him.* 그것이 그를 죽인 결정적 일발이었다 / *I'm afraid these shoes are done for.* 이 구두는 닳아서 못 신을 것 같다. **b**) act for (something). …의 대신이 되다; 대역을 하다. **c**) manage or provide for (something). …을 돌보다. ¶ *My sister does for my father and me.* 누나가 아버지와 나를 돌보고 있다. **d**) serve the purpose of. …의 구실을 하다. ¶ *This box will* ~ *for a chair.* 이 궤짝은 의자로 쓸만하다.

do someone good, benefit. …을 이롭게 하다; 도움이 되다.

do in, **a**) cheat. …을 속이다. **b**) 《*sl.*》 kill; ruin. …을 해치우다; 죽이다; 파멸시키다; 결딴내다. ¶ ~ *oneself in* 자살하다 / ~ *one's car in* 차를 부수다 / *I'll* ~ *him in.* 그를 해치우겠다. **c**) exhaust. …을 지치게 하다.

do or die, make a supreme effort. 필사적으로 하다; 더 없는 노력을 하다.

do out, sweep out; clean. 쓸어 내다; 청소하다. ¶ ~ *out a room* 방을 청소하다.

do over, **a**) do again; repeat. 다시 하다. **b**) 《*colloq.*》 redecorate. 개장(改裝)하다.

do time, 《*colloq.*》 serve a term in prison. 징역을 살다; 복역하다.

do to 〔***unto***〕 =do by.

do up, **a**) wrap up; tie up; button up; fasten (one's shoes, dress). 싸다; (묶어) 포장하다; 단추를 끼우다; (신발 끈 따위를) 매다. ¶ ~ *up a parcel* 소포를 꾸리다. **b**) pin up or arrange (the hair); clean and prepare. (머리에) 핀을 꽂다; 매만져 다듬다; 치우다. **c**) paint and repair (a house). (집 따위를) 손질하다; 수리하다. **d**) 《*colloq.*》《in *passive*》 tire out; exhaust. 지치게 하다. ¶ *I am completely done up with teaching all day.* 하루 종일 가르치느라 녹초가 되었다.

do something up brown, 《*sl.*》 do completely or very well. …을 완벽하게 하다.

do with, **a**) deal with (something). …을 처치〔처리〕하다; …을 어떻게 하다. **b**) get on with; be satisfied with; endure. …로 해나가다; (불만이지만) …한 대로 참다. ¶ ~ *with two meals a day* 하루 두끼 식사로 때우다 / *Can you* ~ *with cold meat for dinner?* 저녁식사는 냉육인데 그런 대로 잡수시겠습니까. **c**) wish. …면 좋겠다〔좋을 성 싶다〕. ¶ *I could* ~ *with more leisure time.* 여가가 더 있으면 좋겠다.

do without, get along without; dispense with (something). …없이 때우다〔지내다〕. ¶ *We can't* ~ *without books, can we?* 우리는 책없이 지낼 수 있을까 / *We must* ~ *without a holiday this year.* 올해에는 휴일없이 지내야 한다.

have 〔***be***〕 ***done with,*** **a**) cease to have any connection with (someone). …와 관계를 끊다. ¶ *I have done with her.* 그녀와 관계를 끊었다. **b**) finish doing or using (something). …을 끝내다. ¶ *Have you done with the newspaper?* 신문 다 보셨습니까.

have to do with (=*have relation with or to*) *something.* …와 관계가 있다. ¶ *I have nothing to* ~ *with him.* 그와 아무런 관계도 없다 / *The book has to* ~ *with religion.* 그 책은 종교와 관계가 있다.

make do (=*get along or manage*) ***with*** *something.* (불충분하지만) …로 때우다; …로 만족하다〔견디다〕. ¶ *make* ~ *with an old coat* (다른 것이 없어서) 헌 코트로 만족하다.

—*auxil. v.* (P25) **1** 《in *interrogative*》 ¶ *Do you like apples?* 사과를 좋아하십니까 / *When does he leave for London?* 그는 언제 런던으로 떠납니까. **2** 《in *emphasizing a verb*》 ¶ *I* ~ *want to go.* 가기를 원한다 / *Do tell me.* 말해다오. **3** 《in *negative*》 ¶ *I* ~ *not know it.* 그것을 모른다 / *Little did I dream that you would return.* 네가 돌아오리라고는 꿈에도 생각 못했다. [語法] not 이외의 부정어일 때에는 도치(倒置)됨.

—*substitute v.* (P1) 《used as *substitute* for other *verbs*》 ¶ *"Do you like sports?" "Yes, I* ~ *."* "스포츠를 좋아하십니까" "네 좋아합니다" / *She plays the piano as well as you* ~ . 그녀는 피아노를 너만큼 잘 친다. [參考] 동일한 동사 및 그 어군의 반복을 피해 쓰임.

—*n.* (*pl.* **do's** or **dos**) **1** 《*sl.*》 a trick. 사기; 야바위. ¶ *He was a fool not to see that it was a* ~ . 그는 그것이 속임수라는 것을 알 수 없을 만큼 바보였다. **2** 《Brit. *colloq.*》 a feast; a party; an entertainment. 축연(祝

宴); 연회; 파티. [E.]
do's and don'ts, customs, rules, or regulations. 지켜야 할 사항; 습관; 규칙; 규정.
Fair do's! Share fairly.; Play fair. 공평히 분배해라; 공평히 해라. [E.]
do. ditto(It.=the same).
D/O, d.o. delivery order. 화물 인도 지시서.
D.O.A. dead on arrival. 도착했을 때 이미 사망함.
do·a·ble [dúːəbəl] *adj.* that can be done. 할 수 있는. [*do*]
do-all [dúːɔːl] *n.* Ⓒ a general helper. 잡역부.
doat [dout] *vi.* =dote.
dob·bin [dábin / dɔ́b-] *n.* Ⓒ **1** a nickname for a slow, gentle horse. 온순하고 일 잘하는 말. **2** 《*D-*》 =Robert. [*Robin*]
doc. document.
doc·ile [dásəl / dóusail] *adj.* **1** obedient. 유순[온순]한; 고분고분한. ¶ *a ~ child* 고분고분한 아이. **2** easy to teach; teachable. 가르치기 쉬운. ● **doc·ile·ly** [-i] *adv.* [L. *doceo* teach]
do·cil·i·ty [dasíləti, dou-] *n.* Ⓤ the state of being docile. 고분고분함; 순종함; 가르치기 쉬움.
*__dock__[1] [dak / dɔk] *n.* Ⓒ **1** a platform where a ship may be repaired, built, or loaded. 선거(船渠); 독. ¶ *a wet* 〔*floating*〕 *~* 계선(繫船)〔부(浮)〕독. **2** 《U.S.》 a wharf; a pier. 선창; 부두. —*vt.* (P6) bring (a ship) into a dock. (배)를 독에 넣다. —*vi.* **1** (P1) come 〔go〕 into a dock. (배가) 독에 들어오다〔가다〕. **2** (P1,4) (of two spaceships) join together in outer space. (우주선이) 도킹〔결합〕하다. [→duct]
dock[2] [dak / dɔk] *n.* Ⓒ the solid part of an animal's tail. (동물의) 꼬리심《털 난 부분과 구별하여》. —*vt.* (P6) **1** cut (a tail, etc.) short. (꼬리 따위)를 짧게 자르다. **2** reduce (wages, etc.), usu. temporarily. (임금 따위)를 깎다; 삭감하다. ¶ *The company docked the men's wages.* 회사는 종업원들의 임금을 깎았다. [E.]
dock[3] [dak / dɔk] *n.* Ⓒ 《*the ~*》 a place in a law court where a prisoner stands or sits. (법정의) 피고석(席). ¶ *be in the ~* 피고인석에 앉아 있다; 재판을 받고 있다. [E.]
dock[4] [dak / dɔk] *n.* Ⓒ 《bot.》 a tall coarse weed. 수영. [E.]
dock·age[1] [dákidʒ / dɔ́k-] *n.* Ⓤ **1** a place to dock a ship. 독〔선거(船渠)〕 설비. **2** a charge for using a dock. 독 사용료. **3** the docking of ships. (선박의) 입거(入渠). [→dock[1]]
dock·age[2] [dákidʒ / dɔ́k-] *n.* Ⓤ **1** curtailment, as of wages. (임금 따위의) 삭감. **2** waste matter in grain. (곡물에 섞인) 잡물; 반지기. [*dock*[2]]
dock·et [dákit / dɔ́k-] *n.* **1** a list of lawsuits to be tried by a court. 소송 사건 일람표. **2** a list or calendar of matters to be done. 처리 예정 사항표. **3** a ticket or label attached to a package, document, etc. giving brief information as to its contents. (화물의) 꼬리표; (서류의) 내용 적요; 부전. —*vt.* (P6) **1** enter on a docket. 내용 적요를 쓰다. **2** make a list or summary of. 적요를 만들다. **3** put a docket or label to. 꼬리표를〔부전을〕 붙이다. [*dock*[2]]
·**dock·yard** [dákjàːrd / dɔ́k-] *n.* Ⓒ 《U.S.》 a place where war ships are built and repaired. 조선소; 해군 공창(工廠)(=《U.S.》 navy yard). [→dock[1]]
:**doc·tor** [dáktər / dɔ́ktər] *n.* Ⓒ **1** a person who practices medicine; a physician; a surgeon. 의사. ¶ *one's family ~* 단골 의사 / *see* 〔*consult*〕 *a ~* 의사의 진찰을 받다 / *be under the ~* 의사의 진료를 받고 있다 / *send for the ~* 의사를 부르러 보내다. **2** the highest degree given by a university or college; a person who has received such a degree. 박사 학위; 박사. 參考 Dr.로 생략함. ¶ *Doctor of Law* 〔*Literature, Medicine*〕 법학〔문학, 의학〕 박사 / *a Doctor of the Church* 교회 박사《학덕이 뛰어난 성직자에게 주는 칭호》. **3** 《*arch.*》 a learned man. 학자.
—*vt.* (P6) 《*colloq.*》 **1** treat diseases in (someone). …를 진료하다. ¶ *She doctored her child for a cold.* 그녀는 자기 아들의 감기를 치료했다. **2** repair; mend. …을 수리하다; 고치다. ¶ *~ a watch* 시계를 수리하다. **3** mix with other things of bad quality; put drugs in. 이물(異物)을 섞다; 섞음질하다. **4** falsify. 속이다. ¶ *~ accounts* 회계를 속이다.
—*vi.* 《*colloq.*》 **1** be a doctor. (의사가) 개업하다; 의사 노릇을 하다. **2** take medicine. 약을 먹다. [→docile]
doctor up, make (something) inferior, etc. by adding a poor ingredient. 섞음질하다.
doc·tor·ate [dáktərit / dɔ́k-] *n.* Ⓒ a degree of doctor given by a university or college. 박사 학위.
doc·tri·naire [dàktrənέər / dɔ̀k-] *n.* an impractical theorist; a person who tries to apply his theory or doctrine regardless of the actual circumstances. 순이론가; (탁상) 공론가. [→doctor]
doc·tri·nal [dáktrənəl / dɔktráinəl] *adj.* of doctrine; instructive. 교의(敎義)〔주의〕의; 학리적인; 교훈적인.
:**doc·trine** [dáktrin / dɔ́k-] *n.* ⒸⓊ **1** something taught as the belief of a church, nation, etc.; belief; principle. 교의(敎義); 교리; 주의; 신조; 학설. ¶ *Every religion has its own ~.* 모든 종교는 각기 그 교리를 가지고 있다. **2** what is taught; 《*collectively*》 teachings. 가르쳐지는 것; 가르침; 교훈.
·**doc·u·ment** [dákjəmənt / dɔ́k-] *n.* Ⓒ anything written, printed, etc., that gives information or proof; anything served as evidence. 문서; 서류; 기록; 증서. ¶ *human documents* 인간 기록 / *official documents*

공문서 / *a diplomatic* ~ 외교 문서. — [dάkjəmènt / dɔ́k-] *vt.* (P6) **1** provide (someone) with documents. 증거(자료)를 제공하다; 전거를 들다. **2** prove or guarantee (something or someone) by documents. 증거 서류로 입증하다. ¶ ~ *a case* 사건을 증거 서류로 입증하다 / *The lawyer's arguments were well documented.* 변호인의 변론은 증거 서류로써 잘 뒷받침되었다.
● **doc·u·men·ta·tion** [dὰkjəmentéiʃən / dɔ̀k-] *n.* [→docile,-ment]

doc·u·men·ta·ry [dὰkjəméntəri / dɔ̀k-] *adj.* **1** in the form of a document. 문서(서류)의; 기록(자료)에 의한; 증서의. ¶ ~ *evidence* 증빙서류. **2** recording an actual event in an artistic fashion. (영화 따위가) 사실을 기록한. ¶ *a* ~ *film* 기록영화. — *n.* Ⓒ (*pl.* **-ries**) a documentary motion picture. 기록 영화; 다큐멘터리.

dod·der [dάdər / dɔ́dər] *vi.* (P1,2A) shake or tremble as from old age or weakness. (노령·병약으로) 비틀거리다; 떨다. ¶ *The old man doddered along.* 노인은 비틀거리며 걸었다. [E.]

do·dec·a·gon [doudékəgὰn / -gɔ̀n] *n.* 《geom.》 a polygon having twelve angles. 12각형. [Gk. *dōdeca* twelve, *gōnia* angle]

do·de·ca·hed·ron [doudèkəhíːdrən] *n.* 《geom.》 a solid figure having twelve faces. 12면체. [↑, *hedra* face]

***dodge** [dαdʒ / dɔdʒ] *vi.* (P1,2A,3) **1** move quickly aside. 잽싸게 움직이다(몸을 비키다). ¶ ~ *about* 요리조리 피하다 / ~ *behind* …뒤로 재빨리 숨다 / ~ *into* …속으로 재빨리 몸을 숨기다 / *They dodged around the corner.* 그들은 재빨리 구석으로 몸을 비켰다. **2** escape (one's duty, etc.) by some trick. 교묘히 둘러대다; 피하다.
— *vt.* (P6) **1** move quickly to avoid (a blow, someone, etc.). 몸을 홱 돌려 …을 피하다. ¶ ~ *a blow* 맞지 않으려고 몸을 홱 피하다. **2** avoid (a question, etc.) by some trick. …을 교묘히 피하다. ¶ ~ *a direct answer* 직답을 피하다 / ~ *one's responsibility* 책임을 교묘히 회피하다 / ~ *a question* 질문을 피하다.
— *n.* Ⓒ **1** a quick movement to one side. (옆으로) 몸을 홱 피하기. **2** 《*colloq.*》 a trick. 속임(수); 술책. **3** 《*colloq.*》 a clever plan or device. 고안; 묘안. ¶ *a* ~ *for remembering names* 이름을 기억하기 위한 묘안. [?]

dodg·er [dάdʒər / dɔ́dʒər] *n.* Ⓒ **1** a person who dodges. 몸을 홱 비키는(피하는) 사람. **2** a dishonest person. 속이는 사람. **3** 《U.S.》 a small handbill. 작은 광고 쪽지.

dodg·y [dάdʒi / dɔ́dʒi] *adj.* ingenious. 교묘한. [?]

do·do [dóudou] *n.* (*pl.* **-dos** or **-does**) 《bird》 a large, short-legged bird not able to fly, now extinct. 도도《지금은 멸종한 큰 새》. [Port.]

doe [dou] *n.* Ⓒ a female deer, rabbit, or hare. 암사슴; 암토끼. [E.]

do·er [dúːər] *n.* Ⓒ a person who does something. (행)하는 사람; 행동자. ¶ *a* ~ *of good* (*evil*) 선행(못된 짓)을 하는 사람 / *He is a* ~ *, not a talker.* 그는 실행가이지 말만 하는 사람이 아니다 / *John is a dreamer, and his brother is a* ~ . 존은 몽상가이고, 그의 형은 행동가이다. [*do*]

:does [dʌz] *v.* the third person, singular, present, indicative form of **do**.

doe·skin [dóuskìn] *n.* Ⓒ the skin of a female deer. 암사슴 가죽. [*doe*]

:does·n't [dʌ́znt] =does not.

do·est [dúːist] *v.* 《*arch.*》 the second person, singular, present form of **do**. ¶ *thou* ~ =you do. [E.]

do·eth [dúːiθ] *v.* 《*arch.*》 the third person, singular, present form of **do**. ¶ *he* (*she*) ~ =he (she) does. [E.]

doff [dαf, dɔ(ː)f] *vt.* (P6) **1** take off or remove (one's hat, clothing, etc.). (모자·옷 따위)를 벗다. ¶ ~ *one's hat to a lady* 숙녀에게 모자를 벗고 인사하다. **2** throw (one's habit, etc.) aside; give up. (습관 따위)를 버리다; 그만두다. ¶ ~ *one's professional manner* 직업적인 태도를 버리다. [*do, off*]

:dog [dɔ(ː)g, dαg] *n.* Ⓒ **1** a common domestic animal, kept as a pet, for hunting, etc. 개. ¶ 《*prov.*》 *Every* ~ *has his day.* 개똥밭에도 이슬 내릴 때가 있다 / 《*prov.*》 *Give a* ~ *a bad name and hang him.* 한 번 낙인(烙印) 찍히면 마지막이다 / 《*prov.*》 *Love me, love my* ~ . 며느리가 미우면 손자까지 밉다 / 《*prov.*》 *Let sleeping dogs lie.* 긁어 부스럼 만들지 마라. **2** any animal of the same family as the dog; a male dog, fox, wolf, etc. 개과(科)의 동물; 수캐; (여우, 이리 따위의) 수컷. **3** a low, worthless man; a fellow. 데데한 인간; 놈; 자식; 녀석. ¶ *You* ~ *!* 이놈의 새끼; 개자식 / *a lucky* ~ 운좋은 녀석 / *a dirty* ~ 깡패. **4** 《*pl.*》 any device to hold or grip something. 무집게; 쇠갈고리. **5** 《*the D-*》 either of two star groups near Orion, Canis Major (the Great Dog) or Canis Minor (the Little Dog). 큰개자리; 작은개자리.

a dog in the manger, a person who prevents others from enjoying something. 짓궂은 심술쟁이.

die a dog's death, die in misery. 비참한 죽음을 하다.

die like a dog =die a dog's death.

die the death of a dog =die a dog's death.

give (***throw***) *something* ***to the dogs,*** throw something aside as worthless. (하찮은 것으로서) 내버리다.

go to the dogs, be ruined. 파멸하다; 타락(영락)하다.

help a lame dog over a stile, help (someone) in trouble. (아무가) 어려움에 처해 있을 때 도와 주다.

lead a dog's life, 《*colloq.*》 live or exist unhappily. 비참한 생활을 하다.

put on the dog, 《*colloq.*》 make a show of being elegant, etc. 허세를 부리다; 고상한〔잘난〕 체하다.

teach an old dog new tricks, induce an old person to adopt new methods, etc. 노인에게 새로운 방법 따위를 가르치다《이제 와서 그런 것은 할 수 없다》.

***treat** someone **like a dog** 〔**worse than a dog**〕,* treat him very badly. …를 개처럼 처우하다.

— *vt.* (**dogged, dog·ging**) (P6) follow or hunt (a person or an animal) like a dog. (개처럼) …을 미행하다; …의 뒤를 밟다; …에게 붙어다니다. [E.]

dog** someone's **steps, follow someone closely. …의 뒤를 밟다.

dog·cart [dɔ́(ː)gkὰːrt, dάg-] *n.* Ⓒ **1** a small cart pulled by dogs. 개가 끄는 수레. **2** a small, open carriage, usu. with two wheels. 2륜 마차《등을 맞댄 좌석이 둘 있음》. [*dog*]

dog·catch·er [dɔ́(ː)gkæ̀tʃər, dάg-] *n.* a person employed or elected to pick up and impound stray dogs. 들개 포획인.

dog·cheap [dɔ́(ː)gtʃíp, dάg-] *adj.* very cheap. 매우 싼; 갯값의.

dog collar [⌐⌐–] *n.* **1** a collar for a dog. 개 목걸이. **2** 《*colloq.*》 a clergyman's collar fastening at the back. (목사가 입는) 뒤에서 잠그는 목닫이.

dog days [⌐⌐] *n. pl.* the very hot and uncomfortable days in July and August. 복중; 삼복.

doge [doudʒ] *n.* the chief magistrate in the old republics of Venice and Genoa. 도제《옛날 Venice와 Genoa 공화국의 수장》. [→duke]

dog-ear [dɔ́(ː)gìər, dάg-] *n.* Ⓒ a turned-down corner of a page in a book. 책장 모서리의 접힌 곳. ¶ *make a* ~ 책장 한 귀퉁이를 접다. — *vt.* turn down the corner of (a page of a book). (책장)의 귀퉁이를 접다. 參考 dog's-ear로도 씀. [*dog*]

dog-eared [dɔ́(ː)gìərd, dάg-] *adj.* in the state of having dog-ears; well worn or well-used. 책장 귀가 접힌; 낡은; 오래 써 닳은. ¶ ~ *furniture* 오래 사용한 가구.

dog-eat-dog [dɔ́(ː)gìːtdɔ́(ː)g, dάgìːtdάg] *adj.* marked by ruthless self-interest; cutthroat. 사리 사욕에 눈이 먼; 격렬한 경쟁의; 인정 사정 없는. — *n.* killing or injuring one another. 동족 상잔.

dog·face [dɔ́(ː)gfèis, dάg-] *n.* 《*sl.*》 a soldier in the U.S. Army; esp., an infantryman. 육군 병사; 보병.

dog·fight [dɔ́(ː)gfàit, dάg-] *n.* **1** a fight between dogs. 개싸움. **2** 《*colloq.*》 a violent battle between fighter planes. 전투기의 맹렬한 공중전〔접근전〕.

dog·fish [dɔ́(ː)gfìʃ, dάg-] *n.* a small kind of shark. 돔발상어류의 일종.

dog·ged [dɔ́(ː)gid, dάg-] *adj.* not easily giving up; steady; fixed in opinion; stubborn. 쉽게 굴하지 않는; 완고한; 끈질긴. ¶ *a* ~ *scholar* 좀처럼 자설(自說)을 굽히지 않는 학자 / *resume one's* ~ *efforts* 불굴의 노력을 다시 계속하다.

It's dogged that 〔***as***〕 ***does it.*** 《*prov.*》 Resolution and concentration can overcome difficulties. 정신일도 하사불성(精神一到何事不成). ● **dog·ged·ly** [-li] *adv.* [*dog*]

dog·ger·el [dɔ́(ː)gərəl, dάg-] *n.* Ⓤ very poor poetry; irregular verse. (운이 맞지 않는) 졸렬한 시(詩). — *adj.* of or like doggerel; comic. 시가 서투른; 빈약한; 우스꽝스러운. [*dog*]

dog·gie [dɔ́(ː)gi, dάg-] *n.* Ⓒ a little dog; a pet name for a dog. 강아지; 멍멍《애칭》.

dog·gie-bag [dɔ́(ː)gibæ̀g, dάg-] *n.* a bag provided by a restaurant to a customer for carrying home leftover food. (레스토랑에서) 먹다 남은 고기 따위를 담아 가는 봉투.

dog·gish [dɔ́(ː)giʃ, dάg-] *adj.* **1** of or like a dog. 개 같은. **2** mean; of uncertain temper. 비열한; 찌무룩한. **3** 《U.S. *colloq.*》 stylish and showy. 멋지고 화려한. [*dog*]

dog·go [dɔ́(ː)gou, dάg-] *adv.* in hiding and without moving; out of sight. 가만히 숨어서; 보이지 않는 곳에. [*dog*]

lie doggo, 《Brit. *sl.*》 lie or hide quietly without moving or making a noise. 가만히 숨어 있다. ¶ *Lie* ~ *until the excitement blows over.* 소동이 가라앉을 때까지 가만히 숨어 있거라.

dog·gone [dɔ́(ː)ggɔ́(ː)n, -gαn, dάg-] *adj., interj.* 《U.S. *sl.*》 Damn!; Darn! 지겨운; 저주할; 빌어먹을.

dog·gy [dɔ́(ː)gi, dάgi] *adj.* (**-gi·er, -gi·est**) like a dog; fond of a dog. 개 같은; 개를 좋아하는. — *n.* Ⓒ (*pl.* **-gies**) 《*child's word*》 a little dog; a doggie. 강아지; 멍멍.

dog·house [dɔ́(ː)ghàus, dάg-] *n.* a small house or shelter for a dog. 개집.

in the doghouse, 《*colloq.*》 in a state of disfavor or shame. 면목을 잃고; 인기가 떨어져; 눈총을 맞고.

dog-lat·in, dog Lat·in [dɔ́glæ̀tin, dάg-] *n.* rough, incorrect Latin. 변칙〔파격〕 라틴어.

dog·ma [dɔ́(ː)gmə, dάg-] *n.* Ⓒ (*pl.* **-mas** or **-ma·ta**) **1** a belief, principle, or doctrine taught or held as truth by some authority. 교의; 교리; 정리; 정설; 원칙. ¶ *a political* ~ 정치상의 원칙 / *the* ~ *that might makes right* 힘이 정의라는 정설. **2** an opinion strongly supported by those who believe it. 독단적 주장〔견해〕; 도그마. [Gk. *dokeō* seem]

dog·ma·ta [dɔ́(ː)gmətə, dάg-] *n.* pl. of **dogma.**

dog·mat·ic [dɔ(ː)gmǽtik, dαg-] *adj.* **1** of or like dogma; very strong in support of and belief in one's opinions. 교의(상)의; 교리에 관한. **2** believed as truth without proof. 독단적〔독선적〕인. ¶ *a ~ statement* 독단적인 언설.

dog·mat·i·cal [dɔ(:)gmǽtikəl, dɑg-] *adj.* = dogmatic. ● **dog·mat·i·cal·ly** [-kəli] *adv.*

dog·ma·tism [dɔ́(:)gmətìzəm, dɑ́g-] *n.* Ⓤ the quality of being dogmatic. 독단론; 독단〔교조〕주의; 독단적 태도. ¶ *a hasty ~* 성급한 독단.

dog·ma·tist [dɔ́(:)gmətist, dɑ́g-] *n.* Ⓒ a person who is dogmatic or who states dogmas. 독단적인 사람; 독단론자; 교조주의자.

dog·ma·tize [dɔ́(:)gmətàiz, dɑ́g-] *vt.* (P6) express (a principle, etc.) as a dogma. 독단적으로 말하다; 정리〔교리〕로서 주장하다. — *vi.* (P1) speak or write dogmatically; lay down the law. 독단적인 주장을 하다; 독단적으로 말하다〔쓰다〕.

do·good·er [dú:gùdər] *n.* 《*colloq.*》 a person who is excessively eager to correct or set things right; esp. a person who tries to correct social evils by charitable actions. 공상적인 사회 개량가. [*do, good*]

dog rose [ㅗ ㅡ] *n.* 《bot.》 the common wild rose. 찔레나무의 일종. [*dog*]

dog's age [ㅗ ㅡ] *n.* 《*colloq.*》 a long time. 오랜 기간; 오랫동안.

dog's chance [ㅗ ㅡ] *n.* a chance with little probability of being realized. 극히 적은 가망성; 가망성이 거의 없음.

Dog star [ㅗ ㅡ] *n.* a popular name for Sirius. 큰개자리; 시리우스.

dog tag [ㅗ ㅡ] *n.* **1** a small metal plate on the collar of a dog, usu. indicating ownership. 개패《개목걸이에 다는 감찰(鑑札)》. **2** 《U.S. *sl.*》 a soldier's identification tag, worn on a chain around the neck. (군인의) 인식표. [*dog*]

dog·teeth [dɔ́(:)gtì:θ, dɑ́g-] *n.* pl. of **dog-tooth**.

dog-tired [dɔ́(:)gtáiərd, dɑ́g-] *adj.* very tired; worn out. 몹시 지친; 녹초가 된. [*dog*]

dog·tooth [dɔ́(:)gtù:θ, dɑ́g-] *n.* (*pl.* **-teeth**) a canine tooth. 송곳니; 견치(犬齒).

dog·watch [dɔ́(:)gwɑ̀tʃ, dɑ́g- / -wɔ̀tʃ] *n.* 《naut.》 the shortest watch on a ship, either from 4:00 to 6:00 p.m. or from 6:00 to 8:00 p.m. in the evening. 절반 당직《오후 4-6시와 6-8시의 두 시간 교대》.

dog·wood [dɔ́(:)gwùd, dɑ́g-] *n.* Ⓒ 《bot.》 a tree with white or pink flowers in the spring and red fruit in the autumn. 말채나무.

doi·ly [dɔ́ili] *n.* Ⓒ (*pl.* **-lies**) a small napkin or mat of linen, paper, etc., used under plates, vases, etc. 작은 냅킨; (접시·꽃병 등의) 장식 받침. [Person]

do·ings [dú:iŋz] *n.* *pl.* deeds; actions; behavior; conduct; happenings; events. 행위; 행동; 행실; 일; 사건; 행사. ¶ *daily ~* 매일 하는 일 / *the day's ~* 그 날의 사건 / *his ~ in England* 영국에서의 그의 행적 / *~ for the month* 이 달의 행사 / *give an interesting account of one's ~* 자기 행위에 관해서 재미있는 이야기를 하다. [*do*]

doit [dɔit] *n.* **1** a small copper coin formerly used by the Dutch. 네덜란드의 옛 동전. **2** a very small sum; a bit. 소액; 조금. ¶ *not worth a ~* 한푼의 가치도 없는 / *He did not care a ~ what anybody thought.* 그는 누가 어떻게 생각하든 조금도 개의치 않았다. [Du.]

do-it-your·self [dù:ətjərsélf] *adj.* designed to be used or done by anyone. (아마추어가 특별한 훈련 없이) 스스로 할〔조립할, 사용할〕 수 있게 설계된. [*do*]

dol. dollar(s).

dol·ce [dóultʃei / dɔ́ltʃi] *adj., adv.* 《It.》《mus.》 sweet and soft. 감미로운〔롭게〕; 부드러운〔럽게〕. [→dulcet]

dol·drums [dóuldrəmz, dɑ́l-] *n. pl.* 《*the ~*》 **1** 《naut.》 the part of the ocean near the equator with very little wind. (적도 부근 해상의) 열대 무풍대. **2** dullness; low spirits. 침체; 무기력; 우울. [? Imit.]
in the doldrums, in a low and sad state of mind. 몹시 우울〔울적〕해.

dole[1] [doul] *n.* Ⓒ **1** a portion of money, food, etc., given in charity; alms. 시주; 보시; 시여(施與)(물). **2** 《Brit.》《*the ~*》 a weekly payment given by the government to unemployed workers. 실업 수당.
be* 〔*go*〕 *on the dole, receive these weekly payments from the government. 실업 수당을 타다.
— *vt.* (P7) give out (something) in portions to the poor, etc.; give (something) in small portions. (가난한 사람 등에게) …을 나누어〔베풀어〕 주다; 조금씩〔아까운 듯이〕 주다. [E.]
dole out, measure out sparingly. 조금씩 내다.

dole[2] [doul] *n.* Ⓤ 《*poet.*》 sorrow; grief. 슬픔. [L. *doleo* grieve]
make one's dole, show great grief. 비탄에 젖다.

dole·ful [dóulfəl] *adj.* sad; mournful; melancholy. 슬픈; 비탄에 젖은; 애처로운; 우울한. ¶ *a ~ tale* 〔*look*〕 슬픈 이야기〔표정〕. [*dole*[2]]

:doll [dɑl, dɔ(:)l] *n.* Ⓒ **1** a child's toy made to look like a baby, a child, etc. 인형. ¶ *a doll's face* 인형 같은 얼굴; 예쁘긴 하나 표정이 없는 얼굴. **2** ⓐ a pretty but rather stupid girl or woman. 아름다우나 이지적이 아닌 여자; 백치미(美)의 소녀〔여자〕. ⓑ 《*colloq.*》 an attractive preson. 매력적인 사람. **3** 《U.S. *sl.*》 a woman. 여자. ¶ *guys and dolls* 젊은 남녀. — *vi., vt.* 《*up*》《*sl.*》 dress smartly. 아름답게 차려 입다. ¶ *be dolled up* 아름답게 차려 입고 있다 / *~ (oneself) up* 차려 입다. ● **doll·like** [dɑ́llàik, dɔ́(:)l-] *adj.* [*Dorothy*]

:dol·lar [dɑ́lər / dɔ́lər] *n.* Ⓒ **1** a unit of money in the United States and some other countries; a hundred cents. 달러. 參考 기호는 $, $. **2** a coin or piece of paper money worth one dollar. 1달러 화폐[지폐]. **3** 《Brit. *sl.*》 5 shillings. 5실링. [Gk. *thaler* the unit of money]

bet one's bottom dollar, 《U.S. *colloq.*》 be absolutely certain. 확신하고 있다.

dollars, the almighty dollar, money; wealth. 돈; 부(富).

feel* [*look*] *like a million dollars, 《U.S. *colloq.*》 feel or look extremely well. 극히 건강하게 느끼다[건강해 보이다].

dol·lop [dáləp / dɔ́l-] *n.* clumsily served lump of food, etc. (치즈·버터 등의) 덩어리.

dol·ly [dáli / dɔ́li] *n.* Ⓒ (*pl.* **doll·ies**) **1** a child's word for a doll. 인형; 각시《소아어》. **2** a small, low frame on wheels, used for moving heavy objects, esp. a cinecamera or TV camera. (무거운 물체 이동용의) 낮고 작은 바퀴 달린 수레; 영화·TV 카메라 이동 대차(臺車). [*doll*]

dol·man [dóulmən, dál- / dɔ́l-] *n.* a long Turkish outer robe; a jacket. 터키인이 입는 긴 외투; (경기병이 어깨에 걸쳐 입는) 상의. [Turk. *dōlāmān* a winding]

dol·men [dóulmen, dálmən / dɔ́l-] *n.* a prehistoric megalithic structure. 돌멘; 고인돌. [F.]

do·lo·mite [dóuləmàit, dálə- / dɔ́lə-] *n.* a rock composed largely of calcium magnecium carbonate. 고회석(苦灰石); 백운석(白雲石). [Person]

do·lor, 《Brit.》 **-lour** [dóulər] *n.* 《*poet.*》 grief; sorrow; distress. 슬픔; 고뇌. [→dole[2]]

dol·or·ous [dálərəs, dóulə- / dɔ́lə-] *adj.* 《*poet.*》 sad; mournful; painful. 슬픈; 애처로운; 고통에 찬. ¶ ~ *news* 슬픈 소식 / *the* ~ *day* 고통스러운 날. [→dole[2]]

dol·phin [dálfin, dɔ́(:)l-] *n.* Ⓒ **1** a sea animal related to the whale, but smaller. 돌고래. **2** a sea-fish which changes color when dying. 만새기; 황새치. [Gk. *delphis*]

dolt [doult] *n.* Ⓒ a dull, stupid fellow. 멍청이; 얼간이. ● **dolt·ish** [dóultiʃ] *adj.* [? *dull*]

dom. domestic; dominion.

do·main [douméin] *n.* Ⓒ **1** the territory under the control of one government or ruler. 영토; 영지. ¶ *the* ~ *of Great Britain* 대영 제국의 판도. **2** the land owned by one person or family; an estate. (개인의) 소유지; 땅. **3** 《*fig.*》 a field or sphere of knowledge, thought, activity, etc. (지식·사상·활동 따위의) 분야; 영역; 범위; …계(界). [→dominate]

·**dome** [doum] *n.* Ⓒ **1** a large, rounded roof. 돔; 둥근 천장. **2** something high and rounded like a dome; 《*fig.*》 the sky. 둥근 천장 모양의 것; 하늘. ¶ *the blue* ~ *above us* 머리위의 창공 / *the* ~ *formed by the trees' branches* 뭇나무의 가지들이 어우러져 이룬 돔. **3** 《*poet., arch.*》 a building; a palace. 궁전. — *vt.* cover (something) with a dome; shape (something) like a dome. …에 돔[둥근 천장]을 달다; …을 돔[반구] 모양으로 하다. — *vi.* rise or swell out like a dome. 반구형으로 부풀다[내밀다]. [L. *domus* house]

domed [doumd] *adj.* rounded; of or like a dome. 돔[반구]형의; 둥근 천장의. ¶ *a* ~ *forehead* 반구형으로 쑥 내민 이마.

:**do·mes·tic** [douméstik] *adj.* **1** of the home, family, or household affairs. 가정의; 가족의; 가사의. ¶ ~ *affairs* 집안일; 가사 / ~ *science* (교과의) 가정과 / ~ *industry* 가내 공업 / ~ *life* 가정 생활 / *Cooking and sewing are* ~ *tasks.* 밥짓기와 바느질은 가정의 일이다. **2** of one's own country; not foreign. 자국의; 국내의(opp. foreign). ¶ ~ *and foreign news* 국내외 뉴스 / ~ *trade* 국내 무역. **3** made in one's own country; native; home-made. 국산의; 자가제(自家製)의(opp. imported). ¶ ~ *goods* [*products*] 국산품. **4** (of animals) not wild; tame. 길러서 길들인(opp. wild). ¶ *a* ~ *animal* 가축; 가금(家禽). **5** fond of home and family life or household affairs. 가정적인; 집안일을 좋아하는. ¶ *a* ~ *man* 가정적인 남자; 외출을 싫어하는 남자.
— *n.* Ⓒ **1** a servant in a household. 하인. ¶ *a female* ~ 가정부. **2** 《*pl.*》 native products. 국산품. [→dome, -ic]

do·mes·ti·cal·ly [douméstikəli] *adv.* **1** in a domestic way. 가정적으로; 국내용으로. **2** in domestic territory. 국내에서. **3** with respect to domestic affairs. 국내 문제에 관하여.

do·mes·ti·cate [douméstəkèit] *vt.* (P6) **1** ⓐ tame (animals, etc.) for domestic use; change (a plant, etc.) from a wild to a tame state. (동물 따위)를 길들이다; (식물 따위를) 순화(馴化)시키다. ⓑ civilize. (야만인)을 교화시키다. **2** make (someone) fond of family life; make (someone) domestic. …에게 가정을 좋아하게 하다; …을 가정적으로 만들다. **3** naturalize. (외국어·습관 따위를) 받아들이다.

do·mes·ti·ca·tion [doumèstəkéiʃən] *n.* Ⓤ the action of domesticating; the state of being domesticated. 길들임; 길듦; 순화(馴化); 교화.

do·mes·tic·i·ty [dòumestísəti] *n.* (*pl.* **-ties**) **1** Ⓤ home and family life; love of home and family life. 가정 생활; 가정(생활)을 사랑함. **2** 《usu. *pl.*》 domestic affairs. 가사(家事).

dom·i·cile [dáməsàil, -səl / dɔ́m-] *n.* Ⓒ **1** house; home; residence. 주소; 주거; 집. **2** 《law》 the place of permanent residence. 본적지. ¶ *one's* ~ *by birth* 본적지. — *vt.* (P6, 13) settle (someone) in a domicile. …의 주소를 정하다; …를 정주(定住)시키다. ¶ *be domiciled at* [*in*] …에 정주하다. — *vi.* (P3) dwell; reside. 살다; 거주[정주]하다. ● **dom·i·cil·i·ar·y** [dàməsílièri / dɔ̀m-] *adj.* [→dome]

dom·i·nance [dámənəns / dɔ́m-] *n.* Ⓤ the state of being dominant; rule; control. 권세; 우세; 지배; 통치. [↓]

dom·i·nant [dάmənənt / dɔ́m-] *adj.* **1** most influential; ruling; governing. (가장) 우세한; 지배적인. ¶ *the ~ party* 제1당; 다수당 / *play a ~ role* 지배적인 역할을 하다. **2** rising high above others. 높이 솟은; 높은. ¶ *a ~ mountain peak* 최고봉; 주봉(主峰). **3** 《biol.》 being the one of a pair of (genes determining) contrasting inherited characteristics that predominates. 우성(優性)의. **4** 《mus.》 based on or having to do with the fifth note of a scale. 제 5도 음의; 딸림음의.
— *n.* Ⓒ 《mus.》 the fifth note in a scale. 딸림음. ●**dom·i·nant·ly** [-li] *adv.* [↓]

dom·i·nate [dάmənèit / dɔ́m-] *vt.* (P6) **1** control or rule (someone, etc.) by strength or will. …을 지배하다; 제어(억제)하다; 좌우하다. ¶ *~ a country commercially* 일국을 상업적으로 지배하다 / *~ one's feelings* 감정을 억제하다 / *The boy dominates his smaller friends.* 그 아이는 꼬마 친구들을 지배하고 있다. **2** rise high above (others); overlook from a height. …위에 우뚝 솟다; …을 굽어보다. ¶ *The high mountain dominates the town.* 그 높은 산은 시(市)를 굽어보고 있다 / *The lighthouse dominates the sea for several miles.* 등대는 바다를 몇 마일이나 굽어보는 위치에 있다.
— *vi.* (P1,3) **1** 《*over*》 have or exercise control over; occupy a commanding position. 지배하다; 우위를 차지하다. ¶ *~ over the weak* 약자를 지배하다. **2** be higher than surrounding objects. 우뚝 솟다. [L. *dominus* load]

dom·i·na·tion [dὰmənéiʃən / dɔ̀m-] *n.* Ⓤ control; rule. 통치; 지배.

dom·i·neer [dὰməníər / dɔ̀m-] *vi.* (P1,3) 《*over*》 rule at one's own will; behave like a tyrant. 독재적으로 지배하다; 폭군처럼 굴다; 압제하다. ¶ *~ over the inferior* 아랫사람들에게 거드름 피우다. [→dominate]

dom·i·neer·ing [dὰməníəriŋ / dɔ̀m-] *adj.* inclined to domineer; masterful. 거만한; 뽐내는; 압제적인.

Dom·i·nic [dάmənik / dɔ́m-], **Saint** *n.* (1170-1221) a Spanish priest. 스페인의 성직자. 參考 도미니크회의 개조.

do·min·i·cal [dəmínikəl] *adj.* **1** belonging to our Lord (=Christ). 주 예수 그리스도의. ¶ *the ~ year* 서력(西曆). **2** having to do with Sunday or the Lord's day. 주일의; 일요일의. [L. *dominus* load]

Do·min·i·can [dəmínikən] *adj.* **1** of Saint Dominic. 도미니크회의. ¶ *the ~ order* 도미니크회. **2** of the Dominican Republic in the West Indies. 도미니카 공화국의. — *n.* Ⓒ **1** a friar or nun of the Dominican order. (도미니크회의) 수사; 수녀. **2** a person of the Dominican Republic. 도미니카 공화국 사람.

Dominican Republic [-ˊ-- -ˊ-], **the** *n.* a country in the West Indies. 도미니카 공화국. 參考 수도는 Santo Domingo.

dom·i·nie [dάməni / dɔ́m-] *n.* **1** 《Sc.》 a schoolmaster. 교장. **2** [*also* doum-] 《U.S. and Brit. *arch.*》 a clergyman. 목사. [→dominate]

·**do·min·ion** [dəmínjən] *n.* **1** Ⓤ power to rule; sovereignty. 지배권; 주권. ¶ *have* (*hold*) *~ over* …을 지배하다 / *be under the ~ of* …의 지배하에 있다 / *bring someone under ~* …을 복종시키다 / *exercise ~ over a country* 나라를 지배하다. **2** ⓊⒸ a territory under the control of a ruler or government. 영토. ¶ *the overseas dominions* 해외 영토. **3** 《*the D-*》 a self-governing part of the British Commonwealth. (영연방의) 자치령. [↑]

dom·i·no [dάmənòu / dɔ́m-] *n.* Ⓒ (*pl.* **-noes** or **-nos**) **1** a loose cloak with a mask, worn at masquerades. (가장 무도회용의) 가면이 달린 겉옷. **2** a person wearing a domino. 그 착용자. [F.]

dom·i·noes [dάmənòuz / dɔ́m-] *n. pl.* **1** flat pieces of bone, wood, etc. with dots on one side and used in playing dominoes. (주사위 같은) 도미노 패. **2** 《used as *sing.*》 a game played with such pieces. 도미노 놀이. [F.]

domino theory [ˊ--- ˋ--] *n.* the theory that if one country is taken over by a Communist regime, the neighboring countries will soon be overrun in turn. 도미노 이론《한 나라가 공산화되면 주변국이 차례차례 공산화된다는 이론》.

Don [dɑn / dɔn] *n.* **1** a nickname for Donald. Donald의 애칭. **2** 《*the ~*》 the river flowing through the European part of the Russia. 돈강(江)《러시아의 모스크바 남쪽 이반 호에서 발원하여 Azov해로 흘러듦》.

·**don**[1] [dɑn / dɔn] *n.* Ⓒ 《Sp.》 **1** 《*D-*》 Mr.; Sir. 군; 씨《스페인어에서 남자 이름 앞에 붙이는 명칭》. **2** a Spanish gentleman; a Spaniard. 스페인 신사; 스페인 사람. **3** an important man. 명사; 거물. **4** 《Brit. *colloq.*》 a head, tutor, or fellow of any college as at Oxford or Cambridge University. 학감; 개인 지도 교사; 특별 연구원. [→dominate]

don[2] [dɑn / dɔn] *vt.* (**donned, don·ning**) (P6) put on (clothing, etc.). (옷 따위)를 입다; 걸치다; (신)을 신다; (모자)를 쓰다 (opp. doff). ¶ *~ one's clothes.* 參考 do on의 단축형. [*do, on*]

do·ña [dóunjɑː] *n.* a Spanish woman of rank, used as a title prefixed to the Christian name. 스페인의 신분 있는 부인. 參考 기혼 여성 이름 앞에 붙이는 경칭. [Sp.]

Don·ald [dάnəld / dɔ́n-] *n.* a man's name. 남자 이름. 參考 애칭은 Don.

do·nate [dóuneit, -ˊ] *vt.* (P6,13) 《orig. U.S.》 make a gift of; give; contribute. …을 주다; 기부(기증)하다. ¶ *~ funds to a university* 대학에 기금을 기부하다 / *~ 5,000 dollars to an orphanage* 고아원에 5천 달러를 기부하다. [L. *dono* give]

do·na·tion [dounéiʃən] *n.* **1** Ⓤ 《sometimes *a ~*》 the act of giving. 기부; 기증; 증

여. ¶ *a blood* ~ 헌혈 / *make*〔*give*〕 *a* ~ 기부를 하다. **2** Ⓒ something given; a gift; a contribution. 기부금; 기증품. ¶ *donations to the school* 학교에의 기증품 / *ask for* 〔*invite*〕 *donations* 모금하다.

do·na·tive [dóunətiv, dán-] *n.* ⟪esp. Church of England⟫ an official gift; a donation. 기부금; 기증품. — *adj.* of the nature of a donative. 기부의; 기부의 성질을 지닌.

:done [dʌn] *v.* pp. of **do.** — *adj.* **1** completed; finished. 완성한; 끝난. ¶ *be* ~ *with something* …을 끝내다〔마치다〕. **2** ⟪*colloq.*⟫ tired out. 몹시 지친. ¶ *You look* ~. 몹시 지쳐 보인다. **3** cooked enough. (음식이) 잘 익은. ¶ *under-done* 설익은〔구운, 끓은〕 / *half-done* 반익은〔구운, 끓은〕 / *over-done* 너무 익은〔구워진, 끓은〕. **4** socially acceptable. 유행〔취미, 예절〕에 맞는. ¶ *It isn't* ~ *to put your knife in your mouth when you eat.* 먹을 때 나이프를 입안에 가져가는 것은 좋지 않다. [*do*]

don·jon [dʌ́ndʒən, dán- / dɔ́n-] *n.* Ⓒ the keep of a castle or a large, strongly-built tower (of a castle). 아성(牙城)의 망루. [→dungeon]

·don·key [dáŋki, dɔ́(:)ŋ-] *n.* Ⓒ **1** a small animal like a horse; an ass. 당나귀. **2** a silly or foolish person. 바보; 얼간이. [? *dun* horse, mon*key*]

don·nish [dániʃ / dɔ́n-] *adj.* **1** of or suggestive of a university don. (영국 대학의) 학감 같은. **2** formal; pedantic. 짐짓 점잔 빼는; 학자연하는. [*don*[1]]

do·nor [dóunər] *n.* Ⓒ a person who donates; a giver. 기부자; 기증자; 제공자; 시여자(施與者). [→donate]

do-nothing [dú:nʌ̀θiŋ] *adj.* idle. 아무 것도 하지 않는. — *n.* an idle person. 아무 것도 하지 않으려는 사람; 게으름뱅이. [*do*]

Don Quix·o·te [dànkihóuti, -kwíksət / dɔ̀nkwíksət] *n.* a person who attempts impossible, romantic deeds, hero of a novel by Cervantes. 돈키호테⟪비현실적인 엉뚱한 행동을 하는 사람⟫. [Sp.]

:don't [dount] =do not.
— *n.* ⟪usu. *pl.*⟫ rules or customs that forbid something. 금지 조항집(集). [→donate]

doo·dad [dú:dæ̀d] *n.* Ⓒ ⟪*colloq.*⟫ **1** a small ornament; bauble. 작은 장식물; 싸구려 장식. **2** a doohickey. (그 뭔가 하는) 물건; 장치. [*dad* piece]

doo·dle [dú:dl] *vi., vt.* (P1; 6) scrawl in an aimless way. (회의 등에서 딴 일에 정신이 팔려) 낙서하다. — *n.* Ⓒ **1** a scrawl. (그런) 낙서. **2** a silly person. 바보. [Amer. =fool]

·doom [du:m] *n.* Ⓤ **1** an unhappy or tragic fate; ruin; death. (나쁜) 운명; 파멸; 죽음. ¶ *go to* 〔*meet, know*〕 *one's* ~ 죽다 / *His* ~ *was to be poverty.* 가난한 것이 그의 운명이었다. **2** ⟪*arch.*⟫ a judgment; a sentence. 재판; 판결; 선고. ¶ *pass* 〔*pronounce*〕 ~ *of death on* 〔*upon*〕 *a political offender* 정치범에게 사형 판결을 내리다. **3** God's Last Judgment of mankind; the end of the world. (하느님의) 최후의 심판; 이 세상 최후의 날. ¶ *the day of* ~ / *till the crack of* ~ 세상의 마지막까지.
— *vt.* (P6,13) ⟪*to*⟫ **1** sentence. 형(刑)을 …에게 선고하다. ¶ ~ *someone to death* 아무에게 사형을 선고하다. **2** ⟪chiefly in *passive*⟫ destine. …을 운명지우다. ¶ *the doomed ship* 침몰할 운명에 있는 배 / *be doomed to fail* 〔*failure*〕 실패하게 돼 있다. [E. statute]

dooms·day [dú:mzdèi] *n.* Ⓒ ⟪often *D-*⟫ the end of the world; the day of God's Last Judgment of mankind. 이 세상 마지막 날; 최후 심판의 날.
till doomsday, for ever. 영원히.

:door [dɔ:r] *n.* Ⓒ **1** an entrance to a building or room; a doorway. 출입구; 현관. ¶ *enter by* 〔*at*〕 *the front* ~ 현관으로 들어가다 / *see someone to the* ~ 아무를 현관까지 배웅하다 / *There is someone at the* ~. 현관에 누가 와 있다. **2** a movable barrier through which one enters a house, room, cupboard, etc. 문. ¶ *bang a* ~ 문을 쾅하고 닫다 / *shut* 〔*open*〕 *the* ~ 문을 닫다〔열다〕 / *shut the* ~ *behind* 〔*after*〕 *one* 들어가〔나와서〕 문을 닫다 / *knock at the* ~ 도어를 노크하다. **3** a room, house, or building that a door belongs to. (출입구가 있는) 집〔방〕; 한집. ¶ *from* ~ *to* ~ 한집 한집; 이집 저집; 집집이 / *My house is next* ~ *but one to his.* 우리 집은 한 집 걸러 그의 이웃이다. **4** ⟪*fig.*⟫ any means of attaining something. …에 이르는 길; 문호. ¶ *a* ~ *to success* 성공에의 길. [E.]
answer 〔***go to***〕 ***the door,*** answer the bell. 내객을 맞으러 나가다〔나오다〕.
at death's door, near death; dying. 죽을 때가 가까워져; 죽음에 직면하여.
at the door of, on the point of. 바야흐로 …하려고 하여.
close the door upon, do not allow to enter. …을 안에 들이지 않다.
darken *someone's* ***door***(***s***) ⇨darken.
lay *a mistake* ***at*** *someone's* ***door,*** blame someone for a mistake. 과오를 아무의 탓으로 돌리다.
lie at *someone's* ***door*** =***lie at the door of*** *someone,* attribute to; be imputable to. (죄책 따위가) …에게 있다.
next door, (in) the next house or apartment. 이웃(집)에. ¶ *the people next* ~ 이웃집 사람들.
next door to, very nearly; almost. …와 같은; 거의. ¶ *That is next* ~ *to murder.* 그건 살인이나 매한가지다.
open a 〔***the***〕 ***door to*** 〔***for***〕, welcome. …에 문호를 개방하다; …을 가능케 하다.
out of doors, in the open air; outside. 집밖〔야외〕에서; 밖에서.
show *someone* ***the door,*** tell someone to leave; turn him out of the house. …에게 나가라고 하다; 내쫓다.
shut 〔***close***〕 ***the door to*** 〔***on***〕, make impos-

sible. …을 불가능케 하다.

with an open door, in public. 문호를 개방하여; 공개로.

within doors, 《*arch.*》 in the house; inside. 옥내〔실내〕에(cf. now *indoors*).

:door·bell [dɔ́:rbèl] *n.* Ⓒ a bell at or near a door, rung by someone wishing to have the door opened. 현관의 벨〔초인종〕.

door·frame [dɔ́:rfrèim] *n.* Ⓒ a wooden frame within which a door (*n.* 2.) is hung. 문틀; 문얼굴.

door·keep·er [dɔ́:rkì:pər] *n.* Ⓒ a person who guards a door; a doorman. 수위; 문지기.

door·knob [dɔ́:rnɑ̀b / -nɔ̀b] *n.* Ⓒ a small knob or handle on a door. 문의 손잡이.

door·man [dɔ́:rmæ̀n, -mən] *n.* Ⓒ (*pl.* **-men** [-mèn, -mən]) **1** a man whose work is opening the door of a hotel, store, etc. for those who enter or leave. (호텔·백화점 따위에서) 문 열어주는 사람. 參考 짐 운반, 택시를 잡아주기도 함. **2** a doorkeeper. 문지기.

door·mat [dɔ́:rmæ̀t] *n.* Ⓒ **1** a mat usu. placed before a door on which one can wipe one's shoes. (현관의) 흙털이 매트. **2** 《*sl.*》 a dominated person. (학대를 받는 따위로) 짓밟혀도 잠자코 있는 사람.

door money [´ ´–] *n.* a payment made for admission to a place of entertainment. 입장료.

door·nail [dɔ́:rnèil] *n.* Ⓒ a nail with a large head used for decorating doors. 문에 박은 대갈못《장식용》.

(*as*) *dead as a doornail,* entirely dead. 완전히 죽어. ¶ *The bear was dead as a* ~. 곰은 완전히 죽어 있었다.

door·plate [dɔ́:rplèit] *n.* Ⓒ a metal plate on a door with a name, house number, etc. on it. 문패.

door·post [dɔ́:rpòust] *n.* Ⓒ either of the two sidepieces of a doorframe. (문틀 양측의) 옆기둥.

as deaf as a doorpost, quite deaf. 찰귀머거리인.

door·sill [dɔ́:rsìl] *n.* =threshold.

door·step [dɔ́:rstèp] *n.* Ⓒ a step leading to the outer door of a house. 현관 정면의 계단.

door·stop [dɔ́:rstɑ̀p / -stɔ̀p] *n.* Ⓒ a device to keep a door open. 문을 연 위치에서 고정시키는 장치.

***door·way** [dɔ́:rwèi] *n.* Ⓒ the entrance to a building, room, etc. closed and opened by a door. (집·방의) 출입구; 문간.

door·yard [dɔ́:rjɑ̀:rd] *n.* Ⓒ 《U.S.》 a yard in front of the door of a house. 출입구〔현관〕의 앞뜰.

dope [doup] *n.* Ⓤ **1** ⓐ a harmful drug which makes a person feel dull or sleepy. 마약; 마취제; 수면제. ⓑ any stimulant given to a horse before a race. (말의) 흥분제. ⓒ Ⓒ a person who takes such drugs. 마약 중독자. **2** oil, grease, etc. used to make something run smoothly. 윤활제. **3** a thick liquid used as protection on the cloth parts of an airplane. 도프 도료(塗料)《비행기 익포(翼布)에 바르는 방수·강화용 니스》. **4** 《U.S. *sl.*》 information. 정보. ¶ *Give me the* ~. 정보 좀 알려주게. **5** Ⓒ 《U.S. *sl.*》 a very stupid person. 바보. **6** 《*fig.*》 something which dulls or deceives the conscience. 양심을 마비시키는 것.

— *vt.* (P6,7) **1** 《*sl.*》 give dope (*n.* 1.) to (someone). …에게 마약을 주다〔먹이다〕. ¶ ~ *a horse* 말에 흥분제를 먹이다. **2** 《*sl.*》 predict; forecast. …의 예상을 하다. **3** apply dope (*n.* 2., 3.) to (something). …에 도프 도료〔윤활제〕를 바르다. **4** 《*fig.*》 deceive. …을 속이다; 기만하다. [Du. =sauce]

dope out, 《*sl.*》 find out; figure or work out. …을 알아내다; 고안해 내다; 추측하다.

dope fiend [´ ´] *n.* 《U.S.》 a drug addict. 마약 중독자.

dope·y, dop·y [dóupi] *adj.* (**dop·i·er, dop·i·est**) 《U.S. *sl.*》 **1** under the influence of drugs. (상습적인 마약·술로) 기능이 둔화된; 활발치 못한; 나른한. **2** stupid. 어리석은; 바보 같은.

Dop·pler effect [dɑ́plər- / dɔ́p-] *n.* 《phys.》 a change in the apparent frequency of sound, light, or other waves when there is relative motion between the source and the observer. 도플러 효과. [Person]

Do·ra [dɔ́:rə] *n.* a nickname for Dorothea, Dorothy, or Theodora. Dorothea, Dorothy, Theodora의 애칭.

Dor·ic [dɔ́(:)rik, dɑ́r-] *adj.* **1** of Doris or its people (*n.* 1.). 도리스 지방의; 도리아인(人)의. **2** 《archit.》 of the architectural style of Doris or its people (*n.* 1.). 도리아식의. [Gk.]

Dor·is [dɔ́(:)ris, dɑ́r-] *n.* **1** a country in ancient Greece. 고대 그리스의 한 지방; 도리스. **2** a woman's name. 여자 이름.

dorm [dɔ:rm] *n.* 《*colloq.*》 =dormitory.

dor·man·cy [dɔ́:rmənsi] *n.* Ⓤ the quality or state of being dormant. 수면〔휴면〕 상태; 휴지〔정지〕 상태; 동면. [↓]

dor·mant [dɔ́:rmənt] *adj.* **1** sleeping, or as if asleep. 잠자는 (듯한). ¶ *Bears are* ~ *during the winter.* 곰은 겨울 동안 동면한다. **2** inactive. 활동치 않는; 휴지해 있는; 잠복의. ¶ *a* ~ *volcano* 휴화산 / *lie* ~ 잠복해〔휴지하고, 동면하고〕 있다; (기계·자금 따위가) 사용되고 있지 않다; (권리 따위가) 미발동이다. [L. *dormio* sleep]

dor·mer [dɔ́:rmər] *n.* Ⓒ《archit.》an upright window in a sloping roof. 지붕창(窓); 천창. [↑]

dor·mice [dɔ́:rmàis] *n.* pl. of **dormouse.**

***dor·mi·to·ry** [dɔ́:rmətɔ̀:ri / -təri] *n.* Ⓒ (*pl.* **-ries**) **1** 《U.S.》 a building containing a number of sleeping rooms. 기숙사; 생활관. **2** 《Brit.》 a sleeping room containing a number of beds. 공동 침실. [→dormant]

dor·mouse [dɔ́ːrmàus] *n.* Ⓒ (*pl.* **-mice**) 《animal》 a small animal that looks somewhat like a squirrel. 산쥐류(類). [↑, *mouse*]

dor·my, -mie [dɔ́ːrmi] *adj.* 《golf》 being in the lead as many holes as there are holes to play. 남은 홀의 수만큼 이긴. [→dormant]

Dor·o·the·a [dɔ̀ːrəθíːə, dɑ̀r-] *n.* a woman's name. 여자 이름.

Dor·o·thy [dɔ́ːrəθi, dɑ́r-] *n.* a woman's name. 여자 이름.

dorothy bag [⌐--⌐] *n.* lady's open-topped handbag. (아가리를 끈으로 죄는) 여성용 핸드백.

dor·sal [dɔ́ːrsəl] *adj.* of or on the back. 등(쪽)의; 등에 있는; 배면의. ¶ *a* ~ *fin* 등지느러미. [L. *dorsum* back]

do·ry[1] [dɔ́ːri] *n.* Ⓒ (*pl.* **-ries**) a rowboat with a flat bottom. 밑이 평평한 작은 배. 參考 미국 New England 지방에 많음. [Amer. Ind.=dugout]

do·ry[2] [dɔ́ːri] *n.* Ⓒ (*pl.* **-ries**) 《fish》 a small sea fish that can be eaten. 달고기류(類). [→John Dory]

dos·age [dóusidʒ] *n.* **1** Ⓒ the quantity of a medicine to be taken at one time. 1회분의 투약[복용]량. **2** Ⓤ the administration of medicine in doses. 조제(調劑); 투약. [↓]

dose [dous] *n.* Ⓒ **1** the quantity of a medicine to be taken at one time; dosage. (약의 1회분) 복용량. ¶ *a lethal* 〔*fatal*〕 ~ 치사량 / *take medicine in small doses* 소량씩 약을 먹다 / *administer a* ~ 투약하다. **2** 《*fig.*》 an amount of something given. (아첨·벌·경험 따위의) 어떤 분량. ¶ *administer doses of punishment* 약이 되도록 때때로 벌을 주다.

a dose of, a bit of. 소량의; 약간의. ¶ *a* ~ *of flattery* 약간의 아첨.

have a regular dose of, have too much of. 너무 많다.

— *vt.* (P6,13) **1** 《*with, to*》 give medicine to (someone) in doses. …에게 약을 주다; (약)을 복용시키다. ¶ ~ *aspirin to a patient* = ~ *a patient with aspirin* 환자에게 아스피린을 주다. **2** 《*with*》 blend.…에 섞다. ¶ ~ *wine with sugar.* [Gk. *dosis* giving]

Dos Pas·sos [dòus pǽsous], **John Roderigo** *n.* (1896-1970) an American novelist. 도스 패소스《미국의 소설가》.

doss house [⌐⌐] *n.* 《Brit. *sl.*》 an inn for the very poor. 값싼 여인숙. [→dorsal]

dos·si·er [dɑ́sièi, dɔ́(ː)si-] *n.* 《F.》 a collection of papers containing information about some particular person or an event. 일건 서류. [F. =bundle of papers]

*__dost__ [dʌst, dəst] *v.* 《*arch.*》 =do. ¶ *Thou* ~. =You do.

:**dot**[1] [dɑt / dɔt] *n.* Ⓒ **1** a small round mark; a point; a period. 점; 작은 점; 마침표. ¶ *put a* ~ *on the i,* i의 점을 찍다. **2** anything like a dot in size or appearance. 점 같은 것; 얼룩; 반점. ¶ *The ship became a mere* ~ *on the horizon* 배는 수평선 위에 한 낱 점으로 변했다. **3** a short signal (·) in the Morse code. (모스 부호의) 도트; 점 (cf. *dash*(—)).

off one's dot, 《Brit. *sl.*》 very stupid; crazy. 멍텅구리의; 머리가 돈.

on the dot, 《*colloq.*》 at the exact time; on time. (정확히) 제시간에. ¶ *arrive at six o'clock on the* ~ 정확히 6시에 도착하다.

to a dot, 《U.S. *colloq.*》 correctly; precisely. 정확히; 완전히; 아주. ¶ *be correct to a* ~ 아주 정확하다.

— *vt.* (**dot·ted, dot·ting**) (P6,13) **1** mark (something) with a dot or dots. …에 점(點)을 찍다. ¶ ~ *an 'i',* 'i'의 점을 찍다. **2** 《esp. in *pp.*》 draw by means of dots; cover (something) with dots. 점으로 그리다; 점으로 덮다. ¶ *a dotted line* 점선. **3** scatter here and there on. (여기저기) 점재(點在)시키다. ¶ *a field dotted with sheep* 양들이 점재하는 들판. [E.]

dot and carry one, in addition, mark with a dot and carry one to the higher unit. (더하기에서, 10이 되면)점을 찍고 한 자리 올리다.

dot and go one, walk (lame). 다리를 절다.

dot someone one, 《Brit. *sl.*》 strike him. 아무를 때리다.

dot one's i's, behave carefully. 조심스럽게 행동하다.

dot the i's and cross the t's, 《*colloq.*》 leave nothing unsaid; make a matter perfectly clear. 세세한 점까지 주도 면밀하다; 명확히 설명하다.

dot[2] [dɑt / dɔt] *n.* Ⓒ money, land, etc. that a woman brings to her husband at marriage; dowry. 아내의 지참금[물]; 아내의 자산. [Du.]

DOT 《U.S.》 Department of Transportation.

dot·age [dóutidʒ] *n.* Ⓤ a feeble and childish condition caused by old age. 노망; 망령. ¶ *be in one's* ~ 망령이 들어 있다. [E.]

do·tard [dóutərd] *n.* Ⓒ a person who is feeble and childish because of old age. 노망난〔망령든〕 사람. [↑]

dote [dout] *vi.* (P1,3) **1** be feeble and childish because of old age. 노망나다; 망령들다. **2** 《*on, upon*》 be foolishly fond of someone; love blindly or excessively. 익애(溺愛)하다; 무턱대고 귀여워하다. ¶ ~ *on* 〔*upon*〕 *one's son* 아들을 무턱대고 귀여워하다. [M.E. *doten* behave foolishly]

*__doth__ [dʌθ, dəθ] *v.* 《*arch.*》 =does.

dot·ing [dóutiŋ] *adj.* foolishly fond; weak-minded. 익애(溺愛)하는; 망령든. ● **dot·ing·ly** [-li] *adv.* [→dote]

dot·ty[1] [dɑ́ti / dɔ́ti] *adj.* (**-ti·er, -ti·est**) 《*colloq.*》 weak-minded; crazy. 노망한; 머리가 돈.

dot·ty[2] [dɑ́ti / dɔ́ti] *adj.* (**-ti·er, -ti·est**) marked with dots; dotted. 점을 찍은; 점점이 있는; (여기저기) 점재하는. [*dot*]

:**dou·ble** [dʌ́bəl] *adj.* **1** twice as much or as many. (2)배의; 곱절의. ¶ *a ~ amount,* 2배의 양 / *a ~ portion* 두 사람 분〔몫〕/ *the ~ number* 갑절의 수 / *~ pay* 두 배의 급료 / *The beauty of this poem is ~ that of the poet's earlier work.* 이 시의 아름다움은 시인의 초기 작품의 그것보다 배나 된다. 參考 본디 명사로서, double of의 형태로 사용되었었음. **2** made of two like parts. 쌍〔짝〕의; 두 개 한조의; 복(식)의. ¶ *~ doors* (좌우) 여닫이문 / *a ~ track* (철도의) 복선 / *a knife with a ~ edge* 양쪽 날의 나이프 / *a ~ blanket* 두 장으로 된 담요. **3** twofold. 이중의. ¶ *a ~ chin* 이중턱 / *a ~ bottom* (방주(方舟)의) 이중 바닥. **4** serving for two persons or things; used for two purposes. 2인용의; 양용(兩用)의. ¶ *a ~ bed* 2인용 침대 / *a ~ use* 두 가지 용도 / *It would serve a ~ purpose.* 일석이조일 게다. **5** having two meanings or characters; insincere; false. 두가지 의미로 받아들일 수 있는; 표리 있는; 성의 없는; 거짓의. ¶ *~ personality* 이중 인격 / *~ conduct* 양다리 걸친 행위 / *a ~ meaning* (어느 쪽으로도 취할 수 있는) 모호한 의미 / *a ~ life* 표리 있는 생활 / *He is a ~ face.* 그는 두 얼굴을 가진 인물이다. **6** (of flowers) having more than one set of petals. 꽃잎이 (여러) 겹의(opp. single). ¶ *a ~ rose* 겹장미.

— *adv.* **1** twice. 2중으로; 2배로. **2** in two; in a pair; two together. 두 개로; 쌍〔짝〕으로. ¶ *ride ~* 같은 말에 둘이 타다.

— *n.* Ⓒ **1** an amount that is twice as much. 배(倍); 배액; 2배의 수〔양〕. ¶ *pay ~* 배액을 지불하다 / *4 is the ~ of 2.* 4는 2의 두 곱이다. **2** a thing or person that looks like another. 꼭 닮은 것〔사람〕; 빼쏜 사람〔것〕. ¶ *meet one's ~* 빼쏜 듯이 닮은 사람을 만나다. **3** 《*pl.*》 a game played by two players on each side. (테니스 따위의) 복식 경기. **4** 《mil.》 a running pace about twice the speed of ordinary marching. 구보(驅步). ¶ *advance at the ~* 구보로 전진하다. **5** a rapid turn made while running, as by a hunted animal. (여우 따위, 쫓기는 짐승의) 역주(逆走); 급회전(急回轉).

on the double, 《U.S.》 quickly; in a slow run. 급속 보로; 구보로.

— *vt.* (P6) **1** ⓐ make (something) twice as much or as many; add an equal amount to (something). …을 (2)배로 하다; 배가(倍加)하다. ¶ *~ one's fortune* 재산을 배가하다 / *~ a sum* 액수를 배로 하다 / *~ one's efforts* 갑절의 노력을 하다. ⓑ be or have twice as much as. …의 두배〔갑절〕이다. ¶ *Their fortune doubles ours.* 그들의 재산은 우리의 두 배이다. **2** fold or bend (something) in two. …을 둘로 접어〔꺾어〕 겹치다. ¶ *~ a piece of paper* 종이를 접어 겹치다 / *~ a blanket* 담요를 둘로 접어 개키다. **3** close tightly together. …을 꼭 쥐다. ¶ *~ one's fists* 주먹을 불끈 쥐다. **4** 《naut.》 sail round. (곶 따위)를 돌다; 회항(回航)하다. **5** act (two parts). …의 두 역(役)을 하다. ¶ *~ the parts of a maid and a cook* 하녀와 숙수의 두 역할을 하다.

— *vi.* (P1,2A) **1** increase twice as much or as many. 2배가 되다; 배가(倍加)〔배증(倍增)〕하다. ¶ *The money doubled in three years.* 돈이 3년(만)에 배가 되었다. **2** be folded or bent in two. 둘로 접혀 겹치다〔구부러지다〕. ¶ *~ over with pain* 고통으로 몸을 구부리다. **3** 《often *back*》 turn back suddenly on the same course. 갑자기 되돌아 뛰다. ¶ *The rabbit doubled (back) on its tracks to escape the dogs.* 토끼는 개를 피하기 위해 오던 길로 되돌아 뛰었다. **4** 《mil.》 run. 구보로 가다. **5** play two parts. 1인 2역을 하다. ¶ *The maid doubled as cook.* 하녀는 요리사 일까지 아울러 했다. [L. *duplus*]

double back, **a**) fold over. 접어 젖히다. **b**) go back the same way that one came. 왔던 길을 되돌아 가다.

double for, take the place of (someone); substitute for (someone). …의 대신〔대역〕을 하다.

double in, fold or turn inwards. (안쪽으로) 접어 넣다.

double up, **a**) 《*colloq.*》 fold up; curl up. 접어〔꺾어〕 젖히다; 말아 올리다. **b**) draw the knees up to the chest; collapse. 몸을 바싹 구부리다; 쓰러지다. ¶ *be doubled up with pain* 고통으로 몸이 구부러지다. **c**) hurry. 서두르다. **d**) share a room with someone else. (둘이서) 방을 같이 쓰다.

dou·ble-bar·reled [dʌ́bəlbǽrəld] *adj.* **1** having two barrels. (2연발 총·쌍안경 따위의) 쌍통(雙筒)의; 쌍총열〔총신〕의. **2** having two purposes. 이중 목적의. **3** 《Brit. *colloq.*》 (of a surname) made up of two names. 성이 쌍으로 된. ¶ *a ~ surname* 복합성(姓) 《e.g. Douglas-Home, Baden-Powell》.

double bass [⌐-⌐] *n.* 《mus.》 a musical instrument of the violin family. 더블 베이스. 參考 최저음을 냄.

double bassoon [⌐--⌐] *n.* 《mus.》 a large bassoon. 더블 바순《오보에 속(屬)의 최저음 악기》.

dou·ble-breast·ed [dʌ́bəlbréstid] *adj.* (of a coat, etc.) overlapping at the front and having two rows of buttons. (양복 상의의) 더블의(opp. single-breasted).

dou·ble-deal·er [dʌ́bəldíːlər] *n.* Ⓒ a deceiver. (언행에) 표리가 있는 사람.

dou·ble-deal·ing [dʌ́bəldíːliŋ] *n.* ⓊⒸ the act of cheating or deceiving. 표리있는 언행; 부정(不正) 행위. — *adj.* deceitful. (언행에) 표리가 있는.

dou·ble-deck·er [dʌ́bəldékər] *n.* Ⓒ 《Brit.》 a ship or a bus with an upper deck or floor. 이중 갑판의 배; 2층 버스〔전차〕.

dou·ble-Dutch [⌐-⌐] *n.* a language that cannot be understood at all. 통 알아들을 수 없는 말.

dou·ble-edged [dʌ́bəlédʒd] *adj.* **1** having

two edges; two-edged. 양날의. **2** 《*fig.*》 (of an argument, etc.) cutting both ways; that can be understood in two ways. (의론 따위가) 찬부 어느 쪽으로도 취할 수 있는; 두 가지로 작용하는.

double en·ten·dre [dú:bl ɑːntɑ́:ndrə, dʌ́bl-] *n.* 《F.》 a word or expression capable of two interpretations one of which is usu. risqúe. 이중의 (특히 한쪽은 외설한) 의미를 함유한 어구(의 사용); 이중 뜻.

double entry [⌐–⌐–] *n.* 《book-keeping》 a method of bookkeeping in which each transaction is written twice. 복식 기장법(記帳法); 복식 부기.

dou·ble-faced [dʌ́bəlféist] *adj.* **1** deceitful; insincere; hypocritical. (언행에) 표리가 있는; 두 마음이 있는; 위선적인. **2** having two faces or aspects. 양면이 있는.

dou·ble-head·er [dʌ́bəlhédər] *n.* two games played consecutively on the same day by the same teams or by different pairs of teams. 더블헤더.

double indemnity [⌐– –⌐––] *n.* a clause in a life insurance policy by which a payment of double the face value of the policy is made in the event of accidental death. (보험금) 배액(倍額) 보상 조항.

double play [⌐– ⌐] *n.* a play in baseball by which two players are put out. (야구에서) 병살(併殺); 더블플레이.

dou·ble-quick [dʌ́bəlkwik] *n.* [U][C] a very fast step in marching. (군대에서의) 구보. — *adj., adv.* **1** at the double; in double time. 구보의(로). **2** very quick(ly). 매우 빠른(빠르게); 급속한(히). — *vi., vt.* (P1;6) march in double-quick step. 구보로 행진하(게 하)다.

dou·blet [dʌ́blit] *n.* [C] **1** a man's close-fitting jacket worn from 15th century to 17th century. (몸에 꼭 끼는) 남자용 상의(上衣); 더블렛. **2** one of a pair of two similar things; a pair. 아주 비슷한 것의 한쪽; 한 짝 (쌍)의 것. **3** one of two or more words in a language having the same original but a different form or meaning. 이중어(二重語); 자매어(語). [參考] fashion 과 faction 따위. [*double*]

double take [⌐–⌐] *n.* a delayed reaction to a surprising or significant situation after an initial failure to notice anything unusual. (무심히 지나쳤던 일·의미에 대한) 뒤늦은 깨달음(반응); …을 뒤늦게 깨닫고 다시 봄.

dou·ble-talk [dʌ́bəltɔ̀:k] *n.* **1** language that appears to be meaningful but in fact is a mixture of sense and nonsense. 그럴 듯한 말 속에 무의미한 소리가 섞인 말. **2** ambiguous talk meant to deceive. (속이기 위한) 애매한 말.

double time [⌐– ⌐] *n.* **1** 《mil.》 a running pace. 구보. **2** double wages paid to people who work at weekends or on public holidays. 배액 지급《휴일 등의 초과 근무 수당》.

doub·loon [dʌblú:n] *n.* a former Spanish gold coin. 옛 스페인의 금화 이름.

dou·bly [dʌ́bəli] *adv.* twice. 두 배로(이중으로); 둘로. ¶ *Your responsibility is ~ heavy.* 너의 책임은 두 배나 무겁다.

:doubt [daut] *vt.* (P6,11,12) 《*that, if, whether, when, what; doing*》 be difficult to believe; be not sure of (something). …을 의심하다; 미심쩍게 여기다; …에 의혹을 품다. [語法] 의문문·부정문에는 that절, 긍정문에는 if, whether, when절 따위를 사용함. ¶ *~ my own eyes* 내 눈을 의심하다 / *~ the existence of God* 신이 존재하는지 어떤지 의심스럽다 / *~ the truth of the story* 그 이야기의 진실성을 의심하다 / *I ~ if he will succeed.* 그가 성공할지 어떨지 의심스럽다 / *I ~ whether it is possible.* 그것이 가능한지 의심쩍다 / *I don't ~ that he is honest.* 그가 정직하다는 것을 의심하지 않는다.
— *vi.* (P3) 《*of*》 be not sure; be not decided. 의심하다; 의심스럽게 여기다; 미심쩍다. ¶ *He doubted of his son's ability.* 아들의 능력이 미심쩍었다 / *I have never doubted of her success.* 그녀의 성공을 의심해 본 적이 없다.
— *n.* [U][C] a feeling of doubting; lack of belief; uncertainty. 의문; 의혹; 불신; 불확실성. ¶ *have grave doubts about it* 그것에 관해 크게 의심을 품다. [→dubious]
beyond* (*no, without*) *doubt, surely; certainly. 의심할 여지 없이; 확실히; 명확히.
give someone the benefit of the doubt, believe the best of him till the opposite is proved. 선의(善意)로 해석하다.
have one's doubts, doubt. 의심하다.
in doubt, not sure; uncertain. 의심하여; 불확실하여.
make no doubt of, do not doubt. …을 전혀 의심하지 않다; 확신하다.
no doubt, **a**) =beyond doubt. **b**) probably; very likely. 아마; 필시; 틀림없이.
out of doubt, doubtless(ly). 의심할 여지가 없는(없이).
throw doubt upon, doubt. …에 의심을 품다.

∙doubt·ful [dáutfəl] *adj.* **1** in doubt; uncertain. (아무가) 의심을 품고; 불확실한. ¶ *I am ~ of the fact.* 그 사실에 의심을 품고 있다 / *He was ~ about her ability to do the work.* 그녀의 일할 능력에 대해서 확신이 없었다. **2** causing or feeling doubt; not clear. 불안한; 확실히 모르는; 분명치 않은. **3** (of a person and his action) suspicious; shady; giving rise to doubt as to integrity. 의심스러운; 수상한. ¶ *a ~ character* 수상쩍은 인물 / *a ~ future* 불안한 장래. ● **doubt·ful·ness** [-nis] *n.*

doubt·ful·ly [dáutfəli] *adv.* in the manner of being doubtful. 의심스럽게; 수상쩍게.

:doubt·less [dáutlis] *adv.* **1** certainly; without doubt. 확실히; 의심할 바 없이. **2** very probably. 아마. ¶ *I shall ~ see you tomor-*

row. 아마 내일 만나뵐 수 있을 테지요. —— *adj.* having no doubts; sure. 의심할 바 없는; 확실한.

douche [du:ʃ] *n.* a jet of water directed on the body (inside or outside) from a pipe. 관수(灌水); 관수욕(浴)(cf. *shower* (*bath*)). ***throw a cold douche upon*** (*a plan etc.*), say that it is useless or impossible. (계획 따위에) 쓸데없다느니 불가능하다느니 말하다; 찬물을 끼얹다. —— *vt.* (P6) apply a douche to. …에 관수욕을 시키다. [→duct]

dough [dou] *n.* Ⓤ **1** the mixture of flour, water, etc. for baking; any soft mass like this. 밀가루 반죽; 부드러운 덩어리. **2** 《*sl.*》 money. 돈. [E.]

dough·boy [dóubɔ̀i] *n.* Ⓒ 《U.S. *colloq.*》 a foot soldier in the United States army. (미군의) 보병.

dough·nut [dóunət, dóunʌ̀t] *n.* Ⓒ a small, brown cake fried in deep fat, usu. in the shape of a ring or a ball. 도넛. 參考 영국에서는 만두형, 미국에서는 고리형.

dough·ty [dáuti] *adj.* (**-ti·er, -ti·est**) brave; strong. 용감한; 강한. ¶ ~ *knights* 용감한 기사들. ● **dough·ti·ness** [-nis] *n.* [E.]

dough·y [dóui] *adj.* (**dough·i·er, dough·i·est**) **1** like dough. (밀)가루 반죽 같은. **2** 《*fig.*》 dull; heavy in the mind; unhealthily pale. (지능이) 둔한; 무딘; 창백하고 늘어진. ¶ *a* ~ *boy* 저능아. [*dough*]

Doug·las [dʌ́gləs] *n.* a man's name. 남자 이름. 參考 애칭 Doug.

dour [dúər, dáuər] *adj.* **1** gloomy; sullen. 음침한; 부루퉁한. **2** 《Sc.》 severe; stubborn. 엄(격)한; 냉혹한; 완고한. ¶ *a* ~ *nature* 완고한 성격 / *a* ~ *warning* 엄한 경고. ● **dour·ly** [-li] *adv.* **dour·ness** [-nis] *n.* [→durable]

douse, dowse [daus] *vt.* (P6) **1** put (something) into water. …을 물에 처넣다. **2** throw water over (something or someone). …에 물을 끼얹다. ¶ ~ *someone with water* …에게 물을 끼얹다. **3** 《*colloq.*》 put out (a light). (불)을 끄다. [E.=beat noisily]

·**dove**[1] [dʌv] *n.* Ⓒ **1** a bird of the pigeon family, but smaller than a pigeon. 비둘기. **2** ⓐ a gentle or loving person. 유순한[귀여운] 사람. ¶ *My* ~. (호칭으로서) 사랑하는 그대여; 여보. ⓑ 《*colloq.*》 a person or group that supports a peaceful policy. 비둘기파(의 사람). 《D-》 the Holy Ghost. 성령. [E.]

dove[2] [douv] *vi.* p. of **dive**[1].

dove·cot [dʌ́vkɑ̀t / -kɔ̀t] *n.* =dovecote.

dove·cote [dʌ́vkòut] *n.* Ⓒ a small house for doves or pigeons. 비둘기장. [E.] ***cause a flutter in the dovecotes,*** excite quiet people. 평지 풍파를 일으키다.

Do·ver [dóuvər] *n.* a seaport in southeast England. 도버항(港). ***the Strait*(*s*) *of Dover,*** a narrow channel between France and England. 도버 해협.

dove·tail [dʌ́vtèil] *n.* Ⓒ 《archit.》 a part or joint shaped like a dove's tail. 열장 이음; 열장장부촉(鏃). —— *vt.* (P6,13) **1** join together by means of dovetails. …을 열장 이음하다. **2** connect precisely or harmoniously. 긴밀히 연결시키다. —— *vi.* (P1,3) fit together exactly or in a harmonious whole. 꼭(들어) 맞다. ¶ *Our schemes dovetailed neatly.* 우리 계획은 멋지게 들어맞았다. [*dove*[1]]

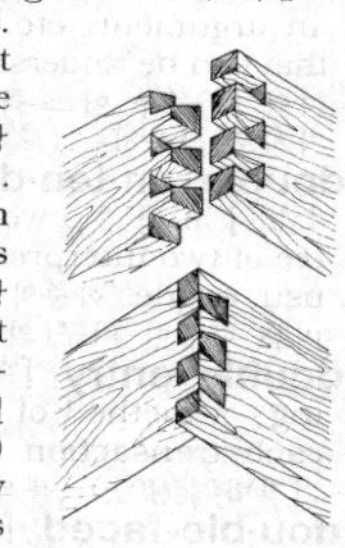
<dovetail>

dow·a·ger [dáuədʒər] *n.* Ⓒ **1** 《law》 a woman who holds a title or property from her dead husband. 귀족 미망인《죽은 남편의 재산과 작위를 이어받은》. ¶ ~ *duchess* (영국의) 공작 미망인 / *the Empress Dowager* 황태후. **2** 《*colloq.*》 an elderly lady with dignity. 점잖은[품위있는] 노부인. [→dower]

dow·di·ly [dáudili] *adv.* in a dowdy manner. 초라하게; 단정치 못하게; 촌스럽게. [↓]

dow·dy [dáudi] *adj.* (**-di·er, -di·est**) badly dressed; not neat; shabby. (복장이) 초라[추레]한; 촌스러운. —— *n.* Ⓒ (*pl.* **-dies**) a dowdy woman. 초라한[단정치 못한] 옷차림의 여자. ● **dow·di·ness** [-nis] *n.* [E.]

dow·el [dáuəl] *n.* a headless peg or round pin that fits into a corresponding hole on another piece, and so forms a joint. 은못. —— *vt.* (**-wel(l)ed**) (P6) fasten with dowels. …을 은못으로 잇다. [G. *dovel* peg]

dow·er [dáuər] *n.* ⓊⒸ **1** a woman's share of her dead husband's property. 과부 상속 재산. **2** =dowry①. **3** a natural gift. 타고 난 것《e.g. beauty, intelligence》. —— *vt.* (P6,13) provide (someone) with a dower. 과부 상속 재산·재능 등을 (아무)에게 주다. ● **dow·er·less** [-lis] *adj.* [L. *dos* dowry]

Dow-Jones [dáudʒóunz] *n.* the publishing company of the Wall Street Journal. 다우존스《'the Wall Street Journal 발간 회사》. ¶ *Dow-Jones Average* 다우존스 평균(주가 지수).

dow·las [dáuləs] *n.* a kind of strong calico. 튼튼한 옥양목. [Place]

:**down**[1] [daun] *adv.* (opp. up) **1** to a lower place; toward the ground. 아래(쪽으)로; 지상으로. ¶ *come* ~ 내려오다 / *pull the blinds* ~ 블라인드를 내리다 / *Tom isn't* ~ *yet.* 톰은 아직 아래층에 내려오지 않았다. **2** in a lower place. 아래(쪽)에서. ¶ *Down in the valley the fog still lingers.* 아래쪽 계곡에서는 안개가 아직도 걷히지 않고 있다. **3** to the lower course of a river. 하류에[로]. ¶ *flow* ~ *the river* 강 하류로 흐르다. **4** to or in a lying or sitting position. 누워; 앉아. ¶ *Sit*

~, *please.* 앉으시오 / *Many people are* ~ (=*ill in bed*) *with a cold.* 많은 사람이 감기로 누워 있다. **5** from a city to the country. 시골로. ¶ *go ~ to the country* 시골로 내려가다 / *go ~ from town* 도시에서 시골로 가다. **6** to or in a place farther south. (멀리) 남쪽으로(에). ¶ *go ~ south* 남쪽으로 가다 / *sail* ~ 배가 남하하다 / *Mrs. Smith lives ~ in Australia.* 스미스씨 부인은 오스트레일리아 남쪽에 살고 있다. **7** from an earlier time (to a later time); to a later period. 초기에서 후기로; 후대에 이르기까지. ¶ *from Chaucer's time ~ to the time of Elizabeth* 초서 시대로부터 엘리자베스 시대에 이르기까지 / *be handed ~ from father to son* 아버지로부터 아들에게 전해지다 / *look ~ through the ages* 전시대를 통해 개관하다. **8** 《expressing a decrease in intensity, amount, bulk, etc.》 ⓐ to a lesser quantity, value, rate, etc. (양·가치·정도·율 따위가) 떨어져; 하락하여; 줄어; 약해져. ¶ *Bread is ~.* 빵값이 떨어졌다 / *The birthrate is considerably ~.* 출산율이 두드러지게 떨어졌다 / *The yield of corn is ~.* 옥수수의 수확량이 줄었다. ⓑ in or to a calmer, less active, or less prominent state. 고요〔평온〕해; 가라앉아. ¶ *The sea has gone ~.* 물결이 잔잔해졌다 / *The wind has died ~.* 바람이 가라앉았다 / *The fire is burning ~.* 불길이 꺼져가고 있다 / *His passions went ~.* 격정이 가라앉았다. **9** really; seriously. 실제로; 본격적으로; 적극적으로. ¶ *get ~ to work* 본격적으로 일에 착수하다 / *wash ~ a car* 차를 샅샅이 닦다. **10** 《with reference to writing》 on paper. 종이에 적어; 문서로. ¶ *write ~ the address* 주소를 쓰다 / *I took his name ~ in my notebook.* 수첩에 그의 이름을 적었다 / *You are ~ for a speech.* 연사 명부에 당신 이름이 적혀 있다. **11** in cash; as immediate payment. 현금으로; 즉전〔맞돈〕으로. ¶ *pay $20 ~ and the rest later* 현금으로 20달러를, 나머지는 나중에 지불하다. **12** 《expressing the lower limit in a series》 …부터 ―(에 이르기)까지. ¶ *read from the beginning ~ to page 50,* 처음부터 50쪽까지 읽다 / *from the king ~ to the humblest of his subject* 위로 왕에서부터 미천한 백성에 이르기까지.

be down on 〔***upon***〕, scold. …을 꾸짖다.

down and out, **a**) 《boxing》 knocked out. 때려눕혀져; 녹아웃을 당하여. **b**) 《*fig.*》 ruined and helpless. 파멸하여.

down at the heel, ⇨heel[1].

down in the mouth 〔***dumps***〕***,*** looking unhappy; discouraged. 슬픈 표정으로; 풀이 죽은〔죽어〕; 낙담하여.

down on one's luck, in difficulties; needing money. 어려움에 처하여; 돈에 궁핍하여.

down on 〔***upon***〕***,*** angry at; feeling ill-will toward. 성이 나; 원한〔적개심〕을 품고.

down to the ground 〔***to earth***〕***,*** completely. 완전히; 철저히; 아주. ¶ *It suits me ~ to the ground.* 그건 내게 아주 잘 맞는다.

Down with …! Overthrow!; Get rid of! 타도하자; 해치우자. ¶ *Down with the tyrant!* 폭군(을) 타도(하자).

hit someone when he is down, show unkindness to him already unfortunate. 이미 불행을 겪고 있는 자에게 가혹하게 대하다.

up and down, to and fro; from side to side. 앞뒤로; 위아래로; 왔다갔다.

— *prep.* down, toward, on, through, along, etc. …을 내려가; …의 아래쪽에〔으로〕; …을 따라. ¶ *go ~ a hill* 산을 내려가다 / *run ~ the stairs* 계단을 뛰어내려가다 / *row ~ a stream* 배를 저어 강을 내려가다 / *live further ~ the river* 강의 훨씬 하류에 살다 / *I went ~ the road.* 길을 따라 내려갔다 / *drive ~ a street* 거리를 따라 차를 몰다 / *The child fell ~ the stairs.* 아이는 계단 아래로 떨어졌다.

— *adj.* **1** in a lower place. 아래(쪽)의. ¶ *a ~ leap* 뛰어내림. **2** (of a train, etc.) downward; going down. (열차 따위의) 아래쪽으로의; 하행의. ¶ *a ~ train* 하행 열차 / *a ~ line* 〔*platform*〕 하행선〔하행선 승강장〕. **3** ill; sick; not active. 병의; 기운없는. ¶ *He is ~ with influenza.* 그는 독감에 걸려 있다. **4** in cash. 현금의. ¶ *~ payment* 현금 지급.

— *vt.* (P6) 《*colloq.*》 **1** bring, or knock down; defeat; overcome; beat. …을 끌어내리다; …을 타도하다; …을 때려눕히다; 지게 하다. ¶ *~ one's opponent* 상대를 쓰러뜨리다 / *~ an enemy* 적을 패배시키다. **2** cause (something) to fall down. …을 떨어뜨리다. **3** drink down. …을 마시다. ¶ *~ a glass of beer* 맥주 한잔을 비우다.

down tools, stop working; begin a strike. 일을 중지하다; 파업을 시작하다.

— *n.* **1** Ⓤ a downward movement. 하강(下降). **2** turn for the worse; reverse. (사업 등의) 악화; 불운. ¶ *The business cycle experienced a sudden ~.* 경기순환은 급속히 악화됐다. **3** 《*colloq.*》 dislike of a person. 혐오. [*adown=off*, →down[3]]

have a down on someone, 《*colloq.*》 dislike him; be prejudiced against him. 아무를 혐오하다; 아무에게 편견을 갖고 있다.

ups and downs, ⇨up (*n.*).

down[2] [daun] *n.* Ⓤ the first soft feathers of young birds, etc. 배냇털; 솜털; 부등깃털. ¶ *a bed of ~* 깃털요. [Scand.]

down[3] [daun] *n.* **1** 《*usu. pl.*》 rolling, grassy, open land. (목양에 적합한) 완만한 기복이 있는 초원지. **2** Ⓒ a treeless mound of sand made by the wind. 사구(砂丘). [E.]

down-and-out [dáunən*d*áut] *adj.* destitute; impoverished; without means of support. 곤궁한; 무일푼의; 영락한. [*down*[1]]

down·cast [dáunkæ̀st, -kɑ̀:st] *adj.* **1** turned downward; looking downward. 고개를 숙인; 눈을 내리깐. ¶ *He spoke with ~ eyes.* 그는 눈을 내리깔고 이야기했다. **2** sad; discouraged. 낙심한; 의기 소침한. ¶ *a ~ expression* 풀죽은 표정 / *The team was ~ over the loss of the game.* 팀은 경기에서 져서 의기 소침했다.

— *n.* Ⓒ a downcast look; ruin. 눈을 내리

깔기; 우울한 표정; 파멸. [*down*[1]]

down·er [dáunər] *n.* 《*sl.*》 **1** a depressant drug. 진정제. **2** a depressing experience or situation. 따분한 경험〔상황〕. [*down*[1]]

down·fall [dáunfɔ̀:l] *n.* Ⓒ **1** 《*fig.*》 ruin; a heavy fall. 파멸; 몰락; 멸망; 급격한 전락(轉落). ¶ *the ~ of an empire* 제국의 몰락 / *bring about one's own ~* 몰락을 자초하다. **2** a heavy rain or snow. 장대비; 큰비; 대설(大雪). [*down*[1]]

down·grade [dáungrèid] *n.* Ⓒ a downward slope. 내리받이; 내리막. — *adj., adv.* downward. 내리받이의〔에서〕; 아래쪽의〔으로〕. — *vt.* (P6) move (someone) to a lower rank with a smaller salary; view (something) in a less favorable way. (급료가 낮은 지위로) 좌천시키다; …을 격하하다.

down·heart·ed [dáunhá:rtid] *adj.* in low spirits; discouraged. 의기소침한; 낙담한; 풀죽은.

down·hill [dáunhìl] *adv.* downward. 비탈을 내려가; 아래(쪽으)로.

go downhill, 《*fig.*》 deteriorate in fortune, character, health; go from bad to worse. 내리막이 되다; 악화하다; 더한층 나빠지다. ¶ *His health went ~ very rapidly.* 그의 건강은 급속도로 악화되었다.

— *adj.* going downward; worse. 내리받이의; 더욱 나빠진. — *n.* Ⓒ a downward slope; a decline. 내리받이; 내리막. ¶ *the ~ of life* 후반생(後半生). [*down*[1]]

down-home [dáunhóum] *adj.* having the worthy simplicity attributed to rural dwellers, esp. in the U.S. South. (미국 남부 특유의 시골 사람같이) 소박한.

Down·ing Street [dáuniŋstrì:t] *n.* **1** a street in London, where government offices and the residence of the prime minister stand. 다우닝가(街). **2** the British government. 영국 정부. [Place]

down·pour [dáunpɔ̀:r] *n.* Ⓒ a heavy rain. 억수; 장대비; 큰비. [*down*[1]]

down·right [dáunràit] *adj.* **1** absolute; thorough. 절대의; 완전한; 순전한. ¶ *a ~ thief* 날강도 / *a ~ lie* 새빨간 거짓말 / *~ nonsense* 터무니 없는 난센스. **2** plain; frank; honest; straightforward. 명백한; 솔직한; 숨김없는. ¶ *a ~ answer* 솔직한 대답 / *a ~ no* 명백한 거부. — *adv.* absolutely; thoroughly. 절대적으로; 완전히; 철저히. ¶ *be ~ unpleasant* 아주 불쾌하다.

down·shift [dáunʃìft] *vi.* shift an automotive vehicle into a lower gear. (자동차의) 기어를 1단 낮추다.

down·stage [dáunstéidʒ] *adv.* toward the front of the stage. 무대의 전방에서〔으로〕.

:down·stairs [dáunstɛ́ərz] (opp. upstairs) *adv.* down the stairs; on or to a lower floor. 아래층에(서); 아래층으로. ¶ *go* 〔*come*〕 *~* 아래층으로 내려가다〔오다〕 / *be waiting ~* 아래층에서 기다리고 있다. — *adj.* on a lower floor. 아래층의; 일층의. — *n.* 《*pl.*》 the lower floor or floors. 아래층.

down·stream [dáunstrí:m] *adv.* in or with the current of a stream. 강을 따라; 강을 내려가; 강하류에.

down-to-earth [dáuntuə́:rθ] *adj.* realistic; practical; unaffected. 현실적인; 실제적인. ¶ *a ~ approach to health care* 건강 관리의 실제적 해결책.

down·town [dáuntáun] *n.* Ⓒ the main business section of a town. (도시의) 상업지구; 도심지(opp. uptown). ¶ *go ~* 시내로 가다; 쇼핑하러 가다. — *adj.* of or in the main business section of a town. 상업지구〔중심지〕의; 시내의. ¶ *a ~ hotel* 시내의 호텔. — *adv.* to, toward, or in the main business section of a town. 상업 지구에(서)〔로〕; 시내〔중심지〕에(서)〔로〕.

down·trod·den [dáuntrὰdn / -trɔ̀dn] *adj.* oppressed; trodden down. 학대〔압박〕 받은; 짓밟힌.

·down·ward [dáunwərd] *adj., adv.* toward what is lower; toward a later time. 아래의〔로〕; 아래로 향한〔향하게〕; 내려가는; …이후의〔에, 로〕(opp. upward). ¶ *a ~ slope* 내리받이 / *lie face ~* 엎드려 눕다 / *from the 18th century ~* 18세기 이래로 / *As the river flows ~, it widens.* 하류로 감에 따라 강폭은 넓어진다.

·down·wards [dáunwərdz] *adv.* =downward.

down·y [dáuni] *adj.* (**down·i·er, down·i·est**) **1** of or like the first soft feathers or hair; soft as down; covered with down. 솜털의; 배냇털의; 솜털처럼 보드라운; 솜털로 뒤덮인. **2** sly; knowing. 방심할 수 없는; 빈틈없는. ● **down·i·ness** [-nis] *n.* [→down[2]]

dow·ry [dáuəri] *n.* Ⓒ (*pl.* **-ries**) **1** the money, property, etc. that a woman brings to her husband at marriage. 신부의 지참금〔물〕. **2** 《*poet., fig.*》 a natural gift. 타고난 재능. [→dower]

dowse[1] [daus] *vt.* =douse.

dowse[2] [dauz] *vi.* use a divining-rod to find underground water or minerals. 수맥이나 광맥을 찾기 위해 점지팡이를 쓰다. [?]

dows·er [dáuzər] *n.* a person who finds water or minerals by means of a divining-rod. 점(占)지팡이를 써서 수맥(水脈)〔광맥〕을 찾는 사람(cf. *diviner*). [?]

dox·ol·o·gy [daksálədʒi / dɔksɔ́l-] *n.* Ⓒ (*pl.* **-gies**) a hymn or prayer praising God. (기독교에서) 찬송가《특히, 영광의 찬미가》. [Gk. *doxa* glory, opinion]

dox·y[1] [dáksi / dɔ́k-] *n.* an opinion; a doctrine of theology. 의견; 교의(教義). [↑]

dox·y[2] [dáksi / dɔ́k-] *n.* **1** 《*sl.*》 a mistress. 정부(情婦). **2** prostitute; a wench. 매춘부. [E. =beggar's wife]

doy·en [dɔ́iən] *n.* Ⓒ the senior member of a group. 고참자; 장로; 수석. ¶ *the ~ of the diplomatic corps* 외교단 수석 대사. [F.]

Doyle [dɔil], **Sir Arthur Conan** *n.* (1859-

1930) an English novelist, and detective story writer. 코넌 도일《영국의 추리 소설가》.

doz. dozen; dozens.

doze [douz] *vi.* (P1,2A) sleep lightly. 졸다; 겉잠자다; 조리치다. ¶ ~ *off* 꾸벅꾸벅 졸다 / ~ *over a book* 책을 읽으며 졸다. — *n.* Ⓒ a light sleep; a nap. 졸음; 겉잠. [Scand.]

:doz·en [dʌ́zn] *n.* Ⓒ (*pl.* **-ens** or **-en**) a group of 12. 1다스; 12(개). ¶ *three ~ eggs* 달걀 3다스 / *some ~ of eggs* 달걀 약 1다스 / *some dozens of eggs* 달걀 두서너 다스 / *half a ~* 반 다스 / *dozens of children* 수십명이나 되는 아이들 / *pack oranges in dozens* 귤을 1다스씩 꾸리다 / *dozens of times* 수십번이나; 몇 번이고 몇 번이고 / *sell by the ~* 다스(단위)로 팔다. [L. *duodecim* twelve]

a baker's* 〔*devil's, long, printer's*〕 *dozen, thirteen. 13개.

talk nineteen* 〔*thirteen*〕 *to the dozen, 《Brit. *colloq.*》 talk incessantly. 쉬지않고 지껄이다.

D.Ph. Doctor of Philosophy.

dr(.) dram(s).

***Dr., Dr** Doctor; debit; debtor.

dr. debtor.

drab[1] [dræb] *adj.* (**drab·ber, drab·best**) **1** dull; monotonous. 우중충한; 단조로운. **2** dull brownish or yellowish gray. 충충한 갈색의; 다갈색의. — *n.* Ⓤ **1** a dull, brownish gray. 충충한 다갈색. **2** monotony. 단조로움. ● **drab·ly** [-li] *adv.* [→drape]

drab[2] [dræb] *n.* Ⓒ **1** a dirty, untidy woman. 추레한 단정치 못한 여자. **2** a slut; a prostitute. 타락한〔방종한〕 여자; 매춘부. [E.]

drachm [dræm] *n.* **1** 《Brit.》 dram. 드램. **2** =drachma.

drach·ma [drǽkmə] *n.* Ⓒ (*pl.* **-mas** or **-mae**) **1** a unit of Greek money. 드라크마《화폐 단위》. **2** an ancient Greek silver coin. (옛 그리스의) 드라크마 은화. **3** a unit of weight in ancient Greece. (옛 그리스의) 무게 단위. [Gk.]

drach·mae [drǽkmi:] *n.* pl. of **drachma.**

***draft,** 《Brit.》 **draught** [dræft, drɑ:ft] *n.* **1** ⓊⒸ a current of air, esp. in a room. 틈새바람; 외풍; 통풍. ¶ *a ~ of air* 틈새바람 / *you may catch (a) cold if you sit in a ~.* 틈새바람 머리에 앉아 있으면 감기에 걸릴 수도 있다. **2** Ⓒ a device for regulating the airflow, as in a stove, etc. (난로 따위의) 통기(通氣)조절장치. **3** Ⓒ a first rough writing (of a book, speech, etc.); a rough plan. 초고; 초안; 설계 도면. ¶ *a rough ~ for a speech* 간단한 연설 초고 / *make out the ~ of the treaty* 조약을 기초하다. **4** ⓐ Ⓤ 《U.S.》 a selection of persons for military service. 징병. ¶ ~ *evasion* 징병 기피. ⓑ Ⓒ persons selected for military service. 징병에 뽑힌 장정들. **5** ⓊⒸ a body of soldiers chosen for a special purpose; detachment. 선발대; 파견(대). **6** Ⓤ the act or quantity of pulling loads, etc. (짐 따위를) 끌기. ¶ *a beast of ~* 짐을 끄는 소〔말 따위〕. **7** 《usu. *draught*》 the pulling in of a fish net; the quantity of fish caught in a net, etc. (그물을) 한번 당겨 올리기; 한 그물의 어획량. ¶ *a ~ of fish* 한 그물의 어획량. **8** Ⓒ an order for the payment of money by a bank, etc. (환)어음. ¶ *a ~ on demand* 일람출급 (환)어음 / *a ~ for $1,000 on* 〔*upon*〕 *the bank* 은행 앞으로 발행된 1,000 달러의 환어음 / *pay by ~* 어음으로 지급하다 / *make a ~ of money* 은행〔자금〕에서 인출하다. **9** Ⓤ 《usu. *draught*》 the depth of water needed to float a ship. (배의) 흘수(吃水). ¶ *a vessel of 20 feet ~* 〔*with a ~ of 20 feet*〕 흘수 20피트의 배. **10** Ⓒ 《usu. *draught*》 the amount taken at one drink; an act of breathing in air, smoke, etc. (약 따위의) 1회분; 한번 복용(량); (공기·연기 따위의) 한 번 들이마심. ¶ *at a ~* 한입〔단숨〕에.

draw a draft on, draw a bill (for a sum) on (someone). …앞으로 어음을 떼다.

— *vt.* (P6) **1** make a sketch of; plan for, or a rough copy of (something). …을 기초하다; 초고〔초안〕을 만들다; …의 밑그림을 그리다. ¶ *He drafted the blueprints for the building.* 그는 건물의 설계도를 그렸다. **2** ⓐ 《U.S.》 select (someone) for military service. …을 징병으로 뽑다. ⓑ select and send (soldiers) on a special duty. …을 선발 파견하다. [→draught]

draft beer [⌐⌐] *n.* beer on tap. 생〔통〕맥주.

draft·ee [dræftí:, drɑ:f-] *n.* Ⓒ 《U.S.》 a person who is drafted for military service. (징병의) 피선발자; 징모병.

draft·ing [drǽftiŋ, drɑ́:f-] *n.* ⓊⒸ the act of drawing up an outline or draft of a bill etc. 기초; 입안; 제도; 어음 발행.

drafts·man [drǽftsmən, drɑ́:fts-] *n.* Ⓒ (*pl.* **-men** [-mən]) **1** a person who draws plans or sketches. 제도자(製圖者). **2** a person who writes out documents, speeches, etc. (공문서·연설문 따위의) 기초자. ● **draft·man·ship** [-ʃip] *n.*

draft·y [drǽfti, drɑ́:fti] *adj.* (**draft·i·er, draft·i·est**) causing a current of air. 틈새바람〔외풍〕이 들어오는; 바람이 통하는. ¶ *a ~ room* 통풍이 잘 되는 방. ● **draft·i·ly** [-li] *adv.*

:drag [dræg] *v.* (**dragged, drag·ging**) *vt.* **1** (P6,7,13) pull or draw (a heavy thing) slowly along the ground; trail (something) on the ground. (무거운 것)을 끌다; …을 질질 끌다. ¶ ~ *a heavy load along* 무거운 짐을 끌다 / ~ *one's skirt* 치맛자락을 질질 끌다 / ~ *oneself through the day's work* 무거운 몸을 끌며 (겨우) 그 날의 일을 마치다 / *They dragged the log out of the forest.* 그들은 통나무를 숲 밖으로 끌어냈다. **2** (P6,13) search the bottom of (a river, lake, etc.) for something with a net or a hook. (그물이나 갈고랑이로 강·호수 따위)의 바닥을 훑다. ¶ *They dragged the lake for his body.* 그의 시체를 찾기 위하여 호수 바닥을 훑었다. **3** (P6) level and smooth (land) with a harrow. 써레로 땅을 고르다. — *vi.* **1** (P1,2) ⓐ trail on the ground; be dragged. (질질) 끌다; 끌리다. ¶ *walk with dragging feet* 발을 질질 끌며 걷다 / *Her skirt dragged.* 그녀 치맛자락이 질질 끌렸다. ⓑ give a feeling of dragging. 질질 끌리듯 괴롭다. ¶ *a dragging pain* 질질 끄는 고통. **2** (P1,2) 《*fig.*》 move slowly; (of time) pass slowly and tediously. 천천히 움직이다〔가다〕; (시간이) 느릿느릿 지나다. ¶ *The minutes dragged like hours.* 일분 일분이 한 시간처럼 길게 느껴졌다 / *The performance dragged on* ~. 공연은 지루하게 오래 끌었다.

drag one's feet, 《often *fig.*》 go forward slowly, unwillingly. 발을 질질 끌며 걷다; 일부러 꾸물거리다.

drag in, bring in. 끌어들이다; 끌어당기다.

drag on 〔***out***〕, make (something) too slow or too long; be too slow; last too long. 오래 끌(게 하)다; 질질 끌다.

drag up, 《*colloq. joc.*》 bring up (a child) in a rough, careless way. (아이)를 거칠게 키우다.

— *n.* Ⓒ **1** a net, hook, etc. used in dragging. (물 속의 바닥을 훑는) 그물; 갈고랑이. **2** the act of dragging. 질질 끌기; 끌어당기기. **3** anything that hinders; an obstruction. 방해(물); 장애. ¶ *She is a* ~ *on my career.* 그녀는 내 출세의 방해물이다. **4** something extremely tiresome. 몹시 따분한 것; 신물이 나는 것. **5** a puff on a cigaret or cigar. 담배 한 모금. **6** an iron shoe to retard wheels and vehicles. 바퀴굄. **7** women's clothes worn by a man. 남자가 입은 여자 복장; 여장(女裝). [*draw*]

drag·ging [drǽgiŋ] *adj.* very slow in walking, developing, etc. 몹시 느린; (발을) 질질 끄는. ¶ *a series of* ~ *speeches* 질질 오래 끄는 일련의 연설 / *the* ~ *hot spell* 언제 끝날지도 모르는 더위의 계속.

drag·gle [drǽgəl] *vt.* (P6) make (something) wet or dirty by dragging through mud, water, etc. (무엇)을 질질 끌어 적시다〔더럽히다〕. — *vi.* (P1,2A) **1** be draggled. 질질 끌어 더러워지다. **2** follow slowly. 천천히 따르다. [*drag*]

drag·gled [drǽgəld] *adj.* dirty, wet, or muddy, as from being dragged through mud. (흙탕에 질질 끌려) 더러운; 젖은; 흙탕투성이의.

drag·net [drǽgnèt] *n.* Ⓒ **1** a net pulled over the bottom of a river, etc. 예인망(曳引網). **2** a network for catching criminals by the police. (경찰의) 수사망(搜査網).

drag·o·man [drǽgəmən] *n.* (*pl.* **-mans, -men** [-mən]) an interpreter in Near East. 근동(近東) 제국의 통역. [Arab.]

·**drag·on** [drǽgən] *n.* Ⓒ **1** 《legend》 a terrible creature like a huge winged snake which often breathed out fire and smoke. 용. 參考 날개와 발톱을 가졌으며 불과 연기를 토한다는 전설상의 괴수(怪獸). **2** a very severe and watchful woman. 엄격한 샤프롱《붙어다니며 감시·시중드는 나이 지긋한 여성》. [Gk. *drakōn* serpent]

·**drag·on·fly** [drǽgənflài] *n.* Ⓒ (*pl.* **-flies**) a large insect, with a long, thin body and two pairs of large wings. 잠자리.

dra·goon [drəgúːn] *n.* Ⓒ **1** a horse-soldier. 기병. **2** 《hist.》 a cavalry man of certain regiments. 용기병《16-17세기 유럽에서 갑옷에 총을 가진 기마병》. — *vt.* (P6) force (someone) (into doing something). 무력으로 박해〔탄압〕하다; 강제하다. ¶ *They dragooned them into working.* 그들은 강제로 그들에게 일을 시켰다. [→dragon]

:**drain** [drein] *vt.* (P6,7,13,18) **1** draw off (water) from a place; make (a place) dry by drawing off water. (…에서 물)을 빼내다; …에서 배수하다. ¶ ~ *water from the road* 도로에서 물을 빼다 / ~ *oil from a crankcase* 크랭크실에서 오일을 빼내다 / ~ *the land* 토지를 간척(干拓)하다 / *They have drained the swimming-pool.* 그들은 수영장의 물을 빼냈다. **2** drink up. …을 다 들이켜다; 비우다. ¶ ~ *a jug dry* 주전자의 물을 비우다 / ~ *a glass of wine* 포도주 한 잔을 들이켜다. **3** 《*of*》 exhaust; use up; deprive. …을 고갈〔소모〕시키다; 빼앗다. ¶ *his face drained of blood* 핏기를 잃은 그의 얼굴 / ~ *someone of money* 아무에게서 돈을 서서히 고갈시키다 / *The war drained the land of its people and wealth.* 전쟁은 그 땅에서 인명과 재산을 앗아갔다. **4** 《esp. in *pp.*》 supply (a house, etc.) with a drainage system. (집 따위)에 배수 시설을 하다. ¶ *Our house is well* 〔*badly*〕 *drained.* 우리 집은 배수 시설이 잘〔안〕 되어 있다. — *vi.* (P1,2A,3) **1** flow gradually. 서서히 흐르다. ¶ ~ *away* 서서히 흘러 없어지다; 물이 빠지다 / *The water drains into a river.* 물은 서서히 강으로 흘러 든다. **2** dry by draining off water. 물이 빠져 〔배수에 의해〕 마르다; 말라붙다; 배수하다. ¶ *The dishes are put on the shelf to* ~. 접시는 물기를 빼기 위해 선반에 놓아둔다 / *The dishes will* ~ *soon.* 접시는 곧 물기가 빠져 마를 게다 / *This land won't* ~. 이 땅은 물이 잘 안 빠진다. **3** 《*fig.*》 disappear or exhaust gradually; fade. 서서히 사라지다; 다 써버리다; 차츰 스러지다. ¶ *His courage drained away.* 그의 용기는 서서히 사라졌다 / *He felt his anger* ~ *from him.* 그는 노여움이 점차 스러져 가는 것을 느꼈다 / *Hope and energy* ~ *away over the years.* 희망도 정력도 세월이 감에 따라 고갈된다.

drain dry 〔***to the dregs***〕, drink up completely. 한 방울도 남김없이 다 마시다.

drain the cup of sorrow to the dregs, experience the greatest sorrow. 슬픔의 쓴 잔을 마시다; 인생의 쓴 맛을 다 맛보다.

— *n.* Ⓒ **1** a ditch or pipe for carrying off water. 배수구〔로, 관〕; 홈통; 하수구. **2** a cause of weakening or loss; a gradual or continuous outflow or expenditure. 유출〔소

비, 소모, 소실]의 원인; (점차적인·끊임 없는) 유출; 출비(出費); 소비; 소모. ¶ *the ~ of specie* 정화의 유출 / *a ~ on one's strength* 체력의 소모 / *the economic ~ of war* 전쟁의 경제적 소모 / *Working too hard is a ~ on a person's strength.* 과로는 체력 소모의 원인이 된다 / *Medical expenses were a ~ on his bank account.* 의료비가 예금 감소의 원인이었다. **3** 《*colloq.*》 a very small amount of liquid, esp. for drinking. (술의) 한 모금; 소량. ¶ *have a ~ with* …와 한잔하다. [E.; *dry*]

go down the drain, **a**) used wastefully or brought to nothing. 낭비되어 없어지다; 헛되이 되다; 수포로 돌아가다. ¶ *Years of work went down the ~ in the fire.* 다년간의 노력이 화재로 수포로 돌아갔다. **b**) grow worse and worse. 점점 나빠지다.

laugh like a drain, 《Brit. *sl.*》 laugh noisily. 큰 소리로 웃다.

drain·age [dréinidʒ] *n.* **1** Ⓤ the act or process of draining. 배수; 방수(放水). ¶ *~ work* 배수 공사. **2** Ⓒ a system of drains. 배수 장치[조직]. **3** Ⓒ that which is drained off. (배수된) 물이나 오물; 하수. **4** Ⓒ an area that is drained. (하천의) 배수 구역; 유역(流域).

drain·pipe [dréinpàip] *n.* Ⓒ a large pipe for carrying off water, etc. 배수관; 하수관; 토관.

drake [dreik] *n.* Ⓒ a male duck. 수오리. [Teut.]

dram [dræm] *n.* Ⓒ **1** a unit of weight. 드램《형량(衡量)의 단위》. **2** a small drink, esp. of whisky; a small quantity. (특히 위스키의) 한 모금; 한 잔; 미량. ¶ *a ~ of whisky* 위스키 한 잔 / *be fond of a ~* 술을 좋아하다 / *have not one ~ of learning* 조금도 배운 것이 없다. [→drachm]

***dra·ma** [drá:mə, drǽmə] *n.* **1** Ⓒ a play for the theater. 희곡; 각본. ¶ *make a novel into a ~* 소설을 희곡화하다. **2** Ⓒ a series of happenings as interesting as such a play. 극적인 사건. ¶ *the ~ of a murder trial* 살인 재판이라는 극적인 사건. **3** Ⓤ 《often *the ~*》 the branch of literature having to do with plays. 극문학; (연)극. ¶ *Elizabethan ~* 엘리자베스조(朝)의 연극. **4** the art of writing and performing plays. 극작법; 연출법. [Gk. *draō* do]

***dra·mat·ic** [drəmǽtik] *adj.* **1** of drama; having to do with plays. (연)극의; 희곡의. ¶ *~ art* 극예술 / *a ~ performance* 연기; 연극 / *a ~ right* 흥행권. **2** (of an event, etc.) seeming like a drama; (of manner, mode of speech, etc.) filled with emotion or exciting qualities; vivid; impressive. 극적인; 연극 같은; 약동적인; 감동적[인상적]인. ¶ *a ~ event* [*speech*] 극적인 사건[연설].

dra·mat·i·cal·ly [drəmǽtikəli] *adv.* **1** in a dramatic manner. 극적으로. **2** from a dramatic point of view. 연극의 입장에서.

dra·mat·ics [drəmǽtiks] *n. pl.* **1** 《used as *sing.*》 the art of acting or producing plays. 연기술; 연출법. **2** plays produced by amateurs. (아마추어의) 연극.

dram·a·tis per·so·nae [drǽmətis pə:r-sóuni:, drá:mətis pə:sóunai:] *n. pl.* 《L.》 the characters in a play; a list of these. 등장 인물; 배역표.

dram·a·tist [drǽmətist] *n.* Ⓒ a writer of plays. 극작가; 희곡 작가.

dram·a·ti·za·tion [drӕmətizéiʃən] *n.* ⓊⒸ the act of dramatizing; that which is dramatized. 각색; 희곡화; 각색 작품.

dram·a·tize [drǽmətàiz] *vt.* (P6) **1** put (a story, etc.) into the form of a play. …을 극화하다; 각색하다. ¶ *~ a novel* 소설을 극화하다. **2** express (something) in a dramatic way. …을 극적으로 표현하다.

dram·a·turge [drǽmətə̀:rdʒ], **-tur·gist** [drǽmətə̀:rdʒist] *n.* =dramatist.

dram·a·tur·gy [drǽmətə̀:rdʒi] *n.* the art of composing dramas or producing them on the stage. 극작술[법]; 연극의 구성법; 연출법.

***drank** [dræŋk] *v.* p. of **drink.**

drape [dreip] *vt.* (P6,13) **1** cover (something) with cloth or hang cloth around (something) in loose folds. (늘어뜨린 천 따위로 무엇)을 주름잡아 덮다. ¶ *~ with red hangings* 붉은 벽걸이 천으로 (아름답게) 덮다. **2** arrange (clothes, etc.) in graceful folds. (옷 따위)를 우아하게 걸치다. ¶ *~ the robe around the model's shoulder* 모델의 어깨에 겉옷을 보기 좋게 걸치다. —*n.* Ⓒ 《often *pl.*》 cloth hung in folds; a curtain. 벽걸이 천; 커튼. [F. *drap* cloth]

drap·er [dréipər] *n.* Ⓒ 《Brit.》 a dealer in cloth or dry goods. 포목상(商).

dra·per·y [dréipəri] *n.* (*pl.* **-per·ies**) **1** 《often *pl.*》 clothing or hangings arranged in graceful folds. (주름이 진) 휘장[벽걸이 천, 커튼]. **2** Ⓤ materials used for curtains, garments, etc. 포목; 피륙. **3** Ⓤ 《Brit.》 the business of a draper. 포목업[상].

dras·tic [drǽstik] *adj.* acting with a strong or violent effect; violent. 격렬한; 맹렬한; 철저한. ¶ *~ measures* 비상 수단; 발본책 / *a ~ debate* 격론 / *a ~ reform* 근본적 개혁 / *apply a ~ remedy* 거친 치료를 하다.
● **dras·ti·cal·ly** [-kəli] *adv.* [→drama]

drat [dræt] *vt.* (P6) 《*vulg.*》 confound, curse, bother (as woman's imprecation). 저주하다; 매도하다. [(*Go*)*d rot*]

Drat (*it*)***!*** Bother (it)! 성가셔; 쳇.

Drat you! Confound you! 이놈의 자식.

drat·ted [drǽtid] *adj.* 《*colloq.*》 cursed. 지겨운; 지긋지긋한. ¶ *This dratted car won't start.* 빌어먹을, 이놈의 차가 도무지 움직이지 않네. [↑]

***draught** [dræft, dra:ft] *n., v.* =draft.
● **draught·er** [-ər] *n.* [→draw]

draughts·man [drǽftsmən, drá:fts-] *n.*

(*pl.* **-men** [-mən]) =draftsman.

draught·y [drǽfti, drɑ́:fti] *adj.* (**draught·i·er, draught·i·est**) =drafty.

:draw [drɔ:] *v.* (**drew, drawn**) *vt.* (P6,7,13) **1** ⓐ cause to move toward or in the same direction as oneself; pull or drag along. (…쪽으로, 같은 방향으로) …을 끌다; (끌어)당기다; 다가놓다. ¶ ~ *a net* 그물을 당기다 / ~ *a cart* 〔*wagon*〕 짐마차를 끌다 / ~ *a book toward one* 책을 앞에 끌어다 놓다 / ~ *one's seat up to a table* 의자를 테이블 쪽으로 끌어당기다 / ~ *something along* …을 질질 끌고 가다 / ~ *someone into the room* 아무를 방으로 끌어들이다 / *They drew her aside.* 그들은 그녀를 곁으로 끌어당겼다. ⓑ cause to move along with one's hand; pull or drag (in any direction). (손으로) 움직이게 하다; 끌다; 치다. ¶ ~ *a curtain over window* 창문에 커튼을 치다 / ~ *down a window shade* 창문에 차양〔블라인드를〕 내리다 / ~ *a hat over the face* 모자를 깊숙히 눌러 쓰다 / ~ *a sail* 돛을 올리다 / 《*fig.*》 ~ *a veil over* (*a subject*) …에 대해 입을 다물다. **2** ⓐ take or pull out. …을 꺼내다; 뽑아〔빼〕내다. ¶ ~ *a pipe from one's pocket* 주머니에서 담배 파이프를 꺼내다 / ~ *out a handkerchief from a bag* 백에서 손수건을 꺼내다 / ~ *a cork* 〔*tooth*〕 (*out*) 코르크 마개〔이〕를 뽑다 / ~ *one's gun and start shooting* 권총을 뽑아들고 쏘기 시작하다. ⓑ pull (a cutting tool) from its sheath. (집에서) 날붙이를 뽑다; 빼다. ¶ ~ *a knife* 〔*one's sword*〕 나이프를〔칼을〕 뽑다. ⓒ take out the bowels or contents of. …의 창자를 빼내다; 내용물을 빼내다; 말리다. ¶ ~ *a chicken* 닭의 창자를 빼내다 / ~ *a pond* 물을 빼내어 연못을 말라붙게 하다. ⓓ bring or take out (liquid); cause to flow. (물 따위)를 퍼〔떠〕내다; (피 따위)를 뽑다; 흘리게 하다. ¶ ~ *water from a well* 우물물을 푸다〔뜨다〕 / ~ *beer from a barrel* 통에서 맥주를 퍼내다 / ~ *blood* 피를 뽑다; 상처입히다; 고통을 주다 / ~ *first blood* 선제 공격을 하다; (상대보다) 우위를 점하다. **3** attract; charm; allure. (주의·흥미 따위)를 끌다; 끌어〔꾀어〕들이다. ¶ ~ *someone's attention* 아무의 주의를 끌다 / ~ *crowds* 〔*audience*〕 군중〔청중〕을 끌어 모으다 / *Honey draws flies.* 꿀은 파리를 꾀어 들인다 / *He was drawn by her soft voice.* 그는 그녀의 부드러운 목소리에 끌렸다. **4** get or receive from a source. 얻다; 받다; 타다. ¶ ~ *money from a bank* 은행에서 돈을 찾다 / ~ *one's pay* 〔*a big salary*〕 봉급〔많은 월급〕을 받다 / ~ *out $ 5,000 at a bank* 은행 예금 5천 달러를 전액 인출하다. **5** ⓐ bring or force out (information, etc.); obtain. …을 얻(어 내)다; (강제로) 알아내다. ¶ ~ *information from* …로부터 정보를 얻다 / ~ *facts from someone* 아무에게서 사실을 알아내다. ⓑ force information, opinion, etc. out of. (의견 따위)를 말하게 하다. ¶ ~ *someone on a subject* 주제에 관해 아무에게 의견을 말하게 하다. **6** form (one's opinion); make; formulate. (결론 따위)를 얻다; (구별·비교 따위)를 하다. ¶ ~ *a conclusion from the facts* 이 사실로부터 결론을 내다 / ~ *a clear distinction between A and B,* A와 B 사이의 구별을〔비교를〕 명확히 하다. **7** take or suck in (air); breathe in; take (a breath). (숨)을 쉬다; 들이마시다〔쉬다〕. ¶ ~ *a long* 〔*deep*〕 *breath* 심호흡을 하다 / ~ *air into the lungs* 공기를 폐 속으로 들이마시다 / ~ *one's last* 〔*first*〕 ~ 숨을 거두다〔이 세상에 태어나다〕 / ~ *a sigh* 한숨을 쉬다. **8** make (a line, figure, etc.) with a pencil, pen, etc., sketch in lines; make a picture in lines. (연필·펜 따위로) …을 그리다; 선으로 그리다; 스케치하다; 선을 긋다. ¶ ~ *a straight line* 직선을 긋다 / ~ *a picture* 〔*map*〕 그림을〔지도를〕 그리다. **9** ⓐ write in full; write out. (문서)를 쓰다; (어음·수표)를 떼다〔발행하다〕. ¶ ~ *a check* 수표를 발행하다 / ~ *a bill of exchange* 환어음을 발행하다 / 《*fig.*》 ~ *on someone for money* 〔*help*〕 아무에게 돈〔도움〕을 요구하다. ⓑ 《*up*》 compose; make out. …을 작성하다. ¶ ~ *up a report* 〔*document, program, plan*〕 보고서를〔문서를, 프로그램을, 계획을〕 작성하다. **10** cause to come forth; bring (about); excite; produce. …을 가져오다; 일으키다; 생기게 하다. ¶ ~ *trouble* 말썽을 일으키다 / ~ *rust* 녹이 나다〔슬다〕 / ~ (*forth*) *applause* 갈채를 받다 / ~ *ruin upon oneself* 자신의 파멸을 초래하다 / ~ *forth laughter* 웃음을 자아내다 / *The deposits* ~ *interest.* 예금에는 이자가 붙는다 / *Her account drew tears from us.* 그녀의 이야기는 우리의 눈물을 자아냈다. **11** finish (a game) undecided. (게임)을 무승부로 끝내다. ¶ *a drawn game* 무승부의 경기 / *The game was drawn.* 그 경기는 비겼다. **12** pull out; stretch out; extend. …을 잡아늘이다; 펴 늘이다. ¶ ~ *a rope tight* 밧줄을 팽팽히 켕기다 / ~ *metal out into a wire* 금속을 잡아뽑아 철사를 만들다. **13** bend (a bow) by pulling back the string; shoot an arrow. 활의 시위를 당기다; 화살을 쏘다. ¶ ~ *a bow* 활을 당기다. **14** ⓐ pack out at random. (많은 중에서 하나)를 뽑다. ¶ ~ *lots* 제비를 뽑다 / ~ *a blank* 꽝을 뽑다 / ~ *a card from the pack* 카드 뭉치에서 카드패 하나를 뽑아내다. ⓑ obtain by lot or chance. (제비)를 뽑아 맞히다; 당첨하다. ¶ ~ *a prize in a lottery* 복권에서 상품에 당첨하다. **15** pull (the face) twisted; distort. 옥죄다; (얼굴)을 찡그리다; 일그러뜨리다. ¶ *a face drawn with pain* 고통으로 일그러진 얼굴. **16** 《naut.》 (of a ship) need (a certain depth of water) to float in. …의 흘수(吃水)가 一이다. ¶ *This boat draws two feet.* 이 배는 흘수가 2피트이다. **17** extract the essence. (더운 물에 달여) 찻물을 우려내다. ¶ *let the tea* ~ 열탕에 홍차가 우러나게 하다.

— *vi.* (P1,2A,3) **1** move; come; go; be moved. (끌리듯이) 움직이다; 오다; 가다; 끌리다. ¶ *This cart draws easily.* 이 짐마차는 쉽게 끌린다 / *She drew back* 〔*aside*〕. 그녀는 뒤

로 물러섰다〔옆으로 비켜섰다〕. **2** approach; come near. 다가 가다〔오다〕; 접근하다. ¶ ~ *together* 한데 모이다 / ~ *to an end* 〔*a close, a finish*〕 끝나다 / *Winter is drawing near.* 겨울이 다가오고 있다 / *This year drew to its close.* 올해도 끝났다 / *A car drew up behind him.* 차 한 대가 그의 뒤에 바짝 다가갔다 / *As she approached, he also drew near.* 그녀가 접근함에 따라 그 역시 가까이 다가갔다. **3** make a picture with a pen, a pencil, chalk, etc. (펜·연필·분필 따위로) 그리다. **4** finish a game undecided. 무승부로 끝나다. **5** cause air to flow. 공기가 통하게 하다. **6** take out a pistol, sword, etc. 권총〔칼〕 따위를 뽑다. **7** attract people. 사람을 끌다. ¶ *The play is drawing very well.* 이 극은 입장 관객을 많이 끌고 있다.

draw a full house, have a crowded attendance. 입장객들로 초만원을 이루다.

draw back, retreat; hesitate (to do some work). 뒤로 물러서다; …하기를 망설이다.

draw down, **a**) pull down. (커튼 따위)를 끌어내리다; 치다. **b**) attract; invite; cause. …을 초래하다; 야기시키다. ¶ ~ *down blame on our heads* 우리 머리 위에 당장 비난을 초래하다.

draw in, **a**) (of a day) become dark. (날이) 저물다; 어두워지다. **b**) become shorter. (해가) 짧아지다. **c**) arrive. 도착하다. ¶ *The train drew in.* 열차가 들어왔다. **d**) move to one side of the road. 길 한 옆으로 비키다. ¶ *The bus drew in to let the car pass.* 버스는 차가 통과하도록 한 옆으로 비켰다. **e**) reduce (expenses); economize. 지출을 줄이다; 절약하다.

draw it mild, 《Brit. *colloq.*》 be moderate; not exaggerate. 과장하지 않다.

***draw level* (*with*),** gain on. 따라 붙다; …와 동점이〔동등하게〕 되다.

draw off, **a**) remove. 제거하다; 없애다. ¶ ~ *off pain* 통증을 없애다. **b**) cause to flow away. 물을 빼다. ¶ ~ *off water from a tank* 〔*the field*〕 물탱크〔밭〕에서 물을 빼다. **c**) pull or take off. 잡아빼다〔뽑다〕. ¶ ~ *off one's gloves* 장갑을 벗어 빼다. **d**) move away. 철수시키다. ¶ *The enemies' losses forced them to ~ off.* 적군에 손실을 가해 퇴각하지 않을 수 없게 했다.

draw out, **a**) pull out; stretch out; extend; prolong. 팽팽히 켕기다; 잡아 펴다〔늘이다〕; 오래 끌게 하다. **b**) encourage (someone) to talk. …를 (살살 꾀어) 말하게 하다. **c**) become longer. 길어지다. ¶ *The days are drawing out.* 낮이 길어지고 있다.

draw up, **a**) arrange (troops, etc.) in order; stand in regular order. (군대를) 정렬시키다. ¶ *The soldiers drew* 〔*were drawn*〕 *up in line.* 군인들은 열을 지어 섰다. **b**) compose; make out. (문서·계획을) 작성하다; (표·지도 따위를) 그리다. **c**) bring or come to a stop. 멈춰 세우다〔서다〕. **d**) 《*reflexively*》 pull up oneself straight; stand straight and stiff. 몸을 곧추 세우다; 꼿꼿이 서다.

— *n.* Ⓒ **1** the act of drawing. 끎; 끌기; (잡아)당김; 뺌; 뽑음. **2** something that attracts, esp. a popular entertainment; an attraction. (주의·흥미·사람 따위를) 끄는 것; 인기 있는 것. ¶ *The new play is a great ~.* 그 새 연극은 대단한 인기를 끌고 있다〔대성공이다〕. **3** a game that ends in a tie. 무승부의 경기. ¶ *The match was* 〔*ended in*〕 *a ~.* 경기는 무승부로 끝났다. **4** drawing of lots. 제비뽑기; 추첨. **5** a movable part of a drawbridge. 도개교(跳開橋)의 개폐부. [A.S. *dragan*, M.E. *drawen* drag]

draw·back [drɔ́ːbæ̀k] *n.* Ⓒ **1** something that causes trouble; a disadvantage; a hindrance. 장애; 지장; 결점; 불이익. ¶ *a ~ to success* 성공을 방해하는 것 / *The ~ to my house is that it faces north.* 내 집에 대한 결점은 그것이 북향집이라는 것이다. **2** money paid back from a charge previously made. 환급금〔세〕; 공제.

draw·bridge [drɔ́ːbrìdʒ] *n.* Ⓒ a bridge that can be lifted, lowered, or moved to one side. 도개교(跳開橋).

〈drawbridge〉

draw·ee [drɔːíː] *n.* Ⓒ a person for whom an order or draft to pay money is written. 환어음 지급인(opp. drawer). [*draw*]

***draw·er** [drɔ́ːər] *n.* Ⓒ **1** a person or thing that draws. 끄는〔당기는〕 사람〔것〕; 제도사. **2** a person who draws an order to pay money. 어음 발행인(opp. drawee). **3** [drɔːr] a box that slides in and out of a chest, table, etc. 서랍. ¶ *a chest of drawers* 장롱. **4.** 《*pl.*》 [drɔːrz] an undergarment for the lower part of the body. 속바지; 속옷; 드로어즈; 팬츠.

draw·ing [drɔ́ːiŋ] *n.* **1** Ⓤ the act of a person or thing that draws. 끎; 꺼냄; 잡아늘임. **2** Ⓤ the art of representing objects by lines. 제도(製圖). **3** Ⓒ a picture, design, sketch, etc. drawn with a pencil, chalk, etc. (연필·분필 따위에 의한) 그림; 선화(線畫); 데생; 스케치; 도면. ¶ *make a rough ~* 밑그림을 그리다.

in drawing, correctly drawn. 정확히 그려져.

out of drawing, **a**) incorrectly drawn. 부정확하게 그려져. **b**) out of keeping. (주위와) 조화되지 않아.

drawing board [⌐–⌐] *n.* a board on which paper is placed for drawing. 제도판(板); 화판(畫板).

drawing card [⌐–⌐] *n.* 《*colloq.*》 a show or performer that attracts a large audience. 인기 있는 흥행〔배우〕.

drawing knife [⌐–⌐] *n.* =drawknife.

drawing pen [⌐–⌐] *n.* a ruling pen.

(제도용) 펜[가막부리]; 오구(烏口).

drawing pin [∠-∠] *n.* 《Brit.》 a short pin with a large flat head, for fastening paper on a board. (제도용) 압정(押釘)(=《U.S.》 thumbtack).

drawing room [∠-∠] *n.* **1** a room in which guests are received. 객실; 응접실. **2** 《U.S.》 a private compartment in a sleeping car. (침대차의) 특별 전용실.

draw·knife [drɔ́:nàif] *n.* (*pl.* **-knives**) a knife with a handle at each end of the blade, used to shave off surfaces. 당겨 깎는 칼《양쪽에 손잡이가 있음》.

draw·knives [drɔ́:nàivz] *n.* pl. of **drawknife.**

drawl [drɔ:l] *vi., vt.* (P1;6,7) speak in a slow, lazy way. 느릿느릿 말하다. — *n.* Ⓒ a slow, lazy way of speaking. 느린 말투. ● **drawl·er** [-ər] *n.* [→draw]

:drawn [drɔ:n] *v.* pp. of **draw.** — *adj.* **1** left undecided. 승부가 나지 않은; 비긴. ¶ *a ~ game* 비긴 경기. **2** twisted out of shape. 일그러진; 찡그린; 뒤틀린. ¶ *a ~ face with pain* 고통으로 일그러진 얼굴. **3** disemboweled, as a fowl prepared for cooking. (닭 따위의) 내장을 빼낸. **4** (of a sword) pulled out of its sheath. (칼집에서) 빼낸; 뽑은. [*draw*]

draw·shave [drɔ́:ʃèiv] *n.* =drawknife.

draw well [∠∠] *n.* a well with rope and bucket. 두레 우물.

dray [drei] *n.* Ⓒ a low, strong cart for carrying heavy loads. 대형 짐마차. — *vt.* carry (something) on a dray. …을 대형 짐마차로 나르다. [→draw]

dray·man [dréimən] *n.* Ⓒ (*pl.* **-men** [-mən]) a man who drives a dray. 짐마차꾼 [마부].

:dread [dred] *vt.* (P6,8,9,11) **1** fear greatly; look forward to (something) with fear. …을 몹시 두려워하다; 극도로 걱정하다. ¶ *~ visits to the dentist* 치과에 가는 것을 두려워하다 / *~ to think what may happen* 무슨 일이 일어날지 생각하기를 두려워하다 / *Cats ~ water.* 고양이는 물을 두려워한다 / *He dreads the coming of winter.* 다가오는 겨울을 걱정하고 있다 / *I ~ that he might come.* 그가 오지나 않을까 걱정하고 있다 / *I ~ going there alone.* 혼자 가는 것이 두렵다. **2** be reluctant to do, meet, etc. …하고 싶지 않다; 싫어하다. ¶ *He dreaded meeting her.* 그는 그녀를 만나고 싶어하지 않았다.

— *vi.* (P1) be in great fear. 몹시 두려워하다.

— *n.* Ⓤ 《sometimes *a ~*》 **1** fear; anxiety. 공포; 두려움; 불안; 걱정. ¶ *be* [*live*] *in ~ of the house catching fire* 집에 화재나 나지 않을까 늘 두려워하다 / *have a ~ of being asked to speak in public* 대중 앞에서의 연설 요청을 받는 것을 두려워하고 있다. **2** a person or thing regarded with fear or awe. 두려워하는 사람[것]; 공포[두려움]의 대상.

— *adj.* 《*arch.*》 dreadful; dreaded; awful. 두려운; 무서운. ¶ *a ~ plague* 무서운 전염병. [E.]

dread·ed [drédid] *adj.* looked with fear or anxiety; greatly feared. 두려워한; 걱정한; 매우 두려운.

:dread·ful [drédfəl] *adj.* **1** causing dread; fearful; terrible. 무서운; 무시무시한. ¶ *a ~ story* [*face, voice*] 무서운 이야기[얼굴, 목소리]. **2** 《*colloq.*》 very bad; very disagreeable. 지독한; 몹시 싫은; 볼썽 사나운. ¶ *~ weather* [*cooking*] 지독한 날씨[요리] / *a ~ hat* 꼴불견인 모자.

dread·ful·ly [drédfəli] *adv.* **1** in a dreadful manner. 무섭게; 무시무시하게. **2** 《*colloq.*》 very; extremely. 몹시; 지독히. ¶ *a ~ long lecture* 몹시 긴 강의 / *a ~ bad pudding* 지독한 푸딩 / *be ~ tired* 몹시 지치다.

dread·nought, dread·naught [drédnɔ̀:t] *n.* **1** a big heavily armed battleship. 노급전함(弩級戰艦). ¶ *a super-dreadnought* 초노급함(超弩級艦). **2** a kind of heavy cloth used for coats. (코트용의) 두꺼운 천 [나사]. [E.]

:dream [dri:m] *n.* Ⓒ **1** an image or a thought passing through a sleeping person's mind. 꿈. ¶ *have a dreadful* [*strange, bad*] *~* 무서운[이상한, 나쁜] 꿈을 꾸다 / *awake from a ~* 꿈에서 깨다 / *go to one's ~* 꿈길을 더듬다; 자다. **2** a fancy; an imagination; a vision; a daydream. 환상; 공상; 백일몽. ¶ *live in a ~* 공상 속에 살다. **3** ⓐ a hope for the future; what one wants to realize. 희망; 이상; 꿈. ¶ *He realized his ~ of becoming a professor.* 그는 교수가 되겠다던 꿈을 실현했다. ⓑ a vain hope. 헛된 희망; 꿈. ¶ *I'll tell you my hopes and dreams.* 나의 희망과 꿈을 이야기하지. **4** a thing or person so charming that it seems dreamlike. 꿈속에서처럼 아름다운 것[사람]. ¶ *a ~ of a dress* 꿈인가 싶은 아름다운 옷 / *She looked a perfect ~.* 그녀는 절세의 미인이었다.

— *vi., vt.* (**dreamed** [dri:md, dremt] or **dreamt**) (P6,7,10,11,12;1,3) **1** have dreams during sleep. 꿈을 꾸다. ¶ *~ a beautiful and happy dream* 아름답고 행복한 꿈을 꾸다 / *I dreamed about my father.* 아버지의 꿈을 꾸었다 / *I dreamed that I was in Paris.* 내가 파리에 있는 꿈을 꾸었다. **2** 《in *negative*》 suppose; think of (something) as possible. 생각하다; 있을 수 있다고 생각하다. ¶ *I never dreamed that he would come to such an end.* 그가 이와 같은 종말을 고하게 되리라곤 꿈에도 생각하지 않았다 / *He little dreamed that he would hurt her.* 그녀에게 상처를 주리라곤 꿈에도 생각 못했다. **3** imagine; hope. 공상[상상]하다; 희망하다. [E.]

dream away, pass one's time idly. (꿈결처럼) 멍하게 때를 보내다. ¶ *~ away one's life* (꿈결처럼) 생애를 허송하다.

dream of, **a**) have dreams of (something). …의 꿈을 꾸다. **b**) indulge in daydreams of (something). …의 몽상에 빠지다. **c**) 《in *negative*》 think of (something) as possible. …이 있을 수 있다고 생각하다. ¶ *Little did I ~ of meeting you.* 너를 만나리라곤 꿈에도 생각지 못 했다.

dream up, **a**) 《*colloq.*》 think out; create; devise. (계획 따위를) 생각해내다. **b**) conceive of; imagine. 몽상〔상상〕하다.

dream·er [dríːmər] *n.* Ⓒ a person who dreams; a person who does not have practical ideas. 꿈꾸는 사람; 몽상가.

dream·i·ly [dríːmili] *adv.* like one in a dream; as if in a dream. 꿈꾸는 사람같이; 꿈을 꾸듯이.

dream·land [dríːmlæ̀nd] *n.* **1** ⓊⒸ a place which a person feels to be unreal. 꿈나라. **2** ⓊⒸ a utopia. 이상향(理想鄕); 유토피아. **3** Ⓤ sleep. 잠.

dream·less [dríːmlis] *adj.* without dreams. 꿈을 꾸지 않는; 꿈이 없는.

dream·like [dríːmlàik] *adj.* like a dream. 꿈과 같은; 어렴풋한.

dreamt [dremt] *v.* p. and pp. of **dream.**

dream·y [dríːmi] *adj.* (**dream·i·er, dream·i·est**) **1** full of dreams. 꿈이 많은. ¶ (*a*) ~ *slumber* 꿈이 많은 잠. **2** like something in a dream; vague; dim. 꿈 같은; 막연한; 어렴풋한. ¶ *a ~ scheme* 꿈과 같은 계획. **3** (of a person) fanciful; unreal; impractical. 환상적인; 비현실적인. ● **dream·i·ness** [-nis] *n.* [E.]

drear [driər] *adj.* 《*poet.*》 =dreary.

·**drear·y** [dríəri] *adj.* (**drear·i·er, drear·i·est**) **1** dull; cheerless; gloomy; making low-spirited. 따분한; 쓸쓸한; 음산한; 음울한. **2** sad; sorrowful. 슬픈. ● **drear·i·ly** [-li] *adv.* **drear·i·ness** [-nis] *n.* [E.]

dredge[1] [dredʒ] *n.* Ⓒ **1** a machine for digging out the bottom of a river, harbor, etc. 준설기(機). **2** a device with a net for catching shellfish, etc. from the bottom of the sea. 훑이 그물《조개 따위를 잡는 저인망의 일종》. — *vt.* (P6,7) **1** clean out (a harbor, etc.) with a dredge. (항구 등)을 준설하다; (물바닥)을 치다. ¶ ~ *up the river* 강바닥을 준설하다. **2** gather (shellfish, etc.) with a dredge. (조개 따위)를 훑이 그물로 훑어모으다. — *vi.* (P1,3) use a dredge. 준설하다; 훑이 그물로 잡다. [E.]

dredge[2] [dredʒ] *vt.* (P6,13) 《*with, over*》 scatter; sprinkle. (가루 따위)를 뿌리다; 살포하다. ¶ ~ *sugar over a cake* 케이크에 설탕을 뿌리다 / ~ *meat with flour* 고기에 밀가루를 바르다. [Gk. *tragēma* sweetmeat]

dredg·er[1] [drédʒər] *n.* Ⓒ **1** a person who operates a dredge. 준설자; 훑이 그물〔저인망〕 사용자. **2** a ship with a dredge; a dredge machine. 준설선(船); 준설기. [→dredge[1]]

dredg·er[2] [drédʒər] *n.* a container used for sprinkling flour, sugar, etc. over food. 음식에 가루를 치는 그릇. [→dredge[2]]

dreg [dreg] *n.* Ⓒ 《usu. *pl.*》 matter which is found at the bottom of a liquid; the most worthless part of anything. (바닥에 남는) 찌끼; 앙금; 쓰레기; 시시한 것. ¶ *the dregs of society* 사회의 최하층; 인간 쓰레기. [Scand.]

drain 〔***drink***〕 ***to the dregs,*** drink leaving nothing. 한방울도 남김없이 다 마시다.

not a dreg, not a bit. 조금도 …않다. ¶ *He left not a ~ in the cup.* 그는 술잔의 술을 조금도 남기지 않았다.

drench [drentʃ] *vt.* (P6) **1** make (something) thoroughly wet; soak. …을 흠뻑 적시다; 물에 잠〔담〕그다. ¶ *be* 〔*get*〕 *drenched* (*to the skin*) *with* 〔*by*〕 *rain* 비에 흠뻑 젖다. **2** force (a sick animal) to take a dose. (마소에) 억지로 물약을 먹이다. — *n.* Ⓒ **1** the act of drenching. 흠뻑 젖음; 물에 담금. ¶ *a ~ of rain* 억수. **2** a draft of medicine given to a sick animal. (마소에 먹이는) 물약. [E.; →drink]

drench·er [dréntʃər] *n.* **1** a heavy rainstorm. 큰 비. **2** an appliance for dosing a beast. 투약기(投藥器).

⁑**dress** [dres] *n.* **1** Ⓤ clothes; costume. 옷; 복장; 의복. ¶ *in Korean ~* 한복을 입고 / *try on a ~* 옷을 입어보다 / *spend much money on ~* 많은 돈을 옷에 쓰다. **2** Ⓤ formal clothes. 정장(正裝). ¶ *in full ~* 정장하고〔으로〕 / *in evening ~* 야회복으로〔을 입고〕. **3** Ⓒ an outer garment for women, girls, and babies; a gown. (여성·아기의) 옷《흔히 원피스형》. ¶ *put on a clean ~* 깨끗한 옷을 입다 / *This ~ is tight on me.* 이 옷은 꼭 낀다. **4** Ⓤ outer covering; external appearance. 겉옷; 외관. ¶ *trees in their spring ~* 봄옷을 입은 나무들.

— *vt.* (P6,7,13) **1** ⓐ put clothes on (someone). …에게 옷을 입히다. ¶ ~ *a child* / ~ *oneself hastily for shopping* 쇼핑 나가기 위해 서둘러 옷을 입다 / *She is dressed in white* 〔*her best*〕. 그녀는 흰옷〔나들이옷〕을 입고 있다. ⓑ provide with clothing. 옷을 마련해 주다. ¶ ~ *one's wife and daughter on $ 500 a year* 아내와 딸 자식을 입히는 데 연(年) 5백달러 들다. **2** adorn; decorate. …을 아름답게 꾸미다; 장식하다. ¶ ~ *a store window* 진열창을 아름답게 장식하다 / ~ *a Christmas-tree* 크리스마스 트리를 꾸미다 / ~ *the street with flags* 거리를 깃발로 장식하다. **3** set in order; brush and arrange (hair). (머리)를 매만져 다듬다; 빗질〔솔질〕하다. ¶ ~ *one's hair* 머리를 빗다. **4** apply medicine and bandages to. (상처)에 약을 바르다; 붕대를 감다. ¶ ~ *a sore* 아픈 곳에 약을 바르다 / ~ *one's wounds* 상처에 붕대를 감다. **5** prepare for use or sale; make suitable or ready to eat by adding sauce, etc. (사용·판매를 위해) …을 다듬다; 조제하다; (먹기 좋게) 준비하다. ¶ ~ *timber* 목재를 다듬다 / ~ *leather* 가죽을 무두질하다 / ~ *fowls for the market* (시장에

내다팔기 위해) 닭의 깃털〔내장〕을 뽑다 / ~ *fish for the table* 식탁에 올리기 위해 생선을 조리하다. **6** arrange (troops) in straight lines. 열을 똑바로 하다; 정렬시키다. ¶ ~ *the ranks* 대열을 나란히 맞추다. — *vi.* (P1,2A,3) **1** put on clothes; wear clothes. 옷을 입다; 옷을 입고 있다. ¶ *He dressed quickly.* 재빨리 옷을 입었다 / ~ *well* 〔*badly*〕 옷차림이 좋다〔좋지 않다〕 / ~ *in good taste* 복장의 취미가 좋다. **2** 《*for*》 put on formal clothes. 정장(正裝)하다. ¶ ~ *for dinner* 만찬을 위해 정장하다 / ~ *for the opera* 오페라에 가기 위해 차려 입다. **3** 《mil.》 get into a straight line. (군대 따위가) 정렬하다. ¶ ~ *to* 〔*by*〕 *the right* 오른쪽을 기준으로 정렬하다. [→direct]

dress down, 《*colloq.*》 scold; beat; thrash. 꾸짖다; 때리다; 매질하다.

dress out, **a**) attire conspicuously; adorn. 차려입다. **b**) treat (a wound). 치료하다.

dress up, put on one's best clothes; put on formal clothes. 차려입다; 성장(盛裝)하다; 정장하다. ¶ ~ *up in one's best* 나들이옷으로 차려입다 / *be dressed up to the nines* 성장(盛裝)을 하고 있다.

dress circle [ˊ ˊ–] *n.* the section of seats in a theater, etc., which has the best, most expensive seats. (극장의) 특등석 《2층 정면으로, 이 좌석에서는 evening dress를 입는 관례가 있었음》. [*dress*]

dress coat [ˊ ˊ] *n.* an evening coat. 남자용 야회복의 상의(上衣); 연미복.

dress·er[1] [drésər] *n.* Ⓒ **1** a person who dresses elegantly or in a certain way. 잘 차려 입는 사람. **2** a person who assists another person to dress. 옷을 잘 입혀주는 사람; (배우의) 의상 담당원. **3** a person or thing that dresses stone, wood, a store window, etc. 다듬는〔마무르는〕 사람〔용구〕; 꾸미는 사람. [*dress*]

dress·er[2] [drésər] *n.* Ⓒ **1** 《U.S.》 a piece of furniture with drawers for clothes and with a mirror; bureau. 경대가 있는 장롱. **2** 《Brit.》 a piece of kitchen furniture with shelves for dishes. 찬장; 찻장. [↑]

dress·ing [drésiŋ] *n.* **1** Ⓤ the act of putting on clothes. 옷입음; 매무새. **2** ⓊⒸ the material used to dress. 마무리 재료. **3** Ⓤ arrangement; preparation; adornment. 매만져 다듬기; 손질; 준비; (식품을) 대강 조리해두기; 장식. ¶ *hair-dressing* 결발; 조발 / *window-dressing* 진열창 장식. **4** ⓊⒸ a sauce for salads, fish, etc. 드레싱 소스. **5** Ⓤ stuffing for a roast fowl, fish, etc. (닭·생선 따위의) 속. **6** ⓊⒸ medicines and bandages to put on wounds, etc. (고약·붕대 따위) 치료용품. **7** Ⓤ chemical plant food. 화학 비료. ¶ *give a field a ~ of lime* 밭에 석회 비료를 주다. [*dress*]

dressing case [ˊ– ˋ] *n.* a small case for toilet articles, used, esp. when traveling. (여행용의) 화장품 주머니〔통, 가방〕.

dress·ing-down [drésiŋdáun] *n.* 《*colloq.*》 a severe scolding; a beating. 호되게 꾸짖음; 야단; 매질.

dressing gown [ˊ– ˋ] *n.* 《chiefly Brit.》 a loose gown worn over night clothes. 화장옷; 실내복(=《U.S.》 bathrobe).

dressing room [ˊ– ˋ] *n.* a room for dressing. 화장실《옷 갈아입는 방》.

dressing table [ˊ– ˋ–] *n.* a low table with a mirror; a dresser. 경대; 화장대.

dress·mak·er [drésmèikər] *n.* Ⓒ a person who makes women's dresses, etc. (여성복 따위의) 양재사(cf. *tailor*). — *adj.* (of women's clothing) having soft lines and subdued decoration. (여성복이) 부드러운 선과 차분한 장식을 살린. [*dress*]

dress·mak·ing [drésmèikiŋ] *n.* Ⓤ **1** the art or process of making women's clothes. (여성복) 제조; 양재(술). **2** the business of a dressmaker. 양재업; 여성복 제조업.

dress rehearsal [ˊ –ˊ–] *n.* the final rehearsal of a play with costumes. (의상을 입고 하는) 최후의 무대 연습; 총예행 연습.

dress suit [ˊ ˊ] *n.* men's formal suit worn in the evening. (남자의) 야회복.

dress·y [drési] *adj.* (**dress·i·er, dress·i·est**) 《*colloq.*》 fond of wearing showy clothes; stylish. 옷치장을 좋아하는; 복장이 멋진. ● **dress·i·ness** [-nis] *n.* [*dress*]

·**drew** [druː] *v.* p. of **draw.**

drib·ble [dríbəl] *vi.* (P1) **1** fall drop by drop; trickle. (물방울이) 뚝뚝 떨어지다〔듣다〕; 뚝뚝〔줄줄〕 흐르다. ¶ ~ *from the leak in the tank* 물 탱크의 새는 틈에서 떨어지다. **2** (of babies, etc.) let saliva run from the mouth. 침을 흘리다. — *vt.* (P6) **1** let (liquid) fall drop by drop. …을 뚝뚝 떨어지게 하다. **2** 《sports》 move (a ball) forward by repeated bounces. (공)을 드리블하다. — *n.* ⓊⒸ **1** the act of dropping; trickle. (물방울의) 뚝뚝 떨어짐; 점적(點滴); 물방울. **2** a very light rain. 가랑비. **3** the act of dribbling a ball. (공의) 드리블. [*drip*]

drib·let [dríblit] *n.* Ⓒ a small amount; a small quantity at a time. 소량; (한번에) 조금. ¶ *give money in driblets* 돈을 찔끔찔끔 주다 / *by* 〔*in*〕 *driblets* 조금씩; 찔끔찔끔. [↑]

dri·er [dráiər] *n.* Ⓒ **1** a person or thing that dries. 말리는 사람〔것〕. **2** a device that removes water by heat, etc.; a dryer. (열 따위에 의한) 건조기(器); 드라이어. **3** a substance that makes something dry quickly. 건조제(劑)(=dryer). [*dry*]

:**drift** [drift] *vi.* (P1,2A,3) **1** be carried along by an air or water current. 떠돌다; 표류하다. ¶ ~ *out to sea* 바다로 표류하다 / ~ *about in the sea* 바다를 이리저리 떠돌다 / ~ *with the current* 흐르는 대로 떠돌다. **2** be carried along by circumstances; go along without aim. 환경에 따라〔되어 가는 대로〕 움직이다; 정처없이 헤매다. ¶ ~ *along through life* 삶을 어영부영 보내다〔지내다〕/ ~ *into war* 부지불식간에 전쟁에 빠지다 / ~ *toward ruin* 서서히 파멸로 향하다 / *He drifts from town to town.* 마을에서 마을로 정처없이 헤맨다. **3** be heaped by force of wind or water. 바람·물에 밀려 쌓이다; 퇴적하다. ¶ *drifting sand* 바람에 불려 쌓인 모래 / *The snow has drifted badly.* 눈이 바람에 불려 많이 쌓였다. — *vt.* (P6,7,13) cause (something) to drift. …을 표류시키다〔떠돌게 하다〕; 떠내려 보내다; 바람에 불려 쌓이게 하다. ¶ ~ *a boat out to sea* 배를 바다로 떠내려 보내다 / *The wind has drifted a mass of snow in the corner of the garden.* 바람이 불어 마당 구석에 큰 눈더미가 쌓이게 했다.

drift apart, 《*fig.*》 gradually become estranged. 점차 소원해지다.

— *n.* Ⓒ **1** ⓊⒸ the state of being drifted; the direction of drifting. 표류; 흐름의 방향. **2** tendency; trend. 경향; 동향; 추세. ¶ *the ~ of public opinion* 여론의 향방. **3** general meaning; intent. 취지; 주된 뜻. ¶ *the ~ of a speech* 〔*conversation*〕 연설의 취지 / *catch the ~ of someone's words* 아무의 말의 취지를 이해하다 / *I don't understand your ~.* 말씀하시는 것의 뜻을 모르겠습니다. **4** snow, sand, etc. heaped up by the wind or water. 바람에 불려〔물에 떠밀려〕 쌓인 것; 퇴적물. ¶ *a ~ of snow* 바람에 불려 쌓인 눈. [*drive*]

drift·er [driftər] *n.* **1** a person or thing that drifts. 표류자〔물〕; 표류선. **2** a fishing boat equipped with drift nets. 유자망(流刺網) 어선. **3** a person who moves aimlessly from one job to another. 직업을 자주 바꾸는 사람.

drift ice [ㅗㅡ] *n.* floating masses of ice (in the sea or a river), carried along by currents of water or air. 유빙(流氷); 성엣장.

drift net [ㅗㅡ] *n.* a net which is allowed to drift with the tide. 유자망(流刺網).

drift·wood [dríftwùd] *n.* Ⓤ wood drifting in the water or washed up on beaches. 유목(流木); 표목(漂木).

***drill**[1] [dril] *n.* Ⓒ **1** a tool or a machine for making holes. 송곳; 천공기; 드릴. **2** military or physical exercises. 교련; 연습(演習); (체육) 훈련. ¶ *soldiers at ~* 훈련중의 병사. **3** the process of teaching or training by repetition. 교육; 연습(練習).

— *vt.* (P6,13) **1** make a hole in (something) with a drill. …에 송곳으로 구멍을 뚫다. **2** 《*in*》 train; teach (someone) by repetition. …을 훈련하다; …에게 반복하여 가르치다〔교육하다〕. ¶ ~ *boys in grammar* 학생들에게 엄격하게 문법을 가르치다.

— *vi.* (P1) **1** make a hole with a drill. (송곳으로) 구멍을 뚫다. **2** be taught or trained by repetition. 교련〔훈련〕을 받다; 맹연습하다. ● **drill·er** [-ər] *n.* [Du.]

drill[2] [dril] *n.* Ⓒ **1** a machine for planting seeds. 파종기. **2** a small and long cut made in the ground to plant seeds in; a row of planted seeds. 파종골; 이랑; (이랑에 심은) 씨의 한 이랑. — *vt.* (P6) plant (seeds, etc.) in drills. (씨)를 파종기로 이랑에 뿌리다. ¶ ~ *wheat* 밀을 심다 / ~ *a field with wheat* 밭에 밀을 심다. [Du.]

drill[3] [dril] *n.* Ⓤ a strong, twilled cotton or linen cloth. 능직(綾織) 무명. [L. *trilix*]

drill·mas·ter [drílmæ̀stər, -mɑ̀:s-] *n.* Ⓒ **1** an officer who leads military drill. 교련 교관. **2** a person who teaches by drilling. 엄하게 가르치는 사람. [Du.]

dri·ly [dráili] *adv.* =dryly.

:drink [driŋk] *v.* (**drank, drunk**) *vt.* (P6,7) **1** take (liquid) into the mouth and swallow. …을 마시다; 마셔 비우다. ¶ ~ *water* 물을 마시다 / ~ *a cup of coffee* 커피 한 잔을 마시다 / ~ *a jug of beer empty* 맥주 한 조끼를 비우다 / ~ *off* 〔*up*〕 *a glass of whisky* 위스키를 단숨에 들이켜다 / ~ *a glass dry* 잔을 비우다 / ~ *wine from* 〔*out of*〕 *a glass* 잔의 포도주를 마시다 / ~ *the cup of joy* 〔*sorrow*〕 기쁨〔슬픔〕을 다 맛보다 / ~ *oneself drunk* 취하도록 마시다 / *He doesn't smoke or ~.* 그는 담배도 술도 안 한다. **2** drink in honor of; drink a toast. …을 위해 축배를 들다. ¶ ~ *someone's health* 아무의 건강을 위해 건배하다 / ~ *a toast to someone* 아무를 위해 축배를 들다 / ~ *success to someone* 〔*a business*〕 아무〔사업〕의 성공을 위해 축배를 들다 / ~ *the Queen* 여왕을 위해 건배하다. **3** suck up; absorb. …을 빨아들이다; 흡수하다. ¶ ~ (*in*) *the fresh mountain air* 신선한 산공기를 들이마시다 / *The soil drinks water.* 땅은 물을 흡수한다. **4** 《often *in*》 take in eagerly through the senses or mind. …을 탄상(嘆賞)하다; 황홀히 보다; 빨려들다. ¶ *Our ears drank in the music.* 우리들의 귀는 음악 소리에 빠져들었다 / *He drank in the beauty of the scene.* 그는 아름다운 경치를 넋을 잃고 바라보았다.

— *vi.* (P1,2A,3) **1** swallow liquid. 물을 마시다. ¶ ~ *from a well* 우물에서 물을 퍼마시다 / ~ *at a spring* 샘물을 떠마시다 / ~ *out of a pail* 통의 물을 마시다. **2** drink alcoholic liquor habitually or too much. (습관적·과도하게) 술을 마시다; 음주벽이 있다. ¶ ~ *deep* 〔*hard, like a fish*〕 과음하다; 통음하다 / ~ *by the lips* 술을 찔끔찔끔 마시다 / ~ *to one's heart's content* 실컷 마시다. **3** absorb. 흡수하다. **4** (of liquid) taste. (마실 것이) …한 맛이 있다〔나다〕. ¶ *This whisky drinks well.* 이 위스키는 맛이 괜찮다.

drink away, lose or spend (money, etc.) by drinkng. …을 술을 마셔 없애다〔소비하다〕. ¶ ~ *away one's fortune* 술 때문에 재산을 날리다.

drink down, **a**) swallow. …을 삼키다; 마시다. **b**) make oneself forget (an unpleasant matter) by drinking wine. 술로 …을 잊다〔달래다〕.

drink in, **a**) absorb. …을 흡수하다. **b**)

take in (something) eagerly through the eyes, etc. (감각을 통해) …을 받아들이다. **c**) be charmed with (beauty). …에 도취되다.
drink off, drink the whole of at once. 단숨에 들이켜다[술잔을 비우다].
drink to, drink in order to show one's respect or hope to (someone or something). …를 위해 축배를 들다.
drink up, **a**) drink off. 꿀꺽 들이켜다; 단숨에 비우다. **b**) suck up; absorb. 빨아 올리다[들이다]; 흡수하다.
—*n.* UC **1** any liquid for drinking; alcoholic liquors. 마실 것; 음료; 술. ¶ *soft drinks* 청량 음료수 / *strong* ~ 술; 화주 / *food and* ~ 음식물 / *be fond of* ~ 술을 좋아하다 / *be given to* ~ 술에 빠지다 / *take to* ~ 술꾼이 되다. **2** U the state of being drunk. 취함; 명정(酩酊). **3** C a draft; a potion. (술) 한 잔. ¶ *have a* ~ 한잔하다 / *stand him a* ~ 그에게 한잔 사다. **4** 《usu. *the* ~》《*sl.*》 a large body of water. (호수·바다·강 따위의) 물. ¶ *jump into the* ~ 물 속에 뛰어들다. [E.]
a drink of, a mouthful of; a cup, glass, etc. of. 한입의; 한모금의; 한잔의.
in drink, drunk. (술에) 취하여.
on the drink, giving way to drinking. 항상 술을 마시고. ¶ *be on the* ~ 술취해 있다.

drink·a·ble [dríŋkəbəl] *adj.* suitable for drinking. 마셔도 좋은. —*n.* 《usu. *pl.*》 something to drink. 마실 것; 음료.

drink·er [dríŋkər] *n.* C **1** a person who drinks. 마시는 사람. **2** a person who drinks alcoholic liquor habitually or too much. (상습적인) 음주가; 술꾼. ¶ *a hard* [*heavy*] ~ 술고래; 주호(酒豪).

drink·ing [dríŋkiŋ] *n.* U the habit of taking alcoholic liquor. 음주. ¶ *be given to* ~ 술에 빠지다 / *give up* ~ 술을 끊다 / *be too fond of* ~ 술을 너무 좋아하다.

drink·ing-foun·tain [dríŋkiŋfàuntin] *n.* a device for providing a supply of drinking-water in public places. (분수식) 물 마시는 곳.

·**drip** [drip] *v.* (**dripped** or **dript, drip·ping**) *vi.* (P1,2A,3) **1** 《*from*》 let drops fall; fall in drops. (물방울이) 똑똑 떨어지다; 물방울이 떨어지다. ¶ ~ *from the trees* 나무에서 물방울이 듣다 / *Your umbrella drips.* 네 우산에서 물방울이 떨어진다. **2** be wet enough to shed drops. 물방울이 떨어질 정도로 흠뻑 젖다. ¶ *His coat was dripping.* 그의 코트가 흠씬 젖어 물방울이 떨어지고 있었다. —*vt.* (P6) let (liquid) fall in drops. …을 똑똑 떨어뜨리다. ¶ *her finger dripping blood* 피가 똑똑 떨어지는 손가락.
dripping wet, very wet. 흠뻑 젖은.
—*n.* C a falling in drops; 《often *pl.*》 liquid that falls in drops. 방울져 떨어짐; 물방울. [E.]

drip·ping [drípiŋ] *n.* CU anything that drops; 《often *pl.*》 the fat and juices melted from roasted meat. 똑똑 떨어지는 것; (불고기에서) 똑똑 떨어지는 국물. [↑]

dripping pan [⌐-⌐] *n.* a shallow pan in which meat is roasted; a pan for catching the dripping from roasting meat. (얇은) 고기구이판; (불고기의) 기름받이.

drip·stone [drípstòun] *n.* 《archit.》 projections over or round windows or door to prevent drip. 빗물막이돌.

dript [dript] *v.* p. and pp. of **drip.**

⁑**drive** [draiv] *v.* (**drove, driv·en**) *vt.* (P6,7,13,18,20) **1** cause to move by force; compel to go onward; send; expel. (마소 따위)를 몰다; 앞으로 가게 하다; 몰아[쫓아]내다. ¶ ~ *cattle to pasture* 소를 목장으로 몰다 / ~ *away flies* 파리를 쫓다 / ~ *the enemy out of the town* 시에서 적군을 물리치다 / ~ *someone to the wall* [*into a corner*] 아무를 궁지로 몰(아 넣)다 / *He was driven from* [*out of*] *the house.* 그는 집에서 내쫓겼다. **2** put (a car, carriage, etc.) in motion; operate; control. …을 운전[조종]하다; 몰다. ¶ ~ *a horse* 말을 몰다 / ~ *a car* [*lorry, bus*] 차[트럭, 버스]를 몰다 / ~ *a train* 열차를 운전하다. **3** take or carry (someone or something) in a vehicle [car]; convey. …을 차로 나르다; 태우다. ¶ ~ *one's produce to market* 농산물을 시장까지 운반하다 / *I'll* ~ *you home* [*to your house*]. 집에까지 태워다 주지. **4** force; compel; bring to a state or condition. …하지 않을 수 없게 하다; …한 상태로 만들다. ¶ ~ *someone mad* [*to madness*] 아무를 미치게 하다 / ~ *someone to desperation* 아무를 자포자기가 되게 하다 / *Hunger drove her to steal.* 굶주림이 그녀로 하여금 도둑질을 하게 했다 / *Ambition drove him to crime.* 야심이 그를 범죄로 이끌었다. **5** 《usu. in *passive*》 (of steam, gasoline, etc.) make (a machine) move. (동력 따위가 기계)를 움직이다. ¶ *a machine driven by steam* [*electricity*] 증기[전동]식 기계 / *A motorboat is driven by a gasoline engine.* 모터보트는 휘발유 발동기로 움직인다 / *Wind drives the mill.* 제분기는 풍력으로 가동된다. **6** force (someone) to work very hard. …를 무리하게 부려먹다; 혹사하다. ¶ ~ *someone hard* [*unmercifully*] 아무를 혹사하다. **7** cause to go into or through; force into. (못)을 쳐박다; (머리)에 주입시키다; 찌르다. ¶ ~ *a nail into a board* 널빤지에 못을 박다 / ~ *a lesson into a child's head* 아이 머리 속에 학과를 주입시키다 / ~ *a dagger into someone's back* 아무의 등을 단도로 찌르다. **8** dash; throw. …을 부딪치다; 내동댕이치다. ¶ *The wind drove the ship onto the rocks.* 바람으로 배가 암초에 부딪쳤다. **9** carry on with vigor; carry through. (사업 따위)를 활발히 하다; 운영하다; 추진하다. ¶ ~ *a roaring trade* 번창하는 장사를 하다 / ~ *a good bargain* 괜찮은 흥정을 하다. **10** make by digging, breaking, leveling, etc.; construct. (굴·갱 따위)를 파다; 뚫다; (철도)를 부설하다. ¶ ~ *a tunnel* 터널을 뚫다 / ~ *a* *well* 우물을 파다 / ～ *a railway through the desert* 사막을 질러 철도를 부설하다. **11** 《sports》 strike (a ball) with force. (볼)을 강타하다. ── *vi.* (P1,2A,3) **1** go in a car, etc. 차로 가다; 드라이브하다. ¶ ～ *away* 차로 떠나다 / ～ *to the lake* 차를 타고 호수로 드라이브하다 / *Will you walk or* ～ *?* 걷겠나 차로 가겠나 / *They got into a car and drove off.* 그들은 차에 올라타고 떠났다. **2** drive a car. 차를 운전하다. ¶ *learn how to* ～ 운전하는 법을 배우다 / *Can you* ～ *?* 차를 운전할 줄 아나. **3** dash; rush; go forward violently. 돌진하다; 질주하다. ¶ *The ship drove across the waves.* 배는 물결을 헤치며 나아갔다.

drive at, mean; intend; aim at. …을 의미하다; 의도하다; 겨냥하다. ¶ *I cannot understand what you are driving at?* 무슨 말씀을 하시려는 건지 이해 못 하겠습니다.

drive away, **a**) send off. 쫓아버리다. **b**) go away in a car. 차를 몰고 가다.

drive away at, 《*colloq.*》 work very hard at. …을 열심히 하다.

drive home, **a**) strike in (a nail) as far as it can go. (못을) 깊이 박다. **b**) impress (an argument) on the mind of a hearer or reader. 충분히 납득시키다; 통감시키다. ¶ ～ *the point home to someone* 요점을 아무에게 잘 이해시키다.

drive out, **a**) go out in a car. 차〔마차〕를 타고 가다. **b**) push away. 밀어제치다.

drive up, come or go up (in a car, etc.); approach; come alongside. (차 따위를 타고) 오다; 가다; 다가오다. ¶ *He drove up (to a hotel).* (호텔로) 차를 몰고 왔다.

let drive at, aim (a blow or shot) at; strike or shoot at. …을 노리어 치다〔발포하다〕; …을 공격하다. ¶ *He let* ～ *at me with a book.* 그는 나에게 책을 던졌다.

── *n.* **1** Ⓤ the act of driving. 차를 몲〔달림〕. **2** ⓊⒸ a fast, hard blow. 타격. **3** Ⓒ a trip in a car, carriage, etc. 드라이브(여행). ¶ *a three hours'* ～, 3시간의 드라이브 / *take* 〔*go for*〕 *a* ～ 드라이브를 하다〔드라이브 여행을 떠나다〕 / *enjoy one's* ～ 드라이브를 즐기다. **4** Ⓒ a short road for cars. 차도(車道). 參考 문에서 현관까지의 짧은 길. **5** Ⓤ energy; vigor. 기력; 활력. ¶ *a man with* ～ 진취적 기상이 넘치는 사람. **6** Ⓤ an effort for some special purpose; Ⓒ a campaign. (특별 목적을 위한) 노력; …운동. ¶ *start a* ～ *to raise money for charity* 자선 기금 모집을 위한 운동을 시작하다. [E.]

drive-in [dráivìn] *n.* Ⓒ 《U.S.》 a place where people can eat, shop, attend movies, etc. while in their cars. 차 탄 채 들어가게 된 곳《식당·영화관 따위》; 드라이브인. ── *adj.* of, pertaining to, or characteristic of such an establishment. 드라이브인 식의. ¶ *a* ～ *theater* 〔*bank*〕 차를 탄 채 들어가는 극장〔은행〕.

driv·el [drívəl] *vi.* (**-eled, -el·ing** or 《Brit.》 **-elled, -el·ling**) (P1,2A,3) **1** let liquid run from the mouth; flow from the mouth like liquid. 침〔콧물〕을 흘리다; 침처럼 흘리다. **2** talk childish nonsense. 철부지〔어린애〕 같은 소리를 하다. ¶ *a driveling idiot* 완전한 바보. ── *n.* Ⓤ **1** liquid running from the mouth. 흐르는 침. **2** stupid, foolish talk. 바보 같은 소리; 잠꼬대. ¶ *say endless* ～ 잠꼬대 같은 소리를 장황하게 늘어놓다. [E.]

driv·el·er, 《Brit.》 **-el·ler** [drívələr] *n.* Ⓒ a person who talks nonsense. 잠꼬대 같은 소리를 하는 사람; 바보.

:driv·en [drívən] *v.* pp. of **drive.**

:driv·er [dráivər] *n.* Ⓒ **1** a person who drives a car, carriage, railway engine, etc. 모는 사람; 운전사; 마부; 조종자; 기관사. **2** a person who makes other people work hard. (아랫사람을 혹사하는) 감독; 우두머리. **3** a golf club with a wooden head. 드라이버《장타를 날리는 골프채》. **4** 《mech.》 a wheel which drives. 동륜(動輪); 구동륜(驅動輪). **5** =pile driver; screwdriver. [*drive*]

drive·way [dráivwèi] *n.* Ⓒ 《chiefly U.S.》 **1** a road for automobiles to drive on. 자동차 도로; 드라이브 웨이. **2** a private road leading from a garage, house, or other building to the street. (차고·집에서 큰 거리로 통하는) 사도(私道).

driv·ing belt [dráiviŋ bèlt] *n.* Ⓒ 《mech.》 a belt that carries motion from an engine to machinery. (기계의) 벨트; 피대.

driz·zle [drízl] *vi.* (P1) rain in as small drops as mist. 이슬비가 내리다〔부슬부슬 오다〕. ── *n.* Ⓤ a rain of this kind. 이슬비; 가랑비. ● **driz·zly** [-i] *adv.* [E.]

droll [droul] *adj.* queer; funny; amusing. 기묘한; 진묘(珍妙)한; 우스운; 재미있는. ¶ *a* ～ *expression* 괘사스러운 표현. ── *n.* Ⓒ a droll person. 익살맞은 사람. [F.]

droll·er·y [dróuləri] *n.* ⓊⒸ laughable talk or tricks; a doll quality or manner. 우스운 이야기〔짓거리〕; 우스움; 익살(맞음). [↑]

drom·e·dar·y [drámidèri, drʌ́m- / drɔ́m-] *n.* Ⓒ (*pl.* **-dar·ies**) a swift camel for riding, usu. with one hump. 단봉(單峯) 낙타. [Gk. *dromas* runner]

drone[1] [droun] *n.* Ⓒ **1** a male honeybee. (꿀벌의) 수펄. **2** a person who does not like to work. 빈둥대는 사람; 게으름뱅이. ── *vi.* spend time idly. 빈둥거리며 시간을 보내다. [E.]

drone[2] [droun] *vi.* (P1,2A,3) **1** make a low, continuous, humming sound. 윙윙거리다. ¶ *droning bees* 윙윙대는 벌. **2** talk in a monotonous voice. 단조로운 목소리로 이야기하다. ── *vt.* (P6,7) utter (words) in a low, monotonous voice. …을 청승맞은 소리로 이야기〔노래〕하다; 단조롭게 말하다. ── *n.* Ⓒ a low, continuous humming sound. 윙윙거리는 소리; 단조로운 저음(低音). [E.]

droop [dru:p] *vi.* (P1,2A,3) **1** hang down;

sink down. 고개를 떨구다; 고개를 숙이다; 축 늘어지다. ¶ *The flowers drooped in the sun.* 꽃들이 햇볕에 축 늘어졌다 / *The heavy snow made the branches* ~. 많은 눈으로 나뭇가지가 축 처졌다. **2** become weak; lose strength; become discouraged. 약해지다; 기운이 없어지다. ¶ *Children* ~ *in hot weather.* 아이들은 더운 날씨에 기운을 잃는다 / *The girl drooped with sorrow.* 소녀는 슬퍼서 맥이 풀렸다.
— *vt.* (P6) let (one's eyes, neck, etc.) hang or sink down. (눈)을 내리깔다; (고개 따위)를 숙이다〔떨구다〕; 처지게 하다. ¶ *She drooped her head.* 그녀는 고개를 숙였다.
— *n.* Ⓒ the state of drooping. 수그러짐; 축 처짐; 의기 소침.
●**droop·ing·ly** [-iŋli] *adv.* [Scand.]

:drop [drɑp / drɔp] *v.* (**dropped, drop·ping**) *vi.* (P1,2A,3,5) **1** fall. 떨어지다. ¶ *An apple dropped from the tree.* 사과가 나무에서 떨어졌다. **2** fall in drops. (물방울이) 뚝뚝 떨어지다; 적하(滴下)하다. ¶ *Rain drops from the clouds.* 비는 구름에서 내린다 / *The tears dropped from her eyes.* 그녀 눈에서 눈물이 흘러 떨어졌다. **3** ⓐ fall suddenly; fall dead, wounded, etc. (죽음·부상 따위로) 픽 쓰러지다; 죽다. ¶ *The wounded man dropped dead.* 부상자는 픽 쓰러져 죽었다 / ~ *with tiredness* 피로로 쓰러지다. ⓑ let oneself fall gently; sit. 넘어지다; 주저앉다. ¶ ~ *to the ground* 〔*floor*〕 땅〔바닥〕에 넘어지다 / ~ *on* 〔*to*〕 *one's knee*(*s*) 맥없이 무릎을 꿇다 / ~ *into the chair* 의자에 주저앉다. **4** have a sudden fall or decent. 갑자기 떨어지다. ¶ ~ *off a cliff* 벼랑에서 굴러떨어지다 / *A pin could* 〔*might*〕 *be heard to* ~. 핀이 떨어져도 들릴 만큼 조용하다. **5** go down. 내려가다; 내리다. ¶ ~ *safely from a window* 창문에서 안전하게 내리다. **6** become lower in amount, degree, etc. 내려가다; 떨어지다; 낮아지다. ¶ *The temperature suddenly dropped.* 기온이 갑자기 떨어졌다 / *The price* 〔*wind*〕 *dropped.* 값이〔풍세(風勢)가〕 떨어졌다 / *Her voice dropped to a whisper.* 그녀의 목소리는 속삭임으로 낮아졌다. **7** come to an end; stop. 끝나다; 멈추다. ¶ *There the matter dropped.* 거기서 일은 끝났다 / *Let the quarrel* ~. 말다툼을 그만두자. **8** come into a certain state. (어떤 상태로) 되다. ¶ ~ *asleep* 잠에 빠지다 / ~ *into oblivion* 잊혀지다 / ~ *into a habit* 부지중 버릇이 붙다. **9** drop behind. 낙오하다; 뒤처지다. — *vt.* (P6,13) **1** let (something) fall. …을 떨어뜨리다. ¶ ~ *a book* 〔*cup*〕 책〔컵〕을 떨어뜨리다 / ~ *one's purse* 돈지갑을 떨어뜨리다. **2** let (liquid) fall in drops. …을 뚝뚝 떨어뜨리다; 주루루 흘리다. ¶ ~ *lemon juice into tea* 레몬즙을 홍차에 몇 방울 넣다 / ~ *sweat* 〔*blood*〕 땀을〔피를〕 흘리다 / *She dropped tears over his death.* 그녀는 그의 죽음에 눈물을 흘렸다. **3** cause to fall by a blow, shot, etc. …을 때려눕히다; 쏘아 떨어뜨리다. ¶ ~ *someone with a blow* 일격에 쓰러뜨리다 / ~ *a couple of birds* 새 몇 마리를 쏘아 떨어뜨리다. **4** ⓐ put an end to; give up; stop. …을 끝내다; 단념하다; 그만두다; 멈추다. ¶ ~ *one's plan* 계획을 단념하다 / ~ *one's conquering air* 위압적인 태도를 버리다 / ~ *the habit of smoking* 담배 피우는 버릇을 버리다 / ~ *the subject* 그 화제를 그만두다 / *His sponsors dropped him.* 후원자들은 그를 포기했다. ⓑ cease to keep up or have to do with; dismiss. …와 관계를 끊다; 해고〔퇴학〕시키다. ¶ ~ *an acquaintance* 절교하다 / *be dropped from the club* 클럽에서 내쫓기다. **5** write or send hastily. …을 써 보내다; 전하다. ¶ *Drop me a line.* 몇 자 소식 좀 보내 주십시오. **6** let fall by chance; say casually. 넌지시 입밖에 내다. ¶ ~ *a comment* 무심코 비평하다 / ~ *a hint* 〔*suggestion*〕 넌지시 힌트〔암시〕를 주다. **7** make lower in amount, degree, etc. …을 낮추다. ¶ *He dropped his voice to a whisper.* 그는 목소리를 낮춰 속삭였다. **8** let (someone) out of car. …를 차에서 내리다; 하차시키다. ¶ *Drop me* (*off*) *at the next corner.* 다음 길 모퉁이에서 내려 주시오. **9** fail to pronounce or write; omit. (발음·철자에서 어떤 음·글자)를 빠뜨리다; 빼먹다. ¶ ~ *a letter from a word* 낱말에서 글자 하나를 빠뜨리다 / ~ *one's h's in speaking* 말할 때 'h'를 발음하지 않다. **10** 《*sl.*》 lose (money, esp. in gambling). (도박 따위에서 돈)을 잃다. **11** (of animal) give birth to. (새끼)를 낳다.

be ready* 〔*fit*〕 *to drop, be exhausted. 몹시 지치다; 녹초가 되다.

drop across, **a**) meet (someone) by chance; come across (someone). 우연히 …와 만나다. **b**) scold. …을 꾸짖다.

drop away, drop off. 한 사람 한 사람 떠나버리다; 점차 없어지다.

drop behind, be left behind; fall behind. 뒤떨어지다; 낙오〔낙후〕하다.

drop down, **a**) fall to the rear; cease. 쓰러지다; 그치다. **b**) move down a stream with the current. (조류나 순풍을 타고) …을 내려가다; 강을 내려가다.

drop in* 〔*by*〕*, pay a sudden, unexpected visit (to someone). 불쑥 들르다.

drop in on, visit (someone) without warining, informally. …을 불시에 방문하다; 불쑥 들르다.

drop in with, meet (someone) by chance. …을 우연히 만나다.

Drop it ! Stop it ! 이제 그만 해라.

drop off, **a**) go away one by one; disappear. 한 사람 한 사람씩 떠나버리다; 사라지다. **b**) become less; decrease. 점차 줄다. ¶ *The audience began to* ~ *off.* 관중이 줄어들기 시작했다 / *Sales are dropping off.* 매상이 줄고 있다. **c**) fall asleep. 잠들다. **d**) get down from a vehicle. 차에서 내리다. **e**) fall down one after another and die. 차례로 쓰러져 죽다.

drop on [***upon***], scold (someone) severely; blame. 호되게 견책하다[꾸짖다]; 비난하다.
drop out, **a**) stop coming to class. (학생이) 탈락하다. **b**) disappear from; leave. 사라지다; 떠나다. **c**) stop being a member of; cease to take part in. …에서 손을 떼다; 그만두다.
— ***n.*** Ⓒ **1** a small fall of liquid. (똑똑 떨어지는) 물방울. ¶ ~ *by* ~ 한 방울 한 방울씩 / *a ~ of rain* [*dew, blood*] 비[이슬, 피] 한 방울. **2** a very small quantity. 미량; 극히 조금. ¶ *I have not taken a ~ of water.* 물 한 방울 안 마셨다. **3** anything like a drop in shape. 물방울 모양의 것. ¶ *fruit drops* 과일 드롭스. **4** a sudden fall. 급락(急落); 갑자기 낮아짐. ¶ *a ~ in prices* 물가의 급락 / *a sudden ~ in one's voice* 목소리가 갑자기 낮아짐. **5** the length of a fall. 낙하 거리. ¶ *a ~ of 250 feet,* 250 피트의 낙차. [E.]
a drop in the ocean [***bucket***], a very small amount compared to the whole; an insignificant contribution. 창해 일속(滄海一粟); 극소량; 극히 미미한 공헌.
at the drop of a hat, at once; without delay. (극히 작은 자극·도발에도) 즉각; 지체없이.
get [***have***] ***the drop on,*** **a**) draw a gun and point it at someone. 상대보다 권총을 먼저 뽑아들다. **b**) get quickly into a more favorable position than someone. 기선을 잡다; (상대)보다 우위에 서다.
have a drop in one's eye, show signs of having drunk. 얼굴에 취기가 돌다.
take a drop, have a drink. 한잔하다. ¶ *have* [*take*] *a ~ too much* 술에 취하다

drop curtain [⌐ ⌐–] ***n.*** 《theatr.》 a painted curtain lowered from a roller. (무대의) 현수막.

drop·let [drάplit / drɔ́p-] ***n.*** Ⓒ a small drop. 작은 물방울.

drop-off [drάpɔ̀:f / drɔ́pɔ̀f] ***n.*** **1** a steep or perpendicular descent. 급사면(急斜面); 수직적인 하강(下降). **2** a marked decline. 두드러진 감소. ¶ *a ~ in attendance* 참석자의 뚜렷한 감소.

drop·out [drάpàut / drɔ́p-] ***n.*** Ⓒ a person who drops out, esp. a student who leaves college before completing it. 탈락자; 탈퇴자; (특히) 중도 퇴학자.

drop·ping [drάpiŋ / drɔ́p-] ***n. pl.*** **1** something which is dropped. 똑똑 떨어지는[듣는] 것. **2** dung of animals. (새·짐승의) 똥; 분(糞).

drop·si·cal [drάpsikəl / drɔ́p-] ***adj.*** 《med.》 of or like dropsy; suffering from dropsy. 수종(水腫)의[같은]; 수종[부종]에 걸린. [Gk.]

drop·sy [drάpsi / drɔ́p-] ***n.*** Ⓤ 《med.》 an unnatural collection of watery fluid in some part of the body. 수종(水腫). [↑]

drosh·ky [drάʃki / drɔ́ʃ-], **dros·ky** [drάski / drɔ́s-] ***n.*** **1** a light, low, four-wheeled open carriage used in Russia. (러시아의) 무개(無蓋) 4륜 마차. **2** a light two-wheeled carriage in German Towns. (독일의) 경장(輕裝) 2륜 마차. [Russ.]

dross [drɔ:s, drαs / drɔs] ***n.*** **1** Ⓤ waste material formed on the surface of melting metals. (녹은 주물에) 뜬 찌끼; 불순물. **2** worthless stuff. 무가치한 것. [E.]

dross·y [drɔ́:si, drάsi / drɔ́si] ***adj.*** worthless. 무가치한.

drought [draut] ***n.*** ⓊⒸ **1** a long period of dry weather. 가뭄; 한발. ¶ *a prolonged ~* 오래 계속되는 가뭄. **2** Ⓤ lack of water; dryness. (대기 따위의) 건조; 마름. [*dry*]

drought·y [dráuti] ***adj.*** (**drought·i·er, drought·i·est**) **1** suffering from drought. 가뭄의. **2** dry; lacking water. 건조한; 말라붙은.

drouth [drauθ] ***n.*** 《*poet.*》 =drought.

:**drove**[1] [drouv] ***v.*** p. of **drive.**

drove[2] [drouv] ***n.*** Ⓒ **1** a large group of cattle, sheep, etc. moving together. (무리를 지어 움직이는 소·양 따위) 가축의 떼. **2** a crowd of people. 군중. [*drive*]

dro·ver [dróuvər] ***n.*** Ⓒ a man who takes cattle, sleep, etc., to market; a dealer in cattle. (소·양 따위) 가축을 시장으로 몰고 가는 사람; 가축상(商).

:**drown** [draun] ***vi.*** (P1) die under water. 물에 빠져 죽다; 익사하다. ¶ *fall in the water and ~* 물에 빠져 익사하다. — ***vt.*** (P6,7,13) **1** ⓐ kill (someone) by keeping him under water. …을 익사시키다. ¶ *~ a cat* 고양이를 익사시키다 / *get* [*be*] *drowned* 익사하다 / *~ oneself in the river* 강에 투신자살하다 / *He was drowned while trying to rescue the boy from the river.* 그는 강에 빠진 아이를 구출하려다가 익사하였다. ⓑ cover with or as if with a liquid. 물 따위로 적시다; 흠뻑 젖게 하다. ¶ *eyes drowned in tears* 눈물에 젖은 눈 / *like a drowned rat* 물에 빠진 생쥐처럼; 흠뻑 젖어. **2** cause (a sound) not to be heard by making a larger sound. (소리)를 들리지 않게 하다. ¶ *His voice was drowned by the coughing of the audience.* 그의 목소리는 청중의 기침 소리로 들리지가 않았다. **3** cause oneself to forget (something) by drinking. …을 술로 달래다[잊다]. ¶ *~ one's sorrows in drink* 슬픔을 술로 달래다. [E.]

drowse [drauz] ***vi.*** (P1) be sleepy; be half asleep; doze. 졸리다; 꾸벅꾸벅 졸다. ¶ *~ during class* 수업 시간에 졸다. — ***vt.*** (P6,7) 《*away*》 make (someone) sleepy; spend (time) in drowsing. …을 졸리게 하다; 꾸벅꾸벅 졸게 하다; (시간)을 흐리멍덩하게 보내다. ¶ *~ away the summer afternoon* 여름 오후를 어물어물 보내다. — ***n.*** Ⓤ 《sometimes *a* ~ 》 the condition of being half asleep; doze. 졸음; 겉잠. [E.]

drow·sy** [dráuzi] ***adj. (**-si·er, -si·est**) **1** half asleep; sleepy. 졸린; 졸음이 오는. ¶ *feel ~* 졸리다. **2** making half asleep. 졸리게 하는. **3** caused by sleepiness. 잠에 기인하는. ● **drow·si·ly** [-li] ***adv.*** **drow·si·ness**

[-nis] *n.* [↑]

drub [drʌb] *vt.* (**drubbed, drub·bing**) (P6, 13) **1** beat (someone) with a stick; beat. …을 막대기[몽둥이]로 치다; 때리다. **2** defeat (someone) soundly in a fight, game, etc. …을 패배시키다. ●**drub·ber** [drʌ́bər] *n.* [Turk.]

drub·bing [drʌ́biŋ] *n.* Ⓤ Ⓒ **1** a beating. (몽둥이로) 때려 누임; 몹시 때림. **2** a thorough defeat. (게임·경기 따위에서의) 결정적 패배; 대패.

drudge [drʌdʒ] *n.* Ⓒ a person who works hard at tiresome, unpleasant tasks. (고되고 재미없는) 일을 꾸준히 해내는 사람. —*vi.* (P1,2A,3) 《*at*》 work like a drudge. (고된 일에) 꾸준히 정진하다. ¶ ~ *at dictionary-making.* 사전 편찬에 정진하다. [? E.]

drudg·er·y [drʌ́dʒəri] *n.* Ⓤ (*pl.* **-er·ies**) hard, uninteresting, or unpleasant work. 고된 일; 싫은 일. [↑]

***drug** [drʌg] *n.* Ⓒ **1** any substance used as a medicine. 약(품). **2** a habit-forming medical substance used to lessen pain or cause sleep. 마약; 마취제. ¶ *a ~ addict* 마약 중독자 / *go on drugs* 마약을 계속하다. **3** an article which is no longer in demand because it is too plentiful. (공급이 수요를 웃돌아) 팔리지 않는 물건.

—*vt.* (**drugged, drug·ging**) (P6) **1** mix harmful drugs in (food, etc.). (음식 따위)에 독약[마약]을 타다[섞다]. ¶ ~ *someone's wine* 아무의 포도주에 독약을 넣다. **2** give (harmful) drugs to (someone). …에게 독약[마약]을 먹이다. **3** affect (the body or senses) in an unnatural way. …을 마비[마취]시키다.

—*vi.* (P1) be in the habit of taking drugs. 마약을 상용하다. [F. *drogue*]

drug·get [drʌ́git] *n.* a coarse woolen floor-covering. (깔개용) 거친 직물《조모(粗毛)에 솜·황마 따위를 섞어 짬》. [F.]

drug·gist [drʌ́gist] *n.* Ⓒ **1** a person who sells drugs, medicines, etc. 약종상(藥種商). **2** 《U.S.》 a person who has a license to make medicine according to a doctor's direction. 약사(藥師) (cf. 《Brit.》 *chemist*).

drug·store [drʌ́gstɔ̀:r] *n.* Ⓒ 《U.S.》 a store where drugs, cigarettes, ice cream, etc. are sold. 드러그스토어《약 외에 화장품·담배·잡지 등을 팔며, 가벼운 식사·음료 따위를 마시는 설비가 되어 있음》.

dru·id, Dru·id [drúːid] *n.* one of an order of priests among the ancient Celts of Britain, Ireland, and France. 드루이드《Britain, Ireland 및 프랑스의 옛 켈트족 사이에 신앙된 드루이드교의 사제》. [Celt.]

:drum [drʌm] *n.* Ⓒ **1** a musical instrument that makes a sound when beaten. 드럼; 북. ¶ *beat a march on the ~* 진군의 북을 울리다. **2** the sound made by a drum; any sound like this. 북 소리; 그 비슷한 소리. **3** any drumlike object. 북 같은 것. **4** a drumlike part of a machine. (기계의) 원통부(圓筒部).

—*vt.* (**drummed, drum·ming**) (P6,7,13) **1** play (music, etc.) on a drum. (곡)을 드럼으로 연주하다. **2** beat, tap, or strike again and again. …을 둥둥 두드리다. ¶ ~ *the table with one's fingers* 손가락으로 테이블을 통통 두드리다. **3** 《*into*》 train by repeating. …을 (귀가 아프도록) 되풀이해 주입시키다. ¶ ~ *complaints into someone's ears* 시끄럽게 잔소리를 퍼붓다 / ~ *Latin into a boy('s head)* 아이 머릿속에 라틴어를 주입시키다.

—*vi.* (P1,2A,3) **1** beat a drum. 북을 치다. **2** beat rhythmically over and over again. 둥둥 두드리다. **3** make a sound like that of a drum. 북과 같은 소리를 내다. [E.]

drum someone out of, send someone away from (a club, etc.) in disgrace. …를 (클럽 따위)에서 쫓아내다; 추방[제명]하다. ¶ *The beggars were drummed out of town.* 거지들은 마을에서 쫓겨났다.

drum up, call (customers, etc.) together by drumming; collect; gather. 북을 울려 …을 모으다.

drum·beat [drʌ́mbìːt] *n.* Ⓒ a sound produced by beating a drum. 북 소리.

drum·fire [drʌ́mfàiər] *n.* heavy continuously rapid artillery fire. 연속 집중 포화.

drum·head [drʌ́mhèd] *n.* the skin of a drum. 북 가죽.

drum major [⌐ ⌐] *n.* a person who leads a marching band. 군악대장; (연대의) 고수장(鼓手長).

drum·mer [drʌ́mər] *n.* Ⓒ **1** a person who plays a drum. 고수(鼓手); 드럼 연주자. **2** 《U.S.》 a traveling salesman. 지방 순회 판매원.

drum·stick [drʌ́mstìk] *n.* Ⓒ **1** a stick for beating a drum. 북채. **2** the lower part of the leg of a cooked chicken, turkey, etc. (요리한 닭·칠면조 따위의) 아랫다리.

***drunk** [drʌŋk] *v.* pp. of **drink.**

—*adj.* 《as *predicative*》 **1** overcome by alcoholic drink; intoxicated. 술 취한. ¶ *get ~* 취하다 / *be beastly (blind, dead) ~* 억병으로 취해 있다 / *He was so ~ that he could not stand up.* 몹시 취해 일어설 수가 없었다. **2** deeply moved; very excited. (강렬한 감정·감동으로) 도취한; 흥분한. ¶ *be ~ with success* 성공에 도취해 있다 / *He is ~ with power.* 권력에 도취되어 있다.

(***as***) ***drunk as a lord (fiddler, fish, pig),*** very drunk. 곤드레만드레 취한.

—*n.* Ⓒ **1** a drunken person. 취한(醉漢); 술고래. **2** a drinking party. 술잔치; 주연(酒宴). [*drink*]

drunk·ard [drʌ́ŋkərd] *n.* Ⓒ a person who is often drunk or who drinks too much. 대주가(大酒家); 모주(꾼); 주정뱅이. [↑]

·drunk·en [drʌ́ŋkən] *adj.* 《as *attributive*》 **1** drunk. 술 취한; 모주의(opp. sober). ¶ *a ~ driver* 음주 운전자 / *a ~ old scoundrel* 술 취한 악한. **2** caused by or resulting from a drunken condition. 술로 인한. ¶ *a ~ brawl* 취중(醉中)에 벌어진 싸움. ●**drunk·en·ly** [-li] *adv.*

drunk·en·ness [drʌ́ŋkənnis] *n.* Ⓤ the state or habit of being drunk. 취태(醉態); 대취; 명정(酩酊).

drunk·om·e·ter [drʌŋkámitər / -kɔ́mi-] *n.* Ⓒ a breath analyser. (날숨에 의한) 음주〔량〕 측정기. [*drink*]

drupe [dru:p] *n.* Ⓒ 《bot.》 a fruit with a hard, stone-like seed surrounded by a soft, fleshy part, such as plums and peaches. 핵과(核果); 다육과(多肉果). [Gk.]

:dry [drai] *adj.* (**dri·er, dri·est**) **1**. ⓐ not wet; not moist. 마른; 건조한. ¶ *~ air* 건조한 공기 / *~ fish* 건어(乾魚) / *a ~ towel* 마른 수건 / *a ~ cough* 마른 기침 / *~ provisions* 건성(乾性) 식료품(食料品). ⓑ not using water. 물을 사용치 않는. ¶ *~ cleaning* 드라이 클리닝 / *a ~ shaver* 전기 면도기. **2** (of a well or cow) not yielding water or milk. 물이 말라붙은; 젖이 안 나오는. ¶ *a ~ cow* 젖이 안 나오는 젖소 / *a ~ river* 말라붙은 강 / *run ~* 물이 마르다 / *The well is ~.* 우물이 말라붙었다 / *The cow has gone ~.* 소의 젖이 말라 안 나온다. **3** (of climate, weather) without rain. 비가 오지 않는; 건조한. ¶ *a ~ season* 갈수기(渴水期); 건조기 / *a ~ climate* 비가 적은 기후 / *a ~ winter* 이상 건조의 겨울. **4** 《*colloq.*》 (of men) thirsty; wanting a drink. 목마른; 목이 타는. ¶ *feel ~* 목이 마르다. **5** not shedding tears; showing no feeling. 눈물을 흘리지 않는; 감정을 나타내지 않는. ¶ *a ~ sob* 눈물을 흘리지 않고 우는 흐느낌 / *with ~ eyes* 눈물을 흘리지 않고 / *~ thanks* 인사 치레로 하는 감사. **6** (of wine) not sweet. (포도주가) 달지 않은. ¶ *~ sherry* 쌉쌀한 셰리. **7** ⓐ not interesting; dull. 재미없는; 따분한; 무미 건조한. ¶ *a ~ book* 〔*lecture*〕 재미없는 책〔강의〕 / *a ~ subject* 무미 건조한 화제. ⓑ (of jests, humor, etc.) quiet; made to appear accidental. 짐짓 시치미 떼고 말하는; 태연한 얼굴로 하는. ¶ *~ humor* 모르는 체하고 말하는 유머 / *a ~ jest* 짐짓 진지한 얼굴로 하는 농담. **8** (of facts, manner, etc.) plain; unadorned. 꾸밈없는; 있는 그대로의. ¶ *~ facts* 적나라한 사실. **9** without butter, jam, etc. on it. 버터를〔잼을〕 바르지 않은. ¶ *~ toast* 버터를 안 바른 토스트. **10** ⓐ marked by the absence of alcoholic beverages. (파티 따위에) 술이 안 나오는. ⓑ 《U.S.》 forbidding the sale of alcoholic drinks. 금주(禁酒)의; 금주법 시행의(opp. wet). ¶ *a ~ state* 금주법 시행의 주(州) / *go ~* 금주하다; 금주법을 실시하다 / *stay ~* 금주를 지키다.

(as) dry as a bone, absolutely dry. 바싹 마른 (=bone-dry).

die a dry death, die naturally, not by drowning or bloodshed. 자연사(自然死)하다; 제명에 죽다.

— *vt.* (P6,7) make (something) dry; wipe away moisture from (something). …을 말리다〔건조시키다〕; …의 수분을 닦다. ¶ *~ one's eyes* 눈(물)을 닦다 / *~ oneself* 몸을 닦다 / *~ a shirt in the open air* 한데에서 셔츠를 말리다 / *~ one's feet with a towel* 수건으로 발을 닦다 / *~ one's hands on a napkin* 냅킨으로 손을 닦다 / *~ clothes by the fire* 옷을 불에 말리다. **—** *vi.* (P1,2A) become dry; lose moisture. 마르다; 건조하다; 말라붙다. [E.]

dry up, **a**) become completely dry; become intellectually unable to produce. 바싹 마르다; (지식 따위가) 고갈되다. ¶ *The well has dried up.* 우물의 물이 말라붙었다 / *My imagination has not dried up yet.* 나의 상상력은 아직도 고갈되지 않고 있다. **b**) 《*colloq.*》 stop talking 〔speaking〕. 이야기를 그치다.

dry·ad, Dry- [dráiəd, -æd] *n.* Ⓒ (*pl.* **-ads** or **-a·des** [-ədì:z]) 《Gk. myth.》 a goddess who lives in a tree; a spirit of the forest. 숲의 여신; 수목의 정(精). [Gk.]

dry battery [∠∠–] *n.* a dry electric battery. 건전지. [*dry*]

dry-clean [dráiklí:n] *vt.* (P6) clean (clothes etc.) with chemical solvents and not with water. …을 드라이 클리닝하다; 건식 세탁을 하다. [*dry*]

dry cleaning [∠∠–] *n.* the cleaning of cloth without water. 드라이 클리닝; 건식 세탁법.

dry dock [∠∠] *n.* a dock from which the water can be pumped. 드라이〔건(乾)〕독 (cf. *wet dock*).

dry·er [dráiər] *n.* =drier.

dry farming [∠∠–] *n.* a way of farming land in regions where there is no irrigation and little rain. 건지(乾地) 농법《비가 적거나 수리(水利)가 좋지 않은 토지의 경작법》.

dry goods [∠∠] *n.* non-liquid groceries, as cereals; 《U.S.》 drapery; woven fabrics. 곡류(穀類); 잡화류; 직물류; 포목.

dry ice [∠∠] *n.* solidified carbon dioxide. 드라이 아이스《고형(固形) 이산화탄소; 냉각제》.

dry land [∠∠] *n.* land as opposed to sea. 육지.

dry law [∠∠] *n.* 《U.S.》 a law prohibiting the making and selling of alcoholic liquor. 금주법(禁酒法); 알코올 음료 판매 금지법.

dry light [∠∠] *n.* absence of bias. 공평 무사(公平無私).

dry·ly, dri·ly [dráili] *adv.* without emotion; in a dry manner. 냉담하게; 무미 건조하게.

dry measure [∠∠] *n.* a measure of bulk, used esp. for grain. 건량(乾量)《곡물의 계량》.

dry·ness [dráinis] *n.* Ⓤ the state of being dry; lack of emotion. 건조; 냉담; 무미 건조.

dry nurse [´ ˊ] *n.* Ⓒ a nurse who looks after a child without suckling it. 보모(保母)(cf. *wet nurse*).

dry plate [´ ˊ] *n.* 《photog.》 a photographic plate with sensitized film hard and dry. (사진) 건판.

dry·point [dráipɔ̀int] *n.* **1** Ⓤ an engraving made with a hard etching needle that incises fine lines on a metal plate without the use of acid. (조각침(針)에 의한) 동판 조각. **2** Ⓒ a print made from such an engraving. 드라이포인트 동판화.

dry rot [´ ˊ] *n.* **1** 《bot.》 a fungous disease of timber, causing it to crumble to a dry powder. 건부병(乾腐病). **2** any moral decay. (도덕의) 퇴폐.

dry-shod [dráiʃɑ̀d / -ʃɔ̀d] *adj.* without wetting the feet or shoes. 발을〔구두를〕 적시지 않고. ¶ *go* ~ 발을 적시지 않고 가다.

d.s. 《comm.》 days after sight(일람후 …일).

D. Sc. Doctor of Science.

D.S.T., DST Daylight Saving Time(일광 절약 시간).

D-trap [dí:træ̀p] *n.* 《mech.》 a trap of D shape. D형 방취판(防臭瓣).

du·al [djú:əl] *adj.* of two; showing two; having two parts; double; twofold. 둘의; 이중(체)의; 이중성의; 이원적(二元的)인. ¶~ *control* 이중 제어 / *the* ~ (*number*) 쌍수 (cf. *plural*) / *a* ~ *personality* 이중 인격. [L. *duo* two]

dual flying [´– ˊ–] *n.* flying with passengers. 동승(同乘) 비행.

du·al·ism [djú:əlìzəm] *n.* **1** Ⓤ the state of being dual; duality. 이중성(二重性); 이원성(二元性). **2** 《philos.》 the theory that the world can be explained in terms of two basic substances or principles, such as mind and body. 이원설; 이원론.

du·al·ist [djú:əlist] *n.* a believer in dualism. 이원론자.

du·al·i·ty [dju:ǽləti] *n.* ⓊⒸ (*pl.* **-ties**) a dual condition or quality. 이중(성); 이체(二體); 이원성.

dub[1] [dʌb] *vt.* (**dubbed, dub·bing**) **1** (P19) make (someone) a knight by touching him on the shoulder lightly with a sword. 검으로 어깨를 가볍게 두드려 …에게 나이트작(爵)을 수여하다. ¶ ~ *a man knight* 어떤 사람에게 나이트작을 수여하다. **2** (P18, 19) give (someone) a title, nickname, etc. to; call. …에게 칭호를〔별명을〕 주다; …을 —라고 부르다. ¶ ~ *someone a scholar* 아무를 학자라고 부르다. **3** (P6,7) smear (leather) with grease. …에 기름칠을 하다. **4** (P7) dress. 마무르다. [E.]

dub in, insert. 삽입하다.

dub out, make smooth. 매끄럽게〔반드럽게〕 다듬다.

dub[2] [dʌb] *n.* Ⓒ 《sl.》 an awkward, unskillful person. 서투른 사람; 데퉁바리. [E.]

dub[3] [dʌb] *vt.* (**dubbed, dub·bing**) (P6) make a new recording on or for (a film) by adding music, speech, etc. (필름에 음악 따위의) 새 녹음을 하다; 더빙하다. ¶ ~ *a film into Korean* 필름에 한국어 대사를 재녹음하다. — *n.* Ⓤ the sound thus added or altered. 더빙. [*double*]

du·bi·ety [dju(:)báiəti] *n.* Ⓤ the quality or state of being doubtful; uncertainty. 의심스러움; 의념(疑念); 불확실함. [↓]

du·bi·ous [djú:biəs] *adj.* **1** doubtful; uncertain; ambiguous. 의심스러운; 확실치 않은; 애매한(opp. clear, simple). ¶ *a* ~ *answer* 애매한 대답 / ~ *weather* 불안한 날씨 / *The result is still* ~. 결과는 아직 확실치 않다 / *He felt* ~ (*about*) *what to do.* 그는 무엇을 해야 할지 갈피를 못 잡았다. **2** questionable; causing suspicion. 의문의 여지가 있는; 의아〔수상〕한; 의혹을 낳는. ¶ *a* ~ *character* 수상한 인물 / *a* ~ *transaction* 수상한 거래. ●**du·bi·ous·ly** [-li] *adv.* [L. *dubius*]

du·bi·ta·tive [djú:bətèitiv / -tə-] *adj.* **1** doubting. 의심하고 있는; 의아스러운. **2** expressing doubt or hesitation. 의심〔망설임〕을 나타내는. [↑]

Dub·lin [dʌ́blin] *n.* the capital of the Irish Republic. 더블린《아일랜드의 수도》.

du·cal [djú:kəl] *adj.* of a duke or dukedom. 공작(公爵)의; 공작령(領)의. [*duke*]

duc·at [dʌ́kət] *n.* **1** Ⓒ a coin of gold or silver formerly used in Europe. (중세 유럽의) 금화; 은화. **2** 《*pl.*》 money. 돈; 금전. [↑]

du·ce [dú:tʃei / -tʃi] *n.* 《Ital.》 a leader; chief. 지도자; 수령. [↑]

·duch·ess [dʌ́tʃis] *n.* Ⓒ **1** the wife or widow of a duke. 공작 부인; 공작 미망인. **2** a woman with a rank equal to a duke's. 여공작. [*duke*]

duch·y [dʌ́tʃi] *n.* Ⓒ (*pl.* **duch·ies**) the land ruled by a duke or duchess; dukedom. 공국(公國); 공작령(領). [↑]

:duck[1] [dʌk] *n.* Ⓒ **1** a wild or domestic swimming bird; the female duck. (집)오리; 암오리(cf. *drake*). **2** Ⓤ the flesh of a duck. 오리 고기. **3** 《*colloq.*》 a nice, delightful person. 귀여운 사람; 애인. ¶ *What a* ~ *of a child!* 정말이지 귀여운 아이군. **4** 《*sl.*》 a person; a fellow. 놈; 녀석. **5** 《cricket》 zero. (득점) 제로; 영점(=duck's-egg). ¶ *be out for a* ~ 득점치 못하고 아웃이 되다 / *break one's* ~ 최초의 1점을 올리다 / *make a* ~ 무득점으로 아웃이 되다. [E.]

a fine day for (***young***) ***ducks,*** rainy weather. 우천(雨天).

duck(***s***) ***and drake***(***s***)***,*** a game in which flat stones are made to skip along the water. 물수제비뜨기.

in two shakes of a duck's tail, instantly. 순식간에.

like a duck to the water, as a matter of course. 당연히.

like a (***dying***) ***duck in a thunderstorm,*** astonished, with the eyes turned up; helpless. 놀라서; 눈을 희번덕거리며; 당황하여.

like water off a duck's back, with no effect. 아무 효과 없이; 마이 동풍격으로.

make ducks and drakes of money, waste money wildly. 돈을 낭비하다.

take to** something **like a duck to water, learn something naturally and very easily. 극히 자연스럽게 배우다; 수월하게 익히다. ¶ *He took to Latin like a ~ to water.* 그는 수월하게 라틴어를 익혔다.

:duck[2] [dʌk] *vi.* (P1,3) **1** dip suddenly (under water, etc.) for a short time. (물 속에) 쑥 잠기다; 무자맥질하다. **2** lower or move to one side suddenly. 홱 몸을 굽히다 〔피하다〕; 머리를 홱 낮추다. —*vt.* (P6,13) **1** dip (the body, head, etc.) under water for a short time. (몸·머리 따위)를 물 속에 쑥 잠그다. **2** lower (the head, body, etc.) suddenly. (머리·몸 따위)를 홱 낮추다〔숙이다〕.

duck out of, 《*colloq.*》 escape one's responsibility for. …에 대한 책임을 회피하다.

—*n.* Ⓒ the act of ducking. 쑥 무자맥질하기; 홱 낮추기. [E.]

duck[3] [dʌk] *n.* **1** Ⓤ strong cotton or linen cloth. 일종의 즈크. **2** 《*pl.*》 trousers or slacks made of duck. 즈크제(製)의 바지 〔슬랙스〕. [Du. *doeck* linen cloth]

duck[4] [dʌk] *n.* Ⓒ an army truck which can be used both on land and in water. (수륙 양용의) 군용 수송 트럭. [alter. of DUKW, code name]

duck·bill [dʌ́kbìl] *n.* Ⓒ 《zool.》 a small, bird-like water mammal of Australia that lays eggs. 오리너구리. [*duck*[1], *bill*]

duck·board [dʌ́kbɔ̀ːrd] *n.* Ⓒ a board or boardwalk which is laid across wet or muddy ground. 진창에 건너질러 깐 널판자(길). [*duck*[1], *board*]

duck·ing [dʌ́kiŋ] *n.* **1** ⓊⒸ the manner of ducking. 물 속에 처박음; 머리를〔몸을〕 홱 숙임. ¶ *get a good ~* 흠뻑 젖다 / *give someone a ~* 아무를 물 속에 처박다; 아무를 흠뻑 젖게 하다. **2** Ⓤ the sport of hunting wild ducks. 오리 사냥. [*duck*[1]]

duck·ling [dʌ́kliŋ] *n.* Ⓒ a young duck. 새끼오리. [*duck*[1]]

duct [dʌkt] *n.* Ⓒ **1** a tube for carrying water, air, wires, etc. (수송)관(管). **2** 《physiol.》 a tube in the body carrying a bodily liquid like tears. 도관(導管); 샘; 선(腺). ¶ *a tear ~* 눈물샘. [L. *duco* lead]

duc·tile [dʌ́ktil] *adj.* **1** (of metals) that can be drawn out into the form of a wire. 잡아늘일 수 있는; 전성(展性)이 있는. ¶ *Copper is highly ~.* 구리는 전성이 크다. **2** (of clay, etc.) that can be easily shaped. (찰흙 따위가) 어떤 형태로도 되는. **3** 《*fig.*》 (of a person, his character) easily influenced or led. (성질이) 유연한; 유순한; 고분고분한. [→duct]

duc·til·i·ty [dʌktíləti] *n.* Ⓤ the quality of being ductile. 연성(延性); 유연성; 고분고분함.

duct·less [dʌ́ktlis] *adj.* having no ducts. 도관(導管)이 없는. ¶ *the ~ glands* 내분비선.

dudg·eon [dʌ́dʒən] *n.* Ⓤ anger. 노여움; 화; 분개. ¶ *be in high* 〔*great, deep*〕 *~* 격분해 있다. [? Anglo-F.]

:due [djuː] *adj.* **1** (of a debt, bill, etc.) scheduled or expected to be paid or to be ready. (부채 따위가) 지급하기로 돼 있는; 지급 기일이 된; 만기의. ¶ *the ~ date* 지급 기일; 만기일 / *become* 〔*fall*〕 *~* (어음 따위가) 만기가 되다 / *The bill is ~ on the 26 th inst.* 그 어음은 이 달 26일이 만기일이다 / *When does the bill fall ~ ?* 그 어음은 언제 만기가 됩니까. **2** (of non-material obligations) that ought to be given, shown, or observed; suitable; proper; rightful. 당연히 주어져야〔표해야, 지켜져야〕 할; 적당한; 당연한; 정당한. ¶ *~ care* 당연한 배려 / *a ~ reward for the work* 노동에 대한 정당한 보수 / *the obedience ~ to parents* 부모에 대한 당연한 순종 / *in ~ form* 정식으로 / *in ~ time* 때가 되면; 머지 않아 / *with ~ respect to* …에게 마땅한 경의를 표하여 / *without ~ cause* 정당한 이유 없이 / *It is ~ to him to say that....* …라고 그가 말하는 것은 당연하다. **3** fair; considerable. 상당한; 충분한. ¶ *after* 〔*on*〕 *~ consideration* 충분한 고려를 한 뒤에 / *a ~ margin for delay* 지체할 것을 고려하여 충분히 잡은 예비 시간. **4** 《as *predicative*》 ⓐ arranged, engaged (to do something); expected. …하기로 마련된〔예정된, 되어 있는〕. ¶ *He is ~ to speak this evening.* 그는 오늘밤 연설하기로 되어 있다. ⓑ (of a train, etc.) expected to arrive. 도착하기로 되어 있는; 도착 예정인. ¶ *When is the train ~ ?* 열차는 언제 도착합니까 / *He was ~ at my place at 7:30.* 그는 우리 집에 7시 반에 오기로 되어 있었다.

be due to, **a**) be owing to; be caused by (something). …에 의하다; …탓〔때문〕이다. ¶ *The accident was ~ to his carelessness.* 사고는 그의 부주의로 인한 것이었다 / *The delay is ~ to a shortage of hands.* 지체는 일손 부족 때문이다. **b**) should be given to (someone). …에게 당연히 주어져야 하다. ¶ *Half the money is ~ to me.* 돈의 절반은 내게 주어야 한다 / *Punishment is ~ to him.* 그에겐 마땅히 처벌이 가해져야 한다.

due from, payable from. …로부터 지급(支給)받아야 할.

in due course, in good time; at the proper time. 적당한 때에; 때가 되면.

—*n.* **1** Ⓒ 《*sing.* only》 that which is owed, or which is required as a right. 당연히 치러져야〔받아야〕 할 것; 당연한 권리. ¶ *the tendency to give the upper classes more than their ~* 상류 계급의 사람들을 과대하게 평가하고 싶어하는 경향 / *take good luck as one's ~* 행운을 당연한 것으로 받아들이다 /

He accepted the present as if it were his ~. 그는 당연하다는 듯이 선물을 받았다 / *Courtesy is his ~ while he is your guest.* 손님으로서 맞이하고 있을 동안엔 당연히 그에게 예의를 다해야 한다. **2** 《usu. *pl.*》 a regular fee; tax; charge. 회비; 세(稅); 사용료. ¶ *harbor dues* 입항세 / *membership dues* 회비.

for a full due, for good; thoroughly; completely. 충분히.

give someone his due, **a**) give someone what is right, fair. (아무)를 공평히 다루다. **b**) admit someone's good points, even if one does not like him. (싫어하는 사람이라도) 인정할 것은 인정해 주다.

give the devil his due ⇨devil.

— *adv.* (of direction) exactly. (방위가) 정(正)…. ¶ *sail ~ south* 정남으로 항해하다 / *The wind is ~ west.* 바람이 정서(正西)에서 불어온다. [L. *debeo* owe]

du·el [djúːəl] *n.* Ⓒ **1** a private fight between two men with swords or pistols. 결투. ¶ *fight a ~ with someone* 아무와 결투하다. **2** (*fig.*) any fight between two persons. (두 사람간의) 싸움; 겨루기; 승부; 경기. ¶ *a ~ of wits* 지혜 겨루기 / *a ~ of words* 말다툼; 언쟁. — *vi., vt.* (**-eled, -el·ing** or 《Brit.》 **-elled, -el·ling**) (P1;6) fight a duel; fight in a duel. 결투를 하다. [L. *duellum* war]

du·el·ist, 《Brit.》 **-el·list** [djúːəlist] *n.* Ⓒ a man who fights a duel. 결투자.

du·en·na [djuːénə] *n.* an elderly woman in charge of young girls, esp. in a Spanish family. 소녀 감독부《젊은 아가씨에 붙어 보호·감독하는 중년의 부인》. [→dominate]

du·et [djuét] *n.* Ⓒ **1** 《mus.》 a tune or song for two players or singers. 이중창(곡); 이중주(곡). **2** (*joc.*) a conversation in which only two people take part. (두 사람만의) 대화. [L. *duo* two]

duff [dʌf] *n.* **1** a stiff flour pudding boiled in a cloth bag; a currant-pudding. (건포도를 넣은) 푸딩의 일종. **2** 《Brit. *sl.*》 dough. 밀가루 반죽. [*dough*]

duf·fel, -fle [dʌ́fəl] *n.* **1** coarse woollen cloth with a thick nap on both sides. 더플《양쪽에 보풀이 있는 거칠게 짠 나사》. **2** 《U.S.》 an outfit or equipment for camping. 캠프용품. [Dut.]

duff·er [dʌ́fər] *n.* Ⓒ 《Brit. *sl.*》 a useless or foolish person. 바보; 얼간이; 무능자; 깡패. [Cant.]

:dug [dʌg] *v.* p. and pp. of **dig.**

du·gong [dúːgaŋ, -gɔːŋ] *n.* Ⓒ a large fish-like animal living in tropical seas. 듀공《열대 바다의 포유 동물》. [Malay]

dug·out [dʌ́gàut] *n.* Ⓒ **1** 《mil.》 a shelter dug in a hillside or the ground. 대피호; 방공호. **2** 《baseball》 a small shelter at the side of a baseball field, used by the players when not playing. 더그아웃《야구장의 선수 대기소》. **3** a boat made of a large log. 통나무배; 마상이. **4** 《Brit. *sl.*》 an old army officer called up again for war service. (퇴역 후 재소집된) 복직 장교. [*dig*]

:duke [djuːk] *n.* Ⓒ **1** 《Brit.》 a nobleman of the highest order, next below a prince. 공작(公爵)(cf. *duchess*). **2** a prince who rules a small state in some parts of Europe. 공(公); 대공(大公). [L. *dux* leader]

duke·dom [djúːkdəm] *n.* **1** Ⓒ a small state ruled by a duke. 공국; 공작령(領). **2** Ⓤ the title or rank of a duke. 공작의 지위(위계).

dul·cet [dʌ́lsit] *adj.* sweet; pleasing, esp. to the ear. (특히 음색이) 고운; 감미로운; 듣기 좋은. [L. *dulcis* sweet]

dul·ci·mer [dʌ́lsəmər] *n.* Ⓒ an old musical instrument with metal strings, which is played by striking the strings with two small hamers. 덜시머《금속현을 때려 소리내는 악기의 일종으로 피아노의 원형》. [↑]

:dull [dʌl] *adj.* **1** not sharp or pointed. (칼이) 들지 않는; 무딘; 날카롭지 않은. ¶ *a ~ pencil* (*edge*) 무딘 연필(날) / *a ~ knife* 날이 들지 않는 칼. **2** stupid; slow to learn or understand. (머리가) 둔한; 우둔한. ¶ *a ~ mind* 둔한 머리 / *a ~ student* 우둔한 학생. **3** ⓐ not bright or clear. 흐린; 칙칙한; 맑지 않은. ¶ *a ~ color* 칙칙한 빛깔 / *a ~ sound* 둔탁한 소리 / *a ~ day* (*sky*) 잔뜩 찌푸린 날(하늘, 날씨). ⓑ not sensitive; not intense. (감각이) 둔한; 심하지 않은; 약한. ¶ *~ pain* 둔통(鈍痛) / *~ sight* 약한 시력 / *be ~ of hearing* 귀가 잘 안 들리다. **4** not interesting or pleasant. (단조롭고) 재미 없는. ¶ *a ~ book* 재미 없는 책 / *a ~ speech* (*story*) 따분한 연설(이야기). **5** not active. 활발치 않은; 부진한; 침체된. ¶ *Trade is ~ this spring.* 올봄엔 상황(商況)이 활발치 못하다.

(***as***) ***dull as ditch water*** (***dishwater***), 《*colloq.*》 very dull or uninteresting. 몹시 단조로운; 매우 따분한.

— *vt.* (P6) make (something) dull. …을 무디게(둔하게) 하다. ¶ *~ the blade* 날을 무디게 하다 / *~ a razor's edge* 면도날을 들지 않게 하다 / *~ the pain* 통증을 완화하다. — *vi.* (P1) become dull. 무디어(둔해)지다. [E.]

dull the edge of, reduce; spoil. …을 감소시키다; 떨어뜨리다; 잡치다. ¶ *~ the edge of one's appetite* 식욕을 감소시키다.

dull·ard [dʌ́lərd] *n.* Ⓒ a dull or stupid person. 멍텅구리; 바보. [↑]

dull·ish [dʌ́liʃ] *adj.* somewhat dull. 좀 둔한.

dull·ness [dʌ́lnis] *n.* Ⓤ the state of being dull. 무딤; 둔함; 활발치 못함; 단조(로움).

dul·ly [dʌ́li] *adv.* in a dull manner. 둔하게; 무디게; 활발치 못하게.

du·ly [djúːli] *adv.* **1** according to what is right; rightly; properly. 정식으로; 당연히; 적절히. **2** sufficiently. 충분히. **3** on time. 제시간(때)에; 시간대로. [*due*]

duly to hand, properly received. 틀림없이 받음. ¶ *Your letter is ~ to hand.* 귀한(貴翰)

틀림없이 받았습니다.

:dumb [dʌm] *adj.* **1** having no power of speech; not able to speak. 말을 못 하는; 벙어리의. ¶ *a* ~ *man* 벙어리 / *deaf and* ~ 농아자의 / *be* ~ *from birth* 선천적인 벙어리이다. **2** not speaking; silent at a given moment. (일시적으로) 말을 하지 않는; 말을 못 하는; 침묵의. ¶ *remain* ~ 침묵한 채 있다. **3** 《U.S. *colloq.*》 stupid; dull. 얼간이의; 우둔(愚鈍)한. [E.]

be struck dumb with (= *cannot speak for the moment because of*) *horror, surprise, etc.* …때문에 아연해지다[말도 못 하다].

strike someone dumb, make someone speechless with surprise. …을 깜짝 놀라게 하다; 아연케 하다.

dumb·bell [dʌ́mbèl] *n.* Ⓒ **1** a short bar with a heavy ball at each end, used for exercising. 아령. ¶ ~ *exercise* 아령 체조 / *a pair of dumbbells* 한 쌍의 아령. **2** 《*sl.*》 a dolt. 바보; 어리석은 사람. [E.]

dumb·found [dʌ̀mfáund] *vt.* =dumfound.

dumb show [∠ ∠] *n.* **1** a gesture without speech. (무언의) 몸짓; 손짓. ¶ *talk in* ~ 몸으로 이야기하다. **2** a part of a play given in gestures; a pantomime. 무언극.

dumb·wait·er [dʌ́mwèitər] *n.* Ⓒ **1** a portable serving table or stand often with revolving shelves, placed near a dining-table. 이동 회전식 식품대(臺). **2** 《U.S.》 a box with shelves which can be pulled up or down a shaft and which is used to carry food, rubbish, etc. from one floor to another. 덤웨이터 리프트《음식·쓰레기 따위를 각 층간에 운반하는 수동이나 전동식 소형 엘리베이터》. [E.]

dum·found [dʌmfáund] *vt.* (P6) make (someone) unable to speak because of surprise. …을 아연케 하다. [E.]

dum·my [dʌ́mi] *n.* Ⓒ (*pl.* **-mies**) **1** 《*sl.*》 a person who is dumb; a mute. 벙어리; 말 없는 사람. **2** 《U.S.》 a stupid person. 바보; 멍텅구리. **3** a figure made in human form, used for showing clothes, etc. (진열창 따위의 의상 전시용) 인체 모형; 마네킹. ¶ *a tailor's* ~ (양복점의) 마네킹. **4** a person who acts for another, who seems to be acting for himself. 대역(代役); 대리; 앞잡이. **5** an imitation; a sham. 모조품; 가짜. ¶ *a* ~ *horse* 목마. **6** 《Brit.》 a baby's rubber teat. (아기의) 고무 젖꼭지(=comforter; 《U.S.》 pacifier).

sell the dummy, deceive the opponent by feigning to pass the ball. 볼을 패스하는 척하여 상대를 속이다.

— *adj.* (**-mi·er, -mi·est**) sham; looking like a real one. 가짜의; 가장[의장(擬裝)]의. [*dumb*]

dump [dʌmp] *vt.* (P6,7) **1** let (something) fall in a mass; throw (something) down. …을 털썩 내려[떨어]뜨리다; (쓰레기 따위)를 버리다. ¶ *She dumped all her rubbish in front of our house.* 그녀는 쓰레기를 몽땅 우리 집 앞에 버렸다. **2** 《comm.》 sell (large quantities of goods) at excessively low prices, esp. in a foreign country. (대량의 상품)을 덤핑[투매(投賣)]하다. — *vi.* (P1) fall in a mass. 털썩[쿵] 떨어지다.

— *n.* Ⓒ **1** ⓐ a place where rubbish is thrown away; a heap of rubbish; a place where loads are emptied out. 쓰레기 버리는 곳; 쓰레기 더미; 짐 부리는 곳. ⓑ 《mil.》 a place in the open for storing goods. 임시 야적장(野積場). **2** a sound which is made when something falls down in a mass. 털썩[쿵]하는 소리. **3** 《*colloq.*》 a small coin. 잔돈. **4** a kind of sweetmeats. 당과(糖菓). **5** a short stout person. 땅딸보. **6** a short thick object of various kind. 굵고 짧은 것. [? N.]

do not care a dump, do not care at all. 조금도 개의[상관]치 않다.

dump·ing [dʌ́mpiŋ] *n.* Ⓤ the act of selling goods at excessively low prices. 덤핑; 투매(投賣).

dump·ish [dʌ́mpiʃ] *adj.* morose; depressed in spirits. 우울한; 울적한.

dump·ling [dʌ́mpliŋ] *n.* Ⓒ a pudding of dough, often folded over and containing fruit or meat. (고기·사과가 든) 찐 경단; 가루 반죽 푸딩. [*dump*]

dumps [dʌmps] *n., pl.* a gloomy state of mind; melancholy. 우울. ¶ *be in the* ~ 우울하다. [*dump*]

dump truck [∠ ∠] *n.* a truck for hauling gravel, coal, etc., that unloads by tilting back the cargo bin and opening the tailboard. 덤프 트럭.

dump·y [dʌ́mpi] *adj.* (**dump·i·er, dump·i·est**) short and thick. 땅딸막한; 뭉뚝한. [*dump*]

dun[1] [dʌn] *vt.* (**dunned, dun·ning**) (P6,13) repeatedly demand that (someone) pay a debt. …에게 빚 갚을 것을 성가시도록 재촉하다. — *n.* Ⓒ **1** a person who duns. (끈질기게 빚 독촉하는) 성가신 채권자. **2** a repeated demand for payment of a debt. 빚 독촉. [E.]

dun[2] [dʌn] *n.* Ⓤ a dull grayish-brown. 암갈색. — *adj.* of a dull grayish-brown. 암갈색의. [E.]

dunce [dʌns] *n.* Ⓒ a stupid person who is not clever at learning; a stupid pupil. 머리 나쁜 학생; 열등생; 바보. [Person]

dun·der·head [dʌ́ndərhèd] *n.* Ⓒ a stupid person. 바보; 멍텅구리. [Person]

dune [djuːn] *n.* Ⓒ a low sand hill heaped up by the wind, esp. near a shore. 사구(砂丘). [F.; →down[2]]

dung [dʌŋ] *n.* Ⓤ the waste matter of animals; manure. (마소 따위의) 똥; 거름. — *vt.* (P6) manure (the ground) with dung. (땅)에 거름을 주다. [E.]

dun·geon [dʌ́ndʒən] *n.* Ⓒ **1** a dark

underground prison, esp. in an old castle. 토굴〔지하〕 감옥. **2** a great tower of a castle. 아성(牙城). [→dominate]

dung·hill [dʌ́ŋhìl] *n.* Ⓒ **1** a heap of waste matter from animals. (동물의) 똥더미; 퇴비. **2** a wicked place or person. 지저분한〔더러운〕 곳〔사람〕. [*dung*]

dunk [dʌŋk] *vt.* 《U.S.》 dip (bread, etc.) into one's drink or soup. (빵 따위)를 음료에 적시다〔담그다〕. [G. *dunken* dip]

dun·nage [dʌ́nidʒ] *n.* **1** 《naut.》 mats and loose wood used to protect cargo. 짐밑받이《뱃짐 밑에 깔거나 사이에 끼움》. **2** baggage. 수화물; 소지물. [L.]

du·o·dec·i·mal [djù:oudésəməl] *adj.* of twelve or twelfths. 12의; 12분산(分算)의; 12진의. ¶ *the ~ system,* 12진법. [↓]

du·o·dec·i·mo [djù:oudésəmòu] *n.* **1** a form of book for which the printer's paper is folded into twelve. 12절판(折判); 사륙판(四六判)(abbr. 12mo). **2** a book of this size. 12절판의 책. [L. *duodecim* twelve]

du·o·de·na [djù:oudí:nə, dju:ɑ́dənə] *n.* pl. of **duodenum.**

du·o·de·num [djù:oudí:nəm, dju:ɑ́dənəm] *n.* (*pl.* **du·o·de·na**) the first portion of the small intestine below the stomach. 십이지장(十二指腸). [↑]

du·o·logue, 《U.S.》 **-log** [djú:əlɔ̀(:)g, -lɑ̀g] *n.* a dramatic piece for two actors; a conversation between two persons. (두 사람의) 대화극; (두 사람간의) 대화(cf. *monologue*). [Gk.]

dup. duplicate.

dupe [dju:p] *n.* Ⓒ a person who is easily tricked or who believes everything. 잘 속는 사람; 봉. ¶ *a ~ of the communists* 공산주의 맹종자. — *vt.* (P6) trick; deceive; cheat. …을 속이다. [F.]

du·ple [djú:pəl] *adj.* **1** double. 2배의; 이중의. **2** 《mus.》 having two beats to the bar. 짝수 박자의; 2박자계(系)의. ¶ *~ time,* 2박자. [L. *duplus* twofold]

du·plex [djú:pleks] *adj.* double; twofold. 2배의; 이중의. ¶ *a ~ lamp* 이중 램프. [↑]

duplex apartment [ˊ– –ˊ–] *n.* 《U.S.》 an apartment having rooms on two floors connected by an inner staircase. 복층 아파트《아래·위층을 한 가구에서 사용하는》.

du·pli·cate [djú:pləkit] *adj.* **1** double; consisting of two equal parts. 이중의; 중복의; 한 쌍의. ¶ *Man's lungs are ~.* 사람의 폐는 쌍으로 돼 있다. **2** exactly like another. (다른 하나와) 완전히 같은; 베낀; 부(副)의; 복제의. ¶ *a ~ key* 곁쇠; 여벌쇠 / *a ~ copy* 부본; 복제품 / *a ~ action* 똑같은 동작 / *~ copies of a map* 지도의 복사.

— *n.* Ⓒ something made exactly like another; a copy. 부본; 사본; 복사; 복제.

in duplicate, in two copies. 정부(正副) 2통으로. ¶ *type a letter in ~* 편지를 2통 타이프로 치다.

— [-kèit] *vt.* (P6) **1** make an exact copy of (something). …을 복사하다. **2** make double; increase by the same amount. 2배로〔이중으로〕 하다. [→duple]

du·pli·ca·tion [djù:pləkéiʃən] *n.* **1** Ⓤ the act of duplicating; the state of being duplicated. 복제; 복사; 이중. ¶ *save time by avoiding ~ of effort* 이중의 수고를 피함으로써 시간을 절약하다. **2** Ⓒ a copy. 복제물; 복사물.

du·pli·ca·tor [djú:pləkèitər] *n.* Ⓒ a machine or person that makes copies. 복사기; 복사하는 사람.

du·plic·i·ty [dju(:)plísəti] *n.* Ⓤ the act of doing something in two different manners to deceive others. (언행 따위의) 표리부동; 속과 겉이 다름; 두 마음.

du·ra·bil·i·ty [djùərəbíləti] *n.* Ⓤ the quality of lasting long; ability to continue long in the same state. 영속성; 내구〔지속〕성. [↓]

du·ra·ble [djúərəbəl] *adj.* lasting a long time; able to continue long in the same state. 오래 가는; 마딘; 내구성이 있는. ¶ *~ friendship* 오래도록 변치 않는 우정 / *a ~ cloth* 튼튼한 천 / *a ~ color* 바래지 않는 색 / *~ goods* (소모품에 대하여) 내구 소비재(材).

● **du·ra·bly** [-bli] *adv.* [L. *durus* hard]

du·ra·ble·ness [djùərəbəlnis] *n.* =durability.

durable press [ˊ–– ˊ] *n.* the process of treating fabrics with chemicals (as resin) and beat for setting the shape and for aiding wrinkle resistance. DP가공《섬유를 화공약품으로 처리해 의류의 모양이 일그러지거나 주름지는 것을 방지하는 가공법》.

du·ral·u·min [djuərǽljəmin] *n.* Ⓤ a light, strong metal that is an alloy of aluminum, copper, manganese, etc., used in aircraft, etc. 두랄루민. [G. *Düren, Aluminum*]

du·ra ma·ter [djúərə méitər] *n.* 《L.》 《anat.》 the outermembrane of the brain. 경뇌막(硬腦膜). [→durable]

dur·ance [djúərəns] *n.* 《*arch.*》 imprisonment. 투옥; 수감(收監); 감금. ¶ *in ~ (vile)* (부당) 감금되어. [↑]

du·ra·tion [djuəréiʃən] *n.* Ⓤ **1** the state of continuing in time. (시간의) 지속; 계속. ¶ *holidays of three week's ~,* 3주간에 걸친 휴가. **2** the period of time during which anything lasts. 지속〔존속〕 기간. ¶ *the ~ of life* 생존 기간 / *be of long* 〔*short*〕 *~* 오래 가다〔가지 않다〕; 오래 지속하다〔하지 않다〕. [↑]

dur·bar [də́:rbɑ:r] *n.* in India, a prince's audience room, or an official audience or reception. (인도에서) 제후의 궁전; 토후나 영국 총독 등에 의한 공식 회견; 접견. [Hind.]

du·ress [djuərés, djúəris] *n.* Ⓤ **1** imprisonment. 감금. ¶ *be held in ~* 감금돼 있다. **2**

threats used to force someone to do something. 협박에 의한 강제; 위압; 강박; 압박. ¶ *under the ~ of dictatorship* 독재 정권의 압정 밑에 / *make a promise under ~* 협박〔강제〕당하여 약속을 하다. [→durable]

:**dur·ing** [djúəriŋ] *prep.* **1** throughout the time of. …동안, …동안〔중〕 내내. ¶ *~ the day* 하룻동안; 하루 종일 / *He slept ~ the lesson.* 수업 중 그는 내내 잤다. **2** at some point of time in. …동안(의 어느 때)에. ¶ *~ my stay in Paris* 파리 체류 중에 / *He left ~ the night.* 그는 밤 사이에 떠났다. [→durable]

durst [dəːrst] *v.* 《*arch.*》 p. of **dare.**

*****dusk** [dʌsk] *n.* Ⓤ **1** a state between darkness and light; time just before it gets quite dark. 어둑어둑함; 어스레함; 땅거미(opp. dawn). **2** shade. 그늘; 어둠.

at dusk, at the time just before dark. 해질 녘에; 땅거미질 때에.

— *adj.* **1** dark; dusky. 어두운; 어두컴컴한; 어스레한. **2** 《*poet.*》 dark-colored. 거무스름한.

— *vt., vi.* make (something) dim or dark; become or look dark. 어두컴컴하게〔어둡게〕 하다; 어두워〔어두컴컴해〕지다. [E.]

dusk·i·ness [dʌ́skinis] *n.* Ⓤ the state of being dusky. 어두움; 어두컴컴함; 어스름.

dusk·y [dʌ́ski] *adj.* (**dusk·i·er, dusk·i·est**) somewhat dark; shady. 어두운; 어두컴컴한; 그늘진; 거무스름한. ¶ *a ~ brown* 암갈색 / *a ~ skin* 거무스름한 피부.

:**dust** [dʌst] *n.* Ⓤ **1** very small pieces of waste matter; powder of earth. 먼지; 티끌. ¶ *a cloud of ~* 자욱한 먼지 / *a thick coating of ~* 두껍게 쌓인 먼지 / *gather ~ in the window* 창문에 먼지가 끼다 / *sweep up ~* 먼지를 말끔히 쓸어내다. **2** earth; soil. 흙; 땅. **3** any powder. 가루; 분말. ¶ *gold ~* 금가루 / *~ tea* 분말차 / *be crushed into ~* 부숴져 가루가 되다 / *The bee is covered with yellow ~ from the flowers.* 벌이 노란 꽃가루를 뒤집어 쓰고 있다. **4** 《*the ~*》 《*poet.*》 a dead and decayed human body. 썩어 흙이 된 유해(遺骸). **5** 《Brit.》 rubbish. 쓰레기.

(as) dry as dust, very dull; uninteresting. 매우 무미 건조한.

bite the dust, **a**) die, get wounded. 죽다; 부상하여 쓰러지다. **b**) suffer defeat; fail 일패도지하다; 패배하다; 실패하다.

in the dust, dead; humbled. 죽어; 굴욕을 당하고.

lick the dust, **a**) =bite the dust. **b**) humble oneself like a slave. 비굴하게 스스로를 낮추다; 굽실거리다.

make* 〔*raise, kick up*〕 *a dust, 《U.S. *sl.*》 make a disturbance. 소동을 일으키다.

shake the dust off one's feet, go away in anger or with feelings of contempt. 분연히〔경멸하여〕 자리를 박차고 일어서다; 결연히 떠나다.

throw dust in someone's eyes, deceive; mislead. 아무를 현혹시키다; 속이다.

— *vt.* (P6,13) **1** cover (something) with powder; sprinkle (powder) over something. …을 가루로 뒤덮다; …에 (가루)를 뿌리다. ¶ *~ a cake with sugar* 케이크에 설탕을 뿌리다 / *~ sand over the ground* 땅에 모래를 뿌리다. **2** take the dust off (something). …의 먼지를 없애다. ¶ *~ a room* 방의 먼지를 청소하다 / *~ a table* 식탁을 훔치다 / *~ off the table cloth* 테이블보의 먼지를 떨다 / *~ oneself down* 〔*off*〕 몸의 먼지를 떨다 / *~ the snow from one's knees* 무릎의 눈을 떨다. [E.]

dust someone's jacket* 〔*coat*〕 *for him, give him a beating. 아무를 후려치다; 두들겨 패다.

dust bin [∠∠] *n.* 《Brit.》 a can or box in which ashes and household rubbish are kept. 쓰레기통.

dust bowl [∠∠] *n.* 《U.S.》 an area once fertile but now a desert. 황진(黃塵) 지대; 건조 평원지대.

dust cart [∠∠] *n.* 《Brit.》 a cart in which rubbish is collected from dustbins. 쓰레기 운반차.

dust coat [∠∠] *n.* 《Brit.》 =duster 3.

dust color [∠∠–] *n.* dull light brown color. 칙칙한 연다갈색.

dust cover [∠∠–] *n.* **1** a cloth or plastic covering used to protect furniture or equipment. (가구 따위에 덮어 씌우는) 먼지 막이 커버. **2** a cover for a book. 책 커버.

dust devil [∠∠–] *n.* a small whirlwind containing sand and dust. (열대 사막 따위의) 회오리바람; 모래 회오리.

dust·er [dʌ́stər] *n.* Ⓒ **1** a person who takes off dust. 청소인; 먼지를 터는 사람. **2** a thing which takes off dust; a cloth or brush for removing dust. 총채; 청소기; 걸레. **3** 《chiefly U.S.》 a long, light, coat worn to keep dust off or out. 더스터 코트; 방진(防塵)용 외의(外衣). **4** a machine for scattering dust or powder on something. 뿌리는 기구; 살포기(=《Brit.》 dust-coat). ¶ *a pepper ~* 후추 뿌리는 기구. [*dust*]

dust·man [dʌ́stmən] *n.* Ⓒ (*pl.* **-men** [-mən]) 《Brit.》 a man employed to remove rubbish. 쓰레기꾼〔운반인〕; 쓰레기 청소부.

dust·pan [dʌ́stpæ̀n] *n.* Ⓒ a flat, broad pan in which dust is collected and removed. 쓰레받기.

dust storm [∠∠] *n.* a dust-laden whirlwind moving across an arid region. 사진(砂塵) 회오리《한발 지역의 광대한 경작지에서 볼 수 있음》; 먼지보라; 모래보라.

dust·up [dʌ́stʌ̀p] *n.* a quarrel; row. 말다툼; 싸움.

*****dust·y** [dʌ́sti] *adj.* (**dust·i·er, dust·i·est**) **1** full of dust; covered with dust. 먼지 많은; 먼지투성이의. ¶ *a ~ road* 먼지 많은 길. **2** like dust in appearance. 먼지 모양의〔같은〕; 분말상(狀)의. **3** having a color similar to that of dust. 먼지빛의; 회색의.

not so dusty, 《Brit. *sl.*》 not so bad; fairly

good. 그리 나쁘지 않은; 괜찮은.
•**dust·i·ly** [-li] *adv.* **dust·i·ness** [-nis] *n.*

•**Dutch** [dʌtʃ] *adj.* **1** ⓐ of the Netherlands, its people, or their language. 네덜란드의; 네덜란드 사람〔말〕의. ⓑ made in Netherland. 네덜란드산〔제(製)〕의. ¶ *a ~ clock / ~ cheese.* **2** 《hist.》 German. 독일의. ¶ *~ blood* 독일계 혈통.
talk to someone like a Dutch uncle, preach to or scold (someone) severely. 준엄하게 타이르다〔꾸짖다〕. ¶ *He talked to me like a ~ uncle.* 그는 준엄하게 나를 꾸짖었다.
— *n.* **1** Ⓤ ⓐ the language of the Netherlands. 네덜란드 말. ⓑ 《hist.》 the language of Germany, including the Netherlands. 네덜란드어(語)가 포함된 독일어. **2** 《*the* ~》 ⓐ the people of the Netherlands. 네덜란드 사람〔국민〕. ⓑ 《U.S.》 a descendant of German immigrants. 독일계 이민의 자손. [Du.]
beat the Dutch, be very surprising. 남을 깜짝 놀라게 하다.
go Dutch on (=*have each person pay his own expenses for*) *a meal, etc.* (식사비 따위)를 각추렴하다; 각자 부담으로 하다.
in Dutch, 《*sl.*》 in trouble, in disgrace. 혼이 나; 창피를 당하여; 노여움을 사; 눈 밖에 나.

Dutch auction [ㅗㅗ—] *n.* a sale where the price gradually comes down until a buyer is found. 값을 깎아내리는 경매.

Dutch bargain [ㅗㅗ—] *n.* an agreement about buying and selling settled while drinking; a wet bargain. 한잔하면서 맺는 매매 계약〔흥정〕.

Dutch comfort [ㅗㅗ—] *n.* a comfort which is not really a comfort to the person to whom it is given. 조금도 고맙지 않은 위로〔위안〕.

Dutch courage [ㅗㅗ—] *n.* courage produced under the influence of alcohol. 술기운에 내는 용기.

Dutch door [ㅗㅗ] *n.* a door consisting of two units. 상하 2단으로 된 문《따로따로 여닫는》.

Dutch·man [dʌ́tʃmən] *n.* Ⓒ (*pl.* **-men** [-mən]) **1** a person of the Netherlands; a Hollander. 네덜란드 사람. **2** a Dutch ship. 네덜란드 배. **3** 《U.S. *sl.*》 a German. 독일 사람.
I'm a Dutchman (*if I do*), 《*colloq.*》 I'll never do…. 결코〔절대〕 …않다〔아니다〕; …이면 성을 갈겠다.

Dutch treat [ㅗㅗ] *n.* 《U.S. *colloq.*》 a meal or entertainment in which each person pays for himself. (회식비의) 각추렴; 각자 부담.

du·te·ous [djúːtiəs] *adj.* 《*poet.*》 obedient; dutiful. 충실한; 본분을 잘 지키는; 순종하는. ¶ *a ~ servant* 〔*wife*〕 충실한 하인〔아내〕. [→duty]

du·ti·a·ble [djúːtiəbəl] *adj.* (of imported goods) on which a tax must be paid. (수입품 등이) 관세가 과해지는; 세금이 붙는(opp. duty-free). ¶ *~ articles* 과세품. [→duty]

du·ti·ful [djúːtifəl] *adj.* performing the duties of one's position; obedient to one's parents or elders. 의무를 다하는; 충실한; 순종하는; 효도의. ¶ *a ~ son* 효자. •**du·ti·ful·ly** [-fəli] *adv.* **du·ti·ful·ness** [-nis] *n.*

:**du·ty** [djúːti] *n.* (*pl.* **-ties**) **1** Ⓒ what a person ought to do; an obligation. 의무; 본분. ¶ *one's ~ to one's parents* (자식의) 부모에 대한 도리〔본분〕 / *do one's ~* 본분을〔의무를〕 다하다 / *It's your ~ to do this work.* 이 일을 하는 것이 너의 의무다 / *He only did his ~ to his country.* 국가에 대해 해야 할 그의 의무를 다했을 뿐이다. **2** 《often *pl.*》 service that a person ought to do in his position. 임무; 직무. ¶ *a ~ of a policeman* 경찰관으로서의 임무 / *A postman's duties are to sort and deliver letters.* 우편 집배원의 직무는 편지를 분류하고 배달해 주는 것이다. **3** Ⓤ respect; obedience. 존경; 복종. ¶ *pay one's ~ to one's teacher.* 선생님께 존경을 표하다. **4** Ⓒ a tax. 세(稅); 《usu. *pl.*》 tax, on articles of foreign trade. 관세. [L. *debeo* owe, -ty]
do duty for, serve instead of. …의 대용이 되다; …의 역(役)을 하다.
on 〔***off***〕 ***duty,*** at 〔not at〕 one's work. 근무 중〔비근무중〕에; 당번〔비번〕인.

du·ty-free [djúːtifríː] *adj.* (of goods) free of customs duty. 관세를 물리지 않는; 무(관)세의; 면세의.

D.V. Deo volente 《L. *God* willing》.

D-valve [díːvælv] *n.* a valve of D shape. D형판(瓣).

DVM doctor of veterinary medicine.

•**dwarf** [dwɔːrf] *n.* Ⓒ (*pl.* **dwarfs** or **dwarves**) **1** a person, an animal, a plant, etc. much smaller than the usual size. 난쟁이; 보통보다 작은 동물〔식물〕. **2** (in fairy tales) a small ugly man with magic powers. (동화 속의 주인공인) 난쟁이(opp. giant).
— *adj.* much smaller than the usual size; checked in growth. 왜소한; 주접든; 지지러진. ¶ *a ~ car* 소형차.
— *vt., vi.* become smaller; make (something) smaller; keep (something) from growing large. 왜소해지(게 하)다; …의 발육을 방해하다; …을 위축시키다. ¶ *The skyscraper dwarfs the church.* 마천루가 교회를 작아보이게 한다. [E.]

dwarf·ish [dwɔ́ːrfiʃ] *adj.* like a dwarf; much smaller than usual. 난쟁이 같은; 왜소한; 소형의.

dwarf tree [ㅗㅗ] *n.* a tree which has been checked in its growth. 분재(盆栽).

dwarves [dwɔːrvz] *n.* pl. of **dwarf.**

:**dwell** [dwel] *vi.* (**dwelt** or 《rare》 **dwelled**) **1** (P2A,3) 《*arch.*》 《*at, in*》 live; make one's home. 거주하다; 살다. ¶ *~ abroad* 해외에 거주하다 / *~ in the country* 시골에(서) 살다. **2** (P3) exist; be present. (어떤 상태로) 있다; 지내다; 머물다; 존재하다. ¶ *~ in happi-*

ness 행복하게 지내다 / *His memories still ~ in her mind.* 그에 대한 추억은 아직도 그녀의 마음에서 사라지지 않고 있다. [E.=lead astray]

***dwell on* 〔*upon*〕,** think, write, or speak about (something) for a long time; put emphasis on (something). …을 곰곰〔깊이〕 생각하다; …을 길게 얘기하다〔쓰다〕; …을 역설〔강조〕하다. ¶ *~ on one's past failures* 과거의 실패를 곰곰 되새기다 / *~ on the pleasures of the past* 과거의 즐거웠던 추억에 잠기다 / *~ on the necessity of something* …의 필요성을 역설하다 / *~ on every detail of someone's appearance* 아무의 용모를 자세히 설명하다.

dwell·er [dwélər] *n.* Ⓒ a person who lives in a place. 거주자; 사는 사람. ¶ *a cave ~* 혈거 생활자 / *city and town dwellers* 도시 거주자.

***dwell·ing** [dwéliŋ] *n.* Ⓒ a house; a place in which one lives. 집; 주거; 주택. ¶ *a portable ~* (차 따위로 운반되는) 이동식 주택 / *change one's ~* 전거(轉居)하다.

dwelling house [⌐–⌐] *n.* a house in which one lives. 주거; 주택.

***dwelt** [dwelt] *v.* p. and pp. of **dwell.**

dwin·dle [dwíndl] *vi.* (P1,2A,3) become smaller and smaller; waste away; lose importance. (점점) 작아지다; 감소하다; (명성 따위가) 떨어지다. ¶ *a dwindling reputation* 떨어져가는 명성 / *His fortune dwindled rapidly.* 그의 재산은 급속히 줄었다. [E.]

dwindle away into nothing, waste away into nothing. 점점 줄어 없어지다.

dwt. denarius weight.

dy·ad [dáiæd] *n.* a group of two; a pair; two. 2개 1조; 2개군(群); 한쌍; 둘. [Gk.]

***dye** [dai] *n.* ⓊⒸ the material used to color cloth, hair, etc.; a color produced by such matter. 염료; 물감; 염색; 색깔; 물(든 색). ¶ *take ~ well* 물이 잘 들다; 염색이 쉽다.

a crime of the blackest* 〔*deepest*〕 *dye, a crime of the worst kind. 최악질의 범죄.

— *vt.* (P6,18) color (something) with a dye. …을 물들이다; 염색〔착색〕하다. ¶ *~ a white dress blue* 흰옷을 청색으로 물들이다 / *~ the stream with blood* 냇물을 피로 물들이다 / *have a dress* 〔*one's hair*〕 *dyed* 옷을〔머리를〕 염색시키다.

— *vi.* (P1) become colored. 물들다. ¶ *~ well* 〔*badly*〕 물이 잘〔잘 안〕 들다 / *Wool dyes readily with acid dyes.* 양털은 산성 염료에 쉽게 물든다. [E.]

***dye something in the grain* 〔*in the wool*〕,** 《U.S.》 dye something before weaving; make something fixed or unchangeable. (직물로 짜기 전에) 실에 물들이다; (사상 따위를) 깊이 물들게 하다〔침투시키다〕.

dye·ing [dáiiŋ] *n.* the process or art of fixing colors firmly to a fabric (=woven material); the business of a dyer. (섬유·옷감·실 따위의) 염색(일).

***dy·er** [dáiər] *n.* Ⓒ a person whose business is to dye cloth. 염색하는 사람; 염색공.

dye·stuff [dáistʌ̀f] *n.* ⓊⒸ a material giving, or used as, a dye. 염료; 물감.

dye·works [dáiwə̀ːrks] *n. pl.* 《used as *sing.* and *pl.*》 a factory where cloth is dyed. 염색 공장.

:dy·ing [dáiiŋ] *adj.* **1** near to death; about to die. 빈사(瀕死)의; 죽어가는. ¶ *a ~ man* 죽어가는 사람 / *the dead and the ~* 죽은 사람들과 죽어가는 사람들. **2** ⓐ associated with (the hour of) death. 죽음의; 임종의. ¶ *one's ~ bed* 임종의 자리 / *a ~ hour* 임종 때 / *one's ~ confession* 임종의 고백. ⓑ said or done at the time of death. 죽음에 임하여 (말)한. ¶ *one's ~ wish* 임종시에 남기는 마지막 소원. **3** coming to an end; drawing to a close; (of the sun) about to sink. 끝나려고 하는; 꺼져가는; 저물어가는; 지는. ¶ *the ~ year* 저물어가는 한 해 / *the ~ moon* 지는 달 / *a ~ fire* 꺼져가는 불 / *a ~ state* 멸망해 가는 국가. **4** 《*sl.*》 anxious. 몹시 …하고 싶어하는. ¶ *She is ~ to go.* 그녀는 몹시 가고 싶어한다. **5** 《*sl.*》 languishing. 풀없는; 번민(煩悶)하는; 우울한. ¶ *a ~ look* 번민하는 표정.

one's ***dying words,*** words spoken by one who is about to die. 유언.

till* 〔*to*〕** *one's* ***dying day, till 〔to〕 the day when one dies. 죽는 날까지.

— *n.* Ⓤ death. 죽음; 임종; 종말. [*die*]

dyke [daik] *n., v.* =dike.

dy·nam·ic [dainǽmik] *adj.* **1** having to do with force. 동적(動的)인(opp. static(al)). **2** producing force or power. 동력의. **3** (of a person) active; forceful; energetic. 활력 있는; 힘찬; 정력적인. ¶ *a ~ personality* 활동적인 성격. **4** of dynamics. 역학(상)의. [Gk. *dunamai* have power]

dy·nam·ics [dainǽmiks] *n. pl.* 《phys.》 **1** 《*sing.* in use》 a branch of physics dealing with forces. 역학; 동역학(opp. statics). **2** the energy, force, or forces producing activity in any form. 동력; 원동력.

***dy·na·mite** [dáinəmàit] *n.* Ⓤ a kind of high explosive used in blasting rock, hard earth, etc. 다이너마이트. — *vt.* (P6) blow up (something) with dynamite. …을 다이너마이트로 폭파하다.

dy·na·mo [dáinəmòu] *n.* Ⓒ (*pl.* **-mos**) a machine for changing mechanical power into electric current. 발전기. [→dynamic]

dy·na·mo·e·lec·tric [dàinəmouiléktrik] *adj.* pertaining to the conversion of mechanical energy into electric energy, or vice versa. 기계 에너지를 전기 에너지로 바꾸는; 전기 에너지를 기계 에너지로 바꾸는.

dy·na·mom·e·ter [dàinəmámitər / -mɔ́m-] *n.* an apparatus designed to measure force or power. (기계적인 힘을 측정하는) 역량계(力量計); 동력계. ¶ *squeeze ~* 악력계.

dy·nast [dáinæst, -nəst / dínæst] *n.* **1** a member of a dynasty. (왕조의) 군주. **2** any ruler. 통치자. [→dynamic]

dy·nas·tic [dainǽstik / di-], **-ti·cal** [-tikəl] *adj.* of or belonging to a dynasty. 왕조의; 왕가(王家)의.

dy·nas·ty [dáinəsti / dí-] *n.* Ⓒ (*pl.* **-ties**) a series of rulers of the same family; the period during which a number of kings from the same family rule a country. 왕조; 왕조 시대. [↑]

dyne [dain] *n.* 《phys.》 the unit of force in the centimeter-gram-second system. 다인《힘의 cgs 단위》. [↑]

dys- [dis-] *pref.* bad; difficult. '악화, 곤란'의 뜻. [Gk. dus-]

dys·en·ter·y [dísəntèri] *n.* Ⓤ 《med.》 a disease of the bowels, accompanied by bloody discharges. 적리(赤痢); 이질. [Gk. *entera* bowels]

dys·func·tion [disfʌ́ŋkʃən] *n.* 《med.》 impaired functioning, as of bodily organ. 기능 장애〔이상, 부전〕. [dys-, →function]

dys·lex·i·a [disléksiə] *n.* 《med.》 a disturbance of the ability to read. 독서 장애; 실독증(失讀症). [dys-, Gk. *léxis* a reading]

dys·pep·si·a [dispépʃə, -siə] *n.* Ⓤ poor digestion. 소화 불량. [Gk. *pessō* digest]

dys·pep·tic [dispéptik] *adj.* suffering from dyspepsia. 소화 불량의; 위병(胃病)에 걸린. —*n.* Ⓒ a person suffering from dyspepsia. 소화 불량인 사람. [↑]

dys·pho·ni·a [disfóuniə] *n.* Ⓤ difficulty in producing speech sounds. 언어 곤란; 발성 장애. [dys-; →phone]

dysp·ne·a [dispníːə] *n.* Ⓤ 《med.》 difficult breathing. 호흡 곤란. [dys-; →*pneō* breathe]

dys·tro·phy [dístrəfi] *n.* Ⓤ 《med.》 faulty nutrition. 영양 장애; 발육 이상(異常). [dys-; →trophy]

dys·u·ri·a [disjuəríə, disjúriə] *n.* Ⓤ difficult urination. 배뇨(排尿) 곤란〔장애〕. [dys-; →urine]

dz. dozen(s).

e E

E, e [iː] *n.* Ⓒ (*pl.* **E's, Es, e's, es**) **1** The fifth letter of the English alphabet. 영어 알파벳의 다섯째 글자. **2** 《mus.》 the third tone or note in the C major scale. 마음(音)《고정 도창법의 '미'》; 마조(調). **3** (in Lloyd's register) a second class. (로이드 선급(船級) 협회의) 제 2 등급. **4** 《math.》 the base of the system of natural logarithms, approximately 2.718. 자연 로그의 밑《값은 대략 2.718》.

E, E., e, e. [iː] east; eastern.

E. Earl; Earth; English; Elizabeth.

e. eldest; engineer; engineering; entrance; 《baseball》 errors.

e. 《phys.》 erg. 에르그.

ea. each.

:each [iːtʃ] *adj.* every one of. 각각〔각기〕의; 각자의. ¶ ~ *person* 각 사람 / *on* ~ *occasion* 일이 있을 때마다 / *Each pupil has his own desk.* 각(各) 학생들은 제각기 자기 책상이 있다 / *Each boy and* ~ *girl has the license.* 남자 아이도 여자 아이도 각자 면허증을 갖고 있다. ── *pron.* **1** each person; each thing. 각자; 각기; 각각. ¶ ~ *of us* 우리들 각자 / *Each went his way.* 각자 자기의 길을 갔다. **2** all. 각자 모두. ¶ *We* ~ *tried, but in vain.* 우리들 모두는 해보았으나 소용 없었다.

each and all, all. 각자 모두.

each and every, any and every. 어느 …도; 모두; 모조리; 죄다.

each other, each the other; one another. 서로. ¶ *They helped* ~ *other.* 그들은 서로 도왔다 / *They hate* ~ *other.* =*Each hates the other.* 두 사람은 서로 미워하고 있다.

── *adv.* to or for each. 각각; 각기; 각자; 하나〔한 사람〕에 대해. ¶ *They cost a penny each.* 그것들은 한 개에 1페니씩 한다. [E.]

:ea·ger [íːgər] *adj.* desiring very much; anxious; zealous. 몹시 …하고 싶어하는; 열심인; 열망하는. ¶ *an* ~ *look* 열망하는 표정 / ~ *in one's studies* 면학에 열심인 / *He is* ~ *to work.* 그는 일을 무척 하고 싶어한다 / *We are* ~ *for* 〔*after*〕 *peace.* 우리는 평화를 갈망하고 있다. [L. *acer* keen]

•ea·ger·ly [íːgərli] *adv.* in a desirous manner; zealously. 열심히; 열렬히; 간절히.

•ea·ger·ness [íːgərnis] *n.* Ⓤ the state of being eager. 열심; 열망. ¶ *In his* ~ *to go abroad, he violated the law.* 외국에 나가고 싶은 나머지 그는 법을 어겼다.

be all eagerness (=*be anxious*) ***to do.*** …하고 싶어 못 견디다.

with eagerness, eagerly. 열심히.

:ea·gle [íːgəl] *n.* Ⓒ **1** 《bird》 a large bird with sharp eyes, powerful wings and hooked bill. (독)수리. **2** a symbol using the eagle. 수리표〔문장〕; 수리인(印). **3** 《U.S.》 an old gold coin worth 10 dollars. 옛 10달러 금화. [L. *aquila* eagle]

ea·gle-eyed [íːgəlàid] *adj.* having very keen eyes, like an eagle; able to see clearly. 관찰안(觀察眼)이 날카로운; 시력이 뛰어난.

ea·glet [íːglit] *n.* Ⓒ a young eagle. 새끼(독)수리.

E. & O.E. errors and omissions excepted.

:ear[1] [iər] *n.* Ⓒ **1** the organ, power, or sense of hearing. 귀; 청력(聽力); 청각; 음감. ¶ *a keen* ~ 예민한 청각 / *the external* 〔*internal, middle*〕 ~ 외〔내, 중〕이(耳) / *cover* 〔*stop*〕 *one's ears* 귀를 막다 / *learn by* ~ 귀로 들어 익히다 / *play by* ~ 악보 없이 연주하다; 악보를 외워 연주하다 / *speak in someone's* ~ 아무의 귀에 속삭이다 / *split one's ears* (큰 소리 따위가) 귀청을 찢다 / *strain one's ears to catch words* 말을 들으려고 온 신경을 귀에 집중시키다 / *A word in your* ~. 잠깐 할 말이 있습니다 / *Were your ears burning last night?* 간밤에 귀가 간질간질하지 않았던가요《당신 이야기를 하고 있었죠》/ *catch the* ~ *of the public* 세상 사람들의 주의를 끌다 / 《*prov.*》 *Walls have ears.* 낮말은 새가 듣고 밤말은 쥐가 듣는다. **2** anything shaped like an ear. 귀같이 생긴 것; 손잡이; 귈손. ¶ 《*prov.*》 *Little pitchers have long* 〔*wide*〕 *ears.* 애들은 귀가 밝다.

be all ears, listen eagerly or attentively. 열심히 듣(고 있)다; 경청하다.

by the ears, in close struggle. 드잡이하여.

fall on deaf ears, not to be listened to; be ignored. (상대가) 들으려 하지 않다; 무시되다.

give one's ears, make any sacrifice for; be anxious. 어떤 희생이라도 치르다; 어떻게든 하려고 하다.

go in one ear and out the other, have no effect or make no impression. 한쪽 귀로 듣고 한쪽 귀로 흘려버리다; 감명〔인상〕을 주지 못하다.

have an 〔***no***〕 ***ear for,*** can 〔cannot〕 judge the worth of (music). (음악 따위를) 들을 줄 아는 귀를 갖다〔갖지 못하다〕.

have 〔***gain, win***〕 ***someone's ear***(***s***)***,*** have his favorable attention. 아무의 주의를 끌다; 아무를 움직일 수가 있다.

have 〔***keep, hold***〕 ***one's ear to the ground,*** pay careful attention to public opinion or situation of something. 여론에 귀를 기울이다; 정세〔동향〕에 주의하다.

have itching ears, be very eager to hear a

rumor, etc. 소문 따위를 몹시 듣고 싶어하다.
have the ear of =have [gain, win] someone's ear(s).
head over ears in =over (head and) ears in.
lend [give] an ear, listen; pay attention. …을 경청하다; …에 귀를 기울이다; …에 주의하다.
over (head and) ears (in) =up to the ears (in).
play it by ear, 《*colloq.*》 act as things develop from moment to moment, rather than making plans in advance. 복안 없이 하다; 즉석에서 하다.
prick up *one's* ***ears*** ⇨prick.
set *someone's* ***by the ears,*** cause someone to quarrel. (아무에게) 말다툼을 하게 하다; 싸움을 일으키게 하다.
tickle *someone's* ***ears,*** flatter. 아무의 마음에 드는 소리를 하여 기쁘게 하다; 아무에게 아첨하다.
turn a deaf ear, refuse to listen; ignore. …을 들으려 하지 않다; 무시하다.
up to the ears (in), deeply engaged, esp. in debt, etc. (빚 따위로) 움쭉 못 하게 되어; 깊이 빠져들어.
wet behind the ears, not experienced; immature. 경험이 없는; 미숙한.
●**ear·like** [-lἀik] *adj.* [E.]

ear² [iər] *n.* Ⓒ the head or spike of grains. 이삭. ¶ ~ *of wheat* 밀의 이삭 / *in* ~ 이삭이 나와[패어] / *come into ears* 이삭이 나오다[패다]. —*vi.* grow or form ears. (곡식이) 패다; 이삭이 나오다. [E.]

ear·ache [íərèik] *n.* ⒸⓊ pain in the ear. 귓병; 이통(耳痛). ¶ *have an* ~ 귀가 아프다. [*ear¹*]

ear·drum [íərdrʌ̀m] *n.* the tympanic membrane of the ear. 고막; 귀청. [*ear¹*]

•**earl** [əːrl] *n.* Ⓒ 《Brit.》 a nobleman ranking between marquis and viscount. 백작(伯爵). 參考 유럽 대륙의 count 에 해당. [E.]

earl·dom [ə́ːrldəm] *n.* **1** Ⓒ the land owned or ruled by an earl. 백작령(伯爵領). **2** Ⓤ the rank or title of an earl. 백작의 지위[신분]. [↑]

:**ear·ly** [ə́ːrli] *adj.* (**-li·er, -li·est**) **1** before the usual time. 이른; 빠른. ¶ *an* ~ *riser* (아침) 일찍 일어나는 사람 / *in the* ~ *morning* 이른 아침에 / *have an* ~ *dinner* 이른 저녁 식사를 하다 / *It is too* ~ *to go to bed.* 취침하기에는 너무 이르다. **2** near the beginning of. 초기의; 조기(早期)의; 첫 …의. ¶ ~ *fruits* 첫물[햇] 과일 / ~ *spring* 이른[초]봄 / *an* ~ *marriage* 조혼(早婚) / *an* ~ *death* 요절 / *in the* ~ *Renaissance* 초기 르네상스 시대에 / *in the* ~ *part of the 20th century,* 20세기 초기에 / *in my* ~ *years* 나의 젊었을 때(에) / *The* ~ *chapters of this book are very interesting.* 이 책의 초장(章)들은 아주 재미있다. **3** in the near future. 가까운 장래의; 머지 않아. ¶ *at the earliest* 빨라야[도] / *on an* ~ *day* 일간; 머지 않아.
at one's earliest convenience, as soon as it is convenient for one to do so. 될 수 있는 대로 빨리; 형편이 닿는 대로.
early in life, when young. 어렸을 때에. ¶ *He learned it* ~ *in life.* 그것을 어렸을 때 배웠다.
early or late, sooner or later. 조만간.
It is early days yet to *do,* …too soon to do. …하기에는 이르다. ¶ *It is* ~ *days yet to make up one's mind.* 결심하기엔 아직 이르다.
keep early hours, rise and go to bed early. 일찍 자고 일찍 일어나다.
— *adv.* **1** before the usual time. 여느때보다 일찍[이르게]. ¶ *go to school* ~ 일찍 등교하다 / *Don't come too* ~. 너무 일찍 오지 마시오. **2** near to the beginning of a period of time. 초기[조기]에; 처음에. ¶ ~ *in the year* 연초에 / ~ *in 1988,* 1988년초에 / ~ *in his diplomatic career* 그의 외교관으로서의 경력 초기에. [→ere]

early bird [⌐-⌐] *n.* 《*colloq.*》 an early riser. 아침 일찍 일어나는 사람.

ear·mark [íərmὰːrk] *n.* **1** Ⓒ a mark put on the ear of a domestic animal to show the owner of it. 귀표《임자를 나타내기 위해 가축의 귀에 표시함》. **2** any mark put to show what the thing is; a sign. 안표; 표(지); 책장의 귀접은 곳. —*vt.* (P6) **1** make with an earmark. …에 표를 하다. **2** set aside or reserve (something) for special purposes. (특정 용도를 위해) 따로 떼어두다; 따로 책정하다. ¶ ~ *the money for traveling* 여행을 위해 돈을 떼어두다 / ~ *sum of money for research work* 연구비로 얼마의 금액을 따로 책정하다. [*ear¹*]

:**earn** [əːrn] *vt.* (P6) **1** receive (money) for work, service, etc. (돈)을 벌다; …의 수입을 얻다. ¶ ~ *50,000 won a day* 하루 5만 원을 벌다 / ~ *one's living* 생계비를 벌다 / ~ *a good monthly income* 꽤 많은 월수가 있다. **2** get (a good name, fame, etc.). (명성 따위)를 얻다. ¶ ~ *a reputation for honesty* 정직하다는 평판을 얻다. **3** be worthy of (something); deserve. …을 받을 가치가 있다[받을 만하다]. ¶ *You have earned our praise.* 네 행위는 칭찬받을 만하다. [E.]

:**ear·nest¹** [ə́ːrnist] *adj.* **1** ⓐ serious and intense; sincerely zealous. 진지한; 열심인. ¶ *an* ~ *effort* 진지한 노력 / *an* ~ *believer* 경건한 신자 / *an* ~ *worker* 열심히 일하는 사람. ⓑ hearty. 마음으로부터의; 진심에서의. ¶ *an* ~ *words* 진심으로 하는 말 / *an* ~ *desire* 충심으로의 소망. **2** important. 중요한; 진지하게 고려해야 할; 엄숙한. [E.]
in earnest, serious(ly); not joking(ly); sincere(ly) and zealous(ly). 진지한[하게]; 본심의[으로]; 본격적인[으로]. ¶ *He set to work in* ~. 그는 본격적으로 일에 착수했다.

ear·nest² [ə́ːrnist] *n.* Ⓒ 《usu. *an* ~》 **1** money partly paid in advance. 계약금; 증거금; 보증금. **2** a sign of what is to come; a token. 전조; 조짐. [L. *arrha*]

ear·nest·ly [ə́:rnistli] *adv.* in an earnest manner. 진지하게; 열심히; 본심으로. [*earnest*[1]]

ear·nest·ness [ə́:rnistnis] *n.* Ⓤ the state of being earnest. 진심; 진지함. [↑]

earn·ing [ə́:rniŋ] *n.* **1** Ⓤ the act of earning. (일해서) 벎. **2** 《*pl.*》 money earned by labor, etc.; gains; profits. 소득; 벌이; 임금; 이익; 수익. [*earn*]

ear·phone [íərfòun] *n.* Ⓒ a headphone. 이어폰; 청취기(cf. *headphone*). [*ear*[1]]

ear·ring [íəriŋ] *n.* Ⓒ an ornament for the ear. 이어링; 귀고리. [↑]

ear·shot [íərʃàt / -ʃɔ̀t] *n.* Ⓤ the distance over which a sound, esp. of the human voice, can be heard; the range of hearing. ((목)소리 따위가) 들리는 거리. ¶ *be out of* 〔*within*〕 ~ 들리지 않는〔들리는〕 곳에 있다 / *We are within ~ of the church bell.* 우리는 교회 종소리가 들리는 곳에 있다. [↑]

:earth [əːrθ] *n.* (*pl.* **earths**) **1** 《*the* ~》 the planet we live on. 지구. ¶ *on the surface of the ~* 지구의 표면에 / *The moon goes round the ~.* 달은 지구 주위를 돈다. **2** Ⓤ the world we live in. 이 세상; 이승. ¶ *while he was on ~.* 그가 살아 있었을 때 / *create a hell on* (*the*) *~.* 생지옥을 만들다. **3** 《*the* ~》 the people who live on the earth. 지구상의 사람들. ¶ *The whole ~ rejoiced.* 전 세계의 사람들이 기뻐했다. **4** Ⓤ 《often *the* ~》 land; ground. 육지; 대지; 지면; 땅. ¶ *The arrow fell to* (*the*) *~.* 화살은 땅에 떨어졌다. **5** ⓊⒸ soil. 흙. ¶ *cover the roots with ~.* 뿌리를 북주다 / *a soft ~* 부드러운 흙. **6** Ⓒ the hole of a fox, etc. (여우 따위의) 굴.

come back* 〔*down*〕 *to earth, return to reality; stop dreaming. 현실로 돌아오다; 몽상을 버리다.

down to earth, practical; realistic. 현실적인; 실제적인.

move heaven and earth, make every effort to gain some aim. 온갖 노력을 다해 보다.

on earth, **a**) living; on the face of the earth. 살아; 지구상에서. **b**) in this world. 이 세상에서. **c**) =why 〔what, where, how〕 on earth.

run to earth, **a**) discover after a long search; trace (something) to its source. (탐색 끝에) 찾아〔알아〕내다; 붙잡다. **b**) run into the hole. (여우가) 굴 속으로 도망쳐 들어가다.

why* 〔*what, where, how*〕 *on earth, What in the world... 도대체; 대관절. ¶ *How on ~ did you find it?* 대관절 어떻게 그것을 찾았나 / *Where on ~ have you been?* 도대체 어디 있었나.

— *vt.* cover (roots) with earth. (뿌리)에 흙을 덮다; 북주다. [E.]

earth·en [ə́:rθən] *adj.* made of earth or baked clay. 흙으로〔오지로〕 만든.

earth·en·ware [ə́:rθənwɛ̀ər] *n.* Ⓤ anything made of baked clay. 토기(土器); 도기(陶器); 오지그릇.

·earth·ly [ə́:rθli] *adj.* (**-li·er, -li·est**) **1** of the earth. 지구의; 지상의(opp. heavenly). **2** of this world; worldly. 현세의; 이승의; 속세의. ¶ *~ joys* 이승의 기쁨 / *~ affairs* 속된 일. **3** 《*colloq.*》 that may be thought or expected; possible. 가능한. ¶ *have no* 〔*not an*〕 *~ chance* 전혀 가망이 없다 / *something of no ~ use* 전혀 소용이 없는〔도움이 되지 않는〕 것 / *What ~ use can it be?* 도대체 무엇에 소용이 되는가.

earth·nut [ə́:rθnʌ̀t] *n.* 《bot.》 an underground part of certain plants, such as a root, tuber, etc. (열매·줄기·뿌리가) 땅 속에 있는 부분《땅콩 따위》.

·earth·quake [ə́:rθkwèik] *n.* Ⓒ **1** a sudden violent shaking of the earth's surface. 지진. ¶ *feel an ~* 지진을 느끼다. **2** 《*fig.*》 any great disturbance of a social or political nature. 대변동; 대동란. ¶ *the political and social ~ in Ireland* 아일랜드의 정치적 사회적 격동.

earth·ward [ə́:rθwərd] *adv.* toward the earth. 지구〔대지, 땅〕쪽으로 (향하여). — *adj.* at or toward the earth's surface. 지구〔땅〕 쪽으로 향(하게) 한.

earth·wards [ə́:rθwərdz] *adv.* =earthward.

earth·work [ə́:rθwə̀:rk] *n.* 《mil.》 a bank of earth piled up as a fortification. 보루(堡壘); 토루.

earth·worm [ə́:rθwə̀:rm] *n.* Ⓒ a worm living in the soil. 지렁이.

earth·y [ə́:rθi] *adj.* (**earth·i·er, earth·i·est**) **1** of or like earth. 흙의; 흙 같은. **2** of this world; worldly. 현세의; 속세의. **3** unrefined; coarse. 속악(俗惡)한; 조야(粗野)한. ¶ *an ~ novel* 저속한 소설.

ear trumpet [ㅅㅅ-] *n.* a trumpet-shaped tube held to the ear, used by a partially deaf person as a hearing aid. 보청기. [*ear*[1]]

ear·wax [íərwæ̀ks] *n.* cerumen. 귀지.

:ease [iːz] *n.* Ⓤ the state of being free from pain, worry, trouble, difficulty, etc. 안락; 안심; 편안; 용이. ¶ *~ of body and mind* 심신의 편안함 / *a life of ~* 여유 있는 안락한 생활 / *pass one's day in ~* 편안히 지내다.

at* (*one's*) *ease, comfortable; relaxed. 편안한〔히〕. ¶ *be at ~ about one's health* 건강에 걱정이 없다 / *feel at ~* 마음을 놓다; 안심〔편안〕하다 / *sit at ~* 편히 앉다 / *ill at ~* 마음을 놓지 못하고; 불안〔불편〕하여 / *set someone's mind at ~* 안심시키다 / *Stand at ~.* 열중 쉬어《구령》.

take one's ease, relax and make oneself comfortable. (몸·마음을) 편안히 하다.

with ease, easily. 어려움 없이; 쉽게. ¶ *He speaks English with ~.* 영어를 어려움없이 말한다.

— *vt.* (P6,7,13) **1** 《*of*》 make (someone) free from pain, etc.; make (pain, difficul-

E

ty, etc.) less. …을 편안히 하다; (고통·어려움 따위)를 완화시키다. ¶ ~ *oneself* 기분 전환을[안심] 하다; 배변[배뇨]하다. **2** 《*away, down, off*》 make (a belt, etc.) loose; loosen. …을 늦추다; 느슨하게[헐겁게] 하다. ¶ ~ *one's hold* 움켜쥔 손을 늦추다 / ~ *a rope* (켕긴) 밧줄을 늦추다. **3** move carefully. …을 조심스레[신중하게] 움직이다. ¶ ~ *one's car into a narrow street* 차를 조심조심 좁은 길 안으로 몰다. — *vi.* (P2A) (of pain, speed, etc.) become less gradually; relax slowly. (아픔 따위가) 가벼워지다; 느그러지다; (속도 따위가) 떨어지다; 줄다. [F.]

ease off, become less severe. 누그러지다; 완화되다.

ease out, 《U.S.》 **a**) gradually force (someone) out of a job. (압력을 넣어) …을 사직시키다. **b**) 《sports》 win easily. 쉽게 이기다.

ea·sel [íːzəl] *n.* Ⓒ an upright frame to hold a canvas for painting, a blackboard, etc. 화가(畫架); 칠판걸이. [Du. *ezel* ass]

E

:eas·i·ly [íːzəli] *adv.* **1** in an easy manner; with ease; without effort; smoothly. 편안히; (손)쉽게; 용이하게. ¶ *catch cold* ~ 감기에 잘 걸리다 / *live* ~ 안락하게 살다 / *The door shuts* ~. 문이 쉽게 닫힌다 / *These shoes fit me* ~. 이 구두가 낙낙하게 잘 맞는다. **2** very likely. 아마; 필시. ¶ *He may* ~ *change his mind.* 아마도 그는 생각을 바꿀게다. [*easy*]

eas·i·ness [íːzinis] *n.* Ⓤ **1** the state of being easy. 쉬움; 평이함. **2** carelessness; indifference; ease of manner. 부주의; 무(관)심; 편안함; 침착.

:east [iːst] *n.* 《usu. *the* ~》 **1** the direction where the sun rises. 동쪽. ¶ *The sun rises in the* ~ *and sets in the west.* 해는 동쪽에서 뜨고 서쪽에서 진다 / *Korea is in the* ~ *of Asia.* 한국은 아시아 동쪽에 있다. **2** 《also *E-*》 an eastern region or district in the world, in a country, etc. 동부. ¶ *The Far East* 극동 / *the Middle East* 중동 / *the Near East* 근동. **3** 《the *E-*》 the Asiatic countries; the Orient; 《U.S.》 the eastern part of the United States. 동양; (미국의) 동부.

to the east of, further east than. …의 동방[동쪽]에. ¶ *The city is 30 miles to the* ~ *of Seoul.* 그 시는 서울 동쪽 30마일 되는 곳에 있다.

— *adj.* of, to, from, or in the east. 동쪽(에서)의; 동쪽(으로(부터)의). ¶ *the* ~ *side of the street* 길의 동쪽.

— *adv.* **1** toward the east. 동쪽으로. ¶ *sail* ~ 동쪽으로 항해하다. **2** on the east. 동쪽에. ¶ *lie* ~ (*of us*) (우리의) 동쪽에 있다. [E.]

East·er [íːstər] *n.* a Christian festival celebrating Christ's coming to life again. 부활절(復活節). ¶ ~ *Day* [*Sunday*] 부활 주일. [E.]

east·er·ly [íːstərli] *adj., adv.* of, toward, or from the east. 동쪽의[으로]; 동쪽으로부터. ¶ *an* ~ *wind* 동풍 / *The wind blows* ~. 바람이 동쪽으로부터 분다. [*east*]

:east·ern [íːstərn] *adj.* **1** of, toward, from, or in the east. 동쪽(으로)의; 동쪽으로부터의. ¶ *the* ~ *side of a building* 건물의 동쪽. **2** of the east portion of the world. 세계의 동부의. ¶ *the Eastern hemisphere* 동반구.

east·ern·er [íːstərnər] *n.* **1** a native or inhabitant of the east. 동부의 주민[사람]. **2** 《*E-*》 《U.S.》 a person of or from the eastern U.S. 미국 동부 제주(諸州)의 사람.

East Indies [´ ´–] *n.* **the,** southeast Asia, including India, Indonesia, and the Malay Archipelago. 동인도《인도·인도네시아·말레이 군도를 포함한 지역의 총칭》.

east·ward [íːstwərd] *adj., adv.* toward the east. 동쪽[동방]으로(의). ¶ *He walked* ~. 그는 동쪽으로 걸었다 / *The orchard is on the* ~ *slope of the hill.* 과수원은 산의 동쪽으로 경사진 곳에 있다.

east·wards [íːstwərdz] *adv.* = eastward.

:eas·y [íːzi] *adj.* (**eas·i·er, eas·i·est**) **1** not difficult. 쉬운; 수월한. ¶ *an* ~ *problem* 쉬운 문제 / *an* ~ *victory* 낙승 / *The work is* ~. 일이 쉽다 / *It is* ~ *for you to say so.* 네가 그렇게 말하기는 쉽다 / *He is* ~ *to deal with.* 그는 다루기가 쉽다. **2** free from pain, worry, etc.; comfortable. 고통이나 걱정이 없는; 안락한; 편안한. ¶ *be* ~ *in one's mind* 마음 편하다; 안심하고 있다 / *lead an* ~ *life* 여유 있는 생활을 보내다 / *He is in* ~ *circumstances.* 유복하게 살고 있다 / *Make yourself* ~ *about it.* 그 일에 관해선 안심하시오 / *I feel* ~ *about the matter.* 그 건에 관해선 안심이다. **3** pleasing; pleasant. 쾌적한. **4** ⓐ not strict; lenient. 엄하지 않은; 관대한. ¶ *an* ~ *master* 너그러운 주인. ⓑ not stiff, but smooth and pleasant. (태도, 말투 따위가) 딱딱하지 않은. ¶ *an* ~ *posture* 여유있는 자세[태도] / *be* ~ *in conversation and graceful in manner* 대화가 딱딱하지 않고 태도는 우아하다. **5** loose. (옷 따위가) 꼭 끼지 않는; 낙낙한. ¶ *an* ~ *coat* / *an* ~ *pair of slippers* 꼭 끼지 않는 슬리퍼.

— *adv.* in a comfortable manner. 쉽게; 편안[안락]하게. [→ease]

Easy does it. Go gently. Take your time. (당황하지 말고) 신중히 하는 게 좋다; 주의해서 천천히 해라.

go easy, go on at ease. 마음 편히 하다; 신중히 하다.

Take it easy! **a**) Be easy! 서두르지 말고[느긋한 마음으로] 해라; 걱정하지 마라. **b**) Good-by! 안녕.

easy chair [´– ´] *n.* an arm chair designed for comfort. 안락 의자.

eas·y·go·ing [íːzigóuiŋ] *adj.* not worrying; taking matters easily. 태평한; 무심한; 안이한. ¶ *an* ~ *person* 마음 편한[태평한] 사람. [→ease]

easy mark [∠– ∠] *n.* 《U.S.》 a person who is easily imposed on. 다루기 쉬운 사람; 얼간이.

:eat [iːt] *v.* (**ate, ea·ten**) *vt.* **1** (P6,7,18) take (food) in through the mouth. …을 먹다. ¶ *something to* ~ 먹을 것 / ~ *one's dinner* [*a meal*] 식사를 하다 / ~ *soup* 수프를 먹다 / ~ *cabbage raw* 양배추를 날것으로 먹다 / *be good to* ~ 먹을 수 있다 / *There is nothing to* ~. 아무것도 먹을 것이 없다. **2** (P6,7) waste, consume, or destroy as if by eating. …을 (서서히) 파괴[소모, 마멸]시키다; …을 부식[침식]하다. ¶ *Acid eats metal.* 산(酸)은 금속을 부식시킨다. **3** make or cause by or as by eating. (갉아먹거나 부식하거나 하여) 먹어 들어가다; 구멍을[통로를] 뚫다; 먹어서 …상태로 하다. ¶ ~ *oneself sick* 과식하여 병이 나다 / *The acid ate a hole in the metal.* 산이 금속에 구멍을 뚫었다. **4** 《*colloq.*》 annoy; trouble. …을 귀찮게 하다; 괴롭히다. ¶ *What's eating on him?* 무엇이 그를 괴롭히는가. — *vi.* **1** (P1,2A,3,4) take food or a meal. 음식을 먹다; 식사를 하다. ¶ ~ *to excess* 과식하다 / ~ *against time* 허둥지둥 먹다 / *be too ill to* ~ 병으로 먹을 수가 없다. **2** (P2A,3) consume something gradually. 부식하다; 침식하다. [E.]

eat away [***into***], destroy gradually; wear away. (부식·침식 따위로) 서서히 파괴하다; 먹어들어가다. ¶ *The river ate away the banks.* 강물에 개개여 둑이 서서히 붕괴되었다 / *Small expenses ate into my money.* 자잘한 지출이 나의 돈을 잠식했다 / *The hard work ate into her.* 고된 일이 그녀의 건강을 파괴했다.

eat one's head off, eat a great deal and do very little work. (말이) 먹일 만큼의 가치가 없다; 먹기만 하고 일을 하지 않다.

eat one's heart out, be very sad; worry oneself secretly. 매우 슬퍼하다; 남몰래 고민하다.

eat out, **a**) use up. …을 다 써버리다. **b**) take a meal at a restaurant, etc.; dine away from home. 외식하다.

eat out of someone's hand, do whatever one wishes. 아무가 바라는[하라는] 대로 하다; 아무에게 굴종하다.

eat someone out of house and home, ruin someone by relying on him so much for support. 너무 기대어 아무를 재정적으로 곤경에 빠뜨리다.

eat up, **a**) eat or use up wholly. (남김없이) 다 먹어치우다; (돈·시간 따위를) 다 써버리다[소비하다]. ¶ ~ *up one's dinner* 음식을 다 먹어치우다. **b**) 《usu. in *passive*》 make (someone) interested in something. (아무)를 열중[도취]하게 하다. ¶ *He is eaten up with success.* 그는 성공에 도취되어 있다.

eat one's words, take back what one has said. 전언(前言)을 취소하다; 식언하다.

eat·a·ble [íːtəbəl] *adj.* fit to eat. 먹을 수 있는; 식용의. — *n.* 《*pl.*》 anything fit to eat; food. 먹을 수 있는 것; 음식.

:eat·en [íːtn] *v.* pp. of **eat.**

eat·er [íːtər] *n.* Ⓒ a person who eats. 먹는 사람. ¶ *a big* ~ 대식가(大食家).

eat·ing [íːtiŋ] *n.* **1** the act of taking food. 먹음; 먹기. ¶ *be fond of* ~ *and drinking* 먹고 마시기를 좋아하다. **2** food. 음식; 먹거리. ¶ *Quails are excellent* ~. 메추라기는 좋은 음식이다.

eating house [∠–∠] *n.* a shop where food is sold ready cooked to be eaten on the spot; a restaurant, usu. an inexpensive or inferior one. 음식점; 값싼 식당. [E.]

EATS European Air Transport Service. 유럽 항공 수송편.

eau de Co·logne [óu də kəlóun] *n.* a sweet-smelling toilet water; cologne. 오드콜론《Cologne 원산의 향수》. [F.]

eau de vie [òu də víː] *n.* 《F.》 =brandy.

eaves [iːvz] *n. pl.* the edges of a roof projecting beyond the sides of a building. 처마. [E.]

eaves·drop [íːvzdràp / íːvzdrɔ̀p] *vi.* (**-dropped, -drop·ping**) (P1) listen secretly to the private talk of other people. (남의 이야기를) 엿듣다.

eaves·drop·per [íːvzdràpər / -drɔ̀p-] *n.* a person who listens secretly to private conversation. (남의 이야기를) 엿듣는 사람.

ebb [eb] *n.* Ⓒ **1** the flowing back of the tide away from the shore toward the sea; the low tide. 썰물; 간조(opp. flood). ¶ ~ *and flow* 조수의 간만. **2** decline; decay. 쇠퇴; 쇠미; 쇠망. ¶ *the* ~ *and flow of life* 인생의 성쇠 / *be at an* ~ 쇠퇴해 있다 / *Crime is on the* ~. 범죄가 감소되고 있다 / *His courage was at its lowest* ~. 그의 용기는 극도로 떨어져 있었다.
— *vi.* (P1,2A,3) **1** flow back or out, go back. 조수가 써다; 물이 빠지다. **2** (of power, etc.) weaken; decline. (세력 따위가) 쇠퇴하다. ¶ *Daylight is ebbing fast.* 햇빛이 급격히 약해지고 있다 / *His life was ebbing away.* 그의 인생은 쇠퇴의 길을 걷고 있었다. [E.]

ebb tide [∠∠] *n.* the tide at ebb. 썰물; 간조(opp. flood tide).

eb·on [ébən] *adj.* **1** 《*poet.*》 made of ebony. 흑단(黑檀)으로 된. **2** very black. 새까만. ¶ ~ *hair* 흑발. [Gk.]

eb·on·ite [ébənàit] *n.* Ⓤ black material used for combs, fountain pens, etc.; hard rubber. 에보나이트; 경화(硬化) 고무.

eb·on·y [ébəni] *n.* **1** Ⓤ the hard black wood used for furniture, etc. 흑단(黑檀)목재. **2** Ⓒ tropical trees that yield this wood. 흑단나무. — *adj.* **1** made of or like ebony. 흑단으로 된; 흑단 같은. **2** deep black. 새까만. [Gk.]

e·bul·lient [ibúljənt, -bʌ́l-] *adj.* **1** boiling. 끓고[비등하고] 있는. **2** full of a happy feeling, enthusiasm, etc.; high-spirited. (열정·흥분·기운이) 넘치는; 용솟음치는; 열광적인. [→boil[1]]

eb·ul·li·tion [èbəlíʃən] *n.* UC **1** the state of boiling or bubbling up. 끓음; 비등. **2** a sudden outburst of feeling, etc. (감정 따위의) 격발. ¶ *an ~ of rage* 격노.

ec- [ek-, ək-, ik-] *pref.* =ex-.

Ec·ce Ho·mo [éksi hóumou, éksei-] *n.* 《L.》 a picture of Christ with crown of thorns. 가시 면류관을 쓴 예수의 초상화. [L.=behold the man (John xix 5)]

ec·cen·tric [ikséntrik, ek-] *adj.* **1** unusual; queer; odd. 색다른; 야릇한; 괴상한; 괴짜의. **2** (of the two circles) not having the same center. 중심을 달리하는. **3** not placed in the center. 중심에서 벗어난(opp. concentric). —— *n.* C **1** an eccentric person. 괴짜; 기인(奇人). **2** the device for changing round motion into back-and-forth motion. 편심기(偏心機). [ex-, →centre]

ec·cen·tric·i·ty [èksentrísəti] *n.* (*pl.* **-ties**) **1** U the state of being eccentric; oddity. 야릇함; 이상함; 색다름. **2** C an odd act or characteristic; peculiarity. 기벽(奇癖); 기행(奇行).

eccl., eccles. ecclesiastical.

Eccle., Eccles. Ecclesiastes.

Ec·cle·si·as·tes [iklì:ziǽsti:z] *n.* C a book of the Bible. 전도서《구약 성서 중의 한 편》. [↓]

ec·cle·si·as·tic [iklì:ziǽstik] *n.* C a clergyman or priest. 성직자. —— *adj.* = ecclesiastical. [Gk. *ekklēsia* assembly]

ec·cle·si·as·ti·cal [iklì:ziǽstikəl] *adj.* of the church or the clergy. 교회의; 성직의 (cf. *secular*). ¶ *~ discipline* 성직자의 계율 / *~ history* 교회사(史). [↑]

ech·e·lon [éʃəlàn / -lɔ̀n] *n.* C **1** the troops, airplanes, etc., arranged like steps. (부대·함선·비행기의) 제형(梯形) 편성; 제대(梯隊); 제진(梯陣). ¶ *an airplane ~* 항공기의 제형 편대. **2** 《often *pl.* with *sing.* meaning》 a level of command (in a group of people or organization). (지휘 계통·조직의) 단계; 계급. ¶ *the top ~ of city officials* 시 관료의 최상층. —— *vt.* (P6) form or move (airplanes, etc.) in echelon. (비행기 따위를) 제형으로 편성하다[움직이다]. [L. *scala* ladder]

Ech·o [ékou] *n.* 《Gk. myth.》 a nymph who loved Narcissus. 숲의 여신.

:ech·o [ékou] *n.* C (*pl.* **-oes**) **1** the state of repeating a sound by reflection. 메아리; 반향. ¶ *an ~ among the hills* 산울림. **2** the act of repeating or imitating another person's thoughts or views. (남의 생각·견해 따위의) 되풀이; 모방. **3** a person who imitates another person's acts, etc. closely. 모방자.

—— *vi.* (P1,2A) 《*with*》 repeat in sound; sound again. 반향하다; 메아리치다. ¶ *His voice echoed through the hall.* 그의 목소리는 홀에 메아리쳤다.

—— *vt.* (P6,7) **1** reflect (sounds). …을 반향시키다; 메아리치게 하다. **2** repeat (another person's words, opinion, etc.); imitate (another person's acts, etc.). (남의 말)을 되뇌다; (남의 의견·감정에) 공명하다; (남의 행동)을 모방하다. ¶ *~ someone's sentiment* 아무의 감정에 공명하다 / *He echoes his wife in everything.* 그는 만사를 아내가 하는 대로 한다. [Gk.]

e·clair [eiklɛ́ər, ik-, ⌐–] *n.* C a finger-shaped cake filled with cream. 에클레어《크림이 든 슈크림 비슷한 과자》. [F.]

e·clat [eiklɑ́:, ⌐–] *n.* 《F.》 great success; applause; renown; fame. 대성공; 대갈채; 명성. ¶ *the ~ of a great achievement* 훌륭한 〔눈부신〕 위업 / *a performance of great ~* 대단한 연기. [F.]

ec·lec·tic [ekléktik] *adj.* choosing and using the best from various sources; made up of things selected from various sources; selecting. (취사) 선택하는; 절충하는; 절충적인. ¶ *an ~ painter* 각종의 기법을 받아들이는 화가 / *an ~ reader* 좋은 작품을 취사 선택해서 읽는 독자 / *Her taste in music is ~.* 그녀의 음악 취미는 어느 한쪽에 치우쳐 있지 않다. —— *n.* C a person who uses eclectic methods in philosophy, etc. 절충학파〔주의〕의 사람. [Gk. *legō* pick]

e·clipse [iklíps] *n.* 《astron.》 C entire or partial cutting off of the light of the sun, moon, etc. by some other heavenly body. (해·달의) 식(蝕). ¶ *solar ~* 일식 / *lunar ~* 월식 / *a partial* 〔*total*〕 *~* 부분〔개기(皆旣)〕식 / *annular ~* 금환(金環)식 / 《*fig.*》 *go into ~ =suffer an ~* (신분·명성 따위가) 실추하다; 빛을 잃다.

—— *vt.* (P6) **1** cause an eclipse of (the sun, moon, etc.); darken. (천체가) …을 가리다; 어둡게 하다. **2** obscure the fame of (someone); surpass. (…의 명성)을 희미하게 하다; 빛을 잃게 하다; 능가하다. ¶ *a soprano whose singing eclipsed that of her rivals* 경쟁 상대를 무색게 할 정도로 잘 부른 소프라노 / *~ someone's reputation* 아무의 명성을 빛 바래게 하다 / *In sports he quite eclipsed his brothers.* 스포츠에서 그는 그의 형들을 능가했다. [Gk. *leipō* leave]

e·clip·tic [iklíptik] *n.* 《astron.》 《*the ~*》 the path which the sun appears to follow among the stars in a year. 황도(黃道). —— *adj.* of eclipses or the ecliptic. 식(蝕)의; 황도의. [↑]

ec·logue [éklɔ:g / -lɔg] *n.* C a short poem of shepherds and their life, often in the form of a conversation between shepherds. 목가(牧歌); 전원시. [→eclectic]

e·col·o·gy [ikɑ́lədʒi / -kɔ́l-] *n.* a branch of biology that deals with the relation of living things to their environment and to each other. 생태학. ● **e·col·og·i·cal** [èkəlɑ́dʒikəl, i:kə-/-lɔ́dʒ-] *adj.* [Gk. *oikos* house]

:ec·o·nom·ic [ì:kənɑ́mik, èkə-/-nɔ́m-] *adj.* **1** of economics. 경제학의. ¶ *an ~ principles* 경제학상의 법칙. **2** of the management of income, expenses, etc; having to do with economy. 경제(상)의. ¶ *an ~ crisis* 경제 위기 / *give up a large house for ~ reasons* 경제적 이유로 큰 집을 내놓다. [→ economy]

***ec·o·nom·i·cal** [ì:kənɑ́mikəl, èk-/-nɔ́m-] *adj.* **1** careful not to waste money, time, goods, etc.; thrifty. (사람이) 검약하는; 절약하는 (opp. extravagant). ¶ *an ~ housewife* 알뜰한 주부 / *be ~ of one's time* 〔*money*〕 시간〔돈〕을 절약하다. **2** not wasteful; using up little. (물건이) 경제적인. ¶ *an ~ stove* (연료 소모 따위가) 경제적인 스토브. **3** of economics. 경제(학)의.

ec·o·nom·i·cal·ly [ì:kənɑ́mikəli, èkə-/-nɔ́m-] *adv.* **1** in an economical manner. 경제적으로; 절약하여. **2** from the viewpoint of economics. 경제학(상)으로 보아.

ec·o·nom·ics [ì:kənɑ́miks, èkə-/-nɔ́m-] *n. pl.* 《used as *sing.*》 the social science that treats the production, distribution, and consumption of wealth. 경제학.

e·con·o·mist [ikɑ́nəmist/-kɔ́n-] *n.* Ⓒ **1** a person who studies economics. 경제학자. **2** an economical person. 절약가; 알뜰한 사람. ¶ *economists even to stinginess* 인색하다고 할 수 있을 정도의 절약가들.

e·con·o·mize [ikɑ́nəmàiz/-kɔ́n-] *vi.* (P1) be economical or careful in spending money; avoid useless expenses. 절약하다; 낭비를 피하다. ¶ *~ in time* 시간을 절약하다 / *~ on half-pay* 절약하여 급료의 반으로 지내다. — *vt.* (P6) spend (money, time, etc.) or use (goods, etc.) without waste. …을 경제적으로 사용하다; 절약하다; 낭비를 피하다. ¶ *This month I must ~ time as much as I can.* 이 달엔 될 수 있는 대로 시간을 절약해야 한다.

***e·con·o·my** [ikɑ́nəmi/-kɔ́n-] *n.* (*pl.* **-mies**) **1** Ⓤ the management of the income, expense, goods, etc. of a household, private business, community, society, etc. 경제; 이재(理財). ¶ *national ~* 국민 경제 / *rural ~* 농촌 경제 / *social ~* 사회 경제. **2** ⓊⒸ the state of being free from waste of money, time, labor, etc. by careful planning and use. 절약. ¶ *~ of time and labor* 시간과 노력의 절약 / *~ in expenditure* 경비의 절약 / *live with rigid ~* 지독히 조리차하며 살다 / *It is an ~ of labor and time to work hard for a limited time.* 제한된 시간에 열심히 일하는 것은 노력과 시간의 절약이 된다. **3** Ⓒ an organization; a system. (유기적인) 조직(체). [Gk. *oikos* house *nemō* manage]

e·cru, é·cru [ékru:, éi-] *n., adj.* 《F.》 pale brown. 담갈색(의).

ec·sta·sy [ékstəsi] *n.* Ⓒ (*pl.* **-sies**) **1** a feeling of great joy; great delight; rapture. 큰 기쁨; 환희; 열광. ¶ *He was speechless with ~.* 기쁨으로 설레어 말도 하지 못했다. **2** the state of being beside oneself with some emotion, esp. joy. 무아경; 황홀 상태. ¶ *listen with ~* 도취되어 듣다 / *He is in ecstasies over the new work.* 그는 새 작품에 열중〔몰두〕해 있다. [Gk. =standing out of oneself]

be thrown ecstasies over, = go 〔get〕 into ecstasies over.

go* 〔*get*〕 *into ecstasies over, be enraptured. …에 황홀해지다〔도취되다〕.

in an ecstasy of joy, beside oneself with joy; absorbed in joy. 기쁜 나머지 자신을 잊고; 환희에 젖어.

ec·stat·ic [ekstǽtik] *adj.* of or in ecstasy; rapturous. 광희의; 황홀 상태의. — *n.* Ⓒ a person who is in the state of ecstasy. 황홀 상태에 도취해 있는 사람. ● **ec·stat·i·cal·ly** [-kəli] *adv.*

Ec·ua·dor [ékwədɔ̀:r] *n.* a country on the northwestern coast of South America. 에콰도르《남아메리카 서북부의 나라; 수도는 Quito》.

Ec·ua·do·ri·an [èkwədɔ́:riən] *adj.* of Ecuador. 에콰도르의. — *n.* Ⓒ a person of Ecuador. 에콰도르 사람.

ec·ze·ma [éksəmə, égzi-, igzí:mə] *n.* Ⓤ a disease of the skin with pain, itching, fever, swelling, etc. 습진. [Gk. =out-boil]

Ed [ed] a petname of Edgar, Edmond, Edmund, Edward, and Edwin. 남자의 이름 《Edgar, Edward... 따위의 애칭》.

ed. editor; edition; edited.

ed·dy [édi] *n.* Ⓒ (*pl.* **-dies**) (of water, smoke, etc.) a round or coiled movement against the main current. 소용돌이; 회오리. ¶ *get into* 〔*get caught up by*〕 *an ~* 소용돌이에 말려들다〔휘말리다〕; 회오리에 휘말리다. — *vi., vt.* (**-died**) (P1,2A; 6) move round and round in small circles; whirl or cause (water, etc.) to whirl; 《*fig.*》 (of people) wander about in circles. 회오리〔소용돌이〕치(게 하)다; (사람들이) 빙빙 돌아다니다; 배회하다. [N.]

e·del·weiss [éidlvàis, -wàis] *n.* a small Alpine plant. 에델바이스. [G. *edel* noble; *weiss* white]

e·de·ma [idí:mə] *n.* (*pl.* **-ma·ta**) a watery swelling in the tissues of the body. 부종(浮腫); 수종(水腫). [Gk.]

e·de·ma·ta [idí:mɑtə] *n.* pl. of **edema.**

E·den [í:dn] *n.* **1** 《Bible》 the garden where Adam and Eve lived at first. 에덴의 동산. **2** a delightful place. 낙원. [Heb. =delight]

Ed·gar [édgər] *n.* a man's name. 남자의 이름. 參考 애칭은 Ed.

:edge [edʒ] *n.* Ⓒ **1** a sharp, cutting side of

a blade. (칼 따위의) 날. ¶ *blunt the ~ of a knife* 나이프의 날을 무디게 하다 / *This knife has a keen ~.* 이 나이프는 잘 든다. **2** the border (of anything); the part that is farthest from the middle. 가; 가장자리; (어떤 면의) 끝; 변두리; 경계. ¶ *the ~ of a plate* 〔*table*〕 접시〔테이블〕의 가장자리 / *the edges of a road* 길의 양단(兩端) / *on the ~ of the forest* 숲가에 / *We live at the ~ of the town.* 시 변두리에 살고 있다.

be on edge, be excited. 몹시 흥분해 있다.

give an edge to, sharpen. (칼 따위에) 날을 세우다〔버리다〕. ¶ *give a sharp and keen ~ to a sword* 칼에 예리한 날을 세우다.

give** someone **the edge of** one's **tongue, 《*sl.*》 speak sharply (to); speak angrily and roughly (to). …에게 성이 나서〔난폭하게〕 말하다; …를 호되게 야단치다.

have the edge on, surpass; be impatient for. (…보다) 좀 우세하다; 신경이 날카로워져 있다; 초조해〔조마조마해〕하고 있다.

***on the edge of** (doing),* on the point of. 이제 막 …하려는 참에; …지경에 이르러.

put an edge on, 《*colloq.*》 sharpen. …을 날카롭게 하다; 날을 세우다〔버리다〕.

put to the edge of the sword, slain. 살해하다.

set** someone's **nerves on edge, cause him to be on edge. …의 신경을 자극하다. ¶ *His voice sets my nerves on ~.* 그의 목소리는 나의 신경을 건드린다.

set** something **on edge, irritate. …을 자극〔초조하게〕 하다.

set 〔***put***〕 ***someone's teeth on edge,*** induce an unpleasant sensation; give an unpleasant feeling to. 불쾌감을 자아내다; 불쾌하게 하다.

***take the edge off** (a knife, argument, etc.),* make less sharp; take away the sharpness or force of. (날·기세를) 무디게 하다; (감흥 따위를) 꺾다.

— *vt.* **1** (P6) give an edge to (a knife); sharpen. …에 날을 세우다; (날붙이)를 갈다. ¶ *~ a knife* 칼의 날을 세우다. **2** (P6) put a border on (something). …에 테를 달다, 테두리를 두르다. ¶ *~ a curtain with lace* 커튼에 레이스를 두르다. **3** (P6,13) move along the edge or border; move sideways. 한발 한발 가를 따라〔옆으로, 비스듬히〕 나아가다; 서서히 움직이다. ¶ *~ a chair forward* 의자를 조금씩 앞으로 당기며 나아가다 / *~ oneself through a crowd* 몸을 옆으로 하여 군중 속을 헤치고 나아가다 / *~ oneself into the conversation* 조금씩 이야기에 끼어들다. — *vi.* (P2A,3) move carefully. 조심스럽게 움직이다. [E.]

edge away 〔***off***〕, move away gradually and carefully. (조금씩) 천천히 떨어지다〔떠나다, 멀어지다〕.

edge into, enter cautiously sideways. 옆으로 끼어들다.

edge out, **a**) gradually remove; move out gradually. 서서히 이전시키다〔물러나게 하다〕; (조심해서) 천천히 나오다. **b**) defeat (someone) by only a small amount. 근소한 차로 이기다; 신승하다.

edge·ways [édʒwèiz] *adv.* with the edge forward; on, by, or toward the edge. 날을 앞으로 향하게 하고; 가(장자리)를 따라〔쪽으로〕; 끝(쪽)에〔으로〕.

get a word in edgeways, say a few words in a conversation when the other person is, for a moment, silent. (이야기가 잠시 끊겼을 때) 교묘히 끼어들다; 곁에서 말참견을 하다.

edge·wise [édʒwàiz] *adv.* =edgeways.

edg·ing [édʒiŋ] *n.* ⓤⓒ narrow border which forms an edge. 가선 두름〔붙이기〕; 가장자리 장식.

ed·i·ble [édəbəl] *adj.* fit to eat; eatable. 식용의; 먹을 수 있는. ¶ *~ oil* 식용유 / *~ frogs* 식용 개구리. — *n.* 《*pl.*》 eatable things; food. 식료품; 음식. [L. *edo* eat]

e·dict [í:dikt] *n.* ⓒ the official public order sent out by authority; decree. 포고(布告); 칙령. [L. *dico* say]

ed·i·fi·ca·tion [èdəfikéiʃən] *n.* ⓤ spiritual instruction; moral improvement. 교훈; 덕성의 함양; 교화. ¶ *for one's own ~* 자기 계발(啓發)을 위하여; 후학을 위하여 / *Good books give ~.* 양서는 교훈을 준다. [→edify]

ed·i·fice [édəfis] *n.* ⓒ **1** a building, esp. a large one. 건물; (특히 궁전·사원 같은) 대건축물. **2** 《*fig.*》 something formed in the mind. (추상적인) 구성물〔조직〕; (사상의) 체계. ¶ *Comte's ~* 콩트의 학문 체계.

ed·i·fy [édəfài] *vt.* (**-fied**) (P6) improve morally; give moral instruction to. …의 덕성을 기르다; …을 계발〔향상〕하다; …을 교화(教化)하다. ¶ *Good deeds ~ us more than words.* 선행은 말보다 더 우리를 교화한다. [L. *aedes* house, -fy]

Ed·in·burgh [édinbə̀:rou, -bə̀:rə] *n.* the capital of Scotland. 에딘버러《Scotland 의 수도》.

Ed·i·son [édəsən], **Thomas Alva** *n.* (1847-1931) an American inventor. 에디슨《미국의 발명가》.

ed·it [édit] *vt.* (P6,13) **1** read, correct, and put (an author's writings, etc.) into a suitable form for publication. (책을) 편집하다. **2** direct the publication of (a newspaper or magazine). (주필이)(신문·잡지)를 편집 발행하다. [L. *do* give]

ed·it. [édit] edition; edited; editor.

·e·di·tion [idíʃən] *n.* ⓒ **1** (of a magazine, book, newspaper, etc.) the number of copies printed at one time; an issue. (잡지·책·신문 등이) 한 번에 간행된 발행 부수; 간행본; 판(版). ¶ *the first* 〔*second*〕 *~* 제1〔2〕판 / *a limited ~* 한정판 / *The book reached a tenth ~.* 그 책은 10판이나 간행되었다. **2** the form in which a book, etc. is published. (책의) 판형(版型); 판(版)《인쇄물의 제본·양식·체재·간행 연도 따위, 출판 형태에 따른 구분》. ¶ *a cheap ~* 염가판 / *a pocket ~* 포켓

판 / *the Sunday* ~ (신문의) 일요판. **3** 《*fig.*》 a repetition of something in a slightly different form. 복제(물). ¶ *He's an inferior ~ of his father.* 그는 생긴 것이 아버지만 못하다. [→edit]

:ed·i·tor [édətər] *n.* Ⓒ **1** a person who edits a newspaper, etc. (신문 따위의) 편집자(인). **2** one having charge of a publication; a person who has charge of a newspaper and decides what shall be printed in it. 편집장; (신문의) 편집 발행인. **3** a person who writes editorials. 논설 위원.

·ed·i·to·ri·al [èdətɔ́:riəl] *adj.* of an editor or editing; by an editor. 편집인의[에 의한]; 편집상의. ¶ ~ *policies* 편집 방침 / *the ~ staff* 편집부원. — *n.* Ⓒ a leading article in a newspaper, etc. in which an editor gives opinions. 논설; 사설(cf. *leader*).

ed·i·to·ri·al·ize [edətɔ́:riəlàiz] *vi.* (P1,3) **1** express editorial opinions in a newspaper, etc. 사설(社說)로 논하다. **2** put (editorial opinions) into an article, etc. (논설을) 싣다.

Ed·mond, -mund [édmənd] *n.* a man's name. 남자 이름. 參考 애칭은 Ed.

·ed·u·cate [édʒukèit] *vt.* (P6,13) **1** teach; train. …을 교육하다; 훈련하다. ¶ ~ *a child* 아이들을 교육시키다 / ~ *someone's taste in literature* 아무의 문학 감상력을 기르다 / ~ *a dog to jump through a hoop* 고리의 구멍을 뛰어넘도록 개를 훈련시키다. **2** send (someone) to school. …을 학교에 보내다. ¶ *be educated at a college* 대학 교육을 받다 / *He educated his brothers after his father's death.* 그는 아버지가 돌아가신 후에 아우들을 학교에 보냈다. [L. *edūco* rear]

ed·u·cat·ed [édʒukèitid] *adj.* having education or a cultivated mind, etc.; trained. 교육을 받은; 교양 있는; 훈련된. ¶ *an ~ man* 교육을 받은 사람 / ~ *classes* 지식 계급.

:ed·u·ca·tion [èdʒukéiʃən] *n.* **1** ⓊⒸ the process of developing knowledge, skill, ability, character, etc. by teaching or training. 교육. ¶ *technical* ~ 기술 교육 / ~ *for citizenship* 공민 교육 / *compulsory* ~ 의무 교육 / *higher* ~ 고등 교육 / *get* [*receive*] ~ 교육을 받다. **2** Ⓤ the knowledge, skill, etc. developed by such training. 교양; 지식; 기술. ¶ *show one's* ~ 교양을 발휘하다. **3** Ⓤ science that deals with the principles, etc., of teaching and learning. 교육학. **4** Ⓤ an organized system of instruction as existing in a given state. 교육 제도.

·ed·u·ca·tion·al [èdʒukéiʃənəl] *adj.* of education; instructive. 교육의; 교육적인. ¶ *an ~ film* 교육 영화 / ~ *expenses* 교육비 / *an ~ system* 교육 제도. ● **ed·u·ca·tion·al·ly** [-i] *adv.*

ed·u·ca·tion·al·ist [èdʒukéiʃənəlist] *n.* a person concerned with the theory, practice, or organization of education. 교육 전문가; 교육학자.

ed·u·ca·tion·ist [èdʒukéiʃənist] *n.* =educationalist.

ed·u·ca·tive [édʒukèitiv / -kə-] *adj.* having the power of educating; instructive. 교육에 도움이 되는; 교육적인.

ed·u·ca·tor [édʒukèitər] *n.* Ⓒ a person who educates; a teacher. 교육자; 교사.

e·duce [idjú:s] *vt.* (P6,13) draw or bring out (a hidden power or quality); draw (a conclusion) from facts. (잠재된 능력·재능 따위)를 끌어내다; 추론(推論)[연역]하다. [L. *dūco* draw]

e·duc·tion [i:dʌ́kʃən] *n.* **1** educing. 추출; 추단; 연역. **2** that which is educed. 끌어낸 [추출한] 것; 추론된 것.

Ed·ward [édwərd] *n.* a man's name. 남자 이름. 參考 애칭은 Ed, Ned.

e. e. errors excepted. 오기(誤記)는 제외하고.

EEC European Economic Community.

EEG electroencephalogram. 뇌파도.

eel [i:l] *n.* Ⓒ a long, smooth, snake-like fish living in a lake or the sea. (뱀)장어. [E.]

(**as**) ***slippery as an eel,*** very slippery; difficult to hold 《also *fig.*》. 매우 미끄러운; 미끄러워 붙잡을 데가 없는.

e'en [i:n] 《*poet.*》 *adv.* =even. — *n.* =evening.

e'er [ɛər] *adv.* =ever.

ee·rie [íəri] *adj.* **1** causing a mysterious feeling or fear; strange. 사위스러운; 무시무시한; 불길한. **2** timid or uneasy because of superstition. (미신적으로) 겁나는; 겁먹은. ● **ee·ri·ly** [-li] *adv.* **ee·ri·ness** [-nis] *n.* [E.]

ee·ry [íəri] (**-ri·er, -ri·est**) *adj.* =eerie.

ef·face [iféis] *vt.* (P6) **1** rub or wipe out (bad memories, etc.). …을 지워[닦아] 없애다. ¶ ~ *the memory of the past* 과거의 기억을 지워 없애다 / *Time cannot ~ us from his heart.* 세월이 흘러도 그의 마음 속에서 우리를 지워 없앨 수는 없다. **2** keep (oneself) from being noticed. …을 눈에 띄지 않게 하다. ¶ ~ *oneself* 자신을 드러내지 않다; 자신을 멸각(滅却)하다. ● **ef·face·a·ble** [-əbl] *adj.* [ex-, →face]

:ef·fect [ifékt] *n.* **1** ⒸⓊ the result of a cause. 결과; 영향. ¶ *cause and* ~ 원인과 결과 / *the effects of light upon the eye* 눈에 미치는 빛의 영향 / *suffer from the effects of the cold* 추위 탓으로 병을 앓고 있다 / *His failure is the ~ of idleness.* 그의 실패는 게으른 탓이다. **2** ⒸⓊ an impression on the mind. 인상; (심적) 효과. ¶ *a dramatic* ~ 극적인 효과. **3** Ⓤ the power which produces some results. 효력; 효능. ¶ *the effects of electricity* 전기의 여러 가지 작용 / *with* ~ 효과적으로; 유효하게 / *without* [*to no*] ~ 아무 효과도 없이. **4** ⒸⓊ influence; the state of being influenced. 영향. ¶ *the effects of heat* 더위먹음 / *have an ~ on* …에 대하여 영향을 미치다 / *exercise a marked ~ upon the body* 몸에

E

강한 영향을 미치다. **5** Ⓤ the main idea; meaning. 취의(趣意); 취지; 의미. ¶ *to this* ~ 이러한 취지로 / *speak to the same* ~ 같은 취지의 말을 하다. **6.** 《*pl.*》 goods or things belonging to someone. 동산(動產); 가재(家財).

bring to effect =***carry into effect,*** put into practice; carry out. 실행에 옮기다; 실시하다.

come* 〔*go*〕 *into effect, (of a law) become effectual; be enforced. 시행되다.

for effect, in order to produce an effect; for show. 효과를 노리어; 남의 눈을 끌기 위해. ¶ *talk merely for* ~ 단지 남을 의식해서 말을 하다.

give effect to, put (a plan) into practice. …을 실행에 옮기다.

in effect, **a**) in fact; really. 사실상; 실제로는. **b**) having legal force. (법적) 효력을 가진. ¶ *The law is still in* ~. 이 법은 아직도 유효하다. **c**) basically; essentially. 근본적〔기본적〕으로는.

of no effect, in vain. 효과 없이; 헛되이. ¶ *be of no* ~ 아무 효과도 없다; 무효이다.

take effect, **a**) become active; come into force. (법률 따위가) 효력을 발생하다; 실시가 되다. **b**) prove to be successful. 효과를 나타내다; (약이) 듣다. ¶ *The medicine failed to take* ~. 약이 듣지 않았다.

to the effect that, having the essential meaning that… …이라는 뜻〔취지〕의.

— *vt.* (P6,13) produce (something) as a result; cause; bring about. 결과로서 …을 낳다; 가져오다. [→fact]

***ef·fec·tive** [iféktiv] *adj.* **1** having an effect; producing the expected or desired effect. 유효한; 효과가 있는. ¶ ~ *steps toward world peace* 세계 평화를 위한 효과적인 조처 / *take* ~ *measures* 유효한 수단을 취하다 / *The medicine was* ~. 약이 효력을 나타냈다. **2** producing a remarkable or striking impression. 효과적인; 눈에 띄는. ¶ *make an* ~ *speech* 효과적인 연설을 하다 / *The dress is* ~. 그 복장은 눈에 띈다. **3** actual or existing. 실제의; 사실상의.

become effective, come into effect. 효력을 발생하다. ¶ *The peace treaty is expected to become* ~ *on May 1.* 평화 조약은 5월 1일 발효한다.

— *n.* 《*pl.*》 soldiers equipped and ready for fighting. 동원할 수 있는 병원(兵員); 실병력(實兵力).

ef·fec·tive·ly [iféktivli] *adv.* in an effective manner. 유효하게; 사실상.

ef·fec·tu·al [iféktʃuəl] *adj.* **1** able to produce the expected effect; adequate. 효과적인; 효력 있는; 적절한. ¶ ~ *measures* 효과적인 조치 / *The punishment was* ~ *and the offence was not repeated.* 처벌이 효과적이어서 불법 행위는 되풀이 되지 않았다. **2** having legal force. (법령이) 유효한. [→effect]

ef·fec·tu·al·ly [iféktʃuəli] *adv.* in an effectual manner; effectively. 유효하게; 효과적으로.

ef·fem·i·na·cy [ifémənəsi] *n.* Ⓤ the state of being effeminate; unmanly weakness. 여자 같음; 유약(柔弱). [↓]

ef·fem·i·nate [ifémənit] *adj.* lacking in manly qualities; unmanly. 여자 같은; 나약한. — *vt., vi.* (P6; 1) make (someone) effeminate; become effeminate. 여자같이 되게 하다〔되다〕. [L. *femina* woman]

ef·fer·ent [éfərənt] *adj.* conveying outward from a central organ or point. 원심성(遠心性)의. ¶ ~ nerves 원심성 신경. [ex-, L. *fero* carry]

ef·fer·vesce [èfərvés] *vi.* (P1) **1** (of liquids or gas) give or send out bubbles of gas; bubble up; come away in bubbles. 거품이 일다; 부글거리다. **2** (of a person) be full of life; be gay; be excited. 활기에 넘치다; 쾌활하다; 흥분하다. [ex-, →fervent]

ef·fer·ves·cence [èfərvésns] *n.* Ⓤ the act of bubbling; the state of being effervesced; excitement; liveliness. 부글거림; 비등(沸騰); 흥분; 활기. [↑]

ef·fer·ves·cent [èfərvésnt] *adj.* sending out bubbles of gas; showing great excitement; lively. 발포성(發泡性)의; 쾌활한; 활기찬.

ef·fete [efíːt] *adj.* worn out; tired out; not able to produce. 정력이 다한; 쇠잔한; 생산력이 없는. ¶ *an* ~ *civilization* 쇠퇴한 문명. [L.]

ef·fi·ca·cious [èfəkéiʃəs] *adj.* able to produce the expected results; effective. 유효한; 효과가〔효능이〕 있는. [→effect]

ef·fi·ca·cy [éfəkəsi] *n.* Ⓤ the state of being efficacious. 유효; 효능; 효력.

ef·fi·cien·cy [ifíʃənsi] *n.* Ⓤ the state of being efficient; effectiveness. 유능; 유효; 능률; 효율. [↓]

·ef·fi·cient [ifíʃənt] *adj.* able to produce the desired results; able. 효과 있는; 능률적인; 유능한. ¶ *an* ~ *man* 유능한 사람 / *the* ~ *cause* 동인(動因) / ~ *machines* 효율적인 기계 / *be* ~ *in doing something* 무엇을 하는 데 유능하다. [→effect]

ef·fi·cient·ly [ifíʃəntli] *adv.* in an efficient manner. 유효하게; 능률적으로.

ef·fi·gy [éfədʒi] *n.* Ⓒ (*pl.* **-gies**) a portrait, statue, or image of a person. 초상; 상(像); 우상. [L. *fingo* fasion]

burn* 〔*hang*〕 *a person in effigy, burn a person's effigy as a sign of hatred. 증오하는 사람의 형상을 만들어 불에 태우다《증오의 표시》.

ef·flo·resce [èflərés / -lɔː-] *vi.* (P1) **1** blossom out; flower. 꽃이 피다. **2** 《chem.》 turn to powder. 풍해(風解)하다. **3** be covered with a powdery crust. 백분(白粉)을 내뿜다. [→flower]

ef·flo·res·cence [èflourésns] *n.* Ⓤ the act of efflorescing; the time of flowering. 개화(開花); 개화기.

ef·flu·ence [éfluəns] *n.* **1** Ⓤ the act of flowing out or forth 방출; 유출; 발산. **2** Ⓒ a thing that flows out or forth. 방출〔유출〕물; 발산물. ¶ *an ~ of light from an open door* 열린 문에서 흘러 나오는 불빛. [ex-, L. *fluo* flow]

ef·flu·ent [éfluənt] *adj.* flowing out. 방출〔유출〕하는; 발산하는. —*n.* **1** something that flows out or forth. 방출〔유출〕물. **2** a stream flowing out from another stream, lake, etc. (강·호수 따위에서) 흘러 나오는 줄기; 지류.

ef·flu·vi·a [eflú:viiə] *n.* pl. of **effluvium.**

ef·flu·vi·um [eflú:viəm] *n.* (*pl.* **-vi·a**) exhalation or vapor, esp. one that is disagreeable. 악취. [→effluence]

ef·flux [éflʌks] *n.* Ⓤ the act of flowing out; Ⓒ a thing that flows out. 유출; 유출물. [ex-, →flux]

:ef·fort [éfərt] *n.* ⒸⓊ **1** the act of putting forth energy and strength; vigorous attempt. 노력; 수고. ¶ *by ~* 노력하여 / *after all one's ~* 온갖 노력에도 불구하고 / *make an ~* 〔*efforts*〕 *to do something* …하려고 노력하다 / *Climbing hills is too great an ~ for old people.* 등산은 노인들에게는 지나치게 힘든 일이다. **2** Ⓒ a result of effort; a thing done with effort. 노력의 결과〔성과〕; 역작. ¶ *literary efforts* 문학 작품 / *The painting is one of his finest efforts.* 그 그림은 그의 최고 걸작중의 하나다. [L. *fortis* strong]

make every effort, do all one can. 온갖 수단〔노력〕을 다하다.

with (***an***) ***effort,*** with great pains; with difficulty. 힘들여; 애를 써서.

without effort, quite easily. 수월히; 힘 안 들이고.

ef·fort·less [éfərtlis] *adj.* making no effort; easy. 노력하지 않는; 힘 안 드는; 용이한.

ef·fron·ter·y [efrʌ́ntəri] *n.* ⓊⒸ (*pl.* **-ter·ies**) shamelessness; boldness; a shameless act. 뻔뻔함; 수치를 모르는〔철면피한〕 행위. ¶ *have the ~ to do something* 뻔뻔스럽게도 …하다. [L. *frons* forehead]

ef·ful·gence [efʌ́ldʒəns] *n.* Ⓤ the state of being effulgent; brightness; radiance. 빛남; 찬연히 빛남; 광휘. [L. *fulgeo* shine]

ef·ful·gent [efʌ́ldʒənt] *adj.* shining brightly; radiant. 빛나는; 광휘 있는.

ef·fuse [efjú:z] *vt., vi.* (P6;1) pour out or forth; gush out. 방출하다; 발산하다; 흘러나오다. —[efú:s] *adj.* spread out. 벌어진; 열린. [L. *fundo* pour]

ef·fu·sion [efjú:ʒən] *n.* **1** Ⓤ the act of effusing; Ⓒ something that effuses. 유출; 방출; 유출물. ¶ *~ of blood* 출혈; 유혈 / *the ~ of lava* 용암의 분출 / *be guilty of ~ of blood* 살상의 죄를 범하다. **2** ⓊⒸ a free outpouring of thought or feeling. (감정·사상 따위의) 토로; 발로. ¶ *poetic effusions* 용솟음치는 감정의 시적 표현.

ef·fu·sive [efjú:siv] *adj.* expressing too much feeling or emotion; demonstrative; poured out. 심정을 토로하는; 감정을 드러낸; 넘치는. ¶ *~ emotion* 넘치는 감정 / *be ~ in one's gratitude* 여러 가지 말로 감사하다.

e.g. [í:dʒí:, fərigzǽmpəl, -zá:m-] for example. 예를 들면. [L.]

:egg[1] [eg] *n.* Ⓒ a round body laid by birds or other animals, from which the young come out. 알; 달걀. ¶ *lay an ~* 〔*eggs*〕 알을 낳다 / *sit on eggs* (닭이) 알을 품다 / *I'll have fried eggs, please.* 달걀 프라이를 먹겠습니다. [E.]

a bad egg, 《*colloq.*》 a worthless person. 쓸모없는 놈; 깡패.

(***as***) ***sure as eggs is*** 〔***are***〕 ***eggs,*** 《*colloq.*》 for certain. 확실히.

in the egg, at an early stage. 초기에.

put 〔***have***〕 ***all one's eggs in one basket,*** risk all on a single attempt. 한 가지 일에 모든 것을 걸다.

teach one's grandmother to suck eggs, teach someone who is wiser than oneself. 부처에게 설법하다; 주제넘게 굴다.

egg[2] [eg] *vt.* (P7) 《*on*》 urge, encourage (someone to do something). …을 부추기다; 선동하다; 격려하다. [N.]

egg·beat·er [égbì:tər] *n.* Ⓒ an instrument used for beating eggs. 거품기(器); 달걀 교반기(攪拌器). [*egg*[1]]

egg·cup [égkʌ̀p] *n.* Ⓒ a small cup for holding a boiled egg. (식탁 위의) 삶은 달걀 담는 그릇.

egg·head [éghèd] *n.* 《*sl.*》 an intellectual person. 지식인; 인텔리. [*egg*[1]]

egg·plant [égplæ̀nt, -plà:nt] *n.* Ⓒ 《bot.》 a plant with eatable egg-shaped, purple fruit; the fruit of this plant. 가지.

egg·shell [égʃèl] *n.* Ⓒ the shell of an egg. 알 껍데기; 난각(卵殼).

egg·whisk [éghwìsk] *n.* 《Brit.》 =eggbeater.

egg white [⌐⌐] *n.* the albumen of an egg. 알의 흰자위.

eg·lan·tine [égləntàin, -tì:n] *n.* Ⓒ a sweet-smelling wild rose with pink flowers and a prickly stem. 들장미의 일종(=sweetbrier). [L.]

e·go [í:gou, égou] *n.* Ⓒ (*pl.* **-gos**) **1** the self. 자아; 자기. **2** 《*colloq.*》 conceit. 자부(自負). [L.=I]

e·go·cen·tric [ì:gouséntrik] *adj.* self-centered, egoistic. 자기 중심(주의)의.

e·go·ism [í:gouìzəm, égou-] *n.* Ⓤ **1** the theory that self-interest is the proper goal of all human actions. 이기주의(opp. altruism). **2** selfishness. 이기심; 아욕(我慾).

e·go·ist [í:gouist, égou-] *n.* Ⓒ **1** a believer in egoism. 이기주의자. **2** a selfish person. 제멋대로 구는 사람.

E

e·go·is·tic [ìːgouíst, ègou-], **-ti·cal-** [-tikəl] *adj.* selfcentered; selfish. 이기적인; 제멋대로의.

e·go·tism [íːgoutìzəm, égou-] *n.* Ⓤ **1** the habit of talking or writing too much about oneself. 자기중심벽(癖). **2** self-conceit; selfishness. 자부; 아욕(我慾).

e·go·tist [íːgoutìst, égou-] *n.* Ⓒ a person who shows egotism; a selfish person. 자기 본위의 사람; 자기 중심주의자.

e·go·tis·tic [ìːgoutístik, èːgou-], **-ti·cal** [-tikəl] *adj.* showing or characterized by egotism; selfish. 자기 본위〔중심〕의; 이기적인.

e·gre·gious [igríːdʒəs, -dʒiəs] *adj.* remarkably bad; shocking; notorious. 실로 지독한; 엄청난; 악명 높은. ¶ *an ~ lie* 〔*fool*〕 지독한 거짓말〔바보〕. ● **e·gre·gious·ly** [-li] *adv.* [L.=out of the flock]

e·gress [íːgres] *n.* **1** Ⓤ the act of going out. (밖으로) 나감. **2** Ⓒ a way out; an exit. 출구. **3** Ⓤ the right to go out. (밖으로) 나갈 권리(opp. ingress). [ex-, L. *gradior* go]

e·gret [íːgrit, ég-, iːgrét] *n.* Ⓒ 《bird》 a large wading bird of the heron family; its long, beautiful plumes. 백로; 백로의 깃털 《장식용》. [→aigrette]

·**E·gypt** [íːdʒipt] *n.* a country in northeastern Africa. 이집트. 參考 수도는 Cairo.

·**E·gyp·tian** [idʒípʃən] *adj.* of Egypt or its people or their language. 이집트(사람·말)의. — *n.* **1** Ⓒ a person of Egypt. 이집트사람. **2** Ⓤ the language of the ancient Egyptians. 이집트 말.

·**eh** [ei] *interj.* an exclamation to express surprise or doubt, or to invite agreement. 어; 뭐; 그렇지; 안 그래. ¶ *You're angry with me, ~?* 자네 내게 성을 내고 있지, 그렇지. [E.]

ei·der [áidər] *n.* Ⓒ 《bird》 a large, northern sea duck with soft, downy breast feathers. (북해 연안의) 물오리의 일종. [Icel.]

ei·der·down [áidərdàun] *n.* **1** Ⓤ soft feathers from the breasts of eiders. eider 앞가슴의 솜털. **2** Ⓒ a bed-covering filled with eiderdown. (특히 eider 솜털로 속을 넣은) 깃털 이불. [↑]

:**eight** [eit] *n.* **1** Ⓤ the number between seven and nine. 여덟; 8. **2** Ⓒ any group or set of eight persons or things. 8인〔개〕 한조〔벌〕. ¶ *the Eights* 옥스퍼드 대 케임브리지 대학 보트레이스. **3** Ⓒ anything shaped like 8. 8자 모양의 것.
a figure* (*of*) *eight, 《skating》 movement following the shape of an 8. 8자형(型) 활주.
— *adj.* of 8. 여덟의; 8의. [E.]

:**eight·een** [éitíːn] *n.* Ⓤ the number between seventeen and nineteen; 18. 열 여덟; 18. — *adj.* of 18. 열 여덟의; 18의. ¶ *in the eighteen-nineties,* 1890년대(代)에.

:**eight·eenth** [éitíːnθ] *n.* **1** 《*the* ~》 next after the 17th; 18th. 열여덟(번)째; 제18. **2** Ⓒ one of 18 equal parts of anything. 18분의 1. — *adj.* of 18th. 18의; 18분의 1의.

eight·fold [éitfòuld] *adj.* having eight times as much or as many. 8 배의; 여덟겹의. — *adv.* eight times as much or as many. 8 배로; 여덟 겹으로.

:**eighth** [eitθ] *n.* **1** 《*the* ~》 number 8; 8th. 여덟(번)째; 제8. **2** Ⓒ one of 8 equal parts of anything. 8분의 1. — *adj.* of 8th. 제8의; 8분의 1의.

eighth note [ㅗㅗ] *n.* 《U.S. mus.》 = quaver 2.

:**eight·i·eth** [éitiiθ] *n.* **1** 《*the* ~》 number 80; 80th. 여든(번)째. **2** Ⓒ one of 80 equal parts of anything. 80분의 1. — *adj.* of 80th. 80번째의.

:**eight·y** [éiti] *n.* Ⓒ eight times ten; 80. 여든; 80. — *adj.* of 80. 80의; 80세의; 80개의.

Ein·stein [áinstain], **Albert** *n.* (1879-1955) a German-American physicist. 아인슈타인《독일 태생의 미국 물리학자》.

Eir·e [ɛ́ərə] *n.* the former name of the Republic of Ireland. 에이레《아일랜드 공화국의 구칭》.

:**ei·ther** [íːðər, áiðər] *adj.* **1** one or the other of two. (둘 중) 어느 한 쪽의. ¶ *take ~ road* 어느 한 쪽 길을 택하다 / *You may sit on ~ side of the table.* 식탁의 어느 한 쪽에 앉으셔도 됩니다 / *Will you give me ~ picture?* (둘 중) 어느 쪽 그림이든 주지 않겠나. **2** one and the other of two; each. 양쪽의. ¶ *There are shops on ~ side of the road.* 길 양쪽에 가게들이 있다 / *The flowers are blooming on ~ side of the walk.* 보도 양옆엔 꽃들이 피어 있다.
— *pron.* one or the other. 어느 한 쪽. ¶ *Either of the pencils is mine.* (두개 중) 한 쪽 연필이 내것이다 / *Do you like ~ of the pictures?* (둘중) 어느 쪽 그림이 마음에 드십니까 / *Here are two apples; take ~ of them.* 여기 사과 두개가 있다. 어느 것이든 하나 골라 가져라.
— *conj., adv.* **1** 《used as *either... or—*》 …거나 또는 —거나. ¶ *Either you or I am to go.* 너나 나 둘 중에 누군가 가야 한다 語法 동사는 가까운 쪽 주어에 일치시킨다 / *I want to go to ~ America or England.* 미국이나 영국 중 어느 쪽이든 가고 싶다 / *not wise or handsome ~* 현명하지도 잘생기지도 않은. **2** 《used after a *negative*》 also. 또한 … 않다〔아니다〕. ¶ *If you don't go, I shall not go, ~.* 네가 가지 않으면 나도 안 간다. [E.]

e·jac·u·late [idʒǽkjəlèit] *vt.* (P6) **1** say suddenly and briefly. …을 돌연 외치다. **2** eject. (액체 특히 정액)을 사출(射出)하다. [L. *jaculum* javelin]

e·jac·u·la·tion [idʒæ̀kjəléiʃən] *n.* ⓊⒸ **1** something said suddenly and briefly; exclamation. 갑작스러운 외침. **2** ejection; liquid thrown out suddenly. 사출(액).

e·ject [idʒékt] *vt.* (P6) throw out; force

out; emit; discharge. …을 내쫓다; 배출〔사출〕하다. ¶ ~ *an agitator from a meeting* 회의에서 선동자를 쫓아내다 / ~ *smoke* 연기를 내뿜다. [L. *jacio* throw]

e·jec·tion [idʒékʃən] *n.* **1** Ⓤ Ⓒ the act of ejecting; the state of being ejected. 쫓아냄; 추방; 배출. **2** Ⓒ something ejected. 배출물; 분출물.

ejection seat [–⌐–⌐] *n.* an emergency escape seat for propelling an occupant out of an airplane. (비행기의) 비상 사출(射出) 좌석(=ejector seat).

eke[1] [iːk] *vt.* (P7) ⟪*out*⟫ add to; increase; make (a living, etc.) with difficulty. (부족)을 보충하다; 늘리다; (생계 따위를) 어렵게 꾸려 나가다. ¶ ~ *out one's livelihood* 생계를 꾸려나가다 / *She eked out her income with a second job.* 그녀는 부업으로 수입을 보태었다. [E.]

eke[2] [iːk] *adv.* ⟪*arch.*⟫ also. 또한. [E.]

EKG electrocardiogram.

el [el] *n.* **1** =ell[2]. **2** ⟪U.S. *colloq.*⟫ an elevated railway. 고가 철도.

***e·lab·o·rate** [ilǽbərit] *adj.* worked out with great care and in great detail; complicated. 공들여〔면밀히〕 만든; 정교한; 복잡한. ¶ ~ *preparations* 면밀 주도한 준비 / *an* ~ *design* 정교한 디자인 / *an* ~ *contrivance* 복잡한 장치 / *make an* ~ *plan* 면밀한 계획을 짜다. —[ilǽbərèit] *vt.* (P6) work out (something) with great care; produce (something) by effort. …을 공들여 만들다; 고심하여 마무르다. — *vi.* (P3) ⟪*on, upon*⟫ talk or write in detail. 상세히 말하다〔논하다, 쓰다〕. ¶ ~ *upon an idea* 어떤 생각에 대해서 상술(詳述)하다. [ex-, →labor]

e·lab·o·rate·ly [ilǽbəritli] *adv.* in an elaborate manner. 공〔정성〕들여; 정교하게.

e·lab·o·ra·tion [ilæ̀bəréiʃən] *n.* **1** Ⓤ the act of elaborating; the state of being elaborated. 공들여 함; 정성; 정교. **2** Ⓒ something elaborated. 고심의 작품; 역작.

e·lapse [ilǽps] *vi.* (P1) (of time) slip away; pass. (때가) 경과하다; 지나다. [→lapse]

***e·las·tic** [ilǽstik] *adj.* **1** able to spring back to its original size, shape, or position after being pulled or pressed. 탄력성〔신축성〕 있는; 신축 자재의; 부드러운. ¶ ~ *force* 탄력성 / ~ *limit* 탄력 한도 / *an* ~ *string* 〔*cord*〕 고무끈 / *an* ~ *cane* 낭창낭창한 지팡이. **2** able to recover quickly from depression; flexible; adaptable. (사소한 일 따위에) 구애되지 않는; 융통성 있는. ¶ *an* ~ *conscience* 구애되지 않는 마음 / *an* ~ *rule* 융통성 있는 규칙 / *He possesses an* ~ *temperament.* 그는 사소한 일에 구애되지 않는 기질을 지니고 있다.
— *n.* **1** Ⓤ tape, cloth, etc. given an elastic quality by partly weaving rubber into it. 고무끈. **2** Ⓒ a rubber band. 고무 밴드〔줄〕. [Gk. *elaunō* drive]

e·las·tic·i·ty [ilæstísəti, ìːlæs-] *n.* Ⓤ **1** the state or quality of being elastic. 탄력(성); 신축성. **2** flexibility; adaptability. 융통성; 순응(성).

e·late [iléit] *vt.* (P6) make (someone) high-spirited; make (someone) proud or joyful. …에게 기운을 북돋우다; …을 우쭐하게 하다. ¶ *be elated by one's success* 성공으로 우쭐해지다 / ~ *someone over* 〔*with*〕 아무를 …로 우쭐하게 하다. [L.=brought out]

e·lat·ed [iléitid] *adj.* in high spirits; proud joyful. 의기왕성한; 우쭐한; 몹시 기뻐하는. ¶ *an* ~ *winner of a contest* 경연 대회에 우승하여 우쭐해 있는 사람.

e·la·tion [iléiʃən] *n.* Ⓤ high spirits; joyous pride. 의기양양; 우쭐함.

E layer [⌐⌐–] *n.* a layer of the ionosphere able to reflect radio waves. E층(層)⟪100-120km 상공의 전리층으로 장파·중파를 반사함⟫.

***el·bow** [élbou] *n.* Ⓒ **1** the joint between the upper and lower arm. 팔꿈치. **2** anything bent like an elbow, as a sharp turn in a road, etc. 팔꿈치 모양의 것. ¶ *the* ~ *of a pipe* 파이프의 L 자형 이음관.

at one's elbow, close by; near by. 바로곁에; 아주 가까이.

bend 〔***lift***〕 ***one's elbow,*** ⟪*colloq.*⟫ drink too much alcohol. (과도하게) 술을 마시다; 과음하다.

out at (***the***) ***elbows,*** **a**) (of clothes) worn out; ragged. (옷의) 팔꿈치가 해지어. **b**) badly dressed; shabby. 복장이 빈약한; 초라한. **c**) poor. 가난하여.

rub elbows with, associate with (famous people). (유명인)과 교제하다; 접촉하다.

up to the elbows, (in work) very busy; deeply engaged. 다망(多忙)하여; 몰두하여.

— *vt.* (P7,13) push (something) with the elbows; make (one's way) by pushing. …을 팔꿈치로 밀어젖히다; 밀어젖히고 나아가다. ¶ ~ *someone off* 아무를 (팔꿈치로) 밀어젖히다; 밀어내다 / ~ *oneself into the room* (사람들을) 팔꿈치로 헤치며 방으로 들어가다 / ~ *one's way through a crowd* 군중을 헤집고 나아가다 / ~ *someone out of society* 아무를 사교계에서 쫓아내다 / *He got elbowed into the roadway.* 사람들에 밀려 차도로 나왔다.
— *vi.* make one's way by pushing. 밀어젖히고 나아가다. [*ell, bow*[2]]

el·bow·chair [élboutʃὲər] *n.* Ⓒ a chair with supports on which the elbows may rest. 팔걸이 의자.

elbow grease [⌐–⌐] *n.* Ⓤ hard work; powerful activity. 고된 육체 노동; 맹렬한 노력〔끈기〕.

el·bow·room [élbourù(ː)m] *n.* Ⓤ enough space to move or work in. 활동할 수 있는 여지; 여유.

:eld·er[1] [éldər] *adj.* (*compar.* of **old**) older; senior. 연상의; 고참의; 선배의. ¶ *my* ~ *sister* 누님; 누나 / *My* ~ *brother is two*

E

years older than I. 형은 나보다 두살 위다 (opp. younger). 語法 *elder*는 형제 자매의 관계를 나타내며 *older*는 일반적으로 연상(年上)을 나타냄.

— *n.* Ⓒ **1** an older person; an aged person. 연장자; 노인. **2** an ancestor. 조상. **3** one of the older and more powerful men in a community, etc. 원로. **4** an official of certain churches. (장로 교회의) 장로. [→ old]

el·der[2] [éldər] *n.* Ⓒ 《bot.》 a low tree with white flowers and purple berries. 양딱총나무. [E.]

el·der·ber·ry [éldərbèri] *n.* the berry of the elder used in medicine and in making wine. 양딱총나무의 열매.

eld·er·ly [éldərli] *adj.* somewhat old; past middle age. 나이가 지긋한; 초로의. [→old]

***eld·est** [éldist] *adj.* (*superl.* of **old**) oldest; first born. 가장 연상(年上)의; 장자의. ¶ *my ~ son* 맏아들; 장남. [↑]

EL Do·ra·do [èl dərɑ́:dou] *n.* (*pl.* **-dos**) Ⓤ an imaginary country with much gold in South America, sought by early Spanish explorers; Ⓒ 《also *Eldorado*》 any unbelievably rich place. 황금의 나라; 보물산. [Sp. =the gilded country]

elec., elect. electric; electrical; electrician; electricity.

:**e·lect** [ilékt] *vt.* **1** (P6,13,19,21) choose; select by vote. …을 선거하다; 선임하다; 투표로 뽑다. ¶ *~ a president* 대통령을 선거하다 / *~ someone to a post* 〔*an office*〕 아무를 자리〔직책〕에 선임하다 / *be elected to Congress* 국회의원에 뽑히다 / *He was elected mayor.* 시장에 당선됐다. **2** (P8) decide. 결정하다. ¶ *He elected to stay at home.* 그는 집에 머물러 있기로 정했다.

— *adj.* chosen; elected but not yet in office. (아직 취임 전이지만) 선거로 뽑힌; 당선된. ¶ *the bride ~* 약혼녀 / *the mayor ~* 시장 당선자. 語法 흔히 명사 뒤에 옴.

— *n.* 《*the ~*》 **1** persons belonging to a group with special rights. 선택받은 사람들. **2** those chosen by God for eternal life because of their merit. 선민(選民). ¶ *God's ~* 하느님의 선민《이스라엘 국민》. [L. *lego* pick]

:**e·lec·tion** [ilékʃən] *n.* ⒸⓊ the act of electing, esp. by vote. 선거; 선임. ¶ *a general ~* 총선거 / *an ~ for the National Assembly* 국회의원 선거 / *an ~ campaign* 선거전〔운동〕 / *carry an ~* 당선되다 / *stand for ~* (선거에) 입후보하다.

e·lec·tion·eer [ilèkʃəníər] *vi.* (P1) work for the success of a candidate or party in an election. (후보자·당을 위해) 선거 운동을 하다.

e·lec·tive [iléktiv] *adj.* **1** chosen or appointed by election. 선거에 의해 뽑힌〔임명된〕; 선거에 의한. ¶ *The office of President of the United States is ~.* 미국의 대통령직은 선거로 뽑는다. **2** having the right or power to elect. 선거권이 있는. ¶ *an ~ body* 선거단체 / *one's ~ franchise* 선거권. **3** 《U.S.》 open to choice; not required; optional. 선택의; 필수가 아닌(opp. compulsory, required). ¶ *an ~ subject* 선택 과목. — *n.* Ⓒ 《U.S.》 an elective subject or course of study. 선택 과목.

e·lec·tor [iléktər] *n.* Ⓒ **1** a person who has the right or power to elect. 선거인; 유권자. **2** 《U.S.》 one of the persons chosen to elect the President and Vice-President of the United States. 대통령 및 부통령 선거 위원.

e·lec·tor·al [iléktərəl] *adj.* **1** of an election or electors. 선거(인)의. ¶ *an ~ district* 선거구. **2** made up of electors. 선거인으로 구성된.

electoral college [-´-- ´--] *n.* 《U.S.》 an assembly of electors chosen by the voters to elect the President and the Vice-President of the United States. (미국 각 주의) 대통령〔부통령〕 선거인단.

e·lec·tor·ate [iléktərit] *n.* Ⓒ 《*collectively*》 the body of persons having the right to vote in an election. 선거민; 유권자(전체). [*elect*]

:**e·lec·tric** [iléktrik] *adj.* **1** of electricity. 전기의. ¶ *an ~ current* 전류 / *an ~ shock* 감전 / *an ~ wave* 〔*wire*〕 전파〔전선〕 / *~ power* 전력 / *~ discharge* 방전 / *an ~ chair* 전기 의자 / *~ appliances* 전기 기구. **2** exciting; thrilling. 전격적〔자극적〕인; 흥분시키는. ¶ *have an ~ effect* 전격적인 효과를 미치다. [Gk. *ēlektron* amber]

e·lec·tri·cal [iléktrikəl] *adj.* =electric.

e·lec·tri·cal·ly [iléktrikəli] *adv.* by or with electricity. 전기로; 전기학상.

e·lec·tri·cian [ilèktríʃən, ì:lek-] *n.* Ⓒ a person who makes, repairs, or sells electric apparatus; an expert in the science of electricity. 전기 기사; 전기 기술자〔기사〕; 전기학자.

***e·lec·tric·i·ty** [ilèktrísəti, ì:lek-] *n.* Ⓤ **1** a form of energy that is produced by the flow of electrons. 전기. ¶ *This typewriter works by ~.* 이 타자기는 전기로 작동한다. **2** an electric current. 전류. **3** the science of electricity. 전기학.

e·lec·tri·fi·ca·tion [ilèktrəfikéiʃən] *n.* Ⓤ the act of electrifying; the state of being electrified; the state of being struck by electricity. 대전(帶電); 충전; 전화(電化); 감전.

e·lec·tri·fy [iléktrəfài] *vt.* (**-fied**) (P6) **1** put electricity into (something). …에 전기를 통하게 하다; 충전하다; 대전(帶電)시키다. ¶ *an electrified body* 대전체(帶電體). **2** make (a railway, etc) able to use electricity. …을 전화(電化)하다. ¶ *~ a railway system* 철도 체계를 전화하다. **3** 《*fig.*》 surprise greatly; excite; thrill. …을 깜짝 놀라게 하다; …을 감동[흥분]시키다. ¶ *His words electrified the audience.* 그의 말은 청중을 감동시켰다.

e·lec·tro- [iléktrou-] *pref.* a word element meaning electricity. '전기'의 뜻. [Gk. *ēlektron* amber]

e·lec·tro·car·di·o·gram [ilèktroukɑ́:r-di:əgræ̀m] *n.* the curve traced by an electrocardiograph. 심전도(心電圖). [electro-]

e·lec·tro·car·di·o·graph [ilèktroukɑ́:r-di:əgræ̀f, -grɑ̀:f] *n.* an instrument for recording action currents in the heart. 심전계(心電計).

e·lec·tro·chem·is·try [ilèktroukémis-tri] *n.* a branch of chemistry that deals with chemical changes produced by electricity and the production of electricity by chemical action. 전기 화학.

e·lec·tro·cute [iléktrəkjù:t] *vt.* (P6) kill (a criminal, etc.) by an electric current, as in an electric chair. …을 전기 사형에 처하다.

e·lec·tro·cu·tion [ilèktroukjú:ʃən] *n.* Ⓤ the act of electrocuting; the state of being electrocuted. 전기 사형.

e·lec·trode [iléktroud] *n.* Ⓒ either of the two terminals of a battery, etc. 전극(電極). [electro-]

e·lec·tro·en·ceph·a·lo·gram [ilèk-trouenséfələgræ̀m] *n.* a graphic record of the electrical activity of the brain as recorded by the electroencephalograph. 뇌파도(腦波圖).

e·lec·tro·en·ceph·a·lo·graph [ilèk-trouenséfələgræ̀f, -grɑ̀:f] *n.* an instrument used for making electroencephalogram. 뇌파 기록 장치.

e·lec·tro·lier [ilèktroulíər] *n.* a chandelier or other support for electric lights. 샹들리에.

e·lec·trol·y·sis [ilèktrɑ́ləsis / -trɔ́l-] *n.* Ⓤ the separation of a substance into its chemical elements by electricity. 전기 분해; 전해.

e·lec·tro·lyte [iléktroulàit] *n.* a substance which is broken up by an electric current; a solution carrying an electric current. 전해질[액].

e·lec·tro·lyze [iléktroulàiz] *vt.* (P6) decompose by electrolysis. 전해(電解)하다.

e·lec·tro·mag·net [ilèktroumǽgnit] *n.* Ⓒ a piece of iron that becomes a strong magnet when an electric current is passed through wire coiled around it. 전자석(電磁石). ● **e·lec·tro·mag·net·ic** [-mæg-nétik] *adj.*

electromagnetic wave [–⌣–⌣⌣–⌣–] *n.* 《phys.》 any of a class of waves propagated by a system of electric and magnetic fields and including all forms of radiant energy. 전자기파(電磁氣波); 전자파.

e·lec·tro·mag·net·ism [ilèktroumǽg-nətìzəm] *n.* the study of the relations between electricity and magnetism. 전자기학(電磁氣學).

e·lec·tro·mo·tive [ilèktroumóutiv] *adj.* producing a flow of electricity. 전동(電動)의; 기전(起電)의. ¶ ~ *force* 기전력(起電力).

e·lec·tron [iléktrɑn / -trɔn] *n.* Ⓒ the smallest unit of matter having negative electricity. 전자(電子)(cf. *proton*). [electro-]

e·lec·tron·ic [ilèktrɑ́nik / -trɔ́n-] *adj.* of an electron, electrons or electronics. 전자(공학)의. ¶ *an* ~ *calculator* [*computer*]전자계산기 / ~ *music* 전자 음악.

e·lec·tron·ics [ilèktrɑ́niks / -trɔ́n-] *n. pl.* 《used as *sing.*》 the science of the systems and phenomena of electrons. 전자공학; 일렉트로닉스.

e·lec·tro·plate [iléktroupléit] *vt.* (P6) cover (something) with a thin coating of metal by electrolysis. …에 전기 도금하다. — *n.* Ⓒ something covered in this way. 전기 도금한 것.

e·lec·tro·scope [iléktrəskòup] *n.* a device for detecting the presence of electricity. 검전기(檢電器).

e·lec·tro·ther·a·py [ilèktrouθérəpi] *n.* 《med.》 Ⓤ treatment of disease by electricity. 전기 요법.

e·lec·tro·type [iléktroutàip] *n.* 《print.》 electroplated facsimile copy. 전기판(版). [electro-]

el·e·gance [éligəns] *n.* **1** Ⓤ the quality of being elegant or refined. 우아; 고상함. **2** Ⓒ something elegant. 우아한[세련된, 고상한] 것. [L.]

el·e·gan·cy [éligənsi] *n.* (*pl.* **-cies**) =elegance.

·el·e·gant [éləgənt] *adj.* having or showing good taste; refined; graceful. 우아[고상]한; 점잖은. ¶ ~ *dress* 우아한 옷 / *an* ~ *young woman* 점잖은 젊은 여성 / *an* ~ *style* 격조 높은 문체 / ~ *manners* 세련된 태도 / ~ *arts* 고아한 예술. ● **el·e·gant·ly** [-li] *adv.* [L.]

el·e·gi·ac [èlədʒáiək, ilí:dʒiæ̀k] *adj.* **1** of or fit for an elegy. 만가(輓歌)의; 애가조(哀歌調)의. **2** sad; mournful. 애수(哀愁)를 띤. — *n.* 《*pl.*》 a series of elegiac verses. 애가[만가] 조의 시. [↓]

el·e·gy [élədʒi] *n.* Ⓒ (*pl.* **-gies**) a poem expressing sorrow, esp. for the dead. 애가(哀歌); 비가(悲歌); 만가. [Gk.]

:el·e·ment [éləmənt] *n.* Ⓒ **1** 《chem.》 a substance that cannot be separated into simpler substances. 원소. **2** a simple and essential thing of which anything is made up. 요소; 성분; 구성 분자. ¶ *discontented elements of society* 사회의 불평 분자 / *The story has in it something of the* ~ *of tragedy.* 그 이야기에는 무언가 비극적인 요소가 있다. **3** earth, air, fire, or water. 기본 물

질《땅·공기·불·물》. 參考 고대 철학에서 자연을 구성하는 근본 요소로 생각했음. **4** 《*the* ~ *s*》 the forces of nature, such as rain and wind. 자연의 힘. ¶ *the fury of the elements* 자연의 맹위 / *exposed to the elements* 비바람에 노출되어 / *the four elements* 사(四)원소《땅·물·불·바람》. **5** 《*the* ~ *s*》 the steps that must be learnt first. 초보; 기본. ¶ *the elements of physics* 물리학의 초보. **6** the surrounding conditions best suited to someone or thing. (본디 적합하다고 보는) 고유의 환경; (활동) 영역; 본령. ¶ *Poetry was his proper* ~. 시는 그의 본령으로 하는 바였다. **7** 《usu. *an* ~》 a very small amount; a trace. 극히 조금; 흔적. ¶ *There is an* ~ *of truth in it.* 그것에는 얼마쯤의 진리가 있다. [L.]

be in* [*out of*] *one's element, be [be not] in the surroundings where one can show at one's best. 본령을 발휘할 수 있는 영역 안[밖]에 있다.

el·e·men·tal [èləméntl] *adj.* **1** of an element; essential; basic. 원소의; 요소의; 기본적인. **2** of the four elements; of the forces of nature. 사(四)원소《땅·물·불·바람》의; 자연력[현상]의. ¶ ~ *forces* 자연력 / ~ *strife* 대폭풍우 / ~ *worship* 자연력 숭배. **3** simple but powerful. 천한. **4** =elementary.

·el·e·men·ta·ry [èləméntəri] *adj.* **1** of the first steps; necessary to be learned first; of the beginning. 초보의; 기본의. ¶ ~ *education* 초등 교육 / *an* ~ *school* 소학교; 초등 학교. **2** of a chemical element or elements. 원소의. ¶ *an* ~ *substance* 단체(單體).

:el·e·phant [éləfənt] *n.* Ⓒ (*pl.* **-phants** or *collectively* **-phant**) a large, heavy animal with a thick skin, long nose, and tusks. 코끼리. [Gk.]

el·e·phan·tine [èləfǽntain, -ti(:)n] *adj.* **1** of or belonging to an elephant. 코끼리의. **2** like an elephant in size or movement; very large and clumsy. 코끼리 같은; 거대한; 볼꼴 사나운.

·el·e·vate [éləvèit] *vt.* (P6,13) **1** lift up; raise. …을 올리다; …을 높이다. ¶ ~ *a weight* 무거운 것을 들어 올리다 / ~ *a balloon* 기구를 올리다 / ~ *one's mind* 마음을 고상하게 하다 / ~ *someone to the post of president* 아무를 사장 자리로 승진시키다 / *The former consul was elevated to the rank of ambassador.* 전(前)영사는 대사로 승진했다. **2** put (someone) in high spirits; encourage. 기운을 북돋우다; 고무하다. [L. *levo* lift]

el·e·vat·ed [éləvèitid] *adj.* **1** raised; high. 높여진; 높은. ¶ *an* ~ *railroad* [*railway*] 고가 철도. **2** (of thoughts, way of writing, etc.) noble; lofty. 고상한; 고결한. ¶ ~ *thoughts* 고상한 사상. **3** in high spirits. 의기왕성한. **4** 《*colloq.*》 slightly drunk. 술이 약간 취한.

el·e·va·tion [èləvéiʃən] *n.* **1** Ⓤ the act of elevating; the state of being elevated. 높임; 향상; 승진. **2** Ⓒ a raised place; a high place. 고지(高地). **3** Ⓒ a height; a height above sea level. 고도; 해발. ¶ *an* ~ *of 3,000 feet* 해발 3천 피트. **4** Ⓤ dignity; nobility. 위엄; 고상; 고결. **5** Ⓒ 《archit.》 a plan showing one side of a building. 입면도(立面圖).

:el·e·va·tor [éləvèitər] *n.* Ⓒ **1** 《U.S.》 a machine to carry people and things up and down in a building. 엘리베이터; 승강기 (cf. 《Brit.》 *lift*). **2** a building for storing grain. (양곡기(揚穀機)가 있는) 큰 곡물 창고.

:e·lev·en [ilévən] *n.* Ⓒ **1** Ⓤ the number between ten and twelve; 11. 열하나; 11. **2** any group or set of eleven persons or things; a football or cricket team. (11명의 선수가 하는) 축구·크리켓 팀. ¶ *be in the* ~ 축구[크리켓] 선수이다.

an eleven, a football or cricket team. 축구[크리켓] 팀.

— *adj.* of 11. 11의. [O.E. *endleofon*]

:e·lev·enth [ilévənθ] *n.* **1** 《*the* ~》 number 11; 11th. 제11; 열한번째. **2** Ⓒ one of 11 equal parts of anything. 11분의 1. — *adj.* of 11th. 제11의; 열한번째의; 11분의 1의.

at the eleventh hour, at the last possible moment. 마지막 순간에; 고빗사위에; 막판에.

elf [elf] *n.* Ⓒ (*pl.* **elves**) **1** a tiny, harmful fairy. 꼬마 요정. **2** a harmful or mischievous child. 장난이 심한 아이; 개구쟁이. ● **elf·like** [⌐làik] *adj.* [O.E. *ælf*]

elf·in [élfin] *adj.* =elfish. — *n.* =elf.

elf·ish [élfiʃ] *adj.* like an elf; mischievous. 꼬마 요정 같은; 못된 장난을 하는.

elf·lock [élflὰk / -lɔ̀k] *n.* a tangled lock of hair. 헝클어진 머리.

e·lic·it [ilísit] *vt.* (P6,13) 《*from*》 draw forth; cause. …을 이끌어내다. ¶ ~ *a laugh from someone* 아무를 웃기다 / ~ *a response with a question* 질문을 해서 대답을 이끌어 내다 / ~ *applause* [*the truth*] 박수 갈채를[진실을] 이끌어내다. ● **e·lic·i·ta·tion** [ilìsətéiʃən] *n.* [L. *elicitum*]

e·lide [iláid] *vt.* (P6) omit (a vowel, syllable). (모음·음절)을 생략하다. [L. *laedo* strike]

el·i·gi·bil·i·ty [èlidʒəbíləti] *n.* Ⓤ the state of being eligible. 적격(성); 적임(성). [↓]

el·i·gi·ble [élidʒəbəl] *adj.* fit to be chosen; suitable. 뽑힐 자격이 있는; 적격의; 알맞은. ¶ *marry an* ~ *bachelor* 적당한 독신 남과 결혼하다 / *He is* ~ *for the position.* 그는 그 직책에 적임이다. — *n.* Ⓒ an eligible person. 적격자; 적임자. [→elect]

·e·lim·i·nate [ilímənèit] *vt.* (P6,13) **1** get rid of (something); remove; take out. …을 제거[배제, 삭제]하다; 지워 없애다. ¶ ~ *danger* 위험을 제거하다 / ~ *useless words* 쓸데 없는 말을 없애다. **2** remove from further competition, esp. by defeating in a contest. (예선에서) 탈락시키다. ¶ ~ *competitors in a* *contest* 경연에서 경쟁 상대를 물리치다. [L. *limen* threshold]

e·lim·i·na·tion [ilìmənéiʃən] *n.* Ⓤ the act of eliminating; the state of being eliminated. 제거; 배제; 삭제. ¶ *the* ~ *of social ills like drug addiction and gambling* 마약 중독이나 도박과 같은 사회악의 제거.

e·lim·i·na·tor [ilímənèitər] *n.* Ⓒ **1** a person who eliminates. 제거하는 사람. **2** 《electr.》 a device that operates from a power line to supply current and voltage to a circuit designed to be operated by a battery. 일리미네이터《직류를 얻는 장치》.

e·lite, é·lite [eilí:t, i-] *n.* 《F.》 《*the* ~, *collectively*》 chosen people; the best people. 엘리트; 선발된 사람들; 정화(精華); 선량. ¶ *the* ~ *of society* 명사; 높은 사람들.

e·lix·ir [ilíksər] *n.* Ⓒ a medicine that cures all ills. 만능약; 영약(靈藥). ¶ *the* ~ *of life* 불로 불사의 영약. [Arab.]

Eliz. Elizabeth; Elizabethan.

***E·liz·a·beth** [ilízəbəθ] *n.* a woman's name. 여자 이름. 參考 애칭은 Beth, Betty 등.

E·liz·a·be·than [ilìzəbí:θən, -béθ-] *adj.* of the time of Queen Elizabeth I (1558-1603). 엘리자베스 여왕 시대의; 엘리자베스조(朝)의. ¶ ~ *literature* 엘리자베스조(朝) 문학. — *n.* Ⓒ a person, esp. a writer or an artist, of the Elizabethan time. 엘리자베스 시대의 문학자나 예술가.

elk [elk] *n.* Ⓒ (*pl.* **elks** or *collectively* **elk**) a large deer of northern Europe, Asia, and America. 큰사슴. [E.]

ell[1] [el] *n.* 《rare》 Ⓒ an old measure of length, used chiefly in measuring cloth, equal to 45 inches. 엘《척도》. ¶ 《*prov.*》 *Give him an inch and he'll take an* ~. 봉당을 빌려주니 안방까지 달란다; 손자를 귀애하니 할아비 상투 꺼든다. [E.=forearm]

ell[2] [el] *n.* Ⓒ **1** the letter L, l. L자(字). **2** something shaped like L. L자형의 것. [↑]

El·len [élən] *n.* a woman's name. 여자 이름.

el·lipse [ilíps] *n.* Ⓒ a shape like an egg; an oval. 타원(형). [Gk. *leipō* leave]

el·lip·ses [ilípsi:z] *n.* pl. of **ellipsis.**

el·lip·sis [ilípsis] *n.* ⓊⒸ (*pl.* **-ses**) the omission of a word or phrase; 《print.》 marks showing omission. 생략(법); 생략 기호《—, …, *** 따위》. [→ellipse]

el·lip·tic [ilíptik], **-ti·cal** [-tikəl] *adj.* **1** shaped like an ellipse. 타원(형)의. **2** 《gram.》 having a word or phrase omitted. 생략의. ¶ *an* ~ *phrase* 생략 구. [↑]

***elm** [elm] *n.* Ⓒ a tall, graceful tree planted chiefly for shade; Ⓤ the hard, heavy wood of this tree. 느릅나무; 느릅나무재(材). [E.]

el·o·cu·tion [èləkjú:ʃən] *n.* Ⓤ the art or manner of speaking or reading clearly and effectively in public. 웅변술; 낭독법; 연설(조). [L. *loquor* speak]

el·o·cu·tion·ar·y [èləkjú:ʃənèri / -əri] *adj.* of elocution. 웅변술의; 낭독법의.

el·o·cu·tion·ist [èləkjú:ʃənist] *n.* Ⓒ a person skilled in elocution; a person who teaches elocution. 웅변가; 낭독가; 연설〔낭독〕법의 교사.

e·lon·gate [ilɔ́:ŋgeit / í:lɔŋgèit] *vt.* (P6) make (something) longer; lengthen; stretch. …을 늘이다; 길게 하다; 연장하다. — *vi.* (P1) become longer. 길어지다. — *adj.* lengthened; long. 늘어난; 긴. [L. *longus* long]

e·lon·ga·tion [ilɔ̀:ŋgéiʃən / ì:lɔŋ-] *n.* **1** Ⓤ the act of lengthening; extension. (잡아)늘임; 연장; 신장(伸長). **2** Ⓒ a lengthened part. 연장부〔선〕.

e·lope [ilóup] *vi.* (P1,2A,3) **1** run away with a lover. (애인과) 사랑의 도피를 하다. **2** escape secretly. 달아나다; 도망하다. ●**e·lop·er** [-ər] *n.* [e-, *leap*]

e·lope·ment [ilóupmənt] *n.* ⓊⒸ the act of eloping. 사랑의 도피; 도망.

***el·o·quence** [éləkwəns] *n.* Ⓤ fluent and forceful speaking; the art or power to win something by speaking. 웅변; 웅변술. ¶ *a flow of* ~ 유창한 변설(辯舌). [→elocution]

***el·o·quent** [éləkwənt] *adj.* **1** ⓐ (of a speaker or writer) having or showing eloquence; fluent. 웅변의; 능변의; 유창한; 잘 쓰는. ¶ *a very* ~ *speaker* 능변의 변설가. ⓑ fluent and persuasive. 설득력 있는. ¶ *an* ~ *speech* 설득력 있는 연설. **2** (of a speech, writing, etc.) very expressive; moving. 생생히 표현하는; 사람을 감동시키는. ¶ *looks* ~ *of disgust* 혐오를 생생하게 나타낸 표정.

El Sal·va·dor [el sǽlvədɔ̀:r] *n.* a small country in western Central America, on the Pacific side. 엘살바도르《중앙 아메리카 서부 태평양 연안의 소국》. 參考 수도는 San Salvador.

:else [els] *adj.* 語法 some-, any-, no-가 붙는 말, 또는 의문 대명사 뒤에 옴. **1** other; different. 다른. ¶ *anybody* ~ 누군가 딴 사람 / *somebody else's book* 누군가 다른 사람의 책 / *What* ~ *could I say?* 달리 어떻게 말할 수 있었을 것인가《그렇게 말할 수밖에 없었다》. **2** additional; more. 그 밖의. ¶ *Who* ~ *is there in the room?* 방 안에 그 밖에 누가 있나 / *Do you have anything* ~ *to tell me?* 그 밖에 내게 말할 것이 있는가 / *There is no one* ~ *who knows about it.* 그것을 아는 사람은 그 밖에 아무도 없다.

— *adv.* **1** in a different way. 다르게; 다른 방법으로. ¶ *How* ~ *can I solve the problem?* 달리 어떻게 문제를 풀 수 있을 것인가. **2** besides; in addition. 그 밖에. ¶ *Did you see anyone* ~ *?* 그 밖에 누구 딴 사람을 보았나 / *Where* ~ *did you go?* 그 밖에 어디를 갔었나. [O.E. *elles*]

or else, otherwise; if not. 그렇지 않으면. ¶ *Take care, or ~ you will fall.* 조심해라, 그렇지 않으면 넘어진다.

:else·where [élshwὲər] *adv.* in, at, or to some other place. 다른 곳에〔으로〕; 어딘가 딴 곳에〔에서, 으로〕. ¶ *as ~* 다른 곳과 같이 / *live ~* 어디 다른 곳에 살다.

e·lu·ci·date [ilú:sədèit] *vt.* (P6) make (something) clear; clarify; explain. …을 분명히 하다; 설명하다. ¶ *~ a difficult point* 어려운 점을 설명하다. ● **e·lu·ci·da·tor** [-ər] *n.* [→lucid]

e·lu·ci·da·tion [ilù:sədéiʃən] *n.* Ⓤ the act of making clear; explanation. 명시(明示); 해설; 설명. ¶ *~ of the theory* 이론의 해명.

e·lude [ilú:d] *vt.* (P6) get away from (something); escape; avoid. …을 (모)면하다; (회)피하다. ¶ *~ a blow* 일격을 피하다 / *~ pursuers* 추적자를 따돌리다 / *The meaning eludes me.* 나는 그 뜻을 모르겠다. [L. *ludo* play]

e·lu·sion [ilú:ʒən] *n.* Ⓤ the act of eluding; escape. 피함; 회피. [↑]

e·lu·sive [ilú:siv] *adj.* **1** (of words, etc.) difficult to understand or remember. 이해하기 어려운; 기억하기 힘든. ¶ *an ~ word* 〔*meaning*〕 이해하기 어려운 말〔뜻〕. **2** inclined to escape. 잘 도망치는〔빠져 나가는〕; 기억에서 사라지기 쉬운. ¶ *an ~ memory* 분명치 않은 기억 / *a fish too ~ to catch* (미꾸라지처럼) 하도 빠져나가기를 잘해서 잡기 어려운. ● **e·lu·sive·ly** [-li] *adv.* **e·lu·sive·ness** [-nis] *n.*

elves [elvz] *n.* pl. of **elf.**

E·ly·sian [ilí(:)ʒiən] *adj.* of or like Elysium; heavenly; happy; delightful. 극락의〔같은〕; 행복한; 즐거운. ¶ *the ~ fields* 극락 정토.

E·ly·si·um [ilíʒəm, -ziəm] *n.* 《Gk. myth.》 a place where virtuous people went after death; paradise; the place of perfect happiness. 극락; 낙토; 이상향; 더없이 행복한 곳.

EM Enlisted Man〔Men〕. 사병.

'em, em [əm] *pron.* 《*colloq.*》 =them.

e·ma·ci·ate [iméiʃièit] *vt.* (P6) make (someone or something) thin. …을 여위게 하다; 수척하게 하다. ¶ *He was emaciated by hunger and fatigue.* 그는 굶주림과 피로로 수척해졌다. —*vi.* become thin. 야위다; 마르다. [L. *macies* leanness]

e·ma·ci·at·ed [iméiʃièitid] *adj.* very thin through loss of flesh. 몹시 여윈; 수척한.

e·ma·ci·a·tion [imèiʃiéiʃən] *n.* excessive thinness from loss of flesh. 몹시 야윔〔마름〕.

em·a·nate [émənèit] *vi.* (P3) 《*from*》 come out; issue. 흘러나오다; 나오다; 생기다; 발(산)하다. ¶ *Various ideas ~ from the brain.* 여러 가지 생각이 머리에서 나온다 / *Fragrance emanates from flowers.* 꽃에서 향기가 난다. [L. *mano* flow]

em·a·na·tion [èmənéiʃən] *n.* **1** Ⓤ the act of emanating; flowing forth. 유출; 발산. **2** Ⓒ something emanated. 유출물; 방산〔방사〕물.

e·man·ci·pate [imǽnsəpèit] *vt.* (P6,13) 《*from*》 set (someone) free; release. …을 해방하다; 석방하다. ¶ *~ slaves* 노예를 해방하다 / *~ someone from anxiety* 아무를 걱정에서 해방하다 / *~ the mind from prejudice* 마음에서 편견을 없애다 / *~ oneself from debt* 빚의 굴레에서 벗어나다. [L. = free from possession]

e·man·ci·pa·tion [imæ̀nsəpéiʃən] *n.* Ⓤ the act of emancipating; the state of being emancipated. (노예 등의) 해방; 석방. ¶ *~ from superstition* 미신으로부터의 해방.

e·man·ci·pa·tor [imǽnsəpèitər] *n.* Ⓒ a person who emancipates. 해방자. ¶ *the Great Emancipator* 위대한 해방자《Abraham Lincoln을 가리킴》.

e·mas·cu·late [imǽskjəlèit] *vt.* **1** remove the male organs of (an animal); castrate. …을 거세하다. **2** weaken. 약하게 하다. —[imǽskjulit, -lèit] *adj.* weakened. 거세된; 약한; 힘 없는. [→masculine]

e·mas·cu·la·tion [imæ̀skjəléiʃən] *n.* Ⓤ the act of emasculating; the state of being emasculated. 거세; 골자를 뺌〔가 빠짐〕.

em·balm [imbɑ́:m] *vt.* (P6) **1** keep (a dead body) from decaying. (사체)를 방부(防腐)하다〔방부 처리하다〕. **2** keep (something) in memory. …을 오래 기억하다. **3** fill (something) with a sweet scent. …을 향기로 채우다; 향기나게 하다. ● **em·balm·er** [-ər] *n.* [→balm]

em·bank [imbǽŋk] *vt.* (P6) protect, enclose, or confine with a raised bank of earth, stones, etc. 둑〔제방〕을 쌓아 두르다. [em-]

em·bank·ment [imbǽŋkmənt] *n.* Ⓒ a bank or wall of earth, stones, etc. used to keep back water. 둑; 방축; 축제(築堤); 제방.

em·bar·go [embɑ́:rgou] *n.* Ⓒ (*pl.* **-goes**) **1** a government order that ships must not enter or leave its ports; a restriction put on trade by law. (선박의) 출항〔입항〕 정지; 수출〔수입〕 금지; 통상 정지. ¶ *lay* 〔*put, place*〕 *an ~ on* (선박)에 입출항 금지를 명하다 / *lift* 〔*raise, take off, remove*〕 *an ~ on* (선박에) 입출항 금지를 풀다 / *be under an ~* 통상 정지 중이다. **2** any restriction. 제한; 억제; 금지. ¶ *lay* 〔*impose*〕 *an ~ on* 〔*upon*〕 *free speech* 언론의 자유를 억압하다.

—*vt.* (P6) **1** lay (ships, etc.) under an embargo; put an embargo on (trade). (선박)의 출〔입〕항을 정지하다; (통상)을 금지하다. **2** seize (ships, etc.) for the service of the state. (선박 따위)를 징발하다(cf. *requisition*). [Sp. *embargar* arrest]

em·bark [embɑ́:rk, im-] *vi.* **1** (P1,3) 《*for*》 go on board a ship. 배에 타다; 승선하다; 출항하다. ¶ *~ for England* 영국을 향해 출항하다. **2** (P3) 《*in, on, upon*》 set out; start. (…

E

에) 나서다; 시작[착수]하다. ¶ ~ *on a new career* 새로운 생활에 들어가다 / ~ *upon a new adventure* 새 모험을 시작하다. — *vt.* **1** (P6) take (someone or something) on board a ship. …을 배에 태우다; 탑재하다. **2** (P13) engage. …에 종사시키다. ¶ ~ *oneself in an enterprise* 사업에 투신하다. [em-]

em·bar·ka·tion [èmbɑːrkéiʃən] *n.* Ⓤ the act of embarking. 화물의 적재[실음]; 승선.

·**em·bar·rass** [imbǽrəs, em-] *vt.* (P6,13) **1** disturb (someone); confuse. …을 곤혹스럽게 하다; 당황[당혹]하게 하다; 혼란시키다. ¶ *feel* [*be*] *embarrassed* 당황하다 / *Don't* ~ *me with difficult questions.* 어려운 질문으로 나를 쩔쩔매게 하지 마라. **2** prevent; hinder. …을 방해하다. ¶ ~ *someone's movements* 아무의 움직임을 방해하다. **3** make difficult or intricate. (문제 따위)를 어렵게 하다; 복잡하게 하다. ¶ ~ *a case* 사건을 복잡하게 하다. **4** 《esp. in *passive*》 burden with debt. 빚을 지게 하다. [→bar]

em·bar·rass·ing [imbǽrəsiŋ, em-] *adj.* confusing; difficult. 당황케[곤혹스럽게] 하는; 성가신.

em·bar·rass·ment [imbǽrəsmənt, em-] *n.* **1** Ⓤ the state of being embarrassed. 당혹; 곤혹; 갈팡댐. ¶ *to one's* ~ 당혹스럽게도. **2** Ⓒ a thing that embarrasses. 당혹게 하는 것. **3** 《*pl.*》 financial difficulties. 재정 곤란.

em·bas·sa·dor [embǽsədər] *n.* =ambassador.

em·bas·sy [émbəsi] *n.* Ⓒ (*pl.* **-sies**) **1** an ambassador and his assistants. 대사; 대사관원. **2** the official building where an ambassador lives. 대사관. **3** a position or duties of an ambassador. 대사의 임무[직]. ¶ *carry out one's* ~ 대사로서의 역할을 다하다. [→ambassador]

em·bat·tle [imbǽtl, em-] *vt.* (P6) prepare or arrange (something) for battle. 전투대형을 갖추게 하다; 포진하다. [em-]

em·bat·tled [imbǽtld / em-] *adj.* drawn up and ready for battle. 전투대형을 취한; 전진(戰陣)을 편. ¶ *an* ~ *line* 전투 진열(陣列).

em·bed, im- [imbéd] *vt.* (**-bed·ded, -bed·ding**) (P6,13) 《usu. in *passive*》 put (something) in a bed; fix or set deeply. …을 묻다[심다]; 끼워 넣다; …을 (기억 따위에) 깊이 간직하다. ¶ ~ *stones in cement* 돌을 시멘트 속에 넣다 / *The incident is embedded in my memory.* 그 사건은 내 기억 속에 간직되어 있다 / *He embedded the seeds in a box of sand.* 씨를 모래통에 심었다 / *A thorn was found embedded in the finger.* 손가락에 가시가 박혀 있었다. [em-]

em·bel·lish [imbéliʃ, em-] *vt.* (P6,13) **1** make (something) more beautiful; decorate. …을 아름답게 하다; 장식하다. ¶ ~ *a dress with lace and ribbons* 옷을 레이스와 리본으로 꾸미다. **2** make (a story, etc.) more interesting. (이야기 따위)를 윤색하다. [L. *bellus* beauty]

em·bel·lish·ment [imbéliʃmənt, em-] *n.* ⓊⒸ **1** decoration. 장식. **2** addition to make (a story, etc.) interesting. 윤색; 문식(文飾).

em·ber [émbər] *n.* 《usu. *pl.*》 pieces of wood or coal still glowing in the dying fire; ashes in which there is still some fire. 타다 남은 것; 깜부기[잉걸]불; 여신(餘燼). [E.]

Ember days [⏑-⏑] *n.* 《Cath.》 12 days of fasting and prayer. 사계 재일(四季齋日).

em·bez·zle [embézl, im-] *vt.* (P6,13) steal (money, etc. given into one's care). (돈 따위)를 착복하다; 횡령하다. ¶ ~ *the school's money* 학교 돈을 횡령하다. [F. *besiler* ravage]

em·bez·zle·ment [embézlmənt / im-] *n.* ⓊⒸ the act of embezzling. 착복; 횡령.

em·bit·ter [imbítər] *vt.* (P6) make (someone) bitter. …을 쓰라리게[비참하게, 분하게] 하다. ¶ *She was embittered by his death.* 그의 죽음으로 그녀는 쓰라림을 겪었다 / *His scolding embittered her because it was unjust.* 그의 질책은 부당했기 때문에 그녀는 몹시 분했다. [em-]

em·bla·zon [embléizən, im-] *vt.* (P6,13) **1** picture in bright colors; decorate. 화려하게 그리다; (화려한 빛깔로) 장식하다. **2** make known the fame of; extol; celebrate. (명성 따위)를 높이다; 찬양하다; 기리다. ¶ *The hero's deeds were emblazoned by a poet.* 영웅의 행위가 시인에 의해서 찬양되었다. ● **em·bla·zon·ment** [-mənt] *n.* [em-]

em·bla·zon·ry [embléizənri, im-] *n.* **1** emblazoning; heraldic decoration. 문장(紋章) 묘화(描畫); 문장 장식. **2** gay decoration. 화려한 장식.

em·blem [émbləm] *n.* Ⓒ a symbol; a badge. 상징; 휘장; 배지. ¶ *The lily is the* ~ *of purity.* 백합은 순결의 상징이다. [Gk. =insertion]

em·blem·at·ic [èmbləmǽtik], **-i·cal** [-ikəl] *adj.* symbolical. 상징적인. ¶ *The cross is* ~ *of Christianity.* 십자가는 기독교를 상징한다.

em·bod·i·ment [embádimənt / -bɔ́d-] *n.* **1** Ⓤ the act of embodying; the state of being embodied. 형체를 부여함; 구체화. **2** Ⓒ something embodied; something that embodies. 구체화된 것; 구체화하는 것; 화신; 권화(權化). ¶ *He is the* ~ *of greed.* 그는 탐욕의 화신이다. [↓]

em·bod·y [embádi / -bɔ́di] *vt.* (**-bod·ied**) (P6,13) **1** ⓐ express (ideas, etc.) in a real form. …을 구체적으로 나타내다; 구체화하다. ¶ ~ *one's views in a speech* 연설에서 자신의 견해를 구체화하다. ⓑ make corporeal; incarnate. 육체를 갖추게 하다; 육체화하다. ¶ ~ *a spirit* 영혼에 육체를 주다. **2** collect (matters) into a book, etc.; include (things) in a body. …을 (책 따위에) 담다; 수록하다; 포함하다. ¶ *This book embodies*

E

all the rules of the University. 이 책에는 대학의 모든 학칙이 담겨 있다. [em-]

em·bold·en [embóuldən] *vt.* (P6,20) make (someone) bold; give courage to. …을 대담하게 하다; 용기를 주다. [em-]

em·bo·li [émbəlài] *n.* pl. of **embolus.**

em·bo·lism [émbəlìzəm] *n.* 《med.》 obstruction by a blood clot. (혈관의) 색전증(塞栓症). [↓]

em·bo·lus [émbələs] Ⓒ (*pl.* **-li**) *n.* 《med.》 a foreign body that forms an obstruction in a blood vessel, as a blood clot or an air bubble. (혈관 어딘가에 막힌) 이물(異物); 색전(塞栓). [Gk. *embolos*]

em·bon·point [ɑ̃:mbɔ(:)mpwǽŋ] *n.* 《F.》 Ⓤ plumpness. (여자의) 비만(肥滿).

em·bos·om [embú(:)zəm] *vt.* (P6) **1** 《usu. in *passive*》 surround. 둘러싸다. ¶ *a small village embosomed in hills* 산에 둘러싸인 작은 마을. **2** take or press (a child, etc.) to one's bosom. 꽉 껴안다. [em-]

em·boss [embás, em-, -bɔ́(:)s] *vt.* (P6,13) decorate (paper, leather, etc.) with a design, figures, etc., that are raised on the surface; cause (a design, figure, etc.) to raise on the surface. …을 돋을새김으로 하다; 도드라지게 하다. ● **em·boss·ment** [-mənt] *n.* [em-]

em·bow·er [imbáuər] *vt.* (P6) enclose with trees, etc. as in a bower; cover. (나무숲으로) 가리다; 나무 그늘이 지게 하다; 우거져 뒤덮다. ¶ *a house embowered in trees* 나무에 가려진[둘러싸인] 집. [em-]

:em·brace [embréis] *vt.* (P6) **1** hold (someone) in one's arms. …을 꼭 껴안다; 포옹하다. ¶ ~ *one's child* 아이를 껴안다. **2** surround or encircle. …을 둘러[에워]싸다. ¶ *an island embraced by the sea* 바다에 둘러싸인 섬. **3** seize; make use of (an opportunity, offer, etc.). (기회 따위)를 잡다; 포착하다; 이용하다. ¶ ~ *an opportunity* 기회를 잡다 / ~ *an offer* 제의에 응하다. **4** contain; include. (많은 것)을 포함하다; 담다; (광범위에) 걸치다. ¶ ~ *the whole field* 전분야에 걸치다 / *An encyclopedia embraces a great number of subjects.* 백과 사전은 많은 항목을 담고 있다. **5** adopt (a faith, opinion, etc.); take (a belief) as one's own. (교의(敎義)·사상·의견 따위)를 받아들이다; 신봉하다. ¶ ~ *Christianity* 기독교에 귀의(歸依)하다. **6** engage in; set out on. (직업에) 종사하다; (생활에) 들어가다. ¶ ~ *a new profession* 새로운 직업에 취업하다 / ~ *a sailor's life* 해원(海員) 생활에 들어가다.

— *vi.* (P1) hold one another in the arms. 서로 부둥켜안다; 포옹하다. ¶ *They met and embraced.* 그들은 만나자 부둥켜안았다.

— *n.* Ⓒ the act of embracing. 포옹.

● **em·brace·a·ble** [-əbəl] *adj.* [→brace]

em·bra·sure [embréiʒər] *n.* Ⓒ **1** an opening in a wall for a gun. 총안(銃眼); 성가퀴. **2** a window or door with sloping sides, as in an old stone castle. (창이나 문의 측면이) 비스듬히 벌어진 것; 사벽(斜壁). [F. *braser* splay]

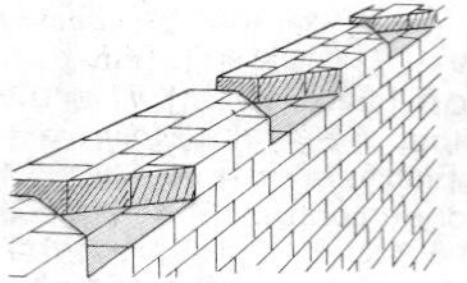

〈embrasure 1〉 〈embrasure 2〉

em·bro·cate [émbroukèit] *vt.* (P6) moisten and rub (a bruised or injured part) with a liniment. (바르는 약·로션제)를 바르다; 발라 문지르다. [Gk. *brekhō* wet]

·em·broi·der [embrɔ́idər] *vt.* (P6,13) **1** decorate (cloth, leather, etc.) with a needlework design; put (a figure) on cloth, etc. …에[을] 수놓다; 자수를 하다. ¶ ~ *a pattern on a handkerchief* = ~ *a handkerchief with a pattern* 손수건에 무늬를 수놓다. **2** improve (a story, etc.) by adding something fanciful; touch up. (이야기 따위)를 윤색하다; 살을 붙이다; 과장하다. — *vi.* (P1) do embroidery. 자수를 하다. ● **em·broi·der·er** [-rər] *n.* [F. *bord* edge]

em·broi·der·y [embrɔ́idəri] *n.* (*pl.* **-der·ies**) **1** Ⓤ the act or art of embroidering; an ornamental needlework. 자수; 수놓기. **2** Ⓒ an embroidered work or material. 자수품. **3** Ⓤ ornamentation. (이야기·작품 따위의) 윤색; 분식(粉飾).

em·broil [embrɔ́il] *vt.* (P6,13) **1** make (someone) take part in a quarrel, etc. (말싸움 따위에) 말려들게 하다. ¶ *become embroiled in a dispute* 논쟁에 말려들다. **2** throw (something) into a confusion. …을 혼란케[복잡하게] 하다. ¶ ~ *a story* 이야기를 복잡하게 하다. ● **em·broil·ment** [-mənt] *n.* [→broil]

em·bry·o [émbriòu] *n.* Ⓒ (*pl.* **-os**) **1** an animal before birth. 태아(胎兒). **2** ⓐ a plant within a seed. 배아(胚芽). ⓑ a beginning or undeveloped stage. (발달의) 초기; 미발달의 단계; 맹아(萌芽).

in embryo, not yet developed. 미발달의; 초기의; 미숙한. ¶ *a plan in* ~ 아직 준비중인 계획.

— *adj.* undeveloped; not mature. 미성(未成)의; 미숙한; 맹아기의. [Gk.]

em·bry·ol·o·gist [èmbriáləʤist / -ɔ́l-] *n.* Ⓒ a specialist in embryology. 발생학자; 태생학자.

em·bry·ol·o·gy [èmbriáləʤi / -ɔ́l-] *n.* Ⓤ the science of embryos. 발생학; 태생학.

em·bry·on·ic [èmbriánik / -ɔ́n-] *adj.* **1** of or like the embryo. 태아의[같은]; 배아(胚芽)의[같은]. **2** undeveloped; not mature. 미발달의; 초기의; 미숙한.

em·cee [émsíː] 《U.S. *colloq.*》 *n.* Ⓒ a master of ceremonies. 사회자. — *vt.* (P6) act as a master of ceremonies for (a radio program, television show, etc.). (라디오 프로·텔레비전 쇼 등)의 사회를 보다. — *vi.* (P1) act as a master of ceremonies. 사회를 보다. 參考 *M*aster of *C*eremonies 의 생략형 M.C.에서.

e·mend [iménd] *vt.* (P6) **1** free from faults or mistakes; correct. (잘못을) 바로잡다. **2** amend (a text) by removing errors. 교정(校訂)하다. ● **e·mend·a·ble** [-əbəl] *adj.* [e-, L. *menda* fault]

e·men·da·tion [ìːmendéiʃən, èmən-] *n.* **1** Ⓤ the act of emending. 바로잡음; 교정(校訂). **2** Ⓒ an emended passage, etc. (in a text). 수정; 정정(訂正)된 곳.

em·er·ald [émərəld] *n.* **1** Ⓒ a bright green precious stone. 에메랄드. **2** Ⓤ bright green. 에메랄드 빛; 밝은 녹색; 선녹색. — *adj.* of or like emerald; bright-green. 에메랄드(빛)의; 밝은 녹색의. [Gk. *smaragdos*]

Emerald Isle [́–– ́], **the** *n.* Ireland. 아일랜드.

***e·merge** [imə́ːrdʒ] *vi.* (P1,3) **1** come out; appear. 나오다; 나타나다. ¶ ~ *from behind the clouds.* 구름 뒤에서 나타나다. **2** come into view; become known (as a result of inquiry). 눈에 들어오다; 분명해지다. ¶ *a ghost emerging from the grave* 무덤에서 나타나는 유령 / *New facts have emerged as a result of inquiry.* 조사 결과 새로운 사실들이 드러났다. [→merge]

e·mer·gence [imə́ːrdʒəns] *n.* Ⓤ the act of emerging; appearance. 출현; 발생.

***e·mer·gen·cy** [imə́ːrdʒənsi] *n.* ⒸⓊ (*pl.* **-cies**) a sudden, unexpected happening. 비상사태; 돌발사고. ¶ *an ~ case* 〔*box*〕 구급 상자 / *an ~ door* 비상구 / *an ~ landing* 불시착 / *~ measures* 비상 수단; 응급 조치 / *in case of* 〔*in an*〕 ~ 긴급한 경우에; 비상시에 / *ready for all emergencies* 모든 비상 사태에 대비가 된.

e·mer·gent [imə́ːrdʒənt] *adj.* happening suddenly and unexpectedly. 돌발적인; 불시의.

e·mer·i·tus [imérətəs] *adj.* retired but holding one's rank or title. 명예 퇴직의. ¶ *an ~ professor* = *a professor ~* 명예 교수. [L.=that has served his time]

Em·er·son [émərsn], **Ralph Waldo** *n.* (1803-82) an American essayist, poet, and philosopher. 에머슨(미국의 수필가·시인·철학자).

em·er·y [éməri] *n.* Ⓤ a hard mineral, used for grinding, smoothing, and polishing. 금강사(金剛砂). [Gk. *smýris* rubbing powder]

e·met·ic [imétik] *adj.* causing to throw up food. 구토를 일으키는; 느글거리는. — *n.* Ⓒ a medicine that causes someone to throw up food. 구토제(劑). [Gk. *emeō* vomit]

em·i·grant [éməgrənt] *n.* Ⓒ a person who emigrates. 이민(opp. immigrant). — *adj.* emigrating. 이민의; 이주하는. [↓]

em·i·grate [éməgrèit] *vi.* (P1,3,4) leave one's own country to live in another. (타국·타향으로) 이민하다; 이주하다(opp. immigrate). ¶ ~ *from England to America* 영국에서 미국으로 이민하다. — *vt.* cause (someone) to emigrate. …을 이주시키다. [e-, →migrate]

em·i·gra·tion [èməgréiʃən] *n.* **1** Ⓤ the act of emigrating. 이주; 이민(移民). **2** Ⓒ a group of emigrants. 이민(단).

é·mi·gré [émigrèi, èiməgréi] *n.* (*pl.* **-grés**) 《F.》 an emigrant, esp. one who fled during the French Revolution. 국외 이주자; (정치적) 국외 망명자. [*emigrate*]

Em·i·ly [éməli] *n.* a woman's name. 여자 이름.

em·i·nence [émənəns], **-nen·cy** [-nənsi] *n.* **1** Ⓤ highness in rank or position; greatness. (지위 따위의) 높음; 탁월; 고명(高名). ¶ *a man of ~* 명사(名士) / *attain ~ as a lawyer* 변호사로서 유명해지다 / *He won ~ as a doctor.* 의사로서 명성을 얻었다. **2** Ⓒ a high place. 고소(高所); 고대(高臺). ¶ *on an ~* 고소(高所)에. **3** 《*E-*》 the title of honor given to a cardinal. 예하(猊下)《cardinal에 대한 존칭》. [L. *emineo* project]

***em·i·nent** [émənənt] *adj.* high; great; remarkable; famous. 높은; 뛰어난; 현저한; 유명한. ¶ ~ *services* 현저한 공로 / ~ *statesmen* 유명한 정치가들 / *a lady ~ for her piety* 두터운 신앙으로 알려진 부인 / *be ~ as a scientist* 과학자로서 저명하다.

em·i·nent·ly [émənəntli] *adv.* in an eminent manner. 뛰어나게; 현저히.

e·mir [əmíər] *n.* Ⓒ **1** an Arabian ruler, prince, etc. (아랍족 국가의) 수장(首長); 왕족. **2** a title of the descendants of Muhammad. 마호메트 자손의 존칭. [Arab.]

em·is·sar·y [éməsèri / -səri] *n.* Ⓒ (*pl.* **-sar·ies**) a person or secret agent sent on a special mission; a spy. 밀사(密使); 밀정; 간첩. ¶ *an ~ of the Devil* 악마의 밀사. [↓]

e·mis·sion [imíʃən] *n.* **1** Ⓤ the act of emitting or sending out. 방사; 방출; 발산. ¶ *the ~ of fragrance* 방향(芳香)의 발산 / *the ~ of light and heat from the sun* 태양으로부터의 빛과 열의 방출. **2** Ⓒ something emitted. 방사물; 방출물. **3** Ⓤ issuing. 발행. [→emit]

e·mit [imít] *vt.* (**e·mit·ted, e·mit·ting**) (P6) **1** give off; send forth (light, smell, etc.); discharge. (빛 따위)를 방사하다; 분출하다; 발하다; 내다. ¶ ~ *a sound* 소리를 발하다 / *a fountain emitting clear water* 맑은 물이 솟아나오는 샘 / *Fire emits heat and smoke.* 불은 열과 연기를 낸다. **2** issue (paper money, etc.). (지폐 따위)를 발행하다. ¶ ~ *paper money* 지폐를 발행하다 [e-, L. *mitto* send]

Em·ma [émə] *n.* a feminine personal name. 여자 이름.

e·mol·lient [imáljənt / imɔ́l-] *adj.* **1** making (the skin etc.) soft. (피부 따위)를 부드럽게(연하게) 하는. ¶ ~ *lotions for the face* (얼굴용) 화장수. **2** 《*fig.*》 tending to soothe the mind. 달래는; 위안하는. ── *n.* Ⓒ a medicine which makes the skin soft. 피부연화제(軟化劑). [L. *mollis* soft]

e·mol·u·ment [imáljəmənt / imɔ́l-] *n.* Ⓒ 《usu. *pl.*》 profit from a job; gain; payment; salary; fees. 보수; 수당; 이득; 급료; 임금. [L.]

:e·mo·tion [imóuʃən] *n.* ⓊⒸ a strong feeling; an excitement. 감정; 정서; 흥분; 감격; 감동. ¶ *with* ~ 감동하여; 감정을 담아 / *without* ~ 감동 없이; 태연히 / *primitive emotions such as fear and anger* 공포와 노염과 같은 소박한 감정 / *betray one's emotions* 감정을 겉에 나타내다 / *suppress one's emotions* 감정을 누르다 / *appeal to one's* ~ *rather than to one's reason* 이성보다 감성에 호소하다. [→ move]

·e·mo·tion·al [imóuʃənəl] *adj.* **1** of or showing the emotions; appealing to the emotions. 감정(정서)의; 감정에 호소하는. **2** easily excited 흥분하기 쉬운. ¶ *an* ~ *nature* 감정에 움직이기 쉬운 성질 / *an* ~ *woman* 감정적인 여자. **3** exciting the emotions. 감동적인. ¶ ~ *music* 감동적인 음악.

e·mo·tion·al·ly [imóuʃənəli] *adv.* in an emotional manner. 정서적으로; 감정에 호소하여.

e·mo·tion·less [imóuʃənlis] *adj.* expressing no emotion. 감정이 없는; 무감정의.

Emp. Emperor; Empress.

em·pan·el, im- [impǽnəl] *vt.* (-(l)ed) (P6) form; call together (a jury). (배심원)을 소집하다. [em-]

em·pa·thy [émpəθi] *n.* 《psych.》 the complete understanding of another's feelings, motives, etc. 감정 이입(移入). [em-, → pathos]

:em·per·or [émpərər] *n.* Ⓒ a man who rules an empire. 황제; 제왕(opp. empress). ¶ *His Majesty the Emperor* 황제(천황) 폐하. [L. *impero* command]

em·pha·ses [émfəsi:z] *n.* pl. of **emphasis.**

·em·pha·sis [émfəsis] *n.* ⓊⒸ (*pl.* **-ses**) **1** (of expression, thought, etc.) special force; importance. 강조; 역설; 중요시. ¶ *lay* (*place, put*) *special* ~ *on* (*upon*) …을 특히 강조(중요시)하다. **2** special force given to syllables, words, or phrases, etc.; an accent. 강세; 어세(語勢). [↓]

·em·pha·size [émfəsàiz] *vt.* (P6) **1** (in speech) give special force to (words, a word, or a part of a word); put emphasis on (something). …을 힘주어 말하다; …을 강조(역설)하다. ¶ ~ *a point* 어떤 점을 강조하다 / ~ *the three principles of democracy* 민주주의의 3원칙을 강조하다. **2** call into special notice; lay special weight on. …을 중시하다. ¶ ~ *the value of education* 교육의 가치를 중시하다. [em-, Gk. *phainō* show]

em·phat·ic [imfǽtik, em-] *adj.* strongly expressed; stressed; speaking with force; striking. 강조된; 어세가 강한; 힘주어 말하는; 두드러진. ¶ *an* ~ *denial* 단호한 거부 / *an* ~ *opinion* 강한 의견 / ~ *words* 강조된 낱말 / ~ *syllables* 강세가 있는 음절.

em·phat·i·cal·ly [imfǽtikəli, em-] *adv.* in an emphatic manner; decidedly. 강조하여; 힘주어; 단호히.

:em·pire [émpaiər] *n.* **1** Ⓒ a group of countries under one ruler. 제국(帝國). ¶ *Empire City* (*State*) 뉴욕시(주)의 별명 / *the Roman Empire* 로마 제국. **2** Ⓤ absolute power or control. 절대권; 제권(帝權). [→ emperor]

em·pir·ic [empírik, im-] *n.* Ⓒ **1** a person who does not believe in theory and who relies on practical experience. 경험주의자. **2** a person who has no regular or proper training; a quack. 돌팔이; 가짜 의사. ── *adj.* = empirical. [Gk. *en* in, *peirao* try = try in]

em·pir·i·cal [empírikəl] *adj.* based entirely on experiment or practical experience. 실험(경험)에 의한. ● **em·pir·i·cal·ly** [-kəli] *adv.*

em·pir·i·cism [empírisìzəm] *n.* 《philos.》 the theory that experience is the only source of knowledge. 경험주의; 경험론(cf. *rationalism*).

em·place·ment [empléismənt] *n.* **1** Ⓤ putting in a place; a location. 정치(定置); 설치. **2** Ⓒ the place in a fortification for heavy guns. 포좌(砲座); 포상(砲床). [*place*]

:em·ploy [emplɔ́i] *vt.* (P6,7,13) **1** get (someone) to work by paying wages or a salary; hire; give work to (someone). …을 고용하다; …에게 일을 주다. ¶ ~ *a new secretary* 새 비서를 쓰다 / ~ *someone as gardener* 아무를 정원사로 고용하다 / *be employed in a bank* 은행에 고용돼 있다 / *This task will* ~ *20 men.* 이 일에는 20명의 일손이 필요할 게다. **2** ⓐ make use of; use. 이용하다; 사용하다. ¶ ~ *a knife to cut bread* 빵을 자르는데 나이프를 쓰다 / ~ *a hammer to drive a nail* 못을 박는데 망치를 사용하다 / ~ *dishonest means in business* 장사에 부정 수단을 쓰다. ⓑ spend; take up. 쓰다; 소비하다; (시간 따위)를 잡다. ¶ ~ *one's spare time in reading books* 여가를 독서에 충당하다 / *Reading books employs much of his time.* 독서는 그의 많은 시간을 차지한다. **3** 《*reflexively*》 spend one's time. 시간을 보내다. ¶ *How do you* ~ *yourself of an evening?* 저녁엔 시간을 어떻게 보내십니까.

— *n.* Ⓤ the act of employing; the state of being employed; service; use. 고용; 근무; 이용. ¶ *I'm in his* ~. 나는 그에게 고용돼 있다 / *I have him in my* ~. 나는 그를 고용하고 있다. [→implicate]

em·ploy·é [emplɔ́iː/ɔmplɔ́iei] *n.* 《F.》 = employee.

•**em·ploy·ee** [implɔ́iː, èmplɔiíː/èmplɔiíː] *n.* Ⓒ a person who is employed by another and paid wages. 사용인; 종업원(opp. employer). ¶ *This firm treats its employees very badly.* 이 회사는 종업원에 대해 대우가 아주 나쁘다.

•**em·ploy·er** [emplɔ́iər] *n.* Ⓒ a person or firm that employs others. 고용주; 사용자; 회사(opp. employee).

:**em·ploy·ment** [emplɔ́imənt] *n.* **1** Ⓤ the act of employing; the state of being employed. 사용; 고용; 근무. ¶ *full* ~ 완전 고용 / *begin* 〔*terminate*〕 ~ 근무를 시작하다〔그만두다〕. **2** ⓊⒸ work; occupation. 일; 직업. ¶ *an* ~ *agency* 〔*bureau, office*〕 직업 안정소〔소개소〕/ *be in* ~ 일하고〔취업해〕 있다 / *be out of* ~ 실직해 있다 / *lose one's* ~ 일자리를 잃다; 실직하다 / *in the* ~ *of someone* 아무에게 고용되어 / *take someone into* ~ 아무를 고용하다 / *throw someone out of* ~ 아무를 해고하다〔실직시키다〕. **3** use. 사용. ¶ *the* ~ *of machinery* 기계의 사용.

em·po·ri·um [empɔ́ːriəm] *n.* **1** a center of commerce; a marketplace. 상업의 중심지; 중앙 시장. **2** 《*colloq.*》 a large shop. 큰 가게; 백화점. [Gk. *emporos* merchant]

em·pow·er [empáuər] *vt.* (P20) **1** give power or authority to (someone); authorize. …에게 권능〔권한〕을 주다. ¶ *I* ~ *you to sign the document on my behalf.* 자네에게 나를 대신해서 문서에 서명할 권능을 위임하네. **2** enable; permit. …할 수 있게 하다; 가능케 하다; 허락하다. ¶ ~ *man to control nature* 인간이 자연을 지배할 수 있게 하다. [em-]

:**em·press** [émpris] *n.* Ⓒ the wife of an emperor; a woman ruler of an empire. 황후; 여제(女帝). ¶ *Her Majesty the Empress* 황후 폐하. [→emperor]

emp·ti·ness [émptinis] *n.* Ⓤ the state of being empty. 공허; 무지. [↓]

:**emp·ty** [émpti] *adj.* (**-ti·er, -ti·est**) **1** holding nothing within itself; unoccupied. 빈; 사람이 없는. ¶ *an* ~ *bottle* 〔*house*〕 빈병〔집〕/ *a room* ~ *of furniture* 가구가 없어 휑뎅그렁한 방. **2** without meaning; vain. 무의미한; 공허한. ¶ *an* ~ *promise* 성의없는 약속; 공수표 / ~ *pleasures* 공허한 쾌락 / *Life is but an* ~ *dream.* 인생은 공허한 꿈에 지나지 않는다. **3** 《*colloq.*》 hungry. 배고픈. ¶ ~ *stomachs* 굶주린 사람들 / *on an* ~ *stomach* 배고픈 배를 움켜쥐고 / *feel* ~ 배고프다.

empty of, lacking; without. …이 없는; …을 결한. ¶ *a life* ~ *of happiness* 행복이 없는 생활.

— *n.* Ⓒ (*pl.* **-ties**) anything empty. 빈 것.

— *v.* (**-tied**) *vt.* (P6,7) **1** ⓐ make (something) empty or vacant. …을 비우다. ¶ ~ *one's cup* 〔*a bottle*〕 술잔〔병〕을 비우다 / ~ *a purse upon a table* 돈지갑의 내용물을 테이블 위에 쏟아놓다. ⓑ take or pour out (the contents) from a vessel. (그릇에서) 꺼내다; 따라 옮기다. ¶ ~ *water out of a glass* 잔에서 물을 따르다 / ~ *the milk from a bottle* 병에서 우유를 따르다 / ~ *a bottle into a cup* 병에서 술잔에 따르다. **2** cause to leave. 떠나게 하다. ¶ *The building was emptied in five minutes.* 5분후엔 그 건물은 (전원이 빠져나가) 완전히 비워졌다.

— *vi.* (P1,2A,3) **1** become empty or vacant. 비워지다. ¶ *The room emptied readily after the lecture.* 교실은 강의가 끝나자 곧 비워졌다. **2** (of a river) flow out. (강이) 흘러들다. ¶ *The Mississippi empties (itself) into the Gulf of Mexico.* 미시시피 강은 멕시코 만으로 흘러든다. [E.]

emp·ty-hand·ed [émptihǽndid] *adj.* having or carrying nothing in the hands. 빈손의; 빈손〔맨손〕으로.

emp·ty-head·ed [émptihédid] *adj.* stupid; silly; ignorant. 머리가 텅빈; 무지한; 어리석은.

em·py·re·al [empíriəl, èmpairíːəl] *adj.* **1** of the empyrean. empyrean의. **2** formed of pure fire or light. 깨끗한 불이나 빛으로 된; 정화(淨火)의. [Gk. *en* on, *pur* fire]

em·py·re·an [èmpəríːən, -pai-, empíriən] *n.* **1** the highest heaven. 최고천(最高天). **2** the heavens; the sky. 하늘; 천공(天空).

— *adj.* =empyreal.

e·mu [íːmjuː] *n.* Ⓒ 《bird》 a large Australian bird closely resembling the ostrich, but smaller. 에뮤《타조 비슷한 새》. [? Port.=crane.]

em·u·late [émjəlèit] *vt.* (P6) **1** try to equal or be better than (someone). …에 지지 않으려고 하다. ¶ ~ *the industry of the ant* 개미의 부지런함에 지지 않으려고 하다. **2** imitate. 모범으로 삼다; 흉내내다. [L. *aemulus* rival]

em·u·la·tion [èmjəléiʃən] *n.* Ⓤ the act of emulating; an imitation. 경쟁(의식); 모범으로 하기. ¶ *in a spirit of* ~ 경쟁심으로. ●**em·u·la·tive** [émjəlèitiv/-lətiv] *adj.*

em·u·lous [émjələs] *adj.* **1** wishing to equal or be better than another. 남에게 지지 않으려는; 남을 능가하려는. ¶ ~ *of another's courage* 남의 용기에 지지 않으려는. **2** (not implying rivalry) eager for. …을 열망하는. ¶ ~ *of fame* 명성을 열망하는.

e·mul·si·fy [imʌ́lsəfài] *vt.* (**-fied**) (P6) change (something) into an emulsion. …을 유화(乳化)하다; 유제(乳劑)로 하다.

●**e·mul·si·fi·er** [-ər] *n.* [↓]

e·mul·sion [imʌ́lʃən] *n.* ⓊⒸ an oily, milky liquid, containing very tiny drops of fat, oil, etc. 유탁액(乳濁液); 유제(乳劑). [L. *mulgeo* milk]

en- [in-, en-] *pref.* 《used to form *v.* from *n.*

& *adj.*》 **1** put into. '…안에 넣다'의 뜻. ¶ *encase.* **2** cause to become. '…으로[하게]하다'의 뜻. ¶ *endear.* [Gk.; L. *in-, im-* in, into]

-en [-ən] *suf.* **1** become or cause to be. '…(하)게 하다[되다]'의 뜻. ¶ *deepen/shorten.* **2** made of; resembling. '…의[로 된]'의 뜻. ¶ *wooden / golden.* [E.]

:en·a·ble [enéibəl] *vt.* (P20) make (someone or something) able; give (someone or something) ability, means, etc. …을 가능케 하다; …에게 힘·수단 따위를 주다. ¶ *His help enabled me to finish the work.* 그의 도움은 내가 그 일을 마치는 것을 가능케 했다 / *The scholarship enabled him to go to college.* 장학금은 그의 대학 진학을 가능케 했다 / *His money enables him to buy anything he likes.* 돈은 그가 좋아하는 것을 무엇이나 살 수 있게 한다. [en-]

en·act [enǽkt] *vt.* **1** (P6,11) make (a bill) into a law. (법률)을 제정하다. ¶ *an enacting clause* 새 규정 조항 / *as by law enacted* 법률이 규정하는 바와 같이. **2** play the part of (someone); act. …의 역(役)을 맡아 하다; 상연하다. **3** 《chiefly in *passive*》 (of events, etc.) come to pass; take place. 일어나다. ¶ *the scene where the robbery was enacted* 강도 사건이 벌어졌던 장면. [en-]

en·act·ment [enǽktmənt] *n.* **1** Ⓤ the act of enacting; the state of being enacted. (법의) 제정. **2** Ⓒ a law. 법령; 조령(條令).

e·nam·el [inǽməl] *n.* Ⓤ **1** a hard glasslike substance; a smooth, hard, glossy coating. 에나멜; (도기(陶器)의) 유약; 법랑. ¶ ~ *paint* 광택(光澤) 페인트. **2** any smooth, hard, enamel-like substance. (치아 따위의) 법랑질. — *vt.* (**-eled, -el·ine** or 《Brit.》 **-elled, -el·ling**) (P6) cover of decorate (something) with enamel. …에 에나멜[유약]을 입히다. ¶ *enameled leather* 칠피. [en-, F. *esmail* →smelt]

en·am·or, 《Brit.》 **-our** [inǽmər] *vt.* (P6) 《chiefly in *passive*》 charm; fascinate; fall in love with (someone); …을 매혹하다; …에 반하다[열중하다]. ¶ *be enamored of a girl* 여자에 마음을 빼앗기다 / *be enamored of the mountains* 산에 매혹되다 / *be enamored with a story* 이야기에 반하다. [en-]

enc., encl. enclosed; enclosure.

en·camp [enkǽmp] *vi.* (P1,2A,3) 《*in*》 stay or settle in a camp. (텐트를 치고) 야영하다. ¶ *We encamped in a valley.* 우리는 계곡에서 야영을 했다. — *vt.* (P6,13) put (someone) in a camp. …을 야영시키다. ¶ ~ *troops* 병사들을 야영시키다. [en-]

en·camp·ment [enkǽmpmənt] *n.* **1** Ⓤ the act of encamping; the state of being encamped. 야영(野營); 노영(露營)(함). **2** Ⓒ a camp. 야영(지).

en·case [enkéis] *vt.* (P6,13) put (something) into a case; enclose. …을 케이스[상자]에 넣다; 싸다. [en-]

en·caus·tic [inkɔ́ːstik] *adj.* burn in. 소작화(燒灼畫)의; 납화(蠟畫)의. — *n.* an encaustic painting. 소작화; 납화. [en-]

en·ceinte [enséint, ɑːnsǽnt] *adj.* 《F.》 pregnant. 임신한. — *n.* an enclosure. 둘러싸인 곳; 구내; 성벽; 성곽. [L. =gird about]

en·ceph·a·li·tis [insèfəláitis] *n.* 《med.》 inflammation of the brain. 뇌염. [Gk.]

encephalitis lethargica [-‐‐‐‐ ‐‐‐‐] *n.* 기면성(嗜眠性) 뇌염.

en·chain [entʃéin] *vt.* (P6) **1** put or bind (something) with a chain. 사슬로 매다. **2** 《*fig.*》 (of the mind, thought, etc.) attract the complete attention of (someone); keep fixed. …의 주의 따위를 끌다[붙들어 매다]; 고정하다. [en-]

·en·chant [entʃǽnt, -tʃɑ́ːnt] *vt.* (P6,13) **1** use magic on (someone); bewitch. …에게 마법을 걸다. ¶ *The witch enchanted all that came near her.* 마녀는 가까이 온 모든 사람에게 마술을 걸었다. **2** delight; charm; fascinate. …을 기쁘게 하다; 매료[매혹]하다; 황홀케 하다. ¶ *be enchanted by her singing* 그녀의 노래에 넋을 잃다 / *be enchanted with the flowers* 꽃에 마음을 빼앗기다. [en-]

en·chant·er [entʃǽntər, -tʃɑ́ːnt-] *n.* Ⓒ a person who enchants; a magician. 마법사 (opp. enchantress).

en·chant·ing [entʃǽntiŋ, -tʃɑ́ːnt-] *adj.* delightful; very attractive; charming. 기쁜; 매혹적인; 넋을 잃게 하는.

en·chant·ment [entʃǽntmənt, -tʃɑ́ːnt-] *n.* **1** Ⓤ the act of enchanting; the state of being enchanted. 마법(을 씀); 매력; 매혹; 마법에 걸린 상태; 황홀. **2** Ⓒ a thing that enchants. 매혹시키는 것. ¶ *the* ~ *of her smile* 매혹적인 그녀의 미소.

en·chan·tress [entʃǽntris, -tʃɑ́ːnt-] *n.* Ⓒ **1** a woman who enchants; a witch. 여자마법사; 마녀(opp. enchanter). **2** a very fascinating, charming woman. 매혹적인 여자; 요염한 미인.

en·cir·cle [ensə́ːrkl] *vt.* (P6,13) **1** make a circle around (someone or something); surround. …을 (빙) 둘러싸다; 에워싸다. ¶ *a lake encircled by woods* 숲에 둘러싸인 호수. **2** move in a circle around (someone or something). …의 주위를 돌다. ¶ ~ *the globe* 지구의 둘레를 돌다. [en-]

·en·close [enklóuz] *vt.* (P6,13) **1** shut (a place) in on all sides; surround. …을 둘러싸다. ¶ *a valley enclosed by tall mountains* 높은 산들로 둘러싸인 계곡 / *The orchard is enclosed with hedges.* 과수원은 산울타리로 둘러싸여 있다. **2** put (something) in an envelope. …을 봉투에 넣다; 동봉(同封)하다. ¶ ~ *a check for $300,* 3백 달러의 수표를 동봉하다 / *I'll* ~ *your letter (along) with mine.* 내 편지에 자네 편지를 동봉한다. **3** contain; hold; shut up. …을 넣다; 밀폐하다. [en-]

en·clo·sure [enklóuʒər] *n.* **1** Ⓤ the act of enclosing; the state of being enclosed. 포

위; 둘러 싸임. **2** Ⓒ something that is enclosed; something that encloses, as a wall or fence. 봉입된〔하는〕 것; 울타리; 담; 벽. [en-]

en·com·pass [inkʌ́mpəs] *vt.* (P6) **1** surround entirely; encircle. …을 둘러〔에워〕싸다. ¶ *a castle encompassed with high walls* 높은 담벽에 둘러싸인 성 / *encompassed with perils* 위험에 싸이다. **2** enclose; contain. …을 봉해 넣다; 포함하다. ● **en·com·pass·ment** [-mənt] *n.* [en-]

en·core [áŋkɔːr, ankɔ́ːr / ɔŋkɔ́ːr] *interj.* 《F.》 Once more !; Again ! 재청이오; 앙코르. — *n.* Ⓒ **1** a demand of 'Encore !'. 앙코르; 재연(再演)의 요청. ¶ *The singer received* 〔*got*〕 *many encores.* 그 가수는 많은 앙코르를 받았다. **2** an additional song, etc., given in reply to such a demand. (앙코르에 응한) 재연; 재주(再奏). ¶ *give* 〔*sing*〕 *three encores* 앙코르로 세 곡을 연주〔노래〕하다. — *vt.* (P6) call for an encore to (someone). …에게 앙코르를 요청하다. [F. =again]

:en·coun·ter [enkáuntər] *vt.* (P6) **1** come upon (someone). …와 우연히 만나다; 조우하다. ¶ ～ *a friend* 뜻하지 않게 친구를 만나다 / *He once encountered a lion in the jungle.* 그는 전에 밀림에서 사자를 만났다. **2** meet (an enemy, etc.). (적과) 충돌〔교전〕하다. **3** meet with (difficulties, etc.). (곤란 따위)를 만나다; 직면하다. ¶ ～ *difficulties* 어려움에 직면하다.
— *vi.* (P1,3) **1** meet unexpectedly with someone. 뜻밖에 만나다; 마주치다. **2** 《*with*》 meet in a fight. (적과) 조우하다; 교전하다.
— *n.* Ⓒ **1** a sudden, unexpected meeting with someone or something. 뜻밖의 만남; 해후. ¶ *an unexpected* ～ 예기치 않은 만남. **2** a battle. 조우전(遭遇戰). [en-, →contra]

:en·cour·age [enkə́ːridʒ, kʌ́r-] *vt.* (P6,13, 20) **1** 《*to do*》 give courage to (someone); inspire. …에게 용기를 주다; …을 북돋다 (opp. discourage). ¶ ～ *a boy to study* 〔*in his studies*〕 소년을 격려하여 공부시키다 / *be encouraged by someone's success.* 아무의 성공에 용기를 얻다 / *Your words* ～ *me greatly.* 자네의 말은 나에게 크나큰 용기를 주네. **2** help; support; promote. …을 조장(助長)하다; 장려하다; 촉진하다. ¶ ～ *learning* 〔*farming*〕 학문〔농업〕을 장려하다 / ～ *a man in his idleness* 사나이의 나태를 조장하다 / *Sunlight encourages the growth of plants.* 햇빛은 식물의 발육을 촉진한다. ● **en·cour·ag·er** [-ər] *n.* **en·cour·ag·ing·ly** [-iŋli] *adv.* [en-]

en·cour·age·ment [enkə́ːridʒmənt, -kʌ́r-] *n.* Ⓤ the act of encouraging; the state of being encouraged; Ⓒ something that encourages. 격려; 장려; 조장; 격려〔조장〕하는 것. ¶ *take* ～ *from his words* 그의 말에 힘을 얻다 / *give someone* ～ *to study* 공부하도록 아무를 격려하다.

en·cour·ag·ing [enkə́ːridʒiŋ, -kʌ́r-] *adj.* giving courage. 용기를 북돋는; 격려〔장려〕하는.

en·croach [enkróutʃ] *vi.* (P2A,3) 《*on, upon*》 go beyond proper limits; intrude upon the rights or property of another. 침입〔침해〕하다; 침식하다. ¶ ～ *on* 〔*upon*〕 *a neighboring land* 이웃의 토지를 침범하다 / ～ *upon others' rights* 〔*privacy*〕 타인의 권리를〔사생활을〕 침해하다 / *The sea encroaches on* 〔*upon*〕 *the land.* 바다가 육지를 침식한다. [F. *croc*→crook]

en·croach·ment [enkróutʃmənt] *n.* Ⓤ Ⓒ the act of encroaching; something taken by encroaching. 침입(지); 침식(지); 침해. ¶ *the* ～ *of a river* 강의 침식.

en·crust [enkrʌ́st], **in-** [in-] *vt.* (P6,13) **1** cover as with a crust. 외피〔껍데기〕로 덮다. ¶ *encrusted snow* 표면이 단단하게 굳은 눈. **2** ornament (a surface) with a crust of precious metal. (보석 따위로) 표면을 장식하다. ¶ *a box encrusted with jewels* 겉을 보석으로 장식한 상자. — *vi.* (P1) form into a crust. 외피〔겉켜〕가 되다. [en-]

en·cum·ber [enkʌ́mbər] *vt.* **1** get in the way of (someone or something); make it difficult for someone to act; hinder. (활동 따위)를 방해하다; 거치적거리게 하다. ¶ ～ *someone's movements* 아무의 움직임을 방해하다 / ～ *trade with heavy taxes* 중세로 무역을 방해하다 / *She was encumbered by her long skirts while running.* 달리는 동안 그녀의 긴 치맛자락이 거치적거렸다. **2** choke up; fill. (장소)를 막다; 가득하게 하다. ¶ *a corridor encumbered with furniture* 가구들로 꽉 들어찬 복도. **3** burden with weight, difficulties, cares, debts, etc. (무거운 짐·부채·어려움 따위)를 짊어지우다; 떠맡게 하다. ¶ *a farm encumbered with mortgages* 저당을 잡힌 농장 / *be encumbered with debts* 빚을 짊어지다. [en-, →cumbrance]

en·cum·brance [inkʌ́mbrəns, en-] *n.* Ⓒ anything that encumbers; obstruction; burden 방해물; 성가신 것; 거치적거림; 무거운 짐. ¶ *a man without encumbrances* 자식이 없는 사람 / *A heavy coat is an* ～ *in walking.* 두꺼운 코트는 걷는 데 거치적거린다. [↑]

Ency(c).Brit. Encyclopaedia Britannica (대영(大英) 백과 사전).

en·cyc·lic [ensíklik, ensáiklik], **-li·cal** [-kəl] *n.* a letter addressed by the Pope to all the bishops of the Roman Church. 동문통달(同文通達)《특히 로마 교황이 모든 성직자에게 보내는 회칙》. — *adj.* having to do with such a document; general. 회칙의; 일반을 대상으로 한. [→cycle]

***en·cy·clo·pe·di·a, -pae-** [ensàikloupíːdiə] *n.* Ⓒ a book or series of books about all branches of knowledge. 백과 사전; 백과 전서. ¶ *Encyclopaedia Britannica* 대영(大英) 백과 사전. [Gk. =all-round education]

en·cy·clo·pe·dic, -pae- [ensàikloupíːdik] *adj.* **1** of or like an encyclopedia. 백과

사전의〔과 같은〕. **2** about all branches of knowledge. 넓은 지식의; 박학의. ¶ *an ~ mind* 박식한 사람.

:end [end] *n.* Ⓒ 《often *the* ~》 **1** the last point or part; the finish. 끝; 종말; 말미. ¶ *a pointed ~* 뾰족한 끝 / *one's journey's ~* 여행의 끝 / *the ~ of the year* 연말(年末); 세밑 / *the ~ of a speech* 연설의 말미 / *~ up* 끝을 위로 하여; 거꾸로 / *bring to an ~ = make an ~ of =put an ~ to* …을 끝내다; 마치다 / *draw to an ~* 마지막이 다가오다. **2** ⓐ the limit or limiting part of a place; a boundary. (장소의) 경계(선); 한계(선). ¶ *both ends of the table* 탁자의 양끝 / *the ~ of the street* 거리의 끝 / *walk from ~ to ~ of a city* 시의 끝에서 끝까지 걷다. ⓑ 《*fig.*》 the limit in degree; bounds. (정도의) 한도. ¶ *be at the ~ of one's patience* 더 이상 참을 수가 없다. **3** an aim; a purpose. 목적; 목표. ¶ *means to an ~* 목적을 위한 수단 / *to* 〔*for*〕 *this ~* 이 목적을 위해 / *to no ~* 헛되이 / *to the ~ that* …하기 위해 / *gain one's end(s)* 목적을 이루다 / *The ~ justifies the means.* 목적은 수단을 정당화시킨다. **4** death; ruin. 죽음; 끝장; 파멸. ¶ *one's latter ~* (아무의) 최후 / *the ~ of feudalism* 봉건제의 종언 / *be near one's ~* 죽어 가고 있다; 죽음이 임박해 있다 / *meet one's ~ bravely* 최후를 용감히 맞이하다 / *come to an untimely ~* 젊어 죽다; 요절하다 / *It was the ~ of him.* 그것이 그의 끝장이었다. **5** conclusion. 결론. **6** the result; the issue. 결과; 결말. ¶ *It is difficult to see the ~.* 결과는 알기 어렵다. **7** a small part that remains; a broken piece. 지스러기; 나부랭이. ¶ *a cigarette ~* 담배 꽁초.

at a loose end = ***at loose ends,*** 《*colloq.*》 unoccupied; having nothing to do. 일이 없는; 할 일이 없는.

at one's wit's end, not knowing what to do; very anxious. 어찌 할 바를 몰라; 몹시 걱정하고.

be at an end, have finished. …해 버렸다; 끝냈다.

come to an end, end; be over. 끝나다.

end for end, contrarywise. 거꾸로; 역으로.

end on, with the end facing or fronting one. 끝을 앞〔정면〕으로 향하여.

end to end, with the two ends facing or together. 끝과 끝을 연결하여.

get (***hold of***) ***the wrong end of the stick,*** get a wrong idea which is exactly opposite to the right idea; misunderstand completely. (의도·의미를) 잘못 생각하다; 완전히 오해하다.

go (***in***) ***off the deep end,*** 《*colloq.*》 **a**) 《Brit.》 lose one's temper. (자제력을 잃고) 흥분〔격앙〕하다. **b**) 《U.S.》 act recklessly or rashly. 무모한 짓을 하다.

in the end, finally; at last. 결국; 마침내.

keep one's end up, **a**) do one's share; fulfil one's responsibility. 자기 책임을 다하다. **b**) hold one's position. 제 위치를 지키다; 끝까지 버티다.

make an end of 〔***with***〕, put an end to; abolish. …을 끝내다; 폐지하다.

make both ends meet, get just enough money for one's needs; manage to live within one's income. 수지 균형을 맞추다; 수입의 범위 내에서 살다.

meet one's end, die. 죽다.

no end, 《*colloq.*》 very much. 많이.

no end of, a large number 〔amount〕 of. 많은; 끝없는. ¶ *no ~ of trouble* 끝이 없는 분규.

on end, **a**) standing on one end; standing 〔unnaturally〕 upright. 한 끝을 아래로 하여; 곧추 세워. **b**) without stopping; continuously. 계속해서. ¶ *It has been raining for three days on ~.* 사흘 동안이나 계속해서 비가 내리고 있다.

play both ends against the middle, make two persons contend with each other for one's own benefit. 양자를 다투게 하여 어부지리를 얻다.

put an end to, stop; abolish something. …을 멈추게 하다; 끝내다; …을 폐지하다.

to no end, uselessly; in vain. 무익하게; 헛되이.

to the (***bitter, very***) ***end,*** until the end arrives; until someone reaches the end. 마지막〔최후〕까지.

to the end that, in order that. …하기 위하여.

— *vt.* (P6,7) bring (something) to an end; put an end to (something). …을 끝내다. — *vi.* (P1,2A,3) come to an end. 끝나다. [E.]

end by doing, do something last. 마지막으로 …하다.

end in, have (something) as a result; lead to (something) at the end. 결국 …이 되다; …로 끝나다. ¶ *The argument between the two men ended in a fight.* 두 사람의 말다툼은 마침내 싸움이 되었다.

end in smoke, have no result; come to nothing. 헛되이 되다; 수포로 돌아가다.

end off, bring to a finish. 끝내다.

end up, finish; die. 끝나다; 죽다. ¶ *~ up in prison* 옥사하다.

end (=*be finished*) ***with something.*** …로 끝나다.

en·dan·ger [endéindʒər] *vt.* (P6) put (someone or something) in danger; expose (someone or something) to danger. 위태롭게 하다; 위험에 드러내다〔빠뜨리다〕. ¶ *~ one's life* 생명을 위태롭게 하다. [en-]

en·dear [endíər] *vt.* (P13) 《*reflexively*》 make (oneself) dear; cause (oneself) to be loved. …을 그립게 하다; 애정을 느끼게 하다. ¶ *an endearing smile* 귀여운 미소 / *She endeared herself to the children.* 그녀는 아이들로부터 사랑을 받았다 / *Her kindness endeared her to all.* 그녀는 친절해서 모두로부터 사랑을 받았다. [en-]

en·dear·ment [endíərmənt] *n.* **1** Ⓤ the act of endearing; the state of being endeared. 친애; 애정. **2** Ⓒ something that endears; an act or word that expresses affection. 사랑을 느끼게 하는 것; 애정의 표현; 애무(愛撫). ¶ *I got tired of her endearments.* 그녀의 애정 표시에 지쳤다.

:en·deav·or, 《Brit.》 **-our** [endévər] *vi.* (P3,4) 《*after*》 try hard; make an effort; strive. 노력하다; 애쓰다. ¶ *~ to compose oneself* 마음을 가라앉히려고 애쓰다 / *~ after fame* 명성을 얻으려고 노력하다. — *n.* Ⓒ an earnest attempt. 시도; 노력. ¶ *do one's best endeavors* 온갖 노력을 다하다 / *make every ~ to succeed* 성공하기 위해 온갖 노력을 다하다 / *His endeavors were in vain.* 그의 노력은 헛되었다. [→devoir]

en·dem·ic [endémik] *adj.* (of a disease) found in a certain nation or area. 한 지방〔민족〕 특유의; 풍토의(cf. *epidemic*). ¶ *a fever ~ to the tropics* 열대 지방 특유의 열병. — *n.* Ⓒ an endemic disease. 풍토병; 지방병. [en-, → demos]

·end·ing [éndiŋ] *n.* **1** the end; the last part. 종지(終止); 종결; 종말; 결말; 최후의 부분. ¶ *a story with a happy ~* 행복한 결말로 끝나는 이야기. **2** death. 죽음. ¶ *His ~ was peaceful.* 그의 죽음은 평화스러웠다. [*end*]

·end·less [éndlis] *adj.* **1** having no end; lasting or going on forever. 끝없는; 무한한; 영구한(opp. limited). **2** very frequent. 끊임없는. ¶ *an ~ tattle* 끊임없는 수다 / *~ cares* 끊임없는 걱정거리 / *He made ~ attempts.* 끊임없는 시도를 했다. **3** joined in a circle; without ends. (사슬 따위 끝과 끝이 이어져) 고리가 되어 있는; 순환의. ¶ *an ~ chain* 〔*belt*〕 순환 사슬〔피대〕. ● **end·less·ness** [-nis] *n.* [*end, -less*]

end·less·ly [éndlisli] *adv.* in an endless manner. 끝없이; 끊임없이.

end·most [én*d*mòust] *adj.* nearest to the end; last; farthest. 제일 끝의; 가장 먼. [*end*]

en·do·crine [éndo*u*kràin, -krì(:)n] *adj.* 《med.》 of a gland which produces certain important secretions. 내분비의. ¶ *an ~ gland* 내분비샘. [endo-, Gk. *krino* shift]

en·dog·a·my [endágəmi / -dɔ́g-] *n.* a custom of marrying only within the tribe. 족내혼(族內婚); 동족 결혼(cf. *exogamy*). ● **en·dog·a·mous** [-məs] *adj.* [endo-, Gk. *gamos* marriage]

en·dorse [endɔ́:rs] *vt.* (P6) **1** write one's name, comment, etc. on the back of a check, etc. (수표 따위)에 배서(背書)하다. ¶ *~ a check* 수표에 배서하다. **2** 《*fig.*》 make sure of; approve. …을 확인하다; …을 인정〔승인, 시인〕하다. ¶ *~ a statement* 진술에 틀림없음을 인정하다 / *I ~ everything that the speaker has said.* 나는 연사가 말한 모든 것을 시인한다. [→dorsal]

en·dor·see [endɔ:rsí:, ⌐–⌐, –⌐⌐] *n.* Ⓒ a person to whom a check, note, etc. is assigned by endorsement. 피배서인(被背書人).

en·dorse·ment [endɔ́:rsmənt] *n.* ⓊⒸ **1** the act of endorsing. 배서(背書). **2** approval; support. 시인; 승인; 지지.

en·dor·ser, -sor [endɔ́:rsər] *n.* Ⓒ a person who endorses. 배서인(背書人); 보증인.

·en·dow [endáu] *vt.* **1** (P6) give a large sum of money to (a school, etc.) as the source of permanent income. …에 기금으로 기부하다. ¶ *~ a college* 대학에 기금을 기부하다 / *He endowed the hospital with a large fortune.* 그는 병원에 많은 재산을 기부했다. **2** (P13) 《in *passive*》 《*with*》 provide. (재능·자질 따위)를 부여하다. ¶ *a meagerly endowed island* 자원이 없는 섬 / *Man is endowed with reason.* 인간에게는 이성이 부여되어 있다. [→dower]

en·dow·ment [endáumənt] *n.* **1** Ⓤ the act of endowing. 기금 기부; 기증. **2** Ⓒ money or property endowed. 기부금; 기본재산. **3** 《usu. *pl.*》 a gift of nature; talent. 천성; 재능. ¶ *natural endowments* 천부의 재능 / *mental endowments* 정신적 자질.

endowment insurance 〔《Brit.》 **assurance**〕 [⌐–⌐ –⌐–〔–⌐–〕] *n.* a form of insurance providing for the payment of a fixed sum at a specified time or at his death. 양로 연금 특약 보험.

end paper [⌐ ⌐–] *n.* a blank leaf at the beginning or the end of a book. (책의) 면지. [*end*]

en·due [indjú:, en-] *vt.* (P13) 《*with*》 provide with a quality or power. (자질·재능·권리 따위)를 주다; 부여하다. [→induce]

en·dur·a·ble [ind*j*úərəbəl, en-] *adj.* that can be endured; likely to last a long time. 참을〔견딜〕 수 있는; 오래가는〔지속하는〕. [→endure]

en·dur·ance [ind*j*úərəns, en-] *n.* Ⓤ the act or power of enduring; patience. 지구력; 내구성; 인내(력); 참음. ¶ *~ flying* 체공 비행 / *with ~* 참을성 있게 / *a man of great ~* 참을성이 많은 사람 / *try one's ~* 인내력을 시험하다.

beyond* 〔*past*〕 *endurance, to an extent that one can no longer endure. 인내력의 한계를 넘어; 참을 수 없을 정도로.

:en·dure [end*j*úər] *vt.* (P6,8,9) put up with; bear; suffer. (고통 따위에) 견디다; 참다; (고난 따위)를 견뎌 내다. ¶ *~ cold* 추위를 참다 / *~ much pain* 많은 고통을 참다 / *~ great difficulties* 큰 어려움을 견뎌 내다 / *~ a variety of torture* 여러 가지 고문에 견디다 / *I can't ~ it any more.* 더는 못 참겠다. — *vi.* **1** (P1,2B) last; continue. 오래가다; 지속하다. ¶ *as long as life endures* 생명을 부지하는 한 / *His fame endures forever.* 그의 명성은 영원히 지속된다. **2** (P1,2A) bear or put up with pain, etc. 참다; 견디다. ¶ *~ to the last* 끝까지 견디다. [→duration]

en·dur·ing [ind*j*úəriŋ, en-] *adj.* long-suffering; lasting. 참을성[인내력]이 강한; 지속하는; 영속적인 ¶ ~ *fame* 불후의 명성 / *an ~ peace* 영속적인 평화.

end·ways [éndwèiz], **end·wise** [-wàiz] *adv.* with the end forward; on end. 수직으로 (세워); 거꾸로. [*end; ways, wise*]

ENE east-northeast.

en·e·ma [énəmə] *n.* 《med.》 **1** washing away of bowels by injecting a liquid. 관장(灌腸). **2** a fluid injected into the rectum. 관장제(劑). [Gk. *enema*]

:en·e·my [énəmi] *n.* (*pl.* **-mies**) Ⓒ **1** a person or group that fights against another. 적(敵); 적병. ¶ *a lifelong ~* 평생의 적 / *a mortal ~* 불구대천의 적. **2** 《*the ~*》 a military force, nation, etc. at war with another. 적군; 적국. ¶ *attack the ~* 적군을 공격하다 / *go over to the ~* 적군에 넘어가다[붙다] / *The ~ was forced to retreat.* 적군은 퇴각하지 않을 수 없었다. **3** anything harmful like an enemy. 해를 끼치는 것; 원수; 적 (opp. friend). ¶ *an ~ of freedom* 자유의 적 / *an ~ to success* 성공을 방해하는 적 / *Frost is an ~ of flowers.* 서리는 꽃의 적이다. [L. *in-* not, *amicus* friend]

be an enemy to, do harm to (someone); hate. …을 해하다; 미워하다.

be one's own enemy, injure oneself. 자신을[스스로를] 해치다.

How goes the enemy? 《*colloq.*》 What time is it? 지금 몇 시인가.

the* (*old*) *Enemy, the Devil. 악마; 사탄.

en·er·get·ic [ènərdʒétik], **-i·cal** [-ikəl] *adj.* full of energy; vigorous; forceful. 정력적인; 원기 왕성한; 힘찬; 강력한. ¶ *an ~ leader* 정력적인 지도자 / *take ~ measures against crime* 범죄 방지의 강력한 조치를 취하다. [→energy]

en·er·get·i·cal·ly [ènərdʒétikəli] *adv.* with energy. 정력적으로; 원기 왕성하게.

en·er·gize [énərdʒàiz] *vt.* (P6) give energy to (someone or something); make (someone or something) active. …에게 정력을 주다; 활기 띠게 하다. ¶ ~ *the spirit with brave words* 용감한 말로 기분을 분발시키다. — *vi.* put forth energy; be active. 힘을 내다; (정력적으로) 활동하다. ● **en·er·giz·er** [-ər] *n.* [↓]

en·er·gy [énərdʒi] *n.* Ⓤ **1** strength; force; power; vigor. 힘; 기운; 정력; 원기; 활기. ¶ *with ~* 원기 왕성하게 / *be full of ~* 정력이 왕성하다 / *brace one's energies* 힘[기운]을 내다. **2** 《*pl.*》 (a person's) active power. 활동력. **3** 《phys.》 the capacity for doing work. 에너지; 세력. ¶ *kinetic* [*motive*] ~ 운동 에너지 / *radiant ~* 복사 에너지 / *latent* [*potential*] ~ 잠재 에너지. [Gk. *ergon* work]

devote* [*bend, apply*] *one's energies* (=*give one's all active power*) *to something. …에 온 정력을 쏟다.

en·er·vate [énərvèit] *vt.* (P6) lessen the vigor or strength of (someone or something); weaken physically or mentally. …에게서 기운[활력]을 빼앗다; …을 약하게 하다. ¶ *Hot weather enervates people who are not strong.* 더운 날씨는 강하지 못한 사람들의 체력을 약화시킨다. ● **en·er·va·tion** [ènərvéiʃən] *n.* [→nerve]

en·fant ter·ri·ble [ɑ̃fɑ̃ teribl] *n.* 《F.》 **1** a child who asks awkward questions. (거북한 질문 따위로 어른을 쩔쩔매게 하는) 깜찍한[무서운] 아이. **2** a person who is indiscreet or lacks a sense of responsibilities. 경솔한 사람; 무책임한 사람.

en·fee·ble [infí:bəl, en-] *vt.* (P6) make feeble; weaken. 약하게 하다; 약화시키다. [en-]

en·fold [enfóuld] *vt.* (P6) **1** fold or wrap up. …을 싸다; 접다. ¶ ~ *someone in a cloak* 아무를 외투로 감싸다. **2** clasp in one's arms; embrace. 안다; 포옹하다. [en-]

·en·force [enfɔ́:rs] *vt.* (P6,13) **1** put (something) into force; make (a law, etc.) effective. …을 힘써 행하다; (법률 따위)를 실시[시행]하다. ¶ ~ *laws* [*rules*] 법률[규칙]을 시행하다. **2** 《*upon*》 force; compel. …을 강요[강제]하다. ¶ ~ *obedience* [*silence*] 복종[침묵]을 강요하다 / ~ *one's will on a child* 자기의 의사를 아이에게 강제하다. ● **en·force·a·ble** [-əbəl] *adj.* [en-]

en·force·ment [enfɔ́:rsmənt] *n.* Ⓤ enforcing or putting into force. 시행; 실행; 강제; 강요. ¶ *strict ~ of the law* 법의 엄격한 시행.

en·fran·chise [enfrǽntʃaiz] *vt.* (P6) **1** grant someone a franchise. …에게 공민권[참정권]을 주다. ¶ *In England women were enfranchised more than half a century ago.* 영국에서는 여성에게 반세기나 전에 참정권이 주어졌다. **2** set (slaves, etc.) free. (노예 등)을 해방하다. ● **en·fran·chise·ment** [-tʃizmənt, -tʃaiz-] *n.* [en-]

eng. engine; engineer; engineering; engraved; engraver; engraving.

:en·gage [engéidʒ] *vt., vi.* **1** ⓐ (P8,11,20) bind (oneself) with a promise; promise. 약속하다; 언질을 주다; 꼭 …하다. ¶ ~ (*oneself*) *to do something* 무엇을 하기로 약속하다 / *If you are not engaged for tomorrow….* 내일 선약이 없으시다면 … / *I'll ~ to finish it by five.* 다섯 시까지는 꼭 마치도록 하죠. ⓑ (P8,11;3) say firmly; assure. …을 단언하다; 보증하다. ¶ *I'll ~ that he is very faithful.* 그가 매우 성실한 사람임을 보증합니다. **2** 《usu. in *passive*》 promise to marry. 약혼하다. ¶ *He and she are engaged.* 그와 그녀는 약혼해 있다 / *He has engaged himself* [*is engaged*] *to a charming girl.* 매력적인 처녀와 약혼했다. **3** (P6,13) employ; hire. 고용하다; 빌리다. ¶ ~ *a workman* 노동자를 쓰다 / ~ *a car by the day* 하루 얼마로 차를 빌리다 / *We engaged him as a translator.* 그를 번역사로 고용했다. **4** (P6,13) cause to be kept apart for one's use; reserve. 예약하다. ¶ ~ *a* *seat* 좌석을 예약하다 / ~ *a room at a hotel* 호텔의 방을 예약해 두다. **5** (P6,13; 3) 《usu. in *passive*》 《*in*》 fill up the time of; keep busy. (시간 따위)를 차지하다; (시간 따위가) 차 있어 여유가 없다; (일 따위에) 종사하다; 사용하다. ¶ *have one's time fully engaged* 시간이 꽉 차 있다《틈이 나지 않다》/ ~ *oneself in* …에 종사하다 / ~ *in business* 사업에 종사하다 / ~ *the line for five minutes,* 5분 동안 전화로 이야기하다 / *The line is engaged.* 《Brit.》 (전화에서) 통화중입니다(=《U.S.》 The line is busy.) / *I'm engaged (for) this evening.* 오늘 저녁엔 시간이 없다 / *He is engaged in writing a letter.* 그는 편지를 쓰고 있다. **6** (P6,13) attract (someone's attention, etc.); draw (someone, etc.) into. (주의 따위)를 끌다; (아무)를 …에 끌어들이다. ¶ *He tried to ~ her attention.* 그는 그녀의 주의를 끌려고 애썼다 / *We engaged him in conversation.* 그를 이야기에 끌어들였다. **7** (P6,13; 1,3) join battle (with); attack. …과 교전(交戰)하다. ¶ ~ *the enemy* 적과 교전하다. **8** (P6; 1,3) interlock. 맞물(리)다. ¶ *This wheel engages with that wheel.* 이 바퀴는 그 바퀴와 맞물린다. [F. *engage* under pledge]

be engaged (=*have promised to marry*) ***to** someone.* …와 약혼해 있다〔약혼했다〕.

engage on (=*start; begin*) *something.* …에 착수하다.

***engage** oneself **to** someone,* promise to marry. …와 약혼하다.

en·gaged [engéidʒd] *adj.* **1** promised to marry. 약혼중의; 약혼한. ¶ *an ~ girl* 약혼한 처녀. **2** having one's time filled up; busy; occupied. 바쁜; 틈이 없는; 사용중의. ¶ *be ~ in writing letters* 편지 쓰기에 몰두해 있다 / *I am ~ for the next three days.* 다음 사흘 동안 시간이 꽉 차 있다. **3** ⓐ (of a seat, etc.) promised; reserved. 예약된. ⓑ hired. 고용된; 빌린. **4** fitted together. 맞물린. **5** fighting. 교전중인.

·en·gage·ment [engéidʒmənt] *n.* Ⓒ **1** ⓐ a promise; a promise to marry. 약속; 약혼. ¶ *an ~ ring* 약혼 반지 / *break off an ~* 파혼〔파약〕하다. ⓑ a promise to meet or go out with someone at a certain time somewhere; an appointment. (회합 따위의) 약속. ¶ *make an ~* 약속을 하다 / *have a dinner ~ with* …와 식사 약속이 있다. **2** employment; a period of being employed; time of use. 고용(기간); 사용 기간. ¶ *six months' ~,* 6개월의 사용 기간. **3** fight; battle. 교전(交戰).

be under engagement, have a contract. 계약이 있다.

enter into 〔***make***〕 ***an engagement with,*** promise; contract. …와 약속하다; 계약하다.

meet one's engagements, pay one's debts. 채무를 이행하다.

en·gag·ing [engéidʒiŋ] *adj.* attractive; pleasing; charming. 마음을 끄는; 애교 있는; 매력적인. ¶ *an ~ manner* 〔*smile*〕 애교 있는 태도〔미소〕. ● **en·gag·ing·ly** [-li] *adv.*

en·gen·der [endʒéndər] *vt.* (P6) produce; cause. …을 일으키다; 일어나게 하다. ¶ *Sympathy often engenders love.* 동정은 흔히 애정을 낳는다. [en-, →genus]

:en·gine [éndʒən] *n.* Ⓒ **1** a machine that produces power or motion. 기관; 발동기. ¶ *internal combustion ~* 내연 기관. **2** a machine that pulls a train, etc.; a locomotive. 기관차. **3** a machine; a device. 기계; 장치. ¶ *a dental ~* 치과용 기계. [L. *ingenium* inborn qualities]

engine driver [ˊ- ˋ-] *n.* 《Brit.》 an engineer on a machine. 기관사(cf. 《U.S.》 *engineer*).

:en·gi·neer [èndʒəníər] *n.* Ⓒ **1** a person who designs machines, roads, bridges, etc. 기사; 공학자. ¶ *an electrical* 〔*civil*〕 ~ 전기〔토목〕 기사. **2** 《U.S.》 a driver; a mechanic. 기관사; 기관공(cf. 《Brit.》 *engine driver*). **3** 《mil.》 a member of a group that does engineering work. 공병. — *vt.* (P6) manage or guide skillfully. …을 공작하다; 교묘히 처리하다. ¶ ~ *a plot* 음모를 꾸미다. — *vi.* (P1) work as an engineer. 기사로서 일하다. [*engine*]

·en·gi·neer·ing [èndʒəníəriŋ] *n.* Ⓤ the science, work, or job of an engineer. 공학; 공사; 기관학. ¶ *aeronautical ~* 항공 공학 / *civil* 〔*electrical, mechanical*〕 ~ 토목〔전기, 기계〕 공학.

en·gine·ry [éndʒənri] *n.* 《rare》 engines; machines. 기관; 기계류.

:Eng·land [íŋglənd] *n.* **1** the largest division of Great Britain. 잉글랜드. **2** Great Britain. 영국. [E.]

:Eng·lish [íŋgliʃ] *adj.* of England, its people, or their language. 영국(인)의; 잉글랜드(사람)의; 영어의. — *n.* **1** 《*the ~, collectively*》 the people of England. 영국인; 영국민. **2** Ⓤ the English language. ¶ *speak in ~* 영어로 말하다 / *What is the ~ for 'bal'?* '발'을 영어로 뭐라고 하는가. [E.]

:Eng·lish·man [íŋgliʃmən] *n.* (*pl.* **-men** [-mən]) Ⓒ **1** a person of England. 영국인. **2** an English ship. 영국 배.

Eng·lish·wom·an [íŋgliʃwùmən] *n.* Ⓒ (*pl.* **-wom·en** [-wìmin]) a woman of England. 영국 여자.

en·gorge [engɔ́ːrdʒ] *vt., vi.* **1** 《med.》 《usu. in *passive*》 fill with blood, as an artery. (혈액 따위로) 가득하게 하다; 충혈하다. **2** devour or swallow greedily. 걸신들린 듯이〔게걸스럽게〕 먹다. [F. *engorger;*→ en-, gorge]

en·graft [engrǽft, -grάːft] *vt.* (P6,13) **1** insert (a part of one tree) into another tree; implant. …을 접목하다. ¶ ~ *peach (up) on the plum* 복숭아를 자두에 접목시키다. **2** fix (something) in someone's mind, soul, etc. …을 마음에 심다〔새기다〕; 명심하다. ¶ *Patriotism was engrafted in his soul.* 그의

마음에는 애국심이 심어졌다 / *Honesty is engrafted in his character.* 성실함이 그의 인품에 배어 있다. [en-]

en·grain [engréin] *vt.* ⇨ingrain.

en·grave [engréiv] *vt.* (P6,13) **1** cut (letters, figures, etc.) on metal, stone, or wood. …을 새기다; 조각하다. ¶ ~ *a name on a stone* = ~ *a stone with a name* 돌에다 이름을 새기다. **2** 《*on*》 impress deeply. …을 마음에 깊이 새기다; 명기하다. ¶ ~ *the sight on one's memory* 그 광경을 마음 속에 깊이 새기다. [→grave[3]]

en·grav·er [engréivər] *n.* Ⓒ a person who engraves. 조각가; 조판공(彫版工).

en·grav·ing [engréiviŋ] *n.* **1** Ⓤ the art of an engraver. 조각(술). **2** Ⓒ an engraved design, plate, etc.; a picture printed from an engraved block or plate, etc. 조판(彫版); 판화.

en·gross [engróus] *vt.* (P6,13) 《chiefly in *passive*》 **1** occupy or absorb wholly (someone's time, etc.). (시간 따위)를 빼앗다; 열중[몰두]하게 하다. ¶ *an engrossing story* 몹시 재미있는 이야기 / *be engrossed in an exciting story* 재미있는 이야기에 열중해 있다 / *This business engrosses my whole time.* 이 사업은 내 시간을 전부 빼앗는다 / *She was engrossed in her work.* 그녀는 일에 몰두해 있었다. **2** write (something) in large letters or in legal form. …을 큰 글자로 쓰다; 정식으로 쓰다. ● **en·gross·ment** [-mənt] *n.* [F.]

en·gulf [engʌ́lf] *vt.* (P6) swallow up; submerge. …을 삼키다; 말려들게 하다. ¶ *The boat was nearly engulfed in the wild sea.* 배는 사나운 바다에 거의 휩쓸렸다 / 《*fig.*》 *Sorrow engulfed him.* 슬픔이 그를 덮쳤다. [en-]

en·hance [enhǽns, -hɑ́:ns] *vt.* (P6) heighten or increase (the value, etc.). (가치·미(美) 따위)를 높이다; 증대시키다; 늘리다. ¶ ~ *the difficulty of* …의 어려움을 더하다 / *Health enhances beauty.* 건강은 아름다움을 증대시킨다. **en·hance·ment** [-mənt] *n.* ⓊⒸ [F. < L. *altus* high]

e·nig·ma [inígmə] *n.* Ⓒ **1** a riddle. 수수께끼. **2** a puzzling person or thing. 이해할 수 없는 사람[사물]. [Gk.]

en·ig·mat·ic [ènigmǽtik, ì:n-], **-i·cal** [-ikəl] *adj.* puzzling; mysterious; perplexing. 수수께끼 같은; 불가해한; 풀기 어려운. ¶ *his* ~ *behavior* [*character*] 그의 수수께끼 같은 태도[성격].

en·join [endʒɔ́in] *vt.* (P6,11,13,20) **1** command; order. …에게 명령하다. ¶ ~ *silence on the children* 아이들에게 침묵할 것을 명하다 / ~ *a student to be diligent* 학생에게 공부를 하도록 이르다. **2** 《law》 《*from*》 prohibit. …을 금하다. ¶ ~ *an action* 행위를 금하다 / ~ *someone from infringing a right* 아무가 권리를 침해하는 것을 금하다. [en-]

:en·joy [endʒɔ́i] *vt.* (P6,9,13) **1** be happy with (something); take delight in (something); make (someone) pleased. …을 기뻐하다, 즐기다; (아무)를 기쁘게 하다. ¶ ~ *a few beers* 몇 잔의 맥주를 즐겁게 마시다 / ~ *reading* [*dancing*] 독서를[춤을] 즐기다 / ~ *the pleasure of life* 인생의 즐거움을 맛보다 / ~ *oneself* 즐기다; 유쾌히 지내다 / *How did you* ~ *your trip?* 여행은 어떠셨습니까. **2** have (something) as one's strong point; have the use of (something). 향유하다; 누리다. ¶ ~ *good health* [*a happy life*] 건강을[행복한 생활을] 누리다 / ~ *a comfortable income* 충분한 수입이 있다 / 《*iron.*》 ~ *a bad reputation* 악명을 드날리다. [en-]

en·joy·a·ble [endʒɔ́iəbəl] *adj.* giving joy; able to be enjoyed; pleasant. 즐거운; 즐길 수 있는; 유쾌한. ¶ *a very* ~ *film* 매우 재미있는 영화 / *have an* ~ *journey* 즐거운 여행을 하다. ● **en·joy·a·bly** [-əbəli] *adv.*

·en·joy·ment [endʒɔ́imənt] *n.* Ⓤ **1** the act of enjoying; happiness; joy; pleasure. 즐김; 즐거움; 쾌락. ¶ *take* ~ *in something* …을 즐기다 / *get* ~ *out of life* 삶에서 즐거움을 얻다. **2** the state of having as one's strong point; use. 누림; 향유(享有). ¶ *the* ~ *of property* 재산의 향유 / *be in the* ~ *of good health* 건강을 누리고 있다. **3** Ⓒ something that gives joy or satisfaction. 기쁨[만족]을 주는 것. ¶ *His visit was a great* ~ *to me.* 그의 방문은 내게 큰 기쁨이었다.

en·kin·dle [enkíndl] *vt.* (P6) **1** (of fire) light up; set (something) on fire. …에 불을 붙이다; …을 불타게 하다. **2** 《*fig.*》 make (passion, etc.) active; excite. (정열 따위)를 타오르게 하다. ¶ ~ *a desire for liberty* 자유에 대한 욕망을 불태우다. [en-]

·en·large [enlɑ́:rdʒ] *vt.* (P6) **1** make (something) larger; increase (something) in size; expand. …을 크게 하다; 늘이다; 확대[확장, 증대]하다. ¶ *a revised and enlarged edition* (책의) 개정 증보판 / ~ *one's house* [*coat*] 집을[코트를] 늘이다 / ~ *the understanding* 이해를 넓히다. **2** 《photog.》 reproduce (a print) on a larger scale. (사진)을 확대하다. ¶ *an enlarged photograph* 확대(擴大) 사진. — *vi.* (P1) become larger. 커지다; 넓어지다. [en-]

enlarge on [***upon***], speak or write more about (something). …을 상설(詳說)하다. ¶ *I need not* ~ *further on* [*upon*] *this point.* 이 점에 대해서는 더 이상의 상세한 설명을 필요로 하지 않는다.

en·large·ment [enlɑ́:rdʒmənt] *n.* **1** Ⓤ the act of enlarging; the state of being enlarged. 확대; 증대; 확장; 상설(詳說). ¶ *the* ~ *of a house* 집의 확장. **2** Ⓒ anything enlarged; an addition. 증가[확대]물; 증축; 증보판. ¶ *make an* ~ *from* …을 확대하여 인화하다.

·en·light·en [enláitn] *vt.* (P6,13) **1** give more knowledge to (someone); instruct. …에게 지식을 주다; …을 가르치다; 계몽[교화]하다. ¶ ~ *the ignorant* 무지한 사람들을 계몽하

다. **2** inform; make clear the meaning to (someone). …에게 알리다; 뜻을 밝히다. ¶ *~ someone as to one's intentions* 아무에게 자신의 의향을 밝히다. **3** 《*poet.*》 shed light upon. …에 빛을 비추다. ● **en·light·en·er** [-ər] *n.* [en-]

en·light·ened [enláitnd] *adj.* cultivated; civilized; well-informed. 계발(啓發)된; 계몽〔개화〕된; 문명화한; (내용을) 잘 알고 있는. ¶ *an ~ age* 개화된 시대 / *be ~ on* …에 관해 잘 알고 있다.

en·light·en·ment [enláitnmənt] *n.* Ⓤ the act of enlightening; the state of being enlightened. 계몽; 개화; 교화. ¶ *carry ~ to* …을 교화하다 / *seek ~ on* …에 관해서 가르침을 청하다 / *work for the ~ of mankind* 인류의 교화를 위해 일하다.

en·list [enlíst] *vt.* (P6,13) **1** get (someone) to join the military service. …을 병적에 편입하다; 징집하다. ¶ *~ men for the army* 장정들을 육군에 편입하다. **2** get the support or help of (someone). …의 지지를〔협력을〕얻다. ¶ *~ someone's aid in* …에서 아무의 도움을 얻다 / *~ someone in an enterprise* 아무를 사업에 참여시키다. — *vi.* (P1,3) **1** join the military service. 입대하다. ¶ *~ in the army* 육군에 입대하다. **2** 《*in*》 give one's support to something; join a movement. 협력〔참가〕하다. ¶ *~ under the banner of freedom* 자유의 기치 밑에 참가하다 / *~ in a cause* 어떤 주의에 참가하다. [en-]

en·list·ed man [enlístid mǽn] *n.* Ⓒ 《U.S.》 a man in the armed forces who is not a commissioned officer or a warrant officer. (장교 이하의) 사병. 參考 E.M.으로 생략함.

en·list·ment [enlístmənt] *n.* ⓊⒸ **1** the act of enlisting; the state of being enlisted. (병사의) 징모; 병적 편입. **2** the period for which a man enlists. 군재적(軍在籍) 기간. [en-]

en·liv·en [enláivən] *vt.* (P6) make (someone) lively or cheerful. …을 활기 띠게 하다. ¶ *His wit enlivened the conversation.* 그의 재치는 대화를 활기 있게 했다 / *Spring enlivens all nature.* 봄은 삼라만상을 생동하게 한다. [en-]

en masse [en mǽs, ɑːŋ mɑ́ːs] *adv.* in a group; all together. 일단이 되어; 함께; 같이. [F. =in a mass]

en·mesh [enméʃ] *vt.* (P6,13) catch as in a net; entangle. …을 그물로 잡다; 망에 걸려들게 하다; (곤란 따위에) 빠뜨리다. [en-]

en·mi·ty [énməti] *n.* Ⓤ strong dislike; hatred. 증오; 적대. ¶ *at ~ with* …와 반목하고; …에게 적의(敵意)를 품고 / *have ~ against someone* 아무에게 적대감을 품다. [→enemy]

en·no·ble [enóubl] *vt.* (P6) **1** give (someone) a rank or title of nobility. …에게 작위를 주다; …을 귀족으로 만들다. **2** make (someone) noble in nature, etc. …을 높이다; 고상하게 하다. ¶ *a character ennobled by suffering* 고난에 의해 높여진 품성. [en-]

en·nui [ɑːnwíː] *n.* 《F.》 Ⓤ weariness of mind; boredom. 권태; 따분함. [→annoy]

e·nor·mi·ty [inɔ́ːrməti] *n.* ⓊⒸ (*pl.* **-ties**) extreme wickedness; a serious crime. 극악성; 흉악; 흉악 범죄. ¶ *the ~ of an offence* 〔*a crime*〕 범죄의 흉악성. [↓]

:e·nor·mous [inɔ́ːrməs] *adj.* very large; huge; immense. 엄청나게 큰; 거대한; 막대한. ¶ *~ profits* 막대한 이득 / *a man of ~ strength* 엄청난 힘을 가진 사람 / *the ~ sum of money* 막대한 액수의 돈 / *Long ago ~ animals lived on the earth.* 태고적에는 거대한 동물이 지상에 살고 있었다. [→normal]

e·nor·mous·ly [inɔ́ːrməsli] *adv.* in an enormous manner; extremely; vastly; unreasonably. 매우; 엄청나게; 막대하게; 터무니없이. ¶ *He is ~ rich.* 그는 엄청난 부자이다.

:e·nough [inʌ́f] *adj.* as much or many as necessary; sufficient. (…하기에) 족한; 충분한; …할 만큼의. ¶ *We have time ~ for the purpose.* 목적을 이루기 위한 시간은 충분히 있다 / *That's ~!* 그만하면 됐다 / *I have ~ money to buy the car.* =*I have money ~ to buy the car.* 차를 살 만한 돈은 있다. 語法 명사 앞에 오는 것이 뜻이 강함.

— *adv.* **1** to the necessary degree; until no more is needed or desired. 충분히; (…하기에) 충분할 정도로. ¶ *Are you warm ~?* 춥지는 않으십니까 / *The meat is done ~.* 고기가 잘 익었다〔구워졌다〕 / *I can't thank you ~.* 아무리 감사를 드려도 모자랍니다 / *He was kind ~ to lend me the book.* 그는 친절하게도 나에게 책을 빌려 주었다 / *He was fool ~ to marry her.* 그는 어리석게도 그녀와 결혼했다. **2** quite; fully. 아주. ¶ *This is good ~.* 이건 아주 좋다.

oddly enough, strange to say. 이상하게도; 묘하게도.

sure enough, certainly; indeed. 틀림없이; 반드시; 참말로.

well enough, fairly well; perfectly. 아주; 꽤; 완전히. ¶ *He plays well ~.* 연주〔연기〕를 아주 잘 한다 / *He could do it well ~ if he liked.* 하려고 하면 충분히 잘 해낼 수 있는 사람인데.

— *n.* Ⓤ the amount necessary. 충분한 양〔수〕. ¶ *more than ~* 충분히 / *have ~ to eat* 먹기에 충분할 만큼 있다 / *~ and to spare* 남아돌 만큼 / *I have had ~.* 실컷 먹었다 / *Enough of that!* 이제 그만. [E.]

have enough to *do*, can barely do. 간신히 …할 수 있다; …하는 것이 고작이다.

have had enough (=*be sick; be tired*) **of** *something.* …에 넌더리가 나다. ¶ *I have had quite ~ of your impudence.* 너의 뻔뻔스러움에는 이제 질렸다.

:en·quire [enkwáiər] *v.* =inquire.

***en·quir·y** [enkwáiəri] *n.* (*pl.* **-quir·ies**) =inquiry.

en·rage [enréidʒ] *vt.* (P6) put (someone) into a rage; make (someone) very angry. …을 격노하게 하다; 화나게 하다. ¶ *be enraged at an insult* 모욕을 당하고 성나다 / *be enraged with* 〔*against*〕 *a haughty person* 오만한 사람에게 몹시 화를 내다. [en-]

en·rap·ture [enrǽptʃər] *vt.* (P6) fill (someone) with great delight or joy. …을 몹시 기쁘게 하다; 도취하게 하다. ¶ *be enraptured with* 〔*over*〕 *good fortune* 행운에 미칠 듯이 기뻐하다 / *The travelers were enraptured with the beautiful scenery.* 여행객들은 아름다운 경치에 도취되었다. [en-]

•**en·rich** [enrítʃ] *vt.* (P6) **1** make (someone or something) rich or splendid; (of land) fertilize. …을 부유하게 하다; 풍부하게 하다; (땅)을 비옥하게 하다. ¶ ~ *land* 땅을 비옥하게 하다 / ~ *someone* 아무를 부유하게 하다 / ~ *the mind* (지식으로) 마음을 풍부하게 하다. **2** improve or raise the value of (something). …의 질〔가치, 효용〕을 높이다. ¶ *enriched food* 강화 식품 / ~ *a food with a seasoning* 조미료로 음식의 맛을 좋게 하다. [en-]

en·rich·ment [enrítʃmənt] *n.* **1** Ⓤ the act of enriching; the state of being enriched. 풍부; 비옥. **2** Ⓒ a thing that enriches. 풍부〔부유, 비옥〕하게 하는 것.

•**en·roll,** 《Brit.》 **-rol** [enróul] *vt.* (**-rolled, -roll·ing**) (P6,13) **1** write (someone's name) in a list; enlist. …을 명부에 올리다; 등록하다. ¶ ~ *men for the army* 장정들을 육군 병적에 넣다 / *be enrolled in a school* 학교에 등록되다 / ~ *oneself* 지원병이 되다; 징집(徵集)에 응하다. **2** make (someone) a member. …을 회원으로 하다. **3** 《*arch.*》 wrap up. 싸다. [→roll]

en·roll·ment, 《Brit.》 **-rol-** [enróulmənt] *n.* ⓊⒸ the act of enrolling; the state of being enrolled; a number enrolled. 기재; 기록; 등록; 입학; 입대; 등록자 수.

en route [ɑːn rúːt] *adv.* 《F.》 on the way. 도중에; 도상(途上)에. ¶ *be* ~ *to* 〔*for*〕 *New York* 뉴욕으로 가는 도중이다. [→en]

en·san·guined [insǽŋgwind, en-] *adj.* **1** stained with blood. 피투성이의. **2** red like blood. 진홍(색)의. [en-]

en·sconce [inskɑ́ns / -skɔ́ns] *vt.* (P13) **1** settle comfortably. (몸)을 편히 안좌(安坐)시키다; 안치(安置)하다. ¶ *I found him reading, ensconced in an armchair before the fire.* 나는 그가 벽난로 앞 안락의자에 자리잡고 독서하는 것을 보았다. **2** hide. …을 숨기다. [en-, *sconce* fortification]

ensconce oneself in, sit in; settle in. …에 자리잡다; 앉다.

en·sem·ble [ɑːnsɑ́ːmbəl] *n.* 《F.》 Ⓒ **1** all the parts of a thing viewed together; the total effect. 총체(總體); 전체적 효과. **2** 《mus.》 a performance of the entire group of singers, musicians, etc. 중창; 협주(곡); 앙상블. **3** all the parts of a woman's harmonious costume designed to be worn together. 갖춘 한 벌의 여성복; 앙상블. [L. *in-, simul* at the same time]

en·shrine [enʃráin] *vt.* (P6,13) **1** keep (someone or something) in a shrine. …을 사당에 모시다; 안치하다. **2** 《*fig.*》 keep (something) sacred; cherish. …을 마음속에 간직하다; 비장(秘藏)하다. ¶ *memories enshrined in one's heart* 가슴 속에 간직된 추억. [en-]

en·shroud [enʃráud] *vt.* (P6,13) **1** cover with a shroud. …에 수의를 입히다. **2** envelop; wrap. …을 싸다. ¶ *be enshrouded in darkness* 어둠에 싸이다. [en-]

•**en·sign** [énsain] *n.* Ⓒ **1** a flag; a banner. 기(旗); 국기. ¶ *the national* ~ 국기. **2** [énsn] 《U.S.》 a navy officer who ranks next below a lieutenant junior grade. 해군 소위. **3** 《Brit.》 a former army officer carrying a flag. 기수(旗手); (연대·중대의 기수를 맡은) 보병 소위. **4** a badge showing one's rank, position, etc. (관직·지위 따위를 나타내는) 기장(記章). [→insignia]

en·si·lage [énsəlidʒ] *n.* **1** the preservation of green fodder in a pit or a silo. 생(生)목초 보존(법). **2** fodder thus preserved; silage. 이렇게 보존된 생목초. — *vt.* (P6) store by ensilage. …을 생목초로 저장하다. [→silo]

en·sile [ensáil] *vt.* (P6) put into a silo. …을 사일로에 저장하다. [↑]

en·slave [ensléiv] *vt.* (P6,13) make (someone) a slave; take away freedom from (someone). …을 노예로 하다; 포로로 하다. ¶ ~ *someone to superstition* 아무를 미신의 노예로 하다 / ~ *oneself to avarice* 탐욕의 노예가 되다 / *He was enslaved by her beauty.* 그는 그녀의 아름다움에 사로잡혔다. [en-]

en·snare [ensnέər] *vt.* (P6,13) catch (an animal) in a trap; capture (someone) by a trick. …을 덫에 걸리게 하다; 함정에 빠뜨리다. ¶ *be ensnared by lies* 거짓말에 걸려들다. [en-]

•**en·sue** [ensúː] *vi.* (P1,3) 《*from, on*》 come after; follow; result. 뒤에〔계속해서〕 일어나다; 결과로서 일어나다. ¶ *What will* ~ *from* 〔*on*〕 *this?* 이제부터는 무슨 일이 일어날까 / *Great excitement ensued when he hit a home run.* 그가 홈런을 치자 관중들의 대흥분이 뒤따랐다. [en-]

en·su·ing [ensúːiŋ] *adj.* following as a result; next. 결과로서 일어나는; 다음의. ¶ *in the* ~ *year* 이듬해에.

en·sure [enʃúər] *vt.* **1** (P6,13) make (something) sure or certain. …을 보증하다; 확실히 하다. ¶ ~ *someone a decent living* 아무에게 상당한 생활을 보장하다 / *measures to* ~ *the success of an undertaking* 사업의 성공을 확실히 하는 방책 / *I cannot* ~ *his being there in time.* 그가 제때에 그곳에 도착할지 보장할 수 없다. **2** (P6,11,13,14) 《*against, from*》 make (someone or something) safe; protect. …을

안전하게 하다; 지키다; 보호하다. ¶ *I could have ensured myself against* 〔*from*〕 *the risk.* 그 위험으로부터 몸을 지킬 수 있었을 텐데. [en-]

en·tab·la·ture [entǽblətʃər, -tʃuər] *n.* Ⓒ 《archit.》 a horizontal part of a building supported by the top of columns. 기둥 위에 건너지른 수평부(部). [→table]

en·tail [entéil] *vt.* **1** (P6,13) 《*on, upon*》 make (something) necessary; impose; require. …을 필요로 하다; …을 과(課)하다. ¶ *Success entails hard work.* 성공에는 노력이 필요하다 / *Such a manner of living entails great expense.* 그러한 생활 태도는 엄청난 지출을 요한다 / *It is entailed on man to observe the law.* 사람은 법을 지켜야 한다. **2** (P6) 《law》 leave (land, money, etc.) to be passed from father to son so that it cannot be sold to anyone. 한정 상속을 시키다. —*n.* **1** Ⓤ entailing; being entailed. 한정 상속. **2** Ⓒ an entailed estate. 한정 상속 재산. [→tail]

en·tan·gle [entǽŋgl] *vt.* (P6,13) **1** ⓐ 《*in*》 catch (something) in a net, vine, etc. …을 엉키게〔얽히게〕 하다. ¶ *Threads get easily entangled.* 실은 잘 엉킨다 / *He entangled his feet in a net.* 그의 발이 그물에 걸려 얽혔다. ⓑ ensnare. 덫〔계략〕에 걸리게 하다. ¶ *be entangled by intrigue* 음모에 걸려들다. **2** put (someone) into difficulty; involve. (곤란 따위에) 빠뜨리다; 말려들게 하다. ¶ *be entangled with someone* 아무와 연루〔관련〕되다. [en-]

en·tan·gle·ment [entǽŋglmənt] *n.* **1** ⓐ Ⓤ the act of entangling. 얽히게 함. ⓑ Ⓒ the state of being entangled; something that entangles. 얽힌 상태; 연루; 혼란; 분규. **2** Ⓒ 《usu. *pl.*》 a barrier of barbed wire. 철조망.

en·tente [ɑːntɑ́ːnt] *n.* 《F.》 Ⓒ an agreement between two or more governments. (국가 간의) 협정; 협약; 협상.

entente cor·diale [ɑːntɑ́ːnt kɔːrdjɑ́ːl] *n.* a friendly agreement. 협상; 협정.

:en·ter [éntər] *vt.* (P6,13) **1** come or go into (a place). …에 들어가다. ¶ ~ *a room* 〔*house*〕 방〔집〕으로 들어가다. **2** ⓐ join; become a member of; be admitted into. (단체 따위)의 일원이 되다; …에 입회하다; 참가하다. ¶ ~ *a club* 클럽에 입회하다 / ~ *a college* 대학에 입학하다 / ~ *the army* 〔*church*〕 군인이〔목사가〕 되다. ⓑ cause to be admitted. …을 입회〔참가, 가입〕시키다. ¶ ~ *a boy in* 〔*at*〕 *a school* 아이를 학교에 넣다 / ~ *a horse in a race* 말을 레이스에 출장시키다. **3** make a beginning of; begin upon; start. …을 시작하다; 착수하다. ¶ ~ *business* 〔*the legal profession*〕 사업〔변호사업〕을 시작하다 / ~ *married life* 결혼 생활로 들어가다 / *He has entered his tenth year in politics.* 그는 정계에 든 지 10년째로 접어들었다. **4** write (something) in a list, book, etc. …을 기입〔기록〕하다; 등록하다. ¶ ~ *a name on a list* 이름을 명단에 기재하다 / ~ *an event* 〔*the facts*〕 *in the book* 책에 사건〔사실〕을 쓰다. **5** make a way into; pierce. …에 박히다; 꿰뚫다; 관통하다. ¶ *The bullet entered the flesh.* 탄알이 살에 박혔다. **6** come into the mind or feeling. (머리·마음속)에 떠오르다. ¶ *A new idea entered my head* 〔*mind*〕. 새로운 생각이 머릿속에 떠올랐다. —*vi.* (P1,3) **1** ⓐ come or go in. 들어가다〔오다〕. ¶ ~ *at* 〔*by*〕 *the door* 문으로 들어가다 / *May I* ~ ? 들어가도 됩니까. ⓑ 《theatr.》 appear on the stage. (무대)에 등장하다. ¶ *The King enters.* 왕 등장. **2** come into a group; join. 참가하다. **3** make a beginning. 시작하다. [L. *intro*]

enter an action against, sue. 고소(告訴)하다.

enter an appearance, appear. 모습을 나타내다; 출두하다.

enter into, **a**) begin; start. 시작〔착수〕하다; 들어가다. ¶ ~ *into business* 사업을 시작하다 / ~ *into a new enterprise* 새 사업에 들어가다 / ~ *into an inquiry* 조사에 들어가다. **b**) take part in; engage in. …에 참가〔참여〕하다; 종사하다. ¶ ~ *into a discussion* 〔*negotiations*〕 토론〔협상〕에 들어가다. **c**) go into a state. (특정한) 상태로 되다. ¶ ~ *into a state of war* 〔*suspended animation*〕 전쟁〔가사(假死)〕 상태로 들어가다 / ~ *into agreement* 〔*a contract*〕 협약〔계약〕을 맺다 / ~ *into relations with* …와 관계를 맺다. **d**) deal with; treat; talk about. 다루다; 설명하다. ¶ ~ *into details* 상술(詳述)하다. **e**) feel sympathy with; understand; share in. (남의 감정)을 헤아리다; 이해〔동정〕하다; …에 공감하다. ¶ ~ *into someone's feeling* 아무의 기분을 헤아리다 / ~ *into the spirit of a poem* 시(詩) 정신을 이해하다. **f**) form a part of. …의 일부를 이루다; 구성 요소가 되다.

enter on 〔***upon***〕***,*** **a**) take possession of (something). …의 소유권을 얻다. **b**) begin; start; set out on. …을 시작하다; …에 들어가다. ¶ ~ *upon a voyage* 항해를 시작하다 / ~ *on a new life* 〔*stage*〕 새로운 생활〔단계〕로 들어가다.

enter up, complete the writing of (an account, etc.). (장부의 셈 따위)를 기장(記帳)하다; 빠짐없이 적다.

en·ter·ic [entérik] *adj.* of the bowels. 장(腸)의. ¶ ~ *fever* 장티푸스. [→entrails]

en·ter·i·tis [èntəráitis] *n.* the inflammation of intestines. 장염(腸炎). [↑]

:en·ter·prise [éntərpràiz] *n.* **1** Ⓒ a plan that requires much money and courage to carry it out; a project. 기업; 기획; 모험적인 사업. ¶ *a private* ~ 사(私)〔민간〕 기업. **2** Ⓤ courage and willingness to start such projects. 모험심; 기업심; 진취의 기상. ¶ *a spirit of* ~ 기업심 / *have no* ~ 진취의 기상이 없다. [L. inter-, *prehendo* grasp]

en·ter·pris·ing [éntərpràiziŋ] *adj.* showing enterprise; courageous; willing to take risks. 기업적인; 기업심이 있는; 용감한; 진취적인. ¶ *an ~ foreign policy* 진취적인 외교 정책 / *an ~ man* 기업가 / *an ~ spirit* 진취의 기상.

:en·ter·tain [èntərtéin] *vt.* **1** (P6,13) please; amuse. …을 즐겁게 하다; …에게 위안을 주다. ¶ *be entertained by a show* 쇼를 보고 즐거워하다 / *The play entertained us very much.* 연극은 우리를 매우 즐겁게 했다. **2** (P6,13) 《*with*》 receive (someone) as a guest; give food and drink to (guests). …을 환대〔대접, 접대〕하다. ¶ *~ one's guests handsomely* 〔*coldly*〕 손님들을 따뜻이〔소홀히〕 대접하다 / *She entertained six people at* 〔*to*〕 *dinner.* 그녀는 여섯 사람을 저녁 식사에 초대했다 / *I was entertained with fruit.* 과일 대접을 받았다. **3** (P6) ⓐ hold (something) in mind. …을 생각하다; 마음에 품다. ¶ *~ a doubt* 〔*hope*〕 의심〔희망〕을 품다. ⓑ consider favorably. (제안 따위)를 받아들이다; …에 응하다. ¶ *I cannot ~ such a proposal.* 그러한 제안은 받아들일 수가 없다. —*vi.* (P1,2) be in the habit of showing hospitality. 환대하다; 대접하다. [L. *teneo* hold]

en·ter·tain·er [èntərtéinər] *n.* Ⓒ a person who entertains, esp. a dancer, singer, etc. at night clubs, etc. 즐겁게 하는 사람; 접대자; 연예인.

en·ter·tain·ing [èntərtéiniŋ] *adj.* interesting; amusing. 재미있는; 즐거운; 유쾌한. ¶ *The traveler was an ~ storyteller.* 나그네는 재미있는 이야기꾼이었다.

·en·ter·tain·ment [èntərtéinmənt] *n.* **1** ⓊⒸ the act of entertaining; the state of being entertained; hospitality. 향응; 환대; 성찬; 연회. ¶ *~ expenses* 접대비 / *a house of ~* 여관; 선술집 / *give an ~ to* …에게 성찬을 대접하다. **2** Ⓒ something that interests, pleases, or amuses. 여흥; 연예. ¶ *an ~ tax* 흥행세. **3** Ⓤ amusement. 위로; 오락. ¶ *find ~ in reading* 독서에서 즐거움을 찾다.

en·thrall, -thral [enθrɔ́:l] *vt.* (P6) charm; captivate; enslave. …을 매혹하다; 사로잡다; 노예로 하다. ¶ *be enthralled by a woman's beauty* 미색에 도취되다. ●**en·thral(l)·ment** [-mənt] *n.* [en-]

en·thrall·ing [enθrɔ́:liŋ] *adj.* very interesting. 매우 재미있는. ¶ *an ~ story* 무척 재미있는 이야기.

en·throne [enθróun] *vt.* (P6) **1** place (a king, bishop, etc.) on a throne. …을 왕위〔주교의 자리〕에 오르게 하다. **2** place (someone) highest of all. …을 우러러 받들다; 깊이 존경하다. ¶ *a queen enthroned in the hearts of her people* 국민들이 진심으로 존경하는 여왕. [en-]

en·throne·ment [enθróunmənt] *n.* ⓊⒸ the act of enthroning; the state of being enthroned. 즉위(식); 주교 취임(식); 숭배.

en·thuse [inθú:z, en-] *vi.* (P1) 《*colloq.*》 《usu. *over*》 become enthusiastic over; show enthusiasm for. 열광하다; 감격하다; 열의를 보이다. [↓]

:en·thu·si·asm [enθú:ziæ̀zəm] *n.* **1** Ⓤ very strong interest; eagerness; zeal. 열광; 열중; 감격(opp. indifference). ¶ *~ for baseball* 야구에 대한 열광 / *with ~* 열광하여; 열심히. **2** Ⓒ an object of enthusiasm. 열광의 대상; 열중시키는 것. ¶ *Golf is his latest ~.* 그는 최근 골프에 열중해 있다. [Gk. *entheos* possessed by a god]

en·thu·si·ast [enθú:ziæ̀st] *n.* Ⓒ a person full of enthusiasm. 열중해 있는 사람; 열광자; 팬; …광(狂). ¶ *an ~ for baseball* 야구광(狂)〔팬〕.

·en·thu·si·as·tic [enθù:ziǽstik] *adj.* full of enthusiasm; zealous; eager. 열심인; 열렬한; 열광적인. ¶ *an ~ supporter* 〔*welcome*〕 열렬한 지지자〔환영〕 / *an ~ collector of stamps* 광적인 우표 수집가 / *be ~ about baseball* 야구에 열광적이다.

en·thu·si·as·ti·cal·ly [enθù:ziǽstikəli] *adv.* with enthusiasm. 열심히; 열광적으로.

en·tice [entáis] *vt.* (P6,7,13,20) tempt (someone) away by arousing hopes or desires; allure. …을 유혹하다; 꾀다; 부추기다. ¶ *~ a girl away from home* 소녀를 집에서 꾀어 내다 / *~ a dog in the garden* 개를 뜰로 유인해 들이다 / *She enticed the bird to eat from her hand.* 자기 손의 것을 먹도록 그녀는 새를 꾀었다. [L. *titio* firebrand]

en·tice·ment [entáismənt] *n.* **1** Ⓤ the act of enticing; the state of being enticed. 유혹; 부추김. **2** Ⓒ something that entices. 유혹물; 미끼.

:en·tire [entáiər] *adj.* **1** not lacking anything; whole; not broken. 빠짐없이 갖춘; 전부〔전체〕의; 손상되지 않은. ¶ *the ~ population of the island* 섬의 전(全)주민 / *The vase was found ~.* 꽃병은 온전한 채로 발견되었다. **2** complete; utter. 완전한. ¶ *~ ignorance* 완전한〔지독한〕 무지 / *an ~ failure* 완전한 실패 / *my ~ support* 나의 전적인 지지. **3** not castrated. 거세되지〔불까지〕 않은. ¶ *an ~ horse* 불까지 않은 말. [→integer]

:en·tire·ly [entáiərli] *adv.* **1** wholly; completely; fully. 전연; 완전히. ¶ *~ bad* 완전히 나쁜 / *~ forgotten* 완전히 잊혀진. **2** solely; only. 오로지; 전적으로. ¶ *work ~ for money-making* 오로지 돈을 벌기 위해 일하다 / *This is ~ my affair.* 이것은 오로지 나만의 문제다.

en·tire·ty [entáiərti] *n.* Ⓤ 《usu. *the ~, its ~*》 the state of being entire; wholeness; completeness; the whole. 완전히 그대로임〔의 상태, 의 것〕; 완전; 전체. [→entire]

in its* 〔*their*〕 *entirety, wholly; completely. 전체로서; 완전히; 온전히 그대로.

·en·ti·tle [entáitl] *vt.* **1** (P19) give a title or name to (someone or something); call (someone or something) by name. …에 제목을 붙이다; …라고 칭하다. ¶ *a book entitled 'On Liberty'* '자유에 관하여' 라는 표제의 책. **2**

(P13,20) give a claim or right to (someone). …에게 권리를[자격을] 주다. ¶ *His learning entitles him to respect.* 그는 학식이 많아 존경받을 만하다 / *I was entitled to my pension.* 연금을 탈 자격이 있었다 / *A woman is just as entitled to enjoy oneself as a man.* 여자도 남자와 똑같이 즐길 권리가 있다. [en-]

en·ti·ty [éntiti] *n.* (*pl.* **-ties**) Ⓒ something that has a real existence; Ⓤ being; existence. 실재(물); 실체; 실재; 존재. [L. *ens* being]

entom. entomology.

en·tomb [entúːm] *vt.* (P6) place (someone) in a tomb; bury. …을 무덤에 묻다; 매장하다. ● **en·tomb·ment** [-mənt] *n.* [en-]

en·to·mol·o·gy [èntəmálədʒi / -mɔ́l-] *n.* Ⓤ the science of insects. 곤충학. [Gk. *temno* cut, →insect]

en·tou·rage [ɑ̀nturáːʒ] *n.* 《F.》 **1** ⓊⒸ environment, esp. social environment; surroundings. 주위; 환경. **2** Ⓒ 《*collectively*》 a group of attendants or associates, esp. of high rank. 주위 사람들; 측근자.

en-tout-cas [ɑ̃ːntuːkáː] *n.* Ⓒ **1** a combination parasol and umbrella. 청우(晴雨) 겸용 양산. **2** an all-weather tennis court. 전천후 옥외 테니스코트. [F. =in any case]

en·tr'acte [ɑntrǽkt / ɔn-] *n.* 《F.》 Ⓒ **1** the time between two acts of a play. 막간(幕間). **2** music, a dance, etc. performed during such an interval. 막간극[무용]; 간주곡. [F. =between-act]

en·trails [éntreilz, -trəlz] *n. pl.* the inner parts of a man or animal; bowels; inner parts. 내장; 창자; 내부. [L. *intra* within]

en·train [entréin] *vt., vi.* (P6; 1,3) 《*at, for*》 put [get] into a train. 열차에 타다[태우다]. [en-]

:en·trance[1] [éntrəns] *n.* **1** ⓊⒸ the act of entering. 들어감; 입장. ¶ ~ *into a port* 입항 / *an ~ examination* 입학[입사] 시험 / *one's ~ into a new life* 새로운 삶의 시작 / *make* [*effect*] *one's* ~ 들어가다 / *make one's ~ into office* 관직에 취임하다 / *Entrance free.* 입장 무료 / *No* ~. 입장 사절 ; 출입 금지. **2** Ⓒ a place by which to enter; a gate; a door. 입구; 문. ¶ *the ~ to the station* 역의 입구 / *at the* ~ 입구[문, 현관]에서 / *at the ~ of the river into the sea* 강물이 바다로 들어가는 곳에. **3** ⓊⒸ a right or permission to enter. 입장권(權); 입장 허가. ¶ *have free ~ to* …에 마음대로 들어갈 수 있다. [F. *entrer* enter]

en·trance[2] [entrǽns, -tráːns] *vt.* (P6) put (someone) into a wonderful state; fill (someone) with joy or delight; charm. 기뻐 어쩔 줄 모르게 하다; 황홀하게 하다; 도취시키다. ¶ *be entranced with music* 음악에 도취되다 / *be entranced at the sight* 경치에 넋을 잃다. ● **en·tranc·ing·ly** [-iŋli] *adv.* **en·trance·ment** [-mənt] *n.* [en-]

en·trant [éntrənt] *n.* Ⓒ a person who enters; a new member in a club, university, etc.; a person taking part in a contest. 들어가는 사람; 입장자; 입회자; 입학자; 참가자. ¶ *an illegal ~ into the country* 불법 입국자. [*entrance*[1]]

en·trap [entrǽp] *vt.* (**-trapped, -trapping**) (P6,13) catch (someone) in a trap; bring (someone) into difficulty or danger; deceive. …을 덫에 걸리게 하다; (함정·곤란·위험 등)에 빠뜨리다; 속이다. ¶ ~ *someone to destruction* 아무를 속여 파멸시키다. [en-]

·en·treat [entríːt] *vt.* (P6,13,15,20) ask earnestly; beg; implore. …에게 간청[탄원]하다. ¶ ~ *someone for* [*to show*] *mercy* 아무에게 자비를 애원하다 / *I ~ you to save his life.* 제발 그의 목숨을 구해 주십시오 / *I ~ this favor of you.* 부디 이 청을 들어주십시오. [en-]

en·treat·y [entríːti] *n.* ⒸⓊ (*pl.* **-treat·ies**) an earnest request; prayer; appeal. 간청; 탄원; 애원. ¶ *make entreaties* 여러 차례 탄원하다 / *deaf to all entreaties* 어떤 탄원에도 귀를 기울이지 않고.

en·tree, en·trée [áːntrei, ─⌐] *n.* 《F.》 **1** Ⓤ a right or freedom to enter. 입장권(權); 입장 허가. ¶ *have* [*enjoy*] *the ~ of the club* 클럽에 마음대로 출입하는 것이 허용되어 있다. **2** Ⓒ 《U.S.》 the main dish of food in a meal. 앙트레《구운 고기 이외의 주(主)요리》. **3** Ⓒ 《Brit.》 a dish of food served before the roast or between the main courses. 앙트레《생선이 나온 다음, 구운 고기가 나오기 전에 나오는 요리》.

en·trench [entréntʃ] *vt.* (P6) **1** surround (something) with a trench; protect; defend. …을 참호로 두르다; 지키다; 방비하다. ¶ ~ *oneself* 자기의 입장을 지키다. **2** establish firmly. …을 확립하다. ¶ *a custom entrenched by tradition* 전통에 의해 확립된 관습. ── *vi.* (P3) 《*on, upon*》 encroach upon (the rights or property of another). 침해하다; 잠식하다. [en-]

en·trench·ment [entréntʃmənt] *n.* ⓊⒸ the act of entrenching; the state of being entrenched; a trench made for defense. 참호파기 (작업); 참호(선); 보루.

en·tre·pre·neur [ɑ̀ːntrəprənə́ːr] *n.* 《F.》 Ⓒ a person who organizes and manages an enterprise. 기업가[주]; 흥행주. [→enterprise]

en·trust [entrʌ́st] *vt.* (P13) 《*to, with*》 charge (someone) with a trust. …을 ─에게 맡기다; 위임하다; 위탁하다. ¶ ~ (*the care of*) *children to a nurse* 아이들 (돌보는 것)을 보모에게 맡기다 / ~ *one's life to a doctor* 생명을 의사에게 맡기다 / ~ *a matter to someone* 일을 아무에게 위임하다. [en-]

·en·try [éntri] *n.* Ⓒ (*pl.* **-tries**) **1** ⒸⓊ the act of entering; entrance. 들어감; 입장; 등장; 가입. ¶ *Korea's ~ into the UN* 한국의 유엔 가입 / *be forbidden* ~ 입장이 금지되다. **2**

Ⓒ permission or right to enter. 입장 허가; 입장권(權). **3** a place or way by which to enter. 입구; 현관; 문간. **4** ⒸⓊ the act of recording something in a book, etc.; something written of printed in a book, etc. 기입; 기입〔기재〕 사항; (사전의) 표제어. ¶ *double* 〔*single*〕 ~ (부기의) 복식〔단식〕 기장 / *an* ~ *in the family register* 입적(入籍). **5** a person or thing taking part in a contest. (경기의) 참가자; 출품물. **6** 《law》 the act of taking possession of lands, buildings, etc. by entering or setting foot in or on them. (토지·가옥에의) 침입; 점유. [F. *entrer* enter]

make an entry of (=*write down; record*) *something.* (어떤 사항)을 기입〔등록〕하다.

make one's entry, enter. 입장〔등장〕하다.

en·twine [entwáin] *vt.* (P6) 《*round, with*》 twine; twist; wind. 뒤엉키게〔얽히게〕 하다; 휘감다. ¶ ~ *a creeper round a pillar* 덩굴 식물이 기둥을 휘감게 하다. [en-]

en·twist [entwíst] *vt.* twist (things) together. (몇 가닥)을 합쳐서 꼬다; 꼬다. [en-]

e·nu·mer·ate [injú:mərèit] *vt.* (P6) name (persons or things) one by one; mention; count. …을 열거하다〔들다〕; 세다. ¶ ~ *someone's weak points* 아무의 약점을 하나하나 들다. ● **e·nu·mer·a·tor** [-ər] *n.* [→ number]

e·nu·mer·a·tion [injù:məréiʃən] *n.* **1** Ⓤ the act of enumerating. 하나하나 들기; 열거. **2** Ⓒ a list; catalog. 일람표; 목록; 세목.

e·nun·ci·ate [inʌ́nsièit, -ʃi-] *vt.* (P6) state definitely; pronounce (words) clearly. …을 명확히 진술〔언명〕하다; 분명히 발음하다. ● **e·nun·ci·a·tor** [-ər] *n.* [L. *nuntius* messenger]

e·nun·ci·a·tion [inʌ̀nsiéiʃən] *n.* ⓊⒸ the act of enunciating; the state of being enunciated; a definite statement; announcement. 발음(하기); 이야기투; 어조; 선언; 언명.

e·n·ure [injúər] *vt., vi.* =inure.

en·u·re·sis [ènjurí:sis] *n.* 《med.》 involuntary emission of urine. 야뇨증(夜尿症). [en-, Gk. *ouron* urine]

en·vel·op [envéləp] *vt.* (P6,13) wrap up; cover up; surround. …을 싸다; 덮다; 덮어 가리다; 둘러싸다. ¶ *be enveloped in flames* 불길에 휩싸이다 / ~ *oneself in a blanket* 담요를 뒤집어 쓰다. [F.]

***en·ve·lope** [énvəlòup, á:n-] *n.* Ⓒ **1** a paper cover for letters, etc. 봉투. **2** covering; wrapper. 덮개; 싸개; 가리개. **3** the bag that holds the gas in a balloon. (기구의) 기낭(氣囊). [↑]

en·vel·op·ment [envéləpmənt] *n.* **1** Ⓤ the act of enveloping; the state of being enveloped. 쌈; 봉함; 포위. **2** Ⓒ something that envelops; a wrapper. 싸개; 포장지. [*envelop*]

en·ven·om [invénəm] *vt.* (P6) **1** put poison on or into (something). …에 독을 넣다. **2** fill (something) with hate. …에 독기를 품게 하다. ¶ *envenomed words* 독설 / *a countenance envenomed with jealousy* 질투로 일그러진 얼굴. [en-]

en·vi·a·ble [énviəbəl] *adj.* to be envied; very desirable. 부러운; 샘나는; 몹시 바람직한. ¶ *an* ~ *position* 부러운 지위. ● **en·vi·a·ble·ness** [-nis] *n.* **en·vi·a·bly** [-bli] *adv.* [→envy]

en·vi·ous [énviəs] *adj.* full of envy; feeling or expressing envy. 부러워하는; 샘내는; 질투〔시기〕하는. ¶ *an* ~ *glance* 부러워하는 눈 / ~ *of another's success* 남의 성공을 부러워하는. ● **en·vi·ous·ness** [-nis] *n.* [→envy]

en·vi·ous·ly [énviəsli] *adv.* in an envious manner. 부러운 듯이; 시기하여.

en·vi·ron [inváiərən] *vt.* (P6,13) surround; encircle. …을 둘러〔에워〕싸다; 포위하다. ¶ *be environed with* 〔*by*〕 *the enemy* 적군에 의해 포위되다. [F.=round about]

***en·vi·ron·ment** [inváiərənmənt] *n.* ⓊⒸ **1** the act of surrounding; the state of being surrounded. 에워쌈; 포위. **2** all the conditions that influence something; surroundings. 주위; 환경. ¶ *social* 〔*moral*〕 ~ 사회적〔도덕적〕 환경 / *A child's character is greatly influenced by his home* ~. 아이의 성격은 가정 환경에 큰 영향을 받는다.

***en·vi·rons** [inváiərənz, énviərənz] *n. pl.* the districts surrounding a town or city; suburbs. (도시의) 부근; 근교; 교외. ¶ *Paris and its* ~ 파리와 그 근교.

en·vis·age [invízidʒ] *vt.* (P6) **1** 《rare》 face (danger, etc.); look in the face of. (위험 따위)에 직면하다; 직시하다. **2** form an image of (something or someone) in one's mind; contemplate. …을 마음 속에 그리다; 계획하다; 꾀하다. ¶ ~ *a plan* 계획을 세우다. [en-]

en·voy[1] [énvɔi, á:n-] *n.* Ⓒ **1** an agent; a messenger. 사절(使節). **2** a government official sent on a diplomatic mission; esp. a minister plenipotentiary. 외교 사절; 전권 공사. 參考 대사의 아래, 공사의 위임. [L. *via* way]

en·voy[2] [énvɔi, á:n-] *n.* Ⓒ 《*poet.*》 a short concluding section in a poem. (시의) 맺음구(句).

***en·vy** [énvi] *n.* (*pl.* **-vies**) **1** Ⓤ a feeling of discontent or ill will against another's good fortune; jealousy. 선망; 시새움; 질투. ¶ *become an object of* ~ *of one's companions* 동료들의 선망〔질투〕의 대상이 되다. **2** Ⓒ 《usu. *the* ~》 the object of such feeling. 선망〔질투, 시새움〕의 대상. ¶ *She was the* ~ *of the young girls.* 그녀는 젊은 아가씨들의 부러움의 대상이었다.

be in envy (=*be jealous*) ***of*** *something.* …을 시새우다〔질투하다, 부러워하다〕.

out of envy, driven by jealousy. 질투심에 이

끌려; 시새운〔부러운〕 나머지.
— *vt.* (**-vied**) (P6, 14) feel envy toward (someone). …을 시기〔부러워〕하다. ¶ *I don't ~ you your fortune.* 네 재산을 부러워〔시기〕하지 않는다 / *I ~ (you) your many books.* 당신의 많은 책이 부럽습니다 / *How I ~ you!* 정말이지 자네가 부럽다. [L. *invidia*]

en·wrap [inrǽp] *vt.* (**-wrapped**) (P6,13) wrap up. …을 싸다; 휩싸다. [en-]

en·zyme [énzaim] *n.* 《chem.》 Ⓒ a chemical substance, formed in living cells, that can cause changes in other substances. 효소. [Gk. *enzumos* leavened]

e·on [íːən] *n.* =aeon.

E·os [íːɑs / -ɔs] *n.* 《Gk. myth.》 the goddess of the dawn. 에오스《새벽의 여신; 로마 신화의 Aurora에 해당》.

ep·au·let, -lette [épəlèt, -lit] *n.* Ⓒ the shoulder ornament of a uniform. 견장. ¶ *win one's epaulets* (하사관이) 장교로 승진하다. [Gk. *spathē* shoulder blade]

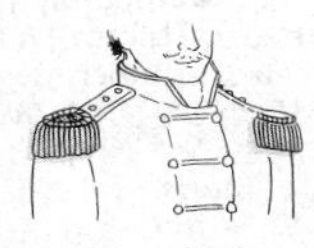
〈epaulet〉

é·pée, e·pee [eipéi, épei] *n.* 《F.》 a thin pointed sword. 에페《뾰족한 가는 펜싱용 검》. [L.]

e·pergne [ipə́ːrn, eipɛ́ərn] *n.* an ornamental dish. 장식 접시《꽃·과일 따위를 담아 식탁에 놓는》. [F.]

e·phem·er·a [ifémərə] *n.* **1** 《insect》 an insect that lives only for a day. 하루살이. **2** 《*fig.*》 a short-lived thing. 매우 단명인 것; 덧없는 것. [epi-, Gk. *hēmera* day]

e·phem·er·al [ifémərəl] *adj.* lasting only a day; very short-lived. 하루살이 목숨의; 단 하루뿐인; 단명의; 덧없는. ¶ *~ pleasures* 덧없는 쾌락 / *an ~ flower* 하루만 피는 꽃.

ep·i- [épi, épə] *pref.* upon; at; on the ground; in addition. '위, 그 위, …외'의 뜻. [Gk.]

ep·ic [épik] *n.* Ⓒ a long poem of the adventures of a hero. 서사시; 사시(史詩). — *adj.* of or like an epic. 서사시의; 서사시적인. [→epos]

ep·i·cen·ter, 《Brit.》 **-tre** [épisèntər] *n.* 《geol.》 Ⓒ a point directly above the true center of the earthquake. 진원지; 진앙(震央). [epi-, →center]

ep·i·cure [épikjùər] *n.* Ⓒ a person who finds pleasure in eating and drinking. 식도락가; 미식가(美食家). [L.]

ep·i·cu·re·an [èpikjuríːən, -kjú(ː)ri-] *adj.* **1** of or like an epicure; fond of pleasure and luxury. 식도락의; 쾌락〔향락〕주의의. **2** 《*E-*》 of Epicurus or his philosophy. 에피쿠로스(주의)의. — *n.* Ⓒ **1** a person who likes pleasure and luxury; an epicure. 쾌락주의자; 미식가. **2** 《*E-*》 a person who believes in the philosophy of Epicurus. 에피쿠로스학파의 사람. [L.]

Ep·i·cu·re·an·ism [èpikjuríːənìzəm, -kjú(ː)ri-] *n.* Ⓤ **1** the philosophy or principles of Epicurus (342?-270 B.C.) or his followers. 에피쿠로스 철학. 參考 쾌락을 인생의 최고선(善)으로 침. **2** 《*e-*》 the taste of an epicurean. 미식주의; 쾌락〔향락〕주의. [L.]

ep·i·dem·ic [èpədémik] *n.* Ⓒ **1** a disease that spreads rapidly among many people in one area. 유행병; 전염병. **2** 《*fig.*》 anything temporarily widespread, as a fad. (일시적) 유행; 보급. ¶ *an ~ of riots* 폭동의 만연 / *an ~ of cheap books* 값싼 책의 보급. — *adj.* **1** (of a disease) spreading rapidly and widely. 전염성의; 유행성의(cf. *endemic*). **2** (of ideas, etc.) widely spread; current. (사상 따위) 유행하고 있는; 퍼져 있는. [Gk. *epi-* among, *demos* people]

ep·i·der·mis [èpədə́ːrmis] *n.* 《anat.》 the outer layer of the skin or of the leaf. 표피. [Gk. *derma* skin]

ep·i·glot·tis [èpəglɑ́tis / -glɔ́t-] *n.* 《anat.》 the cartilage at the root of the tongues. 후두개(喉頭蓋). [Gk. *glōtta* tongue]

ep·i·gone [épəgòun] *n.* an obscure imitator of an important writer or painter. (주요 작가·화가 등의) 모방자; 아류(亞流). [L.]

ep·i·gram [épigrӕ̀m] *n.* Ⓒ a short, witty saying or poem. 경구(警句); 풍자시. ¶ *"Speech is silver, silence is golden." is an ~.* "웅변은 은이요, 침묵은 금이다"란 말은 경구이다. [Gk. *graphō* write]

ep·i·gram·mat·ic [èpigrəmǽtik] *adj.* of or like an epigram; short and witty. 경구의〔적인〕; 풍자적인.

ep·i·gram·ma·tize [èpigrǽmətàiz] *vi.,vt.* make epigrams (of). 경구〔풍자시〕로 표현하다; 경구〔풍자시〕를 짓다.

ep·i·graph [épigrӕ̀f, épigrɑ̀ːf] *n.* Ⓒ **1** carved words on a statue or building. 비명(碑銘); 제명(題銘). **2** a quotation or motto at the beginning of a book or chapter. (권두의) 제사(題詞); 인용구. [*epigram*]

e·pig·ra·phy [epígrəfi] *n.* **1** the study of epigraphs. 비문 연구; 금석학(金石學). **2** epigraphs collectively. 비명(碑銘); 금석문.

ep·i·lep·sy [épəlèpsi] *n.* Ⓤ 《med.》 a nervous disease in which a person loses consciousness for a while. 간질. ¶ *a fit of ~* 간질의 발작. [Gk. *lambanō* seize]

ep·i·lep·tic [èpəléptik] *adj.* of epilepsy. 간질의. ¶ *an ~ patient* 간질 환자. — *n.* Ⓒ a person who has epilepsy. 간질 환자.

ep·i·log, 《Brit.》 **-logue** [épilɔ̀ːg, -lɑ̀g / épilɔ̀g] *n.* Ⓒ **1** the last part of a novel, poem, etc. (소설 작품 따위의) 맺음; 결어. **2** a speech given to the audience at the end of a play. (연극의) 끝맺음말; 에필로그(opp. prolog). [→logos]

E·piph·a·ny [ipífəni] *n.* 《Cath.》 **1** the manifestation of Christ to the Magi. 예수의 공현(公顯). **2** the festival on January 6 celebrating this. 공현 축일(祝日). [Gk.

phaino show]

e·pis·co·pa·cy [ipískəpəsi] *n.* Ⓤ Ⓒ **1** the government of a church by bishops. (영국 국교의) 감독〔주교〕 제도. **2** the position of a bishop. 감독〔주교〕직(職). [↓]

e·pis·co·pal [ipískəpəl] *adj.* **1** of bishops; governed by bishops. 주교의; 감독(제도)의. **2** 《*E-*》 of the Church of England, or of certain Protestant churches of the United States. 감독(교회)파의. ¶ *the ~ Church* 영국 성공회 / *the Protestant ~ Church* 미국 성공회. [Gk. *epi-* upon, *skōpeo* look]

E·pis·co·pa·lian [ipìskəpéiljən, -liən] *n.* Ⓒ a member of the Protestant Episcopal Church. 미국 성공회 회원. — *adj.* = Episcopal; 《*e-*》 =episcopal.

e·pis·co·pate [ipískəpit, -pèit] *n.* an episcopalian office. 감독〔주교〕의 직(위)〔임기〕.

ep·i·sode [épəsòud] *n.* Ⓒ **1** an interesting event or experience in someone's life or history. 삽화적인 사건〔일〕; 에피소드; 일화. **2** an event or action separate from the main plot of a novel or play. (소설·극 중의) 삽화(揷話). [Gk. =coming in besides]

e·pis·tle [ipísl] *n.* Ⓒ **1** a letter, usu. a long, instructive letter. 편지; 서한. 參考 현재는 우스꽝스러운 뜻으로 쓰임. **2** 《*E-*》 a letter written by one of Christ's Apostles. 사도(使徒) 서간. ¶ *the Epistles of St. Paul* 바울의 편지. [Gk. *stello* send]

e·pis·to·lar·y [ipístəlèri / -ləri] *adj.* of, for, or carried on by, letters. 서한〔편지〕의. [↑]

ep·i·taph [épətæ̀f, -tɑ̀:f] *n.* Ⓒ words written on a tombstone in memory of a dead person. 묘비명; 비문(cf. *hic jacet*). [Gk. *taphos* tomb]

ep·i·tha·la·mi·on [èpəθəléimiən] *n.* a song in honor of a bride and bridegroom. 축혼가. [Gk. =nuptial]

ep·i·thet [épəθèt] *n.* Ⓒ an adjective, or an added name expressing some quality, as in 'Richard the Lion-Hearted'. 성질을 나타내는 형용사〔구〕; 통칭; 별명. ●**ep·i·thet·ic** [èpəθétik] *adj.* [Gk. *tithēmi* place]

e·pit·o·me [ipítəmi] *n.* Ⓒ **1** a summary; an outline. 요약; 대강; 개요. **2** a representative of some quality. 전형(적인 예); 축도; 화신. ¶ *the ~ of a perfect soldier* 나무랄 데 없는 군인의 전형 / *He is the ~ of goodness.* 그는 바로 선인(善人) 그 자체이다. [Gk. *temnō* cut]

·**ep·och** [épək / í:pɔk] *n.* Ⓒ a period of time, esp. when some important events happened; the beginning of such a period. (중요한 사건이 일어났던) 시대; 한 시대의 시작; 신기원. ¶ *make* 〔*mark*〕 *an ~ in something* …에 있어서 신기원을 이루다. ●**ep·och·al** [épəkəl / épɔk-] *adj.* [Gk. =pause]

ep·och-mak·ing [épəkmèikiŋ / í:pɔk-] *adj.* beginning an epoch; very important. 신기원의; 획기적인; 중대한. ¶ *an ~ discovery* 획기적인 발견 / *Darwin's 'Origin of Species' was an ~ work in biology.* 다윈의 '종의 기원'은 생물학에 있어 획기적인 연구였다.

ep·os [épɑs / -ɔs] *n.* an early unwritten epic poetry. 구전(口傳) 서사시. [Gk.]

Ep·som salt(**s**) [épsəm sɔ̀:lt(s)] *n.* magnesium sulfate. 황산 마그네슘. [Place]

E.Q., EQ 《psych.》 educational quotient. 교육 지수(cf. *I.Q.*).

eq. equal; equalizer; equation; equivalent.

eq·ua·bil·i·ty [èkwəbíləti, ì:kwə-] *n.* Ⓤ the state of being equable. 한결같음; 균등〔평등〕성; 평정. [↓]

eq·ua·ble [ékwəbəl, í:k-] *adj.* changing little; unvarying; even; calm. 변화가 없는〔적은〕; 한결같은; (마음이) 고요한; 평온한. ¶ *an ~ temper* 〔*climate*〕 온화한 성질〔기후〕. ●**eq·ua·bly** [-bli] *adv.* [→equal]

:**e·qual** [í:kwəl] *adj.* **1** of the same amount, size, number, degree, value, etc. …와 같은; 동일〔동등〕한. ¶ *two officers of ~ rank* 계급이 같은 두 사람의 장교 / *divide the cake into two ~ parts* 케이크를 절반으로 가르다 / *Twice 3 is ~ to 6.* 3의 두배는 6《3×2=6》 / *All men are ~.* 모든 사람은 평등(平等)하다 / *He speaks English and French with ~ ease.* 그는 영어와 프랑스어를 똑같이 잘한다 / *on an ~ footing with* …와 동등한 입장에 서서; 동격으로 / *on ~ terms with* …와 동등한 조건으로; 대등하게. **2** able to; fit for. …할 능력이 있는; 감당할 수 있는; …에 적당한; 걸맞는. ¶ *be ~ to doing the work* 일을 감당할 수 있다 / *be ~ to the occasion* (위험·어려움 따위)를 당하여 동요하지 않다; 훌륭히 일을 처리할 수 있다 / *Being ill, I am not ~ to the journey.* 병이 나서 여행을 할 수가 없다 / *He is ~ to this work.* 그 사람이라면 이 일을 해낼 수 있다 *The soil is ~ to the pasture.* 땅은 목축에 적합하다. **3** (of the mind) not easily moved; calm. (마음이) 평정한. ¶ *preserve an ~ mind amid dangers and anxieties* 위험과 걱정 속에도 마음의 평온을 유지하다.
— *n.* Ⓒ a person or thing equal to another; a rival. 동등한 사람〔것〕; 대등한 사람〔것〕; 필적하는 사람〔것〕. ¶ *one's equals and one's betters* 신분이 같은 사람들과 위의 사람들 / *one's equals in learning* 학문상 동등한 사람 / *The boy has no ~ in mathematics.* 그 아이는 수학에서는 아무도 따를 만한 이가 없다.
— *vt.* (**e·qualed, e·qual·ing** or 《Brit.》 **e·qualled, e·qual·ling**) (P6,13) be equal to (someone or something); be the same as; match. …와 같다〔같아지다〕; 같게 하다; …에 필적하다. ¶ *Three and two equal*(*s*) *five.* 3 더하기 2는 5《3+2=5》 / *This wine does not ~ the first.* 이 포도주는 처음 것만 못하다 / *Nobody equal*(*s*) *him in strength.* 힘에서 그를 당할 사람은 아무도 없다. [L. *aequus*]

e·qual·i·ty [i(:)kwɑ́ləti / -kwɔ́l-] *n.* Ⓤ the state of being equal. 같음; 동등; 평등; 균등. ¶ *~ of educational opportunity* 교육의 기회 균등.

on an equality with, on equal terms with. …와 동등하게.

e·qual·i·za·tion [ìːkwəlaizéiʃən] *n.* Ⓤ the act of equalizing; the state of being equalized. 동등〔동일〕(화); 평등〔균등〕(화).

e·qual·ize, 《Brit.》 **-ise** [íːkwəlàiz] *vt.* (P6,13) 《*to, with*》 make (something) equal or uniform. …을 같게 하다; 동등〔평등, 균일〕하게 하다.

:e·qual·ly [íːkwəli] *adv.* in an equal manner; to an equal degree; uniformly. 같게; 동등〔평등〕하게; 같은 정도로〔범위로〕. ¶ *The sun shines ~ on all.* 태양은 모두에게 똑같이 비춘다 / *The two sisters are ~ pretty.* 두 자매는 똑같이 예쁘다.

e·qua·nim·i·ty [ìːkwənímәti, èk-] *n.* Ⓤ calmness. (마음의) 평정; 냉정; 침착. ¶ *He could face old age with ~.* 평정한 마음으로 노년을 맞이할 수가 있었다. [L. *aequus* even, *animus* mind]

e·quate [ikwéit] *vt.* (P6,13) **1** make (something) equal. …을 같게 하다. **2** consider or treat (something) as equal. 대등한 것으로 보다; 동등하게 다루다. ¶ *~ lunar seas with oceans on earth* 달의 바다를 지구상의 대양에 해당하는 것으로 보다. [→equal]

e·qua·tion [i(ː)kwéiʒən, -ʃən] *n.* **1** Ⓤ the act of equating; the state of being equated. 같게 하기; 동등〔평등〕(화). **2** Ⓒ 《math.》 a statement that two quantities are equal. 방정식; 등식. ¶ *an algebraic ~* 대수방정식 / *a linear* 〔*quadratic, cubic*〕 *~*, 1차〔2차, 3차〕 방정식.

e·qua·tor [ikwéitər] *n.* 《*the ~*》 an imaginary line lying around the middle of the earth, equally distant from the North Pole and the South Pole. 적도(赤道).

e·qua·to·ri·al [èkwətɔ́ːriəl, ìːkwə-] *adj.* of, near, or at the equator. 적도(부근)의. ¶ *an ~ climate* 열대 기후.

eq·uer·ry [ékwəri] *n.* an officer of a royal family who has charge of the horses, or who attends on his master. 왕실의 말을 관리하던 관리; 시종 무관. [Teut. *schiure* a shed]

e·ques·tri·an [ikwéstriən] *adj.* **1** of horses or horse-riding. 말의; 승마〔기마〕의. ¶ *~ skill* 승마술 / *~ feats* 곡마. **2** on horseback. 마상(馬上)의. ¶ *~ knights* 마상의 기사들. — *n.* Ⓒ a person skilled in horse-riding. 승마에 능한 사람. [L. *equus* horse]

e·qui- [ìːkwi-, -kwə-, èkwi-, -kwə-] *pref.* equal. '같은'의 뜻. [L.]

e·qui·an·gu·lar [ìːkwiǽŋgjələr] *adj.* having all angles equal, as a square. 등각(等角)의. [equi-, →angular]

e·qui·dis·tant [ìːkwidístənt] *adj.* equally distant. 등거리의. [equi-, →distant]

e·qui·lat·er·al [ìːkwəlǽtərəl] *adj.* having all sides equal. 등변(等邊)의. ¶ *an ~ triangle* 등변삼각형. — *n.* Ⓒ a figure having all sides equal. 등변형. [equi-, →lateral]

e·quil·i·brate [ìːkwíləbrèit, ìːkwəláibreit] *vt., vi.* balance. 평형시키다〔잡히다〕; 균형을 유지시키다. [→deliberate]

e·qui·lib·ri·um [ìːkwəlíbriəm] *n.* **1** ⓊⒸ a balanced state or condition. 평형; 균형. **2** Ⓤ calmness of mind. 마음의 평정. [↑]

e·quine [íːkwain, ék-] *adj.* of or resembling a horse. 말의; 말 같은. [L. *equus* horse]

e·qui·noc·tial [ìːkwənɑ́kʃəl / -nɔ́k-] *adj.* **1** of the equinox. 주야 평분의; 춘분〔추분〕의. ¶ *the ~ line* 주야 평분선. **2** near or at the equinox. 춘〔추〕분 (부근)의. — *n.* Ⓒ a storm occurring near or at the equinox. 춘〔추〕분(무렵)의 폭풍. [↓]

e·qui·nox [íːkwənɑ̀ks / -nɔ̀ks] *n.* Ⓒ 《usu. *the ~*》 the time in a year when night and day are equal of length. 춘〔추〕분(점). ¶ *the vernal* 〔*autumnal*〕 *~* 춘〔추〕분. [equi-, L. *nox* night]

***e·quip** [ikwíp] *vt.* (**e·quipped, e·quip·ping**) (P6,13) 《*with*》 cause (someone or something) to have necessary things. …에 (필요물을) 갖추다; 채비〔준비〕시키다; 장비하다. ¶ *~ oneself* 몸차림하다 / *~ someone for a journey* 아무에게 여행 채비를 시키다 / *~ someone with learning* 아무에게 학문을 갖추게 하다 / *those equipped with special skills* 특수 기능을 갖춘 사람들 / *I equipped my son with a sound education.* 나는 아들에게 훌륭한 교육을 받게 했다. [N. (→ship)]

eq·ui·page [ékwəpidʒ] *n.* **1** a carriage with its horses and driver. (마부가 딸린) 마차. ¶ *A splendid ~ drove up to my door.* 훌륭한 마차 한 대가 우리집 현관 쪽으로 달려왔다. **2** a collection of various small useful things suitable for a particular purpose. (여러 목적의) 용구 세트. ¶ *a dressing ~* 화장 도구 한 세트 / *a tea ~* 다구(茶具) 한 벌. [↑]

:e·quip·ment [ikwípmənt] *n.* Ⓤ **1** the act of equipping; the state of being equipped. 준비; 채비. **2** 《often *pl.*》 a collection of necessary things furnished for some purpose. 장비; 설비; 비품. ¶ *laboratory ~* 실험실의 설비〔장치〕 / *a soldier's ~* 군인의 장비 / *the necessary equipments for a voyage* 항해에 필요한 비품.

e·qui·poise [ékwəpɔ̀iz, íːk-] *n.* Ⓤ the state of being balanced. 균형; 평형. — *vt.* (P6) **1** counterbalance. 균형을 잡다. **2** hold in suspense. 마음을 졸이게 하다. [equi-]

eq·ui·ta·ble [ékwətəbəl] *adj.* fair; just. 공평한; 정당한. ●**eq·ui·ta·ble·ness** [-nis] *n.* **eq·ui·ta·bly** [-bli] *adv.* [↓]

eq·ui·ty [ékwəti] *n.* Ⓤ fairness; justice. 공평; 공정. [→equal]

e·quiv·a·lence [ikwívələns], **-len·cy** [-lənsi] *n.* Ⓤ the state of being equivalent. 동등; 등가(等價); 같은 값. [↓]

•e·quiv·a·lent [ikwívələnt] *adj.* equal in value, measure, amount, force, meaning, etc. 같은; 동등〔대등〕한; …에 상당하는.

¶ *Cheating is ~ to lying.* 속이는 것은 거짓말과 같다 / *What is $1 ~ to in Korean money?* 1달러는 한국 돈으로 얼마에 상당합니까.
— *n.* Ⓒ something equivalent. 동등물; 상당하는 것. ● **e·quiv·a·lent·ly** [-li] *adv.* [→value]

e·quiv·o·cal [ikwívəkəl] *adj.* **1** having two or more meanings; not clear; vague. 두 가지 뜻으로 취할 수 있는; 분명치 않은; 모호한(cf. *ambiguous*). ¶ *an ~ answer* 〔*expression*〕 모호한 대답〔표현〕. **2** uncertain; doubtful. 확실치 않은; 의심스러운. ¶ *an ~ success* 확실치 않은 성공 / *an ~ mode of life* 의심스런 생활 방식. ● **e·quiv·o·cal·ly** [-kəli] *adv.* [L. *voco* call]

e·quiv·o·cate [ikwívəkèit] *vi.* (P1) use vague expressions. 애매한 말을 쓰다; 말을 얼버무리다. ● **e·quiv·o·ca·tor** [-ər] *n.* [↑]

e·quiv·o·ca·tion [ikwìvəkéiʃən] *n.* ⒸⓊ **1** the use of equivocal expressions. 모호한 말을 씀; 얼버무림. **2** an equivocal expression. 모호한 표현.

•**e·ra** [íərə, érə] *n.* Ⓒ an age or a period in history (marked by some important event). (두드러진 성격·사건 따위로 특징지어진) 시대; 시기; 연대; 기원. ¶ *the Christian ~* 서력 기원. [L.=number, pl. of *aes* money]

e·rad·i·cate [irǽdəkèit] *vt.* (P6) get rid of (something) completely; destroy. …을 완전히 없애다; 근절하다. ¶ *~ an army* 군대를 전멸시키다 / *~ weeds* 잡초를 뿌리째 뽑다 / *Illiteracy has been almost eradicated in Korea.* 한국에서는 문맹이 거의 없어졌다. ● **e·rad·i·ca·tor** [-ər] *n.* [L. *radix* root]

e·rad·i·ca·tion [iræ̀dəkéiʃən] *n.* Ⓤ the act of eradicating; destruction. 완전한 제거; 근절; 멸절(滅絕).

e·rase [iréis / iréiz] *vt.* (P6,13) rub out. …을 지우다〔지워 없애다〕; 삭제하다. ¶ *~ chalk marks from a blackboard* 칠판에서 분필 자국을 지우다 / *~ a name from a list* 명단에서 이름을 삭제하다. ● **e·ras·a·ble** [-əbəl] *adj.* [→raze]

e·ras·er [iréisər / -zər] *n.* Ⓒ a thing that erases; a wiper. 지우개. ¶ *a pencil ~* 고무 지우개 / *a blackboard ~* 칠판 지우개.

e·ra·sure [iréiʃər] *n.* Ⓤ **1** the act of erasing. 지움; 말소; 삭제. **2** Ⓒ an erased word, letter, etc. 지운 낱말〔글자〕(따위). **3** Ⓒ the place where a word, letter, etc. has been erased. 지운 자리〔자국〕.

•**ere** [ɛər] *prep., conj.* 《*poet., arch.*》 (of time) before. …전(前)에. [E.]

:**e·rect** [irékt] *adj.* straight up; upright; directed upward. 곧추선; 직립의; 똑바른. ¶ *an ~ figure* 직립상(像) / *stand ~* 곧추서다; 직립하다 / *with head ~* 머리를 똑바로 쳐들고 / *hold oneself ~* 자세를 똑바로〔꼿꼿이〕하다; 가슴을 펴다.
— *vt.* (P6) **1** put (someone or something) straight up. …을 직립시키다; 곧추세우다. ¶ *~ oneself* 몸을 일으키다〔똑바로 하다〕 / *~ a telegraph pole* 전봇대를 똑바로 세우다. **2** build. (건물 따위)를 세우다. ¶ *~ a house* 〔*tower*〕 집〔탑〕을 세우다. **3** set up; establish. …을 조립하다; 수립하다. ¶ *~ a machine* 기계를 조립하다 / *~ a new government* 새 정부를 세우다. ● **e·rect·ly** [-li] *adv.* **e·rect·ness** [-nis] *n.* [L. *rego* direct]

e·rec·tile [iréktil, -tail] *adj.* capable of being erected. 곧추세울〔직립시킬〕 수 있는; 직립성의.

e·rec·tion [irékʃən] *n.* **1** Ⓤ the act of erecting; the state of being erected. 직립; 기립; 건립. **2** Ⓒ a thing which is erected; a building. 직립물; 건조물; 건설〔건축〕물; 건물. ¶ *The new bank was a handsome ~.* 새 은행은 훌륭한 건물이었다.

ere·long [ɛ̀ərlɔ́(:)ŋ] *adv.* 《*arch.*》 before long; soon. 머지않아; 곧. [E.]

er·e·mite [érəmàit] *n.* 《*arch.*》 =hermit.

ere·while [ɛərhwáil] *adv.* 《*arch., poet.*》 a short time ago; a little before. 조금 전에. [E.]

erg [əːrg] *n.* 《phys.》 the unit of work or energy in cgs. system. 에르그. [Gk. *ergon* work]

er·go [ə́ːrgou] *ad.* 《L.》 《*joc.*》 therefore. 그러므로.

E·rie [íəri], **Lake** *n.* one of the five Great Lakes, between the United States and Canada. 이리 호(湖)《미국과 캐나다 사이에 있는 오대호의 하나》.

er·mine [ə́ːrmin] *n.* (*pl.* **-mines** or *collectively* **-mine**) **1** Ⓒ a kind of weasel whose fur turns white in winter. 산족제비. **2** Ⓤ the soft, white fur of this animal. 위의 모피. **3** Ⓤ the office or rank of a judge (because ermine is worn by judges in England). 판사의 지위〔신분〕. [F.]

Er·nest [ə́ːrnist] *n.* a man's name. 남자 이름.

e·rode [iróud] *vt.* (P6) eat or wear away gradually. …을 침식하다; 부식하다. ¶ *~ the freedom* 자유를 침해하다 / *Acids ~ metal.* 산(酸)은 금속을 부식시킨다 / *Running water erodes soil and rock.* 흐르는 물은 땅과 바위를 침식한다. [→rodent]

E·ros [íərɑs, érɑs / íərɔs, érɔs] *n.* 《Gk. myth.》 the god of love. 사랑의 신《로마 신화의 Cupid에 해당》.

e·ro·sion [iróuʒən] *n.* ⓊⒸ the act of eroding; the state of being eroded or eaten away. 침식; 부식. ¶ *the ~ of a cliff by the action of the waves* 파도의 작용에 의한 단애의 침식. [→erode]

e·ro·sive [iróusiv] *adj.* eroding; causing erosion. 침식하는; 부식적인.

e·rot·ic [irátik / irɔ́t-] *adj.* **1** pertaining to or concerned with sexual love; amorous. 연애〔성애(性愛)〕의; 호색적인. ¶ *an ~ man* 호색가. **2** designed to arouse sexual desire. 성욕을 자극하는. [Gk.*erōs* love]

·**err** [əːr, εər] *vi.* (P1) **1** make mistakes; be wrong. 잘못〔실수〕하다; 틀리다; 그르치다. ¶ ~ *in one's judgment* 판단을 그르치다. **2** do wrong; sin. 잘못을〔죄를〕 저지르다; 그릇된 길에 빠지다. ¶ ~ *from the truth* 진리에서 벗어나다 / *To ~ is human, to forgive divine.* 잘못은 인지상사요, 용서는 신의 소관이다. [L. *erro* stray, →error]

·**er·rand** [érənd] *n.* Ⓒ **1** a short trip for a special purpose, esp. for someone else. 심부름. ¶ *a gawk's ~* 헛걸음; 헛수고 / *send a someone on an ~* 아무를 심부름 보내다 / *make an ~* 잠깐 볼일 보러 나가다; 갈 구실을 만들다 / *The boy was sent on an ~ to the office.* 아이를 회사에 심부름으로 보냈다. **2** the purpose of such a trip. (심부름의) 목적; 볼일. ¶ *I have an ~ to do in town.* 시내에 볼일이 있다. [E.]

go on a fool's errand, **a)** make vain efforts. 헛수고하다. **b)** be taken in. 속다.

go on* 〔*run*〕 *an errand, do an errand. 심부름 가다.

er·rand-boy [érəndbɔ̀i] *n.* a boy employed by a shop or firm to run errands. (가게·회사에서) 심부름하는 소년.

er·rant [érənt] *adj.* **1** wandering; traveling about looking for adventure. (중세 기사가) 모험을 찾아 헤매는〔편력하는〕(cf. *knight-errant*). **2** (of thought, etc.) wandering from the right way; erring. 정도에서 벗어난; 그릇된; 잘못된. [*err; errant* partly from L. *iter* journey]

er·ra·ta [eráːtə, ir-, iréi-] *n.* pl. of **erratum.**

er·rat·ic [irǽtik] *adj.* **1** not steady; wandering; irregular. 일정치 않은; 변하기 잘하는; 변덕스러운. ¶ *~ winds* 풍향이 일정치 않은 바람 / *be emotionally ~* 정서가 불안정하다. **2** unusual; queer. 별난; 야릇한; 엉뚱한. ¶ *~ behavior* 엉뚱한 행동. [→errant]

er·ra·tum [eráːtəm, ir-, iréi-] *n.* Ⓒ (*pl.* **-ta**) an error or mistake in writing or printing. 오자(誤字); 오식(誤植). ¶ *a list of errata* 정오표(正誤表). [L. neut. pp. of *errare* err]

er·ro·ne·ous [iróuniəs] *adj.* mistaken; incorrect. 잘못이 있는; 잘못된; 틀린. ¶ *hold an ~ opinion* 잘못된 생각을 품다. ● **er·ro·ne·ous·ly** [-li] *adv.* [↓]

:**er·ror** [érər] *n.* ⒸⓊ **1** something wrong; a mistake; the state of being wrong or mistaken. 잘못; 실수; 틀림. ¶ *an ~ in calculation* 계산의 잘못〔틀림〕/ *do* 〔*commit, make*〕 *an ~* 잘못을 저지르다 / *be in ~* 잘못되어 있다. **2** a mistaken idea. 잘못된 생각. **3** a misplay in baseball. 에러; 실책. [→err]

er·satz [érzaːts, -saːts] *adj., n.* 《G.》 substitute. 대용〔모조〕의; 대용품. ¶ *~ rubber* 합성 고무 / *~ mink* 대용 밍크. [G. *ersetzen* to replace]

erst [əːrst] *adv.* 《*arch.*》 formerly; long ago. 전에; 오래 전에; 이전에. [→ere]

erst·while [ə́ːrsthwàil] *adv.* 《*arch.*》 formerly; in time past. 이전에; 옛날에.

e·ruct [irʌ́kt] *vt., vi.* (P6; 1) belch forth; emit. 트림하다; 뿜어내다. [L.]

e·ruc·tate [irʌ́kteit] *vt., vi.* =eruct.

er·u·dite [érjudàit] *adj.* of knowledge; learned. 학식이 있는; 박식한. ¶ *an ~ professor* 학식이 풍부한 교수. ● **er·u·dite·ly** [-li] *adv.* [→rude]

er·u·di·tion [èrjudíʃən] *n.* Ⓤ wide knowledge or learning. 깊은 지식; 학식; 박식. ¶ *a man of great ~* 학식이 풍부한 사람.

e·rupt [irʌ́pt] *vi.* (P1,2A,3) break out; burst through or out. 분화(噴火)〔분출〕하다; (감정 따위가) 터지다; (이가) 나다. ¶ *Ashes and lava erupted from the volcano.* 화산에서 재와 용암이 분출했다 / *New teeth ~ when they break through the skin of the gums.* 새 이는 그것이 잇몸의 살갗을 뚫을 때 나게 된다. [L. *rumpo* break]

e·rup·tion [irʌ́pʃən] *n.* ⓊⒸ **1** the act of erupting. 분출; 분화; 폭발; 돌발. ¶ *an ~ of laughter* 웃음의 폭발. **2** smoke, ashes, etc. which is erupted from a volcano. 분출물; 내뿜는 연기; 화산재. **3** 《med.》 a rash on the skin. 발진. ¶ *an ~ on the face* 얼굴에 난 발진.

e·rup·tive [irʌ́ptiv] *adj.* **1** 《geol.》 tending to erupt; bursting forth. 분출하는; 분화성의. **2** of or caused by eruptions. 분출〔분화〕에 의한. ¶ *an ~ rock* 분출암. **3** marked by breaking out. 발진성(發疹性)의.

er·y·sip·e·las [èrəsípələs, ìːr-] *n.* 《med.》 a disease producing deep red color on the skin. 단독(丹毒). [Gk.]

es·ca·drille [éskədrìl] *n.* **1** a squadron of airplanes. 비행대. **2** a small naval squadron. 소함대(小艦隊). [L.]

es·ca·lade [èskəléid] *n.* the act of getting up a wall by means of ladders; an attack on (a fortress etc.) by this means. 사다리로 오르기; (이런 수단에 의한) 요새·성벽의 공격. — *vt.* (P6) 사다리로 오르다. [↓]

es·ca·late [éskəlèit] *vt., vi.* (P6; 1) make or become larger in degree, scale, etc.; increase. 단계적으로 늘(리)다; 확대하다〔되다〕. ¶ *~ a war* 전쟁을 확대하다. [→scale[1]]

es·ca·la·tion [èskəléiʃən] *n.* ⓊⒸ the act of increasing; a gradual increase in military forces, etc. 증가; 증대; (군사력 따위의) 단계적 확대. ¶ *~ of a war* 확전(擴戰).

es·ca·la·tor [éskəlèitər] *n.* Ⓒ a moving stairway for carrying people up or down. 에스컬레이터.

escalator clause [ˊ---ˋ] *n.* a clause in a contract allowing an increase or decrease in pay under specified conditions. 에스컬레이터 조항.

es·ca·pade [éskəpèid, ˋ-ˊ] *n.* Ⓒ 《*arch.*》 an escape from rules or restraint; a mischievous or wild adventure. (규칙·제약으로부터의) 일탈; 도피; 분방한 행위. [↓]

:**es·cape** [iskéip] *vi.* (P1,2A,3) **1** 《*from, out of*》 get free; slip. 도망〔도피〕하다; 탈출하다.

¶ ~ *with bare life* (죽지 않고) 간신히 도망치다 / ~ *from a lonely life* 고독한 생활에서 탈출하다 / *Three prisoners escaped from the prison.* 세 명의 죄수가 탈옥했다. **2** avoid a danger, punishment, disease, pain, etc. (위험·처벌·질병·고통 따위를) 모면하다; 피하다. ¶ *Three members of this family were killed in the war, but one escaped.* 이 집안의 가족 중 세 사람이 전쟁에서 죽었으나 하나는 모면했다. **3** 《*from*》 come out through a hole; leak. 새다. ¶ *The gas is escaping.* 가스가 새고 있다. — *vt.* (P6,9) **1** keep away from (danger, etc.); avoid; elude. …을 (모)면하다; 피하다. ¶ ~ *the danger* 위험을 피하다 / ~ *a task* 작업을 면하다 / ~ *being punished* 처벌을 모면하다 / *He escaped being killed in the battle.* 그는 전사(戰死)를 모면했다. **2** (of a word, sigh, etc.) come out from (lips, etc.) carelessly. (말·탄식 따위가) …로부터 (새어)나오다. ¶ *Angry words escaped his lips.* 분노의 말이 뜻하지 않게 그의 입에서 나왔다. **3** do not come into the notice or memory of (someone). (아무의 주목이나 기억에서) 벗어나다. ¶ ~ *being noticed* 주목받지 못하다 / *His name escaped her.* 그의 이름이 떠오르지 않았다.

cannot escape, cannot help; cannot avoid. …하지 않을 수 없다.

escape someone's memory, be forgotten; cannot be remembered. 잊히다; 생각[기억]에 남지 않다.

— *n.* **1** Ⓒ Ⓤ the act or fact of escaping. 도망; 탈출; 도피. ¶ *a daring* ~ *from prison* 대담한 탈옥. **2** Ⓒ (of water, gas, etc.) the act of escaping from a pipe, etc.; leakage. (수돗물·가스 따위의) 새나옴; 누출. ¶ *There is an* ~ *of gas somewhere.* 어딘가 가스 새는 데가 있다. [→cape[1]]

effect one's escape, be safe from pursuit. 무사히 도망치다.

make one's escape, run away; escape. 달아나다; 도망치다.

make good one's escape =effect one's escape.

narrow escape ⇨narrow.

es·cape·ment [iskéipmənt] *n.* Ⓒ a device in a clock or watch for controlling the movement. (시계 톱니바퀴의) 지동(止動) 기구; 탈진기(脫進機).

es·cap·ism [iskéipìzəm] *n.* Ⓤ a habitual avoidance of unpleasant realities by recourse to imagination and fiction. 현실도피.

es·carp·ment [iskáːrpmənt] *n.* Ⓒ a steep slope; a cliff. 급사면(急斜面); 단애(斷崖); 벼랑. [→scarp]

es·cha·tol·o·gy [èskətálədʒi / -tɔ́l-] *n.* Ⓤ the branch of theology that treats of last or final things, as death. 종말론. [Gk. *éskhatos* last, →-logy]

es·cheat [istʃíːt] *n.* 《law》 reversion of property to the state or to the crown in default of legal heirs or other qualified claimants. (주인 없는 재산의) 국가[주(州)·국왕 등에의] 복귀; 귀속; 몰수. — *vi., vt.* revert or cause to revert to the state, etc., by escheat. (주인 없는 재산·토지 따위)를[가] 복귀[귀속]되다; 복귀[귀속]시키다. [L. *excido* to fall out]

es·chew [istʃúː] *vt.* (P6) keep away from (something); avoid; shun. …을 멀리하다; 피하다. ¶ *This word should be eschewed in polite conversation.* 점잖은 대화에서는 이 말을 피해야 한다. [→shy[1]]

·es·cort [éskɔːrt] *n.* Ⓒ **1** a person or persons going along with another or others to protect or guide. 호위자(들); 호송자. **2** a group of warships or airplanes protecting unarmed ships. 호위함; 호송기(機).

under escort, accompanied by police for protection. 호위된[되어].

— [eskɔ́ːrt] *vt.* (P6,7) go along with (someone) as an escort. …을 호위하다; 곁에 모시고 가다. ¶ ~ *the girls to their homes* 여자들을 그들 집에까지 바래다 주다 / *Warships escorted the steamer.* 군함들이 기선을 호송했다. [ex-, cor-, L. *rego* direct]

es·cu·lent [éskjələnt] *adj.* suitable for food; edible. 먹을 수 있는; 식용의. ¶ *Many types of fish are not* ~. 많은 종류의 물고기가 먹을수 없다. — *n.* something suitable for food. 식용이 되는 것. [L. *esca* food]

es·cutch·eon [iskʌ́tʃən, es-] *n.* Ⓒ a shield on which a family mark is put. 방패 모양의 가문(家紋) 바탕. [L. *scutum* shield]

a blot on one's escutcheon, a stain on one's name or honor; disgrace to one's reputation. 불명예; 오명(汚名).

〈escutcheon〉

Es·ki·mo [éskəmòu] *n.* (*pl.* **-mos** or **-mo**) **1** Ⓒ a member of a North American Indian race living in the extreme north of America and Greenland. 에스키모 사람. **2** Ⓤ the language of this race. 에스키모 말. — *adj.* of the Eskimos or their language. 에스키모 사람[말]의. [Native]

e·soph·a·gi [isáfədʒài / -sɔ́f-] *n.* pl. of **esophagus.**

e·soph·a·gus [isáfəgəs / -sɔ́f-] *n.* (*pl.* **-gi**) a tube connecting the mouth with the stomach. 식도(食道). [Gk. *oiso* carry, *phagein* eat]

es·o·ter·ic [èsoutérik] *adj.* understood only by a small number of people. 비전(祕傳)의; 비밀의. ¶ ~ *Buddhism* 밀교(密敎). [Gk. *eso* within]

ESP extrasensory perception. 초감각적 지각.

esp., espec. especially.

·es·pe·cial [ispéʃəl] *adj.* special; exceptional; particular. 특별한; 특수한; 각별한.

¶ *my ~ aversion* 내가 몹시 싫어하는 것 / *an ~ friend* 각별한 친구 / *of no ~ importance* 특별히 중요하지는 않은. [→special]
in especial, in particular; above all. 특히; 그 중에서도.

:es·pe·cial·ly [ispéʃəli] *adv.* particularly; chiefly. 특히; 각별히; 그 중에서도. ¶ *an ~ careful approach to danger* 위험에 대한 특별히 조심스러운 접근 / *The country prospered, ~ after the war.* 그 나라는 특히 전후에 번영했다.

Es·pe·ran·to [èspərǽntou, -rá:n-] *n.* Ⓤ an artificial language for international use. 에스페란토어(語). 參考 Dr. L. L. Zamenhof 가 창안했음. [L. *spero* hope]

es·pi·al [espáiəl] *n.* an espying. 정탐(偵探); 간첩 행위. [→espy]

es·pi·o·nage [éspiənà:ʒ, -niʒ, ⌐—ná:ʒ] *n.* Ⓤ **1** the act of spying. 간첩 행위. **2** the systematic use of spies by a government to learn the secrets of other nations. 간첩 조직(망). [→espy]

es·pla·nade [èsplənéid, -ná:d, ⌐—⌐] *n.* Ⓒ a level space used for public walks or drives. (산책·드라이브를 위한) 평지; 산책〔드라이브〕길. [→explain]

es·pous·al [ispáuzəl, -səl] *n.* **1** Ⓤ the act of espousing. (주의 따위의) 옹호. **2** Ⓒ 《*arch.*》《usu. *pl.*》 a marriage ceremony. 결혼(식). [↓]

es·pouse [ispáuz, es-] *vt.* (P6) **1** give support to (something); take (an idea, etc.) as one's own; adopt. …을 지지〔옹호〕하다; 채용〔신봉〕하다. ¶ *~ a democratic principle* 민주주의를 지지하다 / *~ a new religion* 새 종교를 신봉하다. **2** 《*arch.*》 (usu. of a man) marry. 장가들다; 아내로 맞이하다. [L. *spondeo* betroth]

es·prit [esprí:] *n.* 《F.》 spirit; wit. 정신; (번득이는) 재치; 기지(機智).

esprit de corps [-də kɔ́:*r*] *n.* 《F.》 the spirit of loyalty among the members of a group, devotion to the honor and well-being of the group. 단체 정신; 단결심.

es·py [espái] *vt.* (**-pied**) (P6) see; catch sight of. …을 발견하다. [Teut.]

Esq., Esqr. Esquire.

Es·qui·mau [éskimòu] *n.* =Eskimo.

es·quire [eskwáiə*r*, ⌐—] *n.* 《Brit.》 **1** 《*E-*》 the title of respect, placed after a man's last name. 님; 귀하. 語法 특히 편지에서 남자 이름 뒤에 Esq.로 생략해서 씀. **2** a member of the upper class ranking next below a knight. 향사(鄕士)《나이트작(爵) 다음 위치의 사람》. [L. *scutum* shield]

***es·say** [ései] *n.* Ⓒ **1** a short literary composition. 수필; 평론; 소론(小論). ¶ *an ~ on modern music* 근대 음악론. **2** an attempt; a trial. 시도; 기도. — [eséi] *vi., vt.* (P1,4;6) **1** make trial of; try; attempt. 시도하다; 해 보다. ¶ *He will not ~ the high jump.* 높이 뛰기는 하지 않을 게다. **2** prove. 증명하다. [→assay]

es·say·ist [éseiist] *n.* Ⓒ a person who writes essays. 수필가.

***es·sence** [ésəns] *n.* Ⓤ **1** the fundamental nature of a thing. 본질; 핵심. ¶ *the very ~ of democracy* 민주주의의 진수(眞髓) / *Health is the ~ of happiness.* 건강은 행복의 요체이다. **2** Ⓒ 《philos.》 true substance. (현상에 대하여) 실재(實在); 본체. **3** ⒸⓊ extract. 정(精); 익스트랙트; 엑스. ¶ *meat ~* 고기의 엑스. **4** ⒸⓊ a pleasant smelling liquid; a perfume. 향수; 향료. [L. *sum* am]
in essence, essentially; in fact. 본질에 있어서; 요컨대.
of the essence, very important. 극히 중요한; 절대 불가결의.

:es·sen·tial [isénʃəl] *adj.* absolutely necessary; very important; fundamental. 없어서는 안 될; 매우 중요한; 필수의; 본질적인. ¶ *things ~ for daily life* 일상의 생활 필수품 / *an ~ difference* 본질적인 차이 / *Water is ~ to life.* 물은 생명에 꼭 필요하다 / *It is to do…* 〔*that…*〕. …하는 것이 긴요하다. — *n.* Ⓒ 《usu. *pl.*》 absolutely necessary elements or qualities. 본질적〔불가결의〕 요소; 주요점. ¶ *the essentials of life* 생명 유지에 불가결한 것 / *~ to happiness* 〔*success*〕 행복〔성공〕에 없어서는 안 될 것. [→essence]

es·sen·tial·ly [isénʃəli] *adv.* in essence; in essentials; fundamentally. 본질적〔근본적〕으로; 본래. ¶ *They are ~ a peace-loving people.* 그들은 본래 평화 애호 민족이다.

EST Eastern Standard Time. 《U.S.》 동부 표준시.

:es·tab·lish [istǽbliʃ] *vt.* (P6,7,13) **1** found; build up. …을 설립〔수립, 창설〕하다; 건조하다. ¶ *~ a school* 학교를 설립하다 / *~ a ship* 배를 건조하다 / *~ a government* 정부를 세우다. **2** set up (something) on a permanent basis; constitute. …을 확립하다; 제정하다. ¶ *~ a theory* 이론을 세우다 / *~ the constitution* 헌법을 제정하다. **3** 《*in*》 ⓐ settle (someone) in a position, business, etc. (지위·직업 따위에) 안정시키다; 취임〔취업〕시키다. ¶ *He established his son in trade.* 아들을 실업에 종사케 했다. ⓑ place; settle. 자리잡게 하다. ¶ *~ oneself in the country* 〔*in a new house*〕 시골에〔새로운 집에〕 자리잡다 / *He retired and established himself on his island.* 그는 은퇴하여 향리의 섬에 정착했다. **4** get (something) generally accepted; prove. …을 납득시키다; 인정케 하다; 입증하다. ¶ *~ a custom* 관습을 확립하다 / *an established repute* 확립된 평판 / *~ the facts of the matter* 그 문제의 사실을 입증하다 / *~ oneself as a leading surgeon* 일류 외과의로서의 기반을 굳히다. [→stable[1]]

***es·tab·lish·ment** [istǽbliʃmənt] *n.* **1** Ⓤ the act of establishing; the state of being established. 확립; 설립; 창설. **2** Ⓒ something established, such as a household, a business, etc. 설립물; 가구; 회사. ¶ *keep a large* ~ 대가족을 거느리고 있다. **3** a department of state for special purposes. 제도; 조직; 편성. **4** all the persons belonging to such a department. 직원; 정원. **5** 《*the E-*》 ⓐ the Church of England. 영국 국교. ⓑ 《esp. Brit.》 the ruling class; the existing power structure in society. 지배 계층; 권력 구조〔기구〕; 체제.

·es·tate [istéit] *n.* Ⓒ **1** a large house and lands as one's property. 가옥; 토지; 소유지. **2** everything belonging to someone; property; possessions. 소유물; 재산. ¶ *real* 〔*personal*〕 ~ 부동산〔동산〕. **3** Ⓤ a certain period in life. (인생의) 시기; 시대. ¶ *reach* 〔*attain to*〕 *man's* 〔*woman's*〕 ~ 성년이 되다. **4** a class or group of people in a nation. (정치상·사회상의) 계급. **5** a condition of worldly prosperity. (세속적 지위·신분과 관련지어서의) 경제〔생활〕 상태; 사회적 지위. ¶ *suffer in one's* ~ 생활이 어렵다. [→state]

estate agent [–´–´–] *n.* 《Brit.》 the manager of real estate of a great house; a person who buys and sells real estate for others (=《U.S.》 realtor). 토지〔부동산〕 관리인; 부동산 중개인.

estate car [–´–´] *n.* 《Brit.》 =station wagon.

·es·teem [istí:m] *vt.* (P6,7,21) **1** have a very favorable opinion of (something); value highly; respect. …을 존경〔존중〕하다; 중시하다. ¶ ~ *courage* 용기를 존중하다 / *I* ~ *him for his honesty.* 정직하니까 그를 좋아한다 / *I* ~ *him highly.* 그를 크게 존경한다 / *Your esteemed letter has just reached me.* 혜신(惠信) 방금 받아 보았습니다 / *I* ~ *it a privilege* 〔*an honor*〕 *to do such a thing.* 저는 그러한 일을 하는 것은 영광이라고 생각합니다. **2** think; consider; regard. …을 (—하다고) 간주하다; (…라고) 생각하다; 믿다. ¶ ~ *oneself lucky* 스스로를 운이 좋다고 생각하다 / *I* ~ *it worthless.* 그것을 무가치하다고 여긴다 / *I do not* ~ *riches a worthy aim.* 나는 부(富)를 추구할 가치가 있는 것으로 생각지 않는다.
— *n.* Ⓤ an opinion, usu. very favorable; high regard. 호의적 의견; 존중; 존경; 경의. ¶ *hold him in high* 〔*great*〕 ~ 그를 크게 존경하다. [→estimate]

es·ter [éstər] *n.* 《chem.》 a compound ether derived from an oxygenated acid. 에스테르. [G.]

es·thete [ésθi:t] *n.* =aesthete.

es·thet·ic [esθétik] *adj.* =aesthetic.

es·ti·ma·ble [éstəməbəl] *adj.* **1** worthy of esteem. 존경〔존중〕할 만한. **2** can be estimated or calculated; calculable. 평가할 수 있는; 어림할 수 있는. [↓]

:es·ti·mate [éstəmèit] *vt.* (P11,13) **1** determine the value of (something); judge. …을 평가하다; 판단하다. ¶ ~ *someone's character high*(*ly*) 아무의 인격을 높이 평가하다. **2** find out the value, size, cost, etc. of (something). …을 어림하다; 개산하다. ¶ *He estimated his losses at 50,000 dollars.* 그는 손실을 5만 달러로 어림했다.
— *vi.* (P3) calculate the value, size, cost, etc. 어림을 하다; 견적서를 만들다. ¶ ~ *for the repair of a house* 집 수리비의 견적을 내다.
— [éstəmit, -mèit] *n.* Ⓒ the act of estimating; a rough calculation; a statement of the probable cost of a job. 평가; 어림; 견적(서). ¶ *the builder's* ~ 건축업자의 견적 / *my* ~ *of him as a poet* 시인으로서의 그에 대한 나의 평가 / *by* ~ 대충 어림하여 / *at a moderate* ~ 줄잡아 어림하여 / *in the* ~ *of the world* 세상의 눈으로 보면 / *the Estimates* 《Brit.》 (재무상이 의회에 제출하는) 세출 세입 예산 / *make* 〔*form*〕 *an* ~ *of* …을 어림잡다〔평가하다〕. [L. *aestimo*]

es·ti·ma·tion [èstəméiʃən] *n.* **1** ⓊⒸ the act of estimating; judgment; opinion. 어림; 견적; 평가; 판단; 의견. ¶ *in my* ~ 내 의견으로는 / *an* ~ *of the cost* 생산 원가의 개산. **2** Ⓤ esteem; respect. 존중; 존경. ¶ *hold someone in high* ~ 아무를 크게 존경하다 / *win someone's* ~ 아무의 호평을 얻다 / *stand high in public* ~ 세평이 높다.

es·trange [estréindʒ] *vt.* (P6,13) **1** separate (someone) because of a loss of feeling or affection. …을 소원하게 하다; 사이가 멀어지게 하다. ¶ *be estranged from one's friends* 친구들과 소원해지다 / *Their quarrel estranged the two lovers.* 말다툼이 원인이 되어 그 연인들은 사이가 나빠졌다. **2** 《*from*》 keep (someone) apart or away. …을 멀리하다; 떼다(cf. *alienate*). [→strange]

es·trange·ment [estréindʒmənt] *n.* ⓊⒸ the act of estranging; the state of being estranged. 소원(疏遠); 이간; 불화(cf. *alienation*). ¶ *cause* ~ *between old friends* 두 옛 친구 사이를 이간하다.

es·trus [éstrəs] *n.* the period of heat or rut; the period of maximum sexual receptivity of female. 발정기. [L.]

es·tu·ar·y [éstʃuèri] *n.* Ⓒ (*pl.* **-ar·ies**) **1** a wide mouth of a river into which the tide flows. (너비가 넓은) 강어귀; 하구 **2** an inlet of the sea. 바다의 후미〔내포〕. [L. *aestus* tide]

et al. [et ǽl, -á:l, -ɔ́:l] 《L.》 **1** et alibi (=and elsewhere). 및 그 밖의 곳에. **2** et alii (=and others). 또한 그 밖.

:etc. [etsétərə, ənsóufɔ̀:rθ] =et cetera.

et cet·er·a [et sétərə] 《L.》 and so on; and so forth. …따위; 등등; 기타(abbr. etc., &c.).

etch [etʃ] *vt., vi.* (P6,13; 1) make (pictures, etc.) by engraving designs on a metal plate with acids. (산류(酸類)로 금속판에 그림 따위)를 에칭하다; 식각법(蝕刻法)을 쓰다. ● **etch·er** [étʃər] *n.* [G. →eat]

etch·ing [étʃiŋ] *n.* Ⓒ **1** a picture, design, etc. printed from an etched plate. 에칭; 동판화; 부식판쇄(刷). **2** Ⓤ the art of an etcher. 부식법; 식각술(蝕刻術).

***e·ter·nal** [itə́ːrnəl] *adj.* **1** everlasting; timeless; unchangeable. 영원[영구]한; 불멸의; 불변의. ¶ ~ *truth* 불변의 진리 / ~ *life* 영원한 생명 / *the Eternal City* 로마. **2** 《*colloq.*》 too frequent, endless. 끊임없는; 끝없는. ¶ ~ *chatter* 끝없는 수다. —*n.* 《*the E-*》 God. 신(神). [L.]

e·ter·nal·ly [itə́ːrnəli] *adv.* **1** forever. 영원히. **2** unchangeably. 변함없이. **3** constantly. 끊임없이.

e·ter·ni·ty [itə́ːrnəti] *n.* (*pl.* **-ties**) Ⓤ **1** the state of being eternal; all time; endlessness. 영구; 영원; 무한; 불멸. **2** the endless period after death; future life. 영세; 내세. ¶ *hover between time* [*this life*] *and* ~ 이승과 저승 사이를 헤매다《죽어 가다》. **3** Ⓒ a period of time that seems endless. 끝없이 계속되는 긴 시간. ¶ *wait an* ~ 오랜 시간 기다리다. **4** 《*the eternities*》 the eternal truths. 불변의 사실[진리]. [L.]

through all eternity, forever. 영원히.

eth·ane [éθein] *n.* 《chem.》 an odorless, gaseous hydrocarbon. 에탄. [↓]

e·ther [íːθər] *n.* Ⓤ **1** 《chem.》 a colorless, strong smelling liquid produced from alcohol. 에테르. **2** 《phys.》 an assumed medium filling all space, through which light waves and wireless waves are transmitted. 에테르《빛·열·전기·자기의 가상적 매체》. **3** 《*poet.*》 the upper sky; the clear sky. 하늘; 창공. [Gk. *aithēr*]

e·the·re·al [iθíːriəl] *adj.* **1** light; airy. 가벼운; 공기같은. **2** not of the earth; extremely delicate or refined. 극히 아름다운; 절묘[영묘]한. ¶ ~ *beauty* 이승에서는 볼 수 없는 아름다움. **3** 《*poet.*》 heavenly. 천상[하늘]의. ● **e·the·al·ize** [-riəlaiz] *vt.* (P6) [↑]

eth·ic [éθik], **-i·cal** [-ikəl] *adj.* of ethics; moral. 윤리(학)의; 도덕의. [→ethos]

eth·ics [éθiks] *n. pl.* **1** 《used as *sing.*》 the study of standards of right and wrong in human behavior. 윤리학. ¶ *Ethics deals with moral conduct.* 도덕적 행위를 다루는 윤리학. **2** individual or professional morals. (사람·직업상의) 도덕; 도의(道義).

E·thi·o·pi·a [ìːθióupiə] *n.* a republic in East Africa. 에티오피아. 參考 수도는 Addis Ababa. ● **E·thi·o·pi·an** [-n] *adj., n.* ⒸⓊ

eth·nic [éθnik], **-ni·cal** [-nikəl] *adj.* **1** of racial groups. 인종의. **2** neither Christian nor Jewish; pagan. 이교도의; 이방인의. ● **eth·ni·cal·ly** [-nikəli] *adv.* [Gk. *éthnos* nation]

eth·nog·ra·phy [eθnágrəfi / -nɔ́g-] *n.* the scientific description and classification of the various races of people. 민족지(民族誌). [↑]

eth·nol·o·gy [eθnálədʒi / -nɔ́l-] *n.* Ⓤ the science of the various races of mankind. 인종학; 민족학(cf. *folklore*). [↑]

eth·yl [éθəl] *n.* 《chem.》 an organic radical of paraffin series. 에틸(cf. *methyl*). [→ether]

eth·y·lene [éθəlìːn] *n.* 《chem.》 a colorless, flammable, gaseous hydrocarbon, used as an anesthetic and in organic syntheses. 에틸렌.

e·ti·ol·o·gy [ìːtiálədʒi / -ɔ́l-] *n.* **1** 《med.》 ⓐ the study of causes or origins, esp. of disease. 병인학(病因學). ⓑ the cause of diseases. 병인(病因). **2** the study of causes. 원인 연구. [Gk.]

et·i·quette [étikèt, -kit] *n.* Ⓤ the customs or formal rules of behavior in polite society, a profession, an official ceremony, etc. 예절; 예법; 에티켓. ¶ *It is against* ~ *to do so.* 그렇게 하는 것은 예의에 어긋난다. [→ticket]

E·ton [íːtn] *n.* a town in South Buckinghamshire, in south England, on the Thames River. 이튼《잉글랜드 남부 템스강에 면한 Buckinghamshire 남부의 도시》. 參考 Eton College의 소재지. [Place]

et seq. 《L.》 et sequens (=and the following); et sequentia or et sequentes (=and those that follow). 및 그 다음(의 말·행(行)·페이지 등) 참조.

é·tude [eitjúːd] *n.* Ⓒ 《F. mus.》 a piece of music intended to give some technical practice. 에튀드; 연습곡.

etym., etymol. etymological; etymology.

et·y·mo·log·i·cal [ètəməládʒikəl / -lɔ́dʒ-] *adj.* of etymology. 어원(語源)의; 어원학상의. ¶ *an* ~ *dictionary* 어원 사전. [↓]

et·y·mol·o·gist [ètəmálədʒist / -mɔ́l-] *n.* Ⓒ a person skilled in etymology. 어원학자.

et·y·mol·o·gy [ètəmálədʒi / -mɔ́l-] *n.* (*pl.* **-gies**) **1** Ⓤ the study of linguistic changes, esp. of word origins. 어원학. **2** Ⓒ an account or explanation of the origin and history of a word. 어원(語源); 어원의 설명. [Gk. *etumos* true]

eu- [ju(ː)-] *pref.* good, well. '양(良), 호(好), 우(優)'의 뜻.

eu·ca·lyp·ti [jùːkəlíptai] *n.* pl. of **eucalyptus.**

eu·ca·lyp·tus [jùːkəlíptəs] *n.* Ⓒ (*pl.* **-tus·es** or **-ti**) 《bot.》 any of the tall, evergreen trees. 유칼립투스; 유칼리. 參考 오스트레일리아산의 상록 고목. [Gk.=well-covered]

Eu·cha·rist [júːkərist] *n.* 《*the* ~》 **1** the Lord's Supper. 성찬(聖餐)(식). **2** the bread and wine taken at the Lord's Supper. (성찬용의) 빵과 포도주; 성체(聖體). [Gk.=thanksgiving]

eu·chre [júːkər] *n.* Ⓤ a variety of card game. 유커《카드놀이의 일종》. —*vt.* (P6) 《U.S. *colloq., fig.*》 outwit. (계략 따위로) 상대의 의표를 찌르다. [G.]

Eu·clid [júːklid] *n.* **1** (300 B.C.?) a Greek mathematician. 유클리드. **2** a form of geometry based on Euclid's work. 유클리드 기하학.

eu·gen·ic [juːdʒénik], **-i·cal** [-kəl] *adj.* **1** having to do with improvement of the race; improving the race. 우생학상의; 인종 개량의. **2** possessing good inherited characteristics. 뛰어난 성질을 이어받은. [↓]

eu·gen·ics [ju:dʒéniks] *n. pl.* 《used as *sing.*》 the science of improving the human race. 우생학(優生學). [Gk. *eugenēs* well-born]

eu·lo·gis·tic [jù:lədʒístik], **-ti·cal** [-tikəl] *adj.* praising highly. 높이 칭찬〔찬양〕하는; 기리는. [*eu-*]

eu·lo·gize [jú:lədʒàiz] *vt.* (P6) praise highly. …을 칭찬〔찬양〕하다; 기리다.

eu·lo·gy [jú:lədʒi] *n.* (*pl.* **-gies**) **1** Ⓒ a speech or writing in praise of a person, esp. a dead person, a thing, etc. 찬사(讚辭); (특히 죽은 이에 대한) 추도 연설. ¶ *The general pronounced a ~ upon the dead soldier.* 장군은 죽은 군인에 대한 추도의 연설을 했다. **2** Ⓤ high praise. 기림; 칭찬; 찬양. [eu-]

eu·nuch [jú:nək] *n.* a castrated man employed in a harem. 환관(宦官); 내시. [Gk. =bedkeeper]

eu·pep·si·a [ju(:)pépʃə, -siə] *n.* Ⓤ 《med.》 good digestion. 정상 소화(消化)(opp. dyspepsia). [eu-, Gk. *pessō* digest]

eu·phe·mism [jú:fəmìzəm] *n.* Ⓤ the use of a mild or indirect expression or word instead of a coarse or unpleasant one; Ⓒ an example of this. (노골적인 말을 피하는) 완곡 어법; 완곡한 어구〔표현〕. ¶ *'Pass away' is a ~ for 'die'.* 'pass away'는 'die'에 대한 완곡한 표현이다. [↓]

eu·phe·mis·tic [jù:fəmístik], **-ti·cal** [-tikəl] *adj.* of or showing euphemism. 완곡 어법의; 완곡한. ¶ *He always uses ~ expressions.* 그는 늘 표현을 완곡하게 한다. [eu-, Gk. *phēmi* say]

eu·phon·ic [ju:fánik / -fɔ́n-], **-i·cal** [-ikəl] *adj.* **1** having to do with euphony. 발음 편의상의. **2** =euphonious. [*euphony*]

eu·pho·ni·ous [ju:fóuniəs] *adj.* sounding well; pleasing to the ear. 음조(音調)〔어조〕가 좋은.

eu·pho·ny [jú:fəni] *n.* ⓊⒸ (*pl.* **-nies**) the state of having a pleasant sound; agreeableness of sound; a pleasing sound. 호음조(好音調); 상쾌한 어조(語調). [eu-, Gk. *phōnē* sound]

eu·pho·ri·a [ju:fɔ́:riə] *n.* **1** a feeling of great happiness. 대단한 행복감. **2** 《psychoanal.》 an exaggerated sense of wellbeing. 다행증(多幸症). [Gk., ↑]

Eu·phra·tes [ju:fréiti:z], **the** *n.* a river flowing through Mesopotamia. 유프라테스 강. 參考 그 유역은 고대 문명의 발상지.

Eur·a·sia [juəréiʒə, -ʃə] *n.* Europe and Asia. 유라시아; 구아(歐亞)(대륙). [*Europe, Asia*]

Eur·a·sian [juəréiʒən, -ʃən] *adj.* **1** of Eurasia or its people. 유라시아 (사람)의; 구아(歐亞)(인)의. **2** of mixed European and Asiatic blood. 유라시아 혼혈의. —— *n.* Ⓒ a person of mixed European and Asiatic blood. 유라시아 혼혈아.

eu·re·ka [juərí:kə] *interj.* 《Gk.》 I have found it! 알았다; 됐다; 이거다《아르키메데스가 왕관의 순금도를 재는 방법을 발견했을 때 지른 소리》.

eu·rhyth·mics [juəríðmiks] *n.* the study or art of rhythmical bodily movement, esp. as physical training. 유리드믹스《음악의 리듬을 몸의 움직임으로 표현하는 리듬 교육법》. [Gk. *eū-* good, →rhythm]

Eu·ro·dol·lars [júərədàlərz / -dɔ̀l-] *n. pl.* 《econ.》 US dollars deposited in European banks and used for international credit for increasing trade. 유로달러. [*Europe, dollar*]

:Eu·rope [júərəp] *n.* a continent to the west of Asia. 유럽. [Gk.]

:Eu·ro·pe·an [jùərəpí:ən] *adj.* of Europe or its people. 유럽(사람)의. —— *n.* Ⓒ a person of Europe. 유럽 사람.

Eu·ro·pe·an·ize [jùərəpí:ənàiz] *vt.* (P6) make (something) European style. …을 유럽식으로 하다; 유럽화하다.

European plan [–––́–̀] *n.* lodging and services only. 식사없는 숙박《유럽 방식의 호텔 요금제》.

eu·tha·na·sia [jù:θənéiʒiə, -ziə] *n.* Ⓤ the method of causing death easily and painlessly; an easy, painless death. 안사술(安死術); 안락사. [eu-, Gk. *thanatos* death]

eu·then·ics [ju:θéniks] *n. pl.* a science or art of improving living conditions. 환경 개선학; 우경학(優境學)《환경 개선으로 인류 개량을 꾀하는 학문》. [Gk. *euthēnéin* thrive]

e·vac·u·ate [ivǽkjuèit] *vt.* (P6,13) **1** move (someone or something) to a safe place. (군대)를 철수시키다; 소개〔피난〕시키다. **2** make (a house, etc.) vacant; make (something) empty. (집 따위)에서 물러나다; …을 비우다. ¶ *~ an area threatened by a forest fire* 산불로 위험해진 지역에서 주민을 피난시키다 / *The soldiers will ~ the town today.* 군인들은 오늘 시에서 철수할 게다. **3** let (waste matter) out from the body. (대소변)을 배출〔배설〕하다. ¶ *~ the bowels* 배변하다. [→vacuum]

e·vac·u·a·tion [ivæ̀kjuéiʃən] *n.* ⓊⒸ the act of evacuating; withdrawal; removal; discharge. (군대의) 철수; 철군; 소개; 물러남; 배설(물).

e·vac·u·ee [ivæ̀kjuí:] *n.* Ⓒ a person who is moved to a safe place in war time. (전시 위험 지역에서의) 소개자(疏開者); 피난자.

e·vade [ivéid] *vt.* (P6,9) get away from (something); escape; avoid. …을 (모)면하다; (회)피하다. ¶ *~ an attack* 공격을 피하다 / *~ pursuit* 추적을 피하다 / *~ the law* 법망을 뚫다 / *~ a duty* 〔*an obligation*〕 의무를〔책임을〕 회피하다 / *~ a question* 질문을 어물어물

넘기다. [L. *vado* go]

e·val·u·ate [ivǽljuèit] *vt.* (P6) find or decide the value or the amount of (something); estimate. …의 가치를 검토하다; …을 평가[어림]하다. ¶ ~ *an old house* 낡은 집의 가격을 평가하다 / ~ *an argument* 의론을 면밀히 검토하다. [→value]

e·val·u·a·tion [ivæ̀ljuéiʃən] *n.* Ⓤ the act of evaluation; the state of being evaluated; valuation. 평가; 감정; 어림.

ev·a·nesce [èvənés, ⌐—⌐] *vi.* (P1) disappear gradually like smoke; vanish; fade away. 점차 사라져 가다; 스러지다. [→vanish]

ev·a·nes·cence [èvənésns, ⌐—⌐] *n.* disappearance; vanishing; evanescent quality. 사라져 없어짐; 스러짐. ¶ ~ *of vapor* 김의 소실(消失).

ev·a·nes·cent [èvənésənt] *adj.* soon passing away; quickly disappearing. 곧 사라지는; 순식간의. ¶ *The joys of life are* ~. 인생의 기쁨이란 덧없는 것이다.

e·van·gel [ivǽndʒəl] *n.* **1** ((*arch.*)) ((*E-*)) any of the Gospels. 복음서. **2** a political or other creed. (정치상·도덕상의) 지도 원리; 정책. [eu-, →angel]

e·van·gel·ic [ìːvændʒélik, èvən-], **-i·cal** [-ikəl] *adj.* of, based on, or according to the teachings of the Gospels or the New Testament. 복음[전도]의; 복음주의의.

e·van·gel·ist [ivǽndʒəlìst] *n.* Ⓒ **1** a preacher of the Gospel, esp. a traveling preacher. (복음의) 선교사; 전도자. **2** ((*E-*)) one of the four writers of the Gospels, Matthew, Mark, Luke, or John. 복음서 저자.

e·van·ge·lize [ivǽndʒəlàiz] *vt.* (P6) preach the gospel to; convert to Christianity. …에게 전도(傳道)하다; 기독교로 개종시키다.

e·vap·o·rate [ivǽpərèit] *vi.* (P1) **1** change into vapor; become vapor and disappear. 증발하다. ¶ *All the water in the dish has evaporated.* 접시 안의 물이 모두 증발해 버렸다. **2** ((*fig.*)) vanish; disappear; die. 사라지다; 죽다. ¶ *His hopes evaporated when he saw his enemies.* 적들을 보았을 때 그의 희망은 무산되었다. —*vt.* (P6) **1** cause (a liquid) to change into gas. …을 증발시키다. ¶ *Heat evaporates water.* 열은 물을 증발시킨다. **2** remove water from (fruit, etc.). (과일 따위)의 수분을[물기를] 빼다. ¶ *evaporated milk* 농축 우유; 연유(煉乳) / ~ *fruit* 과일을 건조시키다. [→vapor]

e·vap·o·ra·tion [ivæ̀pəréiʃən] *n.* ⓊⒸ the act of evaporating. 증발; 탈수.

e·va·sion [ivéiʒən] *n.* **1** Ⓤ the act of evading; escape; esp. an avoiding of a duty. 도피; (책임의) 회피; 탈세. ¶ *the* ~ *of one's duties* 자기 책임의 회피 / *Legal non-payment of tax is called 'tax avoidence', illegal non-payment is 'tax* ~*'.* 세금의 합법적 체납은 과세 회피[절세]라 하고, 불법적인 것은 탈세라 한다. **2** Ⓒ a means of evading; a trick to avoid something. 어물쩍 넘김; 둔사(遁辭); 발뺌. ¶ *His answer was a mere* ~. 그의 대답은 발뺌에 불과했다. [→evade]

e·va·sive [ivéisiv] *adj.* tending or trying to evade. 회피적인; 둔사[구실]의; 발뺌의; 둘러대는. ● **e·va·sive·ly** [-li] *adv.* **e·va·sive·ness** [-nis] *n.*

·**eve** [iːv] *n.* Ⓒ **1** evening or day before a holiday or some other special day. (축제일 따위의) 전야; 전날; 이브. ¶ *Christmas Eve* 크리스마스 이브 / *New Year's Eve* 섣달 그믐날. **2** time just before some event. (어떤 일의) 직전. ¶ *on the* ~ *of the event* 사건의 직전에; 막 …하려는 순간에. **3** ((*poet.*)) evening. 저녁; 밤. [E.]

Eve [iːv] *n.* ((Bible)) the first woman, Adam's wife. 이브. [Heb. = life]

a daughter of Eve, a woman. 여성.

:e·ven[1] [íːvən] *adj.* **1** (of a surface) flat; smooth. 평평한; 평탄한; 반반한; 반드러운. ¶ *an* ~ *surface* 평평한 표면 / *an* ~ *country* 평지 / *as* ~ *as glass* 유리처럼 반드러운 / *The country is* ~*, with no hills.* 국토는 산이 없고 평탄하다. **2** (of motion, quality, etc.) regular; not changing; uniform. 규칙적인; 불변의; 한결같은. ¶ *an* ~ *color* 채지지 않은 색; 고른 빛깔 / *an* ~ *tempo* 일정한 박자 / *the* ~ *beat of the heart* 심장의 규칙적인 고동 / *keep at an* ~ *temperature* 일정한 온도를 유지하다 / *I could hear her* ~ *breathing.* 그녀의 고른 숨소리가 들렸다. **3** (of temper, etc.) calm; peaceful. 평정[고요]한; 평화로운. ¶ *an* ~ *temper* 차분한 기질 / *He returned to his* ~ *way of life.* 다시 이전의 평온한 생활로 돌아갔다. **4** (of a line) on the same line; at the same level. 같은 선[면]상의; 같은 높이의. ¶ *houses* ~ *with each other* 같은 높이의 집들 / *The snow was* ~ *with the roof.* 눈은 지붕 높이까지 쌓였다. **5** equal; equally balanced. 같은; 균등한; 호각의; 대등한. ¶ ~ *scores* 동점 / *an* ~ *contest* 대등한 시합 / ~ *quantities of two substances* 같은 양의 두 물질 / *They had* ~ *shares of the profit.* 그들은 이익을 같은 몫으로 나눠 가졌다. **6** fair; impartial. 공정[공평]한; 공명 정대한. ¶ *an* ~ *bargain* 공정한 거래 / ~ *treatment* 공평한 취급 / ~ *justice* 공정한 재판. **7** exact; precise. 끝수[우수리] 없는; 정확한; 엄밀한. ¶ *an* ~ *hundred* 딱 100달러 / *It cost an* ~ *$8.* 정확히 8달러 들었다. **8** (of a number) that can be divided by two. 짝수의(opp. odd, uneven). ¶ *Eight is an* ~ *number.* 8은 우수[짝수]다.

break even, ((*colloq.*)) neither gain nor lose. 득실 없이 되다; 수지 균형이 맞게 되다.

get [***be***] ***even with,*** (*have one's revenge on*) *someone.* …에게 대갚음하다; 보복[복수]하다.

of even date, ((comm.)) of the same date. 같은 날짜의.

The odds* 〔*chances*〕 *are even. The chances are the same for or against. 승산은 반반이다.

— *vt.* (P6,7) 《*up*》 make (something) level, equal, or balanced. …을 평평하게〔같게, 균등하게〕 하다. ¶ *You've paid for the meal, so if I pay for the taxi that'll ~ things up.* 네가 식대를 냈으니, 내가 택시 요금을 낸다면 공평하게 된다.

— *vi.* become level, equal, or balanced. 평평해〔같아, 평등해〕지다.

even up on, 《U.S.》 =get even with.

— *adv.* **1** in an even manner; equally. 평평〔평탄〕하게; 같게; 대등〔균등〕하게. **2** 《with *comperative degree*》 still; yet. 더; 더욱(더); 더 한층. ¶ *His error was ~ worse.* 그의 잘못은 더욱 나빴다 / *This book is ~ better than that.* 이 책은 그것보다 더 낫다. **3** though it would not be expected. …조차; …도; (설사) …라도. ¶ *He loves ~ his enemies.* 그는 자신의 원수들조차 사랑한다 / *Even now it is too late.* 이제라도 너무 늦다 / *Even young children can understand it.* 어린애들이라도 그것은 알 수 있다 / *He never ~ opened the letter.* 그는 편지를 뜯지도 않았다. **4** indeed; truely. 정말이지; 확실히; 게다가 그것도. ¶ *He is ready, ~ eager to fight it.* 그는 각오가 그것도 싸울 각오가 돼 있다. **5** 《*arch.*》 just; precisely. 바로; 바로 …처럼. ¶ *It turned out ~ as I expected.* 바로 예상했던 대로 되었다. [E.]

even as, **a**) just as; just like. …와 마찬가지로; …와 같이. **b**) at the very time. 바로 그 때. ¶ *She left ~ as you came.* 그녀는 네가 오던 바로 그 때 떠났다.

even if 〔***though***〕, in spite of the fact that…. 비록 …할지라도; …라고 하더라도. ¶ *I'll do ~ if I get scold.* 욕은 먹더라도 나는 하겠다.

e·ven² [íːvən] *n.* Ⓒ 《*poet.*》 evening. 저녁; 밤. [E.]

e·ven-hand·ed [íːvənhǽndid] *adj.* fair; just. 공평한; 공명 정대한. ¶ *~ justice* 공정한 재판. [*even¹*]

:eve·ning [íːvniŋ] *n.* Ⓒ 《sometimes *sing.* without *art.*》 **1** the last part of a day; time between sunset and night. 저녁(때); 해질녘; 밤. ¶ *in the ~* 저녁에; 밤에 / *early* 〔*late*〕 *in the ~* 초저녁에〔저녁 늦게〕 / *musical evenings* 음악의 밤 / *this* 〔*tomorrow, yesterday*〕 *~* 오늘〔내일, 어제〕 저녁 / *on Friday ~* 금요일 밤에 / *at six-thirty in the ~ on December 4th* 12월 4일 저녁 6시 30분에 / *as the ~ proceeds* 저녁이 깊어짐에 따라. **2** the last part of one's life, etc. 늘그막; 만년; 쇠퇴기. ¶ *the ~ of one's life* 인생의 황혼기; 만년 / *People look forward to security in the ~ of their lives.* 사람들은 자신들의 노후가 무사 안이하기를 바란다.

— *adj.* in, of, or for the evening. 저녁(때)의. [E.]

evening dress [⌐–⌐] *n.* formal clothes worn in the evening. 야회복.

evening star [⌐–⌐] *n.* 《*the ~*》 the star to be noticed clearly in the west after sunset, usu. Venus. 개밥바라기; 태백성(太白星); 금성.

e·ven·ly [íːvənli] *adv.* in an even manner. 평평〔평탄〕하게; 같게; 균등하게. [→even¹]

e·ven·song [íːvənsɔ̀ːŋ, -sɔ̀ŋ] *n.* a church service said or sung in the late afternoon or early evening. 만도(晩禱); 저녁기도. [→even²]

:e·vent [ivént] *n.* Ⓒ **1** an important happening; an occurrence. 생긴〔벌어진〕 일; 사건. ¶ *a historical ~* 역사상의 사건 / *school events* 학교 행사 / *a chain of events* 일련의 사건들 / *It was quite an ~.* 꽤 큰 사건이었다. **2** a result; an outcome. 결과; 결말. **3** one of a series of matches in a program of sports. (경기 프로 중의) 한 경기. ¶ *a main ~* 주요 종목; 본경기 / *The next ~ will be the 100 meters race.* 다음 경기는 백미터 경주다. [L. *venio* come]

at all events =***in any event,*** in any case; no matter what happens. 좌우간; 어쨌든; 여하튼. ¶ *He is not clever, but at all events he works well.* 똑똑지는 않지만 어쨌든 그는 일을 잘한다.

in either event, whichever happens. 어떻든; 어차피. ¶ *I'm going by car or by foot, but in either ~ I'll need money.* 타고 가든 걸어가든 하겠다. 그러나 어떻든 돈이 필요하다.

in that event, then; in that case. 그 경우에는; 그렇게 되면.

in the event, as it happened; when it actually happened. (결과로서) 실제는; 결국. ¶ *We're afraid he would be nervous on stage. But in the ~ he performed beautifully.* 우리는 그가 무대에서 흥분하지 않을까 걱정했다. 그러나 결국 훌륭하게 연기를 해냈다.

in the event of, in case of; if there is; if there should happen to be. 만일 …한 경우에는. ¶ *In the ~ of rain, the party will be held indoors.* 비가 올 경우엔 파티는 실내에서 개최될 것이다.

e·vent·ful [ivéntfəl] *adj.* **1** full of events, esp. important events. 사건이 많은; 다사(多事)한. ¶ *He's led quite an ~ life.* 파란 많은 생애를 보냈다. **2** having important results; important. 중대한 (결과를 가져오는); 중요한.

e·ven·tide [íːvəntàid] *n.* Ⓤ 《*poet.*》 evening. 저녁; 밤. [*even²*]

e·ven·tu·al [ivéntʃuəl] *adj.* **1** coming as a result of a series of events; final. 결과로서 일어나는; 종국의; 최후의. ¶ *the ~ reform of society* 결국은 일어날 사회 개혁. **2** depending on future events; possible. (추세에 따라) 일어날 수 있는; 있을 수 있는. ¶ *his ~ death* 그의 우발적인 사망. [*event*]

e·ven·tu·al·i·ty [ivèntʃuǽləti] *n.* (*pl.* **-ties**) **1** Ⓒ an event or a condition that may happen. 예측 못할 사건; 장래 일어날

수 있는 사건. ¶ *We must be prepared for all eventualities.* 우리는 일어날 수도 있는 모든 일에 대비해야 한다. **2** Ⓤ the state of being eventual; possibility. 일어날〔있을〕 수 있음; 우발성.

*__e·ven·tu·al·ly__ [ivéntʃuəli] *adv.* in the end; at last; finally. 마침내; 최후에는; 언젠가는. ¶ *He will be caught* ~. 그는 언젠가는 잡힌다.

e·ven·tu·ate [ivéntʃuèit] *vi.* (P2A,3) come out in the end; happen finally; result. …한 결과가 되다; 결국 …이 되다. ¶ ~ *well* 좋은 결과로 끝나다 / *A rapid rise in prices soon eventuated in mass unemployment.* 물가 폭등은 마침내 대량 실업을 가져왔다. [*event*[1]]

:**ev·er** [évər] *adv.* **1** at any time; until now. 언젠가; 이제까지; 일찍이. ¶ *Nothing* ~ *happens in the town.* 그 마을엔 결코 아무 일도 일어나지 않는다 / *Have you* ~ *been there ?* 그 곳에 가 본 적이 있나 / *Did you* ~ *hear such stuff ?* 그런 것을 들어 본 적이 있는가 / *Is he* ~ *at home ?* 그녀석 집에 붙어 있는 적이 있는지 모르겠어 / *He is working as hard as* ~. 이제까지와 같이 열심히 일하고 있다 / *It was the best thing I* ~ *saw.* 일찍이 본 것 중 가장 좋은 것이었다 / *He is a liar if* ~ *there was one.* 거짓말쟁이라는 게 있다면 그 자야말로 거짓말꾼이었다 / *He is the greatest poet that* ~ *lived in England.* 이제까지 영국 시인으로서는 그가 최대의 시인이다. **2** 《emphasizing a word or phrase》 ¶ *Why* ~ *don't you eat your dinner ?* 대체 식사를 왜 안 하는 거지 / *What* ~ *do you mean ?* 도대체 무슨 말이야 / *When* ~ *will he come ?* 대관절 그 사람 언제 온다는 거지 / *Who* ~ *can it be ?* 대체 누구일까 / *Be as quick as* ~ *you can.* 될 수 있는 대로 빨리 해라. **3** 《*arch.*》 at all times; always. 언제나; 항상. ¶ *repeat* ~ *the same words* 늘 같은 말을 되풀이하다 / *He is* ~ *the same.* 그는 여전하다. [E.]

Did you ever ? Did you ever hear or see the like ? 이런 것 본〔들은〕 적이 있는가; 참말인가; 이거 놀랍군.

ever after, continuously from that time. 그 후 죽; …한 이래 내내. ¶ *They lived happy* ~ *after.* 그들은 이후 내내 행복하게 살았다.

ever and anon, 《*arch.*》 from time to time. 이따금; 가끔.

ever since, from that time until now. 그 후 죽〔내내〕. ¶ *It has rained* ~ *since.* 그 후 죽 비가 내렸다.

ever so, **a**) 《in a *concessive clause*》 however. 비록 …할지라도(cf. *never so*). ¶ *Be it* ~ *so humble, there is no place like home.* 비록 아무리 보잘것없어도 내 집만한 곳은 없다. **b**) very. 매우. ¶ *Thank you* ~ *so much.* 대단히 감사합니다.

for ever (***and ever***) = ***for ever and a day,*** always; eternally. 언제나; 영원히.

hardly 〔***scarcely***〕 ***ever,*** very seldom. 아주 드물다; 좀처럼 …하는 일이 없다.

seldom if ever = ***seldom or never,*** very seldom. 좀처럼 …않다〔없다〕.

Ev·er·est [évərist], **Mount** *n.* the highest mountain in the world, in Nepal and Tibet. 에베레스트산. 參考 해발 8,848m.

ev·er·green [évərgrì:n] *adj.* (of trees, shrubs, etc.) having green leaves throughout the year. 상록(常綠)의(cf. *deciduous*). — *n.* Ⓒ **1** an evergreen plant. 상록수(樹)〔식물〕. **2** 《*pl.*》 evergreen twigs or branches used for decoration, esp. at Christmas. (크리스마스의 장식용) 상록수의 나뭇가지. [*ever*]

*__ev·er·last·ing__ [èvərlǽstiŋ, -lá:s-] *adj.* **1** lasting forever; eternal. 영원한. ¶ ~ *fame* 불후의 명성 / *the* ~ *verities* 영구 불변의 진리. **2** lasting a long time. 영속성의. **3** lasting indefinitely; repeated too often; tiresome. 끝없는; 끊임없는; 따분한. ¶ *an* ~ *noise* 끊임없는 소음 / *I can't stand his* ~ *jokes.* 나는 그의 따분한 농담엔 넌더리가 난다.

— *n.* **1** Ⓤ eternity. 영구; 영원. **2** 《*the E-*》 God. 신(神); 하느님. [*ever*]

ev·er·last·ing·ly [èvərlǽstiŋli, -lá:st-] *adv.* in an everlasting manner. 영원〔영구〕히; 끝없이.

ev·er·more [èvərmɔ́:r] *adv.* always; continuously; forever. 항상; 끊임없이; 영원히. ¶ *He swore to love her* (*for*) ~. 그녀를 영원히 사랑하겠다고 맹세했다. [*ever*]

for evermore, forever. 영원히.

:**eve·ry** [évri:] *adj.* **1** each of all. 각 …마다; 누구나 모두. ¶ ~ *one of you* 너희들 모두 / *They listened to* ~ *word of his lecture.* 그들은 그의 강연의 말을 한마디한마디 놓치지 않고 모두 들었다 / *Every man cannot be a Newton at will.* 모든 사람이 마음대로 뉴튼 같은 사람이 될 수 있는 건 아니다. **2** all possible; the greatest. 가능한 한의; 온갖. ¶ *I have* ~ *confidence in him.* 나는 그를 아주 신임하고 있다 / *He showed me* ~ *kindness.* 그는 내게 온갖 친절을 다했다. **3** each. 각기. ¶ ~ *other day* 이틀마다; 하루 걸러 / *He comes* ~ *third day.* 그는 사흘마다 온다. [*ever, each*]

every bit, **a**) quite; equally. 아주; …와 같이. ¶ *I am* ~ *bit as pleased as you are.* 선생과 마찬가지로 저도 기쁩니다. **b**) =every inch.

every inch, in all respects; completely. 어느 모로 보나; 어디까지나. ¶ *He is* ~ *inch a gentleman.* 그는 어디까지나 신사다.

every now and then = ***every now and again,*** from time to time; occasionally. 때때로; 가끔. ¶ *I write him* ~ *now and then.* 가끔 그에게 편지를 보낸다.

every time, **a**) always; without exception. 언제나; 항상. **b**) 《as *conjunction*》 whenever. …할 때마다. ¶ *Every time I went to his house, he was out.* 집으로 찾아갈 때마다 그는 나가고 없었다.

every which way, 《*colloq.*》 in all directions; in complete disorder. 사방 팔방에; 혼

란에 빠져.

:eve·ry·bod·y [évribàdi, -bʌ̀di / -bɔ̀di] *pron.* everyone; every person. 누구나; 모두; 모든 사람. ¶ *Everybody has the right to speak his mind.* 모든 사람은 자기 생각을 말할 권리가 있다.

:eve·ry·day [évridèi] *adj.* **1** daily; of every day. 매일의; 날마다의. ¶ ~ *life* 나날의 생활. **2** for ordinary days. 일상의; 평상의. ¶ ~ *clothes* 평상복(cf. *Sunday clothes*). **3** ordinary; not new. 보통의; 평범한; 예사로운. ¶ ~ *affairs* 평범한 일 / *a placid,* ~ *scene* 잔잔하고도 평범한 풍경.

:eve·ry·one [évriwʌ̀n, -wən] *pron.* everybody; each person. 누구나; 모두. ¶ *I stayed at work after* ~ *else had gone home.* 모두가 귀가한 다음 나는 남아서 일을 했다.

:eve·ry·thing [évriθìŋ] *pron.* **1** all things. 모든 것; 만사. ¶ *know* ~ 무엇이나 알다 / *Everything has its drawback.* 모든 건 각기 결점이 있기 마련이다. **2** the most important thing. 가장 중요한 것. ¶ *Honor is* ~ *to him.* 그에겐 명예가 무엇보다도 소중한 것이다 / *Money is not* ~. 돈이 전부는 아니다.

and everything, and so on. 그 밖의 이것저것. ¶ *She's worried about her work and* ~. 그녀는 자기 일과 그 밖의 것들로 고민했다.

before everything, first of all. 우선 첫째로; 무엇보다 먼저.

:eve·ry·where [évrihwὲər] *adv.* in all places; wherever. 어디에나; 도처에(서). ¶ *He was welcomed* ~ *he went.* 그는 어디에 가서나 환영을 받았다 / *Clean the house* — ~ *looks so dirty!* 집을 청소해라. 어디건 너무 지저분하다.

e·vict [ivíkt] *vt.* (P6,13) make (someone) go away from land, a building, etc. by the power of law; expel. …을 퇴거시키다; 쫓아내다. ¶ *If you don't pay your rent you'll be evicted.* 집세를 안 내면 쫓아 내겠소. [L. *vinco* conquer]

e·vic·tion [ivíkʃən] *n.* Ⓤ Ⓒ the act of evicting; the state of being evicted; expulsion. 내쫓음; 퇴거; 추방.

:ev·i·dence [évidəns] *n.* Ⓤ Ⓒ anything that makes clear the truth; ground for belief; a proof. 증거; 표시; 흔적. ¶ *the* ~ *of sight* 목격에 의한 증거 / *the* ~ *for* 〔*against*〕 *the accused* 피고인에게 유리〔불리〕한 증거 / *collect* ~ 증거를 수집하다 / *give* 〔*hear*〕 ~ 증언을 하다〔듣다〕 / *give false* ~ *on* …에 관하여 위증하다 / *There is enough* ~ *to prove him innocent.* 그의 무죄를 증명할 증거는 충분하다 / *Her flushed look was visible* ~ *of her fever.* 벌겋게 상기된 그녀의 얼굴은 그녀가 열이 있다는 명백한 증거였다.

bear* 〔*give*〕 *evidence (= *show signs*) ***of*** *something.* …의 흔적을 보이다.

in evidence, easily seen or noticed; clear. 뚜렷이 보이어; 두드러진.

— *vt.* (P6) make (something) clear by evidence; prove. …을 입증하다. ¶ *His genius was evidenced in his first novel.* 첫 소설에서 그의 천재성이 역력했다. [L. *video* see]

·ev·i·dent [évidənt] *adj.* easy to see or understand; plain; clear. 분명한; 명백한. ¶ *Her dislike of me was* ~. 그녀가 나를 싫어하는 것이 명백했다.

:ev·i·dent·ly [évidəntli, èvidént-, évidènt-] *adv.* plainly; clearly. 분명히; 명백히. ¶ *He was* ~ *not well.* 분명히 그는 좋지 않았다.

:e·vil [í:vəl] *adj.* **1** morally bad or wrong; sinful; wicked. (도덕적으로) 못된; (사)악한. ¶ ~ *conduct* 못된 행실; 비행 / *an* ~ *life* 부도덕한 생활 / *the Evil One* 악마. **2** harmful; injurious. 해악을 끼치는; 유해한. ¶ ~ *laws* 악법. **3** unfortunate. 불운한; 수사나운; 불길한. ¶ ~ *news* 〔*tidings*〕 흉보(凶報). **4** very unpleasant. 아주 불쾌한. ¶ *What an* ~ *smell!* 고약한 냄새구나.

fall upon* 〔*on*〕 *evil days, have ill luck. 불운을 만나다.

in an evil hour, unfortunately. 운 나쁘게; 불행히도.

— *n.* **1** Ⓤ something bad; sin; wickedness. 악(惡); 사악; 악행. ¶ *good and* ~ 선악 / *the spirit of* ~ 악령(惡靈). **2** Ⓒ a thing that causes harm or injury. 해악; 악폐; 재해; 불운. ¶ *wish someone* ~ 아무를 저주하다.

●**e·vil·ly** [-vəli] *adv.* **e·vil·ness** [-nis] *n.* [E.]

e·vil·do·er [í:vəldù:ər, ⌐—⌐—] *n.* Ⓒ a person who does evil. 나쁜 짓을 하는 사람; 악인.

evil eye [⌐—⌐] *n.* 《usu. *the* ~》 (a spell put on someone with) a look believed to be capable of inflicting harm. 흉안(凶眼)《한번 노려보면 재앙이 미친다고 함》.

e·vil-look·ing [í:vəllú:kiŋ] *adj.* having a disagreeable appearance; ill-looking. 인상이 좋지 않은.

e·vil-mind·ed [í:vəlmáindid] *adj.* having an evil mind; wicked. 악한 마음이 있는; 사악한; 못된.

e·vince [ivíns] *vt.* (P6) show clearly (one's quality, feeling, etc.); prove. (성질·기분 따위)를 분명히 나타내다; 증명하다. ¶ ~ *great sorrow at parting* 이별에 즈음하여 크게 슬퍼하다 / ~ *one's desire to go home* 귀향의 희망을 밝히다. [→evict]

e·vis·cer·ate [ivísərèit] *vt.* (P6) disembowel. 창자를 빼어내다. ¶ ~ *a chicken* 닭의 창자를 꺼내다. ●**e·vis·cer·a·tion** [ivìsəréiʃən] *n.* [→viscera]

e·voke [ivóuk] *vt.* (P6) call forth; bring out; summon. …을 불러일으키다; 환기(喚起)하다; 불러내다. ¶ *That old film evoked memories of my childhood.* 그 옛 영화를 보니 내 어릴 적 생각이 났다 / ~ *a laugh* 〔*admiration*〕 웃음〔경탄〕을 자아내다. ●**ev·o·ca·tion** [èvəkéiʃən] *n.* [L. *voco* call]

ev·o·lu·tion [èvəlú:ʃən / ì:və-] *n.* Ⓤ **1**

the process of being formed; growth; development. 진전; 발전; 전개; 진화. ¶ *the ~ of the drama* 극의 전개 / *the ~ of a chicken from an egg* 알에서 병아리로의 생육. **2** 《biol.》 the process that all living things have developed from lower and simpler forms of life. 진화(론). ¶ *the ~ of man* 인류의 진화 / *the theory of ~* 진화론. **3** Ⓒ 《mil.》 a movement of ships or of soldiers, planned beforehand. 기동 연습(機動演習). [→evolve]

ev·o·lu·tion·al [èvəlúːʃənəl / ìːvə-] *adj.* =evolutionary.

ev·o·lu·tion·ar·y [èvəlúːʃənèri / ìːvə-] *adj.* **1** of evolution; developed step by step. 발전〔발달〕의; 전개의. **2** agreeing with the theory of evolution. 진화(론)의.

ev·o·lu·tion·ist [èvəlúːʃənist / ìːvə-] *n.* Ⓒ a person who believes the theory of evolution. 진화론자.

e·volve [ivɑ́lv / ivɔ́lv] *vt.* (P6) **1** develop gradually. …을 전개하다; 발전시키다. ¶ *~ a plan* 계획을 발전시키다 / *They evolved a new system for running the factory.* 그들은 공장 조업을 위한 새로운 조직을 전개해 갔다. **2** develop (a living thing) to a higher state. …을 진화시키다. **3** give off (heat, gas, etc.). (열·가스 따위)를 방출하다. — *vi.* (P1) **1** be developed. 발전하다; 전개하다. **2** reach a more highly organized state by a process of growth and change. 진화하다.

● **e·volve·ment** [-mənt] *n.* [L. *volvo* roll]

ewe [juː, jou] *n.* Ⓒ a female sheep. 암양(羊)(opp. ram). [E.]

ew·er [júːər] *n.* Ⓒ a wide-mouthed water pitcher. (아가리가 넓은) 물병. [→aquarium]

〈ewer〉

Ex. Exodus.

ex- [eks-] *pref.* **1** out of; from; out. '…으로부터, …에서, 밖으로'의 뜻. ¶ *exit.* **2** utterly; thorough. '철저하게'의 뜻. ¶ *exterminate.* **3** beyond. '…의 한계 이상으로'의 뜻. ¶ *excess.* **4** former; formerly. '전(前)…, 전의'의 뜻. ¶ *ex-governor* 《보통 하이픈을 붙임》. [L.]

:ex·act [igzǽkt] *adj.* accurate; strictly correct; precise. 정확한; 정밀한. ¶ *an ~ memory* 정확한 기억 / *an ~ observer* 정확한 관측자 / *the ~ sum* 〔*figure*〕 정확한 액수〔숫자〕 / *~ instruments* 〔*sciences*〕 정밀 기계〔과학〕 / *an ~ ear for music* 음악을 듣는 정확한 귀 / *It was sometimes last week, but I can't remember the ~ day.* 지난 주 언제였는데 정확한 날짜는 기억이 안 난다.
— *vt.* (P6,13) require; claim; insist upon. …을 요구하다; 강제〔강요〕하다. ¶ *~ money of* 〔*from*〕 *someone* 아무에게서 강제로 돈을 거두다 / *~obedience and respect from one's children* 자식들에게 순종과 존경을 강요하다 / *This work exacts the closest attention.* 이 일은 아주 세심한 주의가 요구된다. [L. *exigo* require]

ex·act·ing [igzǽktiŋ] *adj.* **1** making rigorous demands; requiring much; severe; strict. 가혹한; 엄한. ¶ *an ~ teacher* 엄한 선생님 / *an ~ employer* 가혹한 고용주. **2** requiring great care, effort, or patience. 힘드는. ¶ *an ~ task* 힘든 일.

ex·ac·tion [igzǽkʃən] *n.* **1** Ⓤ the act of exacting. 강제; 강요; 가혹한 요구. ¶ *the exactions of the teaching profession* 교직의 강요. **2** Ⓒ something exacted, esp. a tax, etc. which a person is forced to pay. 강제로 받아낸 돈; 가혹한 세금.

ex·act·i·tude [igzǽktətjùːd] *n.* =exactness.

:ex·act·ly [igzǽktli] *adv.* **1** in an exact manner; accurately; precisely. 정확히; 엄밀히. ¶ *not ~ the same* 반드시 똑같지는 않은 / *It is now ~ ten o'clock.* 정확히 열 시다 / *That's ~ what he said.* 바로 그가 말한 대로다. **2** just; quite. 바로. ¶ *The doctor told him not to smoke, but he did ~ the opposite.* 의사는 담배를 끊도록 일렀으나, 그는 바로 그 반대되는 짓을 했다. **3** just so; quite right. (동의·찬성을 나타내어) (바로) 맞아; 맞았어.

ex·act·ness [igzǽktnis] *n.* Ⓤ the quality of being exact; precision. 정확; 엄정.

·ex·ag·ger·ate [igzǽdʒərèit] *vt.* (P6) **1** think of or express (something) as greater than it really is; go beyond the truth; overstate. …을 과장하다; 침소 봉대하다 (opp. understate). ¶ *~ one's own importance* 자기를 과대시하다; 우쭐해 하다 / *~ the difficulties of a situation* 상황의 어려움을 과장해 말하다 / *an exaggerated account of one's sufferings* 과장된 고난 이야기 / *It is impossible to ~ the importance of health.* 건강의 중요성은 아무리 과장해도 족하지 않다. **2** increase or enlarge abnormally. 비정상으로 크게 하다.
— *vi.* (P1) give an exaggerated thought or expression of something. 과장해서 말하다〔쓰다〕.

● **ex·ag·ger·a·tor** [-ər] *n.* [L. *agger* heap]

ex·ag·ger·a·tion [igzæ̀dʒəréiʃən] *n.* **1** Ⓤ the act of exaggerating; the state of being exaggerated. 과장(됨). ¶ *To call it a mountain would be an ~; it's more of a hill.* 그것을 산이라 하기엔 좀 과장이고 구릉보다는 좀 크다. **2** Ⓒ an exaggerated statement. 과장된 이야기; 침소 봉대한 말.

·ex·alt [igzɔ́ːlt] *vt.* (P6,13) **1** make (someone) higher in rank, honor, power, character, quality, etc. (명예·품위 따위)를 높이다. ¶ *He was exalted to the position of president.* 그는 사장으로 승진했다. **2** fill (someone) with pride, joy, or noble feeling; praise. …을 우쭐하게 하다; 높이 칭찬하다. ¶ *~someone to the skies* 아무를 극구 칭찬하다〔치켜세우다〕. [L. *altus* high]

ex·al·ta·tion [ègzɔːltéiʃən] *n.* Ⓤ **1** the act of exalting; the state of being exalted. 높임; 고양(高揚). **2** feeling of great joy, pride, etc. 우쭐함; 득의; 의기 양양; 광희(狂喜). ¶ *with great* ~ 의기 양양해서; 우쭐해서.

ex·alt·ed [igzɔ́ːltid] *adj.* **1** elevated in rank, honor, etc. (지위·신분이) 높은. ¶ *an* ~ *personage* 고귀한 사람. **2** noble; elevated; lofty. 고상한; 숭고한. ¶ *an* ~ *style of writing* 격조 높은 문체.

ex·am [igzǽm] *n.* Ⓒ 《*colloq.*》 examination. 시험.

·**ex·am·i·na·tion** [igzæ̀mənéiʃən] *n.* **1** Ⓤ Ⓒ the act of examining; the state of being examined. 검사; 조사; 검열. ¶ *make an* ~ *of* …을 조사하다/ *an* ~ *of a botanical specimen* 식물 표본의 검사. **2** Ⓒ a careful test of someone's knowledge, ability, etc.; an inquiry into someone's physical condition. 시험; 고사; 진단; 진찰. ¶ *an entrance* ~ 입학 시험 / *a physical* ~ 건강 진단 / *pass* 〔*fail in*〕 *an* ~ 시험에 합격〔실패〕하다 / *take an* ~ *in English* 영어 시험을 보다 / *The teacher gave us an* ~ *in history.* 선생님은 우리에게 역사 시험을 치르게 했다. **3** Ⓒ 《law》 a questioning (of a witness). 심문. [↓]

sit for 〔***take***〕 ***an examination,*** take or undergo an examination. 시험을 치르다.

under examination, being examined. 조사〔시험〕 중에.

:**ex·am·ine** [igzǽmin] *vt.* (P6,13) **1** look at or into (something) carefully to find out the facts and learn about them; inspect; investigate. …을 조사〔검사〕하다; 심사하다. ¶ ~ *oneself* 자성(自省)하다 / *have one's health examined* 건강 진단을 받다 / ~ *old records* 옛 기록을 조사하다. **2** 《*in*》 test (a pupil, etc.) by questions. …을 시험하다. ¶ ~ *pupils in history* 학생들에게 역사 시험을 뵈다. [L. *examen* a weighing]

examine into, inquire into. …을 조사하다. ¶ ~ *into a matter* 문제를 조사하다.

ex·am·i·nee [igzæ̀məníː] *n.* Ⓒ a person who is being examined. 수험자; 심리를 받는 사람.

ex·am·in·er [igzǽmənər] *n.* Ⓒ a person who examines. 시험관; 심사원; 조사원.

:**ex·am·ple** [igzǽmpəl, -zɑ́ːm-] *n.* Ⓒ **1** one part that shows what the whole is like; a sample; a specimen. 견본; 표본; 보기. ¶ *a good* ~ *of Shakespeare's verse* 셰익스피어 시(詩)의 좋은 예 / *a classic* ~ *of medieval architecture* 중세 건축의 전형적인 보기. **2** one thing or event that agrees with the general rule. 실례. ¶ *an* ~ *of his work* 그가 한 일의 한 예 / *give an* ~ *of the rule* 규칙의 일례를 들다 / *by way of* ~ 한 예를 들면. **3** a fact in the past used as a key to decide matters in the present. 전례; 선례. ¶ *an action without* ~ 전례가 없는 행위. **4** a person or thing to be copied a model. 모범; 본보기. ¶ *follow someone's* ~ 아무를 본보기로 삼다 / *set a good* ~ *for* 〔*to*〕 …에게 좋은 모범을 보이다 / *He is following his father's* ~. 그는 아버지를 본받고 있다 / *He is an* ~ *for all of us.* 그는 우리 모두에게 모범이다. **5** a warning; a lesson. 본때; 경고. ¶ *Let this punishment be an* ~ *to you.* 이 처벌이 너희들에게 교훈이 되도록 해라. [→exempt]

beyond 〔***without***〕 ***example,*** having no example in the past. 전례 없는.

make an example of someone, punish someone as a warning to others. 본보기로 아무를 벌하다.

ex·as·per·ate [igzǽspərèit, -rit] *vt.* (P6) **1** 《*against*》 irritate very much; make (someone) angry. …을 약올리다; 신경을 자극하다; 성나게 하다. ¶ *The sound exasperated him.* 그 소리는 그의 신경을 건드렸다. **2** make (disease, ill feeling, etc.) worse. …을 더한층 나쁘게 하다. ¶ *Her haughty temper was exasperated by disease.* 그녀의 오만한 성품은 병으로 해서 더 심해졌다. [→asperity]

be exasperated by 〔***at***〕, get angry at. …에 화를 내다.

ex·as·per·a·tion [igzæ̀spəréiʃən] *n.* Ⓒ extreme annoyance or irritation; anger. 격노; 분격.

ex·ca·vate [ékskəvèit] *vt.* (P6) make (a hole) in the ground, etc.; dig; make (something) hollow by taking out the inner part; get or uncover (something) by digging. (구멍)을 파다; …에 구멍을 내다; (속엣것을 빼내어) 텅 비우다; …을 우벼 내다; 발굴하다. ¶ ~ *ruins* 고적을 발굴하다 / ~ *a trench* 〔*tunnel*〕 참호를〔터널을〕 파다 / *Workmen are excavating a cellar.* 인부들이 지하실을 파고 있다. [→cave]

ex·ca·va·tion [èkskəvéiʃən] *n.* **1** Ⓤ the act of excavating. 발굴; 구멍뚫이. **2** Ⓒ a hole or hollow made by digging. (파서) 우묵한 곳; 공동. **3** Ⓒ something dug up, brought to light, by excavation, as a building that had been buried. 발굴물.

ex·ca·va·tor [ékskəvèitər] *n.* Ⓒ a person or thing that excavates. 굴착자; 굴착기.

·**ex·ceed** [iksíːd] *vt.* (P6,13) **1** go beyond the limit of (something). …의 한도를 넘다. ¶ ~ *the speed limit* 제한 속도를 초과하다. **2** be more or greater than (someone); excel; surpass. …을 능가하다; …보다 낫다. ¶ ~ *someone in knowledge* 지식이라는 점에서 아무보다 낫다. [L. *cedo* go]

ex·ceed·ing [iksíːdiŋ] *adj.* very great; extreme; unusual. 과도의; 대단한; 지나친; 유다른. ¶ *an* ~ *grief* 유다른 슬픔 / *a girl of* ~ *beauty* 대단한 미모의 여자. — *adv.* 《*arch.*》 exceedingly. 몹시; 대단히.

·**ex·ceed·ing·ly** [iksíːdiŋli] *adv.* more than others; very greatly; extremely; unusually. 대단히; 몹시; 크게; 극히. ¶ *She is* ~ *beautiful.* 그녀는 대단히 아름답다.

•**ex·cel** [iksél] *v.* (**-celled, -cel·ling**) *vt.* (P6,7,13) 《*in, at, as*》 do better than (someone); surpass. …보다 낫다; 탁월하다. ¶ ~ (*another*) *in courage* 〔*as a soldier*〕 용기에서〔군인으로서〕 남보다 낫다 / ~ *others at sports* 스포츠에서 남보다 뛰어나다 / *You* ~ *me in historical knowledge.* 그는 역사 지식에서 나를 능가한다. — *vi.* (P1,2A,3) 《*in, at, as*》 be remarkably good. 뛰어나다. ¶ *He excels in mathematics.* 그는 수학에 뛰어난 실력이 있다. [L.]

ex·cel·lence [éksələns] *n.* **1** Ⓤ the state of being excellent; superiority. 탁월; 우수; 걸출. ¶ *his* ~ *in baseball* 야구에서의 그의 발군의 실력. **2** Ⓒ an excellent quality or feature. 장점; 미점(美點). [↑]

ex·cel·len·cy [éksələnsi] *n.* Ⓤ **1** 《*arch.*》 =excellence. **2** 《*E-*》 a title of honor given to an ambassador, governor, president, bishop, etc. 각하. 語法 Your 〔His, Her〕 Excellency로 쓰임.

:**ex·cel·lent** [éksələnt] *adj.* unusually good; better than others; superior. 특히 뛰어난; 탁월한; 발군의. ● **ex·cel·lent·ly** [-li] *adv.*

ex·cel·si·or [iksélsiər, ek-] *adj.* ever upward; higher still. 보다 높이; 더 높게. 參考 미국 뉴욕주(州)의 표어. — *n.* Ⓤ 《U.S.》 soft, fine, curled shavings of wood used for stuffing or packing. (채워 넣거나 짐 포장용의) 대팻밥. [L.]

:**ex·cept** [iksépt] *prep.* apart from; other than; not including. …을 제외하고; …외에는. ¶ *He works every day* ~ *Sunday.* 그는 일요일 외엔 매일 일한다 / *Everyone* ~ *her answered the question correctly.* 그녀 외엔 모두가 질문에 정확히 대답했다 / *Nothing remains for us to do,* ~ *to enjoy the fruits of our labors.* 이제 우리가 할 일은 남아 있지 않다, 다음은 그저 그 성과를 즐길 따름이다.

except for, but for; if it were not for. …가 아니라면〔아니었다면〕; …외엔. ¶ *It is good* ~ *for a few mistakes.* 몇 개의 잘못 외엔 좋다.

except that, apart from the fact that. …하다는 것 외에는. ¶ *I know nothing* ~ *that he left home early that morning.* 그 날 아침 일찍 그가 떠났다는 것 외에는 아무것도 모른다.

— *vt.* (P6,13) leave out; omit; exclude. …을 제외하다; 빼다; 생략하다.

— *conj.* 《*arch.*》 if not; unless. …이 아니면. [L. *capio* take]

ex·cept·ing [ikséptiŋ] *prep.* 《usu. *not* ~》 except; leaving out. …을 제외하고; …외에는. ¶ *We must all obey the law, not* ~ *the king.* 왕을 포함한 우리 모두 법에 따라야 한다.

:**ex·cep·tion** [iksépʃən] *n.* **1** ⒸⓊ the act of leaving out. 제외. ¶ *by way of* ~ 예외로서 / *liable* 〔*subject*〕 *to* ~ 이의를 제기할 수 있는 / *make an* ~ *of* …을 제외하다; 특별 취급하다 / *make no exceptions* 특별 취급으로 하지 않다 / *with the* ~ *of* …을 제외하고. **2** Ⓒ a person or thing left out; an unusual instance. 예외; 이례(異例). **3** objection. 반대; 이의(異議). [→except]

take exception to 〔***against***〕, object to; angry at. …에 이의를〔불복을〕 말하다; 화를 내다; 성내다. ¶ *He took* ~ *to* 〔*against*〕 *my proposal.* 그는 나의 제안에 대해 이의를 말했다.

ex·cep·tion·a·ble [iksépʃənəbəl] *adj.* liable to exception; objectionable. 반대할 수 있는; 이의를 제기할 수 있는.

ex·cep·tion·al [iksépʃənəl] *adj.* out of the ordinary; unusual; uncommon. 예외적인; 보통이 아닌. ¶ *an* ~ *promotion* 이례적인 승진 / *an* ~ *use of a word* 낱말의 예외적인 사용 / *This warm weather is* ~ *for January.* 이같이 따뜻한 날씨는 정월달치고는 이례적이다.

ex·cep·tion·al·ly [iksépʃənəli] *adv.* in an exceptional manner or way. 예외적으로; 특히; 매우.

ex·cerpt [iksə́ːrpt, ek-] *vt.* (P6,13) take (a passage) from a book, film, etc.; quote. (일부)를 발췌〔인용〕하다. — [éksəːrpt] *n.* Ⓒ a selected passage; a quotation; an extract. 발췌; 인용; 초록(抄錄). ● **ex·cerp·tion** [-pʃən, ek-] *n.* [L. *carpo* pluck]

•**ex·cess** [iksés, ékses] *n.* **1** Ⓤ too much; more than enough. 과도(함); 초과. ¶ *the* ~ *of liberty* 과도의 자유. **2** Ⓒ the amount greater than is necessary; surplus. 초과량〔액〕; 과잉(opp. lack). ¶ *an* ~ *of blood to the head* 머리에 과다한 피 / *an* ~ *of kindness* 과잉 친절 / *have an* ~ *of energy* 정력이 너무 많다. **3** Ⓤ《often *pl.*》 eating or drinking too much; immoderation. 폭음; 폭식; 부절제.

go 〔***run***〕 ***to excess,*** overdo; go too far. 과도해지다; (도를) 지나치다.

in excess of, more than. …보다 이상으로; …을 초과하여.

to 〔***in***〕 ***excess,*** too much. 극단으로. ¶ *carry something to* ~ …을 극단적으로〔지나치게〕 하다 / *eat* 〔*drink*〕 *to* ~ 과식〔폭음〕하다.

— [ékses, iksés] *adj.* beyond what is allowed; extra. 제한 밖의; 초과된; 여분의. ¶ ~ *baggage* 제한 초과 수하물 / *an* ~ *fare* 거리 초과 요금. [→exceed]

•**ex·ces·sive** [iksésiv] *adj.* too much; beyond due measure; immoderate; extreme. 과도의; 극단의.

ex·ces·sive·ly [iksésivli] *adv.* in an excessive manner; too much; too greatly. 과도하게; 극단으로.

exch. exchange; exchequer.

:**ex·change** [ikstʃéindʒ] *vt.* (P6,13) 《*for*》 give and receive; barter. …을 주고받다; 교환하다. ¶ ~ *gifts* 선물을 교환하다 / ~ *a watch for a camera* 시계를 카메라와 바꾸다 / ~ *blows* 〔*words*〕 주먹〔말〕을 주고받다; 싸우다 / *Will you* ~ *seats with me?* 저와 자리 좀 바꾸시지 않겠습니까.

— *n.* **1** Ⓤ the act of exchanging. 교환; 주고받음. ¶ *an* ~ *of prisoners* 포로의 교환 / *the* ~ *of country life for city life* 시골 생활을

버리고 도시 생활을 함 / *in ~ for a guarantee of security* 신변의 안전을 보장해 주는 대신. **2** Ⓤ a money-changer's trade. 환전업. **3** Ⓒ something exchanged for another thing. 교환물〔품〕. **4** Ⓤ mode of settling debts between different countries without use of money. 환(換); 환 시세. ¶ *a bill of ~* 환어음 / *What is the ~ today?* 오늘 환시세는 어떤가. **5** Ⓒ a place where men trade. 거래소. ¶ *the Stock Exchange* 증권 거래소. [ex-]

in exchange (for...), by way of exchange; instead of. (…와) 교환〔상환〕으로; (…의) 대상(代償)으로; …대신.

make an exchange, exchange. 교환하다.

ex·change·a·ble [ikstʃéindʒəbəl] *adj.* can be exchanged. 교환할 수 있는. ¶ *~ value* 교환 가치〔가격〕.

ex·cheq·uer [ikstʃékər, ékstʃekər] *n.* Ⓒ **1** a place where public money is kept; the Treasury. 국고(國庫). **2** 《*colloq.*》 finances; funds. 재정; 자력; 자금. **3** 《*the E-*》 《Brit.》 a department of the government which deals with public money. (영국의) 재무부. ¶ *the Chancellor of the Exchequer* (영국의) 재무부장관. [from the chequered tablecloth in the old Exchequer]

ex·cise[1] [éksaiz, -s] *n.* ⓊⒸ tax on certain articles made, sold, or consumed within a country. 물품세; 소비세(cf. *custom*). ¶ *the ~ on tobacco.* — *vt.* (P6) put an excise duty on. 소비세〔물품세〕를 과하다. [→census]

ex·cise[2] [iksáiz] *vt.* cut out; remove. …을 잘라 내다; 삭제하다. ¶ *~ passages from a book* 책에서 몇 구절 삭제하다 / *~ a tumor* 종양을 잘라 내다. [L. *caedo* cut]

ex·ci·sion [eksíʒən] *n.* **1** Ⓤ the act of excising; removal. 절제; 절단; 삭제. **2** Ⓒ something excised. 절제〔절단, 삭제〕한 것. [↑]

ex·cit·a·ble [iksáitəbəl] *adj.* can be excited; easily excited. 격하기 쉬운; 곧 흥분하는. [↓]

:ex·cite [iksáit] *vt.* (P6,7,13) **1** stir up the feelings of (someone); stimulate. …을 흥분시키다; 자극하다. ¶ *~ the audience* 청중을 흥분시키다 / *~ oneself* 흥분하다 / *~ someone to anger* 아무를 성나게 하다 / *become 〔get〕 excited at 〔by, about, over〕 his words* 그의 말에 흥분하다〔화를 내다〕 / *The patient must not be excited.* 환자는 흥분해서는 안 된다 / *Don't excite (yourself)!* 《*colloq.*》 흥분치 마시오; 냉정하시오. **2** cause (something) to awake; make (something) active. …을 불러일으키다; …을 부추기다. ¶ *~ a smile* 미소를 자아내다 / *The news excited envy in her.* 그 소식은 그녀의 부러움을 부추겼다.

● **ex·cit·er** [-ər] *n.* [L. *cieo* stir up]

ex·cit·ed·ly [iksáitidli] *adv.* in an excited manner. 흥분하여.

:ex·cite·ment [iksáitmənt] *n.* **1** Ⓤ the act of exciting; the state of being excited. 자극; 격려; 흥분. ¶ *in ~* 흥분하여 / *throw someone into ~* 아무를 흥분시키다. **2** Ⓒ a thing that excites. 흥분시키는 것; 자극물.

·ex·cit·ing [iksáitiŋ] *adj.* stirring; stimulating; thrilling. 자극적인; 흥분시키는; 흥미진진한. ¶ *an ~ story* 재미있는 이야기.

:ex·claim [ikskléim] *vi., vt.* (P1;6) cry out suddenly in surprise, fear, etc.; shout. 부르짖다; 소리치다; 절규하다. [L. *clamo* shout]

exclaim against, criticize (something) loudly. …을 크게 비난하다.

exclam. exclamation.

excl. exclusive.

ex·cla·ma·tion [èkskləméiʃən] *n.* **1** ⓊⒸ the act of exclaiming. 외침; 절규. **2** Ⓒ a cry or word(s) spoken suddenly with strong feelings. (급격한 강한 감정에 의한) 외침(소리). ¶ *an ~ of pain* 고통으로 인한 소리침. [→exclaim]

·exclamation mark [--ˊ-- ˋ] *n.* a mark (!) in writing or printing to show surprise, sorrow or other strong feeling. 감탄 부호; 느낌표. 參考 exclamation point 라고도 함.

ex·clam·a·to·ry [iksklǽmətɔ̀ːri / -təri] *adj.* of, expressing, using, or containing exclamation. 감탄의; 절규적인. ¶ *an ~ sentence* 감탄문.

·ex·clude [iksklúːd] *vt.* (P6,13) (opp. include) 《*from*》 **1** shut out; keep out. …을 제외하다; 들이지 않다; 배제하다. ¶ *a nation excluded from the United Nations,* UN 에서 제외된 국가. **2** force out; expel; reject. …을 쫓아내다; 거절하다. ¶ *~ someone from membership* 아무를 회원에서 제명하다 / *~ someone from a house 〔position〕* 아무를 집〔자리〕에서 쫓아내다 / *~ the possibility of going back* 되돌아오는 것을 불가능케 하다. [→close]

ex·clu·sion [iksklúːʒən] *n.* Ⓤ the act of excluding; the state of being excluded. 제외; 배제; 축출; 배척; 거절(opp. inclusion). [↑]

to the exclusion of (=*so as to shut out*) *something.* …을 제외하고.

·ex·clu·sive [iksklúːsiv] *adj.* **1** shutting out others; trying to shut out others. 제외적인; 배타적인. ¶ *mutually ~ plans of action* 서로 용납이 안 되는 행동 계획 / *He was very ~ in his manner.* 그는 태도가 몹시 배타적이었다. **2** leaving out. 포함시키지 않는(opp. inclusive). ¶ *The price ~ of tax is $ 5.* 세금이 포함되지 않은 가격은 5달러이다. **3** not shared or divided with others; single; sole. 독점적인; 전유적(專有的)인; 유일한. ¶ *~ use* 전용 / *one's ~ hobby* 유일한 취미 / *an ~ agent* 총대리점 / *an ~ right to film the novel* 그 소설의 영화화의 독점권. [↑]

exclusive of, excluding; excepting. …을 제외하고.

ex·clu·sive·ly [iksklúːsivli] *adv.* in an exclusive manner; solely. 배타적으로; 독점

적으로.

ex·com·mu·ni·cate [èkskəmjú:nəkèit] *vt.* (P6,13) shut out (someone) from membership in a church. …을 파문하다; 제명하다. [ex-]

ex·com·mu·ni·ca·tion [èkskəmjù:nəkéiʃən] *n.* **1** Ⓤ the act of excommunicating; the state of being excommunicated. 파문. **2** Ⓒ a formal statement announcing this. 파문 선고.

ex-con·vict [ékskánvikt / -kɔ́n-] *n.* Ⓒ a person with a criminal record; an old offender. 전과자. [ex-]

ex·co·ri·ate [ikskɔ́:rièit] *vt.* (P6) **1** rub or cut the skin of. 피부를 까지게 하다. **2** denounce. 통매(痛罵)하다; 비난하다. [L. *corium* hide]

ex·cre·ment [ékskrəmənt] *n.* Ⓤ waste matter that is sent out from the body. 배설물; 대변(大便)(cf. *excreta*). ●**ex·cre·men·tal** [èkskrəméntl] *adj.* [L. *cerno* sift]

ex·cres·cence [ikskrésns] *n.* **1** Ⓒ something growing out from something else. 생성물(生成物). ¶ *Hair is an ~ from the scalp.* 머리카락은 두피(頭皮)로부터 자연히 나는 것이다. **2** an unnatural growth on the surface. 이상(異常) 생성물. ¶ *warty excrescences* 사마귀 같은 것 / *A corn is an ~ on a toe.* 티눈은 발가락에 생기는 이상 생성물이다. **3** a projection. 돌기. [↓]

ex·cres·cent [ikskrésnt] *adj.* growing abnormally; redundant. 이상(異常) 발육의; 군. [L. *cresco* grow]

ex·cre·ta [ikskrí:tə] *n. pl.* waste matter passed out of the body. 배설물(cf. *excrement*). [↓]

ex·crete [ikskrí:t] *vt.* (P6) **1** send out (waste matter) from the body. …을 배설하다(cf. *secrete*). **2** take away (waste matter) from the blood or tissues. …을 분비하다. [→excrement]

ex·cre·tion [ikskrí:ʃən] *n.* **1** Ⓤ the act of excreting. 배설; 분비. **2** ⒸⓊ that which is excreted. 배설물; 분비물.

ex·cre·to·ry [ékskritɔ̀:ri / ekskrí:təri] *adj.* of excretion. 배설의; 분비의. ¶ *an ~ organ* 배설 기관.

ex·cru·ci·ate [ikskrú:ʃièit] *vt.* (P6) inflict extreme pain or agony upon. (육체적으로) 격통(激痛)을 주다; 고문하다. [→crux]

ex·cru·ci·at·ing [ikskrú:ʃièitiŋ] *adj.* (of a wound, anguish, etc.) very painful; agonizing; torturing. 몹시 고통스러운; 고문을 당하는 것 같은.

ex·cul·pate [ékskʌlpèit, ikskʌ́l-] *vt.* (P6, 13) free from blame; hold and pronounce to be guiltless. 무죄로 하다[를 증명하다]; 변명하다(opp. inculpate). [→culpable]

***ex·cur·sion** [ikskə́:rʒən, -ʃən] *n.* Ⓒ **1** a short journey or trip, esp. for pleasure. 소풍. ¶ *go on* 〔*for*〕 *an ~* 소풍을 가다 / *make* 〔*take*〕 *an ~ to the lake* 호수로 소풍 가다. **2** a digression. 탈선. [L. *curro* run]

ex·cur·sive [ikskə́:rsiv] *adj.* **1** of excursions. 유람의. ¶ *~ trips* 유람(遊覽) 여행. **2** off the subject; wandering. 본제(本題)에서 벗어난; 산만한. ¶ *~ reading* 남독(濫讀). ●**ex·cur·sive·ly** [-li] *adv.*

ex·cus·a·ble [ikskjú:zəbəl] *adj.* pardonable; permissible. 용서할 수 있는; 변명이 서는. [↓]

:ex·cuse [ikskjú:z] *vt.* (P6,9,13) **1** ⓐ regard (a fault, offense) as unimportant; pardon; overlook. (과실 따위를) 그대로 넘기다; 눈감다; 용서하다. ¶ *~ someone's rudeness* 아무의 무례를 눈감다 / *I find it hard to ~ his conduct.* 그의 행동을 그대로 보아 넘기기가 어렵다. ⓑ free (someone) from blame; pardon; forgive. 비난하지 않다; 용서하다. ¶ *~ one's friend for being late* 친구가 늦은 것을 비난하지 않다 / *I ~ you this time, but next time you will be punished.* 이번엔 용서하지만 다음번엔 처벌될 게다. **2** ⓐ give a reason or explanation for (a fault or error); apologize for. 변명하다; 이유를 말하다. ¶ *~ one's conduct by telling the reasons* 이유를 대어 행동의 변명을 하다 / *~ having kept someone waiting for a long time* 아무를 오랫동안 기다리게 한 것을 변명하다. ⓑ serve as an apology or explanation. 변명〔구실〕이 되다. ¶ *Ignorance of a law does not ~ a man for acting against it.* 법을 모른다는 것이 위법(違法)에 대한 구실은 되지 않는다. **3** make (someone) free from duty, etc. …을 면제하다. ¶ *be excused from military service* 병역이 면제되다. **4** 《*reflexively*》 ask to be forgiven; apologize. …의 용서를 빌다; …을 사과하다. ¶ *I excused myself for my rudeness.* 나의 무례함을 사과했다.

excuse oneself, **a**) try to free oneself from blames; make excuse (for one's action). …을 변명하다; 사죄하다. **b**) ask for permission to leave. 떠나는 것을 허가해 달라고 요청하다.

— [ikskjú:s] *n.* Ⓒ **1** an explanation of one's conduct; an apology; a pretext. 변명; 구실; 사죄. ¶ *make an ~ for one's conduct* 자신의 행동에 대해 변명을 하다 / *I have no word to say in ~.* 사죄할 말도 없다 / *on one ~ or another* 이 핑계 저 핑계로. **2** a pardon. 용서. **3** release from duty, etc. 면제. [→cause]

exec. executive; executor.

ex·e·cra·ble [éksikrəbəl] *adj.* **1** deserving to be cursed, very hateful; abominable. 저주할 만한; 혐오할; 지겨운. **2** 《*colloq.*》 very bad. 매우 서투른. ¶ *a picture in ~ taste* 아주 서투른 취미의 그림. [↓]

ex·e·crate [éksikrèit] *vt., vi.* (P6; 1) dislike very much; curse. 몹시 싫어하다; 저주(의 말을) 하다. ●**ex·e·cra·tion** [eksikréiʃən] *n.* [L. *sacer* sacred, accursed]

***ex·e·cute** [éksikjù:t] *vt.* (P6) **1** carry out; perform; do. …을 (행)하다; 수행〔실

행, 집행]하다. ¶ ~ *a plan* [*an order*] 계획[명령]을 수행하다 / ~ *a purpose* 목적을 달성하다 / ~ *a maneuver* 작전 행동을 전개하다. **2** put (a law, etc.) into effect; enforce. (법률·판결 따위를) 발효시키다; 집행[시행]하다. ¶ ~ *a decree* 판결을 집행하다. **3** ⓐ perform by singing, playing, acting, etc. (곡을) 연주하다; 노래를 하다; (역을) 연기하다. ¶ ~ *a piece of music admirably* 악곡을 훌륭히 연주하다 / ~ *the part of Hamlet fairly well* 햄릿 역을 훌륭히 연기하다. ⓑ make (fine arts, etc.) according to a plan. (계획대로 미술품 따위를) 완성하다. **4** put (someone) to death according to law. …를 사형으로 하다. ¶ ~ *a murderer* 살인범을 사형에 처하다. [L. *sequor* follow]

***ex·e·cu·tion** [èksikjú:ʃən] *n.* Ⓤ **1** the act of executing; the state of being executed; performance. 집행; 수행; 사형 집행; 실행; 실시; 완성. ¶ *the* ~ *of one's purpose* 목적의 수행 / *put* [*carry*] *a plan into* ~ 계획을 실천에 옮기다 / *put to* ~ 처형하다. **2** the way of executing; skill. (만드는, 연주·연기하는) 솜씨; 수법; 기법. ¶ *wonderful* ~ 놀라운 기법 / *The* ~ *of the work leaves much to be desired.* 작품 제작의 기법은 아직도 충분치가 않다. **3** Ⓒ a written order issued by a court to put a judgment into effect. 집행 영장.

carry* [*put*] *into execution, carry out. 실행하다.

do execution, have an effective action; take effect. 위력을 발휘하다. ¶ *A nuclear bomb would have done great* ~. 핵폭탄이었다면 엄청난 위력을 발휘했을 게다.

ex·e·cu·tion·er [èksikjú:ʃənər] *n.* Ⓒ a person whose job is to put criminals to death according to law. 사형 집행인.

:ex·ec·u·tive [igzékjətiv] *adj.* of or carrying out management; having the power of putting the laws into effect. (사무)집행의; 집행권[력] 있는. ¶ ~ *ability* 실무적 재능 / *an* ~ *board* 이사회 / *an* ~ *officer* 행정관; 집행관리 / *an* ~ *committee* 집행 위원회 / *the Executive Mansion* (미국의) 대통령 관저; 주(州)지사 관저.

— *n.* Ⓒ **1** a person who carries out or manages affairs. 지배인; 이사; 행정관. **2** 《*the* ~》 the branch of a government that carries out the laws. 행정부. ¶ *the* (*Chief*) *Executive* (미국의) 행정 수반; 대통령.

ex·ec·u·tor *n.* Ⓒ **1** [igzékjətər] a person who is named to carry out the provisions of another's will. (지정) 유언 집행자. **2** [éksikjù:tər] a person who performs things. 집행자.

ex·ec·u·tri·ces [igzèkjətráisi:z] *n.* pl. of **executrix.**

ex·ec·u·trix [igzékjətriks] *n.* (*pl.* **-tri·ces** or **-es**) a woman executor. 여성 유언 집행자. [→execute]

ex·e·ge·ses [èksədʒí:si:z] *n.* pl. of **exegesis.**

ex·e·ge·sis [èksədʒí:sis] (*pl.* **-ses**) *n.* exposition esp. of the Scripture. (성서·경전의) 주석. [Gk.]

ex·em·plar [igzémplər, -plɑ:r] *n.* Ⓒ **1** a person or thing worth imitating; a model. 모범; 범례. **2** a sample; an example. 견본; 표본; 실례. [ex-, L. *emo* take]

ex·em·pla·ry [igzémpləri] *adj.* **1** worth imitating; serving as a model or pattern. 모범으로 삼을 만한; 좋은 본보기가 되는. ¶ ~ *conduct* 모범적인 행위. **2** serving as a warning to others. 본때가 되는. ¶ ~ *punishment* 징계 처벌.

ex·em·pli·fi·ca·tion [igzèmpləfikéiʃən] *n.* **1** Ⓤ the act of showing by example. 예증; 예시. **2** Ⓒ an example; an illustration. 호례(好例); 적례(適例). [→exemplar]

ex·em·pli·fy [igzémpləfài] *vt.* (**-fied**) (P6) show or illustrate (something) by example; be an example of (something). …을 예증[예시]하다; …의 예가 되다. ¶ *a story to* ~ *honesty* 정직을 예증하기 위한 이야기. [↑]

ex·em·pli gra·ti·a [egzémplai gréiʃiə, -zempli: grɑ́:tiɑ̀:] 《L.》 for example. 예를 들면. 參考 e.g.로 생략함.

***ex·empt** [igzémpt] *vt.* 《*from*》 make (someone) free from a duty, rule, etc.; release. …을 면제하다. ¶ ~ *a man from service in the army* 병역을 면제하다 / ~ *foreign tourists from taxes* 외국 관광객의 세를 면제하다. — *adj.* free from a duty, an obligation, a rule, etc.; released. 면제된; 면제의. ¶ *These goods are* ~ *from taxes.* 이 상품은 세금이 면제되어 있다. — *n.* Ⓒ an exempt person. 면세자; 면제된 사람. [ex-, L. *emo* take]

ex·emp·tion [igzémpʃən] *n.* ⓊⒸ the act of exempting; the state of being exempted. 면제; 해제. ¶ ~ *from taxation* 면세(免稅).

:ex·er·cise [éksərsàiz] *n.* **1** Ⓤ the use of body or mind in order to improve it. (심신의) 연마; 수련; 운동; 체조. ¶ *gymnastic exercises* 체조 / *bending exercises* 굽혀펴기 운동 / *do* [*have, get, take*] ~ 운동하다 / *give* ~ *to* …을 훈련하다. **2** ⓐ ⓊⒸ a regular practice or training for skill, learning, etc. 연습. ¶ *exercises on* [*for*] *the piano* 피아노 연습. ⓑ Ⓒ a lesson for practice; a drill. 연습 문제. **3** putting into use; the active use (of). (주의·능력 따위의) 적극적인 사용; (직권 따위의) 행사. ¶ *the* ~ *of caution* (상당히) 주의함 / *the* ~ *of authority* 권력의 행사. **4** 《*pl.*》 ceremonies. 의식. ¶ *graduation exercises* 졸업식.

— *vt.* (P6,13) **1** use (one's body or mind) to improve it. (심신)을 연마하다. **2** give exercise to (one's body, a horse, etc.); drill. …을 훈련하다; 운동시키다. ¶ ~ *a horse* / ~ *one's arms and legs* 팔다리의 운동을 하다. **3** ⓐ carry out (duty, etc.). (의무

따위)를 다하다; 수행하다. ⓑ put into action; make use of; practise. (능력·권력 따위)를 쓰다; 사용〔행사〕하다. ¶ ~ *one's strength* 힘을 쓰다 / ~ *one's talent* 재능을 발휘하다 / ~ *caution* 〔*judgment*〕 주의력〔판단력〕을 발휘하다 / ~ *one's power* 〔*influence*〕 권력〔영향력〕을 행사하다. **4** 《usu. in *passive*》 perplex; worry. …을 괴롭히다; 불안하게 하다. ¶ *be much exercised about one's health* 건강을 매우 걱정하고 있다.

— *vi.* (P1) take exercise. 연습하다; 운동〔체조〕하다. [L. *exerceo*]

*__ex·ert__ [igzə́:rt] *vt.* (P6) **1** use actively; put (something) into action; make (something) active. (지력 따위)를 쓰다; (힘 따위)를 발휘하다. ¶ ~ *every effort* 온갖 노력을 하다 / ~ *oneself for an object* 목적을 향해 노력하다. **2** 《*on*》 have (an influence) on someone. (영향)을 끼치다. ¶ ~ *one's influence* 영향력을 끼치다. [L. *exsero*]

ex·er·tion [igzə́:rʃən] *n.* ⓊⒸ **1** the act of exerting; effort. 노력; 진력. **2** exercise; active use; use. 연마; 발휘; 행사. ¶ *wonderful ~ of will-power* 놀라운 의지력의 발휘.

ex·e·unt [éksiənt, eksiúnt] *vi.* 《L.》 (P1) (in stage direction) they go out. 퇴장하다.

ex·fo·li·ate [eksfóulièit] *vi.* (P1) come off in scales. 벗겨져 떨어지다. ● **ex·fo·li·a·tion** [eksfòuliéiʃən] *n.* [→foliage]

ex·ha·la·tion [èkshəléiʃən, ègzəl-] *n.* ⓊⒸ (opp. inhalation) **1** the act of exhaling. 내뿜음; 숨을 내쉼; 증발. ¶ *the ~ of perfume from a flower* 꽃에서 내뿜는 향기. **2** something exhaled, as air, vapor, steam, etc. 발산물; 증기; 아지랑이. [↓]

ex·hale [ekshéil, igzéil] *vt., vi.* (P6,13; 1) breathe out; give forth (air, vapor, sound, etc.). 숨을 내쉬다〔토해내다〕; (증기 따위를) 발산시키다(opp. inhale). ¶ ~ *a sigh* 한숨을 쉬다 / *The engine exhaled steam.* 기관차는 증기를 내뿜었다. [L. *halo* breathe]

:**ex·haust** [igzɔ́:st] *vt.* (P6) **1** make (something) completely empty; use up; expend completely. …을 비우다; 다 써 버리다. ¶ ~ *a well* 우물을 말리다 / ~ *a tube of air* 관(管)의 공기를 빼다 / ~ *a fortune* 재산을 탕진하다. **2** tire out; make (someone) very tired. (체력 따위를) 다 소모시키다; …를 기진 맥진케 하다. ¶ *be exhausted from* 〔*with*〕 …로 몹시 지치다 / ~ *one's strength* 체력을 완전히 소모하다 / ~ *oneself by hard work* 고된 일로 몹시 지치다. **3** discuss or study thoroughly. (문제 따위)를 철저하게 구명〔연구, 검토〕하다. ¶ ~ *a subject* 문제를 철저히 구명하다.

— *vi.* pass out; escape. 배출〔방출〕되다. ¶ *Steam exhausts.* 증기가 나온다.

— *n.* ⓊⒸ **1** the act of sending out used steam, such gas, gasoline, etc., from a machine. 배출; 배기. **2** a pipe for sending out steam, gas, gasoline, etc. 배기 장치; 배기관. **3** the used steam, gas, gasoline, etc., that is sent out. 배출물. [L. *haurio* draw]

ex·haust·ing [igzɔ́:stiŋ] *adj.* producing much tiredness. (심신)을 지치게 하는.

ex·haus·tion [igzɔ́:stʃən] *n.* Ⓤ **1** the act of exhausting; the state of being exhausted. 배출; 소모; 고갈. ¶ *the ~ of wealth* 부(富)의 고갈. **2** great tiredness. 극도의 피로.

ex·haus·tive [igzɔ́:stiv] *adj.* leaving nothing out; thorough; complete. 남김없는; 철저한. ¶ *an ~ study* 철저한 연구 / *an ~ treatment of a subject* 문제의 철저한 다룸.

ex·haust·less [igzɔ́:stlis] *adj.* that can not be exhausted. 다하지 않는; 무한의; 무진장한.

:**ex·hib·it** [igzíbit] *vt., vi.* (P6; 1) **1** show; display; reveal. …을 보이다; 나타내다. ¶ ~ *anger* 노여움을 나타내다 / ~ *interest* 관심을 보이다 / *The body exhibited signs of decay.* 사체는 부패의 조짐을 보였다. **2** show (pictures, etc.) publicly. (전람회 따위에) …을 전시〔진열〕하다. ¶ ~ *new products for sale* 신상품을 진열하다 / ~ *one's roses in a flower show* 꽃 품평회에 장미를 출품하다. **3** 《law》 show (an evidence, etc.) in court. …을 제출〔제시〕하다. ¶ ~ *one's papers* 서류를 제시하다. — *n.* Ⓒ **1** a thing or things shown publicly. 전시물; 출품물. **2** something shown in court as evidence. 증거 서류〔물건〕. [L. *habeo* hold]

*__ex·hi·bi·tion__ [èksəbíʃən] *n.* Ⓒ **1** the act or fact of showing publicly. 공시; 전람; 전시. **2** a public show of pictures, goods, etc. 전람회; 박람회(cf. *exposition*). **3** pictures, goods, etc. shown publicly. 진열품.

make an* 〔*a regular*〕 *exhibition of oneself, act so badly in public that one receives contempt. 비웃음의 대상이 되다.

ex·hi·bi·tion·ism [èksəbíʃənìzəm] *n.* **1** an excessive tendency to show off one's abilities. 과시벽(誇示癖). **2** tendency to show what should not be shown, esp. indecent exposure. 노출벽(露出癖).

ex·hil·a·rate [igzílərèit] *vt.* (P6) fill (someone) with high spirits; make (someone) cheerful or merry. …의 기분을 북돋우다; …을 명랑하게 하다. [L. →hilarious]

ex·hil·a·ra·tion [igzìləréiʃən] *n.* Ⓤ **1** the act of exhilarating. 기분을 북돋움. **2** the state of being exhilarated; high spirits; liveliness. 들뜬 기분; 유쾌; 명랑.

ex·hort [igzɔ́:rt] *vt., vi.* (P6,13,20; 1) urge strongly; advise or warn earnestly. 권고하다; 충고하다. ¶ *I ~ you not to go.* 가지 말 것을 권한다. ● **ex·hort·er** [-ər] *n.* [L. *hortor*]

ex·hor·ta·tion [ègzɔ:rtéiʃən, èks-] *n.* ⓊⒸ **1** the act of exhorting. 권고; 충고; 장려. **2** a speech, sermon, etc., that exhorts. 훈계; 설교.

ex·hume [igzjú:m, ekshjú:m] *vt.* (P6) **1** take out (a dead body) from a grave, etc.; dig up. (무덤 따위를) 파내다; 발굴하다.

2 《*fig.*》 reveal; disclose. 세상에 드러내다; 빛을 보게 하다. ¶ ~ *some obscure works* 무명의 작품을 발굴하다. [L. *humus* ground]

ex·i·gence [éksədʒəns] *n.* =exigency.

ex·i·gen·cy [éksədʒənsi] *n.* Ⓒ (*pl.* **-cies**) **1** a situation demanding urgent action or attention; an urgent case. 급박; 위급; 긴급한 경우. **2** 《usu. *pl.*》 urgent needs or demands. 급무(急務); 긴급 사태. ¶ *Policemen are trained to meet exigencies.* 경찰관은 긴급 사태에 대처할 수 있게 훈련된다. [→exact]

ex·i·gent [éksədʒənt] *adj.* demanding to act or pay attention at once; urgent; pressing. 긴급한; 절박한.

be exigent of, be requiring. …을 요하다.

ex·ig·u·ous [igzígjuəs, iksíg-] *adj.* scanty (=not enough); small. 부족한; 적은; 얼마 안 되는. [L.]

***ex·ile** [égzail, éks-] *vt.* (P6,13) force (someone) to leave his country or home; banish. …을 추방하다. ¶ ~ *oneself* 유랑하다; 망명하다 / *Many people were exiled from the country for life.* 많은 사람이 영원히 국외로 추방되었다. —*n.* **1** Ⓤ the state of being exiled; banishment. 추방. **2** Ⓒ an exiled person. 추방인; 망명자. [L.]

:**ex·ist** [igzíst] *vi.* (P1,2A,3) **1** have actual existence; be. 존재하다; 있다. ¶ *Do you believe that God exists?* 신(神)이 존재한다고 믿는가. **2** continue to be; live. 생존하다; 살다. ¶ ~ *on one's salary* 월급으로 살다 / *No man can ~ without air.* 아무도 공기 없이는 생존할 수 없다. **3** be found; occur. 있다; 나타나다. ¶ ~ *in solution* 용액으로서 존재하다 / *Lime exists in many soils.* 석회는 많은 흙에 있다 / *Such conditions ~ only in crowded cities.* 그런 상황은 복잡한 도시에서나 있다. [L. *sisto* stand]

:**ex·ist·ence** [igzístəns] *n.* **1** Ⓤ the state of being; existing; real or actual being; being. 존재. ¶ *People no longer believe in the ~ of ghosts.* 사람들은 이제는 유령의 존재를 믿지 않는다. **2** ⓊⒸ living life. 생존; 생활. ¶ *a struggle for ~* 생존 경쟁 / *daily ~* 일상 생활 / *lead a dangerous* 〔*miserable*〕 ~ 위험한 〔비참한〕 생활을 하다 / *Food is necessary for ~.* 음식은 생존을 위해 필요하다. **3** Ⓒ a thing that exists. 생존물.

bring 〔***call***〕 ***into existence,*** give birth to; bring forth. 낳다.

come into existence, be born. 낳다; 생기다; 성립하다.

in existence, existing. 현존의〔하는〕; 존재하는.

ex·ist·ent [igzístənt] *adj.* **1** existing. 실재〔존재〕하는; 생존하는. ¶ *Dinosaurs are no longer ~.* 공룡은 이제 존재하지 않는다. **2** now existing; current. 현존하는; 현행의. ¶ ~ *traffic conditions* 현(행) 교통 상황.

ex·it [égzit, éksit] *n.* Ⓒ **1** a way out; a doorway. 출구(出口)(opp. entrance). ¶ *the ~ from a railway station* 역의 출구 / *an emergence ~ on the left* 왼쪽의 비상구. **2** the act of going out; departure. 퇴출; 퇴거. ¶ *give ~ to someone* 아무를 퇴출시키다. **3** (of actors) the act of leaving the stage. 퇴장. ¶ *make one's ~* 퇴장하다. —*vi.* (of actors) go out; depart. 퇴장하다. ¶ *Exit Macbeth.* 맥베스 퇴장. [L. =He 〔She〕 goes out]

ex·o- [éksou-] *pref.* outside of; external; beyond. '외(外), 외부'의 뜻. [Gk.]

ex·o·bi·ol·o·gy [èksoubaiálədʒi / -ɔ́l-] *n.* the study of life beyond the earth's atomsphere. 우주 생물학. [exo-]

ex·o·dus [éksədəs] *n.* **1** Ⓒ the act of going out; departure. (집단적으로) 나감; 퇴거; (이민 따위의) 출국. ¶ *the summer ~ to the country* 여름철 시골로의 피서. **2** 《*E-*》 《Bible》 the departure of the Israelites from Egypt. 이스라엘인(人)의 이집트 탈출. **3** 《*E-*》 the second book of the Old Testament, that tells of this departure. 출애굽기. [Gk. *hodos* way]

ex of·fi·ci·o [eks əfíʃiòu] *adv., adj.* 《L.》 by virtue of one's office; because of one's office. 직권에 의해서; 직무상. ¶ *be present at a meeting ~* 직무상 모임에 참석하다.

ex·oga·my [ekságəmi / -sɔ́g-] *n.* a legally required marriage outside of the tribe or other social group. 족외(族外) 결혼; 이족(異族) 결혼. [exo-]

ex·on·er·ate [igzánərèit / -zɔ́n-] *vt.* (P6, 13) **1** make (someone) free from blame. (아무)의 결백함을 증명하다. ¶ ~ *oneself from* 〔*of*〕 *a charge of theft* 절도 혐의를 벗다. **2** make (someone) free from obligation, duty, etc. (의무·책임 따위)를 면제하다. [→onus]

ex·or·bi·tant [igzɔ́ːrbətənt] *adj.* (of a price, charge, demand, etc.) unreasonable or extraordinary. (요구가) 엄청난; (가격 따위)가 터무니없는. ¶ *an ~ price* 터무니없는 값. [→orbit]

ex·or·cise, -cize [éksɔːrsàiz] *vt.* (P6) **1** drive out (an evil spirit) by prayers, ceremonies, etc. …의 마귀를 쫓다; 불제(祓除)하다. **2** call up (a spirit). 불러내다. ● **ex·or·cis·er** [-ər] *n.* [Gk. *horkos* oath]

ex·or·di·a [igzɔ́ːrdiə, iksɔ́ːr-] *n.* pl. of **exordium.**

ex·or·di·um [igzɔ́ːrdiəm, iksɔ́ːr-] *n.* (*pl.* **-di·ums, -di·a**) a beginning or introduction to a formal speech, sermon, literary work, etc. 도입부; 서설(序說). [L.]

ex·o·ter·ic [èksətérik] *adj.* (opp. esoteric) **1** not intended for only a chosen few; that can be understood by the public. 일반 대중을 대상으로 한; 대중이 이해할 수 있는. **2** commonplace; popular. 평범한; 보통의; 통속적인. [↓]

ex·ot·ic [igzátik / igzɔ́t-] *adj.* **1** introduced from a foreign country; not native. 외래의; 외국(산)의. ¶ ~ *foods* 외국산의

식품 / ~ *manners* 이국적 풍습. **2** striking or unusual in effect or style; strange. 이국적인; 색다른. ¶ *an ~ note* 이국적인 가락 / *the ~ dress of traditional Korea* 색다른 한국 전통의 복장. —— *n.* Ⓒ anything exotic. 외래의 것《식물·외래어 따위》. ● **ex·ot·i·cal·ly** [-kəli] *adv.* [Gk. *exō* outside]

•**ex·pand** [ikspǽnd] *vt., vi.* (P6,13; 1,2A,3) **1** make or become larger or wider; spread out; unfold. …을 확대[확장]하다; 팽창시키다[하다]; 퍼지다; 넓히다; 넓어지다. ¶ *~ one's knowledge* 지식을 넓히다 / *~ an umbrella* 우산을 펴다 / *~ one's business* 사업을 확장하다 / *Heat expands metal.* 열은 금속을 팽창시킨다 / *A bird expands its wings.* 새는 날개를 편다. **2** develop (something) by adding details. (의론 따위를) 발전시키다. ¶ *He expanded a short story into a novel.* 단편소설을 장편소설로 발전시켰다. [L. *pando* spread]

ex·panse [ikspǽns] *n.* Ⓒ a large, open space or surface. 광활한 공간[장소]. ¶ *an ~ of water* 광대한 물바다. [↑]

ex·pan·si·ble [ikspǽnsəbəl] *adj.* that can be expanded. 펼[늘일] 수 있는; 팽창할 수 있는.

ex·pan·sion [ikspǽnʃən] *n.* ⓊⒸ **1** the act of or process of expanding; the state of being expanded. 팽창; 확장; 확대. ¶ *the ~ of school-building* 학교 건물의 증축 / *Heat causes the ~ of gases.* 열은 가스를 팽창시킨다. **2** development. 발전; 전개.

ex·pan·sive [ikspǽnsiv] *adj.* **1** tending to expand. 신장력(팽창성)이 있는; 퍼지는. **2** wide; vast; spacious. 넓은; 광대한. **3** showing one's feelings freely and openly. 거리낌없는; 개방적인; 대범한. ● **ex·pan·sive·ly** [-li] *adv.* **ex·pan·sive·ness** [-nis] *n.*

ex·pa·ti·ate [ikspéiʃièit] *vi.* (P1,3) 《*on, upon*》 write or speak much. 상술(詳述)하다; 상설(詳說)하다. ¶ *~ on one's favorite subject* 좋아하는 주제에 관해서 상술하다. ● **ex·pa·ti·a·tor** [-ər] *n.* [→space]

ex·pa·tri·ate [ekspéitrièit / -pǽ-] *vt.* (P6) send (someone) out of his native country; give up (one's citizenship); banish; exile. …을 국외로 추방하다; 국적을 버리다. ¶ *~ oneself* 나라를 떠나다; 국적을 버리다. —— *n.* Ⓒ an expatriated person. 국외 추방자; 망명자. [L. *patria* native land]

ex·pa·tri·a·tion [ekspèitriéiʃən / -pæ̀-] *n.* Ⓤ the act of expatriating; the state of being expatriated. 국외 추방; 국적 이탈.

⁑**ex·pect** [ikspékt] *vt.* (P6,8,11,13,20) **1** think of (something) that it will probably happen; look forward to (something); hope. …을 기대하다; 구하다; 바라다. ¶ *I ~ you to help me.* 나를 도와 줄 것을 기대한다. **2** think of (someone) that he will probably come. (올 것)을 기다리다. ¶ *I expected you yesterday.* 어제 올 줄 알고 기다렸네. **3** 《*colloq.*》 think; suppose. …을 생각하다. ¶ *You're tired, I ~.* 피곤하실 것으로 생각합니다 / *Will he come? – I don't ~ so.* 그가 올까 – 나는 그렇게 생각지 않는다. [L. *specto* see]

ex·pect·an·cy [ikspéktənsi] *n.* (*pl.* **-cies**) =expectation.

ex·pect·ant [ikspéktənt] *adj.* looking forward to something. 예기하는; 기대하는. ¶ *an ~ mother* 산월(產月)이 된 임부(姙婦) / *an ~ heir* 추정 상속인 / *be ~ of* …을 고대하고 있다; 기대하고 있다. —— *n.* Ⓒ a person who expects something. 예기자; 기대자. ● **ex·pect·ant·ly** [-li] *adv.*

•**ex·pec·ta·tion** [èkspektéiʃən] *n.* **1** Ⓤ the act or state of expecting; thinking something will come or happen. 기대; 예상; 예기. ¶ *watch in eager ~* 큰 기대를 걸고 지켜보다 / *do something in ~ of a reward* 보상을 바라고 무엇을 하다 / *meet* [*answer, come up to*] *someone's expectations* 아무의 기대에 부응하다 / *fall short of someone's ~* 아무의 기대에 부응치 못하다 / *beyond* [*below*] (*one's*) *~* 예상 이상으로[이하로] / *against* [*contrary to*] *~* 예상에 반하여 / *according to one's ~* 기대했던 대로. **2** 《often *pl.*》 ⓐ something that is expected or looked forward to. 기대되는[대망의] 것; 기대의 대상. ⓑ the prospect of future good, e.g. of money coming. (장차의 좋은 일·이익 따위의) 가망; (특히) 유산 상속의 가망. ¶ *have great expectations from one's uncle* 숙부로부터 막대한 유산을 상속받게 될 것을 기대하다.

ex·pec·to·rant [ikspéktərənt] *n., adj.* (a medicine) helping to expectorate. 가래를 나오게 하는; 거담제(祛痰劑). [↓]

ex·pec·to·rate [ikspéktərèit] *vt., vi.* (P6;1) cough or spit out (matter) from the throat or lungs; spit. (기침하여) 가래를 뱉어내다. [L. *pectus* breast]

ex·pe·di·ence [ikspíːdiəns] *n.* =expediency.

ex·pe·di·en·cy [ikspíːdiənsi] *n.* ⓊⒸ (*pl.* **-cies**) the state of being expedient; self-interest. 편의; 유리; 득책(得策); 사리(私利). [↓]

ex·pe·di·ent [ikspíːdiənt] *adj.* suitable for the purpose; convenient; advisable. (목적 달성에) 도움이 되는; 편의의; 유리한. ¶ *an ~ schedule* 편의적인 계획 / *an ~ politician* 편의주의의 정치가 / *find it ~ to keep silence* 잠자코 있는 것이 득책이라는 것을 알다 / *It is ~ that you go.* 가는 것이 유리하다. —— *n.* Ⓒ a means to a purpose; a shift. 방책; 수단; 편법. ¶ *If you want a fire and have no matches, you can rub two sticks togethers as an ~.* 불은 필요한데 성냥이 없으면 편법으로 두 막대기를 마찰시킬 수 있다. ● **ex·pe·di·ent·ly** [-li] *adv.* [→expedite]

ex·pe·dite [ékspədàit] *vt.* (P6) **1** make (a business, etc.) easy and quick. …을 촉진하다; 진척시키다. ¶ *~ a plan* 계획을 촉진하다 / *~ one's duties* 직무를 신속히 처리하다. **2**

issue or dispatch (an official document). (공문서)를 급송하다; 발송하다. [ex-, L. *ped-, pēs* foot]

:**ex·pe·di·tion** [èkspədíʃən] *n.* **1** Ⓒ a journey for some special purpose, as discovery or battle. 원정; 탐험. ¶ *an arctic ~* 북극탐험 / *go* (*start*) *on an exploring ~* 탐험여행을 떠나다. **2** Ⓒ a group of people, ships, etc., that make such a journey or voyage. 탐험대; 원정대. **3** Ⓤ efficient and prompt action or speed. 신속. ¶ *use all possible ~* 될 수 있는 대로 신속히 처리하다 / *He did his work with ~.* 그는 일을 신속히 처리했다.

ex·pe·di·tion·ar·y [èkspədíʃənèri / -nəri] *adj.* of an expedition. 원정(탐험)의; 파견된.

ex·pe·di·tious [èkspədíʃəs] *adj.* quick; speedy; effective and prompt. 재빠른; 신속한. ●**ex·pe·di·tious·ly** [-li] *adv.*

ex·pel [ikspél] *vt.* (**-pelled, -pel·ling**) (P6,13) drive (someone) out by force; dismiss. …을 몰아(쫓아)내다; 제명하다. ¶ *~ an enemy from a trench* 참호로부터 적을 몰아내다 / *be expelled from school* 퇴학 처분을 받다. [L. *pello* drive]

ex·pel·lent, -lant [ikspélənt] *adj.* expelling. 몰아내는; 쫓아내는. — *n.* an expellent medicine. 구충제(驅蟲劑).

ex·pend [ikspénd] *vt.* (P6,13) **1** spend (money, time, etc.). (돈·시간)을 소비하다. 語法 이 뜻으로는 보통 spend 를 씀. **2** 《*on, in*》 use up (energy, etc.). (노력 따위)를 들이다. ¶ *~ enormous energy and time on work* 일에 막대한 정력과 시간을 들이다. [L. *pendo* weigh]

•**ex·pend·i·ture** [ikspénditʃər] *n.* Ⓤ **1** the act of expending. 지출; 소비. ¶ *at* (*with*) *a minimun ~ of time and effort* 최소한도의 시간과 노력으로 / *be profuse in one's ~* 돈씀씀이가 헤프다. **2** ⓊⒸ the amount of money expended. 지출액; 경비; 비용(opp. income). ¶ *annual ~* 세출(歲出) / *current ~* 경상비 / *~ on education* 교육비.

:**ex·pense** [ikspéns] *n.* **1** Ⓤ 《sometimes *an ~*》 money paid or needed to do something; cost. 출비(出費); 지출; 비용. ¶ *household ~* 가계비(家計費) / *at one's* (*own*) *~* 자비로 / *at an ~ of 50,000 won* 5만원의 비용을 들여. **2** Ⓒ a cause of expense. 출비(出費)의 원인. ¶ *Education is an ~.* 교육에는 비용이 든다. **3** 《usu. *pl.*》 that which is expended. 지출금; 경비; …비(費). ¶ *living expenses* 생활비 / *traveling expenses* 여비 / *cut down* (*curtail*) *one's expenses* 지출을 삭감하다 / *meet one's expenses* 경비를 지불하다. **4** Ⓤ loss; sacrifice. 손실; 희생. [→expend]

at someone's expense, **a**) with someone paying the cost. …에게 비용을 부담시켜. **b**) against someone, so as to make him seem silly. …에게 창피 주어; …을 손상시켜.

at the expense of, with the loss of; causing the loss of; at the cost of. …의 돈(비용)으로; …에게 손해를 끼쳐; …을 희생으로 하여. ¶ *profit at the ~ of another* 남의 돈으로 벌다 / *He made a fortune at the ~ of his health.* 그는 건강을 희생으로 하여 재산을 모았다.

go to the expense of (= *willingly spend money on*) *something.* …에 비용을 들이다. ¶ *go to the ~ of traveling abroad* 비용을 들여 해외 여행을 하다.

put** someone **to expense, force someone to pay expense. …에게 비용을 부담시키다.

:**ex·pen·sive** [ikspénsiv] *adj.* costly; causing expense. 값 비싼; 비용이 드는. ¶ *~ clothes* 비싼 옷.

come expensive, prove to be expensive. 비싸게 치이다.

ex·pen·sive·ly [ikspénsivli] *adv.* in an expensive manner. 비용을 들여; 사치하게.

:**ex·pe·ri·ence** [ikspíəriəns] *n.* **1** Ⓤ the act of gaining knowledge, skill, wisdom, etc. by one's own actions or by practice. 경험; 체험. ¶ *a man of ~* 경험이 풍부한 사람 / *learn something by ~* 경험에 의해서 무엇을 배우다 / *gain ~ in teaching* 가르치는 경험을 얻다 / *Have you had any ~ in this kind of work?* 이런 유(類)의 일을 해 본 경험이 있는가. **2** Ⓒ something experienced. 경험한 것. ¶ *have a pleasant ~* 즐거운 경험을 하다. — *vt.* (P6) have experience of (something). …을 경험(체험)하다. ¶ *~ difficulties* (*pain*) 어려움(고통)을 맛보다 / *be experienced in leading students* 학생 지도에 숙련되어 있다. [L. *experior* try]

•**ex·pe·ri·enced** [ikspíəriənst] *adj.* having much experience; skillful; expert. 경험이 많은; 노련한. ¶ *an ~ teacher* 경험 많은 선생님 / *have an ~ eye* 안식이 높다.

:**ex·per·i·ment** [ikspérəmənt] *n.* ⒸⓊ a trial or a test to find out something. (과학상의) 실험; 시험; 시도. ¶ *an ~ in physics* 물리 실험 / *a chemical ~* 화학 실험 / *make* (*try*) *an ~ in* (*on*) *chemical action* 화학 작용의 실험을 하다 / *conduct a series of experiments on living animals* 일련의 동물 생체 실험을 하다. — [-mènt] *vi.* (P1,3) 《*on, in*》 try tests to find out something. 실험하다; 해 보다. ¶ *~ on chemistry* 화학 실험을 하다. [L. *experimentum* trial, ↑]

ex·per·i·men·tal [ikspèrəméntl / eks-] *adj.* of or based on experiments. 실험(시험)의; 실험에 의거한. ¶ *~ flights* 시험 비행 / *an ~ theater* 실험 극장 / *in the ~ stage* 실험 단계에.

ex·per·i·men·tal·ly [ikspèrəméntəli] *adv.* in an experimental manner. 실험적으로; 실험상.

ex·per·i·men·ta·tion [ikspèrəmentéiʃən] *n.* Ⓤ the act of experimenting; the practice of experiments. 실험; 실지 연습.

ex·per·i·ment·er, -ment·or [ikspérəmèntər] *n.* Ⓒ a person who carries out experiments. 실험자.

:ex·pert [ékspəːrt] *n.* Ⓒ a person who has special knowledge or skill; a specialist. 익수; 노련한 사람; 전문가. ¶ *a technical* 〔*language*〕 ~ 공예〔어학〕의 전문가 / *an ~ in mathematics* 수학 전문가 / *an ~ at one's work* 일에 숙달한 사람. — [ikspə́ːrt, ékspəːrt] *adj.* very skillful; having special skill. 숙련된; 전문의. ¶ *an ~ carpenter* 솜씨 좋은 목수 / *be ~ in* 〔*at*〕 *skiing* 스키에 능숙하다 / *He is ~ in* 〔*at*〕 *driving a car.* 그는 차 운전에 능숙하다. [L.]

ex·per·tise [èkspərtíːz] *n.* skill in or knowledge of a particular field; know-how. 전문적 기술〔지식, 의견〕. ¶ *business ~* 사업의 전문 지식. [↑]

ex·pi·ate [ékspièit] *vt.* (P6) pay for (one's wrong act) by receiving punishment. …의 속죄를 하다; …을 보상하다. ¶ *~ one's sins* 속죄하다 / *The thief expiated his theft by giving back twice as much as he stole.* 도둑은 훔친 것의 배를 되돌려 줌으로써 훔친 보상을 했다. [→pious]

ex·pi·a·tion [èkspəéiʃən] *n.* Ⓤ the act of expiating. 속죄; 보상. ¶ *in ~ of one's sin* 〔*crime*〕 속죄로서; 죄갚음으로.

ex·pi·ra·tion [èkspəréiʃən] *n.* Ⓤ **1** the act of breathing out. 숨을 내쉼; 호기(呼氣). ¶ *the ~ of air from the lungs* 폣속의 공기를 내쉼. **2** end; close. (기한의) 만료; 종결. ¶ *the ~ of a contract* 계약의 만기 / *at the ~ of one's term of office* 임기가 끝나. [↓]

ex·pire [ikspáiər] *vi.* (P1) **1** breathe out. 숨을 내쉬다(opp. inspire). **2** die; (of fire, light, etc.) go out. 죽다; (불 따위가) 꺼지다; 나가다. ¶ *The old man at once expired.* 노인은 갑자기 죽었다. **3** (of a license, etc.) come to an end. 기한이 다 되다; 끝나다. ¶ *My term of office has expired.* 나의 임기가 끝났다. — *vt.* (P6) breathe out (air) from the lungs. 숨을 내쉬다. [L. *spiro* breathe]

:ex·plain [ikspléin] *vt.* **1** (P6,10,11,12,13) tell the meaning of (something); make (something) clear. …을 설명하다; 분명히 하다. ¶ *~ an obscure point* 모호한 점을 분명히 하다 / *~ how to do something* 어떻게 하는지를 설명하다 / *Can you ~ this problem ?* 이 문제를 설명할 수 있나 / *She explained why she was late in getting home.* 그녀는 귀가가 늦은 이유를 설명했다. **2** give reasons for or causes of (something); account for; excuse. 원인·이유를 밝히다; 변명하다. ¶ *~ oneself* 자기의 입장을 설명하다 / *How do you ~ your behavior ?* 네 행동을 어떻게 변명하려 하는가. [→plain]

explain away, make less severe or do away with (a meaning, etc.) by explaining. (의혹·곤란 따위를) 설명하여 제거하다. ¶ *She explained away the child's fears.* 잘 설명하여 그 아이의 두려움을 없애 주었다.

ex·plain·a·ble [ikspléinəbəl] *adj.* that can be explained. 설명〔변명〕할 수 있는.

:ex·pla·na·tion [èksplənéiʃən] *n.* ⒸⓊ **1** the act of explaining. 설명. ¶ *by way of ~* 설명으로써 / *give a satisfactory ~ of* …의 만족스런 설명을 하다 / *Can you say anything in ~ of your conduct?* 너의 행위를 설명할 수 있는가. **2** a statement. 변명. **3** something that explains. 설명이 되는 것. ¶ *The only ~ of* 〔*for*〕 *his behavior is that he's mad.* 그의 행위에 관해 유일하게 설명이 가능한 것은 그가 미쳤다는 것이다. [→explain]

come to an explanation (=*come to a mutual understanding*) ***with*** *someone.* 아무와 상호 이해에 도달하다; 양해가 되다.

in explanation of, explaining. …을 설명하여; 변명하여.

ex·plan·a·to·ry [iksplǽnətɔ̀ːri / -təri] *adj.* serving to make something clear; explaining. 설명의; 변명의; 설명적〔변명적〕인. ¶ *a book with ~ notes* 주석이 붙은 책.

ex·ple·tive [éksplətiv] *adj.* helping to fill up; used merely to fill up. 보충적인; 부가적인. ¶ *~ phrases* 허사(虛辭). — *n.* **1** Ⓒ a meaningless word in a sentence. 허사 《*There* is a book on the table. 의 There 따위》. **2** a meaningless oath. 무의미한 모독·저주의 말《Damn ! 따위》. [L. *pleo* fill]

ex·pli·ca·ble [iksplíkəbəl] *adj.* that can be explained. 설명〔해명〕할 수 있는. [↓]

ex·pli·cate [éksplәkèit] *vt.* (P6) **1** develop (a principle, doctrine, etc.). (원리·이론 따위)를 전개하다. **2** explain. 설명하다; 해명하다. [L. *plico* fold]

ex·plic·it [iksplísit] *adj.* **1** clearly expressed. 명백한; 명확한 (opp. implicit). ¶ *an ~ statement* 명확한 진술. **2** frank. 숨김없는; 솔직한. ¶ *be quite ~ on a point* 어떤 점에 대해서 솔직히 말〔진술〕하다 / *Be ~.* 솔직해라. ● **ex·plic·it·ly** [-li] *adv.* **ex·plic·it·ness** [-nis] *n.* [↑]

•ex·plode [iksplóud] *vt.* (P6) **1** cause (something) to burst suddenly. …을 폭발시키다. ¶ *~ a box of gunpowder* 화약통을 폭발시키다. **2** destroy (a theory, etc.). …을 타파하다. ¶ *~ a theory* 이론을 논박하다 / *~ the old tradition* 낡은 전통을 타파하다. — *vi.* (P1,2A,3) burst suddenly and noisily; burst forth. 폭발하다; (감정 따위가) 터지다. ¶ *~ with* 〔*in*〕 *laughter* 갑자기 폭소가 터지다 / *He exploded with anger.* 그는 노여움으로 불끈했다. [→L. *plaudo* clap]

•ex·ploit [éksplɔit, iksplɔ́it] *n.* Ⓒ a bold or heroic act. 영웅적 행위; 공적; 위업. ¶ *perform a heroic ~* 영웅적 행위를 하다. — [iksplɔ́it] *vt.* (P6) **1** develop. …을 개발하다. ¶ *~ natural resources* 천연 자원을 개발하다. **2** use (something) for one's own purpose; use (something) selfishly. …을 이용하다; (이기적인 목적을 위해) 부당하게 사용하다; 착취하다. ¶ *~ the working classes* 노동자 계급을 착취하다 / *~ a conquered country* 정복한 나라를 착취하다. [L. *plico* fold]

ex·ploi·ta·tion [èksplɔitéiʃən] *n.* Ⓤ **1**

the act of exploiting; the state of being exploited. 개발. **2** selfish use. 이기적 이용; 착취.

·ex·plo·ra·tion [èkspləréiʃən] *n.* UC the act of exploring. 탐험; 탐사; (실지) 답사; 탐구. [↓]

·ex·plore [iksplɔ́ːr] *vt.* (P6) **1** travel through (a little-known land or sea) in order to study it. …을 탐험(답사)하다. ¶ ~ *an uninhabited island* 무인도를 탐험하다. **2** search into; examine closely. …을 조사하다. ¶ ~ *a question* 문제를 조사하다 / ~ *every possibility* 모든 가능성을 검토하다. [L. *exploro* explore]

·ex·plor·er [iksplɔ́ːrər] *n.* C a person who explores. 탐험가; 답사자.

:ex·plo·sion [iksplóuʒən] *n.* C the act of exploding; the state of being exploded. 폭발; 파열; (감정의) 터짐. ¶ *an* ~ *of gunpowder* 화약의 폭발 / *explosions of anger* 노여움의 폭발 / *an* ~ *of laughter* 폭소. [→explode]

ex·plo·sive [iksplóusiv] *adj.* of explosion; tending to burst out with emotion. 폭발(성)의; (감정이) 격하기 쉬운. ¶ ~ *substances* 폭발물. — *n.* C an explosive substance. 폭발물. [↑]

ex·po·nent [ikspóunənt] *n.* C **1** a person or thing that explains. 설명자(물). **2** a symbol; an example. 상징; 전형(典型). ¶ *Lincoln is an* ~ *of self-education.* 링컨은 독학의 전형이다. **3** 《math.》 a number or symbol placed as a superscript to the right of a quantity to indicate a power. 멱(冪)지수. — *adj.* explaining. 설명적인. [→expound]

·ex·port [ikspɔ́ːrt, ∠–] *vt.* send (goods) to another country for sale. (상품)을 수출하다 (opp. import). ¶ ~ *automobiles to a foreign country* 자동차를 외국으로 수출하다. — [∠–] *n.* **1** U the act of exporting goods. 수출. ¶ *ban* 〔*prohibit*〕 *the* ~ *of* …의 수출을 금지하다 / *The* ~ *of wheat is an important industry in the U.S.* 밀의 수출은 미국의 중요한 산업의 하나다. **2** C something exported. 수출품. ¶ *Coffee is a major* ~ *of Colombia.* 커피는 콜롬비아의 주요 수출품이다. [L. *porto* carry]

ex·por·ta·tion [èkspɔːrtéiʃən] *n.* **1** U the act of exporting. 수출(opp. importation). **2** C something that is exported. 수출품. **3** 《*pl.*》 the amount exported. 수출액(량).

ex·port·er [ikspɔ́ːrtər, ∠––] *n.* C a person or company that exports. 수출업자; 수출회사(opp. importer).

:ex·pose [ikspóuz] *vt.* (P6,13) **1** leave (someone or something) unprotected; lay open to. (햇볕·바람 따위에) 쐬다; (비 따위에) 맞히다; (위험 따위에) 노출시키다. ¶ ~ *one's head to the rain* 머리에 비를 맞다 / ~ *one's skin to the sunlight.* 피부를 햇볕에 쬐다 / ~ *oneself to danger* 〔*risk*〕 위험에 노출하다. **2** make (something) known; disclose. …을 알리다; 폭로하다. ¶ ~ *a secret* 비밀을 폭로하다 / ~ *a plot to the police* 음모를 경찰에 알리다. **3** show openly; display. …을 진열〔전시〕하다. ¶ ~ *goods for sale* 상품을 진열하여 팔다 / ~ *new books in a shopwindow* 신간 서적을 진열창에 진열하다. **4** leave (something) open to view; uncover; bare. …을 드러내다. **5** 《photog.》 cause to act on (a film). …을 감광(感光)시키다. **6** abandon. (어린애 따위)를 버리다; 유기하다. [L. *pono* put, →pose]

ex·po·sé [èkspouzéi] *n.* 《F.》 the making public of wrongdoing hitherto kept secret. (추문 따위의) 폭로.

ex·po·si·tion [èkspəzíʃən] *n.* **1** UC the act of exposing; explanation. 설명; 해설. **2** C 《U.S.》 an exhibition of art, industrial products, etc. 박람회; 전시회. 參考 expo로 생략함. ¶ *an art* ~ 미술 전람회 / *an* ~ *of farm products* 농산물 전시회.

ex·pos·i·tive [ikspázətiv / -pɔ́z-] *adj.* descriptive; explanatory. 설명적인; 해설적인.

ex·pos·i·tor [ikspázətər / -pɔ́z-] *n.* C a person who explains; an interpreter. 설명자; 해설자.

ex·pos·i·to·ry [ikspázitɔ̀ːri / -pɔ́zitəri] *adj.* explanatory; expositive. 설명〔해설〕적인.

ex·pos·tu·late [ikspástʃulèit / -pɔ́s-] *vi.* (P1,3) advise earnestly not to do; reason earnestly, esp. to dissuade; remonstrate. 간(諫)하다; 충고하다; 타이르다. ¶ *I expostulated with him in vain.* 그에게 충고했으나 허사였다. [ex-]

ex·pos·tu·la·tion [ikspàstʃuléiʃən / -pɔ̀s-] *n.* U the act of expostulating; C words used in expostulating. 간함; 타이름; 간하는〔타이르는〕 말; 충고의 말.

:ex·po·sure [ikspóuʒər] *n.* **1** UC the act of exposing; the state of being exposed; disclosure of something secret or private, etc. (햇빛·비바람 따위에) 노출(당)함; (숨겨진 일 등의) 폭로. ¶ ~ *to the rain* 비를 맞게 함 / *the* ~ *of one's bare skin to the sun* 맨살의 햇볕에의 노출 / ~ *to danger* 〔*risk*〕 위험에의 노출 / *the* ~ *of an impostor* 사기꾼의 정체폭로 / *the* ~ *of the invasion plans* 침략 계획의 폭로 / *He threatened me with* ~. 그는 폭로하겠다고 나를 협박했다. **2** C (of a house, etc.) direction or location. (집 따위의) 방위. ¶ *a house with a southern* ~ 남향 집. **3** C 《photog.》 the length of time during which film is exposed. (필름의) 노출. ¶ *an* ~ *meter* 노출계(計). **4** UC the act of abandoning a baby, etc. (유아 등의) 유기(遺棄). ¶ *the* ~ *of children* 아이들의 유기. [→expose]

die of exposure, die outdoors because of having no protection from the weather. 한데 죽음을 하다.

ex·pound [ikspáund] *vt.* (P6) explain

(something) in detail. …을 상세히 설명하다. ¶ ~ *one's views* 자신의 견해를 상세히 설명하다. [L. *pono* place]

ex·pres·i·dent [ikspréz̀idənt] *n.* Ⓒ a former president. 전(前)대통령. [ex-, → president]

:ex·press [iksprés] *vt.* **1** (P6,12,13) say or show (a meaning, thought, etc.); make (something) known. …을 표현하다; 나타내다; 발표하다. ¶ ~ *something in words* 〔*drawing, music*〕 무엇을 말로〔그림으로, 음악으로〕 나타내다 / *Words cannot ~ it.* 말로는 그것을 표현할 수 없다 / *Her smile expressed joy.* 그녀의 미소는 기쁨을 나타내고 있었다. **2** (P6) get (juice, etc.) by pressing; squeeze out. 짜(내)다. **3** (P6) send (letters, etc.) by express mail. 급송하다; 속달편으로 보내다. ¶ ~ *a letter* 〔*parcel*〕.

express oneself, make one's meaning, thoughts, or feeling known; say what one means. 생각〔의견, 감정〕을 말하다. ¶ *He is very poor at expressing himself.* 그는 자기 생각을 표현하는 것이 매우 서투르다.

— *adj.* **1** clearly stated; definite. 명확한; 명시〔표명〕된. ¶ *an ~ command* 〔*wish*〕 명확한 명령〔희망〕. **2** speedy; with few stops. 지급(至急)의; 급행의. ¶ *an ~ train* 급행 열차 / *a special* 〔*limited*〕 *~ train* 특급 열차 / *an ~ highway* 고속 도로. **3** exactly like. 빼쏜. ¶ *the ~ image of his father* 자기 아버지를 빼쏨.

— *n.* **1** Ⓒ an express train, bus, etc. 급행. **2** Ⓒ a special messenger. 급사(急使); 특사. **3** Ⓤ a means of carrying mails, etc. speedily. 속달편. ¶ *send a letter by ~* 편지를 속달로 부치다. [ex-, →press]

:ex·pres·sion [ikspréʃən] *n.* **1** Ⓤ the act of expressing; Ⓒ a particular word or phrase; a saying. 표현; (특별한) 어구; 말. ¶ *a happy ~* 교묘한 표현 / *the ~ of a feeling* 감정의 표현 / *a trite and hackneyed ~* 진부한 판에 박힌 말. **2** Ⓒ a look that expresses the feelings; the tone in which a person speaks, reads, or sings. 표정; 어조(語調); 음조. ¶ *a sad ~* 슬픈 표정 / *an ~ of discontent* 불만스러운 얼굴 / *say with no ~ in one's voice* 담담한 어조로 말하다.

beyond* 〔*past*〕 *expression, beyond description; cannot be said in words. 필설로 다할 수 없는; 이루 형언할 수 없는.

find expession (= *be expressed*) ***in*** *something,* …의 형태로 나타나다.

give expression to (= *express; manifest*) *something.* …을 표현하다. ¶ *He gave ~ to his thoughts.* 그는 자신의 사상을 표현했다.

ex·pres·sion·ism [ikspréʃənìzəm] *n.* a movement in arts, especially in drama, to give objective expression to inner experience by the use of symbols, styles, etc. 표현주의.

ex·pres·sion·less [ikspréʃənlis] *adj.* having no expression. 표정이 없는; 무표정한. ¶ *an ~ face* 무표정한 얼굴.

ex·pres·sive [iksprésiv] *adj.* **1** (of the feelings, etc.) expressing. (감정 따위)를 나타내고 있는. ¶ *a look ~ of joy* 〔*sorrow*〕 기쁨〔슬픔〕을 나타내고 있는 표정. **2** full of expression, or meaning; significant. 표정이 풍부한; 의미 있는. ¶ *an ~ face* 〔*voice*〕 표정이 풍부한 얼굴〔목소리〕 / *~ words* 의미 심장한 말. ● **ex·pres·sive·ly** [-li] *adv.*

ex·press·ly [iksprésli] *adv.* **1** clearly. 분명히; 명백히. ¶ *I told you ~ not to touch it.* 그것에 손대지 말라고 자네에게 분명히 일러줬는데. **2** particularly; on purpose. 특별히; 일부러. ¶ *He came ~ to bring the book to me.* 그는 그 책을 내게 갖다 주려고 일부러 왔다.

ex·pro·pri·ate [ekspróuprièit] *vt.* (P6,13) deprive (someone) of property, etc.; take land, etc. from (someone). (재산 따위)를 빼앗다; (토지 따위)를 몰수하다; 강제 수용하다. [→proper]

ex·pul·sion [ikspʌ́lʃən] *n.* ⓊⒸ **1** the act of expelling; the state of being expelled. 추방; 제적; 제명. ¶ *~ from school* 퇴학 / *the ~ of a member from a club* 클럽으로부터의 제명. **2** the act of driving out; the state of being driven out. 몰아냄; 구축(驅逐). ¶ *the ~ of the enemy from their trenches.* 참호로부터 적을 몰아냄. [→expel]

ex·punge [ikspʌ́ndʒ] *vt.* (P6,13) wipe or strike out (words, etc.). …을 지우다; 삭제하다. ¶ *~ a name from a list* 명부에서 이름을 삭제하다 / *~ a word from a sentence* 문장에서 낱말 하나를 지워 없애다. [L. *pungo* prick]

ex·pur·gate [ékspərgèit] *vt.* (P6) remove parts considered improper or objectionable from (a book, etc.). (서책의 부적절한 대목)을 지워 없애다; 삭제하다. ● **ex·pur·ga·tor** [-ər] *n.* [→purge]

·ex·qui·site [ikskwízit, ékskwizit] *adj.* **1** delicately beautiful; excellent; carefully or elaborately made. 절묘한; 더할 나위없는; 정교한. ¶ *~ beauty* 더할 수 없는 아름다움 / *~ designs* 정교한 디자인 / *The girl was an ~ creature.* 그 처녀는 대단한 미인이었다. **2** keenly or intensely felt. 날카로운; 예민한; 격심한. ¶ *an ~ ear for music* 음악에 예민한 귀 / *~ pain* 격통. ● **ex·qui·site·ness** [-nis] *n.* [L. *quaero* seek]

ex·qui·site·ly [ikskwízitli, ékskwizit-] *adv.* in an exquisite manner. 멋지게; 절묘하게; 날카롭게; 정교하게.

ex·tant [ekstǽnt, ékstənt] *adj.* (esp. of old books, etc.) still in existence; existing. (오래된 책·문서 따위가) 현존〔잔존〕하는(opp. extinct). ¶ *None of his letters are ~.* 그의 편지는 하나도 남아있지 않다. [L. *sto* stand]

ex·tem·po·ra·ne·ous [ikstèmpəréiniəs] *adj.* spoken or made without any preparation. 즉석의; 즉흥적인; 임시 변통의. ● **ex·tem·po·ra·ne·ous·ly** [-li] *adv.* **ex·tem·po·ra·ne·ous·ness** [-nis] *n.* [↓]

ex·tem·po·re [ikstémpəri] *adj., adv.*

without any preparation; offhand. 즉석에서(의); 준비없이. ¶ *speak ~ =give an ~ speech* 즉석 연설을 하다. [ex-, L. *tempus* time]

ex·tem·po·rize [ikstémpəràiz] *vt., vi.* (P6; 1) **1** speak, play, sing, etc. extempore. 즉석에서 연설 (따위를) 하다; 즉흥적으로 노래(연주)하다. **2** make for the occasion. 임시 변통으로 만들다; 급조하다. ¶ *~ a shelter* 오두막을 급조하다. •**ex·tem·po·ri·za·tion** [ekstèmpərizéiʃən] *n.*

·**ex·tend** [iksténd] *vt.* **1** (P6,13) stretch or spread out. (팔·손 따위)를 뻗(치)다; 펴다. ¶ *~ the hand* 손을 내뻗다. **2** (P6,13) make longer; continue; carry further. (길게) 늘이다; 연장하다; (줄·철망 따위)를 치다. ¶ *~ a road to the next village* 다음 마을까지 도로를 연장하다 / *~ a wire between two posts* 두 말뚝 사이에 철망을 치다 / *~ one's visit for a few days longer* 체재 기간을 며칠 더 연장하다 / *~ one's hotel reservations* 호텔의 예약을 연장하다. **3** (P6,13) make (something) wider; enlarge; increase (power, influence, etc.). …을 넓히다; 확대(확장)하다. ¶ *~ the city boundaries* 시역(市域)을 넓히다 / *~ a building* 증축하다 / *~ one's operations* (*business*) 사업을 확장하다 / *~ one's knowledge* 지식을 넓히다 / *~ one's power* (*influence*) 세력을 확대하다. **4** (P6,13) give; offer. (은혜·친절 따위)를 베풀다; 주다. ¶ *~ help to the poor* 가난한 사람들에게 도움의 손길을 뻗치다 / *~ a warm welcome* 따뜻이 맞이하다. **5** (P6) give a fuller meaning to. 의미를 확충하다; (법률 따위) 적용 범위를 넓히다. — *vi.* (P2B,3) **1** stretch; reach. 넓어지다; 뻗다; 달하다. **2** continue. …에 이르다; 계속되다. ¶ *My garden extends as far as the woods.* 우리집 정원은 숲에까지 이른다 / *The road extends for miles.* 길은 수 마일이나 뻗어 있다. [ex-, →tend]

ex·tend·ed [iksténdid] *adj.* stretched out; spread out; prolonged. 넓은; 뻗은; 확장된; 연장된.

ex·ten·si·ble [iksténsəbəl] *adj.* capable of being extended. 넓힐(늘일) 수 있는; 신장성(伸張性)의.

·**ex·ten·sion** [iksténʃən] *n.* **1** Ⓤ the act of extending; the state of being extended. 넓힘; 뻗음; 확대; 연장; 연기; 신장. ¶ *the ~ of knowledge* 지식의 확충 / *an ~ of one's holiday* 휴일의 연장 / *the ~ of a railway line* 철도선의 연장. **2** Ⓒ an additional part (of a building, railway line, etc.); an inner telephone line. 연장(증축) 부분; 연장선; (전화의) 내선(內線). ¶ *an ~ lecture* 대학 공개 강좌 / *an ~ table* 신축 자재(自在)의 테이블. **3** 《log.》 denotation. 외연(外延)(cf. *intension*). [→extend]

·**ex·ten·sive** [iksténsiv] *adj.* **1** wide; large; on a large scale. 넓은; 광범한; 대규모의. ¶ *~ knowledge* 넓은 지식 / *an ~ plan* 대규모의 계획 / *an ~ park* 광대한 공원. **2** covering a wide space; coarse. 다방면에 걸친; 조방(粗放)의. ¶ *~ reading* 광범한 독서 / *~ agriculture* 조방 농업. **3** thorough. 철저한. ¶ *~ repairs* (*inquiries*) 철저한 수리(조사). •**ex·ten·sive·ness** [-nis] *n.*

ex·ten·sive·ly [iksténsivli] *adv.* in an extensive manner; widely. 널리; 광범위하게.

·**ex·tent** [ikstént] *n.* **1** ⓊⒸ size; length; height; space; amount. 크기; 길이; 높이; 넓이; 양(量). ¶ *a vast ~ of land* (*sea*) 광대한 토지(바다). **2** Ⓒ the degree; limit. 정도; 범위; 한계. ¶ *to that ~* 그 정도까지 / *reduce the ~ of the law's application* 법의 적용 범위를 제한하다 / *This is the ~ of my ability.* 이것이 내 능력의 한계이다. [→extend]

to a great extent, for the most part; largely. 대부분은; 크게.

to some (***a certain***) ***extent,*** up to a certain degree. 어느 정도까지; 다소.

to the extent of, to a certain degree of. …의 정도까지. ¶ *to the full ~ of one's power* 힘껏 / *to the utmost ~* 극도로.

ex·ten·u·ate [iksténjuèit] *vt.* (P6) make (a crime, etc.) seem less serious by making excuses. (범죄 따위)를 가볍게 하다; 정상을 참작하다. ¶ *extenuating circumstances* 참작할 만한 정황 / *Nothing can ~ his wrong.* 아무 것도 그의 잘못을 가볍게 할 수는 없다. [L. *tenuis* thin]

ex·ten·u·a·tion [ikstènjuéiʃən] *n.* ⓊⒸ the act of extenuating; the state of being extenuated. 정상 참작; 경감.

ex·te·ri·or [ikstíəriər] *adj.* **1** of an outer surface; external; outward. 외면(외부)의; 바깥의(opp. interior). ¶ *the ~ wall of the castle* 성(城)의 외벽 / *~ decorations* 외부의 장식. **2** belonging to the outside. …와 동떨어진; 무관계한. ¶ *His recent behavior is ~ to his real character.* 그의 최근 행동은 그의 본래의 성격과는 무관하다. **3** foreign. 대외적인. ¶ *an ~ policy* 외교정책 / *~ trade* (*commerce*) 대외 무역. — *n.* Ⓒ the outside; an outer surface; a visible appearance. 외부; 외면; 외관. ¶ *He has a rough ~ , but a tender heart.* 그는 외양은 거칠지만 따뜻한 마음을 갖고 있다. [L.]

ex·ter·mi·nate [ikstə́ːrmənèit] *vt.* (P6) destroy (something) completely; root out. …을 전멸시키다; 근절하다. ¶ *This poison will ~ the rats.* 이 독약은 쥐를 전멸시킬 게다. [L. *extermino* banish; →terminus]

ex·ter·mi·na·tion [ikstə̀ːrmənéiʃən] *n.* ⓊⒸ the act of exterminating; the state of being exterminated. 전멸; 근절.

·**ex·ter·nal** [ikstə́ːrnəl] *adj.* **1** on, of, or for the outer part; outward. 밖(겉)의; 외부의; 외면의; 외적인(opp. internal). ¶ *the ~ world* 외계(外界) / *~ influences* 외부의 영향 / *the ~ husk of a fruit* 과일의 겉껍질 / *the enemy both ~ and internal* 내외 양면의 적. **2** outwardly visible; superficial. 표면의; 형식적인. ¶ *~ religion* 형식적 종교. **3**

foreign. 외래의; 대외적인. ¶ *an ~ policy* 대외 정책 / *~ affairs* 외교 문제; 국제 관계 / *the ~ debt of a country* 나라의 외채(外債). **4** 《med.》 used on the outside of the body. 외용(外用)의. ¶ *This alcohol is for ~ use only.* 이 알코올은 외용에 한한다.
— *n.* Ⓒ **1** an outer part. 외부. **2** 《*pl.*》 the outward form or appearance. 외형; 외관. ¶ *judge someone by externals* 아무를 외양으로 판단하다. [L. *exter* outward]

ex·ter·nal·ly [ikstə́ːrnəli] *adv.* from or on the outer part. 외부로부터[에]; 외견상.

ex·ter·ri·to·ri·al [èksteritɔ́ːriəl] *adj.* free from jurisdiction of the territory one resides in. 치외 법권의. [ex-, →territory]

ex·tinct [ikstíŋkt] *adj.* (of a light or fire) no longer burning; gone out; dead; no longer existing. (불이) 꺼진; 활동을 멈춘; (생명 따위가) 끊어진; 멸절(滅絶)된; 스러진. ¶ *an ~ volcano* 사(死)화산 / *an ~ animal* 멸종 동물. [↓]

ex·tinc·tion [ikstíŋkʃən] *n.* ŪC the act of extinguishing; the state of being extinct. 꺼짐; 소화(消火); 끊어짐; 멸절(滅絶); 소멸.

*__ex·tin·guish__ [ikstíŋgwiʃ] *vt.* (P6) **1** put out (a light, fire, etc.). …을 끄다. ¶ *~ a fire* 불을 끄다. **2** destroy (hope, love, life, passions, etc.). …을 소멸시키다; 멸절시키다; 없어지게 하다. ¶ *~ hope* 희망을 잃게 하다 / *~ a race* 민족을 멸종시키다. **3** overcome; make (someone) silent. …을 압도하다; 침묵시키다. **4** pay (one's debts). (부채)를 갚다. ¶ *~ a debt* 빚을 갚다. [L. *stinguo* quench]

ex·tin·guish·er [ikstíŋgwiʃər] *n.* Ⓒ an apparatus for putting out a light, fire, etc. 끄는 것; 소화기; (불꽃 위에 덮어씌우는) 양초 끄개.

ex·tir·pate [ékstərpèit, ekstə́ːrpeit] *vt.* (P6) destroy completely; root out. …을 박멸하다; 근절시키다; 뿌리뽑다. ¶ *~ weeds* 잡초를 뿌리뽑다 / *~ a social evil* 사회악을 근절시키다. [L. *stirps* stem]

ex·tir·pa·tion [èkstərpéiʃən] *n.* ŪC the act of extirpating; the state of being extirpated. 박멸; 근절; 멸절(滅絶).

ex·tol, ex·toll [ikstóul] *vt.* (P6,7) praise (someone) highly. …을 격찬[찬양]하다. ¶ *~ someone's genius* 아무의 재능을 몹시 칭찬하다. [L. *tollo* raise]
extol *someone* ***to the skies,*** speak very highly of someone. …을 몹시 칭찬하다; 치살리다.

ex·tort [ikstɔ́ːrt] *vt.* (P6,13) **1** obtain (money, etc.) from someone by threats, force, etc. …을 공갈하여 빼앗다; 갈취하다. **2** compel (someone) to do something by force. …을 강요하다. ¶ *~ bribes from someone* 아무에게 뇌물을 강요하다 / *~ a confession by torture* 고문으로 자백을 강요하다.
● **ex·tort·er** [-ər] *n.* [L. *torqueo* twist]

ex·tor·tion [ikstɔ́ːrʃən] *n.* ŪC **1** the act of extorting. 갈취; 강요; 강탈. **2** money, etc. obtained in this way. 강탈한 것.

ex·tor·tion·ate [ikstɔ́ːrʃənit] *adj.* demanding unreasonable payment; much too high. 강탈적[강요적]인; (가격 따위가) 엄청난. ¶ *an ~ price* [*charge*] 엄청난 값[요금] / *be ~ in one's demands* 요구가 부당하다.
● **ex·tor·tion·ate·ly** [-li] *adv.*

ex·tor·tion·er [ikstɔ́ːrʃənər] *n.* Ⓒ a person who extorts. 강탈자; 강요자; 착취자.

:**ex·tra** [ékstrə] *adj.* more than usual or expected; additional. 여분의; 임시의; 특별한. ¶ *an ~ edition* 임시 증간(호) / *an ~ pay* 임시 급여 / *an ~ allowance* 임시[특별] 수당 / *an ~ train* 임시 열차 / *an ~ inning game* (야구의) 연장전. — *adv.* more than usually; especially. 여분으로; 특별히. ¶ *an ~ high price* 할증 가격 / *pay ~* 추가로 지급하다.
— *n.* Ⓒ money, newspapers, persons, etc. that are added to the usual number or amount. 할증금; 호외; 임시 고용자. [L.]

ex·tra- [ékstrə-] *pref.* outside (of). '…외(外)의', '범위 밖의'의 뜻. [L.]

*__ex·tract__ [ikstrǽkt] *vt.* (P6,13) **1** pull out or take out (something), usu. with effort. …을 뽑아내다[빼내다]; 꺼내다, 끄집어내다. ¶ *~ a tooth* 이를 뽑다 / *~ a cork from a bottle* 병의 코르크 마개를 뽑다 / *~ a confession* 자백시키다 / *I was not able to ~ any information from him.* 그로부터 어떤 정보도 끄집어낼 수 없었다. **2** obtain (juice, etc.) by boiling, pressing, etc. …을 증류해서[짜내어] 얻다; 추출하다. ¶ *~ oil from olives* 올리브에서 기름을 짜내다 / *~ poisons from plants* 식물에서 독물을 추출하다. **3** choose or copy out (a passage) from a book, etc.; quote. …을 발췌하다; 필요한 것만 뽑아 베끼다; 인용하다. ¶ *~ examples from a story* 이야기에서 보기를 발췌하다.
— [ékstrækt] *n.* **1** ŪC something extracted. 추출물; 엑스. ¶ *~ of beef* 쇠고기 엑스. **2** Ⓒ a passage taken or quoted from a book, etc. (책 따위로부터의) 발췌; 인용구.
● **ex·trac·tor** [ikstrǽktər] *n.* [L. *traho* draw]

ex·trac·tion [ikstrǽkʃən] *n.* ŪC **1** the act of extracting; the state of being extracted. 뽑아냄. ¶ *the ~ of a tooth* 발치(拔齒) / *the ~ of information* 정보를 빼냄. **2** something extracted. 추출물; 엑스; 발췌. **3** origin; family line; birth. 혈통; 가계(家系); 태생. ¶ *people of humble ~* 비천한 태생의 사람들.

ex·tra·cur·ric·u·lar [èkstrəkəríkjələr] *adj.* outside the regular course of study. 과외(課外). ¶ *Football is an ~ activity.* 축구는 과외 활동의 하나다. [extra-, →curricular]

ex·tra·dite [ékstrədàit] *vt.* (P6) **1** give up (a fugitive). (도망범)을 넘겨 주다. **2** obtain the extradition of (such a person). (도망범을) 넘겨받다. [ex-, L. *trado* hand over]

ex·tra·di·tion [èkstrədíʃən] *n.* the handing

over of a fugitive. (도망범의) 인도; 송환.

ex·tra·ne·ous [ikstréiniəs] *adj.* not related to the matter which is being considered; coming from foreign countries. 무관계한; 외래의. ¶ *wash ~ matter away from gold* 금에서 이물질을 씻어내다 / *That question is ~ to the matter in hand.* 그 문제는 당면 문제와는 무관계하다. [→strange]

ex·traor·di·nar·i·ly [ikstrɔ̀:rdənérəli, èkstrəɔ́:rdənèrə- / -dənəri-] *adv.* in an extraordinary manner. 이상(異常)하게; 매우; 엄청나게. [↓]

:ex·traor·di·nar·y [ikstrɔ́:rdənèri, èkstrəɔ́:r- / -dənəri] *adj.* **1** beyond the usual order; unusual; eccentric; remarkable. 이상(異常)한; 보통이 아닌; 비범한; 엄청난; 놀라운. ¶ *an ~ genius* 대단한 재능 / *an ~ man* 비범한 사람 / *~ weather* 이상 기후. **2** additional to the regular staff; special; extra. 정원 외(外)의; 임시의; 특별한; 특명의. ¶ *an ~ general meeting* 임시 총회 / *an ambassador ~* 특명 전권 대사. [extra-]

ex·trap·o·late [ikstræ̀pəlèit] *vt.* (P6) infer (an unknown value, meaning, etc.) from facts that are known; determine from known values. (미지(未知)의 것을 기지(既知)의 것에서) 추정하다; 추론하다. [extra-, →(inter)polate]

extra special [⌐–⌐–] *n.* the lastest edition of an evening paper. 석간의 최종판(版).

ex·tra·ter·ri·to·ri·al [èkstrətèritɔ́:riəl] *adj.* free from the laws of the country that one lives in. 치외 법권의. [extra-]

ex·trav·a·gance [ikstræ̀vəgəns] *n.* **1** Ⓤ the act of being extravagant. 사치; 낭비. **2** Ⓒ a careless or absurd action, idea, speech, etc. 엉뚱한 언동. [↓]

ex·trav·a·gant [ikstræ̀vəgənt] *adj.* **1** spending money, things, etc. carelessly or unreasonably. 사치한; 낭비하는. ¶ *an ~ wife* 돈 씀씀이가 헤픈 아내 / *be ~ in one's way of living* 생활이 사치스럽다. **2** (of speech, action, etc.) beyond the limits of reason. 터무니없는; 무턱댄. ¶ *~ demands* 터무니없는 요구.

load someone with extravagant praise, praise someone to an excessive degree. 마구(과도하게) …를 칭찬하다.

•**ex·trav·a·gant·ly** [-li] *adv.* [→vague]

ex·trav·a·gan·za [ikstræ̀vəgǽnzə] *n.* a play intended to make people laugh; a fantastic composition. 광상극(狂想劇). [↑]

:ex·treme [ikstrí:m] *adj.* (sometimes **-trem·er, -trem·est**) **1** of the highest degree; very great; excessive. 극도의; 극단의; 과도한. ¶ *~ old age* 대단한 고령 / *~ poverty* 극심한 가난 / *the ~ penalty* 극형 / *an ~ case* 극단적인 예 / *~ patience* 극도의 인내 / *an ~ love for one's country* 나라에 대한 극도의 사랑. **2** (of ideas, etc.) radical; advanced. 과격한; 급진의. ¶ *~ people* 과격한 사람들 / *~ opinions* 과격한 의견 / *the ~ Left* 극좌파. **3** at the very end; farthest away. 맨 끝의; (중앙에서) 가장 먼(변두리의). ¶ *the ~ end of the ocean* 대양의 끝 / *the ~ limits of a town* 시의 가장 변두리. **4** last. 최후의; 마지막의. ¶ *~ hopes* 마지막 희망.

in one's extreme moments =***at the extreme hour of life,*** at the end of life. 최후를 맞이하여; 죽음에 즈음하여.

—*n.* **1** Ⓒ an extreme degree, state or act. 극도; 극단. ¶ *be cautious to an ~* 극도로 신중하다. **2** 《*pl.*》 things as different in qualities, etc. as possible. 양극단. ¶ *the extremes of heat and cold* 더위와 추위의 양극단 / 《*prov.*》 *Extremes meet.* 양극단은 일치한다.

go to extremes, take excessive measures; be excessive in speech, action, etc. (언동 따위가) 극단으로 흐르다.

in the extreme, to the utmost degree; very. 극단으로; 매우. ¶ *be showy in the ~* 극도로 야하다.

run to an extreme =go to extremes.

•**ex·treme·ness** [-nis] *n.* [L. *extremus*]

:ex·treme·ly [ikstrí:mli] *adv.* to an extreme degree; very. 극도로; 극단으로; 매우. ¶ *an ~ kind man* 매우 친절한 사람 / *be ~ cold* 무척 춥다.

ex·trem·i·ty [ikstréməti] *n.* Ⓒ (*pl.* **-ties**) **1** the point or end farthest away from the main part. 끝. ¶ *at the ~ of the bridge* 다리 끝에. **2** the state of extreme pain or need; the last stage. (아픔·궁핍 따위의) 극한 상태; 극도; 궁지. ¶ *the ~ of poverty* 극도의 빈곤 / *be in dire ~* 지극한 궁경에 처해 있다 / *expect the ~* 만일을 각오하다; 비상사태를 예상하다 / *to the last ~* 한계점까지. **3** 《sometimes *pl.*》 an extreme measure. 비상 수단. ¶ *go* (*resort*) *to extremities* 비상(최후) 수단에 호소하다. **4** 《usu. *pl.*》 the hands and feet. 손; 발.

ex·tri·cate [ékstrəkèit] *vt.* (P6,13) set (someone) free from danger, difficulty, etc.; release (an animal) from a trap, etc. …을 구출(해방)하다. ¶ *~ oneself from debt* 빚에서 벗어나다 / *Tom extricated the bird from the net.* 톰은 그물에 걸린 새를 풀어 주었다 / *He managed to ~ himself from the difficulties.* 그는 그럭저럭 그 난국에서 벗어날 수가 있었다. [→trick]

ex·tri·ca·tion [èkstrəkéiʃən] *n.* ⓊⒸ the act of extricating; the state of being extricated. 구출; 탈출; 유리(遊離).

ex·trin·sic [ekstrínsik, -zik] *adj.* **1** not belonging to the real character or essence; not essential; not inherent. 본질적이 아닌; 고유하지 않은. **2** external; extraneous. 외부의; 외부로부터의(opp. intrinsic(al)). [L.]

ex·tro·vert [ékstrouvə̀:rt] *n.* a person tending to act rather than think. 외향적인

사람(opp. introvert). [extra-, →introvert]

ex·trude [ikstrúːd] *vt.* (P6) push out; drive out. …을 밀어내다; 몰아(쫓아)내다. — *vi.* (P1) protrude; project. 돌출하다; 밀려나다. [L. *trudo* thrust]

ex·u·ber·ance [igzúːbərəns], **-an·cy** [-ənsi] *n.* ⟪usu. *an* ~⟫ the state of being exuberant; abundance. 무성(함); 풍부; 충만. ¶ *an ~ of foliage* 무성한 가지와 잎 / *an ~ of health* 충만한 건강 / *an ~ of joy* 넘치는 기쁨 / *an ~ of one's youth* 넘쳐 흐르는 젊음. [↓]

ex·u·ber·ant [igzúːbərənt] *adj.* **1** growing plentifully; abundant. 우거진; 풍부한. ¶ *The trees have ~ foliage.* 나무들은 잎이 무성하게 우거져 있다. **2** filled with good health and spirits; full of vitality. 원기가 넘치는. ¶ *The children are in ~ spirits.* 아이들은 활기에 차 있다. [L. *uber* fertile]

ex·ude [igzúːd, iksúːd] *vt.*, *vi.* (P6; 1,2A) send out (something) in drops; (of sweat, etc.) flow out softly. …을 스며나오게 하다; 스며나오다. ¶ *~ an icy sweat* 식은땀을 흘리다 / *Sweat exudes from the pores.* 땀구멍에서 땀이 스며나온다. [L. *sudo* sweat]

ex·ult [igzʌ́lt] *vi.* (P1,3,4) ⟪*at, in, over*⟫ be very glad. 환희하다. ¶ *~ at* 〔*over*〕 *one's success* 성공에 광희(狂喜)하다 / *They exulted in the victory.* 그들은 승리에 환희했다. [L. *salio* leap]

ex·ult·ant [igzʌ́ltənt] *adj.* feeling great joy; triumphant. 크게 기뻐하는; 의기양양한. ¶ *~ over victory* 승리에 의기양양한.

ex·ul·ta·tion [ègzʌltéiʃən, éksʌl-] *n.* Ⓤ the act of exulting; great joy. 몹시 기뻐함; 환희.

:eye [ai] *n.* **1** the organ of sight. 눈. ¶ *the naked ~* 맨눈 / *compound eyes* 겹눈 / *have lovely blue eyes* 사랑스러운 푸른 눈을 가지다 / *hit a man in the ~* 눈을 때리다 / *open* 〔*shut*〕 *one's eyes* 눈을 뜨다〔감다〕 / *from* 〔*out of*〕 *the corner of one's ~* 곁눈질로 / *with one's eyes full of tears* 눈물어린 눈으로 / *meet someone's ~* 아무의 눈에 띄다 / *Where are your eyes?* 눈을 어데 두고 있느냐 ⟪잘 보아라⟫. **2** the power or sense of seeing; eyesight. 시력; 시각(視覺). ¶ *have sharp* 〔*weak*〕 *eyes* 시력이 날카롭다〔약하다〕 / *lose an ~* 한쪽 눈이 실명하다. **3** a look; a gaze. 봄; 눈(길); 시선; 주시; 감시. ¶ *the green ~* 질투의 눈 / *an angry ~* 성난 눈 / *fix one's eyes on* …에 주목하다; …을 응시하다 / *draw the eyes of* …의 눈(길)을 끌다 / *take one's eyes off* 〔*from*〕 …에서 눈을 떼다 / *keep someone under one's eyes* 아무를 감시하다〔지켜보다〕. **4** the power of judging; judgment. 식별력; 감식안(眼); 안식. ¶ *the ~ of an artist* 예술가의 안식 / *have an ~ in one's head* 안식이 있다. **5** ⟪usu. *pl.*⟫ opinion; point of view. 의견; 견해. ¶ *in the eyes of the law* 법률에 비추어 보아; 법의 견지에서 보면 / *You are wrong in my eyes.* 내 견해로는 자네가 나쁘다. **6** an eye-like thing. 눈과 같은 것. ¶ *an ~ of a needle* 바늘귀 / *an ~ of a potato* 감자의 눈〔싹〕. **7** something central. 중심. ¶ *an ~ of a typhoon* 태풍의 눈 / *bull's ~* 과녁의 중심.

an eye for an eye, ⟪Bible⟫ retaliation. 눈에는 눈; 보복.

before one's eyes, in one's presence or sight. …의 면전에서.

black someone's eyes = give someone a black eye.

cast sheep's eyes at =make eyes at.

catch the eye of, attract the attention of. …의 주의를 끌다.

clap eyes on, look at; see. …을 보다. ¶ *I've never clap eyes on him before.* 이제까지 그를 본 일이 없다.

close one's eyes to =shut one's eyes to.

do someone in the eye, ⟪*colloq.*⟫ cheat someone. 아무를 속이다.

dry one's eyes, stop weeping. 울음을 그치다.

feast one's eyes on, look at with delight. …을 보며 즐기다; …로 눈요기하다.

give someone a black eye, hit someone so that there is a discolored area around his eye. 아무를 때려 눈두덩에 멍이 들게 하다.

give an eye to, keep an occasional watch on; give attention to; look after. …을 때때로 지켜보다; …에 주목하다; …을 돌보다.

have an eye for, have the ability to see, judge and understand clearly. …에 대한 감식안〔안목〕이 있다; …을 볼 줄 아는 눈이 있다. ¶ *have an ~ for beauty* 심미안이 있다.

have an eye to, watch for (something) to get; have as one's object. …을 얻으려고 눈독들이다; …을 목적으로〔목표로〕 하다.

have in one's eye(s), have in mind; have a mental picture of. …을 염두에 두고 있다; …을 마음에 그리고 있다.

if you had half an eye, if you were not wholly blind or dull. 조금만 영리했더라면.

in the eye of the wind, in the direction of the wind. 바람 불어오는 쪽을 향해.

in the mind's eye, in imagination. 상상으로.

in the wind's eye =in the eye of the wind.

keep an 〔*one's*〕 ***eye on,*** keep a watch over. …을 지켜보다; …을 감시하다; …에게서 눈을 떼지 않다.

keep one's 〔***both***〕 ***eyes*** (***wide***) ***open,*** watch carefully. 방심 않고 감시하다; 정신 바짝 차리다.

lay eyes on =clap eyes on.

make eyes at, (of a young man) look meaningly or lovingly at (a woman). …에게 추파를 던지다.

make someone open his eyes, surprise someone; make someone wonder. 아무를 깜짝 놀라게 하다.

Mind your eye! Look out! Be careful! 정신 차려; 주의해라.

open one's eyes, look (at) steadily with

astonishment. 놀라서 눈을 크게 뜨다.
open** someone's **eyes to, make someone understand or realize the true state of (something). …의 진상을 깨닫게 하다.
***run** one's **eyes over** 〔**through**〕,* look at hastily; examine quickly. …을 대충 훑어보다; 대충 조사〔검토〕하다.
see eye to eye with, be in complete agreement. 완전히 일치하다. ¶ *I see ~ to ~ with him in that matter.* 그 문제엔 그와 같은 의견이다.
see with half an eye, see or understand (something) easily, because it is so evident. 곧 알다; 쉽게 이해할 수 있다.
set eyes on =clap eyes on.
***shut** one's **eyes to** 〔**on**〕,* refuse to see or consider; disregard. …을 보려고〔생각하려고〕 하지 않다; …을 무시하다; …을 불문에 부치다.
the apple of** one's **eye, the dearest person or thing that one has. 가장 사랑하는〔소중한〕 사람〔것〕.
turn a blind eye to (=*pretend not to see*) *something.* …을 보고도 못 본 체하다.
under** someone's* (very***) ***eyes,*** in someone's presence; with no attempt at secrecy. …의 (바로) 면전〔눈앞〕에서; 공공연히.
up to** one's* 〔the***〕 ***eyes in,*** fully engaged in; very busy with. …에 전념〔몰두〕하고.
with an eye to, with a view to; considering. …할 목적〔마음〕으로; …하려고.
— *vt.* (P6,7) look at; watch. 보다; 주시하다. ¶ *~ someone askance* 아무를 흘겨보다 / *~ with curiosity* 신기한 듯이 보다 / *~ a suspicious person* 수상쩍은 사람을 주시하여 보다. [E.]

eye·ball [áibɔ̀ːl] *n.* Ⓒ the ball-shaped part of the eye. 안구(眼球); 눈알.

•**eye·brow** [áibràu] *n.* Ⓒ the hair above the eye. 눈썹. ¶ *heavy eyebrows* 짙은 눈썹.
knit the eyebrows, bend one's brows. 눈썹을 찌푸리다.

eye·glass [áiglæ̀s, -glɑ̀ːs] *n.* Ⓒ **1** a lens used to help eyesight. 안경 알〔렌즈〕. **2** a cup used for washing eyes. 세안용(洗眼用) 컵. **3** an eyepiece. 접안(接眼) 렌즈. **4** 《*pl.*》 a pair of glass lenses used to improve eyesight. 안경.

eye·lash [áilæ̀ʃ] *n.* Ⓒ a hair or hairs growing on the edge of the eyelid. 속눈썹.

eye·less [áilis] *adj.* blind; without eyes. 눈이 없는; 맹목의. ¶ *an ~ leader* 맹목적인 지도자.

eye·let [áilit] *n.* Ⓒ **1** a small hole to receive a cord, lace, rope, etc. (끈·밧줄 따위를 꿰기 위한) 작은 구멍. **2** a metal ring set in a hole. (운동화 등의 끈 구멍 가장자리의) 테쇠. **3** a hole to peep through; a loophole. 들여다 보는 구멍.

eye·lid [áilìd] *n.* Ⓒ the upper or lower cover of the skin over the eye. 눈꺼풀. ¶ *the upper* 〔*the lower*〕 *~* 윗〔아랫〕눈꺼풀.
hang (***on***) ***by the eyelids,*** just cling to (something). 간신히 매달려 있다; 위험하기 짝없는 상태에 있다.

eye-o·pen·er [áiòupənər] *n.* Ⓒ 《*colloq.*》 **1** something that makes the eyes open in surprise, wonder, etc., such as a piece of news, or a discovery. 당목(瞠目)하게 할 만한 사실; 놀라운 일〔경험〕. **2** a drink of alcohol for waking a person up. 해장술.

eye·piece [áipìːs] *n.* Ⓒ the lens nearest to the eye in a microscope, telescope, etc. 접안 렌즈; 접안경(鏡).

eye·shot [áiʃɑ̀t / -ʃɔ̀t] *n.* Ⓤ the distance at which one can see; the field of vision. 눈이 미치는 곳; 시계(視界). ¶ *beyond* 〔*out of*〕 *~* 눈이 미치지 않는 곳에 / *within* 〔*in*〕 *~ of* 눈이 미치는 곳에 / *come into ~ of* …의 시계〔시야〕에 들어오다.

eye·sight [áisàit] *n.* Ⓤ **1** the power of seeing. 시력; 시각. ¶ *lose one's ~* 실명(失明)하다 / *have good* 〔*poor*〕 *~* 시력이 좋다〔약하다〕. **2** the range of sight. 시계(視界); 시야. ¶ *in one's ~* 안전(眼前)에 / *come within ~* 시계에 들어오다.

eye·sore [áisɔ̀ːr] *n.* Ⓒ a thing unpleasant to look at. 눈에 거슬리는 것; 보아 불쾌한 것.

eye·strain [áistrèin] *n.* Ⓤ a tired or weak condition of the eyes caused by using them too much, reading in a dim light, etc. 안정(眼精) 피로.

eye·teeth [áitìːθ] *n.* pl. of **eyetooth.**

eye·tooth [áitùːθ] *n.* Ⓒ (*pl.* **-teeth**) either of the two pointed teeth in the upper jaw; the canine tooth. 송곳니; 견치.
cut** one's **eyeteeth, grow up; become experienced. 어른이 되다; 경험을 쌓다; 세상을 알다.

eye·wash [áiwɑ̀ʃ, -wɔ̀ːʃ / -wɔ̀ʃ] *n.* Ⓤ **1** a lotion for washing the eyes. 안약; 세안수(水). **2** 《*colloq.*》 a dishonest statement; flattery. 엉터리없는 (거짓)말; 속임수; 아첨.

eye·wit·ness [áiwìtnis, ⌐⌐–] *n.* Ⓒ a person who has actually seen an event and can testify to it. 목격자. ¶ *an ~ of the crime.* 범죄의 목격자.

ey·rie, ey·ry [ɛ́əri, íəri] *n.* (*pl.* **-ries**) = aerie.

f F

F, f [ef] *n.* Ⓒ (*pl.* **F's, Fs, f's, fs** [-s]) **1** the sixth letter of the English alphabet. 영어 알파벳의 여섯째 글자. **2** 《mus.》 the fourth note of the musical scale of C major. 바음(音); 바조(調).

f 《mus.》 forte. 세게.

F. Fahrenheit; February; French; Fellow; Friday.

f. farthing; fathom; feet; feminine; fine; folio; following; foot; franc; frequency.

FA field artillery(야포; 야전포병); Football Association.

FAA 《U.S.》 Federal Aviation Agency. 연방항공국.

Fa·bi·an [féibiən] *adj.* cleverly firing out an enemy by slowness and caution. 지구(持久) 전법을 쓰는. ¶ ~ *tactics* 지구전략. [L. *Fabius*, commander against Hannibal]

Fa·bi·an·ism [féibiənìzəm] *n.* belief in, or the practice of, a Fabian policy. 페이비언주의《페이비언 협회의 주의인 점진적 사회주의》.

Fabian society [∠-- -∠--] *n.* a socialist society favoring the gradual spread of socialism by peaceful means. 페이비언 협회《점진적 사회주의를 주창한 단체》.

•**fa·ble** [féibəl] *n.* **1** Ⓒ a story made up in order to teach a moral. 우화(寓話). ¶ *Aesop's Fables* 이솝 우화. **2** Ⓤ 《*collectively*》 legends; myths. 전설; 신화. **3** Ⓒ an untrue story; a lie. 꾸며낸 이야기; 거짓말. **4** 《rare》 the plot of a drama, narrative poem, etc. (극·서사시 따위의) 줄거리. — *vi.* (P1) tell or write fables; tell false tales. 우화를 이야기하다〔쓰다〕; 거짓말을 하다. [L.]

fa·bled [féibəld] *adj.* told about in fables, legends or myths; having no real existence; fictitious. 우화〔전설, 신화〕로 전해져 내려오는; 꾸며낸 이야기의.

•**fab·ric** [fǽbrik] *n.* **1** Ⓒ a cloth made by weaving. 직물. ¶ *cotton* 〔*silk, woolen*〕 *fabrics* 면〔견(絹), 모〕직물. **2** Ⓤ the style or pattern of weaving; texture. 짠 방식; 짜임새. ¶ *cloths of different* ~ 짜임새가 다른 천. **3** ⓊⒸ a framework; a structure; Ⓒ a building. 구조; 뼈대; 조직; 구조물; 건물. ¶ *the social* ~ 사회 조직 / *the* ~ *of an argument* 의론의 구성〔짜임〕. [L. *faber* artificer]

fab·ri·cate [fǽbrikèit] *vt.* (P6) **1** make; build; construct. …을 만들다; 건조하다; 짜맞추다; 조립하다. ¶ ~ *automobiles* 자동차를 조립하다 / ~ *a bridge* 다리를 건조하다. **2** make up (stories, lies, etc.); make (a false document). …을 날조〔조작〕하다; 위조하다. ¶ ~ *a document* 문서를 위조하다 / ~ *a story* 이야기를 조작하다. [→fabric, -ate]

fab·ri·ca·tion [fæ̀brikéiʃən] *n.* **1** Ⓤ the act of fabricating. 제작; 조립; 구성; 조작; 거짓. **2** Ⓒ something fabricated. 조작한 것; 위조물〔문서〕.

Fab·ri·koid [fǽbrikɔ̀id] *n.* 《trademark》 a waterproof fabric having a cloth foundation and a pyroxylin surface. 패브리코이드《천에 질산 섬유소를 바른 방수 직물; 상표명》.

fab·u·list [fǽbjəlist] *n.* Ⓒ a person who writes or tells fables. 우화 작가; 거짓말쟁이. [→fable]

fab·u·lous [fǽbjələs] *adj.* **1** of or belonging to legends or myths. 전설상〔신화상〕의; 전설적인. ¶ *a* ~ *hero* 〔*story*〕 전설적인 영웅〔이야기〕. **2** far from the truth; hard to believe; enormous. 가공의; 믿기 어려운; 엄청난. ¶ *a* ~ *price* 터무니없는 값. **3** 《*colloq.*》 wonderful; excellent. 놀라운; 굉장한; 멋진. ¶ ~ *jewels* 훌륭한 보석 / *a* ~ *party* 〔*idea*〕 멋진 파티〔착상〕. [→fable]

fab·u·lous·ly [fǽbjələsli] *adv.* extremely; incredibly. 무척; 터무니없이.

fac., facsim. facsimile.

fa·çade [fəsɑ́:d] *n.* Ⓒ **1** the front part of a building. 건물의 정면. **2** a false appearance. 거짓 외관; 가장. [→face]

:face [feis] *n.* Ⓒ **1** the front part of the head. 얼굴. ¶ *a bony* 〔*broad*〕 ~ 뼈만 앙상한〔넓적한〕 얼굴 / *strike someone's* ~ =*strike someone in the* ~ 아무의 얼굴을 때리다 / *hide one's* ~ *with shame* 부끄러워 얼굴을 가리다 / *with a smile on one's* ~ 얼굴에 미소를 띄우고. **2** a look or expression. (표정으로서의) 얼굴; 표정. ¶ *a* ~ *of anger* 성난 얼굴 / *a colorless* ~ 핏기 없는 얼굴 / *wear a sad* ~ 슬픈 표정을 하다 / *put on a grave* ~ 진지한 얼굴을 하다 / *pull* 〔*draw*〕 *a long* ~ 우울한 얼굴을 하다. **3** 《often *pl.*》 《*colloq.*》 an ugly or peculiar look made by moving the mouth, eyes, etc. 찌푸린 얼굴; 혐오의〔비웃는〕 얼굴. ¶ *make a* ~ *at someone* 아무에게 얼굴을 찌푸리다. **4** the outward appearance or aspect. 외견; 외관; 양상. ¶ *the* ~ *of the countryside* 전원의 경관. **5** the surface of something, esp. the front, upper, or outer part. 겉(면); 정면; 표면; 앞면. ¶ *the* ~ *of a card* 카드패의 거죽 / *the* ~ *of a building* 건물의 정면 / *the* ~ *of a dollar bill*

F

달러 지폐의 권면. 6 《*the* ~》《*colloq.*》 rude boldness; impudence. 뻔뻔함. 7 《*fig.*》 self-respect; dignity; good name. 면목; 낯; 위신. ¶ *lose* (*one's*) ~ 면목〔체면〕을 잃다 / *save* (*one's*) ~ 낯〔체면〕을 세우다 / *give a* ~ *to the man* 그 사나이의 낯〔체면〕을 세워주다.

before someone's face, openly. …의 면전에서; 공공연히.

face down 〔***up***〕, with the head or face turned downward 〔upward〕. 얼굴을 숙이고〔쳐들고〕; 겉을 밑으로〔위로〕 하고. ¶ *lie down* ~ *up* 반듯이 눕다.

face to face, a) with faces turned toward each other. (…와) 마주보고. b) 《*with*》 in the actual presence. (…와) 직면하여. ¶ *be* 〔*stand*〕 ~ *to* ~ *with danger* 위험에 직면하다.

fly in the face of, act in opposition to, on purpose; resist openly. …에 정면으로 반대〔도전〕하다; 공공연히 반항하다. ¶ *fly in the* ~ *of the law* 법에 정면 도전하다.

have the face (*to do*), be shameless or bold enough. 뻔뻔하게도 (…하다).

in someone's face, a) in the presence of. …의 면전에서. ¶ *He laughed in my* ~. 내 면전에서 웃었다. b) openly. 공공연히.

in (***the***) ***face of,*** a) in the presence of. …의 면전에서. ¶ *Even in the* ~ *of death he did not hesitate.* 죽음을 눈앞에 두고도 그는 망설이지 않았다. b) in spite of. …에도 불구하고.

in the face of day 〔***the sun***〕, in broad daylight; openly. 대낮에; 공공연히.

lie on one's face, lie with one's face downward; lie with one's back upward. 엎드려 눕다.

look someone in the face, look at someone in a steady manner; meet someone's eyes with no shame or hesitation. …의 얼굴을 정면으로 보다; …의 얼굴을 마주 보다.

make 〔***pull***〕 ***a face*** 〔***faces***〕, 《*at, in*》 show an expression of disgust, pain, etc. 얼굴을 찌푸리다.

make 〔***pull***〕 ***a long face,*** look sad or unhappy. 슬픈〔우울한, 실망한〕 얼굴을 하다.

on the face of it, judging by its outward appearances only. 보기에는; 표면상.

open one's face, 《U.S. *colloq.*》 talk. 입을 열다; 말하다.

put a brave 〔***bold***〕 ***face on*** (*a situation, etc.*), show courage or cheerfulness in the face of difficulties; face courageously. …에 대담한 태도를 가장하다; 짐짓 태연한 체하다.

put a good face on (*a matter*), make (a matter) look well. …의 겉을 꾸미다; 겉바르다.

put a new face on (=*change the aspect of*) *something*. …의 형세를〔국면을〕 일변시키다.

set 〔***put***〕 ***one's face against*** (=*oppose, resist*) *someone* or *something*. …에 반대하다.

show one's face, present oneself; appear. 얼굴을 내밀다; 모습을 나타내다.

to someone's face, a) openly; boldly. 공공연히. b) in someone's presence. …의 면전에서. ¶ *blame* 〔*speak ill of*〕 *someone to his* ~ 아무를 맞대하여 비난〔욕〕하다.

— *vt.* (P6) 1 look or be turned toward or be opposite to (someone or something). …쪽을〔으로〕 향하다; …에 면하다. ¶ ~ *the light* 불빛을 향하다 / *The window faces the sea.* 창문은 바다에 면해 있다 / *The bedroom faces the park.* 침실에서 공원이 보인다 / *My house faces a main street.* 내 집은 중심가를 향해 있다. 2 meet bravely or boldly; confront. …에(게) (용감히) 맞서다; …에 대항하다. ¶ ~ *danger* 〔*the enemy*〕 위험〔적〕에 맞서다 / *I cannot* ~ *him.* 그에게 대항할 수가 없다. 3 (P13) 《*with*》 cover or line (something) with a different material. …을 덧대다; 덧바르다. ¶ ~ *a wall with plaster* 벽을 회반죽으로 덧바르다 / *a coat faced with silk* 비단으로 가선을 두른 상의 / *They faced the wooden house with brick.* 그들은 목조 가옥에 벽돌을 덧대었다. 4 recognize and be prepared to meet; admit. (싫은 것을) 직시하다; 인정하다. ¶ ~ *the situation* 상태를 직시하다 / *We've got to* ~ *facts.* 사실을 인정해야 한다. — *vi.* (P2A,3) 《*on, to, up*》 be turned; look. (얼굴을) 돌리다; 향하다; 면하다. ¶ ~ (*to the*) *north* 북을〔북쪽으로〕 향하다; 북향이다 / *Right* ~! 우향 우 / *About* ~! 뒤로 돌아 / *The hotel faces on a lovely lake.* 호텔은 아름다운 호수에 면해 있다. [L. *facies*]

face (***it***) ***out,*** carry through with courage. 용기있게 밀고 나가다.

face the music ⇨music.

face up to, face (something) with courage; admit (something). …에 대담히 맞서다; …을 인정하다.

face guard [´ˋ] *n.* a mask for protecting the face. (용접공·펜싱 선수 등의) 얼굴 가리개; 마스크.

face powder [´ ˋ-] *n.* a cosmetic powder (e.g. flesh-colored talc) applied to the face. 분.

face-sav·ing [féissèiviŋ] *adj.* serving to save one's dignity or face. 체면을 유지시키는; 체면〔면목〕이 서는. — *n.* an act to save one's dignity. 체면을 유지시키는 행위.

fac·et [fǽsit] *n.* Ⓒ 1 one of the small, flat, polished surfaces of a cut gem or stone. 보석의 작은 평면. 2 an aspect. (사물의) 면; 양상. [→face]

fa·ce·tious [fəsíːʃəs] *adj.* fond of joking; humorous. 농을 좋아하는; 우스(꽝스러)운; 괘사스러운. ¶ *a* ~ *remark* 우스운 말. ●**fa·ce·tious·ness** [-nis] *n.* [L.]

fa·ce·tious·ly [fəsíːʃəsli] *adv.* in a facetious manner; jokingly. 우습게; 우스꽝〔괘사〕스럽게; 농으로.

face-to-face [féistəféis] *adv., adj.* in the presence of each other. 얼굴을 서로 마주 대하여〔대하는〕. [→face]

face value [⸗ ⸗] *n.* **1** the value marked on a piece of money, stamp, etc. 액면 가격. **2** apparent value. 표면상의 가치; 문자〔액면 그〕대로의 의미〔뜻〕. ¶ *take* 〔*accept*〕 *someone* 〔*someone's statement*〕 *at* ~ 아무를〔아무의 진술을〕 액면 그대로 받아들이다.

fa·cia [féiʃə] *n.* a plate over a shopfront with the owner's name, etc. (점두(店頭) 상부의) 간판. [*face*]

fa·cial [féiʃəl] *adj.* of or for the face. 얼굴의. ¶ *a* ~ *expression* 얼굴의 표정 / *a* ~ *spasm* 안면 경련 / ~ *cream* 미안용(美顔用) 크림. — *n.* Ⓤ Ⓒ 《*colloq.*》 a treatment of the face, esp. by massage. 미안술(美顔術).

fac·ile [fǽsil / fǽsail] *adj.* **1** easy to do. 쉽게 할 수 있는(opp. difficult). ¶ *a* ~ *task* 손쉬운 일 / *a* ~ *method* 간편한 방법 / *a* ~ *victory* 낙승. **2** moving or working easily. 술술〔잘〕 움직이는; 경쾌한; 유창한. ¶ *a* ~ *hand* 〔*pen*〕 달필 / *have a* ~ *tongue* 말을 잘하다; 능변이다. **3** gentle; mild. (유)순한; 상냥한. ¶ *have a* ~ *nature* 유순한 성질이다. [L. *facio* do]

fa·cil·i·tate [fəsílətèit] *vt.* (P6) make (something) easy; promote. …을 용이하게〔편하게〕 하다; 촉진하다. ¶ *Airplanes* ~ *travel.* 비행기는 여행을 용이하게 한다. 語法 반드시 무엇을 나타내는 말이 주어가 됨. [→ facile, -ate]

***fa·cil·i·ty** [fəsíləti] *n.* (*pl.* **-ties**) **1** Ⓤ ease. 용이함; 쉬움(opp. difficulty). ¶ *play the piano with* ~ 피아노를 손쉽게 치다. **2** Ⓤ the ability to do something easily. 용이하게 할 수 있는 능력; 솜씨; 능숙; 재능. ¶ *compose with great* ~ 아주 수월하게 만들어 내다 / *have great* ~ *in doing* …을 하는 대단한 재능이 있다 / *He showed wonderful* ~ *in playing difficult music.* 어려운 곡을 연주하는데 놀라운 재능을 보였다. **3** 《*pl.*》 《*for*》 the means which makes an action, etc. easier; something designed to serve a certain function. 편의; 편리; (편의를 주는) 시설; 설비; 기관. ¶ *kitchen facilities* 주방 설비 / *facilities for travel* 여행 기관 / *facilities of civilization* 문명의 이기(利器). [→facile, -ity]

give 〔***offer, afford, accord***〕 ***someone every facility for,*** smooth someone's way for doing something. …에게 —을 위한 온갖 편의를 제공하다.

with facility, with ease. 손쉽게; 용이하게.

fac·ing [féisiŋ] *n.* **1** Ⓒ a covering for the decoration or protection of a building. (건축에서) 마무리 치장한 면; 표면 마무리. ¶ *a wooden house with a brick* ~ 표면 벽돌 마무리 치장의 목조 가옥. **2** 《*pl.*》 material applied along an edge of a garment. (의복의) 가선에 두른 장식; 끝동; (군복의 병과를 나타내는) 깃; 수장(袖章). [*face*]

〈facing 2〉

go 〔***be put***〕 ***through one's facings,*** be thoroughly trained. 충분히 훈련받다.

fac·sim·i·le [fæksíməli] *n.* Ⓒ an exact copy or reproduction of writing, a manuscript, etc. (필적·원고 따위의) 정교한 복제; 모사(模寫). ¶ *make a* ~ *of* …을 모사〔복제〕하다.

in facsimile, exactly; accurately. 정확히.
— *vt.* (P6) make a facsimile of. …을 모사〔복사〕하다. [L. =make like]

:fact [fækt] *n.* **1** Ⓒ something that has happened or been done; an actual event or deed. 실제 있었던 일; 사실. ¶ *a historic* ~ 역사적(인) 사실. **2** Ⓒ ⓐ something known to be true or accepted to be true. 현실에 있는 일; 사실. ¶ *No one can deny the* ~ *that fire burns.* 불이 탄다는 사실을 아무도 부정 못한다. ⓑ something stated to be true or to have happened. 사실〔진실〕이라고 말하는 일; 있었다고 생각되는 일; 사실; 진상. ¶ *tell the facts* 사실을 말하다 / *hear the facts from an eyewitness* 목격자로부터 진상을 듣다. **3** Ⓤ the quality of being real; truth. (이론·의견·상상 따위에 대해서) 현실성; 진실. ¶ *a question of* ~ 현실성의 문제 / *Fact is stranger than fiction.* 사실은 소설보다도 기이하다. **4** Ⓒ 《law》 ⓐ the statement of something that has been done, etc. 말하는〔주장하는〕 사실. ¶ *His facts are doubtful.* 그가 말하는 사실은 의심스럽다. ⓑ 《*the* ~》 something done; a deed; a crime. (사건·상황의) 사실; 범행. ¶ *confess the* ~ 범행을 자백하다 / *be caught in the* ~ 현행범으로 체포되다 / *accessary after* 〔*before*〕 *the* ~ 사후(事後)〔사전〕 종범자. [L. *facio* do, *factum* that which is done]

as a matter of fact, truly; really. 실제로〔상〕; 사실상.

in fact, **a**) =as a matter of fact. **b**) in brief. 요컨대; 결국.

in point of fact =as a matter of fact.

fac·tion [fǽkʃən] *n.* **1** Ⓒ a group of people in a political party, etc. 당파; 파벌; 분파. ¶ *The party has split into two factions.* 당은 두 파로 분열했다. **2** Ⓤ the act of quarreling among the members of a political party, etc. 파벌 싸움; 내분. [↑]

fac·tion·al [fǽkʃənəl] *adj.* of factions. 당파의; 파벌적인.

fac·tious [fǽkʃəs] *adj.* **1** tending to form factions. 당파를 짓고 싶어하는. ¶ *a* ~ *spirit* 당파심. **2** fond of causing trouble. 당파 싸움을 좋아하는; 당쟁〔파벌 싸움〕을 일삼는.
● **fac·tious·ly** [-li] *adv.*

fac·ti·tious [fæktíʃəs] *adj.* not natural; artificial; produced by design. 자연스럽지 않은; 인위적인; 일부러 만든(opp. natural). ¶ ~ *smile* 부자연스런 웃음 / ~ *products* 모조

품; 가짜 / ~ *flowers* 조화(造花). ● **fac·ti·tious·ly** [-li] *adv.* [→fact]

fac·ti·tive [fǽktətiv] *adj.* 《gram.》 (of a verb) taking both an object and a complement. 목적과 보어를 취하는; 작위(作爲)(동사)의. ¶ ~ *verbs* 작위 동사(e.g. He *made* 〔*called, thought*〕 his brother king.).

:fac·tor [fǽktər] *n.* Ⓒ **1** something that helps to bring about a result; an element. (결과를 가져오는) 요인; 요소. ¶ *a principal* ~ 주(主)요인 / *as a* ~ *in the causation of a disease* 병 발생상의 한 요인으로서 / *Effort is an important* ~ *in success.* 노력은 성공을 가져오는 중요한 요인이다. **2** 《math.》 any of the numbers that produce a given number when multiplied together. 인수; 인자. ¶ *a common* ~ 공통 인자; 공인수 / *2 and 3 are factors of 6.* 2와 3은 6의 인수이다. **3** a person who does business for another; an agent. 대리인. [L. *factor* maker, doer; →fact, -or]

:fac·to·ry [fǽktəri] *n.* Ⓒ (*pl.* **-ries**) a building or group of buildings where goods are manufactured. (제조) 공장. [↑]

fac·to·tum [fæktóutəm] *n.* Ⓒ a man who is employed to do all kinds of work. 잡역부(夫). [→fact, total]

fac·tu·al [fǽktʃuəl] *adj.* concerned with fact; based on facts. 사실(상)의; 사실에 의거한(opp. theoretical). [→fact]

·fac·ul·ty [fǽkəlti] *n.* Ⓒ (*pl.* **-ties**) **1** ability to do some special thing. 능력; 재능. ¶ *the limitations of human* ~ 인간 능력의 한계 / *She has a great* ~ *for mathematics.* 그녀는 수학에 대단한 재능이 있다. **2** ⓐ power of the mind. 정신〔지적〕 능력. ¶ *the mental faculties* 지적 제(諸)능력; 지능 / *the* ~ *of memory* 기억력 / *the reasoning* ~ 추리력. ⓑ the natural power of the body. (신체의) 기능. ¶ *the digestive* ~ 소화 기능 / *the faculties of sight and hearing* 시각과 청각. **3** a department of learning in a university. (대학의) 학부. ¶ *the* ~ *of law* 〔*medicine*〕 법〔의(醫)〕학부. **4** 《*the* ~, *collectively*》 the teaching staff in any school. 교직원단(團); 교수단. **5** 《*the F-*》 《Brit. *colloq.*》 doctors as a class. (계층으로서의) 의사들; 의사 동업자. [L. *facio* do]

fad [fæd] *n.* Ⓒ **1** something everybody does or is interested in for a short time. 일시적 유행; 일시적 열중. ¶ ~ *words* 유행어 / *go in fads* 유행하다 / *have a* ~ *for* …에 열중해 있다. **2** something in which a person takes a particular interest; a hobby. 취미; 도락. ¶ *Stamp collecting is his* ~. 우표 수집은 그의 취미이다. [O.E. *ge-fæd* decorum]

fad·dy [fǽdi] *adj.* (**-di·er, -di·est**) given to fads; having special likes and dislikes. 일시적 유행을 좇는; 도락의; 변덕스러운; 까다로운. [↑]

·fade [feid] *vi.* **1** (P1,2A) ⓐ (of a color, a light, etc.) grow pale; lose color. (색·빛 등이) 점차 여려〔희미해〕지다; 빛이 바래다. ¶ *The light was beginning to* ~. 날이 저물기 시작했다 / *My old hat has faded badly.* 내 헌 모자는 빛이 몹시 바랬다. ⓑ (of a sound) grow faint. (소리가) 점차 스러지다. ¶ *The sound of drums faded away.* 북소리의 울림이 점차 사라져갔다. **2** (P1,2A,3) lose freshness or strength. (신선함·힘·활기·건강 등이) 쇠하다; 시들다. ¶ *The flowers* ~ *in autumn.* 꽃은 가을이 되면 시든다 / *A woman's beauty soon fades.* 여자의 아름다움은 곧 쇠퇴한다. **3** (P1,2A,3) go out of sight slowly; die out. (서서히) 모습이 사라지다; 점차 없어지다. ¶ *The stars faded from the sky.* 별들이 하늘에서 점차 사라졌다 / *Anger faded from his eyes.* 그의 눈에서 노여운 빛이 점차 사라졌다 / *All memory of the past has faded.* 과거의 모든 기억이 사라져 없어졌다. — *vt.* (P6,7) cause to fade. …을 바래게〔쇠하게, 시들게〕 하다. ¶ *The sun has faded the* (*color of the*) *curtains.* 햇볕이 커튼을 바래게 했다. [F. *fade* dull]

fade in 〔***out***〕, (of motion pictures, radio, television, etc.) slowly become more 〔less〕 distinct. (소리·영상이) 점차 명료〔불명료〕해지다.

fade into, lose color or strength and become (something else). 약해져〔쇠하여, 희미해져〕 …이 되다.

fad·ed [féidid] *adj.* having lost color or freshness. 퇴색한; 바랜; 시든.

fade-in [féidìn] *n.* Ⓒ (of motion pictures, etc.) a scene that slowly appears. (화면이) 점차 나타나는 장면.

fade-out [féidàut] *n.* Ⓒ (of motion pictures, etc.) a scene that slowly disappears. (화면이) 점차 사라지는 장면.

fae·ces, fe·ces [fí:si:z] *n. pl.* excrement; sediment. 배설물; 분변; 찌끼. [L.]

fa·er·ie, fa·er·y [féiəri, fέəri] *n.* Ⓒ (*pl.* **-er·ies**) 《*arch.*》 **1** fairyland. 요정의 나라; 선경(仙境). **2** a fairy. 요정. — *adj.* 《*arch.*》 fairy. 요정의〔같은〕. [*fairy*]

fag [fæg] *v.* (**fagged, fag·ging**) *vi.* (P1,2A) **1** 《*at*》 work hard until tired. 열심히 (일)하다; 지칠 때까지 일하다. ¶ *He fagged away at physics.* 열심히 물리를 공부했다. **2** 《Brit. *colloq.*》 act as a fag. (하급생이) 상급생의 잔심부름을 하다.

— *vt.* (P6,7) 《usu. in *passive*》 cause to work hard; make (someone) tired out by hard work. 열심히 일하게 하다; (일 따위로) …를 지치게 하다. ¶ *be fagged out* 녹초가 되다.

— *n.* **1** Ⓤ 《often *a* ~》 《chiefly Brit.》 a piece of hard, uninteresting work. 힘든 일. **2** Ⓒ 《Brit.》 a pupil who serves a senior pupil in public schools. 상급생의 잔심부름을 하는 하급생. **3** Ⓒ 《*sl.*》 a cigarette. 담배《궐련》(cf. *gasper*). [? →flag[3]]

fag end [∸∸] *n.* the last, useless part of something. 끄트머리; 끄트러기; 찌꺼기.

fag·ot, 《Brit.》 **fag·got** [fǽgət] *n.* Ⓒ a bundle of sticks bound together and used for firewood. 장작단〔뭇〕; 섶나뭇단. — *vt.* bind or make into a fagot. …을 다발 짓다; 묶다. [F.]

Fahr. Fahrenheit.

Fahr·en·heit [fǽrənhàit] *adj.* of or according to the Fahrenheit scale on which the freezing point is 32° and boiling point of water is 212°. 화씨(華氏)의 (opp. Celsius). 參考 F., Fahr.로 생략함. 고안자인 G.D. Fahrenheit (1686-1736)의 이름에서. [Person]

:fail [feil] *vi.* **1** (P1,3,4) 《*in*》 not succeed; be unable to do. 실패하다(opp. succeed). ¶ ~ *in mathematics* 수학에 낙제하다 / ~ *in business* 사업에 실패하다 / ~ *in finding a work* 일자리를 얻지 못하다 / *The experiment has failed.* 실험은 실패했다. **2** (P1,2A, 3) 《*in*》 be not enough; be wanting; lack. 부족하다; 없다. ¶ ~ *in truthfulness* 진실성이 없다 / ~ *in one's efforts* 노력이 부족하다 / *He fails in courage.* 용기가 부족하다 / *Our water supply failed again.* 수돗물이 또 끊어졌다. **3** (P1,2A) lose power 〔strength〕; grow weak. 쇠하다; 약해지다. ¶ *The patient failed rapidly.* 환자는 급속도로 쇠약해졌다 / *The engine failed.* 엔진이 작동하지 않게 되었다. **4** (P1) lose all one's money in business. 파산하다. — *vt.* (P6) **1** disappoint utterly; neglect to support or help (someone). …을 실망시키다; 못본 체하다. ¶ *When I wanted his help he failed me.* 그의 도움을 원했을 때 그는 외면했다 / *Words failed me.* 말이 입 밖에 나오지 않았다. **2** (P6,8) not do; neglect. …을 하지 않다〔못하다〕; 게을리하다. ¶ ~ *to see the difference* 차이를 보지 못하다 / *He failed to come.* 그는 오지 못했다 / *He never fails to keep his promise.* 그는 결코 약속을 어기지 않는다 / *Don't* ~ *to let me know when you return.* 돌아오면 나에게 꼭 알려주게. **3** 《*colloq.*》 be unsuccessful in (a test, etc.); give the mark of failure to (someone). …에 낙제하다; (시험에서 아무)를 떨어뜨리다.

fail of, be unable to have or get; lack. 달성하지 못하다; …이 없다.

— *n.* Ⓤ failure. 실패. 語法 다음 구로만 쓰임. [L. *fallo* deceive]

without fail, certainly; surely. 틀림없이; 꼭.

fail·ing [féiliŋ] *n.* Ⓒ a fault or weak point; Ⓤ a failure. 결점; 약점; 실패. ¶ *We all have our failings.* 우리는 모두 결점이 있다. — *prep.* in the absence of; without. …이 없으면; …하지 않으면. ¶ *Failing good weather, the picnic will be postponed.* 날씨가 좋지 않으면 소풍은 연기된다 / *Failing his assistance, what would you do ?* 그의 도움이 없으면 어떻게 할 것인가.

:fail·ure [féiljər] *n.* ⓊⒸ **1** lack of success; an unsuccessful effort. 실패(opp. success). ¶ ~ *in a test* 시험의 실패 / *a* ~ *in business* 사업의 실패 / *end in* ~ 실패로 끝나다 / *The attack was a* ~. 공격은 실패였다. **2** the state of being not enough. 부족; 결핍. ¶ *the* ~ *of rain* 비 부족 / *Crop failures resulted in famine.* 농작물의 흉작이 기근을 가져왔다. **3** the act of becoming weak or losing strength. 쇠약; 감퇴. ¶ *heart* ~ 심장마비 / *the* ~ *of one's health* 건강의 쇠약 / *the* ~ *of memory* 기억력의 감퇴. **4** Ⓒ bankruptcy. 파산. ¶ *the* ~ *of a company* 회사의 파산. **5** Ⓒ an unsuccessful person or thing. 실패자; 실패로 끝난 것. ¶ *He was a* ~ *as a teacher.* 교사로서 실패자였다. **6** the act of not doing or failing to do. 불이행; …하지 못함. ¶ *a* ~ *in duty* 의무의 불이행 / ~ *to be on time* 제시간에 대지 못함 / *a* ~ *to appear in the court* 법정에의 불출두. [→fail]

fain [fein] 《*poet.*》 *adj.* 《*to do*》 willing under the circumstances or obliged to do. 기꺼이 …하는. ¶ *They were* ~ *to obey.* 그들은 기꺼이 복종했다. — *adv.* willingly; gladly. 기꺼이. [E.]

would fain, willingly. 기꺼이 …하다. ¶ *I would* ~ *go.* 기꺼이 가겠다.

:faint [feint] *adj.* **1** dim; indistinct; vague. 희미한; 어렴풋한. ¶ *a* ~ *light* 희미한 빛 / *a* ~ *memory* 어렴풋한 기억 / *I have not the faintest idea about it.* 그 일에 관해서는 전연 알지 못하고 있다. **2** (of mental or physical force) weak; almost used up. (체력·기력 따위가) 약한; 기진〔탈진〕한. ¶ *in a* ~ *voice* 약하디 약한 목소리로 / *The traveler was* ~ *from hunger and cold.* 나그네는 허기와 추위로 탈진해 있었다. **3** done without eager interest. 무기력한; 열의없는; 마음 내키지 않는. ¶ *make a* ~ *attempt* 열의없는 시도를 하다. **4** slight; small. 약간의; 미약한; 적은. ¶ ~ *resistance* 미약한 저항 / *There is not the faintest hope.* 실낱같은 희망도 없다. **5** likely to lose consciousness; weak and dizzy. 기절할 것 같은; 어지러운. ¶ ~ *with hunger* 허기져 어지러운 / *turn* ~ 기절하다 / *He felt suddenly* ~. 갑자기 기절할 것 같았다.

— *vi.* (P1,2A,3) lose consciousness. 기절하다; 어지럽다.

— *n.* Ⓒ a loss of consciousness. 기절; 어질증. ¶ *go down in a* ~ 기절하다 / *He fell in a dead* ~. 완전히 의식을 잃고 쓰러졌다. [→feign]

faint-heart·ed [féinthɑ́:rtid] *adj.* lacking courage; timid. 용기가 없는; 겁이 많은.

***faint·ly** [féintli] *adv.* in a faint manner; vaguely; indistinctly. 희미하게; 어렴풋이; 막연히.

faint·ness [féintnis] *n.* Ⓤ the state of being faint; the act of fainting. 희미함; 어렴풋함; (미)약함; 실신; 어지러움.

F

:fair¹ [fɛər] *n.* Ⓒ **1** 《chiefly Brit.》 a gathering to buy and sell things that is held in a particular place at a regular time; a market. 정기시(市); 장(場). **2** an entertainment and a sale of articles, esp. for charitable purposes; a bazaar. 자선시(市); 바자. **3** a display of goods, products, etc. 품평회; 견본시(見本市); 박람회. ¶ *an international trade* ~ 국제 견본시〔박람회〕/ 《U.S.》 *a World's Fair* 만국 박람회. [L. *feria* holiday]

a day after the fair, too late. 이미 때가 늦음; 사후 약방문.

:fair² [fɛər] *adj.* **1** just, honest or right according to the rules. 바른; 공평〔공정〕한; 정당한; 규칙에 따른. ¶ ~ *play* / *a* ~ *judge* 공정한 재판관 / *win in* ~ *fight* 정정당당하게 싸워 이기다 / *It's not* ~. 공정하지가 않다 / *by* ~ *means* 공정한 수단으로. **2** pretty good; average; not bad. 꽤 좋은; 적당한; 나쁘지 않은. ¶ *a* ~ *crop* 평년작 / ~ *health* 괜찮은 건강 / *make* 〔*receive*〕 *a* ~ *grade in arithmetic* 산수에서 '미'의 성적을 받다 / *His knowledge is* ~, *but by no means perfect.* 그의 지식은 괜찮지만 완전하지는 못하다. **3** (of the weather) fine; clear; not rainy or cloudy. (날씨가) 맑은; 갠; 순풍의. ¶ *a* ~ *sky* 맑게 갠 하늘 / *The weather turned* ~. 날씨가 좋아졌다. **4** reasonable; proper. 합당한; 적정한. ¶ *for a* ~ *price* 적정한 가격으로. **5** promising; likely. 유망한; 가망이 있는. ¶ *a* ~ *chance of success* 성공할 것 같은 가능성. **6** light in color; blond. 살빛이 흰; 금발의 (opp. dark). ¶ *a* ~ *man* 살결이 흰 남자 / *She had* ~ *hair.* 그녀는 금발이었다. **7** clean; plain. 깨끗한; (필적 따위가) 또렷한. ¶ ~ *water* 깨끗한 물 / ~ *handwriting* 깨끗한 필적 / *a* ~ *copy* 깨끗한 복사. **8** gentle; polite. 정중한; 공손한. ¶ ~ *words* 공손한 말. **9** 《chiefly *poet.*》 beautiful; lovely. 아름다운; 예쁜; 귀여운. ¶ *a* ~ *young maiden* 예쁜 소녀 / *our* ~ *city* 우리들의 아름다운 도시. **10** (of speeches, promise, etc.) agreeable but false; pleasing but not sincere. 말은 그럴 듯하나 거짓인; 교언(巧言)의. ¶ *He gives us* ~ *words, but does little.* 그럴 듯한 말을 하나 실행하지 않는다. **11** pretty much; abundant. 꽤 많은; 상당한. ¶ *a* ~ *income* 상당한 수입 / *do a* ~ *trade* 꽤 많은 거래를 하다 / *go at a* ~ *pace* 상당한 속도로 가다.

a fair field and no favor, an equal opportunity for each. 각각 공평한 기회.

be in a fair way to do, have a good chance of doing; be likely to do. …할 가망이 있다; …할 것 같다. ¶ *He is in a* ~ *way to make money.* 그는 돈을 벌 가망이 있다.

by fair means or foul, by hook or by crook. 수단을 가리지 않고; 기어코.

fair to middling, 《*colloq.*》 fairy well. 그저 그만한; 좋지도 나쁘지도 않은.

— *adv.* in a fair manner; honestly. 공정〔공평〕하게; 정직하게; 깨끗이; 규칙에 따라; 정중하게.

bid fair (= *have a good chance* = *seem likely*) *to do.* …할 가망이 충분히 있다.

fair and softly, not so fast. 그리 빠르지 않은.

fair and square, 《*colloq.*》 just; honest. 공정한; 정직한; 공명정대한.

— *n.* 《*arch.*》 **1** 《*a* ~ 》 a fair woman. 미인. **2** the fair sex. 여성. [E.]

fair-haired [fɛ́ərhɛ́ərd] *adj.* **1** having light-colored hair; blond. 금발의. **2** 《U.S. *colloq.*》 particularly liked or favored; favorite. (윗사람) 마음에 드는. ¶ *a* ~ *boy* (상사의) 마음에 드는 청년. [*fair²*]

fair·ing¹ [fɛ́əriŋ] *n.* 《Brit.》 a present bought at a fair. 시장에서 산 선물. [*fair¹*]

fair·ing² [fɛ́əriŋ] *n.* the making of an airplane's surface smooth and streamlined. (비행기 기체의) 정형(整形). [*fair²*]

:fair·ly [fɛ́ərli] *adv.* **1** justly; honestly. 공정히; 공평히. ¶ *act* ~ *by all men* 모든 사람에 대해 공평하게 굴다 / *The games were judged* ~. 경기는 공평하게 심판되었다 / *It may* ~ *be said that*…. …라고 해도 부당하지는 않을 것이다. **2** somewhat. 꽤; 상당히. ¶ *Mary plays the piano* ~ *well.* 메리는 피아노를 상당히 잘 친다. **3** 《*colloq.*》 completely; clearly. 완전히. ¶ *be* ~ *beside oneself* 완전히 미치다 / *He was* ~ *caught in the trap.* 그는 완전히 덫에 걸렸다. [*fair²*]

fair-mind·ed [fɛ́ərmáindid] *adj.* not prejudiced; just. 편견 없는; 공정〔공평〕한. [*fair²*]

fair·ness [fɛ́ərnis] *n.* Ⓤ the state of being fair. 공명 정대; 살결의 흼; 아름다움.

fair-spo·ken [fɛ́ərspóukən] *adj.* courteous in speech. 말이 정중한.

fair·way [fɛ́ərwèi] *n.* Ⓒ a passage where ships sail in a river or a harbor. 항로.

fair-weath·er [fɛ́ərwèðər] *adj.* suitable only for fair weather; not helpful in time of need. 청명한 날씨 때만 도움이 되는; 필요한 때 도움이 되지 않는. ¶ *a* ~ *friend* 다급할 때 믿을 수 없는 친구.

:fair·y [fɛ́əri] *n.* Ⓒ (*pl.* **fair·ies**) a tiny imaginary being with magic powers. 요정. — *adj.* of or like fairies; lovely. 요정의; 요정같은; 귀여운. [*fay*]

fair·y·land [fɛ́ərilæ̀nd] *n.* **1** Ⓤ the country of the fairies. 요정〔동화〕의 나라. **2** Ⓒ an enchanting, pleasant and beautiful place. 선경(仙境); 도원경.

fairy tale [⌐–⌐] *n.* **1** a story about fairies. 동화. **2** an untrue story; a lie. 꾸며낸 이야기; 거짓말.

fait ac·com·pli [fet ɑkɔ̃plí: / féit əkɔ́mpli:] *n.* 《F.》 something already done and settled. 기정 사실.

:faith [feiθ] *n.* Ⓤ **1** trust; confidence. 신용; 신뢰. ¶ *lose* ~ *in* …을 신뢰치〔신용하지〕 않게 되다 / *have* ~ *in a friend* 친구를 믿다 / *put one's* ~ *in someone* 아무를 신뢰하

다 / *give ~ to his promise* 그의 약속을 신용하다. **2** belief in God or in the truths of religion; firm belief. 신앙; 신념. ¶ *have ~ in Christianity* 기독교를 믿다. **3** Ⓒ a system of religious belief; a doctrine. 교의(教義); 신조. **4** ⓐ promise to be loyal; loyalty; sincerity. 충실; 성실; 서약. ¶ *act in good ~* 성실히 행동하다. ⓑ a promise. 약속. ¶ *keep ~* 약속을 지키다 / *He has broken ~ with me.* 그는 나와의 약속을 어겼다. [L. *fides*]

in good* (*bad*) *faith, honestly (dishonestly). 성실히(불성실하게, 악의를 가지고).

keep* (*break*) *faith with (=*remain* (*cease to remain*) *loyal to*) *someone* or *something.* …에 대해 신의를 지키다(저버리다).

on the faith of, by warrant of. …의 보증으로.

:faith·ful [féiθfəl] *adj.* **1** 《*to*》 true to one's word, promise, etc.; loyal to someone or something; doing one's duty; reliable. 성실한; 충실한; 신뢰할(믿을) 수 있는. ¶ *a ~ friend* 믿을 수 있는 친구 / *a ~ worker* 성실한 일꾼 / *~ to one's promise* 약속에 충실한 / *be ~ to one's duty* 임무에 충실하다 / *be ~ to God* 신을 깊이 믿다. **2** true to the facts; accurate; without mistakes. 정확한; 틀림이 없는. ¶ *a ~ copy* 정확한 사본(寫本) / *a ~ memory* 정확한 기억력 / *give a ~ account of the course of events* 사건의 경위를 정확하게 설명하다.
— *n.* 《*the ~*》 the people who believe truly or who support loyally. 참된 신자(信者); 충실한 지지자.

·faith·ful·ly [féiθfəli] *adv.* in a faithful manner. 성실히; 충실히; 정확히.

Yours faithfully =***Faithfully yours,*** a common ending of letters to persons other than friends or relations. 여불비례(餘不備禮).

faith·ful·ness [féiθfəlnis] *n.* Ⓤ the state of being faithful; honesty. 성실; 충실; 정확.

faith·less [féiθlis] *adj.* not reliable; unworthy of trust; false. 신용할 수 없는; 신용할 가치가 없는; 부실한.

fake [feik] *vt.* (P6,7) **1** ⓐ 《often *up*》 make up (something false) so as to pass it off as real or genuine; make a false imitation of. …을 위조(조작)하다. ¶ *~ a Picasso* 피카소의 그림을 위조하다 / *~ an alibi* 알리바이를 조작하다. ⓑ change (something) so as to make it look better; touch up. (잘 보이기 위해) 고치다; 손질하다. **2** deceive. 속이다. **3** pretend. …인 체하다; …을 가장하다. ¶ *~ illness* 꾀병을 부리다.
— *n.* Ⓒ **1** something that seems genuine but is not. 위조품; 가짜; 기만. ¶ *His illness was a ~.* 그의 병은 꾀병이었다. **2** a person who tries to deceive; a person who pretends to be what he isn't. 사기꾼.
— *adj.* 《*colloq.*》 false. 위조의; 가짜의. ¶ *a ~ picture* 가짜 그림.

● **fake·ment** [-mənt] *n.* [?]

fa·kir [fəkíər, féikər] *n.* a Mohammedan or Hindu ascetic or monk. (이슬람·힌두교의) 고행승(苦行僧)(=fakeer). [Arab.]

fal·cate [fǽlkeit] *adj.* curved like a sickle; shaped or curved like a hook. 낫 모양의; 갈고리 모양의. [↓]

fal·chion [fɔ́:ltʃən] *n.* Ⓒ **1** a broad, short sword with an edge that curves to a point. 언월도(刀). **2** 《*poet.*》 a sword. 검; 칼. [L. *falx* sickle]

fal·con [fǽlkən, fɔ́:l-] *n.* Ⓒ a hawk trained to hunt other birds and small animals. (사냥용의) 매. [L.]

fal·con·er [fǽlkənər, fɔ́:l-] *n.* Ⓒ a person who hunts with falcons; a trainer of falcons. 매부리.

fal·con·ry [fǽlkənri, fɔ́:l-] *n.* Ⓤ **1** the sport of hunting with falcons. 매사냥. **2** the art of training a falcon. (사냥매의) 훈련.

:fall [fɔ:l] *vi.* (**fell, fall·en**) **1** (P1,2A,2B,3) 《*from, down*》 come down from a higher place; drop; descend. 떨어지다; 낙하(추락)하다; (꽃·잎 따위가) 지다(opp. rise). ¶ *~ from a tree* 나무에서 떨어지다 / *A boy fell from a window* (*bridge*). 아이가 창문(다리)에서 추락했다 / *The roof fell down.* 지붕이 내려앉았다 / *Rain began to ~.* 비가 내리기 시작했다. **2** ⓐ (P1,2A,2B,3) come down suddenly from a standing or sitting position. 넘어지다; 쓰러지다; 구르다. ¶ *~ down on the floor* 마룻바닥에 쓰러지다 / *~ downstairs* 아래층으로 굴러 떨어지다 / *~ to the ground* 땅에 넘어지다 / *~ on one's back* 자빠지다 / *~ face down* 엎어지다 / *~ on one's knees* 무릎을 꿇다 / *Trees fell in the storm.* 나무들이 비바람에 쓰러졌다. ⓑ (P1,2A,3) drop down wounded or dead; be killed. (부상 또는 죽어) 쓰러지다; 죽다. ¶ *~ in battle* 전사하다. **3** ⓐ (P1,2A,3) break down; be destroyed. 쓰러지다; 무너지다; 붕괴하다. ¶ *A bridge fell.* 다리가 무너졌다 / *Many houses fell in the earthquake.* 많은 집들이 지진으로 도괴(倒壞)했다. ⓑ (P3) be taken or conquered; be captured. 함락하다; 빼앗기다. ¶ *~ into the hands of …* …의 수중에 떨어지다 / *The fortress* (*castle*) *fell* (*to the enemy*). 요새는(성은) 적군에게 함락됐다. ⓒ be overthrown. (국가·정권 따위가) 전복되다; 쓰러지다; 망하다. ⓓ 《*pl.*》 yield to temptation or sin. (유혹 따위에) 굴하다; 타락하다. ¶ *~ into bad habits* 못된 습관에 빠지다 / *He was tempted and fell.* 유혹당하여 타락했다. **4** (P3,5) become lowered or directed downward. (눈 따위가) 아래를 향하다; (광선·시선 등이) 향해지다; …에 쏠리다. ¶ *Her eyes fell to the ground.* 그녀의 시선이 땅에 쏠렸다 / *Her eyes fell before his steady gaze.* 그의 지그시 쳐다보는 눈길 앞에서 그녀는 눈을 내리깔았다 / *The light* (*sun*) *fell full on his face.* 불빛(햇빛)이

그의 얼굴 가득히 쏟아졌다. **5** (P1,2) 《*over, upon*》 (of hair, curtains, etc.) hang down. 아래로 내리다; 늘어지다. ¶ *The curtain falls.* 막이 내리다 / *Her hair fell on* 〔*upon, over*〕 *her shoulders.* 그녀의 머리가 어깨 위에 늘어졌다. **6** (P1,2A,2B,3) become lower or less in number, amount, degree, value, etc. 내리다; 낮아지다; 저하하다; 줄다. ¶ ～ *in number* 수가 줄다 / *Prices are falling.* 물가가 떨어지고 있다 / *The temperature fell ten degrees.* 기온이 10도 내려갔다. **7** 《*down, into*》 (of land) slope; (of rivers) flow. (토지가) 경사지다; 내려앉다; (강물 따위가) 흘러들다. ¶ *The river falls to the sea.* 강물은 바다로 흘러든다. **8** (P3) lose position, reputation, etc. (지위·신분·명성 따위를) 잃다; 실각〔몰락〕하다. ¶ ～ *from the people's favor* 대중의 인기를 잃다 / ～ *from power* 권력을 잃다 / ～ *in one's circumstances* 생활 형편이 나빠지다. **9** (P3,5) become or pass into a certain mental or physical state. (어떤 상태에) 빠지다; …하게 되다. 語法 보어 또는 구(句)가 따름. ¶ ～ *in love* 사랑에 빠지다 / ～ *a victim to* …의 희생이 되다 / ～ *asleep* 잠들다 / ～ *ill* 병이 나다 / ～ *into difficulties* 곤란에 빠지다 / ～ *into mistakes* 잘못을 범하다 / ～ *into ruin* 멸망〔파멸〕하다 / *He fell silent.* 그는 갑자기 입을 다물었다. **10** (P1, 2A,3) ⓐ come down, as if by dropping. (떨어지듯) 닥쳐오다; 엄습하다. ¶ *Sleep* 〔*Fear*〕 *suddenly fell on him.* 그에게 갑자기 졸음이〔공포가〕 엄습했다 / *Darkness fell.* 어둠이 깔렸다 / *Night is falling fast.* 급속히 밤의 장막이 덮이고 있다. ⓑ (of speech) be spoken. (말이) 새어나오다. ¶ *Not a word fell from his lips.* 그의 입에서 한마디의 말도 새어 나오지 않았다. **11** (P3) ⓐ come by chance or lot. (우연히) …에게 떨어지다; …의 부담·책임이 되다. ¶ *The duty fell to him.* 임무는 그가 맡게 되었다 / *The cost fell to me.* 비용은 내가 부담하게 되었다. ⓑ come or pass by right. (유산 따위가) …의 것이 되다. ¶ *The estate fell to her.* 재산은 그녀에게 돌아갔다. **12** (P3) happen; occur. (사건 따위가) 일어나다; …이 되다. ¶ *On what day does Christmas* ～ *this year?* 올해 크리스마스는 무슨 요일이 되는가. **13** (P3) be placed. …위치에 오다. ¶ *The accent falls on the last syllable.* 악센트는 마지막 음절에 온다. **14** (P3) ⓐ be divided into. …로 나뉘다. ¶ *The book falls into two parts.* 그 책은 두 부분으로 나뉜다. ⓑ be classified; be included in. 분류되다; 포함되다. ¶ *The specimen falls under this category.* 표본은 이 범주 속에 포함된다.

fall among, come among by chance. 우연히 …속에 들어가다〔섞이다〕. ¶ ～ *among bad people* 못된 사람들과 섞이다.

fall away, **a**) take away support, etc.; separate; desert. 지지를 하지 않게 되다; 버리다. ¶ *His supporters fell away.* 그의 지지자들은 떨어져 나갔다. **b**) disappear; vanish. 사라지다. **c**) become less or small; decline. 줄다; 감소〔저하〕하다. ¶ *The sale has fallen away.* 판매량이 줄었다. **d**) grow thin and weak. 야위다; 약해지다. ¶ *His flesh fell away.* 그는 여위었다〔살이 빠졌다〕.

fall back, move back or away; withdraw; give way. (뒤로) 물러나다; 후퇴하다; 굴(屈)하다.

fall back on 〔***upon***〕***,*** **a**) depend on (someone) for support; resort to. …에게 의지〔의존〕하다. **b**) go back to (some place) for safety; retreat to. …로 철퇴하다.

fall behind, **a**) be left behind; drop behind. 뒤(떨어)지다; 낙후하다. **b**) be late in pay (a debt); fail to pay. 제 때에 갚지 못하다; 체납하다.

fall calm, calm down. (바람이) 가라앉다; 자다.

fall down (***on***)***,*** 《*colloq.*》 fail (in a task, in expectation, etc.). (일에) 실패하다; (기대에) 어긋나다.

fall flat, (of a joke, etc.) fail to entertain or interest. (농담 따위가) 실패로 끝나다.

fall for, **a**) fall in love with; be attracted by. 사랑에 빠지다; …에 반하다. **b**) be deceived by (a trick). …에 속다.

fall foul of, (of a ship) come into collision with; quarrel with. …와 충돌하다; …와 말다툼하다.

fall in, **a**) fall or break down; collapse; give way. 도괴(倒壞)하다; 무너지다. **b**) 《mil.》 form ranks. 정렬하다.

fall in 〔***to***〕 ***pieces,*** 산산이 부서지다.

fall in with, **a**) meet or get acquainted by chance. …와 우연히 만나다〔알게 되다〕. **b**) agree with (someone); yield to. …에 동의〔일치〕하다; …에 응하다〔따르다〕.

fall off, **a**) ＝fall away a), c), d). **b**) become bad (in quality). (질이) 떨어지다.

fall on 〔***upon***〕***,*** **a**) attack. …을 공격하다; 덮치다; 덤벼들다. **b**) take place on (something or someone). (축제일 따위가) 바로 …날이 되다; (…에게) 닥치다; …의 임무가 되다.

fall on *one's* ***feet,*** meet with good fortune in difficulties; be lucky. 어려운 가운데도 잘 되다; 용케 궁지를 벗어나다; 운이 좋다.

fall out, **a**) cease to be friends; quarrel. 사이가 틀어지다; 싸우다. ¶ ～ *out over some trifling matter* 사소한 일로 싸우다. **b**) happen; take place. (…한 일이) 일어나다; 생기다. **c**) 《mil.》 leave one's position in line. 대열을 이탈하다.

fall over *oneself,* **a**) fall because one is awkward or clumsy. 쓰러지다. **b**) 《U.S.》 be in a hurry to do something. 몹시 서두르다. **c**) display great eagerness. 기를 쓰다; 격심한 경쟁을 하다.

fall over one another, 《U.S.》 compete. 서로 앞을 다투다.

fall short, **a**) fail to reach. (거리상으로) 미치

지 못하다. ¶ *The arrow fell short.* 화살은 (목표에) 미치지 못했다. **b**) fail to come up to a standard. (기준·기대 따위에) 못 미치다; 미달하다. ¶ *The result fell short of our expectations.* 결과는 우리의 기대에 못 미쳤다. **c**) prove to be lacking; be not sufficient. 결핍하다; 부족하다. ¶ *Supplies of food fell short.* 식량 공급이 부족했다.

fall through, (a plan, etc.) fail to materialize. (계획 따위가) 허사로 끝나다; 실현되지 않다.

fall to, **a**) begin. …을 시작하다. **b**) begin to eat, fight, etc. 식사를〔싸움을〕 시작하다. **c**) close by itself. 자동적으로 닫히다. **d**) be assigned to. …의 임무가 되다.

—*n.* Ⓒ **1** a dropping from a higher place. 떨어짐; 낙하; 추락. ¶ *a ～ from a horse* 낙마 / *the ～ of an apple* 사과의 떨어짐. **2** ⓐ a sudden drop from a standing position. 넘어짐; 쓰러짐; 무너짐. ¶ *the ～ of a tower* 〔*building*〕 탑〔건물〕의 도괴(倒壞) / *He stumbled and had a bad ～.* 돌부리에 걸려 꽈당 나가 자빠졌다. ⓑ downfall; overthrow; ruin. 함락; 몰락; 붕괴; 멸망. ¶ *the ～ of the Roman Empire* 로마 제국의 멸망. ⓒ yielding to temptation; sin. 유혹에 굴함; 타락. ¶ *the Fall of Man* 인간의 타락. **3** the amount that falls; a distance fallen that which falls or has fallen. 강수〔강설〕량; 낙차(落差); 낙하물. ¶ *the ～ of rain* 〔*snow*〕 *for a year,* 1년간의 강우〔강설〕량 / *a two-inch ～ of snow* 적설량 2인치의 눈 / *a ～ of nine feet,* 9피트의 낙차. **4** becoming lower or less; a decrease; a decline; a reduction in value, price, etc. 내림; 저하; 쇠약; 하락; 감소; (명성 따위의) 실추. ¶ *a ～ in prices* 물가의 하락 / *a ～ of temperature* 기온의 하강. **5** (of land) a downward slope. (토지 따위의) 경사. **6** 《usu. *pl.*》 water coming over a cliff; a waterfall. 폭포. ¶ *Niagara Falls* 나이아가라 폭포. **7** ⓊⒸ 《～ or *the* ～》 《chiefly U.S.》 autumn. 가을.

—*adj.* of, for or in the autumn. 가을의; 가을용의. [E.]

fal·la·cious [fəléiʃəs] *adj.* misleading; erroneous; logically unsound. 사람을 미혹시키는; 잘못된; 불합리한. ● **fal·la·cious·ly** [-li] *adv.* [↓]

fal·la·cy [fǽləsi] *n.* (*pl.* **-cies**) **1** Ⓒ a mistaken idea or belief. 잘못된 생각〔신념〕. ¶ *It is a ～ that the rich are always happy.* 부자가 꼭 행복하다는 것은 잘못된 생각이다. **2** Ⓤ unsound or false reasoning. 불합리한〔잘못된〕 추론(推論). ¶ *based on ～* 잘못된 추론에 의거한. **3** 《log.》 a flaw in syllogism. (논증상의) 허위. [L. *fallo* deceive]

:fall·en [fɔ́:lən] *v.* pp. of **fall.**

—*adj.* **1** dropped. 떨어진. ¶ *～ leaves* 낙엽. **2** down flat. 쓰러진. ¶ *a ～ tree* 쓰러진 나무. **3** degraded. 타락한. ¶ *a ～ woman* 타락한 여자. **4** ruined. 멸망한. ¶ *a ～ empire* 멸망한 제국. **5** killed in battle. 전사한. ¶ *the ～* 전몰자. [*fall*]

fal·li·bil·i·ty [fæ̀ləbíləti] *n.* ⓊⒸ the state or quality of being fallible; a fallible quality. 잘못되기 쉬움〔쉬운 것〕. [↓]

fal·li·ble [fǽləbəl] *adj.* liable to err. 잘못을 범하기 쉬운. ¶ *All men are ～.* 사람은 모두 잘못을 저지르기 쉽다. [→fallacy]

fall·ing [fɔ́:liŋ] *n.* ⓊⒸ the act of coming down. 낙하; 하락; 추락; 함락; 타락. —*adj.* descending. 떨어지는; 낙하〔하락〕하는; 감퇴하는(opp. rising). ¶ *a ～ star* 별똥별 / *a ～ stone* 운석. [*fall*]

fall·out [fɔ́:làut] *n.* Ⓤ the radioactive particles and dust that fall to the earth after a nuclear explosion. 방사성 낙하물〔낙진〕; 죽음의 재. [*fall*]

fal·low[1] [fǽlou] *adj.* **1** (of land) plowed, but left unseeded. (땅을) 놀리고〔묵히고〕 있는. ¶ *lie ～* (밭 따위가) 묵고 있다. **2** (of the mind) not trained; not cultivated. (정신면의) 수양을 쌓지 못한; 교양이 없는.

—*n.* Ⓤ land plowed, but left unseeded for a season. 묵히는 땅; 유휴지. —*vt.* (P6) make (land) fallow. 땅을 갈아만 놓고 놀리다〔묵히다〕. [E.]

fal·low[2] [fǽlou] *adj.* yellowish; light-brown 담황색의; 담갈색의 [E.]

fallow deer [∠-∠] *n.* (*pl.* **f- d-**) a small yellow deer spotted with white. 다마사슴《담황갈색에 흰 반점이 있는 사슴; 유라시아산》.

:false [fɔ:ls] *adj.* **1** not true; not correct; wrong. 그릇된; 잘못된; 틀린; 부정의. ¶ *a ～ statement* 〔*idea*〕 잘못된 진술〔생각〕 / *give a ～ report* 틀린 보도를 하다. **2** not trustful; lying. 신용할 수 없는; 허위의. ¶ *a ～ witness* 거짓 증언을 하는 증인(證人). **3** not faithful or loyal. 불성실한; 신의가 없는. ¶ *a ～ friend* 불충실한 친구 / *be ～ to one's country* 조국을 배반하다. **4** not natural; artificial; not real. 모조의; 인조의; 가짜의. ¶ *a ～ diamond* 모조 다이아 / *a ～ coin* 가짜 돈 / *～ teeth* 의치. **5** supplemental. 임시의; 보조의. ¶ *a ～ deck* 보조 갑판.

—*adv.* in a false manner. 불성실〔부정직〕하게; 배반하여. [→fallacy]

play* someone *false, deceive or cheat someone. 아무를 속이다; 배반하다.

false-heart·ed [fɔ́:lshá:rtid] *adj.* unfaithful; disloyal. 불성실한; 신의 없는.

false·hood [fɔ́:lshùd] *n.* **1** Ⓤ the act of telling lies. 거짓말하기. **2** Ⓒ a lie. 거짓말. ¶ *utter* 〔*speak*〕 *falsehoods* 거짓말을 하다.

false·ly [fɔ́:lsli] *adv.* in a false manner. 거짓(으로); 부정하게; 불성실하게.

false·ness [fɔ́:lsnis] *n.* Ⓤ the state or quality of being false. 거짓; 허위; 잘못; 부정; 불성실.

false pretenses [∠-∠] *n.* 《law.》 speech or action intended to deceive. (금품을 사취하려는) 허위 표시.

fal·set·to [fɔ:lsétou] *n.* Ⓒ (*pl.* **-tos**) 《mus.》 an unnaturally high-pitched voice in a man; a person who sings with such a voice. (남성의) 가성(假聲); 가성 가수. [→false]

fal·si·fi·ca·tion [fɔ̀:lsəfəkéiʃən] *n.* UC the act of falsifying; the state of being falsified. 위조; 변조; (사실의) 왜곡; (기대가) 어긋남. [→false]

fal·si·fy [fɔ́:lsəfài] *v.* (**-fied**) *vt.* (P6) **1** change (something) in order to deceive. …을 위조〔변조〕하다; (사실을) 왜곡하다. ¶ ~ *facts* 사실을 왜곡하다 / ~ *evidence* 위증하다 / ~ *someone's will* 유언장을 변조하다. **2** prove (something) to be false. …이 거짓〔잘못〕임을 증명하다. ¶ ~ *a theory* 이론의 허위를 입증하다. — *vi.* make false statements. 거짓 진술〔주장〕을 하다. ●**fal·si·fi·er** [-ər] *n.* [→false]

fal·si·ty [fɔ́:lsəti] *n.* (*pl.* **-ties**) U the state of being false; C an error. 거짓; 허위; 잘못. [↑]

falt·boat [fá:ltbòut, fɔ:lt-] *n.* 《U.S.》 a folding boat. 접이식 보트. [G. *falten* fold]

fal·ter [fɔ́:ltər] *vi.* (P1,2A) **1** hesitate; lose courage. 머뭇거리다; 멈칫〔주춤〕하다; 용기가 꺾이다. ¶ *She faltered for a moment at the door.* 그녀는 문앞에서 잠시 머뭇거렸다. **2** move or act unsteadily; stumble. 비틀거리다; 넘어지다. ¶ *The man faltered away.* 사나이는 비틀거리며 가버렸다. **3** speak hesitatingly or stammeringly; (of the voice) waver. 말을 더듬다; (목소리가) 떨리다. — *vt.* (P7) 《often *out*》 utter hesitatingly or brokenly. …을 멈칫거리며 말하다; 더듬더듬 말하다. ¶ ~ (*out*) *an apology* 더듬더듬 변명을 하다. [N.]

fal·ter·ing [fɔ́:ltəriŋ] *adj.* hesitating; stumbling; stammering. 멈칫〔머뭇〕거리는; 비틀거리는; 더듬거리는. ●**fal·ter·ing·ly** [-li] *adv.*

:fame [feim] *n.* **1** U high reputation; renown. 명성(opp. notoriety). ¶ *gain* 〔*acquire*〕 ~ 명성을 얻다 / *seek after* ~ 명성을 추구하다. **2** U common or public opinion or estimation of someone. 세평(世評); 평판. ¶ *ill* ~ 악평. [L.]

come to fame = ***gain*** 〔***win***〕 ***fame,*** become famous. 유명해지다.

famed [feimd] *adj.* well-known; famous. 잘〔널리〕 알려진; 유명한. ¶ *The lake is* ~ *for its fine scenery.* 이 호수는 아름다운 경치로 널리 알려져 있다.

:fa·mil·iar [fəmíljər] *adj.* **1** well-known; common; seen often. 잘 알려져 있는; 흔한; 눈〔귀〕에 익은. ¶ *a* ~ *scene* 흔히 볼 수 있는 광경 / *a* ~ *story* 흔한 이야기 / *hear a* ~ *voice* 귀에 익은 목소리가 들리다 / *The name sounds* ~ *to me.* 이름이 귀에 설지 않다. **2** having a good knowledge of; well-acquainted. …에 정통한〔환한〕; 익숙한. ¶ *He is* ~ *with French.* 그는 프랑스 말에 익숙하다 / *He is* ~ *with the classics.* 그는 고전에 밝다. **3** friendly; close; intimate. 친(밀)한. ¶ *a* ~ *friend* 친우 / *be on* ~ *terms with* …와 친한 사이이다 / *make* ~ *with* …와 친밀해지다. **4** not formal; easy. 딱딱하지 않은; 스스럼없는; 쉬운. ¶ *write in a* ~ *style* 딱딱하지 않은 문체로 쓰다. **5** too friendly or intimate. 무람없이 구는. ¶ *too* ~ *with a stranger* 손님에게 무람없는 / *The private's* ~ *manner angered the officers.* 졸병의 무람없는 태도는 장교를 노하게 했다. [→family]

make oneself familiar with, become familiar with. …에 익숙해지다.

fa·mil·iar·i·ty [fəmìljǽrəti] *n.* (*pl.* **-ties**) **1** U the state of being familiar; intimacy; friendship. 친밀; 친교. ¶ *have personal* ~ *with* …와 개인적인 친교가 있다 / *I am on terms of* ~ *with him.* 나는 그와 친한 사이다. **2** U full knowledge; close acquaintance. 정통; 훤히 앎. ¶ *show thorough* ~ *with the law* 법률지식에 정통해 있음을 보이다. **3** U lack of formality or ceremony. 무람없음; 스스럼없음. ¶《*prov.*》 *Familiarity breeds contempt.* 지나치게 스스럼없이 굴면 경멸을 자초한다. **4** U 《often *pl.*》 an unduly informal act or expression. 무람없는 언행. ¶ *I don't like such familiarities.* 나는 저렇게 무람없는 언동은 싫다.

fa·mil·iar·i·za·tion [fəmìljərizéiʃən] *n.* U the act of familiarizing; the state of being familiarized. 친밀; 정통; 익숙게 함.

fa·mil·iar·ize [fəmíljəràiz] *vt.* (P6,13) **1** 《*with*》 make (someone) well acquainted with something. …에 익숙하게〔정통케〕 하다. ¶ ~ *oneself with a foreign language* 외국어에 정통하다 / ~ *a girl with the use of a sewing machine* 소녀에게 재봉틀 사용법을 잘 가르치다. **2** make (something) well known to people; popularize. …을 잘 알리다. ¶ ~ *new ideas to the general public* 새로운 생각을 세상에 널리 알리다.

fa·mil·iar·ly [fəmíljərli] *adv.* in a familiar manner; intimately. 친하게; 무람없게.

:fam·i·ly [fǽməli] *n.* C (*pl.* **-lies**) **1** a group of people consisting of parents and their children. 가족; 일가(一家). ¶ *a* ~ *of two* 부부 두 사람만의 가족 / *My* ~ *are all early risers.* 나의 가족은 모두 아침 일찍 일어난다. 語法 전원을 한 집합체로 볼 때에는 단수동사, 가족 개개인에게 중점을 둘 때에는 복수동사로 받음. **2** 《*collectively*》 the children of two parents. (양친과 구별하여) 아이들; 자녀. ¶ *Does he have any* ~ *?* 그는 아이가 있나. **3** a group of persons who are related; all persons descended from a common ancestor. 일족; 일문; 친척. **4** U 《Brit.》 good or noble descent. 좋은 가계(家系); 가문. ¶ *young men of* ~ 명문의 자제. **5** race. 종족; 인종. **6** a group of related plants or animals; a group of closely related things. (동·식물의) 과(科); (분류상의) 계통; 유(類). ¶ *the cat* ~ 고양잇

과 / *a ~ of languages* 어족(語族). — *adj.* of a family. 가족의; 가정의; 일가(일족, 친척)의. [L.]

family man [ㅅ-- ㅅ] *n.* a husband and father; a man inclined to lead a domestic life. 처자식이 있는 남자; 가정적인 남자.

family name [ㅅ-- ㅅ] *n.* a surname. 성(姓).

in a family way, without ceremony. 허물없이; 탁 터놓고.

in the family way, with child; pregnant. 임신하여.

·**fam·ine** [fǽmin] *n.* **1** Ⓤ extreme lack of food; starvation. 기근; 기아(飢餓); 굶주림. ¶ *Thousands of people died of ~.* 몇 천명이나 되는 사람이 기근으로 죽었다. **2** Ⓒ a serious shortage of anything. 대부족; 대결핍. ¶ *a water* (*coal*) *~* 물(석탄) 기근. [L. *fames* hunger]

fam·ish [fǽmiʃ] *vi.* (P1,3) suffer from extreme hunger. 굶주리다. ¶ *be famished* (*to death*) 굶주려 죽다 / 《*colloq.*》 *I am famishing.* 배가 고파 죽겠다. — *vt.* (P6) cause (someone) to suffer from hunger. …을 굶주리게 하다. [↑]

:**fa·mous** [féiməs] *adj.* **1** very well-known; noted. 유명한; 명성 높은(opp. unknown). ¶ *a ~ surgeon* 유명한 외과의(醫) / *This place is ~ for its hot springs.* 이곳은 온천으로 유명하다 / *He was ~ as a performer.* 그는 연주가로서 유명했다. **2** 《*colloq.*》 excellent; first-rate. 훌륭한; 썩 좋은. ¶ *a ~ dinner* 훌륭한 만찬 / *have a ~ appetite* 식욕이 아주 좋다 / *That's ~!* 멋지다. [*fame*]

fa·mous·ly [féiməsli] *adv.* **1** in a famous manner. 유명하게; 이름 높게. **2** 《*colloq.*》 excellently. 훌륭하게; 뛰어나게; 잘. ¶ *He is getting on ~ with his work.* 그의 일이 잘 진척되고 있다.

:**fan**[1] [fæn] *n.* Ⓒ **1** an instrument to make a current of air. 바람을 일으키는 것; 부채. ¶ *a folding ~* 쥘부채 / *an electric ~* 선풍기. **2** something resembling a fan. 부채 모양의 것.

— *vt.* (**fanned, fan·ning**) (P6,7,13) **1** make a current of air flow onto (something). …을 부채질하다; (부채로) 부치다. ¶ *~ oneself with one's hat* 모자로 부채질하다 / *~ a fire* 부채질하여 불을 일으키다. **2** drive away (something) with a fan, etc. …을 부채 따위로 쫓아버리다. ¶ *~ away flies* 부채로 파리를 쫓다. **3** stir up; excite. (감정을) 부채질하다; 부추기다; 선동하다. ¶ *~ a quarrel* 싸움을 부추기다 / *~ the flames* (아무의) 흥분·노여움을 부추기다. **4** separate (grain, etc.) by a current of air; winnow. (곡물을) 키로 까부르다. — *vi.* (P1) 《*out*》 spread out like a fan. 부채꼴로 펼쳐지다. [L. *vannus* winnowing basket]

:**fan**[2] [fæn] *n.* Ⓒ 《*colloq.*》 an enthusiastic supporter; a fanatic. 열렬한 애호자; 열광자; 팬. ¶ *a baseball ~* 야구팬. [↓]

fa·nat·ic [fənǽtik] *n.* Ⓒ a person who is possessed by excessive and unreasonable feelings or beliefs. 열광자; 광신자. — *adj.* =fanatical. [L. *fanum* temple]

fa·nat·i·cal [fənǽtikəl] *adj.* enthusiastic or zealous beyond reason. 열광적인; 광신적인.

fa·nat·i·cal·ly [fənǽtikəli] *adv.* in a fanatical manner; frantically. 열광하여; 광신적으로.

fa·nat·i·cism [fənǽtəsìzəm] *n.* Ⓤ enthusiasm or zeal beyond reason. 열광; 광신.

fan·ci·er [fǽnsiər] *n.* Ⓒ a person who has a special interest in something. 애호가. ¶ *a bird* (*dog, rose*) *~* 새(개, 장미) 애호가. [→fancy]

fan·ci·ful [fǽnsifəl] *adj.* **1** imaginary; unreal. 상상의; 가공의. ¶ *a ~ story* 가공적인 이야기. **2** led by imagination; imaginative. 상상에 이끌린; 공상적인; 비현실적인. ¶ *a ~ writer* 공상적인 작가. **3** (of clothes, decoration, etc.) curiously designed; quaint. (의상·장식·디자인 따위가) 기발한; 기묘한. ¶ *~ drawings* (*patterns*) 기발한 그림(무늬). ● **fan·ci·ful·ly** [-fəli] *adv.*

:**fan·cy** [fǽnsi] *n.* (*pl.* **-cies**) **1** ⓊⒸ the power of the mind to imagine things not present; imagination. 공상(력); 상상(력). ¶ *luxurious in ~* 상상력이 풍부한 / *He is full of ~.* 그는 공상만 하고 있다. **2** Ⓒ an idea, image, or thought so formed. (그렇게 형성된) 심상(心像); 이미지; 생각. **3** 《usu. *a ~* 》 an example of taste or judgment in art, literature, dress, etc.; a liking; a fondness. 애호; 취미; 좋아함. ¶ *have a ~ for kittens* 새끼 고양이를 좋아하다 / *catch* (*strike, suit*) *the ~ of* …의 마음에 들다 / *take a ~ to* …을 좋아하게 되다 / *He has a ~ for traveling.* 그는 여행을 매우 좋아한다. **4** Ⓒ an idea; caprice; whim. (일시적) 생각(기분); 변덕. ¶ *a passing ~* 일시적으로 떠오른 생각 / *follow one's ~* 기분에 따르다; 기분 내키는 대로 하다.

— *adj.* (**-ci·er, -ci·est**) **1** ornamental rather than useful; decorated; made to please the eye. 장식적인. ¶ *a ~ button* 장식 단추 / *a ~ dress* 가장복(服) / *I want to buy a handbag, not ~ but strong.* 겉만 번드르르하지 않고 튼튼한 핸드백을 사고 싶다. **2** based on the fancy; imaginary. 공상(상상)에 의거한; 변덕의; 엉뚱한. ¶ *a ~ picture* 상상화(畫). **3** requiring unusual skill. 곡예의; 묘기의. ¶ *~ skating* 곡예 스케이트. **4** extravagant; above the real value. 터무니없는; 엄청난. ¶ *at a ~ price* 엄청난 값에(으로). **5** 《U.S.》 particularly excellent. 극상의; 특선의.

— *vt.* (**-cied**) **1** (P6,7,9,11,12,20,21) picture to oneself; imagine. …을 공상(상상)하다. ¶ *I can't ~ his saying such a thing.* 그가 그런 말을 했으리라고는 상상도 할 수 없다 / *He liked fancying himself to be*

F

a grown-up. 그는 자신이 어른이라고 공상하기를 좋아했다. **2** (P11,21) believe (something or someone) without being certain; suppose. …하다고 생각하다; (어쩐지) …하다고 여기다; …하다고 우쭐대다. ¶ *I ~ he is in the country.* 그는 시골에 있다고 생각한다 / *I ~ (that) I've met him somewhere.* 어디서 그를 만난 적이 있다고 생각한다 / *They fancied Tom (to be) dead.* 그들은 톰이 죽은 것으로 여겼다 / *She fancies herself beautiful.* 그녀는 자신이 미인이라고 우쭐대고 있다. **3** (P6,9) have a liking for (something or someone); like. …을 좋아하다. ¶ *I ~ rowing more than riding.* 승마보다 보트타기를 더 좋아한다 / *I don't ~ this place at all.* 이 곳이 전혀 마음에 들지 않는다 / *He's not at all the kind of man I ~.* 그는 전혀 내가 좋아하는 유(類)의 남자가 아니다. **4** (P6,9,12) 《*interj.*, expressing surprise》 suppose; it is a surprise. 상상해 보라; 놀랍다. ¶ *Fancy that!* 그런 일이 있다니 이거 놀랐다 / *Fancy his doing a thing like that!* 그 사람이 그런 짓을 하다니 (놀랍지 않은가) / *Just ~ how I felt then!* 그때 내가 어떤 기분이었는지 상상 좀 해보게. [Gk. *phainō* show]

fancy oneself, **a**) ⇨*vt.* 1. **b**) have a high opinion of oneself. 자신을 …이라고 여기다.

F

fan·cy-free [fǽnsifríː] *adj.* free from influence, esp. of love; not in love. 한 가지 일에 집착하지 않는; 자유 분방한; 아직 사랑을 모르는; 순진한.

fan·cy·work [fǽnsiwəːrk] *n.* Ⓤ ornamental needlework; embroidery. 수예품; 편물; 자수.

fane [fein] *n.* 《*poet.*》 a temple; a church. 사원; 교회당. [L. *fanum* temple]

fan·fare [fǽnfɛər] *n.* **1** Ⓒ a short flourish, tune or call sounded by trumpets or bugles. 팡파르. **2** Ⓤ a loud public show; a showy display. 허세; 야단스런 과시. [*fan*[1]]

fang [fæŋ] *n.* Ⓒ **1** a long, pointed tooth of a wild beast, a poisonous snake, etc. (짐승의) 엄니; 송곳니; (뱀의) 독니. **2** the root of a tooth. 이촉; 치근(齒根). **3** something like a fang. 송곳니 같은 것. [E.]

fan·light [fǽnlàit] *n.* Ⓒ a fan-shaped window or sash over a door. (문 위의) 부채꼴의 창문. [*fan*[1]]

〈fanlight〉

fan·tail [fǽntèil] *n.* **1** a tail, end, or part shaped like an open fan. 부채 모양의 꼬리〔끝, 부분〕. **2** a pigeon whose tail spreads out like an open fan. 공작비둘기《집비둘기의 일종》. [*fan*[1]]

fan·ta·si·a [fæntéiʒiə, -ziə] *n.* Ⓒ 《mus.》 a free musical composition not fixed in form or style. 환상곡. [↓]

·**fan·tas·tic** [fæntǽstik], **-cal** [-kəl] *adj.* **1** odd; queer; grotesque. 이상한; 야릇한; 기괴한. ¶ *~ designs* 기상천외의 디자인 / *~ costume* 야릇한 복장 / *~ rock formations* 기묘한 암층. **2** imaginary; unreal; irrational. 상상의; 비현실적인. ¶ *~ fears* 근거 없는 공포. [→fantasy]

fan·tas·ti·cal·ly [fæntǽstikəli] *adv.* in a fantastic manner. 이상〔기괴〕하게; 공상적으로.

fan·ta·sy [fǽntəsi, -zi] *n.* (*pl.* **-sies**) **1** Ⓤ fancy; imagination. 공상; 상상. **2** Ⓒ a product of the fancy; a daydream. 공상의 산물; 백일몽. **3** Ⓒ 《mus.》 a fantasia. 환상곡. 參考 phantasy 로도 씀. [Gk. *phainō* show]

:**far** [fɑːr] (**far·ther** or **fur·ther, far·thest** or **fur·thest**) *adv.* **1** (of space and time) ⓐ 《expressing rest》 at a distance; a long way off. 멀리 (떨어져); 아득히. ¶ *~ away from here* 여기서 먼 곳에 / *~ beyond the sea* 멀리 바다 저쪽에 / *~ above the trees* 나무 위 높은 곳에 / *He lives ~ away* 〔*off*〕. 멀리 떨어져 살고 있다 / *~ back in the past* 아득히 먼 옛날에. ⓑ 《expressing motion》 to a distance; to a remote point. 멀리; …까지〔로〕. ¶ *~ into the air* 공중 높이 / *drive a stake ~ into the ground* 땅 속 깊이 말뚝을 박다 / *swim ~ out* 멀리 헤엄치다 / *look ~ into the future* 멀리 장래를 내다보다 / *sit ~ into the night* 밤이 이슥하도록 자지 않다 / *We have not come very ~.* 썩 멀리는 오지 않았다 / *I can walk no farther.* 더는 걸을 수가 없다. **2** (of a degree) to a great degree. 크게; 매우; 훨씬. ¶ *~ different* 매우 다른 / *~ beyond one's powers* 도저히 힘이 미치지 않는 / *This is ~ better than that.* 이것이 그것보다 훨씬 낫다.

as 〔***so***〕 ***far as,*** **a**) to the distance, extent or degree that. (장소·거리) …까지; (범위) …하는〔인〕 한(에는). ¶ *walk as ~ as the river* 강까지 걷다 / *I will go with you as ~ as Seoul.* 서울까지 모시고 가겠습니다 / *as ~ as I know* 내가 알고 있는 한에는. **b**) the same distance. …와 마찬가지로 멀리(까지); …만큼. ¶ *He didn't go as ~ as the others.* 그는 남들만큼 멀리 가지 못했다.

by far, very much. 매우; 훨씬; 단연. ¶ *by ~ the best* 가장 뛰어난〔좋은〕 / *too expensive by ~* 너무나도 비싼.

far and away, very much. 훨씬; 단연. ¶ *This is ~ and away the best.* 이것이 단연 좋다.

far and near, everywhere. 도처에

far and wide, everywhere. 널리; 두루. ¶ *travel ~ and wide* 널리 여행하다.

far be it from me (=*I do not want*) *to do.* (…하거나 할 마음은) 추호도 없다.

far from it, not in the least. (그런 일은) 전혀 없다; 결코 …하지 않다.

go far, be successful; accomplish a great deal. 상당히 성공을 거두다.

go so far as to *do*, go to the degree that. …까지 하다; …하기조차 하다.
how far, to what extent; at what distance. (거리·정도가) 얼마만큼; 어느 정도; 어디까지. ¶ *How ~ can she be trusted?* 그녀를 얼마나 믿을 수 있는가 / *How ~ is it from here to the park?* 여기서 공원까지는 (거리가) 얼마나되나요 / *How ~ are you going?* 어디까지 가시나요.
in so far as, to the degree that; since. …인 한(限)은; …인 한에 있어서.
so far, to the extent that; up to now. 거기〔그 정도〕까지; 이제까지. ¶ *So ~ she has been lucky.* 이제까지 그녀는 운이 좋았다.
So far so good. Things are satisfactory up to this point, at least. 지금까지는 (그런대로) 괜찮다; 잘 되어 가고 있다.
this 〔***that***〕 ***far,*** to this 〔that〕 point, time or degree. 여기〔거기〕까지는.
— *adj.* **1** distant; not near; remote. 먼. ¶ *a ~ country* 먼 나라 / *the ~ future* 먼 장래. **2** more distant of two; opposite. (둘 중) 더 먼; 먼 쪽의; 맞은 편의. ¶ *on the ~ side of the river* 강 맞은 편에. **3** advanced. 진행된. ¶ *He is ~ on in years.* 그는 노년이다. [E.]
few and far between, rare; not frequent. 극히 드문; 잦지 않은.

far·a·way [fɑ́ːrəwèi] *adj.* **1** distant; remote. 먼; 먼 옛날의. ¶ *live in a ~ spot* 벽지에서 살다. **2** dreamy; vague. 꿈꾸는 듯한; 멍한. ¶ *a ~ look in her eyes* 그녀의 꿈꾸는 것 같은 눈. [*far*]

farce [fɑːrs] *n.* Ⓒ **1** a play intended merely to cause people to laugh. 소극(笑劇); 익살극. **2** an absurd and useless affair. 우스움; 우스운 것; 시시한 일. [L. *farcio* stuff]

far·ci·cal [fɑ́ːrsikəl] *adj.* of or like a farce; absurd; ridiculous. 익살극의〔같은〕; 시시한; 우스운. ●**far·ci·cal·ly** [-kəli] *adv.*

far cry [⌐ ⌐] *n.* a long distance. 원거리. ¶ *It is a ~ to Chicago.* 시카고까지는 멀다. [*far*]

:fare [fɛər] *n.* **1** Ⓒ the money paid to ride on a train, car, bus, etc. 운임; 요금. ¶ *a single* 〔*return*〕 *~* 편도〔왕복〕 요금 / *I paid the taxi ~.* 택시 요금을 냈다. **2** Ⓒ a passenger. 승객. ¶ *There was only one ~ on the train.* 열차에는 승객이 한 명밖에 없었다. **3** Ⓤ food and drink. 음식; 식사. ¶ *good* 〔*bad*〕 *~* 좋은〔나쁜〕 음식 / *thrive on good ~* 좋은 음식을 먹고 잘 크다 / *a bill of ~* 차림표; 메뉴.
— *vi.* (P2A) **1** get along; do. 지내다; 살아가다. ¶ *How did you ~ in Hawaii?* 하와이에서 어떻게 지내셨나요. **2** 《*with*》 turn out; happen. 돼가다; …이 되다. 語法 it를 주어로 함. ¶ *~ well in business* 사업이 잘 되어가다 / *It fared ill with them.* 그들은 잘 되지 않았다. **3** eat food or be entertained. 먹다; 음식 대접을 받다. ¶ *~ ill* 〔*well*〕 음식 대접을 잘못〔잘〕 받다. **4** 《*arch.*》 go; journey. 가다; 여행하다. ¶ *~ forth on one's travels* 여행길을 떠나다. [E.]

Far East [⌐ ⌐], **the** *n.* the part of Asia that includes Korea, China, Japan, India, etc. 극동; 원동. [*far*]

:fare·well [fɛ̀ərwél] *interj.* good-by. 안녕(히 가십시오, 히 계십시오).
— *n.* **1** Ⓒ a salutation at parting. 헤어질 때의 인사. **2** ⓊⒸ the act of parting. 헤어짐; 작별. ¶ *a sad ~* 슬픈 이별.
bid 〔***say***〕 ***farewell to*** =***take*** *one's* ***farewell of*** =***make*** *one's* ***farewell to,*** say good-by to (someone). (…)에게 작별을 고하다.
— *adj.* parting; last. 헤어지는; 작별〔고별〕의. ¶ *a ~ kiss* 작별의 키스 / *a ~ party* 송별회 / *make a ~ address* 고별사를 하다. [*fare*]

far-famed [fɑ́ːrféimd] *adj.* widely-known; well-known. 널리〔잘〕 알려진; 유명한. [*far*]

far-fetched [fɑ́ːrféʧt] *adj.* forced; unnatural. 억지로 갖다붙인; 부자연스러운; 무리한. ¶ *a ~ thought* 〔*simile*〕 무리한 생각〔직유(直喩)〕.

far-flung [fɑ́ːrflʌ́ŋ] *adj.* widely-spread; extensive. 널리 퍼진〔흩어진〕; 광범위한.

far-gone [fɑ́ːrgɔ́ːn] *adj.* far advanced in a certain condition; very ill; very drunk; very much in debt. (어떤 상태가) 꽤 진행된; 몹시 취한; 병이 심한; 빚을 많이 진.

fa·ri·na [fəríːnə] *n.* **1** meal or flour ground from corn, roots, etc. 곡분(穀粉). **2** 《bot.》 pollen. 꽃가루. **3** 《chem.》 starch. 녹말; 전분. [L.]

:farm [fɑːrm] *n.* Ⓒ **1** a piece of land used to raise crops or animals, usu. plus a house and the other necessary buildings belonging to it. 농장. ¶ *a sheep ~* 양목장 / *work* 〔*live*〕 *on a ~* 농장에서 일하다〔살다〕. **2** a place like a farm. 사육장; 양식장. ¶ *a chicken ~* 양계장 / *an oyster ~* 굴양식장. **3** a farm house. 농가. **4** a baby farm. 탁아소. **5** 《U.S.》 a villa. 별장.
— *vi.* (P1) raise crops or animals on a farm. 농업〔농장〕을 하다. ¶ *My uncle is farming in Cheju-do.* 숙부는 제주도에서 농사를 짓고 계시다. — *vt.* (P6,7) **1** cultivate (land). …을 경작하다. ¶ *He farms 250 acres.* 그는 농지 250에이커를 경작하고 있다. **2** raise (crops or animals) on a farm. (농장에서) 농사를 짓다; 동물을 기르다; 사육〔양식〕하다. ¶ *~ sheep* 양을 기르다. **3** pay rent for the right to cultivate (land). (토지의) 경작료를 지급하다. **4** 《also *out*》 let (land) for rent. 토지를 임대하다. **5** agree to take care of (children) for a fixed sum of money. (일정한 요금을 받고) (어린애)를 돌보기〔보호하기〕로 하다. **6** 《*out*》 send out (work) to be done by others or in other places. (공장 따위가) 일감을 도급으로 내다; 외부에 내다. [orig. = fixed payment; →firm]

:farm·er [fɑ́ːrmər] *n.* Ⓒ a person who owns or works on a farm. 농업〔농장〕 경영

자; 농부; 농사꾼.

farm hand [ㅗㅗ] *n.* a person who works on someone else's farm. 농장 노동자; 농장의 일꾼.

·farm·house [fɑ́ːrmhàus] *n.* Ⓒ a dwelling house on a farm. 농장에 있는 주택; 농가. [*farm*]

farm·ing [fɑ́ːrmiŋ] *n.* **1** Ⓤ the business or management of operating a farm; agriculture. 농장 경영; 농업. **2** practice of letting out the collection of public revenue. (조세·요금 따위의) 징수 청부.

farm·stead [fɑ́ːrmstèd] *n.* 《Brit.》 Ⓒ a farm with its buildings. (건물을 포함하여) 농장; 농원.

farm·yard [fɑ́ːrmjɑ̀ːrd] *n.* Ⓒ an area around farm buildings or enclosed by them. 농가의 뜰〔마당〕.

far-off [fɑ́ːrɔ́(ː)f, -ɑ́f] *adj.* (of space or time) remote; distant. 아득히 저쪽의; 먼. [*far*]

far-out [fɑ́ːráut] *adj.* extremely unconventional; weird. 인습에 사로잡히지 않는; 틀에 박히지 않은; 기묘〔기발〕한.

far-reach·ing [fɑ́ːríːtʃiŋ] *adj.* **1** extending far in influence or effect. (효과·영향 따위가) 널리 미치는; 원대한. ¶ *a ~ effect* 광범위하게 미치는 효과. **2** extending a great distance. 멀리까지 미치는; 광역에 걸친.

far·ri·er [fǽriər] *n.* Ⓒ 《Brit.》 **1** a person who shoes horses. 편자공(工). **2** a horse doctor. 수의(獸醫). [L. *ferrum* iron]

far·ri·er·y [fǽriəri] *n.* (*pl.* **-er·ies**) **1** Ⓤ the art or practice of a farrier. 편자술(術); 편자공(工)의 일. **2** Ⓒ a place where a farrier works. 편자 공장.

far·row [fǽrou] *n.* Ⓒ a litter of pigs. 한 배의 돼지 새끼. — *vi.* (of swine) bring forth young. (돼지가) 새끼를 낳다. — *vt.* give birth to (pigs). (돼지 새끼를) 낳다. [E. =pig]

far·see·ing [fɑ́ːrsíːiŋ] *adj.* able to see far into the future. 선견지명이 있는. [*far*]

far-sight·ed [fɑ́ːrsáitid] *adj.* **1** able to see far; seeing distant objects more clearly than near objects. 먼눈이 밝은; 원시의. **2** farseeing; well-planned. 선견지명이 있는; 앞을 내다보는; 신중한. ¶ *a ~ policy* 앞을 내다보는 정책. ● **far-sight·ed·ly** [-li] *adv.*

:far·ther [fɑ́ːrðər] *adj.* (*compar.* of **far**) **1** ⓐ more distant; or remoter. 더 먼; 더 저쪽의. ¶ *the ~ shore* 건너편 강기슭 / *a memory of a ~ childhood* 더 어릴 때의 추억 / *the ~ side of the mountain* 산 너머 저쪽 / *on the ~ side of fifty* 쉰 살 고개를 훨씬 넘어. ⓑ 《now usu. *further*》 more advanced; later. 더 진행〔진보〕된; 나중의. ¶ *a ~ stage of development* 더 진행된 발달 단계. **2** 《now usu. *further*》 additional; more; further. 그 위의; 그 밖의; 그 이상의. ¶ *until ~ notice* 추후 통지가 있을 때까지. — *adv.* **1** to or at a greater distance. 더 멀리. ¶ *go ~* 더(멀리) 가다 / *see ~ than another* 남보다 더 멀리 보다 / *He lives ~ on.* 그는 더 먼 곳에 살고 있다. **2** to or at a more advanced point. 더 나아가; 더 고도로. **3** 《now usu. *further*》 in addition; moreover; also; further. 게다가; 그 위에; 또한. [→further]

far·ther·most [fɑ́ːrðərmòust] *adj.* most remote or distant; farthest. 가장 먼.

:far·thest [fɑ́ːrðist] *adj.* (*superl.* of **far**) most remote or distant. 가장 먼.

at* (*the*) *farthest, at the greatest distance; at most; at latest. 가장 멀리서; 고작; 늦어도.

— *adv.* to or at the greatest distance. 더 멀리; 훨씬 저쪽에.

far·thing [fɑ́ːrðiŋ] *n.* Ⓒ 《Brit.》 **1** (a former British coin worth) a quarter of a penny. 파딩《영국의 구(舊) 최소 화폐 단위; 1/4 페니》; 그 동화. **2** 《*a ~, negative*》 a bit. 조금도. ¶ *not worth a ~* 조금도 가치가 없는 / *It doesn't matter a ~.* 전혀 문제가 안 된다. [*fourth*]

fas·ci·nate [fǽsənèit] *vt.* (P6,13) **1** (of snakes, etc.) hold (frogs, etc.) motionless or powerless by a fixed stare or through terror. (움츠러져) 옴쭉 못 하게 하다; (잔뜩 노려보아) 그 자리에 못박히게 하다. ¶ *The sight of the snake fascinated the rabbit.* 뱀을 보고 토끼는 그 자리에 못박혔다. **2** charm or attract greatly. …의 정신〔넋〕을 빼앗다; 매혹〔뇌쇄〕하다. ¶ *He was fascinated by* 〔*with*〕 *her beauty.* 그녀의 아름다움에 매혹되었다. [L. *fascinum* spell]

fas·ci·nat·ing [fǽsənèitiŋ] *adj.* charming; enchanting. 매혹적인; 황홀케 하는; 도취시키는. ¶ *a ~ young lady* 매력적인 젊은 부인. ● **fas·ci·nat·ing·ly** [-li] *adv.*

fas·ci·na·tion [fæ̀sənéiʃən] *n.* Ⓤ **1** the act of fascinating; the state of being fascinated. 홀림; 도취(된 상태). **2** very strong attraction; the power to fascinate; charm. 매력; 매혹(력).

fas·cism [fǽʃizəm] *n.* Ⓤ **1** 《also *F-*》 a repressive system of government and society established in Italy under the leadership of Mussolini in 1922. 파시즘. **2** any principles or methods like fascism. 파쇼적 지도 정신; 국수주의. [L. *fascis* bundle of sticks]

fas·cist [fǽʃist] *n.* Ⓒ **1** 《*F-*》 a member of the political party established by Mussolini. 파시스트 당원. **2** anyone who belives in fascism. 국수주의자. — *adj.* of or belonging to the Fascists or Fascism. 파시스트 당(원)의; 파시즘적인. [*fascism*]

:fash·ion [fǽʃən] *n.* **1** ⒸⓊ 《often *the ~*》 the accepted style or custom of a certain time, esp. in dress; the current mode or vogue. (특히 의상 따위의) 유행(형); 시류(풍). ¶ *the latest Paris fashions* 최신 파리의 유행(형) / *the latest ~ in hats* 모자의 최신 유행형 / *be in* 〔*out of*〕 *~* 유행하고 있다〔에 뒤지다〕 / *bring* (*something*) *into ~* (…

을) 유행시키다 / *come* 〔*grow*〕 *into* ~ 유행하게 되다 / *go* 〔*get*〕 *out of* ~ 유행이 스러져 가다 / *follow the* ~ 유행에 따르다 / *lead* 〔*set*〕 *the* ~ 유행을 만들어 내다; 유행의 선구가 되다. **2** Ⓒ a manner; a way. 모양; (방)식. ¶ *in this* ~ 이런 식으로 / *climb in zigzag* ~ 갈짓자로 오르다 / *live in* 〔*after*〕 *one's* ~ 자기 방식대로 살다 / *She walks in a peculiar* ~. 그녀는 묘하게 걷는다. **3** 《*collectively*》 those people who act in accord with the current preferences of society; 《*the* ~》 the fashionable world. 유행〔사교〕계의 사람들; 상류 사회.

after 〔***in***〕 ***a fashion,*** in some manner; not very well; to some extent. 그럭저럭; 그저 그런 대로; 어느 정도.

after the fashion (=*following the example*) ***of*** *something.* …에 따라서; …을 본떠서.

be all the fashion, (of a way of dressing, a custom, etc.) be very popular. 대단히 인기가 있다.

in fashion, in accordance with the fashion. 유행되고 있는(opp. out of fashion). ¶ *Such clothes are no longer in* ~. 그런 옷은 이제 유행되지 않는다.

— *vt.* (P6,13) **1** form; shape. …을 만들다. ¶ ~ *a doll from a piece of wood* 나뭇조각으로 인형을 만들다 / *This pipe is fashioned from clay.* 이 파이프는 찰흙으로 만들어져 있다. **2** 《*to*》 fit. …을 적합〔적응〕시키다. ¶ ~ *a student to modern ideas* 신(新)사상에 학생을 적응시키다. [→fact]

·fash·ion·a·ble [fǽʃənəbəl] *adj.* **1** in accord with the current style; in fashion; up-to-date. 유행의; 시류의. ¶ *a* ~ *dress* 〔*hairdo*〕 유행의 드레스〔머리형〕. **2** used by rich, elegant people. 상류 사회의.

fash·ion·a·bly [fǽʃənəbli] *adv.* in a fashionable manner. 유행에 따라; 시류〔현대〕풍으로.

:fast[1] [fæst, fɑːst] *adj.* **1** quick; rapid. 빠른(opp. slow). ¶ *a* ~ *horse* 빠른 말; 준마 / *a* ~ *train* 급행 열차 / *a* ~ *worker* 일을 빨리하는 사람 / *a* ~ *pain reliever* 금세 듣는 진통제. **2** (of a clock or watch) showing a time ahead of the correct time. (시계가) 더 가는; 빠른. ¶ *My watch is two minutes* ~. 내 시계는 2분 빠르다. **3** firmly fixed. 단단한; 꽉 매인〔쥔, 닫힌, 잠긴〕(opp. loose). ¶ *The window is* ~. 창문이 꼭 닫혀 있다 / *the roots* ~ *in the ground* 땅 속에 단단히 박힌 뿌리 / *lay* ~ *hold on something* =*take* (*a*) ~ *hold of something* 무엇을 단단히 쥐고 놓지 않다. **4** not losing color; unfading. (색이) 바래지 않는; 오래가는. **5** not changing one's mind; loyal. (우정 따위가) 변함없는; 성실한. ¶ *a* ~ *friend* 변함없는 친구. **6** fond of pleasure; too gay; wild. 쾌락을 좇는; 방종한; 방탕한. ¶ *a* ~ *woman* 몸가짐이 헤픈 여자 / *He led a* ~ *life.* 그는 방탕한 생활을 했다.

— *adv.* **1** firmly; fixedly. 단단히; 꽉. ¶ *be bound* ~ *by the feet* 발을 단단히 묶이다 / *shut* ~ 꼭 닫다 / *stand* ~ 꽉 버티어 서다 / *a tree* ~ *rooted* 단단히 뿌리를 내린 나무 / *be* ~ *frozen* 단단히 얼어붙다 / *hold* ~ *to* 〔*by*〕 *a parapet* 난간을 붙잡고 늘어지다. **2** soundly. (잠을) 푹; 깊이. ¶ *The child is* ~ *asleep.* 아이는 깊이 잠들어 있다. **3** quickly; rapidly. 빠르게; 빨리. **4** wildly. 방종〔방탕〕하게. ¶ *live* ~ 방탕한 생활을 하다. [E.]

play fast and loose, say one thing and do another. 언행이 일치하지 않다; 무책임한 행동을 취하다.

fast[2] [fæst, fɑːst] *vi., vt.* (P1,2B,3; 6,7) eat no food for a time, esp. as a religious duty. 단식하다. ¶ ~ *on bread and water* 빵과 물만으로 생활하다 / ~ *an illness off* 단식으로 병을 고치다 / *I have been fasting all day.* 하루 종일 단식하고 있다.

— *n.* Ⓒ **1** the act of fasting. 단식. **2** a day or period of fasting. 단식일; 단식하는 기간. [E.]

break one's fast, take a meal for the first time after fasting; eat breakfast. 단식 후 처음으로 식사하다; 아침 식사를 들다.

:fas·ten [fǽsn, fɑ́ːsn] *vt.* (P6,7,13) **1** fix or attach firmly; tie. …을 단단히 정착〔고정〕시키다; 붙들어 매다. ¶ ~ *one's hair* 머리를 단단히 묶다 / ~ *two things together* 두 개의 물건을 한데 묶다 / ~ *a boat to a tree by a rope* 밧줄로 배를 나무에 붙들어 매다. **2** shut; close. 닫다; 잠그다. ¶ ~ *a door* 문에 자물쇠를 채우다. **3** 《*upon*》 direct; fix. …을 향하다〔돌리다〕; (책임 따위를) 강제로 넘겨 씌우다; (별명 따위를) 붙이다. ¶ ~ *one's eyes on* 〔*upon*〕 *her face* 그녀 얼굴에 눈길을 쏟다 / ~ *a crime on someone* 아무에게 죄를 넘겨 씌우다 / ~ *a blame on someone* 아무에게 누명을 씌우다 / *We fastened the nick-name upon him.* 우리는 그에게 별명을 붙였다. — *vi.* (P1,3) **1** become attached, fixed, or joined; catch. 단단히 고정되다; 잠기다; 닫히다. ¶ *The door* 〔*lock*〕 *will not* ~. 문이〔열쇠가〕 잠기지 않는다. **2** 《*on, upon*》 take a firm hold of ; seize upon. 꽉 붙잡다; 매달리다. ¶ ~ *upon one's prey* 먹이를 꽉 잡고 늘어지다 / 《*fig.*》 ~ *upon an idea* 〔*a suggestion*〕 어떤 생각에 집착하다. [*fast*[1]]

fasten a quarrel upon, pick a quarrel with. …에게 싸움을 걸다.

fasten down, make firm. 확정하다; 단단히 못박다; 눌러 고정시키다.

fasten *something* ***up,*** close something and make it fast; tie firmly. …을 단단히 폐쇄하다; 단단히 매다. ¶ ~ *up a parcel* 소포를 단단히 묶다.

fas·ten·er [fǽsnər, fɑ́ːsnər] *n.* Ⓒ **1** a person who fastens. 잠그는〔죄는〕 사람. **2** a thing used to fasten a door, a garment, etc. 잠그개; 죔쇠; 지퍼.

fas·ten·ing [fǽsniŋ, fɑ́ːsniŋ] *n.* Ⓒ a thing used to fasten, such as a lock, a bolt, or a clasp. 잠그개; 죔쇠.

F

fast food [⌐ ⌐] *n.* food such as hamberger and cooked chicken that is quickly and easily prepared, and sold by a restaurant to be eaten at once or taken away. 간이 즉석 식품; 패스트 푸드. ¶ *a well-known chain of ~ restaurant* 이름난 패스트 푸드 연쇄점.

fas·tid·i·ous [fæstídiəs, fəs-] *adj.* hard to please; very careful; very critical. 가리는 것이 많은; 괴까다로운; 매우 비판적인. ¶ *She is ~ about her clothes.* 그녀는 옷에 까다롭다. [L. *fastidium* loathing]

fas·tid·i·ous·ly [fæstídiəsli] *adv.* in a fastidious manner. 괴까다롭게.

fast·ness [fǽstnis, fɑ́:st-] *n.* **1** Ⓒ a strong, secure place; a fortress. 요새; 보루. **2** Ⓤ the quality or state of being fast. 견고; 고정; 신속. [*fast*[1]]

:fat [fæt] *n.* Ⓤ **1** the oily white or yellow part of meat. 비계; 지방. **2** the richest part of anything. 가장 좋은 부분. ¶ *live on* 〔*off*〕 *the ~ of the land* 윤택〔사치〕하게 살다.

chew the fat, 《*sl.*》 grumble; chat. 투덜거리다; 지껄이다; 재잘대다.

The fat is in the fire. The thing has happened and cannot be prevented. 어쩔 수 없게 되었다; (실수로) 일이 엉뚱하게 됐다.

— *adj.* (**fat·ter, fat·test**) **1** ⓐ having much fat. 비계가〔지방이〕 많은. ¶ *~ meat* 비계가 많은 고기. ⓑ well-fed; plump; fleshy. 살이 찐; 뚱뚱한; 비만한. ¶ *a ~ woman* 살찐 여자 / *You are getting too ~.* 살이 너무 찌네그려. **2** ⓐ thick; well-filled; rich. 두툼한; 풍족한. ¶ *a ~ purse* 두둑한 돈지갑. ⓑ productive; fertile. 생산적인; 비옥한. ¶ *~ soil* 기름진 땅. **3** oily; greasy. 기름기 많은. **4** yielding much money; profitable. 돈벌이가 되는; 이득이 있는. ¶ *a ~ job* 돈벌이가 좋은 일.

a fat chance, 《U.S. *sl., iron.*》 a very slight chance. 불안한 전망; 거의 가망 없는 일.

a fat lot, 《*colloq.*》 not at all. 전혀 …않다. ¶ *A ~ lot I care!* 내가 알게 뭐야.

— *vt.* (P6,7) make (someone or something) fat. …을 살찌우다. ¶ *~ a beast for the market* 시장에 팔려고 짐승을 살찌우다.

— *vi.* (P1,2A) become fat. 살이 찌다. [E.]

***fa·tal** [féitl] *adj.* **1** causing death or ruin. 생명에 관계되는; 치명적인; 파멸적인. ¶ *~ accidents* 치명적인 사고 / *a ~ disease* 불치의 병 / *a ~ mistake* 파멸적인 실수 / *The wound proved ~ to him.* 그 부상이 그의 치명상이 되었다. **2** decisive; fateful. 결정적인; 숙명의. ¶ *The ~ day arrived at last.* 숙명의 날은 마침내 왔다. [→fate]

fa·tal·ism [féitəlìzəm] *n.* Ⓤ the belief that everything is determined or controlled by fate. 숙명론; 운명론.

fa·tal·ist [féitəlist] *n.* Ⓒ a person who believes in fatalism. 숙명론자.

fa·tal·is·tic [fèitəlístik] *adj.* of or based on fatalism. 숙명론적인; 숙명론상의.

fa·tal·i·ty [feitǽləti, fət-] *n.* (*pl.* **-ties**) **1** Ⓒ a fatal accident; a misfortune. (숙명적인) 불행; 재난; 참사. **2** Ⓤ the condition or state of being fated; the inevitable course of destiny. 인과; 운명; 숙명. **3** Ⓤ death in war or as a result of an accident or a disaster; Ⓒ a person killed in an accident or a disaster. (전쟁 따위로 인한) 사고사; 사망자.

fa·tal·ly [féitəli] *adv.* in a fatal manner; according to fate. 치명적으로; 불운하게; 숙명적〔필연적〕으로. ¶ *He was ~ wounded by the accidental discharge of a gun.* 총의 오발 사고로 인해 그는 치명적인 부상을 당했다.

:fate [feit] *n.* Ⓤ **1** the power supposed to guide all events beyond any person's control. 숙명; 운명; 천명. ¶ *accept one's ~* 추세에 맡기다; 체념하다 / *sorrow at one's hard ~* 자신의 불운을 한탄하다. **2** death; ruin. 죽음; 파멸. **3** 《*the Fates*》 《Gk. myth.》 the three goddesses of destiny. 운명의 여신. 參考 생명의 실을 잣는 Cloths, 그 실을 재는 Lachesis, 그 실을 끊는 Atropos 3명의 신(神).

as sure as fate, certainly. 아주 확실히.

fix 〔***seal***〕 ***someone's fate,*** decide his future. …의 장래를 결정하다.

meet one's fate, **a**) die. 죽다. **b**) meet a woman who is destined to be his wife. 장차 아내가 될 여자를 만나다.

— *vt.* (P6) 《chiefly in *passive*》 fix what is to happen. (운명에 의해서) 미리 정하다; 운명지우다. ¶ *be fated to be hanged* 교수형을 받도록 운명지워지다 / *It was fated that....* …하도록 운명지워져 있었다. [L. *fatum*]

fat·ed [féitid] *adj.* **1** controlled by fate. 숙명적인. **2** destined, esp. to destruction. 파멸의 운명에 있는.

fate·ful [féitfəl] *adj.* **1** controlled by fate. 숙명적인. **2** having important results; decisive. 중대한; 결정적인. **3** causing death; ominous. 치명적인; 불길한.

fate·ful·ly [féitfəli] *adv.* in a fateful manner. 숙명적으로; 결정적으로.

fath. fathom.

:fa·ther [fɑ́:ðər] *n.* Ⓒ **1** a man parent; 《often *F-*》 one's own father. 아버지; 부친. ¶ *a bereaved ~* 자식을 여읜 아버지. **2** a man like a father. 아버지 같은 사람. ¶ *He was a ~ to the weak.* 그는 약자들에게 아버지와도 같은 존재였다. **3** a founder; an important leader. 창시자; 창도〔주도〕자. ¶ *the ~ of our school* 우리 학교의 창립자 / *the ~ of modern psychology* 근대 심리학의 아버지 / *Chaucer, the ~ of English poetry* 영시의 아버지 초서. **4** a forefather. 선조; 조상. **5** 《often *F-*》 ⓐ a priest, esp. one who belongs to a certain order in

the church; a title of such a man. 신부(의 칭호). ¶ *Holy Father* 교황; 교황성하(聖下) / *Father Brown* 브라운 신부. ⓑ the head of a monastery. 수도원장. **6** 《*Our F-*》 God. 하느님; 조물주.
be gathered to one's fathers, die. 죽다.
sleep with one's fathers, be dead. 죽었다.
— *adj.* **1** that is a father. 아버지인. ¶ *a ~ bird* 아비새. **2** of or like a father. 아버지의; 아버지 같은. ¶ *~ love* 부성애. **3** native. 조국의.
— *vt.* (P6) **1** be the father of (someone); care for (someone) as a father. …의 아버지이다; …을 아버지로서 부양하다[돌보다]. **2** create; invent. …을 창조하다; 발명하다. [E.]

fa·ther·hood [fáːðərhùd] *n.* Ⓤ the state of being a father. 아버지임.

fa·ther-in-law [fáːðərinlɔ̀ː] *n.* Ⓒ (*pl.* **fa·thers-**) the father of one's husband or wife. 시아버지; 장인; 빙부; 계부(繼父).

fa·ther·land [fáːðərlæ̀nd] *n.* Ⓒ a person's native country. 조국.

fa·ther·less [fáːðərlis] *adj.* without a father living. 아버지 없는.

fa·ther·ly [fáːðərli] *adj.* **1** of a father. 아버지의. ¶ *~ responsibility* 아버지의 책임. **2** like a father; kindly. 아버지 같은; 자애로운. ¶ *a ~ smile* 자애로운 미소. ● **fa·ther·li·ness** [-nis] *n.*

fath·om [fǽðəm] *n.* Ⓒ (*pl.* **-oms** or *collectively* **fathom**) a unit of measure equal to 6 feet, used in measuring the depth of water. 길; 패덤《물 깊이 따위를 재는 단위; 6피트; 약 1.8 m》. ¶ *The sea is sixty fathoms deep here.* 여기의 바다 깊이는 60패덤이다. — *vt.* (P6) **1** measure the depth of (water). (물)의 깊이를 재다. **2** reach the bottom of (something); understand completely. …의 밑바닥을 탐색하다; …을 이해하다. [E.]

fath·om·less [fǽðəmlis] *adj.* too deep to be measured; not easily understood; incomprehensible. (깊이를) 헤아릴 수 없는; 불가해한; 이해할 수 없는. ¶ *the ~ depths of the sea* 바다의 헤아릴 수 없는 깊이.

·fa·tigue [fətíːg] *n.* Ⓤ **1** the state of being very tired; weariness. (심신의) 피로. ¶ *brain* [*physical*] *~* 머리[몸]의 피로 / *be suffering from ~* 피로에 시달리다 / *sleep off ~* 잠을 자서 피로를 풀다. **2** the cause of weariness; toil; labor. 피로의 원인; 고된 일. **3** a condition of weakening in metal, wood, etc. after long strain or use. (무리하거나 장기 사용에 의한 금속·목재 등의) 피로; 약화. **4** Ⓒ 《mil.》 the work of cleaning, cooking, etc. (군무 외의) 잡역. ¶ *~ clothes* 작업복. — *vt.* (P6,13) make (someone) weary; tire. …을 피로케 하다. ¶ *feel very fatigued* 몹시 피곤하다 / *The work fatigued him.* 일이 그를 지치게 했다. [L. *fatigo*]
be fatigued with, be worn out with. …로 녹초가 되다.

fat·ling [fǽtliŋ] *n.* a young animal, such as lamb or calf, fattened for slaughter. 어린 비육 가축. [↓]

fat·ten [fǽtn] *vt.* (P6) make (someone) fat. …을 살찌게 하다. — *vi.* (P1) become fat. 살이 찌다. [*fat*]

fat·tish [fǽtiʃ] *adj.* rather or somewhat fat. 좀 비만한; 살찐.

fat·ty [fǽti] *adj.* (**-ti·er, -ti·est**) of fat; containing fat; like fat. 지방(질)의; 지방이[비계가] 많은; 지방 같은. — *n.* a fat child. 뚱뚱한 아이. ● **fat·ti·ness** [-nis] *n.*

fa·tu·i·ty [fətjúːəti] *n.* Ⓤ (*pl.* **-ties**) the state of being foolish; stupidity; foolishness; Ⓒ an example of foolishness, etc. 우둔; 어리석음; 어리석은 언동. [L.]

fat·u·ous [fǽtʃuəs] *adj.* **1** foolish but self-satisfied; silly; foolish. 우둔한; 어리석은; 바보 같은. ¶ *a ~ attempt* 바보 같은 시도. **2** unreal; illusionary. 실제하지 않는; 환상의. ¶ *a ~ fire* 도깨비불. [L.]

fau·ces [fɔ́ːsiːz] *n. pl.* 《anat.》 the cavity at the back of the mouth, leading into the pharynx. 목구멍; 인후; 구협(口峽). [L. =throat]

fau·cet [fɔ́ːsit] *n.* Ⓒ 《esp. U.S.》 an instrument containing a valve for controlling the flow of liquid from a pipe, a cask, etc. (수도·통 따위의) 주둥이; 꼭지; 고동. [F.]

F

:fault [fɔːlt] *n.* Ⓒ **1** a mistake. 잘못; 과실. ¶ *commit a ~* 잘못을 범하다 / *There are a lot of faults in your composition.* 네 작문에는 잘못이 많다. **2** a bad part; a weak point in one's character. 결점; 약점. ¶ *a ~ in one's character* 성격상의 결함 / *a man of many faults* 결점이 많은 사람 / *Carelessness is his ~.* 부주의가 그의 결점이다. **3** 《*sing.* only》 blame; responsibility. (과실·비행의) 책임; 원인. ¶ *It's not your ~.* 그건 자네 탓이 아냐 / *It was my ~ that they were late.* 그들이 늦은 것은 내 탓이었다. **4** (tennis, etc.) a failure to serve the ball correctly. 폴트《서브의 실수》. **5** 《geol.》 a break in strata. 단층(斷層). [→fail]
be at fault, **a**) 《hunting》 lose the scent. 사냥감의 냄새를 놓치다. **b**) 《*fig.*》 not know what to do next; be at a loss. 어찌할 바를 모르다; 망연 자실하다.
find fault with (=*try to find the bad point of*) *someone or something.* …의 흠[탈]을 잡다.
in fault, wrong; guilty. 잘못하여; 죄가 있는.
to a fault, too much; excessively. 극단으로; 몹시. ¶ *be generous to a ~* 지나치게 너그럽다.
without fault, correct(ly); surely; for sure. 틀림없이; 확실히.

fault·find·er [fɔ́ːltfàindər] *n.* Ⓒ a tiresome person who likes to criticize. 흠[탈]잡는 사람; 잔소리가 심한 사람.

fault·find·ing [fɔ́ːltfàindiŋ] *adj.*, *n.* Ⓤ (the act of) finding fault or criticizing. 흠[탈] 잡는; 흠 잡음; 탈 잡기.

fault·i·ly [fɔ́ːltili] *adv.* in a faulty manner. 잘못하여; 불완전하게.

fault·less [fɔ́ːltlis] *adj.* having no fault at all; perfect. 과실 없는; 완전 무결한.

fault·y [fɔ́ːlti] *adj.* (**fault·i·er, fault·i·est**) having faults; wrong; imperfect. 과실(過失)이 있는; 잘못된; 불완전한.
●**fault·i·ness** [-nis] *n.*

faun [fɔːn] *n.* Ⓒ 《Rom. myth.》 a spirit of the woods, with a goat's horns, feet and pointed ears, that helped farmers and shepherds. 폰 《임야·목축의 신으로 반인반양(半人半羊)》. [L. *Faunus*] 〈faun〉

fau·na [fɔ́ːnə] *n.* Ⓒ (*pl.* **-nas** or *collectively* **-nae**) **1** all the animals found in a certain region or period. (한 지방 또는 한 시대의) 동물상(相); 동물군(群). **2** a treatise on the fauna of a given region or period. (어떤 지역·시대의) 동물지(誌). [↑]

fau·nae [fɔ́ːni] *n.* pl. of **fauna.**

F

Faust [faust] *n.* (in German legends) a man who sold his soul to the devil in return for power and knowledge. 파우스트 《Goethe가 비극의 주인공으로 삼았음》. [L. *faustus* fortunate]

:**fa·vor,** 《Brit.》 **-vour** [féivər] *n.* **1** ⒸⓊ (an act of) kindness; friendly regard; good will. 친절(한 행위); 친절한 마음; 호의. ¶ *an unmerited* ~ 과분한 친절 / *treat someone with* ~ 아무를 친절히 대하다 / *bask in someone's* ~ 아무의 호의를 입다 / *do something out of* ~ 호의에서 무엇을 하다 / *enjoy the* ~ *of someone* 아무의 호의를 입다 / *May I ask a* ~ *of you?* 부탁드릴 일이 있는데요 / *I have a* ~ *to ask of you.* 한 가지 부탁이 있는데요 / *Please do me a* ~. 아무쪼록 부탁합니다. **2** ⒸⓊ an approval; a consent; an agreement; support. 찬성; 허가; 동의; 지지. ¶ *grant someone a* ~ 아무에게 승낙하다 / *look with* ~ *on a plan* =*look on a plan with* ~ 계획에 찬성하다 / *win the* ~ *of the voters* 투표자의 지지를 얻다 / *The vote was 87 in* ~ *to 5 against with 15 abstentions.* 투표는 찬성 87, 반대 5, 기권이 15표였다. **3** Ⓤ special kindness to a particular person; unfair partiality. 총애; 편애; 정실. ¶ *without* ~ *or partiality* 편벽됨이 없이; 공평 무사하게 / *win* [*lose*] *high* ~ *of the king* 왕의 총애를 얻다[잃다] / *win a position by* ~ *more than by merit* 실력보다도 정실로 지위를 얻다. **4** Ⓒ a small gift (given as a love token). (애정의 표시로서의) 선물. **5** ⓊⒸ advantageous circumstances; something favorable. 유리한 정황[것]. ¶ *The evidence is in his* ~. 증거는 그에게 유리하다. **6** Ⓒ 《comm.》 a letter. 서한; 편지. ¶ *your* ~ *of yesterday*('*s date*) 어제 날짜의 귀하의 서신.

by* [*with*] *your favor, with your permission. 실례입니다만.

find favor in someone's eyes, be liked by someone. …의 마음[눈]에 들다.

in someone's favor, to someone's advantage. …에게 유리하게[이익이 되게].

in favor of, **a**) (of a person) on the side of. …을 편들어; 지지[찬성]하고. **b**) (of a thing or action) to the advantage of. …에게 유리하게; 이익이 되도록.

out of someone's favor, not favored; not liked. …의 눈 밖에 나; 마음에 들지 않아; …에게 소원(疏遠)되어.

stand* [*be*] *high in someone's favor, be well regarded by someone. …의 마음에 몹시 들어 있다.

under* (*the*) *favor of, under cover of. …을 틈타; 이용하여; …에게 원조를 받아. ¶ *an escape made under* ~ *of the darkness* 야음을 틈타 결행된 탈출.

— *vt.* (P6,13) **1** agree to (something); approve. …에 찬성하다; 동의하다. ¶ ~ *a proposal* 제의에 찬성하다 / *I* ~ *your opinion.* 네 의견에 찬성한다. **2** show a special kindness to (a particular person); prefer unfairly. …을 편애하다; 편벽되게 좋아하다. ¶ *A teacher should not* ~ *one pupil over others in her class.* 교사는 반의 특정한 아이를 편애해서는 안 된다. **3** help; aid; assist. …을 돕다; …의 편을 들다. ¶ *Fortune favors the brave.* 행운은 용감한 자를 돕는다. **4** 《*with*》 do a kindness to (someone); oblige. …에게 친절하게 하다. ¶ *Will you* ~ *me with a song?* 노래 한 곡 불러주시겠습니까. **5** 《*colloq.*》 resemble (someone) in looks. …를 닮다. ¶ *The baby favors his father.* 아기는 아빠를 닮았다. **6** encourage; make easier or possible. …에 유리하게 되어 가다; 용이하게 하다; 촉진시키다. ¶ *The thick fog favored their escape.* 짙은 안개가 그들의 탈출을 용이하게 했다. [L.]

·**fa·vor·a·ble,** 《Brit.》 **-vour-** [féivərəbəl] *adj.* **1** favoring; approving. 호의 있는; 승낙의; 찬성하는. ¶ *a* ~ *answer* 호의적인 대답. **2** affording convenience; suitable; helpful. 순조로운; 유리한; 적합한; 알맞은. ¶ ~ *weather* 순조로운 날씨 / *a* ~ *wind* 순풍 / *a* ~ *opportunity* 호기(好機) / *a* ~ *position* 유리한 입장. **3** promising. 유망한.

fa·vor·a·bly, 《Brit.》 **-vour-** [féivərəbəli] *adv.* in a favorable manner. 순조롭게; 유리하게; 호의를 갖고; 친절히.

fa·vored, 《Brit.》 **-voured** [féivərd] *adj.* **1** treated with favor; with special advantages. 호의를[호감을] 산; 혜택을 받은; 행운의. ¶ *the most-favored-nation clause* (국제법의) 최혜국(最惠國) 조항 / *born into the* ~ *classes* 혜택 받은 계급에 태어나다. **2** 《often in *compounds*》 with a certain appearance. 얼굴이 …한. ¶ *ill-favored* (얼굴이) 못생긴 / *well-favored* 잘생긴; 아름다운 (얼굴의).

:fa·vor·ite, 《Brit.》 **-vour-** [féivərit] *adj.* liked above all others. 무엇보다도〔가장〕 좋아하는. ¶ *one's ~ daughter* 사랑하는 딸. — *n.* Ⓒ **1** a person or thing liked above all others. 가장 마음에 드는 사람; 인기인; 좋아하는 것. ¶ *fortune's ~* 행운아 / *be a ~ with someone* 아무에게 인기가 있다. **2** a person, a horse, etc. expected to win. (경마에서) 우승 예상마; (경기의) 인기 선수.

fa·vor·it·ism, 《Brit.》 **-vour-** [féivəritìzəm] *n.* Ⓤ the act of favoring one person or group above all others; partiality. 편애(偏愛); 정실.

:fa·vour [féivər] *n.* 《Brit.》 =favor.

fawn[1] [fɔːn] *n.* **1** Ⓒ a deer less than one year old. 새끼 사슴. **2** Ⓤ a light, yellowish brown color. 담황갈색. — *adj.* light yellowish-brown. 담황갈색의. — *vi.* (P1) (of a deer) bear a fawn. (사슴이) 새끼를 낳다. [L. *fetus* offspring]

·fawn[2] [fɔːn] *vi.* (P1,3) 《*on, upon*》 **1** seek favor by acting slavishly. 아첨하다; 비위맞추다. ¶ *~ on* 〔*upon*〕 *one's superiors* 상사에게 아첨하다. **2** (of dogs, etc.) show fondness by moving the tail. (개 따위가 꼬리를 치며) 재롱떨다. ● **fawn·ing·ly** [fɔ́ːniŋli] *adv.* [E.]

fay [fei] *n.* Ⓒ 《*poet.*》 a fairy. 요정. [→fate]

faze [feiz] *vt.* (P6) 《U.S. *colloq.*》 disturb; disconcert. …을 당황케 하다; 쩔쩔 매게 하다. [→feeze]

FBI 《U.S.》 Federal Bureau of Investigation (미국 연방 수사국).

f.c. follow copy. (교정에서) 원고를 보라.

FCA 《U.S.》 Farm Credit Administration (미국 농업 금융국).

fe·al·ty [fíːəlti] *n.* Ⓤ **1** 《hist.》 loyalty to one's ruler. (영주에 대한) 충성; 의무. ¶ *do* 〔*swear*〕 *~* 충성을 맹세하다. **2** 《*poet.*》 loyalty; faithfulness. 신의(信義); 성실. [L. *fides* faith]

:fear [fiər] *n.* Ⓤ **1** a feeling caused by danger; terror; dread. 두려움; 공포. ¶ *the ~ of death* 죽음의 공포 / *Fear came over him.* 공포가 그를 엄습했다 / *She turned pale with sudden ~.* 불의의 공포로 그녀는 파랗게 질렸다. **2** anxiety; uneasiness; Ⓒ that which one fears. 걱정; 불안; 두려워하는 것; 근심사(事). ¶ *hesitate for ~ of failure* 실패가 두려워 망설이다 / *I feel no ~ for my future.* 내 장래에 대해 걱정 않는다 / *Fears were felt for their safety.* 그들의 안전이 걱정되었다 / *I had a ~ that you might miss the train.* 열차를 놓치지 않았을까 걱정했다 / *There is no ~ of rain today.* 오늘 비가 올 염려는 전혀 없다 / *in* 〔*for*〕 *~ of one's life* 생명을 잃지나 않을까 두려워서. **3** awe; great respect. 외경(畏敬); 존숭(尊崇). ¶ *a ~ of God* 하느님에 대한 외경 / *put the ~ of God into someone* 아무를 두려움에 떨게 하다; 호되게 꾸짖다; 정신들게 하다.

for fear of something =***for fear*** (***that***) ***… should*** 〔***might***〕 ***do,*** lest … should do; so as not to do. …을 두려워하여; …하지 않도록. ¶ *He took an umbrella for ~ of the rain.* 그는 비가 오지 않을까 걱정하여 우산을 들고 갔다.

without fear or favor, justly. 공평하게.

— *vt.* **1** (P6,8,9,11,13) be afraid of; be frightened by (something). …을 두려워하다; 걱정하다. ¶ *~ death* 죽음을 두려워하다 / *~ for one's health* 건강에 대해 걱정하다 / *I do not ~ his threats.* 그의 협박을 두려워하지 않는다 / *I ~ it's too late.* 너무 늦지 않을까 걱정이다. **2** (P6) have great respect for (God, etc.). …을 외경하다; 두려워 공경하다. [E.]

·fear·ful [fíərfəl] *adj.* **1** terrible; dreadful. 무서운; 끔찍한. ¶ *a ~ accident* 끔찍한 사고. **2** full of fear; afraid. 두려워하여; 걱정하여. ¶ *He was ~ of the consequences.* 그는 결과를 두려워했다. **3** 《*colloq.*》 very great; extreme. 엄청난; 극도의. ¶ *a ~ mess* 극도의 혼란.

fear·ful·ly [fíərfəli] *adv.* in a fearful manner; very much. 무섭게; 흠칫거리며; 몹시. ¶ *I am ~ busy now.* 지금 무척 바쁘다.

·fear·less [fíərlis] *adj.* without fear; brave. 무서워〔두려워〕하지 않는; 대담한. ● **fear·less·ly** [-li] *adv.*

fear·some [fíərsəm] *adj.* **1** frightful; horrible; terrifying. 무서운; 끔찍한. **2** afraid; timid. 두려워하는; 겁많은. ● **fear·some·ly** [-li] *adv.*

fea·si·bil·i·ty [fìːzəbíləti] *n.* Ⓤ the quality of being feasible. 가능성; 실행할 수 있음. [↓]

fea·si·ble [fíːzəbəl] *adj.* **1** capable of being done or carried out; possible; practicable. 실행할 수 있는; 가능성이 있는. ¶ *a ~ plan* 실행 가능한 계획. **2** likely; probable. 그럴 듯한; 있음직한. ¶ *a ~ rumor* 〔*theory*〕 그럴 듯한 소문〔학설〕. **3** suitable; convenient. 적합한; 편리한. ¶ *a road ~ for driving* 드라이브하기에 적합한 도로. ● **fea·si·bly** [-i] *adv.* [→feat]

:feast [fiːst] *n.* Ⓒ **1** a rich and plentiful meal for some special occasion; a banquet. 성찬(盛饌); 향연. **2** anything pleasant; a delight; a pleasure. (눈·귀를) 즐겁게 해주는 것; 즐거움. ¶ *a ~ for eyes* 눈요기. **3** a festival, esp. a religious festival or anniversary. (특히 종교상의) 축제일; 기념제.

— *vi.* (P1,3) 《*on*》 take part in a feast; have a feast. 맛있는 음식〔진수 성찬〕을 먹다. — *vt.* (P6,7) **1** entertain (someone) with a rich meal. …에게 맛있는 음식을 대접하다. **2** give pleasure to (something). …을 즐겁게 하다. ¶ *~ one's ears with good music* 음악을 들어 귀를 즐겁게 하다 / ~

F

one's eyes on rare books 희귀한 책으로 눈요기하다.

•**feast·er** [-ər] *n.* [L. *festus* festal]

·**feat** [fiːt] *n.* Ⓒ a great deed done by extraordinary skill, strength, etc.; a remarkable act. 위업; 공(적); 묘기; 재주; 곡예. ¶ *a ~ of arms* 무공 / *acrobatic feats* (몸을 가볍게 날려서 하는) 곡예 / *a ~ of strength* 힘의 묘기 / *a tightrope ~* 줄타기 / *perform a superhuman ~* 초인적인 곡예를 실연하다. [L. *facio* do]

:**feath·er** [féðər] *n.* Ⓒ **1** one of the light coverings which grow on a bird's skin; 《*collectively*》 the feathers of a bird. 하나의 (새)깃; 깃털. ¶ *as light as a ~* 매우 가벼운 / *ruffled feathers* 곤두세운 깃털 / *trim feathers with beak* 부리로 깃을 다듬다 / 《*prov.*》 *Fine feathers make fine birds.* 옷이 날개. **2** 《*collectively*》 birds, esp. game birds. 조류(鳥類); (특히) 엽조(獵鳥). ¶ *fur and ~* 엽수(獵獸)와 엽조. **3** anything light like a feather. 깃털처럼 가벼운 것.

a feather in one's cap 〔***hat***〕, something to be proud of; a mark of honor. 자랑(거리); 명예.

birds of a feather, persons of similar character. 같은 깃털의 새; 같은 또래〔동아리〕. ¶ 《*prov.*》 *Birds of a ~ flock together.* 유유상종(類類相從).

crop someone's feathers, humble someone's pride. …의 콧대를 꺾다.

do not care a feather, do not care a bit. 조금도 개의〔상관〕치 않다.

in fine 〔***good, high***〕 ***feather,*** in very good humor; in high spirits. 기분이 좋아; 의기가 드높아; 위세 좋게.

in full feather, **a**) with all the feathers grown. (새끼 새가) 깃털이 다 난. **b**) in full dress. 성장(盛裝)하고. **c**) in high spirits. 기분이 좋아.

show the white feather, show signs of being a coward. 겁이 난 기색을 보이다.

— *vt.* (P6) **1** ⓐ cover or adorn (something) with feathers. …을 깃털로 덮다〔장식하다〕. ¶ *~ an arrow* 화살에 살깃을 붙이다. ⓑ form a feathery covering. 깃털처럼 소복히 덮다. ¶ *boughs feathered with frost* 소복히 서리로 덮인 나뭇가지들. **2** make (an oar) go flat over the face of water. (조정(漕艇)에서 노깃을) 수평으로 젓다《공기 저항을 덜 받게》. — *vi.* grow feathers. 깃털이 나다. [E.]

feather one's nest, make oneself rich, usu. at someone else's expense. 사복(私腹)을 채우다.

feather bed [⌐–⌐] *n.* a mattress that is filled with feathers. 깃털요.

feath·er·weight [féðərwèit] *n.* Ⓒ **1** a very light or unimportant person or thing. 매우 가벼운 사람〔것〕; 하찮은 사람〔것〕. **2** a boxer who weighs between 118 and 126 pounds. (권투의) 페더급 선수.

feath·er·y [féðəri] *adj.* (sometimes **-er·i·er, -er·i·est**) **1** covered with feathers. 깃이 난; 깃털로 덮인. **2** soft like feathers. 깃털처럼 보드라운.

:**fea·ture** [fíːtʃər] *n.* Ⓒ **1** a part of the face, such as the eyes, the nose, etc. 얼굴의 일부《눈·코·입·귀 따위》. **2** 《*pl.*》 the face. 얼굴 (생김); 용모. ¶ *handsome* 〔*poor*〕 *features* 잘〔못〕생긴 용모 / *a man of prominent features* 이목구비가 또렷한 사람. **3** a characteristic or distinct part that attracts attention. 특징; 특색; 요점. ¶ *peculiar features of the epoch* 그 시대의 특색 / *a prominent ~ in the landscape* 그 풍경에서 두드러진 점. **4** 《U.S.》 a long, principal motion picture. 특작(장편) 영화. **5** a prominent, special item in a newspaper, magazine, etc.; a popular program on the radio or on television. 인기 기사; 인기 있는 것; 인기 프로. ¶ *make a ~ of* (*something*) …으로 인기를 끌다.

— *vt.* **1** (P6,13) portray or make the features of (something); emphasize. …의 특징을 그리다; …으로 인기를 끌다; …을 두드러지게 하다. ¶ *The newspaper featured the story of the murder.* 신문은 살인 기사를 특종으로 다루었다 / *She was featured in the film.* 그 영화에서 그녀는 인기를 끌었다. **2** (P6) present (someone) as the star actor or actress. …을 주연시키다. [→feat]

fea·ture·less [fíːtʃərlis] *adj.* without characteristic features; not impressive. 특색〔특징〕이 없는.

Feb. February.

feb·ri·fuge [fébrəfjùːdʒ] *adj.* serving to reduce fever. 열을 내리는; 하열(下熱)성의. — *n.* Ⓤ a medicine to reduce fever; a cooling drink. 해열제; 청량 음료. [L. *febris* fever, *fugo* drive away]

fe·brile [fíːbrəl, féb- / fíːbrail] *adj.* of fever; caused by fever. 발열(發熱)(성)의. [↑]

:**Feb·ru·ar·y** [fébruèri / -ruəri] *n.* the second month of the year. 2월. 參考 Feb. 로 생략함. [L. *februa* purification festival]

fec. fecit.

fe·cal, 《Brit.》 **fae-** [fíːkəl] *adj.* of feces. 배설물의; 똥의; 분변(糞便)의. [↓]

fe·ces, 《Brit.》 **fae-** [fíːsiːz] *n. pl.* waste matter discharged through the anus; excrement. 배설물; 똥; 분변(糞便). [L. *feces* dregs]

fe·cit [fíːsit, féikit] *v.* 《L.》 he 〔she〕 make (it). (아무가) 만들다; 그리다; 쓰다. ¶ *John Jones ~.* 존 존스의 작.

feck·less [féklis] *adj.* spiritless; weak; of no use. 무기력한; 약한; 쓸모 없는; 시시한. [*effectless*]

fec·u·lent [fékjələnt / -kju-] *adj.* turbid; muddy; foul. 탁한; 흐린; 더러운. [→feces]

fe·cund [fíːkənd, fék-] *adj.* productive; fruitful. 다산(多産)의; (땅이) 비옥한. ¶ *~ beasts* 다산의 가축 / *a ~ soil* 비옥한 토

야 / 《*fig.*》 *a ~ imagination* 풍부한 상상력. [L. *fecundus*]

fe·cun·date [fíːkəndeit, fék-] *vt.* (P6,13) **1** make fruitful. …을 열매 맺게 하다. **2** fertilize. …을 비옥하게 하다. **3** 《biol.》 impregnate. 수태(受胎)시키다. [↑]

fe·cun·di·ty [fiːkʌ́ndəti] *n.* Ⓤ the quality of being fecund. 다산성; 비옥; 풍요. [↑]

:fed [fed] *v.* p. and pp. of **feed**.

·fed·er·al [fédərəl] *adj.* **1** of or based upon federation, esp. between nations or states. 연합〔동맹〕의. **2** 《usu. *F-*》 《U.S.》 of or supporting the central government as opposed to the individual governments of the separate states. 연방 정부의. ¶ *The Federal Bureau of Investigation* (미국의) 연방 수사국(abbr. FBI). [L. *foedus* covenant]

fed·er·al·ism [fédərəlizəm] *n.* Ⓤ the doctrines of federal union. 연방주의.

fed·er·al·ist [fédərəlist] *n.* Ⓒ a supporter of federalism. 연방제 지지자.

fed·er·ate [fédərèit] *vi., vt.* (P1; 6) unite into a federation. 동맹〔연합〕하다; 연합시키다. ── [fédərit] *adj.* united into a federation. 동맹의; 연합한.

·fed·er·a·tion [fèdəréiʃən] *n.* **1** Ⓤ the act of federating; a political unity composed of a number of separate states, etc. 연맹; 연합; 동맹. ¶ *the Federation of Labor* 노동자 총동맹. **2** Ⓒ a group of nations united into a league; federated body. 연방(정부); 연방체. ¶ *The United States is a ~.* 미합중국은 연방체이다.

fe·do·ra [fidɔ́ːrə] *n.* a soft felt hat. (챙이 젖혀진) 펠트제(製)의 중절모(帽). [*Fedora* drama by Sardou]

·fee [fiː] *n.* Ⓒ **1** a charge; money charged for a service or for a right to do something. 요금; 보수; 입회금; 수수료. ¶ *an admission ~* 입장료 / *school fees* 학비 / *a doctor's ~* 의사의 진찰료 / *a lawyer's ~* 변호사의 보수 / *an insurance ~* 보험료. **2** tip. 팁; 정표. ¶ *a porter's ~* 짐꾼에게 주는 팁. **3** Ⓤ the right to keep and use land. 영구 차지권(借地權). ── *vt.* (P6) give a fee or tip to (someone). …에게 요금을 지급하다; 팁을 주다. [F. *fe, fief, fiu*]

·fee·ble [fíːbəl] *adj.* (**-bler, -blest**) lacking strength, distinctness, brightness, etc.; weak. 약한; 또렷지〔분명치〕 않은; 희미한. ¶ *a ~ voice* 약한 소리 / *a ~ mind* 정신 박약 / *a ~ speech* 박력 없는 연설. ● **fee·ble·ness** [-nis] *n.* [L. *flebilis* lamentable]

fee·ble-mind·ed [fíːbəlmáindid] *adj.* lacking normal mental powers or firmness of mind. 의지 박약한; 저능(低能)한.

fee·bly [fíːbli] *adv.* in a feeble manner. 약하게; 희미하게; 힘없이.

:feed [fiːd] *v.* (**fed**) *vt.* **1** (P6,7,13) ⓐ give food to (a baby or an animal). …에 먹이를〔음식을〕 주다; 먹이다; 기르다; 부양하다. ¶ *~ children* 아이들을 키우다 / *~ a baby with a spoon* 순갈로 아기를 먹이다 / *~ a duck with bread* 오리에게 빵을 주다 / *~ the horses* 말을 먹이다 / *~ the cattle with hay* 소에게 건초를 주다 / *~ one's family* 식구를 부양하다 / *be well* 〔*poorly*〕 *fed* 영양이 좋다〔나쁘다〕. ⓑ 《*reflexively*》 take food with one's own hand. 제 스스로〔손으로〕 먹다. ¶ *A baby cannot ~ himself.* 아기는 스스로 먹을〔식사할〕 수 없다. **2** (P6,13) give (something) as food. …을 먹이로〔음식으로〕 주다. ¶ *~ corn to horses* 말 먹이로 옥수수를 주다 / *~ grain to chickens* 닭 모이로 곡물을 먹이다 / *~ milk to a cat* 고양이에 우유를 먹이다. **3** (P6,13) ⓐ provide (something) with its necessary material. (원료)를 (기계)에 공급하다. ¶ *~ the engine with gasoline* 엔진에 급유하다 / *~ a printing press with paper* 인쇄기에 종이를 삽지하다 / *~ a stove with coal* 난로에 석탄을 지피다 / *~ a computer with data* 컴퓨터에 데이터를 입력하다. ⓑ provide with (material). (기계)에 (원료)를 공급하다. ¶ *~ coal to a stove* 난로에 석탄을 지피다 / *~ data into a computer* 컴퓨터에 데이터를 입력하다. **4** (P6) arouse; increase. 부채질하다; 더하게 하다; 돋우다. ¶ *~ someone's enmity* 아무의 증오심을 자극하다 / *~ the flame of jeolousy* 질투심에 불을 지르다. ── *vi.* **1** (P1,3) take food; eat. 먹다. ¶ *The cows are feeding in the meadow.* 소들이 목장에서 풀을 뜯고 있다 / 《*joc., colloq.*》 *We ~ at seven.* 우리는 7시에 식사를 한다. **2** (P3) 《*on*》 take as food. …을 상식(常食)하다.

be fed up with, have had enough of something; be utterly bored or disgusted with. …에 넌더리 나다; 신물이 나다.

feed on 〔***upon***〕***,*** **a**) take as usual food; be nourished by; live on. …을 상식(常食)하다; …을 먹다; …으로 살다. ¶ *Cattle ~ chiefly on grass.* 소는 주로 풀을 먹고 산다. **b**) get satisfaction from. …에서 만족을 얻다.

── *n.* **1** Ⓤ food for animals. 먹이; 모이. **2** Ⓒ an act of feeding. 사육; 공급. **3** Ⓒ 《*colloq.*》 a meal. 식사. [→food]

be off one's feed, have no appetite. 식욕이 없다.

out at feed, grazing. 방목(放牧)되어.

feed·back [fíːdbæ̀k] *n.* Ⓤ **1** the return of part of the output of a system to the input in order to correct, control or modify the output. 피드백《출력측의 에너지의 일부를 입력측에 되돌리는 조작》. **2** information about the results of a set of actions, passed back to the person in charge, so that changes can be made if necessary. (소비자·사용자측의) 반응; 의견.

feed·er [fíːdər] *n.* Ⓒ **1** a person or an animal that feeds. 먹는 사람〔동물〕; 사육자; 공급자. **2** a device supplying material or fuel to a machine. (기계의) 공급 장치. **3** a stream flowing into the main river; a branch railway, airline, etc. (강의) 지류; (철도·항공의) 지선. **4** ⓐ a baby's feeding bottle. (아기의) 젖병. ⓑ a child's bib. 어린아이의 턱받이.

feeding bottle [⌐- ⌐-] *n.* Ⓒ a bottle from which babies are given milk; a feeder. (아기의) 젖병.

:feel [fi:l] *v.* (**felt**) *vt.* **1** (P6,12) touch; know or find (something) by touching. …을 만지다; 만져[손대서] 알다; 손으로 더듬다. ¶ ~ *the edge of a knife* 칼날을 만져보다 / ~ *a stone with one's hand* 손으로 돌을 만지다 / *The doctor felt Ted's pulse.* 의사는 테드의 맥을 짚어 보았다 / *Feel how cold the water is.* 물이 얼마나 차가운지 만져 보아라. **2** (P6,22,23,24) know by the senses. …을 느끼다. ¶ ~ *the cold* [*heat*] 추위[더위]를 느끼다 / ~ *a pain in the stomach* 위통(胃痛)을 느끼다 / ~ *the earth shake* 땅이 흔들리는 것을 느끼다 / *I felt someone gazing at me.* 누군가 나를 주시하고 있음을 느꼈다. **3** (P6,11,13) ⓐ experience (a sensation). (어떤 감정)을 느끼다; 경험하다; …에 감동하다. ¶ ~ *sorrow* [*pleasure, delight*] 슬픔[즐거움, 기쁨]을 맛보다 / ~ *pity for* …을 가엾게 느끼다 / ~ *music* 음악에 감동하다 / ~ *one's disgrace keenly* 몹시 치욕감을 느끼다 / ~ *a friend's death* 친구의 죽음을 몹시 슬퍼하다. ⓑ perceive a state of mind or condition of body. (…상태)를 깨닫다; (…감정)을 느끼다. ¶ ~ *angry* [*hungry*] 노여움[배고픔]을 느끼다 / ~ *sorry for* …에 대해 미안함을 느끼다 / ~ *ill* [*sick*] 기분이 나쁘다. **4** (P11,21,24) be of the opinion (that); consider. …라고[하다고] 생각하다. ¶ *I* ~ *it to be true.* 사실이라고 생각한다 / *I* ~ *that the point is not so important.* 그 점은 그리 중요치 않다고 생각한다. — *vi.* **1** (P5) have a sense of being; be. 느낌이 들다; …이다; …하다. ¶ *How do you* ~ *on this matter?* 이 일을 어떻게 생각하나. **2** (P2A,5) give a sense of being. (…한) 느낌을 주다. ¶ *The air felt cold and damp.* 공기는 차고도 습한 감을 주었다 / *Velvet feels smooth.* 우단은 감촉이 매끄럽다. **3** (P2A,3) 《*for*》 search by touching. (손으로) 더듬(어 찾)다. ¶ ~ *in one's pocket for one's key* 호주머니를 뒤져 열쇠를 찾다. **4** (P3) 《*for*》 have sympathy with someone. 동정하다. ¶ ~ *for the victim* 희생자에게 동정하다 / *I felt for her deeply.* 그녀에게 깊은 동정을 느꼈다.

feel as if [***though***]**,** have the impression that…. 마치 …처럼 느끼다. ¶ *She felt as if her head were* [*was*] *burning.* 그녀는 머리가 빠개지는 것처럼 느꼈다.

feel free to, be welcome to do (something). 마음대로 …하다; 사양 않고 …하다. ¶ *Please* ~ *free to come any time.* 아무 때고 가벼운 마음으로 오십시오.

feel like, **a**) give a sense of being. …한 느낌을 주다. **b**) 《*colloq.*》 have a desire for; be inclined for. …하고 싶은 마음이 들다. ¶ *I don't* ~ *like going out tonight.* 오늘 저녁엔 외출하고 싶은 마음이 안 난다.

feel someone out, find out cautiously what someone thinks about something. (상대의) 속을 떠보다; 타진해 보다.

feel up to, 《*colloq.*》 feel or be able to (do); be capable of. …을 할 수 있을 것같이 생각하다. ¶ ~ *up to a long walk* 오래 걸을 수 있을 것처럼 느끼다.

feel one's way, **a**) move carefully. 더듬더듬 나아가다. **b**) act slowly and carefully. 조심스럽게 행동하다.

— *n.* Ⓒ 《usu. *the* ~》 **1** the act of feeling. 느낌. **2** the sense of touch. 촉각. [O.E. *felan*]

feel·er [fí:lər] *n.* Ⓒ **1** a specialized organ for touching on an animal's body, esp. an insect's antenna. 더듬이; 촉각; 촉모(觸毛). **2** a proposal, a hint, etc. made in order to find out the opinions or plans of others. (상대 의중을) 떠보기《질문 따위》.

:feel·ing [fí:liŋ] *n.* **1** ⓊⒸ the condition of touching; the power of physical sensation. 촉감; 느낌; 기분. ¶ *a* ~ *of joy* [*sadness*] 기쁜[슬픈]기분 / *a* ~ *of satisfaction* 만족감. **2** ⓊⒸ the sense of touch. 촉각. ¶ *I lost all* ~ *in my fingers.* 손가락의 감각이 전혀 없었다. **3** Ⓤ an emotion; emotional excitement 감동; 정서. ¶ *with* ~ 감동하여. **4** Ⓤ sympathy; pity. 동정(심). ¶ *show a* ~ *for the poor* 가난한 자들에게 동정을 나타내다 / *have great* ~ *for the sufferings of others* 남의 고난에 크게 동정하다. **5** Ⓒ an opinion; a sentiment. 의견; 감상; 소감. ¶ *express one's feelings about* … 에 관해서 소감을 말하다 / *What's your* ~ *about this idea?* 당신은 이 생각에 대해 어떻게 생각하십니까. **6** Ⓤ understanding; sensibility. 이해력; 감각; 감수성. ¶ *have a* ~ *for painting* 그림에 대한 감상력이 있다. **7** 《*pl.*》 emotions; sensibilities. 감정; 정. ¶ *a man of feelings* 감상가 / *appeal to the feelings rather than to reason* 이성보다 감정에 호소하다 / *hurt the feelings of others* 남의 감정을 상하다 / *enter into someone's feelings* 아무의 감정을 헤아리다.

— *adj.* sensitive; emotional; sympathetic. 다감한; 감동적인; 감정적인; 인정이 많은. [O.E. *feling*]

feel·ing·ly [fí:liŋli] *adv.* in a manner showing strong feeling; with emotion. 감동하여; 동정하여; (뼈에) 사무치게.

:feet [fi:t] *n.* pl. of **foot.**

feign [fein] *vt.* **1** (P6,11,21) pretend. …인 체하다. ¶ ~ *illness* 꾀병을 부리다 / *He feigned himself* (*to be*) *mad.* =*He feigned that he was mad.* 그는 미친 척했다. **2** (P6) make up (something) to deceive. …을 조작[날조]하다. ¶ ~ *an excuse* 핑계를 꾸며대다. [L. *fingo* form, feign]

feint [feint] *n.* Ⓒ **1** a false appearance. …

체하기; 가장. ¶ *Jack made a ~ of working hard.* 잭은 열심히 일하는 체했다. **2** ⓐ 《boxing, fencing》 a pretended blow or attack. 공격하는 시늉; 페인트. ⓑ 《mil.》 a sham attack. 양동 작전. —*vi.* (P1,3) make a pretended blow. 짐짓 공격하는 체하다; 양동 작전을 하다. ¶ ~ *with the left hand and strike with the right* 왼손으로 치는 체하면서 오른손으로 가격하다. [↑]

feld·spar [féldspὰːr] *n.* Ⓤ Ⓒ any of several white or light-red minerals. 장석(長石). 參考 felspar 라고도 함. [G. *feld* field, *spat(h)* spar]

fe·lic·i·tate [filísətèit] *vt.* (P6,13) 《*on, upon*》 congratulate; express good wishes to someone. …을 축하하다; …에 축의를 나타내다. ¶ *His friends felicitated him on* 〔*upon*〕 *his success.* 친구들은 그의 성공을 축하했다. [L. *felix* happy]

fe·lic·i·ta·tion [filìsətéiʃən] *n.* Ⓤ **1** congratulation. 축하. **2** 《usu. *pl.*》 an expression of good wishes. 축사(祝辭).

fe·lic·i·tous [filísətəs] *adj.* (of words, etc.) well-chosen; appropriate. 잘 선택된; 적절한. ¶ *a ~ remark* 〔*quotation*〕 적절한 말〔인용〕/ *a ~ writer* 표현을 잘 하는 작가.

fe·lic·i·ty [filísəti] *n.* (*pl.* **-ties**) **1** Ⓤ happiness; good fortune. 행복; 행운. **2** Ⓤ a pleasing aptness in expression; Ⓒ a well-chosen expression. 표현의 교묘〔적절〕함; 적절한 표현. ¶ *express oneself with ~* 말을 교묘히 표현하다.

fe·line [fíːlain] *adj.* **1** belonging to the cat family. 고양잇과의. **2** catlike; sly; stealthy. 고양이 같은; 교활한; 몰래 하는. ¶ *He walked with ~ softness.* 그는 고양이같이 발소리를 죽이고 걸었다.

feline amenities, veiled spite. 음험.

—*n.* Ⓒ any animal belonging to the cat family, such as a lion, a tiger or a leopard. 고양잇과의 동물. [L. *feles* cat]

:fell[1] [fel] *vi.* p. of **fall.**

fell[2] [fel] *vt.* (P6) knock down; cut down (a tree). …을 넘어뜨리다; 쓰러뜨리다; (나무)를 베어 넘기다. ¶ *My blow felled him.* 나의 일격이 그를 쓰러뜨렸다 / *The men were busy felling old trees.* 남자들은 오래된 나무를 베느라고 분주했다. —*n.* Ⓒ all the trees cut down in one season. 한 철의 벌목량. [→fall]

fell[3] [fel] *adj.* **1** cruel; terrible. 잔인한; 무서운; 끔찍한. ¶ *a ~ blow* 무서운 일격 / *with one's ~ look* 무서운 얼굴로. **2** deadly; destructive. 치명적인; 파괴적인. ¶ *~ poison* 맹독 / *a ~ disease* 치명적인 병. [L. *fello*]

fell[4] [fel] *n.* **1** Ⓤ ⓐ an animal's skin with the hair. 수피(獸皮); 모피. ⓑ human skin. (사람의) 피부. **2** Ⓒ a rough, thick mass of hair. 더부룩한 머리털. [E.]

fel·loe [félou] *n.* Ⓒ the circular edge of the framework of a wheel. (차바퀴의) 테. 參考 felly 라고도 함. [E.]

:fel·low [félou] *n.* Ⓒ **1** 《often *pl.*》 a companion; an associate; a partner. 동료; 동아리; 한패. ¶ *fellows in arms* 전우(戰友) / *fellows in crime* 범죄의 한 패거리 / *~ members* 동료 회원 / *pass all one's fellows* 동배(同輩)를 앞지르다. **2** 《*colloq.*》 ⓐ a man or boy; a person. 사람; 사나이; 놈; 녀석. ¶ *a nice, little ~* 착한 아이 / *My dear ~.* 어이〔이봐〕 자네 / *Poor ~!* 불쌍한 놈 / *What a ~!* 거참 좋은〔못된〕 녀석이군 / *He is not a bad ~.* 그 자는 못된 녀석은 아니다. ⓑ one; anybody. (일반적으로) 사람; 누구든…. ¶ *A ~ can't work all day long.* 사람은 누구나 하루 종일 일할 순 없다. **3** a person of the same class or rank; an equal. 견줄 만한 사람; 필적자; 경쟁자; 상대. ¶ *I never saw his ~.* 그에게 필적하는 자는 없었다. **4** one of a pair. (짝을 이루는 것의) 한쪽〔짝〕. ¶ *a shoe without its ~* 한 짝만의 신발 / *Where is the ~ of this glove?* 장갑의 다른 한 짝은 어디 있나 / *The socks are not fellows.* 양말이 짝짝이다. **5** a graduate student who is given money to continue his studies, often with teaching duties. (대학의 장학금을 타는) 특별 연구원. **6** 《*F-*》 an honored member of a learned society. (학술 협회의) 회원. ¶ *a Fellow of the British Academy* 영국 학사원 회원.

—*adj.* belonging to the same class or group; having a similar background. 동료의; 동아리의; 동배(同輩)의. ¶ *~ workers* 동료 근로자들 / *a ~ student* 동급생. [E. =one who lays money in partnership]

fellow feeling [⌐-⌐-] *n.* sympathy. 동정; 공감. ¶ *have ~ for the unfortunate* 불행한 사람들을 동정하다.

·fel·low·ship [félouʃìp] *n.* **1** Ⓤ companionship; friendly association. 동료〔동배〕임; 친교(親交). ¶ *I enjoy his ~.* 나는 그와 친교를 맺고 있다 / *~ in misfortune* 불행을 함께 함. **2** Ⓒ a group of people having similar tastes, interests, etc.; Ⓤ membership in such a group. (동일 취미·관심사의) 협회; 모임; 단체; 회원임. ¶ *admit someone to* 〔*into*〕 *~* 아무를 입회시키다. **3** Ⓒ a position or sum of money given to a graduate student in a university to further his studies. (대학의) 특별 연구원의 지위; 특별 연구원 장학금. ¶ *go abroad on a ~* 특별 연구원 장학금을 받아 해외로 나가다.

fellow travel·er [⌐- ⌐--] *n.* **1** a person traveling with one. 길동무. **2** one sympathizing with a political movement or party (esp. the Communist party). (정당, 특히 공산당의) 동조자.

fel·ly [féli] *n.* =felloe.

fel·on[1] [félən] *n.* Ⓒ 《law》 a person who has committed a serious crime. 중범죄인. —*adj.* 《*arch., poet.*》 wicked; cruel; fierce. 흉악한; 잔인한; 흉포한. [L. *fello*]

fel·on[2] [félən] *n.* Ⓤ 《med.》 a very painful

poisoned place on a finger or toe, usu. near the nail. 표저(瘭疽). [↑]

fe·lo·ni·ous [filóuniəs] *adj.* 《law》 of the nature of a felony; very wicked. 중죄(重罪)의; 흉악한.

fel·o·ny [féləni] *n.* (*pl.* **-nies**) 《law》 Ⓤ very serious crime such as murder; Ⓒ an instance of this. 중죄(重罪); 사죄(死罪). ¶ *commit a* ~ 중죄를 범하다.

fel·spar [félspɑ̀:r] *n.* 《chiefly Brit.》 = feldspar.

·**felt**[1] [felt] *v.* p. and pp. of **feel.**

:**felt**[2] [felt] *n.* Ⓤ cloth made by pressing closely together wool, hair, or fur. 펠트; 모전(毛氈). — *adj.* made of felt. 펠트제(製)의. ¶ *a* ~ *hat* 펠트모(帽). — *vt.* (P6) make into felt; cover with felt. …을 펠트로 만들다; 펠트로 덮다. [E.]

fem. female; feminine.

:**fe·male** [fí:meil] *adj.* (opp. male) **1** of the sex that gives birth to young or eggs; (of plants) fruit-bearing. 여성의; 암컷의; (식물이) 자성(雌性)의. ¶ *a* ~ *child* 여아(女兒) / *a* ~ *flower* 암꽃. **2** of women or girls. 여자의. ¶ ~ *education* 여자 교육. — *n.* Ⓒ a person or animal of this sex. 여자; 동물의 암컷. 參考 경멸적으로도 쓰임. [L. *femina* woman; →feminine]

feme [fem, fi:m] *n.* 《law》 a woman. 여자.

fem·i·nine [fémənin] *adj.* (opp. masculine) **1** of or like women. 여성의; 여자 같은. ¶ ~ *beauty* 여성미(美) / *a* ~ *fashion* 여성의 유행. **2** 《gram.》 of the gender to which the names of females belong. 여성의. ¶ *a* ~ *noun* 여성 명사. — *n.* 《gram.》 the feminine gender. 여성(형). [L. *femina* woman]

fem·i·nism [fémənìzəm] *n.* Ⓤ **1** the theory that women should have rights equal to those of men in all points. 남녀 동권주의(론). **2** the doctrine that favors more rights and activities for women. 여권 확장론.

fem·i·nist [fémənist] *n.* Ⓒ a person who supports feminism. 남녀 동권론자; 여권 확장론자.

fe·mur [fí:mər] *n.* Ⓒ **1** 《anat.》 the thighbone. 대퇴골. **2** the thigh. 허벅지; 넓적다리. [L.]

fen [fen] *n.* Ⓒ 《Brit.》 a low, wet piece of land; a marsh. 늪지대(地帶); 소택(沼澤). ● **fen·ny** [féni] *adj.* of fens. 늪지대의. [E.]

:**fence**[1] [fens] *n.* **1** Ⓒ a wall of stone, wood, wire, etc. to enclose a garden, a farm, etc. 울타리; 담. **2** Ⓤ fencing. 펜싱.

come down on the right side of the fence, support the stronger. 강한 쪽에 붙다.

sit 〔***stand, be***〕 ***on the fence,*** have not made up one's mind which side to take; remain neutral. 형세를 관망하다.

— *vt.* (P6,7,13) **1** enclose (a garden, etc.) with a fence. …에 울타리를〔울짱을〕 두르다. **2** 《rare》 《*from, against*》 protect. …을 보호하다. — *vi.* (P1,3) fight with swords in the sport of fencing. 펜싱을 하다. [*defend*]

fence about 〔***in, round, up***〕***,*** enclose (a garden, etc.) with a fence. (뜰 따위)를 울짱으로 두르다.

fence *something* ***from*** 〔***against***〕***,*** protect something from or against. …을 —로부터 지키다.

fence off 〔***out***〕, avoid; keep off. …을 피하다; …을 접근시키지 않다. ¶ *be fenced off from the rest of the world* 세상으로부터 두절돼 있다.

fence with, avoid answering clearly. (질문 따위)를 교묘히 얼버무려 넘기다.

fence[2] [fens] *n.* Ⓒ a dealer in stolen goods. 장물아비. [↑]

fenc·er [fénsər] *n.* Ⓒ a person who knows how to fight with a sword in the sport of fencing. 펜싱의 검사(劍士).

fenc·ing [fénsiŋ] *n.* Ⓤ **1** the sport of fighting with swords. 펜싱. **2** 《*collectively*》 fences. 울타리; 울짱. **3** material for fences. 울짱의 재료.

fend [fend] *vt.* (P7) keep off; defend oneself from. …을 피하다; (공격 따위)를 받아넘기다. [→defend]

fend for oneself, get along by one's own efforts. 자신의 노력으로 살아나가다; 자활하다. ¶ *You are old enough to* ~ *for yourself.* 스스로의 힘으로 살아가기에 충분한 나이다.

fend off, avoid (a blow, etc.). (치려고 들어오는 가격 따위)를 피하다. ¶ *He fended off the blow with his arm.* 그는 가격을 팔로 받아 넘겼다.

fend·er [féndər] *n.* Ⓒ **1** 《U.S.》 a guard over the wheel of an automobile against splashing mud. (차의) 바퀴 덮개; 흙받기; 펜더 (=《Brit.》 a mud guard). **2** a part on an automobile, ship, locomotive, etc. for preventing damage caused by striking against another thing. (자동차·기관차 등의) 완충 장치; (배의) 방현재(防舷材). **3** 《U.S.》 a frame on the lower part of a locomotive or streetcar to catch or push aside anything hit. (기관차·전차 따위의) 구난기(救難器). **4** a metal guard or screen in front of a fireplace. 난로 울.

fen·nel [fénəl] *n.* 《bot.》 a fragrant yellow-flowered herb used in sauces. 회향풀. [L. *faenum* hay]

fe·ral [fíərəl] *adj.* **1** wild; untamed. 야생의. **2** brutal. 야성을 드러낸; 잔인한. [L. *ferus* wild]

Fer·di·nand [fə́:rdənæ̀nd] *n.* a man's name. 남자 이름.

fer·ment [fə:rmént] *vi.* (P1) **1** (of wine) go through a chemical change in which bubbles of gas are given off because of the presence of yeast or bacteria. 발효하다. ¶ *Grapes* ~ *if they are kept too long.* 포도는 너무 오래 저장되면 발효한다. **2** become excited. 흥분하다.

— *vt.* (P6) **1** make (something) undergo

this chemical change. …을 발효시키다. **2** excite; stir up (emotions, unrest, etc.). …을 흥분시키다; (감정)을 자극하다; (불안)을 조장하다.

— [fə́ːrment] *n.* **1** Ⓒ a substance that produces this chemical change, such as yeast, bacteria, etc. 효소. **2** =fermentation. **3** Ⓤ a state of unrest or excitement. 불안; 흥분. [L. *ferveo* boil]

fer·men·ta·tion [fə̀ːrmentéiʃən] *n.* Ⓤ **1** 《chem.》 the act or process of fermenting. 발효(작용, 과정). **2** excitement. 흥분.

·**fern** [fəːrn] *n.* Ⓒ 《bot.》 any of a group of plants with no flowers but forming their seeds on the back of featherlike leaves. 양치류. ●**fern·y** [fə́ːrni] *adj.* of, like, or containing fern. 양치류의〔같은〕. [E.]

fe·ro·cious [fəróuʃəs] *adj.* savagely cruel. 사나운; 영악한. ¶ *a ~ lion* 사나운 사자. ● **fe·ro·cious·ly** [-li] *adv.* [L. *ferox*]

fe·roc·i·ty [fərάsəti / -rɔ́s-] *n.* (*pl.* **-ties**) Ⓤ savage cruelty; Ⓒ a savagely cruel act. 사나움; 영악함; 흉맹성; 사납고 흉악한 행위; 만행.

fer·ret[1] [férit] *n.* Ⓒ a white, catlike animal used to hunt rats and rabbits. 흰족제비. — *vt., vi.* (P7; 2A,3) hunt (rats, rabbits) with ferrets. (쥐·토끼를) 흰족제비를 이용하여 사냥하다. [L. *fur* thief]

ferret out, search out; discover with difficulty. 찾아내다; 알아내다; 밝히다. ¶ *~ out the facts* 사실을 밝혀내다 / *The detective ferreted out the secret.* 탐정은 비밀을 알아냈다.

fer·ret[2] [férit] *n.* a narrow cotton or silk ribbon. (무명·비단의) 조붓한 리본. [L. *flos* flower]

fer·ric [férik] *adj.* 《chem.》 **1** of or containing iron. 철(鐵)의; 철분이 있는. **2** containing trivalent iron. 3가(價)의 철; 제2철의. [L. *ferrum* iron]

ferric oxide [⌐– ⌐–] *n.* 《chem.》 red compound of iron and oxygen, found in nature as hematite and as rust, used as a pigment and for polishing. 산화제이철(第二鐵).

fer·ro·con·crete [fèroukάnkriːt, -kɔ́ŋ-] *n.* Ⓤ concrete strengthened by a metal framework inside it. 철근 콘크리트. [↓]

fer·rous [férəs] *adj.* of or containing iron. 철(鐵)의; 철을 함유하는. [L. *ferrum* iron]

fer·rule [férəl, férul] *n.* Ⓒ a metal cap put around the end of a stick, an umbrella, etc. to prevent wear or slipping; a metal ring used to strengthen any joint. (단장·우산 끝의) 물미; (이음매 보강용의) 쇠테. [L. *viriae* bracelets]

·**fer·ry** [féri] *n.* Ⓒ (*pl.* **-ries**) **1** a place where boats carry people and goods across a river, a lake, etc. 나루(터). **2** a boat used for carrying people and goods; a ferryboat. 나룻배; 연락선; 페리.

— *v.* (**-ried**) *vt.* (P6,7) **1** 《*across*》 carry (people and goods) in a ferryboat. …을 나룻배로 건네다. ¶ *~ a car across a lake* 나룻배에 차를 싣고 호수를 건너다. **2** cross (a river) in a boat. (강 따위)를 나룻배로 건너다. **3** deliver (an aircraft, a motorcar, etc.) under its own power. (새로 만든 항공기 따위)를 자력 수송하다.

— *vi.* (P1,2A,3) go across in a ferryboat. 나룻배로 건너다. ¶ *We ferried over* 〔*across*〕 *to the island.* 우리는 나룻배로 섬으로 건너갔다. [E.]

fer·ry·boat [féribòut] *n.* Ⓒ a boat used for ferrying. 나룻배; 연락선.

ferry bridge [⌐– ⌐] *n.* Ⓒ a large ferryboat for carrying railway-coaches. 열차 운반용 연락선.

fer·ry·man [férimən] *n.* Ⓒ (*pl.* **-men** [-mən]) **1** a man who owns a ferryboat. 도선업자(渡船業者). **2** a man who works on a ferryboat. 나룻배의 사공.

·**fer·tile** [fə́ːrtl / -tail] *adj.* **1** (of land) producing crops easily. (땅이) 비옥한. ¶ *~ soil* 비옥한 토양. **2** ⓐ (of a plant) able to produce seeds or fruit (식물이) 열매를 맺는. ¶ *a ~ flower* 열매를 맺는 꽃. ⓑ (of an animal) able to produce young. 번식력이 있는. ¶ *a ~ egg* 수정란(卵). **3** 《*fig.*》 producing much. (창조력·창의력이) 풍부한. ¶ *a ~ imagination* 풍부한 상상력 / *a ~ brain* 창의력이 풍부한 두뇌. [L. *fero* bear]

be fertile in 〔***of***〕, produce much. …이 풍부하다〔많다〕. ¶ *He is always ~ in excuses.* 그는 항상 핑계가 많다.

fer·til·i·ty [fəːrtíləti] *n.* Ⓤ the state or quality of being fertile; 《*fig.*》 richness. 비옥; 결실; 번식력; 풍부. ¶ *~ of fancy* 〔*invention*〕 공상〔독창력〕의 풍부함.

fer·ti·li·za·tion [fə̀ːrtəlizéiʃən] *n.* Ⓤ **1** the act of fertilizing; the state of being fertilized. 풍부〔비옥〕(하게 하기). **2** (of a plant or an animal) the change that takes place in a cell or a seed before it starts to grow. (동식물의) 수정(受精); 수분.

fer·ti·lize [fə́ːrtəlàiz] *vt.* (P6) **1** ⓐ cause (land) to produce much. (땅)을 비옥하게 하다. ¶ *~ farm land* 농지를 비옥하게 하다. ⓑ make productive. 풍부하게 하다. ¶ *~ the mind* 정신을 풍부하게 하다. **2** make (a flower or an egg cell) start to grow by combining it with a male flower or a male egg cell. (동식물)을 수정〔수분〕시키다.

fer·ti·liz·er [fə́ːrtəlàizər] *n.* ⓊⒸ material used to make land able to produce more. 비료.

fer·ule[1] [férəl, -ruːl] *n.* =ferrule.

fer·ule[2] [férəl, -ruːl] *n.* a stick or rod for punishing children by striking them on the hand. (어린이의 손바닥을 때려 벌하기

위한) 회초리; 막대기; 나무주걱.

be under the ferule, be in charge of a teacher. 엄격한 교육을 받고 있다.

— *vt.* (P6) strike or punish with a ferule. 나무주걱으로 때려 벌을 주다. [L. *ferula* rod]

fer·ven·cy [fə́:rvənsi] *n.* Ⓤ earnestness; enthusiasm. 열심; 열의; 열성; 열렬. [↓]

fer·vent [fə́:rvənt] *adj.* **1** earnest; enthusiastic. 열심인; 열의있는; 열렬한. ¶ *a ~ admirer* 열렬한 숭배자 / *a ~ desire* 강한 욕망 / *receive a ~ welcome* 열렬한 환영을 받다. **2** hot; burning; glowing. 뜨거운; 불타는; 작열하는. ●**fer·vent·ly** [-li] *adv.* [L. *ferveo* boil]

fer·vid [fə́:rvid] *adj.* intensely emotional; very ardent. 열정적인; 열의에 불타는; 열렬한. ¶ *a ~ speech* 열정적인 연설 / *~ devotion* 열렬한 애착. ●**fer·vid·ly** [-li] *adv.* [↑]

fer·vor, 《Brit.》 **-vour** [fə́:rvər] *n.* Ⓤ intense emotion; ardor. 열정; 열렬(함). ¶ *religious ~* 종교적인 열정 / *speak with ~* 열정을 담아 이야기하다. [→fervent]

fes·tal [féstl] *adj.* of a feast or festival; gay; joyous. 축제의; 명랑한; 즐거운; 경축의. ¶ *be in a ~ mood* 축제 기분에 들떠 있다. [→feast]

fes·ter [féstər] *vi.* (P1) **1** become filled with poisonous matter. 곪다. ¶ *My wound has festered.* 상처가 곪았다. **2** rot; decay. 부패하다. **3** cause a sore or painful feeling. (마음 속이) 쑤시다. ¶ *Anger festered in his mind.* 분노로 마음속이 부글거렸다. — *vt.* (P6) cause to fester. 곪게 하다; 쑤시게[마음 아프게] 하다. — *n.* a festering wound. 화농성의 상처. [→fistural]

∗**fes·ti·val** [féstəvəl] *n.* Ⓒ **1** a day or special time of rejoicing and celebration. 잔치; 축제(일); 축전. ¶ *a Thanksgiving ~* 감사제 / *Christmas is a Christian ~.* 크리스마스는 크리스천의 축제일이다. **2** a season of cultural entertainments, often annual. (정기적으로 열리는) …기념제; …의 잔치. ¶ *a music [cultural] ~* 음악[문화]제 / *the Edinburgh International Festival* 에딘버러 국제 예술제. **3** merrymaking. 법석; 향연. ¶ *hold [keep, make] ~* 향연을 베풀다; 법석을 떨다. — *adj.* of a feast. 축제(일)의; 축제 같은 [→feast]

fes·tive [féstiv] *adj.* of a festival; gay; joyous; merry. 축제의; 명랑한; 즐거운; 유쾌한. ¶ *the ~ season* (크리스마스 때와 같은) 축제의 계절 / *a ~ scence* 즐거운 광경 / *be in a ~ mood* 축제 기분이다 / *A birthday is a ~ occasion.* 생일은 즐거운 날이다. ●**fes·tive·ly** [-li] *adv.*

fes·tiv·i·ty [festívəti] *n.* (*pl.* **-ties**) **1** Ⓤ merrymaking; gaiety. 축제 (같은) [들뜬] 기분; 법석. **2** 《*pl.*》 festive events or activities. 축제[축하]의 행사.

fes·toon [festú:n] *n.* Ⓒ a chain of flowers, leaves, ribbons, etc. which hangs between two points as a decoration. (장식물로서의) 꽃줄. ¶ *a ~ of roses.* 장미의 장식 꽃줄 — *vt.* (P6) **1** decorate (something) with festoons. …을 꽃줄로 장식하다. ¶ *~ a hall* 홀을 꽃줄로 장식하다. **2** form (something) into festoons. …을 꽃줄로 만들다. [It.]

〈festoon〉

:fetch [fetʃ] *vt.* **1** (P6,7,13,14) 《*for, to*》 go for and bring back. (…을)가서 가져[데려, 불러]오다. ¶ *~ the doctor from the next village* 이웃 마을에서 의사를 불러오다 / *He went home to ~ his sister.* 집으로 누이를 데리러 갔다 / *Fetch me a glass of water.* 물 한 컵만 가져다 주게 / *I'll ~ the letter for you.* 자네 편지를 가져다 주지 / *Please ~ the dictionary to me.* 사전을 가져다 주시오. **2** (P6) (of goods) bring (a price, etc); sell for. (상품이 얼마의 돈)을 가져오다; (얼마)에 팔리다. ¶ *This house will ~ (you) a good price.* 이 집은 좋은 값을 받을 게다 / *This won't ~ (you) much.* 이건 대단한 돈은 못 될 게다. **3** (P6,14) 《*colloq.*》 deal; strike. …에게 (타격)을 가하다; 한 대 먹이다. ¶ *~ him a blow on the chin* 그의 턱에 일격을 가하다. **4** (P6,13) utter (a sigh, a groan, etc.); cause (tears, blood, etc.) to come out. (한숨·신음 소리 따위)를 내다; (피 따위)를 나오게 하다; (눈물 따위)를 자아내다. ¶ *~ a groan* 신음 소리를 내다 / *~ a sigh* 한숨을 쉬다; 탄식하다 / *~ a deep breath* 깊은 숨을 내쉬다. **5** (P6,13) 《*colloq.*》 attract; charm. …을 매혹[매료]하다; …의 인기를 끌다. ¶ *~ the audience* 청중을 끌다 / *~ the public* 일반의 인기를 끌다 / *Her beauty fetched him completely.* 그녀의 아름다움은 그를 완전히 매료시켰다. [E.]

fetch and carry, do small job; run errands. 잡일을 하다; 잔심부름 하다.

fetch down, bring down; lower the market price. 떨어뜨리다; (시가(時價)를) 내리다.

fetch up, **a**) 《naut.》 《*colloq.*》 《*at*》 stop; end up; arrive. 멈추다; 끝나다; 도착하다. **b**) 《Brit. *colloq.*》 throw up food, etc. from the stomach through the mouth. …을 게우다[토하다].

fetch·ing [fétʃiŋ] *adj.* 《*colloq.*》 attractive; charming. 매력 있는; 마음을 사로잡는. ¶ *a ~ smile* 매력적인 미소.

fete, fête [feit, fet] *n.* 《F.》 Ⓒ a festival; an outdoor entertainment. 축제; (야외의) 축연(祝宴); 향연. ¶ *held a great ~* 성대한 축연을 베풀다 / *~ day* 축(제)일 — *vt.* (P6) honor (someone) with a fete or party. 축연[향연]을 베풀어 (아무)를 축하하다. ¶ *~ the engaged couple* 약혼한 두 사람을 축하하다.

fet·ich [fétiʃ, fí:t-] *n.* =fetish.

fet·id [fétid, fí:t-] *adj.* smelling very bad; stinking. 악취를 내는[발하는]. [L. *feteo* stink]

fet·ish [fétiʃ, fíːt-] *n.* Ⓒ **1** an object supposed to have supernatural or magic power. 주물(呪物). **2** anything respected or loved to an abnormal degree. 맹목적 숭배물. ¶ *make a ~ of high grades* 고위 고관들을 맹목적으로 숭배하다. ● **fet·ish·ism** [-izəm] *n.* [L. *facio* do]

fet·lock [fétlɑ̀k / -lɔ̀k] *n.* Ⓒ **1** the back part of a horse's leg just above the foot. (말 다리의) 구절(球節)《말굽 뒤쪽 위의 털난 곳》. **2** a tuft of hair on that area. 말굽 뒤쪽의 더부룩한 털. [E.]

fet·ter [fétər] *n.* **1** Ⓒ a chain to bind the feet and so prevent escape. 족쇄(足鎖); 차꼬. **2** 《usu. *pl.*》 anything that binds; a restraint. 구속물; 속박.
in fetters, fettered; restrained. 족쇄가 채워져; 속박[구속]되어.
— *vt.* **1** (P6) bind (the feet) with fetters. …을 족쇄로 묶다. **2** bind; restrain. …을 속박하다. [E.]

fet·tle [fétl] *n.* Ⓤ physical or mental condition. (심신의) 상태. [E.]
in good 〔***fine***〕 ***fettle,*** in good condition both in physically and mentally; in high spirits. 좋은 상태에; 원기왕성하여. [E.]

fe·tus [fíːtəs] *n.* Ⓒ a young animal not yet born. 태아. [L. *fetus* offspring]

feud[1] [fjuːd] *n.* Ⓒ a bitter quarrel between families, tribes, etc., often passed down from generation to generation. (집안·민족간 따위의 여러 대에 걸친) 불화; 숙원(宿怨) [Teut.]
be at feud with, be quarreling with. …와 반목하고 있다; …와 불화하다.

feud[2] [fjuːd] *n.* Ⓒ 《hist.》 an estate granted to a tenant; fief. 봉토(封土); 영지(領地). [↓]

feu·dal [fjúːdl] *adj.* of feudalism. 봉건 제도의. ¶ *a ~ lord* 봉건 영주 / *the ~ age* 봉건 시대 [L. *feudum* fee, fief]

feu·dal·ism [fjúːdəlìzəm] *n.* Ⓤ the social, economic, and political system in Europe during the Middle Ages. (중세 유럽에 있어서의) 봉건 제도.

feu·da·to·ry [fjúːdətɔ̀ːri / -təri] *adj.* owing feudal services to a lord. 영주에게 봉건적 역무(役務)를 짊어지고 있는. — *n.* Ⓒ (*pl.* **-ries**) a person owing feudal services to a lord; a vassal. 봉건 가신(家臣).

:fe·ver [fíːvər] *n.* Ⓤ **1** 《often *a ~*》 a diseased condition with the body temperature higher than usual (병으로 인한 높은)열; 신열(身熱). ¶ *have a high ~* 열이 높다 / *bring the ~ down* 열을 내리다 / *A sick person often has a ~.* 환자는 흔히 신열이 있다. 語法 이 때의 a는 one의 의미가 아니라 some의 뜻임. **2** any disease that causes a high body temperature. 열병. ¶ *scarlet ~* 성홍열 / *typhoid ~* 장티푸스. **3** 《usu. *a ~, sing.* only》 great nervous excitement. 극도의 흥분; 열광. ¶ *gold ~* 황금열 / *be in a ~ of anxiety* 근심 걱정에 싸여있다.
— *vt.* (P6) throw into fever. 발열(發熱)시키다. [L. *febris*]

fe·vered [fíːvərd] *adj.* having fever; excited. 열이 있는; 흥분한.

fever heat [´– ˋ] *n.* **1** a body temperature higher than normal. (평상 체온 이상의 높은) 열. **2** 《*fig.*》 great intensity. 이상 흥분; 열광.

fe·ver·ish [fíːvəriʃ] *adj.* **1** having fever. 열이 있는. ¶ *I am ~ from my cold.* 감기로 열이 있다. **2** causing or caused by fever. 열병을 일으키는; 열병으로 일어난. ¶ *a ~ swamp* 열병이 많은 늪지대. **3** excited; restless. 흥분한; 침착을 잃은. ¶ *~ activities* 열광적인 활동 / *with ~ excitement* 열광하여 / *in ~ haste* 몹시 서둘러. ● **fe·ver·ish·ly** [-li] *adv.* **fe·ver·ish·ness** [-nis] *n.* [*fever*]

:few [fjuː] *adj.* **1** 《used without *a*》 not many; a small, indefinite number of. (수가) 적은; 소수밖에 없는; (부정적으로) 거의 …없는. ¶ *a man of ~ words* 말이 없는[말수가 적은] 사람 / *He has ~ friends in this city.* 그는 이 시(市)에 친구가 거의 없다. **2** 《used with *a*》 not many but some; a small number of. (긍정적으로) 조금은 있는; 소수의(opp. none). ¶ *in a ~ days* 며칠 있으면[후에] / *I have a ~ friends.* 친구가 조금은 있다 / *I know a ~ of them.* 그들 중 몇 사람은 알고 있다 / *A ~ people were present.* 소수의 사람이 출석했다. 語法 few, a few는 모두 복수 명사를 수반함. (a) few는 수에 관해 쓰이며, (a) little은 양(量)에 관해 사용함.
— *n., pron.* **1** a small, indefinite number of people, things, etc. 소수의 사람[것]; 소량[약간]의 것. 語法 부정관사의 유무에 따른 의미의 차이는 형용사에서와 같음. 또 구문상 few, a few는 모두 항상 복수. ¶ *Few believed her story.* 그녀의 이야기를 믿는 사람은 거의 없었다 / *A faithful ~ remained.* 충실한 몇 사람만이 남았다 / *Send me a ~.* 조금 보내 주십시오 / *Very ~ have seen it.* 그것을 본 사람은 거의 없다 / *I went into a pub and had a ~.* 선술집에 들어가 몇 잔 했다. **2** 《*the ~*》 the minority of people. (다수에 대하여) 소수의[선택된] 사람. ¶ *Yachts are for the ~.* 요트는 선택받은 소수의 사람만이 즐길 수 있는 것이다 / *the ~ who have survived* 살아남은 소수의 사람들. [E.]
a good few, a fairly large number (of). 적지 않은; 다수(의). ¶ *He has a good ~ pictures.* 그는 꽤 많은 그림을 갖고 있다.
every few minutes 〔***hours, days, etc.***〕, at intervals of a few minutes 〔hours, days, etc.〕. 2·3분[두세 시간, 2·3일]마다.
few and far between, very few in number; widely separated. 극히 드물게; 긴 시간 간격을 두고; 아주 뜨게. ¶ *Travelers in the desert are ~ and far between.* 사막의 여행자

는 아주 드물다.

no fewer than, as many as. …(만큼)이나. ¶ *There were no ~ than fifty students present.* 50명이나 되는 학생이 출석했다.

not a few =a good few.

quite a few =a good few.

some few, a fair but not large number of. 소수의 (것); 약간(의); 다소(의).

fez [fez] *n.* (*pl.* **fez·zes** [féziz]) Ⓒ a red felt cap ornamented with a long, black tassel. 터키모(帽)《붉은 색에 검은 술이 달렸음》. [Turk.]

〈fez〉

fi·an·cé [fìːɑːnséi, fiɑ́ːnsei] *n.* Ⓒ 《F.》 a man engaged to be married. 약혼자《남자》.

fi·an·cée [fìːɑːnséi, fiɑ́ːnsei] *n.* Ⓒ 《F.》 a woman engaged to be married. 약혼녀.

fi·as·co [fiǽskou] *n.* Ⓒ (*pl.* **-cos** or **-coes**) a complete failure. 대실패. [It.]

fi·at [fíːət, fáiət / -æt] *n.* Ⓒ an authoritative order or command; a sanction. 명령; 엄명; 인가. [L. =be it done]

fib [fib] *n.* Ⓒ a lie about something unimportant. 죄〔악의〕 없는 거짓말. ── *vi.* (**fibbed, fib·bing**) (P1) tell such a lie. 죄〔악의〕 없는 거짓말을 하다. ● **fib·ber** [fíbə*r*] *n.* [*fable*]

·**fi·ber,** 《Brit.》 **-bre** [fáibə*r*] *n.* **1** Ⓒ a single thread of any kind. 섬유. ¶ *nerve* 〔*muscle*〕 *fibers* 신경 섬유〔근(筋)섬유〕. **2** Ⓤ a substance composed of threads. 섬유 제품. ¶ *cotton* 〔*hemp*〕 ~ 면(綿)〔마(麻)〕섬유. **3** Ⓤ 《sometimes *pl.*》 character; nature. 성격; 기질. ¶ *a man of tough* ~ 거친 성격의 사람. [L. *fibra*]

Fi·ber·glas [fáibə*r*glæ̀s / -glɑ̀ːs] *n.* 《trade mark》 a flexible, nonflammable material of glass spun into filaments. 파이버글라스《섬유 유리의 상표명》.

fi·bril [fáibril, -fí-] *n.* a small fiber. 미소(微小) 섬유; 원섬유. [→fiber]

fi·brin [fáibrin] *n.* 《biochem.》 an insoluble protein that promotes the clotting of blood. 피브린; 섬유소. [→fiber]

fi·brous [fáibrəs] *adj.* having, made up of, or like fibers. 섬유(질)의; 섬유 모양의. [↑]

fib·u·la [fíbjulə] *n.* (*pl.* **-lae** or **-las**) 《anat.》 the splint bone on the outer side of a leg. 종아리뼈; 비골(腓骨). [L.= brooch]

fib·u·lae [fíbjulìː] *n.* pl. of **fibula.**

fich·u [fí(ː)ʃuː] *n.* 《F.》 a three-cornered piece of muslin worn by women. (삼각형의) 숄; 피슈《모슬린·레이스 따위의 여성 어깨걸이》. [L. *figo* fix]

fick·le [fíkəl] *adj.* (sometimes **-ler, -lest**) changing; not constant. 변하기 쉬운; 변덕스러운. ¶ ~ *weather* 변덕스러운 날씨 / *a* ~ *lover* 변덕스러운 애인. [E.]

·**fic·tion** [fíkʃən] *n.* **1** Ⓤ anything imagined or made up; Ⓒ a made-up story. 꾸며낸 것; 꾸며낸 이야기; 허구(opp. fact). ¶ *separate fact from* ~ 사실을 허구와 분간하다 / *The story is pure* ~. 그 이야긴 순전히 꾸며낸 이야기다. **2** Ⓤ literary writings about imaginary people and events(opp. nonfiction). 소설. ¶ *Fact is stranger than* ~. 사실은 소설보다도 기이하다. ● **fic·tion·al** [-ʃənəl] *adj.* [→feign]

fic·ti·tious [fiktíʃəs] *adj.* **1** imaginary; made-up 가공의; 꾸며낸; 조작한. ¶ *a* ~ *character* 가공의 인물/*a* ~ *hero* 소설의 주인공 / *a* ~ *narrative* 꾸며낸 이야기. **2** false; not real. 허위의; 거짓의; 가짜의. ¶ *a* ~ *name* 가명. ● **fic·ti·tious·ly** [-li] *adv.*

fid·dle [fídl] *n.* 《colloq.》 Ⓒ a violin. 바이올린; 제금(提琴).

fit as a fiddle, in good health; quite well. 극히 건강한 상태에.

have a face as long as a fiddle, look dismal. 우울한 얼굴을 하고 있다.

play first 〔***second***〕 ***fiddle*** (***to*** …), take a first〔secondary〕 part. 남의 위〔밑〕에 서다; 아무를 지배하다〔아무에게 종속되다〕.

── *vi.* **1** (P1) 《colloq.》 play the violin. 바이올린을 켜다. **2** (P2A,3) 《*with*》 handle aimlessly. 만지작거리다. ¶ ~ *with a pencil* 연필을 만지작거리다. ── *vt.* (P6) 《colloq.》 play (a tune) on the violin. (곡)을 바이올린으로 켜다. [E.]

fiddle away, idle away. 빈둥거리며〔멍하니〕 지내다.

fid·dler [fídlə*r*] *n.* a person who plays the fiddle. 바이올린 켜는 사람.

fid·dle·stick [fídlstìk] *n.* Ⓒ **1** a violin bow. 바이올린을 켜는 활. **2** 《in *negative*》 something unimportant. 시시한 것. ¶ *not care a* ~ 조금도 상관〔개의치〕 않다.

fid·dling [fídliŋ] *adj.* trifling; useless. 시시한; 하찮은. [E.]

fi·del·i·ty [fidéləti, fɑi-] Ⓤ *n.* **1** faithfulness; loyalty. 충실; 충성. ¶ ~ *to one's master* 〔*principles*〕 주인〔주의〕에 대한 충실 / *take the oath of* ~ 충성을 맹세하다. **2** accuracy; exactness. 정확; 정밀. ¶ *report the news with* ~ 소식을 정확히 전하다 / *a high* ~ *radio* 하이파이〔고성능〕 라디오. [L. *fides* faith]

fidg·et [fídʒit] *vi* (P1,2A,3) 《*about*》 be restless and uneasy. 안절부절 못하다; 불안해 하다. ¶ ~ *about oneself* 걱정하다; 끙끙 앓다. ── *vt.* (P6) make (someone) uneasy; worry. …을 안절부절 못 하게〔불안하게〕 하다; 괴롭히다. ¶ *The heat fidgeted me.* 더위가 나를 괴롭혔다. ── *n.* **1** Ⓒ a restless person. 안절부절 못하는 사람. **2** 《often *pl.*》 restlessness. 안절부절 못함; 불안해 함. [N.]

have the fidgets =***be in a fidget,*** be restless. 안절부절 못하고 있다; 불안해 하다.

fidg·et·y [fídʒiti] *adj.* restless; uneasy.

안절부절 못하는; 불안한. ¶ *The noise made him* ~. 그 소리는 그를 불안하게 했다.

fie [fai] *interj.* for shame! 에잇; 쳇; 저런. ¶ *Fie, for shame!* 아이고 꼴도 보기 싫어 / *Oh,* ~ *upon you for lying!* 쳇 거짓말을 하다니. [L. *fi*]

fief [fi:f] *n.* Ⓒ a piece of land held as a feudal estate. 봉토(封土); 영지. [→fee]

:field [fi:ld] *n.* Ⓒ **1** an open land with few or no trees. 들(판); 들녘. ¶ *in the* ~ 들에서 / *They rode through forest and* ~. 그들은 말을 몰아 숲과 들판을 지나갔다. **2** a piece of land used for planting, pasture, etc. 논·밭; 목초지. ¶ *a rice* ~ 논 / *a wheat* ~ 밀밭 / *go out into the fields* 밭으로 나가다. **3** a wide area or expanse. 질펀하게 펼쳐진 곳; 펄. ¶ *an ice* ~ 빙원(氷原) / *a snow* ~ 설원(雪原) / *a* ~ *of sea* 바다 / *a* ~ *of cloud* 운해(雲海). **4** a piece of land used for sports or an other special purpose. 광장; 경기장(cf. *track*). ¶ *a flying* ~ 비행장 / *a baseball* ~ 야구장. **5** a piece of land where some natural product is obtained. (광물 따위의) 산지(産地). ¶ *a coal* ~ 탄전 / *an oil* ~ 유전 / *a gold* ~ 금의 산지. **6** a battlefield; a battle. 전장(戰場); 전투. ¶ *a hard-fought* ~ 격전; 고전 / *be killed on the* ~ 전장에서 죽다 / *win the* ~ 싸움에 이기다 / *lose the* ~ 진지를 잃다; 패전을 초래하다. **7** the general kind of studies which one is studying; the general type of work which one is doing. 범위; 분야; 영역. ¶ *a* ~ *for research* 연구 분야 / *the* ~ *of vision* 시계(視界) / *have a wide* ~ *of activity* 넓은 활동 범위를 가지다. **8** the inside part of an athletic field surrounded by a running track. 필드 경기장. **9** (in baseball) the outfield. (야구에서) 외야.

be in the field, **a**) be at the front. 출정 중이다. **b**) be taking part in a game, etc. 경기 중이다.

fair field and no favor, equal opportunity. 기회 균등.

hold the field, maintain one's position. 진지를 유지하다; 한 발짝도 물러서지 않다.

keep the field, continue operations. 계속해 싸우다; 작전을 계속하다.

take the field, begin a battle, a campaign, a game, etc. 전투〔운동, 경기〕를 시작하다.

— *vt.* (P6) (in baseball, cricket, etc.) stop or catch and return (a ball). (공)을 잡아 되던지다.

— *vi.* (P1) (in baseball, cricket, etc.) play as a fielder. (야수로) 수비를 보다. [E.]

field day [ˊˋ] *n.* Ⓒ **1** 《mil.》 a day when military drills, mock fights, etc. are done, usu. as entertainment. (군대의) 야외 연습일(演習日). **2** 《U.S.》 a day of unusual activity. 특별한 행사가 있는 날. **3** 《U.S.》 a day for outdoor sports, esp. on a large scale. 야외 운동회의 날.

field·er [fí:ldər] *n.* Ⓒ (of baseball or cricket) a player. (야구 등의) 선수; (외)야수.

field events [ˊ-ˋ] *n.* the events at an athletic meet other than races. 필드 경기〔종목〕.

field glass [ˊˋ] *n.* 《usu. *pl.*》 a pair of small telescopes. 쌍안경.

field goal [ˊˋ] *n.* **1** 《football》 a goal earned by a kick from the field. 필드골 《플레이스킥 또는 드롭킥으로 얻은 3득점의 골》. **2** 《basketball》 a goal scored while the ball is in active play. 필드골; 야투(野投) 《필드에서 투사한 2득점의 골》.

field gun [ˊˋ] *n.* 《mil.》 a light gun with wheels. 야포(野砲).

field hospital [ˊˋ--] *n.* a temporary hospital near a battlefield. 야전 병원.

field marshal [ˊˋ-] *n.* 《Brit.》 an army officer ranked just below the commander in chief. 육군 원수(=《U.S.》 General of the Army).

field mice [ˊˋ] *n.* pl. of **field mouse.**

field mouse [ˊˋ] *n.* (*pl.* **-mice**) a small kind of mouse living in fields. 들쥐.

field·piece [fí:ldpì:s] *n.* =field gun.

field sports [ˊˋ] *n. pl.* **1** sports carried on in the open, esp. hunting, shooting, and fishing. 야외 스포츠《사냥, 사격, 낚시 따위》. **2** athletic sports, such as the high and broad jump, putting the weight, etc., which are not held on the track as are the various races. (트랙 경기에 대한) 필드 경기.

field work [ˊˋ] *n.* scientific or technical exploration done outside the school, the office, etc. 현지 조사〔답사〕; 야외 연구.

field·work [fí:ldwə̀:rk] *n.* 《mil.》 a temporary fortification. 야전 축성; 임시 보루.

fiend [fi:nd] *n.* Ⓒ **1** a devil or demon. 악마. **2** a very cruel or wicked person. 악마와 같은 사람. **3** 《*colloq.*》 a person much given to some habit. …광(狂); 탐닉자. ¶ *an opium* ~ 아편 중독자. [E.]

fiend·ish [fí:ndiʃ] *adj.* very cruel; devilish. 잔인한; 극악 무도한; 악마와 같은. ¶ *a* ~ *crime* 극악 무도한 범죄.

:fierce [fiərs] *adj.* **1** savage; wild. 야만스러운; 사나운. ¶ *as* ~ *as a tiger* 호랑이처럼 사나운. **2** violent; raging. (비바람 따위의) 맹렬한; 격렬한; 무서운. ¶ *the* ~ *heat* 혹서 / *a* ~ *look* 무서운 얼굴 / *a* ~ *tempest* 폭풍우 / *be* ~ *with anger* 불같이 성나 있다. **3** very eager or active; intense. 열렬한; 열심인; 강렬한. ¶ ~ *hatred* 강한 증오 / *make* ~ *efforts to win* 승리하기 위해 열심히 노력하다. ●**fierce·ness** [-nis] *n.* [L. *ferus* savage]

fierce·ly [fíərsli] *adv.* violently; wildly. 사납게; 맹렬히.

·fier·y [fáiəri] *adj.* (**fier·i·er, fier·i·est**) **1** like fire; burning; glowing. 불같은; 불타는; 이글거리는. ¶ *a* ~ *sunset* 불타는 듯한 저녁놀 / ~ *eyes* 이글거리는 눈. **2** full of feeling; intensely passionate. (감정이) 격

한; 열정적인; 열렬한. ¶ *a ~ speech* 열변. **3** easily excited or angered; hasty. 격하기 쉬운; 성내기 잘하는; 성급한. ¶ *a ~ nature* 격하기 쉬운 성질 / *with ~ fury* 불같이 노하여. [*fire*]

fi·es·ta [fiéstə] *n.* Ⓒ 《Sp.》 a religious celebration; a holiday. 축제; 휴일. [→ feast]

fife [faif] *n.* Ⓒ a small, shrill-toned musical instrument like a flute. (플루트 같은) 저, 횡적(橫笛). — *vt., vi.* (P6; 1) play on a fife. 저를 불다. ●**fif·er** [-ər] *n.* [Teut.]

:fif·teen [fíftíːn] *n.* Ⓤ the number between fourteen and sixteen. 열다섯; 15. — *adj.* of 15. 열다섯(15)의. [*five*]

:fif·teenth [fíftíːnθ] *n.* **1** 《usu. *the ~*》 the number 15; 15th. 열다섯(번)째; 제 15. **2** Ⓒ one of 15 equal parts. 15 분의 1. — *adj.* of the 15th. 열다섯(번)째의; 15분의 1의.

:fifth [fifθ] *n.* **1** 《usu. *the ~* 》 the number 5; 5th. 다섯(번)째; 제5. **2** Ⓒ one of 5 equal parts. 5분의 1. — *adj.* of 5th. 다섯(번)째의; 제 5의; 5분의 1의. [*five*]

Fifth Avenue [ˊ ˊ ˊ] *n.* a busy street in New York with fine shops and residences. 5번가(街)《뉴욕시의 번화가》.

fifth column [ˊ ˊ ˊ] *n.* a body of persons in a country who assist its enemy. 제 5열; 간첩.

:fif·ti·eth [fíftiiθ] *n.* **1** 《usu. *the ~* 》 the number 50; 50th. 쉰(번)째; 제 50. **2** Ⓒ one of 50 equal parts. 50 분의 1. — *adj.* of the 50th. 쉰(번)째의; 50 분의 1의.

:fif·ty [fífti] *n.* Ⓤ **1** five times ten; 50. 쉰; 50. **2** ⓐ 《*the fifties*》 the years 50 to 59 in a century. (세기의) 50년대. ⓑ 《*one's fifties*》 the years from the age of 50 to the age of 59. (연령의) 50대. ¶ *He is in his fifties.* 그는 나이가 50대이다. — *adj.* of 50. 50(대)의. [*five*]

fif·ty-fif·ty [fíftifífti] 《*colloq.*》 *adv.* with equal shares. 등분하여; 반반으로. — *adj.* shared equally; half likely and half unlikely. 똑같이 나눈; 반반의. ¶ *have a ~ chance of success* [*to succeed*] 성공의 가능성은 반반이다.

***go fifty-fifty* (*with*),** share equally (with). …와 몫을 [부담을] 반반으로 하다; 2등분하다.

***fig**[1] [fig] *n.* Ⓒ **1** a small, sweet fruit grown in warm countries. 무화과. **2** 《*in negative*》 a very small amount; a little bit. 미량; 하찮은[시시한] 것; 사소한 것. [L. *ficus*]

not care a fig for, not care at all; consider (something) as valueless. …을 전연 문제삼지 않다; 조금도 상관[개의]치 않다. ¶ *I don't care a ~ for such nonsense.* 그런 허튼 소리에 전혀 개의치 않는다.

fig[2] [fig] *n.* **1** dress. 의상; 복장; 옷차림. ¶ *in full ~* 성장(盛裝)하고. **2** condition; spirits. 상태. ¶ *feel in fine ~* 원기 왕성한 느낌이다.

— *vt.* (***figged, fig·ging***) (P6,7) 《*out*》 dress (someone) up. …를 성장(盛裝)시키다; 차려입히다. [?]

fig. **1** figure. **2** figurative. **3** figuratively.

:fight [fait] *v.* (**fought**) *vt.* **1** (P6,7) try to overcome; struggle against (someone or something) …와 싸우다. ¶ *~ disease* 병마와 싸우다 / *~ despair* 절망과 싸우다 / *~ a rival for the business* 경쟁 사업자와 싸우다 / *~ the doubt in one's mind* 마음 속의 의혹과 싸우다. **2** (P6,7) try to win (something); take part in (a struggle, etc.) …을 쟁취하려고 하다; 겨루다; 다투다; (싸움)에 참가하다. ¶ *~ a battle* 싸우다 / *~ a desperate fight* 절망적인 싸움을 하다 / *~ an enemy* 적과 싸우다 / *~ a prize fight* 현상 권투 경기를 하다 / *France fought Spain.* 프랑스는 스페인과 싸웠다. **3** (P6) cause (dogs, etc.) to fight. …을 싸우게 하다.

— *vi.* (P1,2A,2B,3,4) 《*against, with*》 struggle; combat. 싸우다; 격투하다. ¶ *~ for one's country* 조국을 위해 싸우다 / *~ for fame* [*existence*] 명성[생존]을 위해 싸우다 / *~ against* [*with*] *an enemy* 적과 싸우다 / *~ against temptation* 유혹과 싸우다.

fight down, repress; overcome 싸워서 제압[압도]하다; 극복하다. ¶ *~ down one's fear* 공포를 이겨내다.

fight it out, continue fighting until one wins; settle by fighting. 끝까지 싸우다; 싸움에 의해 결말을 내다.

fight off, drive off by fighting. 싸워 물리치다; 쫓아 버리다.

fight one's way, advance by fighting or struggling. 싸우며 나아가다. ¶ *~ one's way through the enemy* 싸워 적군을 헤치며 나아가다.

fight shy of (=*keep away from; avoid*) *something.* …을 피하다.

— *n.* Ⓒ **1** an act of fighting. 싸움. ¶ *have* [*put up*] *a severe ~ with the police* 경찰과 격렬한 싸움을 벌이다. **2** a battle; a contest. 전투; 투쟁. ¶ *a ~ between two armies* 두 군대간의 전투. **3** a boxing match. 권투 경기. **4** Ⓤ will or power to fight; fighting spirit. 전투력; 투지. ¶ *show ~* 투지를 보이다; 굴하지 않다. [E.]

·fight·er [fáitər] *n.* Ⓒ **1** a person who fights, struggles, resists, etc. 전사(戰士); 투사. ¶ *a ~ for liberty* 자유의 투사. **2** an airplane designed for attacking enemy airplanes. 전투기.

fig·ment [fígmənt] *n.* Ⓒ something imagined. 꾸며 낸 것; 허구(虛構)(의 이야기). ¶ *figments of the mind* 상상의 산물. [→ feign]

fig·ur·a·tion [fìgjəréiʃən] *n.* ⓊⒸ **1** the act of giving shape to. 모양짓기; 성형(成形). **2** an appearance given by shaping; a shape; a form. 성형된 모양; 형상; 형태. **3** the act of marking with figures (도안 등에 의한) 장식(裝飾); 수식. [→figure]

fig·ur·a·tive [fígjərətiv] *adj.* **1** ⓐ using words out of their ordinary meaning; not literal. 비유적[은유적]인; 전의(轉意)의. ¶ *a ~ expression* 은유적 표현 / *in a ~ sense* 비유적인 의미로. ⓑ having a symbolical meaning. 상징적 의미를 가진. ¶ *the ~ use of a word* 낱말의 상징적 의미로의 사용. **2** ⓐ full of figures of speech. 문식(文飾)이 많은; 비유가 많은. ¶ *a ~ style* 화려한[수식이 많은] 문체. ⓑ fond of using many figures of speech. 비유를[문식을] 좋아하는. ¶ *a ~ writer* 미문가(美文家). **3** emblematic. 상징적인. ¶ *a ~ design* 상징적인 의장(意匠). ●**fig·ur·a·tive·ly** [-li] *adv.*

:fig·ure [fígjər / -gər] *n.* Ⓒ **1** an outer shape; an outline; a form 모양; 외형; 형태. ¶ *be round in ~* 모양이 둥글다. **2** a form of the human body; an appearance. 자태; 모습; 사람 그림자. ¶ *I could see the ~ of a woman against the wall.* 벽 앞에 여인의 그림자를 볼 수 있었다 / *A ~ came out of the darkness.* 어둠 속에서 사람 그림자가 나타났다. **3** an image; a statue. 상(像). ¶ *a ~ on a coin* 주화(鑄貨)에 새겨진 상(像). **4** a person, esp. an important one; a character. (두드러진) 인물; 명사. ¶ *a ~ in society* 사교계의 명사 / *a leading ~ in diplomacy* 외교계의 지도적 인물 / *He was one of the great figures of his age.* 그는 당대의 위대한 인물의 한 사람이었다. **5** a drawing; an illustration; a design; a pattern. 그림; 도형; 도해(圖解); 도안; 무늬. ¶ *a polka-dot ~* 물방울 무늬 / *the figures on the wallpaper* 벽지의 무늬. **6** a symbol which indicates a number, such as 1, 2, 3, etc. 숫자. ¶ *the ~ 6,* 숫자의 6 / *add up figures* 수를 합계하다. **7** an amount or value expressed in figures; a price. 수치; 수량; 가격. ¶ *buy at a high* [*low*] *~* 고가(高價)[싼값]에 사다. **8** 《*pl.*》 calculation. 계산; 산수. ¶ *I'm poor* [*good*] *at figures.* 계산을[산수를] 못[잘] 한다. **9** a form of speech in which words have a meaning that is not usual. 문식(文飾); 비유. ¶ *a ~ of speech* 비유(적 표현).

cut [***make***] ***a fine*** [***poor, etc.***] ***figure,*** produce a certain impression. (자신에 관해) 어떤 인상을 주다; 두각을 나타내다[초라하게 보이다].

do figures, calculate; reckon. 셈하다; 계산하다.

— *vt.* **1** (P6,13) show (something) by a figure. …을 그림으로[숫자로] 나타내다. **2** (P13) imagine; think. …을 상상하다; 생각하다. ¶ *~ something to oneself* …를 마음속에 그리다 / *I ~ it like this.* 나는 이렇다고 생각한다. **3** decorate (something) with a figure or pattern. …을 그림[도안]으로 꾸미다. **4** (P7) calculate. …을 계산하다. ¶ *~ up a total* 계산하여 합계를 내다. — *vi.* (P1,2B) **1** appear as an important part. (어떤 인물로서) 나타나다; 두각을 나타내다; 이채를 발하다. ¶ *~ largely in the account* 이야기 속에서 유달리 두드러지다. **2** make calculations. 계산하다; 세다. [→feign]

figure as (=*play the part of*) *Hamlet.* (햄릿)의 역을 하다. ¶ *He figured as a king in the pageant.* 야외극에서 왕의 역할을 했다.

figure (=*plan*) ***for*** *something.* …을 계획하다; …에 대한 안(案)을 세우다. ¶ *~ for an election* 선거 대책을 세우다.

figure on, **a**) take (something) into consideration. …을 계산에 넣다[고려하다]. **b**) rely on (something) …을 믿다[기대하다]; …에 의지하다.

figure out(= *think out; determine; solve*) *something.* …을 생각해 내다; 결정하다; 해결하다.

figure out at, amount to. …에 달하다.

fig·ured [fígjərd] *adj.* **1** having a design or pattern. 무늬가 있는; 의장(意匠)이 있는. **2** =figurative.

fig·ure·head [fígjərhèd / -gər-] *n.* Ⓒ **1** a person who is important only in name but has no real authority. 이름뿐인[명목만의] 수령[장(長)]; 겉간판. **2** a statue or carving on the bow of a ship. 이물 장식; 선수상(船首像).

fig·u·rine [fìgjurí:n] *n.* Ⓒ a small ornamental figure; a statuette. 소입상(小立像). [→figure]

fil·a·gree [fíləgrì:] *n.* =filigree.

fil·a·ment [fíləmənt] *n.* Ⓒ **1** a very fine, thin thread. 가는 실; 미세한 섬유. **2** a fine metal thread which lights up in an electric bulb. (전구의) 백열선(白熱線); 필라멘트. ¶ *the ~ in an electric-light bulb.* **3** 《bot.》 a slender stalk of a flower stamen. 화사(花絲)《수꽃술의 꽃밥을 가진 가느다란 줄기》. ●**fil·a·men·ta·ry** [fìləméntəri] *adj.* **fil·a·men·tous** [fìləméntəs] *adj.* [L. *filum* thread]

fil·a·ture [fílətʃər] *n.* **1** Ⓤ the act of reeling silk from cocoons. (누에고치에서) 실뽑기. **2** Ⓒ a machine for reeling silk; a factory for reeling silk. 물레; 제사(製絲)공장. [↑]

fil·bert [fílbərt] *n.* Ⓒ 《bot.》 a hazelnut. 개암《개암나무의 열매》. [*St. Filbert*]

filch [filtʃ] *vt.* (P6,7) steal (something of little value). (하찮은 것)을 훔치다; 후무리다. [? F.]

:file[1] [fail] *n.* Ⓒ **1** a folder or a case for keeping papers in order. 서류[편지]꽂이; 서류 정리 보관함. **2** a set of papers kept in order. (서류·신문 따위의) 철(綴); 철한 서류. **3** a line of people or things one behind another. 종렬(縱列); 열(opp. rank).

on file, in a file; put away and kept in order. 철하여; 정리 보관하여. ¶ *keep on ~* 철해 두다.

— *vt.* (P6,7) arrange (papers) in order. (신문·서류 등)을 정리하다; 철하다.

— *vi.* (P2A) march in a file. 종렬로 나아가

다. ¶ ~ *away* 〔*off*〕 종렬로 분열 행진하다. [L. *filum* thread]

file[2] [fail] *n.* Ⓒ a steel tool for smoothing wood or metal. 줄《공구》. [E.]

fi·let [filéi, ⌐–] *n.* Ⓤ a net or lace with a simple pattern of squares. (정 4각형 무늬의) 그물눈; 레이스. [F.]

fil·i·al [fíliəl] *adj.* due from a child to his parents. 자식으로서의; 효성스러운. ¶ ~ *piety* 효도 / ~ *duty* 자식으로서의 의무. [L. *filius* son, daughter]

fil·i·bus·ter [fíləbʌ̀stər] *n.* Ⓒ **1** 《U.S.》 a person who hinders the passage of a bill by making long speeches; a series of such speeches. 의사(議事) 방해(의 장(長) 연설)자. **2** a person who engages in an unlawful fight against another country. 불법 외침자(外侵者); 약탈병. —*vi.* (P1) act as a filibuster. 의사 방해를 하다; 방해 전술을 쓰다. ¶ ~ *against a bill* 법안에 반대하여 의사 방해를 하다. [Du. *vrijbuiter*; →freebooter]

fil·i·gree [fíləgrì:] *n.* Ⓤ ornamental work of gold or silver wire. (금·은 따위의) 가는 줄 세공. [L. *filum* thread, *granum* grain]

fil·ings [fáiliŋz] *n. pl.* small pieces rubbed off by a file. 줄밥. [*file*[2]]

Fil·i·pi·no [fìləpí:nou] *n.* Ⓒ (*pl.* **-nos**) a person of the Philippines. 필리핀 사람. —*adj.* Philippine. 필리핀의.

:fill [fil] *vt.* **1** (P6,7,13,14) take up all the space in 〔of〕; make (a box, a room, etc.) full. …을 그득하게 하다; 채우다; (공간·장소)를 차지하다. ¶ ~ *the bottle with wine* 병을 포도주로 채우다 / ~ *a barrel with apples* 통에 사과를 잔뜩 채워 넣다 / ~ *a room with furniture* 방을 가구로 가득 채우다 / ~ *a hall with people* 홀을 사람들로 꽉 채우다 / *pockets filled with money* 돈이 가득 든 호주머니 / *Her heart was filled with joy.* 그녀의 가슴은 기쁨으로 뿌듯했다 / *Smoke filled the room.* 연기로 방 안이 자욱했다 / *Fish filled the river.* 강엔 물고기가 수없이 많았다 / *His huge body filled the chair.* 그의 거대한 몸뚱이는 의자에 꽉 찼다. **2** (P6) ⓐ hold (a position); perform the duties of. (지위 따위)를 차지하다; (직무)를 수행하다. ¶ ~ *an office* 직위를 차지하다 / ~ *an order* 명령을 이행하다. ⓑ furnish. (빈자리)를 메우다; 보충하다. ¶ ~ *a vacant post* 결원을 보충하다. **3** (P6) stop up or close a hole in (something). …의 구멍〔틈〕을 메우다. ¶ ~ *a tooth* 이를 해 끼우다 / ~ *a well* 우물을 메우다. —*vi.* (P1,2A) **1** become full. 가득해지다; 차다. **2** (of sails) swell. (돛이 바람을 받아) 부풀다.

fill in, **a**) fill (a hole, etc.) with something. (구멍)을 메우다. **b**) make (a document, etc.) complete by putting it the necessary information. (서류 따위)에 필요 사항을 써 넣다. ¶ ~ *in the blanks* 빈 곳에 기입하다 / ~ *in a form* 용지에 써 넣다 / ~ *in the detail into a form* 용지에 자세한 사항을 기입하다.

fill out, **a**) make or grow larger; expand. …을 부풀리다; …이 부풀다. **b**) make (a document, etc.) complete by filling it in; fill it. (서류 따위)에 다 써 넣다.

fill up, **a**) fill completely or excessively. …을 가득 채우다. **b**) make (something) complete by filling it in; fill out. …의 빈 곳을 채우다. **c**) become full. 그득해지다; 꽉 차다.

—*n.* **1** Ⓒ 《*a* ~》 an amount enough to fill. 그릇을 채울 만큼의 양. ¶ *a ~ of tobacco* 담뱃대를 꽉 채울 분량의 담배. **2** 《*one's* ~》 an amount enough to satisfy. 필요량; 실컷; 잔뜩. ¶ *eat* 〔*drink, have, etc.*〕 *one's* ~ 잔뜩 먹다〔마시다〕 / *cry* 〔*weep*〕 *one's* ~ 실컷 울다. **3** anything to fill in a hole, etc. 메우는 것. [E.]

fil·let [fílit] *n.* Ⓒ **1** a ribbon or a narrow band worn around the head. (머리의) 리본; 머리띠. **2** a slice of fish or meat without bones. (가시·뼈를 발라낸) 생선의 저민 고기살; 필레살《소·돼지의 연한 허리 고기》. —*vt.* (P6) **1** bind (a head) with a ribbon or a narrow band. (머리)를 끈으로 동여매다. **2** cut (fish or meat) into fillets; cut fillets from (fish or meat). (생선·고기)를 저미다; 필레살을 발라내다. [L. *filum* thread]

fill·ing [fíliŋ] *n.* Ⓒ a thing used to fill something else. 채워 넣는 것; 충전물. [*fill*]

filling station [⌐–⌐–] *n.* a place where gasoline and oil for automobiles are sold; 《U.S.》 a gas station. 주유소(注油所).

fil·lip [fíləp] *n.* Ⓒ **1** a quick, smart blow with a fingernail. 손가락으로 튀기기. **2** a thing that gives excitements. 자극물. —*vt.* (P6) **1** strike (someone or something) with a fingernail. …을 손가락으로 튀기다. **2** arouse. …을 자극하다; 분발시키다. [*flip*]

fil·ly [fíli] *n.* Ⓒ (*pl.* **-lies**) **1** a young female horse. 암망아지. **2** 《*colloq.*》 a young lively girl. 활발한 소녀. [N.; →foal]

:film [film] *n.* **1** Ⓒ a very thin skin or coating. (표면에 생긴) 얇은 막〔껍질, 층〕; 박피(薄皮); 피막(被膜). ¶ *a ~ of oil on the water* 수면 위에 뜬 기름의 박막(薄膜). **2** ⓊⒸ a strip of thin, flexible material coated with a substance sensitive to light, used in taking photographs. (사진의) 필름. **3** Ⓒ ⓐ a motion picture. (한 편의) 영화. ¶ *a silent* 〔*sound*〕 ~ 무성〔발성〕 영화 / *a ~ actor* 영화 배우 / *go to see a* ~ 영화 보러 가다. ⓑ 《*the ~s*》 a cinema show; the movies. 영화(映畫). **4** Ⓒ ⓐ a mist. (눈의) 흐림; 침침함. ⓑ 《*fig.*》 a slight veil (of haze, mist, etc.). 엷은 안개〔아지랑이 (따위)〕.

—*vt., vi.* (P6; 1,2A) **1** cover (something) or become covered with a film. 박피로 덮(이)다. ¶ *filmed eyes* 흐려 침침한 눈 / *The water filmed over with ice.* 수면에 살얼음이 덮였다. **2** photograph or be photographed for motion pictures. …을 촬영하다; 찍히다. **3** make a motion picture of (something); become a motion picture. …을 영화화하다; 영화가 되다. ¶ ~ *a novel* 소설을 영화화하다. [E.]

film·y [fílmi] *adj.* (**film·i·er, film·i·est**) like a film; very thin. 박피(薄皮) 같은; 매우 얇은.

fil·ter [fíltər] *n.* Ⓒ **1** a device for purifying liquid or gas by separating out any impurities. 여과기[장치]. **2** a material used in such a device. 여과용 물질. **3** 《electr.》 a device for shutting out certain kinds of lights, electric currents, etc. 여광판(濾光板); 여파기(濾波器). — *vt.* (P6,13) purify (liquid or gas) by a filter. …을 거르다; 여과하다. ¶ ~ *water through sand* 모래를 통과시켜 물을 거르다 / ~ *out* [*off*] *impurities* 불순물을 걸러 제거하다. — *vi.* (P2A,3) move or pass very slowly. 침투하다; 스며들다. [→felt²]

filth [filθ] *n.* **1** Ⓤ disgusting dirt. 오물; 때. ¶ *live in* ~ 불결한 생활을 하다. **2** Ⓒ dirty words or thoughts. 추잡한 말[생각]. [*foul*]

filth·y [fílθi] *adj.* (**filth·i·er, filth·i·est**) disgustingly dirty. 더러운; 추악한; 외설한. ● **filth·i·ly** [-li] *adv.* **filth·i·ness** [-inis] *n.*

fil·trate [fíltreit] *vt., vi.* (P6; 1) filter; pass through a filter. 여과하다; 거르다. — [-rit, -reit] *n.* the liquid obtained as a result of filtering. 여과액(液); 걸러낸 물. [→filter]

fil·tra·tion [filtréiʃən] *n.* Ⓤ the act of filtering. 여과 (작용).

fin [fin] *n.* Ⓒ **1** a winglike part of a fish's body which enables the fish to swim and to balance itself in the water. 지느러미. **2** anything used like a fin. 지느러미 모양의 것. ¶ *an airplane* ~ 비행기의 수직 안정판. — *vi.* (P1) move the fins. 지느러미를 움직이다. [E.]

:fi·nal [fáinəl] *adj.* **1** of, coming or happening at the end; last. 최후[최종]의; 마지막의; 종국의. ¶ *the* ~ *chapter of a book* 책의 마지막 장(章). **2** not to be changed; decisive. 최종적인; 결정적인. ¶ *a* ~ *decision* 최종 결정 / *give one's* ~ *reply* 최종 회답을 하다. **3** related to something's purpose. 목적에 관한; 목적을 나타내는. — *n.* Ⓒ **1** 《usu. *the* ~》 something final. 최후의 것. **2** 《*pl.*》 the last event or game in a series. 최종 시험; 결승전 ¶ *take one's finals* 최종 시험을 치르다. **3** 《*colloq.*》 the edition of a newspaper published latest in the day. (신문의 그 날의) 최종판(版). [L. *finis* end]

final cause [∠-∠] *n.* the purpose. 목적.

fi·na·le [finá:li, -nǽli] *n.* Ⓒ 《It.》 **1** the last part of a long piece of music or a play. 종절(終節); 종악장(終樂章); (연극의) 대미(大尾); 종막. **2** the last part. 종국.

fi·nal·i·ty [fainǽləti] *n.* (*pl.* **-ties**) **1** Ⓤ the state of being final; conclusiveness. 종국; 결말; 궁극; 최후. ¶ *an air of* ~ 단호한 태도 / *speak with* ~ 단호하게 말하다. **2** Ⓒ something final. 최종적[결정적]인 언동[것]. [*finale*]

:fi·nal·ly [fáinəli] *adv.* **1** at last. 최후로; 마침내. **2** in a final manner; conclusively. 최종적으로; 결정적으로.

:fi·nance [finǽns, fáinæns] *n.* **1** Ⓤ (the science of) the management of large amounts of money. 재정; 재무; 재정학. ¶ *public* ~ 국가 재정 / *the Ministry of Finance* 재무부. **2** 《*pl.*》 the income of a state or of a private person; funds. 세입; 수입; 재원. — *vt.* (P6) provide money for (a plan, etc.); provide capital for. …에 융자하다; 자금을 공급하다; 출자하다. ¶ ~ *an enterprise* 사업에 출자하다 / *She financed her brother at the university.* 그녀는 대학생인 남동생의 학자금을 댔다. — *vi.* manage money. 재정을 관장하다. [→fine²]

:fi·nan·cial [finǽnʃəl, fai-] *adj.* of finance or the management of money. 재정[금융](상)의; 재무의. ¶ ~ *affairs* 금전상의 일; 재무 / ~ *circle* 재계(財界) / ~ *difficulties* 재정 곤란 / *the* ~ *year* 회계[재정] 연도.

fi·nan·cial·ly [finǽnʃəli, fai-] *adv.* in relation to finances. 재정적으로; 재정상. ¶ *be* ~ *sound* 재정적으로 견실하다.

fin·an·cier [finənsíər, fài-] *n.* Ⓒ **1** a person who is skilled in finance. 재정가; 재무관. **2** a person who engages in a financial operation. 자본가; 금융업자.

fin·back [fínbæ̀k] *n.* a kind of whale with a fin on the back. 긴수염고래. [fin]

finch [fintʃ] *n.* Ⓒ any of various small songbirds such as sparrows, canaries, and cardinals. 참새과(科)의 새들의 총칭. [E.]

:find [faind] *vt.* (**found**) **1** (P6,13,18,23) come up by chance; meet with. …을 (우연히) 발견하다; …을 만나다. ¶ ~ *a purse in a road* 길에서 돈지갑을 발견하다. **2** (P6, 13,14) look for and get back. (찾아서) …을 발견하다; 찾(아 내)다. ¶ ~ *one's missing watch* 잃은 시계를 찾아 내다 / *I can't* ~ *my book.* 책을 찾을 수가 없다 / *Find your father and tell him to come home.* 네 아버지를 찾아 집에 오시라고 일러라. **3** (P11,18, 20,21,23) learn; discover (a fact by test, experience). (시험·경험에 의해서) …을 알다; 깨닫다; 이해하다. ¶ ~ *something to be true* …이 진실임을 알다 / *I found the book easy.* 그것은 읽기 쉬운 책이었다 / *I found him* (*to be*) *honest.* 나는 그가 정직함을 알았다 / *I found him a very sensible man.* =*I found that he was a very sensible man.* 나는 그가 매우 분별있는 사람임을 알았다. / *I found it difficult to explain.* =*I found* (*that*) *it was difficult to explain.* 그것은 설명하기가 어려움을 알았다. **4** (P6) succeed in obtaining; get. …을 (노력해서) 얻다; 획득하다; 찾아 내다. ¶ ~ *time to read* 독서

할 시간을 찾아내다 / *Will you ~ me a job ?* 일자리를 좀 구해 주시지 않겠습니까 / *She found no help from him.* 그녀는 그에게서 아무런 도움도 얻지 못했다. **5** (P6) reach. …에 달하다〔미치다〕. ¶ *The arrow found its target.* 화살이 과녁에 명중하였다. **6** (P7,11, 18,19) 《law》 arrive at (a conclusion); give a decision; judge. (결론)에 도달하다; 판결〔평결〕을 내리다. ¶ ~ *a verdict of guilty* 유죄 판결을 내리다 / *He was found guilty.* 그는 유죄 판결을 받았다. **7** (P6,13) 《*in, with*》 provide; furnish; supply. …을 지급하다; 갖추다; 주다; 공급하다. ¶ ~ *clerks in uniforms* 점원들에게 제복을 지급하다 / ~ *one's son with everything necessary* 아들에게 필요한 모든 것을 대주다 / *The hotel is well found.* 그 호텔은 시설이 좋다. — *vi.* **1** (P3) 《*for*》 judge; reach a decision. 판결하다. ¶ *The jury found for* 〔*against*〕 *the defendant.* 배심은 피고에게 무죄〔유죄〕 평결을 내렸다. **2** 《*pl.*》 discover game. 사냥감을 발견하다.

find oneself, discover one's power or abilities. 자기의 힘〔능력, 천분〕을 알다.

find fault with ⇨fault.

find it in one's heart to do, feel inclined to do. …하고 싶은〔…할〕 마음이 되다.

find one's legs 〔***feet***〕***,*** **a**) be able to rise and walk. (어린 아이·환자 등이) 설 수 있게 되다; 걸을 수 있게 되다. **b**) act for oneself. 독립하다.

find out, **a**) learn, discover by test, experience, etc. (경험 따위로) …을 알다; 발견하다. ¶ *We found out how to do it.* 그것을 어떻게 하는지 알아 냈다. **b**) discover; detect; bring to light (esp. a hidden or unpleasant fact about someone). 발견하다; 간파하다; 밝히다; 폭로하다. ¶ *His sins have found him out.* 그의 죄상은 드러나고 말았다 / *I found out about their quarrel.* 그들이 말다툼한 것에 관해 알아 냈다.

find one's way, discover which way to go; manage to go, advance, or reach. 길을 찾아서 가다; 애를 써서 나아가다; 다다르다. ¶ *How did you ~ your way out of ravine ?* 어떻게 그 협곡에서 빠져 나왔나.

— *n.* **1** Ⓤ discovery. 발견(하기). **2** Ⓒ a thing found, esp. a valuable thing. 발견물; 희한한 발굴물. [E.]

find·er [fáindər] *n.* Ⓒ **1** a person who finds. 발견자. **2** a small lens on a camera to help find objects more easily. (카메라·망원경의) 파인더.

fin de siè·cle [fæ̃n də sjékl] *n.* 《F.》 the end of the century, esp. of the nineteenth century. 세기말《특히 19세기의》.

***find·ing** [fáindiŋ] *n.* **1** Ⓤ discovery. 발견(함). **2** Ⓒ 《often *pl.*》 something found. 발견물; 습득물. **3** Ⓒ 《law》 a decision reached after an examination; a verdict. 판결; 평결; 판정. **4** 《*pl.*》 tools, supplies, etc. 부속품; 자질구레한 도구. [→find]

:**fine**[1] [fain] *adj.* **1** very good; excellent. 매우 좋은; 훌륭한; 양질의; (최)고급의. 參考 빈정대는 뜻으로도 됨. ¶ ~ *wine* 상질의 포도주 / ~ *iron* 양질의 철 / ~ *watches* 고급 시계 / *a ~ character* 훌륭한 인물 / *with ~ obstinacy* 아주 완고히 / *That's ~ a excuse.* 어처구니없는 구실이군. **2** clear; bright. (날씨가) 갠; 맑은. ¶ *a ~ day* 활짝 갠 날. **3** very small or thin. 작은; 미세한; 가는; 고운. ¶ ~ *thread* 가는 실 / ~ *sand* 고운 모래 / ~ *sugar* 정당(精糖) / ~ *rain* 가랑비. **4** perceived only with difficulty; delicate. 알기 어려운; 미묘한. ¶ *a ~ question* 미묘한 문제 / *a ~ sense of humor* 날카로운 유머 감각 / *a ~ shade of meaning* 미묘한 의미의 차이. **5** pure; perfect. 순수한; 섞인 것이 없는; 순도가 높은; 완벽한. ¶ ~ *gold* 순금 / ~ *love* 순수한 사랑. **6** ⓐ sharp; sensitive. 예민한; 감수성이 강한. ¶ *He has a ~ ear for music.* 음악을 듣는 예민한 귀를 가지고 있다. ⓑ sharp; sharp-pointed; keen-edged. 날카로운; 날이 예리한; 뾰족한. ¶ *a ~ edge* 예리한 날 / *a ~ pen* 끝이 뾰족한 펜. **7** (of the touch) delicate in tenure. 감촉이 좋은; 결이 고운. ¶ ~ *silk* 매끄러운 비단 / *a ~ skin* 매끄러운 피부. **8** elegant; refined. 세련된; 점잖은; 우아한. ¶ *a ~ manner* 세련된 태도. **9** well-shaped; handsome; good-looking. 모양이 좋은; 잘 생긴; 미모의. ¶ *a ~ face* 단정한 얼굴 / *a ~ young man* 미모의 청년 / *a ~ pair of horns* 잘 생긴 한 쌍의 뿔.

not to put too fine a point upon it, frankly speaking. 솔직히〔까놓고〕 말하면.

one fine day 〔***morning***〕***,*** one day 〔morning〕. 어느 날〔아침〕.

one of these fine days, before long. 머지않아. ¶ *Jane will be getting married one of these ~ days.* 제인은 머지않아 결혼한다.

— *n.* fine weather. 맑은 날씨; 쾌청. ¶ *in rain or ~* 비가 오든 안 오든.

— *vt., vi.* (P6,7; 1,2A) **1** 《often *down*》 make (beer) clear; become clear. …을 맑게 하다; 맑아지다. **2** 《esp. *away, down, off*》 make or become finer or thinner. 좀더 곱게 〔가늘게〕 하다; 고와〔가늘어〕지다.

— *adv.* 《*colloq.*》 very well; splendidly. 훌륭히; 잘; 멋지게. ¶ *He did ~.* 훌륭히 했다.

cut 〔***run***〕 ***it fine,*** allow too little time. 시간 여유를 조금밖에 주지 않다; 시간을 매우 절약하다. [→finish]

fine[2] [fain] *n.* Ⓒ a sum of money paid as a punishment. 벌금; 과료. — *vt.* (P6,13) cause (someone) to pay a fine. …에게 벌금을 과하다. [F. *fin* settlement of dispute]

fi·ne[3] [fíːnei] *n.* the end. 끝. [→finis]

in fine, in short; finally; at last. 결국; 마침내.

fine-drawn [fáindrɔ́ːn] *adj.* **1** drawn out very thin. 가늘게 (잡아)늘인. ¶ *a ~ wire* 가늘게 뽑아 늘인 철사. **2** very subtle; too subtle. (의론 따위가) 미묘한. [*fine*[1]]

fine-grained [fáingréind] *adj.* having a fine, close grain. 결이 고운; 결이 촘촘한.

*__fine·ly__ [fáinli] *adv.* in a fine manner. 훌륭히; 가늘게; 곱게; 정교하게. [*fine*¹]

fine·ness [fáinnis] *n.* Ⓤ **1** the state or quality of being fine. 훌륭함; 멋짐; 아름다움. **2** the proportion of pure gold or silver in a mixture of metals. 순도(純度); (합금 속의) 함유량의 비율.

fin·er·y [fáinəri] *n.* Ⓤ gay clothes or ornaments. 화려한 옷; 아름다운 장식품. ¶ *a park in its spring* ~ 아름답게 봄 단장을 한 공원 / *in one's best* ~ 가장 멋진 옷을 입고.

fine-spun [fáinspʌ́n] *adj.* **1** spun until very thin. 극히 가늘게 실을 뽑은[자은]. **2** very subtle. (의론 따위가) 지나치게 미묘한; 면밀한; 치밀한.

fi·nesse [finés] *n.* **1** Ⓤ skill, skillful handling, careful and delicate action. 기교; 솜씨; 수완; 교묘한 처리. ¶ *His violin playing showed great* ~. 그의 바이올린 연주는 대단한 솜씨를 보였다. **2** Ⓒ cunning. 책략; 술책. — *vi.* (P1) use finesse. 책략을 쓰다. — *vt.* (P6,7,13) overcome by finesse. …을 책략으로 지게 하다. [F.]

:**fin·ger** [fíŋgər] *n.* Ⓒ **1** one of the five end parts of the hand, usu. except the thumb. 손가락(cf. *toe*). **2** the part of a glove that covers a finger. (장갑의) 손가락. **3** something like a finger in shape or use. 손가락 모양의 것. ¶ *the fingers of a clock* 시계의 바늘.

burn one's fingers, suffer after a foolish act or mistake. 실수로 인해 혼(쭐)나다; 데다.

by fingers breath, by a very narrow margin. 위기 일발에서; 아슬아슬하게.

get one's fingers burnt =burn one's fingers.

give someone the finger, **a**) make someone fail. 아무를 실패하게 하다. **b**) treat someone cruelly. 박정[쌀쌀]하게 대하다[다루다].

have a finger in the pie, take an active part in some affair. (어떤 일)에 관련을 가지다; 관계하다; 참견하다.

have at one's fingers' ends 〔***fingertips***〕, …에 정통해 있다; …에 환하다.

keep one's fingers crossed, hope for the best. (어떤 노력의) 성공을 바라다; 행운을 빌다; 사태의 호전을 기원하다.

lay 〔***put***〕 ***a finger on,*** **a**) touch; harm. (적의를 가지고) …에게 손가락을 대다; 상처를 주다. ¶ *It's not my fault—I never laid a* ~ *on her!* 내 잘못이 아닐세—그녀에게 손가락 하나 대지 않았단 말야. **b**) indicate 〔point out〕 exactly; remember. 정확히 지적하다; 생각해 내다. ¶ *put one's* ~ *on the cause of the trouble* 분규의 원인을 정확히 지적하다.

let slip through one's fingers, miss; let go. 놓치다.

not lift a finger (***to do***), make no attempt; do nothing. …을 하려고 하지 않다; 아무 일도 안 하다.

turn 〔***twist***〕 ***someone round one's*** (***little***) ***finger,*** control someone completely; have a deep influence on someone. 아무를 마음대로 하다; 완전히 좌우하다.

— *vt.* **1** touch or hold (something) with the fingers; turn about (something) in the fingers. …을 손가락으로 만지다; 만지작거리다; 갖고 놀다. **2** accept wrongly. 불법으로 받다. ¶ ~ *a bribe* 뇌물을 받다. [E.]

fin·ger-al·pha·bet [fíŋgərǽlfəbet / -bit] *n.* a method of speaking for the deaf and dumb; alphabet for the blind. 지화(指話); 수화(手話); 점자(點字).

finger board [⏑– ⏑] *n.* 《mus.》 a keyboard. 건반.

finger bowl [⏑– ⏑] *n.* a bowl to hold water for rinsing the fingers at table after eating. 핑거볼《식탁에서 손가락을 씻기 위해 물을 담아 두는 그릇》.

fin·ger·ing [fíŋgəriŋ] *n.* Ⓤ **1** the act of handling with the fingers. 손끝으로 만지작거림; (염주 따위를) 손끝으로 굴려 넘김. **2** the act or technique of using the fingers in playing a musical instrument. 운지법(運指法). **3** signs to show how the fingers are to be used. 운지 기호. [*finger*]

finger language [⏑–⏑–] *n.* (the use of) the finger-alphabet. (농아자의) 지화(指話); 지문자(指文字).

finger mark [⏑–⏑] *n.* a mark or stain left by a finger. 만져 남긴 손가락 자국.

fin·ger·nail [fíŋgərnèil] *n.* the nail at the end of the finger. 손톱.

to the 〔***one's***〕 ***fingernails,*** completely; thoroughly. 손톱 끝까지; 완전히.

finger plate [⏑–⏑] *n.* a metal plate on a door, near the handle, to protect the door from dirty hands, etc. (문 손잡이 따위의) 지판(指板)《손때 묻는 것을 보호함》.

finger post [⏑– ⏑] *n.* a post, often shaped like a finger, to show the direction. (손가락 모양의) 도표(道標); 방향 표시 말뚝.

fin·ger·print [fíŋgərprìnt] *n.* Ⓒ an impression of the lines on the end of a finger used for identifying a person. 지문(指紋). — *vt.* take the fingerprints of (someone). …의 지문을 채취하다. [*finger*]

fin·ger·stall [fíŋgərstɔ̀ːl] *n.* Ⓒ a cover for a injured finger made of leather or rubber. (가죽 또는 고무의) 손가락싸개; 골무.

fin·ger·tip [fíŋgərtìp] *n.* Ⓒ the tip of a finger. 손가락 끝.

to one's fingertips, thoroughly. 완전히.

fin·i·cal [fínikəl] *adj.* **1** too particular or fastidious. 지나치게 까다로운. ¶ *be very* ~ *about food* 음식에 몹시 까다롭다. **2** over-elaborate. 지나치게 공들인[세밀한]. [? fine]

fin·ick·y [fíniki] *adj.* =finical.

fi·nis [fínis, fáinis] *n.* 《L.》 Ⓒ 《*sing.* only》 the end. 끝; 종결; 종말; 죽음. [L. =end]

:**fin·ish** [finiʃ] *vt.* **1** (P6,7,9) bring or

come to an end. …을 끝내다; 마치다. ¶ ~ *one's work* 일을 끝내다 / ~ *school* 학업을 끝내다 / ~ *speaking* 연설을 끝내다 / ~ *one's life* 일생을 마치다 / ~ *writing a letter* 편지 쓰기를 마치다 / ~ *reading a novel* 소설을 다 읽다 / *Have you finished your homework?* 학교 숙제를 마쳤나. **2** (P6,7,9) 《*up*》 make (something) perfect; complete. …을 완성〔완료〕(完成〔完了〕)하다; 마무리하다. ¶ ~ *a picture* 그림을 완성하다. **3** (P6) 《often *up, off*》 use up; eat or drink completely. …을 다 쓰다; (음식물)을 남김 없이 먹어 치우다; 다 마셔 버리다. ¶ ~ *a plate of food* 음식 한 접시를 깨끗이 비우다〔다 먹다〕. **4** (P6,7) 《often *off*》《*colloq.*》 defeat completely; destroy; kill. (상대)를 해치우다; 퇴치하다; 죽이다. — *vi.* (P1,2A,3) come to an end; end. 끝나다; 끝내다.

finish off, bring (something) to the end; give final touches to (something); kill. …을 끝내다; 마무리하다; 죽이다. ¶ *I finished him off.* 녀석을 해치웠다 / *This spray will ~ off the cockroaches.* 이 분무액을 쓰면 바퀴도 완전히 퇴치할 수 있을 게다.

finish up, complete; use up completely; eat the whole of (something). …을 완성하다; 다 써 버리다; (음식)을 남김 없이 먹어 치우다. ¶ ~ *up a can of paint* 페인트 한 통을 다 쓰다 / ~ *up* 〔*off*〕 *the remains of meat* 나머지 고기를 다 먹어 치우다.

finish with, end; complete; stop being friends with (someone). …로써 끝(장)내다; …와 관계를 끊다. ¶ ~ *someone with a single blow* 단 일격에 아무를 쓰러뜨리다.

— *n.* Ⓒ **1** an end; the last stage. 끝; 마지막 단계; 최후. ¶ *fight to a ~* 최후까지 싸우다. **2** a completed state. 완성(상태). **3** a way of finishing. 끝마무리. [L. *finis* end]

:fin·ished [fíniʃt] *adj.* **1** ended; completed; perfect. 끝난; 완성한; 완전한. ¶ *the ~ work* 완성한 일. **2** refined; fine. 세련된; 훌륭한.

fin·ish·er [fíniʃər] *n.* **1** a person or machine that gives the finishing touches to an article. 완성하는 사람; 마무리공(工); 마무리 기계. **2** 《*colloq.*》 a deciding blow. 결정적인 일격.

fi·nite [fáinait] *adj.* having limits; 《gram.》 having definite person, number and tense. 한계가 있는; 한정의; 인칭·수·시제에 제한되는; 정형(定形)의. ¶ *Human understanding is ~.* 인간의 지식은 한계가 있다. [*finish*]

Fin·land [fínlənd] *n.* a country in northern Europe. 핀란드. 參考 수도는 Helsinki.

Finn [fin] *n.* Ⓒ a person of Finland. 핀란드 사람.

Finn·ish [fíniʃ] *adj.* of Finland, its people, or their language. 핀란드(사람·말)의. — *n.* Ⓤ the language of Finland. 핀란드 말.

fin·ny [fíni] *adj.* having fins; like a fin; of fish. 지느러미가 있는〔같은〕; 물고기의. [*fin*]

fiord, fjord [fjɔːrd] *n.* Ⓒ a long, narrow inlet of the sea between high banks, esp. in Norway. 피오르드; 협만(峽灣). [Norw.]

·fir [fəːr] *n.* 《bot.》 Ⓒ an evergreen tree which has cones and needlelike leaves like the pine; Ⓤ its wood. 전나무; 그 재목. [E.]

:fire [faiər] *n.* **1** Ⓤ the heat or light produced by burning flame. 불; 화염. **2** Ⓒ something burning; burning material in a stove, etc. (모닥불·난로 따위의) 불. ¶ *a cheerful ~* 기분 좋게 타는 불 / *bank up a ~* 불씨를 묻다 / *have a ~ in one's room* 방에 불을 피워두다 / *It is cold; please make* 〔*light*〕 *a ~.* 춥습니다, 불 좀 때 주시오. **3** Ⓒ a destructive burning. 화재; 불. ¶ *a big* 〔*large, great*〕 ~ 큰 화재 / *a forest ~* 산불 / *A ~ broke out last night.* 지난 밤에 큰 불이 일어났다. **4** Ⓤ 《often *a ~*》 the discharge of a gun. 발포; 발사; 사격; 포화. ¶ *a covering ~* 엄호 사격〔포화〕 / *open ~ on* …에 사격을 시작하다 / *cease ~* 사격을 그치다 / *pour ~ upon the enemy* 적에게 포화를 퍼붓다. **5** Ⓤ ⓐ any feeling that suggests fire. 불타는 정열; 격정. ¶ *eyes full of ~* 이글거리는 눈. ⓑ passion; spirit. 흥분; 활기. ¶ *speech lacking ~.* 활기 없는 연설.

between two fires, attacked from two sides at once. 양쪽에서 동시에 공격을 받아; 협공을 당하여.

catch 〔***take***〕 ***fire,*** begin to burn. 불이 붙다; 불타기 시작하다.

go through fire and water, face all dangers. 물불을 가리지 않다; 온갖 위험을 무릅쓰고 맞서다.

hang fire, **a**) (of a gun, etc.) not go off at once. 즉각 발사되지 않다; 불발이 되다. **b**) (of an action, event, etc.) be slow in progress; be delayed or postponed. 늑장부리다; 지연되다.

lay a fire, put the paper, sticks, and coal ready for lighting. 불 땔 준비를 하다; (불을 때기 위해) 장작·석탄 따위를 쌓아놓다.

miss fire, **a**) do not go off. 불발로 끝나다. **b**) have no effect; fail. 효과가 없다; 잘못하다; 실패하다.

on fire, **a**) burning. 불타고. ¶ *a house on ~* 불타(고 있)는 집. **b**) 《*fig.*》 eager; excited. (마음이) 불타고; 흥분하고; 기를 쓰고.

play with fire, do something risky. 불장난하다; 위험한 짓을 하다.

pull (*something*) ***out of the fire,*** make something successful in spite of difficulties. …을 어려움을 무릅쓰고 성공시키다.

set fire to =***set on fire,*** cause to burn. …에 불을 지르다〔붙이다〕; 불타게 하다.

set the Thames 〔***the world***〕 ***on fire,*** 《chiefly *negative*》 perform something which causes great surprise. 세상을 경악시킬 일을 하다. ¶ *He will never set the Thames on ~.* 그는 결코 세상의 주목을 끌 만한 일은 하지 못

할 게다.

under fire, **a**) exposed to enemy guns. 적의 포화에 노출되어; 포화의 세례를 받고. **b**) 《*fig.*》 attacked; criticized. 비난[비판]을 받고.

— *vt.* **1** (P6) cause (something) to burn; set fire to. …에 불을 붙이다[지르다]. ¶ ~ *a house* 집에 불을 지르다. **2** (P6) supply fuel to (something). …에 연료를 넣다. **3** (P6) dry (something) by heat; bake. …을 불에 쬐어 말리다; 굽다. ¶ ~ *bricks* 벽돌을 굽다. **4** (P6) excite. (감정)을 자극하다. ¶ ~ *someone's blood* 아무의 피가 끓게 하다. **5** (P6, 7,13) 《*at, on, upon*》 shoot (guns, etc.). …을 발사하다. ¶ ~ *warning shots* 위협 사격을 하다. **6** (P6,13) 《*from*》《*colloq.*》 dismiss (someone) from a post. …을 해고하다.

— *vi.* **1** (P1,2A) burst into flame; catch fire. 불붙다. **2** (P1,2A) grow hot, red, or excited. 격하다; 흥분하다. **3** (P1,2A,3) 《*at, on, upon*》 (of guns) go off; shoot. 발사하다. ¶ ~ *at* [*on*] *the enemy* 적에게 발사하다. [E.]

fire away, 《*colloq.*》 begin; start, esp. talk or ask questions. (질문 따위)를 시작하다; (일)에 착수하다.

fire off, discharge. 발사[발포]하다. ¶ ~ *off a gun* 총을 발사하다 / ~ *off questions* 질문을 발하다.

fire out, 《U.S. *colloq.*》 dismiss. 해고하다. ¶ *He was fired out for dishonesty.* 불성실하여 해고되었다.

fire up, **a**) set on fire. 불을 지르다[붙이다]. **b**) become angry. 격노[격앙]하다.

fire alarm [ˊ-ˊ] *n.* a signal that a fire has broken out; an apparatus that gives such a signal. 화재 경보(기).

fire·arm [fáiərὰːrm] *n.* 《usu. *pl.*》 a small weapon, such as a gun, a pistol, a rifle, etc. 소화기(小火器); 권총; 총.

fire bomb [ˊˋ] *n.* a bomb that burns violently for the purpose of destruction. 소이탄(燒夷彈).

fire·brand [fáiərbræ̀nd] *n.* Ⓒ **1** a piece of burning wood. 불이 붙은 나뭇조각; 타다 남은 것. **2** a person who stirs up strife among a crowd. (소란 따위의) 선동자.

fire·break [fáiərbrèik] *n.* an empty strip of land to prevent a forest fire from spreading. (산불 따위가 퍼지는 것을 막기 위한) 방화대(防火帶).

fire·brick [fáiərbrìk] *n.* Ⓒ a piece of brick made of a special clay that can withstand great heat. 내화(耐火) 벽돌.

fire brigade [ˊ-ˋ] *n.* an organized body of firemen. 소방대(隊); 소방서(署).

fire·clay [fáiərklèi] *n.* a special kind of clay used in making firebricks. 내화 점토(耐火粘土).

fire company [ˊˋ--] *n.* **1** = fire brigade. **2** a fire insurance company. 화재 보험 회사.

fire·crack·er [fáiərkræ̀kər] *n.* Ⓒ 《U.S.》 a roll of paper which contains gunpowder and a fuse. 폭죽; 딱총.

fire·damp [fáiərdæ̀mp] *n.* Ⓤ a gas formed in coal mines which is sometimes explosive. 탄갱 안에 자연적으로 생기는 폭발성 가스.

fire department [ˊ -ˋ-] *n.* 《U.S.》 = fire brigade.

fire·dog [fáiərdɔ̀ːg / -dɔ̀g] *n.* Ⓒ an iron support for logs in a fireplace; an andiron. (벽난로 따위의) 장작 받침(쇠).

fire engine [ˊ ˋ-] *n.* a machine to put out fires, usu. with hoses for throwing water; a truck equipped with such a machine. 소방 펌프; 소방 자동차.

fire escape [ˊ-ˋ] *n.* a stairway, ladder, etc. to give a way of escape from a burning building. 화재 피난 장치《비상 계단·피난 사다리 따위》.

fire extinguisher [ˊ -ˋ--] *n.* a portable metal tank filled with chemicals which extinguish fire. 소화기.

fire·fly [fáiərflài] *n.* Ⓒ (*pl.* **-flies**) a small insect that emits flashes of soft light. 개똥벌레.

fire·guard [fáiərgὰːrd] *n.* Ⓒ a metal screen placed in front of a fireplace as a protection. 난로 울.

fire hose [ˊˋ] *n.* a tube to carry water to put out fires. 소화(消火) 호스.

fire irons [ˊ ˋ-] *n. pl.* the poker, tongs, shovel, etc. which are used in tending for a domestic fireplace. 난로용 제구《부젓가락·부지깽이·부삽 따위》.

fire·less [fáiərlis] *adj.* without a fire; lacking fire. 불이 없는; 불기 없는.

fire·light [fáiərlàit] *n.* ⓊⒸ the light cast by a fire. (난로의) 불빛.

fire·lock [fáiərlὰk / -lɔ̀k] *n.* Ⓒ an early type of gun that was fired by sparks. 화승총(火繩銃).

fire·man [fáiərmən] *n.* Ⓒ (*pl.* **-men** [-mən]) **1** a person who is trained to put out fires. 소방수. **2** a person who takes care of the fire in a furnace, a boiler, etc. (기선 따위의) 기관사; 화부(火夫).

·fire·place [fáiərplèis] *n.* Ⓒ a place to hold a fire, esp. one built at the base of a chimney. 난로; 벽로.

fire·proof [fáiərprùːf] *adj.* made of material that will not burn; fire-resisting. 내화(耐火)의; 방화의. ¶ *a* ~ *building* 내화 건축.

fire-re·sist·ant [fáiərizìstənt] *adj.* meeting standard requirements when exposed to fire. (건조물 따위가) 내화성(耐火性)의.

fire screen [ˊˋ] *n.* a portable screen used for protecting a person from the heat of an open fire in a room (now mostly used as a decoration.). (난로 앞에 세우는) 화열(火熱) 방지 칸막이.

fire·side [fáiərsàid] *n.* Ⓒ **1** 《usu. *the* ~》

the place near a fireplace or hearth. 노변(爐邊). **2** 《*fig.*》 home; home or family life. 가정 (생활).

fire tower [ㅅ ㅡ] *n.* a tower for watching for fires. 화재 감시 망루.

fire·trap [fáiərtræ̀p] *n.* **1** a building hard to get out of when it is on fire. 화재 비상구가 없는 건물. **2** a building that will burn very easily. (화재 발생시 여러 가지 결함으로) 쉽게 타버릴 위험한 건물.

fire·wa·ter [fáiərwɔ̀ːtər] *n.* Ⓤ 《*colloq.*》 any strong spirits. 화주(火酒); 독한 술《위스키·진·럼주 따위》.

fire·wood [fáiərwùd] *n.* Ⓤ wood for use as fuel. 땔나무; 장작.

fire·works [fáiərwə̀ːrks] *n. pl.* **1** firecrackers, rockets, etc. used in celebrations to make a loud noise or a brilliant fiery display of light. 불꽃(놀이). ¶ *let* 〔*set*〕 *off* ~ 불꽃을 쏘아 올리다. **2** 《*fig.*》 a display of temper, wit, etc. (둘 사이의) 격한 감정·재치의 주고받기.

fir·ing [fáiəriŋ] *n.* Ⓤ **1** the act of setting on fire; the act of shooting guns. 불을 땜〔붙임〕; 점화; 발포; 발사. **2** material for fuel. 연료; 땔감. [*fire*]

:firm[1] [fəːrm] *adj.* **1** (of the body, a building, etc.) strong and hard; solid; fixed. 견고한; 단단한; 튼튼한; 고정〔안정〕된. ¶ *a* ~ *muscle* 단단한 근육 / *a* ~ *building* 튼튼한 건물 / *a* ~ *foundation* 튼튼한 토대〔기초〕 / ~ *ground* (바다에 대하여) 육지 / *a tree* ~ *in the earth* 땅에 단단히 뿌리 박은 나무 / (*as*) ~ *as a rock* 반석 같은; 요지(搖之)부동의. **2** (of one's faith, will, etc.) not easily changed or shaken; decided; resolute. (신념·의지 따위가) 굳은; 확고〔단호〕한; 변함 없는. ¶ *a* ~ *belief* 굳은 신념 / ~ *friendship* 변함 없는 우정 / *a* ~ *expression* 단호한 표정. **3** ⓐ (of an act) steady. (동작 따위가) 흔들림 없는; 확실한. ¶ *walk with* ~ *steps* 확실한 발걸음으로 걷다. ⓑ 《comm.》 constant. 변동 없는; 불변의. ¶ *be* ~ *in price* 시세가 안정되다.

— *adv.* firmly; fast. 단단히; 굳게. ¶ *stand* ~ 버티고 서다; 양보하지 않다.

— *vt.* (P6) **1** make firm or solid. …을 단단히 굳히다. ¶ ~ *the ground after planting* 나무를 심은 뒤에 땅을 다지다. **2** fix firmly. …을 단단히 고정시키다; 안정시키다.

— *vi.* (P1) become firm or solid. 굳어지다; 단단해지다; 안정되다. [L. *firmus*]

firm[2] [fəːrm] *n.* Ⓒ a business company or partnership of two or more people. 회사; 상사(商社). [L. *firmo* confirm; ↑]

fir·ma·ment [fə́ːrməmənt] *n.* 《usu. *the* ~》 the sky; the heavens. 하늘; 천계(天界). [↑]

:firm·ly [fə́ːrmli] *adv.* in a firm manner. 단단히; 확고히.

firm·ness [fə́ːrmnis] *n.* Ⓤ the state or quality of being firm. 견고; 확고 부동.

:first [fəːrst] *adj.* **1** before all others in order, time, or place; earliest 제 1 의; 첫(번)째의; 처음의; 최초의(opp. last). ¶ *a* ~ *edition* (책의) 초판 / *the* ~ *impression* 첫인상 / *a* ~ *offender* 초범자 / *the* ~ *coat* (벽 따위의) 밑칠; 애벌칠 / *the* ~ *frost of the winter* 겨울의 첫서리 / *the* ~ *month of the year* 한 해의 첫째 달. **2** most important or highest in rank, quality, etc. 제 1위의; 가장 중요한; 최상의; 1류의. ¶ *the* ~ *officer of a ship* 배의 1등 항해사 / *the* ~ *violin* 제 1바이올린(연주자) / *the* ~ *lady* 대통령 부인 / *goods of* ~ *grade* 일급품 / *the* ~ *hotel in the city* 그 시(市)에서 제일 가는 호텔. **3** 《*the* ~》 even one. 극히 조금의 …(조차)도. ¶ *He doesn't know the* ~ *thing about it.* 그것에 관해 전혀 모른다.

at first hand, directly; from personal knowledge. 직접; 개인적으로.

at first sight 〔***view***〕***,*** at the first glance; upon being first seen. 일견하여; 첫눈에; 언뜻 보아. ¶ *fall in love at* ~ *sight* 첫눈에 반하여 사랑에 빠지다 / *It seemed good at* ~ *sight.* 언뜻 보아 좋아 보였다.

for the first time, before one does anything else. 처음으로.

in the first place, to begin with; firstly. 우선 첫째로.

(***the***) ***first thing,*** 《*colloq.*》 before anything else; at once. 우선 첫째로; 즉시. ¶ *I'll call you* (*the*) ~ *thing when I arrive.* 도착하는 대로 곧 전화하겠습니다.

— *adv.* **1** ahead of any other person or thing in time, rank, or space; to begin with. 첫째로; 최초로; 맨 먼저. ¶ *We must finish our work* ~. 우선 우리 일을 끝내야 한다. **2** for the first time. 처음으로. ¶ *I* ~ *met her two years ago.* 2년 전에 처음으로 그녀를 만났다. **3** rather than anything else. 차라리. ¶ *We will die* ~. 차라리 죽는 게 낫겠다 / *I'll go to jail* ~. 차라리 교도소에 가는 것이 낫겠다.

first and foremost, before all others; first of all. 우선 첫째로; 맨 먼저.

first and last, altogether; on the whole. 전체로 보아; 대체로.

— *n.* Ⓒ 《usu. *the* ~》 **1** the person, thing, place, etc. that is first. 첫째; 처음; 제 1위. ¶ *the* ~ *of the speakers* 맨 첫째의 연사. **2** the first day of a month. 초하루. ¶ *the* ~ *of June* 6월 초하루〔1일〕. **3** ⓐ a place in the first class. (시험의) 제 1위; 1등; 수석. ¶ *take* 〔*get*〕 *a* ~ *in mathematics* 수학에서 1등의 성적을 따다. ⓑ a first prize in a race, etc. 1등상. **4** 《*pl.*》 articles of the best quality. 일등품; 일급품. [E.]

at (***the***) ***first,*** in the beginning. 처음에는. ¶ *I found English difficult at* ~. 처음에는 영어가 어렵다고 생각했다.

be the first (=*do willingly or eagerly*) ***to do something.*** 기꺼이〔자진해서〕 …하다.

from first to last, from beginning to end. 처

음부터 끝까지.
from the first, from the beginning. 처음부터.

first aid [ㅗㅅ] *n.* temporary or emergency treatment given to an injured person before regular medical treatment. 응급 치료[처치].

first-aid [fə́ːrstéid] *adj.* of the first aid. 응급 치료의.

first-born [fə́ːrstbɔ̀ːrn] *adj.* born first; eldest. 맨 처음 태어난; 장남[장녀]의. ¶ *one's ~ child* 첫 아이. — *n.* Ⓒ the first-born child; the eldest. 첫 아이; 큰아이.

First Cause [ㅗㅅ], **the** *n.* the Creator. 조물주; 신.

first class [ㅗㅅ] *n.* **1** the highest, finest or best class or rank. 일류; 일급; 최고급. **2** (of trains, ships, airplanes, etc.) the most expensive and luxurious class of accommodation. (열차·배·비행기 따위의) 1등.

first-class [fə́ːrstklǽs / -kláːs] *adj.* of the highest, finest or best quality; 《*colloq.*》 excellent. 첫째의; 제 1등의; 제 1류의; 최상의; 매우 훌륭한[멋진]. ¶ *a ~ hotel* 일류 호텔 / *The weather was ~.* 날씨는 최상이었다. — *adv.* **1** with the best accommodations. 1등(승객)으로. ¶ *travel ~* 1등으로 여행하다. **2** 《*colloq.*》 excellently; very well. 뛰어나게; 썩 잘. ¶ *He plays ~.* 그는 경기를 뛰어나게 잘 한다.

first floor [ㅗㅅ] *n.* 《Brit.》 the floor just above the ground floor of a building; 《U.S.》 the ground floor. (영국의) 2층; (미국의) 1층.

first fruits [ㅗㅅ] *n. pl.* **1** the earliest products of a harvest or a season. 만물. **2** the first products or results of one's work or activity. 첫 수확; 첫 수익.

first-hand [fə́ːrsthǽnd] *adj.* obtained directly from the original source; direct. 직접의; 직접 입수한. ¶ *have ~ information* 직접 입수한 정보를 갖고 있다. — *adv.* directly. 직접(으로). ¶ *learn something ~* …을 직접 배우다.

first·ling [fə́ːrstliŋ] *n.* Ⓒ **1** the first product or result of a harvest or a season. 만물. **2** the first offspring of an animal. (가축의) 만배. **3** the first result. 최초의 결과(성과).

first·ly [fə́ːrstli] *adv.* in the first place; first of all. 우선 첫째로[먼저].

first name [ㅗㅅ] *n.* Christian name; given name. 세례명(洗禮名); 이름(cf. *surname, family name*).

first-rate [fə́ːrstréit] *adj.* of the highest, best class or rank; excellent. 1등급의; 일류의; 최상의; 훌륭한; 우수한. ¶ *a ~ actor* 일류 배우 / *a ~ dinner* 훌륭한 만찬. — *adv.* 《*colloq.*》 very good; excellently; very well. 훌륭하게; 멋지게; 아주 잘. ¶ *He sings ~.* 그는 노래를 아주 잘 부른다.

firth [fəːrθ] *n.* Ⓒ a narrow arm of the sea; a river mouth. 만(灣); 하구(河口). [N.=fold]

fis·cal [fískəl] *adj.* of the financial matters of a government; financial. 국고(國庫)의; 재정의; 회계의. ¶ *a ~ year* 회계 연도. [L.]

:fish [fiʃ] *n.* (*pl.* **fish·es** or *collectively* **fish**) **1** Ⓒ a cold-blooded animal which lives in water. 물고기; 어류. **2** Ⓤ the flesh of such animals when used for food. 어육(魚肉). ¶ *have ~ for dinner* 저녁 식사에 생선을 먹다. **3** 《*colloq.*》 a person. 사람; 놈; 녀석. ¶ *a cool* [*queer, poor*] *~* 뻔뻔한[이상한, 불쌍한] 녀석 / *a big financial ~* 재계의 거물.
All is fish that comes to his net. 《*prov.*》 He takes everything without choice. 자빠져도 그냥은 일어나지 않는다.
a pretty [***nice***] ***kettle of fish,*** confusion. 대혼란; 분규.
(***as***) ***drunk as a fish,*** very drunk. 억병으로 취한.
drink like a fish, drink a great deal of alcohol. 술을 고래처럼[벌떡벌떡] 마시다.
feed the fishes, **a**) be seasick. 뱃멀미하다. **b**) drown. 물에 빠져 죽다; 고기밥이 되다.
feel like a fish out of water, feel uncomfortable in unsuitable surroundings. 뭍에 오른 물고기처럼 어릿거리다; 낯선 환경 따위에 어울리지 않다.
neither fish, flesh, nor fowl, (of indeterminate character) neither one thing nor another. 이도 저도 아닌; 정체를 모를.
— *vi.* (P1,3) **1** catch or try to catch fish. 물고기를 잡다; 낚시질하다. ¶ *~ with a rod and line* 낚시하다 / *~ in the river* 강에서 낚시질하다. **2** 《*for*》 search for pearls, etc. in water; try to find anything hidden, buried, etc. (진주 따위를) 채취하다; (감춰진 것을) 찾다. ¶ *~ in a pocket for a coin* 동전을 찾기 위해 호주머니 속을 뒤지다. **3** 《*for*》 try to get information, etc., usu. by indirect methods. (간접적 또는 책략을 써서 정보 따위를) 얻어[이끌어]내다; 찾아내다. ¶ *~ for compliments* 유도하여 치렛말을 하게 하다 / *~ for an invitation* 초청하도록 유도하다.
— *vt.* **1** (P6) catch (fish); try to catch fish in (a lake, etc.). (물고기)를 잡다[낚다]; (강·호수 따위)에서 낚시질하다. ¶ *~ salmon* 연어를 잡다 / *~ a river* 강에서 낚시질하다. **2** (P7,13) 《*out, up, from*》 pull or draw out (something or someone) from water or as if from water. …을 물속에서 끌어올리다; 끌어[끄집어]내다. ¶ *~ out a secret* 비밀을 들춰내다 / *~ someone from the water* 아무를 물 속에서 끌어내다. [E.]
fish in troubled waters, try to make profits from the difficulties of others. 혼란을 틈타 도둑질을 하다.
fish out (=*exhaust the fish of, catch all the fish of*) *a pond, etc.* (못 따위)에서 고기를 다 잡아 씨를 말리다.

fish·er [fíʃər] *n.* Ⓒ **1** fisherman. 어부; 낚

시꾼. **2** an animal that catches fish for food. 물고기를 잡아먹는 동물. **3** a fishing boat. 어선(漁船); 낚싯배.

·fish·er·man [fíʃərmən] *n.* Ⓒ (*pl.* **-men** [-mən]) **1** a man who fishes for a living or for sport. 어부; 낚시꾼. **2** 《*arch.*》 a ship used in fishing. 어선; 낚싯배.

fish·er·y [fíʃəri] *n.* (*pl.* **-er·ies**) **1** Ⓤ business of catching fish. 어업(漁業). **2** Ⓒ a fishing ground. 어장(漁場).

fish hawk [∠∠] *n.* a large bird that feeds on fish (also called osprey). 물수리.

fish·hook [fíʃhùk] *n.* Ⓒ a barbed hook for catching fish. 낚시; 낚싯바늘.

·fish·ing [fíʃiŋ] *n.* Ⓤ the act of catching fish for a living or for sport. 낚시질; 고기잡이; 어업. ¶ *go* ~ 낚시질을 하러가다 / *be fond of* ~ 낚시질을 좋아하다.

fishing boat [∠-∠] *n.* a boat used in fishing. 어선; 낚싯배.

fishing line [∠-∠] *n.* a line used in fishing. 낚싯줄.

fishing net [∠-∠] *n.* a net used in fishing. 어망.

fishing rod [∠-∠] *n.* a rod used in fishing. 낚싯대.

fishing tackle [∠- ∠-] *n.* an instrument for fishing. 낚시 도구.

fish·mon·ger [fíʃmʌ̀ŋgər] *n.* Ⓒ 《esp. Brit.》 a person who sells fish; a dealer in fish. 생선 장수.

fish·plate [fíʃplèit] *n.* a steel plate joining rails of railway line. (철로의) 이음판.

fish pond [∠∠] *n.* a pond in which fish are kept or bred. 양어지(養魚池); 양어못.

fish torpedo [∠-∠-] *n.* a torpedo shaped like a fish. 어뢰.

fish·wife [fíʃwàif] *n.* Ⓒ (*pl.* **-wives**) **1** a woman who sells fish. 여자 생선 장수. **2** a vulgar, scolding woman. 입이 건 여자.

fish·wives [fíʃwàivz] *n.* pl. of **fishwife.**

fish·y [fíʃi] *adj.* (**fish·i·er, fish·i·est**) **1** like a fish. 물고기 같은. ¶ ~ *smell* 비린내. **2** full of fish. 물고기가 많은. ¶ *a* ~ *lake* 물고기가 많은 호수. **3** 《*colloq.*》 arousing suspicion; not probable; unlikely. 의심스러운; 있을 법하지 않은. ¶ *a* ~ *story* 의심스러운 이야기 / *His story sounds* ~. 그의 이야기는 의심스럽다. ●**fish·i·ly** [-li] *adv.* [E.]

fis·sile [físəl] *adj.* **1** easily split. 분열하기 쉬운; 분열성의. **2** capable of nuclear fission. 핵분열성의. [↓]

fis·sion [fíʃən] *n.* ⓊⒸ **1** the act of splitting into parts. 분열; 열개(裂開). ¶ *atomic* 〔*nuclear*〕 ~ 원자핵〔핵〕 분열. **2** 《biol.》 a process of reproduction by splitting. 분열; 분체(分體). ¶ *grow by* ~ 분열 증식하다. [L. *findo* cleave]

fis·sion·a·ble [fíʃənəbl] *adj.* capable of nuclear fission. 핵분열을 일으키는; 핵분열성의.

fis·sure [fíʃər] *n.* Ⓒ a long, narrow opening; a crack. 갈라진 틈; 균열. ¶ *a* ~ *in the earth* 땅의 갈라진 데. ― *vi., vt.* (P1; 6) cleave; split. 갈라지다; 금이 가다; 갈라지게 하다. [→fission]

∗fist [fist] *n.* Ⓒ **1** a clenched hand. 주먹. ¶ *He struck with his* ~. 그는 주먹으로 쳤다 / *He shook his* ~ *at me.* 그는 내게 주먹을 휘둘렀다. **2** 《*colloq.*》 a hand. 손. ¶ *Give us your* ~. 악수하세. **3** 《*colloq.*》 handwriting. 필적. ¶ *He writes a good* ~. 그는 필적이 좋다. ― *vt.* (P6) strike (something) with the fist. …을 주먹으로 치다. [E.]

fist·ic [fístik] *adj.* having to do with fighting with the fists. 권투의. ¶ *a* ~ *contest* 권투 경기.

fist·i·cuffs [fístikʌ̀fs] *n. pl.* fighting with the fists. 주먹 싸움; 주먹다짐. ¶ *come to* ~ 주먹 싸움이 되다. [*fist*]

fis·tu·la [fístjulə] *n.* (*pl.* **-las** or **-lae**) a pipe-like organ in various insects and other animals. (곤충 따위의) 누공(瘻孔); 누관(瘻管). [L. =pipe]

fis·tu·lae [fístjuliː] *n.* pl. of **fistula.**

:fit[1] [fit] *adj.* (**fit·ter, fit·test**) **1** 《*for*》 suitable or suited for; good enough. 적합한; 어울리는; 걸맞은. ¶ *food* ~ *for dogs* 개에 적합한 먹이 / ~ *to drink* 마시기에 알맞은 / *a dress* ~ *for a queen* 여왕에게 걸맞은 옷 / *decide on* ~ *time and place* 적당한 때와 장소를 정하다. **2** proper; right. 적절한. ¶ *Do as you think* ~. 네가 옳다고 생각하는 대로 해라 / *It is not* ~ *for me to do such a thing.* 나는 그런 일을 하기에 적절치가 않다. **3** ready; prepared; in suitable condition. 준비가 된; 곧 …할 것 같은. ¶ *crops* ~ *for gathering* 어느 때고 수확할 수 있는 농작물 / *He is* ~ *to go to war.* 그는 어느 때고 출정할 채비가 돼 있다 / *The ship is now* ~ *for sea.* 배는 이제 언제고 항해할 수 있다. **4** in good health or condition. 건강이〔상태가〕 좋은. ¶ *He keeps* ~ *by playing tennis.* 그는 테니스를 함으로써 항상 좋은 건강 상태를 유지하고 있다 / *He's in no* ~ *state to do his job.* 그는 일을 할 수 있는 상태가 아니다 / *I'm feeling as* ~ *as a fiddle now.* 나는 지금은 몸 컨디션이 아주 좋다.

see* 〔*think*〕 *fit (=*consider proper or advisable; decide*) ***to do.*** (…하는 것이) 정당하다고 생각하다; …하기로 정하다.

the survival of the fittest, 《biol.》 the course of events by which plants and animals best suited to the conditions around them live while those not suited to these conditions die. 적자 생존(適者生存).

― *v.* (**fit·ted** or **fit, fit·ting**) *vt.* **1** (P6) be suitable for or to (something or someone); suit. …에 적합하다; 맞다. ¶ ~ *every occasion* 어떤 경우에도 적합하다 / *The name fits him perfectly.* 그 이름이 그에게 꼭 맞는다 / *He fits the description.* 그는 인상서와 꼭 들어 맞는다 / *This coat doesn't* ~ *him well.* 이 코트는 그에게 잘 맞지 않는다. **2** (P7,13,20) 《*to, in, for*》 make (someone or something) suitable; adapt; prepare. …을 맞게〔적합하게〕 하다; (할 수 있도록) …에게 준비시키다. ¶ ~ *oneself for a new job* 새 일에 적응시키다 / ~ *the punishment to the crime* 범죄에 적합하게 처벌을 하다 / *This school fits students for college.* 이 학교는 학생들에게 대학 갈 준비 교육을 시킨다 / *The hard training fitted us to win the championship.* 고된 훈련은 우리들이 우승하는 데 밑거름이 되었다. **3** (P7,13) 《*with*》 furnish; supply; equip. …에 공급하다; …에 갖추다; 설비하다. ¶ ~ *a door with a handle* 문에 손잡이를 달다 / ~ *a library with shelves* 도서실에 서가를 설비하다. — *vi.* (P1,2A) be suitable or proper; agree. 맞다; 적합하다. ¶ ~ *like a glove* 꼭 맞다 / *The door fits badly.* 문이 잘 맞지 않는다.

fit in, 《*with*》 be in harmony; accord. (…와) 일치하다; 조화하다. ¶ *She doesn't* ~ *in with others.* 그녀는 남들과 어울리지를 못한다.

fit out 〔***up***〕, **a**) furnish; prepare for use. 장비하다. ¶ ~ *out a ship for a voyage* 항해를 할 수 있도록 배의 의장(艤裝)을 하다. **b**) get ready; prepare; supply with things necessary or suitable. 준비〔채비〕하다; …에 필요품을 조달하다; 필요한 설비를 하다. ¶ *They were being fitted up with electric light.* 전등불을 달고 있었다.

— *n.* **1** Ⓤ the state or quality of being fit. 적합(성). ¶ *The* ~ *of this coat is perfect.* 이 상의의 맞음새가 완벽하다. **2** Ⓒ a thing that fits. 적합한 것《꼭 맞는 의복 따위》. [M.E. *fitten*; akin to M.D. *vitten* befit]

·fit² [fit] *n.* Ⓒ **1** a sudden, violent attack of disease; loss of consciousness; convulsions. (병의) 발작; 졸도; 경련. ¶ *a* ~ *of epilepsy* 간질의 발작 / *go into fits* 졸도하다 / *He had a* ~ *of coughing.* 그는 기침이 발작했다. **2** a sudden, temporary outburst of emotion. (감정의) 폭발. ¶ *a* ~ *of anger* 발작적인 노여움. **3** a short period of doing one thing. (일시적인) 기분; 변덕. ¶ *when the* ~ *is on* 기분이 내키면. [E.]

by fits (***and starts***)***,*** not regularly; from time to time. 때때로(생각난 듯이); 발작적으로. ¶ *He works by fits and starts.* 그는 때때로 생각난 듯이 일을 한다.

throw a fit, behave as one who is shocked, infuriated, etc. 매우 흥분하다; 격노하다.

fit·ful [fítfəl] *adj.* irregular; changeable. 발작적인; 일시적 기분의; 변덕의. ¶ *a baby's* ~ *crying* 갓난아기의 발작적인 울음. ●**fit·ful·ly** [-i] *adv.* **fit·ful·ness** [-nis] *n.* [*fit²*]

fit·ly [fítli] *adv.* in a suitable manner; at a proper time. 적합하도록; 꼭; 적당히; 적시(適時)에. [*fit¹*]

fit·ness [fítnis] *n.* Ⓤ good condition; suitability. 적당; 적절; 적합성; 건강. [*fit¹*]

fit·ter [fítər] *n.* Ⓒ **1** a person who fits. 적합자. **2** a person who fits dresses, suits, etc. on people. (옷을) 가봉해 주는 사람. **3** a man who fits together or adjusts the parts of a machine. (기계의) 조립공; 정비사. [*fit¹*]

fit·ting [fítiŋ] *adj.* suitable; proper. 어울리는; 적당〔적절〕한. ¶ *come at a* ~ *moment* 적절한 때에 오다. — *n.* Ⓒ **1** the act of trying on clothes to see if they fit. (가봉한 옷을) 입혀보기. **2** 《*pl.*》 necessary fixtures of a house, shop, etc.; furnishings. 세간; 가구〔도구〕류; 부(속)품. ¶ *office fittings* 사무용 기구. [*fit¹*]

:five [faiv] *n.* **1** Ⓤ the number between four and six; 5. 다섯. **2** Ⓒ a group of 5 persons, esp. on a basketball team. 5인 1조; (특히) 농구 팀. — *adj.* of 5. 다섯의; 5의. [E.]

the five senses, sight, hearing, taste, smell, and touch. 오관(五官).

five·fold [fáivfòuld] *adj.* **1** five times as many or much; repeated five times. 5배〔중, 겹〕의. **2** having five parts. 5부분으로 된. — *adv.* **1** five times. 5배로. **2** to a fivefold degree. 다섯 배나; 5배나.

fiv·er [fáivər] *n.* Ⓒ 《U.S. *colloq.*》 a five-dollar bill, 5달러짜리 지폐; 《Brit. *colloq.*》 a five-pound note. 5파운드짜리 지폐.

:fix [fiks] *vt.* **1** (P6,13) make (something) firm; fasten. …을 고정시키다〔달다〕. ¶ ~ *a handle to an ax* 도끼에 자루를 붙박다 / ~ *a feather in one's hat* 모자에 깃털을 달다 / ~ *the date in my mind* 〔*memory*〕 그 날짜를 마음〔기억〕에 단단히 새겨두다. **2** (P6,13) set definitely; determine; establish (one's residence, etc.). …을 결정하다; (주거 따위)를 정하다. ¶ ~ *a price* 가격을 정하다 / ~ *a day for a meeting* 회합의 날짜를 정하다 / *He fixed himself in the city.* 그는 시내에 주거를 정했다. **3** (P6,13) direct (the eyes, one's attention, etc.) steadily; (of an object) attract and hold (one's attention). (눈길·주의)를 돌리다〔쏟다〕; (주의)를 끌다. ¶ ~ *the mind on a book* 정신을 책에 쏟다 / *The sight fixed my attention.* 그 광경이 내 주의를 끌었다. **4** (P6,13) 《esp. U.S.》 arrange; set right; 《U.S.》 prepare. …을 정돈하다; (식사 따위)의 채비〔준비〕를 하다. ¶ ~ *one's hair* (빗질하여) 머리를 비다듬다 / ~ *a room* 방을 정돈하다 / *What time shall I* ~ *supper?* 몇 시에 저녁 식사를 준비할까요. **5** (P6) 《U.S.》 repair. …을 고치다; 조정하다. ¶ ~ *one's car* 차(車)를 수리하다 / *have one's watch fixed* 시계를 수리시키다. **6** (P13) put or place (blame, etc.) on someone. (책임·죄 따위)를 …에게 씌우다; …의 탓으로 돌리다. ¶ *He fixed the blame on the leader.* 그 책임을 지도자의 탓으로 돌렸다. **7** (P6,13) ⓐ 《chem.》 make (a gas, etc.) solid. (가스 따위)를 응고시키다. ⓑ 《photo.》 make (a negative) permanent. (사진)을 정착시키다. ⓒ 《dyeing》 make (a color) fast. (색)을 고착시키다.

— *vi.* (P3) become fixed. 고정하다; 고착되

다; 응고하다.

fix on 〔***upon***〕 (=*decide on; choose*) *something* or *someone.* …으로 (결)정하다; …을 선정하다. ¶ ~ *on a date for a journey* 여행 날짜를 정하다.

fix up, 《orig. U.S. *colloq.*》 **a**) provide suitable arrangements for. (남을 위해) 준비〔마련〕하다; 주선하다. ¶ *I will ~ you up for the night.* 하룻밤 묵으실 준비를 하죠 / *He fixed me up with a job.* 그는 내게 일자리를 마련해 주었다. **b**) settle; arrange. 정하다. ¶ ~ *up a date for* …할 날짜를 정하다. **c**) organize. 조직〔편성〕하다. **d**) come to a friendly understanding. (협조적으로) 해결하다; 타협하다. ¶ ~ *up a quarrel* 〔*differences*〕 분쟁을〔불화를〕 해결하다. **e**) 《U.S. *colloq.*》 mend; repair. 고치다; 수리하다. ¶ *have one's watch fixed up* 시계를 수리시키다.

— ***n.*** Ⓒ 《*colloq.*》 a difficult position. 어려운〔괴로운〕 입장; 궁지. ¶ *I'm in a ~.* 궁지에 빠져 있다. [L. *figo* fasten]

fix·a·tion [fikséiʃən] *n.* Ⓤ the act of fixing; the state of being fixed. 고정; 정착; 고착.

fix·a·tive [fíksətiv] *adj.* serving to prevent fading or change. 정착〔고정〕하는; 고착성의. — *n.* Ⓒ a substance for keeping something from fading or changing. 정착제〔액〕.

•**fixed** [fikst] *adj.* firmly established; not movable; settled; steady. 고정한; 정착한; 확고한; 불변의. ¶ *a ~ price* 정가 / *a ~ income* 고정 수입 / *a ~ fact* 움직일 수 없는 사실 / *a ~ star* 항성 / *a ~ purpose* 확고한 목적 / *a ~ stare* 응시(凝視).

fix·ed·ly [fíksidli] *adv.* in a fixed manner; without change. 고정〔정착〕하여; 확정적으로; 확고히. ¶ *look ~ at someone* 아무를 응시하다.

fix·ture [fíkstʃər] *n.* Ⓒ **1** something permanently put in place. 정착물; 비치품; 비품; 설비. ¶ *electric light fixtures* 전등(電燈)설비. **2** 《*colloq.*》 a person long established in the same place or position. 같은 곳〔자리〕에 오래 붙박혀 있는 사람. [L. *figo*]

fizz [fiz] *vi.* (P1,2A) make a hissing sound. 쉬잇 소리를 내다. — *n.* **1** Ⓒ a hissing sound. 쉬잇 소리. **2** Ⓤ a bubbling drink, such as champagne or soda water. (소다수·샴페인 따위) 거품이 이는 음료수. [Imit.]

fiz·zle [fízl] *vi.* (P1,2) **1** make a hissing sound. 쉬잇하다. **2** 《*colloq.*》 《*out*》 come to a poor end; fail. 흐지부지 끝나다; 실패하다. ¶ *The plans for the picnic fizzled out.* 소풍 계획은 흐지부지되었다. — *n.* Ⓒ **1** a hissing sound. 쉬잇 소리. **2** 《*colloq.*》 a failure. 실패. [Imit.] [↑]

fjord [fjɔːrd] *n.* =fiord.

flab·ber·gast [flǽbərgæ̀st / -gɑ̀ːst] *vt.* (P6) 《*colloq.*》 astonish greatly; amaze. …을 깜짝 놀라게〔당황케〕 하다. [↓, *aghast*]

flab·by [flǽbi] *adj.* (**-bi·er, bi·est**) not firm; soft; weak. 연약한; 축 늘어진; 처진. ¶ ~ *muscles* 늘어진 근육 / ~ *will* 연약한 의지. ● **flab·bi·ly** [-li] *adv.* [*flap*]

flac·cid [flǽksid] *adj.* **1** hanging loosely; soft. (살이) 축 늘어진; 처진; 단단치 못한. ¶ ~ *muscles* 단단치 못한 근육. **2** (of character, etc.) weak; lacking moral force. (사람·성격·언동 따위가) 기력 없는; 연약한; 헤식은; 흐게늦은. [L. *flaccus*]

:flag[1] [flæg] *n.* Ⓒ **1** a piece of cloth with marks or patterns, used as a symbol of a nation, a state, etc. 기(旗). ¶ *a national ~* 국기 / *fly* 〔*hoist*〕 *a ~* 기를 달다〔걸다〕 / *strike one's* 〔*the*〕 ~ 기를 내리다; 항복하다. **2** a piece of cloth with or without a symbol, used to give information. (신호(信號))기. ¶ *hang the white ~* 백기를 걸어 항복하다.

under the flag of, ranged on the side of. …의 깃발〔기치〕 아래 (모여).

— *vt.* (**flagged, flag·ging**) (P6) **1** put a flag on (something); decorate (something) with flags. …에 기를 걸다; …을 기로 장식하다. ¶ ~ *the streets* 거리에 기를 달다. **2** signal or communicate (orders, etc.) by flags. …을 기로 신호하다. [→flap]

flag[2] [flæg] *n.* Ⓒ 《bot.》 a plant with large, showy flowers and sword-shaped leaves; the iris. (황)창포. [Du.]

flag[3] [flæg] *vi.* (**flagged, flag·ging**) **1** hang loosely. 축 늘어지다; 시들다. ¶ *plants flagging from drought* 가뭄으로 축 늘어진 식물. **2** grow weak; die out. 쇠약해지다; 약해지다. ¶ *My interest in the subject is flagging more and more.* 문제에 대한 나의 흥미가 점점 시들해지고 있다. [→flabby]

flag[4] [flæg] *n.* Ⓒ a flat stone for pavement; a flagstone. 포석(鋪石); 판석(板石). — *vt.* (**flagged, flag·ging**) (P6) pave (a road, etc.) with flagstones. …에 포석으로 포장하다. [→flake]

flag·el·late [flǽdʒəlèit] *vt.* (P6) whip. …을 매질〔채찍질〕하다. ¶ ~ *a criminal* 범죄자를 매질하다. [→flail]

flag·el·la·tion [flæ̀dʒəléiʃən] *n.* Ⓤ the act of whipping. 매질; 채찍질; 편달.

flag·ging [flǽgiŋ] *adj.* tired; weak. 지친; 약한. — *n.* **1** Ⓤ flagstones. 포석(鋪石). **2** Ⓒ a pavement made of flagstones. 포석을 깐 길. [*flag*[4]]

fla·gi·tious [flədʒíʃəs] *adj.* shamefully wicked. 흉악한; 극악한; 파렴치한. [L. *flagitium* crime]

flag·man [flǽgmən] *n.* (*pl.* **-men** [-mən]) Ⓒ **1** a person who carries a flag. 기수(旗手). **2** a person who signals at a railroad crossing, etc. (철도의) 신호수; 건널목지기. [*flag*[1]]

flag·on [flǽgən] *n.* Ⓒ a

〈flagon〉

vessel for liquids, usu. having a handle and a spout, and often a lid; a large bottle. (식탁용) 포도주병《귀때·손잡이가 있고 뚜껑이 달려 있음》. [F.]

flag·pole [flǽgpòul] *n.* Ⓒ a pole from which a flag is flown. 깃대. [*flag*[1]]

fla·grant [fléigrənt] *adj.* outrageous; very wicked; scandalous. 언어도단의; 극악무도한; 악명 높은. ¶ *a ~ sinner* 흉악한 죄인. ● **fla·grant·ly** [-li] *adv.* [L. *flagro* blaze]

flag·ship [flǽgʃìp] *n.* Ⓒ a ship that carries the commander of a fleet. 기함(旗艦). [*flag*[1]]

flag·staff [flǽgstæ̀f, -stɑ̀:f] *n.* =flagpole.

flag station [⌐-⌐] *n.* Ⓒ a railroad station at which trains stop only when a signal is given. 신호 정차역《신호가 있을 때만 열차가 섬》.

flag·stone [flǽgstòun] *n.* Ⓒ a large, flat stone for pavements, etc. 판석(板石); 포석(鋪石). [*flag*[4]]

flail [fleil] *n.* Ⓒ an old-fashioned instrument for beating grain by hand. 도리깨. — *vt., vi.* (P6; 1) 《*on*》 use a flail. 도리깨질하다. [L. *flagellum* whip]

flair [flɛər] *n.* **1** Ⓒ keen perception. 직감적 식별력; 날카로운 안목. ¶ *have a ~ for good poetry* 좋은 시를 식별할 수 있을 만큼 예민한 감각을 지니고 있다. **2** Ⓤ natural talent or ability. (타고난) 능력; 재능. [F.]

·flake [fleik] *n.* Ⓒ a small, light mass. (눈·깃털의) 소편(小片); 작은 조각. ¶ *flakes of snow* 눈송이. — *vi.* (P1,2A) 《*off, away*》 fall away in flakes. 박편(薄片)으로 떨어져 내리다; (of snow) fall in flakes. 눈이 펄펄 내리다. — *vt.* (P6) **1** make (snow, etc.) fall in flakes. …을 펄펄 내리게 하다. **2** separate (something) into flakes. …을 박편으로 하다. ● **flake·like** [⌐làik] *adj.* [Scand.]

flak·y [fléiki] *adj.* (**flak·i·er, flak·i·est**) **1** consisting of flakes. 박편(薄片)의; 조각조각의. **2** easily broken into flakes. 부서져 벗겨지기 쉬운. [↑]

flam·beau [flǽmbou] *n.* Ⓒ (*pl.* **-beaux** [-z]) 《F.》 a flaming torch. 불타는 횃불.

flam·boy·ant [flæmbɔ́iənt] *adj.* **1** gorgeously brilliant; excessively decorated. (문체·몸차림이) 야하게 화려한; (장식이) 지나치게 야단스러운. **2** of or having the style of late French Gothic architecture. 플랑부아양 양식의; 불길 모양의. ● **flam·boy·ant·ly** [-li] *adv.* [↓]

:flame [fleim] *n.* **1** ⓊⒸ glowing, red or yellow tongues of light from a blazing fire. 불꽃; 불길; 화염. ¶ *catch ~* 타오르다. **2** Ⓒ a thing or condition like flame. 불꽃 같은 광휘(光輝); 광채. **3** Ⓒ a burning feeling; passion. 정열; 정염; 격정. ¶ *flames of anger* 불길 같은 노여움 / *flames of love* 불같은 애욕. **4** Ⓒ 《*sl.*》 a sweetheart. 연인; 애인. ¶ *an old ~ of mine* 나의 옛 애인.

burst into flame(s), burst out in flames; begin to burn. 확 타오르다; 타기 시작하다.

commit to the flames, burn up; reduce to ashes. 불태우다; 소각하다. ¶ *commit a letter to the flame(s)* 편지를 태워버리다.

fan the flame, stir up someone's feelings or passions. …의 감정〔정열〕을 부채질하다.

in flames, bursting into flames; burning. 불타고.

— *vi* (P1,2A,3) **1** burn with flames; burn as a flame. 불꽃을 올리며 타다; 불꽃처럼 타오르다. ¶ *The western sky flames.* 서쪽 하늘이 벌겋게 불타고 있다. **2** blush deeply or suddenly. (얼굴이) 붉어지다; 홍조를 띠다. ¶ *Her face flamed with excitement.* 그녀 얼굴이 흥분으로 붉어졌다. **3** give out a bright light. (불꽃처럼) 빛나다; 번뜩이다. **4** have or show a burning feeling; burst out quickly and hotly (with anger, etc.). (정열 따위가) 타오르다; 격분하다. [L. *flamma*]

flame out (up), burst out in flame or with anger. 확 불타오르다; 격노하다.

fla·men·co [flɑːméŋkou] *n.* Ⓤ a strongly rhythmic dancing of the Andalusian gypsies. 플라멩코《스페인 Andalusia 지방의 집시 춤》. — *adj.* of the gypsies. 집시의; 플라멩코조(調)의. [Sp.]

flame·throw·er [fléimθròuər] *n.* Ⓒ a weapon that throws a spray of oil that catches fire in the air. 화염 방사기(火焰放射器). [*flame*]

flam·ing [fléimiŋ] *adj.* **1** in a condition of burning with flames. 불타(고 있)는. **2** very bright and hot. 빛나는; 불타는 것 같은; 염열의. ¶ *a ~ August* 찌는 듯한 8월 / *the ~ sun* 불타듯 이글거리는 태양. **3** bright red or bright yellow in color. (빛이) 불타듯이 붉은; 샛노랑의. **4** (of feeling) passionate; ardent. 열렬한; 정열에 불타는. ¶ *~ patriotism* 열렬한 애국심 / *the ~ passion of youth* 청춘의 불타는 정열. [↑]

fla·min·go [fləmíŋgou] *n.* Ⓒ (*pl.* **-gos** or **-goes**) a tropical wading bird with long legs, a long neck and webbed feet. 플라밍고; 홍학(紅鶴). [Port.]

flam·ma·ble [flǽməbəl] *adj.* 《U.S.》 likely to catch fire easily and quickly. 불붙기〔타기〕 쉬운. ¶ *~ gas* 인화성 가스. [*flame*]

flan [flæn] *n.* Ⓒ an open tart containing fruit. 과일이 든 파이. [F.]

flange [flændʒ] *n.* Ⓒ 《mech.》 a projecting rim or collar on a wheel, pipe, rail, etc. for keeping it in place. 플랜지《날밑 모양의 관(管)을 잇기 위해 덧붙인 것》; (차 바퀴의) 테두리; (레일의) 발. [? F.]

⟨flange⟩

·flank [flæŋk] *n.* Ⓒ **1** the fleshy side of an animal or a person between the ribs and the hip; a piece of meat cut from this part. 옆구리; 옆구리살. **2** (of a building, a mountain, etc.) the side. (건물·산 따위의) 측면. **3** the right or left side of an army, a fleet, etc. (군대·함대 따위의) 측면; (좌우의) 익(翼). ¶ *a ~ attack* 측면 공격 / *cover a ~* 측면을 엄호하다 / *turn the ~ of the enemy* 적의 측면을 돌아 배후를 찌르다.

in flank, at, on or from side. 측면에(서); 측면으로부터. ¶ *take in ~* 측면을 찌르다.

— *vt.* (P6) **1** be at the side of (someone or something). …의 옆에 서다; …의 측면에 있다. ¶ *Large trees flanked the road.* 큰 나무들이 길 옆에 늘어서 있었다. **2** get around the right or left side of (someone or something). …의 측면을 우회하다. **3** attack (an enemy, etc.) from the side. …의 측면을 공격하다. **4** protect at the side. …의 측면을 방어하다.

●**flank·er** [⌐ər] *n.* [F.]

flan·nel [flǽnl] *n.* Ⓤ **1** a soft, warm woolen cloth. 플란넬. ¶ *cotton ~* 면(綿)플란넬. **2** 《*pl.*》 clothes made of flannel; woolen underwear. 플란넬제(製)의 의류(衣類); 두툼한 모직의 속옷. ¶ *~ trousers* 플란넬 바지. **3** Ⓒ 《Brit.》 =washcloth. — *adj.* made of flannel. 플란넬제(製)의. [Welsh.]

flan·nel·et, -ette [flæ̀nəlét] *n.* Ⓤ cotton cloth like flannel. 면(綿) 플란넬.

·**flap** [flæp] *v.* (**flapped, flap·ping**) *vi.* (P1,2A) **1** (of wings) move up and down. (새가 날개를) 퍼덕이다. **2** (of a wide, flat object) move lightly with a slight noise. (넓고 얇은 것이) 펄럭이다; 나부끼다. ¶ *A flag flaps in the wind.* 깃발이 바람에 펄럭인다 / *The curtains flapped in the breeze.* 커튼이 미풍에 펄럭였다.

— *vt.* (P6,7) **1** move (the wings) up and down. (새가 날개)를 퍼덕거리다. ¶ *A bird flaps its wings.* 새가 날개를 퍼덕인다. **2** cause (a wide, flat object) to move lightly with a slight noise. …을 펄럭이게 하다. ¶ *The wind flapped the sails.* 돛이 바람을 받아 펄럭거렸다. **3** strike (someone or something) with something broad and flat. …을 탁 때리다. ¶ *~ flies away* 〔*off*〕 딱 때려 파리를 쫓아버리다.

— *n.* Ⓒ **1** a broad and flat object that hangs loosely, attached at one side only. (한 끝만 매달려) 축 늘어진 것; (봉투·호주머니 따위의) 늘어진 닫개. ¶ *the ~ of an envelope* 봉투의 접혀 늘어진 부분. **2** a flapping motion or noise. 퍼덕〔펄럭〕임; 딱 때리기; 그 소리. [Imit.]

flap·jack [flǽpdʒæ̀k] *n.* Ⓒ **1** a kind of large pancake. 핫케이크류의 과자. **2** a flat case for face-powder. (둥근 화장용) 콤팩트. [↑]

flap·per [flǽpər] *n.* Ⓒ **1** something broad and flat used for striking with. 퍼덕〔펄럭〕이는 것; 딱 때리는 것; 파리채. **2** a broad fin. (물고기의 넓은) 지느러미. [↑]

flare [flɛər] *vi.* (P1,2A) **1** burn unsteadily. 불꽃이 흔들거리다. **2** signal by lights. 불빛으로 신호하다. **3** spread out in the shape of a bell. 종 모양으로 벌어지다. **4** burst out into sudden anger. 격노하다. — *vt.* **1** signal (something) by lights. …을 불빛으로 신호하다. **2** spread out. …을 점차 바깥쪽으로 벌어지게 하다.

flare up 〔***out***〕, **a**) burst into flames. 확 타오르다. **b**) get angry suddenly. 격노하다.

— *n.* Ⓒ **1** an unsteady, bright light. 너울〔흔들〕거리는 (불)빛; 확 타오름. ¶ *the ~ of torches in the wind* 바람에 너울거리는 횃불. **2** a dazzling light used for a signal. 섬광 신호. **3** (of anger, etc.) an outburst. (노여움 따위의) 폭발. **4** a part spreading out into a bell shape. (종·나팔 모양의) 벌어짐〔벌어진 부분〕. **5** a part that spreads out or curves. (스커트 따위의) 플레어. ¶ *a ~ skirt* 플레어 스커트. [?]

flare path [⌐⌐] *n.* the area illuminated to guide aircraft on a landing strip. (비행장의) 조명 활주로.

flare-up [flέərʌ̀p] *n.* Ⓒ **1** a sudden outburst of flame or light. (불꽃의) 확 타오르기; (빛의) 번쩍하기. **2** 《*fig.*》 a sudden outburst of anger, violence, fighting, etc. (발작적인) 격노; (가라앉았던 폭력·싸움의) 돌발.

flar·ing [flέəriŋ] *adj.* **1** flaming. 너울너울 불타는. **2** very bright or showy. 눈에 띄게 화려한; 야한. ¶ *a ~ advertisement* 요란한 광고. **3** gradually spreading outward. 나팔꽃 모양으로 벌어진.

:**flash** [flæʃ] *n.* Ⓒ **1** a sudden bright light. 섬광. ¶ *~ burn* (핵폭탄의 폭발시 방사능에 의한) 섬광 화상 / *a ~ of lightning* (번쩍하는) 번개의 섬광. **2** (of wit, anger, genius, etc.) a sudden and brilliant burst. (재치·천재성 따위의) 번득임; (노여움 따위의) 돌발. ¶ *a ~ of hope* (문득 마음속에 떠오르는) 희망의 빛 / *~ of genius* 천재의 번득임 / *feel a sudden ~ of anger* 돌연 치밀어오르는 노여움을 느끼다. **3** a brief news report, esp. one given by radio. (라디오 따위의) 짤막한 속보; 특보. **4** a very short time; a moment. 극히 짧은 동안; 잠깐; 순간. ¶ *I saw it in a ~.* 그것을 언뜻 보았다 / *I'll be back in a ~.* 곧 돌아옵니다. **5** Ⓤ showy display. 야한 장식. **6** 《cinema》 an exposure of a scene. (영화의) 플래시 《회상적인 순간 장면》.

a flash in the pan, a sudden success that offers no promise for the future. 일시적으로 거둔 반짝 성공.

— *vi.* **1** (P1,2A,3) ⓐ give out a sudden and momentary bright ray of light; shine suddenly. 번쩍하다; 번뜩이다. ¶ *The lightning flashed out from the clouds.* 구름 속에서 번개가 번쩍했다 / *Their armor flashed in the sun.* 그들의 갑주가 햇빛을 받아 번쩍번쩍 빛났다. ⓑ (of the eyes) light up. (눈이) 번쩍

빛나다; 이글거리다. ¶ *His eyes flashed with rage.* 그의 눈은 분노로 이글거렸다. **2** (P 2A,3) ⓐ (of thoughts, ideas, etc.) occur suddenly to the mind; pass suddenly through the mind. (어떤 생각 따위가) 문뜩 머릿속을 스치다; 떠오르다. ¶ *A good idea flashed on me.* 문뜩 좋은 생각이 머릿속에 떠올랐다. ⓑ 《*by*》 come or pass quickly. (스치듯) 홱 지나가다. ¶ *A car flashed by.* 차 한 대가 홱 지나갔다.

— *vt.* (P6,7,13) **1** ⓐ give out (fire, light, etc.) in sudden flashes; cause to flash. …을 번쩍하게 하다〔반사시키다〕; 번쩍 발화시키다; 번뜩이다. ¶ *~ a light* 번쩍 불빛을 비추다 / *~ a sword* 검(劍)을 번뜩이다 / *~ powder* 번쩍하고 화약을 폭발시키다 / *~ light with a mirror* 거울로 빛을 반사시키다 / *Her eyes flashed anger.* 그녀의 눈은 불 같은 노여움으로 이글거렸다. ⓑ direct (light) suddenly. …에게〔…쪽에〕 갑자기 불빛을 비추다. ¶ *~ a lantern in a man's face* 등불을 사나이 얼굴에 비추다. **2** send (a signal, etc.) by flashes of light; communicate (news, etc.) in a short period. (신호)를 불빛을 깜박여 보내다; (뉴스)를 속보하다. ¶ *~ the news by radio* 라디오로 뉴스 속보를 하다 / *The lighthouse flashes signals twice a minute.* 등대는 1분에 두 번 신호 불빛을 보낸다. **3** rapidly direct (a glance, a smile, etc.) at someone. (미소 따위)를 언뜻 보이다; 흘끗 보다. ¶ *~ a smile* 미소를 살짝 지어 보이다. **4** 《*colloq.*》 display showily. …을 과시하다; 자랑해 보이다.

— *adj.* **1** too bright and gay to be in good taste. 야한; 난한; 혼란한. **2** sham. 가짜의. ¶ *~ notes* 위조 지폐. **3** belonging to thieves, etc. (도둑·부랑배 따위) 불량 동아리의; 깡패의; 은어의. ¶ *a ~ term* (도둑·깡패의) 은어. **4** 《Brit. *colloq.*》 fast; sporty. 스포티한; 경쾌한. ¶ *a ~ car* 스포티한 차. **5** happening suddenly. 갑자기 일어나는; 돌발의. [Imit.]

flash·back [flǽʃbæ̀k] *n.* Ⓤ 《cinema》 a sudden transition to the earlier part of a story. (영화에서) 플래시백《전에 있었던 일을 현재 장면에 재현시키기》.

flash·i·ly [flǽʃili] *adv.* in a flashy manner. 야하게; 화려하게.

flash·light [flǽʃlàit] *n.* Ⓒ **1** the light sent out by a lighthouse. (등대의) 회전등. **2** a portable electric light. 회중 전등. **3** a sudden, very bright light for taking photographs. (사진 촬영의) 섬광(등). ¶ *a ~ photograph* 섬광 촬영 사진.

flash·y [flǽʃi] *adj.* (**flash·i·er, flash·i·est**) **1** very bright for a moment. 일시적으로 화려한. **2** looking very bright and good, but worthless. 야한; 굴퉁이의. ¶ *~ ornament* 야한 장식.

〈flask 2〉

flask [flæsk, flɑːsk] *n.* Ⓒ **1** a glass bottle with a narrow neck used in chemical laboratories for holding or heating liquids, etc. 플라스크; 병. **2** a small metal or leather bottle for holding liquids or powder. 수통; 화약통. [O.E. *flasce, flaxe* bottle]

:flat¹ [flæt] *adj.* (**flat·ter, flat·test**) **1** having an even surface; smooth and even; level. 편평〔평탄〕한; 반반한; 납작한; 수평의. ¶ *a ~ roof* 편평한 지붕 / *a ~ piece of land* 평지. **2** not very deep or thick. (접시 따위가) 얕은; 두껍지 않은; 납작한. ¶ *a ~ pan* 속이 얕은 냄비 / *a ~ coin* 납작한 주화. **3** 《as *predicative*》 lying at full length; spread out. 가로 누운; 납작 엎드린. ¶ *He lies ~ on his face.* 엎드려 누워 있다 / *He was ~ on the canvas after the knockdown.* 녹아웃당하여 캔버스에 길게 뻗었다. **4** (of a price, etc.) at a fixed rate; uniform. (값 따위가) 균일한. ¶ *a ~ service charge* 균일 서비스 요금. **5** (of life, commerce, etc.) inactive; lifeless; dull. 활발치 못한; 활기〔생기〕 없는; 따분한. ¶ *~ writing* 생기 없는 문장 / *a ~ stock market* 활기 없는 증권 시장. **6** (of drink, food, etc.) having little or no taste or flavor. 김빠진; 맛 없는. ¶ *~ beer* 김빠진 맥주 / *It tastes ~.* 맛이 없다. **7** (of a tire) empty of air; deflated. (타이어가) 바람이 빠진; 찌부러져 납작한. ¶ *a ~ tire* 바람 빠진 타이어. **8** 《mus.》 lowered a half step below the true pitch. 반음 낮은; 변음의. **9** (of painting) lacking depth or distance; without gloss. (그림이) 변화가 없고 단조로운; 광택이 없는. **10** exact; absolute; complete. 딱; 단호한; 완전한. ¶ *a ~ refusal* 단호한 거절 / *a ~ failure* 완전한 실패; 완패 / *That's ~.* 바로 그렇다. **11** 《*colloq.*》 without money; penniless. 무일푼의.

— *adv.* **1** in a flat manner; evenly. 편평〔평탄〕하게; 납작하게. ¶ *fall ~ on one's face* 앞으로 푹 쓰러지다. **2** exactly; absolutely; completely. 정확히; 단연; 완전히. ¶ *10 seconds ~* 딱 10초; 10초 플랫 / *I tell you ~.* 솔직히 말씀드리면. **3** 《mus.》 half a step below the true pitch. 반음 낮추어.

fall flat, **a**) fall suddenly and at full length. 푹 쓰러지다. **b**) (of a joke, etc.) fail to have the desired effect or to impress. (농담 등이) 기대한 효과가 없다; 실패로 끝나다.

— *n.* Ⓒ **1** something flat; a flat part or side. 편평〔평탄〕한 것; 납작한 것; 편평〔납작〕한 쪽〔면〕. ¶ *the ~ of a hand* 손바닥. **2** a flat piece of land; a plain; a marsh. 평지; 늪. **3** 《*pl.*》 shallows. 여울. **4** 《mus.》 a tone a half step below the true pitch; the sign (♭) showing this. 반음내린 음; 변음; 내림표, 플랫(♭) (opp. sharp).

— *vt., vi.* (**flatted**) (P6; 1) 《rare》 make flat; become flat. 편평〔납작〕하게 하다; 편평

[평탄, 납작]해지다. ●**flat·ness** [´nis] *n.* [N.]

•**flat**² [flæt] *n.* Ⓒ 《Brit.》 an apartment or a set of rooms on the same floor for a single family. 같은 층에서 한 가구가 살 수 있는 구획; 아파트. ¶ *a block of flats* 고층 아파트. [↑]

flat·boat [flǽtbòut] *n.* Ⓒ a large flat-bottomed boat used on a river. (대형의) 너벅선(船).

flat·feet [flǽtfiːt] *n.* pl. of **flatfoot.**

flat·fish [flǽtfiʃ] *n.* Ⓒ (*pl.* **-fish·es** or *collectively* **-fish**) any of a group of fishes with flat bodies and with both eyes on the upper side, such as the flounder. 넙치; 가자미.

flat·foot [flǽtfùt] *n.* Ⓒ (*pl.* **-feet**) a foot with a flattened arch. 편평족.

flat·foot·ed [flǽtfútid] *adj.* of a flatfoot; with flatfeet. 편평족의.

flat·i·ron [flǽtàiərn] *n.* Ⓒ an iron with a flat surface, heated for use in pressing or smoothing cloth. 아이론; 다리미; 인두.

flat·let [flǽtlit] *n.* Ⓒ a two-or three-roomed flat. 방 2-3 개의 아파트.

flat·ly [flǽtli] *adv.* in a flat manner. 단호히; 딱 잘라; 납작[편평]하게.

flat·ten [flǽtn] *vt., vi.* (P6,7; 1,2A) **1** make or become flat. 편평[반반, 납작]하게 하다; 편평[반반, 납작]해지다; 쓰러뜨리다; 쓰러지다. ¶ ~ *crumpled paper* 구겨진 종이를 펴다 / *The violent earthquake flattened the whole town.* 격렬한 지진으로 온 시(市)가 도괴(倒壞)되었다. **2** make dull or tasteless. 활기[기운, 재미] 없게 하다.

flatten out, **a**) flatten down by spreading out. 반반하게 펴다. **b**) (of an aircraft) resume horizontal flight after climbing or diving. 상승 또는 급강하 중의 기체를 수평 비행 자세로 고치다.

•**flat·ter** [flǽtər] *vt.* (P6) **1** praise too much; try to please (someone) with compliments. …에게 아첨하다; 치렛말을 하여 기쁘게 하다. ¶ ~ *the powerful* [*rich*] 권문에[부자에게] 아부하다 / *Oh, you ~ me!* 어머, 말씀을 잘도 하시는군요《아첨의 말에 대해 답하는 말》. **2** make (someone) look better than what is true. …을 실제 이상으로 잘 보이게 [묘사]하다. ¶ *The picture flatters her.* 이 그림은 실물인 그녀보다 낫다. **3** satisfy the vanity of (someone). …의 허영심을 만족시키다; …을 기쁘게 하다. ¶ *He was flattered by her invitation.* 그녀의 초청을 받고 기뻤다. **4** please (the senses, the eye, the ear, etc.). (눈·귀 따위)를 즐겁게 하다. ¶ *The music flattered her ears.* 음악이 그녀의 귀를 즐겁게 했다.

flatter oneself (= *venture to think; be pleased to know or think*) **that ...,** 스스로 …라고[하다고] 생각하다; 자부[우쭐해]하다.

●**flat·ter·er** [-ər] *n.* [? E.]

•**flat·ter·y** [flǽtəri] *n.* (*pl.* **-ter·ies**) **1** Ⓤ the act of flattering. 아첨; 빌붙음. **2** Ⓒ praise, usu. insincere and false. (상대를 기쁘게 하는) 겉치렛말; 감언. [↑]

flat·top [flǽttɑ̀p / -tɔ̀p] *n.* Ⓒ 《U.S. *colloq.*》 an aircraft carrier. 항공 모함(航空母艦). [*flat*¹]

Flau·bert [floubέər], **Gustave** *n.* (1821-80) a French novelist. 플로베르《프랑스의 소설가》.

flaunt [flɔːnt] *vt., vi.* (P6,7; 1,2A) **1** display proudly; parade. (…을) 자랑해 보이다; 과시하다. ¶ ~ *one's knowledge* 지식을 과시하다 / ~ (*one's*) *new clothes* 새옷을 자랑해 보이다. **2** wave or flutter in the wind. (기 따위)를 휘날리게[펄럭이게] 하다; (기 따위가) 나부끼다. ¶ *flags flaunting in the wind* 바람에 나부끼는 깃발. [→planet]

flau·tist [flɔ́ːtist] *n.* =flutist.

fla·vin, -vine [fléivin] *n.* 《chem.》 a yellow dye. 황색 염료. [L. *flavus* yellow]

•**fla·vor,** 《Brit.》 **-vour** [fléivər] *n.* ⓊⒸ **1** taste. 맛; 풍미. **2** a characteristic quality. 두드러진 특질; 풍취; 기미. ¶ *a holiday* ~ 축제 기분 / *an autumn* ~ 추색 / *His story has a ~ of the sea.* 그의 소설엔 바다의 정취가 있다. **3** odor. 향기; 냄새. — *vt.* (P6, 13) **1** 《*with*》 give taste to (something); season. …에 맛을[풍미를] 내다. ¶ ~ *soup with garlic* 수프에 마늘로 풍미를 내다. **2** give a characteristic quality to (something). …에 풍취를 더하다. [L. *fragro* smell sweet]

fla·vor·ing, 《Brit.》 **-vour-** [fléivəriŋ] *n.* Ⓒ a thing used to give a special taste to food or drink. 조미료.

flaw¹ [flɔː] *n.* Ⓒ **1** a crack; a fault; an imperfect point. 금(간 데); 흠(집); 결점. ¶ *a ~ in one's character* 성격상의 결함. **2** 《law》 something omitted. 불비한 점. — *vt., vi.* (P6;1) **1** make a flaw in; crack. 금이 가(게 파)다; 흠집이 나(게 하)다. **2** 《*fig.*》 damage. 손상하다; 손상을 입히다. ● **flaw·less** [´lis] *adj.* [Sw. *flaga* flaw, gust]

flaw² [flɔː] *n.* Ⓒ **1** a sudden rush of wind. 돌풍(突風). **2** a brief storm of wind, with snow, hail, or rain. (눈·비 따위를 동반한) 일시적 폭풍. [↑]

•**flax** [flæks] *n.* Ⓤ **1** 《bot.》 a slender, blue-flowered plant grown for its fiber and seeds. 아마(亞麻). **2** the threadlike fibers from the stem of this plant. 아마의 섬유. [E.]

flax·en [flǽksən] *adj.* **1** like flax; of flax. 아마(亞麻) 같은; 아마(제)의. **2** like the color of flax; pale-yellow. 아마빛의; 담황갈색의. ¶ ~ *hair* 담황갈색 머리.

flax·seed [flǽkssìːd] *n.* the seed of the flax, much used in medicine and in the making of linseed oil. (아마인유(亞麻仁油)를 짜는) 아마의 씨; 아마인.

flay [flei] *vt.* (P6) **1** strip off the skin from (something). (가죽·껍질)을 벗기다.

¶ ~ *a dead ox* 죽은 황소의 가죽을 벗기다. **2** scold or criticize severely. …를 혹평하다; 호되게 꾸짖다. **3** 《*fig.*》 plunder. (돈·재산 따위)를 강탈하다. [E.]

·flea [fliː] *n.* Ⓒ 《insect》 a small, wingless insect which can jump and which sucks the blood of human and other animals. 벼룩. [E.]

a flea in one's ear, a sharp rebuke. 듣기 싫은 소리; 고언(苦言); 빗댐.

flea·bite [flíːbàit] *n.* Ⓒ **1** a bite of the flea; a trifling wound. 벼룩에 물린 자국; 사소한 상처. **2** a small inconvenience. 사소한 불편〔고통〕.

flea market [⌐―⌐] *n.* an open-air market where old or used articles are sold; a street market. 도깨비〔고물〕 시장; 벼룩시장.

fleck [flek] *n.* Ⓒ **1** a spot or streak of color, light, etc., esp. one on the skin. (피부의)반점; 주근깨; 광선; 얼룩. ¶ *flecks of sunlight* 어룽진 일광. **2** a particle. 소편(小片); 소량. ¶ *a ~ of snow* 눈의 세편(細片) / *a ~ of dust* 극히 적은 먼지. — *vt.* (P6) spot (something) with flecks. …에 반점을 찍다. [N.]

flec·tion, 《Brit.》 **flex·ion** [flékʃən] *n.* **1** Ⓤ the act of bending; the state of being bent. 굴곡(屈曲)(작용). **2** Ⓒ a bent part. 굴곡부. **3** 《gram.》 =inflection. [L. *flecto* bend]

fled [fled] *v.* p. and pp. of **flee.**

fledge [fledʒ] *vt.* (P6) **1** bring up (a young bird) until it is able to fly. (날 수 있을 때까지 새끼 새)를 기르다. ¶ *The young birds are not yet fledged enough to fly.* 새끼새들은 아직 날 수 있을 만큼 충분히 자라지 못했다. **2** cover (something) with feathers. …에 깃을 달다; 깃털로 덮다. ¶ ~ *an arrow* 화살에 살깃을 붙이다. — *vi.* (P1) (of birds) grow the feathers necessary for flying. 깃이 다 나다; 날 수 있게 되다. [orig. an adj. =fledged. →fly[1]]

fledged [fledʒd] *adj.* with wings fully developed for flight; able to fly; experienced or capable. 날개깃이 다 난; 날 수 있게 된; 제 구실을 할 수 있게 된.

fledg·ling, 《Brit.》 **fledge-** [flédʒliŋ] *n.* Ⓒ **1** a young bird just able to fly. 부등깃을 이제 막 다 갖춘 새끼 새. **2** an inexperienced person. 미숙자; 풋내기. ¶ *a mere ~* 하찮은 풋내기.

·flee [fliː] *v.* (**fled**) *vi.* (P1,2A,3) **1** ⓐ 《*from, to*》 run away. 달아나다; 도망가다. ¶ ~ *from the angry tiger* 성난 호랑이에게서 달아나다 / ~ *for one's life* 필사적으로 도망치다 / *The troops fled in disorder.* 군대는 뿔뿔이 흩어져 달아났다. ⓑ avoid by going away. (안전한 곳으로) 피(난)하다. ¶ ~ *from the plague* 페스트를 피하다. **2** vanish; disappear swiftly; pass away. 사라지다; 죽다. ¶ *Life had* 〔*was*〕 *fled.* 목숨이 끊어져 있었다 / *The clouds fled before the rising sun.* 구름은 아침해를 받고 사라졌다. — *vt.* (P6) run away from (some place); avoid. …에서 도망치다; …을 피하다. ¶ *He fled the country.* 그는 나라에서 탈출했다. [E.]

fleece [fliːs] *n.* **1** Ⓤ the woolly coat covering a sheep or a similar animal. (양 따위의) 털. **2** Ⓒ the amount of wool cut from a sheep at one time. (한 마리에서) 한 번에 깎아내는 양털. **3** Ⓒ something like wool. 양털 같은 것. ¶ *the fleeces of descending snow* 함박눈 / *a snow-white ~ upon one's head* 머리 위의 양털 같은 백발. — *vt.* **1** (P6,13) 《*of*》 rob; cheat. …로부터 빼앗다; 편취〔갈취〕하다. ¶ ~ *someone of all he possesses* 아무가 가진 것을 모두 빼앗다. **2** (P6) remove the fleece of (a sheep). (양)의 털을 깎다. [E.]

fleec·y [flíːsi] *adj.* (**fleec·i·er, fleec·i·est**) **1** like a fleece. 양털과 같은. ¶ ~ *clouds* 양털구름. **2** covered with fleece. 양털로 덮인. **3** made of fleece. 양털로 만든.

·fleet[1] [fliːt] *n.* Ⓒ **1** a group of warships under one command. 함대. ¶ *a combined ~* 연합 함대. **2** a large group of ships, airplanes, automobiles, etc. moving or working together or under a single ownership. (배의) 선단; (비행기·차 따위의) 대(隊). ¶ *a fishing ~* 어선단. **3** the entire naval force of a nation; a navy. 해군. ¶ *an Admiral of the Fleet*=《U.S.》 *a Fleet Admiral* 해군 원수(元帥). [↓]

·fleet[2] [fliːt] *adj.* 《*poet., lit.*》 swift; rapid. 재빠른; 민속〔쾌속〕한. ¶ *a fleeting glance* 일별 / *a ~ horse* 준마 / ~ *of foot* 발이 빠른. — *vi.* (P1,2A) 《rare》 **1** pass away swiftly and silently; move rapidly. 휙〔빨리〕 지나가다; 재빨리 움직이다. ¶ *The hours fleeted by.* 시간이 순식간에 지나갔다. **2** 《naut.》 change from one place to another; shift. 위치를 바꾸다. — *vt.* cause (time) to pass swiftly. (때)를 순식간에 보내다. ¶ ~ *the time carelessly* 시간을 어영부영 보내다. [E. orig.= float, flow]

fleet·ing [flíːtiŋ] *adj.* passing away swiftly and silently. 빨리〔순식간에〕 지나가는. ¶ ~ *years* 덧없는 세월 / *with a ~ smile* 살짝 웃으며.

Flem·ing [flémiŋ] *n.* Ⓒ **1** a native of Flanders. 플랑드르 사람. **2** a Belgian who speaks Flemish. 플랑드르 말을 쓰는 벨기에 사람. [Du.]

Flem·ish [flémiʃ] *adj.* of Flanders, its people, or their language. 플랑드르(사람·말)의. — *n.* Ⓤ the people of Flanders; their language. 플랑드르 사람·말. [↑]

:flesh [fleʃ] *n.* Ⓤ **1** the soft parts of the body that are between the skin and the bones. 살. ¶ *proud ~* (상처가 아문 자리에 생기는) 군살 / *gain* 〔*put on*〕 ~ 살이 찌다 / *lose ~* 살이 빠지다; 야위다 / *in ~ and blood* 육체〔인간으〕로서. **2** meat. 식용육; 고

기. 參考 이 뜻으로는 보통 meat를 씀. **3** 《*the* ～》 body, not the soul or spirit. 육체. **4** 《*the* ～》 physical desires. 육욕; 수성(獸性). ¶ *the needs of the* ～ 정욕. **5** the soft part of fruit. 과육(果肉). **6** the surface of the human body. 인체의 표면; 피부; 살빛. ¶ *a man of dark* ～ 살빛이 검은 사람. **7** the human race; all living creatures. 사람; 살아 있는 것. ¶ *All* ～ *must die.* 모든 사람은 반드시 죽는다.

flesh and blood, **a**) the human body; human nature. (피가 통하는) 육체; 인간; 인간성. **b**) a person closely related to one. 혈육; 육친.

flesh and fell, **a**) the whole body. 전신. **b**) entirely. 완전히; 전적으로.

go in flesh, become fatter. 살찌다.

go the way of all flesh, die. 죽다.

in the flesh, **a**) alive; in bodily form. 살아; 육체의 형태로. **b**) in person. 직접 본인이; 친히; 손수.

make one's flesh creep, fill him with fear or horror. 섬뜩[쭈뼛]하게 하다.

— *vt.* (P6) **1** incite (a hawk or hound) to hunt by feeding it on the flesh of game it has killed. (매나 개)에게 잡은 짐승의 고기를 맛보여 사냥에의 흥미를 자극하다. **2** 《*fig.*》 incite (someone) to bloodshed. …에게 피비린내나는 참살을 부추기다. **3** thrust (a weapon) into flesh. (칼 따위)를 살에 찌르다. ¶ ～ *one's maiden sword* 처음으로 검에 피를 묻히다. **4** cause to put on flesh; fatten. 살찌우다. [E.]

flesh-col·ored [fléʃkʌ̀lərd] *adj.* of yellowish pink. 살색의.

flesh·ly [fléʃli] *adj.* (**-li·er, -li·est**) **1** of the flesh; bodily. 육체의[적인]. **2** sensual. 육욕의; 관능적인. ¶ ～ *pleasures* 관능적 쾌락. ●**flesh·li·ness** [-nis] *n.*

flesh·pot [fléʃpɑ̀t / -pɔ̀t] *n.* Ⓒ **1** a pot for cooking meat. 고기 요리용 냄비. **2** 《usu. *pl.*》 a place for supplying good food, drink, material comforts, etc. 환락경; 미식(美食); 호화 생활.

flesh wound [ˊˋ] *n.* a wound not reaching the bone or vital organs. 뼈까지 미치지 않은 부상; 경상(輕傷).

flesh·y [fléʃi] *adj.* (**flesh·i·er, flesh·i·est**) **1** fat. 살찐; 비만한. **2** of or like flesh. 육체의. **3** pulpy; very soft. 과육 (모양)의; 연한; 보드라운. ●**flesh·i·ness** [-nis] *n.*

fleur-de-lis [flə̀ːrdəlíːs] *n.* Ⓒ (*pl.* **fleurs-de-lis** [flə̀ːrdəlíːz]) **1** 《bot.》 an iris (flower or plant). 붓꽃 속(屬)의 식물(꽃). **2** an ornament like an iris. 붓꽃 모양의 무늬. [F. =lily flower]

:flew [fluː] *v.* p. of **fly**[1].

flex[1] [fleks] *vt., vi.* (P6; 1) **1** 《anat.》 (of joints) bend or curve. …을 굽히다; 굽다. ¶ ～ *the elbow* [*the knees*] 팔꿈치를[무릎을] 구부리다. **2** 《geol.》 fold. (지층이) 습곡(褶曲)하다. [L. *flecto* bend]

flex[2] [fleks] *n.* 《electr.》 Ⓤ insulated wire for electric current. 절연선(絶緣線). [↑]

flex·i·bil·i·ty [flèksəbíləti] *n.* Ⓤ the quality of being flexible. 구부리기 쉬움; 유연(성). [*flex*[1]]

flex·i·ble [fléksəbəl] *adj.* **1** easily bent without breaking. 구부리기 쉬운; 굴신자재(屈伸自在)의. ¶ *a* ～ *willow wand* 낭창낭창한 버들가지. **2** easily managed or led; adaptable. 어거하기 쉬운; 마음대로 할 수 있는; 융통[순응]성 있는; 유연한. ¶ *a* ～ *system* 융통성 있는 제도 / *a* ～ *schedule* 마음대로 바꿀 수 있는 일정 / *a* ～ *personality* 고분고분한 인품.

flex·ion [flékʃən] *n.* =flection.

flex·u·ous [flékʃuəs] *adj.* full of bends; winding. 굴곡이 많은; 구불구불한. [*flex*[1]]

flex·ure [flékʃər] *n.* **1** Ⓤ the act of bending or curving; the state of being bent. 굴곡[만곡] (작용); 굴곡[만곡] 상태. **2** Ⓒ the bent part. 굴곡[만곡]부.

flick [flik] *n.* Ⓒ **1** a quick, light stroke, as of a whip. (채찍 따위로) 철썩 때리기; (손가락으로) 톡 튀기기; 가볍게 치기. ¶ *give a lazy horse a* ～ 게으른 말을 채찍으로 철썩 때리다. **2** the light, snapping sound of such a stroke. 철썩; 탁; 톡(소리). **3** the act of moving suddenly. 갑자기 움직이기. ¶ *a* ～ *of the wrist* 손목을 재빨리 움직이기. — *vt.* (P6,7) **1** strike lightly. …을 가볍게 찰싹 때리다; 톡 튀기다. **2** move quickly and lightly. 재빨리 움직이다 [Imit.]

·flick·er[1] [flíkər] *vi.* **1** (P1) shine or burn unsteadily. (불빛 따위가) 어른거리다; 깜박이다; 명멸하다. ¶ *The candle flickers.* 촛불이 가물거린다. **2** (P1,2A) move back and forth; quiver. 흔들리다; 떨다. ¶ *leaves flickering in the wind* 바람에 흔들리는 나뭇잎 / *The boat flickered on the waves.* 배는 물결을 타고 까불렸다. **3** (P1,2A) 《*fig.*》 shake like an unsteady flame. 가물거리다. ¶ *A last faint hope flickered up and died.* 마지막 한가닥 희망마저 가물거리다 꺼져버렸다.

— *n.* Ⓒ **1** an unsteady light or flame. 깜박이는[가물거리는] 불빛[불꽃]. **2** (of leaves, etc.) a quick and light movement. (나뭇잎 따위의) 흔들림. [E.]

flick·er[2] [flíkər] *n.* Ⓒ a kind of woodpecker of North America with golden-yellow feathers. 딱따구리의 일종《북아메리카산》. [Imit.]

fli·er, fly·er [fláiər] *n.* Ⓒ **1** a person or a thing that flies; an airplane pilot. 날으는 사람[것]; 비행사. **2** a very fast train, ship, bus, etc. 급행 열차; 쾌속선; 고속 버스. [*fly*[1]]

:flight[1] [flait] *n.* Ⓒ **1** ⓊⒸ the act or the manner of flying. 비행; 비상(飛翔). ¶ *be on a training* ～ 훈련 비행중이다 / *make a long night* ～ 장거리 야간 비행을 하다 / *on the* ～ *back to....* …로 비행기로 돌아가는[오

는〕 도중에 / *A bird takes its* ~. 새가 날고 있다. **2** a distance that a bullet, an airplane, etc. can fly over. (탄알 따위의) 날아가는 거리; 비행 거리. ¶ *the* ~ *of an airplane* (비행기의) 비행 거리. **3** a group or birds, insects, etc. flying through the air together. 떼지어 날고 있는 철새·곤충 따위. ¶ *a* ~ *of swallows* 날고 있는 한떼의 제비. **4** the state of swift passing; (of time) a swift passage. 민속한 움직임; (시간·때의) 빨리 지나감. ¶ *the* ~ *of time* 시간이 화살처럼 지나감. **5** an act of passing over or beyond what is ordinary. (공상·야심의) 비약; 고양(高揚). ¶ *a* ~ *of fancy* 〔*imagination*〕 공상〔상상〕의 비약. **6** a group or series of stairs. (두 층계참 사이를 잇는) 연속의 층계. ¶ *a* ~ *of stairs* 한 줄로 이어진 계단. **7** a small group of aircraft. 비행기의 소편대(小編隊). [→fly¹]

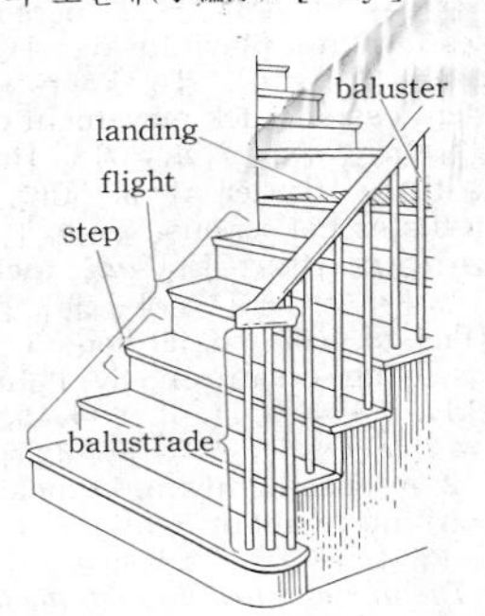

〈flight¹ 6〉

in flight, while flying. 비행중에.
in the first flight, in a leading place; among the best. 선두에 서서; 중요한 위치를 차지하여.
make 〔***take***〕 ***a flight,*** fly. 비행하다; 날다.
take 〔***wing***〕 ***its*** 〔*one's*〕 ***flight,*** fly (off). 날(아가)다; 비행하다.

flight² [flait] *n.* ⓊⒸ the act of fleeing or running away. 도주; 탈주; 패주(敗走). ¶ *a* ~ *from reality* 현실로부터의 도피 / *drive someone to* ~ 아무를 패주시키다. [→flee]
put** the enemy, etc. **to flight, force the enemy, etc. to run away. (적 따위)를 패주시키다.
take to flight =***betake** oneself **to flight,*** run away. 달아나다; 도망가다.

flight deck [ˊ ˋ] *n.* the upper deck of an aircraft carrier, used for taking off from and landing on. (항공 모함의) 비행〔발착〕 갑판. [*flight¹*]

flight·less [fláitlis] *adj.* unable to fly. 날지 못하는.

flight·y [fláiti] *adj.* (**flight·i·er, flight·i·est**) **1** unsteady in character; changeable. 침착하지 못한; 들뜬. **2** slightly crazy. 엉뚱한; 경박한; 변덕스러운.

flim·sy [flímzi] *adj.* (**-si·er, -si·est**) **1** light and thin; easily torn and damaged; weak. 얇은; 부서지기〔깨지기, 찢어지기〕 쉬운; 약한. ¶ ~ *paper* 약한 종이 / *a* ~ *wooden structure* 취약한 목조 건물. **2** lacking seriousness; shallow. 천박한; 하찮은. ¶ ~ *arguments* 하찮은 의론. — *n.* Ⓒ **1** 《*colloq.*》 a thin piece of paper used by reporters. 얇은 종이; (신문 기자가 사용하는) 얇은 복사지. **2** 《*sl.*》 a bank-note; a telegram. 지폐; 전보. [Imit.]

flinch [flintʃ] *vi.* (P1,2A,3) 《*from*》 move back; shrink back. 뒷걸음질치다; 주춤하다. ¶ ~ *from an unpleasant duty* 불쾌한 일에 꽁무니를 빼다 / *bear pain without flinching* 겁내지 않고 고통을 견디다. [F.]

flin·ders [flíndərz] *n. pl.* fragments. 파편; 단편. ¶ *fly in* 〔*be blown to*〕 ~ 산산조각으로 흩어지다 / *break a vase to* ~ 꽃병을 산산조각으로 깨뜨리다. [Norw.]

***fling** [fliŋ] *v.* (**flung**) *vt.* (P6,7,13,18) **1** 《*at*》 throw violently or forcibly. …을 세게 던지다; …을 향해 던지다. ¶ ~ *a stone at a dog* 개에 돌을 던지다 / ~ *one's hat in the air* 모자를 공중에 던지다. **2** move, send, or cast suddenly or angrily. …을 급히 움직이다; 집어〔처〕넣다; 내던지다. ¶ ~ *one's clothes on* 부리나케 옷을 걸치다 / ~ *off one's clothes* 옷을 벗어 던지다 / ~ *someone into prison* 아무를 투옥하다. **3** 《*reflexively*》 ⓐ move oneself violently. 세차게 움직이다; 몸을 내던지다〔날리다〕; 뛰어들다〔나오다〕. ¶ ~ *oneself into a chair* 의자에 털썩 주저앉다 / ~ *oneself into one's clothes* 급히 옷을 걸치다 / ~ *oneself about in his anger* 성이 나서 날뛰다 / *He flung himself into the water.* 그는 물 속에 뛰어들었다. ⓑ enter into, esp. with spirit and determination. 기운차게 착수하다. ¶ ~ *oneself into a task* 기운차게 일에 착수하다. **4** scatter in all directions. 흩뿌리다. ¶ ~ *money to the crowd* 군중에게 돈을 뿌리다. — *vi.* (P1,2A,3) **1** 《*away, off*》 go or rush violently. 돌진하다; 내닫다; 뛰쳐나오다. ¶ ~ *away* 〔*off*〕 *in a rage* 성이 나서 뛰쳐나오다 / ~ *to the door* 문쪽으로 달려가다 / *She flung away from him.* 그녀는 그를 뿌리치고 사라졌다. **2** 《*about*》 (of a horse, etc.) kick or plunge violently. (말 따위가) 날뛰다.
***fling** oneself **into** an enterprise,* take up an enterprise vigorously or ardently. (사업)에 심혈을 쏟다.
fling** oneself* (=*depend*) ***on 〔***upon***〕 *someone,* …에게 의지하다.
fling out, **a**) (of a horse) kick violently. (말이) 날뛰다. **b**) (of a person) act or talk wildly; abuse. (사람이) 거칠게 굴다; 욕설을 퍼붓다.
— *n.* Ⓒ **1** the act of flinging; a sudden throw or movement. (내)던지기; 휘두르기; 내뻗기. ¶ *give a* ~ 내던지다; 발길질하다. **2**

(of a horse) the act of kicking or plunging. (말이) 날뛰기; 발길질. **3** a time of doing as one pleases. 하고 싶은 대로 하기; 방종(의 기간). ¶ *He had his ~ when he was in Paris.* 파리에 있을 때 하고 싶은 대로 놀았다. **4** a scornful or abusive remark; a sneer. 폭언; 욕; 비웃음. [Scand.]

at one fling, with one movement. 단번에; 일거에.

have* 〔*take*〕 *a fling at, **a**) jeer at (someone); abuse. …을 비웃다; 욕하다. **b**) make an attempt at (something). …을 기도〔시도〕하다; 해보다. ¶ *He took a ~ at playwriting.* 그는 극작을 해 보았다.

in full fling, at full speed; impetuously. 전속력으로; 맹렬히.

flint [flint] *n.* **1** Ⓤ Ⓒ a very hard stone that makes a spark when struck against steel; a piece of alloy used in a lighter. 부싯돌; 라이터돌. ¶ *(as) hard as (a) ~* (부싯돌처럼)단단한; 완고한 / *get* 〔*wring*〕 *water from a ~* 기적적인〔불가능한〕 일을 하다. **2** Ⓤ anything that is very hard. 매우 단단한〔완고한〕 것. ¶ *a heart of ~* 냉혹한 마음. [E.]

skin a flint, be extremely stingy. 몹시 인색하다.

flint·lock [flíntlɑ̀k / -lɔ̀k] *n.* Ⓒ **1** a gunlock in which a piece of flint striking against steel produces sparks that set fire to the powder. 부싯돌식 격발 장치. **2** an old-fashioned gun with such a lock. 그러한 구식총; 화승총.

flint·y [flínti] *adj.* (**flint·i·er, flint·i·est**) **1** consisting of or like flint. 부싯돌의〔같은〕. **2** very hard like flint. 매우 단단한; 무정한; 완고한. ¶ *a ~ heart* 냉혹 무정한 마음.

flip [flip] *vt.* (**flipped, flip·ping**) **1** (P6,7,13) toss or move (something) with the fingers; strike lightly. (…을) 손가락으로 튀기다; (…을) 가볍게〔톡〕 치다. ¶ *~ the ash off a cigar* 엽궐련을 톡 쳐서 재를 떨다 / *~ a coin* 주화(鑄貨)를 손끝으로 툭 튀겨 돌게 하다. **2** (P6,7) move about rapidly or sharply; pull suddenly. …을 홱 움직이다〔당기다〕. ¶ *~ a whip* 채찍을 휘두르다 / *~ back several pages* 몇 페이지를 홱 되넘기다. — *vi.* (P1,2A,3) make a quick, light stroke with the finger or a whip. (손가락으로)톡 튀기다; (채찍으로) 철썩 때리다. ¶ *~ at a dog with a whip* 채찍으로 개를 철썩 때리다.

— *n.* Ⓒ **1** a light stroke or tap with the fingers. 손가락으로 튀기기. **2** a sudden, quick movement. 갑자기 홱 움직이기. [Imit.]

flip-flap [flípflæ̀p], **-flop** [-flɑ̀p / -flɔ̀p] *n.* Ⓒ **1** the sound made when a long, loose thing repeatedly hits another object. 퍼덕퍼덕(소리). **2** a kind of jumping; a machine with cars for passengers hung at ends of moving arms. 공중제비; (놀이터의) 공중 회전 시소. [Imit.]

flip·pan·cy [flípənsi] *n.* Ⓤ the state of being flippant. 경솔; 경박(輕薄). [↓]

flip·pant [flípənt] *adj.* not serious; disrespectful to elders. 경솔한; 건방진; 무례한. ¶ *a ~ answer* 무례한 대답 / *a ~ child* 건방진 아이. ●**flip·pant·ly** [-li] *adv.* [Scand.]

flip·per [flípər] *n.* Ⓒ **1** a broad, flat limb of certain sea animals used in swimming. 지느러미 모양의 발; (바다거북·펭귄 따위의) 물갈퀴. ¶ *Sea turtles have flippers.* 바다거북은 물갈퀴가 있다. **2** 《*colloq.*》 a hand. 손. [*flip*]

flirt [fləːrt] *vt.* (P6) **1** throw suddenly. …을 홱 던지다. **2** move (a fan) to and fro quickly. …을 이리저리 홱홱 움직이다; (부채 따위)를 확확 부치다. ¶ *The bird flirts its tail.* 새가 꽁지를 홱홱 움직인다. — *vi.* (P1,3) **1** make love in a playful way. (남녀가) 새롱거리다; 불장난 하다. **2** think playfully; trifle. (반 장난으로)가지고 놀다; 농락하다. — *n.* Ⓒ **1** a person who makes love in a playful way. 사랑을 장난으로 하는 남자〔여자〕; 불장난 하는 사람. **2** a sudden toss; a quick movement of a fan. 홱 던지기; (부채를) 확확 부치기. [Imit.]

flir·ta·tion [fləːrtéiʃən] *n.* Ⓤ Ⓒ a love affair that is not serious. 농탕치기; 불장난.

flir·ta·tious [fləːrtéiʃəs] *adj.* inclined to flirt. 농탕치고 싶어하는; 장난삼아 연애하는.

·**flit** [flit] *vi.* (**flit·ted, flit·ting**) (P2A,3) **1** (of a flying creature) fly lightly and quickly. (새 따위가) 휙 날다. ¶ *~ from tree to tree* (새가) 이 나무에서 저 나무로 날다. **2** ⓐ pass lightly and quickly; (of a person) move about lightly and quietly. 휙 지나가다; (사람이) 조용히〔빠르게〕 움직이다. ¶ *The nurses flitted through the hospital.* 간호사들이 병원 안을 바삐 움직이고 있었다. ⓑ (of a thought, etc.) come and go. (생각 따위가) 머릿속에 스치다. ¶ *~ through* 〔*across*〕 *his mind* (어떤 생각이) 그의 머릿속을 스치다. **3** move, change one's abode, esp. secretly. (몰래)거처를 옮기다; 이사하다. — *n.* Ⓒ **1** a light, quick movement. 가벼운 움직임; 휙 날기. **2** a change of one's abode. 이사; 전거; 야반 도주. [N.→fleet]

flitch [flitʃ] *n.* Ⓒ **1** the side of a hog salted and cured. 소금에 절여 훈제로 한 돼지 허리고기. **2** 《archit.》 a slab of wood. 죽데기. [E.]

flit·ter [flítər] *vi.* (P1,2A) fly about in an irregular way. 날개를 퍼덕이다; 훨훨 날다. [→fleet]

fliv·ver [flívər] *n.* Ⓒ 《U.S. *colloq.*》 a cheap motorcar; a small airplane designed for private use. 싸구려 자동차; 값싼 소형 비행기. [? *flop*]

:float [flout] *vi.* (P1,2A,3) **1** rest or drift on the surface of water or another liquid; be held up or carried along by air, water, etc. (수면·공중 따위에) 뜨다; 떠돌다; 표류하다. ¶ *a leaf floating on the water* 물위에 떠있는 나뭇잎 / *An adballoon* *is floating in the sky.* 기구가 공중에 떠 있다 / *The boat floated down the river.* 배가 강 하류로 떠내려갔다 / *Clouds ~ in the sky.* 하늘엔 구름이 떠다닌다 / *The smell of a rose floated around.* 장미의 향기가 주변에 감돌았다. **2** move in the mind. 생각이 떠오르다. ¶ *ideas floating in the mind* 심중에 떠오르는 생각. **3** move easily or lightly. 가볍고 우아하게 움직이다. ¶ *She floated down the stairs.* 그녀는 계단을 우아하게 내려왔다. — *vt.* (P6) **1** cause (something) to stay on the surface of a liquid; set (something) afloat. …을 뜨게 하다; 띄우다. ¶ *enough water to ~ a ship* 배를 띄우기에 충분한 물 / *The boat was floated on the water.* 수면에 보트가 띄워졌다. **2** cover (a surface) with liquid. (표면을) 액체로 덮다. ¶ *~ oil over the swamp to destroy mosquitoes* 모기 박멸(撲滅)을 위해 늪지대에 기름을 흘리다 / *Her face was all floated with tears.* 그녀 얼굴은 온통 눈물로 젖어 있었다. **3** circulate (rumors, etc.). (소문 따위를) 퍼뜨리다. **4** 《comm.》 ⓐ set going; start; launch. 일으키다; 시작하다; 발족시키다. ¶ *~ a business* 사업을 일으키다 / *~ a company* 회사를 설립하다 / *~ a scheme* 계획을 세우다. ⓑ circulate (securities, etc.). (증권 따위를) 발행하다; 유통시키다. — *n.* Ⓒ **1** something that floats; a buoy. 뜨는 것; 떠도는 것; (낚시)찌. ¶ *a ~ on a fishline.* 낚시찌. **2** a raft; a flat-bottomed boat. 뗏목; 평저선(平底船). **3** a low, flat car used in a parade or pageant. (퍼레이드 따위의) 플로트; 장식(꽃)수레. [E.]

float·age [flóutidʒ] *n.* =flotage.

float·a·tion [floutéiʃən] *n.* =flotation.

float·ing [flóutiŋ] *adj.* **1** that floats. 떠 있는. ¶ *a ~ bridge* 부교(浮橋). **2** not fixed; not staying in one's place. 유동성의; 일정치 않은. ¶ *a ~ vote* 부동표 / *a ~ population* 유동 인구. **3** in use or circulation. 사용되는; 유통 중인.

float·plane [flóutplèin] *n.* an aircraft supported on the water by one or more floats. 플로트가 달린 수상기(水上機).

:flock[1] [flɑk / flɔk] *n.* Ⓒ **1** a group of sheep, goats, or birds living, traveling, or feeding together. (특히 양·염소·새 따위의) 떼. ¶ *flocks and herds* 양떼와 소떼. **2** a crowd. 군중; 많은 사람. ¶ *a ~ of visitors* 많은 방문자. **3** the people of the same church group. 기독교도; 같은 교회의 신도; 회중.

in flocks, in large groups. 떼를 지어; 대거하여.

— *vi.* (P2A,3,4) gather or move in a flock. 떼지어 모이다. [L. *floccus*]

flock[2] [flɑk / flɔk] *n.* Ⓒ **1** a tuft of wool. (양)털뭉치. **2** 《*pl.*》 waste wool or cotton for stuffing mattresses and cushions. 털(솜)부스러기. [↑]

flock·bed [flákbèd] *n.* a bed stuffed with cotton or wool waste. 털부스러기(부스러기솜) 따위로 속을 채운 요가 달린 침대.

floe [flou] *n.* Ⓒ a large sheet or mass of floating ice. 큰 부빙(浮氷); 큰 성엣장. [Scand.]

flog [flɑg, flɔ(:)g] *vt.* (**flogged, flog·ging**) beat (someone) very hard with a whip or a stick. …을 세게 채찍으로(지팡이로) 때리다. ¶ *~ English into a boy* 매질하여 소년에게 영어를 가르치다 / *~ laziness out of a boy* 아이를 회초리로 때려 게으름을 고치다. [L. *flagellum* whip]

flog a dead horse, waste one's efforts. 헛수고를 하다.

flog the water, keep throwing a fishing-line over the water in fishing. (낚시에서) 계속 낚싯줄을 수면에 던지다.

flog·ging [flágiŋ / flɔ́g-] *n.* ⓊⒸ punishment by beating hard. 회초리로 때리는 벌.

:flood [flʌd] *n.* Ⓒ **1** ⓐ a large amount of water covering land that is usu. dry. 홍수; 큰물; 시위. ⓑ 《*the F-*》《Bible》 the water that covered the earth in the days of Noah. 노아의 홍수. **2** the tide flowing toward the shore; the rising tide. 밀물; 만조(滿潮)(opp. ebb). ¶ *ebb and ~* 조수의 간만(干滿) / *The tide is at the ~.* 조수가 밀물 때이다. **3** a great outpouring of anything. (일반적으로 물건의) 홍수; 대범람; 쇄도; 다량의 유출. ¶ *a ~ of words (tears)* 쏟아지는 말(눈물) / *floods of fan letters* 쇄도하는 편지 / *floods of rain* 억수 같은 장대비. **4** 《*poet.*》 the ocean; the sea; a lake; a river. 대양; 바다; 호수; 강.

at the flood, **a**) at the rising tide. 만조(밀물)때에. **b**) 《*fig.*》 at the favorable moment. 바로 좋은 시기에.

— *vt.* **1** (P6) cover (something) with a flood; flow over. …을 홍수로 물에 잠기게 하다; 물이 넘치게 하다. ¶ *The river flooded our fields.* 강이 범람해서 우리 밭들이 물에 잠겼다 / *The river is flooded by the rains.* 비로 인해 강물이 범람했다. **2** (P6,13) cover, fill, or overcome, as if with a flood. (홍수처럼) …을 범람시키다; (빛 따위를) 그득 채우다; 밀려오다; 쇄도하다. ¶ *The room was flooded with moonlight.* 방은 달빛이 비쳐 환했다 / *Applicants flooded the offices.* 응모자들이 사무실에 밀려왔다. **3** (P7) 《*out*》 force to leave because of flood. (홍수로 인해) 물러나게(철수하게) 하다. — *vi.* **1** (of a river, etc.) rise in a flood; become covered with water. 홍수가 나다; 범람하다. **2** (of the tide) rise. 밀물이 들어오다; 만조가 되다. **3** (P2A,3) flow or pour in like a flood. (…이) 범람하다; 쏟아져(밀려) 들어오다; 쇄도하다. ¶ *Fan letters flooded in.* 팬레터가 쇄도했다. [E.]

flood out, force to leave a house because of floods. 홍수로 집을 잃다.

flood control [ˊ-ˋ] *n.* control of rivers that tend to overflow by the use of dams, dikes, reforestation, etc. (강의) 홍수 조절.

flood·gate [flʌ́dgèit] *n.* Ⓒ a gate in a canal, a river, etc. to control the water. (수량 조절을 위한) 수문.

flood·light [flʌ́dlàit] *n.* Ⓒ a lamp that gives a broad beam of light covering a large area; the light provided by such lamps. 투광(投光)조명등; 투광 조명. — *vt.* (**-light·ed** or **-lit**) (P6) light or illuminate (something) by a floodlight or floodlights. …을 투광 조명등으로 비추다.

flood tide [ˊˋ] *n.* the rising tide. 밀물 (opp. ebb tide).

:floor [flɔːr] *n.* Ⓒ **1** the bottom surface of a room; the part of a room on which people walk. (방)바닥. **2** a story of a building. (건물의) 층. ¶ *the first* ~ 《U.S.》 1층; 《Brit.》 2층. **3** the bottom of the ocean or of a cave. (바다·동굴 따위의) 바닥. **4** a part of a room or hall where members of a lawmaking body sit. 의원석(議員席). **5** 《*the* ~》 the right to speak. 발언권. ¶ *get* [*have*] *the* ~ 발언권을 얻다 / *ask for the* ~ 발언권을 요청하다. **6** 《*colloq.*》 (of prices) the lowest level. (가격의) 최저(액). **7** 《cinema, TV》 the part of a film studio where the actors perform. 촬영장. ¶ *on the* ~ (영화를) 제작[촬영] 중에.

mop* [*wipe*] *the floor with, defeat totally. (아무)를 일방적으로 해치우다; 압도하다; 완패시키다.

take the floor, 《chiefly U.S.》 **a**) stand up to speak in a discussion or at a public meeting. 발언을 위해 일어서다. **b**) speak in a debate. 토론에 참여하다. **c**) start dancing, as at a party or in a dance hall. (파티·댄스홀에서) 무도를 시작하다.

— *vt.* (P6) **1** put a floor in or on (a building). …에 바닥을 깔다. ¶ *We will* ~ *this room with oak.* 이 방은 떡갈나무로 바닥을 깔아야겠다. **2** knock down. …을 쓰러뜨리다; 타도하다. ¶ ~ *a man with one's fist* 사내를 주먹으로 때려눕히다. **3** overwhelm; defeat; put to silence. 압도하다; 지우다; 곤혹[침묵]시키다. ¶ *He was floored by the problem.* 그 문제로 당혹했다. [E.]

floor·cloth [flɔ́ːrklɔ̀ːθ] *n.* Ⓒ **1** a cloth for washing floors. 마루 닦는 걸레. **2** a fabric for covering floors. 바닥 깔개.

floor·ing [flɔ́ːriŋ] *n.* **1** Ⓒ a floor. (마룻)바닥. **2** Ⓤ 《*collectively*》 floors; material for making floors. 마루청; 마루 까는 재료.

floor leader [ˊ ˋ-] *n.* 《U.S.》 the member who directs the activities of his party in the floor. (정당(政黨)의) 원내 총무.

floor show [ˊˋ] *n.* an entertainment of music, singing, dancing, etc. at a night club. (호텔·나이트 클럽 따위에서의) 플로어쇼; 여흥.

floor·walk·er [flɔ́ːrwɔ̀ːkər] *n.* Ⓒ a person who oversees sales and direct customers in a large store. (백화점 따위의) 매장(賣場) 감독. [*floor*]

flop [flɑp / flɔp] *v.* (**flopped, flop·ping**) *vt.* (P7,13) drop, throw, or set down heavily and noisily. …을 쿵[쾅] 떨어뜨리다; 툭 던지다; 털썩 내려놓다. ¶ ~ *down a sack of corn* 곡물 푸대를 털썩 내려놓다.

— *vi.* **1** (P1,2A,3) move around heavily and noisily. 쿵쿵 (시끄럽게) 돌아다니다; 퍼덕이다. ¶ *The fish flopped in the boat.* 물고기는 배 안에서 퍼덕였다. **2** fall or drop in this way. 쿵[털썩] 떨어지다. ¶ ~ *into an armchair* 털썩 안락 의자에 주저앉다. **3** change suddenly. 갑자기 변하다. **4** 《*colloq.*》 (of a novel, play, etc.) fail. 실패하다.

— *n.* Ⓒ **1** the act or sound of flopping. 털썩[쿵] 떨어짐[떨어지는 소리]; 털썩[픽] 쓰러짐[쓰러지는 소리]. **2** 《*colloq.*》 a failure. 실패(작). ¶ *The play was a* ~. 연극은 실패였다. [*flap*]

flop·house [flɑ́phàus / flɔ́p-] *n.* Ⓒ a cheap hotel for men only. (남자 전용) 간이[싸구려] 여인숙.

floppy disk [ˊ-ˊ] *n.* 《computer》 a small flexible plastic disk coated with magnetic material on which data for a computer can be stored. 플로피 디스크《플라스틱으로 만든 얇은 외부 기억용 자기(磁氣) 원판》.

flo·ra [flɔ́ːrə] *n.* (*pl.* **-ras** or **-rae**) **1** Ⓤ the plants of a particular area or period of time. (한 지방·한 시대 특유의) 식물(상). **2** Ⓒ a list or description of such plants. 식물지(誌). [L.=goddess of flowers]

flo·rae [flɔ́ːriː] *n.* pl. of **flora.**

flo·ral [flɔ́ːrəl] *adj.* of, made of or like flowers. 꽃의[같은]; 꽃으로 된. ¶ ~ *decorations.*

floral em·blem [ˊ- ˊ-] *n.* a flower or a plant which is the symbol of a country, a state, a city, etc. (나라·주·시 따위를) 상징하는 꽃.

flo·res·cence [flɔːrésəns] *n.* Ⓤ **1** the state of blossoming. 개화(開花). **2** the period of blossoming. 개화기(期); 전성기. [L. *flos* flower]

flo·ret [flɔ́ːrit] *n.* Ⓒ 《bot.》 one of the small flowers which make up the flower head of an aster, a daisy, a dandelion, etc. (국화과 식물의) 작은 (통)꽃. [↑]

flo·ri·cul·tur·al [flɔ̀ːrəkʌ́ltʃərəl] *adj.* of floriculture. 화초 재배(법)의.

flo·ri·cul·ture [flɔ́ːrəkʌ̀ltʃər] *n.* Ⓤ the science or practice of growing flowers. 화초 재배.

flor·id [flɔ́(ː)rid, flɑ́rid] *adj.* **1** (of a face) bright in color; naturally very red. (얼굴빛이) 불그레한; 혈색이 좋은. **2** flowery; richly ornamented. 화려한. ¶ *a* ~ *style* 화려한[미(美)] 문체. ● **flor·id·ly** [-li] *adv.* **flor·id·ness**

[-nis] *n.* [L. *flos* flower]

Flor·i·da [flɔ́(:)ridə, flɑ́r-] *n.* the extreme southeastern State of the United States. 플로리다 주(州). 參考 Fla., Flor.로 생략함. 주도(州都)는 Tallahassee.

flor·in [flɔ́(:)rin, flɑ́r-] *n.* Ⓒ a former English silver coin. 플로린《영국의 옛 은화, 2 실링에 해당》. [→florescence]

flo·rist [flɔ́(:)rist, flɑ́r-] *n.* Ⓒ a person who grows or sells flowers as a business. 꽃집 주인; 꽃 장수; 화초 재배자. [↑]

flo·ru·it [flɔ́(:)rjuit, flɑ́:r-] *n.* the period at which a person lived. 재세기(在世期). [L.=he flourished]

floss [flɔ(:)s, flɑs] *n.* Ⓤ **1** a shiny, untwisted silk thread used for embroidery. (자수용 꼬지 않은) 실; 누에[명주]실; 풀솜. **2** (of plant) the soft, silky fibers of certain pods. (식물의) 명주솜 같은 털; (옥수수 따위의) 수염. [Scand.]

flo·tage [flóutidʒ] *n.* Ⓤ **1** the act of floating. 뜸; 뜨기. **2** the power of floating; anything that floats. 부력(浮力); 떠도는 것. **3** 《*collectively*》 the ships, etc. floating on a river, the sea, etc. (강에 뜨는) 배; 뗏목. **4** the part of a ship above the water line. 흘수선상의 선체(船體). [*float*]

flo·ta·tion, floa- [floutéiʃən] *n.* Ⓤ **1** the act of floating. 뜸; 부양(浮揚). **2** 《comm.》 the act of beginning a business; the act of selling bonds, securities, etc. (회사 따위의) 설립; (채권 따위의) 발행. [→float]

flo·til·la [floutílə] *n.* Ⓒ a small fleet; a fleet of small ships. 소(小)함대; 소정대(小艇隊). ¶ *a destroyer* ~ 구축 함대. [Sp.]

flot·sam [flɑ́tsəm / flɔ́t-] *n.* Ⓤ parts of a wreck found floating on the water. (조난선의) 표류물; 부유(浮遊)짐(cf. *jetsam*). [→float]

flounce[1] [flauns] *vi.* (P2A,3) 《*about, away*》 move suddenly showing anger or impatience, struggle. (성나거나 못 견뎌) 홀쩍 자리를 박차다; 몸부림[발버둥이]치다; 사납게 날뛰다. —*n.* Ⓒ a sudden or jerky movement showing anger or impatience. 몸부림; 발버둥질; 사납게 날뛰기. [Scand.]

flounce[2] [flauns] *n.* Ⓒ an ornamental strip of cloth, gathered and sewed to a dress, a skirt, etc. as trimming. (스커트의 옆으로 여러 겹 댄) 자락 주름 장식. —*vt.* (P6) trim (something) with a flounce. …에 주름 장식을 달다. [F. *fronce* wrinkle]

〈flounce[2]〉

floun·der[1] [fláundər] *vi.* (P1,2A,3) **1** struggle awkwardly and violently, as in mud, water, or snow. 몸부림[발버둥]치다; 허위적[버둥]거리다; 버둥거려 깊이 빠져들다. ¶ *The horse floundered in the deep mud.* 말이 깊은 진창에 빠져 허우적거렸다. **2** make mistakes or stumble, esp. in speaking; hesitate. (연설 따위에서) 실수하다; 말을 더듬다; 망설이다. —*n.* Ⓒ the act of floundering. 몸부림침; 발버둥질; 초조. [Norw.]

floun·der[2] [fláundər] *n.* Ⓒ (*pl.* **-ders** or *collectively* **-der**) any flatfish. 넙치류의 물고기. [Scand.]

:flour [fláuər] *n.* Ⓤ **1** the fine powder made by grinding wheat or grain. 밀가루. 參考 밀가루 외에는 buckwheat flour, rye flour 처럼 나타냄. ¶ *a* ~ *mill* 제분소. **2** any fine powder. 가루; 분말. —*vt.* (P6) **1** put flour on (something); cover (something) with flour. …에 가루를 뿌리다[끼얹다]. ¶ ~ *the fish before frying it* 생선을 튀기기 전에 가루를 뿌리다. **2** 《U.S.》 make (grain) into flour. …을 빻아[갈아, 체로 걸러] 가루로 만들다. [→flower]

∗flour·ish [flə́:riʃ, flʌ́riʃ] *vi.* (P1) **1** (of plants) grow thick; thrive. (식물이) 무성하게 자라다. ¶ *Palm trees do not* ~ *in cold countries.* 야자나무는 추운 나라에서는 무성히 자라지 않는다. **2** be at the peak of life or activity; prosper. 한창 왕성하다; 번창하다; 번영하다. ¶ *My business is flourishing.* 내 사업은 번창하고 있다. **3** write in a decorative style; speak or write with ornamental phrases. 미사 여구를 써서 말하다[쓰다]. **4** 《mus.》 perform a fanfare; play a gay, flowery passage. 화려하게 취주[연주]하다.

—*vt.* (P6) **1** wave (something) in a showy way. …을 흔들(어 보이)다; 휘두르다. ¶ ~ *a handkerchief* 손수건을 흔들다 / ~ *a sword* 칼을 휘두르다 / *John flourished the letters.* 존은 편지를 흔들어 보였다. **2** write, speak or play ornamentally. …을 장식체[문자]로 쓰다; 미사 여구를 늘어놓다; 화려하게 연주하다.

—*n.* Ⓒ **1** the waving motion of a sword, an arm, etc. (손·검 따위를) 휘두르기; 흔들기. ¶ *a* ~ *of one's hat* 모자를 흔듦 / *She laughed with a* ~ *of her hand.* 그녀는 손을 흔들며 웃었다. **2** an extra curved line for decoration in writing. (서명 따위의) 장식체로 쓰기. **3** a showy word or phrase in speech or writing. 미사 여구. ¶ *a letter full of flourishes* 미사 여구로 그득한 편지. **4** 《mus.》 a showy passage or performance. 화려한 연주. ¶ *a* ~ *of trumpets.* [→flour]

in full flourish, very prosperous. 번창하고.

flour·y [fláuəri] *adj.* (**flour·i·er, flour·i·est**) **1** of, consisting of, or like flour. 가루(모양)의; 가루로 된. **2** covered with flour. 가루를 뒤집어 쓴; 가루투성이의. **3** white like flour. (가루처럼) 흰.

flout [flaut] *vt.* (P6) show contempt for (someone or something). …을 조롱하다; 모

욕하다; 비웃다. ¶ ~ *someone's advice* 아무의 충고를 비웃다. — *vi.* (P1,3) 《*at*》 show contempt. 경멸의 태도를 보이다; 우롱하다. — *n.* Ⓒ an act or a speech filled with contempt and insults. 우롱; 모욕; 비웃음. ● **flout·er** [-ər] [→flute]

:flow [flou] *vi.* (P1,2A,3) **1** run along as a stream does. 흐르다. ¶ *Blood flows in the body.* 피는 몸 속을 흐른다 / *Rivers ~ down to the sea.* 강은 흘러 내려가 바다로 간다 / *Tears flowed from her eyes.* 그녀의 눈에서는 눈물이 흘렀다. **2** move easily or smoothly. 물이 흐르듯 나아가다[움직이다]. ¶ *The crowd flowed past the house.* 사람의 물결이 집을 지나갔다 / *The years flowed away.* 세월이 유수와 같이 흘러갔다. **3** move or spring forth smoothly or continuously. (생각·말 따위가) 막힘없이 (술술) 나오다. ¶ *His speech flowed on.* 그의 연설은 청산 유수와 같이 계속되었다. **4** 《*from*》 come from a source; derive. (근원에서) 나오다; 발하다. ¶ *Rivers ~ from the springs and lakes.* 강은 샘이나 호수를 그 원천으로 한다. **5** hang loosely; hang in waves. 멋지게 늘어지다; 늘어져 (물결치듯) 나부끼다. ¶ *Her hair flowed over her shoulders.* 그녀의 머리털은 양어깨에 늘어져 있었다 / *Her long hair flowed in the wind.* 그녀의 긴 머리가 바람에 나부꼈다. **6** (of the tide) rise. (조수가) 밀려오다; 밀물이 들어오다(opp. ebb). ¶ *The tide began to flow.* 밀물이 들어오기 시작하였다. **7** 《*with*》 be full; be plentiful; abound. …로 넘치다; 그득[충만]하다; 많이 있다. ¶ *rivers flowing with fish* 물고기가 많은 강 / *Her heart flowed with gratitude.* 그녀의 가슴은 감사의 마음으로 꽉 찼다.

— *n.* Ⓒ 《*sing.* only》 **1** the act or manner of flowing. 흐름; 흐르기; 유동. ¶ *the ~ of water* [*air*] 물[공기]의 흐름. **2** any continuous movement like water in a river; anything that suggests this. (흐르는 강물 같은 끊임없는) 연속; 거침없는 흐름. ¶ *a rapid ~ of speech* 유창한 변설 / *a ~ of callers* 끊임없는 방문객 / *a ~ of emotion* 감정의 분출 / *the ~ of her hair over her shoulders* 어깨 위에 물결치는 그녀의 머리. **3** the amount that flows. 유출[유입]량. ¶ *a ~ of 100 gallons of oil a second* 1초에 100갤런의 석유의 유출. **4** rise of the tide. 밀물; 만조. ¶ *The tide is on the ~.* 조수가 밀물이 되고 있다. [E.]

:flow·er [fláuər] *n.* **1** Ⓒ the part of a plant which produces the seeds; a bloom; a blossom. 꽃. ¶ *an early* [*a late*] ~ 일찍[늦게] 피는 꽃 / *a bunch of flowers* 한 다발의 꽃; 꽃다발 / *Flowers bloom.* 꽃이 핀다. **2** Ⓒ a flowering plant. 화초; 꽃피는 식물. ¶ *arrange flowers* 꽃꽂이하다. **3** 《*the* ~》 the best part or period. 정화(精華); 정수(精髓); 한창때; 청춘[전성]기. ¶ *the ~ of poetry* 시의 정수 / *the ~ of chivalry* 기사도의 꽃 / *in the ~ of his age* 한창 젊은 때에; 젊음이 한창때에.

a flower girl, a girl who sells flowers. 꽃 파는 아가씨.

a flower show, an exhibition of flowers. 꽃 전시회.

flowers of speech, ornamental or rhetorical phrases. 수사적(修辭的) 어구.

in flower, bearing flowers; blooming. 꽃이 피어 있는.

— *vi.* (P1) **1** bear flowers; bloom; blossom. 꽃이 피다. ¶ *Some roses ~ throughout the growing season.* 어떤 장미는 성장기 동안 내내 꽃이 핀다. **2** come into the finest or fairest condition; flourish. 한창때가 되다; 성숙하다. ¶ *Girls tend to ~ early in the tropics.* 열대에서는 여성이 조숙한 경향이 있다.

— *vt.* (P6) **1** cause or allow to flower. 꽃을 피우다. **2** decorate with flowers or figures of flowers. 꽃으로[꽃무늬로] 장식하다. [L. *flos*]

flower bed [⌐-⌐] *n.* a garden bed in which flowers are grown. 꽃밭; 화단.

flow·ered [fláuərd] *adj.* **1** having flowers. 꽃이 핀. **2** decorated with flowers or patterns of flowers. 꽃으로 꾸민; 꽃 무늬로 장식된.

flow·er·er [fláuərər] *n.* Ⓒ a plant that flowers at a particular time or in a certain manner. 꽃이 피는 식물. ¶ *an early* [*a late*] ~ 꽃이 일찍[늦게] 피는 식물.

flow·er·et [fláuərit] *n.* Ⓒ a small flower. 작은 꽃.

flow·er·ing [fláuəriŋ] *adj.* bearing flowers. 「꽃이 피는.

flow·er·pot [fláuərpàt / -pɔ̀t] *n.* Ⓒ a container, usu. made of clay, in which plants can be grown. 화분.

flower vase [⌐-⌐] *n.* an ornamental vessel of glass, pottery, metal, etc. for containing cut flowers. 꽃병.

flow·er·y [fláuəri] *adj.* (**-er·i·er, -er·i·est**) **1** full of flowers; covered with flowers. 꽃이 많은; 꽃으로 뒤덮인. ¶ *a ~ meadow* 꽃으로 뒤덮인 초원. **2** like flowers. 꽃과 같은. **3** decorated with flowers or patterns of flowers. 꽃으로 장식된; 꽃무늬가 있는. **4** filled with fine words and phrases. 미사여구를 늘어놓은; 화려한. ¶ *a ~ speech* 화려한 말로 꾸민 연설 / *talk in a ~ strain* 미사여구를 늘어놓으며 이야기하다. ● **flow·er·i·ness** [-nis] *n.*

:flown [floun] *v.* pp. of **fly.**

flu [flu:] *n.* 《*colloq.*》 =influenza.

fluc·tu·ate [flʌ́ktʃuèit] *vi.* (P1,2) **1** rise and fall, like waves. (물결처럼) 파동치다. **2** change continually and irregularly. 끊임없이 변동하다; 동요하다. ¶ *fluctuating market* 끊임없이 변동하는 시황(市況) / *The patient's temperature fluctuates.* 환자의 체온이 끊임없이 변동한다. [L. *fluctus* wave]

fluc·tu·a·tion [flʌ̀ktʃuéiʃən] *n.* ⓊⒸ the act of fluctuating; a motion like a wave; continual, irregular change. 파동; (끊임없는) 변동. ¶ *the ~ of the stock market* 증권 시장의 변동.

flue¹ [flu:] *n.* Ⓒ a tube, pipe or other passage for the conveyance of air, smoke, flame, hot air, etc. 작은 굴뚝; 연도(煙道); 염관(炎管). [→flow]

flue² [flu:] *n.* 《*colloq.*》 =influenza.

flu·en·cy [flú:ənsi] *n.* Ⓤ the state or quality of being fluent; the ability to speak easily and well. 유창함; 막힘 없음; 능변. ¶ *with ~* 유창하게 / *speak with great poise and ~* 매우 침착하고도 유창하게 말하다. [↓]

***flu·ent** [flú:ənt] *adj.* **1** flowing smoothly and rapidly. 막힘 없는. **2** able to speak easily and well. 유창한; 능변의. ¶ *a ~ speech* 〔*speaker*〕 능변〔능변가〕 / *a speaker ~ in French* 프랑스어를 유창하게 말할 수 있는 사람. [L. *flou* flow]

flu·ent·ly [flú:əntli] *adv.* in a fluent manner. 막힘 없이; 유창하게.

fluff [flʌf] *n.* Ⓤ **1** very soft and light particles like feathers or hair. 보풀; 괴깔. **2** first soft hair or beard. 솜털; 갓난털; 배내털. — *vt.* (P6,7) **1** shake (something) into the state of fluff. 보풀이 일게 하다; (흔들어) 푸하게〔부풀게〕 하다. **2** 《*colloq.*》 make an error in (spoken lines in a play); misplay (a shot) in a game. (연극 대사를) 틀리다; 잘못〔실수〕하다; (골프 따위에서) 공을 잘못 치다. — *vi.* (P1) become fluffy. 보풀이 일다; 푸해지다. [? *flue*=hairy matter]

fluff·i·ness [flʌ́finis] *n.* Ⓤ the state or quality of being fluffy. 보풀이 읾; 푸함.

fluff·y [flʌ́fi] *adj.* (**fluff·i·er, fluff·i·est**) of fluff; like fluff; covered with fluff. 보풀〔솜털〕의; 푸한; 푹신한; 보풀〔솜털〕로 덮인. ¶ *a ~ little chicken* 솜털로 덮인 병아리.

***flu·id** [flú:id] *adj.* **1** flowing easily, like water or gas. 유동하는; 유동체〔성〕의. ¶ *~ matter* 유동체. **2** changing easily; not fixed or settled. 변하기 쉬운; 고정되어 있지 않은. ¶ *~ opinions* 고정되지 않은 의견. — *n.* ⓊⒸ 《phys.》 a substance that flows like water, gas, etc. 유체(流體); 유동체. ¶ *Water and mercury are fluids.* 물과 수은은 유동체이다. ● **flu·id·ly** [-li] *adv.* [→ fluent]

flu·id·i·ty [flu:ídəti] *n.* Ⓤ the state of being fluid. 유동(성); 유동질(質).

fluid mechanics [⌐— —⌐—] *n.* an applied science dealing with the basic principles of gaseous and liquid matter. 유체 역학.

fluke¹ [flu:k] *n.* Ⓒ **1** a sharp, triangular blade at the end of each arm of an anchor. 닻가지. **2** the barbed head of a spear, a harpoon, an arrow, etc. (창·작살 따위 끝의) 미늘; 살촉. **3** 《*pl.*》 a whale's tail. 고래의 꼬리. [E.]

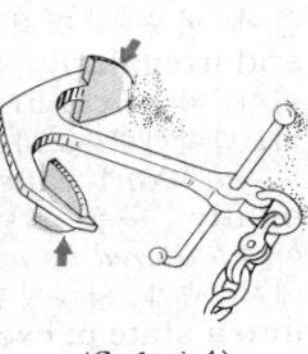
〈fluke¹ 1〉

fluke² [flu:k] *n.* Ⓒ **1** 《*colloq.*》 a lucky chance or accident. 요행; 우연. ¶ *win a game by ~* 요행으로 경기에 이기다. **2** (of billiards, etc.) a lucky stroke or shot. (당구 따위의) 플루크; 어쩌다 맞음. — *vt.* (P6) gain or hit by a fluke. 어쩌다 손에 넣다; 어쩌다 맞히다. [E.]

flume [flu:m] 《U.S.》 *n.* **1** an artificial channel for water. 인공 수로(水路); 홈통식 수로. **2** a deep and very narrow valley containing a stream. (급류가 있는) 협곡(峽谷). — *vi.* (P1) make a flume. 인공 수로를 만들다. — *vt.* (P6) carry by a flume. 홈통식 수로에 흘려 보내 나르다. [L. *flumen* river]

flum·mer·y [flʌ́məri] *n.* Ⓒ **1** kinds of sweet dish made with milk, flour, eggs, etc. 푸딩. **2** empty compliments. 치렛말. **3** nonsense. 헛소리; 잠꼬대. [Welsh *llymru*]

flum·mox [flʌ́məks] *vt.* 《*colloq.*》 puzzle; confuse; perplex. 당황케 하다; 할 바를 모르게 하다. [?]

flung [flʌŋ] *v.* p. and pp. of **fling.**

flunk [flʌŋk] *vi.* (P1) **1** 《U.S. *colloq.*》 《*in*》 get an unsuccessful mark in schoolwork. (시험에서) 낙제점을 따다; 실패하다. ¶ *~ in one's English examination* 영어 시험에서 실패하다. **2** give up. 단념하다. — *vt.* (P6) **1** fail in (schoolwork). …에 낙제하다. ¶ *~ a math examination* 수학 시험에 낙제점을 따다. **2** cause (a student) to fail; give a grade of failure to (a student). (학생)을 낙제시키다; (학생)에게 낙제점을 주다. [*flinch* + *funk*]

flunk·ey [flʌ́ŋki] *n.* 《Brit.》 =flunky.

flunk·y [flʌ́ŋki] *n.* Ⓒ (*pl.* **flunk·ies**) **1** a manservant dressed in a special uniform; a footman. 제복을 입은 하인〔사용인〕. **2** a person who flatters. 아첨쟁이. [Sc.]

flu·or [flú:ɔ:r, -ər] *n.* =fluorite.

flu·o·resce [flùərés, flɔ:r-] *vi.* (P1) emit light by fluorescence. 형광(螢光)을 발하다. [→fluent]

flu·o·res·cence [flùərésəns, flɔ:r-] *n.* Ⓤ 《phys.》 **1** the property of a substance of emitting visible light while exposed to light or X-rays. 형광성(螢光性). **2** light emitted from such a substance. 형광.

flu·o·res·cent [flùərésnt, flɔ:r-] *adj.* **1** emitting fluorescence. 형광(螢光)을 발하는. ¶ *a ~ lamp* 형광등. **2** having the property of fluorescence. 형광성(性).

flu·o·rine [flúəri(:)n, flɔ́:r-] *n.* Ⓤ 《chem.》 a greenish-yellow gas that is a very active chemical element. 플루오르; 불소. [→ fluoresce]

flu·o·rite [flúəràit, flɔ́:r-] *n.* ⓊⒸ a transparent mineral of various colors, used in glassmaking, etc. 형석(螢石). [↑]

flur·ry [flə́:ri / flʌ́ri] *n.* Ⓒ (*pl.* **-ries**) **1** a sudden rush of wind. 돌풍. **2** a sudden gust of rain or snow. (돌풍을 수반한) 소나기; 눈보라. **3** a sudden confusion of the mind. (갑작스런 마음의) 동요; 혼란. ¶ *raise a ~ in an assembly* 집회에 혼란을 일으키다.
in a flurry, in a state of hurry and confusion. 황급히; 허둥지둥; 당황하여.
— *vt.* (**-ried**) (P6) confuse. …을 당황케 하다. ¶ *get* 〔*become*〕 *flurried* 당황하다; 동요하다 / *She was utterly flurried at her error.* 그녀는 실수를 하자 몹시 당황해했다. [Imit.]

·**flush**[1] [flʌʃ] *vi.* **1** (P1) rush out as water does; flow in a large quantity. 왈칵〔쏟아져〕 흐르다〔나오다〕; 분출하다. ¶ *The tide flushed through the narrow inlet.* 조수가 좁은 후미로 쏟아져 밀려왔다. **2** (P1,2A) ⓐ (of blood) rush into the face. (얼굴이 핏기로) 홍조를 띠다; 상기되다. ¶ *He flushed into rage.* 얼굴이 시뻘게져 격노했다. ⓑ 《also *up*》 become red in the face; blush. (얼굴이) 붉어지다; 화끈 달아오르다. ¶ *Her face flushed a rosy red.* 그녀의 얼굴이 확 붉어졌다. ⓒ glow or shine with a reddish brightness. 벌겋게 빛나다; (하늘이) 붉게 물들다. ¶ *The eastern sky was flushing over the hills.* 산 위의 동쪽 하늘이 아침놀로 벌겋게 빛나고 있었다.
— *vt.* **1** (P6) make (someone or someone's face) red. …을 붉히게 하다. ¶ *Shame flushed his cheeks.* 그는 부끄러움으로 얼굴을 붉혔다. **2** (P6,7) cause (something) to rush or flow rapidly. (물을) 왈칵 흐르게 하다. ¶ *~ the water away* 물을 왈칵 흘려보내다. **3** (P6) wash away (something) with a rapid flow of water. …을 물을 쏟아〔뿌려〕 닦다. ¶ *~ the toilet* 변기에 물을 흘려 씻겨 내리게 하다 / *~ the floor with a hose* 바닥을 호스물을 뿌려 닦다. **4** (P6) 《usu. in *passive*》 excite; make (someone) joyful too much. …을 흥분〔상기〕시키다; 의기 양양하게〔우쭐하게〕 하다. ¶ *She was flushed with pride at her son's success.* 그녀는 아들의 성공에 우쭐하고 있었다.
— *n.* Ⓒ **1** ⓐ a rush of blood to the face; a blush. 얼굴 붉힘; 홍조(紅潮); 상기. ¶ *with a quick ~ on one's face* 얼굴을 확 붉히고. ⓑ 《*poet.*》 becoming red. (하늘이) 붉어짐; 놀. ¶ *the ~ of dawn* 아침놀. **2** a sudden rush; a rapid flow (as of water). (물 따위의) 쏟아져 흐름〔나옴〕; 분출; 왈칵 쏟아 흘려보냄. ¶ *a ~ toilet* 수세식 변소. **3** fresh growth. 싹트기. ¶ *the spring ~ of grass* 봄이 되어 풀잎의 싹틈 / *a second ~ of bloom* 제철 아닌 때 꽃이 피기; 철없이 꽃이 핌. **4** glowing vigor. 발랄함. ¶ *a ~ of youthful ardor* 젊은 열정의 발랄함. **5** an excited condition of feeling. (감정의) 격발; 흥분. ¶ *the first ~ of success* 성공하여 최초로 느끼는 흥분 / *the ~ of victory* 승리의 환희. [Imit. *fly rush*]

flush[2] [flʌʃ] *adj.* **1** (of a stream) in a full flow. 물이 그득 찬; 넘칠 것 같은. **2** 《*colloq.*》 having plenty of money; abundant; lavish. 돈을 많이 가진; 많이 있는; 낭비의. ¶ *be ~ with money* 돈을 많이 갖고 있다. **3** making a level surface; even. 같은 높이의; 같은 평면의. — *vt.* (P6) level; make even with a surface. 편평〔평탄〕하게 하다; 고르게 하다.
— *adv.* **1** evenly; on a level. 동일 평면에; 같은 높이로; 평탄하게. **2** directly. 직접. [↑]

flush[3] [flʌʃ] *vi.* (P1) (of birds) fly away suddenly. (새가) 푸르르 날아오르다. — *vt.* (P6) cause (a bird, etc.) to fly away. …을 푸르르 날아오르게 하다. ¶ *Our dog flushed a pheasant in the woods.* 우리 개가 숲속의 꿩을 푸르르 날려보냈다. ●**flush·er** [-ər] *n.* [↑]

flus·ter [flʌ́stər] *vt.* (P6) make (someone) nervous and confused. …을 당황케 하다; 혼란시키다. ¶ *~ oneself* 당황하다; 허둥거리다 / *Jane was flustered by her surprise guest.* 제인은 예기치 않은 손님 때문에 당황하였다.
— *vi.* (P1) become nervous and confused. 당황하다; 혼란하다. — *n.* Ⓒ 《usu. *a ~* 》 the state of being flustered; confusion. 혼란; 당황; 동요. [→flush[1]]
be all in a fluster, be in an extremely confused manner. 몹시 당황해하다.

·**flute** [flu:t] *n.* Ⓒ **1** a long, slender musical instrument with many finger holes, played by blowing into a hole near the upper end. 플루트; 저; 피리. **2** 《archit.》 a long round groove in a column or a pillar. 세로골; 둥근 홈. — *vi., vt.* (P1; 6) **1** play a flute; speak, sing or whistle in a flutelike tone. 플루트를 불다; 플루트 같은 가락으로 말하다〔노래하다, 휘파람을 불다〕. **2** 《archit.》 make a long round groove in a column, a pillar, etc. (기둥 따위에) 세로 홈을 파다. [F.]

flut·ing [flú:tiŋ] *n.* Ⓒ **1** a sound as if produced by a flute. 플루트 같은 소리; 피릿소리. **2** 《archit.》 a decoration made of long round grooves or cords. 세로홈.

flut·ist [flú:tist] *n.* Ⓒ a person who plays on the flute. 플루트 주자(奏者); 피리 부는 사람.

·**flut·ter** [flʌ́tər] *vi.* (P1,2A) **1** (of birds) move the wings lightly up and down. (훨훨) 날갯짓하다; (날개를) 퍼덕이다. **2** wave back and forth lightly and irregularly. (깃발 따위가) 펄럭거리다; 휘날리다; 나부끼다. ¶ *The curtain fluttered in the breeze.* 커튼이 미풍에 펄럭거렸다. **3** beat quickly and irregularly. 불규칙하게 빨리 뛰다〔움직이다〕. **4** be confused or nervous. 갈팡거리다; 당황하다; 조마조마해하다.
— *vt.* (P6) **1** cause (something) to move lightly. …을 퍼덕〔펄럭〕이게 하다. ¶ *The bird fluttered its wings in the cage.* 새장 속에서 새가 날갯짓했다. **2** put (someone) into a state of excitement and confusion. …을 당황케 하다.

—*n.* Ⓒ **1** a quick, fluttering movement. 날갯짓; 펄럭임. ¶ *the ~ of wings* 날갯짓. **2** confusion; excitement. 혼란; 당황; 동요. ¶ *be in a ~ over something* …으로 당황하고 있다. [→fleet]

put someone in a flutter, confuse someone. 당황케 하다.

● **flut·ter·er** [-tərər] *n.*

flut·y [flú:ti] *adj.* (**flut·i·er, flut·i·est**) having clear tones like those of a flute. 플루트〔저〕와 같은; 맑은. [*flute*]

flu·vi·al [flú:viəl] *adj.* produced by a river. 강물의 작용으로 생긴. [L. *fluvius*]

flux [flʌks] *n.* **1** Ⓒ《*sing.* only》 the act of flowing. 흐름; 유출; 유동. ¶ *~ of fluid* 유체의 유동. **2** Ⓤ the rising movement of the tide. 밀물(opp. reflux). **3** Ⓤ constant change or movement. 끊임없는 변화; 변천; 유전(流轉). ¶ *All things are in a state of ~.* 만물은 끊임없이 유전한다. **4** Ⓒ《med.》 an unnatural and abnormal discharge of blood or fluid from the body. (혈액·액체 따위의) 이상(異常) 배출〔유출〕.

the flux and reflux, **a**) ebb and flow. (조수의) 간만. **b**) ups and downs. 부침(浮沈); 영고 성쇠.

—*vt.* (P6) **1** cause to flow. 유출시키다. **2** melt. 녹이다(cf. *fuse*). [L. *fluo* flow]

:fly[1] [flai] *v.* (**flew, flown**) *vi.* (P1,2A,2B,3,4) **1** ⓐ move through the air. 날다. ¶ *A crow is flying.* 까마귀가 날고 있다 / *An arrow flew toward the target.* 화살이 과녁을 향해 날아갔다 / *Fireworks flew up.* 불꽃이 날아올랐다. ⓑ move through the air by mechanical power; operate an airplane. (비행기로) 날다〔가다〕; 비행하다; 비행기를 조종(操縱)하다. ¶ *a plane flying south* 남쪽으로 나는 비행기 / *~ to New York* 뉴욕에 비행기로 가다 / *~ in formation* 편대 비행을 하다 / *He flew back from England.* 영국에서 비행기로 되돌아왔다. **2** float or wave in the air. 공중에 뜨다〔떠돌다〕; 나부끼다; 펄럭이다. ¶ *hair flying in the wind* 바람에 나부끼는 머리카락 / *a flag flying from the tall pole* 높은 깃대에서 휘날리는 깃발 / *A paper kite flies.* 연이 (공중에) 날고 있다. **3** move or pass swiftly. (날아가듯) 달리다; 지나가다. ¶ *The ship flew.* 배가 쏜살같이 달렸다 / *Time flies like an arrow.* 시간은 화살처럼 빨리 지나간다. **4** move or change one's state suddenly. 갑자기 움직이다; 갑자기 상태가 변화하다. ¶ *The door flew open.* 문이 홱 열렸다 / *He flew into a rage.* 그는 불끈 노했다. **5** be carried, blown, or scattered. (바람 따위에) 날리다; 흩어지다. ¶ *Pieces of paper ~ about.* 종잇조각들이 여기저기 흩어져 있다 / *A glass broke and flew about.* 유리가 깨져 사방으로 흩어졌다. **6** hasten; hurry; rush. 급히 서두르다; 급히 달려가다. ¶ *He flew to her aid.* 그녀를 돕기 위해 달려갔다 / *It's getting late, I must ~.* 시간이 늦어지고 있으므로 걸음을 서둘러야겠다. **7** (《Brit.》 **fled**) run away; escape; flee. 달아나다; 도망하다; 피하다. ¶ *~ from danger* 위험을 피하다 / *~ for one's life* 필사적으로 달아나다. —*vt.* (P6) **1** cause (something) to move or float through the air. …을 날리다; …을 공중에 띄우다. ¶ *~ a kite* 〔*a balloon*〕 연을〔기구를〕 띄우다 / *~ a carrier pigeon* 전서구(傳書鳩)를 날리다. **2** operate (an airplane); go across or over (some place) by airplane. (비행기)를 조종하다; …을 비행하다. ¶ *~ a spaceship* 우주선을 조종하다 / *~ the Pacific* 태평양 상공을 날다. **3** allow to stream or wave in the air. (기를) 걸다; 게양하다; 나부끼게 하다. ¶ *~ a flag* 기를 걸다 / *~ a flag of distress* 조난 신호기를 달다. **4** carry (something) by air. …을 비행기로 나르다; 공수하다. ¶ *~ passengers over the Atlantic* 대서양 상공을 날아 여객을 수송하다. **5** escape from (some place); run away from; avoid. …에서 도망하다; 피하다. ¶ *~ the country* 국외로 도망하다 / *The bird has flown its cage.* 새가 새장에서 달아나 없다.

fly at, jump at; attack. …에 덤벼들다; …을 공격하다. ¶ *The dog flew at the thief.* 개는 도둑에게 덤벼들었다.

fly at higher game, have higher ambitions. 더욱 높은 야망〔대망〕을 품다.

fly high, 《colloq.》 have high aims; be ambitious. 야망〔야심〕이 있다; 우쭐하고 있다.

fly in the face of, openly disobey or defy. (정면으로) 맞서다〔도전하다, 반항하다〕.

fly into a rage 〔***passion, temper***〕, become suddenly angry; lose one's temper. 불끈 성내다.

fly low, avoid notoriety. 남의 눈을 거리끼다.

fly off, **a**) run away. 도망하다; 달아나다. ¶ *~ off with public money* 공금을 갖고 달아나다. **b**) take off. 이륙하다.

fly off the handle ⇨handle.

fly out, burst out into angry words (at, against); abuse. …에게 폭언을 하다.

fly to arms, quickly get ready for war. 급히 무기를 들다; 서둘러 전투 준비를 하다.

let fly, **a**) shoot at. (탄알·화살·돌 따위를) 쏘다; 날리다. ¶ *let ~ at a leopard* 표범을 향하여 쏘다 / *let ~ an arrow* 화살을 쏘다 / *let ~ with a rifle* 라이플총으로 쏘다. **b**) use strong language to; abuse; attack. 폭언을 하다; 공격하다.

make the fur 〔***feathers***〕 ***fly,*** cause quarrelling or excitement. 큰 소동을 일으키다.

make the money fly, spend it quickly. 돈을 마구 쓰다.

with flags flying, in triumph. 개가를 올리며.

—*n.* Ⓒ (*pl.* **flies**) **1** the act or process of flying; flight. 날기; 비행; 비상(飛翔). ¶ *have a ~ in an airplane* 비행기로 날다. **2** ⓐ a strip of cloth covering a row of buttons on a dress; a flap. (양복의) 단추 가림. ⓑ a piece of cloth serving as the door of a tent. 천막 출입구의 드림 (자락). **3** a baseball hit high into the air. (야구의) 플라이; 비구(飛球). [E.]

on the fly, **a**) very busily; without resting. 몹시 바쁘게. **b**) while still in the air; before touching the ground. 공중에 떠 있을 동안; 지상에 떨어지기 전에. ¶ *catch a ball on the* ~ 땅에 떨어지기 전에 공을 잡다.

:fly² [flai] *n.* Ⓒ (*pl.* **flies**) **1** a small, two-winged insect, esp. a housefly. 파리. **2** a fishhook with feathers, silk, etc. on it to make it look like a fly. 제물낚시. [↑]

a fly in the ointment, a small thing that spoils something or destroys its value. 옥에 티.

There are no flies on him. ⟪*colloq.*⟫ He is very efficient or no fool. 극히 유능하고 빈틈없는 사람이다.

fly³ [flai] *adj.* ⟪*sl.*⟫ knowing; alert; sharp; quick. 알고 있는; 방심하지 않는; 빈틈없는. [? *fly¹*]

fly·a·way [fláiəwèi] *adj.* flying loose; light and free. 나부끼는; 펄럭이는; 경박한; 마음이 들뜬. [*fly¹*]

fly·blow [fláiblòu] *n.* the egg or young larva of a fly. 쉬⟪파리의 알⟫; 구더기. [*fly²*]

fly·blown [fláiblòun] *adj.* **1** tainted by the eggs or larvae of flies. 파리가 쉬를 슨. **2** spoiled. (명성 따위가) 더럽혀진.

fly-by-night [fláibainàit] *adj.* not reliable. 믿을[신뢰할] 수 없는. —*n.* one who leaves secretly at night. 야반 도주자. [*fly¹*]

fly·catch·er [fláikæ̀tʃər] *n.* **1** an instrument for catching flies. 파리 잡는 기구. **2** a bird that catches insects while flying. 딱새. **3** a spider that catches flies. 깡충거미; 파리잡이거미. [*fly²*]

fly·er [fláiər] *n.* =flier.

fly-fish [fláifìʃ] *vi.* (P1) catch, or try to catch, fish with artificial flies. 제물낚시로 고기를 잡다.

fly·flap [fláiflæ̀p] *n.* Ⓒ an instrument used to kill flies. 파리채.

·fly·ing [fláiiŋ] *adj.* very quick. 나는 듯이 빠른; 몹시 서두르는. ¶ *a* ~ *visit* 황급한 방문. [*fly¹*]

flying boat [⌐-⌐] *n.* an airplane that can float on water. 비행정(艇).

flying column [⌐-⌐-] *n.* ⟪mil.⟫ a military force able to move rapidly. 유격대.

flying disk [⌐-⌐] *n.* =flying saucer.

Flying Dutchman [⌐-⌐-], **the** *n.* ⟪legend⟫ a ghost ship appearing near the Cape of Good Hope. 유령선.

flying field [⌐-⌐] *n.* ⟪U.S.⟫ an airfield. 소(小)비행장.

fly·ing·fish [fláiiŋfìʃ] *n.* a fish that can leap into the air and keep itself up for a time as if flying. 날치.

flying saucer [⌐-⌐-] *n.* an unidentified flying object (often disc-shaped), reported as seen moving in the sky. 비행 접시.

Flying Scotchman [⌐-⌐-] *n.* an express train for Scotland. 스코틀랜드행 급행열차.

flying spot [⌐-⌐] *n.* ⟪TV⟫ a moving beam of light which produces a succession of thin lines against a surface containing an image. 정주사용(定走査用) 광점; 비점(飛點).

flying squad [⌐-⌐] *n.* a police detachment with motor-cars for rapid pursuit. 경찰 기동대.

fly·leaf [fláilìːf] *n.* Ⓒ (*pl.* **-leaves**) a blank leaf or page at the beginning or the end of a book, a pamphlet, etc. (책의 권두·권말의) 면지; 여백의 페이지.

fly·leaves [fláilìːvz] *n.* pl. of **flyleaf.**

fly·o·ver [fláiòuvər] *n.* Ⓒ **1** a low flight by airplanes over a public place. 저공 의례 비행. **2** ⟪Brit.⟫ a highway over or across a road or railway. 고가(高架) 도로.

fly·pa·per [fláipèipər] *n.* ⓊⒸ sticky paper to catch flies. 파리잡이 끈끈이.

fly·speck [fláispèk] *n.* a tiny spot left by a fly. 파리똥 자국. —*vt.* (P6) make flyspecks on. …에 파리똥 자국을 묻히다.

fly·trap [fláitræ̀p] *n.* Ⓒ **1** a trap to catch flies. 파리잡이통. **2** ⟪bot.⟫ a plant that catches insects in its flower. 파리풀.

fly·weight [fláiwèit] *n.* (the class of) a boxer who weighs 112 pounds or less. (권투의) 플라이급 (선수).

fly·wheel [fláihwìːl] *n.* Ⓒ a heavy metal wheel to keep the speed of the machine constant. 플라이휠; 속도 조절 바퀴.

F.M. frequency modulation.

F.O. ⟪Brit.⟫ Foreign Office; ⟪Brit.⟫ Flying Officer(공군 장교).

foal [foul] *n.* Ⓒ a very young horse or donkey. 망아지; 새끼나귀. —*vt., vi.* (P6; 1) give birth to (a foal). (망아지)를 낳다. [E.]

·foam [foum] *n.* Ⓤ **1** ⟪sometimes *a* ~⟫ the mass of small bubbles which forms on the surface of a liquid. 거품. **2** ⟪*poet.*⟫ the sea. (거품 이는) 바다. ¶ *sail the* ~ 바다를 항해하다. —*vi.* (P1,2A,3) **1** produce foam. 거품을 내다. **2** form bubbles on water, etc. 거품이 일다. ¶ *foaming beer* 거품이 이는 맥주. [E.]

foam at the mouth, **a**) produce foam at the mouth when in a fit. 발작이 있을 때 입에 게거품을 뿜다. **b**) ⟪*fig.*⟫ be fiercely angry. 격노하다.

foam·y [fóumi] *adj.* (**foam·i·er, foam·i·est**) **1** foaming. 거품이 이는. **2** filled with foam. 거품투성이의. **3** like foam 거품 같은.
● **foam·i·ly** [-li] *adv.*

fob¹ [fɑb / fɔb] *n.* **1** Ⓒ a small pocket below the waistline of a man's trousers for carrying a watch, etc.; a watch pocket. 바지의 허리 호주머니. **2** ⟪U.S.⟫ a short chain attached to a watch and hanging from such a pocket. (그런 호주머니의) 회중시곗줄(=fob chain). [G.]

fob[2] [fɑb / fɔb] *vt.* (**fobbed**) (P7) 《*arch.*》 deceive; cheat. 속이다. [G.]
fob off, **a**) cheat or deceive (someone) by giving or selling him something of no value. (거짓 약속 따위로 아무를) 속이다. ¶ *She fobbed us off with false promises.* 그녀는 거짓 약속으로 우리를 속였다. **b**) give or sell something of no value. (가짜·엉터리 물건 따위를) 속여 팔다(주다). ¶ *~ off an imitation pearl on someone* 아무에게 가짜 진주를 팔다.

f.o.b., F.O.B. free on board.

fo·cal [fóukəl] *adj.* of a focus. 초점의. ¶ *the ~ length of a lens* 렌즈의 초점 거리. [→ focus]

fo·cal·ize [fóukəlàiz] *vt.* (P6) **1** focus; bring into a focus. 초점에 모으다; 초점에 맞추다. **2** bring to one place. 집중하다.

fo·ci [fóusai] *n.* pl. of **focus.**

·**fo·cus** [fóukəs] *n.* Ⓒ (*pl.* **-cus·es** or **fo·ci**) **1** a point where rays of light meet after being reflected by a mirror or refracted by a lens. 초점. ¶ *a real ~* 실(實)초점 / *a virtual ~* 허(虛)초점 / *out of ~* 초점을 벗어나 / *bring into ~* 초점을(핀트를) 맞추다. **2** the distance to such a point from the center of a lens. 초점 거리. **3** an adjustment of a person's eyes or a camera lens to make an outline into a clear image. 초점을 맞추기 위한 조정. **4** a center of attention, interest, activity, etc. (흥미·관심·주목·활동 따위의) 중심; 초점. ¶ *the ~ of an earthquake* 진앙지(震央地) / *the ~ of interest of the whole world* 전세계의 흥미의 초점.
— *v.* (**-cused, -cus·ing** or 《Brit.》 **-cussed, -cus·sing**) *vt.* (P6,13) **1** bring (something) into focus. …을 초점에 모으다. **2** adjust the distance of (a lens) to make a clear image. (렌즈)의 초점을 맞추다. ¶ *~ the lens of a camera* 카메라 렌즈의 초점을 맞추다. **3** fix (all one's attention) on one thing. (주의)를 집중하다. ¶ *~ one's efforts* 노력을 집중하다 / *~ one's thoughts* (*attention*) *on work* 일에 생각을(주의를) 집중하다.
— *vi.* (P1,2A) **1** come to a focus. 초점에 모이다. **2** adjust one's camera or eyes to make a clear image. (렌즈 따위의) 초점을 맞추다. [L.=hearth]

fod·der [fádər / fɔ́d-] *n.* Ⓤ coarse dried food for horses, cattle, etc. 꼴; 여물; 마초. [E.]

·**foe** [fou] *n.* Ⓒ **1** 《*poet.*》 an enemy, esp. an enemy in war. 적; 원수. **2** 《*fig.*》 something that destroys. 해를 끼치는 것; 파괴하는 것. ¶ *Sloth is the ~ of health.* 나태는 건강의 적. [E.]

foe·man [fóumən] *n.* (*pl.* **-men** [-mən]) 《*arch., poet.*》 an enemy in war; a foe. (전쟁에서의) 적(병). ¶ *a ~ worthy of one's steel* 호적수; 맞수.

foe·tid [fétid / fí:t-] *adj.* =fetid.

foe·tus [fí:təs] *n.* =fetus.

·**fog** [fɔ(:)g / fɑg] *n.* **1** ⓊⒸ very thick mist; a mass of fine drops of water near the earth's surface; a cloud-like mass of smoke, dust, etc. in the air. 안개; 아지랑이; 연무. ¶ *a ~ warning* 안개 경보 / *The ~ has cleared* (*off*). 안개가 걷혔다. **2** Ⓒ mental confusion. 정신적 혼란 상태; 곤혹; 당혹. ¶ *in a ~* 당혹하여 / *out of a ~ of recollection* 어렴풋한 기억으로부터 / *I'm quite in a ~ as to what you mean.* 하시는 말씀을 도무지 이해할 수가 없습니다. **3** ⓊⒸ 《photog.》 a cloud on a print of a photograph. (사진 인화의) 뿌염; 흐림.
— *v.* (**fogged, fog·ging**) *vt.* (P6) **1** cover (something) with fog. …을 안개로 싸다. **2** confuse (one's mind). (마음)을 혼미시키다. **3** produce a cloud in (a photograph). (사진)을 흐리게 하다.
— *vi.* **1** become covered with fog. 안개에 싸이다(덮이다). **2** (of a photograph) become fogged. (사진이) 흐려지다. [E. *foggy* marshy]

fog bank [⌐ ⌐] *n.* a dense mass of fog on the sea. 무봉(霧峰)《멀리 해상에 둑처럼 보이는 짙은 안개의 켜》.

fog·bound [fɔ́(:)gbàund / fág-] *adj.* unable to sail because of heavy fog. (배가) 안개에 발이 묶인; 짙은 안개로 항행 불능의.

fo·gey [fóugi] *n.* =fogy.

fog·gy [fɔ́(:)gi / fági] *adj.* (**-gi·er, -gi·est**) **1** covered with fog. 안개가 낀(자욱한). **2** not clear. 안개 낀 것같이 흐린(어두운); 분명치 않은; 어렴풋한. **3** confused. (사고 따위가) 혼란된; 곤혹의. [*fog*]

fog·horn [fɔ́(:)ghɔ̀:rn / fág-] *n.* Ⓒ a horn blown to warn ships in a fog. 무적(霧笛).

fo·gy [fóugi] *n.* Ⓒ (*pl.* **-gies**) 《usu. *old ~*》 a person who is out of date in thought and action. (생각·행동 따위가) 시대에 뒤떨어진 사람. [E.=marsh]

foi·ble [fɔ́ibəl] *n.* Ⓒ a weak point in a person's character. (성격상의) 약점; 결함. ¶ *an all-too-human ~* 너무나도 인간적인 약점. [→feeble]

foil[1] [fɔil] *vt.* (P6) **1** 《hunting》 spoil or confuse (the scent, etc.). (짐승이 사냥개를 따돌리기 위해) 냄새를 지우다; 자귀를 혼란시키다. **2** prevent someone from being successful in (plans, etc.); baffle. (계획 따위)를 좌절시키다; 허를 찌르다. [orig. = trample, from L. *fullo* fuller]

foil[2] [fɔil] *n.* **1** Ⓤ a very thin, paperlike sheet of metal. 금속의 박편(薄片); 박(箔). ¶ *gold ~* 금박. **2** Ⓒ a person or thing that makes another seem better by contrast. 돋보이게 하는 사람(것). ¶ *play the ~ to someone* 아무를 돋보이게 하는 역을 맡아 하다 / *serve as a ~ to someone's beauty* 아무의 아름다움을 돋보이게 하는 역할을 하다. [L. *folium* leaf]

foil[3] [fɔil] *n.* Ⓒ a long light sword with a button on the point, used in fencing;

《*pl.*》 the act of fencing. 펜싱의 경기검(劍); 펜싱. [?]

foist [fɔist] *vt.* (P7,13) 《*on*》 sell (something worthless) to someone by a dirty trick. (가짜)를 속여 팔다[주다]. ¶ ~ *inferior goods* (*off*) *on someone* 아무에게 불량품을 떠맡기다. [Du. *vuist* fist]

fol. folio; following.

:fold[1] [fould] *vt.* **1** (P6,7) bend and press one part of (something) over another part. …을 접다; 개키다. ¶ ~ *a letter in two* 편지를 반으로 접다 / ~ *up a newspaper* 신문을 접다 / ~ *up beddings* [*one's clothes*] 침구를[옷을] 개키다 / ~ *back the sleeves* 소매를 접어 젖히다 / *A bird folds its wings.* 새가 날개를 접는다. **2** (P6,13) hold (one's arms, hands, etc.) over one another. (팔짱·손 따위)를 끼다; 잡다. ¶ *with folded arms* 팔짱을 끼고. **3** (P13) put the arms around (something) to hold it. …을 (껴)안다. ¶ *She folded her child to her breast.* 그녀는 그녀 아이를 가슴에 껴안았다. **4** (P6,13) wrap, wind, around a thing. …을 싸다; 휘감다. ¶ ~ *one's cloak about oneself* 외투를 걸쳐 입다 / ~ *the blanket round one's naked body* 알몸에 담요를 두르다.

— *vi.* (P1,2A) be folded. 접히다; 포개지다. ¶ *It folds in three.* 그건 셋으로 접힌다.

fold up, **a**) make (something) compact by folding. …을 차곡차곡 개키다; 가지런히 접다. **b**) 《*colloq.*》 fail; collapse. 실패하다; 쓰러지다; 무너지다.

— *n.* Ⓒ **1** a part that is folded. 접힌 부분; 접혀 포개진 데; 켜. **2** a mark made by folding; a hollow made by folded parts. (접은) 금; 주름. ¶ *a* ~ *in a blanket* 담요의 접힌 데[주름]. [E.]

fold[2] [fould] *n.* Ⓒ **1** a small enclosure for sheep. 양 우리. **2** 《*the* ~》 the sheep keep in a fold. (우리 안의) 양떼. **3** the Christian church; the members of a church. 기독교회; 교회 신도들. — *vt.* (P6) keep (sheep) in a fold. (양)을 우리에 가두다. [E.]

-fold [-fould] *suf.* times as many, as much, as great; having many parts. '…배의[로], …중[겹]의'의 뜻. ¶ *manifold* / *threefold.* [↓]

fold·er [fóuldər] *n.* Ⓒ **1** a person or thing that folds. 접는 사람[기구]. **2** a sheet of stiff paper used to cover or hold loose papers. 종이 끼우개. **3** a booklet or pamphlet folded up but not stitched. 접이 책《팜플렛 따위》. **4** 《*pl.*》 a pair of folding eye-glasses. 접는 안경. [*fold*[1]]

fold·ing [fóuldiŋ] *adj.* that can be folded. 접을 수 있는. ¶ *a* ~ *bed* 접침대 / *a* ~ *fan* 접[쥘]부채.

folding doors [⌐⌐ ⌐] *n. pl.* doors with hinged parts so that they can be folded or unfolded. (경첩으로 이어진) 접이문.

fo·li·a·ceous [fòuliéiʃəs] *adj.* **1** of or like a leaf. 잎의; 잎 모양의. **2** having many leaves; covered with leaves. 잎이 많은; 잎으로 뒤덮인. [L. *folium* leaf]

·fo·li·age [fóuliidʒ] *n.* Ⓤ 《*collectively*》 all the leaves of a plant or a tree. 잎. ¶ *two trees with the* ~ *still on them* 아직 잎이 지지 않은 두 그루의 나무. [↓]

fo·li·ate [fóuliit, -lièit] *adj.* having leaves; covered with leaves. 잎이 있는; 잎으로 덮인. — [fóulièit] *vi.* (P1) send out leaves. 잎이 나다. ●**fo·li·a·tion** [fòuliéiʃən] *n.* [L. *folium* leaf]

fo·li·o [fóuliòu] *n.* Ⓒ (*pl.* **-li·os**) **1** a large sheet of paper folded once to make two leaves, or four pages, of a book, etc. 2절지(二折紙). **2** a large book made of sheets of paper folded in this way. 2절판(判)의 책. **3** 《print.》 a page number of a book. 페이지 수; 페이지 매기기. [*fold*[1]]

folio verso [⌐-- ⌐-] *n.* the back of the page. 이면(裏面).

:folk [fouk] *n.* Ⓒ (*pl.* **folks** or *collectively* **folk**) **1** 《often *pl.*》 people in general. 사람들. ¶ *as folks say* (세상) 사람들이 말하듯이 / *city* [*country*] *folk*(*s*) 도시[시골] 사람들 / *old folks* 노인들 / *poor folks* 가난한 사람들. **2** 《usu. *pl.*》《*colloq.*》 the members of one's family. 가족; 일족. ¶ *my folks* 우리 집 식구들. **3** 《*arch.*》 a nation; a race. 국민; 민족; 종족. [E.]

folk dance [⌐ ⌐] *n.* a dance originating among the common people and handed down from age to age; a piece of music for such a dance. 민속[향토] 무용; 그 음악.

folk·lore [fóuklɔ̀:r] *n.* Ⓤ the beliefs, customs and sayings of a people handed down from age to age; the study of these. 민간 전승; 민속학(cf. *ethnology*).

folk song [⌐ ⌐] *n.* a song made and handed down among the common people; a song composed in the style of such a song. 민요; 속요(俗謠); 포크 송.

folk·sy [fóuksi] *adj.* **1** sociable. 사교적인. **2** simple; unpretentious. 소박한. [*folk*]

folk tale [⌐ ⌐] *n.* a story originating among the common people and handed down from age to age. (민간) 전승[전설] 이야기; 민간 설화.

folk·ways [fóukwèiz] *n. pl.* a custom or habit that has grown up with in a social group. 풍습; 민습(民習); 관습.

:fol·low [fálou / fɔ́l-] *vt.* **1** (P6,7) ⓐ go or come after; succeed to (something). …을 따라가다; …의 뒤[다음]에 오다; …에 잇[뒤]따르다. ¶ ~ (*after*) *a guide* 안내자의 뒤를 따르다 / *Spring follows winter.* 봄은 겨울 다음에 온다. ⓑ go after in order to catch; pursue; chase. (잡기 위해) 뒤쫓다; 추적하다. ¶ ~ *a fox* 여우를 뒤쫓다 / ~ *a retreating enemy* 후퇴하는 적을 추적하다 / *I think, we're being followed.* 우리는 추적당하고 있다고 생각한다. ⓒ go along with (some-

one); accompany; attend. (…와) 함께 가다; 수행〔동행〕하다. ¶ ～ *the corpse to church* 교회까지 유해의 뒤를 따르다 / *He followed her home from the party.* 그는 파티장(場)에서 집까지 그녀를 바래다 주었다. **2** (P6) result from (something). …의 결과로서 일어나다〔따르다〕. ¶ *Disease follows intemperance.* 병은 무절제에서 온다 / *Misery follows war.* 전쟁 뒤에는 비참한 상태가 뒤따른다 / *The effect follows the cause.* 원인이 있으면 결과가 있다. **3** (P6) go or walk along (a road, etc.). (길 따위)를 따라서 가다. ¶ *Follow this road for a mile.* 이 길을 따라 1마일을 가시오 / *Follow the river and you'll get to the sea.* 강을 끼고 가시면 바다에 이릅니다. **4** (P6) act according to (something); obey. (관습·규칙·명령 따위)에 따르다; …을 지키다; 복종하다. ¶ ～ *the rules* 〔*someone's directions*〕 규칙〔아무의 지시〕에 따르다 / *Following your advice I kept from saying anything.* 네 충고에 따라 나는 아무 말도 하지 않았다. **5** (P6,13) take the place of in an office, position, etc.; succeed. …의 후임으로 들어앉다; …의 뒤를 잇다. ¶ ～ *one's father in his estates* 아버지의 뒤를 이어 재산을 상속하다. **6** (P6) watch the movements or course of; keep one's eyes on; observe carefully. (움직임·진행·진로 따위)를 지켜 보다; 눈으로 뒤쫓다; 주의를 돌리다. ¶ ～ *a bird in flight* 날고 있는 새를 지켜 보다 / *fail to* ～ *the ball* 공의 방향을 놓치다 / ～ *a departing train with one's eyes* 떠나는 열차를 눈으로 뒤쫓다 / *The medical students kept following the operation.* 의과생들은 수술을 계속 지켜 보고 있었다. **7** (P6) use or take as a model; copy; imitate. …을 모범으로 삼다〔본뜨다〕; …에 따르다; 흉내내다. ¶ ～ *a lead* 앞 사람이 한 대로 따르다 / ～ *someone's example* 아무의 예에 따르다. **8** (P6) understand clearly. (이야기·경과 따위)를 이해하다. ¶ ～ *a play* 연극의 줄거리를 이해하다 / *Do you* ～ *me?* 제 말을 알아듣겠습니까 / *I could not* ～ *his speech.* 그의 연설을 이해할 수가 없었다. **9** (P6) take (something) as one's work. …을 직업으로 하다; …에 종사하다. ¶ ～ *the sea* 뱃사람이 되다 / ～ *the law* 법률에 종사하다; 변호사를 업으로 하다 / ～ *the trade of a carpenter* 목수를 직업으로 삼다.
— *vi.* **1** (P1,2A, 2B) 《*after*》 go or come after. 뒤를 잇다; 다음〔뒤〕에 따르다; 뒤에 오다. ¶ *Go on ahead, and I'll* ～. 앞장 서서 가시오, 따라 갈 테니까 / *The policeman followed after the man.* 경관은 사나이의 뒤를 밟았다. **2** (P1) ⓐ occur later. 나중에 일어나다. ¶ *No one knows what may* ～. 나중에 무슨 일이 있을지 아무도 모른다. ⓑ result logically. 당연히 …한 결과가 되다. ¶ *They are rich but it doesn't* ～ *that they must be happy.* 그들은 부자지만 그렇다고 꼭 행복하다곤 할 수 없다.

as follows, as is written below. 다음과 같이. ¶ *He argued as follows.* 그의 의론은 다음과 같다.

follow home, reason something out to the end. 끝까지 추적하다; 철저하게 추구하다.

follow** one's **nose, go in a straight course. 곧 바로 나아가다.

follow on, follow after an interval. 곧 뒤따르다.

follow out, carry out (something) to the end. 끝까지 해내다; 완수하다. ¶ ～ *out a plan* 끝까지 계획을 완수하다 / ～ *out directions* 지시를 실행하다 / ～ *out the great ideas* 그 위대한 사상을 끝까지 추구하다.

follow through, swing (a bat, racket, etc.) fully. (타구할 때 배트 따위를) 크게 휘두르다.

follow up, **a)** follow closely. 바짝 뒤쫓다. **b)** carry out (something) to the end. …을 철저하게 추구하다. **c)** increase the effect of (something) by doing it more. 효과를 더 올리기 위해 더욱 노력하다.

— *n.* Ⓒ the act or process of following. 뒤쫓음; 뒤따름; 수행; 추구. [E.]

:fol·low·er [fálouər / fɔ́l-] *n.* Ⓒ **1** a person who follows; a servant. 뒤따르는 사람; 종자(從者); 수행원; 부하. **2** a supporter of the beliefs or teachings of another. (신앙·학설 따위의) 추종자; 지지자.

:fol·low·ing [fálouiŋ / fɔ́l-] *adj.* going or coming after; next. 다음의; 다음에 오는; 이하의. ¶ *the* ～ *day* 이튿날 / *in the* ～ *year* ≒ *in the year* ～ 이듬해 / *the* ～ 하기(下記)〔다음〕의 것. — *n.* Ⓒ 《*collectively*》 a group of followers. 전수행원; 부하; 신봉자. ¶ *He has a large* ～. 그는 추종자들이 많다.

:fol·ly [fáli / fɔ́li] *n.* (*pl.* **-lies**) **1** Ⓤ the state of being foolish. 어리석음; 우열(愚劣). ¶ *counterfeit* ～ 짐짓 어리석은 체하다. **2** Ⓒ a foolish act or idea. 우행(愚行); 어리석은 생각. [→fool]

fo·ment [foumént] *vt.* (P6) **1** bathe (a hurt or a painful place) with warm water or medical lotion. (환부)를 찜질하다. **2** help the growth or development of (usu. something undesirable). …을 조장하다. ¶ ～ *a riot* 폭동을 유발하다 / ～ *a revolution* 혁명을 부추기다. [L. *foveo* cherish]

fo·men·ta·tion [fòumentéiʃən] *n.* Ⓤ **1** treatment of a hurt or a painful place with warm water or medical lotion. 찜질. **2** the act of stirring up; encouragement. 조장; 촉진; 자극; 유발.

:fond [fand / fɔnd] *adj.* **1** liking. 좋아하는. **2** affectionate; tender. 애정 있는; 다정한. ¶ *a* ～ *mother* 다정하신 어머니 / ～ *caresses* 애무 / *give someone a* ～ *look* 아무를 애정어린 눈으로 보다. **3** loving too much; foolishly loving. 지나치게 귀여워하는; 정에 무른. ¶ *a* ～ *parent* 자식에게 무른 부모. [M.E. *fonned*]

be fond of, like; love. …을 좋아하다. ¶ *be* ～ *of society* 〔*company*〕 사교를 좋아하다 / *He is* ～ *of drinking.* 그는 술을 좋아한다.

fon·dle [fάndl / fɔ́ndl] *vt.* (P6) touch or stroke (someone or something) gently with love or affection. …을 귀여워하다; 애무하다. ¶ ~ *a kitten* 새끼고양이를 쓰다듬다. [*fond*]

fond·ly [fάndli / fɔ́nd-] *adv.* **1** affectionately; lovingly. 다정하게; 애정을 담아. **2** foolishly; ignorantly. 어리석게도. [*fond*]

fond·ness [fάndnis / fɔ́nd-] *n.* Ⓤ tender liking; doting affection. 애호; 익애(溺愛); 무턱대고 좋아[귀여워]함. ¶ *out of* ~ 좋아서.

fon·due [fάndu:, fandú: / fɔ́ndju:] *n.* ⓊⒸ a dish made of eggs, butter, etc., plus melted cheese. 퐁뒤《버터·치즈를 녹여 달걀을 풀어 만든 요리》. [F.]

font [fant / fɔnt] *n.* Ⓒ **1** a basin to contain the water for baptism. 세례반(盤); 성수반(聖水盤). **2** 《*poet.*》 a fountain. 샘. [L. *fons* fountain]

:food [fu:d] *n.* Ⓤ **1** anything eaten or drunk by a person or an animal, or taken in by a plant to live and grow. 음식; 먹이; 식량; 영양물. ¶ ~ *and drink* 음식물 / ~ *, clothing, and shelter* 의식주 / *daily* ~ 일상의 음식 / *a staple* ~ 주식(主食) / *cook one's own* ~ 자취하다 / *become* ~ *for fishes* 물고기 밥이 되다《물에 빠져 죽다》/ *supply someone with* ~ *and drink* 아무에게 음식을 공급하다. **2** something that serves in any way. (생각 따위의) 양식; (사고·반성의) 자료. ¶ ~ *for thought* 사고의 양식 / ~ *for reflection* 반성의 자료 / *mental* ~ 마음의 양식《독서 따위》. [E.]

be food for worms, be dead. 죽다.

food chain [ˊ ˋ] *n.* a series of organisms ordered according to each organism's use of the next as a food source. 먹이사슬.

food·stuff [fú:dstʌ̀f] *n.* Ⓒ 《often *pl.*》 a material used as food. 식료품; 식량.

:fool [fu:l] *n.* Ⓒ **1** a foolish person. 바보. ¶ *a big* 〔*downright*〕 ~ 지독한 바보 / *a born* ~ 타고난 바보. **2** a person who is tricked. 바보 취급당하는〔만만한〕 사람; 우롱당하는 사람. ¶ *an April* ~ 만우절 바보. **3** a person formerly kept by a king or nobleman to provide amusement. (중세의 궁정 등의) 어릿광대.

be a fool for one's pains, make an effort in vain. 헛수고를 하다; 헛애를 쓰다.

be a fool to, be nothing in comparison with. …와는 비교도 안 되다; …의 발 밑에도 미치지 못하다.

be fool enough to do, do (something) in a very foolish way; do a foolish thing. 어리석게도 …하다; 어리석은 짓을 하다.

be in a fool's paradise, be in happy ignorance of danger. 닥칠 위험을 까맣게 모르고 있다.

be no fool, be clever and capable. 빈틈이 없다.

make a fool of (=*deceive* or *make fun of*) *someone.* …을 속이다; …을 우롱하다〔놀리다〕.

play the fool, **a**) act like a fool; behave like a clown. 바보처럼 행동하다; 어릿광대처럼 굴다. **b**) do silly things; blunder. 바보 같은 짓을 하다; 실수하다.

play the fool with (=*cheat*) *someone.* …을 속이다.

— *vi.* (P1,2A,3) **1** act like a fool. 바보 같은 짓을 하다. **2** joke. 농담을 하다; 장난치다; 까불다. ¶ *Don't* ~ *with the pistol.* 권총 갖고 장난하지 마라. — *vt.* (P6,7,13) **1** make a fool of (someone); deceive. …을 놀리다; 우롱하다; 속이다. ¶ ~ *someone out of his money* 아무에게서 돈을 속여 빼앗다 / ~ *someone to his ruin* 아무를 속여서 파멸시키다. **2** waste in a foolish way. 어리석게 낭비〔허비〕하다. [L. *follis* bellows, windbag]

fool around 〔***about***〕***,*** idle or hang about foolishly and with no set purpose. 목적 없이 어정거리다; 빈둥거리다; 시간을 낭비하다. ¶ *spend much time fooling around* 빈둥거리며 많은 시간을 허송하다.

fool away, spend (time, money, etc.) foolishly. (시간·돈)을 헛되이 쓰다.

fool someone into doing, deceive and so make someone do something. …을 속여 —하게 하다.

fool with, play foolishly with. …을 만지작거리다. ¶ ~ *with a loaded gun* 장전된 총을 만지작거리다.

fool·er·y [fú:ləri] *n.* ⓊⒸ (*pl.* **-er·ies**) a foolish act. 어리석은 행위.

fool·har·dy [fú:lhὰ:rdi] *adj.* (**-di·er, -di·est**) without thought; bold. 무모한. ¶ *pay for a* ~ *act with one's life* 무모한 짓을 하여 목숨을 잃다.

:fool·ish [fú:liʃ] *adj.* without good sense; silly; stupid. 어리석은; 분별 없는. ●**fool·ish·ly** [-li] *adv.* **fool·ish·ness** [-nis] *n.*

fool·proof [fú:lprù:f] *adj.* 《*colloq.*》 so safe or simple that even a fool can use, handle, and understand it correctly. (바보라도 할 수 있는) 간단한; 취급하기 쉬운.

fools·cap [fú:lzkæ̀p, fú:ls-] *n.* Ⓒ a size of writing paper, usu. 13×17 inches. (양지(洋紙)의) 풀스캡판(判); 대판 양지(大判洋紙)《13×17 인치》.

fool's cap [ˊ ˋ] *n.* a cap formerly worn by a clown. (방울 따위가 달린 원뿔형의) 어릿광대모(帽).

〈fool's cap〉

:foot [fut] *n.* Ⓒ (*pl.* **feet**) **1** the end part of a leg on which a person or an animal stands or walks. 발. ¶ *the instep of a* ~ 발등 / *rise to one's feet* 일어서다 / *drag one's weary feet* 피곤한 다리를 질질 끌다 / *stamp one's* ~ *in passion* 성이 나서 발을 동동 구르다 / *He had no shoes on his feet.* 그는 발에 신을 신지 않고 있었다. **2** the lowest part, place, or end of anything; the bottom; the base. (모든 것의) 발에 해당하는 부분; 최저〔최하〕부; 말미; 자락. ¶ *the* ~ *of a mountain* 산기슭 / *the feet of a table* 테이블의 다리. **3** a step or tread. 발걸음. ¶ *a light* 〔*heavy*〕 ~ 가벼운〔무거운〕 발걸음 / *have leaden feet* 발걸음이 무겁다. **4** 《*collectively*》 soldiers who fight on foot; the infantry. 보병. ¶ ~ *and horse* 보병과 기병 / *the 4 th Regiment of Foot* 보병 제4 연대. **5** a measure of length. 피트. 參考 1 foot 는 12인치《약 30센티미터》. **6** one of the parts into which a line of poetry is divided. (시의) 운각(韻脚).

at a foot's pace, at a walking pace. 보행 속도로; 보통 걸음으로.

at someone's feet, under the control of someone; as someone's disciple. …의 말대로; …에게 복종하여〔매료되어〕; …의 제자로서.

be on one's feet, a) be standing; walking, etc. 서 있다; 걷고 있다. b) be well again after illness. 병 후에 건강을 되찾다. ¶ *This medicine will soon have you on your feet again.* 이 약을 쓰면 곧 건강을 되찾을 수 있을 겁니다. c) stand up, esp. in order to speak. (말을 하기 위해) 일어서다. ¶ *No sooner had the question been put than he was on his feet to reply.* 질문이 있자마자 그는 답변을 위해 자리에서 일어섰다.

carry someone off his feet, make someone very enthusiastic; rouse someone's enthusiasm. …을 열중케 하다; 열광시키다.

fall 〔***drop***〕 ***on one's feet,*** come out of a difficult state of affairs without harm; have good luck. 좋지 않은 형편에도 잘 되어 가다; 용케 궁지에서 벗어나다; 운이 좋다.

find one's feet, a) (esp. of a baby or young animal) begin to be able to stand and walk. 설 수 있게 되다. b) learn to manage well. 본래의 특성을 발휘하다.

find 〔***get, have, know***〕 ***the length of someone's foot,*** learn someone's weak points. …의 약점을 알다.

get 〔***have***〕 ***cold feet,*** be too nervous to do something, esp. losing courage just before something. …하기를 겁내다; 걱정하다; 기운을 잃다.

have one foot in the grave, be near death. 다 죽어가고 있다.

jump to one's feet, get up quickly and suddenly. 갑자기〔벌떡〕 일어나다.

keep one's feet, a) continue standing. 곧추 서 있다; 넘어지지 않다. ¶ *keep one's feet on the icy slope* 빙판진 비탈을 넘어지지 않고 걷다. b) act carefully. 신중히 행동하다.

miss one's foot, take a wrong step. 발을 헛디디다.

on foot, a) standing or walking. 서서; 도보로. ¶ *go on* ~ 걸어서 가다. b) (of an enterprise, etc.) in progress. 착수되어; 진행 중에. ¶ *set an enterprise on* ~ 사업을 발족시키다.

put one's best foot forward, a) walk as fast as possible. 될 수 있는 대로 빨리 걷다〔서두르다〕. b) do one's utmost. 최선을 다하다.

put one's foot down, 《*fig.*》 act firmly or decisively, esp. to stop someone else's action. 단호히 행동하다; 단호한 태도를 취하다.

put one's foot in it 〔***one's mouth***〕, say the wrong thing or make an awkward mistake. 실수를 하다.

rush someone off his feet, make someone do too much in too short a time. 단시간 내에 지나치게 많은 일을 하게 하다.

set foot in 〔***on***〕, enter; visit; land. …에 발을 들여놓다; …에 들어가다; 상륙하다. ¶ *since the white man set* ~ *in America* 백인이 아메리카에 발을 들여놓은 이래.

set 〔***put, have***〕 ***one's foot on the neck of,*** utterly subdue. …을 완전히 정복하다.

set someone on his feet, make someone self-supporting. …를 자립시키다.

set on foot, start. 시작하다. ¶ *set negotiations on* ~ 협상을 시작하다.

trample 〔***tread***〕 ***someone or something under foot,*** override; oppress. 짓밟다. ¶ *trample the will of the people under* ~ 민의(民意)를 짓밟다.

— *vt., vi.* (P6,7; 2A,3) **1** walk. 걷다. ¶ ~ *the road* 길을 걷다. **2** dance; kick. 춤추다; (발로) 차다. ¶ ~ *the stage* 스테이지에서 춤추다. **3** make the foot of (a stocking, etc.). (스타킹의) 족부(足部)를 만들다. **4** 《*up*》 add up. 합계하다. ¶ ~ (*up*) *the account.* **5** pay (a bill, expenses, etc.). (셈·비용 따위)를 지불하다. ¶ *I'll* ~ *the bill.* 그 셈은 내가 치르겠다. **6** 《*colloq.*》 amount to. 총계 …에 달하다. [E.]

foot it, a) dance. 춤추다. b) 《*colloq.*》 go on foot. 걸어서〔도보로〕 가다.

foot·age [fútidʒ] *n.* Ⓤ the length in feet. 피트 단위의 길이.

·foot·ball [fútbɔ̀:l] *n.* **1** Ⓤ a field game played with a large leather ball by two teams of 11 players. 축구; 풋볼. ¶ *American* ~ 미식 축구 / *Association* ~ 아식 축구; 사커. **2** Ⓒ a ball of leather used in this game. 축구공.

foot·board [fútbɔ̀:*r*d] *n.* Ⓒ a board or small platform to support the feet. 발판; 디딜판.

foot·bridge [fútbrìdʒ] *n.* Ⓒ a narrow bridge for persons who are walking. 보행자 전용교(橋); 인도교.

foot-can·dle [fútkǽndl] *n.* 《phys.》 the unit for measuring illumination (it was supposed to be the amount of light produced by a standard candle at a distance of one foot). 피트 촉광(燭光).

foot·fall [fútfɔ̀:l] *n.* Ⓒ **1** a footstep. 발자국; 발걸음. **2** the sound of a footstep. 발소리.

foot·gear [fútgìə*r*] *n.* Ⓤ 《*collectively*》 covering for the feet, such as shoes, boots, and slippers. 신발류《신발·양말 따위》.

foot·hill [fúthìl] *n.* Ⓒ 《usu. *pl.*》 a low hill near the base of a mountain or mountain range. 산기슭의 작은 언덕.

foot·hold [fúthòuld] *n.* Ⓒ **1** a place for supporting the feet. 발판. **2** a firm position. 확고한 지위〔기반〕.

foot·ing [fútiŋ] *n.* Ⓒ 《usu. *sing.*》 **1** ⓊⒸ a place supporting the feet. 발판. ¶ *He lost his ~ and fell.* 그는 발판을 헛디뎌 떨어졌다 / *Mind your ~.* 발밑을 조심해라. **2** an established position; a status. (확립된) 기반; 지반; 지위; 자격. ¶ *on an equal ~ with* …와 같은 자격으로 / *get* 〔*gain*〕 *a ~ in the company* 회사에서 확고한 지위를 구축하다. **3** a relationship to others. (남과의) 사이; 관계. ¶ *He is on a friendly ~ with many people.* 그는 사람들과 친밀한 사이다 / *What ~ are you on with her?* 그 여자와는 어떤 관계인가. **4** 《comm.》 the amount obtained by adding up figures. 합계; 총계. **5** the part of a building, etc. which touches the earth. (건물의) 기초. **6** the act of moving on the feet in dancing. 춤의 스텝.

foot·lights [fútlàits] *n. pl.* a row of lights in the front of a stage, nearly on a level with the feet of actors. 각광. ¶ *get across the ~* 두드러지다; 각광을 받다. [*foot*] ***appear*** 〔***come***〕 ***before the footlights,*** attract the attention of people; appear on the stage; be an actor. 각광을 받다; 무대에 서다.

foot·man [fútmən] *n.* Ⓒ (*pl.* **-men** [-mən]) a man servant, usu. in a uniform, who waits on the table, opens the doors, attends his master when driving, etc. (제복을 입은) 종복(從僕); 하인.

foot·mark [fútmὰːrk] *n.* Ⓒ a footprint. 발자국.

foot·note [fútnòut] *n.* Ⓒ a note at the bottom of a page. 각주(脚註). — *vt.* (P6) add such a note to (a text, etc.). …에 각주를 달다.

foot·pad [fútpæ̀d] *n.* Ⓒ a highway robber who goes on foot. (도보의) 노상 강도. 參考 highwayman은 보통 말 탄 강도를 말함.

foot passenger [⌐ ⌐−−] *n.* a person who goes on foot. 보행자; 통행인.

foot·path [fútpæ̀θ / -pὰːθ] *n.* Ⓒ (*pl.* **-paths** [-pæ̀ðz, -pæ̀θs / -pɑːðz]) a narrow path for persons on foot; a sidewalk. 보행자용의 작은 길; 보도(步道).

foot-pound [fútpàund] *n.* 《phys.》 a unit of energy, equal to the amount of energy needed to raise one pound to a height of one foot. 피트 파운드.

foot·print [fútprìnt] *n.* Ⓒ a mark or print made by a foot. 발자국; 족문(足紋); 발자취. ¶ *footprints in snow* 눈 위의 발자국 / *footprints on the sands of time* 역사에 남은 발자취.

foot race [⌐ ⌐] *n.* a contest of speed in running or walking. 경보(競步); 도보〔뜀박질〕 경주.

foot rule [⌐ ⌐] *n.* a measure one foot long made of wood or metal. 1피트 자; 피트자.

foot soldier [⌐ ⌐−] *n.* a soldier who fights on foot; an infantryman. 보병.

foot·sore [fútsɔ̀ːr] *adj.* having sore feet (from excessive walking). 발병이 난; 과도하게 걸어 발에 상처가 난.

***foot·step** [fútstèp] *n.* Ⓒ **1** a person's step. (발)걸음; 보조(步調). **2** the distance covered by a step. 보폭(步幅). **3** the sound made by stepping. 발소리. **4** a footprint. 발자국.
follow 〔***walk***〕 *someone's* ***footsteps,*** do as someone did; imitate what someone else has done; succeed. …의 선례를 따르다; …의 유지(遺志)를 잇다.

foot·stool [fútstùːl] *n.* Ⓒ a low stool on which to rest the feet. 발 올려 놓는 대; 발판.

foot·way [fútwèi] *n.* Ⓒ a footpath; a sidewalk. 보도(步道).

foot·wear [fútwὲər] *n.* Ⓤ 《*collectively*》 anything to be worn on the feet, such as shoes, slippers and boots; footgear. 신발《주로 상업 용어로 구두·슬리퍼·장화 따위》.

foot·work [fútwə̀ːrk] *n.* Ⓤ the use of the feet, as in boxing, tennis, dancing, etc. (구기·권투 따위에서) 발놀림.

foo·zle [fúːzəl] *vt., vi.* (P6; 1) make or do clumsily. 서투르게 하다; 그르치다; 실수하다. — *n.* a foozling. 그르침; 잘못함. [G. *fuscheln*]

fop [fɑp / fɔp] *n.* Ⓒ a man who pays too much attention to his clothes, appearance, etc. 맵시꾼; 멋쟁이. [? →fob²]

fop·per·y [fάpəri / fɔ́p-] *n.* ⓊⒸ (*pl.* **-per·ies**) the behavior, clothes, etc. of a fop. 멋(부림).

fop·pish [fάpiʃ / fɔ́p-] *adj.* having the characteristics of a fop; like a fop. 멋부린; 모양을〔맵시를〕 낸.

:for [fɔːr, fər] *prep.* **1** in support or in favor of; in the interest of. …을 지지하여; …을 위해(opp. against). ¶ *fight ~ one's country* 나라를 위해 싸우다 / *He voted ~ Mr. Smith.* 스미스씨에게 표를 던졌다 / *I am ~ the proposal.* 나는 그 제안에 찬성이다 / *Are you ~ or against it?* 자넨 찬성인가 반대가. **2** in place of; representing. …대신; …을 대표하여. ¶ *use a box ~ a desk* 책상 대신으로 궤짝을 쓰다 / *speak ~ the classmates* 동급생을 대변하다 / *I wrote the letter ~ him.* 그를 대신해서 편지를 썼다. **3** in exchange for; in return for; to the amount of. …의 교환으로서; …에 대하여; …에 달하는. ¶ *a check ~ $1,000,* 1,000 달러의 수표 / *money ~ goods* 상품 대금 / *be* *thanked ~ one's efforts* 수고에 대해 감사를 받다 / *give a cat ~ dog* 개와 교환으로 고양이를 주다 / *These apples are five ~ a dollar.* 이 사과는 1달러에 5개씩이다. **4** ⓐ in order to. …을 위해. ¶ *flee ~ one's life* 필사적으로 도망하다 / *take medicine ~ one's cough* 기침을 멈추기 위해 약을 먹다. ⓑ with the purpose of; as; as being. …목적으로; …로서. ¶ *equipment ~ the army* 군용 장비 / *build a building ~ a church* 교회로 건물을 짓다 / *know a thing ~ a fact* 어떤 일을 사실로서 알고 있다 / *We chose him ~ our leader.* 그를 우리의 지도자로 뽑았다 / *I took him ~ his brother.* 나는 그를 그의 형으로 생각했다. **5** preparing for. …에 대비하여. ¶ *study ~ examination* 시험에 대비하여 공부하다 / *save up ~ a rainy day* 만일의 경우에 대비하여 저축하다. **6** toward; going to. …을 향해; …행의. ¶ *the 10:30 train ~ Pusan,* 10시 30분발 부산행 열차 / *start ~ London* 런던을 향해 떠나다 / *The plane ~ New York took off just now.* 뉴욕행 비행기가 방금 이륙했다. **7** suiting the purposes or needs of; being used by or with; suitable to. …의 목적〔필요, 요구〕에 맞는; …에 적합한; …용의. ¶ *books ~ children* 어린이를 위한 책 / *suits ~ bathing* 수영복 / *horses ~ riding* 승용마 / *words ~ expressing the idea* 그 사상을 표현하는 적절한 말 / *I do not think her the wife ~ you.* 그녀가 자네 부인으로 어울린다고는 생각하지 않는다. **8** because of; by reason of; on account of. …이유로; …때문에. ¶ *~ many reasons* 여러 가지 이유로 / *a city famed ~ its beauty* 아름답기로 유명한 도시 / *shout ~ joy* 기쁜 나머지 소리를 지르다 / *be hospitalized ~ chest pains* 가슴의 통증으로 입원하다 / *She could not speak ~ tears.* 눈물 때문에 말을 할 수가 없었다 / *He was punished ~ stealing.* 그는 훔친 것 때문에 처벌받았다. **9** taking into account; in comparison with. …을 고려하면; …에 비해(서는); …로는. ¶ *It is very warm ~ March.* 3월달치고는 대단히 덥다 / *He is tall ~ his age.* 그는 나이에 비해 키가 크다. **10** ⓐ as long as; during. …동안; …간(間). ¶ *~ life* 일생 동안 / *~ a long time* 오랫동안 / *stay ~ a week,* 1주일간 머무르다 / *We worked ~ ten hours.* 우리는 열 시간 동안 일했다. ⓑ as far as. …의 거리를; …까지. ¶ *He walked ~ a mile.* 1마일 걸었다. **11** 《usu. with *all*》 in spite of. …에도 불구하고. ¶ *For all her faults, I like her.* 결점은 있지만 나는 그녀를 좋아한다 / *He's a decent guy ~ all that.* 그럼에도 불구하고 그는 착실한 사나이다. **12** desirous of; in expectation of. …을 바라는〔구하는〕; …을 기대〔예기〕하여. ¶ *long ~ home* 고향을 동경하다 / *wait ~ an answer* 회답을 기다리다 / *hunger ~ knowledge* 지식을 갈망하다 / *hope ~ the best* 최선을 기대하다. **13** in honor of. …을 기념하여; …에(게) 경의를 표하여; …을 위하여. ¶ *give a dinner ~ someone* 아무를 위하여 만찬회를 열다 / *This monument was built ~ the founder.* 이 기념비는 창립자를 기념하여 세워졌다. **14** in or with regard to; as concerns. …에 관해서(는); …의 점에서는. ¶ *as ~ me* 나로서는 / *(as) ~ the rest* 나머지에 관해서는 / *~ my part* 나에 관한 한 / *good ~ the health* 건강에 좋은 / *He has no equal ~ running.* 달리기에 있어 그와 어깨를 겨룰 수 있는 자는 없다 / *So much ~ today.* 오늘은 이만 끝이다. **15** 《with *n.* or *pron.* and *to do*》 …이 (하여야) 할 일이다; …하는 것은 —에게 어울린다. 語法 'for+(대)명사'의 형태로 뒤에 이어지는 부정사의 의미상 주어가 됨. ¶ *It is time ~ you to go to bed.* 잠잘 시간입니다 / *French is difficult ~ me to learn.* 나는 프랑스어를 배우기가 어렵다.

as for, regarding; in respect of. …에 관해서는.

be for it, 《Brit. *colloq.*》 be about to get into trouble, etc. 난처한 일이 되다; 처벌받게〔야단맞게〕 되다.

be in for, be certain to receive or experience. 아무래도 …을 겪어야만 하다.

be out for, be engaged in seeking. …하는 데 열중하다; …하려고 애쓰다.

for *oneself,* in order to benefit oneself; having no help from others; by one's own efforts. 자신을 위해; 혼자 힘으로.

for all, in spite of. …에도 불구하고; …한데도. ¶ *For all his money, he is not happy.* 돈이 있음에도 불구하고 그는 행복하지 않다.

for all 〔**aught**〕 **I know,** perhaps; probably. (잘은 모르지만) 아마.

for all the world, by any reason. 무슨 일이 있어도.

for better or (**for**) **worse,** whether the results are good or bad. 좋든 나쁘든; 결과가 어떠하든; 어떤 일이 있든.

for certain, certainly. 확실히.

for good (**and all**), permanently. 영원히.

for the life of *one,* if one's life depended on it; by any means. 아무리 해도 (…않다). ¶ *I can't understand it ~ the life of me.* 아무리 해도 그것을 이해할 수가 없다.

Oh 〔**O**〕**, for…!** I wish I had! 있으면 좋을 텐데. ¶ *Oh, ~ a glass of water!* 물 한 컵 마셨으면 좋을 텐데.

—*conj.* because; since. 왜냐하면. ¶ *We can't start out, ~ it is raining hard.* 비가 억수같이 쏟아져서 출발할 수가 없다. [E.]

fo·ra [fɔ́:rə] *n.* pl. of **forum.**

for·age [fɔ́:ridʒ, fάr- / fɔ́r-] *n.* **1** Ⓤ food for horses or cattle. 꼴; 마초; (마소의) 먹이. **2** ⓊⒸ the act of searching for such food. 마초〔사료〕 징발; 마초 구하기. —*vi.* (P1,2A,3,4) **1** wander in search for food. 먹이를〔식량을〕 찾아 헤매다. **2** 《*for*》 search for something one wants. …을 찾아다니다; 뒤적여 찾다. —*vt.* (P6) **1** get food from (someone); plunder. …에게서 양식

을〔마초를〕 징발하다; 약탈하다. **2** supply (horses) with food; feed. (말)에 꼴을〔마초를〕 먹이다. ● **for·ag·er** [-ər] *n.* [Teut. → fodder]

for·as·much [fɔ́ːrəzmʌ́tʃ / fərəz-] *conj.* 《usu. with *as*》 seeing that; since. …이〔하〕므로; …인 까닭에. ¶ ～ *as the time is short* 시간이 짧기 때문에. [→fore]

for·ay [fɔ́ːrei / fɔ́r-] *n.* Ⓒ a sudden attack to steal things by force. (약탈을 목적으로 한) 급습; 침탈; 약탈. — *vt.,vi.* (P6; 1) make a raid. 급습〔습격〕하다; 침략〔약탈〕하다. [→forage]

·**for·bad** [fərbǽd] *v.* p. of **forbid.**

·**for·bade** [fəːrbéid, -bǽd] *v.* p. of **forbid.**

for·bear[1] [fɔːrbέər] *v.* (**-bore, -borne**) *vt.* (P6,8) keep oneself from (something); endure; avoid. …을 삼가다〔피하다〕; 참다; 억제하다. ¶ ～ *angry feelings* 노여움을 억제하다. — *vi.* (P1,3) **1** 《*from*》 hold back. 삼가다; 그만두다. ¶ ～ *from complaining* 불평을 삼가다. **2** control oneself. 참다. [for-]

for·bear[2] [fɔ́ːrbὲər] *n.* =forebear.

for·bear·ance [fɔːrbέərəns] *n.* Ⓤ 《law》 **1** the act of forbearing. 인내. **2** self-control. 자제. [for-]

:**for·bid** [fərbíd] *vt.* (**-bade** or **-bad, -bid·den** or **-bid, -bid·ding**) **1** (P6,9,20) order (someone) not to do; prohibit; not allow (someone, something). …을 금하다; 못하게 하다. ¶ ～ *someone* (*to enter*) *the house* 아무가 집에 들어오는 것을 금하다 / ～ *the use of firearms* 총기의 사용을 금하다 / *Her father forbade her marriage.* 그녀 아버지는 그녀의 결혼을 허락하지 않았다 / *The doctor forbids him wine.* 의사는 그에게 술을 금하고 있다 / *God* ～ *!* 단연코 그런 일은 없다. **2** (P13,14,20) make (something) impossible; prevent. (사정이) …을 허락하지 않다; 불가능하게 하다; 방해하다. ¶ *Time forbids that….* 시간이 …을 허락하지 않는다 / *High walls* ～ *all approach.* 높은 장벽이 접근을 못 하게 한다 / *Smoking is forbidden here.* 여기서는 금연이다. [for-]

·**for·bid·den** [fərbídn] *v.* pp. of **forbid.**

for·bid·ding [fərbídiŋ] *adj.* **1** looking dangerous and disagreeable. 꺼림칙한; 가까이하기 어려운. **2** stern. 험악한; 무서운; 험상궂은. ¶ *a* ～ *look* 험상궂은 얼굴 / ～ *cliffs* 험준한 벼랑.

for·bore [fɔːrbɔ́ːr] *v.* p. of **forbear.**

for·borne [fɔːrbɔ́ːrn] *v.* pp. of **forbear.**

:**force** [fɔːrs] *n.* Ⓤ **1** strength; energy; power. 힘; 에너지. ¶ *the* ～ *of the wind* 풍력(風力) / *the* ～ *of the explosion* 폭발력. **2** ⓐ the strength used upon or against someone or something. 폭력. ¶ *use* ～ *on someone* …에게 폭력을 휘두르다 / *resort to* ～ 폭력에 호소하다. ⓑ physical power or strength. 체력; 힘. ¶ *with all one's* ～ 전력을 다하여 / *He used all his* ～ *in opening the window.* 창문을 여느라고 온 힘을 다했다. **3** mental or moral strength. (정신적·도덕적인) 힘; 기력. ¶ *the* ～ *of one's mind, intellect, or will* 정신력, 지력(知力) 또는 의지력. **4** ⓊⒸ the power to influence, control or persuade; effectiveness. 영향〔지배〕력; 설득력; 효과. ¶ *the* ～ *of public opinion* 여론의 힘 / *a* ～ *for law and order* 법과 질서에 따르게 하는 힘 / *a debater with much* ～ 매우 설득력이 있는 토론가. **5** Ⓒ an organized body of persons for action; the military power; 《often *pl.*》 a body of armed men; troops. (협동 동작을 하는) 집단; 일단; 전원(全員); 병력; 부대; 군대. ¶ *an office* ～ 사무소 전직원 / *the police* ～ 경찰 / *the Air Force* 공군 / *the labor* ～ 노동력 / *in full* ～ 총력으로 / *the armed forces* (한 나라의) 육해공군 / *a small* ～ *of infantry* 보병의 소부대 / *a scout* ～ 정찰대. **6** binding power. 구속력. ¶ *The law no longer has* ～. 그 법은 이제 구속력이 없다. **7** the real meaning (of a word or phrase). (말 따위의) 참뜻; 의미. ¶ *the original* ～ *of words* 말이 갖는 원래의 뜻 / *I don't understand the* ～ *of the word here.* 여기 이 말의 참뜻을 이해 못 하겠다.

by force, forcibly. 우격다짐으로; 강제적으로. ¶ *They made him do it by* ～. 강제로 그가 그 일을 하게 했다.

by force of (=*by means of*) *a habit, etc.* (습관)의 힘으로〔에 의해〕. ¶ *by* ～ *of arms* 무력에 호소하여 / *by the* ～ *of the circumstances* 어쩔 수 없는 사정으로; 부득이.

come into force, (of a law) become effectual. 유효하게 되다; 실시되다.

in force, a) in great numbers. 대거(大擧)하여. b) in effect or operation; valid. 실시중에; 유효하여. ¶ *put in* ～ (법 따위를) 시행〔실시〕하다 / *The law is still in* ～. 그 법은 아직도 유효하다.

— *vt.* (P6,13,20) **1** 《*into*》 make (someone) do something by force; compel; impose. …을 강제하여 —시키다; …을 강제〔강요〕하다; …하지 않을 수 없게 하다. ¶ ～ *a suspect to confess* 〔*into confessing*〕 용의자에게 자백을 강요하다 / *Hunger forced him into a crime.* 굶주림은 그로 하여금 범죄를 저지르지 않을 수 없게 했다. **2** get or take (something) by force. …을 힘으로 빼앗다. ¶ ～ *a bag out of someone's hand* 아무의 손에서 백을 빼앗다. **3** produce or effect (something) by force. (눈물·웃음 따위)를 억지로 자아내다; (목소리·힘 따위)를 애쓰며 내다. ¶ ～ *a smile* 〔*a laugh*〕 억지웃음을 웃다 / ～ *tears* 억지로 울다 / ～ *one's courage* 용기를 불러일으키다. **4** hasten the grown or development of (plants, etc.). (야채 따위의) 촉성(促成) 재배를 하다. **5** use force on. 폭력을 가하다. **6** break open or through by force. …을 억지로 비집어 열다; 억지로 지나가다; 헤치고 나아가다. ¶ ～ *a passage* 억지로 통과하다 / ～ *one's way through the crowd* 군중 속을 헤집고

나아가다. [L. *fortis* strong]

forced [fɔːrst] *adj.* **1** brought about or made by force. 강제적인. ¶ ~ *labor* 강제 노동 / ~ *insurance* 강제 보험 / *a* ~ *march* 강행군. **2** made or kept up by an unnatural effort. 부자연스런; 무리한. ¶ *a* ~ *smile* 억지 웃음 / ~ *tears* 거짓 눈물 / ~ *interpretation* 억지 해석.

force·ful [fɔ́ːrsfəl] *adj.* full of force; powerful. 힘찬; 강력한; 세찬. ¶ *a* ~ *speech* 힘(설득력) 있는 연설. ● **force·ful·ly** [-fuli] *adv.* **force·ful·ness** [-nis] *n.*

for·ceps [fɔ́ːrsəps, -seps] *n.* Ⓒ (*pl.* **-ceps** or **-ci·pes**) a pair of small tongs or pincers used by surgeons, dentists, etc. (외과·치과용의) 겸자(鉗子); 핀셋. [L.]

force pump [ㅅㅡ] *n.* a pump that delivers fluid at increased pressure by means of compressed air. 무자위; 밀펌프.

for·ci·ble [fɔ́ːrsəbəl] *adj.* **1** carried out by force. 힘(폭력)으로 이루어진; 강제적인. ¶ *a* ~ *detention* 억류 / *a* ~ *execution* 강제 집행. **2** having force; powerful. 힘있는; 힘찬. ¶ *a* ~ *style* 힘찬 문체. ● **for·ci·bly** [-bli] *adv.* [*force*]

for·ci·pes [fɔ́ːrsəpìːz] *n.* pl. of **forceps.**

*****ford** [fɔːrd] *n.* Ⓒ a shallow place in a river where a person can cross by walking. (걸어서 건널 수 있는 강 따위의) 얕은 여울. — *vt.* (P6) cross (a stream, a river, etc.) by walking; wade. (…의) 얕은 여울을 건너다. [E.]

fore [fɔːr] *adj.* **1** situated at the front. 앞의; 전방의; 앞에 있는. ¶ *the* ~ *part of the train* 열차의 앞 부분. **2** being or coming first in time, place, etc. 첫째의; 최초의. — *adv.* in the front part, esp. of a ship. 앞쪽에서; 선수(船首)(이물)에.

fore and aft, from bow to stern. 이물에서 고물까지; 배의 앞뒤 방향에.

— *n.* Ⓒ 《*the* ~》 a forward part. 전부(前部); 전면.

to the fore, **a**) at the front. 전면(前面)에. **b**) at hand. 신변 가까이; 곧 소용에 닿게. **c**) into a prominent place or position. 눈에 띄는 곳에; 두드러진 지위에. ¶ *come to the* ~ 지도적 위치에 서다 / *He has come to the* ~. 그는 최근 전면에 부상했다. **d**) alive. 살아(서).

— *interj.* 《golf》 a warning shout to someone in the way. 공 간다 조심해《골프에서 공이 날아가는 방향에 있는 사람에게 외치는 소리》. [E.]

fore·and·aft [fɔ́ːrənǽft, -áːft] *adj.* (of a ship) from bow to stern. 이물에서 고물까지의; 세로의. ¶ *a* ~ *sail* 세로돛 / ~ *rigged* 세로돛 장치의.

fore·arm[1] [fɔ́ːràːrm] *n.* Ⓒ the part of an arm between the elbow and the wrist. 전박(前膊); 팔뚝.

fore·arm[2] [fɔːráːrm] *vt.* (P6) 《chiefly *passive*》 arm (someone or oneself) for a fight or for trouble beforehand. …을 미리 무장하다.

fore·bear [fɔ́ːrbὲər] *n.* Ⓒ 《usu. *pl.*》 an ancestor; a forbear. 조상. [→fore, obs. *beer* (be)]

fore·bode [fɔːrbóud] *vt.* (P6) **1** give (someone) warning of something bad that is going to happen; predict. …의 전조(前兆)를(조짐을) 나타내다; …을 미리 알리다. ¶ *clouds that* ~ *a storm* 폭풍우를 미리 알리는 구름. **2** show a sign of (something bad). …을 예감하다. ¶ ~ *disaster* 재난을 예감하다. ● **fore·bod·er** [-ər] *n.* [*fore*]

*****fore·cast** [fɔ́ːrkæ̀st / -kàːst] *n.* Ⓒ a description of an event which is going to happen in the future. 예보; 예측; 예상. ¶ *make more accurate weather forecasts* 보다 정확한 일기 예보를 하다. — *vt.* (**-cast** or **-cast·ed**) (P6) say in advance (what is going to happen in the future); predict. …을 예보(예상, 예측)하다. ¶ ~ *tomorrow's weather* 내일 날씨를 예보하다 / ~ *the future* 미래를 예측하다. [E.]

fore·cas·tle [fóuksəl, fɔ́ːrkæ̀səl] *n.* Ⓒ **1** the upper deck in the bow of a ship. 앞갑판. **2** the front part of a ship where the sailors live. 앞갑판 밑의 선원실. 參考 fo'c's'le로도 씀. [E.]

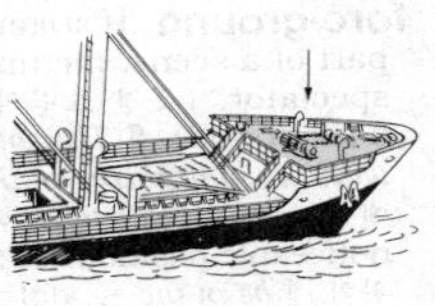
〈forecastle 1〉

fore·close [fɔːrklóuz] *vt.* (P6,13) **1** ⓐ shut out; exclude. …을 제외하다; 배제하다. ¶ *be foreclosed out of the church* 교회에서 내쫓기다. ⓑ prevent from enjoying. …을 방해하다; …못 하도록 하다. **2** 《law》 take away someone's right to take back a mortgage. (…에게 저당물을 되찾는 권리)를 상실케 하다. **3** close beforehand. …을 (미리) 끝내다; 타결(해결)짓다. ¶ *attempt to* ~ *discussion* 토론을 (미리) 끝내려고 하다. [L. *foris* out, →close[1]]

fore·court [fɔ́ːrkɔ̀ːrt] *n.* **1** a court or enclosed space in front of a building. (건물의) 앞뜰. **2** 《tennis, badminton, etc.》 the part of a playing court nearest the net. (테니스 따위의) 포코트. [→fore]

fore·doom [fɔːrdúːm] *vt.* (P6,13) doom beforehand. …의 운명을 미리 정하다. ¶ *efforts foredoomed to failure* 처음부터 실패할 것이 뻔한 노력. [↓]

*****fore·fa·ther** [fɔ́ːrfàːðər] *n.* Ⓒ 《usu. *pl.*》 an ancestor. 조상. ¶ *Forefather's Day* 청교도 미대륙 상륙 기념일《12월 21일》. [→fore]

fore·fin·ger [fɔ́ːrfìŋgər] *n.* Ⓒ the finger next to the thumb; the index finger. 집게손가락.

fore·foot [fɔ́ːrfùt] *n.* Ⓒ (*pl.* **-feet** [-fìːt]) **1** one of the front feet of a four-footed animal, insect, etc. (짐승·곤충의) 앞다리. **2**

the forward end of a keel. (배의) 용골의 전단부.

fore·front [fɔ́ːrfrʌ̀nt] *n.* Ⓒ **1** the foremost position. 최전부(最前部); 선두; 최전면. ¶ *come to the* ~ 세상의 주목을 받다. **2** the center of activity. (활동·흥미·여론 따위의) 중심.

fore·gath·er [fɔːrgǽðər] *v.* =forgather.

fore·go[1] [fɔːrgóu] *v.* =forgo.

fore·go[2] [fɔːrgóu] *vt., vi.* (P6;1) (of degree, time, etc.) go before; precede. …에 앞서다; 선행하다. [*fore*]

fore·go·ing [fɔːrgóuiŋ] *adj.* previous; just before. …에 앞서는; 선행의; 앞(서)의; 전술의. ¶ *The* ~ *are only a few of the instances.* 앞서의 것은 몇 개의 사례에 지나지 않는다 / *the* ~ *chapter* 전장(前章).

fore·gone [fɔːrgɔ́(ː)n, fɔːrgán] *v.* pp. of **forego**[1·2]. — *adj.* that has gone before. 앞(서)의; 앞선; 기지(既知)의.

foregone conclusion [⌐–– –⌐–] *n.* a thing that was never in doubt from the start; an inevitable result. 처음부터 뻔한 결론; 피할 수 없는 결과; 기정 사실.

fore·ground [fɔ́ːrgràund] *n.* Ⓒ **1** the part of a scene, picture, etc. nearest to a spectator. (풍경·그림의) 전경(前景)(opp. background). ¶ *The cottage stands in the* ~ *with the mountains in the background.* 전경엔 오두막이, 배경엔 산이 있다. **2** the most noticeable position. 최전면; 표면; 눈에 띄는 위치. ¶ *be in the* ~ 최전면에 있다; 가장 잘 드러나는 위치에 있다. [*fore*]

fore·hand [fɔ́ːrhæ̀nd] *adj.* ⟪tennis⟫ struck from the racket-holding side of the body. (테니스 따위의) 포핸드의; 전타(前打)의(opp. backhand). ¶ *a* ~ *stroke* 포핸드 스트로크. — *n.* Ⓒ **1** a forehand stroke in tennis. 포핸드; 전타. **2** the part of a horse in front of the rider. 말의 전부(前部).

fore·hand·ed [fɔ́ːrhǽndid] *adj.* ⟪chiefly U.S.⟫ **1** done in good time; timely. 시의(時宜) 적절한. **2** providing for the future; prudent. 장래의 대비가 있는; 알뜰한; 신중한. ¶ *Be* ~ *and save your pennies.* 장래에 대비하여 돈을 저축해 두시오.

:fore·head [fɔ́(ː)rid, fár-, fɔ́ːrhèd] *n.* Ⓒ the part of the face between the eyebrows and the hair. 이마. [*fore*]

:for·eign [fɔ́(ː)rin, fár-] *adj.* **1** of or belonging to another country. 외국〔외래〕의. ¶ *a* ~ *language* 외국어 / ~ *capital* 외자(外資) / ~ *tourists* 외국인 관광객. **2** of another country. 외국에 관한; 외교의. ¶ *a* ~ *policy* 외교〔대외〕 정책 / *the Foreign Ministry* 외무부. **3** ⟪*to*⟫ ⓐ not natural; not belonging or suitable to. 성미에 맞지 않는; 다른; 부적당한. ¶ *Keeping silence is* ~ *to my nature.* 침묵(沈默)을 지키는 것은 내 성미에 맞지 않는다. ⓑ away from the question under consideration. (당면 문제와) 관계 없는; 동떨어진. ¶ ~ *to our discussion* 우리들 토의와는 관계 없는 / *The question is* ~ *to the matter in hand.* 그 문제는 당면한 문제와는 무관하다. **4** introduced from the outside. 외부로부터의. ¶ *a* ~ *substance in the eye* 눈 속에 든 이물질. [L. *foris* outside]

for·eign-born [fɔ́(ː)rinbɔ́ːrn, fár-] *adj.* born in another country. 외국 태생의.

·for·eign·er [fɔ́(ː)rinər, fár-] *n.* Ⓒ a person who belongs to another country; an alien. 외국인.

fore·judge [fɔːrdʒʌ́dʒ] *vt.* (P6, 11, 21) judge or decide beforehand. …을 예단(豫斷)하다; 미리 판단하다. [*fore*]

fore·knew [fɔːrnjúː] *v.* p. of **foreknow.**

fore·know [fɔːrnóu] *vt.* (P6) (**-knew, -known**) have knowledge of (something) beforehand. …을 미리〔사전에〕 알다.

fore·known [fɔːrnóun] *v.* pp. of **foreknow.**

fore·knowl·edge [fɔ́ːrnàlidʒ, –⌐– / -nɔ̀l-] *n.* Ⓤ knowledge of something before it exists or happens. 예지(豫知); 선견(지명); 통찰.

fore·land [fɔ́ːrlənd] *n.* Ⓒ **1** a point of land projecting into the sea; a cape. 곶; 갑(岬). **2** the land along the coast. 해안 지방(opp. hinterland).

fore·leg [fɔ́ːrlèg] *n.* Ⓒ one of the front legs of a four-legged animal or insect. (네발짐승·곤충 따위의) 앞다리.

fore·lock [fɔ́ːrlàk / fɔ́ːrlɔ̀k] *n.* Ⓒ a lock of hair growing above the forehead. 앞머리털. ***take time by the forelock,*** seize an opportunity. 기회를 놓치지 않다.

fore·man [fɔ́ːrmən] *n.* Ⓒ (*pl.* **-men** [-mən]) **1** a man in charge of a group of workers in a factory, etc. 직공 감독; 직공장; 십장. **2** the chairman of a jury. 배심원장.

fore·mast [fɔ́ːrmæ̀st / -màːst] *n.* Ⓒ the mast nearest the front of a ship. 앞돛대.

·fore·most [fɔ́ːrmòust] *adj.* **1** first in place. 맨 첫째의. **2** first in degree, activity, importance, etc. 제 1 급의; 주요한. ¶ *the* ~ *scholar of the age* 당대 제일의 학자. — *adv.* first. 맨 첫째로; 무엇보다 먼저. ***first and foremost,*** first; before all else. 맨 첫째로; 우선〔제일〕 먼저.

fore·name [fɔ́ːrnèim] *n.* a name preceding the surname. (성씨(姓氏) 앞에 붙는) 이름. [*fore*]

fore·noon [fɔ́ːrnùːn] *n.* Ⓤ morning. 오전.

fo·ren·sic [fərénsik] *adj.* **1** of a law court. 법정의. ¶ ~ *medicine* 법의학. **2** of a public debate. 변론〔토론〕의. [→forum]

fore·or·dain [fɔ̀ːrɔːrdéin] *vt.* (P6,11,20) determine the future or fate of (something or someone) beforehand. …의 운명을 미리 정하다. [*fore*]

fore·part [fɔ́ːrpàːrt] *n.* Ⓒ the front part. 전부(前部); 첫 부분.

fore·paw [fɔ́ːrpɔ̀ː] *n.* Ⓒ a front paw of an

animal. (개·고양이 따위의) 앞발.

fore·run [fɔ́ːrrʌ́n] *vt.* (**-ran** [-rǽn], **-run; running**) (P6) **1** precede. …에 앞서다. **2** be a sign or warning of (something to come). 예고(예시, 예보)하다. **3** =forestall. [*fore*]

fore·run·ner [fɔ́ːrrʌ̀nər, –⌐–] *n.* Ⓒ **1** a person who goes or is sent before to pronounce the coming of another. 선구자. **2** a sign that something is to come; an omen. 전조; 조짐. ¶ *Dark clouds were the forerunners of the storm.* 먹구름은 폭풍우가 온다는 전조였다. **3** an ancestor; a predecessor. 조상; 선조; 선인.

fore·sail [fɔ́ːrsèil, 《naut.》 -sl] *n.* Ⓒ the main sail on the foremast of a ship. 앞 돛대의 돛.

fore·saw [fɔːrsɔ́ː] *v.* p. of **foresee.**

***fore·see** [fɔːrsíː] *vt.* (**-saw, -seen**) (P6,7,12) see or know (something) beforehand. …을 미리 알다; 예지(豫知)하다. ¶ ~ *trouble* 곤란을 내다보다 / ~ *what is going to happen* 무엇이 일어날지 예견하다.

fore·seen [fɔːrsíːn] *v.* pp. of **foresee.**

fore·shad·ow [fɔːrʃǽdou] *vt.* (P6) suggest (something) in advance; indicate (something which is going to happen) beforehand. …을 미리 암시하다; 예시하다.

fore·short·en [fɔːrʃɔ́ːrtn] *vt.* (P6) (in drawing or painting) make the lines of (an object) shorter than they really are. (그림 따위)를 원근법에 의해 그리다; (실제보다) 줄이다. [*fore*]

fore·show [fɔːrʃóu] *vt.* (**-showed, -shown** [-ʃóun]) (P6) show (something) beforehand; foretell. …을 미리 보이다; 예고하다.

fore·sight [fɔ́ːrsàit] *n.* Ⓤ **1** the power to see the future. 선견(지명); 통찰(력). ¶ *a man of* ~ 선견지명이 있는 사람; 앞일을 내다보는 사람. **2** careful thought or regard for the future. (장래에 대한) 배려; 심려(深慮); 신중함.

fore·skin [fɔ́ːrskìn] *n.* 《anat.》 the fold of skin which covers the end of the male sexual organ. (음경의) 포피(包皮).

:for·est [fɔ́(ː)rist, fár-] *n.* **1** ⓊⒸ a large area covered with trees. 숲; 산림(지). ¶ *forests stretching for miles* 수 마일이나 뻗친 숲 / *a deep* ~ 깊은 산림 / *primeval forests* 원시림 / *a* ~ *preserve* 〔*reserve*〕 보호림. **2** Ⓒ a large group of trees. 수목. ¶ *land covered with* ~*(s)* 수목(樹木)으로 덮인 땅 / *cut down a* ~ 나무를 베다. **3** Ⓒ something which looks like a forest. 임립(林立)하는 것; 숲처럼 늘어선 것. ¶ *a* ~ *of chimneys* 임립(林立)한 굴뚝. — *vt.* (P6) plant (a place) with trees. 식림(植林)〔식목〕하다. [L. *foris* outside]

fore·stall [fɔːrstɔ́ːl] *vt.* go ahead of or do something before (another) and so prevent another's doing it first; upset a previous plan by doing something before (another). …에 앞서다; 앞지르다; 선수를 치다. ¶ ~ *a riot* 선수를 쳐서 폭동을 막다 / ~ *the opponent* 상대의 기선을 제압하다 / ~ *the enemy's plan* 적의 계획에 선수를 치다. [orig. as n.=ambush (*fore, stall*)]

for·est·er [fɔ́(ː)ristər, fár-] *n.* Ⓒ **1** a person who looks after a forest and the animals there. 산림 간수(看守). **2** a person or an animal living in a forest. 산림에 사는 사람〔동물〕. [*forest*]

for·est·ry [fɔ́(ː)ristri, fár-] *n.* Ⓤ **1** the science of planting and caring for forests. 임학(林學). **2** the management of forests. 산림 관리. **3** 《*collectively*》 forest land. 삼림지; 숲지.

fore·taste [fɔ́ːrtèist] *n.* Ⓒ a previous experience of something that one is to enjoy or suffer in the future; an anticipation. 미리 겪음〔맛봄〕; 예기; 예상. — [–⌐] *vt.* (P6) **1** taste beforehand; have a slight experience of beforehand. …을 미리 맛보다〔겪다〕. **2** anticipate; enjoy (something) by looking forward to it. …을 예기하다; …을 기대하여 즐기다. [*fore, taste*]

fore·tell [fɔːrtél] *vt.* (**-told**) (P6,11,12) tell of (something) beforehand; predict. …을 예고〔예언〕하다. ¶ ~ *the future* 앞날을 예언하다. [*fore, tell*]

fore·thought [fɔ́ːrθɔ̀ːt] *n.* Ⓤ **1** careful thoughts for the future. (장래에 대비한) 고려; 심려. **2** previous planning. (사전의) 계획. [*fore*]

fore·to·ken [fɔːrtóukən] *vt.* (P6) be a sign of (something). …의 전조가〔조짐이〕 되다. — [⌐–⌐] *n.* Ⓒ a sign that something is to happen; an omen. 전조; 조짐.

fore·told [fɔːrtóuld] *v.* p. and pp. of **foretell.**

fore·top [fɔ́ːrtàp, / -tɔ̀p: 《naut.》 -təp] *n.* the platform at the head of a foremast. 앞 돛대의 망루.

:for·ev·er [fərévər] *adv.* **1** for an endless time; for ever. 영원〔영구〕히. ¶ *last* ~ 영원히 계속되다. **2** all the time. 끊임없이; 항상. 參考 영국에선 for ever로 갈라 씀. — *n.* Ⓤ 《*the* ~》 eternity. 영원. [*fore, ever*]

for·ev·er·more [fərèvərmɔ́ːr] *adv.* forever; ever. 영원히.

fore·warn [fɔːrwɔ́ːrn] *vt.* (P6,11,13) give a previous warning to (someone or something). …에게 미리 경고하다〔주의를 주다〕. ¶ *the forewarning hush that comes before an unknown trouble* 예기치 않은 사건의 전조와도 같은 고요. [*fore*]

fore·word [fɔ́ːrwə̀ːrd] *n.* Ⓒ introductory remarks to a book; a preface. 서문(序文).

for·feit [fɔ́ːrfit] *n.* **1** Ⓒ something that is lost or given up because of one's crime, fault, etc.; a fine; a penalty. 몰수물; 벌금. **2** Ⓤ the loss or forfeiting, as a penalty. (권리 따위의) 상실; 박탈. ¶ *the* ~ *of civil rights* 시민권의 박탈. — *adj.* taken away as a forfeit. 몰수된; 상실한. — *vt.* (P6) be deprived of (something) as a forfeit. …을 빼앗기다; 몰수〔상실; 박탈〕되다. ¶ ~ *one's licence* 면허장(狀)을 박탈당하다. ●**for·feit·er** [-ər] *n.* [L. *foris facio* transgress, lit., do outside]

for·fei·ture [fɔ́ːrfətʃər] *n.* **1** Ⓒ something that is lost as a forfeit; penalty. 몰수물; 벌금. **2** Ⓤ loss of rights, etc. (권리 따위의) 상실. [↑]

for·gath·er [fɔːrgǽðər] *vi.* (P1,2A,3,4) **1** meet together; assemble. 모이다. **2** 《*with*》 be friendly; associate. (친하게) 사귀다; 교제하다. **3** meet (someone) by chance. 우연히 만나다. [for-]

:**for·gave** [fərgéiv] *v.* p. of **forgive.**

·**forge**[1] [fɔːrdʒ] *n.* Ⓒ **1** a fireplace where metal is heated and hammered into shape. (대장간·철공장의) 가열로(加熱爐). **2** a place where iron, etc. is melted and hammered into shape. 대장간; 철공장. — *vt.* (P6) **1** heat and hammer (metal) into shape. (쇠)를 불리다; 불려서 만들다. ¶ ~ *an anchor* 닻을 만들다. **2** produce; invent. (거짓말·계획 따위)를 꾸며〔조작해〕 내다; 만들(어 내)다. **3** imitate. …을 위조〔모조〕하다. ¶ ~ *a banknote* 지폐를 위조하다 / ~ *another's signature* 남의 서명을 위조하다. — *vi.* **1** shape metal or iron, as a blacksmith does. 대장장이 일을 하다. **2** make something false to deceive others. 위조하다; 가짜를 만들다. [→fabric]

forge[2] [fɔːrdʒ] *vi.* (P2A) 《*ahead*》 go forward slowly and steadily. (말·사람이) 천천히 나아가다〔전진하다〕; 점진하다. [?]

forg·er [fɔ́ːrdʒər] *n.* Ⓒ a person who imitates something to deceive others. 가짜를 만드는 사람; 위조자. [*forge*[1]]

for·ger·y [fɔ́ːrdʒəri] *n.* (*pl.* **-ger·ies**) **1** Ⓤ the act of forging a signature, a coin, etc. 위조. **2** Ⓒ something produced falsely to deceive. 가짜; 위조물. ¶ *Those documents were all forgeries.* 그 서류들은 모두 가짜였다.

:**for·get** [fərgét] *v.* (**-got, -got·ten** or **-got, -get·ting**) *vt.* (P6,8,9,10,11,12) **1** fail to remember; lose memory of (something). …을 잊다. ¶ ~ *someone's name* 〔*birthday*〕 아무의 이름〔생일〕을 잊다 / *He soon forgets his father's advice.* 그는 아버지의 충고를 곧 잊었다 / *I shall never* ~ *seeing the Swiss Alps for the first time.* 처음으로 스위스 알프스를 본 것을 결코 잊지 못할 게다. **2** omit or neglect (something) without meaning to. (…하는 것)을 깜빡 잊다; …을 태만히〔등한히〕 하다. ¶ *I forgot to close the window.* 창문 닫는 것을 그만 잊어버렸다. **3** leave (something) behind unintentionally. …을 둔 채 잊고 나오다〔가다〕. ¶ ~ *one's umbrella on a bus* 버스에 우산을 둔 채 잊고 내리다. **4** banish (bad memories, etc.) from the mind. (좋지 않은 추억 따위)를 잊어버리다; 마음에 두지 않다; 생각지 않도록 하다. ¶ ~ *and forgive* (원한을) 잊어버리다 / ~ *a bad conduct* 못된 행위를 잊고 용서해주다 / *Forget it!* 그런 일은 잊어버려라; 마음을 쓰지 않아도 좋다. — *vi.* (P1,3) 《*about*》 fail or cease to remember; be forgetful. 잊다. ¶ *I forgot about the holiday tomorrow.* 내일이 휴일이란 것을 깜빡 잊고 있었다. [O.E. *forgietan*]

forget oneself, **a**) behave in an improper manner; lose one's dignity. 분수를 잊다〔모르다〕; 자제력을 잃다. **b**) act unselfishly, not thinking of one's own interests. 사리(私利)를 돌보지 않고 행동하다.

for·get·ful [fərgétfəl] *adj.* **1** 《*of*》 having a poor memory. 잘 잊는; 잊기 잘하는. ¶ *a* ~ *person* 잊기 잘하는〔건망증이 있는〕 사람 / *He is very* ~ *of things.* 그는 건망증이 심하다. **2** apt to neglect. 소홀히〔태만히〕 하기 쉬운. ¶ *be* ~ *of others* 남의 일 따위는 상관하지 않다 / *be* ~ *of one's social obligations* 사회적 의무를 태만히 하기 쉽다. ●**for·get·ful·ly** [-fəli] *adv.*

for·get·ful·ness [fərgétfəlnis] *n.* Ⓤ **1** poor memory. 잘 잊음; 잊기 잘함. **2** carelessness; neglect. 부주의; 등한함.

for·get-me-not [fərgétminɑ̀t / -nɔ̀t] *n.* Ⓒ 《bot.》 a small plant with small blue or white flowers. 물망초.

for·giv·a·ble [fərgívəbəl] *adj.* that can be forgiven. 용서할 수 있는.

:**for·give** [fərgív] *v.* (**-gave, -giv·en**) *vt.* (P6,13,14) **1** 《*for*》 give up the desire to punish (someone). …을 용서하다. ¶ ~ *a sin* 〔*an insult*〕 죄〔무례〕를 용서하다 / *Will you* ~ *me ?* 용서해 주시겠습니까 / *They forgave him his failure.* 그들은 그의 실패를 용서했다 / *Am I forgiven for coming late ?* 늦게 온 것이 용서됩니까. **2** do not demand payment for (a debt, etc.). …을 면제하다. ¶ ~ *a debt* 〔*tax*〕 빚〔세금〕을 면제하다 / ~ *a tenant one hundred dollars in back rent* 밀린 집세 백 달러를 면제해 주다. — *vi.* (P1) show forgiveness. 용서하다. ¶ *My mother doesn't* ~ *easily.* 어머니는 좀처럼 용서를 하지 않는 분이다. [for-]

·**for·giv·en** [fərgívən] *v.* pp. of **forgive.**

for·give·ness [fərgívnis] *n.* Ⓤ the act of forgiving; the state of being forgiven; willingness to forgive. 용서해 줌; 관용; 면제. ¶ *ask* 〔*beg*〕 *someone's* ~ 아무의 용서를 빌다 / *be full of* ~ 매우 관대하다.

for·giv·ing [fərgíviŋ] *adj.* ready to forgive. (쾌히) 용서하는; 관대한. ¶ *a* ~ *soul* 너그러운 사람.

for·go [fɔːrgóu] *vt.* (**-went, -gone** [-gɔ́ːn]) (P6) do without (something); refrain from (something). …없이 때우다; …을 그만두다〔삼가다〕. ¶ *He decided to* ~ *the movies and do his homework.* 가려던 영화 구경을 그만두고 숙제를 하기로 했다. [for-]

:for·got [fərgát/-gɔ́t] *v.* p. of **forget.**

:for·got·ten [fərgátn/-gɔ́tn] *v.* pp. of **forget.**

:fork [fɔːrk] *n.* Ⓒ **1** an instrument with a handle and two or more pointed parts, used for picking up or holding something to eat. 포크; 삼지창. ¶ *a knife and ~* 나이프와 포크. 語法 한 벌을 이루므로 fork 앞의 a는 불필요. **2** ⓐ an instrument like a fork; a garden fork. 포크 모양의 기구; 갈퀴; 쇠스랑. ⓑ a flash of fork-like lightning. 번개. ¶ *jagged forks of lightning* 차상 전광(叉狀電光). **3** a place where a tree, a road, or a stream divides into branches. (나무·길·강 따위의) 갈라진 곳; 아귀; 분기점. ¶ *the ~ of a tree* 나뭇가지의 아귀 / *the ~ of* 〔*in*〕 *a road* 갈림길 / *come to a ~ in a road* 갈림길에 접어들다.

play a good knife and fork, eat heartily. 잔뜩 먹다; 식욕이 왕성하다.

— *vi.* (P1, 2A, 3) (of a tree, river, road, etc.) divide into branches; branch off. 갈라지다; 분기하다. ¶ *The road forks at that point.* 길은 그 지점에서 갈라진다. — *vt.* **1** throw 〔dig〕 (something) with a fork. …을 쇠스랑으로 긁어올리다〔파다〕. **2** make into a fork. 포크 모양으로〔갈라지게〕 하다. [L. *furca*]

fork out 〔***over, up***〕, 《*colloq.*》 pay out or hand over, esp. readily and handsomely. 지불하다; 넘겨〔건네〕주다. ¶ *He had to ~ over sixty dollars to have the car repaired.* 차를 수리하기 위해 60 달러나 지불해야 했다.

forked [fɔːrkt, fɔ́ːrkəd] *adj.* in the shape of a fork; divided into branches. 갈라진; …갈래의. ¶ *~ lightning* 번개 / *a ~ road* 갈림길 / *three-forked* 세 갈래의. [↑]

for·lorn [fərlɔ́ːrn] *adj.* (sometimes **-lorn·er, -lorn·est**) **1** miserable and unhappy. 비참한. **2** left alone; deserted. 고독한; 버림받은. ¶ *a man ~ of his friends* 친구에게 버림받은 사나이. [for-, →lose]

forlorn hope [–́–́] *n.* **1** a very faint hope. 가느다란 희망. **2** a very dangerous plan or enterprise that has little chance of success; a storming party. 절망적인 기도(企圖); 결사대.

:form [fɔːrm] *n.* **1** ⓊⒸ the appearance or outline of anything; a shape; a figure. 외관; 형상; 형체; 모습; 몸; 모양; (사람·물체의) 그림자. ¶ *dark forms of the tree* 나무의 검은 그림자 / *a devil in human ~* 인간의 모습을 한 악마 / *appear in the ~ of a man* 사람의 모습으로 나타나다 / *take the ~ of* … …의 형태를 취하다; …처럼 되다 / *be fair of ~ and face* 용자(容姿)가 단려(端麗)하다 / *A ~ moved in the mist.* 안개 속에서 사람의 그림자가 움직였다. **2** Ⓒ ⓐ a kind or type; a sort. 종류; 품종. ¶ *the lower forms of animal life* 하등 동물 / *the fish and other forms of life in the ocean* 대양의 물고기와 기타의 생물류. ⓑ a particular structure, condition, or pattern in which something appears; a mode. (…이 나타나는) 상태; 성격; 형식; 양식. ¶ *water in the ~ of ice* 얼음의 형태를 취한 물 / *a denunciation in the ~ of a letter* 편지로의 비난 / *a novel ~ of industrial structure* 산업 구조의 새 양식. **3** Ⓒ a thing that gives shape to something; a mold. 형태를 주는〔정하는〕 것; 형(型); 원형. **4** ⓊⒸ set order; method. (어떤 일을 하는 경우의) 정해진 순서·방식; 형식; 폼. ¶ *certain forms of worship* 예배의 제(諸)형식 / *in due ~* 정식으로 / *one's ~ in serving at tennis* 〔*swimming*〕 테니스의 서브〔수영하는〕 폼. **5** Ⓤ 《art, music, etc.》 a manner of arrangement or representation; a style. (표현의) 양식; 형태; 형식 (opp. content). ¶ *in the ~ of a drama* 드라마 형식으로 / *a piece of music in sonata ~* 소나타 형식의 음악. **6** ⓊⒸ behavior according to rule, custom, or etiquette. 예법; 예절; 의례. ¶ *social forms* 사교상의 예절 / *It is not good ~ to pick one's teeth in public.* 대중 앞에서 이를 쑤시는 것은 예절에 어긋난다. **7** ⓊⒸ a formal act (often meaning the lack of substance); formality. (의미 없는) 형식; 의례; 허례. ¶ *as a matter of ~ =for form's sake* 형식상; 의례상 / *attach importance to forms* 형식에 중요성을 두다 / *go through the outward forms of a religious wedding* 종교 결혼이라는 외형만의 형식을 거치다. **8** ⓊⒸ 《gram.》 a shape taken by a word in spelling, sound, or inflection. 형태; 어형. ¶ *the plural* 〔*past*〕 *~* 복수〔과거〕형. **9** Ⓒ 《Brit.》 a grade or class of pupils in a school. (영국의) 학년; 학급(cf. 《U.S.》 *grade*). ¶ *his ~ mistress* 그 아이의 담임 여교사 / *Fred is in the third ~ now.* 프레드는 현재 3학년이다. **10** Ⓒ a set order of words; a printed paper with spaces to be written in. 서식(書式); 신청 용지. ¶ *a tax ~* 납세 용지 / *an order ~* 주문 용지 / *fill in* 〔*out, up*〕 *the ~* 용지에 기입하다 / *after the ~ of* …의 서식에 따라. **11** Ⓤ 《sports》 a bodily condition or fitness. 몸의 컨디션; 《*colloq.*》 good health and spirits. 좋은 건강 상태. ¶ *be in* 〔*out of*〕 *~* 몸 컨디션이 좋다〔나쁘다〕 / *keep in ~* 컨디션을 유지해 두다.

— *vt.* (P6,13) **1** shape; make. …을 모양짓다; 만들다. ¶ *~ a cup out of clay* 찰흙으로 컵을 만들다 / *Water forms ice when it freezes.* 물은 얼면 얼음이 된다. **2** build up (character, etc.); train; develop (habits, etc.). (품성 따위)를 만들다; …을 단련하다; (습관 따위)를 기르다. ¶ *~ one's mind* 수양하다 / *~ good habits* 좋은 습관을 들이다. **3** compose; organize; make up. …을 구성하다; 조직하다; 형성하다. ¶ *~ a club* 클럽을 구성하다 / *~ a committee* 위원회를 조직하다. **4** (P6) frame (ideas, opinions, etc.) in the mind; arrange (someone or something) in some order. (생각·의견 따위)를 정리하다; …을 정렬시키다. ¶ *~ a judgment* 판단을 내리

다 / ～ *an immediate opinion* 의견을 곧 정리하다 / ～ *a regiment into columns* 연대를 종대로 정렬시키다.

— *vi.* (P1,3) take shape; be formed. 모양을 취하다; 모양이〔형태가〕 되다; 형성되다. [L. *forma*]

***for·mal** [fɔ́:rməl] *adj.* **1** of the outward form rather than the content. 형식의; 표면적인. ¶ ～ *resemblance* 외면의 유사 / ～ *logic* 형식 논리 / ～ *obedience* 형식상의 복종. **2** according to strict forms, rules, etc.; regular. 정식의. ¶ *a* ～ *contract* 정식 계약 / *issue a* ～ *protest to the embassy* 정식 항의를 대사관에 내다. **3** ⓐ according to the forms, ceremonies, customs, etc. 형식〔격식〕을 차리는; 의례적인. ¶ *a* ～ *call* 의례적인 방문 / *a* ～ *man* 형식을 차리는 사람. ⓑ stiff. 딱딱한; 경직된. ¶ ～ *manners* = *a* ～ *bearing* 딱딱한 태도. [↑]

formal cause [⌐—⌐] *n.* the idea or definition. 정의(定義).

for·ma·lin [fɔ́:rməlin] *n.* Ⓤ 《chem.》 a liquid used to do away with germs and bad smells. 포르말린. [*formic, aldehyde*]

for·mal·ism [fɔ́:rməlìzəm] *n.* ⓊⒸ excessive attention to forms and customs. 형식주의; 허례. [*form*]

for·mal·i·ty [fɔ:rmǽləti] *n.* Ⓤ (*pl.* **-ties**) **1** the state or quality of being formal; strict adherence to established rules, customs, procedure, etc.; rigidity. 형식적임; 전통적인 규칙〔관습, 절차〕의 엄수; 딱딱함. ¶ *No* ～*, please.* 편히 하시죠. **2** 《usu. *pl.*》 a formal act; a ceremony. 형식적 행위; 의례. ¶ *the formalities of a wedding* 혼례 의식 / *the formalities of a thank-you note* 사례장의 의례적 인사말. **3** 《usu. *pl.*》 an established method of procedure required by custom or rule. 절차. ¶ *the legal formalities* 법률상의 절차 / *go through due formalities* 정식 절차를 거치다. [*form*]

for·mal·ly [fɔ́:rməli] *adv.* in a formal manner; in form. 형식적으로; 정식으로.

for·mat [fɔ́:rmæt] *n.* the shape, size, and general arrangement of a book, magazine, etc. (책·잡지 따위의) 판형; 체재; 구성; 형태. ¶ *a book in a new* ～ 새로운 판형의 책. [*form*]

·**for·ma·tion** [fɔ:rméiʃən] *n.* **1** Ⓤ the process or act of forming; the state of being formed. 형성. ¶ *the* ～ *of character* 인격의 형성〔도야〕 / *the* ～ *of good habits* 좋은 습관의 형성 / *the* ～ *of a Cabinet* 조각(組閣). **2** Ⓤ the way in which something is formed; structure. 구조. ¶ *be of a queer* ～ 기묘한 구조를 이루고 있다. **3** Ⓤ 《mil.》 an arrangement of troops, airplanes, ships, etc. 대형(隊形); 편대. ¶ *close* ～ 밀집 대형 / ～ *flying* 편대 비행 / *in battle* ～ 전투 대형으로. **4** Ⓒ 《geol.》 a series of layers of the same kind of rock or mineral. 암층(岩層); 누층(累層). [*form*]

form·a·tive [fɔ́:rmətiv] *adj.* of forming or developing; forming; shaping. 형성의; 발달의. ¶ ～ *arts* 조형 미술 / ～ *elements* 성어(成語) 요소 / *a child's most* ～ *years* 소아의 최대 발육기(期).

:for·mer [fɔ́:rmər] *adj.* **1** earlier; previous; long past. (이)전의; 앞서의; 과거의. ¶ *a* ～ *president* 전 대통령 / ～ *customs* 옛날의 습관 / *in* ～ *times* 〔*days*〕 옛날엔. **2** before in order; near(er) the beginning. (순서가) 먼저의; 앞선. **3** 《*the* ～》 first of two which were mentioned before. 전자의(opp. latter). ¶ *Of the two men, I prefer the latter to the* ～. 두 사람 중 전자보다 후자를 더 좋아한다. [→fore]

:for·mer·ly [fɔ́:rmərli] *adv.* in the past; in former times; previously. 전에는; 이전은; 옛날엔. ¶ *He* ～ *lived in Japan.* 그는 전에는 일본에서 살았다.

for·mic [fɔ́:rmik] *adj.* of ants; found in ants. 개미의. ¶ ～ *acid* 포름산(酸). [L. *formica* ant]

***for·mi·da·ble** [fɔ́:rmidəbəl] *adj.* **1** causing fear, dread or awe. 무서운; 두려운. ¶ *a* ～ *enemy* 강적 / *a* ～ *opponent in business* 만만치 않은 사업 경쟁자. **2** difficult to overcome or handle. 얕잡을 수 없는. ¶ *a* ～ *task* 벅찬〔힘겨운〕 일. **3** of a surprising number, amount, difficulty, etc. 엄청나게 많은. ¶ *a* ～ *pile of letters* 산더미 같은 편지. **4** ⓐ arousing feelings of awe or admiration. 외경(畏敬)〔경이〕의 마음을 일으키는. ⓑ vastly superior; exceptional. 매우 뛰어난; 각별한. ● **for·mi·da·bly** [-i] *adv.* [L. *formido* fear]

form·less [fɔ́:rmlis] *adj.* having no definite or regular form; shapeless. 형태가 없는; 무형의. [*form*]

For·mo·sa [fɔ:rmóusə] *n.* the old name of Taiwan. 대만(臺灣)의 구칭. ● **For·mo·san** *adj., n.*

***for·mu·la** [fɔ́:rmjələ] *n.* Ⓒ (*pl.* **-las** or **-lae**) **1** a fixed form of words used on certain occasion. (인사 따위의) 틀에 박힌 말; (일반적으로) 상투 어구. ¶ *a magic* ～ 주문. **2** 《med.》 a prescription. 처방(전). ¶ *a* ～ *for a cough* 기침의 처방전. **3** ⓐ 《math.》 a rule expressed in algebraic symbols. 공식; 식. ⓑ 《chem.》 an expression of the composition of a compound by chemical symbols. 식(式). ¶ *a molecular* ～ 분자식 / *a structural* ～ 구조식. **4** a statement of religious belief or doctrine. 신조; 신앙 고백문. **5** a set rule for doing something. 인습적 방식; 전통적 수법. [L. (→form)]

for·mu·lae [fɔ́:rmjəlì:] *n.* pl. of **formula.**

for·mu·la·ry [fɔ́:rmjulèri] *n.* Ⓒ **1** a collection or book of formulas. 공식집. **2** a set form of words; a formula. 상투어. — *adj.* of or in formulas. 공식의; 규정의.

for·mu·late [fɔ́:rmjəlèit] *vt.* (P6) **1**

express (something) in the form of a formula; reduce (something) to a formula. …을 공식으로 나타내다; 공식화하다. **2** express (something) precisely and systematically. …을 정확히 계통적으로 논술하다. ¶ *He finds it extremely difficult to ~ his new theory.* 그는 그의 새 이론을 계통적으로 명확히 논술하기는 매우 어렵다고 느끼고 있다. [L. (→form)]

for·mu·la·tion [fɔ̀ːrmjəléiʃən] *n.* **1** Ⓤ the act of formulating. 공식화; 계통적 논술. **2** Ⓒ an exact and clear expression. 명확한 표현.

for·ni·cate [fɔ́ːrnəkèit] *vi.* (P1) commit fornication. 밀통(密通)〔사통(私通)〕하다. [L. *fornix* brothel]

for·ni·ca·tion [fɔ̀ːrnəkéiʃən] *n.* sexual intercourse between unmarried persons. 밀통(密通); 사통(私通); 간음.

***for·sake** [fərséik] *vt.* (**-sook, -sak·en**) (P6) **1** leave (someone) alone; desert. …를 버리고 돌보지 않다; 내버리다. ¶ ~ *one's children* 〔*friend*〕 자식을〔친구를〕 버리고 돌보지 않다〔모른 체하다〕. **2** give up (a habit, an idea, etc.). (습관 따위)를 버리다; 그만두다. [for-, obs. *sacan* contend]

for·sak·en [fərséikən] *v.* pp. of **forsake.**

for·sook [fərsúk] *v.* p. of **forsake.**

for·sooth [fɔːrsúːθ] *adv.* 《*iron., arch.*》 in truth; truly; no doubt. 참으로; 확실히; 정말이지. [*for, sooth*]

for·swear [fɔːrswέər] *v.* (**-swore, -sworn**) *vt.* (P6) pledge oneself to give up (something). (맹세코) …을 그만두다. ¶ ~ *smoking* 맹세코 담배를 끊다. — *vi.* (P1) make a false statement under oath. 거짓 맹세를 하다; 위증하다. [for-]

forswear oneself, swear falsely; commit perjury. 거짓 맹세하다; 위증(僞證)하다.

for·swore [fɔːrswɔ́ːr] *v.* p. of **forswear.**

for·sworn [fɔːrswɔ́ːrn] *v.* pp. of **forswear.**

***fort** [fɔːrt] *n.* Ⓒ a strong building or place surrounded with defenses against enemies. 보루(堡壘); 요새(cf. *fortress*). ¶ *hold a solitary ~ against the enemy* 외로운 보루를 지키며 적군에 대항하다. [L. *fortis* strong]

hold the fort, **a**) maintain a firm position against attack or criticism. (공격·비판에 대하여) 자기의 입장을 지키다; 굴하지 않다. **b**) keep things going. 현상을 유지해 가다.

forte[1] [fɔːrt] *n.* Ⓒ one's strong point; anything in which one excels or shows particular power. 강점; 장점. ¶ *have a ~ for* …이 강점이다; …을 잘하다. [F. *fort*(→fort) mis-spelt]

for·te[2] [fɔ́ːrti, -tei] *adj.* 《mus.》 loud. 강음(強音)의(opp. piano[2]). — *adv.* loudly. 강하게(abbr. f.). [It.]

:forth [fɔːrθ] *adv.* **1** forward; onward. 앞으로; 전방으로(opp. backward). ¶ *step ~* 앞으로 나오다 / *come* 〔*go*〕 ~ 나오다〔나가다〕 / *stretch ~ one's hand* 손을 내밀다. **2** 《usu. connected with *a verb*》 out into view. 밖으로; 나타나. ¶ *bring ~* 낳다; 일으키다 / *Trees put ~ new leaves in spring.* 나무들은 봄에 싹을 낸다 / *The sun sends ~ light.* 태양은 빛을 발한다 / *Floods of tears burst ~.* 눈물이 왈칵 쏟아져 나왔다. **3** onwards(=further on) in time or order. (시간·순서에 있어) 앞으로; …이후. ¶ *from this day ~* 오늘 이후. [→fore]

and so forth, and so on. …등등; …운운.

back and forth, to and fro. 앞뒤로; 이리저리. ¶ *walk back and ~* 왔다갔다하다.

so far forth, so far. 거기〔그 정도〕까지는.

so far forth as, to whatever extent. …의 정도까지.

forth·com·ing [fɔ̀ːrθkʌ́miŋ] *adj.* **1** about to come; approaching. 앞으로 올; 다가오는. ¶ *a list of ~ books* 근간서(近刊書) 목록 / *in the ~ week* 내주에. **2** at hand when expected or needed. (필요·요구 따위에 대비하여) 준비된; 곧 입수할 수 있는. ¶ *The promised help was not ~.* 약속된 원조의 준비는 없었다. [*forth*]

forth·right [fɔ́ːrθràit] *adj.* **1** frank and outspoken; straightforward. 솔직한. **2** going straight ahead. 똑바른; 직진의. — *adv.* straight; at once. 똑바로; 곧장; 즉시.

●**forth·right·ness** [-nis] *n.*

forth·with [fɔ̀ːrθwíθ, -wíð] *adv.* at once; without delay. 곧; 즉각. ¶ *Tell him to come ~.* 그에게 곧 오라고 해라.

:for·ti·eth [fɔ́ːrtiiθ] *n.* **1** 《usu. *the ~*》 the number 40; 40th. 제40; 마흔(번)째. **2** Ⓒ one of 40 equal parts, 1/40; 40분의 1. — *adj.* of the 40th. 제40의; 마흔(번)째의; 40분의 1의. [*forty*]

for·ti·fi·ca·tion [fɔ̀ːrtəfikéiʃən] *n.* **1** Ⓤ the act or science of fortifying. 요새화; 축성(학). **2** Ⓒ 《usu. *pl.*》 works for defense, such as walls and towers; a fortified place. 방어 공사; 요새. [↓]

for·ti·fy [fɔ́ːrtəfài] *vt.* (**-fied**) (P6,13) **1** 《mil.》 strengthen (a place) with forts, walls, etc. for defense against attack. (공격에 대비하여) 강화하다; 요새화하다. ¶ *a fortified area* 요새 지대. **2** strengthen (someone) physically or mentally. …을 (육체적·정신적으로) 강하게 하다. ¶ ~ *oneself against the cold* 추위에 대비해서 몸을 튼튼히 하다 / ~ *one's courage* 용기를 떨쳐 일으키다. **3** strengthen (wine) by adding alcohol. (술에) 알코올을 더하여 독하게 하다. **4** enrich (food) by adding vitamins and minerals. 식품의 영양가를 높이다〔강화하다〕. ¶ *fortified milk* 강화 우유. [→fort, -fy]

for·tis·si·mo [fɔːrtísəmòu] *adj.* 《mus.》 very loud. 매우 강한(opp. pianissimo). — *adv.* 《mus.》 very loudly. 매우 세게 (abbr. ff.). [It.]

for·ti·tude [fɔ́ːrtətjùːd] *n.* Ⓤ firm courage and endurance in the face of danger, trouble, misfortune, etc. (불행·위험·고통 따위에 견디는) 군센 용기; 불굴의 정신. ¶ *invincible* ~ 견인 불발 / *face death with* ~ 군센 용기로써 죽음에 직면하다. [→fort]

*__fort·night__ [fɔ́ːrtnàit] *n.* Ⓒ 《chiefly Brit.》 two weeks. 2주일간. ¶ *Monday* ~, 2주일 후〔전〕의 월요일 / *today* ~, 2주일 후〔전〕의 오늘 / *stay* (*for*) *a* ~, 2주일간 머무르다. [*fourteen, night*]

fort·night·ly [fɔ́ːrtnàitli] *adv.* once a fortnight. 2주일에 한 번; 2주일마다. — *adj.* appearing once a fortnight. 격주마다의.

FORTRAN [fɔ́ːrtræn] *n.* a computer programing language for problems expressed in algebraic terms. 포트란《과학 기술 계산용의 프로그램 언어》. [*for*mula, *tran*slation]

*__for·tress__ [fɔ́ːrtris] *n.* Ⓒ a place strengthened by military defenses. 보루; 요새(지). ¶ *an impregnable* ~ 난공불락의 요새. [→fort]

for·tu·i·tous [fɔːrtjúːətəs] *adj.* happening accidentally; casual. 우연의; 우발성의. ¶ *a* ~ *encounter* 우연의 만남. ●**for·tu·i·tous·ly** [-li] *adv.* [L. *fors* chance]

for·tu·i·ty [fɔːrtjúːəti] *n.* (*pl.* **-ties**) **1** Ⓤ chance or accident. 우연(성). **2** Ⓒ an accidental happening. 우연의〔우발〕 사건.

*__for·tu·nate__ [fɔ́ːrtʃənit] *adj.* **1** having good luck; receiving some unexpected good; lucky. 운 좋은; 행운의(opp. unfortunate). **2** bringing good luck that was not expected. 행운을 가져오는. ¶ ~ *circumstances* 좋은 결과를 낳는 상황 / *be born under a* ~ *star* 팔자좋게 태어나다. [→fortune]

*__for·tu·nate·ly__ [fɔ́ːrtʃənətli] *adv.* by good fortune; luckily. 다행히(도); 운좋게. ¶ *Fortunately I remembered the address.* 다행히 나는 그의 주소를 기억해 냈다.

:**for·tune** [fɔ́ːrtʃən] *n.* **1** ⓊⒸ great wealth; riches; a great sum of money or property. 부(富); 재산; 대금(大金). ¶ *make a* ~ 재산을 쌓다 / *She has a large* ~. 그녀는 돈이 많다 / *When he died he left a great* ~ *to his son.* 그가 죽었을 때, 아들에게 막대한 유산을 남겼다. **2** ⓊⒸ what happens (good or bad) to someone; luck; chance; destiny; lot. 운; 운세; 운명. ¶ *have one's* ~ *told* 운세를 점쳐받다. **3** Ⓒ good luck; success in general; prosperity. 행운; 성공; 번영. ¶ *seek one's* ~ 행운을 찾다. [L. *fortuna*]

make a fortune, become rich. 부자가 되다.

make one's fortune, prosper. 번영하다.

marry a fortune, marry a wealthy woman. 돈많은 여자와 결혼하다.

tell 〔***read***〕 ***someone's fortune,*** predict one's future. 아무의 운세를 점치다.

try one's fortune, take a chance. 운수를 시험해보다.

fortune hunter [´-- ˋ-] *n.* a person who tries to gain wealth, esp. by marrying a wealthy person. 부자가 되려는 사람; 재산을 노리는 구혼자.

for·tune·tell·er [fɔ́ːrtʃəntèlər] *n.* Ⓒ a person who foretells what will happen to other people in the future. 점쟁이.

for·tune·tell·ing [fɔ́ːrtʃəntèliŋ] *n.* Ⓤ the act of foretelling the future events of other people. 점; 운세 판단.

:**for·ty** [fɔ́ːrti] *n.* **1** Ⓤ four times ten; 40. 마흔; 40. **2** 《*pl.*》 the years of life or century between 39 and 50. (나이의) 40대; (세기의) 40년대. ¶ *Her parents are in their forties.* 그녀의 양친은 40대이다. [→four]

like forty, 《U.S. *colloq.*》 to an extreme degree. 대단한 기세로.

— *adj.* of 40. 40의.

forty winks [´- ˊ] *n.* 《*colloq.*》 a short sleep, esp. by day. (특히 낮의) 얕은 잠; 낮잠.

fo·rum [fɔ́ːrəm] *n.* Ⓒ (*pl.* **-rums** or **fo·ra**) **1** the public square or market place for meeting in an ancient Roman city. (옛 로마의) 집회 광장. **2** a law court. 법정. **3** an assembly for the discussion of a subject of current interest. 토론회. ¶ *an open* ~ 공개 토론회 / *the* ~ *of public opinion* 여론의 비판. [L.]

:**for·ward** [fɔ́ːrwərd] *adj.* **1** situated in the front; moving ahead; onward. 앞의; 전방의; 전진의(opp. backward). ¶ *a* ~ *movement* 전진 운동. **2** advanced; (of plants, children, etc.) well-advanced; early. 나아간; 진행된; 진보적인; 조숙한; 계절에 앞선. ¶ *a* ~ *spring* 이른 봄 / *be* ~ *with one's work* 일이 진척돼 있다 / *She is* ~ *for her age.* 그녀는 나이에 비해 숙성하다. **3** bold; impudent. 주제넘은; 건방진. **4** ready; eager. 자진해〔기꺼이, 곧〕(…하는). ¶ *be* ~ *with one's answer* 즉각 대답하다.

— *adv.* **1** to or toward the front; onward; ahead; toward the future. 앞으로〔에〕; 전방으로〔에〕; 장래에(opp. backward). ¶ *run* ~ 앞으로 달리다 / *rush* ~ 돌진하다. **2** out; into view. 밖으로; 시야 속에. ¶ *come* ~ 앞으로 나오다; (표면에) 나서다.

bring forward, produce. 제출하다.

look forward to, wait for or expect (something) with pleasure. …을 기대하다.

set 〔***put***〕 ***oneself forward,*** try to make oneself great. 중뿔나게 굴다.

— *vt.* **1** (P13) 《*to*》 send (a letter, etc.) to a new address; dispatch (cargo, etc.). (편지)를 전송(轉送)하다; 송부(送付)하다. ¶ ~ *letters to a new address* 편지를 새 주소로 전송하다 / ~ *goods by passenger train* 화물을 객차편으로 보내다. **2** (P6) advance; promote; hasten. …을 진척시키다; (식물 따위

의) 성장을 빠르게 하다. ¶ ~ *the growth of vegetables* 야채를 촉성 재배하다.
— *n.* Ⓒ《sports》one of the players in the front line. 전위(前衛). [→fore, ward]

forwarding agent [⌐— ⌐—] *n.* a person or business company that delivers goods. 운송업자.

for·ward·ness [fɔ́:rwərdnis] *n.* Ⓤ **1** advanced state of development. 진보의 빠름. **2** eagerness. 자진해서 하고 싶은 마음; 열심; 적극성. **3** lack of modesty; boldness. 중뿔남; 뻔뻔스러움; 건방짐.

:for·wards [fɔ́:rwərdz] *adv.* =forward.

for·went [fɔ:rwént] *v.* p. of **forgo.**

fos·sil [fásl / fɔ́sl] *n.* Ⓒ **1** the hardened remains or traces of animals or plants of prehistoric ages found in rock formations in the earth. 화석. ¶ *hunt for* ~ 화석을 찾다. **2** 《*fig.*》a person who is old-fashioned or has out-of-date, fixed ideas. 시대에 뒤진 사람(것); 구식인 사람. — *adj.* **1** having the nature of a fossil; like a fossil. 화석(성)의; 화석 같은. ¶ *a* ~ *plant* (*fish*) 화석 식물(물고기). **2** old-fashioned; out of date. 시대에 뒤(떨어)지는; 낡은; 구식의. ¶ ~ *ideas* 시대에 뒤떨어진 생각 / *a* ~ *approach to teaching* 시대에 뒤진 교수법. [L. *fodio* dig]

fos·sil·i·za·tion [fàsələzéiʃən / fɔ̀silai-] *n.* Ⓤ the act of fossilizing; the state of being fossilized; Ⓒ something fossilized. 화석 작용; 화석화; 화석.

fos·sil·ize [fásəlàiz / fɔ́sil-] *vt.* (P6) **1** make (something) into a fossil. …을 화석으로 하다. **2** make (ideas or opinions) out-of-date. …을 시대에 뒤떨어지게(구식이 되게) 하다. — *vi.* (P1) **1** become fossilized. 화석이 되다. **2** grow old-fashioned. 시대에 뒤지게 되다.

Fos·ter [fɔ́(:)stər, fás-], **Stephen Collins** *n.* (1826-1864) an American composer who is famous for "My Old Kentucky Home", "Old Folks at Home", etc. 포스터《미국의 작곡가》.

·fos·ter [fɔ́(:)stər, fás-] *vt.* **1** (P6) bring up; make grow; care for as one's own child. …을 기르다; 돌보다. ¶ ~ *a child* 아이를 양육하다 / ~ *the sick* 환자의 병구완을 하다. **2** (P6) help the growth or development of; encourage. …을 조성(조장)하다; 촉진하다. ¶ ~ *foreign trade* 해외 무역을 촉진하다 / ~ *musical ability* 음악적 재능을 조장하다. **3** (P13) keep (ambitions, etc.) in one's mind. (야심 따위)를 마음에 품다. ¶ ~ *a hope* 희망을 품다 / ~ *evil thoughts* 못된 생각을 마음에 품다 / ~ *a desire for revenge* 복수심을 품다.
— *adj.* 《U.S.》being or having been brought up in the same family, though not related by blood. 기른. ¶ ~ *parents* 수양 부모 / *a* ~ *child* 양자. [→food]

:fought [fɔ:t] *v.* p. and pp. of **fight.**

·foul [faul] *adj.* **1** very dirty; smelling bad; unpleasant. 더러운; 불결한; 불쾌한. ¶ ~ *water* 불결한 물. **2** (of language, etc.) bad or rude; against the rules; unfair. (말 따위가) 더러운; 반칙의; 부정한. ¶ *a* ~ *tongue* 천한 말 / *a* ~ *talk* 음담 패설 / *by fair means or* ~ 수단을 가리지 않고. **3** wicked; evil. 못된; 사악한. ¶ *a* ~ *deed* 추행 / *a* ~ *murder* 사악한 살인. **4** (of weather) rough or stormy; (of wind or tide) contrary. (날씨가) 나쁜; 거친; (바람·조수가) 반대의. ¶ ~ *weather* / *a* ~ *wind* 역풍. **5** choked with dirt, soot, etc.; entangled. 막힌; 얽힌.

fall* (*run, go*) *foul of, **a**) (of a ship) strike against (something). (배가) …와 충돌하다. ¶ *One boat went* ~ *of the other.* 배 한 척이 다른 배와 충돌했다. **b**) (of a person) quarrel with (someone). …와 의견 충돌을 하다; 싸우다; 언쟁하다.
— *adj.* foully; unfairly. 부정하게; 반칙적으로.

hit foul, 《boxing》hit below the belt; act unfairly. 부정하게 치다《특히, 벨트 아래를 치다》; 비열한 수를 쓰다.

play someone foul, treat someone unfairly. 아무에게 부정행위를 하다; 심한 처사를 하다.
— *n.* Ⓒ **1** 《sports》a play or an action which breaks the rules. 규칙 위반; 부정 행위. **2** 《baseball》a ball knocked outside the base line. 파울.

through fair and* (*through*) *foul, through good or bad fortune; through everything. 어떠한 경우에도.
— *vt.* (P6) **1** make (someone or something) foul; dishonor. …을 더럽히다; 불결하게 하다. ¶ ~ *the hands* 손을 더럽히다 / ~ *the air with smoke* 연기로 공기를 오염시키다 / ~ *someone's name* 아무의 이름을 더럽히다; 아무의 욕을 하다. **2** 《sports》commit a foul against (an opponent). (상대에) 반칙을 범하다; 파울하다. **3** block or choke (a chimney, etc.) with soot, etc.; jam (a road crossing, etc.). …을 막히게 하다. ¶ *Soot had fouled the chimney.* 굴뚝은 검댕으로 막혀 있었다 / *A big truck fouled up the traffic.* 큰 트럭 때문에 교통이 막혔다. **4** ⓐ (of ships, etc.) go violently against (something). (배 따위가) …와 충돌하다. ⓑ cause (anchors, nets, etc.) to become entangled. (닻·그물 따위를) 엉키게 하다.
— *vi.* (P1) **1** become foul; become entangled; strike against each other. 더러워지다; 엉키다; 부딪치다. **2** 《sports》commit a foul; break rules; 《baseball》hit a foul. 반칙(을 범)하다; 파울볼을 치다. [E.]

foul up, 《*colloq.*》make a mess of something; cause disorder. 망쳐놓다; 뒤죽 박죽을 만들다.

fou·lard [fu:lá:rd, fəl-] *n.* Ⓤ a soft, light material of silk, usu. with printed patterns; an article made of foulard, such as a necktie, scarf or hankerchief. 풀라(천)《일종의 비단》; 그 천으로 만든 것《스카프·손수건 따위》. [F.]

foul line [⌐⌐] *n.* 《baseball》 either of the two lines extending from the home plate through the first or the third base to the end of the outfield. (야구에서) 파울라인. [*foul*]

foul·ly [fául*l*i] *adv.* in a dirty or immoral manner. 더럽게; 부정하게.

foul·ness [fáulnis] *n.* **1** Ⓤ the quality of being foul. 불결; 악취. **2** Ⓒ an immoral act. 부정 행위.

foul play [⌐⌐] *n.* play against the rules; an unfair action. (경기의) 반칙 (opp. fair play).

foul-spo·ken [fáulspòukən] *adj.* using indelicate language. 입이 건; 입정사나운.

:found[1] [faund] *v.* p. and pp. of **find.**

:found[2] [faund] *vt.* (P6,7,13) **1** start the construction of (something). …을 창립[설립]하다. ¶ ~ *a new city* 새로운 도시를 건설하다 / ~ *a dynasty* 왕조를 창건하다. **2** 《*on*》 lay the base of (something). …을 근거로 하다. ¶ *write a story founded on facts* 사실에 의거한 이야기를 쓰다. [→fund]

found[3] [faund] *vt.* (P6) melt (metal) and form it into some shape by a mold. (금속을) 녹여 붓다; 주조하다. [L. *fundo* pour]

:foun·da·tion [faundéiʃən] *n.* **1** Ⓤ the act of establishing something. 창립; 창건. ¶ *the ~ of a school* 학교의 설립. **2** Ⓒ 《often *pl.*》 a base to support the whole of a building. 기초; 토대. ¶ *the ~ of a house* 집의 기초. **3** ⒸⓊ that on which some belief, idea, etc. is based. 근거. ¶ *the foundations of his belief* 그의 믿음의 근거 / *The rumor has no ~.* 소문은 사실무근이다. **4** Ⓒ a fund to support a school, a hospital, etc. 기금(基金); 재단. **5** an institution or society. 설립물; 협회. **6** a cosmetic cream, liquid, etc. used as a base for facial make-up. 파운데이션《기초 화장품》. [→found[2]]

be on the foundation, receive one's money from some institution. 재단으로부터 급비(給費)를 받고 있다.

·foun·der[1] [fáundər] *n.* Ⓒ a person who founds or establishes something. 창립자; 창건자. [→found[2]]

foun·der[2] [fáundər] *vi.* (P1) **1** fall in. (집 따위가) 무너지다. **2** (of a horse) break down; stumble. (말이) 쓰러지다; 힘이 빠지다. **3** (of a ship) fill with water and sink. (배 따위가) 침수[함몰]하다. ¶ *The ship foundered in the storm.* 배는 폭풍우에 침수되어 가라앉았다. **4** be ruined; fail. 파멸하다; 실패하다. — *vt.* (P6) **1** cause (a house) to fall in. (집 따위)를 무너뜨리다; 붕괴시키다. **2** cause (a horse) to break down. (말)을 쓰러지게 하다; 녹초가 되게 하다. **3** fill (something) with water and sink (it). …을 침수[함몰]시키다. [→fund]

found·er[3] [fáundər] *n.* Ⓒ a person who casts metal. 주물공(鑄物工). [→found[3]]

found·ling [fáundliŋ] *n.* Ⓒ a baby or child found abandoned whose parents are unknown. 기아(棄兒); 버린[주운] 아이. [→find]

foundling hospital [⌐– ⌐––] *n.* an institution where abandoned babies or children are taken in and looked after. 기아(棄兒) 양육원.

found·ry [fáundri] *n.* (*pl.* **-ries**) **1** Ⓤ the process or act of melting and molding metal; Ⓒ things made by this process. 주조; 주(조)물. **2** Ⓒ a place where metal is melted to be put into a mold. 주물 공장. ¶ *an iron ~* 철공소. [*found*[3]]

fount[1] [faunt] *n.* Ⓒ 《*poet.*》 **1** a fountain; a spring. 샘. **2** a source. 원천. ¶ *a ~ of wisdom* 지혜의 원천[샘]. [L. *fons* spring]

fount[2] [faunt] *n.* a set of a printer's type of one size and design. 동일형 활자의 한 벌. [*found*[3]]

:foun·tain [fáunt*i*n] *n.* Ⓒ **1** a stream of water rising up into the air. 분수(噴水). ¶ *rise like a ~* 분수처럼 솟구치다. **2** an artificial spring of water forced out through pipes and falling into a basin. 분수지(池). **3** a device for supplying water. (분수식) 물 마시는 장치. **4** a natural spring of water. 샘. **5** a source of anything. 원천; 근원. ¶ *a ~ of information* 지식의 샘 / *a ~ of pleasure* 쾌락의 원천 / *poison the fountains of trust* 신뢰의 근원을 해치다. [→fount[1]]

foun·tain·head [fáunt*i*nhèd] *n.* Ⓒ **1** a spring from which a stream begins. 수원(水源). **2** an original source of anything. 본원(本源). ¶ *get to the ~* 근원으로 거슬러 올라가다; 전거[당사자]를 밝히다 / *trace an error to its ~* 잘못의 근원을 알아 내다.

·fountain pen [⌐– ⌐] *n.* a pen for writing with a constant supply of ink within its holder. 만년필.

:four [fɔːr] *n.* Ⓤ the number between three and five. 넷; 4. ¶ *a carriage and ~,* 4두 마차 / *in fours,* 4열로 / *form fours,* 4열을 짓다.

on all fours, on hands and knees. 네 발로 기어; 납죽 엎드려.

— *adj.* of four. 넷(4)의; 네 개의. ¶ *a four-cycle engine,* 4주기식 엔진 / *four-dimensional,* 4차원의. [E.]

the four corners of a document, its scope. 문서의 내용 범위.

the four corners of the earth, the remotest parts. 지구의 구석구석.

to the four winds, 《*arch.*》 in all direction. 사방에[으로].

within the four seas, 《Brit.》 in Great Britain; in the world. 영(英) 본국 영토 내

에; 이 세상에.

four·fold [fɔ́ːrfòuld] *adj.* **1** four times as much or as many. 4 배의. **2** having four folds or parts. 4[네] 겹의; 4 중의. — *adv.* four times as much or as many. 4 배로; 4 겹[중]으로.

four-foot·ed [fɔ́ːrfútid] *adj.* having four feet. 네 발의(cf. *quadruped*).

Four Hundred [ˊ ˊˉ], **the** *n.* 《U.S.》 the most exclusive social group. 상류 인사.

four-let·ter word [ˊˉˉ ˊ] *n.* any of English words generally regarded as vulgar or obscene. 4 글자로 된 추잡한 말《fuck, cunt, piss, shit 따위》.

four-o'clock [fɔ́ːrəklɑ̀k / -klɔ̀k] *n.* Ⓒ 《bot.》 a small garden plant with long red, white, or yellow flowers. 분꽃.

four·pence [fɔ́ːrpəns] *n.* Ⓤ 《Brit.》 the sum of four pence. 4 펜스. 參考 4d., 4d 로 생략함.

four·pen·ny [fɔ́ːrpəni] *adj.* totalling or costing fourpence. 4 펜스(값)의.

four·score [fɔ́ːrskɔ́ːr] 《*arch.*》 *adj.* four twenties; 80. 20 의 4 배의; 80 의. ¶ ~ *years,* 80 년. — *n.* the sum of four twenties. 80; 80 개; 80 살.

four·some [fɔ́ːrsəm] *n.* 《golf》 a game played by four people, two on each side. 한 조 각기 2 명씩 4 사람이 하는 골프 경기.

four·square [fɔ́ːrskwέər] *adj.* **1** square. 4 각의; 정4각형의. **2** firm; steady. 견고한; 안정된. **3** frank; forthright. 솔직한.

:four·teen [fɔ́ːrtíːn] *n.* Ⓤ the number between thirteen and fifteen; 14. 열넷; 14. — *adj.* of 14. 14 의. [E.]

·four·teenth [fɔ́ːrtíːnθ] *n.* **1** 《*the* ~》 the number 14. 열넷째; 제 14. **2** Ⓒ one of 14 equal parts of anything. 14 분의 1. — *adj.* of 14th. 제 14 의; 14 분의 1 의.

:fourth [fɔːrθ] *n.* **1** 《*the* ~》 the number 4; 4th. 넷째; 네번째; 제 4. **2** Ⓒ one of four equal parts. 4 분의 1.

the Fourth of July, 《U.S.》 Independence Day. 독립 기념일.

— *adj.* of 4th. 제 4 의; 4 분의 1 의. [*four*]

fourth·ly [fɔ́ːrθli] *adv.* in the fourth place. 넷째로; 네번째로.

·fowl [faul] *n.* (*pl.* **fowls** or *collectively* **fowl**) **1** Ⓒ 《*arch., poet.*》 a bird. 새. ¶ *the fowls of the air* 하늘의 새. **2** Ⓤ 《*collectively*》 any of the larger birds. 큰 조류(鳥類). ¶ *game* ~ 엽조(獵鳥) / *water-fowl* 물새 / *wildfowl* 들새. **3** Ⓒ a domestic bird used for food; a cock or hen. 가금(家禽); 닭. ¶ *domestic* ~ 가금. **4** Ⓤ the flesh of these birds. 새고기; 닭고기.

— *vi.* (P1) hunt or trap wild birds, esp. birds for eating. 들새를 잡다[사냥하다]. [E.]

fowl·er [fáulər] *n.* Ⓒ a person who shoots or catches wild birds. 들새 사냥꾼.

fowl·ing [fáuliŋ] *n.* Ⓤ the act of hunting wild birds. 들새 사냥.

fowling piece [ˊˉ ˊ] *n.* a light gun for shooting wild birds. 새총; 새 잡는 엽총.

·fox [fɑks / fɔks] *n.* **1** Ⓒ a wild animal of the dog family with a bushy tail. 여우. 參考 fox 는 수컷이며 암컷은 vixen. **2** Ⓤ its fur. 여우 모피. **3** Ⓒ a sly and cunning person. 교활한 사람. ¶ *an old* ~ 노회(老獪)한 사람 / *a* ~ *in a lamb's skin* 위선자.

— *vt.* (P6) **1** deceive. 속이다. ¶ ~ *a secret out of someone* 아무에게서 비밀을 눈치채다 / *get someone foxed* 아무를 속이다. **2** 《chiefly in *pp.*》 change or spoil the color of (paper). …을 변색시키다. ¶ *The engraving is badly foxed.* 판화가 몹시 바랬다. **3** make (beer etc.) sour. (맥주 따위)를 시게 하다.

— *vi.* (P1) **1** act cunningly. 교활하게 굴다. **2** become foxed, as paper or beer. 변색하다; 맛이 시어지다. [E.]

fox·glove [fɑ́ksglʌ̀v / fɔ́ks-] *n.* Ⓒ 《bot.》 a plant with large, bell-shaped purple or white flowers. 디기탈리스.

fox·hole [fɑ́kshòul / fɔ́ks-] *n.* 《mil.》 a hole in the ground for protection against enemy fire. 각개 참호.

fox·hound [fɑ́kshàund / fɔ́ks-] *n.* Ⓒ a kind of dog with a keen sense of smell trained to hunt foxes. 폭스하운드《여우 사냥개》.

fox terrier [ˊ ˊˉˉ] *n.* a small dog, formerly used for driving foxes out of holes, but now kept as a pet. 폭스테리어《본래 여우 몰이용 사냥개》.

fox trot [ˊ ˊ] *n.* a dance with a variety of short, quick steps; a piece of music for it. 폭스 트롯《사교춤의 하나》; 그 춤곡(曲).

fox·y [fɑ́ksi / fɔ́ks-] *adj.* (**fox·i·er, fox·i·est**) **1** like a fox; cunning. 여우 같은; 교활한. ¶ *play* ~ 교활한 짓을 하다. **2** of the color of a fox. 엷은 갈색의; 황갈색의. [E.]

foy·er [fɔ́iər, fɔ́iei] *n.* 《F.》 Ⓒ **1** a lobby in a theater or hotel. (극장·호텔 따위의) 휴게실; 로비. **2** an entrance hall in a house. 집 현관 홀.

FPC Federal Power Commission. 연방 동력 위원회.

Fr. 1 France. **2** French. **3** Father. **4** Friday.

fr. 1 franc. **2** from. **3** fragment.

fra·cas [fréikəs / frǽkɑː] *n.* (*pl.* **fra·cas** [-z]) a noisy quarrel or fight. 싸움 소동; 서로 맞고함치기. [It. *fracasso*]

·frac·tion [frǽkʃən] *n.* Ⓒ **1** a very small piece broken off; a fragment. 단편. ¶ *in a* ~ *of a second* 순식간에. **2** 《math.》 a number less than a whole number. 분수(分數). ¶ *a decimal* ~ 소수 / *a proper* [*an improper*] ~ 진[가]분수 / *A half is a* ~, *and so is a fourth.* 2분의 1은 분수이고, 4분의 1도 그렇다. [L. *frango* break]

frac·tion·al [frǽkʃənəl] *adj.* of a fraction. 분수의; 미소한. ¶ *a* ~ *equation* 분수

방정식.

frac·tious [frǽkʃəs] *adj.* **1** easily made angry. 성내기 잘 하는; 괴까다로운. **2** hard to control. 다루기 힘든. ¶ *a ~ child* 다루기 어려운 아이. ● **frac·tious·ly** [-li] *adv.*

frac·ture [frǽktʃər] *n.* **1** Ⓤ the state or process of being broken; Ⓒ a break in a bone. 부숨; 부서짐; 골절. ¶ *He suffered a ~ in the fall.* 그는 떨어져 뼈가 부러졌다. **2** Ⓒ a break; a crack. 터진 데; 갈라진 금. —*vi., vt.* (P1; 6) break; crack. 부수다; 부러지다; 골절하다. ¶ *~ one's leg* 다리뼈를 분지르다 / *~ a pane of glass* 유리 한 장을 깨뜨리다 / *A child's bones ~ easily.* 어린애의 뼈는 잘 부러진다.

frag·ile [frǽdʒəl] *adj.* easily broken or destroyed. 부서지기〔깨지기, 부러지기〕 쉬운; 약한(opp. strong, elastic). ¶ *~ china* 깨지기 쉬운 도자기 / *a ~ boy* 허약 체질의 소년. ● **frag·ile·ly** [-aili] *adv.* [→fraction]

fra·gil·i·ty [frədʒíləti] *n.* Ⓤ the quality or state of being fragile. 부서지기 쉬움; 무름; 허약함.

∗**frag·ment** [frǽgmənt] *n.* Ⓒ **1** a part; a part that is broken off from a thing. 파편; 단편. ¶ *overhear fragments of a conversation* 대화의 단편을 우연히 듣다. **2** an unfinished work. 단장(斷章); 미완성의 유고(遺稿). [L. *frango* break]

frag·men·tar·y [frǽgməntèri / -təri] *adj.* made up of fragments; not complete. 단편(斷片)의; 미완성의. ¶ *a ~ manuscript* 미완성의 유고(遺稿) / *~ memories* 단편적인 기억.

∗**fra·grance** [fréigrəns], **-gran·cy** [-grənsi] *n.* Ⓤ sweetness of smell; a sweet smell. 향기(로움); 방향(芳香). [↓]

∗**fra·grant** [fréigrənt] *adj.* **1** having or giving off a sweet smell. 향기로운; 방향성(芳香性)의. ¶ *a ~ rose* 향기로운 장미 / *be ~ with flowers* 꽃향기가 나다. **2** pleasant. 유쾌한; 즐거운. ¶ *~ memories* 즐거운 추억. [L. *fragro smell* sweet]

fra·grant·ly [fréigrəntli] *adv.* in a fragrant state. 향기롭게.

∗**frail** [freil] *adj.* **1** fragile. 부서지기〔깨지기〕 쉬운; 무른. ¶ *~ china* 깨지기 쉬운 도자기. **2** having a delicate structure. (몸이) 약한. ¶ *a ~ lady* 연약한 여자 / *my ~ build* 나의 빈약한 체격. **3** apt to be tempted easily. 유혹에 지기 쉬운; 성격이 약한; 의지 박약한; (여자가) 부정한. ● **frail·ness** [∠nis] *n.* [L. *frango* break]

frail·ty [fréilti] *n.* (*pl.* **-ties**) **1** Ⓤ the quality of being frail; moral weakness. 깨지기〔부서지기〕 쉬움; 무름; 의지 박약. **2** Ⓒ a fault; a defect. 약점; 결점; 결함. ¶ *frailties of the human flesh* 인간의 약점. [↑]

:frame [freim] *n.* Ⓒ **1** a supporting or shaping structure. 뼈대. ¶ *the ~ of a house* 〔*ship*〕 집〔배〕의 뼈대. **2** the body structure. 골격; 체격. ¶ *a man of unusually large ~* 유난히 큰 체격의 남자 / *a horse with a strong ~* 튼튼한 체격의 말. **3** a border surrounding of a picture, etc. 테두리; (사진)틀. ¶ *a window ~* 창틀 / *make a ~ for a picture* 사진틀을 만들다. **4** the way something is put together; a structure; a system. 구조; 기구; 조직; 제도. ¶ *a ~ of government* 정치 기구 / *the ~ of society* 사회 조직. **5** a state of mind; mood. 마음의 상태; 기분. ¶ *an unhappy ~ of mind* 비참한 기분 / *be in a proper ~ of mind to do* …하기에 알맞은 기분이다.
—*vt.* **1** (P6) ⓐ shape; put together; build up; construct. 뼈대를〔모양을〕 만들다; 세우다; 조립하다. ¶ *~ a boat* 배를 만들다 / *~ a shelter with* 〔*out of*〕 *brushwood* 잡목 가지로 오두막을 짓다. ⓑ express in words. 말로 표현하다. ¶ *~ a sentence* 문장을 조성하다. ⓒ pronounce. 발음하다. ¶ *His lips could hardly ~ the words.* 그의 입술은 그 말을 거의 발음하지 못했다. **2** (P6,7,13) ⓐ plan or put together in the mind; imagine. (생각 따위)를 마음에 품다; 상상하다. ¶ *He never framed such a question in his mind.* 그는 그 같은 의문을 품어 본 적이 없었다. ⓑ compose; invent. …을 구성하다; 고안〔안출〕해 내다; 만들어 내다; 조작하다. ¶ *~ a plan* 계획을 세우다 / *~ a theory* 이론을 구성하다 / *~ a lie* 거짓말을 꾸며 내다 / *They framed up a story.* 그들은 이야기를 조작해 냈다. **3** (P13,20) fit (one thing) to another; fit for some special purpose. …을 —에 맞추다; (목적에) 적합하게 하다. ¶ *a structure framed to resist the fiercest storm* 어떠한 세찬 폭풍우에도 견디게끔 된 건조물 / *a man not framed for trials and hardships* 시련과 어려움을 견뎌 내지 못하게 되어 있는 사람. **4** (P6) ⓐ put a border round; make a frame for. 테(두리)를 두르다; 틀을〔테두리를〕 만들다; 액자에 넣다. ¶ *~ … in red lines* …을 붉은 줄로 두르다 / *have a picture framed* 사진을 사진틀에 끼우다. ⓑ serve as a frame; enclose like a frame. 테두리 같은 역할을 하다; 테두리같이 둘러싸다. ¶ *a lake framed in woods* 숲으로 둘러싸인 호수. **5** (P6,7) 《orig. U.S.》《often *up*》 make (an innocent person) appear guilty by false evidence; devise false evidence for (a case) in order to make an innocent person appear guilty. (거짓 증거 따위로) 억울한 사람에게 죄를 씌우다; 누명을 씌우다. [O.E. *framian* be helpful, make progress]

frame house [∠ ∠] *n.* 《U.S.》 a house constructed with a skelton frame of timber. (목재 뼈대로 세운) 목조 가옥.

fram·er [fréimər] *n.* Ⓒ **1** a person who builds up a plan, etc. 구성자; 기획자. **2** a person who makes frames for pictures. 사진틀을〔액자를〕 만드는 사람.

frame-up [fréimʌ̀p] *n.* Ⓒ 《U.S. *colloq.*》 **1** a secret plan for an evil purpose. 짬짜미. **2** an arrangement to make an innocent person seem guilty. 음모; 흉계.

frame·work [fréimwə̀ːrk] *n.* Ⓒ **1** a support to which a thing is fixed. 틀; 테두리. **2** a way in which something is constructed. 얼개; 뼈대; 기구. ¶ *the ~ of society* 사회의 기구 / *the ~ of a play* 연극의 얼거리.

***franc** [fræŋk] *n.* Ⓒ a unit of money in France, Belgium and Switzerland. 프랑 《프랑스 등지의 화폐 단위》. [F.]

:France [fræns, frɑːns] *n.* a country in western Europe. 프랑스. 參考 수도는 Paris.

Fran·ces [frǽnsis / fráːn-] *n.* a woman's name. 여자 이름.

fran·chise [frǽntʃaiz / -tʃaiz] *n.* Ⓒ **1** a right granted by a government. 특권; 특허. **2** 《usu. *the ~*》 the right to vote; the right of citizenship. 선거권. ¶ *the parliamentary ~* 국회 의원 선거권 / *guarantee the ~ of every citizen* 모든 시민의 선거권을 보장하다. [F. →frank]

Fran·cis [frǽnsis / fráːn-] *n.* **1** a man's name. 남자 이름. 參考 애칭은 Frank. **2 Saint** (1182-1226) an Italian monk who founded the Franciscan order. 성(聖)프란체스코《프란체스코 수도회의 개조》.

Fran·cis·can [frænsískən] *adj.* belonging to the order of St. Francis. 프란체스코 수도회의. **—*n.*** a member of the order of St. Francis. 프란체스코 수도회의 수사. [*Francis*]

:frank[1] [fræŋk] *adj.* free in expressing one's feelings, thoughts, etc.; straightforward; honest. 꾸밈〔숨김〕 없는; 솔직한. ¶ *a ~ look in one's eyes* 숨김 없는 눈의 표정 / *make a ~ confession* 솔직한 고백을 하다.
to be frank with you, plainly speaking. 솔직히 말하면.
●**frank·ness** [´nis] *n.* [L. *francus* free]

frank[2] [fræŋk] *vt.* (P6) send free of charge. 무료로 보내다. ¶ *~ a letter.* **—*n.*** a mark to show that the mail is to be sent free of charge; a letter or parcel thus sent. (우편물 따위) 무료 송달의 서명〔인(印)〕; 무료 송달 우편물. [↑]

frank·furt·er [frǽŋkfərtər] *n.* Ⓒ 《U.S.》 a reddish sausage made of beef and pork; frankfurt sausage. 비엔나 소시지. [Place]

frank·in·cense [frǽŋkinsens] *n.* Ⓤ a sweet-smelling resin from balsam trees, used as incense. 유향(乳香). [*frank* in sense 'luxuriant', *incense*]

Frank·lin [frǽŋklin], **Benjamin** *n.* (1706-90) an American statesman, author, scientist, and inventor. 프랭클린《미국의 정치가·저술가·과학자·발명가》.

frank·lin [frǽŋklin] *n.* 《Brit. hist.》 formerly, an English farmer whose farm was his own. 자유 토지 보유자; 향사(鄕士). [→frank[2]]

:frank·ly [frǽŋkli] *adv.* in a frank manner. 솔직히. [*frank*[1]]
frankly speaking, to be frank with you. 솔직히 말하면.

***fran·tic** [frǽntik] *adj.* very much excited; wild with excitement, pain, etc. 몹시 흥분한; 광란의; 열광한. ¶ *be ~ with pain* 〔*joy*〕 고통〔기쁨〕으로 미칠 것 같다 / *drive someone ~* 아무를 욱하게 하다. ●**fran·ti·cal·ly** [-kəli] *adv.* [Gk. *phrēn* brain]

fra·ter·nal [frətə́ːrnəl] *adj.* of brothers; like brothers; of a society of men banded together like brothers. 형제의; 형제 같은; 우애의; 우애 연합의. ¶ *~ love* 형제애. [L. *frater* brother]

fraternal orders [-´-´-] *n.* 《U.S.》 a group organized for mutual aid and fellowship. 우애(공제) 조합.

fra·ter·ni·ty [frətə́ːrnəti] *n.* (*pl.* **-ties**) **1** Ⓤ the state of being brothers; brotherhood. 형제 관계. **2** Ⓒ 《U.S.》 a social group of young men in a college. 대학의 남학생 사교 클럽(opp. sorority).

frat·er·nize [frǽtərnàiz] *vi.* (P2A,3) 《*with, together*》 meet together in a friendly way. (형제처럼) 친하게 사귀다〔교제하다〕.
●**frat·er·ni·za·tion** [frætərnizéiʃən] *n.*

frat·ri·cide [frǽtrəsàid] *n.* **1** Ⓤ the act of killing one's own brother or sister. 형제〔동기〕 살해. **2** Ⓒ a person who kills one's own brother or sister. 형제〔동기〕 살해자.
●**frat·ri·cid·al** [-sáidl] *adj.* [↑, suicide, patricide]

fraud [frɔːd] *n.* **1** Ⓤ trickery practiced to gain an unfair profit; dishonesty. 속임; 협잡; 부정직. ¶ *pious ~* (종교상의 방편으로서의 거짓말. **2** Ⓒ an act of fraud; a dishonest act; a person who practices fraud. 사기; 부정 행위; 사기〔협잡〕꾼. ¶ *obtain money by ~* 돈을 사취(詐取)하다. [L. *fraus*]

fraud·u·lence [frɔ́ːdʒuləns], **-len·cy** [-lənsi] *n.* Ⓤ the quality of being fraudulent. 사기; 협잡; 부정 행위.

fraud·u·lent [frɔ́ːdʒulənt] *adj.* dishonest; deceitful. 속이는; 사기의; 부정한. ¶ *~ practices* 사기 행위 / *~ gains* 부정 이익 / *a ~ transaction* 부정 거래.

fraught [frɔːt] *adj.* 《*with*》 filled; involving. …으로 충만한〔찬〕; 포함해 있는. ¶ *be ~ with danger.* [→freight]

Fräu·lein [frɔ́ilain] *n.* 《G.》 **1** a German unmarried woman; a title corresponding to Miss. 미혼 여성; 아가씨; …양(孃). ¶ *~ Schmidt* 슈미트 양. **2** a German governess or female teacher of German in England. (영국의) 독일 여자 가정 교사.

fray[1] [frei] *n.* Ⓒ a quarrel; a fight. 시끄러운 싸움; 언쟁. ¶ *be eager for the ~* 일이 터지기를 고대하다; 싸움을 갈망하다. [→affray]

fray[2] [frei] *vt.* (P6) wear or rub off (cloth, rope, etc.) to threads or fibers at the end or the edge. …을 닳게 하다; 비비다; 무지러지게 하다; 너덜너덜 해지게 하다. ¶ *a frayed shirt* 닳아 해진 셔츠. **—*vi.*** (P1) become frayed. 닳아 해지다; 무지러지다. [L. *frico* rub]

fraz·zle [frǽzəl] 《chiefly U.S. *colloq.*》 *vt., vi.* (P6; 1) make or become worn out or physically exhausted. 닳아 해지(게 하)다; 무지러지(게 하)다; 지쳐 빠지(게 하)다. [G.]

to a frazzle, very badly; thoroughly. 기진맥진하게; 늘씬하게. ¶ *worn to a* ~ 녹초가 되도록 지치다.

FRB Federal Reserve Bank. 연방 준비 은행.

freak [fri:k] *n.* **1** Ⓒ an unusual or abnormal person or thing. 기형(의 사람·동물·것); 변형; 이상(異常). ¶ *a* ~ *of nature* 조물주의 장난; 기형 / *a* ~ *of the modern sensibility.* 현대 감각의 변태적인 산물. **2** ⒸⓊ a causeless, sudden fancy or change of mind. 일시적 기분〔일〕; 변덕. ¶ *out of mere* ~ 단순한 변덕에서; 그저 일시적 기분으로.
— *adj.* unusual. 야릇한; 이상(異常)한. [O.E. *frecia* dance]

freak·ish [frí:kiʃ] *adj.* of or like a freak. 색다른; 야릇한; 변덕스러운.

freck·le [frékl] *n.* Ⓒ a small, brownish spot on the skin. (피부의) 반점; 주근깨.
— *vt.* (P6) cover (the face, the hands, etc.) with freckles. ¶ *His face is freckled all over.* 그의 얼굴엔 온통 주근깨가 나 있다. — *vi.* (P1) become spotted with freckles. 주근깨〔기미〕가 생기다. [N.]

Fred [fred] *n.* a nickname of Frederick. Frederick의 애칭.

Fred·er·ick [frédərik] *n.* a man's name. 남자 이름.

:free [fri:] *adj.* **1** not under any control; independent. 자유로운; 속박 없는; 독립한. ¶ ~ *citizen* 자유 시민 / *a* ~ *country* 자유 국가 / ~ *will* 자유 의사 / *a* ~ *action* 자유 행동. **2** not imprisoned; released. 잡혀 있지 않은; 방면된; 석방된(opp. captive). ¶ *set someone* ~ 아무를 석방하다. **3** able to act or think as one pleases. 마음대로 …할 수 있는; 마음대로의. ¶ ~ *to choose* 마음대로 선택할 수 있는 / *You are* ~ *to do what you like.* 좋아하는 것을 마음대로 해도 된다 / *It is* ~ *for him to do so.* 그가 그렇게 하는 것은 자유이다 / *Please feel* ~ *to do….* 마음대로〔거리끼지 말고〕 …해 주십시오. **4** open (to all); allowable. 개방된; 마음대로 드나들〔이용할〕 수 있는. ¶ *a* ~ *port* 자유항 / *a* ~ *market* 자유 시장 / *be* ~ *of a friend's house* 친구 집에 마음대로 드나들 수 있다 / *The beauties of Nature are* ~ *to all.* 자연의 미관은 누구에게나 개방되어 있다. **5** without anything to stop; not hindered. 막는 것이〔장애가〕 없는. ¶ *The road is now* ~ *of fallen rock.* 도로는 이제 낙석이 없어 안전하게 통행할 수 있다 / *The ship had* ~ *passage through the canal.* 그 배는 그 운하를 자유로이 통행할 수 있었다. **6** ⓐ given without payment. 무료의. ¶ *a* ~ *pass* 무료 승차권〔입장권〕 / *Admission Free.* 입장무료 (게시) / *be given a* ~ *ride on a truck* 트럭에 거저 올라타다. ⓑ ⇨free from 〔of〕. ⓒ having no duty or charge. 세금 없는; 면세의. ¶ ~ *imports* 무관세 수입품 / ~ *trade* 자유 무역(cf. *protection*). **7** ⓐ not occupied or busy. (일에서) 해방되어; 틈〔짬〕이 나서; 바쁘지 않아. ¶ *have very little* ~ *time* 일손날 때가 거의 없다; 몹시 바쁘다 / *I am* ~ *this afternoon.* 오늘 오후에는 한가하다〔시간이 난다〕. ⓑ (of things) not in use. (방 따위가) 비어; 사용되지 않는. ¶ *Have you any rooms* ~ *?* 빈 방이 있습니까. **8** not fixed or fastened; loose. 고정되어 있지〔매지〕 않은; 느슨한. ¶ *leave one end of a rope* ~ 밧줄 한끝을 매지 않은 채 놔 두다 / *get one's arm* ~ (붙잡힌) 팔을 뿌리쳐 떼다. **9** not strictly literal or exact. (번역문 따위) 문자에 구애되지 않는. ¶ *a* ~ *translation* 의역 / *a* ~ *interpretation of myths* 신화의 자유로운 해석. **10** not restricted by the usual rules about meter, rhyme, etc. 규칙〔일정한 틀〕에 얽매이지 않는. ¶ ~ *verse* 자유시(詩). **11** 《chem.》 separate. (화학적으로) 화합(化合)하지 않은; 유리된. ¶ ~ *oxygen* 유리 산소. **12** giving or using much, generous; lavish. 활수한; 손이 큰; 아낌없는. ¶ *a* ~ *spender* 활수하게 돈을 쓰는 사람.

free and easy, 스스럼〔거리낌, 허물〕없는; 마음을 터놓는; 격의 없는; 격식〔예절〕에 얽매이지 않는.

free from 〔***of***〕, without; not having; lacking. …이 없는. ¶ *a day* ~ *from wind* 바람이 없는 날 / *No one is* ~ *from fault.* 결점 없는 사람은 없다.

free on board, 《comm.》 delivered free of charge on a train, ship, etc. 본선 적재 인도; 화차 적재 인도《abbr. f.o.b., F.O.B.》.

free with, giving or using much of. …에게 활수한; 손이 큰; 아낌없는.

have one's hand free, **a**) be in a position to do what one likes. 마음대로 행동할 수 있다. **b**) have no work or duties that require attention. 손이 나〔비어〕 있다; 짬이 나다.

make someone free of (*one's house, etc.*), give him full permission to use…. …을 마음대로 사용하게〔드나들게〕 하다.

make free with, take liberties with. …에게 무람없이 행동하다.

set free, make (someone) free; let (someone) loose; release. …을 해방하다; 석방하다.

— *adv.* **1** in a free manner. 자유롭게; 방해 없이. **2** without cost; paying nothing. 무료로; 거저.

— *vt.* (**freed; free·ing**) (P6,13) **1** make (someone or something) free; release. …을 해방〔석방〕하다. ¶ ~ *someone from restraint* 아무를 구속에서 풀어 주다 / ~ *the land from oppression* 국민을 압정에서 해방하다. **2** 《*from, of*》 ⓐ take pains, etc. from (someone). …을 구(출)하다; (모)면하게 하다. ¶ ~ *oneself from responsibility* 책임을

모면하다 / ~ *someone of* 〔*from*〕 *debt* 아무를 빚에서 구해 내다. ⓑ relieve from any kind of hindrance. 벗기다; 떼다. ¶ ~ *one's hand from fetter* 손의 쇠고랑을 풀다. [E.]

free·boot·er [fríːbùːtər] *n.* a plunderer; a piarate. 약탈자; 해적. [E.]

free·born [fríːbɔ̀ːrn] *adj.* born free, not in slavery. 자유의 몸으로 태어난.

free city [ˊ ˊˊ] *n.* a city forming an independent state. 자유시(市).

freed·man [fríːdmən, -mæ̀n] *n.* Ⓒ (*pl.* **-men** [-mən / -mèn]) a man freed from slavery. (노예에서 해방된) 자유민(opp. freedwoman). [*free*]

:free·dom [fríːdəm] *n.* **1** ⒸⓊ the state of being free; liberty. 자유. ¶ ~ *of speech* 언론의 자유. **2** Ⓤ the state of being free from burdens, duties, another's control, etc.; exemption (from). 속박〔구속〕되지 않음; 면제. ¶ ~ *from fear* 공포로부터의 자유〔해방〕/ ~ *of taxes* 세금의 면제. **3** Ⓤ frankness. 숨김없음; 솔직. ¶ *speak with* ~ 숨김없이 이야기하다. **4** Ⓒ free use. 마음대로 사용할〔드나들〕 수 있음. ¶ *the* ~ *of a library* 도서관에 마음대로 드나듦 / *She has* ~ *of the house.* 그녀는 그 집에 자유로이 출입할 수 있다. **5** ⓊⒸ the right of enjoying all privileges accompanying citizenship, membership, etc. 특권; 특전. [*free*]

free-for-all [fríːfərɔ̀ːl] *n.* Ⓒ a fight, a contest, etc. open to everyone or in which everyone may take part. 누구나 참가할 수 있는 경기. — *adj.* open to all. 누구나 참가할 수 있는.

free hand [ˊ ˊ] *n.* right or liberty to act according to one's own judgment. 자유 행동; 자유 재량(권). ¶ *have* 〔*get*〕 *a* ~ 자유 행동을 할 수 있다 / *They gave him a* ~ *in carrying out the plan.* 그들은 그 계획의 실행을 그의 자유 재량에 맡겼다.

free·hand [fríːhæ̀nd] *adj.* done by hand, without any instruments. 손만으로 그린. ¶ ~ *drawing* 자재화(自在畫).

free·hand·ed [fríːhǽndid] *adj.* generous; liberal. 활수한; 손이 큰; 아낌없는; 너그러운.

free·hold [fríːhòuld] *n.* Ⓤ complete ownership of land. 종신〔자유〕 부동산 보유권; Ⓒ a piece of land so owned. 자유 보유지. ● **free·hold·er** [-ər] *n.*

free lance [ˊ ˊ] *n.* **1** a writer, an artist, etc. who does not work for one regular employer. 자유 계약자; 자유 계약 기고가(寄稿家). **2** a soldier in the Middle Ages who sold his service to any ruler or state. (중세의) 용병(傭兵).

free-lance [fríːlǽns, -lɑ́ːns] *vi.* (P1) work as a free lance. 자유 계약자〔자유 계약 기고가〕로서 일하다.

:free·ly [fríːli] *adv.* in a free manner. 자유로이; 마음대로; 구애되지 않고.

free·man [fríːmən] *n.* Ⓒ (*pl.* **-men** [-mən]) **1** a person who is not a slave. 자유민. **2** a person who has civil and political rights; a citizen. 시민; 공민.

Free·ma·son [fríːmèisn] *n.* a member of a secret society united to help each other as brothers. 프리메이슨(회원의 상호 부조·우애를 목적으로 하는 비밀 결사의 회원).

free·ma·son·ry [fríːmèisnri] *n.* Ⓤ the system, principles and practices of Freemasons. 프리메이슨의 주의·관행 및 제도.

free port [ˊ ˊ] *n.* a part of or all of a port open equally to traders of all countries. 자유 무역항.

free·si·a [fríːʒiə / -ziə] *n.* Ⓒ 《bot.》 a plant with clusters of white or yellow flowers. 프리지어. [Person]

free-spo·ken [fríːspóukən] *adj.* speaking freely; out spoken. 마음대로〔거리낌 없이〕 말하는; 솔직히〔가식 없이〕 말하는. [*free*]

free·stone [fríːstòun] *n.* a soft stone composed of sand and easily cut and worked. 무른돌; 사암(砂岩).

free·think·er [fríːθíŋkər] *n.* Ⓒ a person who forms his religious opinions independently of authority or tradition. (종교상의) 자유 사상가.

free trade [ˊ ˊ] *n.* trade free from governmental restrictions, taxes, protective duties, etc. 자유 무역.

free will [ˊ ˊ] *n.* the human will free from any restraints. 자유 의사.

free·will [fríːwíl] *adj.* of one's own will; voluntary. 자유 의사의; 자발적인.

:freeze [friːz] *v.* (**froze, fro·zen**) *vi.* (P1,2A) **1** change into ice. 얼다. ¶ *Water freezes at 32°F.* 물은 화씨 32도에서 언다. **2** become hard or rigid with cold; be killed or damaged with cold. 추위로 딱딱〔뻣뻣〕해지다; 얼어죽다; 추위의 해를 입다. ¶ ~ *to death* 얼어죽다. **3** be covered with ice. 얼음으로 덮이다. **4** feel very cold. 몹시 춥다. ¶ *I'm freezing!* 지독히 춥다. **5** become rigid or motionless with fear, etc. (공포 따위로) 그 자리에 얼어붙다. ¶ *make someone's blood freeze* 등골이 오싹하게 하다 / *She froze in terror at the sight.* 그 광경을 보고 공포로 그 자리에 얼어붙었다. — *vt.* (P6,7) **1** change (water) into ice; cover (something) with ice. …을 얼리다. ¶ *be frozen into ice* 결빙하다. **2** harden (something) by cold. …을 추위로 뻣뻣하게 하다; 냉동하다. **3** kill or damage (something living) by cold. …을 동사시키다; 추위로 해를 입히다. **4** cause (someone) to freeze with fear, etc.; horrify. …을 오싹하게 하다. **5** fix (prices, etc.) at a given level. (물가 따위)를 동결하다.

be frozen to death, **a**) die from freezing; die of cold and freeze. 얼어죽다. **b**) 《*colloq.*》 feel very cold. 몹시 추위를 느끼다.

freeze on (***to***) (*something*), 《*sl.*》 seize and

cling tightly to. 달라붙다; 꼭 매달리다; 붙들고 늘어지다.
freeze out, force (someone) out. …을 몰아내다.
freeze up, stiffen (something) through cold. …을 얼어붙게 하다.
—*n.* Ⓤⓒ **1** the state of freezing or being frozen. 얾; 빙결. **2** a period of freezing weather. 결빙기; 혹한. [E.]

freez·er [frí:zər] *n.* ⓒ **1** a machine to make ice cream or sherbet. 아이스크림[셔벗] 제조기. **2** a refrigerator cabinet for quick-freezing and storage. 냉동기; 냉장고.

free·zing point [⌐–⌐] *n.* the temperature at which a liquid freezes. 어는점.

***freight** [freit] *n.* Ⓤ **1** the ordinary transportation of goods by water, road or air. (보통의) 화물 수송(편) (opp. express). ¶ *send by* ~ 보통 화물편으로 보내다. **2** the amount paid for carrying goods. 수송료; 운임. ¶ ~ *to collect* 운임 선지급 / ~ *paid* 운임 지급필(畢). **3** the goods transported. 운송[적재] 화물. ¶ *a* ~ *of timber* 목재의 적하(積荷). **4** 《esp. Brit.》 the cargo of a vessel; the transportation of goods by water. 뱃짐; 선하(船荷); 수상운송. **5** ⓒ 《U.S.》 a freight train. 화물 열차. [Du. *vracht*]

freight·age [fréitidʒ] *n.* Ⓤ **1** transporting goods by train, ship, etc. 화물 수송; 운송. **2** the charge for this. 운송료; 운임; 선임(船賃). **3** freight; cargo. 화물; 적하(積荷); 선하(船荷).

freight car [⌐⌐] *n.* 《U.S.》 a goods wagon. (철도의) 화차.

freight·er [fréitər] *n.* ⓒ **1** a ship for carrying cargo; a cargo vessel. 수송선; 화물선. **2** a person who receives and forward freight. 운송업자; 화주.

:French [frentʃ] *adj.* of France. 프랑스의.
—*n.* **1** 《*the* ~, *collectively,* used as *pl.*》 the people of France. 프랑스 사람. **2** the language of France. 프랑스어.
take French leave, go away or do something without having asked to be allowed to go; go away without bidding good-bye. 무단으로 물러가다; 말없이[인사도 없이] 나가다.

French horn [⌐⌐] *n.* a brass wind instrument with a long, coiled tube which has a soft tone. 프렌치호른《관악기》.

French·i·fy [fréntʃəfài] *vt.* (P6) make French or like the French. 프랑스화[풍으로] 하다. [→French]

***French·man** [fréntʃmən] *n.* ⓒ (*pl.* **-men** [-mən]) a person of France. 프랑스 사람.

French·wom·an [fréntʃwùmən] *n.* ⓒ (*pl.* **-wom·en** [-wìmin]) a woman of France. 프랑스 여성.

fren·zied [frénzid] *adj.* wildly excited or uncontrolled with joy, fear, pain, etc. 몹시 흥분한; 열광적인. [↓]

fren·zy [frénzi] *n.* Ⓤ the state near madness or of wild feeling. 격앙(激昂); 광포; 광란; 열광. ¶ *in a* ~ *of delight* 기뻐 미친 듯이 되어 / *arouse a* ~ *of passion* 격정의 불길을 일으키다. —*vt.* (P6) make frantic. 격앙시키다. [→frantic]

freq. frequency; frequent(ly).

fre·quen·cy [frí:kwənsi], **-quence** [-kwəns] *n.* Ⓤ **1** the state of being repeated often. 자주 일어남; 빈발. **2** the number of times anything happens. 빈도; 횟수. ¶ *frequency modulation* 주파수 변조; FM 방송 체제. [↓]

:fre·quent [frí:kwənt] *adj.* **1** repeated often. 잦은; 빈번한. ¶ ~ *pain* 잦은 통증 / ~ *visits* 잦은 방문 / *a* ~ *pulse* 빠른 맥박 / *the* ~ *errors made by beginners* 초심자들이 자주 범하는 잘못. **2** regular; habitual. 상습적인. ¶ *a* ~ *theatergoer* 극장에 자주 가는 사람; 연극의 단골. **3** constantly found, seen, etc.; plentiful. 흔히(볼 수) 있는; 많은. ¶ *a coast with* ~ *lighthouses* 등대가 여기저기 있는 해안. —[frikwént] *vt.* (P6) visit often. 자주 찾다[가다]. ¶ *a frequented seaside resort* 사람들이 자주 찾는 해안 휴양지 / *go by the least frequented route* 사람의 왕래가 가장 적은 길을 가다. [L. *frequens* crowded]

fre·quent·er [frikwéntər] *n.* ⓒ a habitual visitor. 자주 찾는[가는] 사람.

:fre·quent·ly [frí:kwəntli] *adv.* often. 자주; 빈번히.

fres·co [fréskou] *n.* ⓒ (*pl.* **-coes** or **-cos**) a picture painted on a wall of a church, etc. (교회 등의) 프레스코 벽화; Ⓤ the method of painting on walls. 프레스코 화법(畫法). —*vt.* (P6) paint in fresco; ornament with a painting in fresco. 프레스코화로 그리다[장식하다]. [It.]

:fresh [freʃ] *adj.* **1** ⓐ new; newly made or obtained. 신선한; 갓 …한; 갓 된[만든, 입수된, 딴, 잡은]. ¶ ~ *eggs* 신선한 달걀 / ~ *herring* (갓 잡은) 싱싱한 청어 / ~ *footprints* 새로 난 발자국 / *lettuce* ~ *from the garden* 채마밭에서 갓 뜯은 상추. ⓑ not known or used before; not experienced. 미지(未知)의; 사용되지 않은; 처음으로 …하는; 경험하지 않은. ¶ *a* ~ *sheet of paper* 사용되지 않은 새 종이 / *break* ~ *ground* 새로운 분야를 개척하다 / *uncover* ~ *facts* 새로운 사실을 폭로하다 / *seek* ~ *experiences* 새로운 경험을 찾다 / *Do you have any* ~ *news?* 무언가 새로운 뉴스 없나. ⓒ another; different; additional. (또)다른; 신규의. ¶ ~ *supplies* 새 공급 / *begin a* ~ *chapter* 새 장(章)을 시작하다 / *make a* ~ *start* 처음부터 새로 다시 하다. **2** not tired out; lively; vigorous. 지치지 않은; 생기 있는; 기운찬. ¶ *a* ~ *complexion* 싱그러운 안색 / ~ *horses* 씽씽한 말 / *I still feel quite* ~. 아직도 지치지 않고 있다. **3** (of colors, the appearance of objects, memory, etc.) clear; bright. (색

따위가) 바래지 않은; 밝은; (기억 등이) 생생한. ¶ *a ~ red* 선명한 빨강 / *~ paint* 갓 칠한 페인트 / *be still ~ in one's memory* 아직도 기억에 새롭다. **4** (of air, water, etc.) clean and new; pure; refreshing. (공기·물 따위가) 맑은; 상쾌한. ¶ *~ air* 상쾌한 공기 / *in the ~ air* 야외에서. **5** raw; green; inexperienced. 미경험의; 생무지의; 풋내기의. ¶ *a ~ hand* 신참; 초심자. **6** (of winds and breezes) moderately strong. (바람 따위가) 좀 센. ¶ *a ~ breeze* 질풍. **7** not preserved by tinning, freezing, salting, etc. 통조림으로 하지 않은; 냉동하지 않은; 소금에 절이지 않은; 보존 가공하지 않은. ¶ *~ meat* 생육 / *~ vegetables* 생야채. **8** (of water) not salty. (물이) 짜지 않은. ¶ *~ water* 민물; 담수 / *~ butter* 무염〔생〕 버터. **9** 《U.S. *colloq.*》 impudent. 뻔뻔스러운; 건방진. ¶ *get ~ to someone* 아무에게 무람없이 굴다 / *talk ~ to someone* 아무에게 건방지게 말하다. **10** excited with drink. 술에 취해 흥분한. [E.]

fresh·en [fréʃən] *vt.* (P6) make (something) fresh. …을 신선〔생생, 싱싱, 청신〕하게 하다. — *vi.* (P1) become fresh. 신선〔생생, 싱싱, 청신〕해지다. ¶ *take a shower to ~ up* 기분 일신을 위해 샤워를 하다 / *Flowers ~ after rain.* 꽃은 비 온 뒤에 싱그러워진다.

fresh·et [fréʃit] *n.* Ⓒ **1** an overflow of a river caused by heavy rain or melted snow. (큰비·눈석임 등에 의한) 증수(增水); 홍수. **2** a stream of fresh water flowing into the sea. 바다로 흘러드는 담수의 흐름.

fresh·ly [fréʃli] *adv.* **1** in a fresh manner. 새로이; 신선하게; 생생히; 싱싱하게; 활발히. **2** 《followed by *pp.*》 newly; recently. 갓 …하여; 새로이; 최근에. ¶ *~ painted* 갓 페인트를 칠한 / *~ washed* 새로 빤.

fresh·man [fréʃmən] *n.* Ⓒ (*pl.* **-men** [-mən]) a student in the first year of high school or college; a beginner. (대학의) 신입생; 신참자; 초심자.

fresh·wa·ter [fréʃwɔ̀:tər, -wá-] *adj.* of or living in water that is not salty. 민물의; 담수의. ¶ *a ~ fish* 민물고기.

·**fret**[1] [fret] *v.* (**fret·ted, fret·ting**) *vt.* **1** (P6,7) worry; irritate. …을 속태우다; 약올리다; 초조하게〔괴롭게〕 하다. ¶ *~ oneself into a fit of nerves* 약이 올라 울화통을 터뜨리다. **2** (P6) eat away; rub away. …을 부식〔침식〕하다; 개먹다; 마멸시키다. — *vi.* (P1,3) be worried; be anxious. 속이 타다; 초조해하다; 약오르다. ¶ *~ and fume* (화가 나서) 안달복달하다 / *You have nothing to ~ about.* 초조해 할 것 아무것도 없네. [O.E. *fretan* eat]

fret[2] [fret] *n.* Ⓒ a bit of wood on the finger board of some musical instruments. (현악기의) 기러기발. [F. *frette* band, ring]

fret[3] [fret] *n.* Ⓒ a decorative design made of straight lines bent or combined at angles. 뇌문(雷文) 격자 세공. [?]

〈fret[3]〉

fret·ful [frétfəl] *adj.* ill-humored; irritable. 초조한; 짜증난. [*fret*[1]]

fret saw [⌐ ⌐] *n.* a saw with a long, slender blade and fine teeth, used to cut ornamental work from thin wood. 실톱. [*fret*[3]]

fret·work [frétwə̀:rk] *n.* Ⓤ ornamental work with frets in wood. 뇌문(雷文) 장식. [*fret*[3]]

Freud [frɔid], **Sigmund** *n.* (1856-1939) an Austrian physician who developed a theory and technique of psychoanalysis. 프로이트 (오스트리아의 의사·정신 분석학자).

:**Fri.** =Friday.

fri·a·ble [fráiəbəl] *adj.* easily broken into powder. 부서지기〔깨지기〕 쉬운; 가루가 되기 쉬운; 무른. ¶ *Biscuits are ~.* 비스킷은 잘 부스러진다. [L. *frio* crumble]

·**fri·ar** [fráiər] *n.* Ⓒ a member of certain religious orders. 수사(修士). [L. *frater* brother]

fri·ar·y [fráiəri] *n.* a convent of friars. (수사(修士)의) 수도원.

fri·cas·see [frìkəsí:] *n.* 《F.》 a French dish of meat cut up into pieces, stewed or fried, and served in a white sauce. 프리카세《닭이나 송아지 고기를 잘게 썰어 삶은 것에 그 국물을 친 요리》. — *vt.* (P6) cook as fricassee. 프리카세로 조리하다.

fric·a·tive [fríkətiv] 《phon.》 *adj.* (of a speech sound) characterized by audible friction produced by forcing the breath through a constricted or partially obstructed passage in the vocal tract; spirant. 마찰음의. — *n.* Ⓒ a fricative sound. 마찰음《[f] [v] [θ] [ð]》. [L. *frico* rub]

fric·tion [fríkʃən] *n.* **1** Ⓤ the rubbing of one thing against another. 마찰. **2** ⓊⒸ disagreement because of differences in ideas, opinions, etc. 불화; 알력; 충돌. ¶ *~ between two countries* 양국간의 알력. [↑]

:**Fri·day** [fráidi, -dei] *n.* the sixth day of the week. 금요일. 參考 Fri.로 생략. [the day of *Frig*(=Venus)]

fried [fraid] *v.* p. and pp. of **fry.** — *adj.* cooked in hot oil. 기름에 튀긴. [*fry*[1]]

fried·cake [fráidkèik] *n.* 《U.S.》 a doughnut. 도넛. [*fry*[1], *cake*]

:**friend** [frend] *n.* Ⓒ **1** a person whom one knows and likes and who is not a lover or relative. 친구; 벗. ¶ *a ~ of mine* 내 친구 參考 one of my friends 는 '친구들 중의 하나'를 가리킴 / *a childhood ~* 죽마고

우 / *a New York* ~ 뉴욕에 있는 친구 / *a close* 〔*bosom*〕 ~ 가까운〔속마음을 주는〕 친구 / *They are good* 〔*great*〕 *friends.* 그들은 사이가 좋은 친구다 / *A ~ in need is a ~ indeed.* 어려운 때의 친구야말로 참된 친구이다. **2** a person who favors and supports; a helper; a patron. 후원〔지원〕자; 지지자. ¶ *a ~ of* 〔*to*〕 *democracy* 민주주의의 옹호자 / *a ~ of the poor* 가난한 사람들의 친구〔편〕 / *You will always find a good ~ in me.* 언제나 힘이 되어 드리겠습니다. **3** a person who belongs to the same group or side; an ally. (한)편; 우군(友軍)(opp. a foe; an enemy). ¶ *a cat and dog who are not friends* 견원지간(犬猿之間)인 두 사람 / *identify oneself as a ~ or foe* 한편이냐 적이냐를 밝히다; 자기의 입장을 분명히 하다. **4** a companion. 동료. ¶ *The prisoner left the court with his friends.* 그 형사 피고인은 동료 피고인들과 함께 법정을 떠났다. **5** 《*F-*》 a member of the Society of Friends; a Quaker. 프렌드파의 일원; 퀘이커 교도. [E.]

a friend at court, a person who can help one with others; an influential friend. (힘이 되어 줄 수 있는) 유력한 지위에 있는 친구; 유력한 연줄.

be 〔***make***〕 ***friends with*** (= *be* 〔*become*〕 *a friend of*) *someone.* 아무와 친구이다〔친구가 되다〕.

make friends again, become friendly again after a quarrel. 싸운 뒤에 다시 친해지다〔화해하다〕.

friend·less [fréndlis] *adj.* without friends. 친구가 없는; 의지할 데 없는.

friend·li·ness [fréndlinis] *n.* Ⓤ friendly feeling and behavior. 우정; 친절; 호의.

:friend·ly [fréndli] *adj.* (**-li·er, -li·est**) **1** having the nature of a friend; like a friend; kindly. 우정 있는; 친구 같은; 친절한. ¶ *a ~ game* 친선 경기 / *in a ~ manner* 친절〔다정, 상냥〕하게 / *do someone a ~ turn* 아무에게 친절을 다하다 / *have ~ relations with* …와 친(밀)한 관계에 있다; …와 친하게 지내다 / *be on ~ terms with* …와 친밀한 사이다. **2** favoring and supporting. 호의적인; 지지〔찬성〕하는. ¶ *a ~ shower* 단비 / *a ~ nation* 우방; 우호국민.

friendly action [ˊ-- ˊ-] *n.* 《law》 an action brought merely to settle a point. 합의상의 소송.

Friendly Society [ˊ-- -ˊ--] *n.* 《Brit.》 a society for the mutual benefit of its members. 공제(共濟) 조합.

:friend·ship [fréndʃìp] *n.* Ⓤ the state of being friends; the feeling that exists between friends. 친구 사이〔관계〕; 우정. ¶ *a ~ of long standing* 다년간의 교우 관계.

frieze[1] [fri:z] *n.* Ⓒ 《archit.》 an ornamented band along a part of wall just below the ceiling. 프리즈(띠 모양의 장식벽). [F.]

frieze[2] [fri:z] *n.* a coarse woolen cloth with nap on one side only. (외투용의) 두껍고 거친 모직물. [F. *friser* curl]

frig [frig] *vi., vt.* have sexual intercourse with; masturbate. (여성과) 성교하다; 수음하다. [?]

frig·ate [frígit] *n.* Ⓒ **1** a fast warship. 프리깃함(艦). **2** a fast sailing warship from 1750 to 1850. 고대의 쾌속 범선(快速帆船). [It. *fregata*]

〈frigate 2〉

:fright [frait] *n.* **1** Ⓤ sudden fear; Ⓒ a state of sudden fear. (갑작스런) 공포; 놀람; 경악; 공포의 상태. ¶ *get* 〔*have*〕 *a ~* 깜짝 놀라다 / *give someone a ~* 아무를 놀라게 하다 / *in a ~* 깜짝 놀라서 / *I nearly died of ~.* 놀라 죽을뻔했다; 소스라치게 놀랐다 / *His hair stood on end with ~.* 공포로 그의 머리털이 곤두섰다〔머리끝이 쭈뼛했다〕. **2** 《*colloq.*》 a person or thing that is very ugly or ridiculous. 깜짝 놀랄 만큼 싫은〔못생긴; 우스운〕 사람〔것〕. ¶ *She is a* (*perfect*) *~.* 그녀는 (지독한) 추물이다. [E.]

take fright at, be surprised at. …에 놀라다. ¶ *We all took ~ at his sudden appearance in the dark.* 우리는 모두 어둠속에 그가 불쑥 나타나서 몹시 놀랐다.

:fright·en [fráitn] *vt.* (P6,7,13) **1** throw (someone or an animal) into a fright; terrify. …을 깜짝 놀라게 하다; 공포감을 주다. ¶ *~ a child with a ghost story* 귀신 이야기로 아이를 무섭게 하다 / *The large noise frightened everyone.* 큰 굉음이 모두를 놀라게 하였다 / *The boy was frightened at the sudden appearance of the big dog.* 아이는 큰 개의 갑작스런 출현에 몹시 놀랐다. **2** set (someone or an animal) in motion by frightening; move (someone or an animal) away by frightening. …을 협박하여〔겁을 주어〕 …하게 하다. ¶ *The speeding car frightened away a cat sitting on the road.* 전속력으로 달려온 차는 길에 앉아 있던 고양이가 놀라 달아나게 했다.

frighten into, drive into a certain condition by frightening. …을 겁주어〔…에 놀라〕 —하게 하다. ¶ *He was frightened into confession.* 그는 겁이 나서 자백했다.

frighten out of, cause to give up through fear. …을 겁주어 —을 단념하게〔그만두게〕 하다. ¶ *~ a man out of drinking too much* 사나이를 겁주어 과음을 하지 않게 하다.

fright·ful [fráitfəl] *adj.* **1** causing great fear; fearful. 놀라운; 무서운. ¶ *a ~ accident* 〔*sight*〕 끔찍한 사고〔광경〕. **2** 《*colloq.*》 shockingly ugly; unpleasant. 보기 흉한; 불(유)쾌한. ¶ *have a ~ time* 불쾌한 꼴을 당하다〔시간을 보내다〕. **3** 《*colloq.*》 extreme; very great. 극도의; 대단한. ¶ *a ~ thirst* 지독한 갈증 / *I'm in a ~ trouble.* 무척 곤란

한 처지에 있다.

fright·ful·ly [fráitfəli] *adv.* **1** in a frightening way. 무섭게. **2** 《*colloq.*》 very. 몹시.

frig·id [frídʒid] *adj.* **1** very cold. (기후가) 한랭한; 몹시 추운. ¶ *the ~ zone* 한대 / *a ~ climate* 극한 기후. **2** ⓐ (of manners, etc.) indifferent. (태도 따위가) 차가운; 냉담한. ¶ *a ~ reaction to the proposal* 제안에 대한 차가운 반응 / *a ~ stare* 차가운 시선. ⓑ (of an expression, etc.) stiff. 딱딱한; 형식적인. ¶ *a ~ bow* 형식적인 인사 / *a welcome that was polite but ~* 정중하지만 서먹서먹한 환영. **3** (of a woman) sexually unresponsive. 성적 불감증의; 냉감증의(cf. *impotent*). [L. *frigus* cold]

frill [fril] *n.* **1** Ⓒ an ornamental edge on a garment. 주름진 가두리 장식; 프릴. **2** 《*pl.*》 useless ornamentation; affectation. 허식(虛飾); 젠체하기.

put on one's frills, put on airs. 젠체하다.

— *vt.* (P6) ornament with a frill. 가두리장식을 달다. ● **frill·y** [fríli] *adj.* [? F.]

∗**fringe** [frindʒ] *n.* Ⓒ **1** an ornamental edge of loose threads. 술; 술장식. **2** the edge of something. 가장자리; 주변. ¶ *a common with a ~ of houses round it* 주변에 집들로 둘러싸인 공유지. **3** hair hanging over the forehead (usu. woman's hair). 이마에 드리운 머리. **4** the extreme outer edge. 변두리; 외연(外緣). ¶ *on the fringe(s) of the forest* 〔*lake*〕 숲〔호수〕 변두리에 / *live on the outer fringes of Seoul* 서울 변두리에 살다.

— *vt.* (P6,13) **1** make a fringe on; provide with a fringe. (가장자리) 술장식을 달다; 가두리〔술〕 장식 같은 것으로 가장자리를 두르다. **2** be a fringe for. (무엇이) …의 가두리(술) 장식이 되다. ¶ *Houses fringed the road on either side.* 길 양 옆에는 집들이 늘어서 있었다. [L. *fimbria*]

frip·per·y [frípəri] *n.* (*pl.* **-per·ies**) Ⓤ unnecessary ornament on a dress, etc. (옷 따위의) 야한 장식; Ⓒ a cheap decoration; useless trifles. 값싸고 번지르르한 것; 시시한 것. [F. *frepe* rag]

frisk [frisk] *vi.* (P1,2A) 《*about*》 jump and run about playfully; behave in a joyful way. 깡충깡충 뛰놀다; 까불다. ¶ *frisking lambs* 깡충거리며 뛰노는 새끼양. — *vt.* (P6) move (something) in a playful manner. …을 가볍게 움직이다. — *n.* a playful jumping about. 깡충깡충 뛰놀기〔뛰어다니기〕. [F. *frisque* lively]

frisk·y [fríski] *adj.* (**frisk·i·er, frisk·i·est**) lively. 뛰노는; 쾌활한.

frit·ter [frítər] *vt.* 《usu. *away, down*》 **1** waste (money, time, strength, etc.) little by little. …을 조금씩 소비〔낭비〕하다. **2** cut (something) into small pieces. …을 잘게 가르다〔자르다, 찢다, 부수다〕. — *n.* a slice of apple, etc. fried in butter. 프리터《기름에 튀긴 과일 조각》. [→fry]

friv·ol [frívəl] *vt., vi.* **1** behave in a frivolous way. 경박한 행동을 하다. **2** 《*away*》 waste (money, time, etc.) foolishly. 낭비하다. [→frivolous]

fri·vol·i·ty [friváləti / -vɔ́l-] *n.* (*pl.* **-ties**) **1** Ⓤ the state of being frivolous. 경박. **2** Ⓒ a frivolous act. 경박한 행동.

friv·o·lous [frívələs] *adj.* not serious; trifling. 경박한; 시시한; 하찮은. ¶ *a ~ issue* 하찮은 문제 / *~ arguments* 시시한 의론. [L. *frivolus*]

friz, frizz [friz] *vt.* (**frizzed, friz·zing**) (P6) form (hair) into small curls. (머리)를 지지다; 곱슬곱슬하게 하다. — *n.* Ⓒ (*pl.* **friz·zes**) curled hair. 지진 머리털; 고수머리. [↓]

friz·zle[1] [frízl] *vt.* (P6) 《*up*》 form (something) into small, crisp curls; curl. …을 지지다; 곱슬곱슬하게 하다. — *n.* Ⓒ a small, crisp curl. 지진 머리털; 고수머리. [F. *friser*]

friz·zle[2] [frízl] *vt.* (P6) fry or broil. …을 기름에 지글지글 튀기다. — *vi.* (P1) make a noise while frying or broiling. (튀김이) 지글지글 소리나다. [→fry[1], sizzle]

friz·zly [frízli] *adj.* full of small, crisp curls; curly. 지진; 곱슬곱슬한. [*frizzle*[1]]

∗**fro** [frou] *adv.* away. 저쪽으로. 語法 다음 성구(成句)로만 씀. [N. (→from)]

to and fro, forward and back again. 이쪽저쪽으로; 앞뒤로; 왔다갔다.

∗**frock** [frak / frɔk] *n.* Ⓒ **1** a long outer garment; a woman's dress. (위아래가 붙은)여성복; 원피스로 된 겉옷. **2** a monk's gown. 성직자의 옷. **3** a long military coat, cut something like a frock coat. 프록코트 같은 군복. **4** a loose coat worn by workmen over their other clothes. 덧입는 일복. **5** =frock coat. — *vt.* (P6) **1** clothe in a frock. 프록을 입히다. **2** 《*fig.*》 make a monk of. 성직에 앉히다. [F.]

frock coat [⌐ ⌐] *n.* a long black coat for men. 프록 코트.

〈frock coat〉

∗**frog** [frɔːg, frag / frɔg] *n.* Ⓒ **1** a small green or brown jumping animal that lives in water and on land. 개구리. ¶ *an edible ~* 식용 개구리 / (*as*) *cold as a ~* 무척 차가운. **2** an ornamental or fastening button on a garment. 장식(裝飾)단추. **3** 《*colloq., contempt.*》 a Frenchman. 프랑스 사람. **4** a horny growth in the middle of the sole of a horse's foot. (말발굽의) 제차(蹄叉); 연갑(軟甲). **5** 《railway》 a plate used to guide the wheels of a railway car where one track crosses another. (철도 교차점의) 철차(轍叉). [E.]

have a frog in the throat, have a rough voice like a frog; be hoarse. 목소리가 쉬어있다.

frog·man [frάgmæ̀n, -mən / frɔ́g-] *n.* (*pl.* **-men** [⌐mèn, ⌐mən]) a diver trained and equipped with an aqualung for underwater operations. 잠수 공작원〔작업병〕.

frol·ic [frάlik / frɔ́l-] *n.* Ⓒ a piece of fun; a mischievous act. 깡충깡충 뛰놂; 들떠 법석을 떪; 장난. ― *vi.* (**-icked, -ick·ing**) (P1) play or jump about happily. 깡충거리며 뛰놀다; 법석을 치다; 까불다. ● **frol·ick·er** [-ər] *n.* [Du.=gladlike]

frol·ic·some [frάliksəm / frɔ́l-] *adj.* full of fun; merry. 들떠 까부는〔떠드는〕; 들뜬; 명랑한.

:from [frʌm, frɑm, frəm / frɔm, frəm] *prep.* **1** (of place or time) starting at. …로부터; …이래. ¶ *～ here to the station* 여기서 역까지 / *a train ～ New York* 뉴욕발 열차 / *～ that time onward* 그때 이래 쭉〔내내〕 / *～ June 1,* 6월 1일부터. **2** beginning with. …이상; 이하. ¶ *There were ～ 10 to 20 boys there.* 그곳엔 10명에서 20명의 아이들이 있었다. **3** out of. …에서 밖으로. ¶ *take a fountain pen ～ one's pocket.* 호주머니에서 만년필을 꺼내다. **4** sent by. …에게서 보낸. ¶ *letters ～ friends* 친구에게서 온 편지. **5** having the origin or source in. …에 근원을 가진; …에서 인용한. ¶ *words ～ Shakespeare* 셰익스피어 작품에서 인용한 말. **6** out of the reach or possession of. 떨어져; (힘·손)이 미치는 범위로부터. ¶ *Take his sword ～ him.* 그에게서 칼을 뺏어라. **7** caused by; because of; by reason of …의 원인으로〔이유로〕; …때문에. ¶ *weak ～ hunger* 굶주려 약한 / *suffer ～ malaria* 말라리아로 고생하다 / *scream ～ fear* 무서워서 소리치다 / *act ～ a sense of duty* 의무감에 행동하다 / *They obey only ～ fear.* 그들은 단지 무서워서 복종한다. **8** being different. …와 구별하여. ¶ *know good ～ bad* 선악을 변별하다 / *tell one thing ～ another* 한쪽의 것을 다른쪽의 것과 구별하다 / *Anyone can tell black ～ white.* 누구라도 흑과 백은 구별할 줄 안다. **9** in imitation of. …을 본떠(서). ¶ *paint ～ nature* 실물을 사생하다 / *paint ～ memory* 기억을 더듬어 그리다. **10** using as material …을 재료로 하여; …로 (cf. *of*). ¶ *make chemical fibers ～ petroleum* 석유(石油)로 화학섬유를 만들다 / *Wine is made ～ grapes.* 포도주는 포도로 만든다. [E.]

from end to end, throughout. 끝에서 끝까지.

from time to time, occasionally. 이따금; 때때로.

live from hand to mouth, live without provision for the future. 그날 벌어 그날 먹는 생활을 하다; 간신히 지내다.

(***news passing***) ***from mouth to mouth,*** (news passing) from one person to another. 입에서 입으로 전달되는 (뉴스).

frond [frɑnd / frɔnd] *n.* Ⓒ 《bot.》 **1** a leaflike part of a seaweed, lichen, etc. 엽상체(葉狀體). **2** a divided leaf of a fern, palm, etc. (양치류·야자 따위의) 갈라진 잎. [L. *frons* leaf]

:front [frʌnt] *n.* Ⓒ **1** 《usu. *the ～*》 the foremost part; the part that faces forward. 앞; 전방; 정면. ¶ *the ～ of a house* 집의 정면 / *be situated in the ～* 맨 앞에 위치해 있다 / *sit in the ～ of the class* 교실의 맨 앞줄 자리에 앉다 / *Look to your ～.* 앞을 봐라. **2** the land that faces a sea, a river, a lake, etc. (바다·호수 따위에 면한) 토지. ¶ *a river* 〔*lake*〕 *～* 강〔호수〕 연변의 토지. **3** 《mil.》 ⓐ the place where actual fighting is going on. 전선(前線); 전장. ¶ *news from the ～* 전선〔일선〕으로부터의 보도 / *go to the ～* 전선으로 나가다. ⓑ the direction a formed line faces. 정면. ¶ *change ～* 공격 정면을 바꾸다. **4** a political movement on a large scale; the forces fighting for some political or social aim. 정치 투쟁〔운동〕; 전선(戰線). ¶ *the popular* 〔*people's*〕 *～* 인민 전선 / *form* 〔*present*〕 *a united ～ against* …에 대하여 공동 전선을 펴다. **5** 《meteor.》 a line between cold and warm air masses. (기류의) 전선(前線). ¶ *a cold* 〔*warm*〕 *～* 한랭〔온난〕 전선. **6** ⓐ a manner or kind of appearance, esp. one not showing proper respect. 뻔뻔한 행동; 오만. ¶ *have the ～ to do* 뻔뻔하게도 …하다. ⓑ bearing; demeanor. 태도. ¶ *with the familiar ～* 여느 때와 같은 태도로 / *put on a calm ～* 침착한 태도를 보이다. **7** 《*poet., arch.*》 a forehead; a face. 이마; 얼굴. ¶ *lie on the ～* 엎드리다.

come to the front, become very noticeable or important. 전면에 나타나다; 두드러지게 되다.

get in front oneself, 《U.S.》 be quick, hasten. 서두르다.

go to the front, join a troop on campaign. 출정하다.

have the front to do, have the impudence to do. 뻔뻔하게도 …하다.

in front, to the fore. 전방에; 앞에〔의〕. ¶ *the enemy in ～* 전면의 적 / *run in ～* 앞서서 달리다.

in front of, before. …의 앞에; …을 마주보고 (opp. behind, at 〔in〕 the rear of).

put a bold front on, face (someone) boldly. …에 대해 대담하게 나오다.

show 〔***present***〕 ***a bold front,*** face boldly. 대담하게 나오다.

― *adj.* of, in, on, or at the front. 앞의, 전면〔정면〕의; 표면의; 선두의. ¶ *a ～ door* 정문.

― *vt., vi.* **1** (P6; 2A,3) stand opposite to (something); face. …에 면하다. ¶ *The hotel fronts* (*on*) *the lake.* 호텔은 호수에 면해 있다. **2** (P6) 《arch.》 confront. 맞서다. ¶ *～ danger* 위험에 맞서다. [L. *frons* forehead]

front·age [frʌ́ntidʒ] *n.* Ⓒ **1** the front of a building. (건물의) 정면. **2** the land facing a street, a sea, a river, etc. (가로나 바다에 면해 있는) 땅.

fron·tal [frʌ́ntəl] *adj.* **1** of, on, in or at the front. 정면의; 전면의; 정면을 향해서의. ¶ *a ~ attack* 정면 공격. **2** 《anat.》 of the forehead. 이마의; 전두부의. ¶ *the ~ bones* 전두골(前頭骨).

***fron·tier** [frʌntíər, frɑn- / frʌ́ntiər, frɔn-] *n.* Ⓒ **1** the part of a country nearest another country. 국경 지방. **2** a boundary-line. 경계선. **3** 《U.S.》 the farthest edge of a country. 변경 지방. **4** a limit; an undeveloped region. 한계; 미개척의 영역 〔분야〕. —— *adj.* of or on the frontier. 변경 〔국경〕의. ¶ *a ~ town* 국경 도시 / *~ spirit* 개척자 정신. [*front*]

fron·tiers·man [frʌntíərzmən / frʌ́n-, frɔn-] *n.* Ⓒ (*pl.* **-men** [-mən]) a man who lives on the frontier. 국경지방의 주민; 개척자.

fron·tis·piece [frʌ́ntispìːs] *n.* Ⓒ **1** a picture facing the first page or the title page of a book. 권두(卷頭) 그림; (책의) 속표지. **2** the front part of a building; a façade. (건물) 정면. [*front*]

:frost [frɔːst / frɔst] *n.* **1** Ⓤ white frozen vapor; Ⓒ a period of cold weather that makes such vapor. 서리; 일회(一回)의 결상기(結霜期). ¶ *~ on the grass* 풀에 내린 서리 / *the first ~ of autumn* 가을의 첫서리 / *There was* 〔*We had*〕 *a heavy ~ this morning.* 오늘 아침 된 서리가 내렸다. **2** Ⓤ ⓐ the state of being frozen. 빙결(氷結). ⓑ extreme cold; freezing weather. 얼어붙는 추위; 혹한. **3** Ⓤ coldness of manner, etc. (태도 따위의) 차가움; 냉랭함; 냉혹. ¶ *melt the ~ from the heart* 차가운 마음을 녹이다. **4** Ⓒ 《colloq.》 a failure. 실패. ¶ *The entertainment turned out a ~.* 여흥은 뜻밖에 실패작이었다.

—— *vt.* (P6) **1** cover (something) with frost. …을 서리로 덮다. **2** ⓐ cover (a cake, etc.) with white sugar. (케이크 따위)에 설탕을 입히다. ⓑ give a frostlike surface to. 표면을 부옇게 하다; 광택을 지우다. **3** ⓐ freeze; kill by freezing. …을 얼리다; 얼려죽이다; 서리해를 입히다. ⓑ 《fig.》 affect with low spirits. …의 기를 꺾다.

—— *vi.* (P1) cover with frost. 서리가 내리다. [→freeze]

frost·bite [frɔ́ːstbàit / frɔst-] *n.* Ⓤ injury caused by cold to a part of the body. 동상(凍傷).

frost·bit·ten [frɔ́ːstbìtn / frɔ́st-] *adj.* injured by severe cold. 동상(凍傷)에 걸린; 서리해를 입은. ¶ *My ears were ~.* 귀가 동상에 걸렸다.

frost·ing [frɔ́ːstiŋ / frɔ́st-] *n.* Ⓤ **1** a mixture of sugar and some liquid used to cover a cake. (과자의) 당의(糖衣). **2** a dull finish on glass, metal, etc. (유리·금속 따위의) 광택 지움.

frost·y [frɔ́ːsti / frɔ́sti] *adj.* (**frost·i·er, frost·i·est**) **1** covered with frost; cold enough for frost. 서리가 내리는; 혹한의. ¶ *a ~ morning* 서리 내린 아침 / *~ weather* 서리가 내리는 추운 날씨. **2** 《fig.》 white or gray from age, etc. (머리가) 반백의; 하얀. ¶ *a ~ head* 하얀 머리. **3** (of character) cold in feeling; unfriendly. 차가운; 냉랭〔냉담〕한. ¶ *a ~ look* 차가운 얼굴 / *a ~ reception* 냉담한 접대.

froth [frɔːθ / frɔθ] *n.* Ⓤ **1** 《collectively》 foam on a liquid; a foam of saliva caused by disease or excitement. 거품; 게거품. ¶ *the ~ on a glass of beer* 맥주잔의 거품. **2** anything trifling or worthless. 시시한〔하찮은〕 것. —— *vi., vt.* (P1,2A; 6) foam or cause to foam. 거품이 일(게 하)다. ¶ *~ at the mouth* 입에 게거품을 뿜다 / *The beer frothed as it was poured out.* 맥주는 따라짐에 따라 거품이 일었다. [? Sc.]

froth·y [frɔ́ːθi / frɔ́θi] *adj.* (**froth·i·er, froth·i·est**) **1** of, like or covered with froth. 거품의; 거품 같은; 거품투성이의. ¶ *~ beer* 거품 많은 맥주 / *~ waves* 거품이 이는 물결. **2** trifling; empty; worthless. 하찮은; 시시한; 공허한; 천박한. ¶ *a ~ conversation* 시시한 대화. ● **froth·i·ness** [-nis] *n.*

***frown** [fraun] *vi.* (P1,3) **1** bend one's brows in deep thought, strong feeling, displeasure, etc. 눈살을 찌푸리다; 얼굴을 찡그리다. ¶ *~ with concern* 근심으로 눈썹을 찌푸리다 / *~ at the interruption* 방해를 받아 얼굴을 찡그리다. **2** 《*at, on, upon*》 look disapprovingly; have a displeased look. 비난하듯이 보다; 난색을 보이다; 불쾌한 얼굴을 하다. ¶ *~ upon a scheme* 계획에 난색을 보이다 / *She frowned at me for laughing.* 내가 웃는다고 그녀는 불쾌한 얼굴을 했다.

—— *vt.* (P6,7) **1** express (displeasure, disapproval, etc.) by frowning. 얼굴을 찡그려 (불쾌·비난의 기분 따위)를 나타내다. ¶ *~ one's displeasure* 눈살을 찌푸려 불쾌한 빛을 나타내다. **2** 《*away, back, off, down*》 reject or force (someone or something) to retire by frowning. 무서운 얼굴을 하여 …시키다〔위압하다〕. ¶ *~ someone away* 노려보아 물리치다 / *~ down the request* 얼굴을 찡그려 요구를 물리치다.

—— *n.* Ⓒ an act of frowning. 눈살을 찌푸림; 찌푸린 얼굴. [F.]

frowz·y [fráuzi] *adj.* (**frowz·i·er, frowz·i·est**) **1** dirty; slovenly. 추레한; 더러운; 흘게 늦은. **2** smelling bad; musty. 악취를 내는; 퀴퀴한. [↑]

***froze** [frouz] *v.* p. of **freeze.**

***fro·zen** [fróuzn] *v.* pp. of **freeze.**

—— *adj.* **1** turned into ice; hardened by cold. 언; 동결한; 냉동한. ¶ *a ~ stream* 얼음이 언 시내 / *~ meat* 냉동육. **2** very cold. 몹시 추운. ¶ *the ~ zone* 한대 / *the ~ regions of the pole* 혹한의 극(極)지방. **3** cold-hearted; unfeeling. 냉혹한; 쌀쌀한; 냉담한. ¶ *a ~ smile* 차가운 미소. [*freeze*]

F.R.S. Fellow of the Royal Society(영국

학사원).

fruc·ti·fy [frʌ́ktəfài] *v.* (**-fied**) *vi.* (P1) bear fruit. 열매를 맺다. — *vt.* (P6) make (something) bear fruit; make (a tree, a plant, a soil, etc.) fruitful. …에 열매를 맺게 하다; …의 열매를 많이 맺게 하다; (땅)을 비옥하게 하다. [L. *fructus*]

fruc·tose [frʌ́ktous] *n.* fruit sugar. 과당(果糖). [↑]

fru·gal [frú:gəl] *adj.* **1** avoiding waste; saving; economical. 검약한; 알뜰한; 절약하는. ¶ *a ~ housekeeper* 알뜰한 주부 / *be ~ of one's time and money* 시간과 돈을 절약하다 / *She is ~ with her money.* 그녀는 자기 돈을 절약한다. **2** costing little. 비용이 들지 않는; 검소한. ¶ *a ~ meal* 검소한 식사. ●**fru·gal·ly** [-gəli] *adv.* [L. *frux* profit]

fru·gal·i·ty [fru:gǽləti] *n.* Ⓤ the avoidance of waste. 검약; 절약; 검소. ¶ *live with great ~* 몹시 절약하면서 지내다.

:fruit [fru:t] *n.* Ⓤ **1** 《usu. *sing., collectively*》 the edible or juicy part of a plant or a tree containing the seeds. 과일. 語法 종류를 나타낼 때에는 a fruit, fruits가 됨. ¶ *fresh ~* 생과일 / *grow ~* 과일을〔청과를〕 재배하다 / *pare a piece of ~* 과일 하나의 껍질을 벗기다 / *fruits in season* 한창 제철인 과일 / *I like ~.* 과일을 좋아한다 / *He bought several kinds of ~.* 과일 몇 종류를 샀다. **2** 《*collectively*》 《bot.》 the part of a plant where seeds are formed. 열매; 과실. ¶ *dry ~* 건과(乾果) / *bear a hard red ~* 단단한 붉은 열매를 맺다. **3** 《usu. *pl.*》 any product of a plant, such as grain, vegetables, etc. (과일·야채·곡물 따위의) 농작물. ¶ *the fruits of the earth* 대지의 농작물 / *the fruits of the field* 논밭의 산물. **4** 《often *pl.*》 《*fig.*》 the result or reward of any action; product; profit. 성과; 결과; 소산(所産); 수익. ¶ *the fruits of one's labors* 노동의 소산 / *the fruits of industry* 노력의 결실 / *His efforts bore little ~.* 그의 노력은 거의 성과가 없었다. **5** 《Bible》 the offspring of human beings or animals. (인간·동물의) 자손. ¶ *the ~ of the body* 〔*loins, womb*〕 자녀.
— *vi.* (P1) produce fruit. 열매를 맺다. [L. *fructus*]

fruit·age [frú:tidʒ] *n.* **1** the bearing of fruit. 결실; 결과. **2** the growing crop; the fruit as a whole. 성과; 과일.

fruit cake [⌐⌐] *n.* a rich cake containing various fruits or nuts. 프루트 케이크《건포도·열매·시트론 따위를 넣은 케이크》.

fruit·er [frú:tər] *n.* **1** a tree that produces fruit. 과수(果樹). ¶ *a good ~* 좋은 과수. **2** a ship for carrying fruit. 과일 운반선(船). [*fruit*]

fruit·er·er [frú:tərər] *n.* Ⓒ a dealer in fruit. 과일 상인.

·fruit·ful [frú:tfəl] *adj.* producing fruit or good results abundantly. 열매가 많이 열리는; 비옥한; 효과적인. ¶ *a ~ tree* 열매를 잘 맺는 나무 / *a ~ soil* 비옥한 땅 / *a ~ plan* 효과적인 계획 / *a ~ occupation* 실수익이 많은 직업.

fru·i·tion [fru:íʃən] *n.* Ⓤ **1** realization of anything desired; fulfillment; attainment. 실현; 성취; 달성. ¶ *come* 〔*be brought*〕 *to ~* 달성되다; 성취하다; 열매를 맺다 / *~ of my longstanding hope* 오랜 숙원의 실현. **2** use or possession accompanied by pleasure. (달성·실현에서 오는) 즐거움; 누림; 향수. ¶ *the ~ of modern life* 현대 생활의 향수. **3** the state of bearing fruit. 결실; 결정. ¶ *the ~ of one's labors* 노력의 결정. [L. *fruor* enjoy]

fruit knife [⌐⌐] *n.* (*pl.* **-knives** [-nàivz]) a knife used at table for peeling and cutting fruit. 과도(果刀). [*fruit*]

fruit·less [frú:tlis] *adj.* **1** bearing no fruit; barren. 열매를 맺지 않는; 불모의. **2** 《*fig.*》 having no results; useless; vain. 성과 없는; 무익한; 헛된. ¶ *a ~ effort* 헛된 노력 / *be ~ of profit* 이익이 생기지 않다. [*fruit*]

fruit·y [frú:ti] *adj.* (**fruit·i·er, fruit·i·est**) **1** of fruit; like fruit. 과일의〔같은〕. **2** like fruit in taste or smell. 과일 맛이〔향기가〕 있는. **3** rich. 진한 풍미(風味)의.

frump [frʌmp] *n.* a woman who is shabby and out of style in dress. 추레하고 홀게늦은 여자; 몸차림이 너절한 여자. ●**frump·ish** [frʌ́mpiʃ], **frump·y** [frʌ́mpi] *adj.* [?]

frus·ta [frʌ́stə] *n.* pl. of **frustum.**

frus·trate [frʌ́streit] *vt.* (P6,13) make of no avail; bring (plans, efforts, etc.) to nothing; prevent (someone) from carrying out a purpose. …을 무효로 하다; …을 꺾다; 실패하게 하다; 헛되게 하다. ¶ *~ one's enemy in his plans* 적의 계획에 의표를 찌르다 / *~ the intention of the speech* 그 이야기의 의도를 꺾다 / *The prisoners were frustrated in their attempt to escape.* 포로들은 탈주 시도에 실패했다. [L. *frustra* in vain]

frus·tra·tion [frʌstréiʃən] *n.* ⓊⒸ **1** the act of frustrating; the state of being frustrated. 좌절; 실패; 낙담. **2** 《psych.》 a condition of insecurity or dissatisfaction caused by frustrated desires, inner conflicts, etc. 욕구 불만.

frus·tum [frʌ́stəm] *n.* (*pl.* **-tums** or **-ta**) 《geom.》 the part of a conical solid or pyramid left after the top has been cut off by a plane parallel to the base. 절두체(截頭體). [L.=fragment]

·fry[1] [frai] *vt.* (**fried**) (P6) cook in hot fat, oil, etc. …을 기름에 튀기다; 튀김으로 하다. ¶ *fried fish* 생선튀김. — *vi.* (P1) be cooked in boiling fat. 튀김이 되다; 튀겨지다. — *n.* Ⓒ (*pl.* **fries**) a dish of something fried. 튀김 (요리); 프라이. [L. *frigo* fry]

fry² [frai] *n.* Ⓤ《*collectively*》 **1** the young of fish or of certain other animals. 물고기(나 기타 동물)의 새끼. **2** small adult fish which swim in groups. 작은 물고기; 소어(小魚); 치어(稚魚). [N.=seed]

fry·er [fráiər] *n.* **1** a person who fries. 튀김 요리를 하는 사람. **2** fowl intended for frying. (영계 따위) 프라이〔튀김〕의 재료. **3** = frying pan. [*fry*¹]

fry·ing pan [∠-∠] *n.* a flat iron pan with a long handle, used for cooking. 프라이팬. [*fry*¹]

leap* [*jump*] *out of the frying pan into the fire, go from bad to worse. 작은 난을 피하여 큰 난에 빠지다; 갈수록 태산.

ft. foot; feet.

fthm. fathom.

ft-lb foot-pound.

fuch·sia [fjú:ʃə] *n.* 《bot.》 a plant with handsome drooping flowers of different colors. 퓨셔《바늘꽃과(科)의 관상용 관목》. [*Fuchs,* botanist]

fud·dle [fʌ́dl] *vt.* (P6,13) **1** make (someone) stupid with drink; intoxicate. …을 취하게 하다. ¶ *be in a ~ state* 억병으로 취해 있다 / *~ oneself with whiskey* 위스키에 취하다. **2** confuse. 혼미〔혼란〕시키다. — *vi.* **1** drink to excess; have a spell of drinking; get drunk. (술을) 지나치게 마시다; 계속해 마시다; 취하다. **2** be confused (as when drunk). (술취했을 때처럼) 혼미해지다. — *n.* a state of confusion, esp. from drink. (술에 취한) 혼란 상태. [G.]

fudge [fʌdʒ] *n.* Ⓤ **1** a kind of soft candy. 퍼지《설탕·버터·우유·초콜릿 따위로 만든 연한 캔디》. **2** a made-up story; nonsense. 꾸며낸 이야기: 허튼 소리. — *vt.* (P6,7) 《*up*》 fake. …을 조작하다 [G.]

***fu·el** [fjú:əl] *n.* Ⓤ **1** any material that can be burned to produce heat or power. 연료. ¶ *oil ~* 석유 / *gaseous ~* 기체 연료 / *~ gas* 연료 가스 / *put on fresh ~* 새로 연료를 채워넣다. **2** Ⓒ anything that keeps or increases a feeling. 정열을 북돋우는 것.

***add fuel to the fire* [*flames*],** make a passion (such as anger or hatred) stronger. 불에 기름을 붓다; 격정에 불을 붙이다.

— *vt.* (**-eled, -el·ing** or 《Brit.》 **-elled, el-ling**) (P6) supply (a car, a ship, etc.) with fuel. …에 연료를 보급하다. ¶ *~ a ship* 배에 연료를 보급하다.

— *vi.* (P1) provide oneself with fuel. 연료를 얻다; 연료 보급을 하다. ¶ *a fueling station* 〔*base*〕 연료 보급소〔기지〕 / *The ship put into port to ~.* 배는 연료를 보급받기 위해 입항했다. [L. *focus* hearth]

fug [fʌg] *n.* 《chiefly Brit.》 stale air, esp. the warm, humid, ill-smelling air of a closed room. (특히 밀폐된 방의) 퀴퀴한 공기. [? →fussy, fog]

fug·gy [fʌ́gi] *adj.* (**-gi·er, -gi·est**) 《chiefly Brit.》 (of air) stale; having a bad smell. (공기가) 퀴퀴한.

fu·gi·tive [fjú:dʒətiv] *n.* Ⓒ a person who is running away. 도망〔탈주〕자; 망명자. ¶ *a ~ from justice* 도망 범인 / *fugitives from the battle* 탈주병. — *adj.* **1** running away; fleeing. 달아난; 도망하는. ¶ *a ~ criminal* 도망 범인. **2** ⓐ wandering; roving. 방랑의. ⓑ lasting a very short time; soon passing away. 일시적인; 덧없는; 곧 스러져 없어지는. ¶ *~ flowers* 덧없이 지는 꽃. [L. *fugio* flee]

fugue [fju:g] *n.* Ⓒ 《mus.》 a piece of music in which the same melody is repeated with variations. 푸가; 둔주곡(遁走曲). [L. *fuga* flight]

Füh·rer [fjú:rər] *n.* 《G.》 **1** a leader. 지도자; 두령(頭領). **2** 《*der ~*》 Adolf Hitler. 히틀러《히틀러의 칭호, 총통》.

-ful [-fəl, -ful] *suf.* **1** full of; abounding in; characterized by. '…이 많은, …으로 찬'의 뜻. ¶ *beautiful.* **2** able to. '…할 수 있는'의 뜻. ¶ *helpful.* **3** (of) a quantity that fills. '…하나 그득한 (양)'의 뜻. ¶ *spoonful.* [→full]

ful·cra [fúlkrə, fʌ́l-] *n.* pl. of **fulcrum.**

ful·crum [fúlkrəm, fʌ́l-] *n.* (*pl.* **-crums** or **-cra**) **1** 《mech.》 an object which supports a lever; the point at which a lever rests when in action. 지레받침; 지점(支點). **2** 《*fig.*》 anything used to attain an end. 목적을 위해 사용되는 것. [L. *fulcio* prop]

***ful·fill,** 《Brit.》 **-fil** [fulfíl] *v.* (**-filled, -fil-ling**) *vt.* (P6) **1** carry out (a promise, duties, etc.). (의무·약속)을 실행하다; 이행하다. ¶ *~ an engagement* 약속을 이행하다. **2** satisfy (a requirement, a condition, etc.). (요구·조건)을 채우다. **3** finish; complete (a period of time, a term of office, etc.). (기간·임기)를 끝내다. ● **ful-fill·ment, ful·fil·ment** [-mənt] *n.* [*full, fill*]

:full [ful] *adj.* **1** 《*of*》 (of a vessel, etc.) holding as much as it can; filled. 그득찬; (하나) 가득한. ¶ *a cup ~ to overflowing* 넘칠 정도로 꽉 찬 술잔 / *a basket ~ of flowers* 꽃이 가득 들어있는 바구니 / *a room ~ of furniture* 〔*people*〕 가구들〔사람들〕로 들어찬 방 / *fill the glass ~* 술잔을 채우다. **2** complete; entire. 완전한; 온 …의. ¶ *a ~ view* 전경(全景) / *a ~ edition* (생략이 없는) 완전판(版) / *in ~ bloom* 만개되어 / *walk a ~ mile* 꼬박 1마일을 걷다 / *acquire ~ citizenship* 완전한 시민권을 획득하다 / *I waited a ~ hour.* 꼬박 1시간을 기다렸다. **3** at the highest degree; reaching the limit. 최대한의; 최고의; 한창의. ¶ *~ speed* 전속력 / *~ strength* 전력 / *~ summer* 한여름 / *~ daylight* 한낮〔대낮〕 / *a ~ mark* 만점 / *a ~ tide* 만조 / *~ moon* 만월 / *lie at ~ length* 발을 쭉 뻗고 눕다 / *make ~ use of it* 최대한으로 이용하다. **4** moved with deep feeling.

(감동으로) 가슴이 벅찬. ¶ *My heart was too ~ for words.* 가슴이 벅차 말이 나오지 않았다. **5** not tight. (옷 따위가) 낙낙한; 헐렁한. ¶ *a ~ sleeve* 낙낙한 소매. **6** plump; round. 풍만한; 투실투실한; 통통한. ¶ *a ~ bust* 풍만한 가슴 / *be ~ in the face* 얼굴이 통통하다. **7** strong; rich. 힘찬; (성량이) 풍부한. **8** furnished; well provided; rich in. 충분한; 많은; 풍부한. ¶ *a river ~ of fish* 물고기가 많은 강 / *a pocket ~ of money* 돈이 많이 든 호주머니. **9** 《*of*》 much concerned with; occupied with. …에 몰두한; …에 전념한. ¶ *be ~ of one's affairs* 일에 몰두해 있다 / *He is ~ of himself.* 자신의 일만 생각하고 있다.

full chisel, 《U.S. *colloq.*》 (at) full speed. 전속력(으로).

full up, 《*colloq.*》 with no room for more. 꽉 들어차; 만원으로.

— *adv.* **1** completely; entirely; quite. 완전히; 아주. **2** exactly. 정확히; 바로. ¶ *hit him ~ on the nose* 바로[정통으로] 코쭝배기를 때리다 / *look ~ at someone* 아무를 정면으로 보다.

— *n.* Ⓤ **1** the whole. 전부. ¶ *Tell me the ~ of it.* 내게 몽땅 말해라. **2** the utmost extent, degree, length, etc. 최고(점); 절정; 한창. ¶ *in the ~ of spring* 한창 무르익은 봄에. [E.]

at the full, at the time or point of fullness. 정점에서; 한창 때에.

in full, completely; (written or said) with all the words. 완전히; 생략하지 않고.

to the full, completely; to the utmost extent; fully. 충분히; 최대한으로; 실컷.

full·back [fúlbæ̀k] *n.* Ⓒ (in football) a player whose position is farthest from the opponent's goal. (축구에서) 풀백.

full-blood·ed [fúlblʌ́did] *adj.* **1** of pure descent; not hybrid. 순종의; 순수한. ¶ *a ~ Chinese* 순수(純粹)한 중국인. **2** vigorous; hearty; sensual. 원기 왕성한; 기운 찬; 마음으로부터의; 관능의.

full-blown [fúlblóun] *adj.* in full bloom; fully expanded; fully developed. 만개된; 터질 것 같은; 완전히 성숙한. ¶ *a ~ flower* 활짝 핀 꽃 / *a ~ sail* 활짝 편 돛.

full dress [∠∠] *n.* the formal style of clothes for ceremonial occasions; formal attire. 정장(正裝). ¶ *in ~* 정장으로[하고].

full-fash·ioned [fúlfǽʃənd] *adj.* knitted to fit the shape of a body part, esp. of a foot or a leg. 몸·발에 꼭 맞도록 짠[뜬]. ¶ *a ~ sweater* 몸에 꼭 맞게 짠 스웨터.

full-fledged [fúlflédʒd] *adj.* **1** fully developed. 충분히 발달한; 다 자란; 제몫을 하게 된. **2** (of a bird) with the feathers fully grown; able to fly. (새가) 깃털이 다 난; 날 수 있는. 「충분히 성장한.

full·grown [fúlgróun] *adj.* fully grown.

full·length [fúlléŋkθ] *adj.* as large as the human body. 등신대(等身大)의. ¶ *a ~ portrait of the queen* 등신대의 여왕 초상(화).

full·ness [fúlnis] *n.* Ⓤ the state of being full. 꽉 참; 충만; 풍부.

full stop [∠∠] *n.* a period. 마침표; 종지부.

full swing [∠∠] *n.* vigorous working. 맹렬한 활동; 한창.

full·time [fúltáim] *adj.* during all normal working hours. 전(全)시간의; 전시간 종사하는; 전임의. ¶ *a ~ nurse* 상근(常勤)간호사 / *a ~ teacher* 전임 교사.

:ful·ly [fúli] *adv.* completely; entirely; wholly. 완전히; 충분히. ¶ *~ paid* 전액 지급필(畢)의 / *~ three days* 꼬박 사흘 / *~ equipped for the journey* 여행 장비를 완전히 갖춘 / *answer the question ~* 질문에 자세히 답변하다. [*full*]

ful·mi·nate [fʌ́lmənèit] *vt., vi.* (P6,13;3) **1** 《*against*》 protest or blame violently. …에게 비난을 퍼붓다. **2** speak loudly and angrily. 고함[호통]치다; 일갈하다. **3** burst suddenly. 폭발하다[시키다]. [L. *fulmen* lightning]

ful·mi·na·tion [fʌ̀lmənéiʃən, fùl-] *n.* ⓊⒸ **1** the act of fulminating; strong criticism; bitter protest. 격렬한 비난; 질책. **2** a violent explosion. 폭발.

ful·some [fúlsəm, fʌ́l-] *adj.* (of flattery) so much as to be unpleasant; disgusting. (아첨 등이 지나쳐) 역겨운; 구역질나는. ¶ *~ praise* 역겨운 찬사 / *Her speech of thanks was a little too ~.* 사의(謝意)를 표하는 그녀의 말은 정도가 좀 지나쳤다. [*full*]

fum·ble [fʌ́mbəl] *vi.* (P1,2A,3) 《*about, for, in*》 use one's hands uncertainly when looking for (something). 손으로 더듬어 찾다. ¶ *~ about in one's pocket for a key* 호주머니 속의 열쇠를 더듬어 찾다 / *~ at the wall in the darkness* 어둠 속에서 벽을 더듬다 / *He fumbled in the darkness for the doorknob.* 어둠 속을 더듬어 문고리를 찾았다.

— *vt.* (P6) **1** handle awkwardly. …을 어설프게 다루다. ¶ *~ one's instrument* 연장을 어색하게 다루다. **2** deal with (a ball) unskillfully. (공)을 헛잡다; 놓치다. ¶ *~ the ball in a game* 경기에서 공을 헛잡다.

— *n.* Ⓒ **1** an awkward attempt to find or handle something. 서투름. **2** (of baseball, etc.) failure to hold or catch a ball properly. (야구 따위의) 펌블; 헛잡음. [N.]

fume [fjuːm] *n.* Ⓒ **1** 《usu. *pl.*》 smoke or gas, esp. that having a strong, unpleasant smell. 연기; 증기; 가스; 후텁지근한 냄새. ¶ *the fumes of choice tobacco* 향기좋은 담배 연기 / *The air was thick with tobacco fumes.* 담배 연기로 공기가 탁했다. **2** a fit of anger; excitement. 흥분 상태; 노기; 화남. ¶ *in a ~ of anger* 울컥 화가 치밀어. — *vi.* (P1,2A,3) **1** give off gas or smoke. (가스·연기 따위를) 내다. ¶ *smoke fuming from an ash tray* 재떨이에서 피어오르는 연기. **2** pass off in fumes. 연기가 되

다; 증발하다.

— *vt.* (P6) **1** treat (something) with smoke, etc. …을 연기에 쐬다; 그을리다. **2** let off one's rage. 성을[화를] 내다. ¶ *fret and* ~ 안달이 나서 화를 내다 / *He fumed about the slowness of the train.* 그는 열차의 느림에 화를 냈다. [L. *fumus* smoke]

fu·mi·gate [fjú:məgèit] *vt.* (P6,13) **1** 《*with*》 smoke (something) heavily. …을 연기에 쐬다; 그슬리다; 그을리다. **2** make (a room, etc.) free from disease, etc. by burning some medicine which gives off a heavy smoke. (방)을 훈증(燻蒸)소독하다. [→fume]

fu·mi·ga·tion [fjù:məgéiʃən] *n.* Ⓤ the act of smoking (something) heavily. 그슬리기.

:fun [fʌn] *n.* Ⓤ merriment; amusement; joking; a person or thing which causes amusement or merriment. 즐거움; 농담; 장난; 재미(있는 사람·있는 것). ¶ *have* ~ *at the picnic* 소풍을 즐기다 / *We had a lot of* ~ *at a swimming pool.* 풀에서 무척 재미있었다 / *I do not see the* ~ *of it.* 나는 그 재미를 모른다 / *What* ~*!* 정말 재미있구나. [E.]

for* [*in*] *fun, as a joke; not seriously. 농(담)으로; 반재미로; 장난으로. ¶ *I only did it for* [*in*] ~. 그저 장난으로 했다.

for the fun of it, for pleasure; without serious purpose. 장난으로; 반재미로. ¶ *I did it for the* ~ *of it.* 장난으로 했다.

like fun, 《*sl.*》 **a**) not at all. 결코[절대로] … 아니다. **b**) very quickly; vigorously. 매우 빨리; 맹렬히.

make fun of* =*poke fun at, **a**) laugh at (someone). …을 비웃다. **b**) bring (someone) into ridicule. …을 놀리다.

:func·tion [fʌ́ŋkʃən] *n.* Ⓒ **1** natural and proper work; a particular purpose. 기능; 작용; 직무; (본래의) 목적. ¶ *the procreative* ~ 생식 기능 / *the* ~ *of criticism* 비평의 구실 / *discharge one's functions* 직무를 수행하다 / *The* ~ *of the stomach is to digest food.* 위의 기능은 음식을 소화하는 것이다 / *The* ~ *of education is to develop the mind.* 교육의 본래 목적은 정신을 발달시키는 일이다. **2** ⓐ a formal public ceremony. 의식; 축전. ⓑ 《*colloq.*》 a large social gathering. (규모가 큰) 사교적 모임; 연회; 행사. ¶ *go to a* ~ *at the palace* 궁중 향연에 가다. **3** 《math.》 a mathematical amount whose value is related to the changing value of some other amount. 함수.

— *vi.* (P1,2A) fulfil a function; work; act. 작용하다; 기능을 다하다; 활동하다. ¶ *This adjective may* ~ *as an adverb.* 이 형용사는 부사로서의 구실을 할 수 있다. [L. *fungor* perform]

func·tion·al [fʌ́ŋkʃənəl] *adj.* **1** having a function; relating to a function. 기능(상)의. **2** working; acting. 작용하는.

func·tion·ar·y [fʌ́ŋkʃənèri] *n.* Ⓒ (*pl.* **-ar·ies**) an official. 직원; 공무원.

— *adj.* =functional.

:fund [fʌnd] *n.* Ⓒ **1** the amount of money put aside for a particular purpose. (어떤 목적을 위한) 자금; 기금(基金). ¶ *scholarship* ~ 장학 기금 / *a retirement* ~ 퇴직 기금 / *a sinking* ~ 감채 자금 / *a* ~ *for missionary purposes* 선교 목적을 위한 자금 / *A relief* ~ *was collected for the sufferers of the flood.* 수재민들을 위해 구제 자금이 걷혔다. **2** 《*pl.*》 financial resources; money in hand. 재원(財源); 소지금. ¶ *be in* [*out of*] *funds* 수중에 돈이 있다[없다]. **3** 《*the* ~*s*》 《Brit.》 national bonds. 공채(公債); 국채. **4** a stock or store (of common sense, knowledge, etc.). 축적; 간직함. ¶ *a* ~ *of knowledge* 지식의 축적 / *The old man has a* ~ *of interesting stories.* 그 노인은 재미있는 이야기를 많이 알고 있다.

— *vt.* (P6) **1** change (a debt) from a short term to long term. (단기 차입금)을 장기 공채로 바꾸다. **2** put in a fund. …을 자금으로 하다. [L. *fundus* bottom]

·fun·da·men·tal [fʌ̀ndəméntl] *adj.* of, relating to or forming the foundation; very important; most necessary. 기본[기초]의; 근본적인; 중요한. ¶ ~ *rights* 기본적 권리 / ~ *principles* 기본 원칙 / *the* ~ *structure* 기초 구조 / ~ *numbers* 기수(基數) / ~ *changes* 근본적 변화. — *n.* 《usu. *pl.*》 something that serves as a basis; an essential. 기초; 기본; 근본; 원리; 원칙. ¶ *the fundamentals of religion* 종교의 원리.

● **fun·da·men·tal·ly** [-təli] *adv.* **fun·da·men·tal·ism** [-təlìzəm] *n.*

:fu·ner·al [fjú:nərəl] *n.* Ⓒ a ceremony performed when a dead person's body is buried or burned. 장례(식). ¶ *a state* ~ 국장(國葬) / *attend a* ~ 장례식에 참석하다 / *hold a* ~ 장례식을 행하다. — *adj.* of a funeral. 장례(식)의; 장례 행렬의. ¶ *a* ~ *director* 장의사 주인 / *a* ~ *march* 장송 행진곡 / *a* ~ *oration* 조사; 추도사. [L. *funus*]

fu·ne·re·al [fju:níəriəl] *adj.* of a funeral; like a funeral; sad and solemn; gloomy. 장례(식)의[같은]; 구슬픈; 음울한. ¶ *a* ~ *expression* 슬픈 얼굴 / ~ *garments* 상복. [↑]

fun·gi [fʌ́ndʒai, fʌ́ŋgai] *n.* pl. of **fungus.**

fun·gi·cide [fʌ́ndʒəsàid] *n.* Ⓒ fungus-destroying substance. 살균제. [↓]

fun·goid [fʌ́ŋgɔid] *adj.* (of or resembling) a fungus. 진균(眞菌)의; 버섯 비슷한; 진균성(性)의. [→fungus]

fun·gous [fʌ́ŋgəs] *adj.* **1** of or like a fungus; spongy. 버섯의; 버섯 같은; 해면 같은; 유연한. **2** springing up suddenly but not lasting. 갑자기 발생하는; 일시적인; 덧없는.

fun·gus [fʌ́ŋgəs] *n.* (*pl.* **-gus·es** or **-gi**) a mushroom. 버섯; 균류. [L.]

fu·nic·u·lar [fju:níkjələr] *adj.* of or worked by a rope or cable. 밧줄[케이블]의;

케이블에 의해 움직이는. ¶ *a ~ railway* 케이블 철도. —*n.* funicular railway. 케이블카. [L. *funis* cord]

funk [fʌnk] *n.* Ⓒ 《*colloq.*》 **1** a great fear; panic. 공황; 겁. ¶ *be in a ~ of* …에 겁먹고 있다; …을 두려워하고 있다 / *put someone in a ~* 아무를 겁주다. **2** a coward. 겁쟁이. ***in a blue funk,*** 《*colloq.*》 in a state of great fear. 겁에 질려.

—*vi.* (P1) shrink in fear; be in a state of cowardly fear. 두려워 움츠러들다(주춤하다); 겁을 먹고 있다. —*vt.* (P6) **1** fear; be afraid of. …을 두려워하다. **2** try to avoid; shrink. …을 회피하다. ¶ *~ a difficulty* 곤란을 피하려 하다. [?, →frantic]

funk·y [fʌ́ŋki] *adj.* (**funk·i·er, funk·i·est**) 《*sl.*》 in a state of funk; frightened. 겁을 먹은; 무서워하는.

fun·nel [fʌ́nl] *n.* Ⓒ **1** a cone-shaped pipe with a wide mouth, for putting liquid or powder into a small opening. 깔때기. **2** anything shaped like a funnel. 깔때기 모양의 것. **3** a pipe for letting out smoke. 연기통; 굴뚝. —*vt.* (P6,13) **1** pass or feed through a funnel. 깔때기로 흘러들게 하다. ¶ *~ the oil into the bottle.* **2** 《*into*》 concentrate. 집중하다. ¶ *~ all one's energy into the work* 모든 정력을 작업에 쏟다. [L.]

:**fun·ny** [fʌ́ni] *adj.* (**-ni·er, -ni·est**) **1** causing laughter; comical; amusing. 우스운; 우스꽝스러운. ¶ *a ~ story* 우스운 이야기 / *It isn't at all ~.* 우스운 것 하나 없다 / *He is very ~ one.* 아주 재미있는 친구다. **2** 《*colloq.*》 strange; odd. 이상한; 기묘한. ¶ *a ~ affair* 이상한 일 / *a ~ kind of woman* 야릇한 여성 / *a ~ way to behave* 이상한 행동.

feel funny =***go all funny,*** feel rather ill. 기분이 좋지 않다.

● **fun·ni·ly** [-li] *adv.* [*fun.*]

:**fur** [fəːr] *n.* Ⓤ **1** the soft, thick hair covering the skin of certain animals. 보드라운 털; 유모(柔毛). **2** Ⓒ the skin of an animal with such hair; 《*usu. pl.*》 an article of clothing made of or trimmed with such skin. 모피; 모피 제품. ¶ *a coat lined with ~* 털가죽 안감을 댄 코트 / *wear very expensive furs* 매우 비싼 모피옷을 입고 있다. **3** Ⓤ 《*collectively*》 the animals with such skin. 모피짐승《밍크·여우 따위》. **4** a coating of various kinds; a coating on the human tongue in illness. 여러 가지 부착물; 설태(舌苔).

fur and feather, rabbits, hares, etc. and birds. 조수(鳥獸).

hunt fur, hunt hares. 산토끼를 사냥하다.

in furs, wearing a fur coat. 털 외투를 입고.

make the fur fly, cause a disturbance; take part in a fight or quarrel. 소동을 일으키다; 대판 싸움을 벌이다.

—*vt.* (**furred, fur·ring**) (P6) make or cover (something) with fur. …을 모피로 만들다; 모피로 덮다. [Teut.]

fur. furlong.

fur·be·low [fə́ːrbəlòu] *n.* **1** a flounce used on women's clothing. (여자 옷의) 옷단 장식. **2** 《*pl.*》 showy ornamentation. 현란한 장식; 분식. [F. *falbala*]

fur·bish [fə́ːrbiʃ] *vt.* (P6,7) 《*up*》 polish; make an old thing like a new one by polishing it. …을 닦다; 닦아서 새것처럼 만들다. ¶ *~ up old furniture* 낡은 가구를 영채가 나게 닦다 / *Before going to France, he furbished up his half-forgotten French.* 프랑스에 가기에 앞서 반은 잊어버린 프랑스어의 복습을 했다. [Teut.]

***fu·ri·ous** [fjúəriəs] *adj.* very violent and angry; strong and uncontrolled. 격노한; 성이 나서 날뛰는; 광포한. ¶ *a ~ quarrel* 격렬한 언쟁 / *a ~ storm* 사나운 비바람 / *be ~ with anger* 격노해 있다.

grow fast and furious, (of mirth, merry-making, etc.) become uproarious. (연회·놀이 등이) 떠들썩해지다; 무르익어가다.

● **fu·ri·ous·ly** [-li] *adv.* **fu·ri·ous·ness** [-nis] *n.* [*fury*]

furl [fəːrl] *vt., vi.* **1** (P6) roll up; fold up. …을 말다(감다); 개키다; 접다. ¶ *~ a sail* 돛을 말다 / *~ the curtains* 커튼을 당겨 묶다. **2** (P1) become furled. 접히다. [L.]

fur·lined [fə́ːrlaind] *adj.* lined with fur. 모피로 안을 댄. [*fur*]

fur·long [fə́ːrlɔ(ː)ŋ, -lɑŋ] *n.* Ⓒ a measure of distance equal to 1/8th of a mile. 펄롱《길이의 단위: 1마일의 1/8》. [orig.=length of furrow]

fur·lough [fə́ːrlou] *n.* ⓊⒸ time of rest from one's work, esp. for a soldier. (군인 등의) 휴가. ¶ *go home on ~* 휴가로 귀성하다 / *have* (*get*) *a month's ~,* 1개월의 휴가를 받다. —*vt.* (P6) 《esp. U.S.》 give a furlough to. …에게 휴가를 주다. [Du. for-, →leave]

***fur·nace** [fə́ːrnis] *n.* Ⓒ a large enclosed fire used to heat a building or to melt metals. 노(爐); 난방로; 화덕; 용광로. ¶ *an electric ~* 전기로(爐). [L. *fornus* oven]

tried in the furnace, severely tested. 혹독한 시련을 겪은.

:**fur·nish** [fə́ːrniʃ] *vt.* (P6,13) **1** supply; provide. …을 공급하다; 주다; 갖추다. ¶ *~ sufficient evidence* 충분한 증거를 제공하다 / *~ a library with books* 도서실에 책을 갖추다 / *~ someone with information* = *~ information to someone* 아무에게 정보를 주다 / *~ servants with money* = *~ money to servants* 하인들에게 돈을 주다. **2** supply (a room, a house, etc.) with furniture, etc. …에 가구를 비치하다; 설비하다. ¶ *~ a room with a beautiful picture* 방을 아름다운 그림으로 장식하다. ● **fur·nish·er** [-ər] *n.* [Teut. →from]

fur·nished [fə́ːrniʃt] *adj.* with furniture. 가

구가 딸린. ¶ *Furnished House to Let.* 가구가 딸린 셋집《광고》.

fur·nish·ings [fə́:rniʃiŋz] *n. pl.* the furniture of a room, a house, etc. 비치된 가구.

:fur·ni·ture [fə́:rnitʃər] *n.* Ⓤ **1** 《*collectively*》 things of daily use in a home, such as beds, tables, chairs, and desks. 가구. ¶ *a set* 〔*suite*〕 *of* ~ 가구 한 벌 / *an article* 〔*an item, a piece*〕 *of* ~ 가구 한 점 / *full of fine old* ~ 훌륭한 고풍의 가구로 가득 찬. **2** that with which anything is furnished. 내용(물); 소양; 지식. ¶ *the* ~ *of a bookshelf* 서가에 꽂힌 책들 / *the* ~ *of one's mind* 교양; 지식. **3** any needed item for a machine, etc. 부속품; 필요 비치품. [→furnish]

fu·ror [fjúrɔ:r], **-ro·re** [fjuərɔ́:ri] *n.* Ⓒ enthusiastic admiration; excitement; an example of such excitement, etc. 절찬; 격렬한 감격; 열광. ¶ *the soccer* ~ 축구열 / *make a* ~ 열광시키다 / *The play created a regular* ~. 그 연극은 여느때와 같이 열광적인 칭찬을 들었다. [It.→fury]

fur·ri·er [fə́:riər / fʌ́riər] *n.* Ⓒ a person who prepares or sells furs. 모피상; 모피 가공업자. [→fur]

fur·row [fə́:rou / fʌ́rou] *n.* Ⓒ **1** a long, narrow line cut in the earth by a plow. 밭고랑. **2** a wrinkle of a face, esp. the forehead. (얼굴의) 주름. — *vt.* (P6) **1** make furrows in (land). (밭)고랑을 만들다; 갈다. **2** wrinkle. …에 주름을 잡다; 주름지게 하다. ¶ *a face furrowed by old age* 늙어서 주름이 진 얼굴 / *She looked at the exam paper with a furrowed brow.* 얼굴을 찌푸리고 시험지를 들여다 봤다. [E.]

fur·ry [fə́:ri] *adj.* (**-ri·er, -ri·est**) **1** covered or trimmed with fur. 모피로 덮인〔장식된〕. ¶ ~ *animals* 모피동물 / *a* ~ *caterpillar* 온몸에 털이 무성한 풀쐐기. **2** of or made of fur. 모피(제)의; 모피가 달린. ¶ *the* ~ *side of a coat* 외투의 모피를 댄 안쪽. ● **fur·ri·ness** [-nis] *n.* [→fur]

:fur·ther [fə́:rðər] *adj.* compar. of **far. 1** more; moreover; additional. 그 위〔이상〕의; 더 한층의; 추가의. ¶ *without* ~ *argument* 더이상의 논의 없이 / *obtain* ~ *information* 그 이상의 정보를 얻다 / *I have nothing* ~ *to say.* 이상 더는 말할 것이 없다. **2** farther; more distant. 더 먼; 더 앞〔저쪽〕의. ¶ *on the* ~ *side of the road* 〔*river*〕 길〔강〕 저쪽에.

for further details, about more details. 더 상세한 것은; 더 자세한 점은.

until further notice, until (we) tell or inform you later. 추후 통지가 있을 때까지.

— *adv.* **1** at or to a greater extent. 더욱; 더. **2** besides; in addition. 그 위에; 게다가; 그 이상으로. ¶ *Let's not discuss it* ~. 이상 논의는 그만두자 / *Let's listen* ~. 그 앞을 들어보십시다. **3** at or to a greater distance. 더 멀리(로); 더 저쪽에〔앞으로〕. ¶ *go* ~ *away* 더 앞으로 가다 / *I'm too tired to go* ~. 지쳐서 더는 갈 수가 없다.

— *vt.* (P6) promote; put forward. …을 추진〔촉진〕하다; 조성하다. ¶ ~ *friendly relation between Britain and Korea* 한영간의 우호 관계를 촉진하다. [→fore]

fur·ther·ance [fə́:rðərəns] *n.* Ⓤ the act of helping forward; advancement. 조장(助長); 조성(助成); 촉진; 증진. ¶ *the* ~ *of social justice* 사회 정의의 조장 / *in* 〔*on*〕 *the* ~ *of* … 을 증진시키기 위해.

·fur·ther·more [fə́:rðərmɔ̀:r] *adv.* moreover; besides. 그 위에; 또한; 더구나.

fur·ther·most [fə́:rðərmòust] *adj.* furthest; most distant. 가장 먼.

fur·thest [fə́:rðist] *adj., adv.* =farthest.

fur·tive [fə́:rtiv] *adj.* **1** (of an action) done secretly; stealthy. 은밀한; 내밀한; 남몰래 하는. ¶ *cast a* ~ *glance at* …을 훔쳐보다. **2** (of a person) given to behaving in a furtive manner; sly. 수상쩍은; 교활한. ¶ *be* ~ *in one's movements* 움직임이 수상쩍다. ● **fur·tive·ness** [-nis] *n.* [L. *fur* thief]

fur·tive·ly [fə́:rtivli] *adv.* secretly. 남몰래; 가만히.

·fu·ry [fjúəri] *n.* (*pl.* **-ries**) **1** Ⓤ fierce anger; violence. 격노; 격분; 격렬; 광포. ¶ *the* ~ *of desire* 욕망의 격렬함 / *the* ~ *of a hurricane* 허리케인의 맹위 / *be full of* ~ 격노하다 / *fly* 〔*get*〕 *into a* ~ 불같이 노하다; 격노하다. **2** Ⓒ an outburst of anger. 노여움의 폭발. **3** 《*F-*》 《Gk. myth.》 one of the three goddesses of revenge. 복수의 3여신의 하나. **4** a fierce, spiteful woman. 앙심 많은 〔표독스런〕 여자. [L. *furo* am mad]

in a fury, in anger; fiercely. 격노하여; 맹렬히.

like fury, 《*colloq.*》 furiously; violently. 맹렬하게. ¶ *work like* ~ 맹렬히 일하다.

furze [fə:rz] *n.* Ⓤ 《bot.》 a prickly evergreen shrub on wasteland. 바늘금작화. [E.]

fuse[1] [fju:z] *n.* Ⓒ **1** 《electr.》 a piece of wire forming a part of an electric circuit to prevent the formation of an excessive current. 퓨즈. ¶ *blow a* ~ 퓨즈를 끊어지게 하다. **2** a tube or cord of explosives for carrying the spark. 도화선; 신관. — *vt.* (P6) fit a fuse to. …에 신관(信管)〔퓨즈, 도화선〕을 달다. [L. *fusus* spindle]

fuse[2] [fju:z] *vt.* (P6,7) **1** melt (metal) by heat; join together by melting. …을 녹이다; 용해시키다. **2** 《*fig.*》 cause to mix together; blend together; unite. …을 융화시키다; 결합시키다. — *vi.* (P1,2A) **1** be melted. 녹다. **2** be blended(into a whole). 융화되다; 결합되다. [L. *fundo* pour]

fu·see [fju:zí:] *n.* **1** a large-headed match for use in wind. (대가리가 큰) 내풍(耐風) 성냥. **2** a red flare light, used as a warning signal. (적색) 섬광 신호. [*fuse*[1]]

fu·se·lage [fjú:səlɑ̀:ʒ, -lidʒ, -zilɑ̀:ʒ] *n.* Ⓒ the main body of an airplane. 비행기의 동체. [→fuse[1]]

fu·sel oil [fjú:zəl ɔ̀il] *n.* 《chem.》 a mixture of amyl alcohols formed in making some spirits. 퓨젤유(油). [G. *fusel* bad spirit]

fu·si·ble [fjú:zəbəl] *adj.* that can be melted. 녹기 쉬운; 융해〔용해〕하는. [*fuse*²]

fu·sil [fjú:zəl] *n.* 《hist.》 an old-fashioned light flintlock musket. 수발총(燧發銃); 화승총. [L. *focus* fire]

fu·si·lier, -si·leer [fjù:zəlíər] *n.* Ⓒ 《hist.》 formerly, a soldier who carried a light gun called a fusil. 수발총병(燧發銃兵).

fu·sil·lade [fjú:səlèid, -lɑ̀:d, -zə-] *n.* Ⓒ the act of continuously firing guns for a long time; something like this. 일제〔연속〕 사격; (야구의) 집중 안타. ― *vt.* (P6) shoot or attack (something or someone) by a fusillade. …을 일제 사격〔공격〕하다.

fu·sion [fjú:ʒən] *n.* **1** Ⓤ the act of melting by heat (into one); the state of being melted (into one). 용해; 융합. ¶ *nuclear* ~ 핵융합 / *the* ~ *of metals* 금속의 융해 / *the total* ~ *of form and content* 형식과 내용의 완전한 융합. **2** Ⓒ something that has been melted (into one). 융해〔융합〕된 것. **3** Ⓒ union. 결합; 합동. [*fuse*²]

fusion bomb [⌐-⌐] *n.* a bomb which employs nuclear fusion, esp. a hydrogen bomb. 수소 폭탄.

fu·sion·ism [fjú:ʒənìzəm] *n.* the policy of political coalition. (정당의) 합병론(論). [fusion]

•**fuss** [fʌs] *n.* **1** ⓐ ⓊⒸ excitement about an unimportant matter; an excited and anxious state of mind. 사소한 일에 안달복달(함); 흥분. ¶ *get into a* ~ 안달복달하다. ⓑ Ⓒ 《*a* ~》 an example of excitement, confusion, etc. 법석; 대소동. ¶ *start a* ~ 법석을 일으키다 / *kick up a* ~ 공연히 법석을 떨다. **2** Ⓒ a fussy person. 수선스러운 사람; 시끄러운 사람.

make a fuss (about), cause trouble; make angry complaints (about). 법석을 떨다; 소동을 일으키다; 불평을 하다. ¶ *make a great* ~ *about nothing* 아무것도 아닌 일에 야단법석을 치다; 헛소동을 부리다.

***make a fuss of** someone,* treat (someone) with marked consideration; be very attentive to (someone). …을 지나치게 대우하다; …에게 몹시 마음을 쓰다.

― *vi.* (P1,2A,3) make a fuss. 안달복달하다; 법석을 떨다; 떠들어대다. ¶ *Don't* ~ *; we'll get there on time.* 안달하지 마라, 제 시간에 도착하게 될테니. ― *vt.* (P6) cause (someone) to get into a fuss. (하찮은 일로) …을 마음졸이게 하다〔괴롭히다〕; …을 소란케하다. [Imit.]

fuss·y [fʌ́si] *adj.* (**fuss·i·er, fuss·i·est**) **1** ⓐ full of fuss. 떠들어대는; 야단법석의. ⓑ (of a person) hard to please; very particular. (몹시) 까다로운. ¶ *be* ~ *about one's food* 음식에 대해 매우 까다롭다. **2** (of clothes, etc.) decorated too much. (옷 따위에) 요란하게 꾸민〔장식한〕. •**fuss·i·ly** [-li] *adv.* **fuss·i·ness** [-nis] *n.* [*fuss*]

fus·tian [fʌ́stʃən] *n.* Ⓤ **1** thick cotton cloth. 퍼스티언 직(織)《능직 무명의 일종》. **2** 《*fig.*》 high-sounding but empty talk or style. 과장된 표현〔언사〕; 호언 장담. ― *adj.* **1** made of fustian. 퍼스티언제(製)의. **2** 《*fig.*》 empty; pretentious. 과장된; 야단스러운. **3** (of a person) worthless. 별볼일 없는; 쓸모 없는. [F.]

fust·y [fʌ́sti] *adj.* (**fust·i·er, fust·i·est**) having a stale smell; old-fashioned. 퀴퀴한; 곰팡내 나는; 숨막힐 것 같은; 낡은. ¶ *a* ~ *book* 고본(古本); 진부한 책. [O.F. *fust* cask]

fut. future.

•**fu·tile** [fjú:tl, -tail] *adj.* useless; worthless; frivolous; trivial. 쓸데없는; 무익한; 시시한; 천박한. ¶ *a* ~ *attempt* 무익한 기도. [L. *futilis* leaky, futile]

fu·til·i·ty [fju:tíləti] *n.* (*pl.* **-ties**) Ⓤ uselessness; Ⓒ a futile action, etc. 무익(한 것); 무익한〔천박한〕 행동.

:**fu·ture** [fjú:tʃər] *n.* Ⓒ **1** 《usu. *the* ~》 the time that is to come after the present; what is to come. 미래; 장래. ¶ *in* 〔*for the*〕 ~ 장래는; 금후에는 / *in the near* ~ 가까운 장래에; 머지않아 / *prepare for the* ~ 장래에 대비하다. **2** a hopeful prospect. (유망한) 전도; 장래성. ¶ *a young man with a* ~ 전도 유망한 청년 / *have no* ~ 장래성이 없다. **3** 《*the F-*》 the future life; the life after death. 내세(來世). **4** 《gram.》 the future tense. 미래 시제. ― *adj.* **1** ⓐ that is to come. 미래의; 장래의. ¶ ~ *events* 장래의 일 / *his* ~ *wife* 미래의 아내; 약혼자 / ~ *ages* 후세. ⓑ relating to the life after death. 사후(死後)의; 내세의. ¶ *the* ~ *life* 내세. **2** 《gram.》 expressing the time to come. 미래(형)의 (cf. *past, present*¹). ¶ *the* ~ *tense* 미래 시제. [L. *futurus*]

fu·tur·ism [fjú:tʃərìzəm] *n.* a movement in art, literature, music, etc. to express movement and growth. (예술의) 미래파.

fu·tu·ri·ty [fju:tjúərəti, -tʃúr- / -tjúəriti] *n.* (*pl.* **-ties**) **1** Ⓤ the future. 미래; 장래. **2** 《*pl.*》 a future event. 미래의 일. **3** the future life; existence after death. 내세(來世); 저승.

fuze [fju:z] *n., vt.* =fuse¹.

fuzz [fʌz] *n.* Ⓤ **1** light, soft fiber of cloth, down or hair. 보풀; 괴깔; 솜털. **2** frizzled hair. 곱슬 털; 고수머리. **3** 《photog.》 indistinctness. 흐림; 희미함. ― *vt.* cover (something) with fuzz; make (something) fuzzy. …을 보풀이 일게 하다. ― *vi.* become covered with fuzz. 보풀〔괴깔〕이 일다. [Du. *voos*]

fuzz·y [fʌ́zi] *adj.* (**fuzz·i·er, fuzz·i·est**) **1** of or covered with fuzz. 보풀〔괴깔〕의; 보풀〔솜털〕이 인. **2** not clear. 희미한; 분명치 않은. ¶ *a* ~ *sound* 분명치 않은 소리 / *a* ~ *photograph* 희미한 사진. [↑]

f.v. 《L.》 folio verso.

g G

G, g [dʒiː] *n.* Ⓒ (*pl.* **G's, Gs, g's, gs** [dʒiːz]) **1** the seventh letter of the English alphabet. 영어 알파벳의 일곱째 글자. **2** 《mus.》 the fifth note in the major scale of C. 사음(音)《고정 도창법의 '솔'》. ¶ ~ *flat* 〔*sharp*〕 내림〔올림〕사조(調).
G 《electr.》 gauss; German; Germany; Gulf.
g 《psych.》 general intelligence; 《phys.》 (acceleration of) gravity.
g. gram; gauge; gender; genitive; guide; guinea(s).
Ga 《chem.》 gallium.
Ga. Gallic; Georgia.
G.A. General Agent. 총대리인〔점〕; General Assembly. 총회; General Average. 공동해손(海損).
GAB General Arrangements to Borrow. IMF의 일반 차입 협정.
gab [gæb] *n.* Ⓒ 《*colloq.*》 chatter; idle talk. (쓸데없는) 수다; 잡담. ¶ *the gift of the* ~ 변재(辯才); 다변(多辯) / *Stop your* ~. 쓸데없는 수다 집어치워라. — *vi.* (**gabbed, gab·bing**) (P1) talk very much; chatter. 쓸데없는 말을 많이 하다; 수다를 떨다. ¶ ~ *about* …에 관해 쓸데없는 말을 하다. [? N.]
gab·ar·dine, -er·dine [gǽbərdìːn, ⌐–⌐] *n.* **1** Ⓤ a kind of woolen, cotton, or rayon cloth used for raincoats, suits, etc. 개버딘 천《얇은 능직 복지·방수포》. **2** Ⓒ 《hist.》 a long cloak worn by the Jews in the Middle Ages. (중세 유대인이 입은) 낙낙한 상의(上衣). [F.]
gab·ble [gǽbəl] *vi., vt.* (P1; 6,7) talk fast without meaning. 빠르게 지껄이다. ¶ ~ *out an apology* 빠르게 사과의 말을 하다. — *n.* Ⓤ rapid talk without meaning. 빠르게 말하는 뜻모를 지껄임. [Imit.]
gab·by [gǽbi] *adj.* talkative. 말 잘하는; 말 많은; 수다스러운. [→gab]
gab·er·dine [gǽbərdìːn, ⌐–⌐] *n.* =gabardine.
ga·bi·on [géibiən] *n.* 《fortif.》 a cylinder of wicker filled with earth or stones. 보람(堡籃)《축성용의 돌망태.》 [→cage]
ga·ble [géibəl] *n.* Ⓒ **1** the triangular part of a building, formed by two opposite slopes of a roof. 박공; 박풍. **2** the wall of a building having a gable in the upper part.

〈gable 1〉

박공벽. — *vt.* (P6) build with gables. 박공식으로 짓다. [N.]
ga·bled [géibəld] *adj.* built in the form of a gable; having gables. 박공이 있는; 박공식으로 지은. ¶ *a* ~ *roof* 박공 지붕.
Ga·bon [gæbɔ́ːŋ] *n.* a republic of west-central Africa. 가봉.
Ga·bri·el [géibriəl] *n.* **1** a man's name. 남자 이름. **2** 《Bible》 one of the archangels, usu. God's messenger of good news or comfort. 천사 가브리엘. 參考 성모 마리아에게 수태를 알렸음. [Heb.]
gad[1] [gæd] *vi.* (**gad·ded, gad·ding**) (P2A) go about restlessly without purpose. 어슬렁거리다; 나돌아〔싸〕다니다. ¶ ~ *about at one's pleasure* 마음내키는 대로 돌아다니다 / ~ *about* 〔*around*〕 *all day* 온종일 싸다니다. [O.E.]
gad[2] [gæd] *n.* =goad.
gad[3] [gæd] *interj.* God. 하느님; 신. [*God*]
gad·a·bout [gǽdəbàut] *n.* 《*colloq.*》 one who wanders about idly. (정처 없이) 여기저기 돌아다니는 사람. [→gad[1]]
gad·fly [gǽdflài] *n.* Ⓒ (*pl.* **-flies**) **1** a fly that stings cattle and horses. (마소 따위에 꾀는) 등에. **2** an annoying person. 귀찮은 사람. [Obs. *gad* spike]
gadg·et [gǽdʒit] *n.* Ⓒ a small mechanical instrument, device, accessory, etc. 기계장치〔부속품〕; 도구(道具). [? →gauge]
Gael [geil] *n.* Ⓒ a Celt born or living in Scotland or in Ireland. 게일인(人). [Gael.]
Gael·ic [géilik] *adj.* of the Gaels or their language. 게일인(人)의; 게일어(語)의. — *n.* Ⓤ language of the Gaels. 게일어(語).
gaff [gæf] *n.* **1** a strong hook attached to a short handle, used for pulling in large fish. (물고기를 뭍으로 끌어올리기 위한) 갈고리. **2** 《naut.》 the spar for the top of the fore-and-aft sail. 사형(斜桁). **3** 《U.S. *sl.*》 hardship; strain. 어려움; 곤경(困境).
blow the gaff, 《*sl.*》 tell a secret. 비밀을 누설하다.
commit a gaff, say or do by accident something which is very displeasing to others. 우연히 남을 불쾌하게 하는 언동을 하다.
stand the gaff, 《U.S. *sl.*》 hold up well under strain or punishment of any kind. 고난(苦難)〔시련〕에 견디다.
— *vt., vi.* (P6; 1) hook or land (fish) with a gaff. (물고기를) 갈고리에 걸다; 갈고리로 끌어올리다. [F.]
gaffe [gæf] *n.* an unintentional social mistake. (사교상의) 실수; 결례.

gaf·fer [gǽfər] *n.* **1** an old fellow, esp. an old countryman. (시골의) 노인. **2** a man in charge of a number of workmen. 인부 우두머리; 모가비. [*godfather*]

gag [gǽg] *n.* Ⓒ **1** ⓐ something put in a person's mouth to keep him from speaking. 재갈; 하무. ⓑ anything that checks speech. 발언을 막는 것. ¶ *place* 〔*put*〕 *a* ~ *upon freedom of speech* 언론의 자유를 탄압하다. **2** a device to hold the mouth open, as in surgical operation. (치과·외과 수술용) 개구기(開口器). **3** ⓐ words added by an actor to get a laugh. (배우가 무대에서) 웃기기 위해 하는 임기 응변의 대사; 개그. ⓑ《*colloq.*》a joke; a trick played for fun. 농담; 익살; 웃기기 위한 짓거리.
— *vt.* (**gagged, gag·ging**) (P6) **1** put a gag into or on the mouth of (someone). …에게 재갈을 물리다. **2** prevent (someone) from speaking freely by force or authority. …의 언론을 탄압하다. **3** (of an actor) add (jokes) to one's speech when acting in a play. (무대에서) 임기 응변의 대사를 넣다. **4** 《*colloq.*》joke; tell lies as a joke. 농담하다; 농담으로 속이다. [Imit.]

ga·ga [gɑ́ːgɑ̀ː] *adj.* 《*colloq.*》dotty; senile; fatuous. 노망한; 망령든; 무감각한. [?]

gage[1] [geidʒ] *n.* Ⓒ **1** a glove thrown down in challenge; a challenge. 도전(挑戰)의 표시로 땅에 던진 장갑; 도전. **2** a thing given to make a promise sure; a pledge. 저당(물).
throw down a gage, challenge. 도전하다.
— *vt.* (P6) give or offer as a security; pledge. 저당에 넣다; 저당잡히다. [Teut. → wed]

gage[2] [geidʒ] *n., v.* 《U.S.》 =gauge.

gai·e·ty [géiəti] *n.* (*pl.* **-ties**) **1** Ⓤ the state of being gay; cheerfulness; merriment. 유쾌; 명랑; 쾌활. **2** 《often *pl.*》gay entertainment; festivities. 즐거운 일; 들뜬〔축제〕 기분; 법석; 환락. ¶ *the gaieties of the New Year season* 새해 때의 축제 기분. **3** bright, gay appearance; showy color. 화려(함); 화미(華美). ¶ ~ *of dress* 복장의 화려함. [*gay*]

gai·ly [géili] *adv.* **1** happily; merrily. 유쾌히; 명랑〔쾌활〕하게; 들떠. **2** (of dress, color, etc.) brightly; showily. 화려하게. ¶ *ladies* ~ *dressed* 화려하게 차려입은 부인들. [*gay*]

:gain [gein] *vt.* **1** (P6) get (something), esp. by effort; acquire; obtain. …을 얻다; 획득하다; 벌다. ¶ ~ *experience* 경험을 쌓다 / ~ *one's living* 생활비를 벌다 / ~ *possession of an object* 갖고 싶은 것을 손에 넣다 / ~ *popularity* 〔*a good reputation*〕 인기를〔좋은 평판을〕 얻다 / ~ *permission to enter a country* 입국 허가를 얻다. **2** (P6) get in competition; win. (경쟁에서) 따다; 이기다. ¶ ~ *a battle* 싸움에 이기다 / ~ *a prize* 〔*victory*〕 상(賞)을〔승리를〕 쟁취하다 / ~ *an advantage over* …보다 유리한 입장에 서다 / ~ *the upper hand* (*of*) 우위에 서다; 이기다. **3** (P6) get as profit. 이익으로서 얻다; 이득을 얻다; 벌다. ¶ ~ *a large sum* 큰돈을 벌다 / *There is nothing to be gained by discussing that.* 그것을 논의해 보았자 아무 것도 얻을 것이 없다. **4** (P6) reach; get to; arrive at (a place). (노력하여) …에 도달하다; 도착하다; (목적을) 달(성)하다. ¶ ~ *the top of a mountain* 산꼭대기에 이르다 / ~ *one's ends* 목적을 달성하다 / ~ *one's destination* 목적지에 도달하다 / *Our car gained the main street.* 우리 차는 큰 거리에 이르렀다. **5** (P6) get as an addition, increase, etc.; add to. …을 늘리다; 더하다. ¶ ~ *strength* 〔*weight*〕 힘이〔무게가〕 늘다 / ~ *speed* 속력이 붙다 / ~ *five pounds in weight* 몸무게가 5파운드 늘다. **6** (of a watch or clock) become fast by (some minutes, etc.); run fast. (시계가) …만큼 더가다(opp. lose). ¶ *My watch gains two minutes a day.* 내 시계는 하루에 2분 더 간다.
— *vi.* (P1,2B,3) **1** become better or greater; advance; make progress; increase or improve (in). 좋아지다; 진보하다; 증가〔증진, 향상〕하다. ¶ ~ *in weight* 체중이 늘다 / ~ *in importance* 중요성을 더하다 / ~ *in reputation* 평판이 높아지다 / ~ *by comparison* 비교에 의해 돋보이다 / ~ *in health* 건강이 증진하다 / ~ *in speed* 속력이 붙다 / *The sick man gained day by day.* 환자는 상태가 나날이 좋아졌다. **2** (P3) 《*on*》 encroach. 침식(浸蝕)하다. **3** (of a watch or clock) go fast. (시계가) 더 가다; 빠르다. ¶ *My watch gains by five minutes a day.* 내 시계는 하루 5분씩 더 간다.
gain ground, make progress. 좋아지다; 진보하다. ¶ *The sick man gained ground daily.* 병자는 나날이 좋아졌다.
gain on 〔***upon***〕**,** **a**) get nearer to someone or something. …을 바짝 뒤쫓다; 접근하다. ¶ ~ *on someone in a race* 레이스에서 아무를 바짝 뒤쫓다. **b**) go or run faster than. …와의 간격을 벌리다; 떼어놓다. ¶ ~ *on one's pursuers* 추적자와의 간격을 벌리다. **c**) 《*fig.*》 win favor with. …의 마음에 들다. **d**) (of the sea) gradually advance upon (the land). (바다가 육지)를 침식하다.
gain someone over, persuade someone to take one's side; win over. …을 설득하여 제편으로 만들다; 포섭하다.
gain time, cause delay on purpose. 일부러 일을 지연시키다; 시간을 벌다.
— *n.* (opp. loss) **1** ⒸⓊ profit; advantage; 《often *pl.*》 something gained. 이익; 이득; 수익(금). ¶ *love of* ~ 이욕(利慾) / *ill-gotten gains* 부정 이득 / *get* 〔*make*〕 *a* ~ *of two thousand dollars,* 2천 달러의 수익을 올리다 / *No gains without pains.* 수고 없이는 이득도 없다. **2** Ⓒ increase; improvement; addition. 증가; 증진; 증대. ¶ *a* ~ *to knowledge* 지식의 증대 / *make a* ~ *of ten pounds in weight* 몸무게가 10파운드 늘다. [Teut. = hunt]

G

gain·er [géinər] *n.* Ⓒ a person who gains. 획득자; 이득자; 승리자(opp. loser).
come off a gainer, make a profit; win. 이득을 얻다; 승자가 되다.

gain·ful [géinfəl] *adj.* profitable; paying. 이익이 있는; 유리한. ¶ ~ *employment* 돈벌이가 괜찮은 일.

gain·ings [géiniŋz] *n. pl.* what is gained; earnings; profits. 소득; 수익.

gain·say [gèinséi] *vt.* (**-said** [-séid, -séd]) (P6) 《*arch., lit.*》 say that something is wrong or false; deny; oppose. 부정하다; 반대〔반박〕하다. [*against, say*]

gainst, 'gainst [genst / geinst] *prep., conj.* 《*poet.*》 =against.

gait [geit] *n.* Ⓒ a manner of walking or running. 걸음걸이; 발걸음; 보조(步調). ¶ *a slow* ~ 느린 발걸음 / *with hurried* ~ 급한 걸음으로 / *The old man walked with a shuffling* ~. 노인은 발을 지척이며 걸었다. [N. =street]

gai·ter [géitər] *n.* Ⓒ **1** 《usu. *pl.*》 a covering of cloth or leather for the lower leg or ankle. 각반. **2** 《U.S.》 a cloth or leather shoe with elastic sides and no laces. 옆이 신축성이 있는 즈크화(靴) 나 가죽신. [F.]

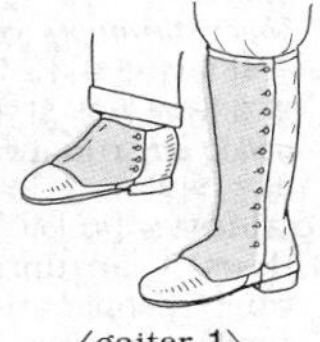
〈gaiter 1〉

gal., gall. gallon; gallons.

ga·la [géilə, gǽlə / gɑ́:lə] *n.* Ⓒ celebration; festival. 축제. ¶ *in* ~ 성장(盛裝)하고; 나들이옷을 입고. —*adj.* festive; showy. 축제(기분)의; 명랑〔유쾌〕한; 화려한. ¶ *a* ~ *day* 축제일 / *a* ~ *dress* 나들이옷 / *Tonight was* ~. 오늘밤은 축제 기분이었다. [It.]
gala night, a night on which there is a specially good show at a theater. 특별 쇼가 있는 밤.

ga·lac·tic [gəlǽktik] *adj.* **1** of milk or stimulating the secretion of milk. 젖의; 최유(催乳)의. **2** of the Milky Way. 은하수의. [*galaxy*]

gal·an·tine [gǽləntì:n] *n.* a dish made of chicken, etc., boned, cut small, usu. rolled, boiled, and served cold. 갤런틴《닭 따위의 뼈를 발라낸 고기로 만든 요리》. [F.]

gal·ax·y [gǽləksi] *n.* Ⓒ (*pl.* **-ax·ies**) **1** a brilliant group of people. (미인·재사 등의) 화려한 대집단; 기라성. ¶ *a* ~ *of movie actresses* 기라성 같은 영화 여배우들. **2** 《*the G-*》 a huge group of stars; the Milky Way. 은하(銀河); 은하수. [Gk. *gala* milk]

∗**gale** [geil] *n.* Ⓒ **1** a strong wind. 강풍; 질풍. **2** 《*poet.*》 breeze. 미풍. **3** an outburst. (웃음·노여움 따위의) 돌발; 폭발. ¶ *a* ~ *of laughter from the spectators* 관객들로부터의 웃음의 폭발. [N.]

ga·le·na [gəlí:nə] *n.* Ⓤ a metallic, gray ore containing much lead sulfide. 방연광(方鉛鑛). [L.]

Gal·i·le·o [gæ̀ləlí:ou, -léiou], **Galilei** *n.* (1564-1642) an Italian astronomer who was the first to prove that the earth goes round the sun. 갈릴레오.

gall[1] [gɔ:l] *n.* Ⓤ **1** ⓐ a bitter fluid made by the liver. 담즙(膽汁). ⓑ gall bladder. 담낭(膽囊). **2** anything bitter or distasteful; hate. 쓰디쓴 것; 증오; 원한. ¶ *vent one's* ~ *on* …에 증오심을 터뜨리다. **3** 《U.S. *colloq.*》 shameless daring; impudence. 뻔뻔스러움; 철면피. ¶ *have the* ~ *to do* … 뻔뻔스럽게도 …하다. [E.]
dip one's pen in gall, write with bitterness; criticize severely. 독필(毒筆)을 휘두르다; 호되게 비평하다.
gall and wormwood, something very bitter; the cause of great anger. 쓰디씀; 몹시 지겨운 것; 깊은 원한〔유한〕.

gall[2] [gɔ:l] *vt., vi.* (P6; 1) **1** make or become sore by rubbing hard. (스쳐서) 피부가 까지(게 하)다; 벗겨지(게 하)다. **2** make (someone) angry; annoy. …을 약올리다; 성나게 하다. ¶ *That remark galled him.* 그 말은 그를 화나게 했다 / *It galls me to think that….* …라는 것을 생각하면 부아가 난다 / *She was galled by his constant criticism.* 그녀는 끊임없는 그의 비판에 화를 냈다. —*n.* **1** Ⓒ a sore spot on the skin caused by rubbing. 찰과상. **2** Ⓤ something irritating; annoyance. 약오름; 화남; 짜증; 고뇌. [O.F. *galer* itch]

gall[3] [gɔ:l] *n.* Ⓒ something like a ball that is formed on leaves by insects, bacteria, etc. 옹두리; 몰식자(沒食子); 오배자. [L.]

∗**gal·lant** [gǽlənt] *adj.* **1** brave; daring. 용감한; 씩씩한. ¶ *a* ~ *knight* 용감한 기사 / *the honorable and* ~ *member* 군인 출신 의원. **2** grand and noble in appearance. 당당한; 장려한. ¶ *a* ~ *pageant* 장려한 행렬 / *a* ~ *sight* 장관 / *a* ~ *ship* 훌륭한 배. **3** gay; showy. 아름답게 차려입은; 화려한. ¶ *in* ~ *attire* 화려하게 차려입고 / *make a* ~ *show* 화려하게 장식하다. **4** [gəlǽnt, gǽlənt] ⓐ very polite and kind to women. (여성에 대해) 친절한; 은근한. ⓑ amorous; of love. 연애의; 엽색(獵色)의. ¶ ~ *adventures* 갖가지 엽색 행각.
—[gǽlənt, gəlǽnt] *n.* Ⓒ **1** a high-spirited or brave man. 씩씩한〔용기 있는〕 남자. **2** a man of fashion. 멋쟁이. **3** ⓐ a man who is very polite and kind to women. 여성에게 친절한 남자. ⓑ (in a good or bad sense) a lover. 정부(情夫). ● **gal·lant·ness** [-nis] *n.* [F. *galer* make merry]

gal·lant·ly [gǽləntli] *adv.* in a gallant manner. 용감〔씩씩〕하게; 화려하게; 친절히.

gal·lant·ry [gǽləntri] *n.* (*pl.* **-ries**) **1** ⓐ Ⓤ bravery; courage. 용감(함); 용기. ⓑ Ⓒ a gallant conduct or speech. 용감한 언동; 무용(武勇). **2** ⓐ Ⓤ very great politeness or kindness to women. 여자에게 은근함. ⓑ Ⓒ

a love-affair. 정사(情事); 염사(艶事). [→gallant]

gall bladder [⌐ ⌐−] *n.* 《anat.》 an organ of the body, like a small bag, in which bile or gall is stored. 쓸개; 담낭. [*gall*¹]

gal·le·on [gǽliən] *n.* Ⓒ a large sailing ship, formerly used as a warship by the Spaniards. 갈레온 선(船)《옛 스페인 군선(軍船)으로 쓰였던 큰 돛배》. [→galley]

〈galleon〉

:gal·ler·y [gǽləri] *n.* Ⓒ (*pl.* **-ler·ies**) **1** a long, narrow hall or passage, often with windows on one side only. 회랑(回廊); 주랑(柱廊). **2** the highest floor of a theater or hall; the people who sit there. (값싼 맨 위층) 관람석(의 관객). **3** a room or building for showing works of art. 화랑(畫廊); 미술품 진열실〔관〕. ¶ *the National Gallery* 런던 국립 미술관. [F.]

bring down the gallery, excite the admiration of the audience. 관중의 인기를 끌다.

play to the gallery, seek the praise of the common people. 대중의 갈채를 노리다; 일반의 속취(俗趣)에 영합하려 하다.

gal·ley [gǽli] *n.* Ⓒ **1** a warship moved by oars and sails, used in ancient times. 갤리배. 參考 옛날 노예·죄수에게 노를 젓게 한 군선(軍船). **2** 《print.》 a tray for holding set-up type; a proof printed from such type. 게라; 교정쇄(刷)(=galley proof). [L. *galea*]

galley proof [⌐− ⌐] *n.* 《print.》 a proof printed from type in a galley so that errors can be corrected. 게라쇄(刷); 교정쇄(刷). ¶ *a ~ marked with the corrections* 교정한 게라쇄.

galley slave [⌐− ⌐] *n.* **1** a slave or prisoner forced to row a galley. 갤리선(船)의 노예. **2** anyone who does very hard work. 고역(苦役)을 하는 사람; 과중 노동을 하는 사람.

Gal·lic [gǽlik] *adj.* **1** of Gaul or its people. 골(Gaul)의; 골 사람의. **2** French. 프랑스(사람)의. [L.]

gall·ing [gɔ́:liŋ] *adj.* vexing; irritating. 짜증나게 하는; 괴롭히는. [*gall*²]

gal·li·pot [gǽləpɑ̀t / -pɔ̀t] *n.* a small earthen pot, used for holding medicine, preserved fruits, etc. 도제(陶製)의 약단지. [*galley, pot*]

gal·li·vant [gǽləvæ̀nt / ⌐−⌐] *vi.* (P1) go about seeking pleasure, esp. with members of the opposite sex. (이성과 함께) 유쾌하게 싸다니다. [→gallant]

***gal·lon** [gǽlən] *n.* Ⓒ a unit of measure for liquids, being equal to 3.785 liters (=the U.S. gallon) and 4.546 liters (=the British gallon). 갤런《용량의 단위》. [F.]

***gal·lop** [gǽləp] *n.* Ⓒ the fastest speed at which horses can run. (말의) 질구(疾驅); 갤럽. ¶ *at a snail's ~* 느릿느릿; 소걸음으로 / *breake into a ~* 갑자기 내달리다.

at a 〔***full***〕 ***gallop,*** at great speed. 질구(疾驅)하여; 전속력으로. ¶ *go* 〔*run*〕 *at a ~* 질주하다.

— *vt.* (P6,7) cause (a horse) to run at full speed. (말)을 전속력으로 달리게 하다.

— *vi.* (P1,2A,3) **1** ⓐ (of a horse) go or move at a gallop. (말이) 전속력으로 달리다. ⓑ (of a rider) ride a horse at its fastest speed. (기수가 말)을 최고 속도로 몰다. **2** 《*over, through*》 read or speak in a hurry. 급히 읽다〔말하다〕. ¶ *~ through* 〔*over*〕 *a letter* 편지를 서둘러 읽다. [F.]

gallop off, run away on horseback. 말을 달려 가버리다.

gal·lows [gǽlouz] *n.* Ⓒ (*pl.* **-lows·es** or **-lows**) **1** an upright wooden framework where people are hanged. 교수대. **2** any similar structure. 교수대 모양의 것; 걸개. **3** 《usu. *the ~*》 death by hanging. 교수형. ¶ *cheat the ~* 어떻게든 교수형을 모면하다 / *come to the ~* 교수형에 처해지다 / *condemn* 〔*send*〕 *someone to the ~* 아무를 교수형에 처하다 / *have a ~ look* 흉악한 인상을 하고 있다. [E.]

gallows bird [⌐− ⌐] *n.* a person who deserves to be hanged. (교수형에 처해야 할) 흉악한 사람.

gallows tree [⌐− ⌐] *n.* =gallows 1.

gall·stone [gɔ́:lstòun] *n.* a hard substance formed in the gall-bladder. 담석(膽石). [→gall¹]

Gal·lup poll [gǽləp pòul] *n.* sampling opinions of the public from which the opinion is deduced. 갤럽 여론 조사. [Person]

ga·lore [gəlɔ́:r] *adv.* in plenty. 많이; 다량으로; 풍부히. ¶ *food and drinks ~* 많은 식품과 음료 / *There were books and magazines ~.* 서적과 잡지가 많이 있었다. [Ir.]

ga·losh [gəlɑ́ʃ / -lɔ́ʃ] *n.* Ⓒ 《usu. *pl.*》 a pair of overshoes, usu. made of rubber or plastic, used on a wet day. 고무덧신; 오버슈즈. [F.]

gals. gallons.

Gal·va·ni [gælvɑ́:ni, gɑ:l-], **Luigi** *n.* (1822-1911) an Italian physicist. 갈바니《이탈리아의 물리학자》.

gal·van·ic [gælvǽnik] *adj.* **1** producing or caused by an electric current. 전류(電流)를 일으키는; 전류에 의한. **2** affecting or affected as if by an electric shock. 경련적인; 발작

적인; 충격적인. ¶ *a ~ smile* 경련적인 웃음 / *the ~ effect of his speech* 청중을 깜짝 놀라게 하는 그의 연설의 효과. [*Galvani*]

gal·va·nism [gǽlvənìzəm] *n.* Ⓤ **1** electricity, esp. produced by chemical action. 전류(電流). **2** 《med.》 application of such electricity to the body as medical treatment. 전기 요법(療法).

gal·va·ni·za·tion [gæ̀lvənizéiʃən] *n.* Ⓤ the act of galvanizing; the state of being galvanized. 전기 요법; 전기〔아연〕 도금.

gal·va·nize [gǽlvənàiz] *vt.* (P6,13) **1** 《med.》 give an electric shock to (muscles or nerves). …에 전기 치료를〔요법을〕 하다 (opp. faradize). **2** stir up; excite or shock, as if by electricity. …을 활기띠우다; 자극하다. ¶ *~ someone to* 〔*into*〕 *life* 아무를 소생시키다〔활기띠우다〕. **3** cover (iron, etc.) with metal to prevent rusting. …에 전기 도금을 하다. ¶ *galvanized iron* 아연 도금판(板); 함석.

gal·va·nom·e·ter [gæ̀lvənɑ́mitər / -nɔ́m-] *n.* an instrument for measuring the strength of an electric current. 검류계(檢流計). [→galvanic]

Gam·bi·a [gǽmbiə] *n.* a republic of western Africa. 감비아《서부 아프리카의 공화국》. 參考 수도는 반줄(Banjul).

***gam·ble** [gǽmbəl] *vi., vt.* (P1,3; 6,7) **1** play for money or some other prize; bet. 도박을 하다; 내기를 하다. ¶ *~ at cards* 카드로 노름을 하다 / *~ away one's fortune* 도박으로 재산을 날리다. **2** risk (something) for some uncertain gain. 투기하다; 모험을 하다; (금품을) 걸다. ¶ *~ on horse races* 경마에 돈을 걸다 / *~ with one's future* 장래를 건 모험을 하다 / *~ one's reputation on* …에 명성을 걸다; 명성을 걸고 …하다. — *n.* Ⓒ 《*colloq.*》 anything that involves risk. 도박; 투기; 모험. ¶ *a ~ with fate* 운명을 건 도박 / *on the ~* 운을 하늘에 맡기고. [*game*]

gam·bler [gǽmbələr] *n.* Ⓒ a person who gambles. 도박꾼.

gam·bling [gǽmbliŋ] *n.* Ⓤ the act of risking money on a game of chance, etc. 도박; 내기. ¶ *indulge in ~* 도박에 빠지다 / *a ~ house* 〔*place*〕 도박장.

gam·boge [gæmbóudʒ, -búːʒ] *n.* a bright yellow color. 자황(雌黃); 치잣빛. [*Cambodia* Place]

gam·bol [gǽmbəl] *n.* Ⓒ 《usu. *pl.*》 playful jumping about, esp. children or animal; frolic. 뛰놀기; (어린이, 새끼양 등의) 장난. — *vi.* (**-boled, -bol·ing** or esp. 《Brit.》 **-bolled, -bol·ling**) (P1,2A) run and jump about. 뛰어다니다; 뛰놀다; 까불다; 장난치다. ¶ *Young lambs ~ in the spring sunshine.* 새끼양들이 봄볕을 받으며 뛰놀고 있다. [It. *gamba* leg]

gam·brel [gǽmbrəl] *n.* Ⓒ 《archit.》 a roof having two slopes on each side. 물매가 2단으로 된 맞배지붕. [F. *jambe* leg]

:game [geim] *n.* **1** Ⓒ any form of play; an amusement; a pastime. 놀이; 오락; 유희. ¶ *children's games* 어린이의 놀이 / *games of cops and robbers* 도둑잡기놀이. **2** Ⓒ ⓐ a certain form of play with special rules. 경기; 게임; 시합. ¶ *athletic games* 체육 경기 / *a ~ at cards* 카드 놀이〔게임〕 / *a drawn ~* 무승부 경기 / *lose a ~* 경기에 지다 / *play a good* 〔*poor*〕 *~* 게임을 잘하다〔게임에 서투르다〕. ⓑ a single round in such a game. (경기 중의 일부를 이루는) 한 승부〔게임〕. ¶ *the final ~ of the season* 시즌 최후의 경기 / *win the three games out of five* 다섯 판 승부에서 3번 이기다. **3** Ⓒ things needed to play a game. 유희〔놀이〕 기구; 게임 용품. ¶ *a store selling toys and games* 장난감과 게임 용품을 파는 가게. **4** Ⓒ ⓐ the condition or the score of a game. 득점; 게임의 형세. ¶ *How* 〔*What*〕 *is the ~?* 게임의 형세는 어떤가 / *The ~ is 4 to 3.* 득점은 4대 3이다 / *The ~ is yours.* 자네 쪽이 우세하다. ⓑ the number of points required to win a game. 이기기 위해 필요한 득점. ¶ *The ~ is 15.* 필요한 점수는 15 득점이다 / *One hundred is* (*the*) *~.* 100점으로 승부는 결정난다. **5** Ⓤ fun; joke; amusement. 농(담); 장난. ¶ *speak in ~* 농으로 말하다. **6** Ⓤ 《usu. *pl.*》 plan; trick; intention. 계획; 계략; 책략; 수(법). ¶ *the same old ~* 예의 같은 수법 / *see through someone's ~* 아무의 계략을 간파하다 / *None of your games.* 이제 그 수(법)에는 넘어가지 않는다 / *The ~ is up.* 만사 끝장이다; 계획은 실패했다. **7** Ⓤ 《*collectively*》 wild animals, birds, or fish that are hunted or caught; the flesh of these animals. 사냥감; 그 고기. ¶ *shoot ~* 사냥감을 쏘다.

a game of chance, a game that depends on luck rather than skill. 기술보다도 운에 달린 경기.

fair game, **a**) the game one is allowed to hunt. 사냥이 허용된 사냥감(opp. forbidden game). **b**) a suitable object of attack, ridicule, etc. 공격·조롱의 적당한 대상.

forbidden game, the game one is not allowed to hunt. 사냥이 금지된 사냥감(opp. fair game).

have the game in one's hands, **a**) be sure of success. 승리가 확실하다. **b**) be able to direct the game. 승패의 열쇠를 쥐고 있다.

make game of, cause people to laugh at; make fun of. …을 놀리다.

play the game, **a**) play according to the rules of the game. 규칙에 따라 행동을〔경기를〕 하다. **b**) 《*fig.*》 be fair and honorable. 정정 당당히 행동하다; 공명 정대하게 행동하다. ¶ *assume to continue to play the ~* 계속 공명 정대하게 하는 척하다.

— *adj.* having enough spirit; ready; willing. …할 마음이〔용기가〕 있는. ¶ *They are ~ for any adventure.* 그들은 어떤 모험이라도 할 각오이다.

— *vi., vt.* (P1,3; 7) 《*away*》 lose in gam-

G

bling. 도박에서 잃다. [E.]

game·bag [géimbæ̀g] *n.* a bag used for carrying game that has been killed. (잡은 사냥감을 담는) 사냥 자루.

game·cock [géimkɑ̀k / -kɔ̀k] *n.* Ⓒ a rooster trained for fighting. 싸움닭; 투계.

game fowl [⌐⌐] *n.* a domestic fowl trained for fighting. 싸움닭.

game·keep·er [géimkìːpər] *n.* Ⓒ 《Brit.》 a person who protects and takes care of wild animals and birds. 사냥터지기. [E.]

game law [⌐⌐] *n.* 《usu. *pl.*》 a law for the preservation of game-birds, etc. 수렵법(狩獵法).

game·ly [géimli] *adv.* like a gamecock; bravely. 싸움닭처럼; 용감히.

game·some [géimsəm] *adj.* full of play; ready to play. 장난치는; 까부는; 놀기 좋아하는.

game·ster [géimstər] *n.* a person who plays cards or other games for money; a gambler. 상습 도박꾼.

gam·in [gǽmin] *n.* 《F.》 a neglected boy, left to run about the streets. 부랑아; 집 없는 아이. [F.]

gam·ma [gǽmə] *n.* Ⓒ the third letter of the Greek alphabet (Γ, γ=English G, g). 감마《그리스어 알파벳의 셋째 글자》. [Gk.]

gamma rays [⌐-⌐] *n.* 《phys.》 one of three kinds of the rays forming part of the radiation of radioactive substance. 감마선.

gam·mer [gǽmər] *n.* an old country-woman. 시골 노파; 할머니(cf. *gaffer*). [*god-mother*]

gam·mon[1] [gǽmən] *n.* Ⓤ 《Brit. *colloq.*》 **1** nonsense. 허튼 소리; 잠꼬대. **2** a trick to deceive. 사기. — *vt., vi.* (P6; 1) deceive with lies; talk gammon. (거짓말로) 속이다. [→game]

gam·mon[2] [gǽmən] *n.* Ⓒ a pig's thigh which is salted and smoked. 돼지 허벅지 고기의 훈제. [F. *gambe* leg]

gam·ut [gǽmət] *n.* Ⓒ **1** the whole series of musical notes that can be produced by the human voice or musical instrument. 전음역(全音域). **2** the major scale. 장음계(長音階). **3** the whole range of anything. 전영역; 전범위; 전반. ¶ *the ~ of dramatic emotion from grief to gaiety* 비창에서 환희에 이르기까지의 온갖 극적인 감동 / *run* [*go*] *the* (*whole*) *~ of experience* 온갖 경험을 다하다. [L. *gamma ut,* words arbitrarily taken as names of notes]

gam·y [géimi] *adj.* (**gam·i·er, gam·i·est**) **1** having the smell of game that has been left uncooked too long. 엽조수육(獵鳥獸肉)의 냄새가 나는. 參考 약간 썩기 시작하여 맛이 좋을 때라고 함. **2** spirited; brave. 용감한; 원기가 좋은. ¶ *a ~ little fellow* 씩씩하고 귀여운 녀석. [*game, -y*]

gan·der [gǽndər] *n.* Ⓒ **1** a male goose. 거위 수컷. **2** 《*colloq.*》 a fool. 바보; 얼간이. **3** 《*sl.*》 a look; a glance. 얼핏 보기; 일별. ¶ *take a ~ at* … …을 힐끗 보다. [E.]

·gang [gæŋ] *n.* Ⓒ **1** a group of people working together for a bad purpose. (악한 따위의) 일단; 갱단. ¶ *a ~ of robbers* 강도단. **2** a group of persons; a group of workmen under one foreman. (사람들의) 집단〔무리〕; (노동자 등의) 한 집단〔팀, 무리〕. ¶ *I am sick of the whole ~ of them.* 녀석들은 모두가 지겹다. **3** a set of tools or machines arranged for use together. (도구의) 한 벌.
— *vi., vt.* (P2A; 6) 《*colloq.*》 **1** form (a gang); group together. 일단이 되다; 폭력단을 만들다. **2** attack in a group. 집단으로 공격하다. [E.]

gang up on, 《*colloq.*》 work together against; attack as a group. …에 대항하여 결속하다; 집단으로 공격하다.

gang·board [gǽŋbɔ̀ːrd] *n.* =gangplank.

Gan·ges [gǽndʒiːz], **the** *n.* a river which flows across North India into the Bay of Bengal. 갠지스 강(江).

gan·gli·a [gǽŋgliə] *n.* pl. of **ganglion.**

gan·gling [gǽŋgliŋ] *adj.* awkwardly tall and slender. 멋쩍게 키가 큰; 껑충한. [? → gang]

gan·gli·on [gǽŋgliən] *n.* (*pl.* **-gli·ons** or **-gli·a**) 《med.》 a group or a meeting-place of nerve. 신경절(神經節). [Gk. = tumor]

gang·plank [gǽŋplæ̀ŋk] *n.* Ⓒ a movable bridge by which people get on and off a ship. (배와 선창을 잇는) 건널판; 트랩. [*gang*]

〈gangplank〉

gan·grene [gǽŋgriːn, ⌐⌐] *n.* the decay of a part of the body caused by lack of blood-supply or by some injury. 괴저(壞疽).
— *vt., vi.* (P6; 1) affect or become affected with gangrene. 괴저에 걸리(게 하)다. [Gk.]

gang·ster [gǽŋstər] *n.* Ⓒ 《U.S. *colloq.*》 a member of a gang of criminals. 갱(의 한 사람); 악한. [*gang*]

gang·way [gǽŋwèi] *n.* Ⓒ **1** a passage between the seats in a theater, etc. (극장 따위) 좌석 사이의 통로. **2** 《naut.》 ⓐ a passage on either side of a ship's upper deck. 배의 상갑판 양쪽의 통로. ⓑ =gangplank. — *interj.* Stand aside and make room! 비켜라. [*gang*]

gan·try [gǽntri] *n.* **1** a four-footed wooden stand for barrels. (목재의) 통받침. **2** a frame for supporting a traveling crane or railway-signals. 갠트리《이동 크레인의 다리 모양의 구조물》; (철도의) 과선(跨線) 신호교(橋). [L. *canterius* nag]

·gaol [dʒeil] *n., vt.* 《Brit.》 =jail.

***gap** [gæp] *n.* Ⓒ **1** an opening. 금; 갈라진 틈; 구멍. ¶ *a ~ in a wall* 벽의 갈라진 틈. **2** ⓐ a period of time which is characterized by silence. (연속성의) 끊어짐; 중단. ¶ *a ~ in the conversation* 대화의 잠시 끊김 / *a momentary ~ in a siren's wailing* 사이렌 소리 사이사이의 끊어짐. ⓑ a space not filled. 빈곳; 공극(空隙). ¶ *a ~ in his memory* 그의 기억이 끊겨 있는 부분 / *a ~ in historical records* 역사 기록의 공백. **3** a difference of opinion, character, etc. (의견 따위의) 차이; 간격. ¶ *the generation ~* 세대간의 격차. **4** a mountain pass. 산길; 산골짜기. [↓]

fill* 〔*stop, supply*〕 *a gap, supply something lacking. 결함〔부족〕을 메우다.

gape [geip] *vi.* (P1,3) **1** ⓐ open the mouth wide; yawn. 입을 크게 벌리다; 하품하다. ⓑ be or become wide open. (구멍·상처 따위가) 벌어지다; 뚫려 있다. ¶ *A large hole gaped on the road.* 도로에 큰 구멍이 뻐끔히 뚫려 있었다. **2** stare with the mouth open as in amazement. (놀라서) 입을 딱 벌리고 보다.

***gape for* 〔*after*〕,** desire eagerly for. …을 갈망하다.

— *n.* Ⓒ **1** the act of gaping; a yawn. 입을 딱 벌리고 보기; 하품. **2** 《*the ~s*》 ⓐ a disease of birds causing them to die with wide-open mouths. (가금의) 부리를 헤벌리는 병. ⓑ a fit of yawning. 하품의 발작. **3** an opening; a gap. 구멍; 터진〔갈라진〕 틈(새).

● **gap·er** [ˊ-ər] *n.* [N. *gapa* yawn]

***ga·rage** [gərɑ́:ʒ, -rɑ́:dʒ / gǽrɑ:dʒ, -ridʒ] *n.* Ⓒ a building or place where automobiles and airplanes are kept or repaired. 자동차 차고; 자동차 수리장; (비행기의) 격납고. ¶ *put a car into a ~* 차를 차고에 넣다 / *take a car out of a ~* 차고에서 차를 꺼내다. — *vt.* (P6) put or keep (an automobile or airplane) in a garage. …을 차고〔격납고〕에 넣다. [F. *garer* protect]

garb [gɑ:rb] *n.* Ⓤ dress, esp. of a priest, judge, or prisoner. (특징 있는) 복장; 의상. ¶ *in the ~ of a sailor* 세일러복을 입고. — *vt.* (P6,13) 《usu. in *passive* or *reflexively*》 clothe. …의 복장을 하게 하다; 입히다. ¶ *be garbed in convict clothes* 죄수복을 입게 되다 / *The priest was garbed in black.* 목사는 검은 복장을 했다. [Teut. → gear]

gar·bage [gɑ́:rbidʒ] *n.* Ⓤ **1** things, esp. food, thrown away from a kitchen, store, etc. (부엌에서 나오는) 지스러기; 찌꺼기; 쓰레기. **2** 《*fig.*》 anything worthless. 무가치한 것; 시시한 것. ¶ *Don't talk such a load of ~!* 그런 시시한 소리 작작 해라. [E.]

gar·ble [gɑ́:rbəl] *vt.* (P6) **1** change (facts, stories, etc.) in a misleading way. (사실)을 굽히다; 왜곡하다. ¶ *a garbled account* 왜곡된 기사 / *~ the facts* 사실을 왜곡하다. **2** quote wrongly from (someone's statements or writings) without ill-will. …을 잘못 인용하다; 오전(誤傳)하다. ¶ *~ a quotation* 멋대로의 인용을 하다. [Arab. *kirbal* sieve]

gar·çon [gɑ:rsɔ̃:, ˊ-ˊ] *n.* 《F.》 (*pl.* *~s*) a waiter in a French restaurant etc. (레스토랑의) 급사; 보이.

:gar·den [gɑ́:rdn] *n.* Ⓒ **1** a place, usu. close to a house for growing vegetables, flowers, fruit, etc. 뜰; 정원; 채원(菜園); 화단; 과수원. ¶ *a flower ~* 꽃밭 / *a front ~* 앞마당 / *a back ~* 뒤뜰. **2** 《often *pl.*》 a park or place for public enjoyment where trees or flowers are planted and often animals are displayed. 공원; 유원지. ¶ *a zoological ~* 동물원 / *a botanical ~* 식물원.

— *adj.* **1** of, for, or found or grown in a garden. 정원의; 정원에 있는〔심는〕. ¶ *~ plants* 원예〔재배〕 식물(cf. *wild plants*) / *a ~ wall* 정원을 둘러싼 담. **2** 《*colloq.*》 of the familiar kind; common; ordinary. 익숙한; 흔한. ¶ *a common or ~ variety* 극히 흔한 재배종.

lead someone up the garden path, 《*sl.*》 deceive him; mislead him. 아무를 속이다; 오도(誤導)하다.

— *vt., vi.* (P6; 1) take care of a garden; work in a garden. 정원을 돌보다; 원예를 하다. [Teut. →yard]

***gar·den·er** [gɑ́:rdnər] *n.* Ⓒ a person who works in a garden or who is hired to take care of it. 정원사; 원정(園丁).

gar·de·ni·a [gɑ:rdí:niə, -njə] *n.* Ⓒ 《bot.》 a sweet-smelling white flower with waxy petals. 치자나무. [Person]

gar·den·ing [gɑ́:rdniŋ] *n.* Ⓤ the art or occupation of cultivating a garden. 원예(기술·직업). ¶ *I am very fond of ~.* 원예를 매우 좋아한다. [*garden*]

garden party [ˊ-ˋ-] *n.* a social gathering held out of doors in a garden or park. 가든 파티; 원유회(園遊會).

garden stuff [ˊ-ˋ] *n.* garden produce; fruit, vegetables, etc. (채원(菜園)에서) 만든 야채류; 청과물.

gar·fish [gɑ́:rfìʃ] *n.* (*pl.* **gar·fish** or **-fish·es**) 《fish》 a long-snouted green-boned fish. 동갈치. [Obs. *gare* spear]

gar·gan·tu·an [gɑ:rgǽntʃuən] *adj.* very large; huge; enormous. 거대한; 엄청나게 큰. ¶ *a ~ amounts of tea* 막대한 양의 차. [*Gargantua,* giant in Rabelais]

gar·gle [gɑ́:rgəl] *vi., vt.* (P6; 1) wash and make clean (the throat) with a liquid which is kept moving at the back of it. 양치질을 하다. ¶ *~ one's throat with salt water* 소금물로 양치질하여 목을 깨끗이 하다. — *n.* Ⓒ a liquid that is used for this purpose. 양치질 약; 양칫물. [↓]

〈gargoyle〉

gar·goyle [gɑ́:rgɔil]

G

n. Ⓒ a pipe for carrying off rain water, often in the form of a grotesque human being or animal. (괴물형상의) 처마 홈통 주둥이; 이무기돌. 參考 고딕 건축에 많음. [F. =throat]

gar·ish [gέəriʃ] *adj.* too bright; showy. 번쩍번쩍거리는; 야한. ● **gar·ish·ly** [-li] *adv.* **gar·ish·ness** [-nis] *n.* [→gaudy]

gar·land [gáːrlənd] *n.* Ⓒ **1** a circle of flowers or leaves to be worn on the head as an honor. 화환(花環); 화관(花冠). ¶ *gain* 〔*get, carry away, win*〕 *the* ~ (경기 따위에서) 승리를 얻다. **2** 《arch.》 a collection of poems or literary pieces. 시문집(詩文集); 선집(選集). — *vt.* (P6) crown or decorate (someone) with garlands. …에게 화관을 씌우다; …을 화환으로 꾸미다. [F.]

gar·lic [gáːrlik] *n.* Ⓤ 《bot.》 a strong-smelling plant of the lily family, used to flavor meats or salads. 마늘. ● **gar·lick·y** [-liki] *adj.* [E. =spear-leek]

·**gar·ment** [gáːrmənt] *n.* Ⓒ **1** any article of clothing, as a dress, coat, or hat. 의복. **2** an outer covering. 외의(外衣); 긴 웃옷; 외피. — *vt.* (P6,13) clothe. …에게 입히다. [→garnish]

gar·ner [gáːrnər] *vt.* (P6,7) gather and store away; get; obtain. …을 저장하다; 축적하다; 얻다; 손에 넣다. ¶ *wisdom garnered from bitter experience* 쓰라린 경험에서 얻은 지혜. — *n.* Ⓒ **1** a storehouse for grain. 곡물 창고. **2** a store of anything. 축적; 저장. [*granary*]

gar·net [gáːrnit] *n.* ⓊⒸ a precious stone, usu. with a deep-red color. 석류석(石榴石). — *adj.* deep-red. 심홍색(深紅色)의. [→(pome)granate]

gar·nish [gáːrniʃ] *n.* **1** Ⓤ something laid around food in a dish as a decoration. (요리에) 장식으로 곁들인 것; 고명. **2** Ⓒ a decoration. 장식(물). — *vt.* (P6,13) 《*with*》 decorate (esp. food). (음식·요리에 장식으로) 야채나 해초 따위를 곁들이다. ¶ ~ *boiled potatoes with chopped parsley* 삶은 감자에 다진 파슬리를 곁들이다. [F. *garnir* fortify]

gar·nish·ment [gáːrniʃmənt] *n.* ⓊⒸ decoration. 장식; 곁들여 꾸밈.

gar·ni·ture [gáːrnitʃər] *n.* ⓊⒸ decoration; garnish. 부속품; 장식물. [→garnish]

gar·ret [gǽrət] *n.* Ⓒ a room just below the roof of a house; an attic. (고미) 다락방. [↓]

be wrong in the garret, be crazy; be queer in the head. 미쳤다; 돌았다; 머리가 이상하다.

from cellar to garret =***from garret to kitchen,*** everywhere in the house. 온 집안 샅샅이〔구석구석〕.

·**gar·ri·son** [gǽrəsən] *n.* Ⓒ **1** a group of soldiers placed in a fort or town. 수비대〔병〕; 주둔군. **2** a place that has a garrison. 주둔지. ¶ *go* 〔*be sent*〕 *into* ~ 수비에 들어가다〔파견되다〕. — *vt.* (P6) **1** place soldiers in (a fort or town). …에 수비대를 두다. **2** defend (a place) by a garrison. …을 수비대로 지키다. [O.F. *garir* defend]

gar·rotte [gərόut, -rát / -rɔ́t] *vt.* (P6) strangle. 목졸라 죽이다. — *n.* strangulation. 교수형(刑). [Sp.]

gar·ru·li·ty [gərúːləti] *n.* Ⓤ the quality of being garrulous. 수다; 다변(多辯). [↓]

gar·ru·lous [gǽrjələs] *adj.* talking too much usu. about unimportant things. 수다스러운; 다변(多辯)의. ● **gar·ru·lous·ness** [-nis] *n.* [L.]

gar·ru·lous·ly [gǽrjələsli] *adv.* in a garrulous manner. 수다스럽게; 재잘재잘.

gar·ter [gáːrtər] *n.* Ⓒ **1** 《usu. *pl.*》 a pair of elastic bands or straps, used to hold up stockings or socks. 양말 대님; 가터. **2** 《*the G-*》 《Brit.》 the highest order of knighthood. 가터 훈장. ¶ *a knight of the Garter* 가터 훈작사(勳爵士) / *the Order of the Garter* 가터 훈위(勳位). — *vt.* (P6) fasten (a stocking or sock) with a garter. 양말 대님으로 (양말)을 고정시키다. [F.]

garter snake [∸–∸] *n.* a harmless snake with yellow stripes, most common in North America. 가터뱀《북아메리카에서 가장 일반적인 독 없는 뱀》.

:**gas** [gæs] *n.* Ⓤ **1** any airlike substance. 가스; 기체. **2** any kind of gas or a mixture of gases, used for lighting or heating. (온열·등(燈)용의) 가스. 語法 종류를 나타낼 때에는 부정관사 또는 복수형을 취함. ¶ *fuel* ~ 연료 가스 / *propane* ~ 프로판 가스 / *a* ~ *lamp* 가스 램프 / *a hotel heated with* ~ 가스 난방의 호텔 / *turn down the* ~ 가스(등) 불(빛)을 약하게 하다 / *turn on* 〔*off*〕 *the* ~ 가스를 틀다〔끄다〕. **3** 《coal mining》 a mixture of explosive gas and air. 폭발 가스. **4** poisonous gas used in warfare. 독가스. ¶ *tear* ~ 최루가스. **5** 《U.S. *colloq.*》 gasoline. 가솔린. ¶ *be out of* ~ 가솔린〔기름〕이 다 떨어지다. **6** 《*sl.*》 empty talk. 헛된〔빈〕 이야기; 허풍. ¶ *Don't pay any attention; it's all* ~*!* 모른체 해라. 거 다 뻥이다.

step 〔***tramp, tread***〕 ***on the gas,*** 《U.S. *colloq.*》 accelerate; speed up. 속력을 내다; 서두르다.

— *vt.* (**gassed, gas·sing**) (P6) **1** supply (something) with gas. …에 가스를 공급하다. **2** attack (the enemy) by poisonous gas. (적)을 독가스로 공격하다. **3** 《*colloq.*》 supply (something) with gasoline. …에 가솔린을 보급하다. — *vi.* (P1,2A) 《*colloq.*》 talk in an empty way; boast. 헛된 이야기를 하다; 허풍을 떨다. [Gk. *kháos chaos*]

gas up, supply one's car with gasoline. (자동차 가솔린 탱크에) 기름을 채우다.

gas·bag [gǽsbæ̀g] *n.* Ⓒ **1** a bag for holding gas. (비행기·기구 따위의) 가스낭(囊). **2** 《*colloq.*》 a person who talks in an empty way. 쓸데없는 말과 허풍이 많은 사람.

gas burner [∸–] *n.* **1** an outlet for gas to be burned. 가스 버너. **2** =gas-stove.

gas chamber [ㅅ̀ㅡ] *n.* a chamber in which people are executed by poison gas. 가스 처형실.

gas cooker [ㅅ̀ㅡ] *n.* a stove for cooking by gas. 가스 레인지.

gas engine [ㅅ̀ㅡ] *n.* one driven by regular explosions of gas in a cylinder. 가스 엔진〔기관(機關)〕.

ga·se·ous [gǽsiəs, -sjəs] *adj.* of or like gas. 가스의; 가스 모양의. ¶ ~ *matter* 기체.

gas fire [ㅅ̀ㅅ] *n.* (a stove for) a fire burning gas to heat a room. 가스불; 가스 난로.

gas fitter [ㅅ̀ㅡ] *n.* a person whose work is putting in and repairing gas-fittings. 가스공(工); 가스 기구〔설비〕 수리〔설치〕인.

gas fittings [ㅅ̀ㅡ] *n. pl.* **1** the work of a gas-fitter. 가스 설비 공사(업). **2** the apparatus such as pipes, burners, etc., for heating or lighting with gas. 가스 기구(器具)(류(類)); 가스등(燈).

gash [gæʃ] *n.* Ⓒ a long, deep wound or cut. 깊은 상처; 중상. ¶ *cut a deep ~ in* … 에 깊은 상처를 입히다. — *vt.* (P6) make a long, deep wound or cut in (something); cut deeply. …에 깊은 상처를 입히다; 깊이 베다. ¶ *He gashed his hand with a sharp knife.* 예리한 칼에 손을 크게 베었다. [F.]

gas helmet [ㅅ̀ㅡ] *n.* =gas mask.

gas·i·fy [gǽsəfài] *vt.* (**-fied**) (P6) change (something) into gas. …을 가스로 바꾸다; 기체로 하다; 기화하다. [*gas*]

gas·ket [gǽskit] *n.* ⓊⒸ **1** 《naut.》 a rope for fastening a sail. 접은 돛을 묶는 밧줄. **2** 《mech.》 any thin material put between metal surfaces in an engine to make the joint tight. 가스켓《기계의 결합부를 메우는 고무·금속 따위의 패킹》. [It.]

gas mantle [ㅅ̀ㅡ] *n.* a lacelike network placed over a gas-burner, which glows and gives off light when heated. 가스 맨틀《가스등·석류 램프 따위의 불꽃 덮개; 점화되면 백열광을 발함》. [*gas*]

gas mask [ㅅ̀ㅅ] *n.* a device that covers nose, mouth, and eyes as a protection against poisonous gases. 방독면.

gas meter [ㅅ̀ㅡ] *n.* an apparatus for measuring the amount of gas that passes through it. 가스 계량기; 가스미터.

***gas·o·line, -lene** [gæsəlíːn, ㅅ̀ㅡ] *n.* Ⓤ a colorless liquid which catches fire very easily, used as fuel for an automobile, etc. 가솔린; 휘발유. 參考 영국에서는 petrol 을 씀, 또 미국에서는 gas 라고도 함. [*gas*]

gas·om·e·ter [gæsɑ́mitər / -ɔ́m-] *n.* Ⓒ **1** an apparatus for holding and measuring gas. 가스 계량기. **2** 《Brit.》 a tank for holding gas. 가스 탱크. 參考 gas holder라고도 함. [*gas*]

***gasp** [gæsp, gɑːsp] *n.* Ⓒ the act of breathing with a quick, painful effort. 헐떡임; 숨막힘; 숨참.

at the* 〔*one's*〕 *last gasp, at the last moment; about to die. 임종〔운명〕시에; 마지막 순간에; 죽어 가고.

— *vi.* (P1,2A) breathe hard; pant. 헐떡이다. ¶ ~ *for breath* 숨이 차 헐떡이다 / ~ *at the sight* 그 광경에 숨이 막히다. — *vt.* (P6,7) 《*out*》 speak breathlessly. 헐떡거리며 …을 말하다. ¶ ~ *out the outline* 헐떡이며 대강을 말하다. [N.]

gasp out* 〔*away*〕 *one's life =***gasp one's last,*** breathe one's last; die. 마지막 숨을 거두다; 죽다.

gas·per [gǽspər, gɑ́ːs-] *n.* 《Brit. *sl.*》 a cheap cigarette. 값싼 궐련(cf. *fag*). [N.]

gas range [ㅅ̀ㅅ] *n.* 《U.S.》 =gas cooker.

gas station [ㅅ̀ㅡ] *n.* 《U.S.》 =filling-station.

gas stove [ㅅ̀ㅅ] *n.* a cooking-stove heated by gas. (요리용) 가스 레인지. [*gas*]

gas·sy [gǽsi] *adj.* (**-si·er, -si·est**) **1** full of gas. 가스로 가득찬. **2** like gas. 가스(질·모양)의; 가스 같은. [*gas*]

gas·ter·o·pod [gǽstərəpɑ̀d / -pɔ̀d] *n.* =gastropod.

gas·tric [gǽstrik] *adj.* of the stomach. 위(胃)의. ¶ ~ *juice* 위액 / ~ *ulcer* 위궤양. [Gk. *gastēr* stomach]

gas·tri·tis [gæstráitis] *n.* inflammation of the stomach. 위염(胃炎).

gas·tro- [gǽstro(u) / -trə] *pref.* (of) the stomach; the stomach and. '복부, 위(胃), 위와 …와의' 의 뜻. 語法 모음 앞에서는 gastr-. [Gk. *gastēr*]

gas·tron·o·my [gæstrɑ́nəmi / -trɔ́n-] *n.* the science or art of cooking and choosing good food. 미식학(美食學). [*gastro-*]

gas·tro·pod [gǽstrəpɑ̀d / -pɔ̀d] *n.* 《zool.》 the class of snails. 복족류(腹足類). [↑, Gk. *pous* foot]

gas·works [gǽswə̀ːrks] *n. pl.* 《usu. used as *sing.*》 a place where gas is made. 가스 제조소. [*gas*]

gat [gæt] *n.* 《*colloq.*》 a gun; a pistol. 권총. [U.S. *Gat*ling gun =machine gun]

⁝**gate** [geit] *n.* Ⓒ **1** ⓐ a part in a wall or fence which can be opened and closed. 문《출입용 대문·성문 따위》. ¶ *open* 〔*close*〕 *the* ~ 문을 열다〔닫다〕 / *enter the front* ~ 정문으로 들어가다 / *go* 〔*pass*〕 *through the* ~ 문을 빠져 나가다 / *at the* ~ *of death* 죽음의 직전에. ⓑ =gateway. **2** a door or valve to control or stop the flow of water in a pipe, canal, etc. 수문; 갑문; (파이프의) 밸브. **3** ⓐ the number of people who pay to see a contest. (운동 경기·연주회 따위의) 유료 입장자 수. ¶ *There was a* ~ *of thousands.* 몇 천이나 되는 입장자가 있었다. ⓑ the amount of money received at the entrance gate. 입장료 총액(=gate money). ¶ *The game had a good* ~. 경기는 많은 입장 수입이 있었다.

get the gate, 《U.S. *colloq.*》 be discharged.

해고되다; 내쫓기다.
give someone the gate, 《U.S. *colloq.*》 discharge. …을 해고하다; 내쫓다.
— *vt.* (P6) confine (a student) to college entirely or after certain hours as a punishment. (영국 대학에서 학생에게) 외출을 금지하다; (벌로서) 금족을 명하다. [E.]

gate-crash·er [géitkræ̀ʃər] *n.* 《*colloq.*》 a person who attends a party, dance, etc. without a ticket or invitation. (초대권·입장권 없이 들어가는) 무단 입장자; 불청객(不請客).

gate·house [géithàus] *n.* Ⓒ a house built at or over a gate. 수위실.

gate·keep·er [géitkìːpər] *n.* Ⓒ a person who is in charge of a gate. 문지기; 수위; 건널목지기.

gate-leg table [géitlèg⌐] *n.* a folding table whose flaps are supported on gate-like legs. 접(摺)탁자.

gate·post [géitpòust] *n.* Ⓒ the post on the side of a gate. 문기둥.
between you and me and the gatepost, speaking as a secret matter between the two of us. 우리끼리의 내밀한 이야기지만.

***gate·way** [géitwèi] *n.* Ⓒ **1** an opening or passage fitted with a gate. 문; 출입구; 현관; 통로. **2** 《*fig.*》 a way of means of approach. (…에) 이르는 길[입구]; 수단. ¶ *a ~ to knowledge* [*success*] 지식[성공]에의 길 / *New York is a ~ to the United States.* 뉴욕은 미국으로 들어가는 길목이다.

G

:gath·er [gǽðər] *vt.* **1** (P6,7) cause (persons or things) to come together in one place or group; assemble; collect. …을 (한 곳·한 무리로) 모으다; 소집하다. ¶ *~ an army* 군을 소집하다 / *~ fragments* 조각들을 모으다 / *~ people about one* 자기 주변에 사람을 모으다 / *Children* (*were*) *gathered about her.* 아이들이 그녀 주위에 모였다 / *We all gathered there after supper.* 저녁을 먹고 우리 모두는 거기에 모였다. **2** (P6,7) ⓐ bring together from various places, sources, etc.; collect. (여기저기서·하나씩) 모으다; 수집하다; 주워 모으다. ¶ *~ shells* [*pebbles*] 조가비를[조약돌을] 주워 모으다 / *~ evidence* 증거를 수집하다 / *~ data from all sources* 모든 출처로부터 자료를 모으다 / *~ sticks for a bonfire* 모닥불을 피우기 위해 나무토막을 모으다. ⓑ select and take in; pick; reap; harvest. 채집하다; 따다; 거둬들이다. ¶ *~ grapes* [*flowers*] 포도를[꽃을] 따다 / *~ crops* 곡물을 수확하다. **3** (P6) collect (oneself or one's energies) for some action; arouse; stir up. (힘 따위를) 모으다; 결집하다; 분발하다. ¶ *~ up one's strength for a task* 일을 위해 힘을 집중하다. **4** (P6,11) 《*from*》 put together in the mind; reason; learn; conclude. 추정[추측]하다; 알다; 결론을 내리다. ¶ *~ the meaning of the remark* 그 말의 의미를 추정하다 / *~ from her tone* [*remark*] *that…* 그녀의 어조[말]로 보아 …로 추찰(推察)하다 / *From this it was gathered that….* 이것으로 미루어 …하다고 추측되었다. **5** (P6,7) ⓐ draw (cloth) in small folds; pull together in folds. (천에) 주름을 잡다. ¶ *a gathered skirt* 주름 치마. ⓑ pull or draw around or close to a person or thing; wrap. (사람·물건 주위에) 당기다; 두르다; 싸다. ¶ *He gathered his scarf around his neck.* 목도리를 당겨 목에 둘렀다 / *She gathered the crying child in her arms.* 그녀는 우는 아이를 두 팔로 가슴에 껴안았다. **6** (P6) draw (the brow) in wrinkle. (눈썹을) 찌푸리다. ¶ *~ one's brows* 눈살을 찌푸리다. **7** (P6) acquire or gain gradually; make (something) greater in amount. …을 서서히 늘리다[더하다]; 증가하다; 조금씩 모으다. ¶ *~ pace* [*speed*] 점차 속도를 더하다 / *~ a million dollars* 백만 달러를 모으다 / *The storm gathered force.* 폭풍우는 점차 그 기세를 더했다. — *vi.* **1** (P1,2A) come together; grow by coming together; assemble; accumulate; increase. 모이다; 모여들다; 집합[집결]하다; 축적하다; 증대하다. ¶ *gathering dark* 점차 더해가는 저녁 어둠 / *the frost that gathers on the windowpane* 창유리에 엉겨붙은 성에 / *at gathering speed* 가속하여 / *~ and go* 집합한 다음 가다 / *Clouds were gathering in the west.* 서쪽 하늘에 구름이 끼고 있었다 / *Suspicion was gathering rapidly in his mind.* 그의 마음 속에 급속히 의혹이 더해가고 있었다. **2** (P1) (of a boil, sore, etc.) swell up with pus; reach the state of bursting. (종기 따위가) 곪다; 곪아 터지게 되다 (cf. *come to a head*). **3** become wrinkled. 주름이 지다[잡히다].
be gathered to one's fathers, die. 죽다.
gather flesh, put on flesh. 살이 붙다.
gather head, **a**) acquire strength. 세력을 증가하다. **b**) swell as a festering sore. 종기가 커지다[곪다].
gather up, **a**) pick up and place together. 주워모으다. ¶ *~ up scattered papers* 흩어진 서류를 주워모으다. **b**) draw together and make more compact; sum up. 요약하다; 개괄(概括)하다. **c**) draw up (one's arms, legs, etc.). (팔·다리 따위를) 오므리다. **d**) ⇨*vt.* 3.
gather oneself up [***together***], get ready to make an effort. 전력을 집중하다.
gather way, (of a ship) begin to move; move with increasing speed. (배가) 움직이기 시작하다; 속력을 더하다.
— *n.* Ⓒ 《usu. *pl.*》 a small fold or pleat made when cloth is gathered. 주름(⇨*vt.* 5 ⓐ). [E.]

***gath·er·ing** [gǽðəriŋ] *n.* Ⓒ **1** a meeting in a group or team. 모임; 집회. ¶ *a social ~* 친목회; 사교적인 모임 / *a political ~* 정치 집회. **2** a collection of money, things, etc. 수금; 채집; 집적(集積). **3** a swelling on the body with pus in it. 화농(化膿); 종기.

GATT, Gatt [gæt] *n.* General Agreement on Tariffs and Trade. 관세 및 무역에 관한 일반 협정; 가트(cf. *WTO*).

gauche [gouʃ] *adj.* 《F.》 awkward; lacking in social ease and grace. 서투른; 어색한; 세련되지 못한; 퉁명스런. [F. =left-handed]

gau·cho [gáutʃou] *n.* (*pl.* **-chos**) a South American cowboy, usu. of mixed European and Indian descent. 남아메리카 대초원의 카우보이《흔히 인디언과 백인과의 혼혈》. [? Sp.]

gaud [gɔ:d] *n.* Ⓒ a cheap, showy ornament. (외양만 번지르르한) 값싼 물건; 싸구려 장식물. [L. *gaudeo* rejoice]

gaud·i·ly [gɔ́:dili] *adv.* in a gaudy manner. 야하게; 상스럽게.

gaud·y [gɔ́:di] *adj.* (**gaud·i·er, gaud·i·est**) too bright and gay; showy. 야한; 화려한; 속악(俗惡)한; 상스러운. ¶ *a ~ dress* 야한 옷. ● **gaud·i·ness** [-nis] *n.*

gauge [geidʒ] *n.* Ⓒ **1** a standard measurement. (포 따위의 구경의) 표준 치수[규격]. **2** an instrument for measuring size, amount, etc. 자; 계기(計器). ¶ *a rain* [*wind*] *~* 우량[풍속]계 / *a pressure ~* 압력계. **3** (of railway lines) the distance between railroad rails. 궤간(軌間). ¶ *broad* [*narrow*] *~* 광궤(廣軌)[협궤(狹軌)]. **4** the depth to which a fully loaded ship goes down to in water. 만재 흘수(滿載吃水). **5** 《*fig.*》 a means of judging or estimating. (판단·평가의) 방법; 수단; 기준. ¶ *the ~ of someone's talents* 아무의 재능의 평가 기준.

take the gauge of, measure; estimate. …을 재다[측정하다]; 평가하다.

— *vt.* (P6) **1** measure accurately. …을 정확히 재다[측정하다]. **2** estimate; judge. …을 평가하다; 판단하다. ¶ *~ someone* [*someone's character*] 아무를[아무의 성격을] 평가하다. [F.]

Gau·guin [gougǽŋ], **Paul** *n.* (1848-1903) a French painter. 고갱《프랑스의 화가》.

Gaul [gɔ:l] *n.* **1** an ancient country in West Europe. 골《서유럽의 고대 국가》. **2** one of the Celtic inhabitants of ancient Gaul. 골의 주민. **3** 《*joc.*》 a Frenchman. 프랑스 사람.

gaunt [gɔ:nt] *adj.* **1** very thin; lean. 몹시 여윈; 마른. ¶ *be ~ from hunger* 굶주려 수척해 있다 / *be ~ with travel* 여행 피로로 여위어 있다. **2** (of a place, etc.) desolate; bleak. 황량한; 쓸쓸한; 음울한. [N.]

gaunt·let[1] [gɔ́:ntlit, gά:nt-] *n.* Ⓒ **1** an iron glove used by soldiers in the Middle Ages to protect the hand. (갑옷의) 철제 장갑. **2** 《fencing, riding》 a heavy glove with a long cuff. (보호용의) 긴 장갑. [Sw. *wante*]

fling [***throw***] ***down the gauntlet,*** make a challenge to (someone). …에게 도전하다.

take [***pick***] ***up the gauntlet,*** accept a challenge. 도전에 응하다.

gaunt·let[2] [gɔ́:ntlit, gά:nt-] *n.* Ⓤ a former military punishment, in which the offender was made to run between two rows of persons who strike with switches or weapons. 옛날 군대의 형벌 《과실을 범한 사람을 두 줄로 선 사람들 사이로 달리게 하여 채찍 따위로 매맞게 함》. [Sw. *gata* street, *lopp* course, run]

run the gauntlet, be criticized severely. 호되게 비평을 받다. ¶ *He ran the ~ of newspapers attacks.* 언론에서 호된 공격을 받았다.

gauss [gaus] *n.* 《electr.》 a unit of intensity of a magnetic field. 가우스《자속 밀도(磁束密度)의 cgs 전자(電磁) 단위》. [Person]

gauze [gɔ:z] *n.* Ⓤ **1** a thin, light cloth which can be seen through. (내비치는) 얇은 직물; 가제. **2** a thin haze. 엷은 안개. **3** a screen of very fine wire. (가는 철사로 짠) 철망(鐵網). [F.]

gauz·y [gɔ́:zi] *adj.* (**gauz·i·er, gauz·i·est**) like gauze; thin and light. 가제 같은; 얇은; 비치는. ¶ *a ~ mist* 엷은 안개. [↑]

:gave [geiv] *v.* p. of **give.**

gav·el [gǽvəl] *n.* Ⓒ a small hammer used by a chairman or an auctioneer to signal for attention or order. (의장·경매인 등의) 망치; 사회봉. ¶ *pound with the ~* = *wield the ~* 의장을 맡아 보다. [Du.]

ga·votte [gəvάt / -vɔ́t] *n.* Ⓒ a lively old French dance; music for this dance. 가보트《프랑스의 활발한 옛 춤》; 가보트 곡(曲). [Prov.]

gawk [gɔ:k] *n.* Ⓒ an awkward, stupid, or bashful person. 멍청이; 얼뜨기; 뱅충이. — *vi.* (P1) 《U.S. *colloq.*》 stare stupidly. 멍청히 바라보다. [N.]

gawk·y [gɔ́:ki] *adj.* (**gawk·i·er, gawk·i·est**) awkward; stupid; bashful. 굼뜬; 멍청한; 데퉁스러운; 뱅충맞은. ● **gawk·i·ly** [-li] *adv.* **gawk·i·ness** [-nis] *n.*

:gay [gei] *adj.* **1** cheerful; merry. 즐거운; 쾌활[명랑]한. ¶ *~ music* 명랑한 음악 / *a ~ laugh* 유쾌한 웃음 / *~ spirits* 들뜬 기분 / *She is as ~ as a lark.* 그녀는 종달새처럼 명랑하다. **2** bright-colored; showy. (색이) 산뜻한; 화려한; 현란한. ¶ *~ colors* 산뜻한 색채 / *~ ornaments* 현란한 장식. **3** fond of pleasures; not moral. 방탕한; 방종한. ¶ *a ~ woman* 몸가짐이 헤픈 여자; 창녀 / *~ quarters* 홍등가; 화류계 / *He is leading a ~ life.* 방탕한 생활을 하고 있다. **4** 《*colloq.*》 homosexual. 동성애의. [F.]

gay·e·ty [géiəti] *n.* =gaiety.

gay·ly [géili] *adv.* =gaily.

:gaze [geiz] *vi.* (P1,2A,3) 《*into, at, on, upon*》 look long and steadily. 한참 바라보다; 눈여겨보다; 응시하다. ¶ *~ at* [*on, upon*] *someone's face* 아무의 얼굴을 응시하다 / *~ up at the stars* 별들을 지그시 한참 바라보다. — *n.* Ⓒ a steady look. 응시; 주시. ¶ *fix one's ~ on someone* 아무를 응시하다 / *stand at ~* 눈여겨보다. [Sw. *gaza* stare]

ga·ze·bo [gəzí:bou, -zéi-] *n.* (*pl.* **-bos**) a shelter or hut, usu. in a garden, where

G

one can sit and look at the view. 전망대; 정자. [?]

ga·zelle [gəzél] *n.* (*pl.* **-zelles** or **-zelle**) any of numerous small, graceful, and swift African and Asian antelopes noted for their soft lustrous eyes. 가젤《작은 영양(羚羊)의 총칭》. [Arab.]

gaz·er [géizər] *n.* a person who gazes. 쳐다보는[응시하는] 사람. ¶ *a star-gazer* 점성가; 천문학자. [→gaze]

ga·zette [gəzét] *n.* Ⓒ **1** a newspaper. 신문. **2** 《Brit.》 a government journal or news sheet. 관보. ¶ *an official* ~ 관보 / *be in the* ~ 관보에 공시되다. — *vt.* (P6) 《usu. in *passive*》 publish (something) in a gazette. …을 관보로 공고하다. ¶ *be gazetted out* 관보로 사직이 보도되다. [It.]

gaz·et·teer [gæ̀zətíər] *n.* Ⓒ **1** a dictionary or an index of geographical names. 지명 사전; 지명 색인. **2** 《*arch.*》 a person who writes for a gazette. 관보 기자.

G.B. Great Britain.

G.C.M. 《math.》 greatest common measure. 최대 공약수.

•**gear** [giər] *n.* Ⓒ **1** a set of metal wheels with teeth in a machine which makes it go faster or slower. 기어; 전동(傳動) 장치; 톱니바퀴. ¶ *a high* [*top*] ~ 고속 기어 / *reduction* ~ 감속 기어 / *put* [*throw*] *the car in* [*into*] ~ 차에 기어를 넣다 / *shift gears* 기어를 바꾸다. **2** 《*collectively*》 a set of things used for some special purpose. (어떤 일·활동에 쓰이는) 장치; 도구; 용구. ¶ *fishing* ~ 어구(漁具); 낚시 도구 / *sporting* ~ 스포츠 용구 / *medical* ~ 의료 기구 / *climbing* ~ 등산 용구. **3** working order or condition. 상태; 컨디션.

all one's worldly gear, all the things which one owns. (가지고 다닐 수 있는) 개인의 소유물.

in gear, with the gears connected in order to work; in working order. 기어가 걸려; 상태가 좋아. ¶ *talk full in* ~ 혀가 아주 매끄럽게 돌다.

out of gear, **a**) with the gears disconnected. 기어가 맞물리지 않아. **b**) 《*fig.*》 (of non-material things) not working smoothly. 상태가 나빠.

— *vt.* (P7) furnish (something) with gear; connect (something) by gears. …에 전동 장치[기어]를 달다; 기어로 연결하다.

— *vi.* (P1,2A) (of gears) fit together. (기어가) 꼭 맞물리다. [Teut. *garwu* ready]

gear·ing [gíəriŋ] *n.* the system of gears. 전동(傳動) 장치; 톱니바퀴 장치.

geck·o [gékou] *n.* (*pl.* **-o(e)s**) 《animal》 도마뱀붙이. [Malay]

gee [dʒiː] *interj.* **1** (to a horse) a word of command to horses, oxen, etc. to turn to the right or go ahead. 어디여; 우(右)로; 이러. [?] **2** 《U.S.》 an exclamation of surprise, etc. 아이고; 깜짝이야. [*Jesus*]

:**geese** [giːs] *n.* pl. of **goose**.

gee·zer [gíːzər] *n.* 《*sl.*》 an old fellow who is often thought to be a little strange. 좀 이상한 사람[노인]. [*guise* mummer]

Ge·hen·na [gihénə] *n.* Hell. 지옥. [Heb.]

Gei·ger(-Mül·ler) counter [gáigər (mjúːlər)-] *n.* 《phys.》 a device used to detect and measure radioactivity. 가이거(뮐러) 계수관(計數管)《방사능 측정기》. [Person]

Gei·gers [gáigərz] *n. pl.* 《*colloq.*》 radioactive particles and radiation collectively. 방사능; 방사성 입자. [Person]

gel [dʒel] *n.* a jellylike or solid material formed from a colloidal solution. 겔《콜로이드 용액의 고체 상태》. — *vi.* (P2A) (**gelled, gel·ling**) form or become a gel. 겔이 되다; 교질화(膠質化)하다. [↓]

gel·a·tin, -tine [dʒélətən] *n.* Ⓤ clear, jellylike substance made from animal bones or hoofs or from vegetables. 젤라틴; 아교. ¶ ~ *paper* (사진의) 젤라틴 감광지 / *vegetable* ~ 우무. [→jelly]

ge·lat·i·nous [dʒəlǽtənəs] *adj.* jellylike; containing gelatin. 젤라틴 모양의[질의].

geld [geld] *vt.* (**geld·ed** or **gelt**) (P6) get rid of the male glands of (a horse or other animal); remove the testicles of. …을 거세하다; 불까다. [N. *geldr* barren]

geld·ing [géldiŋ] *n.* a gelded animal, esp. a horse. 거세된 동물《특히 수말》.

gel·id [dʒélid] *adj.* cold as ice; frozen. 얼음같이 차가운; 극한(極寒)의. [L. *gelu* frost, cold]

gelt [gelt] *v.* p. and pp. of **geld.**

•**gem** [dʒem] *n.* Ⓒ **1** a precious stone; a jewel. 보석; 보옥. **2** anything very valuable and beautiful. 귀중한[아름다운] 사람[것]; 일품; 주옥. ¶ *a literary* ~ 주옥 같은 문학 작품 / *a* ~ *of architecture* 건축의 정수(精粹) / *the* ~ *of the whole collection* 전 소장품 중의 일품. — *vt.* (**gemmed, gem·ming**) (P6) set or adorn (something) with gems. …을 보석으로 장식하다; …에 보석을 박다. ¶ *a ring gemmed with diamonds* 다이아몬드 반지 / *Blossoms* ~ *the tree.* 꽃들은 나무를 보석처럼 치장했다. ●**gem·my** [dʒémi] *adj.* [L. *gemma* bud, gem]

gem·i·nate [dʒémənèit] *vt., vi.* (P6; 1)make or become double. 2배로 하다; 2배가 되다. [-nit, -nèit] *adj.* occurring in pairs. 두 개 한 조의; 쌍생(雙生)의; 한 쌍의. ●**gem·i·na·tion** [dʒèmənéiʃən] *n.* [↓]

Gem·i·ni [dʒémənài, -ni] *n. pl.* 《astron.》 a northern constellation in the zodiac containing two bright stars. 쌍둥이자리. [L. =twins]

gen [dʒen] *n.* 《Brit. *colloq.*》 information published for all ranks. (모든 사람에게 공표되는) 일반 정보. [*general*]

Gen. General; 《Bible》 Genesis.

gen. gender; general; genitive.

gen·darme [ʒɑ́ːndɑːrm] *n.* 《F.》 an armed policeman; an MP. (무장) 경찰관; 헌

병(憲兵).

gen·dar·me·rie [ʒɑːndáːrməri] *n.* 《F.》 a body of gendarmes. 헌병대.

gen·der [dʒéndər] *n.* Ⓤ **1** 《gram.》 the grouping of nouns into three classes, such as masculine, feminine, neuter; Ⓒ one of these classes. (문법에서) 성(性). ¶ *the common* 〔*masculine, feminine, neuter*〕 ~ 통(通)〔남, 여, 중〕성. **2** 《*colloq.*》 sex. 성(性). [→genus]

gene [dʒiːn] *n.* Ⓒ 《biol.》 a small unit in a cell that causes a special characteristic of the parent to pass on to the child; a unit or element of heredity in the chromosome. 유전 원질; 유전(인)자; 염색체. [↓]

ge·ne·a·log·i·cal [dʒìːniəlɑ́dʒikəl / -lɔ́dʒ-] *adj.* of genealogy. 가계〔계보〕의; 계통의; 계도(系圖)의. ¶ *a ~ table* 계도〔족보〕. [↓]

ge·ne·al·o·gist [dʒìːniǽlədʒist] *n.* Ⓒ a person who studies genealogy. 계보학자(系譜學者).

ge·ne·al·o·gy [dʒìːniǽlədʒi] *n.* ⓊⒸ (*pl.* **-gies**) the (science of the) historical development of families and also of animals and plants. 계도; 계통; 가계; 혈통; 계보학(系譜學). [Gk. *genea* race]

gen·er·a [dʒénərə] *n.* pl. of **genus**.

:**gen·er·al** [dʒénərəl] *adj.* **1** of all; for all; common to many or most. 전반적인; 보편적인; 전체의. ¶ *a ~ opinion* 여론 / *a ~ strike* 총파업 / *a ~ election* 총선거(cf. *by-election*) / *a ~ meeting* 총회 / *a ~ examination* 전과목 시험 / *work for the ~ good of society* 사회의 전반적인 이익을 위해서 일하다. **2** ⓐ not limited to one kind, class, etc.; not restricted; not special. 하나로 한정되어 있지 않은; 다방면에 걸친; 제한되지 않은; 전문적이 아닌. ¶ *~ affairs* 총무; 서무 / *~ education* 〔*culture*〕 일반 교육〔교양〕 / *a ~ magazine* 〔*hospital*〕 종합 잡지〔병원〕 / *the ~ public* 일반 대중 / *a general practitioner* 일반의(醫)(cf. *specialist*) / *a ~ dealer* 잡화상(商). ⓑ not limited in application. 대부분에 적용되는〔공통의〕. ¶ *~ truth* 일반 진리 / *~ principles* 일반 원칙; 통칙. **3** common; usual; ordinary. 보통의; 통상의; 널리 행해지는. ¶ *~ pronunciation* 통상의 발음 / *a ~ custom* 널리 행해지는 습관 / *a word in ~ use* 세상에서 널리 쓰이는 말. **4** not detailed; not exact; not definite; vague. 개략의; 대체의; 명확하지 않은; 구체적이 아닌; 막연한. ¶ *a ~ description* 개괄적인 묘사 / *~ instructions* 개략적인〔대충의〕 지시 / *a ~ idea* 막연한 지식 / *speak in ~ terms* 모호한 말을 하다 / *His statement is too ~.* 그의 진술은 너무 애매하다. **5** 《after some official titles》 chief; head; of the highest rank. 총(總)…; …장(長); 최상위의. ¶ *a postmaster ~* 우정 장관 / *the attorney ~* 법무 장관 / *a governor ~* 총독. **6** above the rank of colonel. (대령 계급 이상의) 장성의; 장군의. ¶ *a ~ officer* 장관(將官). — *n.* Ⓒ **1** an army officer of high rank who commands many soldiers. 장군; 육군 대장(cf. *admiral*). **2** a chief; a head. 장(長). [→genus]

as a general rule, in most cases; usually. 대개; 대체로; 일반적으로.

in* (*the*) *general, usually; for the most part; generally. 보통; 대개; 일반적으로. ¶ *Children in ~ are fond of play.* 어린이는 대개 장난을 좋아한다.

in general way, ordinarily. 보통.

gen·er·a·lis·si·mo [dʒènərəlísəmòu] *n.* (*pl.* **-s**) the commander in chief of all or several armies in the field. 대원수. [It. = general]

gen·er·al·i·ty [dʒènərǽləti] *n.* (*pl.* **-ties**) **1** Ⓤ the state of being general. 일반성; 보편성. **2** Ⓤ a general and rather vague statement. 개략; 개설. **3** Ⓒ a general principle or rule. 일반 원칙; 통칙; 통성; 보편적 진리. **4** Ⓤ the great part; the mass. 대부분; 대다수. ¶ *the ~ of people* 대개의 사람들 / *The ~ of the nation were opposed to the policy.* 대다수 국민들은 그 정책에 반대였다. [*general*]

in generalities, vaguely. 막연히.

gen·er·al·i·za·tion [dʒènərəlizéiʃən] *n.* **1** Ⓤ the act of generalizing. 종합; 개괄; 귀납. **2** Ⓒ a general idea or rule. 개념; 통칙.

gen·er·al·ize [dʒénərəlàiz] *vt.* (P6,13) **1** treat (something) as a whole. …을 일반화하다; 일반론으로서 다루다(opp. specialize). **2** form (a general idea or rule) from particular facts. (일반적 법칙)을 얻다; 귀납(歸納)하다. **3** make generally known. …을 널리 보급시키다. — *vi.* (P1) form into a general rule. 개괄(概括)하다; 개론하다.

:**gen·er·al·ly** [dʒénərəli] *adv.* **1** most of the time; usually. 일반적으로; 대개는. ¶ *I ~ get up at seven these days.* 요즈음 나는 대개 7시에 일어난다 / *Dogs ~ love their masters.* 개는 일반적으로 주인을 좋아한다. **2** in most cases; widely. 대체로; 널리. ¶ *The man was ~ respected.* 그 사람은 널리 존경받았다. **3** in a general sense. 대략; 대충. ¶ *~ speaking* 대충〔일반적으로〕 말하면.

gen·er·al·ship [dʒénərəlʃìp] *n.* Ⓤ **1** the military skill or ability of a general. 장군으로서의 기량〔틀〕. **2** the authority of a general. 통솔권. **3** the rank or position of a general. 대장〔장군〕의 직(위).

general strike [⌐—⌐] *n.* a strike by workmen of all or most trades. 총파업.

gen·er·ate [dʒénərèit] *vt.* (P6) **1** produce; be the cause of; bring into being. …을 발생시키다; 가져오다. ¶ *~ electricity* 전기를 발생시키다 / *Fire generates heat.* 불은 열을 발생시킨다 / *Misery often generates crime.* 빈곤은 종종 범죄를 일으킨다. **2** bring (something) into life; bear. …에 생명을 주다; …을 낳다. **3** 《math.》 form (a line, figure, surface, etc.) by moving a point, line, etc. (점이나 선이) …을 형성하다; 그리다. [L. *gigno* beget]

G

:gen·er·a·tion [dʒènəréiʃən] *n.* **1** Ⓒ all the people that are born about the same time. 같은 시대의 사람들; (같은 시기의) 세대. ¶ *the younger* ~ 젊은 세대의 사람들 / *the rising* ~ 젊은 세대; 청년층. **2** Ⓒ a period of time between the birth of one generation and the next; about 30 years. 한 세대; 한 시대《약 30 년간》. ¶ *for generations* 몇 세대에 걸쳐 / *from* ~ *to* ~ 세대에서 세대로 / *A* ~ *ago the mini-skirts were certainly unknown.* 한 시대 전에는 미니스커트는 확실히 (일반에게) 알려져 있지 않았었다. **3** Ⓒ one step in the descent of a family. 일대(一代). ¶ *three generations—grandfather, father, and son.* 할아버지와 아버지, 아들의 3 대. **4** Ⓤ the act of generating; production. 산출; 생식; 발생. ¶ *the* ~ *of heat* 열의 발생.

gen·er·a·tive [dʒénərèitiv, -rətiv] *adj.* **1** producing a child or children. 생식의. ¶ *a* ~ *cell* 생식 세포. **2** having the power of producing. 생산력이 있는; 생식 능력이 있는.

generative grammar [´–––– ´–] *n.* 《linguistics》 a theory of grammar which considers language as consisting of an indefinitely large number of sentences which may be generated by the application of a set of rules. 생성(生成) 문법.

gen·er·a·tor [dʒénərèitər] *n.* Ⓒ a machine that produces electricity, gas, or steam; a dynamo. (가스·증기 따위의) 발생기; 발전기.

ge·ner·ic [dʒənérik] *adj.* **1** 《zool., bot.》 of a genus. 속(屬)의. ¶ *a* ~ *name* 속명(屬名) / *a* ~ *character* 속의 특성. **2** of or common to a class or group; not special. 전체에 관한; 포괄〔일반〕적인. **3** not offering legal protection because of not having a trademark. 상표(商標) 등록에 의한 법적 보호를 받고 있지 않은. ¶ *a* ~ *drug* 상표 등록이 안 된 약품. [L. *genus* race]

***gen·er·os·i·ty** [dʒènərásəti / -rɔ́s-] *n.* (*pl.* **-ties**) **1** Ⓤ the quality of being generous. 너그러움; 관대; 관용. ¶ *He showed* ~ *in his dealings with his enemies.* 적들을 다룸에 있어 그는 관용을 보였다. **2** Ⓒ a generous act. 관대한 행위. [↓]

:gen·er·ous [dʒénərəs] *adj.* **1** willing to give; unselfish. 아끼지 않는; 활수한; 이기적이 아닌. ¶ *a* ~ *patron of the arts* 예술에 대한 아낌없는 후원자 / *be* ~ *with one's money* 돈을 잘 쓰다. **2** willing to forgive; noble. 너그러운; 관대한; 고결한. ¶ *a* ~ *nature* 〔*disposition*〕 관대한 성질 / *be* ~ *to a fault* 잘못에 대해 관대하다. **3** large in amount; plentiful. 큰; 많은; 충분한; 풍부한. ¶ *a* ~ *supply of meat* 고기의 풍부한 공급 / *a* ~ *table* 〔*fare*〕 풍성한 식탁〔음식〕. ● **gen·er·ous·ness** [-nis] *n.* [L. *generosus* well born, generous]

gen·er·ous·ly [dʒénərəsli] *adv.* in a generous manner. 너그럽게; 관대하게; 활수하게; 많이.

gen·e·ses [dʒénəsìːz] *n.* pl. of **genesis.**

gen·e·sis [dʒénəsis] *n.* Ⓒ (*pl.* **-ses**) **1** origin; creation. 기원(起源); 발생; 창시. **2** 《*the G-*》 the first book of the Bible, which includes the story of the creation of the world by God. 창세기. 參考 Gen. 으로 생략함. [Gk.]

gen·et [dʒénit, dʒənét] *n.* **1** a kind of civet cat. 제넷《사향고양잇과(科)》. **2** the fur of this animal. 제넷의 모피. [Arab.]

ge·net·ic [dʒinétik] *adj.* **1** of or relating to genetics. 유전학의. **2** of origin or natural growth. 기원(起源)의; 발생의. [→genesis]

ge·net·ics [dʒinétiks] *n. pl.* 《used as *sing.*》 the science of heredity. 유전학.

***Ge·ne·va**[1] [dʒəníːvə] *n.* a city in southwest Switzerland. 제네바.

ge·ne·va[2] [dʒəníːvə] *n.* a gin flavored with juniper berries, Hollands. (네덜란드제(製)의) 진(술). [→ juniper]

ge·ni·al [dʒíːnjəl, -niəl] *adj.* **1** warm and friendly; kindly. 친절한; 다정한; 상냥한; 온정 있는. ¶ *a* ~ *welcome* 다정한 환영. **2** fit for growth; mild. 성장에 적합한; 온난한; 쾌적한. ¶ *a* ~ *climate* 온난한 풍토 / *enjoy the* ~ *sunshine* 따스한 햇볕을 즐기다. ● **ge·ni·al·ly** [-i] *adv.* **ge·ni·al·i·ty** [dʒìːniǽləti] *n.* [→genius]

ge·nie [dʒíːni] *n.* Ⓒ (*pl.* **-nies** or **ge·ni·i**) (in Arabian fairy tales) a spirit with magical powers. 마신(魔神); 요귀; 정령(精靈). [F. *génie*]

ge·ni·i [dʒíːniài] *n.* pl. of **genius** or **genie.**

gen·i·tal [dʒénətəl] *adj.* having to do with producing offspring. 생식의; 생식기의. ¶ *the* ~ *organs* 생식기. [L. *gigno* beget]

gen·i·tive [dʒénətiv] *n.* Ⓒ 《gram.》 a case indicating possession, origin or source. 속격(屬格); 소유격. — *adj.* of this case; in this case. 속격의; 소유격의. [L. *genitivus* of origin]

:gen·i·us [dʒíːnjəs, -niəs] *n.* Ⓒ **1** Ⓤ very great natural ability. 비범한 재능. ¶ *a man of* ~ 천재 / *have a* ~ *for music* 음악에 천재적인 소질이 있다. **2** a person who has such ability. 천재. ¶ *a* ~ *in physics* 물리학의 천재 / *He is a* ~. 그는 천재다. **3** the special character of a nation, language, or age. 특질; 정신. ¶ *the* ~ *of the English* 〔*our*〕 *language.* 영어〔우리 언어〕의 특질. **4** (*pl.* **ge·ni·i**) a guardian spirit of a place or person. 수호신(守護神); 터주. **5** a person having a great influence over another. (남에게) 큰 영향을 미치는 사람. **6** 《*the* ~》 a general tendency. 풍조. ¶ *the* ~ *of modern civilization* 현대 문명의 경향. [L.]

genius lo·ci [´–– lóusai] *n.* 《L.》 **1** a spirit guarding a place. (그 고장의) 수호신. **2** the particular character of a place felt by a person; the associations of a place. (그 고장의) 기풍; 분위기.

gen·o·cide [dʒénəsàid] *n.* the destroying of the whole race. 전 민족의 근절; 대량

학살. [L. *caedo* kill]

gen·re [ʒáːnrə] *n.* Ⓒ **1** a kind; a style, esp. of art or literature. 종류; 유형; 장르. **2** a style of painting treating scenes and subjects of everyday life. 풍속화(畫)(=genre painting). [F.=kind]

gent [dʒent] *n.* 《*vulg.*》 =gentleman.

gen·teel [dʒentíːl] *adj.* 《usu. *iron.*》 **1** polite; well-bred. 예의바른; 가정 교육이 좋은; 점잖은; 고상한. **2** pretending to be aristocratic. 젠체하는; 고상한〔점잖은〕 체하는. ¶ *They live in ~ poverty.* 가난하면서도 잘 사는 체하다 / *do the ~* 점잔 빼다. ● **gen·teel·ly** [-li] *adv.* **gen·teel·ness** [-nis] *n.* [*gentle*]

gen·tian [dʒénʃiən] *n.* Ⓒ 《bot.》 tall plants with blue, white, red, or yellow flowers; a bitter medicine obtained from its root. 용담속(屬)의 식물; 그 뿌리에서 얻은 쓴 약. [L.]

gen·tile, Gen- [dʒéntail] *n.* Ⓒ **1** a person who is not Jewish. 유태인이 아닌 사람; 이방인. **2** a person who does not believe in the Jewish, Christian, or Mohammedan god. 이교도(異教徒). **3** a person who is not a Mormon. 비(非)모르몬 교도. — *adj.* **1** not Jewish (and, in some cases, not Christian, not Mohammedan). 유태인이 아닌; 이교도(異教徒)의. **2** 《U.S.》 of persons who are not Mormons. 비(非)모르몬 교도의. [L. *gens* clan]

gen·til·i·ty [dʒentíləti] *n.* Ⓤ (*pl.* **-ties**) 《usu. *iron.*》 **1** the state of belonging to the upper class. 좋은 집안 태생. **2** good manners; refinement. 고상함; 점잖음; 세련됨. **3** 《usu. *pl.*》 pretended refinements. 고상한 체하기; 고상한〔점잖은〕 체하는 행위. ¶ *shabby ~* 구차스러운 체면 유지. **4** 《*the ~*》 the upper class. 상류 계급. [↓]

:gen·tle [dʒéntl] *adj.* (**-tler, -tlest**) **1** mild in manner; kindly. 상냥한; 친절한; 부드러운. ¶ *a ~ manner* 부드러운 태도 / *a ~ spirit* 〔*nature*〕 상냥한 마음〔성격〕 / *a ~ mother* 자모(慈母) / *the ~ sex* 여성 / *assuage his anger with ~ words* 부드러운 말로 그의 노여움을 가라앉히다 / *He is ~ to his students.* 그는 학생들에게 친절하다. **2** not rough; not hard; soft. (날씨·언동 따위가) 심하지 않은; 온화한; 가벼운; 조용한. ¶ *a ~ breeze* 산들바람 / *a ~ scolding* 〔*reproof*〕 부드러운 잔소리〔비난〕 / *a ~ punishment* 가벼운 처벌 / *a ~ tap on the shoulder* 어깨를 톡 치기 / *a medicine ~ in its action* 작용이 순한 약. **3** not steep or sharp; gradual. 완만한. ¶ *a ~ slope* 완만한 비탈. **4** of good birth; refined; polite. 집안이 좋은; 고상한; 점잖은; 세련된; 예의바른. ¶ *a man of ~ birth* 〔*blood*〕 좋은 가문 출신의 사람 / *a ~ upbringing* 점잖은 가정 교육. **5** moderate. 알맞은. ¶ *have ~ exercise* 알맞은 운동을 하다. **6** (of animals) easily controlled; not fierce; tame. (동물이) 온순한; 길든. ¶ *a ~ dog* 온순한 개. **7** 《arch.》 noble; chivalrous; courteous. 훌륭한; 기사도에 맞는; 정중한. ¶ *a ~ knight* 용감한 기사. [L. *gens* clan, good family]

gen·tle·folk [dʒéntlfòuk], **-folks** [-fòuks] *n. pl.* people of good family. 지체 있는 사람들; 집안이 좋은 사람들.

:gen·tle·man [dʒéntlmən] *n.* Ⓒ (*pl.* **-men** [-mən]) **1** a man of good taste and manners; a well-bred man; a man of good family. 신사; 집안 좋고 예절바른 사람. **2** a man. 남자. [*gentle, man*]

a gentleman of fortune, a pirate; a sea-robber. 해적.

a gentleman's 〔***gentlemen's***〕 ***agreement,*** an agreement binding as a matter of honor, not by law. 신사 협정.

a gentleman's gentleman, 《*iron.*》 a manservant. 하인; 종복.

gen·tle·man·like [dʒéntlmənlàik] *adj.* like a gentleman; polite. 신사적인; 예의바른.

gen·tle·man·ly [dʒéntlmənli] *adj.* gentlemanlike. 신사다운; 신사적인; 예의바른.

gen·tle·ness [dʒéntlnis] *n.* Ⓤ the quality of being gentle. 온순; 친절; 온화함.

gen·tle·wom·an [dʒéntlwùmən] *n.* Ⓒ (*pl.* **-wom·en** [-wìmin]) a woman of good family; a lady. 좋은 집안의 여성; 귀부인; 숙녀.

:gen·tly [dʒéntli] *adv.* **1** in a gentle manner. 상냥〔다정〕하게; 친절히; 조용히. ¶ *speak ~* 온화하게 이야기하다. **2** after the manner of gentlefolk. 점잖게; 지체 높게; 좋은 집안에. ¶ *~ born* 좋은 집안에 태어나. **3** moderately. 알맞게. **4** gradually. 완만하게. ¶ *a ~ sloping road* 완만히 비탈진 길.

gen·try [dʒéntri] *n.* Ⓤ **1** 《*the ~*》 《Brit.》 people of good family. 상류 가문의 사람들; 신사 계급. 參考 귀족에 버금가는 상류 계급. **2** people (of any class); fellows. (특정 계급·동아리에 속하는) 사람들; 패거리. ¶ *these ~* 이 사람들. [*gentle*]

gen·u·flect [dʒénjuflèkt] *vi.* (P1) bend the knee as act of reverence or worship. (공경하여) 무릎을 굽히다. [L. *genu* knee, *flecto* bend]

·gen·u·ine [dʒénjuin] *adj.* **1** real; true. 진짜의. ¶ *a ~ diamond* 진짜 다이아몬드 / *~ patriotism* 참된 애국심 / *~ Christian spirit* 진짜 기독교 정신 / *~ writing* 친필. **2** sincere; honest; not affected or pretended. 성실한; 진정한; 위선이 없는. ¶ *~ repentance* 마음으로부터의 후회 / *make ~ efforts* 성실하게 노력하다. [L. *genū* knee]

gen·u·ine·ly [dʒénjuinli] *adv.* in a genuine manner. 진정으로; 성실히.

ge·nus [dʒíːnəs] *n.* Ⓒ (*pl.* **gen·er·a** or **ge·nus·es**) **1** a kind; a class. 종류; 유(類). **2** 《biol.》 a group of animals or plants which have a common structure, but are different in important points. 속(屬). 參考 family(과(科))와 species(종(種))와의 중간. ¶ *The tiger and cat belong to different species of the same ~.* 호랑이와 고양이는 속

(屬)은 같지만 종(種)이 다르다. [L. *gigno* beget]

ge·o- [dʒíːə-] *pref.* earth; ground. '지구, 토지'의 뜻. [Gk. *gē*]

ge·o·cen·tric [dʒìːousέntrik], **-tri·cal** [-əl] *adj.* 《astron.》 **1** as viewed or measured from the earth's center. 지구의 중심에서 본〔측정된〕(cf. ***heliocentric***). **2** having or representing the earth as a center. 지구를 중심으로 한; 지구 중심(설)의. ●**ge·o·cen·tri·cal·ly** [-kəli] *adv.* [geo-, →centre]

ge·od·e·sy [dʒiːádəsi / -ɔ́d-], **ge·o·det·ics** [dʒìːoudétiks] *n.* Ⓤ the study of the size and shape of the earth, or large portions of earth's surface. 측지학. [Gk. *daio* divide]

ge·o·det·ic [dʒìːoudétik] *adj.* having to do with geodesy. 측지학의.

geog. geography.

ge·og·ra·pher [dʒiːágrəfər / dʒiɔ́g-] *n.* Ⓒ a person who specializes in geography. 지리학자. [→geography]

ge·o·graph·ic [dʒìːəgrǽfik / dʒiə-], **-i·cal** [-ikəl] *adj.* of geography. 지리학의; 지리의.

ge·o·graph·i·cal·ly [dʒìːəgrǽfikəli / dʒiə-] *adv.* according to geography. 지리적으로; 지리학상.

:ge·og·ra·phy [dʒiːágrəfi / dʒiɔ́g-] *n.* Ⓤ **1** the study of the earth's surface and everything connected with it. 지리학. ¶ *human* ~ 인문 지리학 / *physical* ~ 자연 지리학. **2** the natural features of a place or region. 지리; 지세(地勢); 지형. ¶ *the* ~ *of Africa* 아프리카의 지세. [geo-]

ge·o·log·ic [dʒìːəládʒik / dʒiəlɔ́dʒ-], **-i·cal** [-ikəl] *adj.* of geology. 지질학(상)의.

ge·ol·o·gist [dʒiːálədʒist / dʒiɔ́l-] *n.* Ⓒ a person who specializes in geology. 지질학자.

ge·ol·o·gy [dʒiːálədʒi / dʒiɔ́l-] *n.* Ⓤ **1** the study of the earth's layers and rocks in order to learn their changes and history. 지질학. ¶ *dynamic* 〔*economic*〕 ~ 동력〔경제〕 지질학. **2** the earth's features in a special area. 지질. ¶ *the* ~ *of eastern Kentucky* 켄터기주 동부의 지질. [geo-, -ology]

geom. geometry.

ge·om·e·ter [dʒiːámitər / dʒiɔ́mi-] *n.* **1** a student of geometry. 기하학자(幾何學者). **2** a kind of moth, the worms of which are called measuring worms. 자벌레나방. [geo-]

ge·o·met·ric [dʒìːəmétrik], **-ri·cal** [-rikəl] *adj.* of geometry. 기하학(상)의; 기하학적인. ●**ge·o·met·ri·cal·ly** [-rikəli] *adv.*

geometric progression [–⌐–– –⌐–] *n.* a sequence, such as the numbers 1, 3, 9, 27, 81, in which each term is multiplied by the same factor in order to obtain the following term. 등비수열(等比數列); 기하급수.

ge·om·e·trid [dʒiːámətrid / dʒiɔ́m-] *n.* a measuring worm. 자벌레.

·ge·om·e·try [dʒiːámətri / dʒiɔ́m-] *n.* Ⓤ the branch of mathematics that deals with lines, angles, and solids. 기하학(幾何學). ¶ *analytical* ~ 해석 기하학 / *descriptive* ~ 도형 기하학 / *plane* 〔*space*〕 ~ 평면〔입체〕 기하학. [geo-]

ge·o·phys·ics [dʒìːoufíziks] *n. pl.* 《used as *sing.*》 the physics of the earth. 지구 물리학. [geo-, →physics]

ge·o·pol·i·tics [dʒìːoupálətiks / -pɔ́l-] *n. pl.* 《used as *sing.*》 the study of the relation between politics and geography. 지정학(地政學). [geo-, →politics]

George [dʒɔːrdʒ] *n.* a man's name. 남자 이름.

by George, 《Brit.》 an exclamation of surprise, etc. 정말(이지); 야 그것.

Geor·gia [dʒɔ́ːrdʒə] *n.* a southern State of the United States, on the Atlantic coast. 조지아주(州). 参考 Ga.로 약함. 주도(州都)는 Atlanta.

Geor·gian [dʒɔ́ːrdʒən] *adj.* **1** of the period of the four Georges who were kings of England from 1714 to 1830. 조지왕조의《영국의 조지 1세부터 4세까지의 시대》. **2** of Georgia or its people. 조지아주(州)〔주민〕의. — *n.* Ⓒ a person of Georgia. 조지아주의 주민.

ge·ot·ro·pism [dʒiːátrəpìzəm / dʒiɔ́-] *n.* 《biol.》 response to gravity. 향지성(向地性); 굴지성(屈地性). [geo-]

Ger. German; Germany.

ger. gerund; gerundive.

ge·ra·ni·um [dʒəréiniəm] *n.* Ⓒ a plant with rose-colored flowers. 제라늄; 양아욱. [Gk. *geranos* crane]

ger·i·at·rics [dʒèriǽtriks] *n. pl.* 《used as *sing.*》 《med.》 the study of old age and its diseases. 노인병학. [Gk. *gēras* old age, *iatreia* healing]

germ [dʒəːrm] *n.* Ⓒ **1** a very tiny animal or plant that may cause disease; a microbe. 세균; 병균(cf. ***bacillus, microbe***). **2** a seed; a bud. 종배(種胚); 유아(幼芽). **3** a beginning of anything; an origin. 싹틈; (발생·발달의) 초기; 기원(起源); 본원(本源). ¶ *the* ~ *of an idea* 어떤 생각의 싹틈 / *be in* ~ 아직 초기 단계〔발달되지 않은 상태〕에 있다. [L. *germen*]

:Ger·man [dʒə́ːrmən] *adj.* of Germany, its people, or their language. 독일(사람·말)의. — *n.* **1** Ⓒ a person of Germany. 독일사람. **2** Ⓤ the language of Germany. 독일어(語). [L.]

ger·man [dʒə́ːrmən] *adj.* sprung from the same parents or grandparents. 부모〔조부모〕를 같이하는. ¶ *a brother-german* 친형〔동생〕 / *a cousin-german* 친사촌. [L. =of the same parents]

ger·mane [dʒəːrméin] *adj.* 《as *predicative*》 closely related; to the point. 밀접한 관계가 있는; 적절한. ¶ *What he said was not* ~ *to the question.* 그의 말은 질문과 관련이

없었다. [*german*]

Ger·man·ic [dʒəːrmǽnik] *adj.* German; Teutonic. 독일인(人)의; 튜턴 민족의. — *n.* Ⓤ the language of Teutonic races. 튜턴어(語). [*German*]

German measles [⌐ ⌐–] *n.* 《med.》 a contagious disease; rubella. 풍진(風疹).

:Ger·ma·ny [dʒə́ːrməni] *n.* a country in north central Europe, on the North Sea and the Baltic Sea. 독일. [L.]

germ cell [⌐ ⌐] *n.* 《biol.》 a cell that can produce a new one. 생식 세포. [*germ*]

ger·mi·cide [dʒə́ːrməsàid] *n.* Ⓒ a substance that is used to kill disease germs 살균제. [→germ]

ger·mi·nal [dʒə́ːrmənəl] *adj.* of or belonging to a germ. 배(胚)의; 새싹의; 씨방의.

ger·mi·nant [dʒə́ːrmənənt] *adj.* germinating. 발아(發芽)하는; 싹을 내는; 성장력〔발달력〕이 있는.

ger·mi·nate [dʒə́ːrmənèit] *vi.* (P1) start growing. 발아(發芽)하다; 발생하다. ¶ *Seeds* ~. 씨가 발아하다. — *vt.* (P6) cause (something) to grow or develop. …을 발아(發芽)시키다; 발달〔발생〕시키다. ¶ ~ *seeds* 씨를 발아시키다. [→germ]

ger·mi·na·tion [dʒə̀ːrmənéiʃən] *n.* Ⓤ the act of germinating; the state of being germinated. 발아; 싹〔움〕이 틈.

germ warfare [⌐ ⌐–] *n.* the spreading of germs among the enemy in time of war. 세균전.

ger·on·tol·o·gy [dʒèrəntáləd3i / -tɔ́l-] *n.* = geriatrics.

ger·und [dʒérənd] *n.* Ⓒ 《gram.》 a verb form used as a noun; a verbal noun. 동명사. [L. *gers* carry out]

Ge·stalt [gəʃtáːlt] *n.* 《G.》 form. 형태; 게슈탈트.

Gestalt psychology [–⌐ ⌐––] *n.* psychology that emphasizes the importance of configuration. 형태〔게슈탈트〕 심리학.

ges·tate [dʒésteit] *vt.* (P6) carry in the womb. 임신하다; 회임(懷妊)하다. [L. *gero* carr, do]

ges·ta·tion [dʒestéiʃən] *n.* the period or condition of carrying young in the body. 임신; 회태; 회임 (기간). [↑]

ges·tic·u·late [dʒestíkjəlèit] *vi., vt.* (P1; 6) make gestures; express (something) by gestures. 몸짓〔손짓〕을 하다; 몸짓〔손짓〕으로 말하다〔표시하다〕. [L. *gesus* gesture]

ges·tic·u·la·tion [dʒestìkjəléiʃən] *n.* ⓊⒸ the act of gesticulating. 몸짓; 손짓.

:ges·ture [dʒéstʃər] *n.* **1** ⒸⓊ the movement of the body, esp. the hands and arms, to express an idea or feeling. 몸짓; 손짓; 제스처. ¶ *speak by* ~ 손짓〔몸짓〕으로 이야기하다 / *in a foreign* ~ 외국식의 제스처로 / *make a* ~ *of impatience* 참을 수 없다는 몸짓을 하다. **2** Ⓒ something said or done to impress others. 태도; 거동; 의례적인 동작; 조치. ¶ *a* ~ *of friendship* 우정적 태도〔의사 표시〕/ *a mere* ~ (본심이 아닌) 그저 겉으로만의 행위. — *vi., vt.* (P1; 6) =gesticulate. [L. *gero* conduct]

:get [get] *v.* (**got, got** or **got·ten**) *vt.* **1** (P6, 13,14) come to have; be the owner of; take possession of; obtain. …을 손에 넣다; 소유하다. ¶ ~ *something into one's hands* 〔*possession*〕 무엇을 손에 넣다〔소유하다〕. **2** (P6, 13,14) ⓐ obtain; receive; be given. (…에게서) 얻다; 획득하다; 받다. ¶ ~ *a letter* 편지를 받다 / ~ *orders* 〔*institution*〕 명령을〔지시를〕 받다 / ~ *a telephone call* 전화를 받다. ⓑ obtain (something needed or desired); gain; receive. (필요한 것·바라던 것)을 얻다. ¶ ~ *permission* 〔*a licence*〕 허가〔면허〕를 얻다 / ~ *sleep* 잠을 자다 / ~ *rest* 휴식하다. ⓒ gain as a result of effort; acquire; win. (노력의 결과로) 얻다; 타다; 획득하다. ¶ ~ *a prize* 상을 타다 / ~ *one's liberty* 자유를 획득하다 / ~ *information* 〔*knowledge*〕 정보를〔지식을〕 얻다 / ~ *a good education* 좋은 교육을 받다 / ~ *fame and wealth* 명성과 부(富)를 얻다 / ~ *a good crop* 좋은〔큰〕 수확을 올리다. ⓓ receive as a salary, gift, etc.; earn. (월급·선물 따위)를 받다; 벌다. ¶ ~ *high wages* 높은 임금을 받다 / ~ *a birthday present* 생일 선물을 받다 / ~ *a living* 생활비를 벌다. ⓔ receive as a penalty. (벌로서) 받다. ¶ ~ *15 years in jail,* 15년형(刑)을 받다 / ~ *a whipping* 태형을 받다. **3** (P6,14) ⓐ buy; purchase. …을 사다; …에게 사 주다. ¶ ~ *a son a toy train* 아들에게 장난감 기차를 사 주다 / *He got me a dictionary.* =*He got a dictionary for me.* 그는 내게 사전을 사 주었다. ⓑ engage (someone) for a fee; employ; hire. …을 고용하다. ¶ ~ *one's son a good teacher* 아들에게 좋은 선생님을 붙여 주다. **4** (P6,14) go and take; bring; fetch. …을 가져〔집어〕 오다. ¶ *Get me a chair.* 의자 좀 갖다 주게 / *Go* (*and*) ~ *your umbrella.* 가서 우산을 가져오시오. **5** (P6,13,14) ⓐ seek and find; gain; obtain. 찾(아 내)다; 구하다; 얻다. ¶ ~ *work* 일자리를 얻다 / ~ *a position in a high school* (*as a teacher*) 고등 학교 교사 자리를 얻다 / ~ *one's son a wife* 아들에게 아내를 구해 주다. ⓑ succeed in meeting or reaching (someone); come into contact with; communicate with. …와 연락이 닿다. ¶ *I couldn't* ~ *him, as the line was engaged.* 전화가 통화 중이어서 그에게 연락할 수가 없었다. **6** (P6) catch; become sick with. (붙)잡다; (병에) 걸리다. ¶ ~ *a bad cold* 독감에 걸리다 / *The policemen got a suspect.* 경찰은 용의자를 붙잡았다 / *He got her by the hand.* 그녀의 손을 잡았다. **7** (P6,13) obtain as a result of thinking, investigation, etc.; find out; acquire; learn. (생각·조사의 결과) …을 알아내다; 배우다. ¶ ~ *someone's name* 〔*address*〕 아무의 이름을〔주소를〕 알아 내다 / ~ *a general outline of a case* 사건의 전체 윤곽을

G

알아 내다 / ~ *skill through practice* 실습을 통해 기술을 익히다. **8** (P6) 《*colloq.*》 understand. …을 이해하다. ¶ *I don't ~ what you mean.* 무슨 말씀인지 이해 못 하겠습니다 / *I ~ your point.* 네 생각을 알겠다 / *Did you ~ me ?* 내 말 알겠나. **9** (P6) ⓐ 《*colloq.*》 take as food; eat or drink. …을 먹다; 마시다. ¶ *Did you ~ any lunch ?* 점심은 먹었나. ⓑ 《U.S.》 make ready; prepare. 준비를 하다. ¶ *I'll ~ lunch for you.* 자네 점심을 준비하겠네. **10** (P6,13, 18,20,23,24) ⓐ bring to a state or condition; cause to be; have. …을 어떤 상태로 하다; …하게 하다. ¶ ~ *one's fingers dirty* 손가락을 더럽히다 / ~ *the cards mixed up* 카드 패를 섞다. ⓑ cause; persuade. (설득·권하여 아무)에게 …하게 하다〔시키다〕. ¶ *Please ~ her to come here.* 부디 그녀가 이리 좀 오게 하시오 / *She tried to ~ him to talk.* 그녀는 그가 말을 하게끔 애를 썼다. ⓒ cause (something) to be done. …하게 하다; …해 받다; …당하다. ¶ ~ *one's arm broken* 팔을 부러뜨리다 / ~ *one's feet wet* 발을 적시다 / ~ *someone drunk* 아무를 취하게 하다 / *I got my hair cut yesterday.* 어제 이발을 했다 / *Get your coat mended.* 당신 코트를 수리시키시오 / *I have to ~ my work finished by noon.* 정오까지는 일을 마쳐야 한다. **11** 《have got》 《*colloq.*》 ⓐ have. 가지고 있다. ¶ *I've got nobody to look after me.* 나를 돌봐줄 사람은 아무도 없다 / *She's got an office in the building.* 빌딩 안에 사무실을 갖고 있다 / *I've got things to do this morning.* 오늘 아침엔 할 일들이 있다. ⓑ have to; be obliged to. …하지 않으면 안 되다. ¶ *I've got to go.* 나는 가야 한다 / *You've got to listen to what I say.* 내가 하는 말을 들어야만 한다. **12** (P6) (of animals) beget. (동물이) 새끼를 얻다〔낳다〕. —*vi.* **1** (P2A,4) come (to a place); arrive at; reach. (어떤 장소에) 이르다; 도착하다. ¶ ~ *home late* 늦게 귀가하다 / ~ *to the station* 역에 도착하다 / ~ *to one's destination* 목적지에 이르다〔닿다〕 / *I tried to ~ there before dark.* 어둡기 전에 그곳에 닿으려고 애썼다. **2** (P5) become; grow. (점차) …하게 되다. ¶ ~ *angry* 성나다 / ~ *wet* 〔*dirty*〕 젖다〔더러워지다〕 / ~ *tired in the afternoon* 오후가 되면 피곤해지다. **3** (P5) come to a certain state; come to be. (어떤 상태가) 되다. 語法 be 동사를 대신하여 수동형을 만듦. ¶ ~ *drunk* 술에 취하다 / ~ *promoted* 〔*dismissed*〕 승진〔해고〕되다 / *The days are getting longer.* 낮이 점차 길어진다 / *They got caught in the shower.* 그들은 소나기를 만났다 / *She got married last month.* 그녀는 지난달에 결혼했다. **4** begin. …하기 시작하다; …하게 되다. ¶ ~ *talking* 〔*moving*〕 말하기〔움직이기〕 시작하다 / ~ *discussing together* 토론을 시작하다 / ~ *to know him* 그를 알게 되다. [N.]

get about, **a**) move from place to place. 돌아다니다. ¶ *He gets about with difficulty since his illness.* 앓고 나서 그는 간신히 나다닌다. **b**) become widely known. (소문 따위가) 알려지다; 퍼지다. **c**) 《*colloq.*》 become socially active. 사교적으로 여기저기 돌아다니다. ¶ *She's been getting about much more since her family move to the city.* 가족이 도시로 이사한 이후 그녀는 훨씬 더 많이 나돌아다니게 되었다.

get something across, make something clear or understood. …을 분명히 알게 하다〔이해시키다〕.

get ahead, **a**) succeed. 성공하다; 출세하다. **b**) make progress. 진보하다.

get ahead of, go forward and pass others. …을 앞지르다; …을 능가하다; …보다 낫다.

get along, **a**) manage to make a living. 그럭저럭 살아가다. ¶ *I can't ~ along without his help.* 그의 도움 없이는 살 수가 없다. **b**) 《*with*》 make progress; proceed. 진보시키다; 나아가다. ¶ *How is he getting along with his English ?* 그의 영어는 얼마나 나아졌습니까. **c**) go away; leave. 떠나다; 나가다. ¶ *Get along with you !* 꺼져. **d**) succeed. 성공하다. **e**) 《*with*》 be on good terms; live in harmony. …와 사이좋게 지내다. ¶ ~ *along with one's neighbors* 이웃과 사이좋게 지내다.

get around, **a**), **b**) =get about. **c**) evade some law or rule. 법〔법망〕을 피하다. **d**) avoid an obstacle or difficulty. 곤란 등을 용케 피하다. **e**) 《*colloq.*》 please or flatter (someone) so as to gain what one wants. …을 구워삶다.

get at, **a**) manage to reach; arrive at; approach. …에 도착하다〔닿다〕; 이르다; 미치다; (…에) 연락이 닿다. ¶ *stretch in order to ~ at a top shelf* 맨꼭대기 선반에 닿도록 손을 뻗치다 / *We are trying to ~ at him some way or other.* 어떻게 해서든 그와 연락을 하려고 하고 있다. **b**) manage to find out; understand. …을 발견하다; …을 알아 내다; …을 알다. ¶ ~ *at the root of a problem* 문제의 핵심을 알아 내다 / ~ *at the meaning* 의미를 파악하다. **c**) hint; suggest. …을 암시하다; 넌지시 비추다. ¶ *I can't see what you're getting at.* 당신의 진의(眞意)가 무엇인지 모르겠습니다. **d**) be engaged in (work). …에 종사하다. **e**) 《*colloq.*》 influence by bad means; bribe. 이면 공작으로 (아무)를 움직이다; …을 매수하다. ¶ *The gangsters couldn't ~ at the mayor.* 범죄 조직은 시장을 매수할 수가 없었다.

get away, go away; leave; escape. 떠나다; 달아나다; 도피하다. ¶ ~ *away with stolen money* 훔친 돈을 갖고 달아나다 / ~ *away from the noise of the city* 도시의 소음으로부터 도피하다 / *We cannot ~ away from the true facts.* 우리는 참된 사실을 부정할 수 없다.

get away with, 《*colloq.*》 succeed in doing (something) without being discovered or punished. (벌을 받지 않고) …을 행하다; …을 하고 무사히 끝내다. ¶ *You can't play a dirty trick on me and ~ away with it.* 내게 더러운 수작을 부리지 마, 무사하지 못할 테니.

get back, **a**) (manage to) come back; return. 돌아오다. ¶ *When will you* ~ *back?* 언제 돌아오십니까. **b**) receive back; recover. 되찾다; 회복하다. ¶ ~ *one's money back* 돈을 되찾다 / ~ *back one's health* 건강을 회복하다.

get back at, 《*sl.*》 gain revenge on; get even with. 원한을 풀다; 앙갚음하다; 보복하다.

get by, **a**) pass. 통과하다. ¶ *I moved aside to let the car* ~ *by.* 차를 통과시키기 위해 옆으로 비켜 섰다. **b**) =get away with. **c**) =get along a).

get down, **a**) descend; bring down. 내리다; 내려놓다; 하락시키다. ¶ ~ *down from a horse* 말에서 내리다 / ~ *a book down from a shelf* 서가에서 책을 내려놓다 / *The kitten couldn't* ~ *down from the tree.* 새끼고양이는 나무에서 내려올 수가 없었다. **b**) 《*colloq.*》 depress; discourage. …을 우울하게 하다; 낙담〔실망〕시키다. ¶ *This gloomy house gets me down.* 이 음침한 집은 나를 우울하게 만든다.

get *someone* **or** *something* **down,** **a**) cause something to be down; swallow. …을 내리다; (약 따위)를 삼키다. **b**) make someone depressed or annoyed. …을 의기 소침케 하다.

get down to, begin to consider or act on something. …을 시작하다; 전념하여〔본격적으로〕 착수하다. ¶ ~ *down to one's work* 일에 진지하게〔정력적으로〕 착수하다.

get in, **a**) (manage to) put in or enter (a room, car, etc.). 들어가다. ¶ *I had no key and couldn't* ~ *in.* 열쇠가 없어서 들어갈 수가 없었다. **b**) arrive. 도착하다. ¶ *The train gets in at nine.* 열차는 9시에 도착한다. **c**) manage to join (a club, etc.); (manage to) become a member of. …의 회원이 되다; 뽑히다. **d**) take indoors (in advance). (미리) 집안으로 들여가다. ¶ *I must* ~ *the washing in before it rains.* 비가 오기 전에 빨래를 거둬들여야 한다. **e**) put (words) in; interrupt. (남의 이야기에) 말참견하다.

get into, **a**) (manage to) make one's way into; enter. …에〔로〕 들어가다. **b**) fall into a state or condition; come to. …한 상태가 되다; …하게 되다. ¶ ~ *into a rage* 버럭 성을 내다 / ~ *into debt* 빚을 지다 / ~ *into the first rank* 일류가 되다 / ~ *into a fight* …와 치고받는 싸움이 되다 / ~ *into difficulty with* …와 분쟁을 일으키다. **c**) put into or enter (a car). (차(車) 따위)에 들어가다; 타다. ¶ ~ *someone into a car* 아무를 차 안에 태우다 / *They got into the car and drove off.* 그들은 차에 올라타고 떠났다.

get in with, 《*colloq.*》 become friendly with; begin to associate with. …와 친해지다; 사귀게 되다. ¶ *He got in with a bad crowd.* 나쁜 동아리와 어울리게 되었다.

get it, **a**) understand. 이해하다; 알다. **b**) 《*colloq.*》 be punished or scolded. 벌〔비난〕을 받다; 야단맞다.

get off, **a**) get down; descend. (탈것에서) 내리다. ¶ ~ *off a train* 열차에서 내리다. **b**) (manage to) take off; remove. …을 벗다〔빼다〕; 떼다. ¶ *I can't* ~ *my ring off.* 반지를 뺄 수가 없다 / *Get your wet clothes off, and I'll dry them.* 젖은 옷을 벗어라, 내가 말려 줄게. **c**) start; get away. 떠나다; 출발〔시작〕하다. **d**) (help someone) escape punishment. 벌(罰)을 모면하(게 하)다. ¶ *He got off for £300.* 그는 3백 파운드의 벌금으로 때웠다.

get on, **a**) go on or into (a vehicle); board. (차 따위)에 (올라)타다. ¶ ~ *on a bicycle* 자전거에 올라타다. **b**) (manage to) put on (clothing, etc.). (옷 따위를) 입다; (몸에) 걸치다. ¶ *Get your clothes on.* 옷을 입어라 / *These shoes are tight; I can't* ~ *them on.* 이 신은 발에 꼭 끼여서 신을 수가 없다. **c**) make progress; proceed; advance. (일 따위)를 진척시키다; 나아가게 하다. **d**) continue. 계속하다. **e**) =get along a), b), e). **f**) approach. 가까워지다; 나이를 먹다. ¶ *He's getting on for 60.* 그의 나이도 60에 가깝다.

get onto, 《U.S. *colloq.*》 succeed in understanding; grasp. …을 알다; 이해하다.

get out (of), **a**) go or come out; go away; leave; manage to escape. 가다; 나오다; 떠나다; (모)면하다. ¶ ~ *out of a room* 〔*car*〕 방〔차〕에서 나오다 / ~ *out of prison* 교도소를 나오다 / *Get out (of here)!* (여기서) 나가라; 꺼져. **b**) (manage to) take or pull out; extract. …을 꺼내다; …을 빼다〔뽑다〕. ¶ ~ *out a bottle from one's pocket* 호주머니에서 병을 꺼내다 / ~ *a cork out of a bottle* 병의 코르크 마개를 뽑다 / *Get your books out.* 책을 꺼내시오. **c**) publish; issue; produce. 출판〔발행〕하다; 산출(產出)하다. ¶ ~ *out a book* 책을 출판하다 / ~ *out the coal* 석탄을 산출하다. **d**) complete. …을 완성하다; 끝내다. ¶ *Let's* ~ *this work out.* 자 이 일을 끝내자. **e**) become known. 알려지다; 새다. ¶ *The secret got out.* 비밀이 새었다. **f**) avoid (an unpleasant duty). …을 피하다.

get out of the way, remove (an obstacle). (방해물)을 치우다; 제거하다. ¶ ~ *the chair out of the way* 의자를 치우다.

get over, **a**) manage to go or move over. …을 넘(어가)다; (저쪽으로) 넘어〔건너〕가다. ¶ ~ *over a fence* 울타리를 넘어가다. **b**) overcome. …을 극복하다; 이겨내다. ¶ ~ *over difficulties* 어려움을 이겨내다. **c**) recover from. …에서 회복하다. ¶ ~ *over an illness* 병이 낫다 / ~ *over a shock* 충격에서 헤어나다. **d**) finish; have done with. …을 끝내다; 마치다. ¶ *I would like to* ~ *this over (with) as quickly as possible.* 될 수 있는 대로 빨리 이것을 끝내고 싶다.

get round =get around.

get set! ready! 준비.

get there, **a**) obtain; succeed. 목적을 달성하다; 성공하다. **b**) accomplish. 완성하다.

get through, **a**) manage to come to the end of; finish. …을 완성하다; 끝내다. ¶ ~ *through a task* 〔*a college with honors*〕 일을

G

끝내다〔대학을 우등으로 졸업하다〕. **b**) manage to survive. 살아남다. **c**) bring to or reach the destination. 목적지에 닿다. **d**) succeed in. …에 성공하다. **e**) be passed through Parliament and become law. (의회 등에서 법안이) 통과하다. **f**) =get to b).

get to, **a**) arrive at; reach. (목적지 따위)에 도달하다. **b**) succeed in reaching or communicating with. …와 연락이 닿다. **c**) = get down to.

get together, **a**) come or bring together; collect. 모이다; 집합〔회합〕하다; 모으다. **b**) come to an agreement; agree. (의견이) 일치하다.

get under, control. 진압하다; 이기다.

get up, **a**) rise or rouse from bed. (아침에) 일어나다; 기상하다. **b**) rise from one's seat. (자리에서) 일어서다〔나다〕. **c**) manage to climb; mount. …을〔에〕 오르다; …를 타다. **d**) study hard. (어떤 목적을 위해) 열심히 공부하다. ¶ ~ *up chemistry for an examination* 시험에 대비하여 화학을 공부하다. **e**) prepare; arrange. 준비〔계획〕하다; 마련하다. ¶ ~ *up a pleasant entertainment* 즐거운 여흥을 마련하다. **f**) dress and beautify (oneself) with care. 정성껏 몸치장을 하다; 화장하다. ¶ *She got herself up beautifully.* 그녀는 이쁘게 차려 입었다.

get up to, **a**) arrive at; reach; catch up. …에 도달〔도착〕하다; 따라잡다. **b**) indulge in. …에 몰두하다〔빠지다〕. ¶ ~ *up to mischief* 장난을 일삼다.

G

get·at·a·ble [getǽtəbəl] *adj.* that may be reached; not difficult to see or meet. (도)달할 수 있는; 쉽게 접근할〔얻을〕 수 있는; 손에 넣을 수 있는. [*get*]

get·a·way [gétəwèi] *n.* 《*colloq.*》 an escape (esp. of thieves, etc.). 도망; 탈출. ¶ *make one's* ~ 도주하다.

Geth·sem·a·ne [geθséməni] *n.* 《Bible》 a garden east of Jerusalem where Jesus was finally caught by the Romans. 겟세마네. [Aram.]

get-to·geth·er [géttəgèðər] *n.* 《U.S. *colloq.*》 an informal social gathering or party. (비공식의) 모임; 회합; 간친회. [*get*]

get-up [gétʌ̀p] *n.* Ⓒ 《*colloq.*》 an arrangement; dress; a style. 몸치장; 옷차림. ¶ *a queer* ~ 이상한 옷차림. [*get*]

gew·gaw [gjú:gɔ:] *n.* a small ornament, fine in appearance, but without value. 겉만 뻔드레한 것; 굴퉁이. [E.]

gey·ser [gáizər, -sər] *n.* Ⓒ **1** a hot spring that frequently sends jets of hot water and steam into the air. 간헐천(間歇泉); 간헐 분천(噴泉). **2** [gí:zər] 《Brit.》 an apparatus to heat water quickly by gas. 가스 자동 온수 장치(=《U.S.》 water heater). [Icel. =gusher]

Gha·na [gá:nə] *n.* a country on the coast of West Africa. 가나. 參考 수도는 Accra.

·ghast·ly [gǽstli, gá:st-] *adj.* (**-li·er, -li·est**) **1** horrible; dreadful. 무서운; 무시무시한; 소름끼치는. ¶ *a* ~ *murder* 끔찍한 살인 / *be in a* ~ *frame of mind* 소름이 끼치는 기분이다. **2** like a ghost; pale. 유령〔송장〕 같은; 창백한. ¶ *The sick man looked* ~. 환자는 송장처럼 창백했다. **3** 《*colloq.*》 shocking; very bad. 지독한; 심한. ¶ *a* ~ *mistake* 어이없는 잘못 / ~ *weather* 지독한 날씨. — *adv.* in a ghastly manner; horribly. 무섭게; 송장같이. [E. =ghostly]

gher·kin [gə́:rkin] *n.* a small cucumber used for pickles. 절임용의 작은 오이. [Du.]

ghet·to [gétou] *n.* Ⓒ (*pl.* **-tos** or **-toes**) **1** a special part of a city where Jews live. 게토; 유태인 지구. **2** 《U.S.》 the Negro quarter; a slum. 흑인 지구; 슬럼가(街). [It.]

:ghost [goust] *n.* Ⓒ **1** the spirit of a dead person, supposed to appear before living persons. 유령; 망령. ¶ *be afraid of a* ~ 유령을 무서워하다 / *look like a* ~ (무척 마르고 창백하여) 유령과 같다 / *look as if one had seen a* ~ 유령이라도 본 것처럼 얼굴이 새파랗게 질리다 / *Do you believe in ghosts?* 자네는 유령이 있다고 믿나. **2** a shadowy image; a slight suggestion. 그림자; 환영(幻影); 흔적; 약간의 기색. ¶ *a* ~ *of a smile* 희미한 미소. **3** =ghost writer. **4** a secondary abnormal image or picture which appears on a TV screen, etc. 복상(複像); 고스트. [E.]

give up the ghost, 《*arch.*》 die. 죽다.

have not the ghost of a chance, have no chance at all. 한 가닥의 기회〔가망〕도 없다.

ghost·ly [góustli] *adj.* (**-li·er, -li·est**) **1** of or like a ghost; faint; shadowy. 유령의〔같은〕; 희미한; 그림자 같은. ¶ *our* ~ *enemy* 악마 / *have a* ~ *presence* 유령 같은 존재이다 / *The trees looked* ~ *in the dark.* 나무들은 어둠 속에서 유령처럼 보였다. **2** spiritual. 정신의; 영적(靈的)인. ● **ghost·li·ness** [-nis] *n.*

ghost writer [ㅗ ㅡ] *n.* a person who writes a book for a well-known man who claimes to have written it. (책 따위의) 대필자; 대작자(代作者).

ghoul [gu:l] *n.* Ⓒ **1** (in Oriental folklore) an evil spirit that eats dead bodies. (무덤을 파헤쳐 송장을 먹는다는) 식시귀(食屍鬼). **2** a horrible man. 잔인한 사람. **3** a grave robber. 도굴(盜掘)꾼. ● **ghoul·ish** [gú:liʃ] *adj.* [Arab.]

G.H.Q. General Headquarters. 총사령부.

GI, G.I. [dʒí:ái] *n.* Ⓒ (*pl.* **GI's, G.I.'s, GIs**) 《*colloq.*》 an enlisted soldier in the United States army; a service man. (여군(女軍)까지 포함시켜) 미군 병사. 參考 Government Issue (정부 지급)의 준말. — *adj.* issued by the government; 《*colloq.*》 standardized by the Army. 관급(官給)의; 군(軍) 규격의. ¶ *a* ~ *uniform* 군 규격의 군복〔제복〕.

:gi·ant [dʒáiənt] *n.* Ⓒ **1** an imaginary person who has great size and power. (상상

의) 거인. **2** ⓐ a very large person or thing. 유달리 큰 남자; 거한(巨漢); 거대한 것. ⓑ a great or famous man. 위대한 사람; 유명한 사람. — *adj.* very large; huge. 몹시 큰; 거대한. ¶ *a ~ potato* 매우 큰 감자 / *a man of ~ strength* 괴력의 사나이. [Gk. *gigas*]

gi·ant·ess [dʒáiəntis] *n.* a woman giant. 여자 거인; 왜장녀.

gib·ber [dʒíbər, gíbər] *vi.* (P1) talk fast and meaninglessly. 뜻 모를 소리를 빨리 지껄이다; 불분명한 말을 하다. ¶ *Monkeys ~.* 원숭이들이 꽥꽥거린다. [Imit.]

gib·ber·ish [dʒíbəriʃ, gíbə-] *n.* Ⓤ rapid and not clear talk; meaningless talk. 뜻 모를 빠른 지껄임. ¶ *talk ~* 종잡을 수 없는 말을 하다; 횡설수설하다.

gib·bet [dʒíbit] *n.* Ⓒ a kind of machine with a post and an arm used for hanging a man. 교수대. ¶ *die on the ~* 교수되다. — *vt.* (P6) **1** kill (someone) by hanging on a gibbet. …을 교수형에 처하다. **2** 《*fig.*》 expose (someone) to criticism by the public. …을 대중의 웃음거리로 만들다. ¶ *be gibbeted in the press* 신문에서 지탄당하다. [F. *gibe* club]

gib·bon [gíbən] *n.* Ⓒ a kind of small, long-armed monkey living in southeastern Asia. 긴팔원숭이. [F.]

gib·bos·i·ty [gibásəti / -bɔ́s-] *n.* the quality of being gibbous. 볼록한 원의 성질[상태]; 융기. [↓]

gib·bous [gíbəs] *adj.* **1** convex; curved out. 볼록한 모양의; 융기한. **2** ⓐ (of the moon) between half and full. 반달과 보름달의 중간의. ¶ *a ~ moon* 철월(凸月). ⓑ (of a person) hump-backed. 꼽추의. [L. *gibbus* hump]

gibe [dʒaib] *vi., vt.* (P1,3; 6) 《*at*》 sneer at (someone); make fun of (someone). …을 비웃다[냉소하다]; 놀리다. ¶ *They gibed at his singing.* 그들은 그의 노래에 냉소를 보냈다. — *n.* Ⓒ the act of sneering. 비웃음; 놀림; 우롱. [? F.]

gib·lets [dʒíblits] *n. pl.* the inside parts (i.e. the heart, liver) of a bird which can be cooked and eaten. (닭 따위의) 내장. [F.]

gid·di·ly [gídili] *adv.* in a giddy manner. 현기증이 나서; 어지러워; 경솔히. [↓]

gid·di·ness [gídinis] *n.* Ⓤ the state of being giddy. 현기증; 어지러움; 경솔(함).

•**gid·dy** [gídi] *adj.* (**-di·er, -di·est**) **1** dizzy. 어지러운; 현기증 나는. ¶ *feel ~* 어지러움[현기증]을 느끼다 / *turn ~* 현기증이 나다. **2** causing dizziness. 아찔한; 현기증을 일으키는. ¶ *a ~ cliff* 아찔한 절벽 / *look down from a ~ height* 아찔한 높이에서 아래를 내려다보다. **3** not serious; heedless. 경박한; 경솔한. ¶ *a ~ mind* 들뜬 마음; 경박한 인간 / *a ~ girl* 바람기 있는 여자. [E.]

act* [*play*] *the giddy goat, act foolishly. 어리석은[경솔한] 짓을 하다.

Gide [ʒi:d], **André** (**Paul Guillaume**) *n.* (1869-1951) a French novelist, poet, and critic. 앙드레 지드.

⁝**gift** [gift] *n.* **1** Ⓒ something that is given; a present. 선물; 증여물; 기증품. ¶ *a Christmas ~* 크리스마스 선물 / *send someone a ~* 아무에게 선물을 보내다 / *He made a ~ of ten million won to the old people's home.* 그는 양로원에 천만 원을 기부했다. **2** Ⓤ the power or right to give. 줄 권한; 수여(授與)[증여]권. ¶ *The position is within his ~.* 그 지위를 주는 권리는 그가 쥐고 있다. **3** Ⓒ something one is born with; a natural talent. (천부의) 재능; 자질. ¶ *the ~ of poetry* 시의 재질 / *a person of many gifts* 많은 재능이 있는 사람 / *the ~ of tongues* 어학의 재능 / *have a ~ for music* 음악에 재능이 있다.

at a gift, even as a gift. 거저라도. ¶ *I would not take it at a ~.* 거저 주어도 그건 안 받겠다.

by* [*of*] *free gift, for nothing; free of charge. 거저; 공짜로; 무료로.

— *vt.* (P6) **1** give as a gift. …을 증정[증여]하다. **2** 《usu. in *passive*》 give as a natural gift; endow with a talent, etc. (재능 등)을 주다[부여하다]. ¶ *He is gifted with a keen intellect.* 그는 예민한 지성을 타고났다. [*give*]

gift·ed [gíftid] *adj.* having great natural ability; talented. 타고난[뛰어난] 재능이 있는. ¶ *~ children* 영재아(英才兒).

gig[1] [gig] *n.* Ⓒ **1** an open, light, two-wheeled carriage drawn by one horse. (말 한 필이 끄는) 2륜 경마차. **2** a long, light boat attached to a ship for the captain's use. (배에 실은 선장용의) 소형 보트. [? N.]

gig[2] [gig] *n.* a kind of fish-spear. (고기잡이) 작살. — *vt., vi.* (**gigged, gig·ging**) (P6; 1) fish with a gig. 작살로 찌르다. [Sp. *fisga* harpoon]

•**gi·gan·tic** [dʒaigǽntik] *adj.* very big like a giant; enormous; immense. 거대한; 방대한; 대규모의. [→giant]

gig·gle [gígəl] *vi.* (P1) laugh in a silly manner. 낄낄[킥킥] 웃다. ¶ *Girls giggled at the story.* 소녀들은 그 이야기를 듣고 낄낄거렸다. — *n.* Ⓒ a silly laugh. 낄낄거리는 웃음. ¶ *give a ~* 낄낄 웃다. ● **gig·gler** [-ər] *n.* **gig·gling·ly** [-iŋli] *adv.* [Imit.]

gig·o·lo [dʒígəlòu, ʒíg-] *n.* (*pl.* **-los**) **1** a man who lives at his mistress's expenses. 기둥서방; (여자에게 얹혀 지내는) 놈팡이. **2** a man who dances with ladies for payment. 남자 직업 댄서. [F.]

•**gild**[1] [gild] *vt.* (**gild·ed** or 《rare》 **gilt**) (P6) **1** coat or cover (something) with thin gold. …을 금(金)도금하다; 금박을 입히다. ¶ *~ the frame* 액자에 금박을 입히다. **2** make (something) shine like gold. …을 황금빛으로 빛나게 하다. ¶ *The evening sun was gilding the mountain-tops.* 저녁해가 산꼭대기를 황금빛으로 빛내고 있었다. **3** make (something) seem better and more attractive than it really is. …을 실제보다 좋게 보이게 하다; 겉을 꾸미다. ¶ ~ *a lie* 거짓말을 분식(粉飾)하다 / ~ *someone with virtues* 아무를 미덕으로 꾸미다. [*gold*]

gild the pill, make an unpleasant thing seem acceptable. 언짢은 면을 감추고 좋은 면만을 강조하다.

gild the lily, unnecessarily decorate something that is already beautiful. 이미 완벽한 것에 군손을 대다.

gild[2] [gild] *n.* =guild.

gild·ed [gíldid] *adj.* covered with thin gold. 금을 입힌; 도금한.

gild·ing [gíldiŋ] *n.* Ⓤ **1** the gold leaf or similar material with which a thing is gilded. 도금; 금박. ¶ *chemical* 〔*electric*〕 ~ 전기 도금. **2** the act of gilding. 도금술(術). **3** any coating to give a beautiful appearance. 겉만의 꾸밈; 분식(粉飾); 허식.

gill[1] [gil] *n.* Ⓒ 《usu. *pl.*》 **1** the part of a fish's body for breathing under water. 아가미. **2** the flesh under the chin and jaws of a person. 턱 밑의 군살. **3** the hanging flesh under a fowl's throat. (칠면조 따위의) 목 밑에 늘어진 살. ¶ *turn red in the gills* 성난 얼굴이 되다; 화를 내다. [E.]

look rosy 〔***blue, green***〕 ***about the gills,*** be healthy 〔unhealthy〕-looking. 혈색이 좋다〔나쁘다〕; 기운이 넘치다〔없다〕.

gill[2] [gil] *n.* **1** a deep rocky pass. 깊은 계곡(溪谷); 협곡(峽谷). **2** a narrow stream. 세류(細流). [N.]

gill[3] [dʒil] *n.* a small liquid measure, one quarter of a pint or 0.14 litre. 질《액량의 단위; 1/4 pint; 《英》 0.14*l*》. [F.]

gilt [gilt] *v.* p. and pp. of **gild**[1]. — *adj.* covered with thin gold; gilded. 금도금한; 금을 입힌. ¶ *a book with ~ edges* 가장자리에 금박을 입힌 책. — *n.* Ⓤ a thin layer of gold or gold-colored substance. 금도금; 금가루; 금박. [*gild*]

gilt-edged [gíltèdʒd] *adj.* **1** covered with gold. (종이·서적 따위가) 금테의; 가장자리에 금을 입힌. **2** of the best quality or value. 최상의; 일류의. ¶ ~ *securities* 〔*stocks*〕 우량 증권.

gim·crack [dʒímkræ̀k] *n.* Ⓒ a pretty but worthless thing. 겉만 번지르르한 것; 굴퉁이. — *adj.* pretty but worthless. 허울만 좋은; 굴퉁이의; 속임수의. [? E.]

gim·let [gímlit] *n.* Ⓒ a small tool with a screw point for making small holes. 도래〔나사〕송곳(cf. *auger*). ¶ *eyes like gimlets* 날카로운 눈. [Teut. →wimble]

gim·let-eyed [gímlitàid] *adj.* having eyes that are sharp and piercing. 눈이 날카로운.

gim·mick [gímik] *n.* 《U.S. *colloq.*》 a secret device by which a magician is able to perform a trick; any tricky device. (요술의) 비밀 장치; 트릭. [G.]

·**gin**[1] [dʒin] *n.* Ⓤ a strong, colorless alcoholic drink. 진《증류주의 하나》. [*geneva*[2]]

·**gin**[2] [dʒin] *n.* Ⓒ **1** a machine to separate cotton from its seeds. 조면기(繰綿機); 씨아. **2** an instrument used for pulling up heavy weights. 기중기. **3** a trap; a snare. 덫. — *vt.* (**ginned, gin·ning**) (P6) **1** clear (cotton) of seeds. (씨아로 목화씨)를 빼다; 조면하다. **2** trap; snare. …을 덫으로 잡다. [*engine*]

·**gin·ger** [dʒíndʒər] *n.* Ⓤ **1** a tropical plant from which a strong spicy powder is obtained; its powder. 생강; 그 가루. **2** 《*colloq.*》 energy; force; piquancy. 정력; 기운; 활기; 자극. **3** reddish or brownish yellow color. 황〔적〕갈색. — *vt.* (P7) **1** flavor with ginger. …에 생강을 쳐 맛을 내다. **2** 《*up*》 give more vigor and liveliness to. 활기 띄우다; 기운을 북돋우다. ●**gin·ger·y** [-ri] *adj.* [Skr.=horn body]

ginger ale [⌐-⌐] *n.* a soft drink flavored with ginger. 진저 에일《생강이 든 탄산 청량 음료》.

ginger beer [⌐-⌐] *n.* a sweet drink flavored with ginger. 진저 비어《진저 에일보다 생강 냄새가 더 강한 음료》.

gin·ger·bread [dʒíndʒərbrèd] *n.* **1** Ⓤ a cake or cookie flavored with ginger. 생강이 든 케이크. **2** Ⓒ a pretty but worthless thing. 허울만 번지르르한 것; 굴퉁이.

take the gilt off the gingerbread, show that a thing is not so pleasing as it was thought to be. 표면의 아름다움〔매력〕을 없애 버리다; 정체를 보이다.

— *adj.* showy. 겉만 번지르르한; 야한. ¶ ~ *work* 야한 싸구려 장식.

gin·ger·ly [dʒíndʒərli] *adj., adv.* very careful(ly); cautious(ly). 매우 조심스러운〔스럽게〕. ¶ *in a ~ way* 조심스럽게; 신중하게 / *place something ~ on a desk* …을 책상 위에 조심해서 놓다. [F.]

ging·ham [gíŋəm] *n.* Ⓤ a cotton cloth which is usu. designed in stripes or checks. 깅엄《줄무늬가 있는 무명》. [Malay]

ging·ko [gíŋkou] *n.* (*pl.* **-kos** or **-koes**) = ginkgo.

gink·go [gíŋkou, dʒíŋ-] *n.* Ⓒ (*pl.* **-goes**) a tree found in China and Japan that has fan-shaped leaves and bears eatable nuts. 은행나무. ¶ *a ~ nut* 은행. [Jap.]

gin mill [⌐⌐] *n.* 《U.S. *sl.*》 a saloon. 술집. [*gin*]

gin·seng [dʒínseŋ] *n.* Ⓒ a plant found in China or Korea, whose root is used for medicine. 인삼. [Chinese *jen shen* 人蔘]

gip·sy, Gip·sy [dʒípsi] *n., adj.* 《esp. Brit.》 =gypsy.

gi·raffe [dʒəræ̂f / -rá:f] *n.* Ⓒ an African animal with a very long neck and legs and a spotted skin. 기린; 지라프. [Arab.]

gird[1] [gə:rd] *vt.* (**girt** or **gird·ed**) (P6,7,13) **1** put a belt around (something). (띠·벨트

따위)로 …을 두르다〔매다〕. ¶ ～ *oneself* (*with a belt*) 띠를 매다〔조르다〕/ ～ *the waist* 허리에 띠를 매다 / *be girt about with a rope* 밧줄로 묶이다. **2** surround; encircle. …을 에워〔둘러〕싸다. ¶ ～ *a village* 마을을 포위하다 / *an island girded by the sea* 바다에 둘러싸인 섬. **3** fasten to (someone) by means of a belt, etc. (띠 따위로) …을 채우다. ¶ ～ *someone with a sword* 아무에게 검을 채우다 / *be girded with a sword* 검을 차고 있다. **4** fasten (something) to one's body. (…을) 몸에 차다〔걸치다, 두르다〕. ¶ ～ *a belt* 벨트를 차다; ～ *on one's sword* 칼을 차다; 대검(帶劍)하다. **5** prepare (oneself) for action; make ready for. 준비〔채비〕하다; 긴장하다. [E.]

gird up *one's* ***loins*** ⇨loin.

gird[2] [gəːrd] *vi.* (P3) 《*at*》 laugh at (someone). 비웃다; 놀리다. [E.]

gird·er [gə́ːrdər] *n.* Ⓒ a bar of wood or steel supporting a building, bridge, etc. 도리; 대들보. [*gird*[1]]

***gir·dle** [gə́ːrdl] *n.* Ⓒ **1** something worn around the waist, such as a sash or belt. 띠; 허리띠; 벨트. **2** anything that surrounds. 띠 모양의 것; 둘러싼 것. ¶ *the* ～ *of the sea* 사면을 둘러싼 바다 / *a* ～ *of trees around the lake* 호수를 둘러싼 나무숲. **3** a support like a corset worn about the hips or waist. 거들; 코르셋. — *vt.* (P6,7) **1** encircle. …을 둘러싸다. **2** put a girdle around (the waist). …을 띠로 두르다. [E. →gird[1]]

:girl [gəːrl] *n.* Ⓒ **1** a female child; a young unmarried woman. 계집아이; 소녀; 처녀. ¶ *His first child was a* ～. 그의 첫아이는 계집아이였다 / *the Girl Guides* 소녀단(團)(cf. *Boy Scouts*) / *He married a pretty* ～. 그는 예쁜 처녀와 결혼했다. **2** a young woman who is employed; a maidservant, shopgirl, etc. 여자 피고용자; 하녀; 여점원. **3** 《*colloq.*》 a sweetheart. 연인. **4** 《*colloq.*》 a woman of any age. 여자. [E.]

girl·hood [gə́ːrlhùd] *n.* Ⓤ **1** the time of being a girl. 소녀 시대; 처녀 시절. **2** girls as a class. 소녀들. ¶ *the nation's* ～ 이 나라의 소녀들. [E.]

girl·ie [gə́ːrli] *n.* 《*colloq.*》 a little girl. 여자아이; 아가씨.

girl·ish [gə́ːrliʃ] *adj.* **1** of a girl. 소녀의; 계집아이의. **2** like a girl; suitable for girls. 계집애〔소녀〕 같은; 소녀에 어울리는. ● **girl·ish·ly** [-li] *adv.* **girl·ish·ness** [-nis] *n.* [*girl*]

girt [gəːrt] *v.* p. and pp. of **gird**[1].
— *adj.* surrounded. 둘러싸인. ¶ *a sea-girt island* 바다에 둘러싸인 섬. [*ǵird*[1]]

girth [gəːrθ] *n.* Ⓒ **1** the distance around anything. 주위〔둘레〕의 길이. ¶ *the* ～ *of a tree* 나무의 몸통 둘레 / *measure the* ～ *of someone's waist* 아무의 허리통 치수를 재다. **2** a band around an animal for holding a saddle, pack, etc. in place. (말 따위의) 배띠. — *vt., vi.* (P6; 1) **1** measure the girth of (a tree, etc.). (나무 따위) 둘레의 치수를 재다. **2** put on or tighten up the girth of a horse. 배띠를 두르다〔졸라매다〕. [N. (→gird[1])]

gist [dʒist] *n.* Ⓒ the essential point. 요점; 요지; 골자. ¶ *give a* ～ *of a story* 이야기의 요점을 말하다 / *get* 〔*grasp*〕 *the* ～ *of someone's speech* 아무의 연설의 요지를 파악하다. [L. *jaceo* lie]

:give [giv] *vt.* (**gave, giv·en**) **1** (P13,14) cause (someone) to have; hand over; present. …에게 주다; 증여〔선물〕하다. ¶ ～ *him a book* = ～ *a book to him* 그에게 책을 주다 / *The dog was given to me.* 나는 그 개를 받았다 / *He gave the souvenir to his daughter.* 딸에게 선물을 주었다. **2** (P13,14) hand over in exchange for something; pay. (…와 교환으로) 지불하다. ¶ ～ *5,000 won for this book* 이 책에 5천 원을 지불하다 / ～ *someone 200 dollars for a week's work* 주급(週給) 2백 달러를 지급하다 / *How much did you* ～ *for the coat?* 이 상의에 얼마나 주셨나요 / *Give me a hundred dollars in cash and I'll sign the paper.* 현금으로 백 달러를 주면 서류에 서명하겠습니다. **3** (P13,14) grant; allow; permit. (허가·은혜 따위로서) …을 주다; 인가하다. ¶ ～ *someone a permission* 아무에게 허가를 주다 / ～ *encouragement to* …에게 격려를 주다 / *God* ～ *me wisdom.* 신이여 저에게 지혜를 주소서. **4** (P6,13,14) furnish; provide; supply. …을 제공하다; 제출하다; 공급하다; 투여하다. ¶ ～ *evidence* 증언하다 / ～ *a suggestion* 제안하다 / ～ *a medicine to a patient* 환자에게 약을 주다 / ～ *aid to* …을 원조하다 / *Cows* ～ *us milk.* 젖소는 우리에게 우유를 공급해 준다. **5** (P13,14) yield. 양보하다. ¶ ～ *a point in an argument* 의론에서 한 점을 양보하다. **6** (P6,13,14) pass on; communicate. …을 전(달)하다; 알리다; 전염시키다. ¶ ～ *news* 〔*a message*〕 소식을〔메시지를〕 전하다 / ～ *advice* 충고하다 / ～ *one's name* 이름을 밝히다 / ～ *the driver the name of the hotel* 운전사에게 호텔 이름을 알려 주다 / *You've given me your cold.* 자네 감기를 내게 전염시켰네. **7** (P6,13,14) ⓐ state; put forth. 말하다; 발하다; 내다. ¶ ～ *one's opinion* 의견을 말하다 / ～ *a command* 명령을 내다 / ～ *a cry* 소리치다 / ～ *a cough* 기침을 하다 / ～ *light* 빛을 발하다 / ～ *signs* 신호를 하다. ⓑ show; exhibit. …을 보이다; 나타내다. ¶ ～ *a good example* 좋은 모범을 보이다 / *The thermometer gives 30°C now.* 온도계는 섭씨 30도를 나타내고 있다. **8** (P13) devote. …을 바치다; …에 몰두하다. ¶ ～ *one's mind to one's study* 연구에 몰두하다 / ～ *one's life to music* 음악에 생애를 바치다 / ～ *oneself to one's work* 일에 한 몸을 바치다 / ～ *one's attention to* …에 주의를 기울이다. **9** (P13,14) place in someone's care. …에게 맡기다; 위탁하다. ¶ ～ *something into the hands* 〔*care*〕 *of someone* …을 아무의 관리에 맡기다. **10** (P6,13,14) perform; do; hold. …을 (행)하다;

개최하다. ¶ ~ *a kick* 걷어차다 / ~ *a party* 파티를 열다 / ~ *a play* 연극을 상연하다 / ~ *someone a glance* 아무를 언뜻[흘끔] 보다 / ~ *a blow to someone* 아무에게 일격을 가하다. **11** (P20) cause. …하게 하다. ¶ ~ *someone to know* [*see*] 아무에게 알리다[보게 하다] / ~ *someone furiously to think* 아무로 하여금 크게 생각하게 하다. **12** (P6,13,14) cause; occasion. 생기게[나게] 하다; 일어나게 하다. ¶ ~ *offense* 기분을 상하게 하다 / *She gives me a pain in the neck.* 그녀는 나를 짜증나게 만든다. — *vi.* **1** (P1) make a gift. 주다; 기증을[기부를] 하다. **2** (P1,2A) bend; break down; yield. (힘을 받아) 우그러지다; 휘다; 굽다; 무너지다. ¶ *The cushion gives comfortably.* 쿠션이 푹신푹신해서 기분이 좋다 / *The old chair gave when I sat on it.* 그 낡은 의자는 내가 앉자 찌부러졌다. **3** (P3) 《*on, upon*》 overlook; face. 내려다보다; 면하다. ¶ *The window gives on the sea.* 창문은 바다에 면해 있다. **4** (P1) become mild; melt. (기후 따위가) 온화해[누그러]지다; (얼음·서리 따위가) 녹다. ¶ *The winter is giving.* 겨울의 추위가 누그러져 간다 / *The frost didn't* ~ *all day.* 서리가 온종일 녹지 않았다. [E.]

give a damn [***hoot***], 《usu. *negative*》《*colloq.*》 think as important. 중요하게 생각하다. ¶ *I do not* ~ *a damn.* 조금도 상관[개의]치 않는다.

give and take, exchange on an equal basis. 대등한 입장에서 주고받다.

give away, **a**) give (something) as a present. (선물로서) 주다; 증여하다. **b**) hand over (a bride) to a bridegroom. (신부)를 신랑에게 넘겨[건네] 주다. **c**) 《*colloq.*》 betray; let slip (something secret); reveal; show the true character of (someone). …을 배반하다; (비밀을) 누설하다; …의 정체를 폭로하다.

give back, **a**) return (something) to its owner; restore; reply. 돌려 주다; 되돌리다; 회답하다. ¶ *He gave the papers back to the man.* 서류를 그 사람에게 돌려 주었다. **b**) retire; retreat. 물러서다; 물러나다.

give forth, **a**) send forth; emit; produce. (소리·냄새 따위를) 발(發)하다; 내다. ¶ ~ *forth a sound* 소리를 내다. **b**) make public; spread. 공표하다; 퍼뜨리다.

give in, **a**) stop fighting and admit defeat; yield. 굴복하다. **b**) hand over; deliver. 넘겨[건네] 주다; 제출하다.

give into, (of a passage, window, etc.) lead or open into. …으로 통하다; …에 면하다.

give it to, 《*colloq.*》 punish; scold. …을 벌하다; 책(責)하다; 꾸짖다.

give off, put forth; emit. …을 발(산)하다; 내다. ¶ ~ *off light* 빛을 발하다 / *Boiling water gives off steam.* 끓는 물이 증기를 발산한다.

give out, **a**) become very tired; run short; become used up. 몹시 지치다; 녹초가 되다; 다 써 버리다. ¶ *His money soon gave out.* 그의 돈은 곧 바닥이 났다. **b**) give (things) to others. 도르다; 분배하다. ¶ ~ *out the apparatus required* 필요한 용구를 지급하다. **c**) publish; make known. …을 공표[발표]하다; 고시하다; 알리다. **d**) emit; put forth. …을 발하다; 내다.

give over, **a**) hand over; surrender. 건네[넘겨] 주다. **b**) stop; cease. 그만두다; 멈추다. ¶ ~ *over a bad habit* 못된 버릇을 버리다. **c**) put into another's care. 맡기다. ¶ *He gave it over to my keeping.* 그것을 내가 관리하도록 맡겼다. **d**) indulge in to excess. 몸을 맡기다; 빠지다. ¶ *She gave herself* [*was given*] *over to despair.* 그녀는 깊은 절망에 빠졌다.

give up, **a**) stop trying. 단념하다; 끊다. ¶ *I have given up smoking.* 담배를 끊었다 / *The problem was too difficult for me, so I gave up.* 문제가 너무 어려워서 포기했다. **b**) abandon hope; despair. 절망하다. ¶ *The doctor has given him up.* 의사는 그를 포기했다. **c**) hand over; surrender. 넘겨 주다; 포기하다. ¶ ~ *up one's seat to a lady in a train* 열차에서 숙녀에게 자리를 양보하다 / ~ *up the fort to the enemy* 적군에게 요새를 넘겨 주다. **d**) devote oneself to; indulge in (something). …에 헌신[몰두]하다; 몸을 바치다. ¶ ~ *oneself up to study* 연구에 몰두하다.

give way, **a**) make room for; give place. 자리를[길을] 양보하다. **b**) yield to force. (압력·폭력 따위로) 무너지다; 굴하다; 지다. ¶ ~ *way to temptation* 유혹에 지다 / *The bridge gave way under the heavy load.* 무거운 짐무게를 지탱하지 못하고 다리가 무너졌다.

give-and-take [gívəntéik] *n.* Ⓤ **1** an exchange on an equal basis; mutual cooperation. (타협에 의한) 대등한 주고받기; 호양(互讓); 협조. **2** good-natured exchange of talk, ideas, etc. 의견의 교환.

give·a·way [gívəwèi] *n.* **1** Ⓤ the act of telling a secret carelessly; betrayal. 무심코 비밀을 누설하기. **2** Ⓒ a premium given for promoting sales. 경품. **3** Ⓒ《U.S. *colloq.*》 a question-and-answer game as a radio or television show in which prizes are given away. (라디오·TV의) 퀴즈 프로.

:giv·en [gívən] *v.* pp. of **give.** — *adj.* **1** stated; fixed; appointed. 주어진; 정해진; 일정한. ¶ *under a* ~ *condition* 주어진 조건 밑에서 / *at a* ~ *time* 정해진 시간에 / *within a* ~ *time* 일정한 시간 내에 / *finish the work in a* ~ *time* 정해진 시간 안에 일을 마치다. **2** bestowed as a gift; presented. 선물로 주어진; 증여된. **3** taken as a basis of reasoning; assumed; granted. 전제의; 가정의; 가설의. ¶ *a* ~ *circle* 주어진 원 / *given that* ... 가정하면. **4** 《*to*》 inclined; accustomed. …하고 싶어하는; 탐닉하는; 빠지는; 버릇이 있는. ¶ *be* ~ *to indiscriminate reading* 닥치는 대로 남독(濫讀)하는 버릇이 있다 / *He is* ~ *to drinking.* 그는 음주벽이 있다. [→give]

given name [∠-∠] *n.* 《U.S.》 a name given to a person at his birth. (성에 대한)

이름(=《Brit.》Christian name).

giv·er [gívər] *n.* Ⓒ a person who gives. 주는 사람; 증여자; 기증자.

giz·zard [gízərd] *n.* the second stomach of a bird. 모래 주머니; 사낭(砂囊). [F.]

Gk. Greek.

gla·cial [gléiʃəl] *adj.* **1** of or like ice; very cold; icy. 얼음의(같은); 매우 차가운(추운). **2** of glaciers or the glacial period. 빙하(시대)의. ¶ *the ~ period.* **3** 《chem.》 having an icelike form; crystallized. 빙상(氷狀) 결정의. [L. *glacies* ice]

gla·cier [gléiʃər, gléisjər] *n.* Ⓒ a large riverlike mass of ice which moves slowly down a mountain. 빙하(氷河). [↑]

:glad [glæd] *adj.* (**glad·der, glad·dest**) **1** happy; pleased. 기쁜; 반가운. ¶ *I'm very ~ to see you.* 만나 뵈어 매우 반갑습니다 / *I'm ~ (that) you have come.* 와 주셔서 대단히 기쁩니다 / *I am ~ of* (*about*) *that.* 그거 잘됐군. **2** pleasant; joyful. 즐거운. ¶ *~ news.* [E.]

give the glad eye to, 《*sl.*》 look lovingly at. …에게 다정한 눈길을 주다; 추파를 던지다.

glad·den [glǽdn] *vi., vt.* (P1; 6) become or make happy. 기뻐하다; 기쁘게 하다. [*glad*]

glade [gleid] *n.* Ⓒ an open space in a forest. 숲 속의 빈 터. [↑]

glad hand [ˊˋ], **the** *n.* the hand of welcome. 환대; 겉으로만의 환영. ¶ *give someone the ~* 아무를 (표면적으로는) 따뜻하게 맞이하다.

glad·i·a·tor [glǽdièitər] *n.* Ⓒ **1** (in Ancient Rome) a man trained or hired to fight before the public to entertain them. 검투사. **2** a person who argues with great skill. 논쟁자. [L. *gladius* sword]

glad·i·o·li [glæ̀dióulai] *n.* pl. of **gladiolus.**

glad·i·o·lus [glæ̀dióuləs] *n.* Ⓒ (*pl.* **-lus·es** or **-li**) 《bot.》 a garden plant of the iris family with swordshaped leaves and beautiful flowers. 글라디올러스. [L. =little sword]

·glad·ly [glǽdli] *adv.* in a glad manner. 기꺼이; 즐겁게. [*glad*]

glad·ness [glǽdnis] *n.* Ⓤ the state of being glad. 기쁨; 반가움.

glad rags [ˊˋ] *n.* 《*sl.*》 one's best clothes; evening clothes. 나들이옷; 야회복.

glad·some [glǽdsəm] *adj.* joyful; cheerful; delightful. 기쁜; 유쾌한.

Glad·stone [glǽdstoun, -stən] *n.* a kind of light portmanteau. 여행 가방(=Gladstone bag). [Person]

glad tidings [ˊˋˉ] *n.* the gospel. 복음.

glam·or [glǽmər] *n.* =glamour.

glam·or·ous [glǽmərəs] *adj.* charming; fascinating. 매력이 넘치는; 매력적(매혹적)인. ¶ *a ~ girl* 매혹적인 여자. ● **glam·or·ous·ly** [-li] *adv.* [↓]

glam·our [glǽmər] *n.* Ⓤ 《sometimes *a ~*》 mysterious charm or fascination; enchantment. 매력. ¶ *an actress radiant with ~* 매력이 넘치는 여우(女優).

cast a glamour over, enchant. …에 마법을 걸다; …을 매료하다.

— *vt.* (P6) bewitch. …을 혹하게 하다; 매혹시키다. [corrup. of *grammar*=learning]

:glance [glæns, glɑːns] *n.* Ⓒ **1** a swift look. 언뜻(한번) 봄; 한눈; 일별; 일견. ¶ *at a ~* 일견하여 / *cast a ~ at a report* 보고서를 대충 훑어보다 / *steal a ~ at a pretty girl* 아름다운 소녀를 가만히 훔쳐보다 / *dart a ~ around* 주위를 언뜻 둘러보다 / *They exchanged glances.* 그들은 서로 눈짓을 하였다. **2** a gleam; a flash. 번득임; 섬광.

— *vi.* (P2A,3) **1** 《*at, over, through, into*》 look quickly. 언뜻 보다. ¶ *~ about* (*round*) *the room* 방 안을 재빨리 둘러보다 / *~ over* (*through*) *an account* 계산서를 대충 훑어보다. **2** gleam; flash. 번득이다; 번쩍이다. **3** 《*away, off*》 (of a bullet, etc.) slide off (something); (of a speech, etc.) turn away from the subject. (탄알 따위가) 빗맞다; 빗나가다; (이야기 따위가) 곁가지로 새다. [O.F. *glaichier* slip]

glance back, reflect. …을 반사하다. ¶ *~ back the light* 빛을 반사하다.

gland [glænd] *n.* Ⓒ an organ in the body which gives out some substance. 선(腺); 샘. ¶ *endocrine ~* 내분비선(腺) / *the sweat glands of the skin* 피부의 땀샘. [L. *glans* acorn]

glan·du·lar [glǽndʒələr] *adj.* of or like a gland. 선(腺)(모양)의. [↑]

·glare [glɛər] *n.* Ⓒ 《usu. *sing.*》 **1** a bright and dazzling light. 눈부신 빛; 섬광. ¶ *the ~ of the sun* 이글거리는 햇빛. **2** a fierce and angry look. 노려봄; 쏘아봄. ¶ *the ~ of the lion* 사자의 노려봄 / *look at someone with a ~* 아무를 노려보다. **3** Ⓤ showy appearance or display. 현란함; 야함; 화려.

— *vi.* (P1,2A,3) **1** shine with a dazzling light. 눈부시게 빛나다. ¶ *The hot sun glared down on us.* 뜨거운 햇빛이 우리들을 내리쬐었다. **2** 《*at, upon*》 stare angrily. 노려보다. ¶ *The woman glared at me.* 여자는 나를 쏘아보았다.

— *vt.* (P6,13) express (something) with a fierce look. …을 노려보아 나타내다. ¶ *He glared hatred at me.* 그는 혐오가 담긴 눈길을 나에게 돌렸다. [E.]

glar·ing [glɛ́əriŋ] *adj.* **1** dazzlingly bright. 번쩍번쩍 빛나는; 눈부신. **2** fierce and angry. 몹시 성난. ¶ *~ eyes* 이글거리는 눈. **3** too bright; showy. 야한; 난한. ¶ *~ colors* 야한 빛깔. **4** evident. 두드러진; 명백한. ¶ *a ~ mistake* 두드러진 잘못 / *a ~ lie* 새빨간 거짓말.

Glas·gow [glǽsgou, -kou] *n.* a large seaport in southwest Scotland. 글래스고. 參考 스코틀랜드 남서부의 해항(海港). 조선·섬유·제강(製鋼) 따위의 대중심지.

:glass [glæs, glɑːs] *n.* **1** Ⓤ a hard substance which is usu. clear and easily broken. 유리. ¶ *as clear as* ~ 유리처럼 투명한; 극히 분명한 / *Windows are made of* ~. 창문이 유리로 되어 있다. **2** Ⓤ《*collectively*》 things made of glass. 유리 제품. ¶ ~ *and china* 유리 그릇과 도자기. **3** Ⓒ an object made of glass, such as a drinking vessel, mirror, etc. (유리로 된) 술잔; 컵; 거울 따위(cf. *goblet*). ¶ *enjoy a* ~ *now and then* 가끔 술을 즐기다 / *have a* ~ *with him* 그와 한잔 하다 / *Look at yourself in the* ~. 거울 속의 네 모습을 보라. **4**《*pl.*》ⓐ spectacles; eyeglasses. 안경. ¶ *read without glasses* 안경을 쓰지 않고 읽다. ⓑ binoculars. 쌍안경. **5** a telescope. 망원경. **6** a barometer. 청우계; 기압계. ¶ *The* ~ *is falling.* 기압계가 내려가고 있다.

— *vt.* (P6) **1** fit with glass; cover with glass. 유리를 끼우다; 유리로 덮다. ¶ ~ *a window* 창문에 유리를 끼우다 / ~ *a picture* 그림을 유리에 넣다. **2**《often *reflexively*》 reflect oneself. …의 상(像)을〔그림자를, 모습을〕 비추다. ¶ *The mountains* ~ *themselves in the lake.* 산이 호수에 그림자를 비추고 있다. [E.]

glass blower [ˊ ˋ–] *n.* a person who blows and shapes glass. 유리 부는 직공.

glass cutter [ˊ ˋ–] *n.* a workman or tool that cuts glass. 유리 절단공; 유리칼.

glass·ful [glǽsfùl, glɑ́:s-] *n.* Ⓒ as much as a glass can hold. 잔〔컵〕 하나 가득(한 양).

glass·house [glǽshàus, glɑ́:s-] *n.* Ⓒ (*pl.* **-houses** [-hàuziz]) **1** a place where glass is made; glassworks. 유리 공장. **2** a hothouse; a greenhouse. 온실.

glass paper [ˊ ˋ–] *n.* paper covered with powdered glass, used for making surfaces smooth. 사포(砂布).

glass·ware [glǽswɛ̀ər, glɑ́:s-] *n.* Ⓤ《*collectively*》 articles made of glass, such as glass dishes, pitchers, etc. 유리 제품.

glass·work [glǽswə̀:rk, glɑ́:s-] *n.* Ⓤ **1** the industry manufacturing glass and glassware. 유리(그릇) 제조업. **2** glassware. 유리 제품. **3**《usu. *pl.* used as *sing.*》 a factory where glass is made. 유리 공장.

glass·y [glǽsi, glɑ́:si] *adj.* (**glass·i·er, glass·i·est**) **1** like glass; smooth. 유리 같은; 반드러운; 매끄러운. ¶ *the* ~ *surface of the lake* 거울 같은 호수면(面). **2** (of the eye or look) lifeless expressionless. (눈 따위가) 생기없는; 흐리멍텅한; 멍한; 무표정한. ¶ *give someone a* ~ *eye* 아무를 멍하니 바라보다.

glau·co·ma [glɔ:kóumə, glau-] *n.* Ⓤ《med.》 a disease of the eye. 녹내장. [Gk.]

glau·cous [glɔ́:kəs] *adj.* **1** light bluish-green. 열은 청록색의. **2**《bot.》 covered with whitish powder as plums and grapes are. (자두 따위가) 흰 가루를 뒤집어쓴. [Gk.]

glaze [gleiz] *vt.* **1** (P6,7) put glass in (something). …에 유리를 끼우다. ¶ ~ *a window* 창문에 유리를 끼우다. **2** (P6,7) cover (something) with a glassy surface; give a polished, smooth surface to. …의 표면에 광택을 내다; 유약을 바르다. ¶ ~ *earthenware* 도자기에 유약을 입히다. — *vi.* (P1,2A) become glassy. 유리처럼 되다; 반드러워지다; 광이〔윤기가〕 나다; (눈이) 흐릿해지다. — *n.* **1** Ⓒ a smooth, glasslike surface. 반드러운〔윤기 도는〕 표면. **2** Ⓤ substance used for glazing. 유약; 잿물. [*glass*]

gla·zier [gléizər / -zjər] *n.* Ⓒ a person whose job is to put glass in picture frames, windows, etc. 유리 장수.

:**gleam** [gli:m] *n.* Ⓒ **1** a brief beam or flash of light. 희미한〔어렴풋한〕 빛; 번득임; 섬광. ¶ *the faint* ~ *from a distant church* 멀리 교회에서 새어나오는 희미한 빛. **2** a brief show of feeling or emotion. 감정 따위의 번득임. ¶ *a faint* ~ *of hope* 한 줄기 희미한 희망 / *an occasional* ~ *of intelligence* 이따금 번득이는 지성(知性). — *vi.* (P1,2A) **1** flash with light. 번쩍 빛나다. ¶ *Stars gleamed.* **2** (of emotion, wit, etc.) appear suddenly. 번득이다; 나타나다. ¶ *Wit gleamed in his speech.* 그의 연설에는 재치가 번득였다. [E.]

glean [gli:n] *vi., vt.* (P1; 6) **1** gather what the reapers have left after the harvest in a field. 이삭을 줍다. ¶ ~ *the wheat that is left* 밀의 이삭을 줍다. **2** collect (information, news, etc.) little by little. …을 조금씩 수집하다. ¶ ~ *news* 〔*information*〕 뉴스〔정보〕를 수집하다 / ~ *the data from many books* 많은 책에서 자료를 수집하다. [F.]

glean·ings [glí:niŋz] *n. pl.* things gleaned; collection. 수집한 것.

glebe [gli:b] *n.* **1** Ⓤ《*poet.*》 soil; field. 땅; 토지; 밭. **2**《Brit.》Ⓒ a portion of land owned by a clergyman as part of his living. 목사 영지(領地). [L. *gleba* clod]

glee [gli:] *n.* Ⓤ **1** joy; delight. 기쁨; 환희. ¶ *a shout of* ~ 환성; 환호. **2**《mus.》Ⓒ a part song for three or more voices, usu. without accompaniment of musical instruments. 글리《삼성(三聲) 또는 그 이상의 무반주 합창곡》. [E.]

in high glee, with great joy. 몹시 기뻐하여.

glee·ful [glí:fəl] *adj.* filled with glee; joyous; gay. 매우 기뻐하는; 즐거운. ¶ ~ *news from home* 고향으로부터의 기쁜 소식. ● **glee·ful·ly** [-li] *adv.* **glee·ful·ness** [-nis] *n.*

glee·some [glí:səm] *adj.* =gleeful.

***glen** [glen] *n.* Ⓒ a small, narrow valley. 협곡(峽谷). [Gael.]

glen·gar·ry [glengǽri] *n.* Ⓒ (*pl.* **-ries**) a cap worn by Highlanders in Scotland. (스코틀랜드 고지 사람이 쓰는) 모자.

glib [glib] *adj.* (**glib·ber, glib·best**) speaking smoothly but without much thought or truth. 입심 좋게 지절거리는. ¶ *a* ~ *speech* 유창한 말 / *a* ~ *excuse* 그럴듯한 핑계〔구실〕 / *be of* ~ *tongue* 말을 잘 하다. [Du.]

glib·ly [glíbli] *adv.* in a glib manner. 입심 좋게; 유창하게.

·**glide** [glaid] *vi.* (P1,2A,3) **1** ⓐ move gently and quietly over a smooth surface or through the air. 미끄러지듯 움직이다〔나아가다〕; 활주〔활공〕하다. ¶ *The boat glided through the water.* 배가 물결을 헤치고 미끄러지듯 나아갔다 / *A skater glides on the ice.* 스케이트 선수가 빙판 위를 활주한다. ⓑ (of a person) move along with a smooth, easy walk. 소리 없이〔가만히〕 움직이다. ¶ ~ *in* 〔*out*〕 가만히 들어가다〔나오다〕 / ~ *out of* 〔*into*〕 *the room* 방에서 가만히 나오다〔방으로 가만히 들어가다〕. **2** pass gradually. 서서히〔점차〕 지나가다. ¶ *The hours glided past.* 시간이 어느 틈엔가 지나갔다.
— *vt.* (P6) cause (something) to glide. …을 미끄러지게 하다.
— *n.* Ⓒ **1** a smooth and easy movement. 미끄러짐; 활주. **2** (of an airplane) a slow downward movement without using an engine. 활공(滑空). [E.]

glid·er [gláidər] *n.* Ⓒ an aircraft like an airplane but without an engine. 글라이더; 활공기(滑空機).

glim [glim] *n.* 《*sl.*》 a lamp or other artificial light. 등화(燈火); (등)불. [↓]
douse the glim, put out the light. 등불을 끄다.

glim·mer [glímər] *n.* Ⓒ **1** a faint, wavering light. 희미한〔가물거리는〕 빛. **2** a hint; a faint glimpse. 마음에 짚임; 어렴풋한 인식. ¶ *a ~ of hope* 가냘픈 희망. — *vi.* (P1) **1** shine faintly and waveringly; flicker. 희미하게 빛나다; 명멸(明滅)하다. ¶ *The lights glimmered in the fog.* 안개 속에 등불 빛이 어른거렸다. **2** appear faintly. 희미하게 보이다. [E.]

:**glimpse** [glimps] *n.* Ⓒ **1** a brief, quick view. 언뜻 봄. ¶ *see the Indian ruins by glimpses* 인디언의 유적을 잠깐 보다 / *I caught* 〔*got*〕 *a ~ of her in the crowd.* 군중 속에서 언뜻 그녀를 보았다. **2** a brief appearance; a hint. 어렴풋한 감지(感知)〔깨달음〕. ¶ *a ~ of what is to come* 앞으로 닥쳐올 일의 어렴풋한 감지. — *vt., vi.* (P6; 1) catch a quick view of (something); look briefly. (…을) 언뜻 보다. [E.]

glint [glint] *vi., vt.* (P1; 6) flash; spark; reflect (light). 번쩍 빛나다; 번득이다; 반사하다. ¶ ~ *the lights back* 빛을 반사시키다. — *n.* Ⓒ a flash; a gleam. 번득임; 섬광. ¶ *the ~ of gold* 황금의 번쩍임. [Scand.]

·**glis·ten** [glísn] *vi.* (P1,2A) sparkle; gleam; shine. 번쩍번쩍하다; 빛나다. ¶ *The dewdrops glistened in the sun.* 이슬 방울이 햇빛에 반짝였다 / *Her eyes glistened with curiosity.* 그녀의 눈은 호기심으로 빛났다. — *n.* Ⓒ a gleam. 반짝임; 빛남. [E.]

:**glit·ter** [glítər] *vi.* (P1,2A) **1** shine brightly and at intervals; sparkle. 번쩍번쩍 빛나다. ¶ *stars glittering in the sky at night* 밤하늘에 반짝이는 별들 / 《*prov.*》 *All is not gold that glitters.* 번쩍이는 것이 다 금은 아니다. **2** (of clothes, etc.) be bright and showy. (옷 따위가) 현란하다; 야하다. — *n.* ⒸⓊ **1** a bright, sparkling light. 번쩍이는 빛; 빛남; 광휘. **2** brightness. 현란함; 야함. [N.]

gloam·ing [glóumiŋ] *n.* 《*the ~*》 twilight; dusk. 황혼; 땅거미; 박모(薄暮). [E.]

gloat [glout] *vi.* (P1,3) 《*upon, over*》 look contentedly; feel or show selfish pleasure. 만족스러운 듯이 보다; 고소해하다. ¶ *with a gloating smile* 득의의 미소를 지으며 / ~ *over someone's misfortune* 아무의 불행을 고소해하다 / *sit gloating by oneself* 홀로 득의 만만하여 앉아 있다 / *They gloated over the stolen jewels.* 그들은 만족스러운 듯이 훔친 보석을 보았다. [E.]

glob·al [glóubəl] *adj.* **1** of the earth; worldwide. 지구의; 전세계의. ¶ *our ~ problems* 우리들의 세계적인 문제 / *a ~ war* 세계 전쟁 / *the ~ market* 세계 시장. **2** globe-shaped. 구형(球形)의. [↓]

:**globe** [gloub] *n.* Ⓒ **1** anything shaped like a ball; a sphere. 구체(球體). **2** 《*the ~*》 the earth. 지구. **3** a sphere showing a map of the earth or sky on it. 지구본; 천구의(天球儀). ¶ *a celestial* 〔*terrestrial*〕 ~ 천구의〔지구본〕. [L. *globus*]

globe·fish [glóubfìʃ] *n.* Ⓒ (*pl.* **-fish·es** or *collectively* **-fish**) a fish that can make itself globe-shaped by taking in air. 복어.

globe-trot·ter [glóubtrɑ̀tər / -trɔ̀-] *n.* a person who is always traveling from country to country, esp. a person who travels for amusement. (빈번한) 세계 관광 여행자.

glo·bose [glóubous, -⌐] *adj.* spherical. 구상(球狀)의; 구형(球形)의. [↓]

glob·u·lar [glɑ́bjələr / glɔ́b-] *adj.* **1** shaped like a globe; round. 구형(球形)의; 둥근. **2** consisting of globules. 작은 구체(球體)로 된. [→globe]

glob·ule [glɑ́bjuːl / glɔ́b-] *n.* Ⓒ a very small ball; a tiny drop of liquid. 소구체(小球體); 물방울. ¶ *a ~ of sweat* 땀방울. [↑]

glom·er·ate [glɑ́mərit / glɔ́m-] *adj.* clustered together; collected into a rounded mass. 밀집돼 있는; 구상(球狀)으로 모인. [L. *glomus* ball]

·**gloom** [gluːm] *n.* Ⓤ **1** dimness; darkness. 어둠; 암흑. ¶ *The scenery was enveloped in ~.* 배경은 어둠에 싸여 있었다. **2** 《sometimes *a ~*》 sadness; melancholy. 슬픔; 우울. ¶ *man's future full of ~* 암담한 인류의 장래 / *cast ~ over* 〔*upon*〕 *married life* 결혼 생활에 어두운 그림자를 던지다 / *chase one's ~ away* 우울함을 떨쳐 버리다. — *vt., vi.* (P6;1) make (something) dark; become dark. 어둡게〔우울하게〕 하다; 어두워〔우울해〕지다. [E.]

gloom·i·ly [glúːmili] *adv.* **1** darkly. 어둡게. **2** melancholily. 우울〔음울〕하게.

·**gloom·y** [glúːmi] *adj.* (**gloom·i·er, gloom-**

i·est) **1** dark; dim. 어두운. **2** sad; melancholy. 우울하게 하는; 음울한. ¶ ~ *prospects* 암담한 전망. **3** discouraging. 의기 소침한.
● **gloom·i·ness** [-nis] *n.*

glo·ri·a [glɔ́:riə] *n.* Ⓒ **1** a song of praise to God. 신(神)을 찬양하는 노래. **2** 《*G-*》 one of three Latin hymns of praise to God. 영광송(榮光頌). **3** a halo. 광륜(光輪); 후광(後光). [L.]

glo·ri·fi·ca·tion [glɔ̀:rəfikéiʃən] *n.* Ⓤ **1** the act of glorifying; the state of being glorified. 신(神)의 영광을 기리는 행위. **2** 《*colloq.*》 celebration; festivity. 축연(祝宴). [↓]

glo·ri·fy [glɔ́:rəfài] *vt.* (**-fied**) **1** give glory to (someone); make (someone) glorious. …에 영광을 더하다〔돌리다〕. ¶ ~ *God.* **2** praise; honor. …을 상찬(賞讚)하다. ¶ ~ *the hero* 영웅을 기리다. **3** make (something) more beautiful or splendid. …을 미화(美化)하다. ¶ *Moonlight glorified the running water.* 달빛은 흐르는 물을 아름답게 했다. [→glory]

:**glo·ri·ous** [glɔ́:riəs] *adj.* **1** full of glory. 영광〔광영〕에 찬; 빛나는. ¶ *a* ~ *victory* 빛나는 승리. **2** giving glory. 명예를 주는. **3** magnificent; splendid. 장려〔화려〕한; 장엄한; 찬연한. ¶ *a* ~ *sunset* 장엄한 일몰 / *a* ~ *view* 장관. **4** 《*colloq.*》 thoroughly enjoyable; delightful. 즐거운; 유쾌한. ¶ *have a* ~ *time* 즐거운 시간을 보내다 / *He made a* ~ *mess of the room.* 《*iron.*》 그는 방 안을 온통 난장판을 만들었다.

glo·ri·ous·ly [glɔ́:riəsli] *adv.* **1** magnificently. 장려〔장엄〕하게. **2** 《*colloq.*》 delightfully. 유쾌하게; 즐겁게.

:**glo·ry** [glɔ́:ri] *n.* Ⓤ (*pl.* **-ries**) **1** great praise and honor. 명예. **2** Ⓒ anything bringing this. 명예를〔광영을〕 가져오는 것. ¶ *a* ~ *to someone* 아무에게 자랑이 되는 것. **3** great beauty; splendor. 장관; 미관. ¶ *the* ~ *of the sunset* 일몰의 장려(壯麗)함. **4** ⓊⒸ the best state. 전성(全盛). ¶ *Greece in her* ~ 전성기의 그리스. **5** praise given in worship, esp. of God. 찬미; 영광. ¶ *the* ~ *of God* 신의 영광 / *give* ~ *to God* 신에게 영광을 돌리다; 신을 찬미하다. **6** Ⓒ a halo. 광륜(光輪).

be in one's glory, 《*colloq.*》 be at the best state of one's life. 전성기에 있다.
go to glory, die. 죽다.
return with glory, return in triumph. 개선하다.
send someone to glory, 《*joc.*》 kill. 죽이다.
— *vi.* (**-ried**) (P3,4) 《*in*》 be proud; take delight in. 자랑으로 여기다; 기뻐하다. [L. *glōria* glory, fame]

gloss[1] [glɔ:s, glɑs / glɔs] *n.* Ⓤ 《sometimes *a* ~》 brightness on the surface; a smooth, shining surface. (표면의) 광택; 윤; 광택나는 면. ¶ *the* ~ *of satin* 공단의 광택. — *vt.* (P6,7) **1** make (something) smooth and shining. …의 광(택)을 내다. **2** 《usu. *over*》 make (an error, a fault, etc.) seem right; make (something) seem better than it really is. …을 용케 발뺌하다; 겉을 꾸미다. ¶ ~ *over one's errors* 잘못을 용케 겉바르다. — *vi.* (P1) become shiny. 광택〔윤〕이 나다. [Teut. *gloa* glow]

gloss[2] [glɔ:s, glɑs / glɔ́s] *n.* Ⓒ words inserted in the margin of a text; comment; explanation. 주해; 주석; 설명. — *vt.* (P6) **1** insert glosses in. 주석하다. **2** make an unfavorable comments. 곡해(曲解)하다. [Gk. *glōssa* tongue]

glos·sa·ry [glɑ́səri, glɔ́(:)s-] *n.* Ⓒ (*pl.* **-ries**) a small dictionary or list of special words. (특수어나 술어의) 어해(語解) 사전; 용어〔술어〕 사전. ¶ *a* ~ *to Shakespeare* 셰익스피어 용어 사전. [↑]

gloss·y [glɔ́(:)si, glɑ́si] *adj.* (**gloss·i·er, gloss·i·est**) smooth and shiny. 광택이 있는.
● **gloss·i·ly** [-li] *adv.* **gloss·i·ness** [-nis] *n.* [*gloss*[1]]

glot·ti·des [glɑ́tidì:z / glɔ́t-] *n.* pl. of **glottis.**

glot·tis [glɑ́tis / glɔ́t-] *n.* Ⓒ (*pl.* **-tis·es** or **-ti·des**) an opening between the vocal cords. 성문(聲門). [→gloss[2]]

:**glove** [glʌv] *n.* Ⓒ **1** a covering for the hand to keep it warm. 장갑. ¶ *a pair of gloves* 장갑 한 켤레. **2** a padded covering to protect the hand in some sports, such as boxing, baseball, etc. (야구·권투 따위의) 글러브.

be hand in 〔***and***〕 ***glove*** (= *be very intimate*) ***with someone.*** …와 밀접한 관계가 있다.
fit like a glove, fit perfectly. 꼭 맞다.
handle with 〔***without***〕 ***gloves,*** treat gently 〔roughly〕. …을 부드럽게〔거칠게〕 다루다. ¶ *I handled her with gloves, because she was in deep grief.* 그녀는 깊은 슬픔에 빠져 있었으므로 부드럽게 다루었다.
take off the gloves to, argue or contend seriously. (쟁투(爭鬪)·논쟁)에 본격적으로 나서다.
throw down the glove, challenge. …에게 도전하다.
— *vt.* (P6) cover (a hand) with a glove. 장갑을 끼다. [E.]

:**glow** [glou] *n.* Ⓒ 《usu. *sing.*》 **1** brightness. 빛남; 불빛. ¶ *the* ~ *of sunset* 저녁놀. **2** warmth of the body. (몸의) 달아오름. ¶ *a pleasant* ~ *after a drink* 한잔한 뒤에 기분 좋게 달아오름. **3** flushed look; rosy color of the face. (얼굴의) 홍조; 붉은 얼굴. ¶ *the* ~ *of good health on his cheeks* 불그레한 뺨의 건강색.

all in 〔***of***〕 ***a glow,*** with a flushed look. 빨갛게 달아올라.
— *vi.* (P1,2A) **1** shine with a strong color. (빛이) 불타듯 빛나다. **2** become warm and flushed. 후끈 달아오르다; 홍조를 띠다. ¶ *cheeks that* ~ *with shame* 부끄러워 붉어진

볼. **3** give off light and heat. 빛과 열을 내다. **4** burn with the passion of excitement. (감정이) 불타다; 복받치다. ¶ ~ *with anger* 분노가 복받치다. [E.]

glow·er [gláuər] *vi.* (P1,3) 《*at*》 stare angrily. 노려보다. ¶ *The detective glowered at the robber.* 형사는 그 도둑을 노려보았다. — *n.* Ⓒ an angry look. 성난 얼굴. ● **glow·er·ing·ly** [-əriŋli] *adv.* [Sc.]

glow·ing [glóuiŋ] *adj.* **1** shining with a red or white color of hot metal, etc. 백열의; 벌겋게 달아오른. **2** (of colors, etc.) bright. 불타듯 선명한; 불타는. ¶ *a* ~ *sunset* 붉게 물든 저녁놀. **3** (of the cheeks) appearing warm. 붉게 달아오른; 홍조를 띤. ¶ ~ *cheeks* 홍조를 띤 뺨 / *a* ~ *face* 상기한 얼굴. **4** (of persons or feelings) deeply moved; very enthusiastic. 감동한; 열렬한. ¶ *a* ~ *patriot* 열렬한 애국자 / *in* ~ *terms* 열렬한 말로; 매우 호의적으로. ● **glow·ing·ly** [-li] *adv.* [*glow*]

glow·worm [glóuwə̀ːrm] *n.* Ⓒ an insect that glows in the dark. 개똥벌레(cf. *firefly*).

gloze [glouz] *vt., vi.* (P6,7; 1) **1** 《*over*》 explain away. …을 둘러대다; 말을 꾸며대다. **2** talk flatteringly. 아첨하다. [*gloss*[2]]

glt. 《bookbinding》 gilt. 금테두리의; 금박을 입힌.

glu·ci·num [gluːsáinəm] *n.* Ⓤ 《chem.》 a rare metallic element. 글루시눔. [Gk.]

glu·cose [glúːkous] *n.* Ⓤ a kind of sugar found in fruit or honey. 포도당(糖). [Gk. *glukus* sweet]

***glue** [gluː] *n.* Ⓤ **1** a sticky substance made by boiling the skins and bones of animals. 아교. **2** any similar sticky substance. 접착제; 풀. — *vt.* (P6,7,13) **1** 《*to*》 stick (things) with glue. …을 아교[접착제]로 붙이다; 접착시키다. ¶ ~ *a map to a piece of paper* 종이에 지도를 붙이다 / ~ *two sheets of paper together* 종이 두 장을 한데 붙이다. **2** attach firmly. …을 꼭 붙이다. **3** 《*fig.*》 refuse to leave. 꼭 붙어 떠나지 않다. ¶ *She remained glued to her mother all the evening.* 그녀는 밤새도록 엄마 곁에서 떨어지지 않았다. [L. *glus*]

glum [glʌm] *adj.* (**glum·mer, glum·mest**) gloomy; sullen. 음울한; 울적한; 찌무룩한. [→gloom]

glut [glʌt] *vt.* (**glut·ted, glut·ting**) (P6,13) fill too full; oversupply. 포식[만족]시키다; 과잉 공급하다. ¶ ~ *the appetite* 식욕을 만족시키다 / ~ *one's eyes* 물릴 정도로 바라보다 / ~ *oneself with* …을 실컷 먹다 / ~ *the market* 시장에 과잉 공급하다. — *n.* Ⓒ a full supply; too large a supply. 충분한 공급; 공급 과다. ¶ *a* ~ *of food and cosmetics* 식료와 화장품의 공급 과다. [→glutton]

glu·ten [glúːtən] *n.* Ⓤ a tough, sticky substance found in the flour of wheat. 글루텐; 부질(麩質). [L. =glue]

glu·ti·nous [glúːtənəs] *adj.* sticky. 끈끈한; 점착성의. ¶ ~ *substance* 점착성 물질. [↑]

glut·ton [glʌ́tn] *n.* Ⓒ **1** a person who eats too much. 대식가. **2** a person who has a great desire for something. 끈덕진 사람; 집착심이 강한 사람. ¶ *a* ~ *of books* 책을 탐독하는 사람; 책벌레. [L. *glutio* swallow]

glut·ton·ous [glʌ́tənəs] *adj.* fond of eating too much. 걸신들린.

be gluttonous of, **a**) eat greedily. …을 탐식하다; 식탐하다. **b**) be absorbed in (something). …에 열중하다; 열심이다.

glut·ton·ous·ly [glʌ́tənəsli] *adv.* greedily. 탐욕[게걸]스럽게.

glut·ton·y [glʌ́təni] *n.* ⓊⒸ (*pl.* **-ton·ies**) the act of eating greedily; the habit of eating too much. 대식(大食); 폭식하는 버릇.

glyc·er·in, -ine [glísərin] *n.* Ⓤ a sweet, colorless, thick liquid used in medicines, explosives, etc. 글리세린. [Gk. *glukeros* sweet]

glyc·er·ol [glísəroul, -rɔ̀(ː)l, -ràl] *n.* Ⓤ glycerin. 글리세롤. 參考 글리세린의 학명.

gly·co·gen [gláikədʒən, -dʒèn] *n.* Ⓤ a substance found in an animal's body which is changed into sugar when needed. 글리코겐. [→glycerin]

gm. gram(s); 《Brit.》 gramme(s).

GM General Motors.

G-man [dʒíːmæ̀n] *n.* Ⓒ (*pl.* **G-men** [-mèn]) 《U.S. *colloq.*》 a member of the FBI (=Federal Bureau of Investigation). G맨《미국 연방 수사국의 수사관》. [*Government man*]

G.M.T. Greenwich mean time. 그리니치 표준시.

gnarl [nɑːrl] *n.* Ⓒ a knot on a tree or in wood; a hard, rough lump. 나무의 마디; 혹. [E.]

gnarled [nɑːrld] *adj.* **1** knotted and twisted; full of knots. 뒤틀린; 마디투성이의. **2** 《*fig.*》 having a rugged, weather-beaten appearance. 우락부락한. ¶ *a* ~ *old sea captain* 우락부락하게 생긴 늙은 선장.

gnarl·y [nɑ́ːrli] *adj.* =gnarled.

gnash [næʃ] *vi., vt.* (P1; 6) **1** strike or grind (the teeth) together. 이를 갈다. ¶ ~ *the teeth* 이를 갈다. **2** bite by grinding the teeth. 이를 악물다. [Scand.]

gnat [næt] *n.* Ⓒ **1** a small, two-winged insect that has an itch-causing bite. 각다귀. **2** 《Brit.》 a mosquito. 모기. [E.]

strain at a gnat, stick at trifles. 사소한 일에 구애받다.

·**gnaw** [nɔː] *vi., vt.* (**gnawed, gnawed** or **gnawn**) **1** (P1; 6,7,13) bite off or eat away with teeth bit by bit. 조금씩 물어뜯다[떼다]. ¶ *a dog gnawing at a bone* 뼈다귀를 물어뜯고 있는 개 / ~ *a hole through the wall* 갉작거려 벽에 구멍을 뚫다. **2** (P3; 6) wear away; corrode. 마멸[소모]시키다; 부식시키다. **3** torment. 괴롭히다. ¶ *be constantly gnawed by pain* 끊임없이 고통에 시달리다. [E.]

gnawn [nɔːn] *v.* pp. of **gnaw**.

gneiss [nais] *n.* Ⓤ laminated rock of

quartz, feldspar, and mica. 편마암(片麻岩). [G. *gneistan* sparkle]

gnome [noum] *n.* Ⓒ **1** an imaginary dwarf who guards treasures of gold, silver, and jewels. (지하의 보물을 지킨다는) 난쟁이. **2** a maxim; an aphorism. 격언. [Gk. *gignōskō* know]

GNP [dʒíːènpíː] gross national product. 국민 총생산.

gnu [njuː] *n.* (*pl.* **gnu** or **gnus**) a South African ox-like antelope. 누《남아프리카산 소 비슷한 영양》. [Hottentot]

:go [gou] *vi.* (**went, gone**) **1** (P1,2A,2B,3,4) ⓐ move or pass along; walk; travel. 가다; 걷다; 여행하다. ¶ ~ *up and down* (*a road*) (길을) 왔다갔다 하다 / ~ *on foot* 걸어〔도보로〕 가다 / ~ *by bus* 버스로 가다 / *The train goes* (*at*) *50 miles an hour.* 열차는 시속 50 마일로 간다. ⓑ move from a place; leave; depart. 떠나다. ¶ ~ *on a journey* 여행을 떠나다 / *It's time for us to* ~. 가야 할 시간이다 / *The train has just gone.* 열차는 이제 막 떠났다. ⓒ move to another place, esp. for a particular purpose. (특별한 목적으로) 가다. ¶ ~ *home* 집에 가다 / ~ *upstairs* 위층에 올라가다 / ~ *to school* 학교에 다니다 / ~ *to bed* 잠자리에 들다. ⓓ move away to do something. …하러 가다. ¶ ~ *for a walk* 산책하러 나가다 / ~ *on a picnic* 소풍 가다 / ~ *fishing* 〔*shopping, hiking*〕 낚시〔쇼핑, 하이킹〕 가다 / ~ *searching for someone* 아무를 찾으러 가다 / ~ *to see* 〔*talk with*〕 *a friend* 친구를 만나러〔와 이야기하러〕 가다 / ~ *to the country to live* 시골에 살러 가다. **2** (P1) proceed; advance. 나아가다. ¶ *This car can* ~ *120 kilometers an hour.* 이 차는 시속 120 킬로를 낼 수 있다. **3** (P1) pass; pass away. 지나(가)다. ¶ *Summer is gone.* 여름은 지나갔다. **4** (P3) be spent; be used up. …에 소비되다; 쓰이다. ¶ *His money goes for drink.* 그의 돈은 술값에 쓰인다. **5** (P2A, 2B,3) extend; reach. 뻗다; 달하다; 이르다; 통하다. ¶ *How far does this road* ~ *?* 이 길은 어디까지 뻗어 있나 / *Where does this door* ~ *?* 이 문은 어디로 통해 있나 / *His memory does not* ~ *back that far.* 그의 기억은 거기까지는 미치지 않는다. **6** (P1,2A,3) be in motion or action; work. 움직이다; 돌다; 작동하다. ¶ *The watch* 〔*engine*〕 *won't* ~. 시계가〔엔진이〕 도무지 움직이지 않는다 / *There goes the bell.* 벨이 울리고 있다. **7** (P5) pass from one state to another; become. …하게 되다. ¶ ~ *mad* 미치다 / ~ *blind* 실명하다 / ~ *bankrupt* 파산하다 / *I felt myself going red in the face.* 얼굴이 붉어지는 것을 느꼈다. **8** (P1) ⓐ be broken suddenly; stop being; die. 뚝 부러지다; 소멸하다; 죽다. ¶ *The mast went in the storm.* 태풍에 돛이 뚝 부러졌다 / *He may* ~ *at any time.* 그는 언제 죽을지 모른다. ⓑ break; give away. 무너지다. ¶ *The dike might* ~ *any minute.* 둑은 언제 무너질지 모른다. **9** (P2A,3) end; result. (…한) 결과가 되다; …하게 되다. ¶ *The election went in favor of Mr. Smith.* 선거는 스미스 씨의 승리로 끝났다 / *How did the game* ~ *?* 승부는 어떻게 되었나. **10** (P4) tend; lead. 이바지〔공헌〕하다; 도움을 주다. ¶ *The incident went to show that....* 그 사건은 …하다는 것을 나타내는 데 도움이 되었다 / *This only goes to prove the point.* 이것은 다만 그 점을 증명하는 데 도움이 될 뿐이다. **11** (P3) ⓐ pass into the possession of; be handed to. …의 손에 넘어가다. ¶ *Victory does not always* ~ *to the strong.* 승리는 반드시 강자에게만 돌아가는 것은 아니다. ⓑ turn to certain means; appeal to; resort to. …(수단)에 호소하다; …에 의지하다. ¶ ~ *to war* 전쟁에 호소하다 / ~ *to extremes* 극단으로 흐르다 / ~ *to court* 〔*law*〕 법에 호소하다. ⓒ put oneself to (trouble, expense, etc.). 스스로 …하다; (수고 따위를) 겪다. ¶ ~ *to great expense to accomplish a purpose* 목적을 이루기 위해 크나큰 지출을 하다 / *You don't have to* ~ *to the trouble of making lunch.* 손수 점심을 마련해야 할 수고를 할 것까지는 없다. **12** (P3) be given. 주어지다. ¶ *The first prize went to her.* 1등상은 그녀에게로 돌아갔다. **13** (P2A) be placed; belong. (있어야 할 곳에) 놓이다; 속하다. ¶ *This book goes on the top shelf.* 이 책을 두어야 할 곳은 맨 윗 서가이다 / *Where are the cups to* ~ *?* 컵은 어디다 두는 겁니까. **14** (P3) 《*with*》 harmonize. …와 조화되다. ¶ *Your blue hat doesn't* ~ *with your green gloves.* 자네의 청색 모자는 녹색 장갑과 어울리지 않는군 / *His voice did not* ~ *with his respectable attire.* 그의 목소리는 훌륭한 차림새와는 어울리지 않았다. **15** (P1) be said. …라고(들) 한다. ¶ *It goes that....* **16** (P1,2A) be known; be current. 알려지다; 유통되다; 퍼지다. ¶ *He goes by the name of John.* 그는 존이란 이름으로 통하고 있다. **17** (P3,5) remain; live, or pass in a certain way. (어떤 상태인 채로) 남아 있다; 계속하다; (늘 …하고) 있다. ¶ ~ *naked* 〔*in rags*〕 벌거벗고〔누더기를 걸치고〕 있다 / ~ *barefoot* 맨발로 있다 / *He always goes in plain clothes.* 그는 항상 평복을 입고 있다 / *He is still going strong.* 그는 아직도 건강하다.

be going to do, **a**) be about to do. 이제라도〔금방〕 …할 것 같다. ¶ *It is going to rain.* 비가 올 것 같다. **b**) intend to do; be scheduled to do. …할 예정이다. ¶ *I am going to see him this afternoon.* 오늘 오후 그를 만날 작정이다.

go about, **a**) go here and there. 여기저기 돌아다니다. **b**) turn about. 방향을 바꾸다. **c**) begin; start. …을 시작하다. ¶ ~ *about one's work* 일을 시작하다.

go about to do, try to do; make an effort to do. …을 시도(試圖)하다; …하려고 노력하다.

go after (= *try to get*) *something.* …을 얻으려고 하다.

go against, **a**) resist; oppose. …에 반항하다;

반대하다. **b**) be contrary to (something). …와 상반(相反)하다. **c**) collide with. …와 충돌하다.

go ahead, go on; proceed. 앞서 나아가다; 선행하다.

go along, move along; proceed; advance. 움직이다; (앞으로) 나아가다.

go a long way, be very useful. 매우 도움이 되다〔유익하다〕.

go along with, 《U.S.》 **a**) cooperate with; work together with (someone). …와 협력하다; …와 함께 일하다. **b**) carry out; fulfill. 실행하다. **c**) agree; concur. 찬성하다; 동조(同調)하다.

go around, **a**) be enough for all. 모두에게 충분하다; 모든 필요를 충족시키다. ¶ *The food will just ~ around.* 음식은 모두에게 돌아갈 만큼 있다. **b**) reach one's destination by a way other than the nearest road. 멀리 돌아가다. **c**) be often in company. …와 사귀다; 상종하다; 어울리다. ¶ *~ around with a bad crowd* 불량배들과 어울리다. **d**) be conducted round. (…을) 한 바퀴 돌다. ¶ *~ around a factory* 공장을 한 바퀴 돌다. **e**) pay a visit. 잠깐 들르다. **f**) circulate. (소문·병 따위가) 퍼지다.

go at, **a**) begin; start (work). …을 시작하다. **b**) rush at; attack. 달려들다; 공격하다. ¶ *He went at the man with his fists.* 주먹을 휘두르며 사나이를 공격했다.

go away, leave (for another town, etc.); run away with. 떠나다; 가지고 달아나다.

go back, **a**) return. 돌아가다. **b**) extend backwards in space or time. 거슬러 올라가다. **c**) remember. 회고하다; 되돌아보다. **d**) decline. 쇠하다.

go back on, 《*colloq.*》 break (a promise, etc.); betray (one's friend, etc.). (약속 따위를) 깨뜨리다; 배반〔배신〕하다. ¶ *I don't ~ back on my promises* 〔*word*〕. 난 약속을 어기지 않는다.

go behind, search for a real or hidden meaning of (someone's words). (아무의 말의) 이면의 뜻을 캐다; 숨겨진 의미를〔사실을〕 조사하다.

go between, act as an agent or assistant between two parties. 둘 사이에 중간 역할을 하다; 중재〔중개, 중매〕하다(cf. *go-between*).

go beyond, exceed. …을 넘다; 능가하다; …보다 낫다.

go by, **a**) pass by; elapse. 지나다(cf. *bygone*). ¶ *Years have gone by.* 해가〔세월이〕 지났다. **b**) be guided or led by (something). …에 따라 행동하다.

go down, **a**) sink; descend; (of the sun, etc.) set. 가라앉다; 내려가다; (해 따위가) 지다. **b**) be written as a record; be remembered. 기록되다; 기억되다. ¶ *His name will ~ down in history as a great inventor.* 그의 이름은 대발명가로서 역사에 남을 것이다. **c**) calm down. 조용〔잠잠〕해지다; 가라앉다. ¶ *The wind has gone down.* 바람이 조용해졌다. **d**) be defeated. 패배하다; 타도되다. ¶ *~ down in fighting* 싸움에 지다. **e**) be accepted or believed. 받아들여지다. ¶ *This nonsense goes down as truth with many persons.* 이 바보 같은 소리를 진실이라고 믿는 사람이 많다. **f**) 《Brit.》 leave (a university). (대학을) 떠나다. **g**) (of food) be swallowed. 목구멍을 넘어가다. **h**) become lower in amount, value, power, etc. (양·가치·힘 따위가) 떨어지다; 하락하다; 감소〔저하〕하다.

go far, **a**) last or hold out long. 오래가다; 마디다. ¶ *His money didn't ~ far.* 그의 돈은 오래가지 못했다. **b**) be successful; accomplish much. 성공하다. ¶ *He will ~ far.* 그는 성공할 것이다.

go for, **a**) go in search of; go to fetch; try to get; aim at (something). …을 찾으러〔가지러〕 가다; 얻으려고 하다; 노리다. **b**) serve as; pass for. …의 대용이 되다; …로 통(용)하다. **c**) be taken as (something). …로 생각되다. **d**) be sold at the price of. …값에 팔리다. **e**) 《*colloq.*》 attack with blows or words. …을 공격하다. **f**) 《*colloq.*》 be attracted by; like; favor. …에 끌리다; …을 좋아하다. ¶ *Some women ~ for that type of man.* 어떤 여자들은 그런 타입의 남자를 좋아한다.

go for much, be very useful. 크게 도움이 되다.

go for nothing, have no value. 도움이 되지 않다.

go forth, be made public; be published. 공표〔출판〕되다; (명령 따위가) 나가다.

go hard with, cause much pain or trouble to (someone). …에게 힘겹다; 만만치 않다.

go in, enter; take part in (a game, etc.). …에 들어가다; 참가하다.

go in for, take up (something) as one's business, hobby, etc.; undertake seriously; devote oneself to. …에 종사하다; (시험따위를) 치르다; 열중〔몰두〕하다. ¶ *~ in for an examination* 시험을 치르다 / *~ in for literature* 문학에 열중하다 / *He has gone in for stamp collecting.* 그는 우표 수집에 열중하고 있다.

go in on 〔***with***〕, take part in (something); join. …에 참가하다.

go into, **a**) join; enter. …에 참가〔참여〕하다. ¶ *~ into Parliament* 국회 의원이 되다. **b**) research; examine; study; discuss. …을 조사〔정사(精査)〕하다; 자세히 논(論)하다.

go it, 《*colloq.*》 **a**) behave recklessly or improperly. 무턱대고 하다; 무모하게 굴다. **b**) proceed rapidly or furiously. (맹렬한 기세로) 하다.

go off, **a**) be fired; burst out; explode. 발사되다; 폭발하다. ¶ *A gun went off in the distance.* 멀리서 총소리가 들렸다. **b**) be held; be done; proceed. 행해지다; (일이) 진척되다. **c**) cease. 끝내다. **d**) go away; depart. 떠나다. **e**) fall asleep; become unconscious; die. 잠들다; 의식을 잃다; 실신하다;

죽다. **f**) be extinguished. 꺼지다. **g**) (of food, etc.) become bad. (음식 따위가) 쉬다; 부패하다. ¶ *The milk has gone off.* 우유가 부패했다.

go on [***upon***], **a**) act; behave. 행동하다. **b**) continue. 계속하다[되다]. ¶ ~ *on walking* 계속 걷다 / ~ *on with one's reading* 독서를 계속하다. **c**) happen; take place. 일어나다; 발생하다. **d**) talk effusively; chatter. 기세 좋게 지껄여대다. **e**) elapse; pass away. (시간·세월이) 지나가다. **f**) get along. 지내다.

go out, **a**) come to an end. 끝나다; 없어지다; 유행하지 않게 되다. **b**) go from home; go to parties. 외출하다; 파티에 가다. **c**) stop burning; be extinguished. (불이) 꺼지다. ¶ *The fire* [*light*] *went out.* 불[등불]이 꺼졌다. **d**) go on strike; walk out. 스트라이크를 하다; 동맹 파업[휴학]을 하다. ¶ ~ *out for higher wages* 임금 인상을 요구하며 파업하다. **e**) become outdated. 시대에 뒤떨어지게 되다.

go over, **a**) cross to the other side. 건너다. **b**) study or repeat from beginning to end. 복습하다. ¶ ~ *over one's lessons.* **c**) examine carefully. 정밀하게 조사[검사]하다. **d**) read; scan. 읽다; 대충 훑어보다. **e**) be effective or successful. 효력이 있다; 잘 되다; 성공하다.

go the way of all flesh, die. 죽다.

go through, **a**) experience; endure. (괴로움 따위를) 경험하다; 참다; 견디다. ¶ ~ *through great hardship* 크나큰 어려움을 겪다. **b**) examine carefully; search narrowly. 주의깊게 검토하다; 정사(精査)하다; 주의 깊게 찾다. ¶ ~ *through drawers for a lost purse* 잃어버린 돈지갑이 없는가 서랍을 뒤져 찾다. **c**) spend (money); use up entirely. 다 써버리다. ¶ ~ *through a fortune* 재산을 날리다. **d**) pass; be accepted. 통과하다; 받아들여지다. **e**) carry out; perform. (일·예정·학업 따위를) 끝까지 해내다; 마치다. ¶ ~ *through the schedule for the day* 하루의 예정을 전부 마치다.

go through with, continue to the end; carry out; complete; finish. (끝까지) …을 해내다; 유지[지속]하다; 완성하다.

go together, **a**) go with; accompany. …와 함께 가다; 동행하다. **b**) harmonize; match. 어울리다; 조화하다.

go to pieces, **a**) break up; collapse. 깨지다; 부서지다. **b**) 《*fig.*》 lose one's determination. 결심이 무너지다.

go to sea, **a**) go on a voyage. 출항하다. **b**) become a sailor. 뱃사람이 되다.

go under, **a**) sink. 가라앉다. **b**) fail; be ruined. (사업에) 실패하다; 파멸[파산]하다. ¶ *The firm has gone under.* 회사는 파산했다. **c**) be defeated; succumb. 지다; 굴복하다. ¶ ~ *under in a contest* 경기에 지다. **d**) be known by; go by. …로 통하다.

go up, **a**) rise; mount; increase. 오르다; 늘다. **b**) be destroyed by fire or explosion. (불·폭발에 의하여) 파괴되다. **c**) be ruined. 파멸하다. **d**) be in the process of construction. (건물이) 세워지다.

go with, **a**) accompany; associate. …와 동행하다; 사귀다. **b**) match. …와 어울리다; 조화되다.

go without (=*manage* or *do without*) *something.* …없이 때우다[지내다]. ¶ *Man can not ~ without water.* 인간은 물 없이는 살 수 없다.

It goes without saying that..., It is needless to say that.... …은 말할 것도 없다.

— *n.* Ⓤ **1** the act of going. 감; 떠남. ¶ *the come and ~ of the seasons* 계절의 변화. **2** energy; spirit. 정력; 기력; 활기. ¶ *be full of ~* 정력이[활기가] 넘치다. **3** 《*a ~*》 《*colloq.*》 the state of affairs; the way things are. 사태; 상태. [E. past from *wend*]

on the go, busy; active. 무척 바쁜; 활발한; 활동적인.

G.O. general order(s). 일반 명령.

goad [goud] *n.* Ⓒ **1** a pointed stick for driving cattle. (가축의) 몰이 막대기. **2** anything that drives or urges someone to action. 자극하는 것; 자극물; 격려. ¶ *a necessary ~ for students* 학생에게 필요한 자극. — *vt.* (P6,7,13,20) **1** drive (cattle) with a goad. (가축)을 몰이 막대기로 몰다. **2** 《*into*》 urge (someone) to action. …을 자극[격려]하여 —시키다; 선동하다. ¶ *Hunger goaded her into stealing a loaf of bread.* 그녀는 굶주림 때문에 한 덩어리의 빵을 훔쳤다 / *His laughter goaded me to try.* 그의 비웃음은 나를 분발케 했다. [E.]

go·a·head [góuəhèd] *adj.* 《*colloq.*》 pushing; eager. 진취적인; 적극적인. ¶ *be full of ~ spirit* 진취적 기상이 넘치다. — *n.* permission or a signal to start or continue doing something. (시작·계속하라는) 인가; 승인; 신호. [*go, ahead*]

***goal** [goul] *n.* Ⓒ **1** a place where the course of a race ends. 결승점[선]. ¶ *reach* [*make*] *the ~* 결승점에 이르다; 골인하다 / *He will be the first runner to cross the ~.* 그가 1착으로 골에 들어올 테지. **2** a place through which a ball must be sent in order to score in games, such as football and soccer. (축구 따위의) 골. **3** the score thus made. 득점. ¶ *Our team made a ~.* 우리 팀이 득점했다. **4** an aim or purpose for which an effort is made. 목적; 목표. ¶ *one's ~ in life* 인생의 목표 / *achieve a ~* 목표를 달성하다. •**goal·less** [-lis] *adj.* [? M.E. *gol* boundary]

goal·ie [góuli] *n.* 《*colloq.*》 =goalkeeper.

goal·keep·er [góulkìːpər] *n.* Ⓒ a player who guards a goal in football, soccer, etc. (축구 따위의) 골키퍼; 수문장. [*goal*]

go-as-you-please [góuəzjuplíːz] *adj.* unfettered by regulations. 규칙에 얽매이지 않는. [*go*]

:**goat** [gout] *n.* Ⓒ (*pl.* **goats** or *collectively*

goat) **1** a hairy animal with horns and a beard. 염소. **2** 《U.S. *colloq.*》 a person who is forced to take the blame or punishment for another's deed. 남 대신 죄를 뒤집어 쓰는 사람; 희생양. **3** 《U.S. *colloq.*》 a foolish person. 바보 같은 사람. **4** 《*G-*》 the zodiacal sign, Capricorn. 염소자리.
act 〔***play***〕 ***the*** (***giddy***) ***goat,*** do a foolish thing. 바보 같은 짓을 하다.
get someone's goat, torment; make (someone) angry. …을 괴롭히다; 성나게 하다. ¶ *The constant noisy sounds get my* ~. 끊임없는 잡음이 나를 괴롭힌다.
separate the sheep from the goats, distinguish the good from the bad. 선인과 악인〔유능한 사람과 무능한 사람〕을 구별하다.
● **goat·like** [´-làik] *adj.* [E.]

goat·ee [goutí:] *n.* Ⓒ a pointed hair on a man's chin like a goat's beard. (사람의) 염소 수염.

goat·herd [góuthə̀:rd] *n.* a person who tends goats. 염소지기.

goat·skin [góut-skìn] *n.* Ⓤ the skin of a goat; leather made from the skin of a goat. 염소 가죽.

gob[1] [gɑb / gɔb] *n.* 《*colloq.*》 the mouth. 입; 아가리. ¶ *Stop* 〔*Shut*〕 *your* ~. 아가리 닥쳐. [↓]

gob[2] [gɑb / gɔb] *n.* **1** 《*sl.*》 a clot of slimy substance; spittle. 침. **2** 《U.S. *sl.*》 a sailor of the American navy. 수병(水兵). — *vi.* (P1) spit. 침을 뱉다. [F. *gobe* mouthful]

gob·bet [gábit / gɔ́b-] *n.* a piece of raw flesh or food. (고기·음식 따위의) 작은 조각; 덩어리; 한 입. [*gob*[1]]

gob·ble[1] [gábəl / gɔ́bəl] *vi., vt.* (P1; 6,7) **1** swallow quickly or greedily. 게걸스레 먹다; 통째로 삼키다. **2** 《U.S. *colloq.*》 snatch up. 움켜 쥐다. [*gob*[1]]
gobble up, 《U.S.》 eat up. 다 먹어치우다.

gob·ble[2] [gábəl / gɔ́bəl] *n.* Ⓒ a noise that a male turkey makes in the throat. (칠면조의) 울음 소리. — *vi.* (P1) make this noise. (칠면조가) 꼬록꼬록 울다. [Imit.]

gob·bler [gáblər / gɔ́blər] *n.* Ⓒ a male turkey; a person who gobbles food. 칠면조의 수컷; 게걸스레 먹는 사람. [*gobble*[1]]

go-be·tween [góubitwì:n] *n.* Ⓒ a person who does business for two persons or parties that do not meet each other. 매개자; 주선인; 중매자. [*go, between*]

gob·let [gáblit / gɔ́b-] *n.* Ⓒ a drinking glass with a base and stem, but with no handle. 받침 달린 술잔. [F. *gobel* cup]

〈goblet〉

***gob·lin** [gáblin / gɔ́b-] *n.* Ⓒ (in a fable or myth) a mischievous or evil spirit in the form of an ugly-looking dwarf. (사람을 해친다는) 추한 악귀. [F.]

go-by [góubài] *n.* 《usu. *the* ~》 《*colloq.*》 the act of going by without notice. 짐짓 모르는 체하며 지나감; 몽따며 지나감. [*go*]
give someone the go-by, disregard or neglect intentionally. …을 모르는 체하다; 짐짓 몽따다. [*go*]

go·cart [góukà:rt] *n.* Ⓒ **1** a baby carriage pushed by hand. 유모차. **2** a small structure for teaching children to walk. 보행기. **3** a light carriage. 소형 자동차. [*go*]

⁝**god** [gɑd / gɔd] *n.* Ⓒ **1** 《*G-*》 the maker and ruler of the universe; Supreme Being; Creator. 창조〔조물〕주; 천제(天帝). ¶ *Almighty God* 전능하신 신. **2** a being worshiped as having supernatural powers; a deity; a divinity; a male god. (숭배의 대상으로서의) 신(opp. goddess). ¶ *the* ~ *of day* =*the sun* ~ 태양신 / *the* ~ *of heaven* 하늘의 신; 하느님 / *the* ~ *of the sea* 바다의 신. **3** an image of a god; an idol. 신상(神像); 우상. **4** Ⓒ a person or thing worshipped like a god. (신같이) 숭배되는 사람〔물건〕. [E.]
a (***little***) ***tin god,*** an unimportant official with a very high opinion of himself. 우쭐대는 시시한 관리; 굴퉁이.
by God, upon my word. 맹세코.
for God's sake, with urgent petitions. 제발.
for the gods, very surprising or delightful. 굉장한; 훌륭한. ¶ *a feast for the gods* 훌륭한 성찬 / *a sight for the gods* 굉장한 광경; 장관.
God bless me 〔***my life, my soul***〕***!*** a cry expressing surprise. 아이구 큰일났다.
God forbid! I very earnestly hope not. 그런 일이 있어서야 말이 되는가; 당치도 않다.
God knows (*when, where, why,* etc.).... No one else knows (when, where, why, etc.).... …인지〔하는지〕 신(神)만이 안다; 아무도 모른다.
God knows that.... I call God to witness that.... …임을〔하다는 것을〕 신에게 맹세한다.
God willing, if circumstances allow. 사정이 허락하면.
with God, dead and in heaven. 죽어서 천국에.

god·child [gádtʃàild / gɔ́d-] *n.* Ⓒ (*pl.* **-children** [-tʃìldrən]) a child whom a grown-up person promises, at its baptism to help in its religious training. 대자녀(代子女).

god·daugh·ter [gáddɔ̀:tər / gɔ́d-] *n.* Ⓒ a female godchild. 대녀(代女).

***god·dess** [gádis / gɔ́d-] *n.* Ⓒ **1** a female god. 여신(女神). **2** a very beautiful or charming woman. 절세의 미녀.

god·fa·ther [gádfà:ðər / gɔ́d-] *n.* Ⓒ a man who promises to help someone else's child in its religious training when the child is baptized. 대부(代父).

God-fear·ing [gádfìəriŋ / gɔ́d-] *adj.* fearing God; deeply respectful of God; religious. 신을 두려워하는; 경건한.

God-for·sak·en [gádfərsèikən / gɔ́d-] *adj.*

1 (of a person) abandoned by God; spoiled in character. 신에게 버림받은; 타락한. 2 (of a place) desolate; lonely. 황량한; 쓸쓸한.

God·giv·en [gádgivn / gɔ́d-] *adj.* 1 given by God. 천여(天與)의; 하늘이 준. 2 very welcome. 아주 좋은; 절호(絕好)의.

God·head [gádhèd / gɔ́d-] *n.* 1 《*the* ～》 God. 신. 2 Ⓤ 《*g-*》 divine nature. 신성(神性).

god·hood [gádhùd / gɔ́d-] *n.* Ⓤ divine character. 신(神)임; 신성(神性); 신격.

god·less [gádlis / gɔ́d-] *adj.* 1 not believing in God; not religious. 신을 믿지 않는; 신앙이 없는. 2 wicked. 사악한. ● **god·less·ness** [-nis] *n.*

god·like [gádlàik / gɔ́d-] *adj.* 1 like God or a god; divine. 신과 같은; 신성(神性)의. 2 suitable for God or a god. 신에게 어울리는.

god·ly [gádli / gɔ́d-] *adj.* (**-li·er, -li·est**) obeying God; pious; divine. 신(神)의 법도를 따르는; 경건한; 신앙심이 깊은. ● **god·li·ness** [-nis] *n.*

god·moth·er [gádmʌ̀ðər / gɔ́d-] *n.* Ⓒ a woman who promises, at the baptism of a child, to help in its religious training. 대모(代母).

go·down [goudáun] *n.* a large building for storing goods. 창고. [Malay]

god·par·ent [gádpɛ̀ərənt / gɔ́d-] *n.* Ⓒ a godfather or godmother. 대부(代父); 대모(代母). [*god*]

God's acre [´ ´] *n.* a churchyard. 묘지.

God's Book [´ ´] *n.* the Bible. 성서.

God's earth [´ ´] *n.* the whole world. 전세계.

god·send [gádsènd / gɔ́d-] *n.* Ⓒ a piece of good fortune that comes unexpectedly as if sent by God. 하늘이 주신 것; 뜻하지 않은 행운.

god·ship [gádʃip / gɔ́d-] *n.* the character of a god. 신(神)임; 신격; 신성(神性). 「체.

God's image [´ ´-] *n.* a human body. 인

god·son [gádsʌ̀n / gɔ́d-] *n.* Ⓒ a male godchild. 대자(代子).

God·speed [gádspíːd / gɔ́d-] *n.* Ⓤ (wish for) good fortune of a person going on a journey; success. 여행길의 안전; 성공(의 기원); 행운. 參考 God speed you.의 간약형. ¶ *wish* 〔*bid*〕 *someone* ～ 아무의 여행길의 안전을 빌다. [*god*]

go·er [góuər] *n.* Ⓒ a person or thing that goes. 가는 사람〔것〕. [*go*]

Goe·the [gə́ːtə], **Johann Wolfgang von** *n.* (1749-1832) a German poet, novelist, dramatist and philosopher. 괴테《독일의 시인·소설가·극작가·철학자》.

go-get·ter [góugétər] *n.* 《U.S. *colloq.*》 a pushing and enterprising person. 민완가; 수완가; 정력적인 사람. [*go, get*]

gog·gle [gágəl / gɔ́gəl] *n.* 1 《usu. *pl.*》 large eye-glasses to protect the eyes from light, dust, etc. 보호〔방진(防塵)〕 안경. 2 Ⓒ the act of rolling the eyes to express surprise, fear, etc. (놀람 따위로) 눈을 희번덕거림. — *vi., vt.* roll the eyes. (눈을) 크게 뜨다; (눈알을) 희번덕거리다. [E.]

gog·gle-eyed [gágəlàid / gɔ́gəl-] *adj.* having protruding eyes. 퉁방울눈의.

:**go·ing** [góuiŋ] *n.* Ⓤ 1 departure. 감; 떠남; 출발. ¶ *His ～ was unexpected.* 그의 떠남은 뜻밖이었다 / *Let me know the day of your ～.* 너의 출발 날짜를 알려다오. 2 the condition of ground or land for traveling, walking, riding, etc. 길〔노면〕의 상태. ¶ *The ～ was bad.* 노면 상태가 좋지 않았다. 3 the pace at which one travels. 진행속도〔페이스〕. ¶ *good ～ toward the presidency* 사장 자리로의 순조로운 영진(榮進) / *Fifty miles an hour is pretty good ～.* 시속(時速) 50마일이면 상당한 속도다.
— *adj.* 1 moving; working. (기계 따위가) 활동〔운전, 운동〕중의; 진행중인. ¶ *keep a machine ～* 기계를 계속 움직이다 / *keep the meeting ～* 회의를 속행하다 / *set a clock ～* 시계를 움직이게 하다 / *It easily got ～.* 그것은 수월히 움직였다. 2 current; 《*colloq.*》 existing. 현행의; 현재 있는. ¶ *the ～ price* 〔*rate*〕 현행 가격〔요금〕. 3 doing business successfully. (일·사업 따위를) 잘 하고 있는; 영업중의. ¶ *a ～ business* 순조로운 사업 / *a ～ company* 〔*concern*〕 성업 중인 회사; 계속기업. [*go*]
going on, (of time, etc.) nearly; almost. 거의; 가까이. ¶ *It's ～ on five o'clock.* 거의 다섯 시가 돼간다.
in going order, in a normal condition. 이상 없이.

go·ings-on [góuiŋzɔ́(ː)n] *n. pl.* 《*colloq.*》 behavior; actions. (흔히 비난받을 만한) 행위; 짓.

goi·ter, 《Brit.》 **-tre** [gɔ́itər] *n.* a swelling in the neck caused by disease. 갑상선종(甲狀腺腫). [L. *guttur* throat]

:**gold** [gould] *n.* Ⓤ 1 a shiny, precious metal of bright-yellow color, used for making coins or jewelry. 금; 황금. ¶ *a ring made of pure ～* 순금 반지. 2 《*collectively*》 coins made of gold. 금화. ¶ *pay in ～* 금화로 지급하다. 3 a large sum of money; wealth. 많은 돈; 부(富). ¶ *greed of ～* 금전욕; 물욕. 4 a precious or pure quality. 귀중한 것; 순수한 것. 5 the color of gold. (황)금빛. ¶ *hair of ～* 금발 / *the red and ～ of autumn* 가을의 붉고 누런 황금빛의 단풍.
a heart of gold, (a man of) noble, pure heart. 아름다운〔순진한〕 마음(의 사람).
as good as gold, (usu. of children) very obedient. (흔히 애들이) 매우 고분고분한; 말을 잘 듣는.
the age of gold, the most flourishing age; the golden age. 황금 시대.
— *adj.* (made) of gold; like gold; of the color of gold. 금(제)의; 금 같은; 황금빛의(cf. *golden*). ¶ *a ～ watch* 금시계 / *～ embargo* 금

수출 금지 / *the* ~ *standard* 금본위. [E. → gall[1]]

gold·beat·er [góuldbìːtər] *n.* a person whose trade is to hammer out gold into very thin sheets. 금박사(金箔師).

gold digger [ˊ ˋ–] *n.* **1** 《*colloq.*》 a person who digs or seeks for gold. 금 캐는 사람; 금광을 찾아 헤매는 사람. **2** 《U.S. *sl.*》 a woman who tries to get money from men by tricks. 남자를 속여 돈을 우려내는 여자.

gold-dust [góulddʌ̀st] *n.* Ⓤ gold in the form of a fine powder. 사금(砂金).

:gold·en [góuldən] *adj.* **1** (made) of gold. 금(제)의. ¶ ~ *earrings* 금 귀고리. **2** yielding or containing gold. 금을 산출하는; 금이 함유된. ¶ *The Golden State* 캘리포니아 주(州)의 별명. **3** having the color of gold; shining like gold. 금빛의; 금빛으로 빛나는. ¶ ~ *hair* 금발 / *the* ~ *sun* 금빛으로 빛나는 태양. **4** excellent; beautiful. 뛰어난; 아름다운. ¶ *a* ~ *saying* 금언 / *a* ~ *voice* 아름다운 목소리 / *a* ~ *remedy* 묘약. **5** best; most flourishing. 융성한; 전성의; 번영하는. ¶ *one's* ~ *days* 전성 시대.

golden hours, a happy time. 행복한 때.

golden age [ˊ– ˊ], **the** *n.* the most flourishing period in the history of a nation, literature, etc. 황금[전성] 시대. ¶ *the* ~ *of basketball* 농구의 전성 시대.

golden calf [ˊ– ˊ], **the** *n.* wealth regarded as the greatest object in life. 금력 숭배. ¶ *worship the* ~.

Golden Fleece [ˊ– ˊ], **the** *n.* 《Gk. myth.》 the fleece of gold taken by the Argonauts. 금(金) 양털.

golden mean [ˊ– ˊ], **the** *n.* the principle of avoiding extremes. 중용. ¶ *keep the* ~ 중용을 지키다.

gold·en·rod [góuldnrɑ̀d / -rɔ̀d] *n.* Ⓒ 《bot.》 a tall autumn-blooming plant with many small yellow flowers. 메역취.

golden rule [ˊ– ˊ], **the** *n.* 《Bible》 the rule of doing to others as we would have them do to us. 황금률(律).

golden wedding [ˊ– ˊ–] *n.* the fiftieth anniversary of a wedding-day. 금혼식.

gold·finch [góuldfìntʃ] *n.* Ⓒ 《bird》 a small bright-colored songbird. 검은방울새.

gold·fish [góuldfìʃ] *n.* Ⓒ (*pl.* **-fish·es** or *collectively* **-fish**) a reddish-golden-colored fish living in fresh water. 금붕어.

gold foil [ˊ ˋ] *n.* gold beaten into very thin sheets. 금박(金箔). 參考 gold leaf 보다 두꺼움.

gold leaf [ˊ ˋ] *n.* gold beaten into very thin sheets. 금박(金箔).

gold mine [ˊ ˋ] *n.* **1** a mine that yields gold. 금광; 금갱. **2** 《*fig.*》 a source of something profitable. 보고(寶庫); 부원(富源).

gold plate [ˊ ˊ] *n.* **1** spoons, forks, dishes, etc. made of gold. 금제(金製)의 식기. **2** a covering of gold on top of another metal. 금도금.

gold rush [ˊ ˋ] *n.* a rush of people to newly-found gold-mines. 골드 러시《새로 발견된 금광으로의 쇄도》.

gold·smith [góuldsmìθ] *n.* Ⓒ a person who makes or sells things of gold. 금세공인 [상(商)]. [*gold*]

·golf [gɑlf, gɔ(ː)lf] *n.* Ⓤ an outdoor game played with a small, hard, rubber ball and a set of long-handled clubs. 골프. — *vi.* (P1) play this game. 골프를 치다. [Du. *kolf* club]

golf course [ˊ ˋ] *n.* the ground over which golf is played. 골프장.

golf·er [gɑ́lfər, gɔ́(ː)l-] *n.* Ⓒ a person who plays golf. 골프를 치는 사람.

golf links [ˊ ˋ] *n.* =golf course.

golf widow [ˊ ˋ–] *n.* a woman whose husband spends much leisure time at golf. 골프 미망인《골프를 치느라 자주 집을 비우는 남편을 가진 아내》.

Gol·go·tha [gɑ́lgəθə / gɔ́l-] *n.* **1** the place where Jesus Christ was killed on a cross. 골고다의 언덕. **2** Ⓒ 《*g-*》 a burial place. 매장지; 묘지. [Aram.]

Go·li·ath [gəláiəθ] *n.* **1** 《Bible》 the name of a giant killed by David. 골리앗《다윗에게 죽은 거인》. **2** Ⓒ 《usu. *g-*》 a giant. 거인. **3** Ⓒ 《*g-*》 a powerful traveling crane. 이동식 대형 기중기. [Heb.]

gol·li·wog, -wogg [gɑ́liwɑ̀g / gɔ́liwɔg] *n.* Ⓒ a grotesque doll; a bugbear. 괴기한 인형; 요괴. [?]

gol·ly [gɑ́li / gɔ́li] *interj.* 《*colloq.*》 an exclamation of surprise. 어이구; 어머(나); 저런. [Imit.]

go·losh [gəlɑ́ʃ / -lɔ́ʃ] *n.* =galosh.

G.O.M. Grand Old Man《W. E. Gladstone의 별명》.

go·nad [góunæd, gɑ́n-] *n.* 《anat.》 a gland that produces reproductive cells. 생식선(腺). [Gk. *gonē* seed]

gon·do·la [gɑ́ndələ / gɔ́n-] *n.* Ⓒ **1** a long, narrow boat with high, pointed ends, rowed with an oar, used in Venice. (Venice의) 곤돌라. **2** the boat-shaped car suspended from an airship. (비행선의) 조롱(吊籠). [It.]

〈gondola 1〉

gon·do·lier [gɑ̀ndəlíər / gɔ̀n-] *n.* Ⓒ a person who rows a gondola. 곤돌라 사공.

:gone [gɔːn, gɑn / gɔn] *v.* pp. of **go.** — *adj.* **1** past; lost. 지난; 가버린; 없어진. ¶ *a man* ~ *forty years of age,* 40세를 지난 남자. **2** deceased; dead. 죽은. ¶ *be dead and* ~ 죽어버리다. **3** ruined; hopeless. 영락한;

가망 없는; 절망적인. ¶ *a ~ case* 절망적인 것; 가망 없는 환자. **4** weak and faint. 기력이 쇠한; 아찔해지는. ¶ *a ~ feeling* 아찔해지는 기분. [go]

be gone on (=*be in love with*) *someone.* …에 반해 있다. ¶ *He is ~ on her.* 그는 그녀에게 반해 있다.

far gone, in an advanced stage; deeply involved; dying. 크게 진행되어; 깊이 관련되어; 죽어가고.

gong [gɔːŋ, gɑŋ / gɔŋ] *n.* Ⓒ a bell, shaped like a disc. 징; 공《접시 모양의 종》. [Imit.]

:good [gud] *adj.* (**bet·ter, best**) (opp. bad) **1** excellent; having fine qualities. 좋은; 뛰어난; 훌륭한. ¶ *a ~ tea* (질이) 좋은 홍차 / *a ~ road* 〔*house, picture*〕 훌륭한 도로〔집, 그림〕/ *~ health* 좋은 건강 상태 / *feel ~* 기분이 좋다. **2** well-behaved; honest; dutiful. 예의 바른; 성실〔충실〕한; 정직한. ¶ *a ~ boy* 예절 바른 아이 / *a ~ wife* 충실한 아내 / *lead a ~ life* 도덕적인 생활을 하다. **3** kind; beneficient; favorable. 친절〔다정〕한; 인정 많은; 호의적인. ¶ *a man of ~ reputation* 평판이 좋은 사람 / *do a ~ deed* 친절한 행위를 하다 / *do someone a ~ turn* 아무에게 친절히 하다 / *be ~ to one's neighbors* 이웃에게 친절하다 / *be ~ enough to do* 친절하게도 …하다. **4** happy; enjoyable. 행복한; 유쾌한; 즐거운. ¶ *a ~ joke* 유쾌한 농담 / *have a ~ time* (*of it*) 즐겁게 지내다. **5** ⓐ useful; efficient; suitable. 도움이 되는; 유익〔유리〕한; 적합한. ¶ *a ~ wind* 좋은 바람; 순풍 / *a ~ place to live* (*in*) 살기 좋은 곳 / *be ~ for the health* 건강에 좋다 / *~ for nothing* 아무 쓸모도 없는 / *Milk is ~ for children.* 우유는 어린이에게 좋다 / *Is this water ~ to drink?* 이 물은 마실 수 있습니까. ⓑ valid; reasonable. 유효한; 타당한. ¶ *a ~ excuse* 그럴 듯한 구실 / *The rule holds ~.* 이 규칙은 유효하다 / *He did it for ~ reasons.* 그는 타당한 이유가 있어서 그 일을 했다. **6** thorough; satisfying; considerable. 충분한; 상당한; 어지간한. ¶ *a ~ day's work* 좋이 하루 걸리는 일 / *a ~ half hour* 좋이 반 시간 / *at ~ speed* 상당한 속도로 / *have a ~ meal* 충분한 식사를 하다 / *I gave him a ~ scolding.* 그를 호되게 꾸짖었다. **7** clever; able; skillful. 잘 하는; 유능한; 능숙한. ¶ *a ~ dancer* 능숙한 댄서 / *be ~ at tennis* 〔*mathematics*〕 테니스를〔수학을〕 잘 하다 / *She was not very ~ in her work.* 그녀는 일을 그리 잘 하지 못했다. **8** healthy; strong. 건전한; 튼튼한. ¶ *~ eyesight* 건전한 시력. **9** real. 진짜의. ¶ *tell false money from ~* 가짜 돈을 진짜와 구별하다. **10** reliable; dependable; responsible. 믿을〔신뢰할〕 수 있는. ¶ *~ advice* 신뢰할 수 있는 조언. **11** sound; in perfect condition. 흠집 없는; 완전한; 신선한. ¶ *This egg is not very ~.* 이 달걀은 그다지 신선하지가 못하다. **12** ⓐ (of a person) possessing the necessary amount of strength. 필요한 체력이 있는. ¶ *I am ~ for another ten miles.* 아직 10마일은 더 걸을 수 있다 / *He is ~ for some years more.* 그는 앞으로 몇 해는 더 살 수 있다. ⓑ able and willing to pay. (금전을) 지불할 능력이〔의사가〕 있는. ¶ *He is ~ for a hundred pounds.* 그는 백 파운드를 지불할 의사가 있다. **13** 《*the* ~》 well-behaved people. 선인(善人).

a good deal ⇨deal¹.

a good while, a long time. 오랫동안.

all in good time, at the proper time. 적절한 때에.

as good as, almost; practically. 거의 …나 마찬가지인. ¶ *He is as ~ as dead.* 그는 거의 죽은 거나 같다.

(***as***) ***good as gold,*** **a**) (esp. of a child) very well-behaved. (특히 어린이가) 예의 바른; 점잖은. **b**) trustworthy. 믿을 수 있는. ¶ *His word is as ~ as gold.* 그의 말은 믿을 수 있다.

good and, very; completely; thoroughly. 무척; 매우; 충분히; 아주; 완전히. ¶ *She is ~ and wise.* 그녀는 무척 현명하다.

in good time, punctual. 때맞춰; 제시간에. ¶ *He came in ~ time.* 그는 제시간에 왔다.

make good, **a**) repay; replace. (손해 따위를) 보상하다; 메우다; 지급하다. **b**) perform (a promise); carry out (a purpose). (약속을) 이행하다; (목적을) 달성하다. **c**) succeed in doing. 성공하다. ¶ *He never made ~.* 그는 결코 성공하지 못했다.

not good enough, 《*colloq.*》 not worth doing. …할 가치가 없는.

— *n.* Ⓤ **1** an act that is helpful; benefit; advantage. 이익; 이득; 위함. ¶ *do ~ to* …에게 이득이 되다 / *for the ~ of mankind* 인류를 위해 / *I am saying this for your ~.* 너를 위해서 이 말을 하는 것이다. **2** merit; good point. 장점. ¶ *There is no ~ in her.* 그녀에겐 장점이 없다. **3** 《*pl.*》 things for selling or buying; merchandise. 상품; 물품. ¶ *goods in stock* 재고품 / *canned goods* 통조림류(類) / *dress goods* 드레스 감. **4** 《*pl.*》 ⓐ things owned; possessions; property. 재산; 동산. ⓑ 《Brit.》 any materials or articles, esp. manufactured articles to be transported by rail. 철도 화물. ¶ *by goods* 화차(貨車)로. [E.]

come to no good, end in disaster; come to a bad end. 불행으로 끝나다; 나쁜 결과가 되다.

deliver the goods, do what one promises to do. 약속을 이행하다.

do good, perform virtuous deeds. 선행(善行)을 하다.

for good (***and all***), forever; permanently; finally. 영원히; 이것을 마지막으로. ¶ *He left his country for ~ and all.* 그는 영원히 조국을 떠났다.

to the good, as a profit, benefit, or advantage. 이익이 되어; 흑자로.

:good-by, -bye [gùdbái] *interj.* farewell! 안녕. — *n.* Ⓒ a word spoken when parting from another; a farewell. 작별(作別)

인사; 작별.
say good-by, take leave. 작별을 고하다. ¶ *I must say ~ now.* 이제 작별을 해야겠다.

good-for-nothing [gúdfərnʌ̀θiŋ] *adj.* worthless; useless. 쓸모 없는; 변변치 못한. — *n.* Ⓒ a worthless or useless person. 쓸모 없는〔변변치 못한〕사람.

good-heart·ed [gúdhɑ́ːrtid] *adj.* kind; generous. 친절한; 다정한; 관대한. ● **good-heart·ed·ly** [-li] *adv.* **good-heart·ed·ness** [-nis] *n.*

good-hu·mored, 《Brit.》 **-moured** [gúdhjúːmərd] *adj.* cheerful; amiable. 기분이 좋은; 명랑〔쾌활〕한. ● **good-hu·mored·ly** [-li] *adv.*

good·ish [gúdiʃ] *adj.* pretty good; fairly great; considerable. 꽤〔어지간히〕좋은; 상당한.

good·li·ness [gúdlinis] *n.* Ⓤ the state of being goodly; beauty. 상당함; 아름다움.

good-look·ing [gúdlúkiŋ] *adj.* attractive; beautiful; handsome in appearance. 매력적인; 잘생긴; 미모의.

·good·ly [gúdli] *adj.* (**-li·er, -li·est**) **1** excellent; fine. 훌륭한; 뛰어난. ¶ *a ~ building* 훌륭한 건물. **2** good-looking; handsome. 아름다운; 잘생긴; 미모의. ¶ *a ~ gentleman* 잘생긴 신사. **3** considerable. 상당한. ¶ *a ~ sum of money* 상당한 액수의 돈 / *require a ~ number of calories* 상당한 양의 칼로리를 필요로 하다.

good·man [gúdmən] *n.* (*pl.* **-men** [-mən]) 《*arch.*》 **1** the master of a household. 가장(家長). **2** a husband. 남편.

·good-na·tured [gúdnéitʃərd] *adj.* kindly; cheerful; agreeable. 친절한; 온후한; 기분이 좋은. ● **good-na·tured·ly** [-li] *adv.*

:good·ness [gúdnis] *n.* Ⓤ **1** the state of being good; virtue. 좋음; 선량; 미덕(美德). **2** kindness; friendliness. 친절; 다정함. ¶ *out of the ~ of one's heart* 친절심에서 / *She had the ~ to lend me the money.* 그녀는 친절하게도 돈을 꾸어 주었다. **3** ⓐ the excellence of quality. (질의) 좋음; 우수함. ¶ *the ~ of a material* 재료의 우수함. ⓑ the best part; essence. 가장 좋은 부분; 정수. ¶ *the ~ of meat.*
for goodness' sake, for God's〔Heaven's〕 sake. 제발; 부탁이니까.
Goodness knows, Nobody knows. 아무도 모른다.
Goodness me! expressions of surprise. 아이구; 저런; 어머나.
— *interj.* an exclamation of surprise. 아이구; 저런; 어렵쇼. 參考 God 대신으로 쓰임. ¶ *Goodness (gracious)!* = *Goodness me!* = *Oh my ~!* 저런; 어렵쇼.

good-tem·pered [gúdtémpərd] *adj.* good-natured; amiable. 온후한; 상냥한; 너그러운; 마음씨 좋은.

·good·will [gúdwíl] *n.* **1** kindly or friendly feeling; kindness; willingness. 호의; 친절; 친선; 선의(善意). ¶ *pay a ~ visit to* …에 친선 방문을 하다 / *obtain* 〔*lose*〕 *the ~* 호의를 얻다〔잃다〕. **2** 《comm.》 the popularity or reputation of a business, shop, etc. (영업·점포 따위의) 영업권; 신용; 성가(聲價).

good·y [gúdi] *n.* Ⓒ (*pl.* **good·ies**) **1** 《usu. *pl.*》 something good to eat, esp. a sweet; candy. 맛이 있는 것; 사탕; 캔디. **2** a person who pretends to be virtuous. 도덕가연(然)하는 사람; 선인(善人)인 체하는 사람. — *interj.* an exclamation of pleasure. 기쁘다; 멋지다. — *adj.* (**good·i·er, good·i·est**) pretending to be virtuous. 도덕가연하는; 선인(善人)인 체하는. [*good*]

goof [guːf] *n.* 《*colloq.*》 a silly person; a blunder. 바보; 얼간이; (부주의에 의한) 실책. — *vt., vi.* blunder; spoil; shirk work. 실패〔실수, 실책〕하다; 일을 회피하다. [F. *goffe*]

goof·y [gúːfi] *adj.* 《*colloq.*》 silly. 어리석은; 얼빠진.

:goose [guːs] *n.* Ⓒ (*pl.* **geese**) **1** a web-footed, flatbilled water bird with a long neck; a female goose. 거위; 거위의 암컷. 參考 수컷은 gander. ¶ *a wild ~* 기러기 / *can't say 'bo!' to a ~* 되게 겁쟁이다 / 《*prov.*》 *The ~ hangs high.* 전도 유망하다. **2** 《*fig.*》 a silly person. 바보; 얼간이. ¶ *make a ~ of* … 을 놀리다. **3** (*pl.* **gooses**) a tailor's smoothing iron with a long curved handle like a goose's neck. (양복점의) 다리미. [E.]
cook someone's goose, ruin someone's reputation, plan, etc. …의 평판〔희망·계획〕 따위를 망치다. ¶ *The scandal will cook her ~.* 그 추문은 그녀를 완전히 망칠 게다.
kill the goose that lays the golden eggs, sacrifice future gains to satisfy present needs. 눈앞의 이익을 위해 장래의 이익을 망치다.

goose·ber·ry [gúːsbèri, -bəri, gúːz-] *n.* Ⓒ (*pl.* **-ries**) 《bot.》 a small, sour berry, used to make pies, jam, etc.; the thorny bush that this berry grows on. 구스베리(나무).

goose flesh [⌐⌐] *n.* a rough condition of the skin caused by cold, fear, shock, etc. 소름. ¶ *be ~ all over* 온몸에 소름이 끼치다.

goose skin [⌐⌐] *n.* =goose flesh.

goose step [⌐⌐] *n.* 《mil.》 a way of marching without bending the knees. 무릎을 굽히지 않고 걷는 행진 보조.

G.O.P. Grand Old Party; the Republican Party. 미국 공화당.

go·pher [góufər] *n.* Ⓒ **1** a ratlike animal with large cheek bags. 뒤쥐. **2** a ground tortoise. 육지 거북의 일종. [? F.]

Gor·di·an knot [gɔ́ːrdiən ⌐] *n.* 《*the ~*》 a knot tied by an ancient king to be undone only by the man who should rule Asia. Gordius의 매듭; 어려운 문제; 지난사(至難事). [Gk.]
cut the Gordian knot, settle a most difficult problem in the shortest and

most violent way. 어려운 사태에 신속하고 과감히 대처하다; 문제를 일거에 해결하다.

gore[1] [gɔːr] *n.* Ⓤ thick or clotted blood. 응혈(凝血). [E. =dung]

gore[2] [gɔːr] *vt.* (P6) wound (someone) with a horn or tusk. …을 받다; …을 찌르다. [O.E. *gar* spear]

gore[3] [gɔːr] *n.* Ⓒ a long, triangular piece of cloth put or made in a garment, sail, etc., to change its width or shape. (돛·옷 따위에 대는) 삼각형의 천; 바대; 섶. — *vt.* (P6) put or make a gore in (something). …에 삼각형(形)의 천을 대다. [E. =strip of land]

gorge [gɔːrdʒ] *n.* Ⓒ **1** a deep, narrow valley, usu. with steep, rocky walls. 협곡. **2** the act of eating greedily. 폭식(暴食); 대식(大食). **3** contents of the stomach. (위 안의) 먹은 음식물. ¶ *cast up* 〔*heave*〕 *the* ~ 먹은 것을 토하다. **4** a feeling of disgust. 가슴의 불쾌감. **5** a mass blocking up a passage. 통로를 막는 것.

make someone's gorge rise, cause someone to feel sick with disgust or to feel angry. …을 구역질나게 하다; 성나게 하다.

rouse 〔***stir***〕 ***the gorge,*** make (someone) angry. …을 성나게 하다.

— *vi.* (P1) eat greedily. 게걸스레 먹다

— *vt.* (P6,13) 《usu. *in passive* or *reflexively*》 stuff (one's stomach) with food; swallow (something) greedily. 잔뜩 먹다; …을 걸신들린 듯 삼키다. ¶ ~ *oneself with beefsteak* 비프스테이크를 잔뜩 먹다. [O.F. =throat]

·gor·geous [gɔ́ːrdʒəs] *adj.* rich in color; magnificent. 색채가 현란한; 화려한; 굉장한. ¶ *a* ~ *sunset* 장려한 일몰. ● **gor·geous·ness** [-nis] *n.* [F.]

gor·geous·ly [gɔ́ːrdʒəsli] *adv.* in a gorgeous manner; splendidly; beautifully. 굉장하게; 화려하게; 호화롭게; 아름답게.

gor·get [gɔ́ːrdʒit] *n.* Ⓒ **1** a piece of armor to protect the throat. (갑옷의) 목가리개. **2** a veil to protect the neck and breast worn by women in the Middle Ages. (중세 여자의) 목〔가슴〕가리개. [*gorge*]

go·ril·la [gərílə] *n.* Ⓒ 《animal》 the largest of the manlike apes, living in Africa. 고릴라. [Gk. =wildman]

gor·mand [gɔ́ːrmənd] *n.* =gourmand.

gor·mand·ize [gɔ́ːrməndàiz] *vi., vt.* eat very greedily; gorge. (…을) 걸신들린 듯 먹다; 탐식하다. [*gourmand*]

gorse [gɔːrs] *n.* Ⓤ 《esp. Brit.》 a prickly shrub with yellow flowers. 가시금작화. [E.]

gor·y [gɔ́ːri] *adj.* (**gor·i·er, gor·i·est**) bloody. 피투성이의. ● **gor·i·ly** [-li] *adv.* **gor·i·ness** [-nis] *n.* [*gore*[1]]

gosh [gɑʃ / gɔʃ] *interj.* 《*colloq.*》 《also *by*》 an exclamation of surprise; by God. (놀람·맹세를 나타내어) 아이쿠; 큰일났군; 맹세코. [*God*]

gos·hawk [gáshɔ̀ːk / gɔ́s-] *n.* a powerful, short-winged hawk. 새매류. [*goose, hawk*]

Go·shen [góuʃən] *n.* 《Bible》 a land of plenty and comfort. 고센 땅; 풍요롭고 기름진 땅; 낙토.

gos·ling [gázliŋ / gɔ́z-] *n.* Ⓒ **1** a young goose. 새끼 거위. **2** a foolish, inexperienced person. 어리석은 풋내기. [*goose*]

·gos·pel [gáspəl / gɔ́s-] *n.* Ⓒ **1** the teaching of Jesus and the Apostles. 복음; 기독교의 교의(教義). **2** 《usu. *the G-*》 any one of the first four books of the New Testament. 복음서. 參考 Matthew, Mark, Luke John의 4복음서의 하나. **3** 《usu. *the G-*》 any selected part of these books. 복음서 중의 1절. **4** 《*colloq.*》 anything earnestly believed as a guide for action. 행동에 대한 신조. ¶ *a political* ~ 정치적 신조 / *the* ~ *of temperance* 금주주의. **5** absolute truth. 절대적 진리; 금과 옥조. [*good, spell*]

preach the gospel, give a religious sermon. 전도하다.

take something as gospel, believe something to be true. …을 진실이라고 생각하다; 곧이 곧대로 믿다.

gospel truth [⌐– ⌐] *n.* something absolutely true; truth contained in the gospel. 절대적인 진리〔진실〕; 복음서에 있는 진리.

gos·sa·mer [gásəmər / gɔ́sə-] *n.* **1** Ⓒ a thread of cobweb on grass or in the air. (풀에 걸려 있거나 공중에 부유하는) 거미줄. **2** ⓊⒸ a very thin, light, soft cloth. 가볍고 얇은 천; 사(紗). **3** Ⓒ a coat made of this cloth. 얇은 외투. **4** ⓊⒸ anything very light and thin. 극히 섬세한 것. — *adj.* very light and thin. 얇고 가벼운. ● **gos·sa·mer·y** [-ri] *adj.* [M.E. =goose summer]

·gos·sip [gásip / gɔ́s-] *n.* **1** Ⓤ idle talk and rumors about other people. 잡담; (남의) 소문 이야기. **2** Ⓒ a person who talks idly about other people. 소문을 좋아하는 사람; 수다쟁이. — *vi.* (P1) talk or chatter idly about other people. 소문 이야기를 하다; 잡담을 하다; 수다를 떨다. ¶ ~ *about the neighbors* 이웃에 관한 소문 이야기를 하다. ● **gos·sip·er** [-ər] *n.* [E. =related in God, fellow godparent]

:got [gɑt / gɔt] *v.* p. and pp. of **get.**

Goth [gɑθ / gɔθ] *n.* Ⓒ **1** a member of a Teutonic tribe that conquered the Roman Empire in the third, fourth, and fifth centuries. 고트 사람〔족〕. **2** an uncivilized person; a barbarian. 야만인. [Gk.]

Goth., goth. Gothic, gothic.

Goth·am [gáθəm, góuθəm / gɔ́θ-] *n.* **1** 《U.S.》 New York City. 뉴욕 시. **2** [gátəm, góut- / gɔ́t-] an English village whose inhabitants were said to be very foolish. 바보의 읍(邑)《주민이 모두 어리석었다는 영국 전설의 마을》. [?]

wise men of Gotham, foolish people. 어리석

은 사람들.

Goth·ic [gάθik / gɔ́θ-] *n.* Ⓤ **1** 《archit.》 a style of architecture with pointed arches and high, steep roofs. 고딕식(式) 건축. **2** the language of the Goths. 고트어(語). **3** 《U.S.》 a kind of type used in printing. 고딕체 활자(cf. *Roman, italics*). — *adj.* **1** 《archit.》 of Gothic architecture. 고딕 건축의. **2** of the Goths or their language. 고트(사람·어)의. **3** uncivilized; barbarous. 미개한; 야만의. **4** medieval. 중세의. **5** 《print.》 consisting of German or heavy or black type. 고딕체의. [*Goth*]

got·ten [gάtn / gɔ́tn] *v.* pp. of **get**.

gouge [gaudʒ] *n.* Ⓒ **1** an instrument with a curved blade for cutting holes. 둥근끌. **2** a hole made by a gouge. 둥근 끌로 판 구멍. **3** 《U.S. *colloq.*》 a trick. 사기(詐欺). — *vt.* **1** (P6,7) cut with a gouge. …을 둥근 끌로 파다[쪼다]. **2** (P6,7) 《*out*》 dig out. …을 도려내다. **3** (P6) 《U.S. *colloq.*》 trick. …을 속이다. [L. *gubia*]

gou·lash [gúːlɑːʃ, -læʃ] *n.* a rich stew of meat and vegetables. 쇠고기와 야채의 스튜. [Hung. *gulyás* (*hús*) herdsman's (meat)]

gourd [guərd, gɔːrd] *n.* Ⓒ a hard-shelled fruit of the melon family; the dried shell of this fruit, used for cups, etc. 호리병박(의 열매); (그 열매를 말려서 만든) 호리병. [L. *cucurbita*]

gour·mand [gúərmənd] *n.* Ⓒ a person who is fond of good eating; a glutton. 미식가(美食家); 대식가(大食家). [F.]

gour·met [gúərmei, —´] *n.* a connoisseur of wine or table delicacies. 미식가; 포도주통(通). [F.]

gout [gaut] *n.* Ⓤ 《often *the* ～》 a painful swelling of the joints, esp. of the foot. 통풍(痛風). [L. *gutta* drop]

gout·y [gáuti] *adj.* (**gout·i·er, gout·i·est**) **1** suffering from gout. 통풍(痛風)에 걸린. **2** of gout. 통풍의. **3** causing gout. 통풍을 일으키는. ● **gout·i·ness** [-nis] *n.*

Gov. Governor.

gov. government; governor.

:gov·ern [gʌ́vərn] *vt.* (P6) **1** rule; manage; direct. …을 통치[지배]하다; 다스리다; 관리[운영]하다. ¶ ～ *a country* 나라를 다스리다 / ～ *the people* 국민을 통치[지배]하다 / ～ *a school* 학교를 운영하다 / *Never let your anger* ～ *you.* 분노가 당신을 지배하게 해서는 결코 안 된다. **2** influence; guide; determine. …에 영향을 끼치다; …을 좌우하다; 결정하다. ¶ ～ *someone's decision* …의 결심을 좌우하다. **3** control; restrain. 억제하다. ¶ ～ *one's passions* [*temper*] 격정을[울화를] 억누르다. — *vi.* (P1) be a ruler. 지배 통치하다; 관리하다. ¶ *The queen reigns, but does not* ～. 여왕은 군림은 하지만 정무(政務)는 보지 않는다. [Gk. *kubernaō* steer]

gov·ern·a·ble [gʌ́vərnəbəl] *adj.* able to govern. 다스릴[지배할, 억제할] 수 있는.

gov·ern·ess [gʌ́vərnis] *n.* Ⓒ a woman who teaches children in their own home. 여자 가정 교사.

gov·ern·ing [gʌ́vərniŋ] *adj.* **1** having the right to govern. 통치권을 가진. **2** having the function or property of determining. 지배하는.

:gov·ern·ment [gʌ́vərnmənt] *n.* **1** Ⓤ control; management. 관리; 통치; 통제; 경영. ¶ *school* ～ 학교 운영 / *the* ～ *of one's conduct* 행동의 자제. **2** Ⓒ 《sometimes *G-*》 the body of persons ruling a country. 정부. ¶ *a* ～ *officer* 정부 관리 / *the United States* ～ 미합중국 정부 / *be against the Government* 정부에 반대하다. **3** Ⓒ a system of ruling. 정치 체제; 정체(政體). ¶ *a democratic* ～ 민주 정체 / *parliamentary* ～ 의회 정치. **4** Ⓤ 《gram.》 the influence of one word which determines the case or mood of another. (단어의) 지배.

gov·ern·men·tal [gʌ̀vərnméntl] *adj.* of government. 정치[통치]의; 정부의. [↑]

:gov·er·nor [gʌ́vərnər] *n.* Ⓒ **1** a person who is elected as head of a state of the United States or is appointed head of a British colony. 주(州)지사; 총독. **2** a person who manages or directs a club, society, etc. 총재; 장(長); 관리자. **3** the part of a machine that controls the speed of motion. 자동 조속기(調速機). ¶ *an electric* ～ 전기 조속기. [→govern]

governor general [´-- ´--] *n.* (*pl.* **governors g-** or **g- generals**) a chief of governors. 총독(cf. *viceroy*).

gov·er·nor·ship [gʌ́vərnərʃìp] *n.* Ⓤ the position of a governor. 지사[장관, 총재 등의] 직[지위].

govt., Govt. government.

gowk [gauk, gouk] *n.* a fool. 바보. [N.]

:gown [gaun] *n.* Ⓒ **1** a woman's dress. 부인[여성]복. ¶ *an evening* ～ 여성용 야회복. **2** a long, loose robe which judges, priests, scholars, etc. wear to show their position, profession, etc. (법관·성직자·학자 등의) 정복(正服); 법관복; 가운. **3** a nightgown or a dressing gown. 잠옷; 실내복. **4** 《*collectively*》 members of a university. 대학의 학생과 교수.

arms and gown, war and peace. 전쟁과 평화(平和).

take the gown, become a priest or a lawyer. 목사[변호사]가 되다.

town and gown, persons at Oxford and Cambridge who are not and who are members of the university. (옥스퍼드나 케임브리지의) 시민과 대학측.

— *vi., vt.* put on a gown. 가운을 입(히)다. [L. *gunna* fur]

GPM gallons per minute.

G.P.O., GPO General Post Office. 중앙 우체국.

G.P.U. Gay-Pay-Oo. 구(舊)소련의 비밀 경찰. 參考 1934년 폐지.

Gr. Grecian; Greece; Greek.
gr. grain; gram; gross.
·**grab** [græb] *vt., vi.* (**grabbed, grab·bing**) (P6,13; 1,3) **1** ⟪*at*⟫ seize suddenly; snatch. (…을) 움켜잡다; 잡아채다. ¶ *He grabbed me by the collar.* 그는 내 양복깃을 움켜 잡았다 / *He grabbed at her purse.* 그는 그녀의 돈지갑을 낚아채었다. **2** take possession of (something) by unlawful methods. 가로채다; 횡령〔약탈〕하다. ¶ *a vicious scheme to ~ land* 토지 횡령의 흉계.
— *n.* Ⓒ **1** the act of seizing suddenly. 움켜잡기〔쥐기〕; 잡아채기. **2** something grabbed. 움켜잡은〔낚아 챈, 가로 챈〕 것. **3** a machine used for lifting or moving heavy articles. 그랩⟪무엇을 움켜잡는 장치⟫. [E.]
have the grab on, ⟪*colloq.*⟫ be in a better position than someone else. …보다 유리한 지위를 차지하다.
make a grab at, suddenly seize (something). …을 잡아〔낚아〕채다.
:**grace** [greis] *n.* Ⓤ **1** beauty of action or manner; delicacy; elegance. (성질·태도의) 기품; 우아; 고상함. ¶ *the ~ of action* 〔*bearing*〕 행동〔태도〕의 우아함 / *with ~* 우아하게. **2** good will; kindness. 호의; 선의; 친절. ¶ *an act of ~* 은혜; 특전 / *by special ~* 특별한 호의〔조치〕로. **3** ⓐ the kindness of God. 신의 은총. ¶ *by the ~ of God* 신의 은총으로. ⓑ a virtue, etc. coming from God. 신이 주신 미덕. ¶ *the ~ of humility* 겸손의 미덕. **4** delay granted as a favor. 유예; 지급 유예 (기간). ¶ *give someone two days' ~* 아무에게 이틀의 유예를 주다. **5** ⟪sometimes *a ~*⟫ a short prayer of thanks given before or after a meal. (식전·식후의) 감사의 기도. ¶ *say ~* (식사 전후에) 짤막한 기도를 하다. **6** ⟪*pl.*⟫ good points; charms. 미점(美點); 매력. ¶ *social graces* 사교상의 예절〔매력〕 / *a girl full of pleasant graces* 호감을 주는 매력이 넘치는 아가씨. **7** the title of a duke or an archbishop. 각하⟪공작(부인)·대주교에 대한 존칭⟫. ¶ *His* 〔*Her, Your*〕 *Grace* 각하. **8** ⟪*the Graces*⟫ ⟪Gk. myth.⟫ three sister goddesses, givers of beauty and charm. (세 자매인) 미(美)의 여신들.
fall from grace, do wrong; commit a sin. 못된 짓을 하다; 종교상의 죄를 범하다.
have the grace to *do,* be so kind as to do. 친절하게도〔깨끗이〕 …하다. ¶ *He had the ~ to apologize.* 그는 깨끗이 사죄했다.
in the bad graces of (=*disfavored or disliked by*) *someone.* …에게서 사랑을 못 받고.
in the good graces of (=*favored or liked by*) *someone.* …의 마음에 들어; …의 사랑을 받아.
with (***a***) ***bad grace,*** unpleasantly; unwillingly. 마지못해.
with good grace, pleasantly; willingly. 쾌히; 자진해서; 깨끗이.
— *vt.* (P6,13) give favor or honor to (someone or something). …에(게) 명예를 〔광영을〕 주다. ¶ *She graced the party with her presence.* 그녀가 참석함으로써 그 파티를 빛냈다. [L. *gratus* pleasing]
·**grace·ful** [gréisfəl] *adj.* having or showing grace; elegant. 우아한; 품위 있는; 얌전한. ●**grace·ful·ness** [-nis] *n.*
grace·ful·ly [gréisfəli] *adv.* in a graceful manner. 우아〔단아〕하게; 얌전하게.
grace·less [gréislis] *adj.* **1** without grace. 우아함이〔품위가〕 없는; 촌스러운. **2** ill-mannered; depraved. 예절 모르는; 거친; 타락한.
·**gra·cious** [gréiʃəs] *adj.* **1** graceful; courteous. 우아한; 정중한. **2** winning. 애교있는. **3** merciful; kindly. 자비깊은; 인정많은; 친절한. ¶ *a ~ king* 인자한 왕. — *interj.* an exclamation of surprise. 놀란 외침; 아이구; 저런; 아뿔싸; 어머(나). ¶ *My ~ !* =*Gracious me !* =*Gracious goodness !* 아이쿠; 저런; 아뿔싸.
gra·cious·ly [gréiʃəsli] *adv.* in a gracious manner. 정중히; 자비롭게; 인자하게.
gra·cious·ness [gréiʃəsnis] *n.* Ⓤ elegance; mercy; kindness. 우아; 자비; 친절.
grad. graduate(d); gradient.
gra·date [gréideit / grədéit] *vt., vi.* (P6; 1) **1** (cause to) pass by imperceptible degrees from one shade of color to another. (색조를) 바림하다; 옮어지다. **2** arrange in steps or grades. 순차로 배열하다. [→grade]
gra·da·tion [greidéiʃən / grə-] *n.* ⒸⓊ **1** a gradual change from one thing to another. 점차적 변화. ¶ *the ~ of color in the rainbow* 무지개에서 볼 수 있는 점차적인 빛의 변화 / *change by ~* 서서히 변하다. **2** ⟪usu. *pl.*⟫ steps, stages, or degrees in a series. (점차적 이행 과정에서의) 단계; 순서. ¶ *~ of decay* 부패의 단계 / *~ between right and wrong* 선과 악 사이의 단계. **3** the act of arranging into a series. 순서〔등급〕 매기기.
·**grade** [greid] *n.* Ⓒ **1** ⟪U.S.⟫ a class or year in school. 학년; 학급. ¶ *He is in the fifth ~.* 그는 5학년이다. **2** a step or stage in a course or process. 단계. ¶ *pass through the grades of growing* 점차 성장해 가다. **3** a degree in rank, quality, order, etc. 등급; 계급. ¶ *a poor ~ of wheat* 품질이 낮은 밀 / *A general holds the highest ~ in the army.* 대장은 군대에서 최고 계급이다. **4** a class of persons or things of the same degree. 동일 계급〔등급, 정도〕에 속하는 사람〔것〕. **5** ⟪*the ~ grades*⟫ ⟪U.S.⟫ an elementary school. 국민학교. **6** ⟪U.S.⟫ a number or letter showing a pupil's skill in school work. 성적 (평점); 시험 점수(cf. ⟪Brit.⟫ *mark*). **7** ⟪esp. U.S.⟫ a slope of a road, railroad track, etc. (도로·철도 따위의) 물매; 경사(도). ¶ *a steep ~* 급경사 / *go up the ~* 비탈을 오르다.
at grade, on the same level. 같은 평면에서; 같은 높이의.
make the grade, **a**) ascend a slope. 비탈을 오르다. **b**) overcome difficulties; succeed. 곤란을 이겨내다; 성공하다.

on the down* 〔*up*〕 *grade, **a**) going down 〔up〕. 내리받이〔치받이〕에; 내리막〔오르막〕에. **b**) getting worse 〔better〕. 쇠퇴〔번성〕하여.
— *vt.* (P6) **1** classify. …을 유별하다; 등급별로 분류하다. ¶ ~ *children according to age* 나이에 따라 아동을 분류하다. **2** make (ground, etc.) even or more level. (땅 따위를) 평평하게 하다. ¶ ~ *a road* 길을 고르다. **3** cross with a better breed. (잡종·열등종의 동물을) 순종과 교배시키다.
— *vi.* (P5) take an indicated rank or position. …등급이다. [L. *gradus* step]

grade crossing [ˊ ˊ-] *n.* a place where two roads or tracks cross on the same level. 수평 교차점.

grad·er [gréidər] *n.* Ⓒ **1** a person or thing that grades. 등급을 매기는 사람; 선별인; 선별기. **2** 《U.S.》 a person who is in a certain grade at school. …학년생.

gra·di·ent [gréidiənt] *n.* Ⓒ **1** a slope; the rate of inclination. 경사(도); 물매; 비탈. **2** 《phys.》 the rate at which temperature, pressure, etc. changes. (온도·기압 따위의) 변화도(度). [→grade]

•**grad·u·al** [grǽdʒuəl] *adj.* moving by degrees; gentle and slow. 서서히 이루어지는; 점차적〔점진적〕인. ¶ *a* ~ *slope* 완만한 비탈 / ~ *improvement in health* 건강의 점차적인 회복. [↑]

:**grad·u·al·ly** [grǽdʒuəli] *adv.* little by little. 서서히.

:**grad·u·ate** [grǽdʒuèit, -it] *vt.* **1** (P6,13) permit (someone) to leave school after completing a course of study. …을 졸업시키다. 參考 영국에서는 대학에, 미국에서는 모든 학교의 졸업에 쓰임. ¶ *Seoul University graduated 2,000 students.* 서울 대학교는 2천명의 학생을 졸업시켰다. **2** mark (a flask, tube, etc.) with regular divisions. …에 눈금을 매기다〔붙이다〕. ¶ *a graduated beaker* 눈금이 있는 비커. **3** (P6) classify (things) into grades according to size, quality, etc. …에 등급을 매기다; 등급별로 가르다. **4** (P6) concentrate by evaporation. …을 농축하다. — *vi.* (P1,3) **1** 《*from*》 complete a course of study. 졸업하다. ¶ *He graduated from* 〔《Brit.》 *at*〕 *Yale.* 예일 대학을 졸업했다. **2** receive a degree. 학위를 받다〔따다〕. ¶ *In what year did you* ~? 몇년도에 (학사) 학위를 따셨나요. **3** change gradually into. 점차 변(화)하다. ¶ *The dawn graduated into day.* 밤은 점차 밝아왔다.
— [grǽdʒuit, -dʒuèit] *n.* Ⓒ a person who has graduated and has a degree. 졸업생; (학사) 학위 취득자.
— [grǽdʒuit, -dʒuèit] *adj.* **1** having received a diploma. (대학을) 졸업한; (학사) 학위를 취득한. **2** for a graduate. (대학) 졸업생을 위한. ¶ *a* ~ *school* 대학원 / *do* ~ *work* 대학원에서 공부하다. [*grade*]

•**grad·u·a·tion** [grædʒuéiʃən] *n.* Ⓤ **1** the act of completing a course of study. 졸업. **2** a ceremony at which diplomas are received. 졸업식; 학위 수여식. ¶ ~ *exercises* 졸업식. **3** 《*pl.*》 a mark or marks to show degrees for measuring. 눈금. **4** the act of arranging according to size or kind, etc. (크기·종류에 따른) 분류; 배열.

graft[1] [græft, grɑːft] *vi., vt.* (P1; 6,7,13) **1** insert (a shoot, bud, etc.) into another tree so that it will grow there. 접목〔접붙이기, 꺾꽂이〕하다. **2** 《surg.》 move (a piece of skin, bone, etc.) from one part of the body to another so that it will grow there. (피부·뼈·조직 따위를) 이식(移植)하다. — *n.* Ⓒ **1** the act of grafting. 접목; (조직의) 이식. **2** the part that is grafted. 접목〔이식〕된 부분. ●**graft·er** [-ər] *n.* [Gk. *graphion* stylus]

graft[2] [græft, grɑːft] *n.* ⒸⓊ 《U.S. *colloq.*》 **1** the act of gaining money, etc. through the wrong use of one's position. 독직(瀆職); 부정; 수회(收賄). **2** the money, property, etc. thus acquired. 부정 소득; 뇌물. — *vi., vt.* (P1; 6) obtain (money, property, etc.) by graft. 부정 이득을 취하다; 수회〔독직〕하다. ●**graft·er** [-ər] *n.* [?]

gra·ham flour [gréiəm flàuər] *n.* 《U.S.》 unbolted flour. 전맥(全麥)《체로 기울을 거르지 않은 밀가루》. [Person]

grail [greil] *n.* Ⓒ a cup; a dish. 술잔; 성배(聖杯); 접시. [L.]

:**grain** [grein] *n.* Ⓒ **1** Ⓤ 《*collectively*》 the seed of wheat, corn, oats, or rice. 낟알; 곡물. **2** a very small and hard piece, such as sand, salt and sugar. (모래·소금·설탕 따위의) 알(갱이). ¶ *a* ~ *of sugar* 〔*salt, sand*〕 한 알의 설탕〔소금, 모래〕. **3** the smallest possible amount; any tiny bit. 미량; 극히 조금. ¶ *a* ~ *of hope* 실낱 같은 희망 / *There is not a* ~ *of truth in what he says.* 그가 하는 말에는 아무런 진실도 없다. **4** the small unit of weight; 0.0648 grams. 그레인《무게의 단위; 0.0648 g》. **5** Ⓤ natural character; temper. 기질; 성질; 성벽(性癖). ¶ *a man of coarse* ~ 성격이 거친 사람 / *against* 〔*contrary to*〕 *the* 〔*one's*〕 ~ 기질〔성질〕에 반(反)하여〔맞지 않아〕. **6** Ⓤ ⓐ the little lines and markings in wood, marble, etc. 나뭇결; 돌결. ⓑ a rough surface. 거친 면. ¶ *the* ~ *side of leather.*
in grain, by nature; fundamentally. 타고난; 순전한; 지독한; 근본적으로.
take* 〔*receive*〕 *something with a grain of salt, not believe something all; show caution in accepting something. (남의 말 등을) 에누리해서 〔줄잡아, 비판적으로〕 받아들이다.
without a grain of, have not a bit of. …이 추호〔조금〕도 없이.
— *vt.* (P6) **1** form (something) into grain. …을 낟알 모양으로 만들다. **2** paint in imitation of the grain of wood. 나뭇결 모양으로 칠하다. [L. *granum*]

•**gram,** 《Brit.》 **gramme** [græm] *n.* Ⓒ a

unit of weight in the metric system. 그램《무게의 단위; abbr. g., gm., gr.》. [Gk. *grámma* small weight]

·**gram·mar** [grǽmər] *n.* Ⓤ **1** the study of forms of words and the structure of sentenses. 문법. **2** Ⓒ a treatise or a book on this subject. 문법론(論); 문법서(書). **3** statements about the use of words. 어법. **4** elements of an art, science. 초보; 기초; 기본. [Gk. *graphō* write]

gram·mar·i·an [grəmέəriən] *n.* Ⓒ a person who specializes in grammar. 문법학자.

grammar school [ˊ-ˋ] *n.* **1** 《U.S.》 an elementary school. 초등학교. **2** 《Brit.》 a secondary school preparing for college. 중등 학교. 參考 미국의 high school 에 상당함; 예전에는 라틴어가 주요 학과였으나 지금은 public school 비슷함.

gram·mat·i·cal [grəmǽtikəl] *adj.* **1** according to the rules of grammar. 문법적으로 바른. **2** of grammar. 문법(상)의. ¶ *a ~ mistake* 〔*rule*〕 문법상의 잘못〔규칙〕. ● **grammat·i·cal·ly** [-i] *adv.*

gramme [græm] *n.* 《Brit.》 =gram.

gram·o·phone [grǽməfòun] *n.* Ⓒ 《Brit.》 a machine for reproducing sounds from records. 축음기(cf. 《U.S.》 *phonograph*). [→phonograph]

gram·pus [grǽmpəs] *n.* 《animal》 kinds of dolphin-like cetacean. 범고래. [L. *crassus piscis* fat fish]

gran·a·ry [grǽnəri, gréi-] *n.* Ⓒ (*pl.* **-ries**) **1** a place or building for storing grain. 곡물창고; 곡창. **2** 《*fig.*》 a country or place which produces a large amount of grain, and supplies it to other countries. 곡창 지대. [→grain]

·**grand** [grænd] *adj.* **1** large and fine; splendid; magnificent. 장대〔장려〕한; 웅대한; 훌륭한; 호화로운; 당당한. ¶ *a ~ sight* 장관 / *a ~ house* 〔*party*〕 호화로운 집〔파티〕 / *a ~ mountain scenery* 웅대한 산의 풍경 / *a ~ air* 당당한 풍채 / *speak in a ~ way* 당당히 말하다 / *live in ~ style* 호화로운 생활을 하다. **2** great; important. 큰; 중요〔중대〕한. ¶ *make a ~ mistake* 중대한 실수를〔잘못을〕 하다. **3** main; principal. 주요한; 주된; 으뜸의. ¶ *the ~ ballroom* 대(大)무도실 / *the ~ staircase* 정면 계단 / *the grandstand* 특별 관람석 / *The ~ question we have to decide is ....* 결정해야 할 으뜸 문제는 …이다. **4** dignified; noble; showing high social standing. 위엄 있는; 고귀한; 젠 체하는. ¶ *the ~ style* 장중한 작풍 / *a ~ manner* 젠 체하는〔위엄 있는〕 태도. **5** 《*colloq.*》 very satisfactory or good. 더 없이 좋은; 즐거운. ¶ *in ~ condition* 더 없이 좋은 컨디션으로 / *We had a ~ time yesterday.* 어제는 더없이 즐거운 시간을 보냈다 / *It will be ~ if you can come.* 오실 수 있다면 더없이 좋겠습니다. **6** complete; full. 총괄적인; 전체로서의. ¶ *a ~ total* 총계.

— *n.* **1** a grand piano. 그랜드 피아노. **2** 《U.S. *sl.*》 a thousand dollars. 1,000 달러. [L. *grandis* full-grown]

gran·dad [grǽndæ̀d] *n.* =granddad.

gran·dam [grǽndæm, -dəm] *n.* 《*arch.*》 a grandmother; an old woman. 할머니; 노파. [→grand]

grand·aunt [grǽndæ̀nt, -ɑ̀:nt] *n.* Ⓒ the aunt of one's father or mother. 대고모.

:**grand·child** [grǽn*d*tʃàild] *n.* Ⓒ (*pl.* **-children** [-tʃìldrən]) the child of one's son or daughter. 손자. ¶ *a great-grandchild* 증손 / *a great-great-grandchild* 현손(玄孫).

grand·dad [grǽn*d*dæ̀d] *n.* Ⓒ 《*child's word*》 a grandfather. 할아버지.

:**grand·daugh·ter** [grǽn*d*dɔ̀:tər] *n.* Ⓒ the daughter of one's son or daughter. 손녀(딸).

grand duchess [ˊ-ˊ-] *n.* **1** a wife or widow of a grand duke. 대공비(大公妃); 대공 미망인. **2** a lady equal in rank to a grand duke. 여대공(女大公). **3** a princess of the ruling house of Russia before it became a republic in 1917. (옛 러시아 황제의) 황녀; 황손녀.

grand duchy [ˊ-ˊ-] *n.* a territory under the rule of a grand duke or grand duchess. 대공국.

grand duke [ˊ-ˊ] *n.* **1** the title of the rulers of certain European countries. 대공(大公). **2** formerly in Russia, a son of a czar. (옛 러시아 황제의) 황자(皇子).

gran·dee [grændí:] *n.* Ⓒ a Spanish or Portuguese nobleman of the highest rank; a person of high rank. 대공(大公) 《스페인·포르투갈의 최고 귀족》; 고관; 높은 사람. [→grand]

gran·deur [grǽndʒər, -dʒuər] *n.* ⓊⒸ splendor; magnificence; greatness; dignity; nobility. 장대; 웅대; 장려; 위대; 위엄; 숭고. ¶ *the ~ of Niagara Falls* 나이아가라 폭포의 장관 / *the ~ of his character* 그의 인격의 위대함 / *the architectural ~ of the Baroque* 바로크 건축의 웅대함. [↑]

:**grand·fa·ther** [grǽn*d*fɑ̀:ðər] *n.* Ⓒ the father of one's father or mother. 조부; 할아버지. ¶ *a great-grandfather* 증조부.

gran·dil·o·quence [grændíləkwəns] *n.* Ⓤ the use of lofty or big words. 호언 장담; 큰〔흰〕소리; 호언(豪言). [↓]

gran·dil·o·quent [grændíləkwənt] *adj.* using lofty or big words; speaking boastfully; exaggerated. 대언 장담하는; 과장된; 어마어마한. [→grand, L. *loquor* speak]

gran·di·ose [grǽndiòus] *adj.* grand; seeming grand but not really so; imposing; bombastic. 웅장〔웅대〕한; 당당한; 허세의; 과장된. [→grand]

gran·di·os·i·ty [græ̀ndiɑ́səti / -ɔ́s-] *n.* Ⓤ the state of being grandiose. 웅대; 웅장(함); 어마어마함; 허세.

grand·ly [grǽndli] *adv.* in a grand manner. 웅대[웅장]하게; 장려하게; 숭고하게. [*grand*]

:grand·ma [grǽndmɑ̀:] *n.* Ⓒ《*child's word*》a grandmother. 할머니.

grand·ma·ma, -mam·ma [grǽndmɑ̀:-mə, -məmɑ́:] *n.* =grandma.

:grand·moth·er [grǽndmʌ̀ðər] *n.* Ⓒ the mother of one's father or mother. 할머니.

grand·moth·er·ly [grǽndmʌ̀ðərli] *adj.* of or like a grandmother. 조모[할머니]의; 조모와 같은.

grand·neph·ew [grǽndnèfju:, -nèvju:] *n.* Ⓒ the son of one's nephew or niece. 조카(딸)의 아들; 형제[자매]의 손자.

grand·niece [grǽndnì:s] *n.* Ⓒ the daughter of one's nephew or niece. 조카(딸)의 딸; 형제[자매]의 손녀.

grand opera [⌐⌐–] *n.* a musical drama in which all the speeches are sung to the accompaniment of an orchestra. 그랜드 오페라; 대가극.

:grand·pa [grǽndpɑ̀:, grǽm-] *n.* Ⓒ《*child's word*》a grandfather. 할아버지. [*grand*]

grand·pa·pa [grǽndpɑ̀:pə / -pəpɑ́:] *n.* = grandpa.

:grand·par·ent [grǽndpɛ̀ərənt] *n.* Ⓒ a grandfather or grandmother. 조부; 조모.

grand·sire [grǽndsàiər] *n.* **1**《*arch.*》a grandfather. 조부; 할아버지. **2** an ancestor. 조상. [*grand*]

:grand·son [grǽndsʌ̀n] *n.* Ⓒ the son of one's son or daughter. 손자.

grand·stand [grǽndstæ̀nd] *n.* the main stand for spectators at race, etc. 특별 관람석.

grand·un·cle [grǽndʌ̀ŋkl] *n.* Ⓒ the uncle of one's father or mother. 조부모의 형제; 종조부.

grange [greindʒ] *n.* Ⓒ **1** a farm with its buildings; a farmer's house. 부대 건물이 있는 농장; 호농(豪農)의 저택. **2**《*G-*》《U.S.》an organization of farmers for mutual welfare and advancement. 농민 공제 조합. [→grain]

·gran·ite [grǽnit] *n.* Ⓤ a hard rock used for buildings and monuments. 화강암. ¶ *as hard as* ~ 돌처럼[몹시] 단단한; 완고한. ***bite on granite,*** make a vain effort. 헛수고를 하다; 헛애를 쓰다. [→grain]

·gran·ny, gran·nie [grǽni] *n.* Ⓒ (*pl.* **-nies**)《*colloq.*》a grandmother; an old woman. 할머니《애칭》. [abbr.]

:grant [grænt, grɑ:nt] *vt.* **1** (P6,13,14) ⓐ give one's consent to (something); allow. …을 승낙[동의]하다; 허가[허용]하다. ¶ ~ *someone a favor* [*request*] 아무의 부탁을[요구를] 들어주다. ⓑ bestow; confer. 주다; 수여[교부]하다. ¶ ~ *a degree* 학위를 주다 / ~ *a life annuity* 평생 연금을 주다. ⓒ make over in a legal and formal manner. (증서에 의해) 양도하다. ¶ ~ *the land away* 토지를 양도하다. **2** (P6,11,13,14,20,21) admit; agree. …을 용인[인정]하다; 가정하다. ¶ ~ *the truth of what is said* 한 말이 진실임을 일단 인정하다 / *I had to* ~ (*him*) *the reasonableness of his argument.* 그의 주장이 정당하다는 것을 (그에게) 인정하지 않을 수 없었다 / *granting it to be true* 그것이 사실이라고 하더라도. ***take*** (***it***) ***for granted*** (***that***…)**,** suppose to be true. …을 당연한 것으로 생각하다. ¶ *I take it for granted that man is mortal.* 사람은 누구나 죽는다는 것은 당연하다고 생각한다.

— *n.* **1** Ⓤ the act of granting. 승낙; 허가; 인가; 양도; 수여. **2** Ⓒ something granted; a sum of money given by the authorities. 수여[교부]된 것; 보조금. ¶ *a Government* ~ *to the universities* 대학에 교부되는 정부 보조금. ● **gran·tee** [-í:] *n.* **gran·tor** [grǽntər, græntɔ́:r] *n.* [L. *credo* entrust]

gran·u·lar [grǽnjələr] *adj.* of, like or containing grains or granules. 알갱이(모양)의; 과립상(顆粒狀)의. ● **gran·u·lar·ly** [-li] *adv.* [↓]

gran·u·late [grǽnjəlèit] *vt.* (P6) **1** make or form (something) into small grains. 작은 알갱이로 만들다. **2** make the surface of (something) rough. …의 표면을 까칠까칠하게 하다. — *vi.* (P1) become grains. 알갱이 모양으로 되다. [→grain]

gran·ule [grǽnju:l] *n.* Ⓒ a small grain; a small bit or spot like a grain. 작은 알(갱이); 과립(顆粒); 미립(微粒). [↑]

:grape [greip] *n.* Ⓒ a juicy fruit growing in clusters on a vine; a grapevine. 포도 열매[알]; 포도 나무. [F. =bunch of grapes, hook]

grape·fruit [gréipfrù:t] *n.* Ⓒ a pale-yellow, round fruit like an orange. 그레이프프루트《귤 비슷한 과일》.

grape·shot [gréipʃɑ̀t / -ʃɔ̀t] *n.* a cluster of small iron balls used as a charge for a gun. 포도탄(彈)《여러 개의 작은 철란으로 된 옛 포탄》.

grape sugar [⌐⌐–] *n.* the form of sugar found in ripe grapes; glucose. 포도당(糖) (=dextrose).

grape·vine [gréipvàin] *n.* Ⓒ **1** a vine which bears grapes. 포도 덩굴; 포도나무. **2**《U.S. *colloq.*》a network of rumor; a baseless report. 비밀 정보망; 뜬 소문; 유언비어; 허보(虛報).

graph [græf, grɑ:f] *n.* Ⓒ a drawing that shows the relation between two quantities, the course of change in a thing, etc. 그래프; 도식(圖式); 도표. [Gk. *graphō* write]

graph·ic [grǽfik], **-i·cal** [-ikəl] *adj.* **1** of drawing or painting. 그림의; 도형의. ¶ *the* ~ *arts* 필사(筆寫) 예술; 인쇄 예술. **2** vivid; lifelike. 생생한. ¶ ~ *accounts of the scene* 눈으로 보는 것 같은 광경의 묘사. **3** of or about graphs; shown by a graph. 도식(圖式)의; 그래프의; 도시(圖示)된. ¶ *a* ~ *formula* 구조식 / *a* ~ *curve* 그래프 곡선. [↑]

graph·i·cal·ly [grǽfikəli] *adv.* by graphs or pictures; vividly. 그래프로; 도식으로; 생생히.

graph·ite [grǽfait] *n.* Ⓤ a kind of soft black carbon used in lead pencils. 흑연; 석묵(石墨). [*graph*]

grap·nel [grǽpnəl] *n.* Ⓒ a small anchor with several hooks; an instrument with a hook or hooks for seizing and holding things. (가지가 많은) 소형 닻; (닻 모양의) 걸림 갈고리. [→grape]

grap·ple [grǽpəl] *vt., vi.* (P6,13; 1,2A,3) **1** grip firmly; seize. (…을) 단단히 (붙)잡다; 쥐다. **2** 《*with*》 ⓐ fight; struggle. (…와) 맞붙어 싸우다; 격투하다. ¶ *The two boys grappled with each other.* 두 아이는 서로 맞붙었다 〔드잡이했다〕. ⓑ try hard to find a solution to. 해결을 위해 노력하다. ¶ ~ *with a problem* 문제와 씨름하다. **3** use a grapnel. 걸림 갈고리를 쓰다. — *n.* Ⓒ **1** the act of grappling. (붙)잡기; 맞붙(어 싸우)기; 드잡이; 격투. ¶ *come to grapples with someone* 아무와 맞붙어 싸우게 되다. **2** grapnel. 갈고랑 닻; 걸림 갈고리. [→grape]

:grasp [græsp, grɑːsp] *vt.* (P6) **1** hold firmly; seize. …을 단단히 잡다〔붙들다〕; 쥐다. ¶ ~ *the rope* 밧줄을 꽉 쥐다 / *He grasped my hand.* 그는 내 손을 꽉 잡았다. **2** understand. …을 이해하다. 파악하다. ¶ *I cannot* ~ *your meaning.* 네 말뜻을 이해 못 하겠다. — *vi.* (P3) 《*at*》 try to seize. 잡으려고〔매달리려고〕 하다. ¶ 《*prov.*》 *A drowning man grasps at a straw.* 물에 빠진 자는 지푸라기라도 붙잡으려 한다.

grasp the nettle, tackle difficulty or danger boldly. 감연히 고난과 맞서다〔싸우다〕.

— *n.* Ⓒ 《usu. *sing.*》 **1** the act of grasping. 잡음; 파악. ¶ *make a* ~ *at something* 무언가를 꽉 잡다 / *have a firm* ~ *of a hammer* 해머를 단단히 쥐다. **2** Ⓤ 《often *a* ~》 understanding. 이해. ¶ *a mind of wide* ~ 이해력이 넓은 마음 / *a problem beyond our* ~ 우리들에겐 이해할 수 없는 문제 / *have a good* ~ *of one's subject* 주제를 충분히 이해하고 있다. **3** control; power. 통제; 지배; 권력. ¶ *wrest power from the* ~ *of a usurper* 권력을 강탈자의 손에서 빼앗다. [→grope]

take a grasp on oneself, control one's feelings (of anger, worry, etc.). (노여움·걱정 따위) 감정을 억제하다.

grasp·ing [grǽspiŋ, grɑ́ːsp-] *adj.* greedy; eager to get all one can. 욕심 많은; 탐욕스러운.

:grass [græs, grɑːs] *n.* **1** Ⓤ 《*collectively*》 green plants growing on lawns and in pastures. 풀; 목초. ¶ *a leaf of* ~ 풀잎 하나 / ~ *enough to keep cattle* 소를 먹이기에 충분한 목초. **2** Ⓤ 《usu. *the* ~》 ground covered with grass; a pasture; a lawn. 초지(草地); 풀밭; 목초지; 잔디. ¶ *cut the* ~ 풀밭을 베다 / *Keep off the* ~. 잔디에 들어가지 마시오. **3** Ⓒ any plant that has jointed stems and narrow pointed leaves, such as corn and bamboo. 벼과의 식물.

be* 〔*out*〕 *at grass, a) turn out to pasture. 목장에 있다; 방목되고 있다. b) (of a person) be out of work; take a holiday. 실직하고 있다; (일을) 쉬고 있다.

cut one's own grass, 《*colloq., fig.*》 earn one's own living. 독립된 생계를 꾸리다; 혼자 힘으로 생활하다.

go to grass, a) (of an animal) go to pasture. 목장에 나가다. b) take a holiday; stop or be out of work. (일을) 쉬다; 실직하다. c) retire. (시골에) 은퇴〔은거〕하다. d) be knocked down. 맞아 쓰러지다; 죽다.

let the grass grow under one's feet, 《*nonassertive*》 waste time in doing something. 꾸물거리다; 김이 새게 하다; 노력을 게을리하다.

put* 〔*send, turn out*〕 *to grass, a) send to graze. 목장에 내보내어 풀을 뜯(어 먹)게 하다; 방목하다. b) dismiss. 해고하다. c) knock down. 때려 눕히다.

— *vt.* (P6) **1** cover (land) with grass. …을 풀로 덮다. **2** graze. …에 목초를 (뜯어) 먹이다. [E.]

·grass·hop·per [grǽshɑ̀pər / grɑ́ːshɔ̀pər] *n.* Ⓒ a kind of insect with wings and long, powerful hind legs for jumping. 메뚜기.

grass·land [grǽslæ̀nd / grɑ́ːs-] *n.* Ⓤ land on which grass grows richly, used for pasture. 초원; 목초지; 목장.

grass roots [´ ´] *n.* **1** the rural or agricultural areas of a country. 전원 지대; 농업 지역. **2** the common people, particularly contrasted to the elite. 보통 사람; (일반) 민중. **3** the origin or basis of a thing. 본원(本源); 기초.

grass widow [´ ´-] *n.* a wife whose husband is absent for a time. 남편 부재중의 아내.

grass widower [´ ´--] *n.* a husband whose wife is absent for a time. 아내 부재중의 남편.

grass·y [grǽsi, grɑ́ːsi] *adj.* (**grass·i·er, grass·i·est**) of or like grass; covered with grass. 풀의; 풀 같은; 풀에 (뒤)덮인. ¶ ~ *green* 초록색. [*grass*]

·grate[1] [greit] *n.* Ⓒ **1** a framework of iron for holding coal or wood by a fireplace. (난로 따위의) 쇠살대; 화상(火床). **2** iron bars, such as those over a prison window. 쇠창살. — *vt.* (P6) furnish (something) with iron bars. …에 쇠창살을 달다. [L. *cratis* hurdle]

·grate[2] [greit] *vt.* **1** (P6,7) make (something) into bits by rubbing on a rough surface. …을 갈다; 비비다; 문지르다; 갈아으깨다〔뭉개다〕. **2** (P6,13) rub (something) with an unpleasant sound. …을 삐걱거리(게 하)다. **3** irritate; annoy. 불쾌감을 주다. — *vi.* (P1,3) **1** make a rubbing sound. 삐걱〔끽끽〕거리다. **2** 《*on, upon, against*》 cause an annoyance. 불쾌감을 주다. ¶ *His manner grates on us all.* 그의 태도는 모두에게 불

쾌감을 준다. [Teut.]

:grate·ful [gréitfəl] *adj.* **1** thankful. 고맙게 여기는. ¶ *a* ~ *letter* 감사의 편지 / *I am very* ~ *to you for your help.* 도와 주셔서 매우 감사하게 생각하고 있습니다. **2** pleasant; agreeable. 기분 좋은; 유쾌〔쾌적〕한; 즐거운. ¶ *a* ~ *odor* 상쾌한 향기 / *the* ~ *sound of rain* 기분좋은 빗소리. [L. *gratus* pleasing]

grate·ful·ly [gréitfəli] *adv.* in a grateful manner. 감사하게; 즐겁게; 기쁘게.

grat·er [gréitər] *n.* Ⓒ an instrument with a rough surface on it to grate vegetables, etc. 강판. [*grate*[2]]

grat·i·fi·ca·tion [grӕtəfikéiʃən] *n.* **1** Ⓤ the act of gratifying; the state of being gratified. 만족; 기쁨. ¶ *spiritual* ~ 정신적 만족 / *find one's* ~ *in* …을 기뻐하다 / *To have succeeded in my aims is a source of* ~ *to me.* 목표를 달성했다는 것은 내게 기쁨을 주는 근원이다. **2** Ⓒ something that gratifies. 만족시키는〔기쁨을 주는〕 것. [↓]

·grat·i·fy [grӕtəfài] *vt.* (**-fied**) satisfy; please. …을 만족시키다; 기쁘게 하다. ¶ ~ *one's desire* 욕망을 만족시키다 / *be gratified with the result* 결과에 만족해 하다. [L. *gratus* pleasing, *facio* do, make]

grat·i·fy·ing [grӕtəfàiiŋ] *adj.* satisfying; pleasing. 만족을 주는; 만족스러운.

grat·ing[1] [gréitiŋ] *n.* Ⓒ a framework of bars over a window or opening. 격자(格子); 창살. [→grate[1]]

grat·ing[2] [gréitiŋ] *adj.* harsh; irritating. 삐걱〔끽끽〕거리는; 신경에 거슬리는. ¶ *a* ~ *remark* 신경에 거슬리는 말. [→grate[2]]

grat·is [gréitis, grӕt-] *adv., adj.* for nothing; without charge; free. 무료로〔인〕. ¶ *give away* ~ 무료로 진정(進呈)하다 / *provide a service* ~ 무료로 봉사를 제공하다 / *free,* ~*, and for nothing* 순전히 공짜〔무료〕로 / *Entrance is* ~. 입장 무료. [L.]

·grat·i·tude [grӕtətjù:d] *n.* Ⓤ thankfulness. 감사; 사의(謝意). ¶ *in* 〔*out of*〕 ~ 고마운 생각에서; 고마움에 대한 보답으로 / *with* ~ 감사하여 / *express one's* ~ *for someone's favors* 아무의 호의에 대해 감사의 뜻을 나타내다. [L. *gratus* grateful]

gra·tu·i·tous [grətjú:ətəs] *adj.* **1** given or obtained free. 무료로 얻은〔주어진〕. ¶ ~ *service* 무료 봉사. **2** without reason; unnecessary. 이유〔까닭, 근거〕 없는; 불필요한. ¶ *a* ~ *insult* 까닭 없는 모욕 / *a* ~ *lie* 근거 없는 거짓말. [→gratis]

gra·tu·i·ty [grətjú:əti] *n.* Ⓒ (*pl.* **-ties**) **1** a payment for service; a tip. 정표; 팁. **2** money paid to a soldier when he retires. (제대할 때의) 급여금. [↑]

gra·va·men [grəvéimən / -men] *n.* (*pl.* **-vam·i·na**) **1** grievance. 불평. **2** 《law》 the essential part of a charge, accusation, grievance, etc. (고소·고발·호소 따위의) 주요한 요지(要旨). [L. =*gravis* heavy]

gra·vam·i·na [grəvӕmənə] *n.* pl. of **gravamen.**

:grave[1] [greiv] *n.* Ⓒ **1** a hole in the ground where a dead body is placed; the mound or monument over it; a place of burial. 무덤; 분묘; 묘석(墓石); 묘비; 매장소. ¶ (*as*) *close as the* ~ 절대로 비밀인 / *from the cradle to the* ~ 요람에서 무덤까지; 일생 동안 / *on this side of the* ~ 이승에서 / *find a watery* ~ 물에 빠져 죽다. **2** 《*the* ~》 death. 죽음. ¶ *dread the* ~ 죽음을 두려워하다 / *to one's* ~ 죽을 때까지. [E.]

(as) *silent* 〔*secret*〕 *as the grave,* absolutely silent 〔secret〕. 절대 조용한〔비밀의〕.

beyond the grave, in the next world. 저승에서.

find *one's* ***grave in a place,*** meet one's death in a place; die or be killed in a place. …에서 죽다.

have one foot in the grave, be near death; be very old or sick. 곧 죽을 것 같다; 매우 노쇠하다.

:grave[2] [greiv] *adj.* **1** important; momentous; serious. 중요한; 중대한; 심상치 않은. ¶ ~ *responsibilities* 중대한 책임 / *a* ~ *situation* 심상치 않은 사태 / *a* ~ *defect* 중대한 결함 / *a* ~ *question* 중대한 문제. **2** sober; solemn. 진지한; 침착한; 엄숙한. ¶ *a* ~*, quiet man* 진지하고 조용한 남자 / *as* ~ *as a judge* (재판관처럼) 극히 엄숙한 / *look* ~ 엄숙〔진지〕한 표정을 짓다 / *be* ~ *in manner* 태도가 침착하다. **3** (of color) not gay; dull. (색깔이) 수수한; 충충한. **4** 《phon.》 low in pitch. 저(低)악센트의; 억음(抑音)의. — *n.* Ⓒ the grave accent(`). 억음. [L. *gravis* heavy]

grave[3] [greiv] *vt., vi.* (**graved, graved** or **grav·en**) (P6,13) 《*arch.*》 engrave; carve. 새기다; 파다; 조각하다. ¶ ~ *words in the heart* 말을 가슴 속에 새기다. [E.]

grave·clothes [gréivklòuðz] *n. pl.* clothes in which a dead body is buried. 수의. [*grave*[1]]

grave·dig·ger [gréivdìgər] *n.* Ⓒ a person whose work is digging graves. 무덤 파는 사람.

·grav·el [grӕvəl] *n.* Ⓤ a mixture of small stones and pebbles. 자갈; 밸러스트. — *vt.* (**-eled, -el·ing** or 《Brit.》 **-elled, -el·ling**) (P6) **1** cover (a road) with gravel. (도로)에 자갈을 깔다. ¶ ~ *a walk* 보도에 자갈을 깔다. **2** perplex; nonplus. …을 당혹시키다; 괴롭히다. [F. *grave*]

·grave·ly [gréivli] *adv.* in a grave manner. 중대하게; 진지하게. [*grave*[2]]

grav·en [gréivən] *v.* old pp. of **grave**[3]. — *adj.* carved; sculptured. 새긴; 조각한; 명기(銘記)된.

graven image [⌐– ⌐–] *n.* 우상(偶像).

grav·er [gréivər] *n.* Ⓒ a person or thing that engraves. 조각가; 조각칼. [*grave*[3]]

grave·stone [gréivstòun] *n.* Ⓒ a stone

that marks a grave; a tombstone. 묘비; 묘석(墓石). [*grave*[1]]

grave·yard [gréivjɑ̀ːrd] *n.* Ⓒ a place for burying the dead. 묘지.

grav·i·tate [grǽvətèit] *vi.* (P2A,3) **1** be drawn by gravity; sink. 인력에 끌리다; 가라앉다; 침하(沈下)하다. ¶ ~ *to the bottom* 바닥에 가라앉다 / *The earth gravitates toward the sun.* 지구는 태양에 끌린다. **2** 《*to, toward*》 be attracted. 끌리다. ¶ *In summer people ~ to the seaside.* 여름철이면 사람들이 해변으로 몰려든다. [→grave[2]]

grav·i·ta·tion [grӕ̀vətéiʃən] *n.* Ⓤ **1** the act of gravitating; the force of gravity. 인력(작용). ¶ *the law of ~* 인력의 법칙 / *universal ~* 만유 인력. **2** 《*fig.*》 tendency to move. 경향; 추세. ¶ *the ~ of population toward cities* 인구의 도시 집중 경향.

·**grav·i·ty** [grǽvəti] *n.* Ⓤ **1** the force which draws all bodies on the earth towards the center of the earth. 중력(重力); 지구 인력. **2** the state of being grave; importance; seriousness. 중대; 진지함; 엄숙. ¶ *with ~* 진지〔엄숙〕하게 / *preserve one's ~* 위엄을 유지하다 / *realize the ~ of a situation* 사태의 중대성을 인식하다. **3** heaviness; weight. 무게; 중량. ¶ *the center of ~* 무게 중심(中心); 중심(重心) / *specific ~* 비중. **4** 《phon.》 lowness of pitch. 저음(低音); 억음(抑音). [*grave*[2]]

gra·vure [grəvjúər, grei-] *n.* **1** =photogravure. **2** a plate or print produced by photogravure. 사진 요판(凹版). [→grave[2]]

·**gra·vy** [gréivi] *n.* Ⓤ the juice that comes out of meat in cooking; a sauce made from this juice. (요리할 때의) 고깃국물; 고깃국물 소스. [? O.F.]

:**gray,** 《Brit.》 **grey** [grei] *adj.* **1** having a color between black and white. 잿빛〔회색〕의. ¶ *be ~ as old ash* 아주 창백하다. **2** dark; cloudy 어두운; 흐린. ¶ *a ~ dawn* 어스름 새벽 / *~ skies* 찌푸린 하늘 / *a ~ cloudy* 잔뜩 흐린 음산한 날. **3** gloomy; dismal. 음울〔우울〕한; 쓸쓸한. ¶ *The future looks ~.* 장래가 어둡다. **4** having gray hair. 백발이 성성한; 머리가 희끗희끗한. ¶ *~ hairs* 노년 / *an old ~ man* 머리가 반백의 노인. **5** old; ancient. 오래된; 옛날의; 고대의. ¶ *~ experience* 노련 / *the ~ past* 고대; 태고.

— *n.* Ⓤ **1** gray color. 회색. ¶ *in the ~ of the morning* 어스름 새벽에; 미명에. **2** gray cloth or clothing. 회색의 천〔옷〕. ¶ *a man dressed in ~* 회색옷을 입은 남자.

— *vt., vi.* (P6; 1) make or become gray. 회색으로 하다〔이 되다〕. [E.]

gray·beard [gréibìərd] *n.* Ⓒ an old man. 노인.

gray-eyed [gréiàid] *adj.* having gray eyes. 회색 눈을 가진.

gray·head·ed [gréihèdid] *adj.* having gray hair; old. 백발의; 늙은.

gray·hound [gréihàund] *n.* =greyhound.

gray·ish [gréiiʃ] *adj.* somewhat gray. 회색빛이 도는.

gray mare [ˊˊ] *n.* a wife that rules her husband. 남편을 쥐고 흔드는 아내.

gray matter [ˊˊ—] *n.* **1** 《anat.》 the gray part of the brain. 회백질. **2** intellect. 지력(知力).

·**graze**[1] [greiz] *vi.* (P1,2A) (of cattle, etc.) feed on growing grass. (가축이) 풀을 뜯어 먹다. — *vt.* (P6) put (cattle, etc.) to feed on growing grass. 풀을 뜯어먹게 하다; 가축을 방목하다. [→grass]

graze[2] [greiz] *vt.* (P6) touch (something) lightly in passing; scratch (the skin, etc.). …을 가볍게 스치고 지나가다; (피부를) 스쳐 벗기다. ¶ *She grazed me as she went past.* 그녀가 지나며 나를 가볍게 스쳤다 / *The bullet grazed his thigh.* 탄알은 그의 허벅지에 찰과상을 입혔다. — *vi.* (P1,2A) touch lightly against (something) in passing. 가볍게 스치며 지나가다. — *n.* Ⓒ the act of grazing; a slight wound made by grazing. 가볍게 스치기; 찰과상(傷). [?, ↑]

gra·zier [gréiʒər] *n.* Ⓒ a person who grazes cattle for sale. 목축업자. [*graze*[1]]

gra·zier·y [gréiʒəri] *n.* the business of a grazier. 목축업.

graz·ing [gréiziŋ] *n.* Ⓤ land for cattle, etc. to graze on; a pasture. 목초(지).

Gr. Br., Gr. Brit. Great Britain.

·**grease** *n.* [griːs] Ⓤ **1** melted animal fat. 지방; 굳기름; 수지(獸脂). **2** any thick oily substance. 반고체의 기름 물질; 그리스; 윤활유. **3** the raw state of wool just after shearing and before being cleaned. 깎아낸 채 탈지(脫脂)하지 않는 양털.

in grease =***in pride*** 〔***prime***〕 ***of grease,*** (of deer, etc.) fat; in good condition for killing. (사슴 따위가) 기름이 올라; 먹기 좋은 때인.

— *vt.* [griːs, griːz] (P6) **1** smear (something) with grease; put grease on or in (something). …을 기름으로 더럽히다; …에 기름을 바르다. **2** 《*colloq.*》 bribe or tip. …에 대하여 뇌물을 쓰다. [L. *crassus* fat]

grease the palm of (=*offer bribe to*) ***someone.*** …에게 뇌물을 쓰다〔쥐어주다〕.

grease the wheels, make things run smoothly, esp. by money. (돈을 쓰거나 하여) 일을 원활히 진척시키다.

like 〔***quick as***〕 ***greased lightning,*** 《*colloq.*》 very fast. 번개처럼; 전광 석화와 같이.

grease paint [ˊˊ] *n.* a composition for painting actor's faces. (배우의 화장용) 도란.

greas·y [gríːsi, -zi] *adj.* (**greas·i·er, greas·i·est**) **1** made of or containing grease. 지방이〔기름기가〕 많은. ¶ *The food was ~.* 음식이 기름졌다. **2** covered with grease; full of grease. 기름으로 더러워진; 기름투성이의. ¶ *My hands are ~.* 내 손은 기름투성이다. **3** smooth; slippery. 미끄러운; 매끄러운. ¶ *a ~ road* 미끄러운 길.

:great [greit] *adj.* **1** big; large. 큰; 거대한 (opp. little). ¶ *a ~ river* 〔*mountain, city, building*〕 큰 강〔산, 도시, 건물〕. **2** large in number, quantity. 다수의; 다량의; 많은. ¶ *a ~ many books* 엄청나게 많은 책 / *a ~ crowd* 대군중 / *a ~ majority* 대부분 / *a ~ multitude of flowers* 매우 많은 꽃. **3** (of time) long. 시간이 긴〔오랜〕. ¶ *a ~ while ago* 훨씬〔오래〕 전에. **4** more than usual; in a high degree; extreme. (정도 따위가) 보통이 아닌; 대단한; 엄청난; 지독한. ¶ *a ~ fan* 대단한 팬 / *~ friends* 극친한 친구(사이) / *a ~ danger* 엄청난 위험 / *a ~ fool* 지독한 바보 / *a ~ noise* 지독한 소음; 굉음 / *~ ignorance* 지독한 무식. **5** ⓐ great in ability or power; excellent; famous. 위대한; 뛰어난; 유명〔저명〕한. ¶ *a ~ statesman* 위대한 정치가 / *a ~ soldier* 뛰어난 군인 / *a ~ writer* 유명한 작가. ⓑ important; remarkable. 중대한; 중요한; 주목할 만한. ¶ *a ~ decision* 중대한 결정 / *a ~ occasion* 큰 행사가 있는 날; 대경축일. **6** ⓐ of high rank, birth, or station. (위계·신분·지위 따위가) 높은; 고귀한. ¶ *a ~ noble* 고위의 귀족 / *~ people* 고귀한 사람들 / *the ~ families* 명문. ⓑ noble; lofty; sublime; generous. 숭고한; 고상한; 관대한. ¶ *~ thoughts* 숭고한 사상 / *~ aims* 고상한 목적 / *a man of ~ character* 고상한 인격을 지닌 사람. **7** 《*colloq.*》 grand; splendid; delightful. 훌륭한; 굉장한; 멋진. ¶ *That's a ~ story.* 그건 멋진 이야기다 / *We had a ~ time at the seaside.* 우린 바닷가에서 즐겁게 보냈다. **8** much in use; favorite. 많이〔잘〕 쓰이는; 좋아하는. ¶ *This is a ~ word among school girls.* 이건 여학생들간에 잘 쓰이는 말이다. **9** most important of its kind. (칭호 따위에 쓰이어) 대(大)…. ¶ *the Great War* 세계 〔1차〕 대전 / *Alexander the Great* 알렉산더 대왕. [E.]

a great deal, very much. 많이; 상당히.

be great (=*be skillful*) ***at*** *something.* …에 숙련돼 있다; …을 잘 하다.

be great on (= *be much interested in*) *something.* …에 크게 흥미를 갖다.

Great God 〔***Caesar, Scott***〕***!*** an exclamation of surprise. 아이구〔어머〕 깜짝이야; 이거 큰일 났군; 하느님 맙소사.

have a great mind to, feel very much inclined to. 몹시 …하고 싶어하다; …할〔하고 싶은〕 마음이 대단하다.

no great, not important. 중요하지 않은. ¶ *It's no ~ matter to me.* 그건 내겐 중요하지 않은 문제다.

great-aunt [gréitæ̀nt, -ɑ́:nt] *n.* an aunt of one's father or mother. 부모의 고모; 왕고모.

Great Bear [ㅗㅅ], **the** *n.* 《astron.》 the constellation Ursa Major. 큰곰자리.

Great Britain [ㅗㅅ–] *n.* England, Wales, and Scotland. 대(大)브리튼; 영국.

great·coat [gréitkòut] *n.* Ⓒ 《esp. Brit.》 a heavy overcoat. (감이 두꺼운) 외투.

Great Divide [ㅅ–ㅅ], **the** *n.* the watershed of the Rocky Mountains; death. 로키산맥 분수계(分水界); 죽음.

great-grand·child [grèitgrǽndtʃàild] *n.* (*pl.* **-chil·dren** [-tʃìldrən]) Ⓒ the grandchild of one's son or daughter. 증손.

great-grand·daugh·ter [grèitgrǽnddɔ̀:tər] *n.* Ⓒ the granddaughter of one's son or daughter. 증손녀.

great-grand·fa·ther [grèitgrǽndfɑ̀:ðər] *n.* Ⓒ the grandfather of one's father or mother. 증조부.

great-grand·moth·er [grèitgrǽndmʌ̀ðər] *n.* Ⓒ the grandmother of one's father or mother. 증조모.

great-grand·son [grèitgrǽndsʌ̀n] *n.* Ⓒ the grandson of one's son or daughter. 증손(자).

great gun [ㅅㅅ] *n.* 《*colloq., fig.*》 a person of importance. 높은 양반; 거물.

great-heart·ed [gréithɑ́:rtid] *adj.* **1** brave. 용기 있는; 용감한. **2** noble; generous. 고결한; 관대한.

:great·ly [gréitli] *adv.* **1** very much; highly. 매우; 몹시. ¶ *bother someone ~ with questions* 성가시게 질문하여 아무를 몹시 괴롭히다. **2** in a great manner; nobly; generously. 위대하게; 고결〔고상〕하게; 관대히.

:great·ness [gréitnis] *n.* Ⓤ the quality of being great. 큼; 위대; 거대; 고귀; 관대.

great seal [ㅅㅅ], **the** *n.* **1** the chief seal of a nation or state. 나라〔주〕의 인장. **2** 《*G- S-*》 《Brit.》 state seal. 국새(國璽).

great·un·cle [gréitʌ̀ŋkl] *n.* an uncle of one's father or mother. 증조부.

greave [gri:v] *n.* 《usu. *pl.*》 armor for the leg below the knee. (갑옷의) 정강이받이. [F.=shin]

grebe [gri:b] *n.* Ⓒ a large diving bird; a loon. 농병아리. [F.]

Gre·cian [grí:ʃən] *adj.* Greek. 그리스의. 語法 건축·사람의 얼굴 모양에 관해서 일컬음. ¶ *~ architecture* 그리스(풍의) 건축 / *a ~ nose* 그리스 사람형의 코. — *n.* Ⓒ **1** a Greek. 그리스 사람. **2** a scholar of Greek. 그리스어 학자. [*Greece*]

Gre·co-Ro·man [grì:kouróumən, grìkou-] *adj.* of Greece and Rome. 그리스·로마의. — *n.* a style of wrestling. 그레코로만형 레슬링.

·Greece [gri:s] *n.* a country in southeastern Europe. 그리스. 參考 수도는 Athens. [→Greek]

greed [gri:d] *n.* Ⓤ strong and selfish desire. 욕심(이 많음); 탐욕. ¶ *a miser's ~ for money* 구두쇠의 금전욕. [E.]

greed·i·ly [grí:dili] *adv.* in a greedy manner. 탐욕스럽게; 게걸스럽게. ¶ *eat ~* 걸신 들린 듯이 먹다.

greed·i·ness [grí:dinis] *n.* Ⓤ the quality of being greedy. 탐욕스러움; 욕심부림.

:greed·y [grí:di] *adj.* (**greed·i·er, greed·i·est**) **1** wanting to eat and drink too much;

wanting more than a fair share. 게걸스러운; 탐욕스러운; 욕심 많은. ¶ *a ~ boy* 걸신 들린 아이 / *He is not hungry, merely ~.* 그는 시장하지 않으나 단지 식탐할 뿐이다. **2** wanting strongly; eager. 열망〔갈망〕하는. ¶ *be ~ of* 〔*for*〕 *praise* 상찬(賞讚)을 절실히 바라다 / *be ~ to get a prize* 상타기를 열망하다 / *cast ~ eyes on* 〔*upon*〕 …을 욕심나듯 보다. [E.]

:Greek [gri:k] *adj.* of Greece, its people, or their language. 그리스의; 그리스 사람〔말〕의. — *n.* **1** Ⓒ a person of ancient or modern Greece. 그리스 사람. ¶ *When ~ meets ~, then comes the tug of war.* 두 영웅이 만나면 싸움이 일어난다. **2** Ⓤ ⓐ the Greek language. 그리스말. ⓑ something one cannot under stand. 전연 의미를 모르는 것. [Gk. *Graikoi*]
be Greek (= *be not understandable*) ***to*** someone. 전혀 뜻을 알 수 없다. ¶ *It is* (*all*) *~ to me.* 무슨 말인지 전혀 모르겠다.

Greek calends [ㄹ ㄹ-] *n.* a date or occasion which never comes (for the Greeks had no calends). 절대로 없는 날〔일〕. ¶ *on* 〔*at*〕 *the ~* 절대로〔결코〕 …않는. [L.]

:green [gri:n] *adj.* **1** having the color of growing grass. 초록의; 녹색의; 푸른. ¶ *a ~ jade* 녹색의 비취 / *~ light* 청신호 / *~ food* 푸성귀; 야채. **2** covered with growing grass. 푸른 풀로 덮인. ¶ *~ fields* 푸른 논밭〔들〕. **3** snowless; mild. 눈없는; 온난한(opp. white). ¶ *a ~ Christmas* 〔*winter*〕 눈없는 크리스마스〔겨울〕. **4** not fully developed; not ripe. 익지 않은; 미숙의; 푸른. ¶ *~ fruit* 익지 않은 과일 / *~ wine* 덜 숙성(熟成)된 포도주. **5** raw; not dried; not fired. 생(生)…의; 말리지 않은; 굽지 않은. ¶ *~ timber* 〔*wood*〕 생목(生木) / *~ hide* 날가죽; 생피(生皮) / *~ tobacco* 건조되지 않은 담배 / *~ bricks* 아직 굽지 않은 벽돌. **6** not fully trained; inexperienced (아직) 숙달되지 않은; 미경험의; 미숙의; 풋내기의. ¶ *a ~ hand* 미숙자; 풋내기 / *be ~ and fresh* 풋내기이다 / *be ~ in judgment* 판단이 미숙하다. **7** ⓐ having a pale, sickly color. (안색이) 창백한; 병자와 같은. ¶ *~ with fear* 공포로 새파랗게 질린 / *Her face turned ~.* 그녀의 얼굴이 새파래졌다. ⓑ 《*fig.*》 jealous; envious. 질투로 이글거리는. ¶ *a ~ eye* 질투로 이글대는 눈(cf. *green-eyed*). **8** ⓐ full of vigor; young. 활기 있는; 원기 왕성한; 젊은. ¶ *a man ripe in years but ~ in heart* 나이는 들었지만 마음은 젊은 사람 / *enjoy a ~ old age* 늙어서 더욱 더 원기 왕성하다. ⓑ fresh; new. 새로운; 최신의; 최근의. ¶ *a ~ wound* 새 상처 / *keep one's memory ~* 잊지 않고〔생생히〕 기억에 간직하다 / *be ~ in earth* 매장된 지 얼마 안 되다.
— *n.* Ⓤ **1** green color. 녹색; 초록빛; 푸른 빛. **2** green cloth or clothing. 녹색의 천〔옷〕. **3** Ⓒ a lawn; land covered with grass. 잔디(밭); 풀밭; 초지(草地). **4** 《*pl.*》 green leaves and branches used for decoration. (장식용) 푸른 잎〔가지〕. **5** 《*pl.*》 leaves and stems of plants used for food. 푸성귀; 야채. **6** Ⓤ vigor; freshness; youth. 생기; 활력; 신선함; 젊음. ¶ *in the ~* 혈기〔원기〕 왕성하게. [E.]

green·back [gríːnbæ̀k] *n.* Ⓒ 《U.S. *colloq.*》 a piece of paper money of the United States printed in green. 미국의 달러 지폐.

green·belt [gríːnbèlt] *n.* a strip of open land surrounding a town. 그린 벨트; 녹지대.

green-blind [gríːnblàind] *adj.* suffering from green-blindness. 녹색맹(綠色盲)의.

Greene [griːn], **Graham** *n.* (1904-91) an English novelist. 그린《영국의 소설가》.

green·er·y [gríːnəri] *n.* (*pl.* **-er·ies**) **1** Ⓤ 《*collectively*》 green leaves; green plants. 푸른 잎; 푸른 나무. ¶ *the ~ of the woods in May,* 5월의 신록. **2** Ⓒ a greenhouse. 온실. [E.]

green-eyed [gríːnàid] *adj.* **1** having green eyes. 녹색의 눈을 가진. **2** envious; jealous. 질투〔시기〕가 강한. ¶ *the ~ monster* 질투; 시기.

green·finch [gríːnfìntʃ] *n.* Ⓒ a European bird with green and gold plumage. (유럽산) 방울새.

green fingers [ㄹ ㄹ-] *n.* 《Brit. *colloq.*》 skill in gardening. 원예의 재주〔재능〕. 參考 green thumb이라고도 함.

green·fly [gríːnflài] *n.* Ⓒ a very small green insect which feeds on the juice from young plants. (초록색의) 진딧물의 일종.

green·gro·cer [gríːngròusər] *n.* Ⓒ 《Brit.》 a person who sells fresh vegetables and fruit. 청과물 상인; 야채상(인).

green·gro·cer·y [gríːngròusəri] *n.* (*pl.* **-cer·ies**) 《Brit.》 **1** Ⓒ the business of a greengrocer; a store that sells fresh vegetables and fruit. 청과물상(商)《가게》; 야채 가게. **2** Ⓤ 《*collectively*》 things sold by a greengrocer. 청과물; 야채류.

green·horn [gríːnhɔ̀ːrn] *n.* Ⓒ 《*colloq.*》 a person who has no experience; a person easily fooled. 미숙자; 풋내기; 초심자; 얼간이.

green·house [gríːnhàus] *n.* Ⓒ (*pl.* **-hous·es** [-hàuziz]) a heated building for growing plants. 온실.

green·ing [gríːniŋ] *n.* an apple with a yellowish-green skin when ripe. 청(青)사과 《익어도 껍질이 퍼런》.

green·ish [gríːniʃ] *adj.* somewhat green. 녹색〔초록빛〕을 띤.

Green·land [gríːnlənd] *n.* the largest island in the world, northeast of North America. 그린란드. 參考 덴마크령(領).

green·room [gríːnrù(ː)m] *n.* an actors' resting room in a theater. (극장의) 배우 휴게실〔분장실〕.

green·stuff [gríːnstʌ̀f] *n.* Ⓤ vegetables. 푸성귀; 야채류; 초목.

green·sward [gríːnswɔ̀ːrd] *n.* Ⓤ ground covered thickly with short grass. 잔디밭.

Green·wich [grínidʒ, grén-, -itʃ] *n.* a town

in London. 그리니치《런던 교외의 한 작은 도시》. [Place]

Greenwich Time [∠-∠] *n.* the time measured at Greenwich, used as a basis for the standard time around the world. 그리니치 표준시(時). 參考 Greenwich Mean Time 이라고 하며, G.M.T.로 생략함.

green·wood [grí:nwùd] *n.* Ⓒ a forest when the trees are fully covered with leaves. 우거진 초록의 푸른 숲. [*green*]

go to the greenwood, become an outlaw. 무법자〔추방자〕가 되다; 추방 되어 녹림에 들어가다.

:greet [gri:t] *vt.* (P6,13) 《*with*》 **1** welcome; salute; receive. …을 환영〔맞이〕하다; …에게 인사하다. ¶ *He greeted me with a smile.* 그는 웃으며 나를 맞이했다. **2** receive with a specified reaction. 어떤 반응을 나타내다; …로 응하다. ¶ *They greeted the speech with anger.* 그들은 그 연설에 노여운 반응을 보였다. **3** be seen by (someone's eyes); be heard by (someone's ears); appear before. (눈이나 귀에) 들어오다; 앞에 나타나다. ¶ *The mountain greeted my eyes.* 산이 내 시야에 들어왔다 / *The music of Choping greeted my ear.* 쇼팽의 음악이 들려왔다 / *A view of the sea greeted us.* 바다가 우리 앞에 나타났다. [E.]

***greet·ing** [grí:tiŋ] **1** Ⓒ words of good will; a welcome. 인사. ¶ *clumsy* ~ 어색한 인사 / *parting greetings* 작별 인사 / *exchange greetings* 인사를 주고 받다. **2** 《*pl.*》 a friendly message on a special occasion. 인사의 말. ¶ *send Christmas* 〔*New Year's*〕 *greetings* 크리스마스〔새해의〕 인사장을 보내다 / *with the season's greetings* 계절의 인사를 곁들여.

gre·gar·i·ous [grigέəriəs] *adj.* **1** (of animals or plants) living in groups. (동식물이) 군거(群居)〔군생, 족생(簇生)〕하는; 군집성의. **2** (of persons) fond of being with others. (사람이) 남과 한데 있기〔어울리기〕를 좋아하는; 사교적인. [L. *grex* flock]

Gre·go·ri·an [grigɔ́:riən] *adj.* of Pope Gregory. 교황 그레고리의. [Person]

Gregorian calendar [-∠--∠--], **the** *n.* the calendar we use today which was established by Gregory XIII. 그레고리력(曆).

gre·nade [grənéid] *n.* Ⓒ **1** a small bomb thrown by hand. 수류탄; 투척탄. **2** a round glass bottle containing chemicals, to be thrown to put out a fire. 소화탄. [L. *granum* grain]

gren·a·dier [grènədíər] *n.* a soldier who throws grenades. 척탄병(擲彈兵). ¶ *the Grenadier Guards* 《Brit.》 근위 보병 제 1연대. [↑]

Gresh·am [gréʃəm], **Sir Thomas** *n.* (1519-79) an English financer. 그레셤《영국의 재정가》.

Gresham's law [∠-∠] *n.* the principle that money of lower intrinsic value tends to drive money of equal denomination with higher intrinsic value out of circulation. 그레셤의 법칙《"악화는 양화를 구축한다"는 법칙》.

:grew [gru:] *v.* p. of **grow.**

:grey [grei] *adj.* 《Brit.》 =gray.

grey·beard [gréibìərd] *n.* 《Brit.》 =graybeard.

grey·head·ed [gréihèdid] *adj.* 《Brit.》 = gray-headed.

grey·hound [gréihàund] *n.* Ⓒ a tall, slender, swift dog, used for hunting and racing. 그레이하운드《사냥·경주용 개》.

grey·ish [gréiiʃ] *adj.* 《Brit.》 =grayish.

grid [grid] *n.* Ⓒ **1** a framework of iron bars. 쇠격자; 쇠창살. **2** a wire net that controls the flow of electrons in a vacuum tube. (진공관 속의) 그리드. **3** =gridiron. [↓]

grid·dle [grídl] *n.* a round iron plate for baking cakes on. 과자 굽는 번철. [→gridiron]

gride [graid] *vt., vi.* (P6; 1,2A) 《*along, through*》 cut or grate with a harsh noise. 싸각싸각 베다〔문질리다, 스치다〕. —*n.* such noise. 싸각거리는 소리. [*gird*[2]]

grid·i·ron [grídàiərn] *n.* Ⓒ **1** a framework of metal bars used for broiling meat or fish. 석쇠; 적철(炙鐵). **2** 《U.S.》 a football field. 축구 경기장. [L. *cratis* hurdle]

:grief [gri:f] *n.* (*pl.* **griefs**) Ⓤ deep sorrow; Ⓒ a cause of grief. 깊은 슬픔; 비탄의 원인; 비탄거리. ¶ *be in deep* ~ 깊은 슬픔에 젖어 있다 / *die of* ~ 슬픈 나머지 죽다 / *suffer* ~ *at the loss of one's daughter* 딸을 여의고 비탄에 젖다 / *He is a great* ~ *to his parents.* 그는 부모에게 큰 슬픔거리다. [→grieve]

bring someone to grief, cause someone to meet with misfortune, injury, or ruin. …을 불행을 당하게 하다; 혼나게〔부상을 당하게〕 하다; 파멸시키다.

come to grief, meet with disaster; fail. 재난을 당하다; 불행에 빠지다; 실패〔파멸〕하다.

griev·ance [grí:vəns] *n.* Ⓒ a cause or reason for dissatisfaction or protest. 불만의 씨; 불평의 원인. ¶ *nurse a* ~ 불만〔불평〕을 품다 / *have a* ~ *against someone* 아무에게 불만을 품다. [↓]

:grieve [gri:v] *vt.* (P6) cause (someone) to feel grief; make (someone) very sad. …을 몹시 슬프게 하다; 비탄에 빠뜨리다. ¶ *Your conduct grieves me.* 네 행동은 나를 매우 슬프게 한다. —*vi.* (P1,3,4) 《*at, for, over*》 feel grief. 몹시 슬퍼하다. ¶ ~ *over* 〔*at, for*〕 *the death of one's friend* 친구의 죽음을 몹시 슬퍼하다. [L. *gravis* heavy]

griev·ous [grí:vəs] *adj.* **1** causing grief; showing grief. 슬프게 하는; 슬픈; 비통한. ¶ ~ *news* 비보(悲報) / *a* ~ *mother* 슬픔에 젖어 있는 어머니. **2** causing great pain or suffering; severe. 고통을 주는; 괴롭히는; 심한. ¶ *a* ~ *wound* 몹시 아픈 상처. ●**griev-**

ous·ly [-li] *adv.* **griev·ous·ness** [-nis] *n.*

grif·fin [grífin] *n.* Ⓒ 《Gk. myth.》 an imaginary animal with the head and wings of an eagle and the body of a lion. 그리핀《독수리의 머리, 사자 동체에 날개가 있다는 전설상의 괴수(怪獸)》. [Gk.]

〈griffin〉

grif·fon, griph·on [grífən] *n.* =griffin.

grig [grig] *n.* Ⓒ **1** a small eel. 작은〔새끼〕 뱀장어. **2** a cricket; a grasshopper. 귀뚜라미; 여치. **3** a lively, bright person. 쾌활한 사람. [N.]

grill [gril] *n.* Ⓒ **1** a gridiron. 석쇠. **2** a dish of meat or fish cooked on a gridiron. (석쇠에 구운) 불고기; 생선구이. ¶ *a hot* ~ *of oysters and bacon* 갓 구운 굴과 베이컨 요리. **3** a grillroom. 그릴《식당》. — *vt.* (P6) **1** cook (meat or fish) on a gridiron. (고기·생선)을 석쇠에 굽다. **2** 《U.S.》 put severe questions to (someone). …을 엄중히 심문〔힐문〕하다. ¶ *The police grilled the suspect.* 경찰은 용의자를 호되게 심문했다. — *vi.* (P1) **1** be cooked on a gridiron. (석쇠에) 구워지다; 불〔열〕에 쬐어지다. **2** expose oneself to great heat. 혹서에 노출되다. ¶ ~ *in the sun* 뙤약볕을 그대로 받다. [F.]

grille [gril] *n.* Ⓒ a screen of parallel bars used as a gate, door, or window. 격자; 쇠창살; 창살창〔문〕. [→gridiron]

grill·room [grílrù(:)m] *n.* Ⓒ a restaurant or dining room, esp. one where broiled meat or fish is served. (구운 생선·불고기가 나오는) 그릴《식당》. [*grill*]

grilse [grils] *n.* (*pl.* **grilse** or **grils·es**) a young salmon. 새끼 연어. [?]

***grim** [grim] *adj.* (**grim·mer, grim·mest**) **1** stern; severe. 엄(격)한. **2** without mercy; cruel. 잔인한; 냉혹한; 무자비한. **3** horrible; ghastly; unpleasant. 무서운; 섬뜩한; 불쾌한. ¶ *a* ~ *countenance* 무서운 얼굴 / *a* ~ *smile* 섬뜩한 웃음. **4** fiercely determined. 완강한; 결연한. ¶ *the* ~ *fact* 움직일 수 없는 사실 / ~ *determination* 단호한 결의.

hold on to** something **like grim death, hold on to something very firmly. …에 필사적으로 달라붙다.

● **grim·ly** [grímli] *adv.* **grim·ness** [grímnis] *n.* [E.]

grim·ace [gríməs, griméis / griméis] *n.* Ⓒ the act of twisting the face; an ugly expression of the face. 얼굴을 찡그리기; 찡그린 얼굴. — *vi.* (P1) make grimaces. 얼굴을 찡그리다. [F.]

gri·mal·kin [grimǽlkin, -mɔ́:lkin] *n.* Ⓒ an old she-cat; a spiteful hag. 늙은 암고양이; 앙칼진 할망구. [*grey Malkin*]

grime [graim] *n.* Ⓤ dirt that is hard to take off. 때; 먼지; 검댕. — *vt.* (P6) make (something) dirty with grime; soil. (때·검댕으로) …을 더럽히다. ¶ *The coalminer's hands were all grimed.* 탄광 갱부의 손은 온통 탄의 검정으로 더럽혀져 있었다. [?]

grim·y [gráimi] *adj.* (**grim·i·er, grim·i·est**) full of or covered with grime; very dirty. (때·검댕·먼지 따위로) 뒤덮인; 더러워진; 검댕이 낀.

***grin** [grin] *v.* (**grinned, grin·ning**) *vi.* (P1, 2A,3) **1** 《*at*》 smile broadly. 씩 웃다; 싱글거리다. **2** show the teeth in pain, scorn, anger, etc. (고통·모멸·노여움 따위로) 이를 드러내다. — *vt.* (P6) express (something) by grinning. 싱글싱글 웃어 …을 나타내다. ¶ *He grinned his pleasure.* 그는 기쁜 듯이 이를 드러내며 웃었다.

grin and bear it, endure pain, disappointment, etc., with a broad smile or without complaint. 쓴웃음을 웃으며 참다.

— *n.* Ⓒ a broad smile. 싱긋싱긋〔싱글싱글〕 웃기. ¶ *on the* (*broad*) ~ (이를 드러내어) 씩 웃으며 / *put on a* ~ 싱글싱글 웃다. [E.]

:grind [graind] *v.* (**ground**) *vt.* (P6,7) **1** ⓐ crush (something) into powder or small pieces. …을 갈다; 타다; 바수다; 분쇄하다. ¶ ~ *something to powder* 무엇을 바수어〔으깨어〕 가루로 하다 / ~ (*up*) *wheat into flour* 소맥을 갈아서 가루로 만들다 / ~ (*down*) *rocks* 돌을 잘게 바수다. ⓑ 《often *down*》 crush; oppress. (압제자가) 짓밟아 괴롭히다; 학대하다. ¶ *be ground* (*down*) *by tyranny* 〔*poverty*〕 폭정〔빈곤〕에 시달리다 / ~ *the subjects* (과중한 세금으로) 백성을 괴롭히다. **2** ⓐ wear down or polish the surface of. (표면을) 연마(硏磨)하다; 갈다. ¶ ~ *a lens* 렌즈를 갈다. ⓑ rub on a hard stone to make (a knife, etc.) sharp. (숫돌 따위에) 갈다. ¶ ~ *an ax* 도끼날을 갈다 / ~ *up the tools* 도구의 날을 세우다. **3** work by turning a handle round. (손으로 돌려) 갈다; 소리를 내다. ¶ ~ *a hand-mill* 맷돌을 돌려 갈다 / ~ *a hand organ* 손풍금을 돌려 소리를 내다. **4** rub harshly together. 세게 비벼대다; 맞비비다; 짓밟다. ¶ ~ *one's teeth in anger* 성이 나서 이를 갈다 / ~ *a snake's head under one's heel* 구두 뒤축으로 뱀의 머리를 꽉 밟아 비비다. **5** teach laboriously. 힘들여〔애써서〕 가르치다; (지식을) 주입하다. ¶ ~ *Greek into a boy's head* 소년의 머릿속에 그리스어(語)를 주입시키다.

— *vi.* **1** (P2A) do the act of grinding something. 가루로 타다〔갈다〕. **2** (P1,2A) can be ground. 갈〔탈〕 수 있다; 갈리다. ¶ *This wheat grinds well.* 이 밀은 잘 갈린다. **3** (2A) study hard. 열심히 공부하다. ¶ ~ *for an examination* 열심히 수험 공부를 하다 / *I ground* (*away*) *at my studies.* 공부에 열을 올리고 있었다.

grind down, **a**) make (something) into powder by grinding. …을 갈아 가루로 하다. **b**) wear away; oppress. 마모(磨耗)시키다;

학대〔착취〕하다. ¶ ~ *down the poor* 가난한 사람들을 괴롭히다 / *People are ground down by heavy taxes.* 사람들은 과중한 세금에 시달리고 있다.

grind out, **a**) produce (a tune) by playing musical instruments. 연주하여 (소리를) 내다. ¶ ~ *out a tune on an organ* 풍금으로 곡을 연주하다. **b**) produce (something) with a long effort. 고심하여 만들어 내다.

grind the faces of (=*oppress*) ***the poor,*** 가난한 사람들을 학대하다.

grind up, make (something) into small pieces by grinding. …을 갈아 바수다.

— *n.* Ⓒ **1** the act of grinding. 갈기; 바수기; 으깨기. **2** a long, hard, monotonous task. 힘드는 단조로운 일. **3** 《*colloq.*》 a student who studies hard. (지독히 파는) 공부벌레. [E.]

grind·er [gráindər] *n.* Ⓒ a person or thing that grinds. 가는 사람〔것〕; 숫돌.

grind·stone [gráin*d*stòun] *n.* Ⓒ **1** a flat, round stone which turns on an axle, used for sharpening tools. 회전 숫돌; 연마기(研磨機). **2** =millstone.

keep 〔***hold, have, bring, put***〕 ***someone's nose to the grindstone,*** force someone to work very hard. …을 끊임 없이 혹사하다.

keep 〔***have, hold, put***〕 ***one's nose to the grindstone,*** work hard and continuously. 계속 열심히 일하다.

:grip [grip] *n.* Ⓒ **1** a firm hold. 꽉 쥠〔잡음〕. ¶ *take a* ~ *on a branch* 나뭇가지를 꽉 잡다 / *get a good* ~ *on someone's leg* 아무의 다리를 꽉 잡다. **2** the power of understanding. 이해(력); (정신적) 파악. ¶ *have* 〔*get*〕 *a good of* 〔*on*〕 *a problem* 문제를 잘 이해하(고 있)다. **3** the handle of a tool, etc. 손잡이; 쥘손; 자루. **4** 《U.S.》 a traveler's handbag. 여행 가방. **5** a sudden, sharp pain. 급격한 통증.

be at grips with, be attacking (something) in earnest. 악착같이 맞붙어 있다; …와 씨름하고 있다.

come to grips, **a**) (of wrestler's, etc.) lay hold of each other. (레슬링 선수 등이) 서로 맞붙다. **b**) become involved (with); confront. …에 열중하게 되다; (문제 따위와) 씨름하다; 맞붙다.

— *v.* (**gripped, grip·ping**) *vt.* (P6) **1** grasp firmly; seize. …을 꽉 (붙)잡다〔쥐다〕. **2** ⓐ awake interest; arrest the attention of. (마음·관심 따위를) 끌다; 붙들다. ¶ ~ *someone's attention* 아무의 주의를 끌다 / *He succeeded in gripping his audience.* 관중을 사로잡는 데 성공했다. ⓑ occupy fully. 꽉 차지하다. ¶ *Fear gripped his heart.* 공포가 그의 마음속에 찼다. ⓒ 《rare》 understand; grasp. 이해하다. ¶ *She couldn't* ~ *the point.* 요점을 파악할 수 없었다. **3** (of inanimate things) hold, catch, so as to prevent the motion of. (클러치 따위를) 잡그다; 물리다. ¶ *The brake doesn't* ~ *the wheel properly.* 브레이크가 바퀴에 잘 걸리지 않는다.

— *vi.* (P1) take a fast hold. 꽉 잡다〔쥐다〕. [E.]

gripe [graip] *vt.* (P6) **1** grasp; seize; grip. …을 잡다; 쥐다. ¶ ~ *someone's hand* 아무의 손을 꽉 잡다〔꽉 쥐다〕 / ~ *a sword fast* 칼을 꽉 쥐다. **2** cause (someone) to have pain in the mind; distress. …을 괴롭히다. ¶ *the poverty that gripes the people* 사람들을 괴롭히는 가난. **3** cause (someone) to have pain in the bowels. …을 복통으로 괴롭히다. ¶ *be badly griped* 배가 몹시 아프다.

— *vi.* (P1) **1** feel sharp pains in the bowels. 쿡쿡 찌르듯이 배가 아프다. **2** 《U.S. *colloq.*》 complain constantly; grumble. 끊임없이 불평을 하다; 투덜대다.

— *n.* Ⓒ **1** a firm hold. 꽉 잡기〔쥐기〕; 파악. **2** distress. 괴로움; 괴롭힘. ¶ *be in the* ~ *of hunger* 굶주림에 시달리고 있다. **3** 《*pl.*》 sharp pains in the bowels. 심한 복통. **4** 《U.S. *colloq.*》 a complaint. 불평. [E.]

grippe [grip] *n.* 《F.》 《*the* ~》 influenza. 유행성 감기; 독감.

grip·sack [grípsæ̀k] *n.* 《U.S.》 a valise. 여행용 손가방. [*grip*]

gri·sette [grizét] *n.* 《F.》 a French working-class girl. 일하는 아가씨; 여점원; 여공.

gris·ly [grízli] *adj.* (**-li·er, -li·est**) horrible; ghastly; grim. 무서운; 섬뜩한; 소름끼치는. [E.]

grist [grist] *n.* Ⓤ grain to be ground; grain that has been ground; flour or meal made by grinding. 제분용의 곡물; 빻은 곡물 〔거친 가루〕. ¶ 《*prov.*》 *All is* ~ *that comes to his mill.* 무엇이나 반드시 이용한다. [*grind*]

bring grist to the mill, be profitable; bring in money. 이득이〔돈벌이가〕 되다; 돈이 되다.

gris·tle [grísl] *n.* Ⓤ a cartilage, esp. in cooked meat. (특히 요리한) 연골(軟骨). [E.]

in the gristle, 《*fig.*》 not yet hardened into bone; young; weak. 아직 뼈가 굳지 않은; 미성숙의; 연약한. [E.]

gris·tly [grísli] *adj.* (**-tli·er; -tli·est**) of or like gristle. 연골의〔같은〕.

grist·mill [grístmìl] *n.* a mill for grinding grain. 제분소; 방앗간. [*grind*]

grit [grit] *n.* Ⓤ **1** 《*collectively*》 very tiny pebbles; sand. 자갈; 모래. **2** 《U.S. *colloq.*》 courage. 용기; 불굴의 정신. ¶ *a man of the true* ~ 참다운 용자 / *have* ~ *enough to do* …할 만한 기개가 있다. — *v.* (**grit·ted, grit·ting**) *vt.* (P6) make a noise by rubbing (something). …을 삐걱〔뿌드득〕거리게 하다; 비비대어 소리를 내다. ¶ ~ *the teeth* 이를 갈다. — *vi.* (P1) make a noise by rubbing. 삐걱〔뿌드득〕거리다; 비비대어 소리가 나다. [E.]

grits [grits] *n. pl.* oats, wheat, etc. husked and coarsely ground. (겉겨만 제거한) 거칠게 탄〔빻은〕 곡물《귀리, 밀 따위》. [E.]

grit·ty [gríti] *adj.* (**-ti·er, -ti·est**) **1** of,

like, or containing grit. 모래의〔같은〕; 모래가 있는. 2 《U.S.》 brave. 용감한; 대담한; 굳센. [grit]

griz·zled [grízld] *adj.* gray; gray-haired. 회색의; 백발이 섞인. ¶ ~ *hair hanging over one's face* 얼굴 위로 늘어진 반백의 머리털. [Teut.]

griz·zly [grízli] *adj.* (**-zli·er -zli·est**) gray; grayish. 회색의; 회색을 띤; 회색〔반백〕머리의. — *n.* Ⓒ (*pl.* **-zlies**) a bear found in the Rocky Mountains. (북아메리카 산의) 회색의 큰 곰.

:groan [groun] *n.* Ⓒ a deep sound of pain or sorrow. (고통·슬픔 따위의) 신음 소리. ¶ *give a* ~ 신음 소리를 내다.
— *vi.* (P1,2A) **1** make a groan. 신음하다. ¶ ~ *with pain* 아파서 신음하다. **2** make a sound like a groan. 신음 같은 소리를 내다. ¶ *The steps of the old house groaned under my weight.* 나의 몸무게로 낡은 집의 계단이 삐걱거렸다. **3** suffer deeply. 시달려 신음하다. **4** be overburdened. 과중하게 실리다; 지나치게 얹히다. ¶ *a shelf groaning with books* 많은 책이 과중하게 얹혀 있는 서가. — *vt.* (P6,7) express (something) by groaning. …을 신음 소리로 말하다. [E.]
groan down, silence with sounds of disapproval like groans. 불만〔비난〕의 소리로 침묵시키다. ¶ ~ *down a speaker* 불만의 소리를 질러 연사를 침묵시키다.
groan out, express in a dismal voice, as if with a groan. 신음하듯 슬픈 소리로 말하다.
groan under, suffer deeply from (tyranny, etc.). (압제) 아래에서 신음하다. ¶ ~ *under heavy taxes* 무거운 세금에 시달리다.

groat [grout] *n.* **1** 《Brit. hist.》 an English silver four-penny piece. 그로트 은화《옛 영국의 4 펜스 은화》. **2** a very small sum. (극히) 약간의 액수; 소량. ¶ *don't care a* ~ 조금도 상관않다. [Du. =great]

groats [grouts] *n. pl.* crushed grain, (esp.) oats. 탄 곡물; (특히) 탄 귀리. [E.]

·gro·cer [gróusər] *n.* Ⓒ a person who sells food and household supplies. 식료 잡화상(商)《사람》. [dealer in the *gross*]

·gro·cer·y [gróusəri] *n.* (*pl.* **-cer·ies**) **1** Ⓤ the trade of a grocer. 식료 잡화상(商). **2** 《U.S.》 Ⓒ a grocer's store. 식료 잡화점. **3** 《*pl.*》 things sold by a grocer. 식료 잡화류. [↑]

grog [grɑg / grɔg] *n.* Ⓤ 《esp. Brit.》 a drink of rum or whisky mixed with water. 물을 탄 럼주(酒)〔위스키〕. [Person]

grog blossom [∠ ∠-] *n.* 《*sl.*》 a small red swelling on the nose. (주독으로) 코끝에 생긴 빨간 점; 주부코.

grog·gy [grɑ́gi / grɔ́gi] *adj.* (**-gi·er, -gi·est**) **1** ⓐ unsteady; shaky. 흔들리는; 흔들흔들하는. ¶ *a* ~ *tooth* 흔들리는 이 / *The leg of this chair is* ~. 이 의자의 다리가 흔들거린다. ⓑ weakened and dazed as from exhaustion or a blow. (지쳐 쇠약해지거나 얻어맞은 충격으로) 멍한; 비틀거리는. ¶ ~ *from the lack of sleep* 수면 부족으로 멍한 / *He is* ~ *from his opponent's punches.* 상대의 펀치를 맞고 비틀비틀한다. **2** drunk. 술에 취한. [*grog*]

grog·shop [grɑ́gʃɑ̀p / grɔ́gʃɔ̀p] *n.* a place where strong alcoholic drinks are sold. (특히 싸구려) 술집; 선술집.

groin [grɔin] *n.* Ⓒ **1** the part where the thigh joins the body. 샅; 사타구니; 서혜(鼠蹊). **2** 《archit.》 the curved line where two arched roofs cross. 궁륭(穹窿)《2 개의 vault 의 교차선》. — *vt.* (P6) 《archit.》 form or build (something) with groins. …에 궁륭을 만들다. [? →ground]

·groom [gru(:)m] *n.* Ⓒ **1** a man or boy who takes care of horses. 말구종; 마부. **2** a bridegroom. 신랑. **3** an officer of the English royal household. (영국의) 궁내관(宮內官). — *vt.* (P6,7) **1** feed and take care of (horses). (말)을 보살피다; 손보다. **2** 《chiefly in *passive*》 make (someone) neat. (몸차림)을 단정하게 하다. ¶ *be well-*〔*ill-*〕*groomed* 몸차림이 좋다〔나쁘다〕/ *keep a house well groomed* 집을 깨끗이 해두다 / *a carefully groomed garden* 빈틈없이 손질이 간 정원. [E.]

grooms·man [grú(:)mzmən] *n.* (*pl.* **-men** [-mən]) a man attending on the bridegroom at a wedding. (결혼식의) 신랑 들러리.

groove [gru:v] *n.* Ⓒ **1** a narrow channel, esp. one cut by a tool. 홈. **2** a habitual way of living. 관례; 상궤(常軌). ¶ *deviate from the social* ~ 사회 관습에서 벗어나다 / *get* 〔*fall, drop*〕 *into a* ~ 따분한 틀에 박히다; 천편일률이 되다 / *get out of the* ~ 틀에 박힌 생활에서 벗어나다 / *His life runs in a* ~. 틀에 박힌 생활이 단조롭게 하루하루 계속되고 있다.
in the groove, a) absolutely perfect. 완전 무결의; (컨디션이) 최고조에. b) in the popular fashion. 유행 스타일로.
— *vt.* (P6) make a groove or grooves in (something). …에 홈을 파다. [Du.]

grope [group] *vi., vt.* (P1,2A,3; 6) search for (something) with the hands; search blindly. (손으로) 더듬어 찾다; 모색하다. ¶ ~ *for the switch in the dark room* 어두운 방안을 더듬어 스위치를 찾다 / ~ *deep into someone's soul* 아무의 마음 속을 암중 모색하다. [E.(→gripe)]
grope one's way, a) feel one's way as in the dark. 더듬어 나아가다; 암중 모색하다. b) 《*fig.*》 attempt to settle or overcome difficulties, doubts, etc. by patient thought and inquiry. (곤란·의문 따위를) 해결하려고 시도하다. ¶ ~ *one's way towards clear understanding* 사태를 명확히 이해하려고 노력하다.

gros·beak [gróusbi:k] *n.* 《bird》 a finch with a cone-shaped bill. 콩새류(類) [*gross, beak*]

·gross [grous] *adj.* **1** big; thick; fat. 큰; 두꺼운; 굵은; 살찐. ¶ *a* ~ *stalk* 굵은 줄기 / ~ *features* (몹시) 큰 얼굴 / *a* ~ *girl with small eyes* 눈이 작은 뚱뚱한 여자 아이. **2** very bad. (아주) 심한. ¶ *a ~ mistake* 큰 잘못 / *~ injustice* 〔*immorality*〕 심한 부정〔부도덕〕 / *~ neglect of duty* 심한 직무 태만. **3** full of leaves; dense. (식물이) 우거진; 무성한; (안개 따위가) 짙은. ¶ *a ~ fog* 짙은 안개 / *the ~ vegetation of the tropical jungles* 열대 밀림의 무성한 초목. **4** whole; total. 전체〔전부〕의; 총계의; (무게가) 포장까지 친 (opp. net). ¶ *the ~ amount* 총액; 총량 / *the ~ area* 총면적 / *the ~ income* 〔*earnings*〕 총수입〔수익〕 / *~ weight* 포장까지 포함된 무게 / *~ national product* 국민 총생산《abbr. GNP, G.N.P.》. **5** 《*fig.*》 coarse; vulgar; unrefined 거친; 조야한; 저속한; 세련되지 않은. ¶ *~ manners* 거친 태도 / *~ pleasures* 저속한 오락 / *~ remarks* 상스러운 말 / *a ~ feeder* 조식가(粗食家).

— *n.* **1** Ⓤ 《usu. *the ~*》 the total amount. 총체; 총계. **2** Ⓒ (*pl.* **gross**) twelve dozen; 144. 그로스《12다스; 144개》. ¶ *a great ~*, 12그로스 / *a small ~*, 10다스.

by the gross, **a**) by large amounts. 전체〔모개〕로; 통틀어. **b**) wholesale. 도매로.

in the gross, **a**) as a whole; in large amounts. 전체〔총체〕로서. **b**) wholesale. 도매로.

● **gross·ly** [-li] *adv.* **gross·ness** [-nis] *n.* [L.]

gross ton [ㅅㅅ] *n.* 2,240 pounds. 총톤《중량 「단위》.

grot [grɑt / grɔt] *n.* 《poet.》 = grotto.

gro·tesque [groutésk] *adj.* **1** strange; odd; queer. 그로테스크한; 이상한; 야릇한; 기괴한. ¶ *a ~ appearance* 기괴한 풍모 / *a ~ gesture* 괴이한 몸짓. **2** foolish; absurd. 바보 같은; 어이없는; 당치 않은. ¶ *a ~ mistake* 어이없는 잘못. — *n.* **1** Ⓒ a grotesque person, animal, figure, or design. 괴기한 사람〔것〕. **2** 《*the ~*》 painting, carving, etc., produced in a grotesque style. (그림·조각 따위의) 그로테스크풍(風). ● **gro·tesque·ly** [-li] *adv.* [↓]

grot·to [grɑ́tou / grɔ́t-] *n.* Ⓒ (*pl.* **-toes** or **-tos**) a natural or man-made cave. 작은 동굴; 석굴. [It. *grotta*]

grouch [grautʃ] *n.* Ⓒ 《U.S. *colloq.*》 **1** a habitually bad-tempered person; a person who is apt to complain. 찌무룩한〔부루퉁한, 까다로운〕 사람; 불평가. **2** a fit of bad temper; a discontented feeling. 부루퉁한 기분; 불평; 불만. ¶ *have a ~ against* …에 대해 불평〔불만〕을 품다. — *vi.* (P1) be in a bad temper; complain. 부루퉁해 있다; 불평을 하다 (cf. *grouse*[1]). [*grouse*[1]]

grouch·y [gráutʃi] *adj.* (**grouch·i·er, grouch·i·est**) 《U.S. *colloq.*》 bad-tempered; discontented. 부루퉁〔시무룩〕한; 불평이 있는.

:ground[1] [graund] *n.* **1** Ⓤ 《*the ~*》 the surface of the earth. 땅; 지면; 지표. ¶ *a cell under the ~* 지하실 / *fall to the ~* 땅에 쓰러지다 / *lie on the ~* 땅에 눕다. **2** Ⓤ soil; earth; land. 흙; 토양; 땅; 토지. ¶ *rich* 〔*poor*〕 *~* 비옥〔척박〕한 땅 / *fruits of the ~* 땅의 산물《곡식·야채·과일 따위》 / *till the ~* 땅을 갈다〔경작하다〕. **3** Ⓒ a piece of land for a special use. (어떤 목적을 위한) 장(소); 터; 지역; 운동장. ¶ *a hunting ~* 사냥터 / *a fishing ~* 어장 / *a football ~* 축구장. **4** Ⓤ the bottom of the sea, lake, river, etc. 바다〔물〕 밑; 해저. **5** 《*pl.*》 the gardens around a large house. 뜰; 구내; 부지(敷地). **6** 《usu. *pl.*》 cause; reason; foundation. 원인; 이유; 근거; 기초; 기반. ¶ *grounds for contests* 분쟁의 원인 / *on economic grounds* 경제적 이유로 / *on the ground*(*s*) *of illness* 병 때문에; 병이라는 구실로 / *She has good ground*(*s*) *to say so.* 그녀가 그렇게 말할 근거가 충분히 있다 / *On what ~ do you say that it is true?* 무슨 근거로 그것이 사실이라고 말하는가. **7** Ⓤ position; opinion. 입장; 견지; 의견. ¶ *common ~* 공통의 입장 / *have the ~ on one's side* (경쟁에서) 유리한 입장을 차지하다; 우위에 서다. **8** Ⓤ ⓐ a field of study. (연구의) 분야; 영역. ⓑ a matter for discussion; a topic; a subject. 논제; 화제; 문제. ¶ *touch on forbidden ~* 금제(禁制)된 문제에 언급하다 / *cover a great deal of ~ in an hour's lecture,* 1시간의 강의에서 많은 문제에 관해 이야기하다. **9** Ⓒ a background, as in various arts. 배경; 바탕. ¶ *The cloth has a green pattern on a yellow ~.* 천은 노란 바탕에 녹색 무늬가 있다. **10** 《*pl.*》 small particles that sink to the bottom in coffee or tea. 앙금; 찌끼.

above ground, alive. 살아 있는.

below ground, dead and buried. 죽어서 묻혀 있는.

break fresh 〔***new***〕 ***ground,*** **a**) cultivate new land. 신천지〔처녀지〕를 개척하다. **b**) do something that has not been attempted before. (무언가) 새로운 것을 시작하다.

break ground, till. 땅을 갈다

come 〔***go***〕 ***to the ground,*** be defeated; perish. 지다; 멸망하다.

cover ground, **a**) travel. (어떤 거리를) 가다; 답파하다. ¶ *How much ~ do you cover in a day?* 하루 얼마나 가십니까. **b**) deal with a variety of subjects. 여러 분야를 다루다.

cut the ground from under *someone's* ***feet,*** anticipate and stultify someone's arguments and plans. …의 의표를 찌르다.

down to the ground, thoroughly; in all respects. 철저하게; 모든 점에서.

fall to the ground, fail. 실패로 끝나다. ¶ *The plan fell to the ~.* 계획은 실패로 끝났다.

from the ground up, **a**) extensively. 광범위에 걸쳐; 널리. **b**) completely; thoroughly. 완전히; 철저히.

gain ground, move forward; make progress; win success or an advantage. 전진하다; 진보하다; 우세해지다.

give 〔***lose***〕 ***ground,*** yield; retreat; fail to keep one's position or advantage. 굴하다; 퇴각하다; 불리한 입장에 서다.

hold 〔***keep, stand***〕 *one's* ***ground,*** stand firm;

do not yield; do not retreat. 자기의 입장을 고수하다; 양보하지〔물러서지〕 않다.
on one's own ground, in a familiar situation; on a subject that one knows well; at home. 익숙한〔유리한〕 상황〔장소〕에서; 잘 아는 문제에 대해; 자신의 영역에서.
on the ground of, because of. …의 이유로.
run into the ground, 《*colloq.*》 do too long or too often; overdo. 지나치다.
shift 〔***change***〕 ***one's ground,*** change one's position, point of view, etc. (상황 따위로) 입장을〔견해를〕 바꾸다.
— *vt.* **1** (P13) 《*on, in*》 establish; base. …을 확립〔수립〕하다; …에 기초를 두다〔의거하다〕. ¶ ~ *one's arguments on experience* 논거를 경험에 두다 / *The novel is grounded on fact.* 그 소설은 사실에 의거하고 있다. **2** (P6) cause (a ship) to run aground. (배)를 좌초시키다. **3** (P13) 《*in*》 teach the first principles to. 초보〔기초〕를 가르치다. ¶ ~ *a boy in grammar* 아이에게 문법의 기초 지식을 가르치다. **4** (P6) 《U.S.》 connect (an electric wire) with the ground. …을 접지(接地)하다.
— *vi.* (P1) run aground. 좌초하다. [E.]

ground² [graund] *v.* p. and pp. of **grind.**

ground bait [⌐⌐] *n.* bait thrown into the water to attract fish to that place. (물고기를 유인하기 위한) 밑밥.

ground crew [⌐⌐] *n.* 《U.S.》 a team of mechanics attending to maintenance of aircraft. (비행장의) 지상 정비원(=《Brit》 ground staff).

ground floor [⌐⌐] *n.* **1** 《Brit.》 the first floor. 1층. **2** 《U.S.》 the beginning. 시작.

ground·less [gráundlis] *adj.* without foundation or reason. 근거 없는. ¶ ~ *fear* 근거 없는 공포.

ground·ling [gráundliŋ] *n.* **1** a plant or animal that keeps close to the ground. 지상에〔지표 가까이〕 사는 동물; 지상에〔지표 가까이〕 나는 식물. 「땅콩; 낙화생.

ground·nut [gráundnʌ̀t] *n.* Ⓒ a peanut.

ground plan [⌐⌐] *n.* **1** the plan of a floor of a building. (건축물의) 1층 평면도. **2** any first or essential plan. 기본 계획.

ground rent [⌐⌐] *n.* 《chiefly Brit.》 rent paid to the owner of land on which buildings are constructed. (건물의) 땅세; 땅 임차료(賃借料); 지대(地代).

ground·sel [gráundsəl] *n.* 《bot.》 kinds of weed with yellow flowers. 개쑥갓.

ground staff [⌐⌐] *n.* 《Brit.》 =ground crew.

ground swell [⌐⌐] *n.* the broad, deep waves of the sea caused by a distant storm. (먼 곳의 폭풍 등으로 인한) 큰 놀; 큰 물결.

ground water [⌐⌐–] *n.* water from a spring or well. 지하수.

ground·work [gráundwə̀ːrk] *n.* Ⓤ foundation; basis. 토대; 기초. ¶ *lay the ~ for* … 의 기초를〔기틀을〕 마련하다.

:group [gruːp] *n.* Ⓒ **1** a number of persons or things together. 무리; 떼; 그룹. ¶ *a ~ of persons* 한 떼의 사람 / *a ~ of facts* 일군(一群)의 사실 / *in a ~* 〔*groups*〕 떼를 지어〔이루어〕 / *fall into two groups* 두 그룹으로 나뉘다. **2** a number of persons or things belonging or classed together. (예술·주의·신앙 따위의) 파; (분류학상의) 군(群). **3** 《paint.》 two or more objects forming a complete design. (그림 따위의 구도상의) 군상(群像).
— *vt.* (P6,7) form (persons or things) into a group or groups. …을 무리로〔그룹으로, 집단으로〕 하다; 분류하다. ¶ ~ *the children around the old man* 노인 주위에 어린이들을 끌어모으다.
— *vi.* (2A) gather in a group. 무리를 이루다; 일단(一團)이 되다. ¶ *The men grouped around the fire.* 사람들은 불 주변에 모였다. [It. →crop]

group therapy [⌐⌐––] *n.* 《psychoanal.》 psychotherapy in which a group of patients discuss and share their problems under the leadership of a therapeutist. 집단 요법.

grouse¹ [graus] *vi.* (P1,2A) 《*at, about*》 《*colloq.*》 complain; grumble. 불평을 하다; 투덜거리다(cf. *grouch*). — *n.* a complaint. 불평. [?]

grouse² [graus] *n.* Ⓒ (*pl.* **grouse** or **grous·es**) a game bird with plump body and feathered legs. 뇌조(雷鳥). [?]

:grove [grouv] *n.* Ⓒ a group of trees; a small wood. 나무숲; 작은 숲. [E.]

grov·el [grávəl, grʌ́vəl / grɔ́vəl] *vi.* (**-eled, -el·ing** or 《Brit.》 **-elled, -el·ling**) (P1,2A,3) 《*at, before, under*》 crawl on the ground; humble oneself. 기다; 넙죽 엎드리다; 비굴하게 굴다; 비하(卑下)하다. ¶ ~ *before a king* 왕 앞에 부복하다 / ~ *before* 〔*to*〕 *authority* 권위 앞에 굴하다 / ~ *in the dust* 머리를 조아리다; 비하하다. [N. *a gruffe* on one's face]

:grow [grou] *v.* (**grew, grown**) *vi.* **1** (P1,2A,3) live and become bigger. 성장하다; 자라다; 커지다. ¶ *She has grown into a pretty girl.* 그 아이는 예쁜 처녀로 자랐다 / *Your hair has grown.* 머리가 꽤 길게 자랐군. **2** (P1,2A,3) increase in amount, quality, degree, etc.; develop. (양·크기·정도 따위가) 늘다; 증대하다; 발달하다. ¶ ~ *in strength* 〔*reputation*〕 힘〔명성〕이 증대하다 / *His debts are growing.* 그의 빚이 늘고 있다 / *The storm is growing.* 폭풍우가 거칠어져 간다. **3** (P1,2A,3) come out; spring up; sprout. 나다; 싹〔움〕트다. ¶ *Moss grows on the rock.* 바위에 이끼가 난다. **4** (P4,5) come to be gradually; become; get. 점차 …이 되다; 변하다. ¶ ~ *rich* 〔*poor*〕 부자가 되다〔가난해지다〕 / ~ *pale* 창백해지다 / *The music grew fainter.* 음악 소리가 점점 가늘어졌다 / *It is growing dark* 〔*cold, hotter*〕. 점차 어두워져〔추워져, 더워져〕 간다 / *He grew to know her better.* 그는

점차 그녀를 더 잘 알게 되었다. — *vt.* (P6) cause (an animal or a plant) to grow; raise; cultivate. …을 기르다〔키우다〕; 재배하다. ¶ ~ *roses* 장미를 재배하다. [E.]

grow on 〔**upon**〕**,** become gradually more attractive or effective to (someone). 점차 마음에 들게 되다; 점점 더하게〔높아지게〕 되다. ¶ *This book will soon ~ upon you.* 자넨 이 책을 곧 좋아하게 될걸세 / *A bad habit grew upon her.* 그녀는 못된 버릇이 점점 더해갔다.

grow out of, a) be a result of (something); arise from. …의 결과이다; …에서 생기다〔일어나다〕. ¶ *Invention grows out of necessity.* 발명은 필요에서 생긴다. **b**) become too big for (clothes, etc.). (옷 등)에 비해 너무 커지다. ¶ *~ out of one's clothes* 너무 자라서 옷을 못 입게 되다. **c**) abandon; give up usu. as a result of becoming older. (나이가 들어 못된 버릇 따위에서) 벗어나다. ¶ *He has grown out of his bad habits.* 성장해서 그 나쁜 버릇도 없어졌다.

grow up, a) become fully grown; become an adult. 성인이〔어른이〕 되다. **b**) come into existence; arise; develop. 생기다; 출현하다; 발생하다; 일어나다. ¶ *A new town grew up.* 새 도시가 출현했다.

grow·er [gróuər] *n.* Ⓒ **1** a person who grows something. 재배자; (가축 따위의) 사육자. ¶ *a fruit-grower* 과일 재배자 / *livestock growers* 가축 사육자. **2** a plant that grows in a certain way. 자라는 식물. ¶ *a slow ~* 늦되는〔만생(晩生)〕 식물 / *a quick ~* 일되는〔조생(早生)〕 식물.

•**growl** [graul] *vi.* (P1) **1** ⟪*at*⟫ make a low, angry sound. 으르렁거리다. ¶ *The dog growled at him.* 개가 그를 향해 으르렁거렸다. **2** complain angrily. 불평을 하다; 투덜〔앙알〕거리다. — *vt.* (P6,7) ⟪*out*⟫ express (something) by growling. …을 으르렁거리며 말하다. ¶ *~ out an answer* 불퉁스럽게〔볼멘 소리로〕 대답하다. — *n.* Ⓒ **1** a low, angry sound. 으르렁대는 소리. **2** an angry complaint. 볼멘 소리; 불평; 노성. [Imit.]

:**grown** [groun] *v.* pp. of **grow.** — *adj.* arrived at full growth. 다 자란; 성장한. ¶ *a ~ man* 성인〔어른〕 / *a well-grown tree* 잘 자란 나무. [*grow*]

•**grown-up** [gróunʌ̀p] *adj.* adult; suitable for an adult. 어른〔성인〕이 된; 성인에 적합한; 어른용의. — *n.* Ⓒ an adult. 어른; 성인

•**growth** [grouθ] *n.* **1** Ⓤ the act of growing or developing. 성장; 성육(成育); 발육; 발달. ¶ *the ~ of a plant* 식물의 성장 / *the ~ of education* 교육의 발달 / *the ~ of the nation state* 그 민족 국가의 발전 / *check* 〔*hamper*〕 *~* 성장을 방해하다. **2** Ⓤ increase. 증가; 증대. ¶ *the ~ of power* 권력의 증대 / *the ~ of urban population* 도시 인구의 증대. **3** Ⓤ cultivation. 재배. ¶ *apples of foreign ~* 외국산의 사과. **4** Ⓒ something growing or that has grown. 생장물; 초목. **5** Ⓒ a tumor, cancer, etc. 종양(腫瘍). [*grow*]

grub [grʌb] *n.* Ⓒ **1** a soft, fat insect larva. (갑충 따위의) 유충; 굼벵이; 구더기. **2** a person who works hard at some long, uninteresting work. 고된 일을 열심히 하는 사람. **3** Ⓤ ⟪*colloq.*⟫ food. 음식. ¶ *time for ~* 식사 시간.

— *v.* (**grubbed, grub·bing**) *vt.* (P7) **1** ⟪*up, out*⟫ dig up; dig (roots) out of the ground. …을 파다; (나무 뿌리)를 파내다. **2** ⟪*colloq.*⟫ feed. 음식을 주다; …을 먹이다. ¶ *I have five children to ~.* 먹여 길러야 할 아이가 다섯이다. — *vi.* (2A) **1** dig in the ground; rummage. 땅을 파다; 애써〔샅샅이〕 찾다. ¶ *~ around in one's pocket* 호주머니 속을 샅샅이 뒤지다 / *~ in the earth for potatoes* 흙에서 감자를 캐내다. **2** ⟪*on*⟫ work hard; drudge. 열심히〔뼈빠지게〕 일하다. [E.]

grub along, seek a living day by day. 그날 그날 간신히 살아가다.

grub·by [grʌ́bi] *adj.* (**-bi·er, -bi·est**) **1** having grubs. 구더기가 들끓는. **2** dirty; unwashed. 더러운; 추레한.

•**grudge** [grʌdʒ] *vt.* **1** (P6,13,14) be unwilling to give or allow (someone or something). …을 주기〔내기〕 아까워하다; 내기 싫어하다. ¶ *~ him money* = *~ money to him* 그에게 돈 주기를 꺼리다 / *~ a contribution* 기부를 하기 싫어하다 / *~ no effort* 노력을 아끼지 않다 / *I ~ you nothing.* 당신에겐 아무것도 아깝지 않다. **2** (P14) envy. …을 질투〔시기〕하다; 부러워하다. ¶ *~ him his success* 그의 성공을 질투〔부러워〕하다.

— *vi.* (P1) feel ill-will at; complain. 악의를〔원한을〕 품다; 불평을 하다.

— *n.* Ⓒ a feeling of envy or ill-will. 원한; 악의. ¶ *have* 〔*bear*〕 *a ~ against someone* = *owe* 〔*bear*〕 *someone a ~* 아무에게 원한을 품다 / *work off a ~* 원한을 풀다. [F.]

grudg·ing [grʌ́dʒiŋ] *adj.* unwilling. 마지못한. ● **grudg·ing·ly** [-li] *adv.*

gru·el [grú:əl] *n.* **1** Ⓤ a thin liquid food made by boiling grain in water or milk. (묽은) 죽. **2** ⟪*sl.*⟫ severe punishment. 엄벌. ¶ *give someone his ~* 아무를 호되게 벌하다; 아무를 혼나게 하다〔죽이다〕 / *get* 〔*have, take*〕 *one's ~* 호되게 벌을 받다; 혼나다; 살해되다. [Teut. →groats]

gru·el·ing, ⟪Brit.⟫ **-el·ling** [grú:əliŋ] *adj.* ⟪*colloq.*⟫ exhausting; severe. 녹초를 만드는; (격)심한. ¶ *a ~ game* 격렬한 경기 / *~ tests* 모진 시련. — *n.* ⟪Brit. *sl.*⟫ harsh treatment or punishment. 호된 처사; 엄벌.

grue·some [grú:səm] *adj.* horrible; frightful. 소름끼치는; 무서운. ¶ *a ~ sight* 오싹해지는 광경. [Teut.]

gruff [grʌf] *adj.* **1** harsh; hoarse. 목이 쉰; 탁한 목소리의. ¶ *a ~ voice* 쉰 목소리. **2** rough; rude. 우락부락한; 거친; 퉁명스러운. ¶ *a ~ manner* 거친 태도. ● **gruff·ly** [-li] *adv.* [Du.]

•**grum·ble** [grʌ́mbəl] *vi.* (P1,3) **1** ⟪*at, about,*

over》 murmur discontentedly; growl. 툴툴[투덜]거리다; 으르렁대다. ¶ ~ *at* [*over*] *one's food* 음식 불평을 하다 / *He is always grumbling.* 그는 언제나 투덜거린다. **2** (of distant thunder) rumble. (멀리서 천둥 소리가) 우르르 울리다. — *vt.* (P6,7) express (something) by grumbling. …을 불평스럽게 말하다. ¶ ~ *a reply* 불만스럽게 대답하다. — *n.* Ⓒ **1** complaint. 불평. **2** a rumbling sound. (천둥의) 우르르 소리. [Imit.]

grum·bler [grʌ́mblər] *n.* Ⓒ a person who grumbles. 투덜대는 사람.

grump·y [grʌ́mpi] *adj.* (**grump·i·er, grump·i·est**) ill-tempered; surly. 찌무룩한; (성미가) 까다로운; 뚱한. ¶ *a ~ old woman* 성미 까다로운 노파. [Imit.]

·**grunt** [grʌnt] *vi.* (P1,3) make a noise like a pig; grumble. 툴툴거리다; 불평을 하다. — *vt.* (P6,7) 《*out*》 express (something) by grunting. …을 으르렁[으드등]거리듯 말하다. — *n.* Ⓒ a low, deep, rough sound. 으드등[투덜]거리는 소리. [Imit.]

gr. wt. gross weight.

gryph·on [grífən] *n.* =griffin.

GS, G.S. General Staff; General Secretary; Girl Scouts.

GSO General Staff Officer. 참모 본부; 막료.

g.t.c. 《comm.》 good till canceled. 취소할 때까지 유효.

gua·no [gwɑ́:nou] *n.* Ⓤ dung of sea-birds used for manure. 해조분(海鳥糞). [Native]

·**guar·an·tee** [gæ̀rəntí:] *n.* Ⓒ **1** a promise to cover another's loss. 보증; 담보. **2** a person who gives such a promise. 보증인. **3** a person to whom such a promise is given. 피(被)보증인(opp. guarantor).

stand [***go***] ***guarantee*** (=*promise to pay*) ***for** someone.* …의 보증인이 되다.

— *vt.* (P6,8,11,13,14,21) **1** give a guarantee for (someone). …을 보증하다. ¶ ~ *someone against* [*from*] *loss* 아무에게 손해를 끼치지 않을 것을 보증하다 / ~ *someone's debts* 아무의 빚보증을 서다 / *This watch is guaranteed for one year.* 이 시계는 1년간의 보증이 붙어 있다. **2** 《*colloq.*》 promise; affirm. …을 약속하다; (반드시) …하다. ¶ *I* ~ (that) *he'll come.* 그는 꼭 온다. [→guaranty]

guar·an·tor [gǽrəntɔ̀:r, -tər] *n.* Ⓒ a person who gives a guarantee. 보증인.

guar·an·ty [gǽrənti] *n.* ⓊⒸ (*pl.* **-ties**) **1** a written promise to pay or do something if another fails to do it. 보증(계약)서. **2** something offered as security. 담보. [→warrant]

:**guard** [gɑ:rd] *vt.* (P6,13) **1** keep watch over; take care of; defend; protect. (해·위험 따위에서) …을 지키다; 보호하다. ¶ ~ *life and property* 생명과 재산을 보호하다 / ~ *one's reputation* 명성을 지키다 / ~ *someone from his enemy* [*a danger*] 아무를 적[위험]으로부터 지키다. **2** watch over (a prisoner, etc.) so as to prevent escape, etc. …을 망보다; 감시하다. ¶ ~ *a prisoner* 죄수를 감시하다.

— *vi.* (P3) 《usu. *against*》 prevent by watching; be cautious of. 조심하다; 경계하다. ¶ ~ *against disease* 병을 조심하다 / ~ *against temptation* 유혹에 대비하다.

— *n.* **1** Ⓤ careful watch; caution. 망(보기); 감시; 경계; 조심. ¶ *keep someone under close* ~ 아무를 엄중한 감시 아래 두다. **2** Ⓒ a person or group that guards; a soldier or group of soldiers keeping guard. 망꾼; 감시자; 간수; 보초; 호위병[대]. ¶ *a ~ of honor* 의장병 / *relieve* [*change*] ~ 보초를 교대하다. **3** 《*pl.*》 《Brit.》 troops employed to protect the sovereign. 근위병; 친위대. ¶ *the Guards* 근위 연대 / *the Dragoon Guards* 근위 기병 제 1연대 / *the Grenadier Guards* 근위 보병 제 1연대. **4** Ⓒ 《Brit.》 a person in charge of a railway train. (열차의) 차장(cf. 《U.S.》 *conductor*). **5** ⒸⓊ a position of defense, as in fencing, boxing, etc. 방어 자세. ¶ *a player at open* ~ 방어 자세에 틈이 있는 선수. **6** Ⓒ anything which defends. 방호물(防護物). **7** ⓐ the part of the hilt of a sword which protects the hand. (칼의) 날밑. ⓑ a framework of wire used to keep children out of the fire; a fire-guard. (철망으로 된) 난로의 울. **8** Ⓒ 《football》 either of two players in the line; 《basketball》 either of two players defending the goal. (미식 축구·농구의) 가드. [↑]

keep guard, watch over. 감시[경계]하다.

mount guard, go on duty as a guard. 보초를 서다.

off one's guard, unprepared against attack or danger. 방심하고; 경계를 늦추고. ¶ *throw* [*put*] *someone off his* ~ 아무를 방심케 하다.

on one's guard, prepared against attack or danger; watchful. 조심스럽게; 경계하고. ¶ *on* one's ~ *against depression* 불경기에 대해 만반의 대비를 하고 / *set someone on his* ~ 아무로 하여금 경계심을 품게 하다.

stand guard, act as a guard. 보초를 서다.

guard·ed [gɑ́:rdid] *adj.* **1** defended; protected. 방호[방어]되어 있는. **2** careful; cautious. 조심스러운.

guard·house [gɑ́:rdhàus] *n.* Ⓒ **1** a building used by soldiers on guard. 위병소; 초소. **2** a building used as a jail for soldiers. 구류소; 영창.

·**guard·i·an** [gɑ́:rdiən] *n.* Ⓒ **1** a person who guards. 보호자; 수호자. **2** 《law》 a person who has the care of other person or his property. 후견인. ¶ *act as a ~ for someone* 아무의 후견인이 되다(opp. ward). — *adj.* protecting. 수호하는; 보호하는. ¶ *a ~ angel* 수호 천사.

guard·i·an·ship [gɑ́:rdiənʃip] *n.* Ⓤ the state of being a guardian; the position or office of a guardian. 후견(인의 임무·지위); 보호; 수호.

guard·rail [gɑ́:rdrèil] *n.* Ⓒ a rail for protection. (보호) 난간〔철책〕.

guard·room [gá:rdrù(:)m] *n.* Ⓒ **1** a room used by soldiers on guard. 위병소. **2** a room used as a jail for soldiers. 영창.

guards·man [gá:rdzmən] *n.* (*pl.* **-men** [-mən]) an officer or man of a regiment of the Guards. 근위 연대의 군인.

Gua·te·ma·la [gwà:təmá:lə, -te-] *n.* a country in Central America, south and east of Mexico. 과테말라《멕시코 남동부의 나라》.

gu·ber·na·to·ri·al [gjù:bərnətɔ́:riəl] *adj.* 《usu. U.S.》 of a governor. 주지사(州知事)의; 지방 장관의. ¶ *begin one's ~ campaign* 지사 선거 운동을 시작하다. [L. *gubernator* director]

gudg·eon [gʌ́dʒən] *n.* Ⓒ **1** a small freshwater fish that is easy to catch and is used for bait. 모샘치《잉어과의 작은 담수어》. **2** a person who is easily deceived. (잘 속는) 얼뜨기. [L. *gobio*]

guer·don [gə́:rdən] *n.* Ⓒ 《*poet.*》 a reward. 보수; 포상. — *vt.* reward. 포상을 주다. [G. =repayment]

gue·ril·la, guer·ril- [gərílə] *n.* Ⓒ a person engaged in an irregular war carried on by a small, independent group of fighters; an irregular war so carried on. 게릴라병; 게릴라전. [Sp.]

:guess [ges] *vt.* (P6,10,11,12,21) **1** 《*at*》 form an opinion or idea about (something) without certain reason. …을 추측〔추정〕하다; 짐작을 하다; 알아맞히다. ¶ *~ someone's weight* 아무의 몸무게를 추정하다 / *~ a riddle* 수수께끼를 풀다 / *~ the right answer at once* 정답을 알아맞히다 / *I'm not sure, but I ~ this book is hers.* 자신은 없지만 이 책은 그녀의 것이라고 생각한다 / *I ~ his age at fifty.* =*I ~ his age to be fifty.* =*I ~ that his age is fifty.* 그의 나이를 50살로 추정한다 / *Can you ~ what I have in my pocket?* 내 호주머니에 무엇이 들어있나 알아맞혀 보아라. **2** 《U.S.》 think; suppose; believe. 생각하다; 믿다. ¶ *I ~ we shall miss the train.* 열차 시간에 대지 못할 것으로 생각한다 / *Can you do it? —No, I ~ not.* 그것을 할 수 있나— 아니, 못할 것 같다 / *I ~ not* 〔*so*〕. 그렇지 않을 거다〔그렇다고 생각한다〕. — *vi.* (P1,2A,3) 《*at, about*》 form an opinion without certain reason. 추측〔짐작〕하다; 알아맞히다. ¶ *~ right* 〔*wrong*〕 짐작〔추측〕이 맞다〔틀리다〕.

guess at, attempt to judge rightly; attempt to solve by guessing. 정확히 짐작〔추측〕하다; 짐작으로 알아맞히다. ¶ *We guessed at the height of the building.* 그 건물의 높이를 대중 쳐보았다 / *I can't even ~ at what she wants.* 그녀가 무엇을 원하고 있는지 짐작도 안 간다.

keep** someone **guessing, puzzle someone. 아무를 불안하게〔마음 졸이게〕 하다.

— *n.* Ⓒ **1** an opinion formed without certain reason. 추측; 짐작. ¶ *make a ~ at someone's age* 아무의 나이를 추측하다 / *My ~ is that....* 내 추측으로는〔내가 보는 바로는〕 …이다〔하다〕. **2** an estimate. 평가; 어림. [E.]

at a guess, counting or estimating roughly. 대충 어림〔짐작〕으로.

by guess, making a random guess. 짐작〔추측〕으로. ¶ *write an answer by ~* 답을 추측으로 쓰다.

guess·work [géswə̀:rk] *n.* Ⓤ the act of guessing; the result of guessing. 추측(에 의거한 행위·견해); 억측; 알아맞히기. [↑]

:guest [gest] *n.* Ⓒ **1** a person who is entertained at the house or table of another; a visitor. (초청된) 손님; (빈)객; 내빈. ¶ *a ~ of honor* 주빈(主賓) / *a state ~* 국빈 / *unwelcome guests at a party* 환영받지 못하는 파티의 손님. **2** a person staying at a hotel. 여객; 유숙〔숙박〕객. ¶ *a paying ~* (개인 집의) 하숙인. [E.]

guest room [∠ ∠] *n.* a room set apart for the use of guests. 객실; 사랑(방).

guf·faw [gʌfɔ́:, gə-] *n.* Ⓒ a loud, coarse burst of laughter. 너털웃음; 홍소. — *vi.* (P1) laugh in this way. 너털웃음을 웃다; 홍소하다. [Imit.]

Gui·a·na [giǽnə, gai-, giá:nə] *n.* a region in northern South America. 기아나《남아메리카 북부 지역》. 參考 Guyana, Surinam, 프랑스령 Guiana로 이루어지는 지역.

guid·ance [gáidns] *n.* Ⓤ the act of guiding; the state of being guided; leadership; direction. 안내; 지휘; 지도; 지시. ¶ *vocational ~* 직업 지도 / *under someone's ~* 아무의 지도 밑에〔안내로〕 / *leave a boy without ~* 이끌어 주지 않고 아이를 내버려 두다. [↓]

:guide [gaid] *vt.* (P6,7) **1** show the way; lead; conduct. …을 (길)안내하다; 이끌다. ¶ *~ a ship to a harbor* 배를 이끌어 입항시키다 / *~ tourists through a town* 관광객에게 시내의 길 안내를 하다 / *a blind man guided by a dog* 개에 이끌려가는 맹인. **2** ⓐ supply (someone) with advice; give instruction or help to. 조언하다; 지도하다. ¶ *~ students in English* 학생들에게 영어를 가르치다 / *~ someone to right reading* 바른 독서법을 지도하다. ⓑ influence (someone or his actions); direct. …에게 영향을 주다; (어떤 방향으로) 나아가게 하다. ¶ *~ the young men into the right path* 젊은이를 바른길로 이끌다 / *be guided by one's sense of duty* 의무감에 이끌리다. **3** manage; control. …을 지배하다; 관리〔처리〕하다. ¶ *~ the state* 국가를 통치하다 / *~ the affairs of state* 국무를 처리하다.

— *n.* Ⓒ **1** a person who shows the way. 길 안내자; 길(라)잡이. **2** a person who gives help and advice; an advisor. 지도자; 조언자. **3** a thing that shows the position or direction; a directing principle; a book of information. 길잡이; 지침; 안내서; 입문서. ¶ *a ~ to English studies* 영어 연구의 입문서. [F.]

guide·book [gáidbùk] *n.* Ⓒ a book of information for travelers. 여행 안내서.

guide·line [gáidlàin] *n.* Ⓤ any guide for a future course of action. 미래 행동의 지침.

guide·post [gáidpòust] *n.* Ⓒ a post at crossroads that directs one to places; a sign-post. 길잡이; 이정표.

guild [gild] *n.* Ⓒ **1** 《hist.》 a union of men in the same trade to protect their interests. (중세의) 동업 조합; 길드. **2** an association for the mutual aid and protection of people in a common trade. 동업 조합. [E. →yield]

guil·der [gíldər] *n.* a Dutch silver coin worth about two shillings. 길더《네덜란드의 은화; 약 2 실링》.

guild·hall [gíldhɔ̀:l] *n.* Ⓒ **1** a hall where members of a guild in the Middle Ages met. 중세 길드의 집회소. **2** 《Brit.》 a town hall. 시청; 읍사무소.

guild socialism [⏊⏊––] *n.* an English socialistic theory advocating state-ownership of industries and control and management by guilds of workers. 조합 사회주의.

guile [gail] *n.* Ⓤ cunning; deceit; treachery. 교활함; 기만. [F.]

guile·ful [gáilfəl] *adj.* full of guile; deceitful; crafty. 교활한; 기만적인; 음험(陰險)한. ●**guile·ful·ly** [-fəli] *adv.* **guile·ful·ness** [-nis] *n.*

guile·less [gáillis] *adj.* without guile; honest; frank; innocent. 교활치 않은; 악의 없는; 정직〔솔직〕한; 천진한. ¶ *a ~ child* 천진한 아이. ●**guile·less·ly** [-li] *adv.*

guil·lo·tine [gílətì:n, gì:jə-] *n.* Ⓒ **1** a machine for cutting off a person's head by means of a heavy knife sliding down between two posts. 단두대; 기요틴. ¶ *go to the ~* 단두대에 오르다; 참수형에 처해지다. **2** a machine for cutting paper, metal, etc. (종이·금속 따위의) 절단기. — *vt.* (P6) cut off the head of (someone) with a guillotine. 기요틴으로 …의 목을 자르다. [F. *Guillotin*]

***guilt** [gilt] *n.* Ⓤ crime; sin. 범죄; 죄. ¶ *confess* 〔*deny*〕 *one's ~* 죄를 자백〔부인〕하다 / *charge someone with ~* 아무를 고소하다. [E.]

guilt·i·ly [gíltili] *adv.* in a guilty manner. 「유죄로; 죄가 있는 것처럼.

guilt·i·ness [gíltinis] *n.* Ⓤ the quality or state of being guilty. 죄가 있음; 유죄.

guilt·less [gíltlis] *adj.* **1** not guilty; innocent. 죄 없는; 결백한. **2** having no knowledge or experience. 모르는; 경험이 없는. ¶ *the earth ~ of the plow* 쟁기를 대어본 적이 없는 땅 / *be ~ of the ways of wicked men* 악당들이 항용 쓰는 수법을 모르다.

:guilt·y [gílti] *adj.* (**guilt·i·er, guilt·i·est**) **1** having done wrong; having committed a crime or a sin. 잘못을〔죄를〕 저지른; 유죄의. ¶ *a ~ deed* 범행 / *a ~ mind* 고의(故意) / *be ~ of murder* 살인을 저지르다 / *be declared ~* 유죄로 선고되다 / *plead not ~ to a crime* 무죄를 주장하다. **2** showing or feeling guilt; of guilt. 죄가 있는〔될 것〕 같은; 죄의식이 있는; 죄에 관한. ¶ *a ~ conscience* 양심의 가책 / *a ~ look* 죄지은 얼굴 / *I feel ~ for having left him.* 그를 남겨두고 와서 죄책감을 느끼고 있다. [E.]

Guin·ea [gíni] *n.* **1** a region along the western coast of Africa. 기니. **2** 《*the republic of ~*》 a country in this region. 기니 공화국. 參考 수도는 Conakry.

guin·ea [gíni] *n.* Ⓒ **1** a gold coin, once used in England and worth 21 shillings. (영국의) 기니 금화. **2** the amount of 21 shillings. 21 실링. [Port.]

guinea fowl [⏊–⏊] *n.* 《bird》 a domestic fowl of the pheasant family, with a rounded body and dark feathers spotted with white. 뿔닭《아프리카 원산》.

guinea hen [⏊–⏊] *n.* 《bird》 **1** =guinea fowl. **2** the female of the guinea fowl. 뿔닭의 암컷.

guinea pig [⏊–⏊] *n.* **1** 《zool.》 a short-eared, short-tailed animal like a big, fat, harmless rat. 기니피그《속칭 모르모트》. **2** a living subject for medical or other experiments. 실험 재료(가 되는 사람·동물). **3** one who receives guinea fees for small services. 작은 일을 하고 기니의 보수를 받는 사람.

guise [gaiz] *n.* Ⓒ **1** ⓐ a style of dress. 옷차림; 복장. ¶ *a foreigner in strange ~* 이상한 옷차림의 외국인. ⓑ external appearance; an aspect. 외관; 외견; (겉)모양. ¶ *a fiend in frightful ~* 무시무시한 모양을 한 마귀. **2** pretense. 가장(假裝); 가면. ¶ *in* 〔*under*〕 *the ~ of friendship* 우정을 가장하여. [Teut.]

gui·tar [gitá:r] *n.* Ⓒ a six-stringed musical instrument, played with the fingers. 기타《현악기》. ●**gui·tar·ist** [-rist] *n.* [Gk. *kithara* harp]

gulch [gʌltʃ] *n.* Ⓒ 《U.S.》 a deep, narrow, long valley with steep sides. 골짜기; 협곡(峽谷). [U.S.]

gul·den [gú:ldən] *n.* a Dutch silver coin. 네덜란드의 은화. [Du., G. =golden]

gules [gju:lz] *n., adj.* 《her.》 red. 빨강(의); 적색(의). [F. *goules* ermine dyed red]

:gulf [gʌlf] *n.* Ⓒ **1** a large bay. 만(灣). ¶ *the Gulf of Mexico.* 멕시코 만 / *the Gulf Stream* 멕시코 만류. **2** 《*poet.*》 ⓐ a deep hollow in the earth; an abyss. (지표(地表)의) 깊은 구멍; 심연(深淵). ⓑ a whirlpool. 소용돌이. **3** a wide separation. 큰 격차. ¶ *the ~ between rich and poor* 빈부의 큰 격차 / *The quarrel left a ~ between the two families.* 그 싸움은 두 집안 사이에 깊은 골을 남겼다. — *vt.* (P6) swallow up 삼키다. [Gk. *kolpos*]

gull[1] [gʌl] *n.* Ⓒ 《bird》 a graceful gray-white sea-bird with long wings. 갈매기.

[? Welsh]

gull[2] [gʌl] *n.* Ⓒ a person who is easily deceived or cheated. 잘 속는 사람. — *vt.* (P6,13) deceive; cheat. 속이다. ¶ *They gulled him into going there.* 그를 속여 그 곳에 가게 했다 / ~ *someone* (*out*) *of his money* 아무를 속여 돈을 빼앗다. [↑, Obs. *gull* swallow]

gul·let [gʌ́lit] *n.* Ⓒ **1** the tube from the mouth to the stomach; the throat. 식도(食道); 목구멍. **2** a water channel. 수로(水路); 도랑. [L. *gula*]

gul·li·ble [gʌ́ləbəl] *adj.* easily deceived or cheated. 속(아 넘어가)기 쉬운. [*gull*[2]]

gul·ly [gʌ́li] *n.* (*pl.* **-lies**) Ⓒ a channel for water; a small valley. 도랑; (작은) 협곡(峽谷); 계곡. — *vt.* make gullies in (something). …에 도랑을 만들다. [L. *gula*]

gulp [gʌlp] *vt.* (P6,7) **1** swallow quickly and greedily. …을 꿀꺽꿀꺽 마시다(들이켜다). ¶ ~ *down a glass of water* 물 한 잔을 벌떡벌떡 들이켜다. **2** check; hold back. …을 억제하다; 눌러 참다. ¶ ~ *down a sob* 오열을 삼키다. — *vi.* (P1) make a gulping motion. 꿀꺽 마시다(삼키다). — *n.* Ⓒ the act of gulping; the amount swallowed at one time. 꿀꺽 마시기; 꿀떡 삼키기; 한번 삼킨 양. ¶ (*swallow*) *at one* (*a*) ~ 단숨에 (들이켜다). [Imit.]

⁎**gum**[1] [gʌm] *n.* Ⓤ **1** a sticky substance obtained from certain trees. 고무; 수지(樹脂)(cf. *resin*). **2** chewing gum. 껌. **3** a sticky substance used to fasten papers, etc. together. 고무풀. **4** rubber; 《*pl.*》 rubber overshoes. 탄성(彈性) 고무; 고무(덧)신. **5** Ⓒ a gum tree. 고무나무.

— *v.* (**gummed, gum·ming**) *vt.* (P6,7) stick (things) together with gum; spread gum on the surface of (something). …을 고무풀로 붙이다; …의 표면에 고무를 바르다.

— *vi.* (P1) give off gum; become sticky. 고무를 분비하다; 고무 모양이 되다; 끈적끈적해지다. [Gk. *kommi*]

gum[2] [gʌm] *n.* Ⓒ 《usu. *pl.*》 the flesh around the teeth. 잇몸; 치은(齒齦). [E.]

gum arabic [ˊ ˊ–ˋ] *n.* gum obtained from acacia trees, used in making candy, medicine, etc. 아라비아 고무《수용성 고무질로서 캔디·의약품 제조에 씀》.

gum·boil [gʌ́mbɔ̀il] *n.* a painful swelling inside the mouth. 잇몸 농양(膿瘍).

gum boots [ˊ ˊ] *n.* boots of rubber. 고무 장화; 고무신.

gum·drop [gʌ́mdrɑ̀p / -drɔ̀p] *n.* a small jelly-like sweet. 검드롭《아라비아 고무·젤라틴·그래뉴당(糖)을 재료로 한 젤리 과자》.

gum·my [gʌ́mi] *adj.* (**-mi·er, -mi·est**) sticky; covered with gum; giving off gum. 고무 같은; 끈끈한; 고무로 덮인; 고무를 분비하는. [*gum*[1]]

gump·tion [gʌ́mpʃən] *n.* Ⓤ 《*colloq.*》 the ability, will and courage to do something. 임기(臨機)의 재능; 세재(世才); 수완; 진취성; 용기. [? Scot.]

gum·shoe [gʌ́mʃùː] *n.* **1** a rubber overshoe. 고무 덧신. **2** 《*pl.*》 sneakers. (고무창의) 운동화. **3** 《*sl.*》 a detective. 형사. — *vi.* (P1) 《*sl.*》 go around quietly and secretly. (발소리를 죽여) 가만가만 걷다. [*gum*[1]]

gum tree [ˊ ˊ] *n.* a tree from which gum is got. 고무나무.

be up a gum tree, 《U.S.》 be in difficulties. 어려움[진퇴양난]에 빠져 있다.

⁑**gun** [gʌn] *n.* Ⓒ **1** a weapon that fires a shot, such as a cannon, rifle, pistol, or revolver. 총포(銃砲)《총·권총·대포 따위》. **2** the shooting of a gun as a signal or salute. 대포의 발사. ¶ *a salute of twenty-one guns,* 21발의 예포(禮砲). **3** =gunman.

a son of a gun, a worthless or foolish fellow. 시시한 자식; 바보 같은 녀석.

(***as***) ***sure as a gun,*** without doubt; certainly. 틀림없이; 확실히.

beat (***jump***) ***the gun,*** **a**) start a race before the starting signal is given. (레이스에서) 플라잉을 범하다. **b**) begin any activity prematurely; act hastily. 너무 조급히 시작하다; 성급히 행동하다.

blow great guns, (of the wind) blow very strongly. 바람이 사납게 불다.

stick (***stand***) ***to one's guns,*** be firm; do not yield or retreat. 입장을 고수하다; 굴복하지 않다.

— *v.* (**gunned, gun·ning**) *vi.* (P1) shoot or hunt with a gun; go shooting or hunting. 총으로 쏘다; 총사냥을 하다(가다). — *vt.* (P6,7) shoot (someone). …을 총으로 쏘다; 발포하다. ¶ *be gunned down by assassins* 암살자에게 저격(狙擊)되어 쓰러지다. [*Gunilda,* woman's name applied to war-engines]

gun for, **a**) hunt (animals) with a gun; look for (animals) in order to shoot them. 총으로 …사냥을 하다; …을 쏘려고 찾아다니다. **b**) seek or try earnestly to obtain. …을 얻으려고 노력하다. ¶ *He is gunning for a raise.* 봉급을 올려 받으려고 애쓰고 있다.

gun·boat [gʌ́nbòut] *n.* Ⓒ a small warship carrying heavy guns. (작은) 포함(砲艦).

gun carriage [ˊ ˊ–] *n.* 《mil.》 a wheeled support for a gun. 포가(砲架).

gun·cot·ton [gʌ́nkɑ̀tn / -kɔ̀tn] *n.* Ⓤ an explossive made by treating cotton with nitric and sulfuric acids. 면화약(綿火藥).

gun·fire [gʌ́nfàiər] *n.* Ⓤ the act of shooting with a gun. 포격; 발포; 포화.

gun·lock [gʌ́nlɑ̀k / -lɔ̀k] *n.* the part of a gun which fires the charge. 격발(擊發) 장치; 방아쇠.

gun·man [gʌ́nmən] *n.* Ⓒ (*pl.* **-men** [-mən]) **1** 《U.S. *colloq.*》 ⓐ a man who uses a gun to rob or kill people. 총을 가진 악한; 총잡이. ⓑ an armed civilian. 총기 휴대자. **2** a person who makes guns. 총기 제

조자.

gun metal [ㅗㅗ—] *n.* **1** a dark-gray mixture of metal; a variety of bronze. 암회색의 금속; 포금(砲金); 청동. **2** dark gray. 암회색.

gunned [gʌnd] *adj.* provided with a cannon. 포(砲)를 갖춘.

gun·nel [gʌ́nl] *n.* =gunwale.

gun·ner [gʌ́nər] *n.* Ⓒ **1** a person who works a gun. 포수(砲手); 사격수; 포병. **2** (in the navy) an officer in charge of a ship's guns. 장포장(掌砲長)《준사관》. **3** a person who hunts animals with a gun. 총사냥꾼. [*gun*]

gun·ner·y [gʌ́nəri] *n.* Ⓤ **1** the art and science of making and using heavy guns. 포술(砲術); 포학(砲學). **2** the act of firing heavy guns. 포격; 발포. **3** 《*collectively*》 heavy guns. 포(砲).

gun·ny [gʌ́ni] *n.* (*pl.* **-nies**) **1** Ⓤ a strong, coarse cloth used for sacks and bags. 조제 마포(粗製麻布); 즈크. **2** Ⓒ a sack or bag made of this cloth. 즈크 자루; 마대(麻袋). ¶ *a ~ sack* 〔*bag*〕. [Skr.]

gun·pow·der [gʌ́npàudər] *n.* Ⓤ an bursting powder used in guns, fireworks, etc. 화약. ¶ *smokeless ~* 무연(無煙) 화약. [*gun*]

gun room [ㅗㅗ] *n.* **1** 《nav.》 a room for the use of young officers. (군함의) 하급 장교실. **2** a room in a private house where guns, etc. are kept. 총기실(銃器室).

gun·run·ner [gʌ́nrʌ̀nər] *n.* a person engaged in gunrunning. 총기의 밀수입자.

gun·run·ning [gʌ́nrʌ̀niŋ] *n.* Ⓤ illegally taking guns into a country for the use of rebels. 총기 밀수입.

gun·shot [gʌ́nʃɑ̀t / -ʃɔ̀t] *n.* **1** Ⓒ a bullet or other shot fired from a gun. 발사된 탄환. **2** Ⓒ the shooting of a gun. 사격; 발포; 포격. **3** Ⓤ the distance that a gun will shoot. 사정(射程); 착탄 거리. ¶ *within* 〔*out of*〕 *~* 사정 안〔밖〕에.

gun-shy [gʌ́nʃài] *adj.* (of a hunting dog or horse) afraid of the firing of a gun. (특히 사냥개·말이) 총소리를 겁내는.

gun·smith [gʌ́nsmìθ] *n.* one who makes or repairs guns. 총기 제작〔수리〕자; 총공(銃工).

gun·stock [gʌ́nstɑ̀k / -stɔ̀k] *n.* the wooden support to which the gun-barrel is fixed. 총상(銃床); 개머리판.

gun·wale [gʌ́nl] *n.* Ⓒ 《naut.》 the top edge of the side of a boat. 뱃전의 윗 변죽. 參考 gunnel 로도 씀.

gur·gi·ta·tion [gə̀ːrdʒətéiʃən] *n.* Ⓤ the whirling or eddying of a liquid, as when boiling. (물 따위가) 끓어오름; 비등. [L. *gurges* whirlpool]

gur·gle [gə́ːrgəl] *vi.* (P1) **1** flow with a bubbling sound. 콸콸〔꾸르륵〕 흐르다. **2** make a bubbling sound. 콸콸〔꾸르륵〕 소리를 내다. — *vt.* (P6) express (something) with a gurgling sound. …을 꾸르륵거리며 말하다. — *n.* Ⓒ the act of gurgling; a gurgling sound. 콸콸; 꾸르륵(소리). [Imit. →gargle]

gush [gʌʃ] *vi.* (P1,2A,3) **1** 《*out, forth*》 flow out suddenly with force; pour out. 세차게 흘러 나오다; 분출하다. ¶ *clear water gushing from a spring* 샘에서 솟구쳐나오는 맑은 물. **2** 《*colloq.*》 talk with too much eagerness or admiration. 열심히 지껄여 대다. — *vt.* (P6,7) cause (something) to pour out. …을 유출〔분출〕시키다. ¶ *a wound gushing out crimson blood* 선혈이 철철흐르는 상처.

— *n.* Ⓒ **1** a sudden outflow of water or other liquid. 유출; 분출. ¶ *a ~ of blood* 피의 유출. **2** 《*colloq.*》 a sudden or violent burst (of feeling, etc.); foolish, unrestrained expression of feeling. (감정 따위의) 복받침; 격발; 쏟아져 나오는 말. ¶ *a ~ of rage* 격발된 노여움 / *a ~ of dazzling light* 눈부시게 비추는 광선 / *speak with ~* 거침없이 마구 지껄이다. [E.]

gush·er [gʌ́ʃər] *n.* Ⓒ **1** an oil well with a large natural flow. 분출 유정(噴出油井). **2** a person who gushes. 과장된 감정 표현을 하는 사람.

gush·ing [gʌ́ʃiŋ] *adj.* pouring out; flowing out abundantly. 쏟아져 나오는; 용솟음치는; (감정 따위가) 넘쳐나오는; 분출하는.

gus·set [gʌ́sit] *n.* Ⓒ **1** a triangular piece of cloth let into garment to enlarge or strengthen it. 보강용(補強用) 삼각천; 바대. **2** 《mech.》 a metal bracket for strengthening an angle. 보강용 받침판(板). [F.]

gust [gʌst] *n.* Ⓒ **1** a sudden rush of wind. 돌풍. ¶ *a violent ~ of wind* 세찬 일진의 바람. **2** an outburst of anger or other feeling. (감정의) 격발; 폭발. [N.]

gus·ta·tion [gʌstéiʃən] *n.* Ⓤ **1** the act of tasting. 맛보기; 상미(賞味). **2** the power of tasting. 미각(味覺) [*gusto*]

gus·to [gʌ́stou] *n.* ⓊⒸ (*pl.* **-tos**) **1** taste; liking. 취미; 기호; 애호. ¶ *have a ~ for learning* 학문을 좋아하다. **2** keen enjoyment. 열광적인 즐거움. ¶ *with ~* 매우 즐겁게. [L. *gustus* taste]

gust·y [gʌ́sti] *adj.* (**gust·i·er, gust·i·est**) **1** windy; stormy. 돌풍(突風)의. **2** marked by outbursts of emotion, sound, etc. (감정·소리 따위가) 돌발적인. [→gust]

gut [gʌt] *n.* **1** ⓐ 《*pl.*》 the bowels; intestines. 창자; 내장. ¶ *a pain in the guts* 복통. ⓑ the alimentary canal. 소화관(消化管); 장(腸). ¶ *the large* 〔*small*〕 *~* 대〔소〕장 / *the blind ~* 맹장. **2** 《*pl.*》 the content, esp. the valuable, essential part. 내용; (특히) 본질적인 부분. ¶ *the very guts of a matter* 문제의 본질 바로 그 자체 / *have no guts* 내용이 없다. **3** 《*pl.*》 courage; spirit; endurance. 용기; 기력; 인내력. ¶ *a man with plenty of guts* 용기 있는〔담찬〕 사람 / *work one's guts* *out* 정력을 소모시키다 / *He has no guts.* 그는 용기가 없다〔무력하다〕. **4** Ⓤ a strong cord made from the intestines of animals, used for violin strings and tennis rackets. 장선(腸線). **5** Ⓒ a narrow channel. 좁은 수로(水路); 해협.

— *vt.* (**gut·ted, gut·ting**) (P6) **1** take the intestines out of (a fish). …의 창자를 뽑아내다. **2** remove the entire contents of; plunder; destroy the inside of (a building). …의 내용을〔대요를〕 뽑아내다; 약탈하다; (건물의) 내부를 파괴하다. ¶ *Fire gutted the building.* 화재가 나서 건물 내부를 모두 불태웠다. **3** 《*vulg.*》 eat greedily. 게걸스레 먹다; 탐식하다. [E.]

gut·ta-per·cha [gʌ́təpə́ːrtʃə] *n.* Ⓤ a rubberlike substance made from the juice of certain trees in Malaya. 구타페르카 《말레이지방산 나무의 수지를 말린 고무 비슷한 물질》. [Malay]

gut·ter [gʌ́tər] *n.* Ⓒ **1** a channel under the eaves of a building to carry off rain water. (처마의) 홈통. **2** a channel or ditch along the side of a street to carry off water. (길가의) 도랑; 하수도. **3** 《*the* ~》 a low, poor place. 빈민굴〔가〕. ¶ *people of the* ~ 영세민 / *the language of the* ~ 하층 사회의 말 / *rise from the* ~ 미천한 신분에서 출세하다 / *work one's way up from the* ~ 밑바닥 생활로부터 고생 끝에 신분을 상승시키다.

— *vt.* (P6) furnish (something) with gutters; make gutters in (something). …에 홈통을 달다; 도랑을 만들다〔파다〕.

— *vi.* (P1) become channeled; (of a candle) melt in streams. 도랑이 생기다; 촛농이 흘러 내리다. [L. *gutta* drop]

gut·ter·snipe [gʌ́tərsnàip] *n.* a homeless child or one living mainly in the streets. (거리의) 부랑아. [↑]

gut·tle [gʌ́tl] *vi., vt.* eat greedily. 게걸스럽게 먹다. [→guzzle]

gut·tur·al [gʌ́tərəl] *adj.* **1** of the throat. 목구멍의. **2** produced in the throat. 목구멍에서 나는. ¶ *a* ~ *sound* 후음(喉音). — *n.* Ⓒ 《phon.》 a sound produced in this way, such as [k] and [g]. 후음(喉音). [L. *gutter* throat]

***guy**[1] [gai] *n.* Ⓒ a supporting rope, wire, or chain. 버팀줄. ¶ *the guys of a tent* 천막의 버팀줄. — *vt.* (P6) steady (something) with a guy. …을 버팀줄로 버티다. [F.]

***guy**[2] [gai] *n.* Ⓒ **1** 《U.S. *colloq.*》 a fellow. 사내; 놈; 녀석. ¶ *He's a nice* ~. 그는 좋은 녀석이다. **2** a person of queer appearance or dress. 기이한 옷차림의 사람; 이상한 사람. — *vt.* (P6) make fun of (someone); tease. …을 놀리다. [Person]

Guy·an·a [gaiǽnə, -áːnə] *n.* a republic of northeast-central South America. 가이아나 《남아메리카 동북부의 공화국》. 參考 수도는 조지타운(Georgetown).

guz·zle [gʌ́zəl] *vi., vt.* (P6,7; 1,2A) eat or drink greedily. 폭음(暴飮)〔폭식〕하다. [? O.F. *gosier* throat]

***gym** [dʒim] *n.* 《*colloq.*》 Ⓤ gymnastics; Ⓒ a gymnasium. 체조; 체육관. [*gymnasium*]

gym·na·si·a [dʒimnéiziə] *n.* pl. of **gymnasium.**

gym·na·si·um [dʒimnéiziəm] *n.* Ⓒ (*pl.* **-ums** or **-si·a**) **1** a large room or building for athletic practice. 체육관; 옥내 경기장. **2** 《*G-*》 (in Germany) a secondary school that prepares students for the universities. 대학 예비교(豫備校). [Gk. *gumnos* naked]

gym·nast [dʒímnæst] *n.* Ⓒ an expert in gymnastics. 체육가(家); 체육 교사. [↑]

gym·nas·tic [dʒimnǽstik] *adj.* of physical exercises or activities. 체조의; 체육의. — *n.* the training of the body or mind. 신체〔정신적〕 훈련.

gym·nas·tics [dʒimnǽstiks] *n. pl.* 《used as *sing.*》 physical exercises for devoloping the body. 체조.

gy·ne·col·o·gy, 《Brit.》 **gy·nae-** [gàinikáləd͡ʒi, dʒìn- / -kɔ́l-] *n.* the science of women's diseases. 부인과 의학. [Gk. *gunē* woman]

gy·noe·ci·um [gainíːsiəm, dʒi-, dʒai-] *n.* 《bot.》 a pistil or pistils of a flower. 암술. [↑]

gyp[1] [dʒip] *n.* ***give someone gyp,*** 《Brit. *sl.*》 scold or punish someone; give pain to someone. …를 혼내주다; 몹시 꾸짖다; …에게 고통을 주다. [→gee]

gyp[2] [dʒip] *n.* 《U.S. *sl.*》 a cheat; a thief. 사기(꾼); 도둑. — *vt.* (**gypped, gyp·ping**) 《U.S. *sl.*》 cheat; rob; steal. 속이다; 야바위치다; 훔치다. [↓]

gyp·sy [dʒípsi] *n.* (*pl.* **-sies**) **1** 《often *G-*》 Ⓒ a member of a dark-skinned race of people who originally came from India. 집시(인). **2** Ⓤ the language of the Gypsies. 집시 말〔어〕. — *adj.* of or like a gypsy. 집시의; 집시 같은. 參考 영국에서는 gipsy 로 씀. [*Egyptian*]

gy·rate [dʒáiəreit] *vi.* (P1) move in a circle; whirl. 빙빙 돌다; 선회하다; 소용돌이치다. ¶ *A top is gyrating.* 팽이가 뱅뱅 돌고 있다. [Gk. *guros* ring]

gy·ra·tion [dʒaiəréiʃən] *n.* ⓊⒸ the act of gyrating; a revolution. 회전 (운동); 선회.

gy·ra·to·ry [dʒáiərətɔ̀ːri / -təri] *adj.* turning in a circle. 회전〔선회〕 운동을 하는.

gy·ro·com·pass [dʒáiəroukʌ̀mpəs] *n.* a compass using a motor-driven gyroscope. 회전 나침의. [→gyrate]

gy·ro·scope [dʒáiərəskòup] *n.* Ⓒ a machine with a heavy spinning wheel which helps to keep ships and airplanes balanced. 회전의(回轉儀). [↑]

gyve [dʒaiv] *n.* 《usu. *pl.*》 a chain for the feet; a fetter; a shackle. 차꼬; 족쇄; 고랑. — *vt.* (P6) fasten (the leg) with gyves; fetter. 차꼬를〔고랑을〕 채우다. [E.]

h H

H, h [eitʃ] *n.* Ⓒ (*pl.* **H's, Hs, h's, hs** [éitʃiz]) the eighth letter of the English alphabet. 영어 알파벳의 여덟째 글자.

H **1** hard. 參考 연필의 경도(硬度) 표시. 연도(軟度)는 B(=black)로 표시함. **2** 《electr.》 henry. **3** 《chem.》 hydrogen.

h., H. harbor; high; height; hit; hundred; hour(s).

***ha** [hɑː] *interj.* **1** an exclamation of wonder, surprise, joy, victory, doubt, etc. 하; 허어; 어(이구); 이런. **2** the sound of laughing. 하하《웃음 소리》. [E.]

Ha·ba·ne·ra [hɑ̀ːbənέːərə] *n.* a slow Cuban dance. 하바네라《쿠바의 느린 춤》.

ha·be·as cor·pus [héibiəs kɔ́ːrpəs] *n.* 《L.》《law》 a writ requiring a person to be brought before a judge or into a court to investigate the lawfulness of his restraint. 인신(人身) 제출 영장; 인신 보호 영장. [L.=you must have the body]

hab·er·dash·er [hǽbərdæ̀ʃər] *n.* Ⓒ **1** 《U.S.》 a dealer who sells men's furnishings, such as hats, ties, shirts, etc. 신사용 양품상(商). **2** 《Brit.》 a merchant who sells small goods, such as buttons, needles, and pins, etc. 방물 장수. [Obs. *haberdash* small wares]

hab·er·dash·er·y [hǽbərdæ̀ʃəri] *n.* (*pl.* **-er·ies**) **1** Ⓤ 《U.S.》 men's furnishings, such as hats and shirts. 신사용 장신구류(類). **2** Ⓒ a haberdasher's shop. 신사용 장신구점〔양품점〕.

ha·bil·i·ments [həbíləmənts] *n. pl.* **1** items of clothing. 복장《예복·직업복 등》. **2** 《*joc.*》 clothes. 평상복. [→able]

:hab·it [hǽbit] *n.* **1** ⓊⒸ the tendency to do a certain thing without thought or need for it; a usual way of acting. 습관; 버릇. ¶ *the ~ of smoking* 담배 피우는 버릇 / *be in the ~ of sitting up late* 밤늦도록 안 자는 습관이 있다 / *form a good ~* 좋은 습관을 붙이다 / *fall* 〔*get*〕 *into a bad ~* 〔*into the ~ of smoking*〕 못된 습관〔담배 피우는 버릇〕이 붙다 / *give up* 〔*get rid of, get out of, get over*〕 *a bad ~* 나쁜 버릇을 고치다 / *break someone's ~ =get someone out of a ~ =cure someone of a ~* 아무의 버릇을 고치다 / *Habit is* (*a*) *second nature.* 습관은 제 2의 천성 / *He does it merely out of ~.* 그는 습관상 그렇게 하는 데 지나지 않는다. **2** ⓊⒸ the condition of the body or mind. 체질; 기질. ¶ *a cheerful ~* 쾌활한 기질 / *a man of corpulent ~* 비만형〔성〕의 사람. **3** Ⓒ a special character of an animal or a plant. 습성. ¶ *a twining ~* 휘감기는 습성. **4** Ⓒ ⓐ a special set of clothes, esp. that worn by monks and nuns. (어떤 계층의)복장; 특히, 성직복(聖職服). ¶ *a monk's* 〔*nun's*〕 *~* 수사(修士)〔수녀〕복. ⓑ a woman's riding dress. 여성용 승마복.

break oneself of a habit, become free from one's own habit. (자기)의 버릇을 고치다.

break someone of a habit, cause someone to give up his habit. 아무의 버릇을 고치다.

— *vt.* (P6) put a dress on (someone); clothe(esp. in the dress of a monk). …에 입히다; …을 입다. ¶ *~ oneself in black* 검은 옷을 입다 / *be habited in white* 흰 옷을 입고 있다. [L. *habeo* have]

hab·it·a·ble [hǽbətəbəl] *adj.* fit to live in. 살기에 적합한. ¶ *a ~ house* / *Repairs have made the house ~.* 수리를 해서 집이 살기 좋게 됐다. ● **hab·it·a·bly** [-li] *adv.* [*habitat*]

hab·it·ant [hǽbətənt] *n.* an inhabitant. 사는 사람; 거주자.

hab·i·tat [hǽbətæ̀t] *n.* Ⓒ **1** the natural home of an animal or a plant. (동식물의) 산지(產地); 서식지; 생육지. ¶ *The polar region is the ~ of the polar bear.* 극지방은 북극곰의 서식지다. **2** a living place. 사는 곳; 주소. [L.=it inhabits]

hab·i·ta·tion [hæ̀bətéiʃən] *n.* **1** Ⓒ a place to live in; a dwelling; a home. 주거지; 주소; 주택. **2** Ⓤ the act of inhabiting. 거주. ¶ *a house no longer fit for ~* 더는 살기에 나쁜 집.

***ha·bit·u·al** [həbítʃuəl] *adj.* **1** (of a thing) acting by habit. 습관적인; 예의. ¶ *one's ~ seat* 여느 때와 같은 자리 / *~ morning walks* 습관적인 아침 산책. **2** (of a person) doing something by habit. 상습적인; 습성적인. ¶ *a ~ criminal* 상습범 / *a ~ drunkard* 술꾼; 알코올 중독자. [→habit]

ha·bit·u·al·ly [həbítʃuəli] *adv.* as a habit; regularly. 습관적으로; 늘. ¶ *~ late* 늘 늦는〔지각하는〕.

ha·bit·u·ate [həbítʃuèit] *vt.* (P13) **1** 《*to*》 cause (someone) to form a habit; accustom. …을 익숙게 하다; 습관들이다. ¶ *~ oneself to a cold climate* 추운 기후에 익숙해지다 / *He was habituated to hard work.* 그는 중노동에 익숙해져 있었다. **2** visit (the same place) very often. …에 잘〔자주〕 가다.
● **ha·bit·u·a·tion** [həbìtʃuéiʃən] *n.* [→habit]

hab·i·tude [hǽbitjùːd] *n.* the habitual way of acting; custom. 습관; 습성; 성벽(性癖). [↑]

ha·bit·u·é [həbítʃuèi] *n.* Ⓒ 《F.》 a person who is in the habit of going to a place regularly. 단골 손님. ¶ *a ~ of bars and*

H

nightclubs 바나 나이트 클럽의 단골 손님.

hack[1] [hæk] *vt.* (P6,7) **1** ⓐ cut roughly; cut (something) to pieces. (난폭하게) …을 자르다; 찍다. ¶ ~ *down trees* 나무를 찍어 넘기다 / *The pole was hacked to pieces with an axe.* 전봇대는 도끼로 쳐 토막이 났다. ⓑ sow while breaking up the soil. 흙을 갈아 씨를 뿌리다. ¶ ~ *in wheat* 흙을 갈면서 밀의 파종을 하다. **2** 《Brit.》 kick the shin of. (럭비에서 상대)의 정강이를 까다. —*vi.* (P3) give short, dry coughs. (잦은) 마른기침을 하다. ¶ *a hacking cough* 마른기침. —*n.* Ⓒ **1** a rough cut. 마구 쳐 자르기. **2** a tool for cutting. 도끼·곡괭이류(類). **3** a short dry cough. 마른기침. [E.]

hack[2] [hæk] *n.* Ⓒ **1** 《U.S.》 a coach or carriage for hire. 전세 마차. **2** 《*colloq.*》 a taxi. **3** 《Brit.》 a horse for hire. 임대(賃貸) 말. **4** an old, worn-out horse. 늙다리 말. **5** a horse for riding. 승용마(乘用馬). **6** 《*fig.*》 a person employed to do uninteresting work, esp. writing. (특히) 문필가의 조수; 남의 밑에서 허드렛일을 하는 사람.
—*vi.* (P1) **1** ride a horse. 말을 타다. **2** work as a hack. 남의 밑에서 일하다.
—*vt.* (P6) **1** hire out (a horse). (말)을 세주다. **2** employ (someone) as a hack. (문필가가) …을 조수로 고용하다. **3** make hackneyed. …을 써서 낡게 만들다.
—*adj.* working merely for money; hired. 돈 때문에 일하는; 고용된. ¶ *a ~ writer* 문필가의 조수. [*hackney*]

hack·er [hǽkər] *n.* a person who is able to use or change the information in other people's computer systems without their knowledge or permission. 해커《불법으로 남의 컴퓨터를 작동[조작]하는 사람》. [→hack[1]]

hack·le[1] [hǽkəl] *n.* **1** a comb used in dressing flax, hemp, etc. (삼 따위를) 훑는 빗. **2** one of the long, slender feathers on the neck of a rooster, pigeons, etc. 수탉 따위 목 둘레의 깃털의 하나《제물낚시용》. **3** 《*pl.*》 the neck plumage of certain birds. 수탉 따위의 목둘레의 깃털. ¶ *get one's hackles up about nothing* 아무것도 아닌 일에 성을 내다. [M.E. *hakell*]
with one's hackles up, (of a cock, dog, or man) very angry; ready to fight. 격분해서; 싸울 태세로.

hack·le[2] [hǽkəl] *vt.* (P6) cut roughly. 냅다 자르다; 토막 내다. [→hack[1]]

hack·ney [hǽkni] *n.* Ⓒ **1** a horse used chiefly for riding. (보통의) 승용마(馬). **2** a carriage for hire. 전세 마차. —*adj.* hired; ordinary; not new. 임대의; 평범한; 신선미가 없는. —*vt.* (P6) **1** use (a horse, etc.) too often. …을 혹사하다. **2** make commonplace. 진부하게 만들다. [F.]

hackney carriage [∠- ∠-] *n.* a carriage or coach for hire. 전세 마차.

hackney coach [∠- ∠] *n.* =hackney carriage.

hack·neyed [hǽknid] *adj.* well-worn; used too often; made common. 자주 써서 낡은; 평범한; 진부한. ¶ *a ~ phrase* 진부한 [틀에 박힌] 문구.

·hack·saw [hǽksɔ̀ː] *n.* Ⓒ a narrow, toothed blade with a frame for cutting metal. (금속을 자르는) 쇠톱. [*hack*[1]]

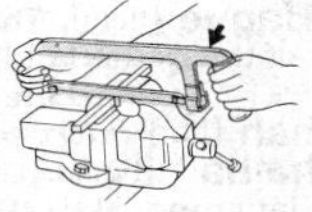
〈hacksaw〉

:had [hæd, həd, əd, d] *v.* p. and pp. of **have.**
be had, be tricked or made a fool of. 속다; 봉변하다. ¶ *I've been ~! Those eggs I bought are all bad.* 당했다, 모조리 상한 달걀을 샀잖아.
had as good [***well***] (*do*), would prefer to do. …하는 편이 좋(겠)다.
(*You*) ***had better*** (*do*), (You) would be wiser to do. …하는 편이 좋(겠)다.
(*You*) ***had better have*** (*done*), (You) would have been wiser to do, but (you) didn't. …하는 편이 좋았다[좋았을걸].
(*I*) ***had rather*** (*do*), (I) would prefer to do. 차라리 …하는 편이 좋다.

Ha·des [héidiːz] *n.* **1** 《Gk. myth.》 the resting place of the dead, below the earth; Pluto, the king of this place. 지하계; 황천; 하이데스《명부의 왕》. **2** Ⓒ 《*h-*》 《*colloq.*》 a hell. 지옥. [Gk. orig. =Pluto]

:had·n't [hǽdnt] had not.

·hadst [hædst, hədst] 《*arch.*》 =had. 語法 주어 thou에 쓰임. ¶ *Thou ~.*

hae·mo·glo·bin [hìːməglóubin] *n.* =hemoglobin.

haem·or·rhage [héməridʒ] *n.* =hemorrhage.

haft [hæft, hɑːft] *n.* Ⓒ the handle of a knife, sword, etc. (칼·검 따위의) 자루; 손잡이. —*vt.* (P6) furnish (a knife, etc.) with a handle. 칼자루를 달다. [E.]

hag [hæg] *n.* Ⓒ **1** a very ugly old woman. 몹시 추한 할멈[노파]. **2** a witch. 마녀. [E.]

hag·gard [hǽgərd] *adj.* worn-out and anxious in appearance from tiredness, worry, etc. (피곤·걱정 따위로) 야윈; 수척한. ¶ *be ~ from overwork* 과로(過勞)로 야위다.
● **hag·gard·ly** [-li] *adv.* **hag·gard·ness** [-nis] *n.* [?↑, F. *hagard*]

hag·gle [hǽgəl] *vi.* (P1,2A,3) 《*about, over*》 talk to someone about a price; dispute or wrangle in bargaining. 쩨쩨하고 성가시게 자꾸 값을 깎다; (가격 때문에) 승강이[입씨름]하다. ¶ *The woman haggled over the price of the butter.* 여인은 성가시게 버터의 값을 자꾸 깎았다. —*n.* haggling. 값을 깎기 위한 승강이; 입씨름; 언쟁. [N.]

hag·i·ol·o·gy [hæ̀giɑ́lədʒi, hèidʒ- / hæ̀giɔ́l-] *n.* literature dealing with the lives of saints. 성인(聖人) 문학; 성인전(傳). [Gk. *hágios* holy]

hag·rid·den [hǽgrìdn] *adj.* annoyed by nightmares or unreasoning fears. (악몽·이유 없는 공포에) 시달리는. [→hag, -ridden]

Hague [heig], **The** *n.* the political capital of the Netherland. 헤이그. 參考 헌법상의 수도는 Amsterdam.

hah [hɑː] *interj.* =ha.

ha·ha [hɑ̀ːhɑ́ː] *interj.* the sound of laughing. 하하(하)《웃음 소리》. [Imit.]

hail[1] [heil] *vt.* **1** (P6,7,19) shout a welcome to (someone); greet. …을 환호하여 맞이하다; …을 환영하다; …에게 인사하다. ¶ *~ someone and give him one's hand* 아무에게 인사하고 악수의 손을 내밀다 / *They hailed him as king.* 그들은 왕이라고 부르며 그를 맞이했다. **2** (P6) call loudly; shout; summon. …을 큰 소리로 부르다. ¶ *~ a taxi* 〔*cab*〕 택시를 부르다 / *~ a passing friend* 지나가던 친구를 부르다.

— *vi.* (P3) **1** 《*from*》 come. …에서 오다; …출신이다. ¶ *He hails from France.* 그는 프랑스 출신이다. **2** 《naut.》 call out or signal to a ship. 배를 향해 부르다; 신호하다.

— *n.* Ⓤ **1** the act of greeting; a shout of welcome. 인사; 환호. **2** a loud call. 소리침; 부르는 소리.

***be hail fellow well met** (**with** someone),* be always friendly with (someone) or pretend to be so. (아무)와 늘 사이가 좋(은 체하)다.

within 〔***out of***〕 ***hail,*** near enough (too far) to be hailed. 목소리가 미치는〔미치지 않는〕 곳에.

— *interj.* an exclamation of greeting. 만세. ¶ *Hail to the king!* 국왕 만세. [N.→hale[1]]

:hail[2] [heil] *n.* **1** Ⓤ small, round bits of ice that fall in a shower. 우박. **2** Ⓒ 《usu. *a ~*》 《*fig.*》 anything that falls like hail. 우박처럼 쏟아지는 것. ¶ *a ~ of bullets* 우박처럼 날아오는 탄알 / *a ~ of questions* 빗발같이 쏟아지는 질문 / *a ~ of blows* 주먹 세례.

— *vi.* (P1) come down in hail. 우박이 내리다. ¶ *It hails.* 우박이 내린다. 語法 비인칭의 it가 주어.

— *vt.* (P6) 《*on, upon*》 pour (something) in a shower like hail. …을 우박처럼 쏟아지게 하다; 빗발처럼 퍼붓다. ¶ *They hailed blows upon him.* 그에게 주먹 세례를 퍼부었다 / *The crowd hailed stones on the thief.* 군중은 도둑에게 마구 돌멩이질을 했다. [E.]

hail·stone [héilstòun] *n.* Ⓒ a small, round ball of ice coming down from thunder clouds. 우박(의 알갱이).

hail·storm [héilstɔ̀ːrm] *n.* Ⓒ a storm with hail. 어지러이 쏟아지는 우박.

:hair [hɛər] *n.* **1** Ⓤ threadlike outgrowths from the skin of man and animals; the growth covering the human head; anything like this. 털; 모발; 털 모양의 것. 語法 집합적으로 '두발(頭髮)'을 전반적으로 가리킬 때에는 불가산어(不可算語). '털 한 가닥, 두 가닥'이라고 할 때에는 a hair, hairs로 됨. ¶ *the ~ of the head* 머리카락 / *wash one's ~* 머리를 감다 / *dress one's ~* 조발(調髮)하다 / *dye one's ~* 머리를 염색하다 / *grow one's ~* 머리를 기르다 / *have one's ~ cut* 머리를 깎다; 이발하다 / *find a ~ in one's soup* 수프 속에서 머리털 하나를 발견하다 / *pluck out a ~* 머리털을 한 가닥 뽑다 / *She has lovely ~.* 그녀는 머리가 아름답다. **2** Ⓒ an extremely small space, distance, degree, etc. (정도·시간적·공간적으로) 극히 조금. ¶ *do not care a ~* 조금도 상관〔개의〕치 않다 / *He missed the target by a ~.* 과녁을 약간 빗맞혔다. **3** Ⓤ cloth made of hair from camels or alpaca. (낙타·알파카 털로 짠) 모직물. [E.]

against the hair, against the grain; contrary to its nature. 성질〔의향〕에 반하여; 본의(本意) 아니게.

***a hair of the dog that bit** someone,* poison which quells poison. 이독 제독(以毒制毒); 해장술.

be not worth a hair, be of no value. 전혀 가치가 없다.

by the 〔***a***〕 ***turn of a hair,*** narrowly. 간신히; 아슬아슬하게.

comb** someone's **hair for him, scold him severely. 아무를 호되게 꾸짖다.

do not turn a hair, give no sign of being troubled. 곤란한 기색이 조금도 없다.

get** someone **by the short hairs, 《*sl.*》 have him at one's mercy; have complete control over him. 아무를 제마음대로 하다; 완전히 지배하고 있다.

get in** someone's **hair, annoy; make (someone) angry. 아무를 괴롭히다〔귀찮게 하다〕; 약올리다. ¶ *I find the children get in my ~ during the school holidays.* 방학 때면 아이들 때문에 성가시다.

keep** one's **hair on, do not get excited. 흥분하지〔화내지〕 않다; 침착을 잃지 않다.

let 〔***put***〕 ***down** one's **hair*** =***let** one's **hair down,*** **a**) (of a woman) allow the hair to fall over the shoulders. (여자가) 머리를 풀어 어깨 위로 늘어뜨리다. **b**) 《*colloq.*》 relax; speak frankly. (마음·몸을) 편히 가지다; 편하게 행동하다; 솔직히 이야기하다.

lose one's hair, **a**) become bald. 머리가 벗어지다. **b**) lose one's temper. 성을 내다; 흥분하다.

make** someone's **hair stand on end, fill (someone) with great fear. …을 머리끝이 쭈뼛하게〔등골이 오싹하게〕 만들다. ¶ *The tales of the jungle made our ~ stand on end.* 밀림의 이야기로 머리끝이 쭈뼛해졌다.

not turn a hair, show no fear in a trying situation; show no fatigue; show no surprise. 태연하다; 피로한〔놀란〕 기색을 보이지 않다.

put 〔***turn***〕 ***up** one's **hair*** =***put** one's **hair up,*** (esp. of a girl) begin to wear her hair rolled up on the head as a woman. (특히 소녀가) 어른처럼 머리를 얹다; 어른이 되다.

split hairs, talk or argue over unimportant points. (대수롭지 않은 것을) 잔달게 논하다(구별하다)(cf. *hairsplitting*).

tear one's hair, show signs of much pain, grief, or anger. 머리를 쥐어뜯다; 몹시 아파(슬퍼)하다; 극도로 분개하다.

to (the turn of) a hair, exactly. 정확히; 딱.

hair·breadth [hέərbrèdθ, -brètθ] *adj.* very narrow; very near. 털끝만한 폭의; 간(위기)일발의; 아슬아슬한. ¶ *a ~ escape* 구사 일생. — *n.* Ⓒ a very narrow space; a very small distance. 털끝만한 폭(간격); 아슬아슬함. ¶ *by a ~* 간일발로; 간신히.

within a hairbreadth of, very nearly; almost. 하마터면; 까딱하면. ¶ *within a ~ of being killed* 하마터면 죽을 뻔하여.

hair·brush [hέərbrʌ̀ʃ] *n.* Ⓒ a brush for hair. 머리솔.

hair·cloth [hέərklɔ̀(ː)θ, -klɑ̀θ] *n.* Ⓤ cloth woven with horsehair, etc. (말·낙타 따위의 털로 짠) 모직천.

hair·cut [hέərkʌ̀t] *n.* Ⓒ the act or style of cutting the hair. 머리깎기; 이발. ¶ *have (get) a ~.*

hair·do [hέərdùː] *n.* Ⓒ (*pl.* **-dos**) 《*colloq.*》 a way of arranging the hair, usu. of women. (여성들의) 머리 스타일; 조발(調髮).

hair·dress·er [hέərdrèsər] *n.* Ⓒ a person who takes care of the hair. 이발사; 미용사 (cf. *barber*).

hair·dress·ing [hέərdrèsiŋ] *n.* Ⓤ **1** the trade of a hairdresser. (여성 머리의) 미용업. **2** the act of dressing the hair. (여성 머리의) 조발(調髮); 머리 치장.

hair·less [hέərlis] *adj.* without hair; bald. 머리가 없는; 벗어진.

hair·line [hέərlàin] *n.* **1** a very thin line. (서화의) 매우 가는 선. **2** the outline of the growth of hair on the head, esp. across the front. (특히 앞이마에 난) 머리선.

hair net [ˊ-ˋ] *n.* a net worn to hold the hair in place. 헤어 네트.

hair oil [ˊ-ˋ] *n.* oil for dressing the hair. 머릿기름.

hair·pin [hέərpìn] *n.* Ⓒ a small, bent pin of wire, shell, etc., to hold the hair in place. 머리핀. — *adj.* U-shaped. U자 모양의. ¶ *a ~ bend (turn),* U 자형으로 구부러진 길 / *a ~ curve in the road* 도로상의 급커브.

hair-rais·ing [hέərrèiziŋ] *adj.* 《*colloq.*》 making the hair stand on end; terrifying. 머리털이 곤두서게 하는; 등골이 오싹하는.

hair's-breadth, hairs·breadth [hέərzbrèdθ] *n., adj.* =hairbreadth.

hair·split·ter [hέərsplìtər] *n.* Ⓒ a person who makes too fine or unnecessary differences. (쓸데없는 일에) 세세한 구별을 하는 사람; 쓸데없이 따지는 사람.

hair·split·ting [hέərsplìtiŋ] *adj., n.* Ⓤ making too fine distinction. 쓸데없는 구별(을 하는); 쓸데없이 따지는.

hair·spring [hέərsprìŋ] *n.* Ⓒ a delicate, hairlike coil spring that controls the balance wheel in a watch. (회중 시계의) 유사(遊絲).

hair·y [hέəri] *adj.* (**hair·i·er, hair·i·est**) **1** covered with hair. 털이 많은; 털로 뒤덮인. ¶ *~ hands* 털 많은 손. **2** of or like hair. 털의; 털 같은. ● **hair·i·ness** [-nis] *n.*

Hai·ti [héiti] *n.* a country in the West Indies. 아이티. 參考 수도는 Port-au-Prince.

hake [heik] *n.* (*pl.* **hakes** or *collectively* **hake**) 《fish》 fish of the cod family. 대구류(類). [? N]

ha·kim [hɑːkíːm] *n.* a physician; a Muslim doctor. (인도·이슬람국의) 의사. [Arab.]

ha·la·tion [heiléiʃən, hæ- / hə-] *n.* Ⓤ 《photog.》 the excessive spread of light in a negative print. 헐레이션; 훈영(暈影). [*hal(o), -ation*]

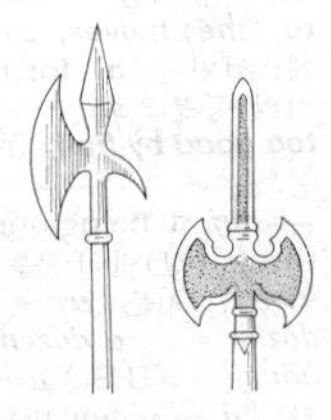

〈halberd〉

hal·berd [hǽlbərd, hɔ́ːl-] *n.* Ⓒ a weapon formed of a spear and an axe, used in the 15th and 16th centuries. 도끼창《창과 도끼를 겸한 무기》. [Teut. =helmet-axe]

hal·bert [hǽlbərt, hɔ́ːl-] *n.* =halberd.

hal·cy·on [hǽlsiən] *adj.* (of the weather) calm; peaceful. (날씨가) 평온한; 평화로운; 잔잔한. ¶ *~ weather* 평온한 날씨 / *a ~ atmosphere* 평화스런 분위기 / *~ days* 평온 무사한 시대. — *n.* a kingfisher that was supposed to calm the waves. 물총새《풍랑을 가라앉힌다는 상상의 새》. [Gk. =kingfisher]

hale[1] [heil] *adj.* healthy; strong and well. 건강한; 정정한. [→whole]

hale and hearty, (esp. of an old person) strong and healthy. (특히 노인 등이) 기력이 왕성한; 정정한.

hale[2] [heil] *vt.* (P6,7) 《*lit., arch.*》 drag by force; bring or take (someone) somewhere by force. …을 세게(거칠게) 끌다; 끌어당기다; (법정)에 끌어내다(cf. *haul*). ¶ *~ someone into court* 아무를 법정으로 끌어내다. [Teut.]

:half [hæf, hɑːf] *n.* Ⓒ (*pl.* **halves**) **1** one of two equal parts, or a quantity equal to such a part. (절)반; 2분의 1. ¶ *~ (of) the boys* 남자 아이들의 반수 / *five miles and a ~* 5마일 반 / *(The) ~ of 4 is 2.* 4의 반은 2다 / *Cut it in ~.* 그것을 반으로 잘라라 / *Half (of) the pear is rotten.* 배의 반은 썩었다(cf. *Half (of) the pears are rotten.* 배의 반수는 썩었다). 語法 관사의 앞에 옴. 뒤에 명사가 계속될 때에는 of를 생략할 때가 많음. 대명사일 때에는 half of it 로 함. 또한 half를 주어로 하는 술어 동사는 half 뒤에 오는 명사

의 수에 의해서 지배됨. **2** either of the two equal periods of a game. 후반 또는 전반전.

by half, **a**) to the extent of half. 반만큼; 반 정도로. ¶ *I will reduce the sum by* ~. 반값으로 깎아 드리죠. **b**) 《*iron.*》 by far; very much. 너무나(도); 매우. ¶ *He is too clever by* ~. 너무나 약다.

by halves, imperfectly. 불완전하게; 중동무이로. ¶ *Don't do things by halves.* 일을 아무렇게나 해서는 안 된다.

cry halves, demand to share equally. (절)반을 요구하다.

cut in half [***into halves***], cut in two. 반으로 쪼개다.

go halves (***with*** *someone* ***in*** *something*), share (something) equally with someone. (둘이서) 절반씩[똑같이] 나누다.

have half a mind to *do,* feel like doing. …하고 싶은 마음이 들다.

to (***the***) ***halves,*** **a**) incompletely. 불완전하게; 절반만. **b**) for half the crop or profits. 이익 등분으로.

too good by half, far too good. 지나치게 좋은.

— *adj.* **1** being one of two equal parts of a thing. (절)반의; 2분의 1의. ¶ *the first* ~ *hour* 최초의 30분 / *a* ~ *share* 절반의 몫 / *a* ~ *dozen* = ~ *a dozen* 반 다스 / ~ *a mile* [*an hour*] = 《U.S.》 *a* ~ *mile* [*hour*] 반 마일[시간] / *a* ~ *moon* 반달 / 《*prov.*》 *Half a loaf is better than no bread.* 반이라도 없는 것보다는 낫다. **2** partial; incomplete. 부분적인; 불충분한; 불완전한. ¶ *a* ~ *knowledge* 어설픈 지식 / ~ *measures* 어정쩡한 조치 / *a* ~ *truth* 반면(半面)만의 진리.

— *adv.* **1** to the degree or extent of a half; partially; almost. 반(쯤); 부분적으로; 일부분; 불충분하게; 거의. ¶ *a biscuit* ~ *done* 설구운 비스킷 / *be* ~ *informed as to* … 에 대해 충분히 알고 있지 못하다 / *It is* ~ *past five.* 다섯 시 반이다 / *He was* ~ *dead from hunger.* 그는 아사(餓死) 직전이었다. **2** to some extent. 어느 정도; 얼마쯤. ¶ *speak* ~ *aloud* 어느 정도 큰 소리로 말하다 / *be* ~ *recovered* 얼마쯤 회복돼 있다. [E.]

half as much [***many***] ***again*** (***as***), one and a half times as much [many] (as). …의 1배 반.

half the time, 《U.S.》 almost always. 거의 언제나.

more than half, very much. 매우; 몹시. ¶ *He was more than* ~ *afraid.* 무척 두려워했다.

not half, **a**) not at all. 조금도 …아니다[…하지 않다]. ¶ *It isn't* ~ *windy today!* 바람이 여간 센 날이 아니다 / *I don't* ~ *like it.* 조금도 좋아하지 않는다. **b**) very much. 매우; 무척. ¶ *Do you like beer? —Oh, not* ~*!* 맥주를 좋아하나—그럼 아주 무척 / *She didn't* ~ *cry.* 그녀는 몹시 울었다.

not half bad, fairly good; actually quite good. 꽤 좋은.

half-a-crown [hǽfəkráun, hɑ́:f-] *n.* **1** Ⓒ a British silver coin worth 2s. 6d. 반(半)크라운의 은화. **2** Ⓤ the amount of 2s. 6d. 2실링 6펜스의 금액(cf. *crown* 6).

half-and-half [hǽfəndhǽf, hɑ́:fəndhɑ́:f] *adj.* **1** half one thing and half another; composed of two parts. 반반의; 두 부분으로 된. ¶ *a* ~ *mixture* 반반의 혼합물. **2** not clearly one thing or the other. 중동무이의; 이도저도 아닌. ¶ ~ *enthusiasm* 어정쩡한 열의. — *adv.* in two equal parts; equally. 반반으로; 같게.

— *n.* Ⓤ **1** 《U.S.》 a mixture of milk and cream. 우유와 크림의 혼합 음료. **2** 《Brit.》 a mixture of ale and porter. (ale 과 porter 의) 혼합주.

half·back [hǽfbæ̀k, hɑ́:f-] *n.* Ⓒ 《football, hockey》 a player whose position is behind the forward line. 하프백; 중위(中衛).

half-baked [hǽfbéikt, hɑ́:f-] *adj.* **1** not completely cooked. 설구워진. **2** 《*colloq.*》 not complete. 불완전[불충분]한. ¶ *a* ~ *plan* 불완전한 계획. **3** 《*colloq.*》 not thorough; socially inexperienced; foolish. 데아는; 무경험의; 미숙한; 어리석은. ¶ *a* ~ *youth* 미숙한 젊은이 / *a* ~ *proposal for tax reform* 신중하지 못한 세제 개혁안(案).

half-blood [hǽfblʌ̀d, hɑ́:f-] *n.* Ⓒ **1** a half-breed. 잡종; 혼혈아. **2** a person related to another by having one common parent. 배다른[각성(各姓)바지] 형제 자매. — *adj.* having only one parent in common with another person. 배다른; 각성바지의. ¶ ~ *brothers.*

half blood [ˊˋ] *n.* the relation between persons who are related through having one common parent. 배다른[각성바지] 형제 자매 관계.

half-boiled [hǽfbɔ́ild, hɑ́:f-] *adj.* not completely boiled. 설익힌; 설끓인; 반숙의.

half boot [ˊˋ] *n.* a boot extending about halfway to the knee. 반장화; 편상화.

half-bred [hǽfbrèd, hɑ́:f-] *adj.* **1** having parents of different races. 잡종의; 혼혈의. **2** ill-bred; rude. 본데[버릇, 예절]없는.

half-breed [hǽfbrì:d, hɑ́:f-] *n.* Ⓒ a person whose parents are of different races. (esp. the offspring of a white man and an American Indian). 튀기; 혼혈아; 잡종. — *adj.* of mixed breed, race, etc. 혼혈의; 잡종의.

half brother [ˊˋˋ] *n.* a brother related through one parent only. 배[씨]다른 형제.

half-caste [hǽfkæ̀st, hɑ́:fkɑ̀:st] *n.* Ⓒ **1** a child of mixed race, esp. of one European parent and one Hindu or Mohammedan parent. 구아(歐亞) 혼혈아. **2** a half-breed person. 혼혈아; 튀기.

half-cooked [hǽfkúkt, hɑ́:f-] *adj.* half-done; not well-cooked. 설익은; 설구운; 반숙의; 미숙의.

half-heart·ed [hǽfhɑ́:rtid, hɑ́:f-] *adj.*

with little interest, eagerness, etc. 마음이 내키지 않는; 열의가 없는; 냉담한. ¶ *He made a ~ attempt to take part with her.* 마지못해 그녀의 편을 들기로 했다. ● **half-heart·ed·ly** [-li] *adv.*

half-hour [hǽfàuər, hɑ́:fàuər] *n.* Ⓒ thirty minutes. 반시간; 30분. — *adj.* of or lasting a half-hour. 반시간의. ● **half·hour·ly** [-li] *adv.*

half-length [hǽflèŋkθ, hɑ́:f-] *adj.* (of a portrait) showing only the upper part of the body. 반신 크기의; 반신상(像)의. ¶ *a ~ portrait / a ~ coat* 반코트. — *n.* Ⓒ a portrait showing only the upper part of the body. 반신상.

half-mast [hǽfmǽst, hɑ́:fmɑ́:st] *n.* Ⓤ (of a flag) the position half-way from the top of a pole, etc. 반기(半旗)의 위치. ¶ *All the flags were at ~ when the king died.* 국왕의 사망으로 모든 기는 반기로 했다. — *adj.* at half mast. 반기의 위치에 단. — *vt., vi.* (P6; 1) fly at half-mast. (반기를) 달다.

half note [ㅅㅅ] *n.* 《U.S. mus.》 a note equal to one half of a whole note. 2분 음표.

half pay [ㅅㅅ] *n.* 《Brit.》 Ⓒ pay given to an officer of the army or navy when not employed or when retired, generally more than half the full pay. (육해군 장교의 감액된) 휴직급(給); 퇴직금.

half·pence [héipəns] *n.* pl. of **halfpenny.**

half·pen·ny [héipəni] *n.* Ⓒ (*pl.* **-pen·nies** or **-pence**) a British bronze coin worth half a penny. 반(半)페니 동화(銅貨); 반페니(의 가치). ¶ *receive more kicks than halfpence* 칭찬은 커녕 혼이 나다.

like a bad halfpenny, turning up when not wanted. 찾지도 않을 때 잘 나타나는.

not have two halfpennies to rub together, be very poor. 피천 한 닢 없다; 알거지가 되다.

— *adj.* **1** worth only a halfpenny. 반페니〔반푼〕의. **2** having little value. 가치 없는; 싸구려의.

half·pen·ny·worth [héipəniwə̀:rθ] *n.* Ⓤ **1** 《*collectively*》 things worth a halfpenny. 반(半)페니 짜리 것. **2** a trifling value; only a little bit. 저(低)가치; 극히 조금; 극소량.

half-price [hǽfpráis, hɑ́:f-] *adv.* at half the usual price. 반액으로.

half sister [ㅅㅅ—] *n.* a sister by one parent only. 배다른〔의붓〕 자매.

half sole [ㅅㅅ] *n.* a sole of a shoe, from the toe to the instep. 구두의 앞창.

half-sole [hǽfsòul, hɑ́:f-] *vt.* repair (a shoe) by putting on a new half sole. (구두에) 새 앞창을 대다.

half sovereign [ㅅㅅ—] *n.* a British gold coin with the value of ten shillings. 반(半)파운드의 금화. 參考 현재는 발행되지 않음.

half-time [hǽftàim, hɑ́:f-] **1** work and pay for the day only. 반일 노동; 반일급(給). **2** the interval between the halves of a game. (경기의) 하프타임.

half·tone [hǽftòun, hɑ́:f-] *n.* **1** a printing process in which a picture reproducing light and dark shades is obtained by means of a screen placed in the camera just in front of the sensitized plate. (사진 제판에서) 망판(網版); 망판 인쇄. **2** 《mus.》 semitone. 반음.

***half·way** [hǽfwéi, hɑ́:f-] *adv.* half the way; in the middle. 중간에〔까지〕; 중도에(서); 도중까지. ¶ *~ up* 〔*down*〕 *the hill* 산 중턱에(서) / *turn back ~* 중도에서 되돌아오다 / *a rope reaching only ~* 중간까지밖에 미치지 않는 밧줄.

meet someone halfway, 《*fig.*》 be ready for compromise with someone. (…와) 타협을 하다.

— *adj.* midway; not complete. 중간의; 중도의; 불완전한. ¶ *~ measures* 철저하지 못한 수단 / *assume a ~ position* 어정쩡한 입장을 취하다.

halfway house [ㅅㅅ] *n.* an inn or other house about midway between two towns. 두 읍내 중간쯤에 있는 여인숙.

half-wit [hǽfwìt hɑ́:f-] *n.* a stupid, foolish person. 정신박약자; 바보.

half-wit·ted [hǽfwítid, hɑ́:f-] *adj.* weak in the mind; very stupid; foolish. 정신박약의; 저능의; 멍텅구리의.

half-year·ly [hǽfjíərli, hɑ́:fjíər-] *adj.* happening every six months. 반년마다의. — *adv.* at six-month intervals. 반년마다.

hal·i·but [hǽləbət, hɑ́l-] *n.* Ⓒ (*pl.* **-buts** or *collectively* **-but**) a large, flat sea fish used for food. 핼리벗《큰 넙치》. [*holy* (as used on holy days) *butt* flat fish]

:hall [hɔ:l] *n.* Ⓒ **1** 《U.S.》 a passageway in a building. 복도. **2** a room at the entrance of a building. 현관(의 공간); 문간. ¶ *Leave your umbrella in the ~.* 우산은 현관에 놔 두시오. **3** a large room for public meetings, parties, etc. 홀; (집회·파티용) 큰 방; 강당. ¶ *a servant's ~* 하인방《하인의 거실·식당용》. **4** a public building. 회관; 공회당. ¶ *a concert ~* 연주회장 / *the Agricultural Hall* 농업 회관 / *a town ~* 읍사무소〔공회당〕. **5** a building of a school, college, or university. 교사(校舍); (대학의) 강당; 집회소. ¶ *the Student's Hall* 학생 회관. **6** the house of an English landowner; a manor house. (지주의) 저택. [E.]

hal·le·lu·jah, -lu·iah [hæ̀ləlú:jə] *interj., n.* an expression in praise of God; a song of praise to God. 할렐루야《신을 찬미하는 말》; 할렐루야 성가(聖歌). [Heb. =praise Jehovah]

hal·liard [hǽljərd] *n.* =halyard.

hall·mark [hɔ́:lmɑ̀:rk] *n.* Ⓒ **1** a mark showing the standard of gold and silver in articles. (금은의) 순분 검증인(純分檢證印). **2** 《*fig.*》 a mark or sign of good quality. 품질 증명; 보증. ¶ *Politeness is the ~ of a gentle-*

man. 예의 바름은 신사임을 증명한다. — *vt.* (P6) put a hallmark on (something or someone). …에 각인(刻印)을 찍다; (…의 품질을) 보증하다. [*hall*]

hal·lo [həlóu, hælóu] *interj., n.* **1** a shout to get attention. 어이; 여보(세요). **2** a call of greeting or surprise; hello. 여; 저런; 어머《인사나 놀람의 소리》(cf. *hello, hullo*). **3** a shout. 소리침; 환호의 외침. ¶ *give a loud* ~ 환호의 소리를 지르다. — *vi.* (P1) shout. 소리치다; 외치다. [? O.F. *halloer*]

hal·loo [həlúː] *interj.* **1** a call to make hunting dogs run faster. 쉿《사냥개를 부추기는 소리》. **2** a shout to get attention. 어이; 여보(세요). — *n.* Ⓒ (*pl.* **-loos**) **1** a call to make hunting dogs run faster. 사냥개를 부추기는 소리. **2** a shout to get attention. 남의 주의를 끌기 위해 외치는 소리. **3** Ⓤ the act of calling in a loud voice. 큰소리로 소리치기. ¶ *cry* ~ 큰소리로 외치다. — *vi., vt.* (P1; 6) shout or call. (사냥개를) 부추기다; 부르다. [↑]

Don't halloo till you are out of wood. Never think you have succeeded till all the difficulties have been got over. 완전히 안심할 수 있을 때까지는 지레 기뻐하지 마라.

hal·low [hǽlou] *vt.* (P6) **1** ⓐ make (something) holy. …을 신성하게 하다. ⓑ devote to some sacred use. 신성한 목적에 바치다. **2** regard 〔honor〕 (something) as holy. …을 신성한 것으로 간주하다〔우러르다〕. [→holy]

Hal·low·een, -e'en [hæləwíːn, hɑ̀l-] *n.* the evening of October 31; the eve of All Saints' Day. 모든 성인(聖人)의 날 전야《10월 31일》.

hall·stand [hɔ́ːlstæ̀nd] *n.* Ⓒ a piece of furniture with a mirror, for hanging coats, hats, etc. 홀스탠드《현관에 두고 코트나 모자를 거는, 거울이 달린 가구》. [*hall*]

hal·lu·ci·nate [həlúːsənèit] *vt.* (P6) affect with hallucination. 환각을 일으키다. ¶ *a hallucinated invalid* 환각을 일으키는 병자. [L.]

hal·lu·ci·na·tion [həlùːsənéiʃən] *n.* ⓊⒸ the act of seeing or hearing things that are not really present; something thus seen or heard; an illusion. 환각; 망상; 환영(幻影); 곡두. ¶ *suffer from hallucinations* 환각에 시달리다 / *cling to a* ~ 망상을 버리지 않고 있다 / *be under no* ~ 잘못 생각을 하고 있지는 않다.

hall·way [hɔ́ːlwèi] *n.* Ⓒ **1** 《U.S.》 a passageway in a building. (빌딩의) 복도; 통로. **2** a room at the entrance of a building. 현관. [*hall*]

hal·ma [hǽlmə] *n.* a game played on a checker-board. 장기의 일종. [Gk.]

ha·lo [héilou] *n.* Ⓒ (*pl.* **-los** or **-loes**) **1** a ring of light around the sun or the moon. (해·달의) 무리; 광관(光冠)(cf. *corona*). **2** ⓐ a bright ring or disk of light drawn or painted around the head of a saint in pictures. (성상(聖像)의) 후광; 광륜. ⓑ 《*fig.*》 glory attached to some idealized person, thing, or institution. (이상화된 인물·사물을 둘러싼) 영광(의 느낌). ¶ *the* ~ *around Shakespear's reputation and works.* 셰익스피어의 명성과 작품을 둘러싼 영광. — *vt.* (P6) surround (something) with a halo. 후광으로 두르다.
— *vi.* (P1) form a halo. 후광이 되다. [Gk. *halōs* threshing-floor, the disk of the sun, etc.]

hal·o·gen [hǽlədʒən, -dʒèn, hél-] *n.* 《chem.》 any one of the chemical elements iodine, bromine, chlorine, and fluorine. 할로겐족 원소《조염(造塩) 원소인 플루오르·염소·브롬·요오드·아스타틴의 총칭》. [*halo, -gen*]

:halt[1] [hɔːlt] *vi., vt.* (P1; 6) stop for a time; cause (something) to stop. 멈추(게 하)다; 정지(하게)하다. ¶ ~ *for breath* 멈춰 서서 숨을 돌리다 / ~ *the engine* 엔진을 정지시키다 / ~ *the advance of the troops* 부대의 진군을 정지시키다 / *The car halted at the crossroads.* 차가 네거리에서 멈춰섰다. — *n.* Ⓒ **1** a stop for a time. (멈춰)섬; 정지; 휴식. ¶ *bring one's horse to a* ~ 말을 멈춰세우다 / *call a* ~ 정지를 명하다 / *come to* 〔*make*〕 *a* ~ 멈춰서다 / *come to a dead* ~ 딱 멈추다. **2** a stopping place (smaller than a station) for trains, trams, etc. (역사(驛舍) 없는) 정거장; 정류소. [G.(→hold)]

halt[2] [hɔːlt] *vi.* (P1,2A,3) 《*between, in*》 **1** 《*arch.*》 be lame. 절뚝거리다. **2** hesitate; walk or speak hesitatingly. 망설이다; 주저하다. ¶ *speak in a halting manner* 멈칫거리며 말하다. — *adj.* lame. 절름발이의. [E.]

hal·ter [hɔ́ːltər] *n.* Ⓒ **1** a rope or strap for leading or fastening an animal. (마소의) 고삐. **2** a rope for hanging criminals. 교수용(絞首用) 밧줄. **3** death by hanging. 교살(絞殺); 교수(형). **4** a backless blouse for women which ties around the neck. 홀터《팔과 등이 드러나게 된 여성용 운동복》.

come to the halter, be hanged. 교수형을 당하다.
— *vt.* (P6) tie (something) with a halter; hang. 목을 매다; 교수형으로 하다. [E.]

halt·ing [hɔ́ːltiŋ] *adj.* **1** limping; lame. **2** (of speech, verse, etc.) hesitating; imperfect. (말이) 막히는; (논리의) 앞뒤가 동닿지 않는; (시 따위가) 불완전한. [*halt*[2]]

halve [hæv, hɑːv] *vt.* (P6) **1** divide (something) into two equal parts. …을 2등분〔반분〕하다. ¶ ~ *the profit with someone* 아무와 이익을 반분하다 / ~ *the work with a colleague* 일을 동료와 똑같이 분담하다. **2** lessen (something) to half. …을 반으로 줄이다; 반감(半減)하다. ¶ *They tried to double the profit by halving the cost.* 생산 코스트를 반감시켜 이익을 배로 하려고 했다. [*half*]

halves [hævz, hɑːvz] *n.* pl. of **half.**

hal·yard [hǽljərd] *n.* 《naut.》 a rope

used to raise or lower a sail, flag, etc. 용총줄(돛·깃발 따위를 오르내리는 밧줄). [orig. *hallyer* (→hale²)]

***ham** [hæm] *n.* **1** Ⓤ the upper part of the leg of a pig, smoked and salted for food. 햄. **2** 《anat.》 Ⓒ the back of the thigh, esp. of animals. (특히 동물의) 넓적다리; 오금. **3** 《*pl.*》 buttocks. 둔부. **4** 《*sl.*》 a poor actor. 서투른 배우. **5** Ⓒ 《*sl.*》 an amateur radio operator. 아마추어 무선사; 햄. [E.]

Ham·burg [hǽmbəːrg] *n.* a port of Germany, on the Elbe. 함부르크(독일 서부 Elbe 강에 위치한 항구 도시).

ham·burg·er [hǽmbəːrgər] *n.* Ⓒ 《U.S.》 ground beef, usu. shaped into a small mass and fried; a sandwich filled with this. 햄버그스테이크(다져 조미(調味)한 쇠고기를 둥글게 구운 것); 이것이 든 샌드위치; 햄버거. [→Hamburg]

Hamburg steak [∠-∠] *n.* =hamburger.

ham-fist·ed [hǽmfístid] *adj.* = ham-handed.

ham-hand·ed [hǽmhǽndid] *adj.* unskillful in using the hands. (솜씨가) 서투른; 손끝이 야무지지 못한; 어색한. [*ham*]

Ham·let [hǽmlit] *n.* a famous tragedy by Shakespeare; the main character in this play. 햄릿(Shakespeare 작의 비극; 그 연극의 주인공).

ham·let [hǽmlit] *n.* Ⓒ a very small village. 작은 마을; 한촌(寒村). [*home*]

:ham·mer [hǽmər] *n.* Ⓒ **1** a tool with a heavy metal head, used to drive nails, break things, etc. (쇠)망치; 마치. ¶ *the ~ and sickle* (구(舊)소련의) 국기 / *a knight of the ~* 대장장이 / *throwing the ~* 해머 던지기. **2** a thing like a hammer in shape or use. 망치 모양의 것. ⓐ the part of a gun used for exploding the charge. (총의) 공이치기. ⓑ a wooden mallet used by an auctioneer. (경매인이 쓰는) 나무망치.

bring* 〔*send*〕 *something* *to the hammer, sell something by public sale. …을 경매에 부치다. 參考 경매할 때 hammer를 두드리는 데서.

come under the hammer, be sold by public sale. 경매에 부쳐지다.

go* 〔*be*〕 *at it hammer and tongs, work, fight with all one's force and strength. 전력을 다해 싸우다〔말다툼하다〕; 맹렬한 기세로 일하다.

go to the hammer =come under the hammer.

up to the hammer, first-class; excellent; perfect. 더할 나위 없는; 일류의; 훌륭한.

— *vt., vi.* (P6,7,18; 1,2A,3) **1** hit (something) with a hammer; work with a hammer; make (a piece of metal) flat with a hammer. (…을) 망치로 때리다〔두드리다〕; …을 두들겨 납작하게 펴다. ¶ *~ a horseshoe* 편자를 쳐서 박다 / *~ a nail into the wall* 벽에 못을 망치로 때려박다 / *~ steel into a sword* 강철을 두드려 칼을 만들다. **2** 《*into*》 force (an idea, etc.) into one's head. (사상·생각 따위)를 주입〔명기〕시키다. **3** 《*at*》 work hard. 꾸준히〔열심히〕 일하다. [E.]

hammer at, **a**) work hard at. …을 열심히 하다. ¶ *~ at a task* 일을 열심히 하다 / *~ (away) at English* 영어 공부를 열심히 하다. **b**) strike repeated blows at. …을 계속해서 두드리다. ¶ *There's somebody hammering at the door.* 누군가 문을 계속 두드리는 사람이 있다.

hammer away, **a**) hit (something) again and again. …을 자꾸 때리다〔두드리다〕. **b**) keep working hard at (a task). …을 꾸준히〔열심히〕 계속하다.

hammer* (*away*) *at =hammer at **a**).

hammer down, fasten down by hammering nails into. …에 못을 박아 고정시키다. ¶ *~ down the lid of a box.* 상자 뚜껑에 못을 박다.

hammer in, force in by hammering. 망치로 쳐서 박아 넣다. ¶ *~ in a nail* =*~ a nail in.*

hammer in* 〔*into*〕 *someone's head, force him to know or see. 머리에 처박아 넣다; 주입〔명기〕시키다 / *I can't ~ anything into his thick head.* 그의 둔한 머리에 아무 것도 이해시킬 수가 없다.

hammer out, **a**) flatten out by hammering. 망치로 두드려 납작하게 펴다. ¶ *~ out metal very thin* 금속을 두드려 얇게 펴다. **b**) work out (an idea, etc.) with much effort; shape out by careful thinking. …을 궁리 끝에 생각해내다; 고심하여 만들어내다.

ham·mer·less [hǽmərlis] *adj.* **1** without a hammer. 망치가 없는. **2** (of small arms) having the hammer inside the lock. (총의) 공이치기가 보이지 않는. ¶ *a ~ pistol* 공이치기가 보이지 않는 권총.

ham·mock [hǽmək] *n.* Ⓒ a hanging bed or couch made of canvas, net, etc. suspended by ropes at both ends. 해먹(매단 침상). [Carib.]

Ham·mond organ [hǽmənd ɔ́ːrgən] *n.* a musical instrument resembling a piano in shape. 해먼드 오르간. [Person]

ham·per¹ [hǽmpər] *vt.* (P6) prevent the free movement of; hinder. …을 저지〔억제〕하다; 방해하다. ¶ *He was hampered by gout.* 그는 통풍(痛風) 때문에 마음대로 움직일 수가 없었다. [? E.]

ham·per² [hǽmpər] *n.* Ⓒ a large basket with a cover, used often to contain food. (식품 등을 담는 뚜껑 달린) 대형 바구니. [F.]

Hamp·shire [hǽmpʃiər] *n.* **1** a county of southern England. 햄프셔(영국 잉글랜드 남부의 주(州)). **2** a kind of large sheep. 영국종(種) 양의 일종. **3** a pig having a black body with a white band. 햄프셔 돼지(영국종 검은 돼지의 일종). [Place]

ham·string [hǽmstriŋ] *n.* 《anat.》 **1** one of the tendons behind the knee. 슬괵근(膝膕筋); 무릎 오금근(筋). **2** the great tendon of a four-footed animal. (네발 짐승의) 퇴근(腿

筋). — *vt.* (**ham·strung** [hǽmstrʌŋ] or **ham·stringed**). (P6) cut a hamstring of and make unable to walk properly. …의 근(筋)〔오금〕을 자르다〔잘라 절름발이를 만들다〕. [*ham, string*]

:hand [hænd] *n.* Ⓒ **1** the part of the body at the end of the arm, used for grasping and holding. 손. ¶ *on one's hands and knees* 납죽 엎드려; 손발로 기어 / *take*〔*lead*〕*someone by the* ~ 아무의 손을 잡다〔손을 잡고 이끌다〕/ *let oneself down* ~ *under hand* (줄을) 타고 내려오다 / *let oneself up* ~ *over hand* (줄을) 잡고 오르다. **2** something like a hand in appearance or use. (모양·기능이) 손 비슷한 것. ¶ *the hands of a clock* 시곗바늘 / *the hour*〔*short*〕~ 시침; 단침(短針) / *the minute*〔*long*〕~ 분침; 장침(長針). **3** 《usu. *pl.*》 keeping; possession; power; control. 소유; 수중; 권력; 권한; 지배; 관리. ¶ *strengthen one's* ~ 지배력을 강화(強化)하다 / *fall into the enemy's hands* 적의 수중에 떨어지다〔넘어가다〕/ *have someone's fate in one's hands* 아무의 운명을 쥐고 있다 / *I have left the matter in my lawyer's hands.* 이 일을 나의 변호사에게 맡겼다 / *The work is in my hands.* 이 일은 나의 관리 아래 있다. **4** side; direction. 쪽; 방향; 방면. ¶ *on every* ~ =*on all hands* 사면(팔방)에서; 사방에서 / *look on either* ~ 좌우 양쪽을 보다 / *He stood at my left* ~. 그는 내 왼쪽에서 있었다. **5** skill; ability. 솜씨; 기량; 수완. ¶ *The picture showed the* ~ *of a master.* 그 그림은 작자의 기량을 나타내고 있었다. **6** ⓐ a style of writing; handwriting. 서체(書體); 필적. ¶ *readable* ~ 읽기 쉬운 서체 / *He writes a good* ~. 글씨를 잘 쓴다. ⓑ a signature. 서명; 사인. ¶ *set one's* ~ *to a document* 문서에 서명하다. **7** aid; assistance; active participation or cooperation. 도움; 조력; 원조; 적극적인 참가〔협력〕. ¶ *lend a* ~ 거들어〔도와〕주다 / *Give*〔*Lend*〕*me a* ~ *with my overcoat.* 외투 입는 것을 거들어 주게 / *a project in which several people had a* ~ 몇 사람이 협력한 계획. **8** a person who does something (with his hands); a hired worker. 일손; 일꾼; 직공; 종업원. ¶ *factory hands* 직공 / *farm hands* 농장 일꾼〔노동자〕/ *all hands* (*on a ship*) (배의) 전(全) 승무원 / *take on hands* 노무자를 고용하다. **9** a person, as the performer of some action or task. 특정한 일을 하는 사람; (어떤 분야의) 전문가. ¶ *a book written by various hands* 여러 전문가가 쓴 책 / *He is an old China* ~. 중국 문제의 전문가이다. **10** a person who has skill or ability enough to do something. (특정한 기술·기량·능력을 가진) 사람. ¶ *a new*〔*green*〕~ 미숙자; 신참 / *an old* ~ 노련한 사람 / *a good*〔*poor*〕~ *at* …을 잘하다〔에 서투르다〕/ *I am not much of a* ~ *at writing letters.* 편지는 그다지 잘 쓰는 편이 못 된다 / *He was a quite* ~ *with the violin.* 그는 바이올린 연주의 명수였다. **11** the breadth of a hand (=4 inches). 손바닥의 폭《4인치》. ¶ *a horse 13 hands high* 키가 4피트 4인치의 말. **12** 《cards》 ⓐ a single round in a game. (카드놀이 승부의) 한 판. ⓑ the cards held by a player. 가진 패. ⓒ a player. 카드놀이를 하는 사람. **13** a source (of knowledge, information). (지식·정보의) 출처; 공급원(源). ¶ *hear something at first*〔*second*〕~ 직접〔간접적으로〕 듣다. **14** instrumentality; agency. (수단·매개로서의) 손; 작용. ¶ *death by his own* ~ 자살. **15** a promise of marriage. 결혼의 언약; 혼약. ¶ *win a lady's* ~ 여성에게서 결혼 승낙을 얻다 / *She gave her* ~ *to him.* 그녀는 그에게 결혼의 승낙을 했다. **16** 《*colloq.*》 applause. 박수 갈채. ¶ *get a* ~ 박수 갈채를 받다.

***ask for** someone's* **hand,** propose marriage. …에게 구혼〔청혼〕하다.

at first hand, directly; from the original source. 직접.

at hand, **a**) within reach; nearby. 손닿는 곳에; 가까이; 근처에. **b**) near in time; about to happen soon. 가까운 장래에; 머지 않아; 곧. **c**) ready for use. 어느 때고 쓸 수 있게 (되어). ¶ *They kept a supply of water at* ~. 물을 언제나 쓸 수 있도록 준비해 두고 있었다.

at second hand, **a**) indirectly. 간접(적)으로. **b**) not new; previously used. 중고(中古)로.

at the hand*(*s*)** (=*through the action*) ***of *something.* …의 손으로〔에서〕; …에 의해.

bear a hand in, take part in. …에 참가하다.

bear*〔*lend*〕*a hand with, help; assist. 돕다; 거들다. ¶ *Please lend me a* ~ *with*〔*in carrying*〕*this baggage.* 이 짐 좀 거들어 주십시오.

be hand*〔*glove*〕 *with, be very intimate with. …와 극히 친밀하다.

***bind** someone* **hand and foot,** make him completely helpless and unable to move. …를 꼼짝달싹 못 하게 하다.

***bite the hand that feeds** one,* do harm to one's benefactor; return evil for good. 은혜를 원수로 갚다.

by hand, **a**) by bottle, not with the mother's milk. (모유 아닌) 우유로. ¶ *bring up a baby by* ~ 갓난아이를 우유로 기르다. **b**) with the hands; not by machinery. (기계가 아닌) 손으로; 수제(手製)로. ¶ *books bound by* ~ 손으로 제본한 책.

by the hands of, by. …의 손으로; …에 의해.

change hands, (of ownership, etc.) pass from one person to another. 임자가 바뀌다; 남의 것이 되다.

come to hand, **a**) come into one's possession; be received; arrived. 입수되다; 받다; 도착하다. **b**) come within one's reach or notice. 손이 미치는〔눈에 띄는〕 범위에 오다.

***eat*〔*feed*〕 *out of** someone's* **hand,** **a**) (of a bird, etc.) be quite tame. 잘 길들어 있다.

H

b) trust someone fully; be willing and ready to obey. 아무를 전적으로 믿다; 무조건 따르다〔복종하다〕.
fight hand to hand, fight at close quarters. 백병전〔접전〕을 벌이다; 격투하다.
for one's own hand, on one's account; for one's own advantage. 자신을 위하여; 자신의 이익을 위하여.
from hand to hand, from one person to another. 이 손에서 저 손으로; 여러 사람의 손을 거쳐.
from hand to mouth, without making any preparation for the future. 그 날 벌어 그 날 먹는. ¶ *They live from ~ to mouth.* 하루 벌어 하루 먹는 생활을 한다.
get one's hand in something, **a**) start something; begin something. …에 손을 대다; 착수하다. **b**) get used to an activity by practising. …에 익숙해지다.
get the upper hand of, win; gain advantage over. …보다 우세해지다.
give one's hand on a bargain, shake hands as a sign that one will keep one's promise. 약속을 지킨다는 표시로 악수하다.
give one's hand to, (of a woman) consent to marry. (여자가) 결혼에 동의하다.
hand and foot, **a**) so that the hands and feet cannot move or escape. 꼼짝 못 하게; 움직일〔달아날〕 수 없도록. ¶ *tie up ~ and foot* 꼼짝하지 못하게 손발을 묶다. **b**) slavishly; diligently. 노예〔수족〕처럼; 충실히. ¶ *wait on someone ~ and foot* 아무를 충실히 섬기다.
hand in hand with, **a**) holding hands with one another. 손에 손을 잡고. ¶ *walk ~ in hand* 손에 손을 잡고 걷다. **b**) together; in co-operation. 협력하여; 공동으로; 제휴하여.
hand over hand 〔***fist***〕, **a**) by using each hand alternately. (줄 따위를) 번갈아 당겨. **b**) quickly and in large amounts. 부쩍부쩍; 신속히.
hand over head, reckless(ly); thoughtless(ly). 무모한〔하게〕; 생각 없는〔없이〕.
hands down, easily; without effort. 손쉽게; 힘 안 들이고. ¶ *win hands down* 쉽게 이기다.
Hands off ! **a**) Don't touch ! 손대지 마시오. **b**) 《*fig.*》 Don't interfere (with). 참견하지 마라; 손을 떼라.
Hands up ! Hold up your hands ! 손들어《항복해라》.
hang on one's hands, (of time) pass slowly and uninterestingly. (시간을) 따분하게 보내다. ¶ *Time hangs heavy on my hands.* 할 일이 없어 따분하다.
have a free hand, be free to act as one chooses. 행동의 자유를 갖다.
have one's hand in (=*be related to; be connected with*) *someone* or *something.* …에 관계〔관여〕하고 있다.
have one's hands full, have more than one can do; be too busy. (바빠서) 손이 나지 않다; 너무 바쁘다.
have something (***heavy***) ***on one's hands,*** don't know what to do with something. 힘겨워하다; 무엇을 해야 할지 모르다.
in hand, **a**) in possession. 갖고〔소유하고〕 있는; 수중에 (있는). ¶ *cash in ~* 수중에 있는 돈 / *We have fifty dollars in ~.* 수중에 50 달러를 갖고 있다 / *We've still five minutes in ~.* 아직 5분의 여유가 있다. **b**) in control or order. 지배〔제어, 억제〕하고; 관리하고. ¶ *keep one's desire well in ~* 자기의 욕망을 잘 억제하다. **c**) under consideration; in readiness. 고려〔심의, 토의〕중에; 준비하고.
join hands, **a**) become associated in some undertaking. 힘을 합치다; 제휴하다. **b**) marry. 결혼하다.
keep 〔***have***〕 ***one's hand in*** =***keep a firm hand on,*** continue practice in order to keep one's skill. (기량이 떨어지지 않게) 계속 연습하다; 기능을 유지하고 있다.
keep one's hand on, exercise control over. 꽉 장악하고 있다.
lay one's hands on 〔***upon***〕, **a**) obtain; acquire. …을 손에 넣다; 제것으로 하다. **b**) seize; get hold of. 붙잡다. **c**) do violence to; attack. 폭행하다; 공격하다. ¶ *lay hands on someone* 아무에게 폭행하다 / *lay hands on oneself* 자살하다.
live from hand to hand, have nothing saved for the future. 하루 벌어 하루 먹는 생활을 하다.
make a hand, gain; succeed. 이익을 얻다; 성공하다.
not lift a hand, make no effort; do nothing. 노력하려고 하지 않다; 수고를 하지 않다.
off hand, at once. 곧; 즉석에서.
off one's hands, out of one's care or control. …의 손을 떠나; …책임에서 해방되어.
on hand, **a**) in one's present possession. 마침 갖고〔수중에〕 있는. ¶ *cash on ~* 갖고 있는 현금 / *with five minutes on ~ before the time* 시간까지는 아직 5분이 있는〔있으므로〕. **b**) be going to happen. 곧 일어날〔있을〕 것 같은; 절박한.
on 〔***upon***〕 ***one's hands,*** under one's care; as one's responsibility. 돌보게〔관리하게〕 되어; …의 책임이 되어. ¶ *She had three invalids on her hands.* 그녀는 3 명의 환자를 돌보고 있었다.
on the one hand…, on the other (***hand***), from one point of view…, from another—, etc. 한편으로는…, 다른 한편으로는—.
on the other hand, on the contrary. 반대로.
out of hand, **a**) out of control. 누를 수 없는; 힘에 겨운; 벅찬. ¶ *let one's temper get out of ~* 부아를 일으키다. **b**) immediately; at once. 곧; 즉각; 즉석에서. **c**) finished. 끝나; 마치어.
play for one's own hand, act so as to benefit oneself. 자기의 이익을 위해 행동하다; 사리를 꾀하다.
play into one another's hands, act for the

advantage of one another. 서로의 이익이 되게 행동하다.

put* 〔*set*〕 *one's hand to, **a**) begin to work at; undertake. …에 착수하다; 일을 시작하다; …에 종사하다. **b**) take hold of. …을 붙잡다.

put in hand, start doing; begin (work, etc.). …하기 시작하다; (일 따위를) 시작하다.

ready to one's hand, convenient; at hand; ready for use. 편리한; 손 가까이 있는; 곧 소용에 닿는.

shake hands, clasp each other's hands as a greeting, agreement, etc. 악수하다.

strike hands, make a contract. 계약을 맺다.

***take a hand at* 〔*in*〕,** 《*fig.*》 join 〔in〕; take part in; be connected with. …에 참가〔참여〕하다; 관여〔관계〕하다.

take in hand, **a**) take charge of. (책임)을 떠맡다. **b**) deal with; handle; treat. 처리하다; 다루다; 논하다.

take one's life in one's hand, take desperate chances. 필사적인 모험을 하다.

throw up one's hands, give up hopelessly 손을 들다; 역부족을〔사태의 악화를, 실패를〕 인정하다.

to hand, at hand; close by. (손) 가까이.

try one's hand, make a trial. 재능을〔적성을, 솜씨를〕 시험해 보다; …을 해 보다.

under one's hand =ready to one's hand.

wash one's hands of, refuse to have anything (more) to do with. …와 관계를 끊다; …에서 손을 떼다.

with a heavy* 〔*an iron*〕 *hand, severely; oppressively. 엄하게; 가혹하게.

with a high* 〔*bold*〕 *hand, with too much pride; not according to rules but according to one's own ideas. 고압적으로; 오만하게.

— *vt.* (P7,13,14) **1** pass (something) with the hand; give; send. …을 집어 주다; (건네) 주다; 보내다. ¶ ~ *someone an enclosed check* 아무에게 수표를 동봉해서 보내다 / *Please ~ me the book.* 그 책 좀 집어 주시오 / *I handed the letter to him.* 그에게 편지를 건네 주었다. **2** lead or help (someone) with the hand. …의 손을 잡고 돕다〔이끌다〕. ¶ ~ *a lady into* 〔*out of*〕 *a bus* 부인에게 손을 빌려 버스에〔에서〕 태워〔내려〕 주다. [E.]

hand down, **a**) pass on to his heir; transmit. (유산)을 남기다; 전하다. ¶ ~ *down one's property to one's children* 자녀들에게 유산을 물려주다 / *a legend handed down through the ages* 대대로 전해 내려오는 전설. **b**) announce (the decision of a court). (평결·판결)을 내리다. ¶ ~ *down a judgment.*

hand in, give; offer; submit. …을 넘겨〔건네〕 주다; 제출하다.

hand it to, 《U.S. *sl.*》 admit the abilities, success, etc. of. …을 정당하게 인정〔칭찬〕하다.

hand off, push away. 밀어 제치다.

hand on, pass along; send from one person to another; transmit. 차례로 넘기다; 다음으로 돌리다; (유산 따위를) 남기다; 전하다. ¶ *When you've finished reading it, kindly ~ it on to your friends.* 다 읽으신 다음엔 친구들에게 차례로 돌려 주십시오.

hand out, **a**) give out; distribute. 주다; (몫을) 나누어 주다; 분배하다. **b**) spend; give out money. (돈을) 쓰다. ¶ *He is quite rich, but he doesn't like handing out.* 그는 아주 부자이지만, 돈을 쓰는 것을 싫어한다.

hand over, **a**) deliver into another's keeping. 남의 보관〔보호, 관리〕에 맡기다. **b**) give up possession of (something). …을 넘겨 주다; 양도하다.

hand round, pass to one person after another; carry round. 차례로 돌리다; 도르다.

hand up, pass up something by hand. 높은 데로 건네 주다. ¶ ~ *up luggage from the hold of a ship* 선창으로부터 짐을 운반해 올리다.

hand·bag [hǽndbæ̀g] *n.* Ⓒ **1** a woman's small bag for money, keys, make-up, etc. (여성용) 핸드백. **2** a small traveling bag. (여행용의 작은) 손가방.

hand·ball [hǽndbɔ̀ːl] *n.* **1** a game played by hitting a small ball against a wall. 벽에 공을 쳐서 되튀는 것을 상대에게 치게 하는 게임. **2** a ball used in this game. 위의 게임에 쓰이는 공.

hand·bar·row [hǽndbæ̀rou] *n.* **1** a frame with two handles at each end by which it is carried. (들것 식의) 운반기. **2** = handcart.

hand·bill [hǽndbìl] *n.* Ⓒ a small printed advertisement to be distributed by hand. (손으로 도르는) 광고 쪽지; 전단.

hand·book [hǽndbùk] *n.* Ⓒ **1** a small book of reference on a special subject; a manual. 안내서; 편람(便覽). ¶ *a ~ on foreign literature* 외국 문학 입문서(書). **2** a guidebook for tourists. 여행 안내.

hand·breadth [hǽndbrèdθ, -brètθ] *n.* (also *hand's-breadth*) the breadth of a hand, used as a measure. 척도로 쓰이는 손의 폭《2 1/2-4 인치(=6-10 cm)》.

hand·cart [hǽndkɑ̀ːrt] *n.* Ⓒ a small cart moved by hand. 손수레.

hand·clap [hǽndklæ̀p] *n.* Ⓒ the act of striking the palms of one's hands together, usu. to show approval. 박수. ¶ *a flurry of handclaps* 우레와 같은 박수.

hand·clasp [hǽndklæ̀sp, -klɑ̀ːsp] *n.* Ⓒ the act of clasping hands by two or more people. 악수(cf. *handshake*).

hand·cuff [hǽndkʌ̀f] *n.* Ⓒ 《usu. *pl.*》 one of a pair of metal bracelets, joined by a short chain, locked around a prisoner's wrist to prevent his escape. 수갑; 쇠고랑(cf. *fetter*). ¶ *get* 〔*put*〕 *handcuffs on* …에게 수갑을 채우다. — *vt.* (P6) hold back (someone) with handcuffs. …에게 수갑을 채우다.

hand·ed [hǽndid] *adj.* 《chiefly in compounds》 **1** having a hand or hands. (…

한) 손을 가진. ¶ *left-handed* 왼손잡이의 / *neat-handed* 손재주 있는 / *heavy-handed* 서투른. **2** played by so many hands or players. …사람이 하는; …명을 필요로 하는. ¶ *a four-handed game at tennis,* 4명이 하는 테니스 경기.

Han·del [hǽndl], **George Frederick** *n.* (1685-1759) a German composer. 헨델《독일의 작곡가》.

∗**hand·ful** [hǽn*d*fùl] *n.* Ⓒ **1** the amount one hand can hold. 손에 가득; 한 움큼; 한 줌(의 양). ¶ *a ~ of sand* 한 움큼의 모래. **2** a very small number or quantity. 소수; 소량. ¶ *a ~ of men* 소수의 사람 / *a ~ of pin money* 약간의 용돈 / *Only a ~ of girls came.* 극히 소수의 소녀만 왔다. **3** 《*colloq.*》 a person or thing that is hard to control. 다루기 힘든 사람〔일〕; 귀찮은 존재. [*hand*]

hand glass [∠∠] *n.* a small mirror with a handle; a magnifying glass to be held in the hand. 손거울; 돋보기; 확대경.

hand·grip [hǽndgrìp] *n.* Ⓒ **1** a handshake, as in greeting. 악수. **2** 《usu. *pl.*》 a handle. 손잡이; 자루; 핸들.

hand·hold [hǽndhòuld] *n.* Ⓒ a place to put the hands. (손으로) 붙잡을〔쥘〕 데.

∗**hand·i·cap** [hǽndikæ̀p] *n.* Ⓒ **1** a disadvantage given to a superior contestant, or an advantage given to an inferior contestant, in order to give both a fair chance of winning in a game, contest, race, etc. 핸디캡《우열(優劣)의 균형을 위해 나은 자에게 지우는 부담》. **2** something which keeps back, such as a difficulty; a disadvantage. 장애; 불리한 조건. ¶ *Lack of education was a ~ to his chances of success.* 무학력(無學力)이 그의 성공의 기회를 가로막는 장애였다. **3** a game or contest in which handicaps are given. 핸디캡이 붙는 경기〔시합〕.

— *vt.* (**-capped, -cap·ping**) (P6) **1** give a handicap to (a racer, contestant, etc.). …에게 핸디캡을 주다. **2** place at a disadvantage; hinder. …을 불리한 입장에 세우다; 방해하다. ¶ *He was handicapped by his age.* 나이를 먹어 불리한 입장에 있었다. [*hand*]

hand·i·craft [hǽndikræ̀ft, -krɑ̀:ft] *n.* **1** Ⓤ skillful use of the hands. (솜씨의) 숙련. **2** Ⓒ any art needing skill with the hands. 수세공(手細工); 수예; 손일; 수공업. [*hand, craft*]

hand·i·crafts·man [hǽndikræ̀ftsmən, -krɑ̀:fts-] *n.* (*pl.* **-men** [-mən]) a person skilled with his hands in a trade or craft. 세공인; 손일하는 장인; 수공업자.

hand·i·ly [hǽndili] *adv.* **1** expertly. 솜씨 좋게; 교묘히. **2** suitably; conveniently. 알맞게; 편리하게. [*handy*]

hand·i·ness [hǽndinis] *n.* Ⓤ the state of being handy; convenience. 솜씨 좋음; 교묘함; 편리.

hand·i·work [hǽndiwə̀:rk] *n.* **1** Ⓤ work done by the hands. 손일; 수세공. **2** Ⓒ one's personal work. 작품; 제작물. ¶ *I suppose this box is your ~.* 이 상자는 너의 작품이라고 생각한다 / *This crisis is our own ~.* 이번 위기는 우리 자신이 만든 것이다. **3** Ⓤ the result of a person's action. 짓; 소행. [*handy, work*]

:**hand·ker·chief** [hǽŋkərtʃif, -tʃì:f] *n.* Ⓒ (*pl.* **-chiefs**) **1** a square piece of cloth for wiping the nose, face, eyes, etc. 손수건. **2** a piece of cloth worn around the neck. 목도리(cf. *neckerchief*). [*hand*]

throw* 〔*drop*〕 *the handkerchief to, **a**) (in games) call upon (a player) to run after the thrower. …에게 손수건을 던지다《술래잡기에서 술래가 자기를 쫓아오라고 하다》. **b**) 《*fig.*》 single out for special favor, by some sign of invitation. (여럿 가운데서) 특별한 호의를 비추다; …에게 의중(意中)을 비추다.

:**han·dle** [hǽndl] *n.* Ⓒ **1** a part of a tool, vessel, etc., grasped by the hand. 핸들; 손잡이; 자루; 곁손. **2** a chance; an opportunity. 편승할〔틈 탈〕 기회; 호기(好機); 호재료; 구실; 계기. ¶ *a ~ for gossip* 소문을 낳는 계기 / *The clue was a ~ for solving the mystery.* 그 실마리가 수수께끼를 푸는 계기가 되었다. **3** 《*colloq.*》 a title added to someone's name. 직함. ¶ *a ~ to one's name* (이름에 붙는) 경칭〔칭호〕.

fly off the handle, 《*colloq.*》 lose one's control; become very angry. 자제심을 잃다; 몹시 성내다〔흥분하다〕.

give a handle to one's enemies, provide them a means of attacking one; provide an excuse. 적에게 공격할 구실을〔핑계를〕 주다.

up to the handle, properly; thoroughly. 충분히; 철저히.

— *vt.* (P6) **1** touch, feel, or use with the hand; use the hands upon. …에 손을 대다; 손으로 만지다; 손으로 다루다. ¶ *~ a gun with precision* 총을 정확히 다루다 / *Please do not ~ the exhibits.* 전시품에 손을 대지 마시오. **2** control; direct. …을 통어하다; 지휘〔감독〕하다. ¶ *~ troops* 〔*men*〕 부대〔부하〕를 지휘하다 / *She was clever enough to ~ her pupils well.* 그녀는 영리해서 학생 아이들을 잘 다루었다. **3** deal with (something or someone); treat. …을 다루다; 처리하다; 논하다. ¶ *~ a subject concisely* 주제를 간단히 논(論)하다 / *The machine handles all our billing.* 청구서의 작성은 모두 기계가 처리한다 / *Don't ~ the animals so roughly.* 동물을 그렇게 거칠게 다루지 마라. **4** deal in (something); buy and sell. …을 매매〔거래〕하다. ¶ *They ~ tobacco in that store.* 그 가게에서는 담배를 판다. [*hand*]

handle bar [∠-∠] *n.* 《often *pl.*》 a curved bar by which a bicycle, motorcycle, etc., is guided. (자전거 따위의) 핸들.

hand·less [hǽndlis] *adj.* having no hands; not skillful; awkward; unhandy. 손이 없는; 서투른; 어색한. [*hand*]

H

hand·made [hǽndméid] *adj.* made by hand. 수제(手製)의; 수세공(手細工)의(cf. *machine-made*).

hand·maid [hǽndmèid] *n.* Ⓒ 《*arch.*》 a female servant or personal attendant. 하녀; 시녀; 몸종.

hand·maid·en [hǽndmèidn] *n.* =handmaid.

hand organ [⌐ ⌐–] *n.* a portable barrel organ that is made to play tunes when a crank is turned. 핸들을 돌려 치는 손풍금.

hand·out [hǽndàut] *n.* **1** something handed out, esp. a statement prepared for journalists. (정부 기관·광고주 등이 신문사에 돌리는) 발표 기사; 보도 자료. **2** a free sample. (무료로 배포되는) 시용(試用) 견본. **3** 《U.S.》 food or clothing given to a beggar or poor person. (거지·가난한 자에게) 베푸는 물건《음식·옷가지 따위》.

hand-picked [hǽndpíkt] *adj.* **1** picked by hand. (과실 따위를) 손으로 딴. **2** carefully selected. 주의 깊게 고른; 정선한. **3** unfairly selected. 멋대로 고른; 불공정하게 고른.

hand·rail [hǽndrèil] *n.* a railing used as a guard or support on a stairway, etc. (계단·승강장 따위의) 난간(cf. *balustrade*).

hand·saw [hǽndsɔ̀ː] *n.* Ⓒ a saw used with one hand. (한 손으로 켜는) 톱.

hand's-breadth [hǽndzbrèdθ, -brètθ] *n.* =handbreadth.

hand·sel [hǽnsəl] *n.* **1** a gift made at New Year's day, or entering upon a new circumstance or enterprise. (새해·개업·결혼 따위의) 선물; 기념품. **2** a first installment. 첫회 불입금. — *vt.* (P6) give handsel to; inaugurate. (새해·개업·취직 따위의) 선물을 주다; 개업하다. [M.E. *handselne* good-luck token]

hand·shake [hǽndʃèik] *n.* Ⓒ an act of grasping and shaking another's hand in greeting. 악수. ¶ *greet someone with a warm* ~ 따뜻한 악수로 아무를 맞이하다. [*hand*]

:hand·some [hǽnsəm] *adj.* (**-som·er, -som·est**) **1** ⓐ (of men) good-looking. (남자가) 잘생긴; 훌륭한(cf. *pretty*). ¶ *a* ~ *young man* 잘생긴 청년; 미남. ⓑ (of women) having beauty and dignity. (여성이) 아름답고 의연(毅然)한; 기품 있는. ⓒ (of things) of fine appearance. (사물이) 훌륭한; 당당한; 아름다운. ¶ ~ *furniture* 훌륭한 가구 / *a* ~ *interior* 〔*silk dress*〕 아름다운 내부〔비단옷〕. **2** fairly large; considerable. 상당한; 어지간한. ¶ *a* ~ *fortune* 〔*salary*〕 상당한 재산〔급료〕. **3** generous. 후한; 활수(滑手)한; 관대한. ¶ ~ *treatment* 후한 대우 / *a* ~ *gift of fifty dollars,* 50달러나 되는 푸짐한 선물.

come down handsome, 《*colloq.*》 behave generously, esp. in money matters. 활수하게 돈을 쓰다〔내다〕.

Handsome is that* (*as*) *handsome does. 《*prov.*》 Handsome is he who behaves handsomely. 외양보다 마음.

● **hand·some·ness** [-nis] *n.* [*hand*]

hand·some·ly [hǽnsəmli] *adv.* in a handsome manner. 훌륭히; 남자답게; 후하게; 관대하게. ¶ *behave* ~ 훌륭히 행동하다 / *be* ~ *rewarded* 후하게 보수를 받다.

hand·spike [hǽndspàik] *n.* a bar of wood used as a lever, esp. on a ship. 나무 지렛대.

hand·spring [hǽndspriŋ] *n.* a spring or leap in which a person turns his heels over his head while balancing on one or both hands. (땅에 손을 짚고 하는) 재주넘기; 공중제비.

hand·stand [hǽndstæ̀nd] *n.* an act of supporting the body on the hands with the trunk and legs balanced in the air. 물구나무서기.

hand-to-hand [hǽndtəhǽnd] *adj.* close together. (상대에) 접근한; 드잡이의; 접전〔육박전〕의. ¶ *a* ~ *combat* 육박전. — *adv.* at close quarters. 접근하다; 육박하다. ¶ *fight* ~ 격투하다; 육박전을 벌이다.

hand-to-mouth [hǽndtəmáuθ] *adj.* not providing for the future; unsettled. 하루벌어 하루 살아가는; 일시 모면의; 불안정한. ¶ *a* ~ *salary* 겨우 먹고 살 정도의 급료 / ~ *employment* 불안정한 직업.

hand·work [hǽndwə̀ːrk] *n.* Ⓤ work done by hand. 손일; 수세공; 수공.

hand·writ·ing [hǽndràitiŋ] *n.* Ⓤ **1** the act of writing by hand. 손으로 씀; 육필(肉筆). **2** a person's way of writing. (개인의) 필적; 서풍(書風); 서체.

∗hand·y [hǽndi] *adj.* (**hand·i·er, hand·i·est**) **1** (of a thing) ⓐ within reach of; at hand; easy to use. 가까이 있는; 편리하게 이용할 수 있는. ¶ *You'd better have a stick* ~. 지팡이는 가까운 곳에 두는 것이 좋다. ⓑ easy to handle; easily managed; convenient. 다루기 쉬운; 간편한; 편리한. ¶ *a* ~ *tool* 쓰기 편리한 도구 / *a* ~ *reference book* 간편한 참고서. **2** (of a person) useful; skilled with the hands. 도움이 되는; 솜씨 좋은; 능숙〔교묘〕한. ¶ *a* ~ *person* 솜씨 좋은 사람 / *be* ~ *with a chisel* 끌을 다루는 솜씨가 능숙하다. **3** (of a place) conveniently located; easily reached. 편리한 곳에 위치한; 근처에 있는. ¶ *The post-office is quite* ~. 우체국은 아주 가까운 곳에 있다. [*hand*]

hand·y·man [hǽndimæ̀n] *n.* (*pl.* **-men** [-mèn]) a man who does various small jobs. (아파트·회사 따위의) 잡역부; 허드레꾼.

:hang [hæŋ] *v.* (**hung**) *vt.* **1** (P6,7) ⓐ fasten or attach to something above; suspend. …위에 (매)달다; 늘어뜨리다. ¶ ~ *a pendulum* 흔들이를 달다 / ~ *a lamp from the ceiling* 천장에 램프를 달다. ⓑ suspend (something) from a nail, book, etc. (못 따위에) 걸다. ¶ ~ *a coat on a nail* 못에 웃옷을 걸다 / ~ *pictures on the wall* 벽에 그림을 걸다 / *Hang your cap on the hook.* 모자는

말코지에 거시오. ⓒ leave hanging. 매달아〔걸어〕 두다. ¶ ~ *meat* (맛이 들 때까지) 고기를 매달아 두다. **2** (P6) fasten or attach (something) by a hinge. (…을 경첩으로) 달다. ¶ ~ *a door on the hinges* 경첩으로 문을 달다. **3** (P6) bend down. …을 숙이다. ¶ ~ *one's head in shame* 부끄러워 고개를 수그리다. **4** (**hanged**) (P6) put (someone) to death by hanging. …을 목매달아 죽이다; 교수형에 처하다. ¶ ~ *someone for murder* 아무를 살인죄로 교수형에 처하다 / ~ *oneself* 목을 매어 자살하다 / *I'm* 〔*I'll be*〕 *hanged if I knew....* …을 알고 있다면 목을 매어도 좋다 《전연 모른다》. **5** (P6) ornament; cover, or furnish (walls) by something suspended. (걸거나 달아) …을 장식하다. ¶ ~ *wallpaper* 벽지를 붙이다 / ~ *the wall with pictures* 벽을 그림으로 장식하다 / ~ *a window with curtains* 창문에 커튼을 치다 / *The room is hung with flags.* 방은 기(旗)들로 장식돼 있다. —*vi.* (P1,2A,3) **1** be suspended; be fastened to something above. 늘어지다; (매)달리다; 걸리다. ¶ *pictures hanging above* 머리 위에 걸려 있는 그림 / *a chandelier hanging from the ceiling* 천장에 늘어져 있는 샹들리에 / ~ *by a rope* 밧줄에 매달리다 / *Her hair hung down on her shoulders.* 그녀의 머리가 어깨 위에 늘어져 있었다. **2** be fastened by a hinge. (경첩 따위로) 자유로이 움직이다. ¶ *a door hanging on its hinges* 경첩에 달려 움직이는 문. **3** (**hanged**) die by hanging. 목을 매어 죽다; 교수형이 되다. ¶ ~ *for one's offense* 범죄로 인해 교수형에 처해지다. **4** ⓐ stick out; lean over. (위에서 덮치듯) 쑥 내밀다; 돌출하다. ¶ ~ *out of the window* 창 밖으로 몸을 쑥 내밀다 / *A cliff hangs over the road.* 벼랑이 위에서 덮치듯 길 위로 돌출해 있다. ⓑ rest or move in the air; float. 공중에 뜨다〔떠돌다〕; 허공에 걸리다. ¶ *A full moon hung in the sky.* 보름달이 허공에 걸려 있었다 / *A heavy smog was hanging over the city.* 짙은 안개가 도시 상공에 자욱히 끼여 있었다 / *a sweet scent of flowers hanging in the air* 대기에 감돌고 있는 꽃향기. ⓒ seem ahead; be near; threaten. 다가〔닥쳐〕오다; 임박해 있다. ¶ *ill luck hanging over him* 그에게 닥쳐오는 불운 / *The examination hangs over us.* 시험이 박두해 있다 / *There's a rainstorm hanging about.* 폭풍우가 닥쳐오고 있다. **5** 《*on*》 be determined by; depend on; rest on. …(여하에) 달려 있다; …나름이다. ¶ *Everything hangs on his answer.* 모든 것은 그의 대답 여하에 달려 있다. **6** be doubtful or undecided; hesitate. 결심〔결정〕을 못하고 있다; 미결인 채로 두다; 망설이다. ¶ ~ *in doubt* 의심하다 / ~ *between staying and going* 갈까말까 망설이다.

hang about 〔***around***〕**,** 《*colloq.*》 **a**) spend time walking slowly or idly in a certain place. 어정거리다; 지정거리다; 헤매다. ¶ ~ *about all day* 온종일 어슬렁대다 / ~ *around* 〔*about*〕 *the seashore* 해변을 어슬렁거리다. **b**) group around; stay near to. 붙어 다니다; 달라붙어 떨어지지 않다.

hang back, be unwilling to do something; hesitate. 꽁무니 빼다; 주춤거리다.

hang by a (***single***) ***hair*** 〔***a thread***〕**,** be in a very dangerous position. 극히 위험하다; 풍전 등화이다.

hang fire, **a**) fail to explode promptly. (화기(火器)가) 발화가 느리다. **b**) be undecided. 결단이 서지 않다; 우물쭈물하다. **c**) be delayed. (일이) 잘 나아가지〔진척되지〕 않다.

hang in the balance 〔***the wind***〕**,** be in doubt or uneasiness. 의심스럽다; 어찌 될지 모르다. ¶ *His life* 〔*fate*〕 *hangs in the balance.* 그의 생명〔운명〕은 불확실하다.

hang off, **a**) cease to cling; leave hold. 손을 놓다〔떼다〕; 떨어지다. **b**) =hang back.

hang on, **a**) grasp or hold firmly. 꽉 붙잡다; 붙들고 늘어지다; 매달리다. ¶ ~ *on like grim death* 필사적으로 매달리다 / *Hang on to me.* 나를 꼭 붙들어라. **b**) depend on. …(여하)에 달리다. **c**) go on doing earnestly; be importunate; persevere. 꾸준히 계속하다; 끈질기다; 참고 견디다. **d**) linger; remain. (병(病) 따위가) 오래 가다; 떨어지지 않다. ¶ *coughs that* ~ *on for months* 몇 달씩이나 오래 끄는 기침.

hang out, **a**) lean toward. 몸을 (앞으로) 내밀다. ¶ *Don't* ~ *out of a train window.* 열차의 차창 밖으로 몸을 내밀지 마시오. **b**) set up (a flag, etc.); suspend out in the open. (남의 눈에 띄도록) 내달다〔걸다〕. ¶ ~ *out a flag.* **c**) 《*sl.*》 live; dwell; lodge. 살다; 거주하다; 묵다. **d**) lean downwards; be suspended. 늘어뜨리다; 처지다; 늘어지다. **e**) hang something out to dry. …을 밖에 널다.

hang over, **a**) project over (something). …위로 쑥 내밀다. **b**) remain to be settled; be postponed. 미결정인 채로 있다; 연기되어 있다. **c**) be close to; threaten. 닥쳐〔다가〕오다; 임박〔박두〕해 있다.

hang the 〔***one's***〕 ***head,*** allow the head to fall forward on the breast. 머리를 수그리다.

hang to, take a firm hold on; hold on to. 꽉 붙잡다; 붙잡고 늘어지다.

hang together, **a**) stay together; remain united. 단결하다. **b**) fit in together; be coherent. (말의) 앞뒤가 맞다; 동이 닿다. ¶ *His story doesn't* ~ *together.* 그의 이야기는 앞뒤가 맞지 않는다.

hang up, **a**) place (something) on hooks or hangers. …에 걸다. **b**) place a telephone receiver on the hook, to break off communication. (전화를 끝내고) 수화기를 걸다. ¶ *He hung up in the middle of conversation.* 통화 도중에 전화를 끊었다. **c**) stop the progress of; delay; interrupt. 진행을 멈추다; 중지하다; 늦어지게 하다. ¶ *The whole business was hung up.* 전(全) 업무가 중단되었다. **d**) 《U.S. *colloq.*》 pawn; buy on credit. 전당(典當)잡히다; 외상으로 사다. **e**)

《Brit. *colloq.*》 rob with violence. 강탈하다. — *n.* Ⓒ 《usu. *the* ~》 **1** the way something hangs. 걸림새; 늘어져〔달려〕 있는 모양. ¶ *the ~ of an overcoat* 체형에 따라 걸쳐진 외투 모양새. **2** 《U.S. *colloq.*》 the way a machine, etc. works; the way of using or handling it well; familiar knowledge gained by practice; knack. (기계 따위가) 작동하는 모양새; 정확한 사용법; 요령. ¶ *see the ~ of a machine* 기계 사용법의 요령을 터득하다. **3** 《*colloq.*》 main thought; meaning. 의미; 취지. ¶ *the ~ of an argument* 논의의 취지. **4** 《*colloq.*》 a bit. 조금; 약간. ¶ *I don't care a ~.* 조금도 개의〔상관〕치 않는다. [E.] ***get the hang of,*** 《*colloq.*》 understand; get the knack of. 이해하다; 요령을 터득하다. ¶ *get the ~ of a tool* 도구의 사용 요령을 터득하다.

hang·ar [hǽŋər] *n.* Ⓒ a shed for airplanes and other aircraft. 격납고.

hang·dog [hǽŋdɔ̀(:)g, -dɑ̀g] *n.* a base person. 비열한 사내. — *adj.* ashamed; base; mean. 부끄러워하는; 비굴한; 초라한.

hang·er [hǽŋər] *n.* Ⓒ **1** a person who hangs something. 거는 사람. **2** ⓐ a tool or machine that hangs things. (무엇을) 거는〔매다는〕 것《(버스·열차의) 손잡이·못·옷걸이·현수막·커튼 따위》; 자재 갈고리. ⓑ 걸려〔매달려〕 있는 것. **3** a hangman. 교수형 집행인. **4** a steep wooded declivity. 급경사지의 숲. **5** a kind of short sword. 단검(短劍). [*hang*]

hang·er-on [hǽŋərɑ́n, -ɔ́(:)n] *n.* Ⓒ (*pl.* **hang·ers-**) **1** a follower. 부하; 아무의 곁을 항상 떠나지 않는 사람; 추종자. **2** an undesirable follower. 식객; (기생충적인) 사람.

·**hang·ing** [hǽŋiŋ] *n.* Ⓤ **1** the act of a person who hangs; the state of being hung or hanged. 걺; 매닮; 걸림; 매달림. **2** death by hanging. 목매어 죽음〔죽임〕; 교살; 교수(絞首). ¶ *a criminal sentenced to ~* 교수형을 선고받은 범인. **3** 《often *pl.*》 a thing that hangs from a wall, bed, etc., such as curtains and draperies. (방의 벽 따위를) 덮어 가리는 것; (벽에) 거는〔다는, 치는〕 것; 족자; 커튼; 벽걸이. — *adj.* **1** deserving punishment by hanging. 교수형에 처할 만한. ¶ *a ~ crime* 교수형에 처할 만한 범죄. **2** fastened to something above. 매달린; 달려 늘어진. ¶ *a ~ lamp* 달려 늘어진 램프. [*hang*]

hang·man [hǽŋmən] *n.* Ⓒ (*pl.* **-men** [-mən]) a public officer who puts criminals to death by hanging them. 교수형 집행인.

hang·nail [hǽŋnèil] *n.* Ⓒ a small piece of loose skin near a fingernail. 손거스러미.

hang·o·ver [hǽŋòuvər] *n.* 《*sl.*》 the unpleasant aftereffects of drunkenness. 숙취(宿醉).

hank [hæŋk] *n.* Ⓒ **1** a circular coil of yarn containing a definite number of yards. (실 따위의) 한 타래〔꾸리〕; 다발. **2** 《naut.》 a ring of rope, iron, etc. used for fastening. (세로돛의) 범환(帆環). [N. *honk* coil]

han·ker [hǽŋkər] *vi.* (P3) 《*after, for*》 long for; wish. 동경하다; 갈망하다. ¶ *~ after one's forbidden pleasures* 금지된 쾌락을 동경하다 / *~ for a foreign-made car* 외제차를 갖고 싶어하다. [? Flem.]

han·ky [hǽŋki] *n.* 《*child's word, colloq.*》 = handkerchief.

han·ky-pan·ky [hǽŋkipǽŋki] *n.* Ⓤ 《*colloq.*》 conduct intended to deceive; trickery. 부정; 사기 (행위); 속임수. ¶ *play ~ with someone* 아무에게 협잡질하다. [Brit. slang]

Ha·noi [hænɔ́i, hə-] *n.* the capital of the Democratic Republic of Vietnam. 하노이 《베트남의 수도》.

Han·sard [hǽnsərd] *n.* the official report of proceedings in the British Parliament. 영국 국회 의사록. [Person]

hanse [hæns] *n.* a medieval guild of a town. (중세 서양의) 상인 조합. [G.]

han·sel [hǽnsəl] *n.* =handsel.

han·som [hǽnsəm] *n.* Ⓒ a two-wheeled covered cab for two passengers, drawn by one horse and with the driver at the back. 말 한 필이 끄는 2인승 2륜마차. [Person]

〈hansom〉

Hants. Hampshire.

hap [hæp] *n.* 《*arch.*》 **1** chance; luck. 운; 행운. ¶ *evil ~* 불운 / *by some ~* 어떤 운명으로 / *It was my good ~ to meet him.* 그를 만나다니 운이 좋았다. **2** a happening. 뜻밖〔우연〕의 일. — *vi.* (P1,4) (**happed**) happen. 우연히 …하다〔일어나다〕. [N. *happ.* good luck]

hap·haz·ard [hǽphæ̀zərd] *n.* Ⓤ mere chance or accident. 단순한 우연. ¶ *at* 〔*by*〕 *~* 우연히. — *adj.* accidental; not planned. 우연의; 무계획한. ¶ *a ~ collection of books* 무계획적인 책 수집 / *a ~ lie* 되는 대로 지껄이는 거짓말. — *adv.* by chance; at random. 우연히; 되는 대로. ●**hap·haz·ard·ly** [-li] *adv.* [→hap, hazard]

hap·less [hǽplis] *adj.* unlucky; unfortunate. 불운한; 불행한. ●**hap·less·ly** *adv.* [*hap*]

:**hap·pen** [hǽpən] *vi.* (P1,3,4) **1** take place; occur. (일·사건이) 일어나다. ¶ *~ what* 〔*whatever*〕 *may ~* 무슨〔어떠한〕 일이 있던 / *I don't know how it happened.* 그것이 어떻게 일어났는지 모르겠다 / *Nothing happened after that.* 그 후엔 아무 일도 없었다 / *Accidents will ~.* 사고는 일어나게 마련이다. **2** be or take place by chance. 우연히 …하다; 뜻하지 않게 …하다. ¶ *I happened to be in the room.* 우연히 방에 있었다 / *I don't ~ to have the money right now.* 지금은 마침 그만큼의 돈을 갖고 있지 않다 / *My attention happened to be drawn to it.* 우연히 내 주의력이 그쪽에 끌렸

다 / *It happens to be a fine day.* 마침 좋은 날씨다. [*hap*]

as it happens, by chance. 우연히; 공교롭게.

happen along, 《*colloq.*》 arrive by chance; drop in. 우연히 다다르다; 불쑥 들르다.

happen in, 《U.S.》 drop in. 들르다.

happen on 〔***upon***〕***,*** meet or find by chance; come upon. …을 우연히 만나다〔발견하다〕. ¶ *~ on an old friend* 뜻밖에 옛 친구를 만나다 / *~ upon the very thing he wants* 그가 원하는 바로 그것을 만나다.

happen to, **a**) come or fall upon unexpectedly; befall. 뜻하지 않게 일어나다; 닥치다. ¶ *Something dreadful must have happened to the airplane.* 비행기에 끔찍한 일이 생겼음에 틀림없다. **b**) become of; be the end of. 되다. ¶ *What has happened to your dog?* 너의 개는 어떻게 되었나.

hap·pen·ing [hǽpəniŋ] *n.* Ⓒ 《often *pl.*》 something that occurs quite unexpectedly; an event. 해프닝; 사건; 일. ¶ *everyday happenings* 매일 일어나는 일 / *have a strange ~* 이상한 일을 만나다. [↑]

:hap·pi·ly [hǽpili] *adv.* **1** in a happy manner; with pleasure or joy. 행복하게; 즐겁게. **2** by a fortunate chance; luckily 다행히(도); 운좋게(도). ¶ *Happily he found the way out.* 다행히도 그는 출구(出口)를 찾았다. [*happy*]

:hap·pi·ness [hǽpinis] *n.* Ⓤ the state of being happy or glad; good fortune. 행복; 행운. ¶ *bring someone ~* 아무를 행복하게 하다 / *have the ~ of seeing someone* 운 좋게도 아무를 만나다.

:hap·py [hǽpi] *adj.* (**-pi·er, -pi·est**) **1** lucky; fortunate. 행복한; 기쁜; 운 좋은. ¶ *a ~ home* 행복한 가정 / *a ~ mood* 행복한 기분 / *be ~ to see someone* 아무를 만나 기쁘다 / *be ~ as a lark* 무척 행복하다 / *Happy are those who are contented.* 만족을 아는 자는 행복하다. **2** enjoying, giving or expressing pleasure; joyous. 즐거운; 유쾌한. ¶ *~ laughter* 즐거운 웃음 / *in a ~ frame of mind* 유쾌한 기분으로. **3** (of language or conduct) well suited; fit; clever; apt. 적절한; 교묘한. ¶ *a ~ way of expression* 적절한〔교묘한〕 표현. **4** 《*sl.*》 slightly drunk. 거나한; 한잔 기분의. [*hap*]

as happy as a king =as happy as the day is long.

as happy as happy can be =as happy as the day is long.

as happy as the day is long, happier than anything else; as happy as possible. 매우〔더없이〕 행복한.

hit 〔***strike***〕 ***the happy mean,*** be or remain moderate. 중용을 지키다.

hap·py-go-luck·y [hǽpigoulʌ̀ki] *adj.* taking things easy; easy-going; thoughtless. 낙천적인; 걱정하지 않는; 되는 대로의. ¶ *in a ~ manner* 마음 편하게. [↑]

ha·rangue [hərǽŋ] *n.* Ⓒ a long, noisy speech, esp. toward a crowd. 열변; 격정적인 연설. — *vi., vt.* (P1;6) make a harangue. 열변을 토하다. ¶ *make a ~ on someone's greatness* 아무의 위대함에 관하여 열변을 토하다. [F.]

har·ass [hǽrəs, hərǽs] *vt.* (P6) **1** 《mil.》 annoy by repeated attacks. …을 쉴새없이 공격하여 괴롭히다. ¶ *Pirates used to ~ the villages along the coast.* 해적들이 연안 마을들을 습격하여 괴롭히곤 했다. **2** trouble; worry. (성가심·걱정 따위로) 괴롭히다. ¶ *be harassed with* 〔*by*〕 *anxieties* 걱정에 시달리다. [F.]

har·bin·ger [hɑ́ːrbindʒər] *n.* Ⓒ a person or thing that goes ahead to announce another's coming; a forerunner. 선구자; 예고(자); 전조. ¶ *a ~ of the middle ages* 중세의 도래를 알리는 것 / *The cuckoo is the ~ of spring.* 뻐꾸기는 봄의 선구자이다. — *vt.* (P6) announce beforehand. …을 미리 알리다〔예고하다〕. [↓]

:har·bor, 《Brit.》 **-bour** [hɑ́ːrbər] *n.* Ⓒ **1** a protected part of a sea, lake, etc., which serves as a shelter for ships and boats. 항구. ¶ *a ~ of refuge* 피난항(港) / *be in ~* 입항중이다. **2** any place of shelter or safety. 피난〔은신〕처; 잠복 장소. ¶ *give ~ to a convict* 죄인을 숨기다.

— *vt.* **1** (P6,13) give shelter to (a ship, etc.); protect. …에게 피난〔은신〕처를 주다; …을 비호하다. ¶ *~ fugitives* 〔*a spy*〕 탈주자를〔간첩을〕 숨기다 / *~ smuggled goods* 밀수품을 은닉하다 / *The woods ~ much game.* 숲에는 많은 사냥감이 살고 있다. **2** (P6) keep (unkind thoughts, etc.) in one's mind; cherish. (마음 속에) 품다. ¶ *~ malice* 〔*a grudge*〕 악의를〔불평을〕 품다 / *~ suspicion against someone* 아무에 대해 의심을 품다 / *~ no hate* 증오심을 품지 않다.

— *vi.* (P1,2A,3) (of ships) take shelter in a harbor. 항구에 정박하다; 입항하다. [E. =army shelter]

har·bor·age [hɑ́ːrbəridʒ] *n.* **1** Ⓤ shelter; protection. 피난; 보호. **2** Ⓒ a place of shelter (for ships); shelter in a port. (배의) 정박처; (항구의) 피난처〔시설〕. [↑]

:hard [hɑːrd] *adj.* **1** firm to the touch; solid. 굳은; 단단한; 딱딱한(opp. soft). ¶ *~ ground* 굳은 땅 / *a ~ bed* 딱딱한 침대 / *an extremely ~ stone* 매우 단단한 돌. **2** firmly formed; tight. 단단히 만들어진; (맨 데 따위가) 꽉 매어진; 꼭〔단단히〕 쥔. **3** powerful; violent; excessive. 강(렬)한; 맹렬한; 극심한; 과도한. ¶ *a ~ blow* 강타 / *a ~ rain* 〔*blizzard*〕 세찬 비〔눈보라〕 / *a ~ drinker* 독한 술을 지나치게 마시는 사람 / *a ~ labor* (형벌로 과하는) 중노동. **4** requiring much effort; difficult; not easy. 노력을 요하는; 어려운; 힘든. ¶ *a ~ problem* 어려운 문제 / *~ work* 힘든 일 / *a ~ hill to climb* 오르기 어려운 산. **5** severe; painful; troublesome. (혹)심한; 혹독〔지독〕한; 괴로운; 귀찮은. ¶ *a ~ winter* 엄

H

동 / *a ~ illness* 중병 / *~ to please* (성미가) 꾀까다로운 / *have a ~ time* (*of it*) 되게 혼나다; 곤욕을 치르다. **6** stern; harsh; cruel; unfriendly. 엄(격)한; 가혹(냉혹)한; 무정한; 친절치 않은; 적의를 품은. ¶ *a ~ teacher* 엄한 선생 / *a ~ official* (*heart*) 냉혹한 관리(마음) / *~ words* 독살스러운 말 / *~ feelings* 악감정. **7** difficult to explain away; undeniable. 변명(부정)하기 어려운; 엄연한. ¶ *~ facts* 엄연한 사실 / *~ proof* 움직일 수 없는 증거. **8** acting with energy; diligent. 열심히 하는; 부지런한; 근면한. **9** harsh or unpleasant to the eye or ear. 눈·귀에 거슬리는; 불쾌한; 거친. ¶ *a ~ voice* 거친 목소리. **10** ⓐ (of water) unfit for washing owing to its mineral salt. 경수(硬水)의; 센물의. ¶ *~ water* 경수. ⓑ 《U.S. *colloq.*》 containing a high percentage of alcohol. (술이) 알코올분이 많은; 독한. ¶ *~ drink* (*liquor*) 독한 술. **11** ⓐ voiceless. 무성 자음의(opp. soft, cf. *strong*). ⓑ pronounced as the stop. 폐쇄음의. **12** 《comm.》 (of markets and prices) high and stable. 강세의; 오름세의(opp. soft, cf. *strong*). ¶ *The prices are ~.* 물가는 오름세에 있다.

***a hard nut* (*to crack*),** 《*fig.*》 a difficult problem; a person hard to understand or influence. 난문제; 다루기 힘든 사람.

a hard row to hoe, a hard task. 어려운 일.

(*as*) *hard as a brick,* very hard. 매우 단단한.

(*as*) *hard as nails,* very hard. 매우 단단한(튼튼한).

be hard on, **a**) treat (someone) severely. …에게 심하게 굴다(대하다). **b**) be difficult, unpleasant, or painful for (someone). …에게 견디기 힘들다.

be hard up for, 《*colloq.*》 **a**) be in great need of (money, etc.). (돈 따위가) 절실히 필요하다; 돈에 궁하다. **b**) be unable to find. 찾을 수가 없다.

do** something **the hard way, learn by experience, not by teaching. 가르쳐서가 아니라 경험으로 배우다.

hard and fast, (of rules, etc.) invariable; strict. (규칙 따위가) 불변의; 엄격한.

hard of hearing, unable to hear properly; rather deaf. 귀먹은; 난청(難聽)의.

— *adv.* **1** firmly; tightly. 굳게; 단단히. ¶ *hold on ~* 단단히 붙들다 / *boil an egg ~* 달걀을 완숙으로 삶다 / *It was frozen ~.* 꽁꽁 얼어붙었다. **2** with great energy or force; earnestly; lively. 열심히; 맹렬히. ¶ *work ~* 열심히 일하다 / *listen ~ to a lecture* 강연에 열심히 귀를 기울이다 / *stare* (*gaze, look*) *~ at someone* 아무를 응시하다. **3** with effort or difficulty. 간신히; 어렵게. ¶ *The cork draws ~.* 코르크 마개가 좀처럼 빠지지 않는다. **4** with vigor, strength or violence. 세(차)게; 격렬하게. ¶ *A storm hit the region ~.* 폭풍이 세차게 그 지역을 덮쳤다. **5** excessively. 지나치게; 매우; 몹시. ¶ *drink ~* 과음하다 / *be ~ sick* 중병이다 / *bear ~ on* …을 몹시 괴롭히다; …에게 큰 타격을 주다. **6** harshly; severely 가혹하게; 심하게. ¶ *work one's maid ~* 가정부를 혹사하다 / *be ~ done by* …에게 심한 취급을 받다; 냉대(冷待)를 받다. **7** 《*after, by, upon*》 close; near. 가까이; 접근하여. ¶ *He followed ~ after me.* 내 바로 뒤에서 따라왔다. [E.]

be hard hit, be severely troubled. 심한 타격을 입다.

be hard put to it, be in great difficulty or trouble. 어려움(곤경)에 빠져(처해) 있다.

go hard with, treat or punish (someone) severely. …에게 고통을 주다; 혼내 주다. ¶ *It will go ~ with you if you are found out.* 발견되면 혼날 게다.

hard by, close by; not far away. 바로 가까이; 극히 접근하여. ¶ *He is ~ by fifty.* 나이가 50에 가깝다.

hard pressed, needing (money) badly. (돈에) 궁핍하여.

It will* (*shall*) *go hard but..., Unless the difficulties are too great. 여간한 장애가 없는(곤란을 만나지 않는) 한. ¶ *It will go ~ but he will succeed.* 여간한 장애가 없는 한 그는 성공할 게다.

take* (*it*) *hard, suffer deeply. (마음에) 괴롭게 생각하다; 통감하다.

hard-bit·ten [hɑ́ːrdbítn] *adj.* stubborn; unyielding. 완고한; 고집이 센; 불굴의.

hard-boiled [hɑ́ːrdbɔ́ild] *adj.* **1** (of an egg) boiled until hard. (달걀을) 완숙으로 삶은. **2** 《*colloq.*》 (of a person) unfeeling; tough. 무감각한; 비정한. **3** 《*colloq.*》 hard; stiff; rough. 완고한; 거친.

hard cash [∠∠] *n.* **1** metal coins. 경화(硬貨). **2** cash. 현금.

hard core [∠∠] *n.* **1** 《Brit.》 heavy materials forming the foundation of a road. (도로 공사에서) 밑에 깔아 노반(路盤)을 다지는 데 쓰이는 경(硬)골재《쇄석(碎石)·벽돌 조각 따위》. **2** nucleus. 핵심.

hard currency [∠∠–––] *n.* 《econ.》 convertible currency. 경화(硬貨)《타국의 통화와 바꿀 수 있는 돈》.

∗**hard·en** [hɑ́ːrdn] *vt., vi.* (P6,13; 1,2A,3) **1** make or become hard. 굳게(단단하게) 하다; 굳어(단단해)지다. ¶ *~ steel* 담금질하여 강철을 경화(硬化)하다 / 《*fig.*》 *~ one's will* 의지를 굳게 하다 / *Clay hardens by drying.* 찰흙은 마르면 굳어진다. **2** make or become firm. 강하게(튼튼하게) 하다; 강해(튼튼해)지다. ¶ *~ the body* (*soldiers*) 몸을(병사를) 단련하다. **3** make or become unfeeling or harsh. 무감각(무정)하게 하다; 무감각(무정)해지다. **4** 《comm.》 (of prices) rise; become stable. (값이) 오르다; 안정되다. [*hard*]

harden off, make (seedlings, etc.) hardy by gradual exposure to cold. (묘목 따위를) 찬 기운을 쐬어 강하게 하다.

hard·head·ed [hɑ́ːrdhédid] *adj.* **1** not easily deceived; practical; shrewd. 냉정

한; 실제적인; 빈틈없는. **2** stubborn; obstinate. 완고한. [*hard*]

hard·heart·ed [há:rdhá:rtid] *adj.* without pity or sympathy; unfeeling. 몰인정한; 잔혹한; 무정한.

har·di·hood [há:rdihùd] *n.* Ⓤ boldness; daring; impudence. 대담(무쌍); 불굴의 정신; 뻔뻔스러움. [*hardy*]

har·di·ly [há:rdili] *adv.* in a hardy manner; boldly. 대담하게; 뻔뻔스럽게.

har·di·ness [há:rdinis] *n.* Ⓤ the quality of being hardy; boldness; hardihood. 강건(强健); 견고; 불굴; 인내력; 대담; 뻔뻔함.

:hard·ly [há:rdli] *adv.* **1** only just; barely; scarcely. 겨우; 거의 …아니다〔않다〕. ¶ *I ~ know him.* 그를 거의 모른다 / *I could ~ understand her.* 도무지 그녀를 이해할 수 없었다 / *Hardly anybody knew it.* 거의 아무도 그것을 몰랐다 / *I need ~ say that I am right.* 내가 옳다는 건 말할 필요도 없을 게다 / *We had ~ got to the station when* 〔*before*〕 *it began to rain.* 정거장에 도착하기가 무섭게 비가 내리기 시작했다. **2** not at all; by no means. 전혀 …않다〔아니다〕; 결코 …않다〔아니다〕. ¶ *You can ~ expect me to help you.* 저의 조력은 전혀 기대하실 수 없을 겁니다 / *His story is ~ true.* 그의 이야긴 전혀 사실이 아니다. **3** probably not. 아마(도) …아니다〔않다〕; 거의 …할 것 같지도 않다. ¶ *He will ~ come today.* 그는 아마 오늘 오지 않을 게다. **4** with difficulty or effort. 힘들여; 어렵게; 고생하여. ¶ *money ~ earned* 어렵게 번 돈 / *Our victory was ~ won.* 우리의 승리는 어렵게 거둔 것이었다. **5** harshly; severely. 엄〔심〕하게; 가혹하게; 호되게. ¶ *treat someone ~* 아무를 심하게 대하다 / *speak ~ of someone* 아무를 혹평하다 / *Don't think so ~ of him.* 그를 그리 나쁘게 생각 마오. [*hard*]

hardly any, little. 거의 …않다〔없다〕.

hardly ever, seldom. 좀처럼 없다〔않다〕. ¶ *He ~ ever goes to bed before midnight.* 자정 전에 잠자리에 드는 일은 좀처럼 없다.

hardly ... when 〔***before***〕***,*** as soon as. …하자마자. ¶ *They had ~* 〔《*lit.*》 *Hardly had they*〕 *gone out when it began to rain.* 그들이 밖에 나가자마자 비가 오기 시작했다.

hard-mouthed [há:rdmàuðd, -màuθt] *adj.* **1** not easily driven or guided. 어거하기 힘든; 힘에 벅찬. **2** using rough speech. 입〔말〕이 거친. [*hard*]

hard·ness [há:rdnis] *n.* Ⓤ the quality of being hard; hardship. 단단함; 견고; 가혹; 난해; 곤란. ¶ *the ~ of rock* 돌의 단단함 / *~ of heart* 마음의 냉혹함.

hard palate [´ ´–] *n.* the front of the palate. 경구개(cf. *soft palate*).

hard-pressed [há:rdprést] *adj.* struggling against great difficulties; short of time, money, etc. (어려움 등에) 압박을 받는; 곤란에 빠진; 돈·시간에 쪼들리는; 절박한.

***hard·ship** [há:rdʃip] *n.* ⓊⒸ something hard to endure, such as hunger, cold, or sickness. 견디기 어려움〔어려운 것〕; 고난; 신고(辛苦); 곤궁; 압제. ¶ *bear ~ without complaint* 불평 없이 어려움을 참고 견디다.

hard·ware [há:rdwὲər] *n.* Ⓤ **1** articles made from metal, such as pots, pans, and knives. 철물류(類). ¶ *a ~ store* 철물점. **2** armaments. 무기 및 전투용 기재(器材). **3** the machinery of an electronic computer. (컴퓨터의) 하드웨어《데이터 처리에 사용되는 기계 설비·장치》(cf. *software*).

hard·wood [há:rdwùd] *n.* Ⓤ any hard, closely packed wood, such as oak, cherry, or maple. 단단한 나무《떡갈나무·벚나무 따위》. — *adj.* made of hardwood. 단단한 나무로 만든.

hard·work·ing [há:rdwə̀:rkiŋ] *adj.* working hard; industrious. 열심히 일하는; 부지런한. ¶ *a ~ student* 부지런한 학생.

***har·dy** [há:rdi] *adj.* (**-di·er, -di·est**) **1** able to bear hardship, fatigue, etc.; vigorous. 어려움에 견디는; 튼튼한; 강한. **2** (of plants) able to survive the cold of winter. 내한성(耐寒性)의. ¶ *~ plants* 내한성의 식물. **3** bold; daring. 대담한; 용감한. [*hard*]

Har·dy [há:rdi], **Thomas** *n.* (1840-1928) an English novelist. 하디《영국의 소설가》.

hardy annual [´– ´––] *n.* **1** the plant lasting for a year that can be grown in the open. 한데에서 자라는 1년생의 내한성(耐寒性) 식물. **2** 《*fig.*》 a question that comes up for discussion yearly. 해마다 되풀이해서 토의 마당에 오르는 문제.

***hare** [hεər] *n.* Ⓒ (*pl.* **hares** or *collectively* **hare**) an animal like a large rabbit. 산토끼 (cf. *rabbit*). ¶ 《*prov.*》 *First catch your ~ (then, cook him).* 떡 줄 놈은 생각도 않는데 김칫국부터 마시지 마라; 우선 사실을〔상대를〕 확인해라. [E.]

as mad as a (***March***) ***hare,*** very wild or mad. 몹시 미쳐 날뛰는; 난폭한《3월 교미기의 토끼같이》.

as timid as a hare, very shy. 몹시 소심한; 겁이 많은.

hare and hounds, a sport in which two persons ('hares') run across country dropping pieces of paper and followed by others ('hounds') who try to catch him. 토끼몰이 술래잡기《두 사람이 종이를 떨어뜨리면서 달아나면 다른 사람들이 뒤쫓아가 잡는 놀이》.

hold 〔***run***〕 ***with the hare and run*** 〔***hunt***〕 ***with the hounds,*** try to serve both sides. 양쪽에 다 좋게 굴다; 팔방미인 노릇을 하다.

make a hare (=*make a fool*) ***of someone.*** 아무를 놀리다.

start a hare, turn aside from the main subject in discussion. 의론에서 주제를 벗어나 지엽으로 흐르다.

hare·bell [hέərbèl] *n.* 《bot.》 a plant with blue bellshaped flowers. 초롱꽃류(類).

hare·brained [hέərbrèind] *adj.* foolish;

thoughtless. 바보 같은; 경박한; 무모한. ¶ *a ~ action* 경솔한 행동.

hare·lip [hέərlìp] *n.* Ⓒ a deformed lip, usu. the upper one. 언청이.

ha·rem [hέərəm] *n.* Ⓒ **1** the part of a Mohammedan house in which the women live. (회교국의) 도장방; 규방. **2** 《*collectively*》 the wives, female servants, etc., living in this part of the house. 위에 사는 처첩들. [Arab. =prohibited place]

har·i·cot [hǽrikòu] *n.* kidney beans. 강낭콩. [F.]

•**hark** [hɑːrk] *vi.* (P1,2A) 《chiefly in *imperative*》 listen. 듣다; 귀를 기울이다.

hark back, go back, return (to a place from which one started, to a subject, etc. about which one was speaking, or to the past). 본디로(원점으로) 되돌아가다(오다). [E.]

hark·en [hɑ́ːrkən] *vi.* =hearken.

Har·lem [hɑ́ːrləm] *n.* the chief negro section in New York. 할렘 《뉴욕시의 흑인 거주 구역》.

har·le·quin [hɑ́ːrlikwin, -kin] *n.* Ⓒ 《often *H-*》 a character in a dumb show, usu. masked and with clothing of varied colors and a wooden sword. (무언극의) 어릿광대역 배우.
— *adj.* varied in color; many-colored. 얼룩빛의; 잡색의. [It. *arlecchino*]

⟨harlequin⟩

har·le·quin·ade [hɑ̀ːrlikwinéid / -kin-] *n.* a scene in a pantomime in which a harlequin plays the leading part. Harlequin 이 주역을 맡은 무언극.

har·lot [hɑ́ːrlət] *n.* a woman who sells herself for money; a prostitute. 매춘부; 창녀. [F. =lad, knave]

ː**harm** [hɑːrm] *n.* Ⓤ injury; damage; evil; wrong-doing. 해; 손해; 손상; 해악; 위해. ¶ *do no ~* 해가 되지 않다 / *do more ~ than good* 유해 무익하다 / *without taking any great ~* 그다지 큰 손해를 입지 않고 / *There is no ~ in trying.* 해 보아도 나쁘지는 않다 / *Where's the ~ in trying?* 해서 나쁠 게 뭐냐.

come to harm, get hurt. 다치다; 혼나다.

do** someone **harm =***do harm to** someone,* hurt. 아무에게 해를 입히다; 아무를 해치다.

no harm done, all is well; no one hurt, etc. 피해 없다; 전원 이상 없다.

out of harm's way, in safety. 해를 입지 않도록; 안전하게. ¶ *keep out of harm's way* 해를 입지 않도록 하다; 화를 피하다.

— *vt.* (P6) damage; hurt; injure. …을 해치다; 손상하다; 다치게 하다. [F.]

har·mat·tan [hɑ̀ːrmətǽn, hɑːrmǽtən] *n.* the parching African land-wind. 하르마탄 《아프리카의 건조한 열풍》. [Negro]

•**harm·ful** [hɑ́ːrmfəl] *adj.* causing damage; injurious; hurtful. 유해한; 해를(해독을) 끼치는. ¶ *a ~ drug* 유해한 약 / *a ~ idea* 위험한 사상. ●**harm·ful·ness** [-nis] *n.* Ⓤ [*harm*]

harm·ful·ly [hɑ́ːrmfəli] *adv.* in a harmful manner. 해롭게; 유해하게.

•**harm·less** [hɑ́ːrmlis] *adj.* causing no harm; having no power to harm anyone or anything. 해를 끼치지 않는; 악의 없는; 천진한. ¶ *a ~ snake* 독 없는 뱀 / *a ~ drug* 무해한 약 / *save someone ~* 아무를 안전하게 구하다 / *The bullet struck a ~ passer-by.* 총탄이 죄 없는 통행인을 맞혔다.

har·mon·ic [hɑːrmɑ́nik / -mɔ́n-] *adj.* **1** having harmony; harmonious; musical. 조화의; 조화된; 화성(和聲)의. **2** 《phys.》 indicating a series of oscillations accompanying a fundamental frequency. 조화 진동의. — *n.* Ⓒ 《mus.》 a fainter and higher tone heard along with the main tone; an overtone. 배음(倍音). [*harmony*]

har·mon·i·ca [hɑːrmɑ́nikə / -mɔ́n-] *n.* Ⓒ a small, musical wind instrument with metal reeds, played by the mouth; a mouth organ. 하모니카.

harmonic progression [-ˊ-ˊ-ˊ-] *n.* = harmonic series.

har·mon·ics [hɑːrmɑ́niks / -mɔ́n-] *n. pl.* 《used as *sing.*》 the science of musical sounds. 화성학(和聲學).

harmonic series [-ˊ-ˊ-] *n.* 《math.》 a series of numbers the reciprocals of which are in arithmetic progression. 조화급수.

•**har·mo·ni·ous** [hɑːrmóuniəs] *adj.* **1** 《mus.》 having or producing harmony; having a sweet sound; melodious. 가락이 맞는; 선율이 아름다운; 화성(和聲)의. **2** (of form) well adapted in size and shape. 조화된; 균형이 잡힌. ¶ *~ colors* 잘 조화된 색채 / *a ~ arrangement of lines* 조화된 선의 배열. **3** getting on well together; free from disagreement. 사이좋은; 화합한; 화목한. ¶ *a ~ family* 화목한 가족 / *~ neighbors* 사이좋은 이웃. [*harmony*]

har·mo·ni·ous·ly [hɑːrmóuniəsli] *adv.* in a harmonious manner. 조화되어; 가락이 맞게; 화목하게.

har·mo·ni·um [hɑːrmóuniəm] *n.* Ⓒ a small organ with metal reeds. (교회 따위에서 볼 수 있는) 작은 오르간.

har·mo·nize [hɑ́ːrmənàiz] *vt., vi.* (P6,13; 1,3) **1** 《*with*》 bring into accord or agreement; be in harmony or agreement. 조화시키다(되다). ¶ *These colors ~ well with the walls.* 이 색들은 벽과 잘 조화된다. **2** add harmony to (a melody). …에 화성(和聲)(조화음)을 가하다.

•**har·mo·ny** [hɑ́ːrməni] *n.* ⓊⒸ (*pl.* **-nies**) **1** ⓐ a due proportion and adaptation of the parts in relation to the whole so as to make a pleasing impression. (각 부분의 전체에 대한) 조화. ¶ *the ~ of motion in dancing*

춤에서 동작의 조화. ⓑ an appropriate or pleasing combination (of colors in a picture, etc.). (색채·형태 따위의) 조화. ¶ *the ~ of colors* 색채의 조화 / *the perfect ~ of mind and body* 심신의 완전한 조화. **2** going on well together; agreement. 화목; 화합; 일치; 협화. ¶ *live in ~ with one's neighbors* 이웃과 사이좋게 지내다 / *work in ~ with one's colleagues* 동료들과 사이좋게 어울려 일하다. **3** 《mus.》 a pleasing combination of notes sounding together in a chord; sweet or pleasing sound; music. 화성(和聲); 해조(諧調); 음악(opp. discord). **4** bringing together of different stories or accounts of the same event or set of events in such a way as to show their essential agreement. (4복음서 따위의) 일치점, 요람(要覽); 공관서(共觀書). [Gk.]

in harmony, harmonious(ly); friendly. 조화를 이루어; 사이좋게; 화목하게.

:har·ness [hɑ́ːrnis] *n.* Ⓤ **1** 《*collectively*》 leather straps, bands, etc., used to attach a horse to a carriage, wagon, plow, etc. (마차, 쟁기 끄는 말의) 마구(馬具). **2** 《*arch.*》 armor for a soldier or horse. 무구(武具); 갑주.

die in harness, die while still working actively. 집무 중에 쓰러지다.

in harness, at one's daily work; in business. (평소의) 일[직무]에 종사하고.

work [***run***] ***in double harness,*** work with a partner; earn a livelihood with one's wife. (부부가) 맞벌이하다.

— *vt.* (P6) **1** put harness on (a horse, etc.). …에 마구를 채우다. ¶ *~ a horse to a carriage* 말에 끌채를 씌워 수레와 연결하다. **2** cause (water, wind, etc.) to produce power. (풍력·수력 따위)를 동력에 이용하다. ¶ *~ the energy of the sun* 태양열을 이용하다. **3** 《*arch.*》 put armor on a soldier, etc. 병사에게 갑주를 입히다. [F.]

Har·old [hǽrəld] *n.* a man's name. 남자의 이름.

·harp [hɑːrp] *n.* Ⓒ a stringed musical instrument set in a triangular frame, played with the fingers. 하프; 수금(竪琴).

— *vi.* (P1,3) **1** play on a harp. 하프를 타다. **2** 《*on, upon*》 keep on talking or writing about; refer constantly to. 같은 일을 되풀이해서 말하다[쓰다]. ¶ *always ~ on the same string* 언제나 같은 말을 되뇌다. [E.]

harp·er [hɑ́ːrpər] *n.* =harpist.

harp·ist [hɑ́ːrpist] *n.* Ⓒ a person who plays the harp. 하프 연주자(演奏者).

har·poon [hɑːrpúːn] *n.* Ⓒ a barbed spear with a rope attached to it, used to catch whales and large fish. (고래잡이용의) 작살. — *vt.* (P6) strike or kill (whales, etc.) with a harpoon. …에 작살을 쏘아 박다; 작살로 잡다. [Gk. *harpē* sickle]

harp·si·chord [hɑ́ːrpsikɔ̀ːrd] *n.* Ⓒ a musical instrument like a piano, used before the piano. 하프시코드《건반 악기의 하나로 피아노의 전신》. [*harp, chord*]

〈harpsichord〉

Har·py [hɑ́ːrpi] *n.* (*pl.* **-pies**) **1** 《Gk. myth.》 a dirty, greedy monster with a woman's head and a bird's body. 여면조신(女面鳥身)의 날개를 가진 괴물. **2** Ⓒ 《*h-*》 a cruel, greedy person who preys upon his or her kind. (동족을 잡아먹는) 잔인하고도 탐욕스러운 사람. [Gk. *harpazo* snatch]

har·que·bus [hɑ́rkwibəs, -kə-] *n.* 《hist.》 an old form of portable gun. 화승총(火繩銃). [Teut. =hook-gun]

har·ri·dan [hǽrədən] *n.* a bad-tempered old woman. 간악한 할멈. [? F.]

har·ri·er[1] [hǽriər] *n.* **1** a small hunting-dog used to hunt hares. 해리어《토끼 사냥에 쓰이는 사냥개》. **2** a cross-country runner. 크로스컨트리 레이스의 주자(走者). [*hare, -ier*]

har·ri·er[2] [hǽriər] *n.* **1** a person who harries. 약탈자; 침략자. **2** a kind of low-flying hawk. 개구리매. [*harry*]

Har·ri·et [hǽriət] *n.* a woman's name. 여자의 이름.

har·row [hǽrou] *n.* Ⓒ an implement with iron teeth or disks which is drawn over plowed land to break up the soil. 써레.

under the harrow, in great pain or difficulty. 괴로움[어려움, 고통]을 당하여; 끊임없이 시달려[압박을 받아].

— *vt.* (P6) **1** draw a harrow over (land, etc.). …을 써레질하다. **2** hurt the feelings of (someone); wound; distress. 감정을 상하게 하다; 괴롭히다. [E.]

Har·row [hǽrou] *n.* an old and famous boys' boarding school near London. 해로교(校). 參考 유명한 퍼블릭 스쿨.

har·row·ing [hǽrouiŋ] *adj.* wounding to the feelings; very painful. 고뇌를 주는; 괴로운. ¶ *a ~ experience* 괴로운 경험. [*harrow*]

Har·ry [hǽri] *n.* a man's name; sometimes a nickname of Henry. 남자의 이름.

har·ry [hǽri] *vt.* (**-ried**) (P6) **1** attack (a place) and rob. …을 약탈하다. **2** torment; worry. …을 괴롭히다. [E.]

·harsh [hɑːrʃ] *adj.* **1** rough to the touch, taste, or hearing; sharp and unpleasant. 거친; 껄껄한; 껄끄러운; 귀[눈]에 거슬리는; 불쾌한(opp. smooth). ¶ *a ~ cloth* 감촉이 껄끄러운 천 / *a ~ odor* 불쾌한 냄새 / *a ~ sound* 귀에 거슬리는 소리 / *a ~ surface* 꺼칠꺼칠한 표면. **2** (of a person) unkind; cruel; severe. 엄(격)한; 가혹한; 냉혹한. ¶ *a ~ life* 험난한 생애 / *a ~ master* 무자비한 주인 / *~ punishment* 호된 벌 / *say a ~ word to one's wife* 아내에게 심한 소리를 하다. [E.]

harsh·ly [háːrʃli] *adv.* in a harsh manner. 거칠게; 엄하게; 귀에 거슬리게; 불쾌하게.

harsh·ness [háːrʃnis] *n.* Ⓤ the quality or state of being harsh; severeness. 엄함; 가혹함; 냉혹함.

hart [haːrt] *n.* Ⓒ (*pl.* **harts** or *collectively* **hart**) a male of the red deer; a stag. 붉은 사슴의 수컷; 수사슴. [E.]

har·um-scar·um [hɛ́ərəmskɛ́ərəm] *adj.* reckless; thoughtless; irresponsible. 무모한; 무분별한; 무책임한. — *adv.* recklessly. 무모〔무분별〕하게; 경솔하게. — *n.* **1** a reckless person. 무분별〔무모〕한 사람. **2** 《*arch.*》 a reckless behavior. 무분별〔무모〕한 행동. [*hare, scare*]

Har·vard [háːrvərd] *n.* the oldest university in the United States. 하버드 대학. 參考 미국에서 가장 오래 된 대학. 1636년 창립됨.

:har·vest [háːrvist] *n.* Ⓒ **1** the act of gathering in crops. 수확; 추수. ¶ *the rice* ~ 벼 수확. **2** the time or season for gathering in crops. 수확기(期). **3** gathered crops. 수확물; 작(作). ¶ *a good* ~ 풍작 / *an average* ~ 평년작 / *a* ~ *of nuts* 수확한 견과. **4** result; reward. 결과; 보수; 댓가. ¶ *the* ~ *of one's mistakes* 잘못의 댓가 / *reap the* ~ *of one's labors* 노동의 보수를 받다. — *vt., vi.* (P6; 1) gather in (a crop of grain, etc.). (…을) 수확하다; 거둬들이다. [E.]

har·vest·er [háːrvistər] *n.* Ⓒ **1** a person who works to gather crops; a reaper. 수확자. **2** a machine for gathering crops. 수확기(機).

harvest festival [⌐–⌐––] *n.* a festival held in Christian churches for thanksgiving after the harvest has been gathered. (교회에서 하는) 수확제; 추수 감사 행사.

harvest home [⌐–⌐] *n.* **1** the end of harvest. 수확의 완료. **2** a festival celebrated at the end of harvest; a harvest song sung at this festival. (수확의 끝남을 축하하는) 수확의 축제; 이 때 부르는 노래.

harvest moon [⌐–⌐] *n.* the full moon at harvest time or in late September. 중추의 만월.

:has [hæz, həz, əz, z] *v.* 3rd person singular present indicative of **have.**

has-been [hǽzbìn] *n.* Ⓒ 《*colloq.*》 a person or thing that is no longer successful or popular. 전성기를 지난 사람〔것〕; 시대에 뒤떨어진 사람〔것〕; 과거의 사람〔것〕. [*has, been*]

hash [hæʃ] *n.* **1** Ⓤ a dish of meat, mixed with potatoes, etc. and cut into small pieces. (야채가 섞인) 잘게 저민 고기 요리. ¶ ~ *and rice* 해시 라이스. **2** Ⓒ a mixture of things used before; a mixture. (뒤)범벅; 그러모음.

make* (*a*) *hash of, 《*colloq.*》 defeat or destroy (an opponent, an argument, etc.); do (something) badly. (상대)를 해치우다; 찍소리 못 하게 하다; …을 망쳐 놓다.

settle someone's hash, 《*colloq.*》 silence or defeat someone completely; put an end to someone. (아무)를 해치우다〔굴복시키다〕; 찍소리 못 하게 하다; 끝장내다.

— *vt.* (P6,7) **1** chop or cut (meat and vegetables) into small pieces. (고기나 야채)를 잘게 저미다. **2** 《*colloq.*》 make a mess of (someone or something). …을 엉망으로 만들다; 망치다. [F. *hache* axe]

hash over, **a**) reconsider. 재고하다. **b**) discuss more than once. 재차〔다시〕 논하다.

hash·eesh [hǽʃiːʃ] *n.* =hashish.

hash·er [hǽʃər] *n.* Ⓒ a person who waits on others sitting at a table. (식당의) 사환; 웨이터. [*hash*]

hash·ish [hǽʃiːʃ] *n.* a preparation made from Indian hemp which causes people to lose their right senses. (인도산 대마(大麻)를 조합한) 마취제; 해시시. [Arab.]

·has·n't [hǽznt] =has not.

hasp [hæsp, haːsp] *n.* Ⓒ a clasp, esp. a hinged metal clasp, used to fasten a door, lid, etc. 문고리; 잠그개. — *vt.* (P6) fasten with a hasp. …을 문고리〔잠그개〕로 잠그다. [E.]

has·sock [hǽsək] *n.* Ⓒ **1** a thick heavy cushion or mat to sit, or kneel on. (꿇어앉을 때의) 무릎 깔개〔방석〕. **2** a tuft of coarse grass. 풀숲. [E.]

·hast [hæst, həst, əst, st] *v.* 《*arch.*》 2nd person singular present indicative of **have.** 語法 주어 thou 에 쓰임.

:haste [heist] *n.* Ⓤ the act of hurrying; quickness of action or movement; rashness. 급함; 서두름; 급속; 신속; 경솔; 당황. ¶ *be in* ~ *to get ahead in the world* 출세하려고 안달하다 / 《*prov.*》 *Haste makes waste.* 서두르면 일을 잡친다.

in haste, in a hurry; rashly. 급히; 서둘러; 경솔히; 당황하여. ¶ *send for a doctor in* (*great*) ~ 급히 의사를 부르러 보내다.

make haste, hurry; be quick. 서두르다; 급히 하다〔가다〕. ¶ *Make* ~ , *or you will miss the train.* 서둘러라, 그렇지 않으면 열차를 놓친다.

— *vt., vi.* (P6; 1) 《rare》 hasten. (…을) 서두르(게 하)다. [Teut.]

haste away, depart with speed. 급히 가다〔떠나다〕.

:has·ten [héisn] *vt.* (P6) cause (someone) to hurry; speed up. …을 서두르(게 하)다; 재촉하다; (속도·일 따위)를 빠르게 하다. ¶ ~ *the growth of plants* 식물의 성장을 촉진하다 / ~ *one's preparations* 준비를 서두르다. — *vi.* (P1,2A,4) be quick; move with speed. 서두르다; 급히 …하다. ¶ ~ *away* 〔*back, down, out, home*〕 급히 가다〔돌아오다, 내리다, 나가다, 귀가하다〕 / *I hastened to change the subject.* 급히 화제를 바꿨다.

·hast·i·ly [héistili] *adv.* in a hasty manner. 급히; 서둘러; 조급히.

hast·i·ness [héistinis] *n.* Ⓤ the quality or

state of being hasty. 급함; 성급함; 경솔.

*__hast·y__ [héisti] *adj.* (**hast·i·er, hast·i·est**) **1** hurried; quick. 급한; 급속한; 신속한. ¶ *a ~ departure* 허둥대는 출발 / *the ~ growth of plants* 식물의 급속한 성장. **2** carelessly said or done; rash. 조급한; 경솔한. ¶ *a ~ judgment* 조급한 판단 / *jump to a ~ conclusion* 성급한 결론을 내리다 / *His ~ remarks caused many misunderstandings.* 그의 경솔한 말은 많은 오해를 낳게 했다. **3** quick-tempered. (기질이) 성급한; 성마른. ¶ *a ~ temper.* [→haste]

:**hat** [hæt] *n.* Ⓒ a covering for the head, usu. with a brim and a crown. 모자. ¶ *a top* 〔*high*〕 *~* 실크 해트 / *have* 〔*keep*〕 *one's ~ on* 모자를 쓰고 있다 / *put on one's ~* 모자를 쓰다 / *Hats off!* 모자를 벗으시오.

(**as**) ***black as one's hat,*** very black. 새까만.

hang up one's hat, pay a long visit (in a house); settle down. 오래 머무르다〔있다〕; 푹 쉬다.

hat in hand, respectfully; humbly. 겸손하게; 공손한 태도로.

My hat! 《*colloq.*》 an exclamation of surprise. 아니; 어머; 이런.

pass 〔***pass*** (**a**)***round, send*** (**a**)***round, go*** (**a**)***round with***〕 ***the hat,*** 《*colloq.*》 ask for contributions of money at a meeting, etc. 모자를 돌려 기부금을 걷다.

raise 〔***take off, touch***〕 ***one's hat to someone,*** greet someone by raising, etc. one's hat. …에게 모자를 들어〔를 벗고, 에 손을 대고〕 인사하다; 경의를 표하다.

talk through one's hat, 《*colloq.*》 talk nonsense. (사실을 모르고) 큰소리치다; 허튼 소리를 하다.

throw 〔***toss***〕 ***one's hat into the ring,*** 《*colloq.*》 enter a competition, esp. an election. 경쟁에 참가하다; 입후보를 선언하다.

under one's hat, 《*colloq.*》 secret; told or written in private. 비밀히; 남몰래.

— *vt.* (**hat·ted, hat·ting**) (P6) cover or provide (someone) with a hat. …에게 모자를 씌우다. [E.]

hat·band [hǽtbæ̀nd] *n.* Ⓒ a band around a hat, just above the brim. 모자의 리본; 테.

*__hatch__[1] [hætʃ] *vt.* (P6) **1** bring forth (young) from eggs. (알·병아리)를 까다; 부화하다. ¶ *~ eggs* 〔*chickens*〕 알을〔병아리를〕 까다 / 《*prov.*》 *Don't count your chickens before they are hatched.* 너구리 굴 보고 피물 돈 내어 쓴다. **2** plot; plan. …을 몰래 꾸미다〔꾀하다〕. ¶ *~ a plot* 음모를 꾸미다 / *~ a scheme* 계획을 세우다. — *vi.* (P1,2A) 《*out*》 bring forth young; come forth from the egg. (알·병아리가) 깨다; 부화하다. — *n.* Ⓒ the act of hatching; all the chickens, etc. hatched at one time. 부화; 한 배의 병아리. [E.]

*__hatch__[2] [hætʃ] *n.* Ⓒ **1** 《naut.》 an opening in a deck. (갑판의) 승강구; 해치. **2** an opening in the floor or roof of a building, etc. (마루·지붕·천장의) 창문; 출입구. **3** a cover for such an opening. 그러한 출입구의 뚜껑. **4** the lower half of a divided door. (상하 두 부분으로 된) 문의 아래짝; 반문(半門). [E.]

under hatches, **a**) put away below deck. 갑판 밑에. **b**) off duty. 비번(非番)인. **c**) put away out of sight; 《*fig.*》 dead and buried. 보이지 않게; 죽어.

hatch[3] [hætʃ] *vt.* (P6) draw, cut or engrave fine parallel lines on. …에 평행선을 긋다〔새기다, 음영(陰影)을 넣다〕. — *n.* Ⓒ one of such a set of lines. 선영(線影); 평행선의 음영. [→hatchet]

hatch·er·y [hǽtʃəri] *n.* Ⓒ (*pl.* **-er·ies**) a place where eggs, esp. those of fish or poultry, are hatched. (물고기·닭 따위의) 부란장(孵卵場); 부화장. [*hatch*[1]]

hatch·et [hǽtʃit] *n.* Ⓒ a small ax with a short handle. 손도끼; 자귀. [→hash]

bury the hatchet, 〈hatchet〉 make peace; agree to end a quarrel. 싸움을 그만두다; 화해하다.

take 〔***dig***〕 ***up the hatchet,*** start fighting; make war. 싸움을 시작하다.

throw the hatchet, 《*sl.*》 talk big; exaggerate. 허풍을 떨다; 어마어마하게 과장하다.

throw the helve after the hatchet, add loss to loss. 손해에 손해를 거듭하다.

hatchet face [⌐-⌐] *n.* a thin narrow face suggesting a hatchet. 뾰족하고 마른 얼굴.

hatch·ing [hǽtʃiŋ] *n.* fine, parallel lines drawn, cut, or engraved close together. (제도·지도 따위에서) 해칭; 음영선(陰影線); 선영(線影). [*hatch*[3]]

hatch·ment [hǽtʃmənt] *n.* 《her.》 a square tablet bearing the coat of arms of a dead person. 상중문장(喪中紋章). 參考 죽은 사람의 무덤이나 문앞 같은 데에 겂. [*achievement*]

hatch·way [hǽtʃwèi] *n.* Ⓒ 《naut.》 an opening in the deck of a ship for going below. (배의) 승강구; 창구(艙口). [*hatch*[2]]

:**hate** [heit] *vt.* (P6,8,9,11,20) dislike very strongly; detest; regret. …을 미워〔증오〕하다; 몹시 싫어하다; 유감으로 여기다(opp. love, like). ¶ *I ~ dogs.* 개를 싫어한다 / *I ~ to do it.* 그런 일은 하고 싶지 않다 / *I ~ troubling* 〔*to trouble*〕 *you.* 폐를 끼쳐 미안합니다 / *I ~ to have you say such a thing.* 자네가 그런 말을 하는 것은 유감이네 / *I ~ that you should think so.* 자네가 그렇게 생각 안 했으면 좋겠네. — *vi.* feel a strong dislike. 싫어하다; 미워〔증오〕하다.

hate out, 《U.S.》 drive out (someone) by a strong dislike. 미워하여 …을 쫓아내다; 따돌리다.

—*n.* Ⓤ very strong dislike. 증오. [E.]

***hate·ful** [héitfəl] *adj.* **1** causing hate; deserving hate. 미운; 증오할 만한; 싫은; 지겨운. ¶ *Murder is a ~ thing.* 살인은 가증할 일이다. **2** full of hate; showing hate. 증오에 찬; 증오를 나타내는. ¶ *a ~ glance* 〔*speech*〕 증오에 찬 눈〔말〕. ● **hate·ful·ly** [-fəli] *adv.* **hate·ful·ness** [-nis] *n.*

hat·ful [hǽtfùl] *n.* as much or as many as a hat will hold. 모자 하나 가득(한 양). [*hat*]

***hath** [hæθ, *h*əθ] *v.* 《*arch.*》 =has.

hat·less [hǽtlis] *adj.* wearing no hat. 모자를 쓰지 않은. [*hat*]

hat·pin [hǽtpìn] *n.* a long, sharp pin worn to fasten a woman's hat to her hair. (여성 모자의) 고정핀.

hat·rack [hǽtræ̀k] *n.* Ⓒ a rack, shelf, hooks, etc. to put hats on. 모자걸이.

***ha·tred** [héitrid] *n.* Ⓤ 《sometimes *a* ~》 very strong dislike; ill will; hate. (강한) 증오; 혐오; 원한. ¶ *a ~ of conventionality* 인습에 대한 강한 반감 / *have a ~ for* 〔*of*〕 *someone* 아무를 미워하다 / *in ~ of someone* 아무를 미워〔증오〕하여 / *He looked at me with eyes full of ~.* 증오에 찬 눈으로 나를 쳐다보았다. [*hate*]

hat·ter [hǽtə*r*] *n.* Ⓒ a person who makes or sells hats. 모자 제조〔판매〕인; 모자상(商). [*hat*]

as mad as a hatter, 《*colloq.*》 very mad or angry. 완전히 미쳐; 격노하여.

hau·berk [hɔ́ːbəːrk] *n.* a coat of chain mail worn in the Middle Ages. (중세의) 사슬 갑옷. [Teut. =neck-cover]

haugh·ti·ly [hɔ́ːtili] *adv.* in a haughty manner. 오만〔거만〕하게; 건방지게; 불손하게. [*haughty*]

haugh·ti·ness [hɔ́ːtinis] *n.* Ⓤ the state of being haughty. 오만〔거만〕함; 불손함; 건방짐.

***haugh·ty** [hɔ́ːti] *adj.* (**-ti·er, -ti·est**) very proud and arrogant. 거만〔오만〕한; 불손한; 건방진. ¶ *be ~ to one's inferiors* 아랫사람에게 거만하다. [L. *altus* high]

***haul** [hɔːl] *vt.* **1** (P6,7) pull or draw (something) with force; tug; drag. …을 세게 잡아 끌다; 잡아〔끌어〕당기다. ¶ *~ a net* 그물을 (잡아)당기다 / *~ a wagon* 짐마차를 끌다 / *~ out a stump* 그루터기를 잡아 뽑다. **2** (P13) move or transport by pulling. …을 끌어 운반하다; 차로 나르다〔수송하다〕. ¶ *~ coal from the mine* 탄광에서 석탄을 운반하다 / *~ timber to a sawmill* 목재를 제재소로 나르다. **3** 《naut.》 change the course of a ship to sail closer to the wind. (배의) 방향을 돌리다. ¶ *~ a ship on as wind.*

—*vi.* (P1,2A,3) **1** pull; tug. 잡아당기다. ¶ *~ at* 〔*upon*〕 *a rope* 로프를 끌어당기다. **2** change the course of a ship; change direction; change one's course of action or opinion. (배가) 방향을 바꾸다; (행동·의견 따위를) 전향하다. ¶ *~ around* 방향을 돌리다 / *The wind has hauled to the west.* 풍향이 서쪽으로 바뀌었다.

haul down one's flag 〔***colors***〕, give in; surrender. 항복하다.

haul in with, 《naut.》 bring up (a ship) close to. …에 접근하도록 뱃머리를 돌리다; …에 배를 접근시키다.

haul off, **a**) turn a ship away from a destination. (피하기 위해) 진로를 바꾸다. **b**) go back; withdraw. 물러나다; 후퇴〔퇴각〕하다. **c**) 《*colloq.*》 draw one's arm back before hitting. (사람을 치려고) 팔을 뒤로 빼다.

haul someone over the coals, scold; criticize; take someone to task. (호되게) 꾸짖다; 비난하다.

haul to 〔***on, onto***〕 ***the wind,*** 《naut.》 head the bow of a ship closer into the wind. 뱃머리를 바람 불어 오는 쪽으로 돌리다.

haul up, **a**) turn a ship nearer to the direction of the wind; change the course of (a ship). 바람 불어 오는 쪽으로 뱃머리를 돌리다; (배의) 침로를 바꾸다. **b**) come to a halt. (배가) 정지하다. **c**) call to account. …을 문책하다; 야단치다.

—*n.* Ⓒ **1** the act of hauling; a strong pull or tug. 세게 끌기; (잡아)당기기; 견인. **2** the distance over which a thing is pulled or drawn. (끌어) 나르는 거리; 운반〔수송〕 거리〔루트〕. ¶ *a ~ of 40 miles* 40 마일의 운송 거리 / *a long ~ on the railway* 철도의 긴 수송 거리. **3** a single pulling of a net; the quantity of fish caught at one time; loot; booty. 한 그물분의 어획(량); 이득. ¶ *get* 〔*make*〕 *a good* 〔*big, fine*〕 *~* 고기를 많이 잡다; 큰 벌이를 하다.

● **haul·er** [-ə*r*] *n.* [*hale*[2]]

haul·age [hɔ́ːlidʒ] *n.* Ⓤ **1** the act of hauling. 끌기; 당기기; 운반(작업). **2** the force used in hauling. 견인력. **3** the charge made for hauling. 운반비; 운임.

haunch [hɔːntʃ, hɑːntʃ] *n.* Ⓒ **1** 《usu. *pl.*》 the parts of an animal's or a man's body round the hips; the hips. 궁둥이; 둔부; 허리. ¶ *squat on one's haunches* 웅크리고 앉다. **2** the leg and loin of an animal, used for food. (식용으로서의) 동물의 허리 부위와 다리 부분. [F.]

***haunt** [hɔːnt, hɑːnt] *vt.* (P6) **1** ⓐ visit (a place) often or repeatedly; visit (someone) frequently. …에 자주〔잘〕 가다; …에 빈번히 들르다; 자주 나타나다. ¶ *~ the theater* 극장에 자주 가다 / *People say ghosts ~ that old house.* 사람들은 그 집에 유령이 자주 나타난다고 한다. ⓑ frequent the company of; be often with. …와 노상 어울리다; 자주 …와 함께 있다. ¶ *~ bad company* 못된 친구들과 자주 어울리다. **2** trouble or bother (someone) by constantly returning to his mind or memory. (기억·생각 따위가 머릿속에서 떠나지 않고) …을 괴롭히다. ¶ *be haunted by fear* 끊임없이 두려움에 시달리다 / *I am haunted with these thoughts.* 이런 생각들이 항상 내

마음에서 떠나지 않는다.
—*n.* Ⓒ **1** 《often *pl.*》 a place often visited. 자주(잘) 가는 곳; 출몰 장소; 소굴. ¶ *a ~ of criminals* 범죄자의 소굴 / *holiday haunts* 휴일의 행락지 / *return to one's old haunts* 옛 소굴로 되돌아오다. **2** 《*colloq.*》 a ghost. 유령. [F.]

haunt·ed [hɔ́:ntid, hɑ́:ntid] *adj.* visited or lived in by ghosts. 유령이 나오는. ¶ *a ~ house* 유령이 나오는 집.

Haupt·mann [háuptmɑ̀:n], **Gerhart** *n.* (1862-1946) a German novelist, dramatist and poet. 하우프트만《독일의 소설가·극작가·시인》.

haut·boy [hóubɔi] *n.* 《mus.》 an oboe. 오보에. [F. =high wood]

hau·teur [houtə́:r] *n.* 《F.》 Ⓤ haughty manner; haughtiness. 오만; 거만.

Ha·van·a [həvǽnə] *n.* **1** the capital of Cuba. 아바나《Cuba 의 수도》. **2** a cigar made in Cuba. 아바나 여송연.

⁑**have** [hæv, həv, əv, v] *v.* (*pres.* 3rd person *sing.* **has** [hæz, həz, əz]; negative **haven't** [hǽvənt], 3rd person *sing.* **hasn't** [hǽznt]; *p.* & *pp.* **had** [hæd, həd, əd]) *vt.* **1** (P6,13) ⓐ possess; hold; own; keep; contain. …을 가지(고 있)다; …이 있다; …을 포함하다. ¶ *I ~ a book.* 책을 가지고 있다 / *He has property.* 그에게는 재산이 있다 / *She has the right to vote.* 그녀에겐 투표권이 있다 / *She had a doll in her hand.* 그녀는 손에 인형을 갖고 있었다 / *Does the house ~ a good garage?* 그 집엔 좋은 차고가 있습니까 / *You ~ my apologies.* 사과드립니다 / *What do you ~ in your pocket?* 호주머니에 무엇이 들어 있나 / *A week has seven days.* 1주일은 7일이다 / *He doesn't ~ any money.* 그는 돈을 갖고 있지 않다. 語法 do not have는 미국 용법, have not는 영국 용법. ⓑ hold or keep in the mind. (마음에) 가지다; 품다; 생각하고 있다. ¶ *~ an idea* (*opinion*) 구상(의견)이 있다 / *~ doubts* 의심을 품다 / *~ no fear* 두렵지 않다 / *Do you ~ any questions?* 질문 있습니까. ⓒ show by action; use; exercise. (행동·말 따위로) 나타내다; 행사하다. ¶ *~ mercy on* …을 가엾이 여기다; …에게 자비를(동정을) 베풀다 / *~ great respect for age* 노인에 대해 크게 경의를 표하다 / *Will you ~ the goodness* (*kindness*) *to do ...?* 부디 …을 해 주시지 않겠습니까. **2** (P6) possess (something) as a mental or physical characteristic. (정신적·신체적 특성)이 있다; 가지다. ¶ *~ a good* (*poor*) *memory* 기억력이 좋다(나쁘다) / *She has red hair.* 그녀는 머리털이 붉다 / *He has only one leg.* 그는 다리가 하나뿐이다. **3** (P6) ⓐ experience; enjoy or undergo. (상태·즐거움·고통 따위를) 경험하다; 즐기다; 당하다; 겪다. ¶ *~ fun* (*a good time*) (시간을) 재미있게 보내다 / *~ a hard* (*trying*) *time* 괴로운 때를(시련을) 겪다; 혼나다 / *I had a terrible dream last night.* 간밤에 무서운 꿈을 꾸었다. ⓑ suffer from. (천재(天災) 따위가) 있다; (병 따위에) 걸리다. ¶ *~ an illness* 병에 걸리다 / *~ a headache* 두통이 있다 / *~ an earthquake* 지진이 나다 / *Do you often ~ colds?* 자넨 감기에 잘 걸리나. **4** (P6) there is; there are. 가지다; 있다. ¶ *I ~ no money left.* 남은 돈이 없다 / *We ~ had much rain this year.* 올해엔 많은 비가 내렸다 / *My room has two windows.* 내 방엔 창문이 두 개 있다 / *He has something strange about him.* 그에겐 이상한 데가 있다. **5** (P6,13) perform; do; engage in; carry on. …에 종사하다; …을 행하다. 語法 동작을 나타내는 목적어를 수반하여 동사의 뜻을 나타냄. ¶ *~ a dance* 춤을 추다 / *~ a talk* 이야기를 하다 / *~ a bath* 목욕하다 / *~ a walk* 산책하다 / *~ a look* 보다 / *~ a smoke* (*drink*) 담배 한 대 피우다(술 한 잔 하다) / *~ a dream* 꿈을 꾸다 / *Let's ~ a try.* 해 봅시다. **6** (P6,13) ⓐ receive; get; take. …을 받다; 얻다. ¶ *~ lessons in dancing* 춤 교습을 받다 / *~ a part in a play* 연극에서 배역을 맡다 / *We had a visitor yesterday.* 어제 방문객이 있었다. ⓑ eat; drink. …을 먹다; 마시다. ¶ *~ a good breakfast* (*a glass of beer*) 훌륭한 아침 식사를(맥주 한 잔을) 하다 / *Will you ~ tea or coffee?* 홍차로 하시겠습니까, 커피를 드시겠습니까. **7** (P24) ⓐ cause it to be done, get it done. …하게 하다; …시키다; …해 받다. ¶ *I must ~ this watch repaired.* 이 시계를 수리시키지 않으면 안 되겠다 / *I had my hair cut.* 머리를 깎게 했다《이발했다》. ⓑ suffer or experience. (좋지 않은 일을) 당하다; 겪다. ¶ *I had my purse stolen.* 돈지갑을 도둑맞았다. ⓒ have finished doing by a certain time. 어느 때까지 끝내고(마치고) 있다. ¶ *You must ~ your homework done by tomorrow morning.* 내일 아침까지는 숙제를 마치고 있어야 한다. **8** (P7,18,23) do and keep done; leave. …을 그냥 그대로 두다. ¶ *~ a baby sleeping* 아기를 그대로 자게 두다 / *Let's ~ a window open.* 창문을 열어 둡시다 / *Let's ~ the light on.* 불을 켠 채로 놔 둡시다. **9** (P22) cause (someone) to do or to be. …로 하여금 —하게 하다; …에게 —시키다; …당하다. 語法 목적어로 '사람'이 온다. ¶ *Have the maid sweep the room.* 가정부에게 방을 청소시켜라 / *She had her son die.* 그녀는 아들을 여의였다 / *I should like to ~ you meet my father.* 우리 아버지를 만나게 하고 싶다 / *He had his sister help him with the work.* 그는 누이로 하여금 자기 일을 돕게 했다 / *We had the boys steal our dog.* 우리들의 개를 아이들에게 도둑맞았다. **10** (P6,7,22,23,24) 《usu. in *negative*》 allow; permit; bear. 허락하다; 용서(용납)하다; 참다. ¶ *~ the girl out after dark* 여자아이에게 일몰 후의 외출을 허락하다 / *I won't ~ this nonsense.* 이 따위 허튼 수작을 용서할 수 없다 / *I will not ~ it.* 용서할 수는 없다 / *I won't have you say such things.* 네가 그런 말을 하면 용서 않겠다. **11** (P6) understand; have knowledge or use of (something). 이해하다; 알(고 있)다; 숙달돼

있다. ¶ *He has no Latin, to say nothing of Greek.* 그는 그리스어는 말할 것도 없고 라틴말도 모른다. **12** (P6,13) retain; keep. 기억하(고 있)다. ¶ *He has the directions in mind.* 지시 사항을 명심하고 있다. **13** (P6,13) 《*colloq.*》 hold at a disadvantage over; defeat. …을 불리한 입장에 두다; 지게 하다. ¶ *You ~ him there.* 그 점에서 자넨 그보다 유리하다 / *He had you completely in the game.* 게임에서 그에게 완전히 지셨군요. **14** (P6,7,15) maintain; assert. (…라고) 하다; 주장〔단언〕하다. ¶ *They will ~ it so.* 그들은 그렇게 주장해 마지않는다 / *Rumor has it that she's going to be married.* 소문에 의하면 그녀는 곧 결혼할 것이라고 한다. 語法 it을 목적어로 함. **15** (P6) 《usu. in *passive*》 ⓐ deceive; cheat. …을 속이다. ¶ *I ~ been had in this trade.* 이 매매에서 나는 감쪽같이 속았다. ⓑ disappoint. …을 실망〔낙담〕시키다. ¶ *He was badly had when he failed in the test.* 테스트에서 실패했을 때 그는 몹시 실망했다. **16** (P6) give birth to. 아이〔새끼〕를 낳다. ¶ *~ a baby / My dog had pubs.* 우리 집 개가 새끼를 낳았다. — *vi.* (P1) be in possession of money or wealth. 돈을 가지고 있다; 재산이 있다.

be had up, be sued. 고소당하다.

had better *do* ⇨had.

had rather ⇨had.

have and hold, possess (something) by law; have permanent possession of (something). …을 보유하다.

have at, 《*arch.*》 **a**) attack. …에게 달려〔덤벼〕들다; …을 공격하다. **b**) go at vigorously. …을 기운차게〔기세 좋게〕 시작하다.

Have done! Stop!; Finish! 멈춰라; 끝내라.

have done with, have finished; have something become unnecessary; make oneself free from someone. …이 끝나다; 필요없게 되다; …와의 관계를 끊다.

have everything *one's* ***own way,*** do everything as one likes. 무엇이건 자기 좋은 대로 하다.

have had it, 《*sl.*》 **a**) become weary of or disgusted with. 싫증나다; 넌더리내다. **b**) suffer defeat; fail. 패배하다; 당하다; 못 쓰게 되다; 실패하다. **c**) have missed one's chance. 기회를 놓치다.

have *someone* ***in,*** have someone in one's room, house, etc.; have someone visit one. (아무를) 집〔방〕에 들이다; 오게 (초대)하다.

have it, **a**) say; declare; tell. 말하다; 주장〔단언〕하다. ¶ *as Plato has it* 플라토가 말하듯이 / *Rumor has it that....* 소문에 의하면 …라고 한다; …라고들 한다. **b**) 《*colloq.*》 beat; defeat; win. 지게 하다; 이기다. **c**) be punished or scolded. 혼나다; 호되게 야단맞다. **d**) 《*colloq.*》 be hopeless. 희망이 없다; 틀렸다. **e**) act. …하다. ¶ *Which way do you want to ~ it?* 어느 쪽으로 하고 싶으십니까 / *Have it your own way.* 마음대로 하시오.

have it coming, 《*colloq.*》 deserve an unpleasant fate. (불행이) 당연한 대갚음으로서 오다; 그건 당연하다〔자업 자득이다〕.

have it in one, 《*colloq.*》 have the courage or ability. (그 사람에게) 그런 용기가 있다; 소질〔역량〕이 있다. ¶ *He has it in him to make his name famous.* 그는 유명해질 소질이 있다.

have it in for, 《*colloq.*》 wish harm to come to (someone); hold ill-will against (someone). …의 불행을 바라다; …에게 원한을〔악의를〕 품다.

have it out of *someone,* return; repay. …에게 보복〔대갚음〕을 하다.

have it out with *someone,* **a**) get a final agreement with someone through fights or discussions. (논쟁 따위에 의해) 최종 합의에 도달하다; 결말을 내다〔짓다〕. **b**) speak out freely. 거리낌없이 말하다.

have no brow of, 《Sc.》 be impressed unfavorably with. …이 싫어지다.

have nothing 〔***something***〕 ***on*** 〔***over***〕 *someone,* **a**) 《U.S.》 have no 〔some〕 advantage or superiority over someone. …보다 나은 데가 없다〔있다〕. **b**) have no 〔some〕 information to the disadvantage of someone. …에게 불리한 정보를 갖고 있지 않다〔있다〕. ¶ *He had something on his teacher.* 그는 자기 선생의 약점을 쥐고 있었다.

have nothing to do with, not concern; not associate with. …와 관계가〔관련이〕 없다. ¶ *~ nothing to do with someone* 아무와 관계가 없다 / *This has nothing to do with you.* 네가 알 바 아니다.

have on, **a**) be wearing; be dressed in. …을 입고 있다. ¶ *He has nothing on.* 그는 아무것도 몸에 걸치지 않고 있다; 알몸이다. **b**) have something arranged. …할 준비가 돼 있다; 계획이 서 있다. ¶ *I ~ nothing on tonight.* 오늘 밤은 아무 계획도 없다.

have *someone* ***on,*** 《*colloq.*》 play a trick on. …에게 장난을 하다; …을 속이다. ¶ *She was having you on when she said that she was married.* 그녀가 결혼을 했다고 했을 때 그녀는 자네를 속이고 있었네.

have only to *do,* need not do anything but... . …하기만 하면 되다.

have *one's* ***own way in everything*** =have everything one's own way.

have to *do,* **a**) be forced to do; must do. …해야(만) 하다. ¶ *I ~ to work hard.* 열심히 일해야 한다 / *You may not want to do, but you'll ~ to.* 하고 싶지는 않을지 모르지만 해야 될 게다 / *My watch will ~ to be mended.* 내 시계는 수리를 하지 않으면 안 되겠다. **b**) 《U.S.》 be certain. 확실하다; 틀림없다. ¶ *He has to be kidding.* 그 사람 농담을 하고 있음에 틀림없다.

have to do with (*=be related to =be connected with =be associated with*) *someone* or *something.* …와 관계가 있다; 관련이 있다.

have someone up, 《usu. in *passive*》 **a**) have someone as a visitor (up to one's room, up from the country, etc.). (위층에서 아래층 사람의) 방문을 받다; (시골로부터 아무를) 초청하다; 올라오게 하다. **b**) bring someone before the authorities, esp. in court; judge someone. …을 법정에 소환하다; 책임을 묻다.

— *auxil. v.* 《with *pp.* of *v.* forming perfects, expressing completion, experience, continuance, or result》 과거 분사와 함께 완료 시제를 만들어, 완료·경험·계속·결과를 나타냄. ¶ *I've just finished it.* 지금 막 끝낸 참이다 / *He has kept it.* 그는 그것을 유지해 왔다 / *When she awoke, the train had already started.* 그녀가 깨었을 때엔 열차는 이미 발차해 버렸다 / *The train will ~ arrived there by ten.* 열차는 10 시까지는 그 곳에 도착해 있을 게다 / *It will ~ been raining a week by tomorrow.* 내일이면 1주일 동안 비가 내린 셈이 된다.

have got, 《*colloq.*》 =have. ¶ *He has* [*He's*] *got a new car.* 새 차를 갖고 있다 / *Have you got the tickets?* 표를 갖고 계십니까(cf. 《U.S.》 *Do you ~ the tickets?*).

***have got to** do,* 《*colloq.*》 =have to do. ¶ *I ~* [*I've*] *got to go now.* 지금 가야만 한다 / *I ~* [*I've*] *got to be at my office at 3 o'clock.* 나는 3 시에 사무실에 있어야 한다.

— [hæv] *n.* Ⓒ **1** 《usu. *pl.*》 《*the ~* 》 a person or country that has much wealth or rich resources. 부자; 부국(富國). **2** 《Brit. *colloq.*》 a trick. 사기. [E.]

haves and have-nots, the rich and the poor; the employers and the employees. 가진 자와 못 가진 자; 경영자와 사용인.

ha·ven [héivən] *n.* Ⓒ **1** a sheltered harbor or port for ships. (피난)항(港). **2** any place of shelter or safety. 피난처. — *vt.* put (a ship) into a port. (배를 항구 따위에) 피난[대피]시키다. [E.]

have-not [hǽvnɑ̀t / -nɔ̀t] *n.* 《usu. *pl.*》 a person or country that has little or no property or wealth. 못 가진 자[나라].

⁝**have·n't** [hǽvənt] =have not.

hav·er·sack [hǽvərsæ̀k] *n.* Ⓒ a bag used by soldiers and hikers for carrying provisions, etc. (병사·여행자의 양식 따위를 넣는) 잡낭(雜囊). [G. =oat-sack]

hav·oc [hǽvək] *n.* Ⓤ very great damage or injury; ruin. (대규모의) 파괴; 황폐. [F.]

cry havoc, 《U.S.》 warn of disaster or danger; 《Brit.》 give the sign to start destroying. 재난[위험]을 예고하다; (군대에) 약탈하라는 신호를 내리다. [F.]

make havoc of =***play havoc among*** [***with***] **a**) destroy; ruin. 파괴하다; 파멸시키다; 망치다. **b**) create disorder or confusion. …을 혼란시키다; 뒤죽박죽을 만들다.

haw[1] [hɔː] *n.* Ⓒ 《bot.》 (the red berry of) a hawthorn. 산사나무(의 열매). [E.]

haw[2] [hɔː] *interj., n.* Ⓒ a stammering sound between words. 어어; 에에《말을 더듬을 때 하는 소리》. — *vi.* (P1) hesitate in speaking. 말을 머뭇거리다; 어어[에에]하다. [Imit.]

haw[3] [hɔː] *interj., n.* Ⓒ a word of command to horses or oxen, directing them to turn to the left or near side. 저라《마소를 "왼쪽으로 돌라"고 할 때의 소리》. — *vt.* turn (horses or oxen) to the left. (마소)를 왼쪽으로 돌게 하다. — *vi.* (of horses or oxen) turn to the left. (마소가) 왼쪽으로 돌다. [M.E. *hawe(n)* look]

Ha·wai·i [həwáiiː, -wɑ́ːjə, hɑːwɑ́ːiː] *n.* the 50th State of the United States. 하와이 주(州). 參考 주도(州都)는 Honolulu.

Ha·wai·ian [həwáiən, həwɑ́ːjən] *adj.* of Hawaii, its people, or their language. 하와이의; 하와이 사람[말]의. — *n.* **1** Ⓒ a person of Hawaii. 하와이 사람. **2** Ⓤ the language of Hawaii. 하와이 말.

haw·berk [hɔ́ːbəːrk] *n.* =hauberk.

haw-haw [hɔ́ːhɔ̀ː] *n.* ha ha. 하하《웃는 소리·웃음》. [Imit.]

·**hawk**[1] [hɔːk] *n.* Ⓒ **1** 《bird》 any of several fierce birds with a strong hooked beak and sharp curved claws. 매. ¶ *a hawk's eye for detecting humbug* 허위를 꿰뚫어 보는 날카로운 눈 / *know a ~ from a handsaw* 판단력이 풍부하다. **2** a person who preys on others. 남을 등쳐먹는 사람; 사기[협잡]꾼. **3** 《*colloq.*》 a person who supports an aggressive or war-like policy. 강경파; 매파 (opp. dove). — *vi.* (P1) hunt with hawks. 매사냥을 하다. — *vt.* (P6) attack (someone or something) as a hawk does. (매처럼) …을 덮치다; …에 덤벼들다. [E.]

hawk[2] [hɔːk] *vt., vi.* try to sell (goods) on the streets by crying out. 외치고 다니며 팔다; 행상하다. [Teut.]

hawk[3] [hɔːk] *vi.* (P1,2A) clear the throat noisily. 헛기침을 하다; (기침을 하여) 담을 내뱉다. — *vt.* 《*up*》 bring up (phlegm) by coughing. (담을) 기침을 해서 내뱉다. — *n.* Ⓒ a noisy effort to clear the throat. (담을 뱉기 위한) 기침. [Imit.]

hawk·er[1] [hɔ́ːkər] *n.* Ⓒ a person who carries about goods for sale and advertizes them by shouting; a peddler. 행상인; 도붓장수. [*hawk*[2]]

hawk·er[2] [hɔ́ːkər] *n.* Ⓒ a person who hunts with a trained hawk. 매부리. [*hawk*[1]]

hawk-eyed [hɔ́ːkàid] *adj.* having sharp eyes like a hawk. 매처럼 날카로운 눈을 가진.

hawk·ing [hɔ́ːkiŋ] *n.* Ⓤ the act of hunting with hawks. 매사냥.

hawse [hɔːz] *n.* the part of a ship's bow having holes for anchor cables to pass through. 선수(船首)의 닻줄 구멍이 있는 부분. [O.N. *hāls* neck]

haw·ser [hɔ́ːzər] *n.* Ⓒ a strong rope or small cable used for mooring or towing ships. (배·계선(繫船)용의) 굵은 밧줄; 묘쇄(錨鎖). [L. *altus* high; orig. =hoister]

haw·thorn [hɔ́:θɔ:rn] *n.* Ⓒ 《bot.》 a thorny shrub or tree of the rose family with white flowers and small red berries. 산사나무. 參考 흰 꽃을 may, 붉은 열매는 haw 라고 함. [*haw*[1]]

Haw·thorne [hɔ́:θɔ:rn], **Nathaniel** *n.* (1804-64) an American writer. 호손《미국의 작가》.

:hay [hei] *n.* Ⓤ **1** grass, clover, etc., cut and dried for use as food for cattle, horses, etc. 건초; 마초. ¶ *make* ~ 벤 풀을 건초용으로 햇볕에 말리다 / 《*prov.*》 *Make* ~ *while the sun shines.* 좋은 기회를 놓치지 마라. **2** grass grown for hay. 건초용의 목초. ¶ *put a field under* ~ 밭을 목초지로 만들다.

hit the hay, 《*colloq.*》 go to bed. 잠자리에 들다.

make hay of, 《*fig.*》 ruin; throw (something) into disorder. …을 혼란시키다; 난잡하게 하다.

— *vi.* (P1) make hay. 건초(乾草)를 만들다.
— *vt.* (P6) supply (horses, etc.) with hay; make (grass, etc.) into hay. …에 건초를 주다; …을 건초로 만들다. [E.]

hay·cock [héikàk / -kɔ̀k] *n.* Ⓒ a small pile of hay shaped like a dome in a field. (원뿔 모양으로) 건초를 모은 더미.

Hay·dn [háidn], **Franz Joseph** *n.* (1732-1809) an Austrian composer. 하이든《오스트리아의 작곡가》.

hay fever [ᐩ ᐩ-] *n.* a disease like a cold affecting the nose, eyes, and throat, caused by the pollen of certain plants. 건초열《일종의 열병》.

hay·field [héifì:ld] *n.* Ⓒ a field where grass, clover, etc., is grown for hay. 건초밭; 목초장. [*hay*]

hay·fork [héifɔ̀:rk] *n.* Ⓒ a fork with a long handle, used to turn or lift hay. 건초용 쇠스랑.

hay·loft [héilɔ̀(:)ft] *n.* Ⓒ a place in a barn where hay is stored. 건초간《건초 두는 곳》.

hay·mak·er [héimèikər] *n.* Ⓒ a person who throws and spreads hay to dry after it has been cut. 건초 만드는 사람.

hay·mak·ing [héimèikiŋ] *n.* Ⓤ the process of making hay. 건초 만들기.

hay·mow [héimàu] *n.* Ⓒ **1** =hayloft. **2** a heap of hay stored in a barn. 헛간에 쌓아둔 건초 더미.

hay·rick [héirìk] *n.* =haystack.

hay·stack [héistæ̀k] *n.* Ⓒ a large heap of hay piled up in the open air. (한데에 쌓인) 건초 더미(가리).

·haz·ard [hǽzərd] *n.* **1** Ⓤ an old gambling game using dice. (주사위로 하는) 도박의 일종; Ⓒ a chance. 운; 우연. **2** Ⓒ a risk; a danger. 위험; 모험. ¶ *run a* ~ 위험을 무릅쓰다 / *It is a* ~ *to drive fast on a rainy day.* 비오는 날 차를 빨리 모는 것은 모험이다 / *The life of a soldier is full of hazards.* 군인의 생명은 위험으로 가득 차 있다.

at all hazards, in spite of great danger or peril. 온갖 위험(만난)을 무릅쓰고.

at* (*by*) *hazard, hazardously; at random. 운을 하늘에 맡기고; 되는 대로.

at the hazard (=*at the risk*) ***of*** *one's life.* 목숨을 걸고; 생명의 위험을 무릅쓰고.

— *vt.* (P6) risk (one's life, fortune, etc.); leave (something) to danger; chance; venture on (a guess, an opinion, etc.). (생명·재산 따위)를 걸다; …을 위험에 드러내다; 운에 맡기고 …을 하다; (억측·의견 따위)를 대담하게 (말)해 보다. ¶ *He hazarded a week's salary on a game of chance.* 위험을 무릅쓰고 1주일분의 급료를 도박에 걸었다. [F.]

haz·ard·ous [hǽzərdəs] *adj.* dangerous; risky. 위험한; 모험적인. ¶ *a* ~ *climb* 위험한 등반.

haze [heiz] *n.* ⓊⒸ **1** a slight mist, smoke, dust, etc., in the air. 아지랑이; 안개; 이내; 연무(煙霧). ¶ *Hills came in sight through a thin* ~. 엷은 안개를 통해 산들이 눈에 들어왔다. **2** vagueness of the mind; confusion of thought. (정신 따위의) 몽롱(함); (지식 따위의) 애매(함); (시력 따위의) 흐림. ¶ *be in a* ~ 몽롱(아련)하다; 애매하다. — *vi., vt.* (P1; 6) become (make) hazy. 희미(흐릿)해지다; 희미(흐릿)하게 하다. [E. *hasu* dusky]

ha·zel [héizəl] *n.* **1** Ⓒ a bushy shrub or small tree whose small rounded nuts are good to eat. 개암(나무). **2** Ⓤ a light brown. 담갈색. — *adj.* light-brown. 담갈색의. [E.]

ha·zel·nut [héizəlnʌ̀t] *n.* Ⓒ a nut of a hazel. 개암.

ha·zy [héizi] *adj.* (**-zi·er, -zi·est**) **1** misty; smoky. 안개가 낀; 흐릿한. ¶ ~ *weather* 안개 낀 날씨. **2** confused; vague; dim. 몽롱한; 희미(막연)한. ¶ *a* ~ *memory* 아련한 기억 / *a* ~ *idea* 막연한 생각 / *one's* ~ *future* 막연한 미래.
● **ha·zi·ly** [-li] *adv.* [*haze*]

Hb hemoglobin.

H.B.M. His (Her) Britannic Majesty. 영국 황제(황후) 폐하.

H-bomb [éitʃbàm / -bɔ̀m] *n.* Ⓒ a hydrogen bomb. 수소 폭탄. [*bomb*]

H.C. House of Commons.

hcf., h.c.f. highest common factor. 최대 공약수.

HE high explosive. 고성능 폭약.

H.E. His Eminence. 예하(猊下) 《Cardinal에 대한 존칭》; His Excellency. 각하.

He 《chem.》 helium.

:he [hi:, i:, hi, i] *pron.* (*pl.* **they**) **1** one particular boy, man, or male animal that has been named just before. 그가; 그는. ¶ *Where is Tom ?—He is in the garden.* 톰은 어디 있나—그는 뜰에 있다. **2** any person whose sex is not known. (성별(性別)을 모르는) 사람. ¶ *Go and see who is there* *and what ~ wants.* 가서 거기 누가 왔는지 무엇을 원하는지 알아보아라. **3** the one who...; anyone. (…하는) 사람. ¶ *He who works hard will certainly succeed.* 노력하는 자는 반드시 성공한다.

— *n.* Ⓒ (*pl.* **hes** [hi:z]) a boy; a man; a male animal. 남자; 수컷. ¶ *both hes and shes* 남자도 여자도; 수컷도 암컷도 / *Is it a ~ or a she ?* 수컷이냐 암컷이냐. [E.]

he- [hi:-] a word element meaning *male.* '남성, 수컷'의 뜻의 결합사. ¶ *a he-goat* 숫양 / *a he-cat* 수고양이. [*he*]

:head [hed] *n.* Ⓒ **1** the part of the body above the neck. 머리; 두부(頭部). ¶ *bow one's ~* (고개를 숙여) 인사하다 / *cut off the ~* 머리를〔목을〕 베다 / *shake one's ~* 머리를 가로젓다 / *lower one's ~* 머리를 수그리다 / *nod one's ~* 고개를 끄덕이다 / *from ~ to foot* 머리끝에서 발끝까지 / *He struck* 〔*hit*〕 *me on the ~.* 그는 나의 머리를 때렸다. **2** mind; intelligence; mental ability. (지능으로서의) 머리; 두뇌; 지능. ¶ *a clear ~* 명석한 두뇌 / *have a good* 〔*poor*〕 *~ for mathematics* 수학의 재주가 있다〔없다〕 / *have a long ~* 선견지명이 있다 / *come into one's ~* (생각 따위가) 머리에 떠오르다; 생각이 나다 / *weak in the ~* 저능이다 / *Use your ~.* 머리를 써라. **3** ⓐ the chief or most important position. 지도자적 지위; 수석. ¶ *at the ~ of* …의 선두에 서서; …의 수위에; …을 통솔하여 / *He is the ~ of the class.* 그는 반의 수석이다. ⓑ a leader; a chief; a director. 지도자; 우두머리; 장; 지휘자. ¶ *a school ~* 교장 / *the ~ of the section* 과장. **4** a person; the head as a symbol for a person. (특질·재능·지위의 상징으로서의) 사람. ¶ *learned heads* 학자들 / *wise heads* 현명한 사람들 / *crowned heads* 고귀한〔왕위에 있는〕 사람들. **5** the top or uppermost part of anything. 최상부; 꼭대기; (무엇의) 머릿부분. ¶ *the ~ of a pin* 〔*nail*〕 핀〔못〕의 대가리 / *the ~ of a ladder* 사다리의 꼭대기 / *the ~ of a lake* (물이 흘러드는) 호수의 물목 / *the ~ of a page* 페이지의 상단 / *the ~ of a mountain* 산꼭대기. **6** the front end; the foremost part. 선두; 맨 앞. ¶ *the ~ of a procession* 행렬의 선두 / *the ~ of a rock* 바위의 돌출부 / *the ~ of a bed* 침대의 머리맡 / *march at the ~ of army* 군대의 선두에서 행진하다. **7** ⓐ (*pl.* **head**) an animal, as one of a number. (마릿수로서의) 한 마리. ¶ *one thousand dollars a ~* 한 마리에 천 달러 / *three ~ of cattle* 소 세 마리. ⓑ a person, as one of a number of individuals. (머릿수로서의) 한 사람. ¶ *dinner at five dollars a* 〔*per*〕 *~* 1인당 5달러의 요리 / *count heads* (출석자·찬성자 따위의) 머릿수를 세다. **8** the front part of a ship. 뱃머리; 이물. **9** the source of a river. 강의 수원(水源). ¶ *the ~ of the Nile* 나일 강의 수원. **10** the foam that rises to the surface of some liquid. (맥주 따위 표면의) 거품. ¶ *the ~ on beer* 맥주의 거품 / *give a ~ to beer* 맥주에 거품이 일게 하다. **11** the heading of a book, composition, chapter, etc.; the title. (책·작문·장(章)·신문 따위의) 표제. **12** a main division of a subject, theme, or topic. (주요) 항목; 제목; 요점. ¶ *a speech arranged under five heads,* 5항목으로 정리된 강연 / *be classified under four heads,* 4항목으로 분류되다. **13** a crisis; a climax. (사태의) 위기; 절정. ¶ *bring matters to a ~* 사태를 위기에 이르게 하다. **14** the point rising from the surface of an inflammatory swelling in the flesh, when about to burst. (곪아서 금세 터질 것 같은) 종기의 대가리. **15** the front surface of a coin. 화폐의 앞면(cf. *tail*). **16** 《*colloq.*》 = headache.

at the head of the list, first in an examination. 시험에서 수석을 차지하여.

at the head of the poll, having the highest number of votes in an election or poll. 선거〔투표〕에서 최다 득표를 하여.

be above** someone's **head = ***be above the heads of** someone,* be beyond someone's power of understanding; be too difficult for (someone). …에게는 너무 어렵다.

beat** someone's **head off, 《U.S.》 beat someone mercilessly. (아무)를 형편없이 패배시키다.

bring (*something*) ***to a head,*** bring to a decisive or critical stage. …을 위기〔중대〕 국면에 이르게 하다.

by a head, by the length of the head. 머리 하나만큼의 차(差)로.

by the head, a little intoxicated. 얼큰히 취하여.

by the head and ears = ***by head and shoulders,*** forcibly. 억지로; 난폭하게.

cannot make head or tail of, cannot understand at all. 도무지 알 수 없다; 뭐가 뭔지 모르다.

come 〔***draw, gather***〕 ***to a head,*** **a**) reach a crisis; reach the highest point. (사태가) 위기에 직면하다; 정점〔절정〕에 달하다. **b**) be about to form pus. (종기 따위가) 곪으려고 하다.

do** something **on** one's **head, do easily; do without effort. 손쉽게 하다; 힘 들이지 않고 하다.

eat** one's **head off, eat a great deal and do very little work. 많이 먹기만 하고 일하지 않다; 무위 도식하다.

get 〔***take***〕 ***a thing into** one's **head,*** have a sudden or obstinate idea or plan of action. 문뜩 (어떤 생각 따위를) 갖게 되다. ¶ *He got it into his ~ that....* 그는 문뜩 …라는 생각이 머리에 떠올랐다.

get** something **out of** one's **head, stop thinking of or believing. …의 생각을 그만두다; …을 믿지 않기로 하다.

give** someone **his head, let someone do as he likes. 마음대로 하게 하다.

go to the 〔*someone's*〕 ***head,*** **a**) confuse or

excite someone; make someone drunk. …을 흥분시키다; (술에) 취하게 하다. **b**) make someone vain or overconfident. 아무를 우쭐하게 하다.
have a head (=*be gifted with talent*) ***for*** *something.* 재능을 타고나다.
have a head on *one's* ***shoulders,*** have practical ability and common sense; be very clever. 실무의 수완〔상식〕이 있다; 매우 총명하다.
head and ears, completely; perfectly. 완전히.
head and shoulders above, considerably higher than (something); better than (something). …보다 훨씬 큰〔뛰어난〕.
head first 〔***foremost***〕, headlong. 곤두박이로. ¶ *fall ~ first* 곤두박이치다.
one's ***head off,*** very much; with all one's strength. 몹시; 극단으로. ¶ *cry one's ~ off* 몹시〔큰 소리로〕 울다.
head on, facing frontward. 정면으로. ¶ *collide ~ on* 정면 충돌하다.
head over ears, (in love, debt, etc.) completely. 완전히; 아주; 푹 빠져.
head over heels =***heels over head,*** **a**) completely; utterly. 완전히; 아주. ¶ *~ over heels in love* 홀딱 반하다. **b**) upside-down 거꾸로. ¶ *turn ~ over heels* 공중제비하다.
hold *one's* ***head high,*** look very proud; give oneself airs. 머리를 잦히고 걷다; 잘난 체하다.
keep *one's* ***head,*** maintain one's self-control; remain calm. 침착을 잃지 않다; 냉정을 유지하다.
keep *one's* ***head above water,*** 《*fig.*》 manage to be out of trouble, esp. debt. (재정적으로) 그럭저럭 해 나가다; 빚을 지지 않고 있다.
lay 〔***put***〕 ***heads together,*** consult or plan together. 머리를 맞대고 상의하다; 협의하다.
lose *one's* ***head,*** **a**) have one's head cut off. 목이 잘리다. **b**) lose one's self-control; get excited. 당황하다; 흥분하다.
make head, go forward; advance. (장애를 헤치고) 나아가다; 전진하다.
make head against, **a**) resist; oppose. …에 저항하여 이겨 내다; 저지하다. ¶ *make ~ against difficulties* 곤란을 극복하다. **b**) rise in surrection against. …에 대하여 반란〔폭동〕을 일으키다.
make neither head nor tail of, be unable to understand; be utterly bewildered at. …을 모르다; …이 이해가 안 되다; 오리 무중이다.
off 〔***out of***〕 *one's* ***head,*** **a**) wildly excited. 몹시 흥분하여. **b**) mad; crazy. 머리가 돌아; 미쳐.
open *one's* ***head,*** 《U.S. *colloq.*》 tell. 이야기〔말〕하다.
out of 〔***on***〕 *one's* ***own head,*** from one's own invention. 자신이 안출〔생각〕하여.
over *someone's* ***head,*** **a**) too difficult for someone to understand. 이해력을 넘어; 이해할 수 없는. ¶ *He talks over our heads.* 그는 우리가 이해할 수 없는 말을 한다. **b**) without consulting someone. (책임 있는 윗사람을) 건너뛰어; 제치고; 상의 없이.
over head and ears =head over ears.
over the head of, in spite of someone's prior or more important claim. …을 앞질러〔제치고〕. ¶ *He was promoted over the ~ of his seniors.* 선배들을 제치고 승진되었다.
put a head on, 《U.S.》 **a**) punch. …을 때리다. **b**) put down. 꺽소리 못 하게 하다; 침묵시키다.
put *something* ***into*** 〔***out of***〕 *someone's* ***head,*** cause someone to remember 〔forget〕 something. (…에게 어떤 일)을 생각나게 하다〔잊게 하다〕.
show *one's* ***head,*** appear. 출두하다.
take it into *one's* ***head,*** form an idea, plan, or intention in one's mind. …할 마음이 들다; …이 생각나다; …하려고 계획하다. ¶ *I took it into my ~ to respect him.* 그를 존경할 마음이 되었다.
take the head, take the lead. 선도(先導)하다.
talk *someon's* ***head off,*** weary someone with talk. 긴 이야기로 …를 넌더리내게 하다.
turn *someone's* ***head,*** cause someone to become conceited or to feel superior. …을 우쭐하게 하다.
turn head over heels, turn a somersault. 재주넘다; 공중제비하다.
— *vt.* **1** (P6) be first on (something). …의 선두에 서다. ¶ *~ a procession* 행렬의 선두에 서다 / *Tom's name headed the list.* 톰의 이름이 명단 필두에 올랐다. **2** (P6) be chief or leader of (a group); lead. …의 장(長)〔우두머리, 지도자〕이다; 지도하다; 거느리다. ¶ *a cabinet headed by him* 그를 수반으로 하는 내각 / *~ a school* 학교의 교장이다 / *~ a revolt* 반란을 지휘하다. **3** (P6) strike or touch (someone or something) with the head. …을 머리로 (받아)치다〔갖다 대다〕. ¶ *~ a ball* 볼을 머리로 받아치다. **4** (P6) 《also *down*》 cut off the head or top of (something). 머리를〔목을〕 베다; 머릿부분〔끝〕을 잘라내다. ¶ *~ (down) a tree* 나뭇가지 끝을 자르다. **5** (P7) 《also *off, back*》 get in front of so as to turn back or aside. 앞을 가로막(아 서)다. ¶ *~ a herd of cattle* 소 떼의 앞을 가로막아 서다. **6** (P7) turn or direct the course of (a ship, etc.). (배 따위를) …로 향하게 하다; …쪽으로 돌리다. ¶ *~ the vessel toward shore* 배를 해안으로 돌리다. — *vi.* (P1,2A,3) **1** go; travel; make for. (어떤 방향으로) 나아가다; 향하다. ¶ *~ home* 집으로 향하다 / *They were heading north.* 북쪽을 향해 나아가고 있었다 / *The dog headed for the woods.* 개가 숲 쪽으로 갔다. **2** grow or come to a head. (식물이) 결구(結球)하다; (종기가 곪아) 근이 생기다. [E.]
be headed for, be destined for. …할 운명에 있다.
head along, go forward. 전진하다.
head back, **a**) interfere; interrupt. …을

방해하다. **b**) go in the opposite direction. 되돌아가다.

head off, interrupt the course of (something) in the middle; get ahead of and cause (something) to stop or turn away. …을 방해하다; (앞을 가로막아) …의 방향을 〔진로를〕 바꾸게 하다.

***head·ache** [hédèik] *n.* **1** ⒸⓊ pain in the head. 두통. ¶ *have a* ~. **2** Ⓒ《U.S. *colloq.*》 a cause of worry, annoyance, or trouble. 고뇌의 원인; 골칫거리.

head·band [hédbæ̀nd] *n.* Ⓒ a band worn around the head. 머리띠.

head·dress [héddrès] *n.* Ⓒ **1** a covering, often ornamental, for the head. (여성의) 머리에 쓰는 것; 머리 장식. **2** the style of wearing or arranging the hair. 조발(調髮) 방식; 머리 스타일.

head·ed [hédid] *adj.* **1** with a head. 머리가 있는. **2** having a heading. 표제가 있는. **3** shaped like a head. 머리 모양을 한. **4**《in compounds》 having a certain kind of head; having a specified number of heads. …한 머리를 가진; 머리가 …개인. ¶ *a slow-headed student* 머리가 둔한 학생 / *a two-headed monster* 머리가 둘인 괴물.

head·er [hédər] *n.* Ⓒ **1**《*colloq.*》 a fall or plunge headfirst. 곤두박이로 뛰어들기〔떨어지기〕. ¶ *take a* ~ *off a ladder* 사다리에서 곤두박이쳐 떨어지다 / *He took a* ~ *into the ditch.* 그는 도랑 속으로 곤두박이쳤다. **2** a machine for cutting off the tops of grain, etc. (곡물 따위의) 이삭을 잘라내는 기계. **3** a brick or stone laid with its length across the thickness of a wall. (벽면에) 마구리가 수평 방향으로 보이게 쌓아올린 벽돌〔돌〕; 인방(引枋)(에 쌓은 벽돌〔돌〕).

head·first [hédfə́ːrst] *adv.* **1** with the head in front. 곤두박이쳐; 거꾸로. ¶ *fall* ~ 곤두박이치다. **2** rashly; thoughtlessly; in haste. 무모하게; 조급하게.

head·fore·most [hédfɔ́ːrmòust] *adv.* = headfirst.

head·gear [hédgìər] *n.* Ⓤ **1** a covering for the head, such as a hat or cap. (머리에) 쓸것; 모자; 헤드기어. **2** the harness for the head of a horse, mule, etc. 말 머리 부분의 마구(馬具)《굴레 따위》.

head·hunt·ing [hédhʌ̀ntiŋ] *n.* practice among some savage tribes of taking the heads of enemies. (미개 야만족의) 머리 베기 사냥《적의 목을 자름》.

head·i·ness [hédinis] *n.* Ⓤ stubbornness; obstinacy. 완고; 고집셈.

head·ing [hédiŋ] *n.* Ⓒ **1** something that serves as a head, top, or front. 머리〔끝〕의 구실을 하는 것. **2** a title or topic at the top of a paragraph, page, chapter, etc. (절·페이지·장(章) 따위의) 표제(表題) (cf. *headline*). ¶ *under the* ~ *of* …라는 표제로; …라는 항목에. **3** Ⓤ《football》 the act of striking the ball with the head. 헤딩.

head·land [hédlənd] *n.* Ⓒ a point of land projecting into water, esp. a cliff. (바다·호수 등에) 삐죽 나온 육지; 갑(岬); 곶.

head·less [hédlis] *adj.* **1** having no head. 머리가 없는. **2** without a leader. 우두머리〔지도자〕가 없는. **3** foolish; stupid. 바보 같은; 어리석은.

head·light [hédlàit] *n.* Ⓒ **1** a bright light on the front of an automobile, a streetcar, etc. (자동차 따위의) 헤드라이트; 전조등(前照燈). **2** a white light at a masthead. (배의) 백색 장등(檣燈).

head·line [hédlàin] *n.* Ⓒ **1** words printed in large type at the top of an article in a newspaper. 신문 따위의 큰 표제(cf. *heading*). ¶ *go into headlines* 신문에 큼직하게 나다. **2** a line at the top of a page which gives the title, page number, etc. 책의 페이지 상란(上欄)《난외 표제·페이지 수 따위가 써 있는 난》. **3**《*pl.*》《Brit.》 a news summary given at the beginning of a news broadcast. (뉴스 방송 전에 말하는) 주요 제목.

hit 〔***make***〕 ***the headlines,***《*sl.*》 become famous. 유명해지다.

— *vt.* (P6) furnish (a news article) with a headline. (신문 기사에) 표제를 붙이다. [E.]

***head·long** [hédlɔ̀ːŋ / -lɔ̀ŋ] *adv.* **1** head first. 곤두박이쳐; 거꾸로. ¶ *fall* ~ 거꾸로 떨어지다 / *plunge* ~ *into the water* 곤두박이쳐 물속으로 뛰어들다. **2** without thinking; rashly; thoughtlessly. 무모〔무분별〕하게; 성급하게; 서둘러. ¶ *rush* ~ *into danger* 앞뒤를 가리지 않고 위험 속에 뛰어들다. — *adj.* **1** having the head first. 곤두박이의; 거꾸로의. **2** rash; violent; reckless. 앞뒤를 가리지 않는; 무모한; 성급한. ¶ *a* ~ *decision* 성급한 결정.

head·man [hédmæ̀n] *n.* Ⓒ (*pl.* **-men** [-mèn]) a leader; a chief. 우두머리; 장.

head·mas·ter [hédmǽstər, -mɑ́ːs-] *n.* Ⓒ the principal teacher, esp. of a private school; a principal. 교장.

head·mis·tress [hédmístris] *n.* Ⓒ the woman who heads a school. 여교장.

head·most [hédmòust] *adj.* first; foremost. 선두의; 첫(번)째의.

head-on [hédɑ́n / -ɔ́n] *adj.* (of two things) meeting front to front; head to head. (두 개의 것이) 정면으로 만나는; 정면 충돌의. ¶ *a* ~ *collision* 정면 충돌. — *adv.* (of ships, vehicles, etc.) directly; head to head in collision. (특히 충돌이) 정면으로. ¶ *strike an iceberg* ~ 빙산을 정면으로 들이받다.

head·phone [hédfòun] *n.* Ⓒ《often *pl.*》 a telephone or radio receiver held over the ears. 헤드폰(cf. *earphone*).

head·piece [hédpìːs] *n.* Ⓒ **1** a piece of armor for the head; a helmet. 투구; 헬멧. **2** a covering for the head, such as a hat or a cap. (머리) 쓰개; 모자. **3** the head; the brain; intellect. 머리; 두뇌; 지능. ¶ *have a good* ~ 머리가 좋다. **4** 《print.》 an ornamental design engraved at the head of a page or chapter. (페이지·장(章) 따위 첫머리의) 꽃 모양 따위의 장식(cf. *tailpiece*).

***head·quar·ters** [hédkwɔ̀:rtərz] *n. pl.* 《used often as *sing.*》 **1** the place from which orders are sent out; the main office; any center of activity or authority. 본부; 사령부(abbr. H.Q.); 활동의 중심; 본거(本據). ¶ *police* ~ 경찰 본부 / *the general* ~ 총사령부. 語法 본부·사령부의 뜻으로는 단수 취급, 그 외엔 복수 취급이 보통. **2** 《usu. *collectively*》 all the people working at such a place. 본부 요원; 사령부원. [E.]

head·set [hédsèt] *n.* =headphone.

head·ship [hédʃip] *n.* Ⓤ the position of a head; chief authority. 우두머리임; 우두머리의〔지도적〕 지위〔권위〕. [*head*]

heads·man [hédzmən] *n.* Ⓒ (*pl.* **-men** [-mən]) a man who puts criminals to death; a public executioner. 사형 집행인.

head·stall [hédstɔ̀:l] *n.* Ⓒ a part of a bridle or halter that fits round a horse's head. (말의) 굴레.

head·stone [hédstòun] *n.* Ⓒ **1** a stone set up at the head of a grave. (무덤 앞에 있는) 묘표(墓標); 묘석. **2** a cornerstone or keystone. 주춧돌; 이맛돌.

head·stream [hédstrì:m] *n.* Ⓒ a stream that is the source of a larger stream. (하천의) 원류(源流).

head·strong [hédstrɔ̀:ŋ / -strɔ̀ŋ] *adj.* determined to have one's own way; obstinate; stubborn; selfish. 고집이 센; 외고집의; 완고한; 멋대로 구는.

head·wa·ters [hédwɔ̀:tərz] *n. pl.* sources of upper parts of a stream. (하천의) 원류; 상류.

head·way [hédwèi] *n.* Ⓤ **1** ⓐ forward motion, as of a ship. (배 따위의) 전진; 진행. ¶ *The ship made* ~ *against the wind.* 배는 바람을 거슬러 나아갔다. ⓑ 《*fig.*》 progress. 진보; 전진. ¶ *make* 〔*gain*〕 ~ *in a career* 출세하다; 승진하다. **2** a clear space overhead permitting passage under a bridge, arch, etc. (다리·아치 따위의 밑에서 위까지의) 간격〔거리〕.

head wind [´ ˋ] *n.* a wind that blows exactly against the front of a ship, an airplane, etc. (배·비행기 따위의) 맞바람.

head·word [hédwə̀:rd] *n.* Ⓒ a word used as a heading, esp. the first word of a dictionary entry. 표제어.

head·work [hédwə̀:rk] *n.* Ⓤ mental work or effort; the act of thinking; thought. 머리를 쓰는 일; 지적〔정신〕 노동; 사고(思考).

head·y [hédi] *adj.* (**head·i·er, head·i·est**) **1** ⓐ willful; hasty; rash. 완고한; 무모한; 성급한. ⓑ violent; destructive. 격심한; 맹렬한; 파괴적인. **2** ⓐ (of liquor) apt to affect or go to one's head; exciting. (술이) 머리에 오르는; 취하게 하는; 흥분시키는. ⓑ 《*fig.*》 tending to disturb the judgment, etc. 판단력을 잃게 하는.

***heal** [hi:l] *vt.* (P6,13) **1** 《*of*》 bring back (the sick) to good health; get rid of (a disease); cure. (병자)를 회복시키다; (병)을 고치다. ¶ ~ *the sick* 병자를 고치다 / ~ *a man of his disease* 그의 병을 고치다 / *be healed of one's wound* 상처가 낫다. **2** bring back to moral or spiritual health or peace of mind; remedy (grief, trouble, etc.). (정신적으로) 고치다; (슬픔·고뇌 따위)를 낫게 하다. ¶ *Time heals most troubles.* 시간이 지나면 대개의 고뇌는 사라진다. — *vi.* (P1,2A) (of wounds, etc.) become sound and well; get well. 회복하다; 낫다. [→whole]

***heal up* 〔*over*〕,** (of a wound) become quite healthy. (상처가) 낫다; 완쾌하다.

heal·er [hí:lər] *n.* Ⓒ a person or thing that heals. (병을) 치료하는 사람〔것〕; 약. ¶ *Time is a great* ~ *of everything.* 시간은 만물의 위대한 치료자이다.

heal·ing [hí:liŋ] *adj.* that heals; getting well; curing. 고치는; 치료의; 나아가고 있는. — *n.* Ⓤ cure. 치유; 치료(법).

:health [helθ] *n.* Ⓤ **1** the state of being well; freedom from sickness. (심신의) 건강; 건전. ¶ (*the*) *public* ~ 공중 위생 / *a bill of* ~ 건강 진단서 / *out of* ~ 건강이 안 좋아. **2** condition of body or mind. (심신의) 건강 상태; 컨디션. ¶ *be in good* 〔*bad, ill, poor*〕 ~ 건강이 좋다〔좋지 않다〕 / *fall into ill* ~ 건강을 해치다. **3** healing power. 치료력. ¶ *There is* ~ *in sea breezes and sunshine.* 바닷바람과 햇빛에는 병을 고치는 힘이 있다. **4** ⓊⒸ in honor of someone's health and happiness. (건강·행복 등을 비는) 축배. ¶ *drink to the* ~ *of someone* = *drink to someone's* ~ = *drink a* ~ *to someone* 아무의 건강을 위하여 축배를 들다 / *To your* ~*!* =*Your* ~*!* 건강을 축하드립니다. [*heal*]

health·ful [hélθfəl] *adj.* giving health; good for the health; wholesome; salutary. 건강〔몸〕에 좋은; 건전한. ¶ ~ *exercise* 〔*diet*〕 건강에 좋은 운동〔식사〕. ●**health·ful·ly** [-li] *adv.* **health·ful·ness** [-nis] *n.*

***health·y** [hélθi] *adj.* (**health·i·er, health·i·est**) **1** ⓐ having good health. 건강한. ¶ *a* ~ *child* 건강한 아이 / ~ *skin* 건강한 피부. ⓑ in sound condition. 건전한. ¶ *a* ~ *mind* 〔*society*〕 건전한 정신〔사회〕. **2** showing good health. 건강해 보이는. ¶ *a* ~ *look* 건강해 뵈는 얼굴. **3** ⓐ good for the mind or spirit. (정신에) 유익한. ¶ ~ *reading for the young* 젊은이들에게 유익한 읽을거리. ⓑ healthful. 건강에 유익한; 위생적인. ● **health·i·ness** [-nis] *n.*

:heap [hi:p] *n.* Ⓒ **1** a number of things lying together; a pile. 쌓아올린 것; 퇴적; 더미.

¶ *a ~ of rocks* 돌더미 / *pile hay in a ~* 건초를 산더미처럼 쌓다. **2** 《*colloq.*》 ⓐ 《often *pl.*》 a large quantity; a great deal; much. 많음; 다량; 다수. ¶ *a ~ of people* 많은 사람들 / *heaps of time* 많은 시간 / *heaps of times* 여러 번; 빈번히 / *make a ~ of money* 한재산 만들다. ⓑ 《*pl.*, as *adv.*》 very much. 매우; 크게. ¶ *feel heaps better* 훨씬 좋게〔낫게〕 느끼다.

all of a heap, **a**) overwhelmed with great surprise; amazed. 깜짝 놀라. **b**) quite suddenly. 갑자기; 느닷없이; 돌연. **c**) prostrated. 쿵; 꽈당; 털석; 푹. ¶ *fall all of a ~* 푹 쓰러지다.

be struck* 〔*knocked*〕 *all of a heap, 《*colloq.*》 **a**) be reduced suddenly to powerlessness. 맥이 쑥 빠지다; 질리다. **b**) be very astonished or confused. 깜짝 놀라다; 크게 당황하다.

in* 〔《rare》 *of*〕 *a heap, in a pile. 산더미처럼 (많이).

— *vt.* **1** (P6,7) 《*up, together*》 ⓐ gather (something) in heaps; pile. …을 쌓아올리다. ¶ *~ (up) stone* 〔*sand*〕 돌을〔모래를〕 쌓아 올리다 / *~ up a mound* 석가산(石假山)〔둑〕을 쌓다. ⓑ collect a large quantity of. …을 많이 모으다; 축적하다. ¶ *~ up riches* 부(富)를 쌓다. **2** (P13) 《*with*》 fill with a heap of something. (그릇·접시 따위에) 수북히 담다; 산더미처럼 쌓다〔싣다〕. ¶ *~ a plate with food* 접시에 음식을 수북히 담다 / *~ a basket with apples* 바구니에 사과를 많이 담다 / *~ a cart with hay* 수레에 건초를 산더미처럼 싣다 / *~ a table with books* 책상에 책을 산더미처럼 쌓다. **3** (P13) give (something) in large amounts to. …을 듬뿍 주다. ¶ *~ gifts upon someone* 아무에게 선물을 산더미처럼 주다 / *~ favors upon someone* = *~ someone with favors* 아무에게 많은 은혜를 베풀다 / 《*fig.*》 *~ insults on someone* 아무에게 갖은 모욕을 주다. [E.]

:hear [hiər] *v.* (**heard**) *vt.* **1** (P6,22,23,24) ⓐ catch (sound) through the ears. …을 듣다; …이 들리다. ¶ *~ the sound of laughter* 웃음 소리가 들리다 / *~ a step on the stairs* 계단의 발소리가 들리다 / *~ one's name called* 자기 이름을 부르는 소리가 들리다 / *I can't ~ you.* (무슨 말인지) 말소리가 안 들린다. ⓑ know the action of (someone or something) by sound. (…이 —하는) 것을 듣다. ¶ *~ something approach* 무엇이 다가오는 소리를 듣다 / *~ someone speaking* 아무가 이야기하는 것을 듣다 / *~ a bird sing* 새가 노래하는 것을 듣다 / *Don't you ~ us calling you?* 우리가 너를 부르는 소리가 안 들리나. **2** (P6,7,22) listen to; pay attention to (something). …에 귀를 기울이다; 경청하다. ¶ *~ music* 〔*a lecture*〕 음악을〔강의를〕 듣다 / *~ someone's story* 아무의 이야기를 듣다 / *~ someone through* 아무의 말을 끝까지 듣다 / *Hear what I say.* 내가 하는 말을 들어라 / *I hardly heard what she said.* 그녀가 하는 말을 거의 듣지 못했다 / *We had better ~ what he has to say.* 그가 하는 말을 잘 듣는게 좋겠다. **3** (P6) listen to (something) officially; give a chance to be heard to (something). …을 공식으로〔정식으로, 직무상〕 듣다; …을 청취하다; (사건)을 심리하다. ¶ *~ the defendant* 피고의 증언을 듣다 / *The judge heard the case in court.* 판사는 법정에서 사건을 심리했다. **4** (P6,7,10,11) be informed of (something); get news of (something). (소식 따위)를 전해 듣다; 보고를 받다. ¶ *~ news* / *I have heard nothing of him since.* 그 후엔 그의 소식을 못 들었다 / *We ~ all kinds of things from villagers.* 우리는 마을 사람들로부터 모든 것을 들어서 알고 있다. **5** (P6) listen to with favor; agree to (something); grant. (소원)을 들어주다. ¶ *~ a prayer* 기도를 들어 주다 / *He heard my plea.* 그는 나의 탄원을 들어 주었다.

— *vi.* **1** (P1) catch or be able to catch sound through the ears. 들리다. ¶ *He can't ~ at all.* 전혀 듣지를 못한다. **2** (P3) 《*from, of, about*》 be told; be informed. 전해 듣다; 소식을 듣다; 보고를 듣다. ¶ *~ from a friend* 친구로부터 소식이 있다 / *~ about someone's doings* 아무의 행위에 대해서 보고를 받다. [E.]

***hear from** someone,* receive news from someone, usu. by letter. …에게서 소식을 듣다; 편지를 받다.

hear of, **a**) get news of (someone or something). …을 소문에 듣다; …의 소식을 듣다. ¶ *I have not heard of him lately.* 최근 그의 소식을 못 듣고 있다. **b**) 《usu. in *negative*》 approve of (something); admit. …에 찬성하다; 허락하다. ¶ *I won't ~ of your request.* 자네의 요구는 들어 줄 수 없다.

hear** someone **out, listen to someone until the end. (…의 말을) 끝까지 듣다. ¶ *Don't interrupt, just ~ me out.* 가만 있어, 끝까지 내 말 들어 봐.

hear say, hear people say; learn by rumor or common talk. (…)을 이야기로〔소문에〕 듣다(cf. *hearsay*).

I hear, It is said that.… …라고(들) 말한다.

make oneself heard, obtain a hearing. 자기의 생각 따위를 듣게 하다. [E.]

:heard [həːrd] *v.* p. and pp. of **hear**.

hear·er [híərər] *n.* Ⓒ a person who hears; a listener. 듣는 사람; 방청인.

:hear·ing [híəriŋ] *n.* **1** Ⓤ the sense by which sound is perceived. 청각. ¶ *be hard of ~* 귀가 어둡다; 난청이다 / *My ~ is getting poor.* 청각이 떨어지고 있다. **2** Ⓒ the act of perceiving sound. 들음; 듣기; 청취. ¶ *At first ~ I didn't like the music.* 처음부터 그 음악은 듣기 싫었다. **3** Ⓒ a chance to be heard; a judicial trial; audience. 들려줌; 들어줌; 심문; 청문회. ¶ *a preliminary ~* 예심(豫審) / *a public ~* 공청회 / *gain* 〔*get*〕 *a ~* 들려주다; 발언의 기회를 얻다 / *give someone a ~* 아무의 우는 소리를 들어 주다 / *hold* 〔*open*〕

hearings 심문을 행하다; 청문회를 열다 / *give someone a fair* ~ 아무의 말을 공평하게 들어 주다. **4** Ⓤ the distance over which sound can be heard. 들리는 거리. ¶ *in someone's* ~ (아무)가 듣는 곳에서 / *out of* 〔*within*〕 ~ 들리지 않는〔들리는〕 곳에서.

hearing aid [ㅅ-ㅅ] *n.* a small electronic device for helping partially deaf people to hear. 보청기.

hear·ken, har·ken [hάːrkən] *vi.* (P1,2,3) 《*lit.*》 listen; hear; attend; take heed. 듣다; 귀를 기울이다. ¶ ~ *to a supplication* 탄원을 듣다. [→hark]

hear·say [híərsèi] *n.* Ⓤ what one has heard about; rumor; gossip. 소문; 풍문. ¶ ~ *evidence* 전문(傳聞) 증거 / *by* 〔*from, on*〕 ~ 소문에 들어; 간접적으로 들어 / *This is mere* ~. 이건 풍문에 불과하다 / *I know* 〔*have*〕 *it only from* ~. 그것은 소문으로 들어 알고 있을 따름이다. [*hear*]

hearse [həːrs] *n.* Ⓒ a car for carrying dead bodies to the grave. 영구차. [L. *hirpex* harrow]

:heart [hɑːrt] *n.* Ⓒ **1** ⓐ a muscular organ that pumps the blood throughout the body. 심장; 염통. ¶ *a* ~ *disease* 심장병 / *a* ~ *patient* 심장병 환자 / *a* ~ *transplant operation* 심장 이식 수술 / *have a weak* ~ 심장이 약하다. ⓑ the part of the body containing the heart. 흉부; 가슴. ¶ *with my hand upon my* ~ 가슴에 손을 얹고; 맹세코 / *clasp* 〔*press*〕 *a child to one's* ~ 아이를 가슴에 바싹 껴안다. **2** feelings; mind; soul. 감정; 마음; (심)정. ¶ *a warm* 〔*cold, brave*〕 ~ 따뜻한〔차가운, 용감한〕 마음 / *with a light* 〔*heavy*〕 ~ 가벼운〔무거운〕 마음으로 / *move* 〔*touch*〕 *the* ~ 마음을 움직이다; 감동시키다 / *My* ~ *leaps up.* 가슴이 기쁨으로 뛴다. **3** emotions of love. 애정; 사랑. ¶ *an affair of the* ~ 연애 사건 / *a woman of one's* ~ 의중의 여인 / *give one's* ~ *to someone* 아무에게 애정을 바치다; 아무를 사랑하다 / *gain* 〔*win*〕 *someone's* ~ 아무의 애정을 얻다. **4** sympathy; kindness; tenderness. 동정심; 인정. ¶ *a man of* ~ 정이〔인간미가〕 있는 사람 / *have no* ~ 인정이 없다 / *Her* ~ *was moved at the sight.* 그 광경을 보고 그녀는 동정했다. **5** courage; spirit. 용기; 기운. ¶ *pluck up* 〔*take, gather*〕 ~ 용기를 불러일으키다; 기운을 내다 / *I haven't the* ~ *to tell her about the news.* 그녀에게 그 소식을 알릴 용기가 없다. **6** ⓐ the center; the central or innermost part. 중심; 중앙부; 속; 오지(奧地). ¶ *the* ~ *of a city* 도심 / *the* ~ *of Africa* 아프리카의 오지 / *the* ~ *of a cabbage* 배추의 고갱이. ⓑ 《*fig.*》 the most important, essential part; the core. 가장 중요한 부분; 핵심; 요점. ¶ *get* 〔*go*〕 *to the* ~ *of the matter* 문제의 핵심을 파악하다. **7** ⓐ 《a way of calling》 a person one loves. 여보; 당신; 내사랑. ¶ *dear* 〔*sweet*〕 ~ 내 사랑하는 사람. ⓑ a person of some particular character (esp. good). 특별한 성격의 사람. ¶ *a noble* ~ 고매한 사람. **8** something shaped like the human heart. 심장 모양의 것; 하트. ¶ *She sent me a Valentine card with a* ~ *on it.* 하트가 그려진 발렌타인 카드를 보내 왔다. **9** 《cards》 a playing card marked with a red figure like a heart. (카드의) 하트. [E.]

***after** one's* (**own**) **heart,** just as one likes it; that suits or pleases one perfectly. (썩) 마음에 드는. ¶ *He's a man after my own* ~. 바로 내가 좋아하는 타입의 사람이다.

***at the bottom of** one's* **heart,** in the depth of one's mind. 내심〔속마음〕으로는.

be of good heart, in the state of being confident, cheerful, courageous. 원기 왕성하다.

***break** someone's* **heart,** crush someone with sorrow or grief. …를 비탄에 젖게 하다. ¶ *His constant unkindness broke her* ~. 그의 한결같은 매정함은 그녀를 슬프게 했다.

by heart, **a**) by memory. 외워서; 암기하여. ¶ *learn* 〔*get*〕 *by* ~ 외다; 암기하다. **b**) perfectly. 완전히.

cry 〔***weep***〕 *one's* **heart out,** weep bitterly without restraint. 목놓아 울다.

devour 〔***eat***〕 *one's* **heart out,** grieve bitterly in secret. 남모르게 비탄에 잠기다.

***do** someone's* **heart good,** give someone joy; make someone cheerful. …을 대단히 기쁘게 하다.

***find it in** one's* **heart to** *do,* feel inclined to do. …하고 싶(은 마음이 되)다; …할 마음이 들다. ¶ *I don't know how you can find it in your* ~ *to do such a thing.* 네가 어떻게 그런 일을 할 마음이 되었는지 알 수가 없구나.

from (***the bottom of***) *one's* **heart,** sincerely; cordially. 마음(속)으로부터; 충심으로.

***give** one's* **heart to,** fall in love with. …을 사랑하다; …에 마음을 빼앗기다.

have (*something*) ***at heart,*** be deeply interested in. …에 열중하다.

have 〔***bring***〕 *one's* **heart in** *one's* **mouth** 〔***boots***〕**,** be very frightened; feel very afraid or worried. 몹시〔깜짝〕 놀라다; 전전긍긍하다.

***have** one's* **heart in the right place,** have a kind heart; to be a kind and generous person. 인정미가 있다; 악의가 없다; 마음이 좋은 사람이다.

***have not the heart to** do,* be too tenderhearted to do. …할 용기가 없다. ¶ *She was sleeping so peacefully, I didn't have the* ~ *to wake her.* 그녀는 매우 평화롭게 자고 있어서 깨울 용기가 나지 않았다. 「인정이 많다.

have (***plenty of***) ***heart,*** be kind and gentle.

heart and soul, with all one's effort, affections, etc.; completely. 열심히; 완전히.

One's **heart sinks.** =《*colloq.*》 *One's* **heart sinks into** *one's* **boots.** One feels suddenly discouraged because of fear. 풀이 죽다; 낙담하다.

heart to heart, intimate; frank; frankly. 속을 털어놓고; 숨김없이(cf. *heart-to-heart*).

¶ *They talked* ~ *to* ~. 그들은 속을 터놓은 솔직한 이야기를 나누었다.
in (***good***) ***heart,*** in a state of cheerfulness or courage. 원기 충만하여; 기운차게.
in one's heart (***of hearts***), in one's deepest feelings. 마음속에[으로]; 가슴 속 깊이.
lay to heart, think over seriously. 마음에 새겨 두다; 진지하게 생각하다.
lose heart, become discouraged. 낙심하다.
lose one's heart to, fall in love with. …와 사랑에 빠지다; …에게 반하다.
near [***next***] ***someone's heart,*** of great value or importance to someone. …에게 소중한; 중요한.
out of heart, **a**) discouraged. 기운 없이; 풀이 죽어. **b**) (of land) in poor condition. (땅이) 메말라; 척박하여.
pluck up [***take***] ***heart,*** take courage; become courageous. 기운을 내다.
put heart into someone, encourage someone. …를 격려하다.
put one's heart into, be absorbed in. …에 열중하다.
rejoice someone's heart =do someone's heart good.
search the [***one's***] ***heart,*** examine the [one's] motives. …의 의중을 떠 보다.
set someone's heart at rest, make someone easy in mind; take away someone's worry. …을 안심시키다; 걱정을 없애다. ¶ *The doctor was able to set her* ~ *at rest.* 의사는 그녀를 안심시킬 수 있었다.
set one's heart on (*something* or *doing something*), make ... the object of one's desire. …에 희망을 걸다; …을 열망하다.
speak to the heart, move the deepest feelings. 마음을 움직이다; 마음에 호소하다.
steal someone's heart, gain someone's affection or love. 아무의 애정을 얻다.
take heart, cheer up; grow braver. 용기를[기운을] 내다.
take heart of grace, pluck up courage to act. 용기를[기운을] 내다.
take something to heart, **a**) be troubled or grieved by something. (손실 따위)를 몹시 괴로워하다. **b**) =lay to heart.
to one's heart's content, as much (many etc.) as one wishes; throughly. 실컷.
wear one's heart on [***upon***] ***one's sleeve,*** **a**) show one's feelings plainly. 심중을 남에게 알리다; 자신의 감정을 숨김없이 드러내다. **b**) fall in love easily. 곧 사랑에 빠지다.
with all one's heart, **a**) sincerely. 마음으로부터; 충심으로. **b**) gladly; willingly. 기꺼이. **c**) with earnestness or zeal. 마음을 담아; 열심히.
with half a heart, without much interest; unwillingly. 내키지 않는 마음으로; 마지못해.

heart·ache [há:*r*tèik] *n.* UC sorrow; grief. 마음 아픔; 상심; 슬픔.

heart·beat [há:*r*tbì:t] *n.* C the movement of the heart; throb. 심장의 고동; 동계(動悸).

heart·break [há:*r*tbrèik] *n.* U deep sorrow or grief; bitter disappointment. 비탄; 실망.

heart·break·ing [há:*r*tbrèikiŋ] *adj.* **1** causing deep sorrow, grief or disappointment; in despair. 가슴이 터질 듯한; 애끊는; 비통한. **2** 《*colloq.*》 causing extreme boredom or fatigue. 질력나는; 따분한. ¶ *a* ~ *job* 따분한 일.

heart·bro·ken [há:*r*tbròukən] *adj.* suffering from deep sorrow or grief; in despair. 비탄에 잠긴; 절망의. ● **heart·bro·ken·ly** [-li] *adv.*

heart·burn [há:*r*tbə̀:*r*n] *n.* U a burning feeling in the stomach after a meal, often rising to the chest and throat. (식사 후의) 명치 쓰림.

heart·burn·ing [há:*r*tbə̀:*r*niŋ] *n.* U concealed jealousy or discontent. 질투; 불만. — *adj.* discontent; jealous. 불만의; 질투의.

heart·ed [há:*r*tid] *adj.* having a specified kind of heart. …의 마음을 가진; …한 마음의. ¶ *sad-hearted* 마음이 슬픈 / *faint-hearted* 마음이 약한.

heart·en [há:*r*tn] *vt.* (P6,7) 《*on, up*》 give courage to (someone); cheer up; encourage. …을 격려하다; 북돋우다. ¶ *be heartened by good news* 반가운 소식에 기운이 솟다.

heart failure [⌐ ⌐] *n.* the stopping of the movement of the heart. 심장 마비.

heart·felt [há:*r*tfèlt] *adj.* with true, warm and deep feelings; sincere. 진심에서의; 마음에 깊이 느낀. ¶ *a* ~ *apology* [*thanks*].

***hearth** [ha:*r*θ] *n.* C **1** the floor of a fireplace. 노(爐); 노상(爐床). **2** the fireside; the home. 노변(爐邊); 가정. [E.]

hearth·rug [há:*r*θrʌ̀g] *n.* C a rug spread out in front of the hearth. 노변(爐邊)의 깔개.

hearth·stone [há:*r*θstòun] *n.* **1** a stone forming a hearth. 노(爐)의 바닥돌. **2** 《*fig.*》 this considered as the center of home life; the home. (가정 생활 중심으로서의) 노변(爐邊); 가정.

***heart·i·ly** [há:*r*t*i*li] *adv.* **1** sincerely; in a warm friendly manner. 마음으로부터; 진정[충심]으로. ¶ *express one's good wishes very* ~ 충심으로 축복의 말을 하다. **2** ⓐ without restraint; vigorously. 실컷; 기운[세]차게. ¶ *laugh* ~ *at someone's jokes* 아무의 농담에 실컷 웃다. ⓑ with a good appetite; much; enough. 식욕 왕성하게; 많이; 충분히. ¶ *eat* ~ 잔뜩[배불리] 먹다. **3** very completely. 완전히; 아주; 철저하게. ¶ *I am* ~ *tired of this work.* 이 일에 아주 질렸다. [*heart*]

heart·i·ness [há:*r*tinis] *n.* U the state of being hearty. 친절; 성실; 원기.

heart·less [há:*r*tlis] *adj.* 《only *fig.*》 without feeling or affection; cruel; pitiless. 무정한; 잔혹한; 무자비한. ¶ *a ~ man* 박정한 사람. ●**heart·less·ly** [-li] *adv.* **heart·less·ness** [-nis] *n.*

heart·rend·ing [háːrtrèndiŋ] *adj.* causing much sorrow or intense distress. 가슴을 찢는 것 같은; 비통한. ¶ *~ news* 비통한 소식. ●**heart·rend·ing·ly** [-li] *adv.*

hearts·ease, heart's-ease [háːrtsìːz] *n.* **1** peace of mind, tranquility. 마음의 평온; 안심. **2** ⟪bot.⟫ a wild pansy. 꼬까오랑캐꽃.

heart·sick [háːrtsìk] *adj.* very unhappy. 몹시 괴로운; 비탄에 잠긴; 비통한.

heart·sore [háːrtsɔ̀ːr] *adj.* feeling or showing grief. 슬픔[비탄]에 잠긴; 마음 아픈.

heart-strick·en [háːrtstrìkən] *adj.* stricken to the heart; full of deep sorrow. 슬픔에 잠긴; 비탄에 젖은.

heart·strings [háːrtstrìŋz] *n. pl.* deepest feelings of love. 마음속 깊은 감정[애정]; 심금(心琴). ¶ *touch the ~ of the audience* 청중의 심금을 울리다.

pull at someone's heartstrings, stir one's deepest feelings. …의 마음속 깊은 곳을 뒤흔들다.

heart-to-heart [háːrttəháːrt] *adj.* without reserve; frank; sincere. 마음을 털어놓은; 숨김없는; 솔직한; 성의 있는. ¶ *a ~ talk.*

heart-whole [háːrthòul] *adj.* **1** not yet in love. 사랑을 모르는; 사랑을 하지 않고 있는. **2** wholly given up to one object. 전념[열중]하는; 한결같은. ¶ *a ~ friendship* 한결같은[진정한] 우정.

heart wood [ㅗㅡ] *n.* the hard, central wood of a tree trunk. (나무의) 심재(心材); 고갱이(cf. *sapwood*).

***heart·y** [háːrti] *adj.* (**heart·i·er, heart·i·est**) **1** friendly; warm-hearted. 마음으로부터의; 마음이 따뜻한; 친절한. ¶ *a ~ welcome* 따뜻한 환영 / *~ approval* 진심으로의 찬성. **2** high-spirited; healthy; cheerful. 기운찬; 건강한; 명랑한. ¶ *He is still hale and ~ at 80.* 그는 나이 80에 아직도 정정하다. **3** (of a meal) plentiful; enjoying plenty of food. (음식이) 푸짐한; 충분한; 배부른; 식욕이 왕성한. ¶ *a ~ appetite* 왕성한 식욕 / *have a ~ meal* 식사를 배불리 먹다. **4** nourishing. 영양이 있는. ¶ *~ beef stock* 영양이 있는 쇠고기 국거리. [*heart*]

:heat [hiːt] *n.* Ⓤ **1** the state of being hot. 열; 더운[따뜻한, 뜨거운] 기운; 염열(炎熱) (opp. cold). ¶ *the ~ of the sun's rays* 태양열 / *the ~ of a fire* 불의 열기 / *enjoy the ~* 따뜻함을 즐기다. **2** fierce feeling; fierceness; excitement. (감정의) 뜨거움; 격렬; 열렬; 흥분. ¶ *with some ~* 좀 흥분하여 / *in the ~ of an attack* 한창 공격중에 / *take ~* 격노하다 / *answer without ~* 열의 없는 대답을 하다 / *He spoke with ~.* 열기를 띠어 이야기했다. **3** hot weather. (자연·환경의) 더위. ¶ *have an unbroken ~* 더위가 계속되고 있다. **4** Ⓒ ⓐ single intense effort. 한번의 노력[활동, 작업]. ⓑ ⟪sports⟫ one trial in a competition or race. (경기의) 1회; 1라운드. ¶ *preliminary [trial] heats* 예선 / *the final ~* 결승전 / *win in the second ~* 제2차 예선에서 이기다. **5** (of a female animal) sexual excitement occurring in a certain season; the period excitement occurring in a certain season. (동물 암컷의) 발정; 암내; 발정[교미]기. ¶ *be on [in, at] ~* 발정하다; 암내를 내고 있다. **6** ⟪*sl.*⟫ pressure. 압력; 강압. ¶ *turn the ~ on someone* 아무에게 압력을 넣다.

at a heat, at a breath. 단숨에; 단번에.

in the heat of, in the act of. 한창 …하는 중에.

on [⟪U.S.⟫ ***in***] ***heat,*** ⟪Brit.⟫ sexually excited. 발정하여.

— *vt.* (P6,7) **1** make (something) hot or warm. …을 가열하다; 따뜻하게 하다; 데우다. ¶ *a room heated by a stove* 난로로 더워진 방 / *~ up cold meat* 냉육을 데우다 / *~ some water* 물을 데우다. **2** excite. …을 흥분시키다. ¶ *a heated brain* 흥분한 머리 / *be heated with argument* 의론으로 격해지다.

— *vi.* (2A) **1** become hot or warm. 뜨거워지다; 따뜻해지다. **2** become excited. 흥분하다. [E.]

heat·ed·ly [híːtidli] *adv.* in an angry, lively, or excited manner. 격(앙)하여; 흥분하여.

heat·er [híːtər] *n.* Ⓒ a thing that gives heat, such as a stove, furnace, or radiator. 가열기(加熱器); 난방 장치; 히터.

heath [hiːθ] *n.* **1** Ⓒ ⟪Brit.⟫ a stretch of waste land covered with heather and low shrubs. 히스 따위가 무성한 황무지. **2** ⓊⒸ ⟪bot.⟫ an evergreen shrub; heather. 히스 ⟪황무지에 자라는 관목⟫. [E.]

***hea·then** [híːðən] *n.* Ⓒ a person who is not a Christian, Jew, or Muhammadan; a very uncivilized person. 이교도(異教徒)(cf. *infidel, pagan*); 야만인. — *adj.* **1** not Christian, Jewish, or Muhammadan. 이교도의. ¶ *a ~ temple* 이교(異教)의 사원. **2** outlandish; barbarous. 이국풍(異國風)의; 미개[야만]의. [E.]

hea·then·dom [híːðəndəm] *n.* Ⓒ heathen lands or people. 이교국(異教國); 이교도(opp. Christendom).

hea·then·ish [híːðəniʃ] *adj.* of the heathen; like the heathen; barbarous. 이교(異教)의; 비(非)기독교적인; 야만스러운.

hea·then·ism [híːðənìzəm] *n.* Ⓤ **1** heathen worship or ways. 이교 (신앙); 우상 숭배. **2** lack of religion; barbarism. 무종교; 야만.

heath·er [héðər] *n.* Ⓤ a rough wild plant with very small red-blue flowers, found on waste land. 히스속(屬)의 식물 (cf. *heath*). [?]

set the heather on fire, make a disturbance. 소동을 일으키다.

take to the heather, become an outlaw.

산적이 되다.

heath·y [híːθi] *adj.* (**heath·i·er, heath·i·est**) **1** of or like a heath. 히스의; 히스 비슷한. **2** covered with heath. 히스가 무성한. [*heath*]

heat·ing [híːtiŋ] *adj.* that heats. 가열하는; 따뜻하게 하는. ¶ *a ~ apparatus* 〔*system*〕 난방 장치. — *n.* Ⓤ the act of making (something) hot. 가열. ¶ *steam ~* 증기 난방. [*heat*]

heat·stroke [híːtstròuk] *n.* ⓊⒸ a sudden illness caused by too much heat; sunstroke. 열사병; 일사병.

heat wave [⌐⌐] *n.* a period of unusually hot weather. (장기간의) 혹서.

***heave** [hiːv] *v.* (**heaved** or 《naut.》 **hove**) *vt.* **1** (P6) raise (something heavy) with effort; lift. (무거운 것)을 올리다; 들어올리다. ¶ *~ an ax* 도끼를 들어올리다 / *~ coal* 석탄을 싣고 부리고 하다; 석탄을 나르다. **2** (P6,7) lift and throw (something), esp. with effort. …을 들어올려 던지다. ¶ *~ an anchor overboard* 닻을 던져 내리다; 투묘하다 / *~ a stone out of the window* 창밖으로 돌을 던지다 / *~ the shot 10 meters* 포환을 10 미터 던지다. **3** (P6) pull (a rope, etc.) with force or effort. (밧줄 따위)를 끌어당기다. **4** (P6) ⓐ cause (something) to swell or rise. …을 부풀게 하다; 융기시키다. ¶ *~ one's chest* 〔*breast*〕 (숨을 들이쉬어) 가슴을 부풀리다. ⓑ cause (something) to rise and fall repeatedly. …을 올라갔다 내려갔다 하게 하다. ¶ *~ one's chest in breathing heavily* 거친 숨결로 가슴을 파동치게 하다 / *The wind heaved the waves.* 바람이 불어 물결이 놀쳤다 / *The waves heaved the ship up and down.* 파도가 배를 위아래로 일렁거리게 했다. **5** (P6) force out (a sigh, etc.) with effort or pain. (한숨 따위)를 내쉬다. ¶ *~ a sigh of relief* 안도의 한숨을 내쉬다 / *~ a groan* 신음소리를 내다. **6** (P6) 《naut.》 move (a ship) into a certain position. (배)를 어떤 위치로 움직이다. ¶ *~ a ship aback* 배를 뒤로 이동시키다. — *vi.* (P1,2A) **1** ⓐ rise, esp. slowly and with difficulty. (서서히 고생하여) 올라가다; 높아지다. ⓑ move up and down as of waves. (물결처럼) 놀지다; 파동치다; 올라갔다 내려갔다 하다. ¶ *heaving billows* 놀치는 물결 / *~ and set* (파도 위의 배가) 일렁거리다 / *a heaving bosom* (흐느낌 따위로) 파동치는 가슴. **2** swell up. 부풀다. **3** breathe with effort, pant. (숨이 차서) 헐떡이다. **4** ⓐ 《naut.》 pull hard at a rope. 밧줄을 세게 끌어 당기다. ⓑ (of ships) be moved by pulling at a rope or otherwise; draw. (배가) 밧줄이나 다른 것에 의해 끌려 이동하다.

Heave away 〔***ho***〕 ***!*** 《naut.》《sailor's call to heave》 pull hard together! 영차 닻 감아라.

heave (*a ship*) ***down,*** turn on one side for cleaning, etc. (청소·수리 따위를 위해) 배를 한쪽으로 기울이다.

heave in 〔***into***〕 ***sight,*** (of a ship, etc.) come into view. (배가) 수평선 위에 나타나다.

heave out, lift up (a flag, etc.). (기(旗) 따위)를 걸다〔올리다〕.

heave (*a ship*) ***to,*** stop by bringing it into the wind etc. (뱃머리를 바람 불어오는 쪽으로 돌려) 정선(停船)하다.

heave up, pull up; retch. 끌어올리다; 토하다.

— *n.* Ⓒ **1** an effort to lift or raise. 무엇을 들어 올리려는 노력. **2** a swell; a stretch, as of sea waves. 부풂; 파도의 놀짐. **3** the distance something is thrown. 던진 거리. [E.]

⁑**heav·en** [hévən] *n.* ⓊⒸ **1** 《chiefly *poet.*》 《often *pl.*》 the sky; the place where God and the angels live. 하늘. ¶ *fowls of ~* 하늘을 나는 새 / *the eye of ~* 태양 / *the starry heavens* 별이 총총한 하늘. **2** 《*H-*》 God. 하느님; 신. ¶ *the justice of Heaven* 하느님의 심판 / *Thank Heaven!* 고마워라 / *Good Heaven(s)!* (아이고) 저런; 이거 큰일이군〔야단났네〕 / *By Heaven(s)!* 신에 맹세코; 반드시 / *Heaven helps those who help themselves.* 하늘은 스스로 돕는 자를 돕는다. **3** the place of greatest happiness. 천국; 극락(opp. hell). ¶ *be in ~* 하늘 나라에 있다; 죽다. **4** 《*fig.*》 a state of extreme happiness. 몹시 행복한 상태. ¶ *a ~ on earth* 지상의 낙원 / *be in the seventh ~* 더없이 행복한 상태에 있다. [E.]

for heaven's sake ⇨sake.

go to heaven, die. 죽다; 승천하다.

Heaven forbid! a solemn expression of desire that something may not happen. 그런 일이 없도록; 그런 일이 있어 되겠는가.

in heaven, dead. 천국에 있는; 죽은.

in heaven's name, 《*emph.*》 on earth. 도대체. ¶ *What in heaven's name are you doing?* 도대체 무얼 하고 있는 건가.

move heaven and earth, do everything possible; make every effort. (…하기 위해) 백방으로 손을 쓰다; 전력을 다하다. ¶ *move ~ and earth to find out the secret* 비밀을 알아내기 위해 온갖 수단을 다 쓰다.

***heav·en·ly** [hévənli] *adj.* **1** of or in heaven. 하늘의. ¶ *The sun, moon, and the stars are ~ bodies.* 태양, 달 및 별들은 천체이다. **2** like heaven; holy; very beautiful. 천국과 같은; 신성한; 아름다운. ¶ *a ~ spot* 천국 같은 곳 / *~ peace* 천국에서와 같은 평화 / *~ daffodils* 아름다운 수선화 / *a ~ mind* (천사와 같은) 거룩한 마음. **3** 《*colloq.*》 very happy; very delightful; excellent. 더없이 행복한; 매우 즐거운; 훌륭한; 멋진. ¶ *have a ~ time* 매우 즐거운 시간을 보내다.

heav·en·ward [hévənwərd] *adj., adv.* toward heaven. 하늘쪽으로 향한〔향해〕.

heav·en·wards [hévənwərdz] *adv.* = heavenward.

⁑**heav·i·ly** [hévili] *adv.* **1** ⓐ with great weight or force. 무겁게. ¶ *a ~ loaded wagon* 무거운 짐을 실은 짐차 / *press ~* 힘주어 누르다 / *weigh ~* 무겁게 중량이 실리다. ⓑ in a heavy manner. (동작 따위가) 무겁게; 답답하게; 느릿느릿; 털썩. ¶ *move ~* 느릿느

릿 움직이다 / *Anxiety presses* 〔*weighs*〕 ～ *on me.* 걱정이 마음을 무겁게 짓누르고 있다 / *He dropped* ～ *into a chair.* 그는 털썩 의자에 주저앉았다. **2** to a high degree; severely. 몹시; (호)되게; (격)심하게. ¶ *be fined* ～ 무거운 벌금이 부과되다 / *be punished* ～ 호되게 처벌되다 / *suffer* ～ 큰 손해〔피해〕를 입다. [→ heavy]

heav·i·ness [hévinis] *n.* Ⓤ the state or quality of being heavy. 무거움; 답답함; 무기력; 침체.

:heav·y [hévi] *adj.* (**heav·i·er, heav·i·est**) **1** weighty; hard to lift or carry. 무거운; 무게가 나가는(opp. light). ¶ *a* ～ *load* 무거운 짐 / *a load too* ～ *to lift* 너무 무거워서 들어올릴 수 없는 짐 / *Gold is heavier than iron.* 금은 쇠보다 무겁다. **2** ⓐ great in quantity or amount; rich. 양(量)이〔액(額)이, 정도가, 규모가〕 큰; 대량의. ¶ *a* ～ *crop* 풍작 / *a* ～ *snowfall* 큰눈 / *a* ～ *loss* 엄청난 손실 / *a* ～ *buyer* 〔*consumer*〕 대량 구입자〔소비자〕 / *a* ～ *drinker* 대주가; 술고래 / *a* ～ *smoker* 줄담배 피우는 사람; 골초. ⓑ large; of more than usual size, force, etc. (보통보다) 큰. ¶ ～ *guns* 〔*artillery*〕 중포(重砲) / ～ *industry* 중공업. **3** grave; severe; hard to do or finish; hard to bear or suffer. 중대한; 심한; 가혹한; 하기〔끝내기〕 힘든; 견디기 어려운. ¶ ～ *news* 중대 뉴스 / ～ *work* 고통스러운 일 / ～ *taxes* 무거운 세금 / ～ *sorrow* 견디기 어려운 슬픔 / *a* ～ *offence* 중죄 / *a* ～ *wound* 중상. **4** ⓐ not easily digested. (음식이) 소화가 잘 안 되는 ¶ ～ *food* 소화가 잘 안 되는 음식. ⓑ which has not risen sufficiently. (빵 따위 구운 것이) 잘 부풀지 않은. ¶ *a* ～ *cake* 잘 부풀지 않은 케이크. **5** forceful; severe; violent. 강한; 맹렬〔격렬〕한. ¶ *a* ～ *blow* 맹타 / *a* ～ *wind* 〔*storm*〕 강한 바람〔사나운 폭풍우〕 / *a* ～ *sea* 거친 바다. **6** loud and intense. (소리 따위가) 큰; 요란한. ¶ ～ *applause* 대갈채. **7** cloudy; gloomy. (하늘이) 잔뜩 흐린〔찌푸린〕; 어둠침침한. ¶ *a* ～ *sky.* **8** ⓐ thick; dense; full of. 짙은; …로 찬〔가득한〕. ¶ ～ *fog* 짙은 안개 / ～ *eyebrows* 짙은 눈썹 / *a heart* ～ *with sorrow* 슬픔으로 가득 찬 마음. ⓑ 《*with*》 weighted down. …로 무거운. ¶ *air* ～ *with moisture* 습기가 차 무거운 공기 / *a tree* ～ *with fruits* 가지가 휘어지게 열매가 달린 나무 / *eyes* ～ *with sleep* 졸려서 개개 풀어진 눈 / *feel* ～ 몸이 느른하다. **9** (of a road) muddy; making traveling difficult. (길이) 질척거리는; 걷기 힘든. ¶ *a* ～ *road.* **10** ⓐ slow in action or in understanding. 굼뜬; (우)둔한. ¶ *a* ～ *fellow* 아둔패기; 느리광이. ⓑ slow and troublesome; clumsy. 느릿느릿한; 어색한. ¶ *a* ～ *manner of speaking* 느린 말투 / *be* ～ *on one's feet* 발걸음이 느리다. **11** feeling sorrow or grief; sad. 슬픈; 기분이 무거운. ¶ ～ *news* 〔*tidings*〕 슬픈 소식 / *with a* ～ *heart* 침울한 마음으로. **12** 《theatr.》 serious; solemn; tragic. 진지한; 엄숙한; 비극적인. ¶ *the part of the* ～ *father* 진지한 아버지역(役). **13** (of writing and writers) dull. 재미없는; 따분한. ¶ *a* ～ *style* 〔*book*〕 따분한 문체〔책〕.

hang heavy on one's hands, (of time) pass slowly and dully. (시간이) 더디고 따분하게 지나가다.

have a heavy hand, **a**) be unskillful; be left-handed. 솜씨가 없다. **b**) be cruel; be overbearing. 잔혹하다; 강압적이다. **c**) be awkward in movement. 동작이 어색하다.

heavy in 〔***on***〕 ***hand,*** **a**) (of a horse) hard to drive. (말 따위가) 어거하기 힘든; 다루기 어려운. **b**) tiresome; dull. 지루한; 따분한.

lie 〔***sit, weigh***〕 ***heavy on,*** **a**) lean on (something). …에 덮쳐 누르듯 압박하다. **b**) cause great pain or trouble to (someone). …을 괴롭히다.

— *adv.* 《now chiefly in *compounds*》 = heavily. [E.]

heav·y-hand·ed [hévihǽndid] *adj.* **1** lacking lightness and fineness of touch, awkward. 솜씨가 서투른; 어색한(opp. light-handed). **2** oppressive. 압제적인.

heav·y-heart·ed [hévihɑ́ːrtid] *adj.* sorrowful; sad; gloomy. 슬픔에 찬; 우울한 (opp. light-hearted).

heav·y-lad·en [hévilέidn] *adj.* heavily loaded. 무거운 짐을 실은〔짊어진〕.

heavy metal [⌐-⌐-] *n.* **1** 《chem.》 metal with heavy-weight. 중금속. **2** 《nav.》 guns or shot of large size. 중포(重砲); 거탄(巨彈). **3** 《*fig.*》 a person or persons having great power or strength. 큰 힘〔영향력〕이 있는 사람.

heavy swell [⌐-⌐] *n.* 《*colloq.*》 a person who appears a man of importance and distinction. 풍채〔태도〕가 당당한 사람.

heavy water [⌐-⌐-] *n.* 《chem.》 water consisting of oxygen and heavy hydrogen. 중수(重水)(D_2O).

heav·y·weight [héviwèit] *n.* Ⓒ **1** a person of much more than average weight. (기수(騎手) 등에서) 평균 체중 이상의 사람. **2** a heavyweight boxer or wrestler. (권투나 레슬링의) 헤비급 선수.

heb·dom·a·dal [hebdɑ́mədl / -dɔ́m-] *adj.* weekly. 7일째마다의; 매주(每週)의. [Gk. *heptá* seven]

He·be [híːbiː] *n.* **1** 《Gk. myth.》 the goddess of youth. 헤베《청춘의 여신》. **2** 《*colloq., joc.*》 a waitress. (술집의) 호스티스; 접대부. [Gk. =youth]

He·bra·ic [hiːbréiik] *adj.* of or having to do with the Hebrews or their language or culture. 헤브라이 사람〔말〕의; 헤브라이 문화의. [*Hebrew*]

He·bra·ism [híːbriìzəm, -brei-] *n.* **1** Hebrew usage or idiom. (헤브라이 특유의) 어법〔관용어〕. **2** Hebrew character, spirit, thought, or practice. (헤브라이 민족 특유의) 성격〔정신, 주의, 풍습〕.

He·brew [híːbruː] *n.* **1** Ⓒ a Jew. 헤브라이

사람; 유대인. 2 Ⓤ ⓐ the ancient language of the Jews; the present-day language of Israel. 고대 헤브라이어(語); 현대 이스라엘어(語). ⓑ 《colloq.》 something one cannot understand. 불가해한 말(cf. *Greek*). ¶ *It's ~ to me.* 그건 나에게 전혀 알아들을 수 없는 말이다. —*adj.* Jewish. 헤브라이 사람〔말〕의. [Heb.]

hec·a·tomb [hékətòum, -tù:m] *n.* **1** (in ancient Greece) a sacrifice of 100 oxen. 신에게 바친 수소 100마리의 희생. **2** a great slaughter. 다수의 희생; 대학살. [Gk. *hekaton* hundred, *bous* ox]

heck [hek] *n.* hell. 지옥.

heck·le [hékəl] *vt.* (P6) trouble (a public speaker) by asking many questions or by making fun of. (연사)에게 어려운 질문을 연달아 퍼부어 괴롭히다. ¶ *The speaker was heckled by the audience.* 연사는 청중의 잇단 질문 공세로 곤욕을 치렀다. [*hackle*[1]]

hec·tare [héktɛər, -tɑ:r] *n.* Ⓒ a unit of area in the metric system; 100 ares. 헥타르《면적의 단위》.

hec·tic [héktik] *adj.* **1** showing signs of a slow wasting disease; feverish. 소모열의〔에 걸린〕; 폐병의〔에 걸린〕; 열이 있는. ¶ *a ~ fever* 소모열 / *a ~ flush* 소모성 홍조. **2** 《colloq.》 very excited. 몹시 흥분〔동요〕한; 열광적인. ¶ *have a ~ time* 몹시 흥분〔열광〕하다; 야단 법석하다 / *a ~ day* 눈코 뜰새없는 하루. [Gk. *hexis* habit of body]

hec·to- [héktou-] *pref.* one hundred. '백'의 뜻. ¶ *hectogram.*

hec·to·gram, 《Brit.》 **-gramme** [héktougræ̀m] *n.* 100 grams. 헥토그램(=3.527 ounces). [Gk. *hekaton* hundred]

hec·to·graph [héktougræ̀f, -grɑ̀:f] *n.* a gelatin pad for making multiple copies. (복사를 위한) 젤라틴판(版).

Hec·tor [héktər] *n.* a Trojan hero, son of King Priam, killed by Achilles in Homer's 'Iliad'. 헥토르《Homer작 'Iliad'에 등장하는 트로이의 용사》.

hec·tor [héktər] *vt., vi.* (P6,13; 1) behave roughly and severely toward a weaker person; scold (someone). 약자를 괴롭히다; 호통치다. —*n.* Ⓒ a person who hectors. 허세부리는 사람; 약자를 괴롭히는 사람. [Gk.]

·**he'd** [hi:d] 《colloq.》 **1** he had. **2** he would.

:**hedge** [hedʒ] *n.* Ⓒ **1** ⓐ a row of bushes forming a fence or dividing line. 산울타리. ¶ *a quickset ~* 산울타리. ⓑ a fence; a wall. 울타리; 담. **2** a barrier. 장벽; 경계. ¶ *a ~ of convention* 인습의 장벽. **3** (in betting, speculation) a second, lesser bet made to guard against loss. (도박·투기에서 위험부담을 줄이기 위해) 양쪽에 걸기; 양다리 걸치기. ¶ *make a ~* 양쪽에 걸다; 양다리 걸다.

be on the hedge, sit on the fence. (유리한 쪽에 붙으려고) 형세를 관망하다; 기회주의적 태도를 취하다.

come down on the wrong side of the hedge, make a wrong decision; do the wrong thing. 결정을 그르치다; 잘못을 저지르다.

take hedge, leave; go away. 떠나다.

—*vt.* (P6,7,13) **1** put a hedge around (something). …에 산울타리를 두르다. ¶ *~ a garden.* **2** 《fig.》 《in, about》 get in the way of; restrict the freedom of action of; hinder as with a hedge. …을 방해하다; (행동의 자유를) 속박〔제한〕하다; (울타리처럼) 에워〔둘러〕싸다. ¶ *~ in the enemy* 적을 포위하다 / *~ students about* 〔*round, in*〕 *with rules* 학생들을 여러 가지 규칙으로 속박하다 / *~ someone's path with difficulties* 아무의 앞길을 어려움으로 가로막다. **3** protect (something) with a hedge, etc.; shelter. (장벽으로) …을 지키다〔보호하다〕; 막다. ¶ *~ someone round with care and affection* 아무를 배려(配慮)와 애정으로 지키다. **4** make (a second, lesser bet) to guard against loss. (도박·투기에서 전액 손실의 방지를 위해) 양쪽에 걸다; 양다리 걸치다. —*vi.* (P1) **1** ⓐ make a hedge. (산)울타리를 만들다. ⓑ cut the edges of a hedge. 산울타리 가지 끝을 자르다. **2** ⓐ allow for escape or retreat; avoid giving a direct answer. 도피구를 마련해 두다; 직접적인 대답을 피하다. ⓑ bet on both sides in order to reduce one's possible losses. (도박에서) 손실의 위험을 줄이기 위해 양쪽에 걸다. **3** hesitate. 망설이다; 주저하다. [E.]

hedge in, **a**) surround. (집 따위를) …로 두르다. **b**) give a limit to (someone). (규율 따위로 사람을) 묶다; 속박〔제한〕하다. ¶ *We ~ him in with rules.* 우리는 그를 여러 가지 규칙으로 얽어맸다.

hedge out, shut out; lock out. (문을 닫고) 안에 들이지 않다; 제외하다.

hedge·hog [hédʒhɑ̀g, -hɔ̀:g / -hɔ̀g] *n.* Ⓒ 《animal》 **1** a kind of rat partly covered with a needle-like skin. 고슴도치. **2** an animal like a rat, covered with something like needles; a porcupine. 호저.

hedge·hop [hédʒhɑ̀p / -hɔ̀p] *vi.* (**-hopped**) 《colloq.》 fly an airplane very low, skimming ground features. (비행기가) 초저공 비행을 하다. [*hedge, hopper*]

hedge·row [hédʒròu] *n.* Ⓒ a row of bushes or small trees forming a hedge. (산울타리를 이루고 있는) 관목의 열(列).

he·don·ism [hí:dənìzəm] *n.* Ⓤ a belief that regards pleasure or happiness as the highest good. 쾌락주의. [Gk. *hēdonē* pleasure]

he·don·ist [hí:dənist] *n.* Ⓒ a person who believes in hedonism. 쾌락주의자.

:**heed** [hi:d] *vt., vi.* (P6; 1) pay attention to (something); take notice of (something). …에 주의하다; 유의〔조심〕하다. ¶ *~ what someone says* 아무가 하는 말에 주의하다 / *~ someone's warning* 아무의 경고에 유의

하다. — *n.* Ⓤ careful attention. 주의; 유의; 조심. [E.(→hood)]
give* [*pay*] *heed to, pay attention to (something). …에 주의하다. ¶ *give ~ to advice* 충고에 유의하다.
***take heed to* [*of*],** take notice of (something). …에 조심하다.

heed·ful [hí:dfəl] *adj.* careful; attentive. 주의깊은; 사려깊은(opp. neglectful).

heed·less [hí:dlis] *adj.* careless; thoughtless. 부주의한; 사려 없는; 경솔한. ● **heed·less·ly** [-li] *adv.*

heed·less·ness [hí:dlisnis] *n.* Ⓤ carelessness; thoughtlessness. 부주의; 사려 없음.

hee·haw [hí:hɔ̀:] *n.* Ⓒ **1** the sound made by a donkey. 나귀의 울음 소리. **2** a loud, rough laugh. (공연한) 큰 웃음; 바보 웃음. — *vi.* make such a sound. 나귀처럼 울다; 공연히 큰 소리로 웃다. [Imit.]

:**heel**[1] [hi:l] *n.* Ⓒ **1** the back part of the foot of a man or an animal. 뒤꿈치. ¶ *He has light heels.* 발이 빠르다. **2** 《usu. *pl.*》 the hind feet of an animal. (동물의) 뒷다리; 뒷굽. **3** the part of a stocking, sock, etc. which covers the heel; the back part attached to the sole of a shoe, supporting the heel. 양말(신발)의 뒤축. ¶ *wear high heels* 하이힐을 신다. **4** anything shaped or used like a heel. (모양·용도가) 발뒤꿈치 모양의 것. ¶ *the ~ of a golf club* (골프채의) 힐. **5** the last best part or remainder. (…의) 나머지; (담배의) 타다 남은 것; 꽁초.
at heel, just behind. 바로 뒤에서.
be at* [*on, upon*] *someone's heels, follow someone closely. …의 뒤를 바싹 뒤쫓다.
come* [*keep*] *to heel, **a**) (of a dog) come close behind one. (개가) 주인의 바로 뒤를 따라오다. ¶ *Come to ~ !* (개를 향해) 따라와. **b**) 《*fig.*》 agree to obey rules, another's will, etc.; cease to oppose. (규칙·명령·타인의 의사)에 따를 것에 동의하다; 반대를 그만두다.
cool* [*kick*] *one's heels, 《*colloq.*》 wait or be kept waiting for a long time. (오랫동안) 기다리게 되다; 기다리다.
down at the heel, having much worn shoes; poorly dressed; shabby. 뒤축이 닳은 신을 신고; (옷이) 초라한.
have* [*get*] *the heels* (=*get ahead*) *of someone. …을 앞지르다.
head over heels = heels over head.
heels over head, **a**) upside down; in jumping, turning the body completely. 거꾸로; 곤두박이쳐서. **b**) in great haste. 허둥지둥; 몹시 당황하여. **c**) completely; utterly. 완전히; 아주. ¶ *heels over head in love* 사랑에 깊이(푹) 빠지다.
kick up one's heels, **a**) jump and make kicking movements in play. 뛰놀다. **b**) have an entertaining time; have fun. 즐거운 때를 보내다. **c**) be lively or merry. 유쾌하게(들떠) 떠들다. **d**) die. 죽다.
kick up someone's heels, **a**) knock down. …를 때려 쓰러뜨리다. **b**) defeat; beat. 지게 하다; 패배시키다.
lay* [*set, clap*] *someone by the heels, **a**) put someone in jail. …를 투옥하다. **b**) overcome. …을 지게 하다; 이기다.
leave the house heels foremost, 《*colloq.*》 be carried out dead. (집에서) 죽어 나가다.
***out at heel*(*s*),** **a**) having holes in the heels of one's shoes or socks. 양말 뒤꿈치가 터져; 구두 뒤축이 닳아 무지러져. **b**) poor; badly dressed. 초라한.
raise* [*lift*] *the heel against, kick; give a kick to (someone). …를 (발로) 차다.
show one's heels* =*show a clean pair of heels* =*take to one's heels, run away. (부리나케) 달아나다.
to heel, **a**) close to one's heels; just behind. 바싹 뒤따라; 바로 뒤에. **b**) under control. 지배되어; 복종하여.
tread on someone's* [*the*] *heels of, come immediately after. 아무를 바싹 뒤따라 오다.
turn on one's heels, turn sharply around. 홱 돌아서다.
turn* [*lay, tip, topple*] *up one's heels, die. 죽다.
turn* [*tumble*] *up someone's heels, **a**) kick down. 차서(때려) 쓰러뜨리다. **b**) kill. 죽이다.
under the heel of* (=*crushed by*) *someone* or *something. …에게 짓눌려(짓밟혀); …에게 학대받아; …에 짓눌려 찌부러져.
with the heels foremost, as a corpse. 사체(死體)가 되어.
— *vt.* (P6) **1** attach the heel to (shoes). …에 굽을 달다. **2** follow (someone) closely. …의 바로 뒤를 따르다; …을 바싹 뒤쫓다.
— *vi.* (P1) **1** follow after someone. (…의) 뒤를 따르다. **2** touch the ground with the heels. 발 뒤꿈치를 지면에 대다. [E.]
heel out, 《rugby》 pass (the ball) out of scrummage with one's heel. 발 뒤꿈치로 공을 차내다.

heel[2] [hi:l] *vi., vt.* (P1,2A; 6) 《*over*》 (of a ship) lean to one side. (배가) 기울다; …를 기울이다. — *n.* Ⓒ a heeling movement. 한쪽으로 기울기. [E.]

heft [heft] *n.* Ⓤ Ⓒ 《*dial.*》 **1** weight. 무게. ¶ *the ~ of a stone* 돌의 무게. **2** importance. 중요함. — *vt.* (P6) 《U.S. *colloq.*, Brit. *dial.*》 judge the weight by lifting. (들어보아) 무게를 알아보다. [→heave]

heft·y [héfti] *adj.* (**heft·i·er, heft·i·est**) **1** heavy. 무거운. **2** big and strong. 크고 탄탄한; 강한.

He·gel [héigəl], **Georg Wilhelm Friedrich** *n.* (1770-1831) a German philosopher. 헤겔 《독일의 철학자》.

he·gem·o·ny [hidʒéməni, hédʒəmòuni] *n.* Ⓤ leadership among a group of nations. 패권; 지도권. [Gk.]

Heg·i·ra [hidʒáirə, hédʒərə] *n.* **1** 《*the H-*》 the flight of Muhammad from Mecca to

Medina in 622 A.D. 헤지라; 마호메트의 도주 《622년》. **2** Ⓤ the Moslem era. 회교 기원; 헤지라 기원. **3** Ⓒ 《*h-*》 escape; flight. 도망; 도피 (여행). [Arab. *hijrah*]

heif·er [héfər] *n.* Ⓒ a young cow. (아직 새끼를 낳지 않은 3살 미만의) 어린 암소. [E.]

heigh [hei, hai] *interj.* an expression to call attention or to show surprise, questioning, pleasure, etc. 어; 여; 에; 야아《주의·놀라움·질문·환희 따위의 뜻을 나타냄》. [Imit.]

heigh-ho [héihóu, hái-] *interj.* an expression of sadness or tiredness. 아아《따분함·슬픔·낙담 따위를 나타냄》. [↑]

:height [hait] *n.* **1** ⓊⒸ ⓐ the state of being high; the distance from the top to the base. 높이(cf. *length, width*). ¶ *the ~ of a box* 〔*tower, mountain*〕 상자〔탑, 산〕의 높이 / *the ~ of a person* 키; 신장 / *six feet in ~* 신장 6피트. ⓑ the distance of anything above the earth or above sea level. (지상·해면에서의) 높이; 고도; 표고; 해발. ¶ *the ~ of an airplane* 비행기의 고도 / *the ~ of 3,000 meters above sea level* 해발 3,000 미터. **2** Ⓒ 《often *pl.*》 a high point or place. 고지(高地); 높은 곳; 산. ¶ *a castle on the heights* 고지 위의 성. **3** 《*the ~*》 the highest point; the utmost degree. 절정; 극치; 한창임. ¶ *the ~ of folly* 더없는 어리석음 / *the ~ of power* 권력의 절정 / *in the ~ of fashion* 한창 유행중에 / *be in the ~ of one's fame* 인기의 절정에 있다. **4** 《*fig.*, Bible》 the heavens. 하늘. [*high*]

at its height = ***at the height of,*** **a)** in the middle of something. 한창 …중에. ¶ *at the ~ of the storm* 폭풍우가 한창일 때에. **b)** at the top of something. …의 정상에서.

in 〔***at***〕 ***the height of summer,*** in the middle of summer. 한여름에. 參考 in the depth of winter 는 '한겨울에'.

height·en [háitn] *vt.* (P6) **1** make (something) higher; increase the height of (something). …을 높게 하다; 높이다. **2** ⓐ make (something) stronger or greater; increase. …을 강하게 하다; 더하다; 증대하다. ¶ *~ anger* 〔*an effect*〕 노여움을〔효과를〕 증대시키다. ⓑ exaggerate. 과장하다. ¶ *~ a description* 묘사를 과장하다. — *vi.* (P1) become higher; increase. 높아지다; 증대하다.

hei·nous [héinəs] *adj.* (of a crime) very bad. (범죄 따위가) 극악한. ¶ *a ~ crime* 가증스럽기 그지없는 범죄. [F. *hair* hate]

:heir [ɛər] *n.* Ⓒ **1** a person who will get someone's property, rank or right when the latter dies. (유산·지위·권리의) 상속인; 법정 상속인. ¶ *a male ~* 남계 상속인 / *an ~ apparent* 추정 상속인 / *an ~ presumptive* 추정 상속인《자기보다 선(先)순위자가 출생한 때에는 상속 자격이 없어지는 사람》/ *~ to one's father's property* 아버지 재산의 상속인 / *fall ~ to* …의 상속인이 되다. **2** a person or group that inherits qualities from others who have lived before. (선대의 특성·정신·전통 따위를) 이어받은 사람〔사회〕; 후계자〔계승자〕. ¶ *an ~ to his mother's grace* 모친의 고상함을 이어받은 사람 / *Englishmen are the heirs of liberty.* 영국인은 자유의 계승자이다. [L. *heres*]

heir·ess [ɛ́əris] *n.* Ⓒ a woman heir. 여자 상속인.

heir·loom [ɛ́ərlùːm] *n.* Ⓒ any valuable thing which is passed on to heirs for generations. 법정 상속 동산; 조상 전래의 가재(家財)〔가보〕.

:held [held] *v.* p. or pp. of **hold**[1].

Hel·en [hélin, -lən] *n.* **1** 《Gk. myth.》 the very beautiful wife of King Menelaus of Sparta and the cause of the Trojan War. 헬레네《트로이 전쟁의 불씨가 된 스파르타 왕 Menelaus 의 아름다운 아내》. **2** a woman's name. 여자의 이름.

hel·i·ces [hélisìːz] *n.* pl. of **helix.**

hel·i·cop·ter [hélikὰptər, híːl- / -kɔ̀p-] *n.* Ⓒ a kind of airplane that is able to go straight up into air by means of horizontal propellers. 헬리콥터. [→helix, Gk. *pteron* wing]

he·li·o·cen·tric [hìːliouséntrik] *adj.* **1** viewed or measured from the sun's center. 태양의 중심에서 본〔관측한〕(cf. *geocentric*). **2** having or representing the sun as a center. 태양을 중심으로 하는〔보는〕. ¶ *the ~ theory of Copernicus* 코페르니쿠스의 태양 중심설. [Gk.]

he·li·o·graph [híːliougræ̀f, -grὰːf] *n.* Ⓒ **1** an instrument used for photographing the sun. 태양 촬영용 사진기. **2** an instrument used for sending messages by means of sunlight. 일광 반사 신호기. **3** an instrument used for measuring the strength of sunlight. 일조계(日照計). — *vt., vi.* signal by heliograph; take a photograph with a heliograph. 일광 반사 신호기로 송신〔촬영〕하다. [Gk.]

he·li·o·trope [híːliətròup / héljə-] *n.* Ⓒ **1** a plant with purple flowers. 헬리오트로프《지칫과(科)에 속하는 다년생의 식물》. **2** Ⓤ light red-blue color. 담자색(淡紫色). [↑]

hel·i·port [héləpɔ̀ːrt, híːlə-] *n.* Ⓒ a landing place for helicopters. 헬리콥터 발착장(發着場). [*heli*copter, air*port*]

he·li·um [híːliəm] *n.* Ⓤ 《chem.》 a very light, colorless and odorless gas which does not burn. 헬륨. 參考 화학 기호는 He. [Gk.]

he·lix [híːliks] *n.* (*pl.* **-lix·es** or **hel·i·ces**) **1** a spiral coil like the thread of a screw. 나선(螺旋); 나선상의 것. **2** a spiral ornament. 나선형 장식. **3** 《anat.》 the rim of the outer ear. 귓바퀴. [Gk.]

·hell [hel] *n.* Ⓤ Ⓒ **1** the place where bad persons are punished after death. 지옥; 명토. **2** a place or state of wickedness or misery. 지옥과 같은 곳〔상태〕; 생지옥. ¶ *make* *someone's life a* ~ 지옥과 같은 생활을 하다 / *suffer* ~ 지옥 같은 괴로움〔고통〕을 겪다. **3** expressing strong feeling, anger, etc. 《강한 감정·노여움·욕 따위를 나타내어》 제기랄; 도대체; 빌어먹을. ¶ *Hell, no!* 당치도 않다 / *Go to* ~*?* 뒈져라; 닥쳐 / *Who the* ~ *are you?* 도대체 넌 누구냐. [E.]

a hell of a (*noise, life, etc.*), 《*colloq.*》 a very unpleasant, unbearable. 몹시 나쁜〔불쾌한〕; 엄청난; 견딜 수 없는.

catch 〔**get**〕 **hell,** 《*sl.*》 receive a severe scolding. 호된 꾸중을 듣다; 되게 야단맞다.

for the hell of it, 《*colloq.*》 just for fun. 장난으로; 농담으로; 반재미로.

give *someone* **hell,** treat someone severely. …를 혼내주다; 못견디게 하다.

hell for leather, at full speed. 전속력으로.

Like hell! 《*sl.*》 Certainly not!; Not at all! 천만에.

like hell, 《*colloq.*》 desperately, very much; very violently. 필사적으로; 몹시.

***he'll** [hiːl] **1** he will. **2** he shall.

hell·cat [hélkæ̀t] *n.* Ⓒ a fierce, violent, bad-tempered woman. 거칠고 심통 사나운 여자; 악녀. [*hell*]

Hel·lene [héliːn] *n.* Ⓒ a Greek. 그리스 사람. [Gk.]

Hel·len·ic [helíːnik, helén-] *adj.* **1** Greek. 그리스의. **2** of the ancient Greek people or language. (고대) 그리스 사람〔말〕의. ¶ ~ *civilization* 고대 그리스 문명. [Gk.]

Hel·len·ism [hélənìzəm] *n.* Ⓤ **1** the ancient culture, ideals, and nationality of Greece. 헬레니즘; 고대 그리스 문화〔정신, 국민성〕. **2** the adoption or imitation of Greek culture. 그리스화(化); 그리스 모방.

Hel·len·ist [hélənist] *n.* Ⓒ a non-Greek who used Greek language, or culture. 그리스 말을〔문화를〕 받아들인 사람.

Hel·len·is·tic [hèlənístik] *adj.* of Greek culture, language and history. 그리스 문화〔말, 역사〕의.

Hel·len·ize [hélənàiz] *vt., vi.* **1** make or become Greek in character. 그리스화(化)하다; 그리스식으로 하다〔되다〕. **2** use or imitate the Greek language, ideals, or customs. 그리스말〔사상, 풍습〕을 쓰다〔모방하다〕.

hell·fire [hélfàiər] *n.* Ⓤ the fire of hell; punishment in hell. 지옥의 불; 지옥의 형벌〔괴로움〕. [*hell*]

hel·lion [héljən] *n.* Ⓒ 《U.S. *colloq.*》 a troublesome, mischievous person. 난폭하여 다루기 벅찬 사람; 무법자. [*hell*]

hell·ish [héliʃ] *adj.* **1** of hell. 지옥의〔같은〕. **2** devilish; very bad; horrible. 악마 같은; 흉악한; 무서운; 소름 끼치는. ¶ *It was* ~ *to see the scene of murder.* 살인 현장은 보기에 끔찍했다. ● **hell·ish·ly** [-li] *adv.* **hell·ish·ness** [-nis] *n.* [*hell*]

***hel·lo** [helóu, ⌐ -, hə-] *interj.* an expression of greeting, as in meeting or calling someone on the telephone; an expression of surprise. 어이; 이봐; 여보; 야; (전화에서) 여보세요; (놀라움을 나타내어) 아니; 저런; 어이구; (흥미를 나타내어) 호. [E.]

***helm**[1] [helm] *n.* Ⓒ **1** the handle of a rudder. 키(자루); 타륜(舵輪). **2** 《*fig.*》 《*the* ~》 a post of control, leadership or guidance. 지도적 지위; 지도; 지배. ¶ *a man of the* ~ 지도자 / *take the* ~ *of state* (*affairs*) 정권을 쥐다〔주도하다〕; 국정을 처리하다. — *vt.* (P6) **1** steer. 키를 잡다; 조타하다. **2** direct. 지도하다. ● **helm·less** [-lis] *adj.* [E.]

helm[2] [helm] *n.* 《*poet.*》 =helmet.

***hel·met** [hélmit] *n.* Ⓒ a strong covering to protect the head, as formerly worn by soldiers in armor, and now worn by people who might hurt their heads in accidents or at work. 투구; 안전모; 헬멧(cf. *headpiece*). [E.]

helms·man [hélmzmən] *n.* Ⓒ (*pl.* **-men** [-mən]) a man who steers a ship or boat. 키잡이; 조타수(操舵手). [*helm*[1]]

Hel·ot [hélət] *n.* Ⓒ **1** a slave in ancient Sparta. 농노(農奴). **2** 《*h-*》 a slave. 노예. [Gk.]

a drunken Helot, 《*fig.*》 a person used as a warning example. …을 경계하기 위해 그 본보기로 사용되는 사람.

:help [help] *vt.* **1** (P6,7,13,20,22) ⓐ do part of the work of (someone) for his advantage; aid; assist. (아무의 일을) 돕다; 거들다. ¶ ~ *someone with his work* 〔*lessons*〕 아무의 일〔학습〕을 돕다 / *I helped mother in her needlework.* 어머니의 바느질을 거들었다 / *Please* ~ *me with* 〔*to carry*〕 *this baggage.* 이 짐 좀 거들어 주십시오 / *Help me* (*to*) *move this desk.* 이 책상 옮기는 일 좀 도와 다오. ⓑ support (someone) in some action or motion; assist (someone) and cause him to do; assist to get (in, out, etc.). (어떤 행동·동작을 하는 데) 손을 빌리다; 거들어 …하게 하다; 도와 들어가게〔타게, 내리게〕하다. ¶ ~ *an old man down* 노인을 도와 내려주다 / ~ *someone to his feet* 손을 빌려 일어서게 하다 / ~ *someone into* 〔*out of*〕 *his clothes* 아무가 옷을 입는〔벗는〕 데 거들어 주다 / *He helped her into the car.* 그녀를 도와 차를 태워주었다 / *He helped her on with her coat.* 그녀를 거들어 외투를 입혀 주었다. ⓒ support (someone) by giving something necessary or by other means. (필요한 것 따위를 주어) 돕다; 구하다. ¶ ~ *someone with money* / *He helps his parents out of his small income.* 얼마 안 되는 수입에서 자기 부모를 돕고 있다. ⓓ get (someone) out of difficulties, etc. (곤란 따위에서) …을 구하다. ¶ ~ *a wounded person* 부상자를 구출하다 / 《*prov.*》 *Heaven helps those who help themselves.* 하늘은 스스로 돕는 자를 돕는다 / *He helped me out of my difficulties.* 그는 곤경에서 나를 구했다. ⓔ 《usu. asking to be saved or rescued》 save from danger or death; rescue. (위험·죽음으로부터) 구(조)하다; 살리

다. ¶ *Help, ~ ; he cried.* '사람 살려, 사람 살려' 하고 그는 소리쳤다. ⓕ make (something) easier to do; promote; contribute; be of use or service. …을 보다 용이하게 하다; 조장〔촉진, 기여〕하다; 도움이 되다. ¶ *~ toward a better understanding* 더 잘 이해하는 데 도움이 되다 / *The accident helped his ruin.* 그 사고가 그의 파멸을 재촉했다 / *The book will ~ to further knowledge.* 이 책은 더 깊은 지식을 얻는 데 도움이 될 것이다. **2** (P6,13) ⓐ make better; cure; relieve. (병·고통 따위)를 완화시키다; 가볍게 하다; 낫게 하다. ¶ *~ the toothache* 〔*a cough*〕 치통〔기침〕을 없애다 / *~ someone of a headache* 두통을 없애 주다. ⓑ serve food to (someone at table); wait on; serve out (food). (식탁에서) 음식 시중을 들다; 권하다; (음식을) 담아주다. ¶ *~ the potatoes* 감자를 담다 / *May I ~ you to some more vegetables ?* 야채를 좀더 드시지 않겠습니까 / *Please ~ yourself to the wine.* 어서 포도주를 마음대로 드십시오. **3** (P6,9) 《with *can, could*》 avoid; refrain from (something). …을 피하다; 아니하다; 그만두다; 참다. ¶ *I can't ~ it.* =*It can't be helped.* (어떻게도) 할 수 없다 / *I could not ~ crying.* 울지 않을 수 없었다 / *I spend no money that I can ~.* 지출하지 않아도 된다면 한푼의 돈도 쓰지 않는다 / *I can't ~ your being a fool.* 네가 바보임은 어쩔 도리가 없다 / *He never said anything if he could ~ it.* 굳이 안 해도 될 경우라면 그는 아무 말도 하지 않았다. — *vi.* (P1) **1** give assistance; be useful. 돕다; 거들다; 도움이 되다. **2** act as a waiter. (식탁에서) 시중 들다.

***cannot help but** do,* cannot fail to do; be compelled or obliged to do. …하지 않을 수 없다.

God help him ! an expression of pity. 가엾어라; 가엾게도.

***help** oneself,* **a**) try to go on without the help of others; do by one's own efforts or judgment. (남의 도움 없이) 자기 스스로 어떻게 해보다. **b**) 《*to*》 serve (food) to oneself; take freely. (음식)을 스스로 제 접시에 담다; 마음대로 집어먹다. ¶ *Please ~ yourself to the fruit.* 과일을 마음대로 드십시오. **c**) 《*to*》 take (anything) for one's own use; take without asking or without permission. …을 자신이 쓰려고 집다; 허가 없이 가지다.

help off, assist in getting off. 거들어 옷(따위)을 벗게 하다; 도와 매듭짓게〔처리하게〕 하다.

help on, help in getting on; help in advancing. 거들어 입혀 주다; 도와 나아가게 하다; 진척시키다.

help** someone **out, help someone in getting or doing something. (곤란한 때에) …을 도와주다. ¶ *~ someone out with his work* 아무의 일을 도와주다.

help** someone **out of, help someone (to) get rid of (difficulty, etc.). …을 도와 (곤경 따위)에서 구출하다.

help** someone **over, aid in surmounting, as some obstacle. …을 도와 장애를 극복하게 하다.

So help me God ! I swear. 하늘에 맹세코.

— *n.* **1** Ⓤ assistance; aid. 도움; 조력(助力). **2** Ⓤ a remedy; relief; an escape. 치료(법); 구제〔방지〕 수단; 도피구. ¶ *There is no ~ for it but to do so.* 그렇게 할 수밖에 달리 길이 없다. **3** Ⓒ a person or a thing that helps. 도움이 되는 사람〔것〕. ¶ *It is a great ~ to me.* 그것은 제게 큰 힘이 됩니다 / *You're no ~ to me.* 너는 내게 아무 도움도 안 된다. **4** Ⓒ 《often *collectively*》 《U.S.》 a hired helper; a part-time servant. 사용인; 시간제 하인〔가정부〕. ¶ *It is hard to find ~ these days.* 요즘은 일손〔사람〕 구하기가 어렵다. [E.]

be of help, be helpful; be useful. 도움이 되다; 유용하다.

***help·er** [hélpər] *n.* Ⓒ a person who helps someone; an assistant. 조력자; 돕는〔거드는〕 사람.

***help·ful** [hélpfəl] *adj.* giving help; useful. 도움이 되는; 유용한. ●**help·ful·ly** [-fəli] *adv.* **help·ful·ness** [-nis] *n.*

help·ing [hélpiŋ] *adj.* assisting. 도움을 주는; 원조의. ¶ *reach out a ~ hand to* …에 원조의 손길을 뻗치다. — *n.* Ⓒ a portion of the food served at a meal. (음식의) 한 그릇. ¶ *a second ~* 두 그릇째; (한 그릇) 더 청해 먹는 음식.

:**help·less** [hélplis] *adj.* **1** not able to help oneself; weak; powerless. 스스로 아무 일도 할〔혼자서 움직일〕 수 없는; 약한; 무력한. **2** lacking help; not helped. 도움이 없는; 의지할 데 없는. **3** not efficient. 무능한.

help·less·ly [hélplisli] *adv.* in a helpless manner. 힘없이; 어찌할 도리없이; 약하게.

help·less·ness [hélplisnis] *n.* Ⓤ the state of being helpless. 도움이 없음.

help·mate [hélpmèit] *n.* Ⓒ a helpful partner, esp. a wife or husband. 협력자; 반려《특히 아내 또는 남편》.

help·meet [hélpmìːt] *n.* =helpmate.

hel·ter-skel·ter [héltərskéltər] *adv.* in a hurry; in disorder. 당황하여; 허둥지둥(어쩔 줄 모르고); 난잡하게. ¶ *run ~* 허둥지둥 뛰(어가)다. — *adj.* hurried and confused; disorderly. 당황한; 난잡한. — *n.* great hurry and confusion. 허둥댐; 당황; 혼란; 난잡. [Imit.]

helve [helv] *n.* Ⓒ a handle of an ax, a hammer, etc. (도끼·망치 등) 자루; 손잡이. [E.]

***hem**[1] [hem] *n.* Ⓒ a fastened edge of cloth. (끝을 접어 감친) 천이나 옷의 가장자리. — *vt.* (**hemmed, hem·ming**) (P6,7) fold over the edge of cloth and fasten it down with needle and thread. 천이나 옷의 끝을 접어 감치다. [E.]

hem in 〔***about, around***〕, surround on all sides. 둘러싸다; 포위하다. ¶ *be hemmed in by enemies* 적군에 포위되다.

hem² [mm, hm] *interj., n.* Ⓒ a sound like clearing the throat, used to attract attention or express doubt or hesitation. 어흠; 에헴《주저·주의를 환기시키기 위한 헛기침》. — *vi.* (**hemmed**) (P1) make this sound. 위의 소리를 내다. [Imit.]

he-man [híːmæ̀n] *n.* Ⓒ (*pl.* **-men** [-mèn]) 《*colloq.*》 a strong, virile man. 강하고 억세어 남성다운 남자. [*he-*]

hem·i- [hémi-] *pref.* half. '반(半)' 의 뜻. [Gk. kemi-]

Hem·ing·way [hémiŋwèi], **Ernest** *n.* (1899-1961) an American novelist, short-story writer, and journalist. 헤밍웨이《미국의 소설가·단편 작가·신문 기자》.

hem·i·sphere [hémisfìər] *n.* Ⓒ a half of a ball or globe; a half of the earth's surface. 반구체; (천체·지구의) 반구(半球). ¶ *the Eastern* (*Western, Northern*) ~ 동(서, 북)반구. ●**hem·i·spher·ic, hem·i·spher·i·cal** [hèmisférik(əl)] *adj.* [hemi-, →sphere]

hem·line [hémlàin] *n.* Ⓒ the lower edge of a dress, skirt, etc. 드레스·스커트 단의 감친 선. [*hem*¹]

hem·lock [hémlɑ̀k / -lɔ̀k] *n.* **1** Ⓒ 《Brit.》 a poisonous plant; Ⓤ a poisonous drink got from this plant. 독당근; 그것에서 채취한 독약. **2** Ⓒ an evergreen tree of the pine family. 솔송나무. [E.]

he·mo·glo·bin [híːməglòubin, hémə-] *n.* Ⓤ the red coloring matter in the blood, serving to carry oxygen to every part of the body. 헤모글로빈; 혈색소. [Gk. *haima* blood]

he·mo·phil·i·a, (Brit.) **hae·mo-** [hìːməfíliə, hèm-] *n.* Ⓤ 《med.》 a hereditary tendency to bleeding even from a slight injury. 혈우병(血友病). [Gk. *haima* blood, *philia* tendency]

hem·or·rhage, 《Brit.》 **haem·or-** [hémərìdʒ] *n.* ⓊⒸ sudden and serious loss of blood; bleeding. 출혈. ¶ *cerebral* ~ 뇌출혈. [Gk. *haima,* blood, *rhēgnumi* break]

hem·or·rhoids, (Brit.) **haem·or-** [hémərɔ̀idz] *n. pl.* 《med.》 piles. 치질. ●**hem·or·rhoi·dal** [hèmərɔ́idl] *adj.* [Gk. *haima* blood, *rheō* flow]

hemp [hemp] *n.* Ⓤ **1** tall annual herbs of a mulberry family. 삼; 대마(大麻). **2** the fiber of this plant for making rope and coarse cloth. 삼의 섬유《밧줄·거친 천을 만듦》. [E.]

hemp·en [hémpən] *adj.* made of hemp. 삼(대마)의.

hem·stitch [hémstìtʃ] *n.* Ⓤ an ornament done with needle and thread, usu. at the edge of cloth. 헴스티치《천 가장자리의 장식 휘갑치기》. — *vt.* (P6) finish (a tablecloth, etc.) with hemstitch. (테이블보 따위의 가장자리)에 휘갑 장식을 치다. [*hem*¹]

〈hemstitch〉

:**hen** [hen] *n.* Ⓒ **1** a female domestic bird esp. a chicken. 암탉(opp. cock). **2** any female bird. 암새. ¶ *a ~ sparrow* 암참새 / *like a ~ with one chicken* 안절부절 못하여; 침착을 잃고. [E.]

hen·bane [hénbèin] *n.* Ⓒ a poisonous plant from which hyoscine is obtained. 사리풀《가짓과의 약용 식물》. [*hen*]

:**hence** [hens] *adv.* **1** 《*arch.*》 from here; away. 여기로부터; 저쪽으로. ¶ *go* (*pass*) ~ 죽다 / *Hence with him.* 그를 데리고 가라. **2** from this time. 지금(이제)부터; 앞으로. ¶ *a year* ~ 지금부터 1년 후에 / *We will leave a week* ~. 우리는 앞으로 1주일이면 떠난다. **3** therefore; for this reason. 그러므로; 고(故)로; 따라서. ¶ *I am ~ unable to help you.* 그러므로 나는 너를 도울 수 없다. [E.]

·**hence·forth** [hènsfɔ́ːrθ] *adv.* from this time on. 이제부터는; 금후(는); 이후.

hence·for·ward [hènsfɔ́ːrwərd] *adv.* = henceforth.

hench·man [héntʃmən] *n.* Ⓒ (*pl.* **-men** [-mən]) a faithful follower; a political supporter who blindly follows his leader. 충실한 추종자; 정치상의 맹목적인 지지자. [E. =horse man]

hen·coop [hénkùːp] *n.* Ⓒ a cage for hens. 닭의 어리; 닭장. [*hen*]

hen·dec·a- [hendékə-] *pref.* eleven. '11' 의 뜻. [Gk.]

hen·house [hénhàus] *n.* Ⓒ a house for domestic birds. 닭장; 계사(鷄舍). [*hen*]

hen·na [hénə] *n.* Ⓒ a small tree growing in Asia and Africa; Ⓤ a red dye got from the leaves of this plant. 헤너《부처꽃과에 속하는 관목》; (그 잎에서 채취하는) 염료·안료. [Arab.]

hen·ner·y [hénəri] *n.* Ⓒ (*pl.* **-ner·ies**) a place where hens are kept. 양계장. [*hen*]

hen party [⌐ ⌐] *n.* 《*colloq.*》 a party for women only. 여자만의 회합(cf. *stag party*).

hen·peck [hénpèk] *vt.* (P6) (of a wife) domineer over (her husband). (남편)을 깔고 뭉개다(손아귀에 쥐다). ¶ *He was henpecked* (*by his wife*). 그는 마누라 손에 꽉 쥐여 지냈다. [*hen*]

hen·pecked [hénpèkt] *adj.* ruled by one's wife. 여편네에게 쥐여 지내는; 엄처시하(내주장)의. ¶ *a ~ husband* 공처가.

·**Hen·ry** [hénri] *n.* a man's name. 남자 이름.

hep·cat [hépkæ̀t] *n.* 《U.S. old *colloq.*》 an expert performer of swing music. 재즈 특히 스윙 음악의 연주자. [?]

He·phaes·tus [hiféstəs / -fíːs-] *n.* 《Gk. myth.》 the god of fire and metalworking. 헤파이스토스《불·대장일을 관장하는 신; 로마 신화의 Vulcan》.

hep·ta- [héptə-] *pref.* seven. '7' 의 뜻. [Gk.]

hep·ta·gon [héptəgɑ̀n / -gɔ̀n] *n.* Ⓒ 《geom.》 a plane figure having seven sides and seven angles. 7각〔7변〕형. **•hep·tag·o·nal** [heptǽgənəl] *adj.* [↑, Gk. *gonia* corner]

hep·tam·e·ter [heptǽmitər] *n.* Ⓤ Ⓒ a verse of seven metrical feet. 칠보격(七步格).

hep·tar·chy [héptɑːrki] *n.* Ⓒ (*pl.* **-chies**) government by seven persons. 칠두(七頭) 정치. [hepta-]

:her [həːr, -əːr, hər] *pron.* **1** the objective form of **she.** 그녀를; 그녀에게. ¶ *We saw ~ this morning.* 오늘 아침 그녀를 만났다 / *They laughed at ~.* 그들은 그녀를 비웃었다 / *He gave ~ a book.* 그녀에게 책을 주었다. **2** the possessive form of **she.** 그녀의. ¶ *Her father is a teacher.* 그녀의 아버지는 교사이다 / *Her coat is the one on the chair.* 그녀의 코트는 의자 위의 것이다. **3** 《used as the *predicate*》《*colloq.*》=she. ¶ *It's ~, sure enough.* 확실히 그녀다. [E.]

He·ra [hírə, hé-] *n.* 《Gk. myth.》 a Greek goddess, wife of Zeus. 헤라《Zeus 신의 아내; 로마 신화의 Juno》.

:her·ald [hérəld] *n.* Ⓒ **1** an officer who announces important news to the public. 전령(傳令). **2** a person who carries news; a messenger. 보도자; 전달자; 사자(使者). ¶ *The cuckoo is a ~ of spring.* 뻐꾸기는 봄의 예고〔선구〕자이다. — *vt.* (P6) bring news of; announce; make known the coming of. …을 알리다〔전달, 보도하다〕; …을 예고하다. ¶ *the song of birds that heralds the dawn* 새벽을 알리는 새들의 노랫소리. [F.]

he·ral·dic [herǽldik] *adj.* of heralds. 전령의. [↑]

her·ald·ry [hérəldri] *n.* (*pl.* **-ries**) **1** Ⓤ science of the special designs used by families as marks of position, history, etc. 문장학(紋章學). **2** Ⓒ a coat of arms. 문장; 가문(家紋). **3** Ⓤ splendid show or ceremony connected with the life of noble families. 어마어마한 의식; 화려한 장관.

***herb** [həːrb] *n.* Ⓒ **1** a plant, with a soft stem, usu. dying down in winter. 초본(草本). **2** a plant used for making medicine. 약용 식물. ¶ *a(n) ~ garden* 약초원(藥草園). [L. *herba* grass]

her·ba·ceous [həːrbéiʃəs] *adj.* **1** of or like an herb. 풀의〔같은〕; 초본의. ¶ *~ plants* 초본 식물. **2** like a leaf; green. 잎과 같은; 초록(색)의. [↑]

herb·age [hə́ːrbidʒ] *n.* Ⓤ **1** 《*collectively*》 green grasses or herbs. 풀; 초본류. **2** 《law》 the right of pasture. 방목권(放牧權).

herb·al [hə́ːrbəl] *adj.* of herbs. 풀의; 초본의. — *n.* Ⓒ a book about herbs. 초본서(書).

herb·al·ist [hə́ːrbəlist] *n.* Ⓒ **1** originally, a botanist. (예전의) 식물학자. **2** now, a person who gathers or deals in herbs; a herb doctor. 식물〔약초〕 채집자; 약초상; 한방의(醫).

her·bar·i·a [həːrbέəriə] *n.* pl. of **herbarium.**

her·bar·i·um [həːrbέəriəm] *n.* Ⓒ (*pl.* **-ums** or **-i·a**) **1** a collection of dried plants systematically arranged. (분류한) 식물 표본집; 석엽집(腊葉集). **2** a room or building where such a collection is kept. 식물 표본실〔관〕. [*herb*]

Her·bert [hə́ːrbərt] *n.* a man's name. 남자 이름.

her·biv·o·rous [həːrbívərəs] *adj.* feeding on plants. 초식(草食)의(opp. carnivorous). ¶ *a ~ animal* 초식 동물. [*herb*]

her·cu·le·an, Her- [hə̀ːrkjəlíːən, həːrkjúːliən] *adj.* **1** of or like Hercules; of great strength or size of body. 헤르쿨레스의〔같은〕; 괴력의; 훌륭한 체격의. ¶ *a man of ~ build* 훌륭한 체격의 사람. **2** needing the strength of a Hercules; very hard to do. 헤르쿨레스와 같은 엄청난 힘을 요하는; 하기가 극히 곤란한. ¶ *a Herculean* 〔*herculean*〕 *task* 몹시 힘이 드는〔어려운〕 일. [↓]

Her·cu·les [hə́ːrkjəlìːz] *n.* **1** 《Gk. myth.》 a hero famous for his great strength. 헤르쿨레스《Zeus의 아들》. **2** Ⓒ a man of extraordinary strength. 괴력 무쌍의 사람; 장사. [Gk. *Hēraklēs*]

:herd [həːrd] *n.* Ⓒ **1** a group of animals, esp. of cows, horses, and elephants. (소·말·코끼리 따위의) 무리; 가축의 떼. ¶ *a ~ of sheep* 양떼. **2** the people; a large crowd of people. 군중; 대중. ¶ *the common* 〔*vulgar*〕 *~* 속중(俗衆); 하층민 / *the ~ instinct* 군중 심리. **3** 《only in *compounds*》 a herdsman. 목자(牧者); 가축을 치는 사람. ¶ *goatherd* / *swineherd.* — *vi.* (P1,2A) 《*together, with*》 flock together. 떼짓다; 모이다. ¶ *~ together.* — *vt.* (P6,7) form (cattle, etc.) into a group. …을 (한데) 모으다. ¶ *~ sheep* 〔*cattle*〕. [E.]

herds·man [hə́ːrdzmən] *n.* Ⓒ (*pl.* **-men** [-mən]) a man who looks after a herd. 목자(牧者); 가축지기.

:here [hiər] *adv.* **1** in or to this place. 여기에(서); 여기〔이리〕로; 이쪽으로(cf. *there*). ¶ *this man ~* 여기(있는) 이 사람 / *We live ~.* 우리는 여기에 살고 있다 / *Here's your hat.* 여기 네 모자가 있다 / *Come ~.* 이리 오너라 / *Here she comes.* 그녀가 온다 / *Here we are.* 자 다 왔다〔도착했다〕 / *Here goes!* 자 간다〔준다, 시작이다〕 / *Here it is.* 자 여기 있다 / *Here you are.* 네 여기 있습니다; 옜다; 옜네; 부디 그렇게 하세요 / *Here, sir!* (점호에 답하여) 네. **2** at this point (in speech, thought, or action); at this time. 이 점에서; 이 때. ¶ *Here I think he is wrong.* 이 점에서 그가 잘못이라고 나는 생각한다 / *Here he paused and looked around.* 여기서 그는 이야기를 멈추고 주위를 둘러보았다. **3** in this life. 이승에서; 현세에서.

here and now, in this place and at this moment. 지금 당장(에); 곧; 즉시(cf. *then and there*). ¶ *I must have it ~ and now.* 지금 당장 그것을 가져야겠다.

here and there, in various places. 여기저기〔이곳저곳〕에서(의).

here below, in this life; on this earth. 이승〔현세〕에; 지상에서.

Here's something for you. I'll give you this. 이것을 드리죠.

Here's to you ! (in a drinking toast) Here's a health to you ! 건강을 위하여 축배.

here, there, and everywhere, in every place. 도처에; 끊임없이 돌아다니녀. ¶ *He is ~, there, and everywhere.* 그는 가지 않는 곳이 없다.

Look here ! Attend to me. 어이; 이봐.

neither here nor there, 《*colloq.*》 not to the point; unimportant. 요점을 벗어나; 문제 밖의; 대수롭지 않은.

— *n.* Ⓤ this place; this point. 이곳; 여기; 이 점. ¶ *from ~ to there* 여기서 거기까지 / *up to ~* 여기까지 / *Do you live near ~ ?* 이 근처에 사니 / *When do we leave ~ ?* 이곳을 언제 떠나나. [E.]

here·a·bout [híərəbàut] *adv.* about this place. 이 근처〔부근〕에. ¶ *He lives ~.* 그는 이 근처 어디에 산다.

here·a·bouts [híərəbàuts] *adv.* =hereabout.

*****here·af·ter** [hiərǽftər, -ɑ́:f-] *adv.* **1** after this time. 금후. **2** in the future life after death. 내세에; 저승에서. — *n.* Ⓤ 《*the ~*》 **1** the future. 금후; 미래. **2** life after death. 내세; 저승. ¶ *in the ~* 내세에서.

here·at [hiərǽt] *adv.* 《*arch.*》 **1** when this happened; at this time. 여기서; 이때. **2** because of this. 이 때문에; 이러므로.

here·by [hìərbái] *adv.* by this means; as a result. 이에 의해서; 이에. ¶ *I ~ resign my office.* 이에 나는 나의 직책을 사임합니다.

he·red·i·ta·ble [hirédətəbəl] *adj.* =heritable.

her·e·dit·a·ment [hèrədítəmənt] *n.* Ⓒ 《law》 property that may be inherited. 상속 (가능) 재산. [↓]

he·red·i·tar·y [hirédətèri / -təri] *adj.* **1** passing naturally from parents to children. 유전하는; 유전성의. ¶ *a ~ disease* 유전성 질환 / *~ characters* 유전 형질. **2** (of rights, property, etc.) coming to one by inheritance; (of a person) holding a hereditary office or title. 상속권에 의한; 세습의. ¶ *~ domains* 세습 영토 / *a ~ monarch* 세습 군주 / *a ~ peerage* 세습의 귀족 지위. **3** (of habits, customs, etc.) learnt, accepted, or made current by continued tradition. 부모로부터 물려받은; 대대로 전해오는. ¶ *a ~ enemy* 숙적 / *~ friendship* 선대로부터의 친교. [→heir]

he·red·i·ty [hirédəti] *n.* Ⓤ **1** the nature or character passed down from parents to children. 유전. **2** the transfer of physical or mental characteristics from parents to offspring. 유전 형질. [↑]

here·in [hìərín] *adv.* in this; in this place. 이 속〔안〕에; 이 곳에. ¶ *the letter enclosed ~* 이 속에 동봉한 편지. [*here*]

here·in·af·ter [hìərinǽftər, -ɑ́:f-] *adv.* 《formal, law》 afterward in this statement. 이하의; 하문(下文)〔하기(下記)〕의.

here·in·be·fore [hìərinbifɔ́:r] *adv.* 《formal, law》 before in this document, statement, etc. (문서·성명 따위에서) 이상〔상문(上文)〕에; 전조(前條)에; 앞에.

here·into [hìəríntu:] *adv.* 《law》 **1** into this place. 이 장소로; 이 안〔속〕으로. **2** into this matter. 이 사항〔사건〕 속으로.

here·of [hìərάv / -rɔ́v] *adv.* 《*lit.*》 of this; about this. 이(것)의; 이에 관해서. ¶ *upon the receipt ~* 이것을 받으시는 대로(즉시) / *more ~ later* 이에 관해 더 상세한 것은 나중에.

here·on [hiərάn / -ɔ́n] *adv.* =hereupon.

here's [hiərz] here is.

her·e·sy [hérəsi] *n.* ⓊⒸ (*pl.* **-sies**) a belief or opinion different from the accepted belief of a religion. (정통 교파·통설에 반하는) 이론(異論); 반론; 이단(異端). [Gk.=choice]

her·e·tic [hérətik] *n.* Ⓒ a person whose belief or opinion is different because of heresy. 이단자(異端者); 이교도.

he·ret·i·cal [hərétikəl] *adj.* of heresy; of a heretic. 이단(異端)의; 이단자의(cf. *heterodox*). ● **he·ret·i·cal·ly** [-kəli] *adv.*

here·to [hiərtú:] *adv.* 《*lit.*》 to this; up to now. 이것〔여기〕에; 이제까지. [*here*]

here·to·fore [hìərtəfɔ́:r] *adv.* **1** before this time; until now. 이제〔지금〕까지. **2** formerly. 이전엔.

here·up·on [hìərəpάn] *adv.* **1** at this point. 여기에 있어서. **2** immediately after this. 바로 이것에 뒤이어; 이 직후에.

here·with [hìərwíð, -wíθ] *adv.* 《*lit.*》 **1** with this. 이와 함께. ¶ *the price list ~ enclosed* 동봉한 가격 일람표. **2** by means of this; hereby. 이 방법으로; 이(것)에 의해.

her·it·a·ble [héritəbəl] *adj.* that can be passed down from parents to children. 상속할 수 있는; 유전성의. [→heir]

her·it·age [héritidʒ] *n.* Ⓒ that which is passed down to a child by his parents. 유산; 세습〔상속〕 재산; 전래의 것; 전통. ¶ *a ~ of disease* 유전병 / *the cultural ~* 문화 유산 / *Debts were his only ~.* 빚이 그가 물려받은 유일한 유산이었다. [↑]

her·maph·ro·dite [hə:rmǽfrədàit] *n.* Ⓒ **1** a person or animal with characteristics of both sexes. 남녀추니; 양성(兩性) 동물〔동체〕. **2** 《bot.》 a plant in which the same flower has stamens and pistils. 자웅 동주(同株); 양성화(花). [→Hermes, Aphrodite]

Her·mes [hə́:rmi:z] *n.* 《Gk. myth.》 the messenger for Zeus and other gods. 헤르메스《신들의 사자(使者)로서 학술·변론의 신; 로마 신화의 Mercury》. [Gk.]

her·met·ic [hə:rmétik] *adj.* **1** closed so tight as to keep out all air or gas. 밀봉한; 밀폐된. **2** of the study aiming to change other materials into gold; of alchemy. 연금

술의. ¶ *the* ~ *art* 〔*science*〕 연금술. ● **her·met·i·cal·ly** [-əli] *adv.* [↑]

***her·mit** [hə́:rmit] *n.* Ⓒ a person who lives by himself, shut off from other people. 은자(隱者); 속세를 버린 사람(cf. *recluse*). ● **her·mit·like** [-làik] *adj.* [Gk. *erēmia* desert]

her·mit·age [hə́:rmitidʒ] *n.* Ⓒ the home of a hermit. 은자(隱者)가 사는 집; 암자.

her·ni·a [hə́:rniə] *n.* ⓊⒸ (*pl.* **-ni·as** or **-ni·ae**) 《med.》 the abnormal state of the pushing out of a part of the bowel through a break in the muscle wall of the abdomen. 헤르니아; 탈장(脫腸). [L.]

her·ni·ae [hə́:rniì:] *n.* pl. of **hernia.**

:he·ro [hí:rou, híə-] *n.* Ⓒ (*pl.* **-roes**) **1** a man admired for his bravery or noble deeds. 영웅; 용사; 위인. ¶ *one of my heroes* 나의 숭배하는 인물 / *make a* ~ *of* …을 영웅시〔영웅 취급〕하다. **2** the chief male person in a story, play, etc. (소설·연극 따위의 남자) 주인공(cf. *heroine*). [Gk. *hērōs*]

***he·ro·ic** [hiróuik] *adj.* **1** of a hero; like or fit for a hero. 영웅의; 영웅적인; 영웅에 걸맞는. ¶ *a* ~ *deed* 영웅적인 행위. **2** courageous. 용감한; 대담한; 모험적인. ¶ ~ *measures* 과감한 수단 / *a* ~ *explorer* 대담한 탐험가. **3** larger than life-size. 실물보다 큰. ¶ *on a* ~ *scale* 실물 이상의 크기로. — *n.* **1** 《usu. *pl.*》 heroic poetry or verse. 영웅시(격). **2** 《*pl.*》 language that sounds too grand and noble; high-flown language. 과장된 언동〔감정〕. ¶ *go into heroics* 감정을 과장해서 말하다.

heroic age [–⌐–⌐], **the** *n.* the time when the heroes of ancient Greece are supposed to have lived. (고대 그리스의) 영웅 시대.

he·ro·i·cal·ly [hiróuikəli] *adv.* in a heroic manner. 영웅적으로〔답게〕; 씩씩하게.

***her·o·in** [hérouin] *n.* Ⓤ medicine which stops the feeling of pain and causes someone to sleep. 헤로인. [*hero*]

her·o·ine [hérouin] *n.* Ⓒ **1** a woman admired for her bravery or noble deeds. 여걸(女傑); 여장부. **2** the chief female person in a story, play, etc. (소설·연극 따위의) 여(女)주인공. [*hero*]

her·o·ism [hérouìzəm] *n.* **1** Ⓤ heroic qualities; great bravery. 영웅적 자질; 용장(勇壯); 장렬. **2** Ⓒ a very brave act. 영웅적 행위.

her·on [hérən] *n.* Ⓒ a large bird with very long legs and neck. 왜가리. [Teut. *heiger*]

Herr [hɛər] *n.* 《G.》 (*pl.* **Her·ren** [hérən]) 《used as a title for a German man》 Mr.; sir. 씨; 님; 선생. ¶ ~ *Brandt* 브란트씨.

***her·ring** [hériŋ] *n.* Ⓒ (*pl.* **-rings** or *collectively* **-ring**) small fish used for food, found in North Atlantic waters. 청어. ¶ *red* ~ 훈제 청어. [E.]

(**as**) ***dead as a herring,*** quite dead. 완전히 죽어〔죽은〕.

packed as close as herrings, packed very close. 꽉 채워져.

her·ring·bone [hériŋbòun] *n.* Ⓒ an ornamental design shaped like the backbone of a fish. 오늬 무늬. —

〈herringbone〉

adj. like or belonging to a herringbone pattern. 오늬 (무늬) 모양의. — *vt.* (P6) work in herringbone. …을 오늬 무늬로 짜다〔수놓다, 쌓다〕.

herring pond [⌐–⌐] *n.* 《*joc.*》 the North Atlantic Ocean. 북대서양.

:hers [hə:rz] *pron.* (the possessive form of **she**) the one or ones belonging to her. 그녀의 것. ¶ *This book is* ~. 이 책은 그녀의 것이다 / *Are you a friend of* ~ ? 그녀의 친구입니까. [*her*]

:her·self [hə:rsélf] *pron.* (*pl.* **them·selves**) ⇨oneself. **1** a reflexive and emphatic form of **she** or **her.** she, her의 재귀 및 강의(強意) 용법. ⓐ 《*emph.*》 그녀 자신; 그녀 스스로. ¶ *She* ~ *will do it.* 그녀 스스로 그 일을 할 것이다 / *Nancy* ~ *bought it for us.* 낸시가 직접 그것을 우리에게 사주었다 / *She wrote the letter* ~. = *She* ~ *wrote the letter.* 그녀 자신이 그 편지를 썼다. ⓑ 《*reflexively*》 그녀 자신을〔에게〕. ¶ *She killed* ~. 그녀는 자살했다 / *She absented* ~ *from the party.* 그녀는 파티에 참석하지 않았다 / *She laughed at* ~. 그녀는 자기 자신을 비웃었다. **2** her normal condition of body or of mind. 본래〔평소〕의 그녀; 정상적인 그녀. ¶ *come to* ~ 의식〔냉정〕을 되찾다 / *She is not* ~ *today.* 그녀가 오늘은 평소의 그녀가 아니다. [*her, self*]

Hert., Herts. Hertfordshire.

Hertz [hə:rts], **Heinrich** *n.* (1857-94) a German Physicist. 헤르츠《독일의 물리학자》.

hertz [hə:rts] *n.* Ⓒ (*pl.* **hertz** or **hertz·es**) the international unit of frequency, equal to one cycle per second. 헤르츠《진동·주파수 단위》. [Person]

Hertz·i·an waves [hə́:rtsiən wéivz] *n. pl.* 《sometimes *h- w-*》 《electr.》 electric waves, as in radio, etc. (first investigated by Heinrich Hertz). 헤르츠파(波); 전자파.

***he's** [hi:z, hiz, iz] he is; he has.

hes·i·tance [hézətəns] *n.* = hesitancy.

hes·i·tan·cy [hézətənsi] *n.* Ⓤ hesitation; doubt; indecision. 주저; 망설임; 우유부단. [↓]

hes·i·tant [hézətənt] *adj.* hesitating; doubtful; undecided. 주저하는; 망설이는; 우유부단한. ● **hes·i·tant·ly** [-li] *adv.*

:hes·i·tate [hézətèit] *vi.* **1** (P1,3,4) ⓐ pause or stop because one is undecided. 주저하다; 망설이다. ¶ ~ *between fighting* *and submitting* 싸우느냐 항복하느냐 망설이다 / *I hesitated (about) what to do.* 무엇을 해야 할지 주저했다 / *Are you still hesitating about buying a car?* 차를 사는 것에 관해 아직도 망설이고 있나. ⓑ be faltering in speech. 말을 머뭇〔멈칫〕거리다. **2** (P4) feel that perhaps one should not do; not wish to do; be unwilling to do. …할 기분이 안 나다; 마음이 안 내키다. ¶ *I ~ to believe it.* 그것은 좀 믿기 어렵다 / *I ~ to take the risk.* 모험을 할 마음이 내키지 않는다. [L. *haereo* stick] ⌈hesitation. 주저하여.

hes·i·tat·ing·ly [hézətèitiŋli] *adv.* with

•**hes·i·ta·tion** [hèzətéiʃən] *n.* ⓊⒸ **1** the act of hesitating; doubt. 주저; 망설임. ¶ *without a moment's* 〔*minute's*〕 ~ 순간의 망설임도 없이 / *After some ~, she bought the red sweater.* 좀 망설이다가 그녀는 그 빨간 스웨터를 샀다. **2** an impediment in speech. 말을 멈칫〔머뭇〕거림; 말을 더듬음.

Hes·per·us [héspərəs] *n.* 《astron.》 the evening star. 개밥바라기; 금성. [Gk.]

Hes·se [hésə], **Hermann** *n.* (1877-1962) a German novelist, awarded 1946 Nobel-prize for literature. 헤세《독일의 소설가. 1946년 노벨 문학상 수상》.

Hes·ti·a [héstiə] *n.* 《Gk. myth.》 the goddess of the hearth. 헤스티아《화덕의 여신; 로마 신화의 Vesta》.

het·er·o- [hétərou-, hétərə-] *pref.* other, different. '딴, 다른'의 뜻(opp. homo-, iso-). [Gk. *heteros*]

het·er·o·dox [hétərədɑ̀ks / -dɔ̀ks] *adj.* **1** (of opinions, beliefs) different from the regularly accepted beliefs or doctrines. 비정통설의; 이설(異說)의; 이단의(cf. *heretical*, opp. orthodox). **2** (of a person) holding such opinions. 비정통설을 신봉하는; 이단의. [Gk. *heteras* other, *doxa* opinion]

het·er·o·dox·y [hétərədɑ̀ksi / -dɔ̀ksi] *n.* ⓊⒸ (*pl.* **-dox·ies**) a belief, doctrine, etc. different from the commonly accepted. 비정통; 이단; 이설(異說)(opp. orthodoxy).

het·er·o·dyne [hétərədàin] *adj.* 《radio》 having to do with the production of sounds by combining radio oscillations of slightly different frequencies. 헤테로다인식의; 주파수 변환식의. [hetero-, →dyne]

het·er·o·ge·ne·ous [hètərədʒíːniəs] *adj.* different in kind; unlike; varied. 이종(異種)의; 이질(異質)의(opp. homogeneous). ¶ ~ *elements in society* 사회의 이질 분자. ● **het·er·o·ge·ne·ous·ly** [-li] *adv.* [Gk. *heteros* other, *genos* kind]

hew [hjuː] *vt., vi.* (**hewed, hewn** or **hewed**) (P6,7,13; 1) **1** cut (something) with an ax, or sword. (도끼·칼 따위로) 자르다. ¶ ~ *to pieces* 잘게 자르다〔토막내다〕/ ~ *a branch off* 나뭇가지를 잘라내다 / ~ *a tree down* 나무를 베어 넘기다. **2** make (something) with cutting blows. 깎아서 …을 만들다. ¶ ~ *a statue from marble* 대리석으로 상(像)을 새기다 / ~ *out a career for oneself* 혼자 힘으로 인생을 개척하다. [E.]

hew one's way, make a path by cutting. 길을 내다; 진로를 개척하다.

hew·er [hjúːər] *n.* Ⓒ a person who hews. 베는〔자르는, 깎는〕 사람.

hewers of wood and drawers of water, 《Bible》 persons who do unpleasant work for little pay; workers of the lowest kind. 천한 일을 하는 사람; 하급 노동자.

hewn [hjuːn] *v.* pp. of **hew**.

hex·a- [héksə-] *pref.* six. '6'의 뜻. [Gk. *hex*]

hex·a·gon [héksəgɑ̀n / -gən] *n.* Ⓒ 《geom.》 a plane figure having six angles and six sides. 6각〔변〕형. ● **hex·ag·o·nal** [heksǽgənəl] *adj.* [↑, Gk. *gonia* corner]

hex·a·gram [héksəgræ̀m] *n.* Ⓒ a six-pointed star formed of two equilateral triangles. 6각〔6선〕 성형(星形). [hexa-]

hex·a·he·dra [hèksəhíːdrə] *n.* pl. of **hexahedron.**

hex·a·he·dron [hèksəhíːdrən] *n.* Ⓒ (*pl.* **-drons** or **-dra**) a solid figure having six faces. 6면체.

hex·am·e·ter [heksǽmitər] *n.* ⓊⒸ 《prosody》 a verse having six feet or measures. 육보격(六步格)(의 시). ¶ *a poem written in hexameters.*

•**hey** [hei] *interj.* a sound made to attract attention, ask a question, or express surprise or joy. 어이; 이봐; 어《놀람》; 야《기쁨》. ¶ *Hey! stop!* 어이, 멈춰 / *Hey? what did you say?* 어엉, 뭐라고 했나. [E.]

hey for..., hurrah for.... …잘한다(잘해).

hey presto, words said when performing a magic trick《therefore used to declare a sudden or unexpected event》. 야앗《요술쟁이의 소리》; 앗《돌발 사태 때의 소리》. ¶ *Hey presto! he escaped.* 앗, 그가 달아났다.

hey·day[1] [héidèi] *n.* Ⓒ 《used as *sing.*》 the time of greatest strength or high spirits. 전성 시대; 절정기; 한창때. ¶ *in the ~ of youth* 한창 젊은 때에. [M.E. *hey* high, *day*]

hey·day[2] [héidèi] *interj.* an expression of joy or wonder. 야아; 아이고 이거《기쁨·놀람의 소리》. [*hey*]

HF, H.F., hf, h.f. high frequency.

hf. half.

Hg 《chem.》 *hydrargyrum* (=mercury).

H.H. His 〔Her〕 Highness.

hi [hai] *interj.* sound made to attract attention, usu. used on meeting. 야아; 어이; 안녕하세요《주의를 촉구하거나 인사할 때의 소리》. [E.]

H.I. Hawaiian Islands; humidity index.

hi·a·tus [haiéitəs] *n.* Ⓒ (*pl.* **-tus·es** or **-tus**) **1** ⓐ a gap or opening. 틈; 벌어진 틈. ⓑ break; interruption. (중도에) 끊어짐; 중절. **2** a gap or break in a manuscript, etc. where some words are lost. (기사·사본 따위의) 결손된〔빠진〕 부분; 탈락; 탈자(脫

字). **3** 《phon.》 a gap separating the sounds of two vowels coming together (e.g. India Office). 모음 접속. [L.]

hi·ber·nal [haibə́:rnl] *adj.* of or having to do with winter; wintry. 겨울의; 겨울 같은. [↓]

hi·ber·nate [háibərnèit] *vi.* (P1) **1** (of some animals) spend the winter in a sleeping or an inactive state. (동물이) 겨울잠자다; 동면하다. **2** ⓐ (of persons) retire into a warm place for the winter. (사람이) 피한(避寒)하다. ⓑ 《*fig.*》 remain inactive. 들어박히다; 은퇴하다. [L. *hibernus* wintry]

hi·ber·na·tion [hàibərnéiʃən] *n.* Ⓤ the state or act of hibernating. 겨울잠; 동면.

Hi·ber·ni·an [haibə́:rniən] *adj., n.* 《*poet.*》 =Irish(man). [Celt.]

hi·bis·cus [hibískəs, hai-] *n.* Ⓒ a plant, shrub, or tree with large, colorful flowers. 무궁화. [Gk. =marsh mallow]

hic·cough [híkʌp] *n., v.* =hiccup.

hic·cup [híkʌp] *n.* Ⓒ 《often *pl.*》 a sudden catching of the breath with a short, sharp sound. 딸꾹질. ¶ *have* 〔*get*〕 *the hiccups* 딸꾹질하다. — *vi., vt.* (P1;7) have hiccups; say with a hiccup or hiccups. 딸꾹질하다; 딸꾹질을 하면서 말하다. [earlier *hicket,* Imit.]

hic ja·cet [hik dʒéisit] *n.* 《L. =here lies》 that which is written on a stone above a grave. 묘비명(墓碑銘)(cf. *epitaph*).

hick·o·ry [híkəri] *n.* Ⓒ (*pl.* **-ries**) a nut-bearing American tree with hard wood; Ⓤ its wood. 히코리《북아메리카산 호두과의 나무》; 그 목재. [Amer-Ind.]

:hid [hid] *v.* p. and pp. of **hide**[1].

hi·dal·go [hidǽlgou] *n.* Ⓒ (*pl.* **-gos**) a Spanish nobleman of the lower class. (스페인의) 하급 귀족. [Sp. =son of something]

***hid·den** [hídən] *v.* pp. of **hide**[1]. — *adj.* put or kept out of sight; secret. 숨겨진; 숨은; 비밀의. ¶ *The story is about ~ treasure.* 이야기는 숨겨진 보물에 관한 것이다. [↓]

:hide[1] [haid] *v.* (**hid, hid·den** or **hid**) *vt.* (P6,13) **1** prevent (something) from being seen or found; put or keep (something) out of sight; cover (something) up; conceal. …이 눈에 띄지〔보이지〕 않게 하다; …을 숨기다; 감추다; 덮어가리다. ¶ *~ money in the ground* 〔*a secret place*〕 돈을 땅속〔비밀 장소〕에 감추다 / *~ something from view* 〔*out of sight*〕 …을 안 보이게 하다 / *~ one's face* 〔*head*〕 얼굴을〔머리를〕 돌리다; (부끄러워) 사람 눈을 피하다 / *Clouds hid the sun.* 구름이 해를 가렸다. **2** ⓐ prevent (something) from being known; keep (something) secret. …을 알지 못하게 하다; …을 비밀로 해두다. ¶ *~ one's feelings* 〔*intentions*〕 감정을〔의도를〕 감추다 / *~ the fact from the world* 세상에 진상을 숨기다 / *I have nothing to ~.* 난 아무 것도 숨길 게 없다. ⓑ prevent from being understood. 이해하지 못하게 하다. — *vi.* (P1,3) hide oneself. 숨다. ¶ *~ behind a door* 〔*in the bushes*〕 문 뒤〔숲속〕에 숨다. [E.]

hide one's ear, take no heed. 유의하지 않다.

hide one's light under a bushel, conceal one's merits. 선행(善行)을 숨기다.

hide out, 《*colloq.*》 go into hiding. 숨다; 잠복하다.

hide[2] [haid] *n.* Ⓒ **1** the skin of an animal, esp. as material for leather. 짐승의 가죽; 수피(cf. *leather*). ¶ *a raw* 〔*green*〕 *~* 생가죽. **2** 《*colloq.*》 the human skin. (인간의) 피부.

have a thick hide, be insensitive to criticism, insults, etc. 낯가죽이 두껍다.

hide and hair, completely. 완전히.

neither hide nor hair, nothing whatever. 전혀 …없는.

save one's hide, evade punishment. 벌을 면하다.

tan 〔***dress***〕 ***someone's hide,*** give someone a beating. …을 갈기다; 매질하다.

— *vt.* (P6) 《*colloq.*》 beat. …을 치다; 갈기다; 때리다. [E.]

:hide-and-seek [háidənsí:k] *n.* Ⓤ a children's game in which one child hides and others try to find him. 숨바꼭질.

hide·a·way [háidəwèi] *n.* Ⓒ a place where one can go to hide. 숨는 곳; 은신〔피난〕처.

hide·bound [háidbàund] *adj.* **1** with the skin sticking close to the bones. (영양 부족으로) 피골이 상접한. **2** 《*fig.*》 very narrow-minded. 편협한; 완고한. ¶ *He was too ~ to accept new ideas.* 그는 너무 완고해서 새로운 사상을 받아들이지 못했다. [*hide*[2]]

***hid·e·ous** [hídiəs] *adj.* **1** very ugly; very unpleasant. 몹시 추한; 추악한; 몹시 불쾌한. ¶ *a ~ face* 추악한 얼굴. **2** horrible; frightful. 무서운; 끔찍한; 소름 끼치는. ¶ *~ cruelty* 끔찍한 잔인성. ●**hid·e·ous·ly** [-li] *adv.* [F. *hisde* fear]

hid·e·ous·ness [hídiəsnis] *n.* Ⓤ the state of being hideous. 무서움; 끔찍함.

hide·out [háidàut] *n.* Ⓒ 《U.S. *colloq.*》 a place for hiding or being alone. (범인 등의) 은신처; 잠복 장소. [*hide*[1]]

hid·ing[1] [háidiŋ] *n.* Ⓤ **1** concealment. 숨음; 숨김; 숨겨〔감춰〕진 상태. ¶ *be in ~* 남의 눈을 피하다 / *remain* 〔*lie*〕 *in ~* 숨어 있다; 잠복해 있다 / *go into ~* 몸을 숨기다; 잠복하다. **2** Ⓒ a place to hide. 숨는 곳; 은신처.

hid·ing[2] [háidiŋ] *n.* Ⓒ 《*colloq.*》 an act of beating. 매질. [*hide*[2]]

hiding place [⌐-⌐] *n.* a place to hide. 숨는 곳; 은신처; 은닉처. [*hide*[1]]

hie [hai] *vi., vt.* (**hie·ing** or **hy·ing**) (P1; 6) 《*arch.,* chiefly *poet.*》 go quickly; hasten. 급히 가(게 하)다; 서두르(게 하)다. [E. =strive, pant]

hi·er·ar·chic [hàiərɑ́:rkik], **-chi·cal** [-əl] *adj.* of, in, or like a hierarchy. 계층제의〔같

은]; 위계 제도[조직]의; 성직자 정치의. [↓]

hi·er·ar·chy [háiərɑ̀ːrki] *n.* Ⓒ (*pl.* **-chies**) **1** an organization (of persons or things) with grades of authority from lowest to highest. 계급[위계] 조직. **2** government by priests. 성직자 정치. [Gk. *hieros* sacred]

hi·er·at·ic [hàiərǽtik] *adj.* **1** of or having to do with priestly caste; used by priests. 성직자의[다운]; 신성한. **2** of or having to do with a form of Egyptian writing used by the early priests in their records. 히에라틱체(體)의; 신관 서체(神官書體)의(cf. *demotic*). [↑]

hi·er·o·glyph [háiərəglìf] *n.* =hieroglyphic.

hi·er·o·glyph·ic [hàiərəglífik] *n.* Ⓒ **1** 《usu. *pl.*》 a picture or symbol standing for a word, an idea, or a sound. 상형 문자 (cf. *ideogram, ideograph*). **2** a secret symbol. 비밀 문자. **3** 《*joc.*》 writing difficult to make out. 판독하기 어려운 악필. — *adj.* **1** of or written in hieroglyphics. 상형 문자의. **2** symbolic. 상징적인. **3** hard to read. 판독하기 어려운. ● **hi·er·o·glyph·i·cal·ly** [-əli] *adv.* [↑, Gk. *gluphō* carve]

hi·er·o·phant [háiərəfæ̀nt] *n.* **1** ⓐ an expounder of sacred mysteries. 밀교(密敎)의 해설자. ⓑ an interpreter; spokesman. 해설자; 대변인. **2** (in ancient Greece) an initiating priest. (고대 그리스의) 신비 의식의 사제[도사(導師)]. [Gk. *hieros* sacred, *phainō* show]

hi-fi [háifái] *n.* 《*colloq.*》 =highfidelity.

hig·gle [hígəl] *vi.* (P1) dispute about prices in a petty way; chaffer. 값을 깎다; 흥정하다. [*haggle*]

hig·gle·dy-pig·gle·dy [hígəldipígəldi] *adv.* in great disorder. 난잡하게; 어수선하게; 엉망진창으로. — *adj.* mixed up; confused. 뒤죽박죽인; 난잡한. — *n.* Ⓤ disorder; confusion. 난잡; 뒤죽박죽. [?]

:high [hai] *adj.* **1** (not of persons or animals) ⓐ tall; lofty. 높은(opp. low). ¶ *a ~ tree* [*mountain*] 높은 나무[산] / *a ~ wall* 높은 담. ⓑ having a certain degree or amount of height. 높이가 …인[되는]. ¶ *How ~ is that tree ?* 저 나무는 높이가 얼마나 되나 / *The wall is six feet ~.* 그 담은 높이가 6 피트이다. ⓒ far above the ground or sea level. 지면[해면]에서 멀리 떨어진; 고공의. ¶ *~ up in the sky* 하늘 높이 / *The sun was ~.* 해가 높이 떠 있었다 / *The cloud is three miles ~.* 구름은 지상 3마일 높이에 있다. **2** exalted in office, rank, or power. (지위·신분 따위가) 높은; 고위의; 고귀한. ¶ *a ~ government official* 정부의 고관 / *a man in ~ position* 지위가 높은 사람 / *~ society* 상류 사회 / *a man of ~ birth* [*descent*] 명문 출신의 사람 / 《Bible》 *the Most High* 하느님. **3** expensive; costly. (값이) 비싼; 고가(高價)의. ¶ *a ~ price* 높은 가격 / *the ~ cost of living* 높은 생활비 / *at a ~ cost* 고가(高價)로. **4** ⓐ chief; main. 주된; 주요한. ¶ *the ~ road* 한길; 주요 도로 / *the ~ altar of a church* (교회의) 주제단(主祭壇). ⓑ important; grave. 중요한; 중대한. ¶ *~ treason* 반역(죄) / *the ~ consequences of such a deed* 그러한 행위가 끼치는 중대한 결과. **5** greater in size, amount, degree, power, etc. than usual. (크기·수량·정도·힘 따위가) 보통 이상의; 높은; 큰; 강(렬)한; 격심한; 고도의. ¶ *a ~ speed* 고속도 / *~ temperature* 고온 / *a ~ wind* 세찬 바람 / *higher education* 고등 교육 / *~ excitement* [*anxiety*] 강한 흥분[불안] / *~ voltage* 고압 / *a ~ rate of interest* 고율의 이자. **6** luxurious. 사치한. ¶ *~ diet* [*living*] 사치한 식사[생활] / *a ~ liver* 사치한 생활을 하는 사람. **7** very good or favorable; excellent. (성질·품질·평가 따위가) 좋은; 고급의; 훌륭한. ¶ *a ~ quality* 좋은 품질 / *a ~ class* 고급 / *have a ~ opinion of someone* 아무를 높이 평가하다. **8** noble; sublime. 고결한; 숭고한. ¶ *a ~ character* 고결한 인격 / *a ~ idea* 숭고한 이상. **9** (of time) fully advanced. (시간·계절 따위가) 한창 …인. ¶ *~ noon* 정오 / *~ summer* 한여름 / *~ tide* 만조. **10** too proud. 오만한; 콧대 높은; 건방진. ¶ *a ~ boast* 큰소리; 호언장담. **11** 《geog.》 far from the equator. (위도가) 높은. **12** upper; inland. 고지(高地)의; 오지(奧地)에 있는. ¶ *~ Asia* 고지 아시아 / *High German* 고지 독일어. **13** extreme in opinion. (정치적·종교적으로) 과격한; 극단의. ¶ *a ~ Tory* 극단적 보수당원. **14** joyful; merry; elated. 즐거운; 유쾌한; 의기가 높은. ¶ *in ~ spirits* 기분이 좋아 / *have a ~* [《*sl.*》 *~ old*] *time* 즐거운 한때를 보내다. **15** ⓐ (of sound) sharp; shrill. (소리가) 날카로운; 새된. ¶ *a ~ voice* 날카로운[새된] 목소리. ⓑ 《phon.》 (of a vowel) pronounced with part of the tongue close to the palate. 고(高)모음의. **16** (of meat) beginning to decay. (고기가) 삭아서 먹기 좋게 된. **17** 《*H-*》 belonging to, characteristic of, the High Church. 고(高)교회파의.

high and dry, **a**) (of a ship) on the shore. (배가) 해안에 얹혀. **b**) alone and helpless; abandoned. 버림받아. **c**) 《*fig.*》 out of the current of events. 시류에 뒤져.

high and low, (people) of all conditions. 상하 귀천의 (모든 사람들)(cf. *adv.*).

high and mighty, 《*colloq.*》 showing too much pride. 오만(불손)한.

in high favor, much liked. 마음에 매우 들어.

— *n.* **1** ⒸⓊ ⓐ something that is of a high level or position. 높은 것. ⓑ heaven. 하늘. **2** Ⓒ an area of high atmospheric pressure. 고기압권. **3** Ⓤ an arrangement of gears giving the greatest speed. (자동차의) 고속 기어.

from (***on***) ***high,*** from heaven. 하늘에서.

on high, high above; in heaven. 높은 곳에[으로]; 하늘에.

— *adv.* **1** to or at a high level, position, degree, etc. 높이; 높은 곳에; 위로; 고위(高

位)에. ¶ *fly* [*climb*] ~ 높이 날다[오르다] / *stand* ~ *in popular esteem* 세상에서 높이 평가[존경]되다. **2** to a high degree, amount, price, etc.; greatly; strongly. (정도·액수·가격 따위가) 높이; 고액으로; 크게; 강하게; 세차게. ¶ *pay* ~ 비싸게 지불하다 / *cost* ~ 비싸게 치이다 / *be sold* ~ 비싸게 팔리다 / *The wind blows* ~. 바람이 강하게 분다. **3** very comfortably; luxuriously. 사치하게. ¶ *live* ~ 사치하게 살다. **4** at or to a high pitch. 음성이 높은 가락으로. ¶ *speak* ~ 큰 소리로 이야기하다. [E.]

high and low, everywhere. 도처에; 온갖 곳을[에(서)] (cf. *adj.*). ¶ *We searched* [*hunted*] ~ *and low for the missing watch.* 없어진 시계를 찾느라고 온갖 곳을 다 찾았다.

hold one's head high, act too proudly. 오만하게[건방지게] 굴다.

play high, play for high stakes. 큰 도박을 하다.

rise high, succeed in life. 출세하다.

run high, **a**) (of the sea) be rough. (물결이) 거칠어지다. **b**) be excited. (감정이) 격해지다.

high-an·gle [háiǽŋgl] *adj.* of a wide angle. 고각(高角)의. ¶ *a* ~ *gun* 고각포(砲); 곡사포.

high antiquity [⌐ –⌐––] *n.* extremely ancient. 아주 옛날; 태곳적.

high·ball [háibɔ̀:l] *n.* Ⓤ Ⓒ 《U.S.》 whiskey, brandy, etc., mixed with soda water. 하이볼《위스키 따위에 소다수를 섞은 음료》.

high·born [háibɔ̀:rn] *adj.* of noble birth. 고귀한 태생의.

high·bred [háibréd] *adj.* **1** born of a good family and well trained. 상류 가정에서 자라난. **2** very elegant. 기품 있는.

high·brow [háibràu] *n.* Ⓒ 《*colloq., often contempt.*》 **1** a person who is interested in intellectual things. 학식이 있는 사람; 지식인. **2** 《*sl.*》 a person who puts on an appearance of great learning. 지식인인 체하는 사람; 인텔리연(然)하는 사람(cf. *lowbrow*). — *adj.* having to do with or characteristic of a highbrow. 지식인의[인 체하는]; 지식인 같은.

High Church [⌐ ⌐], **the** *n.* the party in the Church of England which gives a high place to the authority of the priesthood and various ceremonies in the church. 고교회파(cf. *Low Church*).

high-class [háiklǽs / -klɑ́:s] *adj.* first-class, of high quality. 고급의; 일류의. ¶ *a* ~ *stereo* 고급 스테레오 전축.

high color [⌐ ⌐–] *n.* a red complexion. 좋은 혈색.

High Court [⌐ ⌐], **the** *n.* 《Brit.》 the court in the Supreme Court below the Court of Appeal. 고등 법원.

high day [⌐ ⌐] *n.* festival. (교회의) 축제일.

high explosive [⌐ –⌐–] *n.* a powerful explosive used for its shattering effect. 고성능 폭약.

high·fa·lu·tin [háifəlú:tin] *adj.* =high-flown.

high fidelity [⌐ –⌐––] *n.* the reproduction of sound by a phonograph or radio so that it sounds like the original. 하이파이; 고충실도.

high-fi·del·i·ty [háifidéləti] *adj.* achieving as exact a sound reproduction as possible by using wide ranges of sound waves. 하이파이의; 고충실도의(cf. 《*colloq.*》 *hi-fi*).

high-flown [háiflóun] *adj.* (of ideas, etc.) sounding important, but with little sense. (사상 따위가) 과장된.

high-fre·quen·cy [háifrí:kwənsi] *adj.* of a frequency having from 3 to 30 megacycles per second. 고주파의.

high-grade [háigréid] *adj.* of fine quality; superior. 우수한; 고급의.

high-hand·ed [háihǽndid] *adj.* acting not according to rules but to one's own idea; overbearing. 고압적인; 건방진; 횡포한. ● **high-hand·ed·ly** [-li] *adv.* **high·hand·ed·ness** [-nis] *n.*

high hat [⌐ ⌐] *n.* a top hat. 실크 해트.

high-hat [háihǽt] *n.* Ⓒ 《U.S.》 one affecting superiority. 신사연하는[으스대는] 사람. — *adj.* supercilious; disdainful. 거드름 피우는; 깔보는; 아니꼬운. — *vt., vi.* (P6;1) **1** treat superciliously. 깔보는 투로 대하다; 아랫사람 취급하다. **2** assume a superior attitude. 젠체하다.

high·jack [háidʒæ̀k] *vt.* =hijack.

high jump [⌐ ⌐] *n.* an athletic contest in jumping high. 높이뛰기.

***highland** [háilənd] *n.* **1** 《*often pl.*》 Ⓒ high or mountainous land. 고지(高地); 대지(臺地). **2** 《*the H-s*》 mountainous land in northern and western Scotland. 스코틀랜드 북부와 서부의 고지. — *adj.* of a highland. 고지[산악] 지방의.

High·land·er [háiləndər] *n.* Ⓒ **1** a person who lives in the Highlands of Scotland; a soldier of a Highland regiment. 스코틀랜드 고지 사람; 고지 연대병(兵). **2** 《*h-*》 a person who lives in a highland. 고지 지방의 주민.

high light [⌐ ⌐] *n.* **1** a part of a photograph, etc., in which light is represented as falling with full force. (그림이나 사진 따위의) 강한 빛을 받은 부분. **2** the most interesting scene in a story, etc. (이야기 따위의)가장 흥미 있는 장면.

high·light [háilàit] *vt.* (P6) emphasize; make (something) prominent. …을 강조하다; 두드러지게 하다.

high-lows [háilóuz] *n. pl.* 《*arch.*》 boots reaching over ankles. 편상화(編上靴).

:**high·ly** [háili] *adv.* **1** in a high position or rank. 높은 지위[신분]에[으로]. ¶ *a* ~ *placed official* 고위 관리. **2** in or to a high degree; greatly; very much. 고도로; 크게; 매우. ¶ ~ *advertised goods* 크게 선전된 상품 / *be* ~ *amusing* 무척 재미있다 / *be* ~ *pleased* 크게

기뻐하다. **3** favorably; with honor, praise, or favor. 높이 평가하여; 크게 칭찬〔존경〕하여. ***speak highly*** (=*speak very well*) ***of*** *someone.* …을 격찬하다.
think highly of, respect greatly. …을 크게 존경하다.

high-mind·ed [háimàindid] *adj.* **1** having noble character. 고결한; 고상한. ¶ *a* ~ *ruler* 고결한 통치자. **2** proud. 거만〔오만〕한. ● **high-mind·ed·ly** [-li] *adv.* **high-mind·ed·ness** [-nis] *n.*

***high·ness** [háinis] *n.* Ⓤ **1** the state of being high. (위치·정도·물가·지위 따위가) 높음 (opp. lowness). ¶ *the* ~ *of prices* 〔*of his aims*〕 물가고〔목표의 높음〕 / *the* ~ *of someone's character* 인격의 고결함. **2** 《*H-*》 a title given to people of royal families. 전하. 參考 보통 His, Her, Your 를 앞에 붙임.

high-pitched [háipítʃt] *adj.* **1** of high tone or sound. 가락이〔음조가〕 높은; 새된; (감도 따위가) 높은. **2** having a steep slope. 급경사의.

high-pow·ered [háipáuərd] *adj.* 《as *attributive*》 (usu. of a person) having great power or authority. 정력적인; 강력한. ¶ ~ *executives* 강력한 경영진 / *a very* ~ *professor* 대단히 정력적인 교수.

high-pres·sure [háipréʃər] *adj.* **1** having more than the usual pressure. 고압의. **2** 《*colloq.*》 using strong, vigorous methods. 고압적인.

high-priced [háipráist] *adj.* expensive. 고가의; 비싼.

high-rank·ing [háirǽŋkiŋ] *adj.* high in position. 높은 계급의; 고위의.

high·road [háiròud] *n.* Ⓒ **1** 《Brit.》 a main road; a highway. 주요〔간선〕 도로; 큰길; 공도(公道). **2** 《*fig.*》 a direct way; an easy method. 손쉬운 길; 지름길(=royal road). ¶ *the* ~ *to success* 성공에의 지름길; 출세 가도.

high school [⁄ ⁄] *n.* a school attended after the elementary school. 고등 학교. ¶ *a junior* ~ 중학교 / *a senior* ~ 고등 학교.

high seas [⁄ ⁄] *n.* 《*the* ~》 the open sea not belonging to any country. 공해; 외양.

high-sound·ing [háisáundiŋ] *adj.* (of writing style) written with too much expression. (표현이) 어마어마한. ¶ *a* ~ *title* 어마어마한 직함.

high spirit [⁄ ⁄–] *n.* courageous and enterprising spirit. 불굴의 정신.

high-spir·it·ed [háispíritid] *adj.* **1** courageous; daring. 용감한; 대담한. **2** ⓐ with great liveliness. 기운 찬; 위세 있는; 혈기 왕성한. ⓑ (of a horse) full of spirit. (말이) 팔팔한.

high spot [⁄ ⁄] *n.* an outstanding part or feature. 두드러진 점〔특징〕.

high-strung [háistrʌ́ŋ] *adj.* very sensitive; nervous. 긴장한; 민감한; 몹시 신경질인.

high tea [⁄ ⁄] *n.* 《Brit.》 a meal, usu. in the evening, at which meat is served. 고기 요리가 곁들여지는 저녁 식사.

high-ten·sion [háiténʃən] *adj.* 《electr.》 that can be operated with a high voltage. 고압의. ¶ ~ *currents* 〔*wire*〕 고압 전류〔전선〕.

high-test [háitést] *adj.* **1** passing very difficult requirements and tests. 엄격한 시험을 통과하는. **2** having a very low boiling-point. (휘발유가) 끓는점이 낮은.

high tide [⁄ ⁄] *n.* the time when the tide is highest. 만조시(時).

high time [⁄ ⁄] *n.* a good chance to begin an action. …할 절호의 기회; …할 때. ¶ *It is* ~ *to go.* 이제 가야 할 시간이다.

high-toned [háitóund] *adj.* **1** high in tone or pitch. 가락이 높은. **2** 《U.S.》 dignified. 고결한; 고상한. **3** 《*colloq.*》 fashionable. 상류의; 짐짓 빼는; 멋부리는.

high-up [háiʌ́p] *n., adj.* (a person) of great importance or high rank. 지위가〔신분이〕 높은 (사람).

high water [⁄ ⁄–] *n.* the state of the tidal water at high tide, immediately before it turns; the time of this. 고조(高潮); 만조(때).

high-wa·ter mark [háiwɔ́:tər mà:rk, -wɑ́t-] *n.* **1** the highest level reached by a body of water. 최고 수위(水位)(선). **2** any highest point. 최고점; 절정; 정점. ¶ *reach one's* ~ 절정에 달하다.

:high·way [háiwèi] *n.* Ⓒ **1** a public road; a main road. 공도(公道); 큰길; 주요〔간선〕 도로. ¶ *highways and byways* 큰길 작은 길 / *the king's* ~ 천하의 공도. **2** a direct and easy way. 손쉬운 길. ¶ *a* ~ *to happiness* 행복에의 길.

high·way·man [háiwèimən] *n.* Ⓒ (*pl.* **-men** [-mən]) a man who robs travelers on a highway. 노상 강도.

high words [⁄ ⁄] *n.* an excited argument. 격한 말; 격론. ¶ *High words passed between them.* 격한 말들이 그들 사이에 오갔다.

H. I. H. His 〔Her〕 Imperial Highness. 전하(殿下)〔비(妃)전하〕《왕족에 대한 존칭》.

hi·jack [háidʒæ̀k] *vt.* (P6) 《U.S. *colloq.*》 **1** force the pilot of an aircraft to fly to a different destination. (비행기)를 공중 납치하다. ¶ ~ *an airliner* 정기 여객기를 납치하다. **2** steal goods in transit by force. (수송 중의 물품 따위)를 훔치다〔강탈하다〕. ¶ ~ *goods from a truck* 〔*train*〕 화물을 트럭〔열차〕에서 훔치다. ● **hi·jack·er** [-ər] *n.* [?]

***hike** [haik] *n.* Ⓒ 《*colloq.*》 **1** a long walk in the country for recreation or exercise. (시골의) 도보 여행. ¶ *go on a* ~ 도보 여행을 떠나다. **2** increase; rise. (급료의) 인상; (물가의) 상승. —*vi.* (P1,3) 《*colloq.*》 **1** take a long walk; tramp. 도보 여행하다. **2** 《*up*》 be drawn up unevenly. (셔츠 따위가) 밀려올라가다. —*vt.* (P6) draw or raise with a jerk. 홱 끌어당기다; 끌어올리다. ¶ ~ *a price* 가격을 인상하다. [?]

hik·er [háikər] *n.* Ⓒ a person who hikes. 도보 여행을 하는 사람.

***hik·ing** [háikiŋ] *n.* Ⓤ a hike. 도보 여행; 하이킹.

hi·lar·i·ous [hilɛ́əriəs, hai-] *adj.* (of a person) noisily gay; very merry; cheerful. 들떠서 떠드는; 명랑한; 유쾌한; 즐거운. ● **hi·lar·i·ous·ly** [-li] *adv.* [L. *hilaris*]

hi·lar·i·ty [hilǽrəti, hai-] *n.* Ⓤ merriness; cheerfulness. 들떠 떠듦; 명랑; 유쾌함. [↑]

:hill [hil] *n.* Ⓒ **1** a small and low mountain. 야산; 구릉; 언덕. **2** ⓐ a heap of earth. (두두룩이) 돋운 흙; 흙더미; 무덤. ¶ *an ant* ~ 개밋둑. ⓑ a heap of any kind. 두두룩이 쌓아올린 것. ¶ *a* ~ *of potatoes* 감자 무더기. [E.]

up hill and down dale, **a**) high and low; everywhere. 언덕을 오르고 계곡을 내려가; 도처에; 온갖 곳을. **b**) energetically. 열심히; 정력적으로. **c**) thoroughly. 맹렬히; 철저히.

hill·bil·ly [hílbìli] *n.* Ⓒ (*pl.* **-lies**) 《U.S. *colloq.*》 a person from the mountains of the southern United States. (특히 미국 남부의) 산골 사람; 산사람.

hill·ock [hílək] *n.* Ⓒ a small hill. 좀 높은 구릉(언덕); 야산.

***hill·side** [hílsàid] *n.* Ⓒ the side of a hill. 산의 중턱(사면).

hill·top [híltɑ̀p / -tɔ̀p] *n.* Ⓒ the top of a hill. 야산의 꼭대기.

hill·y [híli] *adj.* (**hill·i·er, hill·i·est**) **1** full of hills; having many hills. 야산(구릉, 기복)이 많은. ¶ *a* ~ *country* 구릉 지방. **2** like a hill; steep. 야산(구릉) 같은; 험한. ¶ *a* ~ *slope* 험한 비탈. ● **hill·i·ness** [-nis] *n.*

hilt [hilt] *n.* Ⓒ the handle of a sword, dagger, etc. (칼·단검 따위의) 자루; 손잡이. [E.]

(***up***) ***to the hilt,*** completely; thoroughly. 완전히; 철저히. ¶ *armed to the* ~ 완전 무장을 하고 / *prove something up to the* ~ 어떤 일을 철저하게 입증하다.

H. I. M. His (Her) Imperial Majesty. 황제(황후) 폐하.

him [him, im] *pron.* **1** the objective form of **he**. 그를(에게). ¶ *I know* ~. 나는 그를 알고 있다 / *I gave* ~ *a book.* 그에게 책을 주었다 / *She went to* ~. 그녀는 그에게로 갔다. **2** 《used as *predicatitive*》 《*colloq.*》 = he. ¶ *That's* ~. 저게 그 사람이다. [*he*]

Him·a·la·yan [hìməléiən, himɑ́:ljən] *adj.* of the Himalayas. 히말라야 산맥의.

Him·a·la·yas [hìməléiəz, himɑ́:ljəz], **the** *n. pl.* a mountain range extending along the north border of India. 히말라야 산맥.

:him·self [*h*imsélf] *pron.* (*pl.* **them·selves**) ⇨oneself **1** a reflexive and emphatic form of **he** or **him**. 그 자신; 그 스스로 (직접); 그 사람 본인이(을); 그 자신을(에게). ⓐ 《*emph.*》: *He* ~ *says so.* =*He says so* ~. 그 자신이 그렇게 말하고 있다 / *Did you see John* ~ *?* 존 그 본인을 직접 만났는가. ⓑ 《*reflexively*》: *He killed* ~. 그는 자살했다 / *He supports* ~. 그는 자활하고 있다 / *John asked* ~ *what he really wanted.* 존은 실제로 자신이 무엇을 원하는가를 자문했다. **2** his usual self. 정상적인 그; 본래(평소)의 그. ¶ *He is not* ~ *today.* 오늘 그는 여느 때의 그와는 다르다 / *He came to* ~. 의식(냉정)을 되찾았다. [E.]

(***all***) ***by himself,*** alone; without any help. 홀로; 혼자 힘으로. ¶ *walk by* ~ 홀로(혼자 힘으로) 걷다.

***hind**[1] [haind] *adj.* (**hind·er, hind·most** or **hind·er·most**) back; rear. 뒤의; 뒤쪽(후부)의(opp. fore). ¶ *the* ~ *legs* (*of an animal*) (동물의) 뒷다리 / *the* ~ *wheels* (*of a cart*) 차의 뒷바퀴. [E.]

hind[2] [haind] *n.* Ⓒ (*pl.* **hinds** or *collectively* **hind**) a female red deer. 암고라니(opp. stag). [E.]

***hin·der**[1] [híndər] *vt.* (P6,13) 《*from*》 prevent; keep back; delay. …을 방해하다; 지체시키다. ¶ *be hindered in one's work* 일을 방해받다 / ~ *a man from committing a crime* 사람이 범죄를 저지르지 못하도록 하다 / *The storm hindered us from starting.* 폭풍우로 출발을 못 했다. [↓]

hin·der[2] [háindər] *adj.* situated at the back. 뒤의; 뒤쪽의; 후부의. ¶ *the hinder parts* (*end*) 후부 / *the* ~ *gate* 뒷문. [→hind[1]]

hind·er·most [háindərmòust] *adj.* = hindmost.

Hin·di [híndi:] *n.* Ⓤ a language of northern India. 북인도어. [→Hindu]

hind·most [háin*d*mòust, -məst] *adj.* furthest behind; last. 가장 뒤의; 최후(부)의. [E.]

Hin·doo [híndu:] *n., adj.* =Hindu.

hin·drance [híndrəns] *n.* Ⓤ the act of hindering; Ⓒ a person or thing that hinders; an obstacle. 방해; 방해자; 방해(장애)물. ¶ *Noise is a* ~ *to studying.* 소음은 공부에 방해가 된다. [*hinder*[1]]

Hin·du [híndu:] *n.* Ⓒ **1** a member of a native race in India. 힌두 사람. **2** a person who believes in Hinduism. 힌두교 신봉자. — *adj.* of the Hindus, their language or religion. 힌두 사람(어, 교)의. [Skr. *Sindhu* river, esp. the Indus]

Hin·du·sta·ni [hìndustǽni, -stɑ́:ni] *n.* Ⓤ a language spoken in most parts of India. 힌두스탄어. [↑]

·hinge [hindʒ] *n.* Ⓒ **1** a tool for joining two parts so that one of them can move, as on a door, gate, or lid. 경첩. **2** 《*fig.*》 a cardinal point. 요체(要諦); 요점; 중심점.

off the hinges, 《*fig.*》 in disorder; in a disturbed condition. 탈(고장)이 나.

— *vt.* (P6) furnish (something) with hinges. …에 경첩을 달다(붙이다). ¶ *a hinged door* 당길문(門).

— *vi.* (P3) 《*on, upon*》 swing or turn on a hinge. 경첩으로 움직이다. [E.]

hinge (=*depend*) **on** *something.* …에 달리다. ¶ *Success mainly hinges on good luck.* (일의) 성패는 주로 행운에 달려 있다.

·**hint** [hint] *n.* Ⓒ a slight sign; an indirect suggestion. 암시; 넌지시 비춤. ¶ *a delicate* 〔*broad*〕 ~ 어렴풋한〔노골적인〕 암시 / *give* 〔*let fall, drop*〕 *a* ~ 힌트를 주다; 넌지시 비추다 / *take a* ~ (약간의 힌트로) 알아차리다.
— *vt., vi.* (P6,11; 3) 《*at*》 give a slight sign of (something); suggest indirectly. 넌지시 비추다; 암시하다. ¶ ~ *at foul play* 부정 행위가 있음을 암시하다 / *He hinted disapproval.* 넌지시 불찬(不贊)의 뜻을 비추었다 / *He hinted that he knew more.* 그는 자신이 좀더 알고 있다는 것을 암시했다. ● **hint·er** [-ər] *n.* [E. var. of obs. *hent* lay hold of]

hin·ter·land [híntərlæ̀nd] *n.* Ⓒ the land or district lying behind a coast. 내지(內地); 내륙 지역; (강안·해안으로부터의) 오지(奧地)(cf. *foreland*). [G.(→ hinder[2])]

·**hip**[1] [hip] *n.* Ⓒ the part of the human body below the waist. 엉덩이; 허리. ¶ *a* ~ *pocket* 뒷주머니 / *with one's hands on one's hips* 두 손을 허리에 대고〔얹고〕. [E.]

have 〔***get***〕 *someone* ***on*** 〔***upon***〕 ***the hip,*** have the advantage over someone in a struggle; get control of someone. 아무보다 우위에 서다; 아무에게 이기다; 아무를 지배하다.

smite hip and thigh, 《Bible》 attack without mercy. 가차 없이 해치우다〔공격하다〕.

hip[2] [hip] *n.* Ⓒ a pod containing the ripe seed of a rose bush. 찔레의 열매. [E.]

hip[3] [hip] *interj.* a sound made twice as a signal for united cheering. (집단 응원 때 등의) 만세, 만세. [?]

hip·pie, -py [hípi] *n.* (*pl.* **-pies**) a young person who rejects established ways of dressing and behaving. 히피(족). [? hip =informed]

hip·po [hípou] *n.* (*pl.* **-pos**) 《*colloq.*》 = hippopotamus.

Hip·poc·ra·tes [hipɑ́krətìːz / -pɔ́k-] *n.* a Greek physician who is considered the Father of Medicine. 히포크라테스《고대 그리스의 의사로서 '의학의 아버지'로 일컬어짐》.

hip·po·drome [hípədròum] *n.* Ⓒ **1** 《Gk., Rom. hist.》 a place for horse races and chariot races in ancient Greece and Rome. (전차 경주·경마를 하던) 경기장. **2** an arena or building for a circus, games, etc. 서커스장(場); 경기장. [Gk. *hippos* horse, *dromos* course]

hip·po·pot·a·mi [hìpəpɑ́təmài / -pɔ́t-] *n.* pl. of **hippopotamus**

hip·po·pot·a·mus [hìpəpɑ́təməs / -pɔ́t-] *n.* (*pl.* **-mus·es** or **-mi**) Ⓒ a very large wild animal with a thick hairless body and short legs, found in African rivers. 하마(河馬). [Gk. *hippos* horse, *potamos* river]

hip·py [hípi] *n.* =hippie.

:**hire** [háiər] *vt.* (P6,7,20) employ (someone) for a fixed payment; pay for the use of (something). …을 고용하다; (무엇)을 임차(賃借)〔임대〕하다; 세내다. ¶ ~ *a man to do a certain piece of work* 어떤 일을 하기 위하여 사람을 쓰다 / *The shopkeeper hired ten girls for the Christmas rush.* 가게 주인은 크리스마스 특수(特需)를 위해 여점원 10명을 고용했다 / *He hired a car and a man to drive it.* 그는 운전사 딸린 차 한 대를 빌렸다.

hire out, give one's work or lend (something) in return for payment. 고용되다; …을 임대하다. ¶ ~ *out horses* 〔*bicycles, boats*〕 *by the hour* 시간당 얼마로 말을〔자전거를, 보트를〕 임대하다.
— *n.* Ⓤ **1** the act of hiring. 임차(賃借); 임대(賃貸); 고용. ¶ *let out on* ~ …을 임대하다. **2** money paid or received for someone's services or for the use of a thing. 임금; 임대〔임차〕료. ¶ *work for* ~ 고용되어〔임금을 받고〕 일하다 / *pay for the* ~ *of a motorcar* 임대 자동차의 사용료를 지불하다. [E.]

for 〔***on***〕 ***hire,*** for use or work in return for payment. 요금을 내면 사용〔이용〕할 수 있는; 임대의. ¶ *a car on* ~ 임대 자동차.

hire·ling [háiərliŋ] *n.* Ⓒ **1** 《*contempt.*》 a person who works only for money. 돈받고〔보수를 목적으로〕 일하는 사람; 고용인; 돈이라면 무엇이나 하는 사람. **2** something hired. 임대한 것; 임대물.

hire-pur·chase [háiərpə́ːrtʃəs] *n.* 《Brit.》 purchase by installments. 분할불식〔할부식〕 구매(=U.S. installment plan).

:**his** [hiz, iz] *pron.* **1** the possessive form of **he.** 그의. ¶ ~ *hat* 그의 모자 / *His name is Bill.* 그의 이름은 빌이다. **2** (*pl.* **his**) the possessive pronoun of **he.** 그의 것; 그의 소유물. ¶ *a friend of* ~ 그의 친구 / *This is mine; that is* ~. 이것은 내 것이고 저것은 그의 것이다 / *His is a timid character.* 그의 성격은 소심하다. [*he*]

·**hiss** [his] *vi., vt.* **1** (P1) make a sound like the [s]. (증기가 분출할 때처럼) 쉿소리를 내다; (노여움·비난 따위를 나타내어) 쉬잇하다. ¶ *A snake hissed away into the grass.* 뱀이 쉿소리를 내며 풀숲으로 들어갔다 / *A pan of meat hissed.* 고기 냄비가 쉿쉿하며 끓었다 / *"Shut up", I hissed at him.* "입 다물어"하고 그에게 속삭였다. **2** (P6,7) 《*away, down, off*》 show dislike by hissing. (혐오·노여움·불만·비난·경멸 따위를 나타내어) 쉬잇하여 제지하다〔꾸짖다〕; 쉬잇하여 물러가게 하다. ¶ ~ *off an actor* 쉬이쉬이 야유하여 배우를 퇴장시키다.
— *n.* Ⓒ a sound like the [s]. 쉿하는 소리. ¶ *the* ~ *of water on a hot stove* 뜨거운 난로 위에서 쉿쉿 물이 끓는 소리 / *Hisses were heard from many who disliked what the speaker was saying.* 연사가 하는 말에 분노한 많은 사람들의 입에서 쉬이 하는 야유 소리가 들렸다. [Imit.]

hist [hist] *interj.* hush. 쉬잇. ¶ *Hist! what was that sound?* 쉬잇. 그게 무슨 소리였지. [?]

his·ta·mine [hístəmì(:)n] *n.* 《chem.》 an amine released by the body in allergic reactions. 히스타민. [↓, *amine*]

his·tol·o·gy [histálədʒi / -tɔ́l-] *n.* 《biol.》 the science of organic tissues. 조직학. [Gk. *histos* tissue, -logy]

***his·to·ri·an** [histɔ́:riən] *n.* Ⓒ a person who writes about history. 역사가; 역사학자. [→*history*]

***his·tor·ic** [histɔ́(:)rik, -tár-] *adj.* **1** having to do with history; historical. 역사의〔에 관한〕(cf. *prehistoric*). **2** famous or important in history. 역사상의; 역사상 유명〔중요〕한. ¶ *a(n)* ~ *event* 역사적 사건 / ~ *scenes* 사적(史跡); 구적(舊跡).

***his·tor·i·cal** [histɔ́(:)rikəl, -tár-] *adj.* of or having to do with history. 역사의〔에 관한〕; 역사적인. ¶ ~ *materials* 사료(史料) / ~ *evidence* 사실(史實) / *a(n)* ~ *method* 역사적 방법 / *a(n)* ~ *novel* 역사 소설. ● **his·tor·i·cal·ly** [-i] *adv.*

:**his·to·ry** [hístəri] *n.* (*pl.* **-ries**) **1** Ⓤ the study or story of past facts and events. 역사. ¶ *ancient* 〔*medieval, modern*〕 ~ 고대〔중세, 근세〕사 / *the* ~ *of England* 영국사. **2** Ⓒ the past story of a man, nation, or thing. (한 개인, 국가, 물건의) 경력; 내력; 유래; 이력. ¶ *medical* ~ *of the patient* 환자의 병력(病歷) / *This sword has a strange* ~. 이 칼에는 기이한 내력이 있다. [Gk. *histōria* inquiry]

become history, become subject matter for history. 역사에 남다.

make history, do such important things as will live long in history. 역사에 남을 만한 일을 하다; 후세에 이름을 남기다.

his·tri·on·ic [hìstriánik / -ɔ́n-] *adj.* **1** of actors or acting. 배우의; 연극의. **2** artificial; not natural. 부자연스러운; 연극 같은. —*n.* 《*pl.*》 the art of acting in plays; dramatics. 연극; 연기. [L. *histrio* actor]

:**hit** [hit] *v.* (**hit, hit·ting**) *vt.* **1** (P6,7,13,14) ⓐ give a blow to (someone); strike; knock. …을 때리다; 치다. ¶ ~ *a ball with a bat* 배트로 공을 치다 / ~ *a nail with a hammer* 망치로 못을 쳐 박다 / ~ *with a stick* 막대기로 때리다 / ~ *someone on the head* 〔*in the ribs*〕 아무의 머리〔옆구리〕를 때리다 語法 hit the someone's head 라고 하지 않음 / *I* ~ *him a blow.* 그에게 일격을 가했다 / *I got mad and* ~ *him hard.* 화가 나서 그를 세게 때렸다. ⓑ come 〔strike〕 against (something); collide with. …을 들이받다; …에 충돌하다. ¶ *get* ~ *by a truck* 트럭에 받혀 나가 떨어지다 / ~ *one's head against the door* 문에 머리를 부딪치다 / *The car* ~ *the mailbox.* 차가 우체통을 들이받았다. **2** (P6) reach (a thing aimed at); succeed in striking with a missile, etc. (겨냥한 것에) 맞히다; 적중〔명중〕하다. ¶ ~ *the target* 과녁을〔목표를〕 맞히다 / ~ *someone with a stone* 돌을 던져 아무를 맞히다 / *We fired and* ~ *the tiger.* 총을 쏘아 호랑이를 맞혔다 / *A bullet* ~ *him.* 총알이 그에게 명중했다. **3** (P6) ⓐ guess right. (바로) 알아맞히다. ¶ *You've* ~ *it.* 맞았어; 바로 맞혔어. ⓑ agree with (something); suit. (취향·목적 따위에) 맞다; 합치하다. ¶ *I'm sure this green shirt will* ~ *Tom's fancy.* 이 파란 셔츠는 틀림없이 톰의 취향에 맞을 게다. **4** (P6) ⓐ reach; arrive at (a place). …에 다다르다; 도착하다. ¶ ~ *town* 시에 도착하다 / *As soon as we* ~ *the hotel, we'll call you up.* 우리가 호텔에 도착하는 대로 자네에게 전화하겠네. ⓑ reach (a certain level). (어떤 수준·정도에) 달하다. ¶ *Prices are expected to* ~ *a new high.* 물가가 전에 없던 최고치를 기록할 것 같다. **5** (P6) have a serious influence upon (someone or something); hurt the feelings of (someone); affect. (…에) 격심한 타격〔영향〕을 주다; (…의) 감정을 해치다. ¶ *He was hard* ~ *by the failure.* 그는 그 실패로 인해 정신적으로 큰 타격을 입었다 / *The crops'll be* ~ *bad(ly).* 농작물이 심한 피해를 입을 것이다 / *The rise of prices has* ~ *our pocket.* 물가의 앙등은 우리들 호주머니에 영향을 끼쳤다. **6** (P6) 《*out*》 assail effectively and sharply; censure. 호되게 비판하다; 비난하다. **7** (P6) (of storms, etc.) attack. (폭풍 따위가) 덮치다; 엄습하다. ¶ *A heavy storm* ~ *the region.* 격심한 태풍이 그 지역을 강타했다. **8** (P6) ⓐ find unexpectedly; discover (something) by chance or after search. 우연히〔찾은 끝에〕 발견하다; 뜻밖에 만나다. ¶ ~ *the right answer* 정답을 알아맞히다 / ~ *a run of bad luck* 잇따라 불운을 만나다 / *We* ~ *the right path at last.* 마침내 바른 길로 나왔다. ⓑ come upon. …에게 생각이 떠오르다. ¶ *An idea* ~ *him.* 문득 어떤 생각이 떠올랐다. **9** (P6) move (someone's feelings); appeal to. …에게 느끼게 하다; 인상을 주다. ¶ *How does that* ~ *you?* 그것을 어떻게 생각하나〔느끼는가〕. **10** (P6) 《baseball》 make (a base hit). 안타를 치다. ¶ ~ *a single* 단타(單打)를 치다 / ~ *a double* 2루타를 치다. —*vi.* (P1,2A,3) **1** deliver a blow. 치다; 때리다. **2** 《*against*》 strike; bump. 부딪치다; 충돌하다. ¶ *I* ~ *against a wall.* 담벽에 부딪쳤다. **3** 《*upon*》 find or come upon something by accident or after searching. 우연히 발견하다〔만나다〕; 생각이 문득 떠오르다. ¶ ~ *on a good plan* 좋은 안이 생각나다 / ~ *upon a solution* 〔*an idea*〕 해결책이〔아이디어가〕 떠오르다.

hit at, **a**) aim a blow at (something). …을 겨냥해 때리다. **b**) attack (someone) in words. …을 비난〔공격〕하다.

hit someone below the belt =hit someone when he's down.

hit one's fancy, appeal to one's fancy. 취향에 맞다.

hit hard (=*put emphasis*) ***on** something.* …을 역설〔강조〕하다.
hit it, guess rightly. 바로 알아맞히다.
hit it off, 《U.S. *colloq.*》 get along well together. 마음이 맞다; 사이 좋게 잘 지내다.
hit off, **a**) follow the example of (someone); write down (something) briefly but well. …를 모방하다; 잘 표현〔묘사〕하다. **b**) produce readily or offhand. 즉석에서 만들다.
hit out, strike forcefully. (힘으로·말로써) 세게 때리다.
hit the ceiling 〔***roof***〕, 《*sl.*》 become very angry. 몹시 성내다.
hit the (***right***) ***nail on the head*** =hit it.
hit up, force 〔speed〕 up. 재촉하다.
hit** someone **when he's down, strike or treat unfairly. 반칙을 하다; 비겁한 짓을 하다.
— *n.* Ⓒ **1** a stroke; a blow; a shot that hits what is aimed at. 타격; 명중; 적중. **2** a stroke of good fortune; a successful and popular song, book, play, etc. 들어맞음; 성공; 히트(곡, 작). **3** an effectively witty or sarcastic remark. 급소를 찌르는 말; 비꼬는 말. **4** 《baseball》 a base hit. 안타; 히트. **5** a collision. 충돌.
hit or miss, without definite direction or plan; aimless. (맞든 안 맞든) 아무렇게나; 되는 대로.
— *adj.* 《*colloq.*》 very popular; very successful. 매우 인기 있는; 몹시 성공적인. [E.]

hit-and-run [hítənrʌ́n] *adj.* (esp. of a driver of a car) causing an accident or damage and running away so as to avoid the penalty. (운전사가) 사람을 치고 뺑소니 치는; 뺑소니 차의. ¶ *a ~ driver* 뺑소니차 운전사.

hitch [hitʃ] *vt., vi.* **1** (P6,7) move or pull suddenly. 홱 움직이다; 홱 당기다〔끌어올리다〕. ¶ *~ one's chair to the table* 의자를 테이블 쪽으로 끌어당기다 / *~ up one's trousers* 바지를 끌어〔치켜〕 올리다. **2** (P13; 1,3) ⓐ fasten or be fastened with a hook, ring, rope, etc. (갈고리·고리·밧줄 따위로) 걸다; 걸리다; 매(어지)다. ¶ *~ a horse to a post* 말을 말뚝에 매다 / *~ a rope over* 〔*round*〕 *a bough* 밧줄을 나뭇가지에 걸다 / *~* (*up*) *a horse* (*to a cart*) 말을 수레에 비끄러매다. ⓑ fasten or be fastened loosely; become fastened; catch. 느슨히 매다〔매어지다〕; 걸리다. ¶ *My dress hitched on a nail.* 옷이 못에 걸렸다.
hitch horses together, 《U.S.》 work together. 협력〔협조〕하다.
hitch** one's **wagon to a star, have a high ambition, ideal, or purpose. 큰 야심〔이상, 목적〕을 품다.
— *n.* Ⓒ **1** a quick, sudden movement; a sudden pull. 급격한 움직임; 홱 당김. ¶ *a ~ of the reins* 고삐를 홱 당김. **2** a kind of knot for fastening rope temporarily. (일시적으로 매어 두는) 느슨한 매듭. **3** something which hinders. 장애; 지장. ¶ *a ~ in one's plans* 계획의 지장〔연기〕. [? O.F. *hocier* jerk]
without a hitch, smoothly; successfully. 지장 없이.

hitch·hike [hítʃhàik] *vi.* 《*colloq.*》 travel by walking and sometimes getting free rides from passing cars. (중도에 지나가는 차 따위에) 편승하여 여행을 하다.

hitch·hik·er [hítʃhàikər] *n.* Ⓒ a person who hitchhikes. 히치하이크를 하는 사람.

***hith·er** [híðər] *adv.* to this place; here. 이곳〔쪽〕으로; 이리로. ¶ *come ~* 이쪽으로 오다.
hither and thither, in various directions. 여기저기에; 이쪽저쪽으로.
— *adj.* on this side. 이쪽의. ¶ *on the ~ side of the bank* 둑 이쪽의. [E.]

***hith·er·to** [hìðərtúː] *adv.* up to this time; until now. 지금〔이제〕까지. ¶ *a fact ~ unknown* 이제껏 알려지지 않은 사실.

Hit·ler [hítlər], **Adolf** *n.* (1889-1945) a German dictator. 히틀러.

***hive** [haiv] *n.* Ⓒ **1** a house or box for bees to live in. (꿀)벌통. **2** a large number of bees living together in this place; 《*fig.*》 busy people living together. (한 벌통에 사는) 벌떼; (함께 사는) 바쁘게 북적이는 사람들. **3** a very busy place. 바쁜 사람들이 떼지어 붐비는 곳; 활동의 중심지. ¶ *a ~ of industry* 산업의 중심지.
— *vt.* (P6) **1** put (bees) into a hive. (벌)을 벌통에 넣다. **2** ⓐ (of bees) store (honey) in a hive. (벌이 꿀)을 벌통에 저장하다. ⓑ 《*fig.*》 store up. 축적하다. — *vi.* (P1,2A) **1** enter or live in a hive. (꿀벌이) 벌통에 들어가다; 벌통에 살다. **2** live close together as bees do. (벌처럼) 군거(群居)하다. ¶ *People ~ in a city.* 사람들이 도시에 밀집해 살고 있다. [E.]

hives [haivz] *n. pl.* 《used as *sing.* and *pl.*》 《med.》 **1** a skin disease. 두드러기. **2** =croup[1]. [Sc.]

H. L. 《Brit.》 House of Lords. 상원.

h'm [hm, mm] *interj.* =hem[2]; hum (*n.* 2).

H. M. His 〔Her〕 Majesty. 폐하.

***ho, hoa** [hou] *interj.* a call to get attention. 호; 야; 어이; 저런《주의·환기·놀람·만족 따위를 나타내는 소리》. ¶ *Ho! ho!* 허허《냉소》/ *Ho, there!* 어이 (이봐). [?]

hoar [hɔːr] *adj.* =hoary.

hoard [hɔːrd] *n.* Ⓒ **1** a store of hidden money; a collection of things esp. those kept secretly for one's own use. 감춘 돈; 비장의 것; 축적물. ¶ *make a ~ of provisions* 식량을 비축하다. **2** 《*fig.*》 a mass of material stored in the memory. (지식 따위의) 온축(蘊蓄). — *vt., vi.* (P6,7; 1) 《*up*》 gather and keep (something) secretly. (무엇을) 남 몰래 저장〔저축, 비장〕하다. ●**hoard·er** [-ər] *n.* [E.]

hoard·ing[1] [hɔ́:rdiŋ] *n.* **1** Ⓤ the act of one who hoards. 저장; 비장(秘藏); 비축(備蓄); 축적. **2** 《*pl.*》 that which is hoarded. 저장〔비장〕물. [↑]

hoard·ing[2] [hɔ́:rdiŋ] *n.* 《Brit.》 Ⓒ **1** a temporary fence enclosing a building during erection. (건축 공사장 따위의) 판장. **2** a billboard. 게시판; 광고판. [Teut. *hurt* hurdle]

hoar·frost [hɔ́:rfrɔ̀(:)st, -fràst] *n.* Ⓤ white frost. (하얀) 서리. [*hoar*]

hoar·hound [hɔ́:rhàund] *n.* = horehound.

hoarse [hɔ:rs] *adj.* sounding rough and deep; having a rough voice; husky. (목이) 쉰; 쉰 목소리의; 귀에 거슬리는. ¶ *grow* ~ 목이 쉬다 / *A bad cold often makes someone* ~. 독감(毒感)은 흔히 사람들의 목을 쉬게 한다. ●**hoarse·ly** [-li] *adv.* **hoarse·ness** [-nis] *n.* [E.]

hoar·y [hɔ́:ri] *adj.* (**hoar·i·er, hoar·i·est**) **1** white or gray, esp. with age; grayish-white; white-haired. (늙어서 머리 따위가) 하얀; 회백색(灰白色)의; 백발의. ¶ ~ *hair* 백발 / *a* ~ *head* 두발이 하얀 머리. **2** 《*fig.*》 ancient; very old; honorable. 고색이 창연한; 매우 오래된; 거룩한. **3** 《bot., insect》 covered with downy hairs. 솜털로 덮인. ● **hoar·i·ness** [-nis] *n.* [*hoar*]

hoax [houks] *n.* Ⓒ the act of playing a trick; a practical joke. 남을 속여먹기; 몹쓸 장난. ¶ *play a* ~ *on someone* 아무를 속여먹다. —*vt.* (P6,13) play a trick on (someone); deceive. …을 (감쪽같이) 속이다. ¶ ~ *someone into thinking* 아무를 속여 …라고 생각하게 하다. [→hocus.]

hob [hab / hɔb] *n.* Ⓒ **1** a metal shelf at the side of a fireplace on which pots are kept warm. 벽난로 내부 양쪽의 시렁《물주전자 따위를 얹음》. **2** a peg used as a target. (고리 던지기에서) 표적 막대. [?]

〈hob 1〉

hob·ble [hábəl / hɔ́bəl] *vi.* (P1,2A) **1** 《*along, about*》 walk with difficulty; limp. 다리를 절다. ¶ *An old man hobbled along the street.* 한 노인이 다리를 절며 거리를 걸어갔다. **2** run lamely. (시구(詩句)가) 딱딱〔어색〕하다. —*vt.* (P6) **1** tie the legs of a horse together to make him walk very slowly. (말이 잘 걷지 못하게) 다리를 한데 묶다. **2** cause (someone) to limp. (아무의) 다리를 절게 하다. **3** hamper; prevent; stop. (진행 따위)를 방해하다. —*n.* Ⓒ **1** a limping walk. 절뚝거리며 걸음. **2** a rope or fetter for hobbling horses. (말의) 다리 묶는 줄; 족쇄. [E.]

·**hob·by** [hábi / hɔ́bi] *n.* Ⓒ (*pl.* **-bies**) a subject which a person studies for pleasure. 취미; 도락. ¶ *Stamp-collecting is her* ~. 우표 수집은 그녀의 취미다. [var. of name *Robin*]

ride a hobby, be too much devoted to one's hobby. 도락에 지나치게 열중하다.

hob·by-horse [hábihɔ̀:rs / hɔ́b-] *n.* Ⓒ **1** a stick with a horse's head used as a toy by children. (끝에 말 머리를 단) 대말. **2** a rocking horse. 흔들 목마.

hob·gob·lin [hábgàlin / hɔ́bgɔ̀b-] *n.* **1** a mischievous imp. 못된 장난하는 꼬마 요귀. **2** an ugly, mischievous child. 선머슴; 개구쟁이. **3** a small ugly person. 못생긴 작은 사람. [→hobby, *goblin*]

hob·nail [hábnèil / hɔ́b-] *n.* Ⓒ a short nail with a large head fixed in the bottoms of shoes. (신창에 박는) 징. [*hob* peg, *nail*]

hob·nob [hábnàb / hɔ́bnɔ̀b] *vi.* (p1,3) **1** be friendly with someone 친하게 사귀다. **2** talk and drink together. 권커니 작커니하다; 허물없이 이야기하다. [*hab nab,* have or not have, give and take]

ho·bo [hóubou] *n.* Ⓒ (*pl.* **-bos** or **-boes**) 《U.S. *colloq.*》 a wandering workman; a tramp; a vagabond. 뜨내기 일꾼; 부랑자; 방랑자. [?<his greeting *ho! beau!*]

Hob·son's choice [hábsənz- / hɔ́bsnz-] *n.* a choice of taking the thing offered or nothing. 선택의 여지가 없는 선택. [Person]

hock[1] [hak / hɔk] *n.* Ⓒ a joint in the hind leg of a cow, horse, pig, etc. (소·말·돼지 따위의) 뒷다리 복사뼈 관절. [E.]

hock[2] [hak / hɔk] *n., vt.* (P6) 《U.S. *colloq.*》 pawn. 전당 (잡히다). [? Du. *hok* prison, debt]

hock[3] [hak / hɔk] *n.* any white Rhine wine. (독일의) Rhine 지방산(産) 백포도주. [*Hochheim* place]

hock·ey [háki / kɔ́ki] *n.* Ⓤ a game played by two teams on grass or ice, using curved sticks and a ball. 하키. ¶ *ice* ~ 아이스하키. [? O.F. *hognet* crook]

ho·cus [hóukəs] *vt.* (P6) **1** play a trick on (someone); cheat. …을 속이다. **2** stupefy with drugs. 마취시키다. **3** put drugs in. …에 마취제를 넣다. [↓]

ho·cus-po·cus [hóukəspóukəs] *n.* Ⓤ **1** a meaningless talk or action intended to deceive or turning someone's attention away from the facts. (…의 주의를 딴 데로 돌리기 위한) 속임수의 무의미한 말〔행동〕. **2** deceiving; trickery. 속임수. —*vt.* (P6) deceive. …을 속이다. [sham L.]

hod [had / hɔd] *n.* Ⓒ **1** a wooden container for carrying bricks or mortar. 호드《벽돌·회반죽을 나르는 긴 자루가 달린 목제 용기》. **2** 《U.S.》 a coal scuttle. 석탄통. [O.F.]

hodge·podge [hádʒpàdʒ / hɔ́dʒpɔ̀dʒ] *n.* Ⓒ 《*sing.* only》 **1** a thick stew of meat and vegetables. (고기와 야채의) 잡탕찜. **2** a mixture of different things. 뒤범벅. [F. = shake pot]

hoe [hou] *n.* Ⓒ a long-handled tool used for loosening the soil or removing weeds. 괭이; (괭이 모양의) 제초기.
— *vt., vi.* (P6,7;1) dig (the soil) or clear (weeds) with a hoe; work with a hoe. 괭이로 파다〔갈다, 제초하다〕. [Teut. (→hew)]
a long* 〔*hard*〕 *row to hoe, a tedious task. 지루한〔따분한〕 일.

·**hog** [hɔ:g, hɑg] *n.* Ⓒ (*pl.* **hogs** or *collectively* **hog**) **1** a pig, esp. castrated male reared for food. 돼지《특히 거세한 식용 수퇘지》. **2** 《Brit. *dial.*》 a young sheep before it is sheared. 첫 털깎기를 하기 전의 어린 양. **3** 《*fig.*》 a greedy or dirty person. 탐욕스러운〔불결한〕 사람. ¶ *eat like a* ~ 돼지처럼 게걸스럽게 먹다 / *get fat as a* ~ 돼지처럼 살찌다.
a hog in armor, a person ill at ease in fine clothes. 값진 옷을 입고도 어색한 사람.
behave like a hog, behave very rudely. 돼지 같이 무례하게 굴다.
go the whole hog, 《*sl.*》 do something thoroughly. 철저하게 하다.
make a hog of oneself, eat greedily. 게걸스럽게 먹다.
— *vt.* (P6) **1** ⓐ seize (food) greedily. (음식)을 돼지처럼 탐하다; 걸근거리다. ⓑ take more than one's share of. 자기 몫 이상을 갖다. **2** cut (the mane) short. (갈기)를 짧게 깎다. [N. (→hew)]

hog·gish [hɔ́:giʃ, hɑ́g-] *adj.* like a hog; greedy, esp. in eating; very selfish; very dirty. 돼지 같은; (특히 음식에) 탐욕스러운; 이기적인; 불결한. ●**hog·gish·ly** [-li] *adv.*

hog·ma·nay [hɑ̀gmənéi / hɔ́g-] *n.* 《Sc.》 **1** New Year's Eve. 섣달 그믐《12월31일》. **2** a gift which children collect on that day. 섣달 그믐날 어린이들이 받는 선물《과자 따위》. [*prob* F.]

hogs·head [hɔ́:gzhèd, hɑ́g-] *n.* Ⓒ **1** a large round wooden container for wine or strong drink. 술을 담는 큰 나무통. **2** a liquid measure equal to U.S. 63, British 52.5 or 54 gallons. 액량 단위《미국 63, 영국 52.5 또는 54갤런》. [*hog*]

hoi pol·loi [hɔ̀i pəlɔ́i] *n.* 《Gk.》 《*the* ~》 the masses; the people. 대중; 민중. [Gk. = the many]

hoist [hɔist] *vt.* (P6,7) raise, pull, or lift up with effort by means of ropes or pulleys. 끌어〔들어〕 올리다; 높이 올리다; 내걸다. ¶ ~ *a flag* 〔*sails*〕 기를〔돛을〕 올리다 / ~ *down* 끌어내리다.
be hoist with one's own petard, be caught and injured by one's own devices against others. 제가 놓은 덫에 제가 걸리다; 자승 자박이 되다.
— *n.* Ⓒ **1** the act of lifting. 들어〔끌어〕올림. **2** an elevator or other apparatus for rasing things. 호이스트; (감아 올리는 소형) 기중기. [Du. *hijschen*]

hoi·ty-toi·ty [hɔ́itiitɔ́iti] *adj.* 《*colloq.*》 arrogant and hard to please. 거만한; 까다로운. [Obs. *hoit* romp]

ho·kum [hóukəm] *n.* 《*colloq.*》 **1** a technique for evoking a desired audience response. (연극 따위에서) 관객의 인기를 노리는 수법. **2** nonsense; claptrap. 되잖은 소리; 엉터리; 홍감. [*hocus-pocus*]

:**hold**[1] [hould] *v.* (**held**) *vt.* **1** ⓐ (P6,7,13) take and keep (something) in the hand; bear or support with the hands, arms, etc.; seize; grasp. …을 손에 가지다; 안다; 잡다; 쥐다. ¶ ~ *a pen* 〔*gun*〕 *in one's hand* 손에 펜을 잡다〔총을 쥐다〕 / ~ *a baby in one's arms* 팔에 아기를 안다 / ~ *someone by the sleeve* 아무의 소매를 잡다 / *The dog held a newspaper between its teeth.* 개가 신문을 한 장 입에 물었다. ⓑ (P7,13,18) keep (something) in a certain position or state. (어떤 위치·상태에) …을 유지하다; …해 두다. ¶ ~ *one's head straight* 〔*on one side*〕 머리를 꼿꼿이 들고〔한쪽으로 기울이고〕 있다 / ~ *one's glance steady* 지그시 응시하다 / ~ *the door open* 문을 열어 두다 / ~ *someone in suspense* 아무를 불안하게 하다; 아무를 마음 졸이게 하다 / ~ *one's judgment in suspense* 판단을 유보하다. **2** (P6,7,13) prevent the movement or escape of (something); support. (움직이거나 달아나지 못하게) …을 붙들다; 버티다. ¶ ~ *someone motionless* 아무를 꼼짝 못하게 붙잡다 / ~ *someone to his word* 〔*terms*〕 아무에게 약속〔조건〕을 지키게 하다 / *Hold him for a minute!* 잠깐 그를 붙들고 있어라 / *He held her so that she couldn't move.* 움직이지 못하게 그녀를 붙잡았다 / *These pillars* ~ *the roof.* 이 기둥들이 지붕을 받치고 있다. **3** (P6,7) restrain (someone or something) from acting or speaking; keep back; control. …을 억제하다; 억누르다; 제지하다. ¶ ~ *one's breath* 숨을 죽이다 / ~ *one's temper* 감정을 억누르다; 화를 내지 않다 / ~ *someone from speaking* 아무가 말하지 못하게 하다 / ~ *inflation in check* 인플레이션을 억제하다 / *Hold your tongue!* 닥쳐. **4** (P6,13) ⓐ contain; have in itself. 들어 있다. ¶ *The bottle holds wine.* 그 병에는 포도주가 들어 있다. ⓑ have room or space for; be capable of containing. 들어가다; 수용할〔들어갈〕 수 있다. ¶ ~ *anything on one's stomach* 무엇이든 뱃속에 넣다 / *eat as much as one can* ~ 먹을 수 있을 만큼 먹다; 많이 먹다 / *The barrel holds ten gallons.* 그 통엔 10갤런이 들어간다 / *The room holds sixty persons.* 이 방은 60명을 수용할 수 있다. **5** (P6,7,11,18,21) ⓐ keep or have (something) in mind; think; believe; maintain (마음에 생각 따위)를 품다〔가지다〕; 생각하다; 믿다; 주장하다. ¶ ~ *a firm belief* 확고한 신념을 가지다 / ~ *no prejudice* 선입견〔편견〕을 갖지 않다 / ~ *the same view as him* 그와 같은 견해를 갖고 있다 / ~ *the opinion that…* …하다는〔이라는〕 생각을 가지다 / *He holds that….* 그는

…라고 주장한다[생각하고 있다] / *The judge held that she was guilty.* 판사는 그녀가 유죄라는 생각이었다. ⓑ regard in a certain manner; consider. …하다고[…로] 보다; …하다고 생각하다. ¶ ~ *someone* (*to be*) *responsible* 아무에게 책임이 있다고 보다 / ~ *someone in esteem* [*contempt*] 아무를 존경[경멸]하다 / *He held himself to be a poet.* 스스로 시인임을 자처했다 / *I* ~ *that she is honest.* 그녀는 정직하다고 생각한다 / *I* ~ *it my duty to inform you.* 귀하에게 알려 드리는 것이 저의 의무라고 생각합니다. **6** (P6) have and keep as one's own; have possession of; own; occupy. …을 (제 것으로) 가지다[소유하다, 보유하다]; (지위 따위)를 차지하다. ¶ ~ *large estates* 많은 땅을 소유하다 / ~ *the first position* 제1위를 차지하다 / *He holds a political office.* 그는 행정관을 하고 있다. **7** (P6,13) 《mil.》 keep against an enemy's attack; defend. (적의 공격으로부터) 지키다; 방어하다; 막다. ¶ ~ *a position* 진지를 지키다 / ~ *a wall gainst invaders* 침공군으로부터 성벽을 지키다 / ~ *one's own position* [*ground*] 자기의 지위를[입장을] 지키다; 굴하지 않(고 버티)다. **8** (P6) have or carry on (a meeting, conversation, etc.); conduct. (모임·식 따위)를 열다; 개최[거행]하다; (대화)를 하다. ¶ ~ *a party* [*meeting*] 파티[회의]를 열다 / ~ *a service* 예배를 보다 / ~ (*a*) *court* 개정(開廷)하다; 재판을 하다 / ~ *a conversation with friends* 친구들과 대화를 가지다 / ~ *classes in the open air* 야외 수업을 하다. **9** (P6) draw and keep (attention); keep the attention of. (주의·관심)을 끌어 붙들어 두다. ¶ ~ *the audience* 청중의 흥미를 끌어 붙들다 / *She failed to* ~ *his attention.* 그녀는 그의 관심을 끌지 못했다. —*vi.* **1** (P1,2A) 《*on, to*》 maintain a grip or grasp. (붙)잡고 있다. ¶ ~ *fast by a piece of rock* 바위를 단단히 붙들다 / *Hold tight!* 단단히 잡아라. **2** (P1, 2A,3) remain or continue unchanged; keep on. 변치 않고 계속되다; …인 체로 있다. ¶ *Please* ~ *still.* 그대로 가만히 있어 주시오 / *The fine weather will not* ~ *long.* 맑은 날씨는 오래 계속되지 않을 게다 / *The weather held warm.* 날씨는 계속 따뜻했다. **3** (P1,2A,3) remain firm or unbroken; not give way. 끊어지지[꺾어지지, 무너지지] 않다; 지탱하다. ¶ *The rope will not* ~ *much longer.* 밧줄이 오래 지탱 못할 게다. **4** (P1,2A,3) continue; proceed. 계속되다; 계속해 나아가다. ¶ ~ *on one's way* 길을 계속해 나아가다. **5** (P1,2A) be in force; be effective; apply. (법률 등이) 효력이 있다; 유효하다; (규칙이) 적용되다. ¶ *The rule still holds* (*good*). 그 규칙은 아직도 유효하다 / *This decision holds in all such cases.* 이 결정은 그와 같은 모든 경우에 적용된다. **6** (P3) 《*from, of*》 have right. …의 권리를 가지다[보유하다]. **7** 《*imperative*》 restrain oneself; check; stop. 삼가다; 멈추다.

hold back, **a**) restrain; check; control. …을 억제하다[누르다]; 제지[자제]하다. ¶ *Police held back the crowd.* 경찰은 군중을 저지했다 / *He could not* ~ *himself back any longer and opened his mouth.* 그는 더는 참지 못하고 입을 열었다. **b**) refrain from (some activity) (어떤 행동)을 삼가다[하지 않다]; 참가하지 않다. **c**) cancel. 취소하다. **d**) refrain from revealing; conceal. 비밀로 하다; 숨겨 두다. ¶ ~ *back information* 정보를 밝히지 않다. **e**) retain possession of (something); keep back. …을 보유하다; 따로 떼어[간직해] 두다.

hold back on, restrain oneself from (doing something). …을 삼가다; 보류하다.

hold by, stick to (something); abide by; maintain. …을 고집[고수]하다; …에 따르다. ¶ ~ *by one's opinion* 자기의 의견을 고수하다 / ~ *by custom* 관습에 따르다.

hold down, **a**) keep (something) under control; check. …을 (억)누르다; 억제하다. ¶ ~ *oneself down* 감정을 억제하다; 마음을 가라앉히다. **b**) 《chiefly U.S. *colloq.*》 continue to hold; have and keep successfully. (일자리·지위 따위)를 계속 유지하다. ¶ ~ *down one's position* 지위를 보존하다.

hold forth, **a**) make a long speech; talk at some length. 길게 이야기하다[늘어놓다]. **b**) propose (a view, etc.). 주다; 제시[제공]하다. ¶ ~ *forth a suggestion* 암시를 주다.

hold good, remain legal or effective. 유효하다. ¶ *This rule holds good in all times and places.* 이 규칙은 언제 어디서나 유효하다.

hold one's hand, be patient; forgive. 참다; 조치를 보류하다; 용서해 주다.

Hold hard! Stop! 멈춰.

hold one's head high, behave proudly. 도도하게[거만하게] 굴다.

hold in, **a**) keep in check; restrain. …을 (억)누르다; 억제하다. **b**) keep oneself in check; control oneself. 참다; 자제하다.

Hold it! Stay like that.; Don't move! 그대로 있어라; 움직이지 마.

hold it [***that***] ***against,*** 《*colloq.*》 think ill of; blame. …을 나쁘게 생각하다; 비난하다. ¶ *She held it against me that I failed to tell her.* 자신에게 말해 주지 않았다고 그녀는 나를 나쁘게 생각했다.

hold off, **a**) resist (the enemy's attack, etc.); keep at a distance; push back. (적의 공격 따위)를 저지하다; 접근시키지 않다; …을 격퇴하다[물리치다]. ¶ ~ *off an enemy.* **b**) keep from acting; delay. (행동)을 지체시키다; 연기하다. ¶ ~ *off starting* 출발을 연기하다 / *Do you think the rain will* ~ *off until after the game?* 경기가 끝날 때까지는 비가 오지 않겠지. **c**) keep or restrain oneself from (doing something). …을 삼가다; 유보하다. **d**) remain at a distance; stay apart. 멀리 떨어져 있다.

hold on, **a**) keep a firm grip on; cling; grip. 꽉 붙잡고 있다; 꼭 매달리다; 달라붙다. ¶ ~ *on to someone's hand* 아무의 손을 꽉 붙

잡다[쥐다]. **b**) keep going; continue. 계속하다; 지속하다. ¶ ~ *on a conversation* 대화를 계속하다. **c**) 《telephone》 not cut off; keep the connection. (전화)를 끊지 않고 두다. ¶ *Hold on a moment, please.* 끊지 말고 잠깐 기다리세요. **d**) 《*colloq.*》 Stop !; Wait ! 멈춰; 기다려.

hold out, **a**) stretch forth; offer (a hand, hope, promise, etc.). 뻗치다; 내(밀다); 제공[제출]하다. ¶ ~ *out a good example* 좋은 보기를 들다 / *She held out her hands to him.* 그녀는 그에게 두 손을 내밀었다. **b**) keep one's position; stand firm; not yield. 굴하지 않다; 버티다. ¶ *The defenders held out for weeks.* 수비대는 몇 주일 동안이나 버텼다. **c**) last to the end; continue; endure. 없어지지 않다; 계속[지속]되다. ¶ *Will the food ~ out ?* 식량이 (떨어지지 않고) 지속될까.

hold over, **a**) keep for future action or decision; postpone. (행동·결정을) 장래로 넘기다; 연기하다. **b**) stay for an additional period or time. 기간 만료 후에도 계속 머물다[재직하다]. **c**) use as a threat; threaten with. (아무)를 …으로 위협하다. ¶ ~ *a stone over someone's head* 아무의 머리를 돌로 위협하다.

hold one's peace [***tongue***], keep silent. 침묵을 지키다.

hold still, remain motionless. 움직이지 않다; 가만히 있다.

hold to =hold by.

hold together, keep or remain united. 단결[결합]하다; 통일을 유지하다. ¶ *The needs of children held their marriage together.* 자식이 있어야 하겠기에 그들의 부부 관계가 유지됐다.

hold up, **a**) support; uphold; endure. …을 지지[유지]하다; 버티다; 지탱하다. ¶ ~ *up the government* 정부를 지지하다 / ~ *up farm prices* 농산물의 가격을 유지하다. **b**) give (an example); show; offer. (본보기로)…을 들다; …을 보이다; 제시하다. **c**) stop; hinder; delay. (멈춰) 서다; 정지하다; …을 저지[방해]하다; 지체시키다. ¶ *They held up at the gate.* 문 있는 데서 멈췄다 / *The storm held us up.* 폭풍이 우리의 전진을 방해하였다. **d**) 《*colloq.*》 stop by force in order to rob. (강도질할 목적으로) 멈춰 세우다. **e**) keep fine; raise; put up. (맑은 날씨가) 계속되다; (들어) 올리다.

hold water, be consistent or logical. 논리가[이론이] 정연하다.

hold with, **a**) agree with (someone) …와 같은 의견이다; …에 동의하다. **b**) approve of (doing something). …을 찬성[승인]하다.

— *n.* **1** ⒸⓊ the act of holding, as with the hands; grasp. 붙잡음; 움켜쥠; 파악. ¶ *have ~ of a rope* 밧줄을 잡다 / *leave ~ of* 잡은 손을 놓다. **2** ⒸⓊ 《*on, over*》 a controlling force; strong influence; authority. 지배[통솔]력; 위력. ¶ *have a ~ on someone* 아무를 지배하는[휘어잡는] 힘이 있다 / *He kept strong ~ on the audience.* 그는 청중들을 강력하게 사로잡고 있었다 / *The government retains its ~ over the country.* 정부는 국가를 지배하는 힘을 보유한다. **3** Ⓒ anything to hold by; a thing with which to grasp something; a place of grasp. 잡는 곳; 붙잡을[발붙일, 매달릴] 데; 버팀; 손잡이. ¶ *The rocks afforded no ~ of for hand or foot.* 암벽에는 붙잡을 데도 발붙일 데도 없었다. **4** Ⓒ a place of security; a fortified place; a strong hold. 안전한 곳; 요새; 성채. **5** Ⓤ grasp with the mind; understanding. (마음으로의) 파악; 이해. ¶ *lay ~ of a writer's ideas* 작가의 사상을[의도를] 파악하다. [E.]

catch [***get, lay, take***] ***hold of,*** take; grasp. …을 붙잡다. ¶ *catch* [*take*] *~ of someone by the arm* 아무의 팔을 잡다 / *Get ~ of the rope.* 밧줄을 붙들어라; 밧줄에 매달려라 / *He felt anger get ~ of him again.* 그는 다시 분노가 치밀어 오르는 것을 느꼈다.

keep hold on (=*hold* or *hang-on to*) *something.* …을 붙잡고 있다; …에 매달려 있다. ¶ *keep a firm ~ on* …을 단단히 붙들고 있다; …을 꽉 잡고 놓지 않다.

lay [***take***] ***hold on,*** seize; grasp. …을 잡다; 장악하다.

let go one's hold (***of***), take one's hands off. 잡은 손을 놓다. ¶ *He let go his ~ of her.* 그는 그녀의 잡은 손을 놓았다.

lose hold of, lose a clue or key to (something); lose all trace of (something). …을 놓치다; …의 단서를[종적을] 잃다.

hold[2] [hould] *n.* Ⓒ a place below deck in which cargo is stored. (배밑의) 선창(船倉). [E.]

hold·back [hóuldbæ̀k] *n.* Ⓒ a thing that holds back; check; restraint; hindrance. 견제물; 속박; 장애. [*hold*[1]]

·hold·er [hóuldər] *n.* Ⓒ **1** a person who holds or owns. 소지인; 소유자. ¶ *a record ~* 기록 보유자. **2** 《in *compounds*》 a thing in or by which something is held. 버티는 것; 넣는[담는] 것. ¶ *a pen-holder* 펜대; 펜걸이 / *a cigarette-holder* 물부리.

hold·fast [hóuldfæ̀st / -fɑ̀ːst] *n.* Ⓒ a thing used to hold something together. 고정시키는 것《죔쇠·꺾쇠·못 따위》.

hold·ing [hóuldiŋ] *n.* ⒸⓊ the act of a person who holds; something owned; property; a piece of land; stocks. 잡음; 쥠; 가짐; 파지(把持); 소유물; 보유지; 소유주(株).

holding company [⌐-⌐--] *n.* a company that owns stocks or bonds of other companies and often controls them. 지주(持株)회사.

hold·up [hóuldʌ̀p] *n.* Ⓒ **1** 《U.S. *colloq.*》 the act of stopping (someone, trains, etc.) by force for the purpose of robbery. 불법으로 정지시켜 금품을 강탈하기; (노상) 강도. ¶ *a ~ man* 강탈자; 노상 강도. **2** delay in traffic. (교통의) 정체(停滯); 지체.

:hole [houl] *n.* Ⓒ **1** a hollow; an empty

place in something; a gap. 구멍; 터진 데; 틈. ¶ *a ~ in the ground* [*in my blouse*] 땅의 움푹 패인 곳[블라우스의 터진 구멍] / *a ~ in one's head* (부상으로) 머리에 난 구멍. **2** ⓐ an open place hollowed out or inhabited by an animal. (짐승)의 굴; 소혈(巢穴). ¶ *a mouse ~* 쥐구멍. ⓑ ((*fig.*)) a small, dark, mean place or house. 비좁고 누추한 집. ¶ *live in a miserable little ~* 초라한 작은 집에 살다. **3** an awkward situation; a predicament. 곤경; 궁지. ¶ *find oneself in a ~* 어찌할 수 없는 처지가 되다 / *put someone in a ~* 아무를 궁지에 빠뜨리다 / *like a rat in a ~* 궁지에 몰린 쥐처럼. **4** ((*colloq.*)) a fault or defect. 결점; 결함. ¶ *point out the holes in an argument* 의론의 결점을 지적하다. **5** ((golf)) ⓐ any of the small hollows into which the ball is to be hit. (골프에서) 홀. ⓑ a score made by so doing. (홀에 공을 넣어서 얻은) 득점.

a square peg in a round hole, a person not fit for his place. 부적임자.

be* (*put*) *in a hole, be in a position from which escape is difficult; be in great difficulty. 어찌할[피할] 수 없는 처지가 되다; 곤경[궁지]에 처해 있다.

burn a hole in someone's pocket, (of money) make someone eager to spend money. 돈이 붙어나지 않다. ¶ *His inheritance was burning a ~ in his pocket.* 그의 상속 재산은 썰물처럼 빠져나가고 있었다.

every hole and corner, every secret place. 구석(에서) 구석(까지).

make a hole in (=*use up a large part of*) *something.* …에 큰 구멍을 내다; (무엇)을 많이 써 버리다[축내다]. ¶ *Traveling made a ~ in the savings.* 여행으로 저금을 많이 축냈다.

pick holes in (=*find fault with*) *someone.* …의 탈을 잡다; …을 흠잡다. ¶ *pick holes in someone's character* 아무의 성격의 흠을 잡다.

— *vt.* (P6,7) **1** make holes in (something); dig (a tunnel, etc.). …에 구멍을 파다; 굴을 뚫다. **2** drive or put (an animal, a ball) into a hole. (동물)을 구멍으로 몰아넣다; (공)을 쳐서 홀에 넣다. ¶ *~ a rabbit* 토끼를 굴에 몰아넣다.

— *vi.* (P2) **1** make a hole or holes. 구멍을 뚫다[내다]. **2** go into a hole. (동면을 위해) 굴에 들어가다. **3** ((golf)) strike the ball into a hole. 공을 홀에 쳐 넣다. [E.]

hole out, ((golf)) hit the ball into a hole. 공을 쳐서 홀에 넣다. ¶ *~ out in one* 한번에 공을 홀에 쳐 넣다.

hole up, spend the winter in sleep; shut oneself in a place; shut up (something or someone). 동면하다; 틀어박히다; 가두다. [E.]

hole-and-cor·ner [hóuləndkɔ́ːrnər] *adj.* (transaction) underhand; shady. 비밀의; 은밀한.

:hol·i·day [hálədèi / hɔ́lə-] *n.* Ⓒ **1** any day of rest; a day of rest from work. 일을 쉬는 날; 휴(업)일(cf. *workday*). ¶ *have a ~ every Sunday* 매(每) 일요일 쉬다 / *Sunday is a ~.* 일요일은 휴일이다. **2** a day, appointed by law or custom, on which general business is stopped, usu. in celebration of some event. (법정) 공휴일; (나라의) 경축일. ¶ *a national ~* 국경일. **3** ((often *pl.*)) ((chiefly Brit.)) a period of leisure or recreation; vacation. 휴가(기(期)); 방학. ¶ *spend the holidays at home* 휴가를 집에서 보내다 / *go on a climbing ~* 휴가를 이용하여 등산을 가다 / *the summer holidays* 여름 휴가(방학). **4** a religious festival; a holy day. (종교 상의) 축제일; 성일(聖日).

make* (*a*) *holiday, rest from work. 일을[업무를] 쉬다.

make a holiday of it, take a holiday and enjoy it. 일을 쉬고 즐기다.

on holiday, having a holiday. 휴가로; 휴가 중에. ¶ *be on ~* 휴가로 쉬고 있다; 휴가 중이다 / *be away on* (*a*) *~* 휴가로 떠나 있다.

take* [*have*] *a holiday, have a day free from work. 휴가를 얻다; 휴업하다. ¶ *take a month's ~,* 1개월의 휴가를 얻다.

— *adj.* **1** fit for a holiday. 휴일다운; 휴일의; 휴가 중의. ¶ *~ dress* 나들이옷 / *a ~ task* 방학 숙제. **2** joyous; gay. 즐거운. ¶ *~ mood* 축제 기분. [*holy, day*]

hol·i·day·mak·er [hálədeimèikər / hɔ́lə-] *n.* Ⓒ a person spending a holiday at an amusement place. (휴일의) 행락객.

ho·li·ness [hóulinis] *n.* Ⓤ **1** the state of being holy. 신성함. **2** ((*His* or *Your H-*)) the title of the Pope. 성하(聖下)((로마 교황의 존칭)). [→holy]

hol·la [hálə, həlɑ́ː / hɔ́lə] *interj., n., v.* = hollo.

:Hol·land [hálənd / hɔ́l-] *n.* the Netherlands. 네덜란드. [Du.(→holt)]

Hol·land·er [háləndər / hɔ́ləndər] *n.* Ⓒ a person of Holland; a Dutchman. 네덜란드 사람.

hol·lo [hálou, həlóu / hɔ́lou] *interj., n.* a shout to attract attention; a cry of greeting or surprise. 어어이; 여어; 여보시오((인사·주의·놀람·환희의 소리)). — *vt., vi.* (P6; 1) call or shout to attract the attention of (someone). (…에게) 어어이 하고 외치다. [var. of *holla*]

hol·loa [hálou / hɔ́l-] *interj., n., v.* =hollo.

:hol·low [hálou / hɔ́l-] *n.* Ⓒ **1** a hole that is wide but no deep. 우묵 패인 데. ¶ *the ~ of the knee* 다리오금 / *the ~ of the hand* 손바닥. **2** a valley; a basin. (산)골짜기; 분지(盆地). ¶ *a wooded ~* 나무가 우거진 골짜기.

— *adj.* **1** ⓐ having an empty space inside; having nothing inside expect air. 속이 (텅) 빈(opp. solid). ¶ *a ~ tree* [*ball*] 속이 빈 나무[공]. ⓑ fallen; sunken. 우묵한; 움푹 패인; 쑥 들어간. ¶ *a ~ surface* 우묵한 표면 / *~ checks* 홀쭉한 볼 / *~ eyes* 우묵한 눈.

2 (of sound) like one made in a large empty space; deep or dull. (소리가) 공허한. ¶ *a* ~ *voice* 공허한〔힘없는〕 목소리 / *hear* ~ *sounds from cave* 굴에서 나는 공허한 소리가 들리다. 3 《*fig.*》 empty; vain; not real or sincere. 실질〔내용〕이 없는; 빈; 헛된; 거짓의. ¶ *a* ~ *promise* 허황된 약속 / *a* ~ *victory* 〔*pleasure*〕 공허〔무의미〕한 승리〔쾌락〕 / ~ *words of praise* 형식적인 칭찬의 말. 4 《*colloq.*》 complete. 완전〔철저〕한.

— *adv.* 1 in a hollow manner. 공허하게. 2 《*colloq.*》 completely; thoroughly. 완전히; 철저히. ¶ *beat someone* (*all*) ~ 아무를 여지없이 해치우다.

— *vt., vi.* (P6,7; 1) 《*out*》 make or become hollow. 속을 비우다; 구멍을〔도려, 파〕내다; 비워지다; 우묵해지다. ¶ *boats hollowed out of logs* 마상이, 통나무 배 / *The river hollows its banks.* 강이 둑을 파들어간다. [E. (→hole)]

hol·low-eyed [hálouàid / hɔ́l-] *adj.* having sunken eyes. 눈이 우묵한.

hol·low·ness [hálounis / hɔ́l-] *n.* Ⓤ 1 the state of being hollow; emptiness. 속이 빔; 우묵함; 공허. 2 lack of sincerity. 불성실; 거짓; 허위.

hol·ly [háli / hɔ́li] *n.* ⓊⒸ (*pl.* **-lies**) 《bot.》 an evergreen shrub or a small tree with hard shiny, prickly leaves and red berries. 호랑가시나무. 參考 크리스마스 장식용. [E.]

hol·ly·hock [hálihàk / hɔ́lihɔ̀k] *n.* Ⓒ 《bot.》 a very tall plant with large flowers of various colors. 접시꽃. [E.=holy mallow]

Hol·ly·wood [háliwùd / hɔ́li-] *n.* a section of Los Angeles where many movies are made. 할리우드.

holm [houm] *n.* 《bot.》 a kind of oak. 너도밤나무류(= ~ oak). [*holly*]

hol·o·caust [hálək ɔ̀:st, hóu-] *n.* Ⓒ 1 an offering all of which is burned. 통째로 구운 제물. 2 a great murder of destruction, esp. by fire. (불에 의한) 대량 학살; 대파괴. [Gk. *holos* whole, *kaiō* burn]

hol·o·graph [hálәgræ̀f, -grɑ̀:f, hóulә-] *n.* 1 a document written wholly by a person under whose name it appears. 자필(自筆)의 서류《증서·유언장·편지 따위》. 2 a type of photograph in which the entire, three dimensional image of the object is recorded. 홀로그래프. [Gk. *holos* whole, -graph]

Hol·stein [hóulstain, -sti:n] *n.* Ⓒ a kind of large black-and-white dairy cattle. 홀스타인종의 젖소. [G.]

hol·ster [hóulstәr] *n.* Ⓒ a leather pistol case, carried at the belt. (혁대에 차는) 가죽제 권총집. [Du.]

holt [hoult / hɔlt] *n.* a copse; a wooded hill. 숲; 잡목이 우거진 야산. [E.]

:ho·ly [hóuli] *adj.* (**-li·er, -li·est**) 1 belonging to or having to do with God; sacred. 신성한. ¶ ~ *ground* 성역 / *a* ~ *vessel* 성기(聖器) / ~ *orders* 성직; 목사직 / *the Holy Bible* 성서 / *the Holy Land* 성지 / *the Holy Office* 종교 재판소 / *the Holy Father* 성하(聖下)《로마 교황》 / *the Holy Week* 부활절의 전주(前週) / *a* ~ *terror* 무서운 사람; 귀찮은 자. 2 like a saint; pure in heart; pious. 성자와 같은; 청순〔지순〕한; 경건한. ¶ *a* ~ *life* 경건한 생활 / *a* ~ *man* 신에게 몸을 바친 사람; 신을 섬기는 사람《성직자·수사 따위》 / *a* ~ *love* 청순한 사랑.

— *n.* a holy place. 신성한 곳. 參考 다음 구로만 쓰임. [→whole]

the holy of holies, a) the inner shrine of the Jewish tabernacle and temple. 유태 신전(神殿)의 지성소(至聖所). b) 《*fig.*》 a very sacred place. 극히 신성한 장소.

Holy Ghost 〔**Spirit**〕 [⌐-⌐〔⌐-〕], **the** *n.* the third person of the Trinity; the spirit of God. 성령.

ho·ly·stone [hóulistòun] *n.* a piece of sandstone used for cleaning the decks of ships. (갑판을 문질러 닦는) 푸석돌. — *vt.* (P6) clean by rubbing with holystone. …을 푸석돌로 문질러 닦다.

·hom·age [*h*ámidʒ / *h*ɔ́m-] *n.* Ⓤ 1 an act of respect or honor (shown to someone or something). 존경; 경의. ¶ *pay* 〔*do*〕 ~ *to someone* 아무에게 경의를 표하다 / *in* ~ *to someone* 아무에게 경의를 표하여. 2 《hist.》 an act of declaring oneself to be the loyal servant of one's lord or king. (봉건 시대의) 충순(忠順)의 맹세; 신종(臣從)의 예(禮). ¶ *do* 〔*render*〕 ~ *to someone* 아무에게 충성을 맹세하고 신하가 되다. [L. *homo* man]

:home [houm] *n.* 1 ⒸⓊ the house where one's family lives. (사는) 집; 주거; 자택. ¶ *one's own* ~ 자기 집; 자택 / *be* (*away*) *from* ~ 집을 비우다; 출타하여 집에 없다 / *make one's* ~ *in the country* 시골에 집을 가지다 / *Every man returned to his own* ~. 모두 제 집으로 돌아갔다. 2 Ⓒ a family circle; household; Ⓤ family life. 가정; 가정 생활. ¶ *a broken* ~ 불행한〔파탄된〕 가정 / *the joys of* ~ 가정 생활의 기쁨 / *keep a happy* ~ 행복한 가정을 갖다. 3 ⒸⓊ one's native place or country. 고향; 본국; 고국. ¶ *one's old* ~ 그리운 고향 / *leave* ~ *for America* 고국을 떠나 미국으로 향하다 / *Where is your* ~ *?* 고향이 어디인가. 4 Ⓒ the place of origin. 발상지; 본고장; 본바닥. ¶ *the* ~ *of jazz* 재즈의 본고장 / *the* ~ *of constitutional government* 입헌 정치의 발상지. 5 Ⓒ the place where an animal, a plant, etc. naturally lives or grows; a habitat. (동물의) 서식지; (식물의) 자생지; 원산지. ¶ *the* ~ *of the crane* 두루미의 서식지. 6 Ⓒ an establishment for the shelter and care of the needy or infirm. 피난〔휴식, 안식〕의 장소; 수용 시설. ¶ *a* ~ *for orphans* 고아원 / *a* ~ *for the aged* 양로원. 7 Ⓒ 《sports》 the goal, esp. the home plate in baseball. 결승점;

(야구에서) 본루(本壘).
at home, **a**) in one's own house, city, or country. (출타하지 않고) 집에 있어; 사는 시(市)에; 본국〔고향〕에. ¶ *Is he (at) ~ ?* 그는 집에 있는가 / *I stay at ~ today.* 오늘은 집에 있다 參考 미국에서는 stay home이라고 함 / *leave something at ~* …을 집에 둔 채 나오다. **b**) as if in one's home; comfortable. 마음편히; 편하게. ¶ *Make yourself at ~.* 내 집처럼 여기세요; 편히 하세요. **c**) well-informed; familiar with. …에 정통〔통달〕하여; …을 잘 하여. ¶ *be at ~ in the classics* 고전에 훤하다 / *He feels at ~ in several European languages.* 그는 유럽 몇 개 국어를 마음대로 구사한다. **d**) 《usu. *negative*》《*fig.*》 prepared to receive visitors. 방문객을 맞아들일 상태에; 면회할 수 있는. ¶ *I am not at ~ to anybody today.* 오늘은 누구와도 만나고 싶지 않다.
one's ***long*** 〔***last***〕 ***home,*** one's grave; one's tomb. 무덤.
— *adj.* **1** of the family. 집의; 가정의. ¶ *~ life* 〔*cooking*〕 가정 생활〔요리〕 / *~ economics* 가정학(家政學). **2** of one's country; domestic. 본국〔고향〕의; 향리의; 국내의(opp. foreign). 語法 '향리, 고향'을 미국에서는 보통 one's home town, 영국에서는 one's native town이라고 함. 단지 home이라고 해도 됨. ¶ *~ industries* 국내 산업 / *~ affairs* 내정(內政) / *the ~ market* 국내 시장 / *~ products* 국산품 / *~ consumption* 국내 소비 / *~ waters* 근해 / *the Home Office* 《Brit.》 내무부(= 《U.S.》 the Department of the Interior). **3** at the place thought of as the base of operation. 본부의. ¶ *the ~ office* 본부. **4** effective; to the point. 효과적인; 급소를 찌르는; 가슴에 찔리는; 통렬한. ¶ *a ~ question* 급소를 찌르는 질문 / *a ~ thrust* 급소를 찌르는 일격; 뜨끔한 평언(評言).
— *adv.* **1** to or at home. 집에〔으로〕; 고국에〔으로〕; 고향에〔으로〕. ¶ *come* 〔*go*〕 *~* 집에 돌아오다〔돌아가다〕; 고향〔고국〕에 돌아오다〔으로 돌아가다〕 / *be ordered ~* 귀국 명령을 받다 / *He is ~ at last.* 드디어 그가 돌아왔다 / *take* 〔*get*〕 *the last bus ~* 막차로 귀가하다 / *on one's way ~ from school* 학교에서 집으로 돌아오는〔가는〕 길에 / *He is ~.* 그는 집에 있다. **2** to the place or point intended; as far as it will go. 겨냥한 곳〔급소〕에; 푹; 철저하게. ¶ *thrust the dagger ~* 비수를 푹 찌르다 / *drive a nail ~* 못을 깊이 처박다 / *drive an argument ~* 철저히 논하여 납득시키다 / *He drove the point ~.* 그는 요점을 철저히 이해시켰다. **3** to the heart of a matter; so as to touch the feeling strongly. 핵심에〔으로〕; 가슴에 찔릴 정도로. ¶ *This comes ~ to me.* 이 말이 내 가슴을 찌른다 / *His words struck ~.* 그의 말은 핵심을 찔렀다.
bring *oneself* ***home,*** recover a loss. 다시 일어서다; 회복하다.
bring *something* ***home to,*** **a**) make (someone) understand clearly. …을 —에게 절실히〔확실히〕 느끼게〔깨닫게〕 하다. ¶ *The scene brought ~ to him what misery really means.* 이 광경은 그에게 가난이라는 것이 실제로 무엇인가를 절실히 깨닫게 했다. **b**) prove a charge against (someone). 아무의 죄상 따위를 입증하다. ¶ *bring a fault* 〔*charge*〕 *~ to someone* 아무의 잘못을〔죄를〕 입증하다.
come home, return, as to one's home. 귀가하다.
come home to, reach (someone's) heart; become completely understood or realized by (someone). (아무)의 가슴에 찡하고 와닿다; 가슴에 찔리다; (아무)에게 완전히 이해되다.
go home, **a**) arrive at home. 집에 닿다. **b**) 《*colloq.*》 die. 죽다.
hit 〔***strike***〕 ***home,*** go directly to the mark. 급소를 찌르다; 적중하다.
see *someone* ***home,*** escort someone to someone's home. …을 집에까지 바래다 주다.
write home about (= *boast; be proud of*) *something.* …에 관해 특별히 언급하다; …을 자랑하다.
— *vi.* (P1) go to a home; fly home. 집에 돌아가다; 보금자리로 날아가다.
— *vt.* (P6) furnish (someone) with a home. …에게 집을 갖게 하다. [E.]

home·bound [hóumbáund] *adj.* going in the direction of one's home or country. 집〔본국〕으로 돌아가는〔오는〕.

home-brewed [hóumbrú:d] *adj.* prepared by mixing at home; homemade. 집에서 만든; 자가제(自家製)의. ¶ *~ beer* 집에서 빚은 맥주.

home·com·ing [hóumkʌ̀miŋ] *n.* **1** Ⓤ the act of coming to one's home. 귀가; 귀성(歸省); 귀국. **2** Ⓒ an event held at a college or university for its graduates every year. 연(年) 1회의 대학 동문회.

home·grown [hóumgróun] *adj.* (of fruits or vegetables) grown at home; domestic; grown or produced for local use. (과일·야채 따위가) 자가 재배의; 국내산의; 지방 소비용의.

home·land [hóumlæ̀nd] *n.* Ⓒ one's native land. 고국; 자국; 본국.

home·less [hóumlis] *adj.* having no home; without a home. 집 없는. ¶ *those left ~ in the war* 전쟁에서 집을 잃은 사람들.

home·like [hóumlàik] *adj.* like home; comfortable; friendly. 내 집 같은; 마음 편한; 편안한; 친근감을 주는. ¶ *a ~ meal* 가정적인 식사.

home·li·ness [hóumlinis] *n.* Ⓤ **1** the state of being simple or plain. 소박; 꾸밈이 없음. **2** the quality of being common. 평범; 통속. **3** the state of being ugly. (용모가) 추함.

***home·ly** [hóumli] *adj.* (**-li·er, -li·est**) **1** like home. 자기 집 같은; 가정적인. **2** plain; simple. 검소한; 질박한; 소박한. ¶ *~ but* *hospitable manners* 소박하지만 환대하는 예절 / *You'll find him a ~ person.* 그가 겸소한 사람임을 알게 될 게다. **3** (of language) familiar; of everyday usage. 통속의; 일상 쓰는. ¶ *if I may use a ~ phrase* 〔*expression*〕 만일 평범한 문구를〔표현을〕 쓴다면. **4** 《U.S.》 not good-looking; ugly. 인물이 없는; 아름답지 못한; 추한. ¶ *a ~ face.*

home·made [hóumméid] *adj.* made at home. 자가제의; 집에서〔손으로〕 만든. ¶ *~ bread* 집에서 만든 빵.

home·mak·er [hóummèikər] *n.* Ⓒ a housewife. 주부(主婦).

ho·me·op·a·thy, 《Brit.》 **-moe-** [hòumiápəθi / -ɔ́p-] *n.* Ⓤ 《med.》 treatment of disease by drugs (usu. in small doses) that, if given to a healthy person, would produce symptoms like those of the disease. 유사 요법(類似療法). [Gk. *homoios* like, *pathos* suffering]

·Ho·mer [hóumər] *n.* a great Greek poet who lived about the ninth century B.C. 호메로스《고대 그리스의 대(大)시인》. ¶ 《*prov.*》 *Even ~ sometimes nods.* 원숭이도 나무에서 떨어질 때가 있다. [Gk.]

hom·er [hóumər] *n.* Ⓒ **1** 《baseball》 a home run in baseball. 홈런. **2** a homing pigeon. 전서구(傳書鳩). [*home*]

Ho·mer·ic [houmérik] *adj.* of Homer; like the style of Homer. 호메로스의; 호메로스풍(風)의. ¶ *the ~ poems.* [*Homer*]

Homeric laughter [–⁄–⁄–] *n.* 홍소(哄笑); 대소.

home run [⁄⁄] *n.* 《baseball》 a hit in baseball that lets the batter run round the bases without a stop. 홈런. [*home*]

home·sick [hóumsìk] *adj.* sad because one is away from home; desiring to go home very much. 고향을 그리는; 집을 그리워하는. ¶ *be* 〔*feel, get, grow*〕 *~* 회향병에 걸리다. [→home]

home·sick·ness [hóumsìknis] *n.* Ⓤ the state of being homesick. 향수; 회향(cf. *nostalgia*).

home·spun [hóumspʌ̀n] *adj.* **1** spun at home. 집에서〔손으로〕 짠; 홈스펀의. **2** plain; simple. 수수한; 소박한; 평범한; 세련되지 않은. ¶ *~ manners* 거친 태도 / *simple, ~ characters* 단순 소박한 인물. —*n.* Ⓤ cloth made of yarn spun at home; a strong, loosely woven cloth. 홈스펀; 수직물.

home·stead [hóumstèd] *n.* Ⓒ **1** a house including the land and other buildings. 부속 건물이 딸린 농가. **2** 《U.S., Brit. colony》 land given to a settler under certain conditions by the government. (정부가 이주민에게 나누어 준) 자작 농장.

home·stretch [hóumstrétʃ] *n.* Ⓒ 《U.S.》 **1** the last part of a race before the goal. (레이스에서) 마지막 직선 코스. **2** the last part of any effort. (여행·일 따위의) 마지막 단계.

·home·ward [hóumwərd] *adj., adv.* toward home. 귀로의; 집〔본국〕을 향해. ¶ *We started ~.* 우리는 귀가〔귀국〕길에 올랐다 / *Our ~ journey was a hard one.* 우리의 귀로 여행은 고생스러운 것이었다 / *The ship is on her ~ course.* 배는 귀항중이다.

home·ward-bound [hóumwərdbáund] *adj.* bound for home; sailing back toward home. 본국행의; 귀항중의.

home·wards [hóumwərdz] *adv.* =homeward.

:home·work [hóumwə̀ːrk] *n.* Ⓤ work, esp. a school lesson, which is to be done at home. 집에서 하는 일; 숙제; 가정 학습. [*home*]

home·y [hóumi] *adj.* (**hom·i·er, hom·i·est**) 《*colloq.*》 of or like home; comfortable; plain and simple. 가정적인〔같은〕; 편안한; 소박한. ¶ *his ~ personality* 그의 소탈한 성품 / *a ~ little inn* 가정적인 자그마한 여관.

hom·i·ci·dal [hàməsáidl / hɔ̀m-] *adj.* of homicide. 살인(범)의. [↓]

hom·i·cide [háməsàid / hɔ́m-] *n.* **1** Ⓤ the act of killing someone. 살인(cf. *murder, manslaughter*). ¶ *justifiable ~* 정당 살인 / *do ~ upon someone* 아무를 살해하다. **2** Ⓒ a person who kills someone. 살인자〔범〕. [L. *homo* man, *caedo* kill]

hom·i·ly [háməli / hɔ́m-] *n.* Ⓒ (*pl.* **-lies**) **1** a talk on a part of the Bible or a religious subject; a sermon. 설교. **2** a serious, dull, moral talk or writing. (따분한) 훈계; 설교. [Gk. *homilos* crowd]

read someone a homily, address such a speech to. …에게 훈계하다; 설교하다.

hom·i·nes [hóuminìːz] *n.* pl. of **homo**[1].

hom·ing [hóumiŋ] *adj.* on the way home; returning home. 집으로 돌아가는〔오는〕; 귀환의. ¶ *Homing pigeons are trained to fly home from a distance carrying messages.* 전서구(鳩)는 먼 곳에서 서신을 가지고 보금자리로 날아오게끔 훈련된다. [→home]

hom·i·ny [háməni / hɔ́m-] *n.* Ⓤ 《U.S.》 dry Indian corn, coarsely ground or broken and boiled as food. 굵게 탄 옥수수(죽). [Amer-Ind.]

ho·mo[1] [hóumou] *n.* Ⓒ (*pl.* **hom·i·nes**) 《L.》 man. 인간《학명》.

ho·mo[2] [hóumou] *n.* (*pl.* **-mos**) 《*sl.*》 =homosexual.

ho·mo- [hóumou / hám-] *pref.* similar. '같은, 같은 종류의' 의 뜻(opp. hetero-). [Gk.]

ho·moe·op·a·thy [hòumiápəθi / -ɔ́p-] *n.* =homeopathy.

ho·mo·ge·ne·i·ty [hòumədʒəníːəti, hàm-] *n.* Ⓤ the state of being homogeneous. 동질; 동성(同性); 동종. [↓]

ho·mo·ge·ne·ous [hòumədʒíːniəs, hàm-] *adj.* of the same kind; made up of similar elements or parts. 동종(同種)의; 동질의 (opp. heterogeneous). ● **ho·mo·ge·ne·ous·ly**

[-li] *adv.* [Gk. *homos* same, *genos* kind]

ho·mog·e·nize [həmádʒənàiz / -mɔ́dʒ-] *vt.* make (something) homogeneous. …을 균질(均質)〔동질〕로 하다. ¶ *homogenized milk* 호모 생유(生乳); 균질 우유.

hom·o·graph [hámәgræ̀f, -grɑ̀:f] *n.* a word with the same spelling as another but with a different meaning and origin. 동형 이의어(同形異義語)(cf. *bow*[1], *bow*[2]). [homo-]

ho·mol·o·gous [həmáləgəs] *adj.* similar; corresponding in structure, position, composition, etc. (구조·위치·성질 따위가) 일치하는; 상응하는. [homo-]

hom·o·nym [hámənim / hɔ́m-] *n.* Ⓒ **1** a word that has the same pronunciation as another, but a different spelling and meaning. 동음 이의어(同音異義語). 參考 see와 sea, air와 heir, dear와 deer 따위. **2** a namesake. 동명 이인〔이물〕. ● **ho·mon·y·mous** [həmánəməs, hou- / -mɔ́n-] [Gk. *homos* same, *onuma* name]

hom·o·phone [hámәfòun, hóumə-] *n.* **1** a letter or character having the same sound as another. 동음 이자(同音異字). **2** =homonym. [Gk. *homos* same, *phōneō* speak]

Ho·mo sa·pi·ens [hóumou séipiənz] *n.* 《L.=man having wisdom》 a man; a human being. 사람; 인류.

ho·mo·sex·u·al [hòuməsékʃuəl] *adj., n.* Ⓒ (one) sexually attracted by persons of one's own sex. 동성애의 (사람)(cf. *lesbian*). ● **ho·mo·sex·u·al·i·ty** [-sekʃuǽləti] *n.* [homo-, *sex*]

hom·y [hóumi] *adj.* (**hom·i·er, hom·i·est**) 《*colloq.*》 like home; comfortable. 자기 집 같은; 편안한. [*home*]

Hon. Honorably; Honorary.

hon. honorably; honorary.

Hon·du·ras [hand*j*úərəs / hɔn-] *n.* a republic in Central America. 온두라스. 參考 수도는 Tegucigalpa. ● **Hon·du·ran** [-rən] *adj., n.*

hone [houn] *n.* Ⓒ a smooth stone on which to sharpen tools, esp. razors. (면도 따위를 가는) 숫돌. —*vt.* (P6) sharpen (something) on a hone. …을 숫돌에 갈다. [E.]

:hon·est [ánist / ɔ́n-] *adj.* **1** not telling lies; not deceiving or stealing; trustworthy. 정직한; 거짓 없는; 믿을 수 있는. ¶ *an ~ man* 정직한 사람 / *an ~ confession* 거짓 없는 고백 / *be ~ in bussiness affairs* 사업상의 일에 속임이 없다 / *It was ~ of you to tell me the truth.* 정직하게 진실을 말씀해 주셨군요. **2** frank; open; sincere. 솔직한; 성실한; 가식 없는. ¶ *an ~ face* 성실해 보이는 얼굴 / *an ~ opinion* 솔직한 의견 / *an ~ countryman* 소박한〔꾸밈 없는〕 시골 사람 / *to be ~ with you* 〔*about it*〕 솔직히〔있는 그대로〕 말씀드리자면. **3** gained by fair means; fair; right. 정직하게 번; 공정한; 정당한. ¶ *~ profits* 정당한 이익 / *an ~ living* 건실한 생계. **4** (of things) not mixed with any foreign substance; pure; real. 섞음질하지 않은; 순수한; 진짜의; 알속의. ¶ *~ milk* 물타지 않은 우유 / *~ wool* 순모 / *give ~ weight* 알속 무게를 달다 / *make an ~ error* 진짜 잘못을 저지르다. **5** 《in a slightly contemptuous sense》 worthy; respectable. 기특한; 칭찬할 만한. ¶ *an ~ fellow* 괜찮은 녀석. [→honor]

be honest (=*be sincere in one's relationship*) ***with*** *someone.* …와 성실히 사귀다.

earn 〔***turn***〕 ***an honest penny,*** make a profit by fair methods. 정당하게 돈을 벌다.

make an honest woman of, marry a woman after seducing her. (관계한) 여자를 정식 아내로 맞이하다.

honest in·jun [ánist índʒən] *adv.* 《also *h- I-*》 《*sl.*》 on my word of honor; honestly. 정직하게 말해서; 정말이지; 틀림없이.

:hon·est·ly [ánistli / ɔ́n-] *adv.* in an honest manner 정직〔성실〕하게; 정말이지. ¶ *Honestly, that's right.* 정말이지 그건 맞다.

:hon·es·ty [ánisti / ɔ́n-] *n.* Ⓤ the quality of being honest; truthfulness; sincerity. 정직; 성실; 솔직(함). ¶ *~ of purpose* 목적의 공명정대함 / *with ~* 정직하게 말해서 / 《*prov.*》 *Honesty is the best policy.* 정직은 최선의 방책.

:hon·ey [hʌ́ni] *n.* **1** Ⓤ a thick, sweet liquid made by bees from the drops which they collect from flowers. 꿀. ¶ *as sweet as ~* 꿀처럼 단 / *Bees store ~ in honeycombs inside hives.* 벌은 벌통 속 벌집에 꿀을 저장한다. **2** Ⓤ 《*fig.*》 anything very sweet or pleasant; sweetness. 달콤한 것; 감미로움. ¶ *Life is not all ~.* 인생은 모든 것이 즐거운 것은 아니다 / *His words were ~ to her.* 그의 말이 그녀에게 감미로웠다. **3** Ⓒ 《*colloq.*》 darling; dear; a sweetheart. 여보; 당신; 연인. 參考 흔히 아내·연인 따위를 부르는 말. ¶ *My ~!* 여보; 당신.

—*adj.* of or like honey; sweet. 꿀 같은; 감미로운.

—*v.* (**-eyed** or **-ied**) *vt.* make (something) sweet with honey. …을 달게 하다. —*vi.* talk sweetly. 교묘한 말로 이야기하다. ● **hon·ey·like** [-làik] *adj.* [E.]

hon·ey·bee [hʌ́nibì:] *n.* Ⓒ a bee that makes honey. 꿀벌.

hon·ey·comb [hʌ́nikòum] *n.* Ⓒ **1** a wax structure containing rows of six-sided cells made by bees to store honey and their eggs. (벌집의) 봉방(蜂房). **2** anything like a honeycomb. 봉방 모양의 것; 와강(窩腔). —*adj.* of or like a honeycomb. 벌집〔봉방〕의; 봉방 같은. —*vt.* (P6) fill (something) with holes. …을 벌집처럼 구멍투성이로 하다. ¶ *The wood was honeycombed by worms.* 나무는 벌레가 먹어 숭숭 구멍이 나 있었다.

hon·ey·dew [hʌ́nidjù:] *n.* **1** Ⓤ a sweet substance formed on the leaves and stems of certain plants in hot weather. 감로(甘露)《식물의 잎·줄기에서 나오는 단물》. **2** Ⓒ a kind of melon with a sweet taste. 감로멜론(=honeydew melon).

hon·eyed [hʌ́nid] *adj.* **1** made sweet with honey; filled or covered with honey. 꿀로 달게 한; 꿀로 뒤덮은〔뒤바른〕; 꿀투성이의. **2** sweet as honey. 꿀처럼 단; 달콤한. ¶ ~ *words* 달콤한 말; 감언.

hon·ey·moon [hʌ́nimùːn] *n.* Ⓒ **1** a holiday spent together by a newly-married couple. 밀월. **2** the first month of marriage. 신혼 첫달. **3** a wedding trip. 신혼〔밀월〕 여행. ¶ *They went on* (*their*) ~. 그들은 신혼 여행을 떠났다. —*vi.* (P1) 《*in, at*》 have a honeymoon. 신혼 여행을 하다. ¶ ~ *in Spain* 스페인에서 신혼 여행을 하다.

hon·ey·suck·le [hʌ́nisʌ̀kl] *n.* Ⓒ 《bot.》 a climbing plant with sweet-smelling white, yellow, or red flowers shaped like trumpets. 인동덩굴.

hong [haŋ / hɔŋ] *n.* a factory; a foreign trading establishment. (중국의) 상관(商館); 외국 상사; 양행(洋行). [Chin.]

Hong Kong, Hong·kong [háŋkáŋ / hɔ́ŋkɔ́ŋ] *n.* a British colony in southeast China (it will be given back to the China in 1997.) 홍콩.

hon·ied [hʌ́nid] *adj.* =honeyed.

honk [hɔːŋk, haŋk / hɔŋk] *n.* Ⓒ **1** the cry of a wild goose. 거위의 울음 소리. **2** any sound like this, as of an automobile horn. (자동차 따위의) 경적 소리. —*vi.* (P1) make such a sound. 거위가 울다; 경적을 울리다. ¶ *Geese* ~. 거위들이 운다. [Imit.]

Hon·o·lu·lu [hànəlúːluː / hɔ̀n-] *n.* the capital of Hawaii on Oahu. 호놀룰루.

:hon·or, 《Brit.》 **-our** [ánər / ɔ́n-] *n.* **1** ⓊⒸ glory; the source of pride and joy. 명예; 광영; 영광. ¶ *the guest of* ~ 주빈(主賓) / *I feel it a great* ~ *to be invited to this party.* 이 파티에 초대되어 큰 영광으로 생각합니다 / *I have the* ~ *to inform you that….* 삼가 …을 알려드립니다. **2** Ⓤ credit; fame; good reputation. 체면; 면목; 신용; 명성; 명예. ¶ *business* ~ 사업상의 신용 / *a matter of* ~ 면목〔체면〕에 관한 문제 / *save* 〔*stain*〕 *one's* ~ 체면을 유지하다〔더럽히다〕 / *die with* ~ *on the battlefield* 명예의 전사를 하다 / *pledge one's* ~ 명예를 걸고 맹세하다 / *Honor is satisfied.* (결투를 하든가 사죄를 받든가 하여) 면목이 섰다. **3** Ⓤ a keen sense of what is right. 도의심; 명예심. ¶ *a man of* ~ 신의를 중히 여기는 사람 / *sell one's* ~ 지조를 팔다 / *conduct oneself with* ~ 훌륭히 행동하다. **4** ⓊⒸ a cause of respect; a thing to which respect should be paid. 존경; 경의; 예(禮). ¶ *a memorial in* ~ *of the dead* 전사자를 위한 위령비(碑) / *be held in* ~ 존경받다 / *have* 〔*hold*〕 *someone in* ~ 아무를 존경하다 / *pay* 〔*give, show*〕 ~ *to* … 에(게) 경의를 표하다 / *pay* 〔*give*〕 ~ *to the national flag* 국기에 대해 경례하다. **5** Ⓤ a high rank or position; 《*H-*》 a title of respect given to certain officials, as judges, mayors, etc., with a possessive pronoun before. 높은 지위; 고위; 각하《판사·시장 등에 대한 경칭; 앞에 Your, His를 붙임》. ¶ *His Honor the Mayor.* 시장 각하. **6** Ⓒ ⓐ 《usu. *pl.*》 a badge; a sign of respect given to a person. 영예의 표창; 명예장(章); 훈장; 서훈. ¶ *a roll of honors* 전사자 방명록 / *birthday honors* 《Brit.》 국왕 탄생일에 행하는 서훈. ⓑ 《*pl.*》 ceremonies of respect. 의식. ¶ *funeral honors* 장례식 / *military honors* 군장(軍葬)의 예 / *render the last honors* 장례식을 행하다〔에 참석하다〕. **7** 《*pl.*》 《univ.》 special rank given to students who graduate or pass examinations with high marks. (대학 따위의) 우등. ¶ *graduate with honors* 우등으로 졸업하다 / *take highest honors in one's class* 반에서 1등을 하다. **8** Ⓒ a person or thing that gives honor to another. 명예가 되는 사람〔것〕; 자랑(거리). ¶ *He is an* ~ *to his family.* 그는 가문의 명예이다.

a code* 〔*law*〕 *of honor, a standard for our usual behavior, manners, etc. 일상 행동·예법 따위의 규범《특히 결투·사교상의》.

a debt of honor, a debt which an honorable person feels he must pay, though it is not held to be a debt by the law. (내기·노름 따위의) 신용빚.

a maid of honor, a maid attending on a great person, esp. a queen or princess. (여왕·왕비 등의) 시녀.

an affair of honor, a duel. 결투.

a point of honor, a question concerning honor; something that affects one's honor. 명예에 관한 일; 체면에 관계되는 일.

be bound in honor to do =***be on one's honor to do,*** be under moral obligation to do. 명예를 걸고 …하지 않을 수 없다. ¶ *I am bound in* ~ *to refuse.* 체면상 거절하지 않을 수 없다.

do someone honor =***do honor to someone*** **a**) show great respect for someone. …을 존경하다; …에게 경의를 표하다. **b**) bring or cause honor to someone. …의 명예가 되다.

***do the honors* (*of*),** act as host or hostess (of). (…의) 주인 역할〔노릇〕을 하다.

for the honor of =***for honor* (*of*),** 《comm.》 in order to save one's credit. …의 신용상.

give someone one's word of honor, state the truth of, or promise to carry out, something on forfeit of one's honor. 명예를 걸고 …에게 말〔약속〕하다.

honor bright, 《*colloq.*》 upon my honor. 맹세코; 확실히.

in honor of someone, showing respect to someone; for the sake of honoring someone; in order to keep the good memory of someone. …에게 경의를 표하여; …을 축하하여; …기념으로.

on 〔***upon***〕 *one's* (***word of***) ***honor,*** risking one's good name; sincerely. 맹세코; 명예를 걸고.

put *someone* ***on his honor,*** put someone under, or trust him on a moral obligation. …에게 명예를 걸고 맹세케 하다.

the honors of war, 《mil.》 privileges granted to a defeated enemy. 항복한 적에게 베푸는 특전.

— *vt.* **1** (P6,13) 《*with*》 give an honor to (someone). …에게 명예를〔영광을〕 주다. ¶ ~ *someone with a visit* 아무에게 방문의 영광을 베풀다 / ~ *someone with the degree* 아무에게 학위를 주다 / *Will you ~ me with a visit?* 왕림의 영광을 베푸시지 않겠습니까. **2** (P6,7) respect highly; worship. …을 크게 존경하다. ¶ ~ *one's parents* 부모를 공경하다. **3** (P6) 《comm.》 accept and pay (a bill, note, etc.) when due. (어음)을 인수해서 (기일에) 지급하다. [L. *honor*]

:hon·or·a·ble, 《Brit.》 **-our-** [ánərəbl/ɔ́n-] *adj.* **1** worthy of honor; to be respected; upright; noble. 존경할 만한; 훌륭한; 올바른; 고결한. ¶ *an ~ man* 존경할 만한 사람 / ~ *conduct* 〔*deeds*〕 훌륭한 행동〔행위〕 / *long years of ~ service* 다년간의 성실한 근무. **2** ⓐ bringing honor to the one who has it. 명예를 가져오는; 명예로운. ¶ ~ *wounds* 명예의 부상 / *an ~ duty* 영직(榮職). ⓑ based on honor. 명예에 입각한; 명예를 손상시키지 않는. ¶ *conclude an ~ peace* 명예로운 평화조약을 맺다. **3** having a title, rank or position of honor. 명예로운 지위·직함을 가진; 현직(顯職)의. **4** 《*H-*, usu. *the H-*》 a title of respect before a name. 각하《사람 이름 앞에 붙이는 경칭》. 參考 Hon. 으로 생략함. ¶ *the Honorable Mr. Justice King* 킹판사 각하. ● **hon·or·a·ble·ness** [-nis] *n.*

hon·or·a·bly, 《Brit.》 **-our-** [ánərəbli/ɔ́n-] *adv.* honestly; as to be worthy of respect. 훌륭히; 부끄럽지 않게; 존경받을 수 있게.

hon·o·rar·i·a [ɑ̀nərɛ́əriə/ɔ̀nə-] *n.* pl. of **honorarium.**

hon·o·rar·i·um [ɑ̀nərɛ́əriəm/ɔ̀nə-] *n.* (*pl.* **-rar·i·ums** or **-rar·i·a**) a fee for professional services on which no fixed price is set. (습관상·예의상 금액을 정하지 않은) 사례; 보수금. [↓]

hon·or·a·ry [ánərèri/ɔ́nərəri] *adj.* **1** given or done as a mark of respect. 명예(상)의. ¶ *an ~ degree* 명예 학위 / *an ~ office* 명예직. **2** having a title or position without receiving pay and often without responsibility. (보수·실권이 없는) 명예직의. ¶ *an ~ consul* 〔*president*〕 명예 영사〔회장〕 / *an ~ member of a club* 클럽의 명예 회원. [*honor*]

hon·or·if·ic [ɑ̀nərífik/ɔ̀n-] *adj.* **1** doing or giving honor. 명예를 주는〔표시하는〕. **2** showing respect. 존경을 나타내는. — *n.* an honorific word or phrase. 경어; 높임말; 경칭. [*honor*]

hooch [hu:tʃ] *n.* 《U.S. *colloq.*》 crude alcoholic liquor. 알코올 음료; 술의 원액; 밀주. [Alaskan]

***hood** [hud] *n.* Ⓒ **1** a soft covering for the head, sometimes part of a cloak. 두건; (외투의) 후드. **2** ⓐ anything like a hood in shape or use. 두건〔후드〕 모양의 것. ⓑ 《U.S.》 a covering over an automobile engine. (자동차의) 엔진 덮개; 보닛. **3** a fold of cloth, banded with distinguishing colors to show what degrees are held, that hangs down over the black gown worn by graduates of universities. (학위의 표상으로서) 대학 졸업식 가운의 등 뒤에 드리운 천《대학에 따라 그 색깔이 각각 다름》.

— *vt.* (P6) **1** cover (something) with a hood. …을 두건으로〔후드로〕 덮어 가리다. **2** 《*fig.*》 cover; veil. …을 가리다; 감추다. ● **hood·less** [´-lis] *adj.* **hood·like** [´-làik] *adj.* [E.]

-hood [-hud] *suf.* **1** the condition, time, or quality of being. '상태·기간·시대·성질'을 나타냄. ¶ *babyhood* 유아기 / *childhood* 유년〔어린〕 시절. **2** the whole group or class of. '집단·계급·신분'을 나타냄. ¶ *priesthood* 성직 / *brotherhood* 형제지간. [E.]

hood·ed [húdid] *adj.* **1** wearing a hood. 두건을〔후드를〕 쓴. **2** shaped like a hood. 두건(후드) 모양의. [*hood*]

hood·lum [hú:dləm, húd-] *n.* Ⓒ 《U.S. *colloq.*》 a rough, lawless fellow; a rough young person on the street. 폭력배의 일원; 불량자; 깡패; 건달. [var. of *Muldoon*]

hoo·doo [hú:du:] *n.* 《U.S *colloq.*》 **1** Ⓤ Negro magic. (북아메리카 인디언·흑인의) 미신; 주술(呪術). **2** Ⓒ a person or thing that brings bad luck. 불길한〔재수 없는〕 사람〔것〕. **3** Ⓤ bad luck. 불길; 불운. — *vt.* (P6) 《*colloq.*》 bring bad luck to (someone); make unhappy. …에게 불운을 가져오다; 불행하게 하다. [*voodoo*]

hood·wink [húdwìŋk] *vt.* (P6,13) **1** mislead (someone) by a trick; deceive. …을 속이다; …의 눈을 현혹(眩惑)시키다. **2** cover the eyes of (a horse, etc.). …의 눈을 가리다. [→hood]

***hoof** [hu:f, huf] *n.* Ⓒ (*pl.* **hoofs** or *rarely* **hooves**) **1** a hard covering for the feet of a horse, cattle, sheep, etc. (마소 따위의) 발굽. **2** 《*sl.*》 a man's foot. 인간의 발.

beat 〔***pad***〕 ***the hoof,*** 《*colloq.*》 walk. 걷다.

on the hoof, alive. (가축이) 도살되지 않고; 살아있는.

under the hoof, trodden down. …에 짓밟혀; 유린되어.

— *vi.* (P1,3) 《*colloq.*》 walk; dance. 걷다; 춤추다.

— *vt.* (P6,13) walk; kick (something) with the hoofs. 걷다; …을 발굽으로 차다. ¶ ~ *it* 걷다.

● **hoof·er** [´-ər] *n.* **hoof·less** [´-lis] *adj.* **hoof·like** [´-làik] *adj.* [E.]

hoof·beat [húːfbìːt] *n.* a sound made by animals' hooves. 발굽 소리.

hoofed [huːft] *adj.* having hoofs. 발굽이 있는. ¶ ~ *animals* 유제(有蹄) 동물.

:**hook** [huk] *n.* Ⓒ **1** a curved or bent piece of stiff material serving to catch, hold, or hang something. 갈(쇠)고리; 걸쇠; 훅. ¶ *a ~ and eye* (옷의) 훅 단추 / *a clothes ~* 옷걸이. **2** a trap; a curved piece of wire for catching fish. 올가미; 낚시 ¶ *a fish ~* 낚시 / *bait a ~* 낚시에 미끼를 달다. **3** a tool shaped like a hook, esp. a sickle. 갈고리 모양의 도구; 특히 낫. **4** ⓐ《boxing》a short and swinging blow. (권투에서) 훅; 휘어치기. ⓑ《cricket, golf》a strike to the left. 좌곡구(左曲球). **5** a sharp curve or bend, as in a road or river. (길·강 따위의) 굴곡부. **6** a headland. 곶《갈고리 모양의》.

above one's hook, beyond one's power. (자신의) 능력을 넘어; 이해할 수 없는.

be 〔***get***〕 ***off the hook,*** **a**) be 〔get〕 out of one's difficulties. 곤란〔곤경, 궁지〕에서 벗어나다〔벗어나 있다〕. **b**) be 〔get〕 free of obligation. 의무〔책임〕에서 해방되다.

by hook or by crook, in one way or another; by any means possible; somehow. 어떻게든; 기어코.

drop 〔***pop, slip***〕 ***off the hooks,*** 《Brit. *colloq.*》 die. 죽다; 뒈지다.

get the hook, 《U.S. *sl.*》 be discharged or dismissed. 목이 잘리다; 해고되다.

go off the hooks, become mad; behave wildly; die. 미치다; 사납게 날뛰다; 죽다.

go on the hook, neglect one's duty. (일·공부에) 게으름을 피우다; 책임을〔의무를〕 태만히 하다.

hook, line, and sinker, 《*colloq.*》 completely. 완전히; 감쪽같이. ¶ *swallow something ~, line, and sinker* 감쪽같이 속다〔당하다〕.

on one's own hook, 《*colloq.*》 by oneself; without the help or advice of others. 혼자 힘으로; 자기 책임으로.

on the hook, be in a position of difficulty, esp. when it is difficult to find a way out. 곤란한 처지에 놓여; 궁지에 몰려; 괴로운 입장에 빠져. ¶ *put someone on the ~* 아무를 궁지에 빠뜨리다.

take 〔***sling***〕 ***one's hook,*** 《*sl.*》 go away. 달아나다; 내빼다.

— *vt.* **1** (P6,7) fasten or attach (something) with a hook. 갈고리로 …을 걸다〔낚아채다, 걸치다〕; 걸쇠〔쇠고리〕로 잠그다; 훅으로 채우다. ¶ ~ *the gate* 문의 쇠고리를 채우다 / ~ *the logs out of the channel* 갈고리로 통나무를 수로에서 끌어내다 / *Will you ~ my dress for me ?* 옷의 훅 좀 채워주겠느냐. **2** (P6) trick. (책략을 써서) 올가미에 걸려들게 하다. ¶ *She hooked herself a husband.* 남자를 낚아서 남편을 삼았다. **3** (P6) make or bend (something) in the shape of a hook. …을 갈고리 모양으로 구부리다. ¶ ~ *one's finger* 손가락을 구부리다. **4** (P6,7) catch (fish, animals, etc.) on or with a hook. (물고기 따위)를 낚시로 잡다. ¶ ~ *a fish* 물고기를 낚다. **5** (P6) 《*sl.*》 steal. 후무리다; 훔치다. **6** (P6) attack with the horns. (소 따위가) 뿔로 받다. **7** (P13) 《boxing》 strike with the arm bent. 훅을 치다; 휘어치기를 넣다. — *vi.* **1** (P1,3) curve like a hook. 갈고리같이 구부러지다. ¶ *This road hooks to the left.* 이 길은 왼쪽으로 구부러져 있다. **2** (P1,2A) be fastened with a hook. 갈고리가 걸리다; 훅이 잠기다〔채워지다〕. ¶ *The door hooks on the inside.* 이 문은 안으로 잠긴다. [E.]

hook one's fish, 《*fig.*》 catch a person for one's own purposes. 노렸던 사람을 용케 낚다; 아무를 잘 설득하다.

hook it, 《*sl.*》 run away. 달아나다; 내빼다.

hook up, **a**) connect (something) with a hook or hooks. 훅으로 잠그다〔잠기다〕. **b**) arrange and connect the parts of (a radio, etc.). (라디오 따위의) 부품을 연결〔조립〕하다.

hook·a, -ah [húkə] *n.* Ⓒ a tobacco-pipe in which the smoke is drawn through water. (물을 통하여 담배를 빠는) 수연통(水煙筒). [Arab.]

hooked [hukt] *adj.* **1** shaped or curved like a hook. 갈고리 모양의; 갈고리처럼 구부러진. ¶ *a ~ nose* 매부리코. **2** supplied with hooks. 갈고리가〔훅이〕 있는. ¶ *a ~ dress* 훅이 달린 옷. **3** made with a hook. 갈고리로 만든. [→hook]

hooked rug [⌐ ⌐] *n.* 《U.S.》 rug made by pulling yarn or strips of cloth through a piece of canvas, burlap, etc. 캔버스나 삼베 따위로 만든 양탄자.

hook-nosed [húknòuzd] *adj.* having a hook-shaped nose. 매부리코의.

hook·up [húkʌ̀p] *n.* Ⓒ 《orig. U.S.》 **1** a diagram of radio apparatus, showing the connection of the different elements. 접속도(圖). **2** a connection of radio and television stations to send out the same program. (TV·라디오 방송국 간의) 중계; 네트워크. ¶ *talk on a national* 〔*nationwide*〕 *TV ~* 전국 TV중계로 이야기하다. **3** a connection between two governments, parties, etc. 제휴; 동맹. ¶ *a ~ between nations* 양국간의 동맹.

hook·worm [húkwə̀ːrm] *n.* Ⓒ a small worm that gets into the bowels and causes a disease. 십이지장충. ¶ ~ *disease* 십이지장충병.

hoo·li·gan [húːligən] *n.* Ⓒ 《Brit. *sl.*》 a rough, lawless fellow; a rough young person. 난폭자; 불량자; 깡패. ¶ *a ~ gang* 폭력단. [Person]

hoo·li·gan·ism [húːligənìzəm] *n.* Ⓤ rough, lawless acts. (깡패의) 난폭한 짓; 행패.

hoop[1] [huːp, hup] *n.* Ⓒ **1** a ring to hold the strips of wood forming the sides of a tubs, barrel or the like. (통 따위의) 테. **2** a large circle to be rolled along the ground

by a child. (어린이가) 굴리는 굴렁쇠. **3** 《*pl.*》 a wire ring used to hold out a woman's skirt. (여자 스커트의) 버팀테. **4** an iron arch in the game of croquet. (croquet의) 아치형 주문(柱門). **5** anything shaped like a hoop. 고리〔테〕 모양의 것.
go through the hoop(s), undergo a trial. 시련을 겪다.
— *vt.* (P6) fasten (something) with hoops; 《*fig.*》 encircle. …에 테를 두르다; 둘러싸다〔치다〕.
●**hoop·like** [⌐làik] *adj.* [E.]

hoop[2] [huːp, hup] *vi.* =whoop.

hoop·er [húːpər] *n.* Ⓒ a person who makes hoops or puts them on tubs, barrels, etc. (통에) 테를 두르는 사람; 통메장이. [→hoop[1]]

hoop·ing cough [húːpiŋ kɔːf, -kɑf / -kɔf] *n.* =whooping-cough.

hoo·poe [húːpuː] *n.* 《bird.》 a bright-colored bird with a fan-like crest. 후투티《유럽산의 새》. [L. *upuna*]

hoo·ray [huréi, huː-] *interj., n., v.* =hurrah.

hoot [huːt] *n.* Ⓒ **1** the cry of an owl. 올빼미의 울음 소리. **2** a shout showing an unfavorable feeling. 야유 (소리); 우우. ¶ *a ~ of rage* 성이 나서 지르는 매도 (소리). **3** a very small bit. (아주) 조금; 약간. ¶ *be not worth a ~* 한 푼의 가치도 없다 / *I don't give a ~.* 조금도 상관 없다 / *I can't sleep a ~.* 조금도 잘 수 없다.
— *vi.* **1** (P1,3) make the sound of an owl. (올빼미가) 울다. **2** 《*at*》 shout to show an unfavorable feeling or scorn. 야유하다; 매도하여 소리치다. ¶ *The audience hooted and jeered at the speaker.* 청중들은 연사에게 우우하며 야유를 터뜨렸다. — *vt.* (P6,7) scorn (someone) by hooting ; drive (someone) away by hooting. …을 조소〔야유〕하다; …을 우우 야유하여 쫓아버리다. [? Imit.]
hoot down, make (someone) silent by hooting. …을 야유하여 침묵시키다.
hoot off (away, out), drive (someone) away by hooting. …을 야유하여 물러나게 하다. ¶ *The audience hooted the actor off the stage.* 관중은 우우 야유를 퍼부어 배우를 무대에서 퇴장시켰다.

hoot·er [húːtər] *n.* Ⓒ **1** an owl. 올빼미. **2** a person who hoots. 야유하는 사람. **3** a siren; a horn. 사이렌; 경적; 기적(汽笛).

Hoo·ver Dam [húːvər dǽm] *n.* a dam on the Colorado River between Arizona and Colorado in the United States. 후버댐 《미국 Colorado강의 댐》.

hooves [huːvz, huvz] *n.* pl. of **hoof.**

:hop[1] [hɑp / hɔp] *v.* (**hopped, hop·ping**) *vi.* (P1,2A,3) move in short jumps with all the feet; jump about on one foot. (두 발로) 깡충 뛰다; (한 발로) 뛰어 다니다. ¶ *Frogs and birds ~.* 개구리와 새는 깡충깡충 뛴다 / *How far can you ~ on your right foot?* 오른발로 얼마나 멀리 뛸 수 있나 / *He came hopping along on one leg.* 그는 한쪽 발로 깡충깡충 뛰면서 왔다. — *vt.* (P6) **1** jump over (a fence, etc.); cross with a hop. (울타리 따위)를 껑충 뛰어넘다; 훌쩍 건너뛰다. ¶ *~ a ditch* 도랑을 건너뛰다. **2** 《*colloq.*》 jump on to. …에 뛰어 올라타다.
hop off, 《*colloq.*》 **a**) (of an airplane) leave the ground; take off. (비행기 따위가) 이륙하다. **b**) depart hastily. 급히 떠나다〔가버리다〕.
— *n.* Ⓒ **1** the act of hopping; a short jump. 깡충깡충 뜀; 앙감질; 토끼뜀. **2** 《*colloq.*》 a dance or dancing party. 댄스(파티). **3** 《*colloq.*》 a flight or short trip in an airplane. (비행기의) 한 항정(航程); 짧은 비행기 여행. [E.]
catch someone on the hop, catch someone at the moment of departure; meet someone when he is unprepared. …를 막 떠나려는 순간에 붙잡다; 불시에 만나다.

hop[2] [hɑp / hɔp] *n.* Ⓒ **1** 《bot.》 a vine with green flowers shaped like cones. 홉. **2** 《*pl.*》 the dried flowers of this vine, used to flavor beer, ale, etc. 건조시킨 홉의 열매〔꽃〕《맥주 따위의 향료로 쓰임》. — *v.* (**hopped, hop·ping**) *vi.* (P1) pick hops. 홉을 따다. — *vt.* (P6) flavor (beer, etc.) with hops. (맥주 따위)에 홉으로 맛을 들이다. [Du.]

:hope [houp] *n.* **1** ⓊⒸ a desire that what one wishes may be gained; expectation; wish. 희망; 기대 (opp. despair). ¶ *give up ~* 희망을 버리다; 절망하다 / *lose all ~* 모든 희망을 잃다 / *set great hopes on a new plan* 새로운 계획에 큰 기대를 걸다 / *cherish high hopes of ...* …의 높은 희망을 가지다〔품다〕 / *I have high hopes that he will succeed.* 그가 성공하는 것을 크게 기대하고 있다 / *There is no ~ of success.* 성공할 가망이 없다 / *He is past ~.* 그는 가망이 없다. **2** Ⓒ a person or thing that gives hope to someone. 희망을 주는 사람〔것, 일〕. ¶ *He is the ~ of our school.* 그는 우리 학교의 희망이다〔호프다〕 / *Success in business was his constant ~.* 사업의 성공이 그의 끊임없는 희망사였다.
be in great hopes that, desire greatly that.... …을 크게 기대하고 있다.
be past (beyond) all hope, be in a hopelessly bad situation. 희망〔가망〕이 전연 없다.
in hopes of = in the hope that (of), in expectation or anticipation of; having hope of. …을 희망〔기대〕하고. ¶ *I live in hopes of seeing him again.* 그를 다시 볼 수 있으리란 기대에 살고 있다 / *I am sending you this book in the ~ that it may be of use to you.* 자네에게 도움이 되기를 기대하면서 이 책을 보내네.
— *vt.* (P6,8,11) desire with a feeling that one's desire may be gained; wish; want. …을 희망〔기대〕하다; 바라다; 생각하다. ¶ *I ~ to see you soon.* 곧 만나기를 바란다 / *I ~ to be able to come.* 나는 갈 수 있기를 바라고 있

다 / *I* ~ *that we shall meet here again.* 여기서 다시 만나기를 희망한다 / *I do* ~ (*that*) *you will soon get well again.* 곧 다시 회복되기를 바랍니다 / *I* ~ *you may succeed.* 당신이 성공하시기를 바랍니다. — *vi.* (P1,3) 《*for*》 have desire or expectation. 바라다; 대망〔기대〕하다. ¶ *I* ~ *for success.* 성공을 기대하고 있다 / *I* ~ *so.* 그러기를 바란다 / *There is nothing to be hoped for.* 아무것도 바랄 것이 없다. [E.]

hope against hope, have hope where there seems to be no ground for hope. 요행을 바라다; 만일을 기대하다.

hope for the best, hope that everything will turn out as well as possible. 낙관하다; 최후까지 희망을 잃지 않다.

hope chest [ˊ ˋ] *n.* 《U.S.》 a box used by a young woman to store things that will be useful after she marries. 처녀의 혼수함(婚需函).

***hope·ful** [hóupfəl] *adj.* (opp. hopeless) **1** 《*of, about*》 feeling or showing hope; full of expectation. 희망하는; 희망을 가진; 희망을〔기대를〕 나타내는; 희망〔기대〕에 찬. ¶ *He is* ~ *that he will succeed.* 그는 성공할 것을 기대하고 있다. **2** causing hope; promising. 희망을 가질 수 있는; 유망한; 가망 있는. ¶ ~ *news* 희망적인 소식 / *a* ~ *pupil* 유망한 학생 / *The weather is* ~. 날씨는 갤 것 같다.

be hopeful about 〔***of***〕, hope; expect. …을 기대하다. ¶ *I am* 〔*feel*〕 ~ *about a settlement.* 해결에 기대를 가지고 있다.

— *n.* Ⓒ a promising young person; a person with a bright future. 전도 유망한 젊은이〔사람〕. ¶ *a young* ~ 젊고 앞길이 유망한 청년. [*hope*]

hope·ful·ly [hóupfəli] *adv.* **1** with hope; in a hopeful manner. 희망을 가지고; 기대를 걸고; 유망하게. **2** it is to be hoped that. 만약 일이 잘되면; …하다는 것이 바람직하다. ¶ *Hopefully he will win.* 잘하면 그가 이길 게다.

hope·ful·ness [hóupfəlnis] *n.* Ⓤ the state of being hopeful; hope. 유망함.

·hope·less [hóuplis] *adj.* (opp. hopeful) **1** 《*of*》 (of a person) without hope; feeling no hope. 희망을 잃은; 절망하고 있는. ¶ ~ *grief* 절망의 비탄 / *I am* ~ *of ever meeting her.* 그녀를 만난다는 따위는 도저히 생각도 할 수 없다. **2** giving no hope; incurable. 가망 없는; 절망적인. ¶ *a* ~ *situation* 절망적인 상황 / *a* ~ *case of cancer* 회복할 가망이 없는 암환자.

be hopeless of (=*do not expect; give up all hope or expectation of*) *something.* …의 희망을 잃고 있다; 절망적이다.

hope·less·ly [hóuplisli] *adv.* without hope. 절망적으로; 희망 없이.

hop garden [ˊ ˋ-] *n.* a field of hops. 홉 재배 농원. [*hop*[2]]

hop·per[1] [hápər / hɔ́p-] *n.* Ⓒ **1** a person or thing that hops. 한 발〔앙감질〕로 뛰는 사람〔것〕. **2** an insect that hops, such as a grasshopper. 톡톡 튀는 벌레《메뚜기 따위》. **3** a box with a wide opening in the top and a small hole in the bottom through which something is carried into a machine. (제분기 따위의) 깔때기 모양의 아가리를 가진 통. [*hop*[1]]

hop·per[2] [hápər / hɔ́p-] *n.* a hop-picker. 홉 채취자〔기〕. [*hop*[2]]

hop·ping [hápiŋ / hɔ́p-] *adj.* moving in short leaps; jumping about; limping. 깡충깡충 뛰는; 바쁘게 움직이는; 절뚝거리는. [*hop*[1]]

hop·scotch [hápskàtʃ / hɔ́pskɔ̀tʃ] *n.* Ⓤ a children's game in which the players hop about in a design drawn on the ground. 오랏말놀이. [*hop*[1]]

Hor. Horace.

Hor·ace [hɔ́:ris / hɔ́r-] *n.* **1** a man's name. 남자 이름. **2** (65-8 B.C.) a Roman lyric poet. 호라티우스《로마의 서정 시인》.

horde [hɔ:rd] *n.* Ⓒ **1** a crowd. 무리; 떼; 대군(大群); 군중. ¶ *a* ~ *of wolves* 이리 떼 / *a* ~ *of insects* 곤충의 대군. **2** a wandering group of people 유목민의 집단. ¶ *a gypsy* ~ 집시의 집단. — *vi.* (P1,3) gather in a horde. 떼지어 모이다; 군집하다. [Turk.=camp]

hore·hound [hɔ́:rhàund] *n.* 《bot.》 a herb with bitter juice. 쓴 박하; 그 즙《기침약》. [E.=hoary herb]

·ho·ri·zon [həráizən] *n.* Ⓒ **1** the line where the earth and sky seem to meet. 지평선; 수평선. ¶ *on the* ~ 지〔수〕평선 위에〔로〕 / *The sun has sunk below the* ~. 해는 지평선 아래로 졌다. **2** 《*fig.*》 the limit of one's thinking, experience, etc. (사고·지식·경험 따위의) 범위; 한계; 시야. ¶ *expand one's* ~ 시야를 넓히다 / *widen the intellectual* ~ 지식의 범위를 넓히다 / *beyond the* ~ *of one's age* 나이의 한계를 넘어 / *Travel broadens one's horizons.* 여행은 사람의 시야를 넓혀 준다. [Gk. *horos* boundary]

·hor·i·zon·tal [hɔ̀:rəzántl / hɔ̀rəzɔ́n-] *adj.* (opp. vertical) **1** running straight and parallel to the horizon. 지평의; 수평의. ¶ *a* ~ *line* 옆으로 그은 선; 수평선 / *a* ~ *plane* 수평면 / *a* ~ *bar* 평행봉; 철봉. **2** flat; level. 평면의; 평평한. — *n.* Ⓒ a horizontal thing or position; a horizontal line. 수평의 것〔위치〕; 수평〔지평〕선.

hor·i·zon·tal·ly [hɔ̀:rəzántli / hɔ̀rəzɔ́n-] *adv.* in a horizontal manner or direction. 수평으로; 가로; 옆으로.

hor·mone [hɔ́:rmoun] *n.* Ⓒ 《physiol.》 a chemical material formed in certain parts of the body and carried by the blood, influencing growth, the action of organs, etc. 호르몬. [Gk. *hormaō* impel]

:horn [hɔ:rn] *n.* Ⓒ **1** ⓐ a hard bone-like material on the heads of cattle, goats, sheep, etc. 뿔. ¶ *a bull with big horns* 큰 뿔

을 가진 황소. ⓑ one of a pair of branched growths on the head of deer, which fall and grow again each year. 사슴뿔. **2** the long, pointed, but not hard objects on the heads of some animals. 촉각(觸角); 더듬이. ¶ *a snail's* ~ 달팽이의 촉각 / *an insect's horns* 곤충의 더듬이. **3** a thing or container made of horn. 뿔로 만든 것; 각제(角製)의 기구. ¶ *a drinking* ~ 뿔로 된 술잔 / *knife with a handle of* ~ 뿔로 된 손잡이가 있는 칼. **4** a musical instrument played by blowing. 호른; 각적(角笛). **5** an instrument that makes a loud sound as a warning signal. 경적. ¶ *blow an automobile* ~ 자동차의 경적을 울리다 / *a fog* ~ 안개 경적; 무적(霧笛) / *Sound the* ~ *to warn that man over there.* 저기 저 사람에게 조심하도록 경적을 울려라. **6** anything shaped like a horn, as a new moon. 뿔 모양의 것 《특히, 끝이 뾰족한 초승달 모양의》. **7** 《as *adj.*》 made of horn. 뿔로 만든〔된〕. ¶ *a* ~ *handle* 뿔로 된 손잡이.

a horn of plenty, a horn-shaped container filled with fruit, vegetables, flower, etc. as a sign of plenty, wealth, etc. 풍요의 뿔 《바라는 대로 음식·과일·꽃 등이 나온다는》.

blow one's own horn, praise oneself; boast. 제자랑하다; 자화자찬하다.

come out of the little end of the horn, 《*colloq.*》 fail or come to grief after boasting. 땅땅 큰 소리를 쳐놓고 실패하다.

draw 〔***pull, haul***〕 ***in one's horns,*** become less eager or active. 슬금슬금 움츠리다〔물러서다〕; 그만두다.

on the horns of a dilemma, forced to chose between two painful situations. 딜레마〔진퇴양난〕에 빠져; 사이에 끼여 난처한 처지에.

show one's horns, show one's real character. 본성을 드러내다.

take the bull by the horns, face a difficult thing or person rather than avoiding them. 감연히〔두려워하지 않고〕 난국에 직면하다〔아무와 맞서다〕.

— *vt., vi.* (P6; 1,2A) hit (something) with horns; provide horns for (something). …을 뿔로 받다; …에 뿔을 달다. [E.]

horn in, 《U.S. *colloq.*》 meddle; intrude. 중뿔나게 나서다; 끼어들다.

horn·bill [hɔ́ːrnbil] *n.* Ⓒ 《bird.》 a large bird having a large bill with a horn or horny lump on it. 코뿔새.

horn·blende [hɔ́ːrnblènd] *n.* Ⓤ a constituent of granite. etc. 각섬석(角閃石).

horned [hɔːrnd, 《*poet.*》 hɔ́ːrnid] *adj.* having a horn or horns; like a horn. 뿔이 있는; 뿔 모양의. ¶ *a* ~ *owl* 부엉이 / *a* ~ *beast* 뿔이 있는 짐승.

hor·net [hɔ́ːrnit] *n.* Ⓒ a large bee-like insect whose sting is very severe. 말벌(류). ¶ *bring* 〔*raise, arouse*〕 *a hornets' nest about one's ears* =*stir up a hornets' nest* = *put one's hand in a hornets' nest* 공연히 벌집을 건드리다; 공연한 말썽을 일으키다. [E.]

horn·less [hɔ́ːrnlis] *adj.* having no horns. 뿔없는. [*horn*]

horn·pipe [hɔ́ːrnpàip] *n.* Ⓒ **1** a lively dance formerly popular among sailors. 활발한 춤. **2** the music for it. 그 춤의 곡(曲). **3** an old musical instrument played by blowing. (양 끝에 뿔이 달린) 나무피리.

horn·y [hɔ́ːrni] *adj.* (**horn·i·er, horn·i·est**) **1** made or consisting of horn; 뿔로 만든〔된〕; 각제(角製)의. **2** hard like a horn. 뿔처럼 딱딱한; 굳은; 각질(角質)의. ¶ *My hands got* ~ *from hard work.* 두 손이 거친 일로 딱딱해졌다. **3** with horns. 뿔이 있는. [*horn*]

horn·y-hand·ed [hɔ́ːrnihǽndid] *adj.* with hands that are hard like horns. 거칠어져 딱딱하게 굳은 손을 가진.

hor·o·loge [hɔ́ːrəlòudʒ, -lɑ̀dʒ / hɔ́rəlɔ̀dʒ] *n.* a time-piece. 측시기(測時器); 시계. [Gk. *hōra* time, *logō* say]

ho·rol·o·gy [hourɑ́lədʒi, hɑr- / hɔrɔ́l-] *n.* Ⓤ the art or science of measuring time or making clocks. 시계 제작 기술; 시계학(學). ● **hor·o·log·ic** [hɔ̀ːrəlɑ́dʒik, hɑ̀r- / hɔ̀rəlɔ́dʒ-], **hor·o·log·i·cal** [-əl] *adj.*

hor·o·scope [hɔ́ːrəskòup, hɑ́r- / hɔ́r-] *n.* Ⓒ 《astrol.》 **1** the position of the stars at the hour of someone's birth, as influencing his life. 12궁도(宮圖); 천궁도(天宮圖). **2** an observation of the sky at a certain time. used in telling fortunes by the stars. 점성; 별점《특정한 때의 별의 위치 관측》. [Gk. *hōra* time, *skopos* observer].

cast 〔***read***〕 ***a horoscope,*** predict someone's future by observing the position of the stars. 별점으로 운세를 점치다.

•**hor·ri·ble** [hɔ́ːrəbəl, hɑ́r- / hɔ́r-] *adj.* **1** causing horror; terrible; dreadful. 무서운; 소름끼치는; 끔찍한. ¶ *a* ~ *sight* 〔*murder*〕 끔찍한 광경〔살인〕. **2** 《*colloq.*》 very unpleasant. 몹시 불쾌한; 지독한; 비참한. ¶ *a* ~ *headache* 지독한 두통 / ~ *weather* 지독한 날씨 / ~ *living conditions* 비참한 생활 조건 / *a* ~ *noise* 지독한 소음. ● **hor·ri·ble·ness** [-nis] *n.* [L. *horreo* bristle, shudder at]

hor·ri·bly [hɔ́ːrəbəli, hɑ́r- / hɔ́r-] *adv.* **1** in a horrible manner; terribly; dreadfully. 무섭게; 무시무시하게; 오싹할〔소름끼칠〕 만큼; 끔찍하게. **2** 《*colloq.*》 very; extremely. 지독히; 극도로.

•**hor·rid** [hɔ́ːrid, hɑ́r-] *adj.* (**-rid·er, -rid·est**) **1** terrible; frightful. 무서운; 무시무시한; 끔찍한. ¶ *a* ~ *monster* 무시무시한 괴물. **2** 《*colloq.*》 very unpleasant. 몹시 불쾌한; 지독한; 지겨운. ¶ ~ *weather* 고약한 날씨.

hor·rif·ic [hɔːrífik, hɑr- / hɔr-] *adj.* 《*lit.*》 horrifying. 몸서리쳐지는; 무서운; 오싹해지는.

hor·ri·fy [hɔ́ːrəfài, hɑ́r-] *vt.* (P6) (**-fied**) **1** fill (someone) with horror. …을 무서워 떨게〔몸서리치게〕 하다; 소름끼치게 하다. ¶ *I was horrified to see the scene.* 그 광경을 보고 등골이 오싹했다. **2** 《*colloq.*》 give a shock to (someone). …을 놀라게 하다; …을 분개해〔어이없게〕 하다. ¶ *I am horrified.* 어처구니가 없다; 놀랐어.

:hor·ror [hɔ́:rər, hár-] *n.* **1** Ⓤ a strong fear or dread. 공포; 전율. ¶ *in* ~ 무서워서; 소름이 끼쳐 / *much to one's* ~ 소름이 끼치게도; 끔찍하게도 / *shrink back from a corpse in* ~ 주뼛해서 시체로부터 뒷걸음치다 / *The story filled her with* ~. 그 이야기는 그녀를 공포에 떨게 했다. **2** ⓊⒸ a strong dislike or disgust. 강한 혐오〔반감, 증오〕. **3** Ⓒ a thing or person that causes horror. 무서운 것〔사람〕; 소름이 끼칠 정도로 끔찍한 것〔일〕; 참사. ¶ *the horrors* (중독의) 발작 / *the horrors of war* 전쟁의 참화. **4** Ⓒ ⓐ 《*colloq.*》 something very bad or unpleasant. 실로 지독한 물건. ⓑ 《*the* ~*s*》 the blues. 우울. [→horrible]

have a horror of, dislike (something) very much. …을 몹시 싫어〔혐오〕하다. ¶ *have a* ~ *of emotional outbursts* 감정의 표출을 극도로 싫어하다 / *have a* ~ *of snakes* 뱀을 극도로 혐오하다.

hor·ror-strick·en [hɔ́:rərstrìkən, hár- / hɔ́r-] *adj.* stricken with horror; horrified. 공포에 휩싸인〔사로잡힌〕.

hor·ror-struck [hɔ́:rərstrʌ̀k, hár- / hɔ́r-] *adj.* =horror-stricken.

hors d'oeu·vre [ɔ:r dɔ́:rv] *n.* (*pl.* ~ **d'oeuvres**) 《F.》 《usu. *pl.*》 light food served before the main courses of a meal. 오르 되브르; 전채(前菜)(cf. *dessert*).

:horse [hɔ:rs] *n.* Ⓒ **1** ⓐ a large, strong animal with four legs, used for carrying loads, riding, etc. 말. ⓑ a full grown male horse. (다 큰) 수말. **2** Ⓤ 《*collectively*》 soldiers on horses; cavalry. 기병(대). ¶ *light* ~ 경(輕)기병 / *There were one hundred horses.* 기병 백기(百騎)가 있었다. **3** 《gym.》 a padded block on legs, used for jumping over. 안마(鞍馬). **4** a frame with legs to support something. (다리가 달린) 받치개; 톱질 모탕; 빨래걸이.

a dark horse ⇨dark horse.

a horse of another 〔***a different***〕 ***color,*** quite a different matter. 전혀 다른〔별개의〕 일.

back the wrong horse, **a**) bet on a horse that loses the race. (판단을 그르쳐) 질 말에 걸다. **b**) give support to the losing side. 패자 쪽을 편들다.

be on one's high horse = mount 〔ride〕 the high horse.

eat 〔***work***〕 ***like a horse,*** eat very much. 엄청나게 먹다〔열심히 일하다〕.

flog 〔***beat, mount on***〕 ***a dead horse,*** argue about a question which has been already settled; waste one's efforts. 끝난 일을 다시 문제삼다; 헛수고하다.

from the horse's mouth, from the most direct and reliable source; not from some third person. 믿을 만한〔확실한〕 소식통〔곳, 사람〕으로부터 (직접).

horse and foot, **a**) horse soldiers and foot soilders. 기병과 보병. **b**) 《*fig.*》 with all one's resources. 전력을 다하여.

horse and horse, 《U.S. *colloq.*》 on even terms. 어슷비슷하게; 비등〔대등, 팽팽〕하게; 피장파장으로.

horse artillery, light artillery with mounted gunners. 기포병(騎砲兵).

horse, foot, and dragoons, **a**) the whole army. 전군(全軍). **b**) unanimously. 일제히.

look a gift horse in the mouth, 《*fig.*》 find fault with a gift or favor received. 받은 선물을 흠〔탈〕잡다.

mount 〔***ride***〕 ***the high horse,*** behave in a very proud manner. 뽐내다; 재다; 거들먹거리다.

pay for the dead horse. 헛돈을 쓰다; 낭비하다.

play horse with, treat (someone) rudely. …을 무례하게 대하다.

pull the dead horse, work for the wages already paid. 선금 받은 일을 하다.

put 〔***set***〕 ***the cart before the horse,*** do or put something in the wrong order; take the effect for the cause. 본말을 전도하다; 거꾸로의 짓을 하다.

spur a willing horse, urge without need. 불필요한 자극을 주다; 쓸데없는 짓을 하다.

take horse, **a**) go riding on horseback. 말을 타고 가다. **b**) (of a mare) permit a horse to cover her. (암말이) 교미하다.

To horse ! Get on your horse ! 승마《구령》.

— *vt.* (P6) **1** ⓐ supply (a carriage) with a horse or horses; put (something) on horseback. (마차)에 말을 매다; …을 말에 태우다〔싣다〕. ⓑ carry (someone) on one's back. …을 업어 나르다. **2** beat (someone) with a whip. …을 채찍으로 때리다. ¶ ~ *a ships crew* 선원들을 매질하다.

— *vi.* (P1) ride on a horse; go on horseback. 말에 올라타다; 말을 타고 가다. [E.]

·horse·back [hɔ́:rsbæ̀k] *n.* Ⓤ the back of a horse. 말의 등. ¶ *go on* ~ 말을 타고 가다.

— *adv.* on the back of a horse. 말을 타고. ¶ *He rides* ~. 말을 타고 있다.

horse·break·er [hɔ́:rsbrèikər] *n.* Ⓒ a person who gives training to horses. 조마사(調馬師).

horse·car [hɔ́:rskɑ̀:r] *n.* 《U.S.》 **1** a streetcar pulled by a horse or horses. 말이 끄는 노면차(路面車). **2** a car used for transporting horses. 마필 수송용 화차〔트럭〕.

horse chestnut [´-´-] *n.* **1** 《bot.》 a spreading shade tree with large leaves, white flowers and reddish-brown seeds. 마로니에. **2** the seed of this tree. 그 열매.

horse dealer [´-´-] *n.* a person who buys and sells horses. 말장수.

horse·flesh [hɔ́:rsflèʃ] *n.* Ⓤ **1** 《*collectively*》 horses. 말. **2** the flesh of horses. 말고기.

horse·fly [hɔ́:rsflài] *n.* Ⓒ (*pl.* **-flies**) a

large fly that bites horses and cattle. 말파리; 쇠등에.

Horse Guards [ᅩᅩ] *n. pl.* 《Brit.》 a cavalry brigade of English Mousehold troops. 근위기병(近衛騎兵).

horse·hair [hɔ́ːrshὲər] *n.* Ⓤ **1** the long hair growing on the neck or tail of a horse. (말의 갈기와 꽁지의) 털; 말총. **2** a hard cloth made of this hair; haircloth. 말총으로 짠 직물.

horse·hide [hɔ́ːrshàid] *n.* **1** the hide of a horse. 마피(馬皮). **2** leather made from this hide. 무두질한 말가죽.

horse·laugh [hɔ́ːrslæ̀f, -làːf] *n.* a loud, rude laugh. 너털웃음; 홍소(哄笑).

***horse·man** [hɔ́ːrsmən] *n.* Ⓒ (*pl.* **-men** [-mən]) **1** a man who rides on horseback. 승마자; 기수(騎手). **2** a man skilled in managing or riding horses. 승마의 명수.

horse·man·ship [hɔ́ːrsmənʃìp] *n.* Ⓤ the art or skill of riding or managing horses. 승마술(乘馬術). ¶ *feasts of* ~ 곡마술(曲馬術).

horse marines [ᅩ ―ᅩ] *n. pl.* **1** 《*joc.*》 an imaginary force of naval cavalry. 기마 수병(騎馬水兵)《있을 수 없는 것》. ¶ *Tell that to the* ~. 되잖은 소리(거짓말) 마라. **2** a person out of his element. 그 자리에 어울리지 않는 사람; 부적격자.

horse opera [ᅩᅩ―] *n.* 《U.S. *colloq.*》 a western film. 서부극 (영화).

horse·play [hɔ́ːrsplèi] *n.* Ⓤ rough, noisy fun. 야단 법석.

horse·pow·er [hɔ́ːrspàuər] *n.* Ⓒ (*pl.* **-pow·er**) a unit of the power of engines, motors, etc. 마력(馬力). 參考 hp., h.p., HP, H.P. 따위로 생략함.

horse race [ᅩᅩ] *n.* a race by horses as a sport. (한 번의) 경마.

horse·rad·ish [hɔ́ːrsræ̀diʃ] *n.* **1** Ⓒ 《bot.》 a tall plant with a white, hot-tasting root. 양고추냉이. **2** Ⓤ the flavor made of this root. 그 뿌리로 만든 조미료.

horse sense [ᅩᅩ] *n.* 《*colloq.*》 plain, practical common sense. 평범하고도 실제적인 상식; 속된 상식.

horse·shoe [hɔ́ːrʃʃùː, hɔ́ːrs-] *n.* Ⓒ **1** a flat, U-shaped metal shoe to protect a horse's hoof. (말)편자. **2** anything shaped like a horseshoe. U자 모양의 것. ¶ *a* ~ *magnet* 말굽 자석. **3** 《*pl.* used as *sing.*》 a game in which the players throw horseshoes at a post 40 feet away. 말굽쇠 던지기 놀이. ― *vt.* (P6) put horseshoes on (a horse's hoof). (말굽)에 편자를 박다.

horse·tail [hɔ́ːrstèil] *n.* Ⓒ **1** a horse's tail. 말꼬리. **2** 《bot.》 a flowerless plant with hollow, jointed stems. 속새.

horse·whip [hɔ́ːrs*h*wìp] *n.* Ⓒ a leather whip for driving or controlling horses. (가죽) 말채찍. ― *vt.* (**-whipped, -whip·ping**) (P6) beat (a horse, man, etc.) with a horsewhip. (말·사람 따위)를 채찍질하다; 징계(응징)하다.

horse·wom·an [hɔ́ːrswùmən] *n.* Ⓒ (*pl.* **-wom·en** [-wìmin]) **1** a woman who rides on horseback. 여성 승마자; 여기수(女騎手). **2** a woman skilled in managing or riding horses. 여성의 승마 명인.

hors·y [hɔ́ːrsi] *adj.* (**hors·i·er, hors·i·est**) **1** of or having to do with horses; like horses. 말의; 말 같은. **2** fond of horses or horse racing. 말을 좋아하는; 경마광(狂)의.

hort. horticultural; horticulture.

hor·ta·tive [hɔ́ːrtətiv], **hor·ta·to·ry** [hɔ́ːrtətɔ̀ːri / -təri] *adj.* giving advice; serving to encourage. 충고의; 권고적(장려적)인. [L. *hortor,* →exhort]

hor·ti·cul·tur·al [hɔ̀ːrtəkʌ́ltʃərəl] *adj.* of the art of gardening. 원예(술)의. [↓]

hor·ti·cul·ture [hɔ́ːrtəkʌ̀ltʃər] *n.* Ⓤ the art or science of growing flowers, fruits, vegetables, etc. 원예; 원예학(술). [L. *hortus* garden, →culture]

hor·ti·cul·tur·ist [hɔ̀ːrtəkʌ́ltʃərist] *n.* Ⓒ a person skilled in gardening. 원예가; 정원사.

ho·san·na [houzǽnə] *interj., n.* Ⓒ a shout of praise to God. 호산나《신을 찬미하는 말》. [Heb. =save, pray[1]]

hose [houz] *n.* ⒸⓊ **1** (*pl.* **hose**) 《*pl.*》 stockings. 목이 긴 양말; 스타킹. **2** (*pl.* **hoses** or **hose**) a tube of rubber, used to carry water, etc., for a short distance. (소방·살수용) 호스. ¶ *by means of a* ~ 호스로 / *a fire* ~ 소방 호스. ― *vt.* (P6,7) put water on (something) with a hose. (호스로) …에 물을 뿌리다. ¶ ~ *the garden* 뜰에 물을 뿌리다 / ~ *the car out* 호스로 물을 뿌려 세차하다 / ~ *down the ship's deck* 호스로 갑판을 닦다. [E.]

ho·sier [hóuʒər] *n.* Ⓒ a person who makes or sells men's socks, underwear, etc. (남자 용품) 양품상(商). [↑]

ho·sier·y [hóuʒəri] *n.* Ⓤ **1** articles sold by a hosier. 양말류; 메리야스류. **2** business of a hosier. (양말·메리야스류) 판매상.

hosp. hospital.

hos·pice [hɑ́spis / hɔ́s-] *n.* Ⓒ **1** a place of shelter for travelers, esp. one kept by a religious order. (순례자 따위를 위한) 숙박(접대)소. **2** a home for the poor, the sick, etc. (빈민·병자 따위의) 수용소. **3** a hospital for people with incurable illness. 호스피스《난치병·말기 환자 등의 수용 시설》. [L. *hospes* guest]

hos·pi·ta·ble [hɑ́spitəbəl / hɔ́s-] *adj.* **1** giving a kind and generous welcome to guests or strangers. (손님이나 타인을) 따뜻하게 대접하는. ¶ ~ *entertainment* 후한(극진한) 대접 / *a* ~ *smile* 따뜻한 미소. **2** favorably receptive or open. 호의로써(진심에서) 받아들이는. ¶ *a climate* ~ *to the raising of corn* 옥수수 재배에 좋은 기후 / *He is* ~ *to new ideas.* 그는 신(新)사상을 쾌히 받아들인

다. [→hospice]

hos·pi·ta·bly [háspitəbəli / hɔ́s-] *adv.* kindly and generously; in a hospitable manner. 친절하게; 따뜻하게; 후(극진)하게.

:hos·pi·tal [háspitl / hɔ́s-] *n.* Ⓒ **1** a place for the treatment and care of the sick or the injured. 병원. ¶ *a general* ~ 종합 병원 / *a mental* 〔*an isolation*〕 ~ 정신(격리) 병원 / *enter* 〔*leave*〕 (*the*) ~ 입원(퇴원)하다 / *He is in* 〔*out of*〕 (*the*) ~. 그는 입원(퇴원)해 있다. 語法 미국에서는 입원·퇴원에 the를 붙일 때가 많음. **2** a similar place for animals. 동물 병원. **3** 《Brit.》 a charitable institution for the poor, the aged, etc. (극빈자·무의탁 노인 등을 수용하는) 자선 시설. 參考 양로원·구빈원·자혜 의원 따위. [L. *hospes* host¹]

·hos·pi·tal·i·ty [hàspitǽləti / hɔ̀s-] *n.* Ⓤ the state of being hospitable; warm, friendly treatment given to guests. 환대; 따뜻한 대접; 후대.

hos·pi·tal·ize [háspitəlàiz / hɔ́s-] *vt.* (P6) put (someone) in a hospital. …을 입원시키다.

·host¹ [houst] *n.* Ⓒ **1** a person who entertains guests warmly at his own house. (연회 등) 주인 (노릇); 접대역(opp. guest). ¶ *a* ~ *country* 주최국 / *act as* ~ (…에서) 주인 노릇을 하다 / *act as* ~ *to a conference* 회의를 주최하다. **2** a keeper of an inn or a hotel. (여관의) 주인. **3** 《biol.》 a plant or an animal in or on which another lives. (기생(寄生) 동식물의) 숙주(宿主); 기주(寄主). [L. *hospes* guest]

reckon* 〔*count*〕 *without one's host, forget to consider the effect of an important thing. 중요한 점(일)을 빠뜨리다; 중대 사항을 고려에 넣지 않고 계획(결정)하다.

·host² [houst] *n.* Ⓒ a great number. 많은 수(사람); 다수. ¶ *a* ~ *of friends* 〔*troubles*〕 많은 친구(말썽) / *despite hosts of difficulties* 수많은 곤란이 있음에도 불구하고. [L. *hostis* stranger, enemy]

be a host in oneself, equal to a host of ordinary persons. 일기 당천(一騎當千)이다.

the host(s) of heaven, **a**) heavenly bodies. 일월 성신(日月星辰). **b**) angels. 천사의 무리.

the Lord* 〔*God*〕 *of hosts, the Lord of armies. 만군(萬軍)의 주(主). 參考 Jehovah를 말함.

host³, Host [houst] *n.* 《*the* ~》 the bread consecrated, or made the body of Christ in the ceremony of the Eucharist. 성체(聖體); 면병(麪餠). [L. *hostia* victim]

hos·tage [hástidʒ / hɔ́s-] *n.* Ⓒ **1** a person held by an enemy as an assurance that certain things will be carried out. 인질; 볼모. ¶ *held someone as a* ~ 아무를 인질로 잡아 두다 / *become a* ~ *in someone's hands* 아무의 인질이 되다 / *Prisoners of war are sometimes held as hostages.* 전쟁 포로들은 가끔 인질이 된다. **2** pledge, security. 저당; 담보. [L. *obses*]

hostages to fortune, persons or things that one may lose (e.g. wife and children). 운명에 맡긴 인질; 언제 잃을는지 모르는 것《처자·재보 따위》.

hos·tel [hástəl / hɔ́s-] *n.* Ⓒ **1** a lodging place, esp. for young people on trips, hikes, etc. (여행하는 청소년을 위한) 숙박소; 유스 호스텔(=youth hostel). **2** 《*arch.*》 an inn. 여관. [*hospital*]

hos·tel·ry [hástəlri / hɔ́s-] *n.* Ⓒ (*pl.* **-ries**) 《*arch.*》 an inn; a hotel. 여인숙; 여관.

·host·ess [hóustis] *n.* Ⓒ **1** a woman who receives and entertaines guests. (연회 따위의) 여주인. **2** a woman who keeps an inn, etc. 여관의 여주인. **3** a woman employed to entertain or dance with guests. 접대부; 호스티스. **4** =air hostess. [→host¹]

·hos·tile [hástil / hɔ́stail] *adj.* of or like an enemy; opposed; unfriendly. 적의; 적의(敵意)가 있는; 반대의; 냉담한; 우호적이 아닌; ¶ *a* ~ *nation* 적국 / *a man* ~ *to reform* 개혁에 반대하는 사람 / *He was* ~ *to our plan.* 그는 우리의 계획에 반대했다. ● **hos·tile·ly** [-i] *adv.* [→ host²]

hos·til·i·ty [hastíləti / hɔs-] *n.* Ⓤ Ⓒ (*pl.* **-ties**) **1** a feeling as an enemy; opposition; unfriendliness. 적의(敵意); 악의; 적개심; 반대; 냉담. ¶ *a personal* ~ *to the system* 제도에 대한 개인적인 반감 / *I feel no* ~ *toward him.* 그에게 아무 적의도 없다. **2** a hostile act; 《usu. *pl.*》 the state of being at war; warfare. 적대 행위; 전쟁 행위; 교전. ¶ *long-term hostilities* 장기 항전 / *cease* 〔*open*〕 *hostilities* 정전(개전)하다 / *suspend hostilities* 전투 행위를 중지하다. [↑]

hos·tler [háslər / ɔ́s-] *n.* Ⓒ a person who takes care of horses at an inn. (여관의) 말을 돌보는 사람. [→hostel]

:hot [hat / hɔt] *adj.* (**hot·ter, hot·test**) **1** having or giving heat; of a high temperature. 더운; 뜨거운(opp. cold). ¶ *a* ~ *day* 더운 날 / *a* ~ *fire* 뜨거운 불 / *a cup of* ~ *tea* 한 잔의 따끈한 홍차 / *a spell of* ~ *weather* 오래 계속되는 더위 / *Running makes me* ~. 달리기는 나를 덥게 만든다 / *The room was as* ~ *as an oven.* 방은 가마솥처럼 뜨거웠다. **2** 《*colloq.*》 new; fresh; recent. 새(로운); 갓…한; 최근의. ¶ ~ *news* 최신 뉴스 / ~ *from the front* 일선에서 갓 돌아온. **3** (of pepper, etc.) producing a burning sensation in the mouth, throat, etc. (입·혀·목이) 화끈거리는; 얼얼한; 톡 쏘는; 매운. ¶ ~ *pepper* 〔*mustard*〕 매운 후추(겨자). **4** eager; keen; zealous. 열렬한; 열광적인; 열중한. ¶ *a* ~ *patriot* 열렬한 애국자 / ~ *on playing tennis* 테니스에 열중하고 있는. **5** excitable; passionate; angry. 흥분하기 쉬운; (성미가) 격렬한; 성난. ¶ *in* ~ *anger* 불같이 노하여 / *get* ~ *over an argument* 의론에 흥분하다. **6** (of a battle, etc.) violent; furious; strenuous. 격렬한; 맹렬한. ¶ *a* ~ *struggle* 격정 / *in* ~

haste 몹시 서둘러 / *the hottest battle of the war* 그 전쟁의 가장 격렬했던 전투. **7** nearing one's object. 목표에 가까운; 거의 알아맞힐〔찾아낼〕 것 같은. ¶ *You are getting* ~. 거의 맞히고 있다. **8** 《*colloq.*》 following very closely; close. 바짝 뒤쫓은; 접근한. ¶ *be* ~ *on someone's heels* 〔*tracks*〕 아무를 바짝 뒤쫓고 있다. **9** (of a performer, feat, etc.) excellent; very good. 뛰어난; 아주 훌륭한. ¶ *not so* ~ 그다지 뛰어나지 않은. **10** (of the scent in hunting) strong. (사냥에서) (냄새가) 강한; 새로운. ¶ *a* ~ *scent.* **11** ⓐ 《electr.》 actively conducting current. 강한 전류가 통하고 있는; 볼트가 높은. ¶ *a* ~ *wire* 열선 / *a* ~ *chair* 전기 사형 의자. ⓑ 《phys.》 charged (with radioactivity); radio active. 방사능이 있는; 방사성의. ¶ ~ *dusts* 방사능진(放射能塵). **12** 《*sl.*》 excellent; good. 근사한; 멋진; 좋은.

be hot on the trail 〔***track***〕 ***of,*** pursue closely. …의 뒤를 바짝 쫓다.

be in hot water, be in trouble, have difficulties. 어려움에 처해 있다.

blow hot and cold, change one's opinions or aittitudes constantly. 의견을〔기분을, 태도를〕 늘 바꾸다; 정견(定見)이 없다; 갈팡질팡하다.

drop like a hot potato 〔***brick, chestnut***〕, 《*colloq.*》 abandon hastily. 황급히 버리다.

get into hot water, 《*colloq.*》 get into trouble. 성가시게 되다; 말썽을 일으키다.

get 〔***catch***〕 ***it hot,*** 《*colloq.*》 be scolded severely. 호되게 꾸중을 듣다〔야단맞다〕; 혼나다.

hot and bothered, excited, aroused or flustered. 흥분해서; (몹시) 당황해서. ¶ *This mistake isn't worth getting* ~ *and bothered about.* 이런 실수로 그렇게 소란떨 것 없다.

hot and heavy, violently; severely. 격렬하게; 맹렬히; 필사적으로.

hot and hot, fresh from an oven, etc. 갓 만들어 따끈따끈한; 갓 요리된.

hot and strong = hot and heavy.

in hot blood, excitedly. 격앙하여.

make it (***too***) ***hot*** (=*make the situation extremely uncomfortable*) ***for*** *someone.* …을 배겨나지 못하게 하다; …을 괴롭히다.

— *adv.* in a hot manner. 뜨겁게; 열렬히; 격렬히; 성이 나서.

give it *someone* ***hot,*** 《*colloq.*》 punish or scold him severely. …를 호되게 꾸짖다〔비난하다〕.

— *vt.* (P6,7) (**hot·ted, hot·ting**) 《usu. *up*》 《Brit. *colloq.*》 warm up food which has become cold. (음식을) 데우다. [E.]

hot air [´ ´] *n.* 《*colloq.*》 an empty, showy talk or writing. 허풍; 헛된〔큰〕 소리; 알맹이 없는 이야기〔문장〕.

hot atom [´ ´–] *n.* an atom whose nucleus is radioactive. 방사성 원자.

hot·bed [hátbèd / hɔ́t-] *n.* Ⓒ **1** a bed of earth usu. covered with glass and kept warm for growing plants out of season. 온상(溫床). **2** 《*fig.*》 any place suitable for the rapid growth of something evil. (범죄·악습 따위의) 온상. ¶ *a* ~ *of juvenile delinquency* 청소년 범죄의 온상.

hot blast [´ ´] *n.* the blast of heated air forced into the furnace. (야금에서) 용광로에 불어넣는 열풍.

hot-blood·ed [hátblʌ́did / hɔ́t-] *adj.* **1** easily excited or made angry. 격하기〔흥분하기, 성내기〕 쉬운. **2** rash; reckless. 성급〔조급〕한; 무모한; 혈기의. **3** passionate. 열렬한; 정열적인.

hot cake [´ ´] *n.* a pancake; a griddlecake. 핫 케이크.

sell 〔***go***〕 ***like hot cakes,*** 《*colloq.*》 be very much in demand; be disposed of rapidly. 수요가 많다; (특히 대량으로) 빠르고 쉽게 처분되다〔팔리다〕.

hot copper [´ ´–] *n.* 《u.s. *colloq.*》 a mouth and throat made hot and dry by drinking too much. (과음 후의 갈증으로) 바짝 타는 입과 목.

hot corner [´ ´–] *n.* 《baseball》 the third base. 삼루(三壘).

hotch·potch [hátʃpàtʃ / hɔ́tʃpɔ̀tʃ] *n.* = hodgepodge.

hot dog [´ ´] *n.* 《U.S. *colloq.*》 sandwich made of a hot sausage in a split roll. 핫 도그.

:ho·tel [houtél] *n.* Ⓒ a house or large building providing lodging, food, etc. 호텔; 여관. ¶ *run a* ~ 호텔을 경영하다 / *put up at a* ~ 호텔에 묵다〔투숙하다〕 / *stay at a* ~ 호텔에 묵고 있다 / *The group of foreign sightseers is staying in the lake-side* ~. 외국 관광단은 호숫가의 호텔에 묵고 있다. [*hospital*]

ho·tel·keep·er [houtélkìːpər] *n.* Ⓒ a person who keeps a hotel. 호텔 경영자〔소유자〕.

hot·foot [hátfùt / hɔ́t-] *adv.* in great haste. 부리나케; 황급히; 서둘러. — *vi.* (P1) 《U.S. *sl.*》 《often ~ *it*》 go in great haste; hurry. 부리나케 가다. ¶ *We hotfooted it over to the street.* 우린 황급히 거리로 뛰어갔다. [*hot*]

hot·head [háthèd / hɔ́t-] *n.* Ⓒ a quick-tempered person. 성급한 사람.

hot·head·ed [háthédid / hɔ́t-] *adj.* quick-tempered; easily excited. 성급한; 격하기〔흥분하기〕 쉬운. ● **hot·head·ed·ly** [-li] *adv.*

hot·house [háthàus / hɔ́t-] *n.* Ⓒ a building covered with glass, kept warm for growing plants; a greenhouse. 온실.

hot line [´ ´] *n.* Ⓒ a direct line of communication by teletype between heads of governments. (국가 수뇌들 간의) 직통 전화; 핫 라인.

hot·ly [hátli / hɔ́t-] *adv.* in a hot manner; with heat. 덥게; 뜨겁게; 격렬히.

hot·ness [hátnis / hɔ́t-] *n.* Ⓤ the quality of being hot; heat. 뜨거움; 열렬; 격렬.

hot pants [´ ´] *n. pl.* **1** 《*vulg.*》 anxious sexual desire. 색정. **2** brief shorts worn by girls and young women. 핫 팬츠.

hot plate [ㅗㅗ] *n.* a small, portable gas or electric cooking stove. (요리용) 가스〔전기〕 레인지.

hot pot [ㅗㅗ] *n.* meat and potatoes cooked together in a tightly covered pot. 뚜껑을 닫고 고기와 감자를 함께 익힌 냄비 요리.

hot seat [ㅗㅗ] *n.* 《*colloq.*》 **1** the electric chair. (사형용) 전기 의자. **2** a difficult situation. 곤란한 입장; 궁지.

hot spring [ㅗㅗ] *n.* a natural spring having waters warmer than 98°F. 온천.

hot·spur [hátspə̀ːr / hɔ́t-] *n.* Ⓒ a thoughtless or reckless person; a hothead. 성급한 사람; 무모한 사람. [*hot*]

hot stuff [ㅗㅗ] *n.* 《*sl.*》 **1** a person of high spirit, vigor, skill, strong will or passions. 원기가 충만한 사람; 정열〔정력〕가. **2** a person or thing of excellent quality. 특히 뛰어난 사람〔것〕.

hot·ten·tot [hátntàt / hɔ́tntɔ̀t] *n.* **1** a member of a South African race. (남아프리카의) 호텐토트 사람. **2** the language of this race. 호텐토트 말. **3** 《*fig.*》 an uncivilized person. 미개인. [Du.]

hot war [ㅗㅗ] *n.* a war characterized by actual fighting. 본격적인 전쟁; 열전(熱戰); 핫 워(opp. cold war). [*hot*]

hot water [ㅗㅗㅡ] *n.* 《*colloq.*》 trouble. (스스로 초래한) 곤란; 어려움; 곤경.

hot-wa·ter bottle [hátwɔ̀ːtər bàtl / hɔ̀t-bɔ̀tl] *n.* a container filled with hot water, used for warming a bed. 탕파.

hot well [ㅗㅗ] *n.* a spring of naturally hot water; the reservoir in condensing steam-engine. 천연 온천; (증기 기관의) 물탱크.

hough [hak / hɔk] *n.* =hock¹.

***hound** [haund] *n.* Ⓒ **1** ⓐ a hunting dog of several breeds, most of which hunt by scent. 사냥개. ¶ *follow hounds* =*ride to hounds* (말을 타고) 사냥개를 앞세워 사냥을 하다. ⓑ 《*the* ~*s*》 a pack of hound. 일단의 사냥개. **2** a scornful person. 비열한 놈.
— *vt.* (P6,7) **1** hunt (an animal, etc.) with hounds; chase. …을 사냥개로 사냥하다; …을 추적하다. **2** 《*on*》 urge. …을 북돋우다; 격려하다. **3** incite (a hound, etc.) to pursuit or attack. …을 —하도록 부추기다. ¶ ~ *a dog at someone* 아무에게 덤벼들도록 개를 부추기다. **4** 《*fig.*》 persecute. 박해하다. ¶ *His enemies hounded him to death.* 적들은 그를 박해하여 죽게 했다. [E.]

⁑**hour** [áuər] *n.* Ⓒ **1** sixty minutes. 1시간; 60분. ¶ *an hour's walk* 〔*work*〕 한 시간의 산책〔일〕 / *a half* ~ 《U.S.》 반 시간 / *a quarter of an* ~, 15분 / *every two hours,* 2시간마다 / *for hours together* 멈추지 않고 여러 시간 동안. **2** the time of day expressed in hours (and minutes). 시각; 때. ¶ *at an early* 〔*a late*〕 ~ 이른〔늦은〕 시간에 / *The* ~ *is 5:30.* 시각은 아침 5시 30분이다 / *The clock has struck the* ~. 벽시계가 때를 알렸다. **3** an appointed or particular time of day. 특정의 시간; 때. ¶ *the* ~ *of his death* 그의 사망 시각 / *the* ~ *of decision* 결단을 내릴 때 / *It was already twenty minutes past the* ~. 이미 정각을 20분 지나 있었다. **4** one's customary and usual time of doing something. (습관적으로 어떤 일을 하는) 여느 때의 시간. ¶ *the* ~ *of lunch* =*the lunch* ~ 점심 시간 / *wait for the opening* ~ *of the museum* 박물관의 개관 시간을 기다리다 / *keep early* 〔*good*〕 *hours* 일찍 자고 일찍 일어나다. **5** 《*pl.*》 a fixed period of time for work, study, etc. (근무·공부 따위의) 시간. ¶ *business hours* 영업(營業) 시간 / *School hours are 9 to 12 and 1 to 4.* 수업 시간은 9시에서 12시 그리고 1시에서 4시까지다 / *The office hours are 9 to 5.* 집무 시간은 9시부터 5시까지. **6** a short or limited period of time; a class period. 짧은〔국한된〕 시간; 1교시(校時). ¶ *enjoy a social evening* ~ 저녁의 사교 시간을 즐기다 / *The* ~ *lasted 50 minutes.* 시간은 50분 끌었다. **7** 《usu. *pl.*》 a period in one's lifetime. (인생의) 한 시기; 때. ¶ *the happiest hours of one's life* 인생의 가장 행복한 시기. **8** an hour's journey or ride. 1시간의 행정(行程)〔거리〕. ¶ *The town is an* ~ *from here.* 시(市)까지는 여기서 1시간 거리이다. **9** the time of death. 죽을 때; 임종. ¶ *His* ~ *has come.* 그의 임종이 다가왔다. [Gk. *hōra*]

after hours, after the regular hours for school, business, etc. 집무〔근무·영업·수업〕 시간이 끝난 후에.

at all hours, at any time. 언제든; 어느 때고.

at the eleventh hour, at the last moment. 위급할 때에.

hour after hour, every hour. 매시간; 몇 시간마다.

hour by hour, each hour; momentarily. 각각(刻刻)으로.

in a good 〔***happy***〕 ***hour,*** fortunately. 운 좋게.

in an evil hour, unluckily. 운 나쁘게; 불행하게도.

keep bad 〔***late***〕 ***hours,*** rise and go to bed late. 밤 늦게 자고 아침 늦게 일어나다.

keep regular hours, rise and go to bed at regular times. 규칙적으로 자고 일어나고 하다.

of the hour, of the present; of this time. 현재의; 지금의. ¶ *the man of the* ~ 시대의 사람 / *the need of the* ~ 목하(目下)의 급무(急務) / *the question of the* ~ 당면 문제.

on the hour, just at a certain o'clock; sharp. 정각〔딱〕 …시에.

hour·glass [áuərglæ̀s, -glɑ̀ːs] *n.* Ⓒ a glass instrument containing water, sand, etc., used for measuring time. 물시계; 모래 시계.

hour hand [ㅗㅗ] *n.* the short hand on a clock or watch to show the hour. (시계의) 시침; 단침. 參考 분침·장침은 minute hand.

hour·ly [áuərli] *adj.* **1** happening every hour. 시간마다의; 매시(每時)의. ¶ *an* ~

train service 매시간마다의 열차 운행 / *medicine to be taken* ~ 매시간 복용하는 약. **2** frequent. 잦은; 끊임없는. —*adv.* **1** every hour; hour by hour; once an hour. 한 시간마다. **2** very often. 자주.

:house [haus] *n.* Ⓒ (*pl.* **hous·es**) **1** a building for people to live in. 집; 주택. 參考 house는 건조물로서의 집. home은 '가정'의 뜻. 미국은 양쪽을 가리지 않고 쓰는 경향이 있음. ¶ *a large* ~ 큰 집 / *a* ~ *in the country* 시골의 집 / *a* ~ *for rent* 〔*to let*〕 셋집 / *Houses are springing up everywhere.* 도처에 집들이 들어서고 있다 / *A man's* ~ *is his castle.* 집은 그 사람의 성채이다《사생활의 침해를 받지않는다》. **2** an inn. 여관; 여인숙. **3** a theater; its audience. 극장; 그 관객; 입장자. ¶ *a full* 〔*good*〕 ~ 만원 / *an empty* ~ 입장자가 적음 / *He spoke to a full* ~. 그는 만당한 청중에게 연설했다. **4** 《usu. in *compounds*》 a building for any purpose. (어떤 목적을 위한) 건물. ¶ *a* ~ *of detention* 유치장 / *a hen-house* 닭장 / *the opera-house* 오페라 극장 / *a schoolhouse* 교사(校舍). **5** home; household; famliy. 가정; 가구; 살림; 가족. ¶ *a cheerful* ~ 밝은 가정 / *receive a stranger in one's* ~ 집에 모르는 사람을 맞아들이다 / *set* 〔*break*〕 *up* ~ 살림을 차리다〔걷어치우다〕 / *Meals are always late in our* ~. 우리 집에서는 항상 식사를 늦게 한다. **6** 《often *H-*》 a line of ancestors and descendants; a family. (선조·자손을 포함한) 가계(家系); 집안; …가(家). ¶ *the House of Hapsburg* 합스부르크가 / *the royal House of England* 영국왕실 / *spring from an ancient* ~ 오래 된 가문의 출신이다. **7** a building or room used for the meeting of public bodies; the members of such a meeting. 의사당; 의원. ¶ *the House of Parliament* (영국의) 국회 의사당. **8** 《*H-*》 a law-making body or group. 의회. ¶ *the House of Representatives* (미국의) 하원 / *both Houses* 양원; 상원과 하원. **9** ⓐ a place of business; a business company. 상사(商社); 회사. ¶ *a publishing* ~ 출판사 / *a stock and bond* ~ 증권 회사. ⓑ 《Brit. *colloq.*》《*the H-*》 the Stock Exchange. 증권 거래소. **10** a boarding-house at a school (usu. one of several); the group of pupils in one such house. (학교의) 기숙사〔생〕.

(**as**) ***safe as a house,*** perfectly safe. 아주 안전한.

bring down the house, 《*colloq.*》 receive loud praise from the audience. 만장의 갈채를 받다.

clean house, **a**) adjust one's household affairs. 집을 정리하다. **b**) do away with undesirable conditions. 바람직하지 않은 요소를 없애다; 숙청하다.

enter the House, become a Member of Parliament. 하원 의원이 되다.

house and home 《*emph.*》 home. 가정.

house of call, a house where carriers call for commissions. (주문 받는 사람의) 단골(처).

house of cards, an immaterial or unsubstantial structure. 취약한〔위험한〕 구조물.

house of god, any place of worship. 교회; 예배당.

house of ill fame, a brothel. 매춘집.

keep a good house, provides the people who live there or one's guests with plenty of good and comfort. 좋은〔호화로운〕 생활을 하다; 손님을 후하게 대접하다.

keep house, **a**) take care of the affairs of a home. 살림을 꾸려 나가다. **b**) start housekeeping. 살림을 차리다.

keep house with *someone,* live in the same house as and share expenses with someone. …와 한집에서 공동 생활을 하다.

keep open house, entertain as guests all those who come at any time. 오는 사람은 언제든지 환영하다.

keep the 〔*one's*〕 ***house,*** always stay at home. 집에 틀어박히다.

like a house on fire 〔***afire***〕, with great speed or energy. 매우 빨리; 신속히; 세차게.

make a house, secure the presence of a quorum. 정족수가 되다.

on the house, free to the customers; paid for by the owner of the business; free. 사업주〔경영자〕 부담으로; 무료로.

set 〔***put***〕 *one's* ***house in order,*** put one's affairs in good condition. 신변 정리를 하다.

the House of Commons, the elective house of the British Parliament. (영국의) 하원.

the House of Lords, the non-elective House of the British parliament. (영국의) 상원.

—[hauz] *vt.* (P6) **1** furnish (someone) with a house. …에게 집을 주다. **2** receive (someone) in a house. …을 집에 받아들이다〔수용하다〕; 집에 재우다. ¶ ~ *flood victims in schools* 수재민을 학교에 수용(收容)하다 / *I housed him for a night.* 그를 하룻밤 집에 재워 주었다. **3** store in a house. …을 저장〔간수〕하다. ¶ *I must find some place where I can* ~ *my books.* 내 책을 간수할 곳을 찾아야겠다.

—*vi.* (P1,2) take shelter; live; dwell. 안전한 곳에 들어가다; 묵다; 숙박하다; 살다. [E.]

house agent [∠∠] *n.* a person who manages the sale or letting of houses. 가옥〔부동산〕 중개업자; 복덕방.

house·boat [háusbòut] *n.* Ⓒ a boat that can be used as a dwelling. (주거용) 집배.

〈houseboat〉

house·break·er [háusbrèikər] *n.* Ⓒ **1** a person who breaks into a house to steal. (낮의) 가택 침입자; 강도(cf. *burglar*). **2** 《Brit.》 a person who dismantles a house. 집을 철거하는 사람.

house·bro·ken [háusbròukən], **-broke** [-bròuk] *adj.* 《U.S.》 trained to live indoors, as a dog. (개 따위가) 집에서 살도록 훈련된.

house builder [∠ ∠–] *n.* a person whose business is to build houses. 건축업자; 목수.

house·coat [háuskòut] *n.* Ⓒ a woman's garment, usu. long with a loose skirt, for in formal wear within the house. (여성의) 실내복《평소 가정에서 입는 원피스》.

house dinner [∠ ∠–] *n.* a specially appointed dinner for members and guests. (클럽 따위에서) 회원·손님을 위해 마련하는 만찬회.

house dog [∠ ∠] *n.* a dog kept in a house; a dog trained to guard a house. (집에서) 기르는 개; 집 지키는 개.

house duty [∠ ∠–] *n.* tax which a person must pay for his own house. 가옥세.

house·fly [háusflài] *n.* Ⓒ (*pl.* **-flies**) a common fly that lives around and in houses. 집파리.

·**house·hold** [háushòuld] *n.* Ⓒ **1** ⓐ all the persons living in a house; family; family and servants. 가족; 한집안 (식구)《고용인 포함》. ⓑ a home and its affairs. 세대; 가구. ¶ *a large* ~ 대세대. **2** 《*the H-*》 such a family or group of royal blood. 왕실; 왕가. — *adj.* of a household; domestic. 가족의; 집안의; 가정의. ¶ ~ *affairs* 가사 / ~ *goods* 살림 도구; 가정용품 / ~ *effects* 가재 도구 / ~ *economy* 가정 경제.

house·hold·er [háushòuldər] *n.* a person who owns a house; the head of a family. 호주; 가구주; 가장(家長).

household word [∠–∠] *n.* a word or phrase in everyday use; a fact well-known to everyone. 일상적으로 잘 쓰이는 말; 잘 알려진 일.

:**house·keep·er** [háuskì:pər] *n.* Ⓒ **1** a woman who takes care of a home and its affairs. 주부. ¶ *a good* ~ 살림 잘 하는 주부. **2** an upper-class servant who directs the housework servants. 가정부; 우두머리 하녀.

house·keep·ing [háuskì:piŋ] *n.* Ⓤ the act of taking care of a household; the act of doing the house work. 살림; 가정(家政); 가사(家事).

:**house·maid** [háusmèid] *n.* Ⓒ a woman servant employed for the housework. 가정부; 하녀.

house·mast·er [háusmæ̀stər / -mà:stər] *n.* Ⓒ the master of a house; the head of a family; a master in charge of a house at a boarding-school. 호주; 집주인; 가장(家長); (영국 사립 남자 학교의) 사감.

house·moth·er [háusmʌ̀ðər] *n.* Ⓒ a woman who takes care of a group of people living together. 여자 사감(舍監).

house party [∠ ∠–] *n.* **1** an entertainment of guests staying overnight or longer. (별장 따위의) 체재객(滯在客)을 위한 접대연(宴). **2** the guests at such a party. 그 체재객 일행.

house physician [∠ –∠–] *n.* a resident physician in a hospital, hotel, etc. (병원·호텔 등의) 입주(入住) 내과 의사.

house·room [háusrù(:)m] *n.* space or accomodation in a room. 집의 수용력; 물건 두는 장소.

house-to-house [háustəháus] *adj.* conducted from one house to the next. 집마다의; 호별(戶別)의. ¶ ~ *visits* 호별 방문.

house·top [háustɑ̀p / -tɔ̀p] *n.* Ⓒ the top or roof of a house. 집 꼭대기; 지붕. ***cry*** 〔***proclaim***〕 ***something from the housetops,*** make something widely known. …을 일반에게〔널리〕 알리다.

house·trained [háustrèind] *adj.* = housebroken.

house·warm·ing [háuswɔ̀:rmiŋ] *n.* Ⓒ a party given on moving into a new house. 집들이 (잔치).

·**house·wife** *n.* Ⓒ **1** [háuswàif] (*pl.* **-wives**) a woman who takes care of a home and its affairs. 주부. **2** [hʌ́zif] (*pl.* **-wifes. -wives**) a small case for needles, thread, etc. 반짇고리.

house·wife·ly [háuswàifli] *adj.* of or like a housewife. 주부의; 주부 같은〔다운〕.

house·wif·er·y [háuswàifəri] *n.* the business of a housewife. 주부의 역할〔일〕; 살림; 가사.

house·wives [háuswàivz] *n.* pl. of **housewife.**

house·work [háuswə̀:rk] *n.* Ⓤ the work of housekeeping, such as washing, cleaning, and cooking. 집안일; 가사.

hous·ing[1] [háuziŋ] *n.* Ⓤ **1** the act of providing houses as home; the act of giving homes to people. 주택 공급. **2** 《*collectively*》 houses. 주택; 집; 주거. ¶ *the* ~ *problem* 〔*question*〕 주택 문제 / *make one's* ~ *more spacious* 집을 확장하다. **3** a cover or shelter. 가리개; 피난처. **4** a protective cover or container of a machine. (케이스; 기계 따위의) 틀; 가구(架構).

hous·ing[2] [háuziŋ] *n.* **1** a cloth covering for horse's body for protection or show. 마의(馬衣). **2** 《*pl.*》 = trappings. [F. *huche*]

Hous·ton [hjú:stən] *n.* a city in Texas. 휴스턴.

Hou·yhn·hnm [hu:ínəm, hwínəm / húihnəm] *n.* a horse with human characterstics. 후이넘《이성(理性)을 갖춘 말》. [from *Gulliver's Travels*]

hove [houv] *v.* p. and pp. of **heave.**

ho·vel [hʌ́vəl, hɑ́vəl] *n.* Ⓒ **1** a small, dirty house; a hut. 작고 더러운〔황폐한〕 집; 오두막집. **2** a shed for cattle, tools, etc. (가축의) 우리; 헛간; 까대기. [M.E.]

·hov·er [hʌ́vər, hάv-] *vi.* (P1,2A,3) **1** 《*about, over*》 (of birds, insects, helicopters, etc.) stay or fly in the air near one place. 하늘을 빙빙 맴돌다; 공중 한 곳에 머물다; 날아다니다. ¶ *The bird hovered over its nest.* 새가 둥지 위를빙빙 맴돌았다. **2** 《*about, around, near*》 (of a person) stay or wait nearby; hang about. …근처를 방황하다〔떠나지 않다〕; 서성거리다. **3** 《*between*》 be in an uncertain condition; hesitate. 망설이다. ¶ ~ *between life and death* 생사의 갈림길을 헤매다 / ~ *on the brink of a decision* 마지막 결단의 순간에 망설이다. [M.E.]

Hov·er·craft [hʌ́vərkræ̀ft, hάvərkrɑ:ft] *n.* a motorized vehicle capable of low-level flight over land and sea by the action of downward directed fans. 호버크라프트 《수면·지면의 몇 피트 위를 떠서 나는 탈것》. [Trade name, *hovor*]

:how [hau] *adv.* **1** 《in *questions*》 ⓐ in what way or manner; by what means. 어떻게 하여; 어떤 (방)식으로. ¶ *How shall we begin it?* 어떻게 시작하면 좋을까 / *How did you do it?* 그것을 어떻게 하였나요 / *How do you say this in English?* 이것을 영어로 어떻게〔무어라고〕 말하나 / *I don't know* ~ *to solve the problem.* 문제를 어떻게 풀어야 할지 모르겠다 / *Be careful* ~ *you act.* 행동에 주의해라 / *How did it happen?* 그것은 어떻게 일어났는가. ⓑ in what state or condition. 어떤 상태〔상황〕에. ¶ *How are you?* 안녕하십니까 / *How are you getting along* 〔*on*〕? 어떻게 지내십니까 / *How's the weather today?* 오늘 날씨가 어떤가 / *How did you find him?* 그의 용태가 어떠했습니까 / *Tell me* ~ *your parents are.* 자네 부모님 건강이 어떠한지 말해 주게 / *How was the party last night?* 간밤의 파티는 어떠했습니까. ⓒ by what name or title. 어떤 이름〔호칭〕으로; 어떻게. ¶ *How is he called?* 뭐라고 부르는가; 이름이 무엇인가 / *I don't know* ~ *to address him.* 그를 어떻게 불러야 할지 모르겠다. ⓓ at what price; in what unit of measurement. 얼마의 값으로; 어떤 단위로; 어떻게. ¶ *How is the dollar today?* 오늘의 달러 시세는 어떻게 되나 / *How is milk sold? —It is sold by the pint.* 우유는 어떻게 파는가—파인트 단위로 판다. ⓔ for what reason; why. 어떤 이유로; 어째서; 왜. ¶ *How comes it that you are here?* 어쩐 일로 여기 와 있나 / *I can't see* ~ *he came to do it.* 그가 어째서 그런 일을 하게 됐는지 알 수가 없다 / *How is it that they are late in coming?* 그들이 늦게 오는 것은 어째서이지. **2** 《with *adj.* or *adv.*》 to what degree, extent, or amount; at what rate. (정도·양·값·율 따위의) 얼마만큼; 얼마나; 어느 정도나. ⓐ 《in *questions*》 *How old is he?* 그는 몇 살인가 / *How long does it take to go there by bus?* 버스로 거기에 가자면 (시간이) 얼마나 걸리는가 / *How far is it from here to the station?* 여기서 정거장까지 (거리가) 얼마나 되나 / *How much did you pay for it?* 그것의 값을 얼마나 주었나 / *How damaged is the car?* 차의 손상은 어느 정도인가. ⓑ 《in *exclamations*》 ¶ *How beautiful* (*she is*)*!* 참 예쁘기도 하다 / *How cold it is!* 정말이지 춥기도 하다 / *How I envy you!* 정말이지 네가 부럽다 / *How she talks!* 정말이지 수다스러운 여자로군. **3** that, …인 것; …하다는 것. ¶ *I was taught how it was wrong to steal.* 훔치는 것은 나쁘다는 가르침을 받았다 / *I told him* ~ *I had read it in the papers.* 신문에서 본 것을 그에게 말했다. **4** to what effect; with what meaning. 어떻게; 어떤 의도로; 무슨 뜻으로. ¶ *How do you mean?* 무슨 뜻입니까; 무슨 말씀인가요 / *How do you say so?* 어떤 의도로 그렇게 말하는가. **5** 《*colloq.*》 What?; I beg your pardon? 뭐라고요. ¶ *How?* 뭐라고요, 다시 한 번 말씀해 주세요. **6** 《in *relative clauses*》 ⓐ the way or manner in which. 어떻게 …인지. ¶ *This is* ~ *it happened.* 일의 발단〔원인〕은 다음과 같다 / *That's* ~ *it is.* 실정은 이상과 같다. ⓑ in whatever way or manner; however. 어떻게든; 아무리 …해도. 語法 이 때 동사+how+형용사〔부사〕+주어+may 〔will〕의 형태를 취하는 수가 많음. ¶ *Work* ~ *hard you may*… 네가 아무리 열심히 일해도… / *Do it* ~ *you can.* 어떻게든 (능력껏) 해 보아라.

and how, 《U.S. *colloq.*》 **a**) of course; certainly. 그렇고말고; 물론. **b**) to a great degree. 무척. ¶ *"Did they enjoy themselves?" "And* ~ *!"* "그들은 즐거워하더냐" "그럼요".

How about …? How would you like…? …하는 것이 어떻습니까; …은 어떤가요. ¶ *How about a little walk?* 잠깐 산책하는 게 어떨까.

How come …? 《U.S. *colloq.*》 Why. 어째서; 왜. ¶ *How come you didn't go with him?* 어째서 그와 함께 가지 않았나.

How comes it that …? How does it happen that …? 어째서 그런가; …하다는 것이 있을 수 있을까.

How do you do [háudjudú:, -djə-]***?*** **a**) 《used in greeting a person or upon being introduced》 안녕하십니까; 처음 뵙겠습니다. **b**) 《*arch.*》 How are you? 안녕하십니까 《상대방의 건강에 관해서》.

How do you like … ? What is your impression of …? …에 대한 인상은 어떠하냐.

How goes it? How are you and your affairs in general progressing? 어떻게 지내나; 경기는 어떤가.

How now? What does this mean? 이건 어찌된 일인가.

How say you? What do you think about it? 너의 생각은.

How so? Why is it so? 어째서 그렇지.

How's that? **a**) What do you think of that? 그것을 어찌 생각하나. **b**) =How so?

How the deuce 〔***the devil, the dickens, ever, on earth***〕***?*** used colloquially to intensify. 도대체 어떻게 해서.

How then? What is the meaning of this? 이건 어찌된 일인가.

No matter how … may, in whatever way

or degree; however... may. 아무리 …해도. ¶ *No matter ~ hard you may work, you will not succeed.* 아무리 열심히 일한다 해도 성공하지 못할 걸세.
—*n.* Ⓒ 《usu. *the* ~》 a manner; means. 방법. ¶ *Tell me the ~ and why of it.* 그 방법과 이유를 말하시오. [E.]

How·ard [háuərd] *n.* a man's name. 남자 「이름.

how·be·it [haubí:it] *conj.* 《*arch.*》 =nevertheless. [E.]

how·dah [háudə] *n.* a railed or canopied seat on the elephant's back. 상교(象轎) 《코끼리 등에 얹은, 닫집이 있는 가마》. [Arab. =litter]

how-d'ye-do [háudidú:] *n.* 《*colloq.*》 an embarrassing situation. 난처〔곤란〕한 일; 괴로운 입장. ¶ *Here's a nice* 〔*pretty*〕 ~. 이것 난처하군. [Abbr. of *how-do-you-do*]

how·e'er [hauέər] *conj., adv.* =however.

:how·ev·er [hauévər] *conj.* nevertheless; though; yet. 그러나; 그렇지만. 語法 접속사로서의 however는 문장의 도중이나 끝에 사용되는 수가 많으며 콤마로 끊어서 삽입됨. ¶ *Later, ~, he decided to go.* 하지만 나중에 그는 가기로 결정했다 / *His mind, ~ did not change.* 그러나 그의 마음은 변하지 않았다 / *It is mine, ~ you may use it.* 그건 내 것이다. 그렇지만 사용해도 좋다 / *Our vacation is not very long; ~ , we plan to go on a trip.* 우리들의 휴가는 그다지 길지는 않다. 하지만 우리는 여행을 할 계획을 하고 있다.
—*adv.* **1** in whatever manner or degree; no matter how. 아무리 …하더라도〔해도〕. ¶ *The work, ~ difficult* (*it may be*), *must be finished by the time fixed.* 이 일은 아무리 어렵더라도 정해진 시간에 끝내야만 한다. **2** in whatever way; by whatever means. 어떻게든. ¶ *Do it ~ you can.* 어떻게든 이 일을 하시오. **3** 《*colloq., emph.*》 《in *questions*》 how in the world. 도대체 어떻게. ¶ *However did you escape?* 도대체 어떻게 도망쳤나. [*how, ever*]

how·itz·er [háuitsər] *n.* a short cannon for firing shells in a high curve. 곡사포(曲射砲). [Boh. =catapult]

:howl [haul] *vi.* (P1,2A) **1** give a long, loud, sad cry, as a dog, a wolf, etc. (개·늑대 따위가) 길게 (여운을 남기며) 짖다. ¶ *Wolves were howling in the distance.* 이리들이 멀리서 길게 짖고 있었다. **2** (of a person) give a long, loud cry of pain, anger or contempt. (고통·노여움 따위로) 울부짖다; 악쓰다; 신음하다; 노호하다. ¶ ~ *like an injured dog* 부상한 개처럼 울부짖다. **3** yell; shout. 소리 지르다. **4** give a long cry like a strong wind. (바람 따위가) 윙윙거리다. ¶ *The wind howled through the trees.* 바람이 나무 사이를 빠져 나가며 윙윙 소리를 내었다.
—*vt.* (P6,7) **1** say (words) in a crying tone. …을 신음하며〔악을 쓰며, 울부짖으며〕 말하다. ¶ ~ (*out*) *obscenities* 추잡한 말을 떠들어대다. **2** make (someone) silent by howling. 고함을 쳐 …을 침묵시키다.
howl down, stop (someone) from speaking by howling or otherwise showing contempt. 소리쳐 …을 침묵시키다. ¶ ~ *down a speaker* 소리를 질러 연사를 침묵시키다.
—*n.* Ⓒ **1** a long, loud, sorrowful cry. (늑대·개 따위의) 길게 짖는 소리. ¶ *the ~ of a dog.* **2** a loud cry of pain, etc. (고통 따위의) 울부짖는〔악쓰는, 아우성, 신음〕 소리; 노호. ¶ *a ~ of pain* / *raise a ~ over high taxes* 높은 세금에 아우성치다. **3** a yell; a shout. 경멸의 웃음 소리; 고함 소리. [Imit.]

howl·er [háulər] *n.* Ⓒ **1** a person or thing that howls. 짖는 짐승; 울부짖는 사람. **2** 《Brit. *colloq.*》 an unreasonable mistake; a foolish mistake., esp. in an examination. 대실책; 큰 실수(=《U.S.》 boner).

howl·ing [háuliŋ] *adj.* **1** producing or uttering a howl. 짖는; 울부짖는; 소리치는. ¶ *a ~ dog* 짖는 개 / *a ~ wind* 윙윙대는 바람 / *a ~ mob* 아우성치는 군중. **2** lonely; lonesome. 외로운; 쓸쓸한. ¶ *a ~ wilderness* 쓸쓸한 황야. **3** 《*colloq.*》 enormous. 엄청난; 굉장한. ¶ *a ~ success* 굉장한 성공.

how·so·ev·er [hàusouévər] *adv.* 《*arch.*》 =however.

hoy·den [hɔ́idn] *n.* Ⓒ a rude, rough-mannered girl; a noisy, active girl. 말괄량이; 덜렁이 처녀. [? Du. *heiden* heathen]

HP, H.P., hp., h.p. horse-power; half pay; high pressure; hire purchase.

HQ, H.Q. headquarters.

hr. hour; hours.

H.R. House of Representatives.

H.R.H. His 〔Her〕 Royal Highness. 전하.

hrs. hours.

hub [hʌb] *n.* Ⓒ **1** the central part of a wheel. (수레바퀴의) 중심; 바퀴통. **2** 《*fig.*》 a center of interest, activity or importance, etc. (흥미·활동·권위 따위의) 중심; 중추. ¶ *the ~ of the universe* 우주의 중심 / *His office is at the ~ of the city.* 그의 회사는 시의 중심에 있다. [→hob]

hub·bub [hʌ́bʌb] *n.* Ⓤ a loud, confused noise; an uproar. 와글와글; 시끌벅적함; 소란. ¶ *The class was in a ~ when the teacher came in.* 선생님이 들어왔을 때 반은 시끌벅적했다. [Icel.]

Hu·bert [hjú:bə(:)rt] *n.* a man's name. 남자 이름.

hu·bris [hjú:bris] *n.* insolent pride. 지나친 자부; 오만. [Gk.]

huck·a·back [hʌ́kəbæ̀k] *n.* Ⓤ a heavy, coarse linen or cotton cloth, used for towels. 허커백직(織)《타월지(地)》. [?]

huck·le·ber·ry [hʌ́kəlbèri] *n.* Ⓒ (*pl.* **-ries**) **1** a small blue-black berry like a blueberry. 월귤. **2** 《bot.》 the shrub that huckleberries grow on. 월귤나무류(類). [E.]

huck·ster [hʌ́kstər] *n.* Ⓒ **1** ⓐ a walking merchant, esp. one who deals in fruits

and vegetables. (과일·야채의) 행상인; 도붓장수. ⓑ a person who sells small articles; a petty trader. (자잘한 물건을 파는) 소매상인; 소상인. **2** a mean person working for money only. 오직 돈만을 위해 일하는 비열한 사람. **3** 《U.S. *colloq.*》 a person who is in the advertising business. 광고[선전]업자.
— *vt., vi.* (P6; 1) **1** carry round (goods) for sale; deal in small articles. (…을) 행상하다; 자잘한 물건을 팔다. **2** haggle. 값을 깎다. [E.]

·**hud·dle** [hʌ́dl] *vi.* **1** (P2A) 《*together, up*》 crowd together in a confused way. (질서 없이) 떼지어 모이다; 여럿이 떼지어 몰려들다. ¶ ~ *together around the fire* 난로 주변에 떼지어 몰려들다. **2** 《football》 gather to get signals. (미식 축구에서) 선수들이 스크럼선 뒤에 집합하다. **3** hunch oneself up in a heap. (몸이) 움츠러들다.
— *vt.* (P7,13) **1** 《*together, up*》 cause (things or persons) to move in a heap or quickly and without order. …을 난잡하게 모으다; 잔뜩 태우다. ¶ *a group of cottages huddled together* 다닥다닥 들어선 일군의 소주택 / ~ *the boys into a bus* 아이들을 버스에 빽빽이 태우다 / ~ *clothes into a trunk* 트렁크에 옷을 잔뜩 쑤셔 넣다. **2** 《*up*》 curl oneself (up). (몸을) 웅크리다; 쭈그리다. ¶ *lie huddled up in bed* 쪼그리고 자리에 눕다. **3** 《*on*》 put on clothes hastily. (옷)을 급히 입다; 걸치다. ¶ ~ *on one's clothes.* **4** 《*through, over*》 do a task, etc. hurriedly or carelessly. (일)을 급히 아무렇게나 하다. ¶ ~ *a job through* 몹시 서둘러 일을 하다 / ~ *over one's duty* 직무를 되는 대로 수행하다.
— *n.* Ⓒ **1** a confused crowd or group of things or persons. 난잡하게 모인 무리. ¶ *huddles of pigs* 빽빽이 들어찬 돼지 떼. **2** disorder; confusion. 혼란; 난잡. ¶ *all in a* ~ 몹시 난잡하게. **3** a grouping of football players before a play to get signals. (미식 축구에서) 선수의 집합. [E.]
go into a huddle, 《*sl.*》 have a secret discussion. 비밀히 상의[협의]하다; 밀의(密議)하다. ¶ *The professors went into a* ~. 교수들은 비밀 회의를 했다.

·**hue**[1] [hjuː] *n.* Ⓒ **1** a particular shade of color; a color; a tint. 색채; 색조; 색; 빛깔. ¶ *a dark* ~ 어두운 색조 / *flowers of every* ~ 여러 가지 색의 꽃 / *The* ~ *of death stole over his features.* 죽음의 빛이 어느 결엔가 그의 얼굴에 나타나 있었다. **2** 《*fig.*》 a variety of opinion. 여러 가지 의견. [E.]

hue[2] [hjuː] *n.* Ⓒ a cry, as in war or pursuit. 고함 소리. 語法 오늘날에는 다음 구에만 쓰임. [F. *huer* shout]
hue and cry, a loud cry of pursuit, alarm, or protest. (추적·놀람·항의의) 외치는 소리. ¶ *raise a* ~ *and cry* '도둑이야, 도둑이야' 하고 소리치다.

huff [hʌf] *n.* Ⓒ a burst of anger. 화냄; 분노. ¶ *take* ~ 버럭 화를 내다 / *get into a* ~ *about nothing* 아무것도 아닌 일에 화를 내다 / *in a* ~ 불끈하여. — *vt.* **1** (P6) make (someone) angry; offend. …을 성나게 하다. ¶ *She was huffed by his rudeness.* 그의 무례함에 그녀는 화가 났다. **2** (P13) 《*into, out of*》 freighten by noisy talk or threats. …을 호통쳐[을러대어] …하게 하다. ¶ ~ *someone into silence* 호통을 쳐 침묵시키다 / ~ *someone out of the room* 호통쳐서 방에서 내쫓다.
— *vi.* (P1) get angry. 성내다. [Imit. of blowing]

huff·ish [hʌ́fiʃ] *adj.* **1** rather angry; irritable; 찌무룩한; 성 잘 내는. **2** insolent; swaggering. 오만한; 뽐내는.

huff·y [hʌ́fi] *adj.* (**huff·i·er, huff·i·est**) **1** offended; keeping silent. 성난; 찌무룩한. **2** easily offended; easily made angry. 화[성]잘 내는. ●**huff·i·ly** [-li] *adv.* **huff·i·ness** [-nis] *n.*

·**hug** [hʌg] *vt.* (**hugged, hug·ging**) (P6) **1** hold (someone) tight in the arms, esp. as a sign of affection. …을 꼭 껴안다; 포옹하다. ¶ *The girl hugged her doll.* 소녀는 인형을 부둥켜안았다. **2** cling to (an idea, etc.). …을 품다; 고집하다. ¶ ~ *a prejudice* 편견을 품다 / ~ *an opinion* 의견을 가지다. **3** (of a ship) keep close to a shore. (배가 해안 근처를) 항행하다.
hug one's chains, be glad of servitude. 속박을 감수하다.
hug oneself on [***for, over***], be pleased with (something). …을 기뻐하다. ¶ ~ *oneself on finding a job* 일자리를 만나 기뻐하다.
— *n.* Ⓒ a tight hold, esp. with the arms. 꼭 껴안음; 포옹. ¶ *a bear* ~ 강한 포옹 / *give mother a* ~ 어머니를 꼭 껴안다. [N.]

:**huge** [hjuːdʒ, juːdʒ] *adj.* (**hug·er, hug·est**) very large; enormous. 매우 큰; 거대[방대]한. ¶ ~ *profits* 막대한 이득 / *a* ~ *building* 거대한 건물 / *a* ~ *difference* 엄청난 차이 / *a* ~ *amount of money* 거금(巨金). ●**huge·ness** [-nis] *n.* [Teut.]

huge·ly [hjúːdʒli] *adv.* to a great extent; very much. 대단하게, 엄청나게.

Hu·go [hjúːgou], **Victor** *n.* (1802-85) a French poet and novelist. 위고《프랑스의 시인·소설가》.

hulk [hʌlk] *n.* Ⓒ **1** the body of an old, wrecked ship. 노후선(老朽船)[폐선]의 선체. **2** a big, badly made ship. 크고 다루기 거북한 배. **3** 《*fig.*》 a big, awkward person or thing. 덩치가 큰 사람[물건]. ¶ *a* ~ *of a man* 거한(巨漢). [E. *hulc*]

hulk·ing [hʌ́lkiŋ] *adj.* bulky; clumsy. 부피가 큰; 몰골스러운. ¶ *We can't move that* ~ *table in our room.* 저 거창한 탁자는 우리 방에 못 들어간다.

hull[1] [hʌl] *n.* Ⓒ **1** the outer covering of a seed, fruit, and vegetable. 껍질; 외피; 꼬투리. **2** any outer covering. (겉을 싸고 있는) 덮개. — *vt.* (P6) remove the hull from (something). …의 껍질을 벗기다; 꼬투리를 까다. ¶ ~ *peas* / *hulled rice* 현미. ● **hull·er** [´-ər] *n.* [E.]

hull² [hʌl] *n.* Ⓒ the body or frame of a ship or an airship. (배·비행선의) 선체.

hull down, so far away that the hull is below the horizon. (배가 돛대만 보일뿐) 선체는 보이지 않는; 아득히 멀리.

— *vt.* strike or pierce the hull of (a ship). (어뢰 따위로 선체)를 관통하다. [↑, G. *hülle*]

hul·la·ba·loo [hʌ́ləbəlù:] *n.* a loud noise or disturbance. 왁자지껄한 시끄러운 소리; 난장판. ¶ *make*〔*raise*〕 *a* ~ 큰 소동을 벌이다; 법석을 떨다. [E.]

hul·lo [həlóu, hʌ́lou, hʌlóu] *interj.* =《Brit.》 hello. [E.]

∗**hum** [hʌm] *v.* (**hummed, hum·ming**) *vi.* (P1,2A) **1** make a continuous sound like that of a bee. (벌 따위가) 붕붕〔윙윙〕거리다. ¶ *The sewing machine is humming.* 재봉틀이 윙윙거린다. **2** make a low [m] sound in thought, hesitation, etc. 말을 우물거리다. **3** sing without opening the lips. (입을 다문 채) 노래를 흥얼거리다. ¶ ~ *a song* 콧노래를 부르다. **4** (of business, etc.) be busy and active. 활기가 있다; 부산하게 움직이다. ¶ *make things* ~ 활기를 띠게 하다 / *The office was really humming* (*with activity*). 종업원들은 아주 분주하게 움직이고 있었다. — *vt.* (P6) **1** sing (a song) without opening the lips. (입을 열지 않고) 흥얼거리다; 콧노래를 부르다. **2** put or bring (someone to do) by humming. 콧노래를 불러 …이 —하게 하다. ¶ *The mother hummed the baby to sleep.* 엄마는 콧노래로 자장가를 불러 아기를 재웠다.

hum along, move along rapidly, esp. in a motorcar etc. (차 따위를 타고) 쌩하고 달리다.

hum and haw 〔***ha***〕, make such sounds through embarrassment when speaking; hesitate; be unable to make up one's mind. (난처해서) 흠 소리를 연발하다; 망설이다; 결심을 하지 못하다.

— *n.* **1** Ⓒ a continuous buzzing sound like that of a bee. (벌 따위의) 윙윙〔붕붕〕 소리. ¶ *the* ~ *of bees.* **2** a low [m] sound uttered in thought, hesitation, etc. (생각·당혹·주저 따위의) 흠〔우물거리는〕 소리. **3** the sound of singing without opening the lips. 콧노랫소리.

— *interj.* a low [m] sound showing surprise, disagreement, doubt, hesitation, etc. 흠; 으응; 어영《놀람·불찬성·의심 따위를 나타내서》.

● **hum·mer** [´-ər] *n.* [Imit.]

⁑**hu·man** [*h*jú:mən] *adj.* **1** of or characteristic of man or mankind. 사람의; 인간의; 인간 특유의. ¶ *a* ~ *being* 인간 / ~ *nature* 인간성 / ~ *progress* 인간의 진보 / *I can't do everything; I'm only* ~. 내가 모든 것을 다할 수는 없다, 나는 그저 인간에 불과하니까 / *He must be less than* ~ *not to be moved by such a story.* 그와 같은 이야기에 감동하지 않는 것을 보니 그는 인간 이하임이 틀림없다. **2** possessed by or suitable for man. 인간에게 흔히 있는; 인간에게 어울리는. ¶ ~ *frailties* 인간의 약함〔약점〕 / *To err is* ~, *to forgive divine.* 잘못을 저지르는 것은 사람이요, 용서함은 신(神)이 하는 일이다. 參考 Pope 의 말.

— *n.* Ⓒ《usu. *pl.*》《*colloq.*》 a person; a human being. 사람; 인간. ¶ *humans and animals* 인간과 동물. [L. *humanus.*]

∗**hu·mane** [*h*ju:méin] *adj.* **1** kind; merciful. 인정 있는; 자비 깊은. ¶ *a man of* ~ *character* 마음씨가 다정한 사람 / *a* ~ *method of killing animals* (짐승의) 무통 도살법. **2** ⓐ tending to be refined; polished. 고상한; 우아한. ⓑ (of studies) concerned with the humanities. 인문학의. ¶ ~ *learning* 고전 문학 / ~ *studies* 인문 과학. ● **hu·mane·ness** [-nis] *n.* [*human*]

hu·mane·ly [*h*ju:méinli] *adv.* kindly; mercifully. 인정 많게; 자비 깊게.

human engineering [´-—-´-] *n.* **1** the industrial management of labor. 인간 관리. **2** the technology of efficient use of machines by human beings. 인간 공학.

∗**hu·man·ism** [*h*jú:mənìzəm] *n.* Ⓤ **1** human nature. 인간성. **2** system of thought or action concerned with human interests. 인본주의. **3** literary culture based on Latin and Greek culture. 인문학; 고전 문학 연구.

∗**hu·man·ist** [*h*jú:mənist] *n.* Ⓒ **1** a person who studies human interests and values. 인간성 연구가; 인본〔인도〕주의자. **2** a person who studies Latin and Greek culture. 고전 문학 연구가.

hu·man·is·tic [*h*jù:mənístik] *adj.* of humanism or humanists. 인간 연구의; 인문학의; 인문주의적인; 고전적인.

hu·man·i·tar·i·an [*h*ju(:)mæ̀nətέəriən] *n.* Ⓒ a person who is devoted to the health, good condition, happiness, etc. of human beings. 인도〔박애〕주의자. — *adj.* devoted to the health, good condition, happiness, etc. of human beings. 인도주의의; 박애(博愛)의.

hu·man·i·tar·i·an·ism [*h*ju(:)mæ̀nətέəriənìzəm] *n.* Ⓤ humanitarian principles. 인도주의; 박애주의.

∗**hu·man·i·ty** [*h*ju:mǽnəti] *n.* (*pl.* **-ties**) **1** Ⓤ《*collectively*》 human beings; mankind. 인간; 인류. ¶ *a friend of* ~ 인류의 벗. **2** Ⓤ the fact of being human; human nature. 인성(人性); 인간성. **3** Ⓤ the quality of being humane; kindness; mercy. 인정; 자애; 친절; 자비. ¶ *a lovely* ~ 아름다운 인간애. **4** 《*the -ties*》 ⓐ the Latin and Greek languages and literatures. 그리스·라틴어학〔문학〕. ⓑ branches of learning concerned with language, literature, philosophy, art, etc. 인문 과학《사회 과학이나 자연 과학에 대한 문학·철학·예술 등》.

hu·man·ize, 《Brit.》 **-ise** [*h*jú:mənàiz] *vt.* (P6) **1** give a human nature to (something). …에게 인간성을 부여하다. **2** make (someone) kind or merciful. …을 인간답게 하다. — *vi.* (P1) become human or humane. 인간다워지다; 자비로워지다.

hu·man·kind [*h*jú:mənkáind] *n.* Ⓤ 《*collectively*》 human beings; mankind. 인간; 인류(=mankind).

hu·man·ly [*h*jú:mənli] *adv.* **1** in a human way. 인간적으로. ¶ *They want to live* ~. 그들은 인간답게 살기를 원한다. **2** in a kind manner. 인정에서; 인간답게. **3** according to the feelings, knowledge, or experience of men. 인간적 견지에서; 인간의 (할 수 있는) 방법으로; 인간의 판단으로; 경험으로; 인력으로. ¶ *It is not* ~ *possible.* 인간의 힘으로는 불가능하다 / *Humanly speaking, he cannot recover.* 인간적인 견지에서 말하자면, 그는 회복할 수 없다 / *We will do whatever is* ~ *possible.* 우리는 인력으로 할 수 있는 것은 무엇이나 하겠다.

:hum·ble [*h*ʌ́mbəl] *adj.* **1** low in position or condition. (비)천한; 변변치 않은; 보잘것 없는. ¶ *a* ~ *cottage* 초라한 집 / *of* ~ *birth* 비천한 태생의 / *a* ~ *income* 하찮은 수입 / *Your* ~ *servant* 여불비례(餘不備禮)《편지의 끝맺음 말》. **2** not thinking of one's own power; not proud. 겸허한; 겸손한; 조심스러운. ¶ *a* ~ *heart* [*person*] 겸손한 마음[사람] / *a* ~ *smile* 수줍은 미소 / ~ *in manner* 태도가 겸손한 / *He became very famous, but remained* ~. 그는 유명해졌지만 교만하지 않았다.

eat humble pie, apologize in a very humble manner. 겸허하게 사과하다.

— *vt.* (P6) make (someone) humble; make (someone) lower in position or pride. …을 천하게 하다; …의 콧대를 꺾다; …의 품위를 떨어뜨리다. ¶ *The failure humbled him.* 그 실패로 그는 한풀 죽었다. [L. *humus* ground]

humble oneself, be modest. 겸손하다.

hum·ble·bee [hʌ́mblbì:] *n.* a bumblebee. 뒝벌. [E. =humming bee]

hum·ble·ness [*h*ʌ́mbəlnis] *n.* Ⓤ the state of being humble. 겸손; 비하(卑下); 비천. [*humble*]

humble plant [⌐-⌐] *n.* 《bot.》 a common sensitive plant. 함수초(含羞草).

hum·bly [*h*ʌ́mbli] *adv.* in a humble manner. 겸손하게[하여]; 스스로를 낮추어; 비천하게.

hum·bug [hʌ́mbʌ̀g] *n.* **1** Ⓒ a dishonest person; a deceiver. 사기꾼; 협잡꾼. **2** ⓊⒸ dishonest behavior or talk; the state of being deceitful. 사기; 협잡; 속임수. — *vt., vi.* (P6,13; 1) 《*into, out of*》 deceive (someone) with dishonest behavior or talk. 속이다; 협잡질하다. ¶ ~ *someone into buying a worthless thing* 아무를 속여 무가치한 것을 사게 하다 / ~ *someone out of his money* 아무를 속여 돈을 빼앗다. — *interj.* Nonsense! 당치 않은. [18c. slang]

hum·drum [hʌ́mdrʌ̀m] *adj.* continuing without change; dull. 단조로운; 따분한. ¶ *a* ~ *life* 따분한 생활. — *n.* **1** Ⓒ a dull person. 따분한 사람. **2** Ⓤ the state of being humdrum. 단조로움; 따분함. [→hum]

hu·mid [*h*jú:mid] *adj.* wet; damp. 습기 있는; 습한; 눅눅[축축]한. ¶ *a* ~ *climate* 습한 기후 / *The air is* ~ *before it rains.* 비오기 전에는 공기가 축축하다. ● **hu·mid·ness** [-nis] *n.* [L. *umeo* be damp.]

hu·mid·i·fy [*h*ju:mídəfài] *vt.* (P6) make humid. 습하게[축축하게] 하다.

hu·mid·i·ty [*h*ju:mídəti] *n.* Ⓤ (P6) **1** the state of being humid; dampness. 습기; 축축함. **2** amount of water vapor in the air. 습도.

hu·mil·i·ate [*h*ju:mílièit] *vt.* (P6) lower the pride of (someone); bring shame to (someone). …의 자존심을 상하게 하다; 면목을 잃게 하다; …에게 굴욕을[창피를] 주다. ¶ *He was humiliated.* =*He humiliated himself.* 그는 창피를 당했다 / *A child who behaves badly before guests humiliates his parents.* 손님들 앞에서 버릇없이 구는 아이는 그 부모를 부끄럽게 한다. ● **hu·mil·i·at·ing·ly** [-iŋli] *adv.* [→humble]

hu·mil·i·a·tion [*h*ju:miliéiʃən] *n.* ⓊⒸ the act of humiliating; the state or feeling of being humiliated. 굴욕(감); 창피; 창피를[굴욕을] 줌[당함].

***hu·mil·i·ty** [*h*ju:míləti] *n.* **1** Ⓤ the state of being humble; modesty. 겸허; 겸손; 스스로를 낮춤. **2** 《usu. *pl.*》 an act showing a humble spirit. 겸손한 행위.

hum·ming [hʌ́miŋ] *adj.* **1** making an unchanging buzzing sound; singing a song without opening the lips. 윙윙[붕붕]거리는; 콧노래를 부르는. **2** quickly active; energetic. 잽싼; 활발한; 활동적[정력적]인. — *n.* Ⓤ a buzzing sound made by a bee; the act of singing with a hum. 윙윙[붕붕]대는 소리; 콧노래(를 부름). [→hum]

hum·ming·bird [hʌ́miŋbə̀:*r*d] *n.* Ⓒ a very small, brightly colored American bird that moves so rapidly as to make a humming sound. (미국산의) 벌새.

hum·mock [hʌ́mək] *n.* Ⓒ **1** a very small, rounded hill or mound. 작은 언덕. **2** a high part of an ice field. 빙원(氷原)의 빙구(氷丘). [? *hump*]

:hu·mor, 《Brit.》 **-mour** [*h*jú:mə*r*] *n.* Ⓤ **1** a funny or amusing quality; the ability to see or express what is funny, amusing, etc. 유머; 해학; 익살; 우스움; 유머를 이해하는 능력. ¶ *He has no sense of* ~. 그는 유머를 모른다[유머 감각이 없다] / *The story is full of* ~. 이 소설엔 유머가 넘쳐 있다. **2** 《often *a* ~》 a mood; a state of mind. (일시적인) 기분; 마음(의 상태). ¶ *please someone's* ~ 아

무의 기분을〔비위를〕 맞추다 / *be in the ~ for...* …할 마음이 내키다 / *be in no ~ for...* …할 마음이 전혀 없다 / *I am in no ~ for talking now.* 지금 이야기할 기분이 아니다 / *He is in a good* 〔*bad*〕 *~ this morning.* 그는 오늘 아침 기분이 좋다〔언짢다〕. **3** a person's natural way of feeling and acting; temperament. 기성(氣性); 기질. ¶ *a man of sanguine* 〔*cheerful*〕 *~* 낙천적인〔밝은〕 기질의 사람 / 《*prov.*》 *Every man has his ~.* 각인각색. **4** liquid inside the eye. (눈알의) 유리액; 수양액(=vitreous ~). **5** Ⓒ 《*arch.*》 any fluid or juice once considered to characterize the nature of an animal or a plant. (동물의) 체액; (식물의) 수액(樹液). ¶ *the cardinal humors,* 4 체액(體液)《혈액·점액·(황)담즙·흑담즙의 네가지》.

out of humor, angry; irritated; in a bad mood. 기분이 언짢아; 성이 나서; 찌무룩하여.

— *vt.* (P6) **1** fit oneself to the mood or wishes of (someone); indulge. …의 비위를 맞추다; 어르다; (사람·취미·기질 따위)를 만족시키다. ¶ *A sick child has to be humored.* 앓는 아이는 비위를 맞춰주어야 한다. **2** act in agreement with the nature of (someone). …와 가락을 맞추다; 동조하다; 잘 다루다. [→humid]

hu·mor·esque [*h*jùːmərésk] *n.* Ⓒ 《mus.》 a light, humorous piece of music. 표일곡(飄逸曲); 유머레스크. [↑]

hu·mor·ist [*h*júːmərist] *n.* Ⓒ a person who writes or says something with a sense of humor. 해학가; 유머 작가.

hu·mor·ous [*h*júːmərəs] *adj.* full of humor; funny; amusing. 유머러스한; 유머가 풍부한; 우스운; 익살스러운; 재미있는. ● **hu·mor·ous·ness** [-nis] *n.*

hu·mor·ous·ly [*h*júːmərəsli] *adv.* in a humorous manner. 우스꽝스럽게; 우습게.

hu·mour [*h*júːmə*r*] *n., v.* 《Brit.》 =humor.

hump [hʌmp] *n.* Ⓒ **1** a rounded, raised-up part like that on the back of a camel. (등의) 혹; 군살. ¶ *Some camels have two humps on their backs.* 어떤 낙타는 등의 혹이 둘이다. **2** a mound; a small, round hill. 원구(圓丘); 야산. **3** 《Brit. *colloq.*》 a fit of depression or melancholy; a feeling of bad temper. 우울; 기분 나쁨; 화. ¶ *get the ~* 우울해〔기분이 나빠〕지다; 화가 나다 / *It gives me the ~.* 우울해진다; 속이 상한다.

get a hump on, 《*colloq.*》 hurry; move fast. 서두르다.

over the hump, past the most difficult part or the crisis; out of danger. 위기를 벗어나; 고비를 넘겨.

— *vt.* (P6,7) raise or bend (the back) into a hump. (등)을 둥그렇게 하다〔구부리다〕; 새우등으로 하다. ¶ *The cat humped her back when she saw the dog.* 고양이는 개를 보자 등을 웅크렸다. [?]

hump·back [hʌ́mpbæ̀k] *n.* Ⓒ **1** a rounded, raised-up back; a crooked back. 곱사등; 새우등. **2** a person with a crooked back. 곱사등이; 꼽추. **3** a large whale that has a humplike fin. 혹등고래.

hump·backed [hʌ́mpbæ̀kt] *adj.* having a humpback. 곱사등(이)의; 꼽추의.

humph [hʌmf, m̥mm̥, mm̥m] *interj.* exclamation uttered in doubt, contempt, etc. 흐응; 흥《의혹·경멸 따위를 나타냄》. — *n.* Ⓒ this kind of exclamation. 흐응; 흥. — *vi.* utter this kind of exclamation. 흐흥〔흥〕하다. [Imit.]

Hum·phrey [hʌ́mfri] *n.* a man's name. 남자 이름.

hump·ty-dump·ty [hʌ́m*p*tidʌ́m*p*ti] *n.* a short dumpty person. 땅딸보. [*hump*]

hu·mus [hjúːməs] *n.* Ⓤ rich soil made from decayed leaves and other vegetable matter. 부식토(腐植土). [L. =ground]

Hun [hʌn] *n.* Ⓒ **1** a member of a warlike, brutal Asiatic people who attacked Europe in the 5th century. 흉노(匈奴). **2** 《often *h-*》 《*fig.*》 a barbarous, destructive person. 야만적인 파괴자; 야만인. **3** 《*contempt.*》 a German soldier; a German. 독일 병정; 독일 사람. [L.]

hunch [hʌntʃ] *vt.* (P6) draw or bend (the back) to form a hump. (등)을 활 모양으로 구부리다. ¶ *He hunched his back to get into the hole.* 그는 구멍 속으로 들어가려고 등을 구부렸다. — *n.* Ⓒ **1** a rounded, raised-up part; a hump. (등의) 혹; 융기. **2** 《U.S. *colloq.*》 a feeling that something will happen. 직감; 예감. ¶ *I have a ~ that something good will happen today.* 오늘은 뭔가 좋은 일이 있을 것 같은 예감이 든다. **3** a thick slice or piece. 두꺼운 조각〔덩어리〕. [? obs. *hinch* push]

hunch·back [hʌ́ntʃbæ̀k] *n.* =humpback.

hunch·backed [hʌ́ntʃbæ̀kt] *adj.* =humpbacked.

:hun·dred [hʌ́ndrəd] *n.* Ⓒ (*pl.* **-dreds** or *after a numeral* **-dred**) **1** ten times ten; 100. 백; 100(개). 語法 1백이면 a를 붙이며, 수사 뒤에서는 -s가 붙지않음. ¶ *a ~ of the men* 부하 백 명 / *four ~ and ten,* 410 / *some ~* 약 100 / *live to a ~* 백살이나 되도록 살다. **2** a large number (of). 많은 수; 많음. ¶ *hundreds of people* 많은 사람 / *have hundreds in the bank* 은행에 많은 돈이 있다 / *People came by* 〔*in*〕 *hundreds.* 많은 〔수백명이나 되는〕 사람들이 왔다. **3** 《hist.》 a division of an English county. (영국의) 백호촌(百戶村). 參考 영국 주(州)의 소 행정 단위.

— *adj.* being ten times ten. 백〔100〕의; 100개〔사람〕의. [E.]

a great 〔***long***〕 ***hundred,*** 120.

a hundred, very many. 아주 많은. ¶ *have a ~ things to do* 할 일이 태산같다.

a hundred and one, a large number of. 다수의; 많은.

a 〔***one***〕 ***hundred percent,*** completely. 완전

히; 백퍼센트로. ¶ *It's a ~ percent useless.* 그건 전혀 소용이 없다.

a hundred to one, almost certainly. 십중 팔구; 거의 확실히. ¶ *A ~ to one it will be a success.* 거의 틀림없이 성공할 게다.

hundreds and hundreds (of), a very large number (of). 매우 많은; (수·양이) 엄청난.

hundreds and thousands, sweets like a small shot used chiefly for decorating cakes, etc. 케이크 장식에 뿌리는 굵은 설탕.

***not a hundred miles from* (*away*),** not very far; at or close to. 그다지 멀지 않은 곳에; …의 가까이.

hun·dred·fold [hʌ́ndrədfòuld] *adj., adv., n.* a hundred times as much or as many. 100배(의, 로). ¶ *a ~ increase in production* 생산의 100 배 증가.

:hun·dredth [hʌ́ndrədθ] *adj., n.* **1** next after the 99th. 백번째(의). ¶ *the ~ day* 백일째. **2** one of 100 equal parts. 100분의 1 (의).

hun·dred·weight [hʌ́ndrədwèit] *n.* Ⓒ (*pl.* **-weights** or *after a numeral* **-weight**) a unit of weight equal to 100 pounds in the United States or 112 pounds in England. 형량(衡量) 단위의 이름《미국은 100 파운드, 영국은 112 파운드》. 參考 cwt.로 생략함.

:hung [hʌŋ] *v.* p. and pp. of **hang.**

Hun·gar·i·an [hʌŋgέəriən] *adj.* of Hungary, its people, or their language. 헝가리(사람, 말)의. — *n.* **1** Ⓒ a person of Hungary. 헝가리 사람. **2** Ⓤ the language of Hungary. 헝가리 말.

Hun·ga·ry [hʌ́ŋgəri] *n.* a country in central Europe. 헝가리. 參考 수도는 Budapest.

:hun·ger [hʌ́ŋgər] *n.* **1** Ⓤ the weak condition caused by lack of food. 기아; 굶주림. ¶ *die of ~* 굶어 죽다. **2** Ⓤ the strong desire for food. 배고픔; 공복(감). ¶ *satisfy one's ~* 허기를 채우다 / *collapse from ~* 배가 고파 쓰러지다 / 《*prov.*》 *Hunger is the best sauce.* 시장이 반찬이다. **3** 《usu. *a ~*》 a strong desire. 열망; 갈망. ¶ *~ for power* 강한 권력욕 / *out of ~ for something to do* 무언가 못견디게 하고 싶어 / *a ~ for change* 변화에 대한 강한 욕구 / *He had a ~ for knowledge.* 그는 지식에 굶주려 있었다.
— *vi.* (P1,3) **1** feel hunger; be hungry. 굶주리다; 배고프다. **2** 《*for, after*》 have a strong desire for something. 열망〔갈망〕하다. ¶ *~ for news* 애타게 소식을 기다리다 / *~ after a little kindness* 작은 친절에 굶주리다.
— *vt.* (P6,13) make (someone) feel hunger; make (someone) do something because of hunger. …을 굶주리게 하다; …을 굶주리게 하여 —하게 하다. [E.]

hunger march [⌐‐ ⌐] *n.* that of unemployed workers who demonstrate because they are starving. (실직자의) 기아 행진.

hunger strike [⌐‐ ⌐] *n.* a refusal to eat until certain demands are granted. 단식 투쟁.

hun·gri·ly [hʌ́ŋgrili] *adv.* **1** in hunger; in a hungry manner. 굶주려; 걸신들린 듯이. **2** with a strong desire. 열망하여; 갈망하여.

:hun·gry [hʌ́ŋgri] *adj.* (**-gri·er, -gri·est**) **1** feeling hunger. 굶주린; 배고픈. ¶ *feel ~* 배고픔을 느끼다 / *He was ~ after the hard work.* 고된 일을 하고 나서 그는 시장했다. **2** showing hunger. 배고픈〔시장한〕 듯한. ¶ *a lean and ~ look* 야위고 배고픈 듯한 얼굴. **3** causing hunger. 배고프게 하는. ¶ *~ work* 배고파지는 일. **4** 《*for*》 having a strong desire; eager. 갈망〔열망〕하는. ¶ *He is ~ for information.* 그는 지식을 갈망하고 있다. **5** (of soil) not rich; poor. (땅이) 척박한; 빈약한; 불모의. ¶ *~ soil* 척박한 땅.

***as hungry as a hunter* (*wolf*),** very hungry. 몹시 배가 고픈.

go hungry, go without food; starve. 먹지않고 있다; 굶(주리)다.

● **hun·gri·ness** [-nis] *n.*

hunk [hʌŋk] *n.* Ⓒ 《*colloq.*》 a big mass or piece. 큰 덩어리; 두껍게 벤 것(cf. *hunch*). [? Flem.]

hunks [hʌŋks] *n. pl.* a miser. 구두쇠. [Du.]

hun·kers [hʌ́ŋkərz] *n. pl.* haunches. 둔부(臀部); 엉덩이.

on one's hunkers, in a squatting position. 쭈그리고; 웅크리고.

:hunt [hʌnt] *vt.* **1** (P6) go after (game or other wild animals) for the purpose of killing or catching them. …을 사냥하다; 수렵하다. ¶ *~ a deer* 사슴사냥을 하다 / *~ big game* 큰 사냥감을 사냥하다 / *go out hunting* 사냥나가다. **2** (P6,7,13) ⓐ search through (a region) looking for wild animals, etc. (사냥거리 등이 있는 지역)을 사냥하며 다니다. ¶ *~ the wood* 숲속을 사냥하며 돌아다니다. ⓑ 《often *up, out, for*》 search (a place) carefully; look for (something); try to find eagerly. (장소)를 샅샅이 찾다; …을 찾다〔구하다〕; 찾으려고〔손에 넣으려고〕 애쓰다. ¶ *~ up words in a dictionary* 사전에서 낱말을 찾다 / *~ for fame* 명성을 추구하다 / *~ out facts* 진실을 찾아내다 / *~ (up) the house for the papers* 집을 샅샅이 뒤져 서류를 찾다 / *go about hunting for a job* 일자리를 찾아다니다. **3** (P6,7,13) ⓐ 《often *from, down*》 chase; drive away; pursue; hound; harry. 몰아내다; 몰이하다; 쫓아버리다; 뒤쫓다; 추적하여 잡다. ¶ *~ a murderer* 살인범을 뒤쫓다 / *~ crows away* 까마귀를 쫓아버리다 / *~ a fox out of its earth* 여우를 굴에서 몰아내다 / *The convict was hunted from the town.* 죄인은 마을에서 추방되었다. ⓑ use (dogs or horses) in hunting. (개·말 따위를) 사냥에 쓰다. ¶ *~ a pack of hounds* 한떼의 사냥개를 부리다.
— *vi.* (P1,3) **1** run after wild animals. 사

냥을 하다. ¶ *go hunting* 사냥하러 가다. **2** 《*for, after*》 seek. 찾다. ¶ ~ *for a lost book* 잃어버린 책을 찾다.
hunt down, **a**) run after (a wild animal, etc.) until successful in killing or catching it; search and find or catch. …을 바짝 뒤쫓아 잡다〔죽이다〕; 찾아 발견하다〔잡다〕. **b**) persecute. 박해하다.
hunt out, find (something or someone) by searching. …을 찾아내다.
hunt up, **a**) search for. …을 찾다. **b**) find (someone) by searching. …을 찾아내다.
— *n.* Ⓒ **1** the act of hunting; a chase. 사냥; 수렵. ¶ *a lion* ~ 사자 사냥 / *have a* ~ 사냥을 하다 / *go on a* ~ 사냥을 가다. **2** a careful search (for something). 찾기; 수색; 탐색; 추구. ¶ *a* ~ *for a job* 일자리 찾기 / *a* ~ *for profit* 이윤의 추구. **3** the act of running after in order to catch something or someone; pursuit. 추적. **4** a group of persons who hunt together. 수렵대(狩獵隊); 수렵 단체. **5** a district for hunting. 수렵 지구; 사냥터. [E.]

hunt ball [⌐⌐] *n.* 《Brit.》 a dancing party given by members of a hunt. 수렵 회원이 개최하는 무도회.

:hunt·er [hʌ́ntər] *n.* Ⓒ **1** a person who hunts. 사냥꾼. **2** a horse or dog trained for hunting. 사냥말; 사냥개. **3** a person who looks for something. (무언가) 찾는 사람; 탐구〔추구〕하는 사람. **4** a kind of watch with a metal cover protecting the dial. 헌터《(사냥꾼용의) 뚜껑이 앞뒤에 달린 회중 시계》.

:hunt·ing [hʌ́ntiŋ] *n.* Ⓤ the act of a person or an animal that hunts. 사냥; 탐구; 수색; 추구. ¶ *be fond of* ~ 사냥을 좋아하다. — *adj.* of or for hunting. 사냥〔수렵〕의. ¶ *a* ~ *dog* 〔*knife*〕 사냥개〔칼〕 / *a* ~ *ground* 사냥터 / *a hunting-cap* 헌팅캡.

hunt·ress [hʌ́ntris] *n.* Ⓒ a woman who hunts. 여자 사냥꾼.

hunts·man [hʌ́ntsmən] *n.* Ⓒ (*pl.* **-men** [-mən]) 《Brit.》 **1** a hunter. 사냥꾼. **2** a man who takes charge of hunting dogs during a hunt. (사냥할 때의) 사냥개 담당자.

hunt-the-slip·per [hʌ́ntðəslípər] *n.* a kind of parlor game. 슬리퍼찾기 놀이.

hur·dle [hə́ːrdl] *n.* Ⓒ **1** a kind of fence to be jumped over in a race. (허들 경기의) 장애물; 허들. **2** 《*pl.*》 a race in which the runners jump over hurdles. 장애물 경주. **3** something that prevents or hinders the action of a person; a difficulty. 장애; 곤란; 난관. **4** a frame made of sticks and used as a fence. (엮어 만든) 임시 울타리. **5** in England, a frame on which criminals used to be dragged. (죄인을 형장으로 이송할 때의) 썰매 모양의 함거(檻車).
— *vt.* (P6) **1** jump over. …을 뛰어넘다. ¶ *He hurdled the last ditch.* 그는 마지막 도랑을 뛰어넘었다. **2** overcome. …을 극복하다. ¶ ~ *a difficulty* 어려움을 이겨내다. **3** enclose (a garden, land, etc.) with a frame of sticks. (정원 따위)에 임시 울타리를 두르다. — *vi.* jump over a hurdle. 장애물〔허들〕을 뛰어넘다. [E.]

hur·dler [hə́ːrdlər] *n.* Ⓒ a person who jumps over hurdles in a race. 장애물 경주자.

hurdle race [⌐⌐ ⌐] *n.* a race in which runners or horses have to jump over hurdles put in the course. 장애물 경주; 허들 레이스.

hur·dy-gur·dy [hə́ːrdigə́ːrdi] *n.* Ⓒ (*pl.* **-dies**) a barrel organ played by turning a handle, often pulled through the streets on wheels. 손잡이를 돌리는 손풍금《노상 따위에서 쓰임》. [Imit.]

·hurl [həːrl] *vt.* (P6,7,13) **1** throw (something) with force. …을 (힘껏) 던지다. ¶ ~ *someone downstairs* 아무를 아래층으로 내던지다 / *The soldiers hurled their spears.* 병사들은 창을 던졌다. **2** utter (hard words, etc.) violently. (욕설 따위)를 퍼붓다〔내뱉다〕. ¶ ~ *abuse at* (*someone*) (아무에게) 욕을 퍼붓다. — *vi.* (P3) 《*colloq.*》 《baseball》 pitch a ball. 볼을 던지다; 투구하다.
hurl oneself at 〔***on, upon***〕 ***something,*** rush. …을 향해 몸을 던지다; …에 달려들다.
— *n.* Ⓒ a violent throw. 세게 내던짐.
● **hurl·er** [⌐ər] *n.* [E.]

hurl·y-burl·y [hə́ːrlibə̀ːrli] *n.* Ⓒ (*pl.* **-burl·ies**) confusion and noise; a disorder. 혼란; 소동. [E.]

Hu·ron [hjúərən], **Lake** *n.* the second largest of the five Great Lakes, between the United States and Canada. (미국과 캐나다 사이의) 휴런 호(湖).

·hur·rah [hərɔ́ː, -rɑ́ː] *interj., n.* Ⓒ a shout of joy, praise, etc. 만세; 후레이《환희·찬탄·격려 따위를 나타냄》. ¶ *Hurrah for the King !* 국왕 만세 / *Hurrah for the holidays !* 휴가 만세 / *Give a hurrah for the hero !* 영웅에게 환호를 보내자. — *vi.* (P1) shout hurrahs; cheer. 만세를 외치다; 환성을 올리다. — *vt.* (P6) meet or encourage (someone) by shouting hurrahs. …을 환호로써 맞이하다〔응원하다〕. [? Du.]

hur·ray, hoo·ray [huréi] *interj., n., v.* =hurrah.

hur·ri·cane [hə́ːrəkèin, hʌ́ri- / hʌ́rikən] *n.* Ⓒ **1** a storm with a violent wind and, usu. very heavy rain. 폭풍; 태풍; 허리케인 (cf. *typhoon*). **2** a sudden, violent outburst (of praise, emotion, etc.). (우레와 같은) 갈채; (감정의) 격발. [Carib.]

hurricane deck [⌐⌐⌐ ⌐] *n.* 《chiefly U.S.》 the deck of a passenger ship. 여객선의 최상갑판(最上甲板).

hurricane lamp [⌐⌐⌐ ⌐] *n.* a lamp designed to resist the wind. 강풍용(強風用) 램프.

·hur·ried [hə́:rid, hʌ́rid] *adj.* forced to hurry; done or made in haste. 재촉받은; 몹시 급한; 서둘러 날림으로 한〔만든〕. ¶ *a ~ meal* 몹시 서두르는 식사. [*hurry*]

hur·ried·ly [hə́:ridli, hʌ́rid-] *adv.* in a hurried manner. 몹시 서둘러〔급히〕; 부리나케; 당황하여.

:hur·ry [hə́:ri, hʌ́ri] *n.* (*pl.* **hur·ries**) Ⓤ **1** haste; rush; eagerness. 서두르는〔허둥지둥하는〕 상태; 매우 급함; 열심. ¶ *Everything was ~ and confusion.* 모든 것이 허둥대는 대법석이었다. **2** 《often *a ~* 》《in *negative* or *interrogative*》 need for hurry. 서두를 필요. ¶ *There is no ~.* 서두를 필요는 없다 / *What's the ~?* 뭣 때문에 그렇게 허둥대는가 / *Is there any ~?* 뭔가 서두를 필요라도 있나.

in a hurry, **a**) anxious to act; quickly. 급히; 서둘러. ¶ *They were in a ~ to set out.* 일각이라도 빨리 떠나려 하고 있었다 / *I am in no ~ for your answer.* 자네의 회답이 급하지는 않다 / *I want to see him in a great ~.* 급히 그를 만나보고 싶다 / *He is in a ~ to get rich.* 그는 빨리 부자가 되려고 초조해 하고 있다. **b**) 《*colloq.*》 willingly; readily. 기꺼이; 자진하여. **c**) 《in *negative*》 easily; soon. 쉽게; 곧. ¶ *They wouldn't forget it in a ~.* 그것을 쉽사리 잊지는 않을겁니다 / *He won't do that again in a ~.* 그는 다시는 그 짓을 않을 게다.

— *v.* (**-ried**) *vt.* (P6,7) cause (someone) to act or move too hastily; hasten. …을 서두르게 하다; 재촉하다; 죄어치다(opp. delay). ¶ *~ one's steps* 발걸음을 재촉하다 / *~ one's movements* 동작을 빨리 하다 / *~ a work* 서둘러 작품을 마무리하다 / *~ someone out* (*of the room*) 아무를 재촉하여 (방에서) 나가게 하다 / *~ someone into a decision* 아무를 재촉하여 결심하게 하다 / *Don't ~ me.* 재촉하지 말아주게 / *~ oneself* 서두르다.

— *vi.* (P1, 2A) act or move rapidly; do (something) quickly. 급히 서두르다〔하다〕. ¶ *~ along* 〔*on*〕 급히 가다 / *~ away* 〔*off*〕 급히 떠나다 / *~ into* 〔*out of*〕 *a bus* 급히 버스를 타다〔에서 내리다〕 / *~ out into the garden* 급히 정원으로 나가다 / *~ downstairs* 급히 아래층으로 내려가다 / *Hurry, or we'll be late.* 서두르지 않으면 늦는다 / *He hurried back to his car.* 그는 급히 자기차(있는 데)로 돌아갔다. [Imit.]

hurry on with, make haste with (something). …을 서두르게 하다; 진척시키다.

hurry up, make haste; cause to act or move with great haste. (급히) 서두르다; 서두르게 하다.

hur·ry-scur·ry, -skur·ry [hə́:riskə́:ri / hʌ́riskʌ́ri] *n.* Ⓒ (*pl.* **-ries**) hurry and confusion. 허둥댐; 혼란. — *adj.* hurried and confused. 허둥대는; 혼란한. — *adv.* with hurry and confusion. 허둥대어; 당황하여. [*hurry*]

:hurt [hə:rt] *vt.* (**hurt**) (P6) **1** cause pain to (someone); give a wound to (someone); injure. 아프게〔다치게〕 하다; 상처를〔부상을〕 입히다. ¶ *The stone ~ his foot badly.* 돌 때문에 그는 발을 크게 다쳤다 / *He was seriously ~ in the accident.* 그 사고로 그는 큰 부상을 입었다 / *My tooth still hurts* (*me*). 이(齒)가 아직도 아프다. **2** give mental pain to; offend; grieve (the feelings of someone). (아무의) 감정〔기분〕을 해치다; 슬프게 하다; 정신적 고통을 주다. ¶ *He was ~ by what was said.* 그 말로 인해 그는 감정이 상했다. **3** do damage or harm to (something). …을 해치다; …에 상해를〔손해를, 손상을, 손실을〕 입히다. ¶ *~ one's reputation* 명성을 손상하다 / *The frost has ~ the crops this year.* 서리는 올해 농작에 피해를 주었다.

— *n.* Ⓤ **1** pain; injury; wound. 고통; 부상; 상처. **2** a bad effect; damage; harm. 해(害); 손상; 손해.

● **hurt·er** [´-ər] *n.* [F. *hurter* knock]

hurt·ful [hə́:rtfəl] *adj.* causing hurt; harmful; injurious. 상처〔손해〕를 주는; 유해한; 해가 되는. ● **hurt·ful·ly** [-fuli] *adv.*

hur·tle [hə́:rtl] *vi.* (P2A,3) **1** 《*arch.*》 《*against*》 crash violently. 소리를 내며〔세차게〕 부딪치다; 충돌하다. ¶ *Spears hurtled against shields.* 창이 (쨍그렁하며) 방패에 부딪쳤다. **2** move with a confused noise; rush, fall, violently or rapidly. 요란한 소리를 내며 〔고속으로〕 움직이다; 세차게 돌진하다〔떨어지다〕. ¶ *The jet plane hurtled through the air.* 제트기가 요란한 소리를 내며 날아갔다.

— *vt.* (P7) dash or drive violently; dash against (something); make (something) meet and strike. …을 내던지다; 맹렬히 돌진시키다; 부딪히다; 충돌시키다.

— *n.* Ⓒ the act or fact of hurtling; a loud, confused noise; clatter. 부딪힘; 충돌(소리). [*hurt*]

:hus·band [hʌ́zbənd] *n.* Ⓒ **1** a man who has a wife. 남편. ¶ *He was a good ~ to her.* 그는 그녀에게 좋은 남편이었다. **2** 《*arch.*》 an economist. 절약가. ¶ *a good* 〔*bad*〕 *~* 절약〔낭비〕가. — *vt.* (P6) **1** manage (money, etc.) with care and economy. (돈 따위)를 알뜰히 관리하다; 절약하다. ¶ *~ one's money* 〔*strength*〕 돈〔힘〕을 절약하다. **2** marry (a woman). (여성과) 결혼하다. [E. =house-dweller]

hus·band·man [hʌ́zbən*d*mən] *n.* Ⓒ (*pl.* **-men** [-mən]) 《*arch.*》 a farmer. 농부.

hus·band·ry [hʌ́zbəndri] *n.* Ⓤ **1** farming. 농업; 경작. **2** domestic management; economical management. 가정(家政); 검약(儉約).

·hush [hʌʃ] *vt.* (P6,7) **1** make (someone) silent or quiet. …을 조용하게 하다; 침묵시키다. ¶ *~ a baby to sleep* 아기를 잠재우다. **2** soothe; calm. …을 달래다; 가라앉히다. — *vi.* (P1) become or keep silent. 조용해지다; 조용히 하다. ¶ *The wind has hushed.*

바람이 조용해졌다.
hush up, **a**) stop discussion of. …을 침묵시키다. **b**) cover up. (사건 따위를) 쉬쉬하여 뭉개다; 흐지부지 숨기다. ¶ *~ up a love affair* 연애 사건을 쉬쉬하여 숨기다.
— *n.* ⓊⒸ silence; stillness. 침묵; 정적. ¶ *in the ~ of the night* 밤의 정적 속에.
— *interj.* [hʌʃ, ʃːː] Be silent !; Keep quiet !. 쉿, 조용히. ¶ *Hush ! Be silent.* 쉿, 조용히 해. [*husht* interj. (Imit.) taken as p.p.]

hush-hush [hʌ́ʃhʌ̀ʃ] *adj.* 《*sl.*》 highly secret. 극비의. ¶ *a ~ report* 극비의 보고서.

hush money [ˊ ˋ–] *n.* money paid to keep someone from telling something. 입씻이; 입막음으로 주는 돈.

husk [hʌsk] *n.* Ⓒ 《usu. *pl.*》 **1** the dry outer covering of certain seeds or fruits. (열매·과실의) 껍질; 껍데기; 깍지; 꼬투리; (옥수수 따위의) 껍질(cf. *grain*). **2** the worthless outer covering of anything. (불필요·무가치한) 겉부분; 외피; 찌꺼기. ¶ *a few husks of reason* 몇마디의 하찮은 이유.
— *vt.* (P6) remove the husk from (something). …의 껍질을〔껍데기를〕 벗기다; 꼬투리를 까다. ● **husk·er** [ˊəɾ] *n.* [Du.]

husk·i·ly [hʌ́skili] *adv.* in a husky voice. 쉰 목소리로.

husk·i·ness [hʌ́skinis] *n.* Ⓤ a low, dry quality of the voice. 쉰 목소리임.

husk·ing bee [hʌ́skiŋ bìː] *n.* 《U.S.》 a gathering or a party of farm families to husk corn. 옥수수 껍질까기(의 모임).

husk·y[1] [hʌ́ski] *adj.* (**husk·i·er, husk·i·est**) **1** dry in the throat; hoarse. 목쉰. ¶ *speak* 〔*sing*〕 *in a ~ voice* 쉰 목소리로 말하다〔노래하다〕. **2** of or like husks. 껍질〔껍데기〕의; 껍질〔꼬투리〕 같은. **3** 《U.S. *colloq.*》 big and strong. 크고 센; 억센; 단단한. — *n.* Ⓒ (*pl.* **husk·ies**) 《U.S. *colloq.*》 a big, strong person. 크고 힘센 사람. [Du.]

hus·ky[2] [hʌ́ski] *n.* an Eskimo; an Eskimo dog. 에스키모인; 에스키모 개. [corrupt of *Eskimo*]

hus·sar [huzáːr] *n.* 《Brit.》 a light cavalry soldier. 경기병(輕騎兵). [→courier]

hus·sy [hʌ́si, hʌ́zi] *n.* Ⓒ (*pl.* **-sies**) **1** a bad-mannered girl; an ill-behaved girl. 말괄량이; 왈가닥. **2** a worthless woman. 닳고닳은〔굴러먹은〕 여자. [→housewife]

hus·tings [hʌ́stiŋz] *n. pl.* 《used as *sing.* and *pl.*》 **1** a platform from which candidates for Parliament are nominated and address the voters. 영국 국회 의원 선거의 연단. **2** 《chiefly Brit.》 a platform from which speeches are made in a political campaign. 선거 운동의 연단. **3** 《*the ~*》 legal actions in an election. 선거 절차; 투표. [E. =house-council]

hus·tle [hʌ́səl] *vt.* (P6,7,13) **1** 《*into doing*》 force (someone) to do something hurriedly or roughly. …을 억지로 하게 하다; 강박하다. ¶ *He hustled the customer into buying more.* 그는 그 손님에게 억지로 더 많이 사게 했다. **2** 《*into, out of*》 push or crowd roughly. …을 거칠게 밀치다; (떠)밀다. ¶ *The other boys hustled him out of the room.* 다른 아이들은 그를 난폭하게 방에서 밀어냈다. **3** 《*colloq.*》 cause (something) to be done quickly. (일 따위)를 빨리 서두르게 하다; 죄어치다. — *vi.* (P1,2A) **1** ⓐ 《*against*》 push roughly; crowd. 거칠게 밀다; 밀치락달치락하다. ⓑ rush roughly; push one's way. 밀치고 나아가다. ¶ *~ through the crowd.* 사람들을 헤집고 나아가다. **2** 《*colloq.*》 work with tireless energy. 정력적으로 일하다; (일을) 척척 해치우다.
— *n.* Ⓤ 《often *a ~*》 **1** rough push. 거칠게 밂; 밀치락달치락. ¶ *~ and bustle* 밀치락달치락; 대혼잡. **2** 《*colloq.*》 energetic activity. (일 따위에서의) 대활동; 대활약. ● **hus·tler** [-əɾ] *n.* [Du. *hutseln* shake up]

:hut [hʌt] *n.* Ⓒ **1** a small, roughly-built house; a small cabin. 오두막; 오막살이집. **2** 《mil.》 a temporary wooden house. 임시 병사(兵舍). — *vt., vi.* (P6;1) lodge in huts. 오두막에 묵다〔숙박시키다〕. [Teut.]

hutch [hʌtʃ] *n.* Ⓒ **1** ⓐ a box or chest to keep things, esp. one used as a home for small animals. 상자; (작은 동물을 기르는) 우릿간. ⓑ a box for grain, etc. 곡물 따위를 담아두는 통〔궤짝〕; 뒤주. **2** 《*colloq.*》 a small cottage. (허술한) 통나무집; 판잣집. [F.]

Hux·ley [hʌ́ksli] *n.* 헉슬리. **1 Aldous**(1894-1963) an English novelist, essayist, and critic. 영국의 소설가·수필가·비평가. **2 Sir Julian Sorell**(1887-1975) an English biologist and writer (brother of 1). 영국의 생물학자·작가《1의 형》. **3 Thomas Henry**(1825-95) an English biologist and writer (grandfather of 1). 영국의 생물학자《1의 조부》.

huz·za,-zah [həzáː] *interj., n., v.* 《*arch.*》 =hurrah.

hy·a·cinth [háiəsinθ] *n.* Ⓒ **1** 《bot.》 a plant of the lily family grown from a bulb. 히아신스. **2** Ⓤ a reddish-orange gem. 히아신스 석(石)《적등색(赤橙色)의 지르콘 광물; 보석으로 침》. ● **hy·a·cin·thine** [hàiəsínθin, -θain] *adj.* [Gk.]

hy·ae·na [haiíːnə] *n.* =hyena.

hy·brid [háibrid] *n.* Ⓒ **1** a plant or an animal produced by parents of different species. (동식물의) 잡종. **2** ⓐ a person of mixed nationality. 혼혈아; 튀기. ⓑ anything made of parts of different origin. 혼성물. ⓒ a word formed with elements of two languages. 혼성어. — *adj.* **1** produced from two different species. 잡종의; 혼혈의. **2** of mixed origin. 혼성의. [L. *hibrida*]

hy·brid·i·za·tion [hàibridizéiʃən / -dai-] *n.* the act or process of producing a hybrid. 잡종 번식(법); 교잡; 교배.

hy·brid·ize [háibridàiz] *vt., vi.* (P6; 1) cause to produce hybrids; produce hybrids. 잡종을 생기게 하다; 잡종이 생기다.

Hyde Park [háid pá:rk] *n.* a park in London, England. 하이드 파크《영국 런던의 공원》.

hy·dra [háidrə] *n.* Ⓒ (*pl.* **-dras** or **-drae**) **1** 《*H-*》《Gk. myth.》 a monstrous snake having nine heads. 히드라《아홉 개의 머리를 가진 괴사(怪蛇)》. **2** 《*fig.*》 any evil difficult to destroy. 근절하기 어려운 난제〔재해〕. **3** 《animal》 a kind of fresh water polyp. 히드라. [Gk.]

hy·drae [háidri:] *n.* pl. of **hydra.**

hy·dran·gea [haidréindʒiə] *n.* Ⓒ 《bot.》 a shrub with large gatherings of small white, pink, or blue flowers. 수국. [Gk. *hudōr* water, *aggos* vessel]

hy·drant [háidrənt] *n.* Ⓒ a large pipe for drawing water directly in order to put out fires. (가로상의) 소화전(消火栓). [↓]

hy·drate [háidreit] *n.* Ⓒ 《chem.》 a kind of material produced when certain substances combine with water. 수화물(水化物). **—** *vi.* become a hydrate; combine with water to form a hydrate. 수화(水化)하다. **—** *vt.* cause (something) to become a hydrate. …을 수화시키다; 수화물을 만들다. [→hydro-]

hy·drau·lic [haidrɔ́:lik] *adj.* **1** having to do with water or liquids in motion. 수력의. **2** worked by the pressure of water in motion. 수압(水壓)의. ¶ *a ~ elevator* 수압식 엘리베이터. **3** hardened with water. 물에서 경화(硬化)하는. ¶ *~ cement* 수경(水硬) 시멘트. [Gk. *hudōr* water, *aulos* pipe]

hy·drau·lics [haidrɔ́:liks] *n. pl.* 《used as *sing.*》 Ⓤ the science of water and other liquids in motion. 수리학.

hy·drid [háidrid], **-dride** [-draid] *n.* 《chem.》 a compound of hydrogen with another element. 수소화물. [hydro-]

hy·dro [háidrou] *n.* Ⓒ (*pl.* **-dros**) 《chem.》 《*colloq.*》 a hydropathic establishment; a house or resting place for people taking mineral-water baths to cure illness. 물치료원; 탕치장(湯治場). [Gk. *hudōr* water]

hy·dro- [háidrou-] *pref.* having to do with water. '물, 수소'의 뜻. [↑]

hy·dro·air·plane [hàidrouέərplèin], 《Brit.》 **-aer·o-** [-έərə-] *n.* =hydroplane.

hy·dro·car·bon [hàidroukáːrbən] *n.* Ⓒ 《chem.》 any of a class of compounds containing only hydrogen and carbon. 탄화수소. [hydro-]

hy·dro·chlo·ric [hàidroukló:rik] *adj.* 《chem.》 containing hydrogen and chlorine. 염화수소의. ¶ *~ acid* 염산.

hy·dro·e·lec·tric [hàidrouiléktrik] *adj.* of or related to the production of electricity by water power. 수력 전기의.

•**hy·dro·gen** [háidrədʒən] *n.* Ⓤ 《chem.》 a very light, tasteless, colorless gas that burns easily. 수소. 參考 화학 기호 H. ¶ *~ bomb* 수소 폭탄(=H-bomb) / *~ peroxide* 과산화수소 / *~ sulfide* 황화수소. [hydro-, Gk. *gignomai* be born]

hy·drol·y·ses [haidrálәsì:z / -drɔ́l-] *n.* pl. of **hydrolysis.**

hy·drol·y·sis [haidrálәsis / -drɔ́l-] *n.* (*pl.* **-ses**) 《chem.》 a decomposition that changes a compound into other compounds by taking out the elements of water. 가수 분해. [hydro-]

hy·drom·e·ter [haidrámitər / -drɔ́-] *n.* Ⓒ an instrument for determining the specific gravity of water or other liquids. (액체) 비중계.

hy·dro·path·ic [hàidroupǽθik] *adj.* of or using hydropathy. 수치료법(水治療法)의. **—** *n.* Ⓒ a sanatorium that specializes in hydropathy. 수치료원.

hy·drop·a·thy [haidrápəθi / -drɔ́p-] *n.* Ⓤ treatment of disease by using water. 수치료법.

hy·dro·pho·bi·a [hàidroufóubiə] *n.* Ⓤ **1** a dreadful disease that a mad dog brings to a person when it bites him; rabies. 공수병; 광견병. **2** a dislike or fear of water. 물에 대한 병적인 공포.

hy·dro·plane [háidrouplèin] *n.* Ⓒ **1** a light motorboat that glides on the surface of water. 수상 활주정(滑走艇). **2** an airplane that lands on and takes off from water; a seaplane. 수상 비행기. **3** the plane which supports a hydroplane. (비행기에 단) 수상 활주 장치.

hy·dro·pon·ics [hàidrəpániks / -pɔ́n-] *n. pl.* 《used as *sing.*》 the growing of plants by only water without any soil. 수경(水耕) 재배; 물가꾸기.

hy·drous [háidrəs] *adj.* containing water. 물을 함유한; 함수(含水)의.

hy·drox·ide [haidráksaid, -sid / -drɔ́k-] *n.* 《chem.》 a compound containing hydrogen in combination with oxygen. 수산화물.

hy·e·na [haiíːnə] *n.* Ⓒ a wolflike, flesh-eating wild animal of Africa and Asia. 하이에나《아시아·아프리카산》. [Gk.]

hy·giene [háidʒi:n] *n.* Ⓤ **1** the science of keeping well. 위생학. **2** rules for keeping good health. 건강법. [Gk. *hugiēs* healthy]

hy·gi·en·ic [hàidʒiénik, -dʒí:n-] *adj.* **1** healthful; concerning health. 건강적〔위생적〕인; 건강에 좋은. **2** related to the science of health. 위생학의.

hy·gi·en·ics [hàidʒiéniks, -dʒí:n-] *n. pl.* 《used as *sing.*》 Ⓤ the science of health. 위생학〔법〕.

hy·gien·ist [haidʒí:nist, háidʒi:-] *n.* Ⓒ a person who is expert in hygiene. 위생학자; 위생 전문가.

hy·grom·e·ter [haigrámitər / -grɔ́m-] *n.* Ⓒ an instrument for measuring the amount of water vapor in the air. 습도계. [Gk. *hugros* wet]

Hy·men [háimən] *n.* **1** 《Gk. myth.》 the god of marriage. 히멘《결혼의 신》. **2** 《*h-*》 《anat.》 a membrane covering the opening of the vagina. 처녀막. [Gk. *Humēn,* (*h-*) skin.]

hy·me·ne·al [hàiməníːəl] *adj.* of or having to do with marriage. 결혼[혼인]의. ¶ ~ *rites* 결혼식. [↑]

*__hymn__ [him] *n.* Ⓒ **1** a song in praise of God. 찬송가; 성가. **2** any song of praise. 찬가. — *vt.* (P6) praise (God) with a hymn. (찬송가(讚頌歌)로 신을) 찬미하다. — *vi.* (P1) sing a hymn. 찬송가를 부르다. ● **hymn·like** [⌐làik] *adj.* [Gk. *humnos*]

*__hym·nal__ [hímnəl] *n.* Ⓒ a book of hymns. 찬송가집. — *adj.* of or having to do with a hymn or hymns. 찬송가[성가]의. [↑]

hy·per- [háipər-] *pref.* over; above; beyond; exceedingly. '…을 넘어, 초과, 과도, 초(超)…'의 뜻. [Gk. *huper*]

hy·per·bo·la [haipə́ːrbələ] *n.* Ⓒ 《geom.》 a curve formed when a cone is cut by a plane at a larger angle with the base than the side of the cone makes. 쌍곡선. [Gk. hyper-, *ballō* throw]

hy·per·bo·le [haipə́ːrbəlìː] *n.* Ⓤ extreme way of expression for more effective writing or speaking. 과장법. [↑]

hy·per·bol·ic [hàipəːrbálik / hàipəːrbɔ́l-], **-bol·i·cal** [-əl] *adj.* **1** of or like hyperbole; exaggeratedly expressed. 과장된; 과대한. **2** of or having to do with hyperbolas. 쌍곡선의.

hy·per·crit·i·cal [hàipəːrkrítikəl] *adj.* too fault-finding; too severe in finding fault with. 혹평하는; 흠[탈]잡는. ● **hy·per·crit·i·cal·ly** [-kəli] *adv.* [hyper-]

hy·per·me·tro·pi·a [hàipərmitróupiə] *n.* a state of being unable to see near objects clearly; far-sightedness. 원시(遠視)(cf. *myopia*). [hyper-]

hy·per·me·trop·ic [hàipərmitrápik- / -trɔ́p-] *adj.* far-sighted. 원시(遠視)의.

hy·per·o·pi·a [hàipəróupiə] *n.* = hypermetropia.

hy·per·op·ic [hàipərápik / -rɔ́p-] *adj.* = hypermetropic.

hy·per·sen·si·tive [hàipərsénsətiv] *adj.* 《med.》 excessively sensitive. 지나치게 민감한; 과민증의. ¶ *be ~ to criticism* 비평에 대해 지나치게 민감하다. [hyper-]

hy·per·ten·sion [hàipərténʃən] *n.* **1** excessive or extreme tension. 과도의 긴장. **2** 《med.》 an abnormally high blood pressure. 고혈압(증). [hyper-]

hy·per·ten·sive [hàipərténsiv] *adj.* of hypertension. 고혈압의; 고혈압을 일으키는. [hyper-]

hy·per·tro·phy [haipə́ːrtrəfi] *n.* 《med.》 growing too big. 비대증(肥大症). — *adj.* of hypertrophy. 이상 비대(증)의. [Gk. hyper-, *trephō* feed]

:**hy·phen** [háifən] *n.* Ⓒ a mark (-) used to join the parts of a compound word. 하이픈. — *vt.* (P6) join (words) with a hyphen; hyphenate. 하이픈으로 연결하다. [Gk. =under one]

hy·phen·ate [háifənèit] *vt.* (P6) join (words) with a hyphen. (두 낱말)을 하이픈으로 잇다.

hy·phen·at·ed [háifənèitid] *adj.* 《U.S. *colloq.*》 joined with a hyphen. 하이픈으로 이은; 하이픈이 붙은.

hyphenated Americans, German-American, Irish-American, etc. 하이픈이 붙은 (외국계의) 미국인《German-American(독일계 미국인), Irish-American(아일랜드계 미국인)과 같이 미국 국적은 갖고 있지만 전(前)국적에 애틋한 감정이 남아있는 사람》.

hy·phen·a·tion [hàifənéiʃən] *n.* Ⓤ the act of hyphenating words. 하이픈으로 연결하기.

hyp·no·ses [hipnóusiːz] *n.* pl. of **hypnosis.**

hyp·no·sis [hipnóusis] *n.* ⓊⒸ (*pl.* **-ses**) the state like sleep in which a person has little feeling and acts by the suggestions of the hypnotizer. 최면 (상태). ¶ *He was under ~.* 그는 최면 상태에 있었다. [Gk. *hupnos* sleep]

hyp·not·ic [hipnátik / -nɔ́t-] *adj.* **1** ⓐ of hypnosis. 최면(술)의; 최면 상태의. ⓑ causing sleep. 잠이 오(게 하)는. **2** easily put into hypnosis. 최면술에 걸리기 쉬운. — *n.* Ⓒ **1** a person who is in the state of hypnosis. 최면 상태에 있는 사람. **2** a drug or other means of causing sleep. 수면제.

hyp·no·tism [hípnətìzəm] *n.* Ⓤ **1** the act or process of hypnotizing. 최면술을 걸기. **2** the science dealing with hypnosis. 최면술.

hyp·no·tist [hípnətist] *n.* Ⓒ a person who hypnotizes. 최면술사.

hyp·no·tize [hípnətàiz] *vt.* (P6) **1** put (someone) into a hypnotic state. …에게 최면을 걸다(cf. *mesmerize*). **2** 《*colloq.*》 rule or control the will of (someone). …을 매혹하다. ● **hyp·no·tiz·a·ble** [-əbəl] *adj.* **hyp·no·tiz·er** [-ər] *n.*

hy·po [háipou] *n.* Ⓤ **1** a colorless salt as clear as crystal, used in photography. 하이포; (사진의) 현상 정착액. **2** =hypodermic. [Abbr. of *hyposulfite*]

hypo- [háipou-] *pref.* less than; under; below. '이하, 밑에'의 뜻. [Gk. *hupo*]

hy·po·chon·dri·a [hàipəkándriə / -kɔ́n-] *n.* Ⓤ abnormal anxiety about one's health; low spirits without any real reason. 건강에 대한 지나친 걱정; 우울증. [Gk. = parts below costal cartilages]

hy·po·chon·dri·ac [hàipəkɑ́ndriæ̀k / -kɔ́n-] *n.* Ⓒ a person suffering from hypochondria. 우울증 환자. —*adj.* of hypochondria; suffering from hypochondria. 우울증의〔에 걸린〕.

hy·poc·ri·sy [hipɑ́krəsi / -pɔ́k-] *n.* ⓊⒸ (*pl.* **-sies**) the act of pretending to have more goodness than one really has. 위선 (행위); 위장. [Gk. ***hupokrinomai*** act in theater]

hyp·o·crite [hípəkrit] *n.* Ⓒ a person who pretends to have goodness which he does not really have. 위선자; 위장〔가장〕자.

hyp·o·crit·i·cal [hìpəkrítikəl] *adj.* of hypocrisy; like a hypocrite; false; dishonest. 위선(僞善)의; 위선(자)적인; 거짓의. ● **hyp·o·crit·i·cal·ly** [-kəli] *adv.*

hy·po·der·mic [hàipədə́:*r*mik] *adj.* **1** of the parts under the skin. 피하(皮下)의; 피하에 있는. **2** injected under the skin through a needle. 피하에 주입되는. ¶ *a ~ injection* 피하 주사. —*n.* Ⓒ **1** an act of putting medicine under the skin. 피하 주사. **2** a medicine that is put under the skin through a needle. 피하 주사약. [hypo-, Gk. ***derma*** skin]

hy·pot·e·nuse [haipɑ́tən*j*ù:s / -pɔ́tənjù:s] *n.* the side of a right-angled triangle opposite the right angle. 빗변. [Gk. =subtending line]

hy·poth·e·cate [haipɑ́θikèit / -pɔ́θ-] *vt.* (P6) 《law》 pledge to a creditor as security. 담보로〔저당에〕 넣다(cf. *mortgage*). [hypo-]

hy·poth·e·ses [haipɑ́θəsì:z / -pɔ́θ-] *n.* pl. of **hypothesis.**

hy·poth·e·sis [haipɑ́θəsis / -pɔ́θ-] *n.* Ⓒ (*pl.* **-ses**) something assumed to be true though it is not proved; an unproved theory. 가설; 억설. [hypo-]

hy·poth·e·size [haipɑ́θəsaiz / -pɔ́θ-] *vi.* (P1) make an hypothesis. 가설〔가정〕을 세우다. —*vt.* (P6) assume. 가정하다. [hypo-]

hy·po·thet·ic [hàipəθétik], **-i·cal** [-ikəl] *adj.* of a hypothesis; not true; supposed. 가설의; 가상의. ● **hy·po·thet·i·cal·ly** [-kəli] *adv.*

hys·sop [hísəp] *n.* a plant of the mint family used in medicine. 히솝풀《약용으로 쓰는 꿀풀과의 식물》. [Gk.]

hys·ter·ec·to·my [hìstəréktəmi] *n.* (*pl.* **-mies**) ⒸⓊ the medical operation for removing the womb. 자궁 절제술(術). [Gk. ***hustera*** womb, →ectomy]

hys·te·ri·a [histíəriə] *n.* Ⓤ a nervous disorder with violent fits of laughing and crying; senseless and uncontrolled excitement. 히스테리; 병적 흥분. [↑]

hys·ter·ic [histérik] *n.* Ⓒ 《usu. *pl.*》 a sudden and violent burst of uncontrolled crying or laughing; hysteria; a person suffering from hysteria. 히스테리의 발작; 히스테리 환자. ¶ *go off* 〔*fall*〕 *into hysterics =take histerics* 히스테리를 일으키다. —*adj.* =hysterical.

hys·ter·i·cal [histérikəl] *adj.* of or like hysteria; abnormally excited; violently uncontrolled. 히스테리의〔적인〕; 병적으로 흥분한.

hys·ter·i·cal·ly [histérikəli] *adv.* in a hysterical manner. 히스테리적으로.

hys·ter·ol·o·gy [hìstərɑ́lədʒi / -rɔ́l-] *n.* 《med.》 the science on the uterus. 자궁학(子宮學). [Gk. ***hustera*** womb]

hys·ter·ot·o·my [hìstərɑ́təmi / -ɔ́t-] *n.* 《med.》 the operation of cutting into the uterus. 자궁 절개술(切開術).

i I

I¹, i [ai] *n.* Ⓒ (*pl.* **I's, Is, i's, is** [aiz]) **1** the ninth letter of the English alphabet. 영어 알파벳의 아홉째 글자. **2** the Roman number 1. 로마 숫자의 1.

:I² [ai] *pron.* (*pl.* **we**) the person who is speaking or writing. 나는; 내가. [E.]

IAEA International Atomic Energy Agency. (유엔) 국제 원자력 기구.

ib. ibidem.

ibid. ibidem.

i·bi·dem [íbidèm, ibáidəm] *adv.* 《L.》 in the same book, chapter, passage, etc. 같은 책[장(章), 절]에. 參考 ib., ibid. 로 생략.

i·bis [áibis] *n.* (*pl.* **i·bis** or **i·bis·es**) 《bird》 a stork-like bird. 따오기. [Gk.]

-i·ble [-əbəl] *suf.* able to. '…할 수 있는'의 뜻. ¶ *visible* 볼 수 있는. [L. *-ibilis*]

IBRD International Bank for Reconstruction and Development. (유엔) 국제 부흥 개발 은행.

IC 《electr.》 integrated circuit (집적 회로); 《gram.》 immediate constituent (직접 구성소(素)).

-ic [-ik] *suf.* **1** of. '…의'의 뜻. ¶ *atomic* 원자의. **2** having the nature of. '…의 성질을 가진'의 뜻. ¶ *heroic* 영웅적인. [Gk. *-ikós*]

-i·cal [-ikəl] *suf.* =-ic. ¶ *hysterical* 히스테리(성)의. [*-ic, -al*]

ICBM intercontinental ballistic missile. 대륙간 탄도탄.

:ice [ais] *n.* **1** Ⓤ frozen water. 얼음. **2** Ⓒ something like ice. 얼음 모양의 것. **3** Ⓒ ⓐ 《U.S.》 a frozen dessert made with fruit juice instead of cream. 셔벗《과즙을 섞은 빙수》. ⓑ 《Brit.》 an ice cream. 아이스 크림.

break the ice a) begin; start something difficult or dangerous. …을 시작하다. b) start being friendly. 스스럼을 없애다; 마음을 터놓다.

cut no ice, 《*colloq.*》 have no effect, influence, or importance. …에 효과가 없다; 쓸모가 없다. ¶ *His argument cuts no ~ with me.* 그가 뭐라 하든 내겐 통하지 않는다.

on thin ice, in a dangerous or difficult position. 살얼음을 밟듯 하는; 위험[불안]한 상태에.

— *adj.* of ice; made of ice. 얼음의; 얼음으로 만든.

— *vt.* **1** ⓐ (P6) cool (something) with ice; put ice in (something). …을 얼음으로 차게 하다; …에 얼음을 채우다. ⓑ (P7) 《*over*》 cover (something) with ice. …을 얼음으로 덮다. ¶ *The shallow pond was soon iced over.* 그 얕은 연못은 곧 얼음으로 덮였다. **2** (P6) freeze; turn to ice. …을 얼리다. [E.]

ice age [스스] *n.* 《geol.》 the period when ice covered a large area of the earth. 빙하 시대.

ice ax [스스] *n.* an ax which is used to break ice when climbing a mountain. (얼음 깨는) 도끼; (등산용) 피켈.

ice·berg [áisbə:rg] *n.* Ⓒ a large mass of ice floating in the sea. 빙산; 유빙.

ice·boat [áisbòut] *n.* Ⓒ **1** a boat used to break a channel in the frozen sea, etc.; an icebreaker. 쇄빙선. **2** a boat built for rapid movement on ice. 빙상선(氷上船).

ice·bound [áisbàund] *adj.* completely frozen; shut in by ice. 얼어붙은; 얼음에 갇힌. ¶ *an ~ harbor* 얼어붙은 항구 / *an ~ ship* 얼음에 갇힌 배.

ice·box [áisbàks / -bɔ̀ks] *n.* Ⓒ 《U.S.》 a box for keeping food cool; a refrigerator. 냉장고; 얼음통.

ice·break·er [áisbrèikər] *n.* Ⓒ 《U.S.》 a strong boat used to break a channel in frozen waters. 쇄빙선.

ice·cap [áiskæ̀p] *n.* Ⓒ a permanent layer of ice over an area. (고산·극지 등의) 만년설[빙].

ice cream [스스] *n.* a frozen dessert made of cream, sugar, eggs, etc. 아이스 크림.

iced [aist] *adj.* **1** cooled with ice. 얼음으로 차게 한. **2** covered with ice. 얼음에 덮인. [*ice*]

ice field [스스] *n.* a large sheet or mass of floating ice; an expanse of ice (in Polar regions). 대부빙(大浮氷); 대빙원(大氷原).

ice floe [스스] *n.* a large sheet of floating ice. 부빙괴(浮氷塊); 판상(板狀)의 대유빙(大流氷).

ice-free [áisfrí:] *adj.* (of a sea, a port, etc.) free of ice. (항만 등이) 얼지 않는; 부동(不凍)의.

ice hockey [스스-] *n.* a game of hockey played on ice. 아이스 하키.

ice·house [áishàus] *n.* (*pl.* **-hous·es**) Ⓒ a building for storing ice. 빙실(氷室); 빙고(氷庫). [*ice*]

Ice·land [áislənd] *n.* a country and large island in the North Atlantic. 아이슬란드.

Ice·land·er [áislæ̀ndər, -ləndər] *n.* Ⓒ a person of Iceland. 아이슬란드 사람.

Ice·lan·dic [aislǽndik] *adj.* of Iceland, its people, or their language. 아이슬란드 사람[어]의. — *n.* Ⓤ the language of Iceland. 아이슬란드어(語).

ice·man [áismæ̀n, -mən] *n.* Ⓒ (*pl.* **-men** [-mèn, -mən]) 《U.S.》 a man who sells or delivers ice. 얼음 장수. [*ice*]

ice pack [´ˏ] *n.* **1** masses of ice floating in the sea. 부빙군(浮氷群). **2** a bag containing ice used to cool the head, etc. 얼음 주머니.

ice skate [´ˏ] *n.* 《usu. *pl.*》 a shoe with a metal blade used for skating on ice. 스케이트 구두.

ice water [´ˏ–] *n.* **1** 《U.S.》 water cooled with ice. (차게 한) 얼음물(=《chiefly Brit.》 iced water). **2** water formed by melted ice. 얼음이 녹은 물.

I.C.F.T.U. International Confederation of Free Trade Unions. 국제 자유 노동자 연맹.

ich·neu·mon [iknjú:mən] *n.* 《zool.》 a small weasel-like animal of Egypt. 몽구스의 일종. [Gk.]

ichneumon fly [–´–ˏ] *n.* 《insect》 any of a large group of insects which lay their eggs upon the larvae of other insects. 맵시벌레.

ich·thy·ol·o·gy [ìkθiálədʒi / -ɔ́l-] *n.* the study of fishes. 어류(魚類)학. [Gk. *ikhthus* fish]

i·ci·cle [áisikəl] *n.* Ⓒ a pointed, hanging piece of ice formed by the freezing of dropping water. 고드름. [→ice, A.S. *isgicel* icicle]

i·ci·ly [áisəli] *adv.* in very cold manner. 차갑게; 냉담하게; 쌀쌀하게. [*icy*]

i·ci·ness [áisinis] *n.* Ⓤ the state of being icy or very cold. (얼음같이) 차가움; 냉랭함; 쌀쌀함.

ic·ing [áisiŋ] *n.* ⓊⒸ **1** a covering of sugar used to cover cakes. (과자의) 당의(糖衣). **2** the formation of ice, esp. on airplane wings. (항공기 날개 등의) 착빙(着氷). [*ice*]

ICJ International Court of Justice. 국제 재판소.

i·con [áikan / -kɔn] *n.* Ⓒ (*pl.* **i·cons** or **i·co·nes**) a picture or image of a sacred person. (그리스 교회의) 성상(聖像)〔성화(聖畫)〕 [Gk. *eikon*]

i·con·o·clast [aikánəklæ̀st / -kɔ́n-] *n.* Ⓒ **1** a person who is opposed to worshiping images of sacred persons. 성상(聖像)〔우상〕 파괴자. **2** a person who attacks traditional beliefs or customs. 인습 타파주의자. [↑, Gk. *claō* break]

•**i·cy** [áisi] *adj.* (**i·ci·er, i·ci·est**) **1** of ice; covered with ice. 얼음의; 얼음으로 덮인. ¶ *the ~ North* 얼음으로 덮인 북부 지방 / *~ waters* 얼음이 깔린 강. **2** very cold like ice. (얼음처럼) 차가운. ¶ *an ~ wind* 몹시 차가운 바람. **3** cold and unfriendly. 냉담한; 차가운. ¶ *an ~ manner* 〔*welcome*〕 냉담한 태도〔환영〕. [*ice*]

ID Infantry Division (보병 사단); Intelligence Department 〔Division〕 (정보부〔과〕).

ID, I.D., i.d. inside diameter. 안지름.

I'd [aid] I should; I would; I had.

id. =idem.

IDA International Development Association. 국제 개발 협회.

I·da·ho [áidəhòu] *n.* a western State of the United States. 아이다호주(州). 參考 Id. 또는 Ida.로 생략함. 주도(州都)는 Boise.

:**i·de·a** [aidí:ə] *n.* Ⓒ **1** a mental image; a thought; an opinion or mental impression; a concept; knowledge. 생각; 의견; 견해; 개념; 지식. ¶ *the Greek ~ of man* 그리스인의 인간관 / *a fixed ~* 고정 관념 / *a man of narrow ideas* 사고(思考) 방식이 편협한 사람 / *tremble of the bare ~ of* …을 생각만 해도 오싹해진다 / *Many do not have a clear-cut ~ of what a university is.* 대학이 무엇인지 명확한 견해를 가진 사람은 적다 / *Have you any ~ of the time ?* 시간이 무엇이라 생각하나. **2** a plan; a design; purpose. 착상; 계획; 의도. ¶ *give up* 〔*hit upon*〕 *the ~ of doing* …하는 것을 단념하다〔생각해 내다〕 / *He is full of new ideas.* 새로운 착상이 많은 사람이다 / *Put your main ideas into words.* 네 생각의 요점을 말로 해 봐라. **3** a fancy; a feeling that something is probable. 상상; …일 것 같다는 느낌; 예감(豫感). ¶ *I have the ~ that he never got undressed for bed.* 그 사람 필시 옷 입은 채로 잘 것이라는 생각이 든다 / *The ~ of such a thing !* 설마. [Gk.=form, kind]

get ideas into one's head, hope for more than will be fulfilled. (실현될 것 같지도 않은) 망상을 가지다.

:**i·de·al** [aidí:əl] *adj.* **1** just as or equal to one's best wish; perfect. 이상의; 이상적인. ¶ *an ~ society* 이상적인 사회. **2** existing only in imagination. 관념적인(opp. real). ¶ *the ~ world* 관념의 세계. — *n.* Ⓒ something looked on as perfect; a perfect type. 이상; 전형(典型). ¶ *realize one's ideals* 이상을 실현하다 / *Ruth's mother is her ~.* 루스의 어머니는 그녀의 이상이다. [→idea, -al]

i·de·al·ism [aidí:əlìzəm] *n.* Ⓤ **1** the practice or effort to live according to one's ideas. 이상주의. **2** (in art, etc.) representing beauty and perfection rather than fact. (예술·문학의) 이상주의. **3** 《philos.》 the theory that reality exists only in the form of ideas. 유심론; 관념론(cf. *materialism,* opp. realism). [→ideal, -ism]

i·de·al·ist [aidí:əlist] *n.* Ⓒ **1** a person who practices or follows his ideals, often neglecting the practical matters. 이상주의자; 관념론자. **2** (in art, philosophy, etc.) a person who believes in idealism. (예술·철학의) 관념론자.

i·de·al·is·tic [aidì:əlístik] *adj.* **1** acting according to ideals. 이상의. **2** of idealism or idealists. 이상주의(자)의; 관념론(자)의.

i·de·al·i·za·tion [aidìːəlizéiʃən] *n.* **1** Ⓤ the act of idealizing. 이상화. **2** Ⓒ a thing idealized; a result of being idealized. 이상화된 것.

i·de·al·ize [aidíːəlàiz] *vt.* (P6) make (something or someone) ideal; look upon (something or someone) as perfect. 이상화하다; 이상적인 것으로 생각하다. ¶ ~ *someone's character* 아무의 성격을 이상적인 것으로 생각하다. —*vi.* (P1) imagine or form an ideal. 이상을 그리다; 이상주의적(的)이다.

i·de·al·ly [aidíːəli] *adv.* **1** according to an ideal; perfectly. 이상적으로. **2** in idea or theory; not practically. 관념적으로; 이론상. ¶ *Ideally we ought to do it, but in practice it is impossible.* 논리상 그 일을 해야 하나 실제로는 불가능하다.

i·dee fixe [iːdéi fíːks] *n.* 《F.》 fixed idea. 고정 관념.

i·dem [áidem] *adv.* 《L.》 in the same writer, etc. 동일 저자〔책〕에. —*n.* the same writer; the same word or book. 같은 저자; 같은 말〔책〕. [L. = the same]

·i·den·ti·cal [aidéntikəl, i-] *adj.* **1** 《*with*》 the same. 같은; 동일한. ¶ *The events happened at the ~ spot.* 사건은 같은 장소에서 일어났다 / *That is the ~ pen I lost.* 저건 내가 잃은 펜과 같은 것이다. **2** exactly alike. 똑같은. ¶ *No two faces are ~.* 똑같은 얼굴이란 없다 / *The two boys took ~ trips last summer.* 두 아이는 지난 여름 똑같은 여행을 했다. ●**i·den·ti·cal·ness** [-nis] *n.* [*idem*]

i·den·ti·cal·ly [aidéntikəli, idén-] *adv.* in an identical manner. 같게; 동일하게.

identical twin [–∠–– ∠] *n.* one of twins, of the same sex, developing from a single fertilized ovum. 일란성 쌍둥이.

i·den·ti·fi·a·ble [aidéntəfàiəbəl, idén-] *adj.* that can be identified. 동일하다고 볼 수 있는. [*identify*]

i·den·ti·fi·ca·tion [aidèntəfikéiʃən, i-] *n.* **1** Ⓤ the act of identifying or being identified. (동일하다는) 증명〔감정, 신원 조사〕. **2** ⓊⒸ anything by which a person or thing is identified. 신원을 증명하는 것.

:i·den·ti·fy [aidéntəfài] *vt.* (**-fied**) (P6,13) **1** 《*with*》 show or recognize (someone or something) to be the same. …을 동일하다고 확인〔인정〕하다 / ~ *the thief* 도둑임을 확인하다. **2** 《~ *A with B,* ~ *A and B*》 treat or consider (something) as the same. …을 같다고 보다; 동일시하다. ¶ *He identified his interests with ours.* 그는 자신의 이해는 우리들의 이해 관계와 동일하다고 보았다. **3** 《*reflexively*》 associate; unite. …와 제휴하다; …와 함께하다. ¶ ~ *oneself* 〔*be identified*〕 *with a movement* 〔*policy*〕. 운동과 행동을 같이 하다〔정책에 제휴하다〕. [↓]

i·den·ti·ty [aidéntəti] *n.* (*pl.* **-ties**) **1** ⒸⓊ the state of being a certain specific person or thing; individuality. 개성; 정체; 신원. ¶ *He did not like the others to know his ~.* 그는 다른 사람에게 자기 신원이 알려지는 것을 꺼렸다 / *reveal someone's ~* 아무의 정체를 폭로하다 / *an ~ card* 〔*disc*〕 신원 증명서〔인식표〕. **2** Ⓤ the state of being the same one; exact likeness; sameness. 동일 (상태); 일치. ¶ *He noticed the ~ of the two papers.* 그는 그 두 서류가 같다는 것을 알아챘다. [L. *idem* same]

id·e·o·gram [ídiəgræ̀m, áid-] *n.* Ⓒ an ideograph. 표의(表意) 문자(cf. *hieroglyph*). [→idea, -gram]

id·e·o·graph [ídiəgræ̀f, áid-, -grɑ̀ːf] *n.* Ⓒ a written character that symbolizes a thing or an idea directly. 표의(表意) 문자. [→idea, -graph]

i·de·o·log·i·cal [àidiəlɑ́dʒikəl, ìd- / -lɔ́dʒ-] *adj.* of or concerned with ideology. 이데올로기의〔에 관한〕. [↓]

i·de·ol·o·gy [àidiɑ́lədʒi, ìd- / -ɔ́l-] *n.* (*pl.* **-gies**) **1** Ⓒ a way of thinking; a set of doctrines or ideas. 이데올로기; 관념〔의식〕 형태. **2** Ⓤ abstract thinking, esp. of a not practical nature. 공리 공론. [→idea, -logy]

id est [íd ést] 《L. =that is》 that is (to say). 즉; 이를테면(abbr. i.e.).

id·i·o·cy [ídiəsi] *n.* (*pl.* **-cies**) **1** Ⓤ the state of being an idiot. 백치. **2** Ⓒ an act like an idiot's. 백치 같은 행위〔언동〕. [*idiot*]

·id·i·om [ídiəm] *n.* Ⓒ **1** a phrase having a particular meaning as a whole. 관용구; 관용어; 이디엄. **2** the language of a certain people or region. 사투리; 방언(方言). ¶ *speak in the ~ of the countryside* 시골 사투리로 이야기하다. **3** a particular or individual way of expression. 특유의 표현; 특색. ¶ *Goethe's ~* 괴테 특유의 표현. [Gk. *idios* own]

id·i·o·mat·ic [ìdiəmǽtik] *adj.* **1** in accordance with idioms. 관용 어법에 맞는. **2** ⓐ using many idoms. 많은 관용어를 사용하는. ⓑ containing or rich in peculiar idioms. 관용어가 많은. ¶ *an extremely ~ language* 관용어가 아주 많은 언어. **3** of an idiom. 관용적인.

id·i·o·syn·cra·sy [ìdiəsíŋkrəsi] *n.* Ⓒ (*pl.* **-sies**) **1** a way of thinking or doing peculiar to one person. (개인의) 특질; 특징. ¶ *It is an ~ of mine not to eat eggs.* 달걀을 안 먹는 것이 내 식성이다. **2** 《med.》 the physical constitution peculiar to a person. 특이 체질. [Gk. *idios* private, *sun* with, *kerannumi* mix]

·id·i·ot [ídiət] *n.* Ⓒ **1** a person born with little mental power. 백치(cf. *imbecile*). **2** 《*colloq.*》 a very stupid person. 바보; 얼간이. [Gk. =private person, ignorant person]

id·i·ot·ic [ìdiɑ́tik / -ɔ́t-] *adj.* of or like an idiot; very foolish. 백치의; 숙맥 같은.

id·i·ot·i·cal·ly [ìdiɑ́tikəli / -ɔ́t-] *adv.* in an idiotic manner; very stupidly. 백치처럼;

천치같이.

:i·dle [áidl] *adj.* (**i·dler, i·dlest**) **1** not willing to work; lazy. 게으른; 나태한(opp. diligent). ¶ *an ~ fellow* 게으름뱅이. **2** not working; not being used; not active. 놀고 있는; 쓰이고 있지〔움직이지〕 않는. ¶ *an ~ workman* 게으른 일꾼 / *in my ~ moments* 내게 시간이 있을 때 / *~ funds* 유휴 자금 / *stand ~* 멍하니 서 있다. **3** useless; worthless; empty. 쓸데없는; 무가치한. ¶ *an ~ attempt* 헛된 기도 / *~ talk* 쓸데없는 이야기; 잡담. **4** without any good reason or foundation. 근거 없는. ¶ *~ fears* 막연한 공포.

— *vi.* (P1,2A) **1** spend time doing nothing; waste time. 게으름피우다; 빈둥거리다. ¶ *~ while others work* 남은 일하는데 빈둥거리다 / *~ about in the room* 방 안에서 빈둥거리다. **2** (of a machine) running, but not engaged in useful work. 기계가 헛돌다. [A.S. *idel* empty]

idle away, let (time) pass without working. (시간을) 헛되이 보내다. ¶ *~ away the afternoon* 오후를 놀고 지내다.

***i·dle·ness** [áidlnis] *n.* Ⓤ the state of being idle or useless. 태만; 무익.

i·dler [áidlər] *n.* Ⓒ a lazy person; a person who wastes time in doing nothing. 나태한 사람; (일하지 않고) 빈둥거리는 사람.

i·dly [áidli] *adv.* in an idle manner; without any particular purpose. 게으르게; 무익하게; 헛되이. ¶ *wander ~* 일없이 돌아다니다.

***i·dol** [áidl] *n.* Ⓒ **1** an image worshipped as a god; a false god. 우상; 신상(神像); 사신(邪神). **2** a person or thing very much loved or admired. 숭배되는 사람〔것〕; 우상. ¶ *a popular ~* 대중의 우상〔숭배 대상〕. **3** 《log.》 a false conception. (선입적) 유견(謬見); 오류. [Gk. *eidos* image, form]

make an idol of, idolize. …을 숭배하다.

i·dol·a·trous [aidálətrəs / -dɔ́l-] *adj.* **1** worshipping idols. 우상 숭배의. **2** blindly admiring. 맹목적으로 숭배하는. ● **i·dol·a·trous·ly** [-li] *adv.* [→idol, Gk. *latreuo* worship]

i·dol·a·try [aidálətri / -dɔ́l-] *n.* Ⓤ worship of idols; much love or admiration for a person or thing. 우상 숭배; 숭배; 심취.

i·dol·ize [áidəlàiz] *vt.* (P6) **1** worship (someone or something) as an idol. …을 우상시〔화〕하다. **2** love or admire extremely. …을 극도로 숭배하다. ¶ *~ a hero* 〔*movie star*〕 영웅을〔영화 배우를〕 극도로 숭배하다.

i·dyll, i·dyl [áidl] *n.* Ⓒ **1** a short poem describing a scene or event in the country. 전원시(田園詩). **2** a scene or event suitable for this. 전원 풍경; 로맨틱한 이야기. [Gk. *eidos* form, picture]

i·dyl·lic [aidílik] *adj.* suitable for an idyll; simple and pleasant like an idyll. 전원시(詩)의; 목가적인.

-ie [-i] *suf.* little, darling. '(애칭으로 쓰여) 작은〔꼬마〕…'의 뜻. ¶ *doggie* 강아지.

i.e. [áiíː, ðǽtíz] that is; that is to say. 이를테면; 즉. [L. *id est*]

-ier [-iər] *suf.* (of an occupation) a person concerned with. '…에 종사하는 사람'의 뜻. ¶ *clothier* 피복〔옷감〕 장수. [L.]

:if [if] *conj.* **1** on condition that; in case that; supposing that. 만약 …이라면. ¶ *If you hit the center of the target, you win a prize.* 과녁의 복판을 맞히면 상을 탄다 / *If she were here, you would notice her.* 그녀가 여기 있으면 당신은 그녀를 알아볼 텐데 語法 현재의 사실에 반대되는 가정. be 동사는 모두 were가 되나 구어에서는 주어에 따라 was도 쓰임 / *If she was here, you would have noticed her.* 그녀가 여기 있었다면 당신은 그녀를 알아봤을 것이오 / *If you wash your hands, I'll give you a piece of cake.* 손을 씻으면 과자를 한 개 주마 / *What shall* 〔*should*〕 *I do ~* (*I should*) *fail again.* 또 실패하면 어쩌지 / *If it had been fine yesterday, we could have reached the summit.* 어제 날씨가 좋았더라면 우린 정상에 닿을 수 있었을 텐데. **2** whether. …일지 어떨지. ¶ *I wonder ~ he will come.* 글쎄 그 사람이 올는지 / *I wanted to see ~ the coat was big enough for me.* 그 코트가 내게 맞을지 어떨지 보고 싶었다. **3** even though; granting that. 비록 …일지라도. ¶ *Even ~ she is tired, she must keep on working.* 피곤할지라도 그녀는 계속 일해야 한다 / 《*emph.*》 *Even ~ I am wrong, you are at least not absolutely right.* 비록 내가 잘못일지 모르지만, 그렇다고 네가 전적으로 옳은 것은 아니다. **4** 《expressing a *wish* or *surprise*》 語法 주절을 생략한 조건절만의 형태가 됨. ¶ *If I only knew!* 내가 알기만 한다면야 / *If he were here with me!* 그가 나와 함께 여기 있다면 좋으련만. **5** whenever. …일 때는 언제나. ¶ *If I don't understand, I ask questions.* 내가 이해를 못 할 때면 언제나 질문을 한다. [A.S. *gif*; G. *ob.*]

as if, as though; as the case would be if. 마치 …처럼. ¶ *He speaks English as ~ he were a native speaker.* 그는 영어를 마치 모국어로 하여 자란 사람처럼 잘 한다.

if anything, somewhat. 어느 정도.

If it had not been for, had it not been for. 만일 …이 아니었다면〔없었다면〕. ¶ *If it had not been for your help, I could not have done it.* 네 도움이 없었다면 나는 그 일을 해내지 못했을 것이다.

If it were nor for, were it not for; but for. 만일 …이 없었다면〔아니라면〕. ¶ *If it were not for the sun, nothing could live.* 태양이 없다면 아무것도 살 수 없을 게다.

I.F., i.f., i-f intermediate frequency. 중간 주파

IFC International Finance Corporation. 국제 금융 공사.

IFTU International Federation of Trade Unions. 국제 노동 조합 연합회.

IGC International Geophysical Cooperation. 국제 지구 관측 협력.

ig·loo [íglu:] *n.* Ⓒ (*pl.* **-loos**) a dome-shaped Eskimo hut of snow. 이글루《에스키모인의 집》. [Esk.]

ig·ne·ous [ígniəs] *adj.* **1** of fire. 불의. **2** produced by fire or volcanic action. 화성(火成)의. ¶ *an ~ rock* 화성암. [L. *ignis* fire]

ig·nes fat·u·i [ígni:z fǽtʃuài] *n.* pl. of **ignis fatuus.**

ig·nis fat·u·us [ígnəs fǽtʃuəs] *n.* 《L. = foolish fire》 (*pl.* **ig·nes fat·u·i**) **1** a will-o'-the-wisp. 도깨비불. **2** 《*fig.*》 a hope eagerly followed and never attained; a mistaken ideal; a delusive hope. 헛된〔잘못된〕 기대. [↑, L. *fatuus* foolish]

ig·nite [ignáit] *vt.* (P6) **1** set fire to (something). …에 불을 붙이다; …을 태우다. ¶ *~ coal* 석탄을 때다. **2** make (something) very hot. …을 고도로 가열하다. — *vi.* (P1) catch fire. 불이 붙다. [→igneous]

ig·ni·tion [igníʃən] *n.* Ⓤ **1** the act of setting on fire. 점화. **2** the act of catching on fire. 인화; 발화. **3** Ⓒ the parts of a gasoline engine that set fire to the fuel. 점화 장치.

ig·no·ble [ignóubəl] *adj.* (opp. noble) **1** mean; of low character. 상스러운; 천한; 비열한. ¶ *To betray one's country is ~.* 나라를 배반하는 것은 비열한 짓이다. **2** of low birth. (태생이) 미천한. ¶ *He comes from an ~ family.* 미천한 집안 출신이다. **3** (of an event) shameful. 수치스러운; 굴욕〔치욕〕적인. ¶ *~ peace* 굴욕적인 강화. [in-¹, →noble]

ig·no·bly [ignóubli] *adv.* in an ignoble manner. 천하게; 상스럽게.

ig·no·min·i·ous [ìgnəmíniəs] *adj.* shameful; dishonorable. 수치스러운; 명예롭지 못한; contemptible. 경멸할(만한). [↓]

ig·no·min·y [ígnəmìni] *n.* (*pl.* **-min·ies**) **1** Ⓤ public shame or dishonor. 치욕; 불명예. ¶ *bring ~ to one's family* 집안을 욕되게 하다. **2** Ⓒ a shameful act. 부끄러운 행위; 추행. [in-¹, L. (*g*)*nomen* name]

ig·no·ra·mus [ìgnəréiməs] *n.* Ⓒ an ignorant person. 무식〔무지〕한 사람. [L. =we know not, →ignore]

***ig·no·rance** [ígnərəns] *n.* Ⓤ lack of knowledge. 무지; 무학. ¶ *be in ~ of* …을 모르다 / *make a mistake out of ~* 무지로 인해 잘못을 저지르다 / *He sinned rather from ~ than from actual wickedness.* 그는 악해서라기보다는 무식한 탓으로 죄를 졌다. [→ ignore]

***ig·no·rant** [ígnərənt] *adj.* **1** knowing little; without knowledge. 무지한; 무식한. ¶ *He may be ~, but he's not stupid.* 그는 무식할지 모르나 바보는 아니다. **2** not aware. 모르는. ¶ *He was ~ of the rule.* 그는 그 규칙을 몰랐다. **3** caused by lack of knowledge; showing ignorance. 무지로 인한; 무지를 드러내는.

ig·no·rant·ly [ígnərəntli] *adv.* because of ignorance; showing ignorance. 무지해서; 몰라서.

***ig·nore** [ignɔ́:r] *vt.* (P6) **1** pay no attention to (something); refuse to notice. …을 무시하다; 모른 체하다. ¶ *~ another's remarks* 남의 의견을 무시하다 / *~ a danger sign* 위험 신호를 무시하다 / *~ someone's presence* 아무의 존재를 무시하다. **2** 《law》 (of a Grand Jury) reject as unfounded. 기각(棄却)하다. [in-¹, L. *gno* know]

i·gua·na [igwá:nə] *n.* Ⓒ 《zool.》 a large, tree-climbing, lizardlike animal in tropical America. 이구아나《열대 남아메리카의, 나무에 오르는 도마뱀의 하나》. [Carib.]

IHP, I.H.P. indicated horsepower. 지시〔실(實)〕마력

IHS, I.H.S. Jesus.

i·kon [áikɑn / -kɔn] *n.* =icon.

il·i·ac [íliæ̀k] *adj.* 《anat.》 of or near the flanks. 장골(腸骨)의. [L. *ilia* flanks]

Il·i·ad [íliəd], **the** *n.* a long Greek narrative poem probably written by Homer. 일리어드《Troy 전쟁을 읊은 서사시》. [Gk. *Ilion* Troy]

an Iliad of woes, a succession of misfortunes 잇단〔연이은〕 불행.

ilk [ilk] *adj.* 《Sc.》 same. 같은.

— *n.* 《*colloq.*》 a family; a kind. 가족; 동류; 동종. ¶ *he and all his ~* 그와 그 가족. [E.]

of that ilk, 《*colloq.*》 of the same place or name; of that kind or sort. 성(姓)과 그 지방 이름이 같은; 동일한; 같은 종류〔종족, 가족〕의.

⁑**ill** [il] *adj.* (**worse** [wə:rs], **worst** [wə:rst]) **1** 《chiefly as *predicative*》 in bad health; sick; not well; having a disease. 병이 든; 건강이 나쁜; 기분이 안 좋은(opp. well). 語法 미국에서는 ill의 뜻으로 sick도 쓰나 영국에서는 ill에 구역질의 뜻이 있어서 잘 안 쓰임. ¶ *He is ~.* 그는 앓고 있다 / *She fell ~.* 그녀는 병이 났다 / *Our cat looks ~.* 고양이가 기분이 안 좋은 모양이다. **2** bad; evil; harmful; unfortunate. 좋지 않은; 사악한; 불길한. ¶ *~ habit* 나쁜 버릇 / *~ company* 나쁜 친구 / *a sign of ~ omen* 불길한 조짐 / *bear someone ~ will* 아무를 좋지 않게 생각하다 / *take something in ~ part* …을 나쁜 뜻으로 해석하다 / 《*prov.*》 *Ill weeds grow apace.* 악사 천리(惡事千里). **3** poor; imperfect. 서투른; 불완전한. ¶ *~ management* 시원찮은 경영 / *~ success* 대단찮은 성공. **4** 《*arch.*》 difficult; hard. 어려운; 까다로운. ¶ *an ~ person to please* 비위 맞추기 어려운 사람.

as ill luck would have it, unfortunately. 불행히도.

be taken ill, fall ill. 병이 나다.

do someone an ill turn, injure someone or someone's interests. 아무를 해치다〔해롭게 하다〕.

— *adv.* badly. 나쁘게; 부정하게. ¶ *speak ~ of someone* 아무를 나쁘게 말하다 / *It goes ~ with me.* 사태가 내게 좋지 않게 되어 간다.

ill at ease, anxious; uneasy. 침착을 잃은; 불

안한.

Ill got, ill spent. 《*prov.*》 부정하게 번 돈은 오래 가지 않는다.

it ill becomes (***you, him, etc.***)***,*** it is unsuitable or proper for (you, him, etc.). …에게 어울리지 않는다.

take** something **ill, be angry at it; be offended by it. …에 화를 내다. ¶ *I took it* ~. 그 일에 화가 났다.

—— *n.* **1** Ⓤ evil; harm. 악; 나쁜 일. ¶ *do* ~ 좋지 않은 짓을 하다. **2** Ⓒ 《usu. *pl.*》 a misfortune; a trouble; a sickness. 불행; 불운; 병. ¶ *experience all the ills of life* 인생의 온갖 고초를 겪다. [N.]

Ill. Illinois.

I'll [ail] I shall; I will.

ill-ad·vised [íladváizd] *adj.* acting or done without proper consideration. 분별 없는; 경솔한. ¶ *an* ~ *remark* 경솔한 말 / *an* ~ *scheme* 현명치 못한 계획. [*ill*]

ill-ad·vis·ed·ly [íladváizidli] *adv.* in an ill-advised manner. 무분별하게.

ill-af·fect·ed [íləféktid] *adj.* not favoring; feeling dislike (for). 호감을〔호의를〕 갖지 않은.

ill blood [∠∠] *n.* hatred. 증오.

ill-bred [ílbréd] *adj.* badly brought up; not polite. 버릇없이 자란; 가정 교육이〔본데〕 없는 (cf. *lowbred*).

ill-con·di·tioned [ílkəndíʃənd] *adj.* bad-natured; in a bad condition. 질〔성질〕이 나쁜; 건강이 좋지 않은.

ill-con·sid·ered [ílkənsídərd] *adj.* not properly considered; unwise. 사려 깊지 않은; 무분별한.

ill-dis·posed [íldispóuzd] *adj.* unfriendly; unfavorable. 악의를 품은; 심사가 나쁜; 짓궂은.

il·le·gal [ilíːgəl] *adj.* not lawful; against the law. 비합법의; 불법의; 위법인(opp. legal). ¶ *It is* ~ *to drive a car without a licence.* 면허 없이 운전하는 것은 불법이다. [in-[1]]

il·le·gal·i·ty [ìliːgǽləti] *n.* (*pl.* **-ties**) **1** Ⓤ the state of being illegal. 불법; 위법. **2** Ⓒ an act against the law. 불법〔위법〕 행위.

il·le·gal·ly [ilíːgəli] *adv.* in an unlawful manner. 불법으로.

il·leg·i·ble [ilédʒəbəl] *adj.* difficult or impossible to read. 읽기〔판독하기〕 어려운. ¶ *The ink had faded so that many words were* ~. 잉크가 바래서 많은 낱말이 판독하기 어려웠다. [in-[1]]

il·le·git·i·ma·cy [ìlidʒítəməsi] *n.* Ⓤ the fact or condition of being illegitimate. 불법; 사생(私生); 불합리. [in-[1]]

il·le·git·i·mate [ìlidʒítəmit] *adj.* (opp. legitimate) **1** against the law; illegal. 불법의. ¶ *an* ~ *action* 비합법 행위 / *an* ~ *business* 불법 영업. **2** born of unmarried parents. 사생(私生)〔서출(庶出)〕의. ¶ *an* ~ *child* 사생아. **3** not logical. 부조리한; 불합리한.

—— [-mèit] *vt.* (P6) declare illegitimate. 불법화〔위법화〕하다; 사생아(私生兒)로 선고하다. [in-[1]]

ill-fat·ed [ílféitid] *adj.* destined to have a bad fate. 운이 나쁜; 불운〔불행〕한. ¶ *an* ~ *suggestion* 불행을 가져오는 제안. [*ill*]

ill-fa·vored, 《Brit.》 **-voured** [ílféivərd] *adj.* (of a person, looks) not pleasant in appearance; having an unpleasant look; ugly. (얼굴이) 못생긴; 추한.

ill-got·ten [ílgátn / -gɔ́t-] *adj.* obtained by dishonest means. 부정한 수단으로 얻은. ¶ *become rich on* ~ *gain* 부정하게 벌어 부자가 되다.

ill-hu·mored, 《Brit.》 **-moured** [ílhjúːmərd] *adj.* bad-tempered; cross; in a bad humor. 기분이 좋지 않은〔언짢은〕; 찌무룩한. [*ill*]

il·lib·er·al [ilíbərəl] *adj.* **1** not liberal; narrow-minded. 너그럽지 않은; 도량이 좁은; 편협한. **2** not generous; stingy. 인색한; 쩨쩨한. **3** without liberal culture. 교양이 없는. [in-[1]]

il·lic·it [ilísit] *adj.* not allowed by law, etc.; illegal; improper. 불법〔위법〕의; 부정한. [in-[1], L. *licet* it is lawful]

il·lim·it·a·ble [ilímitəbəl] *adj.* without limit; immeasurable; endless; vast. 무한의; 끝없는. ¶ ~ *space* 무한한 공간 / *the* ~ *ocean* 광대 무변한 대양. [in-[1]]

Il·li·nois [ìlənɔ́i, -nɔ́iz] *n.* a middle-western State in the United States. 일리노이 주. 參考 Ill.로 생략함. 주도는 Springfield.

il·lit·er·a·cy [ilítərəsi] *n.* Ⓤ the state of being illiterate. 무학; 무교육. [↓]

il·lit·er·ate [ilítərit] *adj.* **1** unable to read or write. 글을 모르는; 무식한; 문맹의. ¶ *the* ~ *voter* 문맹의 유권자. **2** not cultured; uneducated. 교양이 없는; 교육을 못 받은. —— *n.* Ⓒ an illiterate person. 무식한〔교양 없는〕 사람. [in-[1]]

ill-judged [íldʒʌ́dʒd] *adj.* unwise; rash. 분별〔지각〕 없는. [*ill*]

ill-man·nered [ílmǽnərd] *adj.* not polite; rude. 버릇없는; 예절을 모르는.

ill-na·tured [ílnéitʃərd] *adj.* of an ill nature; disagreeable; cross. 근성이 나쁜; 심술궂은; 삐뚤어진.

ill·ness [ílnis] *n.* ⓊⒸ the state of being sick; sickness; an attack or fit of illness. 불건강(상태); 병; 발병. ¶ *feign* ~ 꾀병을 부리다 / *be suddenly seized with* ~ 갑자기 발병하다 / *suffer from a serious* ~ 중병에 걸리다 / *There is no serious* ~ *in the city.* 시중에 심각한 질병은 없다. [*ill*]

il·log·i·cal [iládʒikəl / -lɔ́dʒ-] *adj.* not logical; not well reasoned. 비논리적인; 불합리한. ● **il·log·i·cal·ly** [-i] *adv.* [in-[1]]

ill-o·mened [íloumənd] *adj.* having or attended by bad omens. 불길한; 불운한. [*ill*]

ill-spent [ílspént] *adj.* spent badly; wasted. 잘못 사용된; 낭비된.

ill-starred [ílstá:rd] *adj.* born under an unlucky star; unfortunate. 팔자가 나쁜; 불운한.

ill-tem·pered [íltémpərd] *adj.* having or showing bad temper; cross; quarrelsome. 기분이 좋지 않은[언짢은]; 성마른.

ill-timed [íltáimd] *adj.* coming or done at a bad time. 계제가 나쁜; 시기를 놓친.

ill-treat [íltrí:t] *vt.* (P6) treat cruelly or unfairly. …을 학대[냉대]하다.

ill-treat·ment [íltrí:tmənt] *n.* U cruel, unfair or unkind treatment. 학대; 혹사.

il·lu·mi·nant [ilú:mənənt] *adj.* giving light, illuminating. 빛을 내는[발하는]. — *n.* something that gives light. 발광체. [↓]

•**il·lu·mi·nate** [ilú:mənèit] *vt.* (P6,13) 《*with*》 **1** give light to (something); light up. …을 비추다; 조명하다. ¶ *Candles illuminated the room.* 촛불들이 방을 밝혔다. **2** decorate (something) with colored light. …을 색등으로 장식하다. **3** make (something difficult) clear; explain. …을 밝히다; 설명하다. ¶ *Our teacher illuminated the subject by giving examples.* 선생님은 예를 들어 가며 문제를 우리에게 설명했다. **4** decorate (an initial letter, a word or the border of a page) with colors, pictures, designs, etc. …을 금자(金字)·그림·도안 따위로 꾸미다. **5** give spiritual light to; enlighten. 계몽하다. [in-², L. *lumen* light]

il·lu·mi·na·tion [ilù:mənéiʃən] *n.* **1** U the act of illuminating or lighting up. 조명(照明). **2** U the act of making clear; explanation. 명시; 설명. **3** C 《usu. *pl.*》 decoration with lights. 전광식(電光飾); 일루미네이션. **4** C 《usu. *pl.*》 decoration of initial letters, the borders of pages, etc. with gold and designs. 채식(彩飾). **5** U enlightenment. 계몽; 계시. ¶ *in search of religious* ~ 종교적 계시를 구하여.

il·lu·mine [ilú:min] *vt.* (P6,13) 《*with, by*》 make (something) bright; illuminate; light up. …을 비추다; 밝히다. ¶ *Electric lights ~ our houses.* 전등불이 우리들 집을 밝혀 준다. [*illuminate*]

ill-us·age [íljú:sidʒ, -jú:z-] *n.* U unfair or cruel treatment. 학대; 혹사. [↓]

ill-use [íljú:z] *vt.* (P6) **1** treat badly or cruelly. …을 학대[혹사]하다; 악용하다. **2** make a wrong use of. …을 남용하다.
— [íljú:s] *n.* U bad or cruel treatment. 학대; 혹사; 악용. [*ill*]

•**il·lu·sion** [ilú:ʒən] *n.* UC **1** something which gives a false or misleading appearance or impression. 환상; 착각을 일으키는 것; 환영. **2** a false or mistaken idea, conception or belief; a delusion. 환상; 환각; 착각; 망상. ¶ *produce illusions in someone's mind* 착각을 일으키다 / *be under no ~ about* [*as to*] …에 관해 아무런 착각도 하고 있지 않다. ●**il·lu·sion·ar·y** [-ʒənèri / -əri] *adj.* [in-², L. *ludo* play]

il·lu·sive [ilú:siv] *adj.* of or producing illusion; unreal. 착각의; 착각을 일으키는.

il·lu·so·ry [ilú:səri] *adj.* illusive; unreal. 착각의; 가공의.

:**il·lus·trate** [íləstrèit, ilʌ́streit] *vt.* (P6,13) 《*with, by*》 **1** give (a book, etc.) pictures, diagrams, maps, etc. to help to explain or decorate it. …을 도해(圖解)하다; …에 삽화를 넣다. ¶ *The book is well illustrated.* 이 책은 삽화가 잘 들어가 있다. **2** make (something) clear by stories, examples, etc. …을 실례를 들어 잘 설명[해설]하다. ¶ *~ one's lecture with examples* 예를 들어 강의를 하다 / *Let me ~ how it is so.* 어째서 그런지 실례를 들어 설명 드리죠. [in-², L. *lustro* make bright]

il·lus·trat·ed [íləstrèitid, ilʌ́streit-] *adj.* explained or ornamented by pictures, diagrams, etc. 도해(圖解)된; 삽화가 든.

:**il·lus·tra·tion** [ìləstréiʃən] *n.* **1** C a picture, diagram, map, etc. used to explain or decorate. 삽화; 설명 그림[도표]. **2** C a story, an example, etc. used to explain. (설명을 위한) 실례; 이야기 (따위). **3** U the act of explaining or decorating by the use of pictures or examples. 설명; 예해; 도해.

il·lus·tra·tive [íləstrèitiv, ilʌ́strətiv] *adj.* of or used for illustration. 예증이 되는; 설명적인. ¶ *The example was ~ of the new idea.* 그 실례는 새 구상의 설명에 도움이 되는 것이었다.

il·lus·tra·tor [íləstrèitər, ilʌ́s-] *n.* C **1** a person who makes pictures illustrating books, magazines, etc. 삽화가. **2** a person or thing that explains. 설명[해설]자; 설명이 되는 것.

il·lus·tri·ous [ilʌ́striəs] *adj.* very famous; distinguished. 유명한; 저명[걸출]한.

ill will [∠∠] *n.* unfriendly feeling; unfriendliness. 악의; 적의; 반감; 원한. [*ill*]

ill-wish·er [ílwíʃər] *n.* C a person who wishes misfortune to another. 남을 방자하는[남이 못 되기를 바라는] 사람. [↑]

ILO, I.L.O. International Labor Organization. 국제 노동 기구.

:**I'm** [aim] I am.

im- [im-] *pref.* =in-¹. 語法 p, b, m 앞에 쓰임. ¶ *impossible / imbalance / immoral.*

:**im·age** [ímidʒ] *n.* C **1** ⓐ a thing drawn, painted, sculptured, etc. in the likeness of a person, an animal, etc. 상(像); 화상; 조상(彫像). ¶ *an ~ of the Virgin Mary* 성모 마리아상(像) / *an ~ of a person* 초상. ⓑ an idol. 우상. ¶ *worship an ~* 우상을 숭배하다. **2** a person or thing closely like another; a counterpart. 꼭 닮은 사람[것]. ¶ *She is the ~ of her mother.* 그녀는 제 어머니를 빼쏘았다. **3** 《opt.》 an impression seen in a mirror, through a lens, etc. 영

I

상(映像). ¶ *see one's* ~ *in the mirror* 거울에 비친 자기 모습을 보다. **4** a symbol; a type. 상징; 전형. ¶ *the very* ~ *of laziness* 게으름의 전형〔화신〕. **5**《psych.》 a picture in the mind; a mental conception. 심상(心象); 개념. **6** a figure of speech; a simile; a metaphor. 비유; 직유(直喩); 은유(隱喩). ¶ *speak in images* 비유로 이야기하다.

— *vt* (P6) **1** make a picture or sculpture of (someone or something). …의 상(像)을 그리다〔새기다〕. **2** reflect. (영상 따위)를 비추다. ¶ *The clouds were imaged in the waters of the lake.* 호수면에 구름이 비쳐져 있었다. **3** make a picture of (something) in the mind; imagine. …을 마음에 그리다; 상상하다. ¶ *The boy could* ~ *what his mother was doing at home.* 소년은 어머니가 집에서 무엇을 하고 계신지를 상상할 수 있었다. **4** describe (something) vividly in words. …을 생생하게 묘사하다. **5** symbolize. 상징하다. [L. *imago*]

im·age·ry [ímidʒəri] *n.* Ⓤ 《*collectively*》 **1** pictures in the mind. 심상(心象)《마음에 그리는 상》. **2** figures of speech used to form pictures in the mind. 비유적인 묘사. ¶ *Poetry usually contains much* ~. 시에는 흔히 많은 비유적인 표현들이 들어 있다. **3** 《rare》 images; statues. 상(像); 조상(彫像). [*image*]

i·mag·i·na·ble [imǽdʒənəbəl] *adj.* that can be pictured in the mind; possible. 상상할 수 있는; 생각할 수 있는 한의. ¶ *the greatest joy* ~ 더 없는 큰 기쁨 / *every* ~ *method* 온갖〔모든〕 방법 / *the greatest difficulty* ~ 상상도 못 할 큰 어려움.

***i·mag·i·nar·y** [imǽdʒənèri / -nəri] *adj.* existing only in the imagination; not real. 상상의; 실재하지 않는. ¶ *an* ~ *number* 허수 / *Fairies are* ~. 요정이란 상상의 것이다.

:i·mag·i·na·tion [imæ̀dʒənéiʃən] *n.* Ⓤ **1** the act or power of forming pictures of what is not actually present. 상상(력). ¶ *give full play to one's* ~ 상상의 날개를 펴다 / *beyond all* ~ 전혀 상상도 할 수 없는 / *He sees things in his* ~. 그는 사물들을 그의 상상을 통해서 본다. **2** the ability to create new things or ideas in the mind. 창작력. **3** ⒸⓊ ⓐ something imagined in the mind. 상상의 소산; 공상. ¶ *The story was pure* ~. 이야기는 순전히 상상에서 나온 것이었다. ⓑ a foolish idea. 어리석은 생각.

i·mag·i·na·tive [imǽdʒənətiv, -nèit-] *adj.* **1** of, having or showing imagination. 상상의; 상상적인. ¶ *an* ~ *tale* 상상의 이야기. **2** able to imagine well; creative. 상상력이 풍부한. ¶ *an* ~ *artist* 상상력이 풍부한 예술가.

:i·mag·ine [imǽdʒin] *vt.* (P6,7,10,11,12,20,21,23) **1** form a picture of (something) in one's mind. …을 상상하다; 마음에 그리다. ¶ *such sufferings as we cannot even* ~. 우리가 상상도 할 수 없는 많은 수난들 / *Imagine yourself to be in his place.* 네가 그의 처지에 있다고 생각해 봐라. **2** guess; suppose; think. …을 추측하다; 생각하다. ¶ *I couldn't* ~ *what would be the result.* 결과가 어떻게 될지 짐작도 할 수 없었다 / *I* ~ *that he will come.* 그가 오리라 생각한다.
— *vi.* (P1) use the imagination. 상상(력을 동원)하다. [*image*]

i·ma·gi·nes [iméidʒinìːz] *n.* pl. of **imago.**

i·ma·go [iméigou] *n.* (*pl.* **-gos, -gi·nes**) 《zool.》 the winged stage of insects. 성충(成蟲). [*image*]

im·be·cile [ímbəsil, -sàil / -sìːl] *n.* Ⓒ a person with a very weak mind; a very stupid person. 저능자; 바보(cf. *idiot*). — *adj.* very weak in mind; stupid. 저능한; 어리석은. [L.]

im·be·cil·i·ty [ìmbəsíləti] *n.* (*pl.* **-ties**) **1** Ⓤ the state of being imbecile. 정신 박약; 저능; 치우(癡愚). **2** Ⓒ a foolish action, speech, etc. 어리석은 언행.

im·bibe [imbáib] *vt.* **1** (P6) 《*joc.*》 drink; drink to excess. 과음하다. ¶ *He imbibes too much.* 너무 마신다. **2** (P6) absorb. …을 흡수하다. ¶ *Sponge imbibes water.* 스펀지는 물을 빨아들인다. **3** (P6,13) 《*in*》 《*fig.*》 receive (something) into one's mind. (사상 등을) 받아들이다. ¶ ~ *moral principles* 도의를 받아들이다. **4** (P6,13) 《*from, into*》 take in; inhale. 섭취〔흡입〕하다. [in-[2], L. *bibo* drink]

im·bro·glio [imbróuljou] *n.* Ⓒ (*pl.* **-glios**) **1** a difficult or complicated situation. 분규; 뒤엉킴. **2** a confused or complicated misunderstanding or disagreement. 갈등; 말썽. [in-[2], →broil]

im·brue [imbrúː] *vt.* (P13) make (something) wet, esp. with blood; stain. …을 (피로) 물들이다; 더럽히다. ¶ *His hands were imbrued with blood.* 그의 손은 피로 물들었다. [→imbibe]

im·bue [imbjúː] *vt.* (P6,13) 《*from, into, with*》 **1** impress deeply; inspire. …을 불어넣다; 고취하다. ¶ *The soldiers were imbued with patriotism.* 병사들에게 애국심이 고취되었다. **2** 《*with*》 cause (something) to be full of moisture or color. …에 스며들게 하다; 물들이다. ¶ ~ *a fabric with blue* 천을 파랗게 물들이다. [L.]

***im·i·tate** [ímitèit] *vt.* (P6) **1** do or try to do the same as; follow the example of (someone or something). …을 모방하다; 흉내내다; …을 따르다. ¶ ~ *the ancient wise and good men* 옛 선현(先賢)들을 배우다. **2** make a likeness of (something). …을 모조하다; …와 비슷하게 만들다. ¶ ~ *diamonds in paste* 다이아몬드 모조 보석을 만들다 / *cloth made to* ~ *silk* 비단 비슷하게 만든 천. [L. *imitor*]

I

·im·i·ta·tion [ìmitéiʃən] *n.* **1** Ⓤ the act of imitating. 흉내내기; 모방. ¶ *Children may learn by* ~. 아이들은 모방하면서 배우는지도 모른다 / *Painters lacking originality often spend their lives in the* ~ *of the great masters.* 독창성이 결여된 화가는 왕왕 대가(大家)들의 것을 모방하는 데 세월을 보낸다 / *give an* ~ *of an animal's cry* 짐승 울음소리를 흉내내다. **2** Ⓒ a copy. 모조품; 가짜. — *adj.* made to resemble something real or superior; not real. 모조의; 인조의. ¶ ~ *pearls* 모조 진주.

im·i·ta·tive [ímətèitiv, -tətiv] *adj.* of imitation; not original or real; imitating. 모조의; 가짜의. ¶ ~ *words* 의성어 / ~ *art* 모조 미술 / ~ *poetry* 모방시.

im·i·ta·tor [ímitèitər] *n.* Ⓒ a person who imitates. 흉내내는 사람; 모방자.

im·mac·u·late [imǽkjəlit] *adj.* **1** without a spot or stain; spotless; clean. 더럼이 없는; 얼룩 하나 없는; 깨끗한. ¶ *an* ~ *shirt* 깨끗한 셔츠. **2** without fault or sin; pure. (무결무구의) 완벽한; 순결한. ¶ *His life and conduct were* ~. 그의 생활과 처신은 순결했다. **3** 《zool.》 반점이 없는. [in-[1], L. *macula* spot]

im·ma·nence [ímənəns], **-nen·cy** [-nənsi] *n.* Ⓤ the state of being immanent. 내재(內在)성(性). [↓]

im·ma·nent [ímənənt] *adj.* **1** living or remaining within. 내재하는; 내재적인. **2** (of God) present throughout the universe. (신이) 우주에 편재(偏在)하는. [in-[2], L. *maneo* remain]

im·ma·te·ri·al [ìmətíəriəl] *adj.* **1** not material; not consisting of matter. 비물질적인; 실체가 없는. ¶ *Ghosts are* ~. 유령이란 실체가 없다. **2** not important. 중요하지 않은; 하잘것없는. ¶ *His objections were quite* ~. 그의 반대는 정말 하찮은 것들이었다. [in-[1]]

im·ma·ture [ìmətjúər] *adj.* not fully grown; not mature; not ripe. 미숙한; 미완성의. ¶ ~ *fruit* (*fish*) 풋과일(치어) / *an* ~ *literary words.* [in-[1]]

im·ma·tu·ri·ty [ìmətjú(:)rəti] *n.* Ⓤ the state of being immature. 미숙(상태); 미완성(상태).

im·meas·ur·a·ble [iméʒərəbəl] *adj.* too big to be measured; boundless; vast. 헤아릴 수 없는; 무한(광대)한. ¶ *the* ~ *heavens* 광대 무변의 하늘 / ~ *joy* 한없는 기쁨. [in-[1]]

im·meas·ur·a·bly [iméʒərəbli] *adv.* to an immeasurable extent or degree; vastly. 추측할(헤아릴) 수 없을 만큼; 한없이; 광대하게.

im·me·di·a·cy [imí:diəsi] *n.* Ⓤ the state or quality of being immediate. 직접; 밀접(密接); 즉시. [↓]

:im·me·di·ate [imí:diit] *adj.* **1** happening or coming at once; without delay. 즉시의; 당장의. ¶ *an* ~ *reply* 즉답 / *take* ~ *action* 당장 행동에 옮기다(실행하다). **2** with nothing coming between; direct. 직접의. ¶ *an* ~ *result* 직접적인 결과 / ~ *information* 직접 보도. **3** closest; nearest. 바로 이웃의; 인접한. ¶ *my* ~ *neighborhood* 우리 바로 이웃 / *one's* ~ *family* (친)가족. **4** of the present time; urgent. 현하의; 당면한. [in-[1]]

:im·me·di·ate·ly [imí:diitli] *adv.* in an immediate manner; at once; directly. 즉시; 당장. ¶ *Do it* ~. 지금 즉시 해라 / *I answered his letter* ~. 곧바로 그에게 회답을 썼다. — *conj.* 《chiefly Brit.》 as soon as. …하자마자. ¶ *Immediately he got home, he went to bed.* 그는 집에 돌아오자마자 잠자리에 들었다.

im·me·mo·ri·al [ìmimɔ́:riəl] *adj.* **1** extending beyond reach of memory; very old. 기억에 남지 않는; 아주 오랜; 태고의. ¶ *from time* ~ 먼 옛적부터; 태고 이래. **2** of very great age; very old. 아주 오래 된. ¶ ~ *trees* 고목들. [in-[1]]

:im·mense [iméns] *adj.* **1** very big; huge; vast. 거대한; 광대한. **2** 《*colloq.*》 very good; splendid; excellent. 썩 좋은; 훌륭한. [in-[1], L. *metior* measure]

im·mense·ly [iménsli] *adv.* **1** to an immense degree; enormously. 무한히; 광대하게. **2** 《*colloq.*》 very much. 대단히; 굉장히. ¶ *I enjoyed the party* ~. 파티는 아주 즐거웠다 / *He's* ~ *clever.* 보통 영리한 사람이 아니다.

im·men·si·ty [iménsəti] *n.* Ⓤ **1** very great extent or size; vastness. 광대; 막대. ¶ *the ocean's* ~ 대양의 무변성. **2** infinite space. 무한 공간.

im·merse [imɔ́:rs] *vt.* (P6,13) 《*in*》 **1** dip (something) into a liquid. …을 잠그다; 적시다. ¶ ~ *clothes in water.* **2** baptize (someone) by dipping him under water. …에 침례를 베풀다. **3** involve or absorb deeply. …을 빠지게 하다; 몰두시키다. ¶ *be immersed in one's work* 일에 몰두하다 / *immersed in debts* 빚 때문에 옴짝 못 하다 / *immersed in difficulties* 곤란에 빠져들다. [in-[2], L. *mergo* dip]

im·mer·sion [imɔ́:rʒən, -ʃən] *n.* Ⓤ **1** the act of immersing; the state of being immersed. 침수; 잠김. **2** the state of being deeply engaged or absorbed. 몰입; 몰두; 열중.

·im·mi·grant [ímigrənt] *n.* Ⓒ a person who comes into a foreign country to live there permanently. 이민; 이주자. — *adj.* coming into a country to live. 이민 오는, 이주하는. [in-[2]]

im·mi·grate [íməgrèit] *vi.* (P3) come into a foreign country to live there permanently. 이주하다; 이민 가다 (cf. *emigrate*). — *vt.* (P7) 《*into*》 bring in or send (someone) as an immigrant. 이주시키다. 語法 이주하기 위해 나라를 떠나는 것은 emigrate.

im·mi·gra·tion [ìməgréiʃən] *n.* **1** Ⓤ the

act of coming into a foreign country to live there permanently. 이주; 이민(移民). ¶ *There was ~ to south America from Korea.* 한국에서 남아메리카로 이민이 있었다. **2** Ⓒ the number of immigrants during a certain period. 이민수(移民數).

im·mi·nence [ímənəns] *n.* **1** Ⓤ the state of being imminent. 절박; 긴박(성). ¶ *Dark clouds and thunder show the ~ of a storm.* 검은 구름과 천둥은 곧 폭풍이 분다는 징후이다. **2** Ⓒ something, esp. something evil or dangerous, which is likely to happen soon. 절박한 위험. [↓]

im·mi·nent [ímənənt] *adj.* likely to occur soon; threatening. 절박한; 급박한. ¶ *A storm is ~.* 곧 폭풍우가 닥칠 모양이다. [in-[2], L. *mineo* jut]

im·mo·bile [imóubəl, -biːl] *adj.* **1** not able to move or be moved; firmly fixed. 움직이기 어려운; 고정된. **2** not moving; motionless. 움직이지 않는; 정지된. [in-[1]]

im·mo·bil·i·ty [ìmoubíləti] *n.* Ⓤ the state of being immobile. 부동; 고정; 정지.

im·mo·bi·lize [imóubəlàiz] *vt.* (P6) **1** make (troops, vehicle) immobile. …을 고정시키다; 움직이지 않게 하다. **2** withdraw (coin) from circulation. (화폐의) 유통을 정지시키다.

im·mod·er·ate [imádərit / -mɔ́d-] *adj.* not moderate; extreme; excessive. 중용을 잃은; 극단적인; 과도한. ¶ *~ eating and drinking* 과음 과식하다. [in-[1]]

im·mod·est [imádist / -mɔ́d-] *adj.* not modest. 조심성이 없는; 버릇없는; 건방진. ¶ *~ behavior* 건방진 행동. [in-[1]]

im·mod·es·ty [imádisti / -mɔ́d-] *n.* (*pl.* **-ties**) **1** Ⓤ the state of being immodest; lack of modesty. 조심성이 없음; 뻔뻔스러움; 몰염치. **2** Ⓒ an immodest act or remark. 조심성 없는 언행.

im·mo·late [íməlèit] *vt.* (P6,13) **1** kill or offer (something) as a sacrifice. 죽여서 신에게 바치다; 산제물로 바치다. **2** 《*fig.*》 sacrifice. 희생하다. ¶ *~ one's ambition on the altar of duty* 의리를 위해 대망을 버리다. [L. =sprinkle with meal]

im·mor·al [imɔ́(ː)rəl, imár-] *adj.* **1** not moral. 부도덕한. ¶ *It is ~ to cheat in a test.* 시험의 부정 행위는 옳지 못하다. **2** (of a person, conduct, book, etc.) evil, wicked. (사람·행실 등이) 나쁜; 음란한. ¶ *have ~ relations with many women* 많은 여자들과 불륜의 관계를 가지다. [in-[1], L. *mōs* custom]

im·mor·al·i·ty [ìmərǽləti] *n.* (*pl.* **-ties**) **1** Ⓤ the state of being immoral; wickedness. 불륜; 부도덕; **2** Ⓒ an immoral act. 부도덕한 행위. [↑]

•**im·mor·tal** [imɔ́ːrtl] *adj.* **1** living or lasting forever; never dying. 죽지 않는; 불사의; 불멸의. ¶ *A man's body dies, but his soul may ~.* 사람의 육신은 죽어도 그의 영혼은 죽지 않는다. **2** 《*fig.*》 never to be forgotten; remembered forever. 불후의; 불후의 명성이 있는. ¶ *~ fame* 불후의 명성. — *n.* Ⓒ **1** a person who never dies. 불사신. **2** a person whose fame is remembered forever. 명성이 영원한 사람. **3** 《*pl.*》 the gods, esp. of ancient Greece and Rome. (그리스·로마 신화의) 신들. [in-[1], L. *mors* death]

im·mor·tal·i·ty [ìmɔːrtǽləti] *n.* Ⓤ **1** a life which continues forever; the state of living forever. 불사; 불멸. **2** everlasting fame. 불후의 명성.

im·mor·tal·ize [imɔ́ːrtəlàiz] *vt.* (P6) **1** make (someone) immortal. …을 불사(불멸) 하게 하다. **2** 《*fig.*》 give everlasting fame to (someone). …에게 불후의 명예를 주다. ¶ *Great authors are immortalized by their works.* 위대한 작가들은 그들 작품으로 인해 불후의 명예를 얻은 사람들이다.

im·mov·a·ble [imúːvəbəl] *adj.* **1** not able to move or be moved. 움직이지 않는; 부동의. ¶ *~ estate* (*property*) 부동산. **2** firm; unchanging. 확고한; 흔들리지 않는. ¶ *~ purpose* 확고한 의지. — *n.* Ⓒ 《*pl.*》 immovable property, such as land, buildings, etc. 부동산. [in-[1]]

im·mune [imjúːn] *adj.* **1** 《*from, against, to*》 protected from a particular disease. 면역의. ¶ *I have had that disease and so am ~.* 난 그 병을 앓은 적이 있어 면역이 됐다. **2** safe; free. 면제된. ¶ *He is ~ from punishment.* 그는 벌이 면제되어 있다. [in-[2], L. *munus* public burden]

im·mu·ni·ty [imjúːnəti] *n.* Ⓤ **1** the state of not being affected by a particular disease, poison, etc. 면역(성). ¶ *The injection will give you ~ to the disease.* 이 주사를 맞으면 그 병에 안 걸린다. **2** 《law》 freedom from tax, duty, etc.; exemption. 면제; 면세.

im·mu·nize [ímjənàiz] *vt.* (P6,13) 《*against*》 protect (someone) from a particular disease; give immunity to (someone). …를 면역이 되게 하다. ¶ *~ someone against a disease* 아무를 어떤 병에 면역이 되게 하다.

im·mure [imjúər] *vt.* (P6,13) 《*in*》 shut (someone) up in prison; imprison. …을 유폐하다; 감금하다. ¶ *~ oneself* 들어박히다; 두문 불출하다. [in-[2], L. *murus* wall]

im·mu·ta·bil·i·ty [imjùːtəbíləti] *n.* Ⓤ the state of being immutable. 불변(성); 불역(不易)(성). [↓]

im·mu·ta·ble [imjúːtəbəl] *adj.* never changing; unchangeable. 불변의; 불역(不易)의. [in-[1]]

IMO International Meteorological Organization. 국제 기상학회.

imp [imp] *n.* Ⓒ **1** little devil or demon. 꼬마 도깨비. **2** 《*joc.*》 a mischievous child. 개구쟁이. [E. =young shoot]

im·pact [ímpækt] *n.* ⒸⓊ **1** the act of striking against another; collision. 충돌. ¶ *The ~ of the two cars broke both wind-*

I

screens. 두 차는 충돌하면서 앞 유리들이 모두 깨졌다. **2** strong impression or effect. (강한) 인상; 효과. ¶ *the ~ of a speech on an audience* 청중에게 주는 연설의 큰 감명. [in-², L. *pango* drive (→ impinge)]

im·pair [impέər] *vt.* (P6) lessen the value of (something); make (something) worse; injure. …을 손상하다; 줄이다; 해치다. ¶ *~ one's health* 건강을 해치다. [in-², L. *pejor* worse]

im·pair·ment [impέərmənt] *n.* Ⓤ the act of impairing; the state of being impaired; injury. 손상; 감손; 해침.

im·pale [impéil] *vt.* (P6,13) **1** 《*upon, with*》 pierce through (something) with anything sharp. …을 꿰찌르다. ¶ *He impaled the butterfly on a small pin.* 그는 나비를 작은 핀에다 꽂았다. **2** kill (something) by thrusting upon a sharp stake as capital punishment. (형벌로) 말뚝에 꿰찔러 죽이다. **3** 《*arch.*》 enclose with stakes. 말뚝으로 울을 치다. [in-², L. *palus* stake]

im·pal·pa·ble [impǽlpəbəl] *adj.* **1** ⓐ that cannot be perceived by the sense of touch. 만져도 모르는; 만져서 알 수 없는. ¶ *an ~ pulse* 희미한 맥박. ⓑ not material. 실체가 없는. ¶ *~ forms and shadows* 실체가 없는 모양이나 그림자. **2** not easily grasped by the mind. 이해하기 어려운; 미묘한. ¶ *~ distinctions of meaning* 아주 미묘한 뜻 구별. [in-¹, L. *palpo* touch]

im·part [impɑ́:rt] *vt.* (P6,13) 《*to*》 **1** give a portion of (something); give. …을 (나누어) 주다. ¶ *A teacher imparts knowledge to his pupils.* 교사는 학생들에게 지식을 베푼다. **2** tell; disclose. …을 전하다[알리다]; 폭로하다. ¶ *~ some news* [*a secret*] 소식[비밀]을 알려주다. [in-², →part]

im·par·tial [impɑ́:rʃəl] *adj.* not favoring one side or the other; fair; just. 치우치지 않는; 공평한. ¶ *His judgement is always ~.* 그의 판결은 언제나 공평하다. [in-¹]

im·par·ti·al·i·ty [impɑ̀:rʃiǽləti] *n.* Ⓤ the state or quality of being impartial; fairness; justice. 공평 무사; 불편(不偏).

im·pass·a·bil·i·ty [impæ̀səbíləti] *n.* Ⓤ the state of being impassable. 통행 불능.

im·pass·a·ble [impǽsəbəl] *adj.* that cannot be passed through; not passable. 지나갈 수 없는; 통행 불능의. ¶ *an ~ swamp* [*desert*] 지나갈 수 없는 늪[황무지] / *The road is ~.* 그 길은 통행할 수 없다. [in-¹]

im·passe [ímpæs, -ˊ] *n.* Ⓒ **1** a position or place from which no escape can be made; a deadlock. 막다름; 난국; 곤경. ¶ *The negotiations have reached an ~.* 교섭은 교착 상태에 빠졌다. **2** a road open only at one end. 막다른 골목. [F.]

im·pas·si·ble [impǽsəbəl] *adj.* **1** not capable of suffering. 아픔을 느끼지 않는. **2** impassive; without feeling. 무감각한. [in-¹, L. *patior* suffer]

im·pas·sion [impǽʃən] *vt.* (P6,13) stir the passions of; excite strongly. 흥분시키다. [in-², →passion]

im·pas·sioned [impǽʃənd] *adj.* full of strong emotion; showing deep feeling; passionate. 감격한; 열렬한. ¶ *The statesman made an ~ appeal to the audience.* 그 정치가는 청중을 향해 열의에 찬 호소를 했다.

im·pas·sive [impǽsiv] *adj.* without showing or feeling emotion, pain, etc.; unmoved; insensible. 무감각한; 무감동의; 고통을 느끼지 않는. [in-¹]

im·pa·tience [impéiʃəns] *n.* Ⓤ **1** the state or quality of being impatient; lack of patience. 참을성이 없음; 성마름; 성급함. **2** restless eagerness. (…하고 싶어) 못견딤; 안달. ¶ *She was all ~ to be gone.* 그녀는 가고 싶어 안달이었다. [↓]

·im·pa·tient [impéiʃənt] *adj.* **1** 《*as predicative*》 ⓐ 《*for, at, with*》 not patient; not willing to wait; irritable; restless. 참을성이 없는; 안달하는; 침착하지 못한. ¶ *They were ~ to start.* 떠나고 싶어 안달이었다 / *Don't be so ~!* 좀 참아라 / *be ~ for a friend's arrival* 친구의 도착을 초조하게 기다리다. ⓑ 《*of*》 unwilling to tolerate. 관대하지 않은. ¶ *Our teacher is ~ of carelessness.* 우리 선생님은 부주의에는 아주 엄격하다. **2** 《*as predicative*》 eager to go, do, or act. …하고 싶어 못견디는. ¶ *~ to see one's parents* 부모를 애타게 만나고 싶어하는 / *She is ~ to grow up.* 그녀는 빨리 성인이 되고 싶었다. **3** showing lack of patience. 성마른; 성급한. ¶ *an ~ reply* 성급한 대답. [in-¹, L. *patior* suffer]

im·pa·tient·ly [impéiʃəntli] *adv.* in an impatient manner. 성급[초조]하게; 마음 졸이며.

im·pawn [impɔ́:n] *vt.* (P6) **1** put in pawn. 전당 잡히다. **2** pledge. 언질을 주다. [in-², →pawn]

im·peach [impí:tʃ] *vt.* (P6,13) 《*for, of*》 **1** bring (something) in question. …을 의심하다; 문제삼다. ¶ *~ someone's honor* 아무의 명예를 의심하다. **2** accuse (someone) of wrongdoing. …을 비난하다; 고발하다. ¶ *~ someone of* [*with*] *a crime* [*fault*] 아무의 범죄 행위[과오]를 고발하다. [in-², L. *pedica* fetter]

im·peach·ment [impí:tʃmənt] *n.* ⓊⒸ the act of impeaching; the state of being impeached. 비난; 탄핵; 고소; 의혹.

im·pec·ca·ble [impékəbəl] *adj.* **1** faultless. 결함[나무랄 데] 없는. ¶ *The service was ~.* 서비스는 나무랄 데가 없었다. **2** not doing wrong. 죄를 범하지 않는. ● **im·pec·ca·bly** [-i] *adv.* [in-¹]

im·pe·cu·ni·ous [ìmpikjú:niəs] *adj.* having little money; poor. 돈이 없는; 가난한. [in-¹, →pecuniary]

im·pede [impí:d] *vt.* (P6) obstruct; hinder. …을 방해하다; 막다. ¶ *Snow and ice im-*

peded our progress. 눈과 얼음이 우리의 진행을 가로막았다. [in-², L. *pes* foot]

im·ped·i·ment [impédəmənt] *n.* Ⓒ **1** a thing which hinders; an obstacle. 방해; 장애. **2** a defect in speech. 언어 장애. ¶ *have an* ~ *in one's speech* 말을 더듬다.

im·pel [impél] *vt.* (**-pelled, -pel·ling**) (P13,20) **1** drive; force; compel. …을 강제하다; 어쩔 수 없이 …하게 하다. ¶ *The rain impelled him to give up the plan.* 비로 인해 그는 계획을 단념해야 했다. **2** drive forward; push along. …을 밀고 나아가다; 추진하다. ¶ *The current impelled the boat to shore.* 조류는 배를 해안으로 밀어냈다 / *impelling force* 추진력 / *I felt impelled to say something.* 무엇인가 말을 해야겠다고 느꼈다. [in-², L. *pello* drive]

im·pend [impénd] *vi.* (P1,3) 《*over*》 **1** be about to happen soon; be at hand; threaten. …이 일어나려 하다; 절박해 있다. ¶ *War seemed to* ~. 곧 전쟁이 일어날 것 같았다. **2** hang over. 위에 걸리다. ¶ *Impending cliffs were above us.* 우리들 머리 위에는 비죽이 내민 벼랑들이 보였다. [in-², L. *pendeo* hang]

im·pend·ing [impéndiŋ] *adj.* **1** about to happen soon; threatening. 곧 일어날 것 같은; 절박한. **2** overhanging. 닥쳐오는. ¶ *an* ~ *storm* 〔*disaster*〕 닥쳐올 폭풍우〔재난〕.

im·pen·e·tra·ble [impénətrəbəl] *adj.* **1** ⓐ that cannot be penetrated or pierce. 꿰뚫을 수 없는. ¶ *This wall is* ~ *to shots.* 이 벽은 총알이 안 들어간다. ⓑ that cannot be entered or pass through. 지나갈〔통과할〕 수 없는. ¶ ~ *forests* 발들여 놓을 수 없는 삼림. ⓒ that cannot be seen through. 투시할 수 없는. ¶ ~ *darkness* 칠흑 같은 어둠. **2** (of nonmaterial things) ⓐ not open to reason, sympathy, etc. (사상·감정이) 완고한; 둔감한. ¶ *a mind* ~ *by* 〔*to*〕 *new ideas* 새로운 사상을 받아들이지 않는 완고한 마음. ⓑ that cannot be understood. 이해하기 어려운. ¶ *an* ~ *mystery* 알 수 없는 신비. ⓒ not to be broken through. 깨뜨리지 못 할. ¶ ~ *silence* 범접 못 할 침묵. [in-¹]

im·pen·i·tence [impénətəns] *n.* Ⓤ the state or quality of being impenitent. 회개하지 않음; 완고. [↓]

im·pen·i·tent [impénətənt] *adj.* not penitent; feeling no regret for wrongdoing. 완고한; 뉘우칠 줄 모르는. ● **im·pen·i·tent·ly** [-li] *adv.* [in-¹]

im·per·a·tive [impérətiv] *adj.* **1** that cannot be avoided; necessary. 피할 수 없는; 절대 필요한. ¶ *It is* ~ *that he* (*should*) *stay in bed.* 그는 자리에 누워 있어야 한다. **2** commanding with authority. 명령적인; 권위 있는. ¶ *an* ~ *gesture* 명령적인 제스처. **3** 《gram.》 expressing a command. 명령법. ¶ *an* ~ *sentence* 명령문. —*n.* **1** Ⓒ a command; an order. 명령. **2** Ⓤ 《gram.》 《*the* ~》 the mood expressing command; Ⓒ a form of a verb in this mood. 명령법; 명령형. [L. *impero* command]

im·per·a·tive·ly [impérətivli] *adv.* in an imperative manner. 명령적으로.

im·per·cep·ti·ble [ìmpərséptəbəl] *adj.* too small, slight, slow, etc. to be seen, heard or felt. 미세한; 미미한; 감지할 수 없는. ¶ *the* ~ *growth of a plant from day to day* 식물의 날마다의 미소한 성장 / ~ *shades of meaning* 미미한 뜻의 차이. [in-¹]

***im·per·fect** [impə́ːrfikt] *adj.* **1** ⓐ (of material things) not perfect; not complete. 불완전한; 미완성의. ¶ *This book is* ~, *for the last page is missing.* 이 책은 끝장이 없어서 온전한 것이 못 된다. ⓑ (of non-material things) not reaching a certain standard; not full. 어떤 수준에 미달된; 불비한. ¶ *have an* ~ *knowledge of subject* 주제에 대한 인식이 모자라다. **2** morally imperfect; faulty. 결함〔결점〕이 있는. —*n.* 《gram.》 the imperfect tense. 미완료 시제. [in-¹]

im·per·fec·tion [ìmpərfékʃən] *n.* Ⓤ **1** the state or quality of being imperfect; incompleteness. 미완성; 불완전; 불비. **2** Ⓒ fault; defect. 결점; 단점. ¶ *an* ~ *in his character* 그의 성격(상)의 결함.

im·per·fect·ly [impə́ːrfiktli] *adv.* in an imperfect manner. 불완전〔불충분〕하게.

***im·pe·ri·al** [impíəriəl] *adj.* **1** of an empire or emperor. 제국의; 황제의; 황실의. ¶ *His Imperial Majesty* 황제 폐하. **2** of the rule or authority of a country over its dependents. 지배하는; 지배적인. **3** majestic; magnificent. 장엄한; 위엄 있는; 당당한. **4** of a special (usu. large) size or quality. 우수한; 특대의. —*n.* Ⓒ a small beard beneath the lower lip. 황제 수염. ● **im·pe·ri·al·ly** [-i] *adv.* [→ imperium]

im·pe·ri·al·ism [impíəriəlìzəm] *n.* Ⓤ **1** policy of a country of extending its rule over other countries. 제국주의. **2** imperial power or government. 제정(帝政).

im·pe·ri·al·ist [impíəriəlist] *n.* Ⓒ a person who supports imperialism. 제국주의자.

im·pe·ri·al·is·tic [impìəriəlístik] *adj.* of or supporting imperialism or imperialists. 제국주의(자)의.

im·per·il [impéril] *vt.* (**-iled, -il·ing** or 《Brit.》 **-illed, -il·ling**) (P6) put (someone or something) in danger. …을 위태롭게 하다; 위험(危險)하게 하다. ¶ ~ *one's life to save a child* 아이를 구하기 위해 죽음을 무릅쓰다. [in-²]

im·pe·ri·ous [impíəriəs] *adj.* **1** haughty; arrogant; overbearing. 제왕 같은; 오만한; 전제적인. ¶ *an* ~ *manner* 오만한 태도. **2** necessary; urgent; pressing. 긴급한; 절박한. ¶ *an* ~ *duty* 피할 수 없는 의무. ● **im·pe·ri·ous·ly** [-li] *adv.* **im·pe·ri·ous·ness** [-nis] *n.* [→imperium]

im·per·ish·a·ble [impériʃəbəl] *adj.* not

perishable; everlasting. 불멸〔불사〕의; 불후의. ¶ ~ *glory* 〔*renown*〕 불후의 영광〔명성〕. [in-[1]]

im·pe·ri·um [impíəriəm] *n.* 《L.》 the supreme power. 절대권(絶對權). [L. *impero* command]

im·per·ma·nent [impə́ːrmənənt] *adj.* not permanent; temporary. 일시적인; 영속적이 아닌. [in-[1]]

im·per·me·a·ble [impə́ːrmiəbəl] *adj.* not permitting fluid to pass through; impassable. 침투할 수 없는; 스며들지 않는. [in-[1]]

im·per·son·al [impə́ːrsənəl] *adj.* **1** relating not to any particular person but to all persons or to any person. 개인의 것이 아닌; 비개인적인. ¶ *an ~ point of view* 일반적인 견해 / *write in an ~ manner* 객관적인 글을 쓰다. **2** not existing as a person. 인격을 갖지 않는. ¶ *Nature is an ~ force.* 자연이란 인간 외적(人間外的)인 힘이다. [↓]

im·per·son·ate [impə́ːrsənèit] *vt.* (P6) **1** play (a part) on the stage. …으로 분장하다; …의 역을 맡아 하다. **2** pretend to be (someone or something); imitate. …인 체하다; …을 흉내내다. **3** represent something in the form of a person. …을 의인화(擬人化)하다; 체현(體現)하다. ¶ *Uncle Sam impersonates America.* 엉클 샘은 미국을 의인화한 것이다. [in-[2], →person]

im·per·son·a·tion [impə̀ːrsənéiʃən] *n.* **1** Ⓤ the act of impersonating. 역(役)을 맡아 하기; 분장(扮裝). **2** Ⓒ an impersonated person or thing. 구상화(具象化)된 사람〔물건〕. **3** Ⓤ personification. 인격화; 의인화.

im·per·ti·nence [impə́ːrtənəns] *n.* Ⓤ **1** the state or quality of being impertinent; impudence. 버릇없음; 건방짐. **2** Ⓒ an impertinent person, act or speech. 무례한 사람〔언행〕. **3** Ⓤ unsuitability; inappropriateness. 부적절; 부적당. [↓]

im·per·ti·nent [impə́ːrtənənt] *adj.* **1** impudent; rude. 건방진; 본데없는. ¶ *make an ~ remark* 주제넘게 말하다. **2** not to the point; out of place. 부적절한; 당치 않은. [in-[1]]

im·per·turb·a·ble [ìmpərtə́ːrbəbəl] *adj.* not easily excited; calm. 냉정한; 침착한.

im·per·vi·ous [impə́ːrviəs] *adj.* **1** not allowing entrance or passage. 통과시키지 않는; 스며들게 하지 않는. ¶ *This cloth is ~ to rain.* 이 천은 빗물이 스미지 않는다. **2** 《*fig.*》 that cannot be affected or influenced. 둔감한; 못 알아듣는. ¶ *He is ~ to the argument.* 그에게 그런 말은 통하지 않는다. ●**im·per·vi·ous·ness** [-nis] *n.* [in-[1]]

im·pet·u·os·i·ty [impètʃuάsəti / -ɔ́s-] *n.* (*pl.* **-ties**) **1** Ⓤ impetuous quality. 맹렬함; 성급. **2** Ⓒ an impetuous action. 충동적인 행동. [↓]

im·pet·u·ous [impétʃuəs] *adj.* **1** moving with great force and violence. 맹렬한; 격렬한. ¶ *an ~ wind* 열풍(烈風). **2** ⓐ (of action) performed as a result of sudden feeling and energy. 충동적인. ¶ *make an ~ attack on someone* 느닷없이 아무를 치다. ⓑ (of a person) acting hastily or with sudden feeling. 성급한. ¶ *An ~ person often does things carelessly.* 성급한 사람은 흔히 일에 조심성이 없다. [in-[2], L. *peto* seek)]

im·pet·u·ous·ly [impétʃuəsli] *adv.* in an impetuous manner. 맹렬하게; 성급하게; 충동적으로.

im·pe·tus [ímpətəs] *n.* **1** 《mech.》 Ⓤ the force with which a body tends to move on. 운동량. **2** 《*fig.*》 Ⓒ a forward push; a stimulus. 힘; 관성(慣性); 자극. ¶ *The boy felt no ~ to do well in school.* 소년은 학교에서 잘 하려고 해도 신명이 나지 않았다. [L. =force, attack]

im·pi·e·ty [impáiəti] *n.* (*pl.* **-ties**) **1** Ⓤ lack of respect for God. 불신앙. **2** Ⓤ lack of respect for any usu. honored person, institution, or thing. (윗사람·제도 등에 대한) 불신. **3** Ⓒ an impious act. 불신〔불경〕 행위. [in-[1]]

im·pinge [impíndʒ] *vi.* (P3) **1** 《*against, on, upon*》 hit; strike. 치다; 부딪다. ¶ *He heard the rain ~ upon the earth.* 빗줄기가 땅을 치는 소리를 들었다 / *A strong light impinges on the eyes.* 강한 빛이 눈을 찌른다. **2** 《*upon*》 infringe. 침범하다; 저촉하다. ¶ *~ upon someone's authority* 아무의 권한을 침범하다. [in-[2], L. *pango* drive]

im·pi·ous [ímpiəs] *adj.* **1** not pious; not worshiping God. 신앙심이 없는; 불경한. **2** wicked. 사악한. [in-[1]]

imp·ish [ímpiʃ] *adj.* of or like an imp; mischievous. 꼬마도깨비 같은; 장난기의; 장난 좋아하는. [*imp*]

im·plac·a·ble [implǽkəbəl, -pléi-] *adj.* that cannot be pacified or soothed; relentless. 달래기 어려운; 용서 못 할; 냉혹한. [in-[1]]

im·plant [implǽnt, -plάːnt] *vt.* (P6,13) 《*in*》 **1** instill; fix. (사상 따위)를 불어넣다; 주입하다. ¶ *~ the idea in the student* 학생에게 그 생각을 주입시키다. **2** insert; plant. …을 끼워넣다; 심다. [in-[2]]

●**im·ple·ment** [ímpləmənt] *n.* Ⓒ a tool or an instrument, such as a plow, an ax or a shovel. 도구; 연장. ¶ *surgical implements* 외과용 기구. —[ímpləmènt] *vt.* (P6) **1** put (something) into effect; complete. …을 완성하다. **2** 《Sc. law》 carry out (an engagement, contract, etc.). …을 이행하다. [in-[2], L. *pleo* fill]

im·ple·men·ta·tion [ìmpləmentéiʃən] *n.* Ⓤ the act of implementing; the state of being implemented. 이행; 실행; 성취.

im·pli·cate [ímpləkèit] *vt.* (P6,13) 《*in*》 **1** involve (something or someone); make (someone) concerned. …에 말려들게 하다; …에 관련시키다. ¶ *He is implicated in a crime.* 그는 범행에 관련돼 있다. **2** imply. …

을 함축하다. ¶ *'Parent' implicates 'child'.* '어버이'라고 함은 '자식'이 있음을 암시한다. **3** twist together; entangle. …을 얽히게 하다. [in-², L. *plico* fold]

im·pli·ca·tion [ìmpləkéiʃən] *n.* **1** Ⓤ the act of implying; the state of being implied. 함축; 내포. **2** Ⓒ a thing which is implied; a hint. 암시; 힌트. ¶ *What do you think the ~ of his remarks is?* 너는 그 사람 말을 어떻게 생각하니. **3** Ⓤ the act of implicating; the state of being implicated. 연루; 관련.

im·plic·it [implísit] *adj.* (opp. explicit) **1** without doubt; absolute. 절대의; 맹목적인. ¶ *~ faith* 맹신(盲信) / *He demands ~ obedience.* 그는 절대적인 복종을 요구한다. **2** understood though not clearly expressed; implied. 암시적인; 암묵의. ¶ *He gave us ~ consent to take the apples, for he smiled when he saw us do it.* 그는 우리가 사과를 가져가는 것을 묵인했다, 왜냐하면 우리가 그걸 집을 때 싱긋이 웃었으니까. [→implicate]

im·plic·it·ly [implísitli] *adv.* in an implicit manner. 암암리에; 넌지시; 절대적으로.

·im·plore [implɔ́ːr] *vt.* (P6,13,20) **1** 《*for*》 ask for (something) earnestly. …을 열망하다. ¶ *~ someone's help* 아무의 도움을 열망하다. **2** ask (someone) to do something. …에 애원[탄원]하다. ¶ *~ him to go out* 그에게 나가 주기를 간청하다 / *She implored me to stay with her.* 그녀는 내게 자기와 함께 있어 달라고 애원했다. [in-², L. *ploro* weep]

im·plor·ing·ly [implɔ́ːriŋli] *adv.* in an imploring manner. 애원[간청]하듯이.

·im·ply [implái] *vt.* (**-plied, -ply·ing**) (P6,11) mean (something) without expressing it clearly; suggest indirectly. …을 넌지시 비추다; 암시하다. ¶ *Silence implies consent.* 침묵은 동의를 의미한다. [→implicate]

im·po·lite [ìmpəláit] *adj.* not polite; showing bad manners; rude. 무례한; 버릇없는. ¶ *It is ~ to interrupt the speaker.* 말을 가로막는 것은 무례한 짓이다. ●**im·po·lite·ness** [-nis] *n.* [in-¹]

im·po·lite·ly [ìmpəláitli] *adv.* in an impolite manner. 무례하게; 버릇없이.

im·pol·i·tic [impálitik / -pɔ́l-] *adj.* not politic; unwise. 상책이 아닌; 현명하지 못한; 졸렬한. [in-¹]

im·pon·der·a·ble [impándərəbəl / -pɔ́n-] *adj.* that cannot be precisely determined or measured; very light. 계량할 수 없는; 극미량(極微量)의; 아주 가벼운. [in-¹]

:im·port [impɔ́ːrt] *vt.* **1** (P6,13) 《*from, into*》 bring in (goods) from another country. …을 수입하다(opp. export). ¶ *imported goods* 수입품 / *Most of our coffee is imported from Brazil.* 우리 나라 커피는 주로 브라질에서 수입된다. **2** (P6,11) mean; indicate. …을 의미하다. ¶ *What does this note ~?* 이 기호는 무슨 의미냐 / *I should like to know what his action imports.* 그의 행동이 무엇을 의미하는지 알고 싶군. **3** (P6,11) be important to (someone). …에게 중요한 관계가 있다. ¶ *It is a problem that imports us closely.* 그건 우리들에게 중대한 관계가 있는 문제다. **4** (P6,13) introduce (ideas, etc.). (생각 등)을 전하다. ¶ *~ personal feelings into a discussion* 의론에 사적 감정을 끌어들이다.

—[́–] *n.* **1** Ⓤ the act of importing goods; Ⓒ 《usu. *pl.*》 something imported. 수입; 수입품(opp. export). ¶ *~ duties* 수입세 / *Our imports are made up largely of raw materials.* 우리 수입품의 대부분은 원료가 차지하고 있다. **2** Ⓤ meaning. 의미. ¶ *the ~ of his message* 그의 전언이 의미하는 것. **3** Ⓤ importance. 중요성. ¶ *a matter of great ~* 중대한 일. [in-², L. *porto* carry]

:im·por·tance [impɔ́ːrtəns] *n.* Ⓤ the state of being important; significance. 중요성; 중대성; 유력. ¶ *a person of ~* 유력한 사람 / *a matter of great ~* 아주 중대한 일 / *the ~ of good health* 건강의 중요성 / *attach ~* [*no ~*] *to* …을 중요시하다[하지 않다] / *a position of ~* 중요한 자리 / *with an air of ~* 젠 체하며; 거들먹거리며 / *conscious of* [*knowing, having a good idea of*] *one's own ~* 우쭐해서; 잘난 체하며. [↑]

:im·por·tant [impɔ́ːrtənt] *adj.* **1** (of a thing, ideas, facts, etc.) filled with meaning; worth noticing or considering; serious; valuable. 중대한; 중요한. ¶ *The matter is ~ to us.* 그 일은 우리에게 중요하다 / *It is ~* (*for you*) *to learn to read.* (네가) 읽기를 배우는 것은 중요하다. **2** (of a person) having power or authority. 유력한; 높은. ¶ *an ~ person* 높은 양반; 중요 인사. **3** acting as if important. 젠 체하는; 난 체하는. ¶ *He looks ~.* 그는 거만해 보인다. ●**im·por·tant·ly** [-li] *adv.* [↑]

im·por·ta·tion [ìmpɔːrtéiʃən] *n.* **1** Ⓤ the act of importing. 수입(opp. exportation). **2** Ⓒ a thing which is imported. 수입품. [→import]

im·port·er [impɔ́ːrtər] *n.* Ⓒ a person or company that is engaged in the business of importing. 수입업자; 수입상 (opp. exporter).

im·por·tu·nate [impɔ́ːrtʃənit] *adj.* asking repeatedly; persistent; urgent. 귀찮게 졸라대는. ¶ *an ~ person* 끈질긴 사람. [↓]

im·por·tune [ìmpərtjúːn, impɔ́ːrtʃən] *vt.* (P6,13,20) ask repeatedly or urgently. …을 끈질기게 요구하다; 귀찮게 조르다. ¶ *He is always importuning me to lend him money.* 그는 늘 나에게 돈을 꾸어 달라고 한다. [L. *importunus* inconvenient]

im·por·tu·ni·ty [ìmpɔːrtjúːnəti] *n.* ⓊⒸ (*pl.* **-ties**) the act of asking repeatedly. 귀찮게[끈질기게] 조름.

•**im·pose** [impóuz] *vt.* (P13) 《*on, upon*》 **1** put (a burden, a tax, a punishment, etc.) on (someone). …을 부과하다; 지우다. ¶ *Duties are imposed on wines and spirits.* 주류(酒類)에는 세금이 부과된다. **2** force (something) on another. …을 강요〔강제〕하다. ¶ ~ *one's opinion on others* 남에게 자기 의견을 강요하다. **3** persuade to accept by unfair means; palm off. (가짜 등을) 떠맡기다. ¶ ~ *bad wine on customers* 손님에게 좋지 못한 술을 안기다.
— *vi.* (P3) 《*on, upon*》 **1** take unfair advantage of (a person, his good nature, etc.). (남의 사람 좋음 등을) 악용하다; 기화로 삼다. ¶ *Do not* ~ *upon his kindness.* 그 사람의 친절을 악용하지 마라. **2** deceive; cheat. 속이다; 기만하다. ¶ *His talk completely imposed upon his hearers.* 그의 말에 듣는 이들은 감쪽같이 속았다 / *You have been imposed upon.* 너는 속았단 말이다. **3** 《*colloq.*》 impress with striking character, appearance. 강한 인상을 주다. [in-², →pose]

im·pos·ing [impóuziŋ] *adj.* very impressive; making a strong impression by means of great size, appearance, dignity, etc. 강한 인상을 주는; 이목을 끄는; 당당한. ¶ *an* ~ *building* 으리으리한 건물 / *He talked with an* ~ *attitude.* 그는 당당한 태도로 말했다.

im·po·si·tion [ìmpəzíʃən] *n.* **1** Ⓤ the act of imposing. 부과하기; 과세; 강요; 강제. **2** Ⓒ a tax, task, burden, etc. imposed on someone. 세금; 부담. **3** Ⓒ deception; fraud. 기만; 사기. **4** Ⓤ imposing upon someone by taking advantage of. (아무의 호인됨을) 기화로 삼기; 이용해 먹기. [→impost]

im·pos·si·bil·i·ty [impɑ̀səbíləti / -pɔ̀s-] *n.* (*pl.* **-ties**) **1** Ⓤ the state of being impossible. 불가능(성). **2** Ⓒ a thing which is impossible. 불가능한 일. [↓]

I

:**im·pos·si·ble** [impɑ́səbəl / -pɔ́s-] *adj.* **1** that cannot be done; that cannot happen. 불가능한; …할 수 없는. ¶ *It is* ~ *to live without water.* 물 없이는 살 수 없다 / *It is* ~ *for you to be there on time.* 제시간에 거기에 댈 수는 없다 / *an* ~ *task* 불가능한 일. **2** not easy or convenient. …하기 어려운; 계제가 나쁜. **3** that cannot be true. 있을 수 없는; 믿기 어려운. ¶ *an* ~ *rumor* 〔*story*〕 도무지 믿을 수 없는 소문〔이야기〕. **4** 《*colloq.*》 hard to endure; very objectionable. 참을 수 없는; 불쾌한. ¶ *an* ~ *person* 꼴보기 싫은 놈. **5** absurd. 기묘한. ¶ *an* ~ *hat* 묘한 모자. [in-¹]

im·post [ímpoust] *n.* Ⓒ a tax, esp. one imposed on goods which are imported. 세금; 수입세; 관세. [in-², L. *pono* place]

im·pos·tor [impɑ́stər / -pɔ́s-] *n.* Ⓒ a person who deceives others by assuming a false name or character; a swindler. 이름·신분을 사칭하는 사람; 사기꾼.

im·pos·ture [impɑ́stʃər / -pɔ́s-] *n.* ⒸⓊ deception; fraud. 사기; 협잡.

im·po·tence [ímpətəns] *n.* Ⓤ the state of being impotent; lack of power, esp. of sexual power; helplessness. 무력; 무기력; 허약; 음위(陰痿). [↓]

im·po·ten·cy [ímpətənsi] *n.* =impotence.

im·po·tent [ímpətənt] *adj.* **1** not having physical, mental, or moral power; helpless. 무기력한; 허약한; 줏대없는. **2** (of males) lacking sexual power. 음위(陰痿)의. [in-¹]

im·pound [impáund] *vt.* (P6) **1** shut up (cattle) in a pen. (가축)을 울에 가두다. **2** 《*fig.*》 take (someone or something) into an enclosure. …을 가두다; 처넣다. **3** imprison; take possession of; confiscate. …을 구치하다; 압수〔몰수〕하다. ●**im·pound·ment** [-mənt] *n.* [in-²]

im·pov·er·ish [impɑ́vəriʃ / -pɔ́v-] *vt.* (P6) **1** make (someone) poor. …을 가난하게 만들다. ¶ *an impoverished family* 영락한 집안. **2** use up the resources of (land, etc.). (토지 등)을 메마르게 하다. ¶ ~ *land* 〔*soil*〕 땅을 불모로 만들다 / *an impoverished life* 〔*existence*〕 생기를 잃은 생활. **3** weaken. 허약〔무력〕하게 만들다. ¶ ~ *one's health* 건강을 해치다. [in-², →poor]

im·prac·ti·ca·ble [impræ̀ktikəbəl] *adj.* **1** unsuitable for practical use; that cannot be done. 실행 불가능한. ¶ *This is an* ~ *plan.* 이건실행이 불가능한 계획이다. **2** (of a person or character) difficult to deal with. (사람이) 다루기 힘든; 완고한. **3** (of a road, etc.) not fit to be used. (길이) 다닐 수 없는. [in-¹]

im·prac·ti·cal [impræ̀ktikəl] *adj.* not practical 실용적이 아닌; 비실제적인. [↑]

im·pre·cate [ímprikèit] *vt.* (P6) call down (evil, misfortune, etc.) upon someone. (남에게 불행·재앙이) 내리라고 빌다. ¶ ~ *evil upon someone* 아무에게 재앙이 내리기를 빌다. ●**im·pre·ca·tor** [-tər] *n.* [in-², L. *precor* pray]

im·pre·ca·tion [ìmprikéiʃən] *n.* **1** Ⓤ the act of imprecating. 저주하기. **2** Ⓒ a curse. 저주.

im·preg·na·ble [imprégnəbəl] *adj.* **1** that cannot be overcome by force; strong enough to resist the attack. 난공불락의. ¶ *an* ~ *castle* 난공불락의 성. **2** able to resist persuasion, moral pressure or attack. (설복·압력 등에) 굴하지 않는; 흔들리지 않는. ¶ *an* ~ *argument* 완벽한 이론 / *hold an* ~ *belief* 확고한 신념을 가지다. [in-¹]

im·preg·nate [imprégnèit, ímpreg-] *vt.* (P6,13) **1** make pregnant. …에게 임신시키다. **2** cause (something) to be filled with (something). …에 채우다. ¶ *air impregnated with disease germs* 병균으로 차 있는 공기. **3** 《*with*》 inspire; imbue. …을 불어 넣다; 침투시키다. ¶ ~ *a mind with the new political doctrine* 사람의 마음에 새로운 정치 이론

을 주입하다. — *adj.* impregnated; pregnant. 임신한; 스며든; 주입된. [in-², →pregnant]

:im·press[1] [imprés] *vt.* (P6,13) **1** produce a strong effect on the mind or emotion of (someone). …에게 깊은 감명을 주다; …을 감동시키다. ¶ *His letter impressed us all greatly.* 그의 편지는 우리 모두에게 큰 감명을 주었다 / *He did not ~ me at all.* 그는 내게 아무런 감명을 주지 못했다 / *The speaker impressed the audience.* 그 연사는 청중을 감동시켰다. **2** fix (something) deeply in the mind or memory. …을 명기시키다; 인상지우다; 통감하게 하다. ¶ *The scene was strongly impressed on my memory.* 그 광경은 내게 강한 인상을 주었다 / *I want to ~ upon you the necessity for hardwork.* 네가 근면의 필요성을 통감했으면 싶다. **3** produce (a mark, etc.) on (something) by pressing or stamping. (도장)을 누르다; …에 자국을 남기다. ¶ *~ a mark on the surface = ~ the surface with a mark* 거죽에 표를 하다.

— [∠–] *n.* Ⓒ **1** a mark made by pressure. 각인(刻印). **2** ⓐ the act of pressing; stamping. 날인. ⓑ 《*fig.*》 a result produced on the mind by intellectual or moral force; a characteristic mark. 감명; 인상; 특징. ¶ *leave an ~ upon one's age* 한 시대에 발자취를 남기다 / *a work bearing the ~ of genius* 천재의 특징을 나타내는 작품. [in-², L. *premo*]

im·press[2] [imprés] *vt.* (P6) **1** seize (something) by force for public use. 징발〔징용〕하다. ¶ *~ the school building for the hospital* 교사(校舍)를 병원용으로 징발하다. **2** force (someone) to serve in the navy or army. …을 강제로 군에 징집하다. **3** 《*fig.*》 introduce; bring in; make use of. …을 인용〔이용〕하다. [in-², L. *praesto* furnish (→ press²)]

im·press·i·ble [imprésəbəl] *adj.* impressionable. 다감한; 감수성이 예민한. [↓]

:im·pres·sion [impréʃən] *n.* Ⓒ **1** ⒸⓊ an effect produced on the mind. 인상; 감명. ¶ *He left a good ~ on me.* 그는 내게 좋은 인상을 남겼다 / *the ~ of light on the eyes* 눈에 느끼는 빛의 인상. **2** Ⓒ a vague notion or feeling. (막연한) 느낌; 기분. ¶ *I have an ~ that the plan will never be carried out.* 그 계획은 결코 실현될 수 없을 것이란 느낌이다 / *I have an ~ that we've taken the wrong road.* 우린 길을 잘못 든 모양이다. **3** a mark made by pressing. 날인; 흔적. ¶ *He found an ~ of someone's foot in the ground.* 그는 운동장에서 누군가의 발자국을 발견했다. **4** the act of impressing; the state of being impressed. 인상을 주기; 인상에 남기. **5** an effect or result produced by efforts or labor. (노력 등의) 결과; 효과. ¶ *The efforts of philanthropists and legislators make but little ~ on the mass of human misery.* 박애주의자나 입법가들의 노력은 많은 인류의 불행에는 별반 도움이 되지 못한다. **6** 《print.》 the number of copies of a book printed at one time. 쇄(刷). [→ impress¹]

im·pres·sion·a·ble [impréʃənəbəl] *adj.* easily impressed or influenced; sensitive; impressible. 다감한; 감수성이 많은. ¶ *Youth is an ~ age.* 청춘기란 다감한 시대다 / *Children are more ~ than grown-up people.* 아이들은 성인보다 감수성이 많다.

im·pres·sion·ism [impréʃənìzəm] *n.* Ⓤ the style of painting or writing which expresses general impressions without much attention to details. 인상파; 인상주의.

im·pres·sion·ist [impréʃənist] *n.* Ⓒ an artist, writer, or composer who practices impressionism. 인상파의 화가〔조각가, 작가, 작곡가〕.

·im·pres·sive [imprésiv] *adj.* strongly impressing the mind or feelings. 강한 인상을 주는; 감동적인. ¶ *an ~ speech* 감동적〔인상적〕인 연설 / *He has a very ~ manner.* 그는 태도가 아주 인상적이다. ● **im·pres·sive·ness** [-nis] *n.*

im·print [ímprint] *n.* Ⓒ **1** a mark made by pressing; a print. 각인; 흔적; 자국. ¶ *the ~ of a dirty foot on a floor* 마루 위에 난 더러운 발자국. **2** an impression on the mind; a mark. 인상; 모습. ¶ *an ~ of anxiety on her face* 그녀의 걱정스러운 표정. **3** a listing of the printer's or publisher's name and address and the date and place of publication printed in a book. (책의 끝장에 적은) 간기(刊記).

— [imprínt] *vt.* (P6,13) 《*on, with*》 **1** make a mark on or of (something) by pressing. …을 찍다; 누르다. ¶ *~ the postmark on the envelope* 봉투에 소인을 찍다 / *~ a kiss on someone's forehead* 아무의 이마에 키스하다. **2** fix firmly in the mind; impress. 강한 인상을 주다; 감명(感銘)시키다. ¶ *words* 〔*ideas*〕 *forever imprinted on my heart* 내 마음에 길이 새겨진 말〔사상〕. [in-², L. *premo* press]

·im·pris·on [imprízən] *vt.* (P6,13) 《*for*》 **1** put or keep (someone) in prison. …을 투옥하다. **2** 《*fig.*》 shut up closely; confine. …을 감금하다. ¶ *They were imprisoned in the plane by the hijackers.* 그들은 하이재커들에 의해 비행기 안에 감금되었다. [in-²]

im·pris·on·ment [imprízənmənt] *n.* Ⓤ **1** the act of putting or keeping in prison; the state of being put or kept in prison. 투옥; 구금; 수감. **2** confinement; restraint. 감금; 구속.

im·prob·a·bil·i·ty [imprɑ̀bəbíləti / -prɔ̀b-] *n.* (*pl.* **-ties**) **1** Ⓤ the state of being improbable. 있을 법하지 않음; 믿기지 않음. **2** Ⓒ a thing which is improbable. 있을 법하지 않은 일. [↓]

im·prob·a·ble [imprɑ́bəbəl / -prɔ́b-] *adj.*

not likely to happen or to be true; not probable. 있을 법하지 않은; 믿기지 않은. ¶ *an ~ story* 믿기지 않는 이야기. [in-¹]

im·promp·tu [imprámptjuː / -prɔ́m-] *adv., adj.* without preparation. 즉석의〔에서〕. ¶ *a speech made ~* 즉석 연설. — *n.* Ⓒ a thing which is made or done without preparation. 즉흥적으로 지은〔행하는〕 것; 즉흥시〔곡〕. ¶ *a piano piece that sounds like an ~* 즉흥곡처럼 들리는 피아노곡. [L. *in promptu* in readiness (→prompt)]

im·prop·er [imprápər / -prɔ́p-] *adj.* **1** not proper; not suitable. 부적당한. ¶ *a speech* 〔*behavior*〕 *~ to the occasion* 그 경우에 어울리지 않는 말〔태도〕. **2** wrong; incorrect. 틀린. ¶ *use a word in an ~ sense* 뜻이 틀린 낱말을 쓰다 / *an ~ treatment of a disease* 병의 잘못된 치료. **3** not decent. 온당치 못한; 잡된. ¶ *an ~ word* 〔*book*〕 음란한 말〔책〕/ *an ~ person* 막되먹은 사람. [in-¹]

im·pro·pri·e·ty [ìmprəpráiəti] *n.* (*pl.* **-ties**) **1** Ⓤ the state or quality of being improper; lack of propriety. 부적당; 부정; 어울리지 않음. **2** Ⓒ an improper act, expression, etc. 잘못된 행실; 부적절한 표현. [↑]

:im·prove [imprúːv] *vt.* (P6) **1** make better; increase the value. …을 개선〔개량〕하다; 증진하다. ¶ *He has been improving his English.* 그는 영어 실력을 향상시켜오고 있다 / *I wish you to ~ in your manners.* 네 태도를 좀 고쳤으면 좋겠다. **2** make good use of (something); use well. 이용〔활용〕하다. ¶ *~ one's opportunity* 기회를 이용하다 / *We had two hours to wait, so we improved the time by seeing the city.* 우리는 두 시간을 기다려야 했다. 그래서 그 시간을 이용해서 시내 구경을 했다. — *vi.* (P1,3) become better. 좋아지다; 개량되다. ¶ *His health is improving.* 그의 건강은 좋아지고 있다. [in-², L. *pro* forward]

improve away, get rid of (a good quality) in attempting to improve. 더 좋게 하려다가 망쳐놓다.

improve on 〔***upon***〕***,*** make better; do better than in an earlier attempt. …보다 더 개량하다. ¶ *~ upon the first attempt* 처음의 시도를 개선하다.

:im·prove·ment [imprúːvmənt] *n.* Ⓤ **1** the act of making or becoming better. 개선; 개량; 진보; 향상. ¶ *There is room for ~.* 개선할 여지가 있다. **2** Ⓒ a change or addition which makes something better. 개량 공사; 개량점; 증축. ¶ *I am putting some improvements into my house.* 집을 몇 군데 손보고 있다.

im·prov·i·dence [imprávədəns / -prɔ́v-] *n.* Ⓤ the state of being improvident. 선견지명이 없음; 분별 없는 행동; 낭비. [↓]

im·prov·i·dent [imprávədənt / -prɔ́v-] *adj.* **1** careless in providing for the future; not provident. 선견지명이 없는; 대비가 없는. **2** not thrifty; wasteful. 아낄 줄 모르는; 낭비하는. [in-¹]

im·pro·vi·sa·tion [imprɑ̀vəzéiʃən, ìmprəvi-] *n.* **1** Ⓤ the act of improvising. 즉석에서 만들기. **2** Ⓒ a thing which is improvised. 즉석에서 만든〔행한〕 것《즉흥시·즉흥곡·즉흥 연주 등》. [↓]

im·pro·vise [ímprəvàiz] *vt., vi.* (P6; 1) **1** make (verse, music, etc.) without preparation or plan. (시·음악 등)을 즉석에서 만들다. ¶ *As the singer forgot a part of the words, he had to ~.* 그 가수는 가사를 한군데 잊어버려 즉석에서 지어 불러야 했다. **2** provide (something) roughly for an immediate need. …을 임시변통으로 만들다; 급히 짓다. ¶ *~ a bed out of the leaves and branches* 나뭇잎과 가지로 임시 잠자리를 만들다 / *~ a meal* 있는 재료만으로 식사를 만들다. [in-¹, →provide]

im·pru·dence [imprúːdəns] *n.* **1** Ⓤ the state of being imprudent. 경솔; 무분별. **2** Ⓒ an imprudent behavior, act, etc. 경솔한 행동. [↓]

·im·pru·dent [imprúːdənt] *adj.* not prudent; lacking caution; not careful. 경솔한; 분별 없는. ¶ *It is ~ of you to have done such a thing.* 그런 짓을 했다니 경솔하구나. [in-¹]

im·pu·dence [ímpjədəns] *n.* **1** Ⓤ the state or quality of being impudent; lack of shame or modesty. 뻔뻔스러움; 염치없음. **2** Ⓒ an impudent act or speech. 뻔뻔스러운 언행. ¶ (*Give me*) *none of your ~!* 너무 뻔뻔스럽군. [↓]

im·pu·dent [ímpjədənt] *adj.* **1** without shame or modesty; disrespectful; forward. 뻔뻔스러운; 염치없는; 버릇없는. ¶ *an ~ beggar* 체면도 없는 거지 / *an ~ lie* 뻔뻔스러운 거짓말. **2** insolant; saucy; rude. 건방진. ¶ *~ remark* 건방진 말 / *You ~ hussy!* 요 건방진 계집애. ●**im·pu·dent·ly** [-li] *adv.* [in-¹, L. *pudeo* am ashamed]

im·pugn [impjúːn] *vt.* (P6) attack (someone) by words or arguments; call (something) in question; oppose or challenge as false. …을 논란〔반박〕하다; 비난하다; 문제 삼다. ¶ *Do you ~ my statement?* 내 말이 잘못이란 말이냐. [in-², L. *pugno* fight]

·im·pulse [ímpʌls] *n.* **1** Ⓒ a sudden driving force; the motion or effect caused by such a force. 충격; 추진력; 충동. ¶ *the ~ of hunger* 배고픈 충동 / *The ~ of the propeller drives the aeroplane through the air.* 프로펠러의 추진력이 비행기가 하늘을 날게 한다. **2** ⓊⒸ a sudden desire or inclination to act. 충동. ¶ *Many people are guided more by ~ than by reason.* 많은 사람들이 이성보다는 충동에 지배된다. [→impel]

give an impulse to, stimulate; encourage. …에 충격〔자극〕을 주다; …을 고무하다.

on the impulse of the moment, on the spur

of the moment. 그 때의 일시적 충동으로. ***under the impulse of,*** driven by. …에 이끌려. ¶ *He did so under the ~ of pity.* 그는 동정심에 이끌려 그렇게 했다

im·pul·sion [impʌ́lʃən] *n.* **1** Ⓤ the act of impelling; the state of being impelled. 추진. **2** Ⓒ an impelling force; the effect or motion caused by this force. 추진력; 충격; 충동. ¶ *It was the ~ of hunger that drove the man to steal.* 그 사람이 도둑질을 하게 된 것은 배고픈 나머지였다

im·pul·sive [impʌ́lsiv] *adj.* **1** ⓐ (of a person) acting on or moved by sudden feeling. 충동적인; 일시적 감정에 끌린. ¶ *As he is an ~ person, we never know what he will do next.* 그 사람은 충동적이어서 다음에 무슨 짓을 할지 모른다. ⓑ (of actions) performed as the result of an impulse. 충동적으로 행해지는. ¶ *~ acts* 충동에 의한 행위. **2** driving forward; pushing onward. 추진하는. ¶ *an ~ force* 추진력.

im·pu·ni·ty [impjú:nəti] *n.* Ⓤ freedom from punishment, injury, harm, etc. 벌받지 않음; 무사. ¶ *You cannot break the law with ~.* 법을 어기면 반드시 처벌된다. [in-[1], L. *poena* penalty]

im·pure [impjúər] *adj.* mixed with another substance; not pure; dirty. 잡것이 섞인; 불순(불결)한. ¶ *~ air* 혼탁한 공기 / *The salt we use is slightly ~.* 우리가 먹는 소금은 전혀 깨끗한 것은 아니다 / *~ motives* 이기적인 동기 / *an ~ mind* (*life*) 불순한 마음(생활). [in-[1]]

·**im·pu·ri·ty** [impjúərəti] *n.* (*pl.* **-ties**) **1** Ⓤ the state of being impure; lack of purity. 불순; 불결. **2** Ⓒ 《often *pl.*》 a thing which is or which makes something else impure. 불순물; 잡것; 불결한 것(일). ¶ *impurities in the air* (*food*) 공기(음식물)중의 불순물.

im·pu·ta·tion [ìmpjutéiʃən] *n.* **1** Ⓤ the act of imputing; the state of being imputed. (죄·책임을) 씌우기; 전가하기. **2** Ⓒ a fault or crime imputed. 비난; 비방; 오명(汚名). ¶ *cast an ~ on someone's character* 아무의 사람됨을 비방하다. [↓]

im·pute [impjú:t] *vt.* (P13) 《*to*》 charge (a crime, a fault, etc.) to (someone). …에 (결점·죄 따위)를 씌우다; 지우다; 전가하다. ¶ *~ the accident to the driver's carelessness* 사고를 운전자의 부주의로 돌리다 / *~ one's failure to another* 실패를 남의 탓으로 돌리다 / *I ~ no evil motives or improper conduct to him.* 그에게 그릇된 동기나 행위를 묻고 싶지 않다. [in-[2], L. *puto* reckon]

⁝**in** [in] *prep.* **1** (of position) ⓐ inside of; within; at. …의 안에(서); …에 있어(서). ¶ *live ~ Seoul* 서울에 살고 있다 / *~ school* 학교에서; 재학 중에 / *a wound ~ the head* 머리의 부상 / *sit ~ the shade* 그늘에 앉다 / *I found it ~ the car.* 그걸 차 안에서 찾았다 / *children playing ~ the park* 공원에서 놀고 있는 아이들. ⓑ held by; partly surrounded by; framed by. …에 있는; 갇힌. ¶ *a plant ~ the window* 퇴창(退窓)에 놓인 화분 / *a bird ~ a cage* 새장에 갇힌 새. **2** (of action or motion) into. …의 속에. ¶ *break ~ two* 두 쪽으로 부러지다 / *Put it ~ your pocket.* 그건 주머니에 넣어라 / *He just went ~ the room.* 그는 막 방에 들어갔다. **3** (of condition or situation). …한 상태로(에); …하여. ¶ *~ despair* 절망해서 / *~ a circle* 원을 이루어 / *go out ~ the rain* 비가 오는데 나가다 / *be ~ business* 집무 중이다 / *be engaged ~ reading* 독서하고 있다 / *~ a search for truth* 진리를 찾아서 / *We are ~ good health.* 건강은 좋다. **4** wearing; clothed by. …을 입고; …을 신고. ¶ *a lady ~ white* 흰 옷의 여인 / *a man ~ sandals* 샌들을 신은 남자 / *schoolboys ~ uniform* 교복 차림의 학생들. **5** (of time) ⓐ during; when; within a period of time. …의 동안; …의 사이; …이내에. ¶ *~ the morning* 오전 중에 / *~ (the) future* 장차; 미래에 / *~ the past* 과거에 / *~ his absence* 그가 없는 동안 / *~ crossing the street* 길을 건너고 있는데. ⓑ within the space of. …의 안에; (시간) 이내에. ¶ *I can finish it ~ one day.* 난 그걸 하루에 마칠 수 있다. ⓒ at the end of a period of time; after. …의 다음에; …이 지나면. ¶ *I will come ~ a few minutes.* 몇 분 후에 가마 / *The concert will begin ~ an hour from now.* 연주회는 지금부터 1시간 내에 시작된다. **6** (of sphere of activity or occupation) within the scope of. …의 범위내에; …안에서. ¶ *~ one's sight* 시계(視界) 안에 / *~ my experience* 내 경험으로는 / *~ my opinion* 내 의견으로는. **7** (of material or means) by means of; using; made of. …을 써서; …을 재료로. ¶ *write ~ pencil* 연필로 쓰다 / *a statue ~ bronze* 동상 / *Say it ~ English.* 그걸 영어로 말해라 / *a dress ~ silk* 비단 옷. **8** (of limitation) to physical quality or amount. (수량 따위를 한정하여) …에 있어서; (특정 본위에) 관해서. ¶ *one foot ~ a length* 길이가 1피트 / *seven ~ number* 수는 일곱 / *He is blind ~ one eye.* 한쪽 눈이 어둡다 / *I am weak ~ English.* 나는 영어가 서툴다 / *weak ~ faith* 신앙이 약하다. **9** (of reason or motive) because of; as a result of; for. …으로; …의 결과로; 때문에. ¶ *jump ~ surprise* 놀라서 펄쩍 뛰다 / *cry out ~ alarm* 놀라서 소리치다 / *rejoice ~ someone's recovery* 아무의 회복을 기뻐하다. **10** out of; from among. …당; …에 대하여; …중에서. ¶ *one ~ a hundred* 백에 하나 / *the tallest girl ~ the class* 반에서 제일 큰 소녀. **11** (of mode of arrangement) so as to form. …을 이루어; …으로. ¶ *stand ~ line* 줄서다 / *school boys ~ a row* 한 줄로 선 학생들 / *arranged ~ curls* 곱슬곱슬하게 한. **12** (of direction) toward. …의 쪽으로. ¶ *It flew ~ an easterly direction.* 동쪽으로 날아

갔다.

in that, because. …이므로.

— *adv.* **1** from the outside to the inside; into a place. 속으로; 안에. ¶ *go* ~ 들어가다 / *Please come* ~. 들어오시오. **2** at home, at the office, etc. 집에 (있어); 직장에. ¶ *Is your father* ~*?* 아버지 계시니. **3** in fashion; in season; arrived. 유행하여; 도착하여. ¶ *Summer is* ~. 여름이 되었다 / *Watermelons are* ~. 수박철이 되었다 / *The train is* ~. 기차가 들어왔다. **4** in power; in office. 정권을 잡아; 재직하여. ¶ *The Liberals were* ~. 자유당이 집권했다.

be in for, be certain to receive or experience (esp. something unpleasant). (안좋은 일을) 아무래도 겪어야 하다; 피할 수 없다.

be in for it, be sure to be punished. 처벌을 피할 수 없게 돼 있다.

***be in with** someone,* …와 친하다. ¶ *He is* ~ *with a suspicious character.* 어떤 수상한 인물과 친하게 지낸다.

in and out, alternately; first in, then out. 보였다 안 보였다, 나왔다 들어갔다.

— *adj.* **1** inside; having power, office, etc. 안의; 세력을 잡은. ¶ *the* ~ *party* 집권당; 여당 / *an* ~ *patient* 입원 환자. **2** coming in or turning in. 들어오는. ¶ *an* ~ *train* 도착 열차.

— *n.* 《usu. *the* ~ *s*》 the political party in power. 여당(opp. outs). ¶ *the ins and outs* 여당과 야당. [E.]

ins and outs, **a**) all the details. 상세. ¶ *ins and outs of a question* 〔*situation*〕 문제〔사태〕의 자세한 내용. **b**) twist and turns. (길 따위의) 구불구불함.

in-[1] [in] *pref.* no; not; without; the opposite of. '무(無)…, 불(不)…, 비(非)…'의 뜻. ¶ *incapable.* [L.]

in-[2] [in] *pref.* in; into; within; toward. …의 안에〔속의, 안으로〕의 뜻. ¶ *inhabit* (=live in). [E.]

in. inch; inches.

I

in·a·bil·i·ty [ìnəbíləti] *n.* Ⓤ the state of being unable; lack of ability. 할 수 없음; 불가능; 무능(력). ¶ ~ *to help* 〔*stand, pay*〕 도울〔일어설, 지급할〕 수 없음. [in-[1], *ability*]

in·ac·ces·si·ble [inəksésəbəl] *adj.* **1** (of material things) cannot to be reach. 도달〔접근〕하기 어려운. ¶ *an* ~ *coast* 접근이 어려운 해안. **2** (of non-material things) not easily obtained. 얻기 어려운. ¶ *the* ~ *object of one's ambition* 야망의 이루기 어려운 목적. **3** (of a person) reserved in manner and nature. 가까이하기 어려운; 까다로운. ¶ *an* ~ *fellow* 까다로운 친구. [in-[1], *accessible*]

in·ac·cu·ra·cy [inǽkjərəsi] *n.* (*pl.* **-cies**) **1** Ⓤ the state of being inaccurate. 부정확. **2** Ⓒ an inaccurate thing; an error; a mistake. 과오; 잘못. ¶ *a page full of inaccuracies* 오자 투성이의 페이지. [↓]

in·ac·cu·rate [inǽkjərit] *adj.* not accurate; not exact. 부정확한. ¶ ~ *measurement* 부정확한 측정 / *an* ~ *statement* 불확실한 성명. [in-[1], →accurate]

in·ac·tion [inǽkʃən] *n.* Ⓤ absence of action or motion; idleness. 활동하지 않음; 정지; 나태; 게으름. [in-[1]]

in·ac·tive [inǽktiv] *adj.* that cannot act or move; not active; idle. 활발하지 않은; 나태한. ¶ *He was forced by illness to lead an* ~ *life.* 병 때문에 무위하게 지내야 했다 / *an* ~ *volcano* 휴화산.

in·ac·tiv·i·ty [ìnæktívəti] *n.* Ⓤ absence of activity; idleness. 활동치 않음; 나태.

in·a·dapt·a·ble [ìnədǽptəbəl] *adj.* that cannot be adapted. 적응〔순응〕할 수 없는. [in-[1]]

in·a·dapt·a·bil·i·ty [ínədæ̀ptəbíləti] *n.* Ⓤ lack of adaptability. 비적합성; 적응성이 없음. [↑]

in·ad·e·qua·cy [inǽdikwəsi] *n.* Ⓤ the state of being inadequate. 불충분; 부적당.

in·ad·e·quate [inǽdikwit] *adj.* not equal to the requirements; not sufficient; not enough; not suitable; not adequate. 불충분한; 부적당한. ¶ ~ *resources* 빈약한 자원 / *be* ~ *to do* …할 힘이 없다. ● **in·ad·e·quate·ly** [-li] *adv.* [in-[1]]

in·ad·mis·si·ble [ìnədmísəbəl] *adj.* that cannot be admitted or allowed; not admissible. 허락할 수 없는; 승인할 수 없는. ¶ *an* ~ *point in an argument* 논의에서 한 가지 수용할 수 없는 사항. ● **in·ad·mis·si·bil·i·ty** [-bíləti] *n.* [in-[1]]

in·ad·vert·ence [ìnədvə́ːrtəns] *n.* **1** Ⓤ the state of being inadvertent; lack of attention; carelessness. 부주의. ¶ *The mistake was due to* ~. 틀린 것은 부주의 탓이었다. **2** Ⓒ an inadvertent act; a mistake; an oversight. 잘못; 과오; 실수; 빠뜨림. [in-[1], →advert]

in·ad·ver·ten·cy [ìnədvə́ːrtənsi] *n.* (*pl.* **-cies**) =inadvertence.

in·ad·vert·ent [ìnədvə́ːrtənt] *adj.* **1** not attentive; thoughtless. 부주의한; 소홀한. **2** (of actions) not done on purpose; unintentional. 부주의로 인한; 고의가 아닌. ¶ *an* ~ *insult* 무심코 한 실례 / *My hurting him was quite* ~. 그의 기분을 상하게 한 것은 전혀 고의가 아니었다. ● **in·ad·vert·ent·ly** [-li] *adv.*

in·ad·vis·a·ble [ìnədváizəbəl] *adj.* not wise or prudent; not advisable. 현명하지 못한; 어리석은; 권할 게 못 되는. [in-[1]]

in·al·ien·a·ble [inéiljənəbəl] *adj.* that cannot be given away or taken away. 양보할 수 없는; 빼앗을 수 없는. ¶ *Liberty is an* ~ *right.* 자유는 양도할 수 없는 권리다. [in-[1]]

in·am·o·ra·ta [inæ̀mərɑ́ːtə] *n.* 《It.》 a girl or woman with whom one is in love. 애인; 정부(情婦). [↓]

in·am·o·ra·to [inæ̀mərɑ́ːtou] *n.* (*pl.* **-tos**) 《It.》 a man who is loved. 애인; 정부(情夫). [in-[2], L. *amor* love]

in·ane [inéin] *adj.* **1** silly; foolish. 어리석은. ¶ *an* ~ *question* 〔*remark*〕 어리석은 질문〔소

견]. 2 empty. 공허한. — *n.* 《*the* ~》 infinite space. 허공; 공간. [L. *inanis*]

in·an·i·mate [inǽnəmit] *adj.* **1** without life; lifeless. 생명이 없는; 죽은(opp. animate). ¶ ~ *matter* 무생물 / *an* ~ *human body* 시체. **2** 《*fig.*》 spiritless; dull. 활기 없는. ¶ *an* ~ *face* 생기 없는 얼굴 / ~ *conversation* 지루한 대화. [in-[1]]

in·a·ni·tion [ìnəníʃən] *n.* Ⓤ **1** lack of mental or moral vigor; emptiness. 공허. **2** weakness from lack of food. 영양 실조. [*inane*]

in·an·i·ty [inǽnəti] *n.* **1** Ⓤ the state or quality of being inane. 공허; 우매; 어리석음. **2** Ⓒ something that is inane. 공허한 것; 어리석은 일. ¶ *talk nothing but inanities* 바보같은 소리만 하다. [↑]

in·ap·pli·ca·ble [inǽplikəbəl] *adj.* that cannot be applied; not suitable. 적용할 수 없는; 부적당한. ¶ *The rule is* ~ *in his case.* 그 규칙은 그의 경우에는 적용되지 않는다. [in-[1]]

in·ap·pre·ci·a·ble [ìnəpríːʃiəbəl] *adj.* too small to be noticed or to have any value. 근소한; 사소한. ¶ *an* ~ *difference* 근소한 차이. [in-[1]]

in·ap·pre·hen·si·ble [ìnæprihénsəbəl] *adj.* that cannot be apprehended. 이해할 수 없는; 불가해한. [in-[1]]

in·ap·pro·pri·ate [ìnəpróupriət] *adj.* not suitable; not appropriate. 부적당한; 어울리지 않는. ¶ *Your short dress is* ~ *for a formal party.* 네 짧은 드레스는 공식 파티에는 마땅찮다. [in-[1]]

in·apt [inǽpt] *adj.* **1** not suitable; not apt; unfit. 부적당한. ¶ *He made a very* ~ *remark.* 그의 말은 아주 적절하지 못했다. **2** lacking skill; awkward; clumsy. 서툰(cf. *inept*). ¶ *an* ~ *workman* 서툰 직공. ●**in·apt·ly** [-li] *adv.* [in-[1]]

in·ap·ti·tude [inǽptətjùːd] *n.* Ⓤ **1** lack of suitability; unfitness. 부적절; 부적당. **2** lack of skill; unskillfulness. 서투름; 무재주.

in·ar·tic·u·late [ìnɑːrtíkjəlit] *adj.* **1** (of a person) not able to speak understandably; (of speech) not distinct. 말을 똑똑히 못 하는; 발음이 분명치 않은; (말이) 모호한. **2** unable to speak; dumb. 말을 못 하는; 벙어리의. ¶ ~ *animals* 말 못하는 짐승. **3** unable to express one's thoughts or feelings. 말이 안 나오는. ¶ *Surprise made him* ~. 놀라서 말이 안 나왔다. **4** 《anat.》 not jointed. 무관절(無關節)의. [in-[1]]

in·ar·tis·tic [ìnɑːrtístik] *adj.* **1** not artistic. 예술적이 아닌. ¶ *an* ~ *arrangement* 〔*style*〕 비예술적인 배색(配色)〔문체〕. **2** (of a person, mind, etc.) lacking taste (for art). 예술을 모르는; 몰취미한. [in-[1]]

in·as·much [ìnəzmʌ́tʃ] *adv.* 《used like a *conj.*, followed by *as*》 because; since. …이기 때문에; …이므로. ¶ *She is absent* ~ *as her mother is ill.* 그녀는 어머니가 아파서 결석이다 / *Inasmuch as you wish to, you may go.* 가고 싶다니 가도 좋다. [*in as much as*]

in·at·ten·tion [ìnəténʃən] *n.* Ⓤ lack of attention; carelessness. 부주의. [in-[1]]

in·at·ten·tive [ìnəténtiv] *adj.* not attentive; careless; neglectful. 부주의한; 게으른. ¶ *An* ~ *pupil cannot succeed.* 게으른 학생은 성공을 못한다 / *be* ~ *to a speaker's remark* 연사의 말에 무관심하다.

in·au·di·ble [inɔ́ːdəbəl] *adj.* that cannot be heard. 들리지 않는. ¶ *an* ~ *remark* 들리지 않는 말. [in-[1]]

in·au·gu·ral [inɔ́ːgjərəl] *adj.* of an inauguration. 임관의; 취임(식)의. ¶ *an* ~ *address* 취임사. — *n.* Ⓒ 《U.S.》 a speech made at an inauguration. 취임사〔연설〕. [↓]

in·au·gu·rate [inɔ́ːgjərèit] *vt.* (P6) **1** place (an official) in an important office with a ceremony. …을 취임시키다; …의 취임식을 행하다. ¶ ~ *a president* 대통령〔총장〕 취임식을 거행하다. **2** ⓐ make a formal beginning of (something). …을 정식으로 개시하다. ¶ ~ *a new timetable* 새 시간표로 시작하다. ⓑ open; begin. …을 개시〔시작〕하다. ¶ ~ *a new era* 신기원을 열다. **3** open (a building, exhibition, etc.) for public use with a celebration. 낙성〔제막, 개통〕식을 열다. ¶ ~ *a bridge* 새 다리의 개통식을 하다. [in-[2], →augur]

in·au·gu·ra·tion [inɔ̀ːgjəréiʃən] *n.* Ⓒ **1** an act or ceremony of inaugurating. 취임(식); 개업(식). **2** a formal beginning. 개시.

in·aus·pi·cious [ìnɔːspíʃəs] *adj.* unlucky; unfavorable. 불운한; 불행한; 불길한. ¶ *He chose a very* ~ *moment for making his request.* 그는 아주 나쁜 계제에 요구 사항을 말했다. [in-[1]]

in·be·tween [ìnbitwíːn] *adj.* intermediate. 중간의. — *n.* an intermediate. 중간의 것. ¶ *conservatives, radicals, and inbetweens* 보수, 급진 그리고 중도파. [in-[2], *between*]

in·board [ínbɔ̀ːrd] *adj., adv.* within the ship; towards the center of a ship. 선내의〔로〕; 배의 중심에. [in-[2]]

in·born [ínbɔ́ːrn] *adj.* born with or in a person; natural. 타고난; 생래(生來)의(cf. *inherent*). ¶ *an* ~ *love of music* 선천적인 음악에의 사랑 / *Birds have an* ~ *ability to fly.* 새는 본디부터 나는 재주가 있다. [in-[2]]

in·bred [ínbréd] *adj.* **1** inborn; natural. 생래의; 타고난. ¶ *an* ~ *goodness* 타고난 미덕. **2** bred from parents that are closely related. 동종교배(交配)〔번식〕의. ¶ *Many loyal families are* ~. 왕족의 다수가 혈족 결혼의 가문이다. [in-[2]]

in·breed·ing [ínbrìːdiŋ] *n.* 《biol.》 breeding from closely related ancestors. 근친 교배(近親交配); 동종 번식.

Inc. incorporated.

In·ca [íŋkə] *n.* Ⓒ **1** a member of the group of South American Indians who ruled Peru until the Spanish conquest. 잉카 사람. **2** the ruler of this tribe. 잉카 국왕. [Peruv.]

in·cal·cu·la·ble [inkǽlkjələbəl] *adj.* **1** so great in number that it cannot easily be counted. 헤아릴 수 없는; 무수한. ¶ ~ *stars* 무수한 별들. **2** that cannot be forecast; not to be foretold. 예상할 수 없는. **3** (of a person) that cannot be relied on; uncertain; unsure. 믿을〔신뢰할〕 수 없는. ¶ *a person of ~ moods* 기분파. [in-¹]

in·can·des·cence [ìnkəndésns] *n.* Ⓤ the state of being incandescent. 백열(白熱). [↓]

in·can·des·cent [ìnkəndésnt] *adj.* **1** glowing with heat; red-hot or, esp. white-hot. 백열의. ¶ *an ~ lamp* 백열등. **2** bright; brilliant. 빛나는; 눈부신. [in-², L. *candeo* am white]

in·can·ta·tion [ìnkæntéiʃən] *n.* Ⓒ a set of words sung or spoken to produce a magic effect. 주문(呪文). [in-², L. *canto* chant]

in·ca·pa·bil·i·ty [inkèipəbíləti] *n.* Ⓤ the state of being incapable; incapacity; unfitness. 무능; 부적임. [↓]

***in·ca·pa·ble** [inkéipəbəl] *adj.* lacking ordinary ability; not able; helpless. …을 할 수 없는; 무능한; 무력한. ¶ ~ *of speech* 〔*movement*〕 말〔기동〕을 못하는 / ~ *of telling a lie* 거짓말을 못하는 / *drunk and ~* 고주망태가 된. [in-¹]

in·ca·pac·i·tate [ìnkəpǽsətèit] *vt.* (P6, 13) 《*from, for*》 make (someone) powerless, unfit or unable to act; disqualify. 아무를 못하게 만들다; 무능력하게 만들다; 자격을 빼앗다. ¶ ~ *someone from working* 〔*for work*〕 아무를 일을 못하게 만들다 / *be incapacitated from voting* 선거권을 빼앗기다. [in-¹]

in·ca·pac·i·ty [ìnkəpǽsəti] *n.* Ⓤ **1** lack of ability, ordinary power or fitness. 무능; 부적당. ¶ ~ *for work* 노동〔작업〕 불능 / ~ *for one's position* 부적임(不適任). **2** 《law》 disqualification. 무능; 무자격; 실격.

in·car·cer·ate [inká:rsərèit] *vt.* (P6) 《*lit.*》 shut up (someone) in a prison; imprison; confine. …을 투옥하다; 감금하다. [in-², L. *carcer* prison]

in·car·na·dine [inká:rnədàin, -dì:n] *vt.* 《*poet.*》 make red; dye crimson. 붉게 하다〔물들이다〕. —*adj.* flesh-colored crimson; bloodred. 살빛의; 진홍의; 핏빛의. [↓]

in·car·nate [inká:rnit, -neit] *adj.* appearing in physical form, esp. in human form. 인간의 모습을 한; 화신의. ¶ *an ~ fiend* =*a devil ~* 악마의 화신.
—[inká:rneit] *vt.* (P6,13) 《*as, in*》 **1** provide (something) with flesh or a body; embody. …에 육체를 갖게 하다. ¶ *Medieval belief incarnated the devil in many animal forms.* 중세에는 악마가 여러가지 동물의 모습을 하고 있다고 믿었다. **2** be the type of (something). …의 화신이 되다. **3** put (something) into an actual form; make real. …을 구체화하다; 실현시키다. ¶ ~ *a plan* 〔*an idea*〕. [in-², L. *caro* flesh]

in·car·na·tion [ìnka:rnéiʃən] *n.* **1** Ⓤ the act of taking on human form by a divine being. 육체화; 인간화. **2** 《*the I-*》 the act by Jesus Christ of taking human form. 성육신(成肉身)《예수가 인간으로서 태어남》. **3** Ⓒ any person or thing which represents a principle, a quality, an idea, etc. 화신; 권화(權化). ¶ *He looked* (*like*) *the ~ of health.* 그는 건강의 화신처럼 보였다.

in·case [inkéis] *vt.* =encase.

in·cau·tious [inkɔ́:ʃəs] *adj.* not cautious; careless. 경솔한. [in-¹]

in·cen·di·a·rism [inséndiərìzəm] *n.* Ⓤ **1** the act of willfully setting fire to property. 방화. **2** agitation. 선동. [↓]

in·cen·di·ar·y [inséndièri] *adj.* **1** guilty of purposely setting property on fire. 방화의. **2** causing a fire. 불을 일으키는. ¶ *an ~ bomb* 〔*shell*〕 소이탄. **3** stirring up passion; of agitation. 선동하는. ¶ *an ~ speech* 선동연설. —*n.* Ⓒ (*pl.* **-ar·ies**) **1** a person who sets fire to property purposely. 방화범. **2** a person who stirs up passions; an agitator. 선동자. [L. *incendo* kindle]

***in·cense**¹ [ínsens] *n.* Ⓤ **1** material burned to make a sweet smell. 향; 향료. **2** the smoke or odor given off by such material. 향연기; 향냄새. **3** any pleasant odor. 좋은 냄새; 방향. ¶ *the ~ of flowers* 꽃 향기. **4** flattery. 아첨. ¶ *the ~ of praise* 아첨의 말. —*vt.* (P6) **1** make fragrant with incense. 향을 피우다. **2** offer incense to (a dead person); burn incense in honor of. (죽은 이에게) 분향하다. [↑]

in·cense² [inséns] *vt.* (P6,13) 《usu. in *passive*》《*at, against*》 make (someone) very angry. …을 몹시 화나게 하다. ¶ *Cruelty incenses kind people.* 잔학 행위는 착한 사람들을 격분시킨다. [↑]

in·cen·tive [inséntiv] *adj.* giving a desire to act or work; encouraging. 자극적인; 유발〔고무〕적인. —*n.* ⒸⓊ something which arouses someone to action or effort; a motive. 자극; 동기; 유인. ¶ *The love of money is an ~ to action.* 금전에 대한 사랑이 행위의 한 동기다. [L. =setting the tune]

in·cep·tion [insépʃən] *n.* Ⓒ **1** beginning; start. 처음; 개시; 발단. ¶ *The movement was successful from its ~.* 그 운동은 처음부터 성공적이었다. **2** 《Cambridge univ.》 the taking of a full Master's or Doctor's degree. 학위 취득. [in-², L. *capio* take]

in·cep·tive [inséptiv] *adj.* **1** beginning; marking the beginning. 처음의; 발단의. **2** 《gram.》 expressing the beginning of an action. 기동(起動)(상(相))의. —*n.* an inceptive verb. 기동(起動)동사. (e.g. begin, start)

in·cer·ti·tude [insə́:rtitjù:d] *n.* Ⓤ uncertainty; doubt. (심적인) 불확실(한 상태); 의혹. [in-¹]

in·ces·sant [insésənt] *adj.* not stopping; continuous. 끊임없는; 계속적인. ¶ ~ *noise* 끊임없는 잡음. ●**in·ces·sant·ly** [-li] *adv.* [in-¹, →cease]

in·cest [ínsest] *n.* Ⓤ sexual intercourse or marriage between persons very closely related. 근친 상간(결혼). [in-¹, L. *castus* pure (→chaste)]

:**inch** [intʃ] *n.* Ⓒ **1** a unit of length, equal to 1/12 of a foot. 인치. **2** a very small amount, degree, distance, etc. 소량; 단거리; 소액. **3** 《*pl.*》 height. 신장; 키. 「조금씩. ***by inches,*** little by little; slowly. 서서히; ***every inch,*** in all respects; completely. 모든 점에서; 철두철미. ¶ *Elizabeth I was every ~ a queen.* 엘리자베스 1세는 전형적 여왕이었다. ***to an inch,*** precisely. 정밀하게; 상세히. ***within an inch of,*** very near to; not far from. …에 근접하여; 거의 …할 지경까지. ¶ *come within an ~ of death* 죽을 뻔하다. —*vt., vi.* (P7; 2A) move slowly. 조금씩 움직이(게 하)다. [L. *uncia*]

in·cho·ate [inkóuit / ínkouèit] *adj.* just begun; undeveloped. 초기의; 미발달의. [L.]

in·ci·dence [ínsədəns] *n.* Ⓤ **1** the degree or range of occurrence or influence; extent of influence. 사건(영향)의 정도(범위). ¶ *the ~ of taxation* 세금의 부담 범위 / *the ~ of a disease* 질병의 발생률(이환율). **2** the act of falling upon or influencing. 낙하: 투사(投射); 영향을 끼침. [↓]

:**in·ci·dent** [ínsədənt] *n.* Ⓒ **1** a happening; an event. 생긴 일; 사건. **2** an event unimportant in relation to a large one. 부수적인 사건; 작은 일. **3** 《law》 something attaching to or dependent on something else. 부수적인 것; 부대 조건. —*adj.* **1** 《*to*》 apt to happen. 일어나기 쉬운; 따르는. ¶ *weaknesses ~ to human nature* 인성에 따르는 약점. **2** 《phys.》 of incidence. 낙하의; 투사(投射)의. ¶ *rays of light ~ upon a surface* 표면에 투사되는 광선. **3** 《law》 dependent on, naturally attached to, something else. 따르는; 부수적인. ¶ *rights* (*duties*) *~ to a settled estate* 승계된 부동산에 부수하는 권리(의무). [in-², L. *cado* fall]

in·ci·den·tal [insədéntl] *adj.* 《*to*》 **1** happening with something more important. 부수적인. ¶ *~ expenses* 부대 비용 / *the dangers ~ to a soldier's life* 군인 생활에 따르는 위험. **2** occurring by chance. 우연의; 우발적인. —*n.* Ⓒ an incidental thing. 부수적(우발적)인 일.

in·ci·den·tal·ly [ìnsədéntəli] *adv.* in an incidental manner; by chance; by the way. 우연히; 우발적으로; 부수적으로; 하는 김에.

in·cin·er·ate [insínərèit] *vt.* (P6) burn (something) to ashes. …을 태우다; …을 소각하다. [in-², L. *cinis* ashes]

in·cin·er·a·tor [insínərèitər] *n.* Ⓒ a furnace for burning waste. 쓰레기 소각로.

in·cip·i·ent [insípiənt] *adj.* just beginning. 시초의; 초기의; 발단의. [→inception]

in·cise [insáiz] *vt.* (P6,13) **1** cut into. …을 베다(째다). **2** carve; engrave. …에 조각하다. ¶ *~ a stone surface* 돌 표면에 새기다. [in-², L. *caedo* cut]

in·ci·sion [insíʒən] *n.* **1** Ⓤ the act of cutting into. 베기; 새기기; 째기. **2** Ⓒ a cut made in something. 벰; 쨈. ¶ *a surgical ~* 외과 절개.

in·ci·sive [insáisiv] *adj.* **1** sharp; keen. 날카로운. **2** (of modes of expression) cutting; sharp; sarcastic. 날카로운; 통렬한. ¶ *an ~ remark* (*criticism*) 신랄한 말(비평).

in·ci·sor [insáizər] *n.* Ⓒ a cutting tooth. 앞니.

in·cite [insáit] *vt.* (P6,13,20) stir up; rouse. …을 자극하다; 선동하다. ¶ *~ someone to heroic deeds* 용기 있는 행동을 하도록 아무를 격려하다 / *The captain's example incited the men to fight bravely.* 지휘관의 본보기에 고무되어 사병들은 용감히 싸웠다. [in-², L. *cito* rouse]

in·cite·ment [insáitmənt] *n.* **1** Ⓤ the act of inciting. 격려; 자극; 선동. **2** Ⓒ a thing which stirs up or rouses. 자극(선동)하는 것. ¶ *Interest is an ~ to study.* 호기심은 연구의 한 자극제이다.

in·ci·vil·i·ty [ìnsivíləti] *n.* ⓊⒸ (*pl.* **-ties**) lack of good manners; rudeness; impoliteness. 무례; 버릇없음. [in-¹]

incl. inclusive.

in·clem·en·cy [inklémənsi] *n.* Ⓤ (of weather) the state or quality of being inclement. 험악함; 사나움. ¶ *The ~ of a cold climate kept us indoors.* 어찌나 추운지 우리는 밖에 나가지 못했다. [↓]

in·clem·ent [inklémənt] *adj.* **1** (of weather) rough; stormy. 험악한; 거친. **2** 《rare》 (of character, etc.) severe; cruel. 모진; 잔인한. [in-¹, →clement]

*__in·cli·na·tion__ [inklənéiʃən] *n.* ⒸⓊ **1** the act of bending, leaning or sloping towards something. 기울기; 기대기. **2** the difference in direction between two things as measured by the angle between them. 기욺; 경사. ¶ *the ~ of a roof* 지붕의 물매. **3** 《*for, to*》 a particular tendency of the mind; a liking; a preference. 경향; 성향; 기호. ¶ *an ~ to study* 공부하려는 마음; 연구심 / *an ~ for sports* 운동을 좋아함. **4** a bodily tendency. 체질. ¶ *an ~ to stoutness* 비만 체질. [↓]

:**in·cline** [inkláin] *vt.* **1** (P6) bow; bend; nod; lean. (머리 따위)를 숙이다; 기울이다. ¶ *an inclined plane* 사면(斜面) / *The fair lady graciously inclined her head.* 그 고운 숙녀는 품위 있게 고개를 숙였다. **2** (P13,20) 《usu. in *passive*》 turn (one's mind, etc.) in a certain direction; dispose; favor. (마

음)을 내키게 하다; …하고 싶어지다; …의 경향이 있다. ¶ *I was not inclined to believe the man.* 나는 그 사람을 믿고 싶지 않았다 / *He is inclined to be idle.* 그는 게으른 편이다 / *This inclined her to leave.* 이래서 그녀는 떠나고 싶었다 / *This statement inclines me to believe.* 이 성명은 믿고 싶다 / *I don't feel much inclined to work.* 별로 일할 생각이 안 난다.
— *vi.* **1** (P1) lean; slope; bend. 기울다; 경사지다. **2** (P3,4) tend; have a liking. …하고 싶어하다; …하기 쉽다; …한 경향이 있다. ¶ *I ~ to his opinion.* 그의 의견에 공감이 간다 / *The flowers ~ toward red.* 그 꽃은 붉은 색에 가깝다. **3** (P3) 《*to*》 have a habitual tendency. …한 경향이 있다. ¶ *~ to leanness* 야위는 체질이다.
— *n.* [´–] Ⓒ a slope; an inclined surface. 경향; 사면; 비탈. ¶ *The car went slowly down the ~.* 차는 천천히 비탈을 내려 갔다. [in-², L. *-clino* bend]

in·cli·nom·e·ter [ìnklənámitər / -nɔ́m-] *n.* Ⓒ an instrument that measures the angle of inclination; a dip needle. 경사계. [↑]

***in·close** [inklóuz] *vt.* =enclose.

in·clo·sure [inklóuʒər] *n.* =enclosure.

:in·clude [inklú:d] *vt.* (opp. exclude) (P6,13) 《*in, among*》 **1** put or enclose (something) within limits. …을 포함하다; 포괄하다. ¶ *This volume includes all his works.* 이 책에 그의 작품이 다 있다. **2** contain (something) as a part of the whole; take into account. …를 포함하다; 셈에 넣다. ¶ *Including myself, ten members were present at the meeting.* 나를 포함해서 열 사람이 회의에 참석했다. [in-², L. *claudo* shut]

in·clu·sion [inklú:ʒən] *n.* (opp. exclusion) **1** Ⓤ the act of including; the state of being included. 포함; 포괄. **2** Ⓒ a thing which is included. 함유물.

in·clu·sive [inklú:siv] *adj.* (opp. exclusive) **1** including a great deal; taking everything into account. 일체를 포함한; 포괄적인. ¶ *a party of ten, ~ of the host* 주객(主客)합하여 10 인의 파티 / *~ terms* 식비 기타 일체를 포함한 숙박료. **2** including the mentioned limits. …을 포함하여. ¶ *from Monday to Friday ~* 월요일부터 금요일까지.

in·cog [inkág / -kɔ́g] *adj., adv., n.* 《*colloq.*》 =incognito.

in·cog·ni·ti [inkágniti: / -kɔ́g-] *n.* pl. of **incognito.**

in·cog·ni·to [inkágnitou / -kɔ́g-] *adj., adv.* using a different name so as to escape notice. 익명의(으로); 잠행(미행(微行))의(으로). ¶ *The king traveled ~ to see everything with his own eyes.* 왕은 모든 것을 직접 자기 눈으로 보기 위해 미행했다. — *n.* Ⓒ (*pl.* **-tos** or **-ti**) a person who is incognito. 미행자; 익명의 사람. [It. =unknown (in-¹, → cognition)]

in·co·her·ence [ìnkouhíərəns] *n.* Ⓤ the state of being incoherent; lack of logical connection. 지리멸렬; 조리가 서지 않음. ¶ *an ~ speech* 조리가 없는 연설. [↓]

in·co·her·ent [ìnkouhíərənt, -hér-] *adj.* connected loosely; in bad order; lacking logical connection. 지리 멸렬의; 뒤죽박죽인; 조리가 서지(앞뒤가 맞지) 않는. [in-¹, L. *haereo* stick]

in·com·bus·ti·ble [ìnkəmbʌ́stəbəl] *adj.* that cannot be burned; fireproof. 불연성(不燃性)의. [in-¹]

:in·come [ínkʌm] *n.* ⒸⓊ 《*from*》 the amount of money coming in as payment, interest, profits, etc. 수입; 소득. ¶ *He has a very good ~.* 그는 아주 수입이 좋다 / *earned* (*unearned*) *~* 근로(불로) 소득. [*in, come*]

in·com·ing [ínkʌ̀miŋ] *adj.* **1** coming in. 들어오는. ¶ *~ profits* 수익 / *~ tide* 밀물. **2** following; just entering upon possession, office, etc. 다음에(새로) 오는; 후임의. ¶ *the ~ tenant* 새 차지(借地)(차가(借家))인 / *the ~ president* 후임 대통령. **3** coming; following due. 만기의. ¶ *~ payments* 만기 지급. — *n.* ⓊⒸ 《usu. *pl.*》 the act of coming in; arrival. 도래; 도착. ¶ *the ~ of the tide* 밀물이 듦.

in·com·men·su·ra·ble [ìnkəménʃərəbəl] *adj.* **1** that cannot be compared with each other. 비교할 수 없는. ¶ *Love and money are ~.* 사랑과 돈은 비교의 대상이 아니다. **2** 《math.》 having no common measure. 약분할 수 없는. [in-¹]

in·com·men·su·rate [ìnkəménʃərit] *adj.* **1** not adequate; not enough. 부적당한; 불충분한. ¶ *His strength is ~ to his duties.* 그의 역량은 맡은 일에 맞지 않는다. **2** having no common measure. 같은 표준으로 잴 수 없는. [↑]

in·com·mode [ìnkəmóud] *vt.* (P6) bring discomfort to (someone); inconvenience; trouble. …에 불편을 주다; …을 애먹이다. ¶ *Will it ~ you if I open the window ?* 창문을 좀 열면 안될까요. [in-¹]

in·com·mo·di·ous [ìnkəmóudiəs] *adj.* **1** inconvenient; uncomfortable. 불편한; 불쾌한. **2** inconveniently narrow. 비좁은.

in·com·mu·ni·ca·ble [ìnkəmjú:nəkəbəl] *adj.* that cannot be communicated or told. 전달할 수 없는; 말로 할 수 없는. ¶ *~ joys* 표현할 수 없는 즐거움. [in-¹]

in·com·mut·a·ble [ìnkəmjú:təbəl] *adj.* unchangeable. 불변의.

in·com·pa·ra·ble [inkámpərəbəl / -kɔ́m-] *adj.* that cannot be compared; without equal. 비교할 수 없는; 비길 데 없는; 무비의. ¶ *Cleopatra had ~ beauty.* 클레오파트라는 비길 데 없이 아름다웠다. [in-¹]

in·com·pat·i·bil·i·ty [ìnkəmpæ̀təbíləti] *n.* Ⓤ the state or quality of being incompatible; lack of harmony. 양립할 수 없음; 부조화. [↓]

in·com·pat·i·ble [ìnkəmpǽtəbəl] *adj.* not able to live or act together in harmony; inconsistent. 양립할 수 없는; 조화하기 어려운. ¶ *Excessive drinking is ~ with good health.* 과음은 건강과 양립할 수 없다 / *Fire and water, cats and dogs, are ~.* 물과 불, 고양이와 개는 상극이다. [in-[1]]

in·com·pe·tence [inkámpətəns / -kɔ́m-], **-ten·cy** [-tənsi] *n.* Ⓤ the state of being incompetent. 무능; 무자격. ¶ *the ~ of a worker* 노동자로서의 무자격. [in-[1]]

in·com·pe·tent [inkámpətənt] *adj.* **1** lacking ability, power or fitness; not competent. 무능한. ¶ *an ~ cook* 무능한 요리사 / *a thoroughly ~ person* 정말 무능한 사람. **2** (of work, action, etc.) showing the incompetence. 쓸모 없는. ¶ *an ~ book* 〔*lecture*〕 시시한 책〔강의〕. **3** 《law.》 not qualified. 무능력〔무자격〕의. ── *n.* a person who is without ability. 무자격자; 금치산자.

in·com·pre·hen·si·ble [inkàmprihénsəbəl / -kɔ̀m-] *adj.* **1** that cannot be understood; beyond understanding. 불가해한. **2** infinite. 무한한. [in-[1]]

in·com·press·i·ble [ìnkəmprésəbəl] *adj.* that cannot be compressed. 압축할 수 없는.

in·con·ceiv·a·ble [ìnkənsí:vəbəl] *adj.* **1** that cannot be imagined. 상상할 수 없는. ¶ *It is ~ that a man can live for two hundred years.* 사람이 2백 년간 살 수 있다는 것은 상상할 수 없다. **2** 《*colloq.*》 hard to believe. 믿을 수 없는. ¶ *the ~ story.* [in-[1]]

in·con·ceiv·a·bly [ìnkənsí:vəbli] *adv.* in an inconceivable manner; to an inconceivable degree. 상상을 초월하여; 상상할 수 없을 정도로.

in·con·clu·sive [ìnkənklú:siv] *adj.* not conclusive; not decisive. 결정이 안 된; 요령 부득의. ¶ *~ arguments* 결론에 이르지 못하는 논의. [in-[1]]

in·con·gru·i·ty [ìnkəngrú:əti, -kəŋ-] *n.* (*pl.* **-ties**) Ⓤ the state or quality of being incongruous. 부조화; 불일치. [in-[1]]

in·con·gru·ous [inkáŋgruəs / -kɔ́ŋ-] *adj.* **1** not appropriate; out of place. 적합하지 않은; 어울리지 않는. ¶ *His gloomy face was ~ with the wedding.* 그의 어두운 표정은 결혼식에 어울리지 않았다. **2** lacking in agreement or harmony; not consistent. 조화〔일치〕되지 않는. ¶ *a plan ~ with good sense* 양식에 벗어난 계획.

in·con·se·quent [inkánsikwènt / -kɔ́nsikwənt] *adj.* not logical; not logically connected; not to the point. 논리적이 아닌; 앞뒤가 안 맞는; 모순된. ¶ *an ~ conclusion* 모순된 결론 / *an ~ remark* 〔*reply*〕 엉뚱한 말〔대답〕. [in-[1]]

in·con·se·quen·tial [inkànsikwénʃəl / -kɔ̀n-] *adj.* **1** inconsequent; illogical. 조리가 닿지 않는; 비논리적인. **2** not important. 중요하지 않은; 시시한.

in·con·sid·er·a·ble [ìnkənsídərəbəl] *adj.* not worth consideration; not important. 중요하지 않은; 사소한. ¶ *an ~ difference* 사소한 차이. [in-[1]]

in·con·sid·er·ate [ìnkənsídərit] *adj.* thoughtless of the feelings, wishes or rights of others; careless. 생각이〔배려가〕 없는; 부주의한. ¶ *an ~ remark* 매정한 말.

in·con·sist·en·cy [ìnkənsístənsi] *n.* (*pl.* **-cies**) **1** Ⓤ the state or quality of being inconsistent. 불일치; 모순. ¶ *the ~ of two stories* 두 이야기의 상반〔상충〕. **2** Ⓒ an inconsistent thing. 일치하지 않는 것. ¶ *testimony full of ~* 모순 투성이의 증언. [↓]

in·con·sist·ent [ìnkənsístənt] *adj.* **1** 《*with*》 lacking in agreement or harmony. 일치하지 않는; 조화가 되지 않는. ¶ *His words are ~ with his actions.* 그는 언행이 다르다. **2** not holding together; having contradictions within itself. 모순된; 상반되는. ¶ *an ~ narration* 앞뒤가 안 맞는 이야기 / *a person ~ in argument* 논거에 조리가 없는 사람. **3** not keeping the same principles, etc.; changeable. 잘 변하는; 일관성이 없는. ¶ *You are very often ~.* 너는 너무 변덕이 심하다. [in-[1]]

in·con·sol·a·ble [ìnkənsóuləbəl] *adj.* (of a person or grief) that cannot be consoled; broken-hearted. 달랠 길 없는; 위안이 안 되는. ¶ *The child was ~ at the loss of her doll.* 아이는 인형이 없어져 여간 슬프지 않았다. [in-[1]]

in·con·spic·u·ous [ìnkənspíkju:əs] *adj.* not easily noticed. 두드러지지 않은; 이목을 끌지 않는. ¶ *The woman's dress was plain and ~.* 그 여성의 옷은 평범하고 수수했다. [in-[1]]

in·con·stan·cy [inkánstənsi / -kɔ́n-] *n.* ⓊⒸ (*pl.* **-cies**) the state of being inconstant; changeableness. 변하기 쉬움. [↓]

in·con·stant [inkánstənt / -kɔ́n-] *adj.* **1** not constant; likely to change; fickle. 변하기 잘 하는; 변덕스러운. ¶ *an ~ lover* 바람기 있는 애인. **2** (of things) frequently changing; irregular. 자주 바뀌는; 일정치 않은. ¶ *an ~ style* 변화가 많은 스타일. [in-[1]]

in·con·test·a·ble [ìnkəntéstəbəl] *adj.* that cannot or should not be contested; unquestionable. 논의〔의심〕의 여지가 없는; 명백한. ¶ *~ rights* 부정할 수 없는 권리. [in-[1]]

in·con·ti·nence [inkántənəns / -kɔ́n-] *n.* Ⓤ the state or quality of being incontinent. 자제심이 없음; 무절제. [↓]

in·con·ti·nent [inkántənənt / -kɔ́n-] *adj.* **1** without self-restraint. 자제할 수 없는; 절제 없는. **2** 《med.》 unable to restrain natural discharges. 실금(失禁)의. [in-[1]]

in·con·tro·vert·i·ble [ìnkantrəvə́:rtəbəl / -kɔn-] *adj.* that cannot be disputed; unquestionable. 논의의 여지가 없는; 명백한. ¶ *~ facts* 명백한 사실. [in-[1]]

***in·con·ven·ience** [ìnkənví:njəns] *n.* **1**

Ⓤ the state or quality of being not convenient. 불편; 부자유. ¶ *cause great ~ to someone* 아무를 아주 불편하게 만들다; 아무에게 큰 폐를 끼치다. **2** Ⓒ something which is inconvenient. 폐가 되는 것; 성가신 일. ¶ *The late arrival of the train was an ~ to me.* 기차가 연착해서 애를 먹었다. — *vt.* (P6) put (someone) to trouble or bother. …을 불편하게 하다; 폐를 끼치다. ¶ *You will not ~ me in the least.* 조금도 폐가 되지 않습니다〔개의치 마십시오〕. [in-¹]

·**in·con·ven·ient** [ìnkənvíːnjənt] *adj.* 《*to*》 not convenient; causing difficulty or discomfort. 불편한; 부자유스러운; 성가신. ¶ *If (it is) not ~ to you, I should like to help you.* 괜찮다면 돕고 싶은데 / *It is very ~ if there is no bath in a house.* 집에 욕실이 없으면 몹시 불편하다.

in·con·vert·i·ble [ìnkənvə́ːrtəbəl] *adj.* **1** that cannot be converted or changed. 바꿀 수 없는. **2** (of paper money) not capable of being converted into specie. 태환(兌換)할 수 없는. [in-¹]

in·cor·po·rate [inkɔ́ːrpərèit] *vt.* (P6,13,19) 《*with, into, in*》 **1** join or combine (something) into a whole; make (something) a part of something else. …와 합치다; 합병하다; 편입하다. ¶ *~ another's ideas into one's story* 이야기에 다른 사람의 생각을 짜넣다 / *a book which incorporates the newest information* 최신의 정보를 수록한 책 / *I will ~ your idea in the plan.* 그 계획에 자네 생각을 반영하겠네. **2** ⓐ add or join (a person) to a body or society. (단체의) 일원으로 하다; 가입시키다. ¶ *be incorporated a member of a college* 대학의일원이 되다. ⓑ mix with. …와 섞다. ¶ *~ a chemical substance with others* 화학 물질을 다른 것과 섞다. **3** form (individuals or units) into a legal corporation. …을 법인 조직으로 하다. **4** give a material or physical form to (something). …을 구체화하다.
— *vi.* (P1,3) become combined; form a legal corporation. 통합〔결합〕하다; 법인 조직을 만들다; 법인이 되다.
— *adj.* [inkɔ́ːrpərit] combined into one body. 합쳐진; 합병한. [in-², L. *corpus* body]

in·cor·po·rat·ed [inkɔ́ːrpərèitid] *adj.* **1** combined in one body. 결합된; 합쳐진. **2** 《U.S.》 formed or organized as a corporation. 유한 책임의. ¶ *an ~ company* 유한책임 회사(=《Brit.》 limited (liability) company).

in·cor·po·ra·tion [inkɔ̀ːrpəréiʃən] *n.* ⓊⒸ the act of incorporating; the state of being incorporated. 합체; 결합; 법인 조직.

in·cor·po·re·al [ìnkɔːrpɔ́ːriəl] *adj.* **1** not composed of matter. 실체가 없는; 무형의. ¶ *A ghost is ~.* 유령은 형체가 없다. **2** 《law》 of something not having physical existence, but existing as a right attached to corporeal property. 무체(無體)의. ¶ *~ hereditaments* 무체 유산. [in-¹]

in·cor·rect [ìnkərékt] *adj.* not according to fact or truth; not right; wrong; not proper. 바르지 않은; 틀린; 알맞지 않은. ¶ *an ~ grammatical construction* 문법적으로 틀린 구문 / *an ~ statement* 부정확한 말 / *~ behavior* 부당한 행위. [in-¹]

in·cor·ri·gi·ble [inkɔ́ːridʒəbəl] *adj.* (of a person, a bad habit, etc.) that cannot be made better; hopelessly bad. 고칠 수 없는; 상습의. ¶ *an ~ liar* 〔*drinker*〕 상습적인 거짓말쟁이〔주정뱅이〕. [in-¹]

in·cor·rupt·i·ble [ìnkərʌ́ptəbəl] *adj.* **1** impossible to be made to do wrong, even by the offer of money. (돈으로도) 매수되지 않는. **2** that cannot decay. 부패〔부식〕되지 않는. ¶ *Gold is an ~ metal.* 금은 부식되지 않는 금속이다. [in-¹]

:**in·crease** [inkríːs, ⌐–] (opp. decrease) *vi.* (P1) become greater in number, size, value, etc. 늘다; 붇다. ¶ *His weight has greatly increased.* 그의 체중이 굉장히 불었다 / *The town is increasing in population.* 그 도시는 인구가 늘고 있다. — *vt.* (P6) make (something) greater in number, size, value, etc.; enlarge. 늘리다; 불리다; 증대시키다. ¶ *~ one's wealth* 재산을 늘리다 / *~ one's pace* 더 빨리 걷다 / *~ one's efforts* 더 한층 힘쓰다.
— *n.* [⌐–] **1** ⒸⓊ a growth in number, size, value, etc. 증가. ¶ *an ~ in population* 인구의 증가 / *an ~ in popularity* 인기 상승. **2** Ⓒ the amount that is added. 증대량; 증가액. ¶ *My weight showed an ~ of 5 pounds in a month.* 체중이 한 달 사이 5파운드 늘었다. **3** 《*arch.*》 something that has grown; crops. 곡물; 농산물. ¶ *The earth yields her ~.* 대지에서 곡식이 난다. [in-², L. *cresco* grow]
on the increase, increasing; growing. 느는; 증가하는. ¶ *The membership of the club is on the ~.* 클럽의 회원은 늘고 있다.

in·creas·ing·ly [inkríːsiŋli] *adj.* more and more. 더욱더; 점점.

in·cred·i·bil·i·ty [inkrèdəbíləti] *n.* Ⓤ the state or quality of being incredible. 믿을 수 없음. [↓]

·**in·cred·i·ble** [inkrédəbəl] *adj.* **1** hard to believe; beyond belief. 믿을 수 없는. ¶ *a quite ~ happening* 도무지 믿어지지 않는 사건. **2** 《*colloq.*》 extraordinary; surprising. 거짓말 같은; 엄청난. ¶ *He told us a most ~ story.* 그는 우리에게 아주 놀라운 말을 했다. [in-¹]

in·cred·i·bly [inkrédəbli] *adv.* **1** in an incredible manner; to an incredible degree. 믿기지 않을 정도로; 엄청나게. ¶ *be ~ easy* 믿기지 않을 정도로 쉽다. **2** 《*colloq.*》 very. 매우. ¶ *~ swift* 아주 빠른.

in·cre·du·li·ty [inkridjúːləti] *n.* Ⓤ the state or quality of being incredulous. 의심이 많음; 불신. [*incredible*]

in·cred·u·lous [inkrédʒələs] *adj.* not willing to or not able to believe; doubting. 쉽사리 믿지 않는; 의심 많은. ¶ *Even after the evidence was set before her, she was still ~.* 증거를 제시했는데도 그녀는 믿으려 들지 않았다. [↑]

in·cre·ment [ínkrəmənt] *n.* **1** Ⓤ increase; growth. 증가. **2** Ⓒ the amount of increase; profit. 증가량; 증액; 소득. ¶ *unearned ~* (땅값의) 자연 증가(增價). ● **in·cre·ment·al** [-əl] *adj.* [→increase]

in·crim·i·nate [inkrímənèit] *vt.* (P6) accuse (someone) of a crime; show to be guilt. …에 죄를 씌우다; 고발하다; 유죄임을 보이다. ¶ *~ oneself* 자기의 죄를 인정하다 / *The man said nothing that would ~ his friend.* 그 남자는 친구가 불리해질 어떤 말도 하지 않았다. [in-², →crime]

in·crust [inkrʌ́st] *vt.* cover the surface of (something) with a thin, hard, outer covering. 껍질로 덮다; 외피(外皮)를 형성하다. [in-², *crust*]

in·cu·bate [ínkjəbèit] *vt.* (P6) **1** bring the young out of (eggs) by keeping them warm; hatch. (알을) 부화하다; 까다. **2** hatch (eggs) by artificial heat. 인공 부화시키다. **3** form (a plan) in the mind. (계획 따위를) 생각해내다; 꾀하다. — *vi.* sit on eggs. 알을 품다. [in-², L. *cubs* lie]

in·cu·ba·tion [ìnkjəbéiʃən, ìŋk-] *n.* ⓊⒸ the act of incubating; the state of being incubated. 부화. ¶ *artificial ~* 인공 부화.

in·cu·ba·tor [ínkjəbèitər, íŋk-] *n.* Ⓒ **1** a heated box for hatching eggs. 부화기. **2** an apparatus for rearing a prematurely born child. 인큐베이터; 조산아 보육기.

in·cu·bi [íŋkjəbài, ínk-] *n.* pl. of **incubus.**

in·cu·bus [íŋkjəbəs, ínk-] *n.* Ⓒ (*pl.* **-bus·es** or **-bi**) **1** a nightmare. 악몽; 몽마(夢魔). **2** an oppressive thing; a great worry. 내리누르는 것; (마음의) 부담. ¶ *The examination will be an ~ until I have passed it.* 내가 합격할 때까지 그 시험은 내게 부담이 될 것이다.

in·cul·cate [inkʌ́lkeit, ⌐–⌐] *vt.* (P6,13) 《*on, upon*》 fix (something) firmly in the mind of someone by much repeating. …을 되풀이하여 가르치다; 주입하다. ¶ *~ good manners on a child* 아이에게 예절을 가르치다. [in-², L. *calx* heel]

in·cul·pate [inkʌ́lpeit, ⌐–⌐] *vt.* (cf. *exculpate, incriminate*) **1** blame; accuse. 비난하다; 고발하다. **2** involve in responsibility for wrong doing. 연좌(連坐)시키다. [in-², *culpa* fault]

in·cum·bent [inkʌ́mbənt] *adj.* **1** 《*arch.*》 lying or resting with its weight on something else. 기대는. **2** 《*on, upon*》 pressing as a duty. 의무로서 해야 할. ¶ *It is ~ on you to warn them.* 그들에게 경고하는 일이 네 의무다 / *It is ~ upon me to do it.* 그것이 내가 할 책무다. — *n.* a person who holds an ecclesiastical benefice; a clergyman. 성직록(聖職祿) 소유자; 성직자. [in-², L. *cumbo* lie]

in·cum·ber [inkʌ́mbər] *vt.* =encumber.

in·cum·brance [inkʌ́mbrəns] *n.* = encumbrance.

•**in·cur** [inkə́:r] *vt.* (P6) (**-curred, -cur·ring**) get or fall into (something unpleasant); bring (something unpleasant) upon oneself. (손해·불운 등)을 초래하다; …을 당하다. ¶ *I incurred her anger.* 나는 그녀를 화나게 만들었다 / *The boy incurred great danger in swimming across the river.* 소년은 강을 헤엄쳐 건너다가 엄청난 위험을 겪었다 / *~ debt* 빚을 지다. [in-², L. *curro* run]

in·cur·a·ble [inkjúərəbəl] *adj.* that cannot be cured. 불치의. ¶ *an ~ disease* 불치병. — *n.* Ⓒ a person having an incurable disease. 불치의 병자. [in-¹]

in·cur·sion [inkə́:rʒən, -ʃən] *n.* Ⓒ **1** a sudden attack. 급습. ¶ *The enemy made incursions into their territory.* 적은 갑자기 그들의 영토로 쳐들어 왔다. **2** the act of running or flowing in. 침입; 유입. [→incur]

in·curve [inkə́rv] *vt.* (P6) curve inward. 안으로 굽히다. — [ínkər:v] *n.* 《baseball》 a pitch that curves toward the batter. 인커브. [in-²]

Ind. **1** Indiana. **2** India; Indian.

in·debt·ed [indétid] *adj.* owing money or gratitude. 빚이 있는; 은혜를 입고 있는. ¶ *I am ~ to you for your kindness.* 당신이 잘 해주신 덕분이요 / *I was ~ to the book for most of my information.* 내 지식의 대부분은 책에서 얻었다. [in-², →debt]

in·de·cen·cy [indí:snsi] *n.* (*pl.* **-cies**) **1** Ⓤ the state of being indecent. 무례; 버릇없음. **2** Ⓒ an indecent act or speech. 무례한 언행. [in-¹]

in·de·cent [indí:snt] *adj.* **1** in very bad taste; not suitable. 점잖지 못한; 꼴사나운. ¶ *He spoke and left in ~ haste.* 그는 말을 마치더니 허겁지겁 자리를 떴다. **2** not fit to be seen or heard. 상스러운; 음란한(opp. decent). ¶ *an ~ story* 〔*picture*〕 음란한 이야기〔그림〕.

in·de·ci·sion [ìndisíʒən] *n.* Ⓤ the state or quality of being not able to make up one's mind; lack of decision. 우유부단. [in-¹]

in·de·ci·sive [ìndisáisiv] *adj.* not settling or deciding the matter; indefinite; hesitant. 우유 부단한; 결정적이 아닌. ¶ *an ~ character* 〔*person*〕 우유 부단한 성격〔사람〕 / *an ~ battle* 〔*answer*〕 승패가 안나는 전쟁〔이도저도 아닌 대답〕.

in·de·clin·a·ble [ìndikláinəbəl] *adj.* 《gram.》 not declined. 격변화하지 않는. [in-¹]

in·dec·o·rous [indékərəs, ìndikɔ́:-] *adj.* not suitable; against good manners. 예의없는 ; 점잖치 못한. ¶ *~ speech* 상스러운 말. [→in-¹]

in·de·co·rum [ìndikɔ́:rəm] *n.* **1** Ⓤ the

state or quality of being indecorous. 무례; 버릇없음. **2** Ⓒ an indecorous act or speech. 무례한〔상스러운〕 언행.

:in·deed [indíːd] *adv.* **1** really; certainly. 정말; 확실히. ¶ *Indeed it is true.* 정말, 그건 사실이다 / *You may ~ say so.* 정말 그렇게 말해도 좋다 / *He is ~ a great man.* 확실히 그는 위인이다 / 《*emph.*》 *It's very cold ~.* 실로 대단한 추위이다 / *Thank you very much ~.* 정말 대단히 고맙습니다 / *Yes* 〔*No*〕, *~!* 응〔아니〕 정말이다 / *I met him in the park. — Indeed?* 공원에서 그 사람을 만났다 —정말이냐. **2** in fact; as a matter of fact. 실제로; 사실. ¶ *I think so, ~ I'm sure of it.* 난 실제로 그렇게 생각한다. **3** 《concessive》 it is true; I admit. 정말; 과연. ¶ *I may ~ be wrong.* 과연 내 잘못인지도 모르겠다 / *Indeed he is old, but he is still strong.* 그 사람 늙은 건 사실이나 아직 정정해.
— *interj.* an expression of surprise, irony, or doubt. (놀람·빈정거림·의심 따위를 나타내어) 저런; 설마; 그래요. ¶ *Your sister told me so. — My sister ~!* 당신 누이가 그렇게 말했어요 —설마 내 누이가 / *Indeed! Did he say that?* 내 참, 그가 그랬단 말인가 / *Who is Mr. Smith? —Who, ~?* 스미스씨가 누구지—글쎄 누구일까. [in-[2]]

indef. indefinite.

in·de·fat·i·ga·ble [ìndifǽtigəbəl] *adj.* never getting tired; tireless. 지칠줄 모르는; 물리지 않는. ¶ *~ workers* 근면한 일꾼들. [in-[1], de, →fatigue]

in·de·fea·si·ble [ìndifíːzəbəl] *adj.* (of one's rights, etc.) that cannot be taken away or made void. 파기〔취소〕할 수 없는. ¶ *~ rights to freedom* 빼앗길 수 없는 자유의 권리. [in-[1]]

in·de·fen·si·ble [ìndifénsəbəl] *adj.* **1** that cannot be defended or maintained. 막을〔지킬〕 수 없는. ¶ *an ~ argument* 〔*viewpoint*〕 (비판 따위를 면할 길이 없는) 허술한 논의〔견해〕 / *an ~ town* 방어 불가능한 도시. **2** (of behavior) that cannot be excused. 변명의 여지가 없는; 구실이 안 되는. ¶ *~ behavior* 변명의 여지가 없는 행동. [in-[1]]

in·de·fin·a·ble [ìndifáinəbəl] *adj.* that cannot be difined or described. 정의를 내릴 수 없는; 분명히 나타낼 수 없는. ¶ *an ~ charm* 무어라 형언할 수 없는 매력. [in-[1]]

in·def·i·nite [indéfənit] *adj.* **1** (of modes of expression, ideas, etc.) not exact; not clearly defined. 뚜렷〔분명〕하지 않은. ¶ *an ~ answer* 분명치 않은 대답. **2** (of number, amount, etc.) not strictly limited. 한계가 없는. ¶ *An ~ number of people read Shakespeare.* 헤아릴 수 없이 많은 사람들이 세익스피어를 읽었다. **3** 《gram.》 not limiting or specifying. 부정(不定)의. ¶ *an ~ pronoun* 부정대명사 / *the ~ article* 부정관사. [in-[1], →definite]

in·def·i·nite·ly [indéfənitli] *adv.* in an indefinite manner. 한없이; 애매하게.

in·del·i·ble [indéləbəl] *adj.* **1** that cannot be rubbed out or cleaned. 지워지지 않는. ¶ *an ~ pencil* (지우개로) 지워지지 않는 연필. **2** (of non-material things) not to be done away with. 씻어버릴 수 없는. ¶ *~ shame* 〔*disgrace*〕 씻어버릴 수 없는 수치〔치욕〕. [in-[1], L. *deleo* blot out]

in·del·i·ca·cy [indélikəsi] *n.* (*pl.* **-cies**) **1** Ⓤ the state of being indelicate. 상스러움; 무례; 거칢. **2** Ⓒ an indelicate act or speech. 상스러운 언행. [in-[1]]

in·del·i·cate [indélikit] *adj.* not delicate; shameless. 상스러운; 버릇없는; 무례한.

in·dem·ni·fi·ca·tion [indèmnəfikéiʃən] *n.* ⓊⒸ indemnifying; being indemnified. 보상; 배상; 보장. [↓]

in·dem·ni·fy [indémnəfài] *vt.* (**-fied**) (P6,13) **1** 《*for*》 repay (someone) for loss or damage. …에게 (손해 등의) 배상을 하다. ¶ *He offered to ~ me for my loss of crops.* 그는 내게 농작물의 손실분을 변상하겠다고 했다. **2** give security against (future damage or loss). …을 보장하다. ¶ *~ someone from* 〔*against*〕 *loss* 아무에게 손실에 대한 보장을 해주다. **3** 《law》 give freedom from responsibility or penalty for. …의 책임〔처벌〕을 면제하다. ¶ *~ someone for an action* 어떤 행위에 대한 책임을 묻지 않기로 하다. [in[1]-. L. *damnum* loss, -by]

in·dem·ni·ty [indémnəti] *n.* (*pl.* **-ties**) **1** Ⓤ protection or insurance against loss or damage. 보상; 보장. **2** ⓊⒸ payment for loss or damage. 배상(금). **3** 《law》 exemption from penalty. 형벌의 면제.

in·dent [indént] *vt.* (P6) **1** give a toothlike line to (an edge, etc.). (가장자리를) 들쭉날쭉하게 하다. ¶ *an indented coastline* 들쭉날쭉한 해안선. **2** (in writing or printing) begin (a line) with one or more blank spaces. (패러그래프 첫 행의 시작)을 안으로 한두 자 들여 쓰다〔짜다〕. ¶ *The first word of a paragraph is usually indented.* 패러그래프의 첫자는 흔히 한두 자 들여 쓴다. **3** cut (a document drawn up in duplicate) in two along a zigzag line, so as to form an indenture. (한 장으로 된 두 통의 계약서 등을) 지그재그선〔절취선〕에 따라 자르다. **4** draw up in duplicate. (계약서 등을) 두 통 작성하다. [in-[2], L. *dens* tooth]

in·den·ta·tion [ìndentéiʃən] *n.* **1** Ⓤ the act of giving a toothlike edge to something. (가장자리를) 들쭉날쭉하게 하기. **2** Ⓒ toothlike line. 들쭉날쭉; 톱니 모양.

in·den·tion [indénʃən] *n.* **1** Ⓤ the act of beginning a line with a blank space. 행(行)의 첫자를 들여쓰기. **2** ⓊⒸ indentation. 들쭉날쭉하게 만들기.

in·den·ture [indéntʃər] *n.* Ⓒ **1** 《usu. *pl.*》 a written agreement between a learner of a trade and his master. 도제(徒弟)살이 계약서. ¶ *take up* 〔*be out of*〕 *one's indentures* 도제살이를 마치다. **2** any agree-

ment of which two copies are made. 정부(正副) 2통으로 만든 계약서. **3** the act of making a toothlike line. 톱니 자국을 냄.
— *vt.* (P6) bind (someone) by an indenture. (…의) 고용을 계약서로 약정하다.

:in·de·pend·ence [ìndipéndəns] *n.* Ⓤ the state of being free from the control, influence or support of others. 독립; 자립. [*indent*]

in·de·pend·en·cy [ìndipéndənsi] *n.* **1** Ⓤ independence. 독립. **2** Ⓒ an independent country. 독립국. [↓]

:in·de·pend·ent [ìndipéndənt] *adj.* **1** not under another's control; free from another's influence; not willing to accept help from others. 남의 지배를 받지 않는; 독립의; 독립심이 강한. ¶ *an* ~ *country* 독립국 / *a man of* ~ *mind* 자립심이 강한 사람 / ~ *work* 독자적인 일. **2** not dependent on others for one's living. 자활하는; 남의 신세를 안 지는. ¶ *He is* ~ *of his parents.* 그는 부모에게서 독립해 있다. **3** not needing to work for a living. 일하지 않고도 살 수 있는. ¶ *an* ~ *income* 편히 살 수 있는 수입. **4** voting according to one's own ideas. (투표할 때) 정당에 구애받지 않는. ¶ *an* ~ *voter* 무소속의 선거인[투표자]. **5** not in connection with any other or each other; separate. 관계가 없는; 별개의. ¶ ~ *research* 독자적인 연구.
— *n.* Ⓒ a person who exercises his own will or judgment, esp. in political matters. 독립한 사람; (정치적으로) 무소속인 사람. [in-[1], →dependent]

***in·de·pend·ent·ly** [ìndipéndəntli] *adv.* in an independent manner. 독립해서.

in·de·scrib·a·ble [ìndiskráibəbəl] *adj.* that cannot be described; beyond description. 형언할 수 없는; 필설로 못 다할. ¶ *a strange* ~ *feeling* 형언 할 수 없는 야릇한 느낌 / ~ *charm* 굉장한 매력. [in-[1]]

in·de·struct·i·ble [ìndistrʌ́ktəbəl] *adj.* that cannot be destroyed or broken up. 파괴할 수 없는; 불멸의. [in-[1]]

in·de·ter·mi·nate [ìnditə́ːrmənit] *adj.* **1** not determined; indefinite; vague. 미확정의; 애매한. **2** 《math.》 (of a quantity) not fixed in value. (양이) 부정(不定)한. [in-[1]]

***in·dex** [índeks] *n.* Ⓒ (*pl.* **-dex·es** or **-di·ces**) **1** a thing which points out or indicates; a sign. 가리키는 것; 지표. ¶ *Busy factories are an* ~ *of prosperity.* 공장들이 바쁜 것은 번영의 지표다. **2** an alphabetical list of names or subjects dealt with in a book. 찾아보기; 색인. **3** a pointer on an instrument for indicating measurement. (저울·계기 따위의) 지침(指針). **4** the forefinger. 집게손가락. **5** 《*fig.*》 a guide; a witness. 규준; 징표. ¶ *The face is an* ~ *to character.* 얼굴은 인격을 그대로 나타낸다 / *Style is an* ~ *of the mind.* 글은 마음의 거울이다. **6** 《math.》 an exponent. 지수(指數). ¶ 《econ.》 *an* ~ *number of prices* 물가 지수. **7** 《print.》 a mark used to call attention. 손가락표(☞).
— *vt.* (P6) **1** make an index for (a book). (책)에 색인을 붙이다. **2** enter (a word, etc.) in an index. (말 따위)를 색인에 넣다. [in-[2], L. *dic* point out)]

:In·di·a [índiə] *n.* a country in southern Asia. 인도. 參考 수도는 New Delhi.

:In·di·an [índiən] *n.* **1** Ⓒ a person living in America before the Europeans came; an American Indian. (아메리카) 인디언. **2** Ⓒ a person of India or the East Indies. 인도 사람; 동(東)인도 사람. **3** Ⓤ the language of the American Indians. 아메리카 인디언 말. — *adj.* of India or Indians. 인도의; 인도 사람의; 아메리카 인디언 말의. [→Hindu]

In·di·an·a [ìndiǽnə] *n.* a north central State of the United States. 인디애나 주(州). 參考 약어는 Ind. 주도는 Indianapolis.

Indian corn [ˊ-- ˊ] *n.* a kind of grain that grows on large ears; maize. 옥수수.

Indian file [ˊ-- ˋ] *n.* a single file; one behind the other. 일렬 종대. ¶ *walk in* ~ 일렬 종대로 걷다.

Indian summer [ˊ-- ˊ-] *n.* a period of pleasant, warm days in autumn. (늦가을의) 봄날 같은 화창한 날씨.

India paper [ˊ-- ˋ-] *n.* a thin, tough paper for printing. 인도지.

India(india) rubber [ˊ-- ˊ-] *n.* rubber, esp. in a small piece used for rubbing out pencil marks. 탄성 고무; 지우개.

***in·di·cate** [índikèit] *vt.* (P6,11) **1** ⓐ make known; point out; show. …을 가리키다; 지시하다. ¶ *The arrow indicates the way to the station.* 화살표는 역으로 가는 길을 가리킨다. ⓑ give a sign or hint of. …을 비추다; 암시하다. ¶ ~ *one's intentions* 자기의 의향을 비추다. **2** suggest the necessity of; require. …의 필요를 보이다; …을 필요로 하다. ¶ *Severe illness indicates drastic treatment.* 중증(重症)에는 과감한 요법이 필요하다. **3** be a sign of (something). …의 징후이다. ¶ *Fever indicates illness.* 열은 병의 징후이다. [→index]

in·di·ca·tion [ìndikéiʃən] *n.* **1** Ⓤ the act of indicating. 지시; 지적. **2** Ⓒ a thing which indicates; a sign. 지시한 것; 징후. ¶ *His manner is no* ~ *of his feelings.* 그의 태도가 그의 감정의 표현은 아니다.

in·dic·a·tive [indíkətiv] *adj.* **1** pointing out; showing; suggesting. 나타내는; 표시하는. ¶ *His action was* ~ *of his future intentions.* 그의 행동은 그의 장차의 의도를 말해주는 것이다. **2** 《gram.》 expressing an act, state, or occurrence as actual. 직설법의.
— *n.* 《gram.》 직설법.

in·di·ca·tor [índikèitər] *n.* Ⓒ **1** a person or thing that indicates. 지시자; 지시하는 것. **2** a needle on the dial of an instrument that measures something; a measuring instrument. 지침; 표시기.

in·di·ces [índisì:z] *n.* pl. of **index.**

in·dict [indáit] *vt.* (P6,13) 《*for, as*》 charge (someone) with an offence or crime. …을 고소〔고발〕하다. ¶ ~ *someone for* 〔*on a charge of*〕 *murder* 아무를 살인죄로 기소하다. [in-², →dictate]

in·dict·ment [indáitmənt] *n.* **1** Ⓤ the act of indicting; the state of being indicted; accusation. 기소; 고발. ¶ *bring in an* ~ *against someone* 아무를 기소하다. **2** Ⓒ 《law》 a formal written statement indicting someone. 기소장(起訴狀).

∗**in·dif·fer·ence** [indífərəns] *n.* Ⓤ **1** lack of interest or attention. 무관심. ¶ *The boy's* ~ *to his school-work was a trouble to his parents.* 공부에 대한 소년의 무관심은 부모의 걱정거리였다. **2** lack of importance. 중요치 않음; 사소함. ¶ *It is a matter of* ~. 그건 대단찮은 일이다. [↓]

∗**in·dif·fer·ent** [indífərənt] *adj.* **1** 《*to*》 having or showing no interest or concern. 무관심한. ¶ *be* ~ *to one's clothes* 복장에 무관심하다 / ~ *to pleasure* 〔*the suffering of others*〕 쾌락〔남의 고통〕에 무관심한. **2** not partial; fair; neutral. 공평한; 중립의. ¶ *He maintained an* ~ *attitude.* 그는 중립적 입장을 지켰다. **3** of no importance. 중요하지 않은. ¶ *Success and failure are alike* ~ *to me.* 성공과 실패는 내게는 대단한 것이 아니다. **4** not very good and not very bad; rather bad. 좋지도 나쁘지도 않은; 그저그런. ¶ *He is an* ~ *pianist.* 대단한 피아니스트는 아니다. **5** 《chem. electr.》 neutral. 중성의. [in-¹]

in·di·gence [índidʒəns] *n.* Ⓤ poverty. 빈곤; 가난. [*indigent*]

in·dig·e·nous [indídʒənəs] *adj.* 《*to*》 born or produced in a certain region or country; native. 그 땅에 고유한; 토착의. ¶ *Tigers are* ~ *to Asia.* 호랑이는 원래 아시아산(産)이다. [in-², L. *gen-* be born]

in·di·gent [índidʒənt] *adj.* very poor; living in want. 가난한. [in-². L. *egeo* want]

in·di·gest·i·ble [ìndidʒéstəbəl, -dai-] *adj.* **1** cannot be digested; hard to digest. 소화가 안 되는〔어려운〕. **2** 《*fig.*》 nearly impossible to be understood. 이해하기 어려운. ¶ *an* ~ *fact* 이해가 안 되는 사실. [in-¹]

in·di·ges·tion [ìndidʒéstʃən, -dai-] *n.* Ⓤ the state of being indigestible; difficulty in digesting; pain in the stomach caused by such a difficulty. 소화 불량.

in·dig·nant [indígnənt] *adj.* 《*about, at, over*》 angry at something unfair, unjust or mean. 성난; 분개한. ¶ *He is* ~ *at your dishonesty.* 그 사람은 네 부정직함에 노하고 있다. [in-¹, →deign]

∗**in·dig·na·tion** [ìndignéiʃən] *n.* Ⓤ anger at something unfair, unjust or mean. 분개; 분노.

in·dig·ni·ty [indígnəti] *n.* ⓊⒸ (*pl.* **-ties**) behavior or remark to a person damaging his pride; an insult. 모욕; 경멸. ¶ *be subjected to indignities.* 모욕을 당하다. [L. *indignus* unworthy]

in·di·go [índigòu] *n.* (*pl.* **-gos** or **-goes**) **1** Ⓤ deep blue color. 쪽《물감》; 남색; 인디고(=indigo blue). ¶ *an* ~ *sky* 파란 하늘. **2** Ⓒ a plant from which a blue coloringmatter is obtained. 쪽《식물》. [Gk. *Indikos* Indian]

∗**in·di·rect** [ìndirékt, -dai-] *adj.* **1** not direct; not straight. 곧지 않은. ¶ *an* ~ *route* 돌아가는 길; 우회로. **2** (of expression, etc.) not done by direct means. 에두른; 우회적인. ¶ *make an* ~ *reference to someone* 아무에게 에둘러 말하다 / *She gave an* ~ *answer to my question.* 그녀는 내 질문에 우회적으로 대답했다. **3** not directly connected. 간접적인. ¶ *an* ~ *effect* 간접적인 효과. [in-¹]

in·di·rec·tion [ìndirékʃən, -dai-] *n.* **1** indirect act, means, etc. 간접적인 행동〔방법〕. **2** dishonesty; deceit. 부정직; 사기.

in·di·rect·ly [ìndiréktli, -dai-] *adv.* in an indirect manner. 우회적으로; 간접적으로.

in·dis·creet [ìndiskrí:t] *adj.* not wise or cautious. 무분별한; 경솔한. ¶ *an* ~ *remark* 경솔한 말. [in-¹]

in·dis·creet·ly [ìndiskrí:tli] *adv.* in an indiscreet manner. 분별없이; 경솔하게.

in·dis·cre·tion [ìndiskréʃən] *n.* **1** Ⓤ the state or quality of being indiscreet. 무분별; 경솔. **2** Ⓒ an indiscreet or imprudent act. 무분별한 행동. [in-¹, →discretion]

in·dis·crim·i·nate [ìndiskrímənit] *adj.* not carefully choosing; without distinction; confused. 무차별의; 난잡한; 되는 대로의. ¶ *an* ~ *reader* 남독가(濫讀家) / *He is* ~ *in making friends.* 그는 아무하고나 사귄다 / ~ *blows* 난타. [in-¹]

∗**in·dis·pen·sa·ble** [ìndispénsəbəl] *adj.* **1** 《*for, to*》 absolutely necessary; essential. 필요 불가결의; 없어서는 안 될(opp. dispensable). ¶ *Water is* ~ *to life.* 물은 사는 데 불가결의 것이다 / *Your help is* ~ *to me.* 네 도움이 꼭 필요하다. **2** (of a law, duty, obligation, etc.) that cannot be set aside; unavoidable. (의무 등을) 소홀히 할 수 없는. [in-¹]

in·dis·pose [ìndispóuz] *vt.* (P6,13,20) **1** 《*for*》 make (someone) unwilling. …할 마음이 없게 만들다; …을 싫어지게 하다. ¶ *You are indisposed to make friends with someone who has been unkind to you.* 누구든 자기에게 불친절했던 사람과는 가까이하려 하지 않는다. **2** 《esp. *pp.*》 make (someone) slightly ill. 몸의 컨디션을 좀 나쁘게 하다. **3** 《*for*》 make (someone) unfit or unable. 부적당〔불가능〕하게 만들다. [in-¹]

in·dis·posed [ìndispóuzd] *adj.* **1** slightly ill. 몸이 찌뿌드드한; 기분이 안 좋은. ¶ *I am* ~

with cold. 감기 기운이 있다. **2** unwilling. 마음이 안 내키는; …할 마음이 없는. ¶ *He is ~ to help us.* 그는 우리를 도울 마음이 없다.

in·dis·po·si·tion [ìndispəzíʃən] *n.* **1** Ⓒ a slight illness. 가벼운 병; 찌뿌드드함. **2** Ⓤ unwillingness. 마음이 안 내킴; 싫어함. ¶ *a certain ~ to face the realities of life* 삶의 여러 사실들을 직시(直視)하지 않으려는 마음.

in·dis·put·a·ble [ìndispjú:təbəl] *adj.* that cannot be disputed or doubted; unquestionable. 논의의 여지가 없는; 명백한. ¶ *an ~ fact* 명백한 사실. [in-¹]

in·dis·sol·u·ble [ìndisáljəbəl / -sɔ́l-] *adj.* that cannot be dissolved or destroyed; firm. 분해〔파괴〕할 수 없는; 단단한; 영속하는. ¶ *an ~ friendship* 굳은 우정. [in-¹]

in·dis·tinct [ìndistíŋkt] *adj.* not clear; obscure; vague. 분명치 않은; 희미한. ¶ *an ~ roar from the distant ocean* 먼 바다에서 들려오는 희미한 파도 소리 / *an ~ recollection* 희미한 기억. [in-¹]

in·dis·tinct·ly [ìndistíŋktli] *adv.* in an indistinct manner. 애매하게; 희미하게.

in·dis·tin·guish·a·ble [ìndistíŋgwiʃəbəl] *adj.* that cannot be distinguished. 구분〔분간〕이 안 되는. [↑]

in·dite [indáit] *vt.* (P6) **1** put (something) in words; compose. (시문(詩文) 등을) 짓다; **2** 《usu. *joc.*》 express in writing; write (a letter, etc.). (편지 따위를) 쓰다. ¶ *~ a letter* 〔*a complaint*〕 편지를 쓰다〔불평을 적어 보내다〕. [→indict]

:**in·di·vid·u·al** [ìndəvídʒuəl] *n.* Ⓒ **1** 《*colloq.*》 a person. 사람. ¶ *an agreeable ~* 괜찮은 사람. **2** a single person, animal or thing. 개인; 개체. — *adj.* **1** particular; separate; single. 개개의; 단일의(opp. general). ¶ *each ~ person* 개개인. **2** of or belonging to one person or thing. 일개인의; 개인적인. **3** peculiar to one person or thing; characteristic. 독특한; 특유의; 고유의. [in-¹, →divide]

in·di·vid·u·al·ism [ìndəvídʒuəlìzəm] *n.* Ⓤ the doctrine that the right or welfare of an individual is more important than that of the group; egoism. 개인주의; 이기주의.

in·di·vid·u·al·ist [ìndəvídʒuəlist] *n.* Ⓒ a person who believes in or practices individualism. 개인주의자; 이기주의자.

in·di·vid·u·al·is·tic [ìndəvìdʒuəlístik] *adj.* of individualism or an individualist. 개인주의(자)의; 이기주의(자)의.

in·di·vid·u·al·i·ty [ìndəvìdʒuǽləti] *n.* (*pl.* **-ties**) **1** ⓊⒸ all the characteristics of a person or thing which makes him or it different from others. 개성. **2** Ⓤ the state or quality of being different or apart from others. 개인성(個人性); 개체성(個體性).

in·di·vid·u·al·ize [ìndəvídʒuəlàiz] *vt.* (P6) **1** make (people or things) different from others. …에 개성을 부여하다. ¶ *This school individualizes its course of study.* 이 학교는 그 교과 과정이 특이하다. **2** mark out as an individual; consider (someone or something) one by one. …을 개별화하다; …을 개별적으로 다루다.

in·di·vid·u·al·ly [ìndəvídʒuəli] *adv.* one by one; separately. 개별적으로; 낱낱이. ¶ *The pupils went ~ into their teacher's room.* 학생들은 제각기 선생님 방으로 들어갔다.

in·di·vis·i·bil·i·ty [ìndivìzəbíləti] *n.* Ⓤ the state of being indivisible. 분할할 수 없음. [↓]

in·di·vis·i·ble [ìndivízəbəl] *adj.* that cannot be divided. 분할할 수 없는; 불가분의. [in-¹, →divisible]

in·do·cile [indásil / -dɔ́sil] *adj.* not willing to be taught or trained; difficult to manage. 말을 듣지 않는; 다루기 힘든. [in-¹]

in·doc·tri·nate [indáktrənèit / -dɔ́k-] *vt.* (P6,13) 《*in, with*》 teach particular ideas or beliefs to (someone); cause (someone) to accept particular ideas or beliefs unquestioningly. (사상·교리 따위)를 가르치다〔주입하다〕. ¶ *~ someone with patriotism* 아무에게 애국심을 주입시키다. [in-², L. *doctrina* teaching]

In·do-Eu·ro·pe·an [índoujùərəpí:ən] *n. adj.* (of) the family of languages that includes most of the languages of Europe and Asia. 인도유럽어족(語族)(의). [*India*]

in·do·lence [índələns] *n.* Ⓤ the state or quality of being indolent; laziness; idleness. 나태; 게으름. [in-¹, L. *doleo* grieve]

in·do·lent [índələnt] *adj.* **1** not fond of work; lazy. 게으른. **2** 《med.》 not giving pain. 무통의. ¶ *an ~ abscess* 무통성 농양(膿瘍).

in·do·lent·ly [índələntli] *adv.* in an indolent manner. 게으르게.

in·dom·i·ta·ble [indámətəbəl] *adj.* that cannot be overcome; unconquerable. 굴복하지 않는; 불굴의. ¶ *an ~ will* 불굴의 의지. [in-¹, →daunt]

In·do·ne·sia [ìndouní:ʒə, -ʃə] *n.* a country composed of several islands in the East Indies. 인도네시아. 參考 수도는 Jakarta.

In·do·ne·sian [ìndouní:ʒən, -ʃən] *n.* **1** Ⓒ a person of Indonesia. 인도네시아 사람. **2** Ⓤ the language of Indonesia. 인도네시아어. — *adj.* of Indonesia or Indonesians. 인도네시아의; 인도네시아 사람〔어〕의.

in·door [índɔ̀:r] *adj.* of or done inside a building. 실내〔옥내〕의 (cf. *outside;* opp. outdoor). ¶ *~ games* 실내 경기 / *~ service* 내근(內勤). [→in]

***in·doors** [indɔ́:rz] *adv.* in or into a house or building. 실내〔옥내〕에서(opp. outdoors). ¶ *keep ~* 외출하지 않다.

in·dorse [indɔ́:rs] *vt.* =endorse.

in·dorse·ment [indɔ́:rsmənt] *n.* =endorsement.

in·du·bi·ta·ble [indjú:bətəbəl] *adj.* that cannot be doubted; unquestionable. 의심의 여지가 없는; 명백한. ¶ ~ *proof* 확실한 증거. ● **in·du·bi·ta·bly** [-i] *adv.* [in-¹, →dubitable]

∗**in·duce** [indjú:s] *vt.* **1** (P20) lead on; persuade. 설득〔권유〕하여 …하게 하다. ¶ *I induced father to take me to the theater.* 아버지를 설득해서 나를 극장에 데려가시도록 했다 / *Nothing shall ~ me to go.* 뭐라 하건 나는 안가겠다. **2** (P6) bring about; cause. …을 일으키다; 야기〔유발〕하다. ¶ *Overwork induces illness.* 과로하면 병이 난다 / *Some drugs ~ sleep.* 어떤 약은 잠이 오게 한다. **3** (P13) 《log.》 draw (a general conclusion or principle) from particular facts. 귀납적(歸納的)으로 추론하다. **4** (P6,13) 《electr.》 produce (an electric or magnetic effect) by induction. 유도하다. [in-², L. *duco* lead]

in·duce·ment [indjú:smənt] *n.* **1** Ⓤ the act of inducing. 유도; 권유. **2** Ⓒ a thing which influences or persuades a motive. 유인; 동기. ¶ *Praises are inducements for pupils to learn hard lesson.* 칭찬은 학생들이 열심히 공부하게 되는 자극이 된다.

in·duct [indʌ́kt] *vt.* (P13) **1** bring in; introduce. (자리 등에) …을 안내하다; …을 이끌어 들이다. ¶ ~ *someone into the seat of honor* 아무를 상좌에 이끌어 앉히다. **2** place (someone) in an office, etc. …을 취임시키다. ¶ *He was inducted into the office of the president of the university.* 그는 대학 총장에 취임했다. **3** 《U.S.》 make (someone) a member of the army; enlist. …을 입대시키다; 징집하다. [→induce]

in·duc·tion [indʌ́kʃən] *n.* ⓊⒸ **1** the act or ceremony of inaugurating someone into an office. 취임(식). **2** 《log.》 way of reasoning from many particular facts to one general law; a conclusion reached in this way. 귀납법; 귀납법에 의한 결론(opp. deduction). **3** 《electr.》 the process by which an object having electrical or magnetic property produces similar properties in a nearby object without direct contact. 유도(誘導). **4** the production of facts to support a conclusion. 전제(前提).

in·duc·tive [indʌ́ktiv] *adj.* **1** of induction. 귀납의; 귀납적인(opp. deductive). ¶ ~ *reasoning* 귀납적 추리. **2** 《electr.》 producing electric energy by induction. 유도성의.

∗**in·dulge** [indʌ́ldʒ] *vt.* (P6,13) **1** give way to the wishes of (someone); yield to; spoil. …을 제멋대로 하게 하다; 어하다. ¶ *The parents ~ their child too much.* 그 부모는 자식을 너무 제멋대로 하게 놔둔다. **2** give oneself up to (pleasures, desires, etc.). (환락·욕망 따위)에 빠지다〔열중하다〕. ¶ ~ *oneself in eating and drinking* 먹고 마시는 데에 골몰하다. **3** give pleasure to; favor. …을 기쁘게 하다. ¶ ~ *the company with a song* 한 곡조 불러 동료들을 즐겁게 하다.
— *vi.* (P1,3) **1** 《*in*》 ⓐ give way to one's pleasure; please oneself. 쾌락에 탐닉하다; 한껏 즐기다. ¶ ~ *in tobacco* 〔*golf*〕 담배〔골프〕를 너무 즐기다. ⓑ treat oneself to. 큰 마음 먹고 사다. ¶ ~ *in a new hat* 큰 마음 먹고새 모자를 하나 사다. **2** 《*colloq.*》 drink too much alcohol. 과음하다. ¶ *He indulges too much.* 술을 너무 많이 마신다. [L. *indulgeo*]

in·dul·gence [indʌ́ldʒəns] *n.* **1** Ⓤ the act of indulging. 멋대로 함; 탐닉; 방종. ¶ *Too much ~ in sweets is bad for health.* 단것을 너무 즐기면 건강에 나쁘다. **2** Ⓒ a thing indulged in. 도락; 악습. ¶ *Smoking was his only ~.* 담배는 유일한 그의 도락〔악습〕이었다. **3** ⓊⒸ 《Cath.》 freedom given by a priest from punishment for sin. 면죄(免罪).

in·dul·gent [indʌ́ldʒənt] *adj.* too kind; not critical. 관대한; 멋대로 하게 하는. ¶ *The ~ mother bought her boy everything he wanted.* 지나치게 너그러운 그 어머니는 아들이 원하면 무엇이건 사줬다.

in·du·rate [índjurèit] *vt., vi.* (P6; 1) **1** make or become hard. 굳히다; 굳다. **2** become inveterate. 완고해지다. [in-², L. *durus* hard]

∶**in·dus·tri·al** [indʌ́striəl] *adj.* of industry. 산업의; 공업의. ¶ ~ *workers* 산업 근로자; 공원 / *an ~ school* 실업〔공업〕 학교. — *n.* a person engaged in industry. (산업) 근로자. [L. *industria*]

in·dus·tri·al·ism [indʌ́striəlìzəm] *n.* Ⓤ the system or principle of social and economic organization characterized by large industries. 산업〔공업〕 제도; 산업주의.

in·dus·tri·al·ist [indʌ́striəlist] *n.* Ⓒ a person who owns or nas an important position in an industrial enterprise. 실업가.

in·dus·tri·al·ize [indʌ́striəlàiz] *vt.* (P6) make (something) industrial. 산업〔공업〕화하다.

∗**in·dus·tri·ous** [indʌ́striəs] *adj.* hard-working; diligent. 근면한. ¶ *an ~ wife* 부지런한 아내.

∶**in·dus·try** [índəstri] *n.* (*pl.* **-tries**) **1** Ⓤ steady effort; hard work; diligence. 근면. ¶ *admire his ~* 그의 근면함을 칭찬하다. **2** ⓊⒸ any form of business, trade, or manufacture; the act of manufacturing goods. 산업; 공업. ¶ *the steel ~* 제강업 / *the shipping ~* 해운업. [L. *industria* diligence]

in·e·bri·ate [iní:brièit] *vt.* (P6) **1** make (someone) drunk; intoxicate. (아무를) 취하게 하다. **2** 《*fig.*》 stir strongly with excitement. (자극·흥분 따위로) 도취하게〔어쩔 줄 모르게〕 하다. ¶ *inebriated by success* 성공에 도취된. —[iní:briət] *adj.* drunk; intoxicated. 술에 취한. —[iní:briət] *n.* Ⓒ a habitual drunkard. 주정뱅이. [in-², L. *ebrius* drunk]

in·e·bri·e·ty [ìnibráiəti] *n.* Ⓤ the state of being drunken; drunkenness. 술에 취함; 명정(酩酊).

in·ed·i·ble [inédəbəl] *adj.* not fit to be eaten. 먹지 못하는; 못 먹는. ¶ *an ~ mushroom* 독버섯. [in-¹]

in·ef·fa·ble [inéfəbəl] *adj.* that cannot be expressed in words; beyond description. 이루 말할 수 없는; 말로 표현할 수 없는. ¶ *the ~ beauty of a sunset* 형언할 수 없이 아름다운 해넘이의 장관. [in-¹, ex-, L. *for* speak]

in·ef·fec·tive [ìniféktiv] *adj.* **1** of little use; not effective. 쓸모없는; 무익한. **2** (of a person) incompetent. 무능한. ¶ *an ~ teacher.* [in-¹]

in·ef·fec·tu·al [ìniféktʃuəl] *adj.* without the wanted effect; unsuccessful; useless. 효과가 없는; 실패한; 쓸모없는. ¶ *All his efforts were ~.* 그의 모든 노력은 물거품이었다. [in-¹]

in·ef·fi·cien·cy [ìnifíʃənsi] *n.* Ⓤ the state of being inefficient; inability. 무효; 쓸모없음. [↓]

in·ef·fi·cient [ìnifíʃənt] *adj.* **1** not able to get things done well. 효과없는; 쓸모없는. ¶ *~ labor* 쓸모없는 노력. **2** requiring unnecessary time, energy, etc.; not efficient. 비능률적인; 효율이 낮은. ¶ *an ~ method of production* 비능률적인 생산 방식. **3** (of a person) not skilled. 무능한. ¶ *an ~ workman* 비숙련공. [in-¹, →efficient]

in·el·e·gance [inéləgəns] *n.* **1** Ⓤ the state or quality of being not elegant. 우아하지 못함; 멋이 없음. **2** Ⓒ an inelegant thing. 우아하지 못한 것. [↓]

in·el·e·gant [inéləgənt] *adj.* not in good taste; not elegant; vulgar; crude. 우아하지 못한; 운치가 없는. [in-¹]

in·el·i·gi·ble [inélidʒəbəl] *adj.* 《*for*》 unsuitable; unfit. 자격이 없는; 부적당한. ¶ *A lame man is ~ for an army.* 불구자는 군대에 못간다. —*n.* an ineligible person. 부적격자. [in-¹]

in·ept [inépt] *adj.* **1** not suitable; out of place. 부적당한. **2** absurd; foolish. 어리석은. ¶ *a very ~ remark* 바보같은 소리. [L. *ineptus* (in-¹, → apt)]

in·ept·i·tude [inéptətjù:d] *n.* **1** Ⓤ foolishness. 어리석음; 우매함. **2** Ⓒ a foolish act or speech. 어리석은 언행. ¶ *a speech full of ineptitudes* 도무지 말 같잖은 말.

in·e·qual·i·ty [ìnikwáləti / -kwɔ́l-] *n.* (*pl.* **-ties**) **1** Ⓤ the state of being not equal. 같지 않음; 부동. **2** Ⓤ the state or quality of not being even, regular or uniform. 불균형; 불평등. **3** Ⓒ an example of not being equal, even, etc. 불평등한 것. **4** Ⓒ (of a surface) roughness; irregularity. 우툴두툴함. ¶ *inequalities of the ground* 지면의 기복. [in-¹]

in·eq·ui·ta·ble [inékwətəbəl] *adj.* unfair; unjust. 불공정한; 불공평한. [in-¹]

in·eq·ui·ty [inékwəti] *n.* ⓊⒸ (*pl.* **-ties**) the state or quality of being inequitable; unfairness; injustice. 불공평; 불공정.

in·er·ad·i·ca·ble [ìnirǽdikəbəl] *adj.* 《chiefly *fig.*》 that cannot be rooted out; fixed firmly and deeply; deeply rooted. 근절하기 어려운; 뿌리 깊은. ¶ *~ habits* 〔*hatred*〕 고치기 어려운 습관〔뿌리 깊은 증오〕. [in-¹]

in·ert [inə́:rt] *adj.* **1** 《phys.》 having no power to act or move. 스스로 움직이지 못하는; 활동력이 없는. **2** heavy and dull in mind or body. 굼뜬; 느린. **3** 《chem.》 having no active chemical powers. 화학작용을 일으키지 않는; 비활성의. ¶ *an ~ gas* 비활성 기체. [L. *iners* (in-¹, →art)]

in·er·tia [inə́:rʃiə] *n.* Ⓤ **1** the state of not being willing to move or change. 움직이지〔변하지〕 않으려 함; 불활발. **2** 《phys.》 the force which prevents a thing from being moved when it is still, and keeps it moving when it is moving. 관성(慣性); 타성(惰性). [↑]

in·es·cap·a·ble [ìneskéipəbəl] *adj.* that cannot be escaped or avoided. 피할 수 없는; 벗어날 수 없는. [in-¹]

in·es·sen·tial [ìnisénʃəl] *a.* not essential. 긴요〔중요〕하지 않은. [in-¹]

in·es·ti·ma·ble [inéstəməbəl] *adj.* too great, valuable, etc. to be measured. 잴 수 없는; 평가할 수 없는. ¶ *of ~ value* 더없이 귀중한 / *~ magnitude* 엄청난 크기. [in-¹]

***in·ev·i·ta·ble** [inévitəbəl] *adj.* **1** not avoidable; certain. 피할 수 없는; 필연적인. ¶ *the ~* 필연적인 것 / *Death is ~.* 죽음은 피할 수 없다 / *the ~ hour* 사기(死期). **2** 《*colloq.*》 so frequently seen, heard, etc., that it is familiar and expected. 늘 …해서 이상할 것 없는; (흔히 듣거나 볼 수 있는) 예(例)의. ¶ *an Englishman with his ~ umbrella* 예의 그 우산을 든 영국인. [in-¹, e-, L. *vito* avoid]

in·ex·act [ìnigzǽkt] *adj.* no exact; not accurate. 부정확한. [in-¹]

in·ex·cus·a·ble [ìnikskjú:zəbəl] *adj.* that cannot be excused or justified; unjustifiable. 변명이 안 되는; 용납 못할. ¶ *~ conduct* 용서 못할 짓. [in-¹]

in·ex·haust·i·ble [ìnigzɔ́:stəbəl] *adj.* **1** that cannot be used up; very abundant. 무진장한. ¶ *an ~ supply of water* 무진장한 물의 공급. **2** tireless. 지칠 줄 모르는. ¶ *an ~ boxer* 지칠줄 모르는 권투 선수. [in-¹]

in·ex·o·ra·ble [inéksərəbəl] *adj.* that cannot be moved or influenced by prayers or entreaties; relentless; inflexible. 무정한; 냉혹한; 용서 없는. ¶ *an ~ enemy* 냉혹한 적 / *the ~ laws of nature* 냉엄한 자연의 법칙.

[in-¹, ex-, L. *oro* pray]

in·ex·o·ra·bly [inéksərəbli] *adv.* in an inexorable manner. 냉혹히; 무정하게.

in·ex·pe·di·ent [ìnikspíːdiənt] *adj.* not suitable or wise; not expedient. 부적당한; 좋은 방법이 아닌. ¶ *It would be ~ to increase taxes now.* 지금 세금을 올린다는 것은 현명하지 못하다. [in-¹]

in·ex·pen·sive [ìnikspénsiv] *adj.* costing little; not expensive; cheap. 싸게 먹히는; 비용이 들지 않는; (값이) 싼. [in-¹]

in·ex·pe·ri·ence [ìnikspíəriəns] *n.* Ⓤ the state of being not experienced; lack of experience or practice. 미숙; 무경험. [in-¹]

in·ex·pe·ri·enced [ìnikspíəriənst] *adj.* lacking in knowledge or skill gained from experience or practice; not experienced. 경험이 없는; 미숙한. ¶ *an ~ young salesman* 경험이 없는 젊은 판매원.

in·ex·pert [inékspəːrt, ìnikspə́ːrt] *adj.* not expert; unskilled; clumsy. 미숙한; 서투른. [in-¹]

in·ex·pi·a·ble [inékspiəbəl] *adj.* **1** (of a wrong act) that cannot be paid for. 보상할 수 없는. ¶ *an ~ sin* 속죄 못할 죄. **2** 《*obs.*》 that cannot be appeased. 달랠 수 없는; 누를 길 없는. ¶ *~ hatred* 심한 혐오. [in-¹]

in·ex·pli·ca·ble [inéksplikəbəl, ìniksplík-] *adj.* that cannot be explained or understood; beyond understanding. 설명할 수 없는; 불가해한. ¶ *an ~ mystery* 불가해한 신비. [in-¹]

in·ex·press·i·ble [ìniksprésəbəl] *adj.* that cannot be put into words; beyond expression. 형언할 수 없는. ¶ *~ joy* 말할 수 없는 기쁨. [in-¹]

in·ex·pres·sive [ìniksprésiv] *adj.* lacking in expression; not expressive. 무표정한; 무감동한.

in·ex·tin·guish·a·ble [ìnikstíŋgwiʃəbəl] *adj.* that cannot be put out or stopped. 끌 수 없는; 누를 길 없는. ¶ *~ laughter* 〔*rage*〕 참을 수 없는 웃음〔분노〕. [in-¹]

in·ex·tri·ca·ble [inékstrikəbəl] *adj.* **1** that cannot be gotten free from; that cannot be solved. 헤어날 수 없는; 풀 수 없는; 해결이 안되는. ¶ *~ confusion* 〔*difficulties*〕 어찌 할 수 없는 혼란〔어려움〕. [in-¹]

in·fal·li·bil·i·ty [infæ̀ləbíləti] *n.* Ⓤ the state or quality of being infallible. 절대 확실; 과오가 없음; 무과실성. ¶ *the ~ of the Pope* 교황의 무류성(無謬性). [in-¹]

in·fal·li·ble [infǽləbəl] *adj.* **1** that cannot be mistaken; free from error; absolutely sure. 틀림이 없는; 결코 잘못이 없는; 아주 확실한. ¶ *In some things he is quite ~.* 어떤 점에서 그는 틀림 없는 사람이다 / *an ~ rule* 절대로 확실한 법칙. **2** occurring without fail; always occurring under the given circumstances. 필연적인; 피할 수 없는. ¶ *The ~ result of such conduct will be....* 그런 행위로 인한 필연적인 결과는….

in·fa·mous [ínfəməs] *adj.* **1** having a bad reputation. 악명 높은. ¶ *a name ~ in history* 역사에 남은 악명. **2** shameful; very evil. 수치스러운; 파렴치한. ¶ *an ~ crime* 파렴치죄. **3** very bad of it's kind. 최하의; 열등한. ¶ *an ~ pen* 〔*dinner*〕 형편 없는 만년필〔식사〕. [in-¹, →famous]

in·fa·my [ínfəmi] *n.* (*pl.* **-mies**) **1** Ⓤ bad reputation; dishonor. 악명; 불명예. **2** Ⓤ wickedness. 사악; 부도덕. **3** Ⓒ an infamous act. 비행. [↑]

***in·fan·cy** [ínfənsi] *n.* Ⓤ **1** the state or time of being an infant; early childhood; babyhood. 유소(幼少); 유년(幼年); 어린 시절. **2** the early stage of development. 초기; 초보. ¶ *Eighty years ago the airplane was still in its ~.* 팔십년 전 비행기는 아직 그 요람기였다. **3** 《law》 minority. 미성년. [→infant, -cy]

***in·fant** [ínfənt] *n.* Ⓒ **1** a very young child; a baby. 어린아이; 유아. **2** 《law》 a person who has not yet reached the legal age of majority; a minor. 미성년자. — *adj.* **1** of or for a child; very small or young. 유아(용)의. ¶ *~ food* 유아식. **2** in an early stage. 초기〔초보〕의. [in-¹, L. *for* speak]

in·fan·ti·cide [infǽntəsàid] *n.* **1** Ⓤ the act of killing a baby. 유아 살해. **2** Ⓒ a person who kills a baby. 유아 살해범. [→infant, L. *caedo* kill]

in·fan·tile [ínfəntàil, -til] *adj.* **1** of an infant or infants. 유아의. ¶ *~ diseases* 유아병 / *~ paralysis* 소아 마비. **2** like an infant; babyish. 어린아이 같은. ¶ *~ behavior* 어린애 같은 행동. **3** in an early stage. 초기의. ¶ *an ~ stream* 유년기의 강. [→infant]

in·fan·tine [ínfəntàin, -tìːn] *adj.* infantile; childish. 유아의; 어린이 같은.

in·fan·try [ínfəntri] *n.* 《*collectively*》 foot-soldiers. 보병(cf. *cavalry*). ¶ *mounted ~* 기마 보병. [It. *infante* youth, foot-soldier]

in·fan·try·man [ínfəntrimən] *n.* Ⓒ (*pl.* **-men** [-mən]) a soldier who fights on foot. 보병.

in·fat·u·ate [infǽtʃuèit] *vt.* (P6,13) **1** deprive of sound judgment; fill with blind love; make foolish. 이성을 잃게 하다; 얼이 나가게 하다. **2** arouse a foolish or extreme passion in (someone). (아무에게) 열중하게〔혹하게〕 만들다. [in-², →fatuous]

in·fat·u·at·ed [infǽtʃuèitid] *adj.* showing a foolish fondness. 얼이 나간; 열중해 있는. ¶ *She is ~ with her own beauty.* 그녀는 자신의 아름다움에 취해 있다.

in·fat·u·a·tion [infæ̀tʃuéiʃən] *n.* Ⓤ the state of being infatuated. 열중해 있음; 심취.

***in·fect** [infékt] *vt.* (P6,13) **1** pass on a disease to (someone). …에 병을 옮기다. ¶ *an infected area* 감염 지구 / *~ water with cholera* 콜레라로 물을 오염시키다. **2** affect; influence. …에 영향을 미치다; 감화

시키다. ¶ *His courage* [*fear*] *infected us all.* 그의 용기[공포]가 우리 모두에게 영향을 주었다. **3** 《*fig.*》 affect by example; influence, esp. in a bad way. 나쁜 영향을 주다. ¶ *One bad boy may ~ a whole class.* 나쁜 아이 하나가 온 반을 버려 놓을 수도 있다. [in-², L. *focio* make]

in·fec·tion [infékʃən] *n.* Ⓤ **1** the act of causing disease by the introduction of germs. 전염; 감염. **2** 《*fig.*》 influence spreading from one person to another. (좋지 않은) 영향; 감화. ¶ *the ~ of another's belief* [*excitement*] 다른 사람으로부터의 신념[흥분]의 파급. **3** Ⓒ a disease caused by germs. 전염병(cf. *contagion*). ¶ *Cholera is an ~.* 콜레라는 전염병이다.

in·fec·tious [infékʃəs] *adj.* **1** caused or spread by infection. 전염하는; 전염병의. ¶ *an ~ disease* 전염병. **2** 《*fig.*》 tending to spread to others. 퍼지기 쉬운; 옮기 쉬운. ¶ *Laughter is ~.* 웃음은 옮아간다 / *Habits are ~.* 버릇은 남에게 전염된다.

in·fe·lic·i·tous [ìnfəlísitəs] *adj.* **1** unhappy. 불행한. **2** (of style, speech, etc.) unsuitable. 어울리지 않는; 부적당한. ¶ *an ~ answer* 동문 서답. [in-¹]

in·fer [infə́ːr] *vt., vi.* (**-ferred, -fer·ring**) **1** (P6,11,13,21; 1) reach an idea or conclude by reasoning; conclude (something) from what has been known. 추정[추리, 추론]하다; (결론을) 내다. ¶ *This evidence led him to ~ that we were to blame.* 이 증거로 그는 잘못이 우리에게 있다고 추정했다. **2** indicate; imply; lead to as a conclusion. 의미[암시]하다; (결론으로서) 나타내다. ¶ *Silence often infers consent.* 침묵은 종종 동의의 표시가 된다. [in-², L. *fero* bring]

in·fer·a·ble [infə́ːrəbəl] *adj.* that can be inferred. 추론할 수 있는.

in·fer·ence [ínfərəns] *n.* **1** Ⓤ the act or process of inferring. 추론; 추리. **2** Ⓒ a thing which is inferred; a deduction. 결론. ¶ *What ~ do you draw from these facts?* 이들 사실에서 너는 어떤 결론을 내리겠느냐.

***in·fe·ri·or** [infíəriər] *adj.* (opp. superior) **1** 《*to*》 lower in rank, importance, value, etc. 하급의; …보다 못한. ¶ *A major is ~ to a colonel.* 소령은 대령보다 하위 계급이다. **2** lower or poor in quality; second-rate. (품질이) 못한; 열등한; 떨어지는. ¶ *Foreign mutton is ~ to home-grown in flavor.* 수입 양고기는 국내 것보다 맛이 못하다 / *This wine is very ~ stuff.* 이 포도주는 질이 형편없다. **3** at a lower level in space; beneath. (위치가) 아래의; 밑의. ¶ *the ~ half* [*part*] 하반부[하부]. **4** of low or humble rank. 신분이 낮은. ¶ *the ~ classes* 하층 계급.

— *n.* Ⓒ a person who is lower in rank. 아랫사람; 하급자. ¶ *Be polite to your inferiors.* 아랫사람들을 공손하게 대하여라. [L. *inferus* low]

in·fe·ri·or·i·ty [infìərió(ː)rəti, -ár-] *n.* Ⓤ the state or quality of being below others in rank, quality, importance, etc. 하급; 하위; 열등(opp. superiority).

inferiority complex [-ˊ-ˊ--- ˋ-] *n.* an abnormal feeling of being inferior to others. 열등감.

in·fer·nal [infə́ːrnl] *adj.* **1** of lower world; of hell. 지옥의. ¶ *the ~ region* 하계(下界); 지옥. **2** not human; devilish. 악마 같은. ¶ *The conqueror showed ~ cruelty.* 정복자는 악마같은 잔인성을 보였다. [L. *infernus* underground]

in·fer·no [infə́ːrnou] *n.* Ⓒ (*pl.* **-nos**) **1** hell. 지옥. **2** 《*the I-*》 the first part of Dante's 'Divina Commedia'. 지옥편《단테작(作) '신곡(神曲)'의 제 1부》. **3** a hell-like place or thing. 지옥 같은 곳[것]. ¶ *The burning building became an ~.* 불타는 건물은 지옥을 방불케 했다. [↑]

in·fest [infést] *vt.* (P6,13) (of something harmful) be numerous in (some place). (해충 따위가) …에 들끓다. ¶ *a house infested with rats* 쥐가 들끓는 집. [L. *imfestus* hostile]

in·fi·del [ínfədl] *n.* Ⓒ **1** a person who does not believe in any religion. 무종교자; 무신론자. **2** (of a certain religion) a person who does not believe in the religion. 이교도. ¶ *Mohammedans call Christians infidels.* 회교도는 기독교도를 이교도라 부른다. — *adj.* of an infidel; not believing in religion. 무신론자[이교도]의. [in-¹, L. *fides* faith]

in·fi·del·i·ty [ìnfidéləti] *n.* ⓊⒸ (*pl.* **-ties**) **1** disbelief in religion, esp. in the Christian religion. 신앙이 없음; 기독교를 믿지 않음. **2** unfaithful or disloyal action; unfaithfulness. 불신 (행위); 불성실. [↑]

in·field [ínfiːld] *n.* Ⓒ **1** a baseball diamond. 내야(內野). **2** 《*collectively*》 (in baseball) the infield players. 내야수(cf. *outfield*). **3** the part of a farm nearest the farmhouse. (농가 부근의) 밭; 텃밭. [*in, field*]

in·fil·trate [infíltreit, ˊ-ˋ] *vt., vi.* (P6,13; 1,3) **1** pass or cause (water, etc.) to pass through or into the earth, etc. (물 따위를) 스며들게 하다; 스며들다. ¶ *Water infiltrates sand.* 물은 모래 땅에 스며든다. **2** (of ideas) get into people's minds. (사상 따위가) 침투되다; 감화하다. [in-²]

in·fil·tra·tion [ìnfiltréiʃən] *n.* **1** Ⓤ the act of infiltrating; the state of being infiltrated. 스며듦; 침투. **2** Ⓒ a thing which infiltrates. 스며든 것; 침투물.

***in·fi·nite** [ínfənit] *adj.* **1** without limits; endless. 무한한. ¶ *an ~ space* 무한한 공간 / *~ kindness* [*gratitude*] 한없는 친절[고마움]. **2** extremely great; vast; numerous. 막대한; 무수한. ¶ *~ cases* [*examples*] 허다한 경우[사례]. **3** 《gram.》 not limited by person or number. 부정(不定)의. — *n.* **1** that which is infinite. 무한(한 것). **2** ⓐ 《*the I-*》 God. 조물주(造物主); 신(神). ⓑ 《*the* ～》 infinite space. 무한한 공간. [in-¹, L. *finitus* finite]

in·fi·nite·ly [ínfənitli] *adv.* to an infinite degree. 무한히; 끝없이.

in·fi·ni·tes·i·mal [infìnitésəməl] *adj.* too small to be measured. 극소의; 극미의. — *n.* an infinitesimal amount. 극미〔극소〕량. [↑]

:in·fin·i·tive [infínətiv] *n.* Ⓒ 《gram.》 a form of a verb not limited by person, number, or tense. 부정사(不定詞). ¶ *a split* ～ 분리 부정사. — *adj.* belonging to or formed with the infinitive. 부정사의. ¶ *an* ～ *phrase* 부정사구. [↑]

in·fin·i·tude [infínətjù:d] *n.* **1** Ⓤ the state of being infinite. 무한. **2** Ⓒ an infinite number or extent. 무한량; 무수. ¶ *an* ～ *of stars* 무수한 별들. [↓]

in·fin·i·ty [infínəti] *n.* (*pl.* **-ties**) **1** Ⓤ the state of being infinite; beyond measure in time, number, space, or distance. 무한(無限). ¶ *the* ～ *of God's power* 신의 (능력의) 무궁성(無窮性). **2** Ⓒ an infinite extent, number, amount, quantity, etc. 무한한 수〔양〕. **3** 《math.》 an infinite quantity. 무한대. [→infinite]

in·firm [infə́:rm] *adj.* **1** not strong; weak. 약한; 허약한. ¶ *She was old and* ～. 그녀는 늙고 기력도 없었다 / *an* ～ *gait* 맥없는 걸음걸이. **2** weak in mind or will. 의지가 약한. ¶ *be* ～ *of purpose* 의지가 약하다. [in-¹]

in·fir·ma·ry [infə́:rməri] *n.* Ⓒ (*pl.* **-ries**) a place or room for sick or injured people; a hospital in a school, etc. 진료소〔실〕; 양호실.

in·fir·mi·ty [infə́:rməti] *n.* ⓊⒸ **1** (*pl.* **-ties**) the state or quality of being weak. 허약. **2** a disease. 병; 질병. **3** weakness of character. 심약(心弱); 약점. ¶ *infirmities of purpose* 의지 박약.

***in·flame** [infléim] *vt.* (P6) **1** set (something) on fire. …에 불을 붙이다. **2** 《*fig.*》 arouse passion, desire, etc. in (someone). …를 흥분시키다. ¶ *His speech inflamed the crowd's anger.* 그의 연설은 군중들을 분격하게 했다. **3** stir up (passion, desire, etc.). …을 선동하다; 자극하다. **4** make (someone) hot, red or swollen. …을 달아〔부어〕오르게 하다; 충혈시키다. ¶ *The smoke inflamed my eyes.* 연기로 눈이 충혈되었다. — *vi.* (P1) **1** catch fire. 불이 붙다. **2** 《*fig.*》 become excited. 흥분하다. **3** become hot, red or swollen. 달아〔부어〕오르다; 충혈되다. [in-²]

in·flam·ma·ble [inflǽməbəl] *adj.* **1** easily set on fire. 타기 쉬운; 가연성의. **2** 《*fig.*》 easily aroused or excited. 흥분하기 쉬운. ¶ *an* ～ *temper* 걸핏하면 흥분하는 성미. — *n.* an inflammable substance. 가연성 물질.

in·flam·ma·tion [ìnfləméiʃən] *n.* **1** Ⓤ the act of inflaming; the state of being inflamed. 점화; 연소. **2** ⓊⒸ the condition of any part of the body marked by heat, redness, swelling or pain; such a part. 염증; 염증이 난 데. ¶ ～ *of the lung* 폐렴.

in·flam·ma·to·ry [inflǽmətɔ̀:ri] *adj.* **1** tending to excite or anger. 선동적〔자극적〕인. ¶ *an* ～ *speech* 선동적인 연설. **2** 《med.》 of or causing inflammation. 염증의〔을 일으키는〕.

in·flate [infléit] *vt.* **1** (P6,13) swell (a balloon or tire) with gas or air. …을 공기나 가스로 부풀리다. **2** (P6) 《*fig.*》 cause (someone) to be proud. …을 우쭐하게 만들다. ¶ ～ *someone with pride* 아무를 우쭐거리게 하다. **3** (P6) 《econ.》 increase (prices or the currency) beyond the normal amount or level. (물가를) 올리다; (통화를) 팽창시키다 (opp. deflate). — *vi.* become inflated. 부풀다; (통화가) 팽창하다. [in-¹, L. *flo* blow]

in·flat·ed [infléitid] *a.* **1** distended with air or gas; swollen. (공기 따위로) 부푼; 팽창한. ¶ ～ *ballon* 부푼 풍선. **2** puffed up, as with pride. 우쭐해진. ¶ *an* ～ *conception of one's own talents* 자신은 재능이 있다고 우쭐해하는 생각. **3** turgid or bombastic. 과장된. ¶ ～ *style* 과장된 문체 / ～ *language* 호언장담. **4** 《econ.》 unduly expanded in amount, value, or size; characterized by inflation. (통화가) 팽창된; 폭등한. ¶ ～ *currency* 팽창통화.

in·fla·tion [infléiʃən] *n.* Ⓤ **1** the act of swelling; the state of being swollen. 부풀리기; 부품; 팽창. **2** 《econ.》 the increase in the currency of a country caused by issuing too much paper money or by a sudden increase in prices. 통화 팽창(opp. deflation).

in·flect [inflékt] *vt.* (P6) **1** ⓐ change the pitch or tone of (the voice). (목소리의) 가락을 바꾸다; …에 억양을 붙이다. ⓑ 《mus.》 flatten or sharpen. 반음을 낮추다〔높이다〕. **2** 《gram.》 vary the form of (a word) to show case, number, person, tense, mood, etc. 어형을 변화시키다. **3** bend. …을 구부리다. [in-², L. *flecto* bend]

in·flec·tion [inflékʃən] *n.* **1** Ⓤ change in the pitch or tone of the voice; intonation. (목소리의) 억양. **2** Ⓤ 《gram.》 a variation in the form of a word. 어형 변화; 활용. **3** Ⓒ an inflected form of a word. 변화형; 활용형. **4** Ⓤ the act of bending; the state of being bent. 굴절; 굴곡; 만곡.

in·flex·i·ble [infléksəbəl] *adj.* (opp. flexible) **1** that cannot be bent; stiff. 구부러지지〔굽지〕 않는; 경직된. **2** that cannot be changed; unyielding. 변경할 수 없는; 불굴의. ¶ ～ *courage* 〔*determination*〕 굴하지 않는 용기〔결심〕. [in-¹, →flexible]

in·flex·i·bly [infléksəbli] *adv.* in an inflexible manner. 굽히지 않고.

in·flex·ion [inflékʃən] *n.* 《Brit.》 =inflection.

***in·flict** [inflíkt] *vt.* (P6,13) **1** give or

cause (a wound, pain, etc.). (벌·고통 등)을 주다. ¶ ~ *pain* (*upon*) *someone* 아무에게 고통을 주다. **2** put on or impose (a punishment or anything unwelcome) on someone. (벌금·처벌 등)을 과하다; 부담시키다. ¶ *The teacher inflicts punishment upon lazy pupils.* 선생은 게으른 학생을 처벌한다 / *He inflicts himself on his parents.* 그는 부모에게 누를 끼치고 있다. [in-², L. *fligo* dash]

in·flic·tion [inflíkʃən] *n.* **1** Ⓤ the act of inflicting. (벌·고통 따위를) 과(가)함. ¶ *the ~ of damage on a city by a typhoon* 태풍에 의한 도시의 피해. **2** Ⓒ a thing which is inflicted; suffering; a punishment. 고통; 벌; 폐. ¶ ~ *from God* 천벌.

in·flow [ínflòu] *n.* (opp. outflow) **1** Ⓤ the act of flowing in. 유입(流入). ¶ *The discovery of gold in California caused a great ~ of people.* 캘리포니아에서의 금의 발견으로 엄청난 사람이 몰려들었다. **2** Ⓒ something which flows in. 유입물. [in-²]

:in·flu·ence [ínfluəns] *n.* **1** ⓊⒸ an effect or the result of the use of power or an action toward a person or thing. 영향; 효과; 감화(력). ¶ *the Eastern ~ on the West* 서양에 대한 동양인의 영향 / *under the ~ of alcohol* 술김에 / *Tides are caused by the ~ of the moon and sun.* 조수의 간만은 달과 태양의 작용에 의한다 / *feel the ~ of the music* 음악에 감동하다. **2** Ⓤ the power that comes from wealth, social position, force of character, etc. 영향력; 권위; 세력; 설득력. ¶ *a man of ~* 영향력 있는 사람 / *He exercised his ~ to settle the matter.* 그는 일을 수습함에 있어 영향력을 행사했다 / *The teacher has no ~ over his pupils.* 그 선생은 학생들에게 권위가 없다. **3** Ⓒ a person or thing that has such power. 유력한 사람(것). ¶ *He is an ~ for good.* 그는 선으로 인도하는 사람이다. **4** 《astron.》 an effect supposed to be exerted by the heavenly bodies upon human affairs and character. (천체로부터의) 감응력.
— *vt.* (P6) have an influence on (someone or something); affect. …에 영향을 미치다. ¶ *He was influenced by what he had read.* 그는 그가 읽은 책에 의해 감화를 받았다. [in-², →fluent]

in·flu·en·tial [ìnfluénʃəl] *adj.* **1** having much influence. 영향을 미치는. ¶ *circumstances which were ~ in reaching a decision* 어떤 결정에 이르는 데 작용했던 상황들. **2** possessing and exerting great influence. 영향력이 있는; 유력한. ¶ *an ~ person.*

in·flu·en·za [ìnfluénzə] *n.* Ⓤ an illness like a very bad cold. 인플루엔자; 독감. 參考 흔히 flu로 생략. [→influence]

in·flux [ínflʌ̀ks] *n.* ⓊⒸ the act of flowing or coming in. 유입; 쇄도(opp. efflux). ¶ *an ~ of customers* 천객 만래(千客萬來). [in-², L. *fluo* flow]

in·fold [infóuld] *vt.* (P6) **1** wrap up. …을 싸다. ¶ *He was infolded in an overcoat.* 외투로 몸을 감쌌다. **2** embrace. (끌어)안다. 參考 enfold 라고도 씀. [*enfold*]

:in·form [infɔ́ːrm] *vt.* **1** (P6,13,15,16,17) 《*of*》 give knowledge of something to (someone); make something known to (someone). …에 —을 알리다; (보)고하다. ¶ *He informed me of the news.* 그가 나에게 그 소식을 알려줬다 / *Please ~ me when you arrive.* 도착하시거든 알려주십시오 / *Please ~ us how to find the post-office.* 우체국이 어디 있는지 알려주시오. **2** (P13) inspire; fill. …을 불어넣다; 채우다. ¶ ~ *someone with new life* 아무에게 새로운 생명을 불어넣다 / *I was informed with courage.* 용기가 솟아올랐다.
— *vi.* (P3) 《*against*》 make an accusation. 고발(고소)하다. ¶ *They informed against Tom.* 그들은 톰을 고발했다 / *The thief informed on his accomplices.* 그 도둑은 자기 공범들을 밀고했다. [in-²]

in·for·mal [infɔ́ːrməl] *adj.* (opp. formal) **1** conducted without ceremony or formality. 격식 차리지 않는; 스스럼없는. ¶ *an ~ visit* 개인적(비공식) 방문. **2** (of speech, etc.) suited for everyday, common use; colloquial. 말이 딱딱하지 않은; 구어적인. ¶ *Such an expression as kids for children is ~.* children 을 kids 라 하는 것과 같은 것은 구어적 말씨이다. [in-²]

in·for·mal·i·ty [ìnfɔːrmǽləti] *n.* (*pl.* **-ties**) **1** Ⓤ the state of being informal; the absence of ceremony. 비공식; 약식. **2** Ⓒ an informal act. 형식에 구애받지 않는 행위. ¶ *To walk into a neighbor's house by the back door is an ~.* 이웃집을 뒷문으로 들어가는 것은 스스럼없는 행위이다.

in·for·mal·ly [infɔ́ːrməli] *adv.* in an informal manner. 약식(비공식, 구어적)으로.

in·form·ant [infɔ́ːrmənt] *n.* Ⓒ a person who gives information. 통지(통보)인; 정보(자료) 제공자. ¶ *He is a trustworthy ~ of English.* 그는 영어에 관한 믿을 만한 자료 제공자이다. [*inform*]

:in·for·ma·tion [ìnfərméiʃən] *n.* Ⓤ **1** the act of informing; the state of being informed. 전달; 통보. ¶ *for your ~* (당신에게) 참고가 되시도록; 참고삼아 / *a guidebook for the ~ of tourists* 여행 안내서 / *ask for ~* 문의하다. **2** knowledge given or acquired; facts learnt; news. 지식; 견문; 정보; 자료; 뉴스. ¶ *a man of ~* 사정에 밝은 사람; 소식통 / *get a useful piece of ~* 유익한 정보를 얻다 / *I have no ~ on the point.* 그 일에 대해선 아는 바가 없다. **3** 《law》 accusation. 고발; 고소. ¶ *lay ~ against someone* 아무를 고소하다.

in·for·ma·tion·al [ìnfərméiʃənəl] *adj.* giving information. 정보를(지식을) 제공하는.

in·formed [infɔ́ːrmd] *adj.* having information or knowledge. 지식이 있는; 소식에

밝은. ¶ *a well-informed man* 지식이 많은 사람.

in·form·er [infɔ́:rmər] *n.* Ⓒ **1** a person who informs against others. 고발[밀고]자. ¶ *a common* ~ (경찰내의 직업적) 정보 제공자. **2** a person who informs; informant. 통보[통지]자.

in·fra [ínfrə] *adv.* 《L.》 below or further on in the book, etc. 아래에; 아래쪽에(opp. supra). ¶ *See* ~ *p. 40.* 아래 40 페이지를 보라.

in·fract [infrǽkt] *vt.* (P6) infringe. (법률을) 어기다; 범법하다. [→infringe]

in·frac·tion [infrǽkʃən] *n.* ⓊⒸ the act of breaking a law or rule. (법률·규칙의) 위반; 위반 행위.

in·fra·red [ìnfrəréd] *adj.* 《phys.》 of the invisible rays lying beyond the red end of the visible spectrum. 적외선의(opp. ultraviolet). ¶ ~ *rays* 적외선 / ~ *photography* 적외선 사진술. [*infra, red*]

in·fre·quent [infrí:kwənt] *adj.* seldom happening or occurring; rare. 이따금의; 드문(opp. frequent). ¶ *an* ~ *visitor* 〔*rain*〕 이따금 오는 손님〔비〕. [in-[1]]

in·fre·quent·ly [infrí:kwəntli] *adv.* in an infrequent manner; not often; rarely. 드물게; 이따금; 어쩌다.

in·fringe [infríndʒ] *vt.* (P6) fail to obey or keep; break; violate (a law, rule, or patent). (법률·규칙 등)을 어기다; 위반하다. —*vi.* (P3) 《*on, upon*》 trespass. 범하다; 침해하다. ¶ ~ *upon another person's privacy* 남의 프라이버시를 침해하다 / ~ *a copyright* 저작권을 침해하다. [in-[2]. L. *frango* break]

in·fringe·ment [infríndʒmənt] *n.* ⓊⒸ the act of infringing. 위반; 침해; 위반 행위. ¶ *an* ~ *of copyright* 저작권의 침해.

in·fu·ri·ate [infjúərièit] *vt.* (P6) make (someone) very angry; enrage. …을 몹시 화나게 하다; 격노케 하다. ¶ *Anything of a red color is said to* ~ *a bull.* 무엇이건 붉은색은 투우를 광포하게 만든다고 한다. —[-it] *adj.* very angry. 몹시 화가 난; 격노한. [in-[2], →fury]

in·fuse [infjú:z] *vt.* **1** (P6,13) 《*into, with*》 inspire. …을 불어넣다; 고취하다. ¶ *The teacher infused confidence into Betty.* = *The teacher infused Betty with confidence.* 선생님은 베티에게 자신감을 불어넣어 주었다. **2** (P6,13) put in; pour in. …을 붓다; 주입하다. **3** (P6) soak (something) in hot water. …을 달이다; 우려내다. ¶ ~ *tea* 〔*tea-leaves*〕 차를 달이다. [in-[2], →fuse]

in·fu·sion [infjú:ʒən] *n.* **1** Ⓤ the act of infusing. 주입; 불어넣기. **2** Ⓒ liquid obtained by soaking. 달인 물; 우려낸 즙. **3** something added to or mixed with something else; a mixture. 혼합물.

in·fu·sor·i·a [ìnfjuzɔ́:riə, -sɔ́:-] *n. pl.* 《biol.》 very small living creatures found in water containing decayed vegetable matter. 적충류(滴蟲類)《원생 동물》. [→infuse]

in·gath·er·ing [íngæ̀ðəriŋ] *n.* gathering in. 거둬들임; 수확. [in-[2]]

·in·ge·nious [indʒí:njəs] *adj.* **1** clever; skillful; inventive. 영리한; 재주 있는; 발명의 재능이 있는. ¶ *The boy, being* ~, *quickly made himself some toys.* 소년은 손재주가 있어 재빨리 장난감 몇 개를 만들었다. **2** cleverly made or thought out. 잘 만들어진〔생각해 낸〕. ¶ *an* ~ *device* 정교한 장치 / *an* ~ *excuse* 그럴싸한 핑계. [L. *ingenium* cleverness]

in·ge·nious·ly [indʒí:njəsli] *adv.* in an ingenious manner; cleverly; skillfully. 현명하게; 솜씨 있게; 교묘하게.

in·ge·nu·i·ty [ìndʒənjú:əti] *n.* Ⓤ cleverness in planning, inventing, etc.; creativeness; cleverness. 발명의 재능; 창의성; 재주 있음; 슬기. ¶ *Tom showed* ~ *in making toys.* 톰은 장난감을 만드는 데 창의성을 보였다.

in·gen·u·ous [indʒénju:əs] *adj.* frank; open; simple; innocent. 솔직한; 꾸밈없는; 순진한. ¶ *an* ~ *answer* 〔*smile*〕. 꾸밈없는 대답〔미소〕. [L. = free-born]

in·gen·u·ous·ly [indʒénju:əsli] *adv.* in an ingenuous manner; frankly; innocently. 솔직하게; 꾸밈없이; 순진하게.

in·gen·u·ous·ness [indʒénju:əsnis] *n.* Ⓤ frankness; innocence. 솔직; 순진.

in·gest [indʒést] *vt.* (P6) take (food, etc.) into the body for digestion. 섭취하다. [in-[2], L. *gero* carry]

in·gle [íŋgəl] *n.* a fire or fireplace. 화로; 화롯불. [Sc. -Gael. *aingeal* fire, light]

in·gle-nook [íŋgəlnùk] *n.* =chimney-corner.

in·glo·ri·ous [inglɔ́:riəs] *adj.* **1** without fame or glory; shameful; disgraceful. 수치스러운; 명예롭지 못한. ¶ *an* ~ *defeat* 치욕적인 패배. **2** not famous; unknown. 유명하지 않은; 무명의. [in-[1]]

in·go·ing [íngòuiŋ] *adj.* entering. 들어오는. [in-[2]]

in·got [íŋgət] *n.* mass of metal cast in a mould. 주형(鑄型). [in-[2], A.S. *gotan* pour]

in·grain [ingréin] *vt.* (P6) dye in the fiber before manufacture. (실·섬유)를 짜기 전에 염색하다. —[스스] *adj.* **1** dyed before manufacture. 짜기 전에 염색하는. **2** 《*fig.*》 fixed deeply and firmly. 깊이 물든; 뿌리 깊은. —[스슬] *n.* Ⓤ yarn, wool, etc. dyed before manufacture. 짜기 전에 염색한 면사〔모사〕. [in-[2], →grain]

in·grained [ingréind, ㅅ-] *adj.* deeply fixed in; deep seated. 깊이 배어든; 뿌리 깊은. ¶ ~ *habit* 고질이 된 버릇 / *an* ~ *lier* 상습적인 거짓말쟁이 / *prejudice* ~ *deep in the mind* 뿌리 깊은 편견.

in·gra·ti·ate [ingréiʃièit] *vt.* (P13) bring (oneself) into favor of (someone). …의 환심을 사려들다; 비위맞추다. ¶ *He tried to* ~

himself with his superiors. 상사의 마음에 들려고 애썼다. [in-², L. *gratia* favour]

in·grat·i·tude [ingrǽtətjùːd] *n.* Ⓤ the state of not being thankful; lack of gratitude. 고마움을 모름; 배은망덕. [in-¹]

in·gre·di·ent [ingríːdiənt] *n.* Ⓒ a part of a mixture; element. 혼합물의 성분; 요소. ¶ *the ingredients of candy* 과자의 원료 / *an important ~ in a man's character* 사람의 성격의 중요한 구성 요소. [in-², L. *gradior* go]

in·gress [íngres] *n.* (opp. egress) **1** Ⓤ the act of going in. 들어가기. **2** Ⓒ a place for entering; entrance. 입구. **3** Ⓤ the right to enter. 입장할 권리. [L. *ingredi* enter]

·**in·hab·it** [inhǽbit] *vt.* (P6) live in (a place, a house, etc.); occupy. …에 살다 〔거주하다〕; …을 차지하다. ¶ *Tigers ~ the jungle.* 호랑이는 정글에 서식한다 / *Thoughts ~ the mind.* 생각은 마음 속에 자리를 차지한다 / *Soul inhabits the body.* 영혼은 육신에 깃들인다. [in-², →habit]

:**in·hab·it·ant** [inhǽbətənt] *n.* Ⓒ a person or animal that lives in a place. 거주자; 서식 동물.

in·hab·it·ed [inhǽbitid] *adj.* having inhabitants; lived in. 사람이 살고 있는. ¶ *an ~ house* 사람이 있는 집.

in·hal·ant [inhéilənt] *n.* **1** Ⓤ medicine to be inhaled. 흡입제〔약〕. **2** Ⓒ an apparatus for inhaling it. 흡입기. [→inhale]

in·ha·la·tion [ìnhəléiʃən] *n.* **1** Ⓤ the act of inhaling. 흡입. **2** Ⓒ medicine to be inhaled. 흡입제. [↑]

in·hale [inhéil] *vt.* (P6) draw (air, smoke, etc.) into the lungs. …을 들이마시다 (opp. exhale). ¶ *~ fresh air* 신선한 공기를 들이마시다. — *vi.* (P1) breathe something into the lungs; inhale tobacco smoke. 숨을 들이마시다; 담배 연기를 깊이 빨아들이다. [in-², L. *halo* breathe]

in·har·mo·ni·ous [ìnhaːrmóuniəs] *adj.* not harmonious; unmusical; conflicting. (소리·색깔 등이) 조화되지 않은; 서로 맞지 않는(opp. harmonious). ¶ *~ sounds* 가락이 맞지 않는 소리. [in-¹]

·**in·her·ent** [inhíərənt] *adj.* belonging to someone or something as a natural part; inborn. 본디 갖추어진; 타고난; 고유의. ¶ *Modesty is a virtue ~ in his nature.* 겸양은 그의 타고난 미덕이다 / *an ~ property of matter* 물질 고유의 특성. [in-², L. *haereo* stick]

·**in·her·it** [inhérit] *vt.* (P6,13) **1** ⦅law⦆ receive (property, etc.) at the death of a former owner. (재산 등을) 상속받다〔하다〕. ¶ *Tom inherited his father's farm.* 아버지의 농장을 상속받았다. **2** get (something) from one's ancestors. (성질 등)을 선조에게서 물려받다; 유전하다. ¶ *She inherited her brown hair from her father.* 그녀는 갈색 머리를 아버지로부터 물려받았다. — *vi.* (P1) receive property as an heir; be or become the heir. 재산을 상속받다; 상속인이 되다. ¶ *When he dies, who will ~?* 그가 죽으면 누가 상속을 받지. [in-², L. *heres* heir]

in·her·it·a·ble [inhéritəbl] *adj.* **1** that can be inherited. 상속할 수 있는; 유전하는. **2** able to inherit; qualified to inherit. 상속 자격이 있는.

·**in·her·it·ance** [inhéritəns] *n.* Ⓤ **1** the act of inheriting. 상속. **2** the right of inheriting. 상속권. **3** ⓊⒸ property or qualities inheritied. 유산; 타고난 것. ¶ *an ~ of disease* 병의 유전 / *waste one's ~* 유산을 낭비하다.

in·her·i·tor [inhéritər] *n.* Ⓒ a person who inherits; an heir. 상속인.

in·hib·it [inhíbit] *vt.* (P6) ⦅*from*⦆ restrain; forbid. 억제하다; 금하다. ¶ *~ a selfish desire* 개인적 욕망을 억제하다 / *Shyness inhibited her from speaking up.* 그녀는 부끄러워서 말을 제대로 못했다. [in-², L. *habeo* hold]

in·hi·bi·tion [inhəbíʃən] *n.* ⓊⒸ **1** the act of inhibiting; the state of being inhibited. 억제; 억압; 금지. **2** an inner force that restrains or suppresses actions, emotions or thoughts. 억제력.

in·hos·pi·ta·ble [inhάspitəbəl, ⌐–⌐––/ -hɔ́s-] *adj.* **1** not friendly to visitors. 무뚝뚝한; 불친절한; 대접이 나쁜. ¶ *an ~ host* 불친절한 주인. **2** (of a place, etc.) giving no shelter; barren. 거처할 곳이 없는; 메마른. ¶ *an ~ region* 황야. [in-¹]

in·hos·pi·tal·i·ty [inhὰspitǽləti / -hɔ̀s-] *n.* Ⓤ the state of being inhospitable. 무뚝뚝함; 불친절.

in·hu·man [inhjúːmən] *adj.* not like a human being; unfeeling; cruel; brutal. 사람 같지 않은; 매정한; 잔인한; 야만적인. ¶ *~ treatment* 냉혹한 대우. [in-¹]

in·hu·mane [ìnhjuːméin] *adj.* cruel; unkind. 무정한; 몰인정한.

in·hu·man·i·ty [ìnhjuːmǽnəti] *n.* (*pl.* **-ties**) **1** Ⓤ the state or quality of being inhuman. 몰인정; 잔인. **2** Ⓒ an inhuman or cruel act. 매정〔잔인〕한 행위.

in·im·i·cal [inímikəl] *adj.* **1** like an enemy; unfriendly; hostile. 적의 있는; 비우호적인. ¶ *nations ~ to one another* 서로 적대하는 국가. **2** unfavorable; harmful. 좋지 않은; 해로운. ¶ *Smoking is ~ to (the) health.* 흡연은 건강에 해롭다 / *circumstances ~ to success* 성공하기 힘든 상황. [in-¹, L. *amicus* friend]

in·im·i·ta·ble [inímitəbəl] *adj.* that cannot be imitated; matchless. 모방할 수 없는; 비길 데 없는. ¶ *a man of ~ eloquence* 비길 데 없는 웅변가. [in-¹]

in·iq·ui·tous [iníkwitəs] *adj.* unjust; wicked. 옳지 못한; 사악한. [in-¹, L. *aequus* just]

in·iq·ui·ty [iníkwəti] *n.* (*pl.* **-ties**) **1** Ⓤ the state or quality of being iniquitous; injustice; wickedness. 부정; 사악. **2** Ⓒ an iniquitous act. 옳지 못한 행위; 부도덕한 짓.

·i·ni·tial [iníʃəl] *adj.* at the begining; first; earliest. 모두(冒頭)의; 최초의; 초기의. ¶ *an ~ letter* 머리글자 / *the ~ chapter in a book* 책의 첫 장 / *the ~ stages* 초기; 제1기 / *a ~ attempt* 첫 시도. —*n.* Ⓒ the first letter of a word or name. 머리글자; 이니셜. —*vt.* (P6) (**-tialed, -tial·ing** or esp. Brit. **-tialled, -tial·ling**) mark or sign (something) with one's initial or initials. …에 머리글자로 서명하다. ¶ *~ a report* 보고서에 이니셜의 서명을 하다. [L. *ineo* go in]

i·ni·ti·ate [iníʃièit] *vt.* (P6,13) **1** begin; start. …을 시작[착수]하다. ¶ *~ a reform* 개혁에 착수하다. **2** admit or introduce (someone) into a club, society, etc. …을 가입[입회]시키다. ¶ *~ someone into a society* 아무를 협회에 가입시키다. **3** show (someone) how to do something new. …에 초보를 가르치다. ¶ *~ someone into business method* 아무에게 장사하는 법을 가르치다 / *~ someone into a secret* 아무에게 비밀을 전수하다. —[-ʃiit, -èit] *n.* Ⓒ a person who is initiated. 새 가입자; 새로 시작하는 사람. [↑]

i·ni·ti·a·tion [iniʃiéiʃən] *n.* **1** Ⓤ the act of initiating; the state of being initiated. 착수; 개시; 입회; 입문. **2** Ⓒ the ceremonies by which someone is admitted to a club, a group, etc. 입회식.

·i·ni·ti·a·tive [iníʃiətiv] *n.* **1** Ⓤ 《usu. *the* ~》 the first step; the lead. 제1보; 주도(主導). ¶ *He took the ~ in organizing the group.* 그는 그룹을 조직하는 데 주도했다. **2** Ⓤ the ability to foresee and undertake what ought to be done. 일을 시작하는 능력; 진취의 기상. ¶ *A leader must have ~.* 지도자는 선도(先導)하는 힘이 있어야 한다. **3** 《*the* ~》 the right (of citizens, etc.) to introduce new law. (국민의) 발의권(發議權). ¶ *The Commons have the ~ in respect of money bills.* 하원의원은 재정 법안에 대한 발의권이 있다.

have the initiative, have the right to be the first to do something. 주도권을 가지다.

on one's own initiative, without any orders or suggestions from others. 자발적으로.

in·ject [indʒékt] *vt.* (P6,13) **1** force (something) into some part of the body. …을 주입하다; 주사놓다. ¶ *~ a drug into the arm* 팔에 주사를 놓다. **2** throw in. …을 끼워 넣다. ¶ *~ a suggestion into the conversation* 이야기 중에 한 가지 제안을 하다. [in-[2], L. *jacio* throw]

in·jec·tion [indʒékʃən] *n.* **1** ⓊⒸ the act of injecting. 주입; 주사. **2** Ⓒ liquid which is injected. 주사액.

in·ju·di·cious [ìndʒu(:)díʃəs] *adj.* lacking in judgment; unwise. 생각이 모자라는; 무분별한. ¶ *~ advice* [*remark*] 경솔한 충고[지각없는 말]. [in-[1]]

in·junc·tion [indʒʌ́ŋkʃən] *n.* Ⓒ a command or order, esp. one from a law court ordering someone to do or not to do something. 명령; 지시; (재판소가 내리는) 명령. ¶ *John obeyed his mother's ~ to hurry home.* 존은 어머니 분부에 따라 서둘러 귀가했다 / *issue an ~ against a strike* 파업 금지령을 내리다. [→enjoin]

:in·jure [índʒər] *vt.* (P6) **1** harm; hurt. …을 해치다; 상처내다. ¶ *~ one's hand* 손을 다치다 / *~ picture* 그림을 훼손하다 / *The rain injured our crops.* 비로 농작물이 피해를 입었다. **2** do wrong to; act unjustly toward. (감정 따위)를 해치다; 손상하다. ¶ *~ another's feelings* [*reputation*]. [in-[1], L. *jus* right]

in·jured [índʒərd] *adj.* **1** wronged; having suffered wrong. 해를 입은; 다친. ¶ *the ~ party* 피해자(측). **2** expressing a sense of injury. 감정이 상한. ¶ *an ~ look* [*voice*] 기분 나쁜 듯한 표정[음성].

in·ju·ri·ous [indʒúəriəs] *adj.* **1** harmful; hurtful. 해로운; 유해한. ¶ *a habit ~ to* (*the*) *health* 건강에 좋지 않은 습관. **2** unfair; unjust; insulting. 불공평한; 불법의; 무례한. ¶ *rumors ~ to his reputation* 그의 인망을 헐뜯는 소문들.

·in·jury [índʒəri] *n.* (*pl.* **-ries**) **1** Ⓤ harm; damage. 해; 손해; 부상. ¶ *suffer an ~ to the head* 머리에 부상을 입다 / *an ~ to a picture* [*roof*] 그림[지붕]이 입은 손상. **2** Ⓒ a place that is hurt or wounded. 다친 데; 상처. **3** Ⓒ an act of hurting, or damaging; an insult. 해치기; 모욕. ¶ *an ~ to someone's character* 아무의 인격에 대한 모욕. **4** Ⓒ 《law》 a violation of another's rights, in respect of which legal action can be taken. 권리 침해.

·in·jus·tice [indʒʌ́stis] *n.* **1** Ⓤ the state of being unjust. 부정; 불공평. **2** Ⓒ an unjust act. 부정[불법] 행위. [in-[1]]

do (*someone*) (***an***) ***injustice,*** judge (someone) unfairly. …을 오해하다.

:ink [iŋk] *n.* Ⓤ a colored liquid used for writing or printing. 잉크. ¶ *write with pen and ~* 펜으로 쓰다. —*vt.* (P6,7) mark or stain (something) with ink. …을 잉크로 표하다[더럽히다]. [→encaustic (Gk.= red ink, *caio* burn)]

ink bottle [ㅗ ㅗ] *n.* a bottle for holding ink. 잉크병.

ink·ling [íŋkliŋ] *n.* Ⓒ a hint; a vague noticing. 암시; 어렴풋이 알아차림. ¶ *have an ~ of what is going on* 무슨 일이 일어나는지 어렴풋이 눈치채다. [E.]

ink·pot [íŋkpɑ̀t / -pɔ̀t] *n.* Ⓒ a pot for holding ink. 잉크병. [*ink*]

ink·stand [íŋkstæ̀nd] *n.* Ⓒ a stand for holding ink and pens. 잉크스탠드.

ink·well [íŋkwèl] *n.* Ⓒ an inkpot fitted into a desk or table. (탁상 구멍에 꽂는) 잉크병.

ink·y [íŋki] *adj.* (**ink·i·er, ink·i·est**) **1**

dark or black like ink. 잉크처럼 새까만. ¶ *an ~ sky* 깜깜한 하늘 / *~ darkness* 칠흑 같은 어둠. **2** covered or stained with ink. 잉크로 더러워진. ¶ *an ~ face* 잉크 묻은 얼굴.

in·laid [inléid, ⌐⌐] *adj.* **1** set in the surface as a decoration. (장식으로) 무늬를 박아 넣은; 상감 세공을 한. **2** decorated with a design set in the surface. 상감 무늬가 있는. — *v.* p. and pp. of **inlay.**

***in·land** [ínlənd] *adj.* **1** situated in the interior of a country; away from the sea. (바다에서 먼) 내륙의; 오지의. ¶ *an ~ sea* 내해 / *an ~ town* 내륙 도시. **2** within a country; domestic. 국내의(opp. foreign). ¶ *~ trade* 내륙 무역 / *the ~ revenue* 내국세(稅) 수입. — [ínlæ̀nd, -lənd] *n.* Ⓒ the interior of a country. 국내; 내륙. — [ínlæ̀nd, -lənd / inlǽnd] *adv.* toward the interior. 국내로; 내륙으로. [*in, land*]

in·law [ínlɔ̀:] *n.* 《*colloq.*》 Ⓒ 《often *pl.*》 a relative by marriage. 인척. [in-²]

in·lay [ìnléi, ⌐⌐] *vt.* (**-laid, -lay·ing**) (P6) set (pieces of gold, silver, etc.) in the surface as a decoration; decorate (the surface) with something set in. (장식으로) …을 박아 넣다〔상감하다〕. ¶ *The box was inlaid with silver.* 상자는 은(銀)으로 상감되었다. — [⌐⌐] *n.* ⓊⒸ adesign or pattern made by setting a decoration into a surface. 상감 세공; 상감 무늬. [*in, lay*]

〈inlay〉

in·let [ínlèt] *n.* Ⓒ **1** an arm of the sea reaching inland. 후미. **2** an entrance. 입구(入口)(opp. outlet). **3** something let in. 삽입물. [in-², →let]

in·ly [ínli] *ad.* 《*poet.*》 **1** inwardly. 안에. **2** in the heart; deeply; sincerely. 마음 속에; 깊이; 충심으로. [in-²]

in·mate [ínmèit] *n.* Ⓒ **1** a person kept in a prison, a hospital, etc. (교도소의) 수감자; (병원의) 입원 환자. ¶ *the inmates of a prison* 교도소의 수감자들. **2** a member of a family or other group living under the same roof. 가족; 식구(食口); 동거인. [in-²]

in·most [ínmòust] *adj.* **1** deepest within; most inward. 가장 안쪽의. ¶ *the ~ part of jungle* 정글의 한복판. **2** most secret. (마음 속) 깊이 간직한; 숨겨진; 내심의. ¶ *His ~ desire is to be a politician.* 그의 깊은 속셈은 정치가가 되는 것이다. [in-²]

***inn** [in] *n.* Ⓒ a small hotel where travelers may get food and lodging; a public house; a tavern. 여관; 여인숙; 주막. ¶ *put up* 〔*stay*〕 *at an ~* 여관에 묵다. [in-²]

in·nate [inéit, ⌐—] *adj.* inborn; natural. 타고난; 선천적인(opp. acquired). ¶ *an ~ gift* 천부의 재능. [in-², L. *nāsci* to be born]

***in·ner** [ínər] *adj.* **1** inside; interior. 안의; 내부의(opp. outer). ¶ *an ~ pocket* 안〔속〕주머니. **2** private; secret. 내밀한; 비밀의. ¶ *one's ~ feelings* 〔*thoughts*〕 마음 속 깊이 간직하고 있는 감정〔생각〕. **3** of the mind or soul. 마음〔정신〕의. ¶ *man's ~ life* 사람의 정신 생활.
— *n.* **1** the ring of a target next to the bull's-eye. 과녁의 내권(內圈). **2** a shot hitting this ring. 내권에 맞은 총알〔화살〕. [in-²]

inner man [⌐— ⌐] *n.* 《*the ~*》 **1** man's mind or soul. 마음; 영혼. **2** 《*joc.*》 the stomach. 위; 밥통. ¶ *warm* 〔*satisfy*〕 *the ~* 배를 채우다; 든든히 먹다.

in·ner·most [ínərmòust] *adj.* deepest within; inmost. 가장 안쪽〔내부〕의.

in·ning [íniŋ] *n.* Ⓒ **1** a period in a baseball game during which each team is at bat in turn; a chance to play. 회(回); (공을) 칠 차례; 타순; 이닝. **2** 《*fig.*》 the period when a person or a political party is in power. (개인의) 활동기; 전성기; (정당의) 집권기. ¶ *The Conservatives now have their ~.* 보수당이 현(現) 집권당이다 / *After all, he has had a good long ~.* 어쨌든 그는 복 많은 사람이었다《오래 살았거나 좋은 관직에 오래 있었을 때 하는 말》. 語法 영국에서는 단수든 복수든 innings이며 동사는 단수형으로 받음. [in-²]

inn·keep·er [ínkì:pər] *n.* Ⓒ a person who runs an inn. 여관집 주인.

***in·no·cence** [ínəsns] *n.* Ⓤ **1** the state of being innocent; freedom from sin or guilt. 결백; 무죄. ¶ *The lawyer did his best to prove her ~ of the crime.* 변호사는 그녀의 무죄를 밝히는 데 최선을 다했다. **2** simplicity of heart. 천진난만. [in-¹, L. *noceo* harm]

:**in·no·cent** [ínəsnt] *adj.* **1** free from guilt; doing no wrong. 무죄의; 결백한(opp. guilty). ¶ *He is ~ of the crime.* 그에게는 죄가 없다. **2** knowing no evil; pure in heart and life. 순진〔천진〕한. ¶ *She is as ~ as a baby.* 어린애처럼 순진한 여자다. **3** harmless in meaning and effect. 무해한; 악의가 없는(opp. harmful). ¶ *~ amusements* 해롭지 않은 오락 / *an ~ joke* 악의 없는 농담. **4** simple; foolish. (머리가) 단순한; 어리석은. ¶ *He's not quite so ~ as to believe that.* 그걸 믿을 만큼 그렇게 단순하지는 않다. **5** 《*colloq.*》 lacking. …이 없는. ¶ *hair ~ of pomade* 포마드를 바르지 않은 머리.
— *n.* Ⓒ **1** an innocent person or child. 결백한 사람; 천진한 아이. **2** a fool. 바보. [in-¹, L. *noceo* hurt]

in·no·cent·ly [ínəsntli] *adv.* guiltlessly; harmlessly. 죄없이; 순진하게.

in·noc·u·ous [inɑ́kju:əs / inɔ́-] *adj.* harmless. 무해한. ¶ *an ~ drug* 해가 없는 약. [in-¹, L. *nocuus* harmful]

in·no·vate [ínouvèit] *vi.* (P1,3) introduce something new; make changes. 새로운 것을 도입하다; 쇄신하다. ¶ ~ *on* 〔*upon*〕 *an old custom* 구습을 쇄신하다. [in-², L. *novus* new]

in·no·va·tion [inouvéiʃən] *n.* **1** ⓊⒸ the act of innovating; the introduction of something new. 쇄신; 새로운 것의 도입. ¶ *the ~ of an electronic computer* 컴퓨터의 도입. **2** Ⓒ a thing which is new; a change made in custom or method of doing. 새로운 사물.

in·no·va·tor [ínouvèitər] *n.* Ⓒ a person who makes changes or brings in a new method. 개혁〔혁신〕자; 선구자.

in·nu·en·do [injuéndou] *n.* Ⓒ (*pl.* **-dos** or **does**) an indirect remark or reference critical of somebody. 비꼼; 비아냥거리기; 빈정거림. — *vi.* make innuendoes. 빈정거리다. [L. =by nodding; in-², *nuo* nod]

·in·nu·mer·a·ble [injú:mərəbəl] *adj.* too many to be counted; countless. 헤아릴 수 없는; 무수한. [in-¹, L. *numerus* number]

in·oc·u·late [inákjəlèit / -ɔ́k-] *vt.* (P6,13) **1** inject vaccine, etc. into (a person or animal) to prevent a disease. …에 예방 접종을 하다. ¶ ~ *a child against typhoid* 아이들에게 티푸스의 예방 접종을 실시하다. **2** 《*fig.*》 fill someone's mind with (something). …을 아무의 마음에 불어넣다. ¶ ~ *youth with dangerous ideas* 젊은이들에게 위험한 사상을 불어넣다. **3** insert (a bud, shoot, etc.) into another plant; insert a bud, shoot, etc. into (a plant). 접붙이다; 접목하다. [in-², L. *oculus* eye, bud]

in·oc·u·la·tion [inɑ̀kjəléiʃən, -ɔk-] *n.* ⓊⒸ the act of inoculating. (예방)접종. ¶ *an ~ against cholera* 콜레라에 대한 예방 접종.

in·of·fen·sive [ìnəfénsiv] *adj.* not unpleasant; harmless. 해가 되지 않는; 싫지 않은. [in-¹]

in·op·er·a·tive [inápərèitiv, -ətiv / -ɔ́pərətiv] *adj.* (of laws, etc.) having no effect; not working. 효력이 상실된; 무효의. [in-¹]

in·op·por·tune [inɑ̀pərtjú:n / -ɔp-] *adj.* coming or happening at a bad time; unsuitable. 계제가 나쁜; 부적당한. ¶ *an ~ remark* 시기에 적절하지 못한 말 / *call someone at an ~ time* 계제가 나쁜 때에 아무를 방문하다. [in-¹]

in·or·di·nate [inɔ́:rdənət] *adj.* too much; too great; excessive. 과도한; 지나친. ¶ ~ *demands* 터무니없는 요구 / ~ *pride* 당치 않은 프라이드 / *It took him an ~ amount of time.* 그 일에 엄청난 시간을 빼앗겼다. [in-¹, L. *ordo* order]

in·or·gan·ic [ìnɔ:rgǽnik] *adj.* **1** not made up of plant or animal material. 무기(無機)의. ¶ ~ *chemistry* 무기 화학. **2** (of forms of society, political institutions, etc.) showing the absence of system of structure; lack of proper relation of parts. (사회적·정치적 기관 따위가) 유기적 조직 체계가 없는. [in-¹]

in·pa·tient [ínpèiʃənt] *n.* Ⓒ a person who stays in a hospital and receives treatment. 입원 환자(opp. outpatient). [*in, patient*]

in·put [ínpùt] *n.* Ⓤ the act of putting in; the information fed into a computer. 입력(入力). [*in, put*]

in·quest [ínkwest] *n.* **1** Ⓒ 《law》 a legal examination with the aid of a jury, esp. one to determine the cause of a sudden death. 심리; 검시(檢屍). **2** 《*collectively*》 the jury appointed to make such an examination. 검시 배심원. [→inquire]

in·qui·e·tude [inkwáiətjù:d] *n.* Ⓤ uneasiness; anxiety. 불안; 근심; 걱정. [in-¹, →quiet]

:in·quire, en- [inkwáiər] *vt.* (P6,10,12) seek (imformation) by asking. …을 묻다. ¶ ~ *the way to the station* 정거장 가는 길을 묻다 / *He inquired how to get there.* 그는 그곳에 어떻게 가는지를 물었다. — *vi.* (P3) ask questions. 질문하다; 묻다. ¶ ~ *at the front desk* 프런트에서 묻다 / ~ *of a travel agent as to train scheldules* 여행 안내원에게 열차 시간표를 물어 보다. [in-², L. *quaero* seek]

inquire after (= *ask about the health or welfare of*) someone. 아무의 건강을〔안부를〕 묻다.

inquire for, **a**) try to obtain (something). (가게에서) 물건을 찾다. **b**) ask to see (someone). …에게 면회를 청하다. ¶ ~ *for Mr. Smith at the information desk* 안내소에서 스미스씨의 면회를 청하다.

inquire into a matter, examine; investigate. …을 조사하다. ¶ ~ *into the leak of the examination questions* 시험 문제의 누설을 조사하다.

in·quir·er [inkwáiərər] *n.* Ⓒ a person who inquires. 묻는〔조사하는〕 사람.

in·quir·ing [inkwáiəriŋ] *adj.* seeking information; expressing a desire to learn; questioning. 알고 싶어하는; 미심쩍어하는. ¶ *an ~ look* 미심쩍은 듯한 얼굴.

·in·quir·y, en- [inkwáiəri] *n.* (*pl.* **-quiries**) **1** Ⓤ the act of inquiring. 문의; 조회. ¶ *find out by ~* 문의해서 알다 / *Details will be given on ~.* 자세한 것은 문의하십시오. **2** Ⓒ a question. 질문. ¶ *make inquiries about a subject* 문제에 대하여 질문하다 / *answer someone's ~* 아무의 질문에 대답하다. **3** Ⓒ an examination; an investigation. 조사; 심리. ¶ *an ~ into the truth of a report* 보고의 진위에 대한 조사.

inquiry office [–⏑– –⏑] *n.* a place where information is given. 안내소; 접수구.

in·qui·si·tion [inkwəzíʃən] *n.* **1** Ⓤ thorough examination. 엄중한 조사. **2** Ⓒ an official inquiry before a jury. 심리. **3** 《*the I-*》 《hist.》 a Roman Catholic court to discover and punish those whose beliefs were thought to be wrong. 종교 재판소. [→inquire]

in·quis·i·tive [inkwízətiv] *adj.* **1** eager to learn; curious. 알고 싶어하는; 호기심이 많은. ¶ *Children are* ~. 아이들은 호기심이 많다. **2** fond of learning about other people's affairs. 캐묻기 좋아하는; 꼬치꼬치 캐묻는.

in·quis·i·tor [inkwízətər] *n.* Ⓒ **1** a person who makes an inquisition. 조사〔심리〕관. **2** 《*I*-》 《hist.》 a member of the Inquisition. 종교 재판관.

in·quis·i·to·ri·al [inkwìzətɔ́:riəl] *adj.* of or like an inquisitor. 심문관〔종교 재판관〕 같은.

in·road [ínròud] *n.* Ⓒ a sudden attack. 급습; 기습. ¶ *an* ~ *into the neighboring country* 이웃 나라를 기습하다. [*in, road*]

make inroads (=*move, encroach*) ***into.*** 먹어 들어가다; 잠식하다. ¶ *The city is making inroads into the countryside.* 시(市)는 변두리 시골로 퍼져 나가고 있다 / *make inroads into foreign markets* 외국 시장을 잠식하다.

in·rush [ínrʌ̀ʃ] *n.* Ⓒ the act of rushing in. 난입(亂入); 쇄도. ¶ *the* ~ *of foreign goods* 외국 상품의 쇄도. [*in, rush*]

in·sane [inséin] *adj.* **1** mentally disordered; not sane; mad; crazy. 미친; 미쳐 버린(opp. sane). ¶ *the* ~ 미친 사람. **2** for mad people. 광인을 위한. ¶ *an* ~ *asylum* 정신 병원. **3** very foolish; without common sense. 아주 어리석은; 비상식적인. ¶ *an* ~ *proposal* 아주 어리석은 제안. [in-[1]]

in·san·i·tar·y [insǽnətèri / -təri] *adj.* so dirty as to help the spread of disease. 건강에 좋지 않은; 비위생적인. [↑]

in·san·i·ty [insǽnəti] *n.* (*pl.* **-ties**) **1** Ⓤ the state of being insane; madness; mental disease. 광기; 정신 이상. **2** Ⓒ a mad or foolish act. 미친 짓.

in·sa·tia·ble [inséiʃəbəl] *adj.* that cannot be satisfied; very greedy. 물릴 줄 모르는; 매우 탐욕스러운. ¶ *an* ~ *appetite* 굉장한 식욕 / ~ *of power* 권력에 탐욕스러운. [in-[1]]

in·sa·ti·ate [inséiʃiət] *adj.* =insatiable.

in·scribe [inskráib] *vt.* (P6,13) **1** 《*in, on, with*》 write or engrave. …을 쓰다〔새기다〕. ¶ ~ *a name in a book* 책에 이름을 쓰다 / ~ *a stone with one's name* 돌에 이름을 새기다. **2** impress deeply. …을 마음에 새기다. ¶ *His words are inscribed in my memory.* 그의 말은 내 마음에 깊이 새겨져 있다. **3** address (a book, etc.) to a friend, etc. as a mark of thanks. (책 따위를) 헌정하다. **4** put (a name) on a list. (이름)을 등록하다. ¶ *an inscribed stock* 등록 공채. [in-[2], L. *scribo* write]

·in·scrip·tion [inskrípʃən] *n.* **1** Ⓤ the act of inscribing. 명각(銘刻); 기입(記入). **2** Ⓒ something inscribed esp. words written in a book. etc. or engraved on a monument, a coin, a ring, etc. (기증 도서에의) 제자(題字); 비문(碑文); 명각문.

in·scru·ta·ble [inskrú:təbəl] *adj.* that cannot be understood; hard to understand; mysterious. 이해하기 힘든; 불가해한. ¶ *an* ~ *smile* 뜻 모를 웃음 / *the* ~ *ways of Fate* 불가사의한 운명의 진로. [in-[1], L. *scrutor* search]

:in·sect [ínsekt] *n.* Ⓒ **1** a small animal with three pairs of legs and usu., two pairs of wings. 곤충. **2** 《*colloq.*》 any small creeping or flying animal, such as a spider or a centipede. (거미·지네 따위) 벌레. [in-[2], L. *seco* cut (divided body)]

in·sec·ti·cide [inséktəsàid] *n.* Ⓒ a substance for killing insects. 살충제. [*insect,* L. *caedo* kill.]

in·se·cure [ìnsikjúər] *adj.* (**-cur·er, -cur·est**) **1** not safe; not firm. 불안정한; 든든하지 않은. ¶ *an* ~ *lock* 튼튼하지 못한 자물쇠 / *His position is still* ~. 그의 자리는 아직 불안하다. **2** not to be depended upon. 믿을 게 못되는; 불확실한. ¶ *insecure hopes* 〔*promises*〕 믿을 수 없는 희망〔약속〕. [in-[1]]

in·se·cu·ri·ty [ìnsikjúəriti] *n.* (*pl.* **-ties**) **1** Ⓤ the state of not being secure. 불안전; 위험. **2** Ⓒ a thing which is insecure. 불안전〔위험〕한 것.

in·sen·sate [insénseit] *adj.* **1** without sensation. 감각이 없는. ¶ *the silent* ~ *stones* 무언 무감의 돌. **2** without regard or feeling; cold; cruel. 무정한; 잔인한. **3** senseless; stupid. 분별 없는; 어리석은. ¶ ~ *rage* 공연한 화. [L. *sensus* sense]

in·sen·si·ble [insénsəbəl] *adj.* **1** not able to feel. 무감각한. ¶ *A blind man is* ~ *to colors.* 맹인은 빛을 느끼지 못한다 / ~ *to shame* 수치를 모르는 / *He is* ~ *of the beauties of art.* 예술의 아름다움을 모른다. **2** unconscious. 인사 불성의. ¶ *She fell to the ground* ~. 그녀는 의식을 잃고 땅에 쓰러졌다. **3** not aware; indifferent. 느끼지 않는; 관심이 없는. ¶ ~ *of the danger* 위험을 느끼지 않는. **4** hardly noticeable. 느끼지 못할 정도로. ¶ *by* ~ *degrees* 아주 조금씩. ● **in·sen·si·bly** [-bli] *adj.* [in-[1], sensible]

in·sen·si·bil·i·ty [insènsəbíləti] *n.* Ⓤ **1** the state or quality of being insensible; lack of feeling. 무감각. ¶ ~ *to pain* 통증에 대한 무감각. **2** lack of consciousness. 무의식; 인사 불성. ¶ *in a state of* ~ 인사 불성이 되어. **3** lack of moral feeling. 냉담; 무관심.

in·sen·si·tive [insénsətiv] *adj.* that cannot be impressed or influenced; slow to feel or notice. 둔감한; 감수성이 없는. ¶ ~ *to beauty* 미적 감각이 없는 / ~ *to light* 빛을 느끼지 못하는.

in·sep·a·ra·ble [insépərəbəl] *adj.* that cannot be separated. 떼어놓지 못할; 불가분의. ¶ ~ *friends* 떨어질 수 없는 친구. [in-[1], *separable*]

·in·sert [insə́:rt] *vt.* (P6,13) 《*in, into*》 put in. 끼워넣다; 삽입하다. ¶ ~ *a key in a lock* 자물쇠에 열쇠를 집어넣다 / ~ *a word in a* *line* 행(行) 속에 낱말 하나를 써넣다. —[ㅗ—] *n.* Ⓒ a thing put in, esp. an extra page put in a newspaper, etc. 삽입물; (신문 등의) 삽입 광고. [in-², L. *sero* join]

in·ser·tion [insə́:rʃən] *n.* **1** Ⓤ the act of inserting. 끼워넣기; 삽입. **2** Ⓒ a thing inserted, esp. an advertisement in a newspaper. 삽입물; (신문 등에) 삽입되는 광고물.

in·set [insét] *vt.* (P6,13) (**-set, -set·ting**) put in; insert. …을 끼워넣다; 삽입하다. —[ㅗㅗ] *n.* Ⓒ a thing set in, esp. a smaller map or picture set in the border of a larger one. 삽입된 것; 삽입 도면(지도, 사진). [in-², *set*]

in·shore [ínʃɔ́:r] *adj.* near the shore; moving toward the shore. 해안에 가까운; 해안을 향한. ¶ ~ *fishing* 연안 어업 / *an* ~ *wind* 해안을 향해 부는 바람. — *adv.* toward the shore. 해안을 향하여. ¶ *They went closer* ~. 뭍으로 가까이 다가갔다. [in-², *shore*]

:in·side [ínsáid, ㅗㅗ] *n.* **1** Ⓒ 《usu. *the* ~》 the inner side or part of something. 안쪽; 내부; 내면(opp. outside). ¶ *the* ~ *of a box* 상자의 안쪽 / *the* ~ *of a house* 집의 내부 / *The door is bolted on the* ~. 문은 안에서 잠겨 있다. **2** 《usu. *pl.*》 《*colloq.*》 the stomach and the area near it. 배. ¶ *I have a pain in my inside(s).* 배가 아프다. **3** the contents. 내용. ¶ *the* ~ *of a book* 책의 내용. **4** (of a path) the side remote from the road. 차도에서 먼 쪽. ¶ *walk on the* ~ *of the pavement* 도로의 가장자리 쪽을 걷다.

inside out, **a**) with the inner side turned out. 뒤집어. ¶ *He put on his socks* ~ *out.* 그는 양말을 뒤집어 신었다. **b**) thoroughly. 철저하게; 속속들이. ¶ *He knew the work* ~ *out.* 그는 그 일에 대하여는 아주 밝았다.

on the inside, in a position to know inside affairs. 내부 사정에 밝은 입장에. ¶ *The persons on the* ~ *knew it.* 내막을 알 만한 사람은 알고 있었다.

—[ㅗㅗ] *adj.* **1** inner. 안쪽의. ¶ *Put the money in the* ~ *pocket of your coat.* 돈은 코트 안쪽 주머니에 넣어라. **2** working indoors. 안에서 일하는. ¶ *an* ~ *man* 내근자. **3** private; secret. 개인적인; 비밀의. ¶ *I have* ~ *information of their plans.* 나는 그들 계획의 내막을 알고 있다.

—[ㅗㅗ, ㅗㅗ] *adv.* **1** on or to the inside; within. 내부에; 안쪽에. ¶ *Go* ~. 들어가거라. **2** indoors. 옥내에서.

—[ㅗㅗ, ㅗㅗ] *prep.* within. …의 내부에. ¶ *go* ~ *the gate* 문 안으로 들어가다. [*in, side*]

in·sid·er [ìnsáidər] *n.* Ⓒ **1** a person who belongs to some circle, society, etc. 내부 사람; 회원; 부원(opp. outsider). **2** 《*colloq.*》 a person who is in a position to obtain special information. 내막을 아는 사람; 소식통.

in·sid·i·ous [insídiəs] *adj.* **1** cunning; sly; treacherous. 교활한; 음험한; 방심 못 할. ¶ ~ *wiles* 나쁜 음모. **2** advancing secretly. 모르는 사이에 진행하는. ¶ *an* ~ *disease* 잠행성 질환. [L. *incidiae* ambush]

in·sight [ínsàit] *n.* Ⓤ 《sometimes *an* ~》 the ability to see into the inside or inner parts of something; clear understanding. 사물의 본질을 아는 힘; 통찰력. ¶ *a man of* ~ 통찰력이 있는 사람. [in-²]

gain* [*have*] *an insight into, see the real meaning of. …을 통찰하다. ¶ *He has an* ~ *into character.* 그는 사람을 꿰뚫어 본다.

in·sig·ne [insígni:] *n.* sing. of **insignia.**

in·sig·ni·a [insígniə] *n. pl.* (*sing.* **-signe**) symbols of authority; badges of office or rank. 기장(記章); 훈장. ¶ *army* ~ 육군의 기장 / *the* ~ *of an order* 훈장. [in-², L. *signum* mark]

in·sig·nif·i·cance [ìnsignífikəns] *n.* Ⓤ the state of being insignificant; unimportance; meaninglessness. 하찮음; 무의미. ¶ *rise from* ~ *to fame* 하찮은 신분에서 유명해지다. [↓]

·in·sig·nif·i·cant [ìnsignífikənt] *adj.* having little or no importance; meaningless. 하찮은; 무의미한. ¶ *an* ~ *sum* 하찮은 액수 / *an* ~ *word* 무의미한 말 / *waste time on* ~ *things* 쓸데없는 일에 시간을 들이다. [in-¹]

in·sin·cere [ìnsinsíər] *adj.* not sincere; that cannot be trusted; false. 불성실한; 위선적인. ¶ ~ *praise* 말뿐인 칭찬. [in-¹]

in·sin·cer·i·ty [ìnsinsérəti] *n.* **1** Ⓤ the state or quality of being insincere. 불성실; 위선. **2** Ⓒ an insincere act. 불성실한 행위.

in·sin·u·ate [insínjuèit] *vt.* **1** (P11) hint or suggest indirectly. …을 암시하다; 에둘러 말하다. ¶ *She insinuated that he was wrong.* 그가 나빴다고 그녀는 넌지시 말했다 / *Are you insinuating that I told a lie?* 그래 내가 거짓말을 했다는 거냐. **2** (P13) 《*reflexively*》 put in or introduce (oneself) by clever, indirect means. …에 비집고 들어가다; 교묘히 …하다. ¶ *A cat insinuated itself into the kitchen.* 고양이가 몰래 부엌에 기어들었다 / *He insinuated himself into the king's favor.* 교묘하게 왕의 환심을 샀다. [in-², L. *sinuo* curve, wind]

in·sin·u·a·tion [insìnjuéiʃən] *n.* **1** Ⓤ the act of insinuating. 넌지시 비춤; 교묘하게 들어감. **2** Ⓒ an indirect suggestion critical of someone. 빗댐; 암시. ¶ *That's an evil* ~ *!* 그건 악의적인 비방이다 / *I object to your* ~ *that I have told a lie.* 내가 거짓말했다는 투의 네 말에는 유감이다.

in·sip·id [insípid] *adj.* **1** without taste or flavor. 맛없는; 김빠진. ¶ *an* ~ *drink* 싱거운 음료 / *a rather* ~ *soup* 별로 풍미 없는 수프. **2** dull; uninteresting. 따분한; 재미 없는. ¶ *an* ~ *speech* 지루한 연설. [in-¹, L. *sapio* taste]

in·si·pid·i·ty [ìnsipídəti] *n.* (*pl.* **-ties**) **1** Ⓤ the state or quality of being insipid. 무미(건조); 평범. **2** Ⓒ a thing which is insipid. 평

범〔무미건조〕한 것.

:**in·sist** [insíst] *vi., vt.* (P1,3;11) 《*on, upon*》 **1** declare with force; express one's opinion earnestly; emphasize. 주장하다; 역설〔강조〕하다. ¶ ~ *on the importance of being honest* 정직의 중요성을 강조하다 / *I* ~ *on his innocence.* =*I* ~ *that he is innocent.* 나는 그의 무죄를 주장한다 / *The boy insists that he has a right to do so.* 그 소년은 자기는 그렇게 할 권리가 있다고 고집한다. **2** demand strongly. 강력히 요구하다. ¶ *Mother insists that we (should) wash our hands before eating.* 어머니는 식사 전에 손을 씻을 것을 다짐하신다 / *I* ~ *that you come.* 어쨌든 너는 와야 한다. [in-[2], L. *sisto* stay]

in·sist·ence [insístəns] *n.* Ⓤ the act of insisting; the state or quality of being insistent. 강조; 주장; 강요; 강제적임.

in·sist·ent [insístənt] *adj.* **1** continuing to make a demand or statement. 강요〔주장〕하는. ¶ *Though it was raining, he was* ~ *on going out.* 비가 오는데도 그는 나가겠다고 고집했다. **2** calling attention strongly. 두드러지는; 주의를 끄는. ¶ *an* ~ *knocking on the door* 요란스럽게 문을 두드리는 소리.

in·so·bri·e·ty [ìnsəbráiəti] *n.* Ⓤ lack of restraint, esp. in drinking; intemperance. 자제할 줄 모름; (특히) 과음. [in-[1]]

in·sole [ínsòul] *n.* Ⓒ **1** the inner bottom of a shoe. (구두의) 안창. **2** a removable thin, inner bottom of a shoe used for comfort, etc. (구두의) 깔창. [*in, sole*]

in·so·lence [ínsələns] *n.* **1** Ⓤ the state or quality of being insolent; rudeness. 오만; 건방짐; 무례. **2** Ⓒ an insolent act or speech. 건방진〔무례한〕 언행. [↓]

in·so·lent [ínsələnt] *adj.* very rude to others; insulting. 무례한; 건방진. ¶ *"Shut up!" the* ~ *boy said to his father.* 버릇없는 소년은 아버지에게 "시끄러워요!" 라고 말하였다. ● **in·so·lent·ly** [-li] *adv.* [in-[1], L. *soleo* am accustomed]

in·sol·u·ble [insáljubəl / -sɔ́l-] *adj.* **1** that cannot be melted. 녹지 않는. ¶ *an* ~ *substance.* **2** that cannot be solved or explained. 해결할 수 없는. ¶ *an* ~ *problem* 풀 수 없는 문제. [in-[1]]

in·sol·ven·cy [insálvənsi / -sɔ́l-] *n.* Ⓤ the state of being insolvent. 지불 불능; 파산.

in·sol·vent [insálvənt / -sɔ́l-] *adj.* not able to pay one's debts; bankrupt. 지불 불능의; 파산한. —*n.* Ⓒ an insolvent person. 지불 불능자; 파산한 사람. [→insoluble]

in·som·ni·a [insámniə / -sɔ́m-] *n.* Ⓤ the state of being unable to sleep; sleeplessness. 불면(증). [L. *somnus* sleep]

in·so·much [ìnsoumʌ́tʃ] *adv.* to such an extent or degree. …할 정도까지; …만큼. ¶ *The snow fell heavily,* ~ *that all the traffic was interrupted.* 폭설로 인해 모든 교통이 막혀 버렸다. [*in, so, much*]

*·**in·spect** [inspékt] *vt.* **1** examine carefully and critically. …을 세밀히 조사하다. ¶ *The pupil's teeth are inspected twice a year.* 학생들 치아는 연 2회 검사를 받는다. **2** view or examine officially (troops, etc.). (군대 등)을 시찰하다. ¶ ~ *a factory* 공장을 시찰하다 / *The police inspected the building.* 경찰은 건물을 점검했다. [L. *specio* look at]

in·spec·tion [inspékʃən] *n.* ⓊⒸ **1** the act of inspecting; careful examination. 조사; 검사. ¶ *undergo a medical* ~ 신체 검사를 받다. **2** an official examination or review. 시찰; 검열.

*·**in·spec·tor** [inspéktər] *n.* Ⓒ a person who inspects; an officer appointed to inspect. 조사관; 검사관; 감독관.

*·**in·spi·ra·tion** [ìnspəréiʃən] *n.* **1** Ⓤ the influence of thought and feelings on good actions; any influence arousing the creative power of the mind. 감화; 고무; 격려; 영감; 인스피레이션. ¶ *get* 〔*draw*〕 ~ *from* …에서 영감을 얻다. **2** Ⓒ a person or thing that gives such an influence. 감화·영감을 주는〔고무하는〕 사람〔것〕. ¶ *The captain was an* ~ *to his men.* 선장은 부하의 사기를 고무하는 사람이었다. **3** Ⓒ 《*colloq.*》 a bright idea. 좋은 생각; 명안. ¶ *have a sudden* ~ 갑자기 명안이 떠오르다. **4** Ⓤ the act of drawing air into the lungs. 숨을 들이쉼(opp. expiration). [↓]

:**in·spire** [inspáiər] *vt.* (P6,13,20) **1** affect or encourage (someone) with a noble thought or feeling; produce or arouse (a feeling, a thought, etc.). …을 감동시키다; 고무하다; (사상·감정 등)을 일어나게 하다. ¶ *I inspired him to make greater efforts.* 나는 그에게 좀더 분발하라고 격려했다 / *His success inspired us with new courage.* 그의 성공은 우리에게 새로운 용기를 주었다. **2** give inspiration to (someone); cause, guide or communicate with (someone or something) by divine influence. …에게 영감을 주다. **3** draw (air) into the lungs. (숨)을 들이쉬다(opp. expire). [L. *spiro* breathe]

in·spir·it [inspírit] *vt.* (P6,13,20) encourage; hearten. …에게 용기를 주다; 격려하다. [in-[2]]

inst. instant.

in·sta·bil·i·ty [ìnstəbíləti] *n.* Ⓤ lack of steadiness. 불안정. [in-[1]]

*·**in·stall** [instɔ́ːl] *vt.* (P6,13) **1** put (someone) into office with ceremony. 취임시키다. **2** put (something) into a position or place where it can be used. …을 설치하다. ¶ ~ *a sink* 싱크대를 놓다 / ~ *air-conditioning equipment* 냉난방 장치를 하다. **3** 《*reflexively*》 seat; settle. …을 자리에 앉히다. ¶ *He installed himself in the easy chair.* 그는 안락 의자에 앉았다. [in-[2], L.

stallum stall, seat]

in·stal·la·tion [ìnstəléiʃən] *n.* **1** Ⓤ the act of installing; the state of being installed. 임명; 취임. **2** Ⓒ a system of machinery placed in position for use. 설비; 장치.

in·stall·ment[1], 《Brit.》 **-stal-** [instɔ́ːlmənt] *n.* Ⓒ **1** a part of a debt that is to be paid at a certain time. 분할불; 불입금. ¶ *buy a car on monthly installments* 차를 월부로 사다 / *pay by* 〔*in*〕 *installments* 분할불로 지불하다. **2** any of several parts supplied at successive times. (연속물의) 1회분. ¶ *a story in six installments,* 6회 연속 소설.

in·stall·ment[2] [instɔ́ːlmənt] *n.* 《*arch.*》 =installation.

:in·stance [ínstəns] *n.* Ⓒ **1** a thing offered as an illustration; an example. 예; 실례. ¶ *give an* ~ 예를 들다. **2** a case; an occasion. 경우. ¶ *in this* ~ 이 경우에. **3** a request; a suggestion. 의뢰; 권유. ¶ *She sang at our* ~. 우리 요청으로 그녀는 노래를 불렀다. **4** 《law》 a step in a legal action. 소송 절차.

for instance, as an example. 예를 들면.

in the first 〔***last***〕 ***instance,*** firstly 〔lastly〕. 최초〔최후〕로.

— *vt.* (P6) give or quote (something) as an example. …을 예로 들다. ¶ *He instanced the fly as a dirty insect.* 그는 불결한 벌레의 보기로 파리를 들었다. [→instant]

:in·stant [ínstənt] *n.* Ⓒ **1** a particular moment. 즉시; 즉각. ¶ *At that* ~ *the bell rang.* 바로 그 순간 벨이 울렸다. **2** a short period of time. 순간. ¶ *Don't waste an* ~. 촌각을 아껴라 / *He thought it over for an* ~. 순간 그는 그 일을 다시 생각했다.

in an instant, immediately. 즉시. ¶ *I shall have finished in an* ~. 곧 끝납니다.

on the instant, on the spot. 당장에.

the instant (***that***)***,*** just as soon as. …을 하자마자. ¶ *Let me know the* ~ *he comes.* 그가 오는 대로 내게 알려라.

this instant, instantly. 지금 곧. ¶ *Stop talking this* ~*!* 입 다물어.

— *adj.* **1** immediate; urgent. 즉시의; 긴급한. ¶ *an* ~ *death* 즉사 / *There is an* ~ *need for action.* 즉시 행동할 필요가 있다 / *The medicine showed an* ~ *effect.* 약은 즉효였다. **2** 《comm.》 of this month. 이달의. 參考 inst.로 생략함. ¶ *the 18th* ~ 이 달 18일. **3** (of soup, etc.) ready to be prepared by adding a liquid. 즉석 요리용의; 즉시 사용할 수 있는. ¶ ~ *coffee* 인스턴트 커피. [in-[2], L. *sto* stand]

in·stan·ta·ne·ous [ìnstəntéiniəs] *adj.* occurring or made in an instant or at once. 즉시의; 동시적인. ¶ *an* ~ *photograph* 즉석 사진 / *an* ~ *reply* 즉답 / *The two movements were almost* ~. 그 두 운동은 거의 동시에 일어났다. [↑]

in·stan·ta·ne·ous·ly [ìnstəntéiniəsli] *adv.* immediately; at once. 즉시; 당장에.

:in·stant·ly [ínstəntli] *adv.* at once; immediately. 즉시; 당장에. — *conj.* as soon as. …하자마자. ¶ *I sent a telegram* ~ *I arrived there.* 거기 닿자마자 전보를 쳤다.

:in·stead [instéd] *adv.* in one's or its place. 대신에. ¶ *If you cannot go, let Tom go* ~. 네가 못 가면 대신에 톰을 보내라. [*stead*]

instead of, in place of. …의 대신에. ¶ *Give me this* ~ *of that.* 저것 말고 이걸로 주시오.

in·step [ínstèp] *n.* Ⓒ **1** the upper side of the human foot between the toes and the ankle. 발등. **2** the part of a shoe, a stocking, etc. which covers this area. (구두·양말 등의) 발등에 해당하는 부분. [? *in, step*]

in·sti·gate [ínstəgèit] *vt.* (P6,13,20) urge on; stir up. …을 부추기다; 선동하다. ¶ ~ *a quarrel* 싸움을 붙이다 / *The workers were instigated to go on* (*a*) *strike.* 노동자들은 선동되어 파업을 했다. [L. *stigo* prick]

in·sti·ga·tion [ìnstəgéiʃən] *n.* Ⓤ the act of instigating. 선동; 부추김.

at the instigation of (=*instigated by*) *someone.* …에 선동되어.

in·sti·ga·tor [ínstəgèitər] *n.* Ⓒ a person who instigates. 선동자.

in·still, -stil [instíl] *vt.* (**-stilled, -stil·ling**) (P6,13) 《*into*》 **1** introduce (ideas, etc.) little by little. …을 서서히 주입하다. ¶ ~ *a sense of honor into a child* 아이에게 명예심을 가지게 하다. **2** put in (liquid) drop by drop. …을 방울방울 듣게 하다. [in-[2], L. *stillo* drop]

:in·stinct[1] [ínstiŋkt] *n.* **1** ⓊⒸ a natural feeling or knowledge that one should do a necessary thing without taking conscious thought. 본능. ¶ *act on* ~ 본능대로 행동하다 / *homing* ~ 귀소 본능 / *It is the* ~ *of all animals to fear fire.* 불을 무서워하는 것은 모든 짐승의 본능이다. **2** Ⓒ a natural ability; a talent. 천성; 소질. ¶ *He has an* ~ *for art.* 그는 예술에 대한 소질이 있다. [L. *stigo* prick]

in·stinct[2] [instíŋkt] *adj.* filled with. …으로 가득 찬. ¶ *a picture* ~ *with life and beauty* 생기와 아름다움이 넘치는 그림. [↑]

in·stinc·tive [instíŋktiv] *adj.* caused or done by instinct; not learned; natural. 본능적인; 선천적인. ¶ *Eating is* ~ *in any animal.* 먹는다는 것은 어떤 동물이건 본능적인 것이다 / *an* ~ *taste for art* 천성적인 예술 취미.

in·stinc·tive·ly [instíŋktivli] *adv.* by instinct. 본능적으로.

***in·sti·tute** [ínstətjùːt] *vt.* (P6,13) **1** set up; establish; organize. …을 만들다; 설치하다. ¶ ~ *new rules* 새 규칙을 마련하다 / ~ *a society* 협회를 하나 설립하다. **2** begin; start. …을 시작하다; 개시하다. ¶ *They instituted a search for the missing man.* 행방 불명자의 수색을 시작했다. **3** appoint.

임명하다. ¶ ~ *someone to* 〔*into*〕 *a benefice* 아무를 성직에 임명하다.
—*n.* Ⓒ **1** a thing which is established; an established principle, law, custom, etc. 제도; 관례. **2** a society or organization for some special, esp. public purpose. 협회; 학회. ¶ *an art* ~ 미술 협회. **3** a building used by such a society or organization. 회관; 연구소. ¶ *an* ~ *of music* 음악 연구소 / *the Pasteur Institute* 파스퇴르 연구소. [L. *statuo* set up]

:in·sti·tu·tion [ìnstətjú:ʃən] *n.* Ⓒ **1** a society or organization for some, esp. public, purpose. 회; 협회; 기관. ¶ *an educational* ~ 교육 기관. **2** a building used by such a society or organization. 공공시설; 회관; 연구소. **3** an established law, custom, etc. 제도; 관례. ¶ *the* ~ *of marriage* 결혼 제도. **4** Ⓤ the act of establishing or beginning. 설립; 제정. ¶ *the* ~ *of new rules* 새 규칙의 제정. **5** 《*colloq.*》 a person who is widely known; favorite. 잘 알려진 사람; 명물. ¶ *He is an* ~ *in this town.* 그 사람은 이 마을의 명물이다.

in·sti·tu·tion·al [ìnstətjú:ʃənəl] *adj.* of or like an institution. 제도상의; 공공 기관의; 협회의.

:in·struct [instrʌ́kt] *vt.* **1** (P6,13) 《*in*》 furnish (someone) with knowledge; teach; educate. …을 가르치다. ¶ *He instructs five classes in English.* 그는 5개 반에서 영어를 가르치고 있다. **2** (P20) give orders or directions to (someone). …에게 명령하다; 지시하다. ¶ *I instructed him to come early.* 나는 그에게 일찍 오라고 명령했다 / *We were instructed not to tell about it.* 우리는 그것에 대한 발설을 금지당했다. **3** (P15,16,17) give information to (someone); inform; tell. …에게 통지하다; 알리다. ¶ *Our agent instructed us that we still owed Mr. John 300 dollars.* 대리점에선 우리가 존씨에게 아직 300달러의 미불이 있다고 알려왔다 / *My lawyer instructed me what to say in court.* 변호사는 나에게 법정에서 해야 할 말을 일러주었다. [L. *struo* pileup, excite]

:in·struc·tion [instrʌ́kʃən] *n.* Ⓤ **1** the act of teaching; education. 가르침; 교수; 교육. ¶ ~ *in music* 음악 교육. **2** 《*pl.*》 directions; orders. 지시; 명령. ¶ *follow instructions* 지시에 따르다. **3** knowledge or information given or taught; a lesson. (배운) 지식; 교훈.
give instruction in, teach. …을 가르치다.
give instructions to, order. …에 명령하다.
receive instruction in, learn. …을 배우다.

·in·struc·tive [instrʌ́ktiv] *adj.* giving information or knowledge. 교육적인; 유익한. ¶ *This book is not only interesting but also* ~. 이 책은 재미도 있거니와 유익하다.

in·struc·tor [instrʌ́ktər] *n.* Ⓒ **1** a person who instructs; a teacher; a trainer. 교사; 지도자. **2** 《U.S.》 a lecturer in a university. 대학의 강사.

·in·stru·ment [ínstrəmənt] *n.* Ⓒ **1** a person or thing used by someone to accomplish something; a means. 남의 앞잡이; 수단. ¶ *use someone as an* ~ 아무를 앞잡이로 쓰다 / *The army was the dictator's* ~. 군대는 독재자의 도구였다 / *He is the leader, the others are merely his instruments.* 그가 지도자고 나머지는 그저 앞잡이다. **2** a tool used for delicate or scientific work. 학술용 정밀기기. ¶ *medical instruments* 의료 기구 / *optical instruments* 광학 기계. **3** a device for producing musical sounds. 악기. ¶ *wind instruments* 관악기. **4** 《law》 a piece of formal writing. 증서. [→instruct]

in·stru·men·tal [ìnstrəméntl] *adj.* **1** 《as *predicative*》 serving as a means; helpful. 수단이 되는; 도움이 되는. ¶ *He was* ~ *in obtaining an appointment for his friends.* 그는 친구들이 관직을 얻는 데 힘이 되었다. **2** of or for musical instruments. 악기의〔를 위한〕 (opp. vocal). ¶ ~ *music* 기악곡. **3** of an instrument. 기계(器械)의.

in·stru·men·tal·ist [ìnstrəméntəlist] *n.* Ⓒ a person who plays on a musical instrument. 기악가.

in·stru·men·tal·i·ty [ìnstrəmentǽləti] *n.* Ⓤ help; means. 도움; 수단.
by 〔***through***〕 ***the instrumentality of,*** by means of. …을 수단으로; …의 힘을 빌려.

in·sub·or·di·nate [ìnsəbɔ́:rdənit] *adj.* resisting authority; disobedient. 권위〔권력〕에 반항하는; 고분고분하지 않은. [in-[1]]

in·sub·or·di·na·tion [ìnsəbɔ̀:rdənéiʃən] *n.* Ⓤ resistance to authority; disobedience. 권력〔권위〕에의 반항; 불순종.

in·sub·stan·tial [ìnsəbstǽnʃəl] *adj.* **1** weak; not firm. 약한; 무른. **2** unreal; imaginary. 실재하지 않는; 상상의. [in-[1]]

in·suf·fer·a·ble [insʌ́fərəbəl] *adj.* very hard to endure. 참을 수 없는. ¶ ~ *conduct* 묵과할 수 없는 짓. [in-[1]]

in·suf·fi·cien·cy [ìnsəfíʃənsi] *n.* Ⓤ too small an amount; lack. 불충분; 모자람; 부족. [↓]

in·suf·fi·cient [ìnsəfíʃənt] *adj.* not enough. 불충분한; 불만인. ¶ ~ *light for reading* 독서에 불충분한 조명. [in-[1]]

in·su·lar [ínsələr, -sjə-] *adj.* **1** of islands or islanders. 섬의; 섬 주민의. **2** narrow-minded. 편협한. ¶ ~ *prejudices* 섬나라 근성. [L. *insula* island]

in·su·lar·i·ty [ìnsəlǽrəti, -sjə-] *n.* Ⓤ **1** the state of being an island. 섬(나라)임. **2** narrow-mindedness. 편협; 섬나라 근성.

in·su·late [ínsəlèit, -sjə-] *vt.* (P6,13) **1** set (someone or something) apart; isolate. …을 격리〔고립〕시키다. ¶ ~ *patients with infectious diseases* 전염병 환자를 격리시키다. **2** separate (something) by a material which will not conduct electricity, heat, or sound. (전기·열·소리)를 절연시키다. ¶ ~ *an* *electric wire* 전선을 절연시키다. **3** 《*arch.*》 make (land) into an island; surround by water. (육지를) 섬으로 만들다. [→insular]

in·su·la·tion [ìnsəléiʃən, -sjə-] *n.* Ⓤ **1** the act of insulating; the state of being insulated. 격리; 고립; 절연; 단열; 방음. **2** materials used in insulating. 절연[단열]재.

in·su·la·tor [ínsəlèitər, -sjə-] *n.* Ⓒ a material or device which does not conduct electricity, heat or sound. 절연물; 절연체.

in·su·lin [ínsəlin, -sjə-] *n.* 《med.》 an extract used in treatment of diabetes. 인슐린 《당뇨병약》. ¶ *~ shock* 인슐린 쇼크; 저(低)혈당성(性) 쇼크. [L. *insula* island (of the pancreas)]

•**in·sult** [insʌ́lt] *vt.* (P6) treat (someone or something) with rudeness or contempt. …을 모욕하다. ¶ *She insulted him by calling him a coward.* 그녀는 그를 겁쟁이라고 모욕했다. —[⌐—] *n.* ⒸⓊ a rude or scornful action or speech. 모욕(적인 언행). ¶ *What you say is an ~ to my wife.* 네가 하는 말은 내 아내에 대한 모욕이다. [in-[2], L. *salio* leap]

in·sult·ing·ly [insʌ́ltiŋli] *adv.* in an insulting manner. 무례하게; 모욕해서.

in·su·per·a·ble [insú:pərəbəl] *adj.* that cannot be overcome. 극복할 수 없는. ¶ *~ difficulties* [*grief*] 견딜 수 없는 곤경[슬픔]. [in-[1], L. *supero* overcome]

in·sup·port·a·ble [ìnsəpɔ́:rtəbəl] *adj.* unbearable; unendurable. 참을 수 없는; 견딜 수 없는. [in-[1]]

:**in·sur·ance** [inʃúərəns] *n.* **1** Ⓤ a system of guarding against financial loss from fire, accident, death, etc. 보험. ¶ *life* [*fire*] *~*. **2** Ⓒ a contract insuring property, life, etc.; an insurance policy. 보험 계약; 보험 증서. **3** Ⓤ the amount of money paid for such a system; a premium. 보험료(保險料). **4** Ⓤ the amount of money paid by an insurance company. 보험금. [↓]

•**in·sure** [inʃúər] *vt.* (P6,13) **1** arrange for a money payment in case of accident, damage, injury, to (someone or something) or in case of someone's death. …에 보험을 계약하다; …을 보험에 넣다. ¶ *~ one's house against fire* 집을 화재 보험에 넣다 / *~ one's life for five million won* 5백만 원의 생명 보험에 들다. **2** make sure; make safe; ensure. …을 확인하다; 안전하게 하다. 參考 이 뜻으로는 ensure 가 보통. — *vi.* (P1) issue or procure an insurance policy. 보험 증서를 발행하다; 보험에 가입하다. [→ensure]

in·sur·er [inʃúərər] *n.* Ⓒ a person or company that insures. 보험업자; 보험 회사.

in·sur·gent [insə́:rdʒənt] *n.* Ⓒ **1** a person who rises in revolt; a rebel. 폭도. **2** 《U.S. polit.》 a rebel within a political party. (당내) 반대 분자; 비주류파. — *adj.* rising in revolt. 폭동을 일으키는. [L. *surgo* rise]

in·sur·mount·a·ble [ìnsərmáuntəbəl] *adj.* that cannot be overcome. 극복할 수 없는; 넘지 못할. ¶ *an ~ difficulty* 극복할 수 없는 난관. [in-[1]]

in·sur·rec·tion [ìnsərékʃən] *n.* ⓊⒸ the act of rising against authority; rebellion. 반란; 폭동. [→insurgent]

in·sus·cep·ti·ble [ìnsəséptəbəl] *adj.* not acceptable or sensitive. 느끼지 못하는; 무감각한. [in-[1]]

int. interjection.

in·tact [intǽkt] *adj.* untouched; uninjured; whole. 손대지 않은; 말짱한; 완전한. ¶ *The town was ~ after the earthquake.* 도시는 지진이 나고도 온전했다. [L. *tango* touch]

in·take [íntèik] *n.* **1** Ⓒ a place through which water, air, gas, etc., is brought in. (물·공기 등이) 들어가는 데; 취수구(取水口); 흡입구(opp. outlet). **2** Ⓤ the act of taking in. 받아들임; 취수; 흡입. ¶ *say with a quick ~ of breath* 급히 숨을 들이쉬며 이야기하다. **3** Ⓒ the amount taken in. 취수[흡입]량. **4** 《*dial.*》 a piece of ground, recovered from waste land. 매립지; 간척지. [*in, take*]

in·tan·gi·ble [intǽndʒəbəl] *adj.* **1** that cannot be touched. 만질 수 없는. ¶ *Sound and light are ~.* 소리와 빛은 만져지지 않는다. **2** not easily grasped by the mind; vague. 파악할 수 없는; 막연한. ¶ *an ~ idea* 막연한 구상. — *n.* Ⓒ a thing which is intangible. 막연한 일[것]. [in-[1]]

in·te·ger [íntidʒər] *n.* Ⓒ **1** 《math.》 a whole number. 정수(整數). **2** a thing completed itself; anything entire. 완전한 것; 완전체. [→intact]

in·te·gral [íntigrəl] *adj.* **1** necessary for completeness; essential. 완전하기 위해 필요한; 필수적인. ¶ *~ parts of a machine* / *an ~ part of our plan* 우리 계획에 불가결한 부분. **2** entire; complete. 완전한. **3** 《math.》 of whole numbers; of an integer or integral calculus. 정수의; 적분(積分)의 (opp. fractional). [↑]

in·te·grate [íntəgrèit] *vt.* (P6) **1** bring together (parts) into a whole; make (something) into a whole; complete. …(부분)을 전체에 통합하다; …을 완전한 것으로 하다. **2** 《U.S.》 make (schools, housing, etc.) open to all races on an equal basis. …의 인종 차별을 철폐하다. **3** give the total sum or the average value of. …의 합계를[평균을] 내다. [L. *integro* make whole; *interger*]

in·te·gra·tion [ìntəgréiʃən] *n.* Ⓤ the act of integrating. 통합; 완성; 인종 차별 폐지.

in·teg·ri·ty [intégrəti] *n.* Ⓤ **1** honesty; sincerity. 정직; 성실. ¶ *a man of ~*. **2** wholeness; completeness. 완전; 무결함. [*integer*]

in·teg·u·ment [intégjəmənt] *n.* Ⓒ an outer covering, such as skin or a shell. 외피(外皮). [in-², L. *tego* cover]

in·tel·lect [íntəlèkt] *n.* **1** Ⓤ the power of knowing; understanding. 지성; 지력(知力). ¶ *a man of high* ~ 고도의 지성인. **2** Ⓒ a person who has much mental ability. 지식인. 語法 지식 계급의 뜻으로 집합 명사로도 쓰임. [L. *intelligo* understand (inter-, *lego* read)]

•**in·tel·lec·tu·al** [intəléktʃuəl] *adj.* **1** of the intellect or mind. 지성의; 지력의. ¶ ~ *faculties* 지적 능력. **2** needing intelligence. 지력을 필요로 하는. ¶ *an* ~ *occupation* 지능이 필요한 직업; 지적 직업. **3** having or showing a high degree of intellect. 지성(지력)이 있는; 이지적인. ¶ *an* ~ *face* (*person*) 지적인 용모(사람). — *n.* Ⓒ a person who is well informed and intelligent; a person who is interested in things of the mind instead of practical things. 지식인; 인텔리.

in·tel·lec·tu·al·i·ty [ìntəlèktʃuǽləti] *n.* Ⓤ the state of being intellectual; intellectual power. 지성; 지능; 지력.

in·tel·lec·tu·al·ly [ìntəléktʃuəli] *adv.* **1** in an intellectual manner. 지(성)적으로. **2** so far as intellect is concerned. 지성에 관해서는; 지능상.

:**in·tel·li·gence** [intélədʒəns] *n.* Ⓤ **1** the ability to learn or understand and use what one has learned. 이해력; 지능; 지력. ¶ *The boy has high* ~ *for his age.* 저 아이는 그 나이로서는 지혜롭다 / *A man with* (*of*) *average* (*ordinary*) ~ *will know it.* 웬만한 머리를 가진 사람이라면 그건 안다. **2** news or information, esp. secret information; knowledge. 보도; 정보; 비밀 정보; 지식. ¶ *collect* ~ *of an event* 사건의 정보를 수집하다 / ~ *service* 정보 기관. [*intelligent*]

intelligence department [-ᐩ-- -ᐩ-] *n.* a department of information for the use of army or navy. (군의) 정보부.

intelligence quotient [-ᐩ-- ᐩ-] *n.* a number denoting the ratio of someone's intelligence to the average. 지능 지수. 參考 IQ, I.Q.로 생략함.

intelligence ship [-ᐩ-- ᐩ] *n.* a ship that gathers intelligence for the use of army or navy. 정보 수집함.

intelligence test [-ᐩ-- ᐩ] *n.* a test used to measure mental development. 지능 검사.

•**in·tel·li·gent** [intélədʒənt] *adj.* **1** showing intelligence. 이지적인; 총명한. ¶ *an* ~ *reply* 총명한 대답. **2** able to learn and to use what one has learned and understood. 지능이 있는 영리한. ¶ *an* ~ *child* 영리한 아이 / *Man is* ~ *being.* 인간은 지적인 존재다. [→intellect]

in·tel·li·gent·ly [intélədʒəntli] *adj.* in an intelligent manner. 총명하게; 슬기롭게.

in·tel·li·gent·si·a [intèlədʒéntsiə, -gén-] *n.* 《*the* ~》《*collectively*》 persons who are highly educated and enlightened; the intellectuals. 지식 계급; 인텔리겐치아.

in·tel·li·gi·bil·i·ty [intèlədʒəbíləti] *n.* Ⓤ the quality of being intelligible. 이해할 수 있음; 총명.

in·tel·li·gi·ble [intélədʒəbəl] *adj.* that can be understood; clear. 이해할 수 있는; 명료한. ¶ *an* ~ *explanation* 알기 쉬운 설명.
● **in·tel·li·gi·bly** [-bli] *adv.*

INTELSAT, In·tel·sat [íntelsæ̀t] *n.* International Telecommunications Satellite Consortium. 인텔샛; 국제 상업 통신 위성 기구.

in·tem·per·ance [intémpərəns] *n.* Ⓤ **1** the state of being intemperate; lack of moderation; excess. 절제할 줄 모름; 절도가 없음; 방종. **2** excessive drinking. 과음; 폭음. [↓]

in·tem·per·ate [intémpərit] *adj.* **1** not moderate; lacking in self-control; excessive. 절제 없는; 신중하지 못한; 지나친. ¶ ~ *conduct* 과격한 행동 / ~ *language* 폭언. **2** drinking too much. 폭음(과음)하는. **3** harsh; severe. 사나운; 심한. ¶ ~ *weather* 고약한 날씨. [in-¹]

:**in·tend** [inténd] *vt.* (P6,8,11,13,20) **1** have (something) in mind as a purpose or aim; plan. …할 생각(작정)이다. ¶ *He intended no harm.* 그에게 악의는 없었다 / *I* ~ *to go myself.* =*I* ~ *going myself.* 내가 갈 생각이다 / *Are you going to help her?* — *I* ~ *to* (*do so*). 그녀를 도와주려나 —그래, 그럴 생각이다. **2** 《*for*》 design (someone or something) for a particular purpose. (남)에게 …시키려 하다; (물건)을 어떤 목적에 쓰려고 하다. ¶ *His father intends him for a lawyer.* =*His father intends him to be a lawyer.* =*His father intends that he* (*shall*) *be a lawyer.* 그의 아버지는 그를 변호사로 만들려고 한다 / *The gift was intended for you.* 그건 네게 줄 선물이었다 / *This portrait is intended for me.* 이 초상화는 나를 그린 것이다. **3** mean. …을 뜻하다. ¶ *What do you* ~ *by these words?* 왜 이런 말을 하느냐. [in-², L. *tendo* stretch]

in·tend·ed [inténdid] *adj.* **1** meant; planned. 의도된; 소기의. ¶ *This medicine did not have the* ~ *effect.* 이 약은 기대만큼의 약효를 못 봤다. **2** prospective. 미래의. ¶ *a woman's* ~ *husband* 장차의 남편. — *n.* Ⓒ 《*colloq.*》 a prospective husband or wife. 약혼자. ¶ *his* ~ 그의 약혼자.

•**in·tense** [inténs] *adj.* **1** very great or strong; violent. 심한; 격심(격렬)한. ¶ ~ *cold* 혹한 / *an* ~ *pain* 격통 / ~ *hatred* 격렬한 증오. **2** earnest; passionate. 열렬한; 진지한. ¶ *an* ~ *face* 진지한 얼굴 / *an* ~ *love* 뜨거운 사랑. **3** showing strong feelings. (성격이) 격정적인; 감정적인. ¶ *an* ~ *young lady* 격정적인 아가씨. [→intend]

in·tense·ly [inténsli] *adv.* in an intense manner. 열렬하게; 진지하게.

in·ten·si·fi·ca·tion [intènsəfikéiʃən] *n.* Ⓤ the act of intensifying; the state of being intensified. 강화; 증대.

in·ten·si·fy [inténsəfài] *vt.* (P6) make (something) more intense. …을 강하게 하다; 증대시키다. ¶ *He intensified his efforts.* 가일층의 노력을 했다 / *The strong wind seemed to ~ the cold.* 강한 바람이 추위를 더 심하게 한 모양이었다. — *vi.* (P1) become more intense. 세지다; 격해지다. ¶ *The pain intensified.* 고통이 심해졌다.

in·ten·sion [inténʃən] *n.* **1** Ⓤ a degree (of a quality, etc.). 강도; 세기. **2** vigorous effort (of mind, etc.). (정신적) 노력; 긴장. **3** 《log.》 connotation. 내포(內包)(opp. extension).

·in·ten·si·ty [inténsəti] *n.* Ⓤ **1** the state or quality of being intense. 격렬함; 강렬. ¶ *the ~ of his anger* 그의 심한 분노 / *work* 〔*study*〕 *with ~* 열을 내서 일〔공부〕하다. **2** strength or degree (of heat, sound, etc.). (열·소리 등의) 강도; 세기. ¶ *the ~ of heat* 열의 세기.

in·ten·sive [inténsiv] *adj.* **1** thorough; concentrated. 철저한; 집중적인(opp. extensive). ¶ *an ~ course in English* 영어 집중 강의 / *(an) ~ study* 철저한 연구. **2** 《gram.》 giving force or emphasis. 강의의. ¶ *an ~ prefix* 강의 접두사. **3** 《agriculture》 designed to increase effectiveness. 집약적인. ¶ *~ farming* 집약 농업. **4** 《log.》 contained in a concept. 내포(內包)의; 내포적인.

·in·tent[1] [intént] *n.* ⓊⒸ purpose; intention. 목적; 의지; 의도. ¶ *with good* 〔*evil*〕 *~* 선의〔악의〕로 / *follow someone with ~ to kill* 〔*of killing*〕 아무를 죽이려고 뒤따라가다. [*intend*]

to all intents and purposes, in almost every point; practically. 모든 점에서; 실제로.

·in·tent[2] [intént] *adj.* 《*on, upon*》 earnestly engaged or observed; concentrated. 전념하고 있는; 열중〔몰두〕한. ¶ *I was so ~ on my work that I heard nothing.* 일에 너무 열중해서 아무 것도 못 들었다 / *~ upon a problem* 문제에 골몰해 있는 / *She is ~ on pleasure.* 그녀는 놀이에 열중해 있다. [↑]

·in·ten·tion [inténʃən] *n.* ⓊⒸ **1** a thing which is intended or planned. 목적; 의도; 계획. ¶ *act with good intentions* 선의를 가지고 행동하다 / *I have no ~ of breaking the law.* 법을 어길 생각은 없다. **2** 《*pl.*》 《*colloq.*》 purposes with respect to marrying. 결혼할 의도〔목적〕. ¶ *He has intentions.* 그는 그녀와 결혼할 생각이다. **3** 《surg.》 the course or manner of a wound's healing. 유합(癒合). ¶ *heal with first* 〔*second*〕 *~,* 1차〔2차〕 유합을 하다. [→intend]

by intention, on purpose. 고의로; 일부러.

with the intention of (=*for the purpose of*) *doing something.* …할 생각〔작정〕으로.

in·ten·tion·al [inténʃənəl] *adj.* done on purpose. 고의의(opp. accidental). ¶ *an ~ wrong* 고의적인 잘못. [↑]

in·ten·tion·al·ly [inténʃənəli] *adv.* on purpose. 고의적으로.

in·ter [intə́ːr] *vt.* (**-terred, -ter·ring**) (P6) put (a dead body) into the ground or a tomb; bury. (시체)를 매장하다(opp. disinter). [in-[2], L. *terra* earth]

in·ter- [íntər-] *pref.* **1** one with the other. '상호의'의 뜻. ¶ *intercommunicate.* **2** between; among. '중간의, 사이의'의 뜻. ¶ *international / interpose.* [L.]

in·ter·act [ìntərǽkt] *vi.* (P1) act on each other. 서로 작용하다. ¶ *The two ideas ~.* 그 두 관념은 상호 관계에 있다. [↑]

in·ter·ac·tion [ìntərǽkʃən] *n.* Ⓤ action on each other; the process of interacting. 상호 작용.

in·ter·bred [ìntərbréd] *v.* p. and pp. of **interbreed.**

in·ter·breed [ìntərbríːd] *vt., vi.* (**-bred**) (P6; 1) breed by using different varieties of animals or plants; cross. 이종 교배(異種交配)시키다; 잡종 번식을 하다. [inter-]

in·ter·ca·la·ry [intə́ːrkəlèri, ìntərkǽləri] *adj.* inserted in the calendar as an extra day. 윤(閏)의. ¶ *an ~ month* 윤달. [inter-, L. *calo* proclaim]

in·ter·cede [ìntərsíːd] *vi.* (P3) 《*for, with*》 plead for another; act as peacemaker. 조정하다; 중재하다. ¶ *I interceded for John with his father.* 존을 위해 존의 아버지에게 좋게 말해 줬다. [→cede]

in·ter·cept [ìntərsépt] *vt.* (P6) **1** seize or stop (something or someone) on the way. …을 도중에서 가로채다〔붙잡다〕. ¶ *~ a messenger* 사자(使者)를 중도에서 붙잡다 / *Can we ~ the enemy's attack?* 우리가 적의 공격을 중도에서 저지할 수 있을까. **2** cut off (light, water, etc.). …을 차단하다. ¶ *~ the flow of water.* **3** 《math.》 cut off by two points or lines. 두 점〔선〕을 따라 잘라내다. [inter-, L. *capio* take]

in·ter·cep·tion [ìntərsépʃən] *n.* ⓊⒸ the act of intercepting. 도중에서 가로채기; 차단; 방해.

in·ter·ces·sion [ìntərséʃən] *n.* ⓊⒸ the act of interceding. 중재(仲裁); 조정; 알선. ¶ *through someone's ~* 아무의 주선으로. [*intercede*]

in·ter·change [ìntərtʃéindʒ] *vt.* **1** (P6) put (two or more things or persons) in the place of each other. …을 바꿔놓다〔넣다〕; 교체하다. ¶ *The parts of these machines may be interchanged.* 이들 기계의 부품은 교체할 수 있다 / *~ seats* 〔*places*〕 좌석을〔자리를〕 바꾸다. **2** (P6,13) 《*with*》 make an exchange; alternate. …을 교환하다; 번갈아 하다. ¶ *~ letters* 교신하다 / *~ gifts* 〔*greetings*〕 선물을〔인사를〕 주고 받다 / *You'd better ~ study with play.* 공부도 하고 놀기도 하고 그래라.

— *vi.* (P1) **1** (of two things) take each other's place; exchange. 교환하다. **2** follow one after the other. 번갈아 일어나다.
— [íntərtʃèindʒ, ⌐—⌐] *n.* **1** Ⓤ Ⓒ the act of interchanging. 바꿔놓기; 주고받기; 교환. ¶ *an ~ of calling cards* 명함의 교환 / *the ~ of greetings* 인사의 교환. **2** Ⓒ a junction of two or more highways, usu. express highways, by a system of separate road level. (고속 도로의) 입체 교차점; 인터체인지. [inter-]

in·ter·change·a·ble [ìntərtʃéindʒəbəl] *adj.* that can be interchanged. 교환할 수 있는; 교대〔교체〕할 수있는.

in·ter·col·le·gi·ate [ìntərkəlí:dʒiit] *adj.* between colleges or universities. 대학간의. ¶ *~ (baseball) games* 대학 대항(야구) 시합. [inter-]

in·ter·co·lo·ni·al [ìntərkəlóuniəl] *adj.* between colonies. 식민지간의. ¶ *~ trade* 식민지간 무역. [inter-]

in·ter·com [íntərkàm / -kɔ̀m] *n.* 《*colloq.*》 the intercommunication system. 상호 통신 방식; 인터콤. [inter-]

in·ter·com·mu·ni·cate [ìntərkəmjú:nəkèit] *vi.* (P1) **1** communicate with each other. 서로 왕래〔연락〕하다. **2** lead from one room to the other. (방이) 서로 통하다. ¶ *All three rooms ~ .* 방 세 개는 모두 통하게 되어 있다.

in·ter·com·mu·ni·ca·tion [ìntərkəmjù:nəkéiʃən] *n.* Ⓤ communication with each other. 서로의 왕래; 교제; 상호 연락. ¶ *the ~ system* 상호 통신 방식; 인터콤; 인터폰.

in·ter·con·nect [ìntərkənékt] *vt.* (P6) connect with each other. …을 서로 연결시키다. [inter-]

in·ter·con·ti·nen·tal [ìntərkàntənéntl / -kɔ̀n-] *adj.* that can travel from one continent to another. 대륙간의. ¶ *an ~ ballistic missile* 대륙간 탄도 미사일(abbr. I.C.B.M.). [inter-]

·**in·ter·course** [íntərkɔ̀:rs] *n.* Ⓤ **1** connection or communication between individuals, nations, etc. (개인·국가 간의) 관계; 교섭; 교제. ¶ *commercial ~* 통상 / *social ~* 사교. **2** sexual connection. 성교. [inter-]

in·ter·de·pend [ìntərdipénd] *vi.* (P1) depend upon each other. 서로 의존하다.

in·ter·de·pend·ence [ìntərdipéndəns] *n.* Ⓤ dependence upon each other; the state of being dependent upon each other. 상호 의존. ¶ *the ~ of nations* 국가 간의 상호 의존. [inter-]

in·ter·de·pend·ent [ìntərdipéndənt] *adj.* dependent upon each other. 서로 의존하는. ¶ *Central government and local government are ~ .* 중앙 정부와 지방 정부는 상호 의존 관계에 있다.

in·ter·dict [ìntərdíkt] *vt.* **1** (P6) prohibit; forbid. …을 금지하다. **2** (P13) 《*from*》 restrain. …을 제지〔억지〕하다. **3** (P6) cut off from certain church priviledges. …을 파문하다; …의 성무 수행을 금지시키다. — [⌐—⌐] *n.* Ⓒ a formal prohibition, esp. of certain church privileges. 금지 (명령); (특히) 성무 금지; 파문. [inter-, L. *dico* say]

in·ter·dic·tion [ìntərdíkʃən] *n.* Ⓤ Ⓒ the act of interdicting; the state of being interdicted. 금지; 제지; 성무 금지; 파문.

:**in·ter·est** [íntərist] *n.* Ⓤ **1** Ⓤ Ⓒ the feeling of wanting to know or to do; concern; curiosity. 흥미; 관심. ¶ *I have no ~ in music.* 나는 음악에 흥미가 없다 / *find a fresh ~ in studying languages* 어학 공부에 새로운 흥미를 발견하다. **2** the power to arouse such a feeling. 흥미를 일으키는 힘. ¶ *Local color adds ~ to a story.* 지방색은 이야기에 흥미를 더한다. **3** Ⓒ something in which one has an interest; a hobby; an attraction. 관심사; 흥미의 대상; 취미. ¶ *Volleyball is her chief ~ .* 그녀가 가장 관심을 갖는 것은 배구다 / *Music and painting are his great interests.* 음악과 미술을 그는 가장 좋아한다. **4** importance. 중요성. ¶ *a matter of primary ~* 가장 중요한 일 / *a matter of no ~* 사소한 일. **5** personal influence over the action of others; controlling power. 세력; 지배력. ¶ *have ~ with the authorities* 관계 당국에 영향력이 있다. **6** Ⓒ 《often *pl.*》 advantage; benefit; profit. 이익; 소득. ¶ *common interests* 공통의 이해 / *for one's own ~* 자기 이익을 위해 / *It is (to, for, in) your ~ to do so.* 그렇게 하는 것이 네게 이롭단다. **7** the money paid by a borrower for the use of borrowed money. 이자; 이율. ¶ *He lent her the money at 4 per cent ~ .* 그녀에게 4부 이자로 돈을 빌려주었다. **8** Ⓒ a share or part; a right or claim to something. 주식; 이권; 요구권. ¶ *Father owns an ~ in the farm.* 아버지는 그 농장의 이권을 가지고 있다 / *He has an ~ in the business.* 그는 그 사업에 출자〔관여〕하고 있다 / *buy interests in a company* 어떤 회사의 주식을 사다. **9** 《often *pl.*》 a group of people concerned with some particular kind of work or business. 관계자들; 동업자. ¶ *steel interests* 철강업자 / *the farmming interests* 농장경영자. **10** something added in making a return. 덤. ¶ *He returned the blow with ~ .* 그는 덤으로 주먹을 안겼다.

in the interest*(*s*) *of, on behalf of; for. …을 위해. ¶ *in the ~ of humanity* 인류를 위하여.
— *vt.* (P6,13) **1** cause or arouse the attention or curiosity of (someone). …에 흥미를〔관심을〕 일으키다〔끌다〕. ¶ *Which course interests you most ?* 어느 코스에 가장 관심이있느냐 / *The story interests most boys.* =*Most boys are interested in the story.* 그 이야기에 모든 아이들이 흥미 있어 한다. **2** cause (someone) to take part in something; concern. …을 관계하게 하다; 끌어들

이다. ¶ *try to* ~ *him in the plan* 그 계획에 그가 참여하게 하다 / *He is not interested in the enterprise.* 그는 그 사업에 관계하고 있지 않다. [L. =it matters (inter-, *sum* I am)]

***in·ter·est·ed** [íntəristid, -trəst-, -tərèst-] *adj.* **1** feeling or showing interest or curiosity. 흥미를 가지고 있는; 관심 있는 (opp. uninterested). ¶ *an* ~ *look* 흥미 있어 하는 표정. **2** having a share or part; connected or concerned. 이해 관계가 있는 (opp. uninterested). ¶ *the* ~ *parties* 이해 관계자. **3** influenced by personal interests or considerations. 사심(私心)에 좌우된〔쏠린〕. ¶ ~ *motives* 불순한 동기.

:**in·ter·est·ing** [íntəristiŋ, -trəst-, -tərèst-] *adj.* arousing interest; holding one's attention. 흥미를 일으키는; 주의를 끄는; 재미있는. ¶ *an* ~ *book* / ~ *conversation* / *an* ~ *person* 재미 있는 사람.

in an interesting condition, 《Brit.》 pregnant. 임신하여.

● **in·ter·est·ing·ly** [-li] *adv.*

***in·ter·fere** [ìntərfíər] *vi.* (P1,3) **1** 《*with*》 (of things) come into opposition; obstruct; clash. 방해가 되다; 충돌하다; 대립하다. ¶ *if nothing interferes* 지장이 없다면 / *Their plan interfered with ours.* 그들 계획은 우리의 것과 상충됐다 / *Pleasure must not be allowed to* ~ *with business.* 오락이 일의 방해가 돼서는 안 된다. **2** 《*in, with*》 (of persons) take part in the affairs of others. 간섭하다; 참견하다. ¶ *Don't* ~ *in other people's affairs.* 남의 일에 참견 마라 / *He is always interfering with my work.* 그는 늘 내 일에 간섭하고 있다. **3** 《phys.》 (of heat, light, waves, etc.) strike each other. 간섭하다. [L. *ferio* strike]

***in·ter·fer·ence** [ìntərfíərəns] *n.* [U][C] **1** the act of interfering. 방해; 간섭. **2** 《phys.》 the mutual action of two waves or streams of light, sound, etc. which reinforce or neutralize one another. 간섭. **3** (of radio) the confusion of sounds caused by unwanted signals. 혼신(混信).

in·ter·fuse [ìntərfjú:z] *vt.* (P6,13) cause (things) to mix together. …을 혼합하다. ¶ ~ *one substance with another.* — *vi.* (P1) mix together. 섞이다. [→fuse²]

in·ter·im [íntərim] *n.* 《*the* ~》 the time or period between; the meantime. 사이; 중간 시기.

in the interim, in the meantime; meanwhile. 당분간; 그 동안.

— *adj.* of or for the interim; temporary. 중간의; 잠시〔임시〕의. ¶ *an* ~ *report* 중간 보고. [L. =in the interim]

:**in·te·ri·or** [intíəriər] *n.* [C] 《usu. *the* ~》 **1** the inside. 내부. ¶ *the* ~ *of a building* 건물의 내부. **2** the part of a country away from the sea; inland. 오지; 내륙. **3** the home affairs of a nation. 내정; 내무. ¶ *the Minister of the Interior* 내무 장관.

— *adj.* **1** of the inside of something. 내부의(opp. exterior). ¶ ~ *decoration* 〔*design*〕 내부 장식. **2** away from the sea. 내륙〔내지〕의. **3** of the affairs within a nation; home; domestic. 국내의(opp. foreign). ¶ ~ *trade* 국내 무역. [L.]

in·ter·ject [ìntərdʒékt] *vt.* (P6) throw or put in (a remark, etc.) suddenly; insert. (말 따위)를 갑자기 끼워 넣다. [L. *jacio* throw]

in·ter·jec·tion [ìntərdʒékʃən] *n.* **1** [U] the act of interjecting; exclamation. 갑자기 내는 소리; 감탄. **2** [C] 《gram.》 a word used as an exclamation. 간투사; 감탄사.

in·ter·lace [ìntərléis] *vi.* (P1) cross over and under each other. 섞어짜다; 엇걸리다; 얽히다. ¶ *The branches of the trees interlaced over the path.* 나뭇가지들이 길 위로 엇걸려 있었다. — *vt.* (P6) unite (threads, strips, etc.) by lacing or weaving together. …을 교착(交錯)시키다; 짜맞추다; 섞어 짜다. ¶ ~ *reeds to make a basket* 바구니를 만들려고 갈대를 엮다. [→inter]

in·ter·leaf [íntərlì:f] *n.* (*pl.* **-leaves**) a blank leaf put in and bound up between the pages of a book. 책장에 끼우는 백지; 간지. [→leaf]

in·ter·leave [ìntərlí:v] *vt.* (P6,13) 《*with*》 furnish (a book, etc.) with interleaves. (책장)에 간지를 넣다.

in·ter·line¹ [ìntərláin] *vt.* (P6,13) put a lining between the outer fabric and the ordinary lining of (a garment). (옷의 겉과 안 사이)에 심을 넣다. [inter-]

in·ter·line² [ìntərláin] *vt.* (P6,13) 《*in*》 write (words, etc.) between lines of writing or print. …을 행간에 써 넣다. ¶ ~ *a translation in an text* 원문의 행간에 번역을 써 넣다. [↑]

in·ter·lin·e·ar [ìntərlíniər] *adj.* written between the lines. 행간에 써 넣은. ¶ *an* ~ *note* 행간 주석(註釋).

in·ter·lock [ìntərlák / -lɔ́k] *vi., vt.* (P1; 6) join closely with one another. 맞물리(게 하)다. [inter-]

in·ter·lo·cu·tion [ìntərləkjú:ʃən] *n.* [U][C] interchange of speech; conversation. 말을 주고받기; 대화. [L. *loquos* talk]

in·ter·lop·er [ìntərlóupər] *n.* [C] a person who interferes; an intruder. 중뿔나게 구는〔오지랖 넓은〕 사람. [→leap]

in·ter·lude [íntərlù:d] *n.* [C] **1** a pause between the acts of a play. 막간. **2** an entertainment given during this period. 막간의 연예. **3** a piece of music played between the parts of a song, etc. 간주곡. **4** any event or period of time coming between. 중간참(에 생긴 일). ¶ *an* ~ *of fair weather between storms* 폭풍우 사이의 좋은 날씨. [L. *ludus* play]

in·ter·mar·riage [ìntərmǽridʒ] *n.* [U][C] **1** marriage between different tribes, races, religions, etc. 다른 종족간〔종교간〕의 결혼. **2** marriage between closely-related persons. 근친 결혼. [↓]

in·ter·mar·ry [ìntərmǽri] *vi.* (P1,3) **1** (of people of different tribes, races, religions, etc.) become connected by marriage. (다른 종족·종교끼리) 결혼하다. **2** marry within one's family. 근친 결혼하다. [→inter-]

in·ter·med·dle [ìntərmédl] *vi.* (P3) 《*with, in*》 take part in a matter which really concerns only others; interfere; meddle. 간섭하다; 참견하다. ¶ ~ *with* 〔*in*〕 *other's business* 남의 일에 간섭하다. [inter-]

in·ter·me·di·ar·y [ìntərmí:dièri] *n.* Ⓒ (*pl.* **-ar·ies**) a person who acts between two persons; a go-between. 중개인; 조정자. — *adj.* **1** acting between two persons. 중개하는. ¶ ~ *business* 중개업. **2** being between; intermediate. 사이의; 중간의. [↓]

in·ter·me·di·a·te [ìntərmí:diit] *adj.* being or coming between. 중간에 있는; 중간에 위치한. ¶ *an* ~ *rank* 중간 계급〔계층〕. — *n.* Ⓒ **1** something which lies between. 중간물. **2** a person who acts between others. 중개자. [inter-, L. *medius* middle]

in·ter·ment [intə́:rmənt] *n.* ⓊⒸ the act of interring; burial. 매장. [→inter]

in·ter·mez·zo [ìntərmétsou, -médzou] *n.* **1** a short dramatic or other performance between acts of a play. 막간극. **2** 《mus.》 a short connecting movement in musical work. 간주곡. [It. =intermediate]

in·ter·mi·na·ble [intə́:rmənəbəl] *adj.* very long; endless. 끝없는. ¶ *an* ~ *speech* 지루한 연설. [in-[1]]

in·ter·min·gle [ìntərmíŋgəl] *vt., vi.* (P6; 1) mix together. 섞다; 섞이다. [inter-]

in·ter·mis·sion [ìntərmíʃən] *n.* **1** Ⓒ an interval of time between periods of activity; a break. 중간; 휴식 시간; 중간참. ¶ *pursue one's study without* ~ 쉬지 않고 학문을 추구하다. **2** Ⓤ the act of stopping for a time. 중지; 중단. [↑]

in·ter·mit [ìntərmít] *vt., vi.* (P6; 1) (**-mitted, -mit·ting**) stop for a time. 일시 중단〔중지〕시키다〔하다〕. [L. *mitto* send]

in·ter·mit·tent [ìntərmítənt] *adj.* stopping and beginning again; repeated at intervals. 단속(斷續)하는; 간헐적인. ¶ *an* ~ *rain* 오다 말다 하는 비 / *The* ~ *noise of the railway trains kept me awake.* 이따금씩 들리는 기차 소리에 잠을 못 잤다 / *an* ~ *spring* 간헐천(間歇泉).

in·ter·mit·tent·ly [ìntərmítəntli] *adv.* in an intermittent manner. 단속〔간헐〕적으로.

in·ter·mix [ìntərmíks] *vt., vi.* (P13; 3) mix together. 섞다; 섞이다; 혼합하다〔되다〕. ¶ *Oil does not* ~ *with water.* 기름은 물과 섞이지 않는다. [→inter-]

in·ter·mix·ture [ìntərmíkstʃər] *n.* **1** Ⓤ the act of intermixing; the state of being intermixed. 혼합. **2** Ⓒ a thing made by mixing things together. 혼합물.

in·tern[1] [intə́:rn] *vt., vi.* (P6; 1) force (someone) to stay within a country or definite area. (일정 구역 안에) …을 억류하다. [↓]

in·tern[2] [íntə:rn] 《U.S.》 *n.* Ⓒ a young doctor acting as an assistant in a hospital. 의학 실습생; 인턴. — *vi.* (P1) train or serve as an intern. 인턴으로 근무하다. [F. *interne*]

·**in·ter·nal** [intə́:rnl] *adj.* (opp. external) **1** of or on the inside. 속의; 내부의. ¶ *an* ~ *organ* 내장 / *an* ~ *line* 내선 (전화) / *a medicine for* ~ *use* 내복약. **2** coming from within the thing itself. 내면적인; 본질적인. ¶ ~ *evidence* 내적 증거. **3** within a country; domestic. 국내의; 내정(內政)의 (opp. foreign). ¶ ~ *products* 국내 생산품. [L. *internus*]

in·ter·nal·ly [intə́:rnli] *adv.* in or on the inside. 내부에(서).

:**in·ter·na·tion·al** [ìntərnǽʃənəl] *adj.* between or among nations; concerning several nations. 만국의; 국제간의; 국제적인. ¶ *an* ~ *conference* 국제 회의 / *an* ~ *exposition* 만국 박람회 / *an* ~ *trade fair* 세계 산업 견본시 / ~ *waters* 공해(公海). — *n.* Ⓒ **1** 《*I*~》 one of several international socialist or communist organizations. 국제 노동자 연맹; 인터내셔널. **2** a person who takes part in an international match; an international sporting contest. 국제 경기 참가자; 국제 경기. [inter-]

in·ter·na·tion·al·ism [ìntərnǽʃənəlìzəm] *n.* Ⓤ **1** the principle of co-operation among nations for their common good. 국제주의. **2** international sympathies, ideas, etc. 국제성.

in·ter·na·tion·al·i·za·tion [ìntərnæ̀ʃənəlizéiʃən] *n.* Ⓤ the act of internationalizing; the state of being internationalized. 국제화; 국제 관리(화).

in·ter·na·tion·al·ize [ìntərnǽʃənəlàiz] *vt.* (P6) **1** make (something) international. …을 국제화하다. **2** bring (land, area, etc.) under international control. …을 국제 관리 아래에 두다.

in·ter·na·tion·al·ly [ìntərnǽʃənəli] *adv.* in an international manner. 국제적으로.

in·ter·ne·cine [ìntərní:sin, -sain] *adj.* **1** deadly; destructive. 치명〔살인〕적인; 파괴적인. ¶ *an* ~ *war* 대혈전. **2** deadly or destructive to both sides. 상호 파괴적인; 다같이 망하는〔쓰러지는〕. [L. *neco* kill]

in·tern·ee [ìntərní:] *n.* Ⓒ a person interned. 피(被)억류자. [→intern, -ee]

in·tern·ment [intə́:rnmənt] *n.* Ⓤ the act of interning; the state of being interned. 억류; 수용. [→intern, -ment]

in·ter·pel·late [ìntərpéleit, intə́:rpəlèit] *vt.* (P6) ask (a government Minister, etc.) formally for an explanation of government policy, etc. (장관)에게 정책 등에 대한 설명을 요구하다. [L. =interrupt by speaking]

in·ter·pel·la·tion [ìntərpəléiʃən, intə̀:rpə-] *n.* ⒸⓊ a formal request for an explanation of government policy, etc. 정책 등에 대한 질문.

in·ter·phone [íntərfòun] *n.* an intercommunication system using telephones. 구내 전화; 인터폰. [*phone*]

in·ter·play [íntərplèi] *n.* Ⓤ action or influence on each other. 상호 작용. ¶ *the* ~ *of the parts of a machine* 기계 부품들의 상호 작용. [inter-]

in·ter·pol [íntərpɔ̀(:)l, -pàl] *n.* International Criminal Police Organization. 국제 형사 경찰 기구; 국제 경찰.

in·ter·po·late [intə́rpəlèit] *vt.* (P6,13) **1** alter or corrupt (a text, etc.) by putting in a new word or group of words. …을 개찬(改竄)하다. **2** put in (new or spurious words, etc.). (수정 어구)를 써 넣다. [L.]

in·ter·po·la·tion [intə̀:rpəléiʃən] *n.* **1** Ⓤ the act of interpolating; the state of being interpolate. 개찬. **2** Ⓒ a word, etc. which is interpolated. 써 넣은 어구.

in·ter·pose [ìntərpóuz] *vt.* (P6,13) **1** put in or between. …을 사이에 두다. ¶ ~ *a barrier between two things* 두 물건 사이에 장벽을 두다. **2** insert (a remark or an opinion) into a conversation. …을 끼워 넣다; (말·의견 따위)를 삽입하다. ¶ ~ *an objection at this point* 이 점에 이의를 제기하다. **3** interrupt. …을 방해하다; 훼방놓다. —*vi.* (P1,3) come between parties in a quarrel. 사이에 들다; 중재하다; 말참견하다. [→pose]

in·ter·po·si·tion [ìntərpəzíʃən] *n.* **1** Ⓤ the act of interposing. 삽입; 중재. **2** Ⓒ a thing which is interposed. 삽입물.

·in·ter·pret [intə́:rprit] *vt.* (P6,7) **1** explain the meaning of (something). …을 설명〔해석〕하다. ¶ *I can't* ~ *the passage.* 이 구절은 해석할 수 없다. **2** (in acting or performing) bring out the meaning of (something). …을 연출〔연주〕하다. ¶ *The actor interpreted the part of the soldier wonderfully.* 연기자는 병사역을 훌륭하게 해냈다. **3** consider or understand the meaning of (something). …을 양해〔이해〕하다. ¶ ~ *her silence as consent* 그녀의 침묵을 동의한 것으로 알다.
—*vi.* (P1) 《*for*》 act as an interpreter. 통역〔해설〕하다. ¶ ~ *between two persons* 두 사람의 이야기를 통역하다 / *The student kindly interpreted for me.* 학생이 친절하게 내게 통역을 해 주었다. [L. *interpres* interpreter]

·in·ter·pre·ta·tion [intə̀:rprətéiʃən] *n.* ⓊⒸ **1** the act of interpreting; explanation; translation. 해석(解釋); 설명; 통역. **2** the act of bringing out the meaning of a dramatic part, music, etc. 연출; 연기; 연주.

in·ter·pre·ta·tive [intə́:rprətèitiv / -tətiv] *adj.* used for interpretation; explaining. 해석의; 설명적인; 통역의.

in·ter·pret·er [intə́:rprətər] *n.* Ⓒ **1** a person who translates a conversation or speech into another language. 통역; 통역인. **2** a person who explains. 설명하는 사람; 해설자.

in·ter·pre·tive [intə́:rprətiv] *adj.* =interpretative.

in·ter·reg·na [ìntərrégnə] *n.* pl. of **interregnum.**

in·ter·reg·num [ìntərrégnəm] *n.* Ⓒ (*pl.* **-nums** or **-na**) **1** a period without any ruler between an old ruler and his successor. 공위 기간(空位期間)《새 왕이 즉위할 때까지의》. **2** any period between rulers or activities; a pause. (어떤 정치적인) 공백 기간. [→reign]

in·ter·re·lat·ed [ìntərriléitid] *adj.* having a close connection with each other. 상호 관계가 있는. ¶ *Wages and prices are* ~. 임금과 물가는 상호 관계가 있다. [↓]

in·ter·re·la·tion [ìntərriléiʃən] *n.* ⓊⒸ close connection with each other; mutual relation. 상호 관계. [→inter-]

in·ter·ro·gate [intérəgèit] *vt.* (P6) ask questions of (someone); examine by questioning. …에게 질문하다; …을 심문하다. —*vi.* (P1) ask question. 질문하다. [L. *rego* ask]

in·ter·ro·ga·tion [intèrəgéiʃən] *n.* **1** Ⓤ the act of asking questions. 질문〔심문〕하기. **2** Ⓒ a question. 질문.

interrogation mark [–⏑–⏑ ⏑] *n.* 《gram.》 a question mark. 의문부; 물음표.

in·ter·rog·a·tive [ìntərάgətiv / -rɔ́g-] *adj.* **1** having the form of a question. 의문의. ¶ *an* ~ *sentence* 의문문. **2** questioning; inquiring. 미심쩍어하는. ¶ *an* ~ *look.* —*n.* Ⓒ 《gram.》 a word used to make an interrogative sentence. 의문사. ¶ *'Why', 'who', and 'what' are interrogatives.*

in·ter·ro·ga·tor [intérəgèitər] *n.* Ⓒ a person who asks questions. 질문〔심문〕자.

in·ter·rog·a·tory [ìntərάgətɔ̀:ri / -rɔ́gətəri] *adj.* by questioning; expressing a question. 의문의; 의문을 나타내는. ¶ *an* ~ *method* 문답식. —*n.* Ⓒ (*pl.* **-ries**) a question; an inquiry. 질문; 심문.

:in·ter·rupt [ìntərʌ́pt] *vt.* stop; cut off; hinder. …을 가로막다; 저지〔방해〕하다; 끊다. ¶ ~ *him while he is speaking* 발언 중인 그를 저지하다 / ~ *someone's train of thought* 아무의 일련의 사고를 방해하다 / ~ *electric current* 전류를 끊다 / *That building interrupts the view.* 저 건물이 조망을 가리고 있다 / *Children must learn not to* ~.

아이들은 말참견하지 않게 되도록 배워야 한다. [L. *rumpo* break]

in·ter·rupt·er [ìntərʌ́ptər] *n.* Ⓒ **1** a person or thing that interrupts. 저지하는 사람〔물건〕. **2** 《electr.》 a device for interrupting an electric current. (전류) 차단기.

in·ter·rup·tion [ìntərʌ́pʃən] *n.* **1** Ⓤ the act of interrupting; the state of being interrupted. 차단; 저지; 방해. **2** Ⓒ a thing that interrupts. 차단물.

without interruption, continually. 계속; 간단없이.

in·ter·sect [ìntərsékt] *vt.* (P6) cut across. …을 가로지르다. ¶ *The road intersects the railroad.* 길이 철도를 가로지르고 있다. —*vi.* (P1) cross each other. 교차하다; 엇갈리다. ¶ *a line intersecting another* 다른 선과 교차된 선. [L. *seco* cut]

in·ter·sec·tion [ìntərsékʃən] *n.* **1** Ⓤ the act of intersecting; the state of being intersected. 횡단; 교차. **2** Ⓒ a point or line where two things cross; a place where two streets cross. 교점; 교차선; 교차점.

in·ter·sperse [ìntərspə́ːrs] *vt.* (P6,13) **1** 《*between, among*》 put (something) here and there; scatter. …을 흩뿌리다; 온통 박아넣다; 점재시키다. ¶ *cherry trees interspersed among the pine trees* 소나무 사이에 산재해 있는 벚나무 / ~ *pictures in a book* 그림들을 책의 여기저기에 넣다. **2** 《*with*》 give variety to (something). …에 변화를 주다. ¶ ~ *a book with pictures* 책에 삽화를 넣어 변화를 주다 / *His speech was interspersed with several quotations from Shakespeare.* 그는 연설에서 셰익스피어의 말을 간간이 인용했다. [→sparse]

in·ter·state [íntərstèit] *adj.* 《U.S.》 between states. 각 주(州) 간의. [inter-]

in·ter·stice [intə́ːrstis] *n.* Ⓒ a very small opening; a crack. 틈새기; 갈라진 틈. [L. *sisto* stand]

in·ter·trib·al [ìntərtráibəl] *adj.* between or among tribes. (다른) 종족 간의. [inter-]

in·ter·twine [ìntərtwáin] *vt., vi.* (P6, 13; 1) twine together. 서로 꼬이(게 하)다; 얽히(게 하)다. [inter-]

in·ter·twist [ìntərtwíst] *vt.* (P6,13) twist closely together. 배배 꼬이게 하다.

in·ter·ur·ban [ìntərə́ːrbən] *adj.* between cities. 도시 간의. ¶ *an* ~ *railway* 도시간 철도. [inter-]

:in·ter·val [íntərvəl] *n.* Ⓒ **1** a space between objects. (위치의) 간격; 사이; 거리. ¶ *at intervals of ten feet,* 10 피트 간격으로. **2** a period of time between events. (시간적인) 간격; 사이; 동안. ¶ *after an* ~ *of fifty years,* 50 년이란 세월을 두고 / *at long* 〔*short*〕 *intervals* 이따금〔자주〕 / *at regular intervals* 일정한 간격을〔사이를〕 두고 / *in the* ~ 그 사이에. **3** a pause between two acts of play, opera, etc. (극 따위의) 막간; 휴게 시간. **4** 《mus.》 the difference of pitch between two sounds. 음정(音程). [L. = space between ramparts]

at intervals, **a)** here and there. 여기저기. **b)** now and then. 때때로; 이따금.

***in·ter·vene** [ìntərvíːn] *vi.* **1** come or take place between two events. 사이에 들다〔일어나다〕. ¶ *Years intervened between the two incidents.* 두 사건 사이에는 수 년의 시차가 있다 / *I will see you tomorrow, should nothing* ~. 내일 만나자. 그 사이 아무 일도 없다면. **2** 《*between, in*》 step in; interfere. 중재하다; 간섭하다. ¶ ~ *in the internal affairs of another country* 타국의 내정에 간섭하다. **3** (of things) be placed; lie. 놓이다; 있다. ¶ *A fence intervened between the yards.* 마당 사이에는 울타리가 하나 있었다. [L. *venio* come]

in·ter·ven·tion [ìntərvénʃən] *n.* ⓊⒸ the act of intervening; interference. 개재; 중재; 간섭. ¶ *His* ~ *ended the quarrel.* 그의 중재로 싸움은 끝났다.

***in·ter·view** [íntərvjùː] *n.* Ⓒ **1** a meeting to talk something over. 회견; 회담; 대담. ¶ *Father had an* ~ *with the teacher about John's work.* 아버지는 존의 공부 문제로 선생님과 면담했다. **2** a meeting to give information to the press. (신문 기자 등과의) 회견. **3** an article giving such information. 방문기; 회견기. —*vt.* (P6) have an interview with (someone). …와 회견하다. [inter-]

in·ter·view·er [íntərvjùːər] *n.* Ⓒ a person who interviews; a newspaper reporter, etc. who asks a famous person, etc. questions. 회견자; 탐방 기자.

in·ter·weave [ìntərwíːv] *vt., vi.* (**-wove** or **-weaved, -woven** or **-weaved**) (P6; 1) **1** weave together. 섞어 짜(이)다. **2** mix together. 뒤섞(이)다. [inter-]

in·ter·wove [ìntərwóuv] *v.* p. of **interweave.**

in·ter·wo·ven [ìntərwóuvən] *v.* pp. of **interweave.**

in·tes·tate [intésteit, -tit] *adj.* having made no will. 유언을 남기지 않은. ¶ *die* ~ 유언 없이 죽다. —*n.* Ⓒ a person who has died intestate. 유언을 안 남기고 죽은 사람. [in-[1]]

in·tes·ti·nal [intéstinəl] *adj.* of or in the intestines. 장(腸)의. [↓]

in·tes·tine [intéstin] *n.* Ⓒ 《usu. *pl.*》 the long coiled tube below the stomach through which food passes; the bowels. 장; 내장; 창자. —*adj.* 《*fig.*》 arising from within. 내부의; 국내의. ¶ *an* ~ *war* 내란. [L. *intus* within]

in·ti·ma·cy [íntəməsi] *n.* Ⓤ the state of being intimate; close friendship. 친밀; 친교. [↓]

***in·ti·mate**[1] [íntəmit] *adj.* **1** very familiar; close. 친한; 친밀한. ¶ *be on* ~ *terms with someone* 아무와 친숙한 사이다. **2** coming from close study; deep. 자세한; 깊은. ¶ *an*

~ *knowledge of art* 예술에 대한 해박한 지식. **3** private; personal. 일신상의; 개인적인. ¶ *one's ~ affairs* 개인적인 일. **4** far within; inward. 내심의; 내적인. ¶ *one's ~ feelings* 내적인 감정. — *n.* Ⓒ an intimate friend. 친구. ● **in·ti·mate·ly** [-li] *adv.* [L. *intimus* inmost]

in·ti·mate[2] [íntəmèit] *vt.* **1** suggest; hint. …을 넌지시 비추다; 암시하다. **2** announce. …을 공표하다. [↑]

in·ti·ma·tion [ìntəméiʃən] *n.* **1** Ⓤ the act of intimating. 암시하기; 공표하기. **2** Ⓒ an announcement. 공표; 고시. **3** Ⓒ a hint. 암시.

in·tim·i·date [intímədèit] *vt.* (P6,13) **1** make (someone) afraid; frighten. …을 겁주다; 위협하다. **2** 《*into*》 force (someone) to do something by means of threats. …을 위협해 —시키다. [→timid]

in·tim·i·da·tion [intìmədéiʃən] *n.* Ⓤ the act of intimidating; the state of being intimidated. 위협; 협박; 공갈.

intl, int'l international.

⁝**in·to** [íntu, íntuː, íntə] 語法 [íntu]는 모음 앞, [íntuː]는 문미(文尾)에, [íntə]는 자음 앞에서의 발음. *prep.* **1** to the inside of. (장소)의 안[속]으로. ¶ *put ~ the soup* 수프에 넣다 / *Look ~ this report.* 이 보고서를 보아라 / *She followed him ~ the room.* 그녀는 그를 따라 방으로 들어갔다. **2** toward the middle of (a period of time). (시간)까지. ¶ *He had to work far ~ the night.* 밤늦게까지 일을 해야 했다. **3** to the state or condition of. (상태)로. ¶ *turn water ~ ice* 물을 얼음으로 만들다 / *translate French ~ Korea* 프랑스어를 한역하다 / *Winter passed ~ spring.* 겨울이 가고 봄이 되었다 / *During the night the rain changed ~ snow.* 밤 사이 비는 눈으로 변했다. [*in, to*]

in·tol·er·a·ble [intálərəbəl / -tɔ́l-] *adj.* that cannot be endured; not tolerable; unbearable. 견딜[참을] 수 없는. ¶ *The heat is ~.* 더워서 못 견디겠다 / *an ~ insult* 참을 수 없는 모욕. [in-[1]]

in·tol·er·ance [intálərəns / -tɔ́l-] *n.* Ⓤ **1** unwillingness to allow others' opinions, religious beliefs, etc.; narrow-mindedness. 편협; 도량이 좁음. **2** lack of endurance. 견딜 수 없음.

in·tol·er·ant [intálərənt / -tɔ́l-] *adj.* **1** narrow-minded. 도량이 좁은. **2** 《*of*》 unable or unwilling to endure or allow. 참지 못하는. ¶ *He is ~ of opinions which differ from his own.* 그는 자기와 다른 의견을 용납하지 않는다.

in·to·na·tion [ìntənéiʃən, -tou-] *n.* **1** ⓊⒸ the rise and fall of the voice. 억양; 인토네이션. **2** Ⓤ the act of reciting in a singing voice. 읊음; 영창(詠唱). **3** Ⓤ 《mus.》 the production of musical tones. 발성법. [↓]

in·tone [intóun] *vt., vi.* (P6; 1) **1** recite in a singing voice. (…을) 읊다; 영창(詠唱)하다. **2** give a particular intonation to (something). (…에) 억양을 붙이다. [→tone]

in·tox·i·cant [intáksikənt / -tɔ́k-] *n.* Ⓒ a thing that intoxicates; a strong liquor. 취하게 하는 것; 마취제; 술; 주류. — *adj.* intoxicating. 취하게 하는. [↓]

in·tox·i·cate [intáksikèit / -tɔ́k-] *vt.* (P6,13) **1** make (someone) drunk. …을 취하게 하다. ¶ *He was so intoxicated that he could not walk.* 얼마나 취했던지 걷지도 못했다. **2** excite greatly. …을 도취[흥분]시키다. ¶ *Happiness intoxicated him.* 그는 행복에 도취됐다. [→toxicate]

in·tox·i·cat·ing [intáksikèitiŋ / -tɔ́k-] *adj.* causing intoxication; very exciting. 취하게 하는; 도취시키는.

in·tox·i·ca·tion [intàksikéiʃən / -tɔ̀k-] *n.* Ⓤ **1** the state of being drunk; drunkenness. 취함; 명정(酩酊). **2** great excitement. 흥분; 도취.

in·trac·ta·bil·i·ty [intræ̀ktəbíləti] *n.* Ⓤ the state of being intractable. 다루기[처리하기] 힘듦. [↓]

in·trac·ta·ble [intrǽktəbəl] *adj.* hard to manage; difficult to treat. 다루기 힘든; 처리하기 어려운. ¶ *an ~ horse* 사나운 말 / *an ~ temper* 고집센[고약한] 성미. [in-[1]]

in·tra·mu·ral [ìntrəmjúərəl] *adj.* within a city, a college, a building, etc. 도시[학교, 건물] 안의. [L. *intra* within, *murus* wall]

in·tran·si·tive [intrǽnsətiv] *adj.* 《gram.》 (of verbs) not taking a direct object. 자동(사)의(opp. transitive). [in-[1]]

in·trench [intréntʃ] *v.* =entrench.

in·trep·id [intrépəd] *adj.* bold; brave; fearless. 대담한; 용맹스러운. [in-[1]]

in·tre·pid·i·ty [ìntrəpídəti] *n.* **1** Ⓤ the state or quality of being intrepid. 대담. **2** Ⓒ an intrepid act. 대담한 행위.

in·tri·ca·cy [íntrikəsi] *n.* (*pl.* **-cies**) **1** Ⓤ the state of being intricate. 복잡; 난해. **2** 《*pl.*》 intricate things, events, etc. 복잡한 사물. ¶ *They admired the intricacies of the plot of the drama.* 그들은 그 극의 복잡한 줄거리에 감탄했다. [↓]

in·tri·cate [íntrəkit] *adj.* difficult to understand; complicated. 복잡한; 난해한; 뒤얽힌(opp. simple). ¶ *an ~ knot* 뒤얽힌 매듭 / *~ directions* 복잡한 사용법. ● **in·tri·cate·ly** [-li] *adv.* [in-[2], →trick]

in·trigue [intríːg] *vi.* **1** (P1,3) 《*against*》 carry on a secret plot. 음모를 꾸미다. ¶ *He will fight openly, but he will not ~ against you.* 그는 당당하게 싸울 것이며 네게 음모는 꾸미지 않을 거다. **2** have a secret love affair. 밀통하다. — *vt.* (P6) excite the curiosity or interest of (someone). …의 호기심을[흥미를] 자극하다[돋우다]. — *n.* Ⓒ **1** a secret plot. 음모. **2** a secret love affair. 밀통. [↑]

in·trin·sic [intrínsik] *adj.* belonging to a person or thing naturally; essential. 본디

갖추어진; 본질적인(opp. extrinsic). [L. *intra* within, *secus* apart]

in·trin·si·cal·ly [intrínsikəli] *adv.* naturally; essentially. 본래; 본질적으로.

:in·tro·duce [intrədjúːs] *vt.* (P6,13) ⟪*into, to*⟫ **1** make (someone) known by name; present. (아무)를 (…에게) 소개하다. ¶ ~ *her into* 〔*to*〕 *society* 그녀를 사교계에 데뷔시키다 / *Mr. Brown, may I* ~ *Mr. Smith to you ?* 브라운씨, 스미스씨를 소개합니다 / *Let me* ~ *myself.* 제 소개를 하겠습니다. **2** bring (something) into practice, use, notice, etc.; offer (a new product) for sale. …을 받아들이다; 도입하다; 전하다; (신제품)을 내놓다. ¶ ~ *a new fashion* 〔*custom, method*〕 새로운 유행〔풍습, 방법〕을 소개하다 / ~ *slang into a novel* 소설에 속어를 쓰다 / *The war introduced the jeep.* 전쟁에서 지프가 쓰이게 되었다. **3** give (someone) experience or knowledge of something; lead. …에 경험하게 하다; …을 가르치다; 인도하다. ¶ *We introduced her to city life.* 우리는 그녀에게 처음으로 도시 생활을 경험하게 했다 / *The teacher introduced the new pupils into their classroom.* 선생님은 신입생들을 교실로 데리고 갔다 / ~ *someone to the game of chess* 아무에게 체스 두는 법을 가르쳐주다. **4** bring (a subject, etc.) into conversation, etc.; bring forward. (화제 등)을 꺼내다; …을 제출하다. ¶ ~ *a bill into the Diet* 국회에 의안을 제출하다 / *A new subject was introduced for discussion.* 새로운 의제가 토론에 부쳐졌다. **5** put in; insert. …을 끼워넣다; 삽입하다; 지르다. ¶ ~ *a tube into her windpipe* 그녀의 기관(氣管)에다 튜브를 들이밀다 / ~ *a key into a lock* 자물쇠에 열쇠를 끼우다. **6** begin; open; start. 시작하다. ¶ *He introduced his speech with an anecdote.* 일화를 하나 들면서 연설을 시작했다. [inter-, L. *duco* lead]

:in·tro·duc·tion [ìntrədʌ́kʃən] *n.* **1** Ⓤ the act of introducing; the state of being introduced. 소개; 도입. ¶ *a letter of* ~. **2** Ⓒ the first part of a book, speech, etc. leading up to the main part. 서문; 머리말. **3** Ⓒ an elementary textbook. 입문; 입문서. ¶ *an* ~ *to science* 과학 입문. **4** Ⓒ a thing made known or brought into use. 수입; 도입. ¶ *An electric engine is a later* ~ *than a steam one.* 전기 기관은 증기 기관보다 나중에 들여온 것이다.

in·tro·duc·to·ry [ìntrədʌ́ktəri] *adj.* serving to introduce; beginning. 소개의; 머리말의; 준비의. ¶ ~ *remarks* 머리말 / *an* ~ *chapter* 서장(序章).

in·tro·spect [ìntrəspékt] *vi.* (P1) examine one's own thoughts and feelings. 내성(內省)하다. [L. *specio* look]

in·tro·spec·tion [ìntrəspékʃən] *n.* Ⓤ the act of observing one's own mental processes. 내성(內省); 자기 관찰.

in·tro·spec·tive [ìntrəspéktiv] *adj.* of or inclined toward introspection. 내성적인; 자기 관찰의.

in·tro·vert [íntrəvə̀ːrt, ⌐–⌐] *vt.* direct (one's own mind, thoughts, etc.) inward. (마음·생각 등)을 안으로 돌리다〔향하다〕; 내성(內省)시키다. — [⌐–⌐] *n.* Ⓒ a person who introverts. 내성적인 사람 (opp. extrovert). [L. *verto* turn]

·in·trude [intrúːd] *vt.* (opp. extrude) **1** (P13) ⟪*into*⟫ thrust. …을 밀어넣다. ¶ ~ *political theory into his novel* 자기 소설에 정치 이론을 집어넣다. **2** (P13) ⟪*upon*⟫ force. …을 강제〔강요〕하다. ¶ ~ *oneself into a meeting* 불청객으로 모임에 끼어들다 / ~ *one's opinion upon others* 자기 의견을 남에게 강요하다. — *vi.* (P1,3) ⟪*into, upon*⟫ force or thrust oneself. 밀고 들어가다; (말)참견하다; 방해하다. ¶ *I hope I am not intruding.* 방해가 되지는 않을까요 / ~ *upon another's privacy* 남의 사삿일에 참견하다. [L. *trudo* thrust]

in·trust [intrʌ́st] *vt.* =entrust.

in·tu·i·tion [ìntjuíʃən] *n.* **1** Ⓤ the power to perceive something immediately and without conscious thought. 직각(력); 직관(력). **2** Ⓒ something perceived or learned by this power. 직관적인 지식. [in-[2], L. *tueor* look]

in·tu·i·tive [intjúːitiv] *adj.* of intuition; having intuition; perceived by instinct. 직각의; 직각력이 풍부한; 직감적인; 직감에 의한. ● **in·tu·i·tive·ly** [-li] *adv.*

in·twine [intwáin] *vt., vi.* =entwine.

in·un·date [ínəndèit, -nʌn-] *vt.* (P6) flood; cover (a place) as with a flood. …을 침수시키다; 물에 잠기게 하다; 범람시키다. ¶ *The land was inundated.* 땅은 물에 잠기었다 / ~ *someone with questions* 아무에게 질문 공세를 하다. [in[2]-, L. *undo* wave, water]

in·un·da·tion [ìnəndéiʃən, -nʌn] *n.* ⓊⒸ the act of inundating; a flood. 범람; 홍수.

in·ure [injúər] *vt.* (P13) ⟪*to*⟫ accustom; make (something) tough. …을 익숙하게 만들다; 단련하다. ¶ *be inured to hardship* 곤경에 익숙해 있다. — *vi.* ⟪law⟫ come into operation or use; have or take effect. 효력을 발생하다; 유효하게 되다. ¶ *The fund inured to his benefit.* 기금은 그의 이익에 귀속됐다. ● **in·ure·ment** [-mənt] *n.* [in-[2], L. *opera* work]

:in·vade [invéid] *vt.* (P6) **1** ⓐ enter (a country, etc.) to attack it. …을 침략하다; 침공하다. ¶ *The French army invaded Italy.* 프랑스군이 이탈리아를 침공했다. ⓑ ⟪*fig.*⟫ rush into; crowd into. 밀어닥치다; 쇄도하다. ¶ *My house was invaded by a crowd of people.* 우리 집에는 많은 사람들이 몰려들었다. **2** violate. …을 침해하다. ¶ ~ *the rights of others* 남의 권리를 침해하다. **3** enter and spread through. (병 따위가) 침범하다; 퍼지다. ¶ *a baby invaded by disease* 병에 걸린 아이. [L. *vado* go]

in·vad·er [invéidər] *n.* Ⓒ a person or thing that invades. 침략자; 침입물.

·**in·va·lid**[1] [ínvəlid/-lì:d] *adj.* **1** not strong or healthy; weak. 병약한. **2** of or for a sick person. 환자용의. ¶ *an ~ chair* 환자용 (바퀴 달린) 의자.
— *n.* Ⓒ a sick or weak person. 환자; 병자(cf. *patient*).
— *vt.* (P7,13) **1** make (someone) an invalid. …을 병약하게 만들다. **2** treat (someone) as a sick person; remove (a soldier, etc.) from active service because of illness. …을 병자로 취급하다; 상병(傷病)으로 전역시키다. ¶ *Soldiers are invalided home* 〔*out of the army*〕. 병사들은 상병병(傷病兵)으로 송환〔전역〕되었다.
— *vi.* (P1) become an invalid. 병약해지다. [→valid]

in·val·id[2] [invǽlid] *adj.* not valid; having no value or force. 가치가 없는; 효력이 없는. ¶ *declare a marriage ~* 결혼 무효를 선언하다. [↑]

in·val·i·date [invǽlədèit] *vt.* make (something) valueless or ineffective. …을 무효로 하다. ¶ *~ a claim* 권리를 무효화하다. [↑]

in·va·lid·i·ty [invəlídəti] *n.* Ⓤ lack of validity. 무효.

in·val·u·a·ble [invǽljuəbəl] *adj.* very valuable; very precious; priceless. 아주 귀중한(opp. valueless). [in-[1]]

·**in·var·i·a·ble** [invέəriəbəl] *adj.* never changing. 불변의. [in-[1]]

·**in·var·i·a·bly** [invέəriəbli] *adv.* in an invariable manner; without change; always. 변함 없이; 언제나.

·**in·va·sion** [invéiʒən] *n.* ⓊⒸ the act of invading; the state of being invaded. 침략; 침해. ¶ *the ~ of France by the Germans* 독일인의 프랑스 침략. [→invade]

in·vec·tive [invéktiv] *n.* **1** Ⓤ the act of attacking violently in words. 욕설. **2** Ⓒ 《often *pl.*》 violent words; curses. 악담; 저주. ¶ *a stream of coarse invectives* 한바탕의 온갖 욕설. [↓]

in·veigh [invéi] *vi.* (P3) 《*against*》 attack violently in words. 욕을 퍼붓다. ¶ *~ against militarism* 군국주의를 통렬히 매도하다. [L. *invehor* assail]

in·vei·gle [inví:gəl, -véi-] *vt.* (P13) 《*into, out of*》 trick; deceive; allure. …을 속이다; 유혹하다; 부추기다. ¶ *~ a girl into running away from home* 소녀의 가출을 부추기다. [F. *aveugle* blind (ab-, L. *oculus* eye)]

:**in·vent** [invént] *vt.* (P6) **1** think out; find out; devise. …을 발명하다. ¶ *Marconi invented the radio.* 마르코니가 라디오를 발명했다. **2** make up. 꾸며내다; 날조하다. ¶ *~ an excuse* 구실을 만들다 / *~ an alibi* 알리바이를 조작하다. [in-[2], L. *venio* come]

:**in·ven·tion** [invénʃən] *n.* **1** Ⓤ the act of inventing. 발명. ¶ *the ~ of the steam engine* 〔*gunpowder*〕 증기 기관〔화약〕의 발명. **2** Ⓤ the power of inventing. 발명의 재능. ¶ 《*prov.*》 *Necessity is the mother of ~.* 필요는 발명의 어머니. **3** Ⓒ something invented. 발명품. ¶ *Television is a wonderful ~.* 텔레비전은 놀라운 발명품이다. **4** Ⓒ something made up; a false statement; a lie. 날조; 꾸며낸 이야기. ¶ *an ~ of a weekly magazine* 주간지의 날조 기사 / *The report was an ~.* 보도는 조작이었다.

in·ven·tive [invéntiv] *adj.* of invention; that can invent; creative. 발명의; 발명의 재능이 있는.

:**in·ven·tor** [invéntər] *n.* Ⓒ a person who invents. 발명가〔자〕.

in·ven·to·ry [ínvəntɔ̀:ri/-təri] *n.* Ⓒ (*pl.* **-ries**) a detailed list of goods, furniture, etc.; the goods on such a list. (상품·세간 등의) 명세 목록; 그 목록의 물품. — *vt.* (P6) make an inventory of (things). (물품)의 목록을 만들다. [→invent]

in·verse [invə́:rs, ⌐⌐] *adj.* opposite. 역(逆)의; 반대의. ¶ *in ~ order* 역순으로 / *~ proportion* 〔*ratio*〕 반비례. — *n.* **1** Ⓤ the state of being opposite. 반대; 역(逆). **2** Ⓒ a thing that is the direct opposite of another. 반대의 것. [→invert]

in·verse·ly [invə́:rsli] *adv.* in an inverse manner. 반대로; 거꾸로.

in·ver·sion [invə́:rʒən, -ʃən] *n.* **1** Ⓤ the act of inverting; the state of being inverted. 역; 반대; 전도(顚倒). **2** Ⓒ something inverted. 반대의〔전도된〕 것.

in·vert [invə́:rt] *vt.* (P6) **1** change (something) to its direct opposite; turn upside down. …을 거꾸로 하다; 뒤집다; 반대로 하다. ¶ *~ a glass* 컵을 뒤집다 / *inverted commas* 역(逆)콤마(《" "》 또는 ' '). **2** change the order or position of. (순서·위치)를 바꾸다. [in-[2], L. *verto* turn]

in·ver·te·brate [invə́:rtəbrit, -brèit] *adj.* **1** 《zool.》 having no backbone. 척추가 없는. **2** 《*fig.*》 (of a person) of weak will. 우유부단한. — *n.* Ⓒ **1** an invertebrate animal. 무척추 동물. **2** 《*fig.*》 a person of weak will. 우유 부단한 사람. [in-[1], →vertebra]

·**in·vest** [invést] *vt.* (P6,13) **1** put (money) into a business for profit. …에 투자하다. ¶ *If I had any money, I would ~ it in land.* 돈이 있으면 땅에 투자하겠다. **2** ⓐ clothe. …에 입히다; 두르다. ⓑ 《*fig.*》 envelop or cover. …을 싸다; 에워싸다; 덮다. ¶ *Fog invested the city.* 시내에 안개가 자욱했다 / *The enemy invested the city.* 적군이 도시를 포위했다. **3** install (someone) in office with a ceremony. …을 임명하다. **4** furnish (someone) with power, privilege or authority. (권력·권위·특권 따위를) …에게 주다. — *vi.* (P1,3) 《*in*》 invest money. 투자하다. ¶ *~ heavily in a business* 사업에 거액을 투자하다. [in-[2], L. *vestis* garment, clothes]

·**in·ves·ti·gate** [invéstəgèit] *vt., vi.* (P6.

13; 1) examine carefully. 조사〔연구〕하다. ¶ ~ *the cause of disaster* 참사의 원인을 조사하다. [in-², L. *vestigum* footprint]

*__in·ves·ti·ga·tion__ [invèstəgéiʃən] *n.* ⓊⒸ the act of investigating; careful examination. 조사; 연구. ¶ *on* ~ 조사 결과 / *under* ~ 조사 중.

__in·ves·ti·ga·tive__ [invéstəgèitiv] *adj.* of investigation; inclined to investigate. 조사의; 캐기 좋아하는.

__in·ves·ti·ga·tor__ [invéstəgèitər] *n.* Ⓒ a person who investigates. 조사자; 연구자.

__in·ves·ti·ture__ [invéstətʃər] *n.* **1** Ⓤ the act or ceremony of investing a person with an office, a title, etc. 서임; 임명; 서임식. **2** Ⓒ a thing that covers, clothes, etc. 싸는〔덮는〕 것. [→invest]

*__in·vest·ment__ [invéstmənt] *n.* **1** Ⓤ the act of investing money. 투자. **2** Ⓒ a sum of money invested. 투자 자본; 투자금. ¶ *an ~ in stocks* 주식 투자금. **3** Ⓒ something in which money is invested. 투자의 대상. ¶ *Real estate is sometimes a good* ~. 부동산은 때로는 좋은 투자 대상이다. **4** Ⓤ clothing; covering. 입히기; 씌우기; 덮기. **5** the act of investing (a city, fort, etc.). (시 따위의) 포위. [→invest, -ment]

__in·ves·tor__ [invéstər] *n.* Ⓒ a person who invests money. 투자자. [*invest*]

__in·vet·er·ate__ [invétərit] *adj.* **1** (of a person) firmly fixed in a habit, custom, etc. 고질의; 상습적인. ¶ *an ~ smoker* 골초 / *an ~ liar* 상습적인 거짓말쟁이. **2** deeply rooted. 뿌리 깊은; 만성의. ¶ *an ~ disease* 고질병. [in-², L. *vestus* old]

__in·vid·i·ous__ [invídiəs] *adj.* likely to arouse ill-will or envy. 불쾌한; 시새움을 받기 쉬운. ¶ *an ~ position* 남이 샘내는 지위 / *~ remarks* 듣기 싫은〔기분 나쁜〕 소리. [→envy]

__in·vig·or·ate__ [invígərèit] *vt.* (P6) give vigor or strength to (someone); animate. …에 원기를 주다; …을 격려하다. ¶ *Sea air invigorates the weak.* 바다 공기는 병약한 사람에게 좋다. [in-²]

__in·vin·ci·bil·i·ty__ [invìnsəbíləti] *n.* Ⓤ the state of being invincible. 이길 수 없음; 무적.

__in·vin·ci·ble__ [invínsəbəl] *adj.* 《*lit., fig.*》 that cannot be conquered or overcome; unconquerable. 이길 수 없는; 정복할 수 없는; 무적의. ¶ *an ~ army* 무적의 군대 / *~ opposition* 불굴의 저항. [in-¹, L. *vinco* conquer]

__in·vi·o·la·bil·i·ty__ [invàiələbíləti] *n.* Ⓤ the state of being inviolable. 불가침(성); 신성(神性). [→inviolate]

__in·vi·o·la·ble__ [inváiələbəl] *adj.* that cannot be injured, violated or broken; sacred. 범할 수 없는; 불가침의; 신성한.

__in·vi·o·late__ [inváiəlit] *adj.* uninjured; not violated or broken; kept sacred. 손상되지 않은; 범하여지지 않은; 신성한. ¶ *keep one's promise* 〔*oath*〕 ~ 약속을〔선서를〕 굳게 지키는. [in-¹, L. *violo*]

__in·vis·i·bil·i·ty__ [invìzəbíləti] *n.* Ⓤ the state of being invisible. 눈에 보이지 않음; 불가시(성). [↓]

*__in·vis·i·ble__ [invízəbəl] *adj.* **1** that cannot be seen; out of sight. 눈에 보이지 않는. ¶ *~ to the naked eye* 육안으로 안 보이는 / *The queen kept herself ~ in her palace.* 여왕은 궁정에서 모습을 나타내는 일이 없었다. **2** 《comm.》 not published in financial statements. 재무 제표에 없는. ¶ *~ imports and exports* 무역외 수지. — *n.* 《*the* ~》 **1** that which cannot be seen. 눈에 안 보이는 것. **2** the unseen or spiritual world. 영계(靈界). [in-¹]

__in·vis·i·bly__ [invízəbli] *adv.* in an invisible manner; without being seen. 눈에 안 보이게.

:__in·vi·ta·tion__ [ìnvətéiʃən] *n.* **1** ⓊⒸ the act of inviting. 초대; 안내. **2** Ⓒ a written letter, etc. inviting someone to a party, etc. 초대〔안내〕장. **3** ⓊⒸ attraction; temptation. 유혹; 권유. [↓]

:__in·vite__ [inváit] *vt.* **1** (P7,13) ask (someone) politely to do something or to come somewhere. …을 초대하다. ¶ *~ someone to one's house* 아무를 집에 초대하다. **2** (P20) ask for; request. …에게 청(請)하다. ¶ *He invited her to sing.* 그녀에게 노래를 청했다. **3** (P6) bring on. …을 유발〔초래〕하다. ¶ *That invited the unhappy war.* 그것이 불행한 전쟁을 가져왔다. **4** (P6, 20) attract; tempt. 유혹하다. ¶ *The sea invites us to swim.* 바다를 보니 헤엄치고 싶다 / *The book invites our interest.* 우린 그 책이 보고 싶어졌다. — *vi.* (P1,3) give an invitation. 초대하다. [L. *invito*]

__in·vit·ing__ [inváitiŋ] *adj.* of an agreeable nature; attractive; tempting. 마음을 끄는. ¶ *an ~ meal* 먹음직스러운 식사.

__in·vo·ca·tion__ [invəkéiʃən] *n.* ⓊⒸ **1** the act of calling upon God, a spirit, etc. in a prayer. (신의 도움을 비는) 기도; 기원. **2** the act of calling forth an evil spirit. 주문으로 악마를 불러냄. [→invoke]

__in·voice__ [ínvɔis] *n.* Ⓒ 《comm.》 a list of goods sent to a purchaser with details of prices, quantity, charges, etc. 송장(送狀). — *vt.* (P6) make an invoice of (goods). (상품)의 송장을 만들다. [→envoy]

*__in·voke__ [invóuk] *vt.* (P6) **1** call for (help, protection, etc.) in prayer. (도움)을 기구하다. ¶ ~ *God's blessing* 신의 은총을 빌다. **2** ask for (something) earnestly. …을 간청〔호소〕하다. ¶ ~ *the protection of the law* 법의 보호를 호소하다. **3** call forth (evil spirits, etc.) by magic. …을 주문으로 불러내다. [L. *voco* call]

__in·vol·un·tar·i·ly__ [inválǝntèrili / -vɔ́lən-təri-] *adv.* in an involuntary manner; without a deliberate exercise of the will. 무의식적으로; 모르는 사이에. [↓]

__in·vol·un·tar·y__ [inválǝntèri / -vɔ́ləntə-] *adj.*

(opp. voluntary) **1** done without meaning to do so; unintentional. 무의식적인; 무심결의. ¶ *an ~ action* 무의식적인 행위 / *an ~ sigh* 절로 나오는 한숨. **2** against one's will. 본의 아닌. ¶ ~ *consent* 마지못해 하는 동의. **3** not controlled by the will. 불수의(不隨意)의. ¶ *The beating of the heart is an ~ activity.* 심장의 박동은 불수의 운동의 하나다. [in-[1]]

***in·volve** [inválv / -vɔ́lv] *vt.* **1** (P6,13) cause (someone) to be unpleasantly concerned with; bring (someone or something) into difficulty, danger, etc. …을 (재난·위험 등에) 빠뜨리다; 말려들게 하다. ¶ *be involved in war* 전쟁에 말려들다 / *He is involved in debts.* 그는 빚 때문에 옴쭉을 못 하고 있다. **2** (P6) include (something) as a necessary condition or consequence; imply. …을 (필연적으로) 포함하다. ¶ *Success always involves effort.* 성공하려면 항상 노력해야 한다 / *Living in a hot country always involves some loss of health.* 더운 나라에 사노라면 늘 건강에 좀 무리가 간다. **3** (P13) 《chiefly in *passive*》 take up the attention of (someone); engage completely. …을 열중하게 하다; 몰두시키다. ¶ *be involved in working out a crossword puzzle* 십자말풀이에 열중해 있다. **4** (P6) 《*arch.*》 wrap up; enfold; envelop. …을 싸다; 둘러싸다. ¶ *Fog involved the buildings.* 안개가 건물들을 감쌌다. **5** (P13) bring (something) into a comlplicated form or condition. …을 복잡하게 하다. ¶ *an involved expression* 복잡한 표현 / *His reasoning is very involved.* 그의 추론은 대단히 복잡하다. [L. *volvo* roll]

in·volve·ment [inválvmənt / -vɔ́lv-] *n.* Ⓤ Ⓒ the act of involving; the state of being involved. 말려듦; 연좌; 난처. [↑]

in·vul·ner·a·ble [invʌ́lnərəbəl] *adj.* **1** that cannot be injured; unconquerable. 상처 입힐 수 없는; 지울 수 없는. **2** that cannot be answered or refuted. 반박할 수 없는. ¶ *an ~ opinion* 반박할 수 없는 의견. [in-[1]]

***in·ward** [ínwərd] *adj.* (opp. outward) **1** placed within; internal. 내부의. ¶ ~ *organs* 내장. **2** directed toward the inside or center. 안으로 향하는. ¶ *an ~ voyage* 귀항(歸航) / *an ~ passage* 안쪽으로 난 길. **3** of the inner self; spiritual. 내적인; 정신적인. ¶ ~ *happiness* 마음의 평화 / *His thoughts turned ~.* 그는 깊이 자기를 반성했다. **4** low; muffled. (소리 따위가) 낮은. ¶ *an ~ voice* 입속에서 우물거리는 소리. — *adv.* **1** toward the inside. 안쪽으로. **2** into the spirit or mind. 마음 속으로. [*in, ward*]

in·ward·ly [ínwərdli] *adv.* **1** on or toward the inside. 안에(서). **2** in the mind. 마음 속으로. **3** secretly. 몰래; 비밀히. **4** in low tones. 저음으로.

in·wards [ínwərdz] *adv.* =inward.

in·wrought [inrɔ́:t] *adj.* **1** wrought. 짜[박아]넣은; 수놓은. **2** closely blended. 잘 혼합된[뒤섞인]. [→work]

IOC International Olympic Committee. 국제 올림픽 위원회.

i·o·dine [áiədàin, -dì:n] *n.* Ⓤ a nonmetallic element found in seaweed. 요오드; 옥소(沃素). [Gk. *ion* violet. from color of vapor]

i·o·do·form [aióudəfɔ̀:rm, -ád- / -ɔ́d-] *n.* Ⓤ 《chem.》 an antiseptic. 요오드포름.

i·on [áiən, -ɑn / -ən] *n.* 《phys.》 an electrically charged particle formed in a gas. 이온. ¶ *a negative* [*positive*] ~ 음[양]이온. [Gk. *ion* going]

I·on·ic [aiánik / -ɔ́n-] *adj.* **1** of Ionia or its people. 이오니아의; 이오니아 사람의. **2** 《archit.》 one of the classical orders of Greek architecture. 이오니아식의. — *n.* Ⓤ the Ionian language. 이오니아어. [Gk.]

i·on·ize [áiənàiz] *vt.* (P6) convert into ions. 이온화(化)하다.

i·on·o·sphere [aiánəsfìər / -ɔ́n-] *n.* 《phys.》 the ionized region. 전리층(電離層).

i·o·ta [aióutə] *n.* **1** the Greek letter (Ι, ι (=i)). 이오타《그리스 자모의 아홉째 자》. **2** a very small part or quantity. 극미량(極微量). [Gk. *iōta*]

not an iota, not a bit. 조금도 …않다(cf. *jot*).

IOU, I.O.U. [áioujú:] *n.* Ⓒ (*pl.* **IOUs, IOU's, I.O.U.s, I.O.U.'s**) a note showing a debt, esp. an informal one. 차용 증서《I owe you. 의 발음을 딴 말》.

I·o·wa [áiəwə, -wei] *n.* a state in the central United States. 아이오와 주.

IPA International Phonetic Association [Alphabet]. 국제 음성학 협회[국제 음성 기호].

IPU Inter-Parliamentary Union. 국제 의회 연맹.

IQ, I.Q. intelligence quotient.

ir- [i, ir] *pref.* a form of in- before *r.* r앞에 쓰이는 in-[1]의 변형. ¶ *irresistable* / *irradiate.*

I·ran [iræ̃n, ai-, -rá:n] *n.* a country in southwest Asia; Persia. 이란. 參考 수도는 테헤란(Teheran).

I·raq, I·rax [irá:k] *n.* a country in southwest Asia, centering in the Tigris-Euphrates basin of Mesopotamia. 이라크. 參考 수도는 바그다드(Baghdad).

i·ras·ci·bil·i·ty [iræ̀səbíləti] *n.* Ⓤ the quality or state of being irascible; quickness of temper. 걸핏하면 화냄; 성마름. [↓]

i·ras·ci·ble [irǽsəbəl, air-] *adj.* easily angered; quicktempered. 걸핏하면 성내는; 성마른. [L. *ira* anger]

i·rate [áireit, -ˊ] *adj.* angry; furious. 성난; 화가 난. [↑]

IRBM Intermediate Range Ballistic Missile. 중거리 탄도 미사일.

IRC International Red Cross.

Ire. Ireland.

ire [éiər] *n.* Ⓤ 《*poet.*》 anger. 화; 분노.

ire·ful [áiərfəl] *adj.* angry. 성난; 성마른. [→irate]

∗**Ire·land** [áiərlənd] *n.* **1** the large western island of the British Isles. 아일랜드. **2 the Republic of,** a country in central and southern Ireland. 아일랜드 공화국. 參考 Irish Republic, Eire라고도 함. 수도는 더블린(Dublin).

i·ri·des [írədìːz, ái-] *n.* pl. of **iris.**

ir·i·des·cence [ìrədésəns] *n.* Ⓤ the state or quality of being iridescent; a many-colored appearance. 무지개[진주] 빛깔. [↓]

ir·i·des·cent [ìrədésənt] *adj.* showing rainbowlike colors as an opal; changing in color when light comes from different angles. 진줏빛[무지개 빛깔]의; 반짝거리는. [→iris]

i·rid·i·um [airídiəm, ir-] *n.* Ⓤ 《chem.》 a precious metalic element resembling platinum. 이리듐. [↓]

i·ris [áiris] *n.* Ⓒ (*pl.* **i·ris·es** or **i·ri·des**) **1** 《anat.》 the colored part of the eye around the pupil. (안구의) 홍채(虹彩). **2** 《bot.》 a plant with large flowers and sword-shaped leaves. 붓꽃속(屬)의 식물. **3** a rainbow. 무지개. [Gk.=(goddess of) rainbow]

∗**I·rish** [áiriʃ] *n.* Ⓤ **1** 《*the* ~》 the people of Ireland. 아일랜드인. **2** the language spoken in Ireland. 아일랜드어. — *adj.* of Ireland or the Irish. 아일랜드 (사람·언어)의. [E.]

I·rish·man [áiriʃmən] *n.* Ⓒ (*pl.* **-men** [-mən]) a person of Ireland; a man born in Ireland or of Irish descent. 아일랜드인.

Irish potato [⌐– –⌐–] *n.* the common potato. 감자.

I·rish·wom·an [áiriʃwùmən] *n.* Ⓒ (*pl.* **-wom·en** [-wìmin]) a woman born in Ireland or of Irish descent. 아일랜드 여성.

irk [əːrk] *vt.* (P6) irritate; annoy. 지루하게 하다; 따분하게 만들다. ¶ *It irked him to wait.* 기다리기에 넌더리가 났다 / *It irks me to do that.* 그건 정말 하기 싫다. [E.]

irk·some [ə́ːrksəm] *adj.* so dull as to cause weariness; tedious. 지루한; 따분한.

:**i·ron** [áiərn] *n.* **1** Ⓤ a very common hard metal, from which tools, machines, etc. are made. 철. ¶ *cast* ~ 주철(鑄鐵) / *sheet* ~ (얇은) 철판. **2** Ⓒ a tool, an instrument or a weapon made from this metal. 철제 기구. ¶ *a soldering* ~ 납땜 인두. **3** Ⓒ an instrument made of iron or steel for smoothing or pressing clothes. 아이론; 다리미. ¶ *an electric* ~ 전기 다리미. **4** Ⓒ a golf club with a metal head. 쇠머리 골프채. **5** 《*pl.*》 bands and chains for a prisoner's hands and feet. 수갑; 차꼬. ¶ *The prisoners were put in irons.* 죄수들은 사슬에 매어 있었다. **6** Ⓤ strength; hardness. (쇠 같은) 강함; 견고. ¶ *a man of* ~ 강한 의지의 사람 / *a will of* ~ 무쇠 같은 의지. **7** a preparation of iron as a tonic. 철분이 든 강장제.

have* (*too*) *many irons in the fire, be trying to do (too) many things at once. 한꺼번에 너무 많은 일을 하려 들다.

rule with a rod of iron, control very firmly. 압제(壓制)를 행하다; 가혹하게 다루다.

Strike while the iron is hot. 《*prov.*》 do something at exactly the right moment. 쇠는 뜨거울 때 쳐라《물실 호기(勿失好機)》.

— *adj.* **1** of or made of iron. 철의; 철제의. ¶ *an* ~ *gate* 철문 / *an* ~ *horse* 기관차. **2** like iron; strong; firm. 무쇠 같은; 강한; 불굴의. ¶ ~ *muscles* 단단한 근육 / *an* ~ *will* 불굴의 의지 / 《mil.》 *an* ~ *ration* 휴대용 비상 식량. **3** cruel; severe. 냉혹[무정]한. ¶ *the* ~ *hand of fate* 운명의 냉혹한 손길.

— *vt.* (P6) **1** press (clothes, etc.) with a hot iron. …에 다리미질하다. ¶ *Mother irons the clothes.* **2** cover or furnish (something) with iron. …에 철(판)을 씌우다. **3** put (a prisoner) into irons. 죄수에 차꼬를 [수갑을] 채우다. [E.]

iron out, 《*fig.*》 smooth away; remove. …을 제거하다. ¶ *All the difficulties have now ironed out.* 모든 곤란이 제거[해결]됐다.

i·ron·bound [áiərnbáund] *adj.* **1** bound with iron. 쇠로 덮은[감은]. **2** hard; firm; unyielding. (날씨 따위가) 거친; (규칙 등이) 엄격한; 단호한.

i·ron·clad [áiərnklǽd] *adj.* **1** (of warships, etc.) covered or protected with iron plates. 장갑(裝甲)한. **2** 《U.S.》 unbreakable. 파기[파괴]할 수 없는; 엄한. ¶ *an* ~ *agreement* (파기할 수 없는) 엄한 합의. — *n.* Ⓒ a warship protected with iron plates. 장갑함(艦). 參考 19세기의 용어.

i·ron·gray, 《Brit.》 **-grey** [áiərngréi] *adj.* having the color of freshly-broken iron. 철회색(鐵灰色)의.

i·ron·ic [airánik / -rɔ́n], **-i·cal** [-kəl] *adj.* **1** expressing the opposite of what one really means; of irony. 빈정거리는; 반어적인. ¶ *an* ~ *person* 비꼬기 잘하는 사람. **2** contrary to what was, or might be, expected. 엉뚱한; 얄궂은. ¶ *by an* ~ *chance* 엉뚱하게도; 얄궂게도 / *an* ~ *turn of fate* 얄궂은 운명. [→irony]

i·ron·i·cal·ly [airánikəli / -rɔ́n] *adv.* in an ironical manner. 반어적으로; 얄궂게도.

i·ron·ing [áiərniŋ] *n.* Ⓤ the act of pressing (clothes, etc.) with a heated iron. 다리미질. [→iron]

ironing board [⌐–– ⌐] *n.* a cloth-covered board on which clothes are ironed. 다리미판.

iron lung [⌐– ⌐] *n.* 《med.》 a device by which artificial respiration is given to a patient. 철폐(鐵肺).

i·ron·mon·ger [áiərnmʌ̀ŋgər] *n.* Ⓒ 《chiefly. Brit.》 a dealer in hardware. 철물

상(鐵物商).

i·ron·ware [áiərnwὲər] *n.* Ⓤ articles made of iron; hardware. 철물; 철기.

i·ron·work [áiərnwə̀:rk] *n.* Ⓤ things or parts of a thing made of iron. 철제품; 철제 부분.

i·ron·works [áiərnwə̀:rks] *n. pl.* 《used as *sing.* and *pl.*》 a place where iron is made or worked into iron articles. 제철소; 철공소.

i·ro·ny [áirəni] *n.* ⓊⒸ (*pl.* **-nies**) **1** a way of expressing the direct opposite of the thought in the speaker's mind. 반어(反語); 비꼬기; 풍자. ¶ *The boys called the very thin boy 'Fatty' in ~.* 아이들은 그 말라깽이 친구를 비꼬아 '뚱보'라 불렀다. **2** an event or a situation contrary to what was intended or expected. (사건·운명의) 뜻밖의 결과. ¶ *an ~ of fate* 운명의 장난 / *life's ironies* 인생의 장난. [Gk. *eirōneia,* dissembling, assumed ignorance]

ir·ra·di·ate [iréidièit] *vt.* (P6) **1** direct light upon (something); illuminate. 비추다. ¶ *The sun irradiates the world.* 해가 세상을 비춘다. **2** brighten (something) as if with light. …을 빛나게 하다. ¶ *a face irradiated by a smile* 미소로 빛나는 얼굴. **3** treat (something) by exposing it to X-rays, ultraviolet rays, etc. …을 엑스선, 자외선 등으로 조사(照射)하다. — *vi.* (P1) give out light. 빛나다. [ir-, →radiate]

ir·ra·di·a·tion [irèidiéiʃən] *n.* ⓊⒸ **1** the act of irradiating; the state of being irradiated. 비추기. **2** a ray of light. 광선.

ir·ra·tion·al [irǽʃənəl] *adj.* **1** contrary to reason; unreasonable; absurd. 불합리한; 이치에 안 맞는; 부조리의. ¶ *an ~ fear* 까닭 없는 공포. **2** without reasoning powers. 이성(理性)이 없는. ¶ *an ~ animal* 이성이 없는 동물. **3** 《math.》 not commensurable with the natural numbers. 무리수의(opp. rational). [ir-]

ir·ra·tion·al·ly [irǽʃənəli] *adv.* in an irrational manner. 불합리하게; 이성이 없이.

ir·re·claim·a·ble [ìrikléiməbəl] *adj.* that cannot be reclaimed or reformed. 돌이킬 수 없는. [ir-]

ir·rec·on·cil·a·ble [irékənsàiləbəl] *adj.* that cannot be brought into harmony; opposed. 조화되지 않는; 모순된. ¶ *~ idea* 양립할 수 없는 생각. — *n.* Ⓒ a person who remains opposed to agreement. 비타협적인 사람. [ir-]

ir·re·cov·er·a·ble [ìrikʌ́vərəbəl] *adj.* that cannot be recovered or remedied. 돌이킬 수 없는; 불치의. ¶ *~ debts* 회수 불능의 부채(負債) / *One's lost youth is ~.* 잃어버린 청춘은 돌이킬 수 없다. [ir-]

ir·re·deem·a·ble [ìridí:məbəl] *adj.* **1** that cannot be redeemed. 되돌릴 수 없는. ¶ *an ~ loss* 되돌릴 수 없는 손실. **2** that cannot be exchanged for coins. 불환(不換)의. ¶ *~ paper money* 불환 지폐. **3** hopeless; having no remedy. 가망 없는; 고칠 수 없는. ¶ *an ~ criminal* 교정 불능의 범죄인. ●**ir·re·deem·a·bly** [-i] *adv.* [ir-]

ir·re·du·ci·ble [ìridjú:səbəl] *adj.* **1** that cannot be reduced or lessened. 삭감할 수 없는; 덜 수 없는. **2** that cannot be brought to the desired form, state, degree, etc. (원하는 형식·상태·정도 따위로) 돌릴〔바꿀〕 수 없는. ¶ *~ expenses* 다른 형태로 바꿔 쓸 수 없는 비용.

ir·ref·ra·ga·ble [iréfrəgəbəl] *adj.* that cannot be denied or disproved. 논박할 수 없는; 부정 못 할. [ir-]

ir·ref·u·ta·ble [iréfjutəbəl, ìrifú:t-] *adj.* that cannot be refuted or disproved. 논박〔논파〕할 수 없는. [ir-]

·**ir·reg·u·lar** [irégjələr] *adj.* **1** not following rules; out of the proper order. 불규칙적인. ¶ *at ~ intervals* 불규칙한 간격을 두고 / *~ attendance* 불규칙한 출석 / *an ~ marriage* 정식이 아닌〔내연의〕 결혼 / *~ service* 부정기편(不定期便). **2** uneven; not symmetrical. 고르지 않은; 울퉁불퉁한. ¶ *an ~ group of trees* 〔*buildings*〕 어지러이 선 나무〔건물〕들. **3** 《gram.》 not normally inflected. 불규칙 변화의. ¶ *an ~ verb* 불규칙 동사. **4** 《mil.》 not belonging to the regular army. 정규병(正規兵)이 아닌. — *n.* 《usu. *pl.*》 soldiers not belonging to the regular army. 비(非)정규병; 의용군. [ir-]

ir·reg·u·lar·i·ty [irègjəlǽrəti] *n.* (*pl.* **-ties**) **1** Ⓤ the state of being irregular. 불규칙; 고르지 못함. **2** Ⓒ an irregular act or thing. 고르지 못한〔불규칙한〕 것〔행위〕. ¶ *irregularties in one's conduct* 행위의 불규칙성 / *the irregularities of the earth's surface* 울퉁불퉁한 지구 표면.

ir·rel·e·vant [iréləvənt] *adj.* having no connection with the subject at hand; not to the point. …와 무관계한; 엉뚱한; 잘못 짚은. [ir-]

ir·re·li·gious [ìrilídʒəs] *adj.* not religious; without respect for religion. 무종교의; 신앙이 없는; 경건하지 못한. [ir-]

ir·re·me·di·a·ble [ìrimí:diəbəl] *adj.* that cannot be cured or repaired. 불치의; 고칠 수 없는. ¶ *~ disease* 불치의 병 / *~ defects of character* 고칠 수 없는 인격의 결함. [ir-]

ir·rep·a·ra·ble [irépərəbəl] *adj.* that cannot be repaired or restored. 고칠 수 없는; 회복시킬 수 없는. ¶ *an ~ loss* 회복 불가능한 손실. [ir-]

ir·re·pres·si·ble [ìriprésəbəl] *adj.* that cannot be repressed or held back. 억누를〔억제할〕 수 없는; 제어하지 못하는. ¶ *~ laughter* 억누를 수 없는 웃음. [ir-]

ir·re·proach·a·ble [ìripróutʃəbəl] *adj.* free from blame or fault; blameless; faultless. 결점이 없는; 나무랄 데 없는. ¶ *~ conduct* 나무랄 데 없는 행동. [ir-]

ir·re·sist·i·ble [ìrizístəbəl] *adj.* too great

or strong to be resisted; overwhelming; very convincing. 저항할 수 없는; 억누를 수 없는; 더할 나위 없는. ¶ *an ~ force* 불가항력 / *an ~ desire* 억제할 수 없는 욕망 / *~ proofs* 군소리 할 수 없는 확실한 증거. [ir-]

ir·res·o·lute [irézəlùːt] *adj.* not resolute; undecided. 결단력이 없는; 우유부단한. ¶ *a man ~ in his decision* 결단력이 없는 사람. [ir-]

ir·res·o·lu·tion [irèzəlúːʃən] *n.* Ⓤ the state of being irresolute or undecided. 결단성 없음; 우유부단.

ir·re·spec·tive [irispéktiv] *adj.* 《*of*》 regardless. …와 관계 없는. ¶ *~ of sex or age* 남녀노소를 불문하고 / *~ of what has been said* 무어라 했든간에. [ir-]

ir·re·spon·si·bil·i·ty [ìrispɑ̀nsəbíləti / -pɔ̀n-] *n.* Ⓤ the state of being irresponsible. 무책임. [↓]

ir·re·spon·si·ble [ìrispɑ́nsəbəl / -pɔ́n-] *adj.* **1** not responsible. 책임이 없는. ¶ *an ~ child* 책임이 없는 아이. **2** that cannot be depended on. 무책임한; 믿을 수 없는. ¶ *~ conduct* 무책임한 짓. [ir-]

ir·re·triev·a·ble [ìritríːvəbəl] *adj.* that cannot be recovered; irreparable. 돌이킬 수 없는. ¶ *an ~ loss* 만회할 수 없는 손실. [ir-]

ir·rev·er·ence [irévərəns] *n.* **1** Ⓤ the state of being irreverent. 불경(不敬); 무례. **2** Ⓒ an act or speech showing lack of respect. 불손한〔불경스러운〕 언행. [↓]

ir·rev·er·ent [irévərənt] *adj.* showing no respect; disrespectful. 불손〔무례〕한. [ir-]

ir·re·vers·i·ble [ìrivə́ːrsəbəl] *adj.* **1** that cannot be reversed or turned inside out. 거꾸로 할 수 없는; 뒤집을 수 없는. ¶ *The hands on this clock are ~.* 이 시계의 바늘은 역행(逆行)시킬 수 없다. **2** that cannot be annulled. 취소〔파기〕할 수 없는. ¶ *an ~ decision of the court* 취소할 수 없는 법원의 판결. [ir-]

ir·rev·o·ca·ble [irévəkəbəl] *adj.* that cannot be recalled or undone; not alterable; final. 되불러 올 수 없는; 취소〔변경〕할 수 없는; 최후의. ¶ *an ~ decision* 최종 결정. [ir-]

ir·ri·gate [írəgèit] *vt.* (P6) **1** supply (land) with water for crops from artificial ditches. (땅)을 관개하다. ¶ *a land irrigated by many streams* 많은 개울로 관개된 땅. **2** 《med.》 wash out (a wound, etc.) with a flow of some liquid. (상처 등)을 세척하다. [ir-, L. *rigo* moisten]

ir·ri·ga·tion [ìrəgéiʃən] *n.* ⓊⒸ the act of irrigating; the state of being irrigated. 관개; 세척.

ir·ri·ta·bil·i·ty [ìrətəbíləti] *n.* Ⓤ **1** the quality or state of being irritable. 성마름; 성급함. **2** the quaílty of being excitable by some stimulus. 감수〔흥분〕성. [↓]

ir·ri·ta·ble [írətəbəl] *adj.* **1** easily excited to anger. 걸핏하면 성내는; 성마른. **2** extremely sensitive. 감각이 예민한; 민감한. [→irritate]

ir·ri·tant [írətənt] *adj.* causing irritation. 자극하는; 자극적인. — *n.* Ⓒ something that irritates or excites. 자극물; 자극제. ¶ *Dust is an ~ to the nasal passage.* 먼지는 비강(鼻腔)에 자극이 된다. [↓]

***ir·ri·tate** [írətèit] *vt.* (P6) **1** make impatient or angry. …을 신경질〔안달〕나게 하다; 초조하게 만들다. ¶ *be irritated to be kept waiting long* 장시간 기다리게 해서 신경질이 나다 / *He was irritated against you.* 그는 네게 화를 냈던 거다. **2** cause (a part of the body) to be sore. …을 따끔거리게 하다; …에 염증을 일으키다. ¶ *Smoke irritates the eyes.* 연기 때문에 눈이 맵다. [L. *irrito* annoy]

ir·ri·ta·tion [ìrətéiʃən] *n.* ⓊⒸ the act of irritating; the state of being irritated. 화나게 함; 초조하게 만듦; 자극; 흥분.

ir·rup·tion [irʌ́pʃən] *n.* ⓊⒸ the act of breaking or rushing in. 돌입; 침입. ¶ *an ~ of the enemy* 적의 침입. [L. *rumpo* break]

Ir·ving [ə́ːrviŋ], **Washington** *n.* (1783-1895) an American story writer. 어빙《미국의 작가》.

:is [iz] *vi.* third person, singular, present indicative of **be**.

ISBN International Standard Book Number. 국제 표준 도서 번호.

-ish [-iʃ] *suf.* **1** somewhat; rather. '…기미의, …기미를 띤'의 뜻. ¶ *oldish* 약간 늙은; 예스러운 / *reddish* 불그스레한 **2** having the nature of; like. '…같은, …비슷한'의 뜻. ¶ *boyish* 소년다운. [E.]

i·sin·glass [áiziŋglæ̀s, -glɑ̀ːs] *n.* Ⓤ a kind of gelatine got from a sturgeon. 부레풀; 젤라틴. [Du. *huisenblas* sturgeon's bladder]

Isl(s)., isl(s). island(s).

Is·lam [íslɑːm, íz-, -læm] *n.* Ⓤ **1** the religion of the Moslems; Mohammedanism. 회교; 이슬람교. **2** 《*collectlvely*》 Mohammedans as a group. 회교도. **3** the Mohammedan countries or region. 회교국; 회교권. [Arab. =surrender (to God)]

:is·land [áilənd] *n.* Ⓒ **1** a piece of land surrounded by water. 섬. **2** something like an island. 섬 비슷한 것. ¶ *safety islands in the street* (도로상의) 안전 지대 / *floating islands of ice* 유빙; 성엣장. [E.]

is·land·er [áiləndər] *n.* Ⓒ a person who is living on an island. 섬사람.

:isle [ail] *n.* Ⓒ a small island; an island. 작은섬; 섬. [L. *insula*] 「소도. [↑]

is·let [áilit] *n.* Ⓒ a small island. 작은 섬;

ism [ízəm] *n.* Ⓒ a distinctive doctrine; a theory. 주의. [Gk. *-ismos*]

-ism [-ìzəm] *suf.* **1** doctrine; principle. '…주의, …설(說)'의 뜻. ¶ *socialism.* **2** action; state. '행위, 상태'의 뜻. [↑]

:is·n't [íznt] is not.

ISO International Organization for Standardization. 국제 표준화 기구.

iso- [áisə-] *pref.* equal in value. '같은, 유사한'의 뜻. ¶ *isotope / isomer.* [Gk. *isos* equal]

i·so·bar [áisəbà:r] *n.* Ⓒ (of a weather map) a line that connects places having the same air pressure. 등압선(等壓線). [iso-]

***i·so·late** [áisəlèit, ísə-] *vt.* (P6,13) **1** put apart or alone; separate (something or someone) from others. …을 떼어놓다; 고립시키다. ¶ *The lack of a telephone isolated him.* 전화가 없어서 그는 고립되었다. **2** quarantine. 격리시키다. ¶ *The doctor isolates contagious cases.* 의사는 전염병 환자를 격리시킨다. [→insulate]

i·so·lat·ed [áisəlèitid, ísə-] *adj.* alone; separated. 고립된; 격리된.

i·so·la·tion [àisəléiʃən, ìsə-] *n.* Ⓤ the act of putting apart; the state of being put apart; loneliness. 격리; 분리. ¶ *an ~ hospital* 격리 병원.

i·so·la·tion·ism [àisəléiʃənìzəm, ìsə-] *n.* Ⓤ (of politics, etc.) the principle of keeping out of the affairs of other countries. (정치적인) 고립주의.

i·so·la·tion·ist [àisəléiʃənist, ìsə-] *n.* Ⓒ a supporter of the principle of keeping out of the affairs of other countries. 고립주의자.

i·so·mer [áisəmər] *n.* 《chem.》 a compound having the same molecular formula but having different properties. 이성질체(異性質體). [iso-, Gk. *meros* part]

i·sos·ce·les [aisásəlì:z / -sɔ́s-] *adj.* 《math.》 having two sides equal. 이등변의. ¶ *a ~ triangle* 이등변삼각형. [iso-, Gk. *skelos* leg]

i·sos·ta·sy [aisástəsi / -sɔ́s-] *n.* 《geol.》 the equilibrium of the earth's crust. 지각평형(地殼平衡). [iso-, Gk. *stasis* standing still]

i·so·therm [áisəθə̀:rm] *n.* Ⓒ (of a weather map) a line that connects places having the same average temperature. 등온선(等溫線). [iso-, Gk. *therme* heat]

i·so·ther·mal [àisəθə́:rməl] *adj.* of equality of temperatures. 등온(선)의.

i·so·tope [áisətòup] *n.* Ⓒ 《chem.》 an atom which is of the same chemical element as another, but has a different form. 동위 원소. [iso-, Gk. *topos* place]

Is·ra·el [ízriəl, -reiəl] *n.* **1** 《*collectively*》 the Jews; the Jewish people. 이스라엘 민족; 유태인. **2** a modern country in the Middle East; the Republic of Israel. 이스라엘 공화국. 參考 수도는 Jerusalem. [Heb. *yisrael* striver with God (Gen. XXXII: 28)]

***is·sue** [íʃu: / ísju:] *n.* **1** ⓊⒸ the act of passing or flowing out. 유출. ¶ *the ~ of blood from a wound* 상처에서의 출혈. **2** Ⓒ a thing comes, flows, or is sent out. 유출물(流出物). ¶ *be buried under the ~ from the volcano* 화산의 분출물(噴出物)에 묻히다. **3** Ⓒ exit; the mouth of a river. 출구; 배출구; 강어귀. ¶ *an ~ of water* 배수구. **4** ⓊⒸ the act of publishing or distributing. 발행; 배포. ¶ *the ~ of money* 화폐 발행 / *on the day of ~* 발행일에. **5** Ⓒ that which is published or printed, usu, as a part of a series. 발행〔간행〕물; 인쇄물. ¶ *the October ~ of Reader's Digest* 리더스 다이제스트의 10월호 / *the next ~ of a newspaper* 신문의 다음 호. **6** Ⓒ a point or subject of argument, discussion, etc.; an important problem. 쟁점; (중요한) 문제. ¶ *raise a new ~* 새로운 문제를 제기하다 / *debate an ~* 문제를 토의하다 / *burning issues* 초미(焦眉)의 문제. **7** Ⓒ a result; a conclusion; an end. 결과; 결말. ¶ *the ~ of a fight* 싸움의 결말 / *abide the ~* 결과를 기다리다. **8** ⓊⒸ profits of an enterprise, etc. (사업·부동산 등에서 나는) 이익; 수익. ¶ *the ~ of an estate* 토지 수익. **9** Ⓤ children. 자녀; 자손. ¶ *Elizabeth I died without ~.* 엘리자베스 1세는 자녀를 남기지 않고 죽었다.

at issue, under discussion. 논쟁중인. ¶ *the point at ~* 논쟁중의 문제점.

bring 〔***put***〕 ***a matter to an issue,*** cause a matter to reach the point where a decision can and must be made. (사항)의 결말을 내다.

join issue (=*enter into an argument*) ***with*** *someone.* …와 논쟁하다.

take issue (=*disagree*) ***with*** *someone.* …에 반대하다.

— *vi.* (P1,2A,3) **1** 《*from*》 go or come out; flow out. 나오다; 유출하다. ¶ *The smoke issued from the chimney in rolling clouds.* 연기가 굴뚝에서 뭉게뭉게 굽이치며 올랐다 / *Blood issues from a cut.* 벤 상처에서 피가 나온다. **2** be published. 발행되다. ¶ *a magazine which is issued once a month* 한 달에 한 번 발간되는 잡지. **3** (P1,2A,3) 《*in*》 come to an end; result. 결국 …이 되다. ¶ *The game issued in a tie.* 시합은 비겼다.

— *vt.* **1** (P6) give (something) to the public; publish; send out; put forth. …을 발행〔발간〕하다. ¶ *~ a newspaper* 신문을 내다 / *~ money and stamps* 화폐와 우표를 발행하다. **2** (P6,13) supply (clothing, food, etc.) (의류 등을) 지급〔공급〕하다. ¶ *~ clothing to recruits* 신병에 피복을 지급하다. [→exit]

-ist [-ist] *suf.* **1** a person who does something. '…을 하는 사람'의 뜻. ¶ *pianist / artist.* **2** a person who is skilled in or knows well about some subject. '…에 능한 사람, …가(家)'의 뜻. **3** a person who is occupied with something. '…주의자'의 뜻. ¶ *anarchist / socialist.* [Gk.]

Is·tan·bul [ìstænbú:l, -tɑ:n-] *n.* a city of Turkey. 이스탄불《터키의 옛 수도》.

isth·mi [ísmai] *n.* pl. of **isthmus.**

***isth·mus** [ísməs] *n.* Ⓒ (*pl.* **-muses** or **-mi**) a narrow neck of land joining two large bodies of land. 지협(地峽). ¶ *The Isthmus of Panama* 파나마 지협. [Gk. =neck]

:it [it] *pron.* (*pl.* **they**) **1** anything, except a person, already spoken about. 그것은〔이〕; 그것을〔에〕《앞서 나온 사물을 가리킴》. ¶ *I wrote a letter and sent* ~. 편지를 써서 그것을 부쳤다 / *What is this ? —It is a book.* 이건 무엇이냐 —그건 책입니다 / *She is beautiful, and she knows* ~. 그녀는 미인이며, 자신도 그것을 알고 있다. **2** a baby; a person whose sex is not known. 어린아이; (성별 미상의) 사람. ¶ *The baby cried for its bottle.* 아기는 젖병을 달라고 울었다 / *Go and see who* ~ *is.* 그게 누군지 가보아라 / *Who is that ? —It's a friend of mine.* 저 애는 누구냐 —제 친구입니다. **3** 《as the *subject* of an *impersonal verb*》 語法 비인칭 동사의 주어로서 날씨, 시간, 거리, 그 밖의 어떤 막연한 것을 가리킴. ¶ *It snowed.* 눈이 왔다 / *It grew dark.* 어두워졌다 / *It is four in the morning.* 아침 네 시다 / *It will soon be spring.* 곧 봄이 된다 / *It is fifty feet to the filling station.* 주유소까지 50 피트다 / *It is very hot.* 날씨가 아주 덥다. **4** 《as a *formal subject* or a *formal object*》 語法 형식상의 주어·목적어로서 글의 앞이나 가운데에 둠. ¶ *It is certain that he will succeed.* 그의 성공은 확실하다 / *It is wrong to tell a lie.* 거짓말은 좋지 않다 / *I found* ~ *impossible to sleep.* 잠자기는 틀렸다고 생각했다. **5** 《*It is* 〔*It was*〕... *that* 〔*who, whom, which*〕》 語法 글 가운데의 주어·목적어·부사어구를 강조함. ¶ *It is you that are responsible.* 책임은 네게 있다 / *It was yesterday that he broke the window.* 그가 유리창을 깬 것은 어제였다 / *It is the wife* (*that*) *decides.* 결정은 아내가 한다. **6** 《*idiomatically*》 ¶ *Cut* ~ *out.* 그만둬; 아서라 / *Stick to* ~. 버텨라 / *lord* ~ *over* …에 군림하다 / *brave* ~ *out* 끝까지 해내다.

foot it, walk. 걷다.

Hook it ! Be off ! 도망쳐라.

lord it, play the lord. 뻐기다.

queen it, behave like, play the part of, a queen. 여왕처럼 행동〔군림〕하다.

run for it, run in order to escape, to catch the train, etc. 달아나려고〔기차 시간에 대려고〕 뛰다.

— *n.* 《*colloq.*》 sexual appeal. 성적 매력. [E.]

:I·tal·ian [itǽljən] *adj.* of Italy, its people or their language. 이탈리아의; 이탈리아 사람〔어〕의. — *n.* Ⓒ a person of Italy; Ⓤ the language of Italy. 이탈리아 사람〔어〕. [Gk. *Italia*]

:i·tal·ic [itǽlik] *adj.* 《print.》 of or in the kind of type in which letters slope to the right. 이탤릭체의. — *n.* 《*pl.*》 a sloping kind of letter or printing. 활자의 이탤릭체 (cf. *Gothic, Roman*). [↑]

i·tal·i·cize [itǽləsàiz] *vt.* (P6) print (words, etc.) in a sloping style. …을 이탤릭체로 인쇄하다.

:It·a·ly [ítəli] *n.* a country in southern Europe on the Mediterranean. 이탈리아.

itch [itʃ] *n.* ⓊⒸ **1** a feeling on the skin giving a person a desire to scratch. 가려움. **2** 《med.》 a disease causing that feeling. 옴. **3** 《*fig.*》 a restless and strong desire. 갈망; 열망. — *vi.* (P1,3,4) **1** have an itch. 가렵다. ¶ *My back itches.* 등이 가렵다. **2** 《*fig.*》 have an uneasy longing or desire. …하고 싶어 못견디다〔좀이 쑤시다〕. ¶ *He is itching to find out their secret.* 그들의 비밀이 알고싶어 안달하고 있다. [E.]

have an itching palm ⇨*palm*[1].

itch·y [ítʃi] *adj.* (**itch·i·er, itch·i·est**) itching; like an itch. 옴이 오른; 가려운; 하고 싶어 좀이 쑤시는.

***i·tem** [áitəm, -tem] *n.* Ⓒ **1** (of a list, etc.) a single and separate thing. 항목; 종목. ¶ *number each* ~ *in a catalog* 카탈로그의 항목마다 번호를 매기다. **2** a piece of news. (신문 기사의) 한 절(節); 한 항목. ¶ *Here's an interesting* ~ *from today's newspaper.* 오늘 신문에 재미 있는 기사가 있다. [L. =likewise]

i·tem·ize [áitəmàiz] *vt.* (P6) give the particulars of (something); state (something) by item. …을 종목별로 쓰다; …을 항목으로 나누다.

it·er·ate [ítərèit] *vt.* (P6) say again; repeat. …을 되풀이 말하다. ¶ ~ *an accusation* 비난을 되풀이하다. [L. *iterum* again]

it·er·a·tion [ìtəréiʃən] *n.* ⓊⒸ the act of saying again; repetition. 되풀이; 반복.

it·er·a·tive [ítərèitiv, -rət-] *adj.* repeating; repeated. 되풀이〔반복〕하는.

i·tin·er·an·cy [aitínərənsi, itín-] *n.* ⓊⒸ the act of traveling from place to place. 순회; 순력(巡歷); 편력. [↓]

i·tin·er·ant [aitínərənt, itín-] *adj.* traveling from place to place. 순회하는; 돌아다니는. ¶ *an* ~ *library* 순회 도서관 / ~ *musicians* 순회악단. ● **i·tin·er·ant·ly** [-li] *adv.* [L. *iter* journey]

i·tin·er·ar·y [aitínərèri, itín- / -rəri] *n.* Ⓒ (*pl.* **-ar·ies**) **1** the route of a trip. 여정; 여행 일정. **2** the record of a trip. 여행기. **3** a guidebook for travelers. 여행 안내서.

— *adj.* of traveling or routes of travel. 순회하는; 여로의.

i·tin·er·ate [aitínərèit, itín-] *vi.* (P1) travel from place to place. 순회하다; 여기저기 여행하다.

it'll [ítl] it will.

ITO International Trade Organization. (유엔) 국제 무역 기구.

:its [its] *pron.* the possessive form of **it**; the one or ones belonging to one. 그것〔저것〕의; 그; 저것. ¶ *I don't like* ~ *shape.* 그 모양이 마음에 안 든다 / *This chair has lost one of* ~ *legs.* 이 의자는 다리 하나가 없다.

:it's [its] 《*colloq.*》 it is; it has.

:it·self [it-sélf] *pron.* (*pl.* **them·selves**) **1** a reflexive or emphatic form of **it.** 그 자체; 바로 그것《강조 용법》; 그 자체를《재귀용법》. ¶ *Even the well ~ was empty.* 우물마저 말라 있었다 / *The picture ~ cost ten pounds, without the frame.* 액자 말고 그림만도 10 파운드다 / *The bird hid ~.* 그 새는 숨었다. **2** its normal physical or mental condition. 그 자신. [*it, self*]

by itself, **a**) alone; apart from other things. 홀로. **b**) automatically. 자동적으로.

in itself, independently of outward things. 그 자체; 원래; 본질적으로.

of itself, naturally. 저절로. ¶ *The light went out of ~.* 불은 저절로 꺼졌다.

:I've [aiv] I have.

-ive [-aiv] *suf.* tending to do; having the nature or quality of. '…하는 경향이 있는, …성(性)의'의 뜻. [L. *-ivus*]

i·vied [áivid] *adj.* covered with ivy. 담쟁이로 덮인. [→ivy]

·i·vo·ry [áivəri] *n.* (*pl.* **-ries**) Ⓤ **1** a white bonelike substance forming the long teeth of an elephant, etc. 상아; (해마 등의) 엄니. **2** the color of ivory; creamy white. 상앗빛. **3** 《*pl.*》 things made of ivory. 상아 제품. —*adj.* of or like ivory; made of ivory. 상아의; 상아 같은; 상아로 만든. ¶ *an ~ skin* 상아 같은 피부. [L. *ebur*]

Ivory Coast [´–– ´], **the** *n.* a republic in West Africa. 코트디부아르《서아프리카에 있는 한 공화국》. 參考 수도는 야무수크로(Yamousoukro).

ivory tower [´–– ´–] *n.* the condition of being distant from the actual world; the world of ideas and dreams. 상아탑.

·i·vy [áivi] *n.* ⓊⒸ (*pl.* **i·vies**) 《bot.》 a climbing plant with large, evergreen leaves. 담쟁이. [E.]

IWC International Whaling Convention. 국제 포경 회의.

IWW Industrial Workers of the World. 세계 산업 노동자 동맹.

-ize [-aiz] *suf.* **1** to make or cause to be. '…화(化)하다, …로 하다'의 뜻. ¶ *dramatize.* **2** to become. '…이 되다'의 뜻. ¶ *crystallize.* [Gk. *izo*]

iz·zard [ízərd] *n.* 《*colloq.*》 the letter z. z자.

from A to izzard, from beginning to end. 처음부터 끝까지. [→zed]

j J

J, j [dʒei] *n.* Ⓒ (*pl.* **J's, Js, j's, js** [dʒeiz]) **1** the tenth letter of the English alphabet. 영어 자모의 열째 자. **2** something that has the shape of J. J 모양의 것. ¶ *a J pen,* J 자 표가 있는 끝이 뭉툭한 펜.

jab [dʒæb] *vt., vi.* (P6,13; 1) (**jabbed, jab·bing**) **1** stab (something) with sudden force. …을 쿡 찌르다. ¶ ~ *a big fish with a spear* 작살로 큰 고기를 쿡 찌르다 / ~ *someone with one's elbow* 팔꿈치로 아무를 쿡 찌르다. **2** 《boxing》 give a short, straight blow. 잽을 먹이다. —*n.* Ⓒ a sharp thrust or blow. 쿡 찌르기; 잽. [Imit.]

jab·ber [dʒǽbər] *vi., vt.* (P1,2A; 6) talk very fast and indistinctly; chatter. (알아 듣기 힘들게) 재잘거리다. —*n.* Ⓤ very fast, indistinct talk. (알아 듣기 힘든) 재잘거림. ¶ *the ~ of monkeys* 원숭이들의 캑캑거리는 소리. [Imit.]

ja·bot [dʒæbóu, ʒæbóu] *n.* Ⓒ a frill of lace on the front of a woman's dress. (여성복 앞쪽의) 주름 장식. [F.]

Jack [dʒæk] *n.* a nickname of John. John의 애칭.

·jack [dʒæk] *n.* Ⓒ **1** 《usu. J-》 a man; a fellow. 남자; 녀석; 친구. ¶ *Jack and Jill* 젊은 남녀. **2** 《*colloq.*》 a sailor. 수부; 선원. **3** a male of certain animals. (짐승의) 수컷. **4** a small national flag flown on a ship. (이물에 다는) 작은 국기. ¶ *the Union Jack* 유니언잭. **5** a playing card with a picture of a young man. (카드의) 잭. **6** 《*sl.*》 money. 돈; 금전. **7** a tool for lifting heavy things. 잭. **8** a jackknife. 잭나이프.

before you can* 〔*could*〕 *say Jack and Robinson, very quickly; in a moment, suddenly. 갑자기; 순식간에.

every man jack, 《*colloq.*》 everyone. 누구나.

Jack of all trades, a person who can do many different kinds of work. 무엇이건 다 할 줄 아는 사람; 만능꾼.

—*vt.* (P6,7) **1** 《*up*》 lift (something) with a jack. …을 잭으로 들〔밀〕어올리다. ¶ ~ *up a car to change a tire* 타이어를 갈아 끼우기 위해 차를 잭으로 들어올리다. **2** 《*colloq.*》 abandon; give up (something). …을 포기하다. **3** increase; raise. …을 늘리다; 인상하다. ¶ ~ *price* 〔*wages*〕 값〔임금〕을 올리다. [*John*]

jack·al [dʒǽkɔːl] *n.* Ⓒ **1** a wild, dog-like animal living in Asia and Africa. 자칼 《일종의 들개》. **2** a man who does base work for another. 남의 앞잡이. [Pers.]

jack·a·napes [dʒǽkənèips] *n.* Ⓒ a conceited fellow; a mischievous boy. 제 잘난 줄 아는〔건방진〕 남자; 개구쟁이. [*Jack*]

jack·ass [dʒǽkæ̀s] *n.* Ⓒ **1** a male donkey or ass. 수탕나귀. **2** [-ɑ̀ːs] a stupid person. 바보; 멍청이.

jack·boot [dʒǽkbùːt] *n.* Ⓒ a large boot reaching above the knee. (어부 등이 신는) 긴 장화.

jack·daw [dʒǽkdɔ̀ː] *n.* Ⓒ a black European bird like a crow. 갈가마귀.

:jack·et [dʒǽkit] *n.* Ⓒ **1** a short coat. 재킷. **2** a paper cover for a book, etc. (책의) 커버. ¶ *a book ~* 책 커버. **3** the protective outer covering of a boiler, pipe, etc. (보일러 따위 열의 방산(放散)을 막는) 외피. **4** the skin of a potato, etc. (감자 등의) 껍질. [F. *jaque*]

Jack Frost [⌐⌐] *n.* frost regarded as a person. 서리; 동장군(冬將軍).

jack-in-the-box [dʒǽkinðəbɑ̀ks / -bɔ̀ks] *n.* Ⓒ a toy that springs out of a box when it is opened. (열면 튀어나오는) 장난감. [*John*]

Jack Ketch [⌐⌐] *n.* a common hangman. 교수형 집행자.

jack·knife [dʒǽknàif] *n.* Ⓒ (*pl.* **-knives**) **1** 《U.S.》 a large, strong, folding pocketknife. 잭나이프. **2** a kind of dive in which the diver bends and touches his feet before entering the water. 잭나이프 다이빙《다이빙에서》. [*John*]

jack·light [dʒǽklàit] *n.* 《U.S.》 a light used in hunting for fish at night. (야간의) 고기잡이 횃불.

Jack-of-all-trades [dʒǽkəvɔ́ːltréidz, ⌐—⌐⌐] *n.* ⇨jack.

jack-o'-lan·tern [dʒǽkəlæ̀ntərn] *n.* Ⓒ **1** a pumpkin hollowed out and cut to look like a human face, used as a lantern. (호박의 속을 후벼내고 눈·코·입을 낸) 호박등(燈). **2** a will-o'-the-wisp. 도깨비불.

〈jack-o'-lantern 1〉

jack·screw [dʒǽkskrùː] *n.* Ⓒ a lifting jack worked by the turning of a screw. 나사식(式) 잭.

jack tar [⌐⌐] *n.* a sailor. 수병; 선원.

Ja·cob [dʒéikəb] *n.* 《Bible》 the son of Isaac and father of the twelve tribes of Israel. 야곱. 參考 유대인의 조상. [Heb.]

Jac·o·be·an [dʒæ̀kəbíːən] *adj.* of or belonging to the period of King James I of

J

England, from 1603 to 1625. 영국왕 James 1 세 시대의. ¶ *Jacobean furniture* 〔*drama, poets*〕. [→Jacob, -ean]

jade[1] [dʒeid] *n.* Ⓤ a green stone used for jewels and ornaments. 비취; 옥(玉). [L. *ilia* flank]

jade[2] [dʒeid] *n.* Ⓒ **1** an inferior or overworked horse. 쇠약한〔야윈〕 말. **2** a disreputable woman; 《*iron.*》 any woman. 굴러먹은 여자; 여자; 여인. [? N. =mare]

jad·ed [dʒéidid] *adj.* worn out; exhausted. 지친; 여윈. ¶ *a ~ face* 초췌한 얼굴. [↑]

jag [dʒæg] *n.* Ⓒ a sharp projection. 날카롭게 비어져나온 것. ¶ *a ~ of rock* 삐죽한 바위 모서리. [Imit.]

jag·ged [dʒǽgid] *adj.* with sharp projecting points; cut or torn unevenly. 끝이 뾰족한; 들쭉날쭉한.

jag·uar [dʒǽgwɑːr, -gjuɑ̀ːr / -gjuər] *n.* Ⓒ a fierce animal like a leopard, living in the warmer parts of South America. 재규어; 아메리카표범. [Native]

***jail** [dʒeil] *n.* Ⓒ a prison. 감옥; 교도소. ¶ *break ~* 탈옥하다 / *in ~* 감옥에 들어가서 / *He escaped from ~.* 그는 감옥에서 도망갔다 〔탈옥했다〕. —*vt.* (P6) put (someone) in (a) jail; imprison. …을 투옥하다. 參考 영국에서는 gaol이라 씀. [→cage]

jail·bird [dʒéilbə̀ːrd] *n.* Ⓒ **1** a prisoner in jail. 죄수. **2** a habitual criminal. 상습범.

jail·er, jail·or [dʒéilər] *n.* Ⓒ a person in charge of a jail. 간수; 교도관. 參考 영국에서는 gaoler라 함.

Ja·kar·ta [dʒəkɑ́ːrtə] *n.* =Djakarta.

***jam**[1] [dʒæm] *v.* (**jammed, jam·ming**) *vt.* **1** (P6,7,13) press or squeeze (something) tightly. …을 밀어넣다; 채워넣다. ¶ *~ various things into a suitcase* 갖가지 물건들을 가방에 쑤셔넣다. **2** crush; bruise. …을 으깨다; 멍들게 하다. ¶ *~ a fist into someone's face* 아무의 얼굴을 갈기다 / *~ one's finger in a door* 손가락이 문에 끼이다. **3** (P6) (of a crowd) fill; block. (관중 따위가) …을 막다; 메우다. ¶ *~ a passage* 길을 메우다. **4** (P6) fix or fasten (a part of a machine) so that it cannot be operated. (기계 등의 일부를) 움직이지 못하게 하다. ¶ *The door was jammed.* 문이 끼여 움직이지 않았다. **5** (P6) interfere with radio signals by sending other signals of the same wave length. …을 (같은 파장의 주파를 보내) 방해하다. ¶ *~ the radio* 무선 통신을 방해하다.

—(P1) *vi.* **1** become unworkable or wedged. (물건이 끼여) 움직이지 않게 되다. ¶ *The window jammed.* 창문이 꿈쩍도 하지 않았다. **2** push against something violently. 억지로 밀고 들어가다; 끼어들다. ¶ *People jammed into the train.* 사람들이 기차 안으로 서로 밀치며 들어갔다.

—*n.* Ⓒ the act of jamming; the state of being jammed; a dense crowd; 《*colloq.*》 a difficult situation. 꽉 들어참; 혼잡; 운집; 곤경; 궁지. ¶ *a traffic ~* 교통 체증〔마비〕 / *be in* 〔*get into*〕 *a ~* 궁지에 빠지다. [Imit.]

:**jam**[2] [dʒæm] *n.* Ⓤ a food made by boiling fruit with sugar. 잼. [↑]

Ja·mai·ca [dʒəméikə] *n.* the largest island in the West Indies, south of Cuba. 자메이카. 參考 수도는 Kingstone.

jamb, jambe [dʒæm] *n.* Ⓒ **1** 《*archit.*》 one of the side posts of a doorway, a window, etc. 문설주. **2** 《*pl.*》 stone or brick sides of a fireplace. (벽난로 양쪽의) 돌벽. [F. *jambe* leg]

jam·bo·ree [dʒæ̀mbəríː] *n.* Ⓒ **1** 《*colloq.*》 a noisy, lively party. 떠들썩하고 즐거운 모임. **2** an international meeting of Boy Scouts. 잼버리. [U.S.]

:**James** [dʒeimz] *n.* **1** a man's name. 남자 이름. 參考 애칭은 Jamie, Jim, Jimmy. **2** (in the Bible) the name of one of Christ's disciples; one of the books of the New Testament. 야고보; 야고보서(書).

jam-packed [dʒǽmpǽkt] *adj.* 《U.S. *colloq.*》 filled to the greatest possible extent. 꽉 (들어)찬. [→jam, pack]

:**Jan.** January.

Jane [dʒein] *n.* a woman's name. 여자 이름.

jan·gle [dʒǽngəl] *vi., vt.* **1** (P1; 6) make a harsh noise; cause (something) to sound harshly. 듣기 좋지 않은 소리를 내다; 쩔렁쩔렁 울리게 하다. ¶ *~ a bunch of keys* 열쇠꾸러미를 쩔렁거리다 / *~ a fire bell* 화재의 경종을 울리다. **2** (P1) talk noisily; dispute. 시끄럽게 떠들다; 입씨름하다. —*n.* Ⓒ a harsh sound; a dispute. 귀에 거슬리는 소리; 언쟁. [F. *jangler* chatter, tattle]

jan·i·tor [dʒǽnətər] *n.* Ⓒ **1** 《U.S.》 a person employed to take care of and clean a building, an office, etc. (건물 등의) 관리인. **2** a door-keeper. 문지기; 수위. [L. *janua* door]

:**Jan·u·ar·y** [dʒǽnjuèri / -əri] *n.* the first month of the year. 1월; 정월. 參考 Jan.으로 생략함. [↓]

Ja·nus [dʒéinəs] *n.* 《Rom. myth.》 the god of gates and doors with two faces, one looking forward, one backward. 야누스; 양면신(兩面神). [L. *jānus* doorway]

Jap [dʒæp] *adj., n.* Ⓒ 《*colloq.*》 =Japanese.

Jap. Japan; Japanese.

ja·pan [dʒəpǽn] *n.* Ⓤ **1** a hard, shining lacquer used on wood or metal. 옻칠. **2** articles lacquered in the Japanese manner. 칠기. —*vt.* (P6) (**-panned, -pan·ning**) put japan on (something). …에 옻칠을 하다; 검은 윤을 내다. [↓]

:**Ja·pan** [dʒəpǽn] *n.* a country off the eastern coast of Asia. 일본. [Chin. =sunrise]

:**Jap·a·nese** [dʒæ̀pəníːz, -s] *adj.* of Japan, its people, or their language. 일본의; 일본사람〔어〕의. —*n.* (*pl.* **Jap·a·nese**) **1** Ⓒ a person of Japan; 《*collectively*》 the peo-

J

ple of Japan. 일본인(사람). **2** Ⓤ the language of Japan. 일본어.

***jar**[1] [dʒɑːr] *n.* Ⓒ **1** a wide-mouthed container of glass, earthenware, etc. 항아리; 단지. **2** the amount that a jar can hold. 한 단지의 양. [Arab.]

:jar[2] [dʒɑːr] *v.* (**jarred, jar·ring**) *vi.* **1** (P1) shake harshly; make a harsh, unpleasant noise. 진동하다; 삐걱거리다. **2** (P1) 《*on*》 have an unpleasant effect. (신경에) 거슬리다. ¶ *The sound jars on my ears.* 그 소리는 귀에 거슬린다. **3** (P1,3) 《*with*》 disagree; quarrel. (의견 등이) 다르다; 다투다.
— *vt.* (P6) **1** cause (something) to shake; cause (something) to give a harsh, unpleasant noise. …을 흔들다; 삐걱거리게 하다. ¶ *The wind jarred the whole house.* 바람은 온 집을 흔들었다. **2** cause a shock to. …을 깜짝 놀라게 하다.
— *n.* Ⓒ **1** a harsh, unpleasant noise. 듣기에 불쾌한 소리. **2** a shock. 충격. ¶ *The news gave me a nasty* ~. 그 소식은 내게 역겨운 충격이었다. **3** a dispute; a quarrel. 불화; 다툼. [Imit.]

jar·gon [dʒɑ́ːrgɑn/-gɔn] *n.* Ⓤ **1** meaningless or unintelligible talk. (뜻도 모를) 횡설 수설하는 소리. **2** special or technical words used within a certain profession. 전문어. ¶ *medical* ~ 의학 용어. — *vi.* (P1) talk jargon. 시부렁거리다. [F.]

jar·ring [dʒɑ́ːriŋ] *adj.* sounding harshly and unpleasantly. 귀에 거슬리는 소리를 내는. [*jar*[2]]

jas·mine, -min [dʒǽzmin, dʒǽs-] *n.* **1** Ⓒ 《bot.》 a shrub with fragrant red, white or yellow flowers. 재스민. **2** Ⓤ a perfume made from this flowers. 재스민 향수. 參考 jessamine이라고도 씀. [Pers.]

jas·per [dʒǽspər] *n.* Ⓤ a stone, usu. red, brown or yellow, used for ornamentation. 벽옥(碧玉); 재스퍼. [Gk. *iaspis*]

jaun·dice [dʒɔ́ːndis, dʒɑ́ːn-] *n.* Ⓤ **1** 《med.》 a disease that makes the skin, the eyes, etc. yellow. 황달. **2** a disordered vision. 편견. — *vt.* (P6) effect with jaundice. 황달에 걸리게 하다. [L. *galbus* yellow]

jaunt [dʒɔːnt, dʒɑːnt] *n.* Ⓒ a short pleasure trip; an excursion for pleasure. 소풍. — *vi.* (P1) take such a trip. 소풍 가다. [?]

jaun·ty [dʒɔ́ːnti, dʒɑ́ːn-] *adj.* (**-ti·er, -ti·est**) **1** gay; pleasant. 명랑한; 쾌활한. ¶ *a* ~ *smile* 밝은 미소. **2** stylish. 스마트한. ¶ *a* ~ *hat* 멋있는 모자 / *walk with a* ~ *step* 맵시 있게 걷다. [F. *gentil* (→genteel)]

Jav. Javanese.

Ja·va [dʒɑ́ːvə, dʒǽvə] *n.* **1** an island in the East Indies. 자바. **2** Ⓤ a kind of coffee got from Java. 자바 커피. **3** Ⓤ 《often *j*-》 《U.S. *sl.*》 coffee. 커피. [Place]

Jav·a·nese [dʒɑ̀ːvəníːz] *adj.* of or belonging to Java, its people, or their language. 자바(사람, 말)의. — *n.* (*pl.* **Jav·a·nese**) **1** Ⓒ a native or inhabitant of Java. 자바 사람. **2** Ⓤ the Indonesian language spoken in Java. 자바 말.

jave·lin [dʒǽvəlin] *n.* Ⓒ a light spear thrown by hand, once used as a weapon. (던지는) 창. ¶ *the* ~ *throw* 투창. [F. *javeline*]

***jaw** [dʒɔː] *n.* Ⓒ **1** either of the two bones of the mouth. 턱. ¶ *the upper* (*lower*) ~. **2** 《*pl.*》 a mouth. 입. ¶ *escape the jaws of death* 사지(死地)를 벗어나다. **3** 《*pl.*》 a narrow entrance to a valley. (계곡 등의) 좁은 입구. **4** either of the parts in a machine that hold something. (집게 등의) 무는 부분. **5** 《*sl.*》 a tedious talk. 수다. ¶ *Hold your* ~. 입 닥쳐. — *vt., vi.* (P6; 1) 《*sl.*》 **1** talk tediously. 수다 떨다. **2** scold. 욕지거리하다. [O.F. *joue* cheek (→cheek)]

jaw·bone [dʒɔ́ːbòun] *n.* Ⓒ the bone of the upper or lower jaw. 턱뼈.

jaw·break·er [dʒɔ́ːbrèikər] *n.* Ⓒ 《*colloq.*》 **1** a word or sentence which is hard to pronounce. 발음하기 어려운 말. **2** a kind of very hard candy. 아주 딱딱한 캔디.

***jay** [dʒei] *n.* Ⓒ **1** 《bird》 a noisy American and European bird of the crow family. 어치. **2** 《*colloq.*》 a person who talks too much; a stupid person. 수다쟁이; 바보; 얼간이. [F.]

jay·walk·er [dʒéiwɔ̀ːkər] *n.* 《U.S. *colloq.*》 Ⓒ a person who crosses a street disregarding traffic and traffic lights. (교통 규칙을 아랑곳하지 않는) 무단 횡단자. [↑]

jazz [dʒæz] *n.* Ⓤ **1** lively dance music, originally American Negroes'. 재즈. **2** a dance to such music. 재즈 댄스. — *adj.* of or like jazz. 재즈의. — *vt., vi.* (P6; 1) play jazz; arrange (music) as jazz; dance to jazz. 재즈를 연주하다; …을 재즈 편곡하다; 재즈 댄스를 하다. [U.S.]

***jeal·ous** [dʒéləs] *adj.* **1** 《*of*》 ⓐ feeling fear, suspicion, and hatred towards a rival, esp. in love. 질투심 많은; 시샘하는. ¶ *be* ~ *of someone's success* 아무의 성공을 시샘하다. ⓑ envious. 부러워하는; 선망하는. **2** 《Bible》 (of God) demanding complete faithfulness or worship. (신이 자기만의) 절대적 신앙을 요구하는. **3** careful to protect or keep; watchful. 매우 조심하는; 방심 않는. ¶ *keep a* ~ *eye on someone* 아무에게서 경계의 눈을 떼지 않다 / ~ *of one's rights* (*position*) 자기의 권리(지위)를 잃을까봐 조심하다 (방심 않다). [→zeal]

jeal·ous·ly [dʒéləsli] *adv.* in a jealous manner. 투기(시샘)하여.

***jeal·ous·y** [dʒéləsi] *n.* ⓊⒸ (*pl.* **-ous·ies**) **1** the state of being jealous; jealous feeling. 질투; 시샘; 시기. ¶ *show one's* ~ *of someone's reputation* 아무의 명성을 시기하다. **2** great care, esp. in guarding or watching. 빈틈없는 경계심; 주시(注視).

jean [dʒiːn/dʒein] *n.* **1** Ⓤ a strong cotton

J

cloth. 진. **2** 《*pl.*》 trousers of this cloth. 진으로 만든 바지. [L. *Janua* Genoa]

jeep [dʒiːp] *n.* Ⓒ a small but powerful automobile originally made for military use. 지프차. [Trademark]

jeer [dʒiər] *vt., vi.* (P6; 1,3) 《*at*》 make fun of (someone); sneer at (someone); laugh rudely. (…을) 조롱하다; 놀리다; 조소〔야유〕하다. ¶ *~ at his idea* 그의 발상을 비웃다 / *He was jeered (at) by the audience.* 그는 관중의 야유를 받았다. — *n.* Ⓒ a rude or jeering remark. 조롱; 조소; 야유. [?<cheer]

***Jef·fer·son** [dʒéfərsən], **Thomas** *n.* (1743-1826) the third president of the United States, from 1801 to 1809. 제퍼슨《미국의 제3대 대통령》.

Je·ho·vah [dʒihóuvə] *n.* 《Bible》 the name of God in the Old Testament. 여호와. [Heb. *yahveh*]

je·june [dʒidʒúːn] *adj.* **1** poor; barren. 가난한; 빈약한; 메마른. ¶ *a ~ diet* 악식(惡食). **2** dull; dry; uninteresting. 무미 건조한; 따분한. ¶ *a ~ novel* 〔*style*〕 시원찮은 소설〔문체〕. [L. *jejunus* fasting]

***jel·ly** [dʒéli] *n.* ⓊⒸ (*pl.* **-lies**) **1** a soft, half-solid food made by boiling down fruit juice, meat juice, etc. with sugar. 젤리. **2** a substance like jelly. 젤리 모양의 것.

beat** someone **to a jelly, knock someone down; defeat someone severely. …을 떡이 되도록 패다.

— *vi., vt.* (**-lied**) (P1; 6) become jelly; turn (something) into jelly. 젤리가 되다; 젤리로 만들다. ¶ *~ fruit* 과일을 젤리로 만들다 / *Strong soup will ~ as it cool.* 진한 수프는 식으면 젤리처럼 된다. [L. *gelo* freeze]

jel·ly·fish [dʒélifìʃ] *n.* Ⓒ (*pl.* **-fish·es** or 《*collectively*》 **-fish**) a sea animal with a boneless, umbrella-shaped, partly transparent body like jelly. 해파리.

jen·ny [dʒéni] *n.* Ⓒ (*pl.* **-nies**) **1** a locomotive crane; a machine for spinning several threads at the same time. 이동 기중기; 방적기. **2** a female of some animals. (짐승의) 암컷. ¶ *the ~ ass* 암탕나귀. [<*Jenny, Janet*]

J

jeop·ard·ize [dʒépərdàiz] *vt.* (P6) put (someone or something) in danger; risk. …을 위험에 빠뜨리다; 위태롭게 하다. ¶ *~ one's life* 생명을 위태롭게 하다; 목숨을 걸다. [O.F. = divided game (*joke, part*)]

jeop·ard·y [dʒépərdi] *n.* Ⓤ danger; risk. 위험. ¶ *All at once his life was in ~.* 갑자기 그의 생명이 위험해졌다.

jer·e·mi·ad [dʒèrəmáiəd, -æd] *n.* a mournful complaint. 비탄; 슬픈 하소연. [Lamentations of *Jeremiah,* in Old Testament]

Jer·e·mi·ah [dʒèrəmáiə] *n.* 《Bible》 **1** a great Hebrew prophet. 예레미야. **2** the book of the Old Testament which contains his prophesies. 예레미야서(書). [↑]

Jer·i·cho [dʒérikòu] *n.* an ancient city in Palestine. 예리코《팔레스타인의 고대 도시》.

Go to Jericho! 《*sl.*》 Go to hell!; Get out! 뒈져라; 꺼져.

***jerk**[1] [dʒəːrk] *n.* Ⓒ **1** a sharp, sudden pull, twist, or other movement. 홱 당기는〔비트는, 움직이는〕 일. ¶ *give the rope a ~* 끈을 홱 당기다 / *pull with a ~* 홱 당기다 / *His old car started with a ~.* 그의 고물차가 덜커덩하고 내달았다. **2** a sudden and quick movement of a muscle which cannot be controlled. 근육의 경련.

— *vt.* (P6,7) move or twist (something) suddenly. …을 갑자기 움직이다〔비틀다〕. ¶ *He jerked the stick out of my hand.* 갑자기 내 손에서 지팡이를 뺏었다. — *vi.* (P1,2) move or twist suddenly. 갑자기 움직이다〔비틀다〕. ¶ *The train jerked along.* 열차가 덜컹하며 움직였다. [Imit.]

jerk[2] [dʒəːrk] *vt.* (P6) cut (meat, etc.) into long thin slices and dry it in the sun. (고기)를 얇고 길게 저며 볕에 말리다. ¶ *jerked beef* 쇠고기포(脯). [Peruv.]

jer·kin [dʒə́ːrkin] *n.* Ⓒ 《hist.》 a short, close-fitting, sleeveless coat or jacket often made of leather, worn by men in olden times. 저킨《옛날 남자용 가죽 조끼》. [? O.F. = doublet]

〈jerkin〉

jerk·y [dʒə́ːrki] *adj.* (**jerk·i·er, jerk·i·est**) moving along with sudden starts and stops; full of jerks; not smooth. 갑자기 동작하는; 움찔하는; 경련적인; 고르지 못한. ¶ *a ~ walk* 뒤뚝거리는 걸음걸이 / *a ~ style of writing* 난필(亂筆). [*jerk*[1]]

jer·ry-build [dʒéribìld] *vt.* (P6) build cheaply and flimsily. 날림으로 짓다. [Person]

jer·ry-build·ing [dʒéribìldiŋ] *n.* Ⓤ building of poor quality with cheap materials. 날림 공사; 날림집.

jer·ry-built [dʒéribìlt] *adj.* built cheaply with bad materials. 날림으로 지은.

jer·sey [dʒə́ːrzi] *n.* Ⓒ **1** a close-fitting woolen sweater, worn esp. in athletic exercises. (톡톡하게 짠) 운동 셔츠. **2** a woman's close fitting knitted jacket. 여성용 재킷. [Place]

Jer·sey [dʒə́ːrzi] *n.* **1** one of a group of British islands near the coast of France. 저지 섬《영국 해협에 있음》. **2** Ⓒ a kind of cow originating here. 그 섬에서 나는 소.

Je·ru·sa·lem [dʒirúːsələm, -zə-] *n.* the capital of Israel and ancient Palestine, considered a holy city by Jews, Christians, and Moslems. 예루살렘. 參考 1948년 이스라엘과 요르단 사이에 양분되었다가 1967년 요르단령을 이스라엘이 병합함.

jes·sa·mine [dʒésəmin] *n.* = jasmine.

:jest [dʒest] *n.* **1** Ⓒ a joke. 농담; 농. ¶ *speak* 〔*break, drop*〕 *a* ～ 농담하다; 익살떨다. **2** Ⓤ the act of joking; fun. 조롱; 놀림. ¶ *speak in* ～ 조롱하다.
be a standing jest, be always laughed at. 늘 놀림거리가 되다.
in jest, as a joke; not seriously. 농으로.
— *vi.* (P1,3) **1** joke. 농담하다. ¶ *He has no friends to* ～ *with.* 농담을 나눌 벗이 없다. **2** make fun. 조롱하다. ¶ ～ *at someone* 〔*someone's error*〕 남을〔남의 실수를〕 비웃다. [L. *gero* do]

jest·er [dʒéstər] *n.* Ⓒ a person who jests; (in medieval times) a fool or clown employed by a person of high rank to amuse him. 농담하는 사람; (중세의) 어릿광대. [↑]

Jes·u·it [dʒézuit, -zju-] *n.* Ⓒ a member of the Society of Jesus. 제수이트〔예수회〕의 수사(修士). [*Jesus*]

·Je·sus [dʒí:zəs, -z] *n.* the founder of the Christian religion, called Jesus Christ or Jesus of Nazareth. 예수.

·jet[1] [dʒet] *n.* Ⓒ **1** a stream of water, gas, etc. gushing from an opening. (물·증기 등의) 분출; 사출; 분사. **2** a small opening sending out a jet. 분출구; 주둥이. **3** a jet plane. 제트기. — *vi., vt.* (**jet·ted, jet·ting**) **1** (P2; 7) gush out; send out (water, gas, etc.). 분출하다〔시키다〕. **2** (P2; 6,13) travel by jet plane. 제트기로 여행하다. — *adj.* of or by a jet or jet engine. 분출하는; 제트 엔진의. ¶ *a* ～ *plane* / ～ *propulsion* 제트 추진. [L. *jacio* throw]

jet[2] [dʒet] *n.* Ⓤ **1** a hard black mineral, used for making ornaments, buttons, etc. 흑옥(黑玉). **2** a deep, shining black. 흑옥색. — *adj.* **1** made of jet. 흑옥으로 만든. **2** of deep, shining black. 흑옥색의; 칠흑의. [Place(Gk. *Gagai*)]

jet·lin·er [dʒétlàinər] *n.* Ⓒ a large passengercarrying jet airplane. 제트 여객기. [*jet*[1]]

jet motor [∠ ∠–] *n.* a motor used for jet propulsion. 제트 엔진.

jet·sam [dʒét-səm] *n.* Ⓤ goods thrown overboard to lighten a ship in danger, esp. such goods when washed ashore. 투하(投荷)《조난 때 선박을 가볍게 하기 위해 바다에 던지는》(cf. *flotsam*). [*jet*[1]]

jet·ty [dʒéti] *n.* Ⓒ (*pl.* **-ties**) **1** a structure built out into the water to break the force of the waves and to protect a harbor. 방파제; 둑. **2** a landing place; a pier. 부두; 선창. [*jet*[1]]

·Jew [dʒu:] *n.* Ⓒ a member of the Hebrew race. 유대인. [Heb.]

:jew·el [dʒú:əl] *n.* Ⓒ **1** a precious stone; a gem. 보석. **2** a valuable ornament set with gems. 보석을 박은 장신구. **3** a person or thing of great value. 귀중한 사람; 귀중품. **4** a gem used as a bearing in a watch. (시계에 쓰는) 보석; 경석(硬石). — *vt.* (P6)

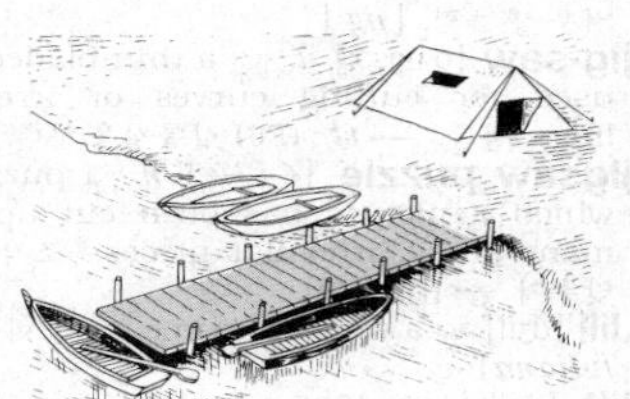
〈jetty 2〉

(**-eled, -el·ing** or esp. 《Brit.》 **-elled, -el·ling**) adorn or set (someone or something) with jewels. …을 보석으로 꾸미다; …에 보석을 박다. ¶ *The sky was jewelled with stars.* 하늘에는 별들이 총총히 박혀 있었다. [F. *joel*]

jew·el·er, 《Brit.》 **-el·ler** [dʒú:ələr] *n.* Ⓒ a person who sells, repairs or makes jewelry. 보석상; 보석공.

·jew·el·ry, 《Brit.》 **-el·ler·y** [dʒú:əlri] *n.* Ⓤ 《*collectively*》 jewels and ornaments containing jewels. 보석; 보석 세공품.

·Jew·ish [dʒú:iʃ] *adj.* of or like the Jews. 유대인; 유대인식의. [Heb.]

jew's-harp, jews'- [dʒú:zhὰ:rp] *n.* Ⓒ a musical instrument held in the mouth and struck by the finger. 구금(口琴). [*Jew, harp*] 〈jew's-harp〉

jib[1] [dʒib] *n.* Ⓒ a three-cornered sail in front of the foremast. (이물의) 삼각돛. [→ gibbet]
the cut of one's jib, 《*colloq.*》 one's appearance. 풍채; 몸차림; 용모.

jib[2] [dʒib] *vi.* (**jibbed, jib·bing**) (P1,3) 《*at*》 (of a horse, etc.) move sideways or backward instead of ahead. (말 따위가) 움직이려 들지 않다; 옆〔뒷〕걸음질하다. [→gibbet]
jib at, hesitate to do; be unwilling to do. 망설이다; …하기를 싫어하다. ¶ ～ *at hard work* 힘든 일을 싫어하다.

jibe [dʒaib] *n.* =gibe.

jif·fy [dʒífi] *n.* (*pl.* **-fies**) 《*colloq.*》 a very short time; a moment. 순간. ¶ *I'll come in* (*half*) *a* ～. 곧 오마. [Mod. E.]

jig[1] [dʒig] *n.* Ⓒ a quick lively dance; the music for it. 지그; 그 곡(曲). — *vi., vt.* (P1,2; 7) (**jigged, jig·ging**) **1** dance a jig. 지그 춤을 추다. **2** move quickly up and down or back and forth. 심하게 상하로 움직이(게 하)다. ¶ *The* ～ *is up.* 《*sl.*》 끝장이다; 다 틀렸다. [G, *geige* violin]

jig[2] [dʒig] *n.* Ⓒ **1** a kind of fishing hook. 낚싯봉 달린 낚시. **2** any of various mechanical devices for guiding a drill, a file, etc. 지그. 參考 천공기나 절삭 공구를 정확히 공작물에 닿게 하는 공구(工具). [↑]

jig·gle [dʒígəl] *vt.* (P6) shake slightly. …을 가볍게 흔들다. — *n.* Ⓒ a slight shake. 가

J

벼운 흔들림. [*jig*[1]]

jig·saw [dʒígsɔ̀ː] *n.* Ⓒ a thin-bladed saw used for cutting curves or irregular lines. 실톱. — *vt.* (P6) 실톱질을 하다. [*jig*[1]]

jigsaw puzzle [⌐–⌐–] *n.* a puzzle in which a picture has been cut up into many small, irregular pieces. 조각 그림 맞추기 놀이[장난감].

Jill [dʒil] *n.* a woman's name. 여자 이름. [L. *Juliana*]

jilt [dʒilt] *vt.* (P6) reject or cast off (a lover). (여자가 남자)를 차버리다. — *n.* Ⓒ a woman who rejects a previously accepted lover. 남자 애인을 차버리는 여자. [↑]

Jim [dʒim] *n.* a nickname of James. James 의 애칭.

Jim Crow [⌐⌐] *n.* 《*contempt.*》 a negro. 흑인; 깜둥이. [U.S. nickname]

Jim Crow car, a car on a railway for negroes. 흑인 전용(열)차.

jim·my [dʒími] *n.* Ⓒ (*pl.* **-mies**) a short crowbar used by burglars to break windows. (도둑이 쓰는) 짧은 쇠지레.

jin·gle [dʒíŋgəl] *n.* Ⓒ **1** a sharp, thinkling sound, as of bells, etc. 짤랑짤랑; 딸랑딸랑. **2** a verse that has a pleasing succession of rhymes. 같은 음이나 유사한 음을 반복하는 시구(詩句). — *vi.* (P1,2A; 2B) **1** make a jingling sound. 짤랑짤랑[딸랑딸랑] 소리내다. ¶ *~ coins in one's pocket* 주머니 속의 동전이 짤랑거리다. **2** (of verse) have a series of simple, pleasing rhymes. (시구의) 어조가 잘 어울리다[압운(押韻)되다]. — *vt.* (P6,7) cause (something) to jingle. …을 짤랑[딸랑]거리다. [Imit.]

jin·go [dʒíŋgou] *n.* Ⓒ (*pl.* **-goes**) a person who supports his own country's warlike policy. 대외 강경론자; 호전론[주전론]자. [conjurer's word]

by (***the living***) ***jingo,*** 《*colloq.*》 by God. 어렵쇼; 절대로.

jin·go·ism [dʒíŋgouìzəm] *n.* Ⓤ the spirit, policy, or practices of jingoes; aggressive patriotism. 외교 정책 강경론; 맹목적 애국주의. [↑]

jin·go·ist [dʒíŋgouist] *n.* Ⓒ a person who believes in jingoism. 대외 강경론자; 국수주의자.

jin·go·is·tic [dʒìŋgouístik] *adj.* of or like jingoes or jingoism. 대외 강경론의; 맹목적 애국주의의.

jinks [dʒiŋks] *n. pl.* 《*colloq.*》 noisy merrymaking. 시끄러운 장난; 법석. ¶ *high ~* 야단법석. [Sc. *Hey Jinks*]

jinn [dʒin] *n.* pl. of **jinnee.**

jin·nee [dʒiníː] *n.* (*pl.* **jinn**) =genie. [Arab.]

jinx [dʒiŋ*k*s] *n.* Ⓒ 《U.S. *colloq.*》 a person or thing that is supposed to bring bad luck. 징크스; 재수 없는 사람[물건]. ¶ *break* [*smash*] *a ~* 징크스를 깨다. — *vt.* (P6) bring bad luck to (someone). …에게 액운을 가져오다. [? Gk. =magic-bird]

jit·ney [dʒítni] *n.* Ⓒ 《U.S. *colloq.*》 an automobile carrying passengers for a small fare, originally five cents. 요금이 싼 합승 버스. [F. *jeter* throw]

jit·ter·y [dʒítəri] *adj.* 《U.S. *colloq.*》 nervous. 신경질의; 신경 과민의.

Jo [dʒou] *n.* a nickname for Joseph or Josephine. Joseph 나 Josephine 의 애칭.

Joan [dʒoun] *n.* a woman's name. 여자 이름.

Job [dʒoub] *n.* 《Bible》 **1** a very patient man in the Old Testament. 욥. **2** the book telling of Job in the Old Testament. 욥기(記). [Person]

⁑job [dʒɑb / dʒɔb] *n.* Ⓒ **1** a piece of work; anything a person must do for pay. 일; 삯일. ¶ *finish one's ~* 일을 마치다 / *give someone an easy ~* …에게 쉬운 일을 주다 / *pay by the ~* 일 단위로 삯을 주다. **2** 《U.S. *colloq.*》 a position; an employment. 일자리; 직업. ¶ *out of a ~* 실직해서 / *He has a ~ as a teacher.* 그는 직업이 선생이다. **3** anything that one has to do; task; duty. 맡은 바 일; 구실; 책무. ¶ *It is your ~ to be in time for school.* 세 시간에 학교에 가는 게 네 할 일이다. **4** 《*colloq.*》 an affair; a matter. 사정; 사건; 일. ¶ *That's a good ~.* 그거 잘했다 / *a bad ~* 불행한 일. **5** 《*colloq.*》 a difficult task. 힘든 일. ¶ *It is a ~ to do the work in a day.* 그 일을 하루에 한다는 것은 여간 일이 아니다. **6** a piece of public work done so as to produce private profit. (공직을 이용한) 독직(瀆職); 부정 행위. **7** 《*sl.*》 a criminal act, as theft, robbery, etc. 범죄; 나쁜 일《도둑질 따위》.

bad job, a hopeless task. 희망 없는 일; 실패.

by the job, (be paid) by contract for each piece of work done. 일 단위로; 도급으로.

do the job for =***do someone's job*** (***for him***), cause (someone) to be ruined. …을 해치우다; 파멸시키다.

lie down on the job, be lazy; fail to do one's work well. 농땡이 부리다; 노력을 아끼다; 실패하다.

make a good job of it, do (something) well; make a profit. 일을 잘 해내다; 벌이가 되다.

on the job, 《*sl.*》 working; diligent at work. 일하고 있는; 열심히 일하는.

— *v.* (**jobbed, job·bing**) *vi.* (P1) **1** do odd jobs; do different kinds of work irregularly. 삯일을 하다; 품팔이하다. ¶ *a jobbing gardener* 임시 고용의 정원사. **2** use an official position to gain private advantage. (공직을 이용해) 부정 행위를 하다. — *vt.* (P6) **1** hire or let for hire (a horse or carriage, etc.). (말·마차 등을) 세주다; 임차하다. **2** divide (work) among several contractors or workers. (일을 나누어) 하도급 주다. ¶ *He jobbed a good deal of the work to smaller firms.* 그는 작은 업체에 하도

급을 많이 주었다. **3** handle (a public matter, etc.) in a dishonest manner. (공직을 이용해) 부정을 하다. ¶ ~ *someone into a post* 직권을 이용해 아무를 어떤 자리에 앉히다. **4** buy in large quantities and sell to dealers in smaller quantities. 중개 매매하다; 도매하다. [Celt. *gob* mouth]

job·ber [dʒábər / dʒɔ́b-] *n.* Ⓒ **1** a wholesaler; a stock-broker. 도매상; 주식 중매인. **2** a person who manages public business for his own profit. 공직을 이용해 개인의 이익을 취하는 자. **3** a person who does odd jobs. 삯일꾼; 날품팔이. [*job*]

job·less [dʒáblis / dʒɔ́b-] *adj.* having no job; out of job. 실직한; 일자리가 없는.

jock·ey [dʒáki / dʒɔ́ki] *n.* Ⓒ a man whose occupation is riding race horses. (경마의) 기수(騎手). — *vi., vt.* (P1; 6) **1** ride (a horse) in a race. 기수 노릇하다. **2** trick; cheat. 속이다; 기만하다. [Sc. *Jock* Jack]

jo·cose [dʒoukóus] *adj.* jesting; playful. 우스꽝스러운; 희롱하는. [L. *jocus* jest]

jo·cos·i·ty [dʒoukásəti / -kɔ́s-] *n.* ⓊⒸ (*pl.* **-ties**) the state of being jocose; a joke. 우스꽝스러움; 익살. [↑]

joc·u·lar [dʒákjələr / dʒɔ́k-] *adj.* funny; joking. 익살스러운; 농담의. [*jocose*]

joc·u·lar·i·ty [dʒàkjəlǽrəti / dʒɔ̀k-] *n.* Ⓤ Ⓒ (*pl.* **-ties**) the state of being jocular; a jocular act or remark. 익살; 익살스러운 언행.

joc·und [dʒákənd, dʒóuk- / dʒɔ́k-] *adj.* 《*poet.*》 cheerful; gay. 쾌활한; 즐거운; 명랑한. [L. *jocundus*]

jo·cun·di·ty [dʒoukʌ́ndəti] *n.* ⓊⒸ (*pl.* **-ties**) the state of being jocund; cheerfulness; gaiety. 쾌활; 명랑; 즐거움.

jodh·purs [dʒádpərz] *n. pl.* breeches for horseback riding. 승마용 긴 바지. [place in India]

Joe [dʒou] *n.* a nickname of **Joseph.** Joseph 의 애칭.

jog[1] [dʒag / dʒɔg] *v.* (**jogged, jog·ging**) *vt.* (P6,7) **1** push (something) slightly; shake with a jerk. …을 살짝 밀다〔찌르다〕. ¶ ~ *someone with one's elbow* 팔꿈치로 살짝 밀다. **2** rouse (one's memory). (기억)을 환기하다. — *vi.* (P1,2A,2B) **1** go slowly and laboriously. 천천히〔터덜터덜〕 걷다. ¶ *The old cart jogged down the road.* 낡은 수레는 천천히 길을 내려갔다. **2** get on slowly, monotonously. 천천히〔단조롭게〕 해나가다. ¶ *Matters jogged along somehow.* 일은 그럭저럭 돼 나갔다.

— *n.* Ⓒ **1** a slight push or shake. 살짝 밀기〔흔들기〕. **2** a hint to awaken attention, etc. 힌트; 암시. **3** a slow and laborious way of walking. 터벅터벅 걷기; 완만한 속보. [Imit.]

jog[2] [dʒag / dʒɔg] *n.* Ⓒ 《chiefly U.S. *colloq.*》 an unevenness or sudden bend in a line or a surface. (선·면의) 고르지 못함; 울퉁불퉁함. [↑]

jog·gle [dʒágəl / dʒɔ́g-] *vi., vt.* (P1; 6) shake or jerk slightly. 가볍게 흔들(리)다. — *n.* Ⓒ a sudden shake. 흔들리기; 진동. [*jog*[1]]

•**John** [dʒan / dʒɔn] *n.* **1** a man's name. 남자 이름. **2** the Apostle John, one of Christ's disciples and supposed to be the author of the Gospel of Saint John, etc.; the Gospel of Saint John. 사도 요한; 요한 복음. [Heb. *yokhanan*]

John Bull [⌐⌐] *n.* **1** a typical Englishman. 전형적 영국인. **2** the English nation. 영국.

John·ny [dʒáni / dʒɔ́ni] *n.* a nickname of John. John의 애칭.

•**John·son** [dʒánsn / dʒɔ́n-], **Samuel** *n.* (1709-84) an English author and dictionary-maker. 존슨《영국의 작가·사전 편집자》.

:**join** [dʒɔin] *vt.* **1** (P6,7,13) put (things) together; unite; be close to (something). …을 잇다; 연결하다; …에 접하다. ¶ ~ *two things together* 두 개를 연결하다 / ~ *one thing to another* 하나를 다른 것에 연결하다 / *His room joins mine.* 그의 방은 내 방 바로 옆이다. **2** (P6,13) bring into close association with. (결혼 따위로) …을 결합시키다. ¶ ~ *two persons in marriage* 두 사람을 결혼시키다. **3** (P6,13) become a member of (a party); associate oneself with (something). …에 가입하다; …의 한 패가 되다. ¶ ~ *the army* 군에 입대하다. **4** (P6,13) enter the company of (someone); do something with (someone). …에 참가하다; …와 협동하다. ¶ *Will you ~ us for a walk?* 같이 산책하지 않겠나. **5** (P6,13) return to (some place). …에 돌아가다. ¶ ~ *one's ship* 〔*regiment*〕 배에〔연대로〕 되돌아가다. **6** (P6,13) meet and form one with. …와 만나다; 합치다. ¶ *The stream joins the river just below the mill.* 그 시내는 물방앗간 바로 밑에서 강과 합친다. — *vi.* **1** (P1,3,4) come together; connect. 합쳐지다; 연결되다. ¶ *The rivers ~ here.* 강들은 여기서 합쳐진다. **2** (P1,4) take part in something. 가입〔참가〕하다. ¶ ~ *in a game* 경기에 참가하다.

join battle, begin fighting. 전투를 개시하다; 교전하다.

join forces (***with…***), unite in action; work together. (…와) 협력하다; 함께 일하다.

join hands, **a**) shake hands. 악수하다. **b**) 《*fig.*》 join with another in a certain action, etc. 제휴하다.

— *n.* Ⓒ a point, line or place where things are joined. 접(합)점; 접합선〔면〕. [L. *jungo* unite]

join·er [dʒɔ́inər] *n.* Ⓒ **1** a person or thing that joins. 결합〔연합〕자; 접합물〔기〕. **2** a workman skilled in making the inside woodwork for houses. 목수; 소목장이.

:**joint** [dʒɔint] *n.* Ⓒ **1** the place where

J

two things join. 이음매; 접합부[점]. ¶ *the ~ of a machine.* **2** the way in which parts are joined. 접합법. **3** 《anat.》 a part of the body where two bones are joined together. 관절. ¶ *the ~ of the leg.* **4** 《bot.》 the part of a stem from which a branch or leaf grows. (가지·잎이 나는) 마디. **5** a large piece of meat with the bone. (뼈가 붙은) 큰 고깃덩이. **6** 《U.S. *sl.*》 ⓐ a cheap, disreputable restaurant, bar, etc. 싸구려식당[술집]. ⓑ any house, building, etc. (일반적으로) 집; 건물. **7** 《*sl.*》 a marijuana cigarette. 마리화나 담배.

out of joint, **a**) (of bones, etc.) dislocated. 탈구하여; 접질려. ¶ *put one's knee out of ~* 무릎 관절을 삐다. **b**) out of order; disordered. 흐트러져; 혼란되어. ¶ *The affairs of the world are out of ~.* 세상의 일들이 뒤죽박죽이다.

— *vt.* (P6) **1** join (something) together. …을 이어맞추다. ¶ *a jointed doll* 조립한 인형. **2** divide (something) at the joints, separate (something) into joints; cut (meat) into joints. …을 이음매에서 나누다; (고기)를 크게[뭉텅뭉텅] 베어내다. **3** plane the joints of (a board). (판자)의 이음매를 대패질하다 [편평하게 하다].

— *adj.* owned or done by two or more persons. 공동의; 합동[연합]의. ¶ *~ ownership* 공유권 / *~ authors* 공동 저자 / *a ~ statement* 공동 성명 / *a ~ convention* 합동회의 / *take ~ action* 행동을 함께 하다. [*join*]

joint·ed [dʒɔ́intid] *adj.* provided with joints. 이음매가[관절이] 있는.

joint·less [dʒɔ́intlis] *adj.* having no joints. 이음매가[관절이] 없는.

joint·ly [dʒɔ́intli] *adv.* in a joint manner; together; in common. 공동으로; 연대하여.

·joint stock [ˊ ˊ] *n.* capital or stock that is held jointly. 공동 자본; 주식 조직. ¶ *a joint-stock company* (미국에서는)합자회사; (영국에서는)주식 회사.

jointure [dʒɔ́intʃər] *n.* money, etc. settled on a wife to be enjoyed after her husband's death. 과부 급여. [→join]

joist [dʒɔist] *n.* Ⓒ 《archit.》 a piece of timber to which the boards of a floor or ceiling are fastened and by which they are supported. 장선; 들보. [L. *jaceo* lie]

:joke [dʒouk] *n.* Ⓒ **1** something said or done to make someone laugh. 농담; 익살. ¶ *make* [*crack*] *a ~* 농담하다; 익살떨다 / *a practical ~* 몹쓸 장난 / *He can't see a ~.* 그 사람은 농담을 알아듣지 못한다 / *It's no ~.* 농담 아니다; 진담이다. **2** a person or thing which is the object of laughter. 웃음가마리; 놀림감.

for a joke, with the intention of causing someone to laugh. 농담삼아.

in joke, not in earnest. 농담으로.

play a joke on, make fun of. …을 놀리다; 조롱하다.

— *vi., vt.* **1** (P1,2A,3) say or do (something) as a joke; jest. 농담하다. ¶ *You are joking.* 농담이겠지 / *joking apart* 농담은 그만하고. **2** (P6,13) make fun of (someone). …을 놀리다; 비웃다. [L. *jocus* jest]

jok·er [dʒóukər] *n.* Ⓒ **1** a person who jokes. 농담하는 사람. **2** 《U.S.》 a hidden clause in a law, a contract, etc. which actually changes the apparent purpose of the whole. 사기 조항. **3** an extra playing card used in some games. (카드놀이) 조커. **4** 《*sl.*》 a man; a fellow. 녀석; 놈.

jok·ing·ly [dʒóukiŋli] *adv.* as a joke. 농담으로; 장난으로.

jol·li·fy [dʒáləfài / dʒɔ́l-] *vt., vi.* (P6; 1) 《*colloq.*》 make (someone) jolly or merry; become gay. …을 즐겁게 하다; 명랑해지다. [→jolly]

jol·li·ty [dʒáləti / dʒɔ́l-] *n.* ⓊⒸ (*pl.* **-ties**) fun; merrymaking. 명랑; 환락; 흥겹게 놀기.

:jol·ly [dʒáli / dʒɔ́li] *adj.* (**-li·er, -li·est**) **1** full of life and fun; merry. 즐거운; 유쾌[명랑]한. ¶ *a ~ fellow* [*party, time*] 유쾌한 친구 [회합, 시간]. **2** 《often *iron.*》 great; thorough. 굉장한; 지독한. ¶ *a ~ fool* 철저한 바보. **3** 《*colloq.*》 agreeable; splendid. 괜찮은; 멋진. ¶ *That's real ~.* 그거 정말 괜찮구나. — *adv.* 《Brit. *colloq.*》 extremely; very; uncommonly. 대단히; 매우. — *vt.* (**-lied**) (P6,7) 《*colloq.*》《*up, along*》 make (someone) cheerful; flatter. …을 기분좋게 해주다; 추어주다. ●**jol·li·ly** [-li] *adv.* **jol·li·ness** [-nis] *n.* [F. *joli* gay]

jolt [dʒoult] *vi., vt.* (P1,2A,2B,3; 6,13) move or shake with a jerk; give (something) a sudden jerk. 덜컹거리(게 하)다; 흔들(리)다. ¶ *The waggon jolted us when it went on the rough road.* 마차는 우리를 뒤흔들면서 험한 길을 굴러갔다. — *n.* Ⓒ a sudden or violent jerk. 급격한 동요; 심한 요동. ¶ *The car stopped with a ~.* 차는 덜커덩하며 섰다 / 《*fig.*》 *The news gave us a ~.* 그 소식은 우리에게 대단한 충격이었다. [?]

jolt·y [dʒóulti] *adj.* moving or shaking with a jerk. 덜컹거리는; 흔들리는.

jon·quil [dʒáŋkwil, dʒán- / dʒɔ́ŋ-] *n.* Ⓒ 《bot.》 a plant of the narcissus family with yellow or white flowers and sword-shaped leaves. 노랑 수선화. [L. *juncus* rush]

Jo·seph [dʒóuzəf] *n.* **1** a man's name. 남자 이름. 參考 애칭은 Jo, Joe. **2** 《Bible》 Jacob's favorite son, who was sold by his jealous brothers into slavery in Egypt. 요셉.

Jo·se·phine [dʒóuzəfìːn] *n.* a woman's name. 여자 이름.

jos·tle [dʒásl / dʒɔ́sl] *vt., vi.* (P6; 2A,3) **1** push against (something); elbow roughly; push one another; make (one's way) through a crowd. 밀다; 찌르다; 팔꿈치로 밀다; 서로 밀치다; 밀치고 나아가다. ¶ *They jostled into the theater.* 그들은 극장에 밀치고

들어갔다. **2** struggle. …와 다투다; 겨루다. ¶ *The candidates jostled with each other in order to win the election.* 후보들은 선거에 이기려고 서로 다퉜다. — *n.* Ⓒ push; knock. 서로 밀치기; 혼잡; 부딪기. [L. *juxta* near]

jot [dʒɑt / dʒɔt] *n.* Ⓒ a little bit; a very small quantity. 조금; 소량. ¶ *I do not know a* ~. 나는 조금도 아는 바 없다. — *vt.* (P7) 《*down*》 write down briefly or quickly. 간단히 적다; 메모하다. ¶ ~ *down his name* 그의 이름을 적어두다.
 ● **jot·ter** [´-ər] *n.* [Gk. *iōta* (*i*, the smallest letter)]

:jour·nal [dʒə́:rnəl] *n.* Ⓒ **1** a daily record of news or events. 일기; 일지. **2** a daily newspaper; a magazine. 일간 신문; 잡지. **3** 《bookkeeping》 a book in which daily business transactions are written down in a systematic form. 분개장(分介帳). **4** = logbook. **5** 《mech.》 a shaft or axle which rests on bearings. 굴대의 목부분; 저널. [→diurnal]

jour·nal·ese [dʒə̀:rnəlí:z] *n.* Ⓤ the style of writing and diction characteristic of many newspapers, magazines, etc. 신문 기사투; 신문 잡지 문체.

·jour·nal·ism [dʒə́:rnəlìzəm] *n.* Ⓤ **1** the work of writing for, editing, or producing a newspaper or periodical. 저널리즘; 신문·잡지(기자)업; 문필업. **2** 《collectively》 newspapers and magazines. 신문 잡지.

jour·nal·ist [dʒə́:rnəlist] *n.* Ⓒ a person who is engaged in journalism. 저널리스트; 신문 잡지업 종사자; 기자.

jour·nal·is·tic [dʒə̀:rnəlístik] *adj.* of or like journalism or journalists. 문필업계의; 신문 잡지류의; 신문 잡지 기자의.

:jour·ney [dʒə́:rni] *n.* Ⓒ **1** a trip, esp. a trip taking a long time or going to a distant place. 여행. ¶ *go on a* ~ 여행을 떠나다 / *make* 〔*have, take, undertake*〕 *a* ~ 여행하다 / *I wish you a safe* ~. 잘 다녀오시오. **2** the distance traveled in a given time. 여정(旅程). ¶ *a day's* ~ *from here* 여기서 하룻길.
be on a journey, be away from home because of traveling. 길을 나서 있다; 여행 중이다.
break one's journey, get off the train, plane, etc. before arriving at one's destination. 여행을 중단하다; 도중 하차하다.
— *vi.* (P1) make a journey; travel. 여행하다. [*journal*]

jour·ney·man [dʒə́:rnimən] *n.* Ⓒ (*pl.* **-men** [-mən]) **1** a person who has mastered his trade or skill and who works for another. 제 구실을 하는 장색(匠色)(cf. *apprentice*). **2** in olden times, a man who was hired to work for another, usu. by the day. (예전의) 날품팔이.

·joust [dʒaust, dʒu:st] *n.* Ⓒ **1** a combat with lances between two knights on horseback. (기사의) 마상 창(槍)시합. **2** 《*pl.*》 a ceremonial contest featuring such a combat. 마상 창시합 대회. — *vi.* (P1) engage in a joust. 마상 창시합을 하다. [L. *juxta* near]

Jove [dʒouv] *n.* **1** 《Rom. myth.》 Jupiter, the chief god in Roman mythology. 조브 신(神). **2** 《*poet.*》 the planet Jupiter. 목성(木星). [L.]
By Jove! an exclamation of surprise, emphasis, etc. 맹세코; 신을 두고; 천만에.

jo·vi·al [dʒóuviəl] *adj.* gay; jolly; merry; good-humored. 쾌활한; 명랑〔유쾌〕한. ¶ *a* ~ *comrade* 유쾌한 친구. [↑]

Jo·vi·an [dʒóuviən] *adj.* **1** of or like the god Jove. 조브 신의〔같은〕. **2** of the planet Jupiter. 목성의.

jowl [dʒaul, dʒoul] *n.* Ⓒ **1** the jaw, esp. the lower jaw. 턱; 아래턱. **2** the cheek. 뺨. ¶ *cheek by* ~ 볼을 맞대고; 밀접하여; 이웃하여. **3** a fold of flesh hanging from the jaw. 아래턱의 늘어진 살. [E.]

:joy [dʒɔi] *n.* **1** Ⓤ a feeling of great pleasure; happiness. 기쁨; 환희. ¶ *He sobbed in his* ~. 기뻐서 흐느껴 울었다 / *She jumped for* ~ *to hear the good news.* 그 희소식에 그녀는 펄쩍 뛰며 기뻐했다. **2** Ⓒ something that causes such a feeling. 기쁨을 주는 것; 기쁨거리. ¶ *His clever child is a* ~ *to him.* 그의 영리한 아이가 그에게는 낙이다. — *vi., vt.* (P3,4; 6) 《*poet.*》 rejoice. 기뻐하다; …을 기쁘게 하다. [L. *gaudium*]

:joy·ful [dʒɔ́ifəl] *adj.* **1** full of happiness or joy. (사람·마음이) 기쁨에 찬. ¶ *a* ~ *day* 아주 기쁜 날. **2** causing joy. 기쁘게 하는. ¶ ~ *news* 기쁜 소식. **3** showing joy. 기쁜〔즐거운〕 듯한. ¶ *a* ~ *look* 기쁜 듯한 표정.
 ● **joy·ful·ness** [-nis] *n.*

joy·ful·ly [dʒɔ́ifəli] *adv.* with joy; in a joyful manner. 기쁜 듯이; 즐겁게.

joy·less [dʒɔ́ilis] *adj.* without joy; dull; dismal. 즐겁지 않은; 우울한.

joy·ous [dʒɔ́iəs] *adj.* joyful; glad; happy. 즐거운; 기쁜 듯한.

joy·ous·ly [dʒɔ́iəsli] *adv.* in a joyous manner. 즐겁게; 희희 낙락하여.

joy·rid·den [dʒɔ́irìdn] *v.* pp. of **joyride.**

joy·ride [dʒɔ́iràid] *n.* Ⓒ 《*colloq.*》 a pleasure ride in a motor car, esp. when the car is driven recklessly or used without the owner's permission. 놀이삼아 하는 드라이브. — *vi.* (**-rode, -rid·den**) 《*colloq.*》 take a joyride. 놀이삼아 드라이브를 하다.

joy·rode [dʒɔ́iròud] *v.* p. of **joyride.**

joy·stick [dʒɔ́istik] *n.* Ⓒ **1** 《*sl.*》 the controlling lever of an airplane. (비행기) 조종간. **2** 《computer》 a lever used to control movement of a cursor or other graphic element for video games and computer graphics. (컴퓨터·비디오 게임의) 조이 스틱; 놀이손; 조작 레버.

J.P. Justice of the Peace.

Jr., jr. Junior.

ju·bi·lant [dʒúːbələnt] *adj.* expressing great joy. 환성을 올리는; 환희에 찬. ¶ ~ *over a victory* 승리의 환희에 찬. ●**ju·bi·lant·ly** [-li] *adv.* [Heb. *yobel* ram, trumpet]

ju·bi·late [dʒúːbəleit] *vi.* (P1) rejoice; jump for joy. 기뻐하다; 기뻐 뛰다. [↑]

ju·bi·la·tion [dʒùːbəléiʃən] *n.* UC a feeling of joy; a joyful celebration of something. 환희; 축제.

ju·bi·lee [dʒúːbəlìː] *n.* C **1** any occasion of exceptional celebration. 축제; 축전. ¶ *hold a ~ over a victory* 승리의 축제를 열다. **2** a 25th or 50th anniversary. 25 년제(祭) 또는 50 년제(祭). ¶ *The school celebrates its ~ this week.* 금주에 학교는 창립 50 주년 기념식을 갖는다. **3** 《Cath.》 a year in which punishment for sin is remitted. 대사(大赦)의 해. [↑]

Ju·dah [dʒúːdə] *n.* **1** 《Bible》 the fourth son of Jacob and Leah. 유다. **2** the powerful tribes of Israel which are composed of his descendants. 유다 종족. **3** an ancient Hebrew kingdom in south Palestine. 팔레스타인의 옛 왕국. [Heb.]

Ju·da·ism [dʒúːdiìzəm, -dei-] *n.* U **1** the religion of the Jews. 유대교. **2** the observance of Jewish rules, customs, etc. 유대주의. [*Jew*]

Ju·das [dʒúːdəs] *n.* **1** 《Bible》 Judas Iscariot, the disciple who betrayed Christ. 가룟 유다《Judah와는 다름》. ¶ ~ *kiss* 배신; 배반. **2** C a treacherous person like Judas Iscariot; a traitor. 반역자; 배신자. [Heb.]

Ju·de·a [dʒuːdíːə] *n.* the southern region of ancient Palestine. 유대《팔레스타인의 남부에 있었던 고대 로마령(領)》.

⁝**judge** [dʒʌdʒ] *n.* C **1** a person who decides right or wrong, good or bad, win or loss, etc. in a law suit or contest; an umpire. 재판관; 판사; 심사원; 심판; 감정가. ¶ *a good ~ of wine* 〔*picture*〕 포도주〔그림〕의 명감식가 / *I am no ~ of music.* 난 음악을 통 모른다. **2** 《*J-s*》 《Bible》 the seventh book of the Old Testament. 사사기(士師記).
— *vt., vi.* (P6,11,12,21; 1,3) **1** decide or give an opinion on (something) as a judge. 판결〔재판〕하다; 심판〔감정〕하다. ¶ *He was judged guilty.* 그에게 유죄가 선고되었다. **2** think; consider; hold an opinion. 생각하다; 판단하다. ¶ *We ~ her story to be false.* 우리는 그녀의 이야기를 거짓이라 생각한다 / *I ~ him to be very honest.* 나는 그가 아주 성실한 사람이라 생각한다. **3** criticize; estimate; form an opinion. 비판하다; 평가하다. ¶ *Don't ~ by appearances.* 외모로 판단하지 마라 / *It is not for me to ~ him.* 내가 그를 평가할 입장은 못된다 / *Try to ~ fairly.* 공정하게 평가하도록 해라. [L. *judex*]

⁝**judg·ment,** 《Brit.》 **judge-** [dʒʌ́dʒmənt] *n.* **1** U the act of judging; the state of being judged. 판단; 감별; 재판; 심판. **2** UC a decision or sentence given by a judge. 판결; 판결문. ¶ *give* (*a*) ~ 판결을 내리다 / *Judgement was deliverd in the Supreme Court.* 대심원에서 판결이 선고되었다. **3** U the power to judge well; good sense. 판단〔비판〕력; 분별; 양식. ¶ *have* 〔*loss*〕 *one's* ~ 판단력이 있다〔을 잃다〕 / *a man of cool* ~ 판단이 냉철한 사람 / ~ *in art* 예술에 대한 견식. **4** C an opinion, estimate or conclusion formed. 의견; 견해; 결론. ¶ *In my ~ he is wrong.* 내 의견으로는 그가 잘못이다. **5** C misfortune regarded as a punishment from God for a sin. 천벌. ¶ *It's a ~ on you for getting up late.* 그건 네 늦잠에 대한 천벌이다. [↑]
pass judgment on, give a decision on (a case, etc.). …에 판결을 내리다.
sit in judgment, judge; criticize. 재판〔비판〕하다.

Judgment Day [⌐-⌐] *n.* the day of the Last Judgment. 최후 심판의 날.

ju·di·ca·ture [dʒúːdikèitʃər] *n.* **1** U duties or authority of a judge. 사법〔재판〕(권). **2** C 《*collectively*》 a body of judges. 사법관; 재판관. **3** C a court of justice. 재판소. [↓]

ju·di·cial [dʒuːdíʃəl] *adj.* **1** of or by courts, judges, etc. 재판관의; 재판상의. **2** ordered or inflicted by a court of justice. 재판소 재결의. ¶ *a ~ decision* 판결 / *a ~ murder* 법의 살인《적법한 판결이지만 부당하다고 여겨지는 사형》/ ~ *process* 소송 절차 / *a ~ separation* (판결에 의한) 부부 별거. **3** suitable for a judge; fair; impartial; critical. 재판관다운; 공평한; 비판적인. ¶ *a ~ mind* 비판적 정신(을 가진 사람). [→judge]

ju·di·cial·ly [dʒuːdíʃəli] *adv.* done by a court of justice; legally; like a judge. 재판상; 공정히; 재판관답게.

ju·di·ci·ar·y [dʒuːdíʃièri, -ʃəri] *n.* C (*pl.* **-ar·ies**) **1** the judicial part of the government; the system of law courts in a country. 사법부; 사법 제도. **2** 《*collectively*》 the judges. 사법관. — *adj.* of law courts or judges. 재판소〔관〕의. ¶ ~ *proceedings* 재판 절차.

ju·di·cious [dʒuːdíʃəs] *adj.* showing good judgment; wise. 사려 분별이 있는; 현명한. ¶ ~ *advice* 현명한 충고 / *a ~ step* 적절한 조치. ●**ju·di·cious·ly** [-li] *adv.*

jug [dʒʌg] *n.* C **1** a vessel for liquids, usu. with a spout or a short neck and a handle. 주전자; 조끼. **2** 《*colloq.*》 a jail. 감옥; 교도소. — *vt.* (P6) (**jugged, jug·ging**) **1** 《*colloq.*》 put (someone) into jail. …을 감옥에 넣다. **2** boil or stew (something) in a jug. …을 항아리에 넣고 삶다. [*Judith*]

jug·gle [dʒʌ́gəl] *vi., vt.* **1** (P1,3) perform tricks with (something); change (something) by means of a trick. 요술을 부리다. ¶ ~ *a handkerchief into a bird* 요술로 손수건을 새로 만들다. **2** (P6,13) give a false account of (facts) to deceive people; cheat; deceive. …을 조작하다; 속이다. ¶ ~ *accounts* 셈을 속이다 / ~ *someone out of his money* 아

J

무의 돈을 사취하다.

juggle with, **a**) perform tricks with (something). …로 요술을 부리다. **b**) cheat (someone); falsify (facts). …을 속이다; (사실)을 조작하다. — *n.* Ⓒ **1** the act of juggling. 요술. **2** a deception; a trick. 사기; 기만. [L. *jocus* jest]

jug·gler [dʒʌ́glər] *n.* Ⓒ **1** a person who performs tricks. 요술쟁이. **2** a person who deceives. 사기꾼. [↑]

:juice [dʒuːs] *n.* Ⓤ **1** the liquid in fruit, vegetables, meat, etc. 즙; 주스. ¶ *tomato* ~ / *apple* ~. **2** 《the *pl.*》 the liquid in the body. 체액. **3** 《*fig.*》 the essence of anything. 정수(精髓); 에센스. **4** ⓐ 《*sl.*》 oil; gasoline. 휘발유. ⓑ electric current. 전류. [L. *jus*]

juic·y [dʒúːsi] *adj.* (**juic·i·er, juic·i·est**) **1** full of juice; having much juice. 즙이 많은. ¶ *a* ~ *orange.* **2** interesting; lively; spicy. 흥미 진진한; 활기찬. ● **juic·i·ly** [-li] *adv.*

juke·box [dʒúːkbɑ̀ks / -bɔ̀ks] *n.* Ⓒ an automatic phonograph that plays after the required coin is put in the slot. 주크 박스; 자동 전축. [Negro]

Jul. July.

Jul·ian [dʒúːljən] *adj.* of Julius Caesar. 율리우스 카이사르의.

:Ju·ly [dʒuːlái] *n.* the seventh month of the year. 7월. 語法 약자는 Jul., Jy.

jum·ble [dʒʌ́mbəl] *vi., vt.* (P1,3; 6,7) 《*up, together*》 mix together; confuse. 뒤죽박죽이 되다[으로 만들다]; 뒤섞(이)다. — *n.* Ⓒ a confused mixture; a medley. 뒤범벅; 엉망; 혼란; 잡동사니. [Imit.]

jumble sale [⌐–⌐] *n.* 《Brit.》 a sale of various cheap secondhand goods to obtain money for charity. (바자에서의) 중고품 특매.

jum·bo [dʒʌ́mbou] *n.* Ⓒ (*pl.* **-s**) **1** a very large person, animal or thing. 점보; 몸집이 큰 사람[짐승]. **2** short for a jumbo jet. 점보 제트기. — *adj.* extremely large. 초대형의. ¶ *a* ~ *jet* 점보 제트기. [? a large elephant in Barnum's show]

:jump [dʒʌmp] *vi.* **1** (P1,2A,3) spring from the ground; spring upward or forward; leap. 도약하다; 뛰어오르다. ¶ ~ *over the fence* 담을 뛰어 넘다 / ~ *on* [*off*] *a car* 차에 뛰어오르다[차에서 뛰어내리다] / ~ *for joy* 덩실거리며 기뻐하다. **2** (P1,2A,3) be surprised; be shocked. 움찔하다; 당황하다. ¶ *The news made me* ~. 그 소식에 깜짝 놀랐다 / *You made me* ~ *when you came in so suddenly.* 네가 그렇게 불쑥 들어왔을 때 나는 섬뜩했었다. **3** (P1,2A,3) rise suddenly. 갑자기 오르다. ¶ *The price of meat has jumped.* 고깃값이 갑자기 올랐다 / *The temperature jumped by five degrees.* 기온이 갑자기 5도나 올랐다. **4** (P1,2A,3) pass or move from one thing to another; skip. (화제 따위가) 비약하다. ¶ *He always jumps from one topic to another.* 그는 언제나 이 이야기했다 저 이야기했다 한다 / ~ *from job to job* 직업을 전전하다. **5** (P3) 《*with*》 agree with. …와 일치하다. ¶ *Your statement doesn't altogether* ~ *with the fact.* 네 말은 사실과 전혀 다르다. — *vt.* **1** (P6) cause (something) to spring, leap, or bound. …을 뛰어오르게 하다. ¶ ~ *a horse over a hurdle* 말이 장애물을 뛰어넘게 하다 / *She jumped her baby on her knee.* 그녀는 애기를 무릎에 놓고 둥개둥개 얼렀다. **2** (P6) leap over. …을 뛰어넘다. ¶ ~ *a stream* 개울을 뛰어넘다. **3** (P6) leave or move from suddenly; be shot away from. …을 벗어나다; 탈선하다. ¶ *The engine jumped the rails.* 기관차가 탈선했다. **4** (P6) pass over; leave out; omit. (책 따위의 일부)를 건너뛰다; 생략하다. ¶ ~ *a chapter in a book* 책에서 한 장을 건너뛰고 읽다. **5** (P6,13) deceive. …을 속이다. ¶ *He was jumped into buying the house.* 그는 그 집을 속아서 샀다. **6** (P6) cook in a frying pan. …을 프라이팬으로 요리하다. **7** (P6) 《U.S.》 leap aboard. …을 뛰어올라 타다. ¶ ~ *a train* [*bus*].

jump at, **a**) spring or leap at; make an attack on. …에 대들다; …을 공격하다. ¶ *A dog jumped at me.* 개가 덤벼들었다. **b**) accept gladly; seize upon with eagerness. …에 쾌히 응하다. ¶ ~ *at an offer* [*the chance*] 제의[기회]에 발바투 덤비다.

jump at [***to***] ***conclusions,*** reach a conclusion hastily without careful consideration. 지레짐작하다; 속단하다.

jump on [***upon***]***,*** **a**) make a sudden attack on. …에 별안간 달려들다. **b**) 《*colloq.*》 scold severely; blame. 심하게 꾸짖다; 비난하다. ¶ ~ *on someone for a fault* [*mistake*] 아무의 잘못을 꾸짖다.

jump up, **a**) leap or spring up quickly. 갑자기 일어나다; 뛰어오르다. ¶ *He jumped up in surprise.* 놀라서 후닥닥 일어났다. **b**) get on a car, train, etc. quickly. (자동차 따위)에 타다.

— *n.* Ⓒ **1** a leap; a bound. 뛰어오름; 도약; 점프. ¶ *a high* ~ 높이뛰기; 하이 점프 / *a* ~ *over the gate* 문을 뛰어넘기. **2** a surprise; a shock. (움찔) 놀람. ¶ *The sound gave her a* ~. 그 소리에 그녀는 흠칫했다. **3** a sudden rise. 급등. ¶ *Prices take a* ~. 물가가 갑자기 오른다. **4** 《*pl.*》《*sl.*》 delirium tremens. (알코올 중독에 의한) 섬망증(譫妄症). [Imit.]

get [***have***] ***the jump on,*** 《*colloq.*》 get [have] an earlier start than; have an advantage over. (일찍 시작해서) …을 앞지르다; …보다 더 낫다. ¶ *We got the* ~ *on our competitors.* 우리는 경쟁자들을 앞질렀다.

on the jump, 《*colloq.*》 busy; busily moving about. 바빠서; 바쁘게 돌아다녀.

jump·er[1] [dʒʌ́mpər] *n.* Ⓒ a person or thing that jumps. 뛰는 사람[것].

jump·er[2] [dʒʌ́mpər] *n.* Ⓒ **1** a loose outer jacket worn by workmen, sailors, etc. 잡

J

바. **2** a woman's sleeveless dress worn over a blouse. (여성용 소매 없는) 잠바 스커트. **3** 《*pl.*》 rompers. 롬퍼스; 아이들의 놀이옷.

〈jumper[2] 3〉

jump·y [dʒʌ́mpi] *adj.* (**jump·i·er, jump·i·est**) **1** moving by sudden, sharp jumps or jerks. 튀어오르는; 도약의. **2** nervous. 흠칫하는.

Jun. June; Junior.

jun. junior.

junc·tion [dʒʌ́ŋ*k*ʃən] *n.* **1** Ⓤ the act of joining; the state of being joined. 접합; 결합; 연접. **2** Ⓒ a place where things join; a place where railroad lines,roads, etc. meet. 접합[연결]점; (길·선로 등의) 합류점; 연락역. [→joint]

junc·ture [dʒʌ́ŋktʃər] *n.* **1** Ⓤ the act of joining; the state of being joined. 결합; 연결. **2** Ⓒ a place where two things join or meet. 이음매; 접합점. **3** Ⓒ a point of time; a crisis; a state of affairs. (어떤) 시기; 위기; 사태. ¶ *at this* ～ 이 (중대한) 때에; 이 참에. [↑]

:June [dʒu:n] *n.* the sixth month of the year. 유월; 6월. [L. *Junius*]

jun·gle [dʒʌ́ŋgl] *n.* Ⓒ **1** any area thickly covered with trees, bushes, vines, etc. 정글; 밀림. **2** 《U.S. *sl.*》 a camp for tramps. 부랑자 숙소. [Hind.]

jungle gym [∠-∠] *n.* an apparatus for playground, consist of bars, ladders, etc. for children to climb on. 정글 짐《둥근 나무나 철봉을 종횡으로 조립하여 만든 어린이들의 운동 시설》.

:jun·ior [dʒú:njər] *adj.* (opp. senior) **1** younger. 연하의; 손아래의; 젊은 쪽의. 參考 Jr., jr.로 생략함. ¶ *John Smith, Jr.* 존 스미스 2세 / *Parker, Junior* 연하인 쪽의 파커. **2** of lower standing or position. 하급의; 후진의. ¶ *the* ～ *partner in a firm* 회사의 하급 사원. **3** youthful. 젊은.

be junior to, younger than. …보다 젊다; 후배이다.

—— *n.* Ⓒ **1** the younger person of two. 손아랫사람. ¶ *I am his* ～ *by two years.* 나는 그보다 두 살 아래이다. **2** one of lower standing or position. 후배; 하급자. **3** 《U.S.》 a student in the third year of a four-year course in high school or college. 4년제 대학·고교의 3학년생. [L. *juvenis* young]

ju·ni·per [dʒú:nəpər] *n.* Ⓒ 《bot.》 an evergreen shrub or tree of the pine family. 노간주나무 종류. [L.]

junk[1] [dʒʌŋk] *n.* Ⓒ a Chinese sailing ship with a flat bottom and three masts. 정크선(船). [Javanese *djong*]

〈junk[1]〉

junk[2] [dʒʌŋk] *n.* Ⓤ objects of no value; things discarded because they are useless; rubbish. 쓰레기; 폐물. [Port. *junco* rush]

jun·ket [dʒʌ́ŋkit] *n.* **1** ⓊⒸ a kind of food made from milk, such as cream, cheese. 유제품; 응유(凝乳) 식품. **2** Ⓒ a feast. 연회; 잔치. **3** Ⓒ a picnic; a pleasure trip. 피크닉; 유람 여행. —— *vi.* (P1) **1** feast. 잔치를 베풀다. **2** picnic. 피크닉 가다. [L. *juncus* rush, from use of rushbasket]

junk·man [dʒʌ́ŋkmæn] *n.* Ⓒ (*pl.* **-men** [-mən]) 《U.S.》 a dealer in junk. 고물상; 폐품업자. [*junk*[2]]

Ju·no [dʒú:nou] *n.* (*pl.* **-nos**) **1** 《Rom. myth.》 the goddess of marriage and the wife of Jupiter. 주노. 參考 그리스 신화의 Hera에 해당. **2** Ⓒ a stately and noble woman. 기품 있는 부인. [L.]

·Ju·pi·ter [dʒú:pətər] *n.* **1** 《Rom. myth.》 the ruler of all the other gods. 주피터. 參考 그리스 신화의 Zeus에 해당. **2** the largest planet in the solar system. 목성(木星). [L.]

ju·rid·i·cal [dʒuərídikəl] *adj.* of the administration of justice. 재판상의; 법률상의. ¶ *a* ～ *person* 법인(法人). [juris-, L. *dico* say]

ju·ris- [dʒúəris-] *pref.* law. '법'의 뜻. [L. *jus* law]

ju·ris·dic·tion [dʒùərisdíkʃən] *n.* Ⓤ **1** the right of administering laws; the authority of a sovereign power. 재판권; 사법권. **2** an extent of authority. 권한이 미치는 범위. **3** Ⓒ the district over which a court has power. 재판 관할구; 관할 구역. ● **ju·ris·dic·tion·al** [-ʃənəl] *adj.* [juris-, L. *dico* say]

ju·ris·pru·dence [dʒùərisprú:dəns] *n.* Ⓤ **1** the science or philosophy of law. 법(률)학; 법리(학). ¶ *medical* ～ 법의학. **2** the state of being well acquainted with laws. 법률에 밝음. **3** the system of laws. 법체계(法體系). [juris-, L. *prudentia* knowledge]

ju·rist [dʒúərist] *n.* Ⓒ an expert in law. 법학자; 법학도. [L. *jūs* law, -ist]

ju·ror [dʒúərər] *n* Ⓒ **1** a member of a jury; a juryman. 배심원. **2** a person who bind himself by an oath. 선서인. [L. *juro* swear]

·ju·ry [dʒúəri] *n.* Ⓒ (*pl.* **ju·ries**) **1** a group of persons, usu. twelve in number, selected to decide whether or not an accused person is guilty in a court of law. 배심(陪審). **2** a group of persons chosen to give a judgment on public matters. (행사 등에서의) 심사원. [↑]

ju·ry·man [dʒúərimən] *n.* Ⓒ (*pl.* **-men** [-mən]) a member of a jury. 배심원.

:just [dʒʌst] *adj.* **1** right; fair. 바른; 공정한. ¶ ～ *conduct* 올바른 행동 / *a* ～ *decision* 공정한 결정. **2** having a right reason or cause;

due; proper. 그럴 만한; 사리에 맞는; 정당한. ¶ *a ~ claim* 〔*reward*〕 당연한 요구〔보수〕/ *~ anger* 무리가 아닌 분노. **3** exact; correct. 바른; 정확한. ¶ *a ~ description* 정확한 묘사. — *adv.* **1** exactly; precisely. 정확히; 바로; 꼭. ¶ *at ~ five* 정각 다섯 시에. 語法 위치에 주의 / *~ one o'clock* 한 시 정각 / *~ then* 〔*here*〕 바로 그때〔여기〕/ *That's ~ what I think.* 그게 바로 내 생각이다. **2** 《often *only ~*》 by a very little margin; barely; narrowly. 아슬아슬하게; 겨우; 가까스로. ¶ *He was ~ in time.* 그는 가까스로 시간에 댔다 / *I ~ caught the train.* 나는 겨우 열차를 탔다. **3** 《in the *perfect* tense》 a moment ago; not long ago. 지금 막; 방금. ¶ *He has ~ come.* 지금 막 왔다. **4** 《*colloq.*》 quite; very. 아주; 정말로. ¶ *The weather is ~ lovely.* 날씨가 정말 좋구나. **5** 《*colloq.*》 only; merely. 단지; 다만; 좀. ¶ *Just a moment.* 좀 기다려라. **6** at this or that exact time. 바로 지금〔그 때〕. ¶ *I'm ~ going.* 지금 곧 간다 / *The train was ~ about to start.* 열차는 그 때 막 떠나려 하고 있었다. [L. *jus* right]

:jus·tice [dʒʌ́stis] *n.* Ⓤ **1** fair dealing; just conduct. 공평; 공정; 정의(opp. injustice). ¶ *treat a man with ~* 남을 공정하게 대접하다. **2** the state of being right or lawful. 정당; 타당; 적법; 합법. ¶ *the ~ of our opinion* 우리들 견해의 정당성 / *He complained with ~ of the bad treatment.* 그가 나쁜 처우에 불평을 한 것은 당연하다. **3** trial and judgment by process of law. 재판. ¶ *a court of ~* 재판소 / *administer ~* 법을 집행하다; 범인을 처벌하다. **4** Ⓒ a judge. 재판관; 판사. ¶ *a ~ of the peace* 치안 판사. [→just]

bring** someone **to justice, legally punish an accused person for his crime. …을 법에 따라 처벌하다.

do** oneself **justice, show one's ability to the full. 역량을 충분히 발휘하다.

***do** someone or something **justice** =**do justice to** someone or something,* treat fairly. …을 공정하게 다루다.

in justice to, in order to be just to; to do someone justice. …을 공정하게 평한다면.

jus·ti·fi·a·ble [dʒʌ́stəfàiəbəl] *adj.* that can be justified. 정당화할 수 있는; 타당한. ● **jus·ti·fi·a·bly** [-i] *adv.* [↓]

jus·ti·fi·ca·tion [dʒʌ̀stəfikéiʃən] *n.* **1** Ⓤ the act of justifying; the state of being justified. 정당화; 변명. **2** ⓊⒸ a good reason. 정당한 이유. ¶ *There is no ~ for your conduct.* 네 행동에는 정당한 사유가 없다.

:jus·ti·fy [dʒʌ́stəfài] *vt.* (**-fied**) **1** show or prove (something) to be right. …을 정당화하다; 정당하다고 하다. ¶ *Can you ~ your absence?* 결근할 만한 이유가 있었나 / *The benefit justifies the cost.* 이익이 생겼다면 비용은 문제삼을것 없다. **2** declare (something done) to have been guiltless. …을 (정당하다고) 변명〔주장〕하다. ¶ *The accused man tried to ~ himself.* 피고는 자기의 무죄를 주장 하려고 했다. [L. *jūstifico*]

just·ly [dʒʌ́stli] *adv.* in a just manner. 바르게; 정당하게.

just·ness [dʒʌ́stnis] *n.* Ⓤ the state of being just. 바름; 공정; 정당. [just]

jut [dʒʌt] *vi.* (**jut·ted, jut·ting**) (P1,2A,3) 《*out, forth*》 stick out; project. 돌출하다; 비어져 나오다. ¶ *The tree branch juts out over the house.* 나뭇가지가 지붕 위로 비어져 나왔다. — *n.* Ⓒ the part which projects; a projection. 돌출(부). [→jet[1]]

jute [dʒu:t] *n.* Ⓤ a strong fiber obtained from tropical plants and used for making burlap, rope, etc. 황마(黃麻)섬유. [Skr.]

ju·ve·nile [dʒú:vənəl, -nàil] *adj.* **1** young; youthful. 젊은; 어린; 연소한. **2** suitable for young people. 소년에 어울리는; 연소자를 위한. ¶ *~ literature* 아동 문학. — *n.* Ⓒ **1** a young person. 소년; 소녀. **2** a book, a magazine, etc. for young people. 연소자를 위한 서적. **3** an actor who plays youthful parts. 아역(兒役). [L. *juvenis* young]

jux·ta·pose [dʒʌ̀kstəpóuz, ⌐-⌐] *vt.* (P6) place (things) side by side. …을 나란히 놓다; 병렬(並列)하다. [L. *juxta* next, →pose]

jux·ta·po·si·tion [dʒʌ̀kstəpəzíʃən] *n.* ⓊⒸ the act of placing side by side; the state of being placed in such a way. 나란히 놓기; 병렬(並列).

J

k K

K, k [kei] *n.* Ⓒ (*pl.* **K's, Ks, k's, ks** [keiz]) **1** the eleventh letter of the English alphabet. 영어 알파벳의 열한째 글자. **2** anything shaped like the letter K. K자 모양의 것.

Kai·ser [káizər] *n.*《G. =emperor》《hist.》 **1** an emperor of Germany or of Austria. 독일 황제; 오스트리아 황제. **2** an emperor of the Holy Roman Empire. 신성 로마제국 황제. [L. *Caesar*]

kale [keil] *n.* Ⓤ **1** a kind of cabbage with curly or wrinkled leaves. 케일《양배추의 일종》(cf. *cole*). **2** cabbage soup. 양배추〔야채〕수프. **3**《U.S. *colloq.*》money; cash. 돈; 현금. [L. *caulis* stem, cabbage]

ka·lei·do·scope [kəláidəskòup] *n.* Ⓒ **1** a tube with mirrors and small, loose pieces of colored glass inside. 만화경(萬華鏡). **2**《*fig.*》any frequent changing scene. 변화 무쌍한 것. ¶ *the ~ of life* (주마등 같은) 인생의 만화경. [Gk. *kalos* beautiful, *eidos* form, *skopeō* look at]

ka·lei·do·scop·ic [kəlàidəskápik / -skɔ́p-] *adj.* of or like a kaleidoscope; continually changing. 만화경 같은; 변화 무쌍한.

:kan·ga·roo [kæ̀ŋgərú:] *n.* (*pl.* **-roos** or *collectively* **-roo**) Ⓒ an Australian animal with powerful hind legs for leaping. 캥거루. [? Native]

kangaroo closure [--ㅅ ㅅ-] *n.* a closure made when chairman in committee selects some amendments for discussion and excludes others. 캥거루식 토론 종결법《의장이 일부 조항만을 토의에 붙이고 여타 조항은 배제함》.

kangaroo court [--ㅅ ㅅ] *n.*《U.S. *colloq.*》an unauthorized or irregular court conducted with disregard to legal procedure. 사적(私的) 재판. ¶ *bring someone to a ~* 아무를 린치하다.

·Kan·sas [kǽnzəs] *n.* a central State in the United States. 캔자스. 參考 Kans., Kan.으로 생략함.

Kant [kænt], **Immanuel** *n.* (1724-1804) a German philosopher. 칸트.

ka·o·lin, -line [kéiəlin] *n.* Ⓤ a white clay used in making fine china. 고령토; 도토(陶土); 카올린. [Chin. *kao-ling* a mountain]

ka·pok [kéipɑk / -pɔk] *n.* Ⓤ the silky fibers obtained from the seeds of a tropical tree. 케이폭; 판야(panja)솜. 參考 이불·베개 등에 채움. [Malay]

kap·pa [kǽpə] *n.* the 10th letter of the Greek alphabet, K, *k*. 그리스어 알파벳의 열째 글자(=k).

kar·at [kǽrət] *n.*《U.S.》=carat.

Kate [keit] *n.* a nickname of Katherine or Catherine. Katherine, Catherine의 애칭.

kay·ak [káiæk] *n.* Ⓒ an Eskimo boat for one person, made of sealskins stretched over a light frame of wood. 카약《에스키모인의 가죽배》. [Eskimo]

Keats [ki:ts], **John** *n.* (1795-1821) an English poet. 키츠.

keel [ki:l] *n.* Ⓒ **1** the lowest timber in the framework of a boat or ship. (배의) 용골(龍骨). **2** a part in an airplane or airship which looks like a ship's keel. (비행기·비행선의) 용골.

lay* (*down*) *a keel, start building a ship. 배를 만들기 시작하다.

on an even keel, **a**) (of a ship) without movement to one side or the other. 배가 수평을 유지하여. **b**)《*colloq.*》steady or steadily. (사람·사태가)안정되어; 원활히; 조용히.

— *vt.* (P6,7) turn (a ship) upside down; upset. (배)를 전복시키다. — *vi.* (P2A) (of a ship) upset. 배가 전복하다. [N.]

keel over, **a**) turn over; upset. 뒤집히다. **b**)《*colloq.*》suddenly lose all feeling because of shock. 기절하다. ¶ *She keeled over in a faint.* 그녀는 혼미해지며 까무라쳤다.

:keen [ki:n] *adj.* **1** sharp. 날카로운. ¶ *a ~ edge* 예리(銳利)한 날 / *a ~ sword* 예리한 칼. **2** eager; ardent; desiring. 열심(熱心)인. ¶ *He is ~ to go.* 가고 싶어서 안달이다. **3** piercing; severe; bitter. 찌르는 듯한; 신랄한; 통렬한. ¶ *a ~ wind* 살을 에는 듯한 바람 / *a ~ pain* 〔*hunger*〕 심한 통증〔허기〕 / *a ~ remark* 신랄한 비평. **4** acute; sensitive. 예민한. ¶ *a ~ sense of smell* 예민한 후각 / *a ~ understanding* 빠른 이해력. **5** strongly felt; intense. 격렬한; 격심한. ¶ *~ pleasure* 〔*sorrow*〕 환희〔비탄〕. [E.]

be keen on doing, be eager to do. 열중하고 있다. *He is very ~ on stamp collecting.* 우표수집에 열중해 있다.

keen·ly [kí:nli] *adv.* sharply. 날카롭게; 예민하게.

keen·ness [kí:nnis] *n.* Ⓤ sharpness. 날카「로움; 예민.

:keep [ki:p] (**kept**) *vt.* **1** (P6) continue (some action or state). (어떤 동작·상태)를 지속하다. ¶ *~ silence* 침묵을 지키다 / *~ step* 계속 걷다. **2** (P7,13,18,21,23) make (someone or something) continue in a certain state. …을 어떤 상태로 두다. ¶ *~ the window open* 문을 열어 놓다 / *~ the house warm* 집을 따뜻하게 해두다 / *~ oneself cool* 냉정을 잃지 않다 / *~ one's car in good condition* 자동차를 잘 정비해 두다 / *I kept him waiting* *for two hours.* 그를 두 시간 기다리게 했다. **3** (P6,13) have (something) for a time in good condition; preserve. …을 보존〔저장〕하다. ¶ ~ *meat* 고기를 상하지 않게 두다 / ~ *old diaries* 옛 일기장을 간직해 두다 / *Keep that in mind.* 그 일을 잊지 마라. **4** (P6) have (something) for sale; deal with (something). (상품으로) …을 갖추다; 매매하다. ¶ *He keeps provisions at his store.* 가게에 식료품을 취급하고 있다 / ~ *a good stock of glassware* 가게에 유리 그릇이 많다. **5** (P6) have and care for (something). …을 돌보다; 보살피다. ¶ ~ *a family* 가족을 부양하다 / ~ *a dog* 개를 기르다 / ~ *a car* 〔*servant*〕 차를〔하인을〕 두다. **6** (P13) 《*from*》 prevent; restrain. …을 방해하다; 제지하다; 막아서 …을 못하게 하다. **7** (P6) write down regularly; record. …을 적다; 기록하다. ¶ ~ *accounts* 기장(記帳)하다 / ~ *a diary* 일기를 쓰다. **8** (P6) obey; follow; fulfill; carry out. …을 지키다; …에 따르다; …을 이행〔실행〕하다. ¶ ~ *the law* 법을 지키다 / ~ *a promise* 약속을 지키다 / *He did not* ~ *faith with me.* 그는 나와의 신의를 지키지 않았다. **9** (P6,13) leave (something) unknown to others; conceal. …을 비밀로 하다. ¶ ~ *a secret* 비밀을 지키다 / *You are keeping something from me.* 내게 뭘 숨기고 있구나. **10** (P6) carry on; manage. …을 경영하다; …에 종사하다. ¶ ~ *a business* 사업을 하다 / ~ *a school* 〔*shop*〕 학교를〔상점을〕 운영하다 / ~ *house* 살림을 꾸리다. **11** (P6) save; hold; possess. …을 소유〔보관〕하다. ¶ *May I* ~ *this book ?—You can* ~ *it for a month.* 이 책을 내가 가질까요—한 달 동안은 괜찮다. **12** (P7,13) detain. 감금하다; 붙들어 두다. **13** (P6,13) guard; protect. 지키다; 보호하다. ¶ ~ *goal* 골을 지키다 / ~ *a town against the enemy* 적으로부터 마을을 지키다. **14** (P6) continue to stay in (a place). …에 오래 있다; 붙박이다. ¶ ~ *one's bed* 〔*room*〕 자리보존하다〔방에만 죽치다〕. **15** (P6) observe; celebrate. (의식)을 거행하다; 축하하다. ¶ ~ *Christmas* 성탄절을 축하하다 / ~ *a feast* 축연을 베풀다. — *vi.* **1** (P2A,3,5) remain in some state. 어떤 상태에 있다. ¶ ~ *well* 건강하게 있다 / ~ *smiling* 계속 웃고 있다 / ~ *quiet* 〔*silent*〕 조용히 하고 있다〔침묵을 지키다〕 / ~ *cool* 〔*calm*〕 냉정〔평온〕을 잃지 않다 / *How are you keeping ?* 어떻게 지내고 있나. **2** (P1,3) remain good. 좋은 상태를 유지하다. ¶ *The meat will* ~ *for two days.* 이 고기가 이틀은 갈 것이다 / *Milk won't* ~ *in this heat.* 이렇게 더워서는 우유가 상하겠다. **3** (P2A,3) remain in a certain place; stay. (어떤 곳에) 머무르다; 죽치다. ¶ ~ *indoors* 〔*at home*〕 집안에만 있다. **4** 《chiefly Brit.》 live; lodge. 살다; 하숙하다.

keep at, **a**) make (someone) remain at work. …을 계속해서 일을 시키다. ¶ *He kept me at it* 〔*the work*〕 *all day.* 그는 나에게 종일 그것〔일〕을 시켰다. **b**) continue doing diligently; persist in. 열심히 하다; 버티다. ¶ *He kept hard at it* 〔*the work*〕 *for weeks.* 그는 몇 주 동안 열심히 그것〔일〕을 했다.

keep away, avoid coming; prevent (someone) from coming. …을 못 오게〔가까이 못하게〕 하다.

keep back, stay or make (someone) stay at a distance; hinder; restrain; conceal; reserve. …을 멀리하다; 근접 못 하게 하다; 방해하다; 숨기다; 간직해 두다. ¶ ~ *back the crowd* 군중의 접근을 제지하다 / ~ *back one's tears* 눈물을 감추다.

keep down, **a**) overcome and control (someone). …을 진압하다. ¶ ~ *down a mob.* **b**) remain sitting or lying down. (적군 등에 안 보이게) 앉아〔엎드려〕 있다.

keep from (= *avoid*) *someone* or *something.* …을 피하다; 제지하다. ¶ ~ *children from going out* 아이들을 못 나가게 하다 / *I cannot* ~ *from saying.* 말하지 않을 수 없다.

keep in, **a**) restrain (a feeling). (감정)을 억누르다. **b**) make (someone) stay in a house, etc.; order (a pupil) to stay in. …을 외출 못 하게 하다; (학생)을 벌로서 남아 있게 하다. ¶ *The doctor kept me in for a week.* 의사가 일 주일 동안 외출을 금했다. **c**) keep (a fire) burning. (불)이 꺼지지 않게 하다.

keep in with *someone,* 《*colloq.*》 remain on good terms with someone. …와 사이 좋게 지내다. ¶ ~ *in with superiors* 〔*ladies*〕 윗사람〔숙녀〕들과 좋게 지내다.

keep it up, continue; not make slower; not loosen. 꾸준히 계속해서 하다.

keep off, refrain from; repel. …을 삼가다; 접근 못 하게 하다. ¶ ~ *off enemy ships* 적함을 격퇴하다 / *Keep off the grass.* 잔디를 밟지 마시오.

keep on, **a**) continue to wear. (옷 따위)를 입은〔걸친〕 채 있다. ¶ ~ *one's hat on* 모자를 벗지 않고 있다. **b**) continue to employ. …을 계속 고용하다. ¶ ~ *on one's cook* 요리사를 계속 있게 하다 / *He was kept on at his old job.* 그는 예전부터의 일에 종사하고 있었다. **c**) continue; go on with; persist. 계속 …하다; 지속하다. ¶ *Don't give up hope;* ~ *on trying.* 희망을 버리지 말고 계속 노력해라.

keep on at, 《*colloq.*》 scold again and again. 잔소리를 하고 또 하다.

keep on with, continue doing. 계속하다.

keep out, **a**) prevent from coming in; shut out. 못 들어오게 하다. ¶ ~ *out foreign goods* 외제품을 못 들여오게 하다. **b**) prevent from doing. …을 못 하게 하다. ¶ ~ *children out of mischief* 아이들이 장난하지 못하게 하다. **c**) remain outside. 참여하지 않다. ¶ ~ *out of quarrels* 싸움에 끼어들지 않다.

keep to, obey; follow. …을 지키다; 따르다. ¶ *Keep to the left.* 좌측 통행.

keep to oneself, **a**) be alone; be unsociable. 남과 어울리지 않다. **b**) not reveal. 남에게 숨

기다. ¶ *He often keeps his opinions to himself.* 그는 자기 의견을 남에게 말하지 않을 때가 종종 있다.

keep under, hold (something) in subjection. …을 억누르다; 복종시키다.

keep up, **a**) keep and continue (an effort, an activity, etc.); prevent from falling or going down. …을 지속하다; 쓰러지거나 내려가지 않게 하다. ¶ ~ *up one's spirits* 〔*trousers, the prices*〕 용기를 잃지 않다〔바지가 흘러내리지 않게 하다; 가격을 유지하다〕. **b**) keep (something) in an efficient state. 좋은 상태에 두다. ¶ *In spite of all this trouble they kept up very well.* 이 모든 어려움에서도 그들은 끄떡 없었다 / ~ *up a car* 차를 잘 정비해 두다 / ~ *up a large house* 대가족을 꾸려가다. **c**) not give way to (grief, etc.). …에 굴하지 않다.

keep up one's end, finish one's part in a common effort. 자기 몫을 해내다.

keep up with, maintain pace with; successfully compete with (something). …에 뒤떨어지지 않다. ¶ ~ *up with* (*the progress of*) *the times* 시대에 뒤지지 않다 / ~ *up with the fashion* 유행에 뒤떨어지지 않다.

keep watch, be alert. 경계하다.

— *n.* Ⓤ **1** maintenance. 유지; 보전. **2** food; cost of living. 식량; 생계비. ¶ *earn one's* ~ 생활비를 벌다. **3** Ⓒ 《hist.》 a tower; a stronghold; a citadel. 탑; 요새(要塞). [E.]

for keeps, 《*colloq.*》 for ever; permanently. 영원히.

·keep·er [kíːpər] *n.* Ⓒ **1** a person who keeps. 지키는 사람; 임자. ¶ *the* ~ *of the dog* 개 임자 / *a coffee-house* ~ 다방 주인. **2** a guard; a watchman. 파수꾼; 경비원. **3** a guardian. 보호자.

keep·ing [kíːpiŋ] *n.* Ⓤ **1** care; charge. 돌봄; 관리. **2** observance; celebration. (의식 등을) 지키기; 축하(행사). **3** harmony; agreement. 조화; 부합. ¶ *His acts are not in* ~ *with his promises.* 그는 약속을 이행하지 않는다 / *This color is out of* ~ *with your room.* 이 색깔은 네 방에 어울리지 않는다.

in someone's (***safe***) ***keeping,*** be kept safely by someone. (안전하게) 보관되어. ¶ *The papers are in my* ~. 서류는 내가 보관하고 있다.

keep·sake [kíːpsèik] *n.* Ⓒ something kept in memory of someone or of some event. 기념품. ¶ *I still have it as a* ~. 기념품으로 그걸 아직 가지고 있다. [E.]

keg [keg] *n.* Ⓒ a small barrel, usu. holding less than 10 gallons. 작은 통. [E.]

kelp [kelp] *n.* Ⓤ **1** any of several kinds of large brown seaweed. 말; 해초. **2** ashes of seaweed, from which iodine is made. 해초의 재; 켈프《요오드의 원료》. [M.E.]

ken [ken] *n.* Ⓤ **1** range of sight. 시계. ¶ *come in* 〔*within*〕 *one's* ~ 시계에 들어오다. **2** range of knowledge. 지식 범위. ¶ *That's beyond my* ~. 그건 내 지력(知力) 밖이다. — *vt.* (P6) 《Sc.》 know; recognize at sight. …을 알다; (보고) 인정하다. [E. =make known]

ken·nel [kénəl] *n.* Ⓒ **1** a house for a dog. 개집. **2** 《often *pl.*》 a place where dogs are bred. 개 사육장. **3** a poor, mean dwelling; a hovel. 누옥; 초라한 집. — *vt., vi.* (**-neled, -nel·ing** or 《Brit.》 **-nelled, -nel·ling**) (P6; 1) put (a dog) into a kennel; keep (a dog) in a kennel; take shelter in a kennel. (개를) 개집에 넣다; 사육장에서 기르다; 개집같은 데서 살다. ¶ ~ *a dog.* [L. *canis* dog]

Kent [kent] *n.* a county in southeastern England. 켄트.

Ken·tuck·y [kəntʌ́ki] *n.* a State in the south central part of the United States. 켄터키. 參考 Ky., Ken.으로 생략함. 주도는 Frankfort.

:kept [kept] *v.* p. and pp. of **keep.**

kerb [kəːrb] *n.* 《Brit.》 =curb 3.

kerb·stone [kə́ːrbstòun] *n.* Ⓒ 《Brit.》 a stone edge of a street; a curbstone. (보도의) 연석(緣石). [→curb]

ker·chief [kə́ːrtʃif] *n.* Ⓒ **1** a piece of cloth worn by women over the head or around the neck. (여성의) 머릿수건; 목도리. **2** a handkerchief. 손수건. [F. *couvrechief* headcover (→cover, →chief)]

〈kerchief 1〉

kerf [kəːrf] *n.* **1** a cut made by a saw or an ax, etc. (칼·도끼 등의) 자국. **2** something cut off. 자른 면; 단면. [→carve]

ker·mis, ker·mess [kə́ːrmis] *n.* a fair to raise money for charity. 바자. [Du.]

ker·nel [kə́ːrnəl] *n.* Ⓒ **1** the soft inner part of a nut or fruit. (과실의) 인(仁); 심(心). **2** a grain of wheat, corn, etc. (곡식) 낟알. **3** the central or important part of anything. (사물의) 중심부; 요점; 핵심. [→corn]

ker·o·sene [kérəsìːn, ⌣–⌣] *n.* Ⓤ a thin oil used in lamps or stoves. 등유(燈油). [Gk. *kēros* wax]

ker·sey·mere [kə́ːrzimìər] *n.* **1** =cashmere. **2** 《*pl.*》 tight-fitting breeches or trousers made of cashmere. 캐시미어 바지. [Place]

ketch [ketʃ] *n.* Ⓒ a small sailing ship with two masts. 작은 두대박이 돛단배. [→catch]

ketch·up [kétʃəp] *n.* Ⓤ a thick sauce made from tomatoes, mushrooms, etc. 케첩. 參考 catchup, catsup 이라고도 씀. [Chin. *kôe-chiap* brine of pickled fish]

·ket·tle [kétl] *n.* Ⓒ a metal pot with a handle and a spout for boiling water. 주전자. [E.]

a pretty kettle of fish, a confused state of affairs. 북새통; 혼란.

ket·tle·drum [kétldrʌ̀m] *n.* Ⓒ a bowl-shaped drum. 케틀드럼; 팀파니. [E.]

:key [kiː] *n.* Ⓒ **1** a metal instrument for opening and fastening a lock; anything like this in shape or use. 열쇠; 열쇠 모양의 것. ¶ *a ~ to a door* 문 열쇠 / *a ~ of a clock* 시계의 태엽 감개 / *turn the ~ in the lock* 자물쇠를 채우다 / *get the ~ of the street* 내쫓기다 / *the ~ to a room* 방문 열쇠. **2** 《*the ~*》 the place or position controlling an entrance or commanding some area. 관문(關門); 요소. ¶ *The Suez Canal is the ~ to the Mediterranean.* 수에즈 운하는 지중해의 관문이다. **3** a guide to solve problems; a clue. 해결책; 실마리. ¶ *a ~ to a puzzle* 수수께끼의 열쇠 / *the golden* 〔*silver*〕 *~* 뇌물. ¶ *He holds the ~ to the political situation.* 그가 정국(政局) 열쇠를 쥐고 있다. **4** the parts of a piano, a typewriter, etc. which the fingers press. (피아노 등의) 키; 건(鍵). **5** a tone or mode thought or expression. (사상·표현의) 기조; 양식; 가락. ¶ *speak in a high ~* 높은 음성으로 얘기하다 / *all in the same ~* 단조롭게; 같은 가락으로 / *The poem is written in a melancholy ~.* **6** 《mus.》 a scale or system of notes in music related to one another in a special way and based on a particular note. 주조(主調); (장단의) 조(調). ¶ *a song written in the ~ of B flat* 내림 나 장조로 된 곡.
— *vt.* **1** (P6) lock (something) with a key. …에 쇠를 채우다. **2** regulate the tone of (a piano, etc.). …의 음조를 맞추다; 조율하다.
key someone up, bring someone into a state of nervous tension; excite; encourage. …을 긴장시키다; 자극하다; 고무하다.
— *adj.* basic; fundamental; essential. 기본적인; 중요한. [E.]

key·board [kíːbɔ̀ːrd] *n.* Ⓒ the row of keys on a piano, an organ, a typewriter, etc. 건반. [*key*]

〈keyboard〉

key·hole [kíːhòul] *n.* Ⓒ a small opening through which a key is inserted to turn a lock. 열쇠 구멍. ¶ *listen at* 〔*spy through*〕 *the ~(s)* 열쇠구멍으로 엿듣다〔엿보다〕. [↑]

key·note [kíːnòut] *n.* Ⓒ **1** 《mus.》 the first note on which a series of tones is based. 주조음(主調音); 기음(基音). **2** the main idea. 주지(主旨); 주안(主眼). ¶ *the ~ of his speech* 그의 연설의 기조 / *a ~ address* 〔*speech*〕 (미국 정당의) 기조 연설.

key·stone [kíːstòun] *n.* Ⓒ **1** 《archit.》 the central stone at the top of an arch. (아치의) 이맛돌; 쐐기돌. **2** the fundamental principle or element. 주지(主旨); 근본 원리.

kg. kilogram; kilograms.

kha·ki [kɑ́ːki, kǽki] *adj.* yellowish brown. 카키색의; 황갈색의. — *n.* **1** Ⓤ a yellowish brown color. 카키색. **2** 《usu. *pl.*》 a military uniform or cloth of this color. 카키색 군복〔천〕. [Hind.=dusty]

Khmer [kméər] *n.* ~ **Republic** the former official name of Cambodia. 크메르 공화국.

:kick [kik] *vt.* (P6,7) **1** strike (something) with the foot. …을 차다; 걷어차다. ¶ *~ a dog* / *~ someone's shin* 아무의 정강이를 차다. **2** 《football》 score (a goal) by kicking the ball. 공을 차서 득점하다. **3** (of a gun) jump back violently. (발사 후 총이) 반동을 주다. **4** 《*colloq.*》 repel; dismiss. …를 퇴짜놓다; 해고하다. — *vi.* (P1,3) **1** strike out with the foot. 차다. **2** 《football》 make a kick. 차다; 킥하다. **3** 《*colloq.*》 resist; object; complain. 반대〔반항〕하다; 불평을 하다. ¶ *If you put up the price of beer, a lot of people will ~.* 맥주 값을 올렸다간 뭇사람들이 불평할 것이다. **4** (of a gun) push or spring back when fired. (총이) 반동하다.
kick against 〔***at***〕, resist. 반항하다.
kick around, **a**) treat (someone) unkindly. …을 박대〔홀대〕하다. **b**) 《*sl.*》 examine (something) from various angles. …을 여러 각도에서 검토하다. **c**) move from place to place. 방랑하다; 돌아다니다.
kick back, get even with. …에게 대갚음하다.
kick downstairs, make (someone) go out of a house. …을 집에서 내쫓다. 「되다.
kick one's heels, be kept waiting. 기다리게
kick off, **a**) start play in football. 킥오프하다. **b**) take off (a shoe) by kicking one's leg. (신을) 차서 벗다. ¶ *~ off one's shoes.* **c**) initiate something. (회합 등을) 시작하다.
kick out, **a**) 《*sl.*》 send (someone) away; send (someone) away from his position. …을 내쫓다; 퇴학〔퇴직〕시키다. ¶ *He was rude, so I kicked him out.* 버릇이 없어 해고했다. **b**) 《football》 kick the ball out of bounds. 공을 라인 밖으로 차내다.
kick over the traces, 《*colloq.*》 become uncontrollable; get out of hand. (말이) 말을 안 듣다; (사람이) 거칠어지다.
kick the bucket, 《*sl.*》 die. 죽다.
kick up a dust 〔***row, shindy, shine***〕, make trouble. 소동〔말썽〕을 일으키다.
kick upstairs, 《*colloq.*》 get rid of by an apparent promotion. …를 한직으로 몰아내다; 승진시켜 파직시키다.
— *n.* **1** Ⓒ a blow with the foot; kicking.

K

(걷어)차기. ¶ *a ~ from a horse* 말의 발길질. **2** Ⓤ the backward spring of a gun, etc. (총의) 반동. **3** Ⓒ 《football》 a person who kicks. 키커. ¶ *He was a splendid ~.* 훌륭한 키커였다. **4** Ⓤ 《*colloq.*》 an objection; a complaint. 반대; 불평. ¶ *have a ~ against the new schedule* 새 스케줄에 반대하다. **5** Ⓤ 《*colloq.*》 ⓐ a stimulating effect; a bite. 자극성; 톡 쏘는 맛. ¶ *This whisky has no ~ in it.* 이 위스키는 쏘는 맛이 없다. ⓑ 《*sl.*》 excitement; thrill. 흥분; 스릴. ¶ *get a ~ out of something* …에서 스릴을 느끼다. ⓒ vigor; energy. 원기; 활력. [E.]

have no kick left, have no power to resist. 반발할 힘도 없다; 힘이 다하다.

kick·off [kíkɔ̀ːf / ⌐ɔ̀f] *n.* **1** Ⓒ 《football》 the act of kicking off to start the game. 킥오프. **2** 《*colloq.*》 any beginning. 시작; 개시.

kick·shaw [kíkʃɔ̀ː] *n.* **1** 《*contempt.*》 a light dish of food elaborately cooked. 공들인 요리. **2** something showy but without value. (쓸데없는) 장식물; 굴퉁이. [F. *quelque chose* something]

:kid [kid] *n.* **1** Ⓒ a young goat. 새끼 염소. **2** Ⓤ flesh of a young goat. 새끼 염소의 고기. **3** Ⓤ leather made from the skin of young goats. 키드 가죽. **4** 《*pl.*》 gloves or shoes made of this leather. 키드 가죽 장갑〔신〕. **5** Ⓒ 《*colloq.*》 a child; a young person. 아이; 젊은이. —*vt.* (P6) joke with; fool; tease. …을 놀리다; 희롱하다. [E.]

kid·dy, -die [kídi] *n.* Ⓒ (*pl.* **-dies**) 《*colloq.*》 a child. 아이; 어린애. [↑]

kid·nap [kídnæ̀p] *vt.* (**-naped, -nap·ing** or **-napped, nap·ping**) (P6) carry off (someone) by force; steal (a baby). …을 납치하다; (어린이)를 유괴하다. [*kid, nab*]

kid·nap·er, -nap·per [kídnæ̀pər] *n.* Ⓒ a person who kidnaps. 납치〔유괴〕범.

kid·ney [kídni] *n.* **1** Ⓒ either of the two bean-shaped organs of the body which take away waste water from the blood. 신장; 콩팥. **2** nature; character; kind. 성질; 기질; 종류. ¶ *a man of my own ~* 나와 같은 기질의 사람 / *two persons of the same ~* 같은 기질의 두 사람 / *a man of the right ~* 착실한 사람; 제대로 된 사람. [E.]

kidney bean [⌐-⌐] *n.* a kind of bean like a kidney in shape. 강낭콩.

:kill [kil] *vt.* **1** (P6,13) cause (a person or an animal) to die. …을 죽이다. ¶ *~ someone by poison* 〔*accident*〕 아무를 독살하다〔사고로 죽게 하다〕 / *The frost has killed all the plants.* 서리로 초목이 다 죽었다 / *Many soldiers were killed.* 많은 병사들이 전사했다 / *~ cows for meat* 고기를 얻기 위해 소를 도살하다. **2** (P6,13) put an end to (something); make useless; destroy; spoil the effect of. …을 끝나게 하다; 못쓰게 만들다; 효과를 약화시키다. ¶ *The wallpaper kills the furniture.* 벽지 때문에 가구가 볼품 없게 된다 / *~ toothache with a medicine* 약으로 치통을 없애다 / *~ someone's love* 〔*hopes*〕 아무의 사랑〔희망〕을 짓밟다 / *~ someone with kindness* 친절이 지나쳐 사람을 못되게〔응석받이로〕 만들다. **3** spend (time) idly. (시간)을 헛되이 보내다. ¶ *I had to ~ an hour until the bus came.* 버스가 올 때까지 한 시간을 헛되이 보냈다. **4** cause (an engine, electric current, etc.) to stop. (엔진·전류 등)을 멈추게 하다; 끊다. **5** ⓐ make a deep impression on; attract much attention. …에 강한 인상을 주다; 주목을 끌다. ¶ *He is dressed to ~.* 그는 기막힌 옷차림을 하고 있다. ⓑ cause strong feelings, laughter, etc. (웃음 등)을 못 참게 하다; 뇌쇄하다. ¶ *The play was so funny that it nearly killed me.* 극이 얼마나 우습던지 배꼽이 빠질 뻔 했다. **6** defeat or veto (a legislative bill). (의안 등)을 부결하다. ¶ *be killed in the committee* 위원회에서 부결되다. **7** 《print.》 cancel (a word, paragraph). …을 삭제하다. [E.]

kill·er [kílər] *n.* Ⓒ **1** a person or a thing that kills. 살인자; 죽이는 것. **2** a person who does not hesitate to kill another; a murderer. 살인광.

kill·ing [kíliŋ] *adj.* **1** deadly; fatal; destructive. 치명적인; 파괴적인. ¶ *a ~ frost* (초목을 얼려 죽이는) 된서리. **2** overpowering; exhausting. 압도적인; 지나친; 지치게 만드는. ¶ *ride at a ~ pace* 무서운 속도로 달리다. **3** 《*colloq.*》 irresistibly funny. 몹시 우스운. ¶ *a perfectly ~ play* 배꼽빼는 농담. **4** 《*colloq.*》 attractive; charming. 매력적인; 뇌쇄시키는. ¶ *She looked ~ in her new coat.* 새 코트를 입은 그녀는 정말 멋있더군. —*n.* **1** the act of taking life; murder. 살인; 살인 행위. **2** 《*colloq.*》 a sudden great financial success. 큰 벌이; 횡재.

kill-joy [kíldʒɔ̀i] *n.* a person who ruins the pleasure of a party. 흥을 깨는 사람.

kiln [kiln] *n.* Ⓒ a furnace or oven for burning or drying something, such as bricks and tiles. 가마; 노(爐). ¶ *a lime* 〔*pottery*〕 *~* 석회〔도기〕 굽는 가마. [L. *culina* kitchen]

ki·lo [kí(ː)lou] *n.* (*pl.* **-los**) Ⓒ **1** =kilogram. **2** =kilometer. [Gk. *khilioi*]

kil·o- [kílə-] *pref.* thousand. '천'의 뜻. [↑]

kil·o·cy·cle [kíləsàikl] *n.* Ⓒ 《electr.》 a unit equal to 1,000 cycles. 킬로사이클. 參考 kc로 생략함. 지금은 kilohertz라고 함.

kil·o·gram, 《Brit.》 **-gramme** [kíləgræ̀m] *n.* Ⓒ a unit of weight equal to 1,000 grams. 킬로그램. 參考 kg으로 생략함.

kil·o·hertz [kíləhə̀ːrts] *n.* a unit of frequency, equal to 1,000 cycles per second. 킬로헤르츠. 參考 kHz로 생략함.

kil·o·li·ter, 《Brit.》 **-tre** [kíləlìːtər] *n.* Ⓒ a unit of capacity equal to 1,000 liters. 킬로리터. 參考 kl로 생략함.

kil·o·me·ter, 《Brit.》 **-tre** [kíləmìːtər] *n.* Ⓒ a unit of length equal to 1,000 meters. 킬로미터. 參考 km로 생략함.

K

kil·o·watt [kíləwɑ̀t/-wɔ̀t] *n.* Ⓒ a unit of electrical power equal to 1,000 watts. 킬로와트. 參考 kw, kW로 생략함.

kilt [kilt] *n.* Ⓒ a short, pleated skirt worn by men in the Scottish Highlands. 킬트. — *vt.* (P6,7) tuck up; form (a skirt, etc.) into pleats. (자락 등)을 걷어올리다; …의 주름을 잡다. [Scand.]

〈kilt〉

***kin** [kin] *n.* Ⓤ **1** 《*collectively*》 one's family or relatives. 가족; 친척. ¶ *My ~ live in Seoul.* 식구들은 서울에 산다. **2** family relationship. 친척 관계. ¶ *What ~ is he to you?* 저 사람과는 어떻게 되나. **3** someone or something of the same kind. 동족; 동류(同類).

near of kin (to), closely related to (someone). (…의) 근친인.

next of kin (to), most closely related to (someone). (…의) 최근친인.

of kin, related; of the same family. 친척의; 동류의.

— *adj.* related; of the same kind. 친척 관계의; 같은 종류의. ¶ *be ~ to him* 그와 친척이다. [E.(→kind²)]

more kin than kind, though related, yet not kindly or friendly. 친척이지만 정은 없는.

:kind¹ [kaind] *adj.* thoughtful of others and their feelings; friendly; gentle. 친절한. ¶ *How ~ you are!* 정말 고맙소. [E.]

Be so kind as to do.* = *Be kind enough to do, Will you kindly do...? (부디) …해주면 고맙겠습니다. ¶ *Be so ~ as to shut the door.* 문 좀 닫아 주면 고맙겠다.

It is kind of you to do, Thank you for *doing*. …해줘서 고맙습니다. ¶ *It is ~ of you to invite me.* 초대해주셔서 고맙습니다.

:kind² [kaind] *n.* **1** Ⓒ ⓐ a race or natural group of animals, plants, etc. with the same general characteristics. 종족《동식물의 유(類)·족(族)·종(種)·속(屬)》. ¶ *the human ~* 인류 / *the cat ~* 고양이속(屬). ⓑ a sort; a variety; a class. 종류; 부류. ¶ *apples of several kinds* 몇 가지 종류의 사과 / *this ~ of book* 이런 종류의 책 / *I like this ~.* 이런 종류가 좋다 / *What ~ of man is he?* 어떤 부류의 사람이냐 / *All kinds of food are sold in the shop.* 이 가게에는 없는 식품이 없다 / *What ~ of house do you live in?* 어떤 집에 살고 있나. **2** Ⓤ natural characteristic. 성질. **3** Ⓤ 《*arch.*》 nature. 자연; 천성. **4** Ⓒ 《*arch.*》 manner. 방식. [E.]

a kind of, something more or less like; vaguely similar. …의 일종; 일종의 …. ¶ *a ~ of gentleman* 〔*essay*〕 일종의 신사〔수필〕.

in kind, **a**) in essential character. 본질적으로. **b**) in goods instead of money. 물건으로. ¶ *payment in ~* 물납(物納). **c**) with something of the same sort. 같은 종류의 것으로. ¶ *repay someone's insult in ~* 아무의 모욕에 대해 모욕으로 갚다.

kind of, 《*colloq.*》 somewhat; rather. 다소; 어느 정도 …같은. ¶ *She looks ~ of tired.* 좀 피곤해 보인다 / *I ~ of thought this would happen.* 어쩐지 이런 일이 일어날 성싶었다.

nothing of the kind, never; nothing at all; never like .... 결코 …이 아니다; 전혀 다르다. ¶ *I shall do nothing of the ~.* 그 따위 일은 죽어도 안 하겠다.

of a kind, **a**) of the same kind. 같은 종류의. ¶ *They are all of a ~.* 다 마찬가지다; 그게 그거다. **b**) of poor quality. 시원찮은; 명색뿐인. ¶ *He is a gentleman of a ~.* 그 자는 사이비 신사다 / *coffee of a ~* 이름뿐인 맛대가리 없는 커피.

something of the kind, something like that. 그저 그 정도의 것. ¶ *He expected something of the ~.* 그 비슷한 것을 기대했다.

kin·der·gar·ten [kíndərgɑ̀ːrtn] *n.* Ⓒ a school that prepares young children for an elementary school. 유치원. [G.=children's garden]

kind·heart·ed [káindhɑ́ːrtid] *adj.* having or showing a kind heart; gentle. 친절한; 착한; 상냥한. [*kind*¹]

***kin·dle** [kíndl] *vt.* **1** (P6,13) set (something) on fire; set fire to (something). …을 태우다; …에 불을 지피다. ¶ *~ straw* 짚을 태우다 / *~ a fire with a match* 성냥을 긋다. **2** (P6) make (something) bright; light up. …을 비추다; 밝게 하다. ¶ *The setting sun kindled the sky.* 석양이 하늘을 붉게 물들였다. **3** (P6,13) excite; stir up. …을 부추기다; 선동하다. ¶ *~ someone with interest* 아무의 흥미를 돋우다 / *His speech kindled their anger.* 그의 연설이 그들의 분노를 부채질했다.

— *vi.* (P1) **1** catch fire; begin to burn. 불이 붙다; 타기 시작하다. ¶ *This wood does not ~.* 이 나무는 잘 타지 않는다 / *The fire is kindling at last.* 겨우 타기 시작하였다. **2** (P3) become bright. 번쩍거리다; 빛나다. ¶ *His eyes kindled with anger.* 눈은 분노로 이글거렸다. **3** 《*at*》 become excited. 흥분하다. ¶ *He kindled at the insult.* 그 모욕적인 말에 그는 불끈했다. [N.]

kind·li·ness [káindlinis] *n.* **1** Ⓤ kindly feeling. 친절한 마음; 친절. **2** Ⓒ a kindly act. 친절한 행위. [*kind*¹]

kin·dling [kíndliŋ] *n.* Ⓤ material for starting a fire, esp. small pieces of dry wood. 불쏘시개. [N.]

:kind·ly [káindli] *adj.* (**-li·er, -li·est**) **1** kind; friendly; gentle. 친절한. ¶ *a ~ heart* 친절한 마음씨 / *a ~ woman* 친절한 여자. **2** pleasant; agreeable; mild. (기후 등이) 상쾌한; 포근한. ¶ *a ~ season* 〔*climate*〕 상쾌한 계절〔온화한 기후〕.

— *adv.* **1** in a kind manner. 친절하게; 부

드럽게; 아무쪼록 (…해 주시오). ¶ *speak* ~ 상냥하게 말하다 / *Would you* ~ *tell me the name of the book?* 그 책의 이름을 좀 말씀해 주시지 않겠습니까. **2** pleasantly; agreeably. 쾌히; 기꺼이. [*kind*[1]]

take kindly to, **a**) be naturally attracted to (something). …을 절로 좋아하다. ¶ *The cat took* ~ *to her warm bed.* 고양이는 따뜻한 그녀의 잠자리를 좋아했다. **b**) adapt oneself to (one's surroundings, etc.). (환경 등)에 정이 들다.

:kind·ness [káindnis] *n.* **1** Ⓤ the state or quality of being good to others. 친절. ¶ *words without* ~ 매정한 말 / *He showed* ~ *by helping her.* 그녀를 도와줌으로써 친절을 나타냈다. **2** Ⓒ a kind act. 친절한 행위. ¶ *do a* ~ *to someone=do someone a* ~ 아무에게 친절을 베풀다 / *He has done me many kindnesses.* 그는 내게 많은 친절을 베풀어 주었다. [*kind*[1]]

have a kindness for, be friendly to (someone). …에 호의를 가지다.

have the kindness to do, be so kind as to do. 친절하게도 …하다.

out of kindness, because of being thoughtful of others. 친절한 마음에서; 선의로.

·kin·dred [kíndrid] *n.* **1** 《*collectively,* used as *pl.*》 relatives; relationship by birth or marriage. 친척; 친척 관계. **2** Ⓤ likeness; resemblance. 유사(類似); 동질. — *adj.* **1** related by birth or marriage. 친족의; 혈연의. **2** of the same kind; like; similar. 유사한; 동류의. ¶ *Pity and love are* ~ *feelings.* 동정과 애정은 같은 감정이다. [E.=kinship]

kin·e·ma [kínəmə] *n.* 《Brit.》 =cinema.

kin·e·mat·o·graph [kìnəmǽtəgræ̀f, kàinə-, -grɑ̀ːf] *n.* =cinematograph.

ki·ne·tic [kainétik, ki-] *adj.* **1** having to do with motion. 운동의. **2** caused by motion. 운동에 의한. ¶ *the* ~ *energy of falling bodies* 낙하하는 물체의 운동 에너지. **3** 《*fig.*》 marked by movement; having moving force. 활동적인. ¶ *a man of* ~ *energy* 활동적인 사람. [Gk. *kineō* move]

ki·net·ics [kainétiks, ki-] *n. pl.* 《used as *sing.*》 the science of motion in relation to force. 동역학(動力學)(opp. statics).

:king [kiŋ] *n.* Ⓒ **1** the male chief ruler of some countries. 임금, 왕; 군주(opp. queen). ¶ *the* ~ *of England* 영국 국왕 / *King George V* 국왕 조지 5세 / *God save the* ~. 국왕 폐하 만세《영국 국가》/ *under Henry I, King of England* 영국 왕 헨리1세 치하에 / *His Majesty the King* 국왕 폐하 / *King's Color* 영국 국기 / 《*prov.*》 *The* ~ *never dies.* 왕은 죽지 않는다《왕정은 영원하다》. **2** 《*colloq.*》 a person who is thought to be very powerful. 제1인자; 거물; 세력가. ¶ *a baseball* ~ 야구왕 / *He is the* ~ *in all kinds of sports.* 어떤 운동에서나 제1인자다. **3** a great merchant, etc. 호상(豪商). **4** a plant, an animal, etc. that is supreme in its class. 최상종(最上種); 왕에 비기는 것. ¶ *the* ~ *of beasts* 백수의 왕《사자》/ *the* ~ *of birds* 백조(百鳥)의 왕《독수리》/ *the* ~ *of the forest* 숲의 왕《떡갈나무》/ *the* ~ *of the jungle* 밀림의 왕《호랑이》/ *an oil* ~ 석유왕 / *the King of Heaven* 신; 하느님 / *the* ~ *of metals* 금속의 왕《금》. **5** a playing card with a picture of a king. (카드의) 킹; 왕. **6** 《chess》 the principal piece. 왕장(王將). [E. *cyning*]

:king·dom [kíŋdəm] *n.* Ⓒ **1** a country ruled by a king or queen. 왕국. **2** a territory where a person has control. 영역. ¶ *the* ~ *of thought* 사고의 영역. **3** one of the three classes into which all natural things are divided. …계(界). ¶ *the animal* 〔*mineral, vegetable*〕 ~ 동물〔광물, 식물〕계.

king·fish·er [kíŋfìʃər] *n.* Ⓒ 《bird》 a bright-colored river bird which feeds on fish and insects. 물총새.

king·like [kíŋlàik] *adj.* like a king; grand. 왕 같은; 당당한.

King Log [⌐⌐] *n.* (from Aesop's fable) king only in name. 이름뿐인 무능한 왕.

king·ly [kíŋli] *adj.* (**-li·er, -li·est**) **1** of or like a king; royal. 왕의; 왕다운. ¶ ~ *power* 제왕 같은 위엄. **2** suitable for a king. 왕에 어울리는; 위엄 있는. ● **king·li·ness** [-nis] *n.*

King of Kings [⌐-⌐], **the** *n.* Jesus Christ; God. 예수; 하느님.

King's Counsel [⌐ ⌐-] *n.* 《Brit.》 a practising barrister appointed as a counsel to the crown. 왕실 고문 변호사(abbr. K.C.). 參考 여왕인 경우에는 Queen's Counsel 이라고 씀.

King's English [⌐ ⌐-], **the** *n.* standard, correct English. 표준 영어.

king·ship [kíŋʃip] *n.* Ⓤ the position, rank, or right of a king. 왕위; 왕권.

kink [kiŋk] *n.* Ⓒ **1** a twist or curl in rope, wire, thread, etc. (밧줄 따위의) 꼬임; 비틀림. **2** a muscular stiffness or pain in some part of the body. 근육의 경련; 쥐. **3** 《*colloq.*》 a mental twist; a strange idea. 변덕; 괴벽. — *vi., vt.* (P1; 6) form a kink; cause (something) to form a kink. 꼬이(게 하)다; 비틀(리)다. [Du.]

kink·y [kíŋki] *adj.* (**kink·i·er, kink·i·est**) full of kinks; tightly-curled; twisted. 꼬인; 비틀린.

kins·folk [kínzfòuk] *n. pl.* 《*collectively*》 relatives. 친척. [*kin*]

kin·ship [kínʃip] *n.* Ⓤ **1** relationship by birth or by marriage. 친척 관계. **2** the state of being similar in qualities. 유사; 근사. ¶ *There is close* ~ *in their ideas.* 그들의 생각은 아주 유사하다. [↑]

kins·man [kínzmən] *n.* Ⓒ (*pl.* **-men** [-mən]) a male relative. 친척〔집안〕의 남성.

kins·wom·an [kínzwùmən] *n.* Ⓒ (*pl.* **-wom·en** [-wìmin]) a female relative. 친척〔집안〕의 여성.

ki·osk [kiɑ́sk / -ɔ́sk] *n.* Ⓒ **1** a small building for selling newspapers, tobacco, etc., or used as a telephone box. 가판대(街販臺); 가두 매점; 공중 전화실. **2** a summerhouse in Turkey, etc. (터키 등지의) 정자. [Turk.]

kirk [kəːrk] *n.* Ⓒ 《Sc.》 a church. 교회. ¶ *go to* ～. [→church]

:kiss [kis] *n.* Ⓒ **1** a touch with the lips as a sign of love, respect, etc. 키스. **2** a slight touch. 가벼운 접촉.
— *vt.* **1** (P6) touch (something or someone) with the lips. …에 키스하다. ¶ ～ *a baby on its cheek* 아이 볼에 입맞추다. **2** touch (something) gently or lightly. 가볍게 닿다〔스치다〕. ¶ *A soft wind kissed the flowers.* 산들 바람이 꽃을 스쳐 갔다. — *vi.* (P1) **1** give a kiss to someone. 키스하다. ¶ *We kissed and parted.* 우리는 키스를 하고 헤어졌다. **2** come in gentle contact. 가볍게 닿다. ¶ *make glasses* ～ 술잔을 가볍게 대다. [E.]
kiss away, remove (something) with kisses. 키스해서 …을 지우다〔없애다〕. ¶ ～ *away a baby's tears* 아이에게 입맞춤해서 울음을 그치게 하다.
kiss one's hand to, wave a kiss to (someone). …에게 키스를 보내다.
kiss the dust 〔***ground***〕, **a)** yield. 항복하다. **b)** be killed. 살해되다.
kiss the rod, accept punishment without resistance. 순순히 벌을 받다.

kit[1] [kit] *n.* Ⓒ **1** a set of tools, materials, etc. for a particular job or purpose. 연장 한 벌. ¶ *a soldier's* ～ 군인의 개인 장비 일습 / *a shoemaker's* ～ 제화공의 연장 일습. **2** the case or bag for carrying or storing these tools. 연장통; 연장 주머니. **3** a circular wooden tub or pail. (둥근) 나무통; 들통. **4** 《*colloq.*》 a collection of persons or things; a set; a lot. (사람·물건의) 일단; 한 패; 한 벌. ¶ *a model airplane* ～ 모형 비행기의 부품 한 벌. [Du.]

kit[2] [kit] *n.* =kitten.

kit·bag [kítbæ̀g] *n.* Ⓒ a knapsack for a soldier; a traveling case. (군인의) 잡낭; (여행용) 행낭. [*kit*[1]]

:kitch·en [kítʃən] *n.* Ⓒ a room where food is cooked. 부엌; 취사장. [L. *coquo* cook]

kitch·en·er [kítʃənər] *n.* **1** a cooking-range. (취사·요리용) 레인지. **2** a person employed in a kitchen. 취사원.

kitch·en·ette, -et [kìtʃənét] *n.* Ⓒ a small, compact kitchen. (아파트 등의) 간이 부엌.

kitchen garden [⌐– ⌐–] *n.* a garden where vegetables and fruit are grown for a family's own use. (가정용의) 채마〔남새〕밭.

kitch·en·maid [kítʃənmèid] *n.* Ⓒ a female servant who helps a cook. (요리사 밑에서 일하는) 식모.

kitch·en·ware [kítʃənwɛ̀ər] *n.* Ⓤ instruments used in a kitchen for cooking, such as pots, pans, and kettles. 부엌 세간; 취사 용구.

***kite** [kait] *n.* Ⓒ **1** a light frame of wood covered with paper or cloth, designed to be flown in the air on the end of a string. 연. ¶ *fly a* ～ 연을 날리다; 여론을 살피다. **2** a bird of the hawk family with long narrow wings. 솔개. **3** someone who plays a trick on another; a rapacious person. 사기꾼; 탐욕스러운 사람. **4** 《*pl.*》 《comm.》 an accommodation bill. 융통 어음. — *vi.* (P1) 《*colloq.*》 fly like a kite. 솔개처럼 날다. — *vt.* (P6) 《comm.》 obtain through kites. 융통어음을 쓰다. [E.]

kite-fly·ing [káitflàiiŋ] *n.* Ⓤ the act of flying a kite. 연날리기.

kith [kiθ] *n.* Ⓤ 《*arch., dial.*》 《*collectively*》 friends; acquaintances. 친구; 아는 사람.
kith and kin, friends and relatives. 친지와 일가붙이. [E. =knowledge (→can)]

:kit·ten [kítn] *n.* Ⓒ a young cat. 새끼고양이. — *vi., vt.* (P1; 6) bear kittens; give birth to (kittens). (고양이가) 새끼를 낳다. [O.F. *chitoun,* →cat]

kit·ten·ish [kítniʃ] *adj.* **1** like a kitten. 고양이 새끼 같은. **2** playful. 까부는; 장난치는.

kit·tle [kítl] *adj.* difficult to deal with; troublesome. 다루기 힘든; 까다로운. [E. *kittle* trickle]

kittle cattle [⌐– ⌐–] *n.* ticklish persons or things. 다루기 힘든 사람〔것〕들.

kit·ty [kíti] *n.* Ⓒ (*pl.* **-ties**) a pet name for a cat or kitten. 고양이(새끼)《애칭》. [→kitten]

klax·on [klǽksən] *n.* a powerful electric horn. 클랙슨. [Trademark]

klep·to·ma·ni·a [klèptəméiniə] *n.* Ⓤ a morbid tendency to theft for its own sake. (병적인) 도벽(盜癖). [Gk. *kleptēs* thief, →mania]

klep·to·ma·ni·ac [klèptouméiniæk] *n.* a person who suffers from kleptomania. 도벽이 있는 사람.

km. **1** kilometer; kilometers. **2** kingdom.

knack [næk] *n.* Ⓒ a special skill or ability needed to do something. 기교; 요령. ¶ *get the* ～ *of serving in tennis* 테니스의 서브 요령을 익히다 / *I can't get the* ～ *of it.* 그 요령을 모르겠다. [M.E. =sharp blow]

knack·er [nǽkər] *n.* 《Brit.》 **1** a person who buys and slaughters useless horses and sells their flesh and skins. 폐마 도살업자. **2** a person who buys and breaks up old houses, ships, etc. and sells their materials. 폐가(廢家)〔폐선〕 처리업자.

knap·sack [nǽpsæ̀k] *n.* Ⓒ a leather or canvas bag for carrying food, clothes, etc. on the back. 냅색; 배낭. [Du. *knappen* bite, →sack]

***knave** [neiv] *n.* Ⓒ **1** a tricky, dishonest person; a rogue. 불량배; 악한. **2** a playing card with a picture of a soldier or ser-

K

vant on it; a jack. (카드놀이의) 잭. **3** 《*arch.*》 a male servant or serving boy. 남자 하인; 사동. [E. =boy, servant]

knav·er·y [néivəri] *n.* (*pl.* **-er·ies**) **1** Ⓤ behavior characteristic of a knave. 못된 짓; 비행(非行). **2** Ⓒ dishonest act. 부정 행위.

knav·ish [néiviʃ] *adj.* dishonest; like a knave. 옳지 못한; 부정한; 악한 같은. ¶ *a ~ trick* 악랄한 수법.

knead [ni:d] *vt.* (P6) **1** mix (dough, clay, etc.) and make into a mass. 반죽해서 (빵·도기(陶器) 등)을 만들다. **2** massage. (근육)을 안마하다. [E.]

:knee [ni:] *n.* Ⓒ the joint between the thigh and the lower leg; a similar joint in an animal; a stifle. 무릎(관절); (짐승의) 뒷다리 관절. ¶ *at one's mother's ~* 어머니 무릎에[슬하에] / *rise on the knees* 무릎으로 서다 / *on one's knees* 무릎 꿇고 / *up to one's knees in water* 무릎까지 물에 잠겨. [E.]

bend the knee to, kneel down to (someone) to beg; yield. …에게 탄원[굴복]하다.

bring someone to his knees, force (someone) to yield. …을 굴복시키다. 「돕다.

give* [*offer*] *a knee to, help (someone). …을

on the knees of the gods, beyond human ability or control; still undetermined. 인력(人力)이 미치지 못하는; 아직 미정의.

knee breeches [ㄹㄹ-] *n. pl.* breeches reaching to the knees. 반바지.

knee·cap [kí:kæ̀p] *n.* Ⓒ **1** the flat, movable bone that covers the front of the knee. 슬개골; 종지뼈. **2** a covering to protect the knee. 무릎받이《보호용》.

knee·deep [ní:dì:p] *adj.* as deep as the knees. 무릎 깊이의. ¶ *~ snow.*

knee·high [ní:hái] *adj.* as high as the knees. 무릎 높이의. ¶ *~ boots.*

***kneel** [ni:l] *vi.* (**knelt** or **kneeled**) (P1,2A, 2B,4) 《*over*》 rest on the bended knees. 무릎을 꿇다. ¶ *~ in prayer* 무릎 꿇고 기도하다 / *~ down to pull a weed* 풀을 뽑으려고 무릎을 굽히다. [→knee]

knell [nel] *n.* Ⓒ 《*a ~* or *the ~*》 **1** the sound of a bell, esp. after a death or at a funeral. 조종(弔鐘). **2** a sign of misfortune, ruin, or failure. 흉조(凶兆). ¶ *sound* [*ring*] *the ~ of the old days* 구시대의 종말을 고하다 / *The decision sounded the ~ of our hopes.* 그 결정으로 우리의 희망은 사라졌다. **3** a mournful sound. 구슬픈 소리. [E.]

knelt [nelt] *v.* p. and pp. of **kneel**.

:knew [nju:] *v.* p. of **know**.

knick·er·bock·ers [níkərbɑ̀kərz / -bɔ̀k-] *n. pl.* short, wide breeches fastened at the knee. 니커보커《무릎 아래서 졸라매는 헐렁한 바지》. [(W. Irving's) *History of New York*]

〈knickerbockers〉

knick·ers [níkərz] *n. pl.* **1** =knickerbockers. **2** a woman's drawers; bloomers. 블루머《니커보커형의 여자 바지》.

knick·knack, nick·nack [níknæ̀k] *n.* Ⓒ **1** a trifle; a toy. 하찮은 물건; 장난감. **2** a small ornamental article. 자질구레한 장신구; 방물. [*knack* in obsolete sense *trinket*]

:knife [naif] *n.* Ⓒ (*pl.* **knives**) **1** a cutting instrument with a sharp-edged blade and handle. 칼; 찬칼; 나이프. ¶ *a table ~* 식탁용 나이프 / *a pocket-knife* 주머니 칼 / *The north wind cuts like a ~.* 북풍이 살을 에는 듯이 차다. **2** a sharp blade forming a part of a tool or machine. (연장의) 날. ¶ *the knives of a lawn-mower* 잔디깎개의 날. **3** ⓐ a cutting instrument used in surgical treatment. 수술칼; 메스. ¶ *the surgeon's ~* 메스. ⓑ 《*the ~*》《*colloq.*》 surgical operations. (외과) 수술. ¶ *be* [*go*] *under the ~* 수술을 받고 있다[받다] / *She died under the ~.* 그녀는 수술 중에 죽었다.

before one could say knife, without a moment's delay; very quickly or suddenly. 느닷없이; 순식간에.

get one's knife into someone, 《*colloq.*》 bear someone ill will. …에게 원한을 품다. ¶ *I got my ~ into him.* 그 자에게 원한이 있다.

play a good knife and fork, eat heartily. 실컷 먹다; 포식하다.

war to the knife, war without mercy; a bitter and unsparing fight. 혈전; 사투.

— *vi.* (P6) cut or kill (something or someone) with a knife. …을 칼로 베다[죽이다]. [E.]

:knight [nait] *n.* Ⓒ **1** a mounted soldier of noble birth who served his king or lord in the Middle Ages. 기사(騎士); 무사. **2** 《Brit.》 a man who has been raised to an honorable rank next below a baronet. 나이트작(爵); 훈작사(勳爵士). 參考 Sir 의 칭호가 허용됨. **3** 《chess》 the piece with a horse's head. 나이트. **4** a man devoted to the service or protection of a lady. 여성에게 헌신적인 남자.

a knight of the pen, a journalist. 기자.

a knight of the road, a highwayman. 노상(路上) 강도.

knight of the shire, 《Brit. hist.》 a person representing a shire in the Parliament. 주(州) 출신 국회의원.

— *vt.* (P6) make a knight of; raise to the rank of knight. …에게 나이트 작위를 수여하다. ¶ *He was knighted by the king.* 그는 왕으로부터 나이트 작위를 받았다. [E. =lad, servant]

knight-er·rant [náitérənt] *n.* Ⓒ (*pl.* **knights-**) a knight traveling in search of adventure in the Middle Ages. (중세의) 무술 수련자; 협객(俠客). [↑]

knight-er·rant·ry [náitérəntri] *n.* Ⓤ the actions of a knight-errant. 무술 수련 행위; 의협적 행위.

knight·hood [náithùd] *n.* Ⓤ **1** the

rank, character, or dignity of a knight. 나이트의 신분·기질·위신; 기사도(騎士道). **2** 《*collectively*》 a body of knights; the class of knights. 기사단.

knight·ly [náitli] *adj.* of or like a knight; brave. 기사의; 기사다운; 의협적인.

:knit [nit] *v.* (**knit·ted** or **knit, knit·ting**) *vt.* (P6,7) **1** make (something) by looping a thread or yarn on needles. …을 뜨다; 짜다. ¶ ~ *a sweater* 스웨터를 뜨다 / ~ *wool into socks* 털실로 양말을 뜨다 / ~ *stockings out of wool* 털실로 스타킹을 뜨다. **2** unite (something) closely; join. …을 밀착시키다; 접합하다; 결합하다. ¶ ~ *one's fingers* 깍지 끼다 / *persons* ~ *together in affection* 〔*by common interests*〕 애정으로〔같은 이해 관계로〕 결합된 사람들 / *A surgeon knits broken bones together again.* 의사가 부러진 뼈를 다시 맞춘다. —*vi.* (P1) **1** make something by looping thread or yarn together. 뜨개질하다. ¶ *She knitted all day long.* 그녀는 온종일 뜨개질을 했다. **2** become united closely. 결합하다. ¶ *A broken bone soon knits.* 부러진 뼈는 쉬 붙는다. [E.]

knit in, mix in knitting. 섞어 짜다. ¶ ~ *in the green with the blue wool* 초록과 남빛 털실을 섞어 짜다.

knit up, **a**) repair (something) by knitting. 짜깁다. **b**) conclude. (토론 등을) 종결하다.

knit·ted [nítid] *adj.* made by knitting. 짠; 뜬.

knit·ting [nítiŋ] *n.* Ⓤ the act of weaving a garment, etc. with needles; knitted work. 뜨개질; 편물.

knitting needle [⌐– ⌐–] *n.* a long needle used for knitting. 뜨개바늘.

:knives [naivz] *n.* pl. of **knife.**

knob [nɑb / nɔb] *n.* Ⓒ **1** a small round lump on a surface; a knot. 혹; 마디; 옹이. **2** the rounded handle of a door, drawer, etc. (문 따위의) 손잡이. [E.]

knob·by [nábi / nɔ́bi] *adj.* (**-bi·er, -bi·est**) covered with knobs; like a knob. 혹이〔마디가〕 많은; 혹 같은.

:knock [nɑk / nɔk] *vt.* **1** (P6,7,13) give a blow to (someone or something); hit. …을 두드리다; 치다. ¶ ~ *a ball hard with a bat* 배트로 공을 세게 치다 / ~ (*at* 〔*on*〕) *a door several times* 문을 여러 번 두드리다 / ~ *something from one's hand* …을 쳐서 손에서 떨어뜨리다. **2** (P13,18) ⓐ hit or strike sharply against (something). …에 부딪치다. ¶ ~ *one's foot against a stone* 발을 돌에 부딪치다. ⓑ make or cause by knocking. 쳐서 …이 되게 하다. ¶ ~ *a hole in a wall* 때려서 벽에 구멍을 내다 / ~ *someone senseless* 아무를 때려서 의식을 잃게 하다. **3** (P6) 《*colloq.*》 find fault with (something); depreciate. …의 흠을 들춰내다; 탈잡다. **4** (P6) 《Brit. *sl.*》 impress greatly; surprise. 감동시키다; 놀라게 하다. ¶ *His rudeness knocked me completely.* 그 자의 방자함에는 두 손 들었다.

—*vi.* (P1,3) **1** strike a blow with something hard. 두드리다; 치다. ¶ ~ *gently on* 〔*at*〕 *the door* 문을 가볍게 노크하다. **2** make a continuous noise by hitting heavily. 연타음(連打音)을 내다; (내연 기관이) 노킹을 일으키다. ¶ *The engine of this car is knocking badly.* 이 차의 엔진은 노킹이 심하다. **3** find fault. 헐뜯다. ¶ *They are always knocking.* 그들은 늘 남을 헐뜯기만 한다.

knock about, **a**) damage (someone or something) with blows or falls. (타격 등으로) …을 못쓰게 만들다; 해치다. **b**) treat or handle roughly. 거칠게 다루다; 학대하다. ¶ *He was badly knocked about.* 그는 몹시 구박받았다. **c**) wander over; lead an unsettled life. 방황하다; 불안정하게 지내다. ¶ *He has knocked about the world a great deal.* 그는 무척이나 세상을 방황했다.

knock at an open door, make useless or unnecessary efforts. 쓸데없는 짓을 하다.

knock down, **a**) knock or strike to the ground. …을 때려눕히다. ¶ *be knocked down by a motorcar* 차에 받혀 넘어지다. **b**) pull down; destroy. …을 분해〔해체〕하다; 때려부수다. ¶ ~ *down a house* 〔*machine*〕 집을 허물다〔기계를 분해하다〕 / ~ *an argument down* 찍소리 못 하게 만들다. **c**) 《*colloq.*》 lower (the price of); reduce. (값)을 깎아 내리다; 감하다. **d**) sell for the highest offer in auction. 낙찰시키다. ¶ *The picture was knocked down to Mr. Wilkinson for a hundred pounds.* 그림은 윌킨슨 씨에게 백 파운드로 낙찰되었다.

knock one's head against, come up against an obstacle; meet with an unexpected opposition. (뜻밖의) 장애물 (등)을 만나다. ¶ ~ *one's head against hard problems* 어려운 문제에 맞닥뜨리다.

knock in 〔***into***〕, **a**) drive or beat (a nail, etc.) in. (못 따위)를 …에 때려박다. **b**) teach (a lesson, rule., etc.) repeatedly so that it shall not be forgotten. (잊지 않게) …을 머리에 주입시키다.

knock into a cocked hat, make (someone) speechless; ruin (a plan, etc.); defeat (an argument) completely. 군소리 못하게 만들다; (계획)을 잡쳐 놓다; 철저하게 논파(論破)하다.

knock into the middle of next week, 《*colloq.*》 beat severely; thrash; punish. …을 두들겨 패다; 매질하다; 처벌하다.

knock off, **a**) strike or brush away. …을 털어〔쫓아〕 버리다. ¶ ~ *a bee off one's hand* 손에서 벌을 쫓아 버리다. **b**) take off from price; deduct. (값)을 깎다. ¶ ~ *off two shillings from the price* 값에서 2실링을 깎다. **c**) 《*colloq.*》 finish quickly or roughly. 급히〔아무렇게나〕 해치우다. ¶ ~ *off a picture* 후딱 그림 한 장 그리다. **d**) 《*colloq.*》 finish or stop (work). (일)을 마치다; 그만두다. ¶ *We usually* ~ *off at one for lunch.* 우리는 점심을 먹기 위해 한 시에는 일을 쉰다.

knock on the head, **a**) kill or make senseless with a blow. …을 때려 죽이다〔기절하게 만들다〕. **b**) destroy, defeat, or ruin. 때려 부수다; 망치다.
knock out, **a**) 《boxing》 defeat (an opponent) by knocking him down to the ground. …을 녹아웃시키다(cf. *knockout*). **b**) strike (someone) senseless. …을 때려 실신하게 만들다.
knock the bottom out of, make of no account (an argument etc.); destroy; defeat. (의논·계획 따위)를 송두리째 뒤엎다; 무효화하다.
knock together, **a**) strike one thing against another. …을 맞부딪치다. ¶ ~ *their heads together* 강경한 수단으로 싸움을 말리다. **b**) build or make up hastily. …을 부랴부랴 만들다.
knock up, **a**) 《Brit. *colloq.*》 rouse from sleep. (문을 두드려) …을 깨우다. ¶ *Knock me up at 7 o'clock.* 일곱 시에 두드려 깨워주시오. **b**) tire out; exhaust. …을 지치게 하다. ¶ *The long climb knocked me up.* 오래 등산했더니 지쳐버렸다. **c**) put together roughly and hastily. 급히〔날림으로〕 만들다. ¶ ~ *up a hut.*
— *n.* Ⓒ **1** (esp. at the door) a blow; a rap. (문을) 두드림; 노크; 그 소리. **2** a severe misfortune or hardship. 큰 타격. [E.]

knock·a·bout [nákəbàut / nɔ́k-] *n.* Ⓒ **1** a small sailing yacht. 소형 돛배. **2** a foolish comedy; a comedian. 우습지도 않은 코미디; 그 연기자. — *adj.* **1** noisy; rough. 시끄러운. **2** (of a garment, etc.) fit for rough use. 막 일할 때 입는.

knock·down [nákdàun / nɔ́k-] *n.* Ⓒ **1** the act of knocking down. 구타; 때려눕힘. **2** something that overwhelms. 압도적인 것. — *adj.* **1** that can knock down; overwhelming. 때려눕힐 수 있는; 압도적인. **2** that can be taken apart. 분해〔해체〕할 수 있는; 조립식의.

knock·er [nákər / nɔ́k-] *n.* Ⓒ a person or a thing that knocks; a small metal striker, etc. fixed to a door. 두드리는 사람〔물건〕; (문의) 노커.

〈knocker〉

up to the knocker, throughly well. 나무랄 데 없이.

knock·out [nákàut / nɔ́k-] *n.* Ⓒ **1** ⓐ the act of knocking out. 때려눕힘; 타도. ⓑ 《boxing》 the final and decisive blow which makes one boxer lose consciousness. 녹아웃. 參考 k.o., K.O.로 생략함. **2** (at an auction) a plot between buyers to secure a lot cheap by avoiding competition and assign it privately afterwards. 서로 짜고 헐값에 낙찰시키는 일. **3** 《*colloq.*》 a very attractive person; a striking thing. 굉장한 사람〔물건〕. — *adj.* 《*colloq.*》 that knocks out; overwhelming. 녹아웃의; 압도적인.

knoll [noul] *n.* Ⓒ a rounded small hill. 둥그런 언덕; 작은 야산. [E.]

·**knot** [nat / nɔt] *n.* Ⓒ **1** the place where two strings, ropes, etc. are tied. 매듭; 고. ¶ *a ~ in a rope* 밧줄의 매듭 / *tie a rope in a ~ =tie a ~ in a rope* 밧줄에 고를 짓다. **2** an ornamental bow of ribbon, etc. (리본 등의) 장식 매듭. ¶ *a shoulder-knot* 견장(肩章). **3** a hard, round lump in a piece of wood, etc. (목재 따위의) 옹이. **4** a group of persons or things. (사람·물건의) 무리; 일단. ¶ *a ~ of people* 일단의 사람들. **5** a difficult or complicated problem. 어려운〔골치 아픈〕 문제. ¶ *tie oneself (up) in* 〔*into*〕 *knots* 골치 아픈 일에 말려들다. **6** a tie; a bond. 인연; 연분. ¶ *the marriage ~* 부부의 인연 / *tie the ~* 짝짓다; 짝지우다. **7** 《naut.》 a unit for measuring the speed of ships at sea. 노트.
cut the knot, solve a problem, etc. quickly by force. 난문제를 대번에 처리하다.
in knots, by twos or threes. 삼삼 오오. ¶ *gather in knots* 삼삼오오 무리지어 모이다.
— *vt., vi.* (**knot·ted, knot·ting**) (P6,7; 1) tie (something) in a knot; tie together (two strings); make or form a knot; tie together. 매듭을 짓다; 매다; 매듭이 되다; 맺어지다. [E.]

knot·hole [náthòul / nɔ́t-] *n.* Ⓒ a round hole in a board where a knot has fallen out. (널판의) 옹이 구멍.

knot·less [nátlis / nɔ́t-] *adj.* without a knot. 매듭이〔옹이가〕 없는.

knot·ted [nátid / nɔ́t-] *adj.* having a knot or knots. 매듭이〔옹이가〕 있는.

knot·ti·ness [nátinis / nɔ́t-] *n.* Ⓤ **1** the state of being full of knots. 매듭이 많음; 옹이투성이. **2** difficulty. 곤란; 어려움.

knot·ty [náti / nɔ́t-] *adj.* (**-ti·er, -ti·est**) **1** full of knots. 매듭이 많은. **2** difficult to solve. 해결이 어려운. ¶ *a ~ problem.*

knout [naut] *n.* Ⓒ a whip formerly used in Russia to inflict punishment upon criminals. 매; 태형구(笞刑具). — *vi.* (P6) whip (criminals, etc.) with a knout. 매질하다; 태형을 가하다. [Russ. *knut*]

:**know** [nou] *v.* (**knew, known**) *vt.* **1** (P6, 10,11,12,21,22) ⓐ be aware, sure, or informed of (something); have knowledge of (something) by experience or study. …을 알다; 알고 있다. ¶ *I ~ nothing about it.* 거기에 대해 아는 바가 없다 / *Do you ~ whether she will come or not?* 그녀가 올지 안 올지 알고 있나 / *I ~ him to be honest.* 나는 그가 정직하다는 것을 알고 있다 / *Every boy knows one and one make two.* 하나 더하기 하나가 둘이라는 것을 모르는 아이는 없다 / *I don't ~ how to spell the word.* 그 낱말을 어떻게 쓰는지 나는 모른다 / *I ~ that he is here.* 그가 여기 있다는 것을 나는 안다. ⓑ have clearly in the mind or memory. …을 기억하고 있다. ¶ *I ~ the poem by heart.* 그 시를 암기하고 있

다. **2** (P6) be acquainted with (someone). …와 아는 사이다. ¶ *Do you ~ Mr. Johnson?* 존슨과는 아는 사이냐 / *He knows his Ch'unch'ŏn very well.* 그는 제고장 춘천 지리에 훤하다. **3** (P6,7) be familiar with; be versed in (something). …을 잘 알다; …에 정통하다. ¶ *I ~ the road.* 이 길은 잘 안다 / *Do you ~ French?* 프랑스 말을 잘 하나. **4** (P6,7,13) 《*from*》 be able to distinguish (something); 《as》 recognize. …을 구별할 줄 알다; 식별할 수 있다. ¶ *I wouldn't ~ him in a crowd.* 군중 속에서 그를 찾아내지 못할 것 같다 / *He knows good poems when he reads them.* 그는 시를 읽으면 그 시의 좋고 나쁜 것을 알아본다 / *It is hard to ~ an Englishman from an American.* 미국인과 영국인을 식별하기는 어렵다. **5** (P6) have experience of. …을 체험하다. ¶ *~ life* 〔*poverty and sorrow*〕 인생〔가난과 슬픔〕을 알다 / *He has known better days.* 그에게도 좋은 시절이 있었다.
— *vi.* (P1,3) be informed. 알고 있다; 알다. ¶ *His father has just died. —Yes, I ~.* 그의 부친이 방금 돌아가셨단다. —응, 안다 / *I ~ of a shop where you can get the things cheaper.* 물건을 더 싸게 살 수 있는 가게를 알고 있다.
***know better** (**than ...**),* be wise enough not to do; be not so foolish as to do. (…할 만큼) 어리석지는 않다. ¶ *I ~ better than to quarrel.* 싸울 만큼 어리석진 않다 / *You ought to ~ better.* 좀더 분별이 있어야지.
know one's own business, not interfere with the affairs of others. 남의 일에 참견하지 않다; 제 분수를 알다.
make oneself known, introduce oneself. 자기 소개를 하다. ┌ken]
— *n.* knowledge. 지식; 앎; 숙지. [E. →can,
be in the know, 《*colloq.*》 have special information. 사정〔내막〕에 밝다.

know·a·ble [nóuəbəl] *adj.* that can be known. 알 수 있는.

know-how [nóuhàu] *n.* Ⓤ 《U.S. *colloq.*》 the knowledge, the ability, the technique, etc. of how to do something. 지식; 능력; 기술; 노하우. ¶ *This business requires a lot of ~.* 이 사업은 많은 노하우가 필요하다.

•**know·ing** [nóuiŋ] *adj.* **1** having knowledge; well-informed. 지식이 있는; 정통한. ¶ *a ~ man* 식자(識者). **2** clever; intelligent; shrewd; showing special knowledge. 영리한; 약은; 빈틈 없는; 아는 체하는. ¶ *a ~ look* 아는 체하는 표정.

know·ing·ly [nóuiŋli] *adv.* **1** in a knowing manner. 아는 체하고. **2** on purpose. 의도적으로. ¶ *He has not ~ hurt my feelings.* 그가 일부러 나를 기분 나쁘게 한 것은 아니다.

:**knowl·edge** [nálidʒ / nɔ́l-] *n.* Ⓤ **1** 《sometimes *a ~*》 what someone knows or acquires through study, experience, etc. 지식. ¶ *He has a lot of ~.* 그는 아는 게 많다 / *gain practical ~* 실제적인 지식을 얻다. **2** learning. 학문; 학식. ¶ *the branches of ~* 학문의 분야 / *the progress of human ~* 인지의 발달 / *build up accurate ~ on a subject* 어떤 문제에 정확한 학식을 쌓아올리다. **3** familiarity; the state or act of knowing; understanding. 익히 앎; 숙지; 이해. ¶ *the ~ of good and evil* 선악의 인식〔판별〕 / *The ~ of his success caused great joy.* 그의 성공을 알고 무척 기뻤다. [→know]
come to someone's knowledge, come to be known. …에게 알려지다.
to (***the best of***) ***one's knowledge,*** as far as one knows. …가 알기로는.
without the knowledge of (= *not being known to*) *someone.* …에게 알리지 않고.

:**known** [noun] *v.* pp. of **know.** — *adj.* familiar. 알려진.

know-noth·ing [nóunʌ̀θiŋ] *n.* Ⓒ an ignorant person. 무식한 사람. — *adj.* completely ignorant. 무지한; 판무식의.

knuck·le [nʌ́kəl] *n.* Ⓒ **1** a finger joint, esp. at the root of a finger of the hand. 손가락 관절. **2** the knee joint of a calf or pig, used as food. (소·돼지의) 무릎 도가니. ¶ *pigs' knuckles* 돼지 족발.
— *vt., vi.* (P6; 2A, 2B) strike or press with the knuckles; strike with a fist; shoot (a marble, etc.) with the fingers. 손가락 마디로 치다〔밀다〕; 주먹으로 때리다; (공깃돌 같은 것을) 손가락으로 튀기다. [E.]
knuckle down, **a**) submit; surrender. 항복하다. **b**) work hard. 열심히 일하다.
knuckle under, 《*to*》 submit; yield; surrender. 굴복〔항복〕하다.

knurl [nəːrl] *n.* Ⓒ **1** a knot on an old tree, etc. 마디; 옹이. **2** a small ridge on the edge of a coin, etc. (동전 가장자리 등의) 깔쭉깔쭉함; 우툴두툴함. [M.E. *knorre*]

knurl·y [nə́ːrli] *adj.* (**knurl·i·er, knurl·i·est**) full of knurls. 마디〔옹이〕가 많은; 혹투성이의.

K.O., k.o. [kéióu] *n.* Ⓒ (*pl.* **K.O.'s** or **k.o.'s**) knockout. 녹아웃.

ko·peck [kóupek] *n.* the 100th part of a ruble, money used in Russia. 코펙(러시아의 동화(銅貨), 1/100 루블). [Russ.]

Ko·ran [kouræ̃n, -rάːn, kɔːrάːn] *n.* 《usu. *the ~*》 the holy book of the Mohammedans. 코란. [Arab.]

:**Ko·re·a** [kəríːə, kouríːə] *n.* a country on a peninsula in east Asia. 한국. [*Koryo* 高麗]

:**Ko·re·an** [kəríːən / kouríːən] *adj.* of Korea; of its people or their language. 한국의; 한국인〔어〕의. — *n.* **1** Ⓒ a person of Korea. 한국인. **2** Ⓤ the language of Korea. 한국어.

kow·tow [káutáu], **ko·tow** [kóutáu] 《Chin.》 *n.* the former Chinese custom of touching the ground with the forehead as a sign of respect. 고두(叩頭). — *vi.* (P1,3) **1** make a kowtow. 고두하다. **2** show submissive respect. 아부하다. ¶ *He'll never ~ to such a man.* 그가 그런 사람에게 아부할 리가 없다. [Chin. *K'ou-t'ou* 叩頭]

kw, kW, kw. kilowatt.

Ky. Kentucky.

L

L, l [el] *n.* Ⓒ (*pl.* **L's, Ls, l's, ls** [elz]) **1** the twelfth letter of the English alphabet. 영어 알파벳의 열두째 글자. **2** anything shaped like the letter L. L자(字) 모양의 것. **3** the Roman numeral for 50. 로마 숫자의 50. ¶ *LVIII,* 58 / *CL,* 150.

L. £. =pound.

la [lɑ(:)] *n.* 《mus.》 the sixth tone of the scale. 라《장음계의 여섯째 음》.

La. Louisiana.

Lab. Labor; Labrador.

lab. laboratory.

*__la·bel__ [léibəl] *n.* Ⓒ **1** a small piece of paper or other material attached to an article and giving information about it. 라벨; 레테르; 찌지; 꼬리표. ¶ *stick labels on the jar* 항아리에 레테르를 붙이다. **2** a short phrase or catchword applied to persons, a theory, etc. 부호; 표지(標識).
— *vt.* (**-beled, -bel·ing** or 《Brit.》 **-belled, -bel·ling**) (P6) **1** put a label on (something). …에 레테르[쪽지]를 붙이다. ¶ *The bottle was labelled 'Poison'.* 그 병에는 '독약'이라는 쪽지가 붙어 있었다. **2** put (something) in a class; call (someone) as…; name. …으로 분류하다; 레테르를 붙이다; …라고 부르다. ¶ ~ *someone a miser* 아무를 구두쇠라고 부르다; 구두쇠란 딱지를 붙이다. [F.]

la·bi·al [léibiəl] *adj.* **1** of the lips. 입술의. **2** 《phon.》 produced by nearly closing, or rounding the lips. 순음(脣音)의. — *n.* Ⓒ 《phon.》 a sound produced in this way, such as p, b, and m. 순음. [L. *labium* lip]

la·bi·o·den·tal [lèibioudéntl] *adj., n.* Ⓒ 《phon.》 (a sound) formed with the lower lip and the teeth, such as f, v. 순치음(脣齒音)(의). [↑]

:__la·bor,__ 《Brit.》 **-bour** [léibər] *n.* **1** Ⓤ work; toil. 노동; 노력; 근로. ¶ *hard* ~ 중노동; 징역 / *with* ~ 힘들여 / *lost* ~ 헛수고. **2** Ⓒ a piece of work; a task. (어떤 하나의) 일. ¶ ~ *of love* (보수 없이) 좋아서 하는 일; 독지사업. **3** Ⓤ persons who work with their own hands; 《*collectively*》 all wage-earning workers. 노동자 (계급); 임금[근육] 노동자. ¶ *a* ~ *and capital* 노동자와 자본가; 노사 / *a Labor Exchange* 직업 소개소 / *the claims of* ~ 노동자의 요구 / *The skilled* ~ *is scarce.* 숙련공이 드물다. **4** 《*pl.*》 ordinary affairs of life. 세상사; 세속의 일. ¶ *His labors are over.* 그의 일생은 끝났다. **5** Ⓤ the pains and efforts of childbirth; the period of these. 진통; 산고(産苦); 진통 기간. ¶ *easy* [*hard*] ~ 순산[난산] / *be in* ~ 산기(産氣)가 있다.
— *vi.* **1** (P1,2A,3,4) do work; work hard; toil. 일하다; 노동하다; 노력하다; 애쓰다. ¶ ~ *after wealth* 부를 얻으려 노력하다 / ~ *to finish a piece of work* 한 가지 일을 마치려 힘쓰다 / ~ *to understand what is said* 무슨 말인지 이해하려고 애쓰다. **2** (P1,2A,3) move slowly and with difficulty; pitch and roll heavily. 애쓰며 나아가다; 배가 난항(難航)하다. ¶ *The old car labored up the hill.* 고물차가 언덕을 힘들게 올라갔다 / ~ *through a heavy sea* 거친 바다를 난항하다. **3** (P1) have the pains of childbirth. 산고를 겪다; 진통하다.
— *vt.* (P6) work out (something) in too much detail; explain in great detail. …을 (지나칠 정도로) 상세히 설명하다; 상론(詳論)하다. [L. *lăbor*]

*__lab·o·ra·to·ry__ [lǽbərətɔ̀:ri / ləbɔ́rətəri] *n.* Ⓒ (*pl.* **-ries**) **1** a place used for scientific work. 실험실; 연구소. **2** a place where drugs, chemicals, etc. are made. 제약소. [↑]

Labor Day [´-`] *n.* 《U.S.》 a legal holiday in honor of labor, in most States of the United States on the first Monday in September. 노동절

la·bored, 《Brit.》 **-boured** [léibərd] *adj.* **1** showing signs of great care or effort. 애쓴 흔적이 있는. ¶ *a very* ~ *poem* 아주 공들여 지은 시. **2** not natural; forced. 부자연한; 억지의. ¶ *a* ~ *smile* 억지 웃음 / *a* ~ *speech* 부자연스런 연설. **3** hard; painful. 힘드는; 곤란한. ¶ ~ *breathing* 가쁜 숨.

·__la·bor·er,__ 《Brit.》 **-bour·er** [léibərər] *n.* Ⓒ a worker, esp. one who works with his hands. (육체) 노동자; 인부.

la·bor·ing, 《Brit.》 **-bour·ing** [léibəriŋ] *adj.* **1** habitually engaged in labor. 노동에 종사하는. ¶ *a* ~ *man* 노동자 / *the* ~ *classes* 노동 계급. **2** troubled. 고생하는; 괴로워하는. **3** rolling or pitching heavily. 몹시 흔들리는.

la·bo·ri·ous [ləbɔ́:riəs] *adj.* **1** requiring hard work; difficult; toilsome. 힘드는; 어려운; 고된. ¶ ~ *work* [*duties*] 힘든 일[임무] / *a* ~ *enterprise* 힘든 사업. **2** hard-working; industrious; diligent. 근면한; 부지런한. ¶ *a* ~ *worker* 근면한 일꾼 / *Ants are* ~ *insect.* 개미는 부지런한 곤충이다. **3** showing signs of effort; labored. 고심한[애쓴] 흔적이 보이는. ¶ *a* ~ *style* 공들인 문체. [*labor*]

la·bo·ri·ous·ly [ləbɔ́:riəsli] *adv.* with great effort. 고생하여; 애써서.

la·bor-sav·ing, 《Brit.》 **-bour-** [léibərsèiviŋ] *adj.* designed to reduce the amount of work required. 노력을 절약하는. ¶ *a* ~ *appliance* 생력(省力) 기구.

labor union [∠– ∠–] *n.* 《U.S.》 an association of workers to protect and promote the welfare, interests, and rights of its members. 노동 조합(cf. 《Brit.》 *trade union*).

:la·bour [léibər] *n., v.* 《Brit.》 =labor.

la·boured [léibərd] *adj.* 《Brit.》 =labored.

la·bour·er [léibərər] *n.* 《Brit.》 =laborer.

la·bour·ing [léibəriŋ] *adj.* 《Brit.》 =laboring.

La·bour·ite [léibəràit] *n.* Ⓒ 《Brit.》 a member of the British Labour Party. 노동당원. [*labor*]

la·bur·num [ləbə́:rnəm] *n.* Ⓒ 《bot.》 a small tree of the pea family with hanging clusters of yellow flowers. 콩과(科)의 낙엽 교목의 하나. [L.]

lab·y·rinth [lǽbərìnθ] *n.* Ⓒ **1** a complex network of winding paths through which it is hard to find one's way; a maze. 미궁(迷宮); 미로(迷路). **2** a complicated affairs. 복잡한〔뒤얽힌〕 사정. [Gk.]

lab·y·rin·thine [læ̀bərínθi(:)n / -θain] *adj.* of or like a labyrinth; confusing; complicated. 미궁 같은; 얽히고 설킨.

lac [læk] *n.* a kind of resinous substance, used in making varnishes, dyes, etc. 랙《니스의 원료》. [Skr.]

:lace [leis] *n.* **1** Ⓤ an ornamental fabric of fine threads made in various designs. (장식용) 레이스. **2** Ⓒ a string or cord passed through holes for fastening shoes, etc. (구두 따위의) 끈; 끈〔엮은〕 끈. ¶ *shoe laces* 구두끈. **3** Ⓤ an ornamental braid of gold or silver. (금·은의) 몰《군복 따위의 장식용 끈》. ¶ *gold* 〔*silver*〕 ～ 금〔은〕몰. **4** Ⓤ a small amount of brandy, gin, etc. added to another liquid. (다른 음료에 섞는) 소량의 브랜디; 진 (따위).
— *vt.* (P6,7) **1** fasten (something) with a lace. …을 끈으로 묶다〔매다〕. ¶ ～ (*up*) *one's shoes* 구두끈을 매다. **2** decorate (something) with lace. 레이스로 장식하다. ¶ *a laced coat* 〔*hat*〕 레이스로 장식한 코트〔모자〕 / *cloth laced with gold* 금몰로 장식한 옷. **3** weave (something) together. …을 섞어 짜다. **4** put (a cord) through a hole. 구멍에 (끈을) 꿰다. **5** add liquor to some drink. (홍차 등)에 알코올 음료를 섞다〔타다〕. ¶ *a cup of tea laced with brandy* 브랜디를 조금 탄 한 잔의 홍차. **6** 《*colloq.*》 lash; beat. …을 채찍질하다; 때리다. **7** compress one's waist. 허리를 졸라매다. — *vi.* (P1,2A) be fastened with a lace. 끈으로 매다〔매어지다〕. [L. *laqueus* noose]
lace into, 《*colloq.*》 **a**) attack physically …을 매질하다. **b**) criticize sharply. …을 매섭게 비난하다.

lace boots [∠∠] *n. pl.* boots fastened with laces. 편상화(編上靴).

lac·er·ate [lǽsərèit] *vt.* (P6) **1** tear (something) roughly. …을 찢다. **2** hurt (the feelings, etc.). (기분 따위)를 상하게 하다. [L.]

lac·er·a·tion [læ̀səréiʃən] *n.* **1** Ⓤ the act of lacerating. (잡아) 찢음. **2** Ⓒ a tear; a wound. 찢어진 상처; 열상(裂傷).

lace·work [léiswə̀:rk] *n.* Ⓤ **1** lace. 레이스 (세공). **2** any openwork like lace. 레이스 모양의 성긴 뜨개질. [*lace*]

lach·ry·mal [lǽkrəməl] *adj.* of or for tears. 눈물의. ¶ *the* ～ *gland* 누선(涙腺); 눈물샘. — *n.* 《*pl.*》 the glands that produce tears. 누선; 눈물샘. [L. *lacrima* tear]

:lack [læk] *vt.* (P6) do not have enough of (something); be without; be short of. …이 없다〔부족하다〕. ¶ *He lacks common sense.* 상식이 모자란다 / *A desert lacks water.* 사막엔 물이 없다. — *vi.* (P1,3) be wanting or missing; be short; be in need. 결핍하다; 모자라다. ¶ *He is lacking in courage.* 용기가 부족하다 / *Money is lacking.* 돈이 달린다.
— *n.* **1** Ⓤ want; shortage. 결핍; 부족. **2** Ⓒ that which is wanted. 부족한 것. ¶ *The plants died for* ～ *of water.* 그 나무는 물이 모자라 죽었다. [E.]
no lack of, enough. 충분한. ¶ *There is no* ～ *of money* 〔*food*〕. 돈〔식량〕은 얼마든지 있다.

lack·ey, lac·quey [lǽki] *n.* Ⓒ **1** a male servant; a footman. 종복(從僕); 마부. **2** a follower who does not have his own will; a servile follower. 추종자; 아첨꾼. — *vt.* (P6) serve (someone) as a lackey. 종복으로서 섬기다; 빌붙다. [F.]

lack·ing [lǽkiŋ] *prep.* without. …없이; …이 없으면. ¶ *Lacking water, we can't live.* 물이 없으면 우리는 못 산다 / *Nothing is* ～ *for your comfort.* 당신의 안락을 위해 부족한 것은 하나도 없다. [*lack*]

lack·lus·ter, 《Brit.》 **-tre** [lǽklʌ̀stər] *adj.* lusterless; dull. 광택이 없는; 활기 없는. [*lack, lustre*]

la·con·ic [ləkɑ́nik / -kɔ́n-] *adj.* using few words; concise. 군말이 없는; 간결한. [Gk.]

la·con·i·cal·ly [ləkɑ́nikəli / -kɔ́n-] *adv.* in a laconic manner; concisely. 말수가 적게; 간결히.

lac·quer [lǽkər] *n.* Ⓤ **1** a hard, bright, smooth varnish shellac made from sap of the sumac tree, etc. used for covering wood, etc. 래커; 옻. **2** 《*collectively*》 wooden articles covered with lacquer. 칠기(漆器). — *vt.* (P6,13,18) cover (something) with lacquer. …에 래커칠을 하다; 옻을 입히다. [Sp. & Port. *lacre*]

lac·quey [lǽki] *n., v.* =lackey.

la·crosse [ləkrɔ́(:)s, -krɑ́s] *n.* Ⓤ an outdoor game, played by two teams of twelve, in which the ball is shot into the opposite goal with a racket called a crosse. 라크로스. 參考 캐나다의 국기(國技)로 되어 있음. [F. *la, crosse* crutch]

lac·tic [lǽktik] *adj.* of or obtained from milk. 젖의; 젖에서 얻는. ¶ ～ *acid* 〔*bacteria*〕

L

〈lacrosse〉

젖산〔젖산균〕. [L. *lac* milk]

lac·tose [lǽktous] *n.* 《chem.》 sugar of milk. 젖당(糖); 락토오스. [↑]

lac·y [léisi] *adj.* (**lac·i·er, lac·i·est**) of or like lace. 레이스의〔같은〕. [*lace*]

:lad [læd] *n.* Ⓒ **1** a boy; a young man. 소년; 젊은이(opp. lass). **2** 《*colloq.*》 a man; a chap. 남자; 녀석; 친구. ¶ *my lads* 제군. [E.]

·lad·der [lǽdər] *n.* Ⓒ **1** a device for climbing up or down consisting of two long sidepieces and many crosspieces. 사닥다리. ¶ *climb up* 〔*down*〕 *a* ~ 사닥다리를 올라가다〔내려가다〕. **2** a means by which a person achieves a purpose. (출세의) 연줄; 수단. ¶ *the* ~ *of success* 성공에의 길〔수단〕 / *climb the* ~ *of fame* 명성이 높아지다. **3** 《Brit.》 a long vertical tear in a woman's stocking. (여자 스타킹의) 세로 올의 풀림(cf. 《U.S.》 *run*). [E.]

get one's foot on the ladder, make a beginning. 일을 시작하다〔착수하다〕.

kick down the ladder, despise the persons or means by which someone has achieved a purpose. 출세에 도움이 됐던 것을〔친구를〕 버리다.

lad·die [lǽdi] *n.* Ⓒ 《Sc.》 a young boy; a lad. 소년; 젊은이. ¶ *Look here,* ~ *what about it?* 이봐 젊은 친구, 어떻게 된 일인가. [*lad*]

lade [leid] *vt.* (***lad·ed, lad·en*** or ***lad·ed***) (P6) **1** put a load on or in; put (goods) into a ship or on a cart. …에 짐을 싣다. ¶ ~ *a ship with cargo* 화물을 배에 싣다 / ~ *hay on a cart* 수레에 건초를 싣다. **2** draw or dip out with a ladle. 국자〔바가지〕로 퍼내다. ¶ ~ *water out of a boat* 보트에서 바가지로 물을 퍼내다. **3** oppress. 괴롭히다. [E.]

·lad·en [léidn] *adj.* **1** loaded. (짐을) 실은; 적재한. ¶ *trees heavily* ~ *with apples* 가지가 휘어지도록 열린 사과나무. **2** burdened; weighed down. 무거운 짐을 진; 짓눌린. ¶ *a mind* ~ *with grief* 슬픔에 가득찬 마음.

lad·ing [léidiŋ] *n.* Ⓤ cargo; freight. 선하(船荷); 뱃짐; 화물. ¶ *a bill of* ~ 선하 증권.

la·dle [léidl] *n.* Ⓒ a cuplike spoon with a long handle, used for dipping out liquids. 국자; (자루 달린) 바가지. — *vt.* (P6,13) **1** dip out (water, etc.) with a ladle. …을 국자〔바가지〕로 퍼내다. ¶ ~ *soup into plates* 접시에 수프를 담다. **2** 《*colloq.*》 give out lavishly or generously. 아낌없이 주다. ¶ ~ *out praise* 마구 칭찬하다. [E.]

:la·dy [léidi] *n.* (*pl.* **-dies**) Ⓒ **1** a well-bred woman; a woman of high social position. 귀부인; 숙녀(opp. gentleman). ¶ *be not* (*quite*) *a* ~ 전혀 숙녀답지 못하다. **2** any woman. 여성; 여인. ¶ *a lady-help* 가정부. **3** 《L-》《Brit.》 a title given to wives or daughters of men with certain high ranks. …마님; …부인; …영애. **4** a wife. 아내. ¶ *the colonel's* ~ 대령 부인. [E. =loaf-kneader]

la·dy·bird [léidibə̀ːrd] *n.* Ⓒ =ladybug.

la·dy·bug [léidibʌ̀g] *n.* Ⓒ a small round beetle with black spots on its back. 무당벌레. 參考 ladybird, lady beetle 이라고도 함.

Lady Day [∠-∠] *n.* a festival on March 25 in honor of the day when the angel Gabriel told Mary that she would be the mother of Jesus; Annunciation Day. 성모 영보(領報) 대축일.

la·dy-in-wait·ing [léidiinwéitiŋ] *n.* Ⓒ (*pl.* **la·dies-**) a lady who is attending on a queen or princess. 시녀; 궁녀.

la·dy·like [léidilàik] *adj.* like or suitable for a lady refined. 귀부인다운; 정숙한. ¶ ~ *manners* 정숙한 태도.

la·dy·ship [léidiʃìp] *n.* Ⓤ **1** the rank of Lady. 귀부인의 신분. **2** 《L-》《Brit.》 a title used in speaking to or of a woman who has the title Lady. Lady 칭호를 가진 부인에 대한 경칭. ¶ *Your* 〔*Her*〕 *Ladyship* 영부인.

lag[1] [læg] *vi.* (**lagged, lag·ging**) (P1,2A) walk or move too slowly; delay; fall behind. 느릿느릿 걷다〔움직이다〕; 늦어지다; 처지다. ¶ ~ *behind in promotion* 진급이 늦다 / *She lagged because she was tired.* 피곤해서 그녀는 느릿느릿 걸었다. — *n.* ⓊⒸ the act of lagging; the amount by which a person or thing falls behind. 지연; 늦어짐; 지체(량). [Dan. =go slowly]

lag[2] [læg] 《Brit. *sl.*》 *vt.* (P6) put in jail; arrest. 투옥하다; 체포하다. — *n.* a convict. 죄인; 죄수. ¶ *an old* ~ 상습범. [↑]

la·ger (beer) [láːgər (bíər)] *n.* Ⓤ a beer which is stored for several months before being drunk. 라거비어; 저장 맥주. 參考 저온에서 6주 내지 6개월 저장 후 출하함. [G.]

lag·gard [lǽgərd] *n.* Ⓒ a person who moves too slowly or who falls behind. 느림보; 굼뜬 사람. — *adj.* falling behind; backward; slow. 느린; 꾸물거리는. [*lag*]

la·goon [ləgúːn] *n.* Ⓒ **1** a small lake or pond, usu. one connected with a larger body of water or the sea. 석호(潟湖); (강·바다로 통하는) 작은 호수〔못〕. **2** the shallow water inside an atoll, or a ring-shaped coral island. 초호(礁湖)《환초(環礁)에 둘러싸인 해면》. [*lacuna*]

L

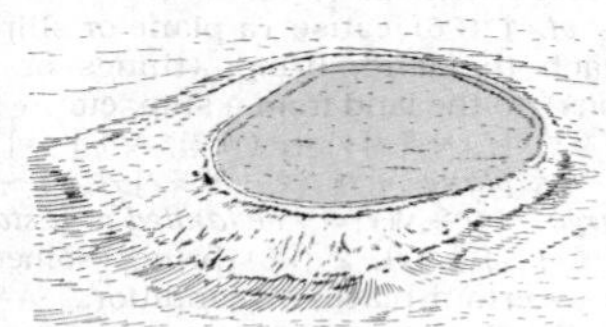
〈lagoon〉

:laid [leid] *v.* p. and pp. of **lay.**

laid paper [⌐ ⌐–] *n.* paper with close parallel lines of the watermark. 평행선 무늬가 내비치는 종이.

:lain [lein] *v.* pp. of **lie.**

lair [lɛər] *n.* Ⓒ **1** a bed or resting-place for a wild animal. 짐승들의 잠자리(굴). **2** any resting place; a shed; a bed; home. 쉬는 곳; 오두막; 잠자리; 집. ¶ *I'll go to my* ~. 나는 집에 가련다. — *vi.* (P1) (of wild animals) go to or rest in a lair. (짐승이) 굴에 들어가다; 굴에서 쉬다. [E.]

lais·sez-faire, lais·ser-faire [lèiseifέər] *n.* Ⓤ the policy of non-interference, esp. in matters of business and economics; the principle of non-interference in the individual matters of others. 불간섭 정책(주의); 자유방임주의. [F. =let act]

la·i·ty [léiəti] *n.* (*pl.* **-ties**) Ⓤ《usu. *the* ~, *collectively*》 **1** laymen of a church. 평신도; 속인(俗人)(opp. clergy). **2** those outside any particular profession. 문외한; 생무지. [*lay*]

:lake [leik] *n.* Ⓒ a large area of water, nearly or entirely surrounded by land. 호수. ¶ *the Great Lakes* (미국과 캐나다 국경에 있는) 오대호 / *the Lake Country* [*District*] (영국 서북부의) 호수 지방. [L. *lacus*]

la·ma [lɑ́:mə] *n.* Ⓒ a Buddhist priest in Tibet or Mongolia. 라마승(僧). [Tibetan]

:lamb [læm] *n.* **1** Ⓒ a young sheep. 어린 양. **2** Ⓤ the meat from young sheep, served as food. 어린 양의 고기. **3** Ⓒ a gentle, innocent person, esp. a child. 천진한 사람; (특히) 어린이. **4** a person who is easily cheated; a simpleton. 잘 속는 사람; 숙맥.

***the Lamb* (*of God*),** Christ. 예수.

— *vt., vi.* (P6;1) (of female sheep) give birth to a lamb or lambs. (새끼 양을) 낳다. [E.]

lam·bent [lǽmbənt] *adj.* **1** (of a flame or light) moving lightly over a surface. (불꽃·빛 따위가) 가볍게 흔들리는. **2** (of the stars or eyes) shining softly and brightly. (별·눈동자가) 부드럽게 빛나는. **3** (of humor, etc.) gentle and bright. (재치 따위가) 경묘한. [L. *lambo* lick]

lamb·kin [lǽmkin] *n.* Ⓒ **1** a little lamb. 어린 양. **2** a young and dear person. 귀여운 아이. [*lamb*]

lamb·skin [lǽmskìn] *n.* **1** Ⓤ the skin of a lamb with the wool still on it. 어린 양의 모피. **2** Ⓒ leather made from the skin of a lamb. 무두질한 어린 양의 가죽.

:lame [leim] *adj.* **1** not able to walk properly as a result of an injury in leg or foot, etc.; crippled. 절룩거리는. ¶ *be* ~ *of* [*in*] *a leg* 한쪽 다리를 절다 / *go* [*walk*] ~ 절룩거리며 걷다 / *a* ~ *duck* 볼장 다 본 사람(사업); 폐선(廢船); 임기가 곧 끝나는 의원(지사, 대통령). **2** unsatisfactory. 불충분한. ¶ *a* ~ *excuse* 서투른 변명. **3** stiff and sore. 뻐근한; 쑤시는. ¶ *a* ~ *arm* [*back*] 쿡쿡 쑤시는 팔(등). — *vt.* (P6) make (someone) lame. …을 절름발이로 만들다. [E.]

·la·ment [ləmént] *n.* Ⓒ **1** an expression of grief. 비탄; 애도. **2** a poem or song that expresses grief; an elegy. 비가(悲歌). — *vt.* (P6) feel or express grief for (something); mourn. …을 슬퍼하다(애도하다). ¶ ~ *someone's death* 아무의 죽음을 애도하다. — *vi.* (P1,3) feel or express grief; mourn. 슬퍼하다; 한탄하다. ¶ ~ *for* [*over*] *someone's death* 아무의 죽음을 슬퍼하다. [L.]

lam·en·ta·ble [lǽməntəbəl] *adj.* sorrowful; mournful. 슬픈; 통탄할.

lam·en·ta·bly [lǽməntəbəli] *adv.* in a lamentable manner; sorrowfully. 슬프게; 슬픈 듯이.

lam·en·ta·tion [læ̀məntéiʃən] *n.* **1** Ⓤ the act of lamenting. 비탄. **2** Ⓒ a lament; an expression of grief. 비탄의 소리; 애가(哀歌).

lam·i·nate [lǽmənèit] *vt.* (P6) **1** ⓐ beat or roll (metal) into thin plates. (금속 등)을 얇은 판으로 만들다. ⓑ make (plywood, plastic, etc.) by uniting layer upon layer. 켜켜이 붙여 (합판 따위를) 만들다. **2** cover (something) with a thin sheet of metal, wood, etc. …에 박판을 씌우다. — *vi.* (P1) split into thin layers. 박편(薄片)으로 쪼개지다; 얇은 판이 되다. — [lǽmənit] *adj.* of or consisting of thin plates or layers. 얇은 판의(으로 된). [L.]

:lamp [læmp] *n.* Ⓒ **1** something that gives light from electricity, oil, etc. 램프; 등(燈). ¶ *an electric* ~ 전등 / *an oil* ~ 석유 램프. **2** the source of knowledge or wisdom. 지식이나 지혜의 샘. ¶ *hand* [*pass*] *on the* ~ 예술(지식) 등을 후세에 전하다. **3** 《*arch.*》 the sun, the moon, a star, etc. 태양, 달, 별 따위. [Gk. *lampas* torch]

smell of the lamp, betray nocturnal study; show signs of much study and effort. 고심한(애쓴)흔적이 보이다.

lamp·black [lǽmpblæ̀k] *n.* Ⓤ **1** fine soot produced by burning oil incompletely. 검댕; 철매. **2** a coloring matter made from this. 그것으로 만든 안료(顔料). [↑]

lamp·light [lǽmplàit] *n.* Ⓒ the light from a lamp. 등불; 호롱불.

lamp·light·er [lǽmplàitər] *n.* Ⓒ a person who went around the streets and lighted street lamps. (가스등(燈)이 있던 시대의) 점등부(夫). ¶ *run like a* ~ 비호같이 달리다.

lam·poon [læmpúːn] *n.* Ⓒ a piece of writing that attacks and laughs at someone. 풍자문(시). — *vt.* (P6) attack (something or someone) by such a piece of writing. …을 풍자하다; 비아냥거리다. [F.]

lamp·post [lǽmppòust] *n.* Ⓒ a post or pillar used to support a street lamp. 가로등의 기둥.

lam·prey [lǽmpri] *n.* Ⓒ a sea animal with gills and an eel-like body. 칠성장어. [L. =lick-rock]

lamp·shade [lǽmpʃèid] *n.* Ⓒ a shade of glass made of cloth, paper, etc. which is placed around a lamp. 램프 갓. [*lamp*]

Lan·ca·shire [lǽŋkəʃìər, -ʃər] *n.* a county in northwestern England. 랭커셔.

•**lance** [læns, lɑːns] *n.* Ⓒ **1** a long wooden weapon like a spear with a pointed steel head. 창. **2** 《*pl.*》 soldiers armed with lances; lancers. 창기병(槍騎兵). **3** a lancet. 랜싯. — *vt.* (P6) **1** pierce or attack (something) with a lance. …을 창으로 찌르다(공격하다). **2** cut (a part of body) open with a lancet. …을 랜싯으로 절개하다. [L.]

〈lance 1〉

Lance·lot [lǽnsələt, -lɑ̀t, lɑ́ːn-] *n.* the bravest of King Arthur's Knights of the Round Table. 랜슬롯《아서 왕의 원탁 기사 중 으뜸가는 용사》.

lanc·er [lǽnsər, lɑ́ːn-] *n.* Ⓒ a cavalry soldier armed with a lance. 창기병. [L.]

lan·cet [lǽnsit, lɑ́ːn-] *n.* Ⓒ a pointed, two-edged knife used by surgeons. 랜싯《외과용 기구》. [L.]

〈lancet〉

⁑**land** [lænd] *n.* **1** Ⓤ the solid part of the earth's surface. 뭍; 육지(opp. sea, water). ¶ *travel by* ~ 육로로 가다 / *make* (*sight*) (*the*) ~ 《naut.》 육지를 확인하다; 육지가 보이는 곳으로 오다 / *the dry* ~ 해안 / *clear the* ~ (배가) 해안의 위험물을 피해 바다로 나가다 / *forest lands* 산림 지대. **2** Ⓤ ⓐ ground; soil. 토지; 지면. ¶ *rich* (*poor*) ~ 비옥(척박)한 땅 / *good corn* ~ 강냉이가 잘되는 토지. ⓑ 《usu. *the* ~》 farm land; agricultural life. 농토; 농경 생활. ¶ *go* (*work*) *on the* ~ 농부가 되다. **3** ⓐ Ⓒ a country; a nation; a region. 나라; 국가; 국토; 지역. ¶ *one's native* ~ 고국 / *visit foreign* (*far-off*) *lands* 외국을 방문하다 / *the* ~ *of the living* 현세. ⓑ Ⓒ a nation's people. 국민. ¶ *The whole* ~ *rejoiced at the news.* 온 국민이 그 소식을 듣고 기뻐했다. **4** 《*pl.*》 the piece of ground considered as property; estate. 소유(사유)지. ¶ *own lands* 땅을 소유하다 / *houses and lands* 가옥과 토지.
— *vt.* **1** (P6) cause (a plane or ship) to reach the land; bring (things or persons) to the land from a ship, etc. …을 상륙시키다; 착륙시키다; (뱃짐 등)을 내리다. ¶ ~ *a plane* 비행기를 착륙시키다 / ~ *the cargo* 뱃짐을 내리다 / *be landed at a station* 역에서 내려지다. **2** (P6) bring (someone) to a certain place, or condition. …을 어떤 특수한 장소(상태)에 이르게(놓이게) 하다. ¶ *This fight landed them both in jail.* 이 싸움으로 둘 다 교도소로 보내졌다 / *This train will* ~ *you in Seoul.* 이 열차는 서울행이다 / *This will* ~ *me in great difficulties.* 이것 때문에 내가 큰 고생을 하게 되었다. **3** (P6) 《*colloq.*》 win; get; secure. 얻다; 손에 넣다. ¶ ~ *a job* 일자리를 얻다 / ~ *a prize* 상을 타다. **4** (P13,14) 《*colloq.*》 deliver a blow; strike. 한 방 먹이다(때리다); 치다. ¶ ~ *someone on the nose* 아무의 콧등에 일격을 가하다.
— *vi.* **1** (P1,3) leave a ship and go on shore; get off from train, etc. 상륙하다; 착륙하다. ¶ ~ *in Pusan* 부산에 상륙하다 / ~ *from a train* 기차에서 내리다. **2** (P1,3) arrive. 도착하다. ¶ ~ *at an inn* 여관에 들다. **3** (P1,3) be in a bad state. (나쁜 상황에) 빠지다. ¶ *He landed in prison.* 그는 감옥에 갔다. **4** (P1) come in first. 일착이 되다. [E.]

lan·dau [lǽndau, -dɔː] *n.* Ⓒ **1** a four-wheeled carriage with two seats and a top made to be folded in two sections. 란다우 마차《포장을 앞뒤로 따로 따로 개폐하게 된 4륜 마차》. **2** an automobile with a similar top. 란다우 자동차. [Place]

land·ed [lǽndid] *adj.* **1** owning land. 땅을 소유한. ¶ *the* ~ *classes* 지주 계급. **2** of or consisting of land. 땅의; 땅으로 된. ¶ ~ *property* 토지 재산; 부동산. [*land*]

land·hold·er [lǽndhòuldər] *n.* Ⓒ a person who owns or rents land. 지주; 토지 소유자; 차지인(借地人).

land·ing [lǽndiŋ] *n.* Ⓒ **1** the act of coming or bringing to land. 상륙; 양륙. ¶ *make a forced* ~ *on an island* 섬에 불시착하다. **2** a place where persons or goods are landed from a ship; landing place. 상륙(양륙)장. **3** a platform between two flights of stairs. (계단의) 층계참. [*land*]

landing craft [⌐– ⌐] *n.* a ship whose bows can be opened up to allow troops and military vehicles to go ashore. 상륙용 주정(舟艇).

landing field [⌐– ⌐] *n.* a field where airplanes can land and take off. 비행장; 이착륙장.

landing gear [⌐– ⌐] *n.* the wheels, floats, etc. of an aircraft, for support on land or water. (항공기의) 착륙(착수) 장치.

landing net [⌐– ⌐] *n.* a small net with a handle for scooping fish up from the water. 사내끼《낚은 물고기를 건져 올리는 그물》.

landing place [⌐– ⌐] *n.* a place where

L

people or goods are landed. 상륙〔양륙〕장.

landing stage [⊂–⊃] *n.* a floating platform used for landing people and goods. 부잔교(浮棧橋).

land·la·dy [lǽndlèidi] *n.* Ⓒ (*pl.* **-dies**) (opp. landlord) **1** a woman who rents her houses or land to others. 여자 지주. **2** the mistress of a boarding house, inn or lodging house. (하숙·여관의) 여주인. [*land*]

land·locked [lǽndlὰkt / -lɔ̀kt] *adj.* (of a bay, harbor, etc.) surrounded or nearly surrounded by land. (항만이) 육지로 둘러싸인.

∗**land·lord** [lǽndlɔ̀ːrd] *n.* Ⓒ (opp. landlady) **1** a person who rents his houses or land to others. 집주인; 지주. **2** the male keeper of a boarding house, inn, or lodging house. (하숙·여관의) 남자 주인.

land·mark [lǽndmὰːrk] *n.* Ⓒ **1** an object that marks the limits of land. 경계표. ¶ *move one's neighbor's landmarks* 이웃과의 경계표를 옮겨 놓다. **2** an easily-seen and well-known mark which serves as a guide to travelers and sailors. (여행자·항해자 등의 길잡이가 되는) 안표(眼標); 육표(陸標). **3** an important fact or event. (역사상의) 획기적인 사건.

land·own·er [lǽndòunər] *n.* Ⓒ a person who owns land. 토지 소유자; 지주.

∗**land·scape** [lǽndskèip] *n.* Ⓒ a piece of inland scenery; a picture showing such a piece of scenery. 풍경; 경치; 풍경화.

land·slide [lǽndslàid] *n.* Ⓒ 《U.S.》 **1** a fall of a mass of earth or rock from the slope of a cliff or a mountain. (산)사태(cf. 《Brit.》 *landslip*). **2** a decisive, overwhelming victory in an election. (선거에서의) 압도적 승리.

land·slip [lǽndslìp] *n.* 《Brit.》 =landslide 1.

lands·man [lǽndzmən] *n.* (*pl.* **-men** [-mən]) Ⓒ **1** a person who lives or works on land. 육상 생활자(opp. seaman). **2** 《naut.》 an inexperienced sailor. 풋내기 선원.

land·ward [lǽndwərd] *adj. adv.* toward the land. 육지쪽의〔으로〕(opp. seaward).

land·wards [lǽndwərdz] *adv.* =landward.

⁑**lane** [lein] *n.* Ⓒ **1** a narrow way between hedges, houses, buildings, etc.; a little, narrow road or street (in a town). 좁은 길; 골목(길); 뒷골목. ¶ *a blind* ~ 막다른 골목 / 《*prov.*》 *It is a long* ~ *that has no turning.* 굽지 않은 길은 없다; 쥐구멍에도 볕들 날이 있다. **2** a course or route used by ships or airplanes. 항로. **3** each of the courses marked out on a road (for a car to follow). (도로의) 차선(車線). ¶ *a four-lane highway* 4차선 도로. [E.]

lang·syne [lǽŋsáin, -záin] *adv.* in the old days; long ago. 오래전에. — *n.* the old days. 그 옛날. [Sc. =long since]

⁑**lan·guage** [lǽŋgwidʒ] *n.* **1** Ⓤ human speech in general; a method of human communication in words. 언어; 말. ¶ *spoken* ~ 구어 / *written* ~ 문어. **2** Ⓒ the speech of one nation or race. 국어. ¶ *the English* ~ 영어 / *a foreign* ~ 외국어 / *a living* 〔*dead*〕 ~ 현대어〔사어〕. **3** Ⓤ the manner of expression or using words; characteric style of a speaker or writer. 어법; 어투; 말씨; 문체. ¶ *bad* ~ 천한 말씨 / *strong* ~ 강경한 말투 / *Shakespeare's* ~ 세익스피어의 문체 / *fine* ~ 아름답게 꾸민 말씨; 화려한 문체. **4** Ⓤ terms and expressions for a special field. 술어; 전문어. ¶ *the* ~ *of science* 〔*poetry, the law*〕 과학 용어〔시어, 법률 용어〕. **5** Ⓒ a method of expression by symbols or gestures. (음성·문자를 쓰지 않은) 말. ¶ *the finger* ~ 수화(手話) / *the* ~ *of flowers* 꽃말. **6** the study of language or languages. 어학; 언어학. ¶ *a* ~ *laboratory* 어학 연습실. [L. *lingua* tongue]

lan·guid [lǽŋgwid] *adj* **1** weak without energy. 기운이 없는; 느른한. **2** without interest; dull; not lively. 무관심한; 활기가 없는; 생기 없는. [L.]

∗**lan·guish** [lǽŋgwiʃ] *vi* **1** (P1) become weak; lose energy; droop. 쇠약해지다; 기운이 없어지다; 시들다. ¶ *The flowers languished in the summer heat.* 여름볕에 꽃들이 시들었다. **2** (P3) live under unfavorable conditions; endure long suffering. 고달픈〔괴로운〕 생활을 하다. ¶ ~ *in prison* 오랜 옥고를 치르다. **3** (P3) 《*for*》 long; pine. 동경하다; 갈망하다. ¶ *He began to* ~ *for fresh air.* 신선한 공기가 몹시도 그리워졌다. **4** (P1) put on a languid look. 우울한〔생각에 잠긴〕 표정을 하다. [L.]

lan·guor [lǽŋgər] *n.* Ⓤ physical or mental weakness; lack of energy, interest, activity, etc.; sluggishness. 무기력; 무관심; 권태. ¶ *the* ~ *of a summer afternoon* 여름 오후의 권태감. [L.]

lan·guor·ous [lǽngərəs] *adj.* bringing about languor; languid. 나른한; 따분한; 울적한.

lan·guor·ous·ly [lǽŋgərəsli] *adv.* in a languorous manner; dully. 나른한 듯이; 귀찮은 듯이. ¶ *lower one's eyelids* ~ 지친 듯이 눈을 내리감다.

lank [læŋk] *adj.* **1** tall and thin; slender; lean. 호리호리한; 여윈; 홀쭉한. ¶ *a* ~ *boy* 가냘픈 소년. **2** (of hair) straight and soft; not curled. 머리카락이 곧고 부드러운. ¶ *a girl with* ~ *blonde hair* 길고 부드러운 금발머리의 소녀. [E.]

lank·y [lǽŋki] *adj.* (**lank·i·er, lank·i·est**) awkwardly tall and thin. 호리호리한; 멀대같은. ¶ *a* ~ *person* 멋없이 키만 큰 사람.

∗**lan·tern** [lǽntərn] *n.* Ⓒ **1** a portable case to protect a light from rain, wind, etc. 랜턴; 등롱; 제등. ¶ *a paper* ~ 등롱; 초롱 / ~ *jaws* 주걱턱 / *parish* ~ 달. **2** the top room of a lighthouse where the light is kept. (등대의) 등실(燈室). [L. *lanterna*]

:lap¹ [læp] *n.* Ⓒ **1** the part of the body from the waist to the knees when a person is sitting; the part of the clothing covering this; the front part of the skirt. 무릎; 옷의 무릎 부분; 스커트의 앞자락. ¶ *sit on one's mother's* ~ 어머니 무릎에 앉다. **2** a loosely hanging edge of clothing; a flap. (옷의) 처진 부분; 옷자락. **3** an overlapping part. 겹쳐진 부분. **4** a complete circuit of racing. (경주로의) 한바퀴; 일주. ¶ *the first* ~ *of the race* 경주의 첫 바퀴 / ~ *time* 랩타임; 도중 계시(計時).

in Fortune's lap = ***in the lap of Fortune,*** fortunate. 운이 좋아서.

in the lap of luxury, in great comfort. 온갖 사치를 다해.

in the lap of the gods, beyond human control or power. 인간의 힘이 미치지 않는 데에.

— *v.* (**lapped, lap·ping**) *vt.* **1** (P7,13) fold; wind or wrap around. …을 접다; 감다. ¶ ~ *a bandage around the wrist* 손목에 붕대를 감다. **2** (P6) put (something) partly over another; overlap. …을 겹치다; 포개다. ¶ ~ *a slate over another* 슬레이트를 다른 슬레이트 위에 겹쳐 놓다. **3** (P7,13) wrap up; enfold; surround. …을 싸다; 둘러싸다. ¶ *He lapped himself in a soft blanket.* 그는 부드러운 담요로 몸을 쌌다 / *Sorrow lapped her over.* 그녀는 슬픔에 싸였다. **4** (P6) enfold caressingly. 안다; 포옹하다. **5** pass by one or more laps. 한바퀴 또는 여러 바퀴 앞서다.

— *vi.* (P1,2A) overlap; be folded over; turn over. 겹쳐지다; 젖혀지다. ¶ *Her reign lapped over into the twentieth century.* 그녀의 치세는 20세기에까지 미쳤다. [E.]

·lap² [læp] *v.* (**lapped, lap·ping**) *vt.* **1** (P6) drink (something) by the tongue, as a cat or dog does; lick. …을 핥다. ¶ *The dog lapped (up) all the milk.* 개가 우유를 깨끗이 핥아 먹었다. **2** (P6) (of water) wash against or beat upon (something) with a light, splashing sound. (파도 등이) …을 철썩철썩 치다[씻다]. ¶ *Waves lapped the shore.* 파도가 해안에 철썩거리며 밀려왔다. — *vi.* (P1,2A) **1** wash or move in small waves with a light sound. 파도가 …을 씻다[치다]; (파도가) 철썩거리며 밀려오다. ¶ *Waves lapped on the beach.* 파도가 해안을 철썩거리고 있었다. **2** lick up liquid with the tongue. 핥다.

lap up, 《*colloq.*》 drink greedily; listen eagerly to (compliments etc.). 게걸스럽게 마시다; (아첨 따위)를 곧이 듣다.

— *n.* Ⓒ **1** an act of lapping. 핥기. **2** the sound of lapping. 해안을 철썩거리는 파도 소리; 핥는 소리. **3** liquid food for dogs. (개의) 유동식(流動食). **4** 《*colloq.*》 a weak beverage. 싱거운 음료. [E.]

la·pel [ləpél] *n.* Ⓒ 《usu. *pl.*》 the front part of a coat that is folded back on the chest. (양복 상의의) 접힌 옷깃. [→lap¹]

〈lapel〉

lap·i·dar·y [lǽpədèri] *n.* Ⓒ (*pl.* **-dar·ies**) a person whose job is to cut, polish, or engrave precious stones. 보석 세공자. — *adj.* **1** of the art of cutting or engraving precious stones. 보석 세공의. **2** engraved on the stone. 돌에 새긴. [L. *lapis* stone]

Lap·land [lǽplæ̀nd] *n.* a region stretching across northern Norway, Sweden, Finland, and northwestern Russia. 라플란드 《노르웨이·스웨덴 등지의 북단 지역》.

Lap·land·er [lǽplæ̀ndər] *n.* Ⓒ a person of Lapland; a Lapp. 라플란드 사람.

Lapp [læp] *n.* **1** Ⓒ a member of a Mongoloid race living in Lapland. (몽고계의) 라플란드 사람. **2** Ⓤ the language of the Lapps. 라플란드어. [Swed.]

·lapse [læps] *n.* Ⓒ **1** (of time) the act of passing away. (시간의) 흐름; 경과. ¶ *the rapid* ~ *of time* 시간의 빠른 경과 / *the* ~ *of centuries* 수 세기의 경과. **2** a slight mistake or error. (사소한) 착오; 실수. ¶ *a* ~ *of memory* 기억 착오 / *a* ~ *of tongue* 실언. **3** the act of falling away from moral standards. 타락. ¶ *a* ~ *from virtue* 타락 / *a* ~ *into crime* 죄를 저지르기. **4** 《*law*》 the loss of a right because it was not used or renewed. 실권; 권리 소멸; 실효.

— *vi.* **1** (P1,3) (of time) glide or slip slowly away; pass away. (때가) 지나다; 경과하다. **2** (P3) make a slight mistake or error. 실수하다; 죄짓다. ¶ ~ *from good behavior* 행실이 나빠지다 / ~ *into crime* 죄를 짓다. **3** (P1,2A,3) 《*into, from*》 fall or slip from moral standards. 타락하다; 나쁜 길로 빠지다. ¶ *He lapsed into bad habits.* 버릇이 나빠졌다 / *I fear he has lapsed again.* 그가 또 나빠졌을까 걱정이다. **4** (P1,3) 《law》 (of a right or privilege) end; pass from one person to another, or become void because it has not been used or renewed. (권리·특권이) 소멸하다; 남의 손에 넘어가다. [L. *lābor* slip]

lap·wing [lǽpwìŋ] *n.* Ⓒ a European bird with a slow irregular flight and a peculiar wailing cry. 댕기물떼새. [*leap, wink*]

lar·board [lá:rbərd] *n.* Ⓒ the left side of a ship as one faces the bow. 좌현(左舷) (opp. starboard). 語法 지금은 흔히 port 라 함. [E.]

lar·cen·ous [lá:rsənəs] *a.* having the character of larceny; committing larceny. 손버릇이 나쁜; 도둑질하는. [↑]

lar·ce·ny [lá:rsəni] *n.* ⓊⒸ (*pl.* **-nies**) 《law》 the act of stealing; theft. 절도(죄); 도둑질. [L. *latro* robber]

larch [lɑːrtʃ] *n.* Ⓒ a tree of the pine family with small cones and needlelike leaves which drop in the fall; Ⓤ the wood of this tree. 낙엽송; 그 재목. [L.]

lard [lɑːrd] *n.* Ⓤ the refined, white fat of pigs, used in cooking. 라드; 돼지 기름. — *vt.* (P6) **1** smear with lard. …에 라드를 바르다. **2** insert strips of bacon in (meat) before cooking. (요리 전에) 베이컨 조각을 넣다. **3** garnish (a talk, etc.) with strange terms, etc. (이야기)를 윤색하다. ¶ *~ one's conversation with quotations* 인용구를 써가며 이야기를 재미있게 꾸미다. [L.]

lar·der [lɑ́ːrdər] *n.* Ⓒ a small room in a house where food is stored; a pantry. 식품 저장실; 찬광. [↑]

la·res, La- [lέəriːz, léir-] *n. pl.* 《Rom. myth.》 the household gods of the ancient Romans. 라레스《가정의 수호신》. [L.]

lar·es and pe·na·tes [lέəriːzəndpənéitiːz] *n.* 《*pl.*》 **1** the gods of the household in ancient Rome. (옛 로마의) 가신(家神). **2** the cherished possessions of a family. 가보(家寶). [L.]

:large [lɑːrdʒ] *adj.* **1** occupying much space; that can hold a great amount; big. 큰; 넓은 (opp. small, little). ¶ *a ~ book* 큰 책 / *a ~ lake* 큰 호수 / *a ~ box* 큰 상자 / *a ~ room* (크고) 넓은 방. **2** great in number or in amount. (수량이) 많은. ¶ *a ~ amount of money* 많은 돈; 거금 / *a ~ supply* 〔*income*〕 대량 공급〔많은 수입〕 / *serve ~ meals* 많은 식사를 제공하다. **3** not little; not confined; far-reaching. 규모가 큰; 광대한; 원대한. ¶ *a ~ idea* 웅대한 사상 / *~ insight* 탁견 / *~ powers* 광대한 권능. **4** 《*fig.*》 broad; generous. 호방한; 관대한(opp. petty, mean²). ¶ *a ~ heart* 큰 도량 / *a ~ tolerance* 관용.
at large, **a)** free; not in prison. 자유로이; 붙잡히지 않고. ¶ *The murderer is still at ~ in this city.* 살인범은 아직 잡히지 않고 시내에 있다. **b)** as a whole; in general. 전체적으로; 일반적으로. ¶ *He is popular with the people at ~.* 그는 널리 사람들에게 인기가 있다. **c)** at full length; in detail. 상세히. ¶ *talk* 〔*write*〕 *at ~* 상세히 말하다〔쓰다〕.
— *adv.* largely; boastfully. 크게; 과장되게. ¶ *talk ~* 허풍치다. [L. *largus* copious]

:large·ly [lɑ́ːrdʒli] *adv.* in great amounts; to a great extent; abundantly; mainly; generously. 크게; 충분히; 주로; 아낌없이. ¶ *He is ~ engaged in writing.* 그가 하는 일은 주로 저술이다 / *give* 〔*spend*〕 *~* 아끼지 않고 주다〔쓰다〕.

large·ness [lɑ́ːrdʒnis] *n.* Ⓤ the state of being large; great size; generosity. 큼; 관대; 위대.

large-scale [lɑ́ːrdʒskèil] *adj.* made or drawn on a large scale; extensive. 대규모의; 대대적인.

lar·gess, -gesse [lɑːrdʒés, lɑ́ːrdʒis] *n.* Ⓤ the act of giving (something) generously; money or other gifts generously given. 아낌없는 증여; 그 금품. [*large, -ess*]

lar·go [lɑ́ːrgou] *adj., adv.* 《mus.》 slow and stately. 느리고 장엄하게. — *n.* Ⓒ (*pl.* **-gos**) a passage or piece of music played in a slow and stately manner. 라르고 조(調)의 악장〔악곡〕. [It.]

lar·i·at [lǽriət] *n., vt.* =lasso.

·lark¹ [lɑːrk] *n.* Ⓒ a small bird with a sweet, clear note; a skylark. 종다리; 종달새. [E. O.N. *lævirki*]
as happy as a lark, very pleasant. 아주 즐거운.
rise with the lark, get up early. 아침 일찍 일어나다.

lark² [lɑːrk] *n.* Ⓒ a bit of fun; a frolic. 농(담); 장난.
for a lark, in joke. 농담으로. ¶ *He only said it for a ~.* 그저 농으로 말했을 뿐이다.
have a lark with, do mischief with. …와 장난하다; 놀리다.
What a lark! How funny this is! What fun! 이거 재미있구나.
— *vi.* (P1,2A) have fun; play pranks; frolic. 장난치다. [Goth. *laikan* hop]
lark about, do mischief and make noise. 장난하며 떠들다.

lark·spur [lɑ́ːrkspə̀ːr] *n.* Ⓒ 《bot.》 a tall garden plant with blue, white, or pink flowers. 참제비고깔속(屬)의 식물. [*lark¹*]

lark·y [lɑ́ːrki] *adj.* (**lark·i·er, lark·i·est**) given to larking; playful. 까부는; 장난치는. [*lark²*]

lar·va [lɑ́ːrvə] *n.* Ⓒ (*pl.* **-vae**) the early form of an insect, the stage between the egg and the pupa. 유충; 애벌레(cf. *pupa*). [L.=ghost]

lar·vae [lɑ́ːrviː] *n.* pl. of **larva.**

lar·val [lɑ́ːrvəl] *adj.* of larvae; in the form of a larva. 유충의.

lar·yn·ge·al [ləríndʒiəl, læ̀rindʒíːəl] *adj.* of the larynx. 후두(喉頭)의. [*larynx*]

la·ryn·ges [ləríndʒiːz] *n.* pl. of **larynx.**

lar·yn·gi·tis [læ̀rindʒáitis] *n.* Ⓤ inflammation of the larynx. 후두염(炎).

la·ryn·go·scope [ləríŋgəskòup] *n.* a mirror apparatus for examining larynx. 후두경(喉頭鏡).

lar·ynx [lǽriŋks] *n.* Ⓒ (*pl.* **-ynx·es** or **la·ryn·ges**) 《anat.》 the upper part of the windpipe, containing the vocal cords. 후두(喉頭). [Gk. *larynx* throat]

las·civ·i·ous [ləsíviəs] *adj.* causing, feeling, or showing lust; lustful. 도발적〔선정적(煽情的)〕인; 음탕한; 호색의. ¶ *a ~ glance* 음탕한 시선. [L.]

la·ser [léizər] *n.* a device that amplifies radiation of frequencies within the range of visible light. 레이저; 광증폭기(光增幅器). [*l*ight *a*mplification by *s*timulated *e*mission of *r*adiation]

·lash [læʃ] *n.* Ⓒ **1** a whip, esp. the string part of it; a stroke or blow with this. 챗열;

L

채찍질. ¶ *receive so many lashes* 난장을 맞다. **2** a sudden, swift movement; the act of violent beating. 급격한 움직임; 심한 타격. ¶ the ~ *of waves against the rock* 바위를 세차게 치는 파도 / *I received a ~ of his hand on my cheek.* 번개처럼 그가 내 뺨을 후려쳤다. **3** a sharp remark. 날카로운 비난. ¶ *under the lashes of critics* 심한 비난을 받고. **4** an eyelash. 속눈썹. ¶ *She has long lashes.* 속눈썹이 길다.

— *vt.* **1** (P6,7) strike (something) with a lash; strike violently. …을 매질하다; 냅다 치다. ¶ *He lashed her across the face.* 그는 그녀의 얼굴을 채찍으로 쳤다 / *The rain lashed the trees.* 비가 세차게 수목을 때렸다. **2** (P6,7) attack (someone) severely with words. 심하게 꾸짖다〔비난하다〕. ¶ ~ *someone to* 〔*into*〕 *fury* 아무를 욕해서 격노케 하다 / ~ *someone with the pen* 글로 아무를 매도하다. **3** (P6,7) wave or beat (something) back and forth; fling quickly. (채찍·꼬리 등)을 세게 흔들다. ¶ *The dog lashed its tail.* 개가 세게 꼬리쳤다 / *The wind was lashing the sails.* 바람이 사납게 돛들을 흔들고 있었다. **4** (P7) fasten (things) with a cord or rope; bind. (밧줄 등으로) …을 잡아매다. ¶ ~ *two pieces together* 두 개를 한데 묶다 / ~ *one piece to another* 하나를 다른 것에 매다. — *vi.* (P2A) **1** move quickly or violently; strike with a whip; strike violently. 급격〔격렬〕하게 움직이다; 매질하다; 세게 때리다. ¶ *The rain lashed hard against the windows.* 빗줄기가 사납게 창문을 때렸다. **2** burst into a sudden, violent attack in words. 마구 욕지거리하다. ¶ ~ *at someone* 아무를 맹렬하게 비난하다. [M.E.]

lash out, **a**) (of a horse) hit; kick; strike. (말이) 발길질하다. **b**) speak bitterly. 폭언을 퍼붓다. ¶ ~ *out against* 〔*at*〕 *the government* 정부를 맹렬히 비난하다.

lash·ing [lǽʃiŋ] *n.* **1** Ⓤ a cord, rope, etc. used for binding. 밧줄; 끈. **2** 《*pl.*》 《*colloq.*》 《*of*》 abundance; plenty. 대량; 풍부. ¶ *lashings of food* 〔*drink*〕 많은 음식〔음료〕 / *apple pie with lashings of cream* 크림을 잔뜩 친 애플 파이. **3** whipping or beating. 매질; 구타. [↑]

•**lass** [læs] *n.* Ⓒ **1** a young woman; a girl. 젊은 여성; 소녀(opp. lad). **2** a sweetheart. 애인; 연인. [O.N.]

las·sie [lǽsi] *n.* Ⓒ **1** a girl. 소녀. **2** a sweetheart. 애인. [↑]

las·si·tude [lǽsitjù:d] *n.* Ⓤ the state of being weary; lack of energy; weariness. 피로; 권태. [L.]

las·so [lǽsou] *n.* (*pl.* **-sos** or **-soes**) a noosed rope used for catching cattle. 고리 밧줄; (휘둘러 던지는) 올무. — *vt.* (P6) catch with a lasso. …을 고리밧줄로 잡다. [→lace]

:**last**[1] [læst, lɑ:st] *adj.* **1** coming after all others; final. 최후의; 맨 마지막의(opp. first). ¶ *the ~ page of this book* 이 책의 맨 끝 페이지 / ~ *but one* 〔*two*〕 끝에서 두〔세〕번째 / *to the ~ man* 최후의 한 사람까지; 전멸할 때까지. **2** the last remaining. 최후로 남은. ¶ *the ~ chance* 마지막 기회 / *I spent my ~ dollar.* 마지막 남은 달러까지 다 썼다. **3** most recent; latest; newest; immediately before this. 최근의; 최신의; 바로 전의. ¶ ~ *night* 어젯밤 / ~ *year* 지난 해 / *the ~ news I heard* 내가 접한 최근의 뉴스 / *the ~ things in hats* 최신 유행의 모자 / *His ~ letter came a week ago.* 그의 마지막 편지를 1 주일 전에 받았다. **4** most unlikely; most unsuitable. 가장 …할 것 같지 않은〔부적당한, 어울리지 않은〕. ¶ *He is the ~ man we want to see.* 그자만은 보고싶지 않다 / *He is the ~ man to accept a bribe.* 그만은 뇌물을 받을 사람이 아니다 / *I shall be the ~ man to think so.* 그런 생각은 하기도 싫다. **5** ⓐ lowest; the most inferior. 최저의; 맨 꼴찌의. ¶ *the ~ boy in the class* 반에서 꼴찌 아이. ⓑ utmost; extreme. 극단의; 극도의. ¶ *It is of the ~ importance.* 그게 가장 중요하다.

— *adv.* **1** finally; after all others. 최후에; 맨 끝에. ¶ *He arrived ~ at the party.* 파티에 맨 나중에 왔다. **2** most lately; most recently. 최근에; 요전에. ¶ *When did you see her ~?* 최근에 그녀를 본 게 언제냐.

— *n.* 《*the ~*, usu. *sing.*》 **1** a person or thing that comes last. 최후의 사람〔것〕. ¶ *the day before ~* 그저께 / *He was the ~ to arrive.* 맨 나중에 그가 도착했다. **2** the end; the last moment; one's death. 최종; 마지막; 임종; 죽음. ¶ *from first to ~* 처음부터 끝까지 / *be faithful to the ~* 끝까지 신의를 지키다 / *I thought every moment would be my ~.* 내 목숨이 경각에 있지 않나 싶었다. [*latest*]

at (***long***) ***last,*** finally. 드디어. ¶ *The holidays came at ~.* 마침내 휴가를 얻었다.

breath one's last, die. 죽다.

hear the last of, hear for the last time. 마지막으로 듣다. ¶ *We shall never hear the ~ of the story.* 그 이야기는 늘 사람들 입에 오르내릴 것이다.

:**last**[2] [læst, lɑ:st] *vi.* **1** (P1,2B) go on; continue in time. 계속되다; 지속하다. ¶ *The fine weather lasted eight days.* 좋은 날씨가 여드레나 계속됐다 / *as long as life lasts* 살아있는 한. **2** (P3) be enough; continue unspent. 족하다; 떨어지지 않다. ¶ *while our money lasts* 돈이 있는 한. **3** (P1,2B) continue in use or alive; endure. 오래가다〔견디다〕. ¶ *He will not ~ (out) till tomorrow.* 그는 내일을 못넘길 것이다 / *This shoes will ~ for a long time.* 이 신은 오래 신겠다. — *vt.* (P7) continue for (someone); suffice. …보다 오래가다; 충분하다. ¶ *The money lasted me (for) two months.* 이 돈으로 두 달은 지낼 것이다. [E.]

last[3] [læst, lɑ:st] *n.* a shoemaker's wooden model for shaping shoes on. 구두골. [E.]

stick to one's last, not meddle with things one does not understand. 모르는 일에 나서지 않다.

·last·ing [lǽstiŋ, lɑ́:st-] *adj.* lasting for a long period or forever; permanent. 영속하는; 내구력이 있는; 영원한(opp. temporary). ¶ *search for a ~ peace* 영원한 평화를 추구하다. ● **last·ing·ly** [-li] *adv.* [*last*[2]]

Last Judgment [⌐ ⌐–], **the** *n.* the final trial of all men by God. 최후의 심판.

last·ly [lǽstli, lɑ́:st-] *adv.* in the end; in conclusion; finally. 최후로; 마지막으로 (opp. first; firstly). [*last*[1]]

last straw [⌐⌐], **the** *n.* a slight addition making a burden no longer tolerable. 인내의 한계를 넘게 하는 것.

latch [lætʃ] *n.* Ⓒ a device for fastening a door, a gate, etc. 빗장; 걸쇠. ¶ *be off the ~* 빗장이 벗겨져 있다 / *The door is on the ~.* 문은 걸쇠만 걸려 있다. — *vt., vi.* (P6; 1) close or fasten (a door, etc.) with a latch. …에 걸쇠를 걸다; 걸쇠가 걸리다. [E.]

latch on to, 《*colloq.*》 **a**) attach (oneself) to. …에 집착하다. **b**) get hold of; obtain. …을 장악하다; 손에 넣다. **c**) understand. …을 이해하다.

latch·key [lǽtʃkì:] *n.* Ⓒ a key for drawing back or unfastening the latch of a door. 걸쇠의 열쇠.

:late [leit] *adj.* (**lat·er, lat·est** or **lat·ter, last**) **1** being after the usual, right or expected time. (시각이) 늦은; 뒤늦은; 지각한(opp. early). ¶ *~ dinner* 늦은 저녁 / *~ spring* 만춘(晩春) / *keep ~ hours* 밤늦게까지 안 자다 / *a ~ marriage* 만혼(晩婚) / *be ~ for school* 학교에 지각하다 / *The train is ten minutes ~.* 기차가 10분 연착이다. **2** toward the end of a certain time; far advanced in a period. 마지막에 가까운; 후기의; 만년의. ¶ *the ~ Middle Ages* 중세 후기 / *in the later part of the year* 그해 말에. **3** recent. 요즈음의; 최근의. ¶ *of ~ years* 요 몇 해 / *the ~ fire* 최근에 난 화재 / *the ~ storm* 요전의 폭풍 / *His latest novel was a success.* 그의 최근의 소설은 큰 호평을 받았다. **4** no longer living; recently dead; former. 최근에 죽은; 고(故)…; 전의. ¶ *my ~ father* 돌아가신 부친 / *the ~ prime minister* 전(前) 수상 / *the ~ government* 이전의 정부. — *adv.* (**lat·er, lat·est** or **last**) **1** after the usual or proper time. 늦게; 더디게. ¶ *come ~* 늦게 오다; 지각하다 / *get up ~* 늦게 기상하다 / *Ten minutes later he came back.* 그는 10분 늦게 돌아왔다 / 《*prov.*》 *Better ~ than never.* 늦더라도 안하느니보다는 낫다. **2** until an advanced hour, esp. of the night; till late. (밤)늦게까지. ¶ *We sat up ~ last night.* 지난 밤 늦게까지 안 자고 있었다. **3** recently; lately. 최근; 요즈음. ¶ *I saw him as ~ as last Sunday.* 바로 지난 일요일에 그를 만났다. [E.]

early and late, from morning till night. 아침부터 밤까지.

·late·ly [léitli] *adv.* 《in *negative* or *interrogative*》 not long ago; recently. 요즈음; 최근. ¶ *Have you seen her ~?* 최근 그녀를 만났느냐 / *She has not been here ~.* 그녀는 요즘 여기 오지 않았다. [*late*]

la·tence [léitəns], **la·ten·cy** [léitənsi] *n.* the quality or condition of being latent. 잠복; 잠재. [L.]

late·ness [léitnis] *n.* Ⓤ the state of being late. 늦음; 지각. ¶ *the ~ of his arrival* 〔*the season*〕 늦은 그의 도착〔때늦게 찾아온 계절〕. [*late*]

la·tent [léitənt] *adj.* existing but not active; concealed; hidden. 잠복성의; 숨어 있는. ¶ *~ ability* 잠재 능력 / *~ heat* 잠열(潛熱) / *the ~ period* 잠복기. [L. →latency]

:lat·er [léitər] *adj.* comparative of **late.** — *adv.* at a later time; after some time. 나중에; 후에. ¶ *five days ~* 닷새 뒤에 / *I will see you ~.* 나중에 만나자 / *I met her two years ~.* 그녀를 2년 후에 만났다. [*late*]

later on, afterward; subsequently. 나중에; 후에(opp. earlier on). ¶ *This happened ~ on.* 이 일은 나중에 일어났다.

sooner or later ⇨soon.

lat·er·al [lǽtərəl] *adj.* of, at, toward, or coming from the side. 옆의; 측면의. ¶ *a ~ branch of a family* 분가(分家) / *a ~ consonant* 설측음(舌側音). — *n.* Ⓒ **1** a lateral part, growth, branch, etc. 옆쪽(에서 생기는 것). **2** 《phon.》 a lateral sound. 측음(側音). [L. *latus* side]

lat·est [léitist] *adj., adv.* superl. of **late;** most recent, newest; last. 최근(의); 최신의; 최후의〔로〕. ¶ *Have you heard the ~ news?* 최근의 소식을 알고 있니 / *the ~ thing* 최신의 발명품. [*late*]

at* (*the*) *latest, not later than (a specified time). 늦어도. ¶ *We must be there by 7 p.m. at* (*the*) *latest.* 늦어도 오후 7시까지는 거기 도착해야 한다.

the latest, the most recent news, fashion, or development. 최근의 소식〔유행, 발전 따위〕.

la·tex [léiteks] *n.* ⓊⒸ (*pl.* **lat·i·ces** or **-tex·es**) a milky liquid found in certain plants and trees, such as the rubber tree, the poppy, etc. 라텍스; 유액(乳液); 수액(樹液). [Gk. *latax* drop]

lath [læθ, lɑ:θ] *n.* Ⓒ (*pl.* **laths**) a thin, narrow strip of wood fastened to the framework of a house to support the plaster. 외(椳); 욋가지. [E.]

as thin as a lath, (of a person) very skinny. 말라빠진.

lathe [leið] *n.* Ⓒ a machine on which articles of wood, metal, etc. are turned to be shaped or polished. 선반(旋盤); 녹로. [M.E.]

lath·er [lǽðər, lɑ́:ð-] *n* Ⓤ《sometimes *a ~*》 **1** the foam or froth produced by soap and water. 비누 거품. **2** foamy sweat, as on a race horse. (경주마의) 거품같은 땀. ¶ *be* (*all*) *in a ~* 땀투성이가 되다. — *vt.* (P6) **1** cover (something) with lather. …에

L

비누 거품을 칠하다. ¶ ~ *one's face before shaving.* 면도하기 전에 얼굴에 비누 거품을 칠하다. **2** 《*colloq.*》 beat severely. …을 마구 때리다〔치다〕. — *vi.* (P1) **1** (of soap) form lather (비누가) 거품이 일다. ¶ *This soap doesn't ~ well.* 이 비누는 거품이 잘 일지 않는다. **2** (of horse) be soaked with sweat. (말이) 땀투성이가 되다. [O.N. =foam]

lath·ing [lǽθiŋ, lɑ:-] *n.* **1** 《*collectively*》 laths. 외. **2** the act of putting laths on walls etc. 외(椳)엮기. [*lath*]

laths [læðz, -θs, lɑ:θs, -ðz] *n.* pl. of **lath.**

lath·y [lǽθi] *adj.* (**lath·i·er, lath·i·est**) like a lath; tall and slender 외 같은; 가늘고 긴. [*lath*]

lat·i·ces [lǽtisi:z] *n.* pl. of **latex.**

:Lat·in [lǽtin] *adj.* **1** of ancient Rome, its people, or their language. 라틴(사람·어)의 (cf. *Romance*). **2** of the languages descended from that of ancient Rome; of the people who speak these languages. 라틴어계(系)의; 라틴 사람 계통의. — *n.* **1** Ⓤ the language of ancient Rome. 라틴어. **2** Ⓒ a member of one of the Latin races. 라틴 사람. [L.]

Lat·in·ism [lǽtənizəm] *n.* a form of expression imitating Latin or derived from Latin. 라틴어풍(風)〔어법(語法)〕.

Lat·in·ist [lǽtənist] *n.* a scholar in Latin. 라틴어 학자.

lat·in·ize [lǽtənàiz] *vt.* (P6) **1** give a Latin form or style to. 라틴어풍으로 하다; 라틴(어)화하다. **2** translate into Latin. 라틴어로 번역하다. — *vi.* (P1) use Latin words or phrases. 라틴어법을 쓰다. [L.] 「(게). [*late*]

lat·ish [léitiʃ] *adj., adv.* rather late. 좀 늦은

·lat·i·tude [lǽtətjù:d] *n.* Ⓤ **1** the distance of a place north or south of the equator as measured in degrees. 위도(opp. longitude). ¶ *at ~ 40°N.* 북위 40도에. **2** 《*pl.*》 regions; districts 지역; 지방. ¶ *cold* 〔*calm*〕 *latitudes* 한대〔무풍대〕/ *high* 〔*low*〕 *latitudes.* 고〔저〕위도 지방. **3** freedom of thought, judgment or action. (사상·판단·행동의) 자유. ¶ *We are allowed some ~ in this work.* 우리는 이 일에 어느 정도의 자유 재량권을 받았다. **4** extent; scope. 범위. [L. *latus* broad]

lat·i·tu·di·nar·i·an [lætitjù:dənέəriən] *adj.* of liberal views, esp. in religious matters; tolerant; broad-minded. 자유주의의; (특히 종파에) 관용적인; 광교파(廣敎派)의. — *n.* Ⓒ a person who is very liberal, esp. in his religious views. 광교파의 사람.

la·trine [lətrí:n] *n.* a place for evacuation of bowels. 변소. [→lave]

L

:lat·ter [lǽtər] *adj.* compar. of **late 1** later; nearer to the end. 뒤쪽의; 끝에 가까운. ¶ *the ~ part of the month* 그 달의 후반. **2** recent 요즘의; 근래의. ¶ *in these ~ days* 요즈음은. **3** 《*the* ~》 the second of two persons or things mentioned; the last mentioned of two. 후자(後者) (opp. former). 參考 형용사의 대명사적 용법. ¶ *Of the two the former is dead, and the ~ is dying.* 그 두 사람 중에서 전자는 죽었고, 후자는 죽어 가고 있다. [=*later*]

one's latter end, one's death; the last moment of life. 임종; 최후. 「즈음; 최근.

lat·ter·ly [lǽtərli] *adv.* of late; recently. 요

lat·tice [lǽtis] *n.* Ⓒ **1** a frame of crossed wooden lathes, or iron bars. 래티스; 격자(格子). **2** a window, a gate, etc. made of a lattice. 격자창〔문〕. — *vt.* (P6) form (a window, etc.) into a lattice; furnish (a gate, etc.) with a lattice. (창 따위)를 격자꼴로 하다; (문 따위)에 격자를 붙이다. [*lath*]

〈lattice〉

lat·ticed [lǽtist] *adj.* made in the form of a lattice; furnished with a lattice. 격자로 된; 격자를 붙인. ¶ *a ~ gate* 격자문.

lat·tice·work [lǽtiswə̀:rk] *n.* **1** Ⓤ 《*collectively*》 lattices. 격자 세공. **2** Ⓒ a lattice. 격자.

laud [lɔ:d] *vt.* (P6) praise; glorify. 칭찬하다; 찬미하다.

laud someone to the skies, speak very highly of someone; praise someone very much. …을 극구 칭찬하다

— *n.* **1** Ⓤ praise. 칭찬; 찬미. **2** Ⓒ any songs or hymns of praise. 찬가; 찬미가. **3** 《*pl.*》 the prayers recited at day break. 새벽 기도. [L.]

laud·a·ble [lɔ́:dəbəl] *adj.* **1** deserving praise; praiseworthy. 칭찬받을 만한; 장한; 기특한. ¶ *a ~ effort.* **2** 《med.》 healthy. 건강한.

lau·da·num [lɔ́:dənəm] *n.* Ⓤ a solution of opium in alcohol used as a medicine. 아편정기(丁幾). [Per.]

lau·da·tion [lɔ:déiʃən] *n.* Ⓤ the act of lauding; the state of being lauded; praise. 칭찬; 칭송; 찬미. [*laud*]

laud·a·to·ry [lɔ́:dətɔ̀:ri / -təri] *adj.* expressing praise. 찬미의; 칭찬의.

:laugh [læf, lɑ:f] *vi.* **1** (P1,2A,3) make sounds of the voice showing pleasure or amusement. (소리내서) 웃다. ¶ *~ merrily* / *~ out loudly* 큰 소리로 웃다 / *~ in someone's face* 아무를 면전에서 비웃다. **2** (P1) be or appear gay and lively. 즐거워하다; (자연계의 움직임 따위가) 홍겨워〔생동하는 것처럼〕 보이다. ¶ *We heard a laughing brook.* 시냇물의 졸졸 소리가 웃음 소리처럼 들렸다.

— *vt.* **1** (P6) express or say (something) with laughter. …을 웃으며 말하다; 웃는 얼굴

로 …을 나타내다. ¶ ~ *a reply* 웃으며 대답하다 / *He laughed his consent.* 그는 웃으며 동의했다. **2** (P7,13,18) influence (someone or something) by laughing. 웃어서 …을 어떤 상태에 이르게 하다. ¶ ~ *someone into silence* 웃어서 아무의 입을 다물게 하다 / *I tried to ~ him out of the foolish belief.* 나는 웃어서 그의 어리석은 생각을 버리게 하려고 했다.

laugh at, **a**) show disrespect to; make fun of (someone). …을 비웃다; 경멸하다. ¶ *Don't ~ at someone in trouble.* 어려운 처지에 있는 사람을 비웃지 마라. **b**) be amused by (something). …을 보고[듣고] 웃다. ¶ ~ *at a joke* 농담에 웃다. **c**) be not moved by; make light of; disregard. 아무렇지 않게 생각하다; 무시하다. ¶ ~ *at danger* 위험을 무시하다.

laugh away, **a**) get rid of (something unpleasant) by laughter. 웃어 …을 떨어 버리다. ¶ *We laughed our fears away.* 우리는 웃음으로 무서움을 달랬다. **b**) keep laughing. 계속 웃다. ¶ ~ *away ones days* 웃으며 지내다.

laugh down, cause (a speech, etc.) to stop by laughing at it. …을 웃어 침묵시키다. ¶ ~ *someone down.*

laugh in [***up***] *one's* ***sleeve,*** laugh secretly or inwardly. 속으로 웃다; 고소해하다.

laugh off, avoid or reject (something) by laughing at it. …을 웃어 넘기다; 일소에 부치다. ¶ ~ *off someone's advice* 아무의 충고를 그저 웃어 넘기다.

laugh on the other [***wrong***] ***side of*** *one's* ***mouth*** [***face***]***,*** be sorry or disappointed after having been pleased; change from joy to sorrow. 좋다가 말다; (웃다가) 울상이 되다; 낙심 천만하다.

laugh over, remember or talk about with laughter. 생각하며 웃다; 웃으며 말하다. ¶ ~ *over a letter* 편지를 보며 웃다.

— *n.* Ⓒ an act or a sound of laughing; laughter. 웃음; 웃음 소리. ¶ *burst into a ~* 웃음을 터뜨리다 / *have a hearty ~* 마음껏[실컷] 웃다 / *give a ~* 웃음 소리를 내다 / *raise a ~* 남을 웃기다 / *give a good ~* 한바탕 웃다. [E.]

have the last laugh on, succeed in (something) after overcoming many difficulties; surprise (someone) by succeeding in doing something he said one couldn't do, etc. 고생 끝에 …에 성공하다; 못 할 거라고 하던 일을 해내서 …을 놀라게 하다.

have [***get***] ***the laugh of*** [***on***] *(someone)****,*** turn the tables on; get the better of (*someone*). 되레 웃어 주다; …을 역전(逆轉)시켜 이기다.

laugh·a·ble [lǽfəbəl, lɑ́:f-] *adj.* causing laughter; amusing. 우스운; 재미있는; 우스꽝스러운. ● **laugh·a·ble·ness** [-nis] *n.* **laugh·a·bly** [-i] *adv.*

laugh·ing [lǽfiŋ, lɑ́:f-] *adj.* **1** that laughs or seems to be merry. 웃고 있는; 기쁜 듯한. ¶ *a ~ face.* **2** causing laughter. 웃기는; 우스운. ¶ *It is no ~ matter.* 웃을 일이 아니다. — *n.* Ⓤ laughter. 웃음. ¶ *hold one's ~* 웃음을 참다.

laughing gas [ˊ-ˋ] *n.* Ⓤ 《chem.》 a colorless gas of nitrous oxide which makes people laugh. 웃음 가스; 소기(笑氣).

laugh·ing·ly [lǽfiŋli, lɑ́:f-] *adv.* with laughter. 웃어; 웃으며.

laugh·ing·stock [lǽfiŋstɑ̀k, lɑ́:fiŋ- / -stɔ̀k] *n.* Ⓒ a person or thing that is laughed at. 웃음거리.

:laugh·ter [lǽftər, lɑ́:f-] *n.* Ⓤ the act or sound of laughing. 웃음; 웃음 소리. ¶ *burst* [*break out*] *into ~* 웃음을 터뜨리다 / *roars of ~* 홍소(哄笑). [*laugh*]

·launch [lɔ:ntʃ, lɑ:ntʃ] *vt.* **1** (P6) cause (a ship) to slide into the water. (배)를 진수시키다. ¶ *A new ship was launched from its supports.* 배는 선거(船渠)에서 진수되었다. **2** (P6) send forth (something) with some force; throw; hurl. …을 밀어내다; 발진시키다; 활공[이륙]시키다; 발사하다. ¶ ~ *a rocket* 로켓을 발사하다 / ~ *an arrow into the air* 화살을 날리다. **3** (P6) ⓐ start; begin. …을 시작하다; 일으키다; 착수하다. ¶ ~ *a new enterprise* 새 사업을 시작하다. ⓑ start (someone) on a new course, career, etc. …을 새로운 길로 내보내다. ¶ ~ *one's son in the world* 아들을 사회로 내보내다 / ~ *a friend in* [*into*] *business* 친구에게 사업을 시작하게 하다. **4** (P6,13) strike; aim. …을 공격하다. ¶ ~ *a blow* 한 대 갈기다. — *vi.* (P2A, 3) **1** put out to sea; go to sea. 바다에 나가다. ¶ ~ *in ocean voyage* 대양에 나아가다. **2** start on a course or career. (사업 등) 새로운 출발을 하다. ¶ ~ *into politics* [*a business career*] 정계에 투신하다[장사길에 나서다].

launch out =***launch*** (***out***) ***into,*** **a**) put to sea. (배가) 바다로 나가다. ¶ ~ *out on a voyage of expedition* 탐험의 항해에 나서다. **b**) start on some new enterprise with enthusiasm. (사업 등)을 열의를 가지고 시작하다. ¶ ~ *(out) into an argument* 활발하게 논의를 개시하다.

— *n.* **1** Ⓤ the act of launching. (배의) 진수. **2** Ⓒ a small open boat driven by an engine. 론치; 기정(汽艇). [*lance*]

laun·der [lɔ́:ndər, lɑ́:n-] *vt.* (P6) wash and iron. …을 빨다; 세탁하다. ¶ *beautifully laundered sheets* 깨끗하게 빤 홑이불. — *vi.* (P2A) be able to be washed. 세탁이 잘 되다. ¶ *This shirt launders well.* 이 셔츠는 세탁이 잘 된다. [L. *lavo* wash]

laun·der·ette [lɔ̀:ndərét, lɑ̀:n-] *n.* a self-service laundry having coin-operated washers, driers, etc. 셀프서비스식 세탁소; 빨래방《코인을 넣어서 작동시키는 세탁기·건조기가 설치돼 있는》.

laun·dress [lɔ́:ndris, lɑ́:n-] *n.* Ⓒ a woman whose work is washing and ironing cloths. 세탁부.

*__laun·dry__ [lɔ́:ndri, lɑ́:n-] *n.* (*pl.* **-dries**) **1** Ⓒ a place where clothes, etc. are washed and ironed. 세탁장; 세탁소. **2** Ⓤ 《*the* ~, *collectively*》 something esp. clothes to be laundered. 세탁물; 빨랫감. [*launder*]

__laun·dry·man__ [lɔ́:ndrimən, lɑ́:n-] *n.* Ⓒ (*pl.* **-men** [-mən]) a man who works in a laundry; a man who collects and delivers laundry. 세탁부(夫).

__lau·re·ate__ [lɔ́:riit] *adj.* crowned with a laurel wreath; honored. 월계관을 쓴. ¶ *a poet* ~ 계관 시인. —*n.* Ⓒ a poet who has been honored. 계관 시인. [↓]

*__lau·rel__ [lɔ́:rəl, lɑ́:r-] *n.* Ⓒ **1** a small evergreen tree with smooth, shiny leaves, used as a symbol of fame and honor. 월계수. **2** a crown of laurel given as a prize or symbol of honor by the ancient Greeks and Romans. 월계관. **3** 《often *pl.*》 honor; fame; victory. 영예; 명성; 승리. ¶ *gain* (*win*) *laurels* 영예를 얻다. [L. *laurus* bay]

look to one's laurels, be careful about one's reputation. 명성을 지키는 데 신경을 쓰다.

rest on one's laurels, be contented with the honors that one has already gained. 이미 얻은 명예에 만족하다.

__lau·reled,__ 《Brit.》 **-relled** [lɔ́:rəld, lɑ́:r-] *adj.* crowned with laurel; honored. 월계관을 쓴; 영예를 얻은.

*__la·va__ [lɑ́:və, lǽvə] *n.* Ⓤ the liquid rock flowing from a volcano; such rock when it has hardened. 용암; 화산암. ¶ ~ *bed* 용암층. [L. *lavo* wash]

__lav·a·to·ry__ [lǽvətɔ̀:ri / -təri] *n.* Ⓒ (*pl.* **-ries**) **1** a room for washing the hands and the face. 세면소; 화장실. **2** a fixed bowl or basin to wash in. 세면대. **3** a toilet. 변소. [L. *lavo* wash, -ory]

__lav·en·der__ [lǽvəndər] *n.* **1** Ⓒ a small plant with pale purple flowers that have a sweet smell. 라벤더. **2** Ⓤ the color of pale purple. 라벤더색; 엷은 자줏빛. [L.]

__lav·ish__ [lǽviʃ] *adj.* **1** very liberal; almost too generous in giving or spending. 활수한; 손이 큰. ¶ *He is* ~ *of* (*with*) *money.* 돈을 잘 쓰는 사람이다 / ~ *hospitality* (너무) 후한 대접 / ~ *expenditure* 낭비. **2** very abundant; excessive. 풍부한. ¶ *a* ~ *supply of food* 풍부(충분)한 식량 공급. —*vt.* (P13) give or spend generously. …을 아끼지 않고 주다; 낭비하다. ¶ ~ *money* (*kindness, praise*) *on someone* 아무에게 아낌없이 돈을(친절을, 찬사를) 주다(베풀다) / ~ *one's money upon one's pleasure* 유흥에 돈을 물쓰듯 하다. [L. *lavo* wash]

__lav·ish·ly__ [lǽviʃli] *adv.* in a lavish manner. 아낌없이; 헙헙하게.

‡__law__ [lɔ:] *n.* **1** Ⓒ Ⓤ a rule made by a government or a ruler; the order produced by it. 법; 법률; 법령. ¶ *the civil* ~ 민법 / *keep* (*break*) *the* ~ 법을 지키다(어기다) / *go to* ~ *against someone* 아무를 고소하다 / *There is a* ~ *against spitting in streetcars.* 전차 안에서 침 뱉는 것을 금하는 법률이 있다. **2** Ⓤ 《often *the* ~》 the profession of lawyers or judges. 사법직(職); 법률업. ¶ *follow the* ~ 변호사가 되다 / *practice* ~ 변호사업을 하다. **3** Ⓤ Ⓒ a rule of a game, trade, etc.; a principle. 규칙; 법칙; 규정. ¶ *the laws of tennis* 테니스 규칙 / *the Law of Moses* 모세의 율법 / *a moral* ~ 도덕률 / *Mendel's* ~ 멘델의 법칙 / *the laws of God* 신의 계율. **4** Ⓤ the branch of knowledge dealing with such rules. 법학. ¶ *study* ~ 법률 공부를 하다. **5** Ⓒ the manner or order in which natural events occur under certain conditions. 법칙. ¶ *the* ~ *of gravitation* 인력의 법칙. **6** the law-court. 법정. [E. =a thing laid down]

be a law to oneself, follow one's own opinion. 자기 생각대로 하다.

be a law unto oneself, disregard convention. 관습을 무시하다.

give the law to, impose one's will upon. …을 마음대로 하다(좌지우지하다).

go to law with = ***have*** (***take***) ***the law of*** bring a suit against. …을 기소(고소)하다.

lay down the law, talk authoritatively. 명령적(독단적)으로 말하다.

read law, study the laws. 법률을 연구하다.

take the law into one's own hands, redress one's wrong by force. (법에 의하지 않고) 멋대로 제재를 가하다; 린치하다.

__law·a·bid·ing__ [lɔ́:əbàidiŋ] *adj.* keeping the law; well behaved. 법을 지키는; 품행이 좋은.

__law·break·ing__ [lɔ́:brèikiŋ] *n.* Ⓤ the act of breaking the law. 위법. —*adj.* violating the law. 위법의.

__law court__ [⌐⌐] *n.* a court of justice; a place where legal cases are judged. 법정(法廷).

*__law·ful__ [lɔ́:fəl] *adj.* **1** according to law; allowed by law; rightful. 합법의; 정당한. ¶ ~ *method* 적법한 방법 / *a* ~ *act* 합법적인 행위. **2** as decided by law. 법정의. ¶ ~ *age* 법정 연령; 성년(成年) / *a* ~ *possessor* (*heir*) 법률상 정당한 소유자(상속자).

__law·ful·ly__ [lɔ́:fəli] *adv.* in a lawful manner; rightly. 합법적으로; 정당하게.

__law·giv·er__ [lɔ́:gìvər] *n.* Ⓒ a man who forms or writes a system of laws; a lawmaker. 입법자.

__law·less__ [lɔ́:lis] *adj.* **1** uncontrolled by the law; breaking the law; unruly. 법을 안 지키는; 무법한; 불법의. **2** without laws. 법률이 없는. ¶ *a* ~ *man* 무법자 / *a* ~ *region* 무법 지대.

__law·less·ly__ [lɔ́:lisli] *adv.* in a lawless manner. 무법(無法)으로; 불법으로; 제어할 수 없이.

__law·mak·er__ [lɔ́:mèikər] *n.* Ⓒ a person who makes or helps to make laws; a leg-

L

islator. 입법자.

:**lawn**[1] [lɔːn] *n.* Ⓒ an area of grass kept closely cut. 잔디(cf. *turf*). ¶ *a tennis* ~ 테니스 코트용 잔디 / *mow* 〔*cut*〕 *the* ~ 잔디를 깎다. [Celt.]

lawn[2] [lɔːn] *n.* Ⓤ a thin cloth of linen or cotton. 론; 한랭사(寒冷紗). [Place]

lawn mower [⌐ ⌐–] *n.* a machine used to cut grass on lawns. 잔디 깎는 기계.

lawn tennis [⌐ ⌐–] *n.* a kind of tennis, usu. played on lawn. 론 테니스《잔디밭에서 하는 정구》; 정구.

law·suit [lɔ́ːsùːt] *n.* Ⓒ a case in a law court. 소송. ¶ *enter* 〔*bring in*〕 *a* ~ *against someone* 아무를 걸어 소송을 제기하다. [*law*]

:**law·yer** [lɔ́ːjər] *n.* Ⓒ a person who advises other persons about matters of law or acts, in a law court; a person skilled or learned in the law. 변호사; 법률가. ¶ *a good* 〔*poor*〕 ~ 법률에 밝은〔어두운〕 사람 / *consult a* ~ 변호사의 의견을 묻다. [*law*]

lax [læks] *adj.* **1** not firm or strict; loose; careless. 애매한. ¶ ~ *in morals* 〔*discipline*〕 소행(素行)이 흐릿한. **2** (of the bowels) loose; having lax bowels. 설사하는. **3** not exact or precise. 정확하지 못한. ¶ ~ *ideas of a subject* 문제에 대한 부정확한 개념 [L.]

lax·a·tive [lǽksətiv] *adj.* making the bowels move or empty. 대변을〔설사를〕 나오게 하는. — *n.* Ⓒ a medicine that does this. 하제(下劑).

lax·i·ty [lǽksəti] *n.* Ⓤ lack of firmness or exactness. 흘게늦음; 방종; 부정확.

:**lay**[1] [lei] *v.* (**laid**) *vt.* **1** (P6,7) ⓐ cause (something) to lie; put or place. …을 눕히다; 누이다; 놓다. ¶ ~ *oneself down* 드러눕다 / *She laid her hands on my shoulder.* 그녀는 내 어깨에 손을 얹었다. ⓑ bury. 묻다; 매장하다. ¶ ~ *someone to rest* 아무를 땅에 묻다. **2** (P7,13) place something in a certain place; set in the proper position. …을 부설하다; 깔다; (벽돌 따위를) 쌓다. ¶ ~ *a cable* 케이블을 부설하다 / ~ *a pavement* 보도를 깔다 / ~ *bricks* 벽돌을 쌓다. **3** (P6,13) knock 〔beat〕 down; deal (a blow) at. …을 때려 눕히다; 쓰러뜨리다; 한 방 갈기다. ¶ *The wind has laid all the crops low.* 바람에 모든 작물이 쓰러졌다 / ~ *a man with a single blow* 한 주먹에 때려눕히다. **4** (P6,13) cover or coat. …을 덮다; 입히다; 칠하다. ¶ ~ *a floor with paint* 마루에 페인트를 칠하다. **5** (P13) say or think that (something) belongs to another; ascribe; impute. …을 비난하다; …을 남에게 돌리다; 남의 탓으로 하다. ¶ ~ *a fault to someone's charge* 실패를 아무의 책임이라 하다 / ~ *a charge of theft against someone* 아무를 도둑으로 몰다. **6** (P6) produce (eggs). (달걀)을 낳다. ¶ *The hens don't* ~ (*eggs*) *in this cold weather.* 이렇게 추워서는 닭이 알을 낳지 않는다. **7** (P6) cause (something) to be quiet; settle; cause to disappear. …을 가라앉히다; 진정시키다; (유령 따위를) 쫓다. ¶ ~ *someone's fear* 아무의 무서움을 진정시키다 / *The shower has laid the dust.* 소나기로 먼지가 가라앉았다 / ~ *a ghost* 귀신을 쫓다. **8** (P6) make (something) ready; prepare. …의 준비를 하다; 마련하다. ¶ ~ *a table for dinner* 저녁상을 차리다 / ~ *a fire* 불을 피우다 / ~ *a trap* 〔*snare*〕 *for foxes* 여우덫을 놓다. **9** (P6, 13) bet; put down as a wager or stake. …을 걸다; 내기에 걸다. ¶ *I* ~ *5 dollars that she will come.* 그녀가 오는 쪽에 5달러 걸겠다 / ~ *on a horse race* 경마에 걸다. **10** (P6,13) 《usu. in *passive*》 locate; situate. …위치를 정하다; 설정하다. ¶ *The scene of the story is laid in Paris in 1927.* 이야기는 1927년의 파리를 무대로 하였다. **11** (P7,18) cause (someone or something) to be in a certain state or condition. …을 어떤 상태로 되게 하다. ¶ ~ *one's chest bare* 모조리 자백하다 / ~ *city waste* 시를 황폐하게 만들다. **12** (P13) put on as a duty; punishment; impose. (의무·벌 등)을 지우다; 과하다. ¶ ~ *heavy taxes on tea* 차에 중과세하다 / ~ *a penalty on someone* 아무를 처벌하다. **13** (P13) bring or place before someone; present. (…을) …에게 제출〔제시〕하다. ¶ ~ *a case before court* 사건을 제소(提訴)하다 / *The bill has been laid before the House of Commons.* 법안은 하원에 제출되었다.

— *vi.* **1** (P1) lay eggs. 알을 낳다. **2** (P3) wager or bet. 걸다; 내기하다. ¶ ~ *on a boat race* 보트 경기에 돈을 걸다. **3** (P3) deal or aim blows. 치다; 때리다. **4** (P3) apply oneself vigorously. 의욕적으로 달라붙다. ¶ *The crew laid to their oars.* 승무원은 일제히 노를 잡았다. **5** (P1) lie. (가로)눕다. [E.]

lay about, 《Brit.》 strike out in all directions; fight fiercely. 전후 좌우로 마구 치다; 맹렬하게 싸우다.

lay aside, put to one side. 치워 두다. ¶ *We cannot* ~ *aside that interesting book.* 그 책이 어찌나 재미있는지 손에서 놓지 못하겠다.

lay away 〔***by, in***〕, **a**) save for future use; store; lay aside. 저축〔비축〕해 두다. ¶ ~ *money by for a rainy day* 궁한 때를 대비해 저축하다 / ~ *in coal for the winter* 겨울을 위해 석탄을 비축해 두다. **b**) give up. 그만두다.

lay before, show; explain to. 보이다; 설명하다. ¶ *He laid before me all the facts.* 모든 사실을 내게 밝혔다〔설명했다〕.

lay down, **a**) place in a lying position; place in a cellar for storing. 눕혀 놓다; 저장하다. ¶ ~ *down wine* 포도주를 저장하다. **b**) give up; sacrifice. 포기하다; 희생하다. ¶ ~ *down* (*one's*) *arms* 무기를 버리다; 항복하다 / ~ *down one's office* 사임하다. **c**) prescribe; declare; assert; state clearly and definitely. 규정하다; 단언하다; 분명히 말하다. ¶ ~ *down a rule* 규칙을 정하다. **d**) begin to build; construct. 기공하다; 건설하다. ¶ ~ *down a ship* 선박을 건조하다 / ~ *down a railway* 철도를 부설하다.

L

lay fast, imprison. 투옥하다.
lay for (=*lie in wait for; wait to attack*) *someone,* 아무를 (치려고) 숨어 기다리다.
lay hands on, grasp; seize. …을 붙잡다, 붙들다.
lay into *someone,* 《*sl.*》 beat. …을 치다, 때리다.
lay it on thick =***lay it on with trowel,*** praise or flatter too much. 너무 칭찬하다; 치살리다 (cf. *trowel*).
lay low, cause to be down; send to the ground. 쓰러뜨리다; 타도하다.
lay off, **a**) take off and put aside. 벗어 놓다(버리다). ¶ ~ *off one's clothes.* **b**) dismiss (someone) during a slack period; discharge for a time. (불황 시에) 일시 해고하다. ¶ ~ *off most of the workers* 노동자의 대부분을 해고하다 / *He was laid off.* 그는 해고당했다. **c**) stop doing (something) (for a time). (얼마간) …을 그만두다; 중지하다.
lay on, **a**) spread; apply. …을 바르다. ¶ *Lay the butter on thick.* 버터를 많이 바르다 / ~ *on paint* 페인트를 칠하다. **b**) strike (a blow); beat. …을 때리다(치다). **c**) make an attack. 공격하다. **d**) supply (water, gas) to a house. 가정에 (물·가스를) 공급하다.
lay open, cut open; expose. …을 절개(切開)하다.
lay *oneself* ***open to,*** expose oneself to (attack, blame, etc.); run the risk of. (비난·공격)에 몸을 드러내다; 위험을 무릅쓰다.
lay out, **a**) arrange in order; plan out. …을 정돈하다; 기획(계획)하다; 꾸미다. ¶ ~ *out a garden for flowers* 정원을 꽃밭으로 꾸미다. **b**) spend carefully. (신중히) 돈을 들이다(쓰다). ¶ ~ *out a large sum of money in purchasing land* 부동산 구입에 거금을 들이다. **c**) prepare for burial. (시체의) 매장 준비를 하다. ¶ ~ *out a dead body.*
lay *oneself* ***out,*** 《*colloq.*》 try one's best; make a great effort. 노력하다; 최선을 다하다. ¶ ~ *oneself out for a prize* 상을 타려고 힘쓰다.
lay over, **a**) 《U.S.》 stop for a short time on one's journey. (여행) 도중 잠시 머무르다. ¶ ~ *over in New York* 뉴욕에서 잠시 머무르다. **b**) delay; postpone. 지연되다; 연기하다.
lay up, **a**) put by; store up; lay aside. 떼어 놓다; 저축하다. ¶ ~ *up food against a day of want* 가난에 대비하여 식량을 마련해 두다. **b**) put (a ship) in dock. (배)를 선거에 매놓다. **c**) 《*passive*》 be ill in bed; be kept indoors. 앓아 눕다; 바깥 출입을 못 하게 되다. ¶ *He is laid up with a cold.* 감기로 누워 있다.

lay² [lei] *vi.* p. of **lie²**.

lay³ [lei] *adj.* **1** of an ordinary person; of a person who is not a clergyman. 속인(俗人)의(opp. clerical). **2** nonprofessional. (전문가가 아닌) 풋내기의. [Gk. *laos* people]

lay⁴ [lei] *n.* Ⓒ a short poem or song; a short narrative poem. (짧은) 시; 노래; (이야기체의) 시(詩). [F.]

lay-by [léibài] *n.* 《Brit.》 a widened section along a main road where vehicles may park without hindering the flow of traffic. (주도로(主道路)에서 판 차의 통과를 기다리는) 대피소. [*lay¹*]

·lay·er [léiər] *n.* Ⓒ **1** a person who lays. 놓는(쌓는) 사람. ¶ *a bricklayer* 벽돌공. **2** one thickness or fold of a material. 켜; 층; 지층. ¶ *a* ~ *of clay between two layers of sand* 두 사구층(砂丘層) 사이의 점토층. **3** a shoot that is grown into a root by bending it over and covering it with earth. (원예의) 휘묻이. [*lay¹*]

lay·ette [leiét] *n.* Ⓒ a collection of clothes, bedding, and other necessary things for a new-born baby. 갓난아이 용품 일습《배내옷, 침구 등》. [F.]

lay figure [´ `–] *n.* **1** a figure of the human body in clay or wax; a plastic model of the human body used for displaying clothes. 인체 모형; 모델 인형. **2** a useless person. 쓸모 없는 사람. **3** an unreal character. 가공의 인물. [Du. *led* joint]

lay·man [léimən] *n.* (*pl.* **-men** [-mən]) Ⓒ **1** a person who is not a priest but who belongs to a church. 평신도; 속인(俗人)(opp. clergyman). **2** a person who is not skilled in some special professions. 전문 지식이 없는 사람; 문외한; 아마추어 (opp. expert). [→lay³]

lay·off [léiɔ̀ːf / -ɔ̀f] *n.* Ⓒ a period during which a workman is temporarily discharged. 일시 해고(기간). [→lay¹]

lay·out [léiàut] *n.* **1** Ⓤ the act of planning or arranging land, streets, etc. (정원·도로 등의) 설계(법). **2** Ⓒ a plan or arrangement, etc. 설계. **3** Ⓒ a plan or design of a book, a newspaper, an advertisement. (서적·광고 등의) 지면 배열; 레이아웃. [→lay¹]

lay·over [léiòuvər] *n.* 《U.S.》 a stop for a time in a place during a journey. (여행 중의) 일시 체재; 도중 하차. [↑]

laze [leiz] *vi.* (P1) be lazy. 게으름을 피우다; 빈둥거리다. [→lazy]

la·zi·ly [léizili] *adv.* in a lazy manner. 게으르게; 빈둥거리며.

la·zi·ness [léizinis] *n.* Ⓤ the state of being lazy. 나태; 게으름.

:la·zy [léizi] *adj.* (**la·zi·er, la·zi·est**) **1** not willing to work; idle. 게으른(opp. diligent). ¶ *a* ~ *fellow* 게으름뱅이. **2** not active; slow. 게으른; 굼뜬. ¶ *a* ~ *correspondent* 편지(글) 쓰기 싫어하는 사람 / *a* ~ *river* 흐름이 느린 강 / *a* ~ *day* 께느른한(여가 있는 나른한) 하루. [G. *lasich* languid, idle]

la·zy·bones [léizibòunz] *n. pl.* 《usu. used as *sing.*》 《*colloq.*》 a lazy person or fellow. 게으름뱅이.

lea [liː] *n.* Ⓒ 《poet.》 a piece of grass land; a meadow. 풀밭, 초원; 목장. [Du.

loo Waterloo]

leach [liːtʃ] *vt.* (P6,7,13) **1** cause (water) to flow through a filter. 여과하다; 거르다. **2** wash (ashes, etc.) to extract some dissolved material. (재 따위로 가용물(可溶物)을 밭다. — *vi.* (P1,2A) (of ashes, etc.) wash to extract some dissolved material. 걸러지다; 녹다; 용해하다. [A.S. =water]

:lead[1] [liːd] *v.* (**led**) *vt.* **1** (P6,7) go before (someone) to show the way. …을 이끌다; 인도하다; 안내하다. ¶ ~ *someone in* 〔*out*〕 아무를 안〔밖〕으로 안내하다 / ~ *someone astray* 아무를 잘못 인도하다. **2** (P6,7) guide (someone or something) by the hand, etc. (소·말 따위를) 끌고 가다. ¶ ~ *the horse by the reins* 말 고삐를 잡고 끌고 가다. **3** (P6) direct; command. …을 지휘〔인솔〕하다. ¶ ~ *troops* 부대를 인솔하다 / ~ *an orchestra* 관현악단을 지휘하다. **4** (P6,16) be at the head of or hold first place in (a parade, a race, etc.). …의 수위를 차지하다; 선두에 서다. ¶ *He leads his class in mathematics.* 그는 반에서 수학을 제일 잘 한다 / *The choir leads the procession.* 합창단이 행렬의 선두에 서 있다. **5** (P7,13) 《*to*》 (of a road, etc.) take (someone) to a place. (도로 따위가 아무)를 …에 이르게 하다; …으로 가게 하다. ¶ *This road will ~ you to the station.* 이 길을 따라 가면 정거장으로 가게 된다 / *Chance led him to London.* 우연히 그는 런던에 가게 되었다. **6** (P13) cause (someone) to be in a certain state. (원인이 어떤 상태·결과)로 …을 이끌다. ¶ *Drink led him to destruction.* 그는 술로 신세를 망쳤다. **7** (P6,20) persuade (someone) to do or believe something; induce. …을 꾀다; 유혹하다; …할 마음이 되게 하다. ¶ *Poverty led him to steal.* 가난이 그를 도둑질을 하게 만들었다 / *I was led to believe that….* 나는 …라고 믿게 되었다. **8** (P6,14) spend; live (a certain kind of life, etc.); cause (someone) to live. (생활)을 하다; 지내다, 살아가게 하다. ¶ ~ *a happy life* 행복하게 살아가다 / ~ *someone a dog's life* 아무가 비참한 생활을 하게 하다 / *She led him a miserable life.* 그녀 때문에 그는 비참한 생활을 하게 되었다.

— *vi.* **1** (P1,2A,3) act as guide or conductor; manage. 안내하다; 선도〔지휘〕하다. ¶ ~ *in prayer* 기도를 인도하다. **2** (P3) act as head; be first; excel. 선두에 서다; 수위를 차지하다. ¶ *She leads in French and English.* 그녀는 프랑스어와 영어에서 일등이다. **3** (P1,2A,3) (of a road, etc.) extend; go; run. (길 따위가 …에) 이르다; 통하다. ¶ *This road leads to the beach.* 이 길을 따라가면 해안에 닿는다. **4** (P3) bring as a result. (결과가 …이) 되다. ¶ ~ *to a good result* 좋은 결과가 되다.

lead away, induce to follow unthinkingly. 꾀어내다; 잘못된 길로 끌어들이다.

lead someone by the nose, have complete control of someone. …을 마음대로 움직이다; 맹종시키다.

lead nowhere, have no result. 헛일로 끝나다.

lead off, make a beginning; begin. 시작하다. ¶ *He led off by making an apology.* 우선 사과의 말부터 시작했다.

lead on, cause (someone) to continue a vain action; mislead. …을 유혹하다; 끌어들이다; …하도록 만들다.

lead out, guide (a lady) from her place to begin a dance, etc. (춤의 파트너로 여자를) 자리에서 끌어내다.

lead the way, go first; show the path. 선두에 서다; 길을 안내하다. ¶ *Lead the way. I am a stranger here.* 앞장 서라. 나는 이 곳이 낯설다.

lead up to, **a**) prepare the way for something. …의 준비를 하다. **b**) direct the conversation toward; approach gradually or evasively. 대화를 …으로 이끌어 가다; …에 점차 접근하다. ¶ ~ *up to one's favorite topic* 자기가 좋아하는 화제로 이끌어 가다 / *What is he leading up to?* 그가 말하려는 속셈은 뭐냐.

— *n.* Ⓒ **1** 《*sing.* only》 the act of leading or conducting. 선도; 지휘; 지도. ¶ *under the ~ of* …의 지도 밑에. **2** 《*the* ~》 the first place or position. 선두; (경기의) 리드. ¶ *gain the ~ in a race* 경주에서 선두에 나서다. **3** 《*sing.* only》 the amount by which one is in front of others. 앞선 거리〔시간〕. ¶ *have a ~ of ten feet,* 10 피트를 리드하다. **4** 《*sing.* only》 example; guidance. 모범; 본보기. ¶ *follow someone's ~* 아무의 본을 따르다. **5** (of a newspaper, etc.) a short introduction to an article. (신문 기사의) 첫머리; 허두. **6** a hint; a suggestion. 실마리; 힌트. ¶ *Please give me a ~ in this business.* 이 장사의 요령을 좀 알려 주시오. **7** a chief part in a play; a chief actor. 주연; 주연 배우. [E.]

take the lead, go into the first or head position; command. 솔선하다; 솔선해서 모범을 보이다.

:lead[2] [led] *n.* Ⓒ **1** Ⓤ a soft, heavy, easily-melted gray metal. 납. ¶ *heavy as ~* 납덩어리처럼 무거운 / *dull as ~* 납처럼 흐릿한 색의. **2** a lump of lead used to measure the depth of water. 측연(測鉛). ¶ *cast* 〔*heave*〕 *the ~* 측연을 던져 수심(水深)을 재다. **3** a long, thin piece of black lead as used in pencils. 연필의 심. **4** 《print.》 a strip of lead used to separate lines of type. 인테르. **5** a ball of lead or other metal fired from a gun. 탄알. **6** 《*pl., collectively*》 strips of lead used to cover a roof, or to frame window glass. (지붕 이는) 함석; 창유리의 납테.

— *vt.* (P6) **1** cover (something) with lead. …에 납을 씌우다. **2** 《print.》 separate (lines of type) with leads. …에 인테르를 끼우다. [E.]

lead·en [lédn] *adj.* **1** made of lead; of the color of lead. 납으로 된; 납빛의. ¶ *a ~*

L

box / ~ *cloud* 납빛의 구름. **2** heavy as lead; oppressive; gloomy. (납처럼) 무거운; 답답한. ¶ *walk at a ~ pace* 터덜터덜 걷다. **3** not active; dull. 무기력한. [↑]

:lead·er [líːdər] *n.* Ⓒ **1** a person who leads; a chief; a guide. 지도자; 선도자; 리더. **2** 《Mus., U.S.》 ⓐ a conductor or director. (관현악단의) 지휘자. ⓑ the principal player of the first violins. 제1 바이올린의 수석 연주자. **3** 《Brit.》 a leading article in a newspaper. (신문의) 논설; 사설. **4** a piece of transparent material used to attach a fishhook to a fish line. (낚시의) 목줄. **5** a thing sold at a low price to attract customers. (손님을 끌기 위한) 특매[특가]품. **6** 《*pl.*》 《print.》 a row of dots or hyphens. 점선(…) 또는 대시선(–). [*lead*[1]]

·lead·er·ship [líːdərʃìp] *n.* Ⓤ **1** the post or duty of a leader. 지도자의 지위[임무]. ¶ *assume the ~ of* …의 통솔 임무를 맡다 / *under the ~ of* …의 지휘 아래. **2** skill in leading; the power to lead. 통솔력. ¶ *able* [*poor*] ~ 유능한[시원찮은] 통솔력.

:lead·ing [líːdiŋ] *n.* Ⓤ the act of guiding; the power or authority to direct. 지도; 통솔; 통솔력. ¶ *men of light and ~* 계몽가들; 지도자들. — *adj.* **1** conducting; at the head. 선도하는; 이끄는. **2** high in rank; important. 수위의; 주된; 중요한. ¶ *a ~ singer* 일류 가수 / *a ~ article* 사설 / *a ~ lady* [*man*] 주연 여우[남우] / *the ~ topics of the day* 오늘의 주요 화제.

:leaf [liːf] *n.* (*pl.* **leaves**) **1** ⒸⓊ one of the flat green parts of a plant. 잎; 나뭇잎. ¶ *be in ~* 잎이 무성하다 / *the fall of the ~* (낙엽지는) 가을 / *In autumn, most trees shed their leaves.* 가을에 대부분의 나무는 잎이 진다. **2** ⒸⓊ a flower petal. 꽃잎. **3** Ⓒ a piece of paper forming, back to back, two printed pages of a book. (책의) 한 장(2 페이지). ¶ *turn over a ~* 책장을 넘기다 / *tear a few leaves out of a book* 책에서 몇 장을 찢어내다. **4** Ⓤ a thin sheet of metal. (금속의) 박(箔). ¶ *gold ~* 금박. **5** a movable board used to extend the top of a desk, a table, etc. (책상·테이블 따위의) 자재판(自在板).

come into leaf, have the leaf buds open. 잎이 나다.

take a leaf out of** someone's **book, follow someone's example; take a hint from another person. …을 본뜨다; (…의 행동)을 모방하다.

turn over a new leaf, make a new start in life; give up bad ways and habits. 새 출발을 하다; 마음을 고쳐먹다.

— *vi.* (P1,2A) form leaves. 잎이 나다. ¶ *The trees ~ (out) in spring.* 나무는 봄에 잎이 난다.

— *vt.* (P6) turn the pages of (a book, etc.). (책 따위)의 페이지를 넘기다. [E.]

leaf bud [∸∸] *n.* a bud which grows into a leaf. 잎눈.

leaf·less [líːflis] *adj.* having no leaves; without leaves. 잎이 없는.

leaf·let [líːflit] *n.* Ⓒ **1** a young leaf; a division of a compound leaf. 작은 잎; 겹잎의 한 조각. **2** a small printed sheet, single or folded; a pamphlet. 낱장으로 된 인쇄물; 전단; 리플릿. ¶ *advertising leaflets* 광고 전단.

leaf·y [líːfi] *adj.* (**leaf·i·er, leaf·i·est**) **1** ⓐ covered with many leaves; having many leaves. 잎이 무성한[많은]. ⓑ produced by leaves. 나뭇잎으로 된. ¶ *a ~ shade* 나무 그늘; 녹음. **2** like a leaf or leaves in shape. 나뭇잎 모양의. ¶ *a ~ design* 나뭇잎 무늬.

:league[1] [liːg] *n.* Ⓒ **1** an agreement between two or more nations or persons for a mutual purpose; the union so formed. 동맹; 연맹. ¶ *the League (of Nations)* 국제 연맹. **2** an association of baseball clubs, etc. (야구 등의) 경기 연맹; 리그. ¶ *a ~ match* 리그전. — *vi., vt.* (P1,2A; 6) unite or combine; join in a league. 동맹하다[시키다]. ¶ *~ together against a common enemy* 공동의 적에 대항해 동맹을 맺다. [L. *ligo* bind]

league[2] [liːg] *n.* Ⓒ an old measure of distance, about three miles. 리그(옛 거리의 단위; 약 3마일). [Celt.]

lea·guer [líːgər] *n.* Ⓒ a member of a league. 동맹국; 맹방; 가맹자[국]. [*league*[1]]

leak [liːk] *n.* Ⓒ **1** a small hole or opening that water, gas, etc. passes through. 새는 구멍; 누출구. ¶ *a ~ in a roof* 지붕의 새는 데 / *stop* [*plug*] *a ~* 누출구를 막다. **2** the act of leaking. 샘; 누출. ¶ *spring* [*start*] *a ~* 새기 시작하다. **3** the amount which leaks out or in. 새는 양.

— *vi.* **1** (P1,2B) ⓐ let water, air, etc. enter or escape slowly through a small hole. (지붕·배 따위가) 새다. ¶ *The boiler is leaking.* 보일러가 새고 있다 / *The roof leaks.* 지붕이 샌다. ⓑ 《*in, out*》 (of a liquid, gas, etc.) enter or escape through a small hole. (액체 등이) 새다. ¶ *Air leaks in through a crack.* 공기가 틈으로 새어 들어간다. **2** (P1,2A) 《*out*》 (of a secret, etc.) become known little by little. (비밀 등이) 서서히 알려지다. ¶ *The secret has leaked out.* 비밀이 새나갔다.

— *vt.* (P6) make (something) pass in or out. 새게 하다. [O.N. *leka* drop]

leak·age [líːkidʒ] *n.* Ⓤ **1** the act or process of leaking; a leak. 샘; 누출. **2** that which leaks in or out. (비밀 등의) 누출; 누설. **3** Ⓒ the amount leaking in or out. 누출량.

leak·y [líːki] *adj.* (**leak·i·er, leak·i·est**) having a leak; leaking out a secret. 새는; (비밀 등을) 누설하기 쉬운.

:lean[1] [liːn] *v.* (**leaned** or **leant**) *vi.* **1** (P2A,3) be not quite upright; incline or bend from a vertical position. 기울다; 구부러지다. ¶ *The tower leaned a little to the right.* 탑이

L

오른쪽으로 좀 기울었다. **2** (P2A,3) 《*on, upon, against*》 bend over; rest on something for support. (사람이) 기대다; 의지하다. ¶ ~ *against the wall* 벽에 기대다 / *She leaned upon my arm.* 그녀는 내 팔에 기댔다 / ~ *on a walking-stick* 지팡이에 의지하다. **3** (P3) 《*on, upon*》 depend; rely on. 의존하다; 의뢰하다. ¶ ~ *on friendship* 우정에 매달리다 / *You must not* ~ *too much on* 〔*upon*〕 *others.* 너무 남을 의존해서는 못쓴다. **4** (P2A, 3) incline in feeling, opinion, action, etc. (마음이) 기울다; 쏠리다. ¶ ~ *toward socialism* 사회주의로 기울다 / *I rather* ~ *to your opinion.* 대체로 네 의견에 찬성이다. **5** (P2A, 3) bend the upper part of the body. 상체를 굽히다. ¶ *He leaned out of the window.* 그는 창 밖으로 상체를 내밀었다.
— *vt.* **1** (P7) cause (something) to lean. …을 기울이다. **2** (P13) place (something) for support. …을 기대게 하다. ¶ ~ *one's stick against the wall* 지팡이를 벽에 세우다.
— *n.* Ⓤ the act of leaning; slope; bend. 기울기; 경사; 치우침. [E.]

:lean[2] [liːn] *adj.* **1** (of a person or animal) thin. (사람·짐승이) 여윈; 마른(opp. fat). **2** (of meat) having little or no fat. (고기가) 기름기가 적은; 살코기의. ¶ ~ *meat* 살코기. **3** not productive; poor in quality. (땅이) 메마른; 수확이 적은. ¶ ~ *years* 흉년 / ~ *crops* 흉작. — *n.* Ⓤ meat without fat. 살코기. [E.]

lean·ing [líːniŋ] *n.* Ⓒ a trend; a fondness. 경사; 경향. ¶ *He has a* ~ *towards pacifism.* 그는 반전론적 경향이 있다. [*lean*[1]]

leant [lent] *v.* p. and pp. of **lean**[1].

lean-to [líːntùː] *n.* (*pl.* **-tos**) Ⓒ a small building built against a main house having a roof with only one slope; a penthouse. 달개집. — *adj.* having supports fixed against a building. 달개 (지붕)의. ¶ *a* ~ *roof* 달개지붕. [*lean*[1]]

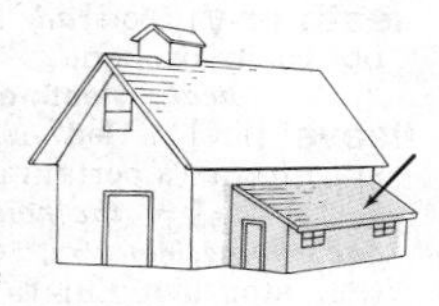
〈lean-to〉

:leap [liːp] *n.* Ⓒ **1** a jump. 뜀; 도약. ¶ *A frog gave a* ~. 개구리 한 마리가 뛰어올랐다. **2** a thing jumped over. 뛰어넘는 것. **3** the height or distance jumped. 한 번 뛰는 높이〔거리〕. **4** a sudden movement upward or forward. 비약; 약진. ¶ *take a* ~ *to fame* 갑자기 유명해지다.
a leap in the dark, an effort to do something recklessly; a rash act. 무모한 행동; 경솔한 짓.
by leaps and bounds, very quickly. 아주 빠르게; 일사천리로. ¶ *Sales are increasing by leaps and bounds.* 매상이 급속히 늘고 있다.
with 〔***at***〕 ***a leap,*** at a bound; suddenly. 단숨에; 별안간.
— *v.* (**leaped** or **leapt**) *vt.* **1** (P6) pass over (something) by a jump or a bound. …을 뛰어넘다. ¶ ~ *a ditch* 도랑을 뛰어넘다. **2** (P6,13) cause (a horse, etc.) to jump or bound. …을 뛰어넘게 하다. ¶ ~ *a horse over a hedge* 말이 울타리를 뛰어넘게 하다.
— *vi.* (P1,2A,3) **1** spring or jump; make a bound. 뛰다; 뛰어오르다; 튀다. ¶ ~ *over a ditch* 도랑을 뛰어넘다. **2** move suddenly, as by jumping. 갑자기 움직이다〔행동하다〕. ¶ ~ *to a conclusion* 단숨에 결론을 내리다. [E.]
leap at, jump at; accept eagerly; seize. …에 냉큼 달려들다; (제안)에 기꺼이 응하다; (기회 따위)를 선뜻 포착하다. ¶ *He leaped at the proposal.* 그는 좋아라 하고 제의에 응했다.
leap for 〔***with***〕 (=*jump for* 〔*with*〕) ***joy,*** 뛸 듯이 좋아하다.
leap out of one's skin, jump suddenly with joy, surprise, fright, etc. 펄쩍 뛰며 좋아하다; 대경 실색하다.
Look before you leap. 《*prov.*》 Think before acting. 잘 생각하고 행동하라.

leap·frog [líːpfrɔ̀ːg, -fràg / -frɔ̀g] *n.* Ⓤ a game in which children jump over each other's backs. 목마뛰기. ¶ *play* ~.

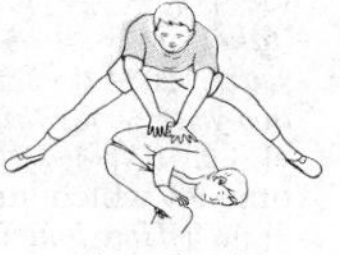
〈leapfrog〉

leapt [liːpt, lept] *v.* p. and pp. of **leap.**

leap year [⌐ ⌐] *n.* a year in which February has 29 days. 윤년.

:learn [ləːrn] *v.* (**learned** or **learnt**) *vt.* (P6,7,8,10,11,12) **1** get knowledge of (something) by study, instruction, or experience. …을 배우다; 익히다; 연습하다; …할 수 있게 되다. ¶ ~ *French* 프랑스어를 배우다 / *She has learned to swim.* 그녀는 헤엄을 칠 수 있게 됐다 / ~ *how to solve the problem* 문제의 해결 방법을 배우다 / *We* ~ *much from experience.* 우리는 경험으로 많은 것을 배운다 / ~ *a lesson by failure* 실패에서 교훈을 얻다. **2** find out; be aware of (something); be informed of (something). …을 알다; 듣다. ¶ *I learned it from her that he had died.* 그녀를 통해 그의 사망을 알게 됐다 / *I learnt that he had been in* (*the*) *hospital.* 그의 입원을 들어서 알았다 / *I learned how they had escaped.* 그들이 어떻게 도망했는지를 알았다 / *I was sorry to* ~ (*from her*) *that he had died.* 그가 죽었다는 것을 (그녀에게서) 듣고 마음이 아팠다. **3** memorize; fix in the mind. …을 외다; 기억하다. ¶ ~ *a poem by heart* 시를 암기하다. **4** gain (a habit, attitude, etc.) by practice. (연습으로) …을 익히다; 체득하다. ¶ *You must* ~ *patience.* 참을성을 길러야 한다.
— *vi.* **1** (P1) get knowledge or skill. 배우다; 익히다; 기억하다. ¶ *The boy learns very fast.* 그 아이는 기억력이 참 좋다. **2** (P3) 《*of*》 hear; be told or informed. 듣다; (들어서) 알

다. ¶ ~ *of the results of the examination* 시험 결과를 알다. [E.; G. *lernen*]

•**learn·ed** [lə́ːrnid] *adj.* **1** having much knowledge or learning. 학식이 있는; 학문적인. ¶ *a ~ man* 학자 / *be ~ in the law* 법률에 밝다. **2** connected with study and learning. 학문적〔학구적〕인. ¶ *a ~ book* 학술 서적 / *the ~ professions* 학문적 직업《원래는 신학·법학·의학의 셋》. ● **learn·ed·ly** [-li] *adv.*

learn·er [lə́ːrnər] *n.* Ⓒ a person who is learning; a beginner. 학습〔수학(修學)〕자, 배우는 사람; 초심자.

:**learn·ing** [lə́ːrniŋ] *n.* Ⓤ the knowledge or skill got by study. 학문; 지식. ¶ *a man of ~* 학자 / 《*prov.*》 *A little ~ is a dangerous thing.* 선무당이 사람 잡는다.

learnt [ləːrnt] *v.* p. and pp. of **learn.**

•**lease** [liːs] *n.* Ⓤ **1** a written agreement for the renting of land or buildings for a certain time in exchange for rent paid; the rights given under such a contract. (토지·건물 등의) 차용 계약; 차용권. ¶ *hold* 〔*take*〕 *on ~* …을 임차하다 / *on a ~ of 20 years,* 20년간 임차 계약으로 / *We signed a two-year ~ for this house.* 이 집을 2년간 빌리기로 계약에 서명했다. **2** Ⓒ the length of time for which such agreement lasts. 차용 기간. ¶ *How long is your ~ on that land?* 그 땅의 임차 기간은 얼마나 됩니까.

by* 〔*on*〕 *lease, by rent. 임대로; 임차로. ¶ *hold the land by* 〔*on*〕 *~* 땅을 임대하다.

take* 〔*get*〕 *a new* 〔*fresh*〕 *lease on life, get a chance to live better or more happily because of recovering one's health, position, money, etc. (건강 등이 회복되어) 수명이 연장되다.

— *vt.* (P6) give or take ownership of (land, a building, etc.), for a certain time, by a contract. (땅, 건물 등)을 임대〔임차〕하다. ¶ *~ land to* 〔*from*〕 *someone* 땅을 아무에게 임대하다〔아무로부터 임차하다〕. [→lax]

lease·hold [líːshòuld] *n.* Ⓤ **1** the right of holding land by lease. 차지권(借地權). **2** lands, buildings, etc. held by lease. 임차물(賃借物). — *adj.* held by lease. 임차한; 조차(租借)의.

lease·hold·er [líːshòuldər] *n.* Ⓒ a person who holds a lease. 임차인(賃借人).

leash [liːʃ] *n.* **1** Ⓒ a chain or strap for holding a dog. (개 등을 매는) 가죽끈; 사슬. ¶ *lead a dog on a ~* 개를 끈에 매어 끌다. **2** Ⓤ control; restraint. 통제; 속박. ¶ *hold in ~* 속박〔지배〕하다. **3** 《*a ~*》《hunting》 a set of three animals, as dogs, foxes, hares, etc. (개·여우 따위를 한데 맨) 세 마리(한 조).

strain at the leash, wait eagerly for permission to do something. 자유를 갈망하다〔얻고자 하다〕.

— *vt.* (P6) fasten or hold (something) with a leash. …을 가죽끈으로 매다. [F.]

:**least** [liːst] *adj.* (superl. of **little**) smallest in size, degree, extent, importance, etc.; slightest; shortest. 가장 작은〔적은〕; 가치가 가장 적은. ¶ *You don't have the ~ chance of success.* 성공할 가망은 조금도 없다 / *There is not the ~ danger.* 적지 않은 위험이 있다. — *adv.* in the smallest or lowest degree. 가장 적게〔작게〕. ¶ *He is ~ wanted here.* 그는 여기서 조금도 쓸모가 없다 / *Those who talk ~ are often the wisest.* 가장 말수 적은 사람이 흔히 가장 현명하다.

least of all, less than any other. 그 중에서도 …아니다.

— *n.* Ⓤ 《usu. *the ~*》 the smallest in size, amount, importance, etc. 최소; 최소량. [*less*]

at* (*the*) *least, at the lowest estimate; at any rate; in any case. 적어도; 어쨌든. ¶ *You might at ~ be polite.* 좀 겸손하면 좋으련만.

not in the least, not at all. 조금도 …아니다. ¶ *It doesn't matter in the ~.* 그건 아무 상관 없다.

to say the least of it, at least. 줄잡아 말해도.

:**leath·er** [léðər] *n.* Ⓤ **1** the skin of an animal prepared for human use. (무두질한) 가죽. ¶ *Morocco ~* 모로코 가죽《염소 가죽으로 만듦》/ *patent ~* 에나멜 가죽. **2** any of various articles made of this material. 가죽〔피혁〕 제품. **3** Ⓒ 《*pl.*》 leather riding breeches. 승마용 가죽 바지. **4** a piece of leather for polishing. 혁지(革砥). — *vt.* (P6) **1** cover or furnish (something) with leather. …에 가죽을 씌우다〔대다〕. **2** strike (someone) with a leather strap. …을 가죽 채찍으로 때리다. [E.]

leath·ern [léðərn] *adj.* **1** made of leather. 가죽으로 된. **2** like leather. 가죽 같은.

leath·er·y [léðəri] *adj.* like leather; tough; not easily broken. 가죽 같은, 가죽처럼 질긴. ¶ *~ meat.* ● **leath·er·i·ness** [-nis] *n.*

:**leave**[1] [liːv] *v.* (**left**) *vt.* **1** (P6) go away or start from (a certain place). …을 떠나다; 출발하다. ¶ *~ the house* 집을 나서다 / *~ one's home* 〔*country*〕 집〔고국〕을 떠나다. **2** (P6) stop living in (a certain place), attending (a school), or belonging to (a club), etc. …을 그만두다; (소속 단체)에서 물러나다; 탈퇴하다; (학교)를 졸업〔퇴학〕하다. ¶ *~ a job* 사직하다 / *~ a political party* 정당에서 탈당하다 / *~ school before graduation* 학교를 중퇴하다. **3** ⓐ (P7,13) forget; fail to take or bring. …을 두고 가다; 잊고 가다. ¶ *~ the book on the desk* 책을 책상 위에 두고 가다. ⓑ (P6) abandon; forsake. 버리다; 방치하다; 저버리다. ¶ *~ one's wife and family* 아내와 가족을 저버리다. **4** (P18, 20,23,24) let (something or someone) be in a certain state or condition; allow (someone, etc.) alone to do something. …한 채로 두다; …하는 대로 내버려 두다; …하게 하다. ¶ *~ the door open* 문을 열어 두다 / ~

L

someone alone 아무를 혼자 내버려 두다 / ~ *work unfinished* 일을 하다가 그냥 두다. **5** (P6,13,14) keep (something) unused; remain; yield as a remainder. …을 남기다; 남겨 두다. ¶ *There was little money left.* 남은 돈이라곤 거의 없었다 / *Leave some milk for the dog.* 개가 마실 우유를 좀 남겨라 / *Three from eight leaves five.* 8에서 3을 빼면 5가 남는다 / *I hope you've left me something to eat.* 내게 먹을 것을 좀 남겨 두었으면 좋겠다. **6** (P6,7,13,14) give (money, etc.) at someone's death; give money, etc. to (someone) at one's death. (재산·처자 등)을 남기고 죽다; 유언으로 남기다; 유증(遺贈)하다. ¶ *The father left his son a large fortune.* 아버지는 아들에게 막대한 유산을 남겼다 / *He left a great name behind him.* 그는 후세에 위대한 이름을 남겼다. **7** (P13,20) cause or allow (something) to be in someone's care or trust; entrust. …을 맡기다; 위임〔일임〕하다; 부탁하다. ¶ *Leave it to me.* 그것은 내게 맡겨라 / ~ *a baby with a woman* 아이를 어떤 부인에게 부탁하다 / *I ~ the matter to you to settle up.* 그 문제를 네게 맡기니 해결해라. **8** (P6, 13,14) deliver; hand over. …을 배달하다; 주다; 두고 가다. ¶ ~ *a message* 메시지를 남기다 / *The postman left two letters for me.* 집배원이 내게 편지 두 통을 두고 갔다. **9** (P7,13) pass; go beyond. …을 지나가다. ¶ ~ *the village on the right* 마을을 오른쪽으로 보며 지나가다. **10** (P7,9) stop 끝내다; 중단하다. ¶ ~ *drinking* 〔*smoking*〕 *for good* 술을〔담배를〕 아주 끊다. — *vi.* (P1,2A,3) go away; depart. 가 버리다; 떠나다; 출발하다. ¶ ~ *for America* 미국으로 가다 / *We are leaving tomorrow morning.* 우린 내일 아침 떠난다. [E.]

be nicely left, be deceived. 속다; 당하다.

be well left, be provided for by legacy. 충분한 유산을 받다.

leave alone, not interfere with. 간섭하지 않다; 내버려 두다.

leave** something **behind, a) forget; go away without something. …을 두고 가다. b) pass by. …을 지나가다.

leave go 〔***hold***〕 ***of,*** relax one's hold; cease to hold. …을 놓다; 손떼다.

leave off, a) stop. 그만두다; 그치다. b) not wear. …을 벗다.

leave out, omit; pass over; neglect. …을 생략하다; 고려하지 않다; 무시하다.

leave over, 《Brit.》 be dealt with another time; let stand over for the time being. 미루다; 연기하다; 남기다.

leave² [liːv] *n.* **1** Ⓤ permission; consent. 허가. ¶ *He gave me ~ to go.* 그는 내게 가는 것을 허락했다 / *ask for ~* 허락해 달라고 하다 / *ask* 〔*get, refuse*〕 *~ to do* …하는 허가를 청하다〔얻다, 거절하다〕 / *May I have your ~ to photograph the place?* 이 곳을 사진 찍어도 괜찮겠습니까. **2** ⓊⒸ permission to be absent from work or duty. 휴가. ¶ *have* 〔*go on*〕 ~ 휴가를 얻다〔가다〕. **3** Ⓒ the period for which such permission lasts. 휴가 기간. ¶ *a three-week ~* (*of absence*) 3주의 휴가. [→life]

by your leave, with your permission. 미안하지만; 실례지만.

on leave, absent from duty with permission. 휴가로.

take French leave, go without asking to be allowed to go. 무단히 자리를 뜨다; 작별 인사 없이 나가다.

take** one's **leave of, say good-bye to (someone) and go; depart. …에게 작별 인사하다.

take leave of** one's **senses, go mad. 미쳐 버리다; 돌다.

leav·en [lévən] *n.* Ⓤ **1** yeast or similar substance used in making bread, etc. 효모; 이스트. **2** anything that causes a general change of the whole; a spiritual influence. 전체적인 변화를 빚어내는 것; 영향·감화를 주는 것; 기운. ¶ *New ~ is working in society.* 사회에 새로운 기운이 일고 있다. — *vt.* (P6,13) **1** make (dough) light. …을 발효시키다. **2** transform (something) with some lightening element. …에 영향을〔변화를〕 미치다. [L. *levo* raise]

leaves [liːvz] *n.* pl. of **leaf.**

leave-tak·ing [líːvtèikiŋ] *n.* Ⓤ the act of taking leave, or saying good-by. 작별; 고별. [*leave²*]

leav·ings [líːviŋz] *n. pl.* what is left as worthless. 나머지; 찌꺼기. ¶ *Give the ~ to the dog.* 찌꺼기는 개에게 줘라. [↑]

le·bens·raum [léibənsràum] *n.* a territory deemed necessary to a nation for its natural development. (영토적 의미의) 생활권(圈). [G. =living space]

lec·tern [léktərn] *n.* Ⓒ a reading desk from which the Bible is read in church. (교회의) 성서대. [L. *lego* read]

:lec·ture [léktʃər] *n.* Ⓒ **1** a speech full of knowledge given to an audience, a class, etc. 강의; 강연. ¶ *give* 〔*deliver*〕 *a ~ on history* 역사 강의를 하다. **2** a scolding; a spoken criticism. 잔소리; 꾸지람. ¶ *read someone a ~* 아무를 꾸짖다. — *vi.* (P1,3) 《*on*》 give a lecture 강의하다. ¶ ~ *on chemistry to a class* 반에서 화학을 강의하다. — *vt.* (P6,13) **1** instruct (someone) by a lecture. …에게 강의하다. **2** scold. …을 꾸짖다. ¶ ~ *someone on his behavior* 아무의 행실을 나무라다. [↑]

lec·tur·er [léktʃərər] *n.* a person who gives a lecture. 강연자; 강사.

led [led] *v.* p. and pp. of **lead¹.**

·ledge [ledʒ] *n.* Ⓒ **1** a narrow shelf projecting out from a wall as under the window. 선반. ¶ *a ~ for chalk at the bottom of a blackboard* 칠판 밑의 분필 놓는 데. **2** a flat area of rock under the sea. 바위 턱; 암초(暗礁). **3** a layer of rock containing metal. 광맥. [*lay*]

ledg·er [lédʒər] *n.* Ⓒ **1** a book in which accounts of money are recorded. 원장(元帳); 원부(原簿). **2** 《archit.》 a horizontal timber of a scaffold. (비계의) 가로장. [↑]

***lee** [liː] *n.* Ⓒ 《usu. *the* ~》 the side protected from the wind; the sheltered side; the direction toward which the wind is blowing. (바람 등을) 피할 곳; 가려진 곳; 바람이 불어가는 쪽.

under* 〔*on*〕 *the lee, of the direction toward which the wind is blowing. 바람 불어가는 쪽에.

under* 〔*in*〕 *the lee of, in the shelter of. …의 그늘에 숨어.

— *adj.* sheltered from the wind; of the part away from the wind. 바람 불어 가는 쪽의(opp. windward). ¶ *the ~ side* 바람이 불어 가는 쪽; 바람을 받지 않는 쪽. [*lay*]

leech [liːtʃ] *n.* Ⓒ **1** a worm living in ponds and streams that sucks the blood of animals. 거머리. ¶ *stick like a ~* 거머리처럼 달라붙다. **2** 《*fig.*》 a person who sucks as much profit as possible out of other. (거머리처럼) 남을 우려먹는 자. [E.]

leek [liːk] *n.* Ⓒ 《bot.》 a vegetable with a white stem which tastes like an onion. 부추. [E.]

leer [liər] *n.* Ⓒ a cunning, mean, sideways look. 곁눈질; 흘겨봄. — *vi.* (P1,3) 《*at*》 look with a leer. 흘겨보다; 곁눈질하다. ● **leer·ing·ly** [líəriŋli] *adv.* [A.S. =look askance]

leer·y [líəri] *adj.* 《*colloq.*》 suspicious; cautious; sly. 의심이 많은; 조심하는; 교활한. ¶ *be ~ of* …을 (의심하여) 조심하다. [↑]

lees [liːz] *n. pl.* the things in a liquid which settle to the bottom; dregs. 찌꺼기; 재강. [F.]

drink* 〔*drain*〕 (*a cup*) *to the lees, **a**) drink to its last drop. (잔)을 깨끗이 비우다. **b**) 《*fig.*》 go through the last extremes of suffering. 갖은 고초를 겪을 대로 겪다.

lee·ward [líːwərd, 《naut.》 lúːərd] *adj., adv.* in the direction toward which the wind blows; opposed to windward. 바람 불어 가는 쪽의〔으로〕(opp. windward). ¶ *It will be warmer on the ~ side of the deck.* 갑판의 바람 불어 가는 쪽이 더 따뜻할 것이다.

— *n.* Ⓤ the direction toward which the wind blows. 바람 불어 가는 쪽. [→lee]

lee·way [líːwèi] *n.* Ⓤ **1** 《naut.》 the sideward drift of a boat caused by the wind. 풍압《항행 중의 배가 바람에 밀려가는 일》. **2** 《*colloq.*》 extra space, time, money, etc. 여유; 여지. **3** loss of time; slowing down of progress. 시간의 손실; 진전의 지체. [→lee]

have leeway, have room for action or freedom. 활동의 여지가 있다.

make up leeway, make up time or distance lost. 늦어진 것을 만회하다.

:left[1] [left] *adj.* the opposite of right. 왼쪽의; 좌측의(opp. right). 語法 한정 용법에만 쓰임. ¶ *the ~ hand* 왼손 / *the ~ fielder* 좌익수 / *on the ~ hand of* …의 왼편〔쪽〕에 / *look* 〔*turn*〕 *neither to the ~ hand nor to the right* 곧장 앞을 보다〔앞으로 돌리다〕.

marry with the left hand, take a wife of a rank lower than one's own. 지체 낮은 여자와 결혼하다.

— *adv.* on or toward the left hand or side. 왼쪽에〔으로〕. ¶ *turn ~* 왼쪽으로 돌다 / *Left turn!* 좌향 좌.

— *n.* Ⓒ **1** 《usu. *the* ~》 the part on the left side. 왼쪽; 좌측. ¶ *to the ~ of* …의 왼쪽에 / *turn to the ~* 왼쪽으로 돌다 / *keep to the ~* 좌측 통행을 하다 / *cannon to the ~ of them* 그들의 좌측을 포격하다 / 《*colloq.*》 *over the ~* 거꾸로 말하면. **2** 《usu. *the L-*》 《polit.》 the socialist and labor parties and their supporters. 사회주의 노동당과 그 추종자들. **3** 《baseball》 a left fielder. 좌익수. **4** 《mil.》 the left wing (of an army). 좌익. [E. =weak]

:left[2] [left] *v.* p. and pp. of **leave.**

left-hand [léfthǽnd] *adj.* on the left; of the left hand. 왼쪽의; 왼손의. ¶ *a house on the ~ side of the street* 길의 왼편에 있는 집. [*left*[1]]

left-hand·ed [léfthǽndid] *adj.* **1** using the left hand more easily or skillfully than the right. 왼손잡이의. **2** done or made with or for the left hand. 왼손으로 한; 왼손용의. ¶ *a ~ blow* 왼손의 강타. **3** going around from right to left. 왼쪽으로 도는. ¶ *a ~ screw* 왼쪽으로 감는 나사. **4** awkward. 서투른. **5** doubtful; questionable. 의심스러운; 불성실한. ¶ *a ~ compliment* 치레뿐인 칭찬.

left·o·ver [léftòuvər] *n.* Ⓒ something left over, as from a meal. 나머지; 먹다 남은 밥. — *adj.* remaining unused, uneaten, etc. 나머지의; 남은 밥의. [*leave*[1]]

:leg [leg] *n.* Ⓒ **1** one of the parts of the body used for walking. 다리(cf. *foot*). ¶ *sit with one's legs crossed* 책상다리를 하고 앉다 / *lame of a ~* 한쪽 다리를 저는 / *He ran off as fast as his legs would carry him.* 걸음아 날 살려라 하고 달아났다. **2** the part of a garment covering a leg. 옷의 다리 부분. ¶ *the ~ of a stocking* 스타킹의 다리 부분 / *the legs of trousers* 바짓가랑이. **3** ⓐ an artificial limb used as a support. 인조 다리; 의족. ¶ *a man with a wooden ~* 나무 의족을 한 사람. ⓑ something like a leg in shape or use; a bar or pole used as a support; one of the branches of a forked or jointed object. (의자·책상 등의) 다리; 버팀대. ¶ *the legs of a chair* 〔*bed*〕 의자〔침대〕의 다리. ⓒ either side of a triangle other than its base. 삼각형의 변《밑변을 제외한》. **4** one section or stage of a journey, etc. (여행의) 한 노정(路程).

feel* 〔*find*〕 *one's legs, (of a baby) get the ability to stand or walk; be able to act

independently. (어린 아이가) 걸을 수 있게 되다; 독립할 수 있게 되다.
get* 〔*be*〕 *on one's* (*hind*) *legs, 《*colloq.*》 **a**) stand up, esp. to speak. (연설하기 위해) 일어서다. **b**) (after an illness) be well enough to walk about again. (건강을 회복해) 걸을 수 있게 되다.
give* (*someone*) *a leg up, **a**) help (someone) to mount a horse or to climb up something. …을 도와서 말에 태우다. **b**) help (someone) in time of need. …가 어려울 때 도와 주다.
have not a leg to stand on, 《*colloq.*》 have no facts or evidence to support an argument. 논거가 빈약하다.
on one's* 〔*its*〕 *last legs, 《*colloq.*》 near one's death; worn out. 죽음이 임박해; 기진해서.
pull* 〔*draw*〕 *someone's leg, make fun of or fool (someone). …을 우롱하다; 속이다.
run someone off his legs, tire (someone) by keeping him constantly busy. (일이 바빠서) 지치게 만들다.
shake a leg, 《*colloq.*》 **a**) hurry. 서두르다. **b**) dance. 춤추다.
shake a loose* 〔*free*〕 *leg, live a fast life. 방탕하다.
show a leg, 《*colloq.*》 get out of bed. 잠자리에서 일어나다.
stand on one's own legs, be independent. 독립하다; 혼자 힘으로 하다.
stretch one's legs, go for a walk, esp. after sitting a long time. (오래 앉아 있다가) 산책하다.
take to one's legs, run away. 도망치다.
try it on the other leg, show one's reserved skill. 비장의 수를 쓰다.
walk off one's legs, walk until one is tired. 지치도록 걷다.
— *vt.* (**-ged**) (P7) push (a boat) with the legs. 발로 (배)를 밀어내다. [N.]
leg it, 《*colloq.*》 walk quickly; run; run away. 빨리 걷다; 뛰다; 달아나다.

leg·a·cy [légəsi] *n.* (*pl.* **-cies**) Ⓒ **1** money or property left to another by someone's will. 유산. ¶ *inherit a* ~ 유산을 물려받다. **2** something handed down from an ancestor. 선조로부터 물려받은 것. ¶ *a* ~ *of hatred* 〔*ill will*〕 대대로 내려오는 원한 (관계). [L. *lēgo* commit]

***le·gal** [líːgəl] *adj.* **1** of law. 법률(상)의. ¶ ~ *affairs* 법적인 일 / *the* ~ *profession* 법조계. **2** of lawyers. 변호사의. ¶ *a* ~ *advisor* 법률 고문. **3** lawful; according to law; admitted by law. 합법의, 적법한. ¶ *a* ~ *fare* 법정 운임 / ~ *tender* 법정 화폐 / *the* ~ *person* 법인 / ~ *limit* 법정 제한 속도. [L. *lex* law]

le·gal·i·ty [liːgǽləti] *n.* (*pl.* **-ties**) Ⓤ the state of being according to the law; the state of being allowed by the law. 적법; 합법(성).

le·gal·ize [líːgəlàiz] *vt.* (P6) make (something) legal; authorize (something) by law. …을 합법화하다; 적법하다고 인정하다.

le·gal·ly [líːgəli] *adv.* **1** in a legal manner. 법률적으로. **2** according to law. 합법적으로.

leg·ate [légət] *n.* an ambassador of the Pope. 로마 교황 사절; 교황 특사. [→legacy]

leg·a·tee [lègətíː] *n.* Ⓒ a person who receives a legacy. 유산 수령인. [↑]

le·ga·tion [ligéiʃən] *n.* **1** Ⓤ 《*collectively*》 a diplomatic minister and his staff. 공사관원 전원(cf. *ambassador, minister*). **2** Ⓒ the official residence of a minister; the position or office of a minister. 공사관; 공사의 직〔직위〕. **3** sending a person for a country, etc. 사절 파견. [L. *lēgo* commit]

le·ga·to [ligáːtou, lə-] *adj., adv.* 《It.》 《mus.》 (performed) smoothly(cf. *staccato*). 레가토; 부드러운; 부드럽게.

***leg·end** [lédʒənd] *n.* **1** Ⓒ a story handed down from the past. 전설. **2** ⓐ a story of the life of a saint. 성인전(聖人傳). ⓑ stories of a famous person; a name famous in such stories. 전설적인 인물〔이야기〕. **3** the words on a coin or medal. (메달·화폐 따위의) 명(銘). **4** a short title or article under a picture, etc. 범례(凡例); (그림의) 제명(題銘). [L. *lego* pick, read]

leg·end·ar·y [lédʒəndèri / -dəri] *adj.* **1** of or like legends. 전설(傳說)의〔같은〕. **2** famous; celebrated. 유명한. ¶ *His deeds became* ~ *throughout the country.* 그의 행위는 전국적으로 유명해졌다. — *n.* Ⓒ a collection of saints' lives. 성인전; 전설집.

leg·er·de·main [lèdʒərdəméin] *n.* Ⓤ **1** sleight of hand. 요술; 속임수. **2** sophistry. 궤변. [F.=light of hand]

legged [légid] *adj.* 《often used in *compounds*》 having legs. 다리가 있는; 다리가 …한. ¶ *thick-legged* 다리가 굵은. [*leg*]

leg·gings [léginz] *n. pl.* a pair of long, heavy coverings to protect legs from mud, cold, etc. 각반; 정강이받이; 게트르. [*leg*]

leg·gy [légi] *adj.* (**-gi·er, -gi·est**) having long legs; having conspicuous or attractive legs. 다리가 긴〔껑충한〕; 매력적인 다리를 가진. ¶ *a* ~ *girl* 다리가 미끈한 여자. [*leg*]

leg·horn [léghɔːrn] *n.* Ⓒ **1** a hat made of Italian straw. 일종의 밀짚모자. **2** [léghɔːrn, légərn] (sometimes L-) a kind of chicken. 레그혼. [Place]

leg·i·bil·i·ty [lèdʒəbíləti] *n.* Ⓤ the state of being easy to read; clearness of print or writing. 읽기 쉬움; 선명도(鮮明度). [L. *lego* read]

leg·i·ble [lédʒəbəl] *adj.* (of handwriting, print, etc.) can easily be read. (필적·인쇄가) 읽기에 쉬운; 명료한(opp. illegible).

***le·gion** [líːdʒən] *n.* **1** Ⓒ 《*collectively*》 (in ancient Rome) a body of from 3,000 to 6,000 soldiers. 옛 로마의 군단《3천-6천 명으로 됨》. **2** Ⓤ an army; a large body of soldiers. 군대; 군단. **3** Ⓤ 《*lit.*》 a great number of persons or things. 다수; 많음. ¶ *My enemies are* ~. 내 적은 헤아릴 수 없다. [L. *lego* pick]

leg·is·late [lédʒislèit] *vi.* (P1,3) make laws. — *vt.* (P6,13) cause (something) to happen by making laws. 법을 만들어 …하게 하다. [L. *lex* law, *lator* proposer]

·leg·is·la·tion [lèdʒisléiʃən] *n.* **1** Ⓤ the act of making laws. 입법. ¶ *the power of* ~ 입법권. **2** 《*collectively*》 the laws that are made. 법률. ¶ *a bill of* ~ 법률안.

·leg·is·la·tive [lédʒislèitiv / -slət-] *adj.* having the power of making laws; of legislation. 입법권이 있는; 입법의. ¶ *a* ~ *body* 입법부.

leg·is·la·tor [lédʒislèitər] *n.* Ⓒ a maker of laws; a member of a legislature. 입법자.

·leg·is·la·ture [lédʒislèitʃər] *n.* Ⓒ the body of persons in a state or country having the power to make or alter laws. 입법부; 입법 기관.

le·git·i·ma·cy [lidʒítəməsi] *n.* Ⓤ the state of being legitimate. 합법; 적법; 정통. [L. *lex* law, *legitimatus* made lawful]

·le·git·i·mate [lidʒítəmit] *adj.* **1** recognized by the law as rightful; lawful. 적법한; 합법적인(opp. illegitimate). **2** reasonable; right. 이치에 닿는; 지당한. ¶ *a* ~ *reason* 그럴 만한 이유. **3** born of parents who are married. 적출(嫡出)의. ¶ *a* ~ *child* 본처 소생. — [-mèit] *vt.* (P6) recognize (something) as lawful; justify; establish (a bastard) as lawfully born. …을 합법으로 인정하다; 정당화하다; (서자)를 적출로 인정하다. ●**le·git·i·mate·ly** [-li] *adv.* [↑]

leg·ume [légju:m] *n.* **1** the seed of a plant bearing pods, as peas, beans, etc.; the plant itself. 콩과의 식물. **2** a pod with the seed inside. 꼬투리. [L. *lego* pick]

le·gu·men [ligjú:mən] *n.* (*pl.* **le·gu·mi·na** or **-mens**) = legume.

le·gu·mi·na [ligjú:minə] *n.* pl. of **legumen.**

le·gu·mi·nous [ligjú:minəs] *adj.* bearing legumes; of legumes; belonging to the same group of plants as beans. 콩의; 콩과(科)의.

:lei·sure [lí:ʒər / léʒ-] *n.* Ⓤ the time free from work or duties; the time when one may rest. 틈; 여가; 레저. ¶ *have no* ~ *for reading* 책 읽을 시간이 없다 / *a man of* ~ 한가한 사람.

at leisure, **a**) not working or busy. 일손이 비어; 실업하여. **b**) without hurrying; slowly. 천천히; 한가하게.

at one's leisure, when one has free time; at one's ease. 한가한 때에.

— *adj.* 《as *attributive*》 free from work; not busy. 한가한; 일이 없는. [L. *licet* it is permitted]

lei·sured [lí:ʒərd, léʒ-] *adj.* **1** having plenty of leisure. 한가한. ¶ *the* ~ *classes* 유한 계급. **2** slow and easy. 느긋한.

lei·sure·ly [lí:ʒərli / léʒ-] *adv.* without hurrying; slowly. 느긋이; 천천히. ¶ *work* ~ / *We strolled* ~ *through the park.* 공원을 천천히 걸었다. — *adj.* not hurried; slow. 느긋한; 여유 있는. ¶ ~ *movement* 느긋한 동작.

:lem·on [lémən] *n.* Ⓒ **1** a small, yellow fruit with a sour juice, related to the orange. 레몬. **2** the tree bearing this fruit. 레몬나무. **3** Ⓤ the color of lemons. 레몬색; 담황색. [Arab.]

lem·on·ade [lèmənéid] *n.* Ⓤ a drink made of lemon juice, water, and sugar. 레모네이드; 레몬수.

lemon squash [⌐-⌐] *n.* a drink made of lemon juice and soda water. 레몬스쿼시.

le·mur [lí:mər] *n.* Ⓒ a kind of monkey with a face like a fox. 여우원숭이《마다가스카르섬의 야행성(夜行性) 원숭이의 하나》. [L. *lemures* ghost]

:lend [lend] *vt.* (**lent**) **1** (P6,7,13,14) ⓐ allow (someone) to have or use something for a time. …을 빌려주다; …에 빌리다(opp. borrow). ¶ *Lend me your book.* 네 책을 좀 빌려다오. ⓑ let out (money) at interest. 이자를 받고 (돈)을 빌려주다. ¶ ~ *out money at high interest* 높은 이자를 받고 돈을 빌려주다. **2** (P6,13,14) 《*to*》 give or provide (assistance, etc.); contribute; give for a time; add. (손·힘을) …에 빌려주다; 제공하다. ¶ ~ *one's aid to a cause* 어떤 운동에 조력하다. **3** (P13,14) afford; add. 주다; 더하다. ¶ *Distance lends enchantment to the view.* 먼데서 보니 경치가 한결 좋다. [A.S. *læn* loan]

lend a (***helping***) ***hand,*** assist; help. 돕다; 조력(助力)하다; 원조하다.

lend ear 〔***an ear, one's ear***〕, listen. …을 들어주다; 경청하다.

lend itself to (= *be suitable for; be useful for*) *something.* (사물이) …에 도움이 되다; …에 적합하다.

lend oneself to, allow oneself to support. …에 도움이 되다; …에 전념하다; 몰두하다.

lend·er [léndər] *n.* Ⓒ a person who lends. 빌려주는 사람; 대금업자.

:length [leŋkθ] *n.* Ⓒ **1** the distance of a thing from end to end. 길이; 세로; 키. ¶ *thirty meters in* ~ 길이 30 미터 / *be of the same* ~ 길이가 같다 / *the* ~ *of a rod* 장대의 길이. **2** the state and quality of being long. 긺; 긴 상태. ¶ *a journey remarkable for its* ~ 아주 장기간에 걸친 여행. **3** ⓐ extent in space, degree, or time. (시간적으로 계속되는) 길이; 범위; 정도. ¶ *the* ~ *of a visit* 방문의 시간 / *He did not go to that* ~. 그는 그렇게까지 하지〔말하지〕 않았다 / *one's* ~ *of life* 〔*days*〕 장수; 장명(長命). ⓑ 《phon.》 vowel quantity or duration. 음의 길이. ¶ *the* ~ *of a syllable* 음절의 길이. **4** a certain measure. 어떤 길이; 일정한 길이의 것. ¶ *a* ~ *of pipe* 일정 길이의 파이프. **5** (of a boat or horse race) its own length. (보트의)

1정신(艇身); (경마의) 1마신(馬身). ¶ *The boat won by two lengths.* 그 보트는 2 정신의 차로 이겼다. [A.S. *lengthu,* →long]

at full length, **a**) with the body fully streched out. 큰대자로 (누워). **b**) in full. 상세히.

at great length, over a very long period. 장황하게. ¶ *He explained it at great* ～. 그는 그것을 장황하게 설명했다.

at length, **a**) at last. 드디어; 마침내. **b**) with details. 상세하게.

at some length, with details. 매우 상세하게.

go all lengths, do anything or everything possible. 어떤 짓도 서슴지 않다.

***go the length of** doing,* go so far as to do. …까지도 하다. ¶ *I will not go the* ～ *of saying such things.* 그런 것까지 말할 생각은 없다.

go the whole length, do as one pleases. 멋대로 놀다.

go to great 〔***any***〕 ***lengths*** ＝go all lengths.

keep** someone **at arm's length, avoid being friendly with someone. …를 경원하다.

know 〔***get, have***〕 ***the length of** someone's* ***foot,*** perceive someone's weak point; have a key to someone's character. …의 약점을 알다; …의 성격을 파악하다.

over the length and breadth of, everywhere; all over; throughout. …을 두루; 샅샅이.

·length·en [léŋkθən] *vt.* (P6,7) make (something) long or longer. …을 길게 하다; 늘이다. ¶ *Ask the tailor to* ～ *the skirt.* 재봉사에게 스커트의 기장을 늘여 달라고 해라. —*vi.* (P1,2A) grow longer. 길어지다. ¶ *The days* ～ *in March.* 3월엔 해가 길어진다.

length·wise [léŋkθwàiz] *adj., adv.* in the direction from end to end. 세로의(로). ¶ *We sleep* ～ *in bed.* 우리는 침대에서 길이로 누워 잔다.

length·y [léŋkθi] *adj.* (**length·i·er, length·i·est**) very long; too long and dull. 기다란; 장시간의; 지루한. ¶ *a* ～ *sermon* 장황한 설교 / *a very* ～ *journey* 실로 기나긴 여정.

le·ni·ence [líːniəns] *n.* Ⓤ ＝leniency.

le·ni·en·cy [líːniənsi] *n.* Ⓤ the state of being mild and gentle; mercy. 관대(寬大); 온화; 자비. [↓]

le·ni·ent [líːniənt] *adj.* mild merciful; not severe; merciful. 관대한; 자비로운. ¶ *a* ～ *punishment* 가벼운 형벌 / *a* ～ *judge* 너그러운 재판관. [L. *lenis* soft]

len·i·tive [lénətiv] *adj.* having the power to ease pain or suffering; soothing; softening. 진통성의. —*n.* Ⓒ a lenitive medicine. 진통제. [↑]

len·i·ty [lénəti] *n.* Ⓤ the state or quality of being lenient. 자비로움; 관대.

·lens [lenz] *n.* (*pl.* **lens·es**) Ⓒ **1** a piece of glass with curved sides used in cameras, etc. 렌즈. ¶ *Lenses are used in cameras, telescopes and other instruments.* 카메라, 망원경 및 그 밖의 기기에 렌즈가 쓰인다. **2** the part of the eye which focuses light. (안구의) 수정체. [→lentil]

Lent [lent] *n.* (in the Christian Church) the 40 days before Easter Sunday, kept in some Christian churches with fasting and regretting for wrongdoing. 사순절《Easter 전의 40일 간》. [E. ＝spring]

:lent [lent] *v.* p. and pp. of **lend.**

len·til [léntil] *n.* Ⓒ 《bot.》 an edible seed shaped like double-convex lens. 렌즈콩; 편두. [L. *lens*]

Le·o [líːou] *n.* 《astron.》 a sign of the zodiac. 사자자리. [→lion]

le·o·nine [líːənàin] *adj.* of or like a lion. 사자의; 사자 같은. [↑]

leop·ard [lépərd] *n.* Ⓒ a fierce animal of the cat family with black spots, found in Asia and Africa. 표범(opp. leopardess). ¶ 《Bible》 *Can the* ～ *change his spots?* 표범이 그 반점을 바꿀 수 있느뇨《성격은 좀처럼 못 고치는 것》. [→lion, pard]

leop·ard·ess [lépərdis] *n.* Ⓒ a female leopard. 암표범.

lep·er [lépər] *n.* Ⓒ a person suffering from leprosy. 나병 환자. [Gk. *lepos* scale]

lep·i·dop·te·ra [lèpidáptərə / -dɔ́p-] *n. pl.* an order of insects, including the butterflies and moths. 인시류(鱗翅類). [↑, Gk. *pteron* wing]

lep·ro·sy [léprəsi] *n.* Ⓤ a disease which slowly eats the body like acid. 나병(癩病). [→leper]

lep·rous [léprəs] *adj.* having leprosy; of or like leprosy. 나병에 걸린; 나병의.

les·bi·an [lézbiən] *adj.* of homosexuality in women. (여성간) 동성애의. —*n.* a homosexual woman. 동성애를 하는 여자. [Gk.]

lese-maj·es·ty [líːzmǽdʒisti] *n.* Ⓤ high treason. 불경(대역)죄. [↓]

le·sion [líːʒən] *n.* Ⓒ **1** a hurt, wound, or injury. 부상; 상처; 손해. **2** an injurious change in an organ; a moral injury. 장애; 정신적 장애. [L. *laedo* hurt]

:less [les] *adj.* (compar. of **little.** cf. *lesser.*) smaller in size, amount, or degree; not so large, great, or much. (수량·크기·정도가) …보다 적은; …보다 작은; …만 못한 (opp. more). 語法 수(數)일 때는 fewer가 더 일반적임. ¶ *of* ～ *value* 〔*importance*〕 그다지 가치가 없는〔중요치 않은〕 / *have* ～ *rain* 비가 덜 오다 / *He spends* ～ *time at work than at play.* 일보다는 노는 시간이 더 많다 / *Less noise, please!* 좀 조용히 해라 / *Eat* ～ *meat and more vegetables.* 고기를 덜 먹고 채소를 더 먹어라.

nothing less (***than***), 《used to emphasize a following adjective or noun》 the same thing as. …와 마찬가지의; 다름 없는. ¶ *It is nothing* ～ *than an invasion.* 그건 바로 침략이다.

something 〔***somewhat***〕 ***less than,*** far from being. (결코) …이 아닌.

— *adv.* to a smaller extent; in a lower degree. 보다 적게; …만 못하게. ¶ *He is ~ fat than he was.* 이전보다는 살이 빠졌다 / *It is ~ important.* 그건 대수롭지 않다 / *He is ~ known.* 그는 별로 알려져 있지 않다.

little less than, almost the same as. 거의 같은 정도. ¶ *It is little ~ than robbery.* 그건 약탈이나 마찬가지다.

more or less, about; rather. 다소; 어느 정도.

no less than, **a**) as much 〔many〕 as...; as ~ as. …와 동수의; …와 마찬가지의. ¶ *She has no ~ than 100 dollars.* 그녀는 백 달러 정도는 가지고 있다 / *No ~ than ten people offered to help us.* 자그만치 열 사람이나 우릴 돕겠다고 나섰다 / *She is no ~ beautiful than her sister.* 그녀는 언니 못지 않게 미인이다. **b**) no other than; just as. …나 다를 바 없는; 바로. ¶ *He is no ~ a person than the prince.* 그는 다른 사람 아닌 바로 왕자다.

none the less, nevertheless; still; for all that. 그럼에도 불구하고. ¶ *Though poor, he is none the ~ happy.* 가난함에도 불구하고 그는 행복하다.

— *n.* Ⓤ a smaller amount, quantity, a time. 보다 적은 양〔수·액〕. ¶ *in ~ than a month* 한 달내에 / *He is ~ of a fool than he looks.* 겉보기처럼 그런 어리석은 사람이 아니다 / *Less than 30 of them remained.* 그들 중에 남은 자는 30명도 안 된다.

in less than no time, 《*joc.*》 very quickly; at once; soon. 당장에; 곧.

— *prep.* minus. …을 빼고; …만큼 모자라는. ¶ *a year ~ six days* 일 년에서 6일을 빼고; 6일이 모자라는 일 년. [E.]

-less [-lis] *suf.* **1** without; lacking. '…이 없는'의 뜻. ¶ *valueless* 무가치한. **2** not be able to do; not become. '…할 수가 없는'의 뜻. ¶ *countless* 헤아릴 수 없는; 무수한. [E.]

les·see [lesíː] *n.* Ⓒ a person who rents land or a house under a lease. 임차인(賃借人) (opp. lessor). [*leaseholder*]

***less·en** [lésn] *vt.* (P6) make (something) smaller or less. …을 줄이다; 적게 하다. ¶ *~ the danger* 위험을 줄이다. — *vi.* (P1) become or grow less. 적어지다; 줄다. ¶ *Light lessens as evening comes on.* 저녁이 되면서 어두워진다. [*less*]

less·er [lésər] *adj.* (compar. of **little**) of a smaller amount; less; smaller; fewer. 적은〔작은〕 쪽의. ¶ *the Lesser Bear* 작은곰자리.

⁝les·son [lésn] *n.* Ⓒ **1** something learned by a pupil or student. 학과. **2** a unit of study taught at one time. (교과서 중의) 과(課). ¶ *Lesson 3,* 제 3 과 / *~ one =the first ~* 제 1 과. **3** 《usu. *pl.*》 instruction in some subject; a course of instruction. 수업; 연습. ¶ *give* 〔*teach*〕 *lessons in music* 음악을 가르치다 / *take* 〔*have*〕 *lessons in Latin from a teacher* 선생한테서 라틴어를 배우다. **4** a part of the Bible read as part of a church service. (교회에서 읽는 성서의) 일과(日課). **5** something learned from experience; a warning example; a scolding. 교훈; 훈계; 질책. ¶ *This failure served as a ~ to him.* 이 실패가 그에게 교훈이 되었다 / *Let this be a ~ to you.* 이것이 네게 교훈이 됐으면 싶다 / *teach* 〔*read*〕 *someone a ~* 아무를 꾸짖다 / *This boy needs a ~.* 이 녀석 혼 좀 나야겠다.

— *vt.* (P6) 《rare》 scold; rebuke; discipline. …을 훈계하다; 꾸짖다; 가르치다. [L. *lego* read, →lecture]

les·sor [lésɔr, -⌐] *n.* Ⓒ a person who gives a lease. 임대인(賃貸人); 빌려준 사람 (opp. lessee).

⁝lest [lest] *conj.* **1** in order that ... not; for fear that. …하지 않도록; …하면 안 되므로. ¶ *You must work hard ~ you* (*should*) *fail.* 실패하지 않도록 열심히 해라 / *Be careful ~ you should fall from the tree.* 나무에서 떨어지지 않도록 조심해라. **2** 《used after words expressing *fear*》 that. …하지나 않을까 하여. ¶ *for fear ~ she should die* 그녀가 죽으면 어쩌나 해서 / *I am afraid ~ he should fail.* 그가 실수할까 봐 걱정이다. [*less*]

⁝let[1] [let] *v.* (**let, let·ting**) *vt.* **1** (P22) permit; allow. …에 시키다; …하게 하다; …을 허락하다. ¶ *Will you ~ me smoke?* 담배 피워도 괜찮을까 / *I'll ~ you do no such thing.* 그런 일을 하면 못쓴다 / *She ~ no one enter the room.* 그녀는 아무도 자기 방에 못 들어오도록 했다. **2** (P22) 《used in the *imperative* with *1st* and *3rd persons* to express a request, a command, a warning, etc.》 …하자; 시키자. ¶ *Let me go home.* 집에 가게 해 주시오 / *Let her do her best.* 그녀가 제 힘껏 하게 두자. **3** (P7,13) allow (someone or something) to pass, go or come. …을 가게〔오게〕 하다; 통과시키다. ¶ *Let the blinds down. =Let down the blinds.* 발을 내려라 / *Let the dog out.* 개를 내보내라 / *I ~ her into my study.* 그녀를 서재에 들어오게 했다 / *~ in light and air* 빛과 공기를 들이다. 參考 목적어 다음에 come이나 go가 생략되어 있음. **4** allow (blood, etc.) to flow out or run out. (액체·기체 따위를) 새게 하다; …을 내다. ¶ *~ someone blood* 아무의 피를 뽑다; 아무로부터 채혈(採血)하다 / *I was ~ blood.* 나는 채혈되었다. **5** (P6,7) 《chiefly Brit.》 rent; hire out. (집·땅 등)을 빌려주다. ¶ *This house is to ~.* 집 세놓음《게시》 / *~ a boat by the hour* (시간당 얼마로) 보트를 빌려주다 / *Rooms to ~.* 셋방 있음《게시》. — *vi.* (P1,3) 《chiefly Brit.》 be rented. 빌려지다; 빌릴 사람이 있다. ¶ *The room lets well.* 그 방은 쉽게 나간다. [E.]

let alone, **a**) not to mention; to say nothing of. 말할 것도 없이; …은 고사하고. **b**) refrain from disturbing; not interfere with. …을 그냥 내버려두다. ¶ *Let me alone.* 내버려두어라; 혼자 있고 싶다.

let be, cease to bother; let alone. …을 내버려두다.

let down, **a**) disappoint; fail; deceive. 실망시키다; 속이다. ¶ ~ *him down* 그를 배반하다[저버리다]. **b**) lower. …을 내리다. **c**) slow down. 속력을 늦추다. **d**) hurt the good name of. …의 위신을 떨어뜨리다.
let drive at *someone,* **a**) aim a powerful blow at. …에게 치고 덤비다. **b**) discharge at. …에 발포하다.
let fall [***drop***], **a**) drop. …을 떨어뜨리다. **b**) say purposely; reveal. …을 무심코 누설하다.
let fly, throw; discharge. …을 던지다; 발사하다.
let go, **a**) set (someone or something) free or allow (someone) to go. …을 해방[방면]하다. **b**) dismiss; fire. 해고하다.
let go of (=*stop holding*) *something,* such *as a rope.* (잡고 있는 밧줄 따위)를 놓다; 놓아주다. ¶ ~ *go* (*of*) *a rope* 밧줄을 놓다 / *Don't* ~ *go of the dog.* 개를 풀어놔선 안된다.
let in, allow (fresh air, etc.) to enter; admit. (빛·공기 등)을 통하게 하다; 들이다.
let *someone* ***in for,*** involve someone in (hard work, difficulty, etc.). (…를 곤란 등)에 빠뜨리다; 말려들게 하다. ¶ *I was* ~ *in for trouble.* 말썽에 말려들었다.
let *someone* ***into,*** **a**) admit someone to. …를 를 —에 들이다; 입회시키다. **b**) make someone acquainted with (a secret, etc.); inform. (남에게 비밀 등)을 알리다. ¶ *I was* ~ *into the secret.* 나는 그 비밀을 알게 됐다. **c**) 《*colloq.*》 attack with blows or words. …을 치다; 욕설하다.
let loose, **a**) free (someone or something) from restraint; set free. …을 놓아주다; 해방시키다. ¶ ~ *a cat loose* 고양이를 놓아주다. **b**) indulge in; do as one wishes. …에 빠지다; 마음대로 하다. **c**) show (one's anger, etc.); give vent to. (노여움 등)을 터뜨리다. ¶ ~ *loose one's fury* 화를 내다.
let me see, let me consider; wait a moment before I think out. 글쎄(다); 잠깐; 저어. ¶ *Let me see; she must be sixteen now.* 글쎄, 그녀 나이가 지금 열여섯일거다 / *Let me see. What was the name?* 그런데, 이름이 뭐더라.
let off, **a**) set (someone) free; excuse; pardon. …을 방면하다; 용서해 주다. **b**) set off; fire (a gun, etc.). 발포하다; 쏘다.
let on, 《*colloq.*》 **a**) reveal. (비밀 등)을 폭로하다; 밝히다. ¶ *He knew the facts, but he never* ~ *on.* 그는 진상을 알고 있었으나 입 밖에 내지 않았다. **b**) 《U.S.》 pretend. …인 체하다.
let out, **a**) permit (someone) to go out. …을 내보내주다. **b**) reveal (a secret) by accident. (비밀)을 어쩌다 누설하다. **c**) make (a garment, etc.) looser; make wider. (옷 따위)를 늘이다; 크게 하다. **d**) lease; rent out. 임대하다; 빌려주다; 세놓다.
let pass, overlook. …을 봐주다; 눈감아 주다; 간과(看過)하다.
let's see 《*colloq.*》 =let me see.
let up, cease; stop; become less strong. 그치다; (비바람 등이) 덜해지다. ¶ *The rains is letting up.* 비가 그치고 있다.

let² [let] *n.* Ⓒ **1** a hindrance; an obstacle. 장애; 방해. **2** Ⓤ 《tennis》 a served ball which touches the net before falling on the other side. 레트《네트를 스치고 들어간 서브》. ***without let or hindrance,*** in perfect freedom. 아무 장애 없이.
— *vt.* (**-ted** or **let**) (P6) 《*arch.*》 《chiefly ~ *and hinder*》 hinder; prevent. 방해하다; 훼방놓다. [E.]

-let [-lit] *suf.* little; small. '작은…, 소(小)…'의 뜻. ¶ *a booklet* 소책자 / *a wavelet* 잔물결 / *a riglet* 작은 고리 / *a streamlet* 실개천. [F.]

let-down [létdàun / ⌐⌐] *n.* Ⓒ **1** a reduction in value, energy, etc. 감소; 감퇴. **2** 《*colloq.*》 a disappointment; a disillusionment. 실망; 환멸. ¶ *His lecture was a* ~. 그의 강연은 한심했다. [*let, down*]

le·thal [líːθəl] *adj.* likely to cause death; fatal. 치사의; 치명적인. ¶ *a* ~ *weapon* 흉기 / *a* ~ *chamber* (개·고양이 등의) 무통(無痛) 도살실; 가스 사형실. [L. *letum* death]

le·thar·gic [leθɑ́ːrdʒik], **-gi·cal** [-dʒikəl] *adj.* **1** sleepy; drowsy; dull. 졸리는; 혼수(상태)의. ¶ *a* ~ *condition* 혼수 상태. **2** producing lethargy. 최면성의. [Gk. *lanthanō* escape notice]

leth·ar·gy [léθərdʒi] *n.* Ⓤ **1** the state of being unnaturally sleepy; abnormal sleep. 혼수 (상태). **2** the state of being slow, lazy or not active; dullness. 무기력.

Le·the [líːθi(ː)] *n.* **1** 《Gk. & Rom. myth.》 a river in Hades, a drink of the water of which causes the dead to forget the past. 망각의 강. 參考 그 물을 마시면 이 세상의 괴로움을 잊게 된다는, 저승에 있는 강. **2** Ⓤ forgetfulness. 망각. [↑]

:let's [lets] let us. …하자.

:let·ter [létər] *n.* Ⓒ **1** ⓐ a (written or printed) mark or sign representing a sound of speech; an alphabetical symbol. 글자; 문자. ¶ *a capital* [*a small*] ~ 대[소]문자. ⓑ a piece of printing type bearing a letter. 활자. **2** written or printed words, usu. sent by mail. 편지. ¶ *a* ~ *of introduction* [*thanks*] 소개[감사]장 / *write a* ~ *to someone* 아무에게 편지를 쓰다 / *post a* ~ 편지를 부치다 / *an open* ~ 공개장. **3** 《often *pl.*》 an official document giving proof, conferring a privilege, etc. 증서; (면허장 등 공식의) 서장. ¶ *a* ~ *of attorney* 위임장 / *letters patent* 특허증; 특허; 개봉 칙허(勅許)장. **4** 《*the* ~》 Ⓤ the outward, literal meaning of words. 글자 자체의 뜻; 자의(字義)(opp. spirit). ¶ *the* ~ *of the law* 법률 조문 / *in* ~ *and in spirit* 형식과 정신 모두; 명실공히. **5** Ⓒ 《*pl.*》 literary culture; literature; learning. 문학; 학문. ¶ *a man of letters* 학자; 문인; 저술가 / *the republic* [*commonwealth*] *of let-*

ters 문단 / *be quick at one's letters* 학문을 빨리 익히다 / *the profession of letters* 문필업. **6** 《*collectively*》 a style of printing type. 자체(字體).

to the letter, according to the literal sense; exactly; precisely. 글자 그대로; 정확히.

— *vt.* (P6) write or engrave letters on (something). …에 글자를 쓰다〔글자를 넣다〕. ¶ *a book cover lettered in gold* 금자(金字)를 넣은 책표지. [L. *littera*]

letter box [∸-∸] *n.* **1** a public box into which letters are put to be delivered by the post office; a pillar-box. 우체통. **2** a private box for letters delivered by a postman. (개인 집의) 우편함.

let·ter·card [létərkɑ̀:rd] *n.* Ⓒ 《Brit.》 a postal card that can be folded and sealed by a gummed edge. 봉함 엽서.

letter carrier [∸-∸--] *n.* a postman; a mail carrier. 우편 집배원.

let·tered [létərd] *adj.* **1** able to read and write; educated; learned. 글을 아는; 학식이 있는. **2** having literary attainments. 문학에 소양이 있는. **3** having letters printed on it; inscribed with letters. 글자를 넣은〔새긴〕. [*letter*]

let·ter·head [létərhèd] *n.* Ⓒ **1** the name and address printed at the top of a sheet of writing paper. (편지지 위쪽에 인쇄된) 주소 성명. **2** a sheet of writing paper so printed. (주소 성명이 인쇄된) 편지지.

let·ter·ing [létəriŋ] *n.* Ⓤ **1** the act of drawing or inscribing letters. 글자를 써〔새겨〕 넣기. **2** the letters so drawn. 쓴 글자.

let·ter·press [létərprès] *n.* Ⓒ the words on a printed page as distinguished from the illustrations. (삽화에 대한) 문자 인쇄면; 본문.

let·tuce [létis] *n.* ⒸⓊ a garden plant with tender, crisp leaves which are much used in salads. 상추; 레터스. [L. *lac* milk (milky juice)]

leu·co·cyte [lú:kəsàit] *n.* 《physiol.》 a white blood corpuscle. 백혈구. [Gk. *leukos* white, *kytos* cuticle]

lev·ee[1] [lévi] *n.* Ⓒ **1** 《U.S.》 a large bank built along a river to prevent overflowing. 호안 제방(護岸堤防). **2** a place for landing passengers and goods from a ship. 부두. [F. *levo* raise, lift]

lev·ee[2] [lévi] *n.* Ⓒ a morning reception held by a king or other ruler for men only (군주 등의) 접견; 《U.S.》 a reception held by the President or another high official. (대통령 등의) 초대회. [F. *levo* a rising]

:lev·el [lévəl] *adj.* **1** having no part higher than any other; perfectly flat and even; smooth; parallel to the surface of still water. 수평의; (수평선에 대하여) 경사가 없는. ¶ *a ~ floor* 판판한 마루. **2** 《*to, with*》 equal; of equal height, importance, degree, etc. 같은 높이〔정도, 중요성〕의; 동등한. ¶ *a ~ race* 호각의 경주 / *The river is now ~ with its banks.* 강은 이제 수위가 둑과 같은 높이다 / *Tom is ~ with John in the class.* 톰은 반에서 존과 같은 성적이다. **3** well-balanced in quality, style, temper, judgment, etc. 균형잡힌; 온건한; 공평한; 이성적인. ¶ *a ~ mind* 안정된 마음 / *have a ~ head* 분별이 있다.

— *n.* Ⓒ **1** an instrument for showing whether a surface is level or not. 수준기. ¶ *take a ~* (토지의) 기복을 재다. **2** something that is level; a flat and even area of land or other surface. 수평(면); 평지; 평면. **3** a height; a horizontal position. 고도; 같은 높이의 면. ¶ *The water rose to a ~ of 20 meters.* 수위는 20미터 높이가 되었다 / *3,800 meters above sea ~* 해발 3,800미터 / *at the ~ of one's eyes* 눈높이로. **4** social, moral or intellectual standard; degree; rank, esp. an equal rank. (사회적·도덕적·지적 등의) 수준; 표준; 동등; 동위. ¶ *rise to higher intellectual levels* 지적 수준이 높아지다.

do one's level best, 《*colloq.*》 do all that one can do. 전력〔최선〕을 다하다.

find one's 〔***its***〕 ***level,*** reach one's 〔its〕 proper or natural place according to one's abilities, etc. 분수에 맞는 지위에 앉다; 마땅한 곳에 자리잡다.

on the level, 《*colloq.*》 honestly; truthfully. 정직하게; 공평하게.

— *v.* (**-eled, -el·ing** or 《Brit.》 **-elled, -el·ling**) *vt.* **1** (P6,7,13) make (something) even, flat or uniform. …을 고르게 하다; 판판하게 하다; 한결같게 하다; 수평되게 하다. ¶ *~ ground* 땅을 고르다 / *~ a road up* 〔*down*〕 노면을 평평하게 깎다〔돋우다〕. **2** (P6,13) aim; direct. (총을) 겨누다; (비난 등을) 퍼붓다. ¶ *~ a satire at* 〔*against*〕 *someone* 아무를 신랄하게 비꼬다 / *~ a gun at a lion* 사자에게 총을 겨누다. **3** (P6,13) 《*to, with*》 bring (something) to the level of the ground; knock down. (건물 등을) 쓰러뜨리다; 무너뜨리다; 때려눕히다. ¶ *~ the tree* 나무를 베어 넘기다 / *~ a building with the ground* 건물을 헐어버리다 / *The first blow leveled him to the ground.* 일격으로 그를 땅에 눕혔다.

— *vi.* **1** (P3) 《*at*》 take aim; direct a gun, etc. 조준하다; 겨누다. **2** (P1,2A) become level. (…와) 같은 수준으로 되다. [L. *levo* lift]

level crossing [∸-∸-] *n.* 《Brit》 a place where a road runs across a railway line. 수평 교차점; 철도 건널목.

lev·el-head·ed [lévəlhédid] *adj.* possessing good common sense and sound judgment; sensible; calm. 분별 있는; 온건한.

lev·er [lévər, lí:vər] *n.* Ⓒ a bar used to move a heavy thing. 지레. ¶ *a control ~* 조정간. — *vt.* (P6,7) 《*out, up*》 move or lift (something) with a lever. …을 지레로 움직이다. — *vi.* (P1,2A) use a lever. 지레를 쓰다. [*level*]

lev·er·age [lévəridʒ, lí:v-] *n.* Ⓤ **1** the action of a lever. 지레의 작용. **2** the advantage or power gained by using a lever. 지레의 비(比). **3** a system or arrangement of levers. 지레 장치. **4** the means of effecting a purpose. 수단. [↑]

le·vi·a·than [liváiəθən] *n.* Ⓒ **1** 《Bible》 a sea animal of a huge size; a water monster. 거대한 해수(海獸). **2** anything enormous, esp. a huge ship. 거대한 것; (특히) 거선(巨船). [Heb.]

lev·i·ty [lévəti] *n.* Ⓤ lack of seriousness, proper behavior or earnestness. 경박스러움; 경솔. [L. *levis* light]

lev·y [lévi] *v.* (**lev·ied**) *vt.* (P6,13) **1** collect (something) by order or force; impose (a tax). …을 거두어들이다; 징수하다; 부과하다. ¶ ~ *a tax on someone* 아무에게 세금을 매기다. **2** call up (a man) for military service; enlist. …을 징집하다. ¶ ~ *troops in time of war* 전시에 군을 소집하다. — *vi.* (P3) impose a tax; get money by authority or force. 과세하다; 압류하다.

***levy war on* 〔*upon, against*〕,** start a war against (a country, etc.). (국가 등에) 도전하다; 싸움을 걸다.

— *n.* (*pl.* **lev·ies**) **1** ⓊⒸ the act of collecting money, a tax, etc. by order or force; the amount so collected. 부과; 징세; 징수액. ¶ *a capital* ~ 자본 과세. **2** Ⓤ the act of calling up men for military service; Ⓒ the number of men so called up. 소집; 징집; 징집병수(數). ¶ ~ *in mass* 국민군 소집. [L. *levo* lift, raise]

lewd [lu:d] *adj.* full of low desire; indecent; immodest. 상스러운; 추잡한. ●**lewd·ly** [-li] *adv.* [E.=unlearned]

lex·i·ca [léksəkə] *n.* pl. of **lexicon.**

lex·i·cal [léksikəl] *adj.* **1** of the vocabulary of a language. 어휘〔어구〕의. **2** of lexicons; of lexicography. 사전(편집)의. [Gk. *lĕgō* speak]

lex·i·cog·ra·pher [lèksəkágrəfər / -kɔ́g-] *n.* Ⓒ a person who makes dictionaries. 사전 편집자. [↑]

lex·i·cog·ra·phy [lèksəkágrəfi / -kɔ́g-] *n.* Ⓤ the act or art of making dictionaries. 사전 편집(술).

lex·i·con [léksəkən] *n.* Ⓒ (*pl.* **-i·ca** or **-cons**) a dictionary, esp. of an ancient language, such as Greek, Hebrew, and Latin. 사전; 고어 사전.

LF low-frequency.

LG Low German.

lg., lge. large.

LH left hand.

LHA local hour angle. 지방 시각(時角).

l.h.b. 《soccer》 left half-back.

L.H.D. 《L.》 *Lit(t)erarum Humaniorum Doctor* (=Doctor of Humanities). 인문학(人文學)박사.

L.I. Long Island.

li·a·bil·i·ty [làiəbíləti] *n.* (*pl.* **-ties**) **1** Ⓤ the state of being liable or under obligation; responsibility. 책임; 의무. ¶ ~ *for debt* 채무 / *limited* 〔*unlimited*〕 ~ 유한〔무한〕 책임. **2** 《*pl.*》 a sum of money that must be paid; a debt. 부채; 빚(opp. assets). ¶ *assets and liabilities* 자산과 부채. **3** Ⓤ the state of being apt to do; tendency. …하기〔빠지기〕 쉬움; (…한) 경향이 있음. ¶ ~ *to disease* 병에 걸리기 쉬움. **4** Ⓒ a thing that works to one's disadvantage. 불리한 일. ¶ *His poor writing is a* ~ *in getting a new job.* 글씨가 서툴러서 새 일자리를 구하기 어렵다. [↓]

***li·a·ble** [láiəbəl] *adj.* **1** 《*to do*》 apt or likely to do; unpleasantly likely. …하기 쉬운; (달갑잖은 일에) 빠지기 쉬운. ¶ *Glass is* ~ *to break.* 유리는 깨지기 쉽다 / *We are all* ~ *to make a mistake.* 사람이란 잘못을 저지르기 쉽다 / *He is* ~ *to catch cold.* 그는 감기에 잘 걸린다. **2** 《*for, to do*》 obliged to take the responsibility for (something); be responsible legally. 책임이 있는〔을 져야 할〕. ¶ *He is* ~ *for damages.* 그에게 손해 배상의 책임이 있다 / *He is* ~ *to pay his wife's debts.* 그가 아내의 빚을 갚아야 한다. [L. *ligo* bind]

li·ai·son [lí:əzàn / li:éizɔ:ŋ] *n.* **1** Ⓤ 《mil.》 a connection or communication between units of a military force. (부대간의) 연락. ¶ *a* ~ *officer* 연락 장교. **2** Ⓒ 《phon.》 (in spoken French) the linking of a silent final consonant to a following word that begins with a vowel or mute *h.* 연결 발음 《프랑스어에서 어미의 자음을 다음 말의 첫 모음에 연결해 발음하는 일》. **3** an illicit amour. 간통. [↑]

***li·ar** [láiər] *n.* Ⓒ a person who tells lies. 거짓말쟁이. ¶ *What a* ~ *he is!* 놈은 순 거짓말쟁이다. [→lie]

Lib. Liberal.

lib. 《L.》 *liber* (=book); librarian; library.

li·ba·tion [laibéiʃən] *n.* Ⓒ **1** the wine offered to a god. 신주(神酒); 제주. **2** 《*colloq.*》 a drinking bout; a merrymaking. 술잔치; 환락. [L.]

li·bel [láibəl] *n.* Ⓒ **1** 《law》 a written or printed statement which injures someone's reputation; Ⓤ the act or crime of publishing such a statement. (남을) 중상하는 글; (문서에 의한) 명예 훼손(죄). **2** 《*colloq.*》 anything that speaks ill of or defames a person's character. (일반적으로) 불명예가〔모욕이〕 되는 것. ¶ *Portraits are often absolute libels upon those whom they represent.* 초상화는 그것이 그려진 사람들에겐 전적으로 모욕일 수가 많다.

— *vt.* (**-beled, -bel·ing** or 《Brit.》 **-belled, bel·ling**) (P6) **1** publish a libel about (someone); make a false statement and defame (someone). …의 명예 훼손 문서를 공개하다; 거짓 표현으로 …의 명예를 훼손하다. **2** 《*colloq.*》 give a damaging picture of; fail to do full justice to (someone). (…의 품성·용모 등)을 그릇되게 그리다. [L. *li-*

bellus a little book]

li·bel·lous [láibələs] *adj.* 《Brit.》 =libelous.

li·bel·ous [láibələs] *adj.* containing that which defames a person; intended to injure a person's reputation. 중상적인; 남을 중상하려 드는. ¶ *a ~ tongue* 독설.

·lib·er·al [líbərəl] *adj.* **1** generous; not sparing. 활수한; 손이 큰; 아끼지 않는. ¶ *a ~ giver* 남에게 인색하지 않은 사람 / *be ~ of* 〔*with*〕 *one's money* 돈에 인색하지 않다. **2** plentiful; abundant; ample. 많은; 풍부한. ¶ *a ~ reward* 많은 보수〔사례금〕/ *a ~ amount* 많은 양 / *a ~ table* 푸짐한 식탁 / *a ~ flow of water* 도도한 물의 흐름. **3** broad-minded; free from prejudice; not narrow in one's ideas. 관대한; 도량이 큰; 공평한. ¶ *a ~ thinker* 편견 없는 사상가. **4** free from literal meaning; not literal; not strict. 자의(字義)에 구애되지 않는; 자유로운. ¶ *a ~ interpretation* 〔*translation*〕 자유역; 의역(意譯). **5** (of an education) fit for a gentleman; of a general and literary kind rather than technical. (교육이) 신사에 적당한〔어울리는〕. ¶ *~ arts* (대학의) 교양 과목 / *~ education* 일반 교양 교육. **6** favoring progress and reforms; liberalistic. 진보적인; 자유주의의(opp. conservative).

— *n.* **1** Ⓒ a person who has liberal political views. 자유주의자. **2** 《usu. *L-*》 《Brit.》 a member of the Liberal Party. 자유당원 [L. *liber* free]

lib·er·al·ism [líbərəlìzəm] *n.* Ⓤ the (belief in) liberal principles. 자유주의.

lib·er·al·i·ty [lìbərǽləti] *n.* (*pl.* **-ties**) **1** Ⓤ the quality of being generous; willingness in giving; large-heartedness. 활수(滑手)함; 관대. **2** Ⓒ 《*pl.*》 a gift, esp. one showing generosity. 선물; 베푼 것.

lib·er·al·ize [líberəlàiz] *vt., vi.* (P6; 1) make or become liberal 자유화하다〔되다〕.

lib·er·al·ly [líbərəli] *adv.* in a liberal manner, generously; abundantly. 관대하게; 아낌없이; 충분〔풍부〕하게; 공평하게.

Liberal Party [∠–– ∠–] *n.* a political party in Great Britian that promotes democratic reforms, etc. (영국의) 자유당.

lib·er·ate [líbərèit] *vt.* (P6,13) **1** set (a prisoner, etc.) free; release. …을 해방하다. ¶ *~ slaves* 노예를 해방하다 / *~ the mind from prejudice* 편견을 제거하다. **2** 《chem.》 allow (gases, etc.) to escape; set free. (가스 따위)를 유리(遊離)시키다. **3** 《phys.》 allow to operate. …을 작용시키다. [→liberal, -ate]

lib·er·a·tion [lìbəréiʃən] *n.* Ⓤ the act of liberating; the state of being liberated. 자유롭게 하기; 해방; 석방.

lib·er·a·tor [líbərèitər] *n.* Ⓒ a person who sets a person or persons free. 해방자.

Li·be·ri·a [laibíəriə] *n.* a republic on the western coast of Africa. 라이베리아. 參考 수도는 Monrovia.

lib·er·tine [líbərtì:n] *n.* Ⓒ a person who leads an immoral life or does shameful conduct. 방탕한 사람; 난봉꾼. [*liberal*]

:lib·er·ty [líbərti] *n.* (*pl.* **-ties**) **1** Ⓤ the state of being free; freedom. 자유. ¶ *Prisoners long for ~.* 수감자들은 자유를 그리워한다. **2** Ⓤ the right to do something without restraint; the freedom of choice. 자유로울 권리; 선택의 자유. ¶ *~ of speech* 〔*the press*〕 언론〔출판〕의 자유 / *have the ~ to do as one pleases* 자기 뜻대로 할 권리를 가지다. **3** 《usu. *pl.*》 the rights and privileges granted by authority. 특권《자치권, 참정권 등》. **4** Ⓒ an improper, excessive freedom or familiarity. 멋대로 함; 방자. [L. *liber* free]

at liberty, **a**) (of a person) free; not busy. 자유로; 한가하여. ¶ *I'm at ~ this afternoon.* 오늘 오후에는 한가하다. **b**) (of a thing) not in use; free to use. 쓰이지 않고〔않는〕; 자유로이 써도 좋은. ¶ *The desk is at ~ (to use).* 이 책상은 써도 된다. **c**) out of employment. 실직해서.

set** someone **at liberty, set someone free; release. …을 해방〔석방〕하다.

take liberties with (=*be too familiar with*) *someone.* …에게 무람없이 굴다. ¶ *take liberties with older people* 어른들에게 방자하게 굴다.

take the liberty of *doing* 〔*to do*〕, do (something) without asking someone's permission. 실례를 무릅쓰고 …하다. ¶ *I took the ~ of reading this letter, even though it was addressed to you.* 네게 온 편지지만 실례인 줄 알면서 내가 읽었다.

li·bid·i·nous [libídənəs] *adj.* lustful; lewd. 음란한; 호색의. ¶ *a ~ person* 〔*book*〕 음탕한 사람〔음란 서적〕. [L. *libido* lust]

li·bi·do [libí:dou] *n.* the instinctive energy; desire derived from id; the sexual instinct. 생명력; 성적 본능. [L.=desire, lust]

li·brar·i·an [laibrέəriən] *n.* Ⓒ a person in charge of a library; a person trained in library service. 도서관원; 사서(司書). [↓]

:li·brar·y [láibrèri / -brəri] *n.* Ⓒ (*pl.* **-braries**) **1** a building or room in which a collection of books is kept for reading. 도서관〔실〕. ¶ *a traveling ~* 순회 도서관. **2** 《*collectively*》 a collection of books belonging to an individual. 장서. ¶ *He has a fine ~.* 훌륭한 장서를 가지고 있다. **3** a series of books of the same kind issued by the same publishing company. (출판사의) 문고; 시리즈. ¶ *The Home University Library.* 가정 대학 문고. **4** a room containing books and used for private study, reading, etc.; a study. 서재. [L. *liber* book]

a walking library, a very well-informed person; a walking dictionary. 박물 군자.

Lib·y·a [líbiə] *n.* a country in northern Africa. 리비아. 參考 수도는 Tripoli.

Lib·y·an [líbiən] *adj.* of Libya or its people.

리비아(사람)의. — *n.* Ⓒ a person of Libya. 리비아인(人).

lice [lais] *n.* pl. of **louse.**

li·cence [láisəns] *n.* =license.

***li·cense** [láisəns] *n.* **1** ⒸⓊ a formal statement of permission to do something granted by law or authority. 면허. ¶ *under ~* 면허를 받고. **2** Ⓒ a written certificate of legal permission. 면허장. ¶ *a ~ to fish* 어업 면허장 / *a ~ to practice medicine* 의사 개업 면장 / *Show me your driver's ~.* 운전 면허증을 봅시다. **3** Ⓤ excessive freedom of action; willful, unruly conduct. 멋대로 함; 방종. ¶ *Little ~ was shown by the occupation forces.* 점령군은 조금도 함부로 행동하는 일이 없었다. **4** Ⓤ freedom from rules in art, etc. 파격(破格). ¶ *poetic ~* 시적 허용《시에서 문법·사실 등을 위반해도 용인되는 일》.
— *vt.* (P6,20) give (someone) permission to do something. …에게 면허〔허가, 인가〕를 주다. ¶ *~ someone to keep beer hall* …에게 맥주집 허가를 내주다. [L. *licet* it is permitted]

li·cen·see [làisənsí:] *n.* Ⓒ a person with a license. 면허〔인가〕 취득자.

li·cen·tious [laisénʃəs] *adj.* ignoring the common rules or principles; sexually immoral; lustful. 행실이 나쁜; 부도덕한; 방탕한; 음란한.

li·chen [láikən, -kin] *n.* ⒸⓊ a mosslike plant without flowers and leaves which grows on rocks, tree trunks, etc. 지의류(地衣類)의 식물; 이끼. [Gk.]

***lick** [lik] *vt.* (P6,7,13,18) **1** pass the tongue over (something). …을 핥다. ¶ *Dogs ~ their wounds.* 개는 다치면 혀로 그 상처를 핥는다 / *The little boy licked his fingers clean.* 그 어린아이는 손가락을 깨끗이 핥았다. **2** (of flames, waves, etc.) move or pass over (something). (파도·불길 등이) …을 씻다; 덮치다; 널름거리다; 뒤덮다. ¶ *The flames were licking the roof of my house.* 불길이 우리 집 지붕에서 널름거리고 있었다. **3** 《*colloq.*》 defeat; overcome. …을 지우다; 이기다. ¶ *Our baseball team can ~ yours.* 우리 야구팀이 너희들 팀을 이길 수 있다 / *I'm licked.* 내가 졌다 / *That licks me.* 그건 내 힘에 부친다〔알 수가 없다〕. **4** 《*colloq.*》 beat; hit. …을 때리다. ¶ *A cowardly boy deserves to be well licked.* 겁쟁이는 좀 맞아도 싸다.
— *vi.* (P1,3) **1** (of flames, etc.) move lightly and quickly. (불길 등이) 널름거리다; 급속히 번지다. ¶ *The waves licked about his feet.* 그의 발밑에서 물결이 남실거렸다. **2** 《*sl.*》 hasten; hurry; speed. 서두르다; 속력을 내다. ¶ *go as hard as one can ~* 쏜살같이 달리다.

***lick one's chops* 〔*lips*〕,** show a desire, esp. for food. …에 입맛을 다시다.

***lick everything* 〔*creation*〕,** surpass everything. 무엇보다도 낫다; 비길 데가 없다.

lick** something or someone **into shape, 《*colloq.*》 make someone or something complete or suitable by training; make more efficient. …을 어연번듯하게 만들다; 제 구실을 하게 만들다.

***lick off* 〔*up*〕,** **a**) take off (something) by licking; drink up or clear by licking. …을 핥아 없애다; 깨끗이 비우다. **b**) destroy. …을 파괴하다; 불태워 버리다.

lick** someone's **shoes, lower oneself before someone. …에게 굴복하다; 빌붙다.

lick the dust, be completely overcome; die, usu. violently. 일패도지(一敗塗地)하다; 살해되다.
— *n.* **1** ⓊⒸ the act of licking with the tongue or an instance of this. (한번) 핥기. **2** Ⓒ a small amount; a bit. 조금; 소량. ¶ *a ~ of butter* 약간의 버터. **3** 《*colloq.*》 ⓐ a sharp blow. 일격; 강타. ⓑ a brief burst of energy; a spurt of speed. 한바탕 용쓰기; 속력. ¶ *at full ~* 전속력으로 / *go at a tremendous ~* 무서운 속도로 달리다. **4** 《U.S.》 a place where salt is found on the surface and where animals come to lick it up. 함염지(含塩池). [E.]

a lick and a promise, a quick, rough washing, sweeping, piece of work, etc. (청소 따위) 겉날리기. ¶ *give the floor a ~ and a promise* 마루를 대강대강 훔치다.

***lid** [lid] *n.* **1** Ⓒ a movable cover for an opening. 뚜껑. ¶ *the ~ of a box* 상자 뚜껑 / *put on* 〔*take off*〕 *the ~* 뚜껑을 닫다〔벗기다〕. **2** an eyelid. 눈꺼풀. **3** 《*sl.*》 a hat; a cap. 모자. [E.]

blow the lid off, 《*sl.*》 expose to public view; reveal. (내막 등)을 폭로하다.

put the lid on, 《Brit. *sl.*》 put a stop to; bring to an end; destroy. …을 끝장내다; 망쳐놓다.

:lie[1] [lai] *vi.* (**lay, lain, ly·ing**) (P1,2A,3,5) **1** be in a flat or horizontal position. (물건이) 가로 놓여 있다. ¶ *a book lying on the table* 탁자에 놓여 있는 책. **2** be or put oneself in a flat or resting position. 드러눕다. ¶ *~ down on the bed* 침대에 눕다 / *~ down and take one's rest* 누워 쉬다. **3** be situated. (토지 등이) …에 있다; 위치하다. ¶ *The lake lies among hills* 〔*to the west of the mountain*〕. 호수는 몇 개의 야산에 에워싸여 있다〔산의 서편에 있다〕. **4** be kept or remain in a specified state. …한 상태에 있다; (어떤 상태로) 누워 있다. ¶ *~ ill in bed* 병석에 있다 / *~ in prison* 옥에 갇혀 있다 / *~ sleeping* 자고 있다 / *~ hidden* 숨어〔잠복해〕 있다 / *The corn lies wasting in the granary.* 강냉이가 창고에 썩고 있었다 / *A happy life lies before you.* 네 앞에는 행복한 생활이 있다. **5** be; exist. (…에) 있다. ¶ *The fault lies here.* 잘못은 여기에 있다 / *Happiness lies in contentment.* 행복은 만족하는 데 있다. **6** be spread out to view; extend in some direction; stretch. (…이) 펼쳐져 있다; (…쪽으로) 뻗어 있다. ¶ *The valley lies at our feet.* 우리들 발밑으로 계곡이 뻗어 있다 / *The path lies along a stream.* 길은

시냇물을 따라 나 있다. **7** be in the grave. (…이) 묻혀 있다. ¶ *His body lies in Boston.* 그의 시신은 보스턴에 묻혀 있다.

as far as in me lies, as well as I can. 내 힘이 미치는 한.

lie at** someone's **door, be someone's responsibility; be attributed to someone. (책임이) …에게 있다. ¶ *The blame lies at his door.* 책임은 그에게 있다.

lie back, get into or be in a resting position. 뒤로 기대다.

lie by, **a**) stop; pause for rest. 쉬다; 휴식하다. **b**) remain unused. 쓰이지 않고 있다.

lie close, be in hiding. 숨어 있다.

lie dog-go, 《*sl.*》 crouch motionless. 웅크리고 있다.

lie down on the job, 《U.S. *colloq.*》 do less than one could or should do; work in a lazy way. 일을 피부리며 하다; 농땡이 부리다.

***lie down under** something,* accept something without protest or resistance. (모욕 등)을 감수하다. ¶ ~ *down under an insult* 모욕을 견디다.

lie in, **a**) remain in bed because of childbirth. 산욕(産褥)에 들다. **b**) consist in (something). …에 있다. **c**) stay late in bed. (평소보다) 늦잠 자다.

lie (=*depend*) ***on** something.* …에 달려 있다; …에 의해 정해지다.

lie over, (of an action) be postponed until some future time; be put off. 연기되다. ¶ *The matter must ~ over.* 그 일은 연기해야 겠다.

lie with, belong to; be the duty of. …에게 있다; …의 책임이다. ¶ *It lies with you to decide.* 네가 결정할 나름이다 / *The fault lies with him.* 잘못은 그에게 있다.

— *n.* the way in which something lies; the direction; lay. 위치; 향; 방향. [E.]

the lie of the land, **a**) the appearance, slope, etc. of an area of land. 지세(地勢). **b**) the state of affairs. 형세; 정세.

:lie² [lai] *v.* (**lied, ly·ing**) *vi.* (P1) speak falsely with intent to deceive; (of things) convey a false impression to a person. 거짓말하다; (물건이) 사람을 헷갈리게 하다; 눈을 속이다. ¶ *Don't ~ about it.* 그 일에 거짓말을 마라. — *vt.* (P7,13) bring, put, etc. (someone or something) by lying. …을 속이다; 현혹시키다. ¶ ~ *someone out of something* 아무를 속여서 …을 빼앗다 / ~ *someone into doing* 아무를 부추겨 …하게 하다.

lie in** one's **throat 〔***teeth***〕, 《*arch., joc.*》 tell gross lies. 터무니없는 거짓말을 하다.

— *n.* Ⓒ a false statement made in order to deceive; a falsehood. 거짓말(opp. truth). ¶ *act a ~* 말이 아닌 행동으로 속이다 / *tell a ~* 거짓말하다 / *That's a ~!* 그건 거짓말이다 / *a barefaced ~* 뻔뻔스러운 거짓말 / 《*prov.*》 *A ~ begets a ~.* 거짓말은 거짓말을 낳는다. [E.]

give the lie to, **a**) openly accuse (someone) of lying. …을 거짓말쟁이라고 비난하다. **b**) prove (something) to be false. …이 거짓임을 입증하다.

lie-a·bed [láiəbed] *n.* 《*sl.*》 a late riser. 늦잠꾸러기. [*lie*¹]

lied [li:d] *n.* 《G.》 Ⓒ (*pl.* **lied·er**) a German song or lyric. 단시(短詩); 가곡; 리트.

lied·er [lí:dər] *n.* pl. of **lied.**

lief [li:f] *adv.* 《*arch.*》 willingly; gladly. 기꺼이; 쾌히. [E.=dear]

would as lief ... as ___=would liefer ... than ___, would rather or more willingly... than ___. —하느니 차라리 …하는 편이 낫다. ¶ *I would as ~ go there as stay.* 여기 있느니 거기로 가는 게 좋겠다 / *I would liefer die than live ashamed.* 부끄럽게 사느니 죽어 버리는 게 낫다.

liege [li:dʒ] *n.* Ⓒ **1** a lord having a right to receive service and devotion from his subject. 군주; 왕후. **2** a person who has been given land from a lord, and therefore must help or give service to him. 가신; 신하. ¶ *His Majesty's lieges* 폐하의 신하.

— *adj.* **1** having the right to receive service and devotion from one's subject. 군주로서의. ¶ *a ~ lord* 군주; 영주(領主). **2** having the duty of giving service and devotion to a lord. 신하로서의. ¶ *a ~ man* 신하. **3** of the relation between a vassel or subject and his lord. 군신(君臣) 관계의; 신종(臣從)의. ¶ ~ *service* 신하로서 섬기기; 신사(臣事). [F.]

liege·man [lí:dʒmən] *n.* Ⓒ (*pl.* **-men** [-mən]) a subject; a faithful dependent; a liege. 신하. [F.]

lien [lí:ən] *n.* Ⓒ 《law》 a claim on possessions or property until the owner's debt to one is paid. 유치권(留置權); 담보권. [L. *ligo* bind]

lieu [lu:] *n.* Ⓤ 《*arch.*》 place. 장소. 語法 다음 구로만 쓰임. [→*locus*]

in lieu, instead. 대신에.

in lieu of, instead of or in place of. …의 대신에.

·lieu·ten·ant [lu:ténənt / 《*army*》 leftén- or 《*navy*》 lətén-] *n.* Ⓒ **1** an officer who assists a commanding officer. 부관. **2** an officer below a captain in the army. 육군 중위. ¶ *a first* 〔*a second*〕 ~ 육군 중위〔소위〕. **3** a junior office below a lieutenant commander in the navy. 해군 대위. ¶ *a ~ junior grade* 해군 중위. [L.=deputy]

lieutenant colonel [-⌐- ⌐-] *n.* an army officer below the rank of colonel. 육군 중령.

lieutenant commander [-⌐--⌐-] *n.* a naval officer in rank next above lieutenant. 해군 소령.

lieutenant governor [-⌐- ⌐--] *n.* **1** 《U.S.》 a vice-governor of a state. (주의) 부지사. **2** 《Brit.》 an official under a governor general of a colony, etc. (식민지 등의) 부총

독(副總督).

:life [laif] *n.* (*pl.* **lives**) **1** Ⓤ the quality that human being, animals, and plants have and that rocks and metals have not; the state of being alive; existence. 생명. ¶ *the struggle for* ~ 생존 경쟁 / *have no regard for human* ~ 인명을 경시하다 / *the origin of* ~ 생명의 기원 / *a matter of* ~ *and deah* 생사가 〔사활이〕 걸린 중대 문제. **2** Ⓒ the period during which a person or thing is alive or useful; the time of being alive. 생애; 수명; (생존) 기간. ¶ *through* ~ 한생애; 평생 / *a machine's* ~ 기계의 수명 / *the* ~ *of a government* 정부의 수명; 집권 기간 / *Shakespear's works have a long* ~. 세익스피어 작품의 수명은 장구하다. **3** Ⓤ 《*collectively*》 living things. 생물. ¶ *animal* 〔*vegetable*〕 ~ 동물〔식물〕 / *minute forms of* ~ 미생물. **4** ⓊⒸ a way or manner of living. 생활 (상태). ¶ *single* 〔*married*〕 ~ 독신〔부부〕 생활 / *city* ~ 도시 생활 / *a* ~ *of poverty* 가난한 생활 / *lead a good* ~ 편안하게 지내다. **5** Ⓤ human social activity and relationship; human existence; human experience. 실〔사회〕 생활; (이) 세상; 세상사; 인생. ¶ *real* ~ 실생활 / *this* ~ 이 세상; 현세 / *get on in* ~ 입신 출세하다 / *see something of* ~ 인생에서 무언가를 알다 / *enter upon* ~ 실사회에 나오다. **6** Ⓒ a biography; an account of a person's life. 전기(傳記); 일대기. ¶ *a* ~ *of Churchil* 처칠전. **7** Ⓤ spirit; energy; vitality; cheering influence. 생기; 활기; 기운; 정력. ¶ *full of* ~ 생기〔활기〕에 찬 / *the* ~ *of the party* 당의 활기 / *Put more* ~ *into your work.* 일에 좀더 힘을 내라. **8** Ⓤ 《art》 living form; life-size figure (as the model). 실물; 원형(原形); 실물 크기(의 모델). ¶ *a portrait* 〔*picture*〕 *drawn from* (*the*) ~ 실물 그대로 그린 초상〔그림〕 / *still* ~ 정물(화). [E.]

bring someone* or *something to life, **a**) bring someone back to consicousness. …의 의식을 되찾게 하다. **b**) cause something to be lively. 활기를 불어넣다.

come to life, recover from a faint; become lively after a dull period. 의식을 회복하다; 제정신이 들다; (침체 후) 활기를 되찾다.

for dear 〔*one's*〕 ***life,*** with desperate energy, as if to save one's own life. 필사적으로; 죽을 힘을 다해.

for life, during one's life. 종신〔무기〕의. ¶ *be imprisoned for* ~ 종신형을 살다 / *an invalid for* ~ 평생 불구(不具).

for the life of me, 《*colloq.*》 《in *negative*》 by any means. 목숨을 걸어서도; 아무리 해도〔도저히〕 (…않다). ¶ *I can't tell you for the* ~ *of me.* 죽어도 말 못 하겠다 / *I can't remember for the* ~ *of me.* 아무리 해도 기억이 안 난다.

have the time of one's life, 《*colloq.*》 enjoy oneself as never before. 난생 처음 즐겁게 지내다.

not on your life, 《*colloq.*》 certainly not. 결코 …않다; 확실히 …않다.

see 〔***learn***〕 ***life,*** have a wide variety of social experience. 세상을 알다; 널리 경험하다.

take someone's life, kill. …을 죽이다.

take one's own life, commit suicide. 자살하다.

to the life, exactly like the living original. 실물 그대로.

true to life, true to reality; as in real life. 실물〔실제〕 그대로.

life belt [ㅅㅅ] *n.* a belt filled with cork, etc., used for making a person float in the water. 구명대(救命帶).

life·blood [láifblʌ̀d] *n.* Ⓤ **1** the blood required to live. 생혈; 생피. **2** something that gives energy or strength. 활력〔생기〕의 근원.

life·boat [láifbòut] *n.* Ⓒ a strong boat for saving persons after an accident at sea. 구명정.

life buoy [ㅅㅅ] *n.* a ring which keeps a person afloat in the water, and so saves his life. 구명 부이〔부대〕.

life·giv·ing [láifgìviŋ] *adj.* that gives or can give life, vitality, or strength; inspiring. 생명〔활력〕을 주는; 기운을 돋우는.

life·guard [láifgɑ̀ːrd] *n.* Ⓒ **1** a swimmer employed to help drowning persons at a swimming pool, a beach, etc. (수영장 등의) 구조원. **2** a bodyguard of soldiers attending a king or some other very important person. 경호원; 친위대.

life insurance [ㅅ—ㅅ—] *n.* **1** the system by which a certain sum of money is paid to a person's family at his death by an insurance company. 생명 보험. **2** the sum thus paid. 생명 보험금.

life jacket [ㅅㅅ—] *n.* a jacket made of material that is able to float a person in the water. 구명 재킷.

〈life jacket〉

life·less [láiflis] *adj.* **1** not living; dead. 생명이 없는; 죽은. ¶ *The* ~ *body floated ashore.* 시체가 해안을 표류했다. **2** not lively; not active. 활기 없는. ¶ *a* ~ *party* 시시한 파티. **3** without life. 생물이 살지 않는. ¶ *a* ~ *planet* 생물이 없는 행성.

● **life·less·ness** [-nis] *n.*

life·less·ly [láiflisli] *adv.* in a lifeless manner. 죽은 듯이; 생기 없이.

life·like [láiflàik] *adj.* looking like a living thing; resembling. 살아 있는 듯한. ¶ *a* ~ *portrait* 실물 그대로의 초상화. ● **life·like·ness** [-nis] *n.*

life line [ㅅㅅ] *n.* a rope used for saving the life of someone who has fallen into deep water, etc. 구명삭; 구명 밧줄.

life·long [láiflɔ̀(ː)ŋ] *adj.* lasting or continuing through a person's life. 평생의. ¶ *a ~ friend* 〔*friendship*〕.

life net [ˊ ˋ] *n.* a strong net used to catch persons jumping from a high, burning building. (소방용의) 구명망.

life-of·fice [láifɔ̀fis] *n.* life insurance business; an office of this. 생명 보험 회사; 그 사무소.

life preserver [ˊ–ˋ–] *n.* **1** 《Brit.》 a loaded cane or other weapon used for self-defence. 호신용 단장. **2** 《U.S.》 something to keep a person afloat in the water 구명구(具).

lif·er [láifər] *n.* 《*sl.*》 a person under life sentence. 무기수(無期囚).

life-size [láifsáiz] *adj.* (of pictures, status, etc.) having the same size as the living model. 실물 크기의. ¶ *a ~ photograph.*

•**life·time** [láiftàim] *n.* Ⓒ the whole time during which a person lives. 일생; 생애. ¶ *spend a ~ for some work* 어떤 일에 생애를 보내다. — *adj.* of the whole time during a person's life; for life. 일생의; 평생의.

life·work [láifwə̀ːrk] *n.* Ⓤ a work to which a person's lifetime is devoted; a work taking the whole life of a person. 일생〔평생〕의 사업.

:**lift** [lift] *vt.* **1** (P6,7) move (something or someone) into a higher position; raise up higher; hold up; take up. …을 들어 올리다; 쳐들다; 안아 올리다. ¶ *~ a chair* 의자를 들어 올리다 / *~ one's arm* 팔을 쳐들다 / *~ a baby* 아기를 안아 들다 / *The mountain lifts its peaks skyward.* 산봉우리들이 하늘 높이 솟아 있다. **2** (P6,7,13) ⓐ raise (something or someone) in rank, level, etc. (지위·상태·정신 등)을 향상시키다; 높이다. ¶ *~ someone from obscurity* 무명인을 출세시키다 / *be lifted up in spirit* 사기가 오르다. ⓑ send up loudly; make louder. 목청을 올리다. ¶ *~ a cry* 소리를 지르다 / *~ (up) one's voice against* …에 항의하다. **3** (P6) take (a crop) from the ground; dig up. (작물)을 파내다. ¶ *~ potatoes* 감자를 캐다. **4** (P6,13) ⓐ remove. …을 치우다; 제거하다. ¶ *~ a tent* 천막을 철거하다 / *~ a worry from one's heart* 근심 걱정을 떨어 버리다. ⓑ put an end to; stop. …을 끝내다. ¶ *~ a blockade* 〔*the siege*〕 봉쇄〔포위〕를 풀다. **5** (P6,13) 《*colloq.*》 use (another's writings) as if they were one's own; 《*sl.*》 steal. …을 표절하다; 훔치다. ¶ *~ a passage from someone's writing* 아무의 글에서 한 구절을 표절하다 / *~ things from a store* 가게에서 물건을 훔치다. **6** (P6) remove wrinkles from someone's face by surgical operation. (성형 수술로 얼굴의) 주름을 없애다. ¶ *~ one's face.*

— *vi.* (P1) **1** move upward; rise; be raised. 오르다; 올라가다. ¶ *The window does not ~.* 창문이 열리지 않는다. **2** (of clouds, fog, etc.) become less thick; pass away. (구름·안개 등이) 걷히다; 개다. ¶ *The fog lifted.* 안개가 걷혔다 / *The gloom lifts.* 표정이 밝아지다.

lift a hand 〔***finger***〕 (=*make a slight effort*) *to do.* …하는 데 좀 수고하다.

lift a 〔*one's*〕 ***hand against*** (=*almost strike*) *someone.* …을 치려고 하다〔으르다〕.

lift** one's **hand, take an oath. 맹세하다.

lift** one's **hat, bow. 인사하다.

lift (***up***) *one's* ***eyes,*** look up. 쳐다보다.

lift (***up***) *one's* ***head,*** appear; show signs of recovering strength; feel pride or self-respect. 나타나다; 원기를 회복하다; 자존심을 갖다.

lift up** one's **heel against, kick. …에게 발길질하다.

— *n.* Ⓒ **1** the act of lifting; an instance of this; a lifting power or influence on the mind; an elevated feeling. 들기; 들어올리기; (정신적인) 고양(高揚); 향상; (감정의) 고조. ¶ *give a stone a ~* 돌을 들(어 올리)다 / *the proud ~ of her head* 고개를 쳐든 그녀의 오만한 태도 / *His visit gave me a great ~.* 그가 방문해 주어 나는 아주 우쭐했다. **2** a piece of help; assistance, esp. by taking someone somewhere by car. 거들기; 돕기; (남을) 차에 태워 주기. ¶ *give someone a ~* 아무를 차에 태워 주다; 아무를 거들다 / *He offered me a ~ to the next city.* 그는 다음 도시까지 나를 태워 주었다 / *Give me a ~ with this job.* 이 일을 좀 도와 다오. **3** a rise to a higher position or rank; promotion. 입신; 출세; 승진. ¶ *a ~ in one's career* 출세; 승진. **4** 《chiefly Brit.》 an elevator. 엘리베이터; 승강기(cf. 《U.S.》 *elevator*). ¶ *go up by ~* 승강기로 오르다. **5** a piece of leather raising the heel of a shoe. 구두 뒤축 가죽의 한 장. [N. *loft* sky, →loft]

lift·man [líftmən] *n.* Ⓒ (*pl.* **-men** [ˊmən]) **1** 《chiefly Brit.》 an operator of an elevator. 엘리베이터 운전 기사. **2** 《*sl.*》 a thief. 들치기; 도둑놈.

lig·a·ment [lígəmənt] *n.* Ⓒ **1** 《anat.》 a band of muscle that joins bones together or that holds an organ of the body in place. 인대(靭帶). **2** a tie; a band. 끈; 띠. [L. *ligo* bind]

lig·a·ture [lígətʃùər, -tʃər] *n.* Ⓒ **1** a thing used for binding up. 끈; 줄. **2** 《surg.》 a piece of thread used to tie up a bleeding vein. 결찰사(結紮絲). **3** the act of binding. 묶기; 매기. **4** 《print.》 a type of two or three letters joined together. 연자(連字); 합자(合字)(《Æ, Œ. ﬁ 등》). **5** 《mus.》 a slur or curved line. 연결선(《⌒》). [↑]

:**light**[1] [lait] *n.* **1** Ⓤ that which makes it possible to see; brightness; radiance. 빛; 광선; 광휘; 밝기; 빛남(opp. darkness). ¶ *~ and shade* 빛과 그늘 / *the ~ of the candle.* **2** Ⓤ daylight; daytime; dawn. 일광; 낮; 새벽. ¶ *get up before ~* 날 새기 전에 일어나다 /

Let's leave before the ~ fails. 어둡기 전에 떠나자. **3** Ⓒ anything that gives light or start something burning; a source of light like a candle, a lamp, a star, or a lighthouse. 발광체; 천체; 광원(光源); 점화물《성냥불 등》; 등대; 등불. ¶ *strike a ~* 성냥을 긋다; 불을 켜다 / *Please give me a ~.* (담뱃)불 좀 빌려 주십시오 / *put* 〔*turn, switch*〕 *on a ~* 불을 켜다 / *turn* 〔*switch*〕 *out* 〔*off*〕 *the ~* 불을 끄다 / *We saw the lights of the city.* 시내의 불빛이 보였다 / *The lights were on* 〔*burning*〕 *in the room.* 방에는 불이 켜져 있었다. **4** Ⓤ the state of being visible; public view or knowledge. 공개된 상태; 공지(公知); 주지(周知). ¶ *bring a matter to ~* 문제를 공개하다〔드러내다〕 / *come to ~* 공개되다. **5** ⓊⒸ illumination of the mind; knowledge or information that helps to explain things. (정신적인) 광명; (문제의 설명에) 도움이 되는 사실. ¶ *throw* 〔*cast, shed*〕 *~ on a subject* 문제를 설명하는 데 도움을 주다. **6** Ⓤ knowledge. 지식; 지성. **7** Ⓒ the aspect in which something is viewed; an appearance from a particular point of view. 견해; 관점; 양상(樣相). ¶ *put things in a favorable ~* 일을 호의적인 입장에서 보도록 하다 / *see someone in a false* 〔*the true*〕 *~* 아무에게 그릇된〔올바른〕 견해를 가지다. **8** Ⓒ a prominent or famous person. 이름난 사람; 현인; 권위자. ¶ *a man of ~ and leading* 선각자. **9** Ⓒ a window or other means of letting in light; a skylight. 채광창; 창(窓).

according to one's lights, according to one's principles, ability, etc. 각자의 주의〔견해, 능력〕에 따라.

between the lights, at dusk or evening. 해질녘에.

between two lights, 《*sl.*》 at night; in the dark. 밤에; 어둠을 타고.

by the light of nature, without the aid of teaching. 직감(直感)으로; 자연히.

get out of the light, 《*colloq., fig.*》 not hinder. 방해하지 않다.

in the light of, with knowledge of; considering. …에 비추어; …을 고려하여.

see the light (***of day***), **a**) be born; come into existence. 태어나다; 세상에 나오다. **b**) understand exactly. 바르게 이해하다.

stand in one's own light, harm oneself or one's reputation by acting foolishly or thoughtlessly. (어리석은 짓이나 실책으로) 불이익을 자초하다.

— *v.* (**light·ed** or **lit**) 語法 형용사적 용법의 과거 분사는 lighted가 흔히 쓰임. *vt.* **1** (P6) set fire to (a candle, a lamp, etc.); cause (a fire) to give off light or burn. …에 불을 붙이다; (불)을 때다. ¶ *~ a fire* 불을 붙이다〔때다〕 / *~ a lamp* 등을 켜다. **2** (P6,7) ⓐ give light to (something); illuminate; brighten. …에 불을 밝히다; …을 비추다; 조명하다. ¶ *~ the streets* 거리를 밝히다 / *~ up a room* 방에 불을 켜다. ⓑ 《*fig.*》 make bright, clear, or cheerful. (얼굴 등)을 밝게 하다; 빛내다. ¶ *A charming smile lighted up his face.* 생긋 웃으면서 그의 표정이 밝아졌다. **3** (P7,13) show the way to (someone) by or as by giving light. 불을 켜서 안내하다. ¶ *~ someone through the dark street* 불을 켜서 어두운 길을 안내하다 / *The girl lighted me downstairs.* 소녀는 불을 들어 아래층으로 나를 안내했다.

— *vi.* **1** (P1,2A) take fire; begin burning. 불이 붙다; 타오르다. **2** (P1,2A) 《*up*》 be lighted; brighten. 밝아지다; 빛나다; 얼굴이 환해지다. ¶ *His face lit up with hope.* 희망으로 그의 얼굴이 빛났다 / *The sky lighted up at sunset.* 하늘은 석양빛으로 붉게 물들었다.

— *adj.* **1** bright; having light; not dark. 밝은(opp. dark). ¶ *a ~ room* 밝은 방 / *It's getting ~.* 날이 밝아 온다. **2** not dark or deep in color; pale; whitish. (색이) 엷은; 연한; 희읍스름한. ¶ *~ green* 연둣빛 / *~ hair* 희끗희끗한 머리. [E.; G. *licht;* L. *luceo* shine]

:light² [lait] *adj.* **1** having little weight; of less than usual weight. 가벼운; 무겁지 않은; (규정보다) 가벼운(opp. heavy). ¶ *a ~ pair of shoes* 가벼운 신발 / *a ~ coin* 함량 미달의 화폐 / *a ~ load* 가벼운 짐. **2** easy to do; not very difficult to bear; not severe. 손쉬운; 어렵지 않은; (벌·부담이) 관대한. ¶ *~ punishment* 가벼운 벌 / *~ work* 쉬운 일 / *~ duties* 가벼운 세금. **3** aiming to entertain; not serious; amusing. 딱딱하지 않은; 오락적인. ¶ *a ~ comedy* 경희극 / *~ reading* 가벼운 읽을거리. **4** (of wine, etc.) containing little alcohol. 알코올분이 적은. ¶ *~ wine* 순한 포도주. **5** active in motion; not moving slowly. 민첩한; 경쾌한. ¶ *~ footsteps* 경쾌한 발걸음. **6** slight; not important. 사소한; 대단찮은. ¶ *a ~ mistake* 사소한 실수 / *~ losses* 가벼운 손실. **7** happy; cheerful; gay. 즐거운. ¶ *with a ~ heart* 쾌활하게 / *in ~ spirits* 마음이 들떠서. **8** ⓐ lightly armed. (군대가) 경장비의. ¶ *~ cavalry* 경기병 / *~ infantry* 경보병. ⓑ producing goods of little weight. 경공업의. ¶ *~ industry* 경공업. **9** less than usual in amount, force, etc.; not violent or intense. (양·정도가) 적은; 경미한. ¶ *a ~ sleep* 옅은 잠 / *a ~ frost* 무서리 / *a ~ snow* 가랑눈 / *a ~ attack of illness* 가벼운 발병. **10** thoughtless; lacking proper seriousness; loose in morals. 경솔한; 몸가짐이 헤픈; 품행이 좋지 않은. ¶ *a ~ woman* 바람기 있는 여자 / *a ~ opinion* 경솔한 판단. **11** (of food) easy to digest. 소화가 잘 되는. ¶ *~ food.*

have a light hand, be skillful; be tactful. 손재간이 있다; 솜씨가 좋다.

light in the head, **a**) dizzy. 어지러운. **b**) silly; foolish. 어리석은. **c**) crazy. 머리가 돈.

make light of, treat (someone or something) as of little importance; pay little or no attention to (someone or something).

…을 얕보다; 무시〔경시〕하다.
— *adv.* lightly; easily. 가볍게; 쉽게; 경쾌하게. ¶ 《*prov.*》 *Light come,* ~ *go.* 쉽게 번 돈은 오래 못 간다 / *sleep* ~ 겉잠 자다 / *travel* ~ 간단한 행장으로 여행하다. [E.; G. *leicht*]
get off light, 《*colloq.*》 escape with a light punishment. 가벼운 처벌로 끝나다.

light³ [lait] *vi.* (**lit** or **light·ed**) **1** (P2A,3) (of a bird) come to rest; land; get down (from a horse, etc.). (새가) 앉다; (말 따위에서) 내리다. ¶ *A bird lighted on the branch.* 새 한 마리가 나뭇가지에 내려앉았다 / ~ *off a horse* 말에서 내리다. **2** (P3) fall suddenly. 불시에 닥치다. ¶ *The blow lit upon his head.* 느닷없이 머리에 주먹이 날아들었다. [→light¹, light²]

***light·en¹** [láitn] *vt.* (P6) make (something) bright or clear. …을 밝게 하다; 밝히다. ¶ *"Lighten our darkness."* 우리를 미망에서 깨어나게 하소서. — *vi.* (P1) **1** become bright. 밝아지다; 깨다. **2** give out flashes of lightning. 번개가 번쩍이다. ¶ *It thundered and lightened all night.* 밤새도록 천둥이 울리고 번개가 쳤다. [*light¹*]

***light·en²** [láitn] *vt.* (P6) **1** reduce (something) in weight. …을 가볍게 하다. ¶ ~ *a ship* 뱃짐을 가볍게 하다. **2** make (someone) more cheerful. …을 기쁘게〔즐겁게〕 하다. ¶ *Her sympathy lightened my trouble.* 그녀의 동정이 내게 위로가 되었다. — *vi.* (P1) become lighter or more cheerful. 가벼워지다; 즐거워지다. ¶ *be lightened at his joke.* [*light²*]

light·er¹ [láitər] *n.* Ⓒ a person or thing that lights to set a fire. 점등부(點燈夫); 라이터. ¶ *a lamp* ~ 가로등 점등부 / *a cigarette* ~. [*light¹*]

light·er² [láitər] *n.* Ⓒ a flat boat for carrying goods in a harbor or a river. 거룻배. — *vt.* (P6) carry (goods) in a lighter. (짐)을 거룻배로 나르다. [*light²*]

light·er·age [láitəridʒ] *n.* **1** the loading, unloading, or carrying of goods in a lighter. 거룻배 쓰기; 거룻배 운반. **2** the price for this. 거룻배 삯.

light-fin·gered [láitfíŋgərd] *adj.* **1** skillful in using the fingers. 손끝이 잰. **2** skillful at stealing. 손버릇이 나쁜; 도벽(盜癖)이 있는. [*light²*]

light-hand·ed [láithǽndid] *adj.* **1** skillful in using the hands or in managing something. 손재주가 있는(opp. heavy-handed). **2** having little in the hands to carry. 손에 든 것이 없는. ¶ *come home* ~ 빈손으로 돌아오다. **3** not having as many men to help as necessary. 일손이 모자라는.

light-head·ed [láithédid] *adj.* **1** ⓐ confused in one's mind. 머리가 이상한. ⓑ thoughtless; forgetful. 지각 없는; 잊기 잘하는. **2** wandering or changeable in one's mind. 변덕이 많은. **3** dizzy; giddy. 머리가 어찔어찔한. ¶ *be* ~ *from fever.*

light-heart·ed [láithá:rtid] *adj.* free from care; merry; cheerful. 걱정거리가 없는; 명랑〔쾌활〕한(opp. heavy-hearted). ● **light-heart·ed·ness** [-nis] *n.*

light·house [láithàus] *n.* Ⓒ a tower with a bright brilliant light at the top to guide ships at night. 등대. [*light¹*]

light·ing [láitiŋ] *n.* Ⓤ **1** the way of using lights (on the stage, etc.); illumination. 조명법; 조명. **2** the act of giving light. 점화.

:light·ly [láitli] *adv.* **1** with little force; softly. 가볍게; 살짝. ¶ *touch a thing* ~. **2** easily. 쉽게. ¶ 《*prov.*》 *Lightly come,* ~ *go.* 쉽게 번 돈 오래 못 간다. **3** quickly, nimbly. 재빨리; 날렵하게. ¶ *leap aside* ~ 냉큼 뛰어 비키다. **4** carelessly; not seriously. 마구; 되는 대로. ¶ *He treats the matter too* ~. 그 일을 되는 대로 마구 한다. [*light²*]

light-mind·ed [láitmáindid] *adj.* thoughtless; lacking seriousness. 경솔한; 경망스러운. [↑]

light·ness¹ [láitnis] *n.* Ⓤ **1** the state or quality of being light in color; brightness. 밝기; 밝음. **2** pale in color. 희읍스름한 색. [*light¹*]

light·ness² [láitnis] *n.* Ⓤ **1** the state of not being heavy. 가벼움. **2** skillfulness. 능란; 솜씨 좋음. **3** delicacy; gracefulness. 우미. **4** cheerfulness. 쾌활. **5** lack of seriousness. 경솔. [*light²*]

:light·ning [láitniŋ] *n.* Ⓤ a flash of light made by electricity in the sky. 번개. ¶ *The house was struck by* ~. 그 집에 벼락이 쳤다. — *vi.* make a flash of light. 번개가 치다. [*light¹*]
like (greased) lightning = with lightning speed, very fast; rapidly. 번개같이; 전광석화처럼.

lightning conductor [⌐-⌐-] *n.* a thin metal bar placed above the top of a building and connected with the earth to prevent a thunderbolt from doing damage. 피뢰침.

lightning rod [⌐-⌐] *n.* =lightning conductor.

light-o'-love [láitəlʌ̀v] *n.* a wanton woman. 바람난 여자; 화냥년. [*light²*]

lights [laits] *n. pl.* the lungs, esp. of sheep, pigs, etc. (양·돼지 등의) 폐장(肺臟). [*light²*]

light·ship [láitʃìp] *n.* Ⓒ a ship with a bright light that anchors in a dangerous place to warn other ships. 등대선. [*light¹*]

light·some [láitsəm] *adj.* 《*poet.*》 **1** light and quick (in movement); nimble. 날랜; 잽싼. ¶ ~ *feet* 잰걸음. **2** merry; gay; cheerful. 쾌활한; 명랑한. ¶ *a* ~ *heart* 즐거운 마음. **3** lacking seriousness. 경박한; 경망스러운. [*light²*]

light·weight [láitwèit] *n.* Ⓒ a boxer or wrestler between a featherweight and a welterweight; esp., a boxer who weights

less than 135 pounds. 라이트급 선수. 參考 아마추어 권투에서는 체중 57-60 kg, 레슬링에서는 64-67 kg, 역도에서는 61-67.5 kg.
— *adj.* **1** below normal weight. 가벼운. ¶ *a* ~ *sweater.* **2** 《boxing》 of or pertaining to a lightweight. 라이트급의. **3** lacking weight and authority; unimportant. 진지하지 못한; 하찮은. [*light*²]

light-year [láitjìər] *n.* an astronomical unit of distance, 5.88 × 10¹² miles. 광년. [*light*¹]

lig·ne·ous [lígniəs] *adj.* of or like wood. 목질의. [L. *lignum* wood; *vitae* of life]

lig·nite [lígnait] *n.* Ⓤ soft, dark-brown coal. 아탄(亞炭); 갈탄. [↑]

lik·a·ble [láikəbəl] *adj.* liked by most people; that can be liked. 호감이 가는; 마음에 드는. [*like*²]

:like¹ [laik] (usu. **more like, most like**) *adj.* **1** having almost or exactly the same in amount, character, form, etc.; similar; equal. (양·성격·모양이) 같은; 같은 액수〔분량〕의; 비슷한; 닮은. ¶ *Our house is* ~ *theirs.* 우리 집은 그들의 집과 같은 모양이다 / *a* ~ *sum* 동액(同額) / *in* ~ *manner* 마찬가지로 / *eyes* ~ *stars* 별 같은 눈 / *Two brother are very* ~ *each other.* 그 두 형제는 똑같이 닮았다 / 《*prov.*》 *Like father,* ~ *son.* 그 아비에 그 아들; 부전자전 / *What is he* 〔*it*〕 ~ ? 그는〔그것은〕 어떤 사람〔물건〕이냐. **2** having the qualities which would be expected; characteristic of. …다운; …에 어울리는. ¶ *It's just* ~ *her to do so.* 그렇게 하는 것은 과연 그녀답다 / *That's just* ~ *your foolishness.* 그건 너 같은 놈이나 할 어리석은 짓이다. **3** in the right condition or mood for; indicate of. …할 것 같은. ¶ *It looks* ~ *rain.* 비가 올 것 같다 / *He feels* ~ *working.* 그는 일하고 싶은 생각이 들었다.

anything like, at all. 조금도; 전혀. ¶ *He does not want anything* ~ *labor.* 노동 따위는 아주 싫어한다.

nothing like, nothing so good as. …을 따를 것이 없다; …만한 것이 없다. ¶ *There is nothing* ~ *leather for shoes.* 구두에는 가죽만큼 좋은 것은 없다.

something like, **a**) almost like; about. 어느 정도 …와 같은; 약; 대략. ¶ *It costs something* ~ *ten pounds.* 비용이 대략 10 파운드 든다. **b**) 《*colloq.*》 《with stress on *like*》 very good; remarkably fine. 썩 좋은〔훌륭한〕. ¶ *This is something* ~ *a dinner!* 이거 진수성찬이구먼.

— *adv.* **1** 《*colloq.*》 《*very* ~ , ~ *enough*》 probably. 아마도. ¶ *Like enough it will rain.* 아마도 비가 올 모양이다. **2** 《*vulg.*》 as it were; so to speak. 마치; 이를테면. ¶ *He was all of a tremble* ~ . 그는 마치 사시나무 떨듯 했다.

— *prep.* in the manner of; to the same degree as. …와 같이; …처럼; …와 마찬가지로. ¶ *speak* ~ *a fool* 바보 같은 소리를 하다 / *work* ~ *a beaver* (비버처럼) 열심히 일하다 / *She sings* ~ *a bird.* 그녀는 새처럼 노래한다.

like anything, 《*colloq.*》 to an extreme degree. 심하게; 매우; 맹렬하게. ¶ *He was proud* ~ *anything.* 그는 기고만장이었다.

— *conj.* 《*colloq.*》 as; in the same way as. …처럼. ¶ *It was just* ~ *he said.* 꼭 그의 말대로였다.

— *n.* Ⓒ a person or thing that is like another; something of a similar nature each other. 닮은 사람; 닮은 것. ¶ *I have never seen the* ~ *of it.* 그런 것은 전혀 본 적이 없다 / *Did you ever hear the* ~ (*of that*)? 그런 것 들어 본 일이 있나 / 《*prov.*》 *Like will to* ~ . 유유상종(類類相從) / *I will never do the* ~ *again.* 그런 짓은 다시 않겠다. [E.]

and the like, and others of the same kind. 그 밖의 같은 것; …따위.

the likes of me 〔***you, him, etc.***〕, people of the same class, rank, etc. as me, you, etc. …같은〔비슷한〕 사람들.

:like² [laik] *vt.* **1** (P6,8,9,18,20) be pleased with or be fond of (something or someone); enjoy. …을 좋아하다. ¶ *I* ~ *fruit.* 난 과일이 좋다 / *He likes sports.* 그는 운동을 좋아한다 / *I* ~ *swimming.* 나는 수영을 좋아한다. **2** (P6,7,8,20,24) wish; wish for; have a preference for (someone or something). …하고 싶다; …하기를 바라다. ¶ *I* ~ *to swim in the river.* 강에서 수영하고 싶다 / *I don't* ~ *to be poor.* 가난해지기는 싫다 / *I don't* ~ *girls to smoke.* 소녀들이 담배 피우는 것은 싫다 / *I* ~ *my tea hot.* 뜨거운 차가 좋다 / *I* ~ *my eggs boiled.* 내 달걀은 삶아 주시오. 語法 부정사를 목적어로 할 때는 특정한 행위를, 동명사를 목적어로 할 때는 일반적인 행위를 말할 때가 많음. **3** (P6) suit the health of (someone). …에 맞다; 적합하다. ¶ *I* ~ *fish but it doesn't* ~ *me.* 나는 생선을 좋아하는데 체질에는 안 맞는다. **4** 《*arch.*》 be pleasing to. …의 마음에 들다. ¶ *It likes me well.* 마음에 든다.

— *vi.* (P1) be pleased; choose. 마음에 들다. ¶ *Do as you* ~ . 좋을 대로 해라 / *Leave whenever you* ~ . 언제든 좋을 때 떠나시오.

should 〔***would***〕 ***like,*** 語法 미국식 영어 또는 영구어(英口語)에서는 1인칭에 would를 씀. **a**) want to have. 갖고 싶다. ¶ *He would* ~ *a cup of tea.* 그는 차 한 잔을 먹고 싶어한다. **b**) wish. …하고 싶다. ¶ *I should* 〔*would*〕 ~ *to go.* 가고 싶군 / *I should* 〔*would*〕 ~ *you to know it.* 네가 그걸 알았으면 좋겠다 / *I should* 〔*would*〕 ~ *to have been there.* 거기에 가 보았더라면 좋았을걸.

— *n.* 《usu. *pl.*》 preferences; tastes; things that one likes. 좋아함; 기호(嗜好); 즐기는 것. ¶ *his likes and dislikes* 그의 호불호(好不好). [E.]

-like [-laik] *suf.* like; suitable for; characteristic of. '… 같은, …의 특징을 지닌, …에 어울리는.' 의 뜻. ¶ *boylike* / *godlike* / *childlike* / *businesslike.* [*like*¹]

like·li·hood [láiklihùd] *n.* Ⓤ probability; something which appears to be probable. 있음직한 일; 가능성. ¶ *In all ~, he will fail.* 십중팔구 그는 실패할 거다 / *Is there any ~ of rain?* 비가 올 것 같지 않으냐 / *There is always a ~ of such a thing to happen.* 그러한 일은 항용 일어날 수 있는 거다. [*like*[1]]

:like·ly [láikli] *adj.* (**-li·er, -li·est**) **1** probable; believable. 있을 법한; 그럴 수도 있는. ¶ *(That's) a ~ story!* 《often *iron.*》 그럴 듯한 얘기군《설마 그럴 수야》 / *I called at every ~ place.* 그럴 만한 데는 다 가 봤다. **2** 《*to do, that*》 to be expected. …할 것 같은. ¶ *It is ~ to rain.* 비가 올 모양이다 / *It is ~ that he will succeed.* 그는 성공할지도 모른다. **3** fitting; proper. 적당한. ¶ *a ~ place to fish* 낚시하기에 좋은 곳 / *I have found a ~ house at last.* 마침내 적당한 집을 찾아 냈다.
— *adv.* 《often used with *very* or *most*》 probably. 아마도; 필시. ¶ *I shall very ~ see you again.* 또 만나게 될 것이다. [*like*[1]]
as likely as not, very probably. 아마도 …이겠지. ¶ *He'll forget all about it as ~ as not.* 아마도 그는 그 일은 모두 잊어버릴 것이다.
likely enough, perhaps. 아마도.

like-mind·ed [láikmáindid] *adj.* with the same opinions, purposes, tastes, etc. 같은 마음〔생각, 목적, 취미〕의. [*like*[1]]

lik·en [láikən] *vt.* (P13) 《*to*》 represent as like; compare. …에 비유하다. ¶ *Life is often likened to a voyage.* 인생을 종종 항해에 비유한다. [*like*[1]]

·like·ness [láiknis] *n.* **1** Ⓤ the state of being like; similarity; Ⓒ a point of resemblance something that is like. 비슷함; 닮음; 유사점〔물〕. ¶ *I can find no ~ between you and your father.* 너희 부자는 전혀 닮은 데가 없다. **2** Ⓒ a picture; a portrait. 사진; 초상. ¶ *I had my ~ painted.* 내 초상을 그리게 했다 / *a good ~* 아주 닮은 그림. **3** Ⓤ appearance; form. 외관; 외양. ¶ *The devil came in the ~ of angel.* 악마는 천사의 모습을 하고 나타났다. [*like*[1]]

:like·wise [láikwàiz] *adv.* in the same manner; in addition; also. 마찬가지로; 또한; 게다가. ¶ *I want to see it ~.* 그것도 보고 싶다 / *He is ~ my classmate.* 그 또한 내 동창이다. [*like*[1]]

***lik·ing** [láikiŋ] *n.* Ⓒ a fondness; preference; a taste. 좋아함; 기호; 취미. [*like*[2]]
have a liking for (=*be fond of*) *something.* …을 좋아하다; 사랑하다. ¶ *have a ~ for apples* 〔*children*〕 사과를〔아이들을〕 좋아하다.
take a liking to (=*be pleased with*) *something.* …이 마음에 들다; 좋아지다. ¶ *I took an immediate ~ to her.* 나는 그녀가 당장에 좋아졌다.
to one's liking, appealing to one's taste. 마음에 들어; 취미에 맞아. ¶ *It is not to my ~.* 난 그거 안 좋아한다.

li·lac [láilək] *n.* **1** Ⓒ a small tree with hanging bunches of fragrant white or pale violet flowers. 라일락. **2** Ⓤ a pale violet color. 연보랏빛. — *adj.* of or having a pale violet color. 라일락〔연보라〕색의. [Pers.]

Lil·li·put [lílipʌ̀t] *n.* the country described by Swift in his 'Gulliver's Travels' where men and women were six inches tall. 소인국(小人國).

Lil·li·pu·tian [lìlipjúːʃən] *adj.* **1** of Lilliput. 소인국(小人國)의. **2** very small. 아주 작은. — *n.* Ⓒ **1** a person of Lilliput. 소인국의 사람. **2** a very small person; a midget. 난쟁이.

lilt [lilt] *vt., vi.* (P6; 1) sing or play (a tune) with a gay, light rhythm. (곡을) 경쾌하게 부르다〔연주하다〕. — *n.* Ⓒ **1** a lively rhythm or movement. 경쾌한 리듬〔동작〕. **2** a gay song. 경쾌한 노래. [M.E. *lilten,* (→lull)]

:lil·y [líli] *n.* (*pl.* **-ies**) Ⓒ a plant with beautiful bell-shaped flowers. 릴리; 나리; 백합. ¶ *the ~ of the valley* 은방울꽃 / *a tiger ~* 참나리 / *water ~* 수련. — *adj.* (white, pure) like a lily. 백합 같은〔처럼 흰, 순결한〕. [Gk.]

:limb[1] [lim] *n.* Ⓒ **1** (of a man or an animal) a leg or an arm; (of a bird) a wing. (사람·짐승의) 팔다리; 수족; (새의) 날개. **2** a main or large branch of a tree; a bough. 나무의 큰 가지. ¶ *a ~ of a tree.* **3** 《*colloq.*》 a person or thing regarded as a part, a branch, a wing, etc. 앞잡이; (수족·날개 같은) 부분. ¶ *a ~ of Satan* 악마의 앞잡이《개구쟁이·장난꾸러기 등》 / *a ~ of the law* 법률의 앞잡이《경찰 등》. **4** 《*colloq.*》 a mischievous child; a naughty boy. 개구쟁이; 장난꾸러기. ¶ *a regular, young ~* 순 개구쟁이 / *You ~!* 요 장난꾸러기.
escape with life and limb, escape without grave injury. 큰 상처 없이 도망치다.
limb from limb, completely separated. 갈기갈기《찢다 등》.
out on a limb, 《*colloq.*》 in a dangerous situation. 아주 위험한 입장에.
— *vt.* cut off a limb from (a body). 팔다리〔날개·가지〕를 자르다. [E.]

limb[2] [lim] *n.* the edge of the disk of the sun, moon, etc. (해·달의) 가장자리. [L. *limbus* hem]

lim·ber [límbər] *adj.* flexible that can easily bend. 유연한; 잘 휘는. ¶ *This wood is very ~.* 이 나무는 아주 잘 휜다. — *vi.* (P2A) become flexible. 유연해지다. — *vt.* (P6,7) make (something) flexible. …을 유연하게 하다. ¶ *Exercise limbers the body.* [? *limb*[2]]

lim·bo [límbou] *n.* Ⓒ (*pl.* **-bos**) **1** 《often *L-*》 a supposed place between hell and heaven where line the souls of unbaptized infants and those of good people who died before Christ's coming. 림보《천국과 지옥 중간에 있다는 가공의 역(域); 세례를 못 받은 유아, 예수 강림 이전의 영들이 머묾》.

2 Ⓤ forgetfulness; oblivion. 망각; 잊혀짐. 3 Ⓒ a prison. 감옥. [→limb[2]]

·**lime**[1] [laim] *n.* Ⓤ 1 a white powder made by burning limestone, sea shells, bones, etc. 석회. ¶ *caustic* 〔*quick*〕 ~ 생석회 / *slaked* ~ 소석회. 2 《rare》 a sticky material used for catching birds; birdlime. 새 잡는 끈끈이; 감탕. — *vt.* (P6) 1 put lime on (a field, etc.). …에 석회를 뿌리다. 2 cover (a twig, a branch, etc.) with birdlime; catch (a bird) with birdlime. (나뭇가지 등)에 감탕을 바르다; (새)를 감탕으로 잡다. 3 treat with lime. 석회로 처리하다. [E.]

lime[2] [laim] *n.* Ⓒ a fruit much like a lemon, but smaller and sourer, its tree. 라임과(果); 라임나무 [→lemon]

lime[3] [laim] *n.* Ⓒ a well-known European tree with small, sweet-smelling flowers; the linden. 린덴《참피나무·보리수 등》. [→linden]

lime·kiln [láimkil*n*] *n.* a kiln for burning lime. 석회 굽는 가마. [*lime*[1]]

lime·light [láimlàit] *n.* Ⓤ 1 a strong light produced by heating lime in a hot flame. 석회등(石灰燈)《이전의 무대 조명용》. 2 《*the* ~》 the center of public attention and interest. 주목의 대상. ¶ *in the* ~ 주목의 대상이 되어 / *fond of the* ~ 남 앞에 나서기를 좋아하다.

·**lime·stone** [láimstòun] *n.* Ⓤ a rock composed chiefly a calcium carbonate, used for road construction, etc. 석회석; 석회암.

lime tree [ˊ ˋ] *n.* =linden.

lime·wa·ter [láimwɔ̀ːtə*r*] *n.* Ⓤ a solution of lime in water, used to counteract an acid. 석회수.

:**lim·it** [límit] *n.* 1 Ⓒ the farthest edge or the boundary; the furthest point or bound in number, amount, degree, etc. 한도; 한계; 극한(極限). ¶ *the* ~ *of human knowledge* 인지(人知)의 한계 / *go beyond the* ~ 한도를 넘다 / 《*colloq.*》 *The sky is the* ~. 무제한이다《무엇이든 주문하라는 뜻》; 기회는 얼마든지 있다. 2 《*pl.*》 bounds; boundary lines. 경계; 범위. ¶ *the city limits* 시계(市界). 3 《*the* ~》 《*colloq.*》 the utmost that one can endure. 인내의 한계. ¶ *the* ~ *of endurance* 인내의 한계 / *That's the* ~*!* 더는 못 참겠다.

off limits, 《U.S.》 outside the limits of the area that one is allowed to enter; out of bounds. 출입 금지 (구역)의; 오프 리미츠. ¶ *Off limits to women.* 부녀자 출입 금지.

to the limit, 《U.S.》 extremely. 극단으로.

within limits, in moderation. 적당히; 정도에 맞게.

without limit, to any extent or degree. 무제한으로; 한없이.

— *vt.* (P6,13) 《chiefly *fig.*》 keep (something) shut within bounds; restrict; set limit to. …을 제한하다. ¶ ~ *the speed of a car to 50 miles an hour* 자동차 속도를 시속 50 마일로 제한하다 / ~ *one's desire* 욕심을 누르다 / *My powers are limited.* 내 힘에는 한계가 있다. [L. *limes*]

·**lim·i·ta·tion** [lìmətéiʃən] *n.* Ⓤ the act of limiting; the state of being limited; Ⓒ a limit of capability. 제한; 한정; (능력·지력 등의) 한계; 범위.

lim·it·ed [límitid] *adj.* 1 kept within certain limits; restricted; narrow. 한정된; 유한의; 좁은. ¶ ~ *ideas* 편협한 생각 / *have a* ~ *intelligence* 두뇌 회전이 나쁘다. 2 《U.S.》 (of a train, a bus, etc.) making only a few stops. 급행의. ¶ *a* ~ *train* 〔*express*〕 급행〔특급〕 열차. 3 《polit.》 restricted by the constitution. 입헌제의.

limited monarchy [ˊ-- ˊ--] *n.* one which is restricted by the constitution. 입헌 군주 정치〔정체〕.

lim·it·less [límitlis] *adj.* without limit; boundless. 무한한; 광대한.

lim·ou·sine [líməzìːn, ˋ-ˊ] *n.* Ⓒ 《F.》 a motorcar with a compartment for from three to five persons, and a separate driver's seat. 리무진.

·**limp**[1] [limp] *n.* Ⓒ a lame way of walking. 발을 절기. ¶ *have a bad* ~ 몹시 절다. — *vi.* (P1,2A) 1 walk lamely. 절룩거리다. 2 move in a rough, irregular manner. 뒤뚝거리다. ¶ *The yacht limped into the harbor with her mast broken.* 요트는 마스트가 부러져 일렁거리며 항구에 들어왔다. [G.]

limp[2] [limp] *adj.* not stiff; weak; lacking strength. 유연한; 약한; 기운 없는. ¶ *a* ~ *collar* 부드러운 칼라 / *I feel as* ~ *as a rag.* 나는 지쳐서 기진맥진이다. [G.]

lim·pet [límpit] *n.* Ⓒ 《shell》 a small shellfish that clings tightly to rocks. 꽃양산조개. [L. *lampreda*]

lim·pid [límpid] *adj.* clear; transparent. 투명한; 맑은. ¶ *a spring of* ~ *water* 맑은 샘물 / ~ *eyes* 맑은 눈 / ~ *language* 〔*style*〕 명석한 말〔문체〕. [L.]

lim·pid·i·ty [limpídəti] *n.* Ⓤ the state of being limpid; clearness 투명; 맑음; 명쾌.

limp·ly [límpli] *adv.* in a limp manner; flexibly; weakly. 유연하게; 힘없이. [→limp[2]]

linch·pin [líntʃpìn] *n.* Ⓒ a pin that is passed through a hole in the end of an axle to keep the wheel in place. 바퀴 멈추개; 바퀴의 비녀장. [E. =axle pin]

:**Lin·coln** [líŋkən], **Abraham** *n.* (1809-65), the 16th president of the Unite States. 에이브러햄 링컨.

lin·den [líndən] *n.* Ⓒ a large tree with heart-shaped leaves and scented yellow flowers. 보리수; 참피나무. [E.]

:**line**[1] [lain] *n.* Ⓒ 1 a string; a cord; a rope; a wire. 끈; 줄; 밧줄; 전선. ¶ *a telephone* ~ 전화선 / *a fishing* ~ 낚싯줄 / *with rod and* ~ 줄 달린 낚싯대를 가지고 / *throw a good* ~ 낚시를 잘 하다 / *a clothes* ~ 빨랫

줄 / *Line engaged* 〔*busy*〕 *!* 통화 중입니다. **2** a very thin, threadlike mark. 선(線). ¶ *a straight* ～ 직선. **3** 《*the* ～》 the equator. 적도. ¶ *cross the* ～ 적도를 지나다. **4** a wrinkle. 주름. ¶ *deep lines in his face* 그의 얼굴에 난 깊은 주름. **5** ⓐ a row of words on a page or in a column; a short letter. (책의) 행(行); 짧은 편지. ¶ *the first* ～ *of the page* 그 페이지의 첫 행 / *Drop me a* ～. 몇 자 적어 보내시오. ⓑ a line of poetry. 시(詩) 한 행; 시구(詩句). ⓒ 《*pl.*》 a piece of poetry; verses. 단시(短詩); 시. **6** a row of things or persons. 열; 줄. ¶ *a* ～ *of trees* 한 줄로 늘어선 나무들 / *stand in* (*a*) ～ (한) 줄로 서다. **7** 《*pl.*》 outline. 윤곽. ¶ *a ship's lines* 배의 윤곽〔외형〕 / *the severe lines of a Gothic church* 간소하고 엄숙한 고딕식 교회의 윤곽 / *He has good lines in his face.* 얼굴의 윤곽이 뚜렷하다. **8** a series of persons in a family; lineage. 가계(家系); 혈통. ¶ *come of a noble* ～ 귀족 집안이다 / *the direct* ～ 직계. **9** a regular course or service of ships, planes, trains, etc. 항로; 노선. ¶ *an airline* 항공로 / *the European* ～ 유럽 항로 / *There are many bus lines in this city.* 이 시에는 버스 노선이 많다. **10** 《mil.》 ⓐ a double row of soldiers. 횡대(橫隊)(cf. *column*). ¶ *draw up in* ～ 횡대로 정렬시키다. ⓑ the area of position closest to the enemy in battle; the front. 전선. ¶ *go into the* ～ 전선에 나가다 / *behind the* ～ 후방에서. **11** 《often *pl.*》 plan; principle; a course of conduct; way of behaving. 계획; 방침. ¶ *on these lines* 이들 방침에서 / *a poor* ～ *to take* 졸책 / *take a strong* ～ 강경 방침으로 나오다. **12** a boundary; a border. 경계(선). ¶ *the state* ～ 주(州) 경계 / *a dividing* ～ 분계선. **13** ⓐ business; profession. 직업; 전문. ¶ *What is your* ～*?* 무슨 일을 하시는지요. ⓑ the field of one's interest, or ability. 취미; 전공; 장기. ¶ *That's not in my* ～. 그 일에는 흥미가 없다 / *Geology is my particular* ～. 지리는 내 전공이다. **14** 《*pl.*》 fate; conditions of life. 운명. ¶ *hard lines* 불운; 불행. **15** a stock of goods of a particular kind offered for sale. 재고 상품; (상품의) 종류〔품목〕. ¶ *The store carries the best* ～ *of shoes in town.* 그 상점은 시내에서 최고급의 신발을 팔고 있다. **16** 《*colloq.*》 a piece of information or knowledge; a clue. (특수한) 정보. ¶ *get a* ～ *on someone's plan* 아무의 계획에 대한 정보를 얻다. **17** 《*pl.*》 a marriage license. 결혼 허가증.

all along the line, everywhere; at every point; completely. 도처에; 모조리.

below the line, not reaching a certain standard. 표준 이하의.

bring into line, **a**) cause to become straight, as in a row. …을 정렬시키다. **b**) persuade or cause him to cooperate or agree. …을 협력하게 만들다.

come into line with (=*agree to*) *something.* …와 일치〔협력〕하다.

draw the 〔***a***〕 ***line,*** set a limit; refuse to go beyond. 한계를 정하다; …이상은 하지 않다. ¶ *know when* 〔*where*〕 *to draw the* ～ 지나친 행동을 하지 않다.

get 〔***have***〕 ***a line on*** (=*get information about*) *something.* …의 정보를 얻다.

give *someone* ***the line enough,*** let him go his own way for a time in order to secure or detect him later(cf. *rope*). …을 한동안 멋대로 하게 내버려 두다.

hit the line, try boldly or firmly to do something. 용감하게 해 보다.

hold the line, stand firmly; permit no retreat. 굳게 지키다; 한 발짝도 양보하지 않다.

in line, **a**) in a straight row. 일직선으로. **b**) in agreement; in harmony. 일치〔조화〕되어. **c**) behaving properly or as required. 자제하여; 정도를 지켜.

in line for, in a position to attain or receive. …을 받을〔얻을〕 입장에 있는. ¶ *in* ～ *for a promotion* 승진 가능성이 있는.

lay it on the line, 《U.S. *sl.*》 **a**) give money; pay. 돈을 치르다. **b**) tell truthfully. 사실대로 이야기하다.

on a line, on the same plane; level. 동등〔대등〕하게.

on the line, not clearly one thing nor the other. 이도저도 아닌; 어중간한.

out of line, not in agreement. 일치되지 않은.

read between the lines, find a hidden meaning or purpose in something written, said, or done. (말·글 또는 행위의) 숨은 뜻을 알아 내다.

shoot a line, 《*sl.*》 boast. 떠벌리다; 큰소리치다.

toe the line, **a**) do exactly what has been commanded. 시킨 대로 하다. **b**) take one's responsibility; do one's duty. 책임을 지다; 할 일을 하다.

—*vt.* **1** (P6,7) draw lines on (paper, etc.); cover (something) with lines. …에 선을 긋다; …을 선으로 덮다. ¶ ～ *the paper* 종이에 줄을 긋다〔치다〕 / *a face lined with pain* 고통으로 찡그린 얼굴. **2** (P6,7,13) form a line along (a place). …에 늘어서다. ¶ *a street lined with trees* 가로수가 줄지어선 길 / *Cars lined the road for two miles.* 길에는 차들이 2마일이나 늘어서 있었다.

—*vi.* (P2A) form a line. 늘어서다; 한 줄이 되다. [L. *linum* flax]

line off, divide with line. 선으로 구획하다. ¶ ～ *off streets on a plan* 계획에 따라 가로(街路)를 구획하다.

line up, place in a line; form a line. 한 줄로 나란히 세우다; 한 줄로 늘어서다.

line² [lain] *vt.* (P6,13) **1** cover the inside of (something). …에 안을 대다. ¶ *My coat is lined with fur.* 내 코트는 안이 털이다. **2** (P6,7,13) 《*with*》 fill; stuff. …을 채워 넣다. ¶ ～ *a purse with money* 지갑에 돈을 채우다 / ～ *one's stomach* 배를 채우다. [↑]

lin·e·age [líniidʒ] *n.* Ⓤ the line of ancestores; ancestry. 혈통; 계통. ¶ *a man of ancient* ~ 구가 출신의 사람. [↑, -age]

lin·e·al [líniəl] *adj.* **1** descending in the direct line of ancestors; ancestral. 직계의; 선조로부터의. ¶ *a* ~ *descendant* 직계 자손. **2** of a line or lines; linear. 선(線)의. [*line*]

lin·e·a·ment [líniəmənt] *n.* 《usu. *pl.*》 **1** the features of the face. 용모. **2** the outline of the body. (몸의) 외형; 윤곽. **3** a distinctive characteristic. 특징. [*line*]

lin·e·ar [líniər] *adj.* of a line; like a line; made of lines. 선의; 선 모양의; 선을 사용한. ¶ *a* ~ *measure* 척도(尺度) / ~ *leaves* 선형 잎.

line·man [láinmən] *n.* Ⓒ (*pl.* **-men** [-mən]) **1** a person who repairs telephone, telegraph or other wires. 보선공《전신·전화의》. **2** 《U.S. football》 a player who plays on the forward line. 전위(前衛). 參考 linesman이라고도 씀.

:lin·en [línin] *n.* **1** Ⓤ cloth made from flax. 아마포(亞麻布); 린네르. **2** 《*collectively*》 articles, such as clothing and sheets made of linen cloth. 린네르 제품《시트·셔츠 등》.

***wash one's dirty linen in public* [*at home*]**, (do not) let people know about one's unpleasant private affairs. 집안의 수치를 외부에 드러내다[숨기다].

— *adj.* made of linen. 린네르(제)의. [*line*]

linen draper [∠- ∠-] *n.* a person who sells linen and cotton goods. 린네르상(商).

lin·er [láinər] *n.* Ⓒ **1** a ship or airplane of a commercial line. 정기선(定期船); 정기 항공기. **2** a person who makes lines. 선[줄]을 긋는 사람. **3** 《baseball》 a straight hit; a line drive. 라이너. [*line*]

lines·man [láinzmən] *n.* Ⓒ (*pl.* **-men** [-mən]) **1** =lineman 1. **2** 《sports》 a person assisting the referee who watches the lines and sees if the ball crosses the line. 선심(線審).

line·up [láinʌ̀p] *n.* Ⓒ an arrangement of the players in certain games; a formation of people into a line; all the members of a group, etc. (구기(球技)의) 라인업; 진용. ¶ *the starting* ~ 시합 개시의 진용[전열].

***lin·ger** [líŋgər] *vi.* **1** (P1,2A) 《*around, about*》 stay on as if unwilling to leave; loiter. 떠나지 않고 꾸물거리다. ¶ ~ *after others have left* 다른 사람들은 갔는데도 안 가고 꾸물거리다. **2** (P3) 《*on, upon, over*》 be too slow; delay. 꾸물거려 시간이 걸리다; 지체하다. ¶ ~ *over one's work* 일을 미적거리다. — *vt.* (P7) pass (time) idly. (시간)을 우물쭈물 보내다. ¶ ~ *out one's life* 빈둥거리며 지내다. [*long*]

lin·ge·rie [lɑ́:ndʒəréi, lǽnʒərì:] *n.* Ⓤ **1** women's underwear. 란제리; 여자 속옷. **2** linen goods in general. 린네르류(類). [F.]

lin·ger·ing [líŋgəriŋ] *adj.* **1** prolonging in time; slow. 오래 끄는; 꾸물거리는. ¶ *a* ~ *disease* 오랜 병. **2** suggesting unwillingness to leave. 떠나기 싫은 듯한. ¶ *a* ~ *look* 가기 싫은 눈치. [*linger*]

lin·go [líŋgou] *n.* Ⓒ (*pl.* **-goes**) language, esp. strange, technical or foreign, that one is not familiar with. (알아듣지 못하는) 뜻 모를 말《술어·외국어 등》. [↓]

lin·gual [líŋgwəl] *adj.* **1** of the tongue. 혀의. **2** 《phon.》 pronounced with the aid of the tongue. 설음(舌音)의. — *n.* 《phon.》 any of the sounds articulated with the tongue. 설음(舌音). 參考 d, t, l, n 등. [L. *lingua* tongue]

lin·guist [líŋgwist] *n.* Ⓒ **1** a person who is skilled in foreign languages. 외국어에 능한 사람. ¶ *He's quite a* ~. 외국어를 썩 잘 하는 사람이다. **2** a person who studies language. 언어학자.

lin·guis·tic [liŋgwístik] *adj.* of language or the study of languages. 언어(학)의; 언어 연구의.

lin·guis·tics [liŋgwístiks] *n. pl.* 《used as *sing.*》 the science of languages. 언어학.

lin·i·ment [línəmənt] *n.* ⒸⓊ a liquid to be rubbed on the skin for easing aches, pains, etc. (액상의) 도포약(塗布藥). [L. *linio* smear]

***lin·ing** [láiniŋ] *n.* **1** Ⓤ the act of covering the inner surface of something; any material used for this purpose. (옷의) 안을 대기; 그 재료. ¶ 《*prov.*》 *Every cloud has a silver* ~. 고생하다 보면 낙도 있다. **2** 《*fig.*》 Ⓒ the contents of something. 내용물. ¶ *the* ~ *of a pocket* 주머니에 든 것. [*line*]

***link**[1] [liŋk] *n.* Ⓒ **1** a ring of a chain. 사슬의 고리. **2** anything that connects two parts, persons, objects, etc. 연결하는 사람[물건]; 연결; 유대. ¶ *a* ~ *with the past* 과거와 연결되는 것 / *Johnsons was a* ~ *between the age of Pope and that of Cowper.* 존슨은 포프 시대와 쿠퍼 시대를 잇는 연결 고리였다. **3** a unit or length. 링크《측량의 단위, 1/100 chain; 약 20 cm》. **4** 《usu. *pl.*》 one of a pair of buttons connected by a chain and used to fasten shirtcuffs. 커프스버튼. — *vt.* (P6,7,13) 《*to*》 connect; unite. …을 잇다; 연결하다. ¶ ~ *the island to the mainland* 섬과 본토를 연결하다 / *These events were all subtly linked together.* 이들 사건은 모두 미묘한 상호 관련이 있었다. — *vi.* (P2A) 《*up*》 join; be connected. 이어지다; 연결되다. ¶ *Our plane links up with that of America in Los Angeles.* 우리 항공기는 로스앤젤레스에서 미국 비행기와 연결된다. [N.]

link[2] [liŋk] *n.* Ⓒ a torch. 횃불. [N.]

links [liŋks] *n. pl.* **1** 《often used as *sing.*》 a golf course. 골프장. **2** a sandy ground by the seashore. (해안의) 모래펄. [E. =ridge]

lin·net [línit] *n.* Ⓒ 《bird》 a small, brown, singing bird. 홍방울새. [→line (flax being its food)]

li·no·le·um [linóuliəm] *n.* Ⓤ a floor covering made of cork and linseed oil. 리놀륨《마루 깔개》. [→line, →oil]

lin·o·type [láinoutàip] *n.*《print.》a typesetting machine that casts each line of type in one piece. 라이노타이프; 자동 주조 식자기(cf. *monotype*). [*line of type*]

lin·seed [línsì:d] *n.* Ⓤ the seed of flax. 아마인(亞麻仁). [→line]

linseed oil [´–´] *n.* a kind of oil made by pressing linseed, used in paints. 아마인유(油)《도료용(塗料用)》.

lint [lint] *n.* Ⓤ **1** a soft cloth made by scraping linen, used for covering wounds. 린트천《붕대·가제용》. **2** bits of thread. 실보무라지. [→line]

lin·tel [líntl] *n.* Ⓒ《archit.》a piece of stone or wood placed above a door or window to support the wall above it. 상인방(上引枋). [→limit]

〈lintel〉

:li·on [láiən] *n.* Ⓒ **1** a large, powerful, flesh-eating animal living in Africa. 사자; 라이온. **2** a brave man. 용맹한 사람. **3** a famous man; a star. 유명한〔인기 있는〕 사람; 명사. ¶ *make a ~ of someone* 아무를 치켜세우다. **4**《*pl.*》《Brit.》noted sights. 명소(名所). ¶ *see* 〔*show*〕 *the lions* 명승지를 구경하다〔시키다〕. **5**《astron.》《*the L-*》the constellation Leo. 사자자리. **6**《*L-*》the national symbol of Great Britain. 영국의 상징. ¶ *the British Lion* 영국(국민). [Gk. *leōn*]

a lion in the path 〔***way***〕**,** an obstacle in the way to overcome. 앞길에 가로놓인 장애물〔난관〕.

beard the lion in his den, meet and challenge someone in his own home, etc. 적지에 뛰어들어 당당히 맞서다.

put one's head into a lion's mouth, take a great risk. 대단한 모험을 하다.

take the lion's share, take the largest or best share. 가장 큰 몫을 차지하다. ¶ *He took the lion's share of the profits.* 그가 그 소득의 알짜를 가져갔다.

twist the lion's tail,《esp. of U.S. journalists》speak ill of Great Britain. 영국 욕을 하다.

li·on·ess [láiənis] *n.* Ⓒ a female lion. 암사자

li·on·heart·ed [láiənhà:rtid] *adj.* brave as a lion. (사자처럼) 용감한.

li·on·hunt·er [láiənhʌ̀ntər] *n.* Ⓒ **1** a person who hunts lions. 사자 사냥꾼. **2** a person who wants to make the acquaintance of many famous people. 유명인들과 사귀고 싶어하는 사람.

li·on·ize [láiənàiz] *vt.* (P6) treat (someone) as a famous or distinguished person. …을 유명인 취급을 하다; 치켜세우다. — *vi.* (P1)《Brit.》see the sights of (a place). 명승지를 구경하다.

:lip [lip] *n.* Ⓒ **1** one of the two edges of the mouth. 입술. **2**《*pl.*》the mouth. 입. ¶ *He refused to open his lips.* 말하려 들지 않았다 / *My lips are sealed.* (알아도) 말 못 하겠다 / *a curl of the ~* 냉소. **3** a projecting edge of an open container that has a hole inside. (그릇의) 주둥이; 귀때. ¶ *the ~ of a bottle* 병의 주둥이.

bite one's lips, hide one's feelings of anger, laughter, etc. 감정을 누르다; 참다.

carry 〔***keep***〕 ***a stiff upper lip,*** do not become discouraged; do not show discouragement. 낙담하지〔겁내지〕 않다.

curl one's lips, laugh scornfully. 냉소하다; 입을 비죽거리다.

hang one's lips, be about to cry; almost cry. 울상을 짓다.

hang on someone's lips, listen attentively. 열심히 듣다; 경청하다.

make (***up***) ***a lip,*** push out the lips as a sign of displeasure. 입을 비죽 내밀다.

smack 〔***lick***〕 ***one's lips,*** show pleasure in food. (맛있어) 입술을 핥다.

— *adj.* not sincere; only on the surface. 말뿐인. [E.]

lip-deep [lípdí:p] *adj.* superficial; expressed but not felt. 천박한; 말뿐인.

lip-lan·guage [líplæ̀ŋgwidʒ] *n.* speech made through the movement of the lips. (농아자의) 시화(視話); 독순(讀脣).

lipped [lipt] *adj.* having (something like) a lip or lips. 입술이〔귀때가〕 있는. ¶ *a ~ pitcher.*

lip reading [´ ´–] *n.* a method of understanding speech by watching the movements of the speaker's lip, which may be learned by deaf people. 독순술(讀脣術).

lip·salve [lípsæ̀v, ´sà:v] *n.* **1** a greasy substance used for healing sore or cracked lips. 입술에 바르는 연고. **2**《*fig.*》flattery. 아첨.

lip·sèrv·ice [lípsə̀:rvis] *n.* insincere expressions of respect, admiration, etc.; insincere promises. 입발매; 말뿐인 약속.

lip·stick [lípstìk] *n.* ⓊⒸ a stick used for coloring the lips. 립스틱; 입술 연지.

liq·ue·fac·tion [lìkwifǽkʃən] *n.* Ⓤ the state or process of changing into a liquid. 액화(液化); 용해. [L.]

liq·ue·fy [líkwifài] *vi.* (**-fied**) (P1) become liquid; melt. 액화(液化)하다; 용해하다. — *vt.* (P6) change (something) into a liquid. …을 액화시키다; 녹이다. ¶ *Gases can be liquified.* 가스는 액화된다. [L.]

li·queur [likə́:r / -kjúər] *n.* Ⓤ a kind of strong and sweet alcoholic drink. 리큐어술. ¶ *~ brandy* 〔*whisky*〕. [L.]

:liq·uid [líkwid] *n.* **1** ⓊⒸ a substance which can flow freely, like water. 액체. **2**《phon.》Ⓒ the sound of [l] or [r]. 유음(流

音). —*adj.* **1** in the form of a liquid; freely flowing. 액체의; 유동적인. ¶ ~ *soap* 물비누 / ~ *food* 유동식 / (*a*) ~ *measure* 액량(단위). **2** clear and bright. 맑은. ¶ ~ *eyes* 맑은 눈 / *the* ~ *sky* 맑게 갠 하늘. **3** 《*fig.*》(of sounds, etc.) smooth; flowing freely. (소리 등이) 흐르는 듯한; 유려한. ¶ *the* ~ *notes of a bird* 새의 유려한 울음소리. **4** (of currency) easy to change into cash. 현금화(化)가 쉬운. ¶ ~ *assets* 〔*capital*〕 유동 자산〔자본〕. **5** not fixed or settled. 불안정한; 유동적인. ¶ *My ideas are still* ~. 내 생각은 아직 유동적이다. [L.]

liq·ui·date [líkwidèit] *vt.* (P6) **1** pay (a debt). …의 빚을 갚다. **2** change (something) into cash. …을 현금으로 바꾸다. **3** ⓐ get rid of (something or someone undesirable). …을 치우다; 제거하다. ⓑ 《*colloq.*》 kill. 죽이다. **4** settle the account of (a business). …을 청산하다. **5** put an end to (something regarded as a public nuisance). …을 일소하다. —*vi.* (P1) fail in business and go bankrupt. 파산하다. [L.]

liq·ui·da·tion [lìkwidéiʃən] *n.* Ⓤ the state of having one's debts paid off. (부채의) 청산.
go into liquidation, go bankrupt. 파산하다.

:liq·uor [líkər] *n.* ⓊⒸ **1** an alcoholic drink. 알코올 음료. **2** Ⓤ a liquid. 액체. [L.]
have 〔***enjoy***〕 ***a liquor,*** have a drink. 한잔하다.
in liquor, drunk. 취해서.
under the influence of liquor, partly drunk. 거나해서.

li·ra [líərə] *n.* Ⓒ (*pl.* **li·re** or **li·ras**) the unit of money in Italy. 리라《이탈리아의 화폐 단위》. [L. *libra* pound]

li·re [lí(:)rei] *n.* pl. of **lira.**

Li·sa [lízə, láizə] *n.* a girl's name, short for Elizabeth. 여자 이름《Elizabeth의 애칭》.

Lis·bon [lízbən] *n.* the capital of Portugal. 리스본.

lisp [lisp] *vi.* (P1) **1** pronounce the sound of [s] or [z] like that of [th]. 틀리게 발음하다《[s, z]를 [θ, ð]로 발음하는 따위》. **2** 《*out*》 speak like a baby. 혀짤배기 소리를 하다.
—*vt.* (P6,7) speak (a word, etc.) imperfectly, like a baby. …을 혀짤배기 소리로 말하다. —*n.* Ⓒ an act of lisping in speaking. 혀짤빼기 소리. ¶ *speak with a* ~.
● **lisp·er** [⌐ər] *n.* [E.]

lis·some, lis·som [lísəm] *adj.* flexible; soft; quick in manner; active. 유연한; 부드러운; 쾌활한. [*lithe*]

:list[1] [list] *n.* Ⓒ a record of names, numbers, words, etc. written in order. 표; 목록; 리스트. ¶ *a price* ~ 가격표 / *make a* ~ *of* (*something*) …의 리스트를 만들다.
be on the sick list, be sick usu. in bed. 앓고 있다; 병중이다.
on the active list, among those who have not retired, esp. in the armed forces. 현역으로.
the free list, **a**) the list of persons who are admitted free to a theater, etc. 무료 입장자 명부. **b**) the list of goods admitted into a country free of tax. 면세품 목록.
—*vt.* (P6) make a list of (something); enlist. …을 리스트에 기입하다. —*vi.* (P3) be recorded. 기록에 실리다. [↓]

list[2] [list] *n.* Ⓒ **1** the edge of cloth. (천의) 가장자리. **2** =lists. —*vt.* (P6) put a border around the edge of (something). …의 가장자리를 대다. [Teut.]

list[3] [list] *n.* Ⓒ a state leaning to one side 한쪽으로의 경사. ¶ *The ship had a bad* ~. 배는 심하게 한쪽으로 기울었다.
—*vi.* (P1,2A) (of a ship) lean to one side. (배가) 한쪽으로 기울다. [*lust*]

:lis·ten [lísən] *vi.* (P1,2A,3) **1** 《*to*》 try to hear; pay attention so as to hear. 주의해서 듣다; 경청하다. ¶ ~ *to the radio* 라디오를 듣다 / *Listen to me carefully.* 내 말을 잘 들어라. 參考 hear 는 '소리가 귀에 들어와 듣다'란 뜻의 말. **2** 《*to*》 obey; follow advice. 귀담아 듣다; 따르다. ¶ ~ *to reason* 순리에 따르다 / *Don't* ~ *to him.* 그 사람 말을 듣지 마라 / ~ *to someone's advice* 아무의 충고에 따르다. [E.]
listen for, wait attentively for (some sound). 어떤 소리에 귀를 기울이다. ¶ ~ *for a footstep* 발자국 소리에 귀를 곤두세우다.
listen in, **a**) listen to radio programs. (라디오를) 청취하다. **b**) listen to another's telephone conversation usu. without his knowledge. (전화를) 도청하다.

lis·ten·er [lísnər] *n.* Ⓒ a person who listens. 듣는 사람; 청취자.

lis·ten·er-in [lísnərìn] *n.* Ⓒ (*pl.* **-ers-in**) a person who listens to the radio. 라디오 청취자.

list·less [lístlis] *adj.* seeming inactive; absent-minded; indifferent. 나른한 듯한; 멍해 있는; 무관심한. [*list*[3]]

list price [⌐ ⌐] *n.* the price given in a list; the official price. 표시 가격; 정가. [*list*[1]]

lists [lists] *n. pl.* a place where knights fought in tournaments. 시합장. [*list*[2]]
enter the lists, take part in a contest. 시합에 참가하다.

·lit [lit] *v.* p. and pp. of **light.**

li·ter, 《Brit.》 **-tre** [lí:tər] *n.* Ⓒ the unit of measure for liquids in the metric system. 리터. 參考 l., lit.로 생략함. [Gk. *litrā*]

lit·er·a·cy [lítərəsi] *n.* Ⓤ the ability to read and write. 읽고 쓰는 능력(opp. illiteracy).

lit·er·al [lítərəl] *adj.* **1** of the letters of the alphabet. 문자의. ¶ *a purely* ~ *error in printing* 단순한 인쇄상의 오식 / ~ *marking* (숫자가 아닌) ABC 따위에 의한 채점. **2** following the given words or the original exactly; word for word. 글자대로의; 축어적인. ¶ *a* ~ *translation* 축어역; 직역 / *in the* ~ *sense of the word* 글자대로의 뜻으로. **3** apt to understand words without imagination or exaggeration. 자구(字句)에 구애된; 상상력이 결여된; 과장이 없는. ¶ *a ~ mind* 융통성이 없는 생각. **4** sticking to the actual fact; perfectly accurate. 사실에 충실한; 정확한. ¶ *the ~ truth* 틀림없는 사실 / *a ~ account of what happened* 사건에 대한 정확한 기사. [→*literary*]

·lit·er·al·ly [lítərəli] *adv.* **1** word for word; exactly. 축어적으로; (글자 뜻) 그대로. ¶ *translate ~* 직역하다 / *interpret a remark ~* 말을 곧이곧대로 듣다. **2** ⟪*emph.*⟫ really; truly. 아주; 정말로. ¶ *I am ~ starving.* 나는 정말로 배가 고프다.

:lit·er·ar·y [lítərèri / -rə-] *adj.* **1** of literature. 문학(상)의. ¶ *~ works* 문학 작품 / *~ property* 저작권; 판권. **2** acquainted with literature. 문학에 통달한. ¶ *a ~ man* 문학자. [L. *littera* letter]

lit·er·ate [lítərit] *adj.* **1** able to read and write. 읽고 쓸 줄 아는; 글을 아는(opp. illiterate). **2** acquainted with literature. 문학에 통한. — *n.* Ⓒ a person who can read and write; a learned person. 글을 아는[학식 있는] 사람. [↑]

:lit·er·a·ture [lítərətʃər, -tʃùər] *n.* Ⓤ **1** ⓐ imaginative writings such as poems, novels, plays, and essays. 문학; 문예. ¶ *Every age produces both good and bad ~.* 어느 시대에나 훌륭한 문학과 그렇지 못한 것이 있다. ⓑ a body of those writings produced by a specified nation, period, etc. (어느 민족·시대 등의) 전체 문헌[문학 작품]. ¶ *Shakespeare is the greatest name in English ~.* 셰익스피어는 영문학상 최대의 인물이다. **2** the study of literature; the occupation of authors. 문학 연구; 저술업. **3** ⟪*collectively*⟫ the writings on a certain subject. (어느 제목에 관한) 저작; 문헌. ¶ *the ~ of music* 음악 문헌 / *the ~ of stamp-collecting* 우표 수집 관계 문헌. **4** ⟪*collectively*⟫ ⟪*colloq.*⟫ any printed material. 인쇄물⟪광고물 등⟫. [→literate, -ure]

lithe [laið] *adj.* bending or twisting easily; flexible. 유연한. [E.]

lith·i·um [líθiəm] *n.* ⟪chem.⟫ a metalic element. 리튬. [↓]

lith·o·graph [líθəgræ̀f, -grɑ̀ːf] *n.* a print made by the process of lithography. 석판 인쇄물; 석판화. — *vt.* (P6) print by the process of lithography. 석판으로 인쇄하다. [Gk. *lithos* stone, -graph]

lith·o·graph·ic [lìθəgrǽfik] *adj.* of a lithograph; made by lithography. 석판화의; 석판 인쇄의. [↑]

lith·o·gra·phy [liθɑ́grəfi / -θɔ́g-] *n.* Ⓤ the process or art of printing from designs on a prepared stone or metal surface. 석판 인쇄(술). [↑]

lith·o·sphere [líθəsfìər] *n.* ⟪geol.⟫ the crust of the earth. 지각(地殼). [↑]

lit·i·gant [lítigənt] *n.* a person or party engaged in a lawsuit. 소송 당사자. — *adj.* engaged in a lawsuit. 소송의; 소송하는. [↓]

lit·i·gate [lítigèit] *vt.* (P6) **1** go to law with (someone); engage in a law case with (someone); contest with (someone) in a law court. …에게 소송을 제기하다; …와 법정에서 다투다. **2** ⟪*fig.*⟫ dispute. 논쟁하다. — *vi.* (P1) go to law. 소송하다. [L.]

lit·i·ga·tion [lìtigéiʃən] *n.* **1** Ⓤ the act of litigating. 소송. **2** Ⓒ a lawsuit. 기소.

li·ti·gious [litídʒəs] *adj.* **1** fond of going to law. 걸핏하면 소송하는. **2** that can be disputed at law. 소송해야 할.

lit·mus [lítməs] *n.* Ⓤ ⟪chem.⟫ a substance that turns red in acid and blue in alkali. 리트머스. [Du.]

litmus paper [⌐-⌐-] *n.* a strip of paper treated with litmus and used to show whether something is acid or alkali. 리트머스 시험지.

li·to·tes [láitətìːz, -tou-, lít-, laitóu-] *n.* ⟪log.⟫ an affirmative expressed by the negative of its contrary. 곡언법(曲言法) ⟪not bad 대신에 very good 하는 따위⟫. [Gk. *litos* plain]

li·tre [líːtər] *n.* =⟪Brit.⟫ liter.

·lit·ter [lítər] *n.* **1** Ⓤ rubbish scattered about; things left in disorder. 쓰레기; 어지러이 흩어진 것. **2** Ⓒ ⟪*a ~*⟫ a condition of disorder. 난잡; 혼란. ¶ *in a ~* 흩어져; 어지럽게. **3** Ⓒ (of some animals) all the young borne at a single birth. (동물의) 한배 새끼. ¶ *a ~ of kittens* 한배의 새끼고양이들. **4** Ⓤ straw, hay, etc. used as bedding for animals. (짐승의) 깔짚. **5** Ⓒ a frame for carrying a sick or wounded person; a stretcher. 들것. **6** Ⓒ a bed enclosed with curtains and carried on men's shoulders or by animals in old times. (지붕·커튼이 있는) 들것 침상.

— *vt.* (P6,7) **1** ⟪*up, with*⟫ make (something) untidy; scatter (things) about. …을 어지럽히다; 흩뜨리다. ¶ *~ (up) a room with papers* 종이로 방을 어지럽히다 / *The lawn was littered with leaves.* 잔디에는 낙엽들이 어지러이 흩어져 있었다. **2** ⟪*down*⟫ scatter straw, hay, etc. to make a bed for (an animal). (짐승)을 위해 깔짚을 깔아주다. ¶ *~ down a horse* 말에게 깔짚을 깔아주다. **3** (of some animals) give birth to (a number of young). (짐승이 새끼)를 낳다. — *vi.* (P1) (of some animals) give birth to a number of young at one time. (짐승이) 새끼를 낳다. [L. *lectus* bed]

:lit·tle [lítl] *adj.* (**less** or **less·er**, **least**; or *colloq.* **lit·tler**, **lit·tlest**) **1** small in size; not great or big; young and small. 작은; 어린 (opp. big, great, large). ¶ *a ~ town* 작은 마을 / *a ~ boy* 어린아이; 꼬마 / *the ~ finger* 새끼손가락 / *~ ones* 아이들; 짐승 새끼들 / *~ rabbits* 새끼토끼 / *a ~ man* 왜소한 사람. **2** ⟪*with a*⟫ ⓐ small in amount, degree, or number. 소량〔조금〕의; 약간의(opp. much). ¶ *a ~ sugar and a ~ butter* 소량의 설탕과 버터 / *have a ~ money* 약간의 돈이 있다 / *drink a ~ wine* 술을 좀 마시다 / *speak a ~ English* 영어를 조금 알다 / *A ~ care would have prevented it.* 좀 조심했다면 그런 일은 없었을 텐데. ⓑ《as a polite formula》 some. 얼마간의; 다소의. ¶ *Let me give you a ~ beer.* 맥주를 좀 드시지요. **3** 《without *a*》 hardly any; no. 거의 없는. ¶ *I eat ~ food for breakfast.* 아침을 굶다시피 했다 / *There is ~ hope.* 거의 절망이다. **4** short in time or distance; not long. (시간·거리가) 짧은. ¶ *Wait a ~ while.* 잠시만 기다려라 / *It is only a ~ distance from here.* 여기서 아주 가깝다. **5** not important; small in value; trivial. 대수롭지 않은; 사소한; 하찮은. ¶ *a ~ matter* 사소한 일 / *Little things amuse ~ minds.* 소인은 하찮은 일을 즐거워한다. **6** narrow-minded; not generous. 도량이 좁은; 인색한. ¶ *a ~ mind* 소견이 좁은 사람 / *~ thoughts* 편협한 생각.

but little, almost no. 거의 없는. ¶ *There is but ~ chance.* 기회는 거의 없다.

no little =***not a little,*** very much. 많은; 적지 않은. ¶ *I took no ~ pains over it.* 그 일로 고생깨나 했다.

only a little, a very small amount of. 조금의; 얼마 안 되는. ¶ *I've only a ~ money with me.* 가진 돈이 얼마 안 된다.

— *adv.* (**less, least**) in a small degree; not much; hardly any; not at all. 조금; 다소; 거의 …않다; 조금도 …않다. 語法 little 은 '거의 …이 아니다', a little 은 '조금 …하다'의 뜻. ¶ *I felt a ~ tired.* 좀 피곤했다 / *Little did I dream that he would succeed.* 그의 성공은 꿈에도 생각 못 했다 / *He is a ~ better today.* 오늘은 좀 낫다 / *It took ~ more than an hour.* 그것은 한 시간 정도밖에 안 걸렸다 / *He ~ knows where you are.* 너 있는 데를 그는 조금도 모른다.

— *n.* Ⓤ **1** a small amount, quantity, or degree. 소량, 소액. ¶ *I have seen ~ of life.* 나는 세상 물정을 거의 모른다 / *He knows a ~ of everything.* 그는 무엇이건 조금씩은 안다 / *Little remains to be said.* 할 말은 거의 다 했다 / *I will do the ~ I can.* 미력이나마 전력을 다 하겠다. **2** 《*a ~*》 a short time or distance. 짧은 시간〔거리〕. ¶ *After a ~ you will feel better.* 조금 있으면 좀 나아질 것이다 / *Please wait a ~.* 잠시 기다려라. [E.]

in little, on a small scale. 소규모로(opp. in large).

little by little, gradually; by degrees. 조금씩.

little or nothing =***little if anything,*** hardly anything. 거의 …없다. ¶ *I know ~ or nothing about it.* 거기 대해 나는 아는 게 거의 없다.

make little of, treat (something) as unimportant. 얕보다; 깔보다.

not a little, much. 적잖은〔상당한〕 양(의 것). ¶ *I lost not a ~ over cards.* 트럼프로 꽤 많은 돈을 날렸다.

Little Corporal [´-- ´--], **the** *n.* the nickname of Napoleon I. 나폴레옹 1세의 별명.

lit·tle·ness [lítlnis] *n.* **1** small size; smallness. 작음. ¶ *the ~ of English mountains compared with the Alps* 알프스에 비한 영국 산들의 왜소함. **2** meanness. 편협; 인색함. ¶ *the ~ of human nature* 인간성의 옹졸함.

lit·to·ral [lítərəl] *adj.* of or on a shore. 해안의. — *n.* Ⓒ a region along a shore. 연해지(沿海地); 연안 지방. [L. *litus* shore]

lit·ur·gy [lítərdʒi] *n.* Ⓒ (*pl.* **-gies**) **1** a form of public worship in a Christian church. 예배식. **2** 《*the L-*》 the Book of Common Prayer used in the Anglican Church. (영국 국교회의) 기도서. [Gk. =public work]

liv·a·ble [lívəbəl] *adj.* **1** (of a house, a climate, etc.) fit to live in. 살기에 좋은. ¶ *a ~ house* 살기에 알맞은 집. **2** (of a person) easy to live with; companionable. 같이 지내기에 좋은; 사교적인. ¶ *He is ~ with.* 함께 지낼 만한 좋은 사람이다. **3** (of life) worth living; endurable. (인생이) 살 보람이 있는; 견딜 만한. ¶ *Such a life is ~.* 그건 보람있는 생활〔인생〕이다. [↓]

:live[1] [liv] *vi.* **1** (P3) dwell; inhabit. 살다; 거주하다. ¶ *I have lived here for the last ten years.* 여기 산 지 10년이 되었다 / *He lives in Seoul.* 그는 서울에 살고 있다 / *The room does not seem to be lived in.* 그 방에는 거처할 수 있을 것 같지 않다. **2** (P1,3) be alive; be living. 살아 있다; 살다. ¶ *~ in water* 물에 살다 / *He still lives.* 그는 아직 살아 있다 / *Live and let live.* 나도 살고 너도 살게 하자《공존공영》. **3** (P1,2A,4) continue to have life; remain alive 생존하다; 오래 살다. ¶ *~ to be old* 장수하다; 오래 살다 / *~ to the age of 85,* 여든다섯까지 (오래) 살다 / *~ to see one's grandchild* 생전에 손자까지 보다. **4** (P2,3) pass one's life in a certain way. …하게 살다. ¶ *~ happily* 행복하게 살다 / *~ high* 호화롭게 지내다 / *~ in comfort* 안락하게 살다 / *~ fast* 방탕하게 살다 / *~ rough* 힘들게〔어렵게〕 살다. **5** (P2A,3) ⓐ keep up or maintain life. 지내다; 생계를 유지하다. ¶ *~ by one's pen* 문필로 생활하다 / *~ on one's salary* 〔*relatives*〕 월급〔친척 도움〕으로 지내다. ⓑ 《*on, upon*》 have as (one's usual) food; depend on for food; feed on. …을 먹고 살다; …을 상식하다. ¶ *~ on rice* 〔*fruit*〕 쌀〔과일〕을 먹고 살다〔상식하다〕 / *Lions ~ upon other animals.* 사자는 다른 짐승을 잡아먹고 산다. **6** (P1) enjoy a full and varied life. 즐겁게 살다; 충실한 인생을 즐기다. ¶ *At 38 she was just beginning to ~.* 나이 서른여덟이 되어 그녀는 비로소 충실한 인생을 시작하고 있었다 / *I lived in those days.* 그 무렵은 살 만했다. **7** (P1) survive; remain in the memory. 존속하다; 살아남다. ¶ *No ship can ~ in such a storm.* 그러한 폭풍에 온전할 배

는 없다 / *His memory lives in my heart.* 그에 대한 추억은 아직도 내 마음에 살아 있다. — *vt.* (P6,7) practice or carry out (something) in one's life; spend or pass (a certain life). …한 생활을 하다〔보내다〕. ¶ ~ *a lie* 거짓된 인생을 살다 / ~ *a life of ease* 안락한 생활을 하다. [E.]

live down, live so as to have others forget one's past mistakes. 그 후의 행위로 불명예 등을 씻다. ¶ *She lived down the scandal.* 그녀는 훌륭한 생활을 해서 그 오명을 씻었다.

live in, dwell at one's place of employment. 주인집에 기거하며 일하다.

live it (***with***)***,*** follow. …을 따라 가다; …에 뒤지지 않다.

live off (=*live at the expense of*) *someone.* …에 기식하다; …의 신세를 지다.

live out, **a**) live until the end of something. 견뎌내다; 살아남다. **b**) dwell away from the house of employment. 집에서 통근하다.

live through, pass through safely; experience and survive; endure. …을 헤쳐 나가다; …을 극복하다; 배겨내다. ¶ ~ *through difficulties* 〔*a crisis*〕 곤란을〔위기를〕 이겨내다.

live up to, act according to (one's ideals, reputation, etc.); fulfill (something expected). …에 따라 살아가다; (주의 등)에 충실히 따르다. ¶ ~ *up to one's income* 수입에 맞게 생활하다 / ~ *up to one's duty* 자기 의무를 완수하다.

live well, live comfortably; lead a virtuous life. 안락하게 지내다; 올바르게 살다.

live with, **a**) accept and endure. …을 견디다; 참다. **b**) live together with. …와 동거하다.

where one lives, 《U.S. *colloq.*》 the vital part. 급소.

live² [laiv] *adj.* 《used only as *an attributive*》 **1** alive; living. 살아 있는. ¶ ~ *fish* 살아 있는 물고기. **2** full of life, energy, or activity; energetic. 활기 있는; 팔팔한. ¶ *a* ~ *man of business* 정력적인 사업가. **3** up-to-date; of present interest. 목하〔당면〕의; 관심사가 되고 있는. ¶ *a* ~ *topic* 오늘의 화제 거리 / *a* ~ *issue* 당면 문제. **4** burning; glowing; ardent. 불타고 있는; 격렬한. ¶ ~ *coals* 타고 있는 석탄 / *a* ~ *hatred* 심한 증오. **5** carrying an electric current. 전류가 통하는. ¶ *a* ~ *wire* 전류가 흐르고 있는 전선 / *a* ~ *machine* 동력이 걸려 있는 기계. **6** fresh; pure. 신선한; 순수한. ¶ ~ *air* 신선한 공기. **7** loaded; not exploded. 장전된; 아직 폭발하지 않은. ¶ *a* ~ *shell* 〔*cartridge*〕 실탄(實彈). **8** broadcast during its occurence (not recorded). 생방송의. ¶ *a* ~ *program* 생방송 프로. [E.]

***live·li·hood** [láivlihùd] *n.* Ⓒ 《usu. *sing.*》 a means of supporting life. 생계; 살림. ¶ *earn* 〔*make, gain*〕 *one's* ~ 생계를 세우다 / *earn* 〔*make*〕 *an honest* ~ 정직하게 일해서 살다.

live·li·ly [láivlili] *adv.* in a lively manner; cheerfully. 원기 있게; 활발하게.

live·li·ness [láivlinis] *n.* Ⓤ the state of being lively; brightness; cheerfulness; gaiety. 생기 있음; 활발; 명랑.

live·long [lívlɔ̀ːŋ / -lɔ̀ŋ] *adj.* 《*poet.*》 **1** long in passing; whole. 꼬박; 내내. ¶ *the* ~ *day* 〔*night*〕 하루 종일〔하룻밤 내내〕. **2** lasting. 영속하는. ¶ *a* ~ *monument* 영원한 기념비.

:live·ly [láivli] *adj.* (**-li·er, -li·est**) **1** full of life; vigorous; active. 활기찬; 기운찬; 활발한. ¶ *a* ~ *discussion* 활발한 토의 / *a* ~ *person* 활동가. **2** (of a color, a light, etc.) bright; vivid. (색이) 선명한; 밝은. ¶ ~ *colors of neon signs* 밝은 네온의 불빛. **3** (of the mind) alive; alert; acute. 활발한; 예민한; 날카로운. ¶ *a* ~ *imagination* 활발한 상상력. **4** cheerful; gay. 즐거운; 쾌활한. ¶ ~ *jazz* 신나는 재즈곡. **5** (of a portrait, a description, etc.) lifelike. 생생한; 박진감 있는. **6** 《*colloq.*》 excitingly or thrillingly dangerous. 아슬아슬한; 위태로운. ¶ *The police had a* ~ *time.* 경찰은 손에 땀을 쥐게 하는 시간을 보냈다. **7** ⓐ bounding back quickly. 탄력이 좋은; 잘 튀는. ¶ *a* ~ *ball.* ⓑ fresh. 신선한. ¶ *a* ~ *breeze* 상쾌한 미풍. **8** strongly felt; powerful. (감정이) 강렬한; 강한. ¶ *a* ~ *sense of gratitude* 진지한 감사의 마음 / *a* ~ *faith* 열렬한 신앙.

liv·en [láivən] *vi.* (P2A) 《*up*》 become cheerful or lively. 쾌활해지다. ¶ *He livened up when he heard the news.* 그 소식에 그는 쾌활해졌다. — *vt.* (P7) make (someone or something) cheerful or lively; brighten. …을 즐겁게 〔쾌활하게〕 하다. ¶ ~ *things* 〔*someone*〕 *up* 일을 즐겁게 하다〔아무를 기분좋게 만들다〕. [→live²]

·liv·er¹ [lívər] *n.* Ⓒ a large organ in the body which produces a liquid which is called bile. 간장(肝臟); 간. [E.]

liv·er² [lívər] *n.* Ⓒ a person who lives in a certain manner. (…하게) 사는 사람; …생활자. ¶ *a fast* 〔*a loose*〕 ~ 방탕자 / *a clean* ~ 청렴 결백한 사람 / *a free* ~ 사치스러운 사람; 미식가. [E.]

liv·er·ied [lívərid] *adj.* dressed in a livery. 제복을 입은. ¶ ~ *waiters.* [→livery]

liv·er·y [lívəri] *n.* (*pl.* **-er·ies**) **1** Ⓤ 《*collectively*》 a uniform for male servants or for the members of any group or profession. 제복. ¶ *in* 〔*out of*〕 ~ 제복을 입고〔사복으로〕 / *the* ~ *of grief* 〔*woe*〕 상복(喪服). **2** Ⓤ 《*collectively*》 characteristic dress; outward appearance. (특수한) 의상〔옷〕; (옷)차림. ¶ *trees in the* ~ *of spring* 봄차림을 한 나무들. **3** Ⓒ the act of keeping horses, vehicles, etc. for pay; the act of hiring out horses, vehicles, etc. 말〔마차〕 대여〔보관〕(업). **4** Ⓒ 《U.S.》 =livery stable. [→delivery]

livery stable [⌐–– ⌐–] *n.* a place where horses and vehicles are kept or let out for pay. 거마 대여소; 말〔보관소〕.

live·stock [láivstɑ̀k / -stɔ̀k] *n.* Ⓤ《*collectively*》 farm animals. 가축. ¶ *The farm was sold with all its* ~. 그 농장은 모든 가축과 함께 팔렸다. [*live*[2]]

liv·id [lívid] *adj.* **1** of a leaden color; black and blue; pale. 납빛의; 검푸른; 창백한. ¶ ~ *marks of blows on the arm* 팔에 난 검푸른 타박상들. **2**《Brit. *colloq.*》 very angry; furious. 무섭게 화난; 격노한. [L.]

:liv·ing [líviŋ] *adj.* **1** having life; alive. 살아 있는. ¶ *all* ~ *things* 살아 있는 모든 것; 생물 / *a* ~ *death* 비참한 생활. **2** still in use; still existing. 지금 쓰이고 있는; 현존하는; 당대의. ¶ *a* ~ *language* 현대어(語) / *the greatest* ~ *writer* 당대 최고의 작가 / *within* ~ *memory* 현존하는 사람들의 기억에 있는. **3** of or for life. 생활의. ¶ ~ *conditions* 생활 상태 / *the* ~ *standard* 생활 수준 / ~ *expenses* 생계비. **4** enough to live on. 생활에 충분한. ¶ *a* ~ *wage* (최저) 생활 임금 / ~ *quarters* 거소; 거주 지역. **5** strong; active. 강한; 활발한. ¶ *a* ~ *faith* 열렬한 신앙 / *a* ~ *discussion* 열띤 토론. **6** lifelike; true to life; real. 실물 그대로의; 빼쏜. ¶ *He is the* ~ *image of his father.* 그는 아버지를 그대로 닮았다. **7** (of rocks) in its natural place. (암석이) 자연 그대로의. ¶ *a* ~ *rock* 천연〔자연〕석.
— *n.* **1** Ⓤ the state of being alive. 살아 있음; 생존. ¶ *The sick man is tired of* ~. 환자는 살기에 지쳐 있다. **2** Ⓒ《usu. *sing.*》 money or things necessary for life; livelihood. 생활비; 생활 필수품; 생계. ¶ *make* 〔*earn*〕 *one's* ~ 생계를 세우다 / *I must work for a* ~. 살기 위해 일해야 한다. **3** Ⓤ manner of life. 생활 양식. ¶ *plain* ~ *and high thinking* 검소하나 철학적인 생활《생활은 낮게 생각은 높게》. [*live*]

living room [ㅅ-ㅅ] *n.* a room designed for general family use; a sitting room. 거실(居室).

liz·ard [lízərd] *n.*《zool.》 kinds of four-legged reptile. 도마뱀. [L. *lacertus*]

lla·ma [lɑ́:mə] *n.* Ⓒ (*pl.* **-mas** or《*collectively*》 **-ma**) an animal like a camel but without a hump, living in South America. 라마; 아메리카 낙타. [Sp.]

LL.B. *Legum Baccalaureus* (L. = Bachelor of Laws).

LL.D. *Legum Doctor* (L. =Doctor of Laws).

lo [lou] *interj.*《*arch.*》 look! see! 보라. ¶ *Lo and behold!* (놀라서) 이 무슨 일이냐. [E.]

:load [loud] *n.* Ⓒ **1** a heavy burden. (무거운) 짐. ¶ *bear a* ~ *on one's shoulders* 짐을 지다. **2**《*fig.*》 something that makes one's mind heavy; a worry. (정신적인) 부담; 걱정. ¶ *a* ~ *of debt* 빚에 대한 부담〔걱정〕 / *That's a* ~ *off my mind.* 마음의 짐하나 덜었다; 시원하다. **3** a bundle of goods to be carried; a piece of cargo. 짐; 화물. **4** a quantity of goods carried at one time. (한 번의) 적재량; 한 바리. ¶ *sell by the* ~ 한 차〔배, 바리〕 얼마로 팔다 / *three truck loads of vegetables* 트럭 세 차분의 채소. **5** the act of putting powder and bullet in a gun; a charge. (화약 등의) 장전; 장탄. **6**《electr., mech.》 the amount of electric current given by a dynamo. 부하(負荷). **7**《*pl.*》《*colloq.*》 a great amount or number. 많은 양〔수〕.
loads of,《*colloq.*》 a lot of; much; many. (수·양이) 많은. ¶ *She has loads of friends.* 친구들이 무척 많다.
— *vt.* **1** (P6,7,13) fill up (a ship, a cart, etc.) with goods; put (goods) on a ship, cart, etc. …에 짐을 싣다. ¶ ~ *a truck with coal* = ~ *coal in a truck* 트럭에 석탄을 싣다. **2** (P6,7,13) pile or heap heavily; fill. …에 잔뜩 싣다〔채워 넣다〕. ¶ *a table loaded with dishes* 상다리가 휘게 음식을 차린 식탁 / *a tree loaded with fruit* 열매가 주렁주렁 달린 나무 / ~ *one's stomach with food* 잔뜩 먹다. **3** (P6,13) give too much; weigh down, burden, or oppress. …을 너무 주다; …에게 짐을 지우다; 괴롭히다. ¶ *He loaded her with compliments.* 그녀에게 그는 마구 칭찬을 해댔다 / *My heart is loaded with sorrow.* 슬픔으로 가슴이 미어지는 것 같다. **4** (P6) put powder and bullet in (a gun); put film in (a camera). (총)에 장전하다; (카메라)에 필름을 넣다. **5** (P6) add (drugs) to drink. (술)에 약품 따위를 넣다; 섞음질하다. ¶ *This wine has been loaded.* 이 포도주는 섞음질이 되어 있다. — *vi.* **1** (P1,2A) put on a load; take on a load; become loaded. 짐을 싣다; 짐을 지다. ¶ *The schoolbus was loading.* 스쿨버스에 아이들이 타고 있었다. **2** (of a gun) receive its charge. (총이) 장전되다. [E. =way]
get a load of,《*sl.*》 listen to; look at (something or someone). …을 듣다〔보다〕.
have a load on,《*sl.*》 be drunk. 취해 있다.
take a load off *someone's* ***mind,*** set someone's heart at ease; relieve someone of anxiety. 마음의 무거운 짐을 벗다; 시름을 덜(어주)다.

load·star [lóudstɑ̀:r] *n.* =lodestar.

load·stone, lode- [lóudstòun] *n.* **1** ⒸⓊ a kind of stone that attracts iron as a magnet; a natural magnet. 천연 자석. **2**《*fig.*》 Ⓒ something that attracts. 흡인력이 있는 것; 사람을 끄는 것. [*load*]

·loaf[1] [louf] *n.* Ⓒ (*pl.* **loaves**) **1** ⓐ bread shaped as one piece. 빵 덩어리. ¶ *a* ~ *of bread* 빵 한 덩어리 / *loaves and fishes* 일신의 이득; 현세적 이득《돈·관직 따위와 같은》/《*prov.*》 *Half a* ~ *is better than none.* 반이라도 없는 것보다 낫다. ⓑ《*the* ~》 (esp. in reference to the price of bread) bread. (상품으로서의) 빵. ¶ *The* ~ *has risen* 〔*fallen*〕 *in price.* 빵값이 올랐다〔내렸다〕. **2** a mass of sugar shaped like a cone. (원뿔 모양의) 사탕 덩어리. **3**《*sl.*》 one's head or brains. 머

리; 두뇌. ¶ *Use your* ~. 머리를 써라. [E.]

loaf² [louf] *vi.* (P1,2A) 《*about*》 live lazily; walk slowly; loiter. 놀고 지내다; 빈둥거리다. ¶ ~ *through life* 평생을 놀고 지내다 / ~ *about* 빈들거리며 돌아다니다. —*vt.* (P7) 《*away*》 waste (time). (시간)을 낭비하다. ¶ ~ *away one's time.* [E.]

loaf·er [lóufər] *n.* Ⓒ **1** a person who loafs; a lazy or idle person. 게으른 사람; 농땡이. **2** a kind of sport shoe. 로퍼《운동화의 일종》. [*loaf²*]

loam [loum] *n.* Ⓤ a mixture of clay, sand, etc. used for plastering. 롬《회반죽 등에 쓰이는》. [E.]

loam·y [lóumi] *adj.* (**loam·i·er, loam·i·est**) of loam; like loam. 롬의; 롬질(質)의.

:loan [loun] *n.* **1** Ⓒ something lent; a sum of money lent at interest. 대여물; 대부금. ¶ *May I have the* ~ *of your umbrella?* 우산 좀 빌려주겠소 / *government* 〔*public*〕 ~ 국채〔공채〕/ 《*colloq.*》 *a* ~ *shark* 고리 대금 업자. **2** Ⓤ the act of lending. 대여. ¶ *ask someone for the* ~ 아무에게 돈을 꾸어 달래다 / *have the* ~ *of something* …을 빌리다.

on loan, lent. 차입으로; 대부로.

—*vt., vi.* (P6; 1) 《chiefly U.S.》 lend. 빌려주다. ¶ *He loaned me some money.* 내게 돈을 좀 빌려줬다. [E.]

loan collection [∠ ―∠―] *n.* a collection of pictures lent for an exhibition. (전시회 목적의) 차용 미술품.

loan office [∠ ∠―] *n.* **1** an office for lending money to private borrower. 대금(貸金)〔금융〕 사무소. **2** a public office for receiving subscriptions to a government loan. 공채 청약 취급소.

loan word [∠ ∠] *n.* a word adopted into one language from another and naturalized. 외래어; 차용어.

loath [louθ] *adj.* 《only as *predicative*》 《*for*》 unwilling; reluctant. 싫어서. ¶ *She was* ~ *for him to go.* 그녀는 그가 가는 것이 싫었다 / *She was* ~ *to leave her native village.* 그녀는 고향을 떠나기가 싫었다. [E.]

nothing loath, with pleasure; willingly. 기꺼이. ¶ *He did it nothing* ~. 싫기는커녕 아주 기꺼이 그것을 했다.

loathe [louð] *vt.* (P6,9,11) **1** feel extreme dislike for (someone or something); hate; detest. 아주 싫어하다; 혐오하다. ¶ *She loathes him.* 그녀는 그라면 꼴도 보기 싫어한다. **2** 《*colloq.*》 expressing mere dislike. (그저) 좋아하지 않다. ¶ *I* ~ *tea for breakfast.* 조반에 차는 좋아하지 않는다. [E.]

loath·ing [lóuðiŋ] *n.* Ⓤ strong dislike or hatred. 혐오.

loath·some [lóuðsəm] *adj.* hateful; detestable; disgusting. 아주 싫은, 지긋지긋한.

loaves [louvz] *n.* pl. of **loaf¹**.

lob [lab / lɔb] *n.* Ⓒ 《tennis》 a ball hit high in the air. 로브《높고 완만하게 쳐보낸 공》. —*vt.* (**lobbed, lob·bing**) *vt.* (P6,7,13) hit (a ball) high in the air. (공)을 높게 치다; 로브로 치다. —*vi.* (P1,2) move, walk or run along with a heavy, clumsy action. 천천히 힘겹고 어색하게 움직이다〔걷다, 뛰다〕. [E. =hanging lump]

lob·by [lábi / lɔ́bi] *n.* Ⓒ (*pl.* **-bies**) **1** an entrance hall or passage; a waiting room. 현관(의 복도); 넓은 대기〔휴게〕실. ¶ *the* ~ *of a theater* 극장의 휴게〔대기〕실. **2** 《*the L-*》 (of the House of Commons 《Brit.》 or the Senate 《U.S.》) a large hall where members interview visitors. (원내(院內)의) 회견실. **3** 《chiefly U.S.》 a group of persons who try to exercise influence over law-makers. 원외 압력 단체. —*vi., vt.* (**lob·bied**) (P1; 6) 《chiefly U.S.》 try to exercise influence over law-makers. (의원에게) 원외에서 압력을 넣다. [Teut., *cf.* lodge & leaf]

lobe [loub] *n.* Ⓒ **1** the lowest, rounded part of the ear. 귓불. **2** anything like this. 귓불 모양의 것. ¶ *a* ~ *of the lungs* 폐엽(肺葉) / *the* ~ *of a leaf* 엽편(葉片); 엽신(葉身). [Gk.]

lob·ster [lábstər / lɔ́b-] *n.* Ⓒ 《zool.》 a shellfish with two large claws and eight legs, used for food. 바닷가재; 대하(大蝦). [→locust]

:lo·cal [lóukəl] *adj.* **1** of a place or places. 장소의. **2** limited to a particular place. 지방(특유)의. ¶ ~ *news* 지방 소식 / ~ *self-government* 지방 자치 단체 / *a* ~ *custom* 지방 풍속. **3** of a certain part of the body. 국부의; 부분적인. ¶ *a* ~ *disease* 국부적 병증(病症). **4** (of a train) stopping at all stations. 역마다 서는〔정차하는〕. ¶ *a* ~ *train* (역마다 서는) 보통〔완행〕 열차. —*n.* Ⓒ **1** a local train. 구간 열차. **2** news of a certain district. 지방 기사. **3** an inhabitant of a particular district. 특정 지방의 사람; 한 고장의 사람. **4** 《Brit. *colloq.*》 a pub in one's own district. 근처의 술집. [→locus]

lo·cal·ism [lóukəlìzəm] *n.* **1** Ⓒ a pronunciation, usage or custom peculiar to a particular district. 지방 사투리; 지방 관습. **2** Ⓤ affection for a particular district; the attachment to one's native place. 지방주의; 향토 편애; 지방 근성.

lo·cal·i·ty [loukǽləti] *n.* (*pl.* **-ties**) **1** Ⓒ a place; a spot where something occurs. 장소; (사건의) 현장. ¶ *the* ~ *of a crime* 범행 장소. **2** Ⓤ the peculiar condition of a place; being local. 장소의 특유한 성질〔상태〕; (어떤 장소에) 위치함. ¶ *a sense of* ~ 장소〔방향〕 감각. **3** a particular district or neighborhood. 어떤 특정 지방〔장소〕. ¶ *the* ~ *of heavy rain* 호우 지대.

lo·cal·ize [lóukəlàiz] *vt.* (P6) **1** limit (something) to a particular place. …을 한 장소에 국한시키다. ¶ ~ *infection* 〔*a disturbance*〕 전염병〔소란〕을 국지화시키다. **2** make (something) local in character. …을 지방화하다.

3 attach (an army, etc.) to a particular district. (군대 등)을 한 지역에 나누어 배치하다.

lo·cal·ly [lóukəli] *adv.* in a local manner; in a particular place. 지방적으로; 위치상. ¶ *Locally this tree is called by another name.* 이 나무는 이 지방에서 이름이 다르다.

:lo·cate [lóukeit, –⌐] *vt.* (P6,13) **1** find out or show the place of (someone or something). …의 장소를 알아내다. ¶ ~ *the source of a pain* 아픈 데를 찾아내다 / *The police tried to* ~ *the haunt of robbers.* 경찰은 도둑들이 잘 가는 곳을 찾아내려고 했다. **2** establish (a building, etc.) in a particular place. (건물 등)을 어떤 위치에 정하다. ¶ *I located my new store in Chongno.* 나는 가게를 종로에 냈다. **3** 《often used as *reflexive* or *passive*》 take up one's residence in (a place); settle. (어떤 장소)에 정착하다. ¶ *be located in Seoul* 서울에 거처를 정하다. — *vi.* (P3) settle down in a place. 거주하다; 살다. [L. *locus* place]

·lo·ca·tion [loukéiʃən] *n.* **1** Ⓒ a place; a position. 장소; 위치. ¶ *This is a good* ~ *for a camp.* 여기가 천막 치기에 좋은 장소이다. **2** Ⓤ the act of locating; the state of being located. 장소에 두기; 위치 선정. **3** ⓊⒸ a place outside of a film studio where a motion picture is filmed. 야외 촬영지; 로케이션. ¶ *a* ~ *scene* 로케이션 장면.

loc. cit [lák sít / lɔ́k -] =loco citato.

loch [lɑk, lɑx / lɔk, lɔx] *n.* Ⓒ 《Sc.》 **1** a lake. 호수. **2** an arm of the sea. 후미; 내포(內浦). [Gael.]

lo·ci [lóusai] *n.* pl. of **locus.**

lock[1] [lɑk / lɔk] *n.* Ⓒ **1** a curl of hair. (머리의) 타래. **2** 《*pl.*》 hair. 두발. ¶ *golden locks* 금발머리. **3** a tuft of wool, silk, etc. (양모, 생사 등의) 술; 타래. [E.]

:lock[2] [lɑk / lɔk] *n.* Ⓒ **1** an instrument for fastening a door, a window, a lid, etc. by using a key. 자물쇠. ¶ *on* 〔*off*〕 *the* ~ 자물쇠를 채워〔열어〕. **2** a part of a canal enclosed by gates at each end so that boats can move up or down from one level to another. (운하의) 수문; 갑문. **3** the part of a gun by which it is fired. (총포의) 발사 장치(cf. *gunlock*). **4** a device to keep a wheel from turning. 제륜(制輪) 장치.

— *vt.* **1** (P6,7) fasten (a door, etc.) with a lock; shut. …에 자물쇠를 채우다. ¶ ~ *a suitcase* 〔*door*〕 슈트케이스〔문〕에 자물쇠를 채우다. **2** (P7,13) ⓐ keep (someone) shut in; confine; imprison. …을 가두다; 구류하다. ¶ ~ *someone* (*up*) *in a room* (밖에서 문을 걸어) 아무를 방에 가두다 / ~ *up a prisoner* 죄수를 감방에 넣다. ⓑ keep firmly fixed in the mind. …을 마음에 깊이 간직하다. ¶ *secrets safely locked in one's breast* 마음속 깊이 간직한 비밀. **3** (P6,7) hold (something) fast; embrace tightly; link; intertwine. …을 움직이지 못하게 잡다; 껴안다; 얽어 짜다. ¶ ~ *a child in one's arms* 아이를 껴안다 / ~ *arms* 〔*fingers*〕 *together* 팔짱을 끼다〔깍지끼다〕 / ~ *one's jaws tightly* 이를 악물다 / *The ship was locked in ice.* 배가 얼음에 갇혔다. — *vi.* (P1) **1** become locked. 자물쇠가 잠기다. ¶ *This door doesn't* ~. 이 문은 잠기지 않는다. **2** become fastened or fixed. 고착되다; 고정되다. [E.]

lock away, store (something) in a locked box, etc. 자물쇠를 채워 …을 저장해 두다.

lock in, keep (someone) in a room etc. by locking the door outside. (아무)를 감금하다. ¶ ~ *someone in the house* 밖에서 문을 잠그고 아무를 집에 가둬놓다.

lock out, shut (something) out by locking the door, etc. …을 못 들어오게 하다; 폐쇄하다.

lock stock and barrel, 《*colloq.*》 completely; entirely. 완전히; 이것저것 모두.

lock up, **a**) imprison (someone) for a crime. 감금〔수감〕하다. **b**) fasten the doors of (a building, etc.) by locking them. (건물의) 출입문을 자물쇠로 잠그다; 문단속을 하다. ¶ ~ *up for the night* 밤에 문단속을 하다.

under lock and key, in a safe place; locked up. 안전한 곳에; 자물쇠를 채워.

lock·er [lákər / lɔ́k-] *n.* Ⓒ **1** a person who locks. 자물쇠 채우는 사람. **2** a cupboard or chest that can be locked. 로커《채우게 된 (찬)장》. **3** a chest; a compartment in a ship's cabin used to keep clothes, ammunition, etc. (선원 각자의 옷 따위를 넣는) 장; 함. ¶ *a shot* ~ 탄약고. **4** a box with a lock for holding private property used by individuals in a public building such as gymnasium. (체육관 등의) 사물함(私物函). [*lock*[2]]

lock·et [lákit / lɔ́kit] *n.* Ⓒ a small case for holding a lock of hair or a picture, usu. worn on a necklace. 로켓. [*lock*[2]]

〈locket〉

lock·jaw [lákdʒɔ̀ː / lɔ́k-] *n.* 《med.》 tetanus. 아관 강직(牙關強直)《파상풍의 일종》. [↑]

lock·out [lákàut / lɔ́k-] *n.* Ⓒ the act of an employer's shutting down a business until the workers accept terms. 공장 폐쇄.

lock·smith [láksmìθ / lɔ́k-] *n.* Ⓒ a person who makes or repairs locks and keys. 자물쇠공(工).

lock·up [lákʌ̀p / lɔ́k-] *n.* Ⓒ **1** the act of locking up; the state of being locked up; a jail. 감금; 유치; 교도소. **2** the time for locking up a store, etc. (점포 등의) 폐문 시간. — *adj.* that can be locked up. 자물쇠가 걸리는〔걸려 있는〕. ¶ *a* ~ *stable* 자물쇠를 건 마구간.

lo·co ci·ta·to [lóukou sitéitou, -sai-]

adv. 《L.》 in the passage already quoted. 위의 인용문 중에서.

lo·co·mo·tion [lòukəmóuʃən] *n.* Ⓤ **1** the act of moving; the ability to move from place to place. 운동; 이동; 운동력. ¶ *the capacity for* 〔*the power of*〕 ~ 보행〔운동〕 능력. **2** means of traveling. 교통 수단〔기관〕. [L. *locus* place, →move]

lo·co·mo·tive [lòukəmóutiv] *n.* Ⓒ a railroad engine that pulls trains. 기관차. ¶ *a steam* ~ 증기 기관차. — *adj.* of locomotion; moving from place to place; movable. 이동의; 이동할 수 있는. ¶ ~ *faculty* 〔*power*〕 이동〔이행〕력 / ~ *organs* 다리.

lo·cum (te·nens) [lóukəm (tí:nenz), -(téninz)] *n.* a substitute physician or clergyman. 대진의(代診醫); 대리 목사. [L. =holding the place]

lo·cus [lóukəs] *n.* Ⓒ (*pl.* **lo·ci**) **1** a position or point, esp. where something happened or found. (사건 등의) 발생 장소; 현장. **2** 《math.》 a curve, surface, or other figure which satisfies a given condition. 궤적(軌跡); 자취. [L. =place]

lo·cust [lóukəst] *n.* Ⓒ **1** a kind of grasshopper which feeds on crops and destroys them. 메뚜기. **2** 《U.S.》 a cicada. 매미. **3** 《*fig.*》 a person of greedy, destructive tendencies. 탐욕스럽고 파괴적인 사람. [L. *locusta*]

lo·cu·tion [loukjú:ʃən] *n.* **1** Ⓤ a style of speech. 말씨, 말투. **2** Ⓒ an idiom. 관용구; 관용어법. [L. *loquor* speak]

lode [loud] *n.* Ⓒ a vein of metal in a rock. 광맥. ¶ *This* ~ *of copper runs for miles.* 이 구리 광맥은 수 마일에 뻗쳐 있다. [→load]

lode·star, load- [lóudstà:r] *n.* Ⓒ **1** a star that shows the way; the North Star. 길잡이가 되는 별《특히 북극성》. **2** 《*fig.*》 a guiding principle. 지도 원리.

lode·stone [lóudstòun] *n.* =loadstone.

:lodge [lɑdʒ / lɔdʒ] *n.* Ⓒ **1** a small house, esp. for hunters, mountaineers, etc.; a hut; a cabin. 오두막; 산막. ¶ *a hunting* ~ 사냥막. **2** a small house used by the gatekeepers or other servants of a great house. 수위실; 경비실. **3** a branch of a certain secret societies; its meeting place; the meeting itself. (비밀 결사의) 지부; 그 집회(소).

— *vi.* **1** (P1,2A,2B) live in a certain place for a time; live in another's house as a paying guest. 하숙〔투숙〕하다. ¶ ~ *at a hotel* 호텔에 투숙하다 / ~ *in a home* 〔*with a family*〕 어떤 집〔가정〕에 하숙하다. **2** (P1,3) come to be placed and fixed firmly. 박히다; 꽂히다. ¶ *The bullet lodged in his arm.* 탄알은 그의 팔에 박혔다 / *The snow lodged on the wall.* 눈이 벽에 붙었다 / *The kite lodged in the branches of a tree.* 연이 나뭇가지에 걸렸다.

— *vt.* **1** (P6) provide (someone) with a house or room to live in for a time; take (someone) into one's house as a paying guest. …을 투숙시키다; 하숙시키다. ¶ *Can you* ~ *us for the night.* 하룻밤 묵을 수 있겠습니까 / *I can* ~ *you for a day or two.* 하루 이틀 우리 집에 머무를 수 있습니다. **2** (P6,13) put (something) into a certain place or position by shooting. (총알 등)을 쏘아 박다. ¶ ~ *a bullet in the wall* 벽에다 총탄을 쏘아박다 / ~ *a blow* 한 방 안기다 / *The hunter lodged an arrow in the tiger's head.* 사냥꾼은 호랑이 머리에 화살을 쏘아 박았다. **3** (P6,13) put or bring (an accusation, a complaint, etc.) before a court or other authority. (법정 등)에 제소하다; (불평 등)을 제기하다. ¶ ~ *a charge* 〔*an accusation*〕 *against someone* 아무를 고발하다 / ~ *a complaint with the police* 경찰에 불평을 제기하다. **4** (P6,13) 《*in, with*》 confer; deposit. …을 맡기다; 일임하다. ¶ ~ *power in* 〔*with, in the hands of*〕 *someone* 아무에게 권력을 맡기다. [→lobby]

lodge·ment [lɑ́dʒmənt / lɔ́dʒ-] *n.* 《Brit.》 =lodgment.

lodg·er [lɑ́dʒər / lɔ́dʒər] *n.* Ⓒ a person living in a rented room; a roomer. 하숙인. ¶ *take in a* ~ 하숙인을 두다.

·lodg·ing [lɑ́dʒiŋ / lɔ́dʒ-] *n.* **1** Ⓒ a place to sleep or live in temporarily. (임시) 숙소. ¶ ~ *for the night* 하룻밤의 숙소. **2** Ⓤ the act of putting someone up in a room for rent. 하숙치기. **3** 《*pl.*》 a room or rooms for rent in a private house. 셋방; 하숙방. ¶ *board and* ~ 식사를 주는 하숙 / *dry* ~ 식사 없는 하숙 / *live in* 〔*look for*〕 ~ 셋방에〔을〕 살다〔을 찾다〕.

lodging house [∠– ∸] *n.* a house which has rooms for rent. 하숙집.

lodg·ment, 《Brit.》 **lodge-** [lɑ́dʒmənt / lɔ́dʒ-] *n.* **1** Ⓤ the act of lodging; the state of being lodged. 숙박; 하숙. **2** Ⓒ something accumulated or deposited. 퇴적〔침전〕물. ¶ *a* ~ *of earth* 토양 퇴적물. **3** Ⓒ ⓐ a foothold gained in a certain place. 발판. ⓑ 《mil.》 a position gained from an enemy. 점령지; 거점.

effect* 〔*make*〕 *a lodgment, gain a foothold. 발판을 마련하다; …에 거점을 구축하다.

lo·ess [lóues, les, lʌs] *n.* Ⓤ a yellowish-brown clay or loam, usu. formed by the wind. 뢰스; 풍적 황토. 參考 중국 북부, 라인강 유역 등지에 있음. [G.]

loft [lɔ:ft / lɔft] *n.* Ⓒ **1** a room directly under the roof of a house; an attic. 고미다락. **2** 《U.S.》 an upper floor of a warehouse, a business building, etc. (창고·상업 빌딩 등의) 맨 위층. **3** 《golf》 the act of hitting a ball high in the air. 공을 올려치기. **4** a house for pigeons. 비둘기집. **5** a gallery in a church or hall. (교회·강당의) 위층. — *vt.* (P6) **1** ⓐ keep (something) in an attic. …을 고미다락에 저장하다. ⓑ

place or keep (pigeons) in a loft. (비둘기를)기르다. **2** 《golf》 hit (a ball) high in the air. 공을 높이 쳐올리다. [N. =sky]

loft·i·ly [lɔ́:ftili / lɔ́ft-] *adv.* in a lofty manner; highly grandly; haughtily. 높게; 웅대하게; 오만하게. ¶ *When I asked for help, he just smiled ~ and turned away.* 도움을 청했더니 그는 그저 거만하게 웃고는 돌아섰다.

loft·i·ness [lɔ́:ftinis / lɔ́ft-] *n.* Ⓤ the state of being lofty; height; grandness, haughtiness. 높음; 고상; 웅대; 오만.

·**loft·y** [lɔ́:fti / lɔ́fti] *adj.* (**loft·i·er, loft·i·est**) **1** (of a hill, a tower, etc.) very high. (산·탑 등이) 아주 높은. ¶ *a ~ mountain* 〔*tree, room*〕. **2** (of principles, aims, style, thought, etc.) nobel; dignified; grand. (주의, 목적, 생각 등이) 고상한; 품위 있는; 웅대한. ¶ *~ language* 〔*style*〕 고상한 말씨〔문체〕 / *the high and ~ aim* 높고 웅대한 목표. **3** (of manners) haughty; proud. (태도가) 오만한. ¶ *in a ~ manner* 오만한 태도로.

:**log** [lɔ(:)g, lɑg] *n.* Ⓒ **1** a round piece of a tree, usu. in its natural state. 통나무. ¶ *a ~ bridge* 통나무 다리 / *Roll my ~, and I'll roll yours.* 나를 도와주면 나도 너를 돕겠다. **2** an instrument for measuring the speed of a ship. (선박 속도를 재는) 측정기(測定器). ¶ *heave* 〔*throw*〕 *the ~* 항해 속도를 재다. **3** a diary about a ship's voyage. 항해 일지. 參考 logbook 라고도 함.

be as easy as rolling off a log, 《U.S.》 be very easy. 아주 쉽다, 식은죽 먹기다.

in the log, rough; not cut. 통나무 그대로.

like a log, quite still; unconscious. 꿈쩍도 않는; 인사불성의. ¶ *sleep like a ~* 정신 없이 자다.

roll logs for (=*endeavor to help*) *someone.* …을 위해 애쓰다.

— *vt.* (**logged, log·ging**) (P6) **1** cut (a tree) into logs. (나무)를 통나무로 자르다. **2** cut down trees on (land). (땅에서) 나무를 벌채하다. **3** enter (something) in a ship's record book. …을 항해 일지에 기입하다. **4** (of ships) cover (so many knots, so much distance) in a day's run. 배가 하루에(몇 노트) 달리다. [E.]

log. logarithm.

log·a·rithm [lɔ́:gəriðəm, lɑ́g- / lɔ́g-] *n.* Ⓒ 《math.》 a figure showing how many times a number called 'the base' must be multiplied by itself to produce a given number. 대수; 로그. [Gk. *logas* reckoning, *arithmos* number]

log·book [lɔ́:gbùk, lɑ́g- / lɔ́g-] *n.* Ⓒ a book in which the events of a ship's voyage are written down every day. 항해 일지. [*log*]

log·ger·head [lɔ́:gərhèd, lɑ́g- / lɔ́gər-] *n.* Ⓒ **1** 《*arch.*》 a stupid person; a blockhead. 멍텅구리; 바보. **2** 《zool.》 a kind of sea turtle chiefly living in the tropical Atlantic. (대서양의) 붉은거북. [*log, head*]

be at loggerheads with, quarrel with. …와 다투다.

log·gia [lɑ́dʒə, lóudʒiə / lɔ́dʒ-] *n.* Ⓒ (*pl.* **-gi·as** or **-gie**) 《It.》 a roofed, with open-sided, gallery or arcade projecting from the side of a building. 로지아《한쪽은 벽이 없는 회랑》. 參考 이탈리아 특유의 건축인데 여름철에 거실로 쓰임.

log·gie [lɑ́dʒe, lóu- / lɔ́-] *n.* pl. of **loggia.**

log·ging [lɔ́:giŋ, lɑ́g- / lɔ́g-] *n.* Ⓤ the work of cutting down trees, making them into logs, and moving them from the forest. 벌목; 또, 그 반출(搬出). [*log*]

·**log·ic** [lɑ́dʒik / lɔ́dʒ-] *n.* Ⓤ **1** the science of reasoning. 논리학. ¶ *deductive* 〔*inductive*〕 *~* 연역〔귀납〕 논리학. **2** a book on logic. 논리학 서적. **3** sound and clear thinking or reasoning; a mode of reasoning. (정확하고도 명석한) 사고; 논리; 논법. ¶ *His ~ is unsound.* 그의 논법은 타당하지가 않다 / *That is no ~.* 그건 조리에 닿지 않는다. **4** a natural and necessary chain of causes and effects. 어쩔 수 없는 필연적인 힘〔결과〕. ¶ *the ~ of fate* 〔*events*〕 운명〔사건〕이라는 거역하지 못할 힘. [→logos]

·**log·i·cal** [lɑ́dʒikəl / lɔ́dʒ-] *adj.* **1** logic; according to the rules of logic. 논리학(상)의. **2** reasonable; reasoning correctly. 조리가 닿는. ¶ *a ~ argument* 논리적인 의론. **3** necessary as the result of what has gone before. 논리상 필연의. ¶ *the ~ result of one's act* 자기가 한 일의 당연한 결과.

log·i·cal·ly [lɑ́dʒikəli / lɔ́dʒ-] *adv.* in a logical manner. 논리상; 논리적으로.

lo·gi·cian [loudʒíʃən] *n.* Ⓒ a person who is skilled in logic. 논리가; 논리학자.

log·os [lóugɑs / lɔ́gɔs] *n.* **1** 《theol.》 the Word. (하느님의) 말씀. **2** Christ. 예수. **3** 《L-》 reason. 이성. [Gk. =word, reason].

loin [lɔin] *n.* **1** 《*pl.*》 the part of the back between the hipbones and the lowest rib. 허리. **2** Ⓤ a piece of meat from this part of an animal. (짐승의) 허리고기; 로인. ¶ *a ~ of mutton* 양의 허리고기. [L. *lumbus*]

gird up one's loins, prepare for journey; make ready for action. (여행)채비를 갖추다; 태세〔자세〕를 취하다.

be sprung from someone's loins, be begotten by someone. 아무의 자식으로 태어나다.

loi·ter [lɔ́itər] *vi., vt.* (P1,2A; 7) 《*away*》 waste time in moving from place to place; pass (time) idly; linger. 어정거리다; 빈둥거리다; 허송 세월 하다. ¶ *~ on the way to school* 지정거리며 학교에 가다 / *He loitered away his time.* 그는 하는 일없이 시간을 보냈다. [Du.]

loi·ter·er [lɔ́itərər] *n.* Ⓒ a person who loiters. 어정거리는 사람; 빈둥빈둥 노는 사람.

loll [lɑl / lɔl] *vi.* **1** (P2A,3) sit or lie in a lazy manner; lean lazily. 축 늘어져 앉다〔기대다〕. ¶ *~ in a chair* 의자에 기대 앉다 / *~ against a wall* 맥없이 벽에 기대다. **2** (P1,2A) (of the tongue, etc.) hang out loosely. (혀 따위가) 축 늘어지다. — *vt.* (P7) allow (the tongue) to hang out loosely. (혀)를 축 늘어뜨리다. ¶ *The hound lolled out his tired tongue.* 그 사냥개는 맥없이 혀를 축 늘어뜨렸다. [Du. *lollen*]

lol·li·pop, lolly- [lálipàp / lɔ́lipɔ̀p] *n.* Ⓒ a kind of hard candy on the end of a small stick. 롤리폽《막대기 끝에 붙인 사탕》. [Dial. *lolly* tongue, *pop*]

lol·ly [láli / lɔ́li] *n.* **1** 《*colloq.*》 =lollypop. **2** 《*sl.*》 money. 돈.

:Lon·don [lʌ́ndən] *n.* the capital of England. 런던.

Lon·don·er [lʌ́ndənər] *n.* Ⓒ a person of London. 런던 사람.

·lone [loun] *adj.* 《used as *attributive*》 alone; lonely; solitary. 혼자의; 쓸쓸한; 외진. ¶ *a ~ house* 외딴 집 / *a ~ traveler* 외로운 나그네. [*alone*]

lone·li·ness [lóunlinis] *n.* Ⓤ the state of being or feeling lonely. 고독; 쓸쓸함.

:lone·ly [lóunli] *adj.* (**-li·er, -li·est**) feeling alone; without companions; solitary. 고독한; 쓸쓸한; 외진. ¶ *feel ~* 쓸쓸하다 / *a ~ road* 인적이 드문 길 / *a ~ house* 외딴 집 / *The friendless boy was ~.* 벗이 없는 그 소년은 고독했다.

·lone·some [lóunsəm] *adj.* feeling lonely; solitary. 고독한; 외딴. ¶ *feel ~* 고독하다 / *a ~ place* 외딴 곳. [*alone*]

:long [lɔːŋ / lɔŋ] *adj.* **1** great in distance or time from end to end. (시간·거리가) 긴 (opp. short). ¶ *a ~ distance* 장거리 / *~ hair* 긴 머리; 장발 / *a ~ war* 오랜 전쟁; 장기전 / *have a ~ wait* 오래 기다리다 / *a ~ spell of rainy weather* 장마 / *a ~ farewell* 긴 이별 / 《*fig.*》 *one's ~ home* 무덤. **2** far-reaching; extending to a great distance. 멀리까지 미치는. ¶ *a ~ memory* (오래 가는) 좋은 기억력. **3** of greater than usual or standard length. 좀 긴; 표준보다 긴. **4** slow; tedious. 느린; 지루한. ¶ *a ~, boring speech* 길고 지루한 연설. **5** having a specific extension in time or space; in length. (시간·거리가) …한 길이의; …길이의. ¶ *thirty feet ~* 30 피트 길이의 / *six hours ~* 여섯 시간 동안의. **6** (of a series, list, etc.) containing many items. 항목이 많은; 다수의. ¶ *a ~ bill* 외상이 많은 계산서 / *a ~ family* (아이가 많은) 대가족. **7** tall. 키가 큰. ¶ *a ~ tree* 키 큰 나무 / *a ~ man* 키다리.

at the longest, to mention the most distant date possible. 아무리 오래 걸려도; 늦어도; 기껏 길어봤자.

be long (*in*) *doing,* take a long time in doing. …하는 데 시간이 걸리다.

have a long arm, can make one's power felt over a wide area. 힘〔세력〕이 널리 미치다.

have a long face, look cheerless or sad. 표정이 침울하다; 시무룩한 표정이다.

have a long head, be clever and sensible. 영리하다; 민감하다.

have long sight, **a**) be able to see distant but not near object cleary. 원시(遠視)다. **b**) 《*fig.*》 be able to foresee things. 선견지명이 있다.

have a long tongue, talk too much. 수다스럽다.

make a long arm, stretch out one's arm as far as possible. 팔을 한껏 뻗다.

— *adv.* **1** for a long time. 오랫동안. ¶ *I have ~ been intending to do it.* 그 일을 하려고 오래 별러왔다. **2** throughout a certain period of time. …부터; 쭉; 내내. ¶ *He lay awake all night ~.* 밤 내내 자지 않고 있었다. **3** far distant from a certain point in time. 오래 전에; 오랜 후에. ¶ *~ before you were born* 네가 태어나기 오래 전에 / *~ after his death* 그가 죽고 오래 지나서.

no longer =***not any longer,*** not now or from now on as in the past. 이젠 …아니다. ¶ *I am sorry I can wait no ~.* 더 기다리지 못해 미안하다.

So long! 《*colloq.*》 Good-by! 안녕 (또 만나).

so 〔***as***〕 ***long as,*** on condition that …; provided that … 혹시 …하다면; …하는 한.

— *n.* Ⓤ **1** a long time. 오랫동안. ¶ *before ~* 머지 않아 / *for ~* 오랫동안 / *It will not take ~.* 오래 걸리지 않을 게다. **2** 《*the ~*》 《Brit. *sl.*》 the long vacation. 여름 휴가.

the long and the short of it, the summary of anything; the gist of it. 결국은; 요컨대.

— *vi.* (P3,4) 《*for*》 wish very much; have a strong desire. 열망하다. ¶ *He longed to see her.* 그녀가 몹시 보고 싶었다. [E.]

long-dis·tance [lɔ́ːŋdístəns / lɔ́ŋ-] *adj.* **1** 《U.S.》 located a long way away. 장거리의. ¶ *a ~ telephone call* 장거리 전화 / *a ~ flight* 장거리 비행. **2** (of weather forecast) made several days in advance. 장기 일기 예보의. — *n.* an operator or exchange that takes care of long-distance calls. 장거리 전화 교환수〔국〕.

long-drawn [lɔ́ːŋdrɔ́ːn / lɔ́ŋ-] *adj.* lasting for a long time; prolonged. 오래 끈; 연기된.

long-eared [lɔ́ːŋíərd / lɔ́ŋ-] *adj.* **1** having long ears. 귀가 긴; 긴 귀를 한. **2** stupid like an ass. (나귀처럼) 멍청한.

lon·gev·i·ty [landʒévəti / lɔn-] *n.* Ⓤ long life. 장수. [L. **longus** long, **aevum** age]

long·hand [lɔ́ːŋhæ̀nd / lɔ́ŋ-] *n.* Ⓤ the usual kind of writing. (속기에 대한) 보통의 쓰기〔서체〕(opp. shorthand). [*long*]

long-head·ed [lɔ́ːŋhédid / lɔ́ŋ-] *adj.* **1** having a long head. 장두(長頭)의. **2** 《*fig.*》 clever; foresighted. 머리가 좋은; 선견지명이 있는.

·long·ing [lɔ́(ː)ŋiŋ, láŋ-] *n.* ⒸⓊ 《*for*》 an earnest desire. 동경; 열망. ¶ *a ~ for home.* — *adj.* having or showing strong desire. 동경〔열망〕하는.

lon·gi·tude [lándʒətjùːd / lɔ́n-] *n.* Ⓤ **1** the distance east or west, measured in degrees, from a line running from the

North to the South Pole through Greenwich near London. 경도(經度). 參考 long.으로 생략되며, 위도는 latitude. ¶ *The ~ of New York is 74 degrees west of Greenwich.* 뉴욕의 경도는 그리니치 서경 74도이다. **2** 《*joc.*》 length. 길이. [L. *longus* long]

lon·gi·tu·di·nal [lɑ̀ndʒətjúːdinəl / lɔ̀n-] *adj.* **1** of longitude. 경도의. **2** of or in length. 길이의. **3** running lengthwise. 세로의. [↑]

long-lived [lɔ́ːŋláivd, -lívd / lɔ́ŋ-] *adj.* **1** living long; old. 장수의. ¶ *a ~ family* 장수하는 집안. **2** lasting. 영속하는; 오래가는. ¶ *~ happiness* 영원한 행복. [*long*]

long·shore·man [lɔ́ːŋʃɔ̀ːrmən / lɔ́ŋ-] *n.* Ⓒ (*pl.* **-men** [-mən]) **1** a man whose work is to load or unload ship. 항만[부두] 노동자. **2** a shore fisherman. 연안 어부.

long-sight·ed [lɔ́ːŋsáitid / lɔ́ŋ-] *adj.* **1** able to see farther than a normal person; far-sighted. 먼 데를 잘 보는; 원시(遠視)의. **2** 《*fig.*》 foreseeing; wise; sagacious. 선견지명이 있는; 현명한; 빈틈없는.

long·stand·ing [lɔ́ːŋstǽndiŋ / lɔ́ŋ-] *adj.* having lasted for a long time. 오래 계속되는; 오랜. ¶ *a ~ conflict* 장기간의 대립.

long-suf·fer·ing [lɔ́ːŋsʌ́fəriŋ / lɔ́ŋ-] *adj.* enduring hardships patiently for a long time. 참을성이 많은; 인내심이 강한. — *n.* Ⓤ patient endurance of hardships. 참을성이 많음.

long·ways [lɔ́ːŋwèiz / lɔ́ŋ-] *adv.* in the direction of the length; along the length; lengthwise. 세로로; 길이로.

long-wind·ed [lɔ́ːŋwíndid / lɔ́ŋ-] *adj.* **1** able to exist for a long time without breathing. 숨[호흡]이 긴; 숨차지 않은. **2** (of a speech, writing, etc.) tiresome; writing or talking tediously. 장황한; 장광설의. ¶ *a ~ speaker.*

long·wise [lɔ́ːŋwàiz / lɔ́ŋ-] *adv.* =longways; lengthwise.

loo [luː] *n.* 《*colloq.*》 a lavatory. 변소. [?]

:look [luk] *vi.* **1** (P1,2A,3) 《*at*》 try to see; direct one's eyes. 보다; 주시하다. ¶ *I looked, but saw nothing.* 보려고 했으나 아무것도 보이지 않았다 / *Look up at the bright stars in the sky.* 하늘의 저 빛나는 별들을 봐라 / *Look this way.* 이쪽을 봐라. **2** 《*(to it) that...*》 (P1,3) be careful; pay attention. 주의[조심]하다. ¶ *Look (to it) that nothing worse happens.* 더 나쁜 일이 일어나지 않도록 유의해라. **3** (P2A,2B,5) ⓐ appear; seem. …하게 보이다; …같다. ¶ *You ~ pale.* 창백해 보인다 / *She never looks her age.* 그녀는 도무지 그런 나이로 보이지 않는다. ⓑ 《*like*》 seem to be; resemble; have the appearance of. …인 것처럼 보이다[생각되다]; …될 것 같다. ¶ *~ like a fool* 바보처럼 보이다 / *It looks like rain.* 비가 올 모양이다. **4** (P2A,3) face. …에 면하다; …쪽을 향하고 있다. ¶ *Our house looks upon a garden [on the road, toward the south].* 우리 집은 정원[길, 남쪽]을 향해 있다 / *My windows ~ out on a garden.* 내 방 문은 정원을 향해 있다. **5** (P3) examine; search. 조사하다; 찾다. ¶ *I have looked everywhere.* 나는 구석구석을 찾아봤다. — *vt.* **1** (P7,13) direct one's eyes on (someone). …을 보다; 주시하다. ¶ *~ him in the face* 그의 얼굴을 정면으로 보다 / *~ someone up and down* 아무를 아래위로 훑어보다. **2** (P12) try to find; seek; search. …을 알아내다; 확인하다. ¶ *Look where you are.* 네가 어디 있는지 알아봐라 / *Look how it rains.* 비가 어느 정도 오느냐. **3** (P6) express (one's mind) by one's looks or appearance. …을 눈으로 나타내다. ¶ *She looked her thanks.* 그녀는 눈으로 감사의 뜻을 나타냈다 / *He looked his despair.* 절망한 표정이었다. **4** (P13) influence by looks. 주시함으로써 …하게 하다. ¶ *~ someone into silence* 아무를 노려보아 입을 다물게 하다.

look about, **a**) glance around; 《*for*》 search about for (something). …을 둘러보다; 둘러보아 찾다. **b**) take care; be on one's guard. 주의하다; 경계하다. **c**) 《*about one*》 study one's surroundings; examine the state of affairs. 주변 상황을 판단[생각]하다. ¶ *I went out to ~ about me.* 내게 무슨 일인가 해서 나가 보았다.

look after, **a**) follow (a departing person or thing) with the eye. …을 눈으로 지켜보다. **b**) take care of; attend to. …을 보살피다. ¶ *~ after a baby* 아기를 보살피다.

look alive, 《*colloq.*》 《usu. as *imperative*》 hurry up; be alert. 서두르다; 조심하다. ¶ *Look alive (there)!* 빨리 빨리 해라.

look at, **a**) observe (something) with attention; pay attention to (something). …을 주시하다. ¶ *Look at that dog.* 저 개를 지켜봐라. **b**) examine. …을 조사하다. ¶ *The doctor looked at my tongue.* 의사가 내 혀를 살폈다.

look away, turn one's face aside. 외면하다.

look back, **a**) 《*on, upon, in, into*》 recall; recollect. …을 회상하다. **b**) 《with *never*》 make progress. 전진하다. ¶ *Since then the industry has never looked back.* 그 이후 산업은 계속 발전했다.

look down on [*upon*] (*=feel superior to*) *someone.* …을 얕보다. ¶ *He looked down upon me as a coward.* 그는 나를 비겁하다고 깔봤다.

look for, **a**) try to find; search for. …을 찾다. ¶ *~ for lost cat.* **b**) expect. …을 기대하다. ¶ *I don't ~ for much profit from the business.* 그 장사에 큰 이문은 바라지 않는다.

look forward to, wait for with pleasure. …을 즐거운 마음으로 기다리다. ¶ *They are looking forward to seeing you.* 그들은 너와 만나길 기쁜 마음으로 기다리고 있다.

look in (on), pay a short visit, usu. without making an appointment. (예고 없이) 잠깐 들르다. ¶ *The doctor looked in on me yesterday.* 의사 선생님이 어제 잠깐 내 집에 들르

셨다.
look into, make an inquiry into; examine. …을 조사하다. ¶ ~ *into the past history* 지나간 역사를 살피다 / ~ *into a matter* 어떤 문제를 조사하다.
look on 〔***upon***〕, **a**) 《*as*》 regard; consider. …이라고 간주하다. ¶ ~ *on a thing as useless* …을 무익하다고 보다. **b**) stand aside and watch; look at. …을 방관하다; 구경하다. **c**) face to. …에 면하다〔향해 있다〕.
look out, **a**) look to the outside, as through a window. (창 따위를 통해서) 내다보다. ¶ *Look out and see if it is raining.* 비가 오고 있는지 좀 내다보아라. **b**) take care; be on guard. 주의하다. ¶ *Look out!* 조심해라.
look out for, **a**) take care of; be on the guard against. …을 조심〔경계〕하다. ¶ ~ *out for a danger* 위험을 경계하다. **b**) be careful about; be concerned about. …을 소중히 하다; 염려하다. ¶ ~ *out for one's health* 건강에 유의하다.
look over, **a**) examine; inspect. …을 조사하다. **b**) overlook. …을 봐주다; 눈감아 주다. ¶ ~ *over a fault.*
look through, **a**) see through (a hole, etc.). …을 통해서 보다. **b**) see or understand perfectly; be visible through. …을 꿰뚫어보다; …을 통해 보이다. ¶ ~ *through a trick* 계략을 간파하다 / *His greed looks through his eyes.* 눈을 보니 탐욕스럽게 생겼다. **c**) read (a book, etc.) through; examine. …을 쭉 훑어보다; 조사하다.
look to, **a**) be careful of; take care of. …을 조심하다. **b**) rely on (someone) for help, advice, etc. …에 의지하다. **c**) face to. …을 향해 있다. **d**) expect. …을 기대하다. ¶ *I* ~ *to you to put everything right.* 네가 모든 것을 정상화시켰으면 한다.
look up, **a**) search for (the meaning of a word, etc.) in a dictionary, etc. …을 (사전 등에서) 찾다. ¶ ~ *up the number in the telephone book* 전화 번호부에서 번호를 찾다. **b**) 《*colloq.*》 pay a visit to (someone). …을 방문하다. ¶ *Look me up when you are in town.* 시내에 나오거든 날 찾아다오. **c**) 《*colloq.*》 become better; improve. 좋아지다; 호전되다. ¶ *Business is looking up.* 사업이 잘 되어 가고 있다. **d**) raise one's eyes. …을 쳐다보다.
look up to, regard (someone) with great respect; admire. …을 존경하다. ¶ *All her pupils* ~ *up to her.* 그녀 반의 학생 모두가 그녀를 존경한다.
— *n.* Ⓒ **1** an act of looking; a glance. 봄; 얼핏 봄. ¶ *have* 〔*get, take, give*〕 *a* ~ *at someone* 아무를 보다〔얼핏 보다〕 / *steal* 〔*cast, shoot*〕 *a* ~ *at someone* 아무를 훔쳐 보다〔흘낏 보다〕 / *He threw me an angry* ~. 성이 나서 나를 째려봤다. **2** 《often *pl.*》 personal appearance, esp. of a pleasing nature. 용모; 생김새; 미모. ¶ *good looks* 미모 / *She has looks and youth.* 그녀는 미모에다 젊음을 간직하고 있다. **3** appearance; aspect; the expression of the eyes or the face. 양상; 외관; 얼굴 표정. ¶ *the* ~ *of the sky* 하늘 모양; 날씨 / *an ugly* ~ *in the eye* 성난 표정 / *He put on a serious* ~. 그는 심각한 얼굴을 했다 / *Affairs took on an ugly* ~. 일이 험악한 양상을 보였다. [E.]

look·er-on [lúkərán / lúkərɔ́n] *n.* Ⓒ (*pl.* **look·ers-**) a person who watches a game, etc. without joining in; an onlooker. 구경꾼; 방관자. ¶ 《*prov.*》 *The lookers-on see most of the game.* 구경꾼이 더 잘 본다. [↑]

look-in [lúkìn] *n.* Ⓒ **1** a glance; a short visit. 일별; 잠깐 들름. **2** 《*colloq.*》 a chance of success. 승산. ¶ *Our team will have a* ~. 우리 팀이 이길 것 같다.

look·ing [lúkiŋ] *adj.* having a certain appearance. …처럼 보이는. 參考 형용사에 붙어 합성어를 만듦. ¶ *angry-looking* 성난 표정의 / *a good-looking girl* 잘생긴 여자.

look·ing-glass [lúkiŋglæ̀s / -glɑ̀ːs] *n.* Ⓒ a mirror. 거울.

look·out [lúkàut] *n.* Ⓒ **1** a careful, sharp watch. 망보기; 감시; 경계. **2** a person who keeps a careful watch. 망보는 사람; 감시인. **3** a place from which to watch. 망보는 데; 망루. **4** 《chiefly Brit.》 ⓐ view. 전망; 경치. ¶ *a beautiful* ~ *over the valley* 계곡 저쪽의 아름다운 경치. ⓑ 《*fig.*》 prospects for the future. 전도(前途). ¶ *It is a bad* ~ *for me.* 앞 일이 걱정이다. **5** 《*colloq.*》 business. 일; 용무. ¶ *That's my* ~. 그건 내 일이다. [E.]
be on the lookout for, watch for (something) carefully. …을 경계하다.
keep a sharp 〔***good***〕 ***lookout for,*** keep a careful watch for (something). …에 주의를 게을리 않다.

***loom**[1] [luːm] *n.* Ⓒ a machine for making cloth. 베틀; 직기(織機). [E.]

loom[2] [luːm] *vi.* (P2A) **1** appear dimly and in a larger form than in reality. 어렴풋이 크게 보이다. ¶ ~ *through the mist* 안개 속으로 어렴풋이 보이다. **2** 《*fig.*》 (of a nonmaterial thing) appear and seem to threaten. (위협하듯이) 모습을 나타내다. ¶ *dangers and anxieties looming ahead* 전도에 닥쳐오는 위험이랑 걱정거리들. [Sw. =come slowly]

loon[1] [luːn] *n.* Ⓒ 《bird.》 a large water bird with a short neck and a pointed bill. 아비(阿比). [O.N. *lomr*]

loon[2] [luːn] *n.* Ⓒ **1** an idler; a scamp. 게으름뱅이; 건달. **2** a boor. 농사꾼. **3** a silly person. 얼간이. [↑]

***loop** [luːp] *n.* Ⓒ **1** a curved line that crosses itself at both ends. (양 끝이 걸리게 된) 고리. **2** anything shaped like this. 고리 모양의 것; 고리. **3** a curve or bend in a river, a road, etc. (강·길 따위의) 굽이; 만곡(부). ¶ *the* ~ *of a river.* **4** a railway that leaves the main line and joints it again. 루프선; 환상선(環狀線).

— *vt.* (P6,7) **1** make a loop of (string, etc.). …을 고리로 만들다[하다]. **2** fasten (something) with a loop or loops. …을 고리로 죄다. **3** encircle (something) with a loop. …을 고리로 싸다[두르다]. — *vi.* (P1) form into a loop. 고리 모양이 되다. [E.]

loop the loop, (of an airplane, etc.) make a vertical loop in the air. (항공기 등이) 공중제비하다.

loop·hole [lú:phòul] *n.* Ⓒ **1** a narrow hole in a wall through which a gun is fired. (성벽 등의) 총안(銃眼). **2** a way of escape. 도피로. ¶ *find a ~ in the law* 법의 허점을 찾아내다. [=hole in a loop]

:loose [lu:s] *adj.* **1** not tight. 헐거운. ¶ *a ~ collar* 헐거운 칼라 / *a ~ coat* (*boot*) 헐렁한 코트[신발]. **2** not fastened; not bound together; not tied up. 고정돼 있지 않은; 매지 않은; 흔들리는. ¶ *~ hair* 풀어진 머리; 산발 / *a ~ window* (*tooth, nail*) 흔들리는 문[치아, 못] / *the ~ end of a rope* 밧줄의 묶지 않은 쪽 / *a ~ package* (*knot*) 느슨한 포장[매듭] / *~ leaves* (*papers*) 제본이 안 된 책장[서류] / 《*fig.*》 *a ~ tongue* 경솔한 입. **3** not put up in a box, can, etc.; not packed. 포장이 안 된; 용기가 없는; 낱개의. ¶ *~ coffee* (*wool*) 달아서 (무게로) 파는 커피[양모]. **4** not controlled; free; not shut in or up. 통제되지 않은; 자유로운; 내놓은. ¶ *let the dog ~ at night* 밤에 개를 풀어놓다 / *~ cash* 잔돈푼 / *The pigs are ~ in the garden.* 돼지들이 마당에서 놀고 있다. **5** not strict or exact. 엉성한; 부정확한; 허술한. ¶ *a ~ translation* 부정확한 번역 / *~ thinking* 산만한 사고. **6** ⓐ not pressed close together. 푸석푸석한. ¶ *~ earth* (*soil*) 푸석푸석한 흙. ⓑ not closely knit. 눈이 성긴; 맺힌 데가 없는. ¶ *a cloth of ~ texture* 올이 성긴 천 / *a ~ (human) frame* 물렁한 체격. **7** careless about morals or conduct. 홀게늦은; 행실이 안 좋은. ¶ *a ~ woman* 바람 난 여자 / *lead a ~ life* 방종하게 지내다. **8** (of the bowels) relaxed. 설사기가 있는. ¶ *have ~ bowels* 설사하다.

at a loose end =***at loose ends,*** 《*colloq.*》 **a**) having nothing to do; without any definite occupation. 아무 하는 일 없이; 일정한 직업이 없이. **b**) in disorder. 무질서하게. **c**) in an uncertain condition. 미정(未定)으로; 불확실하여.

break loose, free oneself by force; escape. 도망치다.

cast loose, become or make loose; untie; unfasten. 풀어지다; 풀다; 풀어놓다.

cut loose, make oneself free from a relation or control; become free. (…에서) 손을 떼다; 자유로워지다.

get loose, escape. 달아나다.

go loose, move about without restriction. 마음대로 돌아다니다.

have a screw loose, 《*colloq., joc.*》 be a little mad; be feeble-minded. (머리가) 좀 돌아 있다[모자라다].

let loose, **a**) release. 놓아주다; 풀어주다. **b**) 《*fig.*》 express without restriction. 거리낌없이 말하다. ¶ *let ~ one's indignation* 벌컥 화내다.

— *adv.* in a loose manner; loosely. 느슨하게.

— *vt.* **1** (P6) make (something) free or loose; untie; unbind; loosen. …을 풀다; 끄르다; 느슨하게 하다. ¶ *~ a knot* 매듭을 풀다 / *~ one's hold of a rope* 밧줄 잡은 손을 놓다 / *~ a boat from its moorings* 뱃줄을 풀다 / 《*fig.*》 *His tongue was loosed by drink.* 그는 술기운에 지껄이기 시작했다. **2** (P6,7) shoot; let fly. (총·활)을 쏘다. ¶ *~ an arrow* 화살을 쏘다.

— *vi.* (P1) relax. 느슨해지다. [N.]

loose fish [⌐⌐] *n.* a dissolute person. 탕아; 난봉꾼.

loose-joint·ed [lú:sdʒɔ́intid] *adj.* **1** having loose joints; loosely built. 관절이[이음매가] 헐거운; 짜임새가 엉성한. **2** able to move freely. 자유로이 움직이는.

loose-leaf [lú:slì:f] *adj.* having pages or sheets that can be taken out and replaced. 가제식(加除式)의; 루스리프식의《서류 등의 낱장을 끼웠다 뺐다 할 수 있는》.

***loos·en** [lú:sən] *vt.* (P6) **1** make (something) loose or less tight; unfasten. …을 느슨하게 하다; 풀다. ¶ *~ a screw* 나사를 풀다 / *~ one's collar* 칼라를 늦추다. **2** make (something) less dense. …을 무르게 하다. ¶ *~ the soil in a garden* 정원의 흙을 부수다. **3** 《*fig.*》 render less strict and severe. 완화하다. ¶ *~ discipline* (*the tension*) 규율[긴장]을 완화하다. [→loose]

loot [lu:t] *n.* Ⓤ 《*collectively*》 things stolen or taken from the enemy. 약탈품; 전리품. — *vt., vi.* (P6; 1) rob (something) by force. 약탈하다. [Hind.]

lop[1] [lɑp / lɔp] *vt., vi.* (**lopped, lop·ping**) (P6, 7; 1) **1** cut away (branches, etc.). (가지를) 치다; 자르다. ¶ *~ (off, away) branches* 나뭇가지를 치다. **2** cut; cut off (an arm, head). (팔·목 등을) 자르다. [? N.]

lop[2] [lɑp / lɔp] *vi.* (**lopped, lop·ping**) (P1) hang down loosely; droop (esp. of an animal's ears). 축 처지다. [? N.]

lope [loup] *vi.* (P1,2A) run or walk with easy and long steps. 성큼성큼 달리다[걷다]. — *vt.* (P6) cause to lope. 성큼성큼 달리게[걷게] 하다. [N. (→leap)]

lo·quat [lóukwɑt, -kwæt / -kwɔt] *n.* Ⓒ 《bot.》 an evergreen tree in Japan, China, etc.; its yellow, edible fruit. 비파(枇杷)나무; 그 열매. [Chin.]

:lord [lɔ:rd] *n.* Ⓒ **1** a ruler; an owner; a master. 지배자; 소유자; 주인. ¶ *the ~ of a mansion* 대저택의 소유주[주인] / *Man is the ~ of creation.* 인간은 만물의 영장. **2** 《usu. *the L-*》 God; the Savior; 《often *Our L-*》 Christ. 신; 하느님; 주; 그리스도. ¶ *the Lord's Prayer* 주기도문 / *Jesus Our Lord* 우리

주 예수 그리스도 / *Lord bless us* (*me*)! = *Lord have mercy* (*upon us*)! 아아, 저런 / *Lord knows who*.... …은 신만이 안다《아무도 모른다》. **3** 《hist.》 a feudal superior. 영주(領主). **4** 《Brit.》 a nobleman; a peer; a member of the House of Lords; a title used in speaking to noblemen of certain ranks. 귀족; 상원 의원; …경(卿). ¶ *make someone a* ~ 아무에게 작위를 수여하다 / *live like a* ~ 떵떵거리고 살다 / *Lord Chamberlain* 궁내(宮內)대신 / *Lord Bishop* 주교《공식 호칭》. **5** 《*poet., joc.*》 a husband. 남편; 서방.

(**as**) ***drunk as a lord,*** very drunk. 만취〔대취〕하여.

be lord of, possess; have. …을 소유하다.

swear like a lord, swear recklessly. 함부로 맹세하다.

— *vi.* (P1,3) act like a lord. 행세하다; 뻐기다. — *vt.* (P6) confer the title of lord upon. …을 귀족으로 만들다. [E.=*loafward*]

lord it over, domineer over. …에 군림하다. ¶ *He lords it over his inferiors.* 그는 부하들에게 상전처럼 군다.

lord·ling [lɔ́:rdliŋ] *n.* Ⓒ a young lord; a petty or minor lord. 젊은 귀족; 소공자(小公子); 소귀족. [↑]

lord·ly [lɔ́:rdli] *adj.* (**-li·er, -li·est**) **1** suitable for a lord; noble and magnificent. 귀족다운; 위엄있는; 당당한. **2** proud; haughty. 오만한. **3** openhanded; generous. 활수(滑手)한; 푸짐한. ¶ *a* ~ *banquet* 대단한 연회.

Lord Mayor [⌐ ⌐–] *n.* 《Brit.》 the title of the mayor of London or of any of several other English cities. (런던, 기타 대도시의) 시장.

Lord's day [⌐ ⌐], **the** *n.* Sunday. 일요일.

lord·ship [lɔ́:rdʃip] *n.* Ⓤ **1** the state or dignity of a lord; rule; command; control. 군주〔귀족〕임; 통치권; 지배; 통제(統制). ¶ *have* ~ *over land and sea* 육지와 바다를 지배하다 / *have* ~ *over self* 자기를 통제하다. **2** 《*His* or *Your L-*》 a term of respect used when speaking to or speaking of a nobleman or a judge. 각하.

lore [lɔ:r] *n.* Ⓤ **1** traditional facts or stories about a certain subject; knowledge of such facts or stories. (특수한 사항에 관한) 전설(집); 민간 전승(傳承)〔구비〕의 학문〔지식〕. ¶ *ghost* ~ 유령에 관한 전승적 지식; 괴담집(怪談集) / *doctor's* ~ 전승의학 / *bird* ~ 조류에 관한 학문 / *herbal* ~ 약초에 관한 지식; 본초학. **2** learning. 지식; 학문. **3** 《*arch.*》 the act of teaching; instruction. 교수(敎授); 교훈. [*learn*]

〈lorgnette 1〉

lor·gnette [lɔ:rnjét] *n.* Ⓒ **1** a pair of eyeglasses with a handle attached. 손잡이 있는 안경. **2** a pair of opera glasses. 오페라 글라스. [F.]

lorn [lɔ:rn] *adj.* 《*poet., joc.*》 **1** having no person who cares for one; forlorn. 의지가지 없는; 고독한. **2** forsaken. 버림받은. [*lose*]

● **lorn·ness** *n.*

lor·ry [lɔ́(:)ri, lári] *n.* (*pl.* **lor·ries**) Ⓒ **1** 《Brit.》 a motor truck; a long low cart for moving heavy goods. 화물차; 트럭(cf. 《U.S.》 *truck*). **2** a railway car used for carrying goods. 화차; 광차(鑛車). [Malay]

Los An·ge·les [lɔ(:)s ǽndʒələs, -li:z] *n.* a large city in California in the United States. 로스앤젤레스.

:lose [lu:z] *v.* (**lost**) *vt.* **1** (P6) ⓐ become unable to find. …을 잃어버리다. ¶ ~ *a key* 열쇠를 잃어버리다 / ~ *one's way* 길을 잃다〔잘못 들다〕 / ~ *one's place in a book* 어디까지 읽었는지 잊어버리다. ⓑ have no longer; have (something) taken away by accident, carelessness, parting, death, etc. (사고·부주의 등으로) …을 잃다; 상실하다; 여의다; 사별하다(opp. gain). ¶ ~ *one's money* 돈을 잃다 / ~ *a friend* 친구를 잃다 / ~ *a son* 〔*one's life*〕 *in the war* 전쟁에서 아들〔목숨〕을 잃다. **2** (P6) get rid of (something); get over. …을 면하다; 벗어나다; 제거하다. ¶ ~ *one's fear* 무섭지 않게 되다 / *I've quite lost my cold.* 감기가 씻은 듯이 나았다. **3** (P6) fail to see, hear, or understand. …을 못 보다; 못 듣다. ¶ *She did not* ~ *a word of his speech.* 그녀는 그의 말을 한 마디도 놓치지 않고 들었다 / *I lost him in the crowd.* 군중 속에서 그를 놓쳤다. **4** (P6) fail to have, get, or catch; be too late for (something); miss. …을 늦어서 못 타다; 못 잡다; 놓치다(opp. catch). ¶ ~ *one's train* 기차를 놓치다. **5** (P6) fail to win or gain. …에서 지다; (상 따위)를 못 타다. ¶ ~ *a game* 〔*a prize*〕 경기에서 지다〔상품을 놓치다〕. **6** (P13, 14) cause (someone) the loss of something; cause someone the loss of (something); cost. …에게 (직업·승리 따위)를 잃게 하다. ¶ *The failure lost him all his fortune.* 그 실패로 전재산을 잃었다 / *The delay lost the battle for them.* 늦었기 때문에 그들은 싸움에 패배했다 / *Illness lost him the job.* 병으로 직장을 잃었다. **7** (P6) 《often in *passive*》 destroy; bring to destruction. …을 망하게 하다; 파괴하다. ¶ *The ship was lost with all its crew.* 배는 전(全)승무원과 함께 침몰했다. **8** (P6,13) spend uselessly; waste. …을 낭비하다. ¶ ~ *one's labor* 노력을 낭비하다 / *We shall* ~ *no time in beginning work.* 일을 지체할 시간이 없다. **9** (P6) (of a clock, etc.) go too slow by (an amount of time). (시계가 …이나) 늦게 가다. ¶ *This watch loses two minutes a day.* 이 시계는 하루 2분씩이나 늦게 간다. — *vi.* **1** (P1) fail to win; be defeated in an election. 지다; 실패하다. ¶ *Our team has lost.* 우리 팀이 졌다 / *He* *lost by 30 votes.* 그는 30표 차로 낙선했다. **2** (P1,3) suffer loss. 손해 보다; 손해 입다. ¶ *I don't care whether I gain or ~.* 이를 보든 손해를 보든 난 상관 없다. **3** (P1) (of a watch or clock) become slow. (시계가) 늦다. ¶ *My watch loses by three minutes a day.* 내 시계는 하루 3분 덜 간다. [E.]

be lost (=*be absorbed or interested*) ***in*** *something.* …에 열중해 있다.

***lose** oneself,* **a**) lose one's way; go astray. 길을 잃다. **b**) become abstracted. 몰두〔열중〕하다. **c**) get confused. 당황하다.

lose by, lose or suffer loss by reason of. …때문에 잃다〔손해 보다〕. ¶ *He lost her by death.* 그는 그녀와 사별했다 / *He is losing by his inefficiency.* 똑똑하지 못해 손해 보고 있다.

lose out, 《*colloq.*》 be defeated. 패배하다.

lose way, stop. (가다가) 서다.

los·er [lú:zər] *n.* Ⓒ **1** a person who loses or fails. 손해 본 사람; 손실자(opp. gainer). **2** a person who is defeated in an election; a person who has failed, lost a game, etc. 실패한 사람; 패자(opp. winner). ¶ *a good* 〔*bad*〕 ~ 패배를 깨끗이 인정하는〔하지 않는〕 사람.

los·ing [lú:ziŋ] *adj.* likely to lose in the end. 손해되는; 될 성싶지 않은. ¶ *play a ~ game* 질 것이 뻔한 경기를 하다. — *n.* **1** the act of one that loses. 실패; 손해. **2** 《*pl.*》 losses by speculation or gambling. (도박 등에서의) 손실.

:loss [lɔ(:)s, lɑs] *n.* **1** Ⓤ the act or fact of losing; state of being lost. 분실; 상실. ¶ *~ of money* 금전의 분실 / *~ of eyesight* 실명 / *the ~ of one's parents* 부모를 여읨. **2** Ⓒ the damage; a thing or amount lost. 손실; 손해; 손실물〔액〕(opp. profit). ¶ *His death is a serious ~ for the country.* 그의 죽음은 나라의 큰 손실이다 / *That will be no ~ to anybody.* 그 때문에 손해 보는 사람은 없다. **3** Ⓒ waste; decrease. 낭비; 감소; 감손(減損). ¶ *~ of blood* 실혈(失血) / *~ in* 〔*of*〕 *weight* 체중 감소〔감량〕. **4** Ⓒ failure to win, get or keep; defeat. 실패; 패배. **5** 《*pl.*》 the number of soldiers lost in battle. 병력 손실; 사상자. **6** 《insurance》 the death of person, destruction of property, insured. (피보험자의) 사망; 손해; 상해. [→lose]

be at a loss, not know what to do or say. 어찌 할 바를 모르다. ¶ *I am at a ~ to explain how he did it.* 그가 어떻게 그것을 했는지 설명하지 못하겠다.

loss leader [⌐ ⌐-] *n.* 《comm.》 an article sold at a loss in order to attract customers. (손해를 보면서 파는) 특매품.

:lost [lɔ(:)st, lɑst] *v.* p. and pp. of **lose.** — *adj.* **1** no longer present; departed. 이미 없는; 사라진. ¶ *a ~ friend* 사별한 친구. **2** missing; no longer possessed. 잃어버린; 분실한. ¶ *a ~ article* 유실물 / *a ~ dog* 잃어버린 개. **3** having gone astray. 길 잃은. ¶ *a ~ child* 미아 / *a ~ sheep* 길 잃은 양《죄인》. **4** not won or gained. (경기에) 진; 놓쳐버린. ¶ *a ~ battle* 패전 / *a ~ cause* 실패〔무위〕로 끝난 주장〔운동〕. **5** wasted; useless. 헛된; 낭비된. ¶ *~ labor* 〔*efforts*〕 헛수고 / *~ time* 낭비된 시간. **6** destroyed; ruined. 파멸된. ¶ *a ~ ship* 난파선 / *a ~ city* 멸망된 도시. **7** hopeless. 가망 없는. ¶ *~ souls* 구할 길 없는 영혼. [→lose]

be lost in, be absorbed in (something); be rapt in. …에 몰두〔골몰〕하다. ¶ *He was ~ in thought.* 그는 생각에 잠겨 있었다.

be lost on 〔***upon***〕, be wasted on (someone); have no influence on. …에게는 소용〔효과〕 없다. ¶ *Your kindness was not ~ on me.* 네 친절이 나에게 힘이 되었다 / *His eloquence was ~ upon his audience.* 그의 웅변이 청중에게 먹혀들지 않았다.

be lost to, **a**) no longer have (any sense of shame, pity, etc.). …에 무신경하다. ¶ *He is ~ to shame.* 그는 창피를 모른다. **b**) (of good luck, happiness, etc.) be no longer approachable to (someone). …에게 다시 오지 않다. ¶ *Hope is ~ to him.* 그에게 이젠 희망이 없다. **c**) do not belong to (someone) any longer. 더는 …의 것이 아니다; …에서 빠져나가다.

:lot [lɑt / lɔt] *n.* **1** Ⓒ a thing used to decide something by chance. 제비. ¶ *draw lots* 제비를 뽑다. **2** Ⓤ such a method for deciding. 제비뽑기; 추첨. ¶ *The committee chose the chairman by ~.* 위원회는 추첨에 의해 위원장을 뽑았다 / *The ~ fell upon him.* 그가 당첨됐다. **3** Ⓒ a share; a portion. 몫. **4** Ⓒ fate; destiny; fortune. 운; 운명. ¶ *a hard ~* 모진 운명; 악운 / *be contented with one's ~* 자기 운명에 만족하다 / *It falls to* 〔*It is*〕 *my ~ to remain here.* 내가 여기 남을 처지가 됐다. **5** Ⓒ a piece of ground. (땅의) 한 구획; 대지; 부지(cf. *allotment*). ¶ *a parking ~* 주차장 / *a building ~* 부지. **6** Ⓒ the whole number or quantity; a group; a collection. 한 무더기; 한 짝; 한 무리. ¶ *the ~ of us* 우리들 모두 / *sell one dollar a ~* 한 무더기 1달러로 팔다 / *They are an interesting ~.* 재미있는 자들이다. **7** Ⓒ 《*colloq.*》 a person of a certain kind. 놈; 친구; 녀석. ¶ *He is a bad ~.* 그는 나쁜 놈이다.

a lot, very much. 대단히; 훨씬. ¶ *Thanks a ~.* 대단히 고맙소 / *It is a ~ better.* 훨씬 낫다.

a lot of =***lots of*** =***a good*** 〔***great***〕 ***lot of,*** many; much. 많은. ¶ *a ~ of books* 많은 책 / *a ~ of food* 많은 음식.

— *vt.* (P6,7) (**-ted**) 《usu. *out*》 divide into lots. 구분하다; 나누다. ¶ *~ out apples by the basketful* 사과를 한 바구니씩 나누다. [E.]

loth [louθ] *adj.* =loath.

lo·tion [lóuʃən] *n.* ⓊⒸ a liquid used for soothing or cleaning the skin, the eyes, etc. 로션; 화장수. [→lave]

lot·ter·y [lɑ́təri / lɔ́t-] *n.* Ⓒ (*pl.* **-ter·ies**) **1** a game of drawing lots in which prizes are given to the lucky numbers. 복권 뽑기. **2** 《*fig.*》 a matter of pure chance. 재수. ¶ *Marriage is a* ~. 결혼은 운이다. [*lot*]

lo·tus [lóutəs] *n.* Ⓒ **1** a water lily. 연꽃. **2** 《Gk. myth.》 a plant whose fruit was supposed to make a person dreamy and forgetful of everything. 로터스; 망우수(忘憂樹)《그 열매를 먹으면 현세의 시름을 잊는다 함》. [Gk.]

lo·tus-eat·er [lóutəsìːtər] *n.* Ⓒ a person living an easy, idle life. 안일을 일삼는 사람. [↑]

:loud [laud] *adj.* **1** (of a sound) strong; not quiet or soft. 소리가 큰; 시끄러운. ¶ *a ~ bell* 소리가 큰 벨 / *in a ~ voice* 큰 소리로; 시끄럽게. **2** insistent. 끈덕진; 성가신. ¶ *He was ~ in denying it.* 그는 그렇지 않다고 우겨댔다. **3** 《*colloq.*》 (of colors, clothes, etc.) too bright; showy; flashy. 야한; 야단스러운(cf. *crude,* opp. quiet). ¶ *a ~ suit* 현란한 옷. **4** 《*colloq.*》 (of behavior) noisy and rude; unrefined; vulgar. 본데 없는; 저속한. — *adv.* in a loud manner; with a loud voice. 야하게; 저속하게; 큰 소리로. [E.]

:loud·ly [láudli] *adv.* **1** in a loud voice. 큰 소리로. **2** in a showy manner; too brightly. 현란[화려]하게; 야하게(cf. *aloud*).

loud-speak·er [láudspìːkər] *n.* Ⓒ an electrical device for making sounds loud enough to be heard. 확성기.

loud-spo·ken [láudspóukən] *adj.* with a loud voice when speaking. 목소리가 큰.

Lou·is [lúːis] *n.* a man's name. 남자 이름. ¶ *Louis XIV* 루이 14세.

lounge [laundʒ] *vi.* (P1,2) **1** 《*along, about*》 walk unhurriedly. 한가하게 걷다; 어슬렁거리다. **2** spend time idly. 빈둥거리다. **3** stand or rest leaning against something in a lazy way. 척 기대다. — *vt.* (P7) 《*away, out*》 spend (time) in idleness. 빈둥거리며 지내다. ¶ *They lounged the summer away.* 그들은 여름을 하는 일 없이 빈들빈들 지냈다. — *n.* Ⓒ **1** the act of lounging. 어슬렁거리기. **2** a place with comfortable chairs for lounging. 휴게실; 라운지. **3** a couch. 안락의자. [? Sc.]

lounge lizard [⌐ ⌐–] *n.* 《*sl.*》 **1** an idle, pleasure-seeking man who spends his time in lounges. 놈팽이; 건달; 제비족. **2** a professional dance-partner for women at dances in hotel lounges. (여성 상대의) 직업적 춤꾼. [↑]

lounge suit [⌐ ⌐] *n.* 《chiefly Brit.》 a man's suit usually worn during the day. 신사복.

lour [láuər] *vi., n.* =lower².

lour·ing·ly [láuriŋli, láuər-] *adv.* =loweringly.

louse [laus] *n.* Ⓒ (*pl.* **lice**) a small insect that lives in dirty hair on dirty skin. 이. [E.]

lous·y [láuzi] *adj.* (**lous·i·er, lous·i·est**) **1** having lice; dirty. 이가 꾄; 더러운. **2** 《*sl.*》 mean; bad; disagreeable. 싫은; 불쾌한. ¶ *I'm having a ~ time these days.* 요즈음 기분이 좋지 않다. **3** 《*sl.*》 well-supplied. 많은; 풍부한. ¶ *~ with money* 돈 많은. [E.]

lout [laut] *n.* Ⓒ a dull and clumsy person. 미련한[투미한] 사람. [M.E. =rag]

lout·ish [láutiʃ] *adj.* unskillful. 미련한; 어줍은.

Lou·vre [lúːvrə, -vər] *n.* 《*the* ~》 a museum in Paris, formerly a royal palace of France. 루브르 박물관. [F.]

lov·a·ble [lʌ́vəbəl] *adj.* worthy of love; amiable. 사랑스러운; 귀여운. ¶ *a ~ child* 귀여운 아이. [↓]

:love [lʌv] *n.* **1** Ⓤ strong affection. 사랑; 애정. ¶ *~ for children* 아이들에 대한 사랑 / *~ of country* 조국애 / *~ toward one's neighbors* 이웃에 대한 사랑 / *a labor of ~* 좋아서 하는 일. **2** Ⓤ 《often *a* ~》 strong liking; a keen interest. 좋아함; 기호. ¶ *a ~ of learning* 향학심 / *a ~ for music* 음악에 대한 사랑. **3** Ⓤ strong and passionate affection between man and woman. (이성간의) 애정; 연애. ¶ *make ~ to* …에 구애하다; …을 애무하다 / 《*prov.*》 *All's fair in ~ and war.* 사랑과 전쟁은 목적을 정당화한다. **4** Ⓒ a person or thing that one loves; a sweetheart. 사랑하는 것; 연인; 애인. 參考 love는 남성이 말하는 애인, lover 는 여성이 말하는 애인. ¶ *my ~* 여보; 당신 / *What a ~ of a cat!* 이 고양이 정말 귀엽군. **5** one's affectionate greeting; a message of affection. 안부를 전한다는 인사말. ¶ *He has sent ~ to my family.* 우리 식구의 안부를 물어 왔다. **6** Ⓤ 《tennis》 no score. 무득점; 영점. ¶ *~ all,* 0 대 0 / *~ game* 러브게임; 영패.

fall in love with (=*come to feel love for*) *someone.* …와 사랑에 빠지다.

for love, **a**) without pay. 무보수로. ¶ *The rich man takes care of a poor boy for ~.* 그 돈 있는 사람은 한 가난한 소년을 무보수로 돌보고 있다. **b**) for pleasure; out of liking. 좋아서. ¶ *play (cards) for ~* 그저 좋아서 (카드)놀이를 하다《판돈없이》.

for love or money, 《in *negative*》 by any means. 도저히 (…않다). ¶ *We can't get it for ~ or money.* 우린 도저히 그걸 구할 수가 없다 / *I wouldn't do such a thing for ~ or money.* 난 그 따위 짓은 도저히 못 하겠다.

for the love (=*for the sake*) ***of*** *something.* … 때문에. ¶ *For the ~ of Mike* [*Pete, heaven*] *do stop it.* 제발 좀 그만 해라.

— *vt.* **1** (P6) have, feel, or show love for (someone). …을 사랑하다. ¶ *~ one's son* [*mother*] 자식을[어머니를] 사랑하다 / *The king was loved by his people.* 왕은 백성들의 사랑을 받았다. **2** (P6,8,9) like very much. …을 매우 좋아하다. ¶ *I should ~ to go with you.* 너와 같이 간다면야 좋고말고 / *I ~ reading* [*skating*]. 난 독서[스케이트]를 좋아한다. [E.]

love·less [lʌ́vlis] *adj.* **1** not loving; feeling no love. 사랑하지 않는; 애정이 없는. ¶ *a ~ union* 사랑 없는 결합. **2** receiving no love. 사랑받지 못하는.

love letter [⌐ ⌐–] *n.* Ⓒ a letter written to express one's love for someone. 연애 편지.

love·li·ness [lʌ́vlinis] *n.* Ⓤ beauty; charm. 아름다움; 매력.

love·lorn [lʌ́vlɔ̀ːrn] *adj.* broken-hearted; suffering from a loss of love, etc. 실연한.

:love·ly [lʌ́vli] *adj.* (**-li·er, -li·est**) **1** beautiful; attractive; charming. 아름다운; 귀여운. ¶ *a ~ sight* 〔*landscape*〕 아름다운 광경〔경치〕. **2** 《*colloq.*》 very enjoyable; delightful. 즐거운; 유쾌한. ¶ *We had a perfectly ~ time.* 정말 즐거웠다. **3** 《*colloq.*》 delicious. 맛있는. ¶ *a ~ taste* 훌륭한 맛.

love match [⌐ ⌐] *n.* a marriage made entirely from motives of love. 연애 결혼.

***lov·er** [lʌ́vər] *n.* Ⓒ **1** a person who loves someone; a man who is in love; a woman's sweetheart. 연인; 애인. ¶ *a ~ and his lass* 서로 사랑하는 두 남녀. **2** 《*pl.*》 a man and woman in love with each other. 연인 사이. ¶ *two happy lovers* 행복한 두 연인. **3** a person who is very fond of something. 애호가. ¶ *a ~ of music* 음악 애호가.

love seat [⌐ ⌐] *n.* a small sofa or double chair for two persons. 러브 시트; 2인용 소파〔의자〕.

love·sick [lʌ́vsìk] *adj.* wasting away or lacking vitality because one is in love. 사랑에 번민하는; 상사병에 걸린.

***lov·ing** [lʌ́viŋ] *adj.* feeling or showing love; affectionate. 사랑하는; 애정이 깊은.

:low[1] [lou] *adj.* **1** not high or tall; near the ground or other base. 낮은. ¶ *a ~ hill* 〔*roof, ceiling*〕 낮은 언덕〔지붕, 천장〕 / *He made a ~ bow.* 그는 허리를 굽혀 인사했다 / *The glass is ~.* 수은주가 내려갔다 / *a ~ temperature* 낮은 온도 / *a ~ dress* 깊이 팬 드레스. **2** below the usual level. 보통 수준보다 낮은. ¶ *The water is ~.* 수위가 얕다 / *The well is ~.* 우물물이 줄었다. **3** small in amount or degree. (양·정도가) 적은. ¶ *a ~ price* 염가 / *~ speed* 느린 속도. **4** not loud; soft. (소리·음성이) 낮은. ¶ *speak in a ~ voice* 낮은 목소리로 말하다 / *~ whisper* 낮은 속삭임. **5** humble; mean; vulgar; poor. 비천한; 하등의; 저속한; 가난한. ¶ *of ~ birth* 태생이 비천한 / *~ life* 하층(민) 생활 / *~ tastes* 저속한 취미 / *~ talk* 상스러운 얘기 / *a ~ fellow* 본데 없는 친구. **6** feeble; weak. 약한; 무력한. ¶ *~ health* 불건강; 허약 / *~ spirits* 무기력; 의기 소침 / *a ~ pulse* 약한 맥박. **7** (of a meal) not rich; plain; simple. 영양가가 낮은; 간소한. ¶ *a ~ diet* 조식(粗食). **8** (of a human race and animal) little advanced. (사람·생물이) 미개한; 미발달의. ¶ *lower tribes* 미개 종족 / *lower animal* 〔*creation*〕 하등 동물. **9** unfavorable; tending to disparage. 반대하는; 비난조의. ¶ *have* 〔*hold, form*〕 *a ~ opinion of* …을 좋지 않게 평가하다; 우습게 보다.

at lowest, to mention the least possible amount, etc. 최하로 잡아도; 적어도.

be in low water, be pinched for money. 돈에 몰리다; 돈 형편이 좋지 않다.

bring low, depress; humble. 쇠하게 하다; 영락시키다; 수모를 주다.

burn low, burn nearly out. 불이 꺼져 가다.

lay low, **a**) overthrow in fight. 쓰러뜨리다; 지게 하다. ¶ *He laid his enemies ~.* 그는 적을 쓰러뜨렸다. **b**) bury. 묻다; 매장하다. **c**) 《*fig.*》 humble. 수모를 주다.

lie low, **a**) crouch. 웅크리다. **b**) lie prostrate or dead. 쓰러져 있다; 죽어 있다. **c**) 《*colloq.*》 keep quiet; remain hidden. 숨죽이고 있다; 숨어 있다. ¶ *You had better lie ~ until the gossip dies down.* 소문이 잠잠해질 때까지 잠자코 있는 게 낫다.

— *adv.* **1** in, to, or toward a low position. 낮게. ¶ *fly* 〔*aim*〕 *~* 낮게 날다〔조준하다〕. **2** quietly; softly; in a low voice. 조용하게; 낮은 소리로. ¶ *speak ~* 작은 소리로 말하다 / *I can't sing so ~ as that.* 난 그처럼 저음으로는 노래를 못 한다. **3** cheaply. 싸게. ¶ *buy* 〔*sell*〕 *~* 싸게 사다〔팔다〕. **4** humbly; meanly. 천하게; 치사하게. **5** on a low diet. 조식(粗食)으로. ¶ *live ~ for a time* 당분간 조식으로 지내다. **6** for low stakes. 판돈을 적게. ¶ *play ~* 적은 판돈으로 하다.

fall low, degrade oneself. 타락하다.

low down, **a**) far from the top. 훨씬 아래에. **b**) meanly. 비열하게.

run low, (of supplies) become exhausted or used up. (공급이) 달리다; 동나다. ¶ *The sands are running ~.* 시간이 다 되어 간다; 목숨이 경각에 있다.

— *n.* Ⓒ that which is low; a low place; the lowest point. 낮은 것; 낮은 데; 저지; 최저점. [N.]

low[2] [lou] *vi.* (P1) make the sound of a cow. (소가) 음매하고 울다. — *vt.* (P6) utter with lowing. 울부짖듯이 말하다. — *n.* Ⓒ the sound made by a cow. (소의) 음매 소리. [E.]

low·born [lóubɔ́ːrn] *adj.* born of humble parents. 태생이 미천한. [*low*[1]]

low·bred [lóubréd] *adj.* ill-mannered; vulgar. 버릇〔본데〕 없는(cf. *ill-bred*).

low·brow [lóubràu] *n.* 《*colloq.*》 a person without intellectual interests or culture. 교양 없는 사람(opp. highbrow). — *adj.* 《*colloq.*》 of a low-brow. 교양 없는. ¶ *such ~ amusements* 그런 저속한 오락.

low-down [lóudáun] *adj.* 《*colloq.*》 not honest; mean. 치사한; 비열한. ¶ *~ behavior* 비열한 짓.

play it low-down, 《*colloq.*》 treat meanly. …을 냉대하다.

— [⌐ ⌐] *n.* Ⓒ 《*the ~*》 《*sl.*》 all the facts; all the truth; secret information. 실상; 진상; 내막. [*low*[1]]

:**low·er**[1] [lóuər] *vt.* **1** (P6) ⓐ let or put (something) down. …을 낮추다; 내리다. ¶ ~ *a flag* 기를 내리다 / ~ *the sails* 돛을 내리다. ⓑ ⟪*sl.*⟫ swallow (food and drink). (음식)을 삼키다. ¶ ~ *a sandwich and a glass of beer* 샌드위치 한 개를 먹고 맥주 한 잔을 마시다. **2** (P6,13) make (a price, a degree, etc.) lower. (값 따위)를 내리다. ¶ ~ *the prices* 가격을 인하하다. **3** (P6,13) reduce the bodily strength and vitality of; weaken. …의 힘〔체력〕을 약화시키다. ¶ ~ *resistance to illness* 병에 대한 저항력을 약화시키다. **4** (P6) make less high; degrade; make humble. (높이)를 낮추다; 한 단 낮추다; 떨어뜨리다; 꺾다. ¶ ~ *a roof* 지붕을 낮게 하다 / ~ *oneself* 자기를 비하시키다; 품위를 떨어뜨리다 / ⟪*fig.*⟫ ~ *one's pride* 자존심을 꺾다. **5** (P6,13) (of voice, pitch, etc.) make lower. (소리·가락)을 낮추다. ¶ ~ *one's voice* 목소리를 낮추다.
— *vi.* (P1) become lower; sink; fall. 낮아지다; 내려가다.
— *adj.* ⟪*compar.* of *low*¹⟫ (opp. upper). ¶ *the* ~ *animals* 〔*creation*〕 (인간 이외의) 하등 동물 / *the Lower House* 〔*Chamber*〕 하원 / *the* ~ *classes* 하층 계급 / *a* ~ *form* 저학년 / *a* ~ *boy* 하급생 / *the* ~ *regions* 〔*world*〕 지옥. [*low*¹]

low·er[2] [láuər] *vi.* **1** (P1,3) ⟪*at, upon, on*⟫ frown; look threateningly. 얼굴을 찌푸리다; 노려보다. ¶ ~ *at someone* 아무에게 못마땅한 얼굴을 하다. **2** (of a sky, clouds, etc.) appear dark and threatening. (날씨가) 험악해지다. ¶ *a lowering sky* 잔뜩 찌푸린 하늘. — *n.* Ⓒ **1** a frowning look; a frown. 찌푸린〔찡그린〕 얼굴. **2** a threatening look. 험악한 날씨. [Du. *loeren* frown]

lower case [⌐–⌐] *n.* ⟪print.⟫ the lower one of a pair of type cases containing small letters. 소문자 활자용 상자(cf. *upper case*). [*lower*¹]

low·er·most [lóuərmòust] *adj.* lowest. 가장 낮은.

low·land [lóulæ̀nd, -lənd] *n.* Ⓒ **1** ⟪usu. *pl.*⟫ land lower than the level of the surrounding land. 저지(低地). **2** ⟪*the L-s*⟫ the southern and eastern regions of Scotland. 스코틀랜드 저지 지방(opp. the Highlands). — *adj.* of, in or from the lowlands. 저지(로부터)의. [*low*¹]

low·land·er [lóuləndər] *n.* Ⓒ a person who lives in a lowland or the Lowlands. 저지인.

low·ly [lóuli] *adj.* (**-li·er, -li·est**) **1** of a low position or rank; of mean or low degree. 지위가 낮은; 비천한. ¶ *a* ~ *occupation* 천직. **2** (of manners, etc.) modest; humble. 겸손(謙遜)한. ¶ *He had a* ~ *opinion of himself.* 그는 스스로를 겸손하게 낮추었다. — *adv.* in a low manner; humbly. 천하게; 겸손하게. [*low*¹]

low-mind·ed [lóumáindid] *adj.* mean; vulgar. 비열한; 속된.

low-necked [lóunékt] *adj.* (of a dress, etc.) cut low so as to lay the neck, shoulders or back bare. (여성복의) 목·어깨·등이 깊이 팬.

low-pitched [lóupítʃt] *adj.* **1** having a low tone. 소리가 낮은. ¶ *a* ~ *voice* 낮은 음성. **2** (of a roof) having little slope; gentle in slope. (지붕의) 물매가 뜬.

low-spir·it·ed [lóuspíritid] *adj.* depressed; spiritless; cheerless. 우울한; 기운이 없는; 풀죽은.

low tide [⌐⌐] *n.* **1** the lowest level reached by the ebbing tide. 썰물(때). **2** ⟪*fig.*⟫ =low water 2.

low water [⌐⌐–] *n.* **1** water at its lowest level, as in a stream. (하천의) 저수위. **2** ⟪*fig.*⟫ the lowest point of decline. 곤궁한〔어려운〕 때.
in low water, short of money. 돈이 궁해.

·**loy·al** [lɔ́iəl] *adj.* **1** faithful to one's king or country. 충성스러운(opp. disloyal). ¶ *a* ~ *subject* 충신. **2** faithful to one's promise, duty or ideals; upright. 성실한; 고결한. ¶ *a* ~ *husband* 성실한 남편. [→legal]

loy·al·ist [lɔ́iəlist] *n.* Ⓒ a person who remains faithful to his king or his country's government, esp. in times of revolt or disturbance. 충신; 왕당파.

loy·al·ly [lɔ́iəli] *adv.* in a loyal manner; faithfully; truly. 충성스럽게; 충실〔성실〕하게.

·**loy·al·ty** [lɔ́iəlti] *n.* Ⓤ the state or quality of being loyal; faithfulness. 충의; 충절; 충실; 성실.

loz·enge [lázindʒ / lɔ́zi-] *n.* Ⓒ **1** a diamond-shaped figure. 마름모(꼴). **2** a small tablet, usu. sweetened and diamond-shaped. 마름모꼴의 정제. **3** any of various lozenge-shaped figures or objects. 마름모꼴의 물건. [F.]

LP [élpí:] *n.* Ⓒ (*pl.* **LPs** or **LP's**) a phonograph record to be played at 33 1/3 revolutions per minute; short for 'Long Playing'. (레코드의) 엘피판.

Ltd., ltd. [límitid] ⟪Brit.⟫ limited. 유한 책임의. ¶ B.T. Batsford Ltd. 비티 배츠퍼드 유한 책임 회사.

lub·ber [lʌ́bər] *n.* Ⓒ **1** a big, slow, careless and rough person. (덩치 큰) 뒤틈바리. **2** an inexperienced and unskilled seaman. 풋내기 선원. [M.E. =sexually impotent(→lob)]

lub·ber·ly [lʌ́bərli] *adj.* clumsy; stupid. 되통스러운; 둔해 빠진. — *adv.* in a lubberly manner. 어설프게.

lu·bri·cant [lú:brikənt] *n.* Ⓤ **1** oil for making the parts of machines work smoothly. 윤활유. **2** ⟪*fig.*⟫ something which makes action, speech, etc. easy. 매끄럽게〔원활하게〕 하는 것. — *adj.* having the property of making (parts of machines etc.) smooth and slippery. 매끄럽게 하는. [L.]

lu·bri·cate [lú:brikèit] *vt.* (P6) **1** make (a machine, etc.) run smoothly by adding oil. …에 기름을 쳐 매끄럽게 하다. **2** 《*fig., colloq.*》 tip; bribe. …에게 팁을 주다; …을 매수하다. ¶ ~ *someone's tongue* 아무를 매수하여 (비밀 따위를) 발설케 하다. — *vi.* (P1) act as a lubricant. 윤활제로 쓰이다. [↑]

lu·bri·ca·tion [lù:brəkéiʃən] *n.* Ⓤ the act of lubricating; oiling. 매끄럽게 하기; 주유(注油).

lu·bri·ca·tor [lú:brikèitər] *n.* Ⓒ **1** a person who lubricates. 기름 치는 사람. **2** a device for oiling machinery. 주유기(注油器).

lu·cent [lú:sənt] *adj.* **1** bright; luminous; shining. 빛나는; 번쩍이는. **2** transparent; clear. 투명한. [→lucid]

lu·cerne, -cern [lu:sə́:rn] *n.* Ⓤ 《chiefly Brit.》 《bot.》 a clover-like plant, grown as feed for cattle; alfalfa. 자주개자리. [F.]

lu·cid [lú:sid] *adj.* **1** easily understood. 알기 쉬운; 명쾌한. ¶ *a ~ explanation* 〔*argument*〕 명쾌한 설명〔논증〕. **2** clearheaded. 머리가 좋은. **3** clear; transparent. 맑은; 투명한. **4** mentally sound; rational; sane. 이성적인; 분별 있는; 건전한. **5** 《*poet.*》 bright; shining. 밝은; 빛나는. [L. *lux* light]

lu·cid·i·ty [lu:sídəti] *n.* Ⓤ the state or quality of being lucid. 명쾌; 명석; 투명; 제정신.

Lu·ci·fer [lú:səfər] *n.* **1** 《*poet.*》 the planet Venus as the morning star. 샛별; 금성. **2** Satan. 사탄; 마왕. ¶ (*as*) *proud a* ~ 마왕처럼 오만한. **3** 《*l-*》 Ⓒ an early type of match. (초기의) 황린 성냥. [L. *lux* light, *fero* bring]

:luck [lʌk] *n.* Ⓤ **1** the force that brings good or bad to someone; fortune; chance. 운; 운수. ¶ *Good* ~ (*to you*)! 행운이 있기를 / *have hard* ~ 운이 나쁘다 / *Bad ~ to you* 〔*him*〕! 이〔저〕 벼락맞을 놈. **2** good fortune. 행운. ¶ *have no* ~ 재수가〔운이〕 없다 / *I had the ~ to find a good job.* 나는 운이 좋아 좋은 일자리를 만났다. [Teut.]

as luck would have it, fortunately (or unfortunately, according to context). 운 좋게도; 다행히; (문맥에 따라) 공교롭게도; 재수 없게.

be down on one's luck, have no luck. 운이 나쁘다.

for luck, in order to bring good luck. 행운을 빌어.

in luck, lucky. 운이 좋아. ¶ *I am in* ~. 난 운이 좋다.

Just my luck ! I am unlucky as usual. 뭐 하나 되는 일이 없단 말이야.

out of luck, unlucky. 운이 없는; 재수 없는.

try one's luck, try to do something just to see what one can do. 되든 안 되든 해보다.

worse luck, unluckily. 재수 없게도. ¶ *And then, worse ~, he came into the room.* 게다가 재수 없게도 그때 그가 방에 들어왔거든.

:luck·i·ly [lʌ́kili] *adv.* by or with good luck; fortunately. 운 좋게. ¶ *Luckily I was out when he called.* 다행히 그가 왔을 때 나는 집에 없었다.

luck·less [lʌ́klis] *adj.* having no good luck; unfortunate. 불운한; 불행한.

:luck·y [lʌ́ki] *adj.* (**luck·i·er, luck·i·est**) **1** (of a person) having good luck; fortunate. 행운의. ¶ *a ~ dog* 〔*beggar*〕 행운아 / *be ~ at games* 시합운이 좋다 / *Third time* ~! (두 번 실패한 사람을 격려해서) 세 번째는 된다. **2** (of events and actions) bringing good luck; likely to bring good luck to the possessor. 행운을 가져오는; (물건이) 재수 좋은. ¶ *a ~ day* 길일(吉日) / *a ~ guess* 〔*hit, shot*〕 어쩌다 들어맞기; 요행수 / *the ~ seventh* (야구의) 러키 세븐 / *a ~ sixpence* 〔*penny*〕 행운의 6펜스〔페니〕《재수 있으라고 갖고 다니는 주화》 / *a ~ number* 재수 좋은 수. [*luck*]

cut one's lucky, 《Brit. *colloq.*》 decamp; run away. 도망 가다.

lu·cra·tive [lú:krətiv] *adj.* producing wealth or profit; bringing money; profitable. 수지 맞는; 돈벌이가〔이익이〕 되는. ¶ *a ~ employment* 〔*trade*〕 괜찮은 직업〔장사〕. [L.]

lu·cre [lú:kər] *n.* Ⓤ 《now always in a bad sense》 profit; money. 이문; 이득; 금전. ¶ *a filthy* ~ 부정한 돈; 악전. [↑]

lu·cu·brate [lú:kjəbrèit] *vi.* (P1) **1** study or write, esp. late at night. (밤 늦도록) 공부하다; 글을 쓰다. **2** write in a scholarly manner. 학구적인 저작을 하다. [→lucid]

lu·cu·bra·tion [lù:kjubréiʃən] *n.* **1** study or writing, esp. late at night. (야심할 때까지 하는) 공부; 저작. **2** (the product of) hard study; a literary work in which the writer shows off his learning. 역작(力作); 노작(勞作).

Lu·cy [lú:si] *n.* a girl's name. 여자 이름.

lu·di·crous [lú:dəkrəs] *adj.* so amusingly silly as to make one laugh; laughable; ridiculous. 익살스러운; 웃기는; 어이 없는. [L. *ludo* play]

lug [lʌg] *v.* (**lugged, lug·ging**) *vt.* (P6,7,13) **1** 《*along, about*》 pull (something heavy) with an effort; drag. …을 힘들여 끌다; 질질 끌다. ¶ ~ *a heavy cart along the streets* 거리를 무거운 달구지를 끌고 가다. **2** 《*in, into*》 《*fig.*》 introduce unnaturally and irrelevantly a subject, name, story, etc. into a conversation. (당치 않은 이야기 따위)를 무리하게 들고 나오다. ¶ ~ *political matters into conversation* 불쑥 정치적인 말을 꺼내다. — *vi.* (P3) 《*at*》 pull hard. 힘껏 잡아당기다. — *n.* Ⓒ the act of lugging; hard pulling. 세게 끌기〔당기기〕. [Sw.]

:lug·gage [lʌ́gidʒ] *n.* Ⓤ 《*collectively*》 《Brit.》 suitcases, bags, etc. of a traveler. (여행용) 가방; 수화물. ¶ *a piece of* ~ 수화물 하나. [↑]

lug·ger [lʌ́gər] *n.* Ⓒ a small boat. 러거《네모꼴 돛을 단 작은 범선》.

lu·gu·bri·ous [lu:gjú:briəs] *adj.* very sad;

gloomy. 아주 슬픈; 애처로운. [L. *lugeo* mourn]

Luke [lu:k] *n.* 《Bible》 **1** **Saint,** one of the early Christian disciples and the author of the Gospel of St. Luke. 성 누가. **2** the Gospel of St. Luke, which is the third book of the New Testament and which tells the story of Jesus' life. 누가 복음.

luke·warm [lú:kwɔ̀:*r*m] *adj.* **1** (of a liquid) slightly warm. (물이) 미지근한. ¶ ~ *water* 미지근한 물. **2** 《*fig.*》 not eager; indifferent. 미온적인; 무관심한. ¶ ~ *agreement* 마지못한 동의 / *He was ~ in his support of the bill.* 그는 그 법안 지지에 미온적이었다. [E. =warm-warm]

·**lull** [lʌl] *vt.* (P6,13) **1** lead (a child) to fall asleep, esp. by singing and rocking it. (어린아이)를 얼러 재우다; 달래다. ¶ ~ *a baby to sleep* 아기를 얼러 재우다. **2** 《usu. as *passive*》 make (a storm, a wind, etc.) quiet. (풍우 등)을 가라앉히다. ¶ *The wind* 〔*sea*〕 *was lulled.* 바람은〔바다는〕 잠잠해졌다. **3** ⓐ make (pain, etc.) less severe; soothe. (고통 따위)를 진정시키다; 덜게 하다. ¶ ~ *pain* 고통을 누그러뜨리다. ⓑ make quiet by deceiving. …을 속여서 —시키다. ¶ ~ *someone's fears* 구슬러서 아무가 무섭지 않게 해주다 / ~ *someone into a false sense of security* 아무를 속여서 안심시키다.
— *vi.* (P1) become calm. 조용해지다; 가라앉다. ¶ *The wind lulled awhile.* 바람은 잠시 조용해졌다.
— *n.* Ⓒ a short period of quietness. 잠시의 고요〔정적〕; 소강(小康). [Imit.]

lull·a·by [lʌ́ləbài] *n.* Ⓒ (*pl.* **-bies**) a song for leading a child to sleep; a cradlesong. 자장가. [Imit.]

lum·ba·go [lʌmbéigou] *n.* Ⓤ rheumatic pain in the lower back and in the loins; backache. 요통(腰痛). [→loin]

:**lum·ber**[1] [lʌ́mbə*r*] *n.* Ⓤ **1** useless things that are stored away; unused furniture; rubbish. 쓰레기; 폐물; 못쓰는 헌 가구. **2** 《U.S.》 wood sawn into planks, boards, etc. (켜낸) 재목; 제재목. — *vt.* **1** (P6,7,13) 《*with*》 fill or obstruct (a place) with useless things. …을 쓸데없는 것으로 꽉 채우다. ¶ *a room lumbered up with old furniture* 헌 가구들로 꽉 찬 방. **2** (P6) 《U.S.》 cut down (trees) as lumber for the market. (내다 팔려고) 재목을 베어내다. [→lumberman]

lum·ber[2] [lʌ́mbə*r*] *vi.* **1** (P2A,2B) walk along heavily and noisily. 터벅거리며 걷다. **2** (P2A) (of a heavy vehicle) roll along with difficulty; move along heavily. (짐수레가) 덜커덩거리며 굴러가다. ¶ *A heavy truck lumbered by* 〔*past, along*〕. 무거운 트럭이 덜커덩거리며 지나갔다. [M.E. *lomeren*]

lum·ber·jack [lʌ́mbə*r*dʒæ̀k] *n.* Ⓒ 《U.S.》 a man who cuts down trees and prepares them for selling; a lumberman. 벌목 인부; 벌채 노동자.

lum·ber·man [lʌ́mbə*r*mən] *n.* Ⓒ (*pl.* **-men** [-mən]) 《U.S.》 **1** =lumberjack. **2** a man whose business is to buy and sell lumber. 목재상. [*n.* < *Lombard* pawn broker's storehouse; *v.* <N.]

lum·ber·mill [lʌ́mbə*r*mìl] *n.* Ⓒ 《U.S.》 a building in which wood is sawn into planks, boards, etc. 제재소.

lum·ber·yard [lʌ́mbə*r*jɑ̀:*r*d] *n.* Ⓒ 《U.S.》 a place where lumber is kept for sale. 목재 적치장(積置場).

lu·men [lú:mən] *n.* (*pl.* **-mi·na** or **-mens**) a unit of light; the light given out by a point source of one candle power. 루멘 《광속(光束)의 단위》. [L. *lumen* light]

lu·mi·na [lú:mənə] *n.* pl. of **lumen.**

lu·mi·nar·y [lú:mənèri / -nəri] *n.* Ⓒ (*pl.* **-nar·ies**) **1** a heavenly body, such as the sun or the moon. (해·달 등) 천체. **2** a body or an object that gives light. 발광체. **3** 《*fig.*》 a learned person with high morals. 선각자; 계몽자. [→lumen]

lu·mi·nos·i·ty [lù:mənɑ́səti / -nɔ́s-] *n.* (*pl.* **-ties**) **1** Ⓤ the quality of being luminous; brightness. 휘도(輝度). **2** Ⓒ a body or an object that gives light. 발광체〔물〕.

·**lu·mi·nous** [lú:mənəs] *adj.* **1** shining by its own light; giving light; bright. 빛을 내는. ¶ *a ~ paint* 발광 도료 / *The sun is a ~ body.* 태양은 하나의 발광체다. **2** full of light. 밝은. **3** 《*fig.*》 easy to understand; clear. 명백한; 선명한. ¶ *a ~ discourse* 명료한 논술. ●**lu·mi·nous·ly** [-li] *adv.*

:**lump**[1] [lʌmp] *n.* Ⓒ **1** a solid mass often with an irregular shape. 덩어리. ¶ *a ~ of sugar* 각사탕 한 개 / *a ~ of clay* 흙덩이 하나; 인간《성서의》 / 《*fig.*》 *He is a ~ of selfishness.* 그는 이기심 덩어리다. **2** a swelling on a body. 혹; 종기. ¶ *a ~ on the forehead* 이마의 혹. **3** 《*colloq.*》 a heavy, clumsy person; a fool. 땅딸보; 멍청이; 바보.
all of a lump, in the mass; all together. 한 덩어리가 되어.
a lump in the 〔*one's*〕 ***throat,*** a feeling of pressure caused by strong emotion. (감동으로) 목이 메는 느낌.
in the lump, as a whole. 통틀어; 일괄해서.
— *vt.* **1** (P6,7,13) 《*together, with*》 make (something) into a lump; put (things) together; deal with (things) in the mass. …을 한 덩어리로 하다; 일괄하다. ¶ ~ *this with that* 이것과 저것을 한데 합치다〔일괄하다〕. **2** (P6,7) dump. …을 털썩 내려놓다.
— *vi.* **1** (P1,2A) form a lump. 한 덩어리가 되다. **2** (P2A) 《*along*》 move heavily. 터벅터벅 걷다. [E.]

lump[2] [lʌmp] *vt.* (P6) 《*colloq.*》 put up with. 꾹 참다. ¶ *If you don't like it, you can ~ it.* 설사 싫더라도 참으시오. [E.]

lump·ish [lʌ́mpiʃ] *adj.* **1** like a lump. 덩어리 같은. **2** dull; stupid. 우둔한; 어리석은.

lump sum [ㅅㅅ] *n.* a sum of money to pay for various things at one time; a gross sum. (일괄해서 한꺼번에 내는) 총액; 일시불 (금액).

lump·y [lʌ́mpi] *adj.* (**lump·i·er, lump·i·est**) **1** full of lumps; clumsy. 덩어리〔혹〕투성이의; 모양새 없는. **2** choppy; rough. 물결이 이는; 거친. ¶ *a ~ sea* 거친 바다.

Lu·na [lúːnə] *n.* 《Rom. myth.》 the goddess of the moon. 루나《달의 여신》. [L. *luna* moon]

lu·na·cy [lúːnəsi] *n.* (*pl.* **-cies**) Ⓤ madness; great foolishness; 《sometimes *pl.*》 a very foolish act. 광기; 정신 이상; 우행(愚行). [↑]

lu·nar [lúːnər] *adj.* **1** of or like the moon. 달의; 달 같은(opp. solar). ¶ *~ calendar* 태음력 / *~ eclipse* 월식 / *a ~ module* 달 착륙선. **2** measured by the moon's revolutions. 달의 운행에 의한. ¶ *a ~ month* 태음월. [L. *lūna* moon]

lu·na·tic [lúːnətik] *n.* Ⓒ **1** a madman. 광인. **2** a foolish person. 바보. — *adj.* **1** mad; crazy. 미친. ¶ *a ~ asylum* 정신 병원. **2** foolish. 어리석은.

:lunch [lʌntʃ] *n.* ⓊⒸ the light midday meal; a light meal. 런치; 점심. — *vi.* (P1) eat lunch. 점심을 먹다. — *vt.* (P6) entertain (someone) with lunch. …에게 점심을 내다. [?]

·lunch·eon [lʌ́ntʃən] *n.* ⓊⒸ a lunch, esp. a formal lunch. 오찬. ¶ *a ~ party* 오찬회.

·lung [lʌŋ] *n.* Ⓒ **1** 《usu. *pl.*》 a breathing organ (of which there are usu. two) in any airbreathing animal. 폐. ¶ *inflammation of the lungs* 폐렴. **2** 《*pl.*》 voice. 목소리. **3** 《*fig.*》 a large open space where people can enjoy pure fresh air, such as a park, esp. in or near a big city. (대도시의 도심 또는 주변의) 공원이나 광장; 쉼터. ¶ *the lungs of London* 런던 시내나 부근의 광장·공원. [E.]

at the top of one's lungs, at the top of one's voice; very loudly. 목청껏.

have good lungs, have a loud voice. 목소리가 크다.

try one's lungs, cry at the top of one's voice; cry loudly. 힘껏 소리치다.

lunge [lʌndʒ] *n.* Ⓒ a sudden thrust. (펜싱의) 찌르기. — *vi.* (P1,2A,2B,3) 《*at*》 plunge; make a sudden thrust. 냅다 찌르다. ¶ *He lunged at me with his sword.* 그는 칼로 나를 찌르려고 덤볐다. [L. *longus* long]

lurch[1] [ləːrtʃ] *n.* Ⓒ a sudden leaning to one side, like that of a ship, a car or a drunken person. (배나 차 따위의) 갑작스러운 기울; 비틀거림. ¶ *The ship gave a sudden ~.* 배가 갑자기 한쪽으로 기우뚱했다. — *vi.* (P1,2A) lean or sway suddenly to one side; stagger. (갑자기) 기울다; 비틀거리다. ¶ *The drunken man lurched down the street.* 취객은 비틀거리더니 땅에 넘어졌다. [? F. *lâcher* let go]

lurch[2] [ləːrtʃ] *n.* Ⓒ 《*arch.*》 a crushing defeat. 대패. 語法 다음 관용구로만 쓰임. [F. *lourche* a game]

leave someone in the lurch, leave someone in a helpless condition or in difficulties. …을 궁지에 내버려두다.

lurch·er [lə́ːrtʃər] *n.* **1** 《*arch.*》 a petty thief. 좀도둑. **2** 《Brit.》 a crossbred hunting dog used, esp. by poachers. (밀렵자가 부리는) 잡종개. [*lurk*]

·lure [luər] *n.* Ⓒ **1** a trained bird or other animal used to attract others. (후림에 쓰이는) 새; 짐승. **2** an artificial bait. 가짜 미끼. **3** anything which attracts; a charm. 유혹하는 것; 매혹. ¶ *Most people feel the ~ of the sea.* 대부분의 사람들은 바다에 매혹을 느낀다. — *vt.* (P6,7,13) **1** call back (a hawk) with a decoy. …을 후림새로 불러들이다. **2** 《*away, into*》 attract; tempt. …을 유인하다; 부추기다. ¶ *~ a fox into a trap* 여우를 유인하여 덫에 빠뜨리다 / *~ someone away from his duty* 아무를 유혹해서 임무를 게을리하게 만들다. [F.]

lu·rid [lúːrid] *adj.* **1** ⓐ glaring in color. 붉게 빛나는. ¶ *the sky ~ with flames* 타는 듯이 붉은 하늘. ⓑ (of a picture) highly colored; gaudy. 야한 색조의. **2** (of the face, skin, etc.) pale. 창백한. **3** terrible; surprising; sensational. 무서운; 놀라운; 요란한; 선정적인. ¶ *a ~ story* 무서운 이야기 / *a ~ career* 기구한 생애. [L.]

·lurk [ləːrk] *vi.* (P2A,3) **1** lie or wait in hide. 숨어 기다리다; 잠복하다. ¶ *A tiger was lurking behind the rock.* 호랑이 한 마리가 바위 뒤에 잠복하고 있었다. **2** 《*fig.*》 exist unsuspected or undiscovered. 잠재해 있다; 눈에 안 띄다. ¶ *A strange beauty lurks in the autumn woodland.* 가을의 숲속에는 불가사의한 아름다움이 있다. — *n.* Ⓒ the act of lurking. 잠행(潛行). ¶ *on the ~* 몰래 엿보고〔노리고〕. [Norw. =sneak off]

lus·cious [lʌ́ʃəs] *adj.* **1** sweet in taste; delicious. 감미로운; 맛있는. ¶ *a ~ pear* 맛있는 배. **2** (of style, etc.) cloying. 야한; 칙칙한. ¶ *~ coloring* 칙칙한 채색 / *a ~ style* 야한 문체. [*delicious*]

lush [lʌʃ] *adj.* **1** fresh and green; growing abundantly. 푸르디푸른; 우거진. **2** abundant; covered with rich growth. 풍성한; 무성한. ¶ *fields ~ with clover* 클로버가 무성한 들판. — *n.* 《U.S. *sl.*》 a drunkard. 주정뱅이. [M.E. =soft]

·lust [lʌst] *n.* ⓊⒸ a strong desire; a sexual desire. (강한) 욕망; 성욕; 색정. ¶ *a ~ for power* 권력에의 집념 / *the lusts of the flesh* 육욕. — *vi.* (P3) 《*after, for*》 have a strong desire, esp. a strong sexual desire. 열망〔갈망〕하다; (특히) 색정을 일으키다. ¶ *~ after money* 돈을 밝히다. [E.]

:lus·ter, 《Brit.》 **lus·tre** [lʌ́stər] *n.* Ⓤ **1** brightness and smoothness of the surface; shine; gloss. 광택; 윤. ¶ *the ~ of silk* 비단의 광택 / *add ~ to the skin* 가죽에 광을 더 내다. **2** fame; glory. 명예; 영광. ¶ *throw ~ on one's name* 이름에 광채를 더하다. [L. *lustro* illumine]

lust·ful [lʌ́stfəl] *adj.* moved by sexual desire; sensual; lewd. 호색의; 육욕의; 음탕한. [*lust*]

lust·i·ly [lʌ́stili] *adv.* in a lusty manner; vigorously. 힘차게; 활발하게.

lus·trous [lʌ́strəs] *adj.* bright; glossy; shining. 광택이 있는; 반짝이는. ¶ *~ pearls* 반짝이는 진주 목걸이.

lust·y [lʌ́sti] *adj.* (**lust·i·er, lust·i·est**) healthy; vigorous. 튼튼한; 원기왕성한. ¶ *a ~ boy* 씩씩한 아이. [*lust*]

lute [lu:t] *n.* Ⓒ stringed musical instrument of olden times. 류트《mandolin 비슷한 14-17세기 경의 현악기》. [Arab.]

〈lute〉

Lu·ther [lú:θər], **Martin** *n.* (1483-1546) the German leader of the Protestant Reformation. 루터.

Lu·ther·an [lú:θərən] *adj.* of Martin Luther; belonging to the Protestant church named for Martin Luther. 루터의; 루터교(파)의. —— *n.* Ⓒ a member of the Lutheran Church; a follower of Martin Luther. 루터교도.

lux·u·ri·ance [lʌgzúəriəns, lʌkʃ-] *n.* Ⓤ the state or quality of being luxuriant; abundant growth; richness. 번성; 다산(多産); 풍부; (문장 등의) 화려함. ¶ 《*fig.*》 *the ~ of man's imagination* 인간의 풍부한 상상력. [→luxury]

lux·u·ri·ant [lʌgzúəriənt, lʌkʃ-] *adj.* growing thick; very productive; rich in decoration. 무성한; 풍요로운; 화려한. ¶ *~ foliage* 무성한 나뭇잎 / *a ~ style* 화려한 문체.

lux·u·ri·ate [lʌgʒúərièit, lʌkʃ-] *vi.* (P1,3) **1** grow more than enough. 번성〔무성〕하다. **2** 《*in*》 take great delight in (something). 즐기다. ¶ *~ in sunshine* 〔*good food*〕 일광욕〔미식〕을 즐기다. **3** feed or live luxuriant. 호사하다; 사치스럽게 지내다.

•**lux·u·ri·ous** [lʌgʒúəriəs, lʌkʃ-] *adj.* **1** (of a person and his habit) fond of luxuries. 사치스러운; 사치를 좋아하는. **2** (of a thing) splendid and comfortable; extravagant. 호사스러운. ¶ *a ~ house* 〔*bed*〕 호화로운 집〔침대〕. ● **lux·u·ri·ous·ly** [-li] *adv.*

:**lux·u·ry** [lʌ́kʃəri] *n.* (*pl.* **-ries**) **1** Ⓤ the state or way of life in which one can enjoy or use expensive things; extravagance. 사치; 호사. ¶ *live in ~* 사치스럽게 지내다 / *in the lap of ~* 온갖 사치에 묻혀. **2** Ⓒ something pleasant but not necessary. 사치품. ¶ *necessaries before luxuries* 사치품에 앞서 우선 필수품. **3** Ⓤ an intellectual or emotional enjoyment. 즐거움; 유쾌; 쾌락(快樂). ¶ *the ~ of leisure* 한가함의 즐거움. [L. *luxus* abundance]

ly·cée [li:séi / lí:sei] *n.* Ⓒ 《F.》 a government-supported secondary school in France. 리세《프랑스의 국립 고등 중학교》. [Gk.]

ly·ce·um [laisí:əm] *n.* Ⓒ **1** 《*L-*》 the small lecture hall in Athens where Aristotle taught. 아리스토텔레스가 철학을 가르친 학원. **2** a lecture hall. 학원; 강당. **3** 《U.S.》 (a building of) an association providing public lectures, concerts, etc. 문화 회관; 강연회; 음악회. [Gk.]

lye, lie [lai] *n.* Ⓤ an alkaline solution of wood-ashes. 잿물. [E.]

:**ly·ing**[1] [láiiŋ] *v.* ppr. of **lie**[1]. —— *n.* Ⓤ the act of telling a lie. 거짓말하기. —— *adj.* false; untruthful. 거짓의; 허위의. ¶ *a ~ story* 거짓 이야기 / *a ~ rumor* 헛소문 / *a ~ prophet* 거짓 선지자.

ly·ing[2] [láiiŋ] *v.* ppr. of **lie**[2].

ly·ing-in [láiiŋín] *n.* the state of attending childbirth; the time spent in bed at childbirth. 해산; 분만; 그 기간. ¶ *a ~ hospital* 산부인과 의원. [*lie*[1]]

lymph [limf] *n.* Ⓤ **1** a colorless fluid in an animal body. 림프액. **2** 《*poet.*》 a pure water. 청수; 맑은 물. [L.]

lym·phat·ic [limfǽtik] *adj.* **1** of or containing lymph. 림프의; 림프를 함유하는. ¶ *a ~ vessel* 〔*gland*〕 림프관〔샘〕. **2** lacking energy; sluggish; slow in thought and action. 나른한; 지둔한; 굼뜬. ¶ *a ~ temperament* 점액질. —— *n.* Ⓒ a tube which carries lymph. 림프관.

lynch [lintʃ] *vt.* (P6) punish (someone) by hanging him to death without a legal trial. …을 린치로 처형하다; …에게 린치를 가하다. ¶ *The crowd lynched him.* 군중은 그에게 린치를 가했다. [Person]

lynx [liŋks] *n.* ⒸⓊ (*pl.* **lynx·es** or *collectively* **lynx**) 《animal》 any of several large wildcats. 스라소니. [Gk.]

lynx-eyed [líŋksàid] *adj.* having very sharp eyes; keen-sighted. 눈이 날카로운〔매서운〕.

lyre [láiər] *n.* Ⓒ a harplike stringed musical instrument in ancient Greece. (고대 그리스의) 수금(竪琴). [Gk.]

lyr·ic [lírik] *n.* Ⓒ a short, musical poem expressing personal emotions. 서정시(敍情詩)(opp. epic). —— *adj.* =lyrical. [Gk.]

lyr·i·cal [lírikəl] *adj.* (of poetry) expressing very personal feelings, like a song; emotional. 서정시조(調)의〔적인〕; 감상적인. ¶ *a ~ poet* 서정시인.

lyr·ist *n.* Ⓒ **1** [láirist] a player on the lyre. 수금(竪琴) 탄주자. **2** [lírist] a lyrical poet. 서정시인.

Ly·sol [láisɔl, -soul] *n.* Ⓤ 《trademark》 a brown liquid, used to prevent the disease germs. 리졸《소독약, 방부제》. [L.]

m M

M, m [em] *n.* Ⓒ (*pl.* **M's, Ms, m's, ms** [emz]) **1** the 13th letter of the English alphabet. 영어 알파벳의 열셋째 자. **2** the Roman number for 1,000. 로마 숫자의 천.

m. married; meter; mile; minute; month; moon; mountain.

∗**ma** [mɑː, mɔː] *n.* Ⓒ《*colloq.*》 mamma; mother. 엄마.

M.A. Master of Arts. 문학 석사.

∗**ma'am** *n.* [mæ(ː)m, mɑːm] Ⓒ **1**《Brit.》 a form of address to the queen or a royal princess. 여왕이나 공주에 대한 존칭. **2** [məm, m] a form of address used by servants to their mistresses, etc. 마님; 아주머님. **3**《U.S.》 a form of address to any woman. 부인; 여사(님); 아주머니. [F. *madame*]

ma·ca·bre [məkɑ́ːbrə, -bər] *adj.* **1** horrible; ghastly. 무서운; 소름끼치는. **2** of death. 죽음의. [F.]

mac·ad·am [məkǽdəm] *n.* Ⓤ broken stones used in making the surface of roads. 머캐덤《도로 포장용의 쇄석(碎石)》. [Person]

mac·a·ro·ni [mæ̀kəróuni] *n.* (*pl.* **-nis** or **-nies**) **1** Ⓤ dried flour paste made into long, thin, hollow tubes. 마카로니《이탈리아 국수》. **2** Ⓒ a dandy. 멋쟁이. [It.]

mac·a·roon [mæ̀kərúːn] *n.* Ⓒ a small, sweet cookie made of egg white, sugar, and crushed almonds or coconut. 마카롱 과자. [↑]

Mac·beth [məkbéθ] *n.* 맥베스. **1** a tragedy by Shakespeare. 셰익스피어 작의 비극. **2** the main character of this play. 그 주인공.

mace [meis] *n.* Ⓒ **1** a large club used as a weapon in the Middle Ages. (중세 때 무기로 쓰인) 철퇴(鐵槌). **2** a staff carried before a mayor, etc. as a symbol of authority. 직장(職杖). [F.]

〈mace 2〉

Mac·e·don [mǽsidɑ̀n / -dən] *n.* =Macedonia.

Mac·e·do·ni·a [mæ̀sədóuniə, -njə] *n.* an ancient kingdom in Europe, in the north of Greece. 마케도니아. ● **Mac·e·do·ni·an** [-n] *adj., n.*

mac·er·ate [mǽsərèit] *vt., vi.* (P6; 1) **1** make or become soft by keeping in water. (물에 담가서) 부드럽게 하다; 부드러워지다. **2** become, or cause to become, lean by fasting, etc.; waste away. (단식 등으로) 야위게 하다; 쇠약해지다. [L.]

Mach, mach [mɑːk, mæk] *n.* Ⓒ Mach number. 마하수(數). [Person]

Mach·i·a·vel·li [mæ̀kiəvéli], **Niccolò** *n.* (1469-1527) an Italian statesman and writer. 마키아벨리. 參考 권모술수 정치의 창도자; 저서 '군주론'.

Mach·i·a·vel·li·an, -vel·i·an [mæ̀kiəvéliən] *adj.* **1** of Machiavelli or his political opinion that rulers should use craftiness to keep their authority. 마키아벨리(주의)의. **2** cunning; crafty. 권모술수의. — *n.* Ⓒ a follower of Machiavelli's principles. 마키아벨리주의자; 권모술수가. [It.]

:**ma·chine** [məʃíːn] *n.* Ⓒ **1** an instrument for doing work consisting of a number of fixed and moving parts. 기계. ¶ *a mowing* ~ 제초기 / *a printing* ~ 인쇄기 / *a sewing* ~ 재봉틀 / *a vending* ~ 자동 판매기 / *the* ~ *age* 기계〔문명〕시대 / *a* ~ *shop* 기계 공장. **2** a mechanism. 기구; 기관. ¶ *the* ~ *of government* 정부 기구 / *the social* ~ 사회 기구. **3** an automobile; an airplane. 자동차; 항공기. **4** leaders of a political party. (정당의) 지배 집단. **5** a person or group that acts like a machine, without thought will or emotion. 기계적으로 움직이는 사람. ¶ *He is a mere* ~. 그는 기계에 지나지 않는다.
— *vt.* (P6) **1** make or shape (something) with a machine. …을 기계로 만들다. ¶ ~ *cloth* 옷감을 짜다. **2** sew with a sewing-machine. …을 재봉틀로 박다. [Gk. *mēkhos* contrivance]

machine gun [–⌐] *n.* a gun that fires bullets continuously. 기관총.

ma·chine-gun [məʃíːngʌ́n] *vt.* (**-ned**) (P6) fire at with a machine gun. 기관총으로 쏘다.

ma·chine-made [məʃíːnmèid] *adj.* made by machinery. 기계로 만든(opp. handmade).

:**ma·chin·er·y** [məʃíːnəri] *n.* Ⓤ **1**《*collectively*》 machines as a group or whole. 기계류. ¶ *a lot of* ~ 수많은 기계. **2** the working parts of a machine. 기계의 운전부. **3** the organization by which something is kept in action. 기구; 조직. ¶ *the* ~ *of government* = *the government* ~ 정치 기구 / *the* ~ *of law* 사법 기관.

ma·chin·ist [məʃíːnist] *n.* Ⓒ **1** a person who controls, makes, and repairs machinery. 기계공; 기계 수리공. **2** a person who is skillful at using machine tools; a person who runs a machine, esp. a sewing-machine. 기계 기술자; 특히 재봉틀

직공.

mack·er·el [mǽkərəl] *n.* Ⓒ (*pl.* **-els** or *collectively* **-el**) an oily seafish with a blue-striped back. 고등어. [F.]

mack·in·tosh [mǽkintɑ̀ʃ / -tɔ̀ʃ] *n.* **1** Ⓒ a waterproof overcoat. 방수 외투; 레인 코트. **2** Ⓤ waterproof cloth used for this overcoat. 방수포(布). [Person]

mac·ro- [mǽkrou-] *pref.* large; long; great. '긴, 큰'의 뜻(opp. micro-). [Gk.]

mac·ro·cosm [mǽkroukɑ̀zəm / -kɔ̀z-] *n.* 《*the* ~》 the universe. 대우주. [Gk. *makros* great, *kosmos* world]

mac·ron [méikrɑn, mǽkrɔn] *n.* a mark over a vowel to show that it is long in quantity. 장음부(長音符)《*ā*, *ē* 따위의 ¯》. [→ macro-]

mac·u·la [mǽkjələ] *n.* (*pl.* **-lae**) **1** a dark spot on the sun. (태양의) 흑점. **2** a stain or spot on the skin. 모반(母斑). [L.]

mac·u·lae [mǽkjəli:] *n.* pl. of **macula**.

:mad [mæd] *adj.* (**mad·der, mad·dest**) **1** out of one's mind; crazy; insane. 미친; 실성한. ¶ *He is quite* ~. 아주 돌아버렸다. **2** greatly excited; wild. 되게 흥분한. ¶ *He is* ~ *with joy.* 그는 기뻐 어쩔 줄 모른다 / ~ *with pain* 아파서 미칠 것 같은. **3** very foolish; reckless. 몹시 어리석은; 무모한. ¶ *a* ~ *plan* 무모한 계획. **4** filled with great eagerness or desire; very fond. 열중한; 빠져버린. ¶ *She is* ~ *about him.* 그녀는 그에게 홀딱 반해 있다 / *He is* ~ *on photography.* 그는 사진에 미쳐 있다 / *The old man is* ~ *for fame.* 그 늙은이는 명예에 안달이 나 있다. **5** 《*colloq.*》《*with, at*》 very angry. 몹시 성난; 격노한. ¶ *She was* ~ *at* 〔*with*〕 *me for saying so.* 내가 그렇게 말했다고 그녀는 몹시 화내고 있었다 / *Don't be mad with* 〔*at*〕 *me.* 나한테 화낼 것 없다. **6** wildly gay or merry. 들뜬. ¶ *in* ~ *spirits* 들떠서 / *be* ~ *with delight* 좋아서 날뛰다. **7** (of animals) having rabies. 광견병에 걸린. ¶ *a* ~ *dog* 미친 개. [E.]

drive someone mad, cause someone to become mad. 아무를 미치게 만들다.

go 〔***run***〕 ***mad,*** become mad. 미쳐버리다.

like mad, wildly or furiously. 미친 듯이. ¶ *run* 〔*work*〕 *like* ~ 미친 듯이 뛰다〔일하다〕.

mad keen, extremely keen. 몹시 …하고 싶어하는. ¶ *The children are* ~ *keen to go to the zoo.* 아이들은 동물원에 가고싶어 안달이다.

Mad·a·gas·car [mæ̀dəgǽskər] *n.* a republican island in the Indian Ocean, off the southeastern coast of Africa. 마다가스카르《아프리카 남동해에 있는 공화국: 섬나라》.

***mad·am** [mǽdəm] *n.* Ⓒ (*pl.* **-ams** or **mes·dames**) **1** a polite word used in speaking or writing to a lady. 아주머님; …부인. **2** 《*colloq.*》 the mistress of a household. 주부. [↓]

mad·ame [mǽdəm] *n.* Ⓒ (*pl.* **mes·dames**) a French form, not British or American, used in speaking or writing to a married woman. 마님; …부인 ¶ ~ *Curie* 퀴리 부인. 參考 Mdme.으로 생략됨. [F. *ma dame* my lady]

mad·cap [mǽdkæ̀p] *n.* Ⓒ a wild and thoughtless person, esp. a girl. 분수 없는 〔무모한〕 사람; 특히 그런 처녀; 왈가닥. — *adj.* thinking nothing of the possible results; mad-brained. 무모한. [*mad*]

mad·den [mǽdn] *vt., vi.* (P6; 1) **1** make or become mad. 미치게 만들다; 미치다. **2** make or become angry. 성나게 하다; 성나다. [*mad*]

mad·den·ing [mǽdniŋ] *adj.* **1** causing to become mad. 미치게 만드는. **2** driving into great anger. 분통을 지르는.

mad·ding [mǽdiŋ] *adj.* **1** 《rare》 mad, or acting madly; furious. 발광한; 미친. ¶ *the* ~ *crowd* 성난 군중. **2** maddening. 미치게 하는.

mad-doctor [mǽddɑ̀ktər / -dɔ̀k-] *n.* 《*arch.*》 a doctor skilled in the treatment of mad persons. 정신과 전문의(cf. *alienist*).

:made [meid] *v.* p. and pp. of **make**.
— *adj.* 《usu. in compounds》 **1** produced or manufactured by men. (인공적으로) 만들어진; 제작한. ¶ *a* ~ *dish* 모듬 요리 / ~ *ground* 매립지 / *American-made articles* 미국제 물건 / *home-made goods* 국산품 / *a* ~ *word* 조어 / *ready-made clothes* 기성복. **2** (of the body) formed; built. (몸집이) …한. ¶ *a well-made man* 체격이 딱 짜인 남자 / *a slightly-made girl* 몸매가 날씬한 처녀. **3** successful; sure of success. 성공하는; 성공이 확실한. ¶ *a* ~ *man* 성공한 사람 / *a self-made man* 자수성가한 사람. **4** created; invented. 만들어낸; 조작한. ¶ *a* ~ *story* / *a well-made play* 그럴 듯한 조작극. [*make*]

ma·de·moi·selle [mæ̀dəmwəzél] *n.* Ⓒ (*pl.* **-selles** or **mes·de·moi·sells**) a French form used in speaking or writing to an unmarried woman. 마드무아젤; 아가씨; …양. 參考 영어의 Miss에 해당. [F.]

made-to-or·der [méidtəɔ́:rdər] *adj.* made according to the customer's wishes. 주문에 의해 만든(opp. ready-made).

made-up [méidʌ́p] *adj.* **1** arranged; put together. 만들어낸; 조립한. **2** not true; invented. 조작한; 꾸며낸. ¶ *a* ~ *story* 꾸며낸 이야기. **3** man-made. 인공의.

mad·house [mǽdhàus] *n.* Ⓒ **1** a hospital or home for insane people. 정신 병원. **2** a place of disorder and uproar. 어수선한 장소; 난장. [*mad*]

mad·ly [mǽdli] *adv.* **1** in a mad manner. 미친 것처럼; 열렬하게. ¶ *be* ~ *in love with him* 그 남자를 죽자사자 좋아하다. **2** wildly; without self-control. 맹렬하게; 무모하게.

mad·man [mǽdmən, -mæ̀n] *n.* Ⓒ (*pl.* **-men** [-mən, mèn]) a crazy person; a lunatic. 미친 사람; 광인. ¶ *become wild like a* ~ 미친 사람처럼 난폭해지다.

:mad·ness [mǽdnis] *n.* Ⓤ **1** the state of being mad. 정신 착란. ¶ *love to* ~ 미친 듯이 사랑하다; 열애하다 / *in one's* ~ 발광해서. **2** great anger. 격노. ¶ *In his* ~ *he tried to kill his best friend.* 얼마나 화가 났던지 그는 가장 친한 친구를 죽이려 했다. **3** a foolish act; a mad action. 무모한〔미친〕 짓. ¶ *It is* ~ *to swim in such weather.* 이런 날씨에 수영하는 건 미친 짓이다.

Ma·don·na [mədánə / -dɔ́n-] *n.* **1** the Virgin Mary (the mother of Jesus Christ). 성모 마리아; 마돈나. **2** Ⓒ a picture or statue of Mary. 성모 마리아 상. [It. = my lady]

Ma·drid [mədríd] *n.* the capital of Spain. 마드리드.

mad·ri·gal [mǽdrigəl] *n.* Ⓒ **1** a sentimental love poem set to music. 짧은 연가(戀歌); 소곡(小曲). **2** a type of song sung in five or six voices without any musical accompaniment. 마드리갈《무반주의 5-6인의 합창곡》. [It.]

mael·strom [méilstrəm] *n.* **1** 《*the M-*》 a great sea current turning around rapidly off the northwestern coast of Norway. 노르웨이 서북 해안의 큰 화방수. **2** Ⓒ a great sea current turning around rapidly. 큰 소용돌이. **3** Ⓒ 《*fig.*》 a violently confused state of mind, affairs, society, etc. (정신적·사회적) 대혼란. ¶ *the* ~ *of war* 전쟁의 소용돌이. [Du.]

:mag·a·zine [mæ̀gəzíːn, ∠-∠] *n.* Ⓒ **1** a collection of various kinds of reading matter regularly published. 잡지. ¶ *edit a* ~ 잡지를 편집하다 / *take a* ~ 잡지를 구독하다. **2** a place for keeping guns and gunpowder. 탄약고; 무기고. ¶ *a powder* ~ 화약고. **3** a space in a gun to hold the cartridges. (총포의) 약실; 탄창. **4** a place in a camera for rolls of film. (카메라의) 필름통. [Arab.]

mag·got [mǽgət] *n.* Ⓒ **1** a wormlike larva of a fly living in decaying flesh, food, etc. 구더기. **2** 《*fig.*》 a strange fancy; a whim. 공상; 일시적 기분. [? N. *mathkr*]

Ma·gi [méidʒai] *n. pl.* (*sing.* **-gus**) 《*the* ~》 《Bible》 the three wise men from the East who came to celebrate the birth of Jesus. 세 동방 박사. [↓]

:mag·ic [mǽdʒik] *n.* Ⓤ **1** the art which makes wonderful things happen by using supernatural power. 마법. ¶ *black* ~ 악마의 마술. **2** a mysterious power. 불가사의한 힘; 마력. ¶ *the* ~ *of music* 음악의 마력. **3** mysterious effects made by tricks. 요술. ¶ *play* ~ 요술을 부리다. — *adj.* 《as *attributive*》 **1** having magic; done as if by magic. 마법의. ¶ *a* ~ *carpet* (하늘을 나는) 마법의 융단 / *a* ~ *wand* 마법의 지팡이 / *a* ~ *lantern* 환등 / ~ *words* 주문(呪文). **2** mysterious. 불가사의한. ¶ ~ *beauty* 기막힌 아름다움 / *the* ~ *influence of past* 과거에 대한 매력. [Pers. *magus* magician]

mag·i·cal [mǽdʒikəl] *adj.* **1** done by magic. 마술의. **2** having magic power. 불가사의한. ¶ *in a* ~ *way* 희한한 방법으로 / *The effect was* ~. 효과는 직방이었다.

mag·i·cal·ly [mǽdʒikəli] *adv.* **1** by means of magic. 마술로. **2** in a magic manner. 불가사의하게.

·ma·gi·cian [mədʒíʃən] *n.* Ⓒ **1** a person who is skilled in magic. 마술사. **2** =conjurer 2.

mag·is·te·ri·al [mæ̀dʒəstíəriəl] *adj.* **1** of a magistrate. 장관의. **2** (of an opinion, etc.) having weight, or authority. (의견 등) 무게 있는; 권위 있는. **3** having a masterful manner or aspect. 거만〔오만〕한 ● **mag·is·te·ri·al·ly** [-li] *adv.* [L. *magister* master]

mag·is·tra·cy [mǽdʒəstrəsi] *n.* ⓊⒸ (*pl.* **-cies**) **1** the position or rank of a magistrate. 장관의 직. **2** 《*collectively*》 a body of magistrates. 행정 장관.

·mag·is·trate [mǽdʒəstrèit, -trit] *n.* Ⓒ **1** a chief officer of the government who has power to apply the law. (사법·행정을 겸한) 장관. ¶ *the chief* ~ 원수; 대통령. **2** a local judge who judges minor law cases; a justice of the peace. 지방 판사; 치안 판사. [→master]

Mag·na Char·ta, Mag·na Car·ta [mǽgnə kɑ́ːrtə] *n.* the great charter of liberties of the English people which King John was forced to accept in 1215. 마그나 카르타; 영국 대헌장. [L. = great charter]

mag·na·nim·i·ty [mæ̀gnənímәti] *n.* (*pl.* **-ties**) **1** Ⓤ the quality or nature of being magnanimous. 도량이 큼; 배짱이 좋음. ¶ *The soldiers showed* ~ *by treating their prisoners well.* 병사들은 그들의 포로들을 다루는 데 관대했다. **2** Ⓒ a magnanimous act. 관대한 행위. [↓]

mag·nan·i·mous [mægnǽniməs] *adj.* noble-minded; generous; not petty. 고결한; 관대한; 너그러운. [magni-, →animus]

mag·nate [mǽgneit, -nit] *n.* Ⓒ **1** a person of high rank. 고관. **2** a rich and powerful person in an industry. (업계의) 거물. ¶ *a financial* ~ 재계의 거물 / *an oil* ~ 석유왕. [L. *magnus* great]

mag·ne·sia [mægníːʃə, -ʒə] *n.* Ⓤ a white, tasteless powder used as a medicine. 산화(酸化) 마그네슘. [Place *Magnesia*]

mag·ne·si·um [mægníːziəm, -ʒəm] *n.* Ⓤ 《chem.》 a light silvery metal element which burns with a bright white light. 마그네슘. [↑]

·mag·net [mǽgnit] *n.* Ⓒ **1** a piece of iron that draws other pieces of iron toward it, or which points north and south. 자석 (cf. *loadstone*). **2** 《*fig.*》 a thing or a person that attracts. 사람의 마음을 끄는 물건〔사람〕. [Gk. *magnētis* stone from *Magnesia*, loadstone]

mag·net·ic [mægnétik] *adj.* **1** having the

qualities of a magnet. 자기(磁氣)를 띤. ¶ *the ~ field* 자장(磁場) / *a ~ needle* 자침 / *the ~ pole* 자극 / *a ~ mine* 자기 기뢰. **2** attractive. 매력 있는. ¶ *a ~ personality* 매력 있는 개성 / *His speech was really ~.* 그의 연설은 정말 훌륭했다.

M

mag·net·ism [mǽgnətìzəm] *n.* Ⓤ **1** the qualities or properties of a magnet. 자기; 자성. **2** the science of magnets. 자기학. **3** 《*fig.*》 attractive power; personal charm. 매력. [*magnet*]

mag·net·ite [mǽgnətàit] *n.* Ⓤ an iron ore having strong magnetic power. 자철광.

mag·net·ize [mǽgnətàiz] *vt.* (P6) **1** make (iron or steel) magnetic; turn into a magnet. (금속)을 자화(磁化)하다. ¶ *become magnetized* 자기(磁氣)를 띠다. **2** attract or influence by personal charm, etc. …을 매혹하다. ● **mag·ne·ti·za·tion** [⌐-nətizéiʃən] *n.*

mag·ne·to [mægní:tou] *n.* Ⓒ (*pl.* **-tos**) a small electric generator with permanent magnets. 자석 발전기.

magni- [mǽgnə-/-ni-] *pref.* great. '큰, 대(大)'의 뜻. [L. *magnus* great]

mag·ni·fi·ca·tion [mæ̀gnəfikéiʃən] *n.* Ⓤ **1** the act of magnifying. 확대. **2** the power of magnifying. 배율(倍率). [magni-]

•**mag·nif·i·cence** [mægnífəsns] *n.* Ⓤ the quality of being magnificent; splendor. 웅대; 장대; 장려(壯麗).

:**mag·nif·i·cent** [mægnífəsənt] *adj.* **1** very fine; splendid; grand. 훌륭한; 굉장한; 장대〔장려〕한. ¶ *a ~ voice* 우렁찬 목소리 / *a ~ building* 굉장한 건물. **2** 《*colloq.*》 excellent; very good. 우수한; 멋진. ¶ *a ~ dinner* 멋진 정찬.

mag·nif·i·cent·ly [mægnífəsəntli] *adv.* in a magnificent manner. 훌륭하게; 멋지게; 당당하게.

•**mag·ni·fy** [mǽgnəfài] *vt.* (P6) (**-fied**) **1** make (something) look larger than its real size. …을 확대하다. ¶ *a magnifying glass* 확대경 / *This microscope magnifies objects five hundred times.* 이 현미경은 물체를 5백배로 확대한다. **2** think or speak of (something) as being much greater than it really is; exaggerate. …을 과장하다. ¶ *~ difficulties* 고난을 과장해서 생각하다. **3** 《*arch.*》 praise highly. 찬미하다; 높이 기리다. [magni-, →-fy]

mag·nil·o·quence [mægníləkwəns] *n.* **1** Ⓤ the state of being too proud of oneself; the act of talking big. 호언장담; 흰소리. **2** Ⓒ speech or writing made up of big words. (말·글 등의) 과장. [↓]

mag·nil·o·quent [mægníləkwənt] *adj.* **1** (of a person) boastful; talking big. 호언장담하는; 흰소리치는. **2** (of language) using big and unusual words. (표현이) 과장된. [→locution]

mag·ni·tude [mǽgnətjù:d] *n.* Ⓤ **1** greatness of size or amount. 큼; 방대; 다량. **2** size. 크기. **3** 《*fig.*》 importance. 중요성. ¶ *a matter of ~* 가장 중요한 일. **4** 《astron.》 the degree of brightness of a star. (별의) 광도; 등급. **5** 《geol.》 the strength of an earthquake. (지진의) 강도. [magni-]

mag·no·li·a [mægnóuliə, -ljə] *n.* Ⓒ a tree with large white or pink blossoms and darkgreen leaves. 목련. [Person, *Magnol*]

mag·num [mǽgnəm] *n.* a two-quart wine or liquor bottle. (2 쿼터들이) 큰 술병; 매그넘. [L. *magnus* great, large, much]

magnum o·pus [mǽgnəm óupəs] *n.* a great work. (예술상의) 대작(大作).

mag·pie [mǽgpài] *n.* Ⓒ **1** a black-and-white bird of the crow family, famous for its noisy chattering. 까치. **2** a person who talks continuously. 수다스러운 사람. [*Margaret, pie ?*]

Ma·gus [méigəs] *n.* sing. of **Magi.**

ma·ha·ra·ja, -jah [mà:hərá:dʒə] *n.* Ⓒ the title of a ruling prince in India. 대왕(大王)《인도 토후국 왕의 존칭》. [Hind.]

ma·hat·ma [məhǽtmə, -há:t-] *n.* Ⓒ a holy person in India who is respected highly for his wisdom, selfishlessness and extraordinary powers. (인도의) 대성(大聖). [Skr. =great soul]

mah-jongg, -jong [má:dʒɔ́:ŋ, -dʒáŋ/-dʒɔ́ŋ] *n.* Ⓤ a Chinese game played by four persons with 136 pieces until one of the players forms winning combinations. 마작. [Chin.]

ma·hog·a·ny [məhágəni/-hɔ́g-] *n.* **1** 《bot.》 a hard reddish-brown wood of a tropical American tree, used to make furniture which can be polished highly. 마호가니 재목. **2** Ⓤ dark reddish-brown. 적갈색; 마호가니색. [Native]

Ma·hom·et [məhámət/-hɔ́m-] *n.* =Mohammed.

Ma·hom·e·tan [məhámətən/-hɔ́m-] *n., adj.* =Mohammedan.

Ma·hom·i·dan [məhámədən/-hɔ́m-] *n., adj.* =Mohammedan.

ma·hout [məháut] *n.* an elephant keeper and driver. (인도의) 코끼리 부리는 사람. [Hind.]

:**maid** [meid] *n.* Ⓒ **1** a young girl. 소녀. **2** an unmarried woman. 미혼의 여성. ¶ *an old ~* 노처녀. **3** a woman servant. 가정부. ¶ *a lady's ~* 시녀 / *a ~ of all work* 잡역부. [E.]

:**maid·en** [méidn] *n.* Ⓒ a girl; a young, unmarried woman. 소녀; 처녀. — *adj.* **1** unmarried. 미혼의. ¶ *a ~ name* 여성의 결혼 전의 성. **2** first; new; untried. 처음의; 처녀…. ¶ *a ~ voyage* 처녀 항해 / *a ~ speech* 처녀 연설 / *a ~ work* 〔*effort*〕 처녀작. [E.]

maid·en·hood [méidnhùd] *n.* Ⓤ the state or time of being a maiden. 처녀성; 처녀 시절.

maid·en-like [méidnlàik] *adj.* =maidenly.

maid·en·ly [méidnli] *adj.* **1** of a maiden. 처녀의. **2** like a maiden; suitable to a maiden; modest. 처녀 같은; 참한; 신중한. ● **maid·en·li·ness** [-nis] *n.*

maid·ser·vant [méidsə:rvənt] *n.* Ⓒ a woman servant. 하녀.

⁑**mail**[1] [meil] *n.* 《esp. U.S.》 **1** Ⓤ 《*collectively*》 letters, papers, parcels, etc., sent through the post office. 우편물(郵便物). ¶ *deliver* ～ 우편물을 배달하다 / *Is the* ～ *in yet?* 편지 왔니 / *The* ～ *is late.* 우편물이 더디다. **2** Ⓤ the government system which carries and delivers such mail. 우편 제도. ¶ *by* ～ 우편으로 / *by air* ～ 항공편으로 / ～ *matter* 우편물 / *a* ～ *order* 우편판매(제). —*vt.* (P6) 《U.S.》 send (letters, etc.) by mail. (편지)를 우송하다(cf. 《Brit.》 *post*). [F. *male* bag]

mail[2] [meil] *n.* Ⓤ a body armor made of steel rings linked together. 쇠미늘 갑옷. —*vt.* (P6) cover, protect with mail. …에게 쇠미늘 갑옷을 입히다. [L. *macula* mesh]

mail·bag [méilbæ̀g] *n.* Ⓒ **1** a mailman's shoulder bag for carrying mail. 우편 가방. **2** a bag for carrying mail. 우편낭. [*mail*[1]]

mail·box [méilbàks/-bɔ̀ks] *n.* Ⓒ 《U.S.》 **1** a public box into which mail is put for collection. 우체통. **2** a private box, as at a home, into which delivered mail is put. (개인 집의) 우편함(cf. 《Brit.》 *letter box*).

mailed fist [∠∠], **the** *n.* armed force; physical force. 무력; 완력.

mail·man [méilmæ̀n] *n.* Ⓒ (*pl.* **-men** [-mèn]) 《U.S.》 a person who collects and carries mail. 우편 집배원(cf. 《Brit.》 *postman*).

maim [meim] *vt.* (P6) cause (someone) to lose the use of a part of the body; cripple. …을 불구로 만들다. ¶ *be seriously maimed by an accident* 사고로 심한 불구가 되다. [F.]

⁑**main** [mein] *adj.* **1** chief; principal; most important. 주요한; 주된; 중요한. ¶ *the* ～ *street* 주요 도로; 큰거리 / *the* ～ *points of an argument* 논의의 요점 / *the* ～ *body of the troops* 주력 부대. **2** largest; of the highest degree. 최고도의. ¶ *by* ～ *force* 〔*strength*〕 전력을 다해. —*n.* Ⓒ **1** a principal pipe for carrying water, gas, etc. (수도·가스 등의) 본관. **2** 《*poet.*》 the wide sea. 대해(大海). [E.]

in the main, for the most part; on the whole. 대체로; 대개. ¶ *The results are, in the* ～*, satisfactory.* 결과는 대체로 만족하다.

with might and main, with all one's strength. 전력을 다해.

main chance [∠∠] *n.* the chance of getting money; one's own interests. 이(利)를 얻을 기회; 사리(私利). ¶ have an eye to the ～ 이끗에 밝다.

main·land [méinlæ̀nd, -lənd] *n.* Ⓒ a large and principal part of a country or broad land, not a small island or peninsula. 본토; (주변의 섬·반도와 구별해) 대륙. ¶ *the U.S.* ～ 미국 본토.

***main·ly** [méinli] *adv.* for the most part; chiefly. 주로. ¶ *You are* ～ *responsible for the trouble.* 그 말썽은 네게 큰 책임이 있다.

main·mast [méinmæ̀st, 《naut.》 -məst] *n.* Ⓒ the chief mast of a ship. 메인마스트; 큰 돛대.

main·sail [méinsèil, 《naut.》 -səl] *n.* Ⓒ the largest sail set from the mainmast. 큰 돛대의 돛; 주범(主帆).

main·spring [méinspriŋ] *n.* Ⓒ **1** the principal spring in a mechanism such as a clock or watch which keeps it going. (시계의) 태엽. **2** 《*fig.*》 the chief cause; the chief motive power. 주요 원인; 원동력.

main·stay [méinstèi] *n.* Ⓒ **1** the strong rope which supports the mainmast of a ship. 큰 돛대의 버팀줄. **2** 《*fig.*》 the main support. 대들보; 의지물(物).

***main·tain** [meintéin, mən-] *vt.* **1** (P6) ⓐ keep up; continue; carry on. …을 지속〔계속 유지〕하다. ¶ ～ *friendly relations* 친선 관계를 계속 유지하다 / ～ *a correspondence* 서신 왕래를 계속하다 / *He maintained a steady speed on the highway.* 그는 고속 도로에서 일정한 속도를 유지해 나갔다. ⓑ preserve. 보전〔보존〕하다. ¶ *Food is necessary to* ～ *life.* 음식은 생명을 보존하는 데 없어서는 안 된다. **2** (P6) support; provide for. …을 부양하다. ¶ ～ *a family* 가족을 부양하다 / ～ *oneself* 자활하다. **3** (P6,11) insist as a belief; assert. …을 주장하다. ¶ *He still maintains that he is innocent.* 그는 여전히 자기 결백을 주장하고 있다. **4** (P6,11) support; back up; defend. 옹호하다; 지키다. ¶ ～ *a cause* 〔*an opinion*〕 주장〔의견〕을 고수하다. **5** (P6) keep in a certain condition. (어떤 상태로) 유지하다. ¶ ～ *a room as it was years ago* 방을 몇 해 전의 상태 그대로 두다. [L. *manus* hand, *teneo* hold]

***main·te·nance** [méintənəns] *n.* **1** Ⓤ the act of maintaining; the state of being maintained. 유지; 보전. ¶ *the cost of* ～ 유지비 / ～ *of peace* 평화 유지. **2** Ⓤ the act of defending. 주장; 옹호. **3** Ⓒ a means of supporting life. 부양; 생계. ¶ *It is hard to get a* ～ *from that little farm.* 저렇게 작은 농토로는 살아가기가 어렵다.

maize [meiz] *n.* Ⓒ a plant that bears grain on large ears; Indian corn. 옥수수; 강냉이. 參考 미국·캐나다 등지에서는 corn이라 함. [Sp.]

Maj. Major.

***ma·jes·tic** [mədʒéstik] *adj.* having a noble and dignified character or appearance. 위엄있는. [→major[2]]

ma·jes·ti·cal [mədʒéstikəl] *adj.* =majestic.

M

ma·jes·ti·cal·ly [mədʒéstikəli] *adv.* in a majestic manner. 위엄 있게; 당당하게.

:maj·es·ty [mǽdʒisti, -dʒəs-] *n.* Ⓤ **1** dignity; nobility. 위엄. ¶ *the ~ of the mountains* 산들의 위용(威容). **2** the supreme power or authority. 권위. ¶ *the ~ of the law* 법의 권위. **3** 《*M*-》 a form in speaking or writing to a king, queen, emperor, or empress. 폐하. 參考 이것을 받는 동사는 3인칭. ¶ *Your ~* 폐하《호칭》/ *His ~* 황제 폐하. [L. *magnus* great]

:ma·jor[1] [méidʒər] *n.* an officer in the army next above a captain. 소령. [↓]

:ma·jor[2] [méidʒər] *adj.* (opp. minor) **1** greater or larger of two things in number, extent, or quality; important. 보다 큰; 많은; 중요한. ¶ *the ~ part of...* …의 대부분 / *~ industries* 주요 산업 / *a ~ poet* 일류 시인 / 《log.》 *the ~ premise* 대전제(大前提). **2** 《Brit.》 senior. 연장(年長)의; 형이 되는. ¶ *Brown ~* 형인 브라운. **3** 《mus.》 of a musical scale which has half-tones between the third and fourth, and seventh and eighth, notes. 장조(長調)의. ¶ *a sonata in C ~* 다장조 소나타 / *the ~ scale* 장음계. **4** 《U.S.》 of the main subject of study. 전공의《과목 등》. **5** of full legal age. 성년(成年)의.
— *n.* Ⓒ **1** 《law》 a person of legal age. 성인(成人). **2** 《U.S.》 the main subject that a student studies; a student of a special subject. 전공 과목〔학생〕. **3** an army officer ranking above a captain. 육군 소령. **4** 《log.》 the major term or subject. 대전제.
— *vi.* (P3) 《U.S.》 study a major subject. 전공하다. ¶ *~ in English literature* 영문학을 전공하다. [L.=greater]

ma·jor-do·mo [mèidʒərdóumou] *n.* Ⓒ (*pl.* **-do·mos**) **1** the chief steward in a great household. 가령(家令); 집사장. **2** 《*joc.*》 a chief servant. 하인 우두머리. [M.L. *mājor domūs* chief officer of the house]

major general [ˊ-ˊ--] *n.* an army officer ranking below a lieutenant general. 육군 소장. [*major*[1]]

***ma·jor·i·ty** [mədʒɔ́(:)rəti, -dʒár-] *n.* (*pl.* **-ties**) **1** Ⓒ 《*collectively*, usu. used as *pl.*》 the greater number or part. 대다수; 대부분; 태반(opp. minority). ¶ *an absolute ~* 절대 다수 / *a ~ party* 다수당 / *a ~ proposal* 다수안(案) / *The (great) ~ of people wish for peace.* 대다수의 사람들이 평화를 바란다 / *The ~ is for him.* 대다수가 그의 편이다 / *be selected by a ~ of 30 to 3,* 30 대 3으로 선출되다. **2** Ⓒ the number of votes by which one side is larger than another. 득표의 (표)차. ¶ *win by a ~ of 50,* 50 표차로 이기다 / *He was returned by a large ~.* 그는 큰 표차로 의원에 선출되었다. **3** Ⓤ full age; the legal age. 성년. ¶ *He will attain* 〔*reach*〕 *his ~ next year.* 그는 내년이면 성년이 된다. **4** Ⓤ the army rank of a major. 소령의 계급. [→major[2], -ity]
go over to* 〔*join*〕 *the majority, 《*fig.*》 die. 죽(은 사람 축에 들)다.

:make [meik] *v.* (**made**) *vt.* **1** (P6,13) put things together so as to produce (a new object); build; form; produce. …을 만들다; 제작하다; 조립하다. ¶ *~ a boat* 〔*dress*〕 보트〔드레스〕를 만들다 / *~ a machine* 기계를 제작하다 / *This box is made of wood.* 이 상자는 목제다 / *~ butter from milk* 버터는 우유로 만든다. 語法 make of 〔out of〕 는 재료의 질이 제품에 남는 경우, make ... from 은 재료·원료가 변형하는 경우. **2** (P13,14) produce something for (someone); produce (something) for someone's use. (아무)에게 …을 만들어 주다. ¶ *~ her a new dress = ~ a new dress for her* 그녀에게 드레스를 만들어 주다. **3** (P7,18,24) cause to grow into; cause to become or be. …을 —하게〔되게〕 하다. ¶ *The news made us happy.* 그 소식은 우리를 행복하게 했다 / *~ a teacher of one's son* 아들을 선생이 되게 하다 / *~ a fool* 〔*monkey*〕 (*out*) *of someone* 아무를 웃음거리로 만들다 / *I could not ~ myself understood in French.* 프랑스 말로는 내 뜻을 알게 할 수 없었다. **4** (P6) cause to develop; build up; form. …을 만들어내다; 발달시키다. ¶ *~ oneself* 독학하다; 자기를 (지적·정신적으로) 형성하다 / *~ one's character* 인격을 도야하다 / *~ one's life* 생활 방도를 정하다. **5** (P6,13) prepare; make ready for use; arrange. …을 마련〔준비〕하다; 정돈하다. ¶ *~ a bed for a guest* 손님을 위해 잠자리를 마련하다 / *~ dinner* 정찬을 준비하다 / *~ a tea* 차를 한잔 내놓다. **6** (P6) get; earn; acquire; win. …을 얻다; 벌다; 획득하다. ¶ *~ money* 돈을 벌다 / *~ a small fortune* 재산을 좀 모으다. **7** (P6) bring about; give rise to; cause to happen. …을 일으키다; 야기시키다. ¶ *~ a noise* 소리를 내다 / *~ a scene* 소란을 피우다 / *She is always making trouble.* 그 여자는 늘 말썽이다. **8** (P6,13) do; execute; effect; perform (an action); carry out. …을 하다; 행하다; 수행하다. ¶ *~ a speech* 연설하다 / *~ an answer* 대답하다 / *~ one's appearance* 얼굴을 내밀다; 출두하다 / *~ war with* 〔*on*〕 *a country* 어느 나라와 전쟁을 치르다 / *~ an escape* 도망치다 / *~ a bargain* 계약을 맺다 / *~ a promise* 약속하다 / *~ a suggestion* 제안하다 / *~ a display of one's knowledge* 실력을 과시하다. **9** (P6) compose; create; write up; draw out. 구성하다; 만들어내다; 저작〔작성〕하다. ¶ *~ a poem* 시를 짓다 / *~ a report* 보고서를 작성하다 / *~ a note* 적어 두다. **10** (P6) equal; amount to; come to. …와 같아지다; 액수가 …이 되다. ¶ *Two and three make(s) five.* 2+3=5 / *Twelve inches ~ a foot.* 12 인치는 1 피트다. **11** (P6,13,14) become; prove to be; develop into. …이 되다. ¶ *He will ~ a good doctor.* 훌륭한 의사가 될 것이다 / *He will ~ her a good husband.* 그는 그녀에게 좋

은 남편이 될 것이다. **12** (P6,19) constitute; appoint. …을 임명하다. ¶ *They made him a judge.* 그들은 그를 심판으로 임명했다. **13** (P6) reach; arrive at. …에 도착하다. ¶ *The ship made port.* 배가 입항했다 / *He made London on the way to Rome.* 로마로 가는 길에 런던에 들렀다. **14** (P6) ⓐ go; travel at a certain speed; cover. …을 가다; 나아가다; …의 속도로 가다. ¶ ～ *one's way on foot* 걸어서 가다 / *This car can* ～ *80 miles an hour.* 이 차는 1시간에 80마일을 간다. ⓑ go on (a journey, etc.). (여행)을 하다. ¶ ～ *an excursion* 소풍가다 / ～ *a European tour* 유럽 여행을 하다 / ～ *two trips to Rome* 로마로 두번 여행하다. **15** (P13,21) judge (something) to be; estimate to be; guess; infer. …을 ―로 어림하다; 판단〔추측〕하다; 추리〔추론〕하다. ¶ *How large do you* ～ *the party?* 파티 규모가 어느 정도라 생각하나 / *I* ～ *it 80.* 80명 규모일 거다 / *What do you* ～ *of this?* 이걸 어떻게 생각하나. **16** (P6) form in the mind; think out. …을 마음으로 정하다; 안출(案出)하다. ¶ ～ *a plan* 계획을 세우다. **17** (P22) cause; force; compel. …을〔에게〕 하게 하다; 강제하다. 語法 수동일 때는 to do가 됨. ¶ *What made you do such a thing?* 왜 이런 짓을 했나 / *I will* ～ *him do it.* 그자에게 그걸 시키고 말겠다 / *You made me miss the train.* 너 때문에 기차를 놓쳤다. ― *vi.* **1** (P4) start; begin an action. …을 하려고 하다. ¶ *She made to go, but I called to her.* 나가려고 하는 그녀를 나는 불렀다 / *He made to answer, when I stopped him.* 그가 대답하려고 할 때 나는 말을 막았다. **2** (P3) ⓐ 《*for*》 go; move toward. 가다; 나아가다. ¶ ～ *for home* 귀로에 오르다. ⓑ 《*to, toward*》 extend to; reach; point. …으로 뻗다; 이르다; 가리키다. ¶ *The road makes toward the sea.* 이 길은 바다에 이른다 / *All the evidence makes in the same direction.* 모든 증거는 한군데로 모아지고 있다. **3** (P2A) 《*as if, as though*》 behave (as if to do). …할 것처럼 행동하다. ¶ *He made as though to strike me.* 그는 나를 칠 듯이 굴었다. **4** (P1,2A) (of tides, etc.) flow; rise. (조수 등이) 밀려오다; 붇다. ¶ *The tide is making fast.* 조수가 빠르게 밀려오고 있다.

make after (=*follow; run after*) *something.* …을 뒤쫓다.

make against (=*be contrary, unfavorable, harmful to*) *something.* …에 불리해지다; …을 방해하다.

make at, go at. …을 향해 가다.

make away with, **a**) steal (something) and go away; run away with. …을 들고〔훔쳐〕 달아나다. **b**) get rid of, kill, or destroy (something). …을 제거하다; 죽이다.

make believe, pretend. 가장하다; …인 체하다. ¶ *Let's* ～ *believe we're Indians.* 인디언을 가장하자.

make *something* ***do*** =***make do with*** *something* ⇨do.

make for, **a**) ⇨*vi.* 2ⓐ. **b**) attack; charge at. …을 공격하다. ¶ *The bull made for him.* 황소가 그에게 덤벼들었다. **c**) help to make; promote. …에 도움이 되다; 조장(助長)하다. ¶ ～ *for world peace* 세계 평화에 이바지하다.

make good (=*pay or compensate for*) *a loss.* (손실)을 메우다.

make it, 《*colloq.*》 succeed; do; achieve. 성공하다; 해내다. ¶ *She was to show up at the place, but she didn't* ～ *it.* 그녀가 그 자리에 나올 터였으나 그렇지 못했다.

make it up (=*become friends again*) ***with*** *someone* (*after quarrel*). …와 화해하다.

make little 〔***much***〕 ***of,*** treat (something) as of little 〔much〕 importance. …을 낮추보다〔중히 여기다〕.

make off, hurry away; run away. 서둘러 떠나다; 도망치다.

make off with, steal. …을 들고 달아나다.

make out, **a**) write out (a list, a check, etc.). …을 쓰다; 기입하다. ¶ ～ *out a receipt* 〔*check*〕 영수증을 쓰다〔수표를 떼다〕. **b**) understand. 이해하다; 뜻을 알다. ¶ ～ *out the meaning.* **c**) see (something) with difficulty; manage to see. 가까스로 알아보다. ¶ *We can't* ～ *out the path in the faint starlight.* 별빛이 흐려 길이 (잘) 안 보인다. **d**) 《*colloq.*》 manage; succeed. 그럭저럭 해나가다; 성공하다. ¶ *He made out very well in his exams.* 시험을 썩 잘 쳤다. **e**) cause (oneself) to appear to be (what one is not). …인 체하다. ¶ ～ *oneself out to be wise* 약은 체하다.

make *something* ***over,*** **a**) make something different. 고쳐 만들다; 개조하다. ¶ ～ *over a dress* 옷을 고쳐 만들다. **b**) hand over (one's property, etc.). …을 양도하다. ¶ ～ *over one's property to one's son* 재산을 아들에게 물리다.

make the best of, use (something) in the best way. …을 최대한 이용하다.

make the most of, use (something) to the greatest advantage. …을 크게 이용하다.

make up, **a**) put together or form (something). 만들다; 짜다. ¶ ～ *up a timetable* / ～ *up cloth into a dress* 천으로 옷을 만들다. **b**) invent (a story, an excuse, etc.). (구실 등)을 꾸며내다; 날조하다. ¶ ～ *up a lie.* **c**) become friends again. 사화(私和)하다. **d**) (of an actor, etc.) put paint, powder, etc. 분장하다(cf. *make-up*). **e**) 《U.S.》 repeat (an examination missed or failed). 추가 시험을 치다; (과목)을 다시 이수하다.

make up (=*pay or compensate*) ***for*** *a loss.* (…의) 벌충을 하다; 메우다. ¶ ～ *up for lost time.* 지연된 시간을 벌충〔만회〕하다.

make up *one's* ***mind,*** decide; make a resolution. 결심하다. ¶ ～ *up one's mind that something must be done* …을 마무리해야겠다고 작정하다.

make up to *someone,* flatter. …의 환심을 사

다. ¶ ~ *up to important people* 명사들의 환심을 사다.

—*n.* Ⓒ **1** the way in which something is made; style; build. 만듦새; 양식; 형(型); 구조. ¶ *a hat of a new* ~ 신식 모자 / *machines of various makes* 각양각색의 기계들. **2** nature; character. 성격; 기질. ¶ *one's mental* ~ 마음씨; 기질 / *a man of quite another* ~ 전혀 다른 성격의 사람. **3** physical build; constitution. 체격; 체질. ¶ *a man of slender* ~ 호리호리한 사람 / *She is slender in* ~. 몸매가 날씬한 여자다. **4** a sort; a brand. 종류; …제. ¶ *This is our own* ~. 이건 국산이다 / *What* ~ *of car is hers?* 그녀 차는 무슨 형이냐. **5** the amount made. 생산고. **6** the act of making. 제조. ¶ *be in the* ~ 제작중이다. [E.]

on the make, 《*colloq.*》 eager to gain money or success. 돈벌이〔출세〕에 열중하여.

make-be·lieve [méikbilìːv] *n.* **1** Ⓤ the act of pretending. 치레; 가장. **2** Ⓒ a person who pretends. …인 체하는 사람. —*adj.* 《as *attributive*》 pretended. …인 체하는; 거짓의. ¶ *a* ~ *sleep* 꾀잠. [E.]

mak·er [méikər] *n.* **1** Ⓒ a person who makes something. 만드는 사람; 제작자; 메이커. **2** Ⓤ 《*the M-*》 God. 신.

make·shift [méikʃift] *n.* Ⓒ a thing used for a time instead of the right thing. (임시의) 대용품. ¶ *use a candle as a* ~ 임시로 양초를 쓰다. —*adj.* temporary. 임시 변통의. [*make, shift*]

make-up [méikʌ̀p] *n.* Ⓒ **1** the way in which a thing is composed; structure. 구성; 구조. ¶ *the mental* ~ *of a man* 인간의 정신적 구조. **2** nature; composition. 성질. ¶ *He is of a nervous* ~. 신경질적인〔소심한〕 사람이다. **3** the way in which an actor paints and powders his face to look his part. 메이크업; 분장. **4** paint and powder put on the face. 화장품. **5** 《print.》 the act of making up. 조판(組版). **6** 《U.S.》 a special examination given to a student who has missed or failed an original one. 추가 시험. [*make, up*]

mak·ing [méikiŋ] *n.* Ⓤ **1** the act or process of making. 만들기; 발전의 과정. **2** structure; make-up. 조립; 구조. **3** cause of success; a means of advancement. 성공·발전의 원인〔수단〕. **4** 《usu. *pl.*》 capacity; talent. 소질; 자질. ¶ *He has the makings of a good teacher.* 훌륭한 선생이 될 자질이 있다. **5** 《*pl.*》 material needed for making something. 원료; 재료. **6** ⓐ Ⓒ something made. 제품; 제작물. ⓑ the amount made at one time. 1회의 생산고. ⓒ 《*pl.*》 earnings; profits. 벌이; 이익.

in the making, in the process of being made; not yet completed. 제작중인; 미완성의. ¶ *a doctor in the* ~ 수련의.

mal- [mæl-], **male-** [mælə-] *pref.* **1** bad; badly. '나쁜, 나쁘게'의 뜻. ¶ *maltreat* 학대하다. **2** not; un-. '불〔비〕…'의 뜻. ¶ *malcontent* 불만인. **3** imperfect. '불완전한'의 뜻. ¶ *malformation* 기형; 불구. [L. *malus* bad]

mal·ad·just·ed [mæ̀lədʒʌ́stid] *adj.* **1** poorly adjusted. 조절이 불충분한. **2** not well fit for one's circumstances. 환경에 적응이 안되는. ¶ *a* ~ *child* 환경에 적응이 어려운 아이.

mal·ad·just·ment [mæ̀lədʒʌ́stmənt] *n.* ⓊⒸ the state of being maladjusted. 조절 불량; 부적응.

mal·a·droit [mæ̀lədrɔ́it] *adj.* **1** not skillful. 솜씨가 없는; 서투른. **2** not clever; not smart. 약지 못한; 어수룩한. [mal-]

mal·a·dy [mǽlədi] *n.* Ⓒ (*pl.* **-dies**) a disease; a sickness; an illness. 병; 질병. ¶ 《*fig.*》 *social maladies* 사회적 병폐. [mal-, L. *habeo* have]

ma·lar·i·a [məlɛ́əriə] *n.* Ⓤ a tropical illness with a high fever, chills, and sweating caused by the bite of a certain kind of mosquito. 말라리아; 학질. [It.=bad air]

ma·lar·i·al [məlɛ́əriəl] *adj.* of malaria. 말라리아의. ¶ ~ *fever* 말라리아 열.

Ma·lay [məléi, méilei] *n.* **1** Ⓒ a group of brown skinned people living on the Malay Peninsula and nearby islands. 말레이 사람. **2** Ⓤ their language. 말레이어(語). —*adj.* of Malay; of the language and people of Malay. 말레이의; 말레이 사람〔어〕의. [Native]

Ma·lay·a [məléiə] *n.* the Malay Peninsula. 말레이 반도.

Ma·lay·an [məléiən] *n., adj.* =Malay.

Ma·lay·sia [məléiʒə, -ʃə] *n.* an independent federation of southeast Asia; the Malay Archipelago. 말레이시아; 말레이 제도.

Ma·lay·sian [məléiʒən, -ʃən] *n.* Ⓒ a person of Malaysia. 말레이 제도인. —*adj.* of Malaysia, its people and their language. 말레이 제도〔사람, 언어〕의.

mal·con·tent [mæ̀lkəntént] *adj.* not contented. 불만의. —*n.* Ⓒ a person who is not contented. 불만〔불평〕자. [mal-]

***male** [meil] *adj.* **1** of the sex such as men, boys, and he-animals. 남성의; 수컷의 (opp. female). ¶ *a* ~ *animal* / *a* ~ *screw* 수나사. **2** of a plant that does not produce fruit. 수술의. ¶ *a* ~ *flower* 수꽃. **3** suitable to or characteristic of a male. 남성에 어울리는; 남성적인(cf. *masculine*). ¶ *a* ~ *voice.* —*n.* Ⓒ **1** a person or an animal of this sex. 남성; 수컷. **2** a male plant. 웅성 식물(opp. female). [→masculine]

male- *pref.* ⇨mal-.

mal·e·dic·tion [mæ̀lədíkʃən] *n.* Ⓒ the act or fact of speaking evil of someone; a curse. 욕설; 악담; 저주(opp. benediction). [mal-]

mal·e·fac·tion [mæ̀ləfǽkʃən] *n.* ⓊⒸ an evil act. 못된 짓; 죄악. [mal-]

mal·e·fac·tor [mǽləfæ̀ktər] *n.* Ⓒ (opp. benefactor) **1** a person who does an evil act. 악인. **2** a person who commits a crime. 범인.

ma·lef·i·cent [məléfəsnt] *adj.* **1** hurtful; harmful. 해로운; 유해한. **2** causing evil. 못된 짓을 하는. [mal-]

ma·lev·o·lence [məlévələns] *n.* Ⓤ the wish that something bad or harmful may happen to others; ill will. 악의; 해칠 마음; 적의(敵意); 저주(詛呪)(opp. benevolence). [↓]

ma·lev·o·lent [məlévələnt] *adj.* showing malevolence; full of ill-feeling. 악의 있는; 악의에 찬. [mal-, L *volo* wish]

mal·fea·sance [mælfíːzəns] *n.* ⓊⒸ 《law》 an evil deed by an official in relation to public affairs. (공무원의) 비행; 독직 행위 (cf. *misfeasance*). [mal-, →fact]

mal·for·ma·tion [mæ̀lfɔːrméiʃən] *n.* Ⓤ the wrong and abnormal structure of a body or a part of it. 기형; 불구(不具). [mal-]

***mal·ice** [mǽlis] *n.* Ⓤ the evil desire to hurt others; ill will. 남을 해칠 마음; 적의; 악의(cf. *malevolence*). ¶ *She didn't do it out of* ~. 그녀가 악의로 그랬던 것은 아니었다. [mal-]

***bear malice to* 〔*toward*〕,** have an evil will toward (someone). …에게 악의〔적의〕를 품다.

ma·li·cious [məlíʃəs] *adj.* showing the desire to hurt others; having ill will. 악의 있는; 남을 해치려는. [↑]

ma·li·cious·ly [məlíʃəsli] *adv.* with the desire to hurt others. 악의를 가지고; 악의로.

ma·lign [məláin] *adj.* filled with harm; having a desire to hurt others; malignant. 유해한; 악성의; 악의 있는(opp. benign). ¶ *have a* ~ *influence* 나쁜 영향이 있다. — *vt.* (P6) speak evil of (someone); curse. …을 헐뜯다; 저주하다. [mal-]

ma·lig·nan·cy [məlígnənsi], **-nance** [-nəns] *n.* Ⓤ **1** the state of being malignant. 악의; 적의. **2** 《med.》 the tendency to cause death. (질병의) 악성. [↓]

ma·lig·nant [məlígnənt] *adj.* **1** showing the desire to hurt others. 악의 있는. **2** 《med.》 dangerous; causing death. 악성의; 생명에 관계된(opp. benignant). ¶ *a* ~ *disease* 난치〔불치〕병. ● **ma·lig·nant·ly** [-li] *adv.* [mal-]

ma·lig·ni·ty [məlígnəti] *n.* (*pl.* **-ties**) Ⓤ **1** the state of being malign. 악의; 적의. **2** 《med.》 the quality of being malignant. (질병의) 악성.

ma·lin·ger [məlíŋgər] *vi.* (P1) pretend to be ill. 꾀병을 부리다. [F. *malingre* sickly]

mall [mɔːl / mæl] *n.* a shaded walk, usu. public. 나무 그늘이 있는 산책길. [*maul*]

mal·lard [mǽlərd] *n.* Ⓒ (*pl.* **-lards** or *collectively* **-lard**) a male wild duck; any common wild duck. 청둥오리. [F.]

mal·le·a·bil·i·ty [mæ̀liəbíləti] *n.* Ⓤ the quality or state of being malleable. (금속의) 가단성(可鍛性); 전성(展性); 유연성. [↓]

mal·le·a·ble [mǽləbəl] *adj.* **1** that can be struck or pressed into various shapes by a hammer without being broken. 가단성〔전성〕이 있는. **2** 《*fig.*》 that can fit oneself to new conditions. 순응하는; 적응성이 있는. [L. *malleus* hammer]

mal·let [mǽlit] *n.* a hammer, usu. with a heavy wooden head. (나무)메. [↑]

mal·low [mǽlou] *n.* Ⓒ 《bot.》 a plant with pink and white flowers and hairy leaves and stems. 당아욱. [L. *malva*]

mal·nu·tri·tion [mæ̀lnjuːtríʃən] *n.* Ⓤ lack of nourishment caused by poor food or wrong diet. 영양 부족〔실조〕. [mal-]

mal·o·dor·ous [mælóudərəs] *adj.* smelling bad. 악취가 나는. [mal-]

mal·prac·tice [mælprǽktis] *n.* Ⓒ **1** 《med.》 a doctor's unlawful and injurious treatment of a patient. (의사의) 부정 치료. **2** 《law》 an official's wrong act or practice. (공무원의) 배임(背任) 행위.

malt [mɔːlt] *n.* Ⓤ **1** barley or other grain which has begun to grow in water, then dried and used in making strong drinks. 맥아; 엿기름. **2** 《*colloq.*》 beer or ale. 맥주. — *adj.* made with malt. 맥아로 만든. ¶ ~ *liquor* 몰트술《ale, beer, stout 등》/ ~ *sugar* 맥아당. — *vt.* (P6) **1** change (grain) into malt. …을 엿기름으로 만들다. **2** make (liquor) with malt. 엿기름으로 (…을) 만들다. — *vi.* (P1) change into malt. 엿기름이 되다. [E.]

mal·treat [mæltríːt] *vt.* (P6) treat or use in a wrong manner; handle roughly. …을 학대〔혹사〕하다. [mal-]

mal·treat·ment [mæltríːtmənt] *n.* Ⓤ rough and unkind treatment. 학대; 혹사.

mal·ver·sa·tion [mæ̀lvəːrséiʃən] *n.* corrupt conduct in an official position. 독직(瀆職); 수뢰(受賂). [mal-, L. *verto* turn]

***ma·ma** [máːmə, məmáː] *n.* = mamma.

:**mam·ma** [máːmə, məmáː] *n.* Ⓒ 《chiefly *child's word*》 a mother. 엄마. [instinctive]

mam·mal [mǽməl] *n.* Ⓒ an animal that has a backbone and feeds its young with its milk, such as human beings, dogs, bats, or whales. 포유 동물. [L. *mamma* breast]

mam·moth [mǽməθ] *n.* Ⓒ a very large, hairy elephant with long curved tusks which disappeared from the earth in prehistoric ages. 매머드. — *adj.* very large; gigantic. 거대한; 매머드 같은. ¶ *a* ~ *enterprise* 거대 기업 / *a* ~ *ship* 거선(巨船). [Russ.]

***mam·my** [mǽmi] *n.* (*pl.* **-mies**) Ⓒ **1** 《*child's word*》 a mother. 엄마(opp. daddy). **2** a Negro woman who looks after white children in the southern States of the United States. (미국 남부의 백인 가정의) 흑인 유모. [*mamma*]

:man [mæn] *n.* Ⓒ (*pl.* **men**) **1** a grown male person. (성인) 남자; 어른(opp. woman; boy). **2** a human being; a person. 사람. ¶ *all men* 모든 사람 / *Any* ~ *can do it.* 그걸 못 하는 사람은 없다 / *What can a* ~ *do in such a case?* 그런 경우 어쩌면 좋단 말인가. **3** 《*sing.*, used without an *article*》 the human race. 인간; 인류. ¶ *Man is mortal.* 인간은 죽게 마련이다. **4** ⓐ a male employee; a manservant or a workman. 고용인; 하인; 머슴; 노동자. ¶ *master and* ~ 주인과 하인. ⓑ 《usu. *pl.*》 soldiers, esp. common soldiers. 군인; 사병. ¶ *officers and men* 장병. **5** a husband. 남편. ¶ ~ *and wife* 남편과 아내; 부부. **6** a person with manly qualities. 남자다운 남자; 대장부; 제구실하는 남자. ¶ *play the* ~ 남자답게 굴다 / *only half a* ~ 나약한 남자; 반쪽 남자 / *He was every inch a* ~. 그는 실로 남자다웠다. **7** one of the pieces used in playing chess or checkers. (체스 등의) 말.

as one man, in complete agreement; with one voice; in chorus. 만장일치로; 일제히; 이구동성으로.

be one's own man, be free to do as one pleases; be in possession of one's senses, energies, etc. 독립해 있다; 자제할 줄 알다; 꿋꿋하다.

make a man of, make (someone) honorable. (아무)를 제몫을 하는 남자로 만들다; 성공시키다.

man and boy, 《as *adv. phrase*》 from boyhood on. 아이적부터.

man of his hands, a man deft of hand. 손재주가 있는 사람.

man of his word, a person who keeps his word. 신의가 있는 사람.

man of parts, an able man. 수완가.

man of the world, an experienced, practical, talented man. 세상 물정에 밝은 사람.

the man in the street, an ordinary person. 일반인; 보통 사람.

to a man, all; without exception. 한 사람 빠짐 없이; 예외 없이. ¶ *We volunteered to a* ~. 우리는 모두 지원했다.

— *vt.* (**manned, man·ning**) (P6) **1** supply (a ship, a fort, etc.) with men. (선박 등)에 인원을 배치하다. ¶ ~ *the ship with 50 sailors* 배에 선원 50명을 두다 / ~ *a fort* 요새에 인원을 배치하다. **2** take (one's place) for work. (선박 등)에 승무(乘務)하다. ¶ *a ship manned by sailors* 선원들이 승선한 배. **3** 《*reflexively*》 make (someone) strong or manly. …을 힘내게 하다. ¶ ~ *oneself* 분발하다. [E.]

man·a·cle [mǽnəkl] *n.* Ⓒ **1** 《usu. *pl.*》 rings or chains to lock about the wrist of a prisoner; a handcuff. 수갑. **2** 《*fig.*》 restriction. 구속; 속박. — *vt.* (P6) **1** put manacles on (someone). …에 수갑을 채우다. **2** place restrictions on (someone). …을 속박하다. [manu-]

:man·age [mǽnidʒ] *vt.* (P6,8) **1** control; direct; handle. …을 제어하다; 다루다; 조종하다; 부리다. ¶ ~ *a boat* 보트를 조종하다 / ~ *one's husband* 남편을 다루다 / ~ *a hotel* 호텔을 경영하다 / *They hired a man to* ~ *the business.* 그들은 그 사업의 경영을 위해 사람을 하나 고용했다. **2** succeed somehow in doing (something). 어떻게든 해서 …하다. ¶ *I think I can* ~ *it.* 어떻게든 그걸 할 수 있다고 생각한다 / *I can't* ~ *it alone.* 나 혼자서는 그 일을 할 수 없다 / *She managed to get what she wanted.* 그녀는 원하는 것을 용케 손에 넣었다. **3** 《*colloq.*》 《often with *can* or *be able to*》 eat. …을 먹다. ¶ *Can you* ~ *another piece of cake?* 과자 한 개 더 먹겠나.

— *vi.* (P1,3) **1** deal with affairs; do business. 일을 처리하다; 사업을 경영하다. ¶ *I won't be able to* ~ *without help.* 도움 없이는 해낼 수 없다. **2** get along. 그럭저럭 해나가다〔살아가다〕. ¶ *I'll* ~ *with the tools I have.* 내게 있는 연장으로 어떻게 해보겠다 / *Does he* ~ *on his monthly income?* 그 사람은 월수입으로 살아가고 있나. [→manual, -age]

man·age·a·ble [mǽnidʒəbəl] *adj.* that can be managed; easily controlled or managed. 다룰 수 있는; 관리〔처리〕하기 쉬운. ¶ *a* ~ *horse* 부리기 쉬운 말.

:man·age·ment [mǽnidʒmənt] *n.* Ⓤ **1** the act of managing; handling; control. 취급; 통어; 처리; 조종. ¶ *The firm is under foreign* ~. 그 회사는 외국인이 경영하고 있다 / *It took a good deal of* ~ *to get him to leave the house.* 그 사람이 집을 비우게 하는 데는 가지가지의 수단을 써야 했다. **2** the managing ability. 경영력; 경영 수완; 지배(력). ¶ *The business failed because of poor* ~. 그 사업은 경영을 잘못해서 망해 버렸다. **3** ⓊⒸ 《*collectively*》 persons who are in charge of a business. 경영자(측(側)). ¶ ~ *and labor* 노사 양측.

:man·ag·er [mǽnidʒər] *n.* Ⓒ **1** a person who is in charge of management. 경영자; 지배인; 감독. ¶ *a stage* ~ 무대 감독 / *the* ~ *of a shop* 상점 지배인. **2** a person who looks after a household skillfully. (가사 등을) 꾸려가는 사람. ¶ *His wife is a poor* ~. 그의 아내는 살림이 서툴다.

man·ag·ing [mǽnidʒiŋ] *adj.* **1** having a power of controlling. 지배〔관리〕하는. ¶ *a* ~ *director* 전무 이사. **2** skillful in managing. 경영을 잘하는. **3** too careful and economical about money. 인색한. **4** wishing to control others. 오지랖 넓은. ¶ *a very* ~ *woman* 너무 오지랖 넓은 여자.

man-at-arms [mǽnətɑ́ːrmz] *n.* Ⓒ (*pl.* **men-** [mén-]) a soldier, esp. a heavily armed soldier on horseback in the Middle

Ages. (중세의) 중기병(重騎兵). [*man, arm*²]

man·a·tee [mǽnətiː] *n.* a seacow. 바다소; 매너티. [Carib.]

Man·ches·ter [mǽntʃèstər] *n.* a town in Lancashire, the center of cotton manufacturing in western England. 맨체스터. ¶ ~ *goods* 맨체스터 면직물. [Place]

man·da·rin [mǽndərin] *n.* **1** Ⓒ a Chinese official of high rank in the old Chinese Empire. (중국 청조(淸朝)의) 관리. **2** Ⓤ 《*M-*》 one of the Chinese dialects spoken by educated Chinese. (중국의) 관화(官話); 북경관화. **3** Ⓒ a kind of small, sweet orange; a tangerine. 만다린 귤. **4** Ⓤ deep orange-colored dye. 등색(橙色) 물감. [Skr. =counsellor]

man·da·tar·y [mǽndətèri / -dətəri] *n.* (*pl.* **-tar·ies**) 《law》 Ⓒ a person or a country that carries out a mandate over another person or country. 수임자(受任者); 위임 통치국. [↓]

man·date [mǽndeit] *n.* Ⓒ **1** an official command. 명령; 훈령. **2** orders from people to those chosen (usu. shown by election). (선거구민의) 요구; 주문. — *vt.* (P6) put (a country or a land) under the rule of another country. …을 위임 통치하에 두다. ¶ *a mandated territory* 위임 통치령. [manu-, L. *do* give]

man·da·to·ry [mǽndətɔ̀ːri / -təri] *adj.* **1** having a nature of command. 명령의. **2** having control over another country or person. 위임의. ¶ ~ *administration* 위임 통치 / *a* ~ *power* 위임 통치국. — *n.* Ⓒ a mandatary. 수임자; 위임 통치국.

man·di·ble [mǽndəbəl] *n.* **1** a jaw, esp. the lower jaw. 턱; (특히) 아래턱. **2** either part of a bird's beak. (새의) 윗[아랫]부리. **3** an organ in insects for seizing and biting. (곤충의) 턱. [L. *mando* chew]

man·do·lin [mǽndəlin], **-line** [mæ̀ndəlíːn] *n.* a musical instrument with four or five pairs of strings, played with a pick. 만돌린. [It.]

mane [mein] *n.* Ⓒ **1** the long hair growing on the back of or about the neck of a horse, lion, etc. 갈기. **2** a person's long and thick hair like mane. (갈기 모양의) 머리털. [E.]

man-eat·er [mǽniːtər] *n.* Ⓒ **1** a person eating human flesh; a cannibal. 식인종. **2** an animal that eats human flesh, esp. a shark, lion, or tiger. 사람을 잡아먹는 짐승 《상어·사자·호랑이 등》. [*man*]

ma·nège, -nege [mænéʒ, -néiʒ] *n.* 《F.》 a riding school; skill in riding; the training of a horse; the action or movements of a trained horse. 승마 학교; 마술(馬術); 말의 조교(調敎).

ma·neu·ver, 《Brit.》 **-noeu·vre** [mənúːvər] *n.* Ⓒ **1** a well-planned movement or change of position of troops or ships. (군대나 함대의) 기동(機動); 작전 행동. **2** 《*pl.*》 a series of military exercises done under conditions like a real war. (군대의) 실전 연습. **3** a skillful movement or plan. 교묘한 행동; 책략. ¶ *a political* ~ 정치 공작 / *a clever* ~ 교묘한 책략.
— *vi.* (P1,2A,2B) (of troops, ships, etc.) move according to a plan. (군대·함대가) 기동 연습하다.
— *vt.* (P6,7,13) **1** cause (troops, ships, etc.) to move or change their position according to a plan. (군대·함대)를 기동 연습시키다. **2** arrange (matters) to suit one's own purposes. 책략으로 …하게 만들다; 책략을 쓰다. ¶ ~ (*someone*) *into* 〔*out of*〕 *a room* 계략을 써서 (아무를) 방으로 끌어들이다〔방에서 내몰다〕. [manu-, →opus]

man Friday [ˊˊ–] *n.* a faithful servant or helper, esp. colored. (특히 흑인) 충복(忠僕)《Robinson Crusoe의 충복의 이름에서》.

man·ful [mǽnfəl] *adj.* showing bravery and determination like a man. 남자다운; 씩씩한. [*man*]

man·ful·ly [mǽnfəli] *adv.* resolutely and bravely like a man. 사나이답게.

man·ga·nese [mǽŋgəniːz, -niːs] *n.* Ⓤ a hard and gray metal element that is easily broken, used in making glass, paint, and medicine. 망간. [→magnesia]

mange [meindʒ] *n.* Ⓤ a skin-disease of animals. (짐승의) 옴. [→mandible]

man·ger [méindʒər] *n.* Ⓒ a box to place hay in for feeding cattle and horses. 여물통; 구유. [→mandible]

a dog in the manger, a person who neither makes use of a thing himself, nor will permit others to do so. 심통 사나운 사람.

man·gle¹ [mǽŋgəl] *vt.* (P6) **1** cut (flesh, etc.) into pieces. (고기 등)을 난도질하다. **2** spoil (a version of a text, a pronunciation, etc.) by mistakes. (실수로) …을 망쳐 놓다. [→maim]

man·gle² [mǽŋgəl] *n.* Ⓒ a machine with rollers for pressing out water from wet clothes and for smoothing them. 압착 롤러; 맹글《세탁물을 탈수하고 주름을 펴는》.
— *vt.* (P6) press (wet clothes, etc.) with a mangle. 맹글로 …의 주름을 펴다. [Gk. =catapult]

man·go [mǽŋgou] *n.* Ⓒ (*pl.* **-goes** or **-gos**) a pear-shaped, juicy, yellowish-red fruit grown in the tropical zone; a tree bearing this fruit. 망고 열매; 망고나무. [Tamil]

man·go·steen [mǽŋgəstiːn] *n.* Ⓒ a juicy, reddish-brown fruit grown in the East Indies; a tree bearing this fruit. 망고스틴 열매; 그 나무. [↑]

man·grove [mǽŋgrouv] *n.* a tropical tree that sends down branches which take root and become new trunks. 홍수림

(紅樹林). [? Port.]

man·gy [méindʒi] *adj.* (**-gi·er, -gi·est**) **1** having the mange. 옴에 걸린. **2** 《*fig.*》 poor and dirty; mean. 초라하고 더러운; 천한. [*mange*]

man·han·dle [mǽnhæ̀ndl] *vt.* (P6) **1** move (something) by human strength. …을 인력으로 움직이다. ¶ *We manhandled the piano up to the stairs.* 우리는 맨손으로 피아노를 계단에 들어 올렸다. **2** treat roughly. …을 거칠게 다루다. ¶ ~ *a prisoner.* [*man, handle*]

Man·hat·tan [mænhǽtn] *n.* the island which contains the main business section of New York City. 맨해튼 섬.

man·hole [mǽnhòul] *n.* Ⓒ a hole through which a man enters an underground pipe or channel to inspect or repair it. 맨홀. [*man*]

***man·hood** [mǽnhùd] *n.* Ⓤ **1** the state or quality of being a man. 남자다움. **2** the time of being a man. 성인. ¶ *be in early* ~ 이제 막 성인이 되었다 / *grow to* 〔*arrive at, come to*〕 ~ 어른이 되다. **3** a manly quality. 남자다움. ¶ *be in the prime of* ~ 남자로서의 한창때다. **4** 《*collectively*》 men. 남자. ¶ *the* ~ *of the country* 한 나라의 남자(전체). [*man*]

manhood suffrage [⌐∸ ∸–] *n.* the right to vote for the adult. 성년 남자 선거권.

man-hour [mǽnàuər] *n.* Ⓒ a time-unit of work equal to an hour of work done by one man. 인시(人時)《1 인당 1 시간의 노동량》. [*man, hour*]

ma·ni·a [méiniə, -njə] *n.* **1** Ⓤ a kind of violent madness and wild excitement. 조병(躁病). **2** Ⓒ a strong liking; unusual, unreasonable enthusiasm. 열광; …광(狂). ¶ *She has a* ~ *for dancing.* 그녀는 댄스광이다. [Gk. *mainomai* be mad]

-ma·ni·a [-méiniə, -njə] *suf.* madness; intense enthusiasm. '…광(狂)'의 뜻. ¶ *kleptomania* 절도광 / *bibliomania* 장서벽〔광〕. [↑]

ma·ni·ac [méiniæ̀k] *adj.* mad; insane. 미친; 발광한. — *n.* Ⓒ a madman; a lunatic. 광인; 미치광이. ¶ *Don't drive so fast, you* ~; *You'll kill us all!* 이 미친 놈아, 그렇게 빨리 몰지 마. 우릴 모두 죽일 참이냐.

ma·ni·a·cal [mənáiəkəl] *adj.* insane; mad; crazy. 실성한; 미친. ¶ ~ *laughter* 실성한 듯한 웃음.

ma·ni·a·cal·ly [mənáiəkəli] *adv.* in a wild and mad way. 미친 듯이.

man·i·cure [mǽnəkjùər] *n.* Ⓤ the act of polishing and cleaning the fingernails. 매니큐어; 미조술(美爪術). — *vt.* (P6) give a manicure to (the fingernails). (손톱)에 매니큐어를 하다; (손톱)을 손질하다. ¶ *have one's fingernails manicured* 손톱 손질을 시키다. [manu-, →cure]

man·i·cur·ist [mǽnəkjù:rist] *n.* Ⓒ a person who manicures others as a profession. 미조사(美爪師).

***man·i·fest** [mǽnəfèst] *adj.* clear to the eye or to the mind; plain. 명백한; 분명한. ¶ *The truth of that statement is* ~. 그 말이 진실임은 명명백백하다. — *vt.* (P6) **1** show clearly. …을 분명히 밝히다. **2** make (something) clear to be true; prove. …을 증명하다. ¶ ~ *the truth* 진실을 증명하다. **3** show (one's feelings). (감정 등)을 나타내다. ¶ ~ *dissatisfaction* 불만을 밖으로 드러내다. — *vi.* (P1) (of a ghost, etc.) appear. (유령 등이) 나타나다. — *n.* a detailed list of a ship's cargo, or passengers carried on an airplane. 적하(積荷) 목록; (비행기의) 승객 명단. [L. *manifestus*]

man·i·fes·ta·tion [mæ̀nəfestéiʃən] *n.* Ⓒ Ⓤ **1** the act of manifesting. 명시. **2** something that manifests; a display; a proof. 표현; 표시; 입증. ¶ *a* ~ *of bad feeling.* **3** a public announcement of policy, etc. (정부·정당의) 정견 발표.

man·i·fes·to [mæ̀nəféstou] *n.* Ⓒ (*pl.* **-tos** or **-toes**) a public declaration of thoughts, plans, etc. by a government or an important person or group. (정책 등의) 선언(서); 성명(서). ¶ *a political* ~ / *issue a* ~ 성명을 발표하다.

***man·i·fold** [mǽnəfòuld] *adj.* **1** of many kinds; various. 다양한; 여러 가지의. **2** having many parts or forms. 다방면의. — *n.* Ⓒ **1** a pipe with several openings used for connecting with other pipes. 다기관(多岐管). **2** one of many copies. 사본; 카피. — *vt.* (P6) make many copies of (something) by means of a duplicating machine. (복사기로) …의 사본을 많이 만들다. [*many*, -fold]

man·i·kin [mǽnikin] *n.* Ⓒ **1** a small man; a dwarf. 난쟁이. **2** an anatomical model of the human body, used for teaching medical students. 인체 해부 모형. **3** a mannequin. 모델 인형; 마네킹. [→man]

Ma·nil·a [mənílə] *n.* **1** a city in the Philippines. 마닐라. 參考 필리핀의 수도. **2** 《often *m*-》 Ⓤ Manila hemp; Manila rope; Manila paper. 마닐라삼; 마닐라 로프; 마닐라 종이. [Place]

ma·nip·u·late [mənípjəlèit] *vt.* (P6) **1** handle (machines) skillfully with the hands. …을 능란하게 다루다. ¶ ~ *handles* 〔*tools*〕 핸들을〔공구를〕 다루다. **2** 《*fig.*》 manage (someone) cleverly by using unfair means. …을 부정 수단으로 교묘히 다루다. ¶ ~ *public opinion* 여론을 조종하다 / *He adores her and she manipulates him shamelessly.* 그는 그녀를 흠모하고 그녀는 파렴치하게 그를 다룬다. **3** treat (an account, etc.) dishonestly for one's own advantage. (장부)를 속이다. ¶ *The accounts were manipulated.* 계산서는 조작된 것들이었다. [*manu-*, L. *pleo* fill]

ma·nip·u·la·tion [mənìpjəléiʃən] *n.* ⓊⒸ

the act of manipulating or handling skillfully; good use of the hands. 능란하게 다루기; 훌륭한 솜씨.

ma·nip·u·la·tor [mənípjəlèitər] *n.* Ⓒ a person who manipulates. 손으로 능란하게 다루는 사람; 조정자.

:man·kind *n.* Ⓤ **1** [mæ̀nkáind] the human race. 인류; 인간. ¶ *the welfare of ~* 인류의 복지. **2** [⌐⌐] the male sex; men. 남자; 남성 (opp. womankind). [*man*]

man·like [mǽnlàik] *adj.* **1** like a man in nature. 남자다운; 남성적인. **2** (of a woman) mannish; masculine. (여자가) 남자 같은.

man·li·ness [mǽnlinis] *n.* Ⓤ the state of being manly. 남자다움.

·man·ly [mǽnli] *adj.* (**-li·er, -li·est**) manlike; as a man should be; strong, brave, noble and honorable. 남자다운; 씩씩한; 용감한 (opp. womanly). ¶ *a ~ man* 남자다운 남자 / *in a ~ way* 남자답게.

man-made [mǽnméid] *adj.* **1** made by man. 인공의. ¶ *a ~ satellite* 인공 위성. **2** made up chemically and not by a natural means. 합성의; 인조의. ¶ *Nylon is a ~ fiber.* 나일론은 합성 섬유다.

man·na [mǽnə] *n.* Ⓒ **1** Ⓤ 《Bible》 the food supplied to the Israelites in the wilderness. 만나《이스라엘인이 광야에서 받았다는 음식》. **2** 《*fig.*》 food for the soul or spirit. 마음〔영혼〕의 양식. **3** something good unexpectedly given. 생각잖은 선물. [Heb.]

man·ne·quin [mǽnikin] *n.* Ⓒ **1** a woman who puts on new clothes and shows them to the customers in a shop. 마네킹 걸. **2** a model or figure of a person. 마네킹. [F.]

:man·ner [mǽnər] *n.* Ⓒ **1** the way in which something happens or is done. 방법; 방식. ¶ *after this ~* 이 같은 방식으로 / *in such a ~* 그 같은 방식으로 / *He is religious after his own ~.* 그는 그 나름대로 성실한 사람이다. **2** the way of acting or behaving. 태도; 거동; 모양. ¶ *a kind ~* 친절한 태도 / *have an awkward ~* 태도가 어색하다. **3** 《*pl.*》 personal behavior in public; polite ways of behaving. 예절; 예의; 좋은 예의 범절. ¶ *have good* 〔*bad*〕 *~* 예의 범절이 좋다〔나쁘다〕 / *It is bad ~ to stare.* 사람을 빤히 보는 것은 예의가 아니다. **4** 《*pl.*》 customs; ways of living. 습관; 풍습. ¶ *manners and customs* 풍속 습관 / *the manners of today* 〔*of our ancestors*〕 오늘날〔우리 선조들〕의 풍습. **5** a style in literature or art. (예술·문학의) 양식; 수법; 작품. ¶ *a picture in the ~ of Picasso* 피카소풍의 그림 / *a novel after the ~ of Dickens* 디킨스 작풍의 소설. **6** 《*arch.*》 (*pl.* **man·ner**) a kind or sort. 종류. ¶ *all ~ of things* 모든 종류의 것들 / *What ~ of man is this ?* 이 사람 뭐하는 사람인가. [L. *manus* hand; →manual]

by all manner of means, 《*arch.*》 most certainly. 확실히; 반드시.

by no manner of means, 《*arch.*》 by no means; not at all. 결코 …아니다.

in a manner, to some degree or extent. 어느 정도; 어떤 의미로는.

in a manner of speaking, 《*arch.*》 so to speak. 이를테면.

in like manner, 《*arch.*》 in kind. 마찬가지로.

no manner of, 《*arch.*》 none at all. 전연 …아니다.

to the manner born, naturally well fitted for (the position, etc.). 타고난; 생래의. ¶ *He was a gentleman to the ~ born.* 타고난 신사였다.

man·nered [mǽnərd] *adj.* **1** 《in compound》 having manners of a certain kind. 행위가 …한. ¶ *well-mannered* 행실이 좋은; 점잖은 / *ill-mannered* 행실이 나쁜. **2** affected; having mannerism. 틀에 박힌.

man·ner·ism [mǽnərìzəm] *n.* **1** Ⓤ too much use of the same style in speaking, writing, behaving, etc. 매너리즘《문체 등이 틀에 박히는 일》. **2** a strange, queer habit. (언어·행동의) 버릇. ¶ *She has this strange ~ of pinching her ear when she talk.* 그녀는 말할 때 귀를 꼬집는 이상한 버릇이 있다.

man·ner·less [mǽnərlis] *adj.* impolite; lacking good manners. 버릇없는.

man·ner·ly [mǽnərli] *adj.* polite; having good manners. 예의바른; 점잖은.

man·ni·kin [mǽnikin] *n.* Ⓒ =manikin.

man·nish [mǽniʃ] *adj.* **1** (of a woman) like a man. 남자 같은. ¶ *a very ~ woman* 흡사 남자 같은 여인. **2** trying to be like a grown-up man. 어른 티를 내는. ● **man·nish·ly** [-li] *adv.* [*man*]

ma·noeu·vre [mənú:vər] *n., v.* 《Brit.》 =maneuver.

man-of-war [mǽnəvwɔ́:r] *n.* (*pl.* **men-**) Ⓒ a warship. 군함. [*man*]

ma·nom·e·ter [mənɑ́mitər / -nɔ́m-] *n.* **1** an instrument for measuring the pressure of gases or vapors. 압력계. **2** an instrument for measuring blood pressure. 혈압계. [Gk. *manos* thin, -meter]

man·or [mǽnər] *n.* Ⓒ a piece of land part of which is used by the owner and the rest is farmed by his peasants. 장원(莊園). [L. *maneo* remain]

ma·no·ri·al [mənɔ́:riəl] *adj.* of a manor. 장원의.

man power [⌐⌐] *n.* **1** man's physical power. 인력(人力). **2** 《mech.》 a unit of power equal to 1/10 horsepower. 공률(工率)의 단위《1/10 마력》. [↓]

man·pow·er [mǽnpàuər] *n.* Ⓤ the total amount of labor force needed for a piece of work; the number of workers needed for such a force. 소요 총인력〔인원〕; 일손. ¶ *a shortage of engineering ~* 기술 인력의 부족. [*man, power*]

M

man·sard [mǽnsɑːrd] *n.* Ⓒ **1** a roof having two slopes on each side. 망사르드 지붕《지붕의 물매가 2 단으로 된》. **2** a room just below the roof; an attic. 고미다락. [Person]

〈mansard 1〉

man·serv·ant [mǽnsəːrvənt] *n.* Ⓒ (*pl.* **men·serv·ants**) a male servant. 하인; 머슴. [*man*]

·**man·sion** [mǽnʃən] *n.* Ⓒ a very large house; a grand residence. 대저택; 맨션. [→manor]

man·slaugh·ter [mǽnslɔ̀ːtər] *n.* Ⓤ **1** the act of killing a person. 살인. **2** 《law》 the act of killing a person unlawfully but without planning to do so. 과실 치사(cf. *homicide, murder*). 參考 murder 보다는 가벼운 죄. [*man*]

man·tel [mǽntl] *n.* =mantelpiece.

man·tel·piece [mǽntlpìːs] *n.* Ⓒ **1** a decorated frame above and around a fireplace. 벽로 장식; 맨틀피스. 參考 미국에서는 흔히 mantel. **2** 《U.S.》 the shelf above a fireplace. 벽로 선반(cf. 《Brit.》 *mantelshelf*). [L. *mantellum* cloak]

man·tel·shelf [mǽntlʃèlf] *n.* (*pl.* **-shelves**) =mantelpiece.

man·tel·shelves [mǽntlʃèlvz] *n.* pl. of **mantelshelf.**

man·tes [mǽntiːz] *n.* pl. of **mantis.**

man·tis [mǽntis] *n.* Ⓒ (*pl.* **-tis·es** or **-tes**) an insect that folds its front legs as if praying and attacks and eats other insects. 사마귀; 버마재비. [Gk.=prophet]

·**man·tle** [mǽntl] *n.* Ⓒ **1** a loose cape or cloak. 망토; 외투. **2** anything that covers like a mantle. 덮개; 씌우는 것. ¶ *The mountain was covered with a ~ of snow.* 산은 눈으로 덮히어 있었다. —*vt.* (P6) **1** cover (something) with a mantle. …에 망토를 씌우다. ¶ *peaks mantled with snow.* **2** conceal. (물건)을 가리다. —*vi.* (P1) **1** (of the face) become red; blush. (얼굴이) 붉어지다. ¶ *Blushes mantled on her cheek.* 그녀의 볼이 확 붉어졌다. **2** spread the wings over the legs. 날개를 펴다. **3** form a coating on a surface. (액체에) 더껑이가 생기다. [*mantelpiece*]

man(·u)- [mǽn(ju)-] *pref.* hand-. '손으로, 손에 의한'의 뜻. [L. *manus* hand]

·**man·u·al** [mǽnjuəl] *adj.* of the hands; done or worked by hand. 손의; 손으로 하는. ¶ *~ crafts* 수공업 / *~ training* (학교의) 공작 / *~ work* 〔*labor*〕 육체 노동 / *a sign ~* 서명. —*n.* Ⓒ **1** a small guide book; a handbook. 편람; 입문서. ¶ *a reference ~ for students* 학생용 참고서 / *a teacher's ~* 교사용 참고서 / *a guitar ~* 기타 교본. **2** 《mil.》 the prescribed drill in handling a rifle. 집총 교범. **3** an organ keyboard. (오르간의) 건반. ●**man·u·al·ly** [-li] *adv.* [manu-]

man·u·fac·to·ry [mæ̀njəfǽktəri] *n.* Ⓒ (*pl.* **-ries**) a factory; a workshop. 제작소; 공장. 參考 지금은 factory를 더 많이 씀. [manu-, →fact]

man·u·fac·tur·al [mæ̀njəfǽktʃərəl] *adj.* relating to the making of articles. 제조(업)의.

:**man·u·fac·ture** [mæ̀njəfǽktʃər] *vt.* (P6) **1** make (things) from raw materials by hand or by machine in a factory. …을 제조하다; 만들다. ¶ *toys manufactured in Korea* 한국제 완구 / *~ cotton goods* 면제품을 만들다. **2** 《*fig.*》 write (novels, etc.) too much or too easily. (소설 등)을 남작하다; 마구 써내다. **3** fabricate; put together. (이야기)를 날조하다. ¶ *~ an excuse* 변명을 꾸며 내다. —*n.* **1** Ⓤ the making of something in a factory, usu. on a large scale. (대규모의) 제조; 제작; 제조업. ¶ *cotton ~* 면직물 제조업 / *home ~* 국내 공업 / *iron ~* 철공업. **2** Ⓒ articles; anything made; the thing manufactured. 제품. ¶ *a Korean ~* 한국산〔제품〕. [manu-, L. *factūra* a making]

:**man·u·fac·tur·er** [mæ̀njəfǽktʃərər] *n.* Ⓒ a person who manufactures, esp. an owner of a workshop. (대규모의) 제조인; 제조업자; 특히, 공장주.

man·u·fac·tur·ing [mæ̀njəfǽktʃəriŋ] *adj.* engaged in manufacture. 제조(업)에 종사하는. ¶ *a ~ industry* 제조 공업.

ma·nure [mənjúər] *n.* Ⓤ material added to or spread over the soil to make it richer. 비료; 거름. ¶ *artificial ~* 인조 비료 / *farmyard ~* 퇴비. —*vt.* (P6) put manure on or in (a place). …에 비료를 주다; 시비(施肥)하다. [→maneuver]

·**man·u·script** [mǽnjəskript] *n.* Ⓒ **1** a book or paper written by hand or on the typewriter, not printed. 사본; 필사본. **2** an author's copy written by hand. 원고. 參考 MS로 생략. 복수는 MSS.

in manuscript, not printed. 인쇄가 안 된. ¶ *a work still in ~* 아직 인쇄가 안 된 작품.

—*adj.* written by hand or with a typewriter. 손으로 쓴; 필사의; 타자한. [manu-]

:**man·y** [méni] *adj.* (**more, most**) a large number of; a lot of. 다수의; 많은. 語法 주어를 수식하는 이외에는 흔히 a large number of, a lot of 등을 씀(opp. few). ¶ *Did you see ~ children there?* 거기에 아이들이 많더냐 / *How ~ sisters do you have?* 누이들이 몇이냐.

a good many, a fair number (of). 꽤 많은. ¶ *A good ~ (people) died of fatigue.* 적잖은 사람이 지쳐서 죽었다.

a great many, a large number (of). 대단히 많은; 엄청난 수의. ¶ *A great ~ people saw him.* 아주 많은 사람들이 그를 보았다 / *There are a great ~ of them.* 그런 것들은 허다하다.

as many as, of the same number as; no less than. …와 같은 수의; …이나 되는. ¶ *You may have as ~ as you want.* 원하는 만큼 가져라 / *As ~ as ten people saw it.* 열 사람이나 그걸 봤다.

as* (*so*) *many, the same in number as. …와 같은 수의; 그만큼의. ¶ *He made five mistakes in as ~ lines.* 다섯 행에서 다섯 개를 틀렸다 / *Those ten days in the town were like so ~ years to me.* 이 마을에서 열흘이 내겐 10년 같았다.

many a, 《lit.》 many. 많은. ¶ *~ a time* 여러 번 / *Many a youth has died of a broken-heart.* 많은 젊은이들이 비탄에 빠진 나머지 죽었다.

many times, often. 몇 번이고.

one too many, not wanted. 불필요한. ¶ *He is one too ~ here.* 그는 여기서 방해만 된다.

one too many for, more than a match for; cleverer than. …의 힘에 겨운; 감당 못 할. ¶ *They are* (*one*) *too ~ for us.* 그들은 우리 힘에 벅차다.

— *n.* 《*collectively,* used as *pl.*》 **1** a great number; many people or things. 다수; 많은 사람〔것〕. ¶ *Many of them are poor.* 그들 중 많은 사람들이 가난하다 / *Many are called but few are chosen.* 청함을 받은 자는 많되 택함을 입은 자는 적다. **2** 《*the ~*》 most people; the public. 대다수의 사람; 민중. [E.]

man·y-head·ed [ménihédid] *adj.* having many heads. 다두(多頭)의. ¶《*contempt.*》 *the ~ beast* 〔*monster*〕 군중; 대중.

man·y-sid·ed [ménisáidid] *adj.* **1** having many sides or aspects. 다방면의. **2** having many interests or abilities. 다재 다능한. ¶ *a ~ man* 재주가 많은 사람.

:map [mæp] *n.* Ⓒ a flat drawing or model of the surface of the earth or part of it, showing countries, rivers, mountains, etc; a similar drawing of the sky, showing position of the stars, planets, etc. 지도; 천체도(cf. *atlas, chart*).

off the map, 《*colloq.*》 out of existence; unimportant. 존재하지 않는; 중요하지 않은.

on the map, 《*colloq.*》 important. 중요한. ¶ *put on the ~* …을 유명하게 만들다.

— *vt.* (**mapped, map·ping**) (P6,7) draw or make a map of (a place). …의 지도를 만들다. [L. *mappa* napkin]

map out, plan; arrange. …의 계획을 세우다; 채비를 갖추다. ¶ *~ out a new city* 신(新) 도시의 계획을 세우다 / *~ out a journey.*

·ma·ple [méipəl] *n.* Ⓤ **1** Ⓒ a kind of tree found in the northern zone with star-shaped leaves and winged seeds. 단풍나무. **2** the wood of this tree. 단풍나무 재목. **3** the sap of certain kinds of maples, used in making sugar and syrup. 단풍당(糖). [E.]

·mar [mɑːr] *vt.* (**marred, mar·ring**) (P6) damage; spoil. …을 손상하다; 못쓰게 만들다. ¶ *~ the beauty of the streets* 거리의 미관을 해치다. [E.]

make* 〔*mend*〕 *or mar, either make a brilliant success of, or ruin completely. 훌륭하게 성공하느냐 아주 결딴나느냐; 흥하느냐 망하느냐.

Mar. March.

mar·a·thon [mǽrəθɑ̀n, -θən] *n.* **1** 《*M-*》 an old battlefield near Athens, in Greece. 마라톤. **2** Ⓒ a long distance foot race of 42.195 kilometers. 마라톤 경주. **3** Ⓒ any long contest or race. (일반적으로) 장거리 경주; 지구전(持久戰); 내구(耐久) 경쟁. ¶ *a dance ~* 댄스의 장시간 경기. [Place]

ma·raud [mərɔ́ːd] *vi.* (P1,3) (as in war) wander about in search of something valuable; plunder. 약탈하다; 노략질하다. ¶ *~ on a town* 노략질하려고 마을을 덮치다 / *Wild beasts ~ at night.* 들짐승은 밤에 설치고 다닌다. — *vt.* (P6) take (something) by force. …을 약탈하다. [F. *maraud* rogue]

ma·raud·er [mərɔ́ːdər] *n.* Ⓒ a person or an animal that marauds. 약탈자; 설치고 다니는 짐승.

:mar·ble [mɑ́ːrbəl] *n.* Ⓤ **1** a white or colored hard limestone used in making statues and buildings. 대리석. **2** 《*pl.*》 a group of sculptures made of marble. 대리석 조각물. **3** Ⓒ a small round piece, esp. of marble or other hard stone used as a child's plaything. 공깃돌. — *adj.* **1** like marble; made of marble; white. 대리석 같은; 대리석으로 만든; 흰. **2** heartless; hard; cold. 무정〔냉정〕한. ¶ *a ~ breast* 냉혹한 마음. — *vt.* (P6) stain in patterns like the markings of marble. …에 대리석 같은 무늬를 넣다. [L. *marmor*]

mar·bled [mɑ́ːrbld] *adj.* colored to look like marble. 대리석 무늬의. ¶ *~ paper* / *the ~ edges of a book* 대리석 무늬의 책 테두리.

mar·ble-heart·ed [mɑ́ːrblhɑ́ːrtid] *adj.* heartless like a stone; having no feeling. (돌처럼) 무정〔냉혹〕한; 모진.

:March [mɑːrtʃ] *n.* the third month of the year. 3월. 參考 Mar.로 생략함. [→Mars]

:march[1] [mɑːrtʃ] *vi.* **1** (P1,2,4) walk with a regular step like soldiers. 행진하다; 행군하다. ¶ *The army marched into the town.* 군대가 마을로 행진해 들어왔다 / *~ away* 〔*off*〕 행진해 가 버리다〔떠나다〕. **2** (P1,2) 《*fig.*》 progress regularly; advance steadily. (착실히) 진전하다. ¶ *Science has marched forward tremendously these past few decades.* 지난 수십 년 동안 과학은 장족의 진보를 했다 / *He marched bravely to his death.* 그는 죽음을 향해 당당하게 걸어갔다 / *March* (*on*)*!* 앞으로 갓.

— *vt.* (P7) cause (someone) to move on. …을 행진시키다; 끌고 가다; 연행하다. ¶ *They marched him off to prison.* 그들은 그를 감옥으로 끌고 갔다.

— *n.* **1** ⓊⒸ 《mil.》 the act of marching. 행군. **2** Ⓒ 《*fig.*》 progress; advance. 진전; 발전. ¶ *the ~ of time* 시간의 진행〔경과〕. **3** Ⓤ

pace; the step of soldiers marching. 보조. ¶ *double* ~ 구보 / *quick* ~ 속보. **4** the distance marched. 행정(行程). ¶ *Our destination is a day's* ~ *away.* 우리 행선지는 걸어서 하룻길이다. **5** Ⓒ 《mus.》 a musical composition for marching. 행진곡. ¶ *a funeral* ~ 장송 행진곡. [F. *marcher*]

be on* 〔*in*〕 *the march, be marching. 진행〔행진〕 중이다.

***steal a march on* 〔*upon*〕,** get a better position over (someone) without being noticed. …을 꼭뒤지르다.

march² [mɑːrtʃ] *n.* (*pl.*) **1** a boundary; a border. 경계. **2** a debatable strip between countries; a border. 경계〔변경〕 지방. — *vi.* (P3) 《*with*》 have a common boundary; border on. 경계를 접하다. [→ mark¹]

mar·chion·ess [mάːrʃənis, mὰːrʃənés] *n.* Ⓒ 《Brit.》 the wife or widow of a marquis. 후작 부인. [→marquis]

march-past [mάːrtʃpæ̀st] *n.* a march of troops which passes in front of an official who looks at it. 분열 행진; 분열식. [*march¹*]

***mare** [mɛər] *n.* Ⓒ a female horse. 암말. [E.]

go on shanks's mare, travel on foot. 걸어가다.

The gray mare is the better horse. The wife is the ruler. 내주장하다.

mare's nest [⌐⌐] *n.* **1** a supposed wonderful discovery which turns out to be illusory. 일대 발견《실은 보잘것 없는》. **2** a very complicated situation. 혼란한 상태.

Mar·ga·ret [mάːrgərit] *n.* a woman's name. 여자 이름.

mar·ga·rine [mάːrdʒərin, -rìːn, ⌐⌐⌐] *n.* Ⓤ imitation butter made from vegetable oils and animal fats. 마가린; 인조 버터. [Gk. *margaron* pearl]

***mar·gin** [mάːrdʒin] *n.* Ⓒ **1** a border; an edge. 가장자리; 가. ¶ *the* ~ *of the lake* 호숫가. **2** the space around the printing or writing on a page. (페이지의) 난외(欄外); 여백. ¶ *a note on* 〔*in*〕 *the* ~ 난외의 주(註). **3** a borderline. 한계. ¶ *be on the* ~ *of bare subsistence* 겨우 입에 풀칠이나 하고 지내다. **4** an extra amount (of money, time); a further amount allowed beyond what is necessary. (시간·돈의) 여유. ¶ *The car passed the child by a narrow* ~. 차는 아이 곁을 아슬아슬하게 비켜 갔다. **5** 《comm.》 the difference between the cost and the selling price. 판매 수익; 마진. ¶ *a narrow* ~ *of profit* 빠듯한 수익〔마진〕. **6** 《stock exchange》 security. 증거금(證據金).
— *vt.* (P6) provide with a border; furnish (something) with a margin. …에 가장자리를 붙이다. [L. *margo*]

mar·gin·al [mάːrdʒənəl] *adj.* **1** written on the margin of a page. 난외(欄外)에 쓴. **2** at the limit. 가장자리의; 가의. **3** of a very narrow margin of profits. 이윤이 빠듯한 〔얼마 안 되는〕. **4** of less importance. 대수롭지 않은. ¶ *a* ~ *interest* 이차적 관심사.

mar·gue·rite [mὰːrgəríːt] *n.* Ⓒ 《bot.》 a kind of daisy with white flowers. 마거리트 《데이지의 일종》. [→margarine]

mar·i·gold [mǽrəgòuld] *n.* Ⓒ 《bot.》 a garden plant with bright yellow or orange flowers. 금잔화; 금송화. [*Mary* (the Virgin), *gold*]

ma·ri·jua·na, -hua·na [mæ̀rə*h*wάːnə, mὰːr-] *n.* the dried leaves and flowers of Indian hemp, smoked in cigarettes as an intoxicant. 마리화나. [Mex.]

ma·rim·ba [mərímbə] *n.* a primitive African musical instrument resembling a xylophone. 마림바. [Afr.]

***mar·ine** [məríːn] *adj.* **1** of the sea; formed by the sea. 바다의; 해산(海產)의. ¶ ~ *cable* 해저 전선 / ~ *products* 해산물. **2** living in the sea. 바다에 사는. ¶ *Seals and whales are* ~ *animals.* 바다표범과 고래는 바다 짐승이다. **3** of sea-trade; nautical. 해상 무역의; 항해의. ¶ ~ *insurance* 해상 보험 / ~ *stores* 낡은 선구류(船具類). — *n.* Ⓒ **1** a sailor serving on land and in the air as well. 해병대원. **2** 《*collectively*》 the navy of a country; all the merchant ships of a country. (한 나라의) 해군; 선박. **3** a picture of the sea. 바다의 그림. [L. *mare* sea]

mar·i·ner [mǽrənər] *n.* Ⓒ 《*poet.*》 a sailor. 선원; 뱃사람.

mar·i·o·nette [mæ̀riənét] *n.* Ⓒ a doll moved by strings or by the hands. 꼭두각시. [F. *Mary*]

mar·i·time [mǽrətàim] *adj.* **1** connected with the sea. 바다의; 해사(海事)의. ¶ ~ *law* 〔*trade*〕 해상법〔해운업〕 / *a* ~ *nation* 해양국(민). **2** bordering on, lying near the sea. 해안의; 연해의. ¶ *a* ~ *town* 해안 도시. **3** of sailing. 항해의. [→marine]

⁑mark¹ [mɑːrk] *n.* Ⓒ **1** a printed or written symbol. 표; 기호; 부호. ¶ *punctuation marks* 구두점 / *a trade* ~ 상표 / *put a* ~ *in pencil* 연필로 표를 하다 / *make one's* ~ *on a document* 문서에 ×표의 서명을 하다. **2** a spot, cut, etc., made on a surface. 반점; 얼룩; 자국; 상처 자국. ¶ *a* ~ *of an old wound* 오래된 상처 자국 / *leave a* ~ *on the new paint* 새로 칠한 페인트 위에 자국을 내다 / *find an ink* ~ *on the carpet* 카펫 위에 잉크 얼룩을 발견하다 / *Who has made dirty marks on this hat?* 이 모자에 누가 얼룩을 냈느냐. **3** a sign of some quality, characteristic, etc. 특징; 징후; 어떤 표시. ¶ *marks of a good breeding* 훌륭한 가정교육을 받고 자란 증거 / *Grey hair is not always a* ~ *of age.* 머리가 희다고 꼭 나이가 많은 것은 아니다. ¶ *marks of old age* 늙은 티. **4** influence; impression. 영향; 감화. ¶ *The doctor left his* ~ *on the thought of his time.* 박사는 당대의 사조에 영향을 남겼다. **5** a target; a goal.

목표; 표적. ¶ *shoot a pistol at a* ~ 표적을 향해 권총을 쏘다 / *beside* [*wide of*] *the* ~ 과녁을 벗어나서; 빗맞아서 / *hit* [*miss*] *the* ~ 성공[실패]하다. **6** Ⓤ importance; fame. 중요성; 명성. ¶ *a man of* ~ 명사(名士) / *make one's* ~ *in literature* 문학에서 이름을 떨치다. **7** a number or letter to show the score. 점수. ¶ *50 marks,* 50 점 / *I got full marks* [*a full* ~] *in mathematics.* 수학에서 만점을 받았다. **8** 《*sing.* only》 what is usual or expected. 표준. ¶ *below* [*beneath*] *the* ~ 표준 이하로 / *up to the* ~ 수준에 달해; 나무랄 데 없이. **9** a line, a dot, etc. to show position; a line to show the starting point. 경계선; 출발점. ¶ *On your marks.* (육상 경기 등에서) 제자리에 / *get off the* ~ 스타트하다; (일을) 시작하다. **10** a person to be laughed at, deceived; an object. 놀림감; 잘 속는 사람. ¶ *He is an easy* ~. 우려먹기 좋은 사람이다; 봉이다.

beyond the mark, too much. 과도하게; 지나치게.

Save the mark! Pardon me for having said such a horrible thing. 말이 지나쳐 미안하다.

toe the mark, follow a rule; do exactly as told. 규칙[관례]에 따르다; 시킨 대로 하다.

— *vt.* **1** (P6,7) ⓐ put or make, leave a mark on (something). …에 표를 하다. ¶ ~ *a river on a map* 지도에 강을 기입하다 / *cloth marked with ink stains* 잉크 얼룩이 있는 천 / *a face marked with small pox* 마맛자국이 있는 얼굴. ⓑ put on (something) with figures, signs, etc. to show the price, name, quality, etc. (가격·제품명·품질 등을 표시하기 위해) …에 가격표·상표·품질 표지(標識) 등을 붙이다. ¶ ~ *goods with price labels* 상품에 가격표를 붙이다 / *a package marked with owner's name* 소유주 이름이 붙어 있는 짐짝. **2** record (the score, etc.); give marks to (examination papers, etc.). …을 기록하다; 채점하다. ¶ ~ *examination papers* 시험지를 채점하다 / ~ *an exercise at 85* 연습 문제에 85 점을 주다. **3** (P6,7) give a character to (something); be a sign of (something); make (someone) distinct. …을 특징짓다; 돋보이게 하다. ¶ *A lot of scientific discoveries marked the century.* 많은 과학상의 발견이 그 세기를 돋보이게 했다 / *His abilities* ~ *him for a leader.* 그의 재능들은 그가 지도자감임을 보여 주었다. **4** (P6,7) show or form (something) by marks. …을 표로 나타내다. ¶ *He marked his pleasure by smiling.* = *His smile marked his pleasure.* 미소가 그의 만족을 말해 주었다 / *The lighted window marked someone's night work.* 불 켜진 창문은 누군가가 밤일을 하고 있음을 나타냈다. **5** (P6,10,12) pay attention to (something); notice. …에 주목하다; …을 주의해 듣다[보다]. ¶ *Mark my words, boys.* 얘들아 내 말 잘 들어라. **6** 《often *out*》 pick out; select; destine. …을 뽑다; 선정하다; 운명짓다. ¶ ~ (*out*) *someone for promotion* 아무를 승진시키기로 하다 / *We are all marked* (*out*) *to die.* 사람은 모두 죽을 운명에 있다. [E.]

mark off [***out***]***,*** show the position of (something) by lines; separate. …에 경계를 짓다; …을 구획하다.

mark time, **a**) move the feet as if marching but without moving forward. 제자리걸음하다. **b**) make no further progress. (일에) 진척이 없다; 교착 상태에 있다.

mark² [mɑːrk] *n.* Ⓒ the German unit of money. 마르크《독일의 화폐 단위》. [G.]

marked [mɑːrkt] *adj.* **1** having a mark. 표[기호]가 있는. ¶ *a* ~ *tree* 표가 있는 나무. **2** ⓐ clear, remarkable. 분명한; 두드러진. ¶ *a* ~ *difference* 현격한 차이 / *show a* ~ *increase* 뚜렷한 증가를 보이다. ⓑ noticeable. 주목할 만한; 이목을 끄는. ¶ *a* ~ *man* 요주의 인물 / *Her coldness was rather* ~. 그녀의 냉랭한 태도는 좀 유난했다.

mark·ed·ly [máːrkidli] *adv.* in a marked manner; remarkably. 현저하게; 두드러지게; 뚜렷이.

mark·er [máːrkər] *n.* Ⓒ **1** a person or a thing that marks. 표를 하는 사람[도구]. **2** a person keeping the score in the game. (게임의) 득점 기록원. **3** a bookmark. 서표(書標). **4** a sign. 표지(標識); 안표(眼標).

:mar·ket [máːrkit] *n.* Ⓒ **1** a meeting of people for buying and selling; the people so gathered. 장; 거기 모인 사람들; 장꾼. **2** a place where goods are bought and sold. 시장. ¶ *a cattle* ~ 우(牛)시장. **3** the trade in particular articles. (특정 상품의) 거래; 매매. ¶ *the corn* ~ 곡물 시장 / *money* ~ 금융 시장. **4** a demand for or opportunity of selling goods in trade. 수요; 판로; 매매의 기회. ¶ *build up markets for new manufactures* 신제품의 판로를 구축하다 / *There is no* ~ *for these goods in Korea.* 한국에선 이런 유(類)의 상품은 팔리지 않는다 / *a good* ~ *for steel* 강철 판매의 호기 / *lose one's* ~ 상기(商機)를 놓치다. **5** the state of trade as shown by prices. 시황(市況); 시세. ¶ *The* ~ *rose* [*fell*]. 시세가 올랐다[내렸다].

at the market, at market price. 시가(時價)로; 시세(時勢)대로.

be in [***on***] ***the market,*** be on sale. 매물로 나와 있다.

bring one's eggs [***hogs, goods***] ***to a bad*** [***the wrong***] ***market,*** miscalculate; fail in one's plan. 오산하다.

come into the market = be in the market.

find a market, be in demand. 판로가 생기다; 살 사람이 나서다.

make a [***one's***] ***market*** (= *make good use*) ***of*** *something.* …을 이용하다. ¶ *make a* ~ *of war* 전쟁을 이용해서 이득을 챙기다.

play the market, 《U.S.》 gamble (in stocks, etc.). (주식 따위에) 투기하다.

put [***place***] *something* ***on the market,*** try

M

to sell something. (물건을) 시장에 내놓다. ***raise the market upon,*** overcharge; ask a high price. …을 (더) 비싸게 부르다.
— *vi.* (P1) buy or sell (something) in a market. 시장에서 매매하다.
— *vt.* (P6) send (something) to market. …을 시장에〔팔려고〕 내놓다. [→merchant]

mar·ket·a·bil·i·ty [mɑ̀ːrkitəbíləti] *n.* Ⓤ the state of being marketable. 시장성(市場性).

mar·ket·a·ble [máːrkitəbəl] *adj.* fit for sale. 팔리는; 시장성이 있는.

mar·ket·er [máːrkitər] *n.* Ⓒ a person who sells or buys in a market. 시장 상인.

mar·ket-gar·den [máːrkitgɑ̀ːrdn] *n.* 《Brit.》 a garden in which vegetables are grown for the market (=《U.S.》 truck farm). (시장에 내기 위한) 채원(菜園).

mar·ket·ing [máːrkitiŋ] *n.* Ⓤ **1** the trade at a market. (시장에서의) 매매. **2** the shopping at a market. 장보기; 쇼핑. ¶ *do one's* ~ 장보다; 물건을 사다.

market place [⌐–⌐] *n.* a place where a market is held. 시장; 장터.

market price [⌐–⌐] *n.* **1** the price of articles when sold in a market. 시장 가격; 시가(市價). **2** the present price. 시세.

mar·ket-ripe [máːrkitràip] *adj.* not quite ripe (but ripe and fit to eat when sold). 아직 덜 익은《시장에 나와 팔릴 때쯤에는 알맞게 익음》.

market town [⌐–⌐] *n.* the town where a market is held. 장이 서는 곳; 장거리.

mark·ing [máːrkiŋ] *n.* **1** Ⓒ a mark. 표; 점. **2** Ⓤ the act of making a mark. 표를 하기. **3** Ⓤ the act of giving marks. 채점. **4** Ⓒ a spot; a dot. 반점; 얼룩; 무늬. [→mark[1]]

marks·man [máːrksmən] *n.* Ⓒ (*pl.* **-men** [-mən]) a person who shoots a rifle, etc. well. 사수; 명사수.

mar·ma·lade [máːrməlèid, ⌐–⌐] *n.* Ⓤ jam made of oranges or lemons boiled with their outer skins. 마멀레이드. [Gk. *meli* honey, *mēlon* apple]

mar·mo·set [máːrməzèt] *n.* a small monkey with a bushy tail. 명주원숭이. [F. =image]

mar·mot [máːrmət] *n.* a small animal with a big tail. 마멋. [↑]

ma·roon[1] [mərúːn] *n.* Ⓤ a dark-red color. 밤색; 적갈색. — *adj.* colored dark-red. 밤색〔적갈색〕의. [It. =chestnut]

ma·roon[2] [mərúːn] *vt.* (P6) **1** leave (someone) on a desert island. …을 무인도에 버리다. **2** isolate (someone) in a place. …을 고립시키다. — *n.* Ⓒ **1** a person whose ancestor was an escaped Negro slave. 탈출한 흑인 노예의 자손. **2** a person left on a desert island. 고도에 버려진 사람. [F.]

mar·quee [mɑːrkíː] *n.* Ⓒ **1** 《esp. Brit.》 a large tent used for garden parties. (옥외 행사용의) 대형 천막. **2** a rooflike shelter projecting over an entrance to a theater, hotel, etc. (극장·호텔 등) 출입구의 차양. [F. *marquise*]

〈marquee 2〉

mar·quess [máːrkwis] *n.* Ⓒ 《esp. Brit.》 =marquis.

mar·que·try [máːrkətri] *n.* Ⓤ (*pl.* **-tries**) thin decorative pieces of wood, ivory, metal, etc. fitted together to form a design, used in furniture or flooring. (가구나 마루 장식의) 쪽매붙임 세공. [→mark[1]]

mar·quis [máːrkwis] *n.* Ⓒ a nobleman below a duke and above an earl. 후작 (opp. marchioness). 参考 영국 이외에서는 duke 와 count 의 중간 작위. [F.]

mar·riage [mǽridʒ] *n.* ⓊⒸ **1** the act of marrying; the state of being married. 결혼. ¶ *communal* 〔*group*〕 ~ 집단 결혼. **2** Ⓒ a wedding ceremony. 결혼식. ¶ *a* ~ *service* (교회에서의) 결혼식. **3** the married life of two persons as husband and wife; the relation between husband and wife. 결혼 생활; 부부 관계. ¶ *break up a* ~ 이혼하다. **4** Ⓒ 《*fig.*》 an intimate union. 밀접한 결합. [→ marital]
give in marriage, give as a husband or wife. 장가〔시집〕 보내다.
take in marriage, …을 남편으로〔아내로〕 맞다.

mar·riage·a·ble [mǽridʒəbəl] *adj.* fit for marriage; old enough to marry. 결혼할 수 있는; 혼기(婚期)의. ¶ ~ *age* 혼기 / *a* ~ *girl* 결혼 적령기의 처녀.

marriage articles [⌐–⌐––] *n.* antenuptial agreement respecting rights of property and succession. 결혼 약정서.

marriage bed [⌐–⌐] *n.* marital intercourse. 부부 동침〔합궁〕.

marriage lines [⌐–⌐] *n.* a certificate of marriage. 결혼 증명서.

marriage portion [⌐– ⌐–] *n.* a dowry. 지참금.

marriage settlement [⌐– ⌐––] *n.* arrangement securing property to wife. 부부 재산 계약.

***mar·ried** [mǽrid] *adj.* **1** joined in marriage; having a husband or wife. 결혼한; 배우자가 있는(opp. single). ¶ *a* ~ *man* 〔*woman*〕 기혼 남성〔여성〕 / *They have been* ~ *for 30 years.* 부부가 된 지 30 년이다 / *Their* ~ *life was happy.* 그들의 결혼 생활은 행복했다. **2** closely united. 밀접하게 결합된. **3** arising from the state of marriage; connected with, enjoyed by, persons joined together in marriage. 결혼으로 생기는; 부부의; 결혼의. ¶ ~ *life* 결혼 생활 / ~ love 부부애 / ~ *happiness* 결혼의 행복. [*marry*[1]]

mar·row [mǽrou] *n.* Ⓤ **1** 《anat.》 the soft substance filling the hollow part of a bone. 골수. **2** 《*fig.*》 the essential part; the

essense. 정수; 진수. ¶ *the ~ of a statement* 말의 핵심. [E.]
to the marrow (***of one's bones***), to one's innermost soul. 뼛속까지; 철저하게. ¶ *frozen to the ~* 뼛속까지 언.

:**mar·ry**[1] [mǽri] (**-ried**) *vt.* **1** (P6) take (a husband or wife) in marriage. …와 결혼하다. ¶ ~ *a fortune* 돈 많은 사람과 결혼하다 / *He married a pretty girl.* 그는 미인과 결혼했다. **2** (P6) (of a priest, etc.) unite (a man and woman) as husband and wife. (목사 등이) …의 결혼을 주례하다. ¶ *They were married by the bishop.* 그들은 주교의 주례로 결혼식을 올렸다 / *The priest married them.* 목사가 그들의 결혼식을 주례했다. **3** (P6,7,13) (of parents, etc.) give (a son or daughter) in marriage. (부모가) …을 장가〔시집〕 보내다. ¶ *He married his daughter to a young lawyer.* 딸을 젊은 변호사에게 시집보냈다 / *He was married to his friend's sister.* 그는 친구 누이와 결혼했다. **4** (P6,13) 《*fig.*》 unite closely. …을 밀착〔결합〕시키다. ¶ ~ *intellect with sensibility* 지성을 감성에 융합시키다.
— *vi.* (P1) enter into a marriage; be married; get married. 결혼하다. ¶ ~ *for money* 돈 때문에 결혼하다 / *When did he get married ?* 그 사람 언제 결혼했지 / ~ *late in life* 늦게 결혼하다. [→marital]
marry off, succeed in arranging a marriage for one's child. 장가〔시집〕 보내다.

mar·ry[2] [mǽri] *interj.* 《*arch.*》 a cry expressing surprise. 어이쿠; 어이구머니; 저런 《놀람·분노 등을 나타냄》. [*Mary* (the Virgin)]

***Mars** [mɑːrz] *n.* **1** 《Rom. myth.》 the Roman god of war. 마르스; 군신(軍神). **2** the planet nearest to the earth. 화성. [L.]

Mar·seil·laise [mɑ̀ːrsəléiz] *n.* the French national song, written in 1792, during the French Revolution. 마르세예즈《프랑스의 국가(國歌)》. [F. *Marseille* Place]

***marsh** [mɑːrʃ] *n.* Ⓒ a piece of low and wet land. 습지; 늪. [E.]

***mar·shal** [mɑ́ːrʃəl] *n.* Ⓒ **1** the highest rank in some armies, esp. of France. (프랑스 등지의) 육군 원수. **2** 《Brit.》 a general of the Air Force. 공군 대장. **3** 《Brit.》 an official who looks after ceremonies, etc. (왕실·궁정의) 전례관(典禮官). **4** 《U.S.》 a national officer having police duty; the head of a fire or police department. 연방 법원의 집행관; 경찰서장; 소방서장.
— *vt.* (**-shaled, -shal·ing** or 《Brit.》 **-shalled, -shal·ling**) (P6,7,13) **1** make (persons) get into a line. …을 정렬시키다. ¶ ~ *the guests at a feast* 손님들을 잔칫자리에 앉게 하다. **2** 《*fig.*》 put (things) in order; arrange clearly. 정리〔정돈〕하다. ¶ ~ *one's facts* 자기 소관사를 정리하다. **3** guide (someone) into a place. …을 안내하다. ¶ ~ *a foreign visitor into the presence of a king* 외국 손님을 왕께 알현시키다.
— *vi.* (P1,2A,3) **1** stand in line. 정렬하다. **2** meet together. 집합하다. [F. *mareschal* farrier]

mar·shal·ing-yard [mɑ́ːrʃəliŋjɑ̀ːrd] *n.* a railway yard where goods trains, etc. are assembled. (철도(鐵道)의) 조차장(操車場).

Marshall islands [ˊ– ˊ–], **the** *n.* a group of islands in the North Pacific. 마샬 군도.

marsh-gas [mɑ́ːrʃgæ̀s] *n.* methane. 메탄; 소기(沼氣). [*marsh*]

marsh mallow [ˊ ˊ–] *n.* 《bot.》 a plant with large pink flowers which grows in marshes. 양아욱.

marsh·mal·low [mɑ́ːrʃmèlou, -mæ̀l-] *n.* Ⓤ a soft, spongy candy with a flavor made from the root of the marsh mallow. 마시맬로 과자.

marsh·y [mɑ́ːrʃi] *adj.* (**marsh·i·er, marsh·i·est**) **1** like a marsh. 늪 같은; 습지의. **2** having many marshes. 습지가〔늪이〕 많은.
● **marsh·i·ness** [-nis] *n.*

mar·su·pi·al [mɑːrsúːpiəl / -sjúː-] *n.* Ⓒ an animal that carries its young in a bag-like part of its body. 유대 동물(有袋動物). [Gk. *marsipos* purse]

mart [mɑːrt] *n.* Ⓒ 《*poet.*》 a market; a trading center. 시장; 상업 중심지. [→merchant]

mar·ten [mɑ́ːrtən] *n.* (*pl.* **-tens** or *collectively* **-ten**) **1** Ⓒ 《animal》 a small brown animal like a weasel. 담비. **2** Ⓤ the fur of this animal. 담비 모피. [F.]

mar·tial [mɑ́ːrʃəl] *adj.* **1** of war. 싸움의; 전쟁의. ¶ ~ *music* 군악. **2** eager to fight. 호전적인. ¶ ~ *spirit* 군인 정신; 사기(士氣). **3** military. 군사의(opp. civil). ¶ ~ *law* 계엄령.
● **mar·tial·ly** [-i] *adv.* [→Mars]

Mar·tian [mɑ́ːrʃən] *adj.* of Mars. 화성의.
— *n.* Ⓒ an imaginary person living on Mars. 화성인. [↑]

mar·tin [mɑ́ːrtən] *n.* Ⓒ 《bird》 a small bird of the swallow family. 흰털발제비. [Personal name]

mar·ti·net [mɑ̀ːrtənét, ˊ–ˊ] *n.* Ⓒ a person who is very strict in training, esp. in the army. 규율이 엄격한 사람. [Person]

***mar·tyr** [mɑ́ːrtər] *n.* Ⓒ **1** a person who dies or suffers pain for his religion, principles, etc. 순교자; 순난자(殉難者). ¶ *die a ~ to principle* 주의를 위해 죽다 / *make a ~ of someone* 아무를 희생시키다. **2** a person who suffers pain for a long time. 늘 시달리는 사람. ¶ *a ~ to gout* 통풍(痛風)을 앓는 사람.
be a martyr to, suffer constantly from. …으로 늘 고생하다.
make a martyr of oneself, victimize oneself ostentatiously. 순교자인 체하다.
— *vt.* (P6) kill or give great pain to

(someone) because of his religion, etc.; cause to suffer. …을 순교자로 만들다; 박해하다; 괴롭히다. [Gk. *martus* witness]

mar·tyr·dom [máːrtərdəm] *n.* Ⓤ death or suffering for the sake of a faith or principle. 순교; 순사(殉死); 고난.

·mar·vel [máːrvəl] *n.* Ⓒ **1** a wonderful thing. 놀라운 일; 경이. ¶ *the latest marvels of science* 최근의 과학의 경이. **2** a person or thing showing some marvelous quality. 비범한 사람〔것〕. ¶ *do marvels* 놀라운 일을 해내다 / *a ~ of beauty* 절세의 미인 / *She is a ~ of patience.* 인내심이 놀라운 여성이다 / 《colloq.》 *He is a perfect ~.* 굉장한 사람이다. — *vi.* (P3) (**-veled, -vel·ing** or 《Brit.》 **-velled, -vel·ling**) 《*at*》 be struck with wonder. 놀라다. ¶ *~ at someone's courage* 아무의 용기에 감탄하다.

— *vt.* (P11,12) 《*why, how, that, etc.*》 wonder. …을 이상하게 여기다. ¶ *I ~ (that) you should say so.* 네가 그런 말을 하다니 모를 일이다. [L. *miror* to wonder] ⌈marvelous.

mar·vel·lous [máːrvələs] *adj.* 《Brit.》 =

:mar·vel·ous [máːrvələs] *adj.* **1** extraordinary; astonishing. 놀라운; 굉장히 좋은. ¶ *a ~ view* 굉장히 좋은 경치. **2** hard to believe. 믿기 어려운.

mar·vel·ous·ly [máːrvələsli] *adv.* in a marvelous manner. 놀랍게; 굉장하게.

Marx [maːrks], **Karl** *n.* (1818-83) a German socialist and political economist. 마르크스 《독일의 사회주의자, 경제학자》.

Marx·i·an [máːrksiən] *adj.* of Marx or his principles. 마르크스(주의)의. — *n.* Ⓒ a Marxist. 마르크스주의자.

Marx·ism [máːrksizəm] *n.* Ⓤ the principles of Marx. 마르크스주의.

Marx·ist [máːrksist] *n.* Ⓒ a follower of the principles of Marx. 마르크스주의자. ⌈이름.

Mar·y[1] [mέəri] *n.* a woman's name. 여자

Mar·y[2] [mέəri] *n.* **1** the mother of Jesus; the Virgin Mary or Saint Mary. 성모 마리아. **2** either of two queens of England, Mary I (1516-58) and Mary II (1662-94). 메리《영국 여왕의 이름》.

Mar·y·land [mérələnd] *n.* an eastern State of the United States. 메릴랜드. 參考 Md.로 생략함. 주도는 Annapolis》. ● **Mar·y·land·er** [-ər] *n.*

mas·cot [mǽskət, -kɑt] *n.* Ⓒ any person, animal, or thing that is supposed to bring good luck; one's pet. 마스코트; 행운을 가져오는 사람〔동물, 물건〕; 행운의 부적. [F.]

·mas·cu·line [mǽskjəlin] *adj.* (opp. feminine) **1** 《gram.》 of the gender of a male. 남성의. **2** of a male; manly. 남자의; 남자다운. — *n.* Ⓤ 《gram.》 the gender of a male. 남성. [L. *mas* male]

mash [mæʃ] *n.* **1** Ⓤ a crushed malt or grain mixed in hot water and used for making beer. 엿기름 물《맥주 원료》. **2** any soft mixture. (감자 따위를 으깬) 질척질척한 것. **3** a mixture of the skins of wheat or meal and warm water and used for feeding horses. (밀기울 같은 것을 더운 물에 갠) 가축사료; 여물죽. — *vt.* (P6) **1** crush (something) into a soft mass. …을 짓이기다. **2** mix with hot water. 더운 물을 섞다〔풀다〕.

be mashed on, be in love with. …에 반하다.
● **mash·er** [´-ər] *n.* [E.]

·mask [mæsk, mɑːsk] *n.* Ⓒ **1** a covering to hide or protect the face. 마스크. ¶ *a flu ~* 감기 예방 마스크 / *a gas ~* 방독면 / *an oxygen ~* 산소 마스크. **2** a false face worn by an actor, etc. (극 등에 쓰는) 가면; 탈. **3** a clay model of someone's face. (점토로 얼굴을 뜬) 데스마스크; 사면(死面). ¶ *a death ~.* **4** pretense; an excuse. 가장; 구실; 핑계. ¶ *under the ~ of charity* 자선을 가장하여 / 《*fig.*》 *hide sorrow under a ~ of laughter* 웃는 얼굴로 슬픔을 감추다. **5** a person who wears a mask. 가장한 사람. **6** a dancing party at which masks are worn. 가면 무도회.

put on a mask, hide one's real feelings. 본심을 감추다.

throw off one's mask, show one's real character. 가면을 벗다; …의 정체를 드러내다.

— *vt.* (P6) cover (a face) with a mask; conceal. …에 가면을 씌우다; 감추다. ¶ *~ one's real character behind an assumed manner* 태도를 꾸며 자기 본성을 감추다.

— *vi.* (P1) put on a mask. 가면을 쓰다.
● **mask·er** [´-ər] *n.* [F. *masque*]

masked [mæskt, mɑːskt] *adj.* **1** putting on a mask; disguised. 가면을 쓴; 변장한. ¶ *a ~ ball* 가면 무도회. **2** hidden; covered. 감춰진; 숨겨진. **3** 《mil》 hidden from the enemy. 차폐된. ¶ *~ guns* 차폐된 포열.

mas·och·ism [mǽsəkìzəm, mǽz-] *n.* Ⓤ the condition in which sexual gratification depends on suffering, physical pain, and humiliation. 마조히즘; 피학대음란증(cf. *sadism*).

·ma·son [méisən] *n.* Ⓒ a builder in stone or brick. 석수; 벽돌공. [F. *maçon*]

ma·son·ic, Ma- [məsánik / -sɔ́n-] *adj.* of Freemasons. 프리메이슨 단(원)의. [↑]

ma·son·ry [méisənri] *n.* Ⓤ (*pl.* **-ries**) **1** the job or skill of a mason. 석공직〔기술〕. **2** something built by a mason. 석조 건축.

masque [mæsk, mɑːsk] *n.* Ⓒ **1** a short play with songs, dances, and a little speaking. 무용 가극. **2** a masked ball. 가장 무도회. [→mask]

mas·quer·ade [mæ̀skəréid] *n.* **1** Ⓒ a dance or party in which people wear masks and fancy dresses. 가면〔가장〕 무도회. **2** Ⓤ change in one's appearance; pretense. 가장; 구실. — *vi.* (P1,2) **1** attend a masquerade party. 가면〔가장〕 무도회에 나가다. **2** 《*as*》 pretend; change one's appearance; disguise oneself. …인 척하다; 가장하다. ¶ *He masqueraded as an*

English lord. 그는 영국 귀족의 행세를 했다. [→mask]

mas·quer·ad·er [mæ̀skəréidər] *n.* Ⓒ a person who masquerades. 가면 무도회 참가자; 가면을 쓴 사람.

:mass[1] [mæs] *n.* Ⓒ **1** a lump; a quantity of matter or collection of things united into one body. 덩어리; 무더기; 일단. ¶ *a ~ of cloud* 〔*earth*〕 한 무더기의 구름〔흙〕/ *a ~ of iron* 쇳덩이. **2** a large number or quantity. 다수; 다량. ¶ *a ~ of people* 많은 사람들〔군중〕/ *a ~ of letters* 산더미 같은 편지 / *a huge ~ of treasure* 막대한 재보. **3** 《*the ~*》 the greater part; the majority. 대부분; 대다수. ¶ *The ~ of opinion is against the plan.* 대다수의 의견은 계획에 반대다. **4** 《*the -es*》 people in general; the lower classes. 일반 대중; 서민 (cf. *the classes*). ¶ *the laboring masses* 근로자 대중.

be a mass of, show large numbers of; be covered with. …투성이다. ¶ *He is a ~ of wounds.* 그는 상처투성이다.

in a mass, altogether. 하나로 합쳐; 통틀어.

in the mass, as a whole; generally. 전체로; 대체로.

— *adj.* on a large scale; for a mass of people or things. 대규모의; 대중을 위한; 다수의. ¶ ~ *communication* 매스컴; 대량 전달 / ~ *production* 대량 생산.

— *vt., vi.* (P6;1) **1** bring or gather into a mass. 한덩어리로 만들다〔되다〕. **2** 《mil.》 bring or come together at one point. 집결시키다〔하다〕. ¶ ~ *troops* 병력을 집결시키다. [L. *massa*]

Mass, mass[2] [mæs] *n.* **1** Ⓤ 《Cath.》 special services and prayers offered in the Roman Catholic Church. 미사. ¶ *attend ~* 미사에 나가다 / *read ~* 미사를 올리다. **2** Ⓒ music to be used for Mass. 미사곡. [L. *mitto* send]

Mass. Massachusetts.

Mas·sa·chu·setts [mæ̀sətʃúːsits] *n.* a northeastern State of the United States, on the Atlantic Coast. 매사추세츠《미 동북부의 주》. 參考 Mass.로 생략함. 주도는 Boston.

mas·sa·cre [mǽsəkər] *n.* Ⓒ the cruel and violent killing of many people or animals. 대량 학살. — *vt.* (P6) kill (people or animals) cruelly and in large numbers. (사람·짐승)을 대량 학살하다. [F.]

mas·sage [məsɑ́ːʒ / mǽsɑːʒ] *n.* ⓊⒸ the act of rubbing the body to lessen pain. 안마; 마사지. — *vt.* (P6) rub (the body) with the hands; treat with massage. …을 마사지〔안마〕하다. ¶ ~ *someone on the shoulders* 아무의 어깨를 안마해 주다 / *Let me ~ your back for you.* 등을 안마해 드리지요. [F.]

mas·seur [mæsə́ːr] *n.* a man who practices massage. 안마사. [↑]

mas·seuse [mæsə́ːz] *n.* a woman who practices massage. 여자 안마사. [↑]

·mas·sive [mǽsiv] *adj.* **1** huge and heavy. (부피가) 큰; 무거운. ¶ *a ~ structure* 크고 육중한 건조물. **2** (of the mind) powerful; solid. (정신이) 강한; 올찬. ¶ *He is a man of ~ character.* 그는 의지가 강한 사람이다. [→mass[1]]

mass media [ˊ ˊ-] *n. pl.* the means of communication used to reach great numbers of people. 매스 미디어; 대중 매체; 대량 전달 매체. [→mass[1]]

mass meeting [ˊ ˊ-] *n.* a large public meeting of people to hear or discuss public affairs, etc. (특히 정치적인) 국민〔민중〕 대회; 대중 집회.

mass production [ˊ -ˊ-] *n.* the production of goods in large quantities by machinery. 대량 생산.

mass·y [mǽsi] *adj.* (**mass·i·er, mass·i·est**) massive; heavy; of great weight. 육중한; 무거운. [→mass[1]]

·mast[1] [mæst, mɑːst] *n.* Ⓒ **1** a tall pole to support the sails of a ship. 돛대; 마스트. **2** any upright pole. 장대; 기둥. ¶ *radio masts* 무전탑(無電塔). [E.]

sail before the mast, be a common sailor. 평선원으로 일하다.

mast[2] [mæst, mɑːst] *n.* Ⓤ the nuts of the chestnut, oak, beech, etc. when used as food for pigs. (돼지먹이인) 밤나무·떡갈나무 등의 열매《밤·도토리 등》. [E.]

:mas·ter [mǽstər, mɑ́ːstər] *n.* Ⓒ **1** a person who rules or commands; an employer; an owner. 주인; 고용주; 임자; 소유주. ¶ *a stationmaster* 역장 / *a ~ of a factory* 공장주 / *A dog knows his own ~.* 개는 주인을 알아본다. **2** the man at the head of a household. 가장(家長). **3** the captain of a merchant ship. (상선의) 선장. **4** 《esp. Brit.》 a male teacher; a schoolmaster. 남자 선생; 교사. **5** a great artist. 대예술가; 거장. **6** a work by a great artist. 대가의 작품. **7** a person who has some special skill or ability in art, work, trade, etc. 숙련자; 달인(達人). ¶ *a ~ of the piano* 피아노 명연주자 / *a great ~ in painting* 그림의 대가 / *a ~ of the situation* 상황 대처에 능한 사람. **8** 《with a boy's name》 young Mr. 도련님; …님. ¶ *Master Tom* 톰 도련님. **9** 《*the M-*》 Christ. 예수 그리스도. **10** 《*M-*》 a degree given at a college or a university. 석사(碩士). ¶ *Master of Arts* 문학 석사《abbr. M.A., A.M.》

be master of, know (a subject) thoroughly; have (a situation) under control. …에 정통해 있다; …을 자유로이 할 수 있다.

be master of oneself, have one's feelings and actions perfectly under the control of one's reason. 자제력이 강하다.

be one's own master, be free to do as one pleases. 마음대로 할 수 있다; 뜻대로 하다.

make oneself master of, learn thoroughly

the facts about (something) or the way to use (it). …에 훤하다; 정통하다.
the master of ceremonies, a person in charge of a ceremony or an entertainment. 사회자. 參考 M.C.로 생략함.
—*adj.* eminently skilled; excellent; chief; of a master. 뛰어난; 주된; 우두머리의. ¶ *a ~ carpenter* 도목수 / *~ minds* 위인〔지도자〕들.
—*vt.* **1** control; govern. …을 억누르다; 지배하다. ¶ *~ one's anger* 노여움을 억누르다 / *~ oneself* 자제하다. **2** become skillful at (something); learn thoroughly. …에 숙달하다; …을 익히다. ¶ *~ an art* 기술을 익히다 / *~ English* 영어를 마스터하다. [L. *magister* he who is greater]

mas·ter·ful [mǽstərfəl, mɑ́:s-] *adj.* **1** fond of gaining control over others. 오만한; 거들먹거리는. **2** skillful; masterly. 교묘한; 능란한. ¶ *a ~ speech* 명연설.

mas·ter·ful·ly [mǽstərfəli, mɑ́:s-] *adv.* too proudly; skillfully. 오만하게.

master key [∸-∸] *n.* a key for opening different sets of locks. 곁쇠; 맞쇠.

mas·ter·ly [mǽstərli, mɑ́:s-] *adj.* very clever; skillful. 교묘한. —*adv.* in a masterly manner. 교묘하게; 노련하게. ●**mas·ter·li·ness** [-nis] *n.*

•**mas·ter·piece** [mǽstərpì:s, mɑ́:s-] *n.* Ⓒ anything made or done in a masterly way; the best piece of work of a writer, painter, etc. 명작; 걸작.

mas·ter·ship [mǽstərʃìp, mɑ́:s-] *n.* **1** Ⓤ the state of being a master. master 임. **2** Ⓒ the position of a master, esp. of a schoolmaster. (특히) 교사직. **3** Ⓤ control; skill. 지배; 숙련.

mas·ter·y [mǽstəri / mɑ́:s-] *n.* Ⓤ **1** control; command; power such as a master has. 지배; 통어(력). ¶ *have the complete ~ over* …을 완전히 통어〔지배〕하다. **2** skill and complete knowledge. 숙달; 정통. ¶ *acquire a ~ of Russian* 러시아어에 숙달되다.

mast·head [mǽsthèd, mɑ́:st-] *n.* Ⓒ **1** the top of a ship's mast. 돛대머리; 장두(檣頭). **2** a sailor who looks out from near the masthead. 돛대머리의 감시인. **3** 《U.S.》 that part of a newspaper or magazine that gives the title, owner, address, rates, etc. 발행인란《신문·잡지의 명칭·발행인·주소·요금 등을 밝힌 난》. —*vt.* (P6) **1** send to the masthead as a punishment. 벌로 돛대머리에 오르게 하다. **2** raise (a sail, flag, etc.) to the top of the masthead. (기 따위)를 장두에 달다. [→mast[1]]

mas·ti·cate [mǽstəkèit] *vt.* (P6) chew. …을 씹다; 저작(咀嚼)하다. [L.]

mas·ti·ca·tion [mæ̀stəkéiʃən] *n.* Ⓤ the act of chewing. 씹기; 저작.

mas·tiff [mǽstif] *n.* Ⓒ a large powerful dog with a broad mouth and hanging lips. 매스티프《큰 맹견의 일종》. [manu-, L. *suesco* grow used]

mas·to·don [mǽstədɑ̀n / -dɔ̀n] *n.* Ⓒ a huge, extinct animal much like an elephant. 마스토돈《코끼리 비슷한 태고의 거대한 짐승》. [Gk. *mastos* nipple, *odous* tooth]

:**mat**[1] [mæt] *n.* Ⓒ **1** a small floor covering. 매트; 돗자리. ¶ *a door ~* (현관의) 신발 흙털개. **2** a flat piece of cloth, etc. for use under a vase, etc. (꽃병 따위의 장식용) 깔개; 받침. **3** an entangled or disorderly mass of hair or grass. (머리카락·풀 따위의) 엉킴; 헝클어짐.
leave someone on the mat, do not allow someone to come into a house. …을 문간에서 쫓아 버리다.
—*v.* (**mat·ted, mat·ting**) *vt.* **1** (P6) cover or supply (something) with a mat. …을 매트로 덮다; …에 매트를 깔다. **2** (P6,7) cause (something) to tangle or become disorderly. …을 엉키게 하다. ¶ *become matted* 엉키다 / *matted hair* 엉킨 머리; 봉두. —*vi.* (P1,2A,2B) become tangled. 엉키다; 엉클어지다. [L. *matta*]

mat[2] [mæt] *adj.* dull; not shining. 광택이〔윤기가〕 없는. ¶ *~ silver* 광택〔윤〕을 없앤 은. —*vt.* (P6) make a surface of (metal, etc.) dull. …의 윤기를 없애다. [Arab. = helpless]

mat·a·dor [mǽtədɔ̀:r] *n.* Ⓒ a man who kills a bull with a sword in a bull-fight; a professional bull-fighter. 투우사(cf. *toreador*). [L. *macto* slaughter]

:**match**[1] [mætʃ] *n.* Ⓒ **1** a game; a contest. 시합; 경기. ¶ *a golf ~* 골프 경기. **2** a person or a thing having equal power to another in a contest; a rival. 필적하는 상대; 호적수. ¶ *You are no ~ for me.* 너는 내 적수가 안 된다 / *meet* 〔*find*〕 *one's ~* 호적수를 만나다 / *be more than a ~ for one* …보다 한 수 위다. **3** a person or a thing exactly like another; one of a pair. 빼쏜 것; 쌍의 한쪽. **4** a person or a thing that is suitable for another. …와 어울리는 것〔사람〕. ¶ *The hat is a very good ~ for your coat.* 그 모자는 네 옷에 썩 잘 어울린다. **5** a person who is suitable as a marriage partner. (결혼 상대로) 걸맞은 사람. ¶ *The girl is a suitable ~ for our son.* 그 처녀는 우리 아이 배필로 안성맞춤인 것 같소. **6** a marriage. 결혼. ¶ *make a ~* 중매를 서다 / *At last they made a ~ of it.* 그들은 마침내 결혼했다.
—*vt.* **1** (P6,13) cause (someone or something) to fight against another. 서로 대항〔경쟁〕시키다. ¶ *~ someone against* 〔*with*〕 *another* 아무를 다른 사람과 경쟁시키다. **2** (P6) be equal to; be a match for (someone or something). …에 필적하다; …의 적수가 되다. ¶ *No one can ~ him in mathematics.* 수학에선 아무도 그의 적수가 안 된다. **3** (P6,13) fit; suit. …에 어울리다. ¶ *His necktie does not ~ his coat.* 그의 넥타이는 옷에 안 어울린다. **4** (P14) find something suit-

able for (another). …에 어울리는 것을 찾다. ¶ *Can you* ~ (*me*) *this cloth?* 이 천에 맞는 걸 찾아 주겠소. **5** (P6,13) cause (someone) to be married. …을 결혼시키다. ¶ *He matched his daughter with* (*to*) *the young man.* 그는 딸을 그 젊은이와 결혼시켰다. — *vi.* (P1) **1** be equal or suitable. 어울리다; 걸맞다. **2** go well together. 조화되다. ¶ *The colors ~ well.* 그 색깔들은 잘 조화된다. [E.]

:match² [mætʃ] *n.* Ⓒ a short piece of wood with a head that catches fire when rubbed. 성냥. ¶ *light* (*strike*) *a ~* 성냥을 긋다. [F. *mesche*]

match·box [mǽtʃbɑ̀ks / -bɔ̀ks] *n.* Ⓒ a small box for matches. 성냥갑.

match·less [mǽtʃlis] *adj.* having no equal; unrivaled. 무쌍의; 비길 데 없는. ¶ ~ *charm* 비길 데 없는 매력. ● **match·less·ly** [-li] *adv.* **match·less·ness** [-nis] *n.* [*match¹*]

match·lock [mǽtʃlɑ̀k / -lɔ̀k] *n.* Ⓒ an old gun with a cord to light the powder. 화승총. [*match²*]

match·mak·er [mǽtʃmèikər] *n.* Ⓒ **1** a person who arranges marriages for others. 결혼 중매인. **2** a person who arranges matches for prize fights, races, etc. 경기의 대전(對戰) 계획을 짜는 사람. [*match¹*]

match·mak·ing [mǽtʃmèikiŋ] *n.* Ⓤ **1** the act of arranging marriages. 결혼 중매. **2** an arranging of prize fights. 경기 대전표 작성.

match·wood [mǽtʃwùd] *n.* Ⓤ **1** small pieces of wood, esp. for making matches. 성냥 개비 재료. **2** very small pieces. 산산 조각들. ¶ *reduce something to ~* …을 산산 조각 내다. [*match²*]

:mate¹ [meit] *n.* Ⓒ **1** (among working men) a companion; a fellow-workman. (직장 · 작업장 따위의) 동료. **2** one of a pair; a husband or wife. 짝의 한쪽; 배우자. ¶ *Where is the ~ to this glove?* 이 장갑 한 쪽은 어디 갔나. **3** a ship's officer below the rank of captain. 항해사; 부선장. ¶ *a chief ~* 일등 항해사. **4** an assistant. 조수. ¶ *a cook's ~* 요리사 조수 / *a surgeon's ~* 외과의 조수. — *vt.* (P6,13) join in marriage; pair (birds). …을 결혼시키다; 교미시키다. — *vi.* (P1) marry; pair. 결혼하다; 교미하다. [? G.]

mate² [meit] *n., v., interj.* =checkmate.

ma·ter [méitər] *n.* Ⓒ 《Brit. *colloq.*》 a mother. 어머니(opp. pater). [L.]

:ma·te·ri·al [mətíəriəl] *n.* **1** ⓊⒸ the substance of which anything is made. 원료; 재료. ¶ *raw ~* 원료 / *clothes made of good ~* 좋은 감으로 만든 옷. **2** Ⓤ that which makes a part of anything, facts, pieces of knowledge, etc.; data. 자료(資料); 제재(題材); 데이터. ¶ *the ~ for a novel* 소설의 자료 / *draw ~ from* …에서 자료를 얻다. **3** 《*pl.*》 tools or articles. 도구. ¶ *writing materials* 필기 도구. **4** Ⓤ cloth. (옷)감. — *adj.* **1** of matter or substance. 물질의; 물질적인(opp. spiritual). ¶ *a ~ being* 유형물 / *the ~ world* 물질계 / ~ *evidence* 물적 증거. **2** ⓐ of the body; rather than the mind or soul; of physical needs. 육체상의. ¶ ~ *comforts* 육체적 쾌락 / *Food is a ~ need.* 음식은 육체상 필요물이다. ⓑ loving things of the senses. 관능(감각)적인. **3** essential; important. 필수의; 중요한. ¶ *be ~ to…* …에 있어서 중요하다 / *a very ~ difference* 매우 중요한 차이. [L. *materia* timber]

ma·te·ri·al·ism [mətíəriəlìzəm] *n.* Ⓤ **1** the theory that nothing exists except matter. 유물론; 유물주의(opp. idealism). **2** the tendency to think more highly of material things than of spiritual things. 물질주의.

ma·te·ri·al·ist [mətíəriəlist] *n.* Ⓒ **1** a person who believes in materialism. 유물론자. **2** a person who values material things more than spiritual things. 물질주의자.

ma·te·ri·al·is·tic [mətìəriəlístik] *adj.* of materialism or materialists. 유물론(자)의.

ma·te·ri·al·i·za·tion [mətìəriəlizéiʃən] *n.* Ⓤ the act of materializing; the state of being materialized. 구체화; 물질화.

ma·te·ri·al·ize [mətíəriəlàiz] *vt.* (P6) **1** give material or concrete form to (something). …에 형체를 주다. ¶ ~ *one's ideas* 자기 생각을 구체화하다. **2** make (something) appear in material form. (영혼 등)을 구체적인 형태로 나타내다. ¶ ~ *a spirit* 영혼을 체현(體現)시키다. **3** make (something) materialistic. …을 물질적(실리적)으로 하다. — *vi.* (P1) **1** (of a wish, hope, plan, etc.) become fact; be carried out. (희망 등이) 실현되다. **2** (of a spirit) appear in material form. 체현되다; 형체로 나타나다.

ma·te·ri·al·ly [mətíəriəli] *adv.* **1** in a material manner. 물질적으로(opp. spiritually). **2** in matter or substance. 실질적으로(opp. formally). **3** considerably; to an important degree. 크게; 현저히. ¶ *differ ~* 크게(현저히) 다르다.

ma·te·ri·a med·i·ca [mətíəriə médikə] *n.* 《L.》 drugs; pharmacology. 약물(藥物); 약물학.

ma·ter·nal [mətə́ːrnl] *adj.* **1** of or like a mother. 어머니의; 어머니 같은(opp. paternal). ¶ ~ *love* 모성애. **2** on the mother's side of the family. 어머니 쪽의. ¶ ~ *relatives* 외가 친척. [→mater]

ma·ter·nal·ly [mətə́ːrnəli] *adv.* **1** in a maternal way. 어머니같이(답게). **2** on the mother's side. 외가 쪽으로.

ma·ter·ni·ty [mətə́ːrnəti] *n.* Ⓤ **1** the state of being a mother. 어머니임. **2** the qualities of a mother; motherhood. 어머니다움; 모성애. — *adj.* for a woman having a baby. 임산부를 위한. ¶ *a ~ hospital* 산부인과 병원 / *a ~ nurse* 조산원; 산파.

math [mæθ] *n.* 《U.S. *colloq.*》 =mathematics.

math·e·mat·i·cal [mæθəmǽtikəl], **-mat·ic** [-mǽtik] *adj.* **1** of the nature of mathematics. 수학적인. **2** very exact; completely accurate. 정확한. [Gk. *manthanō* learn]

math·e·mat·i·cal·ly [mæθəmǽtikəli] *adv.* **1** in a mathematical way. 수학적으로. **2** with accuracy; exactly. 정확하게.

math·e·ma·ti·cian [mæ̀θəmətíʃən] *n.* Ⓒ a person who is skillful in mathematics. 수학자.

•**math·e·mat·ics** [mæ̀θəmǽtiks] *n. pl.* 《used as *sing.*》 Ⓤ the science of space and numbers. 수학. 參考 math.로 생략함. 구어에서는 maths. 또는 math.

maths [mæθs] *n.* 《Brit. *colloq.*》 =mathematics.

mat·i·née, -nee [mæ̀tənéi / mǽtənèi] *n.* Ⓒ 《F.》 a daytime show in a theater. 마티네; 주간 흥행(cf. *soiree*). [F. *matin* morning]

ma·tri·arch [méitriɑ̀ːrk] *n.* **1** the mother who is the ruler of a family or tribe. 여가장(女家長). **2** a venerable old woman. 노부인. [L. *mater* mother, →(patri)arch]

ma·tri·ces [méitrəsìːz, mǽt-] *n.* pl. of **matrix.**

ma·tri·cide [méitrəsàid] *n.* **1** ⓊⒸ the act of killing one's own mother. 모친 살해(행위). **2** Ⓒ a person who kills his own mother. 모친 살해범(opp. patricide). [L. *mater* mother, *caedo* kill]

ma·tric·u·late [mətríkjəlèit] *vt.* (P6) admit (someone) as a student at a university, etc. …에게 대학 입학을 허락하다. — *vi.* (P3) be admitted to a college or university. 대학 입학이 허락되다. [→matrix]

ma·tric·u·la·tion [mətrìkjəléiʃən] *n.* Ⓤ **1** the act of matriculating; the state of being matriculated. 입학 허가. **2** an examination held by colleges or universities which must be passed before a student can be admitted. 대학 입학 시험.

mat·ri·mo·ni·al [mæ̀trəmóuniəl] *adj.* of marriage. 결혼의. ● **mat·ri·mo·ni·al·ly** [-i] *adv.* [↓]

mat·ri·mo·ny [mǽtrəmòuni] *n.* Ⓤ **1** marriage. 결혼. **2** married life. 결혼 생활. [→mater]

ma·trix [méitriks, mǽt-] *n.* Ⓒ (*pl.* **-tri·ces** or **-trix·es**) **1** something from which a thing grows; a place within which something is formed and developed. 모체; 기반. ¶ *the ~ of Western civilization* 서구 문명의 기반. **2** a rock in which a gem, fossil, etc. is enclosed. 모암(母岩); 맥석(脈石). **3** a shape into which hot metal is poured. 주형(鑄型); 거푸집. **4** 《print.》 a piece of metal in which a type is cast. 자모(字母). **5** 《anat.》 the womb. 자궁. [L. =womb]

ma·tron [méitrən] *n.* Ⓒ **1** an elderly married woman. (나이 지긋한) 기혼 부인; 여사. **2** a woman in charge of household affairs in a hospital, school, etc. 가정부; 수(首)간호사; (학교의) 여자 사감 (등). [→mater]

ma·tron·ly [méitrənli] *adj.* **1** of, like a matron. matron 다운. **2** noble and calm. 점잖고 조용한.

Matt [mæt] *n.* a nickname of Matthew. Mattew의 애칭.

mat·ted [mǽtid] *adj.* **1** covered with a mat. 매트를 깐. **2** entangled closely. 엉킨. ¶ *~ hair* 헝클어진 머리. [*mat*[1]]

:mat·ter [mǽtər] *n.* **1** Ⓤ that which all things are made of; substance; material. 물질(opp. mind, spirit). ¶ *solid* 〔*liquid, gaseous*〕 ~ 고체〔액체, 기체〕. **2** Ⓤ stuff; any particular thing. (어떤 특수한)…체(體); …물(物). ¶ *coloring* ~ 색소 / *printed* ~ 인쇄물 / *postal* ~ 우편물. **3** 《*the* ~》 the content of thought, expression or book. (사고·표현 등의) 내용; 제재(題材)(opp. manner, style). ¶ *the ~ of the lecture* 강의 내용. **4** Ⓒ an affair; a subject for discussion; a cause. 사항; 문제; 원인. ¶ *a serious* ~ 심각한 문제 / *money matters* 금전 문제 / *a ~ of* 〔*for*〕 *regret* 유감된 일 / *It's no laughing* ~ 웃을 일이 아니다 / *Matters are quite different here.* 여기서는 사정이 크게 다르다 / *I have no interest in the* ~. 나는 그 문제에 흥미가 없다 / *It's a ~ of* 〔*for*〕 *congratulation.* 그건 축하할 일이군. **5** Ⓤ 《used with *no* or *what*》 importance; significance. 중대한 일; 중요성. ¶ *It's* (*of*) *no* ~. 그건 대수로운 일이 아니다 / *What ~ is it?* 그게 어쨌다는 거냐. **6** 《*the* ~》 difficulty; trouble. 곤란; 지장; 사고. ¶ *What is the ~ with him?* 그 사람에게 무슨 일이 있나. **7** 《usu. *a ~ of*》 an amount, usu. roughly estimated. 약; 대충; 대체적인 양〔수〕. ¶ *a ~ of three days* 약 사흘 정도 / *The loss is a ~ of a hundred pounds.* 손실은 약 백 파운드 정도이다. **8** Ⓤ the yellow liquid which comes out of a wound, etc.; pus. 고름.

a matter of, about. 약; 쯤. ¶ *a ~ of five miles* 약 5마일.

as a matter of course, an event that excites no surprise. 당연한 일로서.

as a matter of fact, in fact; really. 실은; 사실상.

as the matter stands, in the present state of things. 현상태로는.

for that matter, so far as that is concerned. 그 일에 관해서는; 그 일이라면.

in the matter of (=*as regards*) *something.* …에 관해서는.

It is no matter. =***It makes no matter.*** It makes no difference. 그건 아무래도 좋다.

No matter. =What matter?

no matter how 〔***when, which, who, what,*** etc.〕, however 〔whenever, whichever, whoever, etc.〕. 비록 어떻게〔언제, 무엇, 누구〕 … 일지라도. ¶ *No ~ what you may say, I will never believe you.* 네가 무슨 말을 하든 나는 곧이듣지 않겠다.

to make matters worse ⇨ worse.
What matter? It makes no difference. 아무 상관 없다; 아무래도 좋다.
— *vi.* **1** (P1,2A,2B) be important. 중대〔중요〕하다. ¶ *It matters little to me.* 나와는 상관없는 일이다 / *It matters much to us.* 우리로선 문젯거리다. **2** (P1) (of a wound, etc.) form or give out matter. (상처가) 곪다; 고름이 나오다. [→material]

Mat·ter·horn [mǽtərhɔ̀:rn] *n.* a mountain of the Alps. 마터호른《알프스의 고산; 해발 4,478m》.

mat·ter-of-fact [mǽtərəvfǽkt] *adj.* **1** concerned with facts. 사실의. ¶ *a ~ account of the accident* 사고에 대한 사실적인 보고. **2** practical. 실제적인〔상의〕. **3** lacking imagination. 무미 건조한. [*matter*]

mat·ting [mǽtiŋ] *n.* Ⓤ 《*collectively*》 a piece of rough woven fabric used for covering floors, for wrapping things, etc. 매트; 멍석. [→mat[1]]

mat·tock [mǽtək] *n.* Ⓒ a tool with a flat or pointed blade on either side, used for digging, etc. 곡괭이의 일종. [E.]

〈mattock〉

mat·tress [mǽtris] *n.* Ⓒ a cloth-covered pad filled with straw, hair, cotton, etc., used as a bed. 매트리스; 침대요. [It.]

mat·u·rate [mǽtʃərèit] *vt., vi.* (P6;1) **1** discharge pus; suppurate. 화농하다〔시키다〕. **2** ripen; mature. 익다; 성숙하다〔시키다〕.

•**ma·ture** [mətjúər, -tʃúər] *adj.* **1** ⓐ ripe; fully grown. 익은; 여문. ¶ *~ grain* 〔*fruit*〕 여문 곡식〔익은 과일〕. ⓑ (of a person, mind, etc.) having reached a state of full development; adult. 성숙한; 성인이 된. ¶ *a ~ age* 사리를 분별할 수 있는 나이. **2** thought out carefully. 신중한. ¶ *a ~ opinion* 사려 깊은 의견. **3** reached the limit of time for payment. (어음 등이) 만기가 된.
— *vt.* (P6) **1** bring (something) to a fully-grown state; make ripe. …을 성숙시키다; 익히다. ¶ *wine matured by age* 여러 해를 묵어 잘 익은 포도주 / *Suffering matured his understanding.* 고생을 해서 그는 철이 제대로 들었다. **2** work out (something) carefully; develop (something) fully. …을 완성시키다. ¶ *~ one's plans* 계획을 완성하다.
— *vi.* (P1) **1** come to a fully-grown state. 성숙하다. ¶ *These apples are maturing fast.* 이 사과는 조생종이다. **2** reach the limit of time for payment. (어음이) 만기가 되다. ●**ma·ture·ly** [-li] *adv.* [L. *maturus* ripe]

•**ma·tu·ri·ty** [mətjúərəti, -tʃú:- / -tjúərə-] *n.* Ⓤ **1** the state or process of ripening or growing fully. 성숙. ¶ *come to ~* 익다; 성숙해지다. **2** the state of being completed. 완성. **3** the time a debt, note, etc. ought to be paid. (어음의) 만기(일). ¶ *pay at ~* 만기일에 지급하다.

maud·lin [mɔ́:dlin] *adj.* **1** easily moved to tears. 눈물이 헤픈; 잘 우는. ¶ *As soon as he gets drunk he becomes ~.* 취하기만 하면 그는 운다. **2** stupid and sentimental. 쓸데없이 감상적인. ¶ *~ sympathy for criminals* 죄인에 대한 감상적인 동정. [→Magdalen]

maul [mɔ:l] *n.* Ⓒ a large, heavy hammer of wood. 큰 나무망치. — *vt.* (P6,7) **1** do harm to (someone) by beating. …을 때려 상처를 입히다. **2** handle (someone) in a rough way. …을 거칠게 다루다. ¶ *Don't ~ the cat.* 고양이를 거칠게 다루지 마라. **3** damage by criticism. …을 혹평하다. [L. *malleus* hammer]

maun·der [mɔ́:ndər] *vi.* (P1,2A,2B) **1** talk in a foolish and aimless way. 두서없이 말하다. **2** 《*along, about*》 move or act in an aimless way. 헤매다; 헤매고 다니다. [? obs. *maund* beg, →meander]

mau·so·le·a [mɔ̀:səlí:ə] *n.* pl. of **mausoleum.**

mau·so·le·um [mɔ̀:səlí:əm] *n.* Ⓒ (*pl.* **-leums** or **-le·a**) a large, imposing tomb. 능(陵); 영묘(靈廟). [Gk. *Mausōlos,* Person]

mauve [mouv] *n.* Ⓤ a light purple color. 엷은 자주색. — *adj.* of a light purple color. 담자색(淡紫色)의. [→mallow]

maw [mɔ:] *n.* Ⓒ the stomach of an animal. (짐승의) 위; 밥통. [E.]

mawk·ish [mɔ́:kiʃ] *adj.* **1** having a faint, sickly flavor or taste. 속이 느글거리는; 역겨운. **2** sentimental in a silly way. 몹시 감상적인. [N. *madkr* maggot]

•**max·im** [mǽksim] *n.* Ⓒ **1** a short expression of a general truth. 격언. **2** a briefly-expressed rule to guide people. 좌우명; 처세훈(訓)〔술〕. [L. *maximus* greatest]

max·i·ma [mǽksəmə] *n.* pl. of **maximum.**

•**max·i·mum** [mǽksəməm] *n.* Ⓒ (*pl.* **-mums** or **-ma**) the greatest possible number, amount, quantity, degree or point. 최대한; 최대량; 극대(opp. minimum). ¶ *The confusion was at its ~* 혼란은 극에 달했다.
— *adj.* greatest; highest. 최고〔최대〕의; 극한의. ¶ *a ~ thermometer* 최고 온도계. [L. *maximus* greatest]

:**May** [mei] *n.* **1** the fifth month of the year. 5월. **2** 《*fig.*》 youth. 젊음; 청춘. [L. *Maius*]

:**may** [mei] *auxil. v.* (**might**) (P25) **1** be allowed to; be free to. …해도 좋다(opp. must not). ¶ *"May I come in?" —"Yes, you ~* 〔*No, you ~ not*〕*."* 들어가도 되나요. — 그래, 들어오너라〔아니, 들어오지 마라〕 / *I ~ sit down, mayn't* [méiənt, meint] *I?* 앉아도 괜찮겠죠 / *You ~ go if you choose.* 가고 싶으면 가도 좋다. **2** be able to; can. …할 수 있다 (opp. can not). ¶ *It ~ safely be said that….*

…라고 말해도 괜찮다 / *Work hard while you* ~. 일할 수 있을 때 열심히 해라. **3** will possibly. …일지도 모른다. ¶ *It ~ or ~ not be true.* 그게 정말일 수도 혹은 그렇지 않을 수도 있다 / *He ~ come, but I'm not sure.* 그가 올지도 모르겠으나, 장담은 못 하겠다 / *He ~ have called on her.* 그가 그녀를 방문했을지도 모르겠다 / *He ~ have seen it.* 그 사람이 그걸 봤는지도 모른다. 語法 과거의 일을 말할 경우는 may have + *pp.*가 됨. **4** 《used after ask, wonder, etc.; expressing some doubt》 도대체 …일까. ¶ *I wonder who he ~ be.* 그 사람이 대체 누구더라 / *Who ~ you be?* 누구시더라 / *How old ~ he be?* 저 양반 몇 살이나 됐을까. **5** 《expressing wishes》 바라건대 …이기를. ¶ *Long ~ he live!* 그의 장수를 빈다 / *May you succeed!* 성공하시기를(빕니다). **6** 《expressing *a request*》 …해 주시오. ¶ *You ~ stand up, Tom.* 톰, 일어나 보렴. **7** 《in *adv. clause* expressing *purpose*》 …하도록; …하기 위해. ¶ *He works hard* (*so*) *that he ~ succeed.* 성공하기 위해 열심히 일한다. **8** 《in *adv. clause* expressing concession》 비록 …일지라도. ¶ *However* 〔*No matter how*〕 *tired you ~ be, you must do the work.* 아무리 피곤해도 그 일을 해야 한다. [E.]

as best one may, as well as possible. 되도록 잘; 될 수 있는 대로.

be that as it may, although some (contrasting fact) may be true. 그것은 어쨌든.

come what may, whatever may happen. 무슨 일이 있건.

may (***just***) ***as well do,*** have no special reason not to do. …하는 편이 좋다.

may well do, have good reason to do. …하는 것도 무리가 아니다. ¶ *He ~ well be proud of his son.* 자식 자랑을 할 만도 하군.

:may·be [méibi:] *adv.* perhaps; possibly. 아마도. ¶ *Maybe you'll have better luck next time.* 어쩌면 다음엔 더 좋은 일이 있을 거다. [*may, be*]

May Day [스스] *n.* the first day of May, celebrated as a spring festival; nowadays labor parades and meetings are held. 5월제; 메이 데이. [*May*]

may·on·naise [mèiənéiz, 스-스] *n.* Ⓤ 《F.》 a cream-like salad dressing or sauce. 마요네즈 (소스).

:may·or [méiər, mέər] *n.* Ⓒ the chief officer of a city. 시장(市長). [→major]

may·or·al·ty [méiərəlti, mέər-] *n.* Ⓤ the position or term of office of mayor. 시장의 직〔임기〕. [↑]

may·or·ess [méiəris, mέər-] *n.* Ⓒ the wife of a mayor. 시장 부인.

May·pole, may- [méipòul] *n.* Ⓒ a tall pole decorated with ribbons, flowers, etc. around which people dance on May Day. 5월의 기둥《5월제에 꽃 따위를 장식한》. [*May*]

〈Maypole〉

May queen [스스] *n.* a girl, chosen as the queen on May Day. 5월의 여왕; 메이 퀸.

maze [meiz] *n.* Ⓒ **1** a complicated path from which it is hard to find a way out. 미로(迷路). ¶ *a ~ of streets* 아주 복잡한 거리. **2** 《*fig.*》 a confused state of mind. 혼란. ¶ *He is lost in a ~.* 그는 망연 자실해 있다. — *vt.* (P6,13) 《in *passive*》 puzzle; confuse. …을 당황하게 만들다. [E.]

ma·zur·ka, ma·zour·ka [məzə́:rkə, -zúər-] *n.* **1** Ⓒ a lively Polish dance. 마주르카춤. **2** Ⓤ the music for this dance. 마주르카 무용곡. [Pol.]

ma·zy [méizi] *adj.* (**-zi·er, -zi·est**) **1** like a maze. 미로 같은. **2** bewildering; puzzling. 당황한; 혼란한. ● **maz·i·ness** [-nis] *n.* [*maze*]

M.C. master of ceremonies; 《U.S.》 Member of Congress.

M.D. Doctor of Medicine.

:me [mi:, mi] *pron.* **1** the objective case of **I**. 나를; 나에게. ¶ *He saw ~.* 그는 나를 봤다 / *He gave ~ this book.* 그는 이 책을 나에게 주었다. **2** 《as *predicative*》 《*colloq.*》 =I. ¶ *It's ~.* 나다; 접니다. **3** 《in exclamations》 ¶ *Dear ~!* 어머나; 이런 / *Ah ~!* 아아. [E.]

Me. Maine.

:mead·ow [médou] *n.* Ⓤ **1** a field covered with grass which animals eat for food. 목초지. **2** grassy land by the bank of a stream. 강변의 풀밭. [E.]

mead·ow·land [médoulæ̀nd] *n.* Ⓤ meadow. 목초지.

mead·ow·lark [médoulὰ:rk] *n.* Ⓒ 《bird》 a little American song-bird with a yellow breast. 물종다리.

mea·ger, 《Brit.》 **mea·gre** [mí:gər] *adj.* (**-ger·er, -ger·est** or 《Brit.》 **-grer, -grest**) **1** poor. 빈약한. ¶ *a ~ income* 얼마 안 되는 수입 / *a ~ meal* 〔*diet*〕 검소한 식사. **2** lacking in flesh; lean; thin. 마른. ¶ *a ~ face* 야윈 얼굴. [L. *macer*]

mea·ger·ly, 《Brit.》 **-gre-** [mí:gərli] *adv.* in a meager manner. 빈약하게; 말라.

mea·ger·ness, 《Brit.》 **-gre-** [mí:gərnis] *n.* Ⓤ the state or quality of being thin or poor. 빈약; 야윔.

:meal[1] [mi:l] *n.* **1** Ⓒ all the food that is eaten at one time. (1회분의) 식사. ¶ *daily meals* 매일의 식사 / *a square ~* 충분한 식사 / *have* 〔*eat, take*〕 *a ~* 식사하다 / *make a hearty* 〔*good*〕 *~ of* (*something*) 배불리 먹다 / *To be taken two hours after meals.* 식후 2시간 후에 복용할 것. **2** Ⓤ mealtime; the fixed time when the food is taken. 식사 시간. ¶ *the midday ~* 점심 / *at meals* 식사 〔때〕에. [E.]

meal[2] [mi:l] *n.* **1** Ⓤ any eatable grain that is roughly ground, esp. corn meal. 거

칠게 탄 옥수수 (등)(cf. *flour*). **2** grain ground to rough flour. 거친 곡식 가루. [E.]

meal·time [mí:ltàim] *n.* Ⓤ the usual time for eating a meal. 식사 시간; 끼니때.

meal·y [mí:li] *adj.* (**meal·i·er, meal·i·est**) **1** like meal. (탄 곡식) 가루 모양의. **2** covered with meal. 가루로 덮인. **3** (of potatoes) dry and powdery. (찐 감자가) 푸슬푸슬한. ¶ ~ *potatoes.* **4** pale. 창백한. [→meal²]

meal·y-mouthed [mí:limáuðd, -máuθt] *adj.* not willing to tell the truth frankly, esp. when something unpleasant must be said. 완곡하게 말하는; 구변이 좋은. ¶ ~ *politicians* 에둘러〔듣기 좋게〕 말하는 정치가들. [↑]

:mean¹ [mi:n] *v.* (**meant**) *vt.* **1** (P6,7,8,13,14) have (an idea) in mind; intend to do (something); have (a particular intention or purpose) in mind. …을 의도하다; …할 작정이다; …할 뜻을 품다. ¶ *They ~ you no harm.* = *They ~ no harm to you.* 그들은 너를 해칠 생각이 없다 / *She means mischief.* 그녀는 장난칠 생각이다 / *You ~ to say I'm telling a lie?* 너는 내가 거짓말을 한다는 말이냐 / *I don't ~ any harm.* 악의는 아니다 / *Do you ~ to stay long?* 오래 있을 거니 / *I meant to have helped her.* 나는 그녀를 도와 줄 생각이었는데 / *I meant it for your good.* 너를 위해서 그렇게 한 것이다 / *What do you ~ by coming in my room like this?* 이렇게 내 방에 온 목적이 뭐냐. **2** (P20) intend to cause (someone) to do. …에게 —하게 할 생각하다. ¶ *I ~ you to marry him.* 나는 너를 그 사람과 결혼시킬 생각이다 / *He meant his son to obey him.* 그는 아들이 자기 말에 따르게 할 작정이었다. **3** (P6,11) intend to express (something); have as its meaning. …의 뜻으로 말하다. ¶ *What do you ~ by the word?* 그렇게 말하는 의도가 뭐냐 / *I ~ that you are a coward.* 내 말은 네가 겁쟁이라는〔비겁하다는〕 거다. **4** (P6,11) be a sign of (something); signify; express a certain idea. …을 의미하다. ¶ *What does the word ~?* 그 말은 무슨 뜻이냐 / *The red light means 'stop'.* 붉은 신호는 '정지'하라는 뜻이다. **5** (P6) cause (something) to happen; result in (something); come to. …을 초래하다; …하게 되다. ¶ *This means the ruin of me.* 이로써 나는 끝장을 보게 된다 / *Poor digestion means poor nutrition.* 소화가 안 되면 영양실조가 된다. **6** (P13) 《*to*》 have a value equal to (something). …만큼이나 중요하다; …의 가치를 지니다. ¶ *His mother means the world to him.* 그에게는 어머니가 다시없이 귀중하다 / *Money means nothing to me.* 돈 따위는 내게 아무것도 아니다. —*vi.* (P2A) have a certain kind of feeling; be minded. (…에 대해 …한) 기분을 가지다. ¶ *He means kindly by you.* 그 사람은 네게 호감을 가지고 있다. [E.]

be meant for, **a**) have been decided or destined to become (a doctor, etc.). …이기로 되어 있다; 운명적이다. ¶ *She is meant for his wife.* 그녀는 그의 아내가 되기로 되어 있다 / *They are meant for each other.* 그들은 결혼하기로 되어 있다. **b**) have been decided to belong to (someone). …의 것으로 되어 있다. ¶ *This doll is meant for her.* 이 인형은 그녀에게 줄 것이다. [E.]

I mean what I say, I say it seriously. (내 말은) 진담이다.

mean a great deal 〔***much***〕, be significant. 뜻이 깊다; 의미 심장하다.

mean business, be serious. 농담이 아니다; 진심이다.

mean well by 〔***to, toward***〕 *someone,* have good intentions toward someone. …에 호의적이다.

:mean² [mi:n] *adj.* **1** ⓐ low in quality, grade; inferior. (질이) 안 좋은; 뒤떨어지는; 열등한. ¶ *clothes of ~ quality* 감이 좋지 않은 옷 / *a man of ~ understanding* 머리가 안 좋은 사람 / *He is no ~ scholar.* 그는 대단한 학자다. ⓑ of humble birth; of low rank. 천한 태생의; 미천한. ¶ *a man ~ birth.* **2** of poor appearance; shabby. 초라한. ¶ *a ~ house* 〔*street*〕 초라한 집〔거리, 빈민가〕. **3** morally low; base; small-minded; petty. 치사한; 비열한; 인색한. ¶ ~ *thoughts* 〔*motive*〕 비열한 생각〔동기〕 / *a ~ fellow* 치사한 친구. **4** giving or spending very little; not generous; selfish. 쩨쩨한; 이기적인. ¶ *He is ~ about* 〔*over*〕 *money.* 돈 문제에 그는 다랍다. **5** of small importance. 하찮은. ¶ *the meanest flower* 이름도 없는 꽃. **6** unkind; cruel. 매정한. ¶ *That was a ~ remark.* 그 말은 좀 심했다 / *Don't be so ~ to us.* 우리한테 너무 그러지 마시오. **7** 《*colloq.*》 secretly ashamed. 부끄러운; 낯뜨거운. ¶ *You should feel ~ being so stingy.* 그 정도로 인색한 너를 부끄러운 줄 알아라. **8** 《U.S. *colloq.*》 sick; in poor health. 몸이 좋지 않은. [E.]

have a mean opinion of, have contempt for. …을 업신여기다.

no mean, not bad; good. 상당한; 훌륭한. ¶ *Running ten miles is no ~ achievement.* 10마일을 달린다는 것은 대단한 일이다.

***mean³** [mi:n] *adj.* **1** just halfway; middle; average. (수량·거리 등의) 중간인; 평균의. ¶ *the ~ annual temperature* 연간 평균 온도 / *5 is the ~ number between 3 and 7,* 5는 3과 7의 평균치다. **2** ordinary; not too much or too little. 보통의; 중위의. ¶ *take a ~ course* 중도를 택하다. **3** (of the time) between two events. (시간적으로) 사이의. ¶ *for the meantime* 그 동안만; 일시적인 / *in the meantime* 그러는 동안에. —*n.* Ⓤ something that is halfway; the average. 중간; 중위; 중용. ¶ *the happy* 〔*golden*〕 ~ 중도; 중용(中庸). [→medial]

me·an·der [miǽndər] *n.* Ⓒ **1** 《often *pl.*》 the winding course of a stream. (강의) 굽이. ¶ *the meanders of a brook.* **2** a wandering without any special aim. (정처 없이) 어정거림. — *vi.* (P1,2A,2B) **1** follow a winding course. 굽이굽이 흐르다. ¶ ~ *through hills and fields* 언덕과 들판을 굽이쳐 흐르다. **2** 《*along*》 walk about idly or without any special goal. 지향 없이 거닐다. ¶ *We were meandering through the park.* 우린 공원을 이리저리 거닐고 있었다. [Gk. *Maiandros,* the name of a winding river]

·**mean·ing** [míːniŋ] *n.* ⓒⓤ something meant or intended; significance; sense. 의미; 뜻. ¶ *a hidden* ~ 숨은 뜻 / *grasp* (*catch*) *the* ~ *of something* …의 뜻을 파악하다 / *This word has a double* ~. 이 말에는 두 가지 뜻이 있다 / *the* ~ *of her visit* 그녀가 방문한 뜻 / *He misunderstood my* ~. 그는 내 진의를 오해했다.

with meaning, suggesting more than what is actually expressed. 의미 심장하게; 의미 있는 듯이. ¶ *She looked at me with* ~. 그녀는 내게 의미 있는 시선을 보냈다.

— *adj.* full of meaning or significance. 의미 심장한. ¶ *a* ~ *look* 의미 심장한 표정. [*mean*[1]]

mean·ing·ful [míːniŋfəl] *adj.* full of significance. 의미 심장한. ● **mean·ing·ful·ness** [-nis] *n.* [*mean*[1]]

mean·ing·ful·ly [míːniŋfəli] *adv.* in a significant manner. 의미 심장하게.

mean·ing·less [míːniŋlis] *adj.* without meaning; senseless. 무의미한. ¶ *a* ~ *existence.*

mean·ing·ly [míːniŋli] *adv.* in a meaning manner; with meaning or signficance. 의미 있는 듯이.

mean·ly [míːnli] *adv.* **1** in a poor or humble manner; poorly; humbly. 초라하게; 빈약하게. ¶ ~ *dressed* 초라하게 입은 / ~ *born* 미천하게 태어난. **2** in a base or vulgar manner. 치사하게; 비열하게. **3** in a stingy, miserly manner. 인색하게; 다랍게. [*mean*[2]]

think meanly of (=*despise*) *someone.* 아무를 업신여기다.

mean·ness [míːnnis] *n.* ⓤ the state or quality of being mean. 비천; 빈약; 비열; 인색. [↑]

:**means** [miːnz] *n. pl.* **1** 《used as *sing.* or *pl.*》 a way, method, or instrument in which something is done. 수단; 방법. ¶ *a* ~ *to an end* 목적 달성의 수단 / *the* ~ *of communication and transportation* 통신 교통 기관 / *use* (*employ*) *every* ~ 갖은 수단을 쓰다 / *That was the* ~ *of saving his life.* 그것은 그가 살아남는 수단이었다. **2** 《used as *pl.*》 property; wealth; income. 재산; 자력; 수입. ¶ *a man of* ~ 재산가 / *live within one's* ~ 분수에 맞게 살다 / *live above* (*beyond*) *one's* ~ 수입 이상의(분수에 넘는) 생활을 하다. [*mean*[3]]

by all (***manner of***) ***means,*** **a**) without fail; at any cost. 반드시; 무슨 일이 있더라도. ¶ *Do it by all* ~. 반드시 그 일을 해라. **b**) certainly. (대답으로) 아무렴; 좋고말고. ¶ *May I come ? —By all* ~. 가도 좋은가요. —아무렴, 오너라. [→mean[3]]

by any means, somehow; in any way possible; at all. 어떻든; 어쨌든; 도무지. ¶ *He is not by any* ~ *a hero.* 여하간 그를 영웅이라고는 못 한다.

by fair means or foul, by any method; if an honest way is not available. 무슨 수를 쓰더라도.

by means of, through; by using (something); by the use of. …에 의해서; …으로. ¶ *We express our thought by* ~ *of words.* 사상을 말로 나타낸다.

by no (***manner of***) ***means,*** in no way; certainly not. 결코 …않다(아니다). ¶ *He is by no* ~ *equal to the task.* 그 사람은 도저히 그 일을 감당하지 못한다.

by some means or other, somehow or other. 그럭저럭 (해서).

:**meant** [ment] *v.* p. and pp. of **mean.**

:**mean·time** [míːntàim] *n., adv.* (in) the time between two occasions. 그러는 동안(에). ¶ *in the* ~ 그럭저럭하는 동안에 / *Father will be home in the* ~. 그러다 보면 아버지가 오실 테지 / *Meantime, Mother baked bread in an oven.* 그 동안에 어머니가 오븐에다 빵을 구워냈다. [*mean*[3]]

:**mean·while** [míːn*h*wàil] *n., adv.* =meantime.

mea·sles [míːzəlz] *n. pl.* 《used as *sing.*》 an infectious disease which children commonly have, with fever and small red spots on the skin. 홍역. [E.]

mea·sly [míːzli] *adj.* (**-sli·er, -sli·est**) **1** of measles; having measles. 홍역의; 홍역에 걸린. **2** 《*colloq.*》 meager; worthless. 잔단; 하찮은. [↑]

meas·ur·a·ble [méʒərəbəl] *adj.* can be measured. 잴 수 있는. ¶ *within* ~ *distance of* 지척의 거리에. [↓]

meas·ur·a·bly [méʒərəbli] *adv.* to a measurable amount or degree. 잴 수 있을 정도로; 눈에 띄게. ¶ *The sick man has improved* ~ *since yesterday.* 환자는 어제부터 아주 좋아졌다. [↓]

:**meas·ure** [méʒər] *vt.* **1** (P6,13) find out the size, weight, volume, etc. of (something or someone). …을 재다; 측정하다. ¶ ~ *a piece of cloth* 옷감을 재다 / *The tailor measured her for a new dress.* 재단사는 그녀의 새 드레스의 치수를 쟀다. **2** (P6) judge the value of (someone); estimate. …을 판단(평가)하다. ¶ *We can not* ~ *a person at a glance.* 한눈에 사람을 판단할 수는 없다. **3** (P6,13) 《*with, against*》 compare; bring into competition. …을 비교하다; 비교하여 겨루게 하다. ¶ ~ *one's strength with someone* 아무와 힘을 겨루다 / ~ *one's skill against another's* 다른 사람과 솜씨를 겨루어 보다.

— *vi.* **1** (P2A,2B) have a certain size, weight, volume, etc. (크기·길이 등이) 재서

…이다. ¶ *The cloth measures ten yards.* 그 천은 10 야드이다 / *The room measures twenty feet across.* 그 방은 나비 20 피트다. **2** find out sizes or amounts. 재다; 측정하다. ¶ *Can you ~ correctly?* 정확히 잴 수 있겠나.

measure one's length, fall at full length. 벌렁 자빠지다.

measure off, mark off 〔set apart〕 by measuring. …을 재서 자르다; 구획〔구분〕하다. ¶ *~ off a yard of silk* 비단을 1야드 끊다.

measure out, **a**) take a part of (something) by measuring. (어떤 분량을) 재서 떼다. **b**) give (something) to each by measuring. 재서 분배하다. ¶ *~ out food to the people* 사람들에게 음식을 나누어 주다.

measure swords (=*fight*) ***with someone.*** …와 싸우다.

measure someone with one's eye, look over; look up and down. …을 아래위로 훑어보다.

—*n.* **1** Ⓤ the extent, size, volume, etc. of anything. 크기; 치수; 분량; 부피. **2** Ⓒ a tool for measuring. 계량 기구《되·자 따위》. ¶ *a tape ~* 줄자 / *a yard ~* 야드자. **3** Ⓤ a method or system of measuring. 계량〔도량〕법. ¶ *metric ~* 미터법 / *liquid ~* 액량(液量) / *dry ~* 건량(乾量) / *angular ~* 각의 도량법. **4** 《*the ~*》 Ⓒ any standard for measuring; a unit of measuring. 도량 단위. ¶ *An inch is a ~ of length.* 인치는 길이의 단위다. **5** 《*fig.*》 a standard by which a quality of mind or feeling may be measured. (정신·감정의) 척도; 표준. ¶ *Words do not always give the ~ of one's feeling.* 말이 꼭 사람의 감정을 나타내는 척도는 아니다. **6** 《often *pl.*》 a limit. 한도; 정도. ¶ *above* 〔*beyond, out of*〕 *~* 지나치게; 과도하게 / *keep measures* 중용을 지키다 / *You should set ~ to your desire.* 욕심에도 분수가 있어야 한다. **7** Ⓤ quantity; degree. 양; 일정량; 정도. ¶ *a great ~ of truth* 다분한 진실성 / *in a* 〔*some*〕 *~* 어느 정도; 다소 / *a small ~ of pity* 다소의 연민의 정. **8** 《often *pl.*》 a course of action; a step. 조처; 방책. ¶ *foolish measures* 어리석은 방책 / *adopt* 〔*take*〕 *measures* 조처를 취하다. **9** Ⓒ a proposed law; a legislative bill. 법안. ¶ *This ~ has passed the Diet.* 이 법안은 의회를 통과했다. **10** Ⓤ (of poems, music) rhythm in poetry or music. 운율(韻律); 박자. **11** Ⓒ 《math.》 a quantity contained in another an exact number of times. 약수(約數)(cf. *multiple*). ¶ *the greatest common ~* 최대 공약수《abbr. G.C.M.》. [L. *metior*]

give full 〔***short***〕 ***measure,*** give the right 〔less than the right〕 amount. 넉넉하게〔모자라게〕 재어 주다.

give 〔***show***〕 ***the measure of,*** rise to the standard of. …의 표준이 되다.

know no measure, know no bounds. 한이 없다.

take the measure of someone's foot, estimate or gauge someone's character, abilities. 아무의 인격·역량을 저울질하다.

tread a measure, 《*arch.*》 dance. 춤추다.

meas·ured [méʒərd] *adj.* **1** determined by some standard; regular. 표준에 맞는; 정연한. ¶ *the ~ march of the soldiers* 군인들의 정연한 행진 보조. **2** (of speech) careful and considered. (말 따위가) 신중한. ¶ *~ words* 〔*speech*〕. **3** rhythmical. 율동적인. ¶ *walk with ~ tread* 〔*steps*〕 보조를 맞추어 걷다.

meas·ure·less [méʒərlis] *adj.* immeasurable; endless; boundless. 제한 없는; 무한한. ¶ *the ~ ocean* 광대 무변한 대양.

***meas·ure·ment** [méʒərmənt] *n.* Ⓤ **1** the act of measuring. 측량; 측정. **2** 《usu. *pl.*》 the size, volume, weight, etc., found by measuring. 치수; 크기; 부피; 무게 (등). ¶ *inside* 〔*outside*〕 *~* 안〔바깥〕 치수 / *The measurements of this room are 10 by 15 feet.* 이 방 크기는 나비 10 피트, 길이 15 피트다. **3** the way or system of measuring. 측정법. ¶ *liquid ~* 액량 측정법.

:meat [mi:t] *n.* Ⓤ **1** animal flesh used as food; the part that can be eaten, as of shellfish, egg, and fruit. (식용의) 짐승 고기; (조개·달걀·과일 등의) 먹을 수 있는 부분; 속; 살. ¶ *crab ~* 게의 살 / *fat ~* 지육(脂肉) / *lean ~* 살코기 / *the ~ of a nut* 호도 속. **2** 《*arch.*》 food in general; a meal. 음식물. ¶ *green ~* 채소; 푸성귀 / *~ and drink* 음식물 / *white ~* (닭·토끼 따위의) 흰 살 / *before* 〔*after*〕 *~* 식전〔식후〕 / *sit at ~* 식탁에 앉다. **3** 《*fig.*》 the most important part; essence. 내용; 골자. ¶ *the ~ of a story* 이야기의 골자 / *There is not much ~ in the argument.* 그 논의에는 골자가 없다. **4** 《*colloq.*》 something that one is good at. 장기(長技). ¶ *Tennis is my ~.* 정구가 내 장기다. [E.]

as full (***of errors***) ***as an egg is of meat,*** quite full. (잘못) 투성이인. [E.]

be meat and drink to, 《*fig.*》 be a great pleasure to. …에게 대단한 즐거움〔기쁨〕이다.

meat·y [mí:ti] *adj.* (**meat·i·er, meat·i·est**) **1** of or like meat. 고기의; 고기 같은. **2** full of meat. 고기가 많은. **3** substantial; full of substance. 내용이 충실한.

Mec·ca [mékə] *n.* **1** the capital of Saudi Arabia, where Mohammed was born. 메카. 參考 Mekka 로도 씀. **2** Ⓒ 《*m-*》 a place which many people desire to visit. 동경의 땅. ¶ *a tourist ~.* **3** the aim of one's ambitions. 궁극의 목표. [Place]

***me·chan·ic** [məkǽnik] *n.* Ⓒ a worker who is skillful at using or repairing machinery. 기계 수리공; 기술공. ¶ *an auto ~* 자동차 정비공 / *an aviation* 〔*aircraft*〕 *~* 항공기 정비사. [→machine]

***me·chan·i·cal** [məkǽnikəl] *adj.* **1** of or made by a machine. 기계의; 기계로 만든. ¶ *~ power* 기계력 / *~ products* 기계 제품 / *~ engineering* 기계 공학. **2** acting without thinking, like a machine. 기계적인. ¶ *a ~ smile* 무표정한〔의례적인〕 미소 / *greet in a ~*

way 기계적으로 인사하다〔맞다〕.

me·chan·i·cal·ly [məkǽnikəli] *adv.* in a mechanical manner. 기계적으로. ¶ *make one's notes* ~ 기계적으로 메모하다.

me·ch·a·ni·cian [mèkəníʃən] *n.* Ⓒ a worker who is skillful at making or repairing machinery. 기계 기사; 기계공.

me·chan·ics [məkǽniks] *n. pl.* 《used as *sing.*》 **1** the science of machinery. 기계학. **2** the science of forces and motion. 역학.

*__mech·a·nism__ [mékənìzəm] *n.* **1** Ⓒ a machine; the working parts of any machine. 기계 (장치). ¶ *the ~ of a watch* 시계의 기계. **2** Ⓒ any structure or system of parts working together. 기구; 구조. ¶ *the ~ of government* 정부 기구. **3** Ⓤ the mechanical part of an action; technique. 기법; 기교. ¶ *the ~ of playing the violin* 바이올린 연주법. **4** Ⓤ the theory that everything in this universe can be explained by the laws of physics and chemistry. 우주 기계론.

mech·a·ni·za·tion [mèkənizéiʃən] *n.* Ⓤ the act of mechanizing; the state of being mechanized (esp. of an army). 기계화《특히, 육군 부대의》.

mech·a·nize [mékənàiz] *vt.* (P6) perform 〔work〕 by means of machines; make mechanical. …을 기계화하다.

*__med·al__ [médl] *n.* Ⓒ a coinlike piece of metal, marked with a design or words, given as a reward or honor, or for celebrating a great event. 메달; 훈장. ¶ *award a ~* 메달을 받다. [→metal]

the reverse of the question, the other side of the question. 문제의 다른 일면.

me·dal·li·on [mədǽljən] *n.* Ⓒ **1** a large medal. 큰 메달〔상패〕. **2** any round, flat ornament with a design or raised figure on it. 원형의 돋을새김.

med·al·ist, 《Brit.》 **-al·list** [médəlist] *n.* Ⓒ **1** a person who makes medals. 메달 제작자. **2** a person who has been given a medal. 상패 수령자. ¶ *a gold ~* 금메달 수상자.

*__med·dle__ [médl] *vi.* (P1,3) **1** 《*in, with*》 take part in others' affairs unnecessarily. (쓸데없이) 간섭〔참견〕하다(cf. *intermeddle*). ¶ *~ in other people's affairs* 남의 일에 간섭하다. **2** 《*with*》 touch or handle others' things without permission. (무단히) 만지작거리다. ¶ *Don't ~ with my gun.* 내 총 건드리지 마라. [→mix]

med·dler [médlər] *n.* Ⓒ a person who meddles. 간섭하는 사람.

med·dle·some [médlsəm] *adj.* apt to meddle in others' affairs. 간섭하기 좋아하는. ¶ *He is a ~ fellow.* 성가신 놈이다.

me·di·a [mí:diə] *n.* pl. of **medium.**

me·di·ae·val [mì:dií:vəl, mèd-] *adj.* = medieval.

me·di·al [mí:diəl] *adj.* **1** situated in the middle. 중간의. **2** of an average; ordinary. 평균의. [L. *medius* middle]

me·di·an [mí:diən] *adj.* in the middle. 중간의. ¶ *a ~ line* 〔*number, point*〕. — *n.* Ⓒ 《math.》 **1** the middle number of a series. 중앙값; 메디안. **2** a line or point in the middle. 중선; 중점. [↑]

me·di·ate [mí:dièit] *vt.* **1** (P6) settle (something) as a go-between. …을 조정〔중재〕하다. ¶ *~ a dispute* 분쟁을 중재하다. **2** carry (a gift, etc.) from one person to another; communicate (knowledge, etc.) (선물 등)을 중간에서 전해 주다; (사상 등)을 전달하다. — *vi.* (P1,2A,2B,3) 《*between*》 act as a peacemaker between people who quarrel. 조정하다; 중재인 노릇을 하다. — [mí:diət] *adj.* indirect. 간접의(opp. immediate). [L. *medius* middle]

me·di·a·tion [mì:diéiʃən] *n.* Ⓤ the act of mediating; the state of being mediated. 중재.

me·di·a·tor [mí:dièitər] *n.* **1** Ⓒ a person who mediates. 중재자. **2** 《*the M-*》 Christ. 예수.

me·di·a·to·ry [mí:diətɔ̀:ri / -təri] *adj.* of or directed toward mediation. 중재의.

med·ic [médik] *n.* 《U.S. *colloq.*》 **1** a doctor. 의사. **2** a medical student. 의학도. **3** a member of a military medical unit. 위생병. [L. *medicus* doctor]

:**med·i·cal** [médikəl] *adj.* **1** connected with the science or art of medicine. 의학의. ¶ *~ attendance* 진료 / *~ science* 의학 / *~ treatment* 진료; 치료 / *a ~ examination* 〔*checkup*〕 건강 진단. **2** of the treatment of disease by drugs. 내과의(opp. surgical). ¶ *~ ward* 내과 병동 / *~ cases* 내과 환자. [L. *medeor* heal]

med·i·cal·ly [médikəli] *adv.* **1** by medicine. 의학으로. **2** from the medical point of view. 의학적으로.

me·dic·a·ment [mədíkəmənt] *n.* Ⓒ a medicine; a substance used to cure. 의약; 약제(藥劑). [L. *medicā* cure]

med·i·cate [médəkèit] *vt.* (P6) **1** treat with medicine; cure. 약으로 치료하다. **2** put medicine into. …에 약을 섞다. [→medic, -ate]

med·i·cat·ed [médəkèitid] *adj.* having some medical power or properties. 약효를 지닌. ¶ *~ soap* 약용 비누 / *a ~ bath* 약탕(藥湯) / *~ gauze* 치료용 거즈.

me·dic·i·nal [medísənəl] *adj.* **1** of medicine. 약의. **2** useful as medicine. 약용의; 약효가 있는. ¶ *a ~ herb* 약초. ● **me·dic·i·nal·ly** [-nəli] *adv.* [↓]

:**med·i·cine** [médəsən] *n.* Ⓤ **1** ⓊⒸ any drug used to prevent or cure disease. 약; 약제(藥劑); 내복약. ¶ *a patent ~* 매약(賣藥) / *a dose of ~*, 1회분의 약 / *take medicine(s)* 약을 먹다 / 《*prov.*》 *A good ~ tastes bitter.* 좋은 약은 입에 쓰다. **2** the science of preventing, treating, and curing disease. 의학. ¶ *preventive* ~ 예방 의학. **3** a branch of this science making use of treatment by drugs, diet, etc. 내과적 치료(opp. surgery). **4** magical power believed to cure disease among North American Indians, etc. (북아메리카 인디언 등의 치유에 효험이 있다는) 주술(呪術); 주문(呪文); 마술. [L. *medicina* art of healing; →medical, -ine]

take one's medicine, submit to the disagreeable. 싫어도 참다.

medicine ball [⌐−−⌐] *n.* a large, heavy leather ball thrown and caught for physical exercise. (운동용) 큰 가죽공; 메디신 볼.

***me·di·e·val** [mìːdiíːvəl, mèd-] *adj.* of the Middle Ages. 중세의. 參考 A.D. 500-1450 년 경. [→medial, L. *aevum* age]

me·di·o·cre [mìːdióukər, ⌐−⌐−] *adj.* only average; neither very good nor very bad; commonplace. 보통의; 좋지도 나쁘지도 않은; 평범한; 그저 그런. ¶ *a* ~ *story.* [→medial]

me·di·oc·ri·ty [mìːdiákrəti / -ɔ́k-] *n.* (*pl.* **-ties**) **1** Ⓤ the state or quality of being mediocre. 평범. **2** Ⓒ a person of mediocre ability. 평범한 사람.

***med·i·tate** [médətèit] *vi.* (P1,3) 《*on, upon*》 think deeply and seriously. 깊이 생각하다. ¶ ~ *on the meaning of life* 인생의 뜻을 깊이 생각하다. — *vt.* (P6) plan (something) in the mind. …을 계획하다; 꾀하다. ¶ ~ *revenge* 복수를 꾀하다. [L. *meditor*]

med·i·ta·tion [mèdətéiʃən] *n.* Ⓤ the act of meditating; deep thought or reflection. 명상; 묵상.

med·i·ta·tive [médətèitiv] *adj.* of meditation; deep in thought; apt to meditate. 명상의; 묵상에 잠긴; 명상적인.

med·i·ta·tor [médətèitər] *n.* Ⓒ a person who meditates. 명상하는 사람.

***Med·i·ter·ra·ne·an** [mèdətəréiniən], **the** *n.* a large inland sea between Africa and Europe. 지중해. — *adj.* of the Mediterranean Sea or the region around it. 지중해(지방)의. [→medial, →terra]

***me·di·um** [míːdiəm] *n.* (*pl.* **-ums** or **-di·a**) **1** Ⓤ the state or condition of being in the middle; moderateness. 중용. **2** Ⓒ a means by which something is accomplished. 수단. ¶ *an advertising* ~ =*a* ~ *of advertisement* 광고 기관《신문·잡지 등》/ *mass media* 매스 미디어. **3** Ⓒ ⓐ a substance in which something exists. 매개물. ⓑ a substance through which something acts or is carried. 매질(媒質). ¶ *Sound travels through the* ~ *of air.* 소리는 공기라는 매질에 의해 전달된다. **4** Ⓒ a person who is supposed to receive messages from the spirit world. 영매(靈媒); 무당.

by* 〔*through*〕 *the medium of, through the good offices of. …을 통하여; 매개로 하여.

— *adj.* moderate in position, condition, or degree. 중간의. ¶ ~ *quality* 중간의 품질; 중치 / *a medium-range ballistic missile* 중거리 탄도탄. [→medial]

me·di·um-sized [míːdiəmsàizd] *adj.* of a moderate size; neither too large nor too small. (크기가) 중형의; 중간치의. ¶ *a* ~ *hat* 중간 크기의 모자.

med·lar [médlər] *n.* Ⓒ a tree of the rose family or its apple-like fruit. 서양 모과 나무; 그 열매. [Gk. *mespilē*]

med·ley [médli] *n.* Ⓒ **1** a mixture of things of different kinds. 그러모은 것; 잡동사니. **2** a musical piece made up of different parts selected from several pieces. 혼성곡. **3** 《*arch.*》 a literary miscellany. 잡기(雜記). — *adj.* made up of different parts; mixed; varied. 그러모은; 혼합한. ¶ *a* ~ *race* 혼합 경주〔경영(競泳)〕/ *a* ~ *relay* 메들리 릴레이. [→meddle]

me·dul·la [mədʌ́lə] *n.* (*pl.* **-las** or **-lae**) **1** 《anat.》 the marrow of the bones. 골수. **2** 《bot.》 the pith. 고갱이; 수(髓). [L. *medulla* marrow]

me·dul·lae [mədʌ́liː] *n.* pl. of **medulla.**

med·ul·lar·y [médəlèri, -ləri] *adj.* of medulla. 골수의; 고갱이의.

Me·du·sa [mədjúːsə, -zə] *n.* (*pl.* **-sae** or **-sas**) **1** 《Gk. myth.》 one of the three sisters, who had snakes for hair. 메두사《세 자매 괴물 중의 하나》. **2** 《*m-*》 《zool.》 a jellyfish. 해파리. [Gk. *Medousa*]

Me·du·sae [mədjúːsiː] *n.* pl. of **Medusa.**

meed [miːd] *n.* Ⓒ 《*poet.*》 a reward. 보수. ¶ *one's* ~ *of praise* 〔*blame*〕 당연한 칭찬〔비난〕. [E.]

***meek** [miːk] *adj.* mild and gentle; humble in spirit. 순한; 착한. [N.]

(***as***) ***meek as a lamb,*** very mild and gentle. 양처럼 순한.

meek·ly [míːkli] *adv.* in a mild and gentle manner. 순하게; 온순하게.

meek·ness [míːknis] *n.* Ⓤ the state or quality of being meek; mildness; gentleness. 순함; 착함.

meer·schaum [míərʃəm, -ʃɔːm] *n.* **1** Ⓤ a soft, white clay-like stone used to make tobacco pipes. 해포석(海泡石). **2** Ⓒ a tobacco pipe made of this material. 해포석 파이프. [G. =sea foam]

‡**meet** [miːt] *v.* (**met**) — *vt.* (P6) **1** come face to face with (someone); come upon (someone) by chance or arrangement. …을 만나다; …와 마주치다. ¶ *I met Mr. Smith in the park.* 공원에서 스미스씨를 만났다 / *I walked out to* ~ *the officer.* 나는 그 장교를 만나러 밖으로 나갔다. **2** ⓐ be present at the arrival of (someone). …을 마중하다. ¶ *They met the doctor at the airport.* 그들은 박사를 공항에서 마중했다. ⓑ join or go to see (someone) at an appointed place or time. (약속된 장소)에서 …을 만나다. ¶ *I'll* ~

you at your office. 네 사무실에서 만나겠다. **3** be introduced to (someone); become acquainted with (someone). …에 소개되다; …와 아는 사이가 되다. ¶ *When did you first ~ my sister?* 내 누이를 언제 처음 만났던가 / *I am glad to ~ you.* 만나서 반갑습니다. 參考 초대면이 아닐 때는 I'm glad to see you.라고 함. **4** ⓐ experience; suffer; meet with. …을 겪다; 당하다; (곤란 등에) 직면하다. ¶ *~ one's father's death* 부친의 상을 당하다 / *He met his death at the hands of a wicked person.* 그는 흉한의 손에 쓰러졌다. ⓑ fight with; oppose in battle, contest, etc. …에 대항하다; 직면하다; …와 겨루다. **5** face or confront directly or calmly. …에 대처하다; 감내하다. ¶ *~ one's misfortune with a smile* 웃는 낯으로 불행에 대처하다. **6** satisfy (a demand, etc.); pay (a bill, etc.); comply with. …을 충족시키다; …에 응하다; 지급하다. ¶ *~ debts* 빚을 갚다 / *I will do my best to ~ your wishes.* 네 마음에 들도록 최선을 다하겠다. **7** touch; join; reach; flow into at a given point. …에 닿다; 합류하다. ¶ *Her hand met mine.* 그녀의 손이 내 손에 닿았다 / *This road meets the highway.* 이 길은 고속 도로에 합류된다 / *The sound of the sea met the ear.* 바다의 파도 소리가 들렸다. —*vi.* **1** (P1,2A,2B,3) come face to face; come together; get acquainted with each other. 만나다; 회합하다; 아는 사이가 되다. ¶ *They have arranged to ~ at a restaurant.* 그들은 어느 식당에서 만나기로 했다. **2** (P1) (of a meeting, etc.) be held; assemble. (회합 등이) 열리다. ¶ *The committee meets next Monday.* **3** (P1,3) be long enough to touch or join; touch; join. 접촉하다; 합치다; (양 끝 등이) 닿다. ¶ *This belt won't ~ around my waist.* 이 혁대는 짧아서 내 허리에는 맞지 않는다 / *Two telephone lines ~ in this place.* 두 전화선은 여기서 접속된다. **4** (P1,3) make one's means suffice for one's expenses. 수지를 맞게 하다. ¶ *make the two ends ~* 수지를 맞추다; 수입내에서 생활하다.

meet someone halfway, come to compromise with. …와 타협하다. ¶ *She agreed to ~ him halfway.* 그녀는 그와 타협하기로 했다.

meet the case, be adequate. 적절[적당]하다; 괜찮다.

meet trouble halfway, be too much afraid of what may happen. 군걱정을 하다.

meet up with, 《U.S. *colloq.*》 come across; overtake. …와 우연히 마주치다; …을 따라잡다.

meet with, **a**) come across (someone or something) by chance. …와 우연히 만나다. ¶ *~ with a friend in the train* 기차에서 우연히 친구를 만나다. **b**) experience; suffer or gain; receive. …을 겪다; 당하다; 받다. ¶ *~ with an accident* 사고를 당하다 / *~ with a kind reception* 환대를 받다.

—*n.* Ⓒ 《U.S.》 a meeting or gathering as for a sporting event. 회합; 모임; 대회. ¶ *a track-and-field ~* 육상 경기 대회. [E.]

:meet·ing [míːtiŋ] *n.* Ⓒ **1** ⓊⒸ the act or state of coming together, esp. for a special purpose; an assembly. 집합; 집회. ¶ *an athletic ~* 운동회 / *a political ~* 정치적 집회 / *a farewell ~* 송별회 / *a welcome ~* 환영회 / *break up* 〔*dissolve*〕 *a ~* 폐회하다 / *call* 〔*hold*〕 *a ~* 회의를 소집하다〔가지다〕. **2** a point where things come together. 합류점. ¶ *the ~ of waters.* **3** a duel. 결투. **4** 《*the ~*》 persons gathered together at a meeting. 회중(會衆). ¶ *address the ~* 모인 사람들에게 인사하다. **5** an encounter. 만남; 조우. [*meet*]

meeting house [⌐-⌐] *n.* a building used for public worship, esp. by Protestants. 교회; 예배당. 參考 영국에서는 비국교도의 예배당을 말함.

meg·a- [mégə-] *pref.* great; large; a million. '대(大), 큰, 백만'의 뜻. [Gk.]

meg·a·cy·cle [mégəsàikl] *n.* Ⓒ one million cycles. 메가사이클. [mega-, →cycle]

meg·a·lith [mégəliθ] *n.* **1** a very large stone used by prehistoric people. 거석(巨石). **2** an ancient building made of very large stones. 거석 구조물. [Gk. *lithos* stone]

meg·a·lo·ma·ni·a [mègəlouméiniə] *n.* Ⓤ an insane enthusiasm for greatness, power, wealth, etc. 과대 망상증. [Gk. *mania* madness]

meg·a·lop·o·lis [mègəlápəlis / -lɔ́p-] *n.* a single urban complex made up of several large cities and their surrounding areas. 거대(巨帶) 도시. [Gk. *polis* city]

meg·a·phone [mégəfòun] *n.* Ⓒ a large funnel-shaped horn used to make the voice louder. 메가폰; 확성기. —*vt., vi.* (P6;1) announce, speak through a megaphone. 확성기로 알리다〔말하다〕. [Gk. *phōnē* sound]

meg·a·ton [mégətʌ̀n] *n.* Ⓒ a unit of explosive power equal to that of a million tons of T.N.T. 메가톤《핵무기의 폭발력을 재는 단위》. [mega-, *ton*]

me·grim [míːgrim] *n.* **1** a severe headache, usu. on one side of the head only. 편두통. **2** 《*the ~s*》《rare》 low spirits. 우울; 실의. ¶ *have the megrims* 우울해지다. [Gk. *hēmi* half, →cranium]

mel·an·cho·li·a [mèlənkóuliə] *n.* Ⓤ a disordered mental condition marked by extreme depression of spirits and gloomy feelings. 우울증. [Gk. *melas* black, *kholē* bile]

mel·an·chol·ic [mèlənkálik / -kɔ́l-] *adj.* **1** 《rare》 melancholy. 우울한. **2** of melancholia. 우울증의.

·mel·an·chol·y [mélənkàli / -kɔ̀li] *n.* Ⓤ **1** a sad and gloomy state of mind. 우울. **2** melancholia. 우울증. —*adj.* **1** sad and low in spirits; gloomy. 우울한. ¶ *A ~ man is* *not good company.* 우울한 사람은 벗하기가 나쁘다. **2** causing sadness and depression. (풍경 등이) 쓸쓸한. ¶ *a ~ scene* 쓸쓸한 풍경.

Mel·a·ne·sia [mèləníːʒə, -ʃə] *n.* a group of islands in the South Pacific, northwest of Australia. 멜라네시아《오세아니아 중부 섬들의 총칭》.

me·lee, mê·lée [méilei / mélei] *n.* Ⓒ 《F.》 a confused hand-to-hand fight. 난투.

***mel·low** [mélou] *adj.* **1** (of fruit) mature; soft, sweet, and juicy because of ripeness. (과일 등이) 익어 달콤한. ¶ *a ~ peach* 〔*apple*〕. **2** (of wine, etc.) having a rich smell. (포도주 등이) 향기로운. ¶ *~ port* 향기로운 포도주. **3** (of personality) grown wise and gentle by age and experience. (사람됨이) 원만한; 원숙한. ¶ *~ character* 원만한 인격 / *~ wisdom* 온후한 슬기. **4** (of color, sound, etc.) soft, full, and rich. (색깔·소리 따위가) 부드러운. ¶ *~ light* 부드러운 빛 / *a violin with a ~ tone* 음조가 부드러운 바이올린. **5** 《*colloq.*》 pleasant; cheerful; merrily drunk. 기분이 좋은; 거나한.

— *vt., vi.* (P6;1) make (someone or something) become mature, gentle or soft. 익히다; 익다; 원숙하게 하다〔되다〕; 부드럽게 하다〔되다〕. ¶ *Age mellowed her.* 나이를 먹으면서 그녀는 원숙해졌다. [? E.]

mel·low·ly [mélouli] *adv.* in a mellow way. 익어서; 달게.

mel·low·ness [mélounis] *n.* Ⓤ the state or quality of being mellow. 원숙; 감미(甘味).

me·lo·di·ous [milóudiəs] *adj.* **1** sounding agreeable to the ear. 선율이 아름다운. **2** producing sweet melody. 아름다운 선율을 내는. ¶ *a ~ voice* 아름다운 음성. ● **me·lo·di·ous·ly** [-li] *adv.* [→melody]

mel·o·dist [mélədist] *n.* Ⓒ a person who sings or composes melodies. 선율이 아름다운 작곡가〔성악가〕.

mel·o·dra·ma [mélədràːmə, -drӕ̀mə] *n.* **1** Ⓒ a sensational romantic drama. 멜로드라마《해피 엔드로 끝나는 감상적인 통속극》. **2** Ⓒ an event similar to this kind of drama. (멜로드라마 같은) 사건. **3** Ⓤ any sensational writing, speech, or behavior. 신파조의 언동. [Gk. *melos* song, →drama]

mel·o·dra·mat·ic [mèloudrəmǽtik] *adj.* like a melodrama; sensational and exaggerated. 멜로드라마 같은; 신파조의.

***mel·o·dy** [mélədi] *n.* (*pl.* **-dies**) **1** Ⓤ sweet music. 아름다운 가락. **2** Ⓒ a chief part in music; a set of notes arranged to make a pleasing piece of music; an air; a tune. 선율; 멜로디. **3** Ⓒ the leading part in a song or other composition. 가락; 일련의 선율. [Gk. *melos* song, →ode]

mel·on [mélən] *n.* Ⓒ any of the varieties of the muskmelon; a watermelon. 멜론; 수박. ● **mel·on·like** [-laik] *adj.* [L. *melo*]

:melt [melt] *v.* (**melt·ed, melt·ed** or **mol·ten**) *vi.* (P1,2A,2B,3) **1** become a liquid from a solid through heat; dissolve. 녹다; 용해하다. ¶ *Ice melts at 0° C.* 얼음은 섭씨 0도에서 녹는다 / *I'm simply melting.* 더워서 몸이 녹을 지경이다 / *Sugar melts in the mouth.* 설탕은 입에서 녹는다 / *The snow has melted away in the sun.* 눈은 햇볕에 녹아 없어졌다. **2** become mixed or disappear gradually; fade away. 서서히 섞이다〔없어지다〕; 사라지다. ¶ *One color melts into another.* 색은 천천히 다른 색에 섞인다 / *The ocean melts into the sky on the horizon.* 대양은 수평선에서 하늘과 하나가 된다 / *Night melted into day.* 밤이 가고 날이 점점 밝아졌다. **3** (of feelings, heart, etc.) become soft or tender. (감정 등이) 누그러지다. ¶ *Her anger melts under kindness.* 친절 앞에 그녀의 노여움은 풀어졌다.

— *vt.* **1** (P6,13) change (something) from a solid into a liquid state; dissolve. …을 녹이다. ¶ *Heat melts butter.* 열에 버터가 녹는다 / *~ sugar in the mouth* 설탕을 입에 넣어 녹이다. **2** 《*fig.*》 (P6) make (someone) tender or gentle. …을 누그러뜨리다. ¶ *kindness that melts the heart* 마음을 풀어 주는 친절. [E.]

melt·ing [méltiŋ] *n.* Ⓤ the act of melting. 용해. — *adj.* **1** that melts. 녹는. **2** feeling tenderness. 감동적인; 측은해지는. ¶ *a ~ mood* 울고 싶은 심정. **3** languishing; sentimental. 감상적인.

melting point [´-`] *n.* the degree of temperature at which a solid melts into a liquid. 녹는점.

mel·ton [méltən] *n.* Ⓤ a smooth, heavy woolen cloth used for overcoats. 멜턴《모직물의 일종》. [Place]

:mem·ber [mémbər] *n.* Ⓒ **1** a person who belongs to a group, a team, or a society. 일원(一員); 회원. ¶ *a ~ of a club* 클럽 회원 / *a Member of Parliament* (영국의) 국회의원 (abbr. M.P.) / *a Member of Congress* 미국 국회 의원 (abbr. M.C.). **2** a part or an element of a whole. 부분. **3** a part of a person, an animal, or a plant, esp. a leg or arm. 신체〔동식물〕의 일부; (특히) 손발. [L. *membrum*]

***mem·ber·ship** [mémbərʃip] *n.* **1** Ⓤ the state of being a member; the position as a member. 회원임; 회원 지위. ¶ *a ~ card* 회원증 / *a ~ fee* 회비 / *Do you value your ~ in the Senate?* 당신은 상원 의원으로서의 신분을 존중하십니까. **2** Ⓒ the whole group of persons who belong to an organization. 전체 회원. ¶ *have a large ~* 회원이 많다 / *The whole ~ was present.* 전 회원이 출석했다.

mem·brane [mémbrein] *n.* **1** Ⓒ 《biol.》 a thin, sheet-like layer in animals or plants. 박막(薄膜); 막(膜). **2** Ⓤ a writing material made from the skin of an animal; parchment. 양피지(羊皮紙). [*member*]

me·men·to [miméntou] *n.* (*pl.* **-toes** or **-tos**) a thing to remember (something or someone) by; a souvenir; a token. 기념품; 기념물. [L. =remember thou]

mem·o [mémou] *n.* (*pl.* **-os**) 《*colloq.*》 memorandum. 메모. ¶ *make a* ~ 메모를 하다. [↓]

mem·oir [mémwɑːr, -wɔːr] *n.* **1** Ⓒ a biography. 전기(傳記). **2** 《*pl.*》 a written record of events closely connected with one's own experiences. (사건 등의) 회고록; 체험담; 자서전. **3** Ⓒ a record of scientific or academic study. 연구 논문; 보고서. **4** 《*pl.*》 a collection of the studies by a learned society. 학회지(學會誌). [F. *mémoire* memory]

mem·o·ra·ble [mémərəbəl] *adj.* worthy of being remembered; not easily forgotten; very remarkable. 기억할 만한; 잊을 수 없는; 두드러진. [→memory,-able]

mem·o·ran·da [mèmərǽndə] *n.* pl. of **memorandum.**

mem·o·ran·dum [mèmərǽndəm] *n.* Ⓒ (*pl.* **-dums** or **-da**) **1** a short note to remember something by; a short record of something for future use. 메모; 비망록; 간단한 기록. **2** 《diplom.》 a short informal message from one country to other countries. (외교상의) 각서. **3** 《law》 a document recording the terms of a contact. 정관. [→memory]

*__me·mo·ri·al__ [mimɔ́ːriəl] *adj.* **1** in memory of some person or event. 기념의. ¶ *a* ~ *festival* 기념제 / *a* ~ *service* 추도식(追悼式) / *a* ~ *address* 기념 연설. **2** of or connected with memory. 기억의; 기억에 관한. ¶ ~ *power* 기억력. — *n.* **1** Ⓒ something that makes people remember some person or event. 기념물. **2** 《usu. *pl.*》 a record. 기록. **3** a statement sent to a government, etc. 진정서. [→memory]

Memorial Day [-ˊ-- ˋ] *n.* 《U.S.》 a day for honoring dead soldiers, May 30; Decoration Day. 전몰 장병 기념일. 參考 지금은 5월의 마지막 월요일임.

me·mo·ri·al·ize [mimɔ́ːriəlàiz] *vt.* (P6) **1** keep the memory of (someone) by a memorial; commemorate. …을 기념하다. **2** present a memorial to. …에 진정서를 제출하다.

*__mem·o·rize__ [méməràiz] *vt.* (P6) **1** 《chiefly U.S.》 learn (something) by heart. …을 암기하다. **2** note (something) down. …을 기록하다. ● **mem·o·ri·za·tion** [mèmərizéiʃən / -raiz-] *n.* [→memory,-ize]

:**mem·o·ry** [méməri] *n.* (*pl.* **-ries**) Ⓤ **1** the act of remembering; the ability to remember. 기억; 기억력. ¶ *be fresh in one's* ~ 기억에 새롭다 / *commit to* ~ 기억하다 / *bear* 〔*have, keep*〕 *in* ~ 기억하고 있다 / *have a long* ~ 기억력이 좋다 / *have a bad* ~ 기억력이 나쁘다 / *keep one's* ~ *alive* 잊지 않도록 하다 / *to the best of my* ~ 내가 기억하고 있는 한 / *His* ~ *declined.* 그는 기억력이 나빠졌다. **2** Ⓒ things or persons remembered. 기억에 남는 것〔사람〕. ¶ *memories of childhood* 어린 시절의 기억〔추억〕. **3** the length of time during which things are remembered. 기억의 범위. ¶ *beyond the* ~ *of man* 인간의 기억에 없는; 유사 이전의 / *within the* ~ *of man* 인간의 기억에 있는; 유사 이후의. **4** reputation after death. 사후의 명성. ¶ *love someone's* ~ 고인에 대한 추억을 그리다 / *honor the* ~ *of the deceased* 고인의 영혼을 추모하다. [L. *memor* mindful]

in memory (=*in honor* or *remembrance*) ***of someone.*** …을 기념하여.

... of blessed 〔***happy, glorious***〕 ***memory,*** used esp. of deceased princes, etc. 고(故)….

within living memory, within the memory of the living. 지금도 사람들의 기억에 남아.

:**men** [men] *n.* pl. of **man.**

*__men·ace__ [ménəs] *n.* ⓊⒸ a threat. 위협; 협박. ¶ *a public* ~ 공안(公安)에 대한 위협. — *vt.* (P6,13) threaten. …을 위협하다. ¶ ~ *someone with death* 아무를 죽이겠다고 위협하다. [L. *minor* threaten]

men·ac·ing [ménəsiŋ] *adj.* making a menace. 위협적인.

men·ac·ing·ly [ménəsiŋli] *adv.* in a menacing way. 위협적으로.

mé·nage, me- [meinɑ́ːʒ] *n.* 《F.》 **1** a household. 가족; 세대. **2** the management of a household. 살림; 가정(家政).

me·nag·er·ie [minǽdʒəri] *n.* Ⓒ 《F.》 a collection of wild animals kept for exhibition; a place where such animals are kept. (관람을 위한) 야생 동물; 그 동물원.

:**mend** [mend] *vt.* (P6) **1** a bring back (something) to a good condition; repair; set right; patch up. …을 고치다; 수선하다. ¶ ~ *a broken window* 깨진 창문을 고치다 / ~ *a road* 길을 보수하다 / *I had my coat mended.* 코트를 수선시켰다. **2** make (something) better; reform; correct; improve. …을 개선하다; 바로잡다. ¶ ~ *a fault* 결점을 고치다 / ~ *one's ways* 행실을 고치다 / *That won't* ~ *matters.* 그래 봐야 소용 없다 / *Regrets will not* ~ *matters.* 후회한다고 사태가 좋아지는 것도 아니다. **3** increase; quicken. …을 증가시키다; 빨리하다. ¶ ~ *one's pace* 걸음을 재촉하다. **4** add fuel to. 연료를 더하다. ¶ ~ *the fire* 불에 연료를 더 넣다. — *vi.* (P1) become better; improve. (건강·사태가) 좋아지다. ¶ *The patient is mending.* 환자는 회복되고 있다. — *n.* **1** Ⓒ a mended place. 고쳐진〔수선한〕 데. ¶ *a* ~ *in clothes* 옷의 기운 데. **2** Ⓤ (of a person, his health, etc.) the act or state of improving. 고치기; 고쳐지기; 차도(差度). [→amend]

be on the mend, be getting better in health or condition. (건강·상태가) 좋아지고 있다. ¶ *Business is on the* ~. 사업이 호전되고 있다.

men·da·cious [mendéiʃəs] *adj.* **1** false; not true. 거짓의; 허위의. ¶ *a ~ report* 허위 보고. **2** lying. 거짓말을 (잘) 하는. ¶ *a ~ person* 거짓말쟁이. [L. *mendax*]

men·dac·i·ty [mendǽsəti] *n.* (*pl.* **-ties**) **1** Ⓤ the state of being mendacious. 거짓말 하기〔하는 버릇〕. **2** Ⓒ a lie. 거짓말; 허위.

mend·er [méndər] *n.* Ⓒ a person who mends something. 수선〔개선〕자. [*mend*]

men·di·cant [méndikənt] *adj.* begging; living by charity. 구걸하는; 탁발(托鉢)하는. ¶ *a ~ tramp* 구걸하고 다니는 사람 / *a ~ order* (카톨릭의) 탁발 수도회. — *n.* Ⓒ **1** a beggar. 걸인. **2** a begging friar. 탁발 수사(修士). [L. *mendicus* beggar]

men·folk [ménfòuk] *n.* 《use. *pl.*》《*colloq.*》 men, esp. those in a family or community. (가정이나 지역 내의) 남자들(opp. women-folk). [*men*]

me·ni·al [míːniəl] *adj.* suitable for or belonging to a servant; mean; lowly. 하인 노릇하는; 하인의; 천한. ¶ *a ~ task* 하인 노릇 / *~ labor* 하인이 하는 일. — *n.* Ⓒ a servant who does the most lowly tasks. 하인; 종. [→manor]

men·o·pause [ménəpɔ̀ːz] *n.* the final cessation of the menses. 폐경. [Gk. *mēn* month, *pauō* pause]

men·ses [ménsiːz] *n. pl.* the monthly flow of bloody fluid in women. 월경. [L. *mensis* month]

men·stru·al [ménstruəl] *adj.* of or having to do with the menses. 월경의; 월경이 있는. [↑]

men·stru·a·tion [mènstruéiʃən] *n.* the flow of the menses. 월경.

men·sur·a·ble [ménʃərəbəl] *adj.* measurable. 측정할 수 있는. [↓]

men·su·ra·tion [mènʃəréiʃən] *n.* Ⓤ **1** the act of measuring. 측량; 측정. **2** 《math.》 a branch of mathematics dealing with finding size, area, volume, etc. 구적법(求積法). [→measure]

:men·tal [méntl] *adj.* **1** of the mind. 정신의; 마음의(opp. physical). ¶ *~ age* 정신 연령 / *a ~ blow* 정신적 타격 / *a ~ disease* 정신병 / *~ faculties* 지력(知力) / *a ~ test* 지능 검사 / *~ work* 정신〔두뇌〕 노동. **2** done by the mind without the help of writing. 머릿속으로 하는. ¶ *~ arithmetic* 암산. **3** of mental disease. 정신병의. ¶ *a ~ institution* 〔*hospital*〕 정신 병원 / *a ~ case* 정신 질환자 / *a ~ specialist* 정신병 전문의. [L. *mens* mind]

men·tal·i·ty [mentǽləti] *n.* (*pl.* **-ties**) **1** Ⓤ mental ability or power. 지능. ¶ *a man of average ~* 지능이 보통인 사람 / *Persons of very low ~ are called idiots.* 지능이 매우 낮은 사람을 일러 백치라고 한다. **2** Ⓒ a state of mind; a mental attitude. 정신 상태; 심리. ¶ *an abnormal ~* 이상 심리.

men·tal·ly [méntəli] *adv.* in or with the mind. 마음으로; 정신적으로. ¶ *He is strong physically, but weak ~.* 육체적으로는 강한데 정신적으로는 약하다.

men·thol [ménθɔ(ː)l, -θɑl] *n.* Ⓤ a white, waxy substance obtained from the oil of peppermint and used in medicine. 멘톨; 박하뇌(薄荷腦). [→mint[1]]

:men·tion [ménʃən] *vt.* (P6,9,13) speak or write of (someone or something) briefly; refer to; name. …에 대하여 말하다〔쓰다〕; 언급하다; (이름)을 들다. ¶ *as mentioned above* 전기한 바와 같이 / *to ~ a single example* 한 가지 예를 들면 / *Don't ~ it.* 천만에요 / *I mentioned having gone there.* 거기 갔었다고 말했다.

not to mention, to say nothing of (something or someone); besides. …은 말할 것도 없고; …은 물론. ¶ *He can speak French, not to ~ English.* 영어는 말할 것도 없고 프랑스말도 한다.

— *n.* ⓊⒸ a brief, often incidental, reference or statement. 언급; 진술. ¶ *There was no ~ of it in the papers.* 신문에선 그것에 관한 언급이 없었다 / *There is only a bare ~ of him in the book.* 그 책에는 그에 관한 언급이 잠깐 있을 뿐이다. [L. *mentio*]

make mention of (=*speak briefly about*) *someone* or *something.* …에 대해 말하다. ¶ *He made ~ of a tiger he had shot.* 그는 자기가 쏘아 잡은 호랑이 이야기를 했다.

men·tor [méntər, -tɔːr] *n.* a wise and trusted adviser. 현명하고 성실한 조언자. [Gk.]

***men·u** [ménjuː, méi-] *n.* **1** Ⓒ a list of dishes served at a meal. 차림표; 메뉴. **2** Ⓤ the dishes in a meal. 요리; 식사. [F.]

me·ow [miáu, mjau] *n.* Ⓒ the sound a cat or kitten makes. 야옹《고양이 울음 소리》. — *vi.* (P1) make this sound. 야옹하고 울다. [Imit.]

mer·can·tile [mə́ːrkəntìːl, -tàil, -til] *adj.* **1** of merchants or trade. 상업의. ¶ *~ firm* 상사(商社) / *the ~ marine* (한 나라의) 상선 / *~ law* 상법. **2** 《econ.》 of mercantilism. 상업주의의. [→mercer]

mer·ce·nar·y [mə́ːrsənèri] *adj.* **1** working or done for money or reward only; influenced by a desire for gain or reward. 돈을〔보수를〕 목적으로 일하는; 타산적인. ¶ *~ motives* 타산적인 동기. **2** hired in a foreign army. (외국 군대에) 돈으로 고용된. — *n.* a hired soldier. 용병(傭兵). [L. *merces* reward]

mer·cer [mə́ːrsər] *n.* 《Brit.》 a dealer in cloth, esp. silks. 포목상; (특히) 비단 장수. [L. *merx* wares]

***mer·chan·dise** [mə́ːrtʃəndàiz] *n.* Ⓤ 《*collectively*》 articles for sale. 상품. ¶ *No ~ can be returned.* 반품 사절 / *general ~* 잡화. — *vt., vi.* (P6; 1) buy and sell; trade. 매매하다; 거래하다. [→mercer]

:mer·chant [mə́ːrtʃənt] *n.* Ⓒ **1** a person

who buys and sells goods on a large scale. 상인. **2** 《Brit.》 a person who trades on a large scale with foreign countries. 무역상. **3** 《U.S.》 a storekeeper; a retailer. 소매상. **4** a person who is given to. …광(狂). ¶ *a speed* ~ 스피드광. —*adj.* of trade; of commerce. 상업의. ¶ ~ *ships* 상선 / *a* ~ *captain* (상선의) 선장. [L. *merx* wares]

mer·chant·a·ble [mə́:rtʃəntəbəl] *adj.* marketable; that can be sold. 팔리는; 팔릴 수 있는.

mer·chant·man [mə́:rtʃəntmən] *n.* Ⓒ (*pl.* **-men** [-mən]) a merchant ship. 상선.

merchant prince [∠– ∠] *n.* a very rich merchant. 호상(豪商).

merchant service [∠– ∠–] *n.* the merchant navy, which is occupied in trade by sea. (한 나라의) 전(全)상선; 상선대.

***mer·ci·ful** [mə́:rsifəl] *adj.* having or showing mercy; tender-hearted; (of punishment) mild; not severe. 인정 많은; 자비로운; (처벌이) 관대한. ● **mer·ci·ful·ly** [-fəli] *adv.* [→mercy]

mer·ci·less [mə́:rsilis] *adj.* without mercy; cruel. 무자비한; 잔인한. ● **mer·ci·less·ly** [-li] *adv.* **mer·ci·less·ness** [-nis] *n.*

mer·cu·ri·al [mərkjúəriəl] *adj.* **1** of, like, or having mercury. 수은의. ¶ ~ *column* 수은주 / ~ *poisoning* 수은 중독. **2** 《*M-*》 of the god Mercury or the planet Mercury. 머큐리 신의; 수성(水星)의. **3** lively or active; quick witted; clever. 활발한; 재치 있는; 영리한. **4** quickly changing in mind and feeling. 변덕스러운. —*n.* Ⓒ a drug containing mercury. 수은제(劑). [↓]

***mer·cu·ry** [mə́:rkjəri] *n.* (*pl.* **-ries**) **1** Ⓤ a heavy silvery metal element, liquid at ordinary temperatures; quicksilver. 수은. **2** Ⓒ the column of mercury in a thermometer or barometer. 수은주. ¶ *a* ~ *thermometer* 수은 온도계 / *The* ~ *is rising.* 온도가 오르고 있다; 경기가 좋아지고 있다. **3** 《*M-*》 the Roman god of commerce, thieves and eloquence, and the messenger of the gods. 머큐리 신(神). **4** 《*M-*》 the planet nearest to the sun. 수성(水星). **5** Ⓒ a messenger; a guide. 사자(使者); 안내인. [L. *Mercurius*]

:mer·cy [mə́:rsi] *n.* (*pl.* **-cies**) **1** Ⓤ kindness, pity, or forgiveness shown to the weaker; Ⓒ an act of kindness. 친절; 인정; 연민; 자비; 친절한 행위. ¶ *an angel of* ~ 자비의 천사 / *without* ~ 사정없이 / *for mercy's sake* 제발; 아무쪼록 / *have* 〔*take*〕 ~ *on someone* 아무를 가엾이 여기다 / *Mercy on me !* 저런; 어쩌나; 어이쿠 / *throw oneself on an enemy's* ~ 적의 자비에 매달리다 / *He showed no* ~ *to his servants.* 하인들에게 매정했다. **2** Ⓒ something to be grateful for; a blessing. 행운; 고마운 일. ¶ *It's a* ~ *that I've met you.* 너를 만나다니 고맙기도 해라 / *be thankful for small mercies* 적은 것에도 고마워하다; 모자라도 참다. [L. *merces* reward]

at the mercy (=*completely in the power*) ***of*** *a god, etc.* …의 하는 대로. ¶ *at the* ~ *of the waves* 사나운 파도에 내맡겨져.

left to the tender mercies of, in the power of a person who will probably do one harm. …의 하는 대로 내맡겨져; …의 손아귀에 들어.

:mere[1] [miər] *adj.* (superl. **mer·est**) nothing more than; only; simple. …에 불과한; 단순한; 전적인. ¶ *a* ~ *folly* 더 없이 어리석은 짓 / *by* ~ *accident* 아주 우연히 / *a* ~ *child* 아직 어린 아이 / *The* ~ *sight of a snake makes him shudder.* 그는 뱀을 보기만 해도 기겁을 한다. [L. *merus* unmixed]

mere[2] [miər] *n.* 《*poet.*》 a lake; a pond. 호수; 연못. [E.]

:mere·ly [míərli] *adv.* simply; purely. 단순히; 단지; 그저. ¶ *He is not unkind,* ~ *thoughtless.* 그가 몰인정한 것은 아니고 생각이 못미쳤을 뿐이다. [*mere*[1]]

not merely ... but (***also***)..., not only ... but also.... …뿐만 아니라 또. ¶ *He is not* ~ *learned, but also wise.* 그는 배운 것이 많을 뿐 아니라 슬기로운 사람이기도 하다.

mer·e·tri·cious [mèrətríʃəs] *adj.* attractive in a false or showy way; vulgar. 야한; 속된; 뻔드레한. ¶ ~ *jewelery* 야한 장신구. [L. *meretrix* harlot]

merge [mə:rdʒ] *vt.* (P6,7) **1** cause (something) to be absorbed. …을 녹아들게 하다. ¶ *All fear was merged in curiosity.* 호기심으로 해서 모든 무서움이 사라져 버렸다. **2** join together; combine. …을 합병하다. —*vi.* (P1,2A,3) become absorbed or combined. 녹아들다; 합동〔합병〕하다. ¶ *Two small banks merged with a large one.* 두 작은 은행은 한 큰 은행으로 합병했다. [L. *mergo* dip]

merg·er [mə́:rdʒər] *n.* ⓊⒸ the act of combining several companies to make a large one. 합병. ¶ *the* ~ *of small companies* 군소 회사들의 합병. [↑]

me·rid·i·an [mərídiən] *n.* Ⓒ **1** an imaginary line on the earth's surface passing through the North and South Poles. 자오선. **2** noon. 정오. **3** 《*fig.*》 the highest point; a period of great success, happiness, health, etc., in one's life. 전성기. ¶ *the* ~ *of life* 장년기(壯年期); 한창때. **4** the highest point reached by the sun or a star. (태양·별의) 최고점. —*adj.* **1** of a meridian. 자오선의. **2** of midday or noon. 정오의. **3** of the highest point. 정점(頂点)의. **4** of a period of success, happiness, health, etc. in life. 전성기의; 한창때의. [↓]

me·rid·i·o·nal [mərídiənəl] *adj.* **1** of a meridian. 자오선의; 전성기의. **2** of southern Europe, esp. of southern France. 남부 유럽의; (특히) 남부 프랑스의. **3** southern. 남방〔남쪽〕의. —*n.* 《often *M-*》 the people of southern Europe, esp. those of France. 남부 유럽인; (특히) 남부 프랑스인. [→medial, L. *dies,* day]

me·ri·no [mərí:nou] *n.* (*pl.* **-nos**) **1** Ⓒ a kind of sheep with long silky wool. 메리노 양. **2** Ⓤ the wool of this sheep; a soft cloth made from this wool. 메리노 털〔나사〕. [Sp.]

:mer·it [mérit] *n.* **1** ⓊⒸ good points. 장점. ¶ *a man of* ~ 우수한 사람 / *the merits of a book.* **2** Ⓒ something that is worthy of reward. 상 줄 만한 값어치. **3** Ⓒ a reward or punishment. 상벌(賞罰). **4** 《*pl.*》 a quality that is worthy of reward or punishment. 공죄(功罪); 공과(功過). ¶ *I will judge your case on its merits.* 네 경우의 일은 그 시비 곡직에 따라 판단하겠다.

make a merit of (=*take merit to oneself for*) *something.* …을 자랑하다.

— *vt.* (P6) be worthy of (something); deserve. …할 만하다. ¶ *a man who merited respect* 존경받을 만한 사람 / *He merits reward* 〔*punishment*〕. 그는 상〔벌〕받아 마땅하다. [L. *mereor* earn]

mer·i·to·ri·ous [mèritɔ́:riəs] *adj.* worthy of reward or praise. 칭찬할 만한; 기특한. ¶ *have* ~ *features* 많은 가치있는 특색을 지니다.

mer·maid [mə́:rmèid] *n.* Ⓒ **1** an imaginary girl in the sea who is like a fish from the waist down. 인어(人魚). **2** a very good woman swimmer. 헤엄 잘 치는 여자. [→mere²]

mer·man [mə́:rmæ̀n] *n.* Ⓒ **1** an imaginary man in the sea who is like a fish from the waist down. 인어《남자》. **2** a very good swimmer. 헤엄 잘 치는 남자. [↑]

***mer·ri·ly** [mérəli] *adv.* in a merry manner. 즐겁게. ¶ *The birds were singing* ~. 새들이 즐겁게 노래하고 있었다. [merry]

mer·ri·ment [mérimənt] *n.* Ⓤ fun and joy; merry enjoyment. 즐거움; 재미있음; 환락.

:mer·ry [méri] *adj.* (**-ri·er, -ri·est**) **1** full of joy and laughter; cheerful; jolly. 명랑한; 유쾌한. ¶ *I wish you a* ~ *Christmas.* =*Merry Christmas to you.* 성탄을 축하합니다 / ~ *laughter* 즐거운 웃음 (소리) / *Merry England* 즐거운 영국《예부터의 호칭》. **2** 《*colloq.*》 slightly drunk. 거나한. ¶ *be* ~ *in one's cups* 기분좋게 취해 있다. [E.]

(***as***) ***merry as a cricket*** 〔***a grig, a lark***〕, very merry. 아주 명랑한.

make merry, be filled with laughter and gaiety. 흥겨워하다.

make merry over (=*make fun of* or *enjoy*) *someone* or *something.* 놀리다; 조롱하다.

mer·ry-go-round [mérigouràund] *n.* Ⓒ **1** a large round platform with wooden animal-shaped seats, and which goes round to music by machinery. 회전 목마. **2** 《*fig.*》 any rapid round. 급회전; 어지러이 돌아감. ¶ *His holidays were a* ~ *of golf competitions.* 그의 휴가는 여러 골프 경기들로 눈코 뜰 새 없었다.

mer·ry·mak·er [mérimèikər] *n.* Ⓒ a person who shares in merriment and gaiety. 흥겹게 들떠 있는 사람.

mer·ry·mak·ing [mérimèikiŋ] *n.* Ⓤ gaiety; gay entertainment; gay festivities. 환락; 흥겹게 떠들기. — *adj.* jolly; festive. 유쾌한; 축제 기분의.

mes·dames [meidá:m, -dǽm] *n.* pl. of **madam** or **madame.**

mes·de·moi·selles [mèidəmwəzél] *n.* pl. of **mademoiselle.**

mesh [meʃ] *n.* **1** Ⓒ one of the open spaces of a network or wire screen. 그물눈. ¶ *a net of coarse* ~ 눈이 성긴 그물 / *The wire screen has tiny meshes.* 그 철망의 그물눈은 잘다. **2** 《*pl.*》 the threads or cords of a net. 그물실〔철사〕. **3** a net or network. 그물; 그물 세공. **4** 《usu. *pl.*》 a snare. 올가미. **5** Ⓤ the uniting of the teeth of two gear wheels to fit each other. 톱니바퀴의 맞물림.

in mesh, fitted together; in gear. (톱니바퀴가) 맞물려.

— *vi., vt.* **1** (P1;6) catch (something) in a net; be caught in a net. …을 그물로 잡다; 그물에 걸리다. **2** (P1,3) (of gears) fit together. (톱니바퀴가) 맞물리다. [?]

mes·mer·ic [mezmérik, mes-] *adj.* of or caused by mesmerism. 최면술의. [Person]

mes·mer·ism [mézmərìzəm, més-] *n.* Ⓤ **1** the art of causing someone to sleep. 최면술(催眠術)(cf. *hypnotism*). **2** the condition brought on by mesmerism. 최면 상태.

mes·mer·ist [mézmərist, més-] *n.* Ⓒ a person who mesmerizes. 최면술사.

mes·mer·ize [mézməràiz, més-] *vt.* (P6) **1** exercise mesmerism on (someone). …에 최면을 걸다(cf. *hypnotize*). **2** 《*fig.*》 have a powerful influence upon; enchant; fascinate. …을 매료시키다; 홀리게 하다. ●**mes·mer·iz·er** [-ər] *n.* [→mesmeric]

mes·on [mí:zɑn, méz-, -sɑn / mí:zɔn, mésɔn] *n.* 《phys.》 a highly unstable heavy electron found in cosmic rays. 중간자(中間子). [Gk. *mesos* middle]

Mes·o·po·ta·mi·a [mèsəpətéimiə] *n.* a region in Asia between the Tigris and Euphrates rivers. 메소포타미아. ●**Mes·o·po·ta·mi·an** [-ən] *n., adj.*

mes·o·tron [mézətrɑ̀n, més- / -trɔ̀n] *n.* early term for meson. 메손의 구칭. [↑]

Mes·o·zo·ic [mèzəzóuik, mès-] *n.* 《geol.》 《*the* ~》 the geological era of reptiles. 중생대(中生代). — *adj.* of this era. 중생대의. [Gk. =mid-life]

***mess** [mes] *n.* Ⓒ **1** the state of being dirty or confused; a dirty mass of things. 혼란 상태; 불결; 어질러진 것. ¶ *clear away the* ~ 어질러진 것을 치우다 / *I must look a* ~. 몰골이야 말이 아니겠지 / *a* ~ *of clothes* 마구 벗어 던진 옷가지들. **2** a state of difficulty or trouble. 난처한 상태; 곤란. ¶ *get into a* ~ 난처해지다 / *make a* ~ *of* …을 엉망으

로 만들다; 망쳐놓다. **3** a group of people, esp. soldiers or sailors, taking their meals together regularly; the meals of such a group. (군대 등에서) 늘 식사를 함께 하는 동료; 그 식사. ¶ *a ~ hall* (군대·공장 등의) 식당 / *be at ~* 회식〔식사〕중이다 / *go to ~* 회식〔식사〕하다. **4** a dish of soft or liquid food. 한 접시분의 유동식. **5** a quantity of liquid or mixed food for an animal. (가축 한 마리분의) 혼합식.

in a mess, in confusion. 혼란되어; 어질러져.

— *vt.* **1** (P6) supply (someone) with meals. …에게 급식(給食)하다. **2** (P6,7) make a mess of; make dirty. …을 엉망으로 해놓다; 더럽히다. — *vi.* (P2A) eat together in a group; eat at a common table. 회식하다; 함께 식사하다. ¶ *~ together* / *~ with others.* [L. *mitto* send]

mess about 〔***around***〕**,** be busy without doing any real work. 공연히 수선떨다. ¶ *You've messed about all day, and the result is nothing!* 종일 수선만 떨더니 뭣하나 된 일이 없지 않나.

mess up, make (something) dirty or untidy; spoil. …을 더럽히다; 엉망으로 해놓다.

:mes·sage [mésidʒ] *n.* Ⓒ **1** words or news, etc., sent from one person to another. 전언; 전갈. ¶ *I'll give him your ~.* 그분에게 말씀을 전해드리지요 / *leave a ~ with someone* …에게 전언을 부탁하고 가다 / *a ~ form* 전보 용지. **2** 《U.S.》 a formal, official speech or writing. 교서(敎書). ¶ *the President's ~* 대통령 교서. **3** a mission; an errand. 사명; (심부름의) 용건. [↑]

go on a message, go on an errand. 심부름 가다.

:mes·sen·ger [mésəndʒər] *n.* Ⓒ a person who carries a message or does an errand. 사자(使者); 심부름꾼. [→message]

Mes·si·ah [misáiə] *n.* **1** the savior who is expected to set the Jewish people free. (유태인의) 구세주. **2** Jesus the Christ. 예수. **3** Ⓒ 《often *m-*》 a person who saves a people or a nation. (민족·국가의) 해방자; 구제자. [Heb. =anointed]

mes·sieurs [məsjə́:rz] *n.* pl. of **monsieur.**

mess·mate [mésmèit] *n.* Ⓒ a person who regularly eats together with others in the army or navy. (군대 등의) 함께 식사하는 동료; 한솥밥의 친구. [→mess]

Messrs. [mésərz] *n.* =messieurs.

mess·y [mési] *adj.* (**mess·i·er, mess·i·est**) in or like a mess; dirty. 더러운. [*mess*]

mes·ti·zo [mestí:zou] *n.* (*pl.* **-zos** or **-zoes**) a person of mixed blood; a person of Spanish and American Indian blood. 혼혈아. [L. *mixtus* mixed]

:met [met] *v.* p. and pp. of **meet.**

met. metaphor; meteorological; meteorology; metropolitan.

met·a- [métə-] *pref.* after; change; beyond, etc. '뒤에, 변화, 초월하여'의 뜻. [Gk.]

met·a·bol·ic [mètəbálik / -bɔ́l-] *adj.* 《biol.》 of metabolism. 신진 대사의; 물질 교대의. [↑, Gk. *ballō* throw]

me·tab·o·lism [mətǽbəlìzəm] *n.* Ⓤ 《biol.》 the process of changing food into living matter, and then into waste matter, in a living body. 물질 교대; 신진 대사.

:met·al [métl] *n.* **1** ⒸⓊ ⓐ any chemical element, such as iron, gold, tin, silver, etc.; a mixture of such elements. 금속; 합금. ¶ *base metals* 비금속 / *light* 〔*heavy*〕 *metals* 경〔중〕금속 / *noble metals* 귀금속 / *sheet metals* 판금(板金). ⓑ 《chem.》 any element whose atoms tend to lend electrons. 금속 원소. **2** Ⓤ 《Brit.》 broken stones used for roads and road beds. 자갈; 쇄석(碎石). ¶ *road ~* (도로 포장용) 자갈. **3** 《Brit.》 《*the ~s*》 rails of a railway line. 레일; 궤도. ¶ *leave* 〔*run off*〕 *the metals* (열차가) 탈선하다. **4** something made of metal. 금속 제품. **5** material; stuff. 재료; 물질.

— *vt.* (**-aled, -al·ing** or 《Brit.》 **-alled, -al·ling**) (P6) **1** cover (something) with metal. …에 금속을 입히다. **2** make or mend (a road) with metal. (길에) 자갈을 깔다. ¶ *metaled roads* 쇄석을 깐 도로. [Gk. *metallon* mine]

me·tal·lic [mətǽlik] *adj.* of or like metal; made of metal. 금속(성)의; 금속제의. ¶ *~ currency* 경화(硬貨) / *a ~ luster* 금속 광택 / *~ sounds* 금속성의 소리.

met·al·line [métəlin, -làin] *adj.* of or like metal. 금속의; 금속 같은.

met·al·(l)ize [métəlàiz] *vt.* (P6) make metallic; give metallic properties to. …을 금속화(化)하다.

met·al·loid [métəlɔ̀id] *adj.* of or like a metal. 금속의; 금속 같은. — *n.* 《chem.》 an element with characteristic both of metals and non-metals. 메탈로이드; 반(半)금속 원소《비소·규소 따위》.

met·al·lur·gy [métələ̀:rdʒi / metǽlərdʒi] *n.* Ⓤ the science or art of getting metal from ore. 야금(冶金)학〔술〕.

met·al·work [métlwə̀:rk] *n.* Ⓤ **1** things made of metal. 금속 세공품. **2** the making of such things. 금속 세공.

met·al·work·er [métlwə̀:rkər] *n.* Ⓒ a person who works at or in metalworking. 금속 세공인.

met·al·work·ing [métlwə̀:rkiŋ] *n.* Ⓤ the act or process of making things out of metal. 금속 세공.

met·a·mor·phose [mètəmɔ́:rfouz, -fous] *vt., vi.* (P6,13; 1,3) 《*to, into*》 change (something) in form or character; transform. 변형시키다〔하다〕. ¶ *The princess was metamorphosed into a bird by the wicked fairy.* 공주는 마녀에 의해 한 마리의 새로 변했다. [→morphology]

met·a·mor·pho·ses [mètəmɔ́:rfəsì:z] *n.*

pl. of **metamorphosis.**

met·a·mor·pho·sis [mètəmɔ́:rfəsis] *n.* UC (*pl.* **-ses**) a striking change in form or character by natural growth, development, etc. 변형; 변태. ¶ *the ~ of a caterpillar into an insect* 모충(毛蟲)〔풀쐐기〕의 곤충으로의 변태. [↑]

met·a·phor [métəfɔ̀:r, -fər] *n.* UC a way of using a word or phrase to express an idea different from its usual meaning. 은유(隱喩). [Gk. *phero* carry]

met·a·phys·i·cal [mètəfízikəl] *adj.* **1** of metaphysics. 형이상학의. **2** very abstract and difficult to understand. 형이상학적인; 추상적인. ● **met·a·phys·i·cal·ly** [-li] *adv.* [meta-]

met·a·phy·si·cian [mètəfizíʃən] *n.* C a specialist in metaphysics. 형이상학자.

met·a·phys·ics [mètəfíziks] *n. pl.* 《used as *sing.*》 **1** a branch of philosophy that deals with the nature of being, the universe, and the theory of knowledge. 형이상학; 순수 철학. **2** 《*colloq.*》 abstract talk. 추상적 논의; 탁상 공론. [meta-, →physics]

met·a·plasm [métəplæ̀zəm] *n.* 《biol.》 a part of protoplasm containing formative material. 후형질(後形質).

met·a·tar·si [mètətá:rsai] *n.* pl. of **metatarsus.**

met·a·tar·sus [mətətá:rsəs] *n.* (*pl.* **-si**) 《anat.》 bones between tarsus and toes. 척골(蹠骨). [meta-]

mete [mi:t] *vt.* **1** 《*lit.*》 《*out*》 (P7) divide (something) among several persons; give to each his share (of reward, punishment, etc.). (벌·상)을 각기 나누다; 할당하다. ¶ *The king meted out punishments* 〔*rewards*〕. 왕은 각자의 벌〔상〕을 주었다. **2** 《*poet.*》 (P6) measure. …을 재다; 측정하다. [E.]

***me·te·or** [mí:tiər, -tiɔ̀:r] *n.* C a falling star; a piece of matter coming from outer space into the earth's atmosphere at a great speed and burning with a bright glow. 유성; 운석. [Gk. *meteoros* lofty]

me·te·or·ic [mì:tiɔ́(:)rik, -árik] *adj.* **1** of a meteor. 유성의. ¶ *a ~ stone* 운석. **2** 《*fig.*》 brilliant for a short time like a meteor. 유성 같은; 한때는 화려한. ¶ *a ~ career* 한때 화려했던 생애. **3** of atmospheric phenomena. 기상(氣象)의.

me·te·or·ite [mí:tiəràit], **-or·o·lite** [mì:tiɔ́:rəlàit] *n.* C a body of stone or metal that falls to the earth from outer space; a fallen meteor. 운석; 유성.

me·te·or·o·log·i·cal [mì:tiərəládʒikəl / -lɔ́dʒi-] *adj.* of meteorology. 기상(학상)의. ¶ *~ observation* 기상 관측 / *a ~ report* 일기 예보; 기상 통보 / *a ~ chart* 일기도 / *a ~ satellite* 기상 위성 / *a ~ station* 기상 관측소.

me·te·or·ol·o·gist [mì:tiərálədʒist / -rɔ́l-] *n.* C a person who specializes in meteorology. 기상학자.

me·te·or·ol·o·gy [mì:tiərálədʒi / -rɔ́l-] *n.* U the science of the atmosphere, weather, and climate. 기상학.

me·ter[1], 《Brit.》 **-tre** [mí:tər] *n.* **1** C a unit of length in the metric system. 미터 《길이의 단위》. **2** U any poetic rhythm; 《mus.》 a form of rhythm and time. 운율; 박자. [Gk. *metron* measure; mete]

***me·ter**[2] [mí:tər] *n.* C an instrument for measuring. 계량기; 미터. ¶ *an electric ~* 전기 계량기 / *a gas ~* 가스 미터〔계량기〕. [↑]

meth·ane [méθein] *n.* U 《chem.》 a colorless, odorless gas which burns well, produced by the decay of living things. 메탄. [*meth*(*o*)-]

:**meth·od** [méθəd] *n.* **1** C a way of doing something. 방법. ¶ *a teaching ~* 교수법 / *a deductive ~* 연역법. **2** U an orderly arrangement of ideas; an order in getting things done or in thinking. (생각 따위의)조리; 질서; 순서. ¶ *a man of ~* 찬찬한 사람 / *If you used more ~, you wouldn't waste so much time.* 좀 더 체계 있게 했더라면 시간도 절약됐을 텐데 / *There is ~ in his madness.* 보기처럼 그리 무모한 사람은 아니다. [meta-, Gk. *hodos* way]

me·thod·i·cal [məθádikəl / məθɔ́d-] *adj.* **1** arranged or done in an orderly way; systematic. 질서 있는; 조직적인. **2** having a habit of doing things in an orderly way. 차근차근한; 꼼꼼한.

me·thod·i·cal·ly [məθádikəli / məθɔ́d-] *adv.* in a methodical manner. 질서 있게; 정연히.

Meth·od·ism [méθədìzəm] *n.* U the organizations, beliefs, and teachings of the Methodists. 메서디스트파; 감리교파(의 교의). [→method, -ism]

Meth·od·ist [méθədist] *n.* C a member of one of several Protestant religious bodies originally developed from the teachings and work of John Wesley in the 18th century. 메서디스트 교도; 감리교 신자. — *adj.* of the Methodists or Methodism. 감리교도의; 감리교파의.

meth·od·ize [méθədàiz] *vt.* (P6) arrange (work, etc.) in a methodical way. (일 등)을 조직화하다; 순서를 정하다.

meth·yl [méθəl] *n.* U 《chem.》 a kind of alcohol that is poisonous if drunk. 메틸 (cf. *ethyl*). ¶ *~ alcohol* 메틸 알코올. [Gk. *methu* wine, *hulē* wood]

me·tic·u·lous [mətíkjələs] *adj.* extremely careful about small matters. 소심한; 좀스러운. [L. *metus* fear]

me·tic·u·lous·ly [mətíkjələsli] *adv.* in a meticulous manner. 소심하게; 좀스럽게.

mé·tier [méitjei, –⌐] *n.* 《F.》 one's trade or profession; the work that one is specially fitted for. 직업; 전문 기술; 장기. ¶ *Speech is not my ~.* 연설엔 자신 없다.

me·ton·y·my [mitánəmi / -tɔ́n-] *n.* U

《rhet.》 the use of the name of one thing for another with which it is associated, as 'crown' for 'king'. 환유(換喩). [meta-, Gk. *onuma* name]

me·tre [mí:tər] *n.* 《Brit.》 =meter[1].

met·ric [métrik] *adj.* of the measuring system based on the meter. 미터(법)의. ¶ *the ~ system* 미터법 / *a ~ ton* 미터톤 《1,000 kg》. [→meter]

met·ri·cal [métrikəl] *adj.* **1** of or in a rhythm of a poem. 운율(韻律)의. ¶ *a ~ composition* 운문. **2** of or for measurement. 측량(용)의. [↑]

met·rics [métriks] *n. pl.* 《used as *sing.*》 **1** the art of writing in meter. 작시법(作詩法); 운문법. **2** the study of the laws of meter. 운율학(韻律學).

me·trol·o·gy [mitrálədʒi / -trɔ́l-] *n.* the science of weights and measures. 도량형학(度量衡學). [→meter]

met·ro·nome [métrənòum] *n.* Ⓒ 《mus.》 an instrument to beat time, used esp. in practicing music. 메트로놈; 박절기(拍節器). [↑; Gk. *nomos* law]

***me·trop·o·lis** [mitrápəlis / -trɔ́p-] *n.* Ⓒ **1** the capital of a country. 수도. ¶ *Seoul is the ~ of Korea.* 서울은 한국의 수도다. **2** any large city; a principal center of business and culture. 주요 도시; (상업·문화의) 중심지. 語法 capital(수도)과 비교했을 때는 주요 도시의 뜻으로 쓰임. 미국에서 New York은 metropolis이며, capital은 Washington D.C.임. ¶ *a ~ of religion* 〔*commerce*〕 종교〔상업〕의 중심지. **3** 《religion》 the see of a metropolitan bishop. 대주교〔대감독〕교구. [Gk. *mētēr* mother, *polis* city]

***met·ro·pol·i·tan** [mètrəpálitən / -pɔ́l-] *adj.* of a large city or metropolis. 수도의; 대도시의. — *n.* Ⓒ **1** a person living in a capital. 수도의 주민. **2** an archbishop. 대주교.

met·tle [métl] *n.* Ⓤ **1** a state or quality of mind; disposition. 기질; 성미. **2** courage; spirit. 용기; 기개. ¶ *a man of ~* 기개 있는 사람. [→metal]

be on 〔***upon***〕 ***one's mettle,*** prepare to do one's best. 분발하다.

put someone on his mettle, encourage someone. …을 분발하게 하다.

met·tle·some [métlsəm] *adj.* full of mettle; high-spirited; courageous. 씩씩한; 기개 있는; 용기 있는. ¶ *a ~ horse* 팔팔한 말.

mew[1] [mju:] *n.* Ⓒ the cry of a cat. 야옹《고양이 울음소리》. — *vi.* (P1) make this sound. 야옹하고 울다. [Imit.] 「[E.]

mew[2] [mju:] *n.* Ⓒ 《*poet.*》 a gull. 갈매기.

***Mex·i·can** [méksikən] *adj.* of Mexico or its people. 멕시코(인)의. — *n.* Ⓒ a person of Mexico. 멕시코인.

***Mex·i·co** [méksikòu] *n.* a country in North America, just south of the United States. 멕시코. ¶ *the Gulf of ~* 멕시코만.

mez·za·nine [mézənì:n] *n.* Ⓒ **1** a low story between two main stories of a building, often in the form of a balcony. 중이층(中二層). **2** 《Brit.》 the floor below the stage of a theater. 무대 밑. [L. *medianus*]

mez·zo [métsou, médzou] *adj.* 《mus.》 moderate; middle. 적도(適度)의; 알맞은. [→medial]

mez·zo-so·pran·o [métsousəprǽnou, -prá:nou, médzou-] *n.* 《mus.》 **1** Ⓤ a voice between soprano and contralto. 메조소프라노; 차고음(次高音). **2** Ⓒ a singer having such a voice. 메조소프라노 가수.

mfd. manufactured; microfarad.

Mg magnesium.

mg. milligram; milligrams.

mgr. manager; monsignor.

mi [mi:] *n.* Ⓒ 《mus.》 the third tone of the scale. 미《장음계의 제3음》. [→gamut]

mi. mile; miles.

Mi·am·i [maiǽmi] *n.* a city in southeastern Florida. 마이애미.

mi·aow, -aou [miáu, mjau] *n.* the cry of a cat. 고양이 울음소리(cf. *mew*[1]). — *vi.* (P1) cry like a cat; mew. 야옹하다. [Imit.]

mi·as·ma [maiǽzmə, mi-] *n.* (*pl.* **-mas, -ma·ta**) a harmful air arising from marshes. 소기(沼氣); 장기(瘴氣). [Gk. *miainō* pollute] 「**miasma.**

mi·as·ma·ta [maiǽzmətə, mi-] *n.* pl. of

mi·ca [máikə] *n.* Ⓤ 《min.》 a mineral that can be easily separated into thin, partly transparent sheets. 운모. [L. =crumb]

:mice [mais] *n.* pl. of **mouse.**

Mich. Michigan; Michaelmas.

Mi·chael[1] [máikəl], **Saint** *n.* 《Bible》 an archangel who, with the loyal angels, won the war with revolting angels. 대천사 미가엘. 「이름《애칭 Mike》.

Mi·chael[2] [máikəl] *n.* a man's name. 남자

Mich·ael·mas [míkəlməs] *n.* 《Brit.》 the festival of the archangel Michael, held on September 29. 미가엘 축제. 參考 quarter days(사계(四季) 지불일)의 하나. [*Michael,* mass[1]]

Mi·chel·an·ge·lo [màikəlǽndʒəlòu, mìk-], **Buonarroti** *n.* (1475-1564) an Italian sculptor, painter, architect and poet. 미켈란젤로.

***Mich·i·gan** [míʃigən] *n.* a north central State of the United States. 미시간(주). 參考 Mich.로 생략. 주도는 Lansing.

mick·le [míkəl] *n.* 《*arch.*》 great; much. 대량; 다량. ¶ 《*prov.*》 *Many a little* 〔*pickle*〕 *makes a ~.* =*Every little makes a ~* 〔*muckle*〕. 티끌 모아 태산. [E.]

mi·cra [máikrə] *n.* pl. of **micron.**

mi·cro- [máikrou-] *pref.* small; little. '소(小), 미(微)'의 뜻(opp. macro-). [Gk. *mikros* small]

mi·crobe [máikroub] *n.* Ⓒ **1** a very small living thing which can be seen only through a microscope. 미생물. **2** a disease germ. 세균(cf. *germ*). ¶ *a ~ bomb* 세균

탄 / *a ~ hunter* 세균학자. [Gk. *bios* life]

mi·cro·bi·ol·o·gy [màikroubaiάlədʒi / -ɔ́l-] *n.* the study of microorganism. 미생물학(微生物學). [→biology]

mi·cro·cosm [máikroukὰzəm / -kɔ̀z-] *n.* Ⓒ **1** a miniature universe. 소우주(opp. macrocosm). **2** a man or society thought of as a miniature of the universe. (우주의 축도로서의) 인간 (사회). [→cosmos]

mi·cro·far·ad [màikrəfǽrəd] *n.* a unit of electrical capacity, one millionth of a farad. 마이크로패럿《전기 용량의 실용 단위》. [micro-]

mi·cro·film [máikrəfìlm] *n.* Ⓒ a film containing photographs of books, pictures, etc. on a very small scale. 마이크로 필름; 축사(縮寫) 필름. — *vt.* (P6) record on microfilm. …을 마이크로 필름으로 찍다. [↑]

mi·crom·e·ter [maikrάmitər / -krɔ́-] *n.* Ⓒ an instrument for measuring exactly small distances, angles, etc. 마이크로미터; 측미계(測微計).

mi·cron [máikrɑn / -krɔn] *n.* Ⓒ (*pl.* **-cra** or **-crons**) one millionth of a meter. 미크론 《기호: μ》. [micro-]

mi·cro·or·gan·ism [màikrouɔ́:rgənìzəm] *n.* Ⓤ any living thing which can be seen only through a microscope. 미생물.

∗**mi·cro·phone** [máikrəfòun] *n.* Ⓒ an instrument which changes sounds into electric currents to be strengthened and sent out. 마이크(로폰). 參考 mike로 생략함. ¶ a radio ~ 라디오 송화기(送話器). [→phonetic]

∗**mi·cro·scope** [máikrəskòup] *n.* Ⓒ an instrument with several lenses for making very small objects large enough to be seen. 현미경. ¶ *an electron* ~ 전자 현미경 / *under a* ~ 현미경으로. [micro-]

mi·cro·scop·ic [màikrəskάpik / -skɔ́p-], **-i·cal** [-ikəl] *adj.* **1** of a microscope. 현미경의. **2** so small as to be seen only through a microscope. 현미경으로만 볼 수 있는; 미세한; 극미의. ¶ *a ~ organism* 미생물.

mi·cro·scop·i·cal·ly [màikrəskάpikəli / -skɔ́p-] *adv.* **1** with the help of a microscope. 현미경으로. **2** in a minute and careful manner. 현미경으로 보듯이; 미세하게.

mi·cro·wave [máikrouwèiv] *n.* Ⓒ a very short electromagnetic wave. 극초단파.

∗**mid**[1] [mid] *adj.* middle. 중간(중앙)의. ¶ *in ~ summer* 한여름에 / *in ~ career* (*course*) 중도에. [E.]

mid[2], **'mid** [mid] *prep.* 《*poet.*》 =amid.

mid·air [midέər] *n.* Ⓤ any point in the air which does not touch the earth or any other thing. 공중; 허공. ¶ *in ~* 공중에. [→mid[1]]

∗**mid·day** [míddèi, ⌐⌐] *n.* Ⓤ the middle of the day; noon. 정오; 한낮. — *adj.* of midday. 한낮의.

∶**mid·dle** [mídl] *adj.* 《as *attributive*》 halfway between two ends, sides, limits, etc.; in the center. 한가운데의; 중간(중앙)의; 중위의. ¶ *a ~ finger* 가운뎃손가락 / *in one's ~ twenties* 20대 중반에 / *take a ~ point of view* 중도적인 견해를 가지다. — *n.* Ⓒ **1** 《usu. *the* ~》 a point between two ends, sides, limits, etc.; the center. 한가운데; 중앙. ¶ *the ~ of the road* 길의 중간; 길 한가운데 / *in the ~ of a hot day* 더운 한낮에 / *in the ~ of one's work* 한창 일하는 중에. **2** the middle of a body; the waist. (인체의) 몸통; 허리. — *vt.* put (something) in the middle. …을 한가운데에 놓다. [*mid*[1]]

middle age [⌐⌐ ⌐] *n.* the period of life between youth and old age. 중년《약 40세에서 60세》.

mid·dle-aged [mídléidʒd] *adj.* of middle age. 중년의.

Middle Ages [⌐⌐ ⌐], **the** *n. pl.* the medieval period in the history of Europe, from about 500 A.D. to about 1450 A.D. 중세.

middle class [⌐⌐ ⌐] *n.* the social class between the very rich class and the working class. 중류 계급; 중산층.

Middle East [⌐⌐ ⌐] *n.* the lands from the eastern Mediterranean to India. 중동(中東).

mid·dle·man [mídlmæ̀n] *n.* Ⓒ (*pl.* **-men** [-mèn]) **1** a trader who buys goods from the producer and sells them to other merchants or to consumers. 중간 상인. **2** =go-between.

mid·dle·most [mídlmòust] *adj.* =midmost.

Middle West [⌐⌐ ⌐] *n.* the part of the United States between the Appalachian and Rocky Mountains, bounded on the south by Kansas, Missouri, and the Ohio River. 미국의 중서부.

mid·dling [mídliŋ] *adj.* middle or moderate in size, quality, or degree; fairly good; ordinary. 중간 정도의; 보통의; 어지간한. ¶ *a ~ success in business* 장사에서의 그저 그만한 성공 / *The dinner was ~.* 식사는 그저 그만했다 / *feel only ~* 그저 그런 느낌이다. — *adv.* 《*colloq.*》 moderately; fairly. 웬만큼; 상당히. — *n.* 《*pl.*》 products of medium size, quality, or price. 중등품; 이등품; 중간치. [*mid*[1]]

∗**mid·dy** [mídi] *n.* (*pl.* **-dies**) 《*colloq.*》 =midshipman.

middy blouse [⌐⌐ ⌐] *n.* 《U.S.》 a loose blouse with a sailor collar, worn esp. by children and young girls. 미디블라우스. 參考 그냥 middy 라고도 함.

midge [midʒ] *n.* Ⓒ **1** a very small fly, gnat, or similar flying insect. (모기 따위의) 작은 벌레. **2** a very small person. 꼬마둥이. [↓]

midg·et [mídʒit] *n.* Ⓒ **1** a very small person; a dwarf. 꼬마둥이; 난쟁이. **2** anything very small. 아주 작은 물건; 잔챙이. — *adj.* very small. 아주 작은. [E.]

mid·land [mídlənd] *adj., n.* (of) the central 〔middle〕 part of a country. 중부 지방(의). [*mid*[1]]

mid·most [mídmòust] *adj.* being in the middle or nearest the middle; middlemost. 한가운데의. — *adv.* in the midmost part. 한가운데에.

:mid·night [mídnàit] *n.* Ⓤ twelve o'clock at night; the middle of the night. 한밤중. ¶ *at* ~ 오밤중에 / *dark as* ~ 칠흑 같은 어둠. ***burn the midnight oil,*** study till late at night. 밤늦도록 공부하다〔일하다〕.

mid·rib [mídrìb] *n.* Ⓒ 《bot.》 the central vein of a leaf. (잎의) 주맥(主脈).

mid·riff [mídrìf] *n.* Ⓒ a muscular wall between the chest cavity and the abdomen; the diaphragm. 횡경막.

mid·ship [mídʃìp] *adj., n.* (in, of) the middle part of a ship. (선체의) 중앙부(의).

mid·ship·man [mídʃìpmən] *n.* Ⓒ (*pl.* **-men** [-mən]) **1** 《U.S.》 a student at the United States Naval Academy. 해군 사관 학교 생도. **2** 《Brit.》 a graduate from a government naval school. 해군 소위 수습 사관.

:midst[1] [midst] *n.* Ⓒ 《*the* ~》 middle. 한가운데; 중앙. ¶ *out of* 〔*from*〕 *the* ~ *of* …의 한가운데서 / *into* 〔*in*〕 *the* ~ *of* …의 한가운데에〔로〕 / *in* 〔*from*〕 *our* ~ 우리들 중에(서). [*mid*[1]]

midst[2]**, 'midst** [midst] *prep.* 《*poet.*》 = amidst.

mid·stream [mídstríːm] *n.* Ⓒ the middle part of a stream. 흐름의 중앙; 중류(中流).

mid·sum·mer [mídsʌ́mər] *n.* Ⓤ **1** the middle of the summer. 한여름; 성하(盛夏). ¶ *Midsummer Day* 세례 요한 축일《6월 24일; 사계(四季) 지급일의 하나》. **2** the time about June 21st, the longest day of the year. 하지(夏至).

midsummer madness [ㅗ-- ㅗ-], **the** *n.* utter madness or folly. 극도의 광란.

mid·term [mídtə̀ːrm] *n.* 《U.S.》 **1** the middle of a school term, or a political term of office. (학기·임기 따위의) 중간 시기. **2** an examination at the middle of a term. 중간 시험.

mid·way [mídwéi] *adj., adv.* halfway; in the middle of the way. 중도의〔에〕. — *n.* [ㅗㅗ] Ⓒ **1** a half-way point. 중도; 중간. **2** 《U.S.》 the place at a fair for side shows. (박람회 등의) 여흥장.

mid·wife [mídwàif] *n.* Ⓒ (*pl.* **-wives**) a woman whose profession is to help women in childbirth. 조산원; 산파. [E. = with-wife]

mid·wife·ry [mídwàifəri, -wìf-] *n.* Ⓤ the work of helping women in childbirth. 조산술(術). [*midwife, -ery*]

mid·win·ter [mídwíntər] *n.* Ⓤ **1** the middle of winter. 한겨울. **2** the time about December 21st, the shortest day of winter. 동지(冬至). [*mid*[1]]

mid·wives [mídwàivz] *n.* pl. of **midwife.**

mien [miːn] *n.* Ⓤ 《*lit.*》 a person's appearance or manner. 외모; 태도. ¶ *of pleasing* 〔*angry*〕 ~ 즐거운〔화난〕 모습의. [→demean]

:might[1] [mait] *auxil. v.* p. of **may. 1** 《in the *subjunctive*》 …일 것이다; …일지도 모른다. ¶ *Anyone* ~ *do the same, if he had the opportunity.* 기회가 있다면 누구든 그렇게 할 것이다 / *I* ~ *do it if I wanted to.* 내게 생각만 있다면 그것을 할 수 있는데 / *You* ~ *believe me if you read it.* 그것을 읽는다면 너는 나를 믿어 줄 텐데. **2** 《in *requests*》 …해주시지 않겠습니까. ¶ *You* ~ *mail this letter for me.* 이 편지 좀 부쳐주지 않겠느냐 / *You* ~ *shut the window.* 그 창문을 좀 닫아 주지 않겠느냐. **3** 《in *mild blame*》 …해도 좋으련만. ¶ *You* ~ *tell* 〔*have told*〕 *the truth.* 사실대로 말했으면 좋으련만 / *You* ~ *offer to help.* 도움을 청했으면 좋으련만《청하지 않았다》. **4** 《in expressing less *possibility* or *probability* than *may*》 …일지도 모른다. ¶ *You* ~ *get into trouble.* 너(그러다) 난처한 처지에 빠질지도 모른다 / *We* ~ *get there before it rains.* 비가 오기 전에 거기에 도착할 수 있을지도 모른다 / *I'm afraid he* ~ *lose his way.* 그 사람 길이라도 잃지 않을까 걱정이다. **5** 《in *permission*》 …해도 좋다. ¶ *Might I ask you a question?* 뭣 좀 여쭈어 보고 싶은데요 / *I said* (*that*) *he* ~ *go.* 그에게 가도 좋다고 말했다. [*may*]

might as well *do this* ***as*** *do that,* do this is just as good as to do that. …하느니보다 — 하는 것이 낫다. ¶ *You* ~ *as well read some novel as look at the ceiling.* 천장을 쳐다보고 있느니 소설 책을 읽는 편이 낫겠다.

might well *do something,* there is good reason for doing something. …하는 것도 당연하다〔무리가 아니다〕. ¶ *He* ~ *well ask that.* 그가 그렇게 묻는 것도 무리가 아니다.

:might[2] [mait] *n.* Ⓤ great strength of body or mind; power to carry out one's will. 힘; 능력. ¶ 《*prov.*》 *Might is right.* = *Might makes wrong right.* 힘은 정의다; 이기면 충신, 지면 역적. [*may*]

with might and main, with all one's strength. 온 힘을 다해서; 힘껏. [*may*]

might·i·ly [máitili] *adv.* **1** in a mighty manner; powerfully. 힘있게; 힘차게. **2** 《*colloq.*》 very much; extremely. 대단히. ¶ *I pleased him* ~. 그를 아주 기분 좋게 해줬다. [*might*[2]]

might·i·ness [máitinis] *n.* Ⓤ the state or quality of being mighty. 힘참; 강력.

:might·y [máiti] *adj.* (**might·i·er, might·i·est**) **1** showing power; powerful. 힘있는; 강력한. ¶ *a* ~ *wind* 강풍 / *The pen is mightier than the sword.* 문(文)은 무(武)보다 강하다. **2** 《*colloq.*》 very great. 거대한; 대단한. ¶ *a* ~ *hit* 대히트; 대성공 / *a* ~ *bridge* 큰 다리; 대교. — *adv.* 《*colloq.*》 very much; extremely. 대단히; 굉장히. ¶ *He is* ~ *pleased.* 아주 기뻐하고 있다 / *It is* ~ *kind of you.* 정

말 고맙소. [*might*²]
high and mighty, very proud. 아주 교만한 (태도로).
mi·gnon [mínjɑn / -jɔn] *adj.* 《F.》 small and delicately formed. 섬세한.
mi·gnon·ette [mìnjənét] *n.* **1** Ⓒ 《bot.》 a plant with small, sweet-smelling, greenish-white flowers. 목서초(木犀草). **2** Ⓤ grayish green. 회록색(灰綠色). [↑]
mi·graine [máigrein, mí:-] *n.* Ⓤ a periodical headache on one side only. 편두통. [→megrim]
mi·grant [máigrənt] *n.* Ⓒ a person, bird, or an animal that migrates as the seasons change. 이주자; 철새; 이동 동물. — *adj.* moving from place to place; migratory. 이동[이주]하는. ¶ *a ~ worker* 이동[계절] 노동자 / *Swallows are ~ birds.* 제비는 철새다. [L. *migro*]
*__mi·grate__ [máigreit, –ˊ] *vi.* (P1,2) **1** (of a person) leave one's own country and settle abroad. (해외로) 이주하다. **2** (of birds and some fishes) travel from one region to another as the seasonal changes. (새 등이 철따라) 이동하다. ¶ *Some birds ~ north in spring, and south in autumn.* 어떤 새들은 봄에는 북쪽으로, 가을에는 남쪽으로 이동한다. [↑]
mi·gra·tion [maigréiʃən] *n.* Ⓤ the act of migrating; Ⓒ a group of persons, animals, or birds migrating together. 이주; 이동. ¶ *the right of ~* 이주권.
mi·gra·to·ry [máigrətɔ̀:ri / -təri] *adj.* migrating; of migration. 이주하는; 이동의. ¶ *a ~ bird* 철새 / *~ laborers* 계절 노동자 / *a ~ fish* 회유어(回遊魚).
*__mike__ [maik] *n.* 《*colloq.*》 =microphone.
milch [miltʃ] *adj.* **1** kept to provide milk; giving milk. 젖을 짜는; 젖을 내는. **2** 《*fig.*》 a person from whom money is easily drawn; a source of profit. 봉; 수입원(收入源). [*milk*]
:**mild** [maild] *adj.* **1** gentle; kind. 온후한; 친절한. ¶ *be ~ in disposition* 마음씨가 곱다 / *be ~ of manner* 태도가 부드럽다. **2** not severe; calm; warm. 온화한; 따스한. ¶ *~ weather* 따스한 날씨 / *in ~ climates* 기후가 온난한 지방에. **3** not hard, strong, or violent. (병·벌이) 가벼운. ¶ *~ punishment* 가벼운 벌. **4** having a pleasant taste; not bitter. (맛이) 순한; 부드러운. ¶ *a ~ medicine* 쓰지 않은 약 / *~ tobacco* 순한 담배. [E.]
draw it mild, 《*colloq.*》 speak with reserve; not exaggerate. 온건하게[조심스럽게] 말하다; 과장하지 않다.
mil·dew [míldjù:] *n.* Ⓤ any small plant that appears on paper, clothes, leather, etc. in warm and damp weather. 곰팡이. — *vt., vi.* (P6; 1) affect or become covered with mildew. 곰팡나게 하다; 곰팡나다. ¶ *mildewed sheets of paper* 곰팡난 종잇장들. [E.]
mil·dew·y [míldjù:i] *adj.* **1** covered with mildew. 곰팡난. **2** of mildew. 곰팡이의. **3** like mildew. 곰팡이 같은.
mild·ly [máildli] *adv.* in a mild manner; gently. 부드럽게; 온화하게.
to put it mildly, to say the least of it; to speak without exaggeration. 삼가서[과장 없이] 말한다면.
mild·ness [máildnis] *n.* Ⓤ the state or quality of being mild. 온화; 온난.
:**mile** [mail] *n.* Ⓒ a unit of length or distance equal to 5,280 feet. 마일《약 1.6 km.》 (cf. *knot*). [L. *mille* thousand]
mile·age [máilidʒ] *n.* Ⓤ **1** the total distance in miles; the total number of miles covered in a certain time. 총마일수; (일정 기간의) 주행[진행] 거리. ¶ *The ~ of our car this summer was ....* 올 여름의 우리 차 주행 마일수는 …이었다. **2** an allowance for traveling expenses at so much a mile. (마일수에 따른) 여비 수당.
mile·stone [máilstòun] *n.* Ⓒ **1** a roadside stone showing the distance to a certain place. 이정표(里程標). **2** 《*fig.*》 an important event in history, one's life, etc. 획기적 사건.
mil·i·tan·cy [mílitənsi] *n.* Ⓤ the state or quality of being aggressive; fighting spirit. 교전 상태; 호전성; 투지. [↓]
mil·i·tant [mílitənt] *adj.* fighting; anxious to fight. 교전 중인; 호전적인. ¶ *a ~ nation* 교전국. — *n.* Ⓒ a person who is anxious to fight; a militant person. 호전적인 사람; 투사. [L. *miles* soldier]
mil·i·ta·rism [mílitərizəm] *n.* Ⓤ **1** the theory that a nation's safety depends on armed forces. 군국주의. **2** military spirit and ideals. 군국 정신[사상]. [→military]
mil·i·ta·rist [mílitərist] *n.* Ⓒ a supporter of militarism. 군국주의자.
:**mil·i·tar·y** [mílitèri / -təri] *adj.* **1** of, for, by or connected with soldiers, armies. 군대의; 군사의; 군인의(opp. civil). ¶ *the Military Academy* 육군 사관 학교 / *~ affairs* 군사(軍事) / *~ forces* 군세; 병력 / *~ law* 군법 / *~ service* 병역 / *the ~ police* 헌병 / *~ authorities* 군당국 / *~ band* 군악대. **2** of the army. 육군의(opp. naval). — *n.* 《*the ~*》 《*collectively*》 the armed forces; soldiers; the army. 군대; 군인. [→militia, -ary]
mi·li·tia [milíʃə] *n.* Ⓒ 《usu. *the ~*》 a group of citizens trained for defense of their country in war. 민병(民兵); 국민군. [L. *miles* soldier]
mi·li·tia·man [milíʃəmən] *n.* Ⓒ (*pl.* **-men** [-mən]) a member of the militia. 민병(民兵); 국민병.
:**milk** [milk] *n.* Ⓤ **1** the white liquid produced by female animals, esp. cows, for feeding their young. 우유; 밀크. ¶ *a land of ~ and honey* 풍요의 땅 / *~ of human kindness* 따뜻한 인정 / *mother's ~* 모유 / 《*prov.*》 *It is no use crying over spilt ~.* 엎지

른 물은 다시 담을 수 없다. **2** the white juice of some plants; any liquid like milk. 수액(樹液); 유액(乳液); 젖 같은 액체.
as white as milk, pure white. 순백의.
in* (*the*) *milk, yielding milk. 젖을 내는.
milk and water, a feeble discourse or sentiment. 물탄 우유; 맥빠진 강의; 나약한 감상.
— *vt.* (P6) **1** draw milk from (a cow, etc.). …의 젖을 짜다. ¶ *the milking machine* 자동 착유기 / ~ *a cow* 소젖을 짜다. **2** 《*fig., colloq.*》 get all possible profit out of. 착취하다. ¶ ~ *someone dry* 아무를 빈털터리로 만들다. **3** 《*sl.*》 steal a message from. …을 도청하다. **4** extract (something) as if by milking. …에서 즙을 짜다; …에서 정보를 빼내다. ¶ ~ *venom from a snake* 뱀에서 독액을 짜내다 / ~ *information from someone* 아무에게서 정보를 빼내다.
— *vi.* (P1) yield milk. 젖을 내다. ¶ *The cow milks well.* 소에서 젖이 잘 나온다. [E.]

milk·maid [mílkmèid] *n.* Ⓒ a woman who milks cows. 젖짜는 여자.

milk·man [mílkmæ̀n, -mən] *n.* Ⓒ (*pl.* **-men** [-mèn, -mən]) a man selling or delivering milk; a man who milks cows. 우유 장수; 우유 배달원; 젖짜는 사람.

milk·sop [mílksɑ̀p / -sɔ̀p] *n.* Ⓒ a weak, timid boy or man. 소심한 남자; 뱅충이; 겁쟁이.

milk tooth [ˊ ˋ] *n.* one of the first set of teeth of a young child or animal. 젖니(cf. *second teeth*).

milk·white [mílk*h*wáit] *adj.* white as milk. 유백색의.

milk·y [mílki] *adj.* (**milk·i·er, milk·i·est**) of or like milk; yielding milk. 젖 같은; 유백색의; 젖을 내는. ¶ *the Milky Way* 은하수.

:mill [mil] *n.* Ⓒ **1** a machine for grinding grain into flour; any machine for crushing or grinding. 제분기; 분쇄기; 맷돌. ¶ *a hand* ~ 맷돌 / *a coffee* ~ 커피 분쇄기 / 《*prov.*》 *No* ~, *no meal.* 부뚜막엣 소금도 집어넣어야 짜다. **2** a building with such machines. 제분소. ¶ *a water* ~ 물방앗간 / *a windmill* 풍차 / *a flour* ~ 제분소. **3** a machine used in making goods. 제조기. ¶ *a rolling* ~ 압연기. **4** a factory. 공장. ¶ *a cotton* 〔*steel*〕 ~ 방적공장〔제철소〕.
draw water to one's mill, 《*fig.*》 look out for one's own interests. 아전 인수(我田引水)하다; 제 이끗만 노리다.
go through the mill, 《*fig.*》 have hard training or experience. 시련을 통해 수련을 쌓다.
— *vt.* (P6) **1** grind or form (something) by or in a mill; treat in or put through mill. …을 맷돌에 갈다; 제분하다; 기계에 걸다. ¶ ~ *grain* 곡식을 갈다 / ~ *paper* 제지하다 / ~ *timber* 제재하다. **2** 《esp. in *pp.*》 indent the edge of (a coin). (주화 가장자리)를 깔쭉깔쭉하게 하다. ¶ *a milled coin* 가장자리가 깔쭉깔쭉한 돈.
— *vi.* (P2) **1** use a mill. 맷돌질하다; 제분기를 쓰다. **2** 《*about, around*》 (of cattle, crowds of people, etc.) move about in confusion. (가축 떼 등이) 빙빙〔어지러이〕 돌아다니다. ¶ *Cattle sometimes* ~ *about when they are frightened.* 가축은 때로 놀라면 우왕좌왕하며 빙글빙글 돈다. [E.]

mill- [mil-] *pref.* thousand-. '천(千)…'의 뜻. [L. *mille* thousand]

mill·dam [míldæ̀m] *n.* Ⓒ the dam of a millpond. 물방아용 저수지의 둑. [*mill, dam*]

mil·len·ni·a [miléniə] *n.* pl. of **millennium.**

mil·len·ni·um [miléniəm] *n.* Ⓒ (*pl.* **-niums** or **-ni·a**) **1** a period of a thousand years. 천년(간). **2** 《*the* ~》 the period when Christ is to rule on earth. 천년 왕국 《예수가 재림하여 천년 동안 지상을 다스린다는》. **3** a period of justice and great happiness, esp. in the indefinite future. (미래에 예상되는 정의와 지고(至高)의 행복이 있는) 이상적 시대. [→mill-, →annual]

:mill·er [mílər] *n.* Ⓒ a person who owns or works a mill. 방앗간 주인; 제분업자. ¶ 《*prov.*》 *Every* ~ *draws water to his own mill.* 아전 인수 / 《*prov.*》 *Too much water drowned the* ~. 지나침은 모자람만 못하다. [*mill*]

mil·let [mílit] *n.* Ⓤ 《bot.》 a grain-bearing grass grown for its seeds which are used as food. 기장; 수수. [L.]

mill·hand [mílhæ̀nd] *n.* Ⓒ a workman in a mill, esp. a cotton-mill. 제분공; 직공; (특히) 방적공. [*mill*]

mil·li·gram, 《Brit.》 **-gramme** [míləgræ̀m] *n.* Ⓒ one thousandth part of a gram. 밀리그램. 參考 mg.로 생략함. [L. *milli*-thousand]

mil·li·me·ter, 《Brit.》 **-tre** [míləmìːtər] *n.* Ⓒ one thousandth part of a meter. 밀리미터. 參考 mm.으로 생략함.

mil·li·ner [mílənər] *n.* Ⓒ a person who makes and sells women's hats, ribbons, etc. 여성 모자 제조인〔장수〕; 여성 장신구상(裝身具商). [*Milan*]

mil·li·ner·y [mílənèri / -nəri] *n.* Ⓤ **1** 《*collectively*》 women's hats or headdresses. 여성 모자류(類). **2** the business of making and selling women's hats. 여성용 모자 제조 판매업. [↑]

mill·ing [míliŋ] *n.* Ⓤ lines cut on the edge of a coin. (주화 가장자리의) 깔쭉이. [*mill*]

:mil·lion [míljən] *n.* Ⓒ **1** one thousand thousand. 백만. ¶ *many millions of dollars* 수백만 달러. **2** a large number. 다수. ¶ *hundreds of millions of* … 수억의 … / *millions* (*and millions*) *of people* 수없이 많은 사람들. **3** 《*the* ~》 the masses; the majority of people. 일반대중; 민중. ¶ *education for the* ~ 대중을 위한 교육. — *adj.* one thousand thousand; very many. 백만의; 다수의. [mill-]

•**mil·lion·aire** [mìljənέər] *n.* Ⓒ a person having at least a million dollars, etc.; a very rich person. 백만 장자; 거부.

mil·lionth [míljənθ] *adj.* coming last in a series of a million. 백만 번째의. — *n.* Ⓒ one of a million parts. 100만 분의 1.

mil·li·pede [míləpì:d], **-ped** [-pèd] *n.* Ⓒ a small worm with many legs. 노래기. [mill-, →pedal]

mill·pond [mílpɑ̀nd / -pɔ̀nd] *n.* Ⓒ a pond from which water flows to drive a mill wheel. (물방아용) 저수지. [*mill*]

mill·race [mílrèis] *n.* Ⓒ the stream of water flowing to a mill wheel. 물방아(바퀴)를 돌리는 물줄기〔도랑〕.

mill·stone [mílstòun] *n.* Ⓒ **1** one of a pair of round stones for grinding grain. 맷돌짝. **2** 《Bible》 a heavy burden. 무거운 짐; 중하(重荷).

see far into 〔***through***〕 ***a millstone,*** be extraordinarily acute; have very sharp senses, esp. of sight. 감각〔시력, 통찰력〕이 무섭게 날카롭다; 빈틈없다.

mill wheel [ˊˋ] *n.* the wheel supplying power for a mill. 물방아 바퀴.

mill·wright [mílràit] *n.* Ⓒ a person building or repairing water mills. 물방아(만드는) 목수.

Mil·ton [míltən], **John** *n.* (1608-74) an English poet. 밀턴《영국의 시인》.

mime [maim] *n.* **1** a kind of play, with much dancing and mimicry, and little or no speaking. 무언극(cf. *pantomime*). **2** an actor in a mime. 무언극 배우. — *vi.* act in a mime. 무언극을 하다. [Gk. *mimos*]

mim·e·o·graph [mímiəgræ̀f, -grɑ̀:f] *n.* Ⓒ a machine for making copies of written material. 등사판〔기〕. — *vt.* (P6) make (copies) with this machine. …을 등사판으로 인쇄하다. [Gk. *mimeomai* imitate, -graph]

mi·me·sis [mimí:sis, mai-] *n.* 《biol.》 mimicry. 의태(擬態). [Gk. *mimos* mime]

mi·met·ic [mimétik, mai-] *adj.* of imitation; not real; mimic. 흉내내는; 모방의. [→mime]

mim·ic [mímik] *adj.* inclined to imitate; not real. 흉내내는; 모방의. ¶ *~ coloration* 보호색 / *a ~ battle* 모의전(模擬戰) / *~ tears* 거짓 눈물. — *n.* Ⓒ a person who is clever at imitating. 흉내 잘 내는 사람; 모방자.
— *vt.* (**-icked** [-kt], **-ick·ing**) (P6) **1** imitate (something) to make fun of it; copy (something) closely. …의 흉내를 내다; …을 흡사하게 모방하다. ¶ *~ another's voice* 다른 사람의 목소리를 흉내내다 / *We like to get John to ~ our old music teacher.* 우리는 존에게 나이 많으신 음악 선생님의 흉내를 내게 하기를 좋아한다. **2** 《biol.》 have the exact appearance of. …을 의태(擬態)하다. ¶ *There are butterflies which ~ leaves.* 나뭇잎처럼 보이도록 의태하는 나비들이 있다. [*mime*]

mim·icked [mímikt] *v.* p. and pp. of **mimic.**

mim·ick·ing [mímikiŋ] *v.* ppr. of **mimic.**

mim·ic·ry [mímikri] *n.* (*pl.* **-ries**) **1** Ⓤ the act of mimicking. 흉내; 모방. **2** Ⓒ a mimic play or drama. 흉내〔익살〕극. **3** 《biol.》 the resemblance of an animal to its surroundings. 의태(擬態). [→mimic]

mi·mo·sa [mimóusə, -zə] *n.* Ⓒ 《bot.》 a low tree with heads of white or pink flowers. 함수초(含羞草). [↑]

min·a·ret [mìnərét, ˊ-ˋ] *n.* Ⓒ a tall, slender tower of a Mohammedan temple. (회교 사원의) 뾰족탑; 첨탑. [Arab.]

mince [mins] *vt.* (P6) **1** cut (meat, etc.) into small pieces. (고기 따위)를 다지다. ¶ *minced meat* 다진 고기 / *~ onions* 파를 다지다. **2** 《*fig.*》 speak with assumed delicacy; express in a mild way. 에둘러〔조심스럽게〕 말하다. ¶ *do not ~ matters* 〔*one's words*〕 사실대로〔까놓고〕 말하다 / *He minced no words in his accusation.* 사정없이 비난했다. — *vi.* speak or walk in an affected manner. 점잔빼며 말하다〔걷다〕. ¶ *It was a funny sight to see him ~ along.* 그가 점잖게 걸어가는 모양을 보노라니 우스웠다. — *n.* Ⓤ meat which has been minced. 다진 고기. [→minute]

mince·meat [mínsmì:t] *n.* Ⓤ a mixture of apples, raisins, etc., sometimes with meat, used as a filling for pies. 민스미트《파이의 재료》.

make mincemeat of, chop into small pieces; destroy utterly; mangle. …을 잘게 토막치다; 결딴내다; 찍 소리 못 하게 하다.

minc·ing [mínsiŋ] *adj.* pretending; too polite. 점잔빼는; 태깔스러운.

minc·ing·ly [mínsiŋli] *adv.* in a mincing manner. 점잔빼며.

⁑**mind** [maind] *n.* **1** Ⓒ the part of a person that thinks, feels, etc. 마음; 정신(opp. body). ¶ *in the back of one's ~* 마음 속으로 / 《*prov.*》 *A sound ~ in a sound body.* 건전한 정신은 건전한 신체에 깃들인다. **2** Ⓒ the way or process of thinking, feeling, etc. 정신 경향〔형태〕; 사고 방식. ¶ *the English ~* 영국혼 / *a frame of ~* 기분 / *a turn of ~* 마음씨; 기질 / 《*prov.*》 *So many men, so many minds.* 십인 십색; 각인 각색. **3** Ⓤ the mental ability or intellect. 지력(知力); 지성(知性); 지능; 머리(opp. heart). ¶ *a man of strong* 〔*weak*〕 *~* 지력이 강한〔약한〕 사람 / *a man of ~* 지성이 있는 사람 / *have a quick ~* 머리(의) 회전이 빠르다. **4** Ⓤ memory; remembrance. 기억(력). ¶ *Out of sight, out of ~.* 헤어지면 정도 멀어진다 / *bring* 〔*call*〕 *to ~* 기억해내다; 상기하다 / *pass out of ~* 잊어버리다. **5** Ⓒ 《often. *collectively*》 a person who has a mind of a certain kind. (마음의 소유주로서의) 사람; 인간. ¶ *the greatest minds of the world* 세계 최고의 위인들 / *the artistic* 〔*scientific*〕 *~* 예술적〔과학적〕 정신의 소유자. **6** Ⓒ ⓐ what a person thinks, feels, etc.; opinion. 생각; 느낌. ¶ *speak* *one's* ~ 자기 생각을 말하다 / *in my* ~ 내 생각으로는 / *change one's* ~ 생각을 바꾸다 / *open one's* ~ *to someone* 아무에게 생각〔마음〕을 털어놓다 / *meeting of minds* 의견의 일치. ⓑ a liking; a desire; an inclination. 기호; 의향; 희망. ¶ *I have a great* ~ *to do it.* 그렇게 하고 싶은 생각이 굴뚝 같다 / *have half a* ~ *to do* …할 생각이 없는 것도 아니다. **7** Ⓤ sound condition of the mind; reason; health of mind. 제정신; 이성. ¶ *be* 〔*go*〕 *out of one's* ~ 제정신이 아니다〔발광하다〕 / *be in one's right* ~ 정신이 온전하다; 제정신이다 / *Is he in his right* ~ ? 그 사람 제정신이냐.

apply 〔***bend***〕 ***the mind to*** (=*work hard at*) *something.* …에 마음을 쏟다.

bear 〔***have, keep***〕 *something* ***in mind,*** remember something. …을 기억하고 있다; 염두에 두고 있다.

be of a 〔***one***〕 ***mind,*** agree. 같은 의견이다.

give *someone* ***a piece*** 〔***bit***〕 ***of*** *one's* ***mind,*** tell someone bluntly or plainly what one thinks; blame or scold someone. …에게 기탄없이 말하다〔비난하다, 꾸짖다〕.

give *one's* ***mind*** (=*direct one's attention or one's effort*) ***to*** *something.* …에 마음을 쏟다〔전념하다〕.

have a good mind to *do,* be very willing to; be almost resolved to do. …할 생각이 간절하다.

have a mind to *do,* intend to do or think of doing. …할 마음이 있다〔의향이다〕.

have *something* ***on*** 〔***upon***〕 *one's* ***mind,*** be troubled about something. …을 염려〔걱정〕하고 있다. ¶ *I have a lot of trouble on my* ~ . 걱정이 태산 같다.

make up *one's* ***mind*** (=*decide*) ***to*** *do.* …을 하려고 결심〔작정〕하다.

put *someone* ***in mind of,*** remind someone of (something). …에게 —을 기억나게 하다〔상기시키다〕.

take *one's* ***mind off,*** turn one's attention away from (something). …에서 관심을 딴 데로 돌리다.

turn *one's* ***mind*** (=*direct one's attention or thoughts*) ***to*** *something.* …에 주의〔조심〕하다; …에 주의를 돌리다〔관심을 가지다〕.

— *vt.* **1** (P6,12) direct one's mind to; attend to (something); be careful of (something); give head to; obey; follow. …에 주의를 기울이다; 조심하다; …을 지키다〔따르다〕. ¶ ~ *rules* 규칙에 따르다 / *Mind what I tell you.* 내가 한 말을 명심해라 / *Mind your step.* 조심해서 걸어라; 신중히 행동해라 / ~ *one's father* 아버지 말에 따르다 / 《*sl.*》 *Mind your eye!* 잘 봐라; 조심해라 / *Mind your head!* 머리 조심〔숙여라〕《낮은 곳 등에서》 / *Mind the dog.* 개조심《게시》 / *Mind your own business.* 네 할 일이나 해라. **2** (P7) take care of or look after (someone or something); tend. …을 돌보다; 보살피다. ¶ ~ *the baby* 애를 돌보다 / ~ *the house* 가사를 돌보다 / ~ *the shop* 가게를 지키다. **3** (P6,9,12) ⓐ 《chiefly in *negative* or *interrogative*》 be troubled by or feel an objection to (something). …을 귀찮게 여기다; 꺼리다; …에 신경쓰다; …을 싫어하다. ¶ *"Do you* ~ *opening the window?" "No, not at all."* 문 좀 열어도 되겠습니까. 예, 좋습니다 / *"Do you* ~ *my smoking?" "No, I don't* ~ *it."* 담배 좀 피워도 괜찮을까. 응, 괜찮아 〔參考〕 승낙의 대답을 할 때 No(=I don't mind.)가 됨에 주의 / *I will talk with your mother, if you don't* ~. 괜찮다면 자네 어머니와 얘기 좀 할까 한다. ⓑ care 〔worry〕 about; be concerned. …을 염려하다; 걱정하다. ¶ *Never* ~ (*about*) *cost.* 비용은 걱정 마라 / *Don't* ~ *what other people say.* 남들이 뭐라 하든 신경 쓸 것 없다.

— *vi.* (P1) **1** be careful. 주의하다; 조심하다. ¶ *If you don't* ~ , *you will fall down.* 조심하지 않으면 넘어진다 / *Mind and write to me.* 잊지 말고 내게 편지해라 / *Mind out!* 조심해라. **2** feel dislike; care; object. 안 좋아하다; 반대하다; 신경쓰다. ¶ *Never* ~ (*about that*). (그것에 대해선) 걱정할 것 없다 / *Do you* ~ *if I open the window?* =*Would you* ~ *if I opened the window?* 문을 좀 열어도 괜찮을까. 〔參考〕 가정법이 더 공손한 말씨임 / *Come to the party if you don't* ~. 괜찮다면 파티에 나오시오. [E.]

mind you, please note, observe, listen, etc. 알겠나《주의해라, 잘 들어둬 등》.

(-)mind·ed [(-)máindid] *adj.* **1** having a mind to do something; inclined. …하고 싶어하는; …할 마음이 있는. ¶ *He was not so* ~. 그는 그다지 마음이 내키지 않았다 / *be* ~ *to swim* 수영하고 싶어하다. **2** 《in *compounds*》 having a certain kind of mind. …한 마음〔성격〕의. ¶ *high-minded* 고결한 마음의 / *strong-minded* 의지가 강한 / *weak-minded* 심약한. [*mind*]

mind·er [máindər] *n.* Ⓒ 《usu. in *compound*》 a person who takes care. 돌보는〔지키는〕 사람. ¶ *a baby-minder* 아기 보는 사람 / *a machine-minder* 기계 관리인.

mind·ful [máindfəl] *adj.* 《often *of*》 attentive; careful; aware of. 잊지 않는; 주의 깊은; 경계하는.

mind·less [máindlis] *adj.* **1** without mind, thought, or consciousness; senseless. 지각 없는; 어리석은. ¶ *a* ~ *person* 〔*act*〕 어리석은 사람〔짓〕. **2** 《usu. *of*》 careless of; not paying attention to. 조심성 없는; 무관심한. ¶ ~ *of what is going to happen* 무엇이 어떻게 되든 무관심한.

:mine[1] [main] *pron.* a possessive form of **I**; the one or ones belonging to me. 나의 것; 내 것. ¶ *a friend of* ~ 내 친구 / *He was kind to me and* ~. 그는 내게 잘해 줬고 내 친척한테도 그랬다. — *adj.* 《before *a vowel* or *h-*》 《*poet., arch.*》 my. ¶ ~ *eyes* 내 눈 / ~ *heart* 내 마음. [E.]

·mine[2] [main] *n.* Ⓒ **1** a tunnel or deep hole for taking metals, coal, etc., from the earth. 광갱(鑛坑); 광산(cf. *quarry*[1]). ¶ *a coal* ~ 탄광 / *gold* ~ 금광 / *the mines* 광업; 광산업. **2** 《*fig.*》 a rich source. 풍부한 자원; 보고(寶庫). ¶ *a* ~ *of information* 지식의 보고 / *a* ~ *wealth* 부원(富源). **3** a bomb buried under the ground or in the sea. 지뢰; 수뢰; 기뢰(機雷). **4** a secret plot. 비밀 계획.

— *vt.* (P6) **1** dig a passage in. (채굴하려고) …에 갱도를 파다. ¶ ~ *the earth for coal* 〔*gold*〕 석탄〔금〕을 캐려고 땅을 파다. **2** get from a mine. …을 채굴하다; 캐내다. ¶ ~ *coal* 〔*gold*〕 석탄〔금〕을 채굴하다. **3** make an underground passage to and blow up by means of a landmine. …의 밑에 폭발갱(坑)을 파다; …을 지뢰로 폭파하다. ¶ ~ *the wall of a fortress* 성벽을 폭파시키다. **4** lay mines on land or in sea. …에 지뢰〔기뢰〕를 매설하다. ¶ *The navy mined the mouth of the harbor.* 해군은 항구 어귀에 수뢰를 매설했다 / *The ship was mined.* 배는 기뢰로 폭파됐다. **5** 《*fig.*》 destroy (something) by secret means. (은밀한 수단으로) 전복시키다. ¶ *His political career was mined.* (음모 등으로) 그의 정치 생명은 끝장났다.

— *vi.* (Pl,2) **1** dig for coal, etc.; work in a mine. 채탄〔채굴〕하다. ¶ ~ *for gold* 금을 채굴하다. **2** lay mines on land or sea. 지뢰〔기뢰〕를 매설하다. [E.]

mine field [ˊ ˋ] *n.* Ⓒ **1** a land where mines are kept. 광석 매장지. **2** a land or sea where there are explosive mines. 지뢰〔기뢰〕밭. [*mine*[2]]

***min·er** [máinər] *n.* Ⓒ a person working in a mine. 광부; 갱부.

:min·er·al [mínərəl] *n.* Ⓒ **1** a substance having a constant chemical composition; a substance obtained by mining. 광물; 광석. **2** 《usu. *pl.*》 a mineral spring; 《Brit. *colloq.*》 mineral water. 광천; 광천수(鑛泉水); 탄산수. **3** any substance that is neither plant nor animal. 무기물(無機物).

— *adj.* of or containing minerals; not organic. 광물의; 광물을 함유하는; 무기의. ¶ ~ *oil* 광유(鑛油) [*mine*[2]]

min·er·al·ize [mínərəlàiz] *vt.* (P6) **1** convert into mineral substance. …을 광물화〔광화(鑛化)〕하다. ¶ *Coal is mineralized vegetation.* 석탄은 식물이 광물화한 것이다. **2** fill or supply with minerals. …에 광물〔무기물〕을 함유시키다. ¶ *mineralized water* 탄산수.

— *vi.* (Pl,2A,3) search for or collect minerals for study. 광물 채집을〔연구를〕 하다.

min·er·al·o·gist [mìnərǽlədʒist / -lɔ́dʒ-] *n.* Ⓒ a student of mineralogy. 광물학자.

min·er·al·o·gy [mìnərɑ́lədʒi, -rǽlə-] *n.* Ⓤ the science of minerals. 광물학.

Mi·ner·va [minə́ːrvə] *n.* 《Rom. myth.》 goddess of wisdom, defensive of war and arts. 미네르바《지혜·전쟁·기예의 여신》. 參考 그리스 신화의 Athena 에 해당함. [L.]

mine sweeper [ˊ ˋ-] *n.* a ship for removing mines at sea, etc. 소해정(掃海艇). [→mine[2]]

***min·gle** [míŋgəl] *vt.* (P6,13) 《*with*》 combine by mixing; mix. 섞다; 혼합하다. ¶ ~ *wine and water* 포도주와 물을 섞다 / *with mingled feeling* 희비가 엇갈려; 만감이 서려.

— *vi.* 《*in, with*》 mix; join. 섞이다; 사귀다; 참가하다. ¶ *The colors don't* ~ *well.* 색이 잘 배합되지 않는다 / *He mingled in the crowd.* 그는 군중 속으로 사라졌다. [E.]

***min·i·a·ture** [míniətʃər, -tʃùər] *n.* Ⓒ **1** a very small painting, usually a portrait. 세밀화(법); 미니어처. **2** anything represented on a small scale; a small model. 축도; 작은 모형.

in miniature, on a small scale. 소규모로; 소형의; 세밀화로.

— *adj.* done on a small scale. 소형의. ¶ *a* ~ *edition* 축쇄판 / *a* ~ *camera.*

— *vt.* copy (something) on a small scale. …을 축사(縮寫)하다. [L. *minium* red lead]

min·im [mínəm] *n.* 《mus.》 a musical note that has a time value equal to half a semibreve. 2분 음표. [L. *minimus* least]

min·i·ma [mínəmə] *n.* pl. of **minimum.**

min·i·mize [mínəmàiz] *vt.* (P6) **1** make (something) as small as possible; estimate (something) at the smallest degree. …을 최소한으로 하다; 최저로 어림잡다. ¶ *These devices* ~ *the danger of the flight.* 이들 장치는 비행에 따르는 위험을 최소화시킨다. **2** hold (someone) cheap; make the least of. …을 얕보다. ¶ *I don't want to* ~ *your services.* 나는 네 수고를 하찮게 보고 싶지는 않다. [L. *minimus* smallest, least]

***min·i·mum** [mínəməm] *n.* Ⓒ (*pl.* **-mums** or **-ma**) the smallest amount possible; the least. 최소한; 극소(opp. maximum). ¶ *with a* ~ *of effort* 최소의 노력으로 / *The thermometer reached the* ~ *for the year.* 온도계는 그 해의 최저 온도를 기록했다. — *adj.* smallest possible; lowest. 최소〔최저〕의. ¶ ~ *wages* 최저 임금. [↑]

***min·ing** [máiniŋ] *n.* Ⓤ **1** the work of getting coal, etc. from the ground. 채광; 채탄; 광업. ¶ *a* ~ *engineer* 광산 기사. **2** 《mil.》 the act or process of laying mines. 지뢰〔기뢰〕 부설. [*mine*[2]]

min·ion [mínjən] *n.* Ⓒ **1** a favorite. 총아. ¶ *a* ~ *of fortune* 운명의 총아; 행운아. **2** a servant who obeys a master without question. (무조건 복종하는) 하인. **3** a servile follower. 앞잡이. ¶ *a* ~ *of the law* 경관; 간수. [→mignon]

:min·is·ter [mínistər] *n.* Ⓒ **1** 《often *M-*》 the head of a government department. 장관(cf. *secretary*). ¶ *the Prime Minister* 국무 총리; 수상 / *the Ministers* 각료 / *the Minister of* 〔*for*〕 *Foreign Affairs* 외무부 장관. **2** a person representing his own government in a foreign country. 공사(公使)(cf. *ambassador*). **3** a clergyman. 목사. **4**

a servant; an agent. 하인; 대리인; 대행자. ¶ *act as* ~ *of* 〔*to*〕 *another's desires* 〔*pleasures, will*〕 남의 욕구〔의지〕를 위해 힘쓰다. — *vi.* (P3) 《*to*》 give help or service to (someone); contribute. 섬기다; 돕다; 공헌〔이바지〕하다. ¶ ~ *to the sick* 환자를 보살피다 / ~ *to someone's comfort* 아무의 마음을 편하게 해주다. [L. =servant]

min·is·te·ri·al [mìnəstíəriəl] *adj.* **1** of a minister; executive. 장관의; 내각의; 행정상의; 정부의. ¶ *a* ~ *change* 내각의 경질 / *a* ~ *office* 장관직 / ~ *prestige* 정부의 위신 / *the* ~ *party* 여당. **2** serving as a minister or an agent; subordinate. 대리의; 보조의; 종속적인. ¶ ~ *services* 보조적인 일.

min·is·trant [mínistrənt] *adj.* ministering. 섬기는; 봉사의. — *n.* Ⓒ a person who helps or supports. 돕는 사람; 조력〔보조〕자.

min·is·tra·tion [mìnəstréiʃən] *n.* Ⓤ the act of serving as a clergyman. 목사의 직무; 봉사.

***min·is·try** [mínistri] *n.* Ⓒ (*pl.* **-tries**) **1** the office, function, or time of service of a minister or clergyman. 장관·목사의 직무〔임기〕. **2** 《often *M-*》 《*collectively*》 all the ministers of a state; the Cabinet; the department under a minister of government. 각료; 장관(들); 내각; 부(部); 성(省). ¶ *the Ministry of Foreign Affairs* 외무부. [*minister*]

mink [miŋk] *n.* **1** Ⓒ an animal like a weasel living on land and in water. 밍크. **2** Ⓤ its valuable fur. 밍크 모피. [Sw.]

Minn. Minnesota.

Min·ne·so·ta [mìnəsóutə] *n.* a middle northern State of the United States. 미네소타 주(州). 參考 Minn.으로 생략함. 주도는 St. Paul.

Min·ne·so·tan [minəsóutən] *n.* Ⓒ a person of Minnesota. 미네소타 사람. — *adj.* of Minnesota. 미네소타의.

min·now [mínou] *n.* Ⓒ (*pl.* **-nows** or *collectively* **-now**) **1** a small fresh-water fish. 황어·피라미류(類). **2** 《U.S.》 any very small fish. 작은 물고기. ¶ *throw out a* ~ *to catch a whale* 새우로 고래를 낚다; 작은 밑천으로 큰 이득을 얻다. [E.]

***mi·nor** [máinər] *adj.* (opp. major) **1** less; smaller; not important; inferior. 작은 쪽의; 중요하지 않은; 2류의. ¶ *a* ~ *poets* 이류 시인 / *of* ~ *importance* 별로 중요하지 않은 / *a* ~ *premise* 소전제(小前提) / *a* ~ *fault* 사소한 실수. **2** 《mus.》 less by half a tone than the major interval. 단음의; 단조(短調)의. ¶ *the* ~ *scale* 단음계. **3** 《Brit.》 the second or younger. 손아래〔어린 쪽〕의(cf. *junior*). ¶ *Brown* ~ 작은 브라운. — *n.* Ⓒ **1** a person under full legal age. 미성년자. **2** 《log.》 a minor term 〔premise〕. 소명사(小名辭); 소개념; 소전제. **3** 《mus.》 the minor scale. 단음계. ¶ *Violin concerto in E* ~ 마단조 바이올린 협주곡. **4** 《U.S.》 a minor subject or field of study. 부(副)전공 과목. [L. =less]

in a minor key, in a sad mood. 우울한 기분으로.

***mi·nor·i·ty** [minɔ́ːriti, -nάr-, mai-] *n.* (*pl.* **-ties**) **1** Ⓒ the smaller number; the smaller of two parties; less than half of a total. 소수; 소수당; 소수파(opp. majority). **2** Ⓤ the state of being under full legal age. 미성년.

Mi·nos [máinəs, -nαs / -nɔs] *n.* 《Gk. myth.》 a king and lawgiver of Crete. 미노스《크레타 섬의 왕》.

Min·o·taur [mínətɔ̀ːr, máinə-] *n.* 《Gk. myth.》 a monster with the body of a man and the head of a bull. 미노타우로스《인신 우두(人身牛頭)의 괴물》.

min·ster [mínstər] *n.* **1** the church of an abbey or monastery. 수도원 부속의 성당. **2** a large church. 대성당. [→monastery]

min·strel [mínstrəl] *n.* Ⓒ **1** a wandering singer, musician, or poet of the Middle Ages. (중세의) 음유(吟遊) 시인. **2** 《*pl.*》 a group of blackened face performers who sing Negro songs. 흑인으로 분장하여 흑인 노래를 부르는 순회 극단. [→minister]

min·strel·sy [mínstrəlsi] *n.* Ⓤ **1** 《*collectively*》 minstrels. 음유(吟遊) 시인. **2** the art or songs of minstrels. 음유 시인의 연예〔시〕. **3** the singing and poetry of minstrels. (음유 시인의) 시가(詩歌). [↑]

***mint**[1] [mint] *n.* Ⓒ 《bot.》 a sweet-smelling plant whose leaves are used for flavoring. 박하. [Gk.]

mint[2] [mint] *n.* Ⓒ **1** a place where coins are made under government authority. 조폐국. **2** a large sum. 거액; 대량. ¶ *a* ~ *of money* / *a* ~ *of trouble* 허다한 고생. **3** the source of supply or invention. 근원; 재원(財源). — *adj.* new, as if freshly coined. (조폐국 등에서) 갓 나온; 아주 새로운.

in mint state 〔***condition***〕, (of books, stamps, etc.) fresh. 아주 새로운; 갓 만든《책·우표 등》.

— *vt.* (P6) **1** coin (money); (화폐)를 주조하다. **2** 《*fig.*》 invent (new words, idea, etc.). (신어(新語) 따위)를 만들어내다. [L. *Moneta* a goddess]

mint·age [míntidʒ] *n.* Ⓤ **1** the act or process of minting; the product of minting. 화폐 주조; 주조 화폐. **2** the charge for coining. 주화료(鑄貨料). [*mint*[2]]

min·u·et [mìnjuét] *n.* Ⓒ a slow and graceful dance in triple time; the music for this. 미뉴에트《3박자의 우아한 춤》; 그 춤곡(曲). [→minute]

:mi·nus [máinəs] *adj.* less; showing subtraction; negative. 마이너스의; 음(陰)의 (opp. plus). ¶ ~ *electricity* 음전기(電氣). — *prep.* less; wanting; without; taken away from. 마이너스의; …만큼 적은; …이 없는; …을 뺀. ¶ *7* ~ *3 is 4.* / *He came back* ~ *an arm.* 한쪽 팔을 잃고 돌아왔다. — *n.* Ⓒ

1 a minus sign; a negative quantity. 마이너스 부호(−); 음수. ¶ *a grade of A- minus,* A마이너스의 등급. **2** a loss, deficiency, or disadvantage. 손실; 결손. ¶ *a terrible* ~ 대손실. [→minor]

:min·ute[1] [mínit] *n.* Ⓒ **1** sixty seconds; the sixtieth part of an hour or of a degree. (시간·각도의) 분(分). ¶ *a* ~ *hand* (시계의) 분침 / *in a few minutes,* 2·3분내로; 곧 / *ten minutes later,* 10분 후에 / *60 minutes of an angle make one degree* 각도에선 60분이 1도이다 / *five degrees six minutes,* 5도 6분. **2** a moment; an instant. 순간; 잠시. ¶ *in a* ~ 곧; 즉시 / *Wait a* ~. 잠깐 기다려 / *I expect her every*〔*any*〕 ~. 그녀를 이제나 저제나 하고 기다리고 있다 / *Come this* ~*!* 지금 당장 오너라 / *I shan't be a* ~. 곧 돌아오마. **3** a short note or memo. 각서; 메모. ¶ *make a* ~ *of* …의 각서를 만들다; …을 메모해 두다. **4** 《*pl.*》 an official record of a meeting. 의사〔회의〕록. ¶ *keep the minutes of the meeting* 회의록을 적어두다.

the minute (***that***)**,** as soon as. …하자마자; …하자 곧. ¶ *The* ~ (*that*) *I saw him, he ran away.* 내가 보자 그는 달아나버렸다 / *The* ~ *you see him coming, please tell me.* 그가 오는 대로 알려주시오.

to the minute, at the exact time; punctually. 정각에.

up to the minute, up to date. 최신의.

— *vt.* (P6) **1** take the time of exactly. …의 시간을 정확히 재다. ¶ ~ *a race* 레이스 시간을 정밀하게 재다. **2** note down (proceedings). …을 기록하다. [L. *minuo* make small]

***mi·nute**[2] [mainjú:t, mi-] *adj.* **1** (of size, scale, time, etc.) very small; not important. 아주 작은; 사소한. ¶ ~ *particles* 미립자 / *be troubled with* ~ *differences* 하찮은 차이로 고민하다. **2** exact; precise; careful. 정밀한; 자세한; 꼼꼼한. ¶ *a* ~ *inquiry* 자세한 문의 / *give* ~ *instructions* 사용법을 상세히 일러주다. [↑]

min·ute·ly[1] [mínitli] *adv.* every minute; often. 1분마다; 자주. [→minute[1]]

mi·nute·ly[2] [mainjú:tli, mi-] *adv.* in a minute manner or in great detail; precisely. 상세하게; 세세히; 정밀하게. [→minute[2]]

mi·nute·ness [mainjú:tnis, mi-] *n.* Ⓤ the quality of being very small; precise attention; exactness. 자디잚; 미세; 상세.

minx [miŋks] *n.* Ⓒ an impolite or wild girl or woman. 말괄량이; 왈가닥. [G.]

***mir·a·cle** [mírəkəl] *n.* Ⓒ a very marvelous event; any wonderful happening; a remarkable thing. 기적; 불가사의한 사물. ¶ *escape by a* ~ 기적적으로 달아나다 / *work*〔*do, perform*〕 *miracles* 기적을 행하다〔이루다〕 / *to a* ~ 기적적으로 / *a* ~ *skill* 경이적인 기술. [L. *mirus* wonderful]

miracle play [ˊ-- ˋ] *n.* a kind of drama popular in the Middle Ages, based on the life of Christ or the saints. (중세의) 기적극.

mi·rac·u·lous [mirǽkjələs] *adj.* like a miracle; wonderful; supernatural. 기적 같은; 불가사의한.

mi·rac·u·lous·ly [mirǽkjələsli] *adv.* in a miraculous manner; by a miracle. 기적적으로; 불가사의하게; 초자연적으로.

mi·rage [mirá:ʒ / ˊ-] *n.* Ⓒ **1** an image of a distant object, often upside down, seen as if it were near, esp. in the desert. 신기루. **2** 《*fig.*》 an illusion; a deceiving fancy; an unrealizable hope. 몽상; 덧없는 희망. ¶ *pursue the* ~ *of fame* 덧없는 명성을 추구하다. [→miracle]

mire [maiər] *n.* Ⓤ the wet ground; soft, deep mud. 습지; 진창.

drag through the mire, 《*fig.*》 put (someone) to shame; scorn. 아무를 창피주다.

find 〔***stick***〕 *oneself* ***in the mire,*** be in a dilemma. 궁지에 빠지다; 빼도 박도 못하게 되다.

— *vt.* (P6) **1** soil or cover (something) with mud; cause to be stuck in mud. …을 진흙으로 더럽히다; 진창에 빠뜨리다. ¶ ~ *the wheels of a cart* 달구지 바퀴를 진창에 빠지게 하다. **2** 《*fig.*》 involve someone in difficulties. …을 곤경에 몰아넣다.

— *vi.* (P1) get stuck in mire; sink in mud. 진창에 빠지다. [N.]

:mir·ror [mírər] *n.* Ⓒ **1** a looking glass; a surface reflecting an image. 거울. ¶ *a rearview* 〔*driving*〕 ~ (자동차의) 백미러 / *look at oneself in the* ~ 거울에 자기 모습을 비춰보다. **2** anything which gives a true likeness; a model; an example. 모범; 귀감; 본보기. ¶ *a* ~ *of what a man ought to be* 인생살이의 본보기. — *vt.* (P6) reflect (something) in a mirror. …을 비추다; 반영하다. ¶ *Do these opinion polls really* ~ *what people are thinking?* 이들 여론 조사가 진정한 민의를 반영하고 있는가. [→miracle]

***mirth** [mə:rθ] *n.* Ⓤ joyfulness; merriment; gladness. 쾌활; 명랑; 환희; 유쾌. [→merry]

mirth·ful [mə́:rθfəl] *adj.* merry; full of mirth. 유쾌한; 즐거운.

mirth·ful·ly [mə́:rθfəli] *adv.* in a mirthful manner. 즐겁게; 유쾌〔명랑〕하게.

mir·y [máiəri] *adj.* (**mir·i·er, mir·i·est**) muddy; swampy; dirty. 진흙투성이의; 진창의; 더러운. [→mire]

mis- [mis-] *pref.* bad(ly); wrong(ly); misprint. '나쁜, 틀린, 그릇된' 등의 뜻. ¶ *misread / misuse.* [E.]

mis·ad·ven·ture [mìsədvéntʃər] *n.* ⓊⒸ bad luck; a misfortune; an unlucky accident. 불행; 불운; 재난. ¶ *by* ~ 운수 나쁘게; 실수로. [mis-]

mis·al·li·ance [mìsəláiəns] *n.* Ⓒ an improper alliance, esp. in marriage. 지체가 다른〔어울리지 않는〕 결혼. [mis-]

mis·an·thrope [mísənθròup, míz-] *n.* Ⓒ a person who hates or distrusts human beings. 사람을 싫어하는 사람; 염세가(厭世家). [Gk. *miseō* hate, *anthrōpos* man]

mis·an·throp·ic [mìsənθrápik, mìz- / -θrɔ́p-] *adj.* hating or distrusting mankind or human society. 사람을 싫어하는; 염세적인.

mis·an·thro·py [misǽnθrəpi, miz-] *n.* Ⓤ hatred or distrust of human beings or human society. 인간 기피〔불신〕; 염세.

mis·ap·pli·ca·tion [mìsæplikéiʃən] *n.* Ⓤ the act of misapplying; the state of being misapplied. 오용(誤用); 악용. [↓]

mis·ap·ply [mìsəplái] *vt.* (P6) **1** use badly or wrongly; apply dishonestly. …을 잘못 쓰다; 오용〔남용〕하다. ¶ ~ *one's gifts* 〔*opportunities*〕 자기의 재능을〔기회를〕 그릇 쓰다. **2** use dishonestly. …을 악용하다. ¶ ~ *money entrusted to one* 맡긴 돈을 유용하다. [mis-]

mis·ap·pre·hend [mìsæprihénd] *vt.* (P6) misunderstand; apprehend wrongly. …을 오해하다; 잘못 생각하다. [mis-]

mis·ap·pre·hen·sion [mìsæprihénʃən] *n.* Ⓤ the act of misapprehending; Ⓒ a mistaken idea. 오해; 잘못 생각하기. [↑]

mis·ap·pro·pri·ate [mìsəpróuprièit] *vt.* (P6,13) **1** take and use (something) wrongly; use for a wrong purpose. …을 잘못 쓰다; 악용하다. **2** use (another person's money) as one's own. (남의 것)을 횡령〔착복〕하다. ¶ *The treasurer had misappropriated the funds for his own use.* 경리가 그 기금을 착복해 버렸다. [mis-]

mis·ap·pro·pri·a·tion [mìsəpròupriéiʃən] *n.* Ⓤ **1** the act of misappropriating. 남용; 악용. **2** dishonest use (of money, etc.) as one's own. 횡령; 착복. [↑]

mis·ar·range [mìsəréindʒ] *vt.* (P6) arrange (things) improperly. …을 잘못 배열하다.

mis·be·come [mìsbikʌ́m] *vt.* (**-be·came, -be·come**) (P6) be unfit for. 맞지 않다; 어울리지 않다. [mis-]

mis·be·got·ten [mìsbigátn / -gɔ́tn] *adj.* illegitimate; bastard. 서출(庶出)의; 사생아의.

mis·be·have [mìsbihéiv] *vi., vt.* (P1;6) behave badly; conduct oneself badly. 무례한 행동을 하다; 나쁜 짓을 하다. ¶ ~ *oneself* 무례하게〔못되게〕 굴다.

mis·be·haved [mìsbihéivd] *adj.* rough; impolite; rude. 행실이 나쁜; 못된.

mis·be·hav·ior, 《Brit.》 **-iour** [mìsbihéivjər] *n.* wrong or improper behavior. 나쁜 행실; 버릇없음; 부정 행위.

mis·be·lief [mìsbilí:f] *n.* Ⓤ a wrong, false belief or opinion, esp. in religion. 사교(邪敎) 신앙; 그릇된 신앙〔생각〕.

mis·be·liev·er [mìsbilí:vər] *n.* Ⓒ a person who has a wrong belief, esp. in religion. 사교(邪敎)를 믿는 사람; 이교도.

mis·cal·cu·late [miskǽlkjəlèit] *vt., vi.* (P6; 1) **1** calculate (amounts, etc.) incorrectly; miscount. 잘못 계산하다. ¶ ~ *the distance between two cars* 두 차량간의 거리를 잘못 계산하다. **2** form a wrong judgment. 잘못 짚다; 오산하다. ¶ *If she thinks I'll agree to that she's miscalculated badly.* 내가 그것에 동의하리라 생각한다면 그녀의 큰 오산이다. [mis-]

mis·cal·cu·la·tion [mìskælkjəléiʃən] *n.* Ⓤ the act of miscalculating. 잘못 계산함.

mis·call [mìskɔ́:l] *vt.* (P6) call (someone) by a wrong name. …의 이름을 잘못 부르다.

mis·car·riage [mìskǽridʒ] *n.* **1** Ⓤ the state of failure or error; Ⓒ an error; a failure. 실수; 실패; 실책. ¶ *a ~ of justice* 오심(誤審). **2** Ⓤ failure in sending mail, etc. (편지 따위의) 불착(不着); 잘못 배달됨. ¶ *the ~ of goods* 〔*a letter*〕. **3** ⓊⒸ the birth of a baby before it has grown enough to live. 유산. ¶ *have a ~* 유산하다. [mis-, →carriage]

mis·car·ry [mìskǽri] *vi.* (**-ried**) (P1) **1** (of a plan, etc.) fail; go wrong. 실패하다. ¶ *All his plans miscarried.* 그의 계획은 모조리 실패했다. **2** (of a letter, etc.) go astray; fail to reach the destination. (편지 등이) 배달되지 않다. ¶ *My letter to mother must have miscarried.* 어머니에게 부친 편지가 가지 않았음에 틀림없다. **3** give birth to a child before the proper time. 유산하다.

mis·cast [mìskǽst, -ká:st] *vt.* (**-cast**) (P6) give (an actor) a part or role not fit for him. (배우)에게 부적당한 역을 맡기다; 배역을 그르치다. ¶ *He was badly ~ as Julius Caesar.* 율리우스 카이사르역을 그에게 맡긴 것은 아주 잘못이었다. [mis-]

mis·ce·ge·na·tion [mìsidʒənéiʃən] *n.* interbreeding of races, between whites and non-whites. 백인과 유색 인종 간의 결혼〔잡혼〕. [L. *miscere* mix, *genus*]

mis·cel·la·ne·ous [mìsəléiniəs] *adj.* **1** formed of various kinds. 가지가지의; 잡다한. ¶ ~ *goods* 잡화(雜貨). **2** having various qualities; many-sided. 다방면의. ● **mis·cel·la·ne·ous·ly** [-li] *adv.* [↓]

mis·cel·la·ny [mísəlèini / miséləni] *n.* (*pl.* **-nies**) **1** Ⓒ a mixture of various kinds of things. 혼합물. **2** 《often *pl.*》 a book that consists of various authors' writings. 여러 사람의 글을 한데 실은 책; 잡록(雜錄)(cf. *medley*). ¶ *a ~ of American short story* 미국 단편 소설집. [→mix]

mis·chance [mistʃǽns, -tʃá:ns] *n.* **1** Ⓤ bad or hard luck. 불행. **2** Ⓒ a piece of bad luck. 불상사. [mis-]

by mischance, by mistake; unhappily. 잘못돼서; 운 나쁘게; 불행하게(도). ¶ *By sheer ~ the letter was sent to the wrong address.* 불행하게도 편지가 다른 주소로 보내졌다.

•**mis·chief** [místʃif] *n.* (*pl.* **-chiefs**) **1** Ⓤ the act of doing thoughtless tricks. 장난. ¶ *keep children out of ~* 아이들이 장난치지 못하게 해두다 / *Children's ~ may cause* *serious harm.* 아이들의 장난이 큰 일을 낼 수도 있다 / *The boy is up to* ~. 소년은 장난을 꾸미고 있다. **2** Ⓒ 《*sl.*》 a person making mischief. 장난치는 사람. ¶ *You little* ~. 요 장난꾸러기야. **3** Ⓤ harm; damage. 해; 재해. ¶ *do someome a* ~ 아무를 해치다. **4** simple fun; merry teasing. 짓궂음. ¶ *The girl looked at me with her eyes full of* ~. 소녀는 장난기 가득찬 눈으로 나를 보았다. **5** 《*the* ~》 《*colloq.*》 the devil. 도대체. ¶ *Where the* ~ *have you been ?* 도대체 어딜 다녀오는 거냐. [mis-, →achieve]

go* 〔*get*〕 *into mischief, begin to do mischief. 장난을 시작하다.

make mischief between, cause people to quarrel. …의 사이를 이간시키다〔헤살놓다〕.

out of mischief, half in fun. 반장난으로.

play the mischief with, put into disorder; injure. …을 망쳐놓다; (건강 등)을 해치다.

mis·chie·vous [místʃivəs] *adj.* **1** causing injury; harmful. 해로운. **2** playful in an annoying way; teasing. 장난을 좋아하는; 짓궂은; 장난기의. ¶ *a* ~ *boy* 개구쟁이 / *a* ~ *glance* 짓궂은 시선 / *a* ~ *prank* 악의 없는 농담. [↑]

mis·chie·vous·ly [místʃivəsli] *adv.* in a mischievous manner. 해롭게; 장난으로.

mis·con·ceive [miskənsíːv] *vt., vi.* (P6; 1) misunderstand; judge incorrectly. 오해하다; 잘못 생각하다. [mis-]

mis·con·cep·tion [miskənsépʃən] *n.* ⓊⒸ a wrong interpretation; a misunderstanding. 오해; 잘못 생각하기.

mis·con·duct [miskándʌkt / -kɔ́n-] *n.* Ⓤ **1** ⓐ wrong behavior or conduct. 부정 행위. ¶ *The* ~ *of the city treasurer resulted in his being put in prison.* 시 경리의 부정 행위는 그의 철창행으로 끝장났다. ⓑ adultery. 간통. **2** bad or dishonest management. 부당한 조처〔관리〕. ¶ *The general was charged with* ~ *of the war.* 장군은 전쟁 수행의 잘못으로 기소되었다.

— [miskəndʌ́kt] *vt.* (P6) **1** behave badly; behave (oneself) improperly. 행실을 그르치다; 부정 행위를 하다. **2** manage badly. …을 잘못하다. ¶ ~ *a business* 장사를 그르치다.

mis·con·struc·tion [miskənstrʌ́kʃən] *n.* ⓊⒸ the state or act of misunderstanding. 그릇된 해석; 오해. ¶ *She put a* ~ *upon his words.* 그녀는 그의 말을 곡해했다.

mis·con·strue [miskənstrúː, miskɔ́n-] *vt.* (P6) understand (someone's words, acts, etc.) wrongly. …의 뜻을 잘못 알다. ¶ *You* ~ *my words.* 넌 내 말을 오해하고 있구나 / *Don't* ~ *what I am about to say.* 내가 하려는 말을 오해하지는 말게. [mis-]

mis·count [miskáunt] *vt., vi.* (P6; 1) count incorrectly; make an error in counting. 오산하다; 잘못 계산하다. — *n.* Ⓒ an incorrect count. 오산.

mis·cre·ant [mískriənt] *adj.* having no conscience; extremely bad. 사악한; 아주 못된. — *n.* Ⓒ a very wicked person; one guilty of an atrocious crime. 악한; 극악 범죄인. [mis-, →creed]

mis·date [misdéit] *vt.* (P6) put a wrong date on (a letter, etc.). (편지 등)에 날짜를 틀리게 쓰다. [mis-]

mis·deal [misdíːl] *vt., vi.* (**-dealt**) (P6; 1) deal (playing-cards) wrongly. (카드패를) 잘못 도르다. — *n.* Ⓒ a wrong deal at cards. (패를) 잘못 도르기.

mis·deed [misdíːd] *n.* Ⓒ a bad deed; a crime. 악행; 부정 행위; 범죄.

mis·de·mean·or, 《Brit.》 **-our** [misdimíːnər] *n.* Ⓒ **1** 《law》 an unlawful but not very serious act. 경범죄. **2** 《rare》 bad behavior. 비행(非行); 그릇된 행실. [mis-, →demean]

mis·did [misdíd] *vt.* p. of **misdo**.

mis·di·rect [misdirékt] *vt.* (P6) **1** direct badly; give wrong directions or instructions to. …을 그릇 이끌다〔지도하다〕. ¶ *He misdirected the tourist.* 그는 관광객의 인솔을 잘못했다. **2** ⓐ aim badly. …을 잘못 겨냥하다. ¶ *a misdirected arrow* 잘못 쏜 화살. ⓑ use or apply mistakenly. …을 그릇되게 쓰다. ¶ ~ *one's energies* 정력을 헛되게 쓰다. **3** put a wrong address on (a letter, etc.) (편지)의 수취인 주소·성명을 잘못 쓰다. ¶ ~ *a letter.* [mis-]

mis·do [misdúː] *vt.* (**-did, -done**) (P6) do wrongly. 잘못하다; 실수하다. ¶ *We all grieve for things misdone.* 잘못한 일에 대해 우리 모두는 개탄했다. [mis-]

mis·do·ing [misdú(ː)iŋ] *n.* Ⓒ a misdeed. 비행; 범행.

***mis·done** [misdʌ́n] *vt.* pp. of **misdo**.

***mi·ser** [máizər] *n.* Ⓒ a person who loves money too much. 구두쇠. [L. =wretched]

mis·er·a·ble [mízərəbəl] *adj.* **1** very unhappy; sad; wretched. 불행〔불쌍〕한; 슬픈; 비참한. ¶ *feel* ~ 서글퍼지다 / *be made* ~ *by unkindness* 푸대접을 받고 처량해지다 / *a* ~ *life* 비참한 생애. **2** causing trouble or unhappiness. 괴로운; 불행한. ¶ *I have a* ~ *cold.* 지독한 감기가 들었다 / ~ *news.* **3** ⓐ of poor quality; scanty. 빈약한; 불충분한. ¶ *a* ~ *dinner* 초라한 만찬 / *You've made a* ~ *meal, I fear.* 변변치 못한 식사라 미안하오. ⓑ poor; mean. 보잘것 없는; 초라한. ¶ *a* ~ *hovel* 초라한 오두막집. **4** contemptible; shameful. 경멸할 만한; 파렴치한. ¶ *a* ~ *liar* 뻔뻔한 거짓말쟁이. [↑]

mis·er·a·bly [mízərəbəli] *adv.* **1** in a miserable manner. 참혹하게. **2** 《*colloq.*》 very. 대단히; 몹시.

mi·ser·ly [máizərli] *adj.* loving money too much; greedy; stingy. 인색한; 주접스러운. [*miser*]

***mis·er·y** [mízəri] *n.* Ⓤ (*pl.* **-er·ies**) **1** the state of great unhappiness; miserable condition. (참혹한) 불행; 비참; 참상. ¶ *the* ~ *of human life* 인생의 고난 / *the* ~ *of* *the slums* 슬럼가의 참상. **2** extreme pain. 고통. ¶ *suffer great ~ from toothache* 심한 치통에 시달리다. [→miser]

mis·fea·sance [misfí:zəns] *n.* the wrongful performance of a lawful act. 불법 행위; 직권 남용(cf. *malfeasance*). [mis-, →fact]

mis·fire [misfáiər, ⌐⌐] *vi.* (P1) **1** (of a gun, etc.) fail to fire. (총포가) 불발하다. **2** (of an internal combustion engine) fail to start action. (내연 기관이) 점화되지 않다. **3** (of a plan, joke, etc.) fail to gain the desired effect. (계획·농담 등이) 소기의 효과를 못 내다. — *n.* Ⓒ a failure to fire, start action, go off, etc. 불발; 점화되지 않음; 실패. [mis-]

mis·fit [mísfìt, −⌐] *n.* **1** Ⓒ something that does not fit well. 맞지 않는 것. ¶ *Do not buy shoes which are misfits.* 발에 안 맞는 신발은 사지 마라. **2** a person who is not suited to his position or environment. (직책·환경 등에) 적응 못 하는 사람; 부적임자. — *vt., vi.* (**-fit·ted, -fit·ting**) (P6; 1) be too large, or too small for (someone or something). 잘 맞지 않다.

·mis·for·tune [misfɔ́:rtʃən] *n.* ⓊⒸ ill fortune; bad luck; an unhappy accident. 불행; 불운; 불행한 사고; 재난. ¶ *Misfortunes never come singly* 〔*single*〕. 화불 단행(禍不單行) / *It was his ~, not his fault.* 그것은 그가 운이 나빴던 탓이지 잘못은 아니었다.

mis·gave [misgéiv] *v.* p. of **misgive.**

mis·give [misgív] *vt.* (**-gave, -giv·en**) (P6,13, 15) cause (someone) to have doubt, fear, etc. …을 의심〔염려〕하게 하다. ¶ *Her heart misgave her that she might fail.* 그녀는 실패하지나 않을까 불안해졌다. [mis-]

mis·giv·en [misgívən] *v.* pp. of **misgive.**

mis·giv·ing [misgíviŋ] *n.* Ⓒ a feeling of suspicion; Ⓤ doubt. 불안; 의혹.

mis·gov·ern [misgʌ́vərn] *vt.* (P6) govern badly. 악정을 펴다. [mis-]

mis·gov·ern·ment [mìsgʌ́vərnmənt] *n.* Ⓤ bad, evil government. 악정; 실정(失政).

mis·guide [misgáid] *vt.* (P6) 《chiefly in *passive*》 lead (someone) in the wrong way; mislead. …의 지도를 잘못하다. [mis-]

mis·guid·ed [misgáidid] *adj.* wrongly led; led in the wrong way by error or misconduct. 잘못 지도된; 오도(誤導)된. ¶ *a ~ opinion* 그릇된 의견 / *The misguided boy turned to crime.* 그 잘못 키운 아이는 나쁜 길에 들어섰다.

mis·hap [míshæp, −⌐] *n.* Ⓤ the state of bad luck; Ⓒ an unlucky accident. 불행한 사고; 재난. ¶ *without ~* 무사히. [mis-]

mis·in·form [mìsinfɔ́:rm] *vt.* (P6) give incorrect information to (someone). …에게 잘못 전하다; 오보(誤報)하다.

mis·in·for·ma·tion [mìsinfɔ:rméiʃən] *n.* Ⓤ false information or news. 오보(誤報).

mis·in·ter·pret [mìsintə́:rprit] *vt.* (P6) understand or explain wrongly. …을 오해하다, …에 잘못된 해석을 하다.

mis·in·ter·pre·ta·tion [mìsintə:rpritéiʃən] *n.* ⓊⒸ a wrong interpretation; misunderstanding. 오역; 오해.

mis·judge [misdʒʌ́dʒ] *vt., vi.* (P6; 1) judge wrongly. 판단을 잘못하다; 잘못 보다. ¶ *~ someone* 아무를 잘못 보다 / *~ a distance* 거리를 잘못 재다. [mis-]

mis·laid [misléid] *vt.* p. and pp. of **mislay.**

mis·lay [misléi] *vt.* (**-laid**) (P6) **1** put (something) in a place and then forget where it is. …을 두고 잊다〔둔 데를 잊다〕. ¶ *~ a letter* 〔*one's gloves*〕 편지〔장갑〕 둔 데를 잊다. **2** put (something) in the wrong place. …을 잘못 두다.

·mis·lead [mislí:d] *vt.* (**-led**) **1** (P6) lead (someone) in the wrong way. …을 그릇 인도하다. ¶ *The guide misled them in the woods.* 안내인은 숲속에서 그들을 잘못 인도했다. **2** (P6) cause to do wrong. 나쁜 일에 꾀다. ¶ *The boy was misled by bad companions.* 소년은 나쁜 친구들의 꾐에 빠졌다. **3** (P6,13) lead to form a wrong judgment; deceive. …을 현혹시키다; 속이다.

·mis·lead·ing [mislí:diŋ] *adj.* giving a wrong impression; deceiving. 오해하게 하는; 현혹시키는; 속이는.

mis·led [misléd] *vt.* p. and pp. of **mislead.**

mis·man·age [mismǽnidʒ] *vt.* (P6) manage wrongly. …의 조처를 잘못하다; 잘못 관리하다. ¶ *If you ~ the business, you will lose money.* 장사를 잘못했다간 손해 본다. [mis-]

mis·match [mismǽtʃ] *vt.* (P6) match badly or unsuitably. 잘못〔어울리지 않게〕 짝짓다. — *n.* a bad or unsuitable match. 잘못 짝짓기. ¶ *Their marriage was a ~.* 그들의 결혼은 잘못된 것이었다.

mis·name [misnéim] *vt.* (P6) call (someone or something) by a wrong name. …을 틀린 이름으로 부르다.

mis·no·mer [misnóumər] *n.* Ⓒ a wrong name; an incorrect use of a name. 틀린 이름〔명칭〕; 명칭의 오용. ¶ *To call it a hotel is a ~ — it's more like a prison!* 그걸 호텔이라 할 수는 없다. 그건 차라리 감옥 같다.

mi·sog·a·mist [miságəmist, mai- / -sɔ́g-] *n.* a person who hates marriage. 결혼을 싫어하는 사람. [↓]

mi·sog·a·my [miságəmi, mai- / -sɔ́g-] *n.* hatred of marriage. 결혼을 싫어함; 결혼 혐오. [Gk. *miseō* hate, *gamos* marriage, *gune* woman]

mi·sog·y·nist [misádʒənist / -sɔ́dʒ-] *n.* a person who hates women. 여자를 싫어하는 사람. [↑]

mis·place [mispléis] *vt.* (P6) **1** put (something) in a wrong place. …을 잘못 두다. ¶ *~ a book.* **2** 《*colloq.*》 mislay. …을 두고 잊다. ¶ *I've misplaced my glasses again.* 안경 둔 데를 또 잊었다. **3** 《chiefly in *pp.*》 give (one's love, trust, etc.) to an improper person. (애정·신용 등)을 잘못된 사람에게 주다. ¶ *misplaced affection*〔*confidence*〕 잘못 준 애정〔신뢰〕. [mis-]

mis·place·ment [mispléismənt] *n.* Ⓤ the state of misplacing. 잘못 주기〔두기〕.

mis·play [mispléi] *n.* 《U.S.》 a wrong or bad play, as in football or bridge. (경기 등의) 실수; 에러; 미스. — *vt., vi.* (P6; 1) play wrongly or badly. 실수하다; (공)을 잘못 처리하다.

mis·print [mìsprint, -ˊ] *n.* Ⓒ a mistake in printing. 오식(誤植); 미스프린트. — [misprínt] *vt.* (P6) make a mistake in printing of (something). …을 오식하다.

mis·pro·nounce [mìsprənáuns] *vt., vi.* (P6; 1) pronounce (a word) incorrectly. …의 발음을 잘못하다.

mis·pro·nun·ci·a·tion [mìsprənʌ̀nsiéiʃən] *n.* **1** Ⓤ the state of pronouncing incorrectly. 발음의 잘못. **2** Ⓒ a mispronounced word. 틀린 발음.

mis·read [misríːd] *vt.* (**-read** [-réd]) (P6) **1** read or understand incorrectly. …을 잘못 읽다; …의 뜻을 그릇 해석하다. ¶ *~ a letter.* **2** interpret wrongly. …을 오해하다.

mis·rep·re·sent [mìsreprizént] *vt.* (P6) represent wrongly; give a wrong account or impression of (something). …을 잘못 전하다; 틀리게 설명하다. ¶ *He is not so stupid as to ~ the fact.* 그가 사실을 잘못 전할 만큼 어리석지는 않다.

mis·rule [misrúːl] *n.* Ⓤ **1** bad government. 악정; 실정(失政). **2** disorder. 무질서. — *vt.* (P6) rule or govern (people) unjustly. …의 정치를 그르치다.

⁝miss[1] [mis] *n.* **1** Ⓒ a word used in speaking to a girl or a young unmarried woman; a young lady. 소녀; 아가씨; 미혼 여성. **2** 《*M-*》 a title used before the name of a girl or an unmarried woman. …양. 參考 자매가 둘 이상일 경우에는 장녀에게만 Miss Brown처럼 성 앞에, 차녀 이하는 Miss Marie Brown이라고 이름 앞에 붙임. ¶ *Good morning, Miss Kim!* [→mistress]

⁝miss[2] [mis] *vt.* **1** (P6) fail to hit (something). …을 못 맞히다; 빗맞히다. ¶ *~ one's aim* 겨냥이 틀리다 / *He fired at the bird, but missed it.* 새를 쏘았지만 빗맞았다. **2** (P6,9) fail to get, catch, meet or reach (something). …을 획득하지 못하다; …에 못 미치다. ¶ *~ a prize* 상을 놓치다 / *~ a train* 기차를 놓치다 / *~ a good opportunity* 좋은 기회를 놓치다 / *He missed the bank and fell in the water.* 그는 둑에 이르지 못하고 물에 떨어졌다. **3** (P6) fail to see, find, hear, or understand (something). …이 보이지〔들리지〕 않다; …을 이해 못하다. ¶ *~ the point of the joke* 익살의 요지를 이해 못 하다 / *No one will ~ the notice.* 그 공고를 못 보는 사람은 없을 게다 / *I looked for the word in the dictionary, but missed it.* 그 단어를 사전에서 찾았으나 못 찾고 말았다 / *You can't ~ my car; it's a convertible with a green top.* 내 차는 쉽게 찾을 거다. 그건 초록색 포장의 컨버터블이니까. **4** (P6) be absent from (a party, etc.); neglect. …을 결석하다; 빼먹다. ¶ *I missed Mr. Smith's class.* 스미스 선생의 수업에 못 나갔다 / *~ an appointment* 약속을 어기다. **5** (P6,7) leave out; omit; overlook. …을 빠뜨리다; 생략하다; 빠뜨리고 보다. ¶ *Never ~ a word in your reading.* 한 자라도 빠뜨리고 읽으면 안 된다 / *Don't ~ my name out of your list.* 표에서 내 이름이 빠지지 않도록 해라. **6** (P6,9) escape; avoid. …을 피하다; 모면하다. ¶ *He barely missed being run over.* 까딱하면 차에 치일 뻔했다. **7** (P6) become aware of the absence or loss of (something). …이 없는 것을 깨닫다. ¶ *I suddenly missed my bag.* 갑자기 내 가방이 없어진 것을 알았다. **8** (P6) feel sad at the absence or loss of (someone). …이 없어 서운해 하다. ¶ *I will ~ you very much.* 네가 없으면 난 아주 섭섭해 할 거다 / *He's dead and I ~ him.* 그가 죽고 없으니 쓸쓸하구나. — *vi.* **1** (P1) fail to hit. 빗맞다; 빗나가다. ¶ *His shot missed.* 과녁을 빗나갔다. **2** (P1,3) fail to be successful. 실패하다. ¶ *~ in one's attempt* 시도가 실패로 끝나다.

miss fire, **a**) (of a gun) fail to go off. (총이) 불발이 되다. **b**) (of joke, etc.) go unappreciated. (익살 등을) 알아듣지 못하다.

miss *one's* ***footing,*** slip, as in climbing. 발을 헛디디다.

miss the mark, 《*fig.*》 fail to succeed. 빗나가다; 실패하다.

— *n.* Ⓒ **1** a failure to hit, meet, obtain, see, etc. 못〔빗〕맞힘; 못 찾음; 놓침. ¶ *He made more misses than hits.* 맞힌 것보다 헛방이 더 많았다 / 《*prov.*》 *A ~ is as good as a mile.* 오십보 백보다. **2** a failure in an attempt. 실패. ¶ *The play was a sad ~.* 연극은 참담했다. **3** an escape. 모면; 벗어남. ¶ *a lucky ~* 가까스로의 모면. **4** 《*colloq.*》 miscarriage. 유산(流産). [E.]

give *something* ***a miss,*** pass by it; leave it alone; neglect or omit it. 일부러 피하다; 저버리다; 빼다.

Miss. =Mississippi.

mis·shape [misʃéip] *vt.* (**-shaped**; **-shaped** or **-shap·en**) (P6) shape badly; make in the wrong shape. 모양 없게 하다; 잘못 만들다. [mis-]

mis·shap·en [misʃéipən] *v.* pp. of **misshape.** — *adj.* poorly shaped; deformed. 보기 흉한; 잘못 만든; 기형의.

·mis·sile [mísəl / -sail] *n.* Ⓒ a weapon or object that is shot or thrown, such as a stone, an arrow, a bullet, or a rocket. 쏘는〔던지는〕 무기; 미사일; 탄도(彈道) 병기. ¶ *guided missiles* 유도탄 / *an intercontinental* 〔*an intermediate-range*〕 *ballistic ~* 대륙간〔중거리〕 탄도탄. — *adj.* that can be thrown or shot. 던질〔발사할〕 수 있는. ¶ *a ~ weapon* 날아가는 무기. [L. *mitto* send]

:miss·ing [mísiŋ] *adj.* **1** not to be found; failing to appear or return. 행방 불명의. ¶ *The girl is still* ～. 소녀는 아직 행방 불명이다 / *Let's get everyone on deck and see if anyone is* ～. 갑판의 모두를 모이게 하여 누가 안 보이는지 알아봐라 / *He is among the* ～. 그는 행방 불명이다. **2** lacking; lost; absent. 빠져 있는; 없는. ¶ *a* ～ *page* 낙장(落張) / *The money was* ～. 돈이 없어졌다. [*miss*²]

missing link [⌐－⌐] *n.* something necessary for filling a gap or blank in a series. 계열(系列)상 빠져 있는 요소.

·mis·sion [míʃən] *n.* Ⓒ **1** a group of persons sent to another country for a special purpose; 《U.S.》 the diplomatic delegation; the embassy. 외교 사절(단); 재외 공사〔대사〕(관). ¶ *a commercial* 〔*trade*〕 ～ 무역 사절단. **2** business or duty on which one is sent; any errand. (파견되는) 특수 임무. ¶ *be sent on a* ～ 사명을 띠고 파견되다. **3** one's life work; one's calling in life. 천직; 사명. ¶ *have a* ～ *in life* 천직을 가지다 / *It seemed to be her* ～ *to care for her brother's children.* 오빠의 아이들을 돌보는 것이 그녀의 사명 같았다. **4** 《*pl.*》 an organized missionary effort to spread the Christian religion; the district assigned to a priest. (기독교의) 포교; 전도 활동; 전도 지구; 선교지. **5** a group of persons teaching about God in a foreign land. 선교단. ¶ *A* ～ *was sent to Africa.* 선교단이 아프리카에 파견되었다. **6** the station or headquarters of a religious mission. 전도관; 포교(布敎) 본부. [L. *mitto* send]

·mis·sion·ar·y [míʃənèri / -nəri] *n.* Ⓒ (*pl.* **-ar·ies**) a person who works to spread his religious ideas by trying to convert other people. 선교사; 전도사. ¶ *a foreign* ～ 외국인 선교사. —*adj.* of missions, esp. religious missions. 포교〔전도〕의. ¶ ～ *work* 전도 사업.

mis·sis [mísiz, -is], **mis·sus** [mísəz, -səs] *n.* 《*colloq.*》 **1** a wife. 아내; 마누라. **2** 《used by a servant》 the mistress. 마님; 아씨. [→mistress]

·Mis·sis·sip·pi [mìsəsípi] *n.* **1** 《*the* ～》 the large river in North America. 미시시피강《미국 중부를 흐르는 긴 강》. **2** a southern State of the United States. 미시시피 주(州). 參考 Miss.로 생략함.

Mis·sis·sip·pi·an [mìsəsípiən] *adj.* **1** of the Mississippi River. 미시시피 강의. **2** of the State of Mississippi. 미시시피 주(州)의. —*n.* a person of the state of Mississippi. 미시시피 주의 주민.

mis·sive [mísiv] *n.* Ⓒ a letter; a written note esp. a formal one. 서장(書狀); 신서(信書); (특히) 공문서. [→missile]

Mis·sour·i [mizúəri] *n.* **1** a middle western State of the United States. 미주리 주(州). 參考 Mo.로 생략함. **2** 《*the* ～》 a river flowing southwestward from Montana to the Mississippi. 미주리 강.

mis·spell [misspél] *vt.* (**-spelled** or **-spelt**) (P6) spell (a word) wrongly. …의 철자를 잘못 쓰다. ¶ *a misspelt word* 〔*letter*〕 철자가 틀린 말〔편지〕. [mis-]

mis·spelt [misspélt] *v.* p. and pp. of **misspell.** —*adj.* misspelled. 철자가 틀린.

mis·spend [misspénd] *vt.* (**-spent**) spend wrongly; waste. 낭비하다.

mis·spent [misspént] *v.* p. and pp. of **misspend.** —*adj.* used wrongly. 잘못 쓰인; 낭비된. ¶ *a* ～ *youth* 〔*fortune*〕 헛되이 보낸 청춘〔써버린 재산〕. [mis-]

mis·step [misstép] *n.* **1** a wrong or false step. 실족(失足); 헛디딤. **2** an error. 과실.

mis·sus [mísəz, -səs] *n.* =missis.

mis·sy [mísi] *n.* Miss 《a familiar manner of address to a young girl》. 아가씨.

:mist [mist] *n.* **1** ⒸⓊ a thin fog or vapor in the air. (엷은) 안개; 놀. ¶ *The* ～ *has cleared off* 〔*away*〕. 안개가 걷혔다 / *The mist is rising.* 안개가 끼고 있다. **2** Ⓒ something that makes the eye not clear. (눈의) 흐릿함. ¶ *She smiled in a* ～ *of tears.* 그녀는 눈물어린 눈으로 미소지었다. **3** something that darkens the mind. (이해·판단 등을) 흐리게 하는 것.

in a mist, in a puzzle; confused. 어쩔 줄 몰라서; 갈피를 못 잡아.

—*vi.* (P1,2) come down in the form of mist; be covered with mist; become dim. 안개가 끼다〔덮이다〕; 흐릿해지다. ¶ *It is hardly raining, only misting.* 비가 내린다고는 할 수 없고 그저 이슬비다.

—*vt.* (P6) cover or dim (something) with mist; make (something) not clear. …을 안개로 덮다; 흐릿하게 하다. [E.]

mis·tak·a·ble [mistéikəbəl] *adj.* that can be mistaken or misunderstood. 틀리기 쉬운; 오해받기 쉬운. [↓]

:mis·take [mistéik] *vt.* (**-took, -tak·en**) **1** (P6,12) ⓐ take or choose wrongly. …을 잘못 택하다; 선택을 그르치다. ¶ ～ *the road* 길을 잘못 들다 / ～ *one's vocation* 직업을 잘못 택하다. ⓑ understand wrongly; take in a wrong sense. …을 오해하다; 잘못 생각하다. ¶ *There's no mistaking it.* 틀릴 수가 없다 / *He mistook my meaning.* 그는 내 말의 뜻을 오해했다. **2** (P6,13) take (someone or something) for another; regard to be another. …을 잘못 알다; 혼동하다. ¶ *I mistook you for your brother.* 난 너를 네 동생으로 알았다 / ～ *friends for enemies* 친구를 적으로 잘못 생각하다.

—*vi.* (P1) be wrong. 오해하다.

—*n.* ⓊⒸ a misunderstanding; an error; a fault. 틀림; 오해; 실수. ¶ *make a* ～ 잘못하다〔잘못 생각하다〕 / *Don't make any* ～ *about it!* 그 일에 어떤 실수도 없도록 해라. [mis-]

and no mistake, 《*colloq.*》 without doubt; surely; for certain. 틀림없이; 확실히; 절대로

《앞의 말을 강조함》. ¶ *This is good, and no* ～. 이건 좋다. 확실히.

beyond mistake, certainly. 틀림없이.

by mistake, mistakenly. 실수로; 잘못해서. ¶ *take a wrong train by* ～ 잘못해서 딴 차를 타다.

:mis·tak·en [mistéikən] *v.* pp. of **mistake.** — *adj.* wrong; having a wrong opinion; judging wrongly. 틀린; 잘못된; 오해한. ¶ ～ *kindness* 성가신 친절 / *You are* ～. 너는 잘못 생각하고〔오해하고〕 있다 / *Unless I'm* ～, *he is a policeman in plain clothes.* 내 짐작이 틀림없다면 그는 사복을 한 경찰관이다.

mis·tak·en·ly [mistéikənli] *adv.* by mistake. 잘못해서; 오해해서.

mis·ter [místər] *n.* **1** 《usu. *Mr.*》 a title used before a man's name or the name of his office. 군; 씨; 선생; 님; 귀하《Mr.로 생략해서 남자의 성명〔관직명〕 앞에 붙임》. ¶ *Mr. Brown* 브라운씨 / 《U.S.》 *Mr. President* 대통령 각하 / *Mr. Officer* 경찰관님. **2** 《*colloq.*, Brit. *vulg.*》 sir. (호칭으로)선생님; 여보시오. ¶ *Look here,* ～*!* 여보세요, 선생님. [*master*]

mist·i·ly [místili] *adv.* not clearly; in a misty manner. 안개 낀; 흐릿하게. [*misty*]

mis·time [mistáim] *vt.* 《esp. in *pp.*》 say or do (something) out of season or at an unsuitable time. 안 좋은 때에 말하다〔하다〕; 시기를 그르치다. ¶ *mistimed assistance* 때늦은 원조. [mis-]

mis·tle·toe [mísltòu, mízl-] *n.* Ⓒ 《bot.》 a plant growing on the branches and trunks of other trees, often used as a Christmas decoration. 겨우살이《크리스마스 장식용》. [O.E. *mistel* mistletoe+*tan* twig]

:mis·took [mistúk] *vt.* p. of **mistake.**

mis·trans·late [mìstrænsléit, -trænz-] *vt.* (P6) translate incorrectly. …을 잘못 번역하다; 오역(誤譯)하다. [mis-]

mis·trans·la·tion [mìstrænsléiʃən, -trænz-] *n.* ⒸⓊ an incorrect translation. 오역.

mis·treat [mistríːt] *vt.* 《U.S.》 treat wrongly; make a bad use of (something). …을 학대〔혹사〕하다.

mis·treat·ment [mistríːtmənt] *n.* Ⓤ ill treatment. 학대; 혹사.

:mis·tress [místris] *n.* Ⓒ **1** a woman who is at the head of a family and it's servants. 여주인; 주부; 마님(opp. master). ¶ *the* ～ *of a house* 한 집안의 주부. **2** 《often *M-*》《*fig.*》 someone or something regarded as like a female ruler. (여성) 지배자; …의 여왕. ¶ *the* ～ *of the night* 밤의 여왕 《달》 / *the Mistress of the Seas* 바다의 여왕《영국의 별칭》. **3** a woman who has a thorough knowledge or mastery of something. 여류 대가(大家). ¶ *She is a complete* ～ *of the arts of cookery.* 요리술에 있어서는 나무랄 데 없는 대가다. **4** 《Brit.》 a woman teacher in a school. 여선생. ¶ *the French* 〔*a dancing*〕 ～ 프랑스어〔댄스〕 교사. **5** a woman supported by a man but not married to him. 정부; 첩. ¶ *keep a* ～ 첩을 두다. **6** 《*M-*》 a title once used before the name of any woman. …부인〔여사〕. 參考 지금은 Mrs., Miss 를 씀. [→master]

be mistress of the situation, has the power of deciding. 국면을 좌지우지하다.

be one's own mistress, be free to do as one pleases. 자유로운 몸이다.

the Mistress of the Adriatic, another name for Venice. 베니스의 별칭.

mis·tri·al [mistráiəl] *n.* 《law》 a trial of a lawsuit that is void because of errors. 오심(誤審). [mis-]

mis·trust [mistrʌ́st] *vt.* (P6) doubt; suspect. …을 불신하다; 의심하다. ¶ *She mistrusted her ability to learn to swim.* 그녀는 수영을 배울 자신이 없었다. — *n.* Ⓤ lack of trust; suspicion. 불신; 의혹. [mis-]

mis·trust·ful [mistrʌ́stfəl] *adj.* lacking confidence; suspicious. 의심이 많은; 신용하지 않는.

mist·y [místi] *adj.* (**mist·i·er, mist·i·est**) **1** ⓐ covered with mist. 안개 낀. ¶ *a* ～ *morning* 안개낀 아침 / (*the*) ～ *weather* 안개낀 날씨. ⓑ tearful. 눈물어린. **2** not clearly seen; vague. 뚜렷하지 않은; 흐릿한. ¶ *a* ～ *idea* 〔*explanation*〕 확실하지 못한 생각〔설명〕. ● **mist·i·ness** [-nis] *n.* [*mist*]

·mis·un·der·stand [mìsʌndərstǽnd] *vt., vi.* (**-stood**) (P6;1) understand (words or actions) wrongly; gather the wrong meaning from (a remark, etc.). (말·행위)를 오해하다; …에 잘못된 해석을 하다. ¶ *We misunderstood each other.* 우린 서로 오해하고 있었다 / *I misunderstood his meaning.* 나는 그의 말뜻을 잘못 알고 있었다. [mis-]

mis·un·der·stand·ing [mìsʌndərstǽndiŋ] *n.* ⓊⒸ **1** a mistake as to meaning or motive. 오해; 잘못한 해석. ¶ *a* ～ *of a word* 단어의 오역. **2** disagreement; a quarrel caused by a misunderstanding. 의견 차이; (오해로 인한) 불화. ¶ *misunderstandings among* 〔*between*〕 *friends* 친구간의 오해.

mis·un·der·stood [mìsʌndərstúd] *v.* p. and pp. of **misunderstand.** — *adj.* incorrectly understood. 오해한; 뜻을 잘못 해석한.

mis·us·age [misjúːsidʒ, -júːz-] *n.* ⓊⒸ **1** an incorrect usage; misuse (of words, etc.). (말 등의) 오용. **2** ill treatment. 학대; 혹사.

mis·use [misjúːz] *vt.* (P6) **1** use (someone or something) for a wrong purpose. …을 잘못 쓰다; 오용하다. ¶ *He misuses his knife at table by lifting food with it.* 그는 식탁에서 나이프를 잘못 쓰는데 그걸로 음식을 떠 먹는다. **2** treat badly. 학대하다. ¶ *He misuses his laborers by making them work too hard.* 그는 노동자를 중노동시키면서 학대한다. — [misjúːs] *n.* Ⓒ a wrong use. 오용; 악용. [mis-]

mite[1] [mait] *n.* Ⓒ a very small insect

like a spider. 진드기. [E.]

mite[2] [mait] *n.* Ⓒ **1** a very small coin or sum of money. 잔돈; 푼돈. **2** 《*colloq.*》 any small thing, such as a small child. 작은 것; 꼬마. ¶ *What a little ~ she is!* 그 여자는 몸집이 참 작기도 하구나. **3** anything very small; a little bit. 조금; 약간. ¶ *Let me offer my ~ of comfort.* 적으나마 위로가 되었으면 합니다 / 《Bible》 *the widow's ~* 가난한 과부의 한 푼. [E.]

not a mite, not in the least; not at all. 조금도 …않다. ¶ *I couldn't eat a ~ more.* 조금도 더 못 먹겠다.

mi·ter, 《Brit.》 **mi·tre** [máitər] *n.* **1** Ⓒ a kind of crown worn by archbishops and bishops. (카톨릭교의) 주교관(主教冠). ¶ *confer a ~ upon* …을 주교에 앉히다. **2** Ⓤ the rank or position of a bishop. 주교의 신분·지위. [Gk. *mitra* head-band]

mit·i·gate [mítəgèit] *vt.* (P6) soften (anger, pain, etc.); make less severe or painful. …을 누그러뜨리다; 경감시키다. ¶ *~ a punishment* 벌을 가볍게 해주다 / *~ one's anger* 〔*pain*〕 노염〔고통〕을 누그러뜨리다. [L. *mitis* mild]

mit·i·ga·tion [mìtəgéiʃən] *n.* Ⓤ the act of mitigating; Ⓒ anything that mitigates. 완화; 경감; 완화시키는 것.

mi·tre [máitər] *n.* 《Brit.》 =miter.

mitt [mit] *n.* Ⓒ **1** a kind of glove without fingers. 벙어리 장갑. **2** 《*sl.*》 the hand. 손; 주먹. **3** 《*pl.*》 boxing gloves. 권투 장갑. **4** a baseball glove with a thick pad over the palm. (야구용) 미트. [F.]

mit·ten [mítn] *n.* Ⓒ a glove that covers the four fingers together and the thumb separately; a lady's glove that covers the arm and hand. 벙어리 장갑; (여성용) 긴 장갑. [↑]

get the mitten, 《*colloq.*》 **a)** be refused as a lover. (연인에게서) 딱지맞다; 채이다. **b)** be dismissed. 해고되다; 목잘리다.

give the mitten to, reject (someone) as a lover; dismiss. 퇴짜놓다; 차버리다; 해고하다.

handle** someone **without mittens, deal with someone mercilessly. …을 사정 없이 다루다.

:mix [miks] *v.* (**mixed** or **mixt**) *vt.* **1** (P6,13) put (things) together into a single mass or compound; combine. …을 섞다; 혼합하다; 결합하다. ¶ *~ water with wine* 술에 물을 타다 / *~ sand in* 〔*with*〕 *the sugar* 설탕에 모래를 섞다. **2** (P6,13,14) make (something) by blending different things. 섞어서 …을 만들다. ¶ *~ a salad dressing* 샐러드용 드레싱을 만들다 / *~ a poison* 독약을 만들다. **3** (P6,13) cause (persons) to come together. …을 사귀게 하다. ¶ *~ people of different social worlds* 이질 사회의 사람들을 사귀게 하다.
— *vi.* (P1) **1** be mixed. 섞이다. ¶ *Oil and water will not ~.* 물과 기름은 섞이지 않는다. **2** keep company; associate; get along in a friendly way. 교제하다; 사귀다; 사이좋게 지내다. ¶ *~ in society* 사교계에 드나들다 / *~ with others at a party* 파티에서 남들과 잘 어울리다.

mix up, **a)** mix thoroughly. 잘 섞다. **b)** confuse. 혼동하다; 헷갈리다. ¶ *I was so mixed up that I used a wrong method in that problem.* 너무 당황한 나머지 그 문제의 방법을 그르치고 말았다. **c)** involve; concern. 말려들게 하다; 관계하다.
— *n.* Ⓒ **1** mixture. 혼합. **2** 《*colloq.*》 a mixed condition; a mess. 혼란. **3** proportions of a batch of concrete, mortar, etc. 혼합비(混合比). [L. *misceo*]

mixed [mikst] *adj.* **1** made up of different kinds. 섞인; 혼성의; 잡다한. ¶ *a ~ brigade* 혼성 여단 / *a ~ train* 혼합 열차《객차와 화차의》 / *a ~ chorus* 혼성 합창 / *have ~ feelings* 생각이 착잡하다 / *~ marriage* 다른 종교·종족간의 결혼. **2** having both boys and girls; of both women and men. 남녀 공학〔혼합〕의. ¶ *~ bathing* 혼욕(混浴) / *a ~ school* 남녀 공학 학교. **3** mentally confused; confused in mind. 머리가 혼란된. ¶ *~ emotions* 착잡한 심정.

mixed doubles [´ ´–] *n.* a game played by two men and two women. (테니스의) 혼합 복식 경기.

mixed number [´ ´–] *n.* a number consisting of a whole number and a fraction. 대분수(帶分數).

mix·er [míksər] *n.* Ⓒ **1** a mixing machine. 혼합기; 믹서. ¶ *a concrete ~* 콘크리트 믹서. **2** 《U.S. *colloq.*》 a person keeping company with others in society. 교제〔사교〕가. ¶ *He is a good* 〔*bad*〕 *~.* 남과 잘 어울리는 〔교제가 서툰〕 사람이다.

mixt [mikst] *v.* p. and pp. of **mix.**

:mix·ture [míkstʃər] *n.* Ⓒ **1** 《chem.》 something that is mixed. 혼합물(cf. *compound*[1]). ¶ *Air is a ~ of gases.* 공기는 여러 기체의 혼합물이다. **2** Ⓤ the state of being mixed. 혼합. ¶ *speak in a ~ of French and Italian* 프랑스어와 이탈리아어를 섞어서 말하다. **3** two or more substances mixed together but not chemically united. (화합물 아닌) 혼합물. ¶ *a ~ of real and artificial silk* 본견(本絹)과 인견의 혼방사(混紡絲). **4** a combination of various feelings, etc. 착잡한 심경. ¶ *a ~ of grief and anger* 비탄과 분노가 엇갈린 심정. [→mix]

mix-up [míksʌ̀p] *n.* Ⓒ **1** confusion; confused state. 혼란. **2** a fight or quarrel; a confused fight. 싸움; 혼전.

miz·zen [mízən] *n.* Ⓒ a fore-and-aft sail set on the mizzenmast. 뒷돛대의 세로돛. [F. *misaine*]

miz·zen·mast [mízənmæ̀st, -mɑ̀ːst; 《naut.》 -məst] *n.* Ⓒ the rear mast in a two-masted or three-masted ship. (돛대가 둘 또는 셋 있는 배의) 뒷돛대.

Mme. (*pl.* **Mmes.** [meidɑ́ːm]) Madame.

mne·mon·ic [niːmánik / -mɔ́n-] *adj.* helping the memory. 기억을 돕는. ¶ *a ~ system* 기억법. — *n.* 《*pl.*》 the art of helping or improving the memory. 기억술. [Gk. *mnēmōn* mindful]

Mo. 1 molybdenum. 2 Monday. 3 Missouri.

*__moan__ [moun] *n.* Ⓒ a long, low sound of sorrow or pain; any similar sound. (슬픔·고통의) 신음 (소리); 끙끙대기. ¶ *the ~ of the wind* 울부짖는 듯한 바람소리.
— *vt., vi.* (P6;1) make a low sound in pain or sorrow; grieve for. 신음 소리를 내다; 비탄하다(cf. *groan*). ¶ *They moaned their lost ones.* 그들은 죽은 동료를 애통해 했다 / *The wounded moaned ceaselessly.* 부상자의 신음 소리는 끊이지 않았다. [E.]
make one's moan, lament; complain. 슬퍼하다; 투덜거리다.

moan·ful [móunfəl] *adj.* showing sorrow or pain. 한탄하는; 신음하는.

moat [mout] *n.* Ⓒ a deep, wide ditch, usu. water-filled, dug around a castle, etc. as a defense. (성곽 둘레 등의) 해자(垓字); 외호(外濠). — *vt.* (P6) surround (a place) with a moat. …에 해자를 파다. [F. *mote* embankment]

*__mob__ [mɑb / mɔb] *n.* Ⓒ 1 《*collectively*》 a large number of disorderly, rude people; a riotous crowd. 폭도; 난민(亂民). 2 《*the ~*》 the common mass of people. 민중; 대중; 하층민. — *vt.* (**mobbed, mob·bing**) (P6) 1 attack (someone or some place) in a disorderly crowd. 무리지어 …을 습격하다. ¶ *The crowd mobbed the consulate.* 군중들은 일제히 영사관을 습격했다. 2 crowd round in curiosity, anger, etc. …의 주위에 떼지어 모이다. ¶ *The eager girls mobbed the popular singer the moment he appeared.* 열광한 소녀들은 그 인기 가수가 나타나자마자 우우 하고 몰려들었다. [L. *mobile vulgus* the excitable crowd]

mo·bile [móubəl, -biːl / -bail] *adj.* 1 movable; easy to move. 가동성(可動性)의; 이동하기 쉬운. ¶ *~ troops* 기동화부대 / *a ~ camp* 이동 캠프. 2 moving or changing easily. 움직이기 쉬운; 곧잘 변하는. ¶ *a ~ mind* 변덕스러운 마음. [→move]

mo·bil·i·ty [moubíləti] Ⓤ *n.* the state of being mobile. 가동성; 이동성; 변덕. ¶ *social ~* 사회적 이동성.

mo·bi·li·za·tion [mòubiləzéiʃən] *n.* Ⓤ 1 the act of mobilizing. 동원(動員). ¶ *industrial ~* 산업 동원 / *national ~* 국가 총동원. 2 the state of being mobilized. 운용; 유통.

mo·bi·lize [móubəlàiz] *vt.* (P6) 1 call (troops, etc.) into active use. (군대 등)을 동원하다. ¶ *~ armed forces* 군대를 동원하다. 2 put (wealth, etc.) into motion or active use. (부(富) 등)을 유통시키다; 가동성(可動性)을 주다. ¶ *~ the wealth of a country* 일국의 부(富)를 유통시키다. — *vi.* (P1) become organized and ready for war, etc. (군대 등에) 동원되다. [→mobile, -ize]

moc·ca·sin [mákəsin, -zən / mɔ́k-] *n.* Ⓒ 1 a deerskin or other soft leather shoe or sandal. 모카신. 2 a poisonous snake of the southern United States. 독사의 일종. [Amer-Ind.]

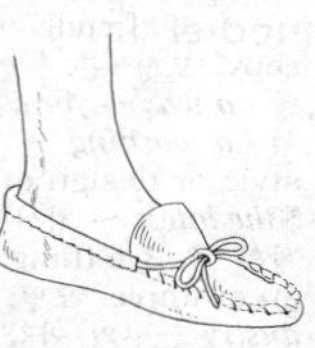
〈moccasin 1〉

:mock [mɑk, mɔ(ː)k] *vt.* (P6) 1 make fun of (someone) by acting in the same way as he; imitate. …을 흉내내며 놀리다. ¶ *The thoughtless children mocked the queer speech of the new boy.* 철없는 아이들은 그 새로 온 아이의 이상한 말씨를 흉내내며 놀렸다. 2 laugh at; scoff at (someone). …을 조롱하다; 비웃다. 3 make light of (someone); cause to become useless; despise. …을 얕보다; 못 쓰게 만들다. ¶ *The river mocked all our efforts to cross.* 강을 건너려고 여러 가지로 애썼으나 허사였다. 4 deceive; disappoint. …을 속이다; 실망시키다. ¶ *He was mocked with false hopes.* 허황된 꿈에 속았다.
— *adj.* not real; false; imitation. 거짓의; 가짜의. ¶ *a ~ trial* 모의 재판 / *a ~ battle* 모의전 / *with ~ modesty* 겸손을 가장하여.
— *n.* Ⓤ an action or a speech that mocks; a thing scorned. 조롱; 경멸. ¶ *make a ~ of someone* 아무를 조롱하다. [F. *mocquer*]

mock·er [mákər, mɔ́(ː)k-] *n.* Ⓒ 1 a person who mocks. 놀리는[흉내내는] 사람. 2 =mockingbird.

mock·er·y [mákəri, mɔ́(ː)k-] *n.* (*pl.* **-er·ies**) 1 Ⓤ the act of mocking; ridicule. 조롱; 놀림. 2 Ⓒ someone or something to be mocked. 놀림감; 웃음가마리. ¶ *His friends made a ~ of him.* 친구들은 그를 웃음거리로 만들었다. 3 Ⓒ an imitation of another's action. 흉내. ¶ *Their ~ of John hurt his feelings.* 그들은 존의 흉내를 내서 그를 기분 나쁘게 했다. 4 a useless or disappointing effort. 헛수고. ¶ *Rain made a ~ of our picnic.* 비 때문에 우리는 소풍을 잡쳤다.

mock·ing·bird [mákiŋbə̀ːrd, mɔ́(ː)k-] *n.* Ⓒ a small songbird of the southern United States. 입내새.

mock·ing·ly [mákiŋli / mɔ́k-] *adv.* in a mocking manner. 조롱하여.

mo·dal [móudl] *adj.* 1 of mode, manner, or form. 모양의; 양식의; 형식의. 2 《gram.》 of the mood of a verb. 법(法)의. [↓]

*__mode__ [moud] *n.* Ⓒ 1 a manner; a fashion; a way; a method; a style. 방법; 양식; 유행; 형식. ¶ *a ~ of life* 생활 양식 / *Miniskirts are the ~ of the moment.* 미니스커트는 한때의 유행이다. 2 《gram.》 mood². (동사의) 법(法); 서법(敍法). 3 《mus.》 a form of scale; one of the two classes of keys in music. 음계; 선법(旋法). [L. *modus* measure]

:**mod·el** [mádl / mɔ́dl] *n.* Ⓒ **1** a small copy. 모형; 본. ¶ *a ~ of a plane* 비행기의 모형 / *a wax ~ for a statue* 밀랍 조상(彫像) 원형 / *a working ~* (기계의) 실용 모형. **2** a style or design of structure. 형(型); 양식. ¶ *the latest ~* 최신형 / *a car of 1990 ~*, 1990년형의 차. **3** a thing or person to be imitated; an example. 모범; 전형; 본보기. ¶ *a ~ of industry* 근면의 귀감 / *the ~ of beauty* 미의 전형. **4** a person who poses for painters, etc. (화가 등의) 모델. ¶ *an artist's ~*. **5** a person, esp. a woman, who wears newly-designed clothes to show people; a mannequin. (양장점 등의) 마네킨. **6** 《*colloq.*》 a person or thing exactly like another. 아주 꼭 닮은 사람〔물건〕. ¶ *The boy is the* 〔*a perfect*〕 *~ of his father.* 그 아이는 제 아버지를 빼쏘았다.

— *vt.* (**-eled, el·ing** or 《Brit.》 **-elled, -el·ling**) (P6,13) **1** make a plan or model of (someone or something); shape; mold; form. …의 모형을 만들다; …을 모델로 제작하다; …의 형을 뜨다. ¶ *~ a horse out of clay* 점토로 말의 상(像)을 만들다 / *~ a figure in wax* 밀랍으로 조상(彫像)을 만들다. **2** plan (something) in a particular way. 설계하다. ¶ *~ a garden after the manner of...* …풍으로 정원을 설계하다. **3** 《*on, upon, after*》 follow as a model. …을 본받다. ¶ *~ oneself on* 〔*upon*〕 *one's father* 아버지를 본받다.

— *vi.* (P1) be a model. 모델이 되다.

— *adj.* serving as a model; worthy of being imitated. 모범의; 전형적인. ¶ *~ behavior* 모범적인 태도 / *Such a ~ wife is rare.* 그만큼 훌륭한 부인은 드물다. [O.F. *modelle*]

mod·el·er, 《Brit.》 **-el·ler** [mádlər / mɔ́dlər] *n.* Ⓒ a person who models. 모형 제작인.

:**mod·er·ate** [mádərət / mɔ́d-] *adj.* **1** (of a person or actions) not extreme; reasonable; calm. 극단으로 흐르지 않는; 적당한; 온화한. ¶ *a ~ man* 온건한 사람 / *~ in temper* 〔*language*〕 기질이〔말씨가〕 부드러운 / *a ~ request* 무리 없는 요구. **2** (of quantity, amount, degree, etc.) medium; average; not large. 보통의; 웬만한. ¶ *~ means* 〔*expenses*〕 그만한 재산〔비용〕 / *at* (*a*) *~ speed* 적당한 속도로.

— *n.* Ⓒ a person holding moderate opinions. 온화한 사람; 온건파의 사람.

— *v.* [mádərèit / mɔ́d-] *vt.* (P6) make (something) less violent, extreme, etc.; cause (something) to become moderate. …을 완화시키다; 적당하게 하다. ¶ *~ one's language* 말을 부드럽게 하다 / *~ one's policy* 〔*views, demands*〕 방도〔견해, 요구〕를 조절하다.

— *vi.* (P1) become less violent, extreme, etc.; become moderate. 부드러워지다; 누그러지다. ¶ *The wind* 〔*sea*〕 *has moderated.* 바람이〔바다가〕 잔잔해졌다. [→mode]

mod·er·ate·ly [mádəritli / mɔ́d-] *adv.* in a moderate manner. 적당히; 알맞게. ¶ *a ~ hot day* 알맞게 더운 날씨.

mod·er·ate·ness [mádəritnis / mɔ́d-] *n.* Ⓤ the state of being moderate. 적당; 온건.

mod·er·a·tion [màdəréiʃən / mɔ̀d-] *n.* Ⓤ temperance; calmness; lack of violence. 적당; 중용; 절제; 온화; 온건. ¶ *in ~* 적당히; 알맞게.

mod·e·ra·to [màdərá:tou / mɔ̀d-] *adj., adv.* 《mus.》 in moderate time. 모데라토; 중간 속도로. [*moderate*]

mod·er·a·tor [mádərèitər / mɔ́d-] *n.* Ⓒ **1** a chairman. 의장; 사회자. **2** a person acting as judge to settle a quarrel. 중재〔조정〕자. **3** a regulator. 조절기.

:**mod·ern** [mádərn / mɔ́d-] *adj.* **1** of the present time; recent. 현대의(opp. ancient). ¶ *~ times* 현대. **2** up-to-date; not old fashion. 신식의; 최신의. ¶ *~ fashions* 최신 유행. — *n.* Ⓒ 《usu. *pl.*》 a person of modern times; a person who has modern tastes. 현대인; 현대적 신사상〔감각〕을 가진 사람. [L. *modo* just now]

mod·ern·ism [mádərnìzəm / mɔ́d-] *n.* **1** Ⓤ a modern view or method. 근대〔현대〕풍; 근대적 방법. **2** Ⓒ a modern thought or practice. 근대〔현대〕 사상; 현대주의. **3** Ⓒ a modern word or phrase. 현대어.

mod·ern·ist [mádərnist / mɔ́d-] *n.* Ⓒ a person who holds modern views, uses modern methods, etc. 근대〔현대〕주의자.

mod·ern·is·tic [màdərnístik / mɔ̀d-] *adj.* modern; of modernism or modernists. 근대적〔현대적〕인; 근대〔현대〕주의(자)의.

mo·der·ni·ty [madə́:rnəti, mou- / mɔd-] *n.* Ⓤ the state of being modern; Ⓒ something modern. 근대〔현대〕성; 근대적〔현대적〕임; 근대적〔현대적〕인 것.

mod·ern·ize [mádərnàiz / mɔ́d-] *vt.* (P6) make (something) modern. …을 근대화〔현대화〕하다. — *vi.* (P1) become modern. 근대적〔현대적〕으로 되다. ● **mod·ern·i·za·tion** [màdərnizéiʃən / mɔ̀dərnai-] *n.* **mod·ern·iz·er** [-ər] *n.*

:**mod·est** [mádist / mɔ́d-] *adj.* **1** not boastful or proud. 겸손한; 삼가는. ¶ *a ~ youth* 겸손한 청년 / *~ behavior* 겸손한 태도. **2** (of a woman) decent in behavior, speech, bearing, dress, etc. 얌전한; 정숙한; 점잖은. **3** not too great; moderate; humble. 적당한; 검소한; 수수한. ¶ *~ expenses* 적절한 지출 / *a ~ demand* 무리 없는 요구 / *a ~ little house* 자그마한 집 / *~ pay* 별로 많지 않은 급료. [→mode]

mod·est·ly [mádistli / mɔ́d-] *adv.* in a modest manner. 겸손하게; 점잖게; 삼가서.

·**mod·es·ty** [mádisti / mɔ́d-] *n.* Ⓤ the state of being modest; humility; moderation. 겸손; 겸양; 조심스러움; 정숙함; 점잖음. ¶ *a woman of great ~* 이를 데 없이 정숙한

부인.

mod·i·cum [mádikəm / mɔ́d-] *n.* Ⓒ《*sing.* only》a small amount or quantity. 소량; 근소; 소액(少額). ¶ *a ~ of sleep* 약간의 수면(睡眠) / *get a ~ of pleasure* 약간의 즐거움을 얻다 / *He is so bright that even with a ~ of effort he does excellent work.* 그는 얼마나 영리한지 적은 노력으로 뛰어난 일을 해낸다. [→mode]

mod·i·fi·ca·tion [màdəfikéiʃən / mɔ̀d-] *n.* **1** Ⓤ the act of modifying or being modified. 가감; 제한; 조절. ¶ *The ~ of his sentence enabled him to leave prison.* 판결의 경감은 그의 석방을 가능하게 했다. **2** Ⓒ a partial change or changing made by modifying. (부분적) 수정; 변경; 수정〔변경〕된 것. ¶ *With some ~ your composition will do for the school paper.* 너의 작문은 조금만 수정을 가하면 학교 신문에 실을 만하다. [→modify]

mod·i·fi·er [mádəfàiər / mɔ́d-] *n.* Ⓒ **1** 《gram.》 a word or group of words that modifies, such as an adjective, adverb, etc. 수식어. ¶ *Adjectives and adverbs are modifiers.* 형용사와 부사는 수식어다. **2** a person or thing that modifies. 수정〔변경〕하는 사람〔물건〕.

***mod·i·fy** [mádəfài / mɔ́d-] *vt.* (P6) **1** change (something) slightly. (부분적으로) 수정〔변경〕하다. ¶ *~ the terms of a contract* 계약 조건을 변경〔수정〕하다 / *~ one's ideas* 〔*opinions*〕 생각을〔견해를〕 고치다〔바꾸다〕. **2** reduce; limit (the meanings of words, etc.); moderate. …을 경감〔완화〕하다; 가감〔조절〕하다. ¶ *~ one's demands* 요구를 조절하다. **3** 《gram.》 qualify. 수식하다. ¶ *Adjectives ~ nouns.* 형용사는 명사를 수식한다. ●**mod·i·fi·a·ble** [-əbəl] *adj.* [→mode,-fy]

mod·ish [móudiʃ] *adj.* fashionable; stylish. 유행의; 현대풍의. ¶ *a ~ hat* 멋진 모자.

mod·u·late [mádʒəlèit / mɔ́-] *vt.* (P6) **1** regulate; adjust; vary; soften. 조정〔조절〕하다. **2** change (the voice, etc.). (음성·음조 등을) 바꾸다. **3** change the frequency of (electrical waves). (주파수)를 변조하다; 바꾸다. — *vi.* (P1) 《mus.》 pass from one key to another. 조(調)바꿈하다. [→mode]

mod·u·la·tion [màdʒəléiʃən / mɔ̀-] *n.* ⓊⒸ the act of modulating or the state of being modulated. 변조; 조절; 조바꿈.

mo·hair [móuhɛər] *n.* Ⓤ **1** cloth made from the hair of the Angora goat. 모헤어《앙고라 염소의 털》. **2** an imitation of such a material. 모조 모헤어. [Arab. =choice]

Mo·ham·med [mouhǽmid, -med] *n.* = Muhammad.

Mo·ham·med·an [mouhǽmidən, -med-] *adj.* of Muhammad or the Moslem religion. 마호메트(교)의; 회교의. — *n.* Ⓒ a follower of Muhammad. 마호메트 교도; 회교도. 參考 Mahometan이라고도 씀.

Mo·ham·med·an·ism [mouhǽmidənìzəm] *n.* Ⓤ the Moslem religion. 마호메트교; 회교.

moil [mɔil] *vi.* (P1) work hard. 억척같이 일하다. ¶ 《*emph.*》 *toil and ~* 뼈 빠지게 일하다. — *n.* Ⓒ hard work. 힘드는 일; 중노동. [L. *mollis* soft]

***moist** [mɔist] *adj.* **1** slightly wet; damp; watery; 습기가 있는; 축축한. ¶ *~ air* 습기 있는 공기 / *a ~ hand* 물기 있는 손. **2** (of season, climate, etc.) rainy. 비가 많은. **3** tearfull. 눈물어린. ¶ *~ eyes.* [F.]

moist·en [mɔ́isən] *vt.* (P6) make (something) moist. …을 축축하게 하다; 적시다. ¶ *~ one's lips* 〔*throat*〕 한잔 하다. — *vi.* (P1) become moist. 축축해지다. ¶ *~ at one's eyes* 눈물을 글썽거리다.

***mois·ture** [mɔ́istʃər] *n.* Ⓤ slight wetness; water vapor in the air or on a surface. 습기; 수증기; 수분.

mo·lar[1] [móulər] *n.* Ⓒ a back tooth used to grind one's food. 어금니. — *adj.* **1** used for grinding. 씹어 부수는. **2** of the molar teeth. 어금니의. [L. *mola* millstone]

mo·lar[2] [móulər] *adj.* **1** 《phys.》 of a mass of matter. 질량(質量)의. **2** 《chem.》 pertaining to gram-molecular weight. 그램 분자의. [→mole[3]]

mo·las·ses [məlǽsiz] *n. pl.* 《used as *sing.*》 a sweet syrup obtained from sugar during the process of manufacture. 당밀(糖密). [L. *mel* honey]

***mold**[1], 《Brit.》 **mould**[1] [mould] *n.* Ⓒ **1** a hollow shape in which anything is cast or formed. 형(型); 금형(金型); 주형(鑄型); 거푸집. ¶ *Hot metal was poured into the ~.* 뜨거운 쇳물이 거푸집에 부어졌다. **2** something formed in a mold. 형에 넣어 만들어진 것 《주물·젤리 등》. ¶ *a ~ of jelly* 젤리 한 개. **3** 《*fig.*》 a pattern; a model. 형(型); 모형. **4** a shape; a form. 형(形); 모습. ¶ *He is manly in ~ and bearing.* 그는 모습이나 태도가 남자답다. **5** ⓊⒸ 《*fig.*》 character; nature. 성격; 성질. ¶ *a man of gentle ~* 점잖은 사람 / *He was cast in a heroic ~.* 영웅 기질의 사람이었다 / *The brothers were cast in the same ~.* 그들 형제는 성격이 똑같았다 / *The two were men of quite different ~.* 그 둘은 성격이 아주 딴판이었다.

— *vt.* **1** (P6,7,13) form or make (something) in a mold; give a shape to (something). …을 틀에 넣어 만들다; 형상짓다. ¶ *~ a statue in* 〔*out of*〕 *clay* = *~ clay into a statue* 점토로 상(像)을 만들다. **2** (P6,13) shape the character of (someone); train; develop. …을 성격지우다; 형성하다; 단련하다. ¶ *~ one's character* 성격을 형성하다; 인격을 도야하다 / *Her character was molded by the trials she went through.* 그녀의 성격은 그녀가 겪은 많은 시련을 통해 형성되었다. [→mode]

mold[2], 《Brit.》 **mould**[2] [mould] *n.* Ⓤ soft, fine, rich soil. 부식토; (자양이 많은) 흙; 경토(耕土). — *vt.* (P7) 《*up*》 cover (something) over with mold. …을 흙으로 덮다. ¶ ～ *up potatoes* 감자를 흙으로 덮다. [E.]

mold[3], 《Brit.》 **mould**[3] [mould] *n.* Ⓤ a wool-like or fur-like tiny plant which grows on wet cloth, old bread, etc. 곰팡이. ¶ *blue* ～ 푸른곰팡이 / *a smell of* ～ 곰팡내 / *gather* ～ 곰팡이가 끼다; 곰팡나다. —*vi.* (P1,2A) become covered with mold. 곰팡나다. —*vt.* cover (something) with mold. …을 곰팡나게 하다; 곰팡이로 덮다. [E.]

mold·er[1], 《Brit.》 **mould·er**[1] [móuldər] *n.* Ⓒ a person or thing that molds or shapes. 금형〔거푸집〕 만드는 사람〔것〕; 주형 제조자. [→mold[1]]

mold·er[2], 《Brit.》 **mould·er**[2] [móuldər] *vi.* (P1,2A) **1** turn into dust; decay; waste away. 썩다; 부서지다. ¶ *Even iron in time molders away.* 쇠도 언젠가는 삭아 없어진다. **2** 《*fig.*》 degenerate, morally and intellectually; pass one's life in idleness. 타락하다; 허송세월하다. ¶ *remain moldering in the country* 시골에서 무위도식하며 지내다. —*vt.* (P6) cause (something) to decay. …을 썩게 만들다. [→mold[3]]

mold·ing, 《Brit.》 **mould-** [móuldiŋ] *n.* **1** Ⓤ the act of shaping. 주조; 소조(塑造). **2** Ⓒ something molded. 주조물. **3** 《often *pl.*》 《archit.》 an ornamental strip used around the upper part of the wall of a room or of a picture frame, etc. (벽의) 장식 쇠시리. [→mold[1]]

mold·y, 《Brit.》 **mould·y** [móuldi] *adj.* (**mold·i·er, mold·i·est** or 《Brit.》 **mould·i·er, mould·i·est**) **1** covered with mold. 곰팡난. ¶ ～ *bread* 〔*cheese*〕. **2** 《*fig.*》 musty; out of date; old-fashioned. 곰팡내 나는; 케케묵은; 진부한. ● **mold·i·ness** [-nis] *n.* [→mold[3]]

***mole**[1] [moul] *n.* Ⓒ a small, dark, slightly raised spot on the skin. (피부의) 점. [E.]

mole[2] [moul] *n.* Ⓒ a small animal that lives chiefly underground. 두더지. ¶ *blind as a* ～ 아주 눈이 먼.

mole[3] [moul] *n.* a big wall of stone laid in the sea. 방파제(防波堤)(cf. *breakwater*). [L. *moles* mass]

mo·lec·u·lar [moulékjulər] *adj.* of or consisting of molecules. 분자(分子)의; 분자로 된. ¶ *a* ～ *formula* 분자식/ ～ *weight* 분자량. [→mass]

mol·e·cule [máləkjùːl / mɔ́l-] *n.* Ⓒ **1** 《chem., phys.》 the smallest particle of an element. 분자(分子). **2** any very small particle. (일반적으로) 미립자(微粒子).

mole·hill [móulhìl] *n.* Ⓒ a small mound of earth raised up by moles. 두더지가 만든 흙두둑. [→mole[2]]

make a mountain out of a molehill, exaggerate; make (something) too important. 침소봉대(針小棒大)하다; 허풍떨다.

mo·lest [məlést] *vt.* 《usu. in *negative*》 annoy; trouble; disturb. …을 괴롭히다; 성가시게 굴다. ¶ *She should not be molested in any way.* 그녀를 가만히 내버려둬라. ● **mo·lest·er** [-ər] *n.* [L. *molestus* troublesome]

mo·les·ta·tion [mòulestéiʃən] *n.* Ⓤ the act of molesting; disturbance. 괴롭힘; 방해.

mol·li·fi·ca·tion [màləfikéiʃən / mɔ̀l-] *n.* Ⓤ the act of mollifying; the state of being mollified. 완화; 누그러뜨림; 진정; 경감; 달램. [↓]

mol·li·fy [málәfài / mɔ́l-] *vt.* (**-fied**) (P6) calm; soften; make (someone or something) quiet. …을 누그러뜨리다; 달래다; 진정시키다. ¶ ～ *someone's anger* (아무의) 화를 진정시키다. [L. *mollis* soft]

mol·lusc [máləsk / mɔ́l-] *n.* 《Brit.》 =mollusk.

mol·lusk [máləsk / mɔ́l-] *n.* Ⓒ any of a large group of animals with soft bodies, usu. covered by a hard shell. 연체(軟體) 동물. [→mollify]

mol·ly·cod·dle [málikàdl / mɔ́likɔ̀dl] *n.* one who is much coddled; a womanish man; a coward. 나약한 사람; 여자 같은 남자; 겁쟁이. —*vt.* (P6) spoil; coddle; take too great care of (a child, etc.). 어하다; 응석받이로〔어해서〕 기르다. [*Molly,* name → coddle]

molt, 《Brit.》 **moult** [moult] *vt., vi.* (P6;1) (of animals) cast off one's feathers, skin, etc. before a new growth; shed (feathers, etc.). 털갈이시키다〔하다〕; 허물을 벗게 하다〔벗다〕. —*n.* Ⓒ the act or season of molting. 털갈이; 허물벗기; 그 시기. [→mutable]

mol·ten [móultn] *v.* pp. of **melt.** —*adj.* **1** melted by heat. 녹은; 용해된. ¶ ～ *steel* 〔*metal*〕 녹인 쇠. **2** made by melting and casting. 주조(鑄造)된. ¶ *a* ～ *image* 주상(鑄像). [O.E. *melten* melt]

mo·lyb·de·num [məlíbdənəm] *n.* Ⓤ 《chem.》 a hard, silverwhite metallic element. 몰리브덴《금속 원소의 하나》. [L.]

mom [mam / mɔm] *n.* Ⓒ 《U.S. *colloq.*》 mother; mamma. 어머니; 엄마. [*mamma*]

:mo·ment [móumənt] *n.* **1** Ⓒ a very short time; an instant. 순간; 찰나. ¶ *in a* ～ 순간에; 곧 / *for a* ～ 잠깐 동안; 잠시 / *Wait a* ～. =*Just a* ～. =*One* ～, *please.* =*Half a* ～. 잠깐만(기다려 주십시오). **2** Ⓤ a special point of time. (어떤) 때; 시기. ¶ *at the* ～ 바로 지금〔그 때〕/ *for the* ～ 우선; 당장은 / *to the very* ～ 정각에 / *He fell down at the last* ～. 그는 막판에 와서 쓰러졌다 / *This is not the* ～ *to discuss it.* 지금 그런 말하고 있을 때가 아니다. **3** 《*the* ～, used as a *conj.*》 as soon as …하자마자. ¶ *He started the* ～ *he got your message.* 그는 네 전갈을 듣자마자 곧 떠났다. **4** Ⓒ the present time. 현재; 지금. ¶ *the question of the* ～ 현하(現下)의 문제. **5** Ⓤ importance. 중요(성); 긴요. ¶ *an affair of great* ～ 중대 사건 / *The chastity of women before marriage will come to be considered of less* ～. 여성의 혼전 순결은 점차로 덜 중요시

하게 될 것이다 / *It is of little* 〔*no*〕 ～. 그건 대단한 일이 아니다. [→move]

at any moment, at all time; very soon. 언제라도; 당장.

at moments, sometimes. 때때로.

not for a moment, not at all. 조금도 …않다. ¶ *I do not for a* ～ *suppose so.* 조금도 그럴 생각이 없다.

of the moment, of the present time. 지금의; 목하〔현재〕의. ¶ *the fashions of the* ～ 지금의 유행물 / *the man of the* ～ 당대의 인물.

this moment, at once. ¶ *Come here this* ～. 당장 오너라.

mo·men·tar·i·ly [móuməntèrəli] *adv.* **1** for a moment. 잠시; 잠깐. ¶ *hesitate* ～ 잠시 망설이다. **2** at every moment. 각일각. ¶ *Our danger is increasing* ～. 위험은 각일각 증대하고 있다. **3** at any moment. 언제라도; 곧.

***mo·men·tar·y** [móumәntèri / -təri] *adj.* lasting for a moment; temporary. 순간의; 한때의. ●**mo·men·tar·i·ness** [-nis] *n.*

mo·men·tous [mouméntəs] *adj.* very important; serious. 중대한; 심각한. ¶ *a* ～ *decision* 중대한 결정. ●**mo·men·tous·ness** [-nis] *n.*

mo·men·tum [mouméntəm] *n.* Ⓤ **1** 《phys.》 the force of motion of a moving object. 운동량. **2** 《*fig.*》 an object's tendency to continue moving forward. 타성(惰性); 여세.

Mon. Monday.

Mon·a·co [mánəkòu / mɔ́n-] *n.* a very small country on the Mediterranean coast. 모나코 공국(公國).

***mon·arch** [mánərk / mɔ́nərk] *n.* Ⓒ **1** a supreme ruler; a sovereign. 군주; 왕. ¶ *an absolute* ～ 전제 군주. **2** a person or thing like a monarch in its class or kind. 왕자; 왕자에 비견할 사람〔짐승〕. ¶ *The lion is the* ～ *of all beasts.* 사자는 동물의 왕이다. [→monad, Gk. *arkhō* rule]

mo·nar·chic [mənɑ́ːrkik], **-chi·cal** [-kikəl] *adj.* of or like a monarch or monarchy. 군주(국)의; 군주 정치의.

mon·ar·chism [mánərkìzəm / mɔ́n-] *n.* Ⓤ the principles of monarchy. 군주주의.

mon·ar·chist [mánərkist / mɔ́n-] *n.* Ⓒ a person who supports or believes in government by a monarch. 군주(제)주의자.

mon·ar·chy [mánərki / mɔ́n-] *n.* Ⓤ government by a monarch; Ⓒ a nation governed by a monarch. 군주 정치; 군주 정체; 군주국.

mon·as·ter·y [mánəstèri / mɔ́nəstəri] *n.* Ⓒ (*pl.* **-ter·ies**) a building for monks to live in. 수도원(cf. *convent, nunnery*). [→monad]

mo·nas·tic [mənǽstik] *adj.* **1** of or like monks or nuns or their way of life; self-denying. 수도원의〔같은〕; 금욕적인; 은둔의. ¶ *lead a* ～ *life* 수도 생활을 하다. **2** of monasteries. 수도원의. ¶ ～ *buildings* 수도원 건물. [↑]

mo·nas·ti·cism [mənǽstəsìzəm] *n.* Ⓤ the system or condition of life according to monastic rules. 수도원 제도; 수도〔금욕〕 생활.

:Mon·day [mʌ́ndi, -dei] *n.* the second day of the week. 월요일. 參考 Mon.로 생략함. [E. =day of the moon]

mon·e·tar·y [mánətèri, mʌ́n- / mɔ́nitəri] *adj.* of money or currency. 화폐의; 금전상의. ¶ *a* ～ *unit* 화폐 단위 / *in* ～ *difficulties* 재정난으로 / *the* ～ *system* 화폐 제도 / *a* ～ *reward* 금전에 의한 보수. [*money*]

:mon·ey [mʌ́ni] *n.* Ⓤ **1** coins; bank notes. 돈; 금전; 화폐《경화·지폐 등》. ¶ *paper* ～ 지폐 / *change* ～ 환전하다 / ～ *out of hand* = *ready* ～ = ～ *down* 현금 / ～ *on* 〔*at*〕 *call* 콜머니 / *have more* ～ *than sense* 생각없이 돈을 뭉텅뭉텅 쓰다. **2** anything used to pay for things, such as precious metals and checks. 통화. **3** wealth; property. 부; 재산. ¶ *lose all one's* ～ 모든 재산을 날리다 / *have plenty of* ～ 많은 재산〔돈〕이 있다. **4** 《*pl.*》 《law》 sums of money. 금액. [→mint]

get one's money's worth, get full value for what one has spent. 쓴 만큼 벌다; 노력한 만큼 얻다.

make money, get money; become rich. 돈을 벌다; 부자가 되다.

marry money, marry a rich person. 부자와 결혼하다.

raise money on, borrow money; secure a loan. 돈을 빌리다; 저당을 넣고 돈을 장만하다.

mon·ey·bag [mʌ́nibæ̀g] *n.* **1** Ⓒ a bag for money. 돈주머니; 지갑. **2** 《*pl.*, used as *sing.*》 《*colloq.*》 wealth; riches; a wealthy person; a rich and greedy person. 부; 재산; 부자; 구두쇠; 수전노.

mon·ey-chang·er [mʌ́nitʃèindʒər] *n.* Ⓒ a person whose business is to exchange money; a machine to exchange money quickly at fixed rates. 환전상; 환전기.

mon·eyed [mʌ́nid] *adj.* **1** wealthy; rich. 돈많은; 부자의. ¶ *a* ～ *man.* **2** of money. 금전상의. ¶ ～ *assistance* 재정적인 원조.

mon·ey·grub·ber [mʌ́nigrʌ̀bər] *n.* Ⓒ a person whose only interest in life is to make money. 돈독이 든 사람; 수전노.

mon·ey·lend·er [mʌ́nilèndər] *n.* Ⓒ a person whose business is to lend money at interest. 돈놀이하는 사람; 대금(貸金)업자.

mon·ey·lend·ing [mʌ́nilèndiŋ] *n.* Ⓤ the act of lending money at interest. 대금(貸金)(업).

mon·ey·mak·er [mʌ́nimèikər] *n.* Ⓒ **1** a person successful at getting money. 축재가. **2** something that produces gain of money. 돈벌이가 되는 일.

mon·ey-mak·ing [mʌ́nimèikiŋ] *n.* Ⓤ the making of money. 돈벌이. — *adj.* profitable. 이익이 생기는; 돈벌이가 되는.

money market [´– ˋ–] *n.* the financial center which decides the rate of interest on borrowed capital. 금융 시장.

money order [´– ˋ–] *n.* an order for the payment of money. 환(換); 우편환. ¶ *a bank* ~ 은행환 / *a telegraphic* ~ 전신환 / *foreign* ~ 외국환.

mon·ger [mʌ́ŋgər] *n.* Ⓒ 《Brit. usu. in compounds》 a dealer or trader in some article. 상인; …상(장수). ¶ *a fishmonger* 어물상; 생선 장수. [L. *mango*]

Mon·gol [mɑ́ŋgəl, -goul / mɔ́ŋgɔl] *n.* **1** Ⓒ a member of the Asiatic race living in Mongolia between China and Siberia. 몽골인. **2** Ⓤ the language of the Mongolians. 몽골어. — *adj.* of the Mongolian people or their language. 몽골인〔어〕의. [Native]

Mon·go·li·a [mɑŋgóuliə / mɔŋ-] *n.* a vast region in Asia between China and Siberia. 몽골.

Mon·go·li·an [mɑŋgóuliən / mɔŋ-] *n.* **1** Ⓒ a person of Mongolia. 몽골인. **2** Ⓤ the Mongolian language. 몽골어. — *adj.* of Mongolia, its people, or their language. 몽골 인종〔어〕의.

mon·grel [mʌ́ŋgrəl, mɑ́ŋ- / mʌ́ŋ-] *n.* Ⓒ **1** an animal, esp. a dog or a plant of mixed breed. 잡종(개). **2** 《*contempt.*》 a person of mixed birth. 혼혈아. — *adj.* of mixed breed, race, etc. 잡종의; 혼혈의. ¶ *a* ~ *dog* 〔*race*〕. [→mingle]

mon·ism [mɑ́nizəm / mɔ́n-] *n.* Ⓤ 《philos.》 the doctrine that the universe can be explained in terms of only one basic substance or principle. 일원론(一元論). ¶ *idealistic* ~ 유심 일원론. [→monad]

mo·ni·tion [mouníʃən] *n.* ⒸⓊ **1** warning; caution. 경고; 주의. **2** an official or legal notice. (정식의) 통고(장); 경고(장). [L. *moneo* warn]

*__mon·i·tor__ [mɑ́nitər / mɔ́n-] *n.* Ⓒ **1** a senior pupil of a school who is given special duties by the teacher. 반장; (교사를 보좌하는) 학급 위원. **2** a person who advises or warns. 훈계〔경고, 권고〕자; 모니터. **3** a receiver used for checking radio or TV programs. 감시 장치〔기〕. **4** a person who is employed to listen to and report on foreign broadcasts, etc. (정보를 얻기 위해 고용된) 외신 방수자(外信傍受者). — *vt., vi.* (P6;1) **1** check (radio or TV programs) by listening in or watching. (라디오·TV를) 모니터하다. **2** listen to and report on (foreign broadcast, etc.). (외신 등을) 방수하다. ¶ ~ *the enemy's radio broadcasts* 적의 라디오 방송을 방수〔청취〕하다. [↑]

mon·i·to·ri·al [mɑ̀nitɔ́:riəl / mɔ̀n-] *adj.* of a monitor; serving to warn; using monitors. 반장의; 권고(자)의; 모니터를 쓰는.

mon·i·to·ry [mɑ́nitɔ̀:ri / mɔ́nitəri] *adj.* warning. 권고〔경고〕의. ¶ *a* ~ *letter* 권고서. — *n.* Ⓒ a letter containing a warning from a bishop. (bishop 의) 계고장(戒告狀).

*__monk__ [mʌŋk] *n.* Ⓒ one of a group of men who give up everything else for religion. 수사(修士); 승려(cf. *nun*). [→monad]

:**mon·key** [mʌ́ŋki] *n.* Ⓒ **1** the animal nearest to man. 원숭이. **2** a mischievous person, esp. a child; an imitating child. 개구쟁이; 남의 흉내를 잘 내는 아이.

get 〔***have***〕 ***one's monkey up,*** 《Brit. *sl.*》 become angry. 화내다.

make a monkey of, make a fool of. …을 웃음거리로 만들다.

put someone's monkey up, 《Brit. *sl.*》 make (someone) angry. …를 화나게 하다.

— *vi.* (P2A,3) 《*colloq.*》 play the tricks; act as a monkey does. 장난치다; 가지고 놀다. ¶ ~ (*about, around*) *with a gun* 총을 가지고 놀다〔만지작거리다〕 / *Stop monkeying* (*about, around*) *with my books.* 내 책 가지고 장난하지 마라. [?]

monkey business [´– ˋ–] *n.* 《U.S. *sl.*》 **1** unfair and secret action. 사기; 기만; 수상한 짓. **2** mischievous behavior. (짓궂은) 장난.

mon·key·ish [mʌ́ŋkiiʃ] *adj.* like a monkey; mischievous. 원숭이 같은; 장난을 좋아하는.

monkey wrench [´– ˋ] *n.* a spanner used for turning nuts, bolts, etc. 멍키렌치. 參考 monkey spanner 라고도 함.

monk·ish [mʌ́ŋkiʃ] *adj.* 《usu. *contempt.*》 of or like a monk; like monks or their way of life. 수사(修士)의; 수사〔중〕 같은. [→monk]

mon·o- [mɑ́nou- / mɔ́nou-] *pref.* one; single. '하나의, 단(單)의' 의 뜻(opp. poly-). ¶ *monorail.* 語法 모음 앞에서는 mon-. [→monad]

mon·o·chro·mat·ic [mɑ̀nəkroumǽtik / mɔ̀n-] *adj.* of one color; of or producing light of one wave length. 단색의; 단채(單彩)의. [↓]

mon·o·chrome [mɑ́nəkròum / mɔ́n-] *n.* Ⓒ a painting or drawing in a single color. 단색화(單色畫). [→chrome]

mon·o·cle [mɑ́nəkəl / mɔ́n-] *n.* Ⓒ an eyeglass to be worn over one eye. 외알 안경. [→ocular]

〈monocle〉

mon·o·cot·y·le·don [mɑ̀nəkɑ̀təlí:dən / mɔ̀nəkɔ̀təlí:-] *n.* Ⓒ a plant with only one leaf growing at first from the seed. 외떡잎〔단자엽(單子葉)〕 식물. [→cotyledon]

mon·o·dy [mɑ́nədi / mɔ́n-] *n.* Ⓒ (*pl.* **-dies**) **1** a sad, mournful song. 애가(哀歌); 만가(輓歌). **2** a poem in which a person feels sorrow for another's death. 애도시(哀悼詩). [→monad, →ode]

mo·nog·a·mist [mənɑ́gəmist / mənɔ́g-]

n. Ⓒ a person who practices or believes in monogamy. 일부 일처주의자(opp. polygamist). [↓]

mo·nog·a·mous [mənágəməs / mənɔ́g-] *adj.* practicing or believing in monogamy; of monogamy. 일부 일처를 지키는; 일부 일처의. [↓]

mo·nog·a·my [mənágəmi / mənɔ́g-] *n.* Ⓤ the act or state of having only one wife or husband at a time. 일부 일처제 〔주의〕(opp. polygamy). [Gk. *gamos* marriage, *gunē* woman, *anēr* man]

mon·o·gram [mánəgræ̀m / mɔ́n-] *n.* Ⓒ a design composed decorative letters, esp. the initials of a name. 모노그램《성명의 첫글자를 도안화하여 짜맞춘 것》. [→gram]

mon·o·graph [mánəgræ̀f, -grɑ̀:f / mɔ́n-] *n.* Ⓒ a book or treatise on one particular subject. 전공 논문; 모노그래프. [→graph]

mon·o·lith [mánəliθ / mɔ́n-] *n.* **1** a single large block of stone. 한 덩어리로 된 큰 돌《건축·조각용》. **2** a monument, statue, etc., formed of a single large block of stone. 돌 하나로 된 기념비 또는 상(像). [Gk. *lithos* stone]

mon·o·logue, 《U.S.》 **-log** [mánəlɔ̀:g, -lɑ̀g / mɔ́nəlɔ̀g] *n.* Ⓒ **1** a long speech by one person in a play, etc. 혼자하는 긴 대사. **2** a dramatic scene for one performer only. 일인극; 독연(獨演). **3** a part of a play in which only one person speaks. 독백; 모놀로그. **4** a long speech or talk by a single person, esp. one that interferes with the general conversation. 장광설(長廣舌). [-logy]

mon·o·ma·ni·a [mɑ̀nəméiniə / mɔ̀n-] *n.* Ⓤ the state of mind in which a person is abnormally interested in one subject or idea only. 한 가지 일에만 열광하기; 편집광(偏執狂). [→mania]

mon·o·ma·ni·ac [mɑ̀nəméiniæ̀k / mɔ̀n-] *n.* Ⓒ a person who is a victim of monomania. 편집광자(偏執狂者); 한 가지 일에만 열광〔집착〕하는 사람.

mon·o·plane [mánəplèin / mɔ́n-] *n.* Ⓒ an airplane with a single wing on its body. 단엽기(單葉機)(cf. *biplane*). [→plane]

mo·nop·o·list [mənápəlist / -nɔ́p-] *n.* Ⓒ a person who has a monopoly or who believes in monopolies. 독점자; 독점 판매자; 전매론자. [*monopoly*]

mo·nop·o·li·za·tion [mənɑ̀pəlizéiʃən / -nɔ̀pəlai-] *n.* Ⓤ the act or the process of monopolizing; the state of being monopolized. 전매; 독점.

mo·nop·o·lize [mənápəlàiz / -nɔ́p-] *vt.* (P6) **1** have or get power strong enough to possess or control (something) while shutting out all others. …의 전매〔독점〕권을 가지다〔획득하다〕. **2** occupy the whole of (something or someone). …을 독점하다. ¶ ~ *the conversation* 대화를 독점하다 / *She will often try to ~ his time.* 종종 그녀는 그의 시간을 독차지하려 든다.

·mo·nop·o·ly [mənápəli / -nɔ́p-] *n.* Ⓒ (*pl.* **-lies**) **1** the shutting out of all others; the control of the entire supply of something. (상품 등의) 전매(권); 독점(권); 시장 독점. ¶ *a ~ on* 〔*of*〕 *tobacco* 담배 전매권. **2** a commercial product or service that is so controlled. 전매품. **3** a person or company that has a monopoly of something. 전매권을 가진 사람〔회사〕; 전매〔독점〕 회사. [Gk. *pōleō* sell]

mon·o·rail [mánərèil / mɔ́n-] *n.* Ⓒ a railway with a single rail. 모노레일; 단궤(單軌)철도. [→rail]

mon·o·syl·lab·ic [mɑ̀nəsilǽbik / mɔ̀n-] *adj.* **1** having only one syllable. 단음절(어)의. **2** speaking in monosyllables; terse or blunt. 단음절어로 말하는; 퉁명스러운. ¶ *a ~ reply* 무뚝뚝한 대답《No, not now. 따위》. [→monad]

mon·o·syl·la·ble [mánəsìləbəl / mɔ́n-] *n.* Ⓒ a word of one syllable. 단음절어.
speak in monosyllables, speak plainly. 퉁명스럽게 말하다.

mon·o·the·ism [mánəθi:ìzəm / mɔ́n-] *n.* Ⓤ the doctrine or belief that there is only one God. 일신교(一神教)(cf. *polytheism*). [→theism]

mon·o·the·ist [mánəθì:ist / mɔ́n-] *n.* Ⓒ a person who believes that there is only one God. 일신교 신자; 일신론자.

mon·o·tone [mánətòun / mɔ́n-] *n.* Ⓒ sameness of tone, style, color, etc. 단조(單調)로움. ¶ *read in a ~* 단조롭게 읽다. — *adj.* =monotonous. — *vt., vi.* (P6;1) repeat monotonously. 단조롭게 반복하다. [→tone]

·mo·not·o·nous [mənátənəs / -nɔ́t-] *adj.* **1** continuing in the same tone; without change. 단조로운; 변화가 없는. ¶ *a ~ voice* 단조로운 목소리. **2** tiresome; dull; uninteresting. 지루한; 따분한. ¶ ~ *work.* 따분한 일. ● **mo·not·o·nous·ly** [-li] *adv.*

mo·not·o·ny [mənátəni / -nɔ́t-] *n.* Ⓤ the state of being monotonous; sameness; dullness. 단조로움; 무변화; 따분함. ¶ *the ~ of the plains* 평야의 단조로움.

mon·sieur [məsjə́:r] *n.* Ⓒ (*pl.* **mes·sieurs**) Mr.; sir. …씨; …님; …귀하. 參考 프랑스어의 경칭. [F.]

mon·soon [mɑnsú:n / mɔn-] *n.* Ⓒ **1** a seasonal wind in the Indian Ocean and in southern Asia. 몬순; 계절풍. **2** a rainy season that comes with the southwest monsoon. 우기; 장마철. [Arab.]

·mon·ster [mánstər / mɔ́n-] *n.* Ⓒ **1** any animal or plant that is unnatural. 괴물. **2** a very big creature or thing; a giant. (괴물 같은) 거대한 짐승〔식물, 물건〕; 거인. **3** a very wicked or cruel person. 극악 무도한 사람. ¶ *a ~ of cruelty* 잔인 무도한 사람. — *adj.*

very big. 거대한. ¶ *a ~ potato* 매우 큰 감자 / *a ~ tree* 거목. [L. *moneo* warn]

mon·stros·i·ty [mɑnstrásəti / mɔnstrɔ́s-] *n.* (*pl.* **-ties**) **1** Ⓒ a monster. 거대한 것; 기형물(奇形物); 포악한 행위. **2** Ⓤ the state of being monstrous. 기형(奇形); 괴이함.

·**mon·strous** [mánstrəs / mɔ́n-] *adj.* **1** very big; not normal; like a monster. 거대한; 기괴한; 괴물 같은. ¶ *a ~ beast* (거대한) 괴수(怪獸). **2** ⓐ very bad; horrible. 아주 고약한; 가공할; 잔혹한. ¶ *a ~ crime* 극악무도한 범죄. ⓑ shocking; outrageous. 아연할; 터무니없는. ¶ *a ~ blunder* 터무니없는 실수. — *adv.* 《*dial.*》 very; extremely. 대단히; 엄청나게.

mon·tage [mɑntáːʒ / mɔn-] *n.* ⓊⒸ **1** the act of making a new picture by arranging several pictures; a picture so made. 몽타주법(法)〔사진〕; 합성 사진. **2** (in motion pictures) the use of a rapid succession of very short scenes. (영화의) 몽타주. [F. *monter* to mount]

Mon·tan·a [mɑntǽnə / mɔn-] *n.* a western State of the United States. 몬태나. 參考 Mont. 로 생략함. 주도는 Helena.

Mon·tan·an [mɑntǽnən / mɔn-] *n.* Ⓒ a person of Montana. 몬태나주(州) 사람. — *adj.* of Montana. 몬태나주의.

:**month** [mʌnθ] *n.* Ⓒ **1** one of the twelve parts into which the year is divided. 달; 월(月). ¶ *last ~* 지난 달 / *next ~* 다음 달 / *~ by* 〔*after*〕 *~* = *~ in, ~ out* 매달; 다달이 / *the ~ before last* 지지난달 / *this day ~* 내달〔전달〕의 오늘 / *this ~* 이달 / *in the ~ of May,* 5월에 / *What day of the ~ is this ?* 오늘이 며칠이냐. **2** the period of time from a day of one month to the same day of the next month. 한달; 1개월. ¶ *a ~ of Sundays* 오랫동안 / *the past ~* 이 한달 (동안). [E.]

·**month·ly** [mʌ́nθli] *adj.* **1** of a month; for a month; lasting a month. 한달 (동안)의; 한 달 계속되는. **2** done, happening, etc. once a month. 월 1회의; 매달의; 월정(月定)의. ¶ *a ~ salary* 월급 / *a ~ visit* 매달의 방문. — *adv.* once a month; every month. 한 달에 한 번; 매달. ¶ *They pay ~.* 월 1회 지불한다. — *n.* Ⓒ (*pl.* **-lies**) a magazine published each month. 월간 잡지.

Mont·re·al [mɑ̀ntriɔ́ːl / mɔ̀n-] *n.* a seaport in Quebec, Canada, on the St. Lawrence River. 몬트리올. 參考 캐나다의 상공업 중심지.

:**mon·u·ment** [mánjəmənt / mɔ́n-] *n.* Ⓒ **1** a building, statue, tomb, etc. set up to keep a person or an event from being forgotten. 기념관〔비〕; 묘비; 기념탑. ¶ *build* 〔*erect*〕 *a ~ to someone's memory* 아무의 추억을 위해 기념비를 세우다. **2** anything that is of special historic interest. (역사적) 기념물; 기념 건축물; 유적. ¶ *an ancient ~* 사적 기념물 / *a natural ~* 천연 기념물. **3** an achievement or work worth remembering. 불후의 업적. ¶ *a ~ of scientific research* 과학적 연구의 불멸의 업적. [→monster]

mon·u·men·tal [mɑ̀njəméntl / mɔ̀n-] *adj.* **1** of a monument. 기념비의. ¶ *a ~ inscription* 비명(碑銘). **2** lasting a long time; important. 불멸의; 기념이 되는. ¶ *a ~ event* 기념비적인 사건 / *a truly ~ work* 실로 기념비적인 작품. **3** (of bad quality) very great; extravagant. 대단한; 터무니없는. ¶ *~ ignorance* 형편 없는 무지.

moo [muː] *n.* Ⓒ (*pl.* **moos**) the sound made by a cow. 음매《소 우는 소리》. — *vi.* (P1) make the sound of a cow. (소가) 음매하고 울다. [Imit.]

·**mood**[1] [muːd] *n.* **1** Ⓒ a state of mind or feeling; a humor. 기분. ¶ *in a merry ~* 즐거운 기분으로 / *I was in the ~ for study.* 공부하고 싶은 기분이었다 / *I am in no ~ for serious music.* 딱딱한 음악은 생각이 없다. **2** 《often *pl.*》 fits of depression or bad temper. 씨무룩함; 짜증; 변덕. ¶ *a man of moods* 변덕스러운 사람. [E.]

·**mood**[2] [muːd] *n.* Ⓒ 《gram.》 one of the forms of a verb that serves to show the speaker's manner. 법; 서법(敍法). ¶ *imperative ~* 명령법 / *subjunctive ~* 가정법. [→mode]

mood·i·ly [múːdili] *adv.* in a moody manner. 씨무룩해서; 뚱해서; 꾀까다롭게. [*mood*[1]]

mood·i·ness [múːdinis] *n.* Ⓤ the state of being moody. 불쾌; 꾀까다로움.

mood·y [múːdi] *adj.* (**mood·i·er, mood·i·est**) **1** having changes of mood. 변덕스러운. **2** often having gloomy moods; gloomy; sad; melancholy. 저기압의; 뚱한; 우울한.

:**moon** [muːn] *n.* Ⓒ **1** 《usu. *the ~*》 the heavenly body which moves around the earth. 달. **2** the moon at a certain period of time; an appearance of the moon. (어떤 시기의) 달; 달의 상(相). ¶ *a full ~* 보름달 / *a half-moon* 반달 / *a new* 〔*the old*〕 *~* 초승〔그믐〕달. **3** the moon as an object that can be seen. (하늘에 뜬) 달. ¶ *Is there a ~ tonight ?* 오늘밤 달이 떴나 / *There is no ~ tonight.* 오늘밤은 달이 없다. **4** the time between one new moon and the next; 《*poet.*》 a month. 태음월(太陰月); 한 달. **5** Ⓤ 《*the ~*》 moonlight. 달빛. ¶ *I walked in the ~.* 달빛 아래를 걸었다. **6** something which looks like the moon. 달 모양의 것. **7** any heavenly body which moves around a planet. 위성.

beyond the moon, far beyond one's reach. 손이 미치지 않는 곳에; 터무니없이.

cry for the moon, desire the impossible. 되지도 않을 일을 바라다.

once in a blue moon, 《*colloq.*》 rarely; seldom; almost never. 아주 드물게; 거의 …않다.

— *vi.* (P2A) move about or look around idly. 멍청하게 돌아다니다〔두리번거리다〕.

— *vt.* (P7) spend (time) idly. (시간)을 허

송세월하다. ¶ ~ *away the holidays* 하는 일 없이 휴일을 보내다. [E.]

moon·beam [múːnbìːm] *n.* Ⓒ a ray of moonlight. 달빛.

moon·calf [múːnkæ̀f, -kɑ̀ːf] *n.* Ⓒ (*pl.* **-calves**) a born fool. (선천적) 백치; 바보.

moon·calves [múːnkæ̀vz, -kɑ̀ːvz] *n.* pl. of **mooncalf.**

moon·less [múːnlis] *adj.* without the moon; lacking the light of the moon. 달이 없는; 달빛이 안 비추는; 어두운.

:moon·light [múːnlàit] *n.* Ⓤ the light of the moon. 달빛. ¶ *in the*〔*under*〕 ~ 달빛 아래. — *adj.* of moonlight; lighted by the moon; performed or happening in the moonlight or at night. 달빛의; 달이 비친; 달밤에 일어난〔일어나는〕. ¶ *a* ~ *ramble* 달밤의 산책 /《*colloq.*》 *a* ~ *flit* 야반 도주.

moon·lit [múːnlit] *adj.* lighted by the moon. 달빛에 비췬; 달빛어린. ¶ *a* ~ *scene* 달빛어린 풍경 / *a* ~ *night* 달밤.

moon·shine [múːnʃàin] *n.* Ⓤ **1** moonlight. 달빛. **2**《*fig.*》 foolish idea or talk; nonsense. 헛소리; 공상; 난센스. ¶ *That's all* ~. 모두가 헛소리다. **3**《U.S. *colloq.*》 strong drink made or sold secretly. 밀조〔밀매〕주.

moon·shin·er [múːnʃàinər] *n.* 《U.S. *colloq.*》 **1** a person who makes alcoholic liquor unlawfully. 밀주 만드는 사람. **2** a person who follows an unlawful trade at night. 밤에 불법 영업하는 사람.

moon·struck [múːnstrʌ̀k] *adj.* crazy; mad. 미친; 머리가 돈.

moon·y [múːni] *adj.* (**moon·i·er, moon·i·est**) **1** of or like the moon. 달의; 달 같은. **2** dreamy; absent-minded. 꿈결같은; 멍청한.

moor[1] [muər] *vt.* (P6,7) fasten (a ship, etc.) with ropes or an anchor; anchor. (배 등)을 잡아매다; 정박시키다; 투묘(投錨)하다. ¶ ~ *a ship at the pier* 배를 부두에 매다. — *vi.* (P1) moor a ship; be made secure by ropes, anchors, etc. (배가) 투묘하다〔정박하다〕; 배를 잡아매다〔계류(繫留)하다〕. [E.]

·moor[2] [muər] *n.* ⓊⒸ 《Brit.》 a wild piece of land covered with grass and heather. 황무지; 광야. [E.]

moor·age [mú(ː)ridʒ / múər-] *n.* ⓊⒸ the act of mooring; the state of being moored; the money charged for mooring a ship; Ⓒ a place for mooring. (선박 등의) 계류(繫留); 정박; 정박〔계류〕료(料); 정박지. [*moor*[1]]

moor·ing [múəriŋ] *n.* **1** the act of mooring. (선박의) 계류(繫留); 정박. **2** 《*pl.*》 the ropes, chains, etc. by which a ship is moored. 계선구(具); 계류 장치. **3** 《*pl.*》 a place where a ship is moored. 정박〔계류〕지.

moor·ish [múəriʃ] *adj.* of or like a moor; abounding in moors. 황야의; 황야에 나는〔사는〕. [moor[2]]

moor·land [múərlæ̀nd, -lənd] *n.* Ⓤ =moor[2].

moose [muːs] *n.* Ⓒ (*pl.* **moose**) a big deer living in the northern part of the United States or in Canada. 큰사슴. [Native]

moot [muːt] *adj.* needing discussion; debatable. 의론의 여지가 있는. ¶ *a* ~ *point* 논쟁점. — *vt.* (P6) **1** discuss; talk about (a question). …을 토의〔논의〕하다. **2** propose (a subject, etc.) for discussion. (문제 등)을 제기하다. ¶ ~ *the question once more* 문제를 한번 더 토의에 부치다. — *n.* Ⓒ a discussion. 토론; 토의. [E.]

moot court [⌐⌐] *n.* a mock court held in a law school to give students practice. 모의 법정〔재판〕.

mop[1] [mɑp / mɔp] *n.* Ⓒ **1** a bundle of many pieces of cloth fastened to the end of a long stick, used for washing floors, etc. 자루〔대〕걸레; 몹. **2** a thick head of hair like a mop. 더벅머리. — *vt.* (**mopped, mop·ping**) (P6,7) **1** wash or clean with a mop. 자루걸레로 …을 청소하다. ¶ ~ *up the floor* 자루걸레로 마루를 닦다. **2** wipe tears or sweat from. (눈물·땀)을 닦다; 씻다. ¶ ~ *one's face with one's handkerchief* 손수건으로 얼굴을 닦다. [→napkin]

mop up, **a**) clean up (spilt water) by mopping. …을 닦다. **b**) finish (work, etc.). …을 끝내다; 마무르다.

mop[2] [mɑp / mɔp] *vi.* (**mopped, mop·ping**) 《*lit.*》 (P1) make faces; grimace. 얼굴을 찡그리다. ¶ ~ *and mow* 얼굴을 찡그리다. — *n.* an ugly twisted face like a monkey. 우거지상. ¶ *mops and mows* 찡그린 얼굴. [→napkin]

mope [moup] *vi.* (P1,2A) be low-spirited; be sad. 의기소침해 있다; 우울해 있다.

mope away one's time, spend one's time in feeling sad or in feeling sorry for oneself. 우울한 나날을 보내다.

— *n.* Ⓒ **1** a person who mopes. 침울해 있는 사람. **2** 《*pl.*》 a gloomy, indifferent state of mind. 우울한 심정; 의기소침. ¶ *have* (*a fit of*) *the mopes* 우울해 있다. ● **mop·er** [-ər] *n.* [*mop*[2]]

mop·ish [móupiʃ] *adj.* gloomy; dejected. 우울한; 풀죽은. [↑]

mop·pet [mɑ́pit / mɔ́p-] *n.* 《*colloq.*》 a child. 어린아이. [L.]

mo·raine [mouréin / mɔ-] *n.* a heap of earth and stones collected by a glacier. 빙퇴석(氷堆石). [F.]

:mor·al [mɔ́(ː)rəl, mɑ́r-] *adj.* **1** good in manner or character; right; virtuous. 도덕적인; 도덕적으로 옳은; 도덕을 지키는(opp. immoral). ¶ *a* ~ *man* 품행이 단정한 사람 / *live a* ~ *life* 바르게 살다. **2** able to understand right and wrong. 도덕 관념이 있는; 선악을 아는(opp. nonmoral). ¶ *Man is a* ~ *being.* 인간은 도덕 관념이 있는 존재다 / ~ *standard* 도덕적 기준 / *the* ~ *sense* 도덕적 감각〔양심〕. **3** of the difference between right and wrong; ethical. 도덕의; 도의상의; 윤리적인. ¶ *a ~ question* 도의상의 문제 / *~ character* 품성 / *~ laws* 도덕률 / *~ philosophy* 〔*science*〕 윤리학. **4** showing examples of right behavior; teaching the principles of good conduct. 교훈적(教訓的)인. ¶ *a ~ book* 교훈적인 책 / *a ~ play* 권선징악극. **5** concerned with the mind and feelings; spiritual. 정신적인(opp. material). ¶ *~ support* 정신적 원조 / *a ~ victory* 〔*courage*〕 정신적 승리〔용기〕 / *use a word in its ~ sense* 말을 (글자대로가 아닌) 정신적 의미로 쓰다. **6** probable. 있을 수 있는. ¶ *a ~ certainty* 거의 틀림없는 일.

— *n.* **1** Ⓒ a moral lesson taught by a fable, an event, etc. (우화·사건 등의) 교훈; 우의(寓意). ¶ *What is the ~ of the story?* 그 이야기의 교훈은 무엇이냐. **2** 《*pl.*, used as *sing.*》 principles of right and wrong; ethics. 도덕; 윤리학. **3** 《*pl.*》 social standards of right and wrong; a manner judged from a moral point of view. (사회적인) 도의; (개인의) 품행; 몸가짐. ¶ *a man of bad morals* 행실이 안 좋은 사람. [L. *mos* custom]

mo·rale [mouræ̃l / mɔrɑ́:l] *n.* Ⓤ the state of mind as regards hope, courage, good spirits, etc. (군대 등의) 사기; 풍기. ¶ *the ~ of an army* 군의 사기. [↑]

mor·al·ist [mɔ́(:)rəlist, mɑ́r-] *n.* Ⓒ a person who lives a moral life; a teacher of or writer on morals. 도덕가; 윤리주의자; 도학자.

mor·al·is·tic [mɔ̀(:)rəlístik, mɑ̀r-] *adj.* moralizing; concerned with morals. 도학적인; 교훈이 되는; 도덕주의의.

mo·ral·i·ty [mɔ(:)rǽləti, mɑr-] *n.* **1** Ⓤ the rightness or wrongness of an action. 도덕(성); 윤리(학). **2** Ⓒ good morals; virtue. 덕성; 덕행; 품행. ¶ *a woman of easy ~* 몸가짐이 헤픈 여자. **3** Ⓒ a moral teaching or lesson. 도덕적 교훈; 훈화. **4** Ⓒ a kind of religious play popular in the 16th century in England. 권선 징악극. [→moral,-ity]

mor·al·i·za·tion [mɔ̀:rəlizéiʃən, mɑ̀r- / mɔ̀rəlai-] *n.* Ⓤ the act of moralizing; the state of being moralized. 설법; 설교; 교화; 도덕적 해석.

mor·al·ize [mɔ́(:)rəlàiz, mɑ́r-] *vt.* (P6) **1** explain (something) in terms of right and wrong. 선악으로 …을 설명하다. **2** talk about morality to (someone); improve the morals of (someone). …에게 도덕을 가르치다; …를 (도덕적으로) 교화하다. — *vi.* (P1) 《*on, upon*》 think, talk, or write about questions of right and wrong. 도리를 가르치다; 설교하다.

mor·al·ly [mɔ́(:)rəli, mɑ́r-] *adv.* **1** in a moral manner; ethically. 도덕상〔도덕적〕으로; 윤리적으로. ¶ *He is a good man ~, but too stupid for his position.* 도덕적으로는 나무랄 데 없는 사람이나 직책을 수행하기에는 무능하다. **2** virtually; practically. 사실상; 실제로. ¶ *I am ~ sure that I locked the door.* 정말 문을 채웠단 말입니다.

mo·rass [məræ̃s] *n.* Ⓒ **1** a piece of soft, wet ground; a swamp. 늪; 습지. **2** 《*fig.*》 a difficult situation. 난국; 곤경. [Teut. (→marsh)]

mor·a·to·ri·a [mɔ̀(:)rətɔ́:riə, mɑ̀r-] *n.* pl. of **moratorium.**

mor·a·to·ri·um [mɔ̀(:)rətɔ́:riəm, mɑ̀r-] *n.* Ⓒ (*pl.* **-ri·ums** or **-ri·a**) 《law》 a government order by which payments of money need not be made for the period during which the order is in effect. 지급 유예령; 지급 연기. [L. *mora* delay]

mor·bid [mɔ́:rbid] *adj.* **1** unhealthy; gloomy, sad and unpleasant. 건전하지 못한; 병적인; 음침한. ¶ *a ~ liking for horrors* 공포에의 병적인 취미. **2** caused by disease; ill. 병으로 인한; 병의. ¶ *Cancer is a ~ growth.* 암은 병적인 형성물이다. [L. *morbus* disease]

mor·bid·i·ty [mɔ:rbídəti] *n.* **1** Ⓤ an abnormal or unhealthy state of mind. (정신적으로) 병적인 상태〔성질〕; 불건전. **2** Ⓒ the rate of disease in a locality. 한 지방의 이환율(罹患率).

mor·bid·ly [mɔ́:rbidli] *adv.* in a morbid manner. 병적으로; 불건전하게.

mor·bid·ness [mɔ́:rbidnis] *n.* Ⓤ the quality of being morbid. 병적 상태; 불건전.

mor·dant [mɔ́:rdənt] *adj.* **1** (of a word) biting; cutting; severe. 신랄한; 매서운. ¶ *a ~ tongue* 독설(毒舌) / *~ criticism* 신랄한 비평. **2** (of a liquid) destroying metal, such as an acid. 부식성의. **3** that fixes colors in dyeing. 매염(媒染)의. — *n.* **1** a substance that fixes colors in dyeing. 매염제. **2** an acid that eats into metal. 금속 부식제. [L. *mordeo* bite]

⁝**more** [mɔ:r] *adj.* (compar. of **many** or **much**) **1** greater in amount or degree. (양·정도가) 더 많은; 더 …한(opp. less). ¶ *I have ~ money than you.* 너보다 돈이 많다 / *He has much ~ ability than I.* 그는 나보다는 훨씬 더 유능하다 / *She is not ~ beautiful than her sister.* 그녀는 제 언니보다 더 예쁘지는 않다. **2** greater in number. (수적으로) 더 많은〔다수의〕(opp. fewer). ¶ *You shouldn't buy ~ books than you can read.* 책을 읽을 수 있을 만큼만 사거라 / *~ people than before* 전보다 더 많은 사람 / *More than ten persons are* 〔*More than one person is*〕 *needed.* 11명〔두 사람〕 이상 필요하다. 語法 영어의 more than ten은 '11 이상' 임. 우리 말의 '10 이상' 은 엄격히는 10 and more 라 함. 또 more than one이 뜻은 복수이나 단수 동사로 받음. **3** further; other; additional. 그 이상의; 그 밖의; 추가〔여분〕의. ¶ *for three ~ days* 사흘 동안 더 / *a little ~ butter* 버터를 좀 더 / *How many ~ boys are there in the garden?* 정원에 아이들이 몇이나 더 있지 / *There is no ~ ink in the bottle.* 병 속에 잉크

가 더는 없다 / *one ~ word* 한 마디만 더 / *a few ~ books* 책 몇 권 더 / *Will you have some ~ tea?* 차 좀 더 들겠나.
— *n.* UC **1** a greater amount, degree, number, etc. 더 많은 양〔정도·수 따위〕 (opp. less). ¶ *He ate much, but I ate ~.* 그가 많이 먹었지만 나는 더 먹었다 / *There is ~ in him than you imagine.* 그에게는 네가 상상도 못 하는 데가 있다 / *Give him some ~.* 조금 더 주어라 / *No ~ of your jokes.* 농담 그만 해라. **2** 《used as *pl.*》 a greater number; a greater number of people. 더 많은 수〔사람들〕(opp. fewer). ¶ *Yesterday half the members were present, but ~ of them are expected today.* 어제는 회원의 반이 출석했으나 오늘은 더 많이 나오리라 생각된다. **3** something in addition; some other things or persons. 그 밖의 다른 것들〔사람들〕. ¶ *More can be said.* 그 밖에도 여러가지로 말을 할 수 있다 / *I should like a little ~ of that meat.* 그 고기를 좀더 먹었으면 좋겠다 / *Did any ~ happen to be there?* 그 밖에도 누구 다른 사람이 거기 있었느냐.
— *adv.* (compar. of **much**) **1** in or to a greater degree or extent. 더욱 많이; 더 크게 (opp. less). ¶ *You should walk ~.* 더 많이 걸어야 한다 / *I love you ~ than any other person does.* 다른 어떤 이가 너를 사랑하는 것보다 더 너를 사랑한다 / *He is ~ clever than honest.* 그는 정직하다기보다는 영리한 사람이다. 語法 A, B 두 형용사를 비교하면서 "오히려 B보다는 A다"라고 할 때는 어미 변화 없이 more 를 쓴다. **2** 《forming the *compar.* of an *adj.* or *adv.*》 더욱 …; 더 …. ¶ *~ careful* 〔*interesting, just*〕 더 조심스러운〔재미있는, 정당한〕 / *~ carefully* 〔*easily, justly*〕 더 조심스럽게〔쉽게, 정당하게〕. **3** in addition. 게다가; 그 위에. ¶ *I could not run any ~.* 더는 뛸 수 없다 / *Do it once ~.* 한 번 더 해라. [E.]
all the more, in that degree; by that amount. 그래서 더; 더욱 더. ¶ *I admired him all the ~ for his honesty.* 그가 정직하기 때문에 한결 더 그를 칭찬했다.
and no more, *that's all.* 그뿐이다. ¶ *It is your imagination and no ~.* 그건 너의 상상일 뿐이다.
be no more, be dead. (이미) 죽고 없다. ¶ *He is no ~.* 그는 이미 죽고 없다.
more and more, to an increasing extent or degree. 더욱 더; 점점 더. ¶ *It is getting ~ and ~ interesting.* 점입가경이다.
more or less, somewhat; about; nearly. 어느 정도; 다소; 거의. ¶ *It is an hour's walk, ~ or less.* 걸어서 한 시간 정도의 거리이다 / *He was ~ or less drunk.* 좀 취해 있었다.
more than all, above all. 특히; 그 중에서도.
never more, never again. 다시 … 않다.
no 〔***not any***〕 ***more than,*** only. 단지. ¶ *He is no ~ than a dreamer.* 그는 단지 공상가일 뿐이다.
no more ... 〔***not ... any more***〕 ***than,*** not ..., nor.... …이 아닌 것처럼 …도 아니다. ¶ *He is no ~ diligent than you are.* 네가 게으른 것처럼 그도 게으르다 / *I am no ~ mad than you (are).* 너처럼 나도 온전한 사람이다.
not more than, at most. 많아야…; 기껏해야. ¶ *She is not ~ than thirty.* 많아야 서른 살이다.
not more ... than, not so ... as.... …이상은 —아니다. ¶ *He is not ~ diligent than you are.* 그도 근면하지만 너 정도는 아니다.
what is more, moreover. 그 뒤에 또; 더군다나.

*__more·o·ver__ [mɔːróuvər] *adv.* also; besides; in addition. 게다가; 더욱이; 또한. ¶ *I don't want to go skating; ~, the ice is too thin.* 스케이트 타러 가고 싶지 않다. 게다가 얼음이 너무 얇다. [E.]

morgue [mɔːrg] *n.* 《F.》 U **1** a place where the bodies of persons found dead are kept until they can be identified. 시체 보관〔공시〕소. **2** a place where material for reference is kept. (신문사 등의) 자료실.

Mor·mon [mɔ́ːrmən] *n.* C a member of a religious organization founded in the United States in 1830 by Joseph Smith (1805-1844). 모르몬 교도. [name of pretended author of 'The Book of Mormon']

Mor·mon·ism [mɔ́ːrmənìzəm] *n.* U the religious system of the Mormons. 모르몬교.

*__morn__ [mɔːrn] *n.* C 《*poet.*》 morning. 아침.

⁑**morn·ing** [mɔ́ːrniŋ] *n.* C **1** the early part of the day; the part of the day not later than noon. 아침; 오전. ¶ *from ~ till night* 아침부터 밤까지 / *in the ~* 아침〔오전〕에 / *this ~* 오늘 아침 / *on the ~ of Monday* 월요일 아침에. 語法 특정한 날은 in the morning of …라고 하지 않고, 전치사 on을 씀. **2** 《*fig.*》 the first or early part of something. 초기. ¶ *the ~ of life* 인생의 초기; 청년기. **3** U 《*poet.*》 dawn. 여명. [E.]
of a morning, often in the morning. 아침에는 흔히. ¶ *I take a walk in a park of a ~.* 아침에는 흔히 산책을 한다.

morn·ing-glo·ry [mɔ́ːrniŋglɔ̀ːri] *n.* C (*pl.* **-ries**) a climbing plant with trumpet-shaped flowers of various colors. 나팔꽃. [↑]

morning sickness [ˊ-ˋ-] *n.* nausea occurring early in the day, usu. as an early symptom of pregnancy. 입덧.

Mo·roc·co [mərákou / -rɔ́k-] *n.* a country in northwest Africa. 모로코.

mo·roc·co [mərákou / -rɔ́k-] *n.* U a fine leather made from goatskin. 모로코 가죽. [Place]

mo·ron [mɔ́ːran / -rɔn] *n.* C a person whose mental ability does not develop beyond that of a child 8 and 12 years old. 지능이 8-12세 정도에 정지한 성인. [Gk. *mōros* dull]

mo·rose [məróus] *adj.* gloomy; ill-humored. 기분이 좋지 않은; 침울한; 까다로운

(opp. amiable; pleasant). • **mo·rose·ly** [-li] *adv.* **mo·rose·ness** [-nis] *n.* [→moral]

Mor·phe·us [mɔ́ːrfiəs, -fjuːs] *n.* 《Gk. myth.》 the god of dreams. 모르페우스《잠의 신 Hypnos 의 아들》. [L.]

mor·phi·a [mɔ́ːrfiə] *n.* Ⓤ =morphine.

mor·phine [mɔ́ːrfiːn] *n.* Ⓤ a drug made from the seed of the white poppy and used to lessen pain. 모르핀. [L.]

mor·phin·ism [mɔ́ːrfənìzəm] *n.* Ⓤ an unhealthy state caused by the habitual use of morphine; the morphine habit. 모르핀 중독.

mor·phol·o·gy [mɔːrfálədʒi / -fɔ́l-] *n.* Ⓤ **1** 《biol.》 a science dealing with the forms and structures of animals and plants. 형태학(形態學). **2** 《gram.》 a science dealing with the forms of words. 언어 형태학; 어형론. [Gk. *morphē* form]

mor·row [mɔ́(ː)rou, mɑ́r-] *n.* Ⓒ **1** 《*poet.*》 the next day or time. 이튿날; 내일. **2** 《*arch.*》 morning. 아침. [→morn]

Morse [mɔːrs], **Samuel F. B.** *n.* (1791-1872) an American inventor. 모스《모스식 전신기의 발명자》. [Person]

mor·sel [mɔ́ːrsəl] *n.* Ⓒ a small piece or bite. (음식의) 한 입〔조각〕. [→mordant]

:**mor·tal** [mɔ́ːrtl] *adj.* **1** be fated to die sometime. 죽을 운명의(opp. immortal). ¶ *Man is* ~. 인간은 죽게 마련이다. **2** causing the death; fatal. 치명적인. ¶ *a* ~ *wound* 치명상 / *a* ~ *disease* 죽을 병. **3** causing the death of the soul. 영원한 죽음을 가져오는. ¶ ~ *sins* (지옥에 떨어질) 대죄(大罪). **4** of death. 죽음의. ¶ *the* ~ *hour* 임종 / ~ *agony* 죽음의 고통 / ~ *remains* 시체; 유해. **5** lasting until death. 필사의. ¶ *a* ~ *enemy* 불구대천의 원수 / *a* ~ *combat* 결투; 사투. **6** of man; human. 인간의. ¶ ~ *power* 인간의 힘 / *this* ~ *life* 이 세상〔인생〕. **7** ⓐ 《*colloq.*》 very great; extreme. 대단한; 극도의. ¶ *in a* ~ *hurry* 너무 급해서. ⓑ long and tiresome. 지루하게 긴. ¶ *The sermon lasted two* ~ *hours.* 설교는 지루하게 두 시간이나 끌었다. — *n.* Ⓒ **1** anything that is to die; a human being. 죽을 운명의 것; 인간. **2** 《*joc.*》 a person. 놈. ¶ *a thirsty* ~ 술망나니; 술꾼. [L. *mors* death]

mor·tal·i·ty [mɔːrtǽləti] *n.* Ⓒ **1** Ⓤ the state of being mortal or subject to death. 죽어야 할 운명〔상태〕. ¶ *None can escape* ~. 누구든 죽음은 피하지 못한다. **2** death on a large scale. 대량 사망. ¶ *the* ~ *from airplane accidents* 비행기 사고로 인한 대량 사망. **3** the death rate. 사망률. ¶ *The* ~ *from typhoid fever is decreasing.* 장티푸스로 인한 사망률은 낮아지고 있다.

mor·tal·ly [mɔ́ːrtəli] *adv.* **1** as causing death; fatally. 치명적으로. ¶ *He is* ~ *wounded.* 그는 치명상을 입었다. **2** 《*colloq.*》 very greatly; bitterly. 대단히; 몹시. ¶ *He was* ~ *offended.* 그는 잔뜩 골이 나 있었다.

mor·tar[1] [mɔ́ːrtər] *n.* Ⓤ a mixture of lime, sand, and water used to hold bricks or stones together. 모르타르; 회반죽. — *vt.* (P6) fasten (bricks, etc.) with mortar; fix (stones, etc.) with mortar; fix (stones, etc.) with mortar. (벽돌·돌 등)을 회반죽으로 붙이다〔굳히다〕. [L.]

mor·tar[2] [mɔ́ːrtər] *n.* Ⓒ **1** a bowl for pressing something to make a powder of it. 절구; 막자사발(cf. *pestle*). **2** a very short cannon. 박격포; 구포(臼砲). [L.]

mor·tar·board [mɔ́ːrtərbɔ̀ːrd] *n.* Ⓒ **1** a board used to hold mortar. 흙받기. **2** 《*colloq.*》 a cap with a flat and square top, worn by teachers and students at school ceremonies. 사각모《대학의 예복용》. [↑]

•**mort·gage** [mɔ́ːrgidʒ] *n.* Ⓒ **1** the right to get another's house, land, etc. as one's own property if a debt is not paid. 저당(권); 담보. ¶ *lend money on a* ~ 저당을 잡고 돈을 빌려 주다. **2** a document that gives such a right. 저당 증서. — *vt.* (P6,13) give (someone) a mortgage; pledge. …을 저당 잡히다; 담보에 넣다. ¶ ~ *a house* 집을 저당 잡히다. [L. *mortuus* dead, →gage[1]]

mor·tice [mɔ́ːrtis] *n., v.* =mortise.

mor·ti·cian [mɔːrtíʃən] *n.* Ⓒ 《U.S.》 an undertaker. 장의사(葬儀士). [L. *mors* death]

mor·ti·fi·ca·tion [mɔ̀ːrtəfikéiʃən] *n.* Ⓤ **1** the feeling of anger and shame. 울분; 굴욕; 치욕. ¶ *shed tears (in one's)* ~ 분해서 눈물을 흘리다. **2** Ⓒ a cause of such a feeling. 울분의 원인; 억울하고 분한 일. **3** the act of mortifying; the state of being mortified. 금욕(禁慾); 고행. ¶ *the* ~ *of the flesh* 금욕; 고행. **4** 《med.》 the death of one part of the body while the rest is still alive. 괴저(壞疽); 괴사(壞死). [↓]

mor·ti·fy [mɔ́ːrtəfài] *vt.* (**-fied**) (P6) **1** overcome (one's physical desires, etc.) by pain and self-denial. (정욕 등)을 억제하다. ¶ ~ *the flesh* 육욕을 억제하다. **2** cause (someone) to feel ashamed; hurt the feelings of (someone). …에게 굴욕감을 주다; …의 감정을 해치다. ¶ *be mortified by* 〔*at*〕 *one's mistake* 실수를 분하게 여기다 / *I was mortified at* 〔*by*〕 *a former friend's neglect.* 옛 친구에게 무시당해서 분했다. **3** cause (a part of the body) to decay. …을 괴저에 걸리게 하다. — *vi.* (P1) 《med.》 (of a part of the body) decay or die. 괴저에 걸리다. [→mortal]

mor·tise [mɔ́ːrtis] *n.* Ⓒ a hole cut in a piece of wood, etc. into which another piece, called a tenon, fits so as to form a joint. 장붓구멍. — *vt.* (P7,13) cut a mortise in (something); fasten (something) securely with a mortise and tenon. …에 장붓구멍을 파다; …을 장부촉이음하다. ¶ ~ *two beams together* 두 도리를 장부촉이음하다. [F.]

mor·tu·ar·y [mɔ́ːrtʃuèri / -tjuəri] *n.* Ⓒ (*pl.* **-ar·ies**) a place where dead bodies may be kept for a short time until burial. 시체 임시 안치소; 영안실. — *adj.* of death or burial. 죽음의; 매장의. [→mortal]

Mo·sa·ic [mouzéiik] *adj.* of Moses. 모세의. ¶ *the ~ law* 모세의 율법.

mo·sa·ic [mouzéiik] *n.* ⓊⒸ a design or picture made by fitting together small pieces of differently colored stone, marble, glass, etc.; anything like mosaic; Ⓒ a piece of such work. 모자이크; 모자이크 그림(무늬); 모자이크 식의 것(물건); 그러모아 만든 작품. — *adj.* made of or like mosaic. 모자이크의; 그러모은. — *vt.* (P6) adorn with mosaics; combine into a mosaic. …을 모자이크로 장식하다; 쪽매붙임하다. [→Muse]

Mo·ses [móuziz, -zis] *n.* **1** 《Bible》 the great leader of the Israelites who led them out of Egypt and gave them laws. 모세. **2** Ⓒ a lawgiver; a leader. 입법자; 지도자. [Heb. =deliverer, savior]

Mos·lem [mázləm / mɔ́zlem] *n.* Ⓒ (*pl.* **-lems** or *collectively* **-lem**) a Mohammedan. 마호메트(이슬람)교. — *adj.* of Mohammedans and their religion. 이슬람교(도)의. [→Islam]

mosque [mask / mɔsk] *n.* Ⓒ a Moslem temple. 이슬람교 사원; 모스크. [Arab.]

·**mos·qui·to** [məskíːtou] *n.* Ⓒ (*pl.* **-toes** or **-tos**) a small flying insect whose female stings the skin of people and animals to suck their blood. 모기. ¶ *Mosquitoes hummed.* 모기가 왱하고 가는 소리를 냈다. [L. *musca* fly]

mosquito boat [-⌐-⌐] *n.* a speedy, unarmored motorboat equipped with torpedoes and small guns. 고속 어뢰정. 參考 지금은 PT boat라 함.

mosquito craft [-⌐-⌐] *n.* a small armed ship capable of moving quickly and making sudden attacks on big ships. 쾌속 소형 함정.

mosquito curtain [-⌐-⌐-] *n.* = mosquito net.

mosquito net [-⌐-⌐] *n.* a net for keeping out mosquitos. 모기장.

·**moss** [mɔ(ː)s, mas] *n.* Ⓤ a small plant with tiny leaves which grows like a thick mat on damp ground, trees, rocks, etc. 이끼. ¶ 《*prob.*》 *A rolling stone gathers no ~.* 구르는 돌에는 이끼가 끼지 않는다. [E.]

moss·grown [mɔ́(ː)sgròun, más-] *adj.* **1** covered with moss. 이끼가 낀. **2** 《*fig.*》 old-fashioned. 구식의.

moss·y [mɔ́(ː)si, mási] *adj.* (**moss·i·er, moss·i·est**) covered with moss; like moss. 이끼가 낀; 이끼 같은. ¶ *a ~ bank*〔*stone*〕 이끼가 낀 둑〔돌〕/ *~ green* 이끼 같은 초록. ●**moss·i·ness** [-nis] *n.*

:**most** [moust] *adj.* (superl. of **much** or **many**) **1** greatest in amount or degree. (양·정도가) 가장 많은〔큰〕(opp. least). ¶ *He has* (*the*) *~ money of the three.* 셋 중에서 제일 돈이 많다 / *He has made* (*the*) *~ mistakes.* 가장 큰 실수를 했다. **2** greatest in number. 가장 수가 많은(opp. fewest). ¶ *Who has* (*the*) *~ books?* 누구한테 책이 제일 많으냐. **3** 《usu. without *definite article*》 almost all. 거의 전부의. ¶ *Most people think so.* 거의 모든 사람이 그렇게 생각한다.

for the most part, mainly; usually; in the main. 대개는.

— *n.* **1** 《*the* ~》 the greatest amount or degree. 최대량; 최대한. ¶ *This is the ~* (*that*) *I can do for you.* 이것이 내가 네게 해줄 수 있는 한도다 / *ask the ~ for it* 최고액을 청구하다. **2** 《*the* ~》 the greatest number. 최대수. **3** 《usu. without *definite article*》 almost all; nearly all people. 대부분; 대개의 사람들. ¶ *Most of the work was done during the day.* 일의 대부분은 그날 끝났다 / *Most like it.* 대부분의 사람들이 그걸 좋아한다 / *Most of the toys are broken.* 장난감들은 대부분 다 부서졌다.

at (***the***) ***most,*** not more than. 기껏해야; 많아야. ¶ *At the ~ five of us will go.* 기껏해야 우리 다섯이 갈 것이다.

make the most of *something,* make the best use of something; use something fully. …을 최대한 이용하다. ¶ *make the ~ of one's opportunity* 기회를 최대한 이용〔활용〕하다.

— *adv.* (superl. of **much**) **1** in or to the greatest extent or degree. 가장; 가장 많이 (opp. least). ¶ *The play which pleased me* (*the*) *~ was 'Hamlet.'* 내가 가장 만족한 연극은 햄릿이었다 / *I like him ~.* **2** 《forming the *superl.* of *adj.* and *adv.*》 가장; 제일. ¶ *~ careful*〔*interesting*〕 가장 신중한〔흥미 있는〕/ *~ carefully* 가장 조심스럽게. **3** very. 대단히; 아주. ¶ *a ~ beautiful girl* 아주 예쁜 소녀 / *He was ~ kind to me.* 내게 아주 친절했다. **4** 《U.S. *colloq.*》 almost. 거의. ¶ *~ all* 거의 모두. [E.]

Most Honorable [⌐⌐---], **the** *n.* the title of a Marquis. 후작의 경칭.

:**most·ly** [móustli] *adv.* chiefly; usually; generally. 주로; 대개.

mote [mout] *n.* Ⓒ a very small particle of dust in the air; 《*fig.*》 a small fault. 티끌; 사소한 결함. [E.]

mo·tel [moutél] *n.* Ⓒ 《U.S.》 a roadside hotel for motorists; a group of cottages for people traveling by car. 모텔《자동차 여행자 숙박소》. [*motor, hotel*]

·**moth** [mɔ(ː)θ, maθ] *n.* Ⓒ (*pl.* **moths** [-ðz, -θs]) **1** a small, four-winged insect very much like a butterfly, usu. most active at night. 나방. **2** an insect of this kind, whose larva feeds on wool, fur, etc. 옷좀나방. [E.]

moth ball [⌐⌐] *n.* a small ball of camphor used to keep moths away from clothing. 좀약.

moth-eat·en [mɔ́(:)θì:tn, mɑ́θ-] *adj.* eaten by clothesmoths; worn-out; 《*fig.*》 out-of-date. 좀먹은; 해어진; 시대에 뒤떨어진; 구식의. [*moth*]

:moth·er [mʌ́ðər] *n.* Ⓒ **1** a woman parent; 《often *M-*》 one's own mother. 어머니; 친어머니. **2** a woman like a mother. 어머니 같은 사람. ¶ *She was a ~ to the poor.* 그녀는 가난한 자의 어머니 같은 여자였다. **3** the head of a convent; Mother Superior. 수녀원장. **4** an old woman. 노부인; 할머니. ¶ *Mother Adams* 아담 할머니《호칭》. **5** 《*fig.*》 the cause or source of something. 출처; 근원. ¶ *Necessity is the ~ of invention.* 필요는 발명의 어머니. **6** 《usu. *the ~*》 a mother's love. 모성애. ¶ *He appealed to the ~ in her.* 그는 그녀의 모성애에 호소했다.

every mother's son, 《*colloq.*》 everybody. 누구나 다; 너나없이.

— *adj.* **1** that is a mother. 어머니인. ¶ *a ~ bird* 어미새. **2** of or like a mother. 어머니의; 어머니다운〔같은〕. ¶ *~ love* 모성애 / *a ~ ship* 모선(母船). **3** native. 모국의; 타고난. ¶ *~ wit* 타고난 재치 / *one's ~ tongue* 모국어.

— *vt.* (P6) **1** take care of (someone) as a mother does. …을 돌보다. **2** adopt (a child) as one's own; acknowledge oneself to be the mother, author, etc. of. …의 어머니가 되다; …의 어머니〔저자〕라고 말하다. **3** 《*fig.*》 give birth to. …을 낳다. [E.]

moth·er·hood [mʌ́ðərhùd] *n.* Ⓤ **1** the state of being a mother. 어머니임. **2** the character or spirit of a mother. 모성. **3** 《*collectively*》 mothers. 어머니.

moth·er-in-law [mʌ́ðərinlɔ̀:] *n.* Ⓒ (*pl.* **moth·ers-**) the mother of one's husband or wife. 장모; 시어머니(opp. father-in-law).

moth·er·land [mʌ́ðərlæ̀nd] *n.* Ⓒ **1** the country of one's birth. 모국. **2** the country where one's parents or ancestors were born. 조국; 조상의 땅.

moth·er·like [mʌ́ðərlàik] *adj.* =motherly.

moth·er·ly [mʌ́ðərli] *adj.* of or like a mother; showing the affection or concern of a mother. 어머니의; 어머니 같은〔다운〕; 다정한.

moth·er-of-pearl [mʌ́ðərəvpə́:rl] *n.* Ⓤ the hard, rainbow-colored lining of some shells, esp. the pearl-oyster. (특히, 진주 조개 안의) 진주층(層); 자개.

mo·tif [moutí:f] *n.* Ⓒ 《F.》 **1** a subject or main idea in a work of literature or music. (문학·음악 등의) 주제. **2** a feature in a decoration or design. 의장(意匠)의 주요소.

mo·tile [móutil / -tail] *adj.* 《biol.》 able to move by itself. 움직일 수 있는; 자동력(自動力)이 있는. [↓]

:mo·tion [móuʃən] *n.* **1** Ⓤ the act of changing from one place or position to another; movement; action. 운동; 이동; 운행; 활동 (opp. rest). ¶ *law of ~* 운동의 법칙 / *the motions of the planets* 행성의 운행 / *It seemed to be in slow ~.* 천천히 움직이는 것 같다. **2** 《usu. *pl.*》 the act of moving the parts of the body, esp. the hand; a gesture. (신체의 일부, 특히 손의) 움직임; 동작; 몸짓. ¶ *Her motions were graceful.* 그녀의 몸놀림은 우아했다 / *a ~ of the hand* 손놀림. **3** Ⓤ a combination of parts in a mechanism; the mechanism. 기계 장치; 기구(機構). **4** Ⓒ a proposal or suggestion, esp. one made at a meeting; 《law》 an application to a court for a ruling, an order, etc. (의회의) 발의(發議); 동의(動議); (원고 또는 피고의) 재정(裁定) 신청. ¶ *second the ~* 동의에 찬성하다 / *on the ~ of…* …의 동의로 / *a ~ to refer to a committee* 위원회에 회부할 동의 / *an urgent ~* 긴급 동의.

go through the motions of, show (something) by gestures; pretend to do (something). …한 시늉〔몸짓〕을 하다.

in motion, moving; traveling; in operation. 움직이고 있는; 운전 중의.

make a motion, propose in a committee meeting or legislative group that a certain action be taken. (의회 등에서) 동의(動議)하다.

of one's own motion, of one's own will. 자진해서.

put* 〔*set*〕 *in motion, start or cause to move. …을 움직이다; 운동〔운전〕하게 하다.

— *vi.* (P3) make a gesture expressing a wish, meaning, etc. 몸짓으로 알리다. ¶ *He motioned for her to be seated.* 그녀에게 앉으라고 손짓했다.

— *vt.* (P7,11,13,20) show (someone) what to do by a gesture. …에게 〔몸짓·손짓으로〕 신호하다; 알리다. ¶ *He motioned me in.* 내게 들어오라고 손짓했다 / *~ the group to go on* 일행에게 계속 가라고 신호하다. [→move]

·mo·tion·less [móuʃənlis] *adj.* not moving; still. 움직이지 않는; 정지한. ¶ *lie ~* 꼼짝 않고 있다. ●**mo·tion·less·ly** [-li] *adv.*

motion picture [ㅗ-ㅗ-] *n.* Ⓒ 《esp. U.S.》 a moving picture; a movie(s). 영화.

mo·ti·vate [móutəvèit] *vt.* (P6) provide (something or someone) with a motive; influence or give a motive to do (something). …에게 동기를 주다; …을 움직이다; 자극하다. [*motive*]

mo·ti·va·tion [mòutəvéiʃən] *n.* Ⓤ the act of motivating; the state of being motivated. 동기를 주는 일; 자극; 유도.

·mo·tive [móutiv] *n.* Ⓤ **1** the inner reason or feeling which makes a person do something. (행동의) 동기; 목적; 자극; 유인. ¶ *the ~ for which they act* 그들 행동의 동기. **2** =motif.

of* 〔*from*〕 *one's own motive, of one's own will. 자진해서; 자의(自意)로.

— *adj.* causing motion; that makes something move. 원동력이 되는; 운동을 일으키는. ¶ *~ power* 원동〔기동〕력.

— *vt.* 《chiefly in *passive*》 move to action. …을 움직이다; 동기를 주다. ¶ *motived by greed* 탐욕에 사로잡혀. [→move]

mot·ley [mátli / mɔ́t-] *n.* Ⓒ a garment of various colors, once worn by clowns; a cloth of mixed colors. (어릿광대의) 얼룩덜룩한 옷; 잡색의 천.

wear (***the***) ***motley,*** play the part of a clown or fool. 어릿광대 역을 하다; 어릿광대 짓을 하다.

— *adj.* of various colors; of various mixed kinds or parts; of varied character. 잡색의; 잡다한; (사람이) 각양각색의. ¶ *a ~ crowd* 잡다한 군중. [E.]

:mo·tor [móutər] *n.* Ⓒ **1** an engine that causes something to move or work; a dynamo; an internal-combustion engine. 모터; 발전기; 원동기; 내연 기관. ¶ *an electric ~* 전동기. **2** an automobile. 자동차. **3** a person or thing that produces motion. 움직이게 하는 사람[물건].

— *adj.* **1** producing or causing motion. 움직이는; 원동력의; 발동의. ¶ *a ~ ship* 발동선 / *~ power* 동력. **2** of, by, or for motor vehicle. 자동차(용)의; 자동차로 하는. ¶ *a ~ trip* [*highway*] 자동차 여행[도로]. **3** 《biol.》 having to do with motion. 운동의. ¶ *a ~ nerve* 운동 신경.

— *vi.* (P1,2A) ride in a motor vehicle; travel by automobile. 자동차에 타다[로 가다]. ¶ *We motored to the station.* 차로 역에 갔다.

— *vt.* (P7,13) carry (something or someone) by automobile. …을 자동차로 나르다. ¶ *Let me ~ you to town.* 읍내까지 태워다 주마. [→move]

motor bicycle [⌐–⌐––] *n.* a bicycle propelled by a motor; a motorcycle. 오토바이; 모터 달린 자전거; 모터바이크.

mo·tor·bike [móutərbàik] *n.* 《*colloq.*》 **1** = motor bicycle. **2** =motorcycle.

mo·tor·boat [móutərbòut] *n.* Ⓒ a boat run by a motor. 모터 보트.

mo·tor·bus [móutərbʌ̀s] *n.* Ⓒ a bus run by a motor. 버스.

mo·tor·car [móutərkɑ̀ːr] *n.* Ⓒ an automobile. 자동차.

motor court [⌐–⌐] *n.* =motel.

***mo·tor·cy·cle** [móutərsàikl] *n.* Ⓒ a two-wheeled vehicle propelled by an internal-combustion engine, resembling a bicycle but usu. larger and heavier. 오토바이.

— *vi.* (P1,2A) ride a motorcycle. 오토바이를 타다.

mo·tor·cy·clist [móutərsàiklist] *n.* Ⓒ a person who rides a motorcycle. 오토바이 타는 사람.

mo·tor·drome [móutərdròum] *n.* Ⓒ a rounded track for automobile or motorcycle racing or testing. 오토바이[자동차] 경주[시험]장.

mo·tor·ing [móutəriŋ] *n.* Ⓤ the act of driving an automobile. 자동차 운전; 드라이브.

mo·tor·ist [móutərist] *n.* Ⓒ a person who drives an automobile or who usu. travels by automobile. 자동차 운전자; 자동차 여행자.

mo·tor·ize [móutəràiz] *vt.* (P6) **1** equip (vehicles) with motors. (차)에 모터를 장착하다. **2** supply (troops, etc.) with motor vehicles. (군대 등)에 자동차를 보급하다.

motor lorry [⌐– ⌐–] *n.* 《chiefly Brit.》 a motor truck. 화물 자동차.

mo·tor·man [móutərmən] *n.* Ⓒ (*pl.* **-men** [-mən]) 《U.S.》 **1** a man who operates a motor, esp. on an electric trolley or train. 전동차 운전사. **2** a man who runs or operates a motor. 모터 담당자.

motor truck [⌐–⌐] *n.* 《U.S.》 a motor-driven truck. 화물 자동차; 트럭.

mot·tle [mátl / mɔ́tl] *n.* ⓊⒸ a large, irregular spot; a spotted pattern or coloring, as of marble. (대리석 등의) 얼룩; 반점; 반문.

— *vt.* (P6) 《usu. in *passive*》 mark (something) with spots of different colors or shades. …을 얼룩덜룩하게 하다. ¶ *a mottled surface* 얼룩덜룩한 표면. [*motley*]

***mot·to** [mátou / mɔ́t-] *n.* Ⓒ (*pl.* **-toes** or **-tos**) **1** a short sentence or phrase used as a rule of conduct. 모토; 좌우명; 금언; 명언. **2** a short sentence, word or phrase written or cut on an object. 제구(題句); 제사(題辭); 명(銘). [L. *muttio* murmur]

***mould** [mould] *n., v.* 《Brit.》 =mold.

mould·er [móuldər] *n., v.* 《Brit.》 =molder.

mould·ing [móuldiŋ] *n.* 《Brit.》 =molding.

mould·y [móuldi] *adj.* 《Brit.》 (**mould·i·er, mould·i·est**) =moldy.

moult [moult] *n., v.* 《Brit.》 =molt.

***mound** [maund] *n.* Ⓒ **1** a bank or heap of earth, stones or sand made by man to mark a grave or to use as a fort. 둑; 석가산(石假山); 흙무덤. **2** a small hill. 작은 언덕[산]. **3** 《baseball》 the pitcher's plate. 마운드; 투수판. — *vt.* surround (something) with a mound; heap up (something) in a mound. …에 둑을 쌓다; 석가산을 만들다. [E.]

:mount[1] [maunt] *vt.* **1** (P6) go up; climb. …에 오르다. ¶ *~ a hill* / *~ a ladder* 사닥다리를 오르다. **2** (P6) get up on (a platform, a horse, etc.). …위에 올라가다; 타다. ¶ *~ a horse.* **3** (P6,13) put (someone or something) on a horse; furnish (someone) with a horse. …을 말에 태우다; …에게 탈 말을 주다. ¶ *He is well mounted.* 좋은 말을 타고 있다 / *My friend was good enough to ~ me for the hunt.* 내 친구는 친절하게도 사냥할 때 탈 말을 나에게 주었다. **4** (P6,13) put (something) in a proper position for use; fix; set. …을 붙박아 놓다; 끼우다; 붙이다. ¶ *~ a specimen on a slide* 표본을 슬라이드에 올려 놓다 / *~ a jewel in gold* 금에 보석

을 박다 / ~ *a picture on cardboard* 대지에 그림을 붙이다 / ~ *a play* 극을 상연하다. **5** (P6,13) have; carry (guns); furnish (a fortress, a ship, etc.) with guns. (포(砲))를 설치〔장비·탑재〕하다. ¶ *a battleship mounting twenty guns* 포 20문을 장착한 군함 / *a tank mounted with four guns* 포 4문을 탑재한 전차. — *vi.* (P1,2A,3) **1** go up; rise; increase. 올라가다; 오르다; 증가하다. ¶ *Prices will* ~. 물가가 오를 게다 / *Debts* ~ *up rapidly.* 빚이 빠르게 불어난다. **2** get on horseback. 말에 타다. ¶ ~ *on a horse* / *The man mounted and rode away.* 그는 말을 타고 가버렸다.

mount guard, act as a guard. 보초 서다; 망보다; 감시하다.

mount guard over, guard; protect. …을 망보다; 지키다.

— *n.* Ⓒ **1** a thing on which anything is mounted; a card for a picture; a setting for a jewel; a carriage for a gun. 물건을 놓는 대; 대지; (보석을 박는) 거미발; 포가(砲架). **2** a horse or other animal for riding. (말 따위와 같은) 탈 것. ¶ *The general had an excellent* ~. 장군에겐 훌륭한 말이 있었다. [L. *mons* mountain]

mount[2] [maunt] *n.* Ⓒ (chiefly *poetic* except in *proper names*) a mountain; a high hill. …산; 산; 언덕. 參考 지금도 고유 명사로 쓰임. Mt.로 생략함. ¶ *Mount Everest* 에베레스트 산 / *the Sermon on the Mount* 산상 수훈(山上垂訓). [↑]

:moun·tain [máuntən] *n.* Ⓒ **1** a very high hill. 산. **2** 《*pl.*》 a chain or group of such hills. 산맥; 연산(連山); 산지. ¶ *the Rocky Mountains* 로키 산맥 / *The mountains are covered with snow.* 산들이 눈에 덮여 있다. **3** 《*fig.*》 anything of great size or amount. 산같이 큰 것; 산적(山積)(한 것); 다량. ¶ *a* ~ *of mail* 산더미 같은 우편물 / ~ *of difficulties* 산적한 난관 / *a* ~ *of flesh* 몸집이 우람한 사람 / *a* ~ *of rubbish* 쓰레기 더미. **4** 《as *adj.*》 of or belonging to a mountain or mountains. 산의; 산에 나는〔속한〕. ¶ ~ *air* 산공기 / ~ *plants.* [*mount*[1]]

moun·tain·eer [màuntəníər] *n.* Ⓒ a person who lives in the mountains; a mountain climber. 산지(山地) 주민; 등산가. — *vi.* (P1) climb mountains for sport. 등산하다.

∗moun·tain·ous [máuntənəs] *adj.* having many mountains; extremely large; huge. 산이 많은; 거대한. ¶ ~ *regions* 산악 지방 / ~ *waves* 큰 물결.

mountain range [∠-∠] *n.* a series of connected mountains considered as a single group. 산맥; 연산(連山).

mountain sickness [∠-∠-] *n.* illness caused by insufficient oxygen in the air at high altitudes. 산악병; 고산병.

moun·tain·side [máuntənsàid] *n.* Ⓒ a slope of a mountain. 산허리; 산중턱.

moun·tain·top [máuntəntàp / -tɔ̀p] *n.* Ⓒ the top of a mountain; the summit. 산꼭대기; 산정(山頂).

moun·te·bank [máuntəbæ̀ŋk] *n.* Ⓒ **1** a person selling worthless medicines, esp. in a public place; a quack doctor. (거리의) 돌팔이 약장수; 돌팔이 의사. **2** a person who deceives people. 사기꾼. [It. =mount on bench]

mount·ed [máuntid] *adj.* **1** seated on horseback. 말에 탄. ¶ ~ *police* 기마 경찰. **2** set up and ready for use; fixed. 설치한; 앉힌; 붙박은. ¶ *a* ~ *gun* 포가(砲架)에 앉힌 포. **3** set or framed in (something). 박아 넣은; 끼워 박은. ¶ *a gold-mounted sword* 금을 박아 넣은 칼. [*mount*[1]]

moun·ting [máuntiŋ] *n.* something that serves as a mount; a support to anything. 대지(臺紙); 받침. ¶ *Her photograph is on a heavy cardboard* ~. 그녀 사진은 두꺼운 판지에 붙어 있다.

:mourn [mɔːrn] *vi., vt.* (P3;6) 《*over, for*》 feel or express sorrow; grieve at someone's death; lament. 슬퍼하다; 애통해 하다; 애도하다. ¶ ~ *over his tragic fate* 그의 비극적 운명을 애도하다 / ~ *the loss of one's mother* 어머니의 죽음을 슬퍼하다. [E.]

mourn·er [mɔ́ːrnər] *n.* Ⓒ **1** a person who mourns. 애도하는 사람. **2** a person who attends a funeral as a friend or relative of the dead person. 회장자(會葬者); 조문객.

∗mourn·ful [mɔ́ːrnfəl] *adj.* **1** sorrowful; sad. 슬픈 듯한; 슬픈. ¶ ~ *songs* 비가(悲歌). **2** causing sorrow. 슬픔을 자아내는. ¶ *a* ~ *scene* 슬픈 정경.

mourn·ful·ly [mɔ́ːrnfəli] *adv.* in a mournful manner. 슬픈 듯이; 비탄에 젖어.

mourn·ing [mɔ́ːrniŋ] *n.* Ⓤ **1** grief; sorrow. 슬픔; 비탄; 애도. **2** an outward expression of sorrow, such as black clothes. 상복(喪服); 상장(喪章). **3** the period during which a person mourns for a dead person. 기중(忌中).

go into* 〔*put on, take to*〕 *mourning, observe mourning; wear mourning for someone's death. 상복을 입다; 몽상(蒙喪)하다.

in mourning, in mourning clothes; in the period of mourning. 상복을 입고; 복상(服喪)하고.

leave off* 〔*go out of*〕 *mourning, stop wearing mourning clothes. 탈상하다.

mourning band [∠-∠] *n.* a black cloth, usu. worn around the arm, to show mourning. 상장(喪章). 參考 mourning badge라고도 함.

:mouse [maus] *n.* Ⓒ (*pl.* **mice**) **1** a tiny, soft-furred animal with a long tail something like, but smaller than a rat. 생쥐. ¶ *a house* 〔*a field, a wood*〕 ~ 생쥐〔들쥐〕. **2** a timid or spiritless person. 겁쟁이; 소심한 사람.

like a drowned mouse, be poor-looking; be wet to the skin. 초라한 몰골로; 물에 빠진 생쥐처럼.

play like a cat with a mouse, make sport of and tease (something or someone). 고양이가 쥐 다루듯 하다; 못살게 굴다.

— [mauz] *vi.* (P1) **1** (of a cat) hunt for. (고양이가) 쥐를 잡다. **2** seek about or search for (something) busily and stealthily. 살금살금 찾아다니다. ¶ *~ about for valuables* 값진 것을 찾아다니다. [E.]

mouse about, search for (something). …을 찾아 다니다.

mouse·trap [máustræ̀p] *n.* Ⓒ a trap for catching mice. 쥐덫.

mous·tache [mʌ́stæʃ, məstǽʃ] *n.* 《Brit.》 =mustache.

mous·y, mous·ey [máusi] *adj.* (**mous·i·er, mous·i·est**) **1** quiet as a mouse. 쥐죽은 듯이 조용한. **2** infested with mice. 쥐가 많은〔꾀는〕. **3** resembling or suggesting a mouse in color, behavior, etc. 쥐 같은; 쥐색의; 쥐같이 구는. [*mouse*]

:mouth [mauθ] *n.* Ⓒ (*pl.* **mouths** [-ðz]) **1** an opening through which an animal takes in food. 입. ¶ *stop someone's ~* 아무의 입을 막다; 말을 못하게 하다 / *Shut your ~!* 입 닫아라 / *have a big ~* 수다스럽다. **2** an opening like a mouth in shape or position. 입 같은 것〔부분〕. ¶ *the ~ of a river* 강 어귀 / *the ~ of a cave* 〔*bottle*〕 굴 입구〔병 주둥이〕. **3** 《usu. *pl.*》 persons to be fed. 식솔; 식구. ¶ *useless mouths* 밥벌레 / *hungry mouths* 굶주린 사람들 / *He has ten mouths to feed.* 식솔이 열이나 된다. **4** a twisted look of the face. 찡그린 얼굴; 우거지상. ¶ *make mouths at someone* 아무를 보고 얼굴을 찡그리다.

down in the mouth, 《*colloq.*》 in low spirits. 낙담해서; 사기가 죽어.

from mouth to mouth, from one speaker to another. 입에서 입으로.

give mouth, (of a dog) bark. (개가) 짖다.

give mouth to (=*speak out*) *something.* …을 입 밖에 내다; 말하다.

in *someone's* ***mouth,*** when said by someone. …가 말하면. ¶ *That sounds funny in your ~.* 네가 그런 말을 하면 우습게 들린다.

put words into *someone's* ***mouth,*** tell someone what to say. 할 말을 일러주다〔가르치다〕.

take the words out of *someone's* ***mouth,*** say what someone was going to say. …이 하려는 말을 앞질러하다.

with one mouth, in chorus. 이구 동성으로.

— *v.* [mauð] *vt.* (P6) **1** take or put (food) into the mouth. …을 입에 넣다; 먹다; 물다. ¶ *A dog mouthed a bone.* 개가 뼈다귀 하나를 물었다. **2** say (something) in a pretended or unnatural way. …을 뽐내며 말하다. ¶ *~ one's words.*

— *vi.* **1** (P1) speak in a pretended or unnatural manner. 뽐내며 말하다. **2** (P1,3) make a twisted look of the face. 얼굴을 찡그리다. ¶ *He mouthed at me.* 나를 보고 상을 찌푸렸다. [E.]

mouth·ful [máuθfùl] *n.* Ⓒ **1** as much as the mouth can hold at one time; the amount the mouth can hold. 한 입 가득; 한 입(의 양). ¶ *take a ~ of dinner* 음식을 한 입 떠먹다 / *at a ~* 한 입에. **2** a small amount of food. 소량의 음식. ¶ *Have a ~ of lunch before you start.* 떠나기 전에 요기를 해라.

mouth organ [⌐ ⌐–] *n.* a harmonica. 하모니카. [E.]

mouth·piece [máuθpìːs] *n.* Ⓒ **1** the part of a pipe, a musical instrument, etc. that is placed against the lips or in the mouth. (파이프 등의) 입에 무는 부분; (물)부리; (악기의) 부는 구멍; (전화의) 송화구. **2** 《*fig.*》 a person, newspaper, etc. expressing the opinions of others; a spokesman. 대변자; (여론의) 대변지(紙)《신문 등》.

mouth·y [máuði, -θi] *adj.* (**mouth·i·er, mouth·i·est**) speaking wildly or loudly; bombastic. 떠벌리는; 큰소리치는. [*mouth*]

mov·a·ble [múːvəbəl] *adj.* that can be carried from one place to another; changing from one state to another; unfixed. 움직일 수 있는; 이동하는; 가동성(可動性)의 (opp. immovable). ¶ *~ prefabricated hospitals* 조립식 이동병원 / *a ~ feast* 해에 따라 날짜가 변하는 축제일《부활절 등》/ *~ property* 동산. — *n.* 《*pl.*》 personal property that can be moved. 동산; 가구(opp. immovables). [↓]

:move [muːv] *vt.* **1** (P6,7,13) change the position of (something); shift; transfer. …을 움직이다; 이동시키다. ¶ *He moved his chair nearer to the window.* 창 가까이로 의자를 옮겼다 / *~ a sick person to another room* 환자를 다른 방으로 옮기다 / *~ troops to the front* 부대를 전선으로 이동시키다. **2** (P6) ⓐ set or keep (something) in motion; stir. 움직이게 하다; 흔들다. ¶ *The wind moved the leaves.* 바람이 나뭇잎을 흔들었다. ⓑ cause (something) to act, work, run, operate. 시동〔작동〕시키다. ¶ *The machine is moved by a spring.* 그 기계는 스프링 식이다 / *The button moves the engine.* 버튼을 누르면 엔진이 작동한다. **3** (P13) stir or arouse the feelings of (someone). …을 감동시키다; …의 마음을 움직여 —하게 하다. ¶ *The story moved her to tears.* 이야기를 듣고 그녀는 감동되어 눈물을 흘렸다. **4** (P6,13,20) cause; persuade. …에게 —할 마음을 가지게 하다. ¶ *Nothing could ~ him to do the work.* 그에게 그 일을 시킬 방도가 없다 / *No argument will ~ him from his opinion.* 무슨 말을 하든 그의 소신을 움직일 순 없다. **5** (P6,11) propose (one's opinion, etc.) formally, as in a meeting. (동의(動議))를 제출하다; 제안하다. ¶ *~ a resolution* 결의안 동의를 제출하다 / *I ~ that the meeting be adjourned.* 나는

회의의 연장을 제의한다. **6** (P6) 《chess》 change (a piece) to a different square. (말)을 쓰다; 움직이다. ¶ ~ *a piece.* — *vi.* (P1,2A,3) **1** change position; change one's place of living. 자리를 옮기다; 이사하다. ¶ *We moved into a new house.* 새 집으로 이사했다 / *Move near this way.* 이쪽으로 더 오시오 / *She moved from her seat to the fire.* 그녀는 좌석에서 난롯가로 갔다. **2** be in motion; be active; act; take part; associate. 활동〔행동〕하다; 간여하다; 교제하다. ¶ ~ *with grace* 점잖게〔우아하게〕 움직이다 / *You should ~ in this matter.* 이 문제의 처리를 강구해라 / *A piston moves by steam pressure.* 피스톤은 증기의 압력으로 움직인다 / *Miss Garner moves in society.* 가너 양은 사교계에 출입하고 있다. **3** ⓐ go or pass on; proceed. 나아가다; 전진하다. ¶ *The crowd moved slowly down the street.* 군중은 천천히 거리를 행진해 내려갔다. ⓑ make progress; advance; develop. 진행〔발전〕하다. ¶ *Events are moving rapidly.* 사건은 급속하게 진전되고 있다 / *The work moves slowly.* 작업이 서서히 진행된다 / *Time moves on.* 시간이 자꾸 지나고 있다. **4** 《*for*》 make a formal request. 신청하다; 제의하다. ¶ ~ *for a new trial* 재심을 요청하다. **5** (of goods) be sold. (상품이) 팔리다. **6** 《chess》 make a move. 말을 쓰다.

feel moved (=*be willing or want*) ***to*** *do*. …할 마음이 내키다. ¶ *I feel moved to read it.* 그걸 읽어 보고 싶구나.

move heaven and earth, try every possible way. 온갖 수단을 다 쓰다.

— *n.* Ⓒ **1** the act of moving; a change of position; the changing of one's place of living. 움직임; 행동; 이동; 이사. ¶ *make a ~ toward a door* 문쪽으로 가다 / *It's time to make a ~.* 이젠 갈 시간이다. **2** an action taken for a certain purpose; a step. 수단; 조치. ¶ *make a clever*〔*shrewd*〕 ~ 영리한〔기민한〕 수단을 쓰다 / *the first*〔*next*〕 ~ (*to make*) 첫째〔다음〕(취할) 조치. **3** 《chess》 the moving of a piece; player's turn. 말 쓰기; 둘 차례. ¶ *It's a nice ~.* 그거 좋은 수다 / *It's your ~ now.* 네가 둘 차례다. [L. *moveo*]

get a move on, 《*sl.*》 **a**) start moving; get going; leave or depart. 출발하다; 떠나다. **b**) hurry. 서두르다.

make a move, go; change one's place; begin to act. 나아가다; 움직이다; 수단을 쓰다.

on the move, **a**) moving from place to place; active; busy. 늘 이동하는; 활동하고 있는; 분주한. ¶ *He is always on the ~.* 그는 항상 바쁘다. **b**) (of affairs, etc.) progressing; advancing. (사건 등이) 진행 중인.

:move·ment [múːvmənt] *n.* **1** Ⓒ the act of moving; action or activity. 동작; 움직임; 운동; 행동. ¶ *We run by movements of the legs.* 다리의 움직임으로 우리는 뛰게 된다 / *the ~ of the waves* 파도의 운동. **2** 《*pl.*》 a particular manner of moving. 태도; 자세. ¶ *His movements are always awkward.* 그 사람 태도는 늘 어색하다 / *Her movements are easy and graceful.* 그녀의 태도는 부드럽고도 우아하다. **3** Ⓒ 《mech.》 the moving parts of a watch, a machine, etc. (시계 등의) 작동 기구; 기계 장치. ¶ *The ~ of a watch is made of many little wheels.* 시계 장치는 많은 작은 톱니바퀴로 되어 있다. **4** Ⓒ a series of organized activities by people for a special purpose. (어떤) 조직적인 운동. ¶ *a temperance ~* 금주 운동 / *a political ~* 정치 운동 / *start a ~ against a policy* 어떤 정책에 대한 반대 운동을 벌이다. **5** Ⓒ ⓐ the act of changing the location; a racial migration. 이사; 이주; (짐승·민족 등의) 이동. ⓑ 《mil.》 a change in the placing of troops or ships. (부대·함선의) 이동; 기동; 작전 행동. **6** Ⓒ the growth of a plant. (식물의) 발아; 성장. **7** Ⓤ a change in the price of stocks or commodities. (시장의) 변동; 가격 변동. **8** Ⓤ the progress of events in a literary work. (사건·이야기 등의) 진전; 변화. ¶ *The play lacks ~.* 그 연극은 변화가 적다. **9** Ⓤ 《mus.》 tempo; rhythm; any of the principal divisions of a symphony. 템포; 율동; 박자; 악장(樂章). ¶ *the first ~ of a sonata* 소나타의 1악장 / *a slow ~* 완서조(緩徐調); 완서 악장. **10** the act of removing unnecessary matter from the bowels. 변통(便通); 통변.

in the movement, keeping up with, not behind the times. 풍조〔시대〕에 뒤지지 않고; 시세를 타고.

mov·er [múːvər] *n.* Ⓒ **1** ⓐ a person or thing that moves or causes (something) to move. 움직이는 사람〔물건〕. ⓑ a person whose work is moving furniture, etc. for those changing residences. 이삿짐 운송업자; 이삿짐 센터. **2** the motive power; a motor. 동력(動力); 발동기. **3** a person proposing a motion; a projector; an originator. 발기인; 동의(動議) 제출자.

:mov·ie [múːvi] *n.* 《U.S. *colloq.*》 Ⓒ 《usu. *pl.*》 a moving picture; a motion-picture theater. 영화; 영화관. ¶ *an 8 mm ~ camera* 8밀리 무비 카메라 / *a movie-goer* 영화팬 / *a ~ house* 영화관 / *go to the movies* 영화 구경 가다.

mov·ing [múːviŋ] *adj.* **1** that moves. 움직이는; 이동하는. ¶ *a ~ object* 움직이는 물체 / *a ~ stairway* 에스컬레이터. **2** causing motion. 움직이게 하는. ¶ *He was the ~ spirit of the undertaking.* 그는 그 기업의 중심 인물이었다. **3** stirring the emotions. 감동시키는. ¶ *a ~ story of human sufferings* 인간 수난의 감동적인 이야기.

mov·ing·ly [múːviŋli] *adv.* in a moving manner. 감동적으로.

mow[1] [mou] *vt., vi.* (**mowed, mowed** or **mown**) (P6,7;1) cut down (grass, grain, etc.) with a scythe or a machine. (풀 따위를) 베다. ¶ ~ *grass* / ~ *a lawn*〔*field*〕 잔디를 깎다〔밭에서 곡식을 베다〕. **2** 《*fig.*》 destroy at a sweep as if by mowing. (일거에) 쓰러뜨

리다; 소탕하다. ¶ *Hundreds of soldiers were mown down by machine-gun fire.* 수백 명의 군인이 기총 소사로 쓰러졌다. [E.]

mow² [mau / mou] *n.* Ⓒ **1** a heap of hay, straw, grain, etc. 건초(곡식) 더미. **2** the part of a barn where hay or grain is stored. 건초(곡식) 두는 곳; 광. [E.]

mow·er [móuər] *n.* Ⓒ a person or machine that mows. 풀 베는 사람; 제초기.

mow·ing [móuiŋ] *n.* Ⓤ the quantity of hay mowed in a single specified period. 한 차례 베어들인 풀의 양.

mown [moun] *v.* pp. of **mow.**

Mo·zart [móutsɑːrt], **Wolfgang Amadeus** *n.* (1756-91) an Austrian composer. 모차르트.

MP, M.P. **1** Member of Parliament. 국회의원. **2** Military Police. 헌병. **3** Metropolitan Police. 수도 경찰. **4** Mounted Police. 기마 경찰.

mp, m.p. melting point. 녹는점; 융해점.

mph, m.p.h. miles per hour. 시속 …마일.

:Mr., Mr [místər] (*pl.* **Messrs.**) Mister, used before the name; the title of a man. …씨; …님; …귀하; …군; …선생. ¶ ~ *Brown* 브라운씨 / ~ *President* 대통령 각하. [*master*]

MRA Moral Re-Armament. 도덕 재무장.

:Mrs., Mrs [mísiz, -is] (*pl.* **Mmes.** [meidɑ́ːm]) Mistress, now used as a title before the name of an married woman. …부인. 參考 미국에서는 흔히 Mrs. 뒤에 남편의 이름을 씀. ¶ ~ *(Alfred L.) Harris* 해리스 부인 / ~ *Kitty Evans* 키티 에번스 부인.

MSS., Mss., mss. [émesés] *pl.* manuscripts. 원고.

:Mt. [maunt] (*pl.* **Mts.**) Mount. 산. ¶ ~ *Everest.*

:much [mʌtʃ] *adj.* (**more, most**) great in quantity, amount, or degree; a lot of. (양·정도가) 많은(opp. little). 語法 긍정문에선 흔히 a lot (of), a great quantity (of), a good deal (of) 등이 쓰임. 그러나 주어를 수식하거나 too, how, as, so 등과 연결될 경우는 긍정문이라도 흔히 much가 쓰임. ¶ *Much time is necessary for me to do it.* 그 일을 하려면 많은 시간이 필요하다 / *There was ~ truth in her speech.* 그녀 말은 다분히 진실이었다 / *She takes too ~ pride in her beauty.* 그녀는 자기 미모에 너무 교만하다 / *Much snow has fallen.* 눈이 많이 내렸다 / *There is not ~ hope.* 그다지 큰 희망이 없다 / 《*iron.*》 *Much right he has to interfere with me!* 제가 나를 간섭할 큰 권리깨나 있는 모양이지《천만의 말씀》.

— *n.* Ⓤ **1** a great quantity, amount, or degree. 대량; 다량. ¶ *Have you learned ~ from that book?* 그 책에서 배운 게 많으냐 / *Much has been said about this.* 여기에 대해서 많은 말이 있어 왔다 / *Too ~ is as bad as none at all.* 너무 많음은 없느니만 못하다 / *So ~ for this story.* 이 이야기엔 이제 멀미가 난다 / *How ~ is it?* 값이 얼마요 / 《*iron.*》 *Much you know about it!* 네가 알긴 뭘 알아. **2** 《chiefly in *negative sense*》 something great, important, etc. 중요한 것; 우수한 것. ¶ *His picture is not ~ to look at.* 그 사람 그림은 그저 그렇다 / *He is not ~ of a scholar.* 대단한 학자는 아니다.

make* 〔*think*〕 *much of, treat or consider (something or someone) as important. …을 중요시하다.

so much, such a quantity; of equal amount. 같은 양의; 그 정도의. ¶ *so ~ brandy and so ~ water* 그만큼의 브랜디와 같은 양의 물.

so much for, that is the end of. 그것으로 끝내다. ¶ *So ~ for today.* 오늘은 그만 끝내자.

this* 〔*that*〕 *much, the amount indicated; so much. 이(그)만큼(은); 여기(거기)까지는. ¶ *Can you spare this ~?* 이렇게까지 줄 수 있나 / *He admitted that ~.* 그는 거기까지는 인정했다.

too much for, superior to (someone) in skill, ability, etc. …의 힘에 겹다; …에게 벅차다. ¶ *He is too ~ for me in mathematics.* 난 그 애한테는 수학에 손들었다 / *The work is too ~ for her.* 그 일은 그녀에게 벅차다.

— *adv.* **1** to a great extent or degree. 대단히; 매우; 퍽(opp. little). 語法 much는 과거분사를 수식하며 또 형용사의 비교급·최상급을 수식하나 원급은 수식하지 않음. ¶ *I like it very ~.* 그것을 몹시 좋아한다 / *I am ~ interested in science.* 나는 과학에 아주 흥미가 있다 / *I arrived ~ too soon.* 나는 너무 일찍 도착했다 / *You can swim ~ better than I.* 너는 나보다 훨씬 헤엄을 잘 친다 / *He is ~ the greatest poet.* 정말로 위대한 시인이다. **2** nearly; about. 거의; 대개. ¶ ~ *the same way* 거의 같은 방법 / *They are pretty ~ alike.* 그들은 아주 비슷하다 / *They are ~ of a size.* 그들은 거의 같은 치수다 / *They are ~ of an age.* 그들은 비슷비슷한 나이다. [E.]

as much again as, twice as much as. …의 두 배.

as much as to say, as if to say. 마치 …라고나 말하려는 듯이.

half as much again as, one and a half times as much as. (양이) …의 한 배 반.

much less, 《preceded by a *negative clause*》 then it is needless to say that the following does not apply. 하물며 (…아니다); 더더욱 (…아니다). ¶ *She does not know English, ~ less French.* 그녀는 영어도 모르는데 하물며 프랑스어를 알겠나.

much more, 《preceded by an *affirmative clause*》 then it is needless to say that the following case applies. 하물며; 항차 (…에 있어서랴). ¶ *A child can do it well, ~ more I.* 아이도 잘하는데 나야 말해서 뭐해.

not so much A as B, B rather than A. A라기보다는 오히려 B이다. ¶ *He is not so ~ a scholar as a writer.* 그는 학자라기보다는 작가다.

not so much as* do *something, not even do

something. …조차 않다. ¶ *He cannot so ~ as write his own name.* 그는 제 이름조차 못 쓴다.
without so much as, not even. …조차 없이〔않고〕. ¶ *He went away without so ~ as saying good-bye.* 그는 인사조차 않고 가버렸다.
much·ness [mʌ́tʃnis] *n.* 《*colloq.*》 greatness in quantity. 많음.
much of a muchness, just about the same; nearly alike. 대동 소이한; 엇비슷한. ¶ *We found it hard to choose a carpet; they were all much of a ~.* 카펫 고르기가 쉽지 않았다. 그것들 모두가 엇비슷했다.
mu·ci·lage [mjúːsəlidʒ] *n.* Ⓤ a sticky, gummy substance used to stick things together, taken from certain plants. 점액(粘液); 고무풀. 參考 영국에서는 gum이라 함. [→mucus]
muck [mʌk] *n.* Ⓤ **1** dirt; moist farmyard manure; a fertilizer. 오물; 거름. **2** 《Brit. *colloq.*》 anything that is unpleasant or untidy; rubbish. 너절한 것; 쓰레기. ¶ *His last book was sheer ~.* 그의 최근작은 시시하기 짝이 없었다.
make a muck of, make (something) dirty or untidy; spoil. …을 더럽히다; 망쳐 놓다.
— *vt., vi.* (P6,7;1) fertilize (the earth) with muck; make (something) dirty; spoil. 거름을 주다; 더럽히다. [Scand.]
muck about, 《*colloq.*》 idle away; loaf about. 빈둥거리다.
muck up, disarrange (a room); spoil (something). …을 어지럽히다; 망쳐 놓다. ¶ *The change in the weather has mucked up our picnic.* 날씨가 달라져 소풍을 잡쳤다.
muck·rake [mʌ́krèik] *n.* **1** 《rare》 a rake for collecting muck. 갈퀴; 쇠스랑《농기구》. **2** 《*the* ~》 the action or practice of looking for scandal, corruption, etc. 추문을 들추기. **3** 《*fig.*》 =muckraker. — *vi.* (P1) hunt for the evil deeds of public men, etc. 추문을 들추다.
muck·rak·er [mʌ́krèikər] *n.* a person who is always looking for scandal, corruption, etc. 남의 추문만을 캐는 사람.
mu·cous [mjúːkəs] *adj.* of, like or producing mucus. 점액(粘液)의〔같은〕; 점액을 분비(分泌)하는. ¶ *the ~ membrane* 점막(粘膜). [E.]
mu·cus [mjúːkəs] *n.* Ⓤ the sticky, slimy substance coming from the mucous membrane of the nose, throat, etc. (동물의) 점액. ¶ *nasal ~* 콧물 / *dried ~* 코딱지. [↑]
:mud [mʌd] *n.* Ⓤ soft, wet earth. 진흙; 진창. ¶ *a mud-caked hand* 진흙투성이의 손 / *His name was ~.* 그의 신용이 땅에 떨어졌다. [E.]
fling 〔***throw***〕 ***mud at,*** speak evil of (someone); try to damage someone's reputation. …을 헐뜯다.
mud in your eye, drink to your health and remember me. 건강을 빕니다《건배 때의 인사》. ¶ *Here's ~ in your eye.* 건배합시다.
stick in the mud, fall in deep mud; reach the end of the road; be very conservative. 진창에 빠지다; 더는 못 가게 되다; 보수적이다.
treat 〔***consider***〕 ***someone as mud*** 〔***as the mud beneath one's feet***〕, treat 〔consider〕 someone as something contemptible. …을 아주 무시하다.
mud·di·ness [mʌ́dinis] *n.* Ⓤ the state of being muddy. 흙투성이; 더러움.
mud·dle [mʌ́dl] *vt.* **1** (P6,7,13) confuse (the brain, etc.); bring (someone) into a state of confusion and disorder. …을 혼란시키다; 당황하게 만들다; (술 따위로 머리)를 멍하게 만들다. **2** (P6) mix up (a drink, etc.). (음료 따위)를 휘저어 섞다. **3** (P6) make a mess of (something). …을 망쳐 놓다. ¶ *~ a piece of business* 〔*a plan*〕 사업〔계획〕을 망쳐 놓다. **4** (P7) 《*away*》 waste. …을 낭비(浪費)하다. ¶ *~ away one's time* 〔*money*〕.
— *vi.* (P2A,3) 《*with*》 act or think in a confused way. 갈피를 못 잡다; 실수(失手)하다. ¶ *~ with one's work* 흐리터분하게 일하다.
muddle about, walk about; work carelessly. 어정거리다; 아무렇게나 일하다.
muddle on 〔***along***〕, struggle on somehow. 그럭저럭 해 나가다.
muddle through, succeed in spite of confusion. 그럭저럭 해내다. ¶ *There were problems, but we muddled through somehow.* 문제가 있었으나 그럭저럭 해냈다.
— *n.* Ⓒ 《usu. *sing.*》 **1** a state of disorder and confusion. 혼란. **2** mental confusion. 어리둥절함; 흐리멍덩한 상태. [E.]
in a muddle, in a puzzle; in disorder. 어리둥절하여. ¶ *Everything was in a thorough ~.* 모든 것이 엉망이었다.
make a muddle of, bungle. …을 엉망으로 만들다; 잡치다.
:mud·dy [mʌ́di] *adj.* (**-di·er, -di·est**) **1** full of mud; covered with mud; filthy. 흙투성이의; 지저분한. ¶ *~ shoes* / *a ~ road* 진창길. **2** ⓐ mentally confused. (머리가) 혼란해진. ¶ *~ thinking.* ⓑ (of liquid) not clear. 맑지 못한. ¶ *~ water* 흙탕물. **3** dark-colored; dull. 충충한; 흐릿한. ¶ *a ~ complexion* 거무한 살갗. — *v.* (**-died**) *vt.* (P6) make (something) dirty with mud; confuse. …에 흙을 묻히다; 혼란시키다. — *vi.* (P1) become dirty with mud. 흙투성이가 되다. [*mud*]
mud·guard [mʌ́dgɑ̀ːrd] *n.* Ⓒ a cover of shield over the wheel of a bicycle, an automobile, etc. to protect against mud flying up from below. (차의) 흙받기. 參考 자전거의 그것은 wing 또는 fender.
mu·ez·zin [mjuːézin] *n.* Ⓒ a Mohammedan official whose job is to announce the hour of prayer. (회교국의) 기도 시각을 알리는 사람. [Arab.]

〈muff[1]〉

muff[1] [mʌf] *n.* a covering of fur, etc. used by women to keep their hands warm. 머프; (여성용) 토시. [→muffle]

muff[2] [mʌf] *n.* Ⓒ **1** any failure; an unskillful fellow; a fool. 실수; 재주 없는 사람; 둔재; 바보. **2** 《sports》 a failure to hold a ball when catching it. 공을 놓치기.
make a muff of (=*make a mistake in*) *something.* …을 실수하다; 잘못하다.
— *vt.* (P6) make an unskillful mistake in (something); miss (a catch). 실수하다; (공)을 놓치다. [↑]

muf·fin [mʌ́fin] *n.* Ⓒ a small, light, round cake, usu. served hot with butter. 머핀《빵의 일종》. [? O.F.]

muf·fle [mʌ́fəl] *vt.* (P6,7) **1** wrap or cover (something) up for warmth. …을 싸다; 덮다. ¶ ~ *one's head* 머리쓰개로 머리를 싸다 / *She muffled* (*up*) *her throat in a warm scarf.* 그녀는 따뜻한 스카프를 목에 둘렀다. **2** wrap up (something) so as to lessen the sound; lessen or dull (a sound). 소리를 죽이기 위해 …을 싸다; 소음(消音)하다. ¶ *Closing the window muffled the noises from the street outside.* 창문을 닫아서 거리의 소음을 막았다. [F. *moufle* mitten]

muf·fler [mʌ́flər] *n.* Ⓒ **1** a scarf worn about the neck for warmth; a hood. 머플러; 목도리; 두건. **2** a device for silencing noises of an automobile, etc. (자동차 등의) 소음기(消音器). ¶ *the ~ in a motor* 내연 기관의 소음기.

muf·ti [mʌ́fti] *n.* Ⓤ the civilian clothes worn by a soldier, sailor, etc. who normally wears a uniform. 평상복; 사복(opp. uniform). ¶ *an officer in ~* 사복 경찰. [Arab.]

mug[1] [mʌg] *n.* Ⓒ **1** a large, heavy cup with a handle. (손잡이 있는 투박한) 컵; 조끼. **2** the amount a mug holds. 그 한 잔의 양. ¶ *drink a ~ of beer* 〔*milk*〕 맥주 한 조끼를〔우유 한 컵을〕 마시다. [N.]

mug[2] [mʌg] *n.* **1** 《*sl.*》 the face; the mouth. 얼굴; 입. ¶ *an ugly ~* 못생긴 상. **2** 《Brit. *sl.*》 a person who is easily deceived; a fool. 어수룩한 사람; 봉. [↑]

mug·gy [mʌ́gi] *adj.* (**-gi·er, -gi·est**) (of the weather) hot, wet, and close; sultry. (무)더운. ¶ ~ *weather* 무더운 날씨. [Scand.]

mug·wump [mʌ́gwʌ̀mp] *n.* 《U.S.》 **1** a person who acts independently, esp. in politics. 당파에 초연한 사람; 무소속 정치인. **2** a conceited person. 자존심이 강한 사람. [N-Amer-Ind. =great chief]

Mu·ham·mad, -med [muhǽməd] *n.* (570-632 A.D.) an Arabian prophet of Islam. 마호메트. 參考 Mahomet, Mohammed 라고도 씀. [Arab.]

Mu·ham·mad·an, -med- [muhǽmədən] *adj., n.* =Mohammedan.

mu·lat·to [mju(:)lǽtou, mə-] *n.* Ⓒ (*pl.* **-toes** or **-tos**) a person who has one white and one Negro parent; any person of mixed white and Negro blood. 백인과 흑인 간의 혼혈아. [→mule]

mul·ber·ry [mʌ́lbèri / -bəri] *n.* (*pl.* **-ries**) **1** Ⓒ a tree with broad, dark-green leaves on which silkworms feed; a sweet, dark-purple, berrylike fruit of this tree. 뽕나무; 오디. **2** Ⓤ a dark, purplish-red color. 짙은 자주색. [L. *morum* mulberry, →berry]

mulch [mʌltʃ] *n.* Ⓒ a layer of dead leaves, straw, etc. spread over the ground to protect the roots of newly-planted trees. (갓심은 나무의) 뿌리 덮개. — *vt.* (P6) cover (roots, etc.) with mulch. …에 뿌리 덮개를 하다. [E. =soft]

mulct [mʌlkt] *n.* Ⓒ the money taken from someone as punishment. 벌금. — *vt.* (P13,14) **1** punish (someone) by means of a mulct. …에 벌금을 물리다. ¶ ~ *someone* (*in*) *£10.* **2** 《*of*》 rob or deprive. …에게서 —을 빼앗다. ¶ *be mulcted of £ 20 by a rascal* 깡패한테 20 파운드를 털리다. [L. *mul(c)ta*]

•**mule**[1] [mju:l] *n.* Ⓒ **1** a strong work animal whose father is a donkey and whose mother is a mare. 노새. **2** 《*colloq.*》 a person having very firm ideas or opinions. 고집쟁이. ¶ *be as stubborn* 〔*obstinate*〕 *as a ~* 아주 고집 불통이다. **3** a kind of spinning machine. 뮬 방적기; 정방기(精紡機). [L. *mulus*]

mule[2] [mju:l] *n.* Ⓒ a heelless slipper. 슬리퍼. [L. *mulleus* shoe of red leather]

mu·le·teer [mjù:lətíər] *n.* Ⓒ a driver of mules. 노새몰이《사람》. [*mule*[1]]

mul·ish [mjú:liʃ] *adj.* **1** like a mule. 노새 같은. **2** fixed in idea or opinion; stubborn; obstinate. 고집센; 완고한. ● **mul·ish·ly** [-li] *adv.* **mul·ish·ness** [-nis] *n.* [↑]

mull[1] [mʌl] *vt., vi.* (P13;3) 《U.S. *colloq.*》 《*over*》 think about for a long time; ponder over. 곰곰이 생각하다. ¶ ~ *over a problem.* [M.E.]

mull[2] [mʌl] *vt.* (P6) heat (wine, etc.) with sugar, spices, etc. …에 향료〔설탕〕 등을 넣어 데우다. [? L.]

mull[3] [mʌl] 《Brit.》 *vt.* (P13) 《*colloq.*》 make a mess of. …을 엉망으로 만들다; 그르치다; 실수하다. ¶ ~ *a catch in cricket* 크리켓의 공을 놓치다. — *n.* a mess. 혼란; 엉망; 실수. [? E.]
make a mull of, fail to do something properly. 실수하다; 망쳐 놓다.

mull[4] [mʌl] *n.* Ⓤ a thin, soft muslin. 얇고 부드러운 무명. [Hind. *malmal*]

mul·lah [mʌ́lə, mú:lə] *n.* a Mohammedan learned man or priest. (회교도의) 식자(識者); 율법 학자. [Arab.]

mul·li·on [mʌ́ljən, -liən] *n.* Ⓒ an upright bar or column between two parts of a window. 세로 창살; 장살대. [F.]

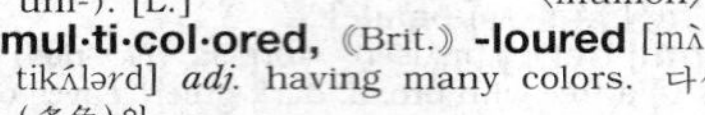
⟨mullion⟩

mul·ti- [mʌ́lti-] *pref.* many. '많은'의 뜻(opp. mono-, uni-). [L.]

mul·ti·col·ored, 《Brit.》 **-loured** [mʌ̀ltikʌ́lərd] *adj.* having many colors. 다색(多色)의.

mul·ti·far·i·ous [mʌ̀ltəfέəriəs] *adj.* many and various. 다양한; 여러 가지의; 다방면의. ¶ ~ *activities* 〔*expenses*〕 다방면에 걸친 활동〔비용〕/ ~ *duties* 여러 가지의 의무. [L. *multifariam* in many way]

mul·ti·foil [mʌ́ltifɔ̀il] *n.* 《archit.》 an ornament consisting of more than 5 foils. 다엽 장식(多葉裝飾). [L. *multus* much]

mul·ti·form [mʌ́ltifɔ̀ːrm] *adj.* having many forms or shapes. 여러 모양의; 다양한.

mul·ti·lat·er·al [mʌ̀ltilǽtərəl] *adj.* **1** many-sided. 다변의. **2** involving two or more nations. 다국간의. ¶ *a* ~ *treaty* 다국간 조약.

mul·ti·mil·lion·aire [mʌ̀ltimìljənέər] *n.* Ⓒ a person whose wealth reaches several millions of dollars, pounds, francs, etc. 억만 장자; 거부(巨富).

mul·ti·par·tite [mʌ̀ltipáːrtait] *adj.* divided into many parts. 많은 부분으로 나뉜.

mul·ti·ple [mʌ́ltəpəl] *adj.* **1** having, or made up of, many parts or elements. 복식(複式)의; 다수의; 다양한; 여러 부분으로 이루어진. ¶ *a man of* ~ *interests* 흥미가 다양한 사람 / ~ *birth* 다태(多胎) 출산《쌍둥이·세쌍둥이 등》/ ~ *shop* 〔*store*〕 연쇄점. **2** 《math.》 repeated many times. 배수(倍數)의. —*n.* Ⓒ 《math.》 a number that can be divided by another number without a remainder. 배수. ¶ *12 is a* ~ *of 3, and also of 2, 4 and 6.* 12는 3의 배수이며 또한 2, 4 그리고 6의 배수이기도 하다 / *the least common* ~ 최소 공배수. [L. *-plex* -fold]

mul·ti·plex [mʌ́ltəplèks] *adj.* multiple; manifold; made up of many parts. 복합의; 다양한; 여러 겹의. [↑]

mul·ti·pli·ca·tion [mʌ̀ltəplikéiʃən] *n.* **1** Ⓤ the act of multiplying; the state of being multiplied; an increase; an abnormal increase of parts. 증가; 증식; 번식. ¶ *the* ~ *of the population.* **2** ⓊⒸ 《math.》 the way of finding the answer when a number is multiplied. 곱셈; 곱하기. ¶ *The result of a* ~ *is called the product.* 곱해서 얻은 답을 곱이라 한다. [→multiply, -ation]

mul·ti·plic·i·ty [mʌ̀ltəplísəti] *n.* Ⓤ 《sometimes *a* ~》 a great number or variety. 다수; 중복; 다양성. ¶ *a* ~ *of errors* 허다한 오류.

mul·ti·pli·er [mʌ́ltəplàiər] *n.* Ⓒ 《math.》 the number by which another number is multiplied. 승수(乘數).

·**mul·ti·ply** [mʌ́ltəplài] *vt.* (**-plied**) **1** (P13) cause (a quantity or number) to increase a certain number of times. …을 곱하다; 곱셈하다(opp. divide). ¶ ~ *three by two,* 3에 2를 곱하다 / *Five multiplied by three is fifteen.* 5곱하기 3은 15다. **2** (P6) increase; add to the number of. 증가시키다; 늘리다. —*vi.* (P1) increase in number or extent; breed; propagate. 증가하다; 번식하다. ¶ *Cares* ~ *as one gets old.* 늙으면 걱정도 많아진다 / *a multiplying glass* 확대경. [→multiple]

·**mul·ti·tude** [mʌ́ltitjùːd] *n.* **1** Ⓤ a great number; Ⓒ a great crowd. 다수; 군중. ¶ *multitudes of admirers* 수많은 팬 / *the stars in* ~ 무수한 별들. **2** 《*the* ~》 the people; the masses. 대중; 민중. [multi-]

a multitude of, a great number of. 많은. ¶ *a* ~ *of flowers* 많은 꽃.

mum[1] [mʌm] *adj.* 《used as *predicative*》 saying nothing; silent. 말이 없는; 무언의. ¶ *stand* ~ 잠자코 서 있다 / *keep* ~ 침묵을 지키다.

as mum as a mouse 〔***mice***〕, speaking nothing at all. 도무지 말이 없는.

sit mum, not joining in a conversation. 이야기에 끼어들지 않다.

—*n.* Ⓒ silence. 침묵.

Mum's the word! Be silent.; Say nothing. 잠자코 있어라.

—*interj.* silence!; hush!; sh! 조용히; 쉿.

—*vi.* (**mummed, mum·ming**) **1** (P1) become silent. 말하지 않다. **2** act in a dumb show. 무언극을 하다. [Imit.]

mum[2] [mʌm] *n.* =mummy[2].

mum·ble [mʌ́mbəl] *vi., vt.* (P1,2A,3;6) speak unclearly or bite (food) as a toothless person. 우물우물 말하다〔씹다〕. ¶ ~ *to oneself* 혼자 중얼거리다. —*n.* Ⓒ an indistinct way of speaking; a mumbled sound. 중얼거림. [→mum[1]]

Mum·bo Jum·bo [mʌ́mbou dʒʌ́mbou] *n.* (*pl.* **M- Jumbos**) **1** an idol or god said to have been worshiped by some West African tribes. 서아프리카인의 우상〔귀신〕. **2** 《*m- j-*》 an object of superstitious awe or reverence. (미신적) 숭배물; 공포의 대상.

mum·mer [mʌ́mər] *n.* **1** a person who acts a silent play. 무언극 배우. **2** 《*colloq., contempt.*》 an actor. 배우; 광대. [→mum[1]]

mum·mer·y [mʌ́məri] *n.* Ⓒ (*pl.* **-mer·ies**) **1** a sort of dumb show. 무언극. **2** a useless or ridiculous ceremony. 허례 허식.

mum·mi·fy [mʌ́mifài] *vt.* (**-fied**) (P6) make (a dead body) into or like a mummy. …을 미라로 만들다. —*vi.* (P1) dry up. 바싹 마르다. [↓]

mum·my[1] [mʌ́mi] *n.* Ⓒ (*pl.* **-mies**) (esp. in ancient Egypt) a dead body kept from decay by chemicals or by being dried. 미라. —*vt.* (**-mied**) (P6) mummify (a dead body). …을 미라로 하다. [Arab. *mum* wax]

mum·my[2] [mʌ́mi] *n.* Ⓒ a child's word for

its mother; a mamma. 엄마. [*mamma*]

mumps [mʌmps] *n. pl.* 《used as *sing.*》 a disease that causes swelling under the ear and difficulty in swallowing. 이하선염(耳下腺炎); 항아리 손님. [Imit.]

munch [mʌntʃ] *vt., vi.* (P6;1) eat (something) noisily and with much movement of the mouth. 우적우적 씹다〔먹다〕. [E.]

mun·dane [mʌ́ndein, –⌐] *adj.* of this world; worldly; earthly. 현세의; 세속의. ¶ *the ~ world* 속세(俗世) / *~ desire* 세속의 욕망. [L. *mundus* world]

Mu·nich [mjúːnik] *n.* a city in southeastern Germany. 뮌헨.

***mu·nic·i·pal** [mjuːnísəpəl] *adj.* of a town or city or its self-government. 시의; 도시의; 자치시의. ¶ *the ~ council* 시의회 / *a ~ office* 시청 / *a ~ undertaking* 시영 사업. [L. *munia* civic offices, *capio* take]

mu·nic·i·pal·i·ty [mjuːnìsəpǽləti] *n.* Ⓤ a town, city, or other district that has local self-government; the governing body of such a town, etc. 지방 자치체; 시 당국.

mu·nif·i·cence [mjuːnífəsəns] *n.* Ⓤ great generosity. 활수(滑手)함; 손이 큼. [L. *munus* gift, -fic]

mu·nif·i·cent [mjuːnífəsənt] *adj.* extremely generous. 활수(滑手)한; 손이 큰. ● **mu·nif·i·cent·ly** [-li] *adv.*

mu·ni·tion [mjuːníʃən] *n.* 《usu. *pl.*》 materials used in war, such as guns, bombs, and other things. 군수품; 무기·탄약 등. ¶ *munitions of war* 군수품〔물자〕/ *a munitions factory* 군수 공장. — *vt.* (P6) provide (someone) with munitions. …에 군수품을 공급하다. ¶ *~ an army* 군을 무장시키다. [L. *munio* defend]

mu·ral [mjúərəl] *adj.* of or like wall; on a wall. 벽의; 벽 위의. ¶ *a ~ painting* 벽화. — *n.* Ⓒ a painting on a wall or ceiling; 《U.S.》 the decoration of a wall. 벽화; 천장 벽화; 벽 장식. [L. *murus* wall]

:**mur·der** [mə́ːrdər] *n.* ⓊⒸ the unlawful killing of a person that is planned beforehand. 살인. ¶ *commit ~* 살인하다 / 《*prov.*》 *Murder will out.* 살인〔악행〕은 반드시 드러난다 / *Murder!* 살인이다; 사람 살려.

cry* (*blue*) *murder, 《*colloq.*》 make an extravagant outcry. 호들갑스럽게 소리 지르다.

— *vt.* (P6) **1** kill (someone) on purpose and unlawfully. 살인하다. **2** 《*fig.*》 spoil (something) because of poor skill or knowledge. …을 망쳐 놓다. ¶ *~ music* 음악을 잡쳐 놓다 / *~ the English language* 엉터리 영어를 하다. [E.]

***mur·der·er** [mə́ːrdərər] *n.* Ⓒ a person who is guilty of murder. 살인자; 살인범.

mur·der·ess [mə́ːrdəris] *n.* Ⓒ a woman murderer. 여성 살인자〔범〕.

mur·der·ous [mə́ːrdərəs] *adj.* **1** of or like murder; that can murder. 살인(용)의. ¶ *a ~ weapon* 흉기 / *a ~ act* 살인 행위 / *a ~ robber* 살인 강도. **2** deadly. 치명적인. ¶ *a ~ blow* 치명적인 일격. **3** brutal; extremely sever. 잔인한; 지독한. ¶ *The heat is ~.* 무섭게 덥다.

mur·der·ous·ly [mə́ːrdərəsli] *adv.* in a murderous or cruel manner. 살인적으로; 흉악하게.

murk [məːrk] *n.* darkness. 암흑. ¶ *the ~ of night* 밤의 어둠. — *adj.* 《*poet.*》 dark. 어두운. [E.]

murk·y [mə́ːrki] *adj.* (**murk·i·er, murk·i·est**) dark; gloomy; heavy and gloomy with mist, etc. 어두운; 음산한; (안개 등이) 자욱한. ¶ *a ~ night* / *a ~ day* 음산한 날.

:**mur·mur** [mə́ːrmər] *n.* Ⓒ **1** a low, continuous, indistinct sound of a running stream. (시냇물 따위의) 졸졸거리는 소리. **2** a whisper. 속삭임. ¶ *the ~ of voices in another room* 옆방에서의 소곤대는 소리. **3** a complaint in a low tone. (낮은) 볼멘소리. ¶ *without a ~* 불평 하나 없이. — *vt., vi.* (P6;1,2A,3) **1** make a low, continuous, indistinct sound like that of stream or wind. 졸졸 소리 내다; (바람이) 살랑거리다. **2** speak in a low voice; whisper. 소곤거리다. **3** 《*at, against*》 complain. 투덜거리다. ¶ *~ at ill treatment* 대우가 나빠 투덜거리다. [L.]

mur·rain [mə́ːrin] *n.* Ⓤ a disease spreading from one animal to another, esp. of cattle. 가축(특히, 소)의 전염병. [F.]

:**mus·cle** [mʌ́səl] *n.* **1** ⒸⓊ a part of the body that can be tightened or loosened to produce movement. 근육. ¶ *an involuntary* 〔*a voluntary*〕 *~* 불수의(不隨意)〔수의〕근 / *He has strong muscles.* 근육이 단단하다. **2** Ⓤ 《*collectively*》 bodily strength. 체력. ¶ *a man of ~* 힘이 좋은 사람.

not move a muscle, be perfectly still. 끄떡도 하지 않다.

— *vi.* (P1,2A) use or appeal to force. 완력을 쓰다〔에 호소하다〕. [L. *mus* mouse]

muscle in, break into another's sphere of influence. 영역을 침범하다.

mus·cle-bound [mʌ́səlbàund] *adj.* having muscles stiff and inelastic through over-exercise. (과도한 운동으로) 근육이 뻣뻣하고 탄력이 없어진. ¶ *a ~ wrestler.*

Mus·co·vy [mʌ́skəvi] *n.* an old name for Russia. 러시아의 옛 이름. [*Moscow*]

mus·cu·lar [mʌ́skjələr] *adj.* of the muscles; having well-developed muscles; strong. 근육의; 근육이 억센; 힘센. ¶ *~ strength* 완력 / *the ~ system.* [*muscle*]

mus·cu·lar·i·ty [mʌ̀skjəlǽrəti] *n.* Ⓤ the state or quality of being muscular; energy. 근육이 늠름함; 억셈; 힘셈.

Muse [mjuːz] *n.* **1** 《Gk. myth.》 any one of the nine sister-goddesses who protected and encouraged the fine arts, poetry, music, etc. 뮤즈신(神)《미술·시·음악 등을 관장하는 아홉 여신 중의 하나》. **2** 《*the m-*》

poetic inspiration or genius; the goddess who inspires a poet. 시상(詩想); 시적 영감; 시흥(詩興); 시신(詩神). **3** 《*m-*》 Ⓒ a poet. 시인. [Gk. *mousa*]

·muse [mju:z] *vi.* (P1,2A,3) **1** 《*on, upon, over*》 think deeply; meditate. 숙고하다; 곰곰이 생각하다; 묵상하다. ¶ ~ *over past memories* 옛 추억에 잠기다 / ~ *on what one has heard* 들은 말을 곰곰이 되새기다. **2** gaze earnestly or wonderingly (on some-one or something). 유심히 바라보다. ¶ ~ *upon a distant view* 먼 데 경치를 찬찬히 바라보다. ●**mus·er** [-*ər*] *n.* [F.]

:mu·se·um [mju:zí:əm / -zíəm] *n.* Ⓒ a building in which objects of all kinds are collected and displayed; 《U.S.》 an art gallery. 박물관; 미술관. ¶ *a* ~ *piece* 진품(珍品). [→Muse]

mush [mʌʃ] *n.* Ⓤ **1** any soft, thick mix-ture or soft mass. 걸쭉한 죽 같은 것. **2** 《U.S.》 corn meal boiled in water. 옥수수죽. **3** 《*colloq.*》 silly talk; sentimentality. 허튼 소리; 괜한 감상(感傷). [var. of mash]

make a mush of (=*spoil*) *something.* …을 엉망으로 해 놓다.

mush·room [mʌ́ʃru(:)m] *n.* Ⓒ **1** a kind of eatable and fast-growing plant with no green leaves and shaped like an umbrella. 버섯; 양송이. **2** 《*fig.*》 an upstart; something but newly risen. 벼락 부자; 새로이 일어난 것. **3** a cloud produced by nuclear explo-sion. 원자운; 버섯 구름. ¶ *a* ~ *cloud.* — *adj.* of or like a mushroom, either in shape or in its rapid growth. 버섯의〔같은〕; 급속히 일어나는. ¶ *a* ~ *millionaire* 벼락 부자; 졸부 / *a* ~ *suburb town* 교외 신흥 도시. — *vi.* (P1) **1** gather mushrooms. 버섯을 따다. ¶ *go mushrooming* 버섯 따러 가다. **2** grow or spread very fast. 급속히 성장하다〔퍼지다〕. [F. *mousseron*]

mush·y [mʌ́ʃi] *adj.* (**mush·i·er, mush·i·est**) **1** like mush. 죽 같은; 질척한. **2** 《*colloq.*》 sentimental; emotional. 감상적인; 정에 약한; 다감한. [Prob. var. of mash]

:mu·sic [mjú:zik] *n.* Ⓤ **1** the art of com-bining and arranging pleasing sounds. 음악. ¶ *a* ~ *band* 악대(樂隊) / ~ *paper* 악보; 오선지 / *the Music of the Spheres* 천상의 묘음(妙音)《천체의 운행에 따라 생긴다고 상상했던》 / *dance to the* ~ 음악에 맞춰 춤추다 / *set a poem to* ~ 시에 곡을 붙이다. **2** a mu-sical score; a musical piece. 악보(樂譜); 악곡. ¶ *Can you read* ~*?* 악보를 볼 줄 아느냐. **3** any pleasing sound; harmony; melody. 듣기 좋은 소리; 묘음(妙音); 가락. ¶ *the* ~ *of the distant breakers* 멀리서 들려오는 바위에 부서지는 파도 소리. [→Muse]

face the music, face one's critics; face a difficult situation boldly. 당당하게 비판을 받다; 감연히 난국에 대처하다.

have no ear for music, have no sense of music. 음악을 모르다.

:mu·si·cal [mjú:zikəl] *adj.* of music; melo-dious; fond of music; skillful in music. 음악의; 선율이 고운; 음악을 좋아하는; 음악에 능한. ¶ *a* ~ *entertainment* 음악의 연주 / *a* ~ *composer* 작곡가 / *a* ~ *director* 지휘자 / *a* ~ *instrument* 악기 / *a* ~ *performance* 연주 / ~ *scales* 음계 / *a* ~ *score* 악보. — *n.* Ⓒ a musical play or comedy. 희가극; 음악극; 뮤지컬.

musical box [⌐-- ⌐] *n.* 《Brit.》 =music box.

mu·si·cale [mjù:zikǽl] *n.* Ⓒ 《U.S.》 a social musical entertainment, usu. held privately. 사교 음악회; (비공개의) 음악회.

music box [⌐- ⌐] *n.* a case or box which produces music mechanically. 오르골; 자명악(自鳴樂); 음악 상자.

music hall [⌐- ⌐] *n.* **1** a hall in which musical performances are held. 음악당; 뮤직 홀. **2** 《Brit.》 a theater for variety shows. 연예관(演藝館).

:mu·si·cian [mju:zíʃən] *n.* Ⓒ a person skilled in music, esp. one who plays music for pay; a composer of music. 음악가; 악사; 작곡가.

music stand [⌐- ⌐] *n.* a stand for holding sheets of music for a player. 악보대.

music stool [⌐- ⌐] *n.* a stool without a back, used while playing a piano. 피아노 의자《등받이가 없는》.

mus·ing [mjú:ziŋ] *adj.* meditative; reflective. 생각에 잠긴. — *n.* Ⓤ the act of meditating; meditation. 묵상; 숙고. [*muse*]

mus·ing·ly [mjú:ziŋli] *adv.* in a musing manner. 생각에 잠겨.

musk [mʌsk] *n.* **1** Ⓤ a strong-smelling substance obtained from the male musk deer and used in perfumes. 사향(麝香). **2** Ⓒ =musk deer. [Gk. *moskhos*]

musk deer [⌐ ⌐] *n.* a small hornless deer living in central Asia. 사향노루.

mus·ket [mʌ́skət] *n.* Ⓒ an old style of gun formerly used by foot-soldiers, now re-placed by the rifle. 구식 소총; 머스켓총. [It. *moschetto* sparrowhawk]

mus·ket·eer [mʌ̀skətíər] *n.* Ⓒ in old days, a foot-soldier armed with a mus-ket. 머스켓 총병(銃兵); 보병. [↑]

mus·ket·ry [mʌ́skətri] *n.* Ⓤ **1** 《*collec-tively*》 muskets; the soldiers armed with muskets. 소총; 소총대(隊). **2** the art of firing or the use of small arms. 소총 사격(술). [↑]

musk·mel·on [mʌ́skmèlən] *n.* Ⓒ any of several sweet, juicy fruits of a trailing plant. 머스크멜론. 參考 참외의 하나로 Can-taloupe라고도 함. [*musk*]

musk·rat [mʌ́skræ̀t] *n.* Ⓒ a rat-like water animal living in North America; its valu-able fur which is used for coats, etc. 사향뒤쥐; 그 모피. [↑]

Mus·lem, -lim [mʌ́zləm, mús-] *n., adj.* =Moslem.

mus·lin [mʌ́zlin] *n.* **1** Ⓤ soft cotton cloth used for dresses, fine curtains, etc. 모슬린; 메린스. **2** 《U.S.》 calico. 캘리코; 옥양목. — *adj.* made of muslin. 모슬린으로 만든. [*Mussolo*, Place]

muss [mʌs] *vt.* (P6,7) 《U.S. *colloq.*》 put into disorder. 엉망[뒤죽박죽]으로 만들다. ¶ *The child's dress was mussed (up).* 아이 옷은 엉망이었다. — *n.* disorder; confusion. 무질서; 혼란; 엉망. [Prob. var. of mess]

mus·sel [mʌ́səl] *n.* Ⓒ an eatable freshwater shellfish whose dark-blue shells are used in making buttons. 홍합《조개》. [→muscle]

Mus·sul·man [mʌ́səlmən] *n.* (*pl.* **-mans**) a Mohammedan. 회교도. [→Islam]

:must[1] [mʌst, məst] *auxil. v.* (**must**) 語法 1, 2, 3의 과거형은 had to. 단, 간접 화법의 종속절에서는 must도 씀. 미래는 will 또는 shall have to. 4의 과거는 'must have + 과거분사'를, 부정형은 영문 주석란(欄)을 참조. **1** 《expressing necessity or obligation》 have to; need (to); be obliged to. …해야 한다; …하지 않으면 안 된다(opp. need not; do not have to). ¶ *One ~ eat to live.* 사람은 살기 위해 먹어야 한다 / *You ~ earn money to support your family.* 가족을 부양키 위해 돈을 벌어야 한다 / *We ~ obey the laws of the country.* 나라의 법을 지켜야 한다 / *Must you see him? —Yes, I ~.* (opp. *No, I don't have to.* =*No, I needn't.*) 그를 꼭 만나야 하나 —응, 만나야 해(opp. 아니, 만날 필요 없어) / *I ~ have my hair cut.* 이발을 해야겠다. **2** 《expressing a command or a strong request》 should; ought to; have to. …해야 한다[마땅하다]; …해라 (opp. must not). ¶ *You ~ do it at once.* 즉시 해야 한다 / *You ~ come and see us sometimes.* 가끔 우리를 만나러 와야 한다 / *Mother said that I ~ do as I was told.* 어머니는 내게 일러 준 대로 해야 한다고 말씀하셨다. **3** 《expressing insistence》 insist that one will. …않고는 못 배긴다; 꼭 …해야 한다. ¶ *She ~ have rings everywhere.* 그녀는 어디건 반지를 끼고 가야 직성이 풀린다 / *I ~ know your reason.* 네 이유를 꼭 알아야겠다. **4** 《expressing certainty or strong probability》 be sure to; be certain to. …임에 틀림없다; 반드시 …이다(opp. cannot). ¶ *He ~ be a good man.* 그는 선량한 사람임에 틀림없다 / *He ~ be mad to do such a thing.* 그런 짓을 하다니 그자는 미쳤군 그래 / *She ~ have been beautiful when young.* 젊어서는 분명히 미인이었을 거다 / *All men ~ die.* 생자 필멸(生者必滅) / *If he says so, it ~ be true.* 그가 그렇게 말한다면 그건 진실이다. **5** unfortunately or unluckily happened to. (과거에) 공교롭게도 …하다. ¶ *As soon as he had recovered from his illness, he ~ break his leg.* 건강을 회복하자마자 재수없게도 다리 하나가 부러졌다.

must needs** do*=needs must** do,* must surely do; cannot help or avoid doing. …하지 않을 수 없다.

— *n.* Ⓒ 《*colloq.*》 something that must be done, had, etc. 절대로 필요한 것; 불가결의 일. ¶ *This book is a ~.* 이 책은 필독서다 / *His attendance is a ~.* 그가 꼭 출석해야 한다. [E.]

must[2] [mʌst] *n.* Ⓤ the juice pressed from grapes before it can cause a slow chemical change; new wine. 포도즙; 새 포도주. [L.]

must[3] [mʌst] *n.* Ⓤ something produced upon decaying organic matter; mold. 곰팡이. ¶ *~ on a cake* 과자의 곰팡이. — *vt., vi.* (P6;1) make or become musty. 곰팡이가 나게 하다; 곰팡이가 나다. [*musty*]

mus·tache, 《Brit.》 **mous-** [mʌ́stæʃ, məstǽʃ] *n.* Ⓒ the hair growing near a man's upper lip; the short, stiff hairs growing near the mouth of an animal. 콧수염; (짐승의 주둥이) 수염. [Gk. *mustax* jaw, upper lip]

mus·ta·chio [məstɑ́ːʃou] *n.* (*pl.* **-chios**) = ⌈mustache.

mus·tang [mʌ́stæŋ] *n.* Ⓒ a small but strong, half-wild horse living on the North American plains. 야생마. [Sp.]

mus·tard [mʌ́stərd] *n.* Ⓤ **1** a plant with yellow flowers and long pods containing seeds. 겨자《식물》; 평지; 갓. **2** the yellow powder made from the seeds of this plant used in cooking because it has a hot taste. 겨자《양념》. ¶ *ground ~* 겨잣가루 / *~ oil* 겨자 기름. [→must[3]]

mus·tard-gas [mʌ́stərdgæ̀s] *n.* an oily liquid of violent irritant and blistering properties; yperit. 겨자탄; 이페리트《독가스》.

mustard plaster [⌐-⌐-] *n.* a paste made with powdered mustard and rubber in solution spread on a cloth and used as a poultice. 겨자 연고《찜질용》.

mus·ter [mʌ́stər] *n.* Ⓤ **1** the act of gathering. (사람·짐승 등의) 집합. **2** an assembly of persons to see if all are present or not. 소집; 점호; 검열.

pass muster, be thought to be satisfactory; be fit for the purpose required. 검열을 통과하다; 합격하다.

— *vi., vt.* (P1;6,7) **1** come together; gather or summon, esp. soldiers, to see if all are present or not. 모이다; (검열, 점호에) 소집하다. ¶ *~ the forces for a struggle* 싸움을 위해 병력을 모으다[집결시키다]. **2** 《*up*》 collect; summon. (용기 등)을 불러일으키다. ¶ *~ up strength* 힘을 내다; 분발하다. [L. *monstro* show]

muster in, 《U.S.》 accept (someone) into military service. …을 입대시키다.

muster out, 《U.S.》 discharge (someone) from military service. …을 제대시키다.

***must·n't** [mʌ́snt] =must not.

mus·ty [mʌ́sti] *adj.* (**must·i·er, must·i·est**) **1** mouldy; having a smell or taste suggesting mould or damp. 곰팡이가 난; 곰팡내가 나는; 축축한. ¶ *a ~ room* 곰팡내가 나는 방 / *~ bread* 곰팡이 핀 빵. **2** 《*fig.*》 out of date. 진부한; 케케묵은. ¶ *~ laws* 구시대의 법률. [*must*[3]]

mu·ta·bil·i·ty [mjù:təbíləti] *n.* the quality of being mutable. 변하기 쉬움; 무상(無常). [→mutate]

mu·ta·ble [mjú:təbəl] *adj.* changeable. 변하기 쉬운; 마음이 잘 변하는. ¶ *~ customs* 잘 변하는 관습 / *a ~ person* 변덕스러운 사람.

mu·tate [mjú:teit] *vt., vi.* (P6;1) **1** change. 변하다. **2** produce mutation. 변종을 낳다. [L. *muto* change]

mu·ta·tion [mju:téiʃən] *n.* UC **1** a change. 변경; 변화. **2** 《biol.》 in plants and animals, the sudden appearance of new, well-marked characteristics which are different from those of the parents. 돌연 변이.

mu·ta·tis mu·tan·dis [mu:tá:tis mu:tǽndis, mju:téitis mju:-] *adv.* 《L.》 with necessary changes. 필요한 변경을 하여; 준용(準用)하여. [→mutate]

***mute** [mju:t] *adj.* **1** not making a sound; silent. 소리가 나지 않는; 무언의. ¶ *stand ~* 묵비권을 행사하다 / *The little girl stood ~.* 소녀는 잠자코 서 있었다. **2** without the power of speech; dumb. 벙어리의. **3** not sounded or pronounced such as the *b* in *dumb.* 묵자(默字)[묵음]의.

— *n.* C **1** a dumb person. 벙어리. **2** a letter that is not sounded. 묵자(默字). **3** a thing put on a musical instrument to soften the sound. (악기의) 약음기(弱音器).

— *vt.* (P6) make the sound of (a musical instrument) less loud; put a mute on. …에 약음기를 대다. ¶ *He played the violin with muted strings.* 그는 바이올린 현에 약음기를 대고 바이올린을 켰다. [L. *mutus*]

mu·ti·late [mjú:təlèit] *vt.* (P6) **1** cut off (a limb, etc.). (수족 따위를) 절단하다. ¶ *man mutilated in hands and feet* 양 수족을 절단당한 사내. **2** make (a story, etc.) imperfect by removing an essential part. (이야기 등의 주요부)를 삭제하여 불완전하게 만들다. ¶ *~ a book* [*speech*] 책[연설]의 골자를 빼서 못쓰게 만들다. [L. *mutilus* maimed]

mu·ti·la·tion [mjù:təléiʃən] *n.* UC the act of mutilating; the state of being mutilated. 수족의 절단; 훼손.

mu·ti·neer [mjù:təníər] *n.* C a person who takes part in a mutiny. 폭도; 반항자. [→mutiny, -eer]

mu·ti·nous [mjú:tənəs] *adj.* (of soldiers, etc.) bold and disobedient; showing a spirit of opposition. 반항적인. ● **mu·ti·nous·ly** [-li] *adv.* [↓]

mu·ti·ny [mjú:təni] *n.* UC (*pl.* **-nies**) resistance by force against someone in authority, esp. that of soldiers or sailors against their officers. 반란; 폭동. ¶ *the Caine ~* 케인호(號)의 반란. — *vi.* (P1,3) (**-nied**) rise against or resist authority by force. 폭동을 일으키다; 반항하다. [L. *moveo* move]

***mut·ter** [mʌ́tər] *vi., vt.* (P1,2A;6,7) 《*at, against*》 speak (something) in a low; indistinct voice; murmur; complain. 중얼거리다; 투덜투덜하다. ¶ *~ curses* 중얼거리며 악담하다. — *n.* C a muttered sound; a murmur. 중얼거림; 투덜거림. [Imit.]

***mut·ton** [mʌ́tn] *n.* U the meat of a sheep. 양고기. ¶ *~ chop* 양고기 갈비; 양의 고깃점. [L. *multo* sheep]

dead as mutton, quite dead. 아주 죽은[숨이 끊어진].

eat [***take***] ***one's mutton with,*** dine with. …와 함께 식사하다.

mutton dressed as lamb, 《Brit. *colloq.*》 an elderly woman dressed in a style suitable for a young woman. 어울리지 않게 젊게 차려 입은 여자.

return to our muttons, (from French) come back to the subject of which we were speaking. 본론으로 돌아가다.

mut·ton-head [mʌ́tnhèd] *n.* 《*colloq.*》 a dull, stupid person. 바보; 멍텅구리.

***mu·tu·al** [mjú:tʃuəl] *adj.* **1** done or felt by each of two toward the other. 서로의; 상호적인. ¶ *~ assistance* [*aid*] 상호 부조 / *a ~ association* 공제 조합. **2** common to two or more persons. 공동[공통]의. ¶ *our ~ friend* 우리 쌍방[공통]의 친구. [L. *mutuus* borrowed]

by mutual consent [***agreement***]***,*** by common consent. 합의에 의해.

mu·tu·al·i·ty [mjù:tʃuǽləti] *n.* U the state of being mutual. 상호 관계; 상관.

mu·tu·al·ly [mjú:tʃuəli] *adv.* each other; one another. 서로; 공동으로.

muz·zle [mʌ́zəl] *n.* C **1** the nose and mouth of a four-footed animal, such as a dog, horse, etc. (개·말 따위의) 입·코 부분; 주둥이. **2** the open end of a pistol [firearm]. 총구; 포구. **3** a guard or cover for the mouth of an animal to prevent its biting. 부리망; 재갈. — *vt.* (P6) **1** put a muzzle on (an animal). …에 재갈을 물리다. **2** 《*fig.*》 prevent (someone) from telling or writing of something. …을 입막음하다; (언론)을 묶어 놓다. [L. *musum*]

muz·zle-load·er [mʌ́zəllòudər] *n.* a gun that is loaded through the muzzle. 전장총(前裝銃).

muz·zy [mʌ́zi] *adj.* dull; confused in mind; stupid from drinking. 멍한; 몽롱한; 술로 멍해진. [?, *mu*(ddy), (*fu*)*zzy*]

⁝**my** [mai, mi] *pron.* belonging to me. 나의. ¶ *~ pen* 나의 펜 / *~ train* 내(가 타고 있는[있던]) 열차 / *This is ~ car.* 이것은 내 차다. — *interj.* an exclamation of surprise, dismay, etc. 친근감·놀람 등을 나타냄. ¶ *Oh, ~ friend!* 어, 여보게 / *My goodness!*

아이고 저런. [→mine]

Myan·mar [mjʌ́nmɑːr] *n.* a country in the southeast Asia. 미얀마. 參考 구칭은 Burma(1989년까지). 수도는 Yangon.

Myan·ma·rese [mjʌ̀nmərí:z] *n.* **1** Ⓒ a person of Myanmar. 미얀마 사람. **2** Ⓤ the language of Myanmar. 미얀마 말.
— *adj.* of Myanmar. 미얀마의.

my·ope [máioup] *n.* a short-sighted person. 근시안인 사람. [Gk. *muō,* shut, *ōps* eye]

my·o·pi·a [maióupiə] *n.* Ⓤ short-sightedness; near-sightedness. 근시(안)(cf. *hypermetropia*).

my·op·ic [maiɑ́pik / -ɔ́p-] *adj.* short-sighted. 근시안의.

myr·i·ad [míriəd] *n.* Ⓒ 《rare》 ten thousand; a very great number. 만(萬); 무수. ¶ ~ *of insects* 〔*stars*〕 무수한 곤충〔별들〕. — *adj.* innumerable; countless. 헤아릴 수 없이 많은; 무수한. ¶ *the ~ stars of a summer night* 여름밤의 헤아릴 수 없이 많은 별들. [Gk. *murioi* 10,000]

myrrh [məːr] *n.* Ⓤ the substance obtained from a tree in Arabia and East Africa, used in medicine or perfumes because of its sweet smell. 미르라; 몰약(沒藥). [Gk. *murra*]

myr·tle [mə́ːrtl] *n.* Ⓒ 《bot.》 **1** an evergreen tree with shiny leaves, white sweet-smelling flowers, and black berries. 도금양(桃金孃)《상록 관목》. **2** a blue-flowered creeping vine. 협죽도과(科)의 식물. [Gk. *murtos*]

:my·self [maisélf] *pron.* (*pl.* **our·selves**) ⇨oneself. **1** a reflexive and emphatic form of **I** or **me.** 나 자신; 자기 자신. ¶ *I did it* ~. 나 자신이 그것을 했다 / *I laid ~ on the grass.* 풀 위에 누웠다 / *I saw it* ~. 내 눈으로 (직접) 그걸 봤다 / *I have hurt* ~. 다쳤다. **2** one's own normal physical or mental condition. 평상시의〔정상적인〕 나. ¶ *I was not ~ yesterday.* 어제는 컨디션이 나빴다. [*me, self*]

(**all**) ***by myself,*** without any help. 내 힘으로; 나 혼자서. ¶ *I cannot do it by* ~. 나 혼자서는 못 한다.

for myself, by my own effort. 혼자 힘으로; 독립해서.

:mys·te·ri·ous [mistíəriəs] *adj.* full of mystery; difficult to understand or explain. 신비한; 불가사의한; 이상한. ¶ *a ~ enemy* 수수께끼의 적 / *a ~ fire* 원인 모를 불〔화재〕/ ~ *murder* 미궁의 살인 사건. ● **mys·te·ri·ous·ly** [-li] *adv.* **mys·te·ri·ous·ness** [-nis] *n.* [↓]

:mys·ter·y [místəri] *n.* Ⓒ (*pl.* **-ter·ies**) **1** ⓊⒸ something strange or secret. 신비; 불가사의. ¶ *a clue to the* ~ 수수께끼를 풀 실마리 / *the mysteries of nature* 자연의 신비. **2** 《*pl.*》 secret religious ceremonies performed in ancient Greeks, Romans, etc. (고대의) 비교(祕敎)〔비밀의〕 의식; 성찬식. **3** a secret principle. (기독교의) 인지를 초월한 교의. **4** secret knowledge or magic. 비법(祕法); 비전(祕傳). **5** a novel designed to excite curiosity by keeping some facts secret until the end. 추리 소설. [GK. *muō* close lips or eyes]

make a mystery of, keep, treat (something) secret; hide what is plain, simple. …을 비밀로 하다; (아무것도 아닌 것)을 신비화하다〔숨기다〕.

mystery play [⌐— ⌐] *n.* a form of drama in the Middle Ages in which scenes from the Bible were shown and performed. 신비극; 기적극.

mys·tic [místik] *adj.* having a spiritual meaning not understood by everybody. 신비(주의)의; 비법의; 비전의. ¶ ~ *arts* 비술(祕術) / ~ *rites* 비교(祕教)의 의식. — *n.* one who believes that truth or God can be known through spiritual insight. 신비가(家). [→mystery]

mys·ti·cal [místikəl] *adj.* =mystic.

mys·ti·cal·ly [místikəli] *adv.* in a mysterious manner. 신비하게; 불가사의하게.

mys·ti·cism [místəsìzəm] *n.* Ⓤ the beliefs of mystics; the belief that knowledge of real truth and of God may be obtained through personal insight and inspiration. 신비주의; 신비교(教). [→mystery]

mys·ti·fi·ca·tion [mìstəfikéiʃən] *n.* Ⓤ the act of mystifying or being mystified; Ⓒ something that mystifies. 신비화; 당혹시킴; 신비적인 것. [↓]

mys·ti·fy [místəfài] *vt.* (**-fied**) (P6) **1** make (something) mysterious. …을 신비화하다. **2** confuse very much; puzzle. …을 어리둥절하게 만들다; 미혹시키다. ¶ *His tricks mystified the children.* 그의 묘기는 아이들을 어리둥절하게 만들었다. [→mistery]

·myth [miθ] *n.* Ⓒ **1** an old story told about persons and events in early history existing only in imagination; Ⓤ 《*collectively*》 such stories. 신화. ¶ *the myths of Greece and Rome* 그리스와 로마의 신화. **2** a person, thing, story or event that is imaginary or invented. 가공의〔신비적인〕 사람〔사물〕. [Gk. *muthos*]

myth·i·cal [míθikəl] *adj.* **1** of myths; existing only in myths. 신화의. ¶ *the ~ age* 신화 시대. **2** unreal; imaginary. 가공의; 공상의. [*myth*]

myth·o·log·i·cal [mìθəlɑ́dʒikəl / -lɔ́-] *adj.* of mythology or myths; unreal; imaginary. 신화의; 신화적인; 신화학의; 실제하지 않는; 상상상의. [↑]

my·thol·o·gist [miθɑ́lədʒist / -θɔ́l-] *n.* Ⓒ a student or writer of mythology. 신화학자〔작가〕.

my·thol·o·gy [miθɑ́lədʒi / -θɔ́l-] *n.* (*pl.* **-gies**) **1** Ⓤ the study of myths. 신화학. **2** Ⓤ 《*collectively*》 myths; Ⓒ a collection of myths. 신화; 신화집. ¶ *Greek* 〔*Roman*〕 ~.

n N

N, n [en] *n.* Ⓒ (*pl.* **N's, Ns, n's, ns** [enz]) **1** the 14th letter of the English alphabet. 영어 알파벳의 열넷째 글자. **2** anything shaped like the letter N. N자 모양의 것. **3** ⟪math.⟫ an indefinite number or quantity. 부정수(不定數); 부정량(不定量).

n. neuter; new; nominative; noon; north; northern; noun; number.

nab [næb] *vt.* (**nabbed, nab·bing**) ⟪*colloq.*⟫ **1** catch suddenly. …을 잡아채다. **2** arrest. …을 체포하다. ¶ *The police nabbed the thief.* [→nap¹]

na·bob [néibɑb / -bɔb] *n.* ⟪hist.⟫ a very rich person, esp. one who had returned from India with a large fortune. (인도에서 돌아온 유럽인) 대부호. [Arab.]

na·celle [nəsél] *n.* the framework containing the engines, etc. of an aircraft; the car of an airship. 나셀⟪항공기의 엔진 수용부(收容部)⟫; (비행선의) 곤돌라. [→navy]

na·cre [néikər] *n.* mother-of-pearl. 진주모(母)〔층(層)〕. [Sp.]

na·dir [néidər, -diər] *n.* Ⓒ **1** the point in the heavens directly beneath the observer. 천저(天底); 척점(蹠點)⟪관측자 바로 밑의 천구점(天球點)⟫ (opp. zenith). **2** ⟪*fig.*⟫ the lowest point; a time of great difficulty. 맨 밑바닥; 구렁텅이. ¶ *the ~ of one's career* 고생하던 밑바닥 생활의 시절. [Arab.＝opposite]

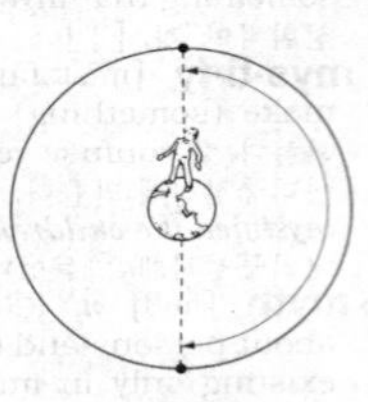

⟨nadir 1⟩

nag¹ [næg] *vi., vt.* (**nagged, nag·ging**) (P1,3; 6,13) constantly find fault with (someone) about little things; trouble (someone) by never-ending complaints. 잔소리하다; 바가지 긁다. ¶ *~ someone to death* 아무를 잔소리로 몹시 괴롭히다 / *She nags from morning till night.* 하루종일 잔소리를 한다. — *n.* Ⓒ **1** an act of nagging. 잔소리. **2** ⟪*colloq.*⟫ a person, esp. a woman, who nags. 잔소리가 심한 사람⟪특히 여자⟫. [Sc.]

nag² [næg] *n.* Ⓒ **1** a small horse; a pony. 작은 말; 조랑말. **2** ⟪*colloq.*⟫ a horse; a poor or inferior horse. 말; 시원찮은 말. [E.]

nai·ad [néiəd, nái-, -æd] *n.* Ⓒ (*pl.* **-ads** or **-a·des**) **1** ⟪Gk. & Rom. myth.⟫ ⟪often *N-*⟫ a fairy girl living in a stream, fountain, etc. 물의 요정. **2** a girl swimmer. 헤엄(잘) 치는 소녀. [Gk.]

:nail [neil] *n.* Ⓒ **1** a metal pin pointed at one end, used to hold separate piece of wood, etc. together. 못; 징. **2** a thin, hard plate on the end of a finger or a toe. 손톱; 발톱.

a nail in one's coffin, ⟪*fig.*⟫ something that shortens one's life. 수명을 줄이는 것. ¶ *Every cigarette you smoke is a ~ in your coffin.* 네가 피우는 담배 하나하나가 네 명을 줄이고 있다.

(*as*) *hard as nails,* **a**) very strong and healthy. 아주 건강한. **b**) pitiless; severe. 냉혹한.

(*as*) *right as nails,* quite right. 올바른; 틀림없는. ¶ *I shall be as right as nails in a few days.* 나는 며칠내로 올바르게 될 것이다.

hit the* (*right*) *nail on the head, get to the root of a matter; touch the exact point in a question. 바로 맞히다; 정곡을 찌르다.

on the nail, at once; on the spot. 곧; 당장. ¶ *pay one's bills on the ~* 청구서를 즉시 지급하다.

tooth and nail, with all one's strength or resources. 필사적으로; 맹렬히.

to the* (*a*) *nail, thoroughly; completely. 철저히; 완전히.

— *vt.* (P7,13) **1** fasten (something) with a nail or nails. 못〔징〕으로 …을 고정시키다. ¶ *~ a notice on* 〔*to*〕 *the door* 문에 게시를 박아붙이다 / *~ down the lid of a box* 상자에 뚜껑을 못박아 고정시키다. **2** hold (something) fast; keep (someone) fixed. …을 움직이지 못하게 하다; …을 꼼짝 못 하게 하다. ¶ *The fire nailed him to the spot.* 화재는 그를 그 자리에서 꼼짝 못 하게 했다. **3** ⟪*colloq.*⟫ catch; seize. …을 붙잡다. ¶ *Nail the man before he leaves!* 놈이 달아나기 전에 붙잡아라. **4** make (a bargain, etc.) certain. (계약 등)을 결정짓다〔체결하다〕. **5** prove (a lie) to be false. (거짓)을 들춰내어 밝히다; 폭로하다. [E.]

nail a lie down to the counter, prove that a thing is not true; expose a lie. 거짓임을 밝히다; 폭로하다.

nail one's colors to the mast, persist; refuse to yield. 고집하다; 양보하지 않다.

nail down, make (something) secure by or as by nailing. 고정시키다; 꼼짝 못 하게 하다.

nail up, fasten (a window, etc.) with nails. (창 따위를) 못질하다. ¶ *~ up a door* (열리지 않도록) 출입문을 못질하다.

nail·brush [néilbrʌ̀ʃ] *n.* Ⓒ a small brush for cleaning fingernails. 손톱 솔.

nail·er [néilər] *n.* **1** a nail-maker. 못 만드

는 사람. 2 《*sl.*》 a first-rate performer of sport, game, etc. (경기 등의) 명인(名人). ¶ *He is a ～ at golf.* 그는 골프의 명인이다.

nail scissors [ˊ ˋ―] *n.* a pair of small scissors used to cut and shape fingernails; a nail clipper. 손톱 가위.

na·ive, -ïve [nɑːíːv] *adj.* simple like a child; innocent. 천진난만한; 순진한. [F.]

na·ive·ly, -ïve- [nɑːíːvli] *adv.* in a naive manner; innocently. 천진난만하게.

na·ive·té, -ïve- [nɑːiːvtéi / nɑːíːvətei] *n.* **1** Ⓤ the quality or state of being naive. 천진난만. **2** Ⓒ a natural action or saying. 순진한 언행.

na·ive·ty, -ïve- [nɑːíːvəti] *n.* =naiveté.

:na·ked [néikid] *adj.* **1** completely undressed; nude. 벌거벗은. ¶ *～ feet* 맨발 / *go* ～ 알몸으로 지내다. **2** without any covering; bare. 노출된. ¶ *a tree ～ of leaves* 낙엽진 나무. **3** without any addition; plain. 꾸밈없는; 적나라한. ¶ *the ～ truth* 〔*facts*〕 있는 그대로의 사실. **4** not helped by glasses. 안경에 의하지 않은. ¶ *the ～ eye* 육안. [E.]

na·ked·ly [néikidli] *adv.* in a naked manner; plainly. 적나라하게.

na·ked·ness [néikidnis] *n.* Ⓤ the state of being naked; plainness; bareness. 벌거숭이; 노출; 적나라; 있는 그대로임.

:name [neim] *n.* Ⓒ **1** a word by which a person or thing is called; a title. 이름; 명칭. ¶ *a family ～ =a surname* 성(姓) / *a middle ～* 중간 이름 / *a first* 〔*a given, a Christian*〕 *～* 세례명 參考 Christina Georgina Rossetti 에서 Christina가 세례명, Georgina가 중간 이름, Rossetti가 성(姓)임 / *He is Bob by ～.* 그는 이름이 봅이다 / *I know the man by ～.* 그 사람의 이름을 알고 있다 / *What ～ shall I say?* 실례지만 성함은. **2** fame; reputation; a well-known person. 명성; 평판; 유명 인사. ¶ *a good* 〔*a bad*〕 *～* 좋은〔나쁜〕 평판 / *He has a ～ for honesty.* 그는 정직하다는 평판이 나 있다 / *make* 〔*win*〕 *a ～ for oneself* 이름을 떨치다; 유명해지다 / 《*prov.*》 *Give a dog a bad ～ and hang him.* 누구든 한번 평이 나빠지면 끝장이다 / *lend one's ～ to an undertaking* 어떤 사업을 위하여 이름을 빌려주다 / *Faulkner is a great ～ in American literature.* 포크너는 미국 문학에 있어서 위대한 인물이다. **3** a group of persons that has one name; a family, a race, etc. 가계(家系); 문중; 씨족. ¶ *the last of his ～* 그의 가문의 마지막 사람 / *the honor of one's ～* 가문의 명예.

by 〔***of, under***〕 ***the name of,*** named. …라는 이름의〔으로〕; …이라고 부르는. ¶ *a man by* 〔*of*〕 *the ～ of Smith* 스미스라는 이름의 사람 / *He goes by* 〔*under*〕 *the ～ of Smith.* 그는 스미스라는 이름으로 알려져 있다.

call someone names, hurt the feelings of someone by using bad names. 아무의 욕을 하다.

get 〔***make***〕 ***oneself a name,*** win reputation. 이름을 날리다; 유명해지다.

Give it a name. Say what you wish (to have). 원하시는 것을 말씀하세요《남을 대접할 때 쓰는 말》.

in the name (= *with the authority*) ***of,*** *someone, God, etc.* …의 이름으로; 권위에 의하여. ¶ *Open in the King's* 〔*Queen's*〕 *～!* 어명이다, 문 열어라 / *in the ～ of God* 신의 이름을 빌려; 맹세코.

put one's name down (=*apply*) ***for*** *something.* …을 신청하다; …에 응모〔가입〕하다.

set 〔***put***〕 ***one's name to,*** sign. …에 서명하다.

take someone 〔***God's***〕 ***name in vain,*** speak disrespectfully of…; use it idly. 함부로〔경솔하게〕 아무〔신〕의 이름을 입에 올리다.

to one's name, belonging to one. 자기 소유의. ¶ *He hasn't a penny to his ～.* 그는 돈 한 푼없는 빈털터리이다.

— *vt.* **1** (P6,19) give a name to (someone or something). …에 이름을 붙이다〔짓다〕; 명명하다. ¶ *We named the dog Ricky.* 개 이름을 리키라고 지었다 / *The baby was named after* 〔*for*〕 *his grandfather.* 아기 이름은 할아버지 이름을 따서 지어졌다. **2** (P6) call (someone or something) by name; mention. …의 이름을 말하다; 지적〔언급〕하다. ¶ *Can you ～ this fish?* 이 물고기의 이름을 아느냐 / *Three pupils were named in the teacher's remarks.* 선생님의 단평 중에서 세 학생의 이름이 거론되었다. **3** (P13,19,21) appoint; choose. …을 ―에 지명〔임명〕하다. ¶ *～ someone as chairman* 아무를 의장에 임명하다 / *He was named president.* 그는 회장에 지명되었다. [E.]

name the day, (of a woman) fix the day for her wedding. 결혼 날짜를 정하다.

Name your price. Say what price you want. 값을 말하시오.

not to be named on 〔***in***〕 ***the same day with,*** quite inferior to. …보다 훨씬 못한.

name·less [néimlis] *adj.* **1** having no name; unknown. 이름없는; 무명의. ¶ *a ～ writer.* **2** impossible to describe clearly. 형언할 수 없는. ¶ *a ～ melancholy* 뭐라 형언할 수 없는 우울. **3** too bad to be spoken of. 입에 담지 못할; 아주 고약한. ● **name·less·ness** [-nis] *n.*

·name·ly [néimli] *adv.* that is to say; in other words. 이를테면; 즉. 參考 접속사의 구실을 함. ¶ *two girls, ～, Mary and Susie* 두 소녀, 즉 메리와 수지.

name·sake [néimsèik] *n.* Ⓒ **1** a person who has the same name as another. 이름이 같은 사람; 동명인. **2** a person named after another. 딴 사람의 이름을 딴 사람.

Nan·cy [nǽnsi] *n.* a woman's name. 여자 이름.

nan·ny [nǽni] *n.* 《Brit.》 a child's nurse. 유모.

nanny goat [ˊ― ˋ] *n.* 《*colloq.*》 a female goat. 암염소(opp. billygoat). [*Ann*]

·**nap**[1] [næp] *n.* Ⓒ a short, light sleep, esp. in the daytime. 겉잠; (특히) 낮잠. ¶ *take a* ~ 낮잠을 한숨 자다.
— *vi.* (**napped, nap·ping**) (P1) **1** sleep for a short time; be half asleep. 졸다; 낮잠 자다. **2** be careless; be off one's guard. 방심하다. [E.]
catch someone napping, 《*fig.*》 find him asleep; catch him off guard; take unawares. (아무의) 방심을 틈타다; 허를 찌르다.

nap[2] [næp] *n.* Ⓤ the short hairs on the surface of cloth. 보풀. — *vt.* (P6) put a nap on (cloth, etc.) by brushing. (천 따위에) 보풀이 일게 하다. [Du.]

na·palm [néipɑ:m] *n.* **1** a chemical substance used to thicken gasoline for incendiary bombs. 소이탄용(燒夷彈用) 가솔린 농축제(濃縮劑). **2** the thickened gasoline. 농축 가솔린. ¶ *a* ~ *bomb* 네이팜탄. [*naph*tha, *palm* oil]

nape [neip] *n.* Ⓒ the back of the neck. 목덜미. [? E.]

naph·tha [nǽpθə, nǽfθə] *n.* Ⓤ a clear liquid got from petroleum, coal tar, etc., used in cleaning and lighting. 나프타유(油); 휘발유; 석유. [Gk.]

naph·tha·lene [nǽfθəlì:n, nɑpθ-] *n.* a disinfectant got in distilling coal tar. 나프탈렌. [↑]

:**nap·kin** [nǽpkin] *n.* Ⓒ **1** a piece of cloth or paper used while eating. 냅킨. **2** 《Brit》. a piece of cloth used as a baby's underclothing; a diaper. 기저귀. [L. *mappa* tablecloth]
lay up in a napkin, neglect to use. 쓰지 않고 치워두다.

napkin ring [⌐-⌐] *n.* a broad ring of metal, ivory, etc., used to hold a folded table napkin. 냅킨링《냅킨을 말아 끼아두는 고리》.

〈napkin ring〉

Na·ples [néiplz] *n.* a city in Italy, famous for its beautiful bay. 나폴리. ¶ 《*prov.*》 *See* ~ *and die.* 나폴리를 보지 않고 경치를 논하지 마라.

·**Na·po·le·on** [nəpóuliən], **Bonaparte** *n.* (1769-1821) a French general and Emperor. 나폴레옹 1세.

Na·po·le·on·ic [nəpòuliɑ́nik / -ɔ́n-] *adj.* of or like Napoleon. 나폴레옹 1세의〔같은〕. ¶ ~ *ambition* 대단한 야심.

nap·py [nǽpi] *n.* Ⓒ 《Brit. *colloq.*》 a baby's napkin; a diaper. 기저귀. [*napkin*]

nar·cis·si [nɑ:rsísai] *n.* pl. of **narcissus.**

nar·cis·sism [nɑ́:rsisìzəm] *n.* Ⓤ morbid self-love or self-admiration. 나르시시즘; 병적인 자기 도취. [↓]

nar·cis·sus [nɑ:rsísəs] *n.* (*pl.* **-sus·es** or **-cis·si**) **1** Ⓒ a spring plant with yellow or white flowers and thin leaves; the flower of this plant. 수선화(cf. *daffodil, jonquil*). **2** 《*N-*》 《Gk. myth.》 a beautiful youth who fell in love with his own image in a spring and changed into the flower of the narcissus. 나르시스. [Gk.]

nar·cot·ic [nɑ:rkɑ́tik / -kɔ́t-] *n.* Ⓒ a drug used to produce sleep or to lessen pain. 나르코틴《마취·수면제》. — *adj.* having the power or effect of a narcotic. 마취성의. ¶ *a* ~ *drug* 마취제. [Gk. *narkē* numbness]

nark [nɑ:rk] *n.* 《*sl.*》 police decoy or spy. 경찰 앞잡이. [Gypsy =nose]

nar·rate [nærέit, ⌐-] *vt.* (P6,13) tell the story of (something); relate. …을 이야기하다; 서술하다. ¶ ~ *one's experiences in a war* 전쟁 경험담을 말하다. — *vi.* (P1) tell stories in speech or writing. 이야기를 말하다〔쓰다〕. [L. *narro*]

·**nar·ra·tion** [nærέiʃən, nə-] *n.* **1** Ⓤ the act or manner of narrating. 서술; 화법. ¶ *Novels, short stories, etc. are forms of* ~. 소설, 단편 등은 서술의 형식을 빌린것이다. **2** Ⓒ a story. 이야기. ¶ *travelers' narrations* 여행담. **3** 《gram.》 a way of telling. 화법. ¶ *direct* 〔*indirect*〕 ~ 직접〔간접〕 화법.

·**nar·ra·tive** [nǽrətiv] *n.* **1** Ⓒ a story. 이야기. **2** Ⓤ the art of telling a story; narration. 설화; 화술. — *adj.* of storytelling; narrating. 이야기체의. ¶ *a* ~ *poem* 설화시.

nar·rat·or [nærέitər, ⌐--] *n.* Ⓒ a person who narrates; a person who reads some passages between the speeches or scenes of a play in a theater, on radio or television. 이야기하는 사람; (극·영화·TV 등의) 해설자.

:**nar·row** [nǽrou] *adj.* (**-row·er, -row·est**) **1** not broad or wide; less wide than usual for its kind. 폭이 좁은(opp. broad, wide). ¶ *a* ~ *road* 〔*ribbon*〕 좁은 길〔리본〕. **2** limited; small. (범위가) 좁은; 한정된; 빠듯한. ¶ *He has a* ~ *circle of friends.* 그는 교우 범위가 좁다〔친구가 별로 없다〕/ *in* ~ *means* 〔*circumstances*〕 궁핍〔곤궁〕해서. **3** with little space, time, etc. to spare; close; near. 가까스로의; 아슬아슬한. ¶ *a* ~ *victory* 신승(辛勝) / *He had a* ~ *escape from drowning.* 하마터면 빠져 죽을 뻔 했다. **4** 《*dial.*》 unwilling to spend or give much money; not liberal; stingy. 인색한; 쩨쩨한(opp. generous). ¶ *He is* ~ *with his money.* 돈에 다라운 사람이다. **5** limited to the point of view; narrow-minded. 시야가 좁은; 편협한. ¶ *take* ~ *views* 편협한 견해를 가지다 / *a* ~ *mind* 좁은 소견(머리). **6** of limited meaning or intent; strict. 협의의. ¶ *in the narrowest sense* 가장 좁은 뜻에서. **7** careful; thorough; minute. 신중한; 정밀한. ¶ *make a*

～ *inquiry* 자세하게 조사하다.
one's narrow bed [***house***], the grave. 무덤.
narrow escape, a hairbreadth escape. 구사일생.
the narrow way, righteousness. 정의.
— *n.* 《usu. *pl.*》 the narrow part of a river, a strait, a valley, etc. (강 따위의) 좁은 곳; 해협; 골짜기.
— *vt.* (P6) make (something) narrower; limit. …을 좁히다; 제한하다. ¶ ～ *an argument* 논의의 범위를 좁히다. — *vi.* (P1) become narrower. 좁아지다. ¶ *The river narrows at this point.* 강은 이 지점에서 좁아진다. [E.]

nar·row·ly [nǽrouli] *adv.* **1** in a narrow or limited manner. 편협하게. **2** with difficulty; barely. 가까스로. ¶ *He ～ escaped death.* 하마터면 죽을 뻔했다. **3** carefully; closely. 주의깊게; 면밀히. ¶ *watch someone ～* 아무를 주의깊게 살피다.

nar·row-mind·ed [nǽroumáindid] *adj.* not having an open mind. 소견이 좁은; 편협한. ● **nar·row-mind·ed·ly** [-li] *adv.* **nar·row-mind·ed·ness** [-nis] *n.*

nar·row·ness [nǽrounis] *n.* Ⓤ the state of being narrow. 좁음; 협소함; 도량이 좁음.

na·sal [néizəl] *adj.* **1** of the nose. 코의. ¶ ～ *inflammation* 비염(鼻炎). **2** coming through the nose. 코에서 나오는. ¶ *a ～ discharge* 콧물. **3** 《phon.》 spoken or pronounced through the nose. 비음의. — *n.* Ⓒ 《phon.》 a nasal sound such as [m] and [n], etc. 비음. [L. *nasus* nose]

na·sal·ize [néizəlàiz] *vt.* (P6) pronounce (a word) through the nose. 콧소리를 내다; 비음화(鼻音化)하다. — *vi.* (P1) talk with a nasal sound. 콧소리로 말하다.

nas·cent [nǽsnt] *adj.* **1** coming into existence. 발생하려고 하는. **2** beginning to grow or develop. (사상·문화 등) 초기의; 발생기의. ¶ *a ～ revolutionary tendency* 혁명 초기의 경향. [L. *nascor* be born]

nas·ti·ly [nǽstili / nɑ́:-] *adv.* in a nasty or offensive manner. 더럽게; 불결하게. [*nasty*]

nas·ti·ness [nǽstinis / nɑ́:s-] *n.* Ⓤ the state of being nasty. 불결; 더러운 것.

na·stur·tium [nəstə́:rʃəm] *n.* Ⓒ 《bot.》 a plant with shieldshaped leaves and yellow, orange or red flowers. 한련(旱蓮). [L.]

∗**nas·ty** [nǽsti / nɑ́:s-] *adj.* (**-ti·er, -ti·est**) **1** very dirty and disagreeable; bad in taste. 더러운; 불쾌한; 역한. ¶ *a ～ food* 메스꺼운 음식 / *a ～ room* 지저분한 방 / *a ～ medicine* 먹기 싫은 약. **2** immoral. 음란한; 저속한. ¶ ～ *language* 상말 / *a ～ book* 음란 서적 / *a ～ person* 비열한 사람 / *a ～ story* 추잡한 이야기 / *leave a ～ taste in the mouth* 뒷맛이 개운찮다. **3** dangerous; threatening. 위험한; 험악한. ¶ ～ *weather* 험악한 날씨 / *Things look ～ for me.* 내게 일이 고약하게 돼 간다. **4** ill-natured; troublesome. 심술궂은; 성가신. ¶ *make a ～ remark* 매정한 말을 하다 / *a ～ temper* 매우 언짢은 기분 / *turn ～* 화내다 / *play someone a ～ trick* 아무에게 비열한 짓을 하다. **5** ⓐ severe; painful. 심한; 고통스러운. ¶ *a ～ cut* 가혹한 처사 / *have a ～ fall* 심하게 낙상하다. ⓑ difficult to deal with. 다루기 어려운. ¶ *a ～ rock to climb* 오르기 힘든 바위. [? E.]

na·tal [néitl] *adj.* of one's birth; 《*poet.*》 native. 출생의; 고향의. ¶ *one's ～ day* 생일 / *one's ～ place* 고향. [→nascent]

⁑**na·tion** [néiʃən] *n.* Ⓒ **1** the people of a country; an independent country. 국민; 국가. ¶ *the French ～* 프랑스 국민 / *Western nations* 서방 제국; 서구. **2** a race of people of the same religion, customs, and language. 민족. ¶ *the Jewish ～* 유태 민족. [→nascent]

⁑**na·tion·al** [nǽʃənəl] *adj.* **1** of a nation. 국민(국가)의. ¶ *a ～ language* 국어 / *a ～ flag* 국기 / ～ *power* 국력 / *the ～ government* 거국 내각. **2** belonging to a nation. 국유의. ¶ *a ～ bank* 국립 은행 / *a ～ park* 국립 공원 / *the ～ forces* (일국의) 육해공군 / *a ～ enterprise* 국영 기업 / ～ *troops* 국군. **3** patriotic; nationalistic. 애국적인; 국가주의(자)의. — *n.* Ⓒ **1** a citizen of a nation. 국민; 동포. **2** 《usu. *pl.*》 citizens of a nation living in foreign countries. 해외 동포.

na·tion·al·ism [nǽʃənəlìzəm] *n.* Ⓤ **1** a strong love for one's country. 애국심; 국가주의. **2** a desire for national independence in a country ruled by another. 독립주의; 자치주의.

na·tion·al·ist [nǽʃənəlist] *n.* Ⓒ a person who supports and fights for nationalism. 국가(민족)주의자. — *adj.* =nationalistic. ¶ *the ～ party* 국민당.

na·tion·al·is·tic [næ̀ʃənəlístik] *adj.* of nationalism or nationalists. 국가주의(자)의.

∗**na·tion·al·i·ty** [næ̀ʃənǽləti] *n.* (*pl.* **-ties**) **1** ⓊⒸ the state of belonging to one nation. 국적. ¶ *the ～ of a ship* 선적 / *What is her ～?* 그녀의 국적은 어디냐. **2** Ⓤ independence as a nation. 국가적 독립; 국가. ¶ *Many African* [*Russian*] *states are obtaining ～.* 아프리카(러시아)의 여러 나라들은 독립해가고 있다.

na·tion·al·i·za·tion [næ̀ʃənəlizéiʃən / -lai-] *n.* Ⓤ the act of nationalizing; the state of being nationalized. 국유화; 국영. ¶ *the ～ of the railways* 철도의 국유화.

na·tion·al·ize [nǽʃənəlàiz] *vt.* (P6) **1** make (a nation); change (a dependent country, etc.) into a nation. …을 독립국으로 만들다. **2** bring(railways, land, industries, etc.) under the control of a nation. (철도·토지 등을) 국유화하다. **3** make into a nation. 귀화(歸化)시키다.

N

national salute [ㅗ-- -ㅗ] *n.* the discharge of guns in sign of respect for the national flag. 국기에 대한 예포(禮砲) 발사.

na·tion·wide [néiʃənwàid] *adj.* stretching throughout the whole nation. 전국적인. ¶ *arouse ~ interest* 전국적인 관심을 불러일으키다.

:na·tive [néitiv] *n.* Ⓒ **1** a person who is born in a certain place or country. …태생(胎生)의 사람. ¶ *a ~ of Seoul* 서울 출신의 사람. **2** a person who lives originally in an uncivilized country. 원주민. ¶ *The natives received him kindly.* 원주민들은 그를 친절하게 맞았다. **3** an animal or a plant found in a particular place. 토착(土着)의 동식물; 자생종(種). — *adj.* **1** of one's birthplace. 출생지의; 자국의. ¶ *one's ~ town* 태어난 도시 / *one's ~ language* 모국어. **2** inborn; not learnt. 타고난; 선천적인. ¶ *~ aptitude* 타고난 기질; 천성 / *~ talent* 천부의 재능. **3** of the original people in any country usu. uncivilized. (백인측에서 보아) 토착의; 원주민의. ¶ *a ~ costume* 민족 의상. **4** (of minerals) found in a natural state. 천연의. ¶ *~ copper* 천연동(銅) / *~ rock* 자연석. **5** (of animals or plants) originally found in a certain place. (동식물이) 재래의. ¶ *a ~ tree* 토착의 나무 / *the ~ British rat* 영국 토종의 쥐. **6** simple; natural. 소박한; 자연 그대로의. ¶ *~ beauty* 소박미(素朴美). [→nation]

go native, (of a European) take up the way of life of a less civilized race among whom one lives. (백인이) 원주민과 같은 생활을 하다. [→nation]

na·tive-born [néitivbɔ́:rn] *adj.* born in a particular place or country. 토박이의. ¶ *a ~ American* 토박이 미국인.

na·tiv·i·ty [nətívəti, nei-] *n.* (*pl.* **-ties**) **1** ⓊⒸ birth. 출생. **2** 《*the N-*》 the birth of Christ. 예수 강탄(降誕). **3** 《*the N-*》 a picture of the birth of Christ. 예수 강탄의 그림.

nat·ty [nǽti] *adj.* (**-ti·er, -ti·est**) neat and smart in clothes or general appearance. 말쑥한; 산뜻한. ¶ *a ~ naval officer* 산뜻한 해군 장교 / *in a ~ business suit* 말쑥한 신사복을 입고. ●**nat·ti·ly** [-li] *adv.* [L.]

:nat·u·ral [nǽtʃərəl] *adj.* **1** of nature. 자연의. ¶ *~ phenomena* 자연 현상 / *~ philosophy* 자연 철학; 물리학 / *~ science* 자연과학 / *~ history* 박물학. **2** in the state produced or provided by nature; not man-made. 천연의; 인공이 아닌. ¶ *~ gas* 천연 가스 / *~ resources* 천연 자원 / *the land in its ~ state* 미개(간)지. **3** belonging to a person by nature; not acquired. 타고난; 천부의. ¶ *a ~ gift* (*poet*) 천부의 재능〔시인〕 / *the ~ color of the hair* 염색을 안한 본래의 모발색 / *a ~ fool* 백치. **4** true to nature; life-like. 꼭 닮은; 흡사한. ¶ *The portrait looks ~.* 초상화가 진짜 사람 같다 / *drawn ~ scale* 실물 크기로 그린. **5** to be expected; normal; ordinary. 당연한; 정상인. ¶ *a ~ death* 자연사 / *It is only ~.* 그건 당연한 일이다 / *He is not in a ~ state of mind.* 여느 때와 다르다; 정상이 아니다 / *It is quite ~ that he should fail.* 그가 실패하는 것은 이상할 것 하나 없다. **6** not pretending; simple; honest. 꾸밈 없는. ¶ *a ~ manner* 꾸밈 없는 태도 / *speak in a ~ voice* 꾸밈 없는 자연스런 음성으로 말하다. **7** 《mus.》 without sharps or flats. 본위의. ¶ *a ~ sign* 본위 기호. **8** illegitimate. 서출(庶出)의. ¶ *a ~ son* 서자.

come natural to (=*be easy for*) *someone.* …에게는 매우 쉽다. ¶ *Swimming comes ~ to him.* 그에게는 수영이 식은 죽 먹기처럼 쉽다.

— *n.* Ⓒ **1** 《*colloq.*》 a fool by birth; an idiot. (타고난) 백치. **2** 《mus.》 a white key on the piano; a musical melody which is not sharp or flat; the sign for this (♮). (피아노의) 흰 건반; 본위음; 제자리표. **3** 《*colloq.*》 a person or thing sure to be successful. 틀림없이 성공하는 사람〔일〕. [→nature]

nat·u·ral·ism [nǽtʃərəlìzəm] *n.* Ⓤ **1** an action or a thought based on natural desire. 자연주의. **2** a theory in literature that wants to show things as they really are. 자연〔사실〕주의. **3** 《philos.》 the belief that there are no supernatural things or events in this world. 자연〔실증〕주의.

nat·u·ral·ist [nǽtʃərəlist] *n.* Ⓒ **1** a person who studies the things of nature, such as plants, minerals and animals. 박물학자. **2** a realist. (예술 등의) 자연주의자.

nat·u·ral·is·tic [nætʃərəlístik] *adj.* **1** having the characteristics of naturalism in art or literature. 자연주의의. **2** of natural history or naturalists. 박물학적인. **3** like nature; realistic. 사실적인.

nat·u·ral·i·za·tion [nætʃərəlizéiʃən / -lai-] *n.* Ⓤ the act of naturalizing; the state of being naturalized. 자연화; 귀화(歸化).

nat·u·ral·ize [nǽtʃərəlàiz] *vt.* (P6) **1** give (a foreigner) citizenship. (외국인을) 귀화시키다. ¶ *a naturalized Korean* 귀화 한국인 / *become naturalized* 귀화하다. **2** accept (a foreign word, custom, etc.). (외국어 등)을 받아들이다. ¶ *a naturalized word* 외래어 / *~ foreign word* 외래어를 자국어화(化)하다. **3** (of animals or plants) introduce and adapt; bring in (a plant or an animal) from another country. …을 이식(移植)하다. ¶ *a naturalized plant* 귀화 식물. **4** make (something) natural. …을 자연적이 되게 하다; 자연에 따르게 하다.

— *vi.* (P1) **1** become naturalized. 귀화하다; 풍토에 순화(馴化)되다. **2** study natural history. 박물학을 연구하다.

:nat·u·ral·ly [nǽtʃərəli] *adv.* **1** in a natural manner. 자연히. **2** by nature. 태어나면서부터; 본디. ¶ *~ curly* 본디부터 고

수머리의 / *a ~ obedient child* 천성이 양순한 아이. **3** of course. 물론; 당연히. ¶ *Yes, ~.* 응, 물론이지.

:na·ture [néitʃər] *n.* **1** Ⓤ the whole material world that is not the work of man. 자연; 자연계. ¶ *a lover of ~.* 자연을 사랑하는 자 / *Nature's engineering* 조화(造化)의 묘(妙) / *All ~ looks gay.* 백화는 기뻐 웃고 새들은 노래한다. **2** Ⓤ《sometimes *N-*》 the powers, forces, etc. that control this material world; the Creator; God. 자연의 힘; 조물주. ¶ *the laws of ~* 자연의 법칙 / *by provision of ~* 자연의 섭리에 의해. **3** Ⓤ the state of man in the earliest times; a condition unchanged from the original state. 자연 그대로임; 원시 상태. ¶ *go back to ~* 자연으로 돌아가다 / *live in a state of ~* 야성 그대로 지내다; 나체로 생활하다. **4** ⓊⒸ the essential quality of a thing; the most important point. 특질; 본질; 성질. ¶ *by the ~ of things* 사물의 본질상; 필연적으로 / *the ~ of gases* (*the soil*) 기체(흙)의 본질 / *Women have kinder natures than men.* 여성은 원래가 남성보다 인정이 많다. **5** ⓊⒸ the mental and spiritual character of a man; a person with a certain character. 성격; 본성; 인간성; 어떤 성질의 사람. ¶ (*a*) *good ~* 착한 성질; 고운 기질; 호인 / *a generous ~* 너그러운 성미(의 사람) / *It is against ~ to kill oneself.* 자살은 인성(人性)에 어긋난다 / *He has* (*He is of*) *a happy ~.* 본시 낙천적인 사람이다. **6** Ⓒ a sort; a kind; a type. 종류; 타입. ¶ *pictures of this ~* 이 종류의 그림 / *Books of that ~ do not interest her.* 그런 책들은 그녀에게 흥미가 없다. [→nascent]

by nature, because of the essential qualities; naturally. 본래; 날 때부터; 본질상.

from (***in, by***) ***the nature of things*** (***the case***), inevitably. 필연적으로.

in a state of nature, completely naked. 벌거숭이로; 나체로.

in the course of nature =from (in, by) the nature of things (the case).

in the nature of, having the character of; of the same kind as; like. …한 성질을 가진; …와 동류의; 비슷한. ¶ *His words were in the ~ of threats.* 그 자의 말은 협박이나 다름 없었다.

pay the debt of nature, die. 죽다.

***naught** [nɔːt, nɑːt] *n.* Ⓤ **1**《*arch.*》 nothing. 무(無). ¶ *bring to ~* (계획 등을) 무효로 하다; 망쳐 놓다 / *come to ~* 수포로 돌아가다; 실패하다. **2** a zero. 제로; 영(0). ¶ *Three thousand is written with a three and three naughts.* 3천은 3에다 영을 3개 붙여 쓴다.

all for naught, in vain; uselessly. 헛되이; 쓸데없이.

set something at naught, make light of something; disregard; ignore. …을 무시하다.

— *adj.*《*arch.*》 useless. 무가치한; 쓸모 없는; 쓸데없는. [O.E. *nā* no, *wiht* thing]

naugh·ti·ly [nɔ́ːtili, nɑ́ːt-] *adv.* in a naughty manner. 장난으로; 짓궂게. [*naughty*]

naugh·ti·ness [nɔ́ːtinis, nɑ́ːt-] *n.* Ⓤ the state of being naughty. 장난. 參考 아이들에게 쓰는 말.

***naugh·ty** [nɔ́ːti, nɑ́ːti] *adj.* (**-ti·er, -ti·est**) causing mischief; behaving badly; harmful. 장난의; 장난꾸러기의; 못된. ¶ *That's very ~ of you.* 그건 좀 심한 장난인데. [E. =never wight]

nau·se·a [nɔ́ːziə, -siə, -ʃə] *n.* Ⓤ **1** a feeling that one is going to throw up food through the mouth. 욕지기; 메스꺼움. **2** seasickness. 뱃멀미. **3**《*fig.*》 a strong dislike; disgust. 혐오. [→nautical]

nau·se·ate [nɔ́ːzièit, -si-] *vi., vt.* (P1; 6) **1**《*at*》 cause (someone) to feel nausea. 욕지기가 나(게 하)다. ¶ *He was nauseated by the sight of blood.* 피를 보고 욕지기가 났다. **2** disgust. 염증이 나다; 정떨어지다. [↑]

nau·se·ous [nɔ́ːʃəs, -ziəs] *adj.* causing nausea or dislike. 욕지기 나는; 싫은.
● **nau·se·ous·ly** [-li] *adv.*

nau·ti·cal [nɔ́ːtikəl] *adj.* of ships, sailors or navigation. 항해의; 배(선박)의. ¶ *a ~ almanac* 항해력(曆) / *a ~ term* 선원 용어.
● **nau·ti·cal·ly** [-i] *adv.* [Gk. *naus* ship]

nautical mile [´-´-´] *n.* a unit of linear measure for ships. 해리(海里)《1,852 미터》.

nau·ti·li [nɔ́ːtəlài] *n.* pl. of **nautilus.**

nau·ti·lus [nɔ́ːtələs] *n.* Ⓒ (*pl.* **-lus·es** or **-li**) any of several tropical shellfish with a spiral shell. 앵무조개. [↑]

***na·val** [néivəl] *adj.* of a navy, warships or ships. 해군의; 군함의; 선박의. ¶ *a ~ battle* 해전 / *a ~ port* 군항 / *a ~ officer* 해군 장교 / *the ~ powers* 해군력; 제해권. [→navy]

nave¹ [neiv] *n.* Ⓒ the central part of a church or cathedral between the side aisles where people sit. 교회의 회중석(會衆席). [↑]

⟨nave¹⟩

nave² [neiv] *n.* Ⓒ the central part of a

wheel. 바퀴통. [E.]

na·vel [néivəl] *n.* Ⓒ **1** the round, small pit in the surface of the belly. 배꼽. **2** 《*fig.*》 the middle; the center. 중심; 한가운데. [E.]

navel orange [´–ˋ–] *n.* a seedless orange with a pit like a navel on the surface. 네이블《과일》.

navel string [´–ˋ] *n.* an umbilical cord. 탯줄.

N

nav·i·ga·ble [nǽvigəbəl] *adj.* **1** (of a river, etc.) able to navigate. 항행할 수 있는. ¶ *The river is not ~ by ocean liners.* 그 강은 원양 여객선이 다닐 수 없다. **2** (of a ship, etc.) fitted for a ship or airplane to navigate. 항행에 적합한. ¶ *This ship is too old and rotten to be ~.* 이 배는 너무 낡고 망가져서 항행하기에 적합하지 못하다. [↓]

nav·i·gate [nǽvəgèit] *vi.* (P1) **1** travel by ship or plane. 항행하다. **2** operate a ship or an aircraft. 조종〔운전〕하다. —*vt.* (P6) **1** direct (a ship or an aircraft). (배·비행기 등)을 조정하다. **2** travel over, through or on (a river, the sea, etc.). (강·바다 등을) 항행하다. ¶ *~ the sea* 항해하다 / *~ the air* 항공하다. [L. *nāvis* ship, *ago* to drive, act]

***nav·i·ga·tion** [næ̀vəgéiʃən] *n.* Ⓤ **1** the act of navigating. 운항; 항행; 항공; 항해. **2** the science of finding out the course or position for ships, airplanes, etc. 항행〔항공〕술. **3** 《*collectively*》 ships. 선박. **4** the passage of ships, etc. over the sea, etc. 항로. ¶ *Ice has stopped all ~.* 얼음으로 모든 항로가 막혔다.

nav·i·ga·tor [nǽvəgèitər] *n.* Ⓒ **1** a person who sails on the sea. 항해자. **2** a person who decides the course of a ship or an airplane. 조종자〔사〕. **3** a person in charge of a ship's or aircraft's navigation. 항해장; 항공사. **4** a person who explores an island, etc. by ship. 해양 탐험가. ¶ *The ~ set out on his long voyage.* 해양 탐험가는 긴 항해에 나섰다.

nav·vy [nǽvi] *n.* Ⓒ (*pl.* **-vies**) 《Brit. *colloq.*》 an unskilled laborer who is employed to dig in making roads, railways or canals. (토목 공사장) 인부. [→navigate]

:na·vy [néivi] *n.* Ⓒ (*pl.* **-vies**) **1** 《*collectively*》 all the warships of a nation; the whole sea force of a nation including ships, officers, men, shipyards, etc. 해군; 해군력. ¶ *the Royal Navy* 영국 해군 / *the ~ yard* 미해군 공창 / *the Navy Department* 미국 해군성. **2** 《*collectively*》 officers and men of the navy; persons engaged in naval work. 해군《군인》. **3** a fleet. 함대. ¶ *the navies of Venice* 베니스의 상선대. [L. *navis* ship]

navy blue [´–ˋ] *n.* very dark blue. 짙은 감청색.

***nay** [nei] *adv.* **1** 《*arch.*》 no. 아니; 부(否) (opp. yes). **2** 《*lit.*》 not only that, but also. …보다는 오히려. ¶ *It's difficult, ~, impossible.* 그건 곤란하다. 아니, 불가능하다. —*n.* Ⓒ **1** a refusal. 거절. ¶ *the yeas and nays* 가부(可否). **2** a negative vote or voter. 반대 투표(자). [N. =not ever]

Naz·a·rene [næ̀zəríːn] *n.* Ⓒ **1** a person born or living in Nazareth; 《*the ~*》 Jesus Christ. 나사렛 사람; 예수. **2** a Christian. 기독교도. —*adj.* of Nazarenes or Nazareth. 나사렛 (사람)의.

Naz·a·reth [nǽzərəθ] *n.* an ancient town in Palestine where Jesus Christ spent his early life. 나사렛 (마을).

naze [neiz] *n.* a headland. 갑(岬); 곶. [E.]

Na·zi [nɑ́ːtsi] *n.* Ⓒ a member of the German fascist political party, found in 1919 by Adolf Hitler; 《*the ~s*》 the party. 나치당원; 나치당. —*adj.* of a Nazi or the Nazis. 나치당(원)의. [G.]

N.B. 《L.》 *nota bene* (=note well). 주의하라.

neap [niːp] *adj.* of a very low tide. 소조(小潮)의. —*n.* a neap tide. 소조(opp. spring tide). ¶ *The tides are at the ~.* 조수는 (지금) 소조다. [E.]

Ne·a·pol·i·tan [nìːəpɑ́lətən / -pɔ́l-] *adj.* of Naples or its people. 나폴리 (사람)의. —*n.* Ⓒ a person of Naples. 나폴리 사람. [Gk.]

:near [niər] *adv.* **1** at a short distance in space or time; not far. 가까이; 접근하여. ¶ *Spring is drawing* 〔*getting*〕 *~.* 봄이 다가오고 있다 / *The new houses are built too ~ to us.* 새로 짓는 집들이 우리 집에서 너무 가깝다. **2** 《*colloq.*》 nearly; almost. 거의. 參考 지금은 흔히 nearly를 씀. ¶ *I was ~ dead with fright.* 무서워 죽을 뻔했다. **3** closely; intimately. (관계가) 가깝게; 밀접하게. ¶ *They are ~ related.* 그들은 서로 가까운 친척이다.

come near to do, almost do. 거의 …할 뻔하다.

come near* (*to*) *doing, almost 〔nearly〕 do. 거의 …할 뻔하다. ¶ *He came ~ to drowning.* 하마터면 빠져 죽을 뻔했다.

far and near, in every direction; everywhere. 도처에.

near at hand, in the near future; within easy reach. 머지 않아; 바로 가까이에.

near by, not far off; near at hand. 가까이에. ¶ *My uncle lives ~ by.* 아저씨는 근처에 사신다.

near upon, almost; not far in time from. (시간적으로) 거의; 거의 …에 가까이. ¶ *It was ~ upon six o'clock.* 거의 여섯 시 가까이 되었었다.

—*adj.* **1** close in distance or time. 가까운; 접근한. ¶ *the ~ future* 가까운 장래 / *the nearest way to the station* 역으로 가는 지름길 / *The park is quite ~.* 공원은 아주 가깝다 / *Spring is ~.* 봄이 가깝다. **2** closely related in blood. 근친의. ¶ *a ~ relative*

가까운 친척 / ~ *and dear* 친숙한. **3** close in friendship; intimate. 친밀한. ¶ *a ~ friend* 친한 친구. **4** close in degree; resembling closely. 가까운 관계의; 흡사한; 모조의. ¶ *a ~ resemblance* 흡사 / *a ~ translation* 원문에 충실한 번역; 축어역(逐語譯) / *a ~ guess* 거의 맞는 추측 / *a ~ escape* 〔*thing, touch*〕 구사 일생. **5** on the left side. 왼쪽의(opp. off, right). ¶ *the ~ side* 좌측; 왼쪽 / *the ~ wheels of a car* 차의 왼쪽 바퀴. **6** unwilling to spend or give money. 인색한. ¶ *You won't get much out of him, he's very ~.* 그에게서 많이는 바라지 말게, 아주 인색하거든.

a near race, a race, in which the two sides are equally matched. 막상막하의 경기.

— *prep.* close to in space, time, degree, or likeness, etc. …의 가까이에; 곁에; 흡사하게. ¶ *~ the river* 강 가까이에 / *He is ~ seventy years of age.* 그는 나이가 일흔에 가깝다 / *The portrait doesn't come ~ to the original.* 그 초상화는 실물과는 꽤 다르다.

— *vt., vi.* (P6; 1) come or draw near to (something); approach. 가까이 가다; 가까워지다. ¶ *The ship neared the dock.* 배가 선착장에 접근했다 / ~ (*to*) *one's end* 임종이 가까워지다. [→nigh]

·near·by [níərbái] *adj., adv.* close at hand; near. 가까이의〔에〕. 語法 부사적 용법일 때 영국에서는 near by 라고 띄어 씀. ¶ *a ~ house* 이웃집 / *A plane lands ~.* 비행기가 부근에 착륙한다.

Near East [∠∠], **the** *n.* the territory including the Balkans, Egypt and the countries of southwestern Asia. 근동(近東).

:near·ly [níərli] *adv.* **1** almost but not quite. 거의; 간신히; 그런 대로. ¶ *It's ~ ten o'clock.* 거의 열 시다 / *He was ~ run over by a car.* 하마터면 차에 치일 뻔했다. **2** closely; intimately. 친밀〔긴밀〕하게. ¶ *It concerns you ~.* 그 일은 네게 깊은 관계가 있다 / *They are ~ related.* 그들은 가까운 친척이다.

not nearly, nothing like; by no means. 도저히 …아니다. ¶ *It's not ~ enough.* 아무래도 모자란다 / *She is not ~ so old as you.* 그녀는 너처럼 그렇게 늙지 않았다.

near·ness [níərnis] *n.* U the state or quality of being near in time, distance, relation, etc. 가까움; 근사; 근친(近親); 친근.

near-sight·ed [níərsáitid] *adj.* able to see things clearly at short distances only; short-sighted. 근시의(opp. far-sighted). ● **near-sight·ed·ly** [-li] *adv.* **near-sight·ed·ness** [-nis] *n.*

:neat[1] [ni:t] *adj.* **1** clean and in order; tidy. 정연한; 깔끔한. ¶ *a ~ room* 〔*desk*〕 (정돈이 잘된) 깨끗한 방〔책상〕 / *a ~ dress* 말쑥한 옷 / ~ *in one's habits* 깔끔한 습성 / *as ~ as a pin* 아주 말쑥한〔산뜻한〕. **2** simple and well-arranged. (외관이) 산뜻한; 균형잡힌. ¶ *He is ~ in his person.* 그는 외관이 단정하다. **3** ⓐ brief and clever in speaking; skillful. (표현이) 적절한; (행동이) 능숙한. ¶ *a ~ reply* 요령 있는 대답 / *a ~ explanation* 적절한 표현 / *make a ~ job of it* 능숙하게 일을 처리하다. ⓑ able and willing to keep things in order. 깔끔한 것을 좋아하는. ¶ *a ~ child* 깔끔한 아이. **4** unmixed with anything; pure. 섞인 것이 없는; 순…. ¶ ~ *weight* 실(實)중량 / ~ *profits* 순익 / *take a drink of whisky ~* 위스키를 스트레이트로 마시다. [L. *niteo* shine]

neat[2] [ni:t] *n.* (*pl.* **neat**) 《*collectively*》 cattle. 축우(畜牛). — *adj.* of the ox kind. 소의. ¶ ~ *cattle* 축우. [E.]

neath, 'neath [ni:θ] *prep.* 《poet.》 =beneath. [Abbr.]

neat·ly [ní:tli] *adv.* in a neat manner. 깨끗이; 말쑥하게. [*neat*[1]]

neat·ness [ní:tnis] *n.* U the state of being neat. 말쑥함; 정연; 능란. [↑]

Ne·bras·ka [nibrǽskə] *n.* a State in the middle west of the United States. 네브래스카. 參考 Nebr.로 생략. 주도(州都)는 Lincoln.

neb·u·la [nébjələ] *n.* C (*pl.* **-lae** or **-las**) 《astron.》 a bright, cloud-like heavenly body composed of a group of stars or burning gas. 성운(星雲). [L. =mist]

neb·u·lae [nébjəli:] *n.* pl. of **nebula.**

neb·u·lous [nébjələs] *adj.* **1** of or like a nebula. 성운 (모양)의. **2** misty; unclear; cloudy. 막연한; 몽롱한. ¶ *a ~ memory* 몽롱한 기억 / ~ *fears* 알 수 없는 막연한 불안.

·nec·es·sar·i·ly [nèsəsérəli, nésisərili] *adv.* as a necessary and sure result; inevitably. 필연적으로; 물론. ¶ *War ~ causes misery.* 전쟁은 반드시 재난을 가져온다 / *It's not ~ interesting.* 꼭 재미있다고는 할 수 없다 / *You don't ~ have to write him.* 그에게 편지할 것까지는 없다. [↓]

:nec·es·sar·y [nésəsèri, nésisəri] *adj.* **1** needed; required; indispensable; essential. 필요한; 없어서는 안 될; 필수의. ¶ *Food is ~ for life.* 삶에 음식은 꼭 필요하다 / *It is ~ that everybody should obey the law.* 누구든 법은 지켜야 한다 / *It is ~ for you to go.* 네가 가 줘야 하겠다. **2** certain to happen; inevitable. 필연적인; 피하기 어려운. ¶ *a ~ conclusion* 필연적인 결과 / *a ~ evil* 필요악(惡).

— *n.* C (*pl.* **-sar·ies**) **1** 《usu. *pl.*》 a necessary or very important thing. 필요한 것; 필수품. ¶ *daily necessaries* 일용품 / *household necessaries* 생활 필수품; 가용품(家用品). **2** 《*the ~*》 《*sl.*》 money or action needed. (어떤 목적을 위해) 필요한 행동; (특히) 돈. ¶ *find* 〔*do*〕 *the ~* 돈 마련을 하다〔필요한 조처를 취하다〕. [L. *necesse* needful]

ne·ces·si·tate [nisésətèit] *vt.* **1** (P6) make (something) necessary; require. …을 필요로 하다. ¶ ~ *an operation* 수술이 필요하다. **2** 《rare》 《usu. in *passive*》 force; compel.

별수 없이 …하게 하다. ¶ *We are necessitated to do so.* 그렇게 할 수밖에 없다.

ne·ces·si·tous [nisésətəs] *adj.* very poor; in great need. 빈곤한; 가난한. ¶ *~ members of the community* 사회의 빈민들 / *be in ~ condition* 곤궁한 처지에 있다.

:ne·ces·si·ty [nisésəti] *n.* (*pl.* **-ties**) **1** Ⓤ the state of being necessary. 필요(성). ¶ *by* 〔*from, out of*〕 *~* 필요해서 / *There is no ~ to do so.* 그렇게 할 필요는 없다 / 《*prov.*》 *Necessity knows no law.* 필요 앞에선 법도 무력; 사흘 굶어 도둑질 안 할 놈 없다. **2** Ⓒ that which comes about or happens as a result of natural law. 필연(성). ¶ *Death is a ~ to life.* 생명에는 죽음이 따르는 법 / *Cause is a ~ to change.* 변경하는 데는 이유가 있어야 한다 / *physical* 〔*logical*〕 *~* 물리적〔논리적〕 필연; 숙명. **3** 《often *pl.*》 something which is greatly necessary for our life. 생활 필수품. ¶ *daily necessities* 일용품. **4** Ⓤ the state of being very poor; need. 빈곤; 궁핍. ¶ *In case of ~, you can call on me.* 돈이 아쉬울 땐 내게 오너라 / *live in ~* 어렵게 지내다.

as a necessity, inevitably. 필연적으로.

***be under the necessity of** doing,* be forced to do. 어쩔 수 없이 …하다.

bow to necessity, do what one is compelled to do. 운명이라고〔어쩔 수 없는 일이라고〕 체념하다.

make a virtue of necessity, **a**) accept without any protest what one is forced to do. 부득이한 일을 군말없이 행하다. **b**) take honor for doing what one has to do. 해야 할 일을 하고도 공치사하다.

of necessity, necessarily; unavoidably; as a matter of course. 필연적으로; 어쩔 수 없이; 당연히. ¶ *I went of ~.* 어쩔 수 없이 갔다.

:neck [nek] *n.* Ⓒ **1** the part of the body between the head and the shoulders. 목. ¶ *risk one's ~* 목숨을 걸고 하다; 위험을 무릅쓰다. **2** the part of the clothes that fits the neck. (옷의) 깃. ¶ *the ~ of a shirt* 셔츠의 깃. **3** anything like a neck in shape or position. 목 모양의 것〔부분〕. ¶ *the ~ of a bottle* 병목. **4** a narrow way or passage of water; a strait; a narrow strip of land. 해협; 지협(地峽).

break one's neck, **a**) make a great effort to accomplish something. 온 힘을 다하다; 굉장한 노력을 기울이다. **b**) be killed by dislocating. 목뼈가 부러져 죽다.

break the neck of, do the hardest part of; get hardest of it over. (일 따위의) 큰 고비를 넘기다. ¶ *break the ~ of the day's work* 하루 일의 어려운 고비를 넘기다.

get it in the neck, 《*sl.*》 suffer a heavy blow. 대타격을 입다; 되게 혼나다.

neck and crop, altogether; completely. 몽땅; 모조리. ¶ *throw someone out ~ and crop* 아무를 가타부타 소리 없이 내쫓다.

neck and neck, running side by side; just even in a contest. (경마 등에서) 나란히; 우열을 가릴 수 없이; 호각(互角)으로.

neck or nothing, taking all possible chances; in a desperate way. 죽기 아니면 살기로; 결사적으로.

save one's neck, **a**) escape hanging. 교수형을 면하다. **b**) escape the consequences of a mistake, error, etc. (과실 등의) 처벌〔책임〕을 면하다.

win 〔***lose***〕 ***by a neck,*** (in a horse race) win by the length on a horse's head and neck. (경마에서) 경주마의 목 하나 차로 이기다〔지다〕; 가까스로 이기다〔아깝게 지다〕

— *vi., vt.* (P1; 6) 《U.S. *sl.*》 clasp one another around the neck; embrace and kiss. (서로) 목을 끌어 안다; 껴안고 키스하다. [E.]

neck·band [nékbæ̀nd] *n.* Ⓒ **1** a band worn around the neck. 목띠. **2** a part of a shirt to which the collar is fastened. (셔츠의) 깃.

neck·er·chief [nékərtʃif] *n.* Ⓒ (*pl.* **-chiefs**) a long piece of cloth worn around the neck. 목도리; 네커치프.

neck·lace [néklis] *n.* Ⓒ a decorative string of jewels, gold, beads, etc., worn around the neck. 목걸이.

neck·tie [néktài] *n.* Ⓒ a narrow band of cloth worn around the neck and tied in front. 넥타이.

neck·wear [nékwɛ̀ər] *n.* Ⓤ articles worn around the neck, such as neck collars, ties, scarfs, etc. 목에 두르는 넥타이·칼라·스카프 류(類).

ne·crol·o·gy [nekrάlədʒi / -krɔ́l-] *n.* **1** a list of persons who have died. 사망자 명단. **2** a notice of a person's death. 사망 통지〔공고〕. [Gk. *nekros* corpse, -logy]

nec·ro·man·cer [nékroumæ̀nsər] *n.* Ⓒ **1** a person who is believed to foretell the future; one who practises necromancy. 점쟁이; 강신술사(降神術師). **2** a magician. 마술사. [Gk. *mantis* seer]

nec·ro·man·cy [nékrəmæ̀nsi] *n.* Ⓤ a foretelling of the future by communicating with the dead. 강신술; 교령술(交靈術).

ne·cro·ses [nekróusi:z] *n.* pl. of **necrosis.**

ne·cro·sis [nekróusis] *n.* ⓊⒸ (*pl.* **-ses**) 《med.》 the death or decay of a part of the living body. 괴저(壞疽); 괴사(壞死). [Gk. *nekros* corpse]

nec·tar [néktər] *n.* Ⓤ **1** 《Gk. & Rom. myth.》 the drink of the gods. 신주(神酒). **2** any sweet drink. 단 음료. **3** 《bot.》 the sweet liquid found in flowers. 화밀(花蜜). [Gk.]

nec·tar·ine [nèktərí:n / néktərin] *n.* Ⓒ a kind of peach that has a smooth, thin skin. 승도복숭아.

nec·ta·ry [néktəri] *n.* 《bot.》 the organ in flowers which produces nectar. 꿀샘; 밀선(蜜腺).

née, nee [nei] *adj.* 《F.》 by birth; born. 구성(舊姓)은…; 친정쪽 성은…. 參考 기혼 여성의 처녀 때 성을 말할 때 쓰임. ¶ *Mrs. Lang, ~ Jones* 랭 부인, 구성은 존스.

:need [ni:d] *n.* Ⓤ **1** 《sometimes *a* ~》 the lack of something necessary. 결핍; 부족. ¶ *the ~ for leadership* 지도력의 부족 / *His novel showed ~ of humor.* 그의 소설에는 해학이 별로 없다 / *He feels the ~ of companionship.* 교우 관계의 결핍을 아쉬워하고 있다. **2** Ⓒ something wanted or necessary. 부족한 것; 필요한 물건. ¶ *our daily needs* 일용 필수품 / *Water was our greatest ~.* 물이야말로 가장 필요한 것이다 / *A small income will satisfy my present needs.* 지금 형편으로는 적은 수입이라도 있으면 좋겠다. **3** necessity. 필요. ¶ *There is no ~ to hurry.* 서두를 필요는 없다 / *He is in ~ of help.* 그는 (지금) 도움이 필요하다 / *fill the ~ for a better education* 더 나은 교육의 필요를 충족시키다 / *You have no ~ to be ashamed.* 부끄러워할 필요가 없다. **4** a situation or time when help is required. 도움이 필요한 때; 어려울 때. ¶ 《*prov.*》 *A friend in ~ is a friend indeed.* 어려울 때의 친구야말로 참다운 친구 / *They failed me in my ~.* 그들은 내가 어려울 때 나를 저버렸다. **5** the state of being very poor. 심한 가난; 궁핍. ¶ *The family's ~ was so great that the children had no shoes.* 그 집은 얼마나 가난했던지 아이들 신발도 없었다.

do** one's **needs, relieve nature. 대소변을 보다.

***had need** do* 〔*to do*〕, 《*lit.*》 ought to do. …해야 하다.

***have need to** do*, must; have to; ought to. …하지 않으면 안 되다.

if need be 〔***were***〕, if it is 〔were〕 necessary. 필요하다면.

in need of, in want of. …이 필요한. ¶ *The house is in ~ of repair.* 그 집은 수리가 필요한 상태이다.

— *vt.* **1** (P6,9) have need of (something); require. …을 필요로 하다. ¶ *This work will ~ a lot of time.* 이 일은 시간이 꽤나 걸리겠다 / *Does she ~ any help?* 그녀에게 도움이 필요한가 / *My shoes ~ mending* 〔*~ to be mended*〕. 내 신은 수선이 필요하다 / 《*iron.*》 *What he needs is a good beating.* 녀석은 된맛을 봐야 한다. **2** (P8) be obliged; be under necessity to (do). …하지 않으면 안 되다; …하여야 한다(⇨*auxil. v.*). ¶ *He needs to be more careful.* 좀더 신중해야 한다 / *He doesn't ~ to see her.* 그는 그녀를 만날 필요가 없다 / *He didn't ~ to be told twice.* 그에겐 되풀이해 말해 줄 필요가 없었다.

— *auxil. v.* 《in *negative* or *interrogative*》 must; have to; should; need to. 《의문문에서》 …해야 하는가; 《부정문에서》 …할 필요가 없다. ¶ *Need she come?* 그녀가 와야 하나 / *You ~ not have done it.* 그걸 할 필요가 없었는데 / *You hardly ~ help him.* 그 사람을 도와줄 건 없다. [E.]

need·ful [ní:dfəl] *adj.* **1** needed; necessary. 필요한. ¶ *all ~ regulations* 모든 필요한 규칙. **2** 《*the* ~》 ⓐ 《*sl.*》 money; cash in hand. 돈; 현금. ⓑ something needed. 필요한 것.

do the needful, do what is necessary. 해야 할 일을 하다.

•**need·ful·ly** [-fəli] *adv.*

:nee·dle [ní:dl] *n.* Ⓒ **1** a thin, sharp-pointed tool for sewing. 바늘. ¶ *a ~ and thread* 실 꿴 바늘. **2** anything like a needle. 바늘 비슷한 것. ¶ *a knitting ~* 뜨개 바늘 / *a phonograph ~* 축음기 바늘 / *the ~ of a compass* 나침반 바늘. **3** a needle-shaped leaf of some trees. (침엽수의 잎) 침엽(針葉); 바늘잎. **4** 《*the* ~》 a fit of nervousness. 초조; 짜증; 화.

a needle's eye, tiny aperture. 바늘귀; (빠끔한) 틈.

as sharp as a needle, very intelligent. 빈틈없는; 아주 영리한〔약은〕.

look for a needle in a haystack, try to look for something which is almost impossible to find. 덤불 속에서 바늘을 찾다《불가능한 일을 시도하다》; 헛수고를 하다.

on the needle, 《*sl.*》 taking drugs by injection, esp. habitually. 마약 상습의.

— *vt., vi.* (P6; 1) **1** sew or pierce with or as if with a needle. 바느질하다; 바늘로〔처럼〕 찌르다. **2** thread (one's way) between or through things. 누비듯 나아가다. [O.E. *nædl*]

nee·dle-bath [ní:dlbæθ, -bɑ̀:θ] *n.* a kind of shower-bath in which the water comes down like needles. 물이 가느다랗게 분출하는 샤워.

nee·dle-book [ní:dlbùk] *n.* a needle-case like a small book. (책 모양의) 바늘겨레.

nee·dle-case [ní:dlkèis] *n.* a case in which sewing needles are kept. 바늘쌈.

needle match [⌐-⌐] *n.* a game closely contested and arousing excitement. 접전(接戰).

•**need·less** [ní:dlis] *adj.* unnecessary. 불필요한; 군. ¶ *~ work* 쓸데 없는 일. [*need*]

needless to say, it is not necessary to say. 말할 필요도 없이.

need·less·ly [ní:dlisli] *adv.* unnecessarily. 쓸데없이.

nee·dle·wom·an [ní:dlwùmən] *n.* Ⓒ (*pl.* **-wom·en** [-wìmin]) a woman who does sewing, esp. to earn money. 바느질하는 여자; 침모(針母). [*needle*]

nee·dle·work [ní:dlwə̀:rk] *n.* Ⓤ the work done with a needle, as sewing, embroidery, etc. 바느질; 자수 (등).

need·n't [ní:dnt] =need not.

needs [ni:dz] *adv.* necessarily. 어떻게든; 반드시; 꼭. 語法 흔히 must의 앞뒤에 쓰임.

N

[*need*]

***needs must** do,* be compelled to do. …하지 않을 수 없다. ¶ *If ~ must, he shall go.* 꼭 그래야 한다면 그를 보내겠소 / *He ~ must come.* 그는 꼭 와야만 한다 / 《*prov.*》 *Needs must (go) when the devil drives.* 억지가 기를 쓰면 이치가 물러선다.

need·y [níːdi] *adj.* (**need·i·er, need·i·est**) very poor; in want. 가난한. ¶ *a ~ family* 가난한 가정. [*need*]

N

ne'er [nεər] *adv.* 《*poet.*》 =never.

ne'er-do-well [nέərduːwèl] *n.* Ⓒ a person who never does anything useful; a worthless fellow. 아무짝에도 못쓸 인간. — *adj.* worthless. 무익한. [Abbr.]

ne·far·i·ous [niféəriəs] *adj.* very evil; unlawful. 사악한; 못된; 무법한. ¶ *a ~ purpose* 악의적인 의도. ●**ne·far·i·ous·ly** [-li] *adv.* [L. *nefas* wrong]

ne·gate [nigeit] *vt.* (P6) deny the existence of (something); say 'no' …을 부정하다. [L. *nego* deny]

ne·ga·tion [nigéiʃən] *n.* Ⓤ **1** the act of denying. 부정(否定)(opp. affirmation). ¶ *double ~* 이중 부정 / *Shaking the head is a sign of ~.* 고개를 가로젓는 것은 부정의 뜻이다. **2** the state of lacking or denying something real or positive. 무(無); 결여; 반대. ¶ *a moral ~* 도덕의 결여 / *Sameness is the very ~ of liberty.* 획일성은 자유의 정반대 / *Death is ~ of life.* 죽음은 삶의 반대.

***neg·a·tive** [négətiv] *adj.* **1** expressing refusal or denial. 부정의; 부인〔취소〕의 (opp. affirmative). ¶ *a ~ answer* 부정적인 대답 / *a ~ order* 금지령. **2** not positive; not active; not forceful. 소극적인(opp. positive). ¶ *~ virtue* (나쁜 짓을 안 하는) 소극적인 덕성 / *a colorless, ~ character* 특징이 없는 소극적인 인물 / *~ kindness* 불친절하지 않을 정도의 친절. **3** 《math.》 less than zero; minus. 부(負)의; 마이너스의. ¶ *the ~ sign* 마이너스 부호. **4** 《electr.》 of the kind of electricity made in silk, etc. by rubbing it on glass. 음전기의(opp. positive). ¶ *the ~ pole* 음극. **5** 《photog.》 of the film or plate in which the lights and shadows are shown in reverse. 음화(陰畫)의(opp. positive). ¶ *a ~ plate* 〔*film*〕 음판; 음화; 네가. **6** (of illness) showing an absence of the germs. (병이) 음성의 (opp. positive).

— *n.* Ⓒ **1** a word showing denial. 부정어 《not, never, no more 등》. **2** the side that stands against something. (논의·투표 등의) 반대측. **3** 《math.》 a minus quality. 음수. **4** 《electr.》 negative electricity. 음전기. **5** 《photog.》 a negative film or plate. 음화(陰畫); 네거(티브).

in the negative, on the side of denying a plan, suggestion, etc.; with a negative or denial answer. 부정적인〔으로〕; 거부〔반대〕하는〔하여〕.

— *vt.* (P6) **1** deny; refuse. …을 부정〔거부〕하다. ¶ *He negatived it.* 그는 그것을 거절했다. **2** make (something) useless; prove (something) false; disprove. …을 무효화시키다; (이론 따위)를 부정하다; 반증하다. ¶ *Experience negatives the theory.* 경험에 의해 그 설이 잘못임을 알다 / *The deep mud negatived all efforts to advance.* 깊은 진창길로 전진하려는 노력은 모두 허사가 되었다.

neg·a·tive·ly [négətivli] *adv.* in a negative manner. 부정적으로(opp. positively).

:ne·glect [niglékt] *vt.* (P6) **1** give no attention to (something); ignore; disregard. …을 무시〔경시〕하다. ¶ *He neglects his family.* 그는 제 가족을 돌보지 않는다 / *~ one's business* 〔*duties*〕 일〔책임〕을 소홀히 하다 / *~ rules* 〔*criticism*〕 규칙〔비판〕을 무시하다. **2** (P8,9) fail to do (something); take no care of (something); omit. …을 게을리하다; (부주의 또는 의도적으로) 해야 할 일을 하지 않고 내버려두다. ¶ *~ writing an answer* 회답을 게을리하다 / *~ to wind up a clock* 시계 밥 주는 것을 잊다 / *Don't ~ paying him a visit now and then.* 이따금씩 그분 찾아뵙는 것을 게을리하지 마라.

— *n.* Ⓤ the act of neglecting; the state of being neglected. 태만; 소홀; 경시; 무시. ¶ *treat with ~* 소홀히 하다 / *the ~ of one's home* 가정을 돌보지 않음 / *Old customs tend to fall into ~.* 옛 풍습들이 무관심으로 스러져 가고 있다. [L. *neglego*]

ne·glect·er, -or [nigléktər] *n.* Ⓒ a person who neglects. 태만한 사람.

ne·glect·ful [nigléktfəl] *adj.* **1** 《*of*》 careless; heedless. 태만한; 게으른. ¶ *lazy and ~* 게을러빠진 / *He is ~ of his duties.* 그는 직무 태만이다. **2** failing to do things habitually. 무관심한. ¶ *He was not ~ and would write to me.* 그는 마음을 써서 자주 편지를 보내곤 했다.

ne·glect·ful·ly [nigléktfəli] *adv.* in a neglectful manner. 태만히; 부주의하게.

neg·li·gee [négliʒèi, ⌐–⌐] *n.* Ⓒ **1** a loose house gown worn by women. (부인용) 실내복; 네글리제. **2** any informal dress. 평상복. [→neglect]

neg·li·gence [néglidʒəns] *n.* Ⓤ the state or quality of being negligent. 태만; 부주의; 흘게늦음. ¶ *His ~ cost him his job.* 게을러서 면직당했다 / *Negligence is often the cause of the child's illness.* 태만으로 해서 어린이 건강을 해치는 일이 흔하다. [→neglect]

neg·li·gent [néglidʒənt] *adj.* 《*of, in*》 lacking care or attention; neglecting one's duty; neglectful; careless. 무관심한; 태만한; 부주의한. ¶ *be ~ in dress.* 옷〔외관〕에 신경을 안 쓰다 / *be ~ of one's duty.* 책임감이 없다.

neg·li·gent·ly [néglidʒəntli] *adv.* in a negligent manner. 태만하게; 무관심하게.

neg·li·gi·ble [néglidʒəbəl] *adj.* that can be easily neglected; of less importance. 무시

해도 좋은; 하찮은 ¶ *a ~ personality* 하찮은 사람 / *a ~ amount* 아주 조금. [→neglect]

ne·go·tia·ble [nigóuʃiəbəl] *adj.* **1** that can be negotiated. 협상[협정]할 수 있는. **2** that can be passed from one person to another in return for money or its equivalent. 양도[유통] 가능한. ¶ *a ~ bill* 유통 어음. **3** (of roads, etc.) that can be passed through or over. (길이) 다닐 수 있는. ¶ *a road ~ by bus* 버스가 다닐 수 있는 길. [↓]

ne·go·ti·ate [nigóuʃièit] *vi.* (P1,2A,3,4) 《*with, for, on*》 discuss and make an agreement with others in political affairs or business deals. 협의[협상]하다; 교섭하다. ¶ *~ with them on a peace treaty* 그들과 평화 조약을 협정하다 / *I want to ~ with him on the matter.* 그와 그 문제를 얘기해 보고 싶다. — *vt.* **1** (P6,13) make arrangements for (something). (협약·거래 등)을 협정하다. ¶ *~ a treaty* 조약을 협정하다 / *~ the terms of peace* 강화 조건을 협정하다. **2** (P6) give or get money for (bonds, stocks, etc.). (어음·증권 등)을 유통[양도]하다; 돈으로 바꾸다. ¶ *~ a bill of exchange* 환어음을 배서하여 양도하다. **3** (P6) 《*colloq.*》 pass over or through (something). (장애물·난관 등)을 통과하다; 뚫고 나아가다. ¶ *The old car can hardly ~ the hill.* 그 고물차가 그 언덕을 넘기는 어렵다. [L. *negotium* business]

***ne·go·ti·a·tion** [nigòuʃiéiʃən] *n.* ⓒⓤ 《often *pl.*》 the act of negotiating. 교섭; 양도; 거래. ¶ *diplomatic negotiations* 외교 절충 / *The negotiations came to an end.* 그 교섭은 끝났다.

ne·go·ti·a·tor [nigóuʃièitər] *n.* ⓒ a person who negotiates. 교섭인; 협상자.

Ne·gress, ne- [ní:gris] *n.* ⓒ a Negro woman or girl. 흑인 여자. [↓]

:Ne·gro, ne- [ní:grou] *n.* ⓒ (*pl.* **-groes**) a person who belongs to the dark African race, with black skin and curly hair. 흑인. — *adj.* of Negroes. 흑인(계)의. ¶ *the ~ question* 흑인 문제. [L. *niger* black]

Ne·groid, ne- [ní:grɔid] *adj.* of or like or related to the Negro race. 흑인의[같은]; 흑인에 관계된. — *n.* ⓒ a person of the Negroid race. 흑인계(系)의 사람.

neigh [nei] *n.* ⓒ a gentle cry of a horse. (말의) 울음 소리. — *vi.* (of a horse) utter a gentle cry. 말이 울다. [E.]

:neigh·bor, 《Brit.》 **-bour** [néibər] *n.* ⓒ **1** a person who lives next to another. 이웃 사람. ¶ *a good* [*bad*] *~* 좋은[나쁜] 이웃. **2** a fellow human being; a member of the society in which one lives. 동포; 동료. ¶ 《Bible》 *Love thy ~ as thyself.* 이웃을 네 몸같이 사랑하라 / *one's duty to one's ~* 박애의 의무. **3** a person, country, or thing that is near another. 이웃하는 사람[나라; 것]. ¶ *a mountain towering above its neighbors* 주변의 산들보다 우뚝 솟은 산 / *one's ~ at dinner* 식탁의 옆자리에 앉은 사람 / *The big tree brought down several of its smaller neighbors as it fell.* 그 큰 나무가 넘어지면서 이웃한 작은 나무 몇 그루를 쓰러뜨렸다. — *vt.* (P6) live or be situated next to (something or someone). …에 인접하다. ¶ *The wood neighbors* (*upon*) *the lake.* 숲이 못에 인접해 있다. — *vi.* (P3) **1** 《*on, upon*》 live or be situated near-by. 가까이에 살다[있다]. ¶ *He neighbors on 5th Street.* 그는 5번가 근처에 산다. **2** 《*with*》 be friendly. 친하게 지내다. ¶ *~ with the Browns* 브라운네와 친하다.

● **neigh·bor·less** [-lis] *adj.* [→nigh, boor]

:neigh·bor·hood, 《Brit.》 **-bour-** [néibərhùd] *n.* **1** ⓤ the state of being neighbors; nearness in position. 이웃하고 있음; 근접. ¶ *The ~ of the railway is a drawback.* 철길에 가까우면 좋지 않다. **2** ⓒ the district near a place or thing. 근처. ¶ *Our ~ has a new supermarket.* 근처에 슈퍼마켓이 있다 / *I'm a stranger in this ~.* 나는 이 지역에 생소하다. **3** 《*collectively*》 people living near one another. 근처의 사람들. ¶ *a friendly ~* 우호적인 인근의 사람들 / *The whole ~ attended the dance.* 근처의 모든 사람들이 댄스파티에 나왔다. **4** ⓒ the part of a country where one lives. (자기가 사는) 지방. ¶ *Our ~ is a beautiful one.* 우리가 사는 데는 아름다운 고장이다.'

in the neighborhood of, ⓐ not far from. …의 근처[가까이]에. ¶ *She lives in the ~ of the mill.* 그녀는 물방앗간 근처에 살고 있다. ⓑ nearly; about. 대략; 약; …정도. ¶ *cost in the ~ of ten dollars* 10 달러 정도의 비용.

:neigh·bor·ing, 《Brit.》 **-bour-** [néibəriŋ] *adj.* living or being near; very near. 근처의; 인접한.

neigh·bor·li·ness, 《Brit.》 **-bour-** [néibərlinis] *n.* ⓤ the state or quality of being neighborly. 이웃다움; 친절함.

neigh·bor·ly, 《Brit.》 **-bour-** [néibərli] *adj.* like a neighbor; kind and friendly. 이웃다운; 친절한.

:neigh·bour [néibər] *n.* 《Brit.》 =neighbor.

:nei·ther [ní:ðər, náið-] *adv.* **1** 《followed by *nor*》 not either; not one and not another. …도 아니고 —도 아니다. ¶ *I saw ~ him nor her.* 나는 그를 못 만났고 그녀도 못 만났다 / *I could ~ move nor utter a word.* 움직이지도 못 하고 말도 한 마디 할 수 없었다 / *Neither he nor I am* [*Neither I nor he is*] *in the wrong.* 그도 나도 잘못이 없다. 語法 주어로 쓰는 경우, 동사는 *nor* 다음 말에 일치시킨다. **2** 《preceded by *a negative clause*》 nor; and not. …도 또한 —아니다[않다]. ¶ *If you do not go, ~ shall I.* 네가 안 간다면 나도 안 가겠다 / *I am not rich, ~ do I wish to be.* 나는 부자가 아니고 또한 되고 싶지도 않다 / *"I am not going."*

"Neither am I." "나는 가지 않겠다." "나도 안 가겠다."

— *adj.* not either. 어느 쪽의…도 —아니다. ¶ *Neither story is interesting.* 어느 얘기도 재미없다 / *I will take ~ side in the dispute.* 그 싸움의 어느 편에도 들지 않겠다 / *I can go in ~ case.* 어떤 경우든 갈 수 없다 / *Neither of the stories is true.* 둘 다 거짓말이다.

— *pron.* 《usu. used as *sing.*》 none of the two; not either. 어느 쪽도 …아니다〔않다〕. 參考 부분 부정은 not both. ¶ *I know ~ of them.* 그들 누구도 나는 모른다 / *Neither of them is drunk.* 둘 다 취하지 않았다 / *He gave me two books, and ~ was satisfactory.* 내게 책 두 권을 주었는데 둘 다 시원치 않았다. [E.=not whether]

Nell [nel] *n.* a woman's name. 여자 이름.

Nel·lie, Nel·ly [néli] *n.* a woman's name. 여자 이름.

Nel·son [nélsn], **Viscount Horatio** *n.* (1758-1805) an English admiral famous for his victory in the battle of Trafalgar. 넬슨《영국의 해군 제독》.

Nem·e·ses [néməsìːz] *n.* pl. of **Nemesis.**

Nem·e·sis [néməsis] *n.* (*pl.* **-ses**) **1** a Greek goddess of punishment and revenge. 인과 응보〔복수〕의 여신. **2** Ⓒ 《*n-*》 ⓐ a person who decides or gives punishment. 벌 주는 사람; 복수자. ⓑ Ⓤ just punishment; inevitable result. 천벌; 응보. ¶ *The nemesis which came to Niobe for boasting was the death of her children.* 큰 소리친 니오베에게 돌아온 응보는 그 자식들의 죽음이었다. [Gk.]

ne·o- [níou-, níːə-] *pref.* new; recent. '새로운, 근대의' 뜻. [Gk. *neos* new]

ne·o·lith·ic [nìːoulíθik] *adj.* of the later part of the Stone Age; of the period when man used polished stone weapons and tools. 신석기 시대의(opp. paleolithic). ¶ *the Neolithic Age* 신석기 시대. [→lithium]

ne·ol·o·gism [niːálədʒìzəm / -ɔ́l-], **-gy** [niːálədʒi / -ɔ́l-] *n.* **1** Ⓤ the use or invention of a new word. 신어(新語)의 사용〔만들기〕. **2** Ⓒ a new word. 신어. [→logos]

ne·on [níːan / -ən] *n.* Ⓤ 《chem.》 a rare gas with no color or smell that gives a glow when electricity passes through it. 네온. ¶ *a ~ sign* 네온사인. [Gk.=new]

ne·o·phyte [níːəfàit] *n.* Ⓒ **1** a person who has recently been admitted to a religion. 새 신자. **2** a beginner in art, business, etc. 초심자(初心者). [neo-, Gk. *phuō* plant]

ne·pen·the [nipénθi] *n.* Ⓒ **1** 《*poet.*》 a medicine believed by ancient Greeks to make a person forget sorrow or trouble. 슬픔·시름을 잊게 하는 약. **2** a pitcher plant. 낭상엽(囊狀葉) 식물《식충(食蟲) 식물의 하나》. [Gk.]

:neph·ew [néfjuː, névjuː] *n.* Ⓒ the son of one's brother or sister. 조카; 생질(opp. niece). [L. *nepos*]

Nep·tune [néptjuːn] *n.* **1** 《Rom. myth.》 the god of the sea. 바다의 신(神). **2** 《astron.》 the third largest planet. 해왕성(海王星). [L.]

〈Neptune 1〉

Ne·re·id, ne- [níəriid] *n.* Ⓒ 《Gk. myth.》 a fairy girl living in the sea; a sea nymph. 바다의 요정. [Gk.]

Ne·ro [níːrou] *n.* (37-68 A.D.) a Roman emperor, famous for his cruelty and tyranny. 네로《로마 제국의 폭군》.

:nerve [nəːrv] *n.* **1** Ⓒ a cordlike part of an animal's body that carries feelings and impulses between the brain and other parts of the body. 신경. **2** Ⓒ a strong cordlike part of the body which joins a muscle to a bone; a sinew. 건(腱); 힘줄; 근육. **3** Ⓤ mental strength; courage. 기력; 용기. ¶ *a man of ~* 배짱 있는 남자 / *recover one's ~* 용기를 되찾다 / *Climbing calls for strength and ~.* 등산에는 체력과 용기가 필요하다. **4** Ⓤ strength; energy. 체력; 정력; 활력. **5** 《*pl.*》 an unhealthy state of mind when a person is easily excited or frightened. 신경 과민. ¶ *have a fit of nerves* 신경 과민이 되다; 신경질을 부리다 / *suffer from ~* 신경 과민이다 / *She is all nerves.* 신경이 곤두서 있다. **6** Ⓤ 《*colloq.*》 rude boldness; impudence. 뻔뻔스러움; 후안무치(厚顔無恥). ¶ *You've got some ~.* 좀 뻔뻔스럽군 / *She had the ~ to say so.* 그녀는 뻔뻔스럽게 그런 말을 했다. **7** Ⓒ 《bot.》 a vein of a leaf. 엽맥(葉脈).

get on someone's nerves, worry or irritate someone. …의 신경을 건드리다.

have the nerve (=*be brave or bold enough*) ***to do.*** …할 용기가 있다; 뻔뻔스럽게도 …하다.

lose one's nerve, become timid or irresolute. 기가 죽다.

strain every nerve, make a great effort. 전력을 다하다; 용쓰다.

— *vt.* (P6,7,13,20) **1** give strength or courage to (someone). …에 힘을 주다; 용기를 북돋우다. ¶ *Her advice nerved him to go his own way.* 그는 그녀의 충고에 용기를 얻어 자기 생각대로 했다. **2** 《*reflexively*》 collect one's energies. 용기를 내다; 분발하다. ¶ *He nerved himself for the task.* 그는 용기를 내어 그 일을 했다. [L. *nervus*]

nerve·less [nə́ːrvlis] *adj.* **1** having no vigor or courage; having no firmness. 용기가 없는; (글에) 짜임새가 없는. ¶ *The gun dropped from his ~ hand.* 손에 힘이 빠지면서 총을 떨어뜨렸다. **2** 《anat., bot.》 without a nerve or nerves. 신경〔엽맥(葉脈)〕이 없는. **3** cool. 냉정한.

nerve·less·ly [nə́ːrvlisli] *adv.* in a nerveless manner. 무기력〔무신경〕하게.

nerve-rack·ing [nə́ːrvrækiŋ] *adj.* extremely irritating, annoying, or trying. 신경을 건드리는〔자극하는, 곤두서게 하는〕. ¶ *a ~ day* 〔*noise*〕 신경질나게 하는 날〔소음〕.

:nerv·ous [nə́ːrvəs] *adj.* **1** of the nerve. 신경의. ¶ *the ~ system* 신경 조직 / *~ breakdown* 〔*prostration*〕 신경 쇠약. **2** having delicate nerves; easily excited; restless and uneasy. 신경질인; 곧잘 흥분하는; 불안〔초조〕한. ¶ *I didn't play well because I was too ~.* 너무 흥분해서 연기를 잘 못했다. **3** strong; having strong and active muscles. 힘찬; 억센. ¶ *~ arms* 억센 팔. **4** 《*fig.*》 lively in style of writing. (문체가) 힘찬. ¶ *a ~ style of writing* 힘찬 필적. [→ nerve]

feel nervous (=*worry much*) ***about something.*** …을 걱정하다.

nerv·ous·ly [nə́ːrvəsli] *adv.* in a nervous manner. 신경질적으로; 힘차게; 늠름하게.

nerv·ous·ness [nə́ːrvəsnis] *n.* Ⓤ the state or quality of being nervous. 신경 과민; 소심.

nerv·y [nə́ːrvi] *adj.* (**nerv·i·er, nerv·i·est**) **1** 《rare》 strong; vigorous. 기골이 장대한; 힘찬. **2** 《U.S. *colloq.*》 rude and bold. 뻔뻔스러운; 대담한. **3** 《Brit.》 nervous; easily got excited or angry. 신경 과민의; 곧잘 흥분하는. [*nerve*]

:nest [nest] *n.* Ⓒ **1** a place where birds or other animals lay eggs and care for their young. 보금자리; 둥우리. ¶ *sit on a ~ of eggs* 알을 품다 / *leave a ~* 둥지를 떠나다. **2** a warm or comfortable place. 안식처. ¶ *a comfortable ~ for one's old age* 노후의 안식처. **3** a secret place where people, esp. thieves, robbers, etc. gather. 소굴. ¶ *a ~ of brigands* 산적의 소굴 / *a ~ of crime* 범죄의 온상. **4** birds or animals living in a nest. (둥우리 속에 있는 새·벌레 등의) 떼; 한배의 새끼. **5** a group of boxes, baskets, etc. which fit into one another. (찬합처럼 차례로 끼우게 된 상자, 바구니 등의) 한 벌.

feather one's nest, get rich in some way or other, usu. by dishonest means. (부정한 수를 써서) 한 재산 모으다.

foul one's own nest, say bad things about one's home. 자기 집〔근무처 (등)〕의 일을 남에게 흉보다.

take a nests, rob it of its eggs, or young birds. 새 보금자리를 털다.

— *vi.* (P1,3) **1** build or live in a nest. 보금자리를 짓다; 보금자리에 들다. **2** hunt for birds' nests. 새 둥지를 찾다. ¶ *The boys have gone nesting.* 아이들이 새 둥지를 찾으러 갔다.

— *vt.* (P6) put (a bird) in a nest; make a nest for (a bird, etc.). (새)를 보금자리에 넣다; (새 따위)에 보금자리를 지어주다. [E.]

nest egg [∠∠] *n.* **1** a real or false egg left in a nest to encourage a hen to go on laying eggs there. 밑알. **2** money that is put aside for future use; money saved as the beginning of a fund. (만일을 위한) 비상금; (저금의) 밑돈.

nes·tle [nésəl] *vi.* (P2A,3) lie or settle down closely and comfortably. 편안하게 눕다〔자리잡다〕. ¶ *a temple nestling among the hills* 산 속에 자리잡은 절 / *A child nestles close to its mother.* 아이가 어머니 곁에 편히 누워 있다. — *vt.* (P13) press (one's head, face, etc.) closely in affection; cuddle. (머리·얼굴 등)을 갖다 대다; 껴안다. ¶ *The little girl nestles her doll at her breast.* 소녀는 인형을 가슴에 꼭 껴안고 있다. [E.]

nest·ling [nés*t*liŋ] *n.* Ⓒ **1** a young newhatched bird unable to leave the nest. 어린〔갓 깐〕 새끼 새. **2** a young child. 유아(幼兒).

:net[1] [net] *n.* Ⓒ **1** woven material of string, cord, thread, wire, etc. with small holes arranged regularly. 그물. ¶ *a tennis ~.* **2** anything made of this material. 그물 모양의 것. ¶ *a mosquito ~* 모기장 / *cast a ~* 그물을 던지다 / *lay a ~* 그물을 치다. **3** a trap. 덫; 함정; 술책. ¶ *He was caught in the ~ of lies.* 그는 거짓말에 넘어갔다.

— *vt., vi.* (**net·ted, net·ting**) (P6;1) **1** make (something) into a net. 그물을 뜨다. **2** catch (something) with a net. 그물로 잡다. ¶ *~ fish* 〔*birds*〕. **3** get (something) with effort. 노력해서 얻다. **4** use a net in (something) to catch or protect. 그물로 덮다; 그물을 치다. ¶ *~ fruit trees* 과일 나무에 그물을 씌우다 / *~ a river* 강에 그물을 치다. [E.]

net[2] [net] *adj.* left over after taking away all necessary expenses. 에누리 없는; 정미(正味)의(opp. gross). ¶ *~ weight* 정미(正味) 중량; 순(純)중량 / *~ price* 정가(正價) / *a ~ profit* 순익. — *vt.* (**net·ted, net·ting**) (P6, 13,14) gain (a certain amount) as a net profit. …의 순익을 얻다. ¶ *~ £10,000 a year* 연 1만 파운드의 순익을 올리다 / *The sale netted me a good profit.* 그걸 팔아서 재미를 좀 봤다. [→neat[1]]

neth·er [néðər] *adj.* 《*arch.*》 lower. 아래의 (opp. upper). ¶ *one's ~ lip* 아랫입술 / *the ~ regions* 〔*world*〕 지옥 / *~ garments* 바지. [E.]

Neth·er·land·er [néðərlændər, -lənd-] *n.* Ⓒ a person of the Netherlands. 네덜란드인(人). [↓]

Neth·er·lands [néðərləndz] *n.* 《*the ~* 》 a country in western Europe, also called Holland. 네덜란드. [E.]

net·ting [nétiŋ] *n.* Ⓤ **1** the act of making nets. 그물뜨기. **2** a netted material. 그물 세공(품). ¶ *wire ~* 철망. [*net*]

net·tle [nétl] *n.* Ⓒ 《bot.》 any wild plant having leaves with stinging hairs. 쐐기풀.

grasp the nettle, 《*fig.*》 take an unpleasant

task in hand boldly. 자진하여 곤란과 싸우다. —*vt.* (P6) **1** sting (someone) with a nettle. …을 쐐기풀로 찌르다. **2** make (someone) angry; irritate; annoy. …을 화[짜증]나게 하다. ¶ *The criticism nettled him.* 그 비평은 그를 화나게 했다. [E.]

net·tle-rash [nétlræʃ] *n.* 《med.》 a skin eruption like nettle-stings. 두드러기. [E.]

·**net·work** [nétwə̀ːrk] *n.* **1** Ⓤ net; netting. 그물 세공품. ¶ *a fine piece of* ~ 고운 망사(網紗) 직물. **2** Ⓒ any net-like system of lines, roads, railways, etc. 망상 조직. ¶ *a* ~ *of railways* 철도망. **3** Ⓒ a group of radio or television stations connected together as a unit. (TV·라디오의) 방송망; 네트워크. ¶ *a radio* ~ 라디오 방송망. [→net[1]]

neu·ral [njúərəl] *adj.* of nerves or the nerve organ. 신경계의. [Gk. *neuron* nerve]

neu·ral·gia [njuərǽldʒə] *n.* Ⓤ a sharp pain in the nerves along the course of a nerve. 신경통.

neu·ron [njúəran, -rɔn] *n.* a nerve-cell with all its processes. 신경 단위.

neu·ro·ses [njuəróusiːz] *n.* pl. of **neurosis.**

neu·ro·sis [njuəróusis] *n.* ⒸⓊ (*pl.* **-ses**) 《med.》 a mental or nervous disorder or disease. 신경증; 노이로제. [→neural]

neu·rot·ic [njuərátik / -rɔ́t-] *adj.* **1** ⓐ of neurosis; suffering from a nervous disease. 신경(계)의; 노이로제의. ⓑ too nervous. 신경 과민의. ¶ *a* ~ *person* 신경이 과민한 사람. **2** (of a drug) acting on nerve. (약이) 신경 안정에 듣는. —*n.* Ⓒ **1** a person suffering from neurosis. 노이로제 환자. **2** a drug that acts on the nerves. 신경 자극제. [↑]

neu·ter [njúːtər] *adj.* **1** 《gram.》 neither masculine nor feminine. 중성(中性)의. **2** 《bot., zool.》 without a sexual organ. 무성(無性)의. **3** 《rare》 taking neither side; neutral. 중립의. —*n.* Ⓒ **1** 《gram.》 a neuter word or gender. 중성. **2** an animal or a plant without sex. 무성 동물[식물]. [L. =neither]

·**neu·tral** [njúːtrəl] *adj.* **1** taking neither side in a war or quarrel. 중립의. ¶ *a* ~ *state* 중립국 / *a* ~ *zone* 중립 지대 / ~ *ships* 중립국 선박. **2** not belonging to any of the two sides. 중립적인. ¶ *a* ~ *opinion* 불편 부당의[공평 무사한] 의견. **3** having no clear and exact quality. 뚜렷하지 않은. ¶ *a* ~ *tint* [*color*] 중간색; 회색. **4** 《chem.》 neither acid nor alkaline; 《electr.》 neither negative nor positive. 중성의; (전하(電荷)가 없는) 중성의. **5** 《biol.》 neuter. 무성(無性)의. —*n.* Ⓒ a country or person that does not take part in a war or quarrel. 중립국; 중립을 지키는 사람. [→neuter, -al]

neu·tral·i·ty [njuːtrǽləti] *n.* Ⓤ **1** a country's policy of not taking part in any war between other nations. 국외(局外) 중립. ¶ *strict* ~ 엄정 중립. **2** 《chem.》 the state or quality of being neutral. 중성.

neu·tral·i·za·tion [njùːtrəlizéiʃən] *n.* Ⓤ the act of neutralizing; the state of being neutralized. 중립; 중화(中和); 불편 부당.

neu·tral·ize [njúːtrəlàiz] *vt.* (P6) **1** make (a country, etc.) neutral. (나라 등)을 중립화하다. ¶ ~ *small nations* 약소국을 중립화하다. **2** 《chem.》 destroy the active or clear nature of (something). …을 중화(中和)하다. ¶ ~ *an acid with a base* 산을 알칼리로 중화시키다. **3** make (something) inactive. …을 무효로 하다. ¶ *One poison sometimes neutralizes another.* 어떤 독은 때로 다른 독의 해독 작용을 한다. ●**neu·tral·iz·er** [-ər] *n.*

neu·tron [njúːtran / njúːtrɔn] *n.* Ⓒ 《phys.》 one of the basic particles in an atom, having the same mass as a proton. 뉴트론; 중성자(中性子). [→neuter]

Nev. Nevada.

Ne·va·da [nivǽdə, -váː-] *n.* a western State of the United States. 네바다. 參考 Nev., NV로 생략함. 주도는 Carson City.

Ne·va·dan [nivǽdən, -váː-] *n.* Ⓒ a person of Nevada. 네바다 주의 사람.

:**nev·er** [névər] *adv.* **1** not ever; not at any time. 일찍이 …없다; 어떤 때든 …않다. ¶ *I have* ~ *heard such a thing.* 그런 일은 들어 본 적이 없다 / *I shall* ~ *forget his kindness.* 그의 친절은 결코 잊지 않겠다 / *Never in my life have I heard such a thing.* 내 일찍이 그런 말은 듣지 못했다. **2** not at all. 결코 …않다; 절대로[조금도] …않다. ¶ ~ *say a word* 한 마디도 않다 / 《*prov.*》 *Better late than* ~. 늦더라도 안 하느니보다는 낫다 / 《*prov.*》 *It is* ~ *too late to mend.* 잘못을 고치는데 늦다는 법은 없다 / *Now or* ~. 지금이 마지막 기회다 / *Never mind.* 걱정 마라; 안심해라. **3** 《*colloq.*》 surely not; you do not mean it. 설마 …은 아니겠지. ¶ *You* ~ *lost my watch.* 설마 내 시계 잃어버린 건 아니겠지. [E. =not ever]

never so, 《*arch.*》 no matter how. 비록 …일지라도. ¶ *Be he* ~ *so rich, she will not marry him.* 아무리 그가 부자일지라도 그녀는 그와 결혼하지 않을 것이다.

Well, I never! I'm surprised! 설마; 어머나; 어유 깜짝이야.

nev·er·end·ing [névəréndiŋ] *adj.* lasting all the time; endless. 끝없는; 한없는.

nev·er·fail·ing [névərféiliŋ] *adj.* lasting all the time; that never changes. 끝없는; (친절 등) 변치 않는.

nev·er·more [nèvərmɔ́ːr] *adv.* never again; never any more. 두 번 다시 …않다.

:**nev·er·the·less** [nèvərðəlés] *adv., conj.* however; in spite of that. 그럼에도 불구하고. ¶ *It was raining;* ~, *we went out.* 비가 오고 있었지만 그래도 우리는 밖에 나갔다 / *It* ~ *makes me anxious.* 그렇지만 나는 걱정하지 않는다.

:new [nju:] *adj.* **1** not known before; discovered or produced for the first time. 처음인; 새로운(opp. old). ¶ *a ~ invention* 새 발견 / *This information is ~ to me.* 이 얘기는 처음 듣는다. **2** recently made or acquired; fresh. 새로 만든; 신선한. ¶ *~ milk* 신선한 우유 / *a ~ suit of clothes* 새로 맞춘 옷 / *go on with ~ courage* 새로운 용기로 다시 시작하다 / *have a ~ teacher* 신임 선생을 맞다. **3** not used before; not worn out. 새것인; 낡지 않은. ¶ *~ furniture* 새 가구 / *This is as good as ~.* 이건 새것이나 마찬가지다. **4** beginning again; following that which has gone before. 새로워진; 거듭난; 새로 시작하는. ¶ *lead a ~ life* 새출발하다 / *a ~ year* 새해 / *a ~ moon* 초승달. **5** different; changed. 전과 달라진. ¶ *I feel like a ~ man.* 난 사람이 달라진 기분이다. **6** not familiar; not yet accustomed. 익숙지 않은; 생소한. ¶ *I am ~ to the work.* 나는 그 일에 서툴다. **7** modern; recent. 신식의; 현대풍의. ¶ *the ~ mode* 신유행; 뉴 모드 / *the ~ woman* 신여성.

make a new man of, improve his character and conduct; restore (=put back) to good health. 새 사람으로 만들다; 다시 건강하게 하다. ¶ *That has made a ~ man of him.* 그 일이 그로 하여금 거듭나게 했다.

new from, freshly arrived from. …에서 새로 온. ¶ *a maidservant ~ from the country* 새로 시골서 온 가정부.

— *adv.* **1** again. 다시; 새로이. **2** 《usu. in *compounds*》 newly; recently. 새롭게; 최근. ¶ *new-fallen snow* 갓 내린 눈. [E.]

new·born [njú:bɔ́:rn] *adj.* **1** recently or just born. 갓 태어난. ¶ *a ~ baby* 신생아. **2** born again. 갱생한; 다시 생긴. ¶ *~ courage* 새로운 용기.

new·com·er [njú:kʌ̀mər] *n.* Ⓒ a person who has just arrived. 신참자.

New England [ˋ ˊ] *n.* the six States in the northeastern United States. 뉴잉글랜드《미국 동북부의 6 개주》.

New Englander [ˋ ˊ--] *n.* a person of New England. 뉴잉글랜드인.

new·fan·gled [njú:fǽŋgəld] *adj.* **1** 《*contempt.*》 of a new fashion; new but somewhat strange. 최신식의; 신기한; 묘한. ¶ *a ~ idea* 묘한 생각. **2** 《rare》 fond of newness and strangeness. 새것〔신기한 것〕을 좋아하는. [E.=new taken]

new-fash·ioned [njú:fǽʃənd] *adj.* of a new fashion; made in a new style. 새 유행의; 신형의; 최신의.

New·found·land [njú:fəndlənd, -lænd / nju:fáundlənd] *n.* **1** a large island just off the eastern coast of Canada. 뉴펀들랜드. **2** Ⓒ a large, long-haired, intelligent dog raised originally in Newfoundland. 뉴펀들랜드 개《헤엄을 잘 침》.

New Guin·ea [njù: gíni] *n.* a large island, north of Australia, also called Papua. 뉴기니 섬.

New Jersey [njù dʒə́:rzi] *n.* an eastern State of the United States. 뉴저지주. 參考 N.J.로 생략함. 주도(州都)는 Trenton.

new look [ˊ ˊ] *n.* new fashion in women's dress; 《*colloq.*》 up-to-date appearance. (여성복의) 새로운 양식; 최신(유행)형《복장 등의》.

·new·ly [njú:li] *adv.* recently; in a new manner or form. 최근; 새로이. ¶ *a newly-built house* 새집 / *a thought ~ expressed* 신사상 / *~ arrived* 새로 도착한. [*new*]

New Mexico [ˋ ˊ--] *n.* a southwestern State of the United States. 뉴멕시코주. 參考 N.Mex., N.M.로 생략함. 주도(州都)는 Santa Fe.

:news [nju:z] *n.* Ⓤ **1** new or recent information. 뉴스; 보도(報道). ¶ *foreign* 〔*home*〕 *~* 해외〔국내〕 소식 / *the latest ~* 최신 뉴스 / *a piece of good ~* 길보(吉報); 희소식. **2** some new or fresh information about something. 색다른 일〔정보〕. ¶ *Is there any ~? =What's the ~?* 뭐 색다른 거 없나 / *That's quite ~ to me.* 그거 금시초문이다 / 《*prov.*》 *No ~ is good ~.* 무소식이 희소식 / 《*prov.*》 *Bad ~ travels quickly.* 악사천리(惡事千里) / *I want to know all your ~.* 어떻게 지내나; 재미는 어떤가 / *That is no ~.* 그건 벌써 들어 안다. **3** 《*N-*》 a newspaper. 신문. [*new*]

***break the news to** someone,* tell someone bad news in a gentle way. …에 좋지 않은 소식을〔흉보를〕 알려주다.

news agency [ˊ ˋ--] *n.* a business organization that gathers and supplies news to newspaper offices or publishing houses. 통신사.

news·agent [njú:zèidʒənt] *n.* 《Brit.》 a person who sells newspapers or magazines. 신문·잡지 판매인.

news·boy [njú:zbɔ̀i] *n.* Ⓒ a boy who delivers or sells newspapers. 신문 배달원; 신문팔이.

news·cast [njú:zkæ̀st, -kɑ̀:st] *vt., vi.* 《U.S.》 broadcast (news) on radio or television. 뉴스 방송을 하다. — *n.* Ⓒ a radio or television program of news reports. 뉴스 방송.

news·deal·er [njú:zdì:lər] *n.* 《U.S.》 = newsagent.

news·man [njú:zmæ̀n, -mən] *n.* Ⓒ (*pl.* **-men** [-mèn, -mən]) **1** =newsboy. **2** a reporter on a newspaper. 취재 기자.

:news·pa·per [njú:zpèipər, njú:s-] *n.* Ⓒ a paper which contains daily news, advertisements, and other pieces of information. 신문. ¶ *a daily ~* 일간 신문 / *take a ~* 신문을 구독하다.

news·print [njú:zprìnt] *n.* Ⓤ a kind of paper used for newspapers. 신문 용지.

news·reel [njú:zrì:l] *n.* Ⓒ a motion picture showing recent events. 뉴스 영화.

news room [ˊ ˋ] *n.* **1** a room where

the news is edited or prepared to be broadcast. 뉴스 편집실. **2** 《Brit.》 a room where newspapers or magazines can be read. 신문·잡지 열람실.

news·stand [njúːzstæ̀nd] *n.* Ⓒ 《U.S.》 a table or stall, e.g. on a street or in a station, where newspapers and magazines are sold. 신문·잡지 판매점〔대〕.

news·ven·dor [njúːzvèndər] *n.* Ⓒ a newspaper seller, esp. on the street. (가두) 신문 판매인; 신문팔이.

news·y [njúːzi] *adj.* (**news·i·er, news·i·est**) having much news or gossip. 뉴스〔화제〕가 많은; 화제가 풍부한. ¶ *a ~ letter* 여러 이야기를 쓴 편지. [*new*]

newt [njuːt] *n.* Ⓒ 《zool.》 a small animal like a lizard which lives both on land and in water. 영원(蠑螈). [=*an* eft]

·**New·ton** [njúːtn], **Isaac** *n.* (1642-1727) an English scientist and mathematician. 뉴턴.

New World [⌐⌐], **the** *n.* North and South America. 신세계; 남북 아메리카 대륙 (opp. the Old World).

:**New York** [⌐⌐] *n.* **1** an eastern State of the United States. 뉴욕주. **2** the largest city in the United States. 뉴욕시.

New Zea·land [njùː zíːlənd] *n.* a country in the South Pacific. 뉴질랜드. 參考 수도는 Wellington.

:**next** [nekst] *adj.* **1** coming immediately after in time, place or order, etc. 다음의; 이번의; 오는··· (opp. last). ¶ *~ week* 〔*month, year*〕 내주〔내달, 내년〕 / *the ~ week* 〔*month, year*〕 그 다음 주〔달, 해〕 語法 현재를 기준으로 할 때는 the를 안 쓰며 과거가 기준일 때는 씀 / *~ Saturday* =*on Saturday ~* 다음 토요일에 / *on Saturday ~ week* 다음 주 토요일에 / *Who is the ~ man to see me?* 다음 분은 누구지《면회 등에서》/ *Not till ~ time.* 다음 이후에는 그만두지《금주·금연의 농담조의 맹세》. **2** nearest in place or position. 가까운; 이웃의. ¶ *the ~ room* 옆방 / *a house ~ to ours* 우리 이웃집. **3** following immediately in rank, importance, etc.; nearest in relation. (순서·가치 등이) 다음〔버금〕가는; 차위(次位)의; (관계가) 가장 가까운. ¶ *the ~ prize* 차위상(次位賞) / *the person ~ to him in rank* 계급이 그의 다음인 사람 / *Ask the ~ person you meet.* 누구든 만나는 대로 물어보시오.

as ... as the next fellow [***man***], 《U.S. *colloq.*》 as ... as anybody. 누구 못지않게. ¶ *He is as clever as the ~ fellow.* 그는 누구 못지않게 영리하다.

get next to, 《U.S. *sl.*》 get to know; get acquainted with; become aware of. ···와 알게〔친하게〕 되다; ···와 가까워지다.

in the next place, secondly, thirdly, etc. 다음에; 둘째로.

next door, (in) the next house. 옆집(에). ¶ *They live ~ door* (*to us*). 그들은 (우리) 옆집에 산다.

next time, 《as *conj.*》 at the next time when .... 다음 번에; 이번에; 다음에 ···할 때.

— *n.* 《usu. *the ~* or *one's ~*》 the next person(s) or thing(s). 다음 사람〔것〕. ¶ *in my ~* (*letter*) 내 다음(편지)에 / *the ~ of kin* 가장 가까운 친척 / *She was the ~* (*person*) *to arrive.* 그녀가 그 다음에 도착했다.

— *adv.* in the nearest time, place, etc.; on the next occasion. 다음에; 이웃에; 이번에는. ¶ *the ~ best thing* 차선(次善)의 것 / *the largest city ~ to Seoul* 서울 다음의 가장 큰 도시 / *Who came ~?* 다음에 누가 왔나.

next to, **a**) 《before a negative word》 almost. 거의. ¶ *The flight is ~ to impossible.* 비행은 거의 불가능하다 / *eat ~ to nothing* 거의 아무것도 못 먹다; 굶다시피하다. **b**) beside. ···의 다음〔이웃〕에. ¶ *She sat ~ to me.* 그녀는 내 곁에 앉았다.

What next! I wonder what will happen next! 다음에는 무슨 일이 일어날까. ¶ *He failed math, then history. What ~!* 그는 수학에 낙제하더니 역사도 낙제했다. 다음엔 또 뭘까.

— *prep.* beside; nearest to. ···의 다음〔곁〕에; ···에 가장 가까운〔가까이〕. ¶ *the seat ~ mine* 내 옆자리 / *the house ~ mine* 우리 옆집 / *Whom did you sit ~ at dinner?* 식사할 때 옆자리에 누구였나. [→nigh]

·**next-door** [néks*t*dɔ̀ːr] *adj.* in the next house. 이웃(집)의. ¶ *a ~ neighbor* 옆집 사람.

nex·es [néksəs] *n.* pl. of **nexus.**

nex·us [néksəs] *n.* Ⓒ (*pl.* **nex·us** or **nex·es**) **1** a connection; a link. 유대; 관계. **2** a connected series or group. (관념·사물 등의) 연쇄적 집단. **3** 《gram.》 a word connected; the relation between a predicate and a subject. 넥서스; 서술적 관계〔표현〕. [L. *necto* bind]

Ni·ag·a·ra Falls [naiǽgərə fɔ́ːlz] *n.* the falls on the Niagara River, which flows from Lake Erie into Lake Ontario. 나이애가라 폭포.

nib [nib] *n.* Ⓒ **1** 《chiefly. Brit.》 a penpoint. 펜촉. **2** a bird's bill. (새의) 부리. **3** the point of anything. 끝; 선단(先端); 첨단. — *vt.* (P6) furnish with a nib. (깃펜의 끝)을 뾰족하게 하다; (펜대)에 펜촉을 끼우다. [→neb]

nib·ble [níbl] *vi., vt.* (P1,3;6,7) **1** bite (food, etc.) away a little at a time as a rabbit or mouse does. (먹을것 등을) 조금씩 물어뜯다. **2** 《*at*》 (of fish, etc.) continue to eat (food) by biting off small pieces. (물고기 등이 미끼를) 입질하다. — *n.* Ⓒ a small bite; the act of nibbling. 조금씩 물어뜯기; (물고기의) 입질. [G. *nibbelen* to pick with the beak]

:**nice** [nais] *adj.* **1** pleasing; agreeable; good. 좋은; 쾌적한; 유쾌한; 훌륭한; 맛있는. ¶ *a ~ room* 쾌적한 방 / *~ weather* 좋은 날

씨 / *a ~ face* 깨끗한〔고운〕 얼굴 / *a ~ child* 상냥한 아이 / *be ~ to the taste* 맛이 훌륭하다. **2** kind; thoughtful. 친절한. ¶ *He is ~ to girls.* 그는 여자들에게 친절하다 / *It is very ~ of you to say so.* 그렇게 말해 주니 친절도 하구나. **3** difficult to explain; minute; delicate. 미묘한; 델리키트한; 미세한. ¶ *~ shades of meaning* 뜻의 미묘한 차이 / *a ~ distinction* 미세한 구분. **4** keen; precise; accurate. 예민한; 치밀한. ¶ *a ~ observer* 예민한 관찰자 / *a ~ sense of color* 예민한 색각(色覺) / *He has a ~ ear for music.* 그는 음악을 아는 사람이다. **5** (in choice or taste) hard to please; not easily satisfied. 까다로운. ¶ *He is ~ in his food.* 그는 식성이 까다롭다 / *She is ~ about the choice of words.* 그녀는 말의 선택에 까다롭다. **6** requiring care or skill. 세심한 주의가〔기술이〕 필요한. ¶ *a ~ problem* 신중해야 할 문제 / *weighed in the nicest scales* 더없이 정밀하게 계량된 / *negotiations needing ~ handling* 진행이 아주 까다로운 협상. **7** refined as to manners, language, etc.; well-bred. 점잖은; 세련된; 본데 있게 자란. ¶ *Nice people would not say such a thing.* 점잖은 사람이라면 그런 소리는 안 한다. **8** 《*iron.*》 difficult; bad; nasty; awkward. 난처한; 성가신. ¶ *a ~ state of affairs* 곤란한 사태 / *You are a ~ fellow, I must say.* 정말 귀찮은 친구로군. **9** 《before *adj.*》 enough. 충분한. ¶ *This is a ~ long stick.* 막대 길이가 이만하면 됐다. [→nescient]

nice and [náisn] ..., nicely; quite; satisfactorily. 기분 좋게; 매우; 더할 나위 없이. ¶ *The car is going ~ and fast.* 차가 기분 좋게 빨리 달리고 있다.

nice-looking [náislúkiŋ] *adj.* having a pretty appearance; agreeable and attractive. 잘 생긴; 애교〔매력〕 있는.

nice·ly [náisli] *adv.* **1** in a nice manner. (기분) 좋게; 훌륭하게. ¶ *do ~* 잘 해내다. **2** 《*colloq.*》 satisfactorily; very well. 만족하게; 아주 잘. ¶ *The dress will suit her ~.* 그 옷이 그녀에게 잘 어울릴 것이다 / *That will suit me ~.* 그건 내게 제격이다.

ni·ce·ty [náisəti] *n.* (*pl.* **-ties**) **1** Ⓤ accuracy; exactness. 정확; 정밀. ¶ *the ~ of observation* 관찰의 정밀도 / *A radio set requires some ~ of adjustment to give the clearest tone.* 라디오는 선명한 소리를 내려면 좀 정확한 조정이 요구된다. **2** Ⓒ a very delicate point. 미묘한 점. ¶ *a ~ of argument* 미묘한 논점 / *I can make my car go, but I have not yet learned all the little niceties of driving.* 차를 가게는 할 수 있지만 운전은 아직 상당히 미숙하다. **3** 《*pl.*》 something refined or elegant. 우아한〔운치 있는〕 것. ¶ *enjoy the niceties of modern life* 현대 생활의 운치를 즐기다. [*nice*]

to a nicety, exactly; precisely. 정확하게. ¶ *The coat fits to a ~.* 그 코트는 꼭 맞는다.

with great nicety, very exactly. 아주 정확하게.

niche [nitʃ] *n.* Ⓒ **1** a hollow in a wall to place a statue, vase, etc. in. 벽감(壁龕). **2** 《*fig.*》 a place suitable for a man or thing. 적소(適所). ¶ *He found his ~ in teaching.* 그는 자신의 적직을 교직(教職)에서 발견했다. — *vt.* place in a niche; settle (oneself) in a niche. …을 벽감에 안치하다; 알맞은 곳에 자리잡다. [It.]

Nich·o·las [níkələs] *n.* **1** (?-342) a patron saint of Russians, young people, sailors, etc. 성(聖)니콜라스《젊은이·뱃사람의 수호성인》. **2** Santa Claus. 산타클로스. **3** a man's name. 남자 이름. 參考 애칭은 Nick.

nick [nik] *n.* Ⓒ a small cut in an edge or surface; a notch. 새김눈; 자른 자리; 이 빠진 데. ¶ *a ~ in the rim of a glass* 컵의 이 빠진 곳 / *a ~ in a ruler* 자의 눈금.

in the nick of time, just in time; in critical or opportune moment. 마침 제때에; 아슬아슬한 때에. ¶ *I saw the baby was about to fall off and caught it just in the ~ of time.* 그 아이가 막 떨어지려는 것을 보고 간신히 붙들었다. — *vt.* (P6) **1** make a small cut or break in (something). …에 새김눈〔눈금, 흠집〕을 내다. ¶ *~ the tree trunk* 나뭇줄기에 (칼)자국을 내다. **2** 《*sl.*》 steal; catch. …을 훔치다. ¶ *~ a watch.* **3** guess exactly. 딱 알아맞히다. [N.]

Nick [nik] *n.* **1** a nickname of Nicholas. Nicholas 의 애칭. **2** the Devil. 악마. 參考 흔히 Old Nick라 함.

***nick·el** [níkəl] *n.* **1** Ⓤ 《chem.》 a hard, silvery-white metallic element. 니켈. 參考 원소기호 Ni. ¶ *~ plate* 니켈 도금 / *~ silver* 양은(洋銀). **2** Ⓒ 《U.S.》 a coin made of nickel worth 5 cents. 5센트짜리 백동화(貨). ¶ *Would you lend me a ~?* 5센트 빌려주겠나. — *vt.* (**-eled, -el·ing** or 《Brit.》 **-elled, -el·ling**) (P6) coat (something) with nickel. …을 니켈 도금하다. [G.]

not worth a nickel, quite worthless. 서푼어치의 가치도 없다.

***nick·name** [níknèim] *n.* Ⓒ **1** a familiar name given to a person or thing in place of a real name. 별명; 애칭. **2** a familiar form of a Christian name. 세례명의 애칭. ¶ *Nick is a ~ for Nicholas.* Nick 는 니콜라스의 애칭이다. — *vt.* (P6,19) give a nickname to (someone). …에 별명을 붙이다. ¶ *The boys soon nicknamed the teacher.* 학생들은 이내 선생에게 별명을 붙였다. [M.E. *an ekename* an additional name]

nic·o·tine [níkəti:n] *n.* Ⓤ a poison, found in tobacco leaves. 니코틴. [Person]

nic·o·tin·ism [níkəti:nìzəm] *n.* suffering from poisoning by nicotine or from the excessive use of tobacco. 니코틴〔담배〕 중독.

:niece [ni:s] *n.* Ⓒ the daughter of one's brother or sister. 조카딸(opp. nephew). [L. *neptice*]

Ni·ge·ri·a [naidʒíəriə] *n.* a country in West Africa. 나이지리아.

nig·gard [nígərd] *n.* Ⓒ a person who is mean in money matters; a person who does not want to spend money for any purpose; a miser. 구두쇠; 노랭이. — *adj.* mean in money matters; miserly. 인색한; 쩨쩨한. [N.]

nig·ger [nígər] *n.* Ⓒ《*colloq., contempt.*》**1** a Negro. 흑인; 검둥이. **2** a member of the black-skinned race. 흑인종. ¶ *a ~ melody* 흑인 노래. [→negro]

***a* 〔*the*〕 *nigger in the woodpile* 〔*fence*〕,** 《U.S. *sl.*》 someone who causes an unexpected problem. 무슨 일을 저지를지 모르는 사람.

work like a nigger, work very hard. 뼈빠지게〔고되게〕 일하다.

nig·gle [nígəl] *vi.* (P1) spend time unnecessarily on small points. 하찮은 일에 시간을 낭비하다. [N.]

nig·gling [níglinŋ] *adj.* trifling; petty; small but persistent; too fussy. 하찮은; 좀스러운; 성가신; 귀찮은. ¶ *a ~ job* 골치 아픈 일.

·**nigh** [nai] *adj., adv.* (**nigh·er** or 《*arch.*》 **near, nigh·est** or 《*arch.*》 **next**) 《*arch., poet.*》 near; nearly. 가까이의〔에〕. ¶ *He is ~ unto death.* 그는 죽어가고 있다. [E.]

:**night** [nait] *n.* Ⓒ **1** the time between evening and morning, or sunset and sunrise. 밤; 저녁(opp. day). ¶ *a dirty ~* 비내리는 밤 / *at nights* 밤마다 / *by ~* 밤에는 / *in the ~* 밤에 / *last ~* 지난 밤. **2** Ⓤ the darkness of night; the dark. (밤의) 어둠. ¶ *escape under cover of ~* 야음을 틈타서 도망가다 / *She went out into the ~.* 밤의 어둠 속으로 걸어 나갔다. **3** a state or time somewhat like night. 암흑 시대〔상태〕《침체, 무지, 불행, 죽음 등》. ¶ *the long ~ of the Middle Ages* 중세의 긴 암흑 시대. **4** 《as *adj.*》 belonging to, used in, or suitable for the night. 야간(용)의. ¶ *~ flying* 야간 비행 / *a ~ breeze* 밤바람 / 《U.S.》 *a ~ letter* (요금이 싼) 야간 전보. [E.]

all night* (*long*)** =all the night,*** throughout the whole night. 밤새도록.

have a good* 〔*bad*〕 *night, sleep well 〔badly〕. 푹 자다〔잠을 설치다〕.

make a night of it, spend the night in enjoyment. 밤새도록 놀다〔술 마시다〕.

night after* 〔*by*〕 *night, every night. 매일밤.

night and day, always; continuously. 밤낮(없이); 노상.

o'* (=*on*) *nights, 《*sl.*》 at night; during the night. 밤에; 밤에 때때로. ¶ *I can't sleep ~.* 밤에 잠이 안 온다.

turn night into day, do at night what is usu. done during the day. 낮에 할 일을 밤에 하다.

night clothes [́ ́] *n. pl.* any kind of clothes to be worn in bed. 잠옷.

night club [́ ́] *n.* a place where people can drink, eat, and enjoy dancing or watching a floor show till late at night. 나이트클럽.

night-dress [náitdrès] *n.* ⒸⓊ a kind of night clothes. 잠옷.

night·fall [náitfɔ̀ːl] *n.* Ⓤ the coming of evening. 해질녘; 황혼.

night·gown [náitgàun] *n.* Ⓒ a long, loose dress for women or children, usu. worn in bed. 잠옷《부인·소아용》.

night·hawk [náithɔ̀ːk] *n.* Ⓒ **1** a kind of American bird that flies and feeds at night. 쏙독새의 일종. **2** 《*colloq.*》 a person who works, studies, or goes about till late at night. 밤늦도록 일〔공부〕하는〔나다니는〕 사람.

night·in·gale [náitəŋgèil, -tiŋ-] *n.* Ⓒ 《Brit.》 a small, reddish-brown bird, the males of which sing sweetly. 나이팅게일《지빠귓과의 작은 새》. [→night, *gale* singer]

night·long [náitlɔ̀(ː)ŋ, -lɑ̀ŋ] *adj.* lasting through the night. 밤새우는; 철야의. ¶ *a ~ festivity* 밤을 새우는 축제. — *adv.* throughout the night. 밤새도록. [*night*]

night·ly [náitli] *adj.* of the night; happening or done every night. 밤의; 밤마다의. ¶ *~ watches* 〔*visit*〕 밤마다의 경비〔방문〕. — *adv.* every night. 밤마다. ¶ *We gathered ~ to talk over the matter.* 우리는 그 문제 때문에 매일 밤 모였다.

night·mare [náitmὲər] *n.* Ⓒ **1** a terrible dream. 악몽; 가위 눌림. ¶ *have a ~* 가위 눌리다. **2** 《*fig.*》 a terrible fear; a terrible experience. 공포; 악몽 같은 경험.

night owl [́ ́] *n.* 《*colloq.*》 a person who regularly stays up late at night. 밤늦도록 안 자는 사람《습관적으로》.

night school [́ ́] *n.* an evening school for persons who work during the day. 야간 학교; 야학(opp. *day school*).

night shift [́ ́] *n.* the night-work hours in a factory; 《*collectively*》 the laborers who work at night. (주야 교대의) 야간 근무(자). ¶ *work on the ~* 야근하다.

night·shirt [náitʃə̀ːrt] *n.* Ⓒ a long, loose dress like a shirt worn by men or boys in bed. (남자용) 긴 잠옷.

night·time [náittàim] *n.* Ⓤ the period of darkness between sunset and sunrise. 야간. ¶ *in the ~* 밤〔야간〕에.

night train [́ ́] *n.* a train that runs at night. 야간 열차.

night·walk·er [náitwɔ̀ːkər] *n.* Ⓒ **1** a person who moves around asleep at night. 몽유병자. **2** a person who walks about at night, such as a thief or someone with other bad purposes. 밤도둑; 매춘부; 야행 동물.

night watch [́ ́] *n.* **1** the act of guarding during the night; a person who is on guard at night. 야경(원). **2** the period when such a guard is kept. (야경의) 근무 시간.

night watchman [ˊ ˋ-] *n.* a watchman who is on duty during the night. 야경원.

ni·hil·ism [náiəlìzəm, ní:ə-] *n.* Ⓤ **1** the complete denial of the meaning of existence. 니힐리즘; 허무주의. **2** the belief of certain Russian revolutionaries, which was against all authority; violent revolutionary beliefs. 폭력 혁명〔무정부〕주의. [L. *nihil* nothing]

ni·hil·ist [náiəlist, ní:ə-] *n.* Ⓒ **1** a person who believes in nihilism. 허무주의자. **2** a person who believes in violent revolution; a terrorist. 폭력 혁명〔무정부〕주의자.

ni·hil·is·tic [nàiəlístik, nì:ə-] *adj.* of nihilism or a nihilist. 허무주의(자)의; 무정부주의(자)의.

Ni·ke [náiki:] *n.* **1** 《Gk. myth.》 the winged goddess of victory. 니케《승리의 여신》. **2** 《U.S.》 an antiaircraft rocket-propelled missile guided by electronic signals from the ground. 나이키《지대공 유도탄의 일종》.

nil [nil] *n.* Ⓤ zero; a score of nothing; none at all. 영; 무. 參考 경기의 득점에 쓰임. ¶ *four goals to* ~, 4 대 0 / *The profits are* ~. 소득은 전무다 / *His influence is now* ~. 그의 영향력은 이젠 없다. [L.]

Nile [nail], **the** *n.* a great river in eastern Africa flowing through Egypt into the Mediterranean. 나일 강.

nill [nil] *vi.* (P1) will not. 바라지 않다. [*ne, will*]

will he, nill he, whether he will or not. 싫든 좋든.

nim·bi [nímbai] *n.* pl. of **nimbus.**

nim·ble [nímbəl] *adj.* **1** quick and swift in movement. 재빠른. ¶ (*as*) ~ *as a goat* 아주 재빠른 / *He is* ~ *on his feet.* 걸음이 재다 / *She is* ~ *in her service.* 바지런하다. **2** quick in understanding; clever. 이해가 빠른; 영리한. ¶ *a* ~ *mind* 예민한 마음. [obs. *nim* take]

nim·bus [nímbəs] *n.* Ⓒ (*pl.* **-bus·es** or **-bi**) **1** a ring of light around the head of a saint or god in a picture; a halo. (성인·불상 등의) 원광(圓光); 후광. **2** a rain cloud. 비구름. [L. =cloud]

Nim·rod [nímrɔd] *n.* **1** 《Bible》 Noah's greatgrandson, known as a great hunter. 니므롯. **2** a devoted hunter. 사냥꾼; 수렵광(狂). [Person in Bible]

nin·com·poop [nínkəmpù:p] *n.* a foolish person. 멍텅구리; 바보. [L.]

⁝**nine** [nain] *n.* **1** Ⓤ the number between eight and ten; 9. 아홉; 9. **2** Ⓒ any group or set of nine persons or things, esp. a baseball team. 아홉 개〔사람〕 1 조(組); (특히) 야구팀.

dressed (***up***) ***to the nines,*** 《*colloq.*》 dressed very smartly and gorgeously. 성장(盛裝)하고; 차려 입고.

— *adj.* of 9. 아홉의; 9 의. ¶ *a* ~ *days' wonder* 남의 소문도 사흘 / ~ *times out of ten* 십중 팔구 / *A cat has* ~ *lives.* ⇨cat. [E.]

nine·fold [náinfòuld] *adj., adv.* **1** nine times as much or as many. 아홉 배의〔로〕. **2** having nine parts. 아홉 겹의〔으로〕.

nine·pins [náinpìnz] *n. pl.* 《used as *sing.*》 《Brit.》 a game played with nine bottle-shaped wooden pins and a ball. 구주희(九柱戱)(=《U.S.》 tenpins). ¶ *fall over like a lot of* ~ 골패짝 무너지듯 하다.

⁝**nine·teen** [náintí:n] *n.* Ⓤ the number between eighteen and twenty; 19. 열아홉; 19. — *adj.* of 19. 19 의.

⁝**nine·teenth** [náintí:nθ] *n.* **1** 《*the* ~》 number 19; 19 th. 제 19. **2** Ⓒ one of 19 equal parts of anything. 19 분의 1. — *adj.* of 19 th. 열아홉째의; 19 분의 1 의.

⁝**nine·ti·eth** [náintiiθ] *n.* **1** 《*the* ~》 number 90; 90 th. 제 90. **2** Ⓒ one of 90 equal parts of anything. 90 분의 1. — *adj.* of 90 th. 제 90 의; 90 분의 1 의.

⁝**nine·ty** [náinti] *n.* Ⓒ nine times of ten; 90. 구십; 90. — *adj.* of 90. 90의.

⁝**ninth** [nainθ] *n.* **1** 《*the* ~》 number 9: 9 th. 제 9. **2** Ⓒ one of 9 equal parts of anything. 9 분의 1. — *adj.* of 9 th. 제 9 의; 9 분의 1 의. [→nine]

Ni·o·be [náiou̯bi] *n.* **1** 《Gk. myth.》 a mother whose fourteen children were killed and herself was turned into a stone from which tears flow forever. 니오베. **2** Ⓒ a woman who weeps for her lost children. 자식을 잃고 비탄 속에 지내는 여인. [Gk.]

nip[1] [nip] *v.* (**nipped, nip·ping**) *vt.* (P6,7) **1** press or pinch (something) tight with the fingers; bite. …을 꼬집다; 물다. ¶ *A crab nipped my toe.* 게가 내 발가락을 물었다. **2** (of frost, wind, etc.) hurt; injure. (바람·서리가 싹 따위)를 해치다; 말리다; 얼게 하다. ¶ ~ *buds on a plant* 나무의 싹을 고사시키다. **3** cut off the end of (something) by biting. …을 따다; 잘라내다. ¶ ~ *off the buds of flowers* 꽃봉오리를 따다. **4** stop the growth of (something). …의 성장을 해치다. **5** 《*colloq.*》 catch suddenly and rudely. …을 잡아채다. — *vi.* (P1,2A) **1** pinch by the fingers; bite. 꼬집다; 따다. **2** (of wind) cause pain on the skin. (바람·추위 등이) 살을 에다. ¶ *The wind nips pretty hard today.* 오늘은 바람이 맵다. **3** 《Brit. *colloq.*》 move off quickly. 서두르다; 빠르게 움직이다. ¶ ~ *on a bus* 버스에 뛰어오르다.

nip along, go hurriedly. 서둘러 가다; 걸음을 재촉하다.

nip and tuck, 《U.S. *colloq.*》 even or close in a contest or race. 막상막하로; 호각(互角)으로.

nip in, **a**) enter hurriedly. 훌쩍 뛰어들다. **b**)

press oneself into (something) by force. …에 비집고 들어가다.

nip in the bud, stop (something) in the very beginning. …을 미연에 방지하다; 화근을 없애다.

— *n.* Ⓒ **1** a tight pinch ; a sudden bite. 꼬집기; 물기. **2** a sharp cold. (바람·추위의) 매서움. ¶ *a nasty ~ in the air* 살을 에는 듯한 냉기. [N.]

nip[2] [nip] *n.* Ⓒ a small amount of liquor. (술) 한잔. ¶ *take a ~ of whisky* 위스키를 한잔하다. — *vi., vt.* (P1; 6,7) drink a little (liquor). (술을) 홀짝거리다. [Du.]

nip·per [nípər] *n.* **1** a person who or that which nips, pinches, or bites. 집는 〔무는, 꼬집는〕 사람〔물건〕. **2** one of the big claws of a lobster or crab. (게 따위의) 집게발. **3** 《*pl.*》 pincers or any tool that nips. 뻰찌; 못뽑이; 족집게 (등). ¶ *a pair of nippers.* **4** 《Brit. *colloq.*》 a young boy. 소년; 아이. [*nip*[1]]

nip·ping [nípiŋ] *adj.* 《chiefly of wind, air, etc.》 very cold. (바람 등이) 살을 에는; 매서운. [*nip*[1]]

nip·ple [nípl] *n.* Ⓒ **1** the pointed part of a breast through which milk is given. 젖꼭지. **2** the rubber mouthpiece of a baby's milk bottle; a pacifier. 고무 젖꼭지. [E. *neble* a small projection]

nip·py [nípi] *adj.* (**-pi·er, -pi·est**) **1** 《Brit. *colloq.*》 quick in movement; swift. 빠른 동작; 민첩. ¶ *You'll have to be pretty ~ if you want to catch the train.* 기차를 타려거든 좀 빨리 움직여라. **2** biting cold. 매서운 추위. [*nip*[1]]

nir·va·na, Nir- [nəːrvάːnə, niər-, nərvǽnə] *n.* Ⓤ 《Buddhism》 a state of perfect happiness gained by devoting oneself to the supreme spirit. 니르바나; 열반. [Skr.]

ni·si [náisai] *adj.* 《law》 not yet final or absolute. 일정 기간 내에 이의를 신청하지 않으면 효력을 발생하는; 가(假)…. [L.]

nit [nit] *n.* the egg of a louse or other verminous insects. (이 따위 해충의) 알; 서캐. [E.]

ni·ter, 《Brit.》 **-tre** [náitər] *n.* Ⓤ 《chem.》 a white crystalline salt used in making gunpowder. 질산 칼륨; 초석(硝石). [Gk. *nitron* natron, native sodium carbonate]

ni·trate [náitreit, -trit] *n.* Ⓤ **1** compound of nitric acid with alkali, etc. 질산염. **2** potassium nitrate or sodium nitrate used as a fertilizer. 질산 칼륨; 질산나트륨. — *vt.* (P6) treat, combine, with nitric acid. …을 질산으로 처리하다. [→niter, -ate]

ni·tric [náitrik] *adj.* **1** 《*arch.*》 of niter. 질소의. **2** 《chem.》 of or containing nitrogen. 질소를 함유하는. [niter, -ic]

nitric acid [⌐-⌐] *n.* a corrosive and caustic liquid. 질산.

•**ni·tro·gen** [náitrədʒən] *n.* Ⓤ a gas without color and smell which forms four-fifths of the air. 질소. [→niter]

ni·trog·e·nous [naitrάdʒənəs / -trɔ́-] *adj.* of or having nitrogen. 질소의.

ni·tro·glyc·er·in, -glyc·er·ine [nàitrouglísərin] [-glísərin, -riːn] *n.* Ⓤ a thick, oily explosive used in dynamite. 니트로글리세린.

ni·trous [náitrəs] *adj.* of or containing nitrogen. 질소의〔를 함유하는〕(cf. *nitric*).

nitrous oxide [⌐-⌐-] *n.* laughing gas. 웃음 가스; 이산화 질소. [→niter, -ous]

nit·wit [nítwìt] *n.* a person with little intelligence. 바보; 멍청이. [*nit* none, →wit]

⁝**no** [nou] *adj.* **1** not a; not any. (사람·물건이) 없는; 한 사람〔하나, 조금〕도 없는(opp. a few). ¶ *There is ~ ink in the bottle.* 병에 잉크가 없다 / *He has ~ brother(s).* 그는 형제가 없다 / *No stars can be seen tonight.* 오늘 밤은 별 하나 안 보인다 / *I saw ~ children in the park.* 공원에서 아이들을 전혀 보지 못했다 / *No other boy could do it.* 다른 소년은 아무도 그렇게 못 했다. **2** not at all; far from being; quite other than. 결코 …않는〔아닌〕. ¶ *It was ~ small loss.* 결코 적은 손실이 아니었다 / *He is ~ scholar.* 그는 결코 학자는 아니다 / *It is ~ distance from here.* 여기서 얼마 안 되는 거리이다. **3** 《as a prohibition》 결코 …해서는 안 되는. ¶ *No smoking.* 흡연 금지 / *No credit.* 외상 사절 / *No admission.* 출입 금지 / *No talking in the class!* 교실에서 잡담 엄금.

There is no *doing.* It is impossible to do. …할 수 없다. ¶ *He is such a strange person; there is no knowing what he'll do next.* 그는 하도 이상한 사람이라서 다음엔 무슨 짓을 할지 모른다.

— *adv.* **1** 《expressing denial, refusal, disagreement》 not so. 아니; 아뇨. 語法 부정으로 묻든 긍정으로 묻든 물음과 상관 없이 대답의 내용이 부정이면 no, 긍정이면 yes를 씀. ¶ *Can't you swim? No(, I can't).* 헤엄 못치나 —그래(, 못 친다) / *Get out of the room.—No, I'll never go out.* 이 방에서 나가거라. —싫다, 절대로 안 나간다. **2** 《used with *comparative*》 not any. 조금도 …아니다〔않다〕. ¶ *He is ~ better than a beggar.* 그는 거지나 진배 없다 / *I could walk ~ further.* 더는 걸어갈 수 없었다. **3** 《used to emphasize a *negative*》 neither. ¶ *One man could not lift it, ~, not half a dozen.* 혼자서는 그걸 못 든다. 아니지, 여섯 사람도 못 들어. **4** 《*or ~*》 not. …든 아니든; …인지 어떤지. ¶ *Cold or ~, you must go today.* 춥든 안 춥든 오늘 가야 한다 / *Unpleasant or ~, it is true.* 불쾌하든 않든 사실이다.

no less than ⇨less.

no more ⇨more.

No sooner … than, as soon as…. …하자마자. ¶ *No sooner had he arrived than he fell ill.* 그는 오자마자 병이 났다.

whether or no, in either case. 어느 쪽이든;

어쨌든. ¶ *Whether or ~ it rains, I'm giving a party tomorrow.* 내일 비가 오든 안 오든 파티는 열겠다.
— *n.* (*pl.* **noes** or **nos**) **1** UC a word used to deny, refuse, or disagree. 부정〔거부〕의 말. ¶ *He said* 〔*answered*〕 *~.* 그는 아니라고 말〔대답〕했다 / *He will not take ~ for an answer.* 그는 싫다는 대답은 못 하게 할 것이다. **2** C 《usu. *pl.*》 a negative vote or voter. 반대 투표; 반대 투표자(opp. aye, yea). ¶ *The noes have it.* 반대 투표 다수《부결됐다》. **3** UC a denial; a refusal. 부정; 거부.

No. **1** north; northern. **2** number. [E.]

No·ah [nóuə] *n.* 《Bible》 the man who survived the Flood with his family and a pair of each animal by means of a big box-like ship. 노아. [*Noah*]

nob [nɑb / nɔb] *n.* C 《*colloq.*》 **1** a head. 머리; 대가리. **2** a person of wealth or high rank in society. 높은 양반; 고관; 부자; 거물. [Sc.]

nob·ble [nábəl / nɔ́bəl] *vt.* 《Brit. *sl.*》 (P6, 13) **1** drug (a horse) to prevent its winning a race. (경마에서) 이기지 못하게 (말)에 약물을 먹이다. **2** convince (someone) by fraudulent method. …을 속이다. [*hobble*]

nob·by [nábi / nɔ́bi] *adj.* (**-bi·er, -bi·est**) 《*sl.*》 very fine; smart. 아주 세련된; 말쑥한; 멋진. [*nob*]

No·bel [noubél], **Alfred Bernhard** *n.* (1833-96) a Swedish inventor of dynamite and the founder of the Nobel prizes. 노벨.

Nobel prizes [ㅅ-ㅅ-] *n.* the six prizes given every year by the Nobel Foundation to those who have done great work in physics, chemistry, literature, medicine, economics and the advancement of peace. 노벨상.

***no·bil·i·ty** [noubíləti] *n.* U **1** the state of being noble in character or mind. 고결〔숭고〕함. ¶ *show great ~ of soul* 영혼의 숭고함을 보여주다〔나타내다〕. **2** the high rank of a person. 고귀한 신분. ¶ *a man of ~* 고귀한 사람 / *the ~ of gold* 금의 지상성(至上性). **3** 《*the ~, collectively*》 people of high rank and noble birth; the whole body of noblemen. 귀족 계급; 귀족. 參考 영국에서 쓰이는 칭호는 duke, marquis, earl, viscount, baron. [↓]

:no·ble [nóubəl] *adj.* (opp. base[1]) **1** great and pure in mind or character. 고상한. ¶ *a man of ~ character* 고매한 인물 / *a ~ soul* 기품이 고상한 사람 / *a ~ poem* 기품 있는 시 / *a ~ deed* 숭고한 행위. **2** high in social rank or title by birth. 신분이〔지체가〕 높은. ¶ *a ~ family* 귀족 / *He is of ~ birth.* 그는 귀족 출신이다. **3** (of a monument, etc.) very splendid; grand. 웅대한; 장엄한. ¶ *a ~ cathedral* 장엄한 대성당 / *a ~ house* 으리으리한 집. **4** (of metal) precious. 귀중한. ¶ *~ metals* 귀금속.
— *n.* C a person of high rank by birth; a peer. 귀족. [L. *nosco* know]

no·ble-look·ing [nóubəllúkiŋ] *adj.* having a noble appearance. 풍채가 훌륭한.

no·ble·man [nóubəlmən] *n.* C (*pl.* **-men** [-mən]) a man of noble rank, title or birth. 귀족.

no·ble-mind·ed [nóubəlmáindid] *adj.* great and noble in mind; magnanimous. 마음이 고상한〔넓은〕.

no·ble-mind·ed·ness [nóubəlmáindidnis] *n.* U the state of being great and noble in mind. 고상〔고결〕함.

no·ble·ness [nóubəlnis] *n.* U the state of being noble. 고결.

no·blesse [noublés] *n.* U **1** noble birth. 귀족. **2** 《*collectively*》 the nobility. 귀족 계급. ¶ 《*prov.*》 *Noblesse oblige* [oublíːʒ]. 특권에는 의무가 따른다. [F.]

no·ble·wom·an [nóubəlwùmən] *n.* C (*pl.* **-wom·en** [-wìmin]) a woman of the nobility. 귀족 《여성형》. [*noble*]

no·bly [nóubli] *adv.* in a noble way; with a noble mind; like a noble. 고귀〔고상〕하게.

:no·bod·y [nóubàdi, -bədi / -bɔ̀di] *pron.* no one; no person. 아무도 …않다. ¶ *Nobody was present.* 아무도 출석하지 않았다 / *Nobody knows it.* 그건 아무도 모른다 / *Nobody ever did his work better.* 자기 일을 더 훌륭하게 한 사람은 일찍이 없었다.
Everybody's business is nobody's business. Responsibility cannot be shared. 책임은 분담이 안 된다; 공동 책임은 무책임.
nobody else, no other person. 그밖에 아무도 …않다. ¶ *Nobody else lives there now.* 거기에는 지금 아무도 다른 사람은 살고 있지 않다.
— *n.* C (*pl.* **-bod·ies**) 《often *sing.* without *an article*》 a man of no importance. 대단찮은 사람. ¶ *I felt ~ in the presence of him.* 나는 그의 면전에서 위축됐다 / *She has married a ~.* 그녀는 대단찮은 남자와 결혼했다. [*no, body*]

noc·tur·nal [nɑktə́ːrnl / nɔk-] *adj.* (opp. diurnal) **1** of the night; done or occurring in the night. 밤의; 밤에 행해지는〔일어나는〕. ¶ *a ~ journey* 야간 여행. **2** 《zool.》 active or busy at night. 밤에 활동하는. ¶ *~ habits* 야행성 / *~ birds* 야행성 조류 / *Bats are ~ animals.* 박쥐는 야행성 동물이다. **3** 《bot.》 open at night and close by day. (꽃이) 밤에 피는. ¶ *a ~ flower.* [L. *nox* night]

noc·tur·nal·ly [nɑktə́ːrnəli / nɔk-] *adv.* at night. 밤에.

noc·turne [náktəːrn / nɔ́k-] *n.* C **1** 《mus.》 a dreamy piece music fit for night. 야상곡(夜想曲). **2** 《paint.》 a painting of a night scene. 야경화(夜景畫). [→nocturnal]

:nod [nɑd / nɔd] *v.* (**nod·ded, nod·ding**) *vi.* (P1,2A,3,4) **1** bend the head forward slightly and quickly, as in agreement, greeting, etc. 고개를 끄덕이다; 끄덕하고 인사하다. ¶ ~ *to* (*at*) *someone in the street* 거리에서 아무에게 끄덕 인사하다. **2** allow the head to bend forward sometimes from sleepiness. 꾸벅꾸벅 졸다. ¶ *sit nodding in a chair* 의자에 앉아 꾸벅꾸벅 졸다. **3** become careless and dull; make a careless mistake. 방심하다; 실수하다. ¶ 《*prov.*》 *Even Homer sometimes nods.* 원숭이도 나무에서 떨어질 때가 있다 / *catch someone nodding* 아무의 방심을 틈타다. **4** swing or move quickly. (나무 따위가) 흔들리다. ¶ *Trees ~ in the wind.* 나무들이 바람에 흔들린다.

— *vt.* (P6,13) **1** bend (the head) forward slightly and quickly. (고개)를 끄덕이다. ¶ ~ *the head.* **2** express (agreement, etc.) by nodding. 끄덕이며 …을 나타내다. ¶ ~ *thanks* 끄덕이며 고맙다고 하다 / *He nodded a greeting to me.* 그는 고개를 끄덕여 내게 인사했다 / *He nodded his head in approval.* 그는 고개를 끄덕여 동의를 표시했다.

have a nodding acquaintance with, know (someone) slightly but not as a friend. (아무와) 인사 정도나 하는 사이다.

— *n.* Ⓒ an act of nodding the head. 끄덕임; 인사; 졸기. ¶ *answer with a ~* 끄덕여 대답하다 / 《Bible》 *the land of Nod* 수면; 졸음 / *He gave me a ~ when he came in.* 그는 들어오면서 끄덕 인사했다. [E.]

node [noud] *n.* Ⓒ **1** 《bot.》 the part of a stem from which leaves come out. 마디. **2** a knot; a round mass. 매듭; 혹; 옹이. **3** 《med.》 a hard swelling on a joint or muscle. 결절(結節). **4** 《phys.》 the point of rest of a vibrating body. 파절(波節). [L. =knot]

nod·ule [nádʒu:l / nɔ́-] *n.* Ⓒ **1** a small round mass, knot or swelling. 작은 마디 (혹). **2** 《bot.》 a small knot on a stem or root. 소결절(小結節); 뿌리혹. **3** a small rounded mass or lump. 작은 덩어리; 단괴(團塊); 노듈. ¶ *nodules of pure gold* 순금덩이. [↑]

no·el [nouél] *n.* **1** Ⓒ a Christmas carol. 크리스마스 축가. **2** 《*N*-》 Christmas. 크리스마스. [F.]

nog [nag / nɔg] *n.* **1** a wooden peg or pin. 나무못(마개). **2** a wooden brick-shaped block. 나무 벽돌. [E.]

no·how [nóuhàu] *adv.* 《*dial.*》 in no wise; by no means. 조금도(결코) …않다. [*no*]

:noise [nɔiz] *n.* ⓊⒸ **1** a confused and unpleasant sound. 소음. ¶ *far from the city ~* 도시의 소음에서 떠나 / *Don't make so much* (*such a loud*) *~.* 그렇게 시끄럽게 떠들지 마라. **2** a sound. 소리.

make a noise, make a sound; complain about something. 떠들다; 투덜거리다. ¶ *He made no ~ about it.* 그는 그 일에 대해 아무 말이 없었다.

make a noise in the world, become famous. 유명해지다.

— *vt.* (P7) 《*abroad*》 spread a rumor about (someone or something). …에 대한 소문을 내다(퍼뜨리다). ¶ *The rumor was noised abroad.* 그 소문은 자자했다. [F.]

It is noised abroad that.... The rumor says...; It is said that.... …라는 소문이 있다.

·noise·less [nɔ́izlis] *adj.* making no noise; quiet; silent. 소리 없는; 조용한. ¶ *a ~ typewriter* / *a ~ revolver* 소음(消音) 연발 권총.

noise·less·ly [nɔ́izlisli] *adv.* silently; quietly. 조용히.

noise·less·ness [nɔ́izlisnis] *n.* Ⓤ the state of being silent or quiet. 고요; 정적(靜寂).

nois·i·ly [nɔ́izili] *adv.* in a noisy manner. 시끄럽게.

nois·i·ness [nɔ́izinis] *n.* Ⓤ the state of being noisy. 시끄러움.

noi·some [nɔ́isəm] *adj.* harmful; unhealthy; disgusting. 해로운; 유해한; 역겨운; 싫은. ¶ *~ odors* 역겨운 냄새. [→annoy]

:nois·y [nɔ́izi] *adj.* (**nois·i·er, nois·i·est**) **1** making much noise. 떠드는; 소리를 많이 내는. ¶ *a ~ crowd* 떠드는 군중 / *a ~ engine* 소음이 많은 엔진. **2** full of confused and unpleasant sound. 시끄러운; 소란스러운; 시끌벅적한. ¶ *a ~ street* (*house*) 시끄러운 거리(집). **3** (of color, style, etc.) too bright. (색깔 등이) 야한; 현란한. [*noise*]

no·mad [nóumæd] *n.* Ⓒ **1** a member of a tribe that moves about from one place to another, such as the Arabs or gypsies. 유랑민(流浪民). **2** a wanderer. 방랑자. — *adj.* **1** moving about from place to place. 유랑하는. **2** wandering in search of pasture. 유목의. [Gk. *nemo* pasture]

no·mad·ic [noumǽdik] *adj.* =nomad.

no·men·cla·ture [nóumənklèitʃər, nouménklə-] *n.* Ⓒ **1** a system of names or words, esp. in the classification of the sciences. (각종 과학 분류학상의) 명명법(命名法). **2** the special words and phrases used to explain things in the various sciences; terminology. 학술 용어; 전문어. ¶ *the ~ of music* (*botany*) 음악(식물학) 용어. [L.]

nom·i·nal [námənl / nɔ́m-] *adj.* **1** not real; existing only in name. 이름뿐인; 유명무실한 (opp. real). ¶ *a ~ king* 이름뿐인 왕 / *The old man is only the ~ head of the business; his daughter makes all the decisions.* 노인은 그 사업의 이름만의 사장이고 모든 것은 딸이 결정한다. **2** of name. 이름의. ¶ *a ~ list* 명부. **3** very small in number, etc.; hardly worth counting. 극히 적은. ¶ *a bird of ~ species* 희귀조(稀貴鳥) / *Food is supplied at a ~ cost.* 음식(식량)은 극히 저렴한 값으로 공급되고 있다. **4** 《gram.》 of a noun; nounlike. 명사(용법)의. [L.]

nom·i·nal·ly [námənəli / nɔ́m-] *adv.* in name only; by name. 이름뿐으로; 명의상.

*__nom·i·nate__ [námənèit / nɔ́m-] *vt.* (P6,13, 19) **1** 《*for*》 name (someone) as a candidate for election, etc. (후보자로) …을 추천하다. ¶ *Three men were nominated for the office of chairman of the council.* 세 사람이 지방 의회의 의장 후보로 추천됐다. **2** appoint (someone) to an office. (관직에) …을 지명하다. ¶ *The governor nominated him to the secretaryship.* 지사는 그를 비서직에 임명했다. [→nominal]

*__nom·i·na·tion__ [nàmənéiʃən / nɔ̀m-] *n.* ⓊⒸ the act of nominating. 추천; 지명; 임명. ¶ ~ *for President* 대통령의 지명.

nom·i·na·tive [námənətiv / nɔ́m-] *adj.* **1** 《gram.》 showing the subject of a verb. 주격(主格)의. ¶ *the* ~ *case* 주격. **2** named or appointed for election or a position. 지명[추천]된. —*n.* Ⓒ 《gram.》 **1** a nominative case. 주격. **2** a word in this case. 주어(主語). [L.]

nom·i·nee [nàməníː / nɔ̀m-] *n.* Ⓒ a person who is nominated. 피(被)지명[추천]자.

non- [nan- / nɔn-] *pref.* 語法 명사·형용사·부사와 같이 쓰임. **1** no; not. '부(否)'의 뜻. ¶ *nonprofessional* 직업적이 아닌. **2** nothing; without. '무(無), 비(非)'의 뜻. ¶ *nonsense* 무의미; 난센스. **3** lacking; before. '결여'의 뜻. ¶ *nonage* 미성년. [L.]

nonce [nans / nɔns] *n.* 《*the* ~》 the present occasion; the one or particular occasion. 목하; 지금; 당분간. [M.E. *for then ones* for the once]

for the nonce, for the time being. 당분간. ¶ *This will do for the* ~. 이걸로 당분간은 괜찮다.

nonce word [⌐⌐] *n.* a word formed and used for a single occasion. (그 때만 쓰는) 임시로 만든 말; 임시어.

non·cha·lance [nánʃələns / nɔ́n-] *n.* Ⓤ the state of being nonchalant. 무관심; 냉담. [↓]

non·cha·lant [nánʃələnt / nɔ́n-] *adj.* **1** showing lack of interest; indifferent. 무관심한. **2** unexcited; without eagerness. 냉정[냉담]한. ¶ *with a* ~ *air* 냉정한 태도로. [non-, L. *caleo* be warm]

non·cha·lant·ly [nánʃələntli / nɔ́n-] *adv.* in a nonchalant manner. 무관심하게.

non·com·bat·ant [nankámbətənt / nɔnkɔ́m-] *n.* Ⓒ **1** a person in a war or an army who does not actually fight in battle, such as a surgeon or nurse. 비전투원. **2** a civilian. 민간인. —*adj.* of noncombatants. 비전투원의. [non-]

non·com·mis·sioned [nànkəmíʃənd / nɔ̀n-] *adj.* not yet appointed to the rank of second lieutenant. (장교에) 임명이 안 된. ¶ *a* ~ *officer* 하사관(abbr. N.C.O.). [↑]

non·com·mit·tal [nànkəmítl / nɔ̀n-] *adj.* giving no clear opinions or purposes. 언질을 주지 않는; 모호[애매]한. ¶ *a* ~ *reply* 모호한 대답. [non-]

non·con·duc·tor [nànkəndʌ́ktər / nɔ̀n-] *n.* Ⓒ 《phys.》 anything that does not let heat, electricity, etc. pass easily through. (열·전기 따위의) 절연체; 부도체(不導體). ¶ *Glass is a* ~ *of electricity.* 유리는 전기의 부도체다.

non·con·form·ist [nànkənfɔ́ːrmist / nɔ̀n-] *n.* Ⓒ **1** a person who does not agree with accepted church belief. (기존의) 교의(教義)에 따르지 않는 사람. **2** 《*N-*》 a Protestant who does not belong to the Church of England. (영국의) 비국교도. [→conform]

non·con·form·i·ty [nànkənfɔ́ːrməti / nɔ̀n-] *n.* Ⓤ **1** 《often *N-*》 refusal to act or believe according to the doctrines, rules, etc. of an established church. (기존의) 교의(教義)의 거부; 국교(國教) 반대. **2** 《often *N-*》 nonconformists as a group. 비(非)국교도들. **3** refusal to obey a rule. (기존의) 규범에 대한 불복종. **4** want of agreement between persons or things. 불일치; 부조화.

non·de·script [nàndiskrípt / nɔ̀n-] *adj.* hard to describe; not clear. 형언하기 어려운; 정체 모를. ¶ *a row of* ~ *humble houses* 한 줄로 늘어선 초라한 정체 모를 집들 / *eyes of a* ~ *shade, neither brown, blue, nor grey* 갈색도 청색도 그렇다고 회색도 아닌 형언키 어려운 색조의 눈. —*n.* Ⓒ a nondescript person or thing. 정체 모를 사람[것]. ¶ *What do you call that* ~*?* 저 사람[것] 말인데, 뭐라고 부르지. [→describe]

none [nʌn] *pron.* **1** 《used as *pl.* and *sing.*》 no one or ones. 아무(것)도 …않다[없다]. ¶ *There were* [*was*] ~ *present.* 출석한 사람은 아무도 없었다 / *None of them has* [*have*] *come.* 그들 중 어느 누구도 오지 않았다 / *None were* [*was*] *left when I came.* 내가 왔을 땐 아무 것도 남아 있지 않았다. **2** not any; nothing. 조금도 …않다[없다]. ¶ *He has much money, but I have* ~. 그에겐 돈이 많으나 내겐 한 푼도 없다 / *There is* ~ *of the water left.* 물이라고는 조금도 남아 있지 않다 / *None of the food was wasted.* 음식은 조금도 낭비되지 않았다 / *It is* ~ *of your business.* 그건 네 알 바 아니다.

none but, no one except. …외에는 아무도 ~ 않다. ¶ *None but fools have ever believed it.* 바보가 아닌 이상 아무도 그것을 믿지 않았다.

—*adv.* not at all; never. 결코[조금도] …않다. ¶ *The price is* ~ *too high.* 값은 절대로 비싸지 않다 / *I slept* ~ *last night.* 간밤에 한잠도 못 잤다 / *She is* ~ *so pretty.* 그녀는 조금도 예쁘지 않다. [E.=not one]

none the better [***worse***]***,*** just the same. 매한가지인. ¶ *He is* ~ *the better for the medicine.* 그는 약 때문에 특별히 나아진 것도 없다.

none the less, nevertheless. 그럼에도 불구하고.

non·en·ti·ty [nanéntəti / nɔn-] *n.* Ⓒ (*pl.*

-ties) **1** a person or thing of no importance. 하찮은 사람〔물건〕. ¶ *The famous singer's husband was a mere* ~. 그 유명한 가수의 남편은 그저 평범한 사람이었다. **2** a thing that does not exist; an imaginary thing. 존재〔실재〕하지 않는 것; 허구. [non-]

non·es·sen·tial [nànisénʃəl / nɔ̀n-] *adj.* not necessary; not very important. 꼭 필요하지 않은; 비본질적인. — *n.* Ⓒ a person or thing that is not essential. 없어도 괜찮은 사람〔것〕.

none·the·less [nʌ̀nðəlés] *adv.* however; nevertheless. 그럼에도 불구하고.

non·ex·ist·ence [nànegzístəns / nɔ̀n-] *n.* Ⓤ **1** the state of not existing. 존재하지 않음; 무(無). **2** a thing that does not exist. 존재하지 않는 것.

non·ex·ist·ent [nànigzístənt / nɔ̀n-] *adj.* not present; not living in the world. 존재하지 않는.

non·in·flam·ma·ble [nàninflǽməbəl / nɔ̀n-] *adj.* not easily set on fire; very hard to burn. 불연성(不燃性)의. [non-]

non·in·ter·fer·ence [nànintərfíərəns / nɔ̀n-] *n.* Ⓤ the act of not taking part in other countries' affairs. (외교상의) 불간섭.

non·in·ter·ven·tion [nànintərvénʃən / nɔ̀n-] *n.* Ⓤ a policy of a country holding back from interference in the affairs of other countries. 내정(內政) 불간섭.

non·me·tal·lic [nànmitǽlik / nɔ̀n-] *adj.* not metallic. 비금속의.

non·moral [nɑnmɔ́:rəl / nɔnmɔ́r-] *adj.* not concerned with morals; neither moral nor immoral. 도덕과 관계가 없는; 초(超)도덕적인.

non·par·ti·san, -zan [nɑnpɑ́:rtəzən / nɔn-] *adj.* not supporting any of the regular political parties. 무소속의. [non-]

non·pay·ment [nɑnpéimənt / nɔn-] *n.* Ⓤ neglect to pay; the condition of being unpaid. 미지급; 체납; 지급 거절〔불능〕.

non·plus [nɑnplʌ́s, ⌐– / nɔnplʌ́s, ⌐–] *vt.* (**-plused, -plus·ing** or 《Brit.》 **-plussed, -plus·sing**) (P6) cause (someone) to be completely puzzled or perplexed. …을 당황하게 하다. ¶ *I was nonplused as to how to settle the quarrel.* 어떻게 싸움을 말릴까 난감했다. — *n.* Ⓒ a state of being nonplused. 당혹; 당황; 난처. ¶ *be* 〔*stand*〕 *at a* ~ 난처해지다; 당황하다. [L. *non plus* not more]

put someone to a nonplus, perplex someone completely. …을 난처하게 하다; 궁지(窮地)로 몰다.

non·res·i·dent [nɑnrézədənt / nɔn-] *adj.* not living in a particular place; living away from one's place of work. 부재(不在)의; 임지(任地)에 거주하지 않는. — *n.* Ⓒ a nonresident person. 부재자; 임지에 거주하지 않는 사람. [non-]

non·re·sist·ant [nànrizístənt / nɔ̀n-] *adj.* making no resistance; not opposing. 무저항의. — *n.* Ⓒ a person who never opposes constituted authority or force. 무저항주의자.

·non·sense [nánsens / nɔ́nsəns] *n.* Ⓤ **1** foolish or meaningless words or actions. 바보 같은〔무의미한〕 말〔행동〕. ¶ *sheer* ~ 순 엉터리 / *talk* ~ 허튼 소리를 하다 / *The plan was all* ~. 그 계획은 정말 터무니 없었다. **2** acts or things of little worth. 허튼 짓; 하찮은 것. — *interj.* what you say, propose, is foolish. 바보 같은 소리, 그만둬. ¶ *Oh,* ~*!* 어이 없군. — *adj.* comic; seeming to have no meaning. 우스운; 무의미한. ¶ ~ *verses* 말같잖은 시. [non-]

non·sen·si·cal [nɑnsénsikəl / nɔn-] *adj.* foolish; full of nonsense. 무의미한; 터무니 없는. ●**non·sen·si·cal·ly** [-kəli] *adv.*

non·stop [nánstáp / nɔ́nstɔ́p] *adj., adv.* without a stop. 도중에 서지 않는〔않고〕; 직행의〔으로〕. ¶ *a* ~ *flight* 직행편 / *talk* ~ 쉴새 없이 지껄이다. — *n.* **1** a nonstop flight. 무착륙 비행. ¶ *make a* ~ *to London* 런던까지 무착륙 비행하다. **2** a nonstop train. 직행 열차.

non·suit [nànsú:t / nɔ̀n-] *n.* 《law》 a decision of a judge stopping a plaintiff's suit 소송 기각(訴訟棄却). — *vt.* (P6,13) stop (a plaintiff's suit). (소송)을 기각하다. ¶ *be nonsuited* 소송이 기각되다. [non-]

non·sup·port [nànsəpɔ́:rt / nɔ̀n-] *n.* lack of support; 《law》 failure or neglect to support someone for whom one is legally responsible. 원조〔지지〕하지 않음; 부양 의무 불이행.

non·un·ion [nɑnjú:njən / nɔn-] *adj.* **1** not belonging to a labor union. 노동 조합에 가입하지〔속하지〕 않은. **2** not recognizing a labor union. 노동 조합을 인정하지 않는.

noo·dle[1] [nú:dl] *n.* 《usu. *pl.*》 a food like macaroni used in soup, etc. 국수의 일종; 누들. [G. *nudel*]

noo·dle[2] [nú:dl] *n.* Ⓒ **1** 《*colloq.*》 a fool. 바보; 멍청이. **2** 《*sl.*》 the head. 머리; 대가리. [?]

nook [nuk] *n.* Ⓒ **1** an inside angle or corner. 구석. **2** a sheltered place. 쑥 들어간 곳. [N]

look in every nook and corner, look everywhere. 샅샅이 뒤지다; 구석구석 찾다.

:noon [nu:n] *n.* Ⓤ **1** twelve o'clock in the daytime; the middle of the day. 낮 12시; 정오. ¶ *at* ~ 정오에. **2** 《usu. *the* ~》 《*fig.*》 the highest point. 절정; 전성기. ¶ *at the* ~ *of life* 장년기에; 한창때에. **3** 《*poet.*》 midnight. 한밤중; 오밤중. [L. *nonus* ninth; orig. of 3 p.m.]

noon·day [nú:ndèi] *n.* Ⓤ noon. 정오; 한낮 (cf. *midday*). — *adj.* of noon. 정오의. ¶ *the* ~ *sun* 한낮의 태양.

noon·tide [nú:ntàid] *n.* =noon.

noose [nu:s] *n.* Ⓒ **1** a loop with a slip knot, which becomes tight when one

end is pulled. 올가미. **2** a trap; a bond; the marriage tie. 덫; 얽매는 것; (부부의) 유대. **3** 《*the* ~》 execution by hanging. 교수형.
put one's neck* 〔*head*〕 *into the noose, allow oneself to be caught in a dangerous position. 자승자박하다.
—*vt.* (P6) catch (something) with a noose; form a noose in or of (a rope, etc.). …을 올가미로 〈noose 1〉 잡다; …로 올가미를 만들다. [L. *nōdus* knot, node]

:nor [nɔːr, nər] *conj.* **1** 《preceded by *neither* or *not*》 and not; and not either. …도 또한 …않다. ¶ *It is neither hot ~ cold.* 춥지도 덥지도 않다 / *Neither she ~ I am happy* 〔*Neither I ~ she is happy*〕. 그녀나 나나 행복하지 않다 語法 동사는 가까운 주어와 일치함 / *She can neither read ~ write.* 그녀는 읽을 줄도 쓸 줄도 모른다 / *They had neither food ~ drink.* 그들에겐 먹을 것도 마실 것도 없었다 / *Not I, ~ anybody else, saw it.* 나도 그렇지만 누구도 그걸 못 봤다. **2** 《preceded by a *negative clause*》 and not. 또한 …않다. ¶ *I said that I had not bought it, ~ had I.* 그걸 사지 않았다고 말했고, 또 사실 사지 않았다 / *I don't know, ~ can I guess.* 알지도 못하거니와 짐작도 안 간다 / *His speech was long, ~ did they listen.* 그의 말은 길었고 듣는 사람도 없었다. **3** 《at the beginning of a sentence》 and not. …도 않다. ¶ *Nor will I deny the fact.* 나도 그 사실은 부인하지 않는다. **4** 《*arch.*》 =neither. ¶ *Nor silver ~ gold can buy it.* 은으로도 금으로도 그것은 못 산다. [E. = never whether]

Nor. Norway; North.

Nor·dic [nɔ́ːrdik] *adj.* of or belonging to the blond-races of northwestern Europe. 북유럽 사람의《특히 스칸디나비아의 금발의 인종》. —*n.* Ⓒ a member of the Nordic races. 북유럽인. [N.]

Nor·folk [nɔ́ːrfək] *n.* **1** a seaport in southeastern Virginia. 미국 Virginia 주의 항구 도시. **2** a county in eastern England. 영국 동부의 주.

norm [nɔːrm] *n.* Ⓒ **1** a standard, model or pattern for a group. 표준; 기준; 규범. ¶ *agree with the ~* 기준에 맞다. **2** a daily standard of output to be reached by a worker. 1일 책임 생산량; 노르마. ¶ *fulfill the ~* 책임량을 해내다. [L. *norma*]

:nor·mal [nɔ́ːrməl] *adj.* **1** of the ordinary standard; regular; natural; usual; not mad. 표준〔보통〕의; 정상적인(opp. abnormal). **2** 《geom.》 being at right angles. 수직의. —*n.* **1** Ⓤ anything normal; the ordinary state, condition, quantity, etc. 표준적인 것; 정상. ¶ *The rain raised the river two feet above ~.* 비로 인해 강물은 정상보다 2피트 불었다. **2** Ⓒ 《geom.》 a line that is at an angle of 90 degrees. 수직선; 법선(法線). [↑]

nor·mal·cy [nɔ́ːrməlsi] *n.* =normality.

nor·mal·i·ty [nɔːrmǽləti] *n.* Ⓤ the state of being normal. 정상 (상태).

nor·mal·ize [nɔ́ːrməlàiz] *vt.* (P6) **1** make (something) normal. 정상화하다. **2** bring (something) into agreement with a standard, pattern, rule, etc. …을 표준에 일치시키다. ● **nor·mal·i·za·tion** [nɔ̀ːrməlizéiʃən] *n.* **nor·mal·iz·er** [-ər] *n.*

nor·mal·ly [nɔ́ːrməli] *adv.* in a normal manner; ordinarily. 보통은; 정상적으로. ¶ *a ~ educated person* 정상적인 교육을 받은 사람 / *A child ~ begins to lose his first teeth at six years.* 아이는 보통 여섯 살이 되면 젖니가 빠지기 시작한다.

normal school [⌐-⌐] *n.* a school where high-school graduates are trained to become teachers. 사범 학교《교육 대학의 구칭》.

Nor·man [nɔ́ːrmən] *n.* **1** Ⓒ ⓐ a person of Normandy, in France. 노르망디 사람. ⓑ descendant of the mixed Scandinavian and Frankish race established there in the 10th century. 노르만 사람. **2** Ⓤ the language of the Normans. 노르만어. —*adj.* of Normandy or the Normans. 노르망디(사람)의; 노르만 사람〔언어〕의. ¶ *~ architecture* 노르만 건축. [=*Northman*]

Norman Conquest [⌐-⌐-] *n.* the conquest of England by the Normans in 1066. 노르만인의 영국 정복.

Nor·man·dy [nɔ́ːrməndi] *n.* a district on the English Channel in northern France. 노르망디《프랑스 북부의 영국 해협에 면한 지방》.

Norman French [⌐-⌐] *n.* French spoken by the Normans in England after the Conquest. 노르만 프랑스어.

Norse [nɔːrs] *adj.* of ancient Scandinavia, esp. of Norway, its people or their language. 고대 스칸디나비아(사람, 언어)의; 노르웨이(사람, 언어)의. —*n.* **1** 《*the N-*》 《used as *pl.*》 the people of ancient Scandinavia. 고대 스칸디나비아인(人). **2** Ⓤ the Norwegian language. 노르웨이어. [Du.=north]

Norse·man [nɔ́ːrsmən] *n.* Ⓒ (*pl.* **-men** [-mən]) a person of ancient Scandinavia or Norway; a Northman. 고대 스칸디나비아인; 노르웨이인.

:north [nɔːrθ] *n.* 《usu. *the ~*》 **1** one of the four main points of the compass, opposite to the south. 북; 북쪽; 북부. ¶ *in the ~ of* …의 북쪽에. **2** 《*N-*》 any part of the earth toward north; the northern part of the United States. 북반구; 북극 지방; 미국 북부의 여러 주. —*adj.* being in the north; coming from the north; toward the north. 북쪽에 있는; 북으로부터의; 북향의. ¶ *a ~ wind.* —*adv.*

to the north. 북(쪽)으로. ¶ *northbound traffic* 북상하는 차. [E.]

North Carolina [ˊ——ˊ—] *n.* a southeastern State of the United States, on the Atlantic coast. 노스캐롤라이나 주. 參考 N.C.로 생략함. 주도는 Raleigh.

North Da·ko·ta [nɔ́:rθdəkóutə] *n.* a north central State of the United States. 노스다코타. 參考 N.Dak. 로 생략함. 주도는 Bismarck.

:north·east [nɔ̀:rθí:st, 《naut.》 nɔ̀:rí:st] *adj.* **1** halfway between north and east. 북동의. **2** directed toward, facing or coming from the northeast. 북동에 면한; 북동으로부터의. — *n.* Ⓤ 《usu. *the* ～》 a northeast direction; a part or place that lies in this direction. 북동; 북동부 (지방). — *adv.* to or toward the northeast. 북동으로[에]. [*north*]

north·east·er [nɔ̀:rθí:stər, 《naut.》 nɔ:rí:st-] *n.* Ⓒ a strong wind or storm from the northeast. 북동풍.

north·east·er·ly [nɔ̀:rθí:stərli, 《naut.》 nɔ:rí:-] *adj.* moving toward or in the northeast; coming from the northeast. 북동의; 북동으로부터의. — *adv.* toward the northeast. 북동에[으로].

north·east·ern [nɔ̀:rθí:stərn, 《naut.》 nɔ:rí:-] *adj.* **1** of the northeast. 북동의. **2** at, in, from, or toward the northeast. 북동에 있는[으로부터의, 에의].

north·east·ward [nɔ̀:rθí:stwərd, 《naut.》 nɔ:rí:-] *adv., adj.* =northeasterly.

north·er [nɔ́:rðər] *n.* Ⓒ a cold, strong wind or storm from the north, esp. in Texas and on the Gulf of Mexico. 노더《가을·겨울에 Texas 나 Mexico 만 일대에 부는 강한 북풍》. [*north*]

north·er·ly [nɔ́:rðərli] *adj.* moving toward the north; coming from the north; of the north. 북으로의; 북으로부터의. ¶ *a ～ breeze* 북풍. — *adv.* toward or from the north. 북(쪽)으로; 북(쪽)으로부터. ¶ *The wind blew ～.* 바람은 북쪽에서 불어왔다.

:north·ern [nɔ́:rðərn] *adj.* **1** of the north. 북쪽의. **2** at, in, or toward the north; from the north. 북(쪽)에 있는[으로 향하는, 으로부터]. ¶ *the ～ hemisphere* 북반구 / *the ～ lights* 북극광. **3** 《*N-*》 《U.S.》 of or in the North of the United States. 북부 지방의. ¶ *～ customs* 북부 지방의 풍속·관습. — *n.* Ⓒ 《*N-*》 a person who lives in a northern area; a northerner. 북부 지방인.

north·ern·er [nɔ́:rðərnər] *n.* Ⓒ **1** a person living in the north. 북국인. **2** 《usu. *N-*》 《U.S.》 a person living in or coming from the northern part of the United States. 미국 북부의 사람[출신자](opp. southerner).

north·ern·most [nɔ́:rðərnmòust, -məst] *adj.* farthest north. 가장 북쪽의; 최북의.

north·land [nɔ́:rθlənd] *n.* Ⓒ the northern part of a country or an area; the land or region in the north. 북부 지방[지대]; 북방에 있는 나라; 북국(北國).

North·man [nɔ́:rθmən] *n.* Ⓒ (*pl.* **-men** [-mən]) **1** one of the ancient Scandinavians. 고대 스칸디나비아인. **2** a person or people of northern Europe. 북유럽 사람.

North Pole [ˊˊ] *n.* the nothern end of the earth's axis. 북극.

North Star [ˊˊ], **the** *n.* =polar star.

north·ward [nɔ́:rθwərd] *adv.* to or toward the north. 북쪽으로. ¶ *He walked ～.* — *adj.* moving to or toward the north. 북쪽으로의; 북향의. ¶ *take a ～ direction* 방향을 북쪽으로 잡다 / *The orchard is on the ～ slope of the hill.* 과수원은 언덕의 북쪽 비탈에 있다. — *n.* Ⓤ the north. 북방; 북부. ¶ *The river flows to the ～.* 강은 북쪽으로 흐르고 있다.

north·wards [nɔ́:rθwərdz] *adv.* =northward.

·north·west [nɔ̀:rθwést, 《naut.》 nɔ̀:rwést] *n.* 《usu. *the* ～》 the point or direction halfway between north and west; an area that lies in this direction. 북서(쪽, 지방). — *adj.* being in the northwest; moving toward the northwest; coming from the northwest. 북서의; 북서로의; 북서로부터의. — *adv.* to the northwest. 북서에(로).

north·west·er [nɔ̀:rθwéstər, 《naut.》 nɔ̀:rwést-] *n.* Ⓒ a strong wind or storm from the northwest. 북서풍.

north·west·er·ly [nɔ̀:rθwéstərli, 《naut.》 nɔ:rwést-] *adj.* moving toward or in the northwest; coming from the northwest. 북서의[로부터의]. — *adv.* toward the northwest. 북서로(에).

north·west·ern [nɔ̀:rθwéstərn, 《naut.》 nɔ̀:rwést-] *adj.* **1** of the northwest. 북서의. **2** at or in the northwestern; coming from the northwest; moving toward the northwest. 북서로부터의; 북서로의; 북서에.

·Nor·way [nɔ́:rwei] *n.* a country in northern Europe. 노르웨이.

Nor·we·gian [nɔ:rwí:dʒən] *adj.* of Norway, its people or their language. 노르웨이 사람[언어]의(cf. *Norse*). — *n.* Ⓒ **1** a person of Norway. 노르웨이 사람. **2** Ⓤ the language of Norway. 노르웨이어. [*Norway*]

Nos. numbers.

:nose [nouz] *n.* **1** Ⓒ an organ on the face with which people and animals smell. 코. ¶ *an aquiline ～* 매부리코 / *blow one's ～* (흔히, 눈물을 감추려고) 코를 풀다 / *hold one's ～* (구려서) 코를 싸쥐다[막다] / *pick one's ～* 코를 후비다. **2** Ⓒ anything like a nose in shape or position. (코 모양의) 돌출부. ¶ *a ～ of an airplane* 기수(機首). **3** 《usu. *a* ～》 the sense of smell. 후각. ¶ *have a good ～* 냄새를 잘 맡다. **4** the ability to find out or discover as if by the sense of smell. 깜새

등을 알아내는 능력; 직감력; 육감. ¶ *a good ~ for a mystery* 비밀에 대한 예민한 육감 / *have a good ~* (형사 등이) 육감이 예민하다; 눈치가 빠르다.
as plain as the nose in one's face, very clear; obvious. 명명백백하여.
bite* 〔*snap*〕 *someone's nose off, speak or answer sharply to someone. …에게 퉁명스럽게 대답하다; …을 쏘아붙이다.
by a nose, by a very narrow margin. 근소한 차로. ¶ *win a race* 〔*the election*〕 *by a ~* 경기〔선거〕에서 근소한 차로〔간신히〕 이기다.
cannot see beyond* 〔*the length of*〕 *one's nose. 《*fig.*》 have no imagination, foresight, etc. 상상력이 없다; 앞일을 내다보지 못하다.
count* 〔*tell*〕 *noses, count the number (esp. of votes). (찬성자 따위의) 인원수를 세다.
cut off one's nose to spite one's face, do harm to one's own cause or interests when angry with others. 홧김에 제게 손해될 짓을 하다.
follow one's nose, go straight ahead. 곧장 가다.
keep* 〔*have, hold, put*〕 *someone's nose to the grindstone ⇨grindstone.
lead someone by the nose, have complete control over. …을 마음대로 부리다.
nose to nose, face to face. 얼굴을 맞대고.
on the nose, precisely; exactly. 정확히; 딱 떨어지게.
pay through the nose, pay far too much. 터무니 없는 돈을 치르다.
put* 〔*poke*〕 *one's nose into, interfere with (something) esp. when it is not one's business. …에 쓸데 없이 간섭하다
put someone's nose out of joint, take someone's place in another's love or favor; upset or spoil someone's plan. …을 밀어내고 대신 차지하다; 남의 일을 잡쳐 놓다.
turn up one's nose at, treat (someone or something) with contempt; despise. …에 코방귀 뀌다; 멸시하다.
under someone's* (*very*) *nose, directly in front of someone; plainly visible. …의 코앞에서; 면전에서.
— *vt.* **1** (P7) discover (something) by smell; search for (something). …을 냄새 맡다; 낌새채다; 찾아내다. ¶ *The dog nosed out a rat.* 개는 쥐를 찾아냈다 / *He'll ~ out a scandal anywhere.* 그는 어디서건 추문을 들춰낸다. **2** (P6) press the nose against (something); touch (something) with the nose. 코를 비비다. ¶ *Horses ~ each other.* 말이 서로 코를 비빈다. **3** (P6,7,13) move cautiously forward. 조심스럽게 나아가다. — *vi.* (P2A,3) **1** smell at or about an object. 냄새 맡다; 냄새 맡고 다니다. ¶ *The dog kept nosing about the room.* 개는 킁킁거리며 방안을 돌아다녔다. **2** pry. 참견하다. ¶ *~ into another's affairs* 남의 일에 간섭하다. **3** push one's way carefully. 조심스럽게 전진하다. ¶ *The ship nosed carefully into the harbor.* 배는 조심스레 항구에 전진해 들어갔다. [E.]
***nose down* 〔*up*〕,** (of an airplane) turn down 〔up〕 the nose. (비행기가) 기수를 숙이다〔위로 하다〕.
nose one's way, (of a ship, etc.) move or push forward slowly. 전진하다; 나아가다. ¶ *The ship nosed her way through the winding channel.* 배는 조심스럽게 구불구불한 수로를 지나갔다.

nose bag [ㅡㅡ] *n.* a bag with food to be hung over a horse's head. (말 목에 거는) 꼴 주머니.

nose·bleed [nóuzblìːd] *n.* Ⓤ bleeding from the nose. 코피.

nose dive [ㅡㅡ] *n.* **1** a head-on dive of an airplane. 급강하. **2** any sudden and sharp drop. (주가·물가 등의) 폭락.

nose-dive [nóuzdàiv] *vi.* (P1) (of an airplane, etc.) make a nose dive. (비행기 따위가) 급강하하다; 폭락하다.

nose·gay [nóuzgèi] *n.* Ⓒ a beautifully-arranged bunch of sweet-smelling flowers. (향기 좋은) 꽃다발.

nose ring [ㅡㅡ] *n.* **1** a ring passed through the nose of an animal for leading it. (소 따위의) 코뚜레. **2** a ring worn in the nose as an ornament. 코걸이.

no side [ㅡㅡ] *n.* the call of time at Rugby football game. 타임 아웃.

nos·tal·gia [nɑstǽldʒiə / nɔs-] *n.* Ⓤ **1** homesickness. 향수〔회향〕(병). **2** a strong desire for something in the past. (과거에 대한) 그리움; 동경. [Gk. *nostos* return home, *algos* pain]

nos·tal·gic [nɑstǽldʒik / nɔs-] *adj.* of nostalgia. 향수에 잠기는; 과거를 그리는.

·nos·tril [nástril / nɔ́s-] *n.* Ⓒ one of the two outer openings in the nose. 콧구멍. [E. =nose-hole]
the breath of one's nostrils, something which one regards with delight. 사람이 즐기는〔좋아하는〕 것; 없어서는 안 될 것.

nos·trum [nástrəm / nɔ́s-] *n.* Ⓒ a medicine sold at a drugstore, etc., the effect of which is doubtful; a quack medicine. (약효가 의심스러운) 만능〔비방〕약; 가짜약. [L. =our thing]

nos·y, nos·ey [nóuzi] *adj.* (**nos·i·er, nos·i·est**) 《*colloq.*》 **1** inquisitive; eager to know other people's affairs. 캐묻길 잘하는; 남의 일에 덥적거리는. **2** having a large nose. 코가 큰. [*nose*]

Nosy Par·ker [nóuzi páːrkər] *n.* one who interferes with others' business. 남의 일에 중뿔나게 구는 사람.

:not [nɑt, nt, n / nɔt, nt, n] *adv.* 《used to make meaning *negative*》 …이 아니다; …않다. ¶ *I'm ~ a child.* 나는 어린애가 아니다 / *I can't stay.* 나는 기다릴 수가 없다 / *He will ~* 〔*won't*〕 *come.* 그는 오지 않을 게

다 / *It isn't true.* 그건 사실이 아니다 / *I haven't a watch* =《U.S.》 *I don't have a watch.* 내게는 시계가 없다 / *Won't you join the party?* 파티에 참석하지 않을래 / *Don't come nearer.* 가까이 오지 마라 / *He advised me ~ to go there.* 내게 거기 가지 말라고 충고했다 / *It's your fault (and) ~ mine.* 그건 내가 아니고 네 잘못이다 / *Not everybody can be a poet.* 누구나 시인이 되는 것은 아니다 / *It's mine, ~ yours.* 그건 내 것이지 네 것은 아니다 / *Not a cloud was seen in the sky.* 하늘엔 구름 한 점 없었다 / *I told her ~ to go.* 그녀에게 가지 말라고 했다 / *He is ~ my son, but my brother.* 그는 내 아들이 아니고 내 동생이다 / *Is he coming?—Perhaps ~.* 그가 올까 —아마 오지 않을 게다 / *~ a few* (수가) 적지 않이 / *Not knowing, I can't say.* 아는 바 없으니 할 말이 없다 / *If he asks I shall give, if ~, ~.* 달라면 줄 것이고, 달라지 않으면 주지 않겠다 / *Right or ~, it is a fact.* 옳건 그르건 그건 엄연한 사실이다 / *I know ~.* 나는 모른다 / *Say ~ so.* 그런 말 하는 게 아니다 / *He did wrong in ~ speaking.* 말을 안한 것이 잘못이었다 / *I insist that you ~ be late.* 내가 이르노니 늦지 않도록 해라 / *He hasn't any money.* =《U.S.》 *He does ~ have any money.* 그에겐 돈이 전혀 없다 / *He'll never pay, ~ he!* 그는 결코 갚지 않을 게다, 갚을 리가 없지. [E. =nought]

not a, not one. 하나의 …도 없다. ¶ *Not a dog would bark at him.* 개 한마리도 그에게 짖지 않는다.

not at all ⇨all.

not but what [《formal》 ***that***], nevertheless; although. 단…; 그러나; 하긴 …이기는 하지만. ¶ *I cannot do it; not but what a stronger man might.* 나는 못한다; 나보다 힘센 사람은 몰라도.

not half ⇨half (*adv.*).

not only [***merely, simply***] ***... but*** (***also***)***...,*** …뿐만 아니라 —도 (또한). ¶ *This book is ~ only interesting but (also) instructive.* 이 책은 재미있을 뿐 아니라 교훈적이다.

not that ..., (though) it is not suggested that... …이라는 것은 아니나.

nota bene [nóutə bíːni] note well; take notice. 주의하라. 參考 N.B.로 생략함. [L.=mark well]

no·ta·bil·i·ty [nòutəbíləti] *n.* (*pl.* **-ties**) **1** Ⓤ the state of being notable. 유명; 저명. **2** Ⓒ an important or distinguished person. 저명 인사. [→note]

•**no·ta·ble** [nóutəbəl] *adj.* worthy of notice; remarkable. 주목할 만한; 현저한; 두드러진. ¶ *a ~ increase of population* 현저한 인구증가 / *a ~ event* 주목할 사건 / *His deed was very ~.* 그의 공적은 가히 주목할 만했다. —*n.* Ⓒ a notable person. 저명 인사. ¶ *Many notables were present at the meeting.* 많은 저명 인사들이 그 회합에 나왔다. [→note]

no·ta·bly [nóutəbli] *adv.* in a notable way; remarkably; strikingly. 현저하게; 뚜렷이. ¶ *Sugar consumption was ~ higher.* 사탕 소비가 현저하게 증가했다.

no·ta·ry [nóutəri] *n.*Ⓒ (*pl.* **-ries**) a public official who makes certain the truthfulness of documents. 공증인. [→note]

no·ta·tion [noutéiʃən] *n.* ⒸⓊ **1** a set of signs, symbols or letters used to represent numbers, quantities, etc. 표기; 기호. **2** the act of recording by such symbols or signs. 표시〔기호〕법. ¶ *musical* 〔*chemical*〕 *~* 음악〔화학〕 기호법 / *the Roman ~* 로마 숫자법《Ⅰ, Ⅱ, Ⅲ, Ⅳ 따위》. **3** Ⓒ a brief written record. 기록. ¶ *He made a ~ on the margin of the paper.* 종이 여백에다 몇 자 적었다. [→note]

•**notch** [nɑtʃ/nɔtʃ] *n.* Ⓒ **1** a V-shaped cut in an edge or on a surface. (V자 꼴의) 새김눈. ¶ *The Indians cut notches on a stick to keep count of numbers.* 인디언들은 숫자를 기록하기 위해 막대기에 새김눈을 냈다. **2** a deep, narrow pass between mountains. 산골짜기. **3** 《*colloq.*》 a step; a grade; a degree. 단(段); 단계; 급(級). ¶ *top notch* 일급 / *He is a ~ above the others.* 그는 다른 사람들보다 한수 위다. —*vt.* (P6) make a notch on (something). …에 새김눈〔금〕을 내다. ¶ *~ wood with a knife* 나무에 금을 내다. [F. *hoche* (*an hoch* 〉 *a notch*)]

:**note** [nout] *n.* Ⓒ **1** ⓐ a memo; a memorandum. 메모; (간단한) 기록. ¶ *notes for a speech* 연설 원고 / *speak without a ~* 〔*from notes*〕 메모 없이〔메모를 보며〕 연설하다. ⓑ 《*pl.*》 a record of experience, etc. (경험 등의) 기록. ¶ *the notes of a journey* 여행기. **2** a comment; an explanation; a short remark concerning a word or passage in a book. 주석; 주(註). ¶ *a ~ on* 〔*to*〕 *the text* 본문에 단 주석 / *The notes make the book clearer.* 주석이 있어서 책이 이해하기 쉽다. **3** a short letter; a letter from one government to another. 짧은 편지; (외교상의) 통첩. ¶ *a ~ of invitation* 초대장 / *a diplomatic ~* 외교 문서 / *Drop me a ~ about your plan.* 네 계획에 대해 간단히 적어 보내라. **4** paper money; a bank note; a check. 지폐; 어음; 수표. ¶ *a ~ of hand* 약속 어음. **5** Ⓤ greatness; fame; importance. 저명; 명성; 중요성. ¶ *a person of ~* 저명 인사. **6** Ⓤ notice; attention. 주의; 주목; 중요성. ¶ *be worthy of ~* 주목할 만하다. **7** any sign or mark. 표; 기호; 부호. ¶ *a ~ of exclamation* 느낌표(!) / *a ~ of interrogation* 물음표(?). **8** 《mus.》 a musical sound or tone; a sign to show the pitch and length of a sound; a key of a piano, etc. 음표; (피아노 따위의) 건; 키(key). ¶ *a whole ~* 온음표(𝅝) / *a half ~* 2분음표(𝅗𝅥) / *strike the notes* 건반을 두드리다 / *the funeral ~ of a bell* 장송(葬送)을 알리는 종

소리. **9** the way of speaking. 어조(語調). ¶ *change one's* ~ 어조를 바꾸다. **10** 《*fig.*》 a characteristic; a distinguishing quality. 특색; 특징. ¶ *There was a* ~ *of pessimism in his writing.* 그의 글에는 염세적인 데가 있었다.

compare notes, exchange ideas or opinion. 의견을 교환하다.

make* 〔*take*〕 *a note* 〔*notes*〕 *of, write down (things) to be remembered. …을 메모하다; 적어두다.

strike* 〔*sound*〕 *a false note, (of an act, speech, etc.) be not suitable to the conditions, etc. 당치 않은〔어림없는〕 행동〔말〕을 하다.

strike a note, convey a certain impression, feeling, etc. (어떤 인상·느낌 등을) 전하다; 나타내다.

strike the right note, 《*fig.*》 say, write, or do what is suitable or pleasing. 적절한 말을 하다〔글을 쓰다, 처신을 하다〕.

take note of, take notice of; give attention to. …에 주목하다; 관심을 가지다.

— *vt.* **1** (P6,7) make a note of (something). …을 적어두다; 메모하다. **2** give attention to (something); notice; observe. …을 주의〔주목〕하다. [L. *nota* a mark]

note down, write down (something) as a memo. …을 메모하다. ¶ *I noted down every word he said.* 나는 그가 말한 것은 모두 적어두었다.

:note·book [nóutbùk] *n.* Ⓒ a book for taking notes or opinions. 노트; 공책; 수첩.

***not·ed** [nóutid] *adj.* well-known; distinguished; famous. 유명〔저명〕한; 이름있는. ¶ *a* ~ *poet* 저명한 시인 / *He was* ~ *for his bravery.* 그는 용감해서 유명했다.

note·paper [nóutpèipər] *n.* Ⓤ paper for writing letters; writing paper. 편지지; 메모용지.

note-tak·ing [nóuttèikiŋ] *n.* Ⓤ the act of taking notes. 노트하기; 적기.

note·wor·thy [nóutwə̀ːrði] *adj.* worthy of note; remarkable. 주목할 만한. ¶ *make a* ~ *contribution to the state* 나라에 주목할 만한 공헌을 하다.

:noth·ing [nʌ́θiŋ] *pron.* not anything. 아무것도 없다; 아무 것〔일〕도 …않다〔아니다〕. 語法 형용사는 뒤에 옴. ¶ *There is* ~ *new in his story.* 그의 이야기에는 새로운 것이 아무 것도 없다 / *There's* ~ *like home.* 내 집보다 좋은 데는 없다 / *Nothing could be more strange.* 신기하기 짝이 없다 / *I can give you* ~ *but this.* 네게 줄 건 이것뿐이구나 / *Nothing great is easy.* 큰 일치고 쉬운 것은 없다 / *Nothing venture,* ~ *have* 〔*win*〕. 범의 굴에 들어가야 범을 잡는다.

— *n.* **1** Ⓤ a thing that does not exist; zero. 무(無); 공; 《math.》 영; 제로. ¶ *Now that he is dead, he is* ~. 그는 죽었으니 이제 그는 없다 / *He is six feet* ~. 정확히 6 피트다 / *Multiply 6 by* ~, *and the result is* ~. 6에 0을 곱하면 0이 된다 / *Twice* ~ *is* ~. 0의 두 배는 0이다 / *Of* ~, *comes* ~. 무(無)에서 유(有)는 생기지 않는다. **2** Ⓒ 《sometimes *pl.* or *a* ~》 a thing, event or person that is not important; trifling conversation. 하찮은 물건〔일, 사람〕; 쓸데없는 대화. ¶ *the little nothings of life* 이 세상의 사소한 일들 / *He is* ~ *without his money.* 돈이 없다면 그는 하찮은 사람이다 / *His wife is a* ~. 그의 아내는 아무 짝에도 못 쓴다 / *soft* 〔*sweet*〕 *nothings* 연인들끼리의 그렇고 그런 얘기.

all to nothing, supremely; completely. 더할 나위 없이; 충분히.

come to nothing, fail; turn out useless. 실패하다; 헛일이 되다.

for nothing, **a**) without payment; free. 무료로; 거저. ¶ *I got* 〔*did*〕 *it for* ~. 공짜로 얻었다〔무보수로 했다〕. **b**) in vain; uselessly. 헛되이; 쓸데 없이. ¶ *He has not traveled the world for* ~. 그는 쓸데 없이 세계를 돌아다니지는 않았다《소득이 있었다》. **c**) without reason. 까닭 없이. ¶ *They quarreled for* ~. 그들은 이유도 없이 싸웠다.

have nothing to do with, have no connection with something; avoid dealing with something. …와 상관이 없다; …와 접촉을 피하다. ¶ *It has* ~ *to do with me.* 그건 나와 상관 없다 / *You had better have* ~ *to do with him.* 그 사람과는 멀리 하는 게 좋다.

make nothing of, **a**) treat or regard (something) as unimportant. …을 우습게 여기다〔보다〕. ¶ *make* ~ *of one's illness* 자기 병을 대수롭지 않게 여기다. **b**) 《preceded by *can*》 can not understand (a question, etc.). …을 이해하지 못하다. ¶ *I can make* ~ *of what he says.* 그가 무슨 말을 하는지 모르겠다. **c**) 《preceded by *can*》 fail to use (one's talents, etc.); fail to do (a job, etc.). …을 이용하지 못하다; 해내지 못하다. ¶ *He could make* ~ *of his talents.* 그는 자기 재능을 발휘할 수 없었다.

next to nothing, almost nothing; very little. 없는 거나 진배없는.

nothing but, only; merely. 다만 …뿐; …에 불과한. ¶ *It's nothing but a joke.* 그저 농담일 뿐이다.

Nothing doing! 《*colloq.*》 an expression of failure or disappointment; an expression indicating a refusal of a request. 틀렸다; 젠장; 싫다; 거절한다.

***nothing else* 〔*other*〕 *than* 〔*but*〕** =nothing but.

nothing if not, very; excessively; above all else. 대단히; 더없이; 무엇보다도 …. ¶ *She's* ~ *if not polite.* 공손하기 이를데 없는 여인이다.

There is nothing for it but to do. We can only do. …하는 수 밖에 없다; 다른 도리가 없다. ¶ *There was* ~ *for it but to obey.* 복종할 수 밖에 없었다.

There is nothing in it. It is not true or important. It is easy. 그건 거짓말이다〔아무것도 아니다〕; 쉬운 일이다.
think nothing of, consider or treat (someone or something) as unimportant. …을 우습게 보다; 멸시하다.
to say nothing (=*not to speak*) ***of*** *something.* …은 말할 것도 없고.
— *adv.* not at all; in no manner or degree. 조금도 …이 아니다. ¶ *It helps me* ~. 내겐 아무 도움도 안 된다 / *He cares* ~ *how he looked.* 그는 외관에는 조금도 신경을 안 쓴다 / *She is* ~ *wiser than before.* 그녀의 분별없기는 예나 마찬가지다 / *This poem is* ~ *like so good as that one.* 이 시는 저 시보다 훨씬 못하다. [M.E. =*no thing*]
nothing less than =***nothing short of,*** just the same as. …나 다름 없는. ¶ *It is* ~ *less than madness.* 미친짓이나 다름 없다.

noth·ing·ness [nʌ́θiŋnis] *n.* UC **1** the state of being nothing; non-existence. 무; 없음; 공(空). **2** the state of no value. 무가치(한 것). **3** unconsciousness. 인사 불성.

:no·tice [nóutis] **1** U attention; heed. 주의. ¶ *attract* ~ 주의를 끌다; 눈에 띄다 / *escape one's* ~ 눈에 띄지 않다 / *not worth* 〔*beneath*〕 *one's* ~ 보잘것 없는; 고려할 가치가 없는 / *A sudden sound caught our* ~. 갑작스런 소리가 우리의 주의를 끌었다. **2** CU an announcement; an information. 통지(서); 정보. ¶ *issue a* ~ 통지를 내다 / *till further* ~ 추후 통지 있을 때까지 / *I must have* ~ *of that question.* 그 문제에 대해서는 통지해 주길 바란다. **3** U warning; caution beforehand; a formal statement, esp. of one's intention to end an agreement, relation, or contract at a given time. 경고; 예고; (해약·해직 따위의) 통고. ¶ *at a moment's* ~ 당장에; 즉석에 / *give a month's* ~ 한 달 후에 해약할 것을 통고하다 / *without* ~ 예고 없이; 무단으로 / *at short* ~ (기간의) 충분한 예고 없이 / *give a servant* ~ 하인에게 해고를 통고하다. **4** C a short article that gives some news; a review of a book or play. (신문 등의) 짧은 기사; 공고; 서평(書評). ¶ *The play got a favorable* ~. 그 극은 호평을 받았다 / *There is a* ~ *in the paper describing Mary's birthday party.* 신문에 메리의 생일기념 파티가 있다는 기사가 실렸다. **5** C a paper fixed up in a public place giving information, direction, etc. 게시(揭示). ¶ *put up* 〔*post*〕 *a* ~ *on the door of the church* 교회 문에 게시를 붙이다.
bring to someone's notice, make someone notice. …의 주의를 끌게 하다; 눈에 띄게 하다.
come into notice, attract attention. 주의를 끌다.
give notice, warn; inform; tell. …을 알리다; 통고하다. ¶ *The driver sounded his horn to give* ~ *that he was going to turn the corner.* 운전자는 모퉁이를 돈다는 것을 알리기 위해 경적을 울렸다.
have notice (=*be told*) ***of*** *something.* …의 통지를 받다.
serve notice, give warning; inform. 경고하다; 예고하다; 알리다.
take notice, become aware; give attention; observe. 알게 되다; 주의〔주목〕하다. ¶ *Take* ~ *that everything is ready.* 만반의 준비를 갖추도록 해라 / *The baby is beginning to take* ~. 어린애가 지각이 들기 시작했다.
take notice of, pay attention to; show interest in; treat with particular consideration. …을 주목하다; 후대하다. ¶ *He took no* ~ *of what I said.* 그는 내 말을 무시했다.
— *vt.* **1** (P6,10,11,12,22,23) become aware of (something); find. …을 알아채다; 알게 되다. ¶ *I noticed my purse was missing.* 내 지갑이 없어진 것을 알았다 / *Then I noticed that he was very tired.* 나는 그때 그가 몹시 지친 것을 알았다 / *Did you* ~ *anyone come in?* 누가 들어 오는 것을 알았느냐. **2** observe; take notice of; pay attention to (something). …에 주의〔주목〕하다; 관심을 가지다. ¶ *The baby notices everything now.* 아기는 이제 무엇에나 관심을 갖는다. **3** speak or write about (something). …에 언급하다. ¶ ~ *a book in a newspaper* 신문에 책을 소개하다. **4** give notice to. …에 통고〔예고〕하다. **5** give a sign of recognizing. 알은 체하다. ¶ *She was too shy to* ~ *him.* 너무 수줍어 그에게 알은 체도 못했다. [L. *nosco* know]

no·tice·a·ble [nóutisəbəl] *adj.* **1** easily observed or noticed; conspicuous. 쉽게 눈에 띄는; 두드러진. ¶ *The torn place wasn't* ~. 찢어진 데는 눈에 띄지 않았다. **2** worthy of attention. 주목할 만한; 중요한.

no·tice·a·bly [nóutisəbəli] *adv.* to a noticeable degree; remarkably. 두드러지게.

notice board [´-`] *n.* 《esp. Brit.》 a board on which notices are shown. 게시판.

no·ti·fi·ca·tion [nòutəfikéiʃən] *n.* **1** U the act of making something known. 통지; 고시. **2** C a notice. 통지서; 공고문. ¶ *a* ~ *of the meeting* 집회 통지서. [↓]

:no·ti·fy [nóutəfài] *vt.* (**-fied**) **1** (P6,13,15) 《*of*》 make (something) known. …을 통지하다; 알리다. ¶ ~ *the post office of one's change of address* 우체국에 달라진 주소를 알려주다. **2** (P6,13) 《*to*》 report; announce. …을 발표하다. [→notice]

:no·tion [nóuʃən] *n.* C **1** a general idea. 개념; 관념. ¶ *I've no* ~ *of the new word.* 그 신어의 뜻을 모르겠다 / *Everyone has a* ~ *of what thirst means.* 갈증이 어떤 것인지는 누구나 안다. **2** an opinion; a belief. 의견; 견해. ¶ *Such is the common* ~. 그게 일반적인 견해다. **3** a natural tendency toward some course of action; an intention. 의향; 생각. ¶ *I got a sudden* ~ *to go out to the country.* 갑자기 시골에 가고 싶어졌다 / *I have no* ~ *of going there.* 거긴 가고 싶

지 않다. **4** 《*pl.*》《U.S.》 small, useful articles, such as pins, needles and thread. 방물; 자질구레한 실용품. [→notice]

no·tion·al [nóuʃənəl] *adj.* **1** of a notion. 개념상의. **2** abstract. 추상적인. **3** imaginary; fanciful. 공상적인.

no·to·ri·e·ty [nòutəráiəti] *n.* (*pl.* **-ties**) **1** Ⓤ the state of being widely known for something bad. (나쁜 뜻의) 평판. **2** Ⓒ a person having ill fame. 악명 높은 사람. [↓]

no·to·ri·ous [noutɔ́:riəs] *adj.* widely known in a bad sense. (나쁜 뜻으로) 소문난. ¶ *a ~ liar* 소문난 거짓말쟁이 / *This district is ~ for smog.* 이 지역은 스모그로 유명하다 / *a ship ~ for ill luck* 악운(惡運)으로 인해 유명한 배. [L. *nōtori-us* well known]

No·tre Dame [nòutrə dɑ́:m] *n.* **1** Our Lady; the Virgin Mary, mother of Jesus. 성모 마리아. **2** a famous cathedral in Paris. 노트르담 성당.

*__not·with·stand·ing__ [nɑ̀twiðstǽndiŋ, -wiθ- / nɔ̀t-] *prep.* in spite of. …에도 불구하고. ¶ *He failed ~ my advice.* 내가 조언을 했는데도 실패했다 / *Notwithstanding his naughtiness, I love my little boy.* 장난이 심하지만 내 어린 놈이 귀엽다. — *conj.* 《*arch.*》 in spite of the fact that…; although. …이라 해도; …함에도. ¶ *He went ~ (that) he was ordered not to.* 못 가게 했는데도 그는 갔다. — *adv.* however; nevertheless. …일지라도. ¶ *Whatever you may say, I will go, ~.* 네가 뭐라 하건 나는 간다. [*not, withstand*]

nou·gat [nú:gət, nú:gɑ:] *n.* Ⓒ a sweet candy made of sugar, nuts, etc. 누가 캔디. [F.]

nought [nɔ:t] *n., adv.* =naught.

*__noun__ [naun] *n.* Ⓒ 《gram.》 a word used as the name of a person, place, condition, etc. 명사. ¶ *an abstract ~* 추상 명사 / *a collective ~* 집합 명사. — *adj.* used as a noun. 명사 (용법)의. ¶ *a ~ clause* 〔*phrase*〕 명사절〔구〕. [→nominal]

*__nour·ish__ [nə́:riʃ, nʌ́r-] *vt.* (P6) **1** give food to (an animal, etc.) to make it grow. (동물 등)을 기르다. ¶ *~ a baby with milk* 아기를 우유로 키우다 / 《*fig.*》 *Good books ~ people's mind.* 좋은 책은 사람의 마음을 살찌운다. **2** have (a hope, an ill feeling, etc.) in mind. (희망·원한 등)을 품다. ¶ *~ a hope* 희망을 품다 / *It has nourished the dream in us.* 그것은 우리들에게 꿈을 가지게 했다. [L. *nutrio*]

nour·ish·ment [nə́:riʃmənt, nʌ́r-] *n.* Ⓤ **1** food; something which helps to improve quality or help growth. 음식; 영양 있는 것; 자양물. ¶ *intellectual ~* 지적(知的) 양식. **2** the act of nourishing; the state of being nourished. 양육; 영양 상태. ¶ *devote oneself to the ~ of education* 교육의 육성에 헌신하다.

nou·veau riche [nú:vou rí:ʃ] *n.* (*pl.* **nou·veaux riches** [nú:vou rí:ʃ]) a person who has lately become rich and does not behave well. 벼락 부자; 졸부. [F. = new rich]

Nov. November.

*__nov·el__[1] [nɑ́vəl / nɔ́v-] *adj.* **1** new; recent. 새로운. **2** strange; unusual. 이상〔신기〕한. ¶ *In 1920, flying was still a ~ method of travel.* 1920년대에, 날아다닌다는 것은 아직 신기한 여행 방법의 하나였다. [L. *novus* new]

:**nov·el**[2] [nɑ́vəl / nɔ́v-] *n.* Ⓒ a long story presenting imaginary characters and events as if they were real. 소설. [↑]

nov·el·ette [nɑ̀vəlét / nɔ̀v-] *n.* Ⓒ a short novel. 단편 소설.

nov·el·ist [nɑ́vəlist / nɔ́v-] *n.* Ⓒ a person who writes novels. 소설가.

*__nov·el·ty__ [nɑ́vəlti / nɔ́v-] *n.* (*pl.* **-ties**) **1** Ⓤ the state of being strange; newness; unusualness. 신기함; 진귀함. ¶ *The new game was fun at first, but the ~ soon wore off.* 새 놀이는 처음에는 재미있었다. 그러나 곧 시들해졌다. **2** Ⓒ something new or unusual. 이상〔신기〕한 것. **3** 《chiefly *pl.*》 small, cheap, but cleverly-made articles such as toys and paper hats. (장난감 따위) 색다른 고안물. [→novel[1]]

:**No·vem·ber** [nouvémbər] *n.* the eleventh month of the year. 11월. 參考 Nov.로 생략함. [L. *novem* nine]

nov·ice [nɑ́vis / nɔ́v-] *n.* Ⓒ **1** an inexperienced person; a beginner. 초심자(cf. *tiro*). **2** a person who begins a life given to God; a person who is to become a monk or a nun. 수련 수사(修士)〔수녀〕. [→novel[1]]

no·vi·ti·ate, no·vi·ci·ate [nouvíʃiit, -èit] *n.* ⒸⓊ the state or the period of being a novice. 초심자임; (수사·수녀의) 수련 기간. [↑]

:**now** [nau] *adv.* **1** at the present time; at this moment. 지금; 이제(opp. then). ¶ *Where is your mother ~?* 지금 어머니는 어디 계시지 / *Tom must be a man ~.* 톰은 이제 어른이 되었을 게다 / *I thought so once, but ~ I know better.* 한때는 그렇게 알았으나 지금은 잘 알게 됐다. **2** at once. 곧; 당장. ¶ *Do it ~.* 지금 곧 해라. **3** under these conditions. 지금(의) 사정으로는. ¶ *I would do anything ~.* 이리 된 마당에 못 할 것이 없다 / *Now what can we do?* 이제 우리는 어쩐다지. **4** since; because. …이므로. ¶ *Let's go for a walk, ~ the rain has stopped.* 산책하러 가자, 비도 그쳤으니. **5** (in a story) and then; after this; next; by that time. 그리고는; 그 때(는 이미). ¶ *Caesar was ~ crossing the river.* 시저는 그때 강을 건너고 있었다. **6** 《used to begin or emphasize a sentence》 그런데; 자. ¶ *Now what do you mean?* 그런데 그게 무슨 말이지 / *Now listen to me.* 자, 내 말 들어봐 / *Now let's go.* 자, 가자.

(*every*) *now and then* 〔*again*〕, sometimes; from time to time. 때때로; 가끔. ¶ *I saw him* (*every*) ~ *and again.* 나는 가끔 그를 만난다.

just now, only a few moments ago. 지금 막.

now ... now 〔***then***〕 ***...,*** sometimes ..., and sometimes .... 때로는 …, 또 어떤 때는…. ¶ *The weather was ~ hot, ~ cold.* 날씨는 더웠다가, 또 때론 추웠다가 했다.

now now, 《expressing a mild warning》 now then. 자 자; 이봐 이봐. ¶ *Now ~, stop quarreling!* 자 자, 그만 싸워라.

now or never, at this moment or not at all. 때는 지금이다; 지금이 절호의 기회다.

— *conj.* 《often followed by that》 as a result of the fact; since. …이니까; …한 이상은. ¶ *Now* (*that*) *you are grown up, you must work harder.* 다 컸으니 더 열심히 일해라 / *Now* (*that*) *you mention it, I do remember.* 네가 그 말을 하니까 생각이 난다.

— *n.* Ⓤ the present; this time. 지금; 현재. ¶ *by ~* 지금쯤은 / *for ~* 지금으로서는 / *from ~ on* 금후; 앞으로는 / *until* 〔*up to*〕 *~* 지금까지(로는) / *Now is the time.* 지금이 때다〔기회다〕. [E.]

***now·a·days** [náuədèiz] *adv.* at the present time; in these days. 지금은; 오늘날에는. — *n.* Ⓤ the present time. 지금; 현재. [E.]

no·way [nóuwèi] *adv.* =noways.

no·ways [nóuwèiz] *adv.* not at all; by no means. 결코 …아니다〔않다〕. [*no*]

:**no·where** [nóuhwɛ̀ər] *adv.* not anywhere; not in, at, to, or from any place. 어디에도 …없다. ¶ *My pen is ~ to be found.* 펜이 간 곳이 없다 / *The book is ~ to be had.* 그 책은 어디서고 파는〔구할〕 데가 없다. [*no*]

be 〔***come in***〕 ***nowhere,*** (in a contest) fail completely to win. (경기에서) 참패하다.

nowhere near, far from. (…와는) 거리가 먼; 아주 …이 아닌. ¶ *It is ~ near finished.* 끝내려면 멀었다.

no·wise [nóuwàiz] *adv.* not at all. 결코 … 않다〔아니다〕. [*no*]

nox·ious [nákʃəs / nɔ́k-] *adj.* poisonous; harmful. 유독한; 해로운. ¶ *~ weeds* 독초 / *a ~ T.V. program* 불건전한 TV 프로. ● **nox·ious·ly** [-li] *adv.* [L. *noxa* harm]

noz·zle [názəl / nɔ́zəl] *n.* the pointed end of a pipe used to direct a stream of water. (파이프의) 뾰족한 끝; 노즐. [→nose]

N.T. New Testament.

nu·ance [njúːɑːns, –⌐] *n.* Ⓒ a delicate difference in tone, color, feeling, expression, meaning, etc. (색·소리·뜻 따위의) 미묘한 차이; 뉘앙스. [F.]

nu·cle·ar [njúːkliər] *adj.* of a nucleus. (세포·원자)핵의. ¶ *a ~ bomb* 핵폭탄 / *~ energy* 원자력; 핵 에너지 / *~ physics* 핵물리학 / *~ fission* 핵분열 / *~ fusion* 핵융합. [L. *nux* nut]

nu·cle·i [njúːkliài] *n.* pl. of **nucleus.**

nu·cle·us [njúːkliəs] *n.* Ⓒ (*pl.* **-cle·i** or **-us·es**) **1** a central part around which other matter is collected or grows. 핵(심); 중심. ¶ *the ~ of a theory* 학설의 중심 / *the ~ of the community* 사회의 중핵(中核). **2** 《biol.》 the central part of a cell of an animal or a plant. 세포핵. **3** 《phys.》 the central part of an atom. 원자핵. **4** 《astron.》 the central part of a comet. 혜성핵(彗星核). [↑]

nude [njuːd] *adj.* **1** naked; bare; without clothes. 벌거벗은; 나체〔알몸〕의. ¶ *a ~ figure* 나체상(像). **2** 《*fig.*》 not hidden; plain. 있는 그대로의. ¶ *a ~ fact* 적나라한 사실. — *n.* **1** Ⓒ 《art》 a naked human figure. 나체화. **2** 《*the ~*》 the state of being naked. 나체(의 상태). ● **nude·ness** [njúːdnis] *n.* [L.]

nudge [nʌdʒ] *vt.* (P6) touch or push (someone) slightly with the elbow to attract attention. (팔꿈치로) 슬쩍 찌르다. ¶ *He nudged me to go ahead.* 앞서 가라고 나를 살짝 찔렀다. — *n.* Ⓒ a slight touch or push with the elbow. (팔꿈치로) 슬쩍 찌르기. [?]

nu·di·ty [njúːdəti] *n.* (*pl.* **-ties**) **1** Ⓤ the state of being naked. 알몸; 적나라. **2** Ⓒ something naked. 벌거벗은 것. [→nude]

nu·ga·to·ry [njúːgətɔ̀ːri / -təri] *adj.* valueless; useless; of no effect. 무효의. [L. *nugae* trifles]

nug·get [nʌ́git] *n.* Ⓒ **1** a lump of gold found in a rock or the earth. (천연의) 금괴. **2** anything precious or valuable. 가치 있는 것. [? E.]

·**nui·sance** [njúːsəns] *n.* Ⓒ a disagreeable thing, person or act that troubles people. 성가심; 성가신 일〔사람〕. ¶ *No Nuisances.* 소변 금지 / *What a ~!* 정말 귀찮군 / *It is a ~ to have a cold.* 감기에 걸리면 정말 골칫거리다 / *You are a ~ to yourself and to everybody else.* 너는 아무짝에도 못쓸 놈이다. [L. *noceo* hurt]

make a nuisance of oneself =***make oneself a nuisance,*** annoy; be troublesome to others. 남에게 폐를 끼치다.

null [nʌl] *adj.* **1** having no legal force; useless in law. (법적으로) 무효의. ¶ *The agreement is ~ unless it is signed.* 그 계약은 서명하지 않으면 무효다. **2** having no value or importance. 쓸모 없는; 무가치한. ¶ *as ~ as nothing* 없는거나 다름 없는; 있으나마나 한. **3** 《math.》 amounting to zero. 영〔제로〕의. [L. *nullus* none]

null and void, having no legal force. 무효의 《강조》.

nul·li·fy [nʌ́ləfài] *vt.* (**-fied**) (P6) make (something) of no value or effect; declare that something is legally useless; cancel. (법적으로) …을 무효화하다; 취소하다. ● **nul·li·fi·er** [-ər] *n.*

nul·li·ty [nʌ́ləti] *n.* (*pl.* -ties) 1 Ⓤ the state of being null. 무효. 2 Ⓒ something or someone null. 쓸모 없는 물건〔사람〕. 3 Ⓒ something with no legal force. (법적으로) 효력 없는 것.

numb [nʌm] *adj.* having lost the sense of feeling or moving. (추위 등으로) 곱은; 감각을 잃은. ¶ *be ~ with cold* 추워서 곱다. — *vt.* (P6) make (something) numb. …의 감각을 없애다; 마비시키다. ¶ *The icy cold numbed our fingers.* 매서운 추위로 손가락에 감각이 없어졌다. [→nimble]

:**num·ber** [nʌ́mbər] *n.* Ⓒ 1 ⒸⓊ a quantity; an amount; the sum. 수; 총수. ¶ *a whole ~* 정수(整數) / *an odd* 〔*even*〕 *~* 홀수〔짝수〕 / *a positive* 〔*plus*〕 *~* 정수(正數) / *a negative* 〔*minus*〕 *~* 음수(陰數) / *cardinal* 〔*ordinal*〕 *numbers* 기수〔(순)서수〕 / *the ~ of books in this library* 이 도서관의 책의 총수 / *They are twenty in ~.* 그들은 수가 20명이다. 2 ⒸⓊ a sign or word that shows how many; a figure; a numeral. 숫자. ¶ *2,7, and 9 are numbers.* 2,7,9 등을 숫자라 한다. 3 the grade, rank, turn, position, etc. in a series. 번호; …번. ¶ *a house ~* (집의) 번지 / *Room No. 312* / *No. 10, Downing Street.* 다우닝가(街) 10번지《영국 수상 관저》. 4 ⓐ a copy of a newspaper, magazine, etc. (신문·잡지 등의) …호. ¶ *the March* 〔*winter*〕 *~ of the magazine* 잡지의 3월〔겨울〕호. ⓑ a single song, dance, etc. in the program of a concert, show, etc. (연주회 등의) 곡목(曲目); (프로그램의) …부(部). ¶ *a ~ from the opera* 오페라 중의 한 곡목. 5 《*pl.*》 a large quantity; a lot; many people; several people. 다수; 많은〔약간의〕 사람들. ¶ *in great* 〔*small*〕 *numbers* 다수〔소수〕로 / *numbers of* 다수의; 많은 / *There are numbers who believe so.* 그렇게 믿는 사람들도 많다. 6 fellows; company. 동료; 패; 동아리. ¶ *the head of our ~* 우리 패거리의 우두머리 / *He is not of our ~.* 그는 우리 패거리가 아니다. 7 《*pl.*》 superiority that is based on quantity. 숫자 상의 우세. ¶ *They were beaten by superior numbers.* 그들은 수적으로 밀려 패배했다. 8 《*pl.*》 arithmetic. 산수. ¶ *He is not good at numbers.* 그는 산수를 잘 못한다. 9 《gram.》 a word form or ending which shows whether one or more than one is meant. 수. ¶ *the singular* 〔*plural*〕 *~* 단수〔복수〕. 10 《*pl.*》 verses. 시행(詩行).

a number of, many; several. 다수의; 얼마간의.

in number, in total; when counted. 총계해서; 수효는. ¶ *The boys were 500 in ~.* 아이들 수효는 500명이었다 / *They exceed us in ~.* 그들은 수적으로 우리보다 우세하다.

in numbers, **a**) in separate forms. (잡지 따위를) 분책(分冊)하여. **b**) in the forms of poetry. 시(詩)의 형식으로.

to the number of, amounting to. …에 달하는〔이르는〕.

without 〔***out of***〕 ***number,*** too many to be counted. 무수한; 헤아릴 수 없는.

— *vt.* 1 (P6) give a number to (something). …에 번호를 매기다. ¶ *~ the pages in a book* 책에 페이지를 매기다. 2 ⓐ (P6) amount to (a certain number). …에 이르다〔달하다〕. ¶ *The visitors numbered fifty.* 방문자는 50명에 이르렀다. ⓑ (P6) contain; comprise. …에 포함하다; …의 수가 있다. ¶ *The class numbers forty boys.* 학급의 학생수는 40명이다. ⓒ (P6,13) count. …을 세다. ¶ *~ the persons in the crowd* 군중의 수효를 세다. 3 (P6) 《in *passive*》 limit the length of (something, esp. one's life). …의 기간을 제한하다. ¶ *His days are numbered.* 여생이 얼마 안 남았다. 4 (P13) include; regard as one of a company. …의 하나로 간주하다. ¶ *~ him among my friends* 그를 내 친구의 한 사람으로 여기다. [L. *numerus*]

num·ber·less [nʌ́mbərlis] *adj.* 1 very numerous; that not be counted. 무수한. ¶ *the ~ sands on the seashore* 해변의 헤아릴 수 없는 모래알. 2 without a number. 번호가 없는. ¶ *a ~ page* 번호가 안 매겨진 페이지.

number one [ˊ-ˊ] *n.* 1 《*colloq.*》 oneself. 자기(자신). ¶ *He always thought first of ~.* 그는 늘 자기 자신을 먼저 생각한다. 2 《U.S. *colloq.*》 the best or most important. 최고의 것; 가장 중요한 것.

numb·ness [nʌ́mnis] *n.* Ⓤ the state of being numb. 저림; 곱음; 무감각. [→numb]

nu·mer·a·ble [njúːmərəbəl] *adj.* that can be counted. 셀 수 있는. [↓]

nu·mer·al [njúːmərəl] *n.* Ⓒ a word, letter, or figure expressing a number. 숫자. ¶ *Arabic numerals* 아라비아 숫자 《1, 2 …》 / *Roman numerals* 로마 숫자《I, II …》. — *adj.* of number; expressing numbers. 수의; 수를 나타내는. [→number]

nu·mer·ate [njúːmərèit] *vt.* (P6) 1 count (something). …을 세다. 2 read (a numerical expression). (숫자)를 읽다.

nu·mer·a·tor [njúːmərèitər] *n.* Ⓒ 1 《math.》 the number above the line in a fraction. 분자(cf. *denominator*). 參考 fraction은 분수; denominator는 분모. 2 a person or thing counts by numbers. 계산하는 사람; 계산기.

nu·mer·i·cal [njuːmérikəl] *adj.* of numbers; expressed in numbers. 수의; 숫자로 나타낸. ¶ *a ~ equation* 수식(數式) / *~ order* 번호순 / *a ~ statement* 통계.

nu·mer·i·cal·ly [njuːmérikəli] *adv.* in a numerical manner; by numbers. 수로; 수적으로; 숫자상으로.

:**nu·mer·ous** [njúːmərəs] *adj.* great in number; very many. 다수로 이루어진; 다수의. ¶ *a ~ family* 대가족 / *make ~ telephone calls* 빈번하게 전화를 걸다.

Nu·mid·i·a [njuːmídiə] *n.* 《geog.》 a very

old kingdom in North Africa. 누미디아(왕국). 参考 아프리카의 옛 왕국. 지금의 Algeria 부근. [L.]

nu·mis·mat·ic [njù:məzmǽtik, -məs-] *adj.* of coins or medals; of numismatics. 화폐의; 화폐〔고전(古錢)〕학의. [Gk. *nomisma* coin]

nu·mis·mat·ics [njù:məzmǽtiks, -məs-] *n. pl.* 《used as *sing.*》 the study of coins or medals. 화폐학; 고전학.

nu·mis·ma·tist [nju:mízmətist, -mís-] *n.* Ⓒ a person who collects coins and medals; an expert in numismatics. 고전(古錢) 수집가; 화폐〔고전〕학자.

num·skull [nʌ́mskʌ̀l] *n.* Ⓒ 《*colloq.*》 a stupid fellow; a fool. 바보. [→numb]

·nun [nʌn] *n.* Ⓒ a woman in a convent who leads a religious life in the service of God. 수녀(修女)(opp. monk). [L. *nonna*]

nun·ci·o [nʌ́nʃiòu] *n.* (*pl.* **-os**) Ⓒ a diplomatic representative of the Pope to a foreign country. 로마 교황 사절〔대사〕. [L. *nuncius* envoy]

nun·ner·y [nʌ́nəri] *n.* Ⓒ (*pl.* **-ner·ies**) a place where nuns live; a convent. 수녀원(修女院). [→nun]

nup·tial [nʌ́pʃəl, -tʃəl] *n.* 《usu. *pl.*》 a wedding. 결혼식. —*adj.* of marriage or wedding. 결혼(식)의. ¶ *the ~ bed* 신방; 신혼 초야. [L. *nubo* marry]

:nurse [nəːrs] *n.* Ⓒ **1** a person who takes care of the sick, the injured, etc. 간호사; 간호인; 간호병. ¶ *a hospital ~* 병원 간호사 / *a Red Cross ~* 적십자사 간호사. **2** a woman who takes care of children. 유모. 参考 a wet nurse 라고 함. a dry nurse는 보모. **3** 《*fig.*》 a person who feeds and protects. 보호자; 보육(保育)하는 사람. **4** 《*fig.*》 a place where something is protected or grows. 양성소; 발상지. ¶ *Ancient Greece was the ~ of learning.* 옛 그리스는 학문의 온상(溫床)이었다 / *This college has been the ~ of many famous men.* 이 대학은 많은 명사들을 배출해왔다.

—*vt.* (P6) **1** ⓐ take care of (the sick, the injured, etc.); try to cure. …을 간호하다; 치료하다. ¶ *~ a sick person through an illness* 환자를 줄곧 간병하다 / *~ a wounded leg* 다친 다리를 치료하다. ⓑ give special care to. …을 소중히 다루다. ¶ *~ a fire* 불이 꺼지지 않도록 잘 지키다. **2** take care of (a baby); give milk to (a baby) at one's breast. (아기)를 돌보다; …에게 젖을 먹이다. **3** ⓐ hold (a baby, a pet, etc.) closely; hold in arms or on the lap. …을 품에 안다〔끌어 안다〕; 어르다. ¶ *~ a child* 〔*cat*〕 어린이〔고양이〕를 끌어 안다 / *~ the fire* (끌어 안 듯하고) 불을 쬐다; 불 곁에 바싹 다가 앉다. ⓑ preserve or cherish. (마음)에 품다; 지니다. ¶ *~ hopes* 〔*hatred*〕 *in one's heart* 마음에 희망〔원한〕을 품다. **4** make (a baby, a plant, etc.) grow with special care. …을 키우다. ¶ *~ a plant* 나무를 잘 자라게 하다.

—*vi.* (P1) **1** be a nurse; act as a nurse. 보살피다; 간호하다. **2** give milk to a baby at one's breast. 젖을 먹이다. **3** (of a baby) be given milk from a mother or a nurse at her breast. (아기가) 젖을 빨다. [→nourish]

nurse·ling [nə́ːrsliŋ] *n.* =nursling.

nurse·maid [nə́ːrsmèid] *n.* Ⓒ a maid hired to look after children. 아이보는 여자; 업저지.

·nurs·er·y [nə́ːrsəri] *n.* Ⓒ (*pl.* **-er·ies**) **1** a room for young children or babies. 아기방; 육아실. ¶ *a ~ governess* 보모겸 가정교사. **2** a place where young plants are grown. 묘상(苗床). **3** a place that helps something to nourish, grow and develop. 사육실(飼育室); 온상.

nurs·er·y·man [nə́ːrsərimən] *n.* Ⓒ (*pl.* **-men** [-mən]) a man who owns a nursery for growing plants to sell. 종묘원 주인.

nursery rhyme [´-- ˋ] *n.* a short, traditional poem or song for small children. 동요.

nursery school [´-- ˋ] *n.* a school for children under the ages of 2-5. 보육원.

nurs·ling [nə́ːrsliŋ] *n.* Ⓒ **1** any baby or infant that is taken care of by a nurse. 유아(乳兒·幼兒). **2** any person or thing that is tenderly cared for, esp. a young tender plant. 귀하게 자란 사람〔나무〕. [→nurse]

nur·ture [nə́ːrtʃər] *n.* Ⓤ **1** anything that gives nourishment. 자양물. **2** the act of bringing up; training; education. 양육; 보육; 교육. ¶ *the ~ of chicks* 병아리 사육. —*vt.* (P6) **1** feed; nourish. …에게 영양물을 주다. ¶ *~ a young plant.* **2** train and teach; promote the development of. …을 양육하다; 발육을 촉진시키다. ¶ *a delicately nurtured girl* 곱게 자란 소녀 / *The music teacher nurtured her voice.* 음악 선생은 그녀에게 발성 연습을 시켰다. ● **nur·tur·er** [-tʃərər] *n.* [↑]

:nut [nʌt] *n.* Ⓒ **1** a dry fruit with a hard shell and seeds inside it that may be eaten. 나무 열매; 견과《호두, 밤 따위》. **2** 《mech.》 a small block with a hole to be screwed on to the end of a bolt. 너트. **3** 《*sl.*》 the head. 머리; 대가리. **4** 《*sl.*》 a crazy or eccentric or foolish person. 미치광이; 괴짜; 바보. **5** 《*colloq.*》 a dandy; a fop. 멋쟁이.

a hard* 〔*tough*〕 *nut to crack, 《*colloq.*》 a very hard problem; a person or thing that is hard to deal with. 난문제; 다루기 힘든 사람.

***be* (*dead*) *nuts on* 〔*about*〕,** **a**) be crazy about (something). …에 열중해 있다. **b**) be good at (something). …을 매우 잘하다; 능하다.

***be nuts to* 〔*for*〕,** be very charming to (someone). …가 아주 좋아하는 것이다.

don't care a nut, don't mind at all. 조금도 개의치 않다.

for nuts, 《*sl.*》 at all. 전혀. 語法 부정사와 함께 쓰임. ¶ *She can't sing for nuts.* 노래는 통 못한다.

off** one's **nut, 《*colloq.*》 **a**) mad. 미쳐서. **b**) drunken. 취해서.

— *vi.* (**nut·ted, nut·ting**) (P1) gather nuts. 나무 열매를 줍다. ¶ *go nutting* 나무 열매를 주우러 가다. [E.]

nut·crack·er [nʌ́tkræ̀kər] *n.* Ⓒ **1** 《often *pl.*》 a tool for cracking nuts. 호두 까는 기구. **2** a bird of the crow family that feeds on nuts. 산갈가마귀. [*nut*]

〈nutcracker 1〉

nut·meg [nʌ́tmeg] *n.* Ⓒ 《bot.》 a hard, nutlike seed of an East Indian tree, used as a spice or as medicine; its tree. 육두구 열매《약용》; 그 나무. [*nut*]

nu·tri·ent [njúːtriənt] *n.* Ⓤ anything that gives nourishment; food. 영양물; 음식. — *adj.* nutritious. 자양분이 많은; 영양이 풍부한. [→nourish]

nu·tri·ment [njúːtrəmənt] *n.* Ⓤ anything that gives nourishment; food. 자양물; 음식물. ¶ *Wheat contains a great amount of* ~. 소맥에는 자양분이 많이 들어 있다.

nu·tri·tion [njuːtríʃən] *n.* Ⓤ **1** the act of nourishing; the state of being nourished. 영양 (작용, 섭취, 상태). **2** nourishment; food. 영양물; 음식. [*nourish*]

nu·tri·tious [njuːtríʃəs] *adj.* having or supplying much nourishment. 자양분이 많은; 영양이 되는. ¶ *a* ~ *diet* 영양식.

nu·tri·tive [njúːtrətiv] *adj.* **1** of nutrition. 영양의. **2** promoting the process of nourishing; nutritious. 영양이 풍부한(되는).

nut·shell [nʌ́tʃèl] *n.* Ⓒ the hard shell of a nut. 견과(堅果)의 껍질. [→nut]

in a nutshell, very clearly and briefly. 아주 간결하게. ¶ *Just tell me the story in a* ~. 얘기를 간단하게 해라.

nut·ty [nʌ́ti] *adj.* (**-ti·er, -ti·est**) **1** having many nuts. 견과(堅果)가 많은. **2** having a taste like nuts; having a good taste. 견과 맛이 나는; 맛이 좋은. **3** 《*colloq.*》 excessively fond of (something); crazy; mad. 열중한; 미친; 미치광이의. ¶ *be* ~ *about sports cars* 스포츠카에 미쳐 있다. **4** 《*colloq.*》 smart; showy. 멋있는; 화려한. [→nut]

nuz·zle [nʌ́zəl] *vt., vi.* (P6; 2A) **1** (of hogs, etc.) root up land with the nose. (돼지 등이) 코로 구멍을 파다. **2** push or rub the nose against (something). …에 코를 비벼대다. ¶ *The pony nuzzled* (*against*) *his shoulder.* 조랑말은 그의 어깨에 코를 비벼 댔다. **3** lie or sleep close together; hold lovingly. 붙어 자다; 끌어 안다. ¶ ~ *oneself against* (*into, up to, etc.*) *something* …에 바싹 다가붙다 / *The puppy nuzzled its mother.* 강아지는 제 어미에게 붙어 잤다. [→nose]

N.Y. New York (State).

N.Y.C. New York City.

nyc·ta·lo·pi·a [nìktəlóupiə] *n.* 《med.》 a condition of the eyes in which light is nearly blind at night or in a dim light. 야맹증(夜盲症). [Gk. *nuktalōps*]

***ny·lon** [náilɑn / -lɔn] *n.* Ⓤ **1** a very strong chemical substance used to make clothes and stockings. 나일론. **2** 《*pl.*》 stockings made of this material. 나일론 양말. [Trade name]

***nymph** [nimf] *n.* Ⓒ **1** 《Gk. & Rom. myth.》 a goddess living in rivers, seas, springs, trees, hills, etc. 님프; 여정(女精). **2** 《*poet.*》 a beautiful girl. 아름다운 소녀. [Gk. *numphē*]

N.Z. New Zealand.

o O

O[1], **o** [ou] *n.* Ⓒ (*pl.* **O's, Os, o's, os**) **1** the 15th letter of the English alphabet. 영어 알파벳의 열다섯째 글자. **2** anything shaped like the letter O. O자 모양의 것. **3** a zero. 영; 제로. ¶ *double o seven,* 007.

:O[2], **oh** [ou] *interj.* **1** an exclamation that shows surprise, terror, wish, joy, etc. 오; 앗; 어머나; 아. ¶ *O dear me!* 저런 / *Oh, I miss you!* 아, 네가 보고 싶구나. 語法 O에는 콤마를 붙이지 않으나 Oh에는 붙임 / *O yes.* 응 그래 / *O no.* 천만에 / *O that I might see him.* 아아 그를 좀 만났으면. **2** 《used before a name in addressing》 아; 어. ¶ *Oh! Mr. Jones* 아 존스 씨 / *O Lord, help us!* 오, 주여 우리를 도와 주소서. [L.]

o' [ə] *prep.* =of; on. ¶ *3 o'clock,* 3시.

oaf [ouf] *n.* (*pl.* **oafs** or **oaves**) **1** an ugly child. 못생긴 아이. **2** a very stupid child or man. 멍청이; 바보; 멍청한 아이〔어른〕. [N. (→elf)]

:oak [ouk] *n.* Ⓒ **1** a tree with hard, tough wood and nuts called acorns. 오크《떡갈나무·참나무·가시나무 무리; 과실은 acorn》. **2** a leaf of this tree. (장식용) 오크 잎. **3** the wood of this tree. 오크 재목. — *adj.* (made) of oak. 오크의; 오크제의; 오크 재목의. [E.]

oak·en [óukən] *adj.* made of oak. 오크제(製)의.

oa·kum [óukəm] *n.* Ⓤ the loose fiber of old hemp used for filling up the cracks of a ship. (틈새를 메우는) 뱃밥《낡은 밧줄을 푼 것》. [E. =off-comb]

·oar [ɔːr] *n.* Ⓒ **1** a long pole with a flat end, used for rowing a boat. 노; 오어. **2** a person who uses an oar; an oarsman. 노 젓는 사람. ¶ *He is the best* ~ *in the crew.* 그는 노잡이로서는 선원 중에서 최고다. [E.]

be chained to the oar, 《*fig.*》 be forced to do hard work. 중노동을 강요당하다.

have an oar in every man's boat, put a word in about everything. 무슨 일에나 참견하다.

lie 〔***rest***〕 ***on one's oar,*** stop work for a time and rest. 잠시 쉬다.

pull a good oar, row skillfully. 노질을 잘하다.

put in one's oar, 《*colloq.*》 interfere in other people's business. 남의 일에 간섭하다.

oar·lock [ɔ́ːrlɑ̀k / -lɔ̀k] *n.* Ⓒ a U-shaped metal support on the side of a boat in which an oar is rested; a rowlock. 노받이; 놋좆.

oars·man [ɔ́ːrzmən] *n.* Ⓒ (*pl.* **-men** [-mən]) a person who uses an oar. 노 젓는 사람; 노잡이.

o·a·ses [ouéisiːz] *n.* pl. of **oasis.**

o·a·sis [ouéisis] *n.* Ⓒ (*pl.* **-ses**) **1** a place in a desert where there are trees and water. 오아시스. **2** 《*fig.*》 a beautiful sight, place, etc. among ugly surrounding. (좋지 않은 환경 등에서의) 휴식처; 위안의 장소. [Gk.]

·oat [out] *n.* 《usu. *pl.*》 a plant or its grain, used as food, esp. for horses. 귀리; 메귀리. — *adj.* made of oats or oat straw. 귀리로 만든; 귀리짚으로 만든. [E.]

feel one's oats, 《U.S. *colloq.*》 be in high spirits; feel important. 원기 왕성하다; 잘난 체하다.

sow one's wild oats, lead a gay or immoral life while young and before marriage. 젊어서 난봉 부리다〔방탕한 생활을 하다〕.

oat·en [óutn] *adj.* of or made of oats or an oat straw. 귀리로〔귀리짚으로〕 만든. ¶ *an* ~ *pipe* 〔*flute*〕 보리 피리.

·oath [ouθ] *n.* Ⓒ (*pl.* **oaths** [ouðz, ouθs]) **1** a solemn statement or promise to God, expressing that something is true. 맹세. ¶ *a false* ~ 거짓 맹세 / *an* ~ *of office* =*an official* ~ 취임 선서 / *on* 〔*upon*〕 *my* (*Bible*) ~ 맹세코 / *make* 〔*swear, take*〕 *an* ~ 맹세〔선서〕하다. **2** a curse; a swearword. 저주; 악담; 욕설. ¶ *He threw a stone at the dog with an* ~. 그는 '망할 놈의 개' 하며 돌을 던졌다. [E.]

put someone on oath, cause someone to make an oath. …을 맹세하게 하다.

take one's oath that .... =***take one's oath on something,*** promise or declare something by making an oath; swear solemnly. …은 확실하다고 맹세하다; …을 선서하다. ¶ *I'll take my* ~ *that I was there.* 내가 분명히 거기 있었다고 맹세하겠다.

oat·meal [óutmiːl] *n.* Ⓤ the meal made from oats. 오트밀; 귀리죽. [*oat*]

oaves [ouvz] *n.* pl. of **oaf.**

ob·bli·ga·to [ɑ̀bligáːtou / ɔ̀b-] *adj.* 《It. mus.》 (of part or accompaniment) essential; indispensable; inseparable. (반주 따위가) 반드시 따르는; 생략할 수 없는. — *n.* 《mus.》 an instrumental accompaniment to the voice and another instrument. 오블리가토; 조주(助奏).

ob·du·ra·cy [ɑ́bdjurəsi / ɔ́b-] *n.* Ⓤ the quality or state of being obdurate; stubbornness. 완고; 외고집; 냉혹. [↓]

ob·du·rate [ɑ́bdjurit / ɔ́b-] *adj.* hard-hearted; stubborn; obstinate. 완고한; 고집 센; 냉혹한. ¶ *an* ~ *old man* 완고한 늙은이 / *an* ~ *refusal* 완강한 거절. ●**ob·du·rate·ly** [-li] *adv.* **ob·du·rate·ness** [-nis] *n.* [→duration]

·o·be·di·ence [oubíːdiəns] *n.* Ⓤ the act of obeying what is told or ordered; the state of being obedient; submission; faithfulness. 복종; 순종; 충실. ¶ *blind* ~ 맹종(盲從) / *reduce to* ~ 복종시키다. [→obedient]

in obedience to, in accordance with. …에 복종하여; …에 따라서. ¶ *in* ~ *to someone's orders* 아무의 명령에 따라서〔복종하여〕.

:o·be·di·ent [oubíːdiənt] *adj.* willing to obey; eager to do what is told or ordered. 순종하는; 말 잘 듣는; 착한. ¶ ~ *to one's parents* 부모에게 순종하는 / *The* ~ *dog came at his master's whistle.* 그 말 잘 듣는 개는 주인의 호각 소리를 듣고 왔다.

Your obedient servant, 《Brit.》 an expression used at the end of a formal or official letter. 근배(謹拜)《공문서 등의 끝맺는 말》. [→obey]

o·be·di·ent·ly [oubíːdiəntli] *adv.* in an obedient manner; faithfully. 공손하게.

o·bei·sance [oubéisəns, -bíː-] *n.* **1** Ⓒ a low bow that expresses respect. 인사; 경례; 절. ¶ *make an* ~ *to someone* 아무에게 절하다; 경례하다. **2** Ⓤ homage; obedience; submission. 존경; 복종. ¶ *do* 〔*make, pay*〕 ~ *to someone* 아무에게 경의를 표하다. [→obey]

ob·e·lisk [ábəlìsk / ɔ́b-] *n.* Ⓒ **1** a high, four-sided stone pillar, pointed at the top, set up as a monument. 방첨탑(方尖塔); 오벨리스크. **2** 《print.》 a dagger. 단검표; 칼표(†). [Gk.]

〈obelisk 1〉

o·bese [oubíːs] *adj.* very fat; stout. 뚱뚱한. [L. *edo* eat]

o·bes·i·ty [oubíːsəti] *n.* Ⓤ the quality or state of being obese. 뚱뚱함; 비대; 비만.

:o·bey [oubéi] *vt., vi.* (P6;1) **1** do what is told or ordered; follow the rules. (명령 등에) 복종하다; (법령 등을) 지키다. ¶ ~ *one's parents* 부모에게 순종하다 / ~ *the orders of one's superiors* 상관의 명령에 따르다 / ~ *rules* 규칙을 지키다. **2** act according to (an instinct, etc.); react or respond to. (양심·본능 등에) 따라 행동하다; …에 반응하다. ¶ *Animals* ~ *their instincts.* 짐승은 본능대로 행동한다 / *The motorcar promptly obeys its wheel.* 자동차는 핸들 조작에 따라 신속하게 움직인다. [ob-, L. *audio* hear]

o·bit·u·ar·y [oubítʃuèri] *n.* Ⓒ **1** a notice of someone's death in a newspaper, often with a short account of his life. 사망 기사〔광고〕. **2** 《religion》 a list of dead members of a religious community. 과거장(過去帳). — *adj.* of death. 사망(자)의. ¶ *an* ~ *ceremony* 장례식 / *an* ~ *notice* 사망 기사. [L. *obitus* death]

:ob·ject [ábdʒikt / ɔ́b-] *n.* Ⓒ **1** anything that can be seen or touched; a material thing. 사물; 물체. ¶ *What is that* ~ *by the fence?* 담 옆에 있는 저게 뭐냐. **2** a person or thing to which people direct their feeling, thought, or action. (감정, 사상, 동작 등의) 대상. ¶ *an* ~ *of love* 사랑의 대상 / *He was an* ~ *of hatred.* 그는 증오의 대상이었다. **3** 《colloq.》 a pitiful or funny person or thing. 불쌍한 놈; 이상한 물건. ¶ *What a funny-looking* ~ *he is!* 참 묘하게도 생긴 놈이군. **4** an aim; a purpose; a goal; an end. 목표; 목적. ¶ *I came here with the sole* ~ *of making money.* 오로지 돈 벌기 위해 나는 여기에 왔다. **5** 《gram.》 a word or group of words to which the action of the verb is directed or to which a preposition expresses some relation. 목적어(cf. *subject*). **6** 《philos.》 something toward which a cognitive act is directed. 객체(客體); 객관(opp. subject).

— *v.* [əbdʒékt] *vi.* (P1,2A,3) 《*to*》 protest; be opposed; feel dislike. 항의하다; 이의를 제기하다; 싫어하다. ¶ *She objected to being treated like a child.* 그녀는 자기를 어린애 취급한다고 항의했다 / *Do you* ~ *to my smoking?* 나 담배 좀 피우면 안 될까 / *I don't* ~ *to a good glass of whisky.* 좋은 위스키 한 잔 하는 것은 나쁘지 않다 / *I* ~ *to that question being asked.* 그 문제의 질문은 받고 싶지 않다.

— *vt.* (P11) give as a reason against (something); oppose. 반대의 이유로 …을 말하다. ¶ *They objected that he was dishonest.* 그들은 그가 정직하지 못하다고 반대를 했다 / *He objected two facts against* 〔*to*〕 *the theory.* 그는 그 이론에 반하는 두 가지 사실을 반대 이유로 들었다. [L. *ob-* toward, against, *jacio* throw, put]

I object. I have and express an objection. 나는 불찬성이오.

ob·jec·ti·fy [əbdʒéktəfài] *vt.* (P6) make objective. 객관화〔구체화〕하다.

·ob·jec·tion [əbdʒékʃən] *n.* **1** ⒸⓊ the act of objecting; opposition; disapproval; dislike. 반대; 이의(異議); 불복. ¶ *feel an* ~ *to going* 가고 싶지 않다 / *I have no* ~ *to going there.* 나는 거기에 가는 것을 반대하지 않는다. **2** Ⓒ something objected to; an obstacle; a defect; hindrance. 반대 이유; 난점; 결함; 장애. ¶ *the chief* ~ *to the novel* 그 소설의 주된 난점 / *I wish to make a strong* ~ *against….* 나는 …에 대해 강한 이의를 제기하고자 한다 / *There is no* ~ *to your leaving at once.* 지금 곧 떠나도 지장이 없다.

take objection (***to***), **a**) express disapproval (of). (…을) 반대하다. **b**) feel dislike (for). (…이) 싫다. ¶ *I take* ~ *to his arrogant behavior.* 나는 그 자의 거들먹거리는 꼴이 마음에 안 든다.

ob·jec·tion·a·ble [əbdʒékʃənəbəl] *adj.* **1** tending to cause objection. 반대할 만한. **2** unpleasant; undesirable. 마음에 안 드는;

불쾌한. ¶ *He has many ~ habits.* 그에게는 마땅찮은 버릇이 많다.

ob·jec·tive [əbdʒéktiv] *n.* Ⓒ **1** 《gram.》 the objective case. 목적격. **2** the object or purpose which is aimed at. 목표; 목적. ¶ *with no special ~* 이렇다 할 목적 없이. **3** the lens of a microscope which is nearest to whatever one is looking at. 대물(對物) 렌즈. — *adj.* **1** of the outward things. 외계(外界)의. **2** 《philos.》 really existing outside the mind; real. 실재하는; 객관적인(opp. subjective). ¶ *an ~ method* 객관적 방법. **3** of the object or purpose of an action or thought. 목적〔목표〕의. ¶ 《mil.》 *an ~ point* 목표 지점. **4** 《gram.》 of the object of a verb or preposition. 목적격의. ¶ *~ genitive* 〔*possessive*〕 목적 소유격.

ob·jec·tive·ly [əbdʒéktivli] *adv.* in an objective manner. 객관적으로; 객관적 견지에서.

ob·jec·tiv·i·ty [àbdʒektívəti / ɔ̀b-] *n.* Ⓤ the state of being objective; impersonal or impartial judgment. 객관성; 객관적 타당성.

object lesson [´-- ˋ--] *n.* a lesson taught or learnt by means of examples or specimens. 실물 교육.

ob·jec·tor [əbdʒéktər] *n.* Ⓒ a person who objects or protests. 반대자.

ob·jet d'art [ɔbʒɛ dɑːr] *n.* 《F.》 (*pl.* **ob·jets d'-**) a small picture, vase, etc. of some artistic value. 작은 미술품; 골동품. [F. =object of art]

ob·jur·gate [ábdʒərgèit / ɔ́b-] *vt.* (P6) scold; abuse; blame. …을 꾸짖다; 야단치다; 비난하다. [L. *jurgo* quarrel]

ob·jur·ga·tion [àbdʒərgéiʃən / ɔ̀b-] *n.* Ⓤ the act of objurgating; abuse. 힐책; 비난.

ob·la·tion [abléiʃən / ɔb-] *n.* **1** the act of offering worship or sacrifice to God or a god. (성체의) 봉헌. **2** the thing offered, esp. the bread and wine of Holy Communion. (성찬식의) 봉납물. **3** a gift for religious uses. (교회에의) 헌금; 기부. [L. *latus* (pp.) brought]

ob·li·gate [ábləgèit / ɔ́b-] *vt.* (P6,20) 《chiefly in *pp.*》 bind by law; bind by a sense of duty or a promise; oblige. …에게 의무를 지우다; 고맙게 여기게 하다. ¶ *I am obligated to you for your help.* 도와 주신 데 대해서 감사드립니다 / *The law obligates a father to support his children.* 법은 아버지가 어린 자식을 부양하도록 되어 있다. [→ligament]

***ob·li·ga·tion** [àbləgéiʃən / ɔ̀b-] *n.* **1** ⓊⒸ a duty; the binding power of a duty, law, moral feelings, promise, etc. 의무; 책임. ¶ *Taxes are an ~ which may fall on anybody.* 세금이란 누구나 져야 할 의무다 / *~ of conscience* (의무가 따르는) 양심의 구속력 / *discharge one's obligations* 책임을 다하다 / *lay an ~ upon someone* 아무에게 의무를 지우다. **2** Ⓤ a sum which one must pay; a debt. 채무; 빚. ¶ *The firm was unable to meet its obligations.* 그 회사는 채무의 상환이 불가능했다. **3** a debt of gratitude. 은의(恩誼); 의리.

be under an obligation to (=*must do something for*) *someone.* …에게 할 의무〔의리〕가 있다. ¶ *be under an ~ to care for someone* 아무를 보살필 의무가 있다.

of obligation, required. 의무적인.

repay an obligation, return another's kindness. 은혜에 보답하다.

ob·lig·a·to·ry [əblígətɔ̀ːri, áblig- / əblígətəri, ɔ́blig-] *adj.* of the nature of an obligation; required; compulsory. 의무적인; 필수의. ¶ *Attendance at primary school is ~.* 국민 학교에 다니는 것은 의무적이다 / *It is ~ for us to obey the laws.* 법을 준수하는 것이 우리의 의무다.

:o·blige [əbláidʒ] *vt.* **1** (P20) force or compel a person to act. …을 의무적으로 …하게 하다; 강제하다. ¶ *I won't ~ you to stay here any longer.* 여기에 더 있지 않아도 괜찮다 / *I am obliged to leave early to catch my train.* 기차를 타려면 일찍 떠나야 한다. **2** (P6,7,13) do a kindness to (someone); satisfy a desire of (someone). …에게 친절을〔은혜를〕 베풀다; …의 소원을 들어주다. ¶ *Oblige me by shutting the door.* 문을 닫아 주면 고맙겠다 / *Will any gentleman ~ a lady?* 여성에게 자리를 양보해 주실 분은 안 계십니까 / *She obliged me with a song.* 그녀는 나에게 노래를 한 곡 불러 주었다 / *I am much obliged to you.* 정말 고맙습니다 / *Could you ~ me with 10,000 won?* 제게 만 원을 (빌려) 주실 수 있습니까.
— *vi.* (P1,3) 《*colloq.*》 be kind enough to do something. 호의를 보이다; 은혜를 베풀다. ¶ *Can you ~ with a song?* 노래 한 곡 들려 주겠습니까. [*obligate*]

o·blig·ing [əbláidʒiŋ] *adj.* willing to do favors; kind. 친절한. ¶ *an ~ neighbor* 친절한 이웃. ●**o·blig·ing·ly** [-li] *adv.*

ob·lique [əblíːk, ou-, 《U.S. mil.》 əbláik] *adj.* **1** ⓐ slanting. 비스듬한; 기울어진; 기운. ⓑ 《math.》 neither vertical nor horizontal. 사선(斜線)의; 빗각의. ¶ *~ lines* 사선 / *~ angle* 빗각. **2** 《*fig.*》 not frank; indirect. 에두른; 간접적인. ¶ *~ praise* 넌지시 하는 칭찬. — *adv.* 《mil.》 with a change of direction of approximately 45 degrees. 45도 각도로. — *vi.* (P1,2A,3) **1** slant; turn aside. 기울다; 구부러지다; 빗나가다. **2** 《mil.》 march or advance obliquely. 반좌〔우〕향으로 가다. ●**ob·lique·ly** [-li] *adv.* [L.]

ob·liq·ui·ty [əblíkwəti] *n.* ⓊⒸ **1** the state of being oblique. 경사; 기울기. **2** ⓐ turning aside from good behavior, etc. 부정(不正); (행위가) 바르지 못함. ¶ *~ of conduct* 행위의 바르지 못함. ⓑ turning aside from sound judgment. 사곡(邪曲). ¶ *~ of mind* 마음의 요사스러움.

ob·lit·er·ate [əblítərèit] *vt.* (P6) rub or

blot out (something); remove all traces of (something); destroy. …을 말소하다; 지워 버리다; 흔적을 없애다. ¶ *The earthquake obliterated an entire city.* 지진으로 시 전체가 흔적도 없이 사라졌다 / *One bomb will be enough to ~ the whole town.* 단 한 발의 폭탄이면 온 도시가 쑥대밭이 된다 / *~ one's signature* 서명을 지워버리다 / *Time obliterates sorrow.* 시간이 지나면 슬픔은 사라진다. [→letter]

ob·liv·i·on [əblíviən] *n.* Ⓤ the state of being forgotten; the act of forgetting. 망각. ¶ *in utter ~ of something* …이 완전히 잊혀진 / *be buried in ~* 잊혀지다. [L. *obliviscor* forget]

fall* 〔*sink, pass, go*〕 *into oblivion, become forgotten; die from the memory of the world. (세상에서) 잊혀지다. ¶ *Many ancient cities have long since passed into ~.* 많은 옛 도시들이 세상 사람들의 기억에서 잊혀진 지 오래다.

ob·liv·i·ous [əblíviəs] *adj.* forgetful; not mindful. 잊기 쉬운; 부주의한; 멍한. ¶ *be ~ of something* …을 잊어버리다 / *~ of the consequences of one's actions* 자기 행위의 결과에 대하여 등한한. ● **ob·liv·i·ous·ly** [-li] *adv.* **ob·liv·i·ous·ness** [-nis] *n.*

ob·long [ábləːŋ, -laŋ / ɔ́blɔŋ] *adj.* greater in length than in breadth. 직사각형의; 타원형의. —*n.* Ⓒ a figure longer than it is broad; a rectangle. 직사각형; 타원형. [L. *longus* long]

ob·lo·quy [ábləkwi / ɔ́b-] *n.* Ⓤ bad words spoken of a person or thing; ill repute; disgrace. 욕(설); 악담; 오명(汚名); 불명예. ¶ *heap ~ upon* 갖은 욕설을 하다. [L. *loquor* speak]

ob·nox·ious [əbnákʃəs / -nɔ́k-] *adj.* very unpleasant; disagreeable; hateful. 기분 나쁜; 불쾌한; 미움받는. ¶ *an ~ odor* 구린 내 / *His way of talking was quite ~ to those attending the meeting.* 그의 말투는 모임에 참석한 사람들에게 아주 불쾌하게 들렸다. ● **ob·nox·ious·ly** [-li] *adv.* **ob·nox·ious·ness** [-nis] *n.* [L. *obnoxius* exposed to harm]

o·boe [óubou] *n.* Ⓒ a wind musical instrument made of wood. 오보에《목관 악기의 하나》. [It.]

ob·scene [əbsíːn] *adj.* (**-scen·er, -scen·est**) filthy; not decent; impure. 음란한; 추잡한. ¶ *~ language* 〔*books*〕 음탕한 말〔음란 서적〕. [L. *obsc(a)enus*]

ob·scen·i·ty [əbsénəti, -síːn-] *n.* Ⓤ the state of being obscene in language or action. 음란; 외설.

ob·scur·ant [əbskjúərənt] *n.* a person who prevents progress and advance in knowledge. 개화 반대론자; 반계몽주의자. [*obscure*]

ob·scur·ant·ist [əbskjúərəntìst] *n.* = obscurant.

ob·scu·ra·tion [àbskjuəréiʃən / ɔ̀b-] *n.* the action of darkening; an act of obscuring or being obscured. 어둡게 함; 몽롱(한 상태).

***ob·scure** [əbskjúər] *adj.* **1** ⓐ not easily understood; not clear in meaning; vague. 이해하기 어려운; 분명하지 않은; 애매(모호)한. ¶ *an ~ meaning* 〔*answer, argument, explanation*〕 분명하지 않은 뜻〔대답, 논거, 설명〕 / *His part in the affair remains ~.* 그 사건에서의 그의 역할은 아직 모호하다. ⓑ not clear to the senses. (소리·형체 따위가) 희미한; 선명하지 않은. ¶ *an ~ form* 희미한 형체 / *~ sounds* 희미한 소리. **2** not well known; not famous; remote; hidden. 잘 알려져 있지 않은; 무명의; 숨겨진; 외딴. ¶ *an ~ scholar* 무명(無名)의 학자 / *of ~ origin* 〔*birth*〕 기원〔태생〕이 불확실한 / *an ~ poet* 무명 시인 / *an ~ mountain village* 외진 산간의 마을. **3** ⓐ dim; dark; gloomy. 어두컴컴한. ¶ *an ~ corner of the back room* 뒷방의 어두침침한 한쪽 구석. ⓑ (of color) not bright; dull; darkish. (색깔 등이) 침침한; 흐릿한. ¶ *~ color* 흐릿한 빛깔.

—*vt.* (P6) **1** darken; hide. …을 어둡게〔흐리게〕 하다; 덮어 감추다; 가리다. ¶ *The sun was obscured by clouds.* 구름에 가려 태양은 희미하게 보였다 / *His fame was obscured by that of his greater father.* 그의 명성은 그보다 한층 위대했던 아버지 때문에 빛을 잃었다. **2** make (something) less clear; make (something) difficult to be understood. …을 모호〔애매〕하게 하다. ¶ *His difficult style obscures his meaning.* 그의 난해한 문체가 글의 뜻을 모호하게 한다. [L.]

ob·scure·ly [əbskjúərli] *adv.* in an obscure manner. 어둡게; 흐릿하게; 이름 없이.

ob·scu·ri·ty [əbskjúərəti] *n.* (*pl.* **-ties**) **1** Ⓤ the state of being obscure; darkness; dimness. 불명료; 어둠; 몽롱. ¶ *~ of style* 문체의 모호성. **2** Ⓒ an obscure or indistinct thing. 분명치 못한 점〔곳〕. **3** Ⓒ an unknown person or place. 이름 없는 사람〔곳〕. ¶ *rise from ~ to fame* 무명인에서 출세하다. [obscure]

sink into obscurity, be buried without ever having become famous. 세상에서 잊혀지다; 초야에 묻히다.

ob·se·quies [ábsəkwiz / ɔ́b-] *n. pl.* the funeral ceremonies. 장례식. [L. *sequor* follow]

ob·se·qui·ous [əbsíːkwiəs] *adj.* eager to obey and serve, esp. in expectation of reward. 빌붙는; 아첨하는. ● **ob·se·qui·ous·ly** [-li] *adv.* **ob·se·qui·ous·ness** [-nis] *n.*

ob·serv·a·ble [əbzə́ːrvəbəl] *adj.* **1** that can be seen or noticed. 보이는; 관찰할 수 있는. **2** remarkable; noticeable. 주목할 만한; 눈에 띄는. **3** deserving to be kept. 지켜야 할. [→observe]

***ob·serv·ance** [əbzə́ːrvəns] *n.* **1** Ⓤ the act of observing or keeping a law, custom, etc. (법률·습관 등의) 준수. ¶ *the ~ of Sundays* 주일을 지키기. **2** Ⓒ a religious ceremony; a custom. (종교적인) 의식; 관례. ¶ *Church services are religious observances.* 교회의 예배는 종교적 의식이다. **3** 《*arch.*》 respectful attention or service. 경의(敬意); 공경(恭敬). ¶ *pay humble ~* 공경하다.

ob·serv·ant [əbzə́:rvənt] *adj.* **1** quick to pay attention; watchful; attentive. 주의 깊은; 관찰력이 날카로운. ¶ *An ~ boy soon noticed the mistake.* 주의 깊은 아이는 잘못을 곧 알아차린다. **2** careful in keeping a law, rule, custom, etc. 준수하는. ¶ *~ of laws* 법을 지키는. ● **ob·serv·ant·ly** [-li] *adv.*

O

:ob·ser·va·tion [àbzərvéiʃən / ɔ̀b-] *n.* **1** Ⓤ the act of observing; careful notice; the state of being observed. 관찰; 관측; 주목. ¶ *escape ~* 남의 눈을 벗어나다(피하다) / *keep a patient under ~* 환자를 잘 관찰하다 / 《mil.》 *~ post* 관측소 / *He tried to avoid ~.* 그는 남의 눈에 띄지 않도록 노력했다. **2** the power of noticing. 관찰력. ¶ *a man of no ~* 관찰력이 없는 남자. **3** ⓐ Ⓒ a result or fact obtained by observing; something noticed. (관찰에 의해 얻은) 지식(결과). ⓑ 《*pl.*》 the notes, remarks, or records of what is observed. 관찰 기록. ¶ *As a student of bird life he kept a record of his observations.* 조류 생태 연구자로서 그는 관찰한 것들을 기록해 두었다. **4** Ⓒ a remark or comment based on observing. 관찰에 의거한 소견(의견); 평(評). ¶ *make an ~ about something* …에 대하여 소견을 말하다.

come 〔**fall**〕 **under** *someone's* **observation,** catch someone's attention. …의 눈에 띄다. ¶ *An unlawful act has come under the policeman's ~.* 어떤 부정 행위가 경찰관의 눈에 띄었다.

ob·serv·a·to·ry [əbzə́:rvətɔ̀:ri / -təri] *n.* Ⓒ (*pl.* **-ries**) a building for observing and studying the sun, stars, etc.; a place for observing the weather, etc. 천문대; 기상대; 관측소.

:ob·serve [əbzə́:rv] *vt.* **1** (P6,10,11,12,17,22,23) watch carefully. …을 관측(관찰)하다; 잘 (살펴)보다. ¶ *~ the stars* 별을 관측하다 / *Observe how to do that.* 그걸 어떻게 하는지 잘 봐라 / *~ the behavior of birds* 새들의 생태를 관찰하다 / *~ the height of the sun* 태양의 높이를 관측하다. **2** (P6,11,22,23) be aware of (something); notice. …을 알아채다; (관찰에 의해) …을 인지하다(보다). ¶ *I observed something queer in his behavior.* 나는 그의 행동에서 어딘가 이상한 점을 알게 됐다 / *I observed him open* 〔*opening*〕 *the door.* 나는 그가 문 여는 것을 봤다 / *He observed that it had suddenly become much colder.* 그는 갑자기 몹시 추워진 것을 알게 되었다 / *Then I observed that she had turned pale.* 그 때 나는 그녀의 얼굴이 창백해진 것을 봤다. **3** (P6) keep; follow; obey. (법률 등)을 지키다. ¶ *~ a rule* 규칙을 지키다 / *~ silence* 〔*the time*〕 침묵(시간)을 지키다. **4** celebrate; keep. (의식)을 거행하다; (명절·생일 따위)를 축하하다. ¶ *~ Christmas* 〔*someone's birthday*〕 크리스마스를〔아무의 생일을〕 축하하다. **5** (P6,11) remark; say. …을 (의견으로) 진술하다; …라고 말하다. ¶ *She observed that we might have rain soon.* 곧 비가 올 거라고 그녀는 말했다 / *He observed nothing on the subject.* 그는 그 문제에 대해 한 마디의 의견도 말하지 않았다.

— *vi.* **1** (P1) take notice; act as an observer. 알아차리다; 관찰하다. ¶ *He observed keenly but said nothing.* 그는 예의 관찰했으나 말은 없었다. **2** 《*on, upon*》 say; remark. 의견을 말하다. ¶ *No one observed on that subject.* 그 문제에 대해 아무도 말을 안 했다. [L. *servo* keep]

·ob·serv·er [əbzə́:rvər] *n.* Ⓒ **1** a person who watches. 관찰(관측)자. ¶ *an ~ of the stars.* **2** a person who follows certain rules or customs. (규칙 등의) 준수자. ¶ *an ~ of his promises* 약속을 잘 지키는 사람. **3** a person who attends a meeting, etc. but has no part in it. 입회인; 옵서버.

ob·serv·ing [əbzə́:rviŋ] *adj.* observant; quick to notice. 관찰력이 날카로운; 주의 깊은.

ob·sess [əbsés] *vt.* (P6) 《usu. *in passive*》 fill the mind with (a fear, a wild fancy, etc.) completely. (근심, 망상 등이) 들리다; 붙다; 괴롭히다; 사로잡히다. ¶ *be obsessed by a demon* 귀신이 들리다(붙다) / *be obsessed with a fixed idea* 고정 관념에 사로잡히다 / *She is always obsessed by* 〔*with*〕 *the idea of her own inferiority.* 그녀는 늘 자기 자신의 열등감에 사로잡혀 있다. [L. *sedeo* sit]

ob·ses·sion [əbséʃən] *n.* **1** Ⓤ the state of being ruled by a fixed idea. (고정 관념 등에) 사로잡혀 있음. **2** Ⓒ a fixed idea which takes possession of one's mind. 강박 관념.

ob·so·les·cent [àbsəlésənt / ɔ̀b-] *adj.* **1** going out of use; becoming obsolete. 소용없게(쓰이지 않게) 된; 쇠퇴해 가고 있는. ¶ *This word is now ~.* 이 말은 요즘 쓰이지 않는다. **2** 《biol.》 gradually disappearing. 퇴행성의. [L. *soleo* be accustomeld]

ob·so·lete [àbsəlí:t, ⌐–⌐/ɔ́bsəlì:t] *adj.* out of date; no longer used or in fashion. 쓸모없게 된; 쓰이지 않는; 구식의. ¶ *~ firearms* 구식 화기 / *an ~ word* 폐어. [↑]

·ob·sta·cle [ábstəkəl / ɔ́b-] *n.* Ⓒ something that stands in the way and stops progress; hindrance. 방해물; 장애(물). ¶ *an ~ race* 장애물 경주 / *High tariffs are the chief obstacles to free trade.* 높은 관세는 자유 무역의 큰 장애다. [L. *sto* stand]

ob·stet·ric [əbstétrik] *adj.* of the care of women in childbirth. 산과(産科)의; 조산(助産)의. ¶ *an ~ nurse* 산과 간호사 / *an ~*

operation 산과 수술. [↑]

ob·stet·ri·cian [àbstətríʃən / ɔ̀b-] *n.* a medical doctor specializing in obstetrics. 산과 의사.

ob·stet·rics [əbstétriks] *n. pl.* 《used as *sing.*》 the branch of medicine which deals with childbirth. 산과학(産科學)(cf. *midwifery*).

ob·sti·na·cy [ábstənəsi / ɔ́b-] *n.* (*pl.* **-cies**) Ⓤ the state of being obstinate; stubbornness; Ⓒ an obstinate act or attitude. 완고; 고집; 완고한 행위[태도]. [↓]

·ob·sti·nate [ábstənit / ɔ́b-] *adj.* **1** not giving up one's opinion; unwilling to obey; stubborn. 완고한; 외고집의. ¶ *an ~ person* 고집쟁이 / *The ~ child refused to answer.* 그 고집센 아이는 대답을 하려 들지 않았다. **2** (of disease) hard to recover from. (병이) 난치의; 잘 낫지 않는. ¶ *an ~ cough* 잘 낫지 않는 기침 / *She is in bed with an ~ disease.* 그녀는 난치병을 앓고 있다. [→obstacle]

ob·sti·nate·ly [ábstənitli / ɔ́b-] *adv.* in an obstinate manner. 완고하게; 외고집으로.

ob·strep·er·ous [əbstrépərəs] *adj.* noisy; wild; unruly. 시끄러운; 난폭한. ¶ *an ~ child* 장난이 심한 아이. [L. *strepo* make noise]

ob·struct [əbstrʌ́kt] *vt., vi.* (P6;1) make (progress, development, etc.) difficult; disturb; hinder. (진로 등을) 막다; 방해하다. ¶ *Dirt obstructs the drains.* 쓰레기로 하수구가 막혔다 / *~ the traffic* 교통을 방해하다 / *A strike obstructed the work of the factory.* 파업으로 공장이 가동을 못 했다. [L. *tsruo* pile]

ob·struc·tion [əbstrʌ́kʃən] *n.* Ⓤ the act of obstructing; Ⓒ something that obstructs. 방해; 장애; 장애물. ¶ *an ~ on the railroad* 철로 위의 장애물 / *Prejudices are a great ~ to progress.* 편견은 발달에 큰 장애물이다.

ob·struc·tive [əbstrʌ́ktiv] *adj.* causing or likely to cause obstruction. 방해하는; 장애가 되는. ¶ *The noises from the streets are ~ to his study.* 거리의 소음이 그의 공부를 방해하고 있다. —*n.* Ⓒ a person or thing that obstructs. 방해자[물].

:ob·tain [əbtéin] *vt.* (P6) **1** get or gain (something) through effort. 얻다; 획득하다. ¶ *~ a reward* 보상을 받다 / *~ a livelihood* 생계 수단을 얻게 되다 / *He finally obtained a copy of the book he was looking for.* 마침내 그가 찾던 책을 하나 입수했다. **2** accomplish; fulfill. …을 달성하다; 이루다. —*vi.* (P1) be established; be in fashion; prevail. 행해지다; 유행[통용]되다. ¶ *The custom still obtains in some districts.* 그 풍습은 아직도 몇몇 지방에서는 행해진다 / *The theory no longer obtains.* 그 이론은 이젠 통하지 않는다. [→tenant]

ob·tain·a·ble [əbtéinəbəl] *adj.* that can be obtained. 얻을 수 있는; 이룰 수 있는.

ob·trude [əbtrú:d] *vt., vi.* (P13;1) push (oneself, one's opinions, etc.) forward against other's will; force oneself upon others. (자기 의견 등을 남에게) 강요하다; 억지쓰다; 중뿔나게 굴다. ¶ *~ on someone's privacy* 남의 사삿일에 나서다 / *Don't ~ your opinions upon others.* 네 생각을 남에게 강요하지 마라. [L. *trudo* push]

ob·tru·sive [əbtrú:siv] *adj.* inclined to obtrude; undesirably noticeable or showy. 강요하는; 중뿔나게 나서는; 눈에 거슬리는. [↑]

ob·tuse [əbtjú:s] *adj.* **1** (of a knife, etc.) not sharp or pointed; blunt. (칼 따위) 무딘 (opp. sharp). **2** (of an angle) having between 90° and 180°. 둔각(鈍角)의(opp. acute). ¶ *an ~ angle* 둔각. **3** slow to understand; dull. (머리가) 둔한. ¶ *An ~ person is slow in understanding a joke.* 머리 둔한 사람은 농담을 이해 못 한다 ●**ob·tuse·ly** [-li] *adv.* [L. *tundo* beat]

ob·verse [ábvə:rs / ɔ́b-] *n.* Ⓒ 《usu. *the ~*》 (opp. reverse) **1** the side of a coin or medal which has the main design. (화폐·메달 등의) 표면. **2** the counterpart of a fact. (사실 등의) 역(逆). —[ɑbvə́:rs, ɑ́bvə:rs / ɔ́bvə:rs] *adj.* **1** facing the obverse. 겉의. **2** being the counterpart of a fact. 반면(反面)의; 역의. [→versatile]

ob·vi·ate [ábvièit / ɔ́b-] *vt.* (P6) remove; clear away; prevent (an disease, etc.). (곤란 등)을 제거하다; (질병 등)을 미연에 방지하다. ¶ *~ a difficulty* [*danger, objections*] 어려움을[위험을, 장애를] 피하다. [→via]

·ob·vi·ous [ábviəs / ɔ́b-] *adj.* **1** easy to see; evident at a glance; clear. 명백한; 뚜렷한. ¶ *It is ~ that you are in the wrong.* 네가 잘못인 것은 자명하다 / *That a blind man ought not to drive a car is too ~ to need proof.* 소경이 차를 운전해선 안 된다는 것은 두말 할 나위 없다. **2** too apparent; obtrusive. 너무 뚜렷한; 눈에 거슬리는. ¶ *His polite manners were a little ~.* 그의 공손한 태도는 좀 눈에 거슬렸다. **3** too simple. 빤한. ¶ *The joke is too ~.* 참 시시한 농담이다. [↑]

:ob·vi·ous·ly [ábviəsli / ɔ́b-] *adv.* clearly; evidently. 명백히.

oc·a·ri·na [ɑ̀kərí:nə / ɔ̀k-] *n.* an egg-shaped musical wind-instrument, usu. made of terracotta. 오카리나《도기제의 타원형 취주 악기》. [It.]

:oc·ca·sion [əkéiʒən] *n.* **1** Ⓒ a particular time esp. marked by certain circumstance; an event. (어떤 특정한) 때; 경우; 일. ¶ *on this ~* 이 때; 이 경우 / *on one ~* 언젠가; 전에 / *on such an ~* 그 경우 / *on the ~ of his death* 그의 사망시에 / *They met on several occasions.* 그들은 여러 번 만났다 / *This is not an ~ for laughter.* 이것은 웃을 일이 아니다. **2** Ⓒ a good chance;

O

an opportunity. 호기(好機); (…할) 기회. ¶ *improve the ~* 기회를 이용하다 / *on the first ~* 기회 있는 대로. **3** Ⓒ a special event or ceremony; celebration. 행사; 의식; 축전(祝典). ¶ *A wedding is a very happy ~.* 결혼식은 아주 기쁜 행사다 / *The coronation of the king was a great ~.* 대관식은 성대했다. **4** Ⓤ reason; cause; need. 근거; 이유; 필요. ¶ *have no ~ to do* …할 이유[필요]가 없다 / *There is no ~ for you to get excited.* 네가 흥분할 필요는 없다.

on [***upon***] ***occasion***(***s***), sometimes; now and then. 때로; 이따금. ¶ *On ~ we have a picnic in the country.* 이따금 시골에 놀러 간다.

rise to the occasion, do whatever suddenly becomes necessary. 임기 응변의 조치를 취하다.

take [***seize***] ***the occasion to*** *do,* avail oneself of the opportunity to do. 기회를 이용하여 …하다.

— *vt.* (P6,13,14,20) cause; bring about. …의 원인이 되다; …을 초래하다. ¶ *Her behavior occasioned her parents much anxiety.* 그녀의 행실은 부모의 큰 걱정거리였다. [→case[1]]

·**oc·ca·sion·al** [əkéiʒənəl] *adj.* **1** happening sometimes; coming now and then. 이따금의. ¶ *an ~ earthquake* 이따금 있는 지진 / *an ~ visitor* 가끔 오는 손님. **2** used or designed for a special event or time. 특별한 경우를 위한; 임시의. ¶ *~ verses* [*music*] 특별한 경우를 위해 만든 시[음악] / *a ~ table* 임시 탁자.

:**oc·ca·sion·al·ly** [əkéiʒənəli] *adv.* now and then; sometimes. 이따금; 때때로.

Oc·ci·dent [áksədənt / ɔ́k-] *n.* **1** 《*the ~*》 the West; Europe and America. 서양; 구미(歐美)(opp. Orient). **2** 《*the o-*》 the west. 서쪽; 서방. [L. *occido*]

Oc·ci·den·tal [àksədéntl / ɔ̀k-] *adj.* **1** of the Occident. 서양의(opp. Oriental). **2** 《*o-*》 western. 서방의. — *n.* Ⓒ a person of Occidental countries. 서양인.

oc·cult [əkʌ́lt, ákʌlt / ɔkʌ́lt] *adj.* **1** concealed; hidden; secret. 숨은; 비밀의. **2** supernatural; magical; mysterious. 초자연적인; 마법의; 신비한. ¶ *Alchemy is one of the ~ sciences.* 연금술은 일종의 신비학이다. — *vt., vi.* hide or become hidden from view. …을 숨기다; 숨다. [L. *occulo* hide]

oc·cu·pan·cy [ákjəpənsi / ɔ́k-] *n.* Ⓤ the act of occupying; the period during which a house, etc. is occupied. 점유; 점유 기간. [→occupy]

oc·cu·pant [ákjəpənt / ɔ́k-] *n.* Ⓒ **1** a person who holds a house, land, office, etc. 점유자. **2** a person who is living in a place. 거주자. ¶ *Who is the ~ of this hut?—Rats are the only occupants.* 이 오두막엔 누가 살고 있소. —쥐뿐이오.

:**oc·cu·pa·tion** [àkjəpéiʃən / ɔ̀k-] *n.* **1** Ⓒ a business; a profession; Ⓤ employment. 직업; 업무; 일. ¶ *a man out of ~* 실업자 / *He has no fixed ~.* 고정직이 없다. **2** Ⓤ the act of occupying; the state of being occupied. 점유; 점령; 거주. ¶ *an ~ army* =*an army of ~* 점령군 / *the ~ of a house by a family* 한 가족이 집에 들어 살기. **3** Ⓤ the period during which a land, a house, etc. is occupied. 점유 기간.

oc·cu·pa·tion·al [àkjəpéiʃənəl / ɔ̀k-] *adj.* of an occupation. 직업의. ¶ *an ~ disease* 직업병 / *~ therapy* 작업 요법(療法)《심신(心身) 장애자에게 가벼운 작업을 시키면서 행하는 치료법》.

:**oc·cu·py** [ákjəpài / ɔ́k-] *vt.* (**-pied**) (P6,13) **1** take possession of (land, etc.); live in (some place). …을 점유[점령]하다; …에 거주하다. ¶ *~ the enemy's territory* 적의 영토를 점령하다 / *~ a house* 집을 차지하고 살다 / *~ rooms* [*an office*] 방[사무실]을 쓰고 있다. **2** take up or fill (a certain amount of space, time, position, etc.). (장소·시간 등)을 차지하다; 요하다. ¶ *Mr. Jones occupies an important position in this company.* 존스 씨는 이 회사의 요직을 차지하고 있다 / *His speech occupied more than one hour.* 그의 연설은 한 시간 이상 걸렸다 / *It occupies 3 hours to go there.* 거기 가려면 세 시간 걸린다 / *Many cares and anxieties occupied his mind.* 많은 근심 걱정이 그의 마음에서 떠나지 않았다. [L. *capio* take]

occupy oneself in [***about, with***] = ***be occupied in,*** engage in (something); be busied with. …에 종사하다; …에 전념하다. ¶ *He occupied himself with solving the problem.* 그는 그 문제를 푸는 데 골몰했다 / *We were occupied in building a new bridge.* 우리는 새 다리를 놓는 일을 했다.

:**oc·cur** [əkə́ːr] *vi.* (**-curred, -cur·ring**) **1** (P1) happen; take place. (일이) 생기다; 발생하다. ¶ *Several fires have occurred lately.* 최근 여러 건의 화재가 있었다. **2** (P1,2A) exist; be found. 있다; 보이다; 눈에 띄다. ¶ *Several misprints ~ on the last page.* 끝 장에 몇 자의 오식이 있다 / *Such plants ~ in Africa.* 그런 식물은 아프리카에 있다. **3** (P3) 《*to*》 come into one's mind. 생각이 나다. ¶ *It occurred to me that I should call on him.* 그를 찾아봐야겠다는 생각이 났다 / *Did it ~ to you to visit him?* 그를 찾아볼 생각을 했느냐. [→current]

·**oc·cur·rence** [əkə́ːrəns, əkʌ́r-] *n.* **1** Ⓤ the act or fact of occurring. (사건 등의) 발생. ¶ *The ~ of thunder in winter is comparatively rare.* 겨울철의 천둥은 비교적 드물다. **2** Ⓒ a happening; an event; an incident. 생긴 일; 사건. ¶ *an everyday ~* 일상사(日常事) / *an ~ of no importance* 대수롭지 않은 일 / *a most mysterious ~* 아주 신기한 일.

be of frequent [***rare***] ***occurrence,*** occur frequently [rarely]. 자주[드물게] 일어나다.

:o·cean [óuʃən] *n.* Ⓒ **1** the sea. 대양; 해양; …양(洋). ¶ *the Pacific Ocean* 태평양. **2** 《*fig.*》 a vast expanse of something. 광대무변(廣大無邊); …의 바다. ¶ *an ~ of light* 빛의 바다; 광대한 빛 / *an ~ of tears* 〔*difficulties*〕 끝없는 눈물〔난관〕/ *a vast ~ of foliage* 수해(樹海). **3** 《use. *pl.*》 《*colloq.*》 great quantity; plenty. 많음; 다량; 풍부. ¶ *oceans of money* 엄청난 돈; 거금(巨金) / *oceans of time* 많은 시간. [Gk.]

o·ce·an·ic [òuʃiǽnik] *adj.* **1** of or like the ocean. 바다의; 바다 같은. **2** living in or produced by the ocean. 바다에서 나는. ¶ *~ fish* 바닷물고기. **3** vast. 광대한. **4** 《*O-*》 of Oceania. 대양주(大洋洲)〔오세아니아〕의.

o·cher, o·chre [óukər] *n.* Ⓤ **1** a yellowish clay, used for making yellow-brown paint. 황토(黃土)《그림물감 원료》. **2** a yellow-brown color. 황토색; 오커. **3** 《U.S. *colloq.*》 money. 돈. [Gk. yellow]

:o'clock [əklák / -lɔ́k] *adv.* of the clock; according to the clock. …시(時). ¶ *at three ~,* 3시에. [abbr. of the clock]

Oct. October.

oc·ta·gon [áktəgàn, -gən / ɔ́ktəgən] *n.* Ⓒ a plane figure with eight sides and eight angles. 8변형; 8각형. [Gk. *oktō*, L. *octo* eight]

oc·tag·o·nal [aktǽgənl / ɔk-] *adj.* of an octagon. 8변형의; 8각형의.

oc·tave [áktiv, -teiv / ɔ́k-] *n.* Ⓒ **1** 《mus.》 the eighth note in the musical scale; a distance of eight notes on a scale; all the notes within this distance. 옥타브; 1음계 《제8음; 8도 음정》. **2** 《*poet.*》 the first eight lines of a sonnet. 8행 연구(聯句)《sonnet 의 처음 8행》. [L. *octo* eight]

oc·ta·vo [aktéivou / ɔk-] *n.* (*pl.* **-vos**) a size of a book in which each sheet is folded into eight leaves or sixteen pages. 8절판(切版)(cf. *folio*). 參考 8vo 로 생략. ¶ *a book in 8vo,* 8절판의 책. — *adj.* having this size. 8절판의. ¶ *an ~ edition* 8절판.

oc·tet(te) [aktét / ɔk-] *n.* **1** 《mus.》 eight singers or players. 8중주〔중창〕단. **2** =octave 2.

:Oc·to·ber [aktóubər / ɔk-] *n.* the tenth month of the year. 10월. [L. *octo* eight]

oc·to·pi [áktəpài / ɔ́k-] *n.* pl. of **octopus.**

oc·to·pus [áktəpəs / ɔ́k-] *n.* Ⓒ (*pl.* **-puses** or **-to·pi**) **1** 《animal》 a sea animal with a soft body and eight long arms. 낙지; 문어. **2** 《*fig.*》 any powerful organization or influence with wide-reaching branches. 다방면에 세력을 떨치는 연합 조직. [octo-, L. *poús* foot]

oc·tu·ple [áktjupəl, aktjúː-] *adj.* eightfold. 8배의. — *vt.* (P6) multiply by eight. 8배하다. [octo-, L. *-plus* -fold]

oc·u·lar [ákjələr / ɔ́k-] *adj.* of the eyes or sight. 눈의; 시력의. ¶ *an ~ witness* 목격자. [L. *oculus* eye]

:odd [ad / ɔd] *adj.* **1** a little more (than what is needed); left over. 여분의; 나머지의; …여(餘)의. ¶ *three hundred (and) ~ pupils,* 3백 명 남짓한 학생 / *the ~ money* 우수리 돈 / *It cost six dollars ~.* 6달러 남짓 들었다 / *twenty ~ years,* 20여 년 / *You may keep the ~ money.* 우수리는 그냥 가지시오. **2** not paired; missing a part of a set. 외짝의; 짝이 모자라는. ¶ *an ~ stocking* 〔*glove, shoe*〕 한 짝뿐인 양말〔장갑, 신발〕/ *~ volumes* 낙질본(落帙本). **3** extra; for a short time; occasional. 임시의; 단기의. ¶ *~ jobs* 임시〔뜨내기〕 일 / *an ~ hand* 〔*man, lad*〕 임시 고용인 / *at ~ moments* 짬짬이 / *at ~ times* 간혹; 이따금. **4** ⓐ (of numbers) not even; not able to be divided by two. 홀수〔기수〕의. ¶ *One, three, five, and seven are ~ numbers.* 1, 3, 5, 7은 홀수다. ⓑ called or known by an odd numbers. 홀수 번호의. ¶ *the ~ houses in a street* 거리의 홀수 번호의 집들 / *the ~ months* 큰달. **5** strange; queer; peculiar. 별난; 이상〔기묘〕한. ¶ *an ~ habit* 묘한 버릇 / *an ~ fish* 괴짜 / *It is ~ that you did not know it.* 네가 그걸 모른다니 이상하다. [N. *oddi* point, angle]

odd·i·ty [ádəti / ɔ́d-] *n.* (*pl.* **-ties**) **1** Ⓤ the state of being odd; strangeness. 기묘; 별남. ¶ *the ~ of his dress and manners* 그의 묘한 복장과 거동. **2** Ⓒ a queer person, thing or act. 괴짜; 묘한 물건. ¶ *He looks a regular ~.* 정말 괴짜군. [↑]

odd·ly [ádli / ɔ́d-] *adv.* in an odd manner. 기묘하게; 별나게; 기이하게.

odd·ment [ádmənt / ɔ́d-] *n.* Ⓒ 《usu. *pl.*》 something left over; an odd piece. 남은 물건; 짝이 안 맞는 물건; 잡동사니.

odds [adz / ɔdz] *n. pl.* 《sometimes used as *sing.*》 **1** things which are not equal; inequalities. 불평등(한 것·일); 차이. **2** advantages; chances in favor of one side and against another. 승산. ¶ *fight against longer ~* 강적과 싸우다 / *The ~ are in our favor* 〔*against us*〕. 우리에게 승산이 있다〔없다〕. **3** a quarrel. 싸움; 다툼. **4** the ratio of the money staked on a chance to that which will be paid if the chance succeeds. (도박에서) 지른 돈의 비율. ¶ *The ~ are 5 to 1.* 비율은 5대 1이다《상대방이 이기면 지른 돈의 5배를 내줌》. **5** an extra allowance given to the weaker side in a game, etc. 핸디캡; 접어주기. [→odd]

be at odds (=*quarrel*) ***with someone.*** …와 싸우고 있다.

by long 〔***all***〕 ***odds,*** by far; certainly. 훨씬; 분명히. ¶ *This is by all ~ the easier way.* 이게 훨씬 쉬운 방법이다.

make no odds, keep balanced. 균형을 이루다.

make odds even, make equal. 우열을 없애다.

odds and ends, useless things left over.

O

나머지; 잡동사니.

set at odds, make (someone) quarrel. …을 다투게 하다; 싸움을 붙이다.

ode [oud] *n.* Ⓒ a poem which expresses noble feelings in a solemn style, usu. in honor of a person or event. 송시(頌詩); 부(賦). [Gk. *aeidō* sing]

o·di·ous [óudiəs] *adj.* hateful; unpleasant; ugly. 밉살스러운; 불쾌한; 추한. ¶ *His conduct was* ~. 그 자의 행동은 불쾌했다. ●**o·di·ous·ly** [-li] *adv.* **o·di·ous·ness** [-nis] *n.* [L.=hatred]

o·di·um [óudiəm] *n.* Ⓤ hatred; ill feeling. 증오; 혐오. ¶ *I shall get the* ~ *of it.* 그 때문에 욕깨나 먹게 됐다. [↑]

O

***o·dor,** 《Brit.》 **-dour** [óudər] *n.* **1** Ⓒ smell; scent; fragrance. 냄새; 향내. **2** Ⓤ reputation. 평판; 인기. ¶ *He is in bad* ~. 평판이 나쁘다. [L. *odor*]

o·dor·ous [óudərəs] *adj.* having an odor; sweet-smelling; fragrant. 향내나는; 향기로운.

O·dys·se·us [oudísiəs, -sju:s] *n.* =Ulysses.

Od·ys·sey [ádəsi / 5d-] *n.* an epic poem about Odysseus, a Greek hero, written by Homer. 오디세이. [Gk.]

***o'er** [ɔ:r, ouər] *prep., adv.* 《*poet.*》=over.

oe·soph·a·gus [isáfəgəs / -sɔ́f-] *n.* = esophagus.

⁝of [av, ʌv / ɔv, əv] *prep.* **1** belonging to. …의; …에 속하는. ¶ *the men* ~ *that time* 그 시대의 사람들 / *a leg* ~ *a table* 탁자 다리 / *a friend* ~ *mine* 내 친구. **2** out of; from among; parted from. …의 중(안)의; …의 일부(분)의. ¶ *some* ~ *us* 우리 중의 몇 사람 / *Take part* ~ *it, not the whole* ~ *it.* 그 중에서 일부만 가져라, 전부는 말고. **3** containing; having. …이 든. ¶ *a cup* ~ *tea* 차 한 잔 / *a house* ~ *six rooms* 방 여섯 있는 집. **4** made of or from; using as the material. …으로 만든; …을 재료로 한. ¶ *a house* ~ *wood* 목조 가옥 / *made* ~ *brick* 벽돌로 지은 / *a piece* ~ *paper* 종이 한 장. **5** about; concerning. …에 대하여(는); …에 관하여(는). ¶ *be hard* ~ *hearing* 잘 듣지 못하다 / *be sixty years* ~ *age* 나이는 60세 / *tell someone* ~ *an accident* …에게 사고에 관해 이야기하다 / *be quick* ~ *eye* 눈치가 빠르다 / *be afraid* ~ *dying* 죽음을 두려워하다. **6** that is (the same as); named. …라고 하는; …하다는. ¶ *the city* ~ *New York* 뉴욕이라는 도시 / *(the) three* ~ *us* 우리들 셋 / *an angel* ~ *a girl* 천사 같은 소녀 / *the fact* ~ *my having done it* 내가 그렇게 한 사실. **7** away from. …에서 (떨어져). ¶ *three miles west* ~ *the river* 강에서 서쪽으로 3마일 / *rob him* ~ *a purse* 그에게서 지갑을 털다 / *borrow money* ~ *one's brother* 동생에게서 돈을 빌리다 / *within ten minutes* ~ *the station* 역에서 10분 이내의 (거리에). **8** caused by. …로 인한; …때문에. ¶ *die* ~ *heart failure* 심장 마비로 죽다 / *die* ~ *sorrow* 상심으로 죽다. **9** having; being. …을 가진; …한. 參考 of+명사로 형용사구를 만듦. ¶ *a man* ~ *ability* 재능 있는 사람 / *a girl* ~ *twelve* 열두 살 난 소녀 / *a look* ~ *pity* 측은해하는 표정. **10** produced, written, etc., by. …의 손에 의한. ¶ *the works* ~ *Shakespeare* 세익스피어의 작품. **11** toward; directed to. …에의; …에 대한. ¶ *the love* ~ *God* 하느님에 대한 사랑 / *the fear* ~ *God* 신에의 두려움. **12** (of time) on; during. …의 때(에)는; …의 동안. ¶ ~ *recent years* 근년 / ~ *old* 옛날에는 / ~ *late years* 최근 몇 해 / 《*colloq.*》 *We usually go to church* ~ *a Sunday.* 일요일엔 대개 교회에 간다. **13** 《U.S. *colloq.*》 (of time) before; to. …(분) 전(opp. after). ¶ *at ten minutes* ~ *six,* 6시 10분 전에. [E.]

⁝off [ɔ:f, af / ɔf] *prep.* **1** ⓐ not on; away from. …에서 떨어져(벗어나). ¶ *three miles* ~ *the road* 길에서 3마일 떨어져 / *A button is* ~ *your coat.* 코트의 단추 하나가 떨어졌다 / *He fell* ~ *his horse.* 말에서 떨어졌다 / *He pushed me* ~ *my seat.* 그는 자리에서 나를 밀어냈다 / *go* 〔*get*〕 ~ *the subject* 본제(本題)에서 벗어나 있다 / *She took the ring* ~ *her third finger.* 그녀는 약손가락에서 반지를 뽑았다. ⓑ remove from. (있던 자리에서) 떨어져. ¶ *The wheel was* ~ *the car.* 차바퀴가 빠졌다. **2** seaward from. …의 앞〔난〕바다에. ¶ ~ *the coast of Alaska* 알래스카의 앞바다에(서) / ~ *the harbor* 항구를 벗어나. **3** less than. …에서 할인하여; 에누리해서. ¶ *It was sold at ten percent* ~ *the usual price.* 그것은 1할 할인해서 팔렸다.

—*adv.* **1** away. 저쪽으로; 떨어져; 벗어져. ¶ *take* ~ *one's hat* 모자를 벗다 / *work with one's coat* ~ 겉옷을 벗고 일하다 / *go* ~ *on a journey* 길을 나서다 / *She stood a few yards* ~. 그녀는 몇 야드 떨어져 있었다 / *Off we go!* 자, 떠나자〔가자〕. **2** distant in time or space. (시간·거리가) 떨어져. ¶ *The holidays are a week* ~. 앞으로 1주일이면 휴가다 / *far* ~ 멀리 떨어져 / *three miles* ~, 3마일 밖에. **3** so as to stop or make less; not connected. 줄어; 정지하여; 끊어져. ¶ *turn the water* ~ 물을 잠그다 / *leave* ~ *work* 일을 그만두다 / *The radio was* ~ *all day.* 라디오는 종일 꺼져 있었다. **4** in full; wholly; completely. 전부; 완전히; 끝까지. ¶ *drink* ~ 단숨에 마셔 버리다 / *clear* ~ *the table* 식탁을 깨끗이 치우다 / *be* ~ *with* …와 손을〔관계를〕 끊다. **5** without work; away from the work. 일을 쉬어. ¶ *We were* ~ *for the afternoon.* 오후에 일이 없었다 / *He is* ~ *duty.* 그는 비번이다 / *He took a day* ~. 그는 하루 휴가를 냈다.

be badly* 〔*well*〕 *off, in a bad 〔good〕 condition. 어렵게〔유복하게〕 지내다.

be off, go away; leave quickly; run away. 떠나다; 도망치다.

Keep off! Don't come near! 접근 금지.

off and on, now and then. 이따금. ¶ *He*

comes here ~ and on. 가끔 여기에 온다.
Off with you ! Go away ! Depart ! 꺼져.
on and off =off and on.
— *adj.* **1** ⓐ farther; far. 먼 쪽의; 저쪽의. ¶ *on the ~ side of the wall* 벽의 저쪽에. ⓑ (of horses, carriages, etc.) on the right-hand side. (말 따위) 오른쪽의(opp. near). ¶ *the ~ horse of a pair* 두 말 중 오른쪽 말. ⓒ away from a main line. (본 길에서) 갈라진; 지엽적인. ¶ *an ~ road* 옆길 / *an ~ issue* 지엽적인 문제. **2** away from work; not busy; not active. 쉬는; 한가한; 한산한. ¶ *during ~ hours* 한가한 시간에 / *an ~ day* 쉬는 날 / *an ~ season in the trade* 경기가 안 좋은 철; 불황기. **3** wrong; in error; not normal. 틀린; 상태가 나쁜; 정상이 아닌. ¶ *You are ~ on that point.* 그 점에서 틀려 있다 / *He is a little ~, but he's really harmless.* 그는 좀 이상하지만 별탈은 없다 / *I am feeling rather ~ today.* 왜 그런지 오늘은 기분이 별로다. **4** (of food) no longer fresh. (음식이) 상한. ¶ *The fish is a bit ~.* 고기가 좀 상했다. **5** on the way; beginning; starting. 떠나는; 시작하는. ¶ *The train started and we were ~ on our trip.* 기차가 떠나고 우리 여행이 시작됐다. [→of]

of·fal [ɔ́(:)fəl, ɑ́fəl] *n.* Ⓤ the useless parts of fish or other animals killed for food; waste and worthless matter. (생선 등의 버린) 내장 (등); 쓰레기. [=off-fall]

off chance [∠∠] *n.* a slight possibility. 만의 하나의 기회. ¶ *There is an ~....* 잘만 되면 …될지도 모른다. [*off*]

off-col·or [ɔ́:fkʌ́lər, ɑ́f- / ɔ́f-] *adj.* **1** defective in color. 안색이 나쁜. **2** somewhat improper. 점잖지 못한. [*off*]

:of·fence [əféns] *n.* 《Brit.》 =offense.

***of·fend** [əfénd] *vt.* (P6) **1** hurt the feelings of (someone); make (someone) angry or displeased. …의 감정을 해치다; 화나게 하다; 불쾌하게 만들다. ¶ *I am sorry if I've offended you.* 기분 나쁘게 했다면 미안하다 / *I was offended at* 〔*by*〕 *his rude manners.* 그의 무례한 태도에 화가 났다 / *My friend was offended by my laughter.* 내가 웃었더니 친구는 화를 내더군 / *Some music offends, rather than pleases, the ear.* 어떤 음악은 듣기 좋다기보다 귀에 거슬린다. **2** cause (someone) to sin. …을 죄짓게 하다. ¶ 《Bible》 *If thy right eye ~ thee, pluck it out.* 만일에 네 오른 눈이 너를 실족게 하거든 빼어내 버려라.
— *vi.* (P3) **1** commit a crime; break a law, custom, religious code, etc. 죄를 짓다; 법(규) 따위를 어기다; 위반하다. ¶ *~ against custom* 〔*the law*〕 관습〔법〕을 어기다. **2** hurt someone's feelings; commit an offense. 기분을 해치다. ¶ *In what have I offended ?* 저 때문에 기분이 상하셨나요. [L. *fendo* strike]

of·fend·er [əféndər] *n.* Ⓒ a person who breaks a law or rule. 범법자; 위반자. ¶ *a first ~* 초범(자) / *an old* 〔*a repeated*〕 *~* 상습범 / *Offenders will be fined 5 dollars.* 위반자는 5달러의 과료에 처함.

:of·fense, 《Brit.》 **-fence** [əféns] *n.* **1** Ⓒ the act of breaking a law or rule; sin; crime. 위반; 반칙; 죄; 범죄. ¶ *an ~ against good manners* 무례 / *Driving while drinking is a serious ~.* 음주 운전은 중대한 범죄다. **2** Ⓤ attack. 공격(opp. defense). ¶ *The most effective defense is ~.* 가장 효과적 방어는 공격이다. **3** Ⓒ something that hurts a person's mind; insult; displeasure. 기분 상하게 하는 것; 불쾌한 일; 모욕. ¶ *No ~ was meant.* 악의는 아니었다. **4** Ⓤ the state of being offended; anger. 기분이 상함; 화남. [→offend]
commit* 〔*do*〕 *an offense, offend. …을 위반하다; 범법하다.
give offense to, make (someone) displeased; insult. …을 기분 나쁘게 하다; 모욕하다.
take offense (=*become displeased*) ***at*** *something.* …에 불쾌해지다; 화내다.

***of·fen·sive** [əfénsiv] *adj.* **1** unpleasant; disgusting. 불쾌한; 싫은. ¶ *~ to the eye* 보기 싫은 / *That smell is ~.* 냄새가 역하다. **2** insulting; not respectful. 무례한; 기분 나쁜. ¶ *~ language* 무례한 언사. **3** attacking; aggressive. 공격적인; 공격용의(opp. defensive). ¶ *~ weapons* 〔*arms*〕 공격 무기.
— *n.* Ⓒ 《often *the ~*》 an attack; an aggression. 공격; 공세.
take the offensive, be aggressive. 공세로 나오다; 공세를 취하다.

:of·fer [ɔ́(:)fər, ɑ́f-] *vt.* **1** (P6,13,14) give (someone) a chance to get; present; hold out. …에 신청〔제출〕하다; 제공하다; (손 따위)를 내밀다. ¶ *~ a gift to someone* 아무에게 선물을 내놓다 / *~ one's hand* (악수를 위해) 손을 내밀다; 청혼하다 / *~ a bribe* 뇌물을 주다 / *She offered me her help.* 나를 도와 주겠노라 했다. **2** (P6,13) present (something) to God. …을 신에게 바치다; 드리다. ¶ *~ a prayer* (*to God*) 기도를 드리다 / *~ up sacrifices* 제물을 바치다. **3** (P6,8) propose; suggest. …을 제의〔제안〕하다. ¶ *Everyone offered his own solution.* 제각기 나름대로의 해결책을 내놨다 / *He offered to accompany me home.* 나를 집까지 바래다 주마고 했다. **4** (P6,8,13) try; attempt; make a show of. …하려고 하다; 시도하다. ¶ *He offered to strike me.* 나를 때리려고 했다 / *~ resistance* 〔*violence*〕 저항〔폭력〕을 시도하다. **5** (P6,13,14) show (something) for sale; bid (an amount of money) as a price. …을 팔려고 내놓다; …의 값을 부르다. ¶ *He offered* (*me*) *forty dollars for the goods.* 그 물건을 40 달러에 사겠다고 했다 / *~ goods at low price* 물건을 싼 값에 내놓다.
— *vi.* (P1) **1** occur; be proposed. 나타나다; 일어나다; 제공되다. ¶ *I shall seize the first opportunity that offers.* 첫번째의 기회를

잡을 것이다. **2** sacrifice in worship. (제물로) 바치다.

— *n.* Ⓒ **1** the act of offering; something offered; a suggestion; a proposal. 신청; 제공; 제의. ¶ *an ~ of help* 돕겠다는 제의 / *make an ~ of money* 돈을 기부하겠다고 하다 / *She has declined several offers of marriage.* 여러 번의 청혼을 거절해 왔다. **2** a price offered. 부르는〔사는〕 값; 오퍼. ¶ *an ~ of $ 35,000 for a house* 집 한 채 값으로 35,000 달러의 제의. **3** putting forward for sale. 팔려고 내놓기. ¶ *This house is on ~.* 매물로 나온 집이다. [L. *fero* bring]

goods on offer, goods for sale at a certain price. 매물.

O

·**of·fer·ing** [ɔ́(:)fəriŋ, ɑ́f-] *n.* **1** Ⓤ the act of making a proposal. 신청; 제공. **2** Ⓒ a gift esp. to the church. 제물; 봉납물(奉納物); (교회에의) 헌금. **3** Ⓒ a gift; a present. 선물.

off·hand [ɔ́(:)fhǽnd, ɑ́f-] *adj.* made or done without preparation; careless. 즉석의; 준비 없이 하는; 되는 대로의. ¶ *an ~ remark* 되는 대로 하는 말. — *adv.* in an offhand manner; without preparation. 즉석에서; 되는 대로. ¶ *translate ~* 즉석에서 번역하다 / *reply ~* 적당히 대답하다. [*off*]

off·hand·ed [ɔ́(:)fhǽndid, ɑ́f-] *adj.* =offhand.

:**of·fice** [ɔ́(:)fis, ɑ́f-] *n.* Ⓒ **1** a building or room used as a business place. 사무실; 회사; 일터. ¶ *a lawyer's ~* 법률〔변호사〕 사무소 / *a dentist's ~* 치과 진료실 / *be* 〔*work*〕 *in an ~* 회사에 근무하고 있다 / *a branch ~* 지점(支店). **2** ⒸⓊ a public position; a post. 관직; 지위. ¶ *hold* 〔*take*〕 *~* 관직에 있다 / *accept* 〔*resign*〕 *~* 취임〔사직〕하다 / *The President holds the highest public ~ in the United States.* 합중국에서 대통령은 최고의 지위다. **3** a government department. 관청; 국; 부; 성. ¶ *the Foreign Office* 외무부. **4** a duty; a task; a job. 임무; 직무; 소임. ¶ *A teacher's ~ is teaching.* 선생의 소임은 가르치는 일이다 / *The ~ of the ears is to hear.* 귀의 역할은 듣는 일이다. **5** 《*the ~*》 all the people working in an office. (사무실의) 전직원. ¶ *The whole ~ was at the wedding.* 직원들은 모두 결혼식에 갔다. **6** 《usu. *pl.*》 an act of kind or unkind services; an attention. 친절〔불친절〕한 행위; 주선. ¶ *by her good offices* 그녀의 호의로 / *He did me many good offices.* 나를 위해 이것저것 애를 많이 썼다. **7** a religious ceremony or prayer. (종교적) 의식; 기도. ¶ *the last offices* 장례식. **8** 《*pl.*》 《Brit.》 rooms in a house used for household work, such as the kitchen, cellar, or bathroom. (부엌, 광, 욕실 등) 가사실(家事室). [L. *facio* do]

office boy [⌐–⌐] *n.* a boy employed in an office to do small jobs. 사환.

of·fice·hold·er [ɔ́(:)fishòuldər, ɑ́f-] *n.* Ⓒ a person holding an office, esp. a public office; a public servant. 공무원; 관리.

:**of·fi·cer** [ɔ́(:)fisər, ɑ́f-] *n.* Ⓒ **1** a person whose business is to perform a public duty. 공무원; 관리. **2** a person who is appointed to manage the affairs of an organization. 임원; 직원. **3** 《mil.》 a person who is appointed to command others. 장교. ¶ *a commanding ~* 사령관. **4** 《naut.》 the captain; a person below the rank of captain. 선장; 고급 선원. ¶ *a first* 〔*a second, a third*〕, 1〔2, 3〕등 항해사.

— *vt.* (P6) 《usu. in *passive*》 furnish with officers; act as an officer to. 장교를〔고급 선원을〕 배치하다; 지휘하다. ¶ *The army was well officered.* 군은 잘 통솔되어 있었다.

:**of·fi·cial** [əfíʃəl] *adj.* **1** of an office or a position of authority. 관(官)의; 직무(職務)〔공무(公務)〕상의(opp. private). ¶ *~ responsibilities* 직무상의 책임 / *an ~ report* 공보(公報) / *an ~ position* 관직; 공직. **2** approved by authority; authorized. 공인된; 공식적인. ¶ *~ discount rate* 공정 할인율 / *~ statement* 공식 성명 / *The news is not ~.* 그 뉴스는 비공식적인 것이다. **3** suitable for a person in office; formal. (사람이) 관료적인; 의례적(儀禮的)인. ¶ *an ~ manner* 딱딱한〔관료적〕 태도 / *an ~ reply* 의례적인 답변.

— *n.* Ⓒ a person who works in a public office; an officer. 관리; 공무원; 임직원. ¶ *a government* 〔*a public*〕 *~* 관리.

of·fi·cial·ism [əfíʃəlìzəm] *n.* **1** an official system; formality. 관료〔형식〕주의. **2** excessive attention to official rules. 지나친 형식 의존; 번문 욕례(繁文縟禮)(cf. *red tape*).

·**of·fi·cial·ly** [əfíʃəli] *adv.* in an official manner. 관리로서; 공무〔직무〕상.

of·fi·ci·ate [əfíʃièit] *vi.* (P2A,3) **1** carry out the duties of an office. 직무를 수행하다. **2** carry out the duties in a religious service. (사제(司祭)가) 의식을 행하다. ¶ *~ at a marriage* 결혼식을 집행하다. **3** serve as referee, umpire in a sport contest or game. (경기의) 심판을 보다. [→office]

of·fi·cious [əfíʃəs] *adj.* very fond of giving unwelcome service or advice. (공연히) 참견〔간섭〕하는. ¶ *an ~ manner.* ● **of·fi·cious·ly** [-li] *adv.*

off·ing [ɔ́(:)fiŋ, ɑ́f-] *n.* Ⓒ 《usu. *the ~*》 the distant part of the sea as far as can be seen from the land. 난바다. [*off*]

in the offing, **a**) (of a ship) at some distance from the shore but still in sight. (배가) 난바다에; 멀리 아득히 보여. **b**) 《*fig.*》 (of an event) near; which will probably happen soon. 가까이에; 곧 일어날 것 같아.

off·ish [ɔ́(:)fiʃ, ɑ́f-] *adj.* 《*colloq.*》 cold or distant in manner. (태도가) 쌀쌀한.

off-li·cence [ɔ́(:)flàisəns, ɑ́f-] *n.* 《Brit.》 a

licence to sell beer and other alcoholic liquors for consumption off the premises; the place where such sales are conducted. 주류 판매 허가; 그 점포《점내에서의 음주는 불허》. [*off*]

off·print [ɔ́:fprìnt, ɑ́f-] *n.* Ⓒ a reprint of an article from a magazine, etc. (잡지 등에서의) 발췌 인쇄. [↑]

off·set [ɔ́(:)fsèt, ɑ́f-] *n.* Ⓒ **1** something which makes a balance between loss and gain; compensation. 상쇄하는 것; 차감(差減) 계산; 벌충. **2** Ⓤ 《print.》 a kind of printing process. 오프셋 인쇄(印刷). **3** ⓐ something developed or set off from something else. 분파(分派). ⓑ 《bot.》 a side shoot from a main stem or root; a branch; an offshoot. 곁눈; 분지(分枝). **4** the beginning; the start. 시작; 출발.
— [ɔ̀(:)fsét, ɑ̀f-] *vt.* (**-set, -set·ting**) (P6,13) make up for (something); balance. …을 메우다; 상쇄하다. ¶ *Part of the profit ~ the loss.* 이익의 일부로 손실을 메우다.

off·shoot [ɔ́(:)fʃù:t, ɑ́f-] *n.* Ⓒ anything of secondary development from a main part or source; a shoot from a main stem; a branch; a separate family. 분지(分枝); 지파(支派); 분파; 분가(分家).

off·shore [ɔ́(:)fʃɔ́:r, ɑ́f-] *adv.* away from the shore. 앞바다에[쪽으로]. ¶ *A wind is blowing ~.* 바람이 바다쪽으로 불고 있다 / *They pushed the boat ~.* 그들은 보트를 바다로 밀어넣었다. — *adj.* **1** coming from the shore; moving towards the sea. 앞바다의[로 향한]. ¶ *an ~ wind* 바다쪽으로 부는 바람. **2** at a distance from the shore. 해안에서 떨어진. ¶ *~ fisheries* 근해 어업.

·**off·spring** [ɔ́(:)fspriŋ, ɑ́f-] *n.* Ⓒ (*pl.* **off-spring** or **-springs**) **1** a child or children; descendants. 자식; 자녀; 자손. **2** 《*fig.*》 a result; product; something created. 결과; 소산(所産). ¶ *the ~ of a vivid imagination* 왕성한 상상력이 낳은 소산[작품].

off·stage [ɔ́(:)fstéidʒ, ɑ́f-] *adj.* away from the part of the stage that the audience can see. 무대 뒤의《객석에서 안 보이는》.

off-the-rec·ord [ɔ́:fðərékərd, ɑ́f-] *adj.* (of a statement) made in confidence; not to be recorded. (성명 등이) 비공개의; 내밀한; 기록에 남기지 않은. [*off*]

off·year [ɔ́(:)fjìər, ɑ́f-] *adj.* **1** of a year without a major election. 중간 선거의 해의. **2** of a year marked by inferior production. 작황(作況)이 나쁜 해의.

·**oft** [ɑft, ɔ(:)ft] *adv.* 《*arch., poet.*》 =often.

⁝**of·ten** [ɔ́(:)ftən, ɑ́f-] *adv.* many times; frequently. 종종; 자주. ¶ *I ~ see him.* =*I see him ~.* 자주 그를 만난다 / *It very ~ rains here.* 여긴 비가 아주 잦다. [E.]
as often as, each time that. …할 때마다. ¶ *As ~ as he sees me, he asks for money.* 나를 만날 때마다 돈 얘기다.
as often as not =***more often than not,*** frequently. 자주; 빈번히. ¶ *More ~ than not, he visited the village.* 자주 시골에 간다.
every so often, from time to time. 이따금; 때때로.
once too often, once more than is wise, safe, etc. 공연히 한번 더; 도를 지나쳐; 너무 자주. ¶ *He exceeded the speed limit once too ~ and was fined* £5. 꽤나 속도 위반을 하더니 끝내는 벌금 5파운드를 물었다.

of·ten·times [ɔ́(:)ftəntáimz, ɑ́f-] *adv.* 《*arch., poet.*》 =often.

oft·times [ɑ́fttàimz, ɔ́(:)ft-] *adv.* =often.

o·gle [óugəl] *vi., vt.* (P1;6) look at (someone) meaningly. (…에게) 추파를 보내다. — *n.* an ogling glance. 추파. [G. *auge* eye]

o·gre [óugər] *n.* Ⓒ (in fairy tales) a monster or giant who eats people; a cruel, ugly man. (동화의) 사람 잡아먹는 귀신; 잔인하고 무서운 사람. [F.]

o·gre·ish [óugəriʃ] *adj.* like an ogre. 사람 잡아먹는 귀신 같은

⁝**Oh, oh** [ou] *interj.* =O².

O·hi·o [ouhàiou] *n.* a northeastern State of the United States. 오하이오 주. 參考 O.로 생략함. 주도는 Columbus.

ohm [oum] *n.* Ⓒ a unit of resistance to an electric current. 옴《전기 저항의 단위》. [Person]

o·ho [ouhóu] *interj.* a cry of pain, surprise, etc. 아야; 아; 어. [*o, ho*]

⁝**oil** [ɔil] *n.* **1** ⓊⒸ a thick, greasy liquid used for fuel, cooking, driving machinery, etc. 기름. ¶ *machine ~* 기계유 / *mineral ~* 광유(鑛油) / *whale ~* 고래 기름. **2** 《*pl.*》 an oil painting; an oil color. 유화; 유화 그림 물감. **3** 《*pl.*》 =oilskins.
burn [***consume***] ***the midnight oil,*** sit up late at night working or studying. 밤늦게까지 일[공부]하다.
pour [***throw***] ***oil on the flame,*** make a quarrel worse; agitate. 싸움을 부채질[선동]하다.
pour [***throw***] ***oil on*** (***troubled***) ***waters,*** put down a quarrel, etc. (싸움 등을) 가라앉히다; 진정시키다.
strike oil, **a**) discover a source of mineral oil. 유맥(油脈)을 찾아내다. **b**) 《*fig.*》 gain profit; suddenly become rich. 노다지를 잡다; 벼락 부자가 되다.
— *vt.* (P6) **1** put oil in or on (a machine, etc); supply (something) with oil. (기계 따위)에 기름을 바르다[치다]. **2** bribe (someone) …에게 뇌물을 주다. — *vi.* (P1) become oil by melting. 녹아 기름이 되다. ¶ *Be careful not to allow butter to ~.* 버터가 녹지 않게 조심해라. [L. *olea* olive]
have a well-oiled tongue, be very talkative. 구변이 좋다.
oil someone's hand [***palm***], give (someone) a bribe. …에게 뇌물을 (쥐어)주다.
oil one's [***the***] ***tongue,*** flatter. 아첨하다;

알랑거리다.
oil the wheels, make things go smoothly (by bribes). (뇌물을 써서) 일이 잘 돌아가게 하다.
smell oil, bear traces of much labor. 애쓴 흔적이 (엿)보이다.

oil cake [´ ˌ] *n.* cattle food made from crushed oil seeds. 깻묵《사료》.

oil·can [ɔ́ilkæ̀n] *n.* Ⓒ a can with a long narrow projecting tube, used for pouring oil into machines. 주유기(注油器).

oil·cloth [ɔ́ilklɔ̀(ː)θ, -klɑ̀θ] *n.* Ⓤ cotton cloth waterproofed with oil paint. 유포(油布).

O

oil·col·or [ɔ́ilkʌ̀lər] *n.* 《usu. *pl.*》 paint ground in oil. (유화용) 그림 물감.

oil·er [ɔ́ilər] *n.* Ⓒ **1** a person who pours oil on machinery. 기름치는 사람; 주유자 (cf. *oilman*). **2** an oilcan. 주유기. **3** a ship built for carrying oil; a tanker. 유조선; 탱커. **4** 《U.S. *colloq.*》 an oilskin coat. 방수복.

oil field [´ ˌ] *n.* an area where mineral oil is found. 유전(油田).

oil·man [ɔ́ilmæ̀n, -mən] *n.* (*pl.* **-men** [´mèn, -mən]) **1** a maker or seller of oil. 제유업자; 기름 장수. **2** a person who oils machines. 주유원(注油員)(cf. *oiler*).

oil painting [´ ˌ-] *n.* **1** the art of painting in oilcolors 유화 그리는 법. **2** a picture painted in oilcolors. 유화(油畫).

oil·skin [ɔ́ilskin] *n.* **1** Ⓤ cloth waterproofed with oil. 유포(油布); 방수천. **2** 《*pl.*》 a coat or pair of trousers made of oilskin. 방수복.

oil well [´ ˌ] *n.* a well yielding oil. 유정(油井).

oil·y [ɔ́ili] *adj.* (**oil·i·er, oil·i·est**) **1** of or like oil; covered with oil. 기름의; 기름 같은; 기름이 밴; 기름투성이의. **2** 《*fig.*》 (of manner or speech) smooth-tongued; flattering. (언행이) 매끄러운; 겉발림말을 잘하는. ¶ *Politicians often have an ~ manner.* 정치가들은 흔히 겉발린 말을 잘한다.

oint·ment [ɔ́intmənt] *n.* ⓊⒸ a greasy substance often used as skin medicine. 연고; 고약. ¶ *Cold cream is an ~.* 콜드 크림은 연고의 일종이다. [L. *unguo* anoint]

OK, O.K. [òukéi, ´ ˌ] *adj., adv.* 《U.S. *colloq.*》 all right; correct(ly); approved. 오케이; 좋아; 틀림 없는; 검사필의. 參考 okay, okeh, okey 라고도 씀. ¶ *Everything's OK.* 만사 오케이 / *OK, I'll do it.* 좋아, 그거 내가 하지. —*n.* Ⓒ (*pl.* **OK's** or **O.K.'s**) 《originally U.S. *informal*》 an approval. 동의; 인가; 승인. —*vt.* (**OK'd** or **O.K.'d, OK'ing** or **O.K.'ing**) (P6) approve. …을 승인하다. ¶ *get an OK on a proposal* 제안을 승인받다. [all correct의 발음 철자인 oll korrect에서]

o·kay [òukéi] *adj., adv., vt., n.* 《U.S. *colloq.*》 =O.K.

Ok·la·ho·ma [òukləhóumə] *n.* a southwestern State of the United States. 오클라호마. 參考 Okla.로 생략함. 주도는 Oklahoma City.

:old [ould] *adj.* (**old·er** or **eld·er, old·est** or **eld·est**) **1** having lived or existed for a long time; aged. 늙은; 나이 먹은(opp. young). ¶ *grow* 〔*get*〕 *~* 나이를 먹다; 늙다 / *the ~* 늙은이들 / *young and ~* 늙은이나 젊은이나; 남녀 노소 / *be prematurely ~* 겉늙다 / 《*colloq.*》 *one's ~ man* 〔*wife*〕 자기 서방〔마누라〕 / *He looks ~ for his age.* 그는 나이보다 늙어 보인다 / *He is the oldest boy in the class.* 그는 반에서 제일 나이가 많다. **2** of age; in age. …살의. ¶ *How ~ is he?* / *a girl* (*of*) *twelve years ~* 스무 살 된 처녀 / *He is three years older than I.* 그는 나보다 세 살 많다 / *a baby ten days ~* 태어난 지 열흘된 아기. **3** not new; made long ago; much used. 낡은; 오래된; 닳은. ¶ *~ clothes* 헌옷 / *an ~ ruin* 폐허; 옛터; 유적 / *one's ~ school* 모교. **4** former; past. 이전의; 본디의; 과거의. ¶ *the ~ year* 지난해 / *an ~ pupil of his* 그의 제자 / *an ~ boy* 졸업생 / *an ~ soldier* 고참병. **5** ancient; of a time long past. 예전의; 고대의; 역사 있는(opp. new, modern). ¶ *~ civilizations* 옛 문명 / *Old English* 고대 영어 / *an ~ family* 구가(舊家) / *the ~* 오래된 것 / *an ~ school* 보수 집단. **6** experienced. 노련한. ¶ *~ in crime* 상습범의 / *an ~ bird* 노련한 사람 / *He is an ~ hand at this work.* 그는 이런 일에는 노련한 사람이다. **7** familiar; long known or in use. 낯익은; 예(例)의; 이전부터의. ¶ *~ friends* 오랜 친구 / *~ familiar faces* 그 전부터 아는 사이 / *one of his ~ trick* 그가 늘 하는 수작 / *It is the ~ story.* 흔한〔진부한〕 얘기다. **8** 《*colloq.*》 dear. 친애하는; 정든. ¶ *~ boy* 〔*bean, chap, fellow*〕 여보게 / *my dear ~ fellow* 내 친애하는 벗 / *the ~ country* 고향; 고국.
any old, 《*sl.*》 any ... whatever. 어떤 …라도. ¶ *Any ~ hat will do.* 어떤 모자라도 좋소 / *Come at any ~ time.* 언제든 오게나.
(*as*) ***old as the hills*** 〔***world***〕, very old. 매우 오래된.
have a fine 〔***good, high***〕 ***old time,*** 《*sl.*》 enjoy oneself very much. 한껏 즐기다.
have an old head on young shoulders, be very wise for one's age. 나이에 비해서는 썩 영리하다.
the Old Lady of Threadneedle Street, 《Brit.》 the Bank of England. 잉글랜드 은행.
—*n.* Ⓤ former times; the past. 옛날. 語法 전치사 뒤에 쓰임. ¶ *days of ~* 옛날 / *the men of ~* 구시대의 사람 / *our fathers of ~* 옛 우리 조상. [E.]
in days of old, in former times. 옛날에.
of old, **a**) formerly. 예전에. ¶ *Of ~ there were giants.* 예전에 거인들이 있었다. **b**) 《*arch.*》 from long ago. 오래 전부터. ¶ *I have known him of ~.* 예전부터 안다.

old Adam [´ ´-], **the** *n.* the natural

tendency toward sin. 악한 인성(人性).

old·en [óuldən] *adj.* 《*arch.*》 old; ancient. 오래된; 옛날의. ¶ *in the* ~ *days* =*in* ~ *times* 옛날엔.

·old-fash·ioned [óuldfǽʃənd] *adj.* keeping to old ways, customs, ideas, etc.; out of date. 고풍〔구식〕의; 유행〔시대〕에 뒤진. ¶ *an* ~ *dress* 〔*idea*〕 구식 옷〔생각〕 / *an* ~ *housekeeper* 보수적인 주부.

Old Glory [ˊ ˊˋ] *n.* the Stars and Stripes, the national flag of the United States. 미국 국기; 성조기.

old·ish [óuldiʃ] *adj.* somewhat, rather old. 예스러운.

old·line [óuldláin] *adj.* conservative; established. 보수적인; 확립된; 전통 있는. ¶ *an* ~ *shop* 〔*store*〕 노포(老鋪).

old maid [ˊ ˋ] *n.* an elderly woman who had never married. 노처녀; 올드 미스.

old·maid·ish [óuldméidiʃ] *adj.* like or characteristic of an old maid. (성격이) 노처녀 같은; 잔소리가 심한.

old man [ˊ ˊ], **the** *n.* **a**) 《naut. *sl.*》 the captain of a ship. 선장. **b**) =old Adam.

old·ster [óuldstər] *n.* 《*colloq.*》 an old or older person. 늙은이; 나이가 지긋한 사람.

old-time [óuldtáim] *adj.* of past times. 옛날의; 예전부터의.

old-tim·er [óuldtáimər] *n.* Ⓒ 《*colloq.*》 a person who has been a resident, member, worker, etc. for a long time; a veteran; an old-fashioned person. 오래 전부터 거주〔근무〕하던 사람; 고참; 구식 사람.

old-wom·an·ish [óuldwúməniʃ] *adj.* of or like an old woman; fussy. 노파의〔같은〕; 잔소리가 심한.

old-world [óuldwə́ːrld] *adj.* **1** of or belonging to the ancient world. 고대(세계)의; 고풍의. **2** 《often *O- W-*》 of the Old World. 구세계의. ¶ ~ *customes* 구세계 관습.

·Old World [ˊ ˊ], **the** *n.* Europe, Asia, and Africa; the Eastern Hemisphere. 구세계; 동반구(東半球)(opp. the New World).

Old Year's Day [ˊ ˊ ˋ], **the** *n.* New Year's Eve; the last day of the year. 섣달 그믐날.

o·le·an·der [òuliǽndər, ˊˊˋ] *n.* Ⓒ 《bot.》 a poisonous evergreen shrub with rose-colored or white flowers. 서양협죽도. [L.]

ol·fac·to·ry [ɑlfǽktəri / ɔl-] *adj.* of the sense or organ of smell. 후각(嗅覺)의. ¶ *the* ~ *nerve* 후각 신경 / *the* ~ *organ* 후각 기관. —*n.* Ⓒ (*pl.* **-ries**) 《usu. *pl.*》 an olfactory organ; the sense of smell. 후각 기관; 후(嗅)신경; 후각. [L. *oleo* smell, *facio* make]

ol·i·garch [ɑ́ləgɑ̀ːrk / ɔ́l-] *n.* Ⓒ one of the rulers of an oligarchy. 과두 정치의 집정자. [Gk. *oligoi* few, *arkhō* rule]

ol·i·gar·chy [ɑ́ləgɑ̀ːrki / ɔ́l-] *n.* (*pl.* **-chies**) Ⓤ the form of government ruled by a few powerful persons; Ⓒ a country governed in this way. 과두 정치; 과두정치 국가.

:ol·ive [ɑ́liv / ɔ́l-] *n.* **1** Ⓒ an evergreen tree that grows near the Mediterranean Sea; the tree itself; the fruit of this tree. 올리브; 올리브 나무; 그 열매. **2** Ⓤ the wood of this tree. 올리브 목재. **3** Ⓤ a dull yellowgreen color. 올리브색; 연둣빛. —*adj.* of an olive; of a dull yellowishgreen. 올리브의; 올리브색의. [L. *oliva*]

O·lym·pi·a [əlímpiə, ou-] *n.* a plain in Greece where the ancient Olympic Games were held. 올림피아. [→Olympus]

O·lym·pi·ad, o·lym- [əlímpiæ̀d, ou-] *n.* Ⓒ **1** a period of four years between celebrations of the Olympic Games in ancient Greece. (옛 그리스의) 올림피아기(紀)《4년간》. **2** the modern Olympic Games. 국제 올림픽 대회.

O·lym·pi·an [əlímpiən, ou-] *adj.* **1** of Olympia or Mt. Olympus. 올림피아의; 올림포스산의. **2** like an Olympian god; godlike; magnificent. 올림포스신 같은; 거룩한; 위풍 당당한. **3** of the Olympic Games of ancient Greece. 고대 올림픽 경기의. —*n.* Ⓒ **1** one of the twelve major Greek gods who were supposed to live on Mt. Olympus. 올림포스 12 신(神)의 하나. **2** a player taking part in the ancient or modern Olympic Games. 올림픽 경기 출전 선수.

·O·lym·pic [əlímpik, ou-] *adj.* of Olympia. 올림피아의. —*n.* 《*the* ~*s*》 Olympic Games. 올림픽 경기.

Olympic Games [ˊˊˋ ˊ], **the** *n. pl.* **1** the festival with contests in athletics, music, poetry, etc. held every four years at Olympia in ancient Greece. 고대 올림픽 경기. **2** the international sports contest of modern times held every four years in a different country. 국제 올림픽 경기.

O·lym·pus [əlímpəs, ou-] *n.* the mountain in Greece where the gods were supposed to live. 올림포스 산(山). [Gk. *Olumpos*]

o·meg·a [oumíːgə, -méi-, -mé-] *n.* Ⓒ **1** the last letter of the Greek alphabet (Ω, ω). 그리스 알파벳의 끝자. **2** 《*fig.*》 the last; the end. 최후; 마지막; 죽음. ¶ *alpha and* ~ 처음과 끝; 전체. [Gk. =great O]

om·e·let, -lette [ɑ́məlit / ɔ́m-] *n.* Ⓒ a dish made of eggs, milk, and other materials, cooked and folded in a pan. 오믈렛. ¶ 《*prov.*》 *You cannot make an* ~ *without breaking eggs.* 부뚜막엣 소금도 집어 넣어야 짜다《목적을 위해서는 그 나름의 노력이 필요하다》. [F.]

o·men [óumən] *n.* ⒸⓊ a sign that something good or bad is going to happen. 전조(前兆); 징조(cf. *presage*). ¶ *an* ~ *of misfortune* 흉조 / *be of good* 〔*bad*〕 ~ 좋은〔나쁜〕 징조다 / *A red sunset is an* ~ *of good weather.* 석양이 붉으면 (다음날) 날씨가 좋을 징조다. [L.]

O

om·i·nous [ámənəs / ɔ́m-] *adj.* of an evil omen; unlucky. 불길(不吉)한; 징조가 나쁜. ¶ *Those clouds look ~ for our hiking.* 저 구름들을 보니 우리 하이킹은 안 좋을 것 같다. ●**om·i·nous·ly** [-li] *adv.* **om·i·nous·ness** [-nis] *n.* [↑]

o·mis·sion [oumíʃən] *n.* **1** Ⓤ the act of omitting; the state of being omitted. 태만; 소홀; 탈락; 유루(遺漏). ¶ *sins of ~* 태만죄. **2** Ⓒ something which is omitted or neglected. 생략된〔빠뜨린〕 것. ¶ *There are some omissions in this report.* 이 보고서에는 몇 군데 빠진 데가 있다. **3** neglect or failure to do something required. 불이행. [↓]

·**o·mit** [oumít] *vt.* (**-mit·ted, -mit·ting**) **1** (P8,9) fail to do; neglect. …을 잊다; …을 태만히 하다. ¶ *I omitted to lock the window.* 내가 창문을 잠그는 일을 잊었다 / *He omitted doing his homework.* 숙제를 소홀히 하였다. **2** (P6,13) 《*from*》 fail to include (something); leave out. …을 빼다; 생략하다. ¶ *~ a word from a sentence* 문장에서 한 낱말을 생략하다 / *This part of the book may be omitted.* 책에서 이 부분은 빼도 좋다. [L. *omitto*]

om·ni- [ámni- / ɔ́m-] *pref.* all; every. '전부; 모두'의 뜻. [L. *omnis* all]

om·ni·bus [ámnəbʌ̀s / ɔ́m-] *n.* Ⓒ a large vehicle which carries many passengers; a bus. 승합 마차〔자동차〕; 버스. 參考 bus, 'bus로 생략함. —*adj.* including many different items; used for several purposes. 다수 항목을 포함하는; 총괄적인. ¶ *an ~ bill* 일괄 법안. [L. =for all]

om·nip·o·tence [amnípətəns / ɔm-] *n.* Ⓤ **1** infinite power; unlimited power. 전능. ¶ *the ~ of God* 신의 전능. **2** 《*the O-*》 God. 신. [↓]

om·nip·o·tent [amnípətənt / ɔm-] *adj.* having infinite or unlimited power; all-powerful. 전능한; 힘이 무한한. ¶ *the Omnipotent* 전능의 신. [omni-]

om·ni·pres·ence [àmnəprézəns / ɔ̀m-] *n.* Ⓤ the state of being present everywhere at the same time. 편재(遍在); 무소 부재(無所不在)(cf. *ubiquity*). ¶ *God's ~* 신의 편재.

om·ni·pres·ent [àmnəprézənt / ɔ̀m-] *adj.* present everywhere at the same time. 편재하는.

om·nis·cience [amníʃəns / ɔm-] *n.* Ⓤ **1** complete or unlimited knowledge. 전지(全知). **2** 《*the O-*》 God. 신. [L. *scio* know]

om·nis·cient [amníʃənt / ɔm-] *adj.* knowing all; having complete or infinite knowledge. 전지(全知)의; 박식(博識)한. [↑]

om·niv·o·rous [amnívərəs / ɔm-] *adj.* **1** eating both animal and vegetable food; eating any kind of food. 잡식(雜食)의; 무엇이나 먹는. ¶ *an ~ animal* 잡식 동물. **2** taking in everything; reading at random. 무엇이든 탐하는; 남독(濫讀)하는. ¶ *He is an ~ reader.* 남독가이다. [L. *voro* devour]

:on [an, ɔːn / ɔn] *prep.* **1** in the state of touching the surface of; upon. …의 표면에; …위에; …에 접해서(opp. off). ¶ *a book ~ the table* 탁자 위의 책 / *flies ~ the ceiling* 천장에 붙어 있는 파리들 / *She put the ring ~ her finger.* 손가락에 반지를 끼었다 / *He has a hat ~ his head.* 머리에 모자를 쓰고 있다 / *hang a picture ~ the wall* 벽에 그림을 걸다. **2** close to; near; along or by. …에 근접해서; …에 따라서; …의 가에. ¶ *a house ~ the river* 강변에 있는 집 / *a farm ~ the road* 도로 연변에 있는 농장 / *Paris is ~ the Seine.* 파리는 센 강변에 있다 / *The sun shone ~ the porch.* 햇볕이 현관에 내리쬐고 있었다. **3** to the surface of; onto …의 위(쪽)에. ¶ *drop a fork ~ one's lap* 무릎에 포크를 떨어뜨리다. **4** toward; in the direction of; 《U.S.》 against. …을 향해서; …쪽으로. ¶ *have pity ~ the poor* 가난한 자에게 동정하다 / *call ~ someone* 아무에게 전화하다 / *~ your right hand* 네 오른쪽에 / *hit someone ~ the head* 아무의 머리를 때리다 / *The typhoon was ~ us.* 태풍이 이 쪽으로 오고 있었다 / *march ~ Paris* 파리를 향해 진격하다 / *The feeling stole ~ me.* 그런 느낌이 나를 엄습했다. **5** about; concerning; relating to. …에 대한〔관한〕. ¶ *a lecture ~ Shakespeare* 세익스피어에 관한 강의 / *talk ~ many subjects* 많은 문제에 관해 이야기하다 / *I congratulate you ~ your success.* 자네 성공을 축하한다. **6** upon the basis of. …에 의거해; …에 따라. ¶ *act ~ someone's advice* 아무의 조언에 따라 행동하다 / *a story based ~ fact* 사실에 근거한 이야기 / *rely ~ something* …에 의지하다 / *the tax ~ tobacco* 담배에 매긴 세금 / *~ authority* 직권에 의해 / *~ my honor* 내 명예를 걸고. **7** at the time of; during; after (thinking, etc.). …의 때에; …동안; …한 뒤에. ¶ *~ examination* 시험해 보고 / *~ Christmas Eve* 크리스마스 이브에 / *~ arriving at the station* 역에 도착하는 대로 / *pay the bill ~ leaving* 떠날 때 지불하다. **8** in a condition or state of. …한 상태에; …로. ¶ *~ sale* 판매 중 / *~ fire* 불이 붙어 / *travel ~ the cheap* 적은 돈으로 여행하다 / *He is always ~ the move.* 그는 늘 한자리에 붙어 있지 못한다 / *The workers are ~ strike.* 노동자들은 파업 중이다. **9** by means of; by the use of. …에 의해; …을 써서. ¶ *go ~ foot* 걸어서 가다 / *wipe one's hands ~ a towel* 수건에 손을 닦다 / *play a waltz ~ the piano* 피아노로 왈츠를 치다 / *We went ~ the bus.* 버스를 타고 갔다. **10** added to. …에 더하여. ¶ *errors ~ errors* 실수 위에 또 실수 / *loss ~ loss* 손해에 손해를 거듭해. **11** for the purpose of. …의 목적으로; …을 위해. ¶ *go to New York ~ urgent business* 급한 일로 뉴욕에 가다 / *go ~ fishing* 〔*hunting*〕 낚시〔사냥〕하러 가다. **12** connected with; employed in. …에 관계하여; 종사하고. ¶ *~ duty* 근무 중

에 / *He is ~ the committee.* 그는 위원회에 관계〔근무〕하고 있다. **13** 《*colloq.*》 paid by. …의 부담으로. ¶ *The drinks are ~ me.* 술은 내가 낸다.

— *adv.* **1** forward; ahead; onward. 앞쪽으로; 전방(前方)으로. ¶ *further ~* 더 앞으로 / *march ~* 진군(進軍)하다 / *move ~* 계속 전진〔진행〕하다 / *from that day ~* 그날 이후. **2** lastingly; continuously; in progress. 계속해서; 진전해서. ¶ *sleep* 〔*work*〕 *~* 계속 자다〔일하다〕 / *go ~* 계속 가다 / *Go ~ with the story.* 이야기를 계속해라 / *The battle is now ~.* 전투는 지금 계속되고 있다. **3** in the state of touching, covering, or being supported. 접해서; 덮여; 쓰고; (떠)받쳐져(opp. off). ¶ *Put your shoes ~.* 신을 신어라 / *Is the tablecloth ~ ?* 테이블보는 덮여 있나 / *Put the coat ~.* 코트를 입어라 / *He had nothing ~.* 그는 아무것도 걸치고 있지 않았다. **4** in use or action. 사용〔작동〕 중에. ¶ *The radio was ~.* 라디오는 켜져 있었다 / *The brakes are ~.* 브레이크가 걸려 있다 / *Switch ~ the light.* 불을 켜라 / *The movie was already ~ when we arrived.* 우리가 도착했을 때 영화는 이미 상영되고 있었다 / *The water is ~.* 물이 나오고 있다. [E.]

and so on, and more of the same; and so forth. 그 밖에 여러가지; 기타 …등등.

neither off nor on (***to***)***,*** indifferent to; changeable; wavering. 무관심한; 변하기 쉬운; 결단을 못 내리는.

off and on, =***on and off,*** not continuously; intermittently. 이따금; 간간이.

on and on, without stopping; continuously. 계속; 끊임없이. ¶ *talk ~ and ~* 계속해서 길게 이야기하다.

:once [wʌns] *adv.* **1** one time; one time only. 한 번; 일 회(만). ¶ *~ a week* 일주일에 한 번 / 《*prov.*》 *Once bit*(*ten*) *twice shy.* 자라 보고 놀란 가슴 소댕 보고 놀란다 / *He comes ~ every day.* 그는 매일 한 번씩 온다. **2** 《usu. in *negative*》 ever; at all. 한번도 (…않다). ¶ *I haven't seen her ~.* 그녀를 만난 적이 없다 / *He didn't ~ offer to help.* 그는 한 번도 돕겠다고 제의하지 않았다. **3** even one time; at any time. 한 번이라도; 일단 (…하면); 언제든. ¶ *When ~ he understands, he will never make a mistake.* 일단 이해만 하면 다시는 틀리지 않는다. **4** formerly; some time ago. 일찍이; 이전에; 언젠가. ¶ *I have seen him ~.* 그를 한 번 만난 적이 있다 / *a once-powerful nation* 한때의 강국 / *He ~ lived in Paris.* 파리에 거주한 적이 있다. **5** at some time in the future; at any time. 언제고 (한 번). ¶ *I should like to see him ~ before I go.* 떠나기 전에 그를 한 번 만났으면 좋겠다.

not once, never; not at all. 한 번도 … 않다. ¶ *Not ~ has he kept his promises.* 그는 약속이라곤 지켜본 일이 없는 사람이다.

once again =once more.

once and again, repeatedly; time after time. 재차; 여러 번; 몇 번이고. ¶ *He has been told ~ and again not to tell lie.* 거짓말을 하지 말라는 말을 누차 들어왔다.

once (***and***) ***for all,*** finally; decisively; conclusively 마지막으로; 단호히. ¶ *Let's settle this question ~* (*and*) *for all.* 이 문제를 깨끗이 결말냅시다.

once in a while 〔***way***〕***,*** now and then. 때때로. ¶ *I still see my ex-wife ~ in a while.* 지금도 가끔 전처(前妻)를 만나고 있다.

once or twice, not often; a few times. 한두 번; 드물게. ¶ *I've seen him in the pub ~ or twice.* 술집에서 그를 한두 번 만났다. 「에.

once upon a time, long ago; once. 옛날(옛적)

once more, again; another time. 한 번 더; 또 한 번. ¶ *Say it ~ more.* 그거 한 번 더 말해 봐라.

— *conj.* if ever; whenever; as soon as; if once; when once. 한 번 …하면; …하자마자. ¶ *Once you cross the river, you are safe.* 이 강을 일단 건너기만 하면 산다 / *Once you hesitate you are lost.* 망설였다가는 끝장이다.

— *n.* Ⓤ one time; a single occasion. 한번; 일회; 한 차례. ¶ *Once is enough for you* 〔*me*〕. 네겐〔내겐〕 한 번으로 족하다.

all at once, **a**) suddenly. 별안간; 갑자기. ¶ *All at ~ we heard a loud noise.* 별안간 큰 소리가 들려왔다. **b**) all at the same time. 모두 동시에. ¶ *Don't all speak at ~.* 한꺼번에 들 얘기하지 마라.

at once, immediately; at the same time. 곧; 동시에. ¶ *Come here at ~.* 즉시 오너라 / *He is at ~ stern and tender.* 엄하면서도 부드러운 데가 있다.

for once, for one time at least; as an exception. 적어도 한 번은; 예외적으로. ¶ *He was right for ~.* 옳았던 적도 있었다.

for this 〔***that***〕 ***once,*** this 〔that〕 time only. 이번〔그 때〕만은. ¶ *you may do so for this ~.* 이번만은 그래도 좋다.

— *adj.* former. 이전의. ¶ *my ~ friend* 한때〔예전〕의 친구 / *his ~ master* 그의 전 주인. [→one]

on·com·ing [ánkʌ̀miŋ, ɔ́(:)n-] *adj.* coming nearer; approaching. 다가오는. ¶ *~ winter* 오는 겨울. — *n.* Ⓤ an approach 접근. ¶ *the ~ of the storm* 폭풍의 접근. [*on*-]

:one [wʌn] *adj.* **1** a single; the only. (단)하나의. ¶ *~ dollar,* 1 달러 / *~ pair of shoes* 신 한 켤레 / *~ man ~ vote,* 1인 1표(주의) / *with ~ voice* 이구 동성으로 / *This is the ~ way to learn foreign languages.* 이것이 외국어 학습의 한 가지 방법이다 / *No ~ man can do it.* 그걸 할 수 있는 사람은 없다. **2** a certain; some. 어떤 (하나의); 어느. ¶ *~ day* 어느날 / *~ Brown* (어떤) 브라운이라는 분 / *from ~ side to the other* 한 쪽에서 다른 쪽으로 / *I met him ~ night.* 어느 날 밤 그를 만났다 / *I will take you there ~ day.* 언제고 거기에 너를 데리고 가겠다. **3** same; unchanging; united; undivided. 같은; 불변의; 일체(一體)의; 불가분의. ¶ *of ~ height* 같

O

은 키[높이]의 / *The class was ~ in its approval.* 학급 전체가 찬성했다 / *We held ~ opinion.* 우리는 의견이 일치했다.
become [***be made***] ***one,*** be united; be married. 하나가 되다; 결혼하다.
for one thing, for one reason. 한 가지 이유로는. 「똑같은.
one and the same, exactly the same. 아주
one or two, a few. 한 둘의; 두서넛의. ¶ *~ or two people* 한두 사람 / *~ or two days* 이삼일.
— *n.* **1** Ⓤ the first and smallest number. 하나; 1. ¶ *lesson ~* 제1과 / *Book One* 제1권 / *I'll meet you at ~.* 한 시에 만나자. **2** 《*~, the ~*》 a single person or thing. 한 사람; 한 개. ¶ *~ of these days* 일간; 머지않아 / *a nest with young ones* 새끼들이 있는 보금자리 / *He gave me the ~ I wanted.* 그는 내가 원하던 것을 한 개 주었다 / *He is not ~ to be easily frightened.* 여간해서 놀라는 사람이 아니다. **3** 《*the O-*》 Ⓤ God. 신. ¶ *the Holy One =the One above* 신 / *the Evil One* 악마; 사탄.
all in one, combined; all together. 겸하여; 함께. ¶ *He is cook, gardener and chauffeur all in ~.* 그 자신이 요리사에, 정원사에, 운전사로서 혼자서 다 한다.
all one, **a**) united or agreed. 일치해서. **b**) all the same; indifferent. 마찬가지인; 아무래도 좋은. ¶ *It is all ~ to me.* 난 아무래도 좋다.
at one (*=in agreement*) ***with*** *someone.* …와 일치해서; 동의(同意)하여. ¶ *We are all at ~ about the plan for the picnic.* 우리는 소풍가는 데 대해 모두 동의한다.
by ones and twos, singly or in pairs. 한 사람씩 또는 두 사람씩. ¶ *They came by ones and twos.* 그들은 한두 사람씩 나타났다.
for one, at least; personally. 적어도; 개인적으로는. ¶ *I, for ~, don't like it.* 내 개인적으로는 그건 싫다.
one and all, everybody. 모두; 누구나.
one by one, one after another 하나씩; 차례로. ¶ *He counted out the coins ~ by ~.* 동전을 하나씩 세어서 냈다. 「대체로.
one with another, on the average. 평균해서;
— *pron.* some person or thing; any person or thing; the same person or thing. 어떤 사람[물건]; (일반적으로) 사람; 물건; 세상 사람; 동일한 사람[물건]. ¶ *One must do one's* [*his*] *best.* 사람은 모름지기 자기 최선을 다해야 한다 / *I'll choose this ~.* 이걸로 하겠다 / *Would you like an apple* [*some apples*]*? —Yes, I'd like ~* [*some*]. 사과 하나[몇 개] 줄까 —그래, 하나[몇 개] 줘 / *The problem was not an easy ~.* 문제는 쉬운 게 아니었다. [E.]
one another, mutually. 서로.
the one ... the other, the former ... the latter. 전자는 … 후자는.

one-eyed [wʌ́náid] *adj.* having only one eye. 애꾸(눈)의.

one-horse [wʌ́nhɔ́ːrs] *adj.* **1** drawn by or made to be drawn by a single horse. 말 한 필이 끄는. **2** 《*colloq.*》 unimportant; minor. 하찮은; 작은. ¶ *a ~ town* 작은 동네 / *a ~ paper,* 3류 신문.

one-legged [wʌ́nlégid] *adj.* having only one leg; leaning to one side. 외다리의; 한쪽에 치우친; 일방적인.

one-man [wʌ́nmæ̀n] *adj.* of one man; done by one man. 한 사람의; 혼자서 하는. ¶ *a ~ job* 혼자서 하는 일.

one·ness [wʌ́nnis] *n.* Ⓤ the state of being one or single; unity; agreement; sameness. 하나임; 단일; 일치; 동일(성).

on·er·ous [ɑ́nərəs, óu-/ɔ́n-] *adj.* making many troubles; burdensome. 성가신; 달갑잖은. ¶ *an ~ duty* 달갑잖은 일. [→ onus]

·one·self [wʌnsélf] *pron.* **1** 《a reflexive and emphatic form of **one**》 one's own self. 자기 자신; 스스로. ¶ *amuse ~* 재미있어하다 / *kill ~* 자살하다 / *speak to ~* 혼잣말하다 / *teach ~* 독학하다 / *write a letter ~* 자신이 (직접) 편지를 쓰다 / *It is important to do it ~.* 스스로 그 일을 하는 것은 중요하다 / *At the age of seven one ought to dress ~.* 나이 7살이면 스스로 옷을 입어야 한다. **2** one's normal physical or mental condition. (심신의) 정상적 상태. [*one*]
be oneself, **a**) be normal in mind or body. 심신이 정상이다. **b**) have full control of one's mind or body. 자제하다. **c**) act naturally. 자연스럽게 행동하다.
beside oneself, mad; lost in something. 미쳐서; 이성을 잃고. ¶ *be beside ~ with anger* 화가 나서 이성을 잃다.
by oneself, **a**) alone. 혼자서; 홀로. ¶ *He lives* (*all*) *by himself.* 그는 혼자 지낸다. **b**) without help from others. 혼자 힘으로. ¶ *You'll have to solve that problem by yourself.* 그 문제는 네 혼자 힘으로 해결해야 한다. 「신이 들다.
come to oneself, recover one's senses. 제정
for oneself, **a**) without help from others. 혼자 힘으로; 스스로. ¶ *You must see it for yourself.* 너 자신이 직접 확인해라. **b**) for one's own use. 자신이 쓰기 위해; 자기를 위하여[위한]. ¶ *He built a house for himself.* 그는 자기가 살 집을 지었다.
in spite of oneself, without consciousness. 자기도 모르게.
of oneself, of its own accord; automatically. 저절로; 제물로.
to oneself, not shared by anyone else. 자기만의. ¶ *have a large room to ~* 자기만 쓰는 큰 방이 있다.

one-sid·ed [wʌ́nsáidid] *adj.* **1** having only one side. 한쪽만의; 한쪽의. **2** seeing only one side of something; unfair; prejudiced. 한쪽으로 치우친; 불공평한. ¶ *a ~ view* 편견 / *a ~ judgment* 불공정한 판단. **3** not even; not equal. 불균등한; 일방적인. ¶ *a ~ game* 일방적인 경기. [*one*]

one-time [wʌ́ntàim] *adj.* of the past; former. 과거의; 이전의. ¶ *a ~ teacher of history* 전직 역사 교사.

one-track [wʌ́ntræ̀k] *adj.* **1** having only one track. (철도가) 단선(單線)인. **2** narrow; interested in one thing only. 편협한; 하나밖에 모르는. ¶ *a ~ mind* 편협한 마음.

one-up [wʌ́nʌ́p] *adj., adv.* **1** having gained an advantage in some way. 한 발 앞서(는). **2** one each. 서로 1 점씩(의).

one-up·man·ship [wʌ̀nʌ́pmənʃìp] *n.* Ⓤ 《*colloq.*》 the technique of keeping one step ahead of a competitor. (경쟁 상대보다) 한 발 앞서는 수〔기술〕.

one-way [wʌ́nwéi] *adj.* moving or proceeding in only one direction. 일방 통행의; 편도(片道)의. ¶ *~ traffic* 〔*street*〕 일방 통행〔통로〕. ── *n.* Ⓒ a single ticket. 편도 차표.

on·go·ing [ángòuiŋ, ɔ́(:)n-] *adj.* continuing without termination or interruption. 계속〔진행〕 중인. ¶ *~ research projects* 진행 중인 연구 계획. ── *n.* **1** the action of going on. 진행; 계속. **2** strange doings; strange behavior. 야릇한〔괴상한〕 행위(cf. *goings-on*). [*on-*]

*__on·ion__ [ʌ́njən] *n.* Ⓒ a plant of the lily family, the bulblike root of which is eaten. 양파. ● **on·ion·like** [-làik] *adj.* [L. *unio*]

know one's onions, 《*sl.*》 be good at one's job. 자기 일에 정통하다.

on·look·er [ánlùkər, ɔ́(:)n-] *n.* Ⓒ a person who looks on at something happening without taking part in it; a watcher; a spectator. 방관자; 목격자; 구경꾼. [*on-*]

:__on·ly__ [óunli] *adj.* **1** sole; single. 단 한 사람〔하나〕의; 유일(唯一)한; …뿐인. ¶ *an ~ daughter* 〔*son*〕 외딸〔외아들〕 / *my one and ~ friend* 내 유일한 친구 / *It was his one and ~ hope.* 그것이 그의 유일 무이한 희망이었다. **2** the best of its kind. 가장 좋은; 최고〔최상〕의. ¶ *He is the ~ man for the position.* 그 자리엔 그가 안성맞춤이다.

── *adv.* merely; solely; and no one or nothing more. 단지; 오직 …뿐. ¶ *Only I can do it.* 나만이 그 일을 할 수 있다 / *She was ~ doing it to please him.* 오로지 그를 기쁘게 하려고 그렇게 하고 있었다 / *I saw her three times ~.* 그녀를 단지 세 번 만났다 / *You can ~ guess* 〔*guess ~*〕. 너는 추측만 할 수 있을 따름이다.

if only, I wish that …. …하기만 하면. ¶ *If ~ it would stop snowing!* 눈이 그치기만 한다면 (좋을 텐데).

not only A but (***also***) ***B,*** B as well as A. A뿐만 아니라 B도.

only just, barely. 겨우; 가까스로. ¶ *He has ~ just come.* 그는 지금 막 왔다 / *I was ~ just in time.* 간신히 시간에 댔다.

only too, very. 대단히; 아주. ¶ *I'm ~ too glad to see you.* 만나서 너무 기쁘구나.

── *conj.* but then; except that. …이기는〔하기는〕 하지만; …이 아니라면〔없으면〕. ¶ *I would do that with pleasure, ~* (*that*) *I am too busy.* 기꺼이 하고 싶기는 하나 너무 바빠서… / *He would have started, ~ it rained.* 비가 내리지만 않았더라면 출발했을 것이다. [*one*]

only for, but for. …이 아니라면. ¶ *Only for my tea, I should have had the headache.* 차를 안 마셨더라면, 예의 그 두통이 났을 것이다.

on·rush [ánrʌ̀ʃ, ɔ́(:)n-] *n.* Ⓒ a strong or violent rush forward. 돌진; 돌격. [*on-*]

on·set [ánsèt, ɔ́(:)n-] *n.* Ⓒ **1** an attack. 공격. ¶ *the violent ~ of the enemy* 적의 맹공격. **2** a first step forward; a start; a beginning. 시작; 개시; 착수. ¶ *at the first ~* 시작으로 / *at the ~ of the journey* 여행 시초에.

on·shore [ánʃɔ́:r, ɔ́(:)n-] *adj., adv.* moving toward the shore; situated on the land; toward the shore. 뭍의〔으로〕; 육상에서(의).

on·slaught [ánslɔ̀:t, ɔ́(:)n-] *n.* Ⓒ a furious or violent attack. 맹공격. ¶ *The natives made an ~ on the settlers.* 원주민들은 식민자(植民者)들에게 맹공격을 가했다. [*on-*]

*__on·to__ [ántu:, ɔ́(:)n-, -tə] *prep.* on; upon; to a place. …의 위에; …을 향해서. ¶ *get ~ a horse* 말에 올라타다 / *throw a ball ~ the roof* 지붕 위로 공을 던지다.

o·nus [óunəs] *n.* Ⓒ a burden; a task; duty; responsibility. 부담; 의무; 책임. ¶ *The ~ of proof lies with you.* 증거를 제시할 책임은 너에게 있다. [L.]

*__on·ward__ [ánwərd, ɔ́(:)n-] *adv.* forward; to the front. 앞으로; 나아가서; 전방으로. ¶ *move ~* 전진하다 / *They marched ~.* 그들은 앞으로 행진하였다. ── *adj.* moving toward the front; going forward; advancing. 전진하는; 향상적인. ¶ *Their help is necessary for our ~ movement.* 우리가 진보하려면 그들의 도움이 필요하다. [*on*]

*__on·wards__ [ánwərdz, ɔ́(:)n-] *adv.* =onward.

on·yx [ániks / ɔ́n-] *n.* Ⓤ a kind of stone in layers of various colors. 얼룩마노(瑪瑙) 《보석》. [Gk. *onux*]

oo·long [ú:lɔ̀(:)ŋ, -làŋ] *n.* Ⓤ a Chinese black tea. 오룡차(烏龍茶). [Chin. *wulung* = black dragon]

ooze [u:z] *vi.* (P2A,3) **1** flow gently; leak out gradually. 스며나오다. ¶ *Blood oozed out of the wound.* 상처에서 피가 스며나왔다 / *boots oozing* (*with*) *water* 물이 새는 구두. **2** (of secrets, etc.) be disclosed or revealed. (비밀 등이) 새다; 누설되다. ¶ *The secret information began to ~.* 비밀 정보가 누설되기 시작했다. **3** disappear gradually. 서서히 사라지다. ¶ *His hope is oozing away.* 희망이 스러져가고 있다.

── *vt.* (P6) **1** give off (water, etc.) slowly. (물 따위)를 스며나오게 하다. ¶ *He was oozing sweat.* 땀이 나고 있었다. **2** disclose; reveal. (비밀 등)을 누설하다.

── *n.* ⒸⓊ **1** a soft mud, esp. at the bottom of a river. (강바닥 같은 데의) 개흙. **2** a slow flow; something that flows. 스며나옴; 분비(물). [E.]

oo·zy [ú:zi] *adj.* (**-zi·er, -zi·est**) **1** flowing or leaking out gently; muddy. 스며나오는; 새는; 개흙〔진흙〕의. **2** damp with moisture. 눅눅한; 습한. ●**oo·zi·ly** [-li] *adv.*

o·pac·i·ty [oupǽsəti] *n.* UC (*pl.* **-ties**) **1** the state of being opaque; something opaque. 불투명(체). **2** 《*fig.*》 lack of clearness; dullness of mind. 흐리터분함; 우둔. [→opaque]

o·pal [óupəl] *n.* C a precious stone which shows beautiful changes of color. 오팔; 단백석. [Skr.]

O

o·pal·esce [òupəlés] *vi.* (P1) exhibit a play of colors like that of the opal. 오팔 비슷한 빛을 내다.

o·pal·es·cent [òupəlésənt] *adj.* of or like an opal. 오팔의〔같은〕.

o·paque [oupéik] *adj.* **1** not allowing light to pass through; not transparent. 불투명한. **2** 《*fig.*》 dark; dull; stupid. 어두운; 흐릿한; 칙칙한; 우둔한. —*n.* 《*the* ～》 something opaque. 불투명체; 암흑(opp. transparent). ● **o·paque·ness** [-nis] *n.* **o·paque·ly** [-li] *adv.* [L. *opacus* shaded]

ope [oup] *vi., vt.* 《*poet.*》 =open.

:o·pen [óupən] *adj.* (**o·pen·er, o·pen·est**) **1** not closed; not shut. 열린; 열려 있는. ¶ *an ～ door* 열린 문 / *keep* 〔*hold*〕 *a door ～* 문을 열어 두다 / *push* 〔*pull*〕 *a door ～* 문을 밀어서〔당겨서〕 열다 / *throw a door ～* = *throw ～ a door* 문을 활짝 열어 놓다 / *keep one's eyes* 〔*ears*〕 *～* 방심하지 않고 지켜보다〔귀를 기울여 듣다〕 / *The lid of this watch flies ～.* 이 시계의 뚜껑은 열어 젖히게 되어 있다. **2** spread out; extended; not folded. 펼쳐진; 벌린; 편. ¶ *an ～ book* 〔*newspaper*〕 펼쳐진 책〔신문〕 / *an ～ flower* 피어 있는 꽃 / *welcome with ～ arms* 양팔을 벌리고 맞아들이다. **3** ⓐ not enclosed; free for (people, traffic, etc.) to go in or out, clear. 개방된; 출입이 자유로운. ¶ *an ～ field* (울타리·수목이 없는) 넓은 들판 / *an ～ moor* 광활한 황무지 / *a vast, ～ ocean* 광막한 대양 / *The road is ～ for traffic.* 길은 통행이 자유롭다 / *The coast is ～.* 해안은 항해에 지장(支障)이 없다. ⓑ ready to admit persons, customers, etc. (상점 등이) 열려 있는; 영업 중인. ¶ *The shop is ～ now.* 가게는 지금 영업하고 있다 / *keep the electric lift ～ eleven hours a day* 승강기를 하루 11시간 가동시키다. **4** not covered or protected; exposed. 덮개가 없는; 노출된. ¶ *an ～ boat* 갑판이 없는 배 / *an ～ car* 무개차(車); 오픈 카 / *an ～ bottle* 마개 없는 병 / *～ wiring* 나선(裸線). **5** ⓐ not decided; pending. 미결〔미정〕의. ¶ *an ～ question* 미해결의 문제 / *leave a matter ～* 문제를 뒤로 미루다; 보류하다. ⓑ not hidden; not secret. 공공연한; 다 아는. ¶ *an ～ secret* 공공연한 비밀 / *an ～ scandal* 모두가 아는 스캔들 / *treat someone with ～ contempt* 아무를 뭇사람 앞에서 창피를 주다. **6** unfilled; vacant. 비어 있는; 공석인. ¶ *The position is still ～.* 그 자리는 아직 공석이다. **7** public; free to all. 공개적인; 참가 자유의. ¶ *an ～ meeting* 〔*lecture, library*〕 공개 경쟁〔강의; 도서관〕. **8** ⓐ not prohibited. 해금(解禁) 중인. ¶ *an ～ season for hunting* (수렵 등의) 해금기. ⓑ free from snow or frost; warm or mild. 눈·서리가 내리지 않는; 춥지 않은. ¶ *The winter was ～.* 따뜻한 겨울이었다 / *The weather was fair and ～.* 날씨는 청명하고 따스했다. **9** frank; liberal; generous. 솔직한; 관대한. ¶ *an ～ manner* 솔직한 태도 / *an ～ mind* 편견 없는 마음. **10** not healed over. (상처가) 아물지 않은; 낫지 않은. ¶ *an ～ wound* 아물지 않은 상처.

be open to, a) willingly receive. 기꺼이 받아들이다. ¶ *He is ～ to persuasion.* 그는 남의 말을 고분고분 잘 듣는다. b) be not protected against (something); liable to receive; subject to. …에 보호되어 있지 않다; (위험 등에) 노출되어 있다; …을 받기 쉽다〔면할 수 없다〕. ¶ *be ～ to an attack* 공격에 노출되어 있다 / *be ～ to an air raid* 공습을 받기 쉽다 / *be ～ to temptation* 유혹에 약하다.

be open with (=*speak frankly to*) *someone.* …을 솔직하게 말하다. ¶ *I will be ～ with you about it.* 그 일을 탁 털어 놓고 이야기하겠다.

in the open (***air***), outdoors. 야외에서.

keep open house, be prepared to entertain visitors at any time. 언제든 내객을 환대하다.

open and shut, easily decided; clear; simple. 명명 백백한; 간단〔단순〕한. ¶ *an open-and-shut case* 지극히 간단한 일〔사건〕.

—*vt.* **1** (P6,7,13) make open; cause (something) to be open. …을 열다; 펴다. ¶ *～ a door* 문을 열다 / *～ a book* 책을 펴다 / *～ a letter* 편지를 뜯다 / *Open the box for me.* 그 상자를 열어다오 / *He didn't ～ his lips.* 그는 입을 열지 않았다〔한 마디도 안 했다〕. **2** (P6,7) unfold; spread out. …을 펼치다〔펴다〕. ¶ *～ an umbrella* 〔*a book, a map*〕 우산을〔책을, 지도를〕 펼치다. **3** (P6) make (something) known or public; reveal. …을 공개하다; 밝히다. ¶ *～ one's design* 계획을 밝히다 / *He opened his heart to his mother.* 자기 심중을 어머니에게 털어놓았다. **4** (P6) begin; start; begin to use. …을 시작〔개시〕하다; 이용하기 시작하다. ¶ *～ a new store* 새 가게를 내다 / *～ an acount* 계좌를 트다; 거래를 시작하다 / *～ a library* 도서관을 개관하다 / *～ fire on the enemy* 적에게 사격을 개시하다. **5** (P6,7) make an opening in. …을 절개하다. ¶ *～ (up) a wound* 상처를 째다. **6** (P6) make or force a passage, etc. (길 따위를) 개설하다; 뚫다. ¶ *～ a road* 도로를 개설하다 / *～ one's way through the crowd* 군중 속을 비집고 나아가다. —*vi.* **1** (P1) become open; be opened. 열리다. ¶ *The door opened easily.* 문은 쉽게 열렸다 / *The door will ~ inward.* 문은 안쪽으로 열린다. **2** (P1) begin. 시작하다; 개점[개업]하다. ¶ *School opens at eight.* 수업은 8시에 시작한다 / *A new store opens next week.* 새 가게가 다음 주(週)에 문을 연다. **3** unfold; bloom. 벌어지다; (꽃이) 피다. ¶ *The flowers in the garden are opening.* 정원의 꽃들이 피기 시작했다. **4** (P3) 《*to, into*》 lead into; face to. (문이) 통하다; 면하다; 향하다. **5** (P1,2A) come into view. 보이기 시작하다. ¶ *A wide view opened below us.* 아래에 광활한 시계(視界)가 펼쳐졌다.

open one's eyes, express surprise. (놀라서) 눈이 휘둥그레지다.

open someone's eyes, inform someone of, undeceive or enlighten someone; rouse someone to facts. …를 눈뜨게[깨닫게] 하다; 계발하다.

open fire, begin to shoot. 발포하다; 포격을 개시하다.

open into, lead to. …로 통하다.

open on, give or have view of. …에 면(面)[향]하다. ¶ *The room opens on the lawn.* 방문을 열면 잔디밭을 향하게 된다.

open out, **a**) unfold; expand. 열리다; (꽃이) 피다; 펼(쳐)지다. **b**) develop; become communicative; enlighten. 마음을 터놓다; 계몽하다. **c**) accelerate. 속도를 가하다.

open the door to, give opportunity for. …에게 기회를 주다.

open to, open into. …쪽으로 통하다. ¶ *The window opens to the south.* 문이 남향이다.

open up, set free; begin; start; make accessible; reveal 개방하다; 시작하다; 개통하다; 폭로하다.

— *n.* 《*the* ~》 Ⓤ **1** the outdoors; open or clear space; opening; the open sea. 옥외; 노천; 공터; 광장; 넓은 바다. **2** the condition of being publicly known. 공개된[주지(周知)의] 상태; 공공연함. ¶ *come into the ~* 공개되다 / *The secret is now in the ~.* 그 비밀은 이제 공공연한 것이 되어 있다. [E.]

come out into the open, come into public view; make one's ideas or plans known. 밝혀지다; …을 공표[공개]하다.

o·pen-air [óupənέər] *adj.* outdoor. 옥외[야외]의. ¶ *an ~ theater* 노천 극장 / *~ treatment* 외기(外氣) 요법 / *an ~ school* 임간(林間) 학교.

o·pen-armed [óupənά:rmd] *adj.* extending one's hands; hearty; sincere. 양팔을 벌린; 진심에서의. ¶ *an ~ welcome* 마음으로부터의 환영.

open circuit [ˊ-- ˊ-] *n.* 《electr.》 an electric circuit that is broken and thus carries no current. 개회로(開回路) (cf. *closed circuit*).

open door [ˊ- ˊ] *n.* 《*the* ~》 the policy of trading with any country freely and on equal terms; a policy of admission without any limit. 기회 균등; 문호 개방.

o·pen·er [óupənər] Ⓒ *n.* a person who opens; a thing that opens, such as a can opener, a bottle opener, etc. 여는 사람; 개시자(開始者); (병·깡통 따위의) 따개. ¶ *a tin* [*can*] *~* 깡통 따개.

o·pen-eyed [óupənáid] *adj.* **1** having the eyes wide open, as in surprise. 눈을 크게 뜬. ¶ *~ astonishment* 깜짝 놀람; 기절초풍. **2** watchful. 방심하지 않는. ¶ *~ attention* 세심한 주의.

o·pen-faced [óupənféist] *adj.* **1** having a gentle, honest look. 부드러운[착한] 얼굴의. **2** with the face uncovered. 맨얼굴의.

o·pen-hand·ed [óupənhǽndid] *adj.* willing to give; generous. 손이 큰; 활수(滑手)한.

o·pen-heart·ed [óupənhά:rtid] *adj.* frank; generous. 솔직한; 관대한.

:o·pen·ing [óupəniŋ] *n.* Ⓒ **1** a gap; a hole; an open space; an open piece of land in the forest; a passage. 구멍; 열린 데; (빈)틈; 공지; 숲 속의 빈터; 통로. ¶ *an ~ in a wall* [*fence*] (벽·울타리의) 개구멍. **2** a beginning; a start. 시초; 개시. ¶ *the ~ of Parliament* (의회의) 개원(開院) / *the ~ of a speech* 연설의 첫머리. **3** a chance; an opportunity; a vacant position. 좋은 기회; 취직 자리; 공석. ¶ *an ~ for trade* 거래의 호기 / *a fine ~ for a young man* 젊은이에게 알맞은 좋은 취직 자리. — *adj.* first; beginning. 처음의; 시작하는. ¶ *the ~ words of his speech* 그의 연설 서두. [*open*]

·o·pen·ly [óupənli] *adv.* frankly; publicly. 공개적으로; 내놓고; 공공연히. ¶ *speak quite ~ to someone* 아무에 대해 까놓고 얘기하다 / *be ~ known for a scoundrel* 악당으로 널리 알려지다.

o·pen-mind·ed [óupənmáindid] *adj.* willing to listen to new ideas or arguments; unprejudiced. 마음이 넓은; 허심탄회한.

o·pen-mouthed [óupənmáuðd, -máuθt] *adj.* **1** having one's mouth open. 입을 벌린. **2** showing greed (for food, etc.). 탐욕스러운; 게걸스러운. **3** showing wonder or amazement. (놀라서) 입을 딱 벌린.

o·pen·ness [óupənnis] *n.* Ⓤ **1** the state of being open. 개방 상태. **2** frankness; willingness to listen to new ideas or arguments; lack of prejudice. 솔직; 관대; 무사(無私).

open shop [ˊ- ˊ] *n.* 《U.S.》 a factory or shop which employs both members and nonmembers of labor unions. (비(非)노조원도 채용하는) 개방주의 공장.

:op·er·a[1] [άpərə / ɔ́p-] *n.* **1** ⒸⓊ a play in which actors sing their parts to the accompaniment of an orchestra. 오페라; 가극. ¶ *a comic ~* 희(喜)가극 / *a grand ~* 대(大)가극; 그랜드 오페라《비극적 줄거리가 많음》 / *a light ~* 경가극. **2** Ⓒ a theater where operas are played. 오페라 극장. [L.=work]

o·per·a[2] [oupərə, άp- / ɔ́p-] *n.* pl. of **opus.**

op·er·a·ble [ápərəbəl / ɔ́p-] *adj.* admitting of a surgical operation; practicable. 수술이 가능한; 실행 가능한. [→opus]

opera glasses [⌐--⌐-] *n. pl.* small glasses for both eyes used in theaters. 오페라 글라스. [→opera]

opera hat [⌐--⌐] *n.* a man's tall, black silk hat which may be folded flat. 오페라 해트《접을 수 있는 실크 해트》.

opera house [⌐--⌐] *n.* a theater where operas are played. 가극장(歌劇場).

:op·er·ate [ápərèit / ɔ́p-] *vt.* (P6) **1** cause (a machine, etc.) to work; run. (기계 등)을 움직이다; 조종[조작]하다. ¶ ~ *the machine* 기계를 조작하다. **2** 《U.S.》 manage. …을 경영[관리]하다. ¶ ~ *a hotel* [*school*] 호텔을[학교를] 경영하다. **3** bring about (an effect); accomplish. (효과 등)을 가져오다; 낳다; …을 이루다[일으키다]. ¶ *Energy operates changes.* 에너지는 변화를 일으킨다. **4** perform an operation. …을 수술하다. ¶ *an operated arm* 수술한 팔. —*vi.* (P1,2A,3,4) **1** (of a machine, etc.) work; act. (기계 등이) 움직이다; 작동하다; 작용하다. ¶ *The machine operates automatically.* 기계는 자동식이다 / *The tax operates to our disadvantage.* 세금은 우리에게 불이익을 가져온다. **2** (of medicines, etc.) produce a certain effect. (약이) 듣다. ¶ *Some drugs* ~ *harmfully on the human body.* 어떤 약은 인체에 해롭다 / *The drug operated well.* 약효가 좋았다. **3** perform a surgical operation to cure disease. 수술을 하다. ¶ *The doctor operated on my stomach.* 그 의사가 내 위를 수술했다. **4** carry on military activity. 군사 행동을 취하다. **5** (of a stockbroker) buy and sell, esp. in order to influence prices. (시세 변동을 노려) 매매하다; 주가를 조작하다. [L. *opus* work]

op·er·at·ic [àpərǽtik / ɔ̀p-] *adj.* of or like an opera 가극(풍)의. [→opera]

:op·er·a·tion [àpəréiʃən / ɔ̀p-] *n.* **1** Ⓤ action; (the process of) working; the way a thing works. 작업; 가동; 작용; 작업[공작] 과정; 조작. ¶ *The* ~ *of this machine is simple.* 이 기계의 조작[운전]은 간단하다 / *the* ~ *of nature* 대자연의 작용 / *the* ~ *of thinking* [*breathing*] 사고[호흡] 작용 / *a delicate* ~ *in watchmaking* 시계 제조의 정교한 작업. **2** Ⓒ the activity in the way of business; management. 운영; 운용(법); 경영; 시행. ¶ *building* ~ 건축 공사 / *the* ~ *of hotels* [*railroads*] 호텔[철도]의 경영[운영] / *the cost of* ~ 운영비 / *the rate of* ~ 조업률. **3** Ⓒ《often *pl.*》a series of movements of an army or a fleet; a plan of action. 군사 행동; 작전. **4** Ⓒ a surgical treatment. 수술. ¶ *perform an* ~ *on* [*upon*] *a patient* 환자를 수술하다. **5** Ⓒ 《math.》 addition, multiplication, division, and other such work. 계산; 운산. **6** financial transaction meant to affect prices. 시장[가격] 조작. [→operate]

come* [*go*] *into operation, begin to be operated. 작동[실시, 개시]되다.

get into operation, cause (a machine, etc.) to work. …을 가동[활동]시키다.

in operation, working; in effect or use. 작업[운전, 시행] 중.

put into operation, execute; start. (법률 「등)을 시행[실시]하다.

op·er·a·tion·al [àpəréiʃənəl / ɔ̀p-] *adj.* **1** of or for an operation. 작동상[조작상]의. **2** of or ready for use in a military operation. 작전상의. **3** in use; operating. 사용하는; 사용 중의.

op·er·a·tive [ápərətiv, -rèi- / ɔ́p-] *adj.* **1** operating; working; in effect. 작용[활동]하는; 효과 있는. ¶ *Such a law will not be* ~ *any more.* 그런 법률은 이젠 죽은 법이나 다름없다. **2** of surgical operations. 수술의. ¶ ~ *surgery* 수술(외과)학.

·op·er·a·tor [ápərèitər / ɔ́p-] *n.* Ⓒ a person who operates a machine, etc. 조작자; 기사; 기술자; 교환원; 경영자; 수술자. ¶ *a telephone* [*an X-ray, a hotel*] ~ 교환수[엑스선 기사, 호텔 경영자].

op·er·et·ta [àpərétə / ɔ̀p-] *n.* Ⓒ a short opera. 오페레타. [→opera]

oph·thal·mi·a [ɑfθǽlmiə, ɑp- / ɔf-] *n.* an inflammation of the eyes. 안염(眼炎). [↓]

oph·thal·mic [ɑfθǽlmik, ɑp- / ɔf-] *adj.* of the eye. 눈의; 안과의; 안염(眼炎)의(cf. *optic*). [↓]

oph·thal·mol·o·gy [àfθælmálədʒi, àp- / ɔ̀fθælmɔ́l-] *n.* 《med.》 a branch of medical science that deals with the structure, functions and diseases of the eye. 안과학. [Gk. *ophthalmos* eye]

oph·thal·mol·o·gist [àfθælmálədʒist, àp- / ɔ̀fθælmɔ́l-] *n.* a physician who specializes in ophthalmology. 안과 의사.

o·pi·ate [óupiit, -èit] *n.* Ⓒ **1** a drug containing opium that brings sleep or rest. 아편제(劑). **2** anything that brings sleep or rest. (일반적으로) 마취약. —*adj.* 《*arch.*》 **1** containing opium. 아편이 든. **2** tending to bring sleep. 졸리게 하는. [→opium]

o·pine [oupáin] *vt., vi.* (P11; 1,3) think; suppose; have or express an opinion. 생각하다; …라고 여기다; (의견을) 말하다. ¶ *He opined that the weather would get better by night.* 그는 밤이 되면서 날씨는 좋아질 것이라고 말했다. [L. *opinor*]

:o·pin·ion [əpínjən] *n.* **1** ⒸⓊ what one thinks about a subject; 《*pl.*》 views; beliefs. 의견; 견해; 소신. ¶ *political* [*religious*] *opinions* 정치적[종교적] 견해 / *public* ~ 여론 / *a matter of* ~ (각자의) 견해상의 문제 / *have the courage of one's opinions* 소신을 피력하고 이를 내세우다 / *I am of* (*the*) ~ *that….* 내 의견은 …이다. **2** Ⓒ a judgment about someone or something. 평가; 평판. ¶ *What is your* ~ *of him?* — *I have a high* [*no*] ~ *of him.* 그 사람을 어떻게 평가하느냐 —나는 그 사람을 높이[대단치 않게] 평가한

다 / *In my ~, she is a fool.* 내 판단으로는 그녀는 어리석다. **3** Ⓒ a formal statement by an expert. (의사·법률가 등의) 전문적인 의견; 감정. ¶ *a doctor's* 〔*medical*〕 *~* 의사의 소견 / *get another* 〔*a second*〕 *~* 다른 사람의 의견을 구하다. [→opine]

act up to one's opinions, act according to what one thinks right. 소신대로 행하다.

in the opinion of someone = ***in someone's opinion,*** as it seems to someone. 아무의 의견〔견해〕에 의하면.

o·pin·ion·at·ed [əpínjənèitid] *adj.* obstinate. 자기 의견을 고집하는; 완고한.

o·pi·um [óupiəm] *n.* Ⓤ a powerful drug made from a certain kind of poppy and used to cause sleep and make less pain. 아편. [Gk. *opos* juice]

opium den [∠-- ∸] *n.* a place where opium can be bought and smoked. 아편굴(阿片窟).

o·pi·um-eat·er [óupiəmì:tər] *n.* one who takes opium as a habit. 아편 중독자.

o·pos·sum [əpásəm / əpɔ́s-] *n.* Ⓒ 《zool.》 a small American tree animal which pretends to be dead when captured. 주머니쥐《아메리카산》. [Amer-Ind.]

play opossum, pretend to be dead, ill, ignorant, etc. 죽은 체하다; 꾀병 앓다; 몽따다.

·**op·po·nent** [əpóunənt] *n.* Ⓒ a person who takes the other side in a game, discussion, or fight. (시합·논쟁 등의) 반대자; 적수; 상대. — *adj.* acting against each other; opposing. 반대의; 적대하는. ¶ *on the ~ bank* 대안(對岸)에. [L. *pono* put]

op·por·tune [àpərtjú:n / ɔ́pər∸] *adj.* (of time) good; right for the purpose; (of an event or action) happening or done at the right time; timely. (때가) 적절한; 알맞은; (사건·행위 등이) 시의(時宜) 적절한. ¶ *He appeared at a most ~ moment.* 그는 아주 알맞은 때에 왔다. ● **op·por·tune·ly** [-li] *adv.* **op·por·tune·ness** [-nis] *n.* [L. *portus*]

op·por·tun·ism [àpərtjú:nìzəm / ɔ̀pərtjù:-] *n.* Ⓤ the policy or manner of making decisions on the basis of the circumstances of each particular time. 임기 응변주의; 편의〔기회〕주의.

op·por·tun·ist [àpərtjú:nist / ɔ̀pərtjù:-] *n.* Ⓒ a person who practices opportunism. 기회주의자.

:**op·por·tu·ni·ty** [àpərtjú:nəti / ɔ̀pər-] *n.* ⒸⓊ (*pl.* **-ties**) a good chance; time and circumstance that are good for a purpose. 좋은 기회; 호기. ¶ *equality of ~* 기회균등 / *afford* 〔*give*〕 *an ~* 기회를 주다 / *at* 〔*on*〕 *the first ~* 기회 있는 대로 / *find* 〔*miss*〕 *an ~* 기회를 만나다〔놓치다〕 / *His life has been deficient in opportunities.* 그에게는 기회라는 게 별로 없었다.

take 〔***seize***〕 ***the opportunity,*** make use of a particular moment. 기회를 잡다〔포착하다〕.

op·pos·a·ble [əpóuzəbəl] *adj.* **1** that may be opposed. 반대〔대항〕할 수 있는. **2** that may be put opposite to something else. 마주보게〔맞서게〕 할 수 있는. [↓]

:**op·pose** [əpóuz] *vt.* **1** (P6,13) stand or fight against somebody or something; resist. …에 반대〔저항〕하다. ¶ *~ the enemy with determination* 적(敵)에게 단호히 맞서다 / *~ a bill in the Diet* (의회에서) 의안에 반대하다 / *It is the duty of an opposition to ~.* 반대하는것은 야당의 본분이다. **2** 《*with*》 (P13) contrast; set against. …와 대립〔대조〕시키다; 마주보게 하다. ¶ *~ anger with good nature* 화낸 사람에게 웃는 낯으로 대하다 / *~ force with reason* 폭력에 대하여 이성으로 대하다 / *~ black with white* 흑을 백과 대비하다 / *The thumb can be opposed to any of the fingers.* 엄지손가락은 어느 손가락과도 서로 맞댈 수 있다. [→pose]

be opposed to, be hostile to; be the opposite of. …에 반대하다; …의 반대다. ¶ *Night is opposed to day.* 밤은 낮의 반대다.

:**op·po·site** [ápəzit / ɔ́p-] *adj.* **1** facing; front to front or back to back. …에 면하고 있는; 마주보는; 등을 맞댄. ¶ *the ~ side of the road* 길의 저쪽〔맞은편〕 / *the tree ~ my house* 우리 집 앞에 있는 나무 / *the houses ~* 맞은쪽의 집들. **2** just contrary; entirely different. 정반대의; 역(逆)의. ¶ *go in the ~ direction* 정반대쪽으로 가다 / *hold ~ opinions* 반대 의견을 가지다.

— *adv., prep.* in front of; in the opposite position. …의 맞은쪽〔편〕에. ¶ *a storehouse ~ the postoffice* 우체국 맞은편의 가게 / *There was an accident ~.* 맞은쪽에 사고가 있었다.

sit opposite to, sit face to face. 마주 앉다; 대좌하다.

— *n.* Ⓒ 《often *the ~*》 a thing or person that is opposite. 반대되는 사람〔사물〕. ¶ *White is the ~ of black.* 백은 흑과 반대다〔반대색이다〕 / *It is just the ~ of what he says.* 그의 말과는 정반대다. [L. *pono* put]

op·po·site·ly [ápəzitli / ɔ́p-] *adv.* in an opposite manner; face to face with. 반대로; 거꾸로; 마주 보고.

opposite number [∠-- ∠-] *n.* 《chiefly Brit.》 a person or thing occupying the same or similar position in another group, etc. (다른 직장·집단 등에서) 같거나 비슷한 지위에 있는 사람〔사물〕.

:**op·po·si·tion** [àpəzíʃən / ɔ̀p-] *n.* ⓊⒸ **1** the act of opposing; the state of being opposite to another object or person; resistance; hostility. 반대; 대립; 저항 (행위); 대치. ¶ *~ to authority* 권위에 대한 저항 / *The police met with fierce ~.* 경찰은 격렬한 저항에 부딪쳤다. **2** contrast. 대조. **3** 《often *the O-*》 Ⓒ an opposing political party. 반대당; 야당. ¶ *the leader of the Opposition* 야당의 지도자.

have an opposition to (= *stand against* or *oppose*) *someone or something.* …에 반대이다.

in opposition to, against. …에 반대하여;

…에 반항하여.
offer opposition to (=*oppose*) *someone or something.* …에 반대〔저항〕하다.

·op·press [əprés] *vt.* (P6) **1** treat (someone) harshly; rule (a nation) unjustly or cruelly. …을 억압하다; 학대하다. ¶ *The tyrant oppressed his poor subjects.* 폭군은 그의 가난한 백성들을 탄압했다. **2** weigh heavily on the mind of (someone); distress. (마음)을 무겁게 억누르다; 괴롭히다. ¶ *Care and sorrow oppressed her.* 근심과 슬픔이 그녀를 괴롭혔다. **3** make (someone) weary. …을 시달리게〔지치게〕하다. [→ob-]

·op·pres·sion [əpréʃən] *n.* ⓊⒸ **1** the act of oppressing; cruel or severe treatment; a burdening. 억압; 탄압; 학대. **2** a heavy feeling; a feeling of discomfort; weariness. 중압감; 불안감; 지침.

op·pres·sive [əprésiv] *adj.* **1** tyrannical; unjust; severe. 포악한; 압제적인; 가혹한. ¶ *an ~ ruler* 폭군. **2** (of weather) heavy; sultry. 답답한; 무더운; 찌는 듯한. ¶ *The air is very ~.* 바깥 공기가 찌는 듯이 덥다. ● **op·pres·sive·ly** [-li] *adv.* **op·pres·sive·ness** [-nis] *n.*

op·pres·sor [əprésər] *n.* Ⓒ a person who is cruel or severe to his inferiors. 압제자; 폭군; 박해자.

op·pro·bri·ous [əpróubriəs] *adj.* **1** showing scorn or reproach; insulting; abusive. 욕지거리하는; 모욕적인; 상스러운. ¶ *use ~ language* 입정 사납게 지껄이다. **2** deserving opprobrium; disgraceful. 욕먹을 만한; 불명예스러운. ¶ *~ conduct* 파렴치한 짓. [L. *probrum* disgrace]

op·pro·bri·um [əpróubriəm] *n.* Ⓤ reproach or disgrace because of shameful conduct; scorn; dishonor. 비난; 욕설; 불명예. [↑]

op·tic [áptik/5p-] *adj.* of the eye or the sense of sight. 눈의; 시각(視覺)〔시력〕의 (cf. *ophthalmic*). ¶ *the ~ angle* 시각(視角) / *The ~ nerves go from the eyes to the brain.* 시신경은 눈에서 뇌로 연결된다. [Gk. *optos* seen]

op·ti·cal [áptikəl/ɔ́p-] *adj.* **1** of the eye; of (the sense of) sight. 눈의; 시력〔시각〕의. ¶ *an ~ defect* 시각 장애; 시력의 결함 / *What you have seen is an ~ illusion.* 네가 본 것은 환상(幻想)일 뿐이다. **2** made to help eyesight. 시력을 돕는; 광학의. ¶ *an ~ instrument* 광학 기계. ● **op·ti·cal·ly** [-kəli] *adv.*

op·ti·cian [aptíʃən/ɔp-] *n.* Ⓒ a maker or seller of spectacles, telescopes, and other optical instruments. 안경상(商); 광학 기구 제작자〔판매상〕.

op·tics [áptiks/ɔ́p-] *n. pl.* 《used as *sing.*》 the science of light and vision. 광학.

op·ti·ma [áptəmə/ɔ́pt-] *n.* pl. of **optimum.**

op·ti·mal [áptəməl/ɔ́pt-] *adj.* most favorable. 최적〔최선〕의. [L. *optimus* best]

op·ti·mism [áptəmìzəm/ɔ́p-] *n.* Ⓤ **1** a habitual state of mind of looking on the bright side of things. 낙천주의. **2** the belief that everything in life will end happily. 낙천; 낙관(opp. pessimism). [↑]

op·ti·mist [áptəmist/ɔ́p-] *n.* Ⓒ a person who always looks on the bright side of things; a believer in optimism. 낙천가; 낙천주의자(opp. pessimist).

op·ti·mis·tic [àptəmístik/ɔ̀p-] *adj.* disposed to look on the bright side of things; of optimism. 낙천적〔낙관적〕인; 낙천주의의(opp. pessimistic). ● **op·ti·mis·ti·cal·ly** [-kəli] *adv.*

op·ti·mum [áptəməm/ɔ́pt-] *n.* (*pl.* **-mums** or **-ma**) 《biol.》 the most favorable or natural conditions (for growth, reproduction, etc.). (성장·번식 등의) 최적 조건.

op·tion [ápʃən/ɔ́p-] *n.* ⓊⒸ **1** the right or power of choice; the act of choosing; choice. 선택의 자유; 선택권; 선택. ¶ *Leave it to her ~.* 그녀 선택에 맡겨라 / *We had no ~ but to obey him.* 그를 따를 수밖에 없었다. **2** 《comm.》 the right to buy or sell something at a fixed price within a fixed date. 매매선택권; 옵션. [L. *opto* choose]
at one's option, as one pleases; at will; freely. 임의로; 마음대로.
make one's option, choose. 선택하다.

op·tion·al [ápʃənəl/ɔ́p-] *adj.* left to one's choice; free (to be chosen). 임의의; 자유 의사의. ¶ *an ~ subject* 선택 과목 / *Attendance is ~.* 출석은 자의(自意)이다. ● **op·tion·al·ly** [-əli] *adv.*

op·u·lence [ápjələns/ɔ́p-] *n.* Ⓤ wealth; riches; abundance. 부유; 풍부. [↓]

op·u·lent [ápjələnt/ɔ́p-] *adj.* wealthy; rich; abundant. 부유〔풍부〕한. ¶ *~ sunshine* 눈부신 햇빛. [L. *opulens*]

o·pus [óupəs] *n.* Ⓒ (*pl.* **o·pe·ra** or **o·pus·es**) a work; a composition; a musical composition. 저작; 작품. 參考 op.로 생략함. ¶ *Beethoven op.15,* 베토벤 작품 15번. [L.= work]

:or [ɔːr, ər] *conj.* **1** a word used to express a choice or difference. 혹은; 또는; …이나 —나. 語法 or 로 주어가 결합됐을 때 동사는 가까운 쪽의 인칭·수에 일치. ¶ *You can go ~ stay.* 가거나 또는 있어도 된다 / *You ~ I am to go.* 너나 내가 가야 한다 / *Will you walk ~ ride?* 걸어가겠나 타고 가겠나 / *It must be either black ~ white.* 그건 검거나 희어야 한다 / *Whether he speaks ~ not, the result will be the same.* 그가 말을 하건 안 하건 결과는 마찬가지다. **2** that is; in other words. 즉; 바꾸어 말하면. ¶ *botany, ~ the science of plants* 식물학, 즉 식물에 관한 학문 / *a negro ~ a black man* 니그로, 바꾸어 말하면 흑인. **3** and if not; otherwise. 그렇지 않으면. ¶ *Work hard, ~ you'll fail.* 열심

히 공부해라, 안 그러면 실패한다 / *Ask him whether he wants it ~ not.* 그가 그걸 원하는지 아닌지 물어 봐라 / *It must be my uncle, ~ I am a Dutchman.* 분명히 내 삼촌이야, 아니라면 내 목을 주마. **4** or so; about. …쯤; …정도. ¶ *It is about three ~ four miles away.* 3·4마일쯤 떨어져 있다. [E.]

o·ra·cle [ɔ́(:)rəkəl, ár-] *n.* Ⓒ **1** (in ancient Greece) the answer of a god given to a question about future. 신탁(神託); 탁선(託宣). **2** a place where a god gives answers; 《*pl.*》 the Scriptures. 신탁소(所); 성서(聖書). **3** a person who gives a god's answers; a prophet; a very wise person. 신탁을 전하는 사람; 예언자; 선지자. [L. *oro* speak]

o·rac·u·lar [ɔːrǽkjələr / ɔr-] *adj.* **1** of or like an oracle. 신탁의; 신탁 같은. **2** mysterious; obscure. 수수께끼 같은. **3** solemn; dogmatic; wise. 엄연한; 독단적인; 현명한.

o·ral [ɔ́ːrəl] *adj.* **1** spoken; not written; using speech. 구두(口頭)의; 구술의. ¶ *an ~ examination* 구두 시험 / *~ instruction* 구두 지시 / *~ pleadings* 〔*proceedings*〕 구두 변론. **2** 《anat.》 of the mouth. 입의; 구부(口部)의. ¶ *~ hygiene* 구강(口腔) 위생 / *the ~ cavity* 구강 / *~ contraceptive* 경구(經口) 피임약. [L. *os* mouth]

o·ral·ly [ɔ́ːrəli] *adv.* by spoken words; by word of mouth. 구두로.

:or·ange [ɔ́(:)rindʒ, ár-] *n.* **1** Ⓒ a reddish-yellow, round, juicy fruit; an evergreen tree that bears this fruit. 오렌지; 등자(橙子); 오렌지나무. ¶ *the bitter ~* 등자나무 / *the mandarin ~* 만다린귤《중국산》. **2** Ⓤ a reddish-yellow color. 오렌지색; 주황색. — *adj.* of oranges; reddish-yellow. 오렌지(색)의. [Arab. *naranj*]

or·ange·ade [ɔ̀(:)rindʒéid, àr-] *n.* Ⓤ sweet drink made by mixing sugar, orange juice, and water. 오렌지에이드; 오렌지즙.

or·ange·ry [ɔ́(:)rindʒəri, ár-] *n.* Ⓒ an orchard or glass-house where orange trees are grown and cultivated. 오렌지밭〔온실〕.

o·rang-u·tan, -ou·tang [ɔːrǽŋutæ̀n / ɔ́ːrəŋúːtæn], [-tæ̀ŋ] *n.* Ⓒ a large, long-armed ape living in Borneo and Sumatra. 오랑우탄; 성성(猩猩)이. [Malay]

o·rate [ɔːréit] *vi.* (P1) make an oration. 연설조로 말하다. [L. *oro* speak]

o·ra·tion [ɔːréiʃən] *n.* **1** Ⓒ a formal public speech, usu. one given on a special occasion. 연설; 식사(式辭). ¶ *a funeral ~* 조사(弔辭); 추도 연설. **2** Ⓤ 《gram.》 narration. 화법. ¶ *direct* 〔*indirect, oblique*〕 *~* 직접〔간접〕 화법.

or·a·tor [ɔ́(:)rətər, ár-] *n.* Ⓒ a person who speaks very fluently in public; a skillful public speaker. 연설자; 변사; 웅변가.

or·a·tor·i·cal [ɔ̀ːrətɔ́ːrikəl / ɔ̀rə-] *adj.* of or like oratory or an orator; rhetorical. 연설의; 연설자의; 웅변조의; 수사적(修辭的)인.

or·a·to·ri·o [ɔ̀(:)rətɔ́ːriòu, àr-] *n.* Ⓒ (*pl.* **-os**) a musical composition, usu. on a sacred, religious theme, sung with orchestral accompaniment. 오라토리오; 성담곡(聖譚曲).

or·a·to·ry[1] [ɔ́ːrətɔ̀ːri / ɔ́rətəri] *n.* Ⓤ the art of public speaking; eloquence; rhetoric. 웅변술; 웅변; 수사.

or·a·to·ry[2] [ɔ́ːrətɔ̀ːri / ɔ́rətəri] *n.* Ⓒ (*pl.* **-ries**) a small chapel in a church or a private house. 기도실; 작은 예배당.

orb [ɔːrb] *n.* Ⓒ a sphere; a round body such as the sun or the moon. 구(球); 천체《태양·달 따위》. — *vt.* 《*poet.*》 form into a circle or globe; enclose; encircle. 공 모양으로 하다; 에워싸다. [L. *orbis*]

·or·bit [ɔ́ːrbit] *n.* Ⓒ **1** 《astron.》 the path of a star or other heavenly body moving round another; the path in which a man-made satellite moves about a heavenly body. (천체·인공 위성의) 궤도(軌道). ¶ *put a rocket into ~* 로켓을 궤도에 쏘아 올리다. **2** 《*fig.*》 the regular course of life; the extent or sphere of activity, experience, or influence. 생활의 궤도; 활동〔경험·세력〕 범위. **3** 《anat.》 the eye socket. 안와(眼窩); 눈구멍. — *vi.* (P1) (of a satellite, etc.) move in an orbit. 궤도를 돌다. ¶ *The spaceship orbited for four days.* 우주선은 4일 동안 궤도를 돌았다. [↑]

or·bit·al [ɔ́ːrbitl] *adj.* of an orbit. 궤도의.

·or·chard [ɔ́ːrtʃərd] *n.* Ⓒ a field where fruit trees are grown and cultivated; 《*collectively*》 fruit trees. 과수원(果樹園); 과수. [E.]

·or·ches·tra [ɔ́ːrkəstrə] *n.* Ⓒ **1** a group of musicians who play together on their instruments, esp. stringed instruments. 오케스트라; 관현악단(원). **2** the place in front of the stage where these musicians play together. (극장의) 관현악단석(席). ¶ *~ stalls* (극장의) 일층 앞자리. [Gk. *orkheomai* dance]

or·ches·tral [ɔːrkéstrəl] *adj.* of an orchestra. 오케스트라(용)의.

or·ches·trate [ɔ́ːrkəstrèit] *vt.* (P6) compose or arrange for performance by an orchestra. …을 관현악용으로 작곡〔편곡〕하다.

or·ches·tra·tion [ɔ̀ːrkəstréiʃən] *n.* Ⓤ the act of arranging music for an orchestra. 관현악 작곡〔편곡〕(법).

or·chid [ɔ́ːrkid] *n.* 《bot.》 **1** Ⓒ a plant with beautiful, colorful flowers having three petals. 난초. **2** Ⓤ a light purple color. 연한 자주색. — *adj.* light purple. 연한 자주색의. [Gk.]

·or·dain [ɔːrdéin] *vt.* **1** (P7,11) give orders to (someone); (of God, destiny, a law, etc.) decide; appoint; regulate. …에게 명령하다; (신·운명·법률 등이) …라고 (규)정하다; …을 제정(制定)하다. ¶ *God has ordained that….* 신은 …이라고 정하셨

다 / *The law ordains that murderers shall be hanged.* 법은 살인한 자들은 교수형에 처해진다고 규정하고 있다. **2** (P6,19) appoint (someone) a minister in a Christian church. …을 목사로 임명하다. ¶ *be ordained priest* 목사가 되다. [→order]

or·deal [ɔːrdíːəl, ɔ́ːrdiːl] *n.* **1** Ⓤ (in former times) a method to decide whether someone is guilty or not by having him pass through fire, take poison, etc. (고대의) 범죄 유무 판별법. **2** 《*fig.*》 Ⓒ a severe test; a difficult or painful experience. 가혹한 시련; 고된 체험. ¶ *the ~ of taking three examinations in a day* 하루에 시험을 세 번 치르는 고된 시련. [E.]

:or·der [ɔ́ːrdər] *n.* **1** Ⓤ regular arrangement; the way one thing comes after another. 순서. ¶ *names arranged in alphabetical ~* 알파벳 순으로 배열된 이름 / *in due ~* 순서에 따라 / *in ~ of age* 〔*size, scores*〕 나이〔치수; 득점〕 순으로 / *follow the ~ of events* 사건의 순서를 좇다. **2** Ⓒ a social rank, grade, or class. 계급; 등급; 석차. ¶ *the lower* 〔*higher*〕 *orders* 하층〔상류〕 계급 / *the ~ of knights* 기사 계급 / *all orders of society* 사회의 모든 계층. **3** ⓐ Ⓤ rightly arranged conditions. 정돈. ¶ *put* 〔*set*〕 *things in ~* 물건을 정돈하다 / *put one's ideas in ~* 생각을 정리하다 / *The room is out of ~.* 방이 정돈돼 있지 않다. ⓑ Ⓒ 《mil.》 arrangement of troops; formation. 대형(隊形). ¶ *a battle* 〔*close*〕 *~* 전투〔밀집〕 대형. **4** Ⓤ the way or condition in which things happen according to law or rule. 질서; 치안. ¶ *peace and ~* 안녕 질서 / *public ~* 치안; 공안(公安) / *the ~ of nature* 〔*things*〕 자연계〔만물〕의 질서 / *keep* 〔*restore*〕 *~* 치안을 지키다〔회복하다〕. **5** Ⓒ 《often *pl.*》 a strict instruction; a command. 명령. ¶ *give strict orders* 엄명을 내리다 / *receive orders* 명령을 받다 / *strict orders to keep the secret* 비밀 유지의 엄명 / *They are under orders to search the house.* 그 집을 수색하라는 명령을 받고 있다. **6** Ⓒ a request for goods or services; goods ordered. 주문(품). ¶ *mail an ~* 우편으로 주문하다 / *send an ~ to a shop* = *place an ~ with a shop* 가게에 주문하다 / *give a waitress an ~ for coffee* 웨이트리스에게 커피를 주문하다 / *That book is on ~.* 그 책은 주문되어 있다 / *He gave an ~ for 15 tons of coal.* 석탄 15톤을 주문했다. **7** Ⓒ a written or printed paper directing someone to pay money. 환(어음). ¶ *draw a money ~* 환어음을 발행하다 / *send a postal money ~* 우편환을 보내다. **8** Ⓤ condition; state. 상태; 컨디션. ¶ *The machine is in good ~.* 기계는 잘 돌아가고 있다 / *This watch easily gets out of ~.* 이 시계는 고장이 잘 난다 / *The engine is out of ~.* 엔진이 고장이다. **9** Ⓒ a kind; a sort. 종류. ¶ *talents of a high ~* 뛰어난 재능 / *This is a matter of quite another ~.* 이건 전혀 별개의 문제다. **10** Ⓤ a fixed method of conduct or action in a meeting, parliament, etc.; the customary practice. 관습; 정례(定例); 의사 진행 절차. ¶ *His remarks are in* 〔*out of*〕 *~.* 그의 발언은 의사 규칙에 맞는다〔위배된다〕 / *rise to a point of ~* (의원이) 기립하여 연설자의 의사 규칙 위반을 의장에게 항의하다. **11** Ⓒ the course of things now moving; the established system or regime. (시대의) 추세; 주조; 체제. ¶ *a new ~ of things* 사물의 새로운 추세 / *the new ~ in linguistics* 언어학의 새로운 추세〔경향〕 / *the present social* 〔*economic*〕 *~* 현재의 사회〔경제〕 체제 / *a new* 〔*an old*〕 *~* 신〔구〕체제 / *The old ~ should be changed.* 구체제는 변경되어야 한다. **12** 《biol.》 a group in the plant or animal world between family and class. (동식물 분류상의) 목(目). **13** 《Brit.》 Ⓒ a pass admitting the bearer gratis or cheap to a theater, etc. 무료 입장권; 할인권. ¶ *an ~ for the play* 그 연극의 특별 입장권. **14** Ⓒ a religious body or society. 수도회. ¶ *the Franciscan ~* 프란체스코회. **15** Ⓒ a badge worn by persons of high rank. 훈장. ¶ *the Order of the Garter* 가터 훈장.

by order of (=*according to an order given by*) *someone.* 아무의 명령에 따라.

in order, **a**) in the right position. 순서 있게; 차례대로. **b**) in good condition; suitable. 순조로운; 적절한.

in order of (=*arranged according to*) *something.* …의 순으로.

in order that one may …, so that one may…. …할 수 있도록. ¶ *They are looking out in ~ that an accident may not happen again.* 다시 사고가 나지 않게 조심하고 있다.

in order to do, for the purpose of doing. …하기 위하여. ¶ *She worked hard in ~ to win the prize.* 상을 타려고 열심히 일했다.

in short order, 《U.S.》 quickly; in a short time. 곧; 지체없이.

on order, having been ordered, but not yet received (by the dealer). 주문해 둔. ¶ *The books you ordered are not in stock, but* (*they are*) *on ~.* 주문하신 책은 지금 품절입니다. 그러나 주문해 두었습니다.

on the order of, like; similar to; belonging to the class or kind of. …와 비슷한; …와 같은; …의 종류에 속하는.

out of order, not in order. 어긋나; 고장이 나; 규칙을 벗어나.

take order with, dispose of. …을 처분하다; 치우다.

the order of the day, **a**) the daily business set down for consideration or discussion (as in a meeting). (그 날의) 의사 일정. **b**) the current fashion. 유행; 풍조. ¶ *Winter sports are the ~ of the day.* 동계 운동이 유행이다.

to order, according to the buyer's wishes. 주문에 의해〔따라〕.
— *vt.* **1** (P6,7,11,20) command; bid; tell what to do. …을 명령〔지시〕하다. ¶ *He ordered me back* 〔*home, away*〕. 그는 내게 돌아가라고〔집에 가라고; 가라고〕 명령했다 / *She ordered the book* (*to be*) *brought to her.* 그 책을 가져오라고 명했다 / *He ordered that the windows* (*should*) *be locked.* 그는 창문을 잠그라고 명했다 / *He ordered silence.* 조용히 하라고 했다 / *The doctor ordered absolute quiet.* 의사는 절대 안정을 명했다 / ~ *someone out of the country* 아무에게 국외 추방을 명하다 / *I am not a dog to be ordered in and out.* 나는 사사건건 지시를 받아야 하는 개가 아니다. **2** (P6,13,14) 《*from*》 request (something) to be supplied, made, or furnished. …을 주문하다; 맞추다. ¶ ~ *a new book from America* 미국에 신간 서적을 주문하다 / ~ *a pair of shoes* 구두 한 켤레를 맞추다 / *She ordered her daughter a new dress.* 딸에게 새 옷을 한 벌 맞춰 주었다. **3** (P6,7) keep or put (something) in order; manage; arrange. …을 정리〔처분; 정돈〕하다. ¶ ~ *one's life for greater leisure* 생활을 훨씬 여유 있게 하다 / ~ *one's affairs* 신변을 정리하다.
— *vi.* (P1) give an order. 명령〔주문〕하다. ¶ *He wanted to* ~, *but the waiter was busy.* 주문을 하고 싶었으나 웨이터가 바빠서 못 했다. [L. *ordo*]
order about 〔***around***〕, send (someone) here and there; often give orders to (someone). …을 마구 부리다; 사방으로 심부름 보내다. ¶ *I don't like to be ordered around.* 혹사당하기는 싫다.

or·der·li·ness [ɔ́ːrdərlinis] *n.* Ⓤ **1** the state of being in order. 질서 정연. **2** orderly behavior. 순종.

·or·der·ly [ɔ́ːrdərli] *adj.* **1** tidy; well arranged; in order. (정리) 정돈된; 질서 정연한. ¶ *an* ~ *arrangement of dishes on the shelves* 시렁에 놓인 접시들의 가지런한 정돈 상태 / *an* ~ *room* 깔끔히 정돈된 방. **2** keeping order; obedient and quiet; well behaved. 질서 있는; 규율이 바른; 순종하는; 정숙한. ¶ *an* ~ *class* 〔*crowd*〕 질서 있는 학급〔군중〕 / ~ *conduct* 〔*behavior*〕 범절 있는 행동 거지. **3** being on duty. 당번〔당직〕의. ¶ *an* ~ *man* 당번병; 전령.
— *n.* Ⓒ (*pl.* **-lies**) 《mil.》 **1** a soldier who attends on an officer to carry out his orders. 연락병; 전령. **2** a military hospital attendant who works to keep things clean and in order. (군 병원의) 위생병; 잡역부(夫).

or·di·nal [ɔ́ːrdənəl] *adj.* showing order in a series. 순서의〔를 나타내는〕(opp. cardinal). ¶ *First, second, third, etc. are* ~ *numbers.* 첫째, 둘째, 셋째 등은 서수(序數)라고 한다. — *n.* Ⓒ an ordinal number. 서수. [→order]

ordinal number [⌐-- ⌐-] *n.* any of the numbers that express degree, quality, or position in a series. 서수.

or·di·nance [ɔ́ːrdənəns] *n.* Ⓒ a rule or law made by the authorities of a town or city. 조례; 법령; 포고. ¶ *a city* ~ *against excessive horn blowing* 지나친 경적을 규제하는 시조례(市條例). [*order*]

or·di·nar·i·ly [ɔ̀ːrdənérəli, ⌐-⌐--/ɔ́ːdənrili] *adv.* usually; commonly. 통상적〔보통〕으로. [↓]

:or·di·nar·y [ɔ́ːrdənèri / ɔ́ːdənri] *adj.* **1** usual; normal; customary; of a kind usually met with. 보통의; 평범한; 흔히 있는. ¶ *an* ~ *meeting* 정례회(定例會) / *in an* 〔*the*〕 ~ *way* 보통으로; 여느 때 같으면 / *an* ~ *man* 보통 사람 / *in an* ~ *dress* 평복으로 / *The* ~ *traffic will be stopped because of the parade.* 퍼레이드 때문에 통상적인 교통은 정지당하게 될 게다. **2** somewhat below the average. 평균 이하의; 좀 떨어지는. ¶ *a man of very* ~ *ability* 재주가 메주 같은 사람 / *a very* ~ *wine* 맛대가리 없는 술. [→order, -ary]
above the ordinary, better than usual. 뛰어난; 비범한.
by ordinary, ordinarily. 보통; 흔히.
in ordinary, in regular service. 상임(常任)의.
out of the ordinary, unusual; not regular or customary. 이상한; 예외적인.

or·di·na·tion [ɔ̀ːrdənéiʃən] *n.* Ⓤ the ceremony of admitting a person as a Christian priest or minister. 성직(聖職) 수임식; 서품식. [→ordain]

ord·nance [ɔ́ːrdnəns] *n.* Ⓤ 《*collectively*》 the cannon; the heavy guns; the military weapons. 대포; 무기; 화기. [→ordinance]

·ore [ɔːr] *n.* ⓊⒸ the rock or earth from which metal is obtained. 조광(粗鑛); 광석. [E.]

Or·e·gon [ɔ́ːrigàn, -gən, ár- / ɔ́rigən, -gɔ̀n] *n.* a northwestern State of the United States, on the Pacific coast. 오리건 주(州).

:or·gan [ɔ́ːrgən] *n.* Ⓒ **1** a musical wind instrument played by touching keys and pressing pedals. 오르간. 參考 미국에서는 흔히 교회의 pipe organ을 이름. **2** the part of an animal or plant that has a special function and duty, such as an eye or a stomach. (생물의) 기관(器官). ¶ *digestive* ~ 소화 기관 / *a sense* ~ 감각 기관. **3** a means of expressing or communicating public opinion, thoughts, etc.; a newspaper or magazine that makes known what people think. (의견 발표의) 기관; 기관지(機關紙)《신문·잡지 따위》. ¶ *the* ~ *of the government* 정부 기관지. **4** a means of action; an instrument. (정치적인) 기관. ¶ *an* ~ *of government* 정치 기관. [Gk. *organon* tool]

organ grinder [⌐- ⌐-] *n.* a person

who plays a barrel-organ in the street by turning a handle. 거리의 악사; 풍각쟁이.

or·gan·ic [ɔːrgǽnik] *adj.* **1** 《med.》 of some organs of the body. 기관(器官)의. ¶ ~ *disease* 기질성(器質性) 질병. **2** 《biol.》 having an organized structure, such as plants or animals. 유기체〔유기물〕의(opp. inorganic). ¶ *an ~ body* 유기체 / *Fossils are remains of ~ bodies.* 화석은 유기물의 시체다. **3** of a chemical compound which contains carbon. (화학에서) 유기(有機)의 (opp. inorganic). ¶ *an ~ compound* 유기 화합물 / ~ *chemistry* 유기 화학. **4** made up of related parts; systematic; essential; fundamental. 조직〔체계〕적; 본질적. ¶ *an ~ whole* 유기적 통일체. [→organ]

or·gan·i·cal·ly [ɔːrgǽnikəli] *adv.* by or through organization; in an organic manner. 기관에 의해; 유기적으로.

·or·gan·ism [ɔ́ːrgənìzəm] *n.* Ⓒ **1** a living thing with organs or an organized structure; an animal or a plant. 유기체〔물〕; 동식물; 생물. ¶ *microscopic organisms* 미생물. **2** 《*fig.*》 an organized body or system which has many parts dependent upon each other. 유기적 조직체. ¶ *A nation is a political ~.* 국가란 정치적인 유기적 조직체다.

or·gan·ist [ɔ́ːrgənist] *n.* Ⓒ a person who plays an organ. 오르간 연주자. [→organ]

:or·gan·i·za·tion [ɔ̀ːrgənəzéiʃən / -nai-] *n.* **1** Ⓤ the act of organizing; the state of being organized. 조직; 편성; 기구(機構). ¶ *The ~ of the human body is very complex.* 인체의 조직은 아주 복잡하다. **2** Ⓒ a group of persons united for some purpose or work, such as a club or a church. 조합; 단체; 협회. **3** Ⓒ a thing made up of related parts, each having a special duty. 유기체(有機體). ¶ *A tree is an ~ of roots, trunk, branches, leaves and fruits.* 나무는 뿌리, 줄기, 가지 그리고 잎과 열매들로 된 하나의 유기적 조직체다.

:or·gan·ize [ɔ́ːrgənàiz] *vt.* (P6) **1** get together and arrange (things) in order; establish. …을 편성〔조직〕하다. ¶ ~ *a baseball team* 〔*an army, a government, a party*〕 야구팀〔군대, 정부, 당〕을 조직하다. **2** 《esp. used in *pp.*》 furnish (something) with organs; give organic structure to (something). …에 기관(器官)을 부여하다; 유기체(有機體)로 하다. ¶ *an organized body* 〔*matter*〕 유기체 / *A rose is a highly organized plant.* 장미는 고도의 유기 식물이다. **3** arrange; make preparations for and carry out. (행사 등)을 계획〔준비〕하다; 마련하다. ¶ ~ *an entertainment* 여흥을 꾸미다〔준비하다〕. — *vi.* (P1) become organized. 조직화〔유기화〕하다. [→organ, -ize]

or·gan·iz·er [ɔ́ːrgənàizər] *n.* Ⓒ a person who organizes things, such as a party, a factory, or a company. 조직〔편성〕자; 창립자.

or·gy [ɔ́ːrdʒi] *n.* (*pl.* **-gies**) **1** Ⓒ party with wild merrymaking; a drunken revel. 진탕 마시고 떠드는 주연(酒宴); 야단 법석. **2** excessive indulgence in any activity. (어떤 일에) 지나치게 탐닉하기. ¶ *an ~ of reading* 독서 삼매. **3** 《*pl.*》 (in ancient Greece and Rome) secret ceremonies in honor of the gods, esp. of wine. (고대 그리스·로마의) 비밀 주신제(酒神祭). [Gk. *orgia* pl.]

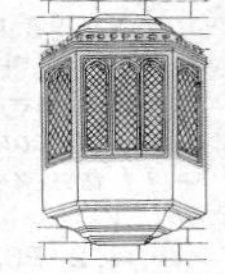
〈oriel〉

o·ri·el [ɔ́ːriəl] *n.* Ⓒ a window projecting from an upper story. 퇴창(退窓); 출창(出窓). [F. *oriol*]

·o·ri·ent [ɔ́ːriənt, -ènt] *n.* **1** 《*the O-*》 the East; the countries of Asia. 동양; 아시아의 여러 나라(opp. Occident). **2** Ⓤ 《*poet.*》 the east. 동쪽.
— *adj.* **1** 《*O-*》 《*poet.*》 eastern; of the countries of Asia. 동방의; 동양의. **2** bright or shining like pearls; of the finest kind. (보석 등이) 찬란히 빛나는; 최고의. ¶ *an ~ pearl* 최량의 진주. **3** rising; dawning. (태양 등이) 솟는; 떠오르는. ¶ *the ~ sun* 떠오르는 태양.
— [ɔ́ːriènt] *vt.* (P6) **1** place or turn toward the east. 동쪽으로 향하게 하다. **2** 《*reflexively*》 make (oneself) fit for one's surroundings. (환경에) 적응시키다. ¶ ~ *oneself to a new school* (전학한) 새 학교에 적응시키다. **3** place in the right position. 바른 위치에 놓다; 방위를 바로 하다. **4** direct to a particular object. (특정한 목표나 대상에) 방향을 잡다; 지향(志向)하다. [L. *orior* rise]

·o·ri·en·tal [ɔ̀ːriéntl] *adj.* **1** 《*O-*》 of the Orient. 동양의(opp. Occidental). ¶ *Oriental civilization* 동양 문명. **2** eastern. 동쪽〔동방〕의. — *n.* Ⓒ 《*O-*》 a person of the Orient. 동양인.

O·ri·en·tal·ist, o- [ɔ̀ːriéntəlist] *n.* Ⓒ a person who studies or knows Oriental languages, literature, art, etc. 동양학자; 동양통(通).

o·ri·en·tate [ɔ́ːrientèit] *vt.* =orient.

o·ri·en·ta·tion [ɔ̀ːrientéiʃən] *n.* Ⓤ **1** 《archit.》 the act of placing a church so that the altar end points to the east. (교회를) 성단이 동쪽이 되도록 세움. **2** determination of one's true position in relation to circumstances, etc. (새로운 환경 등에의) 자기 위치 정착; 적응. **3** a period or process of introduction and adjustment. 진로 지도; 오리엔테이션. **4** 《zool.》 homing instinct. 귀소(歸巢) 본능.

or·i·fice [ɔ́ːrəfis, ɑ́rə- / ɔ́ri-] *n.* Ⓒ a mouth of a cave, pipe, tube, etc.; an opening. (동굴·관(管) 등의) 뚫린 입구; 구멍. [L. *os* mouth, *facio* make]

orig. original; originally.

:**or·i·gin** [ɔ́ːrədʒin, ɑ́rə-] *n.* UC **1** the source from which anything comes; the beginning. 기원(起源); 발단; 출처. ¶ *the ~ of a word* 말의 기원 / *the ~ of a quarrel* 언쟁의 발단 / *of ancient ~* 기원이 오래 된 / *the ~ of the rumor* 소문의 출처. **2** birth; family; background; parentage. 출생; 가문; 태생. ¶ *a man of noble ~* 귀한 집안의 출신 / *by ~* 태생은. [L. *origo*]

:**o·rig·i·nal** [ərídʒənəl] *adj.* **1** of the beginning or origin; existing from the first; not translated; not copied; newly-created. 본디의; 원작[원문]의; 최초[고유]의. ¶ *the ~ plan* 원안(原案) / *the ~ settlers of America* 미국의 초기의 개척자[이민] / *the ~ edition of a book* 초판본 / *an ~ painting* 원화 / *I read the story in the ~ Russian.* 나는 그 소설을 러시아어 원서로 읽었다. **2** able to create; new and fresh. 독창적인; 참신한. ¶ *an ~ writer* 독창적인 작가 / *an ~ idea* 신안 / *an ~ work* 창작.
—*n.* C **1** the first model from which another is copied or translated. 원형; 원물; 원문. ¶ *read in the ~* 원문으로 읽다 / *The ~ of this picture is in Rome.* 이 그림의 원화는 로마에 있다. **2** ⓐ an unusual person. 기인(奇人); 괴짜. ⓑ a person who is original in his ways of thinking and acting. 독창적인 사람. [↑]

•**o·rig·i·nal·i·ty** [ərìdʒənǽləti] *n.* (*pl.* **-ties**) **1** U the ability to create something new. 독창력. ¶ *the ~ of an inventor* 발명가의 독창력 / *a man of great ~* 독창력이 뛰어난 사람. **2** U freshness; novelty. 참신(斬新); 새로움. ¶ *a work of no great ~* 그다지 독창성이 안 보이는 작품. **3** C a queer person; a curious thing. 기인; 진품(珍品).

•**o·rig·i·nal·ly** [ərídʒənəli] *adv.* **1** by origin; at first. 본디; 처음에는. ¶ *a house ~ small* 원래 작았던 집 / *a plant ~ African* 아프리카 원산의 식물. **2** in an original manner. 독창적으로; 기발하게. ¶ *I want this room decorated ~.* 이 방을 독특하게 꾸며 주시오.

•**o·rig·i·nate** [ərídʒənèit] *vt.* (P6) bring (something) into being; create; invent. …을 일으키다; 시작하다; 창작[창설]하다; 발명하다. ¶ *What originated the Great War?* 세계 대전은 무엇 때문에 일어났나. —*vi.* (P2A,3) 《*from, in, with*》 start; begin; begin to exist. 시작되다; 발생하다. ¶ *The quarrel originated in rivalry between two tribes.* 싸움은 두 종족 간의 불화로 시작됐다 / *The fire originated in the bathroom.* 불은 욕실에서 났다.

o·rig·i·na·tion [ərìdʒənéiʃən] *n.* UC **1** the act of originating; the state of being originated; origin. 개시; 시작; 창작; 발명; 기인(起因). **2** the power of originating. 독창력.

o·ri·ole [ɔ́ːriòul] *n.* C an American song-bird with yellow and black feathers. 꾀꼬리의 일종. [L. *aurum* gold]

O·ri·on [əráiən] *n.* **1** 《Gk. myth.》 a handsome hunter with a belt around his waist and a sword by his side. 오리온. **2** 《astron.》 a group of bright stars near the equator of the heavens named for this hunter. 오리온자리. [Gk.]

or·i·son [ɔ́ːrəzən, ɑ́rə- / ɔ́ri-] *n.* C 《usu. *pl.*》 a prayer. 기도. [L. *oro* pray]

:**or·na·ment** [ɔ́ːrnəmənt] *n.* **1** U adornment; decoration. 장식. **2** C something to add beauty, such as furniture, vases, or pieces of china. 장식물. ¶ *personal ornaments* 장신구. **3** 《*fig.*》 C a person or his act that adds honor or grace to his society. (사회 등에) 명예를 가져오는 사람; 명예로운 행위. ¶ *He is an ~ to his profession.* 그는 동업자들 사이의 자랑거리다. **4** 《*pl.*》 things used in church services, such as vestments, plates, bells, etc. 교회의 예배용품. —[ɔ́ːrnəmènt] *vt.* (P6,13) 《*with*》 make (something) beautiful; decorate. …을 장식하다. [→ornate]

•**or·na·men·tal** [ɔ̀ːrnəméntl] *adj.* of ornament; decorative. 장식의; 장식이 많은.

or·na·men·ta·tion [ɔ̀ːrnəmentéiʃən] *n.* U **1** the act of ornamenting; the state of being ornamented. 장식; 수식(修飾). **2** 《*collectively*》 decorations; ornaments. 장식품.

or·nate [ɔːrnéit] *adj.* adorned or decorated too much; excessively decorated. 너무 장식한; 화려하게 꾸민. [L. *orno* adorn]

or·ni·thol·o·gist [ɔ̀ːrnəθɑ́lədʒist / -θɔ́l-] *n.* C a person who studies birds. 조류학자.

or·ni·thol·o·gy [ɔ̀ːrnəθɑ́lədʒi / -θɔ́l-] *n.* U the study of birds. 조류학. [Gk. *ornis* bird, *rhugkhos* bill]

•**or·phan** [ɔ́ːrfən] *n.* C a child who has lost both or one of his parents by death. 고아(cf. *foundling*). —*adj.* of or for orphans; being without one or both parents. 고아의; 부모의 한[양]쪽이 없는. ¶ *an ~ asylum* 고아원. —*vt.* (P6) deprive (a child) of one or both parents. …을 고아로 만들다. ¶ *He was orphaned by the war and brought up in a public institution.* 그는 전쟁으로 고아가 되어 공공 시설에서 자랐다. [Gk. =bereaved]

or·phan·age [ɔ́ːrfənidʒ] *n.* **1** U the state of being an orphan. 고아임. **2** C a home for orphans. 고아원.

Or·phe·us [ɔ́ːrfiəs, -fjuːs] *n.* 《Gk. myth.》 a musician who charmed even birds and beasts by playing his lyre sweetly. 오르페우스. [Person]

or·tho·dox [ɔ́ːrθədɑ̀ks / -dɔ̀ks] *adj.* **1** generally accepted, esp. in religion. (종교상의) 정설(正說)의; 정통파의(opp. heterodox). **2** approved; usual; customary. 옳다고 인정된;

인습적인; 전통적인. [Gk. *doxa* opinion]

Orthodox Church [∠−− ∠], **the** *n.* the group of Eastern or Greek Catholic churches that recognizes a head other than the Pope in Rome. 동방 정교회《그리스·러시아 등 동방 제국에 신자가 많음》.

or·tho·dox·y [ɔ́:rθədàksi / -dɔ̀k-] *n.* U C (*pl.* **-dox·ies**) the state of being orthodox belief; orthodox practice. 정설; 정교(正教); 정설 신봉; 정통파; 일반적인 설에 따름 (opp. heterodoxy).

or·thog·ra·phy [ɔːrθágrəfi / -θɔ́g-] *n.* U **1** the art of writing words with the right letters; correct spelling. 철자법; 정자법. **2** the science which treats of spelling and letters. 문자론(文字論); 철자론. [ortho-]

or·tho·pe·dics, -pae- [ɔ̀:rθoupí:diks] *n. pl.* 《used as *sing.*》 the branch of medicine which deals with deformities, esp. in young children. (소아) 정형외과. [Gk. *pais* child]

Os·car [áskər / ɔ́s-] *n.* 《cinema》 a small golden statue awarded annually in the U.S. for achievements in motion-pictures. 오스카상(像).

os·cil·late [ásəlèit / ɔ́s-] *vi.* (P1,3) **1** swing to and fro like a pendulum. (시계추처럼) 흔들리다; 진동하다. **2** be very changeable in one's states, opinions or purposes. (의견 등이) 흔들리다; 동요하다. ¶ *They oscillated in their opinion.* 그들의 의견은 수습이 되지 않았다. — *vt.* (P6) cause (someone or something) to oscillate. 진동[동요]시키다. [L.]

os·cil·la·tion [àsəléiʃən / ɔ̀s-] *n.* U C **1** the act of oscillating; a single swing of a pendulum, etc. 진동; 흔들림; (시계추 등이) 한 번 흔들림. ¶ *the* ~ *of an electric current* 전파의 진동. **2** the state of being changeable in one's states, opinions, etc. (의견 등의) 동요.

os·cil·la·tor [ásəlèitər / ɔ́s-] *n.* 《wireless》 an instrument producing electromagnetic waves. 발진기(發振器).

os·cil·la·to·ry [ásələtɔ̀:ri / ɔ́sələtəri] *adj.* marked by or involving oscillations. 진동하는; 흔들리는.

os·cil·lo·graph [əsíləgræ̀f, -grɑ̀:f] *n.* 《electr.》 an instrument for recording oscillations of an electric current. 오실로그래프.

os·prey [áspri / ɔ́s-] *n.* C 《bird》 a large fish-eating bird of the hawk family. 물수리. [L. *os* bone, *frango* break]

os·se·ous [ásiəs / ɔ́s-] *adj.* made of bone; having bone. 뼈의; 뼈로 된; 골질(骨質)의. [L. *os* bone]

os·si·fi·ca·tion [àsəfəkéiʃən / ɔ̀s-] *n.* U the process of ossifying; the state of being ossified; C the part that is ossified; bone structure. 뼈로 변함; 그 부분; 골격. [↓]

os·si·fy [ásəfài / ɔ́s-] *vi., vt.* (P1;6) **1** change into bone. 뼈로 변하다; 골화(骨化)하다. **2** become hard or fixed like bone; make (something) hard; 《*fig.*》 become hard-hearted, or conservative. 굳어지다; 경화(硬化)하다; 보수적으로 되다. [L. *os* bone, →-fy]

os·ten·si·ble [asténsəbəl / ɔs-] *adj.* on the surface only; apparent; pretended. 표면상의; 겉치레의(opp. real; actual). ¶ ~ *purpose* 표면상의 목적[의도]. [L. *ostendo* show]

os·ten·si·bly [asténsəbli / ɔs-] *adv.* in an ostensible manner; apparently. 표면상.

os·ten·ta·tion [àstentéiʃən / ɔ̀s-] *n.* U vain or unnecessary display of wealth, knowledge, etc. to attract others; boastful exhibition. 겉치장; 과시. ¶ *the* ~ *of a rich, vain man* 돈 많고 허영심 많은 자의 허세.

os·ten·ta·tious [àstentéiʃəs / ɔ̀s-] *adj.* done for unnecessary display; liking to attract notice. 과시하는; 허식의. [→ostensible]

os·ten·ta·tious·ly [àstentéiʃəsli / ɔ̀s-] *adv.* in an ostentatious manner. 여봐란 듯이.

ost·ler [áslər / ɔ́s-] *n.* =hostler.

os·tra·cism [ástrəsìzəm / ɔ́s-] *n.* U the act of ostracizing; the state of being ostracized. (고대 그리스의) 도편(陶片) 추방; 배척; 추방. ¶ *suffer political* ~ 정치적 추방을 당하다. [↓]

os·tra·cize [ástrəsàiz / ɔ́s-] *vt.* (P6) **1** (among the ancient Greeks) banish a marked citizen for a time by popular vote. (고대 그리스에서) …을 도편(陶片) 추방하다. **2** banish (someone) from society; shut (someone) out from privileges. …을 추방[배척]하다. [Gk. *ostrakon* potsherd(used in voting)]

os·trich [ɔ́(:)stritʃ, ás-] *n.* C a very large, fast-running African bird which cannot fly. 타조. [L. *avis* bird & Gk. *strouthos* ostrich]

an ostrich belief [***policy***], belief or policy that is founded on self-delusion or a refusal to accept facts. (쫓기면 머리만 감추는 식의) 자기 기만의 얕은 지혜; 눈 가리고 아웅하기. ***have the digestion of an ostrich,*** can digest any food. 위장이 튼튼하다.

O·thel·lo [ouθélou] *n.* **1** a play by Shakespeare. 오셀로《셰익스피어작의 비극》. **2** the hero of this play. 그 극의 주인공.

:oth·er [ʌ́ðər] *adj.* **1** different; not the same. 다른. ¶ *any* ~ *girl* 어느 다른 소녀 / *any person* ~ *than yourself* 네가 아닌 어떤 다른 사람 / *in* ~ *words* 다른 말로 / *Come some* ~ *day.* 언제고 다른 날에 오너라. **2** more; further. 그 밖의; 그 위의. ¶ *Have you any* ~ *questions ?* **3** 《with *the* or *one's*》 of the rest; remaining; another. 나머지의; 다른 또 하나의. ¶ *the* ~ *girls* 그 외의 다른 소녀들 / *Give me the* ~ *coat, not this one.* 이거 말고 다른 코트를 주시오 / *Take it in your* [*the*] ~ *hand.* 다른 한쪽 손

으로 그걸 들어라. **4** opposite; reverse. 역(逆)의; 반대의. ¶ *the ~ side of the road* 길 저쪽 / *the ~ thing* 그 반대(의 것) / *the ~ end of the table* 테이블 저쪽 끝. **5** former. 이전의. ¶ *people of ~ days* 이전 사람들 / *in ~ times* 이전에는.

every other day, every second day. 하루 걸러; 격일로.

other things being equal, if conditions are [were] the same except for the point under discussion. 다른 조건이 같다면.

the other day, a day recently passed; a few days ago. 일전에; 며칠 전. ¶ *I saw your mother in town the ~ day.* 나는 며칠 전에 시내에서 네 어머니를 봤다.

— *pron.* **1** 《*the ~*》 the other one; the second of two. 다른〔딴〕 사람; 다른〔딴〕 것; 다른 한쪽. ¶ *Each loved the ~.* 서로 사랑했다 / *one or the ~ of us* 우리 둘 중의 어느 하나. **2** 《*pl.*》 other persons or things; the rest. 다른 사람〔물건〕; 다른 것; 나머지. ¶ *Be kind to others.* 남에게 친절해라 / *Show me some others.* 다른 몇 가지를 보여 주시오 / *After we left the others played cards.* 우리가 간 다음 남은 사람들은 카드놀이를 했다.

one after the other, in succession. 차례로; 번갈아.

one from the other, apart. 구별하여. ¶ *I can't tell the twins one from the ~.* 나는 그 쌍둥이를 구별 못 하겠다.

some day [***time***] ***or other,*** at some period in the future not clearly stated. 후일; 언젠가. ¶ *He hopes to go to Greece some day or ~.* 그는 언제고 그리스에 다녀오기를 바라고 있다.

someone [***something***] ***or other,*** a person [thing] unknown. 누군가가〔무엇인가가〕.

— *adv.* differently; otherwise. 다른 방법으로; 달리. [E.]

other than, except for. ¶ *I could not do ~ than love her.* 나는 그녀를 사랑하지 않을 수 없었다.

:oth·er·wise [ʌ́ðərwàiz] *adv.* **1** in another manner; differently. 다른 방법으로; 달리. ¶ *or ~* 또는 그 반대로 / *You should have done ~.* 다른 방법으로 했어야 했다 / *I think ~.* 내 생각은 다르다 / *I could not do ~.* 나는 달리 방도가 없었다. **2** in other respects. 다른 점에서는. ¶ *They are noisy, but ~ very nice boys.* 수선스럽지만 그 밖의 점에서는 아주 좋은 아이들이다. **3** or else; or; if not. 그렇지 않으면. ¶ *Work hard, ~ you shall not eat.* 열심히 일해라, 안 그러면 굶기겠다 / *I went at once, ~ I would have missed her.* 나는 곧 갔다. 그러지 않았다면 그녀를 놓쳤을 거다.

— *adj.* different; in another condition; of another nature. 다른; 다른 종류의. ¶ *How can it be ~ than harmful ?* 해롭지 않고 무어란 말이냐. [*other, wise*]

and otherwise, and others. 기타. ¶ *books political and ~* 정치 및 그 밖의 책.

other world [⌐–⌐], **the** *n.* the world after death; the future world. 저승; 내세.

oth·er·world·ly [ʌ́ðərwə́:rldli] *adj.* of another world, as the world of imagination or the world to come. 내세의; 저승의; 공상적인. [*other*]

o·ti·ose [óuʃiòus, óuti-] *adj.* **1** serving no practical use; not effective; unnecessary. 소용 없는; 불필요한. ¶ *His remarks were quite ~.* 그의 말은 전혀 필요 없는 것이었다. **2** 《rare》 idle. 게으른; 한가한. [L. *otium* leisure]

Ot·ta·wa [átəwə / ɔ́t-] *n.* the capital of Canada. 오타와.

ot·ter [átər / ɔ́t-] *n.* Ⓒ (*pl.* **-ters** or 《*collectively*》 **-ter**) 《zool.》 a fisheating animal that lives in and near the water; Ⓤ its fur. 수달; 수달피. [E.]

Ot·to [átou / ɔ́t-] *n.* a man's name. 남자 이름.

Ot·to·man [átəmən / ɔ́t-] *n.* **1** Ⓒ a Turk. 터키 사람. **2** 《*o-*》 Ⓒ a cushioned seat like a sofa or chair without back or arms. 오토만 의자. — *adj.* Turkish. 터키의. [Person]

ouch [autʃ] *interj.* an exclamation expressing sudden pain. 아야. [Imit.]

:ought[1] [ɔ:t] *auxil. v.* 《used with *to do*》 **1** have a duty to; should. …해야만 하다; …함이 당연하다. ¶ *You ~ to pay your debts.* 빚을 갚아야지 / *I ~ to have told you.* 나는 네게 말을 했어야 했다 / *You ~ to have been there.* 거기 다녀왔어야 하는데 / *You ~ to have done it.* 마땅히 그래야 했다. **2** need; had better. 필요하다; …하는 편이 좋다. ¶ *You ~ to start before it rains.* 비 오기 전에 떠나는 게 좋겠다. **3** be almost sure; be expected. 아마도 …일 것이다; 틀림없이 …할 것이다. ¶ *I ~ to be through with it by Sunday.* 그걸 일요일까지는 끝낼 거다 / *It ~ to be a fine day tomorrow.* 내일 날씨는 좋을 게다 / *He ~ to have arrived by this time.* 이 때쯤은 도착했어야 하는데. [= *owed*]

ought[2] [ɔ:t] *n.* 《*colloq.*》 nothing; a zero; 0. 영(零); 제로(cf. *naught*). [E.]

·ounce [auns] *n.* Ⓒ **1** a unit of weight equal to 1/16 of a pound. 온스. 參考 oz. 로 생략. **2** a very small amount; a little bit. 조금; 소량. ¶ *He hasn't got an ~ of sense.* 눈치라고는 없는 사람이다. [L. *uncia*]

:our [auər, ɑ:r] *pron.* (the *possessive* case of **we**) **1** of us; belonging to us. 우리들의. ¶ *~ country* [*language*] 우리 나라〔말〕/ *Our Father* (아버지) 하느님. **2** 《used by a king, an editor, etc.》 my. (국왕·신문 사설 등에서) 짐(朕)의; 필자의. ¶ *~ loyal subjects* 짐의 충성스러운 백성들 / *This is a mistake in our opinion.* 이것은 필자의 잘못된 생각입니다. [E.]

:ours [auərz, ɑ:rz] *pron.* anything that belongs to us. ¶ *this house of ~* 우리들의 집 / *Ours is a big school.* 우리 학교는 크다.

our·self [àuərsélf, ɑːr-] *pron.* myself. 내 스스로. [*our, self*]

:our·selves [àuərsélvz, ɑːr-] *pron.* a reflexive and emphatic form of **we** or **us.** 우리 자신; 우리 자신을〔에게〕. ¶ (*all*) *by* ~ 우리들만으로; 우리 힘으로 / *We had better do it* ~. 우리가 하는 것이 낫겠다 / *We dressed* ~. 우리 손으로 치장했다 / *We* ~ *will do the work.* 우리 스스로가 그 일을 하겠다 / *Let us go* ~. 우리 스스로 가자. [*our, self*]

oust [aust] *vt.* (P6,13) **1** 《*from*》 drive out (someone), esp. by unfair means. (부당하게) …을 내쫓다. ¶ ~ *someone from office* 아무를 해고하다 / *He was ousted from this country.* 그는 이 나라에서 추방됐다. **2** 《*of*》 dispossess. …을 빼앗다. ¶ *The Government ousted him of his passport.* 정부는 그의 여권을 몰수했다. [F. *oster, ōter* take away]

:out [aut] *adv.* **1** ⓐ not present; away from home or inside. 부재중인; 집에 없는; 밖에 나가. ¶ *He is* ~. 그는 외출 중이다 / *She is* ~ *shopping.* 그녀는 장보러 나갔다 / *Throw him* ~ *!* 놈을 쫓아내라 / *We are dining* ~ *this evening.* 오늘 저녁은 밖에 나가 식사한다. ⓑ away from a usual place; far away. (여행 등으로) 멀리 떠나; 외국에. ¶ *His son is* ~ *in Canada.* 그의 아들은 캐나다에 가 있다 / *He lives* ~ *in the country.* 그는 시골에 가 살고 있다. **2** outdoors; outside. 문 밖에; 바깥에. ¶ *go* ~ *for a walk* 산책하러 나가다 / *They are* ~ *in the garden.* 그들은 정원에 나가 있다 / *He is* ~ *just now.* 그는 방금 나갔다. **3** in public; in or into existence, notice, or clearness. 발표되어; 알려져; 나타나서; 눈에 띄어. ¶ *The secret is* ~ *at last.* 마침내 비밀이 드러났다 / *The rose is* ~. 장미가 피었다 / *The sun* 〔*moon*〕 *came* ~. 해가〔달이〕 떴다 / *War broke* ~. 전쟁이 발발했다 / *His new book is* ~. 그의 새 저서가 출판됐다 / *The chicken is* ~. 병아리가 깨었다. **4** completely; to an end; thorough. 완전히; 최후〔끝〕까지. ¶ *be tired* ~ 지쳐 버리다 / *argue it* ~ 결론이 날 때까지 논의하다 / *Play the game* ~. 끝까지 경기를 해라 / *I had my sleep* ~. 실컷 잤다. **5** aloud or loudly. 큰 소리로. ¶ *sing* 〔*shout, cry*〕 ~ 큰 소리로 노래하다〔소리치다; 울부짖다〕 / *Speak* ~ *so that all can hear.* 모두가 듣게 크게 말해라. **6** not at work; on strike. 일을 않고; 파업하여. ¶ *The workers are* (*going*) ~ *again.* 노동자들이 또 파업에 들어간다 / *He is* ~ *on account of illness.* 그는 병으로 쉬고 있다. **7** ⓐ to a state of no longer existing. 없어져; 다하여; 떨어져. ¶ *The fire is* ~. 불이 꺼졌다 / *blow* ~ *the light* 불을 불어 끄다 / *die* ~ 소멸하다 / *The wine has run* ~. 술이 동났다. ⓑ not in the right or normal state; not correct. 정상을 벗어나; 틀려. ¶ *My watch is three minutes* ~. 내 시계는 3분이 빠르다〔늦다〕 / *My arm is* ~. 팔이 퉁겨졌다 / *I was* ~ *in my calculations.* 내 계산이 틀렸다. **8** no longer in fashion or use. 유행이 지나; 쓰이지 않아. ¶ *Long skirts have gone* ~. 롱 스커트는 유행이 지났다. **9** off the coast. 난바다에. ¶ *be* ~ *at sea* 항해 중이다; 바다에 나가 있다 / *row* ~ 난바다로 저어 나가다. **10** ⓐ in the state of being excluded. 제외되어; 아웃되어. ¶ *lock* ~ 내쫓다 / *The batter is* ~. 타자가 아웃됐다. ⓑ out of office; not in power. 정권을 떠나; 재야(在野)에. ¶ *The Socialists is* ~. 사회당은 야당이 됐다. **11** to others. 남에게. ¶ *let* ~ *horses* 말을 빌려 주다 / *give* ~ *the books* 배본(配本)하다. **12** from among others. 많은 것 중에서. ¶ *pick* ~ 골라내다 / *find* ~ 찾아 내다. **13** (of a girl) into society. (여자가) 사교계에 나와. ¶ *This girl has just come* ~. 이 처녀는 막 사교계에 나왔다.

all* 〔*flat*〕 *out, 《*colloq.*》 with utmost speed or strength. 전속력으로; 전력을 다해. ¶ *His car was going all* ~. 차가 쏜살같이 달리고 있었다.

be out and about ⇨about.

be out for* 〔*to do*〕*, 《*colloq.*》 make efforts to get or to do (something). …을 얻으려고〔하려고〕 힘쓰다. ¶ *I am not* ~ *for compliment.* 칭찬받고 싶지 않다.

out and away, by far; without comparison. 훨씬; 비길 데 없이. ¶ *She was* ~ *and away the prettiest girl in the room.* 그녀는 그 방에서 단연 뛰어난 미인이었다.

out and out, completely; thoroughly. 완전히; 철저히. ¶ *He is a scoundrel* ~ *and* ~. 그는 진짜배기 악당이다.

out from under, 《*colloq.*》 away from difficulty or danger. 곤경〔위험〕을 벗어나〔피하여〕. ¶ *He's finally* ~ *from under financially.* 마침내 그는 재정 위기를 벗어났다.

out of, **a**) away from inside. …의 밖으로. ¶ *go* ~ *of the house* 외출하다 / *look* ~ *of the window* 창밖을 보다. **b**) beyond. …을 넘어. ¶ ~ *of control* 제어할 수 없어 / ~ *of patience* 참을 수 없는 / *He went* ~ *of the yard.* 그는 마당 밖으로 나갔다. **c**) lacking. …이 없어〔떨어져〕. ¶ ~ *of money* 돈이 없어 / ~ *of breath* 숨이 차서. **d**) because of. …때문에. ¶ *cry* ~ *of joy* 기뻐서 소리치다.

out of it, **a**) not included; sad for this reason. 제외되어; 외로운. ¶ *Among those ladies in fine clothes, she felt quite* ~ *of it.* 그 화려한 의상을 한 부인들 속에서 그녀는 심한 소외감을 느꼈다. **b**) mistaken. 틀린. ¶ *You are absolutely* ~ *of it!* 너는 완전히 착각하고 있구나. **c**) not concerned with. 관여하지 않고. ¶ *I'm glad to be* ~ *of it.* 나는 관여되지 않아서 다행이다.

Out upon you! Get away! 꺼져.

Out with him! Turn him out! 놈을 쫓아내.

Out with it! **a**) Take it out! 끄집어 내라. **b**) Speak it out! 말해 봐.

—*prep.* 《U.S.》 out of. …밖으로. ¶ *throw*

something ~ *the window* …을 문 밖으로 집어 던지다 / *come* ~ *the door* 문 밖으로 나오다.
— *adj.* **1** outer; on the outside. 밖의; 바깥쪽의. ¶ *an* ~ *island* 외딴 섬. **2** beyond the usual size. (크기가) 특대의. ¶ *an* ~ *size* 특대형(特大型). **3** (of a match) played away from the home ground. (경기가) 홈 그라운드 아닌 데서 치러지는. ¶ *an* ~ *match* 원정 경기〔시합〕.
— *vi* (P1) become known; go or come out. 알려지다; 드러나다. ¶ *Truth will* ~ *soon.* 진상은 곧 드러난다.
— *vt.* (P6) 《*colloq.*》 **1** put out by force. 밀어내다. ¶ *Out that man !* 저자를 끌어내라. **2** 《boxing》 knock out. 때려 눕히다. ¶ *He was outed in the first round.* 그는 첫 라운드에 녹아웃되었다.
— *n.* **1** 《*the* ~*s*》 the party which is out of office. 야당(opp. ins). **2** 《U.S.》 a fault. 잘못; 결점. [E.]
be at* 〔*on*〕 *outs, be at odds. 사이가 나쁘다.
make a poor out, be unsuccessful. 신통치 않다.
the ins and outs, **a**) both the party in power and the party out of office. 여당과 야당. **b**) turns and twists. 구불구불. **c**) the whole story. 자초지종.

out- [aut-] *pref.* **1** outward; forth. '밖으로; 밖에서'의 뜻. ¶ *outburst* 폭발; 돌발 / *outgoing* 떠남; 출발. **2** outside; at a distance. '…의 밖에; 떨어져서'의 뜻. ¶ *outbuilding* 만채 / *outlying* 떨어져 있는. **3** more or longer than. '…보다 많은〔긴〕'의 뜻. ¶ *outbid* …보다 비싸게 부르다 / *outlive* …보다 오래 살다. **4** better than. '…보다 나은'의 뜻. ¶ *outdo* …을 능가하다 / *outrun* …을 앞지르다. [E.]

out·and·out [áutndáut] *adj.* complete; thorough. 완전한; 철저한. ¶ *an* ~ *refusal* 단호한 거절. [*out-*]

out·bal·ance [àutbǽləns] *vt.* =outweigh.

out·bid [àutbíd] *vt.* (**-bid, -bid·den** or **-bid, -bid·ding**) (P6) offer to pay more than someone else. …보다 비싼 값을 매기다. ¶ ~ *each other* 서로 경쟁하다 / *He* ~ *all other bidders at the auction.* 그는 경매에서 최고가를 불렀다. [*out-*]

out·bid·den [àutbídn] *v.* pp. of **outbid.**

out·bound [áutbàund] *adj.* outward bound; not homeward bound. 외국으로 가는. ¶ *a ship* ~ *for Africa* 아프리카행 선박.

out·brave [àutbréiv] *vt.* challenge bravely; excel in bravery. …에 용감하게 맞서다; …보다 용감하다.

***out·break** [áutbrèik] *n.* Ⓒ **1** the act of breaking out; outburst. (전쟁·유행병 등의) 발발; 창궐; (감정의) 폭발. ¶ *an* ~ *of sorrow* 설움의 복받침 / *an* ~ *of war* 〔*anger*〕. **2** a riot; a revolt; a rebellion. 반란; 폭동.

out·build [àutbíld] *vt.* (P6) build more or better than. …보다 많이〔낫게〕 짓다. [*out-*]

out·build·ing [áutbìldiŋ] *n.* Ⓒ a building separate from a main building. 바깥채; 헛간. [*out-*]

out·burst [áutbə̀ːrst] *n.* Ⓒ the act of bursting forth; an eruption; a sudden intense expression of feelings. (화산의) 폭발; (감정의) 폭발. ¶ *an* ~ *of anger* 분노의 폭발.

out·cast [áutkæ̀st, -kɑ̀ːst] *adj.* exiled; driven out; homeless; friendless. 추방된; 집 없는; 버림받은. — *n.* Ⓒ a person or animal driven away from home or from his country. 추방된 사람; 집 없는 사람; 부랑인.

out·class [àutklǽs, -kláːs] *vt.* (P6) excel in skill, quality, class, etc.; be much superior to (someone or something). …보다 뛰어나다; …을 능가하다; …보다 윗길이다.

***out·come** [áutkʌ̀m] *n.* Ⓒ the result; the consequence. 결과; 성과.

out·crop [áutkrɑ̀p / -krɔ̀p] *n.* Ⓒ (of a layer or vein) the part of a mineral vein that appears on the surface of the ground. (광맥의) 노출; 노두(露頭). ¶ *the* ~ *of a vein of gold* 금광맥(金鑛脈)의 노두. — *vi.* (**-cropped, -crop·ping**) (P1) appear; crop out. (지층 등이) 노출하다; 드러나다. [*out-*]

out·cry [áutkrài] *n.* Ⓒ (*pl.* **-cries**) **1** a loud cry or shout; a sudden cry or uproar; a confused noise. 부르짖음; 고함 소리; 소음. **2** an auction. 경매.

out·date [àutdéit] *vt.* (P6) make old-fashioned. …을 구식이 되게 하다.

out·did [àutdíd] *v.* p. of **outdo.**

out·dis·tance [àutdístəns] *vt.* (P6) leave (something or someone) behind by going or running faster. …을 (훨씬) 앞지르다.

out·do [àutdúː] *vt.* (**-did, -done**) (P6) do better than someone else; surpass; excel. …보다 낫다; …을 능가하다. ¶ ~ *oneself* 이제까지보다 더 잘 하다〔열심히 하다〕 / *She will outdo me in most things.* 그녀는 나보다 모든 면에서 낫다.

out·done [àutdʌ́n] *v.* pp. of **outdo.**

***out·door** [áutdɔ̀ːr] *adj.* **1** in the open air; open-air. 집 밖의; 한데의(opp. indoor). ¶ ~ *games* 옥외 경기 / *an* ~ *life* 야외 생활. **2** 《Brit.》 outside of a poorhouse, hospital, etc. (고아원·양로원 등) 복지 시설 외의. ¶ ~ *relief* (사회 복지 시설 밖에 있는 사람을 위한) 구조 사업.

***out·doors** [àutdɔ́ːrz] *adv.* in the open air; outside a building. 옥외〔야외〕에서. — *n.* 《*the* ~》 the world outside of houses; the open air. 옥외; 야외.

***out·er** [áutər] *adj.* **1** near the outside; exterior. 밖의; 바깥쪽의. ¶ *the* ~ *world* 외부 세계; 세상; 자기와 무관한 일반 사람들 / *an* ~ *wall* 외벽 / ~ *space* 외계; 우주. **2** objective; physical or material. 객관적인; 실재(實在)의. [→out, -er]

outer man [´-´] *n.* 《*the* ~》 a man's outward personal appearances. 외모; 풍채 (cf. *inner man*).

out·er·most [áutərmòust, -məst] *adj.* farthest outside. 가장 바깥(쪽)의.

out·face [àutféis] *vt.* (P6) stare at (someone) boldly; face up to (someone) without fear. …을 째려 보다; …에 태연히 맞서다.

out·fall [áutfɔ̀:l] *n.* Ⓒ the mouth of a river, etc. 강어귀.

out·field [áutfì:ld] *n.* Ⓒ **1** farm-land lying away from the home farm. 멀리에 있는 밭. **2** 《*the* ~》 ⓐ 《baseball and cricket》 the part of the field beyond the infield or diamond. 외야(外野). ⓑ 《*collectively*》 the outfielders. 외야수(cf. *infield*). [*out-*]

out·field·er [áutfì:ldər] *n.* Ⓒ 《baseball》 a player who is stationed in the outfield. 외야수.

***out·fit** [áutfit] *n.* Ⓒ **1** 《*collectively*》 all the articles necessary for a special purpose; a set of clothes; equipment. 도구 일습; 복장 일습; 장비. ¶ *a baseball* ~ 야구 비품 / *a carpentry* ~ 목수의 연장 일습 / *a sailor's* ~ 선원 장비 / 《*fig.*》 *one's mental* ~ 마음가짐. **2** 《*colloq.*》 a group of people associated for a certain purpose. (여행단·기술자 등의) 집단; 일단. ¶ *The whole* ~ *was against him.* 모두가 그에게 반대했다. — *vt.* (**-fit·ted, -fit·ting**) (P6,13) furnish (something) with an outfit; equip. …의 채비를 하다; …에게 공급하다. ¶ ~ *an expedition to the Antarctic zone* 남극 탐험의 채비를 갖추다 / *Every family was outfitted with shoes.* 모든 가족에게 신발이 지급되었다. [*out-*]

out·fit·ter [áutfìtər] *n.* Ⓒ a shopkeeper dealing in an outfit. 장신구상; 여행 용구상. ¶ *a sporting* ~ 운동 용품점.

out·flank [àutflǽŋk] *vt.* (P6) **1** 《mil.》 go beyond, move to the outside of, the enemy's flank. (적)의 측면을 포위하다. ¶ ~ *the enemy* 적의 측면을 포위하다. **2** 《*fig.*》 get the better of. 선수를 쓰다; …을 앞지르다.

out·flow [áutflòu] *n.* Ⓒ the act of flowing out. 유출; 내뿜음. ¶ *the* ~ *of water* 물의 유출.

out·gen·er·al [àutdʒénərəl] *vt.* (P6) defeat by superior strategy. 작전으로〔전술로〕 이기다.

out·go [àutgóu] *n.* Ⓒ (*pl.* **-goes**) the amount of money that is spent or paid out; expenditure. 비용(費用); 지출(opp. income). ¶ *The* ~ *was greater than the income.* 수입보다 지출이 많았다.

out·go·ing [áutgòuiŋ] *adj.* going out; departing. 나가는; 떠나는. ¶ *the* ~ *tide* 썰물 / *an* ~ *ship* 떠나는 배. — *n.* **1** ⓊⒸ the act of going out; departure. 출발. **2** 《*pl.*》 expenditure; expenses. 지출; 비용(opp. incoming).

out·grew [àutgrú:] *v.* p. of **outgrow.**

out·grow [àutgróu] *vt.* (**-grew, -grown**) (P6) **1** become too big for (something). 커져서 입지〔들어가지〕 못하게 되다. ¶ ~ *one's clothes* 몸이 커져 옷을 못 입게 되다 / *My family has outgrown our house.* 식구가 늘어 집이 좁아졌다. **2** grow away from (something). (성장해서) …을 벗어나다〔잃다〕. ¶ ~ *a bad habit* 〔*fairy tales*〕 나이가 들어 나쁜 버릇이 없어지다〔동화를 듣지 않게 되다〕 / *She outgrew her impudent nature.* 그녀는 자라더니 건방진 데가 없어졌다. **3** become taller or bigger than (someone). …보다 커지다. ¶ *My sister has outgrown me.* 누이동생이 나보다 더 커졌다. [*out-*]

out·grown [àutgróun] *v.* pp. of **outgrow.**

out·growth [áutgròuθ] *n.* ⒸⓊ **1** a natural development or result. 자연적인 발전〔결과〕. ¶ *The present success is the* ~ *of his diligence for years.* 오늘날의 그의 성공은 여러 해 동안의 근면의 소산이다. **2** something that has grown out of something else; an offshoot. 파생물; 부산물; 분지(分枝); 가지. ¶ *an* ~ *of new shoots on a branch* 가지에 난 새싹. **3** the act of growing forth. 성장; 싹틈. ¶ *the* ~ *of a tree* 〔*new leaves*〕 나무〔새 잎〕의 성장.

out·guess [àutgés] *vt.* (P6) get the better of. …을 앞지르다〔능가하다〕.

out-Her·od [àuthérəd] *vt.* (P6) surpass Herod in cruelty, etc. …보다 포학하다. ¶ *"It out-Herods Herod."* 잔인하기가 헤롯왕 뺨친다. [*out-*]

out·house [áuthàus] *n.* Ⓒ a building belonging to a main building; a detached shed. 딴채; 헛간. ¶ *Near the farm-house were sheds and outhouses.* 농장 안채 옆에 몇 채의 부속 건물과 헛간이 있었다.

out·ing [áutiŋ] *n.* Ⓒ a pleasure trip; a walk; a hike; an excursion. 행락; 소풍; 산놀이. [*out-*]

out·laid [autléid] *v.* p. and pp. of **outlay.**

out·land·ish [autlǽndiʃ] *adj.* **1** strange; queer; unfamiliar. 이상한; 묘한. ¶ *He uses many* ~ *words in his speech.* 말할 때 그는 생소한 낱말을 많이 쓴다. **2** looking like something foreign. 이국풍(異國風)의.

out·last [àutlǽst, -lɑ́:st] *vt.* (P6) last longer than (something); outlive (someone). …보다 오래 가다〔살다〕. ¶ *These shoes will* ~ *the others.* 이 신발들은 다른 것보다 질기다.

out·law [áutlɔ̀:] *n.* Ⓒ **1** a person deprived of the protection of the law. 법의 보호를 박탈당한 사람. **2** a lawless wanderer; a habitual criminal. 부랑자; 상습범. — *vt.* (P6) **1** take legal protection away from (someone). …에서 법익(法益)을 박탈하다. **2** take legal force away from (something). …에서 법적인 효력을 없애다. **3** 《*fig.*》 expel (someone) from society. …을 사회에서 추방〔매장〕하다. **4** make (something) unlawful; prohibit. …을 불법화하다.

out·law·ry [áutlɔ̀:ri] *n.* Ⓤ the act of outlawing; the state of being outlawed. 사회적 매장; 불법화. [*out-*]

out·lay [áutlèi] *n.* Ⓒ expense; expenditure. 비용; 지출(支出). ── [⌐⌐] *vt.* (**-laid**) (P6,13) spend (money). …을 지출하다. ¶ *~ money in improvement* 개량 공사에 돈을 들이다. [*out-*]

***out·let** [áutlet, -lit] *n.* Ⓒ **1** a way out; a passage; a means of expression. 출구; 배출구; 방출구. ¶ *an ~ for the youth's energy* 젊은 혈기의 배출구 / *the ~ of a lake* 호수의 배수구. **2** a market for goods. 판로. ¶ *We have many commercial outlets for new products to South Africa.* 우리는 남아프리카에 신제품의 여러 판로를 갖고 있다.

***out·line** [áutlàin] *n.* Ⓒ **1** a line that forms or traces the outer limits of an object. 윤곽(선); 외형(外形). ¶ *the ~ of an egg* 달걀의 외형 / *The ~ of Italy suggests a boot.* 이탈리아의 지형은 구두를 연상시킨다. **2** a brief sketch or draft. 약도; 밑그림. ¶ *This is the ~ of a house.* 이건 어떤 가옥의 약도다. **3** a short summary; a general plan. 개요; 요강; 초안. ¶ *in ~* 개략적인 / *an ~ of world history* 세계사의 개요. **4** 《*pl.*》 a statement of general principles and main facts only. 요점; 주안점. ¶ *They agreed as to the grand outlines.* 그들은 주된 사항에는 동의했다.

give an outline of, describe (something) in general terms. …의 개요를 설명하다.

── *vt.* (P6) **1** draw or trace the outer line of (something or someone); sketch. …의 윤곽(약도, 밑그림)을 그리다. ¶ *~ the shape of a mountain* 산의 윤곽을 그리다. **2** describe or state (something) in a few words. …의 대요를 말하다; …을 약술(略述)하다.

out·live [àutlív] *vt.* (P6) live or last longer than (someone or something); survive; outlast. …보다 오래 살다; 살아남다; 오래 살아 …을 잃다. ¶ *She outlived her elder sister by ten years.* 그녀는 언니보다 10 년을 더 살았다 / *~ disgrace* 오래 살아서 불명예도 잊혀졌다.

out·look [áutlùk] *n.* ⒸⓊ **1** view. 전망; 조망. ¶ *This room has an ~ on a beautiful lake.* 이 방에서는 아름다운 호수가 내다보인다. **2** prospect for the future. 장래의 전망; 전도. ¶ *a hopeful ~* 희망적인 전도 / *The weather ~ for today is wet and windy.* 오늘의 일기는 습하고 바람이 불겠다. **3** a point of view. 견해; 견지. ¶ *a cheerful ~ on life* 즐거운 인생관 / *a narrow* (*prejudiced*) *~* 좁은(편파적인) 견해. **4** the place from which such a view is obtained. 전망대. ¶ *an ~ tower* 전망탑.

out·ly·ing [áutlàiiŋ] *adj.* far from the center; distant; remote. 중심에서 멀리 떨어진; 외진. ¶ *an ~ district of the city* 시의 외곽지대.

out·ma·neu·ver [àutmənúːvər] *vt.* (P6) surpass (the enemy) in maneuvering; get an advantage over (the enemy) by maneuvering. …을 책략으로 이기다; …의 허를 찌르다.

out·ma·noeu·vre [àutmənúːvər] *vt.* 《Brit.》 =outmaneuver.

out·match [àutmǽtʃ] *vt.* (P6) be superior to (someone or something); excel. …보다 한수 위다; …을 능가하다. ¶ *He outmatches any player in our school.* 그는 우리 학교의 가장 우수한 선수다. [*out-*]

out·mod·ed [àutmóudid] *adj.* out-of-date; out of fashion. 구식의; 유행이 지난.

out·most [áutmòust / -məst] *adj.* outermost; farthest out. 제일 바깥의; 가장 먼.

out·num·ber [àutnʌ́mbər] *vt.* (P6) be greater in number than (someone or something). …에 수적으로 우세하다. ¶ *The enemy outnumbered us by 5,000.* 적의 병력은 우리보다 5,000 명이 더 많았다 / *The women outnumbered the men five to two.* 여성 숫자는 남성보다 5 대 2 로 더 많았다.

out-of-date [áutəvdéit] *adj.* old-fashioned; not up-to-date. 구식의(cf. *up-to-date*). ¶ *~ styles in dress* 구식 복장. [*out-*]

out-of-door [áutəvdɔ́ːr] *adj.* =outdoor.

out-of-doors [áutəvdɔ́ːrz] *adj.* outdoor. 문밖의; 한데의. ── *n., adv.* outdoors. 한데(에서); 야외(에서).

out-of-the-way [áutəvðəwéi] *adj.* **1** remote; hidden. 외진; 궁벽한. ¶ *an ~ village* 외딴 마을. **2** unusual; strange. 별난; 이상한. ¶ *~ events* 이상한 사건들 / *an ~ proposed* 별난 제안.

out·pa·tient [áutpèiʃənt] *n.* Ⓒ a person who comes to a hospital to receive treatment. (병원의) 외래(外來) 환자(opp. in-patient).

out·play [àutpléi] *vt.* (P6) play better than (someone); beat. (경기에서) …을 이기다.

out·point [àutpɔ́int] *vt.* (P6) score more points than. (경기에서) …보다 많이 득점하다.

out·post [áutpòust] *n.* Ⓒ **1** a military guard stationed at a distance from the main body of soldiers. 전초(前哨); 전초부대. **2** the place so occupied. 전초 기지. **3** any distant settlement. (타국내의) 재외기지(거류지). ¶ *the outposts of the Empire* 제국의 재외 기지.

out·pour [áutpɔ̀ːr] *n.* Ⓒ that which is poured out. 유출(물). ── [⌐⌐] *vi., vt.* (P1;6) pour out. 흘러나오(게 하)다.

out·pour·ing [áutpɔ̀ːriŋ] *n.* **1** Ⓒ anything that is poured out. 유출물. **2** 《usu. *pl.*》 outflow of thoughts or feelings. (감정의) 토로; 발로.

***out·put** [áutpùt] *n.* Ⓤ **1** the work done or amount produced; the act of producing. 생산품; 생산고; 생산. ¶ *the daily ~ of motorcars* 차량의 1일 생산량. **2** 《electr.》 the information produced from a computer. 출력(出力); 발전력(opp.

input). [*out-*]

·out·rage [áutrèidʒ] *n.* Ⓒ Ⓤ **1** a violent or cruel act; an act against law or morality. 폭행; 불법 행위. ¶ *The angry crowd committed many outrages.* 성난 군중은 갖은 난동을 부렸다. **2** insult. 모욕. —*vt.* (P6) **1** do violence to (someone or something); break (the law, etc.); harm. …을 폭행〔학대〕하다; 위법〔범법〕 행위를 하다. ¶ ~ *public opinion* 여론을 짓밟다. **2** insult. …을 모욕하다. [L. *ultra* beyond]

out·ra·geous [autréidʒəs] *adj.* violent; immoral; cruel; extremely offensive; insulting. 난폭한; 부도덕한; 잔인한; 무법한.

out·ra·geous·ly [autréidʒəsli] *adv.* in an outrageous manner. 난폭〔잔인〕하게; 무법하게.

out·ran [àutræ̀n] *v.* p. of **outrun.**

out·range [àutréindʒ] *vt.* (P6) (of guns, etc.) have a greater or longer range than (something). …보다 착탄(着彈) 거리가 멀다. [*out-*]

out·rank [àutræ̀ŋk] *vt.* (P6) 《U.S.》 be superior to; rank above. …보다 계급이 위다.

out·reach [àutríːtʃ] *vt.* (P6) reach farther than; do better than. …보다 멀리 미치다; …을 능가하다.

out·rid·den [àutrídn] *v.* pp. of **outride.**

out·ride [àutráid] *vt.* (**-rode, -rid·den**) (P6) ride faster or farther than (something or someone); reach faster than (something or someone); ride past. (타고) …보다 빨리〔멀리〕 가다; …보다 빨리 닿다; …을 타고 지나치다.

out·rid·er [áutràidər] *n.* Ⓒ a servant who rides on a horse before or beside a carriage. (기마(騎馬)의) 마차 시종(侍從).

out·rig·ger [áutrìgər] *n.* Ⓒ **1** a projecting device fastened at the side of a boat. (보트의) 현외(舷外) 장치. **2** a boat with such a device. 그 (장치를 한) 보트. **3** a projecting board or beam attached for temporary or special use. (돛 아랫단을 받치는) 현외 부재(舷外浮材). [*out-*]

out·right [áutráit] *adv.* **1** completely; entirely; utterly. 철저히; 완전히; 한껏. ¶ *be* ~ *lazy* 여간한 농땡이가 아니다. **2** openly; frankly. 공공연히; 기탄없이. ¶ *He told him* ~ *what he thought of him.* 그에 대한 감정을 기탄없이 말했다. **3** at once; immediately; at one time. 곧; 즉시. ¶ *He bought the house and contents* ~. 그는 그 집을 샀는데 당장에 마음에 들었다. —[ㅗㅗ] *adj.* **1** frank; straightforward; direct. 솔직한; 직선적인. ¶ *an* ~ *refusal* 일언지하의 거절. **2** complete; thorough. 철저한; 충분한. ¶ *an* ~ *rogue* 철저한 깡패.

out·ri·val [àutráivəl] *vt.* (**-valed, -val·ing** or 《Brit.》 **-valled, -val·ling**) (P6) beat (others) in a race; defeat; excel. …을 이기다; …보다 낫다.

out·rode [àutróud] *v.* p. of **outride.**

out·run [àutrʌ́n] *vt.* (**-ran, -run, -run·ning**) (P6) **1** go or run faster than (something or someone). …보다 빨리 가다〔달리다〕. ¶ *He can* ~ *his elder brother.* 형보다 잘 뛴다. **2** go beyond; exceed; pass the limits of. …을 초과하다. ¶ *His expenses* ~ *his income.* 나가는 돈이 수입보다 많다. [*out-*]

out·set [áutsèt] *n.* 《*the* ~》 the beginning; the start. 최초; 시작.

at* 〔*in*〕 *the outset, firstly; in or at the beginning. 처음에.

from the outset, from the beginning. 처음부터. ¶ *From the* ~ *the prospects were poor.* 처음부터 전망은 어두웠다.

out·shine [àutʃáin] *vt.* (**-shone**) (P6) shine more brightly than; excel. …보다 빛나다〔밝다〕; …보다 낫다. ¶ *He outshines the rest in arithmetic.* 산술에선 단연 선두다.

out·shone [àutʃóun / -ʃɔ́n] *v.* p. and pp. of **outshine.**

out·shoot [àutʃúːt] *vt.* (**-shot**) (P6) **1** shoot faster or better than (someone). …보다 빨리〔잘〕 쏘다. **2** shoot out or send forth (something). (싹·가지)를 내다. —[ㅗㅗ] *n.* **1** Ⓒ projection; offshoot. 돌출; (싹·가지를) 냄; 출수(出穗). **2** 《baseball》 a pitched ball that curves away from the batter. 아웃슈트.

out·shot [àutʃát / -ʃɔ́t] *v.* p. and pp. of **outshoot.**

:out·side [áutsáid, ㅗㅗ] *n.* Ⓤ **1** outer side or part. 바깥(쪽); 외부. ¶ *the* ~ *of a box* 상자의 겉 / *open the door from* ~ 밖에서 문을 열다 / *ride on the* ~ *of a bus* 버스 옥상석(席)에 타고 가다. **2** appearance. 외관; 겉보기. ¶ *He has a rough* ~ *but a good heart.* 보기에 거칠게 생겼으나 마음은 곱다. **3** 《*the* ~》 the outside world. 외부 세계. ¶ *a prisoner about to resume life on the* ~ 머지않아 바깥 세상에 나가 살게 될 죄수. **4** the condition of not being a member of a body, society, etc. 국외(局外). ¶ *It is difficult for those on the* ~ *to understand the inner life of a college.* 대학 밖에 있는 사람이 그 곳 생활을 알기는 어렵다. **5** the farthest limit. 극한.

at the outside, at most. 고작. ¶ *I expected twenty people at the* ~. 기껏해야 20명이리라고 예상했다.

—[ㅗㅗ, ㅗㅗ] *adj.* **1** on or of the outside. 외부의. ¶ ~ *repairs* 외부 수리. **2** coming from the outside. 외래(外來)의; 밖으로부터의; 타인(他人)의. ¶ *You should not expect* ~ *help.* 남의 도움을 기대해서는 안 된다. **3** not main; not regular. 부(副)의; 본업 이외의. ¶ *an* ~ *job* 부업 / ~ *activities* 여가의 활용. **4** extreme; greatest possible. 극한의; 한도에 달하는. ¶ *an* ~ *estimate* 최대 견적. **5** (of a chance) very unlikely. 있음직하지 않은. ¶ *an* ~ *chance of saving him* 그를 살릴지도 모를 만의 하나의 가능성.

—[ㅗㅗ] *adv.* **1** outdoors; in the open

air. 밖에(서). ¶ *Run ~ and play.* 밖에 나가 놀아라. **2** to or on the outside. 밖에; 밖으로. ¶ *Put these flowers ~.* 이 꽃들을 밖에 내다 놓아라 / *The vase is black both ~ and in.* 이 꽃병은 안팎이 검다.
— [⌐⌐, ⌐⌐] *prep.* **1** at or on the outside of. …의 밖의[밖에]. ¶ *Play ~ the house.* (집) 밖에 나가 놀아라. **2** beyond; except. …의 한도를 넘어; …을 제외하고. ¶ *No one knew it ~ us.* 그건 우리밖에 아는 사람이 없다. [*out-*]

out·sid·er [àutsáidər] *n.* Ⓒ **1** a person who does not belong to a special group or class; a stranger. 국외자(局外者); 문외한; 조합[당(黨)] 외의 사람(opp. insider). **2** a horse not considered to have any chance of winning a race. (경마에서) 승산이 없는 말. **3** 《*colloq.*》 a person who has very bad manners. 무지막지한 사람.

out·size [áutsàiz] *adj.* larger than the usual size. 특대(特大)의. — *n.* a garment of such a size. (옷 따위) 특대품.

out·skirts [áutskə̀ːrts] *n. pl.* **1** the outer edge of a town or place. (도시 등의) 변두리; 교외. ¶ *She lives on the ~ of the town.* 그녀는 교외에 살고 있다. **2** the fringe of a subject. (문제 등의) 주변. ¶ *the ~ of history* 역사의 주변.

out·spo·ken [áutspóukən] *adj.* speaking or spoken openly; frank. 기탄없이 말하는; 솔직한. ¶ *He is very ~.* 아주 솔직한 사람이다. ● **out·spo·ken·ly** [-li] *adv.*

out·spread [àutspréd] *vi., vt.* (**-spread**) (P1;6) spread out; extend. 퍼지다; 펼치다.
— *adj.* [⌐⌐] spread out; extended. 퍼진; 뻗친. ¶ *an eagle with ~ wings* 날개를 편 독수리.

***out·stand·ing** [àutstǽndiŋ] *adj.* **1** standing out. 돌출한; 튀어나온. ¶ *a high ~ tower* 높게 우뚝한 탑. **2** distinguished; well-known. 걸출한; 두드러진. ¶ *an ~ figure* 걸출한 인물. **3** unpaid; unsettled; undone. 미불(未拂)의; 미해결의. ¶ *He had a lot of work ~.* 못 다한 일이 많다 / *~ debts* 밀린 빚. ● **out·stand·ing·ly** [-li] *adv.*

out·stay [àutstéi] *vt.* (P6) stay longer than (someone). …보다 오래 머무르다(cf. *overstay*). ¶ *~ the other guests* 다른 손님보다 오래 있다. [*out-*]

outstay** one's **welcome, stay longer than one is wanted. 밑이 질겨[오래 눌러 앉아] 미움받다.

out·stretched [àutstrétʃt] *adj.* stretched out or spread. 편; 벌린. ¶ *~ arms* 벌린 팔.

out·strip [àutstríp] *vt.* (**-stripped, -strip·ping**) (P6) **1** go or run faster than (others) as in a race. …을 앞지르다. **2** do something better than (someone else); excel. …보다 낫다; …을 능가하다. ¶ *He can ~ his friend both in sports and in study.* 운동에서나 공부에서나 친구들보다 낫다.

out·vote [àutvóut] *vt.* (P6) defeat (someone) in voting. 투표수로 …을 이기다.

***out·ward** [áutwərd] *adj.* **1** going toward the outside; going away from one place. 밖으로 향하는; 밖으로의. ¶ *an ~ motion* 바깥쪽으로의 움직임 / *the ~ course of a ship* 외항로(外航路). **2** of or on the outside; external. 외부[바깥쪽]의(opp. inward). ¶ *the ~ appearance of the buildings* 건물의 외관. **3** that can be seen. 눈에 보이는. ¶ *~ show* 외관; 겉치레 / *to all ~ appearance* 겉보기에는. **4** physical; bodily. 물질[육체]의. ¶ *the ~ eye* 육안(肉眼).

to outward seeming, apparently. 보기에는; 외견상.

— *adv.* toward the outside; away from the port; on the outside; in appearance. 밖에; 밖으로; 국외[해외]로; 바깥쪽에; 외관상. ¶ *the branches spreading ~* 바깥쪽으로 뻗는 가지 / *face ~* 밖을 향하다 / *The ship was ~ bound.* 선박은 외국행이었다. [*out-*]

out·ward·ly [áutwərdli] *adv.* on the outside; in appearance. 외부[외면]에; 외관상. ¶ *Though frightened, the boy remained ~ calm.* 무서웠지만 소년은 겉으로는 침착했다.

***out·wards** [áutwərdz] *adv.* =outward.

out·wear [àutwέər] *vt.* (**-wore, -worn**) (P6) **1** last or wear (something) longer than another. …보다 오래 가다. ¶ *Old handmade work will ~ machine-made stuff.* 오래 된 수제품이 기계 제품보다 튼튼하다. **2** wear out (something); use up (something). 입어서 낡게 하다; …을 써서 낡게 하다. **3** pass (time) away by endurance. …을 참고 견디다.

out·weigh [àutwéi] *vt.* (P6) be greater than (something or someone) in weight, value, importance, etc. …보다 무겁다; (가치·중요성 등에서) …보다 더하다. ¶ *No other idea could ~ yours.* 아무도 네 생각보다 낫지 않다.

out·wit [àutwít] *vt.* (**-wit·ted, -wit·ting**) (P6) excel (someone) in wit; beat (someone) by cunning. 지혜가 …을 앞서다; …을 속여 넘기다. ¶ *The thief outwitted the policeman and run away.* 도둑은 경찰을 따고 달아났다.

out·wore [àutwɔ́ːr] *v.* p. of **outwear.**

out·work [áutwə̀ːrk] *n.* Ⓒ **1** 《mil.》 a defensive wall or ditch built away from the center of the defenses. 외보(外堡); 외루(外壘). **2** work done away from a workroom. 직장 밖에서의 일; 외근. — [⌐⌐] *vt.* (P6) work harder or faster than (another). …보다 열심히[빨리] 일하다.

out·worn [áutwɔ́ːrn] *adj.* **1** that is worn out. 닳은; 해어진. ¶ *~ clothes* 해진 옷. **2** out-of-date. 시대에 뒤진; 구식의. ¶ *an ~ fashion* 구식 유행 / *~ opinions* 진부한 생각.
— [⌐⌐] *v.* pp. of **outwear.** [*out-*]

o·val [óuvəl] *adj.* egg-shaped. 달걀꼴의.
— *n.* Ⓒ something egg-shaped. 달걀꼴의 물건; 타원체. [→ovum]

o·va·ry [óuvəri] *n.* Ⓒ (*pl.* **-ries**) **1** the organ of the female body in which eggs are produced. 난소. **2** 《bot.》 the part of a plant in which seeds are produced. 씨방. [↑]

o·va·tion [ouvéiʃən] *n.* Ⓒ an enthusiastic applause; a hearty public welcome. 대단한 갈채; 열렬한 환영. [L. *ovo* exult]

·ov·en [ʌ́vən] *n.* Ⓒ an enclosed space in a stove for baking food. 솥; 오븐. [E.]

:o·ver [óuvər] *prep.* (opp. under) **1** above; higher than. …의 (바로) 위에; …보다 높이. ¶ *the sky ~ our heads* 우리 머리 위의 하늘 / *a lamp ~ the table* 식탁 위의 램프. **2** so as to cover; on; upon. …을 덮어〔가려〕; …에 덮어씌워. ¶ *put one's hands ~ one's face* 손으로 얼굴을 가리다 / *a blanket lying ~ a bed* 침대에 씌운 담요 / *wear a cape ~ one's shoulders* 어깨에 망토를 걸치다 / *water running ~ a rock* 바위 위를 흐르는 물. **3** across; from one side to the other side of; on the other side of. …을 넘어 저쪽에; …건너〔너머〕에. ¶ *fly ~ the lake* 호수 저쪽으로 날아가다 / *lands ~ the sea* 바다 저쪽의 나라들 / *climb ~ a wall* 담을 타고 넘다 / *a bridge ~ a river* 강을 가로지른 다리. **4** here and there in; through all parts of. 전면에; 온…에; 온통. ¶ *travel all ~ the country* 나라 방방곡곡을 다니다 / *spread butter ~ bread* 빵 거죽에 버터를 바르다 / *show someone ~ the town* 아무에게 시내 곳곳을 보여 주다. **5** more than. …이상(以上). ¶ *~ 30 miles,* 30 마일 이상 / *remain ~ a month at the seashore* 해변에서 한 달 이상을 지내다. **6** above in authority, power, position, etc. …보다 힘있어; …을 지배하여. ¶ *reign ~ a country* 일국을 지배하다 / *Mr. Smith is ~ me in the office.* 스미스 씨는 내 상사다 / *They want a strong man ~ them.* 그들은 힘있는 분을 모시고 싶어한다. **7** during; through; until after. …에 걸쳐; …동안 내내; …죽. ¶ *stay ~ the night* 하룻밤 묵다 / *keep a diary ~ many years* 여러 해 동안 일기를 적다. **8** concerning; about. …에 대〔관〕하여. ¶ *talk ~ the matter* 그 문제를 이야기하다 / *quarrel ~ a matter* 어떤 일로 말다툼하다. **9** while doing or engaged in. …을 하면서; …에 종사하여. ¶ *fall asleep ~ work* 일하면서 졸다 / *Let us discuss the matter ~ dinner.* 그 일은 식사하면서 이야기하자. **10** by means of. …에 의해; …로. ¶ *She told me ~ the phone.* 전화로 내게 이야기했다 / *I heard it ~ the radio.* 라디오에서 그걸 들었다. **11** along. …을 따라. ¶ *drive ~ a highway* 하이웨이를 드라이브하다.

— *adv.* **1** ⓐ above. 위(쪽)에; 머리 위에; 높이. ¶ *A flock of birds flew ~.* 한 떼의 새가 머리 위로 날아갔다. ⓑ beyond the top or upper surface or edge of something. 쑥 나와; 돌출하여; 내밀어. ¶ *a roof that hang ~* 쑥 내민 지붕 / *She bent ~.* 그녀는 몸을 굽혔다. **2** completely; all through; covering the entire area. 전면에; 온통; 도처에. ¶ *be covered ~ with paint* 전면(全面)에 페인트 칠이 되다 / *a landscape dotted ~ with trees* 일대에 나무들이 점점이 있는 풍경 / *be fomous all the world ~* 전세계적으로 유명하다. **3** across; to or on the other side; at some distance. 넘어서; 건너서; 저쪽에; 떨어진 데에. ¶ *~ here* 이쪽으로; 이쪽에서(는) / *go ~ to America* 미국으로 가다 / *go ~ to the enemy* 적쪽으로 넘어가다〔붙다〕 / *hand the money ~* 돈을 건네 주다 / *He came to a wall and jumped ~.* 벽에 다가오더니 훌쩍 뛰어 넘었다. **4** down from a standing position; upside down; into an opposite position. 넘어져; 쓰러져; 거꾸로; 뒤집어. ¶ *roll ~ and ~* 데굴데굴 구르다 / *turn ~ the pages* 책장을 넘기다 / *knock something ~* 무엇을 뒤집어엎다 / *turn a coin ~* 동전을 뒤집다 / *He fell ~ on the ice.* 그는 얼음 위에 넘어졌다. **5** finished; at an end. 끝나서. ¶ *All is ~.* 만사는 끝났다 / *The game is ~.* 경기가 끝났다 / *Our holidays will soon be ~.* 휴가도 이제 곧 끝난다 / *It is all ~ with him.* 그 사람 이젠 끝장났다. **6** through; from start to finish; from beginning to end. 처음부터 끝까지; 완전히. ¶ *all the year ~* 일 년 내내 / *read a newspaper ~* 신문을 끝까지 다 읽다 / *He took out his money and counted it ~.* 그는 돈을 꺼내서는 그걸 모조리 셌다. **7** again; once more; another time. 되풀이하여; 다시. ¶ *Try it ~.* 다시 해라 / *six times ~* 여섯 번이나 되풀이해서 / *many times ~* 몇 번이고 되풀이해. **8** more; too; in excess; besides. 더; 지나치게; 게다가. ¶ *I have six dollars and ~.* 6 달러 이상 가지고 있다 / *We have only three days ~.* (이제) 사흘밖에 남지 않았다 / *He is ~ polite.* 그는 너무 점잖다. [OE. *ofer*]

all over, **a**) on or in every part; throughout. 온통; 도처에. ¶ *travel all ~* 두루 다니다. **b**) finished. 끝나서. ¶ *It is all ~ now.* 이제 다 끝났다. **c**) characteristic of. …다운; …특유의. ¶ *That is Jones all ~.* 과연 존스답다〔다운 수법이다〕.

all the world over, all over the world. 전세계에.

go over, examine carefully. 검토하다; 잘 조사하다. ¶ *go ~ a report* 보고서를 검토하다.

over again, once more. 다시 한 번.

over against, opposite to or in contrast with. …의 맞은편에; …와 대조하여.

over all, from end to end; as a whole. 끝에서 끝까지; 전체로서.

over and above, in addition to; more than; besides. 게다가.

over and over 〔***again***〕, again and again; repeatedly. 몇 번이고; 되풀이하여.

o·ver- [òuvər-] *pref.* **1** too much; too long, etc. '너무(…하게), 과도히'의 뜻. ¶ *overcrowded.* **2** extra. '…범위 밖의, 여분의'의 뜻. ¶ *oversize.* **3** over, in the senses of the prep. '넘어서, 지나서' 따위의 뜻. ¶ *overland.* [↑]

o·ver·act [òuvərǽkt] *vt., vi.* (P6;1) act to excess; act (one's part) in an exaggerated way. 지나치게 하다; (연극에서) 과장된 연기를 하다. ¶ ~ (*in*) *a play.* [over-]

o·ver·ac·tive [òuvərǽktiv] *adj.* too active. 활동이 지나친.

o·ver·all [óuvərɔ̀:l] *adj.* **1** including all; whole. 전체적; 전부의. ¶ *the* ~ *expenses* 총경비. **2** from end to end. 끝에서 끝까지. ¶ ~ *length* 전장(全長). — *adv.* throughout; entirely. 전체적(전면적)으로. — *n.* **1** 《Brit.》 Ⓒ a loose outer garment slipped on over other clothes. 헐렁한 겉옷. **2** 《*pl.*》 loose trousers to be pulled over ordinary trousers. (가슴받이가 있는) 작업 바지. [over-]

o·ver·anx·ious [óuvərǽŋkʃəs] *adj.* too anxious. 너무 걱정하는.

o·ver·arch [òuvərɑ́:rtʃ] *vt.* hang or spread over like an arch. …위에 아치를 이루다. ¶ *The rainbow overarched the mountain.* 무지개가 산 위에 아치를 이루었다.

o·ver·arm [óuvərɑ̀:rm] *adj.* =overhand.

o·ver·ate [òuvəréit / òuvərét] *v.* p. of **overeat.**

o·ver·awe [òuvərɔ́:] *vt.* (P6) overcome (someone) with awe; strike fear into. …을 위압하다; 겁주다. ¶ *His manner overawed us.* 행동이 위압적이었다.

o·ver·bal·ance [òuvərbǽləns] *vt.* (P6) **1** be greater than (something) in weight, value, influence, etc. 무게(가치)가 …보다 더하다. ¶ *The expenses overbalanced the profit.* 지출이 수익을 앞질렀다. **2** cause (someone or something) to lose balance. 균형을 잃게 하다. ¶ *His weight as he leaned over the side overbalanced the boat and it upset.* 그가 뱃전에 기대자 그 무게로 배가 중심을 잃어 전복했다. [over-]

o·ver·bear [òuvərbɛ́ər] *vt.* (**-bore, -borne**) overcome; bear down. …을 압도(위압)하다. ¶ *He overbore my protest.* 내 항의도 그의 앞에서 무력했다.

o·ver·bear·ing [òuvərbɛ́əriŋ] *adj.* haughty; self-important. 오만한.

o·ver·bid [òuvərbíd] *vt., vi.* (P6;1,3) exceed in bidding; bid more than the real value. (…보다) 비싸게 부르다. ¶ ~ *for stock* 주가를 높게 매기다.

o·ver·blown [òuvərblóun] *adj.* **1** blown off. 날려가 버린. **2** more than full-blown. (꽃이) 한창때를 지난. ¶ *an* ~ *flower.*

o·ver·board [óuvərbɔ̀:rd] *adv.* from a ship into the water. 배 밖으로; (배에서) 물속으로. ¶ *fall* ~ (배에서) 물에 빠지다 / *Throw that box* ~. 그 상자를 물에 버려라. ***throw overboard,*** 《*fig.*》 abandon. 저버리다.

o·ver·bold [òuvərbóuld] *adj.* too bold; reckless. 무모한.

o·ver·bore [òuvərbɔ́:r] *v.* p. of **overbear.**

o·ver·borne [òuvərbɔ́:rn] *v.* pp. of **overbear.**

o·ver·bur·den [òuvərbə́:rdn] *vt.* (P6) load (someone or something) with too great a burden; overload. …에 과중한 부담을 주다; 과도하게 하다. ¶ *The president is overburdened with responsibilities.* 대통령은 책임이 너무 무거웠다. [over-]

·**o·ver·came** [òuvərkéim] *v.* p. of **overcome.**

o·ver·care·ful [òuvərkɛ́ərfəl] *adj.* too careful. 너무 조심하는(신중한).

o·ver·ca·pi·tal·ize [òuvərkǽpətəlàiz] *vt.* (P6) fix the capital of (a company, business, etc.) at too high an amount; overestimate the capital value (of a company, etc.). …에 과대한 자본을 가지게 하다; …의 자본을 과대 평가하다.

o·ver·cast [óuvərkǽst, -kɑ́:st, ⌐–⌐] *adj.* cloudy; dark. 흐린; 음산한. ¶ *an* ~ *sky* 음산한 하늘. — [⌐–⌐, ⌐–⌐] *vt.* (**-cast**) (P6) **1** cover (the sky) with clouds; make (the sky) dark. …을 구름으로 덮다(어둡게 하다). ¶ *The fair sky was soon* ~. 맑던 하늘은 이내 어두워졌다. **2** sew over (the edges of a seam) to prevent the cloth from separating into threads. …을 휘갑치다; 감치다. [over-]

o·ver·charge [òuvərtʃɑ́:rdʒ] *vt., vi.* (P6, 13;1) **1** load (something) too heavily. 짐을 너무 싣다. **2** put too much loading in (a gun); charge too heavily with electricity. (총)에 너무 장전(裝塡)하다; 과충전(過充電)하다. **3** ask (someone) for too much money as payment for something. 부당한 값을 요구하다. ¶ *I was overcharged for a meal here.* 식대를 가당찮게 물었다. **4** exaggerate. 과장하다. — [⌐–⌐] *n.* ⓊⒸ **1** too heavy a load. 장전 과다; 과충전(過充電). **2** too great a request of money for something. (요금 등의) 과다 청구; 바가지 씌우기.

o·ver·cloud [òuvərkláud] *vt.* (P6) **1** cover (the sky) with clouds. …을 구름으로 덮다; 흐리게 하다. **2** 《*fig.*》 make (someone) gloomy. …을 우울하게 만들다.

·**o·ver·coat** [óuvərkòut] *n.* Ⓒ a heavy coat worn over ordinary clothes in cold weather. 외투.

:**o·ver·come** [òuvərkʌ́m] *vt.* (**-came, -come**) (P6) **1** defeat; conquer. …에 이기다; …을 압도(정복)하다. ¶ ~ *the enemy* 적을 정복하다 / ~ *a difficulty* (*one's fault*) 난관(자기 결함)을 극복하다. **2** 《usu. in *passive*》 make (someone) weak or exhausted. …을 지치게 하다. ¶ *He was* ~ *by* (*with*) *hunger.* 그는 허기를 이길 수 없었다 / *The child was* ~ *by weariness and slept.* 아이는 피곤해서 잠이 들었다.

o·ver·con·fi·dence [òuvərkɑ́nfədəns / -kɔ́n-] *n.* Ⓤ too much self-reliance. 과신; 자만.

o·ver·con·fi·dent [òuvərkɑ́nfədənt / -kɔ́n-] *adj.* too confident. 과신(자만)하는.

o·ver·crowd [òuvərkráud] *vt.* (P6) crowd (a hall, bus, etc.) too much. …에 너무 넣다(태우다). ¶ ~ *a bus* (*theater, train*).

o·ver·de·vel·op [òuvərdivéləp] *vt.* 《photog.》 develop (film) too long. …을 지나치게 현상하다. ¶ ~ *a photograph.*

o·ver·did [òuvərdíd] *v.* p. of **overdo.**

o·ver·do [òuvərdú:] *vt.* (**-did, -done**) (P6) **1** do (something) too much. …을 지나치게 하다; 도를 지나치다. ¶ ~ *the joke* 지나친 농담을 하다. **2** exaggerate; carry too much. …을 과장하다. ¶ ~ *one's part* 과장된 연기를 하다. **3** 《usu. in *passive*》 cook (food, etc.) too much. …을 너무 삶다(굽다)(cf. *overdone*). **4** exhaust (몸)을 과로하게 하다. ¶ *You mustn't ~ it.* 과로하지 마라.

o·ver·done [òuvərdʌ́n] *v.* pp. of **overdo.** — *adj.* done too much; cooked too much. 지나치게 한; 너무 삶은〔구운〕 (cf. *underdone*). ¶ *He likes his meat ~.* 바싹 구운 고기를 좋아한다. [over-]

o·ver·dose [òuvərdóus] *vt.* (P6) cause (someone) to take too much medicine. 약을 너무 많이 넣다〔먹이다〕. — *n.* [⌐–⌐] Ⓒ too large a dose. (약의) 과다 투여.

o·ver·draw [òuvərdrɔ́:] *vt.* (P6) **1** draw more money from (a bank account) than one has in the bank. (어음)을 너무 발행하다; (예금)을 너무 많이 찾다; 차월(借越)하다. **2** exaggerate. …을 과장하다.

o·ver·dress [òuvərdrés] *vt., vi.* (P6;1) dress too richly or extravagantly. 옷치장을 지나치게 하다. — *n.* [⌐–⌐] Ⓒ a woman's dress worn over the main dress. (여성의 얇은) 웃옷.

o·ver·drive [òuvərdráiv] *vt.* (P6) overwork; exhaust by forcing to work too hard; drive too hard. …을 혹사하다〔너무 부려먹다〕. ¶ ~ *a horse* 〔*workmen*〕 말〔일꾼들〕을 혹사하다.

o·ver·due [òuvərdjú:] *adj.* unpaid at the time expected for payment; behind time fixed for arrival. (지불) 기한이 지난; (기차·기선이) 연착한. ¶ *an ~ check* 기한 경과 수표 / *The train is already half an hour ~.* 기차가 벌써 반 시간 연착이다. [over-]

o·ver·eat [òuvərí:t] *vi.* (**-ate, -eat·en**) (P1) eat too much. 과식하다.

o·ver·eat·en [òuvərí:tn] *v.* pp. of **overeat.**

o·ver·es·ti·mate [òuvəréstəmèit] *vt.* (P6) estimate at too high (a number, value, amount, etc.); overvalue. …을 과대 평가하다. ¶ *He overestimates his own ability.* 자기 역량을 과신하고 있다. — *n.* [óuvəréstimit] Ⓒ an estimate that is too high. 과대 평가.
● **o·ver·es·ti·ma·tion** [óuvərèstəméiʃən] *n.*

o·ver·ex·pose [òuvərekspóuz] *vt.* (P6) 《photog.》 expose (film) too much or for too long. (필름)을 너무 노출시키다.

o·ver·ex·po·sure [òuvərekspóuʒər] *n.* Ⓤ too much or too long an exposure (of photographic film). (필름의) 노출 과도.

o·ver·fed [òuvərféd] *v.* p. and pp. of **overfeed.**

o·ver·feed [òuvərfí:d] *vt., vi.* (P6;1) (**-fed**) feed (someone) to excess; eat too much. 너무 먹이다; 과식하다. ¶ ~ *oneself* 과식하다.

•**o·ver·flow** [òuvərflóu] *vt.* (P6) **1** flow over or beyond the poroper limits; flood. …을 넘쳐 흐르게 하다; 범람시키다. ¶ *The river often overflowed its banks.* 강은 자주 둑을 넘치곤 했다. **2** flow over the top of (something). …에서 넘치다. — *vi.* (P1,3) 《*with*》 flow over; abound. 충만하다; 넘치다. ¶ *The glass was full to overflowing.* 잔이 철철 넘치고 있었다 / *I overflowed with joy.* 나는 기쁨에 넘쳐 있었다. — *n.* [⌐–⌐] Ⓒ **1** the act of flowing over; an excessive amount. 홍수; 범람; 충만; 과잉. ¶ *an ~ of population* 인구 과잉. **2** an outlet for overflowing liquid. 배수구; 배수로.

o·ver·grew [òuvərgrú:] *v.* p. of **overgrow.**

o·ver·grow [òuvərgróu] *vi., vt.* (**-grew, -grown**) (P1;6) **1** grow over. (…에) 온통 자라다; 만연하다. ¶ *a garden overgrown with weeds* 잡초가 무성한 정원 / *The wall is overgrown with ivy.* 담은 온통 담쟁이로 덮여 있다. **2** outgrow; grow too fast. …보다 더 자라다; 너무 빨리 자라다. ¶ ~ *a coat* 너무 자라서 코트를 못 입게 되다. [over-]

o·ver·grown [òuvərgróun] *v.* pp. of **overgrow.** — *adj.* grown too big; covered with grass, leaves, etc. 너무 자란; (식물이) 무성한.

o·ver·growth [óuvərgròuθ] *n.* **1** Ⓤ too great growth. 너무 자람; 무성함; 만연. **2** Ⓒ something that has grown or spread too much. 온통 나있는〔뒤덮인〕 것.

o·ver·hand [óuvərhæ̀nd] *adj., adv.* 《sport》 (played) with the hand raised above the shoulder; down from above. 팔을 어깨 위로 들어 던지는〔던져〕; (공을) 내리치는〔쳐〕. ¶ *an ~ service* 공을 내리치는 서브 / *pitch ~* 팔을 들어 던지다.

o·ver·hang [òuvərhǽŋ] *vt., vi.* (**-hung**) (P6;1,2B) **1** hang or project over (something). …위에 쑥 내밀다. ¶ *The trees ~ the street to give good shade in summer.* 수목들은 길 위로 뻗어나와 여름에 그늘을 만들어 준다 / *The cliff overhangs the stream.* 벼랑이 시냇물 위에 쑥 나와 있다. **2** threaten. …을 위협하다. ¶ *Danger overhangs us.* 우리에게 위험이 닥치고 있다. — *n.* [⌐–⌐] Ⓒ something that is projecting over. 쑥 내민 것; 돌출. [over-]

o·ver·haul [òuvərhɔ́:l] *vt.* (P6) **1** examine (something) thoroughly in order to repair and improve it. …을 정밀 검사하다. ¶ ~ *the state of a business* 업무 상태를 철저히 파악하다 / *He was overhauled by a doctor.* 의사의 정밀 검사를 받았다. **2** (of a ship, etc.) catch up with (something); overtake. (배 따위가) …을 따라잡다; 추월하다. ¶ ~ *another vessel* 다른 배를 앞지르다. — [⌐–⌐] *n.* Ⓒ a thorough examination. 정밀 검사.

•**o·ver·head** [óuvərhéd] *adv.* in the sky;

above one's head; on the floor above. 상공에; 머리 위에; 위층에. ¶ *the stars* ~ 하늘의 별들 / *the family* ~ 위층에 사는 가족.
— [ˊ-ˋ] *adj.* being or passing overhead; placed overhead. 머리 위의[를 지나는]; 고가(高架)의. ¶ *an* ~ *railway* 고가 철도 / ~ *wires* 가공선(架空線).

o·ver·hear [òuvərhíər] *vt.* (**-heard**) (P6) hear (something) by accident or when one does not mean to hear it; hear (something) without the speaker's notice. …을 어쩌다[귓결에] 듣다; 엿듣다. ¶ *I accidentally overheard what they were saying.* 우연히 그들의 하는 얘기를 듣게 되었다.

o·ver·heat [òuvərhí:t] *vt.* (P6) heat (something) to excess. …을 너무 뜨겁게 하다; 과열시키다. — *vi.* (P1) become overheated. 과열하다. [over-]

o·ver·hung [òuvərhʌ́ŋ] *v.* p. and pp. of **overhang.** — [ˊ-ˋ] *adj.* hung from above. 위에서 매어단. ¶ *an* ~ *door* 내리닫이 문.

o·ver·in·dulge [òuvərindʌ́ldʒ] *vt.* (P6) indulge (someone) to excess. …을 너무 방임하다; 어해서 기르다. ¶ ~ *one's children* 아이를 어해서 키우다.

o·ver·joy [òuvərdʒɔ́i] *vt.* (P6) 《chiefly in *passive*》 make extremely joyful. 몹시 기쁘게 하다. ¶ *I am overjoyed today to find you just the same as ever.* 옛 모습대로의 너를 만나니 오늘은 정말 기쁘다.

o·ver·joyed [òuvərdʒɔ́id] *adj.* 《*at*》 very pleased. 몹시 기쁜. ¶ *We were* ~ *to hear that they wore safe.* 그들이 무사하다는 소식에 우리는 몹시 기뻤다.

o·ver·lad·en [òuvərléidn] *adj.* overburdened; overloaded; excessively covered (with ornament). (짐을) 너무 실은; (장식 등이) 요란한; 지나친. [over-]

o·ver·laid [òuvərléid] *v.* p. and pp. of **overlay.**

o·ver·land [óuvərlæ̀nd, -lənd] *adv., adj.* on land; by land. 육상에서(의); 육로로(의). ¶ *an* ~ *journey* 육로 여행 / *We travelled* ~ *from New York to Florida.* 육로로 뉴욕에서 플로리다로 갔다.

o·ver·lap [òuvərlǽp] *vi., vt.* (**-lapped, -lap·ping**) (P1;6) **1** lap or project over (something); lie so as to cover a part. 겹치다; 겹쳐지다; 포개(지)다. ¶ *The roofing slates are laid to* ~ *each other.* 슬레이트 지붕이 서로 겹쳐져 깔려 있다. **2** extend over part of (a period of time, spare of activity, etc.) (시간 등이) 부분적으로 일치하다; 중복되다. ¶ *Your visit and mine will just* ~. 너와 나의 방문은 똑같은 시간대가 될 것이다.

o·ver·lay [òuvərléi] *vt.* (**-laid**) (P6,13) **1** place (something) over another thing; spread over. …에 씌우다; 깔다; 바르다. ¶ *The dome is overlaid with gold.* 돔은 금으로 도금되어 있다. **2** make (something) dark or gloomy. …을 흐리게[어둡게] 하다. **3** weigh down. …을 압도하다.
— [ˊ-ˋ] *n.* Ⓒ something laid over something else. 덮어씌우는 것; 위에 까는 것.

o·ver·leap [òuvərlí:p] *vt.* (P6) leap over (something); jump too far; disregard. …을 뛰어넘다; 너무 멀리 뛰다; 무시하다.
overleap oneself, go beyond one's power and miss what one aims at. 도가 지나쳐 실패하다. [over-]

o·ver·lie [òuvərlái] *vt.* (**-lay, -lain**) (P6) lie over or upon; suffocate by lying upon. …위에 눕다; 위에 누워 질식시키다. ¶ ~ *a baby* 끼고 자다가 아기를 질식시키다.

o·ver·load [òuvərlóud] *vt.* (P6) put too much load on (something). …에 너무 싣다.
— [ˊ-ˋ] *n.* Ⓒ too great a load. 너무 실음; 과적(過積).

***o·ver·look** [òuvərlúk] *vt.* (P6) **1** (of a place or building) look down on (something) from above. …을 내려다보다. ¶ *My study window overlooks a flower garden.* 내 서재 창문에서 화원이 내려다보인다. **2** ⓐ fail to see; miss. …을 빠뜨리고 보다. ¶ ~ *the mistake* 틀린 데를 못 보고 지나다 / *In her hurry she overlooked a passage in the letter.* 서두른 나머지 그녀는 편지의 한 줄을 빠뜨리고 읽었다. ⓑ pay no attention to; fail to punish. …을 눈감아 주다; 용서하다. ¶ ~ *bad conduct* 비행을 묵인해 주다 / *Please* ~ *his behavior this time.* 이번에는 그의 행실을 눈감아 주시오. **3** oversee; supervise. …을 감독하다. ¶ *be overlooked by one's manager* 지배인의 감독을 받다.

o·ver·mas·ter [òuvərmǽstər / -mɑ́:s-] *vt.* (P6) overcome; conquer; overpower. …을 이기다; 정복하다. ¶ *an overmastering love* [*hate, passion*] 억제할 수 없는 사랑[증오; 격정]. [over-]

o·ver·match [òuvərmǽtʃ] *vt.* (P6) be more than a match for; surpass. …보다 우수(우세)하다; …보다 낫다. [↑]

o·ver·much [óuvərmʌ́tʃ] *adj., adv.* too much. 과다한[하게]; 지나친; 지나치게. ¶ *work* ~ 너무 일하다 / *He doesn't like me* ~. 그다지 나를 좋아하지 않는다.

o·ver·nice [óuvərnáis] *adj.* too nice or fastidious; too particular. 너무 까다로운[꼼꼼한]; 결벽증이 있는.

***o·ver·night** [óuvərnáit] *adv.* **1** during or through the night. 밤새도록; 밤새껏. ¶ *stay* ~ *with a friend* 친구와 하룻밤을 지내다 / *This fish won't keep* ~. 이 생선은 아침까지 못 간다. **2** on or during the night before. 전날 밤에. ¶ *It happened* ~. 그건 간밤의 일이었다. — [ˊ-ˋ] *adj.* **1** of only one night; lasting through a night. 하룻밤의; 밤새껏의. ¶ ~ *guests* 일박하는 손들 / *an* ~ *conversation* 밤을 새는 대담. **2** of a short journey. 짧은[일박] 여행의.

o·ver·pass [òuvərpǽs, -pɑ́:s] *vt.* (**-passed** or **-past**) (P6) **1** pass over (a river, bounds, etc.). (강 따위)를 건너다; 넘다; 통과하다. **2** overlook; miss. …을 빠뜨리고 보다. **3** exceed; surpass. …을 능가하다; 초월하다. ¶ *It overpasses endurance.* 그건 참을 수가 없다 / *He overpassed all competitors.* 모든 경쟁자를 물리쳤다. ―[ˊ-ˋ] *n.* Ⓒ a bridge over a road, railroad, etc. 고가 도로[철도]; 육교. 「pp. of **overpass.**

o·ver·past [òuvərpǽst, -pɑ́:st] *v.* p. and

o·ver·pop·u·la·tion [òuvərpɑpjəléiʃən / -pɔp-] *n.* Ⓤ too much population. 인구 과잉. [over-]

o·ver·pow·er [òuvərpáuər] *vt.* **1** overcome; defeat; conquer. …에 이기다; …을 제압하다. ¶ ~ *the enemy* 적을 무찌르다. **2** affect greatly; be too strong or intense for. (정신적으로) …을 압도하다; …의 힘에 겹다. ¶ *be overpowered by* [*with*] *grief* 슬픔을 가눌 길 없게 되다 / *The anger overpowered her.* 화가 치밀어 견딜 수 없었다.

o·ver·pro·duc·tion [òuvərprədʌ́kʃən] *n.* Ⓤ too much production. 생산 과잉.

o·ver·ran [òuvərǽn] *v.* p. of **overrun.**

o·ver·rate [òuvəréit] *vt.* (P6) estimate (something) too highly; put too high a value on. …을 과대 평가하다. ¶ ~ *one's capacities* 자기 능력을 과신하다.

o·ver·reach [òuvərí:tʃ] *vt.* (P6) **1** ⓐ reach or extend over (something); reach too far. …을 지나치다; 너무 뻗다; 넘다. ⓑ miss by reaching too far; overshoot. (목표 등)을 넘어가다; 지나쳐 가다. ¶ ~ *a goal.* **2** cheat (someone) by cunning. …을 속이다. **3** 《*reflexively*》 fail or miss by trying to get too much or trying to do more than one can. 무리하여 실패하다. ¶ *His cunning overreached itself.* 그는 지나치게 잔꾀를 부리다가 실패했다.

o·ver·ride [òuvəráid] *vt.* (**-rode, -rid·den**) (P6) **1** ⓐ ride over or across. …을 말타고 지나가다[넘다]. ⓑ trample or crush under foot. …을 짓밟다; 유린하다. ¶ ~ *an enemy in one's path* 앞길의 적을 무찌르다. **2** 《*fig.*》 refuse; disregard. …을 거절하다; 무시하다. ¶ ~ *advice* [*objection*] 충고[반대]를 무시하다. **3** prevail over; take the place of. …을 뒤엎다; 대신하다. ¶ ~ *all the previous rules* 이전의 규칙들을 엎어버리다. **4** tire out (a horse) by riding it too much. (말)을 너무 타서 지치게 만들다. ¶ *an overridden horse* 기진맥진한 말. [over-]

o·ver·rode [òuvəróud] *v.* p. of **override.**

o·ver·rule [òuvərú:l] *vt.* (P6) **1** decide against (someone's idea, etc.); set aside. …을 각하[파기]하다. ¶ *He overruled their suggestion.* 그는 그들의 제안을 물리쳤다 / *The claims were overruled.* 요구는 묵살되었다. **2** rule over (someone); govern; prevail over; defeat. …을 지배하다; …에 이기다. ¶ *His greed overruled his caution.* 그는 탐욕 때문에 신중하지 못했다.

o·ver·run [òuvərʌ́n] *vt.* (**-ran, -run, -run·ning**) (P6) **1** spread over in great numbers. (잡초 등이) 퍼지다; 우거지다. ¶ *Weeds overran his garden.* 정원에는 잡초가 무성했다. **2** run over so as to harm; invade. …을 망쳐놓다; 침략하다. ¶ *The enemy troops overran the country.* 적군이 그 나라를 유린했다. **3** run beyond (something). …을 넘어[지나쳐]가다; 오버런하다. ¶ ~ *second base* 2루를 오버런하다 / *His speech overran the time allowed.* 그의 연설은 허용 시간을 초과했다.

o·ver·saw [òuvərsɔ́:] *v.* p. of **oversee.**

o·ver·sea [óuvərsí:] *adv., adj.* =overseas.

o·ver·seas [òuvərsí:z] *adv.* across the sea; abroad. 해외로; 외국에. ¶ *go* ~ 해외로 나가다. ―[ˊ-ˊ] *adj.* of countries across the sea; foreign. 해외(로부터)의; 외국의. ¶ ~ *markets* 해외 시장 / *an* ~ *broadcast* 대외 방송 / *We enjoyed our* ~ *travel.* 해외 여행을 즐겼다.

o·ver·see [òuvərsí:] *vt.* (**-saw, -seen**) (P6) keep watch over and direct (someone); manage. …을 감독하다. ¶ ~ *the work* [*workers*] 일[일꾼들]을 감독하다.

o·ver·seen [òuvərsí:n] *v.* pp. of **oversee.**

o·ver·se·er [óuvərsì:ər] *n.* Ⓒ a person who keeps watch over the work of others. 감독; 직공장; 관리인.

o·ver·set [òuvərsét] *vt., vi.* (**-set, -set·ting**) (P6;1) overturn; overthrow; upset. 뒤집어 엎다; 뒤집히다. ¶ ~ *a boat* [*plan*] 배를[계획을] 뒤집다 / ~ *the government* 정부를 전복시키다. [over-]

o·ver·shad·ow [òuvərʃǽdou] *vt.* (P6) **1** cast a shadow on (something); darken; make (someone) gloomy. …을 그늘지게 하다; 어둡게 하다; 우울하게 하다. **2** 《*fig.*》 become more important than (something); make insignificant; lessen the importance of by contrast. …보다 낫다; …의 빛을 잃게 하다. ¶ *Her new book will* ~ *all her earlier ones.* 그녀의 새 책은 이전의 모든 책보다 나을 것이다 / *His early success was overshadowed by his later failure.* 후일의 실패로 인해서 그의 초기 성공은 빛바랜 것이 되었다.

o·ver·shoe [óuvərʃù:] *n.* Ⓒ 《usu. *pl.*》 a waterproof rubber shoe worn over another shoe for protection against getting wet. 덧신; 오버슈즈.

o·ver·shoot [òuvərʃú:t] *vt.* (**-shot**) (P6) **1** shoot over or beyond (something). (과녁)을 넘게 쏘다. **2** 《*fig.*》 go beyond (what is proper or right); go too far. …의 도를 지나치다. [over-]

overshoot oneself [***the mark***], do something too much; exaggerate. …을 지나치게 하다; 과장하다.

o·ver·shot [òuvərʃɑ́t / -ʃɔ́t] *v.* p. and pp. of **overshoot.**

―[ˊ-ˋ] *adj.* driven by water passing over from above. (물레방아가) 위로부터 물을 받는.

o·ver·sight [óuvərsàit] *n.* ⓊⒸ **1** failure

to notice because of carelessness or idleness. (부주의로 인한)간과; 빠뜨림; 실수. ¶ *Through an ~, the kitten got no supper last night.* (주인의) 실수로 인하여 고양이는 간밤에 저녁을 굶었다. **2** supervision; watchful care. 감독; 감시. ¶ *While children are at school they are under their teacher's ~ and direction.* 아이들은 학교에 있는 동안 선생의 감독과 지시를 받는다.

o·ver·size [óuvərsáiz] *adj.* larger than the proper or usual size. 보통 것보다 큰; 특대의. —[ˊ-ˋ] *n.* **1** a size larger than the proper or usual size. 보통 이상의 큰 치수; 특대품. **2** something larger than is necessary. 쓸데 없이 크기만 한 것.

o·ver·sleep [òuvərslíːp] *vt., vi.* (**-slept**) (P6;1) sleep beyond the time set for rising. 너무 오래 자다. ¶ *I overslept (myself) this morning.* 오늘 아침은 늦잠을 잤다. [over-]

o·ver·slept [òuvərslépt] *v.* p. and pp. of **oversleep.**

o·ver·spread [òuvərspréd] *vt.* (**-spread**) (P6) spread over; cover. …을 온통 덮다; …에 온통 펴다. ¶ *Black clouds soon ~ the whole sky.* 이윽고 검은 구름이 온 하늘을 덮었다.

o·ver·state [òuvərstéit] *vt.* (P6) state or express too strongly; exaggerate. 허풍떨다; 과장하다(opp. understate). ¶ *~ one's case* 자기 주장을 떠벌리다.

o·ver·state·ment [òuvərstéitmənt] *n.* UC extravagant statement; exaggeration. 과장.

o·ver·stay [òuvərstéi] *vt.* (P6) stay beyond the expected time. 너무 오래 머무르다 (cf. *outstay*).

overstay* one's *welcome, stay so long that one is no longer a welcome guest. 너무 오래 머물러 있어 미움을 사다.

o·ver·step [òuvərstép] *vt.* (**-stepped, -step·ping**) (P6) step over or beyond; exceed. …을 밟고 넘다; 지나가다; …의 한도를 넘다. ¶ *~ one's authority* 월권하다 / *~ the limits* 한계를 넘다.

o·ver·stock [òuvərsták / -stɔ́k] *vt.* (P6) stock too much; supply with more than is needed. …을 너무 사들이다〔공급하다〕. ¶ *an overstocked shop* 물건을 너무 많이 들여놓은 가게. —[ˊ-ˋ] *n.* UC too great a supply or stock. 공급 과다; 과잉 재고.

o·ver·strain [òuvərstréin] *vt.* (P6) stretch too tightly; overwork. …을 너무 긴장시키다; 무리하게 쓰다. ¶ *~ one's eyes* 〔*nerves*〕 시력〔신경〕을 너무 쓰다. —[ˊ-ˋ] *n.* U too excessive a tension; overwork. 과도한 긴장; 과로.

***overstrain* oneself,** use one's strength too much; work too hard. 과로하다.

o·ver·sup·ply [òuvərsəplái] *vt.* (**-plied**) (P6,13) supply too much. …을 지나치게 공급하다. —[ˊ--ˋ] *n.* UC (*pl.* **-plies**) an excessive supply. 공급 과잉.

o·vert [óuvəːrt, -ˊ] *adj.* open; public; evident; not hidden. 명백한; 공공연한; 숨김 없는(opp. covert). ¶ *a market ~* 공개 시장 / *The bombing of the city was an ~ act of war.* 도시의 폭격은 명백한 전쟁 행위였다.

● **o·vert·ly** [-li] *adv.* [L. *aperio* open]

***o·ver·take** [òuvərtéik] *vt.* (**-took, -tak·en**) (P6) **1** come up or catch up with (something or someone). (사람·뒤진 일 등)을 따라잡다; 추월하다; 만회하다. ¶ *I ran to ~ him.* 그를 따라잡기 위해 뛰었다. **2** (of trouble, storms, etc.) come upon (someone) suddenly or unexpectedly. (폭풍·재난 등이) …을 갑자기 덮치다. ¶ *A storm overtook the ship.* 폭풍이 배를 덮쳤다. **3** overcome. …을 압도하다. ¶ *be overtaken by terror* 공포에 휩싸이다. [over-]

be overtaken in 〔***with***〕 ***drink,*** be drunk. 취해 있다. 「take.

o·ver·tak·en [òuvərtéikən] *v.* pp. of **over-**

o·ver·task [òuvərtǽsk, -táːsk] *vt.* (P6) give too great or too heavy tasks to (someone). …에게 무리한 일을 시키다; …을 혹사하다.

o·ver·tax [òuvərtǽks] *vt.* (P6) **1** tax too much. …에 세금을 너무 물리다. ¶ *This country is overtaxed.* 이 나라는 중과세에 시달리고 있다. **2** lay too heavy a burden on (someone or something). …에 과중한 부담을 주다; 무리를 강요하다. ¶ *~ someone's patience* 아무를 못 견디게 굴다 / *Don't ~ yourself!* 과로는 금물이다.

o·ver·threw [òuvərθrúː] *v.* p. of **overthrow.**

***o·ver·throw** [òuvərθróu] *vt.* (**-threw, -thrown**) (P6) **1** overturn; upset. …을 뒤집어 엎다; 쓰러뜨리다. ¶ *The heavy winds overthrew numorous telephone poles and trees.* 강풍은 무수한 전주와 나무들을 쓰러뜨렸다. **2** overcome the power of (someone or something); defeat. (국가·정부 등)을 전복시키다; 무너뜨리다. ¶ *The people overthrew the king.* 국민들은 왕을 내몰았다 / *~ a government* 정부를 전복시키다. **3** 《baseball》 throw above and beyond (where the player is aiming). 폭투(暴投)하다; 너무 높이 던지다.

—[ˊ-ˋ] *n.* C **1** the act of overthrowing or the state of being overthrown; ruin; defeat. 전복; 멸망; 패배; 타도. ¶ *The ~ of his plans left him much discourage.* 계획이 좌절되어 그는 몹시 실의에 빠졌다. **2** 《baseball》 a throw above and beyond where it is aimed. 높이 던지기; 폭투.

give 〔***have***〕 ***the overthrow,*** overturn; be overturned; ruin; be ruined. 전복하다〔되다〕; 멸망시키다〔하다〕.

o·ver·thrown [òuvərθróun] *v.* pp. of **overthrow.**

o·ver·time [óuvərtàim] *n.* U **1** extra time; time worked beyond the regular hours. 규정 외의 노동 시간; 초과 근무 시간.

¶ *You ought to be paid for* ~ . 초과 근무 수당을 받아야 한다. **2** extra work done after regular working hours are over; very much work. 시간외 노동; 초과 노동. ¶ *He's on ~ tonight.* 오늘 밤 그는 야근이다. — *adv., adj.* beyond the regular working hours. 규정 시간 외에(의). ¶ ~ *pay* 초과 근무 수당 / *work* ~ 초과 근무하다. — [⌐—⌐] *vt.* give too much time to (something). …에 너무 시간을 들이다. [over-]

o·ver·tone [óuvərtòun] *n.* **1** Ⓒ a fainter and higher tone than the main tone. 배음(倍音); 상음. **2** 《usu. *pl.*》 an additional meaning; a hint. (말 등의) 암시; 부수적 의미. ¶ *His words were polite, but there were overtones of anger in his voice.* 그의 말씨는 정중했으나 음성엔 노기가 있었다.

o·ver·took [òuvərtúk] *v.* p. of **overtake.**

o·ver·top [òuvərtáp / -tɔ́p] *vt.* (**-topped, -top·ping**) (P6) rise over or above the top of (something or someone); surpass; excel. …보다 높다; …의 위에 솟다; …을 능가하다. ¶ *The new building will ~ all the others.* 새 건물이 여타 건물들보다 높을 것이다.

o·ver·ture [óuvərtʃər, -tʃùər] *n.* Ⓒ 《often *pl.*》 **1** a proposal; an offer. 제안; 제의. ¶ *overtures of peace* 강화 제의. **2** 《mus.》 music played as an introduction to an opera, oratorio, etc. 서곡; 전주곡. [→vert]

make overtures to, **a**) make on offer to (someone). …에게 제안하다. ¶ *The enemy made us peace overtures.* 적은 우리에게 강화를 제의해 왔다. **b**) begin to deal with (someone) in the hope of reaching an agreement. …와 교섭을 시작하다. [→overt]

***o·ver·turn** [òuvərtə́ːrn] *vt.* (P6) **1** turn over; upset. …을 뒤집어엎다. ¶ *The boat was overturned.* 배가 뒤집혔다. **2** cause (someone or something) to fall down; destroy. …을 멸망시키다; 파괴하다. ¶ *The government was overturned.* 정부가 전복됐다. — [⌐—⌐] *n.* Ⓒ the act of overturning; the state of being overturned. 전복; 와해; 멸망. [over-]

o·ver·value [òuvərvǽljuː] *vt.* (P6) value above its true worth. …을 과대 평가하다.

o·ver·watch [òuvərwátʃ, -wɔ́tʃ] *vt.* (P6) watch over. …을 감시하다.

o·ver·ween·ing [òuvərwíːniŋ] *adj.* haughty; arrogant; conceited; self-confident. 오만한; 자부심이 강한; 뽐내는. ¶ ~ *pride* 오만한 자존심.

o·ver·weigh [òuvərwéi] *vt.* (P6) **1** be heavier than (something or someone); overbalance. …보다 무겁다; 중요하다. **2** oppress. …을 압박하다; 누르다.

o·ver·weight [óuvərwèit] *n.* Ⓤ too much weight; extra weight. 초과 중량. ¶ *pay for the ~ of a letter* 편지의 중량 초과분 요금을 치르다. — [⌐—⌐] *adj.* weighing more than is normal, necessary, or allowed; having too much weight. 중량이 초과된; 너무 무거운. ¶ *The boy is ~ for his age.* 아이가 그 나이엔 너무 무겁다.

***o·ver·whelm** [òuvərhwélm] *vt.* (P6) **1** crush or destroy utterly; overcome completely; overpower. …을 눌러 찌그러뜨리다; (감정 등이) 압도하다. ¶ *be overwhelmed with grief* 비탄에 빠지다. **2** (of a flood, waves, etc.) cover completely and swallow up (something) (홍수 등이) …에 덮치다; …을 침몰시키다. ¶ *The boat was overwhelmed by the high waves.* 배는 높은 파도에 휩쓸렸다.

o·ver·whelm·ing [òuvərhwélmiŋ] *adj.* too powerful or too much to be resisted; overpowering. 압도적인; 저항할 수 없는. ¶ ~ *majority* 압도적인 다수 / ~ *grief* 가눌 길 없는 슬픔. ● **o·ver·whelm·ing·ly** [-li] *adv.*

***o·ver·work** [òuvərwə́ːrk] *vt., vi.* (**-worked, -wrought**) (P6;1) work or cause (someone or something) to work too much or too hard. …을 과로하게 하다; 혹사하다; 과로하다. ¶ ~ *a horse* 말을 너무 부려먹다. — [⌐—⌐] *n.* Ⓤ **1** too much or too hard work. 과로; 지나친 노동. **2** extra work. 초과 노동(근무).

o·ver·wrought [òuvərɔ́ːt] *v.* p. and pp. of **overwork.** — *adj.* **1** very excited; overworked. 잔뜩(너무) 긴장한; 과로한. ¶ ~ *nerves* 과민해진 신경. **2** decorated to excess. 온통 치장한; 너무 공들인.

***owe** [ou] *vt.* (P13,14) **1** must pay; be in debt to (someone). …에게 빚이 있다. ¶ *I ~ ten dollars to the baker.* =*I ~ the baker ten dollars.* 빵집에 10 달러 빚지고 있다. **2** ⓐ 《*fig.*》 feel bound to express. (어떤 감정)을 표시해야 하다. ¶ *I ~ you my best thanks.* 당신에게 감사한 마음 이를 데 없소 / *I ~ no thanks to him.* 그에게 감사할 까닭이 없다. ⓑ 《*to*》 be obliged or indebted for (something). …에게 은혜를 입고 있다; …의 덕분이다. ¶ *I ~ my success to you.* 네 덕분에 성공했다 / *He owed his success to luck more than to capacity.* 그는 재능 때문이라기보다 운이 좋아서 성공했다 / *We ~ a great deal to our parents.* 우리는 부모님께 막대한 은혜를 입고 있다.

— *vi.* (P3) be in debt. 빚지고 있다. ¶ *She still owes for what she bought last summer.* 지난 여름에 산 물건 값을 아직 안 갚고 있다. [E.]

:ow·ing [óuiŋ] *adj.* due as a debt; owed; not paid. 빚지고 있는; 미불의. ¶ *This will pay what is ~ .* 이로써 대가는 치르게 된다 / *How much is ~ to you?* 네게 갚을 게 얼마지 / *We must pay what is ~ .* 갚을 건 갚아야 한다.

owing to, **a**) because of; on account of. …때문에; …이 원인으로. ¶ *Owing to careless driving, he had an accident.* 난폭한 운전으로 그는 사고를 냈다. **b**) as a result of. …에 의한; …로 인한. ¶ *His death was ~ to an ac-*

cident. 그의 사망은 사고 때문이었다. [*owe*]

:**owl** [aul] *n.* Ⓒ **1** a bird with great, round eyes which eats small animals and which is active at night. 올빼미. **2** 《*fig.*》 a wise-looking stupid person. 약은 체하는 바보. [E.]

as blind* 〔*stupid*〕 *as an owl, very blind 〔stupid〕. 전혀 앞을 못 보는〔숙맥인〕.

owl·et [áulət] *n.* Ⓒ a small owl; a young owl. 올빼미 새끼.

owl·ish [áuliʃ] *adj.* like an owl; trying to look wise. 올빼미 같은; 약은 체하는.

:**own** [oun] *adj.* **1** belonging to oneself; peculiar to oneself. 자기 자신의; 고유한. ¶ *my ~ children* 내 아이들 / *He has his ~ troubles.* 그 사람 나름의 고민이 있다 / *I saw it with my ~ eyes.* 내 눈으로 그걸 봤다 / *He did it in his ~ way.* 그는 그걸 자기 방식대로 했다. **2** done, produced, etc. by and for oneself. 자기 힘으로〔자신이〕 하는. ¶ *make one's ~ clothes* 자기 옷을 제 손으로 만들다 / *He cooks his ~ meal.* 그는 손수 음식을 만든다. **3** related directly to. (혈연 관계가) 친(親)…. ¶ *one's ~ brothers* 친형제 / *She is his ~ mother.* 그녀는 그의 친어머니다.

be one's own man ⇨man.

— *n.* 《*one's ~* 》 that which belongs to oneself. 자신의 것. ¶ *He claims it as his ~.* 그는 그것이 제 것이라고 주장한다 / *Keep it for your (very) ~.* 네가 가져라.

come into one's own, receive what properly belongs to one; get the credit, fame, etc. that one deserves. (명예·신용 따위) 당연히 받을 만한 것을 받다.

hold one's own, **a**) keep one's position against an attack; be not forced back. 자기 입장을 지키다; 굴(屈)하지 않다. **b**) (in illness) not lose strength. 기운을 잃지 않다.

of one's own, belonging to oneself. 자기 소유의. ¶ *I have no house of my ~.* 내겐 집이 없다.

on one's own, 《*colloq.*》 by one's own efforts; by oneself. 자기 힘으로; 스스로. ¶ *do something on one's ~* 혼자서 무엇을 하다.

— *vt.* **1** (P6) have; possess. …을 가지고 있다; 소유하다. ¶ *He owns much land.* 그에게는 땅이 많다. **2** (P6,11) recognize (something) as one's own. …을 자기 것이라고 인정하다. ¶ *He refused to ~ her.* 그는 그녀를 제 자식이 아니라고 했다. **3** (P6,11) admit; acknowledge; confess; recognize. …을 인정하다; 승인하다; 털어놓다. ¶ *At last he owned his guilt.* 끝내는 자기 죄를 시인했다 / *~ oneself in the wrong* 자기 잘못을 인정하다 / *Do you ~ the story to be a lie?* 그 이야기가 거짓임을 인정하겠나 / *He owned that I was in the right.* 그는 내가 옳았다고 했다.

— *vi.* 《*to*》 (P2A,3) confess; make a clean breast. 고백〔자인〕하다; 실토하다. ¶ *He owned to many faults.* 그는 많은 과오를 인정했다 / *The boy owned to having stolen the book.* 아이는 그 책을 훔친 것이라고 실토했다. [E. =possess]

:**own·er** [óunər] *n.* Ⓒ a person who owns or possesses. 소유주; 임자.

own·er·less [óunərlis] *adj.* without an owner; not belonging to anybody. 임자가 없는. ¶ *an ~ house* 임자 없는 집.

own·er·ship [óunərʃip] *n.* Ⓤ the state or condition of being an owner; the right of possession. 소유자임; 소유권.

:**ox** [ɑks / ɔks] *n.* Ⓒ (*pl.* **ox·en**) a full-grown male of cattle. (불깐) 수소(cf. *bull*[1], *cow*, *steer*[2]). ¶ *as strong as an ~* 힘이 장사인. [E.]

ox·cart [ákskὰ:rt / ɔ́ks-] *n.* Ⓒ a cart drawn by oxen. 우차(牛車); 달구지.

ox·en [áksən / ɔ́ksən] *n.* pl. of **ox**.

ox·ford [áksfərd / ɔ́ks-] *n.* 《usu. *pl.*》 a kind of low shoe. 옥스퍼드 슈즈《단화의 일종》.

•**Ox·ford** [áksfərd / ɔ́ks-] *n.* **1** a city in southern England. 옥스퍼드 시(市). **2** the famous university located in Oxford. 옥스퍼드 대학. [Place]

ox·i·da·tion [ὰksədéiʃən / ɔ̀ks-] *n.* Ⓤ 《chem.》 the action or procss of oxidizing. 산화(酸化) (작용). ¶ *Burning is one kind of ~.* 연소는 산화 작용의 한 형태다. [↓]

ox·ide [áksaid / ɔ́ks-] *n.* ⒸⓊ 《chem.》 a compound of oxygen with some other element. 산화물. [F (→oxygen)]

ox·i·dize [áksədàiz / ɔ́ks-] *vt.* (P6) **1** combine (something) with oxygen. …을 산화시키다. **2** rust. …을 녹슬게 하다. — *vi.* (P1) be combined with oxygen; become rusty. 산화되다; 녹슬다. [↑]

ox·y·a·cet·y·lene [ὰksiəsétilì:n / ɔ̀ks-] *adj.* of a mixture of oxygen and acetylene. 산소 아세틸렌 혼합물의. [↓]

oxyacetylene blowpipe 〔torch〕 [–––⌐–– ⌐–〔⌐〕] *n.* a tool with a very hot flame for welding or cutting metals. 산소(아세틸렌) 용접기. [↓]

•**ox·y·gen** [áksidʒən / ɔ́ks-] *n.* Ⓤ a gas without color, smell, or taste, which is essential to life and to burning. 산소(酸素). [Gk. *oxus* sharp, *gignomai* become]

ox·y·gen·ate [áksidʒənèit / ɔ́ks-] *vt.* (P6) 《chem.》 treat or combine with oxygen; oxidize. 산소로 처리하다〔화합시키다〕. [↑]

•**oys·ter** [ɔ́istər] *n.* Ⓒ an edible shellfish living in shallow sea water and which has a rough shell. 굴. ¶ *as dumb as an ~* 통 말이 없는. [Gk. *ostreon*]

oz. ounce; ounces.

o·zone [óuzoun, –⌐] *n.* Ⓤ **1** 《chem.》 a form of oxygen which is produced in the air after thunderstorms. 오존. **2** 《*colloq.*》 very pleasant, fresh air, e.g. at the seaside. 신선한 공기. [Gk. *ozō* smell]

P p

P, p [piː] *n.* Ⓒ (*pl.* **P's, Ps, p's, ps** [piːz]) **1** the 16th letter of the English alphabet. 영어 알파벳의 열여섯째 글자. **2** anything shaped like the letter P. P자 모양의 것.
mind one's P's and Q's, be careful what one does or says. 언행을 조심하다.

pa [pɑː] *n.* Ⓒ 《*child's word*》 papa; father. 아빠.

:pace[1] [peis] *n.* Ⓒ **1** a single step; the length of a single step. 한 걸음; 1보폭(步幅)《약 2 1/2 피트》. ¶ *There were perhaps ten paces between me and the bear.* 곰과 나와의 거리는 열 발짝 정도였다. **2** the rate of speed. 걷는 속도; 보조(步調). ¶ *go at a good* ~ 상당한 속도로 가다; 잰걸음으로 가다 / *a* ~ *of three miles an hour* 한 시간 3마일의 속도 / *at a snail's* ~ 거북이걸음으로. **3** a way of stepping. 걸음걸이. ¶ *an alderman's* ~ 당당한 걸음걸이. **4** a particular pace of a horse in which it lifts both feet on the same side at once. (말의) 측대보(側對步)《한쪽의 앞뒷다리를 동시에 드는 2박자의 걸음걸이》.
go the pace, **a**) go at great speed. 아주 빠르게 걷다. **b**) 《*fig.*》 spend money freely; live a wasteful or wild life. 돈을 물쓰듯 하다; 방탕한 생활을 하다.
keep pace (=*get into step*) ***with*** *someone.* …와 보조를 같이 하다.
put *someone* ***through his paces,*** test someone's knowledge, ability, etc. (…의) 기량을 시험하다.
set 〔***make***〕 ***the pace,*** **a**) set an example of speed for others to keep up with. (선두에서) 보조를 정하다. **b**) be an example or a model for others to follow. 모범을 보이다.
— *vi.* (P1,2A) **1** walk with slow, regular steps. 천천히〔보조를 맞추어〕 걷다. ¶ *He paced slowly toward the gate.* 문으로 천천히 걸어갔다 / ~ *back and forth a room* 방 안을 왔다갔다하다. **2** (of a horse) go at the pace. (말이) 측대보로 걷다(cf. *amble*).
— *vt.* (P6,7) **1** 《*out, off*》 measure by counting the number of paces. 보측(步測)하다. ¶ ~ *off the ground* 〔*the distance*〕 지면을〔거리를〕 보측하다. **2** set the pace for (a runner in a race). (경주에서) …에게 보조〔속도〕를 보여 주다〔조절해 주다〕. **3** walk with slow, regular steps in. …을 천천히 걷다. ¶ ~ *a room* 방 안을 천천히 왔다갔다하다. [L. *passus*]

pa·ce[2] [péisi] *prep.* by leave of. …에게는 실례지만. ¶ ~ *Mr. Jones* 존스씨에게는 실례지만. [L. *pax* peace]
pace tua [´-tjúːei], by 〔with〕 your leave. 실례지만.

pace·mak·er [péismèikər] *n.* **1** a person who sets the pace for another. 보조〔속도〕 조정자. **2** a machine that regulates the beat of the heart. 심장 박동 조절 장치. [→ pace[1]]

pac·er [péisər] *n.* **1** Ⓒ a pacing horse. 측대보(側對步)로 걷고 있는 말. **2** =pacemaker. [↑]

:pa·cif·ic [pəsífik] *adj.* **1** peaceful; making peace; loving peace. 평화로운; 평화를 사랑하는. ¶ ~ *words* 타협적〔화해적〕인 말 / ~ *waters* 고요한 바다. **2** 《*P-*》 of, on, or near the Pacific Ocean. 태평양(연안)의. ¶ *the Pacific* (*Ocean*) 태평양. [L. *pax* peace]

pac·i·fi·ca·tion [pæ̀səfəkéiʃən] *n.* Ⓤ the act of pacifying; the state of being pacified. 강화; 화해; 진정.

pac·i·fi·er [pǽsəfàiər] *n.* **1** a person who pacifies. 분쟁 조정자; 화해자. **2** 《U.S.》 a baby's rubber teat. 고무 젖꼭지(=《Brit.》 comforter, dummy).

pac·i·fism [pǽsəfìzəm] *n.* Ⓤ the principle that military force should never be used. 평화주의; 반전론(反戰論); 무저항주의.

pac·i·fist [pǽsəfist] *n.* Ⓒ a believer in pacifism. 평화주의자; 반전론자.

pac·i·fy [pǽsəfài] *vt.* (**-fied**) (P6) **1** make (someone) peaceful or calm. …을 진정시키다; 달래다. ¶ ~ *a baby* 아기를 달래다 / ~ *anger* 노여움을 진정시키다. **2** bring peace to (a country, etc.). …에 평화를 가져오다.

:pack [pæk] *n.* Ⓒ **1** a set of things tied together to be carried. 포장한 짐; 짐짝; 꾸러미; 배낭. ¶ *The soldier carried a* ~ *on his back.* 병사는 배낭을 메고 있었다. **2** a lot; a group; a group of animals hunting together. 다수; 다량; 일단의 사람들; 한 패거리; (사냥개 따위의) 한 떼. ¶ *a* ~ *of thieves* 도둑떼 / *He often tells a* ~ *of lies.* 그는 곧잘 거짓말을 늘어 놓는다 / *a* ~ *of hounds* 한 무리의 사냥개 / *Lions do not hunt in packs, but alone.* 사자는 무리짓지 않고 홀로 사냥한다. **3** a set of playing cards. (카드의) 한 벌. **4** 《U.S.》 a small package or container. 한 갑. ¶ *a* ~ *of cigarettes* 담배 한 갑. **5** large pieces of ice floating together. 부빙군(浮氷群). ¶ *The ship forced its way through the* ~. 배는 부빙군을 헤치고 전진하였다. **6** a soft mixture used by a woman to make her face beautiful. (화장용) 팩. **7** a wet cloth used for a sick or injured person. (찜질하는) 습포.
— *vt.* **1** (P6,7,13) put (things) into a bag, box, etc.; put things into (a bag, box,

etc.). …을 꾸리다〔싸다, 묶다〕; …에 채워 넣다. ¶ ~ *a suitcase with clothes* 여행 가방에 옷을 챙겨넣다 / *get* 〔*have*〕 *one's things all packed up* 소지품들을 모두 꾸리다 / *He packed* (*up*) *his clothes for the trip.* 여행을 떠날 짐꾸리기를 마쳤다. **2** (P6,7,13) make (something) into a wrapped parcel. …을 포장하다. ¶ ~ *a lunch* 도시락을 싸다. **3** (P6,13) put (something) into tins, etc. for shipping or marketing. (시장 등에 내려고) …을 통조림 따위로 하다. ¶ *be packed in cans* 통조림으로 하다 / ~ *fruit* 〔*meat*〕 *in cans* 과일을〔고기를〕 통조림으로 만들다. **4** (P6,7,13) press or crowd closely together; fill (a place) closely. (사람이) …을 꽉 채우다; 들어차다. ¶ *People were packed into the small room.* 사람들이 좁은 방에 꽉 들어찼다 / *People packed the hall.* 사람들이 홀을 꽉 메웠다 / *The theater was packed with a large audience.* 극장은 많은 관중으로 꽉 찼다. **5** (P6) make tight with something that water, steam, air, etc. cannot leak through. (물·증기 따위가 새지 않게) 틈막이를 하다; 패킹하다. ¶ ~ *a joint of a water pipe* 송수관의 이음매를 패킹하다. **6** (P6) wrap (the body, etc.) in wet cloth; surround with wet sheets. …에 찜질〔습포〕하다. **7** (P6) fill (a jury, committee) with partisans. (배심원 등)을 자기 패거리로 구성하다. ¶ ~ *a jury.* **8** (P6,13) put a load on. …에 짐을 싣다.

— *vi.* **1** (P1,2A) become packed. 짐을 꾸리다; 포장하다. **2** (P1,2A,3) be filled; become firmly pressed. 채워지다; 꽉 차다; 몰려들다. **3** (P1,2A) leave in haste. (짐을 싸서) 서둘러 가버리다. [E.]

pack someone off, send someone away. …을 해고하다〔내쫓다〕.

pack up, **a**) put one's things into a pack, bag, etc. for a journey. (여행을 떠나려고) 짐을 꾸리다. ¶ *Let's ~ up and start at once.* 짐을 싸서 빨리 떠나자. **b**) stop working. 일을 끝내다〔그만두다〕.

send someone packing, send someone away at once. …을 지체 없이 내쫓다〔해고하다〕.

:pack·age [pǽkidʒ] *n.* Ⓒ a bundle of things packed together; a parcel; Ⓤ the act of packing. 보따리; 소포; 꾸러미; 포장.

pack animal [´ ˋ—] *n.* an animal used to carry goods, such as a horse and camel. (마소 등) 짐 나르는 짐승.

pack·er [pǽkər] *n.* Ⓒ **1** a person or machine that packs. 짐꾸리는 사람〔기계〕. **2** a person who packs meat, fruit, etc. for sale. 포장 출하업자.

pack·et [pǽkit] *n.* Ⓒ **1** a small bundle; a parcel. 한 다발〔묶음〕; 소포. ¶ *a ~ of letters* 편지 한 묶음. **2** a small ship used to carry mail, message, etc. 우편선; 정기선《우편·여객·화물용》.

pack·ing [pǽkiŋ] *n.* Ⓤ **1** any material used in packing. 포장재(包裝材); 충전물; 패킹. **2** the act of putting clothes, etc. into trunks or bags, ready for a journey. (길 떠날 채비로) 짐꾸리기. ¶ ~ *charges* 짐꾸리기 요금; 포장비 / *begin* 〔*get on with*〕 *one's ~* (길 떠날 채비로) 짐꾸리기를 시작하다.

pack·man [pǽkmən] *n.* Ⓒ (*pl.* **-men** [-mən]) a person who goes from place to place selling goods; a peddler. 행상; 도붓장수.

pact [pækt] *n.* Ⓒ an agreement between persons or nations. 협정; 협약; 계약. ¶ *a peace ~* 평화 협정. [L. *pacisco* agree]

***pad** [pæd] *n.* Ⓒ **1** a soft mass used for comfort, protection, or filling out. (푹신하게) 덧대는〔메워 넣는〕 것; 패드; 쿠션. ¶ *a shoulder ~* (웃옷의) 어깨심 / *a ~ of wool on a wound* (상처에 댄) 거즈 / *The baby's carriage has a ~ made to fit it.* 유모차에는 푹신한 방석이 설치되어 있다. **2** the soft underpart of the foot of some animals; the foot of a fox, hare, etc. (짐승의) 발바닥살; 육지(肉趾); (여우·토끼 등의) 발(cf. *paw*). **3** a number of sheets of writing or blotting paper fastened together along one edge. (한 장씩 떼어 쓰게 된) 종이철(綴). ¶ *a writing ~* 편지지 철. **4** 《U.S.》 a large floating leaf (of the waterlily, etc.). (수련 따위의) 부엽(浮葉).

— *vt.* (**pad·ded, pad·ding**) **1** (P6,13) fill or stuff (something) with something soft. …에 패드를〔푹신한 속을〕 대다〔채워넣다〕. ¶ ~ *a cushion with wool* 방석에 양털을 채워넣다 / *a padded chair* 푹신한 의자 / *padded field uniform* 방한복(防寒服). **2** (P6,7) 《*out*》 expand (a speech, a piece of writing, etc.) by using unnecessary words. (연설·문장 등)에 군말을 넣어 길게 늘이다. ¶ ~ *out a sentence* 〔*book, an article*〕. [*pod*]

pad·ding [pǽdiŋ] *n.* Ⓤ any soft material used to pad. (푹신하도록) 채워넣는 것; 충전물. [*pad*]

***pad·dle**[1] [pǽdl] *n.* Ⓒ **1** a short broad oar used without a rowlock to propel a small boat, etc. (뱃전에 고정시키지 않고 사용하는) 노(櫓). **2** a flat instrument used to mix, stir, or beat. (휘젓거나 섞는 데 쓰는) 넓적한 주걱. **3** one of the broad boards fixed around a waterwheel or a paddle-wheel. (외륜선(外輪船) 등의) 물갈퀴.

— *vt., vi.* (P6; 1) move (a boat or canoe) with a paddle or paddles; stir (something) with a paddle. (…을) 노로 젓다; 노를 젓다; (…을) 주걱으로 휘젓다. ¶ ~ *a boat* 배를 노로 젓다. [? *padell* small spade]

paddle one's own canoe, do (something) without depending on others. 혼자서 해내다; 독립 독행하다.

pad·dle[2] [pǽdl] *vi.* (P1,2A,3) **1** move the hands or feet about in water; walk in shallow water with bare feet. 물에서 철벅거리다; 얕은 물을 맨발로 걷다. **2** 《*arch.*》 touch with the fingers. 만지작거리다. [?]

〈paddle steamer〉

paddle steamer [ˊ-- ˋ--] *n.* a steamer propelled by paddle wheels. 외륜선.

paddle wheel [ˊ-- ˋ] *n.* a wheel with paddles fixed around it, used to propel a boat. (외륜선의) 외륜.

pad·dock [pǽdək] *n.* Ⓒ **1** a small grass field used for exercising or keeping horses. (마구간 곁의) 작은 방목장; 조마장(調馬場). **2** an enclosed place near a race track where horses are assembled before a race. (경주마의) 출전 대기소. [E.]

pad·dy [pǽdi] *n.* (*pl.* **pad·dies**) **1** Ⓤ rice, esp. in the husk. (쓿지 않은) 쌀; 벼. **2** Ⓒ a rice field. 논. [Malay]

pad·lock [pǽdlɑ̀k / -lɔ̀k] *n.* Ⓒ a lock that can be put on and taken off. 맹꽁이 자물쇠. —*vt.* (P6) fasten (something) with a padlock. …에 맹꽁이 자물쇠를 채우다. [M.E.]

pae·an, pe·an [píːən] *n.* Ⓒ a song of joy, praise or thanksgiving for victory. 기쁨의 노래; 찬가. [Gk. *paiān* hymn to Apollo under name of *Paiān*]

pae·o·ny [píːəni] *n.* =peony.

pa·gan [péigən] *n.* Ⓒ **1** a person who is not a Christian, a Moslem, or a Jew; a heathen. 이교도. **2** a person without any religion. 신앙이 없는 사람. —*adj.* of pagans or paganism; not religious. 이교도의; 무신앙의. ¶ *~ gods* 이교도의 신(神)들. [L. *pagus* country district]

pa·gan·ism [péigənìzəm] *n.* Ⓤ the state of being pagan; pagan beliefs, attitudes and customs. 이교 (신앙).

:page[1] [peidʒ] *n.* Ⓒ **1** one side of a leaf of paper in a book. 페이지; 면; 쪽. ¶ *open a book at* 〔*to*〕 *~ 15,* 책의 15 페이지를 펼치다 / *turn over the ~* 책장을 넘기다. **2** 《often *pl.*》 a record; an episode. 기록; 삽화(插話). ¶ *the pages of history* 역사의 기록. **3** 《*fig.*》 an important event or period. (역사상 주목할) 사건; 시기. ¶ *a new ~ in one's life* 인생의 새로운 장(章). —*vt.* (P6) number the pages of (a book, etc.). …에 페이지를 매기다. ¶ *~ a book.* [L. *pagina*]

page[2] [peidʒ] *n.* Ⓒ **1** a boy who does errands in a hotel, club, etc. (호텔 등의) 급사; 사환; 보이. ¶ *The pages at hotels usually wear uniforms.* 호텔 보이는 대개 제복을 입는다. **2** a boy attending on a person of high rank. 시동(侍童). **3** 《hist.》 a youth who was preparing to become a knight. 수련 기사(修練騎士).
—*vt.* (P6) **1** attend (someone) as a page. …에게 급사로서 시중들다. **2** try to find (a person) at a hotel, club, etc. by using a page or servant to call his name. (급사를 시켜) 아무의 이름을 불러 찾게 하다. ¶ *Paging Mr. Brown.* 알려드립니다. 브라운씨를 찾습니다《호텔 등에서의 안내 방송》. [F.]

pag·eant [pǽdʒənt] *n.* **1** Ⓒ a splendid colorful show or public performance, esp. a procession of magnificently dressed people on horseback. 화려한 행사〔행렬〕; 패전트. ¶ *a splendid ~ in celebration of the great victory* 위대한 승리를 기념하는 화려한 행사. **2** Ⓒ an outdoor play made up of scenes from the history of a place, etc. (역사적 장면을 나타내는) 야외극; 패전트. [L.]

pag·eant·ry [pǽdʒəntri] *n.* Ⓤ **1** 《*collectively*》 pageants; splendid, colorful display. 화려한 구경거리; 장관(壯觀). **2** empty display. 허식; 겉치레.

pag·i·na·tion [pæ̀dʒənéiʃən] *n.* **1** numbering the pages of books, etc. 페이지 매기기. **2** the figures with which pages are numbered. 페이지를 나타내는 숫자; 페이지수. [→page[1]]

pa·go·da [pəgóudə] *n.* Ⓒ an Oriental towering temple with many stories. (동양식 사찰의) 탑. [Port.]

***paid** [peid] *v.* p. and pp. of **pay.**
—*adj.* **1** receiving money for work; hired. 유급의; 고용된. ¶ *a ~ holiday* 유급 휴가. **2** settled. 지불을 끝낸.

***pail** [peil] *n.* Ⓒ **1** a round, deep vessel of wood, metal, etc. with an arched handle used for carrying liquids; a bucket. 들통; 버킷. **2** a pailful. 한 들통(의 양(量)). ¶ *a ~ of water.* [L. *patella* pan]

pail·ful [péilfùl] *n.* Ⓒ as much as a pail holds. 한 들통 (가득한 양).

:pain [pein] *n.* Ⓤ **1** very unpleasant feeling of body or mind; trouble. (심신의) 고통; 고뇌. ¶ *the ~ of parting* 이별의 아픔 / *The whole matter is a ~ to me.* 모든 일이 내게는 하나의 고통이다. **2** Ⓒ an ache. (국부적인) 통증; 아픔. ¶ *a ~ in the head* 두통 / *bear ~* 아픔을 참다 / *have a ~ in one's neck* 목이 아프다 / *wake in ~* 아파서 잠이 깨다. **3** 《*pl.*》 care; efforts. 고심; 노력. ¶ 《*prov.*》 *No pains, no gains.* =*No gains without pains.* 수고 없이는 이득도 없다 / *reward for one's pains* 수고에 대한 보답. **4** punishment. 벌. ¶ *pains and penalties* 형벌.

be at the pain(s) of doing, take the trouble to do. …하는 수고를 하다.

for someone's pains, as thanks or in return for someone's service. 수고한 보답으로; 수고 값으로.

in pain, feeling pain. 괴로워서.

on* 〔*under*〕 *pain of death, on condition

that someone will be put to death if he breaks his promise, etc. (위약(違約)하면) 사형에 처한다는 조건으로.

take pains, do one's best; make efforts. 전력을 다하다; 애쓰다. ¶ *He takes great pains with his work.* 그는 자기 일에 전력을 다하고 있다.

with pain, because of pain. 고통으로; 고뇌로.

— *vt.* (P6,20) cause (someone) to feel pain; hurt. …을 괴롭히다; 아프게 하다. ¶ *It pains me to walk.* 걸으면 발이 아프다 / *Your disapproval pains me more than I can say.* 네 반대가 내게는 이루 말할 수 없는 고통이다 / *Does your tooth ~ you ?* 이가 아프냐.

— *vi.* (P1) have a feeling of pain. 괴로워하다; 아프다. ¶ *My arm is paining.* 팔이 아프다. [Gk. *poine* penalty]

***pain·ful** [péinfəl] *adj.* **1** feeling or causing pain; full of pain. 아픈; 고통스러운. ¶ *a ~ experience* 쓰라린 경험 / *a ~ illness* 아픈 병. **2** requiring effort; difficult. 힘든; 어려운. ¶ *a ~ duty* 어려운 직책.

pain·ful·ly [péinfəli] *adv.* in a painful manner. 아픈 듯이; 괴롭게.

pain·ful·ness [péinfəlnis] *n.* Ⓤ the state of being painful. 아픔; 고통.

pain·less [péinlis] *adj.* causing no physical pain; without pain. 고통〔통증〕이 없는; 괴롭지 않은.

pains·tak·ing [péinztèikiŋ, péins-] *adj.* taking pain; careful; very industrious. 힘이 드는; 정성들인; 근면한. ¶ *a ~ scholar* 성실한 학자 / *~ work* 힘이 드는 일. [→pain]

:paint [peint] *n.* Ⓤ **1** coloring matter mixed with oil or water that gives color to a surface; 《often *pl.*》 coloring materials in tubes or cakes. 페인트; 도료; 그림 물감. ¶ *Wet* 〔*Damp, Fresh*〕 *~!* 칠 주의《게시》 / *a can of ~* 페인트 한 통 / *a box of paints* 그림 물감 한 상자. **2** the layer or coat of paint put on the surface of a thing. (표면에 착색된) 칠; 도장(塗裝); 채색. ¶ *scrub off ~* 칠을 벗기다 / *The ~ comes off easily.* 칠이 쉬 벗겨진다. **3** cosmetics, as lipstick, rouge, etc. 화장품《루주 따위》.

— *vt.* (P6,7,18) **1** cover or coat (something) with paint, lotion, medicine, etc. …에 페인트를 칠하다; (상처 따위)에 …을 바르다; 화장하다. ¶ *~ the walls* 벽에 페인트를 칠하다 / *~ a car red* 차를 빨갛게 칠하다 / *~ the wound with iodine* 상처에 요오드팅크를 바르다 / *She paints herself thick.* 그녀는 짙은 화장을 한다. **2** picture (something) in colors. (그림 물감으로) …을 그리다. ¶ *~ a landscape on a wall* 벽에 풍경화를 그리다 / *a portrait painted to life* 실물(實物) 크기로 그린 초상화 / *John painted a picture of his mother.* 존은 어머니의 초상화를 그렸다. **3** describe vividly. …을 생생하게 묘사하다. ¶ *He painted his experience in glowing colors.* 그는 자기 경험을 화려한 필치로 서술했다 / *He is not so black as he is painted.* 그는 남들이 말하는 그런 나쁜 사람이 아니다. — *vi.* (P1) practice painting; make a picture. 그림을 그리다. ¶ *~ in water colors* 수채화를 그리다. [L. *pingo*]

paint out something, cover up something with paint. …을 페인트로 지워버리다.

paint box [´ `] *n.* a box with cakes or tubes of paint. 그림 물감 상자.

paint·brush [péintbrʌ̀ʃ] *n.* Ⓒ a brush used for painting. 화필; 페인트 솔.

***paint·er** [péintər] *n.* Ⓒ a person who paints pictures; a workman who paints house, walls, etc. 화가; 페인트공; 도장공(塗裝工).

:paint·ing [péintiŋ] *n.* **1** Ⓒ a painted picture. 그림; 유화; 수채화. **2** Ⓤ the occupation of painting. 그림 그리기; 도장(塗裝)(업).

:pair [pɛər] *n.* Ⓒ (*pl.* **pairs** or **pair**) **1** a set of two things of the same kind. 한 벌〔켤레, 쌍〕. ¶ *a ~ of stockings* 〔*shoes*〕 스타킹〔구두〕 한 켤레 / *These stockings are not pairs.* 이 스타킹은 짝짝이다. **2** a thing with two parts, each of which cannot be used without the other. (따로따로는 못 쓰는) 짝진 것. ¶ *a ~ of glasses* 안경 (하나) / *a ~ of pants* 바지 한 벌 / *a ~ of scissors* 가위. **3** a couple of animals; a married or engaged couple. (짐승의) 한 쌍; 부부; 2인조. ¶ *a ~ of rascals* 2인조 악당 / *a carriage and ~* 쌍두 마차 / *the happy ~* 신랑 신부. **4** the other part of a pair. (짝을 이루는 것의) 한 짝. ¶ *I cannot find out the ~ to this shoe.* 이 신 한 짝이 안 보인다.

another 〔***a different***〕 ***pair of shoes*** 〔***boots***〕**,** another matter. 별개 문제. ¶ *That's another ~ of shoes.* 그건 별개의 문제이다.

— *vt.* (P6) join or unite (persons or things) in couples. …을 짝짓다. — *vi.* (P1,2A) **1** be joined in couples. 짝이 되다. **2** become man and wife; mate. 부부가 되다. [→par]

pair off, **a**) divide into pairs. 두 사람〔개〕씩 떼어놓다. **b**) go off in pairs or couples. 두 사람씩 떠나다〔떨어지다〕. **c**) 《*colloq.*》 marry. 결혼하다.

pa·ja·mas, 《Brit.》 **py·ja·mas** [pədʒɑ́ːməz, -dʒǽməz] *n. pl.* Ⓒ a sleeping suit consisting of a loose-fitting jacket and trousers. 파자마; 잠옷. [Pers. *pā*(*i*) leg, *jāmah* garment]

***pal** [pæl] *n.* Ⓒ 《*colloq.*》 a close friend. 친구; 단짝; 짝궁. ¶ *a pen ~* 펜팔. [Gipsy]

:pal·ace [pǽlis, -əs] *n.* Ⓒ **1** a large, grand house such as that of a king, a nobleman, or a bishop. 궁전; (bishop)의 관저. **2** a very large, fine house. 훌륭한 대저택. [L. *palatium*]

pal·an·quin, -keen [pæ̀lənkíːn] *n.* Ⓒ a covered seat carried on the shoulders of men, usu. used in India, China, etc. (인도·중국 등지의) 가마. [Port.]

P

pal·at·a·ble [pǽlətəbəl] *adj.* having a pleasant taste; delicious; pleasing. 맛이 좋은; 맛있는; 유쾌한. [→palate, -able]

pal·a·tal [pǽlətl] *adj.* **1** of the palate. 구개(口蓋)의; 입천장의. **2** 《phon.》 made by placing the tongue near the hard palate. 구개음(音)의. — *n.* Ⓒ 《phon.》 a palatal sound. 구개음. [↓]

pal·ate [pǽlit] *n.* **1** Ⓒ the roof of the mouth. 구개(口蓋); 입천장. ¶ *the hard* 〔*soft*〕 ~ 경(硬)〔연(軟)〕구개. **2** Ⓤ Ⓒ the sense of taste; liking. 미각; 취미; 기호. ¶ *have a delicate* ~ 식성이 까다롭다 / *suit one's* ~ 구미에 맞다. [L. *palatum*]

pa·la·tial [pəléiʃəl] *adj.* like a palace; magnificent. 궁전 같은; 으리으리한. [→palace]

pa·lav·er [pəlǽvər, -lɑ́:vər] *n.* **1** Ⓒ a conference, esp. with African natives. 교섭; 상담(商談)《특히 아프리카 원주민과의》. **2** Ⓤ idle talk. 쓸데없는 이야기; 수다. **3** smooth talk; flattery. 아첨. — *vi., vt.* (P1; 6) talk idly; use many words. 수다를 떨다. [→parable]

P

:pale[1] [peil] *adj.* **1** having very little color; whitish. 창백한; 핏기 없는. ¶ *go* 〔*grow, turn*〕 ~ 창백해지다 / *You look* ~. 안색이 나쁘군. **2** not bright or brilliant; dim. (색깔이) 엷은; 칙칙한. ¶ *a* ~ *pink* 엷은 분홍색 / ~ *blue* 담청색. — *vi., vt.* (P1; 6) become or make (something) pale. 창백해지다〔하게 하다〕; 엷어지다; 엷게 하다. [→pallid]

pale[2] [peil] *n.* Ⓒ **1** a long, narrow, pointed board used for fences. (울타리용) 말뚝. **2** 《*fig.*》 a fence; a boundary. 경계; 한계. ¶ *within* 〔*out of, beyond*〕 *the* ~ *of the law* 법률의 영역 안〔밖〕의 / *He is beyond* 〔*outside*〕 *the* ~ *of civilized society.* 그는 문명 사회의 영역 밖에 있는 사람이다. — *vt.* (P6) enclose with pales. 울짱을 두르다. [L. *palus*]

pale·face [péilfèis] *n.* Ⓒ a white person. 백인. [→pale[1]]

pale·ness [péilnis] *n.* Ⓤ the state or quality of being pale. 창백함; (색이) 엷음.

pa·le·og·ra·phy, -lae- [pæ̀liɑ́grəfi / -ɔ́g-] *n.* **1** ancient writing or ancient forms of writing. 고문서. **2** a study of ancient writings to determine dates, origins, meaning, etc. 고문서학(學). [Gk. *palaios* ancient]

pa·le·o·lith·ic, -lae- [pæ̀liəlíθik] *adj.* of or having to do with the earlier part of the Stone Age. 구석기 시대의.

pa·le·on·tol·o·gy, -lae- [pæ̀liəntɑ́lədʒi / -tɔ́l-] *n.* the study of ancient forms of life through fossil animals and plants. 고생물학.

Pal·es·tine [pǽləstàin] *n.* a former country in southwest Asia, on the Mediterranean Sea. 팔레스타인.

pal·ette [pǽlit] *n.* Ⓒ a board for mixing colors. 팔레트. [F.]

pal·ing [péiliŋ] *n.* Ⓒ a fence made of pales. 울타리; 울짱. [→pale[2]]

pal·i·sade [pæ̀ləséid] *n.* **1** Ⓒ a long, strong, pointed wooden stake; a pale. 말뚝. **2** a fence of such stakes. 울타리; 울짱. **3** 《*pl.*》 《U.S.》 a line of high, steep cliffs, usu. along a river. (강가의) 벼랑. — *vt.* (P6) surround or fortify (something) with a palisade. …둘레에 울타리를 치다. [→pale[2]]

pal·ish [péiliʃ] *adj.* somewhat pale. 좀 창백한; 파리한. [→pale[1]]

pall[1] [pɔ:l] *n.* Ⓒ **1** a heavy cloth used to cover a coffin, tomb, etc. 관(棺)〔무덤·영구차 등〕을 덮는 보. **2** 《*fig.*》 something which covers, darkens, etc. 휘장; 장막. ¶ *a* ~ *of darkness* 어둠의 장막 / *a* ~ *of smoke* 연막. [L. *pallium* cloak]

pall[2] [pɔ:l] *vi.* (P1,3) become uninteresting; become dull. 시시해지다; 흥미가 없어지다. ¶ *Pleasures soon* ~ *on us.* 즐거움은 곧 시들해졌다. [→appall]

pal·la·di·a [pəléidiə] *n.* pl. of **palladium.**

pal·la·di·um [pəléidiəm] *n.* (*pl.* **-la·di·a**) **1** 《Gk. myth.》 《*the P-*》 a wooden statue of Pallas Athene in Troy, Athena. (Troy 의) Pallas 여신상(女神像). **2** anything regarded as an important safeguard. 수호물(守護物). **3** 《chem.》 a rare metal. 팔라듐. [Gk. =image of Pallas]

pall·bear·er [pɔ́:lbɛ̀ərər] *n.* one of the men who walk with the coffin at a funeral. (장례 때) 관을 메는〔수행하는〕 사람. [*pall*[1]]

pal·let [pǽlit] *n.* Ⓒ a bed of straw; a poor bed. 짚자리; 초라한 잠자리. [L. *palea* straw]

pal·li·ate [pǽlièit] *vt.* (P6) **1** make (pain or a disease) somewhat better without curing it. (고통·질병 등)을 일시적으로 완화시키다. ¶ ~ *a disease.* **2** excuse. 변명하다. ¶ ~ *a crime* 〔*an offence*〕 죄를 변명하다. [L. *pallium* cloak]

pal·li·a·tion [pæ̀liéiʃən] *n.* ⓊⒸ **1** the act of palliating; the state of being palliated. (고통·질병 등의) 일시적인 완화. **2** an excuse. 변명.

pal·li·a·tive [pǽlièitiv, -liə-] *adj.* serving to palliate; excusing. 경감하는; 한때 완화시키는; 변명하는. — *n.* Ⓒ a thing that palliates. 완화제; 변명.

pal·lid [pǽlid] *adj.* (**-lid·er, -lid·est**) pale; bloodless. 창백한; 핏기 없는. ¶ *a* ~ *face* 〔*complexion*〕 창백한 얼굴〔안색〕. [L. *palleo* be pale]

pal·lor [pǽlər] *n.* Ⓤ paleness, esp. of the face. (얼굴이) 창백함; 파리함. [↑]

:palm[1] [pɑ:m] *n.* Ⓒ **1** the inner surface of the hand between the wrist and the fingers. 손바닥. **2** any broad, flat part at the end of an arm, a handle, etc. 손바닥 모양의 것. **3** 《rare》 the length of a hand, 7 to 10 inches, as a measure. 뼘《길이 측정의 단위; 18-25 cm》.

grease 〔***gild, tickle***〕 ***someone's palm,*** pay

someone money to do wrong; bribe. 뇌물을 쓰다.
have an itching palm, be greedy for money; be eager to be bribed. 뇌물을 탐내다.
have* 〔*hold*〕 *someone in the palm of one's hand, control completely. …을 손아귀에 쥐다; 완전히 지배하다.
— *vt.* (P6,7) **1** hide (something) in the palm. …을 손바닥에 감추다. ¶ *~ a card* (요술 등에서) 카드를 손 안에 감추다. **2** touch (something) with the palm. …을 손바닥에 대다. [L. *palma*]
palm off something on someone, give, sell or pass something worthless to someone by a trick or by lies. (가짜 따위를) 속여서 …에게 주다〔팔다, 떠넘기다〕. ¶ *~ off a forgery on someone* 아무에게 가짜를 팔아먹다.

palm² [pɑːm] *n.* Ⓒ **1** a tall tree growing in warm climates, with large leaves at the top. 종려; 야자. **2** a palm leaf, shown as a symbol of victory. 종려 잎《승리의 상징》. **3** 《*the* ~》 victory; triumph. 승리. ¶ *bear* 〔*carry off*〕 *the ~* 이기다; 우승하다. [↑]
yield the palm to, be surpassed by. …에게 지다.

palm·er [páːmər, páːl-] *n.* Ⓒ a pilgrim who had traveled to the Holy Land and brought back a palm leaf as a sign of this. 성지 순례자. [*palm²*]

palm·ist [páːmist] *n.* Ⓒ a person who tells fortunes by examining the palm of the hand. 수상가(手相家); 손금쟁이. [*palm¹*]

palm oil [⌐ ⌐] *n.* the oil obtained from the fruit of the palm tree. 야자 기름. [*palm²*]

palm·y [páːmi] *adj.* (**palm·i·er, palm·i·est**) **1** abounding in or shaded with palms. 종려가 많은〔무성한〕. **2** successful; prosperous. 번창하는; 번영하는. ¶ *one's ~ days* (지나간) 전성기 / *Rome in her ~ state.* 황금시대의 로마.

pal·pa·ble [pǽlpəbəl] *adj.* that can be felt or touched; obvious; evident. 손으로 만질〔촉지(觸知)할〕 수 있는; 뚜렷한; 명백한. ¶ *a ~ error* 명백한 오류. [L. *palpo* touch]

pal·pa·bly [pǽlpəbli] *adv.* in a palpable manner; obviously. 촉지할 수 있게; 명백히.

pal·pi·tate [pǽlpətèit] *vi.* (P1,2A) **1** (of the heart) beat rapidly. (가슴이) 두근거리다. ¶ *of palpitating interest* 가슴이 두근거릴 정도로 흥미있는. **2** quiver; tremble. 떨리다. ¶ *~ with fear* 공포에 떨다. [→palpable]

pal·pi·ta·tion [pæ̀lpətéiʃən] *n.* ⓊⒸ irregular, quickened beating of the heart. 동계(動悸); 가슴의 두근거림.

pal·sied [pɔ́ːlzid] *adj.* having palsy; paralyzed; trembling. 중풍의; 마비된; (수족이) 떨리는. [↓]

pal·sy [pɔ́ːlzi] *n.* ⓊⒸ a disease which causes trembling of the hands and feet. 중풍; 마비. — *vt.* (P6) cause to suffer with palsy. 중풍에 걸리게 하다; 마비시키다. ¶ *a palsied arm* 마비된 팔. [→paralysis]

pal·ter [pɔ́ːltər] *vi.* (P1,3) 《*with*》 **1** talk or act insincerely; trifle deceitfully. 아무렇게나 말하다〔행동하다〕; 속이다. **2** treat or decide lightly or carelessly. 적당히 다루다; 어름어름 넘기다. ¶ *Do not ~ with serious matters.* 중요한 문제를 어름어름 넘겨서는 안된다. **3** bargain; haggle. 값을 깎다. ¶ *~ with someone about the* 〔*a*〕 *price* 값을 깎으려고 흥정하다. [↓]

pal·try [pɔ́ːltri] *adj.* (**-tri·er, -tri·est**) unimportant; mean; worthless. 하찮은; 무가치한. ¶ *a ~ gift* 시시한 선물. [G. *palte* rag]

pam·pas [pǽmpəz, -pəs] *n.* 《usu. *pl.*》 a wide treeless plain of South America, esp. in Argentina. 팜파. [Peruv.]

pam·per [pǽmpər] *vt.* (P6) **1** treat too kindly; satisfy or indulge too much. …에게 너무 잘 해주다; 어하다. ¶ *~ a child* 〔*sick person*〕 아이를 어해서 기르다〔아픈 사람의 온갖 시중을 들다〕. **2** 《*arch.*》 overfeed; glut. 너무 먹이다; 포식하게 하다. ¶ *~ one's stomach* 포식하다. [G. *pampen* cram]

·pam·phlet [pǽmflit] *n.* Ⓒ a small book with a paper cover. 팸플릿. [*Pamphilus* name of a medieval poem]

pam·phlet·eer [pæ̀mflitíər] *n.* Ⓒ a writer of pamphlets. 팸플릿 필자. — *vi.* (P1,3) write or publish pamphlets. 팸플릿을 쓰다〔발행하다〕.

Pan [pæn] *n.* 《Gk. myth.》 the god of woods and fields. 판신(神); 목양신(牧羊神). [Gr. god's name]

:pan [pæn] *n.* Ⓒ **1** a broad, shallow dish for cooking. 납작한 냄비; 팬. ¶ *pots and pans* 취사 도구 / *a frying ~* 프라이팬. **2** anything like a pan in shape; either of the dishes on a pair of scales. 팬 모양의 기물; (저울의) 접시.
— *vt.* (**panned, pan·ning**) (P7) **1** cook (something) in a pan. …을 팬으로 요리하다〔굽이다〕. **2** 《*out, off*》 wash (sand, gravel) in a pan to separate out gold. (모래 등)을 일어 금을 가려내다. **3** 《*colloq.*》 criticize severely. 혹평하다; 깎아내리다. — *vi.* (P2A) 《*out*》 **1** yield gold. 사금이 나다. **2** 《*fig.*》 result; turn out; succeed. …한 결과가 되다; 성공하다. ¶ *~ out well* 〔*bad*〕 잘 돼가다〔안 되다〕 / *How did it ~ out?* (결과가) 어떻게 됐나. [E.]

pan- [pæn-] *pref.* all. '전…, 범(汎)…'의 뜻. ¶ *Pan-American* 범미(汎美)의. [Gr. *pan* all]

pan·a·ce·a [pæ̀nəsíːə] *n.* Ⓒ a remedy for all diseases or ills; a cure-all. 만병 통치약. [Gk. *akos* cure]

·Pan·a·ma [pǽnəmɑ̀ː, ⌐⌐⌐] *n.* **1** a country in central America; its capital. 파나마. **2** 《sometimes *p-*》 a Panama hat. 파나마 모자. [Place]

Pan-A·mer·i·can [pæ̀nəmérikən] *adj.* **1** of all the countries and peoples of North, Central and South America. 범미(汎美)

의. **2** of all Americans. 전(全)미의. [Gk. *pan* all]

pan·cake [pǽnkèik] *n.* Ⓒ a thin, flat cake made of batter and fried in a pan. 팬케이크. [*pan, cake*]

pan·cre·as [pǽŋkriəs, pǽn-] *n.* Ⓒ a part of the body near the stomach producing a digestive juice. 췌장(膵臟)(cf. *sweetbread*). [Gk. *kreas* flesh]

pan·da [pǽndə] *n.* **1** a bear-like animal with black legs and a black and white body that chiefly feeds on bamboo. 판다(giant panda). **2** a small reddish-brown animal that somewhat looks like a raccoon. 완웅(浣熊)(lesser panda). [Nepali]

pan·de·mo·ni·um [pæ̀ndəmóuniəm] *n.* **1** Ⓒ 《*P-*》 the abode of all the demons; the hell. 복마전; 지옥. **2** Ⓤ wild disorder or confusion. 수라장. [→demon]

P

pan·der [pǽndər] *n.* **1** a go-between in secret love-affairs. 뚜쟁이; 포주. **2** a person who helps others to satisfy base desires. (못된 짓의) 중개자. — *vi.* (P3) act as a pander; try to satisfy others' base desires. 뚜쟁이 노릇을 하다; (남의) 저속한 욕망에 영합(迎合)하다. ¶ ~ *to someone's ambition* 아무의 야심에 영합하다 / *Some newspapers ~ to the liking for sensational stories.* 몇몇 신문들은 선정적인 기사에 대한 대중적인 기호에 영합하고 있다. [Person in Boccaccio]

Pan·do·ra [pændɔ́ːrə] *n.* 《Gr. myth.》 a woman sent to the earth to punish mankind for Prometheus having stolen the fire from Heaven. 판도라. [Hesiod, *Op.* 50-105]

***pane** [pein] *n.* Ⓒ a single sheet of glass in a window. (한 장의) 창유리. [L. *pannus* a cloth]

pan·e·gyr·ic [pæ̀nədʒírik, -dʒái-] *n.* Ⓒ a speech or piece of writing to praise a person or thing. 찬사(讚辭). [Gk. *paneguris* festival]

***pan·el** [pǽnl] *n.* Ⓒ **1** a flat piece of wood or other material set into a door, wall, etc. that is distinct from the surrounding areas. 패널; 판벽널; 머름; (벽·천장 따위에 댄) 장식널. **2** a thin board used for oil painting; a picture on such a board. 패널; 화판; 패널화. **3** a list of persons called as a jury; the jury as a whole. 배심원 명부; 배심원 전원. **4** a group formed for discussion. (토론회·좌담회 등의) 위원회. ¶ *a five-man ~,* 5인 위원회 / *a ~ of experts* 전문가들의 위원회 / *a ~ discussion* 공개 토론회; 패널 디스커션.
— *vt.* (**-eled, -el·ing** or 《Brit.》 **-elled, -el·ling**) (P6) cover or decorate (something) with panels. …에 판벽널〔패널〕을 대다; 판벽널〔패널〕로 장식하다. [→pane]

pan·el·ing, 《Brit.》 **-el·ling** [pǽnliŋ] *n.* Ⓤ 《*collectively*》 panels. 판벽널.

***pang** [pæŋ] *n.* Ⓒ a sharp, sudden pain or feeling. 격통; (에는 듯한) 마음의 아픔. ¶ *the pangs of death* 죽음의 고통 / *the pangs toothache* 〔*conscience*〕 격심한 치통〔양심의 가책〕. [E.]

***pan·ic** [pǽnik] *n.* ⓊⒸ **1** a sudden, unreasoning fear spreading among many people. 원인을 알 수 없는 갑작스레 퍼지는 공포〔대혼란〕. ¶ *The fire caused a ~ among the crowd.* 화재로 군중은 대혼란에 빠졌다 / *When I realized the situation, I got* 〔*went*〕 *into a ~.* 사태를 알게 되자 나는 공포에 휩싸였다. **2** 《econ.》 a sudden financial fear which leads to mistrust. (금융) 공황; 패닉(cf. *crisis*). ¶ *a ~ in the market* 시장 공황 / *a stock-exchange ~* 주식공황. — *vt.* (**-icked, -ick·ing**) affect (someone) with panic. …에 공황을〔공포를〕 일으키다. — *adj.* uncontrollable and unaccountable fear. (공포가) 걷잡을 수 없는; 어찌할 수 없는. [Gk. *pānikós* of god Pan]

pan·icked [pǽnikt] *v.* p. and pp. of **panic.**

pan·ick·ing [pǽnikiŋ] *v.* ppr. of **panic.**

pan·ick·y [pǽniki] *adj.* in a panic. 공황(상태)의.

pan·ic-strick·en [pǽnikstrìkən] *adj.* filled with panic; madly frightened. 공포에 질린. ¶ *be* 〔*get*〕 ~ 공포에 휩쓸리다 / ~ *eyes* 공포에 질린 눈.

pan·ni·er [pǽnjər, -niər] *n.* Ⓒ **1** one of a pair of baskets for carrying on the shoulder of a person or on the back of a horse. 등광주리; (말에 지우는) 옹구. **2** a frame used for stretching out the skirt at the hip. 패니어《여자 스커트를 펴지게 버티는 고래뼈 따위의 테》. [L. *panis* bread]

pan·o·ply [pǽnəpli] *n.* Ⓒ (*pl.* **-plies**) a complete suit of armor. 갑옷 투구 한 벌. [Gk. *hopla* arms]

pan·o·ram·a [pæ̀nərǽmə, -rɑ́ːmə] *n.* Ⓒ **1** a wide, unbroken view. 전경(全景). ¶ *The windows opened upon a ~ of beach and sea.* 창문에서 해변과 바다 전경이 바라보이게 돼 있었다. **2** a scene which is constantly changing. 연달아 바뀌는 광경. ¶ *the ~ of city life* 바쁘게 돌아가는〔주마등 같은〕 도시 생활. **3** a continuous series of pictures that is unrolled so that it seems as if a person were looking at it from a central point. 파노라마; 회전 그림. **4** a complete view of some subject. (어떤 문제의) 전모. [Gk. *horaō* see]

pan·o·ram·ic [pæ̀nərǽmik] *adj.* of or like a panorama. 파노라마(식)의. ¶ *a ~ view* 전경.

***pan·sy** [pǽnzi] *n.* Ⓒ (*pl.* **-sies**) a small plant with flowers of several colors. 팬지. [F. *pensée* thought, pansy]

***pant** [pænt] *vi.* (P1,3) **1** breathe rapidly or violently. (숨이 차서) 헐떡거리다. ¶ *The walk uphill made him ~.* 오르막길을 걸으며 그는 몹시 숨이 찼다. **2** 《*for, after*》 long eagerly for; desire greatly. 갈망하다. ¶ ~ *for* 〔*after*〕

liberty 자유를 갈구하다. **3** speak with short, quick breathe. 헐떡이며 말하다. —*vt.* (P6,7) 《*out*》 utter words in short gasps. …을 헐떡이며 말하다. —*n.* Ⓒ a short, rapid breath. 헐떡임; 숨참. [E.]

pan·ta·loon [pæ̀ntəlúːn] *n.* **1** Ⓒ 《*P-*》 a character in Italian comedy, usu. a thin, foolish old man wearing pantaloons. (이탈리아 희극의) 말라깽이 늙은 어릿광대. **2** 《*pl.*》 《U.S.》 a kind of trousers. 판탈롱(바지). [*Pantaone,* trousered character in Italian comedy]

pan·the·ism [pǽnθiìzəm] *n.* Ⓤ **1** the doctrine that God is the universe and the universe is God. 범신론(汎神論). **2** the worship of all the gods. 다신교(多神教). [Gk. *theos* god]

pan·the·ist [pǽnθiist] *n.* Ⓒ a person who believes in pantheism. 범신론자.

Pan·the·on [pǽnθiàn, -ən] *n.* **1** 《*the* ～》 a Roman temple for all the gods, built in 27 B.C. 판테온; 만신전(萬神殿). **2** 《*the* ～》 a building for the burial or commemoration of the famous men of a nation. (한 나라의 위인들을 모신) 사당. **3** 《*p-*》 all the gods of a people. (한 나라 국민이 믿는) 모든 신. [Gk. *pan* all, *theos* god]

pan·ther [pǽnθər] *n.* Ⓒ (*pl.* **-thers,** *collectively* **-ther**) **1** a leopard. 표범. **2** a mountain lion; a puma; a cougar. 아메리카 표범; 퓨마. [Gk. *panthēr*]

pan·to·graph [pǽntəgræ̀f, -grɑ̀ːf] *n.* Ⓒ **1** an instrument for copying a map, drawing, etc. on any scale desired. (신축 자재의) 사도기(寫圖器); 축도기. **2** 《electr.》 device for carring electric current to a vehicle from overhead wires. 팬터그램; 집전기(集電器)《전철 등의》. [Gk. *pan* all, *graphō* draw]

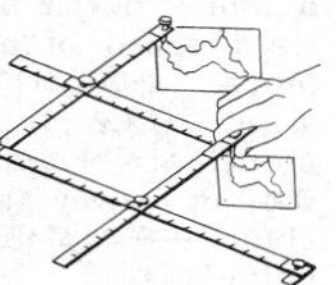
〈pantograph 1〉

pan·to·mime [pǽntəmàim] *n.* Ⓒ **1** a play without words, in which the actors express themselves by gestures. 무언극. **2** 《Brit.》 a play based on a fairy tale. 동화극; 팬터마임. **3** Ⓤ gestures without words. 손짓발짓; 몸짓. ¶ *express oneself in* ～ 몸짓으로 말하다.
—*vt., vi.* express (thought, feeling, etc.) or act in pantomime. 몸짓으로 말하다. [Gk. *pan* all →mime]

·**pan·try** [pǽntri] *n.* Ⓒ (*pl.* **-tries**) a room in which food or tableware is kept. 식품 저장실; 식기실; 팬트리. [→pannier]

pan·try·man [pǽntrimən] *n.* (*pl.* **-men** [-mən]) a man in charge of a pantry. (호텔 등의) 식품실 관리인.

pants [pænts] *n. pl.* **1** 《U.S. *colloq.*》 trousers; drawers. 바지. **2** 《Brit.》 men's underpants. (남성의) 팬츠. [→pantaloon]

pan·zer [pǽnzər] *adj.* 《G.》 armored. 기갑(機甲)〔장갑(裝甲)〕의. ¶ *a* ～ *division* 〔*troop*〕 기갑 사단〔부대〕.

pap [pæp] *n.* Ⓤ soft food for infants or sick persons such as bread soaked in milk. 유동식《유아·환자용》. [E.]

:**pa·pa** [pɑ́ːpə, pəpɑ́ː] *n.* Ⓒ 《*child's word*》 father; daddy. 아버지; 아빠. [L.]

pa·pa·cy [péipəsi] *n.* (*pl.* **-cies**) ⓊⒸ 《usu. *the* ～》 **1** the position, rank, or authority of the Pope. 로마 교황의 직위; 교황권. **2** the period during which a pope rules. 교황의 임기. **3** the papal system. 교황 제도. [L. *pāpa,* →pope]

pa·pal [péipəl] *adj.* **1** of the Pope or the papacy. 로마 교황(권)의. ¶ *a* ～ *letter* 교황 교서(敎書). **2** of the Roman Catholic Church. 카톨릭 교회의. ¶ ～ *ritual* 카톨릭 교회의 의식. [↑]

pa·pay·a [pəpɑ́ːjə, -pái̯ə] *n.* Ⓒ a tropical tree with large leaves and melonlike fruit at the top; its fruit. 파파야나무; 그 열매. [Sp.]

:**pa·per** [péipər] *n.* **1** Ⓤ a thin material made of wood pulp, etc. used for writing, printing, wrapping, etc. 종이. ¶ *a sheet of* ～ 한 장의 종이 / *a piece of* ～ 한 조각의 종이 / *wrapping* ～ =*brown* ～ 포장지 / *ruled* ～ 괘지 / *section* ～ 모눈종이 / *a blank sheet* 〔*piece*〕 *of* ～ 백지 한 장. **2** Ⓒ a newspaper. 신문. ¶ *Bring me today's* ～. 오늘 신문을 가져오너라 / *What do the papers say?* 신문에는 뭐라고 났던. **3** 《*pl.*》 documents carried to prove who or what one is. 신분 증명서. **4** 《often *pl.*》 an official document; a written matter. 서류; 문서. ¶ *state papers* 공문(서) / *important papers* 중요 서류〔문서〕/ *valuable papers* 유가증권. **5** Ⓒ a set of questions for an examination; a student's written answers to the questions. 시험 문제; 답안(지). ¶ *collect the papers* 답안지를 거두다 / *a difficult* ～ *for such young students* 그런 어린 학생에게는 어려운 시험 문제. **6** Ⓒ ⓐ an essay on a particular topic. (연구) 논문. ⓑ 《U.S.》 an essay which a student is required to write. (학생에게 제출하도록 할당된) 논문. ¶ *write a* ～ 논문을 쓰다 / *He read a* ～ *on the teaching of English.* 그는 영어 교수법에 관한 논문을 발표했다 / *collected papers* 논문집. **7** Ⓤ a written promise to pay money; a bank note; paper money. 어음; 지폐.

commit to paper, write down. 글로 적어두다; 기록하다.

on paper, **a**) in writing or print. 종이에 쓰인〔인쇄된〕. **b**) in theory. 이론상으로는.

put pen to paper, begin to write. 붓을 들다; 쓰기 시작하다.

send in one's papers, resign. 사표를 내다.

—*adj.* **1** made of paper. 종이로 된〔만든〕. ¶ *a* ～ *screen* 장지 / ～ *money* 지폐. **2** existing only on paper; little more than a

P

mere name. 지상(紙上)의; 장부상의; 명목만의. ¶ ~ *blockade* 선언〔말〕뿐인 봉쇄 / *a* ~ *war* 〔*warfare*〕 필전(筆戰) / ~ *profits* 장부상의 이익.

— *vt.* (P6,7) **1** cover (something) with paper; put paper on (a wall, etc.). …을 종이로 덮다〔바르다〕. ¶ ~ *a wall* 〔*room*〕 도배하다. **2** write (something) on paper. …을 종이에 쓰다. [→papyrus]

paper up, cover (a window, door, etc.) by pasting paper over. …을 도배하다.

pa·per·back [péipərbæ̀k] *n.* Ⓒ **1** a book bound in a paper cover. 종이 표지의 책; 페이퍼백. **2** a low-priced edition of a book. 염가〔보급〕판.

pa·per-boy [péipərbɔ̀i] *n.* a boy who sells or delivers newspapers. 신문팔이〔배달원〕.

pa·per·hang·er [péipərhæ̀ŋər] *n.* a person whose business is to cover walls etc. with paper. 도배장이.

pa·per-knife [péipərnàif] *n.* (*pl.* **-knives**) a flat, blunt knife made of bone, wood, etc. used for cutting sheets of paper, an envelope, or the leaves of a book. 종이(베는) 칼.

pa·per-knives [péipər nàivz] *n.* pl. of **paper-knife.**

pa·per·mill [péipərmìl] *n.* a factory in which paper is made. 제지 공장.

paper money [ㅅ-ㅅ-] *n.* money made of paper. 지폐(opp. specie).

pa·per·weight [péipərwèit] *n.* a small, heavy object laid upon loose papers to keep them from being scattered. 문진.

pa·per·y [péipəri] *adj.* thin like paper. 종이처럼 얇은.

pa·pist [péipist] *n.* 《usu. *joc., contempt.*》 a Roman Catholic. 천주교인. [→pope]

pa·py·ri [pəpáiərai, -riː] *n.* pl. of **papyrus.**

pa·py·rus [pəpáiərəs] *n.* (*pl.* **-rus·es** or **-ri**) Ⓤ **1** a tall water plant. 파피루스《아프리카산 수초의 하나》. **2** a kind of paper made from this plant by the ancient Egyptians, etc. 파피루스 종이. **3** 《*pl.*》 an ancient document or manuscript on papyrus. 고문서(古文書). [Gk.]

par [pɑːr] *n.* Ⓤ **1** 《sometimes *a* ~》 equal value, level, etc.; equality. 동등; 동가(同價). **2** the average or normal amount, degree, or state. 기준; 정상 상태. **3** 《com.》 the value of stocks, bonds, etc. that is printed on them; the face value. 액면대로의 가치; 액면 가격. **4** the normal value of the money of one country established in terms of that of another country. 환평가(換平價). **5** 《golf》 the number of strokes set as the standard of any given hole or course. 기준 타수(打數).

above par, at a premium; above the face value. 액면가 이상으로. ¶ *This stock is above* ~. 이 주식은 액면가 이상이다.

at par, at its face value. 액면가로.

below par, **a**) at a discount. 액면가 이하로. **b**) slightly out of health. 건강이 좀 나빠. ¶ *Tom has been feeling below* ~ *lately.* 톰은 요즘 건강이 좋지 않다.

on a par (***with***), equal (to). …와 동등한. ¶ *The gains and losses are about on a* ~. 손익이 반반이다 / *His knowledge of English seems on a* ~ *with my own.* 그의 영어 실력은 나와 같은 정도다 / *They are on a* ~ *in ability.* 그들은 능력이 비슷하다.

— *adj.* **1** average; normal. 평균〔표준〕의. **2** of or at par. 평가의; 액면의. ¶ ~ *value* 액면가격. [L.=equal]

para-[1] [pərɑ́ː, pǽrə] *pref.* side-, beside, aside, amiss, beyond. '측면', '근접', '부정', '초월'의 뜻. [Gk.]

para-[2] [pərɑ́ː, pǽrə] *pref.* protection against or for. '방호(防護), 피난'의 뜻. ¶ *parasol.* [L. *paro* prepare]

par·a·ble [pǽrəbəl] *n.* Ⓒ a short story told to illustrate moral teaching. 우화; 비유(담). ¶ *take up one's* ~ 이야기〔설교〕를 시작하다 / *teach in parables* 우화를 들려주어 깨우치다. [L. *parabola,* ↓]

pa·rab·o·la [pərǽbələ] *n.* Ⓒ 《math.》 a curve formed by cutting a cone with a plane parallel to its side. 파라볼라; 포물선(線). [para-[1], Gk. *ballō* throw]

par·a·bol·ic [pæ̀rəbɑ́lik / -bɔ́l-] *adj.* of or like a parabola. 포물선(모양)의.

par·a·chute [pǽrəʃùːt] *n.* Ⓒ **1** an umbrella-like apparatus used for descending from a great height. 낙하산; 파라슈트. **2** a similar device used to reduce the forward speed of an aeroplane when it lands. (항공기의) 제동용(制動用) 낙하산.

— *vi.* (P1,2A,3) descend by a parachute. 낙하산으로 강하하다. — *vt.* (P6) drop or convey (something) by a parachute. …을 낙하산으로 투하하다. [para-[2], →chute]

par·a·chut·ist [pǽrəʃùːtist] *n.* Ⓒ a person who uses a parachute; 《*pl.*》 paratroops. 낙하산 강하자; 낙하산병.

***pa·rade** [pəréid] *n.* Ⓒ **1** a march for display; a procession 행진. ¶ *The Oympic Games began with a* ~ *of all the competing nations.* 올림픽 경기는 모든 참가국들의 행진으로 시작되었다. **2** a review of troops; a place where soldiers drill. 열병식; 열병장. **3** a display; a great show. 과시; 자랑. ¶ *make a* ~ *of* (*one's wealth etc.*) (부)를 과시하다; 자랑하다. **4** a group of people walking for display or pleasure. 행렬; 행진하는 사람들. **5** a public promenade, square, etc. 유보장(遊步場); 산책길; 광장.

— *vt.* (P6) **1** assemble (troops) for review. (열병을 위해 군대)를 정렬시키다; 열병하다. ¶ *Parade the men, sergent-major!* 상사, 병사들을 정렬시켜. **2** march through (some place) with display. …을 대열을

지어 행진하다. ¶ ~ *the streets* 거리를 행진하다. **3** make a display of (something). …을 과시하다. ¶ *He is always parading his knowledge.* 그 친구는 늘 자기의 유식함을 내세운다.
— *vi.* (P1) **1** march in a parade. 행진하다; 누비고 다니다. **2** assemble in military order for review. 정렬하다. [→pare]

par·a·digm [pǽrədim, -dàim] *n.* Ⓒ **1** a pattern; an example. 범례; 모범. **2** 《gram.》 an example of a noun, verb, pronoun, etc. in all its inflections. 어형 변화표; 활용례(活用例). [para-¹, Gk. *deiknumi* show]

:**par·a·dise** [pǽrədàis, -dàiz] *n.* **1** 《*the P-*》 the garden of Eden. 에덴 동산. **2** Ⓤ heaven. 천국. **3** a place or state of great happiness. 낙원; 지복(至福). [Gk.]

*__par·a·dox__ [pǽrədɑ̀ks/-dɔ̀ks] *n.* Ⓒ **1** a statement which seems absurd, but which may be true. 역설(逆說); 패러독스. ¶ *"More haste, less speed" is a* ~. "급할수록 천천히"는 일종의 역설이다. **2** a statement which says two opposite things. 모순된 말; 억지. **3** a person, thing, or situation that seems to show contradiction. 사리를 모르는 사람; 사리에 맞지 않는 일. [para-¹, Gk. *doxa* opinion]

par·a·dox·i·cal [pæ̀rədɑ́ksikəl/-dɔ́ks-] *adj.* of paradoxes; expressing a paradox; fond of using paradoxes. 역설적인; 모순된; 역설을 좋아하는.

par·af·fin, -fine [pǽrəfin] *n.* Ⓤ **1** a white, tasteless substance like wax, used for making candles, etc. 파라핀. **2** oil containing paraffin, used for lighting etc. 파라핀유. [L. *parum* little, *affinis* having affinity]

par·a·gon [pǽrəgɑ̀n, -gən] *n.* Ⓒ a model of perfection or excellence; an example of goodness. 모범; 귀감; 전형. ¶ *a* ~ *of beauty* 미의 전형; 절세의 미인 / *a* ~ *of virtue* 덕의 귀감. [It.]

:**par·a·graph** [pǽrəgræ̀f, -grɑ̀:f] *n.* Ⓒ **1** a distinct section of a piece of writing. (글의) 절; 항(項); 단락. **2** a brief article, item, etc. in a newspaper or magazine. (신문·잡지 등의) 짧은 기사〔글〕. ¶ *an editorial* ~ 짧은 논설. **3** a sign used to show where a paragraph begins. 단락 부호(《 ¶ 》). — *vt.* (P6,13) **1** separate or arrange (a sentence) in paragraphs. (글)을 절(節)로 나누다. **2** write paragraphs about (something). …에 대해 짧은 기사를 쓰다. [para-¹]

Par·a·guay [pǽrəgwài, -gwèi] *n.* a country in central South America. 파라과이. 參考 수도는 Asunción.

par·a·keet [pǽrəkì:t] *n.* Ⓒ any of several kinds of small, long-tailed parrots. (작은) 잉꼬. [F.]

par·al·lax [pǽrəlæ̀ks] *n.* 《astron.》 the change in the direction in which an object is seen, caused by a change in the position of the observer. 시차(視差). [para-¹, Gk. *allassō* change]

*__par·al·lel__ [pǽrəlèl] *adj.* **1** never meeting because always at the same distance from each other. 평행의. ¶ ~ *lines* 평행선 / ~ *bars* (체조용) 평행봉. **2** like; similar; corresponding. 유사〔비슷〕한; 상응하는. ¶ *a* ~ *case* 비슷한 사례; 유례.
— *n.* Ⓒ **1** a parallel line or surface. 평행선〔면〕. **2** a person or thing like or similar to another; similarity; resemblance. 유사(한 물건); 대등(한 사람); 필적(하는 것·사람). ¶ *bear a close* ~ *to* …와 흡사하다 / *without* ~ 무비(無比)의 / *There is no parallel to it.* 그것과 견줄 물건은 없다 / *This case is without* ~. 이런 경우는 그 유례가 없다. **3** comparison. 비교; 대비. ¶ *draw a* ~ *between this winter and last winter* 금년 겨울과 지난 겨울을 비교하다. **4** one of the parallel circles marking the degrees of latitude on a glove. 위선(緯線); 위도권(圈). **5** 《electr.》 an arrangement in an electrical system. 병렬(竝列)(opp. series).
— *vt.* (**-leled, -lel·ing** or 《Brit.》 **-lelled, -lel·ling**) (P6) **1** be parallel with (something). …와 평행하다. ¶ *The road parallels the river.* 길은 강과 평행하여 있다. **2** compare. …을 비교하다. **3** correspond to (something). …에 필적시키다. ¶ *You won't easily* ~ *that.* 그것과 견줄 만한 것은 좀처럼 없을 것이오. [para-¹, Gk. *allēlous* each other]

par·al·lel·ism [pǽrəlèlizəm] *n.* Ⓤ **1** the state of being parallel. 평행(상태). **2** similarity; resemblance. 유사.

par·al·lel·o·gram [pæ̀rəléləgræ̀m] *n.* Ⓒ a four-sided figure whose opposite sides are parallel and equal. 평행 사변형.

par·a·lyse [pǽrəlàiz] *vt.* 《Brit.》 =paralyze.

pa·ral·y·ses [pərǽləsì:z] *n.* pl. of **paralysis.**

pa·ral·y·sis [pərǽləsis] *n.* (*pl.* **-ses**) **1** Ⓤ loss of the power of motion or sensation in any part of the body. 마비; 중풍. ¶ *cerebral* ~ 뇌성 마비 / *facial* ~ 안면 마비. **2** ⓊⒸ 《*fig.*》 the loss of energy, willpower, etc. 무력; 무기력; 무능; 정체. ¶ *a* ~ *of trade* 무역의 정체 / *moral* ~ 도의심의 마비 / *The whole country was in a state of* ~. 온 나라가 마비 상태에 있었다. [para-¹, Gk. *luō* loose]

par·a·lyt·ic [pæ̀rəlítik] *adj.* of paralysis; having paralysis. 마비(성)의; 중풍에 걸린.
— *n.* Ⓒ a person who has paralysis. 중풍 환자.

*__par·a·lyze,__ 《Brit.》 **-lyse** [pǽrəlàiz] *vt.* (P6) **1** affect (someone) with paralysis. …을 마비시키다; 저리게 하다. ¶ *His feet are paralyzed.* 그의 두 다리가 마비되었다. **2** make (someone) powerless; render useless. …을 무력하게 만들다; 쓸모없게 하다. ¶ *He was paralyzed with terror.* 그는 무서워

서 옴쭉을 못했다 / *Business is totally paralyzed.* 영업은 완전히 기능을 상실했다. [→paralysis, -ize]

par·a·mount [pǽrəmàunt] *adj.* 《*to*》 supreme; chief; superior. 최고의; 주요한; 가장 뛰어난. ¶ *This duty is ~ over all the others.* 이 임무는 다른 모든 것에 우선한다 / *of ~ interest* 〔*importance*〕 가장 흥미있는〔중요한〕. — *n.* Ⓒ a person who has supreme power. 최고 권위자; 수령. ¶ *a ~ chief* 군주 / *the lady ~* 여왕. [→per-, ad-, mount]

par·a·pet [pǽrəpit, -pèt] *n.* Ⓒ **1** a low wall or railing at the edge of a roof, bridge, balcony, etc. (지붕·다리·발코니 등의) 난간. **2** a low wall of stone, earth, etc. to protect soldiers. 흉벽(胸壁). [para-[2] →pectoral]

par·a·pet·ed [pǽrəpitid, -pètid] *adj.* having a parapet or parapets. 난간〔흉벽〕이 있는.

par·a·pher·nal·ia [pæ̀rəfərnéiljə] *n. pl.* **1** personal belongings. (자질한) 개인 소지품. **2** 《sometimes used as *sing.*》 equipment; apparatus. 장비; 비품. ¶ *camp ~* 야영 장비. [para-[1], Gk. *phernē*, dower]

par·a·phrase [pǽrəfrèiz] *n.* Ⓒ an expression of the meaning of a passage in other words. (알기 쉽도록) 바꾸어 말하기〔쓰기〕; 의역(意譯). — *vt., vi.* (P6; 1) express (a passage) in a paraphrase. 의역하다; 바꾸어 말하다〔쓰다〕. [para-[1]]

par·a·site [pǽrəsàit] *n.* Ⓒ **1** an animal or a plant which lives on another. 기생 동식물. ¶ *Mistletoe is a ~ on oak-trees.* 겨우살이는 오크나무의 기생 식물이다. **2** a person who lives at another's expense. 식객; 기식자. [para-[1], Gk. *sitos* food]

par·a·sit·ic [pæ̀rəsítik], **-i·cal** [-kəl] *adj.* of or like a parasite; living at another's expense. 기생 동·식물의〔같은〕; 식객 노릇하는.

:par·a·sol [pǽrəsɔ̀:l, -sɑ̀l / -sɔ̀l] *n.* Ⓒ a light umbrella used by women as a sunshade. (여성용) 양산; 파라솔. [para-[2], →sol]

par·a·troop·er [pǽrətrù:pər] *n.* Ⓒ a soldier in the paratroops. 낙하산병(兵). [*para*chute, *troop*]

par·a·troops [pǽrətrù:ps] *n. pl.* troops trained to drop onto a battlefield by parachute. 낙하산 부대.

par·a·ty·phoid [pæ̀rətáifɔid] *n.* Ⓤ a kind of fever like typhoid. 파라티푸스《열병의 하나》. — *adj.* of paratyphoid. 파라티푸스의. [para-[1]]

par·boil [pɑ́:rbɔ̀il] *vt.* (P6) boil (food) for a short time before roasting, etc. …을 살짝 데치다; 반숙하다. [per-]

:par·cel [pɑ́:rsəl] *n.* Ⓒ **1** a small, wrapped bundle; a package. 소포; 소화물. ¶ *~ delivery* 소포 배달 / *send away* 〔*off*〕 *a ~* 소화물을 보내다 / *make a thing into a ~* …을 소포로 만들다 / *do up* 〔*wrap up*〕 *a ~* 소포를 꾸리다 / *by ~ post* 소포 우편으로. **2** 《*arch.*》 a portion; a part. 일부분. ¶ *a ~ of land* 땅 한 뙈기 / *part and ~* 중요한 부분; 요점(要點). — *vt.* (**-celed, -cel·ing** or 《Brit.》 **-celled, -cel·ling**) (P6,7) divide (something) into portions. …을 구분하다; 나누다. ¶ *~ out candy* 과자를 분배하다. [→part]

parcel post [´–´] *n.* a branch of the post office which collects and delivers parcels. 소포 우편(물).

parch [pɑ:rtʃ] *vt.* (P6) **1** roast (something) over a fire. …을 볶다; 굽다. ¶ *~ some peanuts* 땅콩을 볶다. **2** make (something or someone) dry or thirsty by heating. …을 바싹 말리다; 목마르게 하다. ¶ *parched land* 건조한 땅 / *I am parched with thirst.* 갈증이 심하다. — *vi.* (P1) become dry or thirsty. 바싹 마르다; 목마르다; 목이 타다. [E.]

parch·ment [pɑ́:rtʃmənt] *n.* **1** Ⓤ a writing material prepared from the skin of sheep, goats, etc. 양피지(羊皮紙). **2** Ⓒ a manuscript or document written on parchment. 양피지에 쓴 사본〔문서〕. **3** Ⓤ paper that looks like parchment. 모조 양피지. [Place (*Pergamum*)]

:par·don [pɑ́:rdn] *n.* ⓊⒸ **1** forgiveness. 용서; 관용. ¶ *ask for someone's ~* 아무의 용서를 빌다 / *ask ~ for one's fault* 과실에 대해 관용을 빌다 / *I beg a thousand pardons for stepping on your feet.* 다리를 밟아 죄송합니다, 거듭 용서를 빕니다. **2** 《law》 the act of setting someone free from punishment; a document confirming this act. 은사(恩赦); 사면(장). ¶ *particular* 〔*special*〕 *~* 특사 / *general ~* 대사(大赦); 일반 사면.

I beg your pardon, **a**) Please excuse me. 죄송합니다. **b**) I did 〔could〕 not hear what you said. 죄송합니다만 다시 한번 말씀해 주십시오.

— *vt.* (P6,13,14) **1** forgive; excuse. 용서하다; 관대히 봐주다. ¶ *Pardon me, but....* 죄송하지만… / *There is nothing to ~.* 별말씀을; 천만에요 / *You'll ~ me, but I have something to say to this.* 죄송하지만 저는 이에 대해 드릴 말씀이 있습니다 / *He is a mean fellow, if you will ~ the expression.* 실례되는 표현일지 모르지만 그 친구는 치사합니다. **2** 《law》 free from further punishment. …을 사면하다. ¶ *The judge pardoned the crime.* 판사는 죄를 용서해주었다. [per-, →donation]

par·don·a·ble [pɑ́:rdnəbəl] *adj.* that can be pardoned. 용서할 수 있는.

pare [pɛər] *vt.* (P6,7) **1** cut away the outer part of (something). …을 깎다; …의 껍질을 벗기다. ¶ *~ an apple* 사과 껍질을 깎다 / *~ one's nails* 손톱을 깎다. **2** cut away (something) little by little. …을 조금씩 줄이다. ¶ *~ down expenses* 비용을 조금씩 줄여나가다. [L. *paro* prepare]

:par·ent [pɛ́ərənt] *n.* Ⓒ **1** a father or mother. 부모; 양친. **2** an animal or a plant that produces offspring. 동식물의 모체(母

體). ¶ *a* ~ *bird* 〔*company*〕 어미새〔모(母)회사〕. **3** an origin; a source. 원천. ¶ *the* ~ *of vice* 악의 근원 / *Ignorance is the* ~ *of many evils.* 무지는 많은 죄악의 원인이다. [L. *pario* beget]

par·ent·age [pέərəntidʒ] *n.* Ⓤ **1** descent from parents or ancestors; family line; birth. 혈통; 가문; 태생. ¶ *a noble* 〔*mean*〕 ~ 지체 있는〔미천한〕 가문 / *come of good* ~ 양가(良家)의 출신이다; 가문이 좋다 / *His* ~ *is unknown.* 그의 태생은 알려져 있지 않다. **2** fatherhood or motherhood. 어버이임.

pa·ren·tal [pəréntl] *adj.* of a parent. 부모의; 어버이다운. ¶ ~ *love* 〔*care, authority*〕 어버이의 사랑〔배려, 권위〕.

pa·ren·the·ses [pərénθəsìːz] *n.* pl. of **parenthesis.**

pa·ren·the·sis [pərénθəsis] *n.* Ⓒ (*pl.* **-the·ses**) **1** an explanatory word, phrase, sentence, etc. put into an already complete sentence. 삽입어〔구, 문〕. **2** 《usu. *pl.*》 either or both of the curved lines ( ) used to mark off a parenthesis. 괄호. ¶ *the words in parentheses* 괄호 안의 말. **3** an episode. 삽화; (막간의) 여담. [para-, Gk. *en* in]

par·en·thet·ic [pæ̀rənθétik], **-cal** [-kəl] *adj.* **1** placed in parentheses. 괄호에 싸인. **2** using parentheses; explaining. 삽입구를 쓴; 설명적인. ¶ *a* ~ *remark* 설명적인 말.

par·fait [pɑːrféi] *n.* ⓊⒸ a dessert made of ice cream, eggs, syrup, etc. frozen together. 파르페《빙과의 일종》. [F.]

par·i·ah [pəráiə, pǽriə] *n.* Ⓒ **1** a member of a low caste in South India and Myanmar. 남부 인도와 미얀마의 최하층민. **2** a wild dog in India. 인도의 들개. **3** a social outcast. 사회적 폐물; 부랑인. [Tamil]

par·ing [pέəriŋ] *n.* Ⓒ the part pared off. 벗긴〔깎은〕 껍질. [→pare]

***Par·is** [pǽris] *n.* **1** the capital of France. 파리. **2** 《Gk. myth.》 the son of Priam, King of Troy. 파리스《Helen을 빼앗아 Troy 전쟁을 일으킴》. [Place, name]

·**par·ish** [pǽriʃ] *n.* Ⓒ 《Brit.》 a part of a country with one church and one clergyman; the people of a parish. 교구(教區); 교구민. [para-¹, Gk. *oikeō* dwell]

go on the parish, receive financial help from a parish. 교구의 도움을 받다〔신세를 지다〕.

pa·rish·ion·er [pəríʃənər] *n.* Ⓒ a member of a certain parish. 교구민. [↑]

Pa·ri·sian [pərí(ː)ʒiən, pərízian] *adj.* of or like Paris or its people. 파리(식)의. —*n.* Ⓒ a person of Paris. 파리 사람. [*Paris*]

par·i·ty [pǽrəti] *n.* Ⓤ 《sometimes *a* ~》 equality in rank, quality, etc.; resemblance. 동격; 동등; 유사. ¶ ~ *of treatment* 균등 대우. [par]

by parity of reasoning, analogously. 유추(類推)에 의해.

stand at parity, be equal. 동위(同位)〔동격〕이다.

:**park** [pɑːrk] *n.* Ⓒ **1** a large, open space of ground for public recreation. 공원. ¶ *a national* ~ 국립 공원. **2** a large area of woods and fields around a country house. (시골 대저택 주위의) 대정원. **3** 《hist.》 land set apart for wild animals, preserved for hunting. 사냥터. **4** an open space used by the military for artillery, stores, etc. 군수품 저장소. **5** a place where a motorcar may be left for a time. 주차장. ¶ *a car* ~ 주차장.

—*vt.* (P6,7) leave (a motorcar, etc.) in a certain place; put (arms, etc.) in a park. (자동차)를 주차시키다; (포차(砲車) 등)을 한 곳에 정렬시키다. ¶ *No parking here.* 주차 금지 / ~ *guns* 대포를 집결시키다 / *Park yourself here.* 여기 있어라. [F.]

park·way [pɑ́ːrkwèi] *n.* Ⓒ a broad road bordered with grass and trees. 공원 도로; 자동차 전용 도로. [*park*]

par·lance [pɑ́ːrləns] *n.* Ⓤ a way of speaking. 말투; 어조. ¶ *newspaper* ~ 신문 용어 / *in common* ~ 보통말로 (하면). [→parley]

par·ley [pɑ́ːrli] *n.* ⒸⓊ a discussion, esp. with an enemy. (적과의) 담판; 회담. ¶ *The general held a* ~ *with the enemy about exchanging prisoners.* 장군은 적과 포로 교환에 관해 회담했다. —*vi.* (P1,3) have a discussion, esp. with an enemy. 담판〔회담〕하다. [F. *parler* speak]

sound a parley, invite to a parley by trumpet-call. 나팔을 불어 적군에게 화평 교섭을 제의하다.

:**par·lia·ment** [pɑ́ːrləmənt] *n.* ⓊⒸ a meeting or a group of elected persons that makes the laws of a country; 《*P-*》 the legislating body of Great Britain. 의회; 국회; 영국 의회. ¶ *the Houses of Parliament* 영국 의회 양원; 영국 의회 의사당 / *enter* 〔*go into*〕 *Parliament* 하원 의원이 되다 / *a Member of Parliament* 하원 의원. [F. *parlement* speaking]

par·lia·men·tar·i·an [pɑ̀ːrləmentέəriən] *n.* Ⓒ **1** a person who has much knowledge about a parliament and its procedures. 의회법 학자; 의회 법규에 정통한 사람. **2** 《*P-*》 a person who supported Parliament against Charles I. (영국) 의회당원.

par·lia·men·ta·ry [pɑ̀ːrləméntəri] *adj.* **1** of parliament; passed by a parliament; according to the rules and customs of a parliament. 의회의; 의회에서 제정한; 의회법에 의거한. **2** polite. 정중한. ¶ ~ *language* 정중한 말.

:**par·lor,** 《Brit.》 **-lour** [pɑ́ːrlər] *n.* Ⓒ **1** (originally) a room for receiving guests; (now) a living room. 객실; 거실. **2** a semiprivate room in a hotel, and inn, etc. (호텔·여관 등의) 특별 휴게〔담화〕실. **3**

《U.S.》 a decorated room for business; a shop. 가게; …점. ¶ *a beauty* ~ 미장원 / *a tea* ~ 다방. [→parley]

parlor car [⌐— ⌐] *n.* 《U.S.》 a very fine railroad car for day travel. 특별 객차.

pa·ro·chi·al [pəróukiəl] *adj.* **1** of or in a parish. 교구의. **2** 《*fig.*》 narrow in thought. 편협한. ¶ *His point of view was too* ~. 그의 견해는 편협하기 짝이 없었다. [→parish]

parochial school [⌐⌐——⌐] *n.* a school established by a church. 교구 부속 학교.

par·o·dist [pǽrədist] *n.* Ⓒ a writer of parodies. 패러디 작가. [↓]

par·o·dy [pǽrədi] *n.* ⒸⓊ (*pl.* **-dies**) a comic imitation of a serious writing; Ⓒ a poor imitation. (어떤 작품을) 익살스럽게 모방해 쓴 시문(詩文); 패러디; 서투른 모방. —*vt.* (P6) write a parody of; imitate poorly. …을 익살스럽게 모방해 쓰다; 서투르게 모방하다. [para-¹, →ode]

pa·role [pəróul] *n.* Ⓤ **1** a promise by a military prisoner not to try to escape. (포로가 도망하지 않겠다는) 약속; 선서. ¶ *The prisoner broke his* ~. 포로는 선서를 깼다. **2** 《U.S.》 the act of making a prisoner free before his time is up. 가석방. —*vt.* (P6) put (someone) on parole. 가석방하다. ¶ *The judge paroled the boys on condition that they report to him every three months.* 판사는 소년들을 석 달마다 그에게 보고한다는 조건으로 가석방했다. [F.=word, →parabola]

par·ox·ysm [pǽrəksìzəm] *n.* Ⓒ a sudden attack or outburst of pain, laughter, anger, etc. (감정의) 발작; 격발(激發). ¶ *a* ~ *of disease* 병의 발작 / *a* ~ *of pain* 통증의 격발 / *a* ~ *of rage* 분노의 격발. [para-¹, Gk. *oxus* sharp]

par·quet [pɑːrkéi] *n.* Ⓒ **1** a floor of parquetry. 쪽모이 세공을 한 마루. **2** 《U.S.》 the part of the main floor of a theater. 극장의 아래층. —*vt.* (P6) construct a flooring of parquetry. 쪽모이 세공의 마루를 깔다. [→park]

par·quet·ry [pɑ́ːrkitri] *n.* Ⓤ woodwork fitted together to make an ornamental pattern. 쪽모이 세공.

par·ri·cide [pǽrəsàid] *n.* **1** the act of killing a parent or a near relative. 어버이〔근친〕 살해(cf. *matricide*). **2** a person who kills his parent or a near relative. 어버이〔근친〕 살해범. [L. →pater, →(sui)cide]

:par·rot [pǽrət] *n.* Ⓒ **1** a bird that can repeat a person's words. 앵무새. **2** a person who merely repeats others' words or acts. 앵무새처럼 남의 언행을 되풀이하는 사람. —*vt.* (P6) repeat (words, etc.) without understanding. (뜻도 모르고 남의 말 등)을 되풀이하다. [? F.]

par·ry [pǽri] *vt., vi.* (**-ried**) (P6;1) turn (a blow) aside (e.g. with the arm); avoid (a question). (공격을) 받아넘기다; 비키다; (질문을) 피하다. ¶ ~ *a blow* 〔*the blade of an enemy's sword*〕 타격〔적의 칼날〕을 슬쩍 피하다 / ~ *a question* 질문을 어물쩍 피하다. —*n.* Ⓒ (*pl.* **-ries**) the act of parrying, esp. in fencing. 받아넘김《특히 펜싱에서의》. [→pare]

parse [pɑːrs] *vt.* (P6) 《gram.》 explain (a word) grammatically, pointing out its part of speech, case, etc.; explain (a sentence) showing the relationship of the parts. (낱말)의 품사 및 문법적 관계를 설명하다; (글)을 분석 해부하다. [→part]

par·si·mo·ni·ous [pɑ̀ːrsəmóuniəs] *adj.* too economical. 너무 아끼는; 인색한. [↓]

par·si·mo·ny [pɑ́ːrsəmòuni / -məni] *n.* Ⓤ extreme economy. 극도의 검약; 인색. [L. *parco* spare]

pars·ley [pɑ́ːrsli] *n.* Ⓤ 《bot.》 a vegetable with green leaves, used with meat or in salad. 파슬리《식용》. [Gk. *petra* rock, *selinon* parslcy]

pars·nip [pɑ́ːrsnip] *n.* Ⓒ 《bot.》 a vegetable with a long, white root. 양방풍나물 《식용》. [L. *pastinaca*]

·par·son [pɑ́ːrsən] *n.* Ⓒ 《*the* ~》 a clergyman in a parish; 《*colloq.*》 any clergyman. 교구 목사; 목사. [=person]

the parson's nose, 《*colloq.*》 the tailpiece of a cooked chicken. (요리한 닭의) 볼기살; 엉덩이 살.

par·son·age [pɑ́ːrsənidʒ] *n.* Ⓒ a house for a clergyman. 목사관(牧師館).

:part [pɑːrt] *n.* Ⓒ **1** that which is less than the whole; one of the pieces which something is made up of. 일부; 부분. ¶ *a piece of stone which was a* ~ *of a gravestone* 묘석의 일부였던 돌조각 / *the thick* ~ *of the hand* 손의 두툼한 부분 / *Jack ate* ~ *of an apple.* 잭은 사과를 좀 베어먹었다 / *He lost* ~ *of his money.* 그는 돈을 얼마쯤 잃었다 / *(A) great* ~ *of his story is true.* 그의 이야기의 대부분은 진실이다 / *He ran* ~ *of the way.* 그는 길 가던 도중에 좀 뛰었다 / *It is pretty cold here for a great* ~ *of the year.* 여기는 1년의 대부분이 매우 춥다. **2** each of a number of equal portions composing a whole. 율; 비율; (전체의) …분의 1. ¶ *a third* ~, 3분의 1 / *three parts of flour to one of sugar* 밀가루 3에 설탕 1의 비율 / *(The) most* ~ *of the audience slept during the speech.* 연설 동안 대부분의 청중은 잠을 잤다 / *I have finished two of the three parts of the work.* 일의 3분의 2는 끝냈다. **3** an organ of the body; a piece of a machine; a necessary element of a whole. 신체의 기관(器官); (기계의) 부품; 요소. ¶ *the inward parts of the body* 내장 / *spare parts for a machine* 기계의 예비 부품 / *the better* ~ *of a man's nature* 인간의 선성(善性) / *Our experiences are* ~ *of ourselves.* 경험은 인격의 요소이다. **4** a section to which a number is given in a book. (서적 등의) 부; 편. ¶ *a story in three parts* 세

편으로 된 소설 / *The book is divided into three parts.* 그 책은 3부로 나뉘어져 있다. **5** 《*pl.*》 a district. 지방; 지역. ¶ *He has traveled much in foreign parts.* 외지(外地)를 많이 다녔다 / *How long are you staying in these parts ?* 이 지방에 얼마나 계셨소. **6** a person's duty, share, or concern; a share in some job. 직분; 본분; 관계; 역할. ¶ *Everyone must do his* ~. 누구건 자기 본분을 다해야 한다 / *I had no* ~ *in these events.* 나는 이들 사건과는 전연 관계가 없다 / *It is the* ~ *of a wise man to take no notice of such foolish talk.* 슬기있는 사람의 역할이란 그런 객쩍은 말에 귀를 기울이지 않는 것이다. **7** a role of an actor or actress; the words spoken by them. (극에서의) 역(役); 역할; 대사. ¶ *play the* ~ *of Ophelia* 오필리아 역을 하다. **8** one of the sides in a contest, dispute, or transaction. (논쟁·거래 등의) …편; 쪽. ¶ *He always takes his brother's* ~ *in a quarrel.* 싸울 때는 늘 제 동생 편을 든다. **9** 《usu. *pl.*》《*arch.*》 ability; talent. 재능; 능력. ¶ *a man of parts* 유능한 사람 / *of excellent parts* 유능한. **10** 《mus.》 a melody sung by one of a group of singers. 악곡의 일부; 음부(音部). ¶ *sing the bass* ~ 저음부를 부르다 / *The four parts in singing are soprano, alto, tenor, and bass.* 성악의 4부란 소프라노, 알토, 테너 그리고 베이스를 말한다.

for my part, as far as I am concerned. 나로서는. ¶ *I, for my* ~, *have no objection.* 나로서는 이의가 없다.

for the most part, mostly. 대체로; 대개.

in part, partly; to some extent. 부분적으로; 어느 정도. ¶ *His story is true in* ~. 그의 말이 어느 정도는 사실이다.

on one's part =***on the part of,*** **a**) on one's side. …의 편에. **b**) as far as one is concerned. …에 관한 한.

part and parcel, an essential element. 중요 부분.

part of speech, one of the various grammatical classes into which words are grouped. 품사.

play a part (=*have a role*) ***in*** *something.* …의 역(役)을 하다.

take *something* ***in good*** 〔***evil, bad***〕 ***part,*** accept something with a good 〔unfavorable〕 spirit. …을 선의〔악의〕로 해석하다.

take part in, join; help in. …에 가담〔관여〕하다; 편들다. ¶ *I took only a small* ~ *in these events.* 나는 이들 사건에 조금 관여했을 뿐이다.

—*adv.* partly. 일부분은; 어느 정도. ¶ *Your opinion is* ~ *right.* 네 의견에 일리는 있다 / *The box is made* ~ *of iron and* ~ *of wood.* 그 상자는 일부는 쇠, 일부는 나무로 돼 있다.

—*vt.* (P6) **1** divide (something) into two or more pieces; divide (the hair) in opposite directions. …을 (一부분으로) 나누다〔분할하다〕; 가르마를 타다. ¶ ~ *the crowd* 군중을 헤치다 / ~ *one's hair in the middle* 한가운데서 가르마를 타다 / *A smile parted her slip.* 그녀는입술을벌리고 해죽이 웃었다 / *An island parts the river into two branches.* 섬이 강의 흐름을 두 갈래로 가른다. **2** separate; break or tear. …을 분리시키다; 떼어놓다. ¶ ~ *the fighting dogs* 싸우는 개를 갈라놓다. **3** 《*arch.*》 divide into shares. 몫으로 나누다. ¶ ~ *the booty* 장물을 분배하다.

—*vi.* (P1,3) **1** go away; separate. 헤어지다. ¶ *I parted with him on bad terms.* 그와 사이가 틀어져 헤어졌다 / *The lovers parted in anger.* 두 남녀는 화가 나서 갈라섰다 / *Now we must* ~. 이젠 작별 시간이 됐군. **2** come to pieces; break. 나뉘다; 갈라지다; 조개지다; 끊어지다. ¶ *The stream* 〔*road*〕 *parted.* 강〔길〕이 갈라졌다 / *The rope parted.* 로프가 끊어졌다. [L. *pars*]

part company, bring a friendship, an association, etc. to an end. …와 절교하다; 헤어지다.

part from, leave; say good-bye to. …을 떠나다; …와 헤어지다.

part with, **a**) part from. …와 헤어지다. **b**) give up; let (something) go. …을 포기하다; 손 떼다. ¶ ~ *with house* 가출하다 / ~ *with horses* 〔*servant*〕 말을 버리다〔하인을 해고하다〕.

·**par·take** [pɑːrtéik] *v.* (**-took, -tak·en**) *vi.* (P1,3) **1** ⓐ 《*of*》 eat or drink a part of. (…의 얼마 쯤을) 먹다; 마시다; (음식을) 함께 먹다. ¶ ~ *of wine* 포도주를 좀 마시다 / *Will you* ~ *of our breakfast with us ?* 우리와 아침 식사를 함께 하시죠. ⓑ 《*in*》 take part in; share in. (…을) 함께 하다; 참여하다. ¶ ~ *in an enterprise* 사업을 함께 하다 / ~ *in the general rejoicing* 기쁨을 함께 나누다. **2** 《*of*》《*fig.*》 have some of the nature of. 어느 정도 …한 성질〔경향〕이 있다. ¶ *He partakes of the character of his mother.* 성질이 그의 모친 같은 데가 있다 / *His manner partakes of insolence.* 그는 태도가 좀 시건방지다. —*vt.* (P6) take a part of (something). …을 함께 하다. [*part-take*]

par·tak·er [pɑːrtéikər] *n.* Ⓒ a person who partakes. 함께하는 사람; 관계〔분담〕자.

Par·the·non [pɑ́ːrθənɑ̀n, -nən] *n.* 《*the* ~》 the ancient Greek temple of Athena on the Acropolis in Athens. 파르테논 신전. [Gk. *Parthénos* Athene the Virgin]

·**par·tial** [pɑ́ːrʃəl] *adj.* **1** not complete; in part. 불완전한; 부분적인. ¶ 《astron.》 *a* ~ *eclipse* 부분식(部分蝕) / ~ *knowledge* 어설픈 지식 / *a* ~ *loss* 〔*success*〕 부분적인 손실〔성공〕. **2** showing favor to only one side, not both. 편파적인; 불공평한. ¶ *He is always* ~ *to his youngest son.* 그는 늘 막내를 편애한다. **3** 《*to*》 being fond of; having a special liking for. 특히 좋아하는. ¶ *be* ~ *to tomatoes* 토마토를 특히 좋아하다 / *She is particularly* ~ *to sweets.* 그녀는 단것을 아주 좋아한다. [→part, L. *capio* take]

par·ti·al·i·ty [pɑ̀ːrʃiǽləti] *n.* (*pl.* **-ties**) **1** Ⓤ

P

the state or quality of being not fair to both sides. 편파; 불공평. ¶ *without* ~ 공평하게. **2** ⒸⓊ a particular liking. 특히 좋아함. ¶ *have a* ~ *for poetry* 시를 특히 좋아하다.

par·tial·ly [pá:rʃəli] *adv.* not completely; partly; in a partial manner. 불완전하게; 부분적으로; 불공평하게.

par·tic·i·pant [pɑ:rtísəpənt] *n.* Ⓒ a person who participates. 참가〔관계〕자. ¶ *a* ~ *in a game* 경기 참가자. —*adj.* taking part; participating. 관여〔관계〕하는; 참가하는. [→participate, -ate]

par·tic·i·pate [pɑ:rtísəpèit] *vi.* (P1,3) 《*in*》 take part in something; have a share with other people. 참여〔참가, 관여〕하다. ¶ ~ *in a conversation* 대화에 참여하다 / ~ *in another's joy* 〔*in a discussion*〕 남과 기쁨을 나누다〔토론에 참가하다〕. [→part, L. *capio* take]

par·tic·i·pa·tion [pɑ:rtìsəpéiʃən] *n.* Ⓤ the act of participating. 참가; 참여; 관계.

par·tic·i·pa·tor [pɑ:rtísəpèitər] *n.* Ⓒ a person who participates. 관계〔참가〕자.

par·ti·cip·i·al [pɑ̀:rtəsípiəl] *adj.* 《gram.》 of a participle. 분사의. ¶ ~ *construction* 분사구문 / ~ *phrase* 분사구. [↓]

·**par·ti·ci·ple** [pá:rtəsìpəl] *n.* Ⓒ 《gram.》 a word derived from a verb and having the functions of both verb and adjective. 분사(分詞). [→partial]

·**par·ti·cle** [pá:rtikl] *n.* Ⓒ **1** the smallest possible amount; a very small portion; a very little piece. 극미량; 극히 작은 조각. ¶ *particles of sand* 미세한 모래 / *a* ~ *of food* 소량의 음식 / *without a* ~ *of feeling* 〔*truth*〕 추호의 감정〔진실〕도 없이 / *He has not a* ~ *of virtue.* 그에게는 손톱만큼의 미덕도 없다. **2** 《gram.》 a minor part of speech. 불변화사. 參考 관사·전치사·접속사·접두사·접미사 등. [L. *pars* part, -cle]

par·ti-col·ored, 《Brit.》 **-oured** [pá:rtikʌ̀lərd] *adj.* having or showing many different colors. 여러 색으로 된; 잡색의; 다채로운. [→part, →color]

:**par·tic·u·lar** [pərtíkjələr] *adj.* **1** different or distinct from others; special. 다른 것과 다른; 특별〔특수〕한(opp. general). ¶ *on that* ~ *day* 그 날 따라 / *of no* ~ *importance* 특별히 중요치는 않은; 평범한 / *take* ~ *notice* 특별히 주의하다 / *for no* ~ *reason* 특히 이렇다 할 이유 없이 / *I have nothing* ~ *to do now.* 지금(은) 특별하게 (해야) 할 일은 없다. **2** belonging to each single person or thing. 개개의; 독자적인; 독특한. ¶ *my* ~ *interests* 나 개인의 이익 / *do something in a* ~ *way* 독특한 방법으로 …을 하다 / *my own* ~ *faults* 내 특유의〔나만의〕 허물. **3** outstanding. 두드러진; 눈에 띄는. ¶ *There is no* ~ *news today.* 오늘은 이렇다 할 소식이 없다. **4** hard to please; very careful (about one's food, dress, etc.); wanting everything to be just right. (괴)까다로운; 깔끔한; 깐깐한. ¶ *a teacher* ~ *about manners* 예의범절에 까다로운 선생 / *Mrs. Brown is so* ~ *about her housework that servants will not work for her.* 브라운 부인은 집안 일에 어찌나 까다로운지 하인들이 배겨나지 못할게다. **5** telling all without omitting any small thing. 상세한; 꼼꼼한. ¶ *give a full and* ~ *account of* …에 관해 상세히 보고〔설명〕하다.

be particular about, be not easily satisfied with (something); be very careful about. …에 대해 까다롭게 굴다; 깐깐하다.

—*n.* **1** Ⓒ a detail; an item. 세목; 항목. ¶ *be complete in every* ~ 모든 점에서 완전하다 / *His answer was correct in every* ~. 그의 대답은 모든 점에서 정확했다. **2** 《*pl.*》 a full report. 명세(明細); 상세한 사항〔내용〕. ¶ *write the particulars of the case* 사건의 상세한 내용을 쓰다 / *All the particulars of the accident are now known.* 사고의 상세한 내용이 모두 밝혀졌다 / *For further particulars apply to Mr. Harris.* 더 상세한 내용에 관해서는 해리스 씨에게 문의하시기 바랍니다. [L. *particula* particle]

in particular, especially. 특히; 각별히(opp. in general).

par·tic·u·lar·i·ty [pərtìkjəlǽrəti] *n.* (*pl.* **-ties**) ⓊⒸ the state or quality of being particular; 《*pl.*》 something particular. 상세; 면밀; 특별; 까다로움; 상세한 사항.

par·tic·u·lar·ize [pərtíkjələràiz] *vt., vi.* (P6; 1) describe (something) in detail; mention individuals. (…을) 상세히 서술하다; 일일이 열거하다.

:**par·tic·u·lar·ly** [pərtíkjələrli] *adv.* in a particular manner; especially; in detail; one by one. 특히; 상세히; 일일이. ¶ *not* ~ *difficult* 별로 어렵지 않은 / *She mentioned that point* ~. 그녀는 특히 그 점을 자세히 말했다.

part·ing [pá:rtiŋ] *n.* **1** ⓊⒸ the act of taking leave; departure. 이별; 고별. ¶ *on* ~ 이별에 즈음하여 / *at* ~ 헤어질 때에. **2** ⓊⒸ (a point of) separation; division. 분할; 분리; 분기(점). ¶ *at the* ~ *of the ways* 갈림길에서; 기로에 서서. **3** Ⓒ the line from which one's hair is brushed to right and left. (머리의) 가르마. —*adj.* **1** departing. 헤어지는; 떠나는. ¶ *a* ~ *guest* 돌아가는 손님. **2** dividing. 나누는; 분할하는. ¶ *a* ~ *line* 분할선. **3** given, spoken, done, etc. at parting. 이별〔작별〕의. ¶ *a* ~ *gift* 이별의 선물 / *a* ~ *kiss* 이별의 키스. [→part]

·**par·ti·san, -ti·zan** [pá:rtəzən / pɑ̀:rtizǽn] *n.* Ⓒ **1** a strong, eager supporter of a party, group, cause, etc. (당·주의 등의) 지지자. **2** a member of a group of irregular troops engaged in guerrilla fighting. (비정규의) 게릴라 대원; 빨치산. —*adj.* of or like a partisan. 당파의; 당파심이 강한; 게릴라 대원의. [F. *partizane*]

par·ti·san·ship [pá:rtəzənʃìp / pɑ̀:rtizǽnʃìp] *n.* Ⓤ **1** strong support; blind or strong loyalty. 당파심; 맹목적인 충성. **2** taking sides. (당파적) 가담. [→part]

par·ti·tion [pɑːrtíʃən, pər-] *n.* **1** Ⓤ the act of dividing. 분할; 구분; 분배. ¶ *the ~ of a man's wealth when he dies* 사망으로 인한 그의 재산 분배. **2** Ⓒ a part so formed; one of divided parts; a section; a thin wall between rooms, etc. 칸막이; 칸막이한 방; 격벽(隔壁). — *vt.* (P6) divide (something) into sections; distribute. …을 칸막이하다; 분할〔분배〕하다. ¶ *~ an empire among three brothers* 하나의 제국을 세 형제간에 분할하다 / *~ a house into rooms* 집을 몇 개의 방으로 칸막이하다. [→part]

par·ti·zan [pɑ́ːrtəzən / pɑ̀ːrtizǽn] *n., adj.* =partisan.

:part·ly [pɑ́ːrtli] *adv.* in part; to some extent. 부분적으로; 어느 정도. ¶ *I went ~ on business and ~ for pleasure.* 일 반(半), 놀이 반으로 갔다. [→part]

:part·ner [pɑ́ːrtnər] *n.* Ⓒ **1** a member of a company who owns stocks and carries on the business in cooperation with others. 공동 출자자; (출자) 조합원; 사원. ¶ *an acting* 〔*active*〕 *~* 업무 집행 사원 / *a business ~* 동업자 / *sleeping* 〔*silent*〕 *~* 익명 사원 / *a general ~* 무한책임 사원〔조합원〕. **2** a person who shares; an associate. 한패; 동아리. ¶ *His sister was his ~ in the crime.* 그의 누이는 그의 공범이었다. **3** a husband or wife. 배우자. **4** one of two persons who dance together; (in a game, a sport, etc.) a player on the same team; a companion. (댄스의) 파트너〔상대〕; (놀이·운동 따위에서) 같은 팀의 선수〔짝〕.
— *vt.* (P6) join (others) together as partners. …을 제휴시키다; 한패로 만들다. [→part]

·part·ner·ship [pɑ́ːrtnərʃip] *n.* Ⓤ the state of being a partner; Ⓒ a joint business; an association. 공동; 협력; 조합; 회사. ¶ *enter into ~ with one's friend* 친구와 공동 경영을 시작하다 / *in ~ with* (*others*) …와 협력하여 / *take someone into ~* 아무를 공동 경영자로 하다 / *a limited ~* 합자 회사.

par·took [pɑːrtúk] *v.* p. of **partake.**

·par·tridge [pɑ́ːrtridʒ] *n.* Ⓒ (*pl.* **par·tridg·es** or *collectively* **par·tridge**) a game bird of several varieties, smaller than a pheasant; Ⓤ its flesh as food. 자고(鷓鴣)류《메추라기와 비슷한 엽조(獵鳥)》; 그 고기. [Gk. *perdix*]

part song [ˊ ˋ] *n.* a harmonized song in which the parts are sung by different people, often unaccompanied. 합창곡.

part-time [pɑ́ːrttàim] *adj.* working less than the standard hours. 파트타임의; 비상근(非常勤)의(opp. full-time). ¶ *a ~ worker* 시간급 노동자 / *a ~ teacher* 시간 강사.
— *adv.* on a part-time basis. 파트타임으로; 비상근으로. [*part, time*]

part·tim·er [pɑ́ːrttáimər] *n.* Ⓒ a person who is employed to work part-time. 파트타이머; 비상근자.

par·tu·ri·ent [pɑːrtjúəriənt] *adj.* about to give birth. 해산(解産)달의; 만삭의. [→parent]

par·tu·ri·tion [pɑ̀ːrtjuəríʃən] *n.* childbirth. 분만; 해산. [↑]

:par·ty [pɑ́ːrti] *n.* Ⓒ (*pl.* **par·ties**) **1** a group of people united for the same purpose or by the same interest. (목적·관심을 함께 하는) 사람들; 일행; …대(隊). ¶ *a search ~* 수색대. **2** a company met together for pleasure or entertainment; a social gathering. (사교상의) 모임; 회; 파티. ¶ *a garden ~* 가든 파티 / *give* 〔*have, hold*〕 *~* 파티를 열다 / *a dinner ~* 만찬회 / *Jean had a ~ on her birthday.* 진은 그녀 생일에 파티를 열었다. **3** a group of people who share the same political opinions, etc.; a political organization. 당; 당파; 정당. ¶ *the government* 〔*opposition*〕 *~* 여당〔야당〕 / *the Democratic Party* 민주당 / *~ spirit* 당파심; 당파근성 / *the ~ system* 정당 제도. **4** a person interested in or concerned in some affair; one who takes part in something. (소송·계약 등의) 당사자; 상대자; 관계인; 한패; 공범. ¶ *all the parties concerned* 관계자〔당사자〕 일동 / *a third ~* 제3자 / *an interested ~* 이해 관계자 / *He was a ~ to the crime.* 그는 그 범행의 공범이었다. **5** 《*colloq.*》 a person. 사람. ¶ *a funny old ~* 재미있는 늙은이.
— *adj.* **1** of a social gathering. 파티의. ¶ *a ~ dress* 파티 의상. **2** of political organizations. 당파의; 정당의. ¶ *a ~ government* 정당 내각. [→part]

par·ty·col·ored, 《Brit.》 **-oured** [pɑ́ːrtikʌ̀lərd] *adj.* =parti-colored

pa·sha [pɑ́ːʃə, pǽʃə, pəʃɑ́ː] *n.* Ⓒ a former title of high-ranking officers or officials in Turkey. 파샤《터키의 문무 고관의 옛 존칭》. [Turk.]

:pass[1] [pæs, pɑːs] *vi.* (P1,2A,3) **1** ⓐ move from one place to another; go by or past; proceed; leave behind. 지나다; 통과하다; 전진하다; 앞지르다. ¶ *~ along a street* 거리를 지나다 / *~ a shop* = *~ by a shop* 가게 앞을 지나다 / *I saw a party of students ~.* 한 무리의 학생들이 지나가는 것을 보았다 / *The third horse passed the second and neared the first.* 세번째 말이 둘째 말을 앞지르더니 첫째 말에 다가갔다 / *Just let me ~.* 좀 지나가겠습니다. ⓑ go through 〔across, over〕 관통하다; 건너다; 넘다. ¶ *~ over* 〔*across*〕 *the ocean* 대양을 건너가다 / *Some trains ~ through this station.* 이 역엔 정차하지 않고 그냥 통과하는 열차도 있다. **2** change from one state into another. 옮아가다; 변화하다. ¶ *The weather passed suddenly from hot to cold.* 날씨가 덥더니 갑자기 추워졌다. **3** (of time) go by; be spent. (시간이) 경과하다; 지나다. ¶ *~ a night* 〔*the summer at seaside*〕 하룻밤을 〔여름을 해변에서〕 지내다 / *Five years have passed since I last saw him.* 그를

마지막으로 본 지 5년이 지났다. **4** disappear; die; go away; come to an end. 소멸하다; 없어지다; 지나가버리다; 끝나다. ¶ ~ *out of existence* 사라져 없어지다 / *Your trouble will soon ~ away.* 걱정거리는 곧 없어질 것이다 / *The matter had passed from my memory.* 그 일은 내 기억에서 사라졌다 / *She passed away at six o'clock this morning.* 그녀는 오늘 아침 6시에 사망했다. **5** happen; be done or said (between persons). (일이) 발생하다; (말 따위가) 오가다. ¶ *Tell me all that passed.* 있었던 일을 내게 전부 말해라 / *Low whispers passed between them.* 수군대는 말이 그들 사이에 오갔다. **6** 《*as, for*》 be accepted or recognized. …으로 통하다; 통용되다; 인정되다. ¶ ~ *as* 〔*for*〕 *a first-rate artist* 일류 화가로 알려지다 / *He passes by the name of Logan.* 그는 로건이란 이름으로 통한다. **7** go through an examination, etc. successfully; (of a bill or law) be approved by a majority. (시험 등에) 합격하다; (의안이) 통과되다; 제정되다. ¶ *The bill passed.* 의안은 통과됐다 / *He passed first in the examination.* 시험에서 일등으로 합격했다 / *The bill passed the Senate.* 의안이 상원을 통과했다 / *The proposal passed.* 제안이 받아들여졌다. **8** be current; go or be sent about from person to person. 통용되다; (손에서 손으로) 건네지다; 넘어가다. ¶ *The letter passed from hand to hand.* 편지는 이 사람 저 사람에게로 건네졌다 / *Property passes from father to son.* 재산은 아들에게로 상속된다. **9** 《*on, upon, for, against*》 (of a court, etc.) express or pronounce the judgment; (of a judgment, etc.) be expressed or pronounced. (법정 등이) 판결을 내리다; (판결 등이) 내려지다. ¶ *The judgment passed against us.* 우리에게 불리한 판결이 내려졌다 / *The jury passed on the case.* 배심원이 그 사건의 심리에 입회했다 / *Judgment was passed for the defendant.* 판결은 피고에게 유리하게 내려졌다. **10** 《football, etc.》 throw or kick the ball to another player of one's own team. (자기 편에게) 공을 패스하다. **11** 《cards》 refuse one's turn to play, bid, etc. (다음 사람에게 그냥) 패스하다.

— *vt.* (P6,7,13,14) **1** go by, beyond, over, across, through (something or someone); overtake. …을 지나가다; 통과하다; 건너다; 추월하다. ¶ ~ *a house* 집을 지나가다 / ~ *a hill* 언덕을 넘어가다 / ~ *an ocean* 대양을 건너다 / *Have we passed the station yet?* 벌써 역을 지났나. **2** ⓐ allow (someone) to go past or enter; cause (someone) to move past. …을 통과시키다; …에 들이다; …을 열병하다. ¶ *The soldier on guard passed him.* 보초는 그를 들여보냈다 / *The general passed the troops in review.* 장군은 부대를 열병했다 / *They readily passed us through the customs.* 그들은 곧 우리들을 통관시켰다. ⓑ cause to circulate. …을 유통〔통용〕시키다. ¶ ~ *forged notes* 위폐를 유통시키다 / *He passed me a bad check.* 그는 나에게 부도 수표를 발행했다. **3** cause (something) to go through; put (a rope, etc. through). …을 뚫고 지나가게 하다; …을 꿰다; (밧줄 등)을 걸다. ¶ ~ *the liquid through a filter* 액체를 여과기에 부어 거르다 / ~ *a rope around a log* 통나무에 밧줄을 걸다 / ~ *a thread through a hole* 구멍에 실을 꿰다. **4** spend (time, etc.). (시간)을 보내다. ¶ ~ *a pleasant evening* 즐거운 저녁을 보내다 / ~ *the time by reading a book* 책을 읽으면서 시간을 보내다 / *How did you ~ the summer vacation.* 여름 방학을 어떻게 지냈느냐. **5** be successful in (an examination, etc.). (시험 등)에 합격하다. ¶ ~ *an examination* 시험에 합격하다 / *The doctor passed me (as)* fit for work. 의사는 내게 근무처에 나가도 좋다고 했다. **6** (of a committee, law-making body, etc.) approve (a motion, law, etc.). (의회 등이 동의·법안)을 통과시키다; 가결하다. ¶ ~ *the bill* 의안을 통과시키다 / *The bill passed Congress.* 의안은 의회를 통과했다. **7** let go by without care or notice; neglect. …을 눈감아 주다; 무시하다. ¶ *Those words of his won't be passed over in silence.* 그가 한 말들이 그냥 조용히 넘어가지는 못 할 게다. **8** hand (something) from one to another. …을 건네주다; 돌리다. ¶ *Please ~ (me) the butter.* 버터 좀 이리 건네 주십시오 / *Read this and ~ it on to Dick.* 이것을 읽고 다음 차례인 딕에게 건네주시오. **9** 《*on, upon*》 express or pronounce (an opinion or a judgment). (판결)을 선고하다; (판단·평가)를 내리다. ¶ ~ *sentence of death on the criminal* 범인에게 사형을 선고하다. **10** be better than (something); go beyond the limit of (something). …보다 낫다; …을 초월하다. ¶ *His behavior passes my understanding.* 그의 행동을 나는 이해할 수 없다 / *He passes all others in wealth.* 그는 누구보다도 부자다. **11** 《football, etc.》 throw or kick (a ball) to another player of one's own team. (공을) 패스하다.

pass away, **a**) die; come to an end. 죽다; 끝나다. **b**) spend (time); waste. (시간)을 보내다; 낭비하다.

pass by, **a**) go by or past. 옆을 지나가다. **b**) pass by without looking or noticing; neglect; overlook. 못 보고 지나가다; 눈감아 주다.

pass off, **a**) disappear gradually. 차츰 사라지다. **b**) come to an end. 끝나다. ¶ *The storm soon passed off.* 폭풍이 곧 멎었다 / *The meeting passed off successfully.* 회합은 성공적으로 끝났다. **c**) put on a false appearance of (someone else); pretend; deceive someone by giving (a false thing). 짐짓 …인 체하다; …을 속이다. ¶ ~ *oneself off as an artist* 예술가인 체하다. **d**) ignore; treat (something) as unimportant. …을 무시〔경시〕하다.

pass on, **a**) move forward. 나아가다. **b**)

repeat. 되풀이하다. **c**) hand (something) from one to another. 다음으로 넘기다. **d**) die. 죽다.

pass out, 《*colloq.*》 lose consciousness; die. 기절하다; 죽다

pass over, **a**) ignore; fail to notice. …을 무시하다; 간과하다. **b**) go or move from one side to the other. …에 넘겨주다; 양도하다.

pass the buck, 《U.S. *colloq.*》 shift the responsibility on to another. …에 책임을 전가하다.

pass the time of day, say 'Good morning', 'Good afternoon', etc. to someone on meeting him; greet; exchange simple, everyday remarks. (일상적인) 인사를 나누다.

pass through, experience. …을 경험하다.

pass up, refuse; give up. …을 거절하다; 포기하다.

pass water, make water. 소변보다; 오줌누다.

— *n.* Ⓒ **1** the act of passing; success in an examination. 통과; 합격. ¶ *get a* ~ 합격하다; 붙다. **2** a ticket allowing one to go somewhere; a free ticket. 입장권; 허가증; 무료 승차[입장]권; 패스. ¶ *a free* ~ *to a theater* 극장의 무료 입장권. **3** state; condition; crisis; difficult circumstances. 상태; 사태; 위기; 곤경. ¶ *a pretty* ~ 매우 난처한 상태[처지] / *Things have come to a strange* ~. 일이 이상한 사태로 돌아갔다. **4** a trick played by moving the hands quickly and skillfully; a gesture. (손놀림에 의한) 요술[속임수]; 손짓; 몸짓. ¶ *make passes* 손을 놀려 최면을 걸다 / *The magician made passes in doing his tricks.* 요술사는 속임수를 써서 요술을 보였다. **5** 《football, etc.》 an act of passing the ball from one player to another. (공의) 패스. **6** 《cards》 an act of not taking one's turn. (카드놀이의) 패스. **7** 《fencing》 a thrust with the sword. 찌르기. [pace[1]]

bring to pass, **a**) cause to happen. …을 야기시키다. **b**) accomplish. 실현[성취]하다; 이루다. ¶ *bring a reconciliation to* ~ 화해를 성립시키다.

come to pass, take place; happen. 일이 일어나다.

make a pass at, **a**) try to embrace or caress (a girl); court. (여자)에게 구애하다; 지분거리다. **b**) 《fencing》 thrust one's sword at; try to attack. 찌르다; 찌르려 하다.

:pass[2] [pæs, pɑːs] *n.* Ⓒ a narrow way or course, esp. over or through a range of mountains. 산길; 고갯길. ¶ *a teahouse on a* ~ 고갯마루의 찻집 / *a mountain* ~ 산길. [↑]

hold the pass, support as defend some cause. 주의를[이익을] 옹호하다.

sell the pass, betray a cause; yield up a position. 주의를 배반하다; 지위를 양보하다.

pass·a·ble [pǽsəbəl, pɑ́ːs-] *adj.* **1** that can be passed through or over. 통행할 수 있는; 건널 수 있는. ¶ *a* ~ *road* [*river*]. **2** fairly good; moderate. 괜찮은; 웬만한. ¶ *a* ~ *composition* 그런대로 잘된 작문 / *a* ~ *knowledge of geography* 상당한 지리 지식. **3** current. 통용하는; 유통되는. ¶ *a* ~ *coin* 유통 주화. **4** (of a bill, etc.) that may be enacted. (법안 등이) 가결될 수 있는.

pass·a·bly [pǽsəbəli, pɑ́ːs-] *adv.* pretty; fairly; moderately. 그런대로; 꽤; 알맞게.

:pas·sage [pǽsidʒ] *n.* Ⓤ **1** the act of passing or proceeding; movement from one place to another; change from one condition to anotehr. 통행; 통과; (시간 등의) 경과; 추이; 변천. ¶ *the* ~ *of time* 시간의 경과[추이] / *the* ~ *of men and vehicles* 사람과 차량들의 통행. **2** Ⓒ a voyage across the sea from one place to another; a journey. 항해; 도항; 여행. ¶ *birds of* ~ 철새 / *have a smooth* ~ 순탄한 항해를 하다 / *Did you have a pleasant* ~*?* 항해는 즐거웠습니까. **3** a passenger's accommodations on a ship; the payment for this. 배의 수용 설비; 승선료. ¶ *pay one's* ~ 뱃삯을 내다 / *book one's* ~ *on a steamer* 승선 예약을 하다 / *work one's* ~ 뱃삯 대신 배에서 일해주다. **4** ⓐ Ⓒ a long and narrow way, esp. between rooms in a house; a hall; a lobby; the course of a river or sea. (건물 내의) 통로[복도]; 홀; 로비; 수로; 항로. ¶ *We walked through the* ~. 우리는 복도를 따라 걸어갔다 / *a* ~ *into a bay* 만으로 들어가는 입구. ⓑ a way by which one passes; a way through. (통과할 수 있는) 좁은 통로; 길. ¶ *cut a* ~ 길을 내다 / *force a* ~ *through a crowd* 군중을 헤치고 나아가다. **5** ⓐ the right or permission to pass through, over, or into. 통행권; 통행 허가. ¶ *a free* ~ 통행 자유 / *No* ~ *this way!* 이 길은 통행 금지《게시》 / *give* [*refuse*] *a* ~ *through the country* 국내 통과를 허락[거절]하다. ⓑ the sum payable a passage. 통행료. ¶ *pay one's* ~. **6** Ⓒ a piece from a speech or writing. (글·연설 등의) 한 구절. ¶ *a* ~ *from Shakespeare* 셰익스피어에서의 한 인용구. **7** approval of a bill, law, resolution, etc. (의안 등의) 통과; 가결. ¶ *the* ~ *of a bill through Congress* 법안의 의회 통과. **8** Ⓒ what is said or done between two persons. (쌍방간의) 담합; 논쟁; 티격태격. ¶ *a* ~ *of* [*at*] *arms* 주먹다짐; 싸움 / *have stormy passages with someone* 아무와 심하게 다투다. [→pass, -age]

pas·sage·way [pǽsidʒwèi] *n.* Ⓒ a corridor; a passage. 복도; 통로.

pass·book [pǽsbùk, pɑ́ːs-] *n.* a book showing money paid into and taken out of a bank by a customer. 은행 통장(cf. *bankbook*). [*pass*]

pas·sé [pæséi / pɑ́ːsei, pǽs-] *adj.* 《F.》 past; old-fashioned; out of date. 과거의; 구식의; 시대에 뒤진. ¶ *a* ~ *belle* 한물 간 미인.

:pas·sen·ger [pǽsəndʒər] *n.* Ⓒ **1** a person who travels on a train, bus, boat, etc. 승객; 선객. ¶ *a first-class* ~ 일등 승객. **2** a traveler, esp. on foot; a wayfarer. 도보 여행자. **3** 《*colloq.*》 a member of a team, crew, etc. who does no proper work. (팀 등에서) 제몫을 하지 못하는 사람. ¶ 《*fig.*》 *The cabinet carries a few passengers.* 내각에는 짐스러운 무능 각료가 몇 있다. [→pass]

passenger boat [∠-- ∸] *n.* a boat for carrying passengers. 여객선.

passenger car [∠-- ∸] *n.* a railroad car for carrying passengers; an automobile for carrying no more than nine passengers. 객차《열차의》; (승객 9인 이하의) 승용차.

passenger plane [∠-- ∸] *n.* an airplane for carrying passengers. 여객기.

passenger train [∠-- ∸] *n.* a train for carrying passengers. 여객 열차.

pass·er [pǽsər, pɑ́:sər] *n.* Ⓒ a person who passes; a passer-by. 통행인; 길 가는 사람. [*pass*]

pass·er-by [pǽsərbái, pɑ́:s-] *n.* Ⓒ (*pl.* **pass·ers-by**) a person who passes by, usu. by walking. 지나가는 사람; 통행인.

pas·sim·e·ter [pæsímitər] *n.* an automatic machine for supplying railway passengers with tickets. 승차권 자동 판매기. [→pass, -meter]

pass·ing [pǽsiŋ, pɑ́:s-] *adj.* **1** transient; not lasting; incidental. 일시적인; 잠깐〔순간〕의; 우연의. ¶ ~ *pleasure* 순간의 즐거움. **2** current. 현재의. ¶ *the* ~ *day* 현재 / *during the* ~ *year* 금년 내내. **3** going by, beyond, or through. 지나가는; 통과하는. ¶ *a* ~ *car* 지나가는 차 / *the* ~ *hour* 지나가는 시간. — *adv.* 《*arch.*》 very; surpassingly. 대단히; 뛰어나게. ¶ ~ *rich* 〔*strange*〕 아주 돈많은〔이상한〕.

— *n.* Ⓤ **1** going away; disappearance; death. 통과; 가버림; 사라짐; 소멸; 사망. ¶ *with the* ~ *of the years* 해가〔세월이〕 지남에 따라 / *the* ~ *of old system* 구제도의 소멸 / *the* ~ *of a hero* 한 영웅의 죽음. **2** act of going by. 통행; 지나감. ¶ *watch the* ~ *of people* 사람들의 통행을 지켜보다. **3** happening. 발생. ¶ *the* ~ *of great events* 대사건들의 발생. [*pass*]

in passing, by the way; incidentally. …하는 김에; 내친 걸음에.

:pas·sion [pǽʃən] *n.* **1** ⓊⒸ very strong feeling, emotion or enthusiasm; deep love or affection. 열정; 정열; 열성; 열애. ¶ *a leader lacking in* ~ 정열이 없는 지도자 / *one's ruling* 〔*master*〕 ~ 주정(主情); 외곬으로 쏠린 감정 / *be filled with* ~ *for* …을 뜨겁게 사랑하다 / *He has enough* ~ *to make a great poet.* 그에겐 대시인이 되기에 족한 열의가 있다. **2** 《*a* ~》 an outburst of rage. 격노; 격분. ¶ *in a* ~ 격분해서 / *He flew into a* ~ *at my words.* 내 말에 그는 벌컥 성을 냈다. **3** Ⓒ 《*for*》 a very strong liking. 기호(嗜好); 굉장히 좋아하는 것. ¶ *She has a* ~ *for painting.* 그녀는 그림이 대단한 취미다. **4** Ⓤ suffering; 《*the P-*》 the sufferings of Christ on the cross. 고난; 그리스도의 수난. ¶ *a* ~ *play* (예수의) 수난극. [L. *patior* suffer]

***pas·sion·ate** [pǽʃənit] *adj.* easily moved or excited by passion; expressing or having strong feelings; easily get angry. 열렬한; 정열적인; 다정다감한; 성급한; 툭하면 성내는. ¶ *a* ~ *speech* 열변 / *a* ~ *supporter of democracy* 민주주의의 열렬한 지지자 / ~ *love* 〔*desire*〕 뜨거운 사랑〔강한 욕망〕 / *A tiger is a* ~ *animal.* 범은 격해지기 쉬운 짐승이다.

pas·sion·less [pǽʃənlis] *adj.* having no passion; calm. 열정이 없는; 냉정한.

***pas·sive** [pǽsiv] *adj.* **1** being acted upon but not acting. 수동적인. ¶ *in a* ~ *sense* 수동적인 의미에서. **2** 《gram.》 showing that the subject is acted upon by the verb. 수동태의 (opp. active). **3** not resisting; submissive; inactive. 무저항의; 소극적인; 남이 시키는 대로 하는; 활기 없는. ¶ *a* ~ *nature* 소극적인 성격 / *a* ~ *member of a committee* 위원회 활동에 소극적인 위원 / *be* ~ *in an action* 행동이 소극적이다. — *n.* 《*the* ~》 《gram.》 the passive voice. 수동태. [→passion]

pas·siv·i·ty [pæsívəti] *n.* Ⓤ the state or quality of being passive; passiveness; inaction. 수동성; 무저항; 불활동; 복종.

pass·key [pǽskìː, pɑ́:s-] *n.* **1** Ⓒ a key designed to open several locks; a master key. 결쇠. **2** a private key. 사용(私用)의 열쇠. [*pass, key*]

Pass·o·ver [pǽsòuvər, pɑ́:s-] *n.* an annual Jewish holiday in memory of the sparing of the Jewish houses when God killed the first-born children in Egypt. 유월절(逾越節)《1월 14일》. [*pass*]

pass·port [pǽspɔ̀ːrt, pɑ́:s-] *n.* Ⓒ **1** an official document giving permission to travel abroad. 여권; 패스포트. **2** something that enables someone to win or obtain something. (사랑·존경 따위를 얻는) 수단.

pass·word [pǽswə̀ːrd, pɑ́:s-] *n.* Ⓒ a secret word that must be uttered by a person before he passes a guard; a watchword. 암호.

:past [pæst, pɑːst] *adj.* **1** of an earlier time. 과거의; 예전의. ¶ *in time* ~ 과거에는 / ~ *glory* 과거의 영광 / *This picture remind me of my* ~ *days.* 이 사진을 보니 옛날 일들이 생각난다. **2** 《as *predicative*》 gone by; over. 지나간; 끝난. ¶ *Her sorrows are* ~. 그녀의 불행은 끝났다 / *Summer is* ~. 여름은 지났다. **3** just ended; ago. 막 지난; 지금부터 …전. ¶ *the* ~ *week* 지난 주 / (*for*) *ten years* ~ 지난 10년(동안) / *for some time* ~ 얼마 전부터; 요한동안. **4** no longer in office; former. 전임(前任)의. ¶ *a* ~ *chairman* 전(前)의장 / *a* ~ *president of club* 클럽의 전(前)회장. **5**

《gram.》 expressing what is gone by. 과거의. ¶ *the ~ tense* 과거 시제.
— *n.* **1** 《usu. *the ~*》 time gone by. 과거. ¶ *in the ~* 과거(왕년)에 / *in the remote ~* 아주 오래 전에 / *memories of the ~* 추억. **2** Ⓒ a happening in past time; a past life, history, career, etc. 과거지사; 이력; 경력. ¶ *The school has a glorious ~.* 이 학교는 빛나는 과거가 있다 / *We know nothing of his ~.* 그의 과거는 전혀 모른다. **3** Ⓒ 《*a ~*》 one's past life, esp. that which is kept concealed. (좋지 못한 숨겨진) 내력(경력). ¶ *a woman with a ~* 과거가 있는 여자. **4** 《usu. *the ~*》 《gram.》 the past tense. 과거 시제.
— *prep.* **1** beyond in time; after. (시간)을 지나서. ¶ *~ noon* 한낮을 지나 / *at a quarter ~ four.* 4시 15분에 / *My grandmother is now ~ ninety.* 할머님은 지금 아흔이 넘으셨다. **2** beyond in place; going by or beyond. (장소·공간)을 지나서. ¶ *run ~ the post office* 우체국 앞을 지나 달리다 / *Bullets whistled ~ their ears.* 총알이 쌩하고 귓가를 지나갔다 / *I fell asleep and went ~ my station.* 잠에 떨어져 내릴 정거장을 지나갔다. **3** beyond in number, amount or degree. (수량이) …을 넘어; 이상(以上)으로. ¶ *It's ~ three pounds.* 그건 3파운드가 넘는다. **4** beyond the power, reach, scope, or influence of. (정도·범위 따위)를 넘어서; …이 미치지 않는. ¶ *~ endurance* 참을 수 없는 / *~ belief* 믿을 수 없는 / *The problem is ~ understanding.* 그 문제는 이해가 되지 않는다 / *He is ~ praying for.* 그 사람은 구제 불능이다.
— *adv.* so as to pass by. …을 지나(쳐)서. ¶ *walk (go) ~* 스쳐 지나가다 / *hasten (run) ~* 서둘러(뛰어) 지나(쳐)가다 / *drive ~* 차를 몰고 지나가다 / *The years flew ~.* 세월이 빠르게 흘렀다. [→pass]

***paste** [peist] *n.* Ⓤ **1** a mixture of flour, water, etc., used for sticking (paper, etc.) together. 풀. ¶ *scissors and ~* ⇨ scissors. **2** a soft mixture of flour and water with butter, etc. used in making pastry. 가루반죽; 페이스트. **3** a way of preparing foodstuffs by beating them up into a soft and moist mass. 반죽. **4** a soft jelly like candy. (젤리와 같은) 과자의 일종. **5** the glassy substance used in making artificial precious stones. (모조 보석 제조용의) 납유리.
— *vt.* (P6,7,13) 《*up, down, together, on, with*》 stick (something) with paste; cover (a wall, etc.) by pasting things on it. …을 풀로 바르다(붙이다); 도배하다. ¶ *~ up a notice* 벽보를 붙이다 / *~ a wall with paper* 벽을 도배하다 / *She pasted the pictures in her scrapbook.* 스크랩북에 그림들을 붙였다. [Rom.]

paste·board [péistbɔ̀ːrd] *n.* Ⓤ a stiff, boardlike material made by pasting several sheets of paper together. 판지(板紙).

pas·tel [pǽstel / pǽstl] *n.* **1** Ⓤ a kind of crayon made of coloring matter mixed with gum, etc. used in drawing. 파스텔. **2** Ⓒ a drawing made with such crayons. 파스텔화. **3** Ⓤ a method of drawing with such crayons. 파스텔화법. [L. *pasta* paste]

pas·tern [pǽstəːrn] *n.* Ⓒ the part of a horse's foot between the hoof and the fetlock. 발회목. [F.]

pas·teur·ism [pǽstərìzəm, -tʃə-] *n.* **1** a method of preventing hydrophobia. 광견병 예방 접종. **2** a method of keeping milk from spoiling. 저온 살균법. [*Pasteur*]

pas·teur·i·za·tion [pæ̀stərizéiʃən, -tʃə-] *n.* Ⓤ the method of pasteurizing. 저온 살균법.

pas·teur·ize [pǽstəràiz, -tʃə-] *vt.* (P6) heat and suddenly cool (milk, etc.) to destroy harmful bacteria. (우유 등)을 저온 살균하다.

***pas·time** [pǽstàim, pɑ́ːs-] *n.* Ⓒ anything done for amusement or recreation. 오락; 유희. [*pass, time*]

pas·tor [pǽstər, pɑ́ːs-] *n.* Ⓒ a minister in charge of a church or parish; a clergyman; a priest. 목사. [→pasture]

pas·tor·al [pǽstərəl, pɑ́ːs-] *adj.* **1** of shepherds or rural life; rustic; (of land) used for pasture. 양치기의; 전원 생활의; 시골의; (땅이) 목축에 알맞은. ¶ *a ~ life* 전원 생활 / *~ poetry (music)* 전원시(음악). **2** of a priest or his duties. 목사의. ¶ *a ~ staff* 목장(牧杖)《주교가 가지는 지팡이》. — *n.* Ⓒ a poem, play, picture, etc. on rural life. 전원시; 전원극; 목가; 전원화(畫).

***pas·try** [péistri] *n.* (*pl.* **-tries**) Ⓤ paste mixed with flour, oil and water and baked in an oven; piecrust; Ⓤ 《*collectively*》 things made of pastry; Ⓒ one of these things. 가루반죽; 페이스트리; 파이 껍질; 가루반죽으로 만든 과자. [→paste]

pas·tur·age [pǽstʃuridʒ, pɑ́ːs-] *n.* Ⓤ **1** grass used as food for cattle. 목초. **2** grassland for grazing; pasture. 목장. [↓]

:pas·ture [pǽstʃər, pɑ́ːs-] *n.* **1** Ⓤ land on which cattle can feed; Ⓒ a piece of land of this kind. 목장; 목초지. **2** Ⓤ grass used as food for cattle. 목초. ¶ *These lands afford good ~.* 이 지역은 질 좋은 목초를 산출한다.
— *vt.* (P6) **1** put (cattle, sheep, etc.) out to feed in a pasture. (가축)을 방목(放牧)하다. **2** (of cattle, etc.) feed on (grass, etc.). (가축이 목초)를 뜯어먹다.
— *vi.* (P1) feed on growing grass. 풀을 먹다. [L. *pasco* feed]

past·y[1] [péisti] *adj.* (**past·i·er, past·i·est**) **1** like paste. 풀 같은. **2** (of the complexion, etc.) pale. (안색 등이) 창백한. [→paste]

pas·ty[2] [pǽsti, pɑ́ːsti] *n.* ⒸⓊ a pie, esp. a meat pie. 고기파이. [↑]

***pat**[1] [pæt] *v.* (**pat·ted, pat·ting**) *vt.* (P6,13) strike (something) gently with something flat; tap (someone's shoulder, etc.) with the hand, often as a sign of sympathy or affection. …을 가볍게 두드리다(치다); 토닥이다《애정·위안 따위의 표시》. ¶ ~ *someone on the back* (*head, shoulder*) 아무의 등을(머리를, 어깨를) 가볍게 치다 / *He patted the dog with his hand.* 손으로 개를 토닥거렸다.

— *vi.* (P1) **1** walk or run with a patting sound. 가벼운 발소리를 내며 걷다(뛰다). **2** strike gently or lightly. 가볍게 두드리다(치다).

— *n.* Ⓒ **1** a light, quick blow with the hand; the light sound of this. 가볍게 두드리기; 그 소리. **2** a small mass, esp. of butter. (버터 등의) 작은 덩어리. [E.]

pat² [pæt] *adj.* suitable; apt; timely. 적절한; 꼭 맞는. ¶ *a ~ arrival* 아주 제때의 도착 / *a ~ reply* 적절한 대답.

— *adv.* **1** aptly; exactly. 적절하게; 딱 들어맞게. ¶ *The story came ~ to the occasion.* 그 얘기는 그 경우에 딱 들어맞았다. **2** readily; fluently. 즉시; 거침없이. ¶ *answer ~* 즉시 대답하다. [↑]

have (***know***) *something* (***down***) ***pat,*** 《*colloq.*》 know thoroughly. …을 완전히(철저히) 알다.

stand pat on, 《*colloq.*》 refuse to change (one's plans, purposes, etc.). …을 굽히지 않다; 버티다. ¶ *I'm going to stand ~ on what I said before.* 먼저 한 말을 번복할 생각은 조금도 없다.

:patch [pætʃ] *n.* Ⓒ **1** a small piece of cloth, etc. put on to mend a hole. (깁는 데 쓰는) 헝겊 조각. **2** a piece of plaster put over a cut or wound; a pad worn to protect a hurt eye. (상처에 대는) 반창고; 안대. **3** a small plot of ground. 작은 땅뙈기; 한 구획. ¶ *a cabbage ~* (한 뙈기의) 배추밭; 남새밭. **4** a small spot different from the rest in color, appearance, etc. 얼룩; 반점. ¶ *a ~ of brown on the skin* 살갗의 갈색 반점 / *a ~ of sunlight on the floor* 마루에 비친 햇살의 얼룩무늬.

not a patch on, 《*colloq.*》 not equal to someone; very inferior to (someone). …와는 비교가 안 되는; 턱없이 열등한.

strike a bad patch, 《*colloq.*》 experience a period of bad luck or difficulties. 한동안 고초를 겪다.

— *vt.* (P6,7) **1** put a patch or patches on (something); mend (something) with patches. …에 헝겊을 대다(대고 깁다); …을 덧대어 고치다(수선하다). **2** serve as a patch for. (…이) …을 깁는 재료로 쓰이다. **3** make, mend or put together roughly or hastily. 일시적으로 서둘러 만들다(고치다). ¶ *~ up a costume for a play* 서둘러 무대 의상을 만들다. [E.]

patch up, settle (a quarrel, etc.). (분쟁 등)을 수습하다.

patch·work [pǽtʃwə̀ːrk] *n.* ⒸⓊ **1** a fancywork made of pieces of cloth of different colors. 쪽모이 세공《색깔이 다른 헝겊 조각을 여러 모양으로 기워 맞춘 것》. ¶ *a ~ quilt* 쪽모이 누비 이불. **2** anything like this. 위와 같은 것《쪽모이 세공품》. ¶ *a ~ of fields and woods* 쪽모이 같은 밭과 숲들. **3** a rough and disorderly mixture; a jumble. 그러모은 잡동사니.

patch·y [pǽtʃi] *adj.* (**patch·i·er, patch·i·est**) made up of patches; not regular; uneven. 기워맞춘; 그러모은; 불규칙한. ¶ *His knowledge is ~.* 그의 지식은 단편적이다.

pate [peit] *n.* Ⓒ 《*colloq.*》 the head; brains. 머리; 두뇌. ¶ *a bald ~* 대머리. [M.E.]

·pat·ent [pǽtənt, péit-] *n.* Ⓒ an official license giving the sole right to make or sell a new invention; an official document granting such a right; an invention that is patented. 특허(권); 전매 특허증; 특허품. ¶ *apply for a ~* 특허를 신청하다 / *get* (*take out, obtain*) *a ~ for* (*on*) *an invention* 발명품의 특허를 얻다.

— *vt.* (P6) get a patent for (a new invention). …의 전매 특허를 얻다.

— *adj.* **1** given or protected by a patent. 전매 특허의. ¶ *a ~ medicine* 전매 특허약. **2** evident; plain. 명백한; 뻔한. ¶ *a ~ fact* 명백한 사실 / *It is ~ that he hates you.* 그는 분명히 너를 증오하고 있다. **3** open to the public. 공개된. **4** 《*colloq.*》 new, clever and useful; cleverly made or done. 신기한; 신안(新案)의. ¶ *I've got a ~ way of cording a box.* 내 상자 꾸리는 방법은 독특하다. [L. *pateo* be open]

pat·ent·ee [pæ̀təntíː, pèi-] *n.* Ⓒ a person who holds a patent. 특허권자.

patent leather [⌐-⌐-] *n.* leather with a hard, smooth, glossy surface, usu. black. (검정) 에나멜 가죽.

patent medicine [⌐-⌐--] *n.* medicine that is patented. 특허 의약품; 매약(賣藥).

pa·ter [péitər] *n.* Ⓒ 《Brit. *colloq.*》 father. 아버지; 부친(cf. *mater*). [L. =father]

pa·ter·nal [pətə́ːrnəl] *adj.* **1** of or like a father; fatherly. 아버지의; 아버지다운. ¶ *~ care* 아버지로서의 보살핌 / *~ love* 부성애(父性愛). **2** on the father's side of the family. 아버지쪽의; 부계(父系)의. ¶ *a ~ grandmother* 친할머니. **3** received or inherited from a father. 부조 전래(父祖傳來)의. [↑]

pa·ter·ni·ty [pətə́ːrnəti] *n.* Ⓤ **1** the state of being a father; fatherhood. 아버지임; 부성(父性). **2** paternal origin. 부계(父系). ¶ *King Arthur's ~ was unknown.* 아서왕의 부계는 불명했다. **3** origin. 기원.

pat·er·nos·ter [pǽtərnɑ̀ːstər / -nɔ̀s-] *n.* Ⓒ the Lord's Prayer, esp. in Latin. (특히 라틴어의) 주기도문. [L =Our Father]

:path [pæθ, pɑːθ] *n.* Ⓒ (*pl.* **paths** [pæðs, pæðz / pɑːðz]) **1** a way made by the footsteps of men or animals; a foot-path. (작은) 길; 소로; 인도; 보도. **2** a line along which a person or thing moves; a course. 통로; 진로. ¶ *the ~ of the moon* 달의 궤도 / *the ~ of a bird in the air* 하늘의 새가 다니는 길. **3** 《*fig.*》 a course of conduct or action. 행로; 방향. ¶ *a ~ to success* 성공에의 길. [E.]

˙pa·thet·ic [pəθétik] *adj.* arousing sympathy and pity; pitiful. 애처로운; 슬픈; 감상적인. [Gk. *paskhō* suffer]

pa·thet·i·cal·ly [pəθétikəli] *adv.* in a pathetic manner. 애처롭게; 연민의 정이 날 만큼.

path·find·er [pǽθfàindər, pɑ́:θ-] *n.* Ⓒ a person who finds or makes a path or way where none had existed; an explorer. 개척자; 탐험자. [*path*]

path·less [pǽθlis, pɑ́:θ-] *adj.* having no paths; untrodden. 길이 없는; 전인 미답의.

path·o·log·i·cal [pæ̀θəlɑ́dʒikəl / -lɔ́dʒ-] *adj.* **1** of pathology. 병리학의. ¶ *~ studies* 병리학 연구. **2** due to disease. 질병의; 병적인. ¶ *a ~ condition of the blood cells* 혈구의 병적 상태. [↓]

pa·thol·o·gy [pəθɑ́lədʒi / -θɔ́l-] *n.* Ⓤ **1** the science which deals with the causes and nature of diseases. 병리학. **2** all the conditions, processes, or results of a particular disease. 병리; 병상(病狀). [→pathetic]

pa·thos [péiθɑs / -θɔs] *n.* Ⓤ the quality in something spoken, written, etc. that arouses a feeling of pity or sadness. 페이소스; 파토스《언어·작품 등에서 연민의 정을 자아내는 힘》. [→pathetic]

path·way [pǽθwèi, pɑ́:θ-] *n.* Ⓒ a path. 작은 길; 소로. [*path*]

-pa·thy [-pəθi] *suf.* feeling; disease; treatment of disease. '감정, 고통, 요법'의 뜻. [→pathos]

:pa·tience [péiʃəns] *n.* Ⓤ **1** the state, ability, or fact of being patient. 인내(력); 참을성; 끈기(opp. impatience). ¶ *have ~ with* …을 참다 / *lose (one's) ~ with* …을 참을 수 없게 되다; …에 분통이 터지다 / *A cat shows ~ by watching a mousehole.* 고양이는 쥐구멍을 끈기 있게 지킨다. **2** a card game played by one person. 페이션스《혼자 하는 카드놀이의 하나》. [↓]

be out of patience with, be no longer able to endure. …에 더는 참을 수 없게 되다.

have no patience with, be unable to permit or bear. …을 참지 못하다.

the patience of Job, patience without end. (욥과 같은) 대단한 인내심.

:pa·tient [péiʃənt] *adj.* enduring pain, hardship, etc. without complaint. 잘 참는; 인내심이 강한; 끈기 있는(opp impatient). ¶ *be ~ with* 〔*toward*〕 *a troublesome person* 말썽 많은 사람을 참을성 있게 대하다 / *be ~ of difficulties* 어려움을 잘 견디다 / *a ~ worker.* —*n.* Ⓒ a sick person receiving medical treatment. 환자(cf. *invalid*[1]). [→passion]

pa·tient·ly [péiʃəntli] *adv.* in a patient manner. 참을성 있게; 끈기 있게.

pat·i·na [pǽtənə] *n.* **1** a kind of green film on the surface of old bronze. 동녹(銅綠); 녹청(綠青). **2** fine gloss produced by age of old woodwork, furniture, etc. (오랜 가구 따위의) 반들반들한 윤; 고색(古色). [It.]

pa·ti·o [pǽtiou, pɑ́:-] *n.* 《Sp.》 an inner court or yard open to the sky next to a house. 안뜰.

pa·tri·arch [péitriɑ̀:rk] *n.* Ⓒ **1** a father and head of a family or tribe. 가장; 족장(族長). **2** an old and respected man. 원로(元老); 장로. ¶ *a village ~* 마을의 장로. **3** a bishop in the early Christian church. (초기 기독교의) 주교. [Gk. *patēr* father, *arkhō* rule]

pa·tri·ar·chal [pèitriɑ́:rkəl] *adj.* **1** of a patriarch; worthy of respect. 가장〔족장〕의; 존경할 만한. **2** ruled by a patriarch. 가장〔족장〕이 지배하는.

pa·tri·cian [pətríʃən] *n.* Ⓒ **1** a nobleman of ancient Rome. (고대 로마의) 귀족 (opp. plebeian). **2** an aristocrat. (일반적으로) 귀족. —*adj.* of the patricians; aristocratic. 귀족의; 귀족적인. [→pater]

pat·ri·mo·ni·al [pæ̀trəmóuniəl / -mə́-] *adj.* of a patrimony. 조상 전래의; 세습의. [↓]

pat·ri·mo·ny [pǽtrəmòuni / -mə-] *n.* Ⓒ (*pl.* **-nies**) **1** property given by one's father or ancestors. 세습 재산. **2** property belonging to a church, monastery, or convent. 교회〔수도원〕 재산. [→pater]

˙pa·tri·ot [péitriət / pǽtriət] *n.* Ⓒ a person who shows great love for his country. 애국자. [↑]

˙pa·tri·ot·ic [pèitriɑ́tik / pæ̀triɔ́tik] *adj.* having the qualities of a patriot. 애국적인.

˙pa·tri·ot·ism [péitriətìzəm / pǽt-] *n.* Ⓤ the feelings and qualities of a patriot. 애국심.

pa·trol [pətróul] *vi., vt.* (**-trolled, -trol·ling**) (P1; 6) **1** go to (a district or section) regularly and repeatedly for watching or guarding. (…을) 순찰〔순시〕하다. ¶ *The police was patrolling the street.* 경찰이 거리를 순찰하고 있었다. **2** go about; march through. (…을) 무리지어 돌아다니다; 행진하다. ¶ *Bands of unemployed patrolled the town.* 실업자 무리들이 시가지를 누비고 다녔다.

—*n.* **1** Ⓤ the act of patrolling. 순찰; 순시. **2** Ⓒ a person or persons who patrol. 순시자; 순찰병. **3** Ⓒ a group of soldiers, ships, airplanes, etc. sent out for guarding and for getting information about the enemy. 척후; 초계함〔기〕. ¶ *a ~ boat* 초계정. **4** Ⓒ a group of boy scouts. 보이스카웃의 분대. [F. *patrouiller*]

pa·trol·man [pətróulmən] *n.* Ⓒ (*pl.* **-men** [-mən]) a man, esp. a policeman, who patrols. 순시인; 순찰 경관.

·**pa·tron** [péitrən] *n.* Ⓒ **1** a person who gives support to someone. 후원자; 패트런. ¶ *a ~ of the arts.* **2** a regular customer. 단골. **3** a guardian saint or god; a patron saint. 수호 성인; 수호신. [→pater]

pa·tron·age [péitrənidʒ, pǽt-] *n.* Ⓤ **1** support or encouragement given by a patron. 후원; 찬조. ¶ *under the ~ of* …의 후원 아래. **2** regular business given by customers. (상점 등에 대한 손님의) 애고(愛顧); 단골. **3** a patronizing manner. 보호자인 체하는 태도; 생색내기. ¶ *with an air of ~* 은혜라도 베풀 듯이. **4** 《sometimes *contempt.*》 the right to appoint people to important positions, esp. without regard to their ability. (관직 등의) 임명〔서임〕권. ¶ *the ~ of a Congressman* 국회 의원의 관직 임명권.

pa·tron·ess [péitrənis] *n.* Ⓒ a woman patron. patron 의 여성형.

pa·tron·ize [péitrənàiz, pǽt-] *vt.* (P6) **1** act as a patron toward (someone); support; protect. …을 후원〔보호〕하다. **2** be a regular customer of (a shop, etc.). …을 단골로 하다. ¶ *a poorly patronized store* 단골이 적은 가게. **3** treat (someone) as an inferior; treat in a condescending way. …을 아랫사람 취급하다; …에 생색내다. ¶ *We dislike having anybody ~ us.* 선심 쓰는 체하는 사람은 못마땅하다. [→pater]

pat·ter[1] [pǽtər] *vi.* (P1,2A) make sound with rapid taps of the feet. 토닥토닥〔후두두〕 소리가 나다. ¶ *The rain patters on the glass.* 빗방울이 유리창에 후드득거린다 / *The children ~ about the house.* 아이들이 요란하게 집 안을 뛰어다닌다. — *vt.* (P6) cause (something) to make a pattering sound. …에 후두두〔또닥또닥〕 소리를 내다. — *n.* Ⓒ a series of rapid taps. 위의 소리들. [→pat]

pat·ter[2] [pǽtər] *n.* **1** Ⓤ rapid and easy talk. 빠르게 하는 말; 수다. ¶ *a comedian's* 〔*magician's*〕 *~* 코미디언〔요술사〕의 재게 지껄이는 말. **2** Ⓤ the particular dialect or slang of a class or group. 은어. ¶ *thieves' ~* 도둑들의 은어. — *vt., vi.* (P6; 1) talk rapidly with little meaning. 건성으로 빠르게 지껄이다. ¶ *~ prayers.* [*pateruoster*]

:**pat·tern** [pǽtərn] *n.* Ⓒ **1** a fine example meant to be followed. 본보기; 모범. ¶ *a ~ of virtue* 〔*industry*〕 덕〔근면〕의 귀감. **2** an arrangement of forms, figures, colors, etc. used in decoration; a design. 무늬; 도안《장식적인》. ¶ *the patterns of wallpaper* 〔*carpets, rugs, cups*〕 벽지〔양탄자, 컵〕의 무늬 / *the frost ~ on the window* 유리창에 난 성에 무늬. **3** a model or shape that serves as a guide in constructing anything. 형(型); 본; 양식. ¶ *Mary used a paper ~ in cutting out her new dress.* 메리는 새 옷을 마르는데 종이 옷본을 썼다. **4** a habit or a way of acting that does not change. (변하지 않는) 양식; 습성; 형(型). ¶ *the migration ~ of the swallow* 제비들의 이주 습성 / *the behavior patterns of teenagers,* 10 대들의 행동 양식.
— *vt.* (P6,13) **1** decorate (something) with a pattern. …에 무늬를 넣다〔만들다〕. ¶ *a carpet patterned with flower* 꽃무늬를 넣은 카펫. **2** make or do (something) in imitation of a model. …을 본뜨다; 모방하다. ¶ *~ oneself after one's mother* 어머니를 본뜨다 / *~ a dress upon* 〔*after*〕 *a model* 본에 따라 옷을 짓다. [→patron]

pat·ty [pǽti] *n.* ⒸⓊ (*pl.* **-ties**) a small pie containing meat, etc. 작은 고기 파이. [F. *pate*]

pau·ci·ty [pɔ́:səti] *n.* Ⓤ smallness of number or quantity; lack; less than is needed. 소수; 소량; 결핍; 부족. [L. *paucus* scanty]

Paul [pɔ:l] *n.* a man's name. 남자 이름.

Paul·ine [pɔ́:lain] *n.* a woman's name. 여자 이름.

paunch [pɔ:ntʃ] *n.* Ⓒ the belly; the stomach. 배; 위(胃). [L. *pantex*]

pau·per [pɔ́:pər] *n.* Ⓒ a person supported by charity; a very poor person. 극빈자; 피구호 대상자; 빈민. [L. =poor]

pau·per·ism [pɔ́:pərìzəm] *n.* Ⓤ poverty; 《*collectively*》 paupers. 빈곤; 빈민.

pau·per·ize [pɔ́:pəràiz] *vt.* (P6) bring (someone) to the state of being a pauper; make (someone) very poor. …을 생활 보호 대상자로 하다; 가난하게 만들다.

:**pause** [pɔ:z] *n.* Ⓒ **1** a short period during which work or speaking is ceased; a stop; a rest. 휴지(休止); 중지. ¶ *make a ~* 쉬다; 한숨 돌리다 / *a ~ in the wind* 바람의 잠시 멎음 / *He made a short ~ and then went on reading.* 그는 잠시 멈췄다가 계속 읽어나갔다. **2** hesitation; delay. 주저; 망설임. **3** 《mus.》 a sign (𝄐 or 𝄑) over or under a note showing that the note is to be prolonged. 연장 기호; 늘임표.
— *vi.* (P1,3) **1** make a pause; stop for a time. 멈추다; 잠시 정지하다. ¶ *The dog paused when he heard me.* 개는 내 소리를 듣고 멈칫섰다. **2** 《*on, upon*》 hesitate; linger. 망설이다. [Gk. *pauō* stop]

·**pave** [peiv] *vt.* (P6) cover (a road, street, etc.) with stones, asphalt, etc. (길)을 포장하다. [L. *pavio* ram]
pave the way for, prepare for (something); make (something) smooth or easy. …의 길을 열다; …을 가능하게〔쉽게〕 하다. ¶ *Einstein's theory paved the way for the atomic bomb.* 아인슈타인 이론은 원자탄 제조를 가능하게 만들었다.

·**pave·ment** [péivmənt] *n.* **1** Ⓤ the paved surface. 포장면(面). **2** Ⓤ material used in paving. 포장 재료. **3** Ⓒ 《Brit.》 a paved path for foot-passengers. 보도(步道); 인도(cf. 《U.S.》 *sidewalk*).

·**pa·vil·ion** [pəvíljən] *n.* Ⓒ **1** a large tent.

대형 천막. **2** a light and usu. open building used for shelter, performances or exposition. 가건물; 연예장(演藝場); 전시관. **3** a part of a building higher and more decorated than the rest. 누각; 정자. **4** one of a group of buildings forming a hospital. 병동(病棟). [L. *papilio*]

pav·ing [péiviŋ] *n.* Ⓤ pavement; material for pavement. 포장(鋪裝); 포장 재료. [→pave]

:paw [pɔː] *n.* Ⓒ **1** a soft foot of a four-footed animal. (개·고양이 등의 발톱 있는) 발 (cf. *pad, hoof*). **2** 《*colloq.*》 a human hand. (사람의) 손. ¶ *Don't put your dirty paws on me.* 그 더러운 손을 내게 대지 마. —*vt.* (P6) **1** (of animals) touch roughly or beat (something) with the forepaw. …을 앞발로 할퀴다[치다]. ¶ *The cat pawed the mouse she had caught.* 고양이는 잡은 쥐를 앞발로 쳤다 / *The horse pawed the air.* 말은 앞다리를 공중에 쳐들고 내흔들었다. **2** 《*colloq.*》 (of persons) handle wildly or awkwardly. …을 거칠게[서투르게] 다루다. [F.]

pawl [pɔːl] *n.* Ⓒ 《mech.》 a short iron bar on the teeth of a wheel to prevent the wheel from turning back. 톱니멈춤쇠《톱니바퀴의 역회전을 막는》. —*vt.* (P6) secure (a wheel, etc.) with a pawl. …에 톱니멈춤쇠를 걸다. [Du.]

pawn[1] [pɔːn] *vt.* (P6) leave (something valuable) in return for the right to borrow money. …을 전당잡히다. —*n.* **1** Ⓒ something left with a lender of money. 저당물. **2** Ⓤ the state of something being pawned. 저당; 저당잡힘. ¶ *put a ring in* ~ 반지를 저당잡히다 / *take* [*redeem*] *out of* ~ 저당물을 찾다. [F. *pan*]

pawn[2] [pɔːn] *n.* Ⓒ **1** 《chess》 the least valuable piece in the game of chess. (체스의) 졸. **2** 《*fig.*》 an unimportant person used by others for their own purposes as a cat's-paw. (남의) 앞잡이. [L. *pedo* foot-soldier]

pawn·bro·ker [pɔ́ːnbròukər] *n.* Ⓒ a person whose business is to lend money on goods left with him. 전당포 주인. [→pawn[1]]

pawn·shop [pɔ́ːnʃɑ̀p / -ʃɔ̀p] *n.* Ⓒ a pawnbroker's shop. 전당포.

pawn ticket [⌐∸] *n.* a ticket for goods in pawn. 전당표.

:pay [pei] *v.* (**paid**) *vt.* (P6,7,13,14) **1** ⓐ give (someone) money in return for goods or services; give (money) in return for goods or services. …에 돈을 지불하다; (돈)을 치르다. ¶ ~ *him money* = ~ *money to him* 그에게 돈을 치르다 / ~ *cash for one's purchases* 산 물건 값으로 현찰을 주다 / ~ *20 pounds for a room* 방세로 20 파운드를 내다 / ~ *the doctor* 치료비를 내다 / *We are paid by the day* [*month*]. 우리는 일당[월급]을 받고 있다 / ~ *one's servant* 하인에게 삯을 주다 / *You must* ~ *fifty cents to ride the bus.* 버스 요금으로 50 센트를 내야 한다 / *He paid a dime for the ice cream.* 아이스크림 값으로 10 센트를 줬다. ⓑ put or place (money) intrust; deposit. (은행 구좌 등)에 불입하다; 예입[입금]하다. ¶ ~ *money in a bank* [*into one's account*] 은행[자기 구좌]에 불입하다 / ~ *money into the Exchequer* 국고에 납입하다. **2** give (someone) money owed or due; give back (a debt). (빚 따위)를 갚다; 상환하다. ¶ ~ *one's debts* 빚을 갚다 / ~ *a tax* 세금을 내다 / ~ *a lawyer's fee* [*servant's wages*] 변호료[하인 급료]를 치르다. **3** give or offer (a service, a visit, etc.); render. (방문 등)을 하다; (경의 등)을 표하다. ¶ ~ *a visit to* [*on*] *someone* = ~ *someone a visit* 아무를 방문하다 / ~ *attention to what she says* 그녀의 말을 주의깊게 듣다 / ~ *one's respects to someone* 아무에게 경의를 표하다 / *Please* ~ *my compliments to her.* 그녀에게 안부를 전해 주시오. **4** 《*back, out*》 return (someone or something) for favors or hurts; suffer (a penalty, etc.). …에 보복[앙갚음]하다; (벌·고통 등)을 감수하다; 받다. ¶ *He paid her insults in kindness.* 그녀의 모욕에 친절로써 응했다 / *I paid him back blow for blow.* 나를 치기에 나도 그를 갈겼다 / *I will* ~ *him out for all the harm he has done.* 그자가 나를 해친 만큼 몽땅 안겨 줄 테다 / *The one who does wrong must* ~ *the penalty.* 잘못을 한 자는 벌을 받아야 한다. **5** be profitable to (someone); give (profit, interest, etc.). …에게 이익을 주다; …의 벌이가 되다. ¶ *Farming does not* ~ *me.* 농사는 수지가 안 맞는다 / *That stock paid 5% last year.* 그 주식은 지난 해 5%의 이익이 났다 / *The business is just beginning to* ~. 장사가 이제야 이문이 남게 됐다. —*vi.* (P1,3) **1** give money in return for goods or services; give what is owed. 지불하다; 갚다. ¶ ~ *for a book* 책값을 치르다. **2** (of business, etc.) be profitable. (일 등이) 이익이 되다; 벌이가 되다. ¶ *This profession pays well.* 이 직업은 벌이가 괜찮다 / *It pays to be honest.* 정직하면 보답이 있다. **3** 《*for*》 suffer a penalty; make up. 벌을 받다; 벌충하다. ¶ *You must* ~ *for your rudeness.* 건방지다가는 혼날 줄 알아라.

hell to pay = the devil to pay.

pay away, **a**) spend. 돈을 쓰다. **b**) = pay out c).

pay back, **a**) return borrowed money. 빚을 갚다. **b**) give the same treatment as received. 앙갚음하다.

pay down, **a**) pay in cash on the spot. 맞돈을 내다. **b**) pay a part of the payment at the time of purchase, and the remainder later. (월부의) 계약금을 치르다.

pay in, put (money, etc.) into a bank, etc. (돈)을 은행에 입금하다.

pay in kind, pay in goods instead of money. 현물로 갚다.

pay off, **a**) pay (a debt) completely. (빚)을

다 갚다. **b**) give (someone) his wages and discharge (him). 급료를 주고 해고하다. **c**) 《*colloq.*》 result in success; be fully effective. 뜻대로 잘되다; 성과를 거두다. ¶ *The bet on the horse paid off!* 그 말에 걸었더니 들어맞았다.

pay out, **a**) punish (someone) for what he has done. …에 보복하다; 혼내주다. **b**) give out (money). (돈)을 치르다. **c**) 《naut.》 let out (a rope, etc.) by making it looser. (밧줄)을 늦추어 풀어내다.

pay up, pay (a debt) completely or on time. (빚 등)을 모조리 갚다; 기한내에 지불하다.

pay one's way, live without borrowing money. 빚없이 살다.

the devil to pay, a great trouble; commotion. 큰 말썽(거리); 대혼란. ¶ *If the facts are made public, there will be the devil* 〔*hell*〕 *to* ~. 그 일이 알려지면 여간 시끄럽게 되지 않을 게다.

— *n.* Ⓤ **1** the act of paying; money given for things or work; salary or wages. 지불; 임금; 급료. ¶ *What is the* ~*?* 보수는 얼마냐. **2** a return for favors or harms; reward or punishment. 보복; 보수; 대가. [L. *paco* appease]

in someone's pay =in the pay of. ¶ *He has six men in his* ~. 고용인이 여섯 사람 있다.

in the pay of, employed and paid by. …에 고용되어. ¶ *He was in the* ~ *of the firm.* 한때 그 회사에 있었다.

pay·a·ble [péiəbəl] *adj.* **1** that must or can be paid. 지불해야 할; 지불할 수 있는. ¶ ~ *at the bank* 은행 지불의 / *bills* ~ 지불 어음(cf. *bills receivable*). **2** that pays well; profitable. 채산이 맞는; 이익이 나는.

pay·day [péidèi] *n.* ⓊⒸ the day on which a salary is paid. 월급날.

pay dirt [´ ˌ] *n.* **1** 《U.S.》 earth found to contain enough metal to be worth mining. 채산이 맞는〔유망한〕 광산. **2** 《U.S. *colloq.*》 any source of success or wealth; a valuable or useful discovery. 벌이가 되는 일; 노다지. ¶ *hit* ~ 노다지를 찾아내다.

pay·ee [peií:] *n.* Ⓒ a person to whom money is paid or is to be paid. (어음 등의) 수취인.

pay·er [péiər] *n.* Ⓒ a person who pays or is to pay money. 지불인.

pay·mas·ter [péimæ̀stər, -mὰ:s-] *n.* Ⓒ a person whose job is to give out pay. 회계(담당자).

pay·ment [péimənt] *n.* ⓊⒸ **1** the act of paying. 지불. ¶ ~ *by installment* 분할불 / ~ *in advance* 선불 / ~ *in part* 내입(內入); 일부 선불 / ~ *in full* 전액 지불; 청산 / ~ *in kind* 현물 지급. **2** the money or the amount of money paid. 지불액. **3** reward; punishment. 보수; 징벌 ¶ *Baby's good health is* ~ *enough for me.* 아기가 건강해서 내게 큰 보람이다.

pay·off [péiɔ̀(:)f, -ὰf] *n.* **1** a paying of wages. 급료 지불. **2** the time of such payment. 급료 지불일. **3** returns from an enterprise, specification, etc. 이득; 이익. **4** (of a story, situation, etc.) the climax. (이야기 등의) 클라이맥스.

pay packet [´ ˌ–] *n.* 《Brit.》 an envelope or packet containing weekly pay. 급료 봉투.

pay·roll [péiròul] *n.* 《U.S.》 a list of employees and the salary of each; the total amount of their salaries. 임금 대장; (종업원의) 급료 총액.

pay sheet [´ ˌ] *n.* =payroll.

pea [pi:] *n.* Ⓒ (*pl.* **peas** or **pease**) a plant of the bean family; the seed of this plant, used as food. 완두(콩). [→pease (false singular)]

as like as two peas, exactly alike. 빼쏜; 흡사한.

:peace [pi:s] *n.* Ⓤ **1** freedom from war. 평화(opp. war). ¶ *decide between war and* ~ 전쟁과 평화 양단간 결정을 하다. **2** 《usu. *P-*》 an agreement to end war. 강화(조약). ¶ *the Peace of Paris of 1815,* 1815년의 파리 강화 조약 / *a* ~ *conference* 평화 회담. **3** 《usu. *the* ~》 the public order for keeping a quiet and safe state. 치안; 공안. ¶ *a breach of the* ~ 치안 방해 / *keep the* ~ 치안을 유지하다 / *the* ~ *of the country* 나라의 치안. **4** a quiet state; calmness. 평온; 고요. ¶ *disturb the* ~ *of the household* 집안에 분란을 일으키다 / ~ *of mind* 마음의 평정. [L. *pax*]

at peace, free from war; living in harmony; in a quiet state. 평화롭게; 사이좋게; 마음 편히.

break the peace, cause civil disorder, etc. 치안을 어지럽히다.

hold 〔***keep***〕 ***one's peace,*** keep silent. 침묵을 지키다.

keep the peace, obey the laws and avoid civil disorder. 치안을 유지하다.

make peace, stop fighting and come to an agreement. 화해〔강화〕하다.

make one's peace with, be friendly with someone again after a quarrel. …와 화해〔사화(私和)〕하다.

peace·a·ble [pí:səbəl] *adj.* **1** loving peace. 평화를 사랑하는. **2** quiet; calm. 조용한; 평온한. ¶ *a* ~ *temper* 조용한 기질.

:peace·ful [pí:sfəl] *adj.* **1** calm; quiet. 조용한; 고요한. ¶ *a* ~ *death* 편안한 임종. **2** loving peace; free from war. 평화를 사랑하는; 전쟁을 떠난. ¶ ~ *uses of atomic energy* 원자력의 평화적 이용. ● **peace·ful·ness** [-nis] *n.*

peace·ful·ly [pí:sfəli] *adv.* in a peaceful manner. 평화롭게; 조용하게.

peace·mak·er [pí:smèikər] *n.* Ⓒ a person who makes or bring about peace. (분쟁) 조정자; 중재인.

peace·time [pí:stàim] *n.* Ⓤ the period free form war. 평시; 평화시(opp. wartime).

¶ *in* ~ 평(화)시에 / ~ *industries* 평시〔평화〕 산업. — *adj.* of peacetime. 평(화)시의.

:peach[1] [piːtʃ] *n.* **1** Ⓒ a sweet, juicy fruit with a white or yellowish pink skin; the tree bearing this fruit. 복숭아; 그 나무. **2** Ⓤ the color of a peach, usu. a soft, yellowish pink. 복숭아빛. **3** 《*sl.*》 a fresh, beautiful young girl. 발랄하고 예쁜 소녀. — *adj.* yellowish-pink. 복숭아 빛의. [L. *Persicus* Persian]

peach[2] [piːtʃ] *vi.* (P3) 《*against, upon*》 《*sl.*》 inform against (another). 밀고하다. [→impeach]

pea·chick [píːtʃik] *n.* a young peafowl. 공작 새끼. [→peacock]

peachy [píːtʃi] *adj.* (**peach·i·er; peach·i·est**) **1** like a peach. 복숭아 같은. **2** 《U.S. *sl.*》 excellent; fine. 훌륭한; 멋진. [→peach[1]]

·pea·cock [píːkɑ̀k / -kɔ̀k] *n.* Ⓒ (*pl.* **-cocks** or 《*collectively*》 **-cock**) a large bird with beautiful green, blue, and gold feathers. 공작. ¶ *proud as a* ~ 뻐기는; 우쭐거리는 / *play the* ~ 뻐기다. — *vi.* (P1) walk about proudly, throwing out one's feet like a peacock; give oneself airs; show off. 거들먹거리며 걷다; 뻐기다; 허세를 부리다. [L. *pavo*+cock]

pea·fowl [píːfàul] *n.* Ⓒ a peacock or peahen. 공작《암수 모두》. [↑]

pea green [ˊ ˊ] *n.* a bright, light-green color. 황록색. [→pea]

pea·hen [píːhèn] *n.* Ⓒ a female peafowl. 공작《암컷》. [→peacock]

:peak[1] [piːk] *n.* Ⓒ **1** ⓐ the pointed top of a mountain or hill. 산꼭대기. ⓑ a mountain that stands alone. 홀로 우뚝한 산; 고봉(孤峰). **2** the highest point of development, activity, etc. 절정; 최고점. ¶ *the* ~ *hour of traffic volume* 교통량의 피크 때; 러시아워 / *the* ~ *of happiness* / *Sales reached a new* ~. 매상이 신기록을 세웠다. **3** a pointed end or top. 뾰족한 끝. ¶ *the* ~ *of a knife* 〔*beard, roof*〕 칼끝〔수염끝; 지붕 꼭대기〕. **4** (of a cap) the front part over the eyes. (모자의) 앞챙. **5** 《naut.》 the narrow part of a ship's hold, at either end. 이물과 고물의 좁고 뾰족한 끝. — *vi.* reach a peak. 최고도〔최대치〕에 이르다. [=pike]

peak[2] [piːk] *vi.* (P1) (of a person or an animal) grow thin and weak. 여위어 가다; 살이 빠지다. [?]

peaked[1] [piːkt, -kid] *adj.* having a peak. 뾰족한. ¶ *a* ~ *roof* 〔*cap*〕 뾰족한 지붕〔모자〕. [*peak*[1]]

peak·ed[2] [píːkid] *adj.* thin, pale and weak-looking. 여윈; 수척한. ¶ *a* ~ *face* 수척한 얼굴. [*peak*[2]]

·peal [piːl] *n.* Ⓒ **1** a loud sound of gunfire, etc. (포성 등이) 울리는 소리. ¶ *a* ~ *of thunder* 천둥 소리 / *peals of laughter* 폭소. **2** a set of tuned bells; the harmoney of these bells; a chime. (음률을 맞춘) 한 벌의 종; 차임; 그 화음. ¶ *in* ~ 가락을 맞추어. — *vi.* (P1,2A) ring loudly. 울리다. — *vt.* (P6,7) cause (a bell, etc.) to ring loudly. …을 울리다. ¶ ~ (*out*) *a bell* 종을 울리다. [E.]

pe·an [píːən] *n.* =paean.

pea·nut [píːnʌ̀t] *n.* Ⓒ a nut-like seed in a hard shell. 땅콩; 피넛. [*pea*]

·pear [pɛər] *n.* Ⓒ a yellowish, juicy fruit, usu. narrower at the upper part; the tree bearing this fruit. 서양배; 서양배나무. [L. *pirum*]

:pearl [pəːrl] *n.* Ⓒ **1** a round, bright, white jewel found in a certain shellfish. 진주. ¶ *a cultured* ~ 양식 진주 / *an artificial* ~ 모조 진주. **2** something like a pearl, such as a tear. 진주 모양의 것. **3** a valuable thing; a very fine example of a class. 귀중한 것; 전형; 정화(精華). ¶ *She is a* ~ *among women.* 그녀는 전형적인 여성이다. **4** Ⓤ the color of a pearl. 진줏빛. **5** Ⓤ the shiny inside of a certain shellfish containing a pearl; a mother-of-pearl. 진주층(層); 진주모(母).

throw* 〔*cast*〕 (*one's*) *pearls before swine, offer a valuable thing to a person who cannot appreciate it. 돼지에게 진주를 던지다.

— *adj.* of, like, or having pearls. 진주 같은; 진주(색)의.

— *vt.* (P6) adorn with pearls. 진주로 장식하다. [L. *perla*]

pearl diver [ˊ ˊ—] *n.* a person who gathers pearl oysters by diving for them. 진주 캐는 사람.

pearl oyster [ˊ ˊ—] *n.* a kind of shellfish which produces pearls. 진주조개.

pearl·y [pə́ːrli] *adj.* (**pearl·i·er, pearl·i·est**) of or like a pearl; decorated with pearls. 진주의〔같은〕; 진주로 장식한. ¶ ~ *teeth* 진주같은 잇바디.

peas·ant [pézənt] *n.* Ⓒ **1** in Europe, a poor farmer or farm laborer. 농부; 소작농(小作農). ¶ ~ *labor* 농사; 농사일 / *a* ~ *girl* 농촌 소녀. **2** a rustic; a country man. 촌사람. — *adj.* of peasants. 농부의. 參考 영국·미국에는 peasant 가 없음. [→pagan]

peas·ant·ry [pézəntri] *n.* Ⓤ 《usu. *the* ~》 《*collectively,* used as *pl.*》 peasants. 소작농; 소작인 계급.

pease [piːz] *n.* pl. of **pea.**

pea·shoot·er [píːʃùːtər] *n.* Ⓒ a toy consisting of a tube through which dried peas can be shot. 콩알총. [*pea*]

pea soup [ˊ ˊ] *n.* a thick soup made from dried peas. 완두 수프.

pea·soup·er [píːsùːpər] *n.* Ⓒ 《*colloq.*》 a thick, yellow fog, esp. in London. (런던의) 황색의 짙은 안개.

peat [piːt] *n.* Ⓤ a coal-like mass made of decayed plants used for burning. 토탄(土炭) (덩어리)(cf. *turf*). [M.E.]

peb·ble [pébəl] *n.* Ⓒ **1** a small, round

stone worn smooth by water. 조약돌; 자갈. **2** a kind of agate. 마노(瑪瑙). **3** rock-crystal used for lenses. 수정(水晶)《렌즈 제조용》. —*vt.* (P6) cover (a path, etc.) with small stones. …을 자갈로 포장하다. [A.S. *papol-stan*)]

peb·bly [pébli] *adj.* having many pebbles; covered with pebbles. 자갈이 많은; 자갈투성이의. ¶ *a ~ beach.*

pec·ca·ble [pékəbəl] *adj.* tending to sin easily. 죄짓기 쉬운. [L. *pecco* sin]

peck[1] [pek] *n.* Ⓒ **1** a measure for grain equal to 2 gallons. 펙《건량 단위; 약 9리터》. ¶ *a ~ of beans* [*potatoes*]. **2** a lot; a large amount. 많음; 다량. ¶ *a ~ of worries* [*troubles*] 많은 걱정거리[골칫거리] / *a ~ of dirt* 쓰레기 더미. [F. *pek*]

peck[2] [pek] *vt.* (P6,13) **1** (of a bird) strike or pick up (something) with the beak. …을 부리로 쪼다; 쪼아 먹다. ¶ *~ something out of a hole* 구멍에서 무엇을 쪼아내다 / *A pigeon was pecking peas.* 비둘기가 완두콩을 쪼아먹고 있었다. **2** make (a hole) with the beak or a pointed tool. …을 쪼아 파다. ¶ *Woodpeckers ~ holes in trees.* **3** 《*colloq.*》 eat bit by bit. 조금씩 먹다. **4** 《*colloq.*》 kiss briefly and casually. 형식적으로 가볍게 키스하다.
—*vi.* (P3) **1** 《usu. *at*》 aim or strike at (a thing) with the beak. 부리로 쪼다. **2** strike or break (esp. the ground) with a pointed instrument. 뾰족한 것으로 (땅)을 두드리다[파다]. **3** 《*colloq.*》 《*at*》 eat only a little of; eat bit by bit. 조금씩 쪼듯 먹다(cf. *nibble*). ¶ *Because she is not feeling well today, she just pecks at her food.* 그녀는 오늘 입맛이 없어 음식을 깨지락거리기만 한다. **4** 《*colloq.*》 《usu. *at*》 find fault with repeatedly. 자꾸 탈잡다.
—*n.* Ⓒ **1** an act of pecking. 쪼기. ¶ *The hen gave me a ~.* 암탉이 나를 톡 쪼았다. **2** a hole or mark made by the act of pecking. 쪼아서 생긴 구멍[흠집]. **3** 《*colloq.*》 a quick, casual kiss. 형식적인 가벼운 키스. [→ pick]

pec·to·ral [péktərəl] *adj.* of or put on the breast or chest. 가슴의; 가슴에 다는. [L. *pectus* chest]

pec·u·late [pékjəlèit] *vi., vt.* (P1; 6) appropriate to one's own use (money or goods held in trust for others). (맡긴 돈 따위를) 횡령하다; 들어먹다(cf. *embezzle*). [→ peculiar]

pec·u·la·tion [pèkjəléiʃən] *n.* the act of peculating. 횡령; 착복.

:**pe·cu·li·ar** [pikjú:ljər] *adj.* **1** 《*to*》 belonging to one special person, thing or place; individual; special. 고유의; 독특한; 특별한. ¶ *receive ~ attention* 특별한 주의를 받다 / *my own ~ right* [*temperament*] 내 고유의 권한[체질] / *Each person's fingerprints are ~ to himself.* 사람의 지문은 사람마다 특이하다. **2** strange; unusual. 묘한; 별난. ¶ *~ ways* 별난 버릇 / *a ~ sort of man* 별난 부류의 사람 / *look ~* 이상하게 보이다 / *It is ~ that he has not come today, for he usually appears every Tuesday.* 화요일이면 나타나던 그가 오늘은 안 보이니 이상한 일이다 / *What a ~ thing to say!* 별말을 다 하는군.
—*n.* Ⓒ something belonging to one only. 사유 재산. [L. *peculium* private property (*pecu* cattle)]

pe·cu·li·ar·i·ty [pikjù:liǽrəti] *n.* (*pl.* **-ties**) **1** Ⓤ the state of being special or strange. 기묘[독특]함. ¶ *One of his peculiarities is that his two eyes are not the same color.* 그에게서 또 한 가지 묘한 것은 두 눈의 색깔이 다르다는 것이다. **2** Ⓒ a special quality; an odd quality. 버릇; 별남. ¶ *We noticed the ~ of his manner at once.* 우리는 당장 그의 별난 거동을 알아봤다.

pe·cu·li·ar·ly [pikjú:ljərli] *adv.* personally; especially; oddly. 개인적으로; 특히; 기묘하게.

pe·cu·ni·ar·y [pikjú:nièri / -njəri] *adj.* of or concerned with money. 금전(상)의. ¶ *~ affairs* [*assistance, losses*] 금전적인 문제[원조, 손실] / *~ penalty* 벌금. [L. *pecunia* money (*pecu* cattle)]

ped. pedal; pedestal.

ped·a·gog·ic [pèdəgádʒik, -góudʒ-], **-i·cal** [-ikəl] *adj.* of teachers or teaching; of pedagogy. 교육자의; 교수법의; 교육(학)의. [↓]

ped·a·gogue [pédəgàg, -gɔ̀:g] *n.* Ⓒ **1** a teacher. 선생; 교사. **2** 《*contempt.*》 a narrow-minded teacher; a pedantic person. 깐깐한[까다로운] 선생; 유식한 체하는 사람. [Gk. *pais* boy, *ago* lead]

ped·a·go·gy [pédəgòudʒi, -gàdʒi] *n.* Ⓤ the science or art of teaching. 교육학; 교수법.

ped·al [pédl] *n.* Ⓒ (of a bicycle, an organ, etc.) a device operated by the foot. 페달.
—*vt., vi.* (**-aled, -al·ing** or 《Brit.》 **-alled, -al·ling**) (P6,7; 1,2A) move or operate by a pedal or pedals; use the pedals of (something). 페달을 밟아 움직이다; …의 페달을 밟다. ¶ *He pedaled* (*his bicycle*) *slowly up the hill.* 언덕을 향해 천천히 (자전거) 페달을 밟아 올라갔다. —*adj.* **1** of the foot or feet. 발의. **2** of or operated by a pedal or pedals. 페달의. [L. *pes* foot]

ped·ant [pédənt] *n.* Ⓒ a person, esp. a teacher, who shows off his knowledge more than is necessary. 유식한 체하는 사람; 현학자(衒學者). ¶ *A ~ often makes a show of knowledge without knowing how to use it well.* 현학자는 자기 지식을 어떻게 활용할지도 모르면서 유식한 체만 한다. [It.]

pe·dan·tic [pidǽntik] *adj.* showing off one's knowledge more than is necessary. 유식한 체하는; 아는 체하는.

ped·ant·ry [pédəntri] *n.* ⓊⒸ (*pl.* **-ries**)

the act of showing off one's knowledge. 학자인 체함.

ped·dle [pédl] *vi.* (P1) **1** go from place to place selling small articles. 행상(行商)하다; 도부치다. **2** 《*fig.*》 busy oneself with useless things. 쓸데없는 일에 분주떨다. — *vt.* (P6) **1** carry (something) from place to place in order to sell them. …을 팔러 다니다. **2** sell (something) little by little. …을 조금씩 (잘라) 팔다. [? M.E. *ped* basket]

ped·dler, ped·lar [pédlər] *n.* Ⓒ a person who peddles. 행상인; 도붓장수.

ped·es·tal [pédəstl] *n.* Ⓒ **1** a base on which a column or a statue stands. (조상(彫像)의) 대좌(臺座); 기둥받침; 주각(柱脚). **2** a base or foundation for various things. 기초; 토대. [→pedal, →stall]

***put* 〔*set*〕 *someone* on a pedestal,** think someone with great admiration. …을 받들다; 존경하다.

***pe·des·tri·an** [pədéstriən] *n.* Ⓒ a person who is walking. 보행자. — *adj.* **1** going on foot; walking. 도보의; 걷는. **2** (of writing, etc.) without imagination; dull. (문체 등이) 재미가 없는; 평범한. ¶ ~ *argument* 〔*writing*〕. [→pedal]

pe·di·a·tri·cian [pìːdiətríʃən, pèd-] *n.* Ⓒ a doctor who specializes in pediatrics. 소아과 의사. [Gk. *pais* child, *iatreia* treatment]

pe·di·at·rics [pìːdiǽtriks, pèd-] *n. pl.* 《used as *sing.*》 the branch of medicine dealing with children's diseases. 소아과.

ped·i·gree [pédəgrìː] *n.* Ⓒ a list showing the line of a family; ⒸⓊ the line of a family. 계도(系圖); 족보; 가계(家系); 혈통. ¶ *a family of* ~ 명문(名門) / *a family* ~ 가계(보(譜)); 족보. — *adj.* having a known pedigree. 혈통이 좋은. ¶ ~ *cattle* 순종의 소. [L. *pes* foot, *de* of, *grus* crane; describing the arrow-mark denoting descent]

ped·i·greed [pédəgrìːd] *adj.* having a good or famous pedigree. 가문이 좋은; 혈통이 분명한.

ped·i·ment [pédəmənt] *n.* 《Gk. archit.》 Ⓒ a triangular part at the top of a house. 박공. [L.]

ped·lar [pédlər] *n.* =peddler.

pe·dom·e·ter [pidámitər / -dɔ́m-] *n.* an instrument for recording the number of steps taken and thus measuring the distance traveled. 보수계(步數計). [→pedal, -meter]

pe·dun·cle [pidʌ́ŋkəl] *n.* 《bot.》 the main stem of a flower or cluster of flowers. 꽃자루; 화경(花梗). [→pedal]

peek [piːk] *vi.* (P1,2A) look quickly and secretly. 슬쩍 들여다보다; 엿보다. — *n.* Ⓒ a quick, secret look. 엿보기. [*peep*[1]]

***peel** [piːl] *n.* Ⓤ the outer skin of fruit. (과일의) 껍질. — *vt.* (P6,7,13) **1** take the skin off (fruit, etc.). (과일)의 껍질을 벗기다. ¶ ~ *an orange* 오렌지 껍질을 까다. **2** strip off. (껍질)을 벗기다; 까다. ¶ ~ *the bark from* 〔*off*〕 *trees* 나무 껍질을 벗기다. — *vi.* (P1, 2A) come off; become bare. 벗겨지다. ¶ *The wallpaper is peeling* 〔*off*〕. 벽지가 벗겨지고 있다 / *He got sunburnt and his face peeled.* 볕에 타서 얼굴의 살갗이 벗겨졌다. [L. *pilo* strip off hair]

peel·ings [píːliŋz] *n. pl.* parts peeled off (esp. of potatoes). 벗긴 껍질《특히 감자의》.

***peep**[1] [piːp] *vi.* (P1,2A,3) **1** look through a small or narrow opening; look secretly. 훔쳐보다; 엿보다. ¶ ~ *at someone through the keyhole* 아무를 열쇠 구멍으로 들여다보다 / ~ *over a wall* 담장 너머로 엿보다. **2** come slowly or partly into view. 서서히 나타나다. ¶ *The stars were beginning to* ~ (*out*) *through the clouds.* 구름 사이로 별들이 하나 둘씩 나타나고 있었다.
— *n.* Ⓒ **1** ⓐ a secret look. 엿보기; 훔쳐보기. ¶ *take a* ~ *at something* 무엇을 슬쩍 보다 / *Let me have just one* ~ *at the letter.* 그 편지를 한번 슬쩍 보여 주게나. ⓑ a short, quick look; a limited view; a little look. 잠깐〔얼핏〕 보기. ¶ *take a* ~ *into the kitchen* 부엌을 잠깐 들여다보다 / *We can get a* ~ *at the beach from his room.* 우리는 그의 방에서 해변을 좀 내다볼 수 있다. **2** the first appearance. 첫 출현. ¶ *at the* ~ *of day* 새벽〔날 샐녘〕에. **3** Ⓒ a small hole to look through. 들여다보는 구멍〔틈새〕. [E.]

peep[2] [piːp] *n.* Ⓒ a sound made by a young bird, a mouse, etc. 삐악삐악; 짹짹《병아리·쥐 따위의 우는 소리》. — *vi.* **1** make a peep. 삐악삐악 울다; 짹짹거리다. **2** speak in a weak voice. 작은 소리로 말하다. [Imit.]

peep·er [píːpər] *n.* Ⓒ a person who looks secretly. 엿보는 사람. [→peep[1]]

peep·hole [píːphòul] *n.* Ⓒ a hole through which a person can peep. 엿보는 구멍. [↑]

:peer[1] [piər] *n.* Ⓒ **1** a person of the same rank; an equal. 동료; 대등〔동등〕한 사람. ¶ *without a* ~ 비길 데 없는 / *He is so fine a man that it would be hard to find his* ~. 그가 너무 우수한 사람이라 그에게 필적할 만한 인재를 찾기란 어렵다. **2** 《Brit.》 a person who has a title, such as a duke, a marquis, etc.; a nobleman. 귀족. **3** 《Brit.》 a person having the right to sit in the House of Lords. 상원 의원. [L. *par* equal]

:peer[2] [piər] *vi.* (P1,2A,3) **1** 《*into, at*》 look closely, as a near-sighted man does. (근시인 사람처럼) 꼼꼼히 들여다보다; 응시하다. ¶ ~ *into someone's face* 아무의 얼굴을 자세히 보다. **2** appear slightly; come into sight. 나타나다; 보이기 시작하다. ¶ *The sun was peering from behind a cloud.* 구름 사이로 해가 나타나고 있었다. [L. *paro* provide]

peer·age [píəridʒ] *n.* **1** 《*collectively*》 the

whole body of peers. 귀족(계급). **2** Ⓤⓒ the rank of a peer. 귀족의 지위. **3** ⓒ a book giving a list of the peers of a country. 귀족 명부. [*peer*[1]]

peer·ess [píəris] *n.* ⓒ **1** the wife of a peer. 귀족 부인. **2** a woman having the rank of peer in her own right. 여성 귀족.

peer·less [píərlis] *adj.* without equal; matchless. 비할 데 없는; 무쌍한. ¶ *a queen of ~ beauty* 절세의 미인; 경국지색.

peeve [pi:v] *vt.* (P6) 《usu. in *pp.*》 《*colloq.*》 make peevish; annoy. 신경질나게 하다; 화나게 만들다. [M.E.]

pee·vish [pí:viʃ] *adj.* hard to please; irritable; complaining. (사람이) 까다로운; 신경질적인; 불평이 많은. ¶ *a ~ child.* [↑]

pee·vish·ly [pí:viʃli] *adv.* in a peevish manner. 까다롭게; 뚱해서.

pee·vish·ness [pí:viʃnis] *n.* Ⓤ the state of being peevish. 까다로움.

***peg** [peg] *n.* ⓒ **1** a short piece of wood, metal, etc. used to fasten something or to hang something on; a small bolt. (나무·금속제의) 못; 쐐기못; 걸이못. ¶ *hat pegs* 모자걸이. **2** a stick used to hold the ropes of a tent; a piece of wood used to fill a hole in a cask, etc. (천막설치용) 말뚝; (통(桶) 따위의) 마개. ¶ *tent pegs* 천막 말뚝. **3** 《Brit.》 a clothes-pin. 빨래 집게. **4** 《*fig.*》 a subject or an excuse upon which a talk, argument, etc. is based. 핑계; 구실. ¶ *a ~ to hang a claim on* 요구 조건을 내거는 꼬투리 / *a good ~ to hang a sermon on* 잔소리를 시작하는 구실. **5** 《Brit. *colloq.*》 a glass of strong drink. (독한) 술 한잔. **6** 《*colloq.*》 a leg. 다리.

a square peg in a round hole* =*a round peg in a square hole, a person not fitted to his work or position. (일·지위 등의) 부적임자(者).

off the peg, 《Brit.》 (of clothes) ready-made. 기성복의.

take someone down a peg (or two), make someone humble; humiliate. …의 콧대를 꺾다; 끽 소리 못 하게 만들다.

— *v.* (**pegged, peg·ging**) *vt.* (P6,7,13) **1** put a peg into (something); hold (something) with a peg. …에 나무못을 박다; 나무못(말뚝)으로 고정시키다. ¶ *~ down a tent.* **2** fix or maintain (prices, etc.) at a certain level. (가격 등)을 안정(고정)시키다. ¶ *~ the price of beer at 1,000 won* 맥주 한 병 값을 천원으로 고정시키다. — *vi.* (P2A,3) 《*away, at*》 work hard and diligently. 열심히 일하다. [Du.]

peg at, strike or aim at with a peg. 치며 덤비다; 겨누다.

peg away, keep working patiently. 열심히 일하다. ¶ *~ away at English* 영어 공부를 착실히 하다.

peg out, **a**) mark (a boundary, etc.) with pegs. (말뚝)으로 경계를 표시하다. **b**) 《*sl.*》 come to an end; die. 끝장나다; 죽다.

Peg·a·sus [pégəsəs] *n.* **1** 《Gk. myth.》 the winged horse of the Muses. 시신(詩神) 뮤즈의 말; 페가수스. **2** Ⓤ poetic genius; poetic inspiration. 시재(詩才); 시흥(詩興). [Gk.]

〈Pegasus 1〉

peg top [⌐⌐] *n.* **1** a pear-shaped wooden top. 서양배 모양의 나무 팽이. **2** 《*pl.*》 trousers wide at the hips and narrowing to the ankle; peg top trousers. (엉덩이 부분이 넓고 밑이 좁은) 팽이 모양의 바지. [*peg*]

peign·oir [peinwá:r, ⌐—] *n.* 《F.》 a woman's dressing sack or gown. (여성용의) 화장옷; 실내복.

Pei·ping [péipíŋ] *n.* =Peking.

pe·jo·ra·tive [pidʒárətiv, -dʒɔ́:r-, pédʒə-, pídʒə-] *adj.* tending to make worse; disparaging. 퇴화적(退化的)인; 경멸적인. — *n.* a pejorative form or word. 경멸어. [L.]

Pe·king [pí:kíŋ] *n.* the capital of the People's Republic of China. 베이징; 북경.

pe·lag·ic [pəlǽdʒik] *adj.* of the ocean or the open sea. 원양(遠洋)의. ¶ *~ fishery* 원양 어업. [Gk. *pelagos* sea]

pelf [pelf] *n.* Ⓤ 《*contempt.*》 money; riches; wealth. 돈; 금전; 부(富). [F.]

pel·i·can [pélikən] *n.* ⓒ 《bird》 a large waterbird with a baglike part under its huge bill. 펠리컨. [Gk.]

Pelican State [⌐—⌐] *n.* a nickname for Louisiana. 루이지애나 주의 속칭.

pel·let [pélit] *n.* ⓒ **1** a little ball of mud, paper, bread, medicine, etc. (흙·종이·빵 등의) 작은 덩어리; 알약. **2** a small lead ball for a gun; a bullet. 소총탄. [L. *pila* ball]

pell-mell, pell mell [pélmél] *adv.* in a disorderly manner; quickly. 난잡하게; 무턱대고; 황급히. ¶ *The children dashed ~ down the beach and into the waves.* 아이들이 우르르 바닷가로 내달아 바다로 뛰어들었다. — *adj.* disorderly; headlong. 난잡한; 무모한. — *n.* ⓒⓊ disorder; hurry and confusion. 난잡; 혼란; 뒤죽박죽. [F. *pelemele*]

pel·lu·cid [pəlú:sid] *adj.* **1** very clear, like water. 투명한; 맑은. ¶ *a ~ stream* 맑은 시내. **2** (of the mind, style, etc.) easy to understand; expressed clearly. (문체 등이) 간결한; 명석한. ¶ *~ language* 간결한 언어 / *a ~ style of writing* 간결한 문체. [→per]

pelt[1] [pelt] *vt.* (P6,13) throw (something) at (something or someone); throw (objects) continuously. …에 물건을 집어던지다; …을 계속 던지다. ¶ *~ a boy with snowballs* 아이에게 눈뭉치를 던지다 / 《*fig.*》 *~ someone with incessant questions* 아무에게 질문 공세를 펴다. — *vi.* (P2A) **1** beat or strike heavily; fall violently. (비 따위가) 세차게 내리다. ¶ *The rain was pelting down on the pavement.* 비가 차도에 세차게 퍼붓고 있었다. **2** run as fast as possible. 질주하다. — *n.* **1** UC the act of pelting. 집어던짐; 타격; 억수로 퍼붓기. **2** U speed. 속도; 속력. ¶ *at full* ~ 전속력으로. [? *pellet*]

pelt[2] [pelt] *n.* U the skin of a sheep, goat, etc. with the wool or hair left on; rawhide. (양·염소 등의) 생가죽; 모피; 펠트. [L. *pellis* skin]

pel·ves [pélviːz] *n.* pl. of **pelvis.**

pel·vis [pélvis] *n.* C《anat.》(*pl.* **-vis·es** or **-ves**) the basinshaped hollow made by the end of the backbone and the hip bone. 골반. [L. =basin]

pem·mi·can, pem·i- [pémikən] *n.* U dried meat beaten and mixed into cakes. 페미컨《말린 쇠고기 다짐에 지방·과일을 섞어 굳힌 인디언의 휴대 식품》. [Amer-Ind.]

:pen[1] [pen] *n.* C **1** an instrument used for writing with ink. 펜. ¶ *a fountain* ~ 만년필 / ~ *and ink* 필묵(筆墨); 저술. **2** style of writing; writing. 문체; 문필. ¶ *He lives by the* ~. 글을 써서 생활하고 있다 / *The* ~ *is mightier than the sword.* 문(文)은 무(武)보다 강하다. — *vt.* (**penned, pen·ning**) (P6) write. …을 쓰다. ¶ *I penned a few words to Father today.* 오늘 부친께 몇 자 적어 올렸다. [L. *penna* feather]

pen[2] [pen] *n.* C **1** a small yard or enclosure for sheep, pigs, cows, etc. (가축의) 우리. **2** any small enclosed place. (작은) 울을 친 곳. ¶ *a play* ~ *for a baby.* — *vt.* (**penned** or **pent, pen·ning**) (P7,13) shut up (cattle, etc.) in a pen; enclose. (가축 등)을 우리에 넣다 〔가두다〕; 감금하다. ¶ *The boy was penned up in the barn.* 소년은 헛간에 감금되었다. [E.]

pe·nal [píːnəl] *adj.* of punishment; to be punished. 형(刑)의; 형벌의; 형을 받아야 할. ¶ *the* ~ *code* 형법 / *a* ~ *offense* 형사범(犯) / ~ *servitude* 징역형. [→pain]

pe·nal·ize, -ise [píːnəlàiz, pénəl-] *vt.* (P6) **1** declare (an action, etc.) punishable by law or rule; punish. …에 유죄를 선고하다; 처벌하다. ¶ *Our teacher penalizes cheating heavily.* 선생님은 커닝 행위에 대해선 가차 없이 처벌한다. **2** give a penalty to (a player, etc.). …에 페널티를 적용하다. ¶ *The referee penalized the team for unnecessary roughness.* 심판은 팀에게 고의적인 거친 경기에 대한 벌점을 주었다. **3** place at a disadvantage. …을 불리한 입장에 몰아넣다.

***pen·al·ty** [pénəlti] *n.* (*pl.* **-ties**) **1** UC a punishment. 형벌. ¶ *the death* ~ 사형 / *It is forbidden under* ~ *of death* 〔*a fine*〕. 그것을 어기면 사형〔벌금형〕에 처해진다 / *pay the* ~ 벌을 받다. **2** C a fine. 벌금; 과료. **3** C (in sport) a disadvantage to which a player or team must submit for breaking a rule. 반칙에 대한 벌점; 페널티. [*panal*]

pen·ance [pénəns] *n.* U punishment which one imposes upon oneself for sin, esp. at a priest's direction. 속죄; 참회의 고행(苦行). [↑]

pen-and-ink [pénəndíŋk] *adj.* drawn with pen and ink. 펜으로 쓴. [→pen[1]]

***pence** [pens] *n.*《Brit.》pl. of **penny.**

pen·chant [péntʃənt] *n.* a strong taste or liking; inclination. 취미; 기호; 경향. ¶ *have a* ~ *for taking long walks.* 오래 걷기를 무척 좋아하다. [F.]

:pen·cil [pénsəl] *n.* C **1** a pointed instrument for writing or drawing. 연필. **2** 《*fig.*》 the art or style of a painter. 화법(畫法). ¶ *the masterly* ~ *of Rembrandt* 렘브란트의 위대한 화풍. — *vt.* (**-ciled, -cil·ing** or 《Brit.》 **-cilled, -cil·ling**) (P6) write or draw (something) with a pencil. …을 연필로 쓰다〔그리다〕. ¶ ~ *a note* 필기하다 / *a penciled line* 연필로 그은 줄. [→penis]

pencil case [⌐-⌐] *n.* a case for pencils. 필통.

pend·ant [péndənt] *n.* C **1** an ornament hanging from a necklace or bracelet. (목걸이·귀고리 등) 늘어뜨리는 장식; 펜던트. **2** an ornament hanging down from a ceiling or roof. (천장 등에서) 늘어뜨리는 장식《샹들리에 등》. **3** 《naut.》 a long triangular flag used on ships as a signal. (신호용) 삼각기. — *adj.* =pendent. [L. *pendeo* hang]

pend·ent [péndənt] *adj.* **1** hanging; overhanging. 늘어진; 매달린; 돌출한; 쑥 내민. ¶ *a* ~ *lamp* / *the* ~ *branches of willow which touch the water* 늘어져서 수면에 닿은 버들가지들. **2** (of a lawsuit) undecided; pending. 미결(未決)의; 미정의. — *n.* =pendant. [↑]

pend·ing [péndiŋ] *adj.* not yet decided or settled. 미정의. ¶ *a* ~ *question* 현안(懸案)의 문제 / *While the agreement was* ~ … 합의에 이르지 못한 동안은 …. — *prep.* **1** during. …중에. ¶ ~ *investigation* 조사중에. **2** until. …까지. ¶ *Pending his arrival, I was talking with his wife.* 그가 올 때까지 그의 처와 이야기하고 있었다. [→pendent, -ing]

pen·du·lous [péndʒələs] *adj.* hanging loosely; swinging. 매달린; 흔들리는. [↓]

pen·du·lum [péndʒələm, -də-] *n.* C a body hung from a point; swinging to and fro. (시계 따위의) 흔들이. [L. *pendulus* hanging]

pen·e·tra·bil·i·ty [pènətrəbíləti] *n.* U the quality of being penetrable. 침투성; 투과성. [*penetrate*]

pen·e·tra·ble [pénətrəbəl] *adj.* that can be penetrated. 침투〔관입(貫入)〕할 수 있는.

***pen·e·trate** [pénətrèit] *vt.* (P6) **1** ⓐ enter into; pierce. …을 꿰뚫다; 관통하다. ¶ *Its sharp claws penetrated the skin.* 날카로운 발톱이 살갗을 파고들었다 / *Our eyes could not* ~ *the fog.* 안개 때문에 앞이 안 보였다 / *His voice could not* ~ *the walls.* 그의 목소리는 안에서 들리지 않았다. ⓑ force one's

way through and into. …을 뚫고 나아가다. ¶ ~ *a forest* 숲을 헤치고 나아가다. **2** spread through; soak through. …에 침투하다; 스며들다. ¶ *Her clothes are penetrated with a sweet smell.* 그녀의 옷에는 좋은 향내가 스며있다 / *The rain penetrated all our clothes.* 우리들 옷은 비에 흠뻑 젖었다 / *Smoke penetrated the whole building.* 온 건물에 연기가 꽉 찼다. **3** affect or move deeply; inspire. 깊은 감동을 주다; 감명시키다. ¶ *New ideas ~ the minds of most men but slowly.* 새로운 사상은 대개의 사람들에게는 빨리〔금방〕 먹혀들지는 않는다. **4** see through or into; understand. …을 꿰뚫어 보다; 간파하다. ¶ *We soon penetrated his disguise.* 우리는 그의 변장을 곧 알아봤다 / *His mind can ~ the mystery of human nature.* 그는 인간성의 미스터리를 꿰뚫어 볼 수 있다.
— *vi.* (P2A,3) 《*into, through*》 pierce; affect the feelings or mind deeply. 꿰뚫다; 침투하다; 스며들다. ¶ *Revolutionary ideas ~ very slowly in this country.* 혁명적인 사상이 이 나라에서는 잘 먹혀들지 않는다. [L. *penetro*]

pen·e·trat·ing [pénətrèitiŋ] *adj.* **1** sharp; piercing; keen; understanding thoroughly. 침투하는; 스며드는; 통찰력이 날카로운; 꿰뚫어 보는. ¶ *a ~ mind* 통찰력이 예민한 사람. **2** sharp; piercing. 날카로운; 찌르는 듯한. ¶ *a ~ sound* 날카로운 소리.

pen·e·tra·tion [pènətréiʃən] *n.* Ⓤ **1** the act or power of penetrating. 꿰뚫고 들어감; 침투(력). ¶ *peaceful ~ (of revolutionary ideas, etc.)* (혁명적 사상 등의) 평화적 침투. **2** sharpness of mind; insight. 통찰력. ¶ *a man of great ~* 통찰력이 예리한 사람.

pen·e·tra·tive [pénətrèitiv] *adj.* able to penetrate; piercing. 침투하는; 예민한; 통찰력이 있는.

pen·guin [péŋgwin, pén-] *n.* Ⓒ 《bird》 a seabird found around the South Pole. 펭귄. [F.]

pen·hold·er [pénhòuldər] *n.* Ⓒ **1** a handle by which a pen point is held in writing. 펜대. **2** a rack for pens. 펜걸이. [*pen, holder*]

pen·i·cil·lin [pènəsílin] *n.* Ⓤ a very powerful drug for destroying bacteria. 페니실린. [L. *penicillium* mould]

***pen·in·su·la** [pinínsələ, -sjə-] *n.* Ⓒ **1** a long strip of land almost surrounded by water. 반도. **2** 《*the P-*》 ⓐ the Iberian Peninsula. 이베리아 반도《포르투갈과 스페인》. ⓑ Gallipoli (in the first World War). (제1차 세계 대전 때의) 갈리폴리 반도. [L. *paene* almost, *insula* island]

pen·in·su·lar [pinínsələr, -sjə-] *adj.* of or like a peninsula. 반도(모양)의. — *n.* a person who lives in a peninsula. 반도의 주민.

pen·i·tence [pénətəns] *n.* Ⓤ regret for sin or wrongdoing; repentance. 후회; 참회.

pen·i·tent [pénətənt] *adj.* showing penitence. 회오(悔悟)〔참회〕하는. — *n.* Ⓒ a person who is sorry for his sin or wrongdoing. 참회하는 사람. [L. *paenitet* repent]

pen·i·ten·tial [pènəténʃəl] *adj.* of or showing penitence or penance. 회오(悔悟)〔참회〕의; 속죄〔고행〕의. ¶ *the ~ psalms* 참회 시편 / *~ tears* 참회의 눈물.

pen·i·ten·tia·ry [pènəténʃəri] *n.* Ⓒ (*pl.* **-ries**) 《U.S.》 a prison, esp. a state or federal prison; 《Brit.》 a reformatory. 교도소; 감화원. — *adj.* **1** of or for penance or punishment. 후회의; 징벌의. ¶ *~ houses* 감화원. **2** 《U.S.》 making a person liable to punishment. 처벌 받아야 할. ¶ *a ~ offence* (교도소에 수감될 만한) 형사범.

pen·i·tent·ly [pénətəntli] *adv.* in a penitent manner. 회개〔회오(悔悟)〕하여.

pen·knife [pénnàif] *n.* Ⓒ (*pl.* **-knives**) a small pocketknife formerly used for sharpening quill pens. 주머니칼《전에 깃털펜을 깎던》. [*pen*[1]]

pen·knives [pénnàivz] *n.* pl. of **penknife.**

pen·man [pénmən] *n.* Ⓒ (*pl.* **-men** [-mən]) **1** a writer; an author. 작가; 필자. **2** a person skilled in handwriting. 달필가(達筆家). ¶ *a good ~* 서가(書家). [*pen*[1]]

pen·man·ship [pénmənʃìp] *n.* Ⓤ the art, style or practice of handwriting. 서도(書道); 서법(書法); 습자(習字).

pen·name [⌐⌐] *n.* a name used by an author instead of his real name. 필명(筆名); 펜네임.

pen·nant [pénənt] *n.* Ⓒ **1** a long, narrow, triangular flag used on ships, etc. 길고 좁은 삼각기. **2** 《U.S.》 a flag given to a champion team in a sport, esp. baseball. 우승기; 페넌트. ¶ *win the ~* 우승하다. [mixture of *pendant* and *pennon*]

pen·ni·less [pénilis] *adj.* without a penny; very poor. 피천 한닢 없는; 째지게 가난한. [*penny*]

pen·non [pénən] *n.* Ⓒ **1** a long, triangular flag borne on a lance. (중세에) 창(槍) 끝에 달던 길쭉한 삼각기. **2** a flag or banner. 기; 깃발. [→pen[1]]

pen·n'orth [pénərθ] *n.* =pennyworth.

Penn·syl·va·ni·a [pènsilvéiniə, -njə] *n.* an eastern State of the United States. 펜실베이니아 주. 參考 Pa., Penn., Penna.으로 생략. 주도는 Harrisburg.

:**pen·ny** [péni] *n.* Ⓒ (*pl.* **-nies** or *collectively* **pence**) **1** a British bronze coin equal to one-hundredth of a pound. 페니《영국의 청동화(青銅貨)로 1/100 파운드》. ¶ *There are four pennies.* / *It costs four pence.* 비용은 4펜스다 / *Can you give me six pennies for a sixpence?* 6펜스를 줄 테니 페니 동전 여섯 개 주시오 / *It will cost you a pretty ~.* 그러자면 엄청나게 돈이 들 게다 / 《*prov.*》 *A ~ saved is a ~ gained.* 한푼을 아끼면 한푼의 벌이. **2** 《U.S., Can. *colloq.*》 a cent. 1센트. [E.]

penny dreadful [ㅗ–ㅗ–] *n.* 《chiefly Brit.》 a cheap story or book of stories of crime and bloodshed. (범죄·유혈 따위를 다룬) 싸구려 선정 이야기〔소설〕.

pen·ny-wise [péniwáiz] *adj.* economical over small sums. 푼돈을 아끼는. ¶ 《*prov.*》 *Penny-wise and pound-foolish.* 한푼 아끼려다 백 냥 잃기.

pen·ny·worth [péniwəːrθ] *n.* Ⓒ **1** the amount which can be bought for a penny; a small amount. 1페니어치의 양; 소액; 조금. ¶ *a* ~ *of salt* 소금 1페니어치 / *a* ~ *of advice* 간단한 충고. **2** a bargain. 거래.

a good* 〔*bad*〕 *pennyworth, a good〔bad〕 bargain. 유리〔불리〕한 거래; 사서 득을〔손해를〕 본 물건.

pe·nol·o·gy [piːnálədʒi / -nɔ́l-] *n.* the science of punishment of crime and management of prisons. 행형학(行刑學). [→ penal, pain]

***pen·sion**[1] [pénʃən] *n.* Ⓒ a regular payment to a person who has ceased active work because of illness, injury, old age, etc. 연금; 부조금; 노령 연금. ¶ *retire on a* ~ 연금 받고 퇴직하다 / *draw one's* ~ 연금을 타다 / *an old age* ~ 노령 연금. — *vt.* (P6,7) give a pension to (someone). …에게 연금을 지급하다. [L. *pendo* pay, weigh]

pension off, permit to retire from service with a pension. 연금을 주어 퇴직시키다.

pen·sion[2] [pɑːnsjɔ́ːŋ / ㅗ–] *n.* Ⓒ a boarding house or boarding school in France and other Continental countries. 하숙집; 기숙학교. [F.]

pen·sion·er [pénʃənər] *n.* Ⓒ a person who receives a pension. 연금 수령자〔생활자〕. [pension[1]]

pen·sive [pénsiv] *adj.* engaged in serious thought; thoughtful; melancholy. 생각〔시름〕에 잠긴; 구슬픈. [L.]

pent [pent] *v.* p. and pp. of **pen**[2]. — *adj.* shut up; kept in; confined. 갇힌; 감금〔유폐〕된. ¶ *be* ~ *in the house all winter* 겨울 내내 집안에 갇히다 / ~ *up in an office all day* 하루 종일 사무실 밖을 못 나가다. [→pen[2]]

pen·ta·gon [péntəgɑ̀n / -gɔn] *n.* **1** Ⓒ a figure having five sides and five angles. 5변형; 5각형; 5릉보(稜堡). **2** 《*the P-*》 the building in Arlington, Virginia, in which the Department of Defense of the United States is located. 미국 국방부 건물; 펜타곤. [Gk. *pente* five]

pen·tam·e·ter [pentǽmitər] *n.* Ⓒ poetry with five feet in each line in English verse. 5운각시(韻脚詩). [↑]

pen·tath·lon [pentǽθlən, -lɑn] *n.* Ⓒ an athletic contest in which each competitor participates in five events. 5종경기(cf. *decathlon*). [Gk. *pente* five, *athlon* contest]

Pen·te·cost [péntikɔ̀(ː)st, -kɑ̀st] *n.* **1** the Jewish harvest festival, the fiftieth day after the Passover. (유태교의) 오순절(五旬節). **2** Whitsunday; the seventh Sunday after Easter. 성신(聖神) 강림절. [Gk. *pentēkostos* fiftieth]

pent·house [pénthàus] *n.* Ⓒ **1** a small house with a sloping roof projecting from a building; the projecting part of a sloping roof. 외벽에 붙인 비스듬한 지붕을 한 작은 집; 처마; 차양. **2** a shed or a small house built on the top of a building. 건물 옥상에 지은 작은 집; 펜트하우스. [F. *apentis* (L. *ad* to, *pendo* suspend)]

pe·num·bra [pinʌ́mbrə] *n.* Ⓒ (*pl.* **-brae** or **-bras**) 《astron.》 a partially shadowed area around the complete shadow during an eclipse. 반음영(半陰影)《일식·월식 때의 그늘진 부분》. [L. *paene* almost, *umbra* shade]

pe·num·brae [pinʌ́mbriː] *n.* pl. of **penumbra.**

pe·nu·ri·ous [pinjúəriəs] *adj.* poor; scanty. 가난한; 근소한; 인색한. [↓]

pen·u·ry [pénjəri] *n.* Ⓤ extreme poverty; 《*of*》 want. 빈곤; 궁핍; 결핍. [L.]

pe·on [píːən, -ɑn] *n.* **1** a person doing work which needs little skill. 막일꾼. **2** (in Latin America) a worker held as a slave to work off a debt. 빚 때문에 노예로 일하는 사람. [→pawn[1]]

pe·on·age [píːənidʒ, -ɑn-] *n.* **1** the condition of being a peon. peon의 신분. **2** the system of employing peons. peon의 제도. [↑]

pe·o·ny, pae- [píːəni] *n.* Ⓒ (*pl.* **-nies**) 《bot.》 a garden plant bearing large, showy, many-petaled flowers; its flower. 작약(芍藥); 모란. ¶ *a tree* ~ 모란 / *blush like a* ~ 얼굴을 붉히다. [Gk. *paiōnía*]

⁝**peo·ple** [píːpl] *n.* (*pl.* **peo·ple** or (for 1) **-ples**) 《used as *pl.*》 **1** Ⓒ 《chiefly *a* ~ or *peoples, collectively*》 the members of a particular race or nation. 국민; 민족. 語法 단수 취급. 때로 구성원을 고려하여 복수 취급. ¶ *all the peoples of the world* 세계의 모든 민족 / *the peoples of Asia* 아시아의 여러 국민 / *a warlike* ~ 호전적인 민족 / *the chosen* ~ 유태 민족. **2** 《*collectively*》 persons; men, women and children; persons in general. 세인(世人); 세상 사람들. ¶ *What will* ~ *say?* 남들이 뭐라 할까 / *People tell me I speak English well.* 남들이 나더러 영어를 잘 한다는군 / *The streets were crowded with* ~. 거리는 사람들로 북적거렸다 / *There were ten* ~ *present.* 열 사람이 있었다 / *I saw some dogs but no* ~. 개 몇 마리 외에는 사람은 안 보였다 / *I don't mind what* ~ *say.* 남이야 뭐라든 상관없다. **3** 《*collectively*》 persons living in a place or belonging to a group; 《*one's* ~》 one's family or relatives. (한 지역·집단의) 사람들; 가족; 친척; 일가. ¶ *village* ~ 마을 사람들 / *I want you to see my* ~. 우리 식구를 만나 주었으면 좋겠네 / *the* ~ *here* 여기 있는 사람들 / *southern* ~ 남쪽 사람들 / *country*

～ 시골 사람들 / *He spent his holidays with his* ～. 휴가를 식구들과 지냈다 / *How are all your* ～? 식구들 모두 안녕하십니까. **4** 《*the* ～》 persons of the lower classes. 평민; 서민. ¶ *a man of the* ～ 일반민; 평민 / *The French nobles oppressed the* ～. 프랑스 귀족들은 평민을 억압했다. **5** 《*one's* ～ or *the* ～》 persons in relation to a ruler, etc.; one's subjects. 신민(臣民); 아랫사람. ¶ *the king and his people* 왕과 신민 / *a pastor and his* ～ 교구(教區) 목사와 교구민.
— *vt.* (P6) fill (a place, etc.) with people; put people, animals, etc. in (a place, etc.). …을 사람으로 채우다; …에 사람·짐승 등을 살게 하다(cf. *populate*). ¶ *a thickly-peopled country* 인구 밀도가 큰 나라 / ～ *a country* 식민(植民)하다. [L. *populus*]

pep [pep] *n.* Ⓤ 《U.S. *colloq.*》 spirit; energy. 원기; 기운. ¶ *have plenty of* ～ 씩씩하다. — *vt.* (**pepped, pep·ping**) (P6,7) 《*up*》 make (someone) energetic; encourage; stimulate. …을 격려하다. [L. *piper*]

·**pep·per** [pépər] *n.* **1** Ⓤ a seasoning with a hot taste, used for soup, meats, etc. 후추. **2** Ⓒ a plant bearing a somewhat hollow, spicy, green or red fruit; its fruit. 고추. ¶ *green* ～ 피망 / *Chinese* 〔*Japanese*〕 ～ 산초나무 / *red* ～ 고추. **3** Ⓤ keen and bitter criticism. 혹평.
— *vt.* (P6,13) **1** season (food) with pepper. …에 후춧가루로 양념하다. **2** hit with small objects sent thick and fast. …에 퍼붓다; 연발하다. ¶ ～ *a target with bullets* 목표에 총알을 난사하다 / *Hailstones peppered the lawn.* 우박이 잔디에 쏟아져 내렸다 / 《*fig.*》 *The speaker was peppered with awkward questions* 연사는 골치아픈 질문 공세를 받았다. [↑]

pep·per-and-salt [pépərənsɔ́:lt] *adj.* having black and white finely mixed. (천이) 희고 검은 반점이 있는.

pep·per·box [pépərbɑ̀ks / -bɔ̀ks] *n.* = pepper castor.

pepper castor 〔**caster**〕 [⌐– –〔–〕] *n.* a small container with small holes, used for sprinkling pepper on food. 후춧가루병.

pep·per·mint [pépərmìnt] *n.* Ⓤ **1** a strong-smelling plant. 서양 박하. **2** an oil made from this plant. 박하유. **3** Ⓒ a candy flavored with this oil. 박하 사탕. [↑]

pep·sin [pépsin] *n.* Ⓤ a liquid produced in the stomach which helps to digest food; a medicine to help digestion. 펩신《소화제》. [Gk. *pepsis* digestion]

:**per** [pəːr, pər] *prep.* **1** by means of; through. …에 의해; …으로. ¶ ～ *post* 〔*rail*〕 우편〔철도편〕으로 / ～ *J. Jones* 존스씨에 의해. **2** for each. …에 대해; …마다. ¶ *interest* ～ *annum* 연리(年利) / *earn 150 dollars* ～ *week* 주당(週當) 150 달러 벌다. [L.]

per- [pəːr, pər] *pref.* through(out); completely. '완전히, 끝까지…'의 뜻. ¶ *perfect* / *pervade.* [L.]

per·ad·ven·ture [pə̀:rədvéntʃər / pər-] *adv.* 《*arch.*》 **1** perhaps. 아마도. ¶ *Peradventure he will come today.* 아마 오늘 올 것이다. **2** by chance. 우연히; 어쩌다. ¶ *if* 〔*lest*〕 ～ 혹시 …하는 일이 있으면〔없도록〕. — *n.* chance; uncertainty. 우연; 불안; 불확실성. [per-]
beyond 〔***without***〕 ***peradventure,*** certainly; certain. 확실히; 반드시 하는. ¶ *Beyond* ～ *he will come.* 꼭 온다.

per·am·bu·late [pərǽmbjəlèit] *vt., vi.* (P6; 1) walk through or about (a place, etc.); walk through and examine. (…을) 돌아다니다; 답사하다. ¶ ～ *the streets* 거리를 돌아다니다. [L. *ambulo* walk]

per·am·bu·la·tor [pərǽmbjəlèitər] *n.* 《Brit.》 Ⓒ **1** a small, light carriage for a baby, pushed by hand. 유모차. 參考 pram으로 생략함. **2** a person who perambulates. 순시〔답사〕자.

per an·num [pər ǽnəm] *adv.* 《L.》 yearly; by the year. 1년마다.

per cap·i·ta [pər kǽpitə] *adv.* 《L.》 for each person. 각 사람에 대하여. ¶ *the* ～ *income,* 1인당 소득.

:**per·ceive** [pərsí:v] *vt.* **1** (P6,22,23) become aware of (someone or something) through the senses; notice. …을 지각〔인정〕하다; …을 눈치채다. ¶ ～ *someone approach* 누가 다가오는 것을 깨닫다 / *Do you* ～ *a red color or a blue one?* 붉은지 푸른지 알아보겠나. **2** (P6,11,12) understand; take in with the mind. 이해하다; 파악하다. ¶ *I perceived that he would refuse.* 나는 그가 거절할 줄을 알고 있었다 / *He perceived that he could not make her change her mind.* 그녀의 마음이 요지부동이라는 것을 알았다. [L. *capio* take]

:**per·cent, per cent** [pərsént] *n.* Ⓒ (*pl.* **-cent**) one of a hundred parts; percentage. 퍼센트; 100분(分). 參考 기호 %; p.c., per. ct. 로 생략함. ¶ *Six* ～ *of 50 is 3.* 50의 6퍼센트는 3이다. [→cent]

·**per·cent·age** [pərséntidʒ] *n.* ⒸⓊ **1** the rate or proportion of each hundred; a part of each hundred. 백분율. ¶ *What* ～ *of your income do you save?* 수입의 몇 퍼센트를 저금하나. **2** a part or proportion. 비율. ¶ *a small* ～ *of water* 적은 비율의 물 / *A large* ～ *of the students won scholarships.* 많은 비율의 학생이 장학금을 탔다. **3** tax, interest, commission, etc. expressed in percent. (백분율의) 조세; 이율; 수수료(등). ¶ *work for a* ～ 수수료를 받고 일하다.

per cent·um [pər sentəm] *adv.* 《L.》 by the hundred; for or in every hundred. 100에 대해.

per·cep·ti·ble [pərséptəbəl] *adj.* that can be perceived through the senses. 지각할 수 있는; 알 수 있는. [→perceive]

per·cep·ti·bly [pərséptəbəli] *adv.* in a perceptible manner; to a perceptible degree. 지각할 수 있을 정도로; 두드러지게.

per·cep·tion [pərsépʃən] *n.* Ⓤ **1** the act, faculty or power of perceiving. 지각(력); 지각 작용. ¶ *a man of keen* ~ 지각력이 예민한 사람 / *His quick* ~ *of danger prevented the accident.* 그의 빠른 판단으로 사고는 피할 수 있었다. **2** the understanding which is the result of perceiving. 이해; 판단. ¶ *Did you have time to get a clear* ~ *of the accident ?* 사고의 발생 가능성을 어떻게 그리 빨리 알았나. [→perceive]

per·cep·tive [pərséptiv] *adj.* of perception; able to perceive; having the power of perceiving. 지각의; 감지하는[할 수 있는]; 지각력이 있는.

*__perch__[1] [pəːrtʃ] *n.* Ⓒ **1** a bar or branch on which a bird can rest. (새의) 홰. **2** 《*colloq.*》 any high, secure place or position. 안전한 높은 지위. **3** a measure of length equal to 5 1/2 yards; a rod. 퍼치《약 5.03 m》.

Come off your perch, 《*colloq.*》 Don't be so proud ! 그렇게 으스댈 것 없다.

hop [***tip over***] ***the perch,*** 《*colloq.*》 die. 죽다.

— *vi.* (P3) sit on a perch. (홰에) 앉다. ¶ *A bird perched on a twig.* 새 한마리가 나뭇가지에 앉았다 / *He perched on the arm of a chair.* 의자 팔걸이에 앉았다.

— *vt.* (P13) place or set (something) on a perch. …을 (홰에) 앉히다; 놓다. ¶ ~ *one's hat on the side of one's head* 모자를 삐딱하게 쓰다 / *The village is perched on a high hill.* 마을은 높은 언덕 위에 있다. [L. *pertica* pole]

perch[2] [pəːrtʃ] *n.* Ⓒ (*pl.* **perch·es** or *collectively* **perch**) a kind of small fresh-water fish with sharp fins, used for food. 농어류(類)의 식용 담수어. [Gk. *perke*]

per·chance [pərtʃǽns, -tʃάːns] *adv.* 《*arch.*》 by chance; perhaps. 우연히; 아마도. [per-]

per·cip·i·ent [pərsípiənt] *adj.* having the power of perceiving, esp. keenly. 지각력이 뛰어난. — *n.* a percipient person. 지각자; 천리안(千里眼)(의 사람). [→perceive]

per·co·late [pə́ːrkəlèit] *vi.* (P1,3) pass through very small spaces; filter. 여과되다; 삼투(滲透)하다. ¶ *Water percolates through sand.* 물이 모래에 스며든다. — *vt.* (P6) **1** cause (a liquid) to pass through small spaces; filter. …을 여과시키다; 침투시키다. **2** prepare (coffee) in a percolator. 퍼컬레이터로 (커피)를 끓이다. ¶ *I'll* ~ *some coffee for you.* 커피를 끓여 드리겠습니다. [L. *colum* strainer]

per·co·la·tor [pə́ːrkəlèitər] *n.* Ⓒ **1** a thing that percolates. 여과기. **2** a coffee pot in which boiling water filters through ground coffee. 퍼컬레이터; 여과기 달린 커피 끓이개.

per·cus·sion [pərkʌ́ʃən] *n.* **1** Ⓤ the act of striking one thing against another violently. 충격; 충돌. **2** the shock, vibration or noise made by striking. 진동; 격동; 음향. **3** 《*collectively*》 percussion instruments. 타악기(打樂器). [L. *quatio* shake]

percussion cap [–⌐–⌐] *n.* a small container holding a charge that explodes when struck, used as in firing a gun. 뇌관.

Per·cy [pə́ːrsi] *n.* a man's name. 남자 이름.

per di·em [pər díːəm, -dáiəm] *adv.* 《L.》 per day; for each day. 하루에 대하여. — *n.* the allowance of so much every day. 일당(日當).

per·di·tion [pərdíʃən] *n.* Ⓤ **1** ruin; destruction. 파멸. **2** the loss of the soul or of hope for salvation; hell. 영원한 죽음; 지옥. [L. *perdo* destroy]

per·e·grine [pérəgrin, -grìːn], **-grin** [-grin] *adj.* foreign; (of birds) migratory. 외국의; (새가) 이주하는. — *n.* Ⓒ 《bird》 a large, swift falcon. 송골매. [per-, L. *ager* field]

per·emp·to·ry [pərémptəri, pérəmptɔ̀ːri] *adj.* **1** allowing no denial or refusal; leaving no choice. 단호한; 군말하지 못하게 하는. ¶ *a* ~ *command* 엄명. **2** 《law》 final; absolute; decisive. 결정적인; 절대의. ¶ *a* ~ *decree* 확정판결. **3** dogmatic. 독단적인. ¶ *a* ~ *attitude* 고압적인 태도 / *a* ~ *teacher* 위압적인 선생. [L. =destructive]

per·en·ni·al [pəréniəl] *adj.* **1** lasting throughout the whole year; flowing at all seasons of the year. 사철을 통한; 사철 끊이지 않는. ¶ *a* ~ *stream* 연중 마르지 않는 시내. **2** lasting for a very long time. 여러 해 가는; 영구한. ¶ ~ *youth* 영원한 젊음 / *a* ~ *problem* 늘 발생하는 문제. **3** (of plants) living for a number of years. 다년생(多年生)의 (cf. *annual*). ¶ ~ *garden plants* 다년생 정원수. — *n.* a perennial plant. 다년생 식물(cf. *biennial*). [L. *annus* year]

per·en·ni·al·ly [pəréniəli] *adv.* in a perennial manner; perpetually. 다년간에 걸쳐; 부단히.

:**per·fect** [pə́ːrfikt] *adj.* **1** complete; faultless; whole; having all its parts there. 완전한; 결함이 없는; 온전한. ¶ *a* ~ *crime* 완전범죄 / *The set was* ~. 완전한 한 세트였다 / *a* ~ *gentleman* 전형적인 신사 / *a* ~ *life* 나무랄 데 없는 생활 / *The weather was* ~. 날씨는 그만이었다 / *His arithmetic paper was* ~. 산수 답안지는 백점이었다. **2** exact; accurate. 정확한. ¶ *a* ~ *square* 정방형; 정사각형 / *a* ~ *copy of a book* 똑같은 복사본. **3** completely skilled; excellent. 아주 숙달된; 우수한. ¶ ~ *in the use of arms* 무기 사용에 숙달한 / *a* ~ *tennis player* 일류 테니스 선수. **4** entire; utter. 진짜의; 지독한. ¶ *a* ~ *fool* 지독한 바보 / *a* ~ *stranger* 생판 모르는 사람. **5** 《gram.》 of a tense showing an event or action completed at the time of the present, the past or the future. 완료의. ¶ ~ *tenses* 완료시제.

— *n.* Ⓒ 《gram.》 the perfect tense. 완료시제.

— [pə(ː)rfékt] *vt.* **1** (P6) make (something) perfect. …을 완성하다. ¶ ~ *a plan* 계획을 성취시키다 / *She worked to ~ her piano technique.* 피아노 주법의 완벽을 위해 힘썼다. **2** (P6,13) train thoroughly, raise to the highest point. …을 숙달시키다. ¶ ~ *one's skill* 기술을 숙달시키다 / *He perfected himself in English.* 그는 영어에 익숙해졌다. [per-, →fact]

·per·fec·tion [pərfékʃən] *n.* Ⓤ **1** the state of being perfect; completeness. 완전; 완벽. ¶ *come to ~* 완성되다 / *bring something to ~* …을 완성시키다. **2** the act of making something complete; completion. 완성. ¶ *The ~ of our plans will take another week.* 우리 계획이 완성되려면 1주일이 더 걸릴 것이다. **3** the highest excellence. 극치; 탁월. ¶ *His work is always ~.* 그의 작품은 늘 완벽하다.

to perfection, perfectly. 완전히. ¶ *cook to ~* 훌륭하게 요리하다.

:per·fect·ly [pə́ːrfiktli] *adv.* in a perfect manner; completely. 완전하게; 더할 나위 없이.

per·fid·i·ous [pərfídiəs] *adj.* faithless; treacherous. 부실한; 믿을 게 못되는. ¶ *a ~ friend* 불성실한 친구. [↓]

per·fi·dy [pə́ːrfədi] *n.* (*pl.* **-dies**) **1** Ⓤ the act of breaking faith. 부실(不實); 불신(不信). **2** Ⓒ a faithless or treacherous act. 불신 행위. [L. *fides* faith]

per·fo·rate [pə́ːrfərèit] *vt.* (P6) **1** make a hole through (something). …에 구멍을 내다. ¶ *a target perforated by bullets* 총알 구멍이 난 과녁. **2** make a row of holes through (something) so that it can be torn off easily. …에 눈금 바늘 구멍을 내다. ¶ *Computer tapes* 〔*Sheets of postage stamps*〕 *are perforated.* 컴퓨터 테이프〔전지 우표〕에는 눈금 바늘 구멍이 나 있다. [L. *foro* bore]

per·fo·ra·tion [pə̀ːrfəréiʃən] *n.* **1** Ⓤ the act of perforating; the state of being perforated. 구멍내기; 구멍이 남; 관통. **2** Ⓒ a hole or a line of holes bored or punched through something. 구멍; 눈금 바늘 구멍. ¶ *the perforations in a salt-cellar* (식탁의) 소금 용기에 송송 뚫린 구멍.

per·force [pərfɔ́ːrs] *adv.* by or through necessity; necessarily. 부득이; 어쩔 수 없이; 강제적으로. — *n.* Ⓤ compulsion. 강제. ¶ *by* 〔*of*〕 ~할 수 없이; 필연적으로. [per-]

:per·form [pərfɔ́ːrm] *vt.* (P6) **1** do; carry out. …을 시행〔실행〕하다. ¶ ~ *a duty* 책임을 다하다 / ~ *a task* 일을 성취하다 / ~ *a ceremony* 의식을 행하다 / *Perform your promise.* 약속을 지켜라. **2** act (a play, etc.); play (music). …을 연기〔연주〕하다. ¶ ~ *a play* 극을 공연하다. — *vi.* (P1,3) act a part; exhibit skill in public. (극을) 공연하다; 연주하다. ¶ ~ *before the king* 어전에서 공연하다. [per-]

:per·form·ance [pərfɔ́ːrməns] *n.* **1** Ⓤ the act of performing. 실행; 수행; 성취. ¶ *in the ~ of one's regular duties* 일상적인 임무 수행중. **2** Ⓒ a thing performed; an act; a deed. 작업; 행위. ¶ *a fine ~* 훌륭한 성과 / *The child's kicks and screams made a shameful ~.* 그 아이가 발길질하고 울부짖고 하는 것은 못 봐줄 일이었다. **3** Ⓒ a public exhibition; a play; a concert. 공연; 연주; 흥행. ¶ *There are two performances a day.* 하루 두번의 공연이 있다.

per·form·er [pərfɔ́ːrmər] *n.* Ⓒ a person who performs. 실행자; 연기〔연주〕자. ¶ *a ~ on the piano* 피아노 연주자.

·per·fume [pə́ːrfjuːm, pərfjúːm] *n.* Ⓤ **1** a sweet smell. 향기; 향내. **2** a liquid having the sweet smell of a flower. 향수(香水). — [‑ˊ, ˊ‑] *vt.* (P6) fill (something) with a pleasant smell; put a perfume on (something). …에 향기가 나게 하다; 향수를 뿌리다〔바르다〕. ¶ ~ *oneself* 향수를 바르다. [per-]

per·fum·er [pəːrfjúːmər, ˊ‑‑] *n.* Ⓒ **1** a person who makes or sells perfume. 향수 제조인〔판매상〕. **2** a person or thing that gives out a sweet smell. 향내를 풍기는 사람〔물건〕.

per·fum·er·y [pərfjúːməri] *n.* (*pl.* **-er·ies**) **1** Ⓤ a perfume; 《*collectively*》 perfumes. 향수; 향수류. **2** Ⓒ a place where perfumes are made or sold. 향수 제조소; 향수 가게〔판매점〕.

per·func·to·ri·ly [pəːrfʌ́ŋktərili] *adv.* in a perfunctory manner. 적당히; 형식적으로. [↓]

per·func·to·ry [pəːrfʌ́ŋktəri] *adj.* **1** done carelessly only as a form or routine; superficial; hasty. 형식적인; 되는 대로의; 겉치레의. ¶ *a ~ piece of work* 〔*examination*〕 아무렇게나 한 일〔형식적인 시험〕 / *He gave his face a ~ wash.* 그는 세수를 후딱 해치웠다. **2** acting in a superficial or mechanical way. 피상적〔기계적〕으로 하는. ¶ *a ~ workman* 성의가 없는 일꾼. [L. *fungor* perform]

per·go·la [pə́ːrgələ] *n.* Ⓒ a shady place formed by a trellis supported by posts. 퍼골라《덩굴을 지붕처럼 올린 정자》; 덩굴시렁. [It.]

:per·haps [pərhǽps, pəræ̂ps] *adv.* possibly; maybe. 아마도; 어쩌면(cf. *maybe*). ¶ *Perhaps he has* 〔*He has ~*〕 *seen it.* 아마 그것을 봤을 것이다 / *Perhaps so* 〔*not*〕. 어쩌면 그럴 것이다〔그렇지 않을 게다〕. [→hap]

per·i- [pérə-, péri-] *pref.* round; surrounding; near. '둘레, 주변, 부근'의 뜻. [Gk.]

per·i·carp [pérəkàːrp] *n.* Ⓒ 《bot.》 the covering of fruit. 과피(果皮). [Gk. *karpos* fruit]

·per·il [pérəl] *n.* Ⓤ very great danger; risk. 위험; 위기; 모험. ¶ *at one's ~* 위험을 무릅쓰고 / *Storms are a ~ to small boats.* 폭풍우는 작은 배엔 위험이 된다.

in peril of, in danger of losing. …을 잃을 위

험에 빠져. ¶ *He is in ~ of his life.* 목숨이 위태롭게 됐다.
— *vt.* (**-iled, -il·ing** or《Brit.》**-illed, -il·ling**) (P6) put (something) in danger. …을 위험에 빠뜨리다. [L. *periculum*]

per·il·ous [pérələs] *adj.* dangerous; risky. 위험한; 모험적인. ● **per·il·ous·ly** [-li] *adv.*

pe·rim·e·ter [pərímitər] *n.* Ⓒ **1** the outer boundary of a figure. 둘레; 주위; 주변. **2** the length of this line. 주변의 길이. [peri-, →meter]

:pe·ri·od [píəriəd] *n.* Ⓒ **1** a certain length of time; the time after which the same things begin to happen again. (일정한) 기간; 주기. ¶ *the growing ~* 성장기 / *for a short ~ of time* 잠시 동안 / *the ~ I spent at my uncle's* 내가 아저씨 집에 있던 기간 / *I lived in Ireland for a ~ in my youth.* 젊어서는 아일랜드에 살았다. **2** a certain number of years in history, a civilization, etc.; an era. 시대. ¶ *the Caesarian ~* 카이사르 시대 / *the Restoration ~* 왕정 복고기 / *Men will enter a more brilliant ~ in the 21st century.* 인류는 21세기에 더욱 빛나는 시대로 들어설 것이다. **3** a mark (.) at the end of a sentence; a full stop. 마침표; 종지부. **4** one of the parts of time into which a school day, a game, etc. is divided. (학교) 수업 시간; 경기의 구분《전반·후반 따위》. ¶ *We have four periods on Saturday.* 토요일은 수업이 네 시간이다. **5**《*the* ~》the present day or time. 현대; 당대. ¶ *young men of the ~* 현대의 젊은이들. **6** end. 끝; 종결. ¶ *put a ~ to* …을 끝내다 / *The ~ of his rule was soon reached.* 그의 치세는 곧 끝났다. **7**《*pl.*》menses. 월경(주기). [Gk. *hodos* way]

pe·ri·od·ic [pìəriádik / -ɔ́dik] *adj.* **1** occurring, happening, appearing at regular intervals. 주기적인; 정기의. ¶ *a ~ wind* 계절풍 / *~ attacks of malaria* 주기적인 말라리아 발작. **2** occurring occasionally. 단속적인; 어쩌다 생기는. ¶ *a ~ fit of clearing up one's desk* 어쩌다 책상을 정리하고 싶어지는 기분. **3** of a time in history. 시대의.

pe·ri·od·i·cal [pìəriádikəl / -riɔ́di-] *adj.* **1** occurring at intervals. 주기적인. **2** published at regular intervals. 정기 간행의. — *n.* Ⓒ a magazine published at regular intervals. 정기 간행물.

pe·ri·od·i·cal·ly [pìəriádikəli / -riɔ́di-] *adv.* at regular intervals; from time to time. 정기적으로; 단속적으로.

per·i·pa·tet·ic [pèrəpətétik] *adj.* **1** moving from place to place. 돌아다니는; 순회하는. ¶ *a ~ preacher* 순회 전도사. **2**《*P-*》of the philosophy of Aristotle, who walked about while teaching. 소요학파(逍遙學派)의. — *n.* Ⓒ《*P-*》a follower of Aristotle. 소요학파의 학도(學徒). [Gk. *pateo* tread]

pe·riph·er·y [pəríːfəri] *n.* Ⓒ (*pl.* **-er·ies**) a boundary line; an outside surface. 주위; 외면(外面). [Gk. *pherō* carry]

per·i·phrase [pérəfrèiz] *n.* =periphrasis. — *vt., vi.* (P6; 1) express in a roundabout way. 에둘러〔넌지시〕 말하다. [peri-, Gk. *phrázein* speak]

pe·riph·ra·ses [pərífrəsìːz] *n.* pl. of **periphrasis.**

pe·riph·ra·sis [pərífrəsis] *n.* ⓊⒸ (*pl.* **-ses**) a roundabout way of speaking; a periphrastic expression. 완곡법(婉曲法); 에두르는 표현. ¶ *'The answer is in the negative' is a ~ for 'no'.* '대답이 부정적이다'는 '거절'의 에두른 말이다. [Gk. =circumlocution]

per·i·phras·tic [pèrəfrǽstik] *adj.* of or expressed in periphrasis. 에두른; 우회적인. [↑]

per·i·scope [pérəskòup] *n.* Ⓒ an instrument with mirrors and lenses by which the observer can see over an obstacle. 잠망경. [→scope]

per·i·scop·ic [pèrəskápik / -skɔ́p-] *adj.* **1** giving distinct vision all around. 사방(四方)이 보이는. **2** of or by a periscope. 잠망경의.

:per·ish [périʃ] *vi.* (P1,2A) die; be destroyed. 죽다; 망하다. ¶ *~ with hunger* 굶어죽다 / *Flowers ~ when frost comes.* 서리가 내리면 꽃은 진다. — *vt.* (P6) (of cold, etc.) cause to suffer extremely. …을 몹시 괴롭히다. ¶ *We were perished with cold.* 추워서 오금을 못 펴겠다. [per-, L. *eo* go]

Perish the thought! Don't even consider such a possibility! 그만 집어치워라.

per·ish·a·ble [périʃəbəl] *adj.* liable to spoil or decay. 썩기 쉬운; 소멸되기 쉬운. ¶ *Fish is ~.* 생선은 상하기 쉽다. — *n.*《*pl.*》something perishable. 썩기 쉬운 것〔음식〕.

per·ish·ing [périʃiŋ] *adj.* causing extreme discomfort, exhaustion, etc. (추위 따위가) 극심한; 지독한. ¶ *It's really ~ (cold) this morning.* 오늘 아침은 지독히도 춥군.

per·i·to·ni·tis [pèrətənáitis] *n.* Ⓤ《med.》inflammation of the lining of the abdomen. 복막염. [Gk. *teinō* stretch]

per·i·wig [périwìg] *n.* Ⓒ a wig. 가발. [→peruke]

per·i·win·kle[1] [périwìŋkl] *n.* Ⓤ《bot.》a creeping, evergreen plant with blue or white flowers. 협죽도과(夾竹桃科)의 식물. [L. *pervinca*]

per·i·win·kle[2] [périwìŋkl] *n.* Ⓒ a seasnail with a spiral shell. 경단고둥. [E.]

per·jure [pə́ːrdʒər] *vt.* (P6)《*reflexively*》**1** make (oneself) guilty of swearing falsely that something is true. 위증하다. ¶ *The witness perjured himself.* 증인은〔목격자는〕 위증했다. **2** break a solemn promise. 맹세를 깨뜨리다. ● **per·jur·er** [-dʒərər] *n.* [L. *juro* swear]

per·ju·ry [pə́ːrdʒəri] *n.* (*pl.* **-ju·ries**) **1** Ⓤ the act of perjuring oneself. 위증(죄). ¶ *commit ~* 위증죄를 범하다. **2** Ⓒ a willfully false statement. 거짓말. **3** Ⓤ the act of breaking a solemn promise. 맹세를 깨뜨림.

perk [pəːrk] *vi.* (P2A) **1** lift up one's head brisky or spiritedly. (머리를 쳐들고) 거들먹거리다; 뻐기다. **2** become lively or active; recover from sickness. 기운을 되찾다. **3** put oneself forward assertively. 주제넘게 나서다. — *vt.* (P7) **1** raise (the head, etc.) briskly or spiritedly. (머리)를 쳐들고 으쓱대다. ¶ ~ *up one's head* 머리를 쳐들고 으쓱대다. **2** 《*reflexively*》 make (oneself) trim or smart in appearance. 멋내다. ¶ ~ *oneself up* 쪽 빼다. [? O.F.]

perk·y [pə́ːrki] *adj.* (**perk·i·er, perk·i·est**) lively; active; impudent; saucy. 기운찬; 의기 양양한; 멋부리는; 건방진. ● **perk·i·ness** [-nis] *n.* [↑]

perm [pəːrm] *n.* 《*colloq.*》 =permanent wave.

per·ma·nence [pə́ːrmənəns] *n.* Ⓤ the state of being permanent. 영구(永久); 영속; 불변. [→permanent]

per·ma·nen·cy [pə́ːrmənənsi] *n.* (*pl.* **-cies**) **1** =permanence. **2** Ⓒ a permanent person, thing, or position. 변하지 않는 사람; 영구적인 것; 영속적인 지위.

:per·ma·nent [pə́ːrmənənt] *adj.* lasting; continuing in the same state. 영구한; 영속적인(opp. temporary). ¶ ~ *residence* 영주(永住) / *a* ~ *tooth* 영구치 / *the* ~ *way* 궤도(軌道). [L. *maneo* stay]

per·ma·nent·ly [pə́ːrmənəntli] *adv.* in a permanent manner. 영구히; 영속적으로.

permanent wave [ˊ–––ˊ] *n.* a hair wave that is produced as by applying chemical preparations and that remains even after the hair is washed. 퍼머.

per·me·a·bil·i·ty [pə̀ːrmiəbíləti] *n.* Ⓤ the state or quality of being permeable. 투과성(透過性); 침투성. [↓]

per·me·a·ble [pə́ːrmiəbəl] *adj.* that can be permeated. 침투할 수 있는; 투과성이 있는. ¶ *A brick or sponge is* ~ *by water.* 벽돌이나 해면에는 물이 스며든다.

per·me·ate [pə́ːrmièit] *vt.* (P6) pass into (something) and fill every space of it; pass through. …에 스며들다; 골고루 번지다. ¶ *A powerful scent permeated the room.* 독한 냄새가 방안에 퍼졌다 / 《*fig.*》 *The new idea has permeated the people.* 새로운 의식이 사람들에게 퍼져갔다. — *vi.* (P1,3) spread; diffuse. 퍼지다; 침투하다; 보급되다. ¶ ~ *through the soil* 흙에 스며들다 / 《*fig.*》 ~ *among the people* 사람들 사이에 퍼지다. [L. *meo* go]

per·me·a·tion [pə̀ːrmiéiʃən] *n.* Ⓤ the act of permeating; the state of being permeated. 침투; 투과; 보급.

per·mis·si·ble [pəːrmísəbəl] *adj.* able to be permitted; allowable. 허용할 수 있는. ¶ ~ *conduct* 허용할 수 있는 행동. [↓]

·per·mis·sion [pəːrmíʃən] *n.* Ⓤ the act of allowing or permitting. 허가; 허용. ¶ *ask for* ~ 허가를 요청하다 / *grant* 〔*give*〕 ~ 허가하다 / *do something without* 〔*with*〕 ~ 무단히〔허가 받고〕 …을 하다.

per·mis·sive [pəːrmísiv] *adj.* permitting; permitted. 허가하는; 허가 받은.

:per·mit [pəːrmít] *v.* (**-mit·ted, -mit·ting**) *vt.* (P6,8,9,13,14,20) **1** allow; give leave to (someone or something). …을 허용하다; 허가하다. ¶ *Permit me to smoke.* =*Permit my smoking.* 담배 좀 피우게 해 주십시오 / *Permit me a few words.* =*Permit a few words to me.* 몇 말씀 여쭙겠습니다 / *Permit me to finish my statement.* 내 말을 끝까지 들어주십시오 / *We are not permitted to call him on the telephone.* 우리가 그를 전화통에 불러낼 수는 없다. **2** make (something) possible; admit; do not prevent. …을 가능하게 하다; …을 인정하다; …하도록 하다. ¶ ~ *parking* 주차를 허가하다 / *The law does not* ~ *the sale of this book.* 법으로 이 책은 판매가 금지되어 있다 / *No infringement will be permitted.* 위반은 용서되지 않는다.

— *vi.* (P1,3) **1** afford opportunity; make possible. 허용하다; 가능하게 하다. ¶ *I'll go, weather permitting.* 날씨가 좋으면 가겠다 / *Please drop in when time permits.* 시간이 허락하면 들르십시오. **2** 《*of*》 admit of. 여유〔여지〕가 있다. ¶ *The situation permits of no delay.* 사태는 일각을 지체할 수 없다 / *It permits of no excuse.* 변명은 있을 수 없다.

— [pə́ːrmit, pərmít] *n.* Ⓒ a written order allowing someone to do something. 허가증; 면허장; 감찰. ¶ *a* ~ *to hunt* 수렵 허가증 / *get a* ~ *to carry a gun* 무기 휴대증을 받다 / *Do you have a* ~ *to fish in this lake?* 이 연못의 낚시 허가증이 있나. [L. *mitto* send]

per·mu·ta·tion [pə̀ːrmjutéiʃən] *n.* Ⓒ **1** 《math.》 any one of the possible orders in which a number of things can be arranged. 순열(順列). **2** alteration. 변경; 교체; 변환. [→mutable]

per·ni·cious [pərníʃəs] *adj.* destructive; harmful; fatal. 파괴적인; 유해한; 치명적인. ¶ *a* ~ *habit* 나쁜 버릇 / *an ideology* ~ *to young mind* 젊은이에게 해로운 이데올로기 [L. *nex* death]

per·ox·ide [pərɑ́ksaid / -rɔ́k-] *n.* ⓊⒸ an oxide containing a large amount of oxygen. 과산화물; 페록사이드. ¶ *hydrogen* ~ = ~ *of hydrogen* 과산화 수소. [per-]

per·pen·dic·u·lar [pə̀ːrpəndíkjələr] *adj.* **1** upright; at right angles. 직립한; 수직의; 직각의(cf. *horizontal*). ¶ *a* ~ *line* 수직선 / *The floor of a room is* ~ *to the side walls and parallel to the ceiling.* 방바닥은 벽과 직각을 이루고 천장과는 평행한다. **2** very steep. 가파른. ¶ *a* ~ *cliff* 깎아지른 낭떠러지. — *n.* **1** Ⓒ a perpendicular line. 수직선. **2** Ⓤ a perpendicular position. 수직(의 위치). ¶ *out of (the)* ~ 경사져. [L. *perpendiculum* plumb-line]

per·pen·dic·u·lar·ly [pə̀ːrpəndíkjələrli] *adv.* in a perpendicular manner. 수직으로; 아주 가파르게.

per·pe·trate [pə́ːrpətrèit] *vt.* (P6) do or commit (something bad). (나쁜 짓 등)을 하다; 범하다. ¶ *The king's brother perpetrated the cruel murder of the prince.* 왕의 동생은 왕자를 살해하는 잔인한 짓을 했다 / *~ a crime* 죄를 저지르다. [L. *patro* effect]

per·pe·tra·tor [pə́ːrpətrèitər] *n.* Ⓒ a person who perpetrates (something). 못된 짓을 하는 사람; 가해자; 범인.

*__per·pet·u·al__ [pərpétʃuəl] *adj.* **1** lasting forever; eternal. 영구한; 영원한. ¶ *~ snow(s)* 만년설 / *a ~ rose* 사계절 피는 장미. **2** lasting throughout life. 종신의. ¶ *a ~ annuity* 종신 연금 / *~ punishment* 종신형. **3** continuous; frequent. 끊임없는; 빈번한. ¶ *~ change* 끊임없는 변화 / *The house demands ~ care.* 그 집은 자주 손을 봐야 한다 / *~ quarreling* 〔*questions*〕 끊임없는 싸움〔질문〕. [L. *peto* seek]

per·pet·u·al·ly [pərpétʃuəli] *adv.* forever; constantly. 영구히; 간단 없이.

per·pet·u·ate [pə(ː)rpétʃuèit] *vt.* (P6) make (something) perpetual; cause (something) to be remembered forever. …을 영속시키다; 불멸〔불후(不朽)〕케 하다. ¶ *~ one's name* 이름을 길이 (후세에) 남기다 / *The statue was erected to ~ the memory of a benefactor.* 상(像)은 기증자를 영원히 기념하기 위해 세워졌다.

per·pet·u·a·tion [pə(ː)rpètʃuéiʃən] *n.* Ⓤ the act of perpetuating; the state of being perpetuated. 영구화; 불후〔불멸〕케 함.

per·pe·tu·i·ty [pə̀ːrpətjúːəti] *n.* (*pl.* **-ties**) **1** Ⓤ the state of being perpetual. 영속; 불변. **2** Ⓒ something perpetual. 영속하는 것. **3** Ⓤ 《law.》 a perpetual possession. 영구 재산〔소유권〕. **4** Ⓒ a perpetual annuity. 종신 연금.

in* 〔*to, for*〕 *perpetuity, forever. 영구히.

*__per·plex__ [pərpléks] *vt.* (P6,13) 《*about, at, with*》 make difficult for (someone) to understand; puzzle; bewilder; confuse. …을 당혹케 하다; 난감〔난처〕하게 하다. ¶ *~ someone* 〔*someone's mind*〕 아무를〔의 마음을〕 난감하게 만들다 / *feel* 〔*be*〕 *perplexed about something* 어떤 일로 난감해하다 / *He is perplexed with the problem.* 그 문제로 고민하고 있다. [L. *plecto* plait]

per·plexed [pərplékst] *adj.* puzzled; bewildered; confused. 당혹한; 어쩔 바를 모르는; 혼란한; 복잡한. ¶ *a ~ question* 복잡한 질문.

per·plex·ing [pərpléksiŋ] *adj.* puzzling; bewildering; confusing. 난처하게 하는; 당혹케 하는; 복잡한. ● **per·plex·ing·ly** [-li] *adv.*

per·plex·i·ty [pərpléksəti] *n.* (*pl.* **-ties**) **1** Ⓤ the state of being perplexed; puzzlement; bewilderment; confusion. 혼란; 곤혹; 당혹. ¶ *in one's ~* 당혹하여. **2** Ⓒ something that perplexes. 난처한 일. ¶ *to one's ~* 난처하게도.

per·qui·site [pə́ːrkwəzit] *n.* Ⓒ any profit or right added to one's regular pay. 임시 수당; 부수입. ¶ *The maid's perquisites include the old dresses of her mistress.* 하녀의 부수입에는 안주인의 헌 옷가지도 있다. [→quest]

per se [pər séi, -síː] *adv.* 《L.》 in or by itself. 그 자체로서; 본질적으로.

*__per·se·cute__ [pə́ːrsikjùːt] *vt.* **1** (P6) treat (someone) cruelly, esp. because of religious reasons. (이교도 등)을 박해〔학대〕하다. ¶ *The Romans persecuted the Christians.* 로마인들은 기독교도를 박해했다. **2** 《*with*》 treat badly; do harm to again and again; annoy. …을 못 살게 굴다; 괴롭히다. ¶ *~ someone with questions* 아무를 질문 공세하다 / *The cruel boy persecuted the cat by throwing stones at it whenever it came near.* 그 못된 아이는 고양이가 다가올 때마다 돌을 던져 괴롭혔다. [L. *sequor* follow]

per·se·cu·tion [pə̀ːrsikjúːʃən] *n.* ⓊⒸ the act of persecuting; the state of being persecuted. 박해; 학대; 괴롭힘. ¶ *the ~ of the Jews* 유대인 박해.

persecution mania 〔**complex**〕 [—ˊ—ˋ—ˊ—〔ˊ—〕] *n.* an insane delusion that one is persecuted. 피해 망상.

per·se·cu·tor [pə́ːrsikjùːtər] *n.* Ⓒ a person who persecutes. 박해자.

Per·seph·o·ne [pəːrséfəni] *n.* 《Gk. myth.》 the queen of the lower world. 페르세포네《명부(冥府)의 여왕》.

Per·seus [pə́ːrsjuːs, -siəs] *n.* 《Gk. myth.》 the hero who killed Medusa. 페르세우스《Zeus의 아들》.

*__per·se·ver·ance__ [pə̀ːrsəvíːrəns] *n.* Ⓤ the act of persevering; patience; refusal to give up. 인내(력); 불요 불굴(不撓不屈). [↓]

per·se·vere [pə̀ːrsəvíər] *vi.* (P1,3) 《*in, with*》 continue steadily in spite of hardship; persist. 참다; 인내하다; 꾸준히 힘쓰다. ¶ *~ in one's studies* 연구를 꾸준히 계속하다 / *~ with one's task* 꾸준히 일에 힘쓰다. [L. *severus* strict]

per·se·ver·ing [pə̀ːrsəvíəriŋ] *adj.* refusing to give up; keeping on trying; patient. 참을성이 많은; 끈기 있는.

Per·sia [pə́ːrʒə] *n.* a country in southwestern Asia. 페르시아. 參考 1935년에 Iran으로 개칭.

*__Per·sian__ [pə́ːrʒən, -ʃən] *adj.* of Persia, its people, or their language. 페르시아의; 페르시아 사람〔말〕의. ¶ *a ~ carpet* 페르시아 융단. — *n.* Ⓒ **1** a person of Persia 페르시아 사람. **2** Ⓤ the language of Persia. 페르시아 말.

per·si·flage [pə́ːrsəflàːʒ, pɛ̀ərsiflάːʒ] *n.* Ⓤ joking talk; light mockery. 농담; 희롱. [F.]

per·sim·mon [pəːrsímən] *n.* Ⓒ a yellow, sweet fruit; the tree which produces this fruit. 감(나무). [Amer-Ind.]

***per·sist** [pəːrsíst, -zíst] *vi.* **1** (P1,3) 《*in*》 continue steadily in spite of difficulty; insist; say again and again. 고집하다; 주장하다; 우기다. ¶ ~ *in one's opinion* 자기 의견을 고집하다 / *Johnny persists in reading in bed.* 조니는 침대에 누워 책을 보겠다고 고집한다. **2** (P1) last; stay; remain. 살아남다; 존속하다. ¶ *The tendency* 〔*fever*〕 *still persists.* 그 경향〔열〕이 아직 있다 / *The belief persists that killing spiders brings rain.* 거미를 죽이면 비가 온다는 속설이 지금도 있다. [L. *sisto* stand]

per·sist·ence [pəːrsístəns, -zís-], **-en·cy** [-ənsi] *n.* Ⓤ the act of persisting; the state of being persistent. 고집; 버팀; 지속; 영속. ¶ *the* ~ *of a fly buzzing around one's head* 머리 둘레를 파리 한 마리가 윙윙거리며 떠나지 않음 / *the* ~ *of a cough* 기침이 멎지 않음.

***per·sist·ent** [pəːrsístənt, -zíst-] *adj.* persisting; lasting; continuing. 고집하는; 끈질긴; 영속하는. ¶ ~ *attacks* 집요한 공격 / ~ *efforts* 꾸준한 노력 / *a* ~ *headache that lasted for three days* 사흘을 계속한 끈질긴 두통.

per·sist·ent·ly [pəːrsístəntli, -zíst-] *adv.* in a persistent manner; insistently; steadily. 고집해서; 끈질기게; 꾸준히.

:**per·son** [pə́ːrsən] *n.* Ⓒ **1** a man, woman, or child; a human being. 사람《남녀 노소 모두》; 인간(cf. *people*). ¶ *a young* ~ 젊은 사람 《특히 여성에게 쓰임》 / *a nice* ~ 괜찮은 사람 / *Several persons were present.* 몇 사람이 나왔었다. **2** one's body or bodily appearance. 신체; 몸; 모습; 풍채. ¶ *No symptom of disease was observed on her* ~. 그녀의 몸에 병의 증세는 없었다 / *a young woman of an agreeable* ~ 모습에 호감이 가는 젊은 여인 / *The* ~ *of the king was sacred.* 왕의 모습은 거룩했다. **3** a character in a play, etc. (극의) 역; 등장 인물. ¶ *persons of the play* 등장 인물. **4** 《gram.》 one of the three forms of pronouns to show the person speaking (first person), the person spoken to (second person), or the person or thing spoken of (third person). 인칭. ¶ *the first* 〔*the second, the third*〕 ~, 1〔2, 3〕인칭. [L. *persona* player's mask]

in person, **a**) in one's own person; by oneself. 스스로; 자신이. **b**) in the flesh. (사진 등이 아닌) 본인 자신이. ¶ *come* 〔*appear*〕 *in* ~ 본인 자신이 오다〔나타나다〕.

in the person of, named; under the name of. …라는 이름의.

offences against the person, bodily assaults, etc. 신체에 대한 위해(危害); 폭행.

per·son·a·ble [pə́ːrsənəbəl] *adj.* good-looking; handsome. 인상이 좋은; 잘 생긴.

per·son·age [pə́ːrsənidʒ] *n.* Ⓒ **1** a person of importance or high rank. 명사(名士); 요인. **2** a person in a book or play, etc. (극 등의) 역; (등장) 인물.

:**per·son·al** [pə́ːrsənəl] *adj.* **1** individual; of a single person; private. 개인의; 개인적인; 사사로운(opp. public). ¶ *a* ~ *column* (신문의) 인사란 / *a* ~ *letter* 친전(親展) 편지; 사신 / ~ *tastes* 개개인의 취미. **2** done in person or by oneself; directly by oneself. 자신이 행하는; 본인 스스로의. ¶ *a* ~ *interview* 직접 면접 / *a* ~ *call* 직접〔개인〕적인 방문. **3** of a person's body or appearance. 신체〔풍채〕의; 용모의. ¶ ~ *appearance* 용모; 풍채 / ~ *beauty* 용모의 아름다움. **4** about or against a person or persons. 개인에 관한; 인신 공격의. ¶ ~ *abuse* 〔*remarks*〕 인신 공격; 욕설 / *Try not to be* ~. 사적인 것은 말하지〔묻지〕 않도록 해라. **5** 《gram.》 expressing persons. 인칭의. ¶ ~ *pronoun* 인칭 대명사. **6** 《law.》 of all property except land. 인적인; 동산(動産)의. ¶ ~ *property* 동산; 인적 재산. —*n.* 《*pl.*》 《U.S.》 short paragraphs in a newspaper about a particular person or persons. (신문의) 인물 비평; 인사란. [→person]

:**per·son·al·i·ty** [pə̀ːrsənǽləti] *n.* (*pl.* **-ties**) **1** Ⓤ the state, quality, or fact of being a person; one's character. 개성; 인격; 성격. ¶ *a man of strong* ~ 개성이 강한 사람 / *The writer's* ~ *can be seen in what he writes.* 저자의 개성이 그의 작품에 나타난다 / *a double* ~ 이중 인격 / *A pleasing* ~ *helps to sell goods.* 호감이 가는 성격은 장사에 도움이 된다. **2** Ⓤ one's existence as an individual, a person, or personage. 개인으로서의 존재; 사람. **3** Ⓒ a person who is well known in certain circles; a personage. (어느 방면의) 유명 인사. ¶ *a leading* ~ *of the stage* 그 무대에서의 유명인. **4** 《often *pl.*》 unpleasant remarks about a person. 인물 비평; 인신 공격. ¶ *Sharp personalities were exchanged on both sides.* 양쪽에서 심한 말이 오갔다.

***per·son·al·ly** [pə́ːrsənəli] *adv.* **1** without help from others; by oneself. 자신이; 스스로. ¶ *be* ~ *responsible* 스스로 책임을 지다 / *attend to business* ~ 자신이 직접 실무에 임하다. **2** as a person 개인으로서; 인간으로서. ¶ *I dislike the writer* ~, *but I admire his style.* 인간적으론 그 작가가 싫지만 그의 문체는 높이 평가한다. **3** as far as one is concerned; as regards oneself. 자기로서는; 개인으로서는. ¶ *Personally, I think you are right.* 나로서는 네가 옳다고 생각한다.

per·son·ate [pə́ːrsənèit] *vt.* (P6) **1** play a part in a drama, etc. 역을 맡아 연기하다. **2** pretend to be (another person). (남의) 행세를 하다; …인 체하다.

per·son·a·tion [pəːrsənéiʃən] *n.* Ⓤ **1** the act of personating. 역(役)을 맡아 하기. **2** the state of being personated. (신분의) 사칭.

per·son·i·fi·ca·tion [pəːrsɑ̀nəfikéiʃən / -sɔ̀n-] *n.* **1** Ⓤ representing as a person, such as speaking of the sun as he, and the moon as she. 인격화; 의인(擬人)(화). **2**

Ⓤ《rhet.》a figure of speech in which a lifeless thing or quality is spoken of as if alive. 의인법(擬人法). **3** Ⓒ a person or thing imagined as a striking example of some quality. 권화(權化); 화신(化身). ¶ *He is the ~ of selfishness.* 그는 이기주의의 화신이다. [→person]

per·son·i·fy [pəːrsɑ́nəfài / -sɔ́-] *vt.* (P6) (**-fied**) regard or imagine (something) as a person; stand for in one's person; represent. …을 의인화(擬人化)하다; 인격화하다; …의 화신(化身)이 되다. ¶ *Satan personifies evil.* 사탄은 악의 화신이다 / *We often ~ a ship by referring to it as 'she'.* 흔히 우리는 배를 의인화하여 그것을 언급할 때 'she'라고 한다.

per·son·nel [pə̀ːrsənél] *n.* Ⓤ《*collectively*》the persons employed in a company, etc.; a body of employees. 전(全)직원〔사원〕. ¶ *the ~ department* 인사과.

per·spec·tive [pəːrspéktiv] *n.* **1** Ⓤ the art of drawing to show depth and distance. 투시 화법; 원근법(遠近法). **2** Ⓒ a picture so drawn. 투시화. **3** Ⓤ the relationship of objects, scenes, or events. 배경; 원근(遠近); 배합; 관계. **4** Ⓒ a distant view; a view in front. 원경; 조망(眺望). **5** the effect of the distance of events upon the mind. 전망; 예상; 예측.

in perspective, **a**) according to the rules of perspective. 원근법에 의해. **b**) in a true relationship. 올바른 관계에서. ¶ *see things in ~* 사물을 바로 보다.

— *adj.* of or drawn in perspective. 투시 화법의; 원근법에 의한. ¶ *a ~ drawing* 투시 화법. [L. *specio* look]

per·spi·ca·cious [pə̀ːrspəkéiʃəs] *adj.* quick to understand or judge; acute. 이해가 빠른; 총명한. ¶ *a ~ mind* 이해가 빠른 사람. [↑]

per·spi·cac·i·ty [pə̀ːrspəkǽsəti] *n.* Ⓤ the state of being perspicacious; keen perception; acuteness. 안식(眼識); 총명.

per·spi·cu·i·ty [pə̀ːrspəkjúːəti] *n.* Ⓤ the quality of being perspicuous; acuteness; clearness; plainness. 명민(明敏); 명석; 명료.

per·spic·u·ous [pəːrspíkjuəs] *adj.* easy to be understood; clearly expressed; clear. 명료한; 명쾌한. ¶ *~ writing* 명쾌한 필법.

per·spic·u·ous·ly [pəːrspíkjuəsli] *adv.* in a perspicuous manner; clearly. 명료〔명쾌〕하게.

per·spi·ra·tion [pə̀ːrspəréiʃən] *n.* Ⓤ the act of perspiring; sweat. 발한(發汗) (작용); 땀. ¶ *drops of ~* 땀방울. [↓]

per·spire [pərspáiər] *vi., vt.* (P1; 6) sweat; exude. 땀을 흘리다; 발한(發汗)하다; 분비하다; 내다. 參考 sweat 보다 품위 있는 말. ¶ *She perspired heavily when she played volleyball.* 그녀는 배구할 때 몹시 땀을 흘렸다. [L. *spiro* breath]

:per·suade [pəːrswéid] *vt.* (P13,15,20) get (someone) to do as one wishes; cause (someone) to believe; convince. …을 설득해서 —시키다; …을 설득〔납득〕시키다; 믿게 하다. ¶ *~ someone out of these ideas* 아무를 설득해서 이들 생각을 버리게 하다 / *~ someone to come* 아무를 오도록 설득하다 / *~ someone into believing* 아무를 믿게끔 설득하다 / *~ someone of the truth* = *~ someone that it is true* 아무에게 사실임을 납득시키다 / *be persuaded of someone's innocence* = *be persuaded that someone is innocent* 아무가 무죄임을 믿다 / *~ oneself that...* …이라고 믿다. [→suasion]

per·sua·sion [pəːrswéiʒən] *n.* **1** Ⓤ the act or power of persuading; the state of being persuaded; belief; conviction. 설득(력); 신념; 확신. ¶ *He spoke with great ~.* 그는 아주 설득력 있게 말했다 / *It is my private ~ that he is mad.* 나 혼자 생각인데 그는 미쳤다. **2** a religious belief; a religious sect holding a certain belief. 신조; 종파(宗派). ¶ *He is of the Methodist ~.* 그는 감리교파다.

per·sua·sive [pəːrswéisiv] *adj.* having the power to persuade; convincing. 설득력이 있는〔좋은〕. ¶ *a ~ argument* 〔*talker*〕 설득력 있는 논거〔논객〕.

per·sua·sive·ly [pəːrswéisivli] *adv.* in a persuasive manner. 설득력 있게.

PERT [pəːrt] *n.* a method for completing a vast, complex job (such as building a skyscraper) with minimum labor, time and cost, by the aid of computers. 퍼트방식《대규모 프로젝트를 되도록 합리적·신속·경제적으로 완성시키는 방법》. [*P*rogram *E*valuation and *R*eview *T*echnique]

pert [pəːrt] *adj.* rude in speech or manner; impudent. 건방진; 방자한(opp. modest). ¶ *a ~ girl* 되바라진 소녀 / *a ~ reply* 건방진 대답. [L. *apertus* open]

per·tain [pərtéin] *vi.* (P3)《*to*》belong to; refer; be suitable for or to. 속하다; 관계하다; 어울리다. ¶ *a disease which pertains to poverty* 가난에 붙어다니는 질병 / *We own the house and the land pertaining to it.* 우리는 집과 거기 딸린 땅을 소유하고 있다 / *That remark hardly pertains to the matter in hand.* 그 말은 당면 문제와 거리가 멀다 / *It does not ~ to the young to instruct their elders.* 젊은 사람이 윗사람에게 이래라 저래라 해서는 못쓴다. [→tenable]

per·ti·na·cious [pə̀ːrtənéiʃəs] *adj.* holding firmly to an opinion, a purpose, an action, etc.; stubborn; persistent. 굳게 결심한; 완고한; 고집센. ¶ *A bulldog is a ~ fighter.* 불독은 불굴의 투견이다. [L. *pertināx* holding firmly]

per·ti·nac·i·ty [pə̀ːrtənǽsəti] *n.* Ⓤ the state or quality of being pertinacious. 집요; 불굴; 완고.

per·ti·nence [pə́ːrtənəns], **-nen·cy** [-si] *n.* Ⓤ the state or quality of being pertinent; fitness. 적절; 타당. ¶ *the ~ of the evidence* 증거의 타당성. [↓]

per·ti·nent [pə́ːrtənənt] *adj.*《*to*》right

and proper; being to the point. 적절한; 요령 있는. ¶ *be ~ to the subject* 이 문제에 적절하다 / *If your question is ~, I will answer it.* 네 질문이 이치에 맞는다면 내가 대답하지. [per-, L. *teneo* hold]

per·turb [pərtə́:rb] *vt.* (P6) make anxious or afraid; disturb (someone), esp. in mind; agitate. …을 불안하게 만들다; 당황하게 하다; 마음을 어지럽히다. ¶ *Mrs. Smith was much perturbed by her son's illness.* 아들의 병으로 스미스 부인은 크게 당황했다. [L. *turbo* trouble]

per·tur·ba·tion [pə̀:rtərbéiʃən] *n.* **1** Ⓤ the act of perturbing; the state of being perturbed; disturbance. 동요; 낭패; 불안. **2** Ⓒ a thing or cause that perturbs. 불안의 씨.

Pe·ru [pərú:] *n.* a country on the west coast of South America. 페루. 參考 수도는 Lima.

pe·ruke [pərú:k] *n.* Ⓒ a wig worn by men in the 17 and 18 centuries. (남성) 가발. [It.]

〈peruke〉

pe·rus·al [pərú:zəl] *n.* Ⓤ the act of reading carefully. 정독(精讀). ¶ *I have just finished the ~ of your letter.* 막 당신의 편지를 자세히 읽었소. [↓]

pe·ruse [pərú:z] *vt.* (P6) read carefully; examine; look over. 숙독하다; 음미하다. ¶ *~ a book* (*letter*). [→use]

Pe·ru·vi·an [pərú:viən] *adj.* of Peru or its people. 페루 (사람)의. —*n.* Ⓒ a person of Peru. 페루 사람. [*Peru*]

per·vade [pərvéid] *vt.* (P6) spread throughout; penetrate; pass into all parts of. …에 널리 퍼지다; 두루 미치다. ¶ *The strong odor of pines pervades the air.* 진한 소나무 향기가 공기 속에 그득하다 / *He worked so hard that weariness pervaded his whole body.* 그는 과로해서 온 삭신이 노곤했다. [L. *vado* go]

per·va·sion [pərvéiʒən] *n.* Ⓤ the act of pervading; the state of being pervaded. 두루퍼짐; 고루 미침; 보급.

per·va·sive [pərvéisiv] *adj.* tending to spread throughout. 온통 퍼지는; 널리 미치는. ● **per·va·sive·ly** [-li] *adj.* **per·va·sive·ness** [-nis] *n.*

per·verse [pərvə́:rs] *adj.* **1** persisting in doing something undesired; contrary. 외고집의; 심통사나운. ¶ *The ~ man continued to smoke, against his doctor's orders.* 그 심통사나운 사람은 의사의 지시에도 불구하고 계속 담배를 피웠다. **2** persistent in wrong. 완고한; 완미(頑迷)한. **3** ill-tempered; wicked. 사악한. ● **per·verse·ly** [-li] *adv.* [→versatile]

per·ver·sion [pərvə́:rʒən, -ʃən] *n.* **1** Ⓤ the act of perverting; the state of being perverted. (의미 등의) 곡해(曲解); 악용. ¶ *The statement is an audacious ~ of the truth.* 그 성명은 대담하게도 진실을 왜곡한 것이다. **2** Ⓒ an abnormal or wrong form of something. 도착(倒錯); 변태; 전도(轉倒). ¶ *sexual ~* 성욕 도착; 변태 성욕.

per·ver·si·ty [pərvə́:rsəti] *n.* ⓊⒸ (*pl.* **-ties**) the state or quality of being perverse. 사악; 외고집.

per·ver·sive [pərvə́:rsiv] *adj.* tending to pervert. 나쁜 길로 이끄는.

per·vert [pə:rvə́:rt] *vt.* (P6) lead or turn away from the right way or purpose; misuse; twist the meaning of (something). …을 그르치다; 그릇되게 이끌다; 악용하다; 곡해하다. ¶ *~ someone* 남을 그릇 이끌다 / *~ one's mind* 마음을 그릇되게 먹다 / *~ one's judgment* 판단을 그르치다 / *To ~ what someone has said is to give a wrong meaning to it.* 남이 한 말을 곡해한다는 것은 그 말을 잘못 해석한다는 뜻이다. — [pə́:rvə:rt] *n.* Ⓒ a perverted person. 타락한 자; 변절자. [per-, L. *verto* turn]

per·vi·ous [pə́:rviəs] *adj.* **1** 《*to*》 that can be penetrated; giving passage to something. 통하게 하는; 투과시키는. ¶ *Glass is ~ to light.* 유리는 빛을 투과시킨다. **2** 《*to*》 open or accesible to reason, feeling, argument, etc. (도리·말 따위가) 통하는; 아는. ¶ *~ to reason* 도리를 아는. [L. *via* road]

pe·so [péisou] *n.* Ⓒ (*pl.* **-sos**) 《Sp.》 the unit of money and a silver coin used in Latin American countries or in the Philippines. 페소.

pes·si·mism [pésəmìzəm] *n.* Ⓤ the tendency to think the worst of everything; a belief that life is not worth living. 비관(주의); 염세(주의)(opp. optimism). [L. *pessimus* worst]

pes·si·mist [pésəmist] *n.* Ⓒ a person who believes in pessimism. 비관론자; 염세주의자(opp. optimist).

pes·si·mis·tic [pèsəmístik] *adj.* taking the worst view of everything. 염세적인 (opp. optimistic).

pest [pest] *n.* **1** Ⓒ a thing or person that causes trouble or harm. 골치 아픈 사람(물건); 골칫거리. ¶ *Flies an mosquitoes are pests.* 파리와 모기는 성가신 벌레들이다. **2** ⓊⒸ 《*arch.*》 pestilence; the plague. 역병; 흑사병; 페스트. [L. *pestis* plague]

pes·ter [péstər] *vt.* (P6,13) trouble; worry. …을 괴롭히다; 애먹이다. ¶ *~ someone with questions* 아무를 귀찮게 물어대다 / *We were pestered with flies.* 파리 때문에 애먹었다.

pest·house [pésthàus] *n.* Ⓒ (*pl.* **-hous·es**) 《*arch.*》 a hospital for people infected with plague. 격리 병원.

pes·tif·er·ous [pestífərəs] *adj.* **1** spreading diseases or infections. 전염성의. ¶ *Rats are ~.* 쥐는 병을 전염시킨다. **2** bringing moral evil. 도덕적인 해를 가져오는; 불건전한. **3** 《*colloq.*》 troublesome; annoying. 골치 아픈; 성가신. [→pest]

pes·ti·lence [péstələns] *n.* ⓊⒸ any dangerous disease which spreads rapidly. 유행병; 페스트.

pes·ti·lent [péstələnt] *adj.* **1** bad for health; often bringing death. 전염성의; 몸에 해로운; 치명적인. ¶ *Smallpox, yellow fever, and the plague are ~ diseases.* 천연두, 황열병 및 페스트는 전염병이다. **2** morally harmful. 도덕적으로 유해한. ¶ *a ~ den of vice* 악의 소굴. **3** 《*colloq.*》 troublesome; annoying. 성가신; 귀찮은. ¶ *a ~ fellow* 골치 아픈 친구.

pes·ti·len·tial [pèstəlénʃəl] *adj.* **1** carrying dangerous diseases; harmful; dangerous. 역병(疫病)을 가져오는; 유해〔위험〕한. **2** 《*colloq.*》 exciting disgust. 역겨운. ¶ *a ~ nuisance* 역겨운 일.

pes·tle [pésl] *n.* Ⓒ a stick used for breaking things to powder in a mortar. 막자; 공이. — *vt., vi.* (P6;1) pound with pestle; use apestle. 막자로 빻다; 막자를 쓰다. [L. *pinso* pound]

*__pet__[1] [pet] *n.* Ⓒ **1** a small animal, bird, etc. kept in the house. 애완 동물; 페트. ¶ *keep pets / a ~ shop* 애완 동물 가게. **2** a darling; a favorite. 소중한 사람〔물건〕. ¶ *make a ~ of a little girl* 어린 소녀를 귀여워하다. — *adj.* **1** treated as a pet. 애완의; 총애하는. ¶ *a ~ lamb* 애완 동물로 기르는 새끼양. **2** favorite; especially liked. 귀여워하는; 특히 좋아하는. ¶ *Politics is his ~ subject.* 그는 정치학을 특히 좋아한다. — *vt.* (**pet·ted, pet·ting**) (P6) **1** treat (an animal, etc.) as a pet. …을 귀여워하다. ¶ *She petted the little dog.* **2** touch (someone) in a loving way. …을 애무하다; 페팅하다. [Sc.]

one's **pet aversion,** something one esp. dislikes. 아주 싫은 것.

pet[2] [pet] *n.* Ⓒ an unsatisfied state of mind; a burst of ill humor. 기분이 나쁨〔언짢음〕. ¶ *in a ~* 기분이 안 좋아서. [↑]

pet·al [pétl] *n.* Ⓒ 《bot.》 the colored part of a flower. 꽃잎. [Gk.]

pe·tard [pitɑ́ːrd] *n.* 《hist.》 a small bomb for breaking doors or gates; a kind of firework. (성문 파괴용) 폭약; 폭죽. [L. *pedo* break wind]

hoist with *one's* **own petard,** caught and injured with one's own evil plans. 자승자박이 되어.

Pe·ter [píːtər] *n.* a man's name. 남자 이름. ¶ *Peter the Great* 피터 대제(大帝) / *Saint* 〔*St.*〕 *Peter* 성베드로. [Gk. *petra* stone]

rob Peter to pay Paul, take or borrow from one person to pay another. 한쪽에서 빼앗아 다른 쪽에 주다; 빚내서 빚을 갚다.

pe·ter [píːtər] *vi.* (P2A) 《*sl.*》 《*out*》 slowly end or disappear; give out. 서서히 끝나다〔사라지다〕. ¶ *My energy* 〔*enthusiasm*〕 *petered out.* 나는 기운이〔열의가〕 서서히 없어졌다. [↑]

*__pe·ti·tion__ [pitíʃən] *n.* Ⓒ **1** an earnest request; a formal request from a lower to a higher officer; a letter containing such requests. 청원; 신청; 청원서. ¶ *a ~ to the mayor for cleaner streets* 길을 좀 깨끗이 해달라고 시장에게 청원하다. **2** prayer. 기도. ¶ *She made a silent ~ to God for help.* 그녀는 도움을 달라고 조용히 하느님께 기도했다. — *vi., vt.* (P3,4; 6,8,13,20) make a petition to (someone); pray. (…에) 청원하다; 기도하다. ¶ *~ the king* 〔*a court of law*〕 왕〔법정〕에 청원하다. [L. *peto* ask]

pe·ti·tion·er [pitíʃənər] *n.* Ⓒ a person who petitions. 청원자.

pet name [⌐⌐] *n.* one familiarly used as expressing affection. 애칭.

pet·rel [pétrəl] *n.* Ⓒ a black and white sea bird. 바다제비류의 새. [→Peter]

storm(y) petrel, 《*fig.*》 a person whose coming is the cause of disturbance, etc. 오기만하면 궂은 일 등이 생긴다고 하는 사람.

pet·ri·fac·tion [pètrəfǽkʃən] *n.* Ⓤ the act of petrifying; the state of being petrified. 석화(石化) 작용; 망연자실(茫然自失). [↓]

pet·ri·fy [pétrəfài] *v.* (**-fied**) *vt.* (P6,13) **1** turn (something) into stone. …을 돌이 되게 하다. ¶ *There is a petrified forest in Arizona.* 애리조나 주에 석화(石化)한 삼림이 있다. **2** 《*fig.*》 make (someone or something) motionless with fear or surprise. (공포 등으로) …을 돌처럼 굳어지게 하다. ¶ *She was petrified with fear.* 그녀는 무서워서 오금을 펴지 못했다. — *vi.* (P1) **1** become stone. 돌이 되다. **2** be stony or motionless. 돌처럼 굳어지다. [Gk. *petra* stone]

pet·rol [pétrəl] *n.* Ⓤ 《Brit.》 gasoline. 가솔린. [↓]

pe·tro·le·um [pitróuliəm] *n.* Ⓤ a heavy, brown oil obtained from the earth. 석유. ¶ *crude ~* 원유 / *Gasoline, kerosene, and paraffin are made from ~.* 가솔린, 등유 및 파라핀은 석유로 만든다. [Gk. *petra* stone, L. *oleum* oil]

pet·ti·coat [pétikòut] *n.* Ⓒ **1** a underskirt worn by girls and women. 페티코트. **2** 《*colloq.*》 a woman; a girl; 《*pl.*》 female sex. 여자; 소녀; 여성. — *adj.* of or by a woman; feminine. 여자의; 여성에 의한. ¶ *~ government* 내주장; (정계에서의) 여성 정치; 여인 천하. [=*petty coat*]

pet·ti·fog [pétifàg, -fɔ̀(ː)g] *vi.* (P1) be or act like a pettifogger. 궤변을 늘어놓다; 되잖은 말을 하다. [*petty*, ? obs. Du. *focker* cheater]

pet·ti·fog·ger [pétifàgər, -fɔ̀(ː)g-] *n.* **1** an inferior lawyer. 삼류〔엉터리〕 변호사. **2** any inferior person who uses petty, mean, cheating methods. 궤변을 농하는 사람; 협잡꾼.

pet·tish [pétiʃ] *adj.* ill-tempered and complaining; easily angered; peevish. 심술이 난; 걸핏하면 화내는. ¶ *a ~ reply* 퉁명스러운 대답 / *a ~ child* 부루퉁한 아이. [→pet]

*__pet·ty__ [péti] *adj.* (**-ti·er, -ti·est**) **1** small;

unimportant. 작은; 하찮은. ¶ ~ *theft* 좀도둑질 / ~ *cash* 잔돈(푼) / ~ *affairs* 하찮은 일 / *The children's quarrel concerned a ~ problem.* 아이들 싸움은 사소한 문제 때문이다. **2** narrow-minded; mean. 마음이 좁은; 쩨쩨한 (opp. large). ¶ *a ~ grudge* 다라운 앙심 / *Don't be so ~.* 쩨쩨하게 굴지 마. **3** on a small scale. 소규모의. ¶ *a ~ farmer* 소농(小農). ● **pet·ti·ly** [-li] *adv.* **pet·ti·ness** [-nis] *n.* [F. *petit* little]

pet·u·lance [pétʃələns] *n.* Ⓤ the state or quality of being petulant; bad temper. 토라짐; 성마름. [L. *peto* seek]

pet·u·lant [pétʃələnt] *adj.* impatient and ill-tempered. 불끈거리는; 성마른.

pe·tu·ni·a [pitjúːniə, -njə] *n.* **1** 《bot.》 Ⓒ a garden plant with flowers shaped like a trumpet. 피튜니아. **2** Ⓤ purple; a deep violet color. 암자색(暗紫色). [S. Amer. *pety* tobacco]

pew [pjuː] *n.* Ⓒ **1** a fixed wooden bench in a church. 교회의 신도석. **2** the place in a church set apart for the use of a certain family or group of people. (교회의) 가족석. **3** 《*colloq.*》 a seat of any kind; a chair. 의자; 걸상. ¶ *Can't you find a ~ somewhere?* 앉을 데가 없나요 / *Take a ~.* (손님에게) 앉으세요. [Gk. *podion* pedestal]

pew·ter [pjúːtər] *n.* **1** Ⓤ mixture of tin and lead used for making pots, etc. 백랍(白鑞). **2** Ⓒ dishes, pots, etc. made of pewter. 백랍제의 그릇. [? It.]

phag·o·cyte [fǽgəsàit] *n.* 《physiol.》 a sort of white blood corpuscle. 식세포(食細胞)(cf. *leucocyte*). [Gk. *phag-* eat, *kutos* cell]

pha·lan·ges [fəlǽndʒiːz / fə-] *n.* pl. of **phalanx.**

pha·lanx [féilæŋks, fǽl-] *n.* Ⓒ (*pl.* **-lanx·es**) **1** a group of heavily-armed ancient Greek soldiers in close ranks. (옛 그리스의) 밀집방진(密集方陣). **2** ⓐ any tightly massed body of persons, or animals united for one purpose. (사람·동물의) 밀집; 집결. ⓑ a number of persons united for a common purpose. 결사(結社). **3** (*pl.* **-lan·ges**) 《anat.》 a bone of the fingers or toes. 지골(指骨); 지골(趾骨). [Gk.]

phan·tasm [fǽntæzəm] *n.* Ⓒ **1** an imaginary vision. 환영(幻影); 환상. ¶ *the phantasms of dreams* 꿈속의 환상. **2** a ghost. 유령. **3** a deceiving likeness. 착각. [Gk. *phaino* show]

phan·tas·mal [fæntǽzməl] *adj.* of a phantasm; imaginary. 환상(공상)의.

phan·ta·sy [fǽntəsi, -zi] *n.* =fantasy.

phan·tom [fǽntəm] *n.* Ⓒ **1** a ghost; a shadowy appearance. 유령. ¶ *His fevered brain filled the room with phantoms from the past.* 열에 들뜬 그의 머리에는 방안이 과거의 죽은 망령들로 꽉 찼다. **2** something imagined. 환상; 허깨비. —*adj.* **1** of or like a ghost. 유령의(같은). ¶ *a ~ ship* 유령선. **2** imagined. 상상(가공)의. [→phantasm]

Phar·aoh [fέərou] *n.* Ⓒ the title for the kings of ancient Egypt. 파라오《옛 이집트의 왕의 칭호》. [Exod. vii. 9]

Phar·i·sa·ic [fæ̀rəséiik], **-i·cal** [-ikəl] *adj.* **1** of the Pharisees. 바리새파(派)(사람)의. **2** 《*p-*》 thinking a form to be the most important thing of all. 형식을 중시하는. **3** 《*p-*》 pretending to be highly moral without the real spirit; hypocritical. 위선의. [↓]

Phar·i·see [fǽrəsìː] *n.* Ⓒ **1** a member of an ancient Jewish religion. 바리새파의 사람. **2** 《*p-*》 a pharisaic person. 형식주의자; 위선자. [Heb.]

phar·ma·ceu·ti·cal [fɑ̀ːrməsúːtikəl / -sjúːt-] *adj.* of pharmacy. 제약학(製藥學)의; 약제의. [→pharmacy]

phar·ma·cist [fάːrməsist] *n.* Ⓒ a person who prepares medicines; a druggist. 약제사.

phar·ma·col·o·gy [fɑ̀ːrməkάlədʒi / -kɔ́l-] *n.* Ⓤ the science of drugs, their preparation, etc. 약학; 약물학.

phar·ma·co·poe·ia [fɑ̀ːrməkəpíːə] *n.* Ⓒ **1** an official list of medicines and their preparation and use. 약전(藥典); 조제서(調劑書). **2** a stock of drugs. 약물류(藥物類).

phar·ma·cy [fάːrməsi] *n.* (*pl.* **-cies**) **1** Ⓤ the science of making medicines. 조제술; 약학. **2** Ⓒ a shop for selling medicines. 약국; 약방. [Gk. *pharmakon* drug]

pha·ryn·ges [fəríndʒiːz] *n.* pl. of **pharynx.**

phar·ynx [fǽriŋks] *n.* Ⓒ (*pl.* **-ynx·es** or **-ryn·ges**) 《anat.》 the tube at the back of the mouth. 인두(咽頭). [Gk.]

•**phase** [feiz] *n.* Ⓒ **1** a stage or state in the development of events; one side or view of a subject. 단계; 국면. ¶ *The war now entered on its final ~.* 전쟁은 이제 종반전에 들어섰다. **2** one appearance of the moon in its series of changes. (달의) 상(相); 위상(位相). ¶ *The new moon and the full moon are phases of the moon.* 초승달과 보름달은 달의 위상이다. **3** one side, part, or view (of a subject). (문제 등의) 면(面); 상(相). ¶ *the most attractive ~ of her character* 그녀의 특성 중 가장 매력적인 면. **4** 《phys.》 a particular stage. 상(相). [→phantasm]

Ph. D. Doctor of Philosophy. 철학 박사.

pheas·ant [fézənt] *n.* Ⓒ (*pl.* **-ants** or *collectively* **-ant**) a large bird with a long tail and beautiful feathers. 꿩. [Gk. *Phasis*, river]

Phe·ni·cia [finíʃə, -níː- / -ʃiə] *n.* =Phoenicia.

phe·nix [fíːniks] *n.* =phoenix.

phe·nol [fíːnoul, -nɑl, -nɔ(ː)l] *n.* Ⓤ 《chem.》 a poisonous substance produced from coal tar; carbolic acid. 페놀; 석탄산(酸). [F. *phen* derivation from coal tar]

phe·nom·e·na [finámənə / -nɔ́m-] *n.* pl. of **phenomenon.**

phe·nom·e·nal [finámənl / -nɔ́m-] *adj.* **1** of a phenomenon or phenomena. 현상(現象)의. **2** unusual; wonderful. 특이한; 경이적인. ¶ *a ~ memory* 〔*harvest*〕 놀라운 기억력〔수확〕. [→phantasm]

***phe·nom·e·non** [finámənàn / -nɔ́mənən] *n.* Ⓒ **1** (*pl.* **-na**) a natural event, fact, etc. that can be seen. 현상(現象). ¶ *an electrical ~* 전기 현상 / *the phenomena of disease* 병의 현상〔현재 상태〕. **2** 《*pl.*》 something extraordinary or strange. 비범한 물건〔사람〕. ¶ *an infant ~* 신동(神童). [↑]

phew [Φ:, pj:, fju:] *interj.* a sound spoken suddenly with a strong feeling of dislike. 체; 쳇《초조하거나 불쾌할 때 내는 소리》. [Imit.]

phi·al [fáiəl] *n.* Ⓒ a small glass bottle for medicine. 작은 유리병; 약병. ¶ *a medicine ~* 약병. [Gk.]

phil. philology; philosophy.

Phil. Philippine.

phi·lan·der [filǽndər] *vi.* (P1) (of a man) make love without serious intentions. (여자를) 집적거리다; 지분거리다. [Gk. *anēr* man]

phil·an·throp·ic [fìlənθrápik / -θrɔ́p-] *adj.* of philanthropy; kindly. 박애(博愛)의; 인애(仁愛)의; 인정 많은. [Gk. *anthrōpos* man]

phi·lan·thro·pist [filǽnθrəpist] *n.* Ⓒ a person who loves mankind and does good for them. 박애주의자; 자선가.

phi·lan·thro·py [filǽnθrəpi] *n.* **1** Ⓤ the love of mankind; the desire to help mankind. 박애; 자선. **2** 《*pl.*》 an action that serves humanity. 자선 사업. ¶ *A hospital is a useful ~.* 자선 시설은 훌륭한 자선 사업이다.

phi·lat·e·list [filǽtəlist] *n.* Ⓒ a person who collects postage stamps. 우표 수집가. [↓]

phi·lat·e·ly [filǽtəli] *n.* Ⓤ the act of collecting postage stamps. 우표 수집. [Gk. *atelēs* tolltree]

phil·har·mon·ic [fìlhɑ:rmánik, fìlər- / -mɔ́n-] *adj.* loving music. 음악을 애호하는. — *n.* Ⓒ a philharmonic society or concert. 음악 협회; (음악 협회가 개최하는) 음악회. [→harmony]

Phil·ip [fílip] *n.* **1** a man's name. 남자 이름. **2** 《Bible》 one of the twelve persons who served Jesus Christ. 빌립《12 사도의 한 사람》.

***Phil·ip·pine** [fíləpì:n] *adj.* of the Philippine Islands or their people. 필리핀(사람)의.

Philippine Islands [⌐–– ⌐–], **the** *n.* = Philippines.

***Phil·ip·pines** [fíləpì:nz], **the** *n.* a group of islands in the western Pacific Ocean; a country consisting of these islands. 필리핀 군도; 필리핀 공화국《수도는 Manila》.

Phil·is·tine [fíləstì:n, filísti:n, fílistàin] *n.* **1** 《Bible》 one of the warlike people who attacked the Israelites. 필리스틴 사람. **2** a person who is commonplace. 속물(俗物). — *adj.* **1** of the Philistines. 필리스틴(사람)의. **2** lacking culture. 속물 같은. [Assyr.]

philo- [filou-] *pref.* love, loving, a lover of. '사랑하는, 사랑하는 사람'의 뜻. [Gk. *philos* dear]

phil·o·log·i·cal [filəládʒikəl / -lɔ́dʒ-] *adj.* of philology. 언어학〔문헌학〕(상)의. [↓]

phi·lol·o·gist [filálədʒist / -lɔ́l-] *n.* Ⓒ a person expert in philology. 언어〔문헌〕학자. 參考 최근에는 linguist 라고 함.

phi·lol·o·gy [filálədʒi / -lɔ́l-] *n.* Ⓤ **1** the study of the history of language; linguistics. 언어학(cf. *linguistics*). **2** the study of written records. 문헌학. [philo-, →logos]

***phi·los·o·pher** [filásəfər / -lɔ́s-] *n.* Ⓒ **1** a person who studies philosophy. 철학자; 철인(哲人). **2** a person who always faces all events calmly. 현인(賢人); 달관한 사람. ¶ *You are a ~.* 넌 문리(文理)를 깨쳤구나. [→philosopy]

phil·o·soph·ic [fìləsáfik / -sɔ́f-], **-i·cal** [-ikəl] *adj.* **1** of or like philosophy or a philosopher. 철학의; 철학자 같은. **2** devoted to philosophy. 철학에 통달한. **3** calm; reasonable. 냉정한; 이성적인. ¶ *a ~ mind* 이지적인 사람.

phi·los·o·phize [filásəfàiz / -lɔ́s-] *vi., vt.* (P1,3; 6) **1** think or use one's reason like a philosopher. 철학적으로 생각하다; 사색하다. ¶ *~ about life* 〔*death*〕 인생〔죽음〕을 사색하다. **2** make philosophic; treat from the point of view of a philosopher. 철학화하다; 철학적으로 취급하다〔보다〕.

:**phi·los·o·phy** [filásəfi / -lɔ́s-] *n.* (*pl.* **-phies**) **1** Ⓤ a study of the general truth of the universe, life, morals, etc. 철학. **2** ⓊⒸ an explanation or a theory of the universe. 철리(哲理); 원리; 세계〔우주〕관. **3** Ⓤ calmness; a calm manner of accepting things. 냉정; 깨달음. **4** ⓊⒸ a system for guiding life. 인생관. [Gk. *sophos* wise]

phil·ter, phil·tre [fíltər] *n.* a drug or potion used to make a person fall in love. 미약(媚藥)(cf. *aphrodisiac*); 마법(魔法)의 약. [Gk. *phileō* love]

phlegm [flem] *n.* Ⓤ **1** a thick liquid which comes from the nose and throat. 담(痰). **2** a sluggish temperament. 점액질(粘液質). **3** slowness; coolness; calmness. 굼뜸; 느림; 냉담; 무기력. [Gk. *phlegō* burn]

phleg·mat·ic [flegmǽtik] *adj.* **1** of or producing phlegm. 담(痰)의; 담이 많은. ¶ *~ temperament* 점액질(粘液質). **2** slow; cool; calm. 굼뜬; 냉담한. ¶ *He was ~ in the face of danger.* 그는 위험에 처해서도 냉정했다. [↑]

Phoe·ni·cia [finíʃə, -ní:- / -ʃiə] *n.* an ancient country on the coast of Syria. 페니

키아.

Phoe·ni·cian [finíʃən, -níːʃ- / -níʃiən] *adj.* of Phoenicia, its people, or their language. 페니키아(사람, 어)의. — *n.* **1** Ⓒ a person of Phoenicia. 페니키아인(人). **2** Ⓤ the language of Phoenicia. 페니키아어(語).

phoe·nix [fíːniks] *n.* Ⓒ 《Egyptian myth.》 a mythical Arabian bird which burns itself after a long life and rises fresh again from the ashes. 피닉스; 불사조(不死鳥). [Gk. *phoinix*]

·**phone** [foun] *n.* 《*colloq.*》 telephone. 전화(기); 수화기. ¶ *talk on the* ~ / *tell something over the* ~ …을 전화로 얘기하다 / *The* ~ *rang and he hurried to it.* 전화벨이 울리자 그는 급히 가서 받았다 / *The* ~ *lines are engaged.* 통화중입니다 / *Please hold the* ~ *a moment.* (수화기를 놓지 말고) 잠깐만 기다리십시오. — *vt., vi.* (P6; 3) telephone. 전화하다. ¶ *I've got to* ~ *him.* 그에게 전화해야겠다. [Abbr.]

pho·net·ic [founétik] *adj.* **1** of or representing speech sounds. 음성의; 음성을 나타내는. ¶ ~ *symbols* 〔*signs*〕 발음 기호 / *The* ~ *spelling of 'photo' is 'foto'.* 'photo'의 표음 철자는 'foto'다. **2** of phonetics. 음성학상의. [Gk. *phōneō* speak]

pho·ne·ti·cian [fòunətíʃən] *n.* Ⓒ an expert in phonetics. 음성 학자.

pho·net·ics [founétiks] *n. pl.* 《used as *sing.*》 Ⓤ the study of speech sounds and the way of pronunciation. 음성학.

phon·ic [fánik, fóun-] *adj.* of (speech) sounds. 소리의; 음성의. [↓]

pho·no·graph [fóunəgræ̀f, -grɑ̀ːf] *n.* Ⓒ 《U.S.》 a machine that reproduces the sounds of a record; a record player. 축음〔유성〕기(cf. 《Brit.》 *gramophone*). [Gk. *phōnē* sound]

pho·ny [fóuni] *adj.* (**-ni·er, -ni·est**) 《*sl.*》 not real; not true. 가짜의. — *n.* Ⓒ (*pl.* **-nies**) 《*sl.*》 a person or thing that is phony. 가짜; 사기꾼. [Ir.]

phos·phate [fásfeit / fɔ́s-] *n.* Ⓤ **1** a chemical compound containing phosphorus. 인산염(燐酸塩). **2** the substance containing this compound that makes soil fertile. 인산 비료. **3** carbonated beverage of water. 소다수(水); 탄산수(炭酸水). [→phosphorous]

Phos·phor [fásfər / fɔ́s-] *n.* 《*poet.*》 the morning star, esp. Venus. 샛별. [↑]

phos·pho·res·cence [fàsfərésns / fɔ̀s-] *n.* Ⓤ **1** the act or process of giving out light without heat. 인광(燐光)을 냄. **2** the light so produced. 인광. ¶ *the* ~ *of fire-flies* 개똥벌레의 인광. [↓]

phos·pho·res·cent [fàsfərésnt / fɔ̀s-] *adj.* giving out phosphorescence. 인광을 내는; 푸르게 빛나는.

phos·phor·ic [fasfɔ́ːrik, -fár- / fɔsfɔ́rik] *adj.* of or like phosphorus. 인의; 인 같은. ¶ ~ *acid* 인산.

phos·pho·rous [fásfərəs / fɔ́s-] *adj.* containing phosphorus in its lowest valency. 인을 함유한. ¶ ~ *acid* 아(亞)인산. [Gk. *phos* light, *pherō* carry]

phos·pho·rus [fásfərəs / fɔ́s-] *n.* Ⓤ 《chem.》 a yellowish or red material that lights and burns easily, used in making matches, etc. 인(燐). [↑]

:**pho·to** [fóutou] *n.* Ⓒ (*pl.* **-tos**) 《*colloq.*》 a photograph. 사진. — *vt., vi.* (P6; 1) take photographs of. (…을) 사진 찍다. [Abbr.]

photo- [foutou-] *pref.* light-. '빛, 사진'의 뜻. [Gk. *phōs* light]

pho·to·chem·i·cal [fòutoukémikəl] *adj.* of photochemistry. 광화학(光化學)의. ¶ ~ *smog* 광화학 스모그.

pho·to·chem·is·try [fòutoukémistri] *n.* the chemistry of the interactions of radiant energy and chemical systems. 광화학(光化學). [photo-, *chemistry*]

photo finish [ˊ- ˊ-] *n.* (in racing) a close finish that can be decided only from a photograph; any close finish of a game. 사진 판정이 필요한 결승; 대접전.

pho·to·flash lamp [fóutouflæ̀ʃ lǽmp] *n.* an electric bulb which gives a sudden bright light when one takes a photograph. (촬영용) 섬광 전구.

pho·to·gen·ic [fòutədʒénik] *adj.* **1** looking well in a photograph. 사진을 잘 받는 얼굴. **2** 《biol.》 phosphorescent. 인광(燐光)을 내는. [Gk. *-genēs* produced]

:**pho·to·graph** [fóutəgræ̀f, -grɑ̀ːf] *n.* Ⓒ a picture made with a camera. 사진. ¶ *have* 〔*get*〕 *one's* ~ *taken* 사진을 찍어 달래다. — *vt.* (P6) take a picture of (something) with a camera. …을 사진 찍다; 촬영하다. — *vi.* (P1) be photographed. 사진 찍다. ¶ *She photographs well* 〔*badly*〕. 그녀는 사진을 잘 받는다〔안 받는다〕 / *I always* ~ *badly.* 늘 사진이 시원찮다. [photo-, →-graph]

pho·tog·ra·pher [fətágrəfər / -tɔ́g-] *n.* Ⓒ a person who takes photographs. 사진사.

pho·tog·ra·phic [fòutəgrǽfik] *adj.* **1** of or like photography. 사진의; 사진 같은. ¶ ~ *accuracy* 사진 같은 정밀도. **2** used in or produced by photography. 사진에 의한; 사진으로 된. ¶ *a* ~ *record of a trip* 여행의 사진 기록.

pho·tog·ra·phy [fətágrəfi / -tɔ́g-] *n.* **1** taking photographs. 사진 촬영. **2** the science and art of taking photographs. 사진술.

pho·to·gra·vure [fòutəgrəvjúər] *n.* 《print.》 Ⓒ a picture got by etching on a metal, the product of photography. 그라비아(인쇄); 사진 요판화(凹版畵). [F. *gravure* engraving]

pho·tom·e·ter [foutámitər / -tɔ́-] *n.* an instrument that measures intensity of light. 광도계(光度計); 노출계. [→ -meter]

pho·to·mon·tage [fòutoumɑntɑ́:ʒ / -mɔn-] *n.* a composite picture made from several photographs. 포토 몽타주; 합성(몽타주) 사진.

pho·ton [fóutɑn / -tɔn] *n.* 《phys.》 a unit of visible light or of radiant energy. 광자(光子). [photo-]

pho·to·play [fóutəplèi] *n.* Ⓒ a motion-picture play. 극영화.

pho·to·te·leg·ra·phy [fòutoutilégrəfi] *n.* the electric transmission of facsimiles of photographs. 사진 전송(술); 전송 사진.

:**phrase** [freiz] *n.* Ⓒ **1** 《gram.》 a group of words not containing a subject and a predicate, used as a single word. 구; 프레이즈. ¶ *a set* ~ 성구(成句); 숙어 / *a noun* (*an adjective*) ~ 명사(형용사)구. **2** an expression often used as a unit; phraseology. 어법; 말씨. ¶ *He answered in carefully chosen phrases.* 그는 조심스럽게 말을 골라 가면서 대답했다. **3** a short, striking expression. 경구(警句). ¶ *Disraeli was a great maker of phrases.* 디즈레일리는 경구의 대가(大家)였다. **4** 《mus.》 a short part of a music piece. 악구(樂句).
— *vt.* (P6) express (something) in words. …을 말로 나타내다. ¶ *as he phrases it* 그의 말인즉 / *I shouldn't* ~ *it quite like that.* 나라면 그런 식으로 말하지 않는다. [Gk. *phrazō* tell]

phra·se·ol·o·gy [frèiziɑ́lədʒi / -ɔ́l-] *n.* ⓊⒸ (*pl.* **-gies**) the manner of expression; a particular selection and arrangement of words. 어법; 말씨; 문체; 표현법. ¶ *the* ~ *of the Bible* 성경의 문체 / *the* ~ *of the sports page of a newspaper* 신문의 스포츠난의 문체. [↑]

phre·net·ic [frinétik] *adj.* frantic or fanatic. 열광한. [Gk. *phrēn* mind]

phre·nol·o·gy [frinɑ́lədʒi / -nɔ́l-] *n.* the study of the shape of skull, supposed to show a person's mental power. 골상학(骨相學). [↑]

phthi·sis [θáisis, tái-] *n.* tuberculosis of the lungs; consumption. 폐결핵; 폐병. [Gk. *phthinō* decline]

phut [fʌt] *ad., n.* the sound of a bladder collapsing. 뻥(소리). [Hind.]
go phut, collapse; end in nothing. 터지다; 결딴나다; 실패하다.

phys·ic [fízik] *n.* Ⓤ **1** medicine, esp. one that moves the bowels. 약; 하제(下劑). **2** the science of medicine. 의술. — *vt.* (**-icked, -ick·ing**) (P6) **1** give medicine to (someone); cure. …에게 약을 먹이다; …을 치료하다. **2** handle severely. 혼내주다; 해치우다. [Gk. *phusis* nature]

:**phys·i·cal** [fízikəl] *adj.* **1** of nature; of the laws of nature; natural; belonging to the science of physics. 자연의; 자연 법칙의; 자연 과학의. ¶ ~ *science* 자연 과학 / *a* ~ *impossibility* 물리적 불가능. **2** of material things; material. 물질의; 물질적인(opp. spiritual). ¶ *the* ~ *world* 물질계 / *the* ~ *evidence* 물적 증거. **3** of the body. 몸의; 신체의. ¶ ~ *training* 체조. **4** of the science of physics. 물리학의; 물리적인. [↑]

physical anthropology [⌐-⌐-⌐-⌐--] *n.* the physiological and anatomical study of human body. 자연 인류학.

phys·i·cal·ly [fízikəli] *adv.* **1** concerning the body. 신체적으로; 신체상. ¶ ~ *and mentally* 심신(心身) 모두. **2** with reference to the natural world; materially. 자연법칙에 따라; 물질적으로. ¶ *It is* ~ *impossible.* 그건 자연법칙 상 불가능하다.

:**phy·si·cian** [fizíʃən] *n.* Ⓒ a doctor, esp. of medicine. 의사; 내과의(cf. *surgeon*). ¶ *consult a* ~ 의사의 진찰을 받다.

phys·i·cist [fízisist] *n.* Ⓒ a person who studies physics. 물리학자. 「**physic.**

phys·icked [fízikt] *v.* p. and pp. of

pys·ick·ing [fízikiŋ] *v.* ppr. of **physic.**

***phys·ics** [fíziks] *n. pl.* 《used as *sing.*》 the science that studies matter and the forces of the natural world. 물리학. [*physic*]

phys·i·og·no·my [fiziɑ́gnəmi / -ɔ́nə-] *n.* (*pl.* **-mies**) **1** Ⓤ the art of judging the character of a person by his face; Ⓒ the features of a face. 인상(관상)학; 인상술(人相術); 인상. ¶ *Can you read his* ~*?* 그 사람 인상을 말할 수 있느냐. **2** Ⓒ 《*colloq.*》 the face. 얼굴; 상판. **3** Ⓒ the general appearance (of a landscape). 외형; 외관; 지상(地相). ¶ *the* ~ *of a country* (*building*) 국토의 지세(地勢)(건물의 외관(外觀)). [→physic, → gnome]

phys·i·o·log·i·cal [fìziəlɑ́dʒikəl / -lɔ́dʒ-] *adj.* of physiology. 생리학(상)의. ¶ *the* ~ *action of alcohol* 알코올의 생리학적 작용. [↓]

phys·i·ol·o·gist [fìziɑ́lədʒist / -ɔ́l-] *n.* Ⓒ a person who studies physiology. 생리학자.

phys·i·ol·o·gy [fìziɑ́lədʒi / -ɔ́l-] *n.* Ⓤ the science that studies the parts of a living body and their operation. 생리학. [→ physic, -logy]

phys·i·o·ther·a·py [fìziouθérəpi] *n.* 《med.》 treatment of diseases and defects by physical remedies. 물리 치료법. [→physic, →therapy]

phy·sique [fizí:k] *n.* Ⓤ the form and development of the body; bodily structure. 체격. ¶ *a man of strong* (*powerful*) ~ 체격이 튼튼한(강한) 사람. [→physic]

pi·a·nis·si·mo [pìːənísəmòu] *adj.* very soft. 아주 약한. — *adv.* 《mus.》 very softly. 아주 약하게(opp. fortissimo). [It.]

pi·an·ist [piǽnist, píːən-, pjǽn-] *n.* Ⓒ a person who plays the piano. 피아니스트.

***pi·an·o**[1] [piǽnou, pjǽ-] *n.* Ⓒ (*pl.* **-an·os**) a musical instrument with many wires sounded by hammers. 피아노. ¶ *a cottage* ~ 소형 수형(竪型)(업라이트)피아노 / *a grand* ~ 그랜드 피아노 / *an upright* ~ 수형(업라이

트] 피아노. [→pianoforte]

pi·an·o[2] [piɑ́:nou] *adj.* soft. 약하고 부드러운. — *adv.* 《mus.》 softly. 약하게; 부드럽게 (opp. forte[2]). [It. =smooth, flat]

pi·an·o·for·te [piǽnəfɔ̀:rt, piæ̀nəfɔ́:rti] *n.* = piano[1]. [It. *piano* (*e forte*) =soft (& loud)]

pi·az·za [piǽzə / -ǽtsə] *n.* **1** (esp. in Italy) an open public space with houses round it. 광장(cf. *plaza*). **2** 《U.S.》 a large porch along one or more sides of a house. 회랑(回廊). [It.]

pic·a·resque [pìkərésk] *adj.* (of a style of fiction) dealing with the adventures of rogues. (소설이) 악한(惡漢)을 제재로 한. [Sp.]

pic·co·lo [píkəlòu] *n.* Ⓒ (*pl.* **-los**) a small flute. 피콜로《작은 피리의 일종》. [It.]

⁝pick[1] [pik] *vt.* **1** (P6,7) make a hole in (soil, rock, etc.) by striking with a pointed instrument; use a pointed instrument, such as the fingernail, on (something) in order to remove (something). (뾰족한 것으로) …에 구멍을 파다; …을 후비다; 파다; 쑤시다; 우비다. ¶ ~ (*the*) *ground* 땅을 파다 / ~ *one's teeth with a toothpick* 이쑤시개로 이를 쑤시다 / ~ *a thorn out of one's finger* 손가락의 가시를 빼다. **2** (P6,13) remove feathers, etc. from (a cock, hen, etc.); take (flowers, fruit, etc.) from a tree or plant. …의 깃털을 뜯다; (꽃·열매 등)을 따다. ¶ ~ *a chicken* 닭털을 뜯다 / ~ *cotton* 목화를 따다 / ~ *the meat off the bone* 뼈에서 살을 뜯어 내다 / *She likes to* ~ *flowers.* 그녀는 꽃따기를 좋아한다. **3** (P6,7) choose or select carefully. (신중히) …을 골라잡다. ¶ ~ *the best one* 제일 좋은 것을 고르다 / ~ *a partner* 파트너를 고르다 / ~ *a horse in a race* (*to make a bet on it*) (돈을 걸려고) 경마에서 말을 고르다. **4** (P6,13) seek purposely an opportunity or occasion for (something); seek and point out severely; begin (a quarrel, fight, etc.). (기회 등)을 잡다; (흠)을 들추어내다; (싸움 등)을 걸다. ¶ ~ *fault* 결점을 찾아내다 / ~ *holes* 〔*flaws*〕 *in someone* 아무의 흠을 들추다 / *He picked a fight with his brother.* 그가 동생에게 싸움을 걸었다. **5** (P6) take up (bits of food) with the bill or teeth; (of a person) eat in a small quantity. (부리 따위로) …을 쪼(아 먹)다; 조금씩 먹다. ¶ ~ *grains* 낟알을 쪼아먹다 / ~ *a bit of food* 음식을 조금 먹다. **6** (P6,13) open (a lock) with a wire, etc. without using a key (for an unlawful purpose). (자물쇠)를 따다; 열다. ¶ ~ *a lock on the door* 문의 자물쇠를 따다 / *The burglar picked the lock with a wire.* 강도는 철사로 자물쇠를 열었다. **7** (P6) pull apart; loosen. …을 찢다; 뜯다; 째다. ¶ ~ *rags* 〔*fibers*〕 넝마를〔천을〕 찢다. **8** (P6) steal from (someone's pocket); rob; pilfer. …을 훔치다; 소매치기하다. ¶ ~ *a pocket* 〔*purse*〕 주머니의 것〔지갑〕을 소매치기하다 / ~ *pockets* 소매치기하다 / 《*fig.*》 ~ *someone's brains* 아무의 지혜를 빌리다. **9** (P6) play (the guitar, etc.) with the fingers. …을 손가락으로 치다. ¶ ~ *a banjo* 밴조를 치다 / ~ *a guitar* 기타를 치다.

— *vi.* (P1,3) **1** use a pointed instrument on something; dig lightly. 찌르다; 쑤시다. **2** (of a cock, etc.) peck at the ground or take bits of food with the bill; 《*colloq.*》 eat a small quantity of. (닭 따위가) 쪼(아 먹)다; 조금씩 먹다. ¶ *some chickens picking about the yard* 마당에서 모이를 쪼아먹고 있는 몇 마리의 병아리. **3** find fault. 흠을 들추다. **4** choose carefully. 골라내다; 정선(精選)하다.

pick at, **a**) eat (one's food) only a little at a time. …을 조금씩 먹다. ¶ ~ *at the bread* 빵을 조금씩 뜯어먹다 / *She only picked at her food as she didn't like to eat.* 그녀는 먹기 싫어 음식을 그저 깨적거리기만 했다. **b**) find fault with (someone); annoy (someone) by criticizing. …의 흠을 찾다; …에 잔소리를 해대다. **c**) touch; handle; toy with. 손대다; 만지작거리다.

pick off, **a**) shoot or kill one by one. 하나씩 하나씩 저격하다. **b**) take off by picking or pulling. 따다; 뜯다.

pick on, choose or select (someone) as a victim; blame. 희생물로 …을 골라내다; 비난〔혹평〕하다. ¶ *He always picks on small points to criticize.* 그는 늘 시시한 걸 가지고 잔소리한다.

pick out, **a**) choose; select. …을 골라내다. ¶ ~ *out one's successor* 후임자를 물색하다. **b**) distinguish (someone or something) from others. …을 분간〔식별〕하다; 구별하다. ¶ ~ *out a friend from* 〔*in*〕 *the crowd* 군중 속에서 친구를 알아보다. **c**) make out (the meaning). (뜻)을 알다.

pick over, examine (a number of things) to choose from. (골라내려고) …을 점검하다.

pick up, **a**) get or acquire unexpectedly. …을 우연히 손에 넣다. ¶ ~ *a watch up on the street* 거리에서 시계를 줍다 / ~ *up information* 정보를 얻다. **b**) lift or raise (something) with the fingers or hand. …을 집어 올리다; 들다. ¶ ~ *up the ashtray* 재떨이를 집어올리다 / ~ *up a stone* 돌을 들어올리다 / ~ *up a receiver* 수화기를 들다 / ~ *up a newspaper to read* 신문을 보려고 집어들다. **c**) learn or grasp. …을 익히다; 알다. ¶ *She picked up some English words from her music teacher.* 그녀는 음악 선생님에게서 영어를 몇 마디 배웠다. **d**) recover (one's health, etc.); cheer up. (건강)을 회복하다; (기운)을 되찾다. ¶ *He will soon* ~ *up.* 그는 곧 회복될 것이다 / *Business is picking up now.* 사업이 지금 좋아지고 있다. **e**) continue; carry on. 계속하다. ¶ *He picked up where he stopped the day before.* 그는 일전에 그만둔 데서 다시 계속했다. **f**) give a ride to (someone); meet and take along. …을 태워주

다; …와 만나 같이 가다. ¶ *He picked up her on the way to school.* 그는 학교 가는 길에 그녀를 만나 같이 갔다 / *The bus picked up passengers.* 버스가 승객을 태웠다. **g**) happen to make friends with (someone). (아무)와 아는 사이가 되다. ¶ ~ *up new friends in a hotel* 호텔에서 친구들을 사귀다. **h**) increase (speed). (속력)을 더하다. ¶ *The train began to ~ up speed after leaving the station.* 기차는 정거장을 떠나 속력을 내기 시작했다.

pick one's way, select one's way carefully; walk slowly and carefully. 조심해서 걷다; 신중히 길을 찾아 가다.

— *n.* **1** Ⓤ the act or the right of selecting. 선택(권). ¶ *have one's ~ of* …의 선택권을 가지다 / *Take your ~.* 고르시오. **2** Ⓒ a person or thing selected; the best part or example. 선택된 사람〔물건〕; 최상의 것. ¶ *the ~ of the scholars* 학자의 귀감 / *the ~ of the basket* 〔*bunch*〕 정선품(精選品). [E.]

pick[2] [pik] *n.* Ⓒ **1** an iron tool with a sharp point, used for breaking up roads, etc. 곡괭이. **2** ⓐ a small pointed instrument used for cleaning the teeth, the ears, etc. 쑤시는〔후비는〕 물건《이쑤시개 따위》. ⓑ =plectrum. [*pick*[1]]

pick·a·back [píkəbæ̀k] *adv.* (of a child, etc.) on the back or shoulders. 등에 업혀; 목말 타고. ¶ *ride ~* 목말 타다. [*pick*[1]]

pick·ax, -axe [píkæ̀ks] *n.* Ⓒ a tool, having an pointed iron head at one end and the blade. 곡괭이. [*pick*[2]]

picked [pikt] *adj.* **1** especially chosen or selected. 골라 뽑은; 정선한. **2** gathered from plants. 딴; 따낸. **3** cleaned by picking. (깃털 등을) 깨끗이 뜯은. [*pick*[1]]

pick·er [píkər] *n.* Ⓒ a person or tool that gathers, picks, etc. 따는 사람〔기구〕; 곡괭이. [*pick*[1]]

pick·et [píkit] *n.* Ⓒ **1** a post fixed in the ground to make a fence, to tie a horse, etc. 말뚝. **2** 《mil.》 a group of soldiers acting as a guard. 초계병(哨戒兵); 경비대. **3** 《*pl.*》 persons watching at a factory, shop, etc., during a strike. 파업 이탈 감시원; 피킷.
— *vt.* (P6) **1** enclose (a farm, etc.) with pickets; fence. …에 말뚝을 둘러치다. **2** tie (a horse, etc.) to a picket. …을 말뚝에 매다. ¶ *Picket your horse here.* 말을 여기에 매라. **3** place pickets at or near; watch or guard. …에 감시원을 배치하다; …을 감시하다. ¶ *~ a factory* 공장에 피킷을 배치하다. **4** place (someone) as a guard. …을 감시원으로 배치하다. ¶ *Detectives were picketed here and there among the crowd.* 군중 속 여기저기에 밀정이 배치되었다.
— *vi.* (P1) serve as a picket. 감시자가 되다. [F. *piquer* prick]

pick·ing [píkiŋ] *n.* Ⓒ **1** a thing which is picked. 채집물(採集物); 훔친 물건; 장물. **2** 《*pl.*》 a thing left over; gleanings. (따다) 남은 것; 찌꺼기; 이삭. **3** Ⓤ the act of a person who picks. 파기; 따기; 채집; 훔치기. ¶ *~ and stealing* 소매치기와 도둑질. [*pick*[1]]

·**pick·le** [píkəl] *n.* Ⓤ **1** a solution of salt, vinegar, etc. used to keep or give a taste to meat, fish, vegetables, etc. (고기·야채 등을) 절이는 액체《소금물·초 따위》. **2** 《usu. *pl.*》 vegetables, esp. cucumbers, preserved in pickle. 절인 것; 피클즈《오이지 따위》. **3** Ⓒ 《*colloq.*》 a difficult situation. 난처한 입장; 곤경. ¶ *be in a ~* 곤경에 처해 있다. **4** Ⓒ 《*colloq.*》 a mischievous child. 장난꾸러기. ¶ *a regular young ~* 아주 심한 장난꾸러기.

have a rod in pickle for ⇨rod.

— *vt.* (P6) keep (a vegetable) in pickle. (소금·식초에) …을 절이다. ¶ *a pickled radish* 단무지. [Du.]

pick·pock·et [píkpɑ̀kit / -pɔ̀k-] *n.* Ⓒ a person who steals from people's pockets. 소매치기. [*pick*[1]]

pick·up [píkʌ̀p] *n.* ⒸⓊ **1** the part of a record player in which the needle is set. (전축의) 픽업. **2** 《*colloq.*》 an informal acquaintance. 어쩌다 알게 된 사람. **3** Ⓤ increase in speed; speeding up. 가속(加速). **4** 《*colloq.*》 the state of getting better in business, health, etc.; recovery. 개선; 회복. ¶ *a ~ in business* 경기 회복. **5** a small, often open truck. 소형 트럭; 픽업. **6** the person or goods taken into a vehicle. 차에 태운 사람〔실은 물건〕. [*pick*[1]]

*__pic·nic__ [píknik] *n.* Ⓒ **1** a short trip on which someone carries food for an outdoor meal. 소풍; 피크닉. ¶ *go on a ~* 소풍 가다. **2** something specially agreeable or easily done. 유쾌한〔쉬운〕 일. ¶ *no ~* 쉽지 않은 일.
— *vi.* (**-nicked, -nick·ing**) (P1) go on a picnic. 피크닉 가다. [F. *piquenique*]

pic·nicked [píknikt] *v.* p. and pp. of **picnic.**

pic·nick·ing [píknikiŋ] *v.* ppr. of **picnic.**

pic·to·ri·al [piktɔ́:riəl] *adj.* of or like pictures; expressed in pictures. 그림의; 그림 같은; 그림으로 나타낸. ¶ *~ art* 〔*skill*〕 회화술(繪畫術) / *a ~ magazine* 화보(畫報) / *~ description* 그림 같은 묘사. — *n.* Ⓒ a magazine with many pictures. 화보. [L. *pingo* paint]

⁝**pic·ture** [píktʃər] *n.* Ⓒ **1** a painting, drawing, portrait, or photograph. 그림; 초상화; 사진. ¶ *take a ~* 사진을 찍다 / *have one's ~ taken* 사진을 찍게 하다 / *sit for one's ~* 초상화를 그리게 하다. **2** a very beautiful scene, person or thing like a picture. 그림같이 아름다운 경치〔사람, 물건〕. ¶ *She is a perfect ~.* 그녀는 정말 그림처럼 아름답다 / *The trees and brook make a lovely ~.* 나무와 개울이 한 폭의 아름다운 그림을 이룬다. **3** something or someone that resembles another; an image. 똑같이 닮은 것. ¶ *You are the ~ of your cousin.* 너는 네 사촌을 꼭 닮았구나. **4** a type or symbol. 상징; 전형. ¶ *She looks the ~ of health.* 그녀는 건강의 전형이다. **5** a very clear or colorful description. 그림 같은 묘사. ¶ *give realistic pictures of life in colonial days* 식민지 시절의 생활상을 사실적으로 묘사하다 / *Kipling has given us many pictures of Indian life.* 키플링은 우리에게 인디언 생활상을 많이 묘사해 주었다. **6** a mental image or idea. 심상(心像); 상상(想像). ¶ *recall a ~ from the past* 과거를 회상하다 / *It is hard to form a true ~ of conditions in Russia.* 러시아의 진정한 상황을 상상하기는 힘들다. **7** an image on television or in a movie. (TV·영화의) 화상. **8** a motion picture; 《chiefly Brit.》 《*the ~s*》 movies. 영화. ¶ *go to the pictures* 영화 구경 가다.

in the picture, well-informed; important; relevant. 잘 알려져; 중요하여; 관련이 있어.

out of the picture, not in the picture. 관계없는; 중요치 않은; 당치 않은.

— *vt.* (P6,13) **1** paint or draw. …을 그리다. ¶ *~ a country scene* 시골 풍경을 그리다. **2** see (something) in the mind; imagine. …을 마음에 그리다〔상상하다〕. ¶ *I could not ~ him as a cowboy.* 나는 그를 카우보이로 상상할 수가 없다 / *Try to ~ yourself in his situation.* 그와 입장을 바꾸어 생각해보라 / *Picture to yourself what it must be to have no money.* 돈이 없으면 어떠할지 생각해 봐라. [L. *pingo* paint]

picture gallery [ˊ-- ˋ---] *n.* a place for showing pictures. 화랑; 미술관.

·**pic·tur·esque** [pìktʃərésk] *adj.* **1** as beautiful as a picture; vivid. 그림같이 아름다운; 생생한. ¶ *a ~ description of one's travel* 그림같이 묘사된 여행담. **2** suitable for a picture. 화제(畫題)로 삼기 좋은. ¶ *a ~ old mill* 화제로서 좋은 오래된 물방앗간. **3** (of the character of a person) original. 개성이 강한; 독창적인. [→picture, -esque]

picture writing [ˊ-- ˋ--] *n.* a primitive mode of recording events before the introduction of letters. 그림〔상형〕 문자.

·**pie**[1] [pai] *n.* UC a baked dish of fruit or meat enclosed in pastry. 파이. [E.]

(***as***) ***easy as pie,*** 《*colloq.*》 very easy. 아주 쉬운.

have a finger in the pie, be concerned or take an active part in some affair. 관여하다; 간섭하다.

pie[2] [pai] *n.* 《bird》 a magpie. 까치. [L. *pica*]

pie·bald [páibɔ̀ːld] *adj.* **1** having markings in two colors, esp. white and black. (흑백) 얼룩의. ¶ *a ~ horse.* **2** mixed; of mixed birth. 혼합한; 잡종의; 혼혈인. — *n.* C a black and white horse. (흑백의) 얼룩말. [*pie*[2]]

⁑**piece** [piːs] *n.* C **1** a part separated or broken off from a whole. 조각; 단편; 일부; 파편. ¶ *a ~ of cake* 과자 한 조각 / *tear a ~ off a newspaper* 신문지 한 장을 찢다 / *The bottle broke in pieces.* 병이 박살났다. **2** ⓐ a single thing of a set. (세트로 된 것의) 한 개; 하나. ¶ *a dinner service of 60 pieces,* 60 개 한 벌의 정찬용 식기 / *There is one ~ missing.* 한 개가 없어졌다. ⓑ one of a set of chessmen. (장기 등의) 말. **3** a unit of things of a kind; a limited part; a section; a quantity. 한 개; 한 장; 한 덩어리; (땅의) 한 구획. ¶ *a ~ of furniture* 가구 한 점 / *a ~ of road* 길의 한 구간 / *a ~ of land* 한 뙈기의 땅 / *a ~ of bread* 빵 한 덩이. **4** a single and separate instance or example. 한 예; 일례. ¶ *a ~ of advice* 충고 한 마디 / *a ~ of information* 한 가지 정보 / *a ~ of nonsense* 한 토막의 난센스. **5** a coin. 화폐. ¶ *a five-cent ~,* 5 센트짜리 화폐 / *a penny ~,* 1 페니 동전. **6** a musical or literary work, esp. a short one. (예술상의) 작품. ¶ *a Beethoven ~* 베토벤의 곡 / *a ~ of poetry* 시 한 편 / *play a ~* (*of music*) 한 곡 연주하다 / *a sea ~* 바다 그림. **7** a definite size or amount in which various articles are sold; an amount of work forming a single job. 일정량의 거래 단위《한 필, 한 통 등》; 작업량. ¶ *a ~ of wallpaper* 벽지 한 두루마리 《길이 12 야드》 / *A ~ of muslin is ten yards.* 모슬린 한 필은 10 야드다 / *The workmen are paid by the ~.* 노동자들은 작업량에 따라 임금을 받는다. **8** a rifle or gun. 총; 포(砲). **9** 《*contempt.*》 a woman; a girl. 여자; 아가씨. ¶ *a pretty ~.*

all of a piece, consistent. 일련(一連)의; 시종일관한.

give someone a piece of one's mind, scold or criticize someone frankly. …을 솔직하게 나무라다; …에게 직언하다.

go to pieces, become very nervous; lose control. 신경질적으로 되다; 자제심을 잃다.

in one piece, seamless; jointless. 꿰맨〔이은〕 데 없이.

of a piece, of the same kind; alike. 같은 종류의; 한 모양인.

piece by piece, part by part; one piece at a time. 하나씩; 조금씩.

take to pieces, separate. 해체〔분해〕하다.

— *vt.* (P6,7,13) **1** mend or patch (something) by adding a piece. …을 이어서 수선하다. ¶ *Mother pieced a quilt yesterday.* 어제 어머니는 천을 잇대어 누비 이불 하나를 만드셨다. **2** make (something) by joining sections together. …을 결합하다; 접합하다. [Rom. *pettia*; F. *petit*]

piece out, complete (a story, etc.) by joining parts or pieces. …을 이어대서 완전하게 하다.

piece together, join (things) so that they make a whole. …을 이어맞추다. ¶ *~ together the fragments of a broken vase* 깨진 꽃병 조각을 이어 맞추다 / 《*fig.*》 *~ together evidence* 증거를 종합하다.

piece up, repair by adding pieces. …을

이어 맞추어 수선하다.

piece-goods [pí:sgùdz] *n. pl.* textile, fabrics, silk, cotton, etc. made in standard lengths. 피륙.

piece·meal [pí:smì:l] *adv.* **1** piece by piece; a little at a time. 하나씩; 조금씩. ¶ *work done* ~ 조금씩 해서 된 일. **2** to pieces; into fragments. 조각조각으로. ¶ *The lamb was torn* ~ *by the wolves.* 양은 이리들에게 발기발기 찢겼다. — *adj.* coming or done piece by piece. 조각난; 단편적인. ¶ *these* ~ *reforms* 이들 단편적인 개혁.

piece·work [pí:swə̀:rk] *n.* Ⓤ work paid for according to the amount done. 성과에 따라 임금을 주는 일(opp. timework).

pied [paid] *adj.* having many colors; spotted. 얼룩덜룩한; 잡색(雜色)의. ¶ *a* ~ *coat.* [→pie²]

***pier** [piər] *n.* Ⓒ **1** a post for supporting an arch, a bridge, etc. 홍예받이; 교각. **2** a roadway reaching out into the sea from the land. 잔교(棧橋); 부두. **3** the part of a wall between windows, doors, etc. 창[문] 사이의 벽. [L. *pera*]

***pierce** [piərs] *vt.* (P6) **1** make a hole in or through (something). …에 구멍을 내다; …을 꿰찌르다. ¶ *She pierced her ears for earings.* 그녀는 귀고리를 하려고 귀에 구멍을 냈다 / *The rose thorn pierces the finger easily.* 장미의 가시는 손가락을 찌르기 쉽다. **2** go into; go through (something). …을 관통하다. ¶ *This tunnel pierces two mountains.* 이 터널이 두 산을 관통하고 있다. **3** force a way through or into. …에 스며들다; 비집고 들어가다. ¶ *The cold wind pierced our clothes.* 찬 바람이 옷 속에 스며들었다 / *A shriek pierced the night.* 날카로운 비명이 어둠을 갈랐다 / *No ray can* ~ *such darkness.* 빛도 못 들어갈 만큼 칠흑같은 어둠이다. **4** understand; see through or into; move (the feelings, etc.). …을 알아내다; 간파[통찰]하다; 감동시키다. ¶ *a heart pierced with pity* 연민의 정에 찬 마음 / ~ *a disguise* [*mystery*] 변장[비밀]을 간파하다.
— *vi.* (P2A,2B,3) 《*into, through*》 enter; go through; make passage. 들어가다; 관통하다. ¶ *The sun pierced through the clouds.* 구름 사이로 해가 나왔다 / *A point as blunt as this will never* ~. 끝이 이렇게 무디어선 뚫지 못한다 / *Here no light can* ~. 여기엔 빛이 못 들어온다. [F. *percer*]

pierc·ing [píərsiŋ] *adj.* **1** sharp; penetrating. 날카로운; 꿰찌르는. ¶ *a* ~ *glance* 날카로운 시선. **2** (of wind) cold and strong. (바람이) 차고 매서운. ¶ ~ *cold* 살을 에는 추위 / *a* ~ *wind* 매서운 바람.

Pi·er·rot [pí:əròu] *n.* Ⓒ (*pl.* **-rots** [-z]) 《sometimes *p-*》 an actor with a painted white face, amusing people by his foolish movements. 피에로. [F.]

pi·e·ty [páiəti] *n.* ⓊⒸ **1** deep respect for God; reverance felt for God. 경건; 신앙심. ¶ *Nuns live in* ~. 수녀들은 신앙 생활을 한다. **2** deep love and respect for one's parents, ancestors, etc. 효심; 효도. ¶ *filial* ~ 효도. [→pious]

:pig [pig] *n.* **1** Ⓒ a fat animal used for food; Ⓤ its meat; pork. 돼지; 돼지 고기. **2** Ⓒ 《*colloq.*》 a person who seems or acts like a pig; a person having a great desire for food. (돼지처럼) 더러운 사람; (음식에) 탐욕스러운 사람. **3** Ⓤ a small bar or mass of metal. 쇳덩어리; 금속괴(塊).

bring one's pigs to a pretty [***a fine, the wrong***] ***market,*** fail in an adventure [undertaking]. 헛장사하다; 헛짚다.

buy a pig in a poke, buy something which one does not properly know about. 잘 살피지도 않고 사다.

drive one's pigs to market, snore. 코골다.

make a pig of oneself, eat too much. (돼지처럼) 많이 먹다.

Pigs might fly. Wonders might happen. 별 신기한 일도 있군《있을 수 없는 말을 들을 때 씀》.

please the pigs, please God. 운이 좋다면.
— *vi., vt.* (P1; 6) (**pigged**) bring forth (pigs). (돼지가) 새끼를 낳다. [E.]

pig it [***together***], 《*colloq.*》 live together like pigs in a dirty uncomfortable place. 누추한 데서 함께 지내다. ¶ *His family* ~ *it in one room.* 그의 식구들은 한 방에서 우글우글 지낸다.

pig-boat [pígbòut] *n.* 《naut. *sl.*》 a submarine. 잠수함. [*pig, boat*]

:pi·geon [pídʒən] *n.* Ⓒ **1** a bird with the power of finding its way home. 비둘기. ¶ *a carrier* [*homing*] ~ 전서구(傳書鳩) / *a wood* ~ 산비둘기. **2** a clay disk thrown into air as a target for shooting. (사격용) 클레이 피전. **3** 《*sl.*》 a person easily deceived. 잘 속는 사람; 봉. — *vt.* (P6) swindle. 사취하다; 속여먹다. [L. *pipio* cheep]

pigeon breast [⌐-⌐] *n.* a swelling chest like that of a pigeon. 새가슴.

pi·geon·hole [pídʒənhòul] *n.* Ⓒ **1** a hole in which pigeons nest. 비둘기장의 출입구. **2** one of a set of boxes where papers are put. 서류 정리함의 한 칸.

〈pigeonhole 2〉

— *vt.* (P6) **1** place (a paper) in a pigeonhole. (서류)를 정리함에 넣다. **2** classify and lay aside in memory where one can refer to it. (훗날을 위해 머리속에 정리해) 기억해두다. **3** put aside with the idea of dismissing, forgetting, or neglecting. 묵살하다. ¶ *The citizens request for a new road was pigeonholed.* 새 길을 내달라는 시민들의 요청은 묵살되었다.

pi·geon·toed [pídʒəntòud] *adj.* having

the toes or feet turned inward. 발〔발가락〕이 안으로 굽은; 안짱다리의.

pig·gish [pígiʃ] *adj.* like a pig; greedy; dirty. 돼지 같은; 게걸스러운; 불결한. [*pig*]

pig·gy [pígi] *n.* Ⓒ (*pl.* **-gies**) 《*child's word*》 a little pig. 새끼돼지.

pig·gy·back [pígibæ̀k] *adv.* =pickaback.

pig·head·ed [píghèdid] *adj.* unwilling to listen to reason; stupidly stubborn. 고집 센; 완미(頑迷)한. 「(銑鐵).

pig iron [´-`-] *n.* rough iron. 무쇠; 선철

pig·ling [pígliŋ] *n.* Ⓒ a young pig. 새끼돼지. [*pig, =ling*]

pig·ment [pígmənt] *n.* **1** Ⓤ coloring matter to make paints; Ⓒ a paint. 그림물감; 안료(顔料). **2** Ⓤ 《biol.》 a natural coloring matter of a tissue. 색소(色素). ¶ *The color of flowers is due to the cells filled with ~.* 꽃들의 빛깔은 세포 속의 색소 때문이다. [L. *pingo* paint]

pig·my [pígmi] *n.,adj.* =pygmy.

pig·skin [pígskìn] *n.* **1** Ⓤ the skin of a pig; Ⓒ leather goods made from it. 돼지 가죽; 돼지 가죽 제품. **2** Ⓒ 《*colloq.*》 a saddle. 안장. **3** Ⓒ 《U.S. *colloq.*》 a football. 미식 축구공. [*pig*]

pig·sty [pígstài] *n.* Ⓒ (*pl.* **-sties**) **1** an enclosed place for pigs. 돼지 우리. **2** a dirty room or house. 지저분한 방〔집〕.

pig·tail [pígtèil] *n.* Ⓒ **1** a twisted bunch of hair hanging from the back of the head. 땋아 늘인 머리; 변발(辮髮). **2** a tail of a pig. 돼지 꼬리. **3** a twisted roll of tobacco. 가늘게 꼰 담배.

pig·wash [pígwɑ̀ʃ, ´wɔ̀ːʃ / ´wɔ̀ʃ] *n.* Ⓤ waste food for pigs. 돼지 먹이; 꿀꿀이죽.

pike[1] [paik] *n.* Ⓒ 《hist.》 a weapon with a long stick and a pointed metal head. 미늘창(槍). — *vt.* (P6) pierce with a pike; kill with a pike. 창으로 찌르다〔죽이다〕. [F. pic]

pike[2] [paik] *n.* =turnpike.

pike·staff [páikstæ̀f, -stɑ̀ːf] *n.* Ⓒ (*pl.* **-staves**) the stick of a pike. 창자루. [*pike*[1]]

as plain as a pikestaff, very easily seen or understood. 아주 명백한.

pike·staves [páikstèivz] *n.* pl. of **pikestaff.**

pi·las·ter [pilǽstər] *n.* Ⓒ an ornamental rectangular column forming the part of a wall. 벽기둥《장식적인》. [→pillar]

:pile[1] [pail] *n.* Ⓒ **1** a number of things lying one upon another; a heap; a mass. 쌓아올린 것; 더미. ¶ *a ~ of sand* 모래 더미 / *a ~ of hay* 〔*books, wood*〕 건초〔책, 장작〕 더미 / *a funeral ~* 쌓아올린 화장용 장작. **2** 《*colloq.*》 ⓐ a large amount. 대량. ¶ *a ~ of things to do* 산적(山積)한 일거리. ⓑ a large quantity of money; a fortune. 거금(巨金); 재산. ¶ *make one's ~* 한재산 만들다. **3** a large building or group of buildings. 대형 건축물(군).
— *vt.* (P6,7,13) **1** place or throw (something) in a pile. … 겹쳐 쌓다. ¶ *~ books one on top of the other* 책을 쌓아올리다 / *~ bricks* 벽돌을 쌓다 / *~ on coal* 석탄을 쌓다. **2** cover (something) with large amounts; fill. …에 산처럼 쌓다. ¶ *a wagon piled with hay* 건초를 산적한 마차. — *vi.* (P2A,2B,3) **1** form a pile. 쌓이다. ¶ *Snow piled against the fences.* 눈이 울타리에 쌓였다. **2** go confusedly in a group; crowd. 우르르 몰려가다. ¶ *They piled into the car.* 그들은 우르르 차에 올라탔다. [→pillar]

pile arms, 걸어총하다.

pile it on, 《*colloq.*》 exaggerate. 과장하다; 떠벌리다.

pile on* 〔*up*〕 *the agony, 《*colloq.*》 make a description of a painful event more agonizing than is necessary. (경험한 일의) 괴로움〔쓰라림〕을 과장해서 말하다.

pile up, **a**) heap up; store. 쌓(이)다. ¶ *~ up debts* 〔*money*〕 빚이 쌓이다〔돈을 모으다〕 / *The snow is piling up.* 눈이 쌓인다. **b**) 《naut.》 run (a ship) on rocks or aground. 배가 좌초하다. **c**) (of a motorcar) crash into another car. (차가) 연쇄 충돌하다.

pile[2] [pail] *n.* 《usu. *pl.*》 a post put into the earth for supporting a foundation. 말뚝; 파일. — *vt.* (P6) drive piles into (the ground). …에 말뚝을 박다. [L. *pilum* javelin]

pile[3] [pail] *n.* Ⓤ soft, fine hair; short hair on thick cloth or a carpet. 솜털; 보풀. [L. *pilus* hair]

pile[4] [pail] *n.* 《med.》 **1** 《usu. *pl.* used as *sing.*》 a disease with tumors of the rectal veins. 치질(痔疾). **2** such tumor. 수치질; 치핵. [L. *pila* ball]

pile driver [´ `-] *n.* a machine for driving piles into the ground. 말뚝 박는 기계. [*pile*[2]]

pil·fer [pílfər] *vt., vi.* (P6; 1) steal (something) in small amounts. 좀도둑질하다. [→pelf]

·pil·grim [pílgrim] *n.* Ⓒ **1** a person who travels on foot to a holy place. 순례자. **2** a traveler; a wanderer. 나그네; 방랑자. [→peregrinate]

pil·grim·age [pílgrimidʒ] *n.* **1** ⒸⓊ a journey to a holy place. 순례. ¶ *go on a ~* 순례 여행을 떠나다 / *make one's ~ to* …에 참여하다. **2** Ⓒ 《*fig.*》 a human lifetime. 인생행로; 생애. — *vi.* (P1) go on a pilgrimage. 순례길에 오르다.

Pilgrim Fathers [´- ´-], **the** *n. pl.* the Puritans who left England and landed at Massachusetts in 1620. 1620년 Mayflower를 타고 미국에 간 영국 청교도단.

·pill [pil] *n.* Ⓒ **1** a small ball of medicine to be swallowed whole. 알약; 환약. ¶ *a ~ to cure an earthquake* 전혀 쓸모 없는 대책. **2** 《*colloq.*》 something unpleasant but unavoidable; an unpleasant person. 싫은 것〔사람〕. ¶ *It was a bitter ~ for him to swallow.* 그에게 있어 그것은 하기 싫은 일이었다. **3** 《*sl.*》 a very small ball of anything. (야

구·골프 등의) 작은 공. [→pile[4]]

pil·lage [pílidʒ] *n.* **1** Ⓤ the act of taking goods by force, esp. in war. (특히 전시의) 약탈. **2** Ⓒ a thing stolen by force, esp. in war. 약탈품. — *vt., vi.* (P6; 1) rob (something) violently; plunder. (…을) 약탈하다; 노략질하다. ¶ *The invaders pillaged our town.* 침략군은 우리 마을을 노략질했다. [F. *piller* rob]

*__pil·lar__ [pílər] *n.* Ⓒ **1** an upright, ornamental post to support a structure; a column. 기둥. **2** something shaped like a pillar. 기둥 모양의 것. ¶ *a ~ of smoke* 〔*cloud*〕 연기〔구름〕 기둥. **3** 《*fig.*》 a firm, important supporter. 중진(重鎭); 대들보. ¶ *a ~ of the state* 나라의 주석(柱石). [L. *pila*]

pillar box [⌐–⌐] *n.* 《Brit.》 a letterbox in the street. (거리의) 우체통(cf. 《U.S.》 *mailbox*).

pill·box [pílbɑ̀ks / -bɔ̀ks] *n.* Ⓒ **1** a small box for holding pills. 알약통. **2** 《mil. *sl.*》 a small, low, concrete and steel fortress with machine guns. 토치카. [→pill]

pil·lion [píljən] *n.* the seat for a second person on a motor-bicycle, placed behind the seat of the principal rider. (오토바이의) 뒷자리. ¶ *ride ~* 오토바이 뒷자리에 타다. [L. *pellis* skin]

pil·lo·ry [píləri] *n.* (*pl.* **-ries**) **1** Ⓒ 《hist.》 a wooden framework with holes for the head and hands, used to punish criminals in olden days. 칼《옛 형구》. **2** 《*the ~*》 public shame. 웃음거리. ¶ *be in the ~* 웃음거리가 되다. — *vt.* (P6) (**-ried**) put (someone) in the pillory; expose (someone) to public shame. …에 칼을 씌워 대중 앞에 내놓다; …을 웃음거리로 만들다. [F. *pellori*]

〈pillory 1〉

:**pil·low** [pílou] *n.* Ⓒ cushion used to support the head when lying down. 베개. ***take counsel of*** 〔***advise with***〕 ***one's pillow,*** think over a matter during the night. 하룻밤 자며 잘 생각하다.

— *vt.* (P6) place (one's head) on a pillow, etc.; serve as a pillow for (someone). (머리)를 베개에 얹다; …의 베개가 되다. ¶ *~ one's head upon one's arm* 팔베개를 베다 / *The earth shall ~ my head tonight.* 오늘은 한뎃잠을 자야지〔노숙해야지〕. [E.]

pil·low·case [píloukèis] *n.* Ⓒ a removable covering for a pillow. 베갯잇.

pil·low·slip [píl*ou*slìp] *n.* =pillowcase.

*__pi·lot__ [páilət] *n.* Ⓒ **1** a person who guides a ship into or out of a harbor. 수로 안내인. **2** a person who flies a plane. 비행기 조종사; 파일럿. ¶ *a test ~* 시험 조종사. **3** a guide; a leader. 안내인; 지도자.

drop the pilot, abandon a trusted adviser. 좋은 충고자를 버리다.

— *vt.* (P7,13) act as the pilot of (a ship, an airplane, etc.); guide; lead. …의 수로 안내를 하다; …을 조종하다; 안내하다. ¶ *~ a boat through a channel* 운하를 통해 배를 안내하다 / *The aviator pilots his airplane.* 조종사는 자신의 비행기를 조종한다 / *Tom piloted his friends through the large factory and explained each process.* 톰은 친구들에게 큰 공장을 보여 주고 각 공정(工程)을 설명했다. [It. *pilota*]

pi·lot·age [páilətidʒ] *n.* Ⓤ **1** the act or art of piloting. 수로 안내; 항공기 조종(술). **2** the fee paid to a pilot. 수로 안내료.

pilot scheme [⌐–⌐] *n.* a preliminary experimental trial on a project. (계획의) 예비 시행.

pi·men·to [piméntou] *n.* (*pl.* **-tos**) **1** =allspice. **2** =pimiento.

pi·mien·to [pimjéntou] *n.* Ⓒ (*pl.* **-tos**) a sweet pepper. 피망. [Sp.]

pimp [pimp] *n.* a pander. 뚜쟁이; 포주.

— *vi.* act as a pander. 뚜쟁이 노릇하다. [O.F. =allure]

pim·per·nel [pímpərnèl, -nəl] *n.* Ⓒ 《bot.》 a small annual plant with red, white, or blue flowers. 별봄맞이꽃. [F.]

pim·ple [pímpl] *n.* Ⓒ a small, pointed, inflamed swelling on the skin. 여드름. [E.]

pim·pled [pímpld] *adj.* having or covered with pimples. 여드름이 난; 여드름투성이의.

pim·ply [pímpli] *adj.* (**-pli·er, -pli·est**) = pimpled.

:**pin** [pin] *n.* Ⓒ **1** a short piece of wire with a point at one end and a head at the other. 핀. ¶ *a safety ~* 안전핀《수류탄의》/ *a tie ~* 넥타이 핀 / *You might have heard a ~ drop.* 바늘 떨어지는 소리도 들릴 만큼 조용했다. **2** ⓐ anything used to fasten things together; a nail; a bar used for fastening a door. 못; 비녀장; 빗장; 마개. ⓑ a badge or an ornament with a pin or clasp to fasten it to the clothing. (핀이 달린) 기장(記章); 브로치. **3** a peg in a violin etc., to which a string is fastened. (현악기의) 줄감개. **4** 《chiefly in *negative*》 anything of small value; a bit. 하찮은 것; 조금; 소량. ¶ *I don't care a ~* 난 전혀 관심이 없다 / *not worth a ~* 아무 가치도 없는. **5** 《usu. *pl.*》 《*colloq.*》 legs. 다리. ¶ *He is quick on his pins.* 그는 발이 빠르다. **6** 《bowling》 a wooden club used as a target. (볼링의) 핀.

be on one's last pins, be going to die. 죽어 가고 있다.

pins and needles, a prickling sensation felt when the circulation returns to a numb limb. 손발이 저려 따끔따끔한 느낌.

sit 〔***be***〕 ***on pins and needles,*** feel uneasy. 불

안하다; 안절부절 못 하다.

stick pins into (=*trouble*) *someone*. …을 괴롭히다.

— *vt.* (**pinned, pin·ning**) (P7,13) **1** fasten (something) with a pin. 핀으로 꽂다; …에 빗장을 지르다. ¶ ~ *up a notice on the wall* 게시물을 핀으로 벽에 붙이다 / ~ *a flower to one's coat* 핀으로 가슴에 꽃을 달다. **2** hold fast. …을 움직이지 못하게 하다. ¶ *The fallen tree pinned him to the ground.* 쓰러진 나무에 깔려 그는 땅바닥에서 꼼짝 못 했다. **3** bind to (promise). (약속)에 매이다. [E.]

pin someone down (=*make someone stick*) *to something*. …을 옴쭉 못 하게 하다; 속박하다.

pin one's faith on someone, believe someone absolutely. …을 절대적[맹목적]으로 신용하다[믿다].

pin something on someone, put the responsibility of something on someone. …에 —의 책임을 지우다.

pin·a·fore [pínəfɔ̀:r] *n.* Ⓒ a child's or woman's washing overall. (아이·여성의) 앞치마《가슴받이가 있는》. [*pin*, *afore*]

pin·ball [pínbɔ̀:l] *n.* ⒸⓊ 《U.S.》 a game played with small metal balls on an inclined table. 핀볼; 코린트게임(의 공). [*pin*, *ball*]

pince-nez [pǽnsnèi] *n.* (*pl.* **pince-nez** [-nèiz]) 《used as *sing.* and *pl.*》 《F.》 a pair of eyeglasses with a spring clip which grips the nose. 코안경.

〈pince-nez〉

pin·cers [pínsərz] *n. pl.* **1** a tool like scissors, used to grip or draw (something). 펜찌; 못뽑이; 족집게. ¶ *a pair of* ~. **2** the large claws of a crab, a lobster, etc. (게 따위의) 집게발. [↓]

∗**pinch** [pintʃ] *vt.* **1** (P6,7) press (something) between the thumb and a finger or between two hard edges; crush. …을 꼬집다; 집다; 따다; 끼워 으깨다. ¶ ~ *one's nose* 코를 쥐다 / ~ *out young buds* 어린 싹을 따다 / *She pinched her finger in the door.* 문틈에 그녀의 손가락이 끼었다. **2** (P6,7) press on and give pain to (someone or something). …을 꽉 끼게 하다. ¶ *The shoe pinches me at the heel.* 신의 뒤꿈치가 죈다. **3** (P6) 《usu. in *passive*》 cause (someone) to become thin or worn or to be in difficulties. …을 여위게 하다; 위축시키다; 괴롭히다. ¶ *be pinched with cold* 추위에 오그라들다 / *a face pinched by* [*with*] *hunger* 굶어서 마른 얼굴 / *be pinched for money* 돈에 쪼들리다. **4** (P6,7,13) 《*sl.*》 steal; extort. …을 훔치다; 빼앗다. ¶ ~ *money from* [*out of*] *someone* …에게서 돈을 우려내다. **5** (P6) 《*sl.*》 catch; arrest. 붙잡다; 체포하다. — *vi.* (P1) **1** press hard. 죄다. **2** be careful in spending; be mean. 절약하다; 잘게 굴다. ¶ ~ *and save* 인색하게 굴어 돈을 모으다.

where the shoe pinches, where or what the discomfort or trouble is. 고민[괴로움]의 참원인; 곤란한 점. ¶ *That is where the shoe pinches.* 거기가 문제점이다.

— *n.* Ⓒ **1** the act of pinching. 꼬집음; 죔. ¶ *give someone a* ~ 아무를 꼬집다. **2** as much as one can take up with the thumb and a finger; a bit. 엄지와 집게손가락으로 집을 만한 양; 조금. ¶ *a* ~ *of salt* 소량의 소금. **3** something difficult; an emergency. 곤란; 어려움; 위기. **4** 《*sl.*》 theft. 도둑질. **5** 《*sl.*》 an arrest. 체포. [L. *picco* pick]

at [《U.S.》 ***in***] ***a pinch***, in an emergency; if absolutely necessary. 위급한 경우에; 다급하면.

when it comes to the pinch, at the critical moment. 위급할 때.

pinch-hit [píntʃhít] *vt.* (**-hit, -hit·ting**) 《U.S.》 **1** 《baseball》 bat for another when a hit is badly needed. 대(代)타자가 되다. **2** take another's place in an emergency. 대역(代役)을 하다.

pinch hitter [´-´-] *n.* 《baseball》 a person who bats for another player at a critical moment. 핀치 히터; 대(代)타자.

pin·cush·ion [pínkùʃən] *n.* Ⓒ a small cushion to stick pins in. 바늘 겨레. [*pin*]

:**pine**[1] [pain] *n.* Ⓒ **1** an evergreen tree with needle-shaped leaves and cones; Ⓤ the wood of this tree. 소나무; 그 목재. ¶ *a* ~ *cone* 솔방울 / *a* ~ *needle* 솔잎. **2** a pineapple. 파인애플. [L. *pinus*]

pine[2] [pain] *vi.* **1** (P1,2A,2B) 《*away*》 become thin and weak from anxiety, distress, etc. (근심 등으로) 수척해지다. ¶ ~ *away* (*one's health*) 슬픈 나머지 건강을 해치다 / ~ *from hunger* 굶어 수척해지다 / *Abandoned by her lover, she pined away.* 애인에게 버림받고 그녀는 수척해졌다. **2** (P3,4) 《*for, after*》 long eagerly; yearn for. 그리워하다; 갈망하다. ¶ ~ *for one's family* 가족을 그리워하다 / ~ *one's dinner* 허기를 느끼다 / *He pines for a sight of his home.* 그는 고향을 한 번 보고자 한다 / *He is pining to go into the army.* 그는 군(軍)입대를 열망(熱望)하고 있다. [→pain]

∗**pine·ap·ple** [páinæ̀pl] *n.* Ⓒ **1** a tropical plant which bears a large, cone-shaped fruit; the large, juicy fruit of this plant. 파인애플(나무). **2** 《*sl.*》 a bomb. 폭탄. [→pine[1], apple]

pin·feath·er [pínfèðər] *n.* Ⓒ a small undeveloped feather. (새의) 솜털; 잔털. ¶ *Remove all the pinfeathers from the chicken before cooking it.* 요리하기 전에 병아리의 잔털을 모두 뽑아 버려라. [*pin*]

ping [piŋ] *n.* Ⓒ a sharp sound, such as that of a rifle bullet whistling through the air. 핑(하는 소리). — *vi.* (P1) make this sound. 핑 소리가 나다. [Imit.]

ping·pong [píŋpàŋ, -pɔ̀(:)ŋ] *n.* Ⓤ a game somewhat like tennis, played on a table with rackets and a light ball; table tennis. 탁구; 핑퐁. [Imit.]

pin·head [pínhèd] *n.* Ⓒ **1** the head of a pin. 핀의 대가리. **2** a tiny, worthless object. 사소한[하찮은] 것. **3** 《*colloq.*》 a very stupid person. 바보; 어리보기. [*pin*]

pin·hole [pínhòul] *n.* Ⓒ a hole made by a pin; a small hole in which a pin or peg fits. 바늘 구멍; 작은 구멍.

pin·ion [pínjən] *n.* Ⓒ **1** the end joint of a bird's wing; a wing feather. 새의 날개 끝 부분; 날개털. **2** 《*poet.*》 a wing. 날개. **3** any one of the stiff flying feathers of the wing. 칼깃. — *vt.* (P6,13) **1** cut off a pinion of (a bird) to prevent flight. (날지 못하게) 날개 끝을 자르다. **2** bind (someone's hand or arms) tightly to his side; make (someone) powerless by binding his arms (아무의 양팔)을 몸체와 함께 단단히 붙들어 매다; (아무의) 양팔을 (꼼짝 못 하게) 묶다. ¶ ~ *a prisoner to a tree* 죄인을 나무에 붙들어 매다. [L. *penna* feather]

:**pink**[1] [piŋk] *n.* **1** Ⓒ a garden plant like the carnation with flowers of various colors. 패랭이꽃; 석죽. **2** Ⓤ a very pale red color. 연분홍색. **3** Ⓤ the highest degree or condition. 최고도; 극치. ¶ *She is in the* ~ *of health.* 그녀의 건강은 그만이다. — *adj.* **1** of a very pale red color. 연분홍색의. **2** 《*colloq.*》 leftist. 좌경적인. [?]

pink[2] [piŋk] *vt.* (P6,7) **1** prick or pierce (something or someone) with a sword, a spear, etc. …을 찌르다; 꿰뚫다. ¶ ~ *a man through the arm* 아무의 팔을 찌르다. **2** decorate (cloth, leather, etc.) with small holes or by cutting the edges. (천·가죽 등)에 장식 구멍을 뚫다; (가장자리)를 톱니꼴로 자르다. [A.S. *pyngan* prick]

pink[3] [piŋk] *vi.* (P1) (of petrol engines) make a metallic sound, caused by premature explosion; knock. (엔진이) 노킹하다. [Imit.]

pin money [⌐ ⌐-] *n.* the amount of money given to a wife for her own use; pocket money. (아내에게 주는) 용돈. [*pin*]

pin·nace [pínis] *n.* Ⓒ **1** a boat carried on board a larger ship. 함재정(艦載艇). **2** a small sailing ship with two masts. 두대박이 작은 돛배. [→pine[1]]

pin·na·cle [pínəkəl] *n.* Ⓒ **1** a slender, pointed tower. 뾰족탑. **2** a high, slender mountain peak. 산봉우리; 정상. **3** the highest point. 정점; 절정. ¶ *be at the* ~ *of one's fame* 명성의 절정에 있다. — *vt.* (P6) **1** furnish (something) with pinnacles. …에 뾰족탑을 달다. **2** place (something) on a pinnacle. …을 높은 데에 두다. [→pinion]

pin·point [pínpɔ̀int] *vt., vi.* (P6; 1) aim at accurately. 정조준하다. — *adj.* extremely accurate 아주 정확한. ¶ ~ *bombing* 정밀 폭격. — *n.* **1** the point of a pin. 바늘끝. **2** something very small; a trifle. 아주 작은; 하찮은. [*pin, point*]

pin·prick [pínprìk] *n.* Ⓒ **1** a small hole (puncture) made by a pin. 바늘로 찔러 낸 구멍. **2** a minor irritation or annoyance. 귀찮고 성가신 일; 성가시게 굴기. ¶ *a* ~ *policy* 귀찮게 하는 짓궂은 정책. [*pin, prick*]

***pint** [paint] *n.* Ⓒ a measure of capacity equal to half a quart. 파인트《액량 단위의 하나》. 參考 Brit. 약 0.57, U.S. 약 0.47 리터. [F. *pinte*]

pin·up [pínʌ̀p] *n.* Ⓒ 《U.S. *colloq.*》 a picture of a very attractive girl, to be displayed on a wall; a very attractive girl. (벽에 꽂아 두는) 미인 사진; 대단한 미인. — *adj.* very attractive. (벽에 꽂아 둘 만큼) 매력 있는. ¶ *a* ~ *girl.* [*pin*]

***pi·o·neer** [pàiəníər] *n.* Ⓒ **1** a person who does something first to prepare the way for others; a settler in a frontier country; an explorer. 선구자; 개척자; 주창자; 선봉. ¶ *pioneers in the teaching of English* 영어 교육의 선구자. **2** 《mil.》 one of advance corps preparing road for troops. (선발)공병. — *vi.* (P1) act as a pioneer. 개척자가 되다; 솔선하다. — *vt.* (P6) open up (a way, etc.); take the lead in (something). …을 개척하다; 주창[창도]하다. [→pawn]

***pi·ous** [páiəs] *adj.* **1** showing respect for God; religious. 경건한; 믿음이 깊은(opp. impious). **2** done under pretence of religion. 종교를 빙자한; 위선적인. [L. *pius*]

pip[1] [pip] *n.* Ⓒ a small seed, as of an orange or apple. (오렌지·사과 등의) 씨. ¶ *He spat out the pips.* 씨를 뱉어 냈다. [→pippin]

pip[2] [pip] *n.* 《*the* ~》 **1** a disease of fowls characterized by scales in the mouth and throat. 가금(家禽)의 혀·목의 병. **2** 《Brit. *sl.*》 depression; bad temper. 기분이 좋지 않음; 불쾌함. ¶ *It gives me the* ~. 그것은 내 기분을 언짢게 한다. [→pituitary]

pip[3] [pip] *vt.* (**pipped, pip·ping**) (P6) **1** kill by a gunshot. …을 사살하다. **2** blackball; frustrate. …을 배척하다; (계획 등)을 좌절시키다. — *vi.* (P1,2A) peep; 《*out*》 die. 삐악삐악 울다; 죽다. [? →peep]

pip[4] [pip] *n.* Ⓒ 《Brit.》 a short high-pitched sound, usu. mechanically produced. (기계 따위가 내는) '삐' 소리. ¶ *the six pips of the time-signal* 여섯 시를 알리는 삐삐 시보 소리. [Imit.]

:**pipe** [paip] *n.* Ⓒ **1** a tube made of metal, wood, etc. through which water, gas, etc. moves. 파이프; 관(管). ¶ *a water* ~ 수도관. **2** a tube-like organ of the body; 《*pl.*》 such an organ used to breathe. 신체의 관 모양의 기관(器官); 기관(氣管). **3** an L-shaped tube used for smoking tobacco; the amount of tobacco such a tube can be filled with. (담배) 파이프; (파이프 한 대분의) 담배; 담배 한 대. ¶ *He smoked a ~ of tobacco.* 파이프 담배를 한 대 피웠다. **4** a musical instrument played by blowing air into it; a flute; a whistle; 《the ~ *s*》 the bagpipes. 피리; 플루트; 호각; 백파이프. **5** a keen voice like that of a child or bird. (어린애의) 날카로운[새된] 목소리; (새의) 울음[지저귀는] 소리. ¶ *the ~ of a cuckoo* [*lark*] 뻐꾸기[종다리]의 울음소리. **6** a large cask of wine. (포도주의) 큰 술통.

put someone's pipe out, try to keep someone from succeeding. …의 성공을 방해하다.

Put that in your pipe and smoke it. Think it over. 잘[곰곰이] 생각해 보아라.

— *vi.* **1** (P2A) play on a musical pipe; whistle. 피리를 불다; 호각[호적]을 불다. **2** (P1,2A) make a keen voice; (of birds) sing. 날카로운 소리를 내다; (새가) 지저귀다. **3** (P1,2A) weep. 울다.

— *vt.* **1** (P6,7) supply (something) with a pipe. …에 관을 달다. ¶ *~ a boiler for water* 보일러에 급수관을 달다 / *Our street is being piped for gas.* 우리가 사는 거리는 가스관이 설치되어 있다. **2** (P6,20) play (a note) on a musical pipe; 《naut.》 call (someone or something) by a whistle. …을 피리로 연주하다; …을 호적[호각]으로 부르다. ¶ *~ a song* [*tune*] (피리·나팔 따위로) 노래를[곡을] 연주하다 / *~ all hands to work* 호적으로 전 선원에게 작업을 시키다. **3** (P13) move or carry (something) by a pipe. …을 관으로 나르다. ¶ *~ water into a city* 수도관으로 시에 물을 공급하다. [L. *pipo* chirp]

pipe away, give a signal by a whistle for a boat to start. 호적으로 출선(出船)을 지시하다.

pipe down, 《*sl.*》 stop talking; become quiet. 입을 다물다; 조용해지다.

***pipe one's eye*(*s*),** 《*colloq.*》 weep. 울다.

pipe up, **a**) 《*colloq.*》 speak up suddenly. 갑자기 큰 소리를 지르다. **b**) begin to sing or play. 노래[취주]하기 시작하다.

pipe dream [∸∸] *n.* a fantastic idea, vain hope or plan, etc., such as an opium smoker might have. (아편 중독자가 그리는 것 같은) 공상적인 생각[희망, 계획 따위]; 몽상.

pipe·line [páiplàin] *n.* Ⓒ **1** a line of pipes for carrying oil, gas, water, etc., usu. underground. (석유·가스 등의) 도관(導管); 파이프라인. **2** a source of information, usu. secret. (기밀) 정보 루트.

in the pipeline, (of any kind of goods) on the way; about to be delivered. (물건이) 수송[운송] 중인.

pip·er [páipər] *n.* Ⓒ a person who plays on a pipe, esp. a bagpipe. 피리 부는 사람; 백파이프 부는 사람. [*pipe, -er*]

pay the piper, bear the expenses; suffer for one's actions or pleasures. 비용을 부담하다; 응보를 받다. ¶ 《*prov.*》 *He who pays the ~ calls the tune.* 사업 등에 돈을 댄 사람이 그것을 관장한다.

pi·pette [pipét] *n.* Ⓒ a slender tube or pipe used to transfer or measure liquids. 피펫《극소량의 액체를 옮기거나 재는 데 쓰는 화학 실험용 가는 관》. [F.]

pip·ing [páipiŋ] *n.* Ⓤ **1** the sound produced by a pipe; the music of pipes; a shrill voice or call. 피리 소리; 관악(管樂); 가늘고 높은 소리. ¶ *the ~ of frogs* [*birds*] *in the spring* 봄철에 들려 오는 드높은 개구리[새]들의 울음소리. **2** 《*collectively*》 pipes; a system of pipes. 관; 배관(配管). — *adj.* **1** shrill; high-pitched. 날카로운 소리를 내는; 가락이 높은. **2** peaceful. 평화로운. ¶ *the ~ times of peace* 태평 세대. — *adv.* so as to hiss. (몹시 뜨거워) 쉭쉭 소리를 낼 정도로. [→pipe]

pi·quan·cy [píːkənsi] *n.* Ⓤ the state of being piquant. 짜릿함; 얼얼함; 톡 쏘는 맛. [F. *piquer* prick]

pi·quant [píːkənt] *adj.* **1** agreeably sharp or biting to the taste. 짜릿한; 톡 쏘는. ¶ *~ pickles* 짜릿한 맛의 오이지 / *a ~ sauce* 톡 쏘는 맛이 나는 소스. **2** exciting interest. 흥미를 자아내는. ¶ *a ~ bit of news* 흥미 있는 뉴스 한 토막.

pique[1] [piːk] *n.* Ⓤ slight anger or irritation; displeasure. 화; 불쾌. ¶ *in a fit of ~* = *out of ~* 홧김에 / *She went out in a ~.* 그녀는 발끈하여 나가 버렸다.

— *vt.* (P6,13) **1** ⓐ wound the pride of (someone); irritate. …의 자존심을 건드리다; 성나게 하다. ¶ *be piqued at someone* 아무에게 화를 내다 / *He was piqued at her refusal.* 그녀의 거절로 인해 그는 자존심이 상했다. ⓑ excite; stir up. …을 자극하다. ¶ *His curiosity was piqued by Fred's collection of stamps.* 프레드가 수집한 우표를 보고 그는 호기심이 발동했다. **2** 《oneself *on*》 pride (oneself). …을 자랑하다. ¶ *She piqued herself on her skill in making pies.* 그녀는 자기의 파이 만드는 솜씨를 자랑했다. [→piquancy]

pi·que[2] [pi(ː)kéi] *n.* Ⓤ a cotton material with raised stripes. 피케《골지게 짠 피륙》. [F.]

pi·ra·cy [páiərəsi] *n.* ⓊⒸ (*pl.* **-cies**) **1** robbery by pirates. 해적 행위. **2** the act of pirating another's literary work. 저작권 침해. [↓]

***pi·rate** [páiərət] *n.* Ⓒ **1** a sea robber; an armed ship used by pirates. 해적; 해적선. **2** a person who uses another's literary work, etc. without permission. 저작권 침해자. — *vt., vi.* (P6; 1) **1** practice piracy (upon something). 해적질하다. **2** use (a literary work, etc.) without permission. 저작권을 침해하다. ¶ *a pirated edition* 해적판. [Gk. *peiraō* attempt]

pi·rat·i·cal [paiərǽtikəl] *adj.* of or like a pirate; engaged in piracy. 해적의; 저작권 침해의.

pir·ou·ette [pìruét] *n.* Ⓒ a rapid spinning around on one foot or on the toes in dancing. (발레 등의) 발끝으로 돌기. —*vi.* (P1) dance in this way. 발끝으로 선회하다. [F. =top[2]]

pis·ca·to·ry [pískətɔ̀:ri / -təri], **-ri·al** [pìskətɔ́:riəl] *adj.* of fishers or fishing. 물고기의; 어부〔어업〕의. [L. *piscis* fish]

Pis·ces [písi:z] *n. pl.* **1** 《zool.》 the fishes. 어류. **2** 《astron.》 the 12th zodiacal constellation. 물고기자리. [↑]

pis·ci·cul·ture [písəkʌ̀ltʃər] *n.* Ⓤ the act or art of breeding and raising fish. 어류 양식(魚類養殖); 양어(법). [↑]

pish [pí∫] *interj.* an exclamation of contempt or impatience. 피; 쳇; 흥. —*vi.* (P1) make this exclamation. 쳇하다. [Imit.]

piss [pis] *vi.* (P1) urinate; make water. 《*vulg.*》 오줌 누다. —*n.* urine. 소변. [E.]

pis·til [pístəl] *n.* Ⓒ 《bot.》 the seed-bearing part of a flower. 암술(opp. stamen). [→pestle]

***pis·tol** [pístl] *n.* Ⓒ a small, short gun made to be held in one hand. 피스톨; 권총. —*vt.* (**-toled, -tol·ing** or 《Brit.》 **-tolled, -tol·ling**) (P6) shoot (someone or something) with a pistol. …을 권총으로 쏘다. [Place *Pistoia*]

pis·ton [pístən] *n.* Ⓒ 《mech.》 a round piece or cylinder which moves to and fro in a cylinder. 피스톤. ¶ *a ~ rod* 피스톤 로드〔간(杆)〕. [→pestle]

:**pit**[1] [pit] *n.* Ⓒ **1** a hole in the ground. (땅의) 구멍; 구덩이. **2** a covered hole serving as a trap. 함정; 덫. **3** a deep hole made in the earth to dig out coal or other minerals. 채굴갱; 탄갱; 수갱(竪坑); 곧은쌤. ¶ *a coal ~* 탄갱. **4** 《*the ~*》 the ground floor of a theater. 극장의 일층석. **5** a hollow part of the body. 신체의 오목한 곳. ¶ *the ~ of the stomach* 명치. **6** a mark left by smallpox. 마맛자국. **7** 《*the ~*》 hell; the grave. 지옥; 나락; 무덤. ¶ *the ~ of hell* 지옥의 나락. **8** a place where dogs or cocks are made to fight. 투견장; 투계장.

—*vt.* (**pit·ted, pit·ting**) **1** (P6) make a pit in (some place). …에 구멍을 내다. ¶ *a face pitted with smallpox* 마맛자국이 있는 얼굴. **2** (P13) set (one animal) to fight against another; 《*fig.*》 oppose; match with. (두 짐승)을 싸움붙이다; 맞서게 하다; 대항시키다. ¶ *I pitted my dog against the cat.* 내 개를 고양이와 싸우게 했다 / *~ one's strength* 〔*brains, skill*〕 *against that* 〔*those*〕 *of another* 남과 힘〔두뇌, 기술〕을 겨루다. **3** (P6) keep (something) in a pit. …을 구덩이에 저장하다. **4** (P6) entrap. …을 함정에 빠뜨리다. [L. *puteus* well]

pit[2] [pit] *n.* Ⓒ 《U.S.》 the hard seed of a cherry, peach, plum, etc.; a stone. (버찌·복숭아 등의) 씨; 핵(核). —*vt.* (**pit·ted, pit·ting**) (P6) remove pits from (fruit). …의 씨를 빼다. [Du. =pith]

***pitch**[1] [pit∫] *n.* Ⓤ **1** a thick black material made from boiled tar and used to pave roads or to mend holes. (타르에서 채취하는) 피치; 역청(瀝青). **2** the sap of a pine tree. 송진.

as dark as pitch, very black; very dark. 칠흑 같은; 새까만.

—*vt.* (P6) cover (something) with pitch. …에 피치를〔송진을〕 바르다. [L. *pix*]

:**pitch**[2] [pit∫] *vt.* **1** (P6,7,13) ⓐ throw; fling. …을 (집어)던지다. ¶ *~ a stone* 돌을 던지다 / *~ a book out of a window* 책을 창 밖으로 내던지다 / *~ a letter into the fire* 편지를 불 속에 처넣다. ⓑ 《baseball》 throw (a ball) to the batsman. (타자에게) 투구하다. ¶ *~ a ball up* 〔*short*〕 공을 치던지다〔짧게 던지다〕. **2** (P7) 《mus.》 set (a tune, etc.) in a certain key or note. (가락 등)을 조정하다〔맞추다〕. ¶ *~ a tune in a higher key* 음조를 높이다. **3** (P6) lay out (something) for sale. (상품)을 진열하다. **4** (P6) fix (something) in the ground; set up. …을 땅에 고정시키다〔세우다; 설치하다〕. ¶ *~ a tent* 천막을 치다 / *~ one's tent* 주거를 정하다; 자리잡다 / *~ oneself* 좌정하다; 걸터앉다. **5** (P6) 《*sl.*》 tell; narrate; express. 말하다; 이야기하다. ¶ *~ a yarn* 허풍을 치다.

—*vi.* **1** (P1) throw. 던지다. ¶ *He pitched for our team.* 우리 팀의 투수 노릇을 했다. **2** (P1,2A,3) fall headfirst. 거꾸로 떨어지다. ¶ *The boy pitched downstairs.* 아이가 아래층으로 굴러 떨어졌다 / *~ on one's head* 곤두박이치다. **3** (P1) set up a tent. 천막을 치다; 야영하다. **4** (P1,2A) (of a ship) move up and down. 배가 뒷질하다(opp. roll). ¶ *Our ship pitched violently in the storm.* 배는 폭풍에 심하게 앞뒤로 요동쳤다. **5** (P3) 《*on, upon*》 choose or decide without thinking over. (잘 생각하지 않고) 고르다〔정하다〕.

pitch in, 《*colloq.*》 begin to work hard. 열심히 하기 시작하다.

pitch into, 《*colloq.*》 eat (something) as if one is very hungry; blame or scold (someone) in a severe tone. 게걸스레 먹어대다; 마구 비난하다〔꾸짖다〕.

pitch it strong, 《*colloq.*》 talk big; boast. 과장해서 말하다; 허풍치다.

pitch on 〔***upon***〕, **a**) dicide on. 결정하다; 고르다. ¶ *He pitched upon the wrong man for the purpose.* 일을 하는 데 사람을 잘못 골랐다. **b**) encounter. …을 우연히 만나다. ¶ *I pitched upon the very house that suited me.* 내 마음에 드는 바로 그런 집을 우연히 만났다.

—*n.* Ⓒ **1** the act of pitching. 던지기; 배의 뒷질. **2** ⓊⒸ a musical note. 가락; 음의 높낮이. ¶ *at a high* 〔*low*〕 *~* 높은〔낮은〕 가락으로. **3** 《*fig.*》 a certain point; position; degree. (어떤) 점; 도; 정도. ¶ *the lowest ~ of bad fourtune* 불행의 밑바닥 / *All my feelings were excited to a high ~.* 내 기분은 그저 그만이었다. **4** height; top. 높이; 정점. ¶ *at the*

~ *of one's voice* 목청껏. **5** Ⓒ Ⓤ slope. 경사; 물매. ¶ *the ~ of a roof* 지붕의 물매. **6** the place at which a person usu. stays or a thing is usu. fixed. 늘 머무는 거처(居處); 정해진 위치. [E.]

queer the pitch for, spoil (someone's) plans to nothing. …의 계획을 망쳐 놓다.

take up one's pitch, keep one's part. 분수를 지키다.

pitch·blende [pítʃblènd] *n.* Ⓤ a black, shining mineral containing uranium, radium, etc. 역청 우라늄광(鑛). [→pitch[1]]

pitch·dark [pítʃdá:*r*k] *adj.* very dark. 새까만; 칠흑의. [↑]

***pitch·er**[1] [pítʃə*r*] *n.* Ⓒ a large pot with a handle and lip for holding and pouring liquids. (주둥이가 넓은) 물주전자. ¶ 《*prov.*》 *Little pitchers have long* [*big*] *ears.* 애들은 귀가 밝다. [L. *picarium*]

***pitch·er**[2] [pítʃə*r*] *n.* Ⓒ a person who pitches; the player who pitches the ball to the batter. 던지는 사람; 투수(cf. *catcher*). [→pitch[2]]

pitch·fork [pítʃfɔ̀:*r*k] *n.* Ⓒ a large fork with a long handle used for tossing hay or straw. (건초용) 갈퀴; 쇠스랑. — *vt.* (P6,13) toss (hay, straw, etc.) with a pitchfork. (건초 등)을 갈퀴로 긁어 올리다. [*pitch*]

pitch·y [pítʃi] *adj.* (**pitch·i·er, pitch·i·est**) **1** full of pitch. 피치가 많은. **2** like pitch; stickly; black. 피치 같은; 진득진득한; 검은. [→pitch[1]]

pit·e·ous [pítiəs] *adj.* arousing sorrow or pity. 불쌍한; 가엾은. ● **pit·e·ous·ness** [-nis] *n.* [→pity]

pit·e·ous·ly [pítiəsli] *adv.* in a piteous manner. 가엾게도; 불쌍하게.

pit·fall [pítfɔ̀:l] *n.* Ⓒ a hidden pit used to catch animals; a hidden danger or trap. 함정; 뜻밖[의외]의 위험; 덫. [*pit.*]

pith [piθ] *n.* Ⓤ **1** 《bot.》 the soft, spongy material in the center of the stem of certain plants. (초목의) 수(髓); 고갱이. **2** a similar soft tissue. 골; 심. **3** 《*fig.*》 the main part of a thing. 요점; 골자. ¶ *of great ~ and moment* 극히 중대한 / *the ~ of a speech* 연설의 골자. **4** strength; energy. 체력; 정력. [E.]

pith·y [píθi] *adj.* (**pith·i·er, pith·i·est**) **1** having much pith; of or like pith. 골이 있는; 수(髓) 같은. **2** forceful; full of meaning. 힘찬; 함축성 있는. ¶ *a ~ sentence* 힘찬 문장 / *a ~ opinion.* 설득력이 있는 의견. [↑]

pit·i·a·ble [pítiəbəl] *adj.* **1** arousing pity. 불쌍한; 가련한. ¶ *a ~ sight* 가엾은 정경 / *He was in a ~ condition.* 그는 딱한 입장에 처해 있었다. **2** arousing contempt or scorn. 비루한; 치사한. [→pity]

pit·i·a·bly [pítiəbli] *adv.* in a pitiable manner. 가엾게도; 한심하게도.

pit·i·ful [pítifəl] *adj.* **1** arousing pity or sorrow. 불쌍한. **2** feeling or showing pity. 인정이 많은. **3** arousing contempt. 비루한; 비열한. ● **pit·i·ful·ly** [-fəli] *adv.*

pit·i·less [pítilis] *adj.* without pity or mercy. 무자비한; 냉정한.

pit·i·less·ly [pítilisli] *adv.* in a pitiless manner. 무자비[냉정]하게.

pit·man [pítmən] *n.* Ⓒ (*pl.* **-men** [-mən]) a person who works in a pit, esp. in a coal mine. 광원(鑛員); 갱부; 탄광 인부. [→pit[1]]

pit·tance [pítəns] *n.* Ⓒ **1** a small allowance of money. 적은[몇 푼의] 수당. **2** a small amount. 소량. ¶ *a mere ~* 근소; 소량. [→pity]

***Pitts·burgh** [pítsbə:*r*g] *n.* a city in southwestern Pennsylvania. 피츠버그.

:pit·y [píti] *n.* (*pl.* **pit·ies**) **1** Ⓤ the feeling of sorrow over the trouble of others; mercy. 연민의 정; 동정. ¶ *feel* [*have a feeling of*] *~ for someone* 아무를 불쌍히 여기다 / *I did it out of ~ for her.* 그녀가 가엾어서 그랬다. **2** Ⓒ a cause of regret or pity. 애석한[유감스러운] 일. ¶ *The ~ is that he has failed.* 그가 실패했다니 참 안됐다 / *What a ~ you could not go!* 네가 못 간다니 정말 섭섭하구나 / *It is a ~ to give up the attempt.* 그 일을 그만두게 돼서 유감이다 / *More's the pity.* 그래서 더 유감이다.

for pity's sake, an expression of annoyance. 제발; 아무쪼록.

have* [*take*] *pity on (= *show mercy to*) *someone.* …에게 동정하다.

in pity of, feeling pity. …이 가엾어서.

— *vt.* (**pit·ied**) (P6) feel pity for (someone or something). …을 동정하다. ¶ *I ~ those who are out in the cold tonight.* 이 추운 밤에 한데에 있는 이들이 불쌍하다 / *He is to be pitied.* 그는 가엾은 사람이다. [→pious]

piv·ot [pívət] *n.* Ⓒ **1** a shaft, pin or point on which a thing turns. 피벗; 선회축(旋回軸). **2** 《*fig.*》 a thing on which something important depends; the central point. 중심점; 추요부(樞要部). ¶ *the ~ of hope* 희망의 중심점 / *His pitching was the ~ of all our hopes.* 그의 투구가 우리 모두의 희망이었다. **3** 《mil.》 a man round whom a body or troops wheels. (대열의 방향 전환시) 기준이 되는 병사; 향도(嚮導). — *vt.* (P6) place on or supply (something) with a pivot. …을 축 위에 놓다; …에 축을 달다. — *vi.* (P3) turn on a pivot. 추축(樞軸)으로 선회하다. ¶ *~ on one's heel* 뒤꿈치로 빙 돌다. [F.]

piv·ot·al [pívətl] *adj.* of or serving as a pivot. 추축(樞軸)의; 중추의; 중요한.

pix·y, pix·ie [píksi:] *n.* Ⓒ (*pl.* **pix·ies**) a small elf or fairy. 작은 요정(妖精). [E.]

pl. **1** place. 자리; 장소. **2** plural. 복수.

plac·ard [plǽka:*r*d, -kə*r*d] *n.* Ⓒ a poster; a large printed notice. 플래카드; 포스터; 벽보. — *vt.* (P6,13) place placards on or in (some place); advertise (something) by means of placards. …에 포스터를 붙이다; …을 전단(傳單)으로 광고

하다. ¶ *They placarded the fence with advertisement.* 울타리에 광고를 내다 붙였다. [Du. *plakken* to glue]

pla·cate [pléikeit, plækéit] *vt.* (P6) take away the anger of (someone); calm. …을 달래다; 진정시키다. [L. *placo* appease]

:place [pleis] *n.* Ⓒ **1** a part of space where someone or something exists; an area. 자리; 장소; 곳. ¶ *a market* ~ 장터 / *This is no* ~ *for men.* 여긴 남자들이 올 자리가 아니다 / *from* ~ *to* ~ 여기저기로 / *One cannot be in two places at once.* 사람이 동시에 두 곳에 있을 수는 없다. **2** a region; a district. 지역; 지방. ¶ *It snows heavily in this* ~. 이 지방에는 눈이 많이 내린다. **3** a city; a town; a village. 시; 읍; 면. ¶ *What* ~ *do you come from?* 어느 도시에서 왔느냐. **4** a special spot. (신체의) 어느 개소〔부분〕; 국소(局所). ¶ *a sore* ~ *on the arm* 팔이 쑤시는 부분 / *a decayed* ~ *in a tooth* 이의 벌레 먹은 데. **5** a house and its grounds. 집; 주거지. ¶ *Come round to my* ~ *tonight.* 오늘밤 우리 집에 들르시오 / *He has a beautiful* ~ *in Kent.* 그는 켄트주에 좋은 집이 있다. **6** a building or space used for a special purpose. 건물; …소(所); …장(場); …집. ¶ *a* ~ *of business* 사무〔영업〕소 / *a* ~ *of amusement* 오락장 / *There are many nice eating places near our house.* 우리 집 부근엔 음식을 잘 하는 집이 많다. **7** Ⓤ space; room. 여지; 공간. ¶ *leave* ~ *for him* 그의 자리를 남겨 두다 / *There is no* ~ *for doubt.* 의심할 여지가 없다 / *There is a time and* ~ *for everything.* 모든 것엔 때와 장소가 있다. **8** Ⓒ a seat. 좌석; 자리; 위치. ¶ *keep a* ~ *for someone* 아무를 위해 자리를 잡아 두다 / *Go back to your* ~. 네 자리로 돌아가거라 / *We took our places at the table.* 우리는 식탁에 자리잡고 앉았다 / *I changed places with him.* 그와 자리를 바꾸었다. **9** a position; a job; another's state. 지위; 직(職); 입장. ¶ *If I were in your* ~, 내가 네 입장이라면 / *learn one's* ~ 자기 분수를 알게 되다. **10** a duty or piece of business. 직무; 일. ¶ *It's my* ~ *to show you the way.* 당신을 안내하는 것이 제 할 일입니다 / *It is not my* ~ *to make the final decision.* 최후 결정을 내리는 일은 내 직무가 아니다. **11** an order of a discussion, a race, etc. 순서; 단계; 순위. ¶ *in the first* ~ 첫째로 / *win the first* ~ 일등하다. **12** (esp. of servants) work; employment. 일자리; 직(職). ¶ *He was ten years in his last* ~. 마지막 직장에서 10년 있었다. **13** 《math.》 the position of a figure in relation to other figures of a given series or group. 위(位); 자리. ¶ *Answer to four places of decimals.* 소수점 이하 네 자리까지만 답을 내라. **14** a passage in a book. (책의) 한 줄〔구절〕 ¶ *I've lost my* ~. 어디까지 읽었는지 모르겠다.

a place in the sun, an advantage. 우위; 유리한 입장.

find a place, get a job. 취직하다.

give place to (=*make way for*) *someone.* …에 길을〔지위를〕 양보하다. ¶ *The cinema is giving* ~ *to the television.* 영화는 TV에게 그 자리를 물려주고 있다.

in someone's place, instead of someone. …의 대신에.

in place, in the right place; properly. 적절한 위치에; 적절하게. ¶ *Such remarks are not in* ~. 그건 온당한 말이 아니다.

in place of, instead of. …의 대신에.

keep someone in his proper place, make someone do only his own duty. …에게 제 분수를 지키게 하다.

know one's place, be humble enough. 자기 분수를 알다.

out of place, not in the right or proper place or order. 제자리를 떠난; 부적절한.

take place, happen. 일어나다. ¶ *It took* ~ *ten years ago.* 10년 전에 일어났다.

take the place (=*act instead*) ***of*** *someone.* …에 대신하다; …을 대리하다.

— *vt.* (P6,7,13) **1** put (something) in a place. …을 두다〔놓다〕; 배열〔배치〕하다. ¶ *Place them in order.* 그것들을 차례대로 놓아라 / *Place the book on the table.* 책을 탁자 위에 놓아라 / *The house is well* 〔*badly*〕 *placed.* 집의 방위가 좋다〔나쁘다〕. **2** put (someone) in a post, position, etc. …을 (지위 등)에 앉히다. ¶ ~ *her in a key position* 그녀를 요직에 앉히다 / *He has been placed at the head of his department.* 그는 부장에 임명되었다. **3** 《*with*》 order (something) for or from a firm, etc.; 《*in*》 put (money) into a business. (주문)을 내다; (돈)을 투자하다. ¶ ~ *an order with a firm* 어떤 회사에 주문을 내다 / ~ *a book with a publisher* 출판사에 책을 주문하다 / ~ *one's money to the best advantage* 돈을 가장 유리하게 투자하다. **4** know; recognize; estimate. 알다; 인정하다; 평가하다. ¶ *a person difficult to* ~ 정체를 알 수 없는 사람 / *I know his face, but I can't quite* ~ *him.* 그의 얼굴은 알지만 그가 누구인지는 기억해 내지 못하겠다. **5** show the position or order in a race; rank. 순위를 정하다; 등급을 매기다. ¶ *As a novelist I* ~ *him among the first.* 나는 그를 소설가로서는 첫째로 꼽는다. **6** fix; rest. (신용·희망 등)을 두다; 걸다. ¶ ~ *confidence in someone* 아무를 신뢰하다. [Gk. *platus* board]

place-card [pléiskɑ̀ːrd] *n.* a card on which is written the place of a guest at a formal dinner. (공식 연회 등의) 좌석표.

place-kick [pléiskìk] *n.* a kick given a football after it has been put on the ground. 플레이스킥《공을 땅에 놓고 차기》.

place·ment [pléismənt] *n.* Ⓤ **1** the act of placing; the state of being placed. 놓기; 놓이기; 놓임; 배치. **2** the act of finding work or a job for a person. 직업 소개.

plac·er [pléisər] *n.* Ⓒ a place where gold or other minerals can be obtained by washing sand, stones, etc. 사금(砂金)

채취소; 사광(砂鑛).

plac·id [plǽsid] *adj.* calm; peaceful. 조용한; 평온한. ¶ *a ~ lake* 고요한 호수. ●**plac·id·ly** [-li] *adv.* **plac·id·ness** [-nis] *n.* [L. *placeo* please]

plac·id·i·ty [pləsídəti] *n.* Ⓤ calmness; peace. 평온; 평정.

plack·et [plǽkit] *n.* Ⓒ **1** an opening at the top of a skirt to make it easy to put on. (스커트의) 옆의 튼 데. **2** a pocket in a woman's skirt. (스커트의) 주머니. [Du.]

pla·gi·a·rism [pléidʒiərìzəm] *n.* **1** Ⓤ the act of plagiarizing. 표절; 표절 행위; 도작(盜作). **2** Ⓒ a plagiarized idea, passage, etc. 표절한 것. [↓]

pla·gia·rist [pléidʒiərist] *n.* Ⓒ a person who plagiarizes. 표절〔도작(盜作)〕자.

pla·gia·rize [pléidʒiəràiz, -dʒjə-] *vt.* (P6) take and use (the ideas, works, etc. of another) as one's own. (남의 생각·문장 등)을 표절하다. [L. *plagio* kidnap]

***plague** [pleig] *n.* Ⓤ **1** a deadly disease which spreads rapidly; 《*the* ~》 a dangerous disease spread by rats and carried to man by fleas. 역병(疫病); 전염병; 페스트. ¶ *Plague on* 〔*upon*〕 *it* 〔*him, etc.*〕 *!* = *Plague take it* 〔*him, etc.*〕 *!* 염병할; 제기랄. **2** a punishment thought to be given by God. 천벌. **3** Ⓒ 《*colloq.*》 a person or thing that causes great trouble; a nuisance. 골칫거리; 말썽거리. ¶ *That child is the ~ of my life.* 저 아이가 내 골칫거리다 / *The locusts are a regular ~ this year.* 금년엔 메뚜기 떼 때문에 큰일이다.

— *vt.* **1** (P6) cause (someone) to suffer from a plague. …을 역병에 걸리게 하다. **2** (P6,13) trouble; worry. …을 애먹이다; 골치 아프게 하다. ¶ *~ someone with questions* 아무에게 성가시게 물어대다. [L. *plaga* stroke]

pla·guy [pléigi] *adj.* 《*colloq.*》 annoying; troublesome. 골치 아픈; 성가신. [↑]

plaice [pleis] *n.* Ⓒ (*pl.* **plaic·es** or *collectively* **plaice**) a flat sea-fish. 넙치류; 가자미. [L. *platessa*]

plaid [plæd] *n.* **1** Ⓤ woolen cloth with a square pattern of different colors. 격자(格子) 무늬의 스카치 나사. **2** Ⓒ a long piece of this cloth worn over the shoulder and breast by Scottish Highlanders. (격자무늬 스카치 나사의) 긴 어깨걸이. [Gael.]

:**plain** [plein] *adj.* **1** clear; easy to understand; easily seen or heard. 분명한; 알기 쉬운; 잘 보이는〔들리는〕. ¶ *in ~ English* 쉬운 영어로 / *~ writing* 평이한 문장 / *The meaning is ~.* 뜻은 간단하다 / *The matter is quite ~.* 문제는 아주 쉽다. **2** simple; frank; common. 간소한; 솔직한; 수수한; 보통의. ¶ *~ living* 검소한 생활 / *a ~ man of the people* 보통의 평범한 사람 / *in ~ clothes* 평상복으로. **3** not lovely or not pretty. 예쁘지 않은; 못생긴. ¶ *a plump girl with a ~ face* 차마 예쁘다고 할 수 없는 뚱뚱한 소녀. **4** all of one color. 무지(無地)의. ¶ *a ~ wallpaper* 단색의 벽지. **5** flat; level. 판판한.

in plain words = ***be plain with you,*** frankly speaking. 솔직히 말해서.

— *adv.* clearly. 분명히; 알기 쉽게. ¶ *speak ~* 알기 쉽게 말하다.

— *n.* Ⓒ a large field; a large area of open space. 평지; 평원(平原). ¶ *Cattle wandered over the plains.* 소들이 들판을 거닐고 있었다. [L. *planus*]

·**plain·ly** [pléinli] *adv.* in a plain manner. 쉽게; 명백히; 솔직히.

plain·ness [pléinnis] *n.* Ⓤ the state of being plain. 평이; 쉬움; 명백; 솔직; 검소.

plains·man [pléinzmən] *n.* Ⓒ (*pl.* **-men** [-mən]) a person who lives on the plains. 평원의 주민.

plain-spo·ken [pléinspóukən] *adj.* frank in speech. 솔직한. ¶ *a ~ opinion* 솔직한 의견.

plaint [pleint] *n.* ⓊⒸ **1** 《*poet.*》 a lament; lamentation; complaining. 애가(哀歌); 비탄; 불평; 불만. **2** 《law》 a complaint. 고소(장). [L. *plango* beat breast]

plain·tiff [pléintif] *n.* Ⓒ 《law》 a person who brings a suit in a law court. 원고(原告)(opp. defendant). ¶ *The ~ accuses the defendant of injuring him.* 원고가 피고를 상해죄로 고발하다. [↑]

plain·tive [pléintiv] *adj.* showing sorrow or melancholy; mournful. 슬픈 듯한; 애처로운. ¶ *a ~ song* 애가(哀歌). [↑]

plait [pleit, plæt] *n.* Ⓒ **1** 《U.S.》 a flat fold; a pleat. (천 등의) 주름. **2** a strip of woven hair; a braid. 땋은 머리; 변발. ¶ *She wore her hair in a ~.* 머리를 땋았다. — *vt.* (P6) make (something) into a braid or plait. …에 주름을 잡다; …을 땋다; 꼬다. ¶ *a plaited skirt* 주름 치마 / *plaited straw* 꼰 짚. [L. *prico* fold]

:**plan** [plæn] *n.* Ⓒ **1** a map showing the arrangement of the parts of anything. 설계도; 도면. ¶ *a raised ~* 투영도(投影圖) / *a floor ~* 평면도 / *the plans of a house* 가옥 설계도. **2** a way or scheme for making, doing or arranging something. 계획; 설계. ¶ *Everything went according to* (*the*) *~.* 만사가 계획대로 되었다 / *plans for the future* 미래에 대한 설계 / *think out* 〔*form*〕 *a ~* 계획을 세우다 / *I have a ~ for overcoming our difficulties.* 내게 우리 곤경을 이겨 낼 안이 있다. **3** a map of a small district, town, etc. (시가 따위의) 지도; 안내도. ¶ *a town ~* 시가도.

— *vt.* (**planned, plan·ning**) **1** (P6) make a drawing of (a structure). …의 설계도를〔도면을〕 그리다. ¶ *~ a house.* **2** (P6) think out a scheme for doing (something). …을 계획하다. ¶ *Have you planned your trip?* 여행 계획을 세웠나. **3** (P8) 《U.S.》 intend; expect. …할 의향〔작정〕이다. ¶ *I am planning to go to Africa.* 아프리카에 갈 생각이다.

— *vi.* make a plan. 계획을 세우다. [→

plain]

:**plane**[1] [plein] *n.* Ⓒ **1** a surface that is smooth, flat and level. 면; 평면. ¶ *an inclined ~* 사면(斜面). **2** a grade of development; a level. (발달의) 정도; 단계; (지식 따위의) 수준. ¶ *a high ~ of civilization* 고도의 문명 / *His superstition places him on the same ~ as the savage.* 미신을 믿고 있는 그는 야만인과 동열(同列)이다. **3** 《*colloq.*》 an airplane. 비행기. ¶ *go by ~* 비행기로 가다. **4** the surface of the wings of an airplane. (비행기의) 날개.
— *adj.* flat; even. 평면의; 편평한. ¶ *~ geometry* 평면 기하학 / *a ~ figure* 평면도 / *a ~ surface* 평면 / *~ sailing* 평면 항법(航法).
— *vi.* (P1) travel by plane. 비행기로 가다. [→plain]

plane[2] [plein] *n.* Ⓒ **1** a tool to make the surface smooth. 대패. **2** a machine for smoothing metal. 평삭반(平削盤); 플레이너. — *vt.* (P6) smooth (the surface) with a plane. …을 대패질하다. [↑]

plane[3] [plein] *n.* 《also *plane tree*》 a tall spreading broad-leaved tree of the genus Platanus. 플라타너스. [→place]

:**plan·et** [plǽnət] *n.* Ⓒ one of the heavenly bodies which moves around the sun. 행성(行星). 參考 항성은 fixed star. ¶ *inferior* 〔*major*〕 *~* 내(內)〔대(大)〕 행성 / *secondary planets* 위성 / *primary planets* 행성《위성과 구별하여》. [Gk. *planaomai* wander]

plane table [ㄹ ㄹ] *n.* a drawing board placed on a tripod and used by surveyors, etc. (측량용) 평판(平板). [*plane*[1]]

plan·e·tar·i·a [plæ̀nətέəriə] *n.* pl. of **planetarium.**

plan·e·tar·i·um [plæ̀nətέəriəm] *n.* Ⓒ (*pl.* **-i·a** or **-ums**) a room with an apparatus for showing the movements of heavenly bodies. 플라네타륨; 천문관(天文館). [↓]

plan·e·tar·y [plǽnətèri / -təri] *adj.* **1** of a planet or planets. 행성의. ¶ *the ~ system* 태양계. **2** of the earth or this world; terrestrial. 지상(地上)의; 이 세상의. **3** moving like a planet. 궤도를 운행하는. [→planet]

***plank** [plæŋk] *n.* Ⓒ **1** a broad, thick piece of timber, usu. 2 to 6 inches thick. (두꺼운) 널(빤지); 판자. **2** a thing which supports. 의지가 되는 것; 지지물. **3** 《*fig.*》 an article of the statement of principles of a political party. (정당의) 강령의 조목·항목.
— *vt.* **1** (P6) cover (something) with planks. …에 판자를 대다〔깔다〕. **2** (P6,7) 《*down*》 《*colloq.*》 ⓐ put down. …을 (털썩) 내려놓다. ⓑ pay in cash. 맞돈을 내다. ¶ *He planked down ten pounds.* 즉석에서 10 파운드를 냈다. [L. *plax* flat plate]

plank·ing [plǽŋkiŋ] *n.* Ⓤ **1** 《*collectively*》 planks in a floor. 마루청. **2** the act of covering with planks. 판자깔기.

plank·ton [plǽŋktən] *n.* Ⓤ 《biol.》 very small animal and plant organisms floating in water. 플랑크톤. [Gk.]

:**plant** [plænt, plɑːnt] *n.* Ⓒ **1** a living thing that grows usu. from the ground, having a stem, a root, and leaves. 식물. ¶ *Birds are not plants.* 새는 식물이 아니다. **2** such a small organism, in contrast with a tree or shrub. 풀. **3** a young organism ready for putting into other soil. 묘목; 모종. ¶ *tomato plants* 토마토 묘목 / *cabbage plants* 양배추 모종. **4** the building and equipment of a factory, business, etc.; an apparatus used for a mechanical process in a factory, etc. 공장; 공장 설비; 플랜트. ¶ *a water-power ~* 수력 발전소 / *an automobile ~* 자동차 공장. **5** 《*sl.*》 a trap. 함정.
— *vt.* **1** (P6,13) put (young trees, seeds, etc.) in the ground to make them grow; sow. …을 심다; (씨를) 뿌리다. ¶ *~ a tree* 나무를 심다 / *~ seeds* 씨를 뿌리다. **2** (P6,13) 《*with*》 provide (land) with plants. (땅)에 …을 심다; 이식하다. ¶ *~ a garden with roses* 정원에 장미를 (옮겨) 심다. **3** (P6,13) fix (something) in position; put. …을 설치하다; 세우다. ¶ *She planted herself in front of the stove.* 난로 앞에 턱 좌정했다 / *~ a flag in the ground* 땅에 기를 꽂다 / *~ a dagger in someone's heart* 아무의 가슴을 칼로 찌르다. **4** (P6,13) 《*with*》 introduce (young fish, spawn, oysters) in a river, lake, etc. …을 강 (따위)에 방류하다; 양식(養殖)하다. ¶ *~ a river with fish* 고기를 강에 방류하다. **5** (P6,13) introduce (an idea, a feeling, etc.). (주의 등)을 주입하다; 가르치다. ¶ *~ a love for learning* 학문에 대한 사랑을 심어주다 / *Missionaries planted civilization among the savages.* 선교사들은 미개인들에게 문명을 전파했다. **6** (P6) settle (people) in a colony; set up (a colony, a city, etc.). (사람들)을 …에 식민하다; (식민지)를 건설하다. ¶ *~ people in an island* 섬에 사람들을 정주(定住)시키다. **7** (P6,13) aim and strike; deliver (a blow); send (a bomb). 한대 먹이다; 포격하다. ¶ *~ a blow.* **8** (P6) 《*sl.*》 devise. 꾸미다; 꾀하다. **9** (P6,13) 《*sl.*》 conceal (stolen goods, etc.); bury. (장물)을 숨기다; 묻다. [L. *planta* slip, cutting]

plan·tain [plǽntin] *n.* 《bot.》 Ⓒ a common weed with broad leaves. 질경이. [L. *plantago*]

·**plan·ta·tion** [plæntéiʃən] *n.* Ⓒ **1** a large farm in tropical countries where cotton, tobacco, sugar, rubber, etc. are grown. (특히 열대·아열대 지방의 대규모) 농장; 재배장. ¶ *a strike of laborers on the plantations* 농장 일꾼들의 파업 / *He manages a cotton ~.* 면화 농장을 관리하고 있다. **2** a large planting of trees. 식림〔조림〕지. ¶ *a rubber* 〔*coffee*〕 *~* 고무〔커피〕 재배원(園). **3** the act of setting colonists; 《*pl.*》 《hist.》 a colony. 식민; 식민지. [→plant]

plant·er [plǽntər, plɑ́ːntər] *n.* Ⓒ **1** a person who owns or manages a plantation. 농

장주. **2** a person who plants. 심는 사람; 재배〔경작〕자. ¶ *a cotton* ~. **3** a planting machine. 파종기(播種機). ¶ *a corn* ~ 옥수수 파종기. **4** 《hist.》 a colonist. 식민자.

plant louse [ˊ ˋ] *n.* a harmful insect which sucks the sap of plants; an aphid. 진디.

plaque [plæk / plɑ:k] *n.* Ⓒ **1** a thin piece of metal, clay, etc. used as an ornament on the wall. (금속·도자기 등의) 장식판《벽에 거는》. **2** a platelike ornament or badge. (둥그스름한) 배지; 브로치. **3** 《med.》 a patch of eruption, etc. (둥글게 튀어오른) 반(斑); 플라크. [Flem. *placke* a coin]

plash[1] [plæʃ] *n.* Ⓒ **1** a splashing sound of water. 철벙; 철벅《물소리》. ¶ *a* ~ *of oars* 철벅하는 노질 소리. **2** a puddle. 웅덩이. — *vi., vt.* (P1; 6) splash. 철벅거리다. [Imit.]

plash[2] [plæʃ] *vt.* (P6,13) **1** bend and twist together. (나뭇가지 따위를) 서로 얽다; 엮다. ¶ ~ *branches into a hedge* 나뭇가지들을 서로 얽어 울타리를 만들다. **2** make or repair by plashing. …을 얽어 고치다. [→plait]

plash·y [plǽʃi] *adj.* (**plash·i·er, plash·i·est**) **1** ⓐ full of pools or puddles. 웅덩이가 많은. ⓑ marshy; wet. 습지의; 질척질척한. **2** making a sound like a splash of water; splashing. 철벅〔철썩〕거리는. [plash[1]]

plasm [plæzəm] *n.* 《biol.》 protoplasm. 원형질(原形質). [↓]

plas·ma [plǽzmə] *n.* **1** green quartz. 녹옥수(綠玉髓)《짙은 녹색의 반투명 옥수(玉髓)》. **2** 《physiol.》 blood without the corpuscles. 혈장(血漿). **3** 《biol.》 =plasm. [Gk. *plassō* mould]

***plas·ter** [plǽstər, plɑ́:stər] *n.* Ⓤ **1** a mixture of lime, sand, and water used for coating walls and ceilings. 회반죽; 벽토(壁土). **2** a white powder that becomes a thick paste when mixed with water and becomes hard as it dries; plaster of Paris. 석고. **3** ⓊⒸ a substance applied to the body to relieve soreness, etc. 고약. ¶ *an adhesive* ~ 반창고 / *a mustard* ~ 겨자씨 연고《찜질약》.
— *vt.* (P6,7,13) **1** cover (a wall, a ceiling, etc.) with plaster. …에 회반죽을〔벽토를〕 바르다. **2** apply a plaster to (a wound, etc.). …에 고약을 붙이다. **3** spread with anything thickly. …을 두껍게〔더덕더덕〕 바르다. ¶ ~ *a piece of bread with butter* 빵 조각에 버터를 많이 바르다 / *plastered with mud* 진흙을 처바른. **4** stick (something) all over. …에 온통 붙이다. ¶ *plastered with jewels* 온통 보석으로 장식한 / *The wall was plastered with many posters.* 벽에는 온통 포스터투성이였다. [→plasma]

plas·ter·er [plǽstərər, plɑ́:st-] *n.* Ⓒ a person who plasters walls and ceilings. 미장이. [↑]

plas·tic [plǽstik] *adj.* **1** molding or giving form to matter. 조형적(造形的)인. ¶ ~ *images* 소상(塑像) / *the* ~ *arts* 조형 미술. **2** that can be formed or molded easily. 가소성(可塑性)의. ¶ *Clay is a* ~ *substance.* 찰흙은 가소성 물질이다. **3** easily influenced. 감수성이 강한. — *n.* Ⓤ 《often *pl.*》 a substance that is made into various shapes by heat, pressure, etc. 플라스틱; 합성 수지. ¶ *a* ~ *toy* 플라스틱 장난감. [→plasma]

plas·tic·i·ty [plæstísəti] *n.* Ⓤ the quality of being plastic. 가소성(可塑性); 적응성.

plastic surgery [ˊ– ˊ––] *n.* a branch of surgery dealing with the repair of lost or deformed parts of the body, usu. by removing other parts of the body. 성형 외과.

plat [plæt] *n.* **1** a small piece of ground. 작은 땅; 땅뙈기. **2** 《U.S.》 a plan; a map. 도면; 지도. — *vt.* (**plat·ted, plat·ting**) (P6) 《U.S.》 draw a map of. …의 도면을 그리다. [*plot*]

:**plate** [pleit] *n.* Ⓒ **1** a flat, open dish for holding food. 접시. ¶ *a* ~ *for soup* 수프 접시 / *Our food is served on plates.* 음식은 접시에 담아 제공된다. **2** the amount of food a plate will hold; the food contained on a plate. (요리) 한 접시분; (접시에 담은) 요리. ¶ *a* ~ *of soup* 수프 한 접시. **3** food served to one person at a meal. 1인분의 식사. ¶ *two dollars a* ~ 식사 1인분 2달러. **4** Ⓤ 《*collectively*》 dishes, knives, forks, etc. made of gold, silver, or other metals. (금은제의) 식기류. ¶ *a piece of* ~ 금은제 (도금) 식기의 한 개 / *church* ~ 성배(聖杯) / *family* ~ 가문(家紋)을 새긴 가보(家寶)의 식기. **5** a thin, flat piece or sheet of metal, glass, etc. 판금(板金); 판유리. ¶ *a tin* ~ 양철 / *the iron or steel plates on a warship* 군함의 장갑판. **6** a thin, flat piece of metal with someone's name, etc. 금속제의 명찰; 명판(銘板). ¶ *a doorplate* 문패 / *put up one's* ~ (개업의(開業醫)로) 간판을 내걸다. **7** 《print.》 a full-page picture in a book; a sheet of metal used for printing. 1페이지 크기의 도판(圖版); 연판(鉛版); 스테로판. **8** 《photog.》 a thin sheet of glass on which a photograph is taken. 감광판(感光板). ¶ *a dry* 〔*wet*〕 ~ 건(乾)〔습(濕)〕판 / *a negative* ~ 원판(原板). **9** the home base in baseball. (야구의) 본루. **10** a thin piece of plastic material to which artificial teeth are attached. 의치상(義齒床). **11** 《electr.》 the anode. (진공관의) 양극(陽極). ¶ *a positive* ~ 양극판.
— *vt.* (P6,13) **1** cover (esp. a ship) with metal plates for protection. (선박 따위)에 금속판을 씌우다. **2** coat (metal) with gold, silver, etc. (금속)에 도금하다. [F. *plat* flat]

***pla·teau** [plætóu / ˊ–] *n.* (*pl.* **-teaus** or **-teaux**) Ⓒ **1** an elevated, flat piece of land; a tableland. 고원; 대지(臺地). **2** a big dish. 쟁반. **3** a decorative plaque. 장식용 접시. [↑]

pla·teaux [plǽtouz / –ˊ] *n.* pl. of **plateau.**

plat·en [plǽtən] *n.* Ⓤ **1** a flat metal

plate or cylinder of a printing press that presses the paper onto the inked type. (인쇄기의) 압반(壓盤); (윤전기의) 롤러. **2** the roller of a typewriter. (타자기의) 롤러. [*plate*]

:plat·form [plǽtfɔ̀ːrm] *n.* Ⓒ **1** a raised floor or stage for speakers; a raised part of the floor in a school-room on which the teacher stands. 연단; 교단(教壇). **2** a raised level surface beside the track at a railroad station. 플랫폼; (역의) 승강장. ¶ *a ~ ticket* (역의) 입장권. **3** 《U.S.》 a statement of the main principles of a political party. (정당의) 강령; 정강. ¶ *The ~ of the new political party demands lower taxes.* 새 정당의 정강은 조세 인하를 요구하고 있다. [→plate, →form]

plat·ing [pléitiŋ] *n.* Ⓤ **1** the art of coating with gold or silver. 도금술(鍍金術). **2** a thin coating of gold, silver or other metals. (금·은 등의) 도금. **3** the action of one that plates. (금속에 의한) 표면 피복; 금·은을 입히기. [↓]

plat·i·num [plǽtənəm] *n.* Ⓤ a silvery metal used for jewelry, etc. 백금; 플라티나. [→plate]

plat·i·tude [plǽtətjùːd] *n.* **1** Ⓒ a dull or flat remark, esp. one uttered as if it were fresh. 늘 하는 말; 상투어. ¶ *"Nobody lives forever" is a ~.* "누구나 죽게 마련이다"는 (진부한) 상투어다. **2** Ⓤ the quality of being dull and flat. 단조로움; 진부함. [↑]

Pla·to [pléitou] *n.* (427 ?-347 ? B.C.) a Greek philosopher. 플라톤.

Pla·ton·ic [plətɑ́nik / -tɔ́n-] *adj.* **1** of Plato or his philosophy. 플라톤(철학)의. **2** 《also *p-*》 idealistic or impractical; confined to words or theory. 관념적인; 실행이 따르지 않는. ¶ *a ~ scheme* 실행성이 없는 계획. **3** 《also *p-*》 not sensual but spiritual. 순(純) 정신적인. ¶ *~ love* 정신적 연애. [*Plato*]

pla·toon [plətúːn] *n.* Ⓒ **1** a small group of about 60 soldiers acting as a unit. (보병) 소대. ¶ *A ~ is one of the units of a company, usually consisting of two or more squads.* 1소대는 중대의 구성 단위로서 보통 둘 또는 그 이상의 분대로 이루어진다. **2** 《U.S.》 a small unit of policemen. (소규모의) 경찰대. **3** a small group. 일단(一團); 일조(一組). [L. *pila* ball]

plat·ter [plǽtər] *n.* Ⓒ a large, flat dish for serving meat, fish, etc. 큰 접시; 쟁반. [→plate]

plau·dits [plɔ́ːdəts] *n. pl.* **1** the act of clapping hands to show approval. 박수갈채. ¶ *The actress bowed in response to the ~ of the audience.* 여배우는 관중의 박수갈채에 허리를 굽혀 답례했다. **2** the enthusiastic expression of public praise. 칭찬; 절찬. [L. *plaudo* clap (hands)]

plau·si·bil·i·ty [plɔ̀ːzəbíləti] *n.* Ⓤ the state or quality of being plausible. 그럴 듯함; 그럴싸함. [↓]

***plau·si·ble** [plɔ́ːzəbəl] *adj.* **1** (of statements, etc.) specious; seemingly reasonable. (말 따위가) 그럴 듯한. **2** (of persons) fair-spoken. 말솜씨가 좋은. ¶ *a ~ liar* 입담 좋은 거짓말쟁이. [→plaudits]

:play [plei] *vt.* **1** (P6) take part in (a game, a sport, etc.). (놀이 등)을 하다; (시합·경기)에 참가하다. ¶ *~ baseball* 야구를 하다 / *~ bridge* 브리지를 하다 / *~ in a set of tennis* 테니스를 한 세트 치다. **2** (P6,13) take part in a game against (someone or something); fill (a position) or use (a player, etc.) in a game. …을 상대로 시합하다; …을 선수로 쓰다; (포지션)을 맡다. ¶ *~ another team* 다른 팀과 시합하다 / *I played center forward.* 나는 센터 포워드를 맡았다. **3** (P6) act the part of (someone) in a play or in real life; perform (a drama, etc.) on the stage; perform in (a city, etc.). (배역을) 맡아 하다; …처럼 행동하다; (도시 등)에서 공연[흥행]하다. ¶ *~ (the part of) Cinderella* 신데렐라 역을 맡아 하다 / *~ a tragedy* 비극을 상연하다 / *~ the madman* 미친 사람처럼 행동하다 / *~ fair* [*false*] 공정[부당]하게 굴다 / *They played Pusan for a month.* 그들은 부산에서 한 달 동안 공연했다 / *~ a leading* [*principal*] *part* 주역을 하다 / *~ the fool* 바보스레 행동하다 / *He played hero before her.* 그녀 앞에서 영웅처럼 굴었다. **4** (P6) produce music or sound from (a musical instrument, tape recorder, etc.); perform (a piece of music) on an instrument. (악기·곡)을 연주하다. ¶ *~ the piano* 피아노를 연주하다 / *~ a waltz* 왈츠를 연주하다 / *~ a record* 음반을 틀다 / *~ by ear* 악보 없이[보지 않고] 연주하다 / *She is playing a sonata on the piano.* 피아노로 소나타를 치고 있다. **5** (P6,13) do (a trick, joke, etc.) either in fun or to deceive; cause. (장난·농담)을 하다; (해로움 따위)를 끼치다[주다]. ¶ *~ havoc* 해를 끼치다 / *~ someone a mean trick* = *~ a trick on someone* 아무를 속여 먹다 / *They played a joke on him.* 그에게 농지거리를 했다. **6** (P6) imitate or pretend to be (someone) or to do (something) in fun. …의 흉내를 내며 놀다. ¶ *~ house* 소꿉장난하다 / *~ soldiers* 병정놀이하다 / *The children played that they were pirates.* 아이들은 해적놀이를 했다. **7** (P6) cause (something) to move, act, or work; direct (a jet of water, a searchlight, etc.). …을 쓰다[움직이게 하다]; (물·빛 등)을 향하게 하다. ¶ *~ a horse on a lawn* 말을 잔디 위에서 걸리다 / *~ one's stick freely* 지팡이를 휘두르다 / *~ water* [*a hose*] *on a burning house* 타고 있는 집에 물을 끼얹다[호스를 돌리다] / *~ a searchlight upon a ship* 배에 서치라이트를 비추다. **8** (P13) aim and discharge. …을 발사하다. ¶ *~ guns on a fortress* 요새에 포격을 가하다. **9** (P6,7) wear out; tire out. …을 지치게 하다. ¶ *~ a fish on a line* 낚싯줄을 이리저리 당

겨서 고기를 지치게 만들다.
— *vi.* **1** (P1,2B,3) spend time doing something pleasant, not working. 놀다; 장난치다. ¶ ~ *indoors* 실내에서 놀다 / ~ *(at) hide-and-seek* 숨바꼭질하다 / *She likes to ~ with her doll.* 인형과 놀기를 좋아한다 / *The cat is playing with its tail.* 고양이가 제 꼬리를 가지고 놀고 있다. **2** (P1,3) be not at work. 파업하다; 일을 않고 놀다(opp. work). **3** (P3) 《*with*》 toy; fool; trifle; handle. 만지작거리다; 우롱하다; 가지고 놀다. ¶ ~ *with fire* 불장난하다 / ~ *with edged tools* 위험〔무모〕한 일에 손을 내밀다 / ~ *with a woman's affections* 여자의 애정을 우롱하다. **4** (P1,3) do something in sport; take part in a game; gamble. 놀이를 하다; 시합하다; 경기를 하다; 내기를 하다. ¶ ~ *for money* 돈을 걸고 내기하다 / ~ *the horses* 〔*horse races*〕 경마에 걸다 / ~ *high* 〔*low*〕 대판으로〔좀스럽게〕 노름하다. **5** (P1,2A) (of ground) be in a certain condition. (지면의 상태가) … 상태에 있다. ¶ *The ground plays well.* 경기장의 상태는 (운동하기에) 좋다. **6** (P1,2A) act on the stage; (of a play, film, etc.) be performed or be showing. 극에 출연하다; 연기하다; (연극·영화 따위가) 상연〔공연〕되다. ¶ *The actor plays well.* 배우가 연기를 잘 한다 / *What's playing tonight ?* 오늘 밤에는 무엇이 상연되지. **7** (P1,2A,3) perform music on an instrument; (of a musical instrument) sound in performance. (음악·악기가) 울리다; 연주하다. ¶ *The flutes are playing.* 플루트가 취주되고 있다 / *The strings played well.* 현악기의 연주가 좋았다 / *Will you ~ for us ?* 연주〔반주〕해 주겠느냐 / *The band is playing.* 악대가 연주하고 있다. **8** (P2A,5) behave or act in a certain way. 행동하다; 처신하다. ¶ ~ *false with a friend* 친구에게 부정한 짓을 하다 / ~ *fair* 옳게〔깨끗하게〕 처신하다. **9** (P2A,3) (of light, water, etc.) be moving with a dancing motion; (of a fountain, a jet of water, etc.) be in operation. (빛·물 따위가) 흔들리다; 춤추다; (분수 등이) 분출하다. ¶ *Sunlight plays on the water.* 햇볕이 물 위에서 춤을 춘다 / *A smile played upon her lips.* 그녀 입술에 미소가 감돌았다. **10** (P3) be aimed and discharged at in succession. 연속 발사되다; 연발하다. ¶ *Guns ~ on a fortress.* 요새를 향해 포가 계속 불을 뿜는다. **11** (P2A,3) move freely; work. (기계 등이) 잘 움직이다; 가동하다. ¶ *A piston rod plays within a cylinder.* 피스톤 막대는 실린더 안에서 잘 움직인다.

be played out, be exhausted; be worn out; become useless. 다 써 버리다; 지치다; 쓸모 없게 되다.

play at, **a**) do for pleasure. …하고 놀다. **b**) work at playfully. …을 장난삼아 하다. ¶ ~ *at business* 시덥잖게 장사하다.

play down, make light of (something). …을 가볍게 보다.

play into** someone's **hands, plot together. 짜고 하다; 한통속이 되다.

play off, **a**) practice. …을 행하다; 실행하다. **b**) deceive. …을 속이다.

***play off** one person **against** another,* set one person against another for one's own advantage. 아무를 다른 사람과 이간붙여 어부지리를 노리다.

***play on** 〔**upon**〕,* try to make use of (someone's feelings, honesty, etc.) for one's advantage. (…의 감정)을 이용하다; …을 틈타다. ¶ ~ *upon people's fears* 국민의 공포심을 이용하다.

play out, **a**) play to the end. 끝까지 (연주, 경기)하다. ¶ *The actors played out the tragedy.* 배우들은 그 비극을 끝까지 연출했다. **b**) be exhausted. 지치다.

play up, **a**) work hard or perform one's duty. 열심히 하다; 할 일을 다하다. **b**) 《*colloq.*》 advertise. 광고〔선전〕하다.

***play up to** someone,* **a**) 《*colloq.*》 do or say in order to gain favor, etc. …에 아첨하다; 빌붙다. **b**) help; assist. …을 돕다; 지지하다.

— *n.* **1** Ⓤ action or exercise for amusement. 놀이; 유희. ¶ *The boys are at ~.* 아이들이 놀고 있다 / 《*prov.*》 *All work and no ~ makes Jack a dull boy.* 공부만 하고 놀이를 모르는 아이는 바보가 된다《공부도 하고 놀기도 해라》 / *child's ~* 아이들 장난; 식은 죽 먹기. **2** Ⓤ ⓐ a game; sport. 경기; 승부; 시합. ¶ *during ~* 경기 중에 / *Play begins at 10 a.m.* 경기는 10 시에 시작한다. ⓑ gambling; betting money. 도박; 돈내기. ¶ *He lost all money at ~.* 노름으로 돈을 몽땅 날렸다. **3** Ⓒ a turn to play in a game; a move or act in a game. 경기의 순번〔차례〕. ¶ *It's your ~ next.* 다음은 네 차례다. **4** Ⓤ manner of playing; conduct; action. 시합하는 솜씨; 태도; 행동; 움직임. ¶ *fair ~* 페어 플레이 / *foul ~* 반칙; 부정 행위. **5** Ⓒ fun; amusement; joke. 재미; 즐거움; 장난; 농담. ¶ *say something in ~* …을 장난으로 말하다 / *a ~ on words* 말장난《익살 등》. **6** Ⓤ activity; use; operation; freedom or room for movement; scope. 활동; 운용; 작용; 자유로운 활동; 활동의 범위. ¶ *be in full ~* 왕성하게 활동하고 있다 / *give full ~ to one's imagination* 한껏 상상의 날개를 펴게 하다 / *This wheel has too much ~.* 이 바퀴는 움직임이 너무 헐겁다 / *give a wheel more ~ on the axle* 바퀴와 축을 더 헐겁게 하다. **7** Ⓒ a drama; the written text for this. 극; 연극; 희곡; 각본. ¶ *act a ~* 연극을 하다 / *a moral ~* 권선 징악극; 교훈극 / *a ~ of Ibsen* 입센극. **8** Ⓤ light, quick, changeable movement. (빛 따위의) 움직임; 어른거림. ¶ *the ~ of light and shade on a wall* 벽에 어른거리는 명암 / *the ~ of expression in a face* 얼굴 표정의 움직임. [E.]

(as) good as a play, amusing; interesting. 재미있는.

bring** 〔**come**〕 **into play, bring 〔come〕 into use; cause 〔begin〕 to work. …을 이용하다;

쓰이게 되다; 움직이게 하다; 움직이기 시작하다.

make a play for, 《*colloq.*》 use one's arts to win the love or favor of. …을 유혹하려고〔…의 마음에 들려고〕 책략을 쓰다. ¶ *He doesn't like girls who make a ~ for him.* 자기와 사귀려고 요령을 부리는 여자를 그는 싫어한다.

play·back [pléibæ̀k] *n.* Ⓒ **1** the act of reproducing recorded sound. 녹음 재생. **2** the device used for it. 재생 장치.

play·bill [pléibìl] *n.* Ⓒ **1** a poster advertising the performance of a play. 연극의 광고〔전단〕. **2** a program of a play. (극장의) 프로그램.

play·boy [pléibɔ̀i] *n.* Ⓒ 《*colloq.*》 a fellow who is chiefly interested in seeking pleasure. 바람둥이; 플레이보이.

play·day [pléidèi] *n.* Ⓒ a holiday. 휴일.

:play·er [pléiər] *n.* Ⓒ **1** a person who plays a game. 경기자; 운동 선수. ¶ *a ball ~* (야구 등) 구기 선수. **2** a musician. 연주자. **3** an actor. 배우. **4** a device for playing a musical instrument automatically. 자동 연주 장치. ¶ *a ~ piano* 자동 피아노.

play·fel·low [pléifèlou] *n.* Ⓒ a playmate. 놀이 친구.

play·ful [pléifəl] *adj.* **1** fond of playing or fun. 놀기 좋아하는; 쾌활한. ¶ *a ~ kitten* 재롱떠는 새끼고양이. **2** humorous; not serious; joking. 농담〔장난〕의. ¶ *a ~ remark* 익살; 농담.

play·ful·ly [pléifəli] *adv.* gaily; humorously. 쾌활하게; 익살스럽게.

play·ful·ness [pléifəlnis] *n.* Ⓤ the state of being playful. 장난; 농.

play·go·er [pléigòuər] *n.* Ⓒ a person who goes often or habitually to the theater. 연극 구경을 자주 가는〔좋아하는〕 사람.

:play·ground [pléigràund] *n.* Ⓒ a ground for children's play; a place of amusement; any place of recreation. 운동장; 놀이터; 행락지; 휴양지. ¶ *Switzerland, the ~ of Europe* 유럽의 휴양지, 스위스.

play·house [pléihàus] *n.* Ⓒ **1** a theater. 극장. **2** 《U.S.》 a small house for children to play in. (아이들) 놀이집. **3** a toy house. 장난감 집.

playing cards [∸–∸] *n. pl.* cards used in playing games. 트럼프.

playing field [∸–∸] *n.* 《chiefly Brit.》 any official ground where various games are played. (공인·공식의) 경기장.

:play·mate [pléimèit] *n.* Ⓒ a companion in play or games. 놀이 친구.

play·thing [pléiθìŋ] *n.* Ⓒ **1** a thing to play with; a toy. 노리개; 장난감. **2** 《*fig.*》 a person treated as a mere toy. 노리개 취급받는 사람; 놀림감. ¶ *He was just her ~.* 그는 그녀의 노리개에 불과했다 / *Are we the ~ of fate?* 우리는 운명의 노리개인가.

play·time [pléitàim] *n.* Ⓤ a period for play or recreation, esp. in schools. 노는 시간; 휴식 시간.

play·wright [pléiràit] *n.* Ⓒ a person who writes plays for the theater; a dramatist. 극작가.

pla·za [plɑ́:zə, plǽzə] *n.* Ⓒ a public square or open place in a city or town(esp. in Spain). (특히 스페인의) 광장; 플라자(cf. *piazza*). [L.=place]

plea [pli:] *n.* Ⓒ **1** a request; an appeal. 청원. **2** an excuse. 변명; 핑계. ¶ *Her ~ for staying at home was headache.* 그녀는 머리가 아프다는 핑계로 집에 있었다. **3** 《law》 an answer by a defendant to charges in a law court. 항변(抗辯). ¶ *He made a ~ of not guilty.* 그는 무죄를 주장했다. [L. *placeo* please]

on the plea of (=*making an excuse of; on the pretense of*) *something.* …을 구실로.

:plead [pli:d] *vi.* (P1,3) **1** argue or reason for or against something. 변론하다. ¶ *~ for the defendant* 피고를 위해 변호를 하다. **2** make an earnest appeal; beg earnestly. 탄원하다. ¶ *~ for mercy* 자비를 빌다 / *~ for consideration* 관대한 조처를 빌다 / *When the rent was due, the poor man pleaded for more time.* 집세의 만기가 되자 그 가난한 사람은 좀더 시간을 달라고 애원했다. **3** make a plea in a law court. 항변하다. ¶ *The prisoner was held to be insane and therefore unable to ~.* 피고는 미친 사람이라는 판정이 났고 따라서 항변할 수 없었다.

— *vt.* (P6) **1** defend (a case) by arguments in a law court. …을 변호하다. ¶ *He could not find a good lawyer to ~ his case.* 그에겐 사건을 맡길 적당한 변호사가 없었다. **2** answer (something) to a charge. …을 주장하다. ¶ *~ innocence* 결백을 주장하다. **3** offer (something) as an excuse. 핑계로 …라고 말하다. ¶ *She pleaded ignorance of the fact.* 그녀는 그 사실을 몰랐다고 변명했다. [O.F. *plaid* plea]

plead guilty 〔***not guilty***〕 ***to*** (=*admit* 〔*deny*〕 *to be responsible for*) *something.* …에 대한 유죄〔무죄〕를 주장하다.

plead·er [plí:dər] *n.* Ⓒ **1** a person who pleads. 변론자. **2** a lawyer in a court. 변호사.

plead·ings [plí:diŋz] *n. pl.* 《law》 the statements by a plaintiff and a defendant in a court. (원고의) 고소장(告訴狀); (피고의) 항고장.

pleas·ance [plézəns] *n.* 《*arch.*》 **1** pleasure; delight. 향락; 쾌락. **2** a pleasant place, usu. with trees, fountains, and flowers. 유원지. [↓]

:pleas·ant [pléznt] *adj.* **1** delightful; pleasing. 유쾌한; 즐거운. ¶ *have a ~ time* 즐겁게 지내다 / *a ~ voice* 듣기 좋은 음성 / *The sight was ~ to the eye.* 그 광경은 보기에 좋았다 / *It is a ~ day for walking.* 산책하기에 좋은 날이다. **2** having an agreeable or charming manner; amiable. 호감이

가는; 상냥한. ¶ *a ~ companion* 마음에 드는 벗 / *He has a ~ manner.* 그는 매너가 좋다 / *He made himself very ~.* 그는 아주 호감이 가게 행동했다. [→please]

·**pleas·ant·ly** [plézntli] *adv.* in a pleasant manner. 유쾌하게.

pleas·ant·ness [plézntnis] *n.* Ⓤ the state or quality of being pleasant. 유쾌; 즐거움.

pleas·ant·ry [plézntri] *n.* (*pl.* **-ries**) **1** Ⓤ humor; merriment. 익살; 유쾌. **2** Ⓒ a humorous speech; a joke. 농담; 유머러스한 말.

:**please** [pli:z] *vt.* (P6) give pleasure or delight to (someone); satisfy. …의 마음에 들게 하다; …을 기쁘게 하다; 만족시키다. 語法 be pleased at 〔in, with〕의 꼴로 형용사적으로 쓰임. ¶ *~ oneself* 좋을 대로 하다 / *This book will ~ you.* 이 책을 읽으면 마음에 들 거요 / *He is pleased at his son's success.* 그는 아들이 출세해서 기뻐하고 있다 / *She was pleased with the news.* 그 소식에 그녀는 기뻤다 / *It pleased him to go.* 그는 기꺼이 갔다 / *He is a difficult master to ~.* 그는 까다로운 주인이다. — *vi.* **1** wish; desire; like. 바라다; 좋아하다. ¶ *I'll do as I ~.* 내 마음대로 하겠다 / *Take as many as you ~.* 원대로 가져가시오 / *He will come when he pleases.* 그는 마음이 내키면 올 게다. **2** be agreeable; win favor; make oneself pleasant. 남의 마음에 들다; 남을 기쁘게 하다; 호감을 주다. ¶ *the desire to ~* 기쁘게 해 주려는 마음 / *He is anxious to ~.* 그는 남의 호감을 사려고 애쓴다 / *She never fails to ~.* 그녀는 절대로 남의 마음을 상하게 하지 않는다. **3** 《used only as a polite addition to requests or commands》 if you like; if you please. 좋으시다면; 부디. ¶ *Come in, ~.* 어서 들어오세요 / *Please take your seat.* 자아, 앉으세요 / *"Will you have another cup?" "Please."* "한 잔 더 하시겠소." "예, 주십시오." [L. *placeo* to be agreeable, please]

be pleased (=*be glad* or *happy*) *to do.* 기꺼이 …하다. ¶ *I shall be pleased to do so.* 기꺼이 그렇게 하지요.

if you please, **a**) if you wish. 좋다면; 아무쪼록. ¶ *Give me a cup of tea, if you ~.* 차 한 잔 주시면 고맙겠네요. **b**) expressing surprise. 놀랍게도. ¶ *The next moment, if you ~, the man was out of sight.* 다음 순간 놀랍게도 그 남자는 사라지고 없었다 / *He was, if you ~, a thief.* 그 사람은 놀랍게도 도둑이었다네.

please God, if it is God's wish; if it is possible. 신의 뜻이라면; 잘만 되면.

pleased [pli:zd] *adj.* feeling or showing pleasure; glad; satisfied. 기뻐〔좋아〕하는; 만족한. ¶ *She looked ~ with herself.* 그녀는 (자기가 한 일에) 만족해하는 것 같았다 / *She gave a ~ smile.* 그녀는 흡족한 듯이 웃었다 / *He had a ~ look on his face.* 그는 만족스러운 표정을 짓고 있었다.

·**pleas·ing** [plí:ziŋ] *adj.* giving pleasure; agreeable. 기분 좋은. ¶ *a ~ young man* 호감이 가는 젊은이 / *We have made ~ progress in our talks.* 우리는 재미있게 대화를 이끌어 갔다. ● **pleas·ing·ly** [-li] *adv.*

pleas·ur·a·ble [pléʒərəbəl] *adj.* giving pleasure; enjoyable. 즐거운; 유쾌한. ¶ *The old woman spent a ~ time.* 그 노부인은 즐거운 시간을 보냈다. [↓]

:**pleas·ure** [pléʒər] *n.* **1** Ⓤ a feeling of satisfaction; enjoyment. 만족; 즐거움; 기쁨. ¶ *It gave me much ~ to hear the news.* 그 소식을 듣고 매우 기뻤다 / *The boy's ~ in the gift was good to see.* 선물을 받고 좋아하는 소년의 모습은 보기에도 좋았다 / *It gave me great ~ to work for a man like that.* 그런 사람을 위해 힘쓰는 것이 내게는 크나큰 기쁨이었다 / *Will you do me the ~ of coming to dine?* 와서 식사라도 해 주시면 기쁘겠습니다. **2** Ⓒ a thing which gives joy or delight; a source of joy. 즐거움; 즐거운 일. ¶ *It's a ~ to talk to her.* 그녀와의 이야기는 즐겁다 / *It would be a ~ to see you again.* 다시 뵙기를 고대합니다. **3** Ⓤ desire; choice. 욕구; 희망. ¶ *Is it your ~ to go now?* 지금 가고 싶다는 말이냐. **4** Ⓤ physical self-indulgence. (관능적) 쾌락. ¶ *a life given* (*up*) *to ~* 향락에 빠진 생활 / *a man of ~* 난봉꾼 / *seek ~* 쾌락을 좇다. [L. *placeo* please]

at one's pleasure, as one likes. 마음대로; 좋을 대로.

during one's pleasure, as long as one pleases. 마음〔의향〕이 있는 동안에.

for pleasure, for fun. 재미로. ¶ *Did you come here on business or for ~?* 여긴 볼일이 있어 왔나 그냥 놀러 왔나.

take one's pleasure, 《*arch.*》 enjoy oneself. 즐기다. ¶ *He takes his ~ in riding and hunting.* 그는 승마와 사냥을 즐긴다.

take* 〔*find*〕 *pleasure in, enjoy; like. …을 즐기다; 좋아하다.

with pleasure, willingly; gladly 기꺼이.

pleat [pli:t] *n.* Ⓒ a fold made in cloth by doubling it and pressing it down. (치마의) 주름; 플리트(cf. *plait*). — *vt.* (P6) make a pleat in (cloth). …에 주름을 잡다. ¶ *a pleated skirt* 주름치마. [→plait]

plebe [pli:b] *n.* 《U.S. *colloq.*》 a member of the lowest class at the U.S. Military or Naval Academy. 육군〔해군〕 사관 학교의 최하급생. [↓]

ple·be·ian [plibí:ən] *n.* Ⓒ **1** one of the ancient Roman common people. (고대 로마의) 평민(cf. *patrician*). **2** a common person. 서민. — *adj.* **1** of the plebeian. 평민〔서민〕의. ¶ *have ~ taste* (기호·취미 등이) 서민적이다. **2** common. 보통의. [L. *plebs* commons]

pleb·i·scite [plébəsàit, -sit] *n.* Ⓒ a direct vote by the people on some important issue. 국민 투표. [L. *plebs* commons, *scisco* vote for]

plebs [plebz] *n.* 《*collectively,* used as *pl.*》 **1**

the common people in ancient Rome. (고대 로마의) 평민. **2** the common people. 대중. [→plebeian]

plec·tra [pléktrə] *n.* pl. of **plectrum.**

plec·trum [pléktrəm] *n.* Ⓒ (*pl.* **-trums** or **-tra**) a small, thin instrument of metal or ivory used for plucking certain stringed instruments. (기타 따위 현악기의) 채; 픽(= pick). [Gk. *prēsso* strike]

***pledge** [pledʒ] *n.* **1** Ⓒ something given as security or a guarantee; Ⓤ the state of being held as security. 담보물; 담보. ¶ *put in* ~ 저당잡히다 / *hold in* ~ 담보로 잡다 / *He took the watch out of* ~. 그는 저당잡혔던 시계를 찾았다 / *The jewel was kept by the money-lender as a* ~. 보석은 대금업자에 담보로 잡혀 있었다. **2** Ⓒ something given to show love, friendship, etc. (사랑·우정 등의) 증거. ¶ *a* ~ *of friendship* 우정의 징표 / *give a gold ring as a* ~ *of love* 사랑한다는 뜻으로 금반지를 주다 / *a* ~ *of* (*conjugal*) *affection* (부부간) 사랑의 징표《자식》. **3** Ⓒ the act of drinking to someone's health. 건배. **4** Ⓤ an agreement; a promise. 약속; 서약. ¶ *under* ~ *of secrecy* 비밀을 지킨다는 맹세 아래.

take* 〔*sign*〕 *the pledge, promise solemnly not to drink or never to drink again. 금주의 맹세를 하다. ¶ *The drunkard signed the* ~. 그 술꾼은 다시는 술을 안 하겠다고 맹세했다.

— *vt.* (P6,13) **1** give (something) as security; put (something) in pawn. …을 담보에 넣다; 저당잡히다. ¶ *He pledged his watch.* **2** drink a health to (someone). …을 위해 건배하다. ¶ *The knights rose from the banquet table to* ~ *the king.* 기사들은 연회석에서 일어나 왕을 위해 건배했다. **3** make a solemn promise to do (something). …할 것을 서약〔맹세〕하다. ¶ *He pledged* (*himself*) *to stop drinking.* 술을 끊겠다고 맹세했다 / *He pledged* (*his word*) *to do his best.* 최선을 다할 것을 서약했다. ●**pledg·er** [-ər] *n.* [O.F. *plege*]

pledg·ee [pledʒíː] *n.* a person to whom pledge is given. 저당권자(者).

ple·na·ry [plíːnəri, plén-] *adj.* **1** complete; absolute. 완전한; 절대적인. ¶ *The envoy was given* ~ *powers to negotiate with the rebels.* 그 사절은 반역자들과의 협상에 전권을 부여받았다. **2** attended by all the members who are entitled to be present. 전원 출석한. ¶ *a* ~ *session* 본회의. [L. *plenus* full]

plen·i·po·ten·ti·ar·y [plènipəténʃəri, -ʃièri] *n.* Ⓒ (*pl.* **-ar·ies**) a person given full power or authority by his government. 전권(全權) 대사; 전권 위원. — *adj.* having full power and authority. 전권을 가지는. ¶ *The United States usually has a minister* ~ *in every important foreign country.* 미국은 보통 각 주요국마다에 (특명) 전권 공사를 둔다.

[↑, →potent]

plen·i·tude [plénətjùːd] *n.* Ⓤ the state of being full or complete; abundance. 충분; 충만; 절정; 풍부. ¶ *in the* ~ *of his power* 권력의 절정에서 / *a feeling of* ~ *after meals* 식후의 포만감(飽滿感). [→plenty]

plen·te·ous [pléntiəs, -tjəs] *adj.* 《*poet.*》 plentiful; fruitful. 충분한; 결실이 많은; 풍부한. ¶ ~ *crops* 풍작.

***plen·ti·ful** [pléntifəl] *adj.* abundant; great in quantity; more than enough. 풍부한; 충분한(opp. scarce). ¶ *a* ~ *harvest* 풍작 / *a* ~ *land* 비옥한 땅 / *Apples are now cheap because they are* ~. 사과는 (풍작이라) 흔해서 지금 값이 싸다. ●**plen·ti·ful·ness** [-nis] *n.*

plen·ti·ful·ly [pléntifəli] *adv.* amply; abundantly. 풍부하게; 충분히.

:plen·ty [plénti] *n.* Ⓤ a full or sufficient supply; the state of being plentiful. 풍부; 많음. ¶ ~ *of food* 〔*money*〕 풍부한 음식〔돈〕 / *Six will be* ~. 여섯이면 족하다 / *You have* ~ *of time to catch the train.* 기차 시간에는 충분하다. — *adv.* 《*colloq.*》 quite; enough. 아주; 충분히. ¶ *The house is* ~ *large enough.* 집의 크기는 아주 충분하다. [→plenary]

plenty of, much. 많은.

ple·o·nasm [plíːənæ̀zəm] *n.* 《rhet.》 the use of more words than are necessary to express an idea; an instance of this. 용어법(冗語法); 장황한 말. ¶ *'Hear with one's ears' is a* ~. '귀로 듣는다'는 용어(冗語)이다. [Gk. *pleon* more]

pleth·o·ra [pléθərə] *n.* **1** excessive fullness; too much. 과다; 과잉. **2** 《med.》 excess of red corpuscles in the blood. 다혈증(多血症); 적혈구 과다증. [Gk. *plēthō* become full]

pleu·ra [plúərə] *n.* Ⓒ (*pl.* **-rae**) the thin membrane covering the chest. 늑막(肋膜). [Gk. *pleura* rib]

pleu·rae [plúəriː] *n.* pl. of **pleura.**

pleu·ri·sy [plúərəsi] *n.* Ⓤ inflammation of the pleura. 늑막염.

plex·us [pléksəs] *n.* (*pl.* **-us·es** or **plexus**) 《anat.》 a network, as of veins, nerves, etc. (혈관·신경 등의) 망상 조직. ¶ *the solar* ~ 태양 신경총(叢). [→plait]

pli·a·bil·i·ty [plàiəbíləti] *n.* Ⓤ the quality of being pliable. 유연(성); 유순. [↓]

pli·a·ble [pláiəbəl] *adj.* **1** that can be easily bent; flexible. 휘기 쉬운; 유연한. ¶ *Copper wire is* ~. 동선(銅線)은 유연하다. **2** easily influenced or persuaded. 순진〔순직〕한; 유순한. ¶ *a* ~ *person* 〔*disposition*〕 유순한 사람〔성격〕. [→ply[2]]

pli·an·cy [pláiənsi] *n.* =pliability.

pli·ant [pláiənt] *adj.* **1** pliable; bending easily. 잘 휘는. ¶ *a* ~ *twig* 나긋나긋한 가지. **2** (of the mind, character, etc.) easily influenced; yielding. 유순한; 고분고분한. ¶ *He has a* ~ *nature.* 천성이 착하다. [L. *plico* fold]

pli·ers [pláiərz] *n. pl.* 《used as *sing.*》 a kind of small pincers with long jaws, used for bending wires, etc. 집게; 펜치; 플라이어. [↑]

·**plight**[1] [plait] *n.* Ⓒ a state or condition, usu. unfavorable or bad. 좋지 않은 상태; 곤경(cf. *pickle*). ¶ *find oneself in a sorry* ~ 딱한 처지에 놓이다 / *He was in a sad* ~ *when he became ill and had no money.* 병이 나고 돈이 떨어졌을 때 그의 신세는 처량했다. [→plait]

plight[2] [plait] *vt.* (P6) pledge; promise; engage. 맹세하다; 약혼하다. ¶ ~ *one's word* 서약하다 / *plighted lovers* 사랑을 언약한 남녀.
— *n.* a solemn promise; engagement. 서약; 약혼. [E.]

plinth [plinθ] *n.* Ⓒ the square base of a column. 주추; 방형 대좌(方形臺座). [Gk. *plinthos* tile]

plod [plɑd / plɔd] *vi.* **1** (P2A,3) 《*on, along*》 walk or move slowly and heavily. 터벅터벅 걷다. ¶ ~ *on one's way* 터벅터벅 걸어가다 / *The man plodded wearily along the road.* 그는 지친 걸음으로 길을 터벅터벅 걸었다. **2** (P2A,2B,3) 《*fig.*》 work slowly with great effort. 끈기 있게〔꾸준히〕 일하다. ¶ ~ *through a task* 힘들여 일을 해내다 / *The student plodded along in mathematics.* 학생은 꾸준히 수학 공부를 했다. — *vt.* (P6) walk slowly and heavily along or over (some place). …을 따라 터벅터벅 걷다. ¶ ~ *one's weary way* 지친 다리를 끌고 가다. [probably Imit.]

plod·der [plɑ́dər / plɔ́d-] *n.* Ⓒ a walker or worker who plods. 터벅터벅 걷는 사람; 꾸준히 일하는 사람.

plod·ding [plɑ́diŋ / plɔ́d-] *adj.* slow and steady in one's way of walking or working. 터벅터벅 걷는〔꾸준히 일하는〕 사람.

plop [plɑp / plɔp] *n.* Ⓒ a sound of or like something dropping into water without a splash. 퐁당(하는 소리). — *v.* (**plopped, plop·ping**) *vi.* (P1) **1** drop with such a sound. 퐁당 떨어지다. **2** make this sound. 퐁당 소리를 내다. — *vt.* (P6) cause (something) to make or drop with this sound. …을 퐁당 떨어뜨리다. — *adv.* with a plop. 퐁당하고. [Imit.]

:**plot** [plɑt / plɔt] *n.* Ⓒ **1** a secret plan, esp. to do something evil. 음모. ¶ *They formed a* ~ *to overthrow the government.* 그들은 정부를 전복하려는 음모를 꾸몄다 / *The police have uncovered a* ~ *to assassinate the president.* 경찰은 대통령의 암살 음모를 적발했다. **2** the plan or main story of a play, novel, etc. (소설·각본 등의) 구상; 줄거리. ¶ *Boys like plots dealing with adventure and mystery.* 소년들은 모험과 신비를 다룬 줄거리를 좋아한다 / *The* ~ *thickens.* 얘기가 재미있어진다. **3** a small piece of land. 작은 땅; 소구획. ¶ *a* ~ *of potatoes* 감자밭.
— *v.* (**plot·ted, plot·ting**) *vt.* (P6,7,10,12) **1** make a secret plan for (something). …을 꾀하다; 꾸미다. ¶ ~ *the destruction of empire* 제국의 붕괴를 꾀하다 / *His enemies are plotting his downfall.* 그의 적들은 그의 몰락을 꾀하고 있다. **2** (P6) make a map of (something). …의 도면을 그리다. ¶ ~ *the course of the ship* 선박의 항로를 도면에 기입하다. **3** (P6,7) divide (land) into plots. (땅)을 구획하다. ¶ *The old farm was plotted out into house lots.* 오래 된 농장은 택지로 구획되었다.
— *vi.* (P1,3,4) **1** form plans. 계획을 짜다. ¶ *We are plotting as to how we shall spend our holidays.* 여름 방학을 어떻게 보낼 것인가를 구상하고 있다. **2** plan secretly with others to do something wrong; conspire. 음모를 꾸미다; 공모하다. ¶ *The traitors plotted against the government.* 반역자들은 대(對)정부 음모를 꾸몄다. [E.]

plot·ter [plɑ́tər / plɔ́t-] *n.* Ⓒ a person who plots; a conspirator. 음모자.

plotting paper [´-- ⁀-] *n.* Ⓤ paper ruled into small squares of the same size. 모눈 종이; 그래프 용지.

plough [plau] *n.* 《Brit.》 =plow.

plov·er [plʌ́vər, plóuvər] *n.* Ⓒ a shore bird with pointed wings and a short tail. 물떼새. [L. *pluvia* rain]

·**plow,** 《Brit.》 **plough** [plau] *n.* Ⓒ **1** a tool used for cutting and turning up the soil. 쟁기. **2** ⓐ any tool like a plow. 쟁기 모양의 기구. ⓑ a machine for removing snow. 제설기(=snowplow). **3** 《*the P-*》《astron.》 a group of seven stars shaped like a plow. 북두칠성. **4** 《Brit. *colloq.*》 failure to pass an examination. 낙제. ¶ *take a* ~ 낙제하다.

be at* 〔*follow, hold*〕 *the plow, work as a farmer; become a farmer. 농사일하다; 농군이 되다.

be under the plow, be turned up by the plow. (땅이) 경작되어 있다.

put one's hand to the plow, set to work. 일에 착수하다.

— *vt.* **1** (P6,7) cut and turn up (the soil) with a plow. 땅을 갈다; 경작하다. ¶ ~ *a field* 밭을 갈다. **2** (P6) make a long deep cut in (the earth, one's face, etc.). (밭에) 고랑을 파다; (얼굴에) 주름살을 짓다. ¶ *Her face is plowed with wrinkles.* 그녀의 얼굴에 주름이 져 있다. **3** (P6) 《*fig.*》 cut or force a way through (something). …을 헤치고 나아가다. ¶ ~ *the waves* (배가) 파도를 가르고 나아가다 / ~ *one's way through a crowd* 군중을 헤치고 나아가다. **4** (P6) 《Brit. *colloq.*》 refuse to pass in an examination. 낙제시키다. — *vi.* **1** (P1) work with a plow. 쟁기질하다; 갈다. ¶ ~ *and sow* 갈고 씨를 뿌리다. **2** (P2A,3) 《*through*》 cut a way; advance laboriously. 헤치고 나아가다. ¶ ~ *through the mud* 진구렁을 힘겹게 걸어가다 / *The ship plowed through the waves.* 배는 파도를 헤치고 전진했다. **3**

(P1) (of land) be suitable for plowing. (땅이) 경작에 적합하다. ¶ *The land plows hard after the drought.* 가뭄 뒤의 땅은 갈기가 힘들다. [E.]

plow a lonely furrow, 《*fig.*》 take one's own course without others' help or support. 독자적인 길을 걷다.

plow back, **a**) plow (grass, etc.) into the soil to make it fertile. (풀 등)을 쟁기로 도로 묻다《거름이 되게》. **b**) 《*fig.*》 retain profits for reinvestment. (이익을) 재투자하다.

plow the sand(***s***), 《*fig.*》 engage upon a worthless plan; labor uselessly. 헛수고하다.

plow through, work, read, with effort through (a book, etc.). (책 따위)를 애써서 읽다〔공부하다〕. ¶ *He plowed through his exams.* 그는 고생하여 시험에 통과했다.

plow up, turn up with a plow. (땅을) 갈아엎다. ¶ ~ *up roots* 뿌리를 파엎다 / 《*fig.*》 *The engine left the rails and plowed up the track for several yards.* 기관차가 탈선하면서 선로가 몇 야드 뒤집혔다.

plow·boy, 《Brit.》 **plough-** [pláubɔ̀i] *n.* Ⓒ a boy who leads the horses drawing a plow. 쟁기 멘 마소를 끄는 소년.

plow·man, 《Brit.》 **plough-** [pláumən] *n.* Ⓒ (*pl.* **-men** [-mən]) a person who operates a plow; a farmer. 농부.

plow·share, 《Brit.》 **plough-** [pláuʃɛ̀ər] *n.* Ⓒ the sharp blade of a plow. 보습; 쟁기날.

:pluck [plʌk] *vt.* **1** (P6) pick off (flowers, fruit, feathers, etc.); pull out the feathers of (a fowl, etc.). …을 따다; 뜯다; …의 털을 뽑다. ¶ ~ *feathers from a goose* 거위의 털을 뽑다 / ~ *flowers in the garden* 정원의 꽃을 따다. **2** (P6) ⓐ pull at (something) sharply. …을 확 (잡아)당기다. ¶ ~ *a handkerchief from the pocket of a coat* 코트 주머니에서 손수건을 홱 빼다 / *The little boy plucked my shirt.* 그 어린아이는 내 셔츠를 잡아당겼다. ⓑ 《*colloq.*》 plunder; swindle. 등쳐먹다; 사취하다. **3** (P6) 《Brit. *colloq.*》 refuse to pass in an examination. 낙제시키다. **4** (P6,7) summon up (courage, spirit). (용기 등)을 불러일으키다. ¶ *Pluck up your courage! You aren't hurt badly.* 용기 내라, 별로 다치지 않았다. **5** (P6) make a musical sound by pulling at (the strings of a guitar, etc.). (현악기)를 뜯다. ¶ ~ *a harp string.* — *vi.* (P3) 《*at*》 pull suddenly. 홱 잡아당기다.

get plucked, fail in an examination. 낙제하다.

pluck a pigeon, cheat a green, inexperienced youth. 만만한 사람을 속여먹다.

— *n.* Ⓤ **1** courage; spirit. 용기. ¶ *a man of* ~ / *The cat showed* ~ *in fighting the dog.* 고양이는 개와 싸우면서 투지 만만했다. **2** Ⓒ an act of pulling sharply. 확(잡아)당김. **3** 《Brit. *colloq.*》 a failure in an examination. 낙제. **4** something plucked out; the heart, liver, lungs, etc. of an animal, used as food. (요리용으로 발라 낸 짐승의) 내장. [E.]

pluck·y [plʌ́ki] *adj.* (**pluck·i·er, pluck·i·est**) courageous; brave. 용기 있는. ¶ *a* ~ *boy.*

plug [plʌg] *n.* Ⓒ **1** a piece of some material to fit into a hole. 마개. **2** a place where the hose is attached in a fire; a fireplug. 소화전(消火栓). **3** an electrical device for connection. 플러그. **4** a cake or stick of compressed tobacco. (고형(固形)의) 씹는 담배.

— *v.* (**plugged, plug·ging**) *vt.* **1** (P6,7) stop up or fill with a plug; put a plug into. …을 틀어막다. ¶ ~ *a hole* 〔*wall*〕 구멍〔벽의 구멍〕을 메우다. **2** (P6) strike with a missile; shoot. …에 총탄을 쏘아 박다; 쏘다. **3** (P6,7,13) force the attention of the public to by constant repetition, advertising, etc. (TV 등에서) 반복해서 선전〔광고〕하다. — *vi.* (P2A) 《*colloq.*》 plod; work hard. 부지런히 일〔노력〕하다. ¶ ~ *along at a Latin lesson* 끈기 있게 라틴어 공부를 하다. [M. Du. *plugge* block]

plug in, connect (an electric device) with an outlet by inserting a plug. 플러그를 꽂다.

:plum [plʌm] *n.* Ⓒ **1** a small juicy fruit with a smooth red skin; its tree. 플럼; 서양자두; 그 나무. **2** a raisin used in cake. (제과용) 건포도. **3** 《*colloq.*》 something good; the pick; the choicest of its kind; an easy, well-paid job. 가장 좋은 것; 알짜; 일품; 수지 맞는 일(자리). ¶ *This contract will prove to be a rich* ~ *for our firm.* 이번 계약으로 우리 회사는 한밑천 잡을 게다. **4** 《*colloq.*》 an extra dividend. 특별 배당. [→prune[1]]

plum·age [plúːmidʒ] *n.* Ⓤ 《*collectively*》 a bird's feathers. 깃털. [→plume]

plumb [plʌm] *n.* Ⓒ **1** a small weight at the end of a line, used to find the depth of water, the upright line of a wall, etc. 연추(鉛錘); 측연(測鉛). **2** the state of standing upright. 수직.

off 〔***out of***〕 ***plumb,*** not vertical; sloping. 수직이 아닌; 기울어진.

— *adj.* **1** standing upright. 수직의. ¶ *This wall is not exactly* ~. 이 벽은 좀 기울었다. **2** 《*fig.*》 true; complete. 진정한; 순전한. ¶ ~ *nonsense* 순 엉터리.

— *adv.* in a plumb state or manner; directly. 수직으로.

— *vt.* (P6) **1** test the depth of (water) or the upright line of (something) with a plumb line. (수직이나 수심)을 재다. ¶ ~ *the depth of a lake* 호수의 수심을 재다. **2** 《*fig.*》 (of the eye) see to the bottom of; (of the mind) understand fully. …을 꿰뚫어 보다; …의 진상을 알다. ¶ ~ *a mystery* 비밀의 진상을 구명하다. [L. *plumbum* lead]

plumb·er [plʌ́mər] *n.* Ⓒ a person who installs and repairs water or gas pipes in buildings. (수도·가스 등의) 배관공(配管工).

plumb·ing [plʌ́miŋ] *n.* Ⓤ **1** the water or gas pipes in a building. (건물의) 연관류(鉛管類). ¶ *bathroom* ~. **2** the work or trade of a plumber. 배관 공사.

•**plume** [plu:m] *n.* Ⓒ **1** a long, large feather. (크고 긴) 깃털. **2** an ornamental feather worn on a hat. (모자 따위의) 장식 깃털.

borrowed plumes, **a**) a dress which is not one's own. 빌려 입은 옷. ¶ *adorn oneself with borrowed plumes* 빌린 옷으로 꽝내다. **b**) second-hand knowledge, etc. with which a person shows off. 남에게서 빌린 지식.

— *vt.* (P6,13) **1** (of a bird) clean and smooth (feathers). (새가 깃털)을 다듬다. ¶ *The pigeons were pluming their wet wings.* 비둘기들이 젖은 깃털을 다듬고 있었다. **2** decorate (something) with feathers; dress oneself with borrowed plumes. 깃털로 장식하다; 빌린 옷으로 차려 입다. ¶ ~ *arrows with plumes* 화살을 깃털로 장식하다. **3** pride oneself on. …을 자랑하다. ¶ *Mary plumed herself on her skill in dancing.* 메리는 자기의 춤 솜씨를 뽐냈다. **4** pull the feathers out of. …의 깃털을 뽑다. [L. *pluma*]

plum·met [plʌ́mit] *n.* =plumb.

•**plump**[1] [plʌmp] *adj.* fat or rounded out. 통통하게 살찐. ¶ *A healthy baby has* ~ *cheek.* 건강한 아기의 볼이 통통하다. — *vt.* (P6,7) make (someone) fat. …을 살찌게 하다. — *vi.* (P1,2A) become fat. 살이 찌다. [Du. *plomp* blunt, not pointed]

plump[2] [plʌmp] *vi.* **1** (P1,2A) ⟪*down, into, upon*⟫ fall or drop heavily; sit heavily or suddenly. 쿵하고 떨어지다; 털썩 주저앉다. ¶ *He plumped down on a chair.* 의자에 털썩 앉았다. **2** (P3) ⟪*for*⟫ vote for one. 한 사람에게만 투표하다.

— *vt.* (P7) drop, place, or throw heavily or suddenly. …을 털썩 떨어뜨리다[놓다, 던지다]. ¶ *The girl plumped a book on the floor.* 소녀는 책을 털썩 마루에 던졌다.

— *adv.* **1** heavily. 털썩; 쿵. ¶ *The lunch basket fell* ~ *into the pond.* 도시락 바구니가 풍덩 연못에 떨어졌다. **2** suddenly. 갑자기. **3** in plain words; directly; bluntly. 노골적으로; 통명스레. ¶ *I told him* ~ *and plain what I thought of him.* 그에게 대한 내 생각을 까놓고 분명히 말해 줬다.

— *adj.* direct. 노골적인. ¶ *a* ~ *refusal* 일언지하의 거절.

— *n.* Ⓒ ⟪*colloq.*⟫ a sudden, heavy fall. 쿵[털썩] 떨어지기. [probably Imit.]

plum·y [plú:mi] *adj.* (**plum·i·er, plum·i·est**) **1** decorated with plumes. 깃털로 장식한. **2** like a plume. 깃털 같은. **3** having plumes. 깃털이 있는. [→plume]

•**plun·der** [plʌ́ndər] *vt., vi.* (P6; 1) steal (something) by force, esp. in war times. (전시에) …을 약탈하다. ¶ *The pirates entered the harbor and began to* ~ *the town.* 해적들은 항구에 닿자 마을을 약탈하기 시작했다.

— *n.* **1** Ⓤ the act of plundering. 약탈 행위. ¶ *During the* ~ *soldiers arrived.* 약탈이 진행되는 동안 군인들이 도착했다. **2** Ⓒ the things that are plundered. 약탈품. [G.= household stuff]

:**plunge** [plʌndʒ] *vt.* (P7,13) ⟪*into*⟫ **1** throw or push (something) suddenly into something else. …을 던져 넣다; 집어넣다. ¶ ~ *one's hand into hot water* 손을 뜨거운 물에 집어넣다 / ~ *a knife into her heart* 그녀의 가슴에 칼을 꽂다. **2** put (something) into a certain condition. …을 (어떤 상태에) 몰아넣다; 빠뜨리다. ¶ ~ *a room into darkness* 방을 갑자기 어둡게 하다 / ~ *one's family into poverty* 가족을 가난에 빠뜨리다 / *be plunged into the depths of grief* 비탄의 구렁에 빠지다 / ~ *a country into war* 나라를 전쟁의 구렁에 밀어넣다.

— *vi.* **1** (P2A,3) throw oneself (into water, danger, etc.). 잠수하다; 뛰어들다; 떨어지다. ¶ *He plunged into every sort of dissipation.* 그는 온갖 방탕(생활)에 빠져들었다 / ~ *into the river* 강에 뛰어들다. **2** (P2A,3) ⟪*into, in, up, down*⟫ rush; dash. 돌진하다; 뛰어들다. ¶ ~ *into a fight* 싸움에 뛰어들다 / ~ *down a slope* 비탈에 굴러떨어지다. **3** leap with the body forward and the legs up, as a horse does; pitch, as a ship. (말이) 뒷다리를 쳐들며 뛰다; (배가) 뒷질하다. ¶ *The ship plunged about in the storm.* 배는 폭풍을 만나 앞뒤로 흔들렸다. **4** ⟪*colloq.*⟫ spend much money; bet very much money. 돈을 물쓰듯하다; 큰 도박을 하다. ¶ ~ *into debt* 빚을 걸머지다.

— *n.* Ⓒ **1** the act of plunging; a sudden fall; a dive. 뛰어듦; 돌진; 빠져듦. ¶ *a* ~ *into danger* 위험에 빠짐. **2** ⟪*colloq.*⟫ a heavy gamble. 큰 도박. [→plumb]

take the plunge, **a**) venture to do something difficult or new. 모험을 하다; 과감히 하다. **b**) make a fresh start. 새 출발을 하다.

plung·er [plʌ́ndʒər] *n.* Ⓒ **1** a person or thing that plunges. 뛰어드는 사람[것]. **2** a piston in a machine. (피스톤의) 플런저.

plu·per·fect [plu:pə́:rfikt] *n., adj.* ⟪gram.⟫ (the tense) of the past perfect. 과거 완료(의). [L. *plus quam perfectum* more than finished]

:**plu·ral** [plúərəl] *adj.* showing more than one. 복수의(opp. singular). ¶ *the* ~ *number* 복수.

— *n.* **1** Ⓤ ⟪gram.⟫ the plural number. 복수. **2** Ⓒ the form of a noun showing more than one. 복수형(의 말). [→plus, -al]

plu·ral·i·ty [pluərǽləti] *n.* (*pl.* **-ties**) **1** Ⓤ the state or fact of being plural. 복수; 복수형임[상태]. **2** Ⓒ a great number. 다수. **3** Ⓒ ⟪U.S.⟫ (of an election) the difference between the first and the second in the number of votes. 초과 득표수.

plu·ral·ize [plúərəlàiz] *vt.* (P6) make plural; express in the plural form. 복수(형

으)로 하다; 복수로 나타내다.

plural vote [⌐—⌐] *n.* the vote of one person in more than one constituency. (둘 이상 선거구에서의) 복식 투표(권).

***plus** [plʌs] *prep.* (opp. minus) **1** with the addition of. …을 더한. ¶ *Three ~ seven equals ten.* 3에 7을 더하면 10이다. **2** and in addition. …에 덧붙여; …외에. ¶ *The salary was £ 500, ~ commissions.* 봉급은 커미션을 합해서 500 파운드였다. —*adj.* **1** 《math.》 showing addition. 양수〔플러스〕의. ¶ *a ~ sign* 플러스 부호. **2** 《electr.》 showing positive. 양(陽)의. **3** additional; extra. 여분의. ¶ *~ value* 여분의 가치; 부가 가치. **4** 《*colloq.*》 and more. 그 이상의. ¶ *She has personality ~.* 그녀에게는 개성 이상의 무엇이 있다. [L. *plūs* more]

plush [plʌʃ] *n.* Ⓤ a kind of cloth softer and thicker than velvet. 견면(絹綿) 벨벳; 플러시천. [→pile[3]]

Plu·to [plúːtou] *n.* **1** 《Gk. and Rom. myth.》 the god of the underworld. 플루토 《하계(下界)의 신》. **2** 《astron.》 the planet fartherest from the sun. 명왕성(冥王星). [Gk. *Ploutōn*]

plu·toc·ra·cy [pluːtákrəsi / -tɔ́k-] *n.* (*pl.* **-cies**) **1** Ⓤ government by wealthy people. 금권(金權) 정치. **2** Ⓒ a group of wealthy people. 재벌. [Gk. *ploutos* wealth]

plu·to·crat [plúːtoukræ̀t] *n.* Ⓒ **1** a person who is powerful because of his wealth. 부호 정치가; 금권가(金權家). **2** 《*colloq.*》 a rich person. 부자; 부호.

plu·to·ni·um [pluːtóuniəm] *n.* 《chem.》 a radioactive element. 플루토늄. [→Pluto]

***ply**[1] [plai] *v.* (**plied**) *vt.* **1** (P6) work hard at (something). …을 힘써〔열심히〕 하다. ¶ *~ one's book* 책을 정독하다. **2** (P6) use (instruments). (연장 등)을 쓰다; 놀리다. ¶ *The woman plied her needle.* 부인은 부지런히 바느질을 했다 / *He plied his ax in the woods.* 숲 속에서 열심히 도끼질을 했다. **3** (P13) 《*with*》 urge repeatedly. …을 자꾸 권하다〔강요하다〕. ¶ *They plied him with food and drink.* 그들은 그에게 음식을 자꾸 권했다 / *They plied the actor with questions.* 그들은 배우에게 질문을 퍼부었다. **4** (P13) assail vigorously. …을 맹렬하게 공격하다. —*vi.* **1** (P2A,3) (of a bus, boat, etc.) run regularly between two places. 정기적으로 다니다. ¶ *Buses ~ between the two cities.* 버스들이 두 시 사이를 왕래하고 있다. **2** (P1) (of a ship) work against wind. (배가) 바람을 거슬러 항해하다. **3** (P2A,3) wait for customer. (택시 등이) 손님을 기다리다. [→apply]

ply[2] [plai] *n.* Ⓒ (*pl.* **plies**) **1** a layer or thickness of cloth. 주름. **2** a twist in a rope, cord, etc. (밧줄 등의) 가닥. ¶ *a single ~* 외가닥 줄 / *a three ~ rope* 세 가닥으로 꼰 밧줄. [L. *plico* fold]

ply·wood [pláiwùd] *n.* Ⓤ a tough board made of thin layers of wood stuck together in crosswise. 합판; 베니어 판.

:P.M., p.m. afternoon. 오후. 參考 라틴어의 post meridiem 에서. ¶ *at 9 p.m.* 오후 9시.

pneu·mat·ic [njumǽtik] *adj.* **1** of air; filled with air. 공기의; 공기로 채운. ¶ *a ~ pillow* 〔*cushion*〕 공기 베개〔방석〕. **2** worked by compressed air. 압축 공기로 작용하는. ¶ *a ~ brake* 공기 브레이크. —*n.* **1** a pneumatic tire. 공기(가 든) 타이어. **2** 《*pl.*》 《phys.》 the science of mechanical properties of air or other elastic fluids or gasses. 기학(氣學); 공기 역학(力學). [Gk. *pneō* breathe]

pneu·mo·nia [njumóunjə, -niə] *n.* 《med.》 Ⓤ a serious illness of one or both of the lungs. 폐렴. [↑]

P.O. post office.

poach[1] [poutʃ] *vt., vi.* (P6;1,3) **1** hunt or fish in a secret and illegal way. 밀렵〔밀어(密漁)〕하다. **2** 《*fig.*》 encroach on what is another's sphere of action. (남의 영역을) 침범하다. ¶ *~ in another's business* 남의 사업 영역을 침범하다 / *~ for fresh ideas* (남의 저서 따위에서) 새로운 사상을 찾다 / *~ a ball in one's partner's court* 파트너가 칠 공을 자기가 가로채어 치다. **3** 《sports》 take an unfair means. 부정을 하다. ¶ *~ a start in a race* 앞질러 스타트하다. [→poke]

poach[2] [poutʃ] *vt.* (P6) cook (an egg) by breaking it into boiling water. 수란(水卵)을 뜨다. ¶ *poached eggs* 수란《깨어 삶은 달걀》. [→pocket]

P.O. Box, P.O.B. Post Office Box.

pock [pak / pɔk] *n.* Ⓒ a mark on the skin left by some diseases. 마맛자국. [E.]

:pock·et [pákit / pɔ́k-] *n.* Ⓒ **1** a small bag fixed on one's clothing to carry money or other small articles. 포켓; 호주머니. **2** any small bag fixed on something to hold small articles. 작은 주머니. ¶ *A golf bag has a ~ for golf balls.* 골프백에는 골프공을 넣는 포켓이 있다. **3** 《*fig.*》 money; pecuniary resources. 돈; 용돈. ¶ *empty pockets* 빈털터리 / *a deep ~* 충분한 자력(資力); 부. **4** a sack of hops or wool of definite amount (about 168 lb.). (홉·양털 등의) 한 부대. **5** a cavity where a deposit of ore is found. 광혈(鑛穴). ¶ *strike a ~ of gold* 노다지를 만나다. **6** 《U.S.》 glen. 골짜기. **7** a place in the air in which an airplane drops suddenly; an air pocket. 에어 포켓.

be in pocket, have or have obtained money. 돈이 있다; 이득을 보고 있다.

be out of pocket, have not or have lost money. 돈이 없다; 손해를 보고 있다. ¶ *He is 10 dollars out of ~.* 그는 10달러를 손해보고 있다.

have** someone **in** one's **pocket, have someone in one's power. (아무)를 마음대로〔좌지우지〕하다.

keep** one's **hands in** one's **pockets, be

idle. 빈둥거리다.
put** one's **hand in** one's **pocket, spend money; pay. 돈을 쓰다; 지불하다.
put** one's **pride in** one's **pocket, do not show one's pride. 자존심을 누르다.
suffer in** one's **pocket, lose. 손해를 보다.
— *vt.* (P6) **1** put (something) into a pocket. …을 주머니에 넣다. **2** get or take (money, etc.) usu. without right. (돈)을 착복하다; 들어먹다. ¶ *He pocketed our money.* 놈이 우리 돈을 들어먹었다. **3** hide or not show (one's feelings, etc.). (감정 등)을 나타내지 않다; 감추다. ¶ *She pocketed the insult and put on her best smile.* 그녀는 모욕에 대해 내색을 않고 웃어 보였다. **4** 《*colloq.*》 hem in (competitor) in race. (경마 등에서 경쟁자)를 둘러싸고 방해하다.
— *adj.* that can be carried in a pocket; small. 포켓에 들어가는; 작은. ¶ *a ~ edition* 포켓판. [F. *poche*]

pock·et·book [pákitbùk / pɔ́k-] *n.* Ⓒ **1** a small esp. paperback book that can be carried in the pocket. 포켓형의 염가판《문고판 등》. **2** a leather case for carrying money, papers, etc.; a woman's purse. 지갑; 핸드백. **3** 《Brit.》 a small notebook. 수첩. **4** Ⓤ financial resources. 재원(財源); 자력.

pock·et·ful [pákitfùl / pɔ́k-] *n.* Ⓒ the amount a pocket can hold. 한 주머니 가득. ¶ *a ~ of money* 상당한 돈; 한 재산.

pock·et·knife [pákitnàif / pɔ́k-] *n.* Ⓒ (*pl.* **-knives** [-nàivz]) a small knife with blades that fold into the handle. 주머니칼.

pocket money [⌐–⌐–] *n.* money for small expenses. 용돈.

pock·marked [pákmàːrkt / pɔ́k-] *adj.* having pocks. 곰보인; 마맛자국이 있는. ¶ *a ~ face* 얽은 얼굴. [*pock*]

pod [pad / pɔd] *n.* Ⓒ a long seed container of peas, beans, etc. 콩꼬투리. — *v.* (**pod·ded, pod·ding**) *vi.* (P1,2A) 《*up*》 form pods. 꼬투리가 생기다. — *vt.* (P6) take off the pods of (peas, beans, etc.). (콩 등)의 꼬투리를 까다. [?]

podg·y [pádʒi / pɔ́dʒi] *adj.* (**podg·i·er, podg·i·est**) 《*colloq.*》 (of person) fat and short; dumpy. 땅딸막한. [?, →pudgy]

Poe [pou], **Edgar Allan** *n.* (1809-1849) an American poet, critic and writer. 포《미국의 시인; 소설가》.

:po·em [póuim] *n.* Ⓒ a rhythmical composition of words, often expressing deep feeling and great beauty of language or thought. 시; 노래; 시적인 문장. ¶ *compose a ~* 시를 짓다 / *a prose ~* 산문시. [Gk. *poieō* make]

po·e·sy [póuizi, -si] *n.* Ⓤ 《*arch.*》 the art of writing poetry; 《*collectively*》 poetry; poems. 시작법(詩作法); 시.

:po·et [póuit] *n.* Ⓒ a person who writes verses or poems. 시인; 가인(歌人). ¶ *a ~ laureate* 계관 시인. [→poem]

po·et·as·ter [póuitæ̀stər] *n.* Ⓒ a writer of second-rate or poor verse. 삼류 시인.

po·et·ess [póuitis] *n.* Ⓒ a female poet. 여류 시인.

po·et·ic [pouétik], **-i·cal** [-kəl] *adj.* **1** of poets or poetry. 시의; 시인의. ¶ *a ~ romance* 전기시(傳奇詩). **2** showing the characteristics of good poetry. 시적인; 시취(詩趣)가 있는. ¶ *~ fancies* 시적 상상력 / *a ~ person* 시인적인 사람. **3** suitable for poems or poets. 시의 소재가 되는. ¶ *a ~ subject* 시제(詩題) / *~ language* 시적인 언어.

·po·et·ry [póuitri] *n.* Ⓤ **1** 《*collectively*》 poems. 시. ¶ *epic ~* 서정시 / *Most young men write some ~ sooner or later.* 대개의 젊은이들은 이르건 늦건 시를 쓰게 된다. **2** the art of writing poems. 작시(법)(作詩(法)). ¶ *She has no talent for ~.* 그녀는 시재(詩才)가 없다. **3** something poetic. 시적인 것.

poign·an·cy [pɔ́injənsi] *n.* Ⓤ the state or quality of being poignant. 통렬; 매서움. ¶ *~ of flavor* 쏘는 듯한 맛. [↓]

poign·ant [pɔ́injənt] *adj.* **1** sharp or painful to the feelings. (슬픔·뉘우침 등이) 격렬한. ¶ *~ sorrow* 사무치는 슬픔 / *a ~ situation* 아주 괴로운 입장. **2** keen; bitter. 날카로운; 신랄한. ¶ *~ sarcasm* 신랄하게 비꼬는 말 / *~ suffering* 쓰라린 고통. **3** 《rare》 sharp or stinging to the taste or smell. 쏘는 듯한; 코를 찌르는. ¶ *~ sauces* 매운 양념 / *~ perfumes* 자극적인 향기. [→point]

poin·set·ti·a [pɔinsétiə] *n.* Ⓒ a plant with large, scarlet, petal-like leaves and tiny, greenish flowers. 포인세티아; 성성목(猩猩木)《크리스마스 장식용》. [Person *Poinsett*]

:point [pɔint] *n.* Ⓒ **1** a sharp end of a stick, pin, weapon, etc.; a sharp corner or edge. 뾰족한 끝[모서리]. ¶ *the ~ of a needle* [*sword*] 바늘[칼] 끝. **2** ⓐ a place or spot. 장소; 점. ¶ *a ~ on a road* 길의 어느 지점 / *move from ~ to ~* 이리저리 (자리를) 옮기다 / *At this ~ the car stopped.* 여기서 차가 섰다. ⓑ a small mark left on a surface; a dot. 작은 점; 얼룩; 반점. ¶ *several points on the paper made by a pencil* 종이 위의 몇 개의 연필자국. **3** a moment when something important is going to happen. 중대한 순간. ¶ *at the ~ of death* 임종 때 / *a turning ~* 전환점 / *We are coming to the ~ where a decision must be made.* 이제 결정을 내려야 할 때가 되었소. **4** ⓐ 《*the ~*》 a main idea or purpose in a story, joke, etc. (이야기 등의) 요점; 요지; 포인트. ¶ *What is your ~ in saying so?* 무엇 때문에 그 얘기를 하는거냐 / *the ~ in a speech* 연설의 요지 / *a joke without any ~* 싱거운 농담. ⓑ Ⓤ an aim. 목적. ¶ *There is no ~ in doing that.* 그렇게 할 목적이 없다. **5** a characteristic. 특징. ¶ *Kindness is her good ~.* 친절이 그녀의 미점(美點)이다. **6** a full stop or period; a dot used in print, etc. 종지부; (기호로서의) 점. ¶ *ten ~ two,* 10.2. **7** a piece of land going out into the sea; a small cape. 갑; 곶. **8** ⓐ a degree of a thermometer; a score; a mark or grade. (온도계 등의) 눈금; 도; 득점; 등급. ¶ *The temperature has gone up two points.* 기온은 2도 올라갔다 / *gain* 〔*score*〕 *5 points in a game* 경기에서 5점 따다. ⓑ a definite position in a scale, etc.; limit; degree. 한계점; 한계; 정도. ¶ *freezing* 〔*boiling, melting*〕 ~ 어는〔끓는, 녹는〕점 / *be angered to the ~ of madness* 미칠 정도로 화나다. **9** 《Brit.》《*pl.*》 short rails used to enable a train to pass from one track to another. 전철기(轉轍機)(=《U.S.》 switch). **10** 《naut.》 one of 32 marks showing direction on a compass; a direction. 나침반의 방위를 가리키는 32점의 하나; 방위.

at all points, in every respect; completely. 모든 점에서; 완전히. ¶ *be prepared at all points* 완벽하게 준비하다.

beside 〔***away from, off***〕 ***the point,*** not to the point. 예상이 어긋난; 잘못 짚은(opp. to the point).

carry 〔***gain***〕 *one's* ***point,*** succeed; secure one's object. 주장〔목적〕을 관철하다.

come to the point, get to the essential part. 요점에 닿다. ¶ *When it came to the ~, he declined.* 막상 본론에 들어서자 그는 발을 뺐다.

get *someone's* ***point,*** understand someone's purpose. …의 의도를 알게 되다.

give points to *someone,* be able to offer advantages to and yet defeat someone; be better than someone. …에게 핸디캡을 주다; …보다 낫다.

in point of fact, as a matter of fact; to tell the truth; really. 실은; 사실을 말하면.

make a point of *doing* =***make it a point to*** *do* (=*be sure to do*) *something.* 반드시 …하다; 정해 놓고 …하다.

on the point of *doing* (=*just about to do*) *something.* 막 …하려고 하는 차에.

to the point, getting to the essential part; apt. 요령 있는; 적절(適切)한(opp. beside the point).

— *vt.* **1** (P6) make (something) sharp. …을 뾰족하게〔날카롭게〕 하다. ¶ *~ a knife* 칼을 갈다. **2** (P6) emphasize. …을 강조하다. ¶ *He pointed his remarks with illustrations.* 예를 들어가며 자기 말을 강조했다. **3** (P6,7,13) ⓐ 《*at, to, toward*》 direct or aim. (손가락 따위)를 향하게 하다; 겨누다. ¶ *She pointed her finger at me.* 그녀는 손가락으로 나를 가리켰다 / *A boy pointed a toy pistol at me.* 꼬마아이가 장난감 권총을 내게 겨누었다 / *The magnetic needle points to the north.* 자침(磁針)은 북쪽을 가리키고 있다. ⓑ 《*out*》 show, as with a finger. (손가락 따위로) 가리키다. ¶ *~ out an object to someone* 아무에게 한 물건을 가리키다. ⓒ 《*out*》 direct attention to. …을 지적하다. ¶ *They pointed her out as the famous singer.* 유명 가수로 그녀를 지적했다. **4** (P6) ⓐ mark (something) with points. …에 (구두)점을 찍다. ¶ *~ a sentence* 문장에 구두점을 찍다. ⓑ separate by decimal point. 소수점을 찍어 구분하다. — *vi.* **1** (P3) 《*at, to, toward*》 direct the finger, eye, etc. 손가락질하다; 눈을 돌리다; 가리키다. ¶ *Don't ~ at others.* 남을 손가락질하면 안 된다. **2** (P1) (of a dog) show the presence of game by standing and looking toward it. (개가) 사냥감이 있는 곳을 가리키다. [L. *pungo* prick]

point off, divide a sentence by a comma. 콤마로 끊다.

point up, emphasize. 강조하다.

point·blank [pɔ́intblǽŋk] *adj.* **1** aimed directly at the mark. 직사(直射)의. ¶ *a ~ shot* 직사; 수평 사격. **2** direct; plain. 직접적인. ¶ *a ~ refusal* 노골적인 거절. — *adv.* **1** straight. 직선으로; 바로. ¶ *The gun was aimed ~ at his head.* 총은 그의 머리를 바로 겨누고 있었다. **2** directly; without hesitation. 노골적으로; 분명히. ¶ *a ~ question* 단도 직입적인 질문.

:point·ed [pɔ́intid] *adj.* **1** having a sharp point like a needle. 뾰족한. ¶ *a ~ pencil* 뾰족한 연필. **2** sharp; direct; striking. 날카로운; 두드러진. ¶ *a ~ reproof* 신랄한 질책 / *a ~ joke* 뼈있는 농담. **3** clearly aimed at someone. 아무를 분명히 지칭한. ¶ *a ~ remark* 면박(面駁).

point·er [pɔ́intər] *n.* Ⓒ **1** a thing or person that points. 지시하는〔가리키는〕 사람〔물건〕. **2** a long, slender stick used for pointing out things on a map, etc. 지시봉(指示棒); 교편(敎鞭). **3** 《*colloq.*》 a hint. 암시. **4** a short-haired dog trained to point out where hunted birds are hiding, etc. 포인터 개.

point·less [pɔ́intlis] *adj.* **1** having a dull edge. 끝이 무딘. **2** without meaning or sense. 무의미한. **3** (in a game) without a point scored. (경기가) 무득점의.

points·man [pɔ́intsmən] *n.* Ⓒ (*pl.* **-men** [-mən]) 《Brit.》 **1** a railway switchman. 전철수(轉轍手)(=《U.S.》 switchman). **2** a policeman who directs traffic. 교통 경찰.

point switch [´ ˋ] *n.* a device of two movable rails to turn a train from one railroad track to another. 전철기(轉轍機).

·poise [pɔiz] *n.* **1** Ⓤ mental or physical balance. 평형; 균형; (마음의) 평정. ¶ *He walked on the tight rope with perfect ~.* 완전한 균형을 유지하며 팽팽한 밧줄 위를 걸었다 / *He lost his ~ when we laughed at him.* 우리가 웃자 그는 자제력을 잃고 말았다. **2** Ⓒ the manner in which a person moves. 몸가짐새; 자세; 태도.

— *vt.* (P7,13) keep (something) in the state of balance; carry or hold steadily. …을 균형 잡히게 하다; …의 평형을 잡다〔유지하다〕. ¶ *He poised himself on his hands.* 그는 물구나무를 섰다 / *The crane poised itself on*

one leg. 두루미는 다리 하나로 서 있었다.
— *vi.* (P2A) **1** be balanced; remain in balance. 균형이 잡히다. ¶ *A bird poised on the branch.* 새 한 마리가 균형을 잡고 나뭇가지에 앉아 있었다. **2** (of birds, etc.) remain in the air; hover. (새 따위가) 하늘을 맴돌다. [L. *pendo* weigh]

:poi·son [pɔ́izən] *n.* U C **1** a drug or any substance that is dangerous to life if taken into the body. 독약; 독. ¶ *kill oneself by taking* ~ 음독 자살하다 / *a* ~ *shell* 독가스탄(彈) / *slow* 〔*cumulative*〕 ~ 자주 쓰면 독이 되는 것; 효과가 느린 독약. **2** anything dangerous or harmful. 해로운 것; 해독; 폐해. ¶ *Roast pork is* ~ *to some people.* 구운 돼지고기에 중독되는 사람도 있다 / *a moral* 〔*political*〕 ~ 도덕적〔정치적〕 폐해 / *the* ~ *of envy* 질투라고 하는 해독.
hate like poison, hate bitterly. …을 죽도록 미워하다.
One man's meat is another man's poison. 《*prov.*》 갑에게 약은 을에게 독; 사람마다 기호는 각각.
What's your ~ ***?*** 《*colloq.*》 What will you drink? 뭘 마시겠나《술자리에서》.
— *vt.* (P6) **1** kill or injure (someone) by poison; put poison into or on (something). …을 독살하다; …에 독을 넣다〔바르다〕. ¶ *a poisoned arrow* 독화살 / ~ *the well* 우물에 독약을 넣다 / ~ *someone's food* 남의 음식에 독을 타다. **2** 《*fig.*》 have an evil or harmful influence on (someone); destroy by evil suggestion. …에 해독을 끼치다; 망쳐 놓다. ¶ ~ *another's mind* 남을 악에 물들게 하다 / ~ *someone's mind against...* 아무를 …에 대해 감정을 품게 하다. [L. *potio* drink]

poi·son·ous [pɔ́izənəs] *adj.* **1** having poison; dangerous to life if taken into the body. 유독한; 해로운. ¶ *a* ~ *snake* 〔*plant*〕 독사〔독초〕 / ~ *air* 유독한 공기 / *a* ~ *dose* 치사량의 독약. **2** 《*colloq.*》 very unpleasant; disagreeable. 아주 불쾌한; 악취가 나는. ¶ *a perfectly* ~ *fellow* 꼴도 보기 싫은 놈 / *The heat is simply* ~. 끔찍한 더위다.
●**poi·son·ous·ly** [-li] *adv.*

poison gas [⌒–⌒] *n.* a gas which kills or injures, used in chemical warfare. 독가스.

·poke[1] [pouk] *vt.* (P6,7,13) **1** push (someone or something) with a finger, a stick, etc. (막대·손가락으로) …을 (쿡) 찌르다. ¶ *He poked me in the ribs with his elbow.* 그는 팔꿈치로 내 옆구리를 쿡 찔렀다. **2** stir up (a fire). (불)을 쑤석거리다. ¶ ~ *the fire* 불을 쑤셔 일으키다. **3** thrust or intrude (someone or something). …을 들이밀다. ¶ *Don't* ~ *your nose into my affairs.* 내 일에 참견 마라 / *Don't* ~ *your head out of a train window.* 열차 창밖으로 머리를 내밀지 마라.
— *vi.* **1** (P3) 《*at*》 push with a stick, etc. (막대 따위로) 찌르다. **2** (P1,3) look for something; search; meddle. 찾다; 뒤지다; 참견하다. ¶ ~ *into another's private affairs* 남의 사삿일에 참견하다. **3** (P2A) feel one's way. 더듬거리며 가다; 여기저기 찾아 헤매다. ¶ *He is poking around for the lost child.* 그는 잃어버린 아이를 찾아 헤매고 있다.
poke about, search; be eager to know another's private affairs. (남의 일에) 참견하다; 꼬치꼬치 캐다.
poke fun at, make fun of (something); ridicule. …을 놀리다.
— *n.* C a push or thrust. (쿡) 찌르기; 찌름. ¶ *give a* ~ 쿡 찌르다. [E.]

poke[2] [póuk] *n.* 《*dial.*》 a bag; a sack. 주머니; 자루. [Gael. *poca*]
buy a pig in a poke ⇨pig.

pok·er[1] [póukər] *n.* C **1** a person or thing that pokes. 찌르는 사람〔물건〕. **2** an iron bar for stirring a fire. 부지깽이. [E.]
as stiff as a poker, very cold and hard in behavior or manner. (사람이) 아주 딱딱한.

pok·er[2] [póukər] *n.* U a card game in which the players bet on the value of the cards they hold. 포커《카드 놀이》. ¶ *a* ~ *face* 무표정한 얼굴. [F. *poque*]

pok·y, pok·ey [póuki] *adj.* (**pok·i·er, pok·i·est**) **1** slow; dull. 느린; 굼뜬. **2** uncomfortably small; stuffy. 비좁은; 답답한. ¶ *a* ~ *little house* 〔*room*〕 작고 비좁은 집〔방〕. **3** (of dress) shabby. (옷이) 초라한; 꾀죄죄한. [E.]

·Po·land [póulənd] *n.* a country in central Europe bordering on the Baltic sea. 폴란드. 參考 수도는 Warsaw.

·po·lar [póulər] *adj.* **1** of or near the North or South Pole. (남·북)극(極)의; 극지(極地)의. ¶ *a* ~ *bear* 북극곰; 흰곰 / *the* ~ *circle* 극권(極圈) / *the* ~ *lights* 극광(極光) / *in* ~ *regions* 극지에 / ~ *expedition* 극지탐험. **2** 《electr.》 of a magnetic pole. 자(기)극(磁(氣)極)의. **3** opposite in character or action. 정반대의; 역(逆)의. ¶ ~ *personality* 정반대인 (두 사람의) 성격. [→pole[2]]

Po·lar·is [pouléəris, -lǽr-] *n.* the North Star. 북극성.

po·lar·i·ty [poulǽrəti] *n.* U **1** 《phys., electr.》 the magnetic power to point north and south. 극성(極性). ¶ *A magnet has* ~. 자석은 극성이 있다 / *magnetic* ~ 자기극성. **2** the state of showing two opposite qualities, principles, etc. (성질·주의 등의) 정반대; 역; 대립. [→polar, -ity]

polar star [⌒–⌒], **the** *n.* the star just above the North Pole. 북극성.

Pole [poul] *n.* C a person of Poland. 폴란드 사람. [G.]

:pole[1] [poul] *n.* C a long, slender piece of wood or other solid material. 장대; 기둥; 막대기. ¶ ~ *jump* 장대높이뛰기 / *a telegraph* ~ 전신주 / *a flag* ~ 깃대 / *a barber's* ~ (붉고 푸른) 이발소 기둥 간판. — *vt.* (P6) push (a boat, etc.) with a pole. (배 따위)를 상앗대질하다. ¶ *a canoe poled by two men* 두 사

람이 젓는 카누. [L. *palus* stake]

·**pole**² [poul] *n.* Ⓒ **1** one of the two ends of the axis of the earth or other round bodies. (지구·천체의) 극; 자기극(磁氣極). ¶ *the North* 〔*South*〕 *Pole* 북〔남〕극. **2** each of the two terminal points of a magnet or battery. (자석·전지 등의) 극. ¶ *the positive* 〔*negative*〕 ~ 양극〔음극〕. **3** 《*fig.*》 an opposite extreme. 정반대; 극단. [Gk. *polos*]

be poles asunder 〔***apart***〕**,** be widely separated; be in extreme opposition to one another. (성격·견해 등이) 정반대다; 천양지차(天壤之差)다.

pole·cat [póulkæ̀t] *n.* **1** 《Brit.》 a small, dark brown animal with a very disgusting odor. 족제비의 일종. **2** 《U.S.》 =skunk. [G.]

po·lem·ic [poulémik / pɔ-] *n.* **1** an argument; a dispute. 논쟁; 논박. **2** 《*pl.*》 the art or practice of disputation. 논증법(論證法). ¶ *theological polemics* 신학상의 논증. **3** a person who conducts an argument against another. 논객(論客)《특히 신학상의》. — *adj.* of or belonging to argument or dispute; fond of discussion. 논쟁하는〔을 즐기는〕. ¶ ~ *theology* 논증 신학 / *a* ~ *writer* 논객. [Gk. *polemos* war]

po·lem·i·cal [poulémikəl / pɔ-] *adj.* = polemic.

pole·star [póulstɑ̀ːr] *n.* **1** 《*the* ~》 the North Star; Polaris. 북극성. **2** Ⓒ a guiding principle. 지도 원리. **3** Ⓒ a center of attraction. 매력의 중심; 주목의 대상. [*pole*²]

pole vault [⌐ ⌐] *n.* a field event in which a jump is performed over a high crossbar with the aid of a long bar; a pole jump. 장대높이뛰기. [*pole*¹]

:**po·lice** [pəlíːs] *n.* **1** Ⓤ the department of government organized to keep order and enforce law. 경찰. **2** 《*the* ~ ; *collectively*》 the member of this department; policemen. 경찰관. [語法] 항상 복수 동사를 취함. ¶ *the harbor* ~ 수상경찰 / *the Metropolitan Police* 수도경찰 / *a* ~ *court* 즉결 재판소 / ~ *magistrate* 즉결 재판소 판사 / *a* ~ *station* 경찰서 / *The* ~ *are on his track.* 경찰이 그를 추적하고 있다.

— *adj.* of or connected with the police. 경찰의. ¶ *receive* ~ *protection* 경찰의 보호를 받다.

— *vt.* (P6) **1** control or protect (a district, etc.) by means of police. …의 치안을 유지하다. ¶ ~ *the streets* 거리의 치안을 지키다. **2** provide (a district, etc.) with police. …에 경찰을 두다; 경비하다. **3** 《*fig.*》 control; discipline. …을 단속하다; 규제하다. [Gk. *polis* city]

:**po·lice·man** [pəlíːsmən] *n.* Ⓒ (*pl.* **-men** [-mən]) a member of a police force; a police officer. 경찰관; 경관.

po·lice·wom·an [pəlíːswùmən] *n.* Ⓒ (*pl.* **-wom·en** [-wìmin]) a female member of a police force. 여자 경찰관; 여경.

·**pol·i·cy**¹ [pɑ́ləsi / pɔ́l-] *n.* (*pl.* **-cies**) **1** ⒸⓊ a way or principle of action by a person or group, esp. a government. 정책; 방침; 방책. ¶ *foreign* ~ 외교 정책 / *domestic* ~ 국내 정책 / *a* ~ *writer* 정책 입안자 / *It is a good* ~ *to tell the truth.* 사실대로 말하는 것이 좋은 방법이다 / 《*prov.*》 *Honesty is the best* ~. 정직은 최선의 방책. **2** Ⓤ practical wisdom. 지혜; 지략. ¶ *Policy goes beyond strength.* 지혜는 힘보다 낫다. [↑]

pol·i·cy² [pɑ́ləsi / pɔ́l-] *n.* Ⓒ (*pl.* **-cies**) a written contract issued by an insurance company. 보험 증권. ¶ *a life insurance* ~ 생명 보험 증권 / *take out a* ~ *on one's life* 생명 보험에 들다. [Gk. *apodeixis* proof]

po·li·o [póuliòu] *n.* 《*colloq.*》 =poliomyelitis.

po·li·o·my·e·li·tis [pòulioumàiəláitis] *n.* Ⓤ a disease of the nervous system esp. of children. 척수 회백질염(灰白質炎); 소아마비. [Gk. *polios* gray, *muelos* marrow]

·**Pol·ish** [póuliʃ] *adj.* of Poland, its people or their language. 폴란드 사람〔어〕의. — *n.* Ⓤ the language of the Poles. 폴란드어. [*Pole*]

:**pol·ish** [pɑ́liʃ / pɔ́l-] *vt.* (P6,7) **1** 《*up, away, out*》 make (something) smooth and shiny by rubbing. …을 닦다; 광을 내다. ¶ ~ *furniture* 〔*floor, shoes*〕 가구〔마루, 구두〕를 닦다 / ~ *rice* 쌀을 찧다 / ~ *silver* 은그릇을 닦다. **2** 《*fig.*》 make (someone) refined or elegant; bring to a finished, perfect condition. …을 세련되게〔품위 있게〕 하다; 다듬다; 마무리하다; (시문을) 퇴고(推敲)하다. ¶ *a polished gentleman* 세련된〔점잖은〕 신사 / ~ *a set of verses* 시구를 다듬다 / *have polished manners* 태도가 점잖다 / *His essay needs polishing.* 그의 수필은 좀 생경(生硬)하다.

— *vi.* (P1) **1** become smooth and bright. 윤〔광〕이 나다. ¶ *This wood won't* ~. 이 나무는 윤이 안 난다 / *Mahogany polishes beautifully.* 마호가니는 반들반들 윤이 잘 난다. **2** become refined or elegant. 품위 있게 되다.

polish off, 《*colloq.*》 finish or defeat quickly. 재빨리 끝내다〔해치우다〕.

polish up, **a**) make brighter by rubbing. 윤을 내다. **b**) improve. 다듬다; 개량하다. ¶ ~ *up one's French* 불어 실력을 연마하다.

— *n.* Ⓤ **1** the act of polishing; a smooth, shiny surface; gloss. 닦기; 광내기. ¶ *the brilliant* ~ *of silver* 은그릇의 번쩍거리는 광택 / *The table has a nice* ~. 식탁이 반들반들 윤이 난다. **2** a substance for polishing. 닦는〔광내는〕 재료; 광택제. ¶ *boot* 〔*shoe*〕 ~ 구두약 / *metal* ~ 금속 광택제. **3** elegance; culture. 우아; 세련; 교양. ¶ *the* ~ *of cultivated society* 교양 있는 사회의 품위 / *the exquisite* ~ *of Pope's poems* 포프의 시에서 보는 세련된 우아함. [L. *polio*]

pol·ish·er [pɑ́liʃər / pɔ́liʃər] *n.* **1** Ⓒ a person who polishes. 닦는〔윤내는〕 사람. **2** Ⓤ any substance used in polishing. 광택제. [→polish]

:po·lite [pəláit] *adj.* (**-lit·er, -lit·est**) having good manners; refined; cultured. 예의 바른; 세련된; 교양 있는. ¶ ~ *society* 상류 사회 / *a* ~ *man* 〔*remark*〕 교양 있는 사람〔말〕 / *He is always* ~ *to everyone.* 그는 누구에게나 늘 공손하다 / *Mother always warns us to be* ~. 어머니는 예의바르게 행동하라고 늘 주의를 주신다 / ~ *letters* 〔*literature*〕 순문학(純文學). [→polish]

·po·lite·ly [pəláitli] *adv.* in a polite manner; courteously. 점잖게; 공손하게.

·po·lite·ness [pəláitnis] *n.* Ⓤ the state of being polite; Ⓒ a polite act or statement. 정중함; 공손한 태도나 말.

pol·i·tic [pálitik / pɔ́l-] *adj.* **1** cunning. 간사한; 교활한. **2** prudent; tactful. 신중한; 분별 있는; 재치 있는. ¶ *He made a* ~ *answer to her embarrassing question.* 그는 그녀의 난처한 질문에 조심스럽게 대답했다. **3** 《rare》 political. 정치상의. ¶ *a body* ~ 정치적 통일체; 국가. [→policy[1]]

·po·lit·i·cal [pəlítikəl] *adj.* of politics, government or public affairs. 정치(학)상의; 정치에 관한. ¶ ~ *circles* 정계 / *a* ~ *party* 정당 / ~ *science* 정치학 / *a* ~ *view* 정견 / *a* ~ *offence* 정치범.

po·lit·i·cal·ly [pəlítikəli] *adv.* in a political manner; from a political point of view. 정치상; 정치적으로.

·pol·i·ti·cian [pàlətíʃən / pɔ̀l-] *n.* Ⓒ **1** a person who is active in political affairs. 정치가. **2** 《U.S.》 a person who is working for his political party, often as a means of personal gain. 정객(政客); 정상배; 정치꾼 (cf. *stateman*).

:pol·i·tics [pálitiks / pɔ́l-] *n. pl.* **1** 《used as *sing.*》 the study of government; the management of political affairs. 정치; 정치학. ¶ *a matter of high* ~ 고도의 정치(적) 문제 / *enter* ~ 정계에 들어가다; 정치가가 되다. **2** political plans, ideas, etc. 정책; 정견. ¶ *party* ~ 정당 정책 / *the* ~ *of a newspaper* 신문의 기조(基調) / *What are your* ~*?* 당신의 정견(政見)은 어떤 것입니까. **3** 《used as *sing.*》 the management of private affair. 관리; 경영. ¶ *the* ~ *of a business* 사업 경영.

pol·i·ty [páləti / pɔ́l-] *n.* (*pl.* **-ties**) **1** Ⓤ the political condition of being organized as a state. 정치 형태. **2** Ⓒ a state or community having a government. 국가; 정치적 조직체.

pol·ka [póulkə / pɔ́l-] *n.* Ⓒ a lively dance for couples; the music for such a dance. 폴카춤; 폴카곡(曲). [Pol.]

·poll[1] [poul] *n.* Ⓒ **1** the total number of votes at an election. 투표수. ¶ *a heavy* 〔*light, poor*〕 ~ 투표 다수〔소수〕 / *at the head of the* ~ 최고 득표로. **2** ⓐ 《*pl.*》 《U.S.》 a place to vote. 투표소. ¶ *go to the polls* 투표소에 가다. ⓑ the voting at an election. 투표. ¶ *the opening* 〔*close*〕 *of the* ~ 투표 개시〔종료〕. **3** ⓐ a list of voters. 선거인 명부. ¶ *have one's name on the* ~ 선거인 명부에 등록하다. ⓑ a count by heads. 머릿수. **4** 《*dial., joc.*》 the head of a body. 머리; 대가리. ¶ *a snow-white* 〔*gray*〕 ~ 백발〔반백〕의 머리. **5** an inquiry into the opinions, etc. of many people. 여론 조사.

— *vt.* (P6) **1** enter (someone) in a list. …을 명부에 등록하다. **2** obtain (a vote); give (a vote) to (someone). (…표)를 획득하다; 득표하다; …에게 (표를) 던지다. ¶ *We polled only a quarter of the votes cast.* 우리는 투표수의 4분의 1의 득표에 그쳤다. **3** cut off (the head of a tree) short; remove the horns of (cattles, etc.). …의 가지 끝을 치다; …의 뿔을 자르다. ¶ ~ *trees* 〔*cattle*〕. **4** ask the opinions, etc. of others on (something) …에 대한 여론 조사를 하다.

— *vi.* (P1) 《*for*》 give one's vote. 투표하다. [E.]

poll[2] [pal / pɔl] *n.* a parrot. 앵무새.

pol·lard [pálərd / pɔ́l-] *n.* **1** a polled tree. 가지를 친 나무. **2** a polled animal. 뿔이 잘린 짐승《사슴 따위》. **3** bran. 밀기울. — *vt.* (P6) cut off. …을 잘라내다. [→poll]

pol·len [pálən / pɔ́l-] *n.* Ⓤ the powder in a flower carried by bees, etc. 화분(花粉); 꽃가루. [L. =fine powder, flour]

pol·li·nate [pálənèit / pɔ́l-] *vt.* (P6) 《bot.》 (of bees) carry pollen to (other flowers). …에 수분(授粉)하다. ¶ *Insects or wind* ~ *the majority of plants.* 곤충이나 바람이 대부분의 식물에 수분을 한다. [↑]

pol·li·na·tion [pàlənéiʃən] *n.* 《bot.》 the carrying of pollen to the pistils of flowers. 수분(授粉) (작용).

pol·ling-booth [póuliŋbù:θ] *n.* a place where voters go to record votes. (투표소의) 기표장. [→poll]

pol·li·wog, pol·ly·wog [páliwàg / pɔ́liwɔ̀g] *n.* a tadpole. 올챙이. [E.]

poll parrot [⌐ ⌐–] *n.* a parrot; a foolish babbler. 앵무새; 같은 말을〔진부한 어구들을〕 되풀이하는 사람. [*Mary*]

poll·ster [póulstər] *n.* one who takes a public opinion poll. 여론 조사원. [*poll*]

poll tax [⌐⌐] *n.* a tax on every person. 인두세(人頭稅). [*poll*]

pol·lute [pəlú:t] *vt.* (P6) make (something) dirty; make (the mind, morals, etc.) impure. …을 더럽히다; 오염시키다. ¶ ~ *the environment* 환경을 오염시키다 / *Chemical wastes* ~ *the rivers and streams.* 화학 폐기물이 하천을 오염시킨다 / ~ *the mind of a young person* 젊은이를 도덕적으로 타락시키다. [L. *pullo*]

pol·lu·tion [pəlú:ʃən] *n.* Ⓤ the act of polluting; the state of being polluted. 더럽힘; 오염. ¶ *environmental* ~ 환경 오염.

po·lo [póulou] *n.* Ⓤ a game played on horseback with wooden sticks and one

small wooden ball. 폴로 경기. [→Oriental]

〈polo〉

po·lo·naise [pὰlənéiz, pòul-/pɔ̀l-] *n.* Ⓒ a slow, stately Polish dance; the music for this dance. 폴로네즈《폴란드의 춤, 또 그 곡》. [F. (→Polo)]

pol·troon [pɑltrúːn/pɔl-] *n.* Ⓒ a mean coward. 비겁한 사람; 겁쟁이. [It. *poltro* bed]

pol·y- [páli-/pɔ́li-] *pref.* many; much; more than one. '다(多), 중(重), 복(複)'의 뜻. [Gk. *polus* many, much]

pol·y·eth·y·lene [pὰliéθəlìːn/pɔ̀l-] *n.* 《chem.》 one of a group of thermoplastics used in goods packing, insulation, etc. 폴리에틸렌. [poly-]

po·lyg·a·mist [pəlígəmist] *n.* Ⓒ a man who has more than one wife. 일부다처(一夫多妻)론자.

po·lyg·a·mous [pəlígəməs] *adj.* more than one wife to a husband or more than one husband to a wife. 일부다처(一夫多妻)의; 일처다부(一妻多夫)의. [Gk. *gamos* marriage]

po·lyg·a·my [pəlígəmi] *n.* Ⓤ the custom of having more than one wife. 일부다처제(一夫多妻制)(cf. *monogamy*).

pol·y·glot [páliglὰt/pɔ́liglɔ̀t] *adj.* knowing several languages; written in several languages. 수개 국어를 아는; 수개 국어로 쓰인. ¶ *a ~ student* 수개 국어를 말하는 학생 / *a ~ area* 수개 국어가 통하는 지역. [Gk. *glōssa* tongue]

pol·y·gon [páligὰn/pɔ́ligɔ̀n] *n.* 《geom.》 Ⓒ a plane figure with more than four angles. 다각형(多角形). ¶ *a regular ~* 정(正)다각형. [poly-, Gk. *gonia* angle]

pol·y·he·dra [pὰlihíːdrə/pɔ̀l-] *n.* pl. of **polyhedron.**

pol·y·hed·ron [pὰlihíːdrən/pɔ̀l-] *n.* (*pl.* **-s** or **-dra**) a solid figure having many faces. 다면체(多面體); 다면형. [poly-, Gk. *hedra* face]

pol·y·mer [páləmər/pɔ́l-] *n.* 《chem.》 Ⓒ any of two or more polymeric compounds. 중합체(重合體). [↓]

pol·y·mer·ic [pὰləmerik/pɔ̀l-] *adj.* 《chem.》 having the same elements combined in the same proportions by weight, but differing in molecular weight. 중합(체)(重合(體))의. [Gk. *meros* part]

Pol·y·ne·sia [pὰləníːʒə, -ʃə/pɔ̀l-] *n.* a group of many small islands in the Pacific Ocean. 폴리네시아 제도(諸島). [Gk. *nēsos* island]

Pol·y·ne·si·an [pὰləníːʒən, -ʃən/pɔ̀l-] *a.* of Polynesia; of its language or native. 폴리네시아의; 폴리네시아인〔어〕의. — *n.* **1** a native of Polynesia. 폴리네시아인. **2** the language of Polynesia. 폴리네시아어(語).

pol·y·syl·lab·ic [pὰlisilǽbik/pɔ̀l-] *adj.* (of a word) having more than three syllables. 다음절(多音節)의(opp. monosyllabic). [poly-]

pol·y·syl·la·ble [pálisìləbəl/pɔ́l-] *n.* Ⓒ a word made up of more than three syllables. 다음절어(多音節語). [ploy-]

pol·y·tech·nic [pὰliténknik/pɔ̀l-] *adj.* dealing with various arts or sciences. 여러 공예(工藝)의. ¶ *a ~ school* 공예〔종합 공업〕 학교《영국의 과학 기술 전문 학교》. [→technical]

pol·y·the·ism [páliθiːizəm/pɔ́l-] *n.* Ⓤ the belief in many gods. 다신론; 다신교 (cf. *monotheism*). [poly-, Gk. *theos* god]

pol·y·the·ist [páliθiːist/pɔ́l-] *n.* Ⓒ a person who believes in polytheism. 다신론자; 다신교도.

po·made [pɑméid, poumáːd] *n.* Ⓤ a substance containing oil and used for keeping the hair in place. 포마드; 머릿기름. — *vt.* (P6) put pomade on. …에 포마드를 바르다. [↓]

pome [poum] *n.* an apple or any fruit like it. 이과(梨果)《배·사과 따위》. [L. *pomum* apple]

pome·gran·ate [pámәgrӕnit/pɔ́m-] *n.* Ⓒ a fruit having many whitish seeds which are covered with red flesh; the tree bearing this fruit. 석류(의 열매·나무). [↑, →grain]

pom·mel [pʌ́məl, pám-/pɔ́m-] *n.* Ⓒ **1** a round knob on the handle of a sword, etc. 칼의 자루끝. **2** a round part at the front of a saddle. 안장의 앞머리. — *vt.* (**-meled, -mel·ing** or 《Brit.》 **-melled, -mel·ling**) (P6) beat (something or someone) with the hands closed tight. …을 주먹으로 치다〔때리다〕(cf. *pummel*). ● **pom·mel·er** [-ər] *n.* [→pome]

·**pomp** [pamp/pɔmp] *n.* Ⓤ **1** brilliant or splendid display; magnificence. 화려; 장관(壯觀). ¶ *They wondered at the ~ of the coronation.* 그들은 대관식의 장려함에 경탄했다. **2** 《often *pl.*》 a vain show. 허세; 과시. [Gk. *pempō* send]

pom·pon [pámpɑn/pɔ́mpɔn] *n.* Ⓒ **1** an ornamental ball worn on hats, shoes, etc. 방울술《장식용》. **2** 《bot.》 a kind of dahlia or chrysanthemum bearing small, round flowers. 퐁퐁달리아. [F.]

pom·pous [pámpəs/pɔ́m-] *adj.* **1** acting with self-importance. 거만한. ¶ *in a ~ manner* 건방진 태도로; 건방지게 / *a ~ fellow*

시건방진 놈. **2** full of splendor. 화려한. ● **pom·pous·ly** [-li] *adv.* **pom·pous·ness** [-nis] *n.* [→pomp]

pon·cho [pántʃou / pɔ́n-] *n.* Ⓒ (*pl.* **-chos**) a piece of cloth with a hole in the center, worn in South America. 판초《한 장의 천으로 된 남미 원주민이 입는 옷》. [Amer-Sp. *pontho* woolen fabric]

〈poncho〉

:pond [pand / pɔnd] *n.* Ⓒ a small pool of water. 못; 연못. [pound³]

pon·der [pándər / pɔ́n-] *vt.* (P6,10,12) think deeply about (something). …을 깊이 생각하다; 숙고하다. ¶ ~ *a difficulty* 난국을 깊이 생각하다 / ~ *what to do* 무엇을 할 것인가를 깊이 생각한다. — *vi.* (P1,3) 《*on, over*》 consider something carefully. 숙고하다. ¶ ~ *over a matter* 문제를 곰곰 생각하다. [L. *pondus* weight]

pon·der·ous [pándərəs / pɔ́n-] *adj.* **1** very heavy and slow. 아주 무거운. ¶ *a* ~ *axe* 묵직한 도끼. **2** dull in speech or writing. (말·문체 따위가) 답답한. ¶ *in a* ~ *way* 답답한 어조로. **3** giving a feeling of weight; massive. 육중한. ¶ *a* ~ *building* 육중한 건물.

pon·tiff [pántif / pɔ́n-] *n.* Ⓒ **1** the Roman Catholic Pope. 로마 교황. **2** a bishop. 주교(主敎). **3** a high or chief priest. 제사장. [L.=priest]

pon·tif·i·cal [pantífikəl / pɔn-] *adj.* of a pontiff. 로마 교황의; 주교의. — *n.* 《*pl.*》 robes or special objects for bishops, etc. worn in ceremonies. 주교의 제복(祭服) 및 휘장. ● **pon·tif·i·cal·ly** [-kəli] *adv.*

pon·tif·i·cate [pantífikit / pɔn-] *n.* Ⓤ the position of a pontiff; the term of a pontiff. 로마 교황[주교]의 직[직위, 임기].

pon·toon [pantú:n / pɔn-] *n.* Ⓒ **1** a flat-bottomed boat used to support a bridge. (배다리용의) 너벅선. ¶ *a* ~ *bridge* 배다리; 부교(浮橋). **2** a flat-bottomed boat. 평저선(平底船). **3** a device attached to the bottom of an airplane for floating on water. (수상(水上) 비행기의) 플로트(float). [L. *pons* bridge]

:po·ny [póuni] *n.* Ⓒ (*pl.* **-nies**) **1** a horse of a small breed; a small or young horse. 조랑말. **2** 《Brit. *sl.*》 the sum of twenty-five pounds. 25 파운드《도박 용어》. **3** 《U.S. *colloq.*》 a literal translation of a text in a foreign language, used in doing schoolwork, often dishonestly. (외국어 교과서 따위의) 주역서(註譯書). [L. *pullus* foal]

poo·dle [pú:dl] *n.* Ⓒ a pet dog with long hair, usu. cut into some pattern. 푸들《애완견의 하나》. [G.]

pooh [pu:] *interj.* an expression of contempt, impatience, etc. 흥; 피; 쳇《경멸·초조 따위를 나타내는 소리》. ¶ *Pooh! You don't dare jump.* 피, 뛸 용기가 없을게다. [↓]

pooh-pooh [pú:pú:] *vt.* (P6) express contempt for; laugh at. …을 비웃다; 코방귀 뀌다. ¶ *He pooh-poohed the signs of danger.* 그는 위험 신호를 거들떠보지도 않았다. [Imit.]

:pool¹ [pu:l] *n.* Ⓒ **1** a small body of still water. 물웅덩이. ¶ *a* ~ *of water.* **2** a still, deep part in a river. 강의 깊은 곳; 소. **3** a swimming pool. 수영장. [E.]

·pool² [pu:l] *n.* **1** Ⓤ a kind of billiards. 당구의 일종. **2** Ⓒ the things or money gathered by some persons for a common purpose; a combination of corporations in business. 합동 자금; 기업 합동. **3** Ⓒ the total amount of stake in a gambling, etc. (노름 등에) 태운 돈 전부. — *vt.* (P6) put (money) into one common fund. 공동으로 …을 내놓다; 공동 출자하다. ¶ *Let's* ~ *our money to buy a car.* 차를 한 대 사게 돈을 걷자. [F. *poule*]

poop [pu:p] *n.* Ⓒ **1** a raised deck in the back part of a ship. 선미루(船尾樓)갑판. **2** the stern of a ship. 선미; 고물. [L. *puppis*]

:poor [puər] *adj.* **1** having little or no money or goods. 가난한(opp. rich). ¶ *the hungry* ~ 굶주린 가난한 사람들 / *the needy* ~ 극빈한 사람들 / *be born* ~ 가난하게 태어나다 / *a* ~ *prisoner* 변호사가 없는 피고. **2** small in amount; lacking. 적은; 모자라는. ¶ *a* ~ *crop* (*harvest*) 흉작 / ~ *in natural resources* 천연 자원이 빈약한 / *a* ~ *supply* 불충분한 공급. **3** not good; inferior. 서투른; 열등한; 잘 못하는. ¶ *a* ~ *picture* 서투른 그림 / *a* ~ *head for figures* 숫자에 어두운 / *I am a* ~ *hand at playing tennis.* 나는 테니스가 서툴다 / *He is a* ~ *driver* (*speaker*). 그는 운전[연설]이 서투르다. **4** badly made; mean. 빈약한; 초라한. ¶ ~ *clothes* 초라한 옷 / *a* ~ *place* 누추한 곳. **5** not sound or healthy; weak. (몸이) 허약한; (신체의 기능이) 좋지 않은; 건강하지 못한. ¶ *a* ~ *body* 허약한 신체 / ~ *digestion* 소화 불량 / *a* ~ *memory* 나쁜 기억력 / *in* ~ *spirits* 의기 소침하여. **6** needing sympathy or pity; unfortunate. 가엾은; 불행한. ¶ *Poor fellow!* 불쌍한 놈 / *My* ~ *brother died last night.* 내 가엾은 동생은 어젯밤 죽었다. **7** 《often *iron.*or *joc.*》 having little value; worthless. 변변찮은; 하잘것 없는. ¶ *in my* ~ *opinion* 내 어리석은 소견으로는 / *to the best of my* ~ *abilities* 미약하나마 내 힘닿는 데까지. [L. *pauper*]
(**as**) ***poor as Job*** [***a church mouse***], very poor. 몹시 가난한.

poor box [⌐⌐] *n.* a box (in a church) into which people put money to help the poor. (교회의) 헌금함; 자선함.

poor law [⌐⌐] *n.* 《hist.》 Ⓒ a law offering relief to the poor at public expense. 빈민 구제법.

·poor·ly [púərli] *adv.* in a poor manner; not well; badly. 가난하게; 서투르게; 졸렬하게. ¶ *People in this country are poorly off.* 이 나라의 사람들은 가난하다 / *a ~ built house* 날림 집 / *He spoke very ~.* 그는 말이 아주 서툴렀다 / *think ~ of* …을 시답잖게 여기다. — *adj.* sickly; in poor health. 병적인; 허약한. ¶ *I feel ~.* 몸이 찌뿌드드하다.

poor·ness [púərnis] *n.* Ⓤ the state or quality of being poor. 결핍; 불충분; 졸렬; 허약. ¶ *the ~ of his performance* 그의 졸렬한 연기.

poor-spir·it·ed [púərspíritid] *adj.* having or showing a poor spirit; having no courage. 겁이 많은; 소심한.

poor white [´ ´] *n.* 《*contempt.*》 a poor and lazy white person in the southern United States. (미국 남부의) 가난한 백인.

·pop[1] [pɑp / pɔp] *n.* Ⓒ **1** a short, sharp, quick sound. '펑[땅, 쿵]' 하는 짧고 날카로운 소리. ¶ *The cork came out with a ~.* 펑하며 마개가 빠졌다 / *We heard the ~ of a pistol.* 탕하는 권총 소리를 들었다. **2** Ⓤ any kind of sweet bubbling drink. 거품 나는 청량 음료. **3** 《*colloq.*》 a shot. 발사; 발포. ¶ *have a ~ at a rabbit* 토끼에 한 방 쏘다.

— *v.* (**popped, pop·ping**) *vi.* **1** (P1) make a short, sharp, quick sound; burst. 펑 소리가 나다; 펑 터지다[튀다]. ¶ *A balloon pops when it is heated.* 풍선은 가열하면 뻥 터진다. **2** (P2A,3) move, come, enter, or appear suddenly. 불쑥 오다[들어오다, 나타나다]. ¶ *~ in and out the room* 방을 들락거리다. **3** (P1) (of the eyes) stick out or open wide suddenly. 눈이 튀어나오다; 휘둥그래지다. ¶ *His eyes popped (out) in surprise.* 놀라서 눈이 휘둥그래졌다.

— *vt.* **1** (P6,7) cause (something) to make a short, sharp, quick sound; 《U.S.》 heat corn, etc. till it bursts open. …을 펑[탕]하고 터뜨리다; (옥수수 등)을 (볶아) 튀기다. ¶ *~ corn* [*maize*]. **2** (P7,13) place or thrust suddenly. …을 탁 놓다; …을 불쑥 밀어넣다[내밀다]. ¶ *~ a coin into one's pocket* 동전을 주머니에 처넣다 / *She popped her head out through the window.* 그녀는 머리를 불쑥 창 밖으로 내밀었다. **3** (P6,7) 《*colloq.*》 shoot; fire (a gun or pistol). …을 발사하다. **4** (P6) pawn. 저당잡히다.

pop in, **a**) call; pay a visit suddenly; drop in. 예고없이[갑자기] 방문하다[들르다]. **b**) enter a room suddenly. 불쑥 들어가다.

pop off, **a**) (of a gun) be fired. 탕 쏘다. **b**) go away suddenly and in a hurry. 갑자기[서둘러] 가버리다. **c**) 《*sl.*》 die. 죽다.

pop out, **a**) rush suddenly and rapidly from a room, house, etc. (방, 집안에서) 갑자기[재빠르게] 달려 나가다. ¶ *He has just popped out.* 그는 방금 뛰어 나갔다. **b**) be put out suddenly. 갑자기 꺼지다. ¶ *The wind made the candle ~ out.* 바람에 촛불이 갑자기 꺼졌다. **c**) 《*sl.*》 die (suddenly). 급사하다.

pop the question, 《*colloq.*》 propose marriage. 청혼하다.

— *adv.* with a pop; unexpectedly or suddenly. 펑하고; 갑자기; 불쑥. ¶ *a balloon go ~* 풍선이 뻥 터지다. [Imit.]

pop[2] [pɑp / pɔp] *n.* Ⓒ 《usu. *pl.*》 《*colloq.*》 a popular concert; a popular song or piece of music. 대중 음악회; 대중 가요. — *adj.* 《*colloq.*》 popular. 통속적[대중적]인. ¶ *a ~ concert* 대중 음악회; 팝 콘서트. [Abbr.]

pop[3] [pɑp / pɔp] *n.* 《U.S. *sl.*》 a father; any elderly man. 아버지; 아빠; 아저씨. [*papa*]

pop. popular(ly); population.

pop·corn [pɑ́pkɔ̀ːrn / pɔ́p-] *n.* Ⓤ a kind of corn which bursts open when heated. 팝콘; 튀긴 옥수수. [*pop*[1]]

·Pope, pope [poup] *n.* Ⓒ **1** 《*the* ~》 the head of the Roman Catholic Church. 로마 교황. **2** 《*p*-》 《*fig.*》 a person who thinks oneself to be an authority. 자칭 권위자[대가]. [Gk. *pappas* father]

pop-eyed [pɑ́pàid / pɔ́p-] *adj.* 《U.S. *colloq.*》 having bulging eyes; open-eyed (with surprise, etc.) 퉁방울눈의; (놀라서) 눈이 휘둥그래진. [*pop*[1]]

pop·gun [pɑ́pgʌ̀n / pɔ́p-] *n.* Ⓒ a toy gun that shoots a pellet with a loud pop. 장난감 총. [*pop*[1]]

pop·in·jay [pɑ́pindʒèi / pɔ́p-] *n.* Ⓒ a vain, chattering, thoughtless person. 잘난체하고 수다스러운 사람. [Gk. *papagas* parrot]

pop·ish [póupiʃ] *adj.* (unfriendly) of the Pope or the Roman Catholic Church. 로마 교황의; 카톨릭의. ● **pop·ish·ly** [-li] *adv.* [→pope]

pop·lar [pɑ́plər / pɔ́p-] *n.* Ⓒ a tall tree with small heart-shaped leaves; Ⓤ the wood of this tree. 포플라나무; 그 재목. [L. *populus*]

pop·lin [pɑ́plin / pɔ́p-] *n.* Ⓤ a silk and woolen cloth. 포플린《천》. [→papal; =made at papal town of Avignon]

pop·py [pɑ́pi / pɔ́pi] *n.* **1** Ⓒ (*pl.* **-pies**) 《bot.》 a plant with showy flowers of various colors and notched leaves. 양귀비. ¶ *a field* [*red*] *~* 개양귀비. **2** Ⓤ poppy red; scarlet. 심홍색. [L. *papaver*]

pop·u·lace [pɑ́pjələs / pɔ́p-] *n.* Ⓤ 《usu. *the ~, collectively*》 the great mass of common people. 대중; 민중. [↓]

:pop·u·lar [pɑ́pjələr / pɔ́p-] *adj.* **1** liked by many people. 인기 있는. ¶ *The singer is ~ with girls.* 그 가수는 소녀들에게 인기가 있다 / *Professor Smith is ~ among the students.* 스미스 교수는 학생들 사이에 인기가 있다. **2** of, for or by the common people. 대중의[을 위한, 에 의한]. ¶ *the ~ voice* 여론 / *a ~ government* 민주 정치. **3** widespread among people. 유행의; 유행하고 있는. ¶ *a ~ song* 유행가; 팝송. **4** suitable for most people. 대중적인; 통속의. ¶ *a ~ novel* 통속

소설 / *in ~ language* 쉬운 말로; 평이한 말로 이야기하면 / *at ~ prices* 염가로. [L. *populus* people]

·**pop·u·lar·i·ty** [pàpjəlǽrəti / pɔ̀p-] *n.* Ⓤ the state of being liked by many people. 인기; 호평. ¶ *enjoy general ~* 인기가 있다 / *the ~ of sports* 스포츠의 인기.

pop·u·lar·i·za·tion [pàpjələrizéiʃən / pɔ̀p-jələrai-] *n.* Ⓤ the act of making something popular; the state of being popular. 통속화; 보급.

pop·u·lar·ize [pápjələràiz / pɔ́p-] *vt.* (P6) make (something) popular. …을 대중〔통속〕화하다. ¶ *~ science* 과학을 보급시키다.

pop·u·lar·ly [pápjələrli / pɔ́p-] *adv.* **1** in a popular manner. 통속적으로. ¶ *a popularly-written book* 통속적으로 쓰인 책. **2** by the people generally 일반적으로. ¶ *That is ~ known.* 그건 널리 알려져 있다.

pop·u·late [pápjəlèit / pɔ́p-] *vt.* **1** supply (a town, country, etc.) with people. (나라·마을 등)에 사람이 살게 하다; 식민하다. ¶ *Many Englishmen populated America.* 많은 영국인들이 미국에 식민했다. **2** live in (a town or country). …에 거주하다. ¶ *Indians once populated this area.* 이 지역엔 한때 인디언들이 거주했었다 / *Seoul is densely* 〔*thickly*〕 *populated.* 서울은 인구 밀도가 높다. [→ popular, -ate]

:**pop·u·la·tion** [pàpjəléiʃən / pɔ̀p-] *n.* **1** ⓊⒸ the total number of people living in a country, city, etc. 인구; 주민수. ¶ *The area has a large* 〔*small*〕 *~.* 그 지역은 인구가 많다〔적다〕. **2** 《*collectively*》 the people or a group of people in a city, country, etc. (일정 지역의) 주민. ¶ *the adult ~* 성년(成年) 주민 / *the farm ~* 농촌 인구; 농민 / *The rural ~ of Korea is decreasing.* 한국의 농촌 인구는 감소하고 있다.

pop·u·lous [pápjələs / pɔ́p-] *adj.* having many people; thickly populated. 인구가 많은; 인구 밀도가 높은.

por·ce·lain [pɔ́:rsəlin] *n.* Ⓤ **1** fine, white earthenware. 도자기; 자기(磁器). ¶ *Teacups are often made of ~.* 찻잔은 흔히 도자기로 만든다. **2** 《*collectively*》 dishes or ornaments made of the porcelain; china. 자기 제품. [→pork (through the hog-backed shell named in It. *parcella*)]

:**porch** [pɔ:rtʃ] *n.* Ⓒ **1** a covered entrance to a doorway or other building. 현관. **2** 《U.S.》 a veranda. 베란다; (지붕있는) 툇마루. [→portico]

por·cine [pɔ́:rsain, -sin] *adj.* of or like pigs. 돼지의; 돼지 같은. [→pork]

por·cu·pine [pɔ́:rkjəpàin] *n.* Ⓒ an animal with sharp spines on its body to protect it from enemies. 호저(豪猪)《아프리카산》. [→pork, →spine]

pore[1] [pɔ:r] *vi.* (P3) **1** gaze closely and steadily. 자세히 보다; 주시하다. **2** 《*at, on, over*》 think or read earnestly. 곰곰이 생각하다; 몰두하다; 정독하다. ¶ *~ over a problem* 문제를 숙고하다 / *~ over a book* 열심히 책을 읽다. [M.E.(→peer)]

pore[2] [pɔ:r] *n.* Ⓒ a very small opening in the skin of animals or in the surface of leaves. 털구멍; 기공(氣孔). ¶ *Sweat comes through the pores in the skin.* 땀은 피부의 기공을 통해 나온다. [Gk. *poros*]

·**pork** [pɔ:rk] *n.* Ⓤ the meat of pigs used for food. 돼지 고기; 포크. [L. *porcus* pig]

pork·er [pɔ́:rkər] *n.* Ⓒ a pig fattened for food. (식용의) 살찐 돼지.

por·nog·ra·phy [pɔ:rnágrəfi / -nɔ́g-] *n.* Ⓤ obscene writings or pictures. 춘화(春畫); 외설물; 도색〔포르노〕 문학. [Gk. *pornē* harlot]

po·rous [pɔ́:rəs] *adj.* **1** full of pores or very small holes. 구멍이 많은. ¶ *a ~ sponge* 다공성(多孔性)의 스폰지. **2** absorbing a liquid or air. (액체·공기를) 빨아들이는. ● **po·rous·ness** [-nis] *n.* [→pore[2]]

por·poise [pɔ́:rpəs] *n.* Ⓒ (*pl.* **-pois·es** or *collectively* **-poise**) a sea animal of the whale family; a dolphin. 돌고래. [→pork, → piscatory]

por·ridge [pɔ́:ridʒ, pár- / pɔ́r-] *n.* Ⓤ 《chiefly Brit.》 a soft food made of cereal or vegetables boiled in water or milk. 포리지. [= *pottage*]

por·rin·ger [pɔ́:rindʒər, pár- / pɔ́r-] *n.* Ⓒ a small shallow dish for porridge, etc. (작은) 죽그릇. [↑]

:**port**[1] [pɔ:rt] *n.* Ⓒ **1** a place where ships take refuge from storms. 피난항(避難港). **2** a place where ships arrive and depart; a harbor. 선착장; 항구. ¶ *a naval ~* 군항 / *a free ~* 자유항 / *a ~ of call* 기항항(寄航港) / *a ~ of delivery* 화물 인도항 / *a ~ of recruit* 식료품 적재항. **3** a town with a harbor. 항구도시. **4** 《*fig.*》 a shelter; a refuge. 피난처. ¶ *come safe to ~* 무사히 난을 피하다. [L. *portus*]

any port in a storm, any way out of a difficulty, etc. must be accepted. 궁여지책; 그나마 아쉬운 대로 의지가 되는 것.

clear a port, sail from a port. 출항하다.

make (***a***) ***port,*** enter (a) port. 입항하다.

port[2] [pɔ:rt] *n.* Ⓒ the left side of a ship. (선박의) 좌현(左舷)(opp. starboard). ¶ *on the ~ bow* 좌현 고물에. — *adj.* on the left side of a ship. 좌현에. — *vt., vi.* (P6; 1) turn to the left side of a ship; turn the helm to the left. 이물이 왼쪽으로 돌게 하다; 좌현으로 선회하다. [*port*[1]]

port[3] [pɔ:rt] *n.* Ⓤ the way in which a person behaves; bearing. 태도; 거동; 외양. [L. *porto* carry]

port[4] [pɔ:rt] *n.* Ⓤ a strong, sweet, dark-red wine, originally from Portugal. 포트와인《포르투갈 원산의 붉은 포도주》. [Place]

·**port·a·ble** [pɔ́:rtəbəl] *adj.* that can be easily carried or moved. 들고 다닐 수 있는; 휴

대용의. ¶ *a ~ radio* 〔*television*〕 휴대용 라디오〔텔레비전〕. [→port³]

por·tage [pɔ́ːrtidʒ] *n.* **1** Ⓤ the act of carrying. 운반. **2** Ⓤ the act of carrying boats, cargo, goods, etc. overland from one river to another. 연수(連水) 육로 운반. **3** Ⓒ the place where this transportation is done. 연수 육로. [↑]

por·tal [pɔ́ːrtl] *n.* Ⓒ a large gateway or entrance. (으리으리한) 정문; 입구. [L. *porta* gate]

port·cul·lis [pɔːrtkʌ́lis] *n.* Ⓒ a strong iron frame of bars that can be raised or lowered at the entrance of a castle or fort. (성(城) 따위의) 내리닫이 쇠살문. [L. *porta* gate, *colo* percolate]

por·tend [pɔːrténd] *vt.* (P6) give warning or a sign of (something usu. bad) beforehand; foretell. …의 전조(前兆)가 되다; …을 예시(豫示)하다. ¶ *Black clouds ~ a storm.* 검은 구름은 폭풍우를 예시한다. [→pro-, →tend¹]

por·tent [pɔ́ːrtənt] *n.* Ⓒ **1** a sign of some evil to come. 불길한 징조. ¶ *portents of war* 불길한 전쟁의 징조. **2** a marvel. 놀라운 일; 경이. ¶ *the portents of modern science* 현대 과학의 경이. [↑]

por·ten·tous [pɔːrténtəs] *adj.* **1** showing or giving a portent. 불길한; 흉조의. ¶ *~ events* 불길한 사건들. **2** extraordinary; marvelous. 경이적인. ¶ *~ abilities* 놀라운 재능. **3** self-important. 젠 체하는; 거만한. ¶ *a ~ manner*.

:por·ter¹ [pɔ́ːrtər] *n.* Ⓒ **1** a person who carries burdens or baggage, esp. at a station or hotel. 운반인; (역의) 짐꾼; (호텔의) 포터; 보이. ¶ *a ~ at a meat-market* 푸줏간의 배달부 / *Give your bags to the ~* 가방들을 짐꾼에게 맡기시오. **2** 《U.S.》 a person who serves passengers in a railroad parlor car or sleeping car; a waiter. (침대차 등의) 사환〔급사〕. **3** a man employed to clean, sweep, etc. in a place of business. (사업장·건물 등의) 청소부. [L. *porto* carry]

por·ter² [pɔ́ːrtər] *n.* Ⓒ a doorman; a gate keeper. 문지기. ¶ *The ~ let them in.* 수위가 그들을 들여보냈다. [L. *porta* gate]

por·ter³ [pɔ́ːrtər] *n.* a dark-brown or blackish kind of beer. 흑맥주. [*porter¹*]

por·ter·house [pɔ́ːrtərhàus] *n.* Ⓒ **1** a kind of large steak; a porterhouse steak. 고급 비프스테이크. **2** 《U.S.》 formerly, an eating-house, where beefsteaks, beer, porter, etc. were served. (예전의) 간이 식당; 선술집. [→portable]

port·fo·li·o [pɔːrtfóuliòu] *n.* Ⓒ (*pl.* **-li·os**) **1** a case for carrying papers, etc.; a brief case. 손가방; 서류 가방. **2** the position of a minister of state. 각료직. ¶ *hold the ~ of Finance* 재무 장관직에 있다 / *resign one's ~* 장관직을 사임하다 / *a minister without ~* 무임소 장관. [L. *porto* carry, *folium* leaf]

portfolio investment [–⌒⌒–⌒] *n.* investment by purchase of securities. (투자 수익 획득을 위한) 증권 투자; 간접 투자.

port·hole [pɔ́ːrthòul] *n.* Ⓒ **1** a small, round window in the side of a ship. 현창(舷窓). **2** an opening in a ship, fort, etc. through which to shoot. 총안(銃眼); 포안(砲眼). [→portal]

por·ti·co [pɔ́ːrtikòu] *n.* Ⓒ (*pl.* **-coes** or **-cos**) a porch with a roof supported by columns. 주랑(柱廊); 현관. [↑]

:por·tion [pɔ́ːrʃən] *n.* Ⓒ **1** a part of the whole. 부분; 일부분. **2** the quantity of food served to one person. (식사의) 1인분. **3** the part of an estate given to an heir; a share. 상속 재산; 몫. **4** one's fate. 운명. ¶ *our ~ in life* 우리들의 운명.

a portion of, a small amount of (something). 약간의.

— *vt.* **1** (P7) divide (something) into shares. …을 분배하다. ¶ *~ out food* 〔*property*〕 음식〔재산〕을 분배하다. **2** (P6) give a share to. …에 몫을 내주다. ¶ *~ a daughter* 딸에게 지참금을 주다. [L. *portio*]

port·ly [pɔ́ːrtli] *adj.* (**-li·er, -li·est**) **1** fat; stout. 뚱뚱한; 살찐. **2** dignified 풍채가 좋은. ¶ *a ~ man* 풍채 좋은 남자. ● **port·li·ness** [-nis] *n.* [→port³]

port·man·teau [pɔːrtmǽntou] *n.* Ⓒ (*pl.* **-teaus** or **-teaux**) 《Brit.》 a large traveling bag, that opens like a book. 여행 가방. [→port³, →mantle]

port·man·teaux [pɔːrtmǽntouz] *n.* pl. of **portmanteau.**

·por·trait [pɔ́ːrtrit, -treit] *n.* Ⓒ **1** a picture of a person. 초상(화); 인물 사진. **2** a vivid description of a person's appearance or character. 생생한 묘사. [→pro-¹, L. *traho* pull]

por·trai·ture [pɔ́ːrtrətʃər] *n.* **1** Ⓤ the act or art of portraying. 묘사(법); 초상화법. **2** Ⓒ a portrait; 《*collectively*》 a collection of portraits. 초상화; 초상화 콜렉션. ¶ *English ~ of 18th century,* 18세기 영국인 초상화집(集). **3** Ⓤ vivid description of a person's appearance or character. (언어에 의한) 인물 묘사.

por·tray [pɔːrtréi] *vt.* (P6) **1** make a portrait of (someone). …의 초상을 그리다. **2** describe clearly (someone or something) in words. …을 생생하게 묘사하다. ¶ *The book 'Black Beauty' portrays the life of a horse.* '블랙 뷰티'라는 책은 한 마리 말의 일생을 여실하게 묘사한 것이다. **3** play (a part) on the stage. …의 역(役)을 연기하다. ● **por·tray·er** [-ər] *n.* [→portrait]

por·tray·al [pɔːrtréiəl] *n.* **1** Ⓤ the act of portraying. (그림) 그리기; 묘사. **2** Ⓒ a portrait or description. 초상화; 묘사물.

Por·tu·gal [pɔ́ːrtʃəgəl] *n.* a small country in Europe, just west of Spain. 포르투갈

《수도는 Lisbon》.

Por·tu·guese [pɔ̀ːrtʃəgíːz, -gíːs, ⌐⌐] *n.* **1** Ⓒ a person of Portugal. 포르투갈 사람. **2** Ⓤ the language of Portugal. 포르투갈어(語). — *adj.* of Portugal or Portuguese. 포르투갈 (사람·말)의.

pose [pouz] *n.* Ⓒ **1** a position of the body. 자세; 포즈. ¶ *a careful* ~ 신중한 자세 / *The* ~ *in the portrait is very fine.* 초상화에서의 그 자세는 아주 좋다. **2** a mental attitude assumed for effect; a pretense. 마음가짐; 꾸민 태도; 겉치레. ¶ *His friendliness is a mere* ~. 그의 우정은 순전히 겉치레다.
— *vi.* **1** (P1,3) hold a certain position of the body. 포즈를 취하다. ¶ *She posed for a picture.* 그녀는 초상화를 위해 포즈를 잡았다. **2** (P2A) pretend to be what one really is not. …인 체하다; 가장하다. ¶ ~ *as a detective* 형사인 체하다 / *The man poses as an actor.* 그는 배우인 것처럼 행동한다.
— *vt.* (P6) **1** put (someone) in a position suitable for a picture, photograph, etc. …에게 포즈를 취하게 하다. ¶ ~ *a model for a picture* 모델에게 그림의 포즈를 취하게 하다. **2** put (a question, etc.) for consideration. (문제 등)을 제기하다. ¶ ~ *an argument* 〔*a question*〕 논지〔문제〕를 제기하다. [=pause; in compounds and their derivatives, as *compose, composition,* there is confusion with L. *pono* put]

Po·sei·don [pousáidən, pə-] *n.* 《Gk. myth.》 the god of the sea and of horses. 포세이돈; 해신(海神). 參考 로마 신화에서는 Neptune. [Gk.]

pos·er [póuzər] *n.* Ⓒ **1** a difficult question or problem. 어려운 질문; 난문제. **2** an affected person. 젠체하는 사람. [→pose]

:po·si·tion [pəzíʃən] *n.* Ⓒ **1** the place where a thing or person is. 위치. ¶ *The villa has a very good* ~. 별장은 아주 좋은 위치에 있다. **2** Ⓤ the proper place. 적소(適所). ¶ *He is in* ~. 그는 알맞은 자리에 있다 / *the* ~ *of the players on the field* 경기장에서의 선수들의 위치. **3** the way in which a person or thing is placed or arranged; a posture; situation. 자세; 상태; 입장. ¶ *sit in a comfortable* ~ 편한 자세로 앉다 / *The* ~ *is very critical.* 상태는 심각하다 / *I was placed in a awkward* ~. 나는 난처한 입장에 처해 있었다. **4** social rank. (사회적) 지위. ¶ *a high* 〔*low*〕 ~ *in society* 높은〔낮은〕사회적 지위 / *a responsible* ~ 책임 있는 지위 / *a man of* ~ 지위가 있는 사람. **5** a job. 일자리; 직(職). ¶ *He has a* ~ *in a bank.* 그는 은행에 근무하고 있다. **6** a way of thinking; a mental attitude. 견해. ¶ *the conservative* ~ 보수적인 견해. [L. *pono* put]

·pos·i·tive [pázətiv / pɔ́z-] *adj.* **1** clearly expressed; sure; unquestionable; that can not be denied. 명백〔확실〕한; 의심할 여지가 없는; 부정할 수 없는. ¶ *a* ~ *fact* 명백한 사실 / *a* ~ *promise* 확약 / *We have* ~ *knowledge that the earth moves round the sun.* 우리는 지구가 태양의 주위를 돌고 있다는 것을 확실히 알고 있다. **2** ⓐ quite sure; cetain. 확신하는. ¶ *He is* ~ *about his success.* 그는 성공을 확신하고 있다 / *Are you* ~ *that he will come ?* 그가 올 것이라고 확신하느냐. ⓑ too sure; too confident. 자신만만한. ¶ *Her* ~ *manner annoyed us.* 그녀의 자신만만한 태도에 우리는 곤혹스러웠다. **3** real; practical; constructive. 실제적〔현실적〕인; 실증〔건설〕적인. ¶ *a* ~ *mind* 현실적인 사람 / *He gave us* ~ *help.* 실제적으로 우리를 도왔다. **4** showing agreement; approving. 긍정적인. ¶ *a* ~ *answer* 긍정적인 대답. **5** 《phys., electr.》 not negative; plus. 양성(陽性)의; 플러스의(opp. negative). ¶ ~ *electricity* 양전기(陽電氣). **6** 《*colloq.*》 complete; quite. 완전〔순전〕한; 전적인. ¶ *a* ~ *fool* 순전한 바보. **7** 《gram.》 in its simple form, as of an adjective or adverb. 원급(原級)의. ¶ *the* ~ *degree* 원급. **8** 《math.》 plus; greater than zero. 양(陽)의; 플러스의(opp. negative). ¶ *the* ~ *sign* 플러스 기호《+》. **9** 《photog.》 having the lights and shadows in the same position as in the original. 양화(陽畫)의(opp. negative).
— *n.* Ⓒ **1** reality. 실재(實在). **2** 《gram.》 a positive degree. 원급. **3** a positive quantity. 정량(正量). **4** a positive photographic print. (사진의) 양화; 포지티브. [→position]

pos·i·tive·ly [pázətivli / pɔ́z-] *adv.* in a positive manner; absolutely; decidedly. 확실하게; 단호히.

pos·i·tive·ness [pázətivnis / pɔ́z-] *n.* Ⓤ the state of being positive. 결정적임; 적극성.

pos·i·tiv·ism [pázətivìzəm / pɔ́z-] *n.* Ⓤ **1** 《also *P-*》 the philosophical system of Auguste Comte, which rejects any abstract speculation. 실증 철학. **2** the state of being positive. 적극성; 명확성.

pos·i·tron [pázətràn / pɔ́zətrɔ̀n] *n.* a positively charged particle. 양전자(陽電子). [→positive, →electron]

pos·se [pási / pɔ́si] *n.* 《U.S.》 a group of men summoned by a sheriff to help him. (보안관에 의해 소집된) 치안〔수색〕대. [L. =be able]

:pos·sess [pəzés] *vt.* **1** have (something) as one's own; hold. …을 소유하다; 가지다. ¶ ~ *a house* 〔*property*〕 집〔재산〕을 소유하다 / ~ *wisdom* 지혜가 있다. **2** 《usu. in *passive*》 occupy (something) by an evil spirit, etc. (귀신 등이) …에 붙다(cf. *obsess*). ¶ *A demon possessed him.* 그에게 귀신이 씌었다 / *What possessed him to do it ?* 그에게 무엇이 씌어 그랬을까. **3** maintain or control (one's mind). (마음)을 어떤 상태로 유지하다; 자제하다. ¶ ~ *one's mind in peace* 마음을 편안히 가지다. [L. *possideo*]

be possessed by (=*have one's mind occupied by*) *something evil.* (나쁜) …에 사로잡혀〔씌어〕있다.

be possessed of, own or hold. …을 소유하고 있다. ¶ *She is possessed of a large fortune.* 막대한 재산을 가지고 있다.

:pos·ses·sion [pəzéʃən] *n.* **1** Ⓤ the act of possessing; the state of being possessed; ownership. 소유. ¶ *the ~ of property* 재산의 소유 / 《*prov.*》 *Possession is nine points of the law.* 가진 사람이 임자. **2** Ⓒ a thing possessed; 《*pl., collectively*》 wealth. 소유물; 재산. ¶ *a national ~* 국유 재산 / *It was his most treasured ~.* 그것은 그가 가장 소중히 여기는 재산이었다 / *Please move your possessions from my room.* 네 물건들을 내 방에서 옮기도록 해라 / *a man of great possessions* 대단한 재산가. **3** Ⓒ a territory ruled by another country. 영지(領地); 속령(屬領). ¶ *the French possessions in North Africa* 북아프리카의 프랑스 영지. **4** Ⓤ self-control. 자제(自制). [↑]

hold possession of (=*take and keep*) *something.* …을 소유하고 있다.

in 〔***into***〕 ***one's possession,*** owned by; possessed by. …에 소유되어. ¶ *The keys are in his ~.* 열쇠는 그가 가지고 있다.

in 〔***into***〕 ***possession of,*** holding; keeping; possessing. …을 가지고 있는. ¶ *The widow is in ~ of a large fortune.* 미망인은 대단한 재산을 가지고 있다 / *At his father's death he came into ~ of a million dollars.* 부친의 사망으로 그에겐 100 만 달러가 생겼다.

pos·ses·sive [pəzésiv] *adj.* **1** of possession. 소유의. **2** 《gram.》 showing possession. 소유를 나타내는. ¶ *a ~ pronoun* 소유대명사. —*n.* Ⓒ 《gram.》 **1** the possessive case. 소유격. **2** a word in that case. 소유격의 낱말.

pos·ses·sor [pəzésər] *n.* Ⓒ a person who has something; an owner. 소유주; 임자.

:pos·si·bil·i·ty [pɑ̀səbíləti / pɔ̀s-] *n.* (*pl.* **-ties**) **1** Ⓤ the state of being possible. 가능성. ¶ *There is much ~ of his success.* 그가 성공할 가능성은 많다 / *The ~ of flying machines was long denied.* 하늘을 나는 기계의 가능성은 오랫동안 부정되었었다. **2** Ⓒ something that may happen. 일어날〔있을〕 수 있음〔있는 일〕. ¶ *Let's consider the possibilities.* 있을〔일어날〕 수 있는 몇 가지 사태를 생각해 보자 / *Failure is a ~.* 실패도 있을 수 있다. **3** 《usu. *pl.*》 power of favorable development; prospects. 발전 가능성; 가망; 장래성. ¶ *The scheme has great possibilities.* 그 계획은 아주 유망하다. [↓]

:pos·si·ble [pɑ́səbəl / pɔ́s-] *adj.* **1** that can be done; within the limit of one's ability or power. 할 수 있는; 가능한. ¶ *as … as ~* 될 수 있는 한 …하게 / *if ~* 가능하다면 / *a ~ but difficult task* 할 수는 있지만 하기 힘든 일 / *a result not ~ to foresee* 예견할 수 없었던 결과. **2** that may be or happen. 일어날 수 있는; 있음직한. ¶ *Is it ~ that it will rain today?* 오늘 비가 올까 / *Snow is ~ today.* 오늘 눈이 올 것 같다. **3** 《*colloq.*》 that can be considered; that can be put up with. (그런 대로) 고려해 볼 만한; 참을 수 있을 정도의. ¶ *the only ~ man for the position* 유일한 적임자 / *a just ~ meal* 겨우 먹을 만한 식사 / *He is not a ~ person.* 저 사람으론 안 된다. **4** 《used to emphasize *a superlative*》 되도록의; 가능한 한의《최상급과 함께 쓰여 그 뜻을 강조함》. ¶ *the highest ~ speed* 최고 속력 / *the least ~ delay* 되도록 빨리 / *He lives in the simplest ~ way.* 그는 되도록 간소하게 살고 있다.

—*n.* **1** 《*the ~, one's,* or *pl.*》 something that can be done. 가능한 일; 전력. ¶ *I will do my ~.* 힘껏 하겠소 / *It is hard to see the limits of the ~ in modern invention.* 근대 발명에 있어서 그 가능성의 한계는 내다보기 어렵다. **2** the highest possible score in shooting, etc. (사격 등의) 최고점. ¶ *score a ~* 최고점을 따다. [L. *posse*]

:pos·si·bly [pɑ́səbəli / pɔ́s-] *adv.* **1** perhaps; maybe. 아마도. ¶ *He may ~ come.* 아마 그는 올지도 모른다 / *Possibly you are right.* 어쩌면 네가 옳을지 모른다. **2** by any means. 아무리 해도; 도저히. ¶ *I cannot ~ go.* 난 아무리 해도 못 가겠다 / *Come as often as you ~ can.* 어떻게 하든 몇 번이고 자주 오너라.

pos·sum [pɑ́səm / pɔ́s-] *n.* Ⓒ 《zool.》 《U.S. *colloq.*》 an opossum. 주머니쥐《미국산》. [Abbr.]

play 〔***act***〕 ***possum,*** pretend to take no notice; pretend to be sick, ignorant, dead, etc. 모른 체하다; 꾀병부리다; 죽은 체하다. [Abbr.]

:post¹ [poust] *n.* Ⓒ a piece of wood, metal, etc. set upright to hold something up; a pole. 기둥; 말뚝; 푯말. ¶ *a telegraph ~* 전주(電柱).

—*vt.* **1** (P6,7,13) fix or put up a poster, etc. on (a wall, etc.). (벽 따위)에 …을 붙이다. ¶ *Don't ~ this wall.* (여기) 벽보 금지 / *~ (up) an advertisement* 광고를 붙이다. **2** (P7) put (a name, etc.) in a list that is published; bring (something) to public notice. …을 공고〔고시〕하다; 퍼뜨리다. ¶ *~ someone for a robber* 아무를 도둑이라고 소문내다 / *~ a ship as missing* 배는 실종됐다고 공고하다 / *~ a reward* 포상을 내걸다. **3** 《U.S.》 close (a place, etc.) to the public by means of signs or notices. (땅)에 출입금지 게시를 하다. [L. *postis*]

:post² [poust] *n.* Ⓒ **1** a situation; an office; a job. 지위; 직(職); 직장. ¶ *have a ~ in a company* 어떤 회사에 근무하고 있다 / *obtain a ~ in a bank* 은행에 취직하다 / *proceed to one's new ~* 새 직장에 다니기 시작하다. **2** a place where a soldier or policeman is on watch. 초소; 부서; 담당 위치〔장소〕. ¶ *Remain at your ~.* 네 초소를 지켜라 / *the sentry at his ~* 담당 구역에서 근무 중인 보초 / *When the firealarm sounds, each man rushes to his ~.* 화재 경보가 울리면 각자는 자기 위치로 달려간다. **3** a place where soldiers are stationed. 주둔지. **4** a trading place in an uncivilized, unsettled region. (미개지의) 교역소(交易所). ¶ *a ~ for a fur company* 모피 회사의 교역소. **5** the soldiers in a post. 주둔병; 수비대. ¶ *a chain of posts along a frontier* 국경을 따라 배치된 일련의 수비대. **6** 《mil.》 a bugle call giving notice of the hour for retiring. 취침 나팔. — *vt.* (P6) station or assign (someone) at a post. (사람)을 배치하다. ¶ *~ guards at the Diet Building* 의사당에 경비병을 배치하다. [L. *pono* put, place]

:post³ [poust] *n.* **1** Ⓤ 《usu. *the ~*》 《esp. Brit.》 the system of carrying and delivering letters, cards, and parcels. 우편; 우편제도. ¶ *send something by ~* …을 우송하다 / *by return of ~* (답신 따위를) 편지 받는 대로 곧; 지급으로. **2** Ⓒ 《Brit.》 letters. 우편물(cf. 《U.S.》 *mail*). ¶ *Today's ~ has not come yet.* 오늘 우편물은 아직 오지 않았다 / *The ~ has been collected.* 우편물 수집이 완료되었다. **3** Ⓒ 《Brit.》 a post office; a post box; a pillar box. 우체국; 우체통. ¶ *take letters to the ~* 편지를 우체국[우체통]에 가지고 가다. **4** 《hist.》 Ⓒ ⓐ one of a number of men placed with horses at intervals along roads, his duty being to carry letters, etc. on horseback to the next station or state. (역참(驛站)의) 파발꾼. ⓑ the place where horses were kept for such riders. 역참; 역참의 마구간. ⓒ a horse kept at such a place; a post-horse. 역마. — *vt.* (P6) **1** send (a letter, etc.) by mail. …을 우송하다. ¶ *~ a letter* 편지를 우송하다 / *~ a parcel* 소포를 부치다. **2** put (a letter, etc.) into the post; mail. …을 투함하다. **3** 《usu. in *passive*》 inform (someone) of something. …에게 —을 알리다. ¶ *He is well posted in the latest event.* 그는 최근의 사건을 잘 알고 있다. **4** (P6,7) 《bookkeeping》 carry from a day-book to a ledger. (원장에) 전기(轉記)하다; 분개(分介)하다. **5** hasten. …을 서두르게 하다.
— *vi.* (P2A) go or start in haste; travel with haste. 급히 가다[떠나다]; 급하게 여행하다. ¶ *Post off at once and waste no time.* 시간을 아껴 서둘러 여행하다. [L. *pono* put, place]

post- [poust-] *pref.* after; later than; behind. '후, 다음'의 뜻. [L.]

***post·age** [póustidʒ] *n.* Ⓤ the amount charged for sending anything by mail. 우편 요금. ¶ *~ due* [*free*] 우편 요금 부족[무료] / *~ paid* 우편 요금 지불필 / *~ to America on a letter* 미국행 편지의 우편 요금.

postage stamp [´-- ˌ] *n.* Ⓒ a government stamp put on letters or parcels to show that postage has been paid. 우표.

***post·al** [póustəl] *adj.* of mail or post offices. 우편의; 우체국의. ¶ *the ~ charge* 우편 요금 / *~ service* 우편 (업무) / *a ~ order* 우편환 / *the Universal Postal Union* 만국 우편연합. — *n.* Ⓒ 《U.S.》 a post card. 관제 엽서. [→post³]

post bag [´ ˌ] *n.* 《Brit.》 a mailbag. 우편낭; 행낭.

post·bel·lum [pòustbéləm] *adj.* after the war. 전후(戰後)의; (미국의) 남북 전쟁 후의 (opp. antebellum). [post-]

post·box [póustbàks / -bɔ̀ks] *n.* Ⓒ 《Brit.》 a mailbox. 우체통. [→post³]

:post card [´ ˌ] *n.* **1** a card issued by a government on which a postage stamp is printed; a postal card. 관제 엽서. **2** 《U.S.》 a private card to be sent by mail. 사제 엽서.

post-chaise [póusttʃèis] *n.* 《hist.》 a hired carriage used for traveling in the days before there were railways. 역마차.

post-code [póustkòud] *n.* 《Brit.》 a system of letters and numbers added to addresses to speed and simplify the delivery of post. 우편 번호(cf. 《U.S.》 *zip code*).

post·date [pòustdéit] *vt.* (P6) **1** give a later date than the actual date to (a letter, a check, etc.). (편지·수표 등의) 날짜를 실제보다 늦추어 적다[찍다]. **2** follow (something) in time. (시간적으로) …의 뒤에 오다[일어나다]. ¶ *His fame postdated his death.* 그는 사후에 유명해졌다.

post·er [póustər] *n.* Ⓒ **1** a large printed card or notice posted in a public place. 포스터; 벽보. **2** a person who posts bills, etc. 벽보 붙이는 사람. [→post¹]

poste restante [pòust restɑ́:nt / ˌ ˌ-´] *n.* **1** a direction on a letter to show that it should be held at the post office until called for. (우편물의) 국유치(局留置). **2** 《Brit.》 the post office department in charge of such letters. 유치 우편물과(課). [F. =letter(s) remaining]

pos·te·ri·or [pastíəriər / pɔs-] *adj.* **1** back; rear; situated behind. (위치가) 뒤[뒤쪽]의 (opp. anterior). ¶ *the ~ end of a fish* 물고기의 꼬리. **2** later in time or order. (시간적으로) 뒤의; (순서가) 다음의(opp. prior). ¶ *~ events* 그 뒤의 사건들. — *n.* Ⓒ **1** the hinder parts. 후부; 뒷부분. **2** 《often *pl.*》 the parts at the back of the hip, esp. of animals; the buttocks. 미부(尾部); 엉덩이. [post-]

***pos·ter·i·ty** [pastérəti / pɔs-] *n.* Ⓤ **1** 《*collectively*》 those who come after in family line. 자손(opp. ancestry). **2** all future generations. 후세(後世). ¶ *write for ~* 후세를 위해 기록하다.

pos·tern [póustə:rn, pás-] *n.* 《hist.》 a back door or gate; a small side door or gate. 뒷문; 협문(夾門). ¶ *The castle had a ~ door.* 그 성에는 협문이 하나 있었다.

Post Exchange [´ -ˌ] *n.* 《U.S.》 a shop at a military post that sells cigarettes, candy, etc., to soldiers. 매점; 주보(酒保). 參考 P.X.로 생략함.

post·free [póustfríː] *adj.* **1** that can be sent free of postal charges. 우송료 무료의. **2** 《Brit.》 postpaid. 우송료 선불(先拂)의. [*post*[3]]

post·grad·u·ate [póustgrǽdʒuit, -èit] *adj.* 《orig. U.S.》 of a course of study after graduation from a college or university. 대학 졸업 후의; 대학원의. —*n.* Ⓒ a student who studies after graduation at a college or university. 대학원 학생; 연구(과)생 (cf. *undergraduate*). [post-]

post·haste [póusthéist] *adv.* 《*arch.*》 quickly; with great haste; very speedly. 급히; 황급히. ¶ *ride* ~ 급히 달려가다. [*post*[3]]

post horse [ㅗ ㅗ] *n.* a horse for post-chaises or for hire to travelers. 역마; 파발마. [*post*[3]]

post·hu·mous [pástʃuməs / pɔ́s-] *adj.* **1** born after the death of the father. 유복자로 태어난. ¶ *a* ~ *child* 유복자. **2** published after the death of the author. 사후에 출판된. ¶ *a* ~ *work* 유저(遺著). **3** happening after one's death. 사후의. ¶ ~ *fame* 사후의 명성. [L. *postumus* last]

:post·man [póus*t*mən] *n.* Ⓒ (*pl.* **-men** [-mən]) 《Brit.》 a man who works at the post office to collect or deliver mail; a letter carrier. 우편 집배인; 우체부(cf. 《U.S.》 *mailman*). [*post*[3]]

post·mark [póus*t*màːrk] *n.* Ⓒ a post office mark stamped on letters, parcels, etc. giving the place and the date. (우표의) 소인(消印). —*vt.* (P6) stamp (a letter, etc.) with a postmark. …에 소인을 찍다.

post·mas·ter [póus*t*mæ̀stə*r*, -màːs-] *n.* Ⓒ the director of a post office. 우체국장.

postmaster general [ㅗㅡㅡ ㅗㅡㅡ] *n.* (*pl.* **postmasters g-**) **1** 《Brit.》 the Minister in charge of the postal department. 체신 장관. **2** 《U.S.》 the head of a government's postal system. 우정 장관.

post me·rid·i·em [pòust mərídiəm, -diəm] *adj.* of the afternoon. 오후의(opp. ante meridiem). 參考 P.M., p.m. 으로 생략함. [post-]

post·mis·tress [póus*t*mìstris] *n.* Ⓒ a woman director of a post office. 여성 우체국장. [*post*[3]]

post·mor·tem [poustmɔ́ː*r*təm] *adj.* after death. 사후(死後)의. ¶ *a* ~ *examination* 검시(檢屍). —*n.* Ⓒ the examination of a dead body, esp. to find the cause of death. 검시; 시체 해부(cf. *autopsy*). [post-]

:post office [ㅗ ㅗ] *n.* **1** the place where the collection, sorting, delivery of mail is carried out. 우체국. **2** 《often *P- O-*》 the government department in charge of mail. 우정성. [*post*[3]]

post·paid [póustpéid] *adj.* with the postage paid in advance. 우편 요금 선불의.

·post·pone [pous*t*póun] *vt.* (P6) put off (something) till a later time; delay. …을 연기하다. ¶ *Let's* ~ *the meeting.* 회합을 연기하자. [post-, L. *pono* put]

post·pone·ment [pous*t*póunmənt] *n.* ⓊⒸ the act of postponing. 연기. ¶ *The* ~ *of the game disappointed many people.* 경기의 연기는 많은 사람을 실망시켰다.

post·pran·di·al [pòus*t*prǽndiəl] *adj.* after dinner. 식후의. ¶ *a* ~ *nap* 식후의 걸잠 / 《*joc.*》 ~ *oratory* 식후의 연설. [post-]

post·script [póus*t*skrìpt] *n.* Ⓒ **1** a note or message added after the signature of a letter. (편지의) 추신. 參考 P.S.로 생략함. **2** a supplementary part added to a book or an article. 후기(後記). **3** 《Brit.》 a talk at the end of some B.B.C. news bulletine. 뉴스 방송 끝의 해설. [post-]

pos·tu·late [pástʃəlèit / pɔ́s-] *vt.* **1** (P6) demand (something); require. …을 요구하다. ¶ *the claims postulated* 요구 사항. **2** (P6, 11) assume (something) without proof as a basis of reasoning. …을 자명한 이치로 가정하다. —*n.* [-lit, -lèit] Ⓒ something self-evident or assumed without proof as a basis of reasoning. 자명한 이치; 기초 조합; 공리(公理). ¶ *a* ~ *of geometry* 기하학의 공리. [L. *postulo*]

pos·ture [pástʃə*r* / pɔ́s-] *n.* **1** ⒸⓊ the way a person holds himself. 자세; 태도; 포즈. ¶ *in a sitting* ~ 앉은 자세로 / *take the* ~ *of defense* 방어 자세를 취하다 / *Poor* ~ *is unhealthy and unsightly* 나쁜 자세는 건강에도 보기에도 나쁘다. **2** Ⓒ a mental attitude. 마음가짐. **3** Ⓤ the state or condition of affairs. 상태; 사태. ¶ *the military* ~ *of a nation* 한 국가의 군사(軍事) 상황.
—*vi.* (P1) take a certain position, esp. for effect. 포즈를 잡다《효과를 보려고》. ¶ *The dancer postured before a mirror.* 댄서는 거울 앞에서 포즈를 잡았다.
—*vt.* (P6) set (someone) in a particular position. …에게 (어떤) 포즈를 취하게 하다. [L. *pono* put]

post·war [póustwɔ́ː*r*] *adj.* after the war. 전후의(opp. prewar). [post-]

po·sy [póuzi] *n.* Ⓒ (*pl.* **-sies**) **1** a bunch of flowers, esp. one to be used as a sign on the breast. (가슴에 다는) 꽃(다발). **2** 《*arch.*》 a motto or a line of poetry engraved within a ring. (반지 안쪽에 새긴) 기념 문자. [→poesy]

:pot [pat / pɔt] *n.* Ⓒ **1** a round vessel or container, such as a coffeepot or a teapot. 단지; 항아리; 독; 병. ¶ 《*prov.*》 *A little* ~ *is soon hot.* 소인(小人)은 화를 잘 낸다 / 《*prov.*》 *The* ~ *calls the kettle black.* 똥 묻은 개가 겨 묻은 개 나무란다. **2** the amount such a vessel can hold. pot 하나의 양. ¶ *a* ~ *of milk* 우유 한 병. **3** a vessel for holding plants; a flowerpot. 화분. **4** 《*colloq.*》 a large sum of money. 대금; 거금. ¶ *make a* ~ 〔*pots*〕 *of money* 큰돈을 벌다. **5** 《*colloq.*》 a prize, esp. a silver cup. 상

(품); 은배상(銀杯賞). **6** 《*colloq.*》 a person of some importance. 요인(要人); 높은 양반. ¶ *a big* ~ 높으신 양반. **7** a shot aimed at a short distance. 근거리 사격(cf. *pot-shot*). ¶ *take a* ~ *at a bird* 새를 근거리에서 쏘다. ***go to pot,*** 《*colloq.*》 become useless; be ruined. 못 쓰게 되다; 결딴나다; 파멸하다. ***keep the pot boiling,*** make one's living; keep things going. 생계를 세우다[꾸려가다]; 경기 좋게 잘 계속해 나가다.
make the pot boil, earn enough money to live on. 살림을 꾸려가다.
— *v.* (**pot·ted, pot·ting**) *vt.* (P6) **1** put (something) into a pot. …을 단지[항아리, 병 따위]에 넣다. ¶ ~ *flowers* 꽃을 화분에 심다 / ~ *fruit* 과일을 단지에 넣다. **2** keep (something) in a pot. …을 단지[항아리, 병 따위]에 넣어 보존하다. ¶ ~ *jam* / ~ *eggs* 달걀을 물유리에 넣어 두다. **3** shoot. …을 쏘다. **4** 《billiard》 drive (a ball) into a pocket. (공)을 포켓에 쳐서 넣다.
— *vi.* (P3) 《*at*》 shoot. 쏘다. [E.]

pot·ash [pátæʃ / pɔ́t-] *n.* 《chem.》 **1** Ⓤ any of several substances obtained from wood ashes and used in making soap, fertilizers, etc. 잿물; 수산화칼륨; 탄산칼륨. **2** =potassium. [=*pot ashes*]

po·tas·si·um [pətǽsiəm] *n.* Ⓤ 《chem.》 a soft, light, silver-white metal found only in compounds. 칼륨; 포타슘. [↑]

po·ta·tion [poutéiʃən] *n.* Ⓤ **1** the act of drinking. 마시기. **2** 《usu. *pl.*》 a drink, esp. of alcoholic liquor. 음료; 특히 술. [→potable]

:po·ta·to [pətéitou] *n.* Ⓒ (*pl.* **-toes**) **1** a plant with rootlike bulbs, or tubers which can be eaten; one of these tubers. 감자. **2** 《U.S.》 a sweet potato. 고구마. [Haiti]

potato chip [–⌐–⌐] *n.* a thin slice of potato fried crisp and salted. 포테이토칩.

pot-belly [pátbèli / pɔ́t-] *n.* **1** a large round belly. 올챙이배; 똥배. **2** a person who has such a belly. 배불뚝이. [*pot*]

pot·boil·er [pátbɔ̀ilər / pɔ́t-] *n.* Ⓒ 《*colloq.*》 a literary or artistic work produced only to make money; a writer or artist who produce this. 돈벌이 위주의 작품[작가].

pot-bound [pátbàund / pɔ́t-] *adj.* **1** (of a plant) suffering from insufficiency of space for its roots in a pot. 화분에 뿌리가 꽉 찬. **2** 《*fig.*》 suffering from lack of room to expand. 성장[발전]할 여지가 없는.

po·ten·cy [póutənsi] *n.* Ⓤ **1** the state of being potent; power; strength. 힘; 세력. ¶ *the* ~ *of a drug* 약의 효능. **2** capacity of development. 능력. [↓]

po·tent [póutənt] *adj.* **1** having great power; strong. 힘있는; 강력한; 유력한. ¶ *a* ~ *prince* 세력 있는 군주 / *a* ~ *remedy for a disease* 질병 치료에 좋은 요법. **2** having authority and influence. 설득력이 있는. ¶ *a* ~ *reason* 설득력 있는 논리. [L. *posse* be able]

po·ten·tate [póutəntèit] *n.* Ⓒ a powerful person or ruler. 권력자; 세력자; 군주. [→potent, -ate]

po·ten·tial [pouténʃəl] *adj.* that can come into existence, but not in existence at present; able to be developed; latent. 가능한; 잠재적인; 잠재력이 있는(opp. actual). ¶ *a* ~ *genius* 천재의 소질이 있는 사람 / *The seed is the* ~ *flower and fruit.* 씨는 장차 꽃과 열매가 된다.
— *n.* **1** Ⓤ something that is potential; a potentiality; possibility. 가능(성); 잠재력. ¶ *He seems to have* ~ *as a leader.* 그는 지도자로서의 잠재적인 능력을 가진 것 같다. **2** electric potential. 전위(電位). ¶ *a current of high* ~ 고압 전류. [→potent, -ial]

po·ten·ti·al·i·ty [poutènʃiǽləti] *n.* (*pl.* **-ties**) Ⓤ **1** the state or quality of being potential; potential characteristic; hidden power; possibility of development. 가능성; 잠재 능력; 발전의 가능성. ¶ *the potentialities of a political situation* 정국(政局)의 여러 가지 발전 가능성. **2** 《*pl.*》 something potential. 가능한 것.

po·ten·tial·ly [pouténʃəli] *adv.* in a potential state; possibly, but not yet actually. 잠재적으로; 어쩌면; 혹시.

poth·er [páðər / pɔ́ðər] *n.* ⓊⒸ **1** a choking cloud of dust, smoke, etc. 자욱한 먼지[연기]. **2** an uproar; a disturbance. 법석; 소란. ¶ *The children are making a great* ~ *about the picnic.* 아이들이 소풍 문제로 떠들며 야단 법석이다. — *vt.* (P6) disturb; annoy. …을 성가시게 하다; 괴롭히다. — *vi.* (P1) make a noise; make a pother. 떠들다. [?]

pot·herb [páthə̀ːrb / pɔ́t-] *n.* Ⓒ any herb that is boiled and eaten or used to flavor food. 데쳐 먹거나 향미료로 쓰이는 야채. [*pot, herb*]

pot·hole [páthòul / pɔ́t-] *n.* **1** 《geol.》 a deep round hole in the rock of a river bed or cave. 강바닥 암석이나 동굴에 난 구멍; 구혈(甌穴). **2** a hole in the surface of a road made by rain and traffic. 길에 팬 구멍. [*pot*]

pot·hook [páthùk / pɔ́t-] *n.* Ⓒ a hook for hanging a pot or kettle over a fire. 화덕 위에 냄비 등을 매다는 고리. [*pot*]

pot-hunt·er [páthʌ̀ntər / pɔ́t-] *n.* **1** a person who hunts for food or profit, ignoring the rules of sport. 마구잡이 사냥꾼. **2** a person who takes part in contests merely for the sake of prizes. 상품 위주의 경기 참가자.

po·tion [póuʃən] *n.* Ⓒ a dose of liquid medicine or poison. (물약이나 독약의) 한 잔. [L. *potio* drink]

pot·luck [pátlʌ̀k / pɔ́t-] *n.* Ⓤ food which happens to be available for a meal. (손님 접대에) 있는 재료로만 장만한 요리. ¶ *Come into the house and take* ~ *with me.* 들어와

서 아무거나 있는 대로 요기하세. [*pot*]

pot·sherd [pátʃə̀ːrd / pɔ́t-] *n.* Ⓒ a piece of broken earthenware, esp. archaeological value. 질그릇 조각《고고학의 자료》. [*pot, sherd*]

pot-shot [pátʃàt / pɔ́tʃɔ̀t] *n.* **1** shot fired at game without regard to the rules of sport. (잡기만 하면 된다는) 마구잡이 총사냥. **2** a shot aimed at a short distance. 근접 사격. [*pot*]
take a pot-shot at a rabbit, make an attempt of mere chance. 운에 맡기고 한 번 해보다.

pot·tage [pátidʒ / pɔ́t-] *n.* Ⓤ《*arch.*》soup thickened with vegetables and meat; broth. 진한 수프. [*potage*]

pot·ted [pátid / pɔ́t-] *adj.* **1** planted in a pot. 화분에 심은. ¶ *a ~ plant* 화분에 심은 식물. **2** cooked and kept in sealed pots or cans. (조리하여) 단지에 넣은; 통조림한. [*pot*]

pot·ter[1] [pátər / pɔ́-] *n.* Ⓒ a person who makes pots, dishes, vases, etc. 도공(陶工); 도예가. [→pot]

pot·ter[2] [pátər / pɔ́-] *vt., vi.* 《chiefly Brit.》 =putter[2].

potter's clay [⏤⏤] *n.* a clay used or suitable use by potters. 도토(陶土); 질흙.

potter's field [⏤⏤] *n.* a piece of ground used for burying people who have no friends or money. 무연고(無緣故)〔공동〕묘지.

potter's wheel [⏤⏤] *n.* a horizontal revolving disk on which clay is molded into bowls, etc. 녹로(轆轤); 물레.

pot·ter·y [pátəri / pɔ́t-] *n.* (*pl.* **-ter·ies**) **1** 《*collectively*》 things made from clay and hardened in ovens, such as pots and dishes. 도기(陶器); 도자기; 오지그릇. **2** Ⓤ the art of making earthenware. 도기 제조법. **3** Ⓒ a place where earthenware is made. 도기 제조소. [→pot]

pot·ty[1] [páti / pɔ́ti] *adj.* (**pot·ti·er, pot·ti·est**)《Brit. *sl.*》**1** insignificant; trivial. 하찮은; 시시한. **2** foolish; mad; easy; to be accomplished without difficulty. 어리석은; 미친; 쉬운. ¶ *a ~ sort of game* 식은죽 먹기. [?]

pot·ty[2] [páti / pɔ́ti] *n.* 《*colloq.*》 a child's toilet; 《*child's word*》 a toilet. 어린이 변기; 변소. [→pot]

pouch [pautʃ] *n.* Ⓒ **1** a small bag or sack. 가방; 주머니. ¶ *a postman's ~* 우편낭. **2** 《zool.》 a baglike or pocketlike part of some animals. (캥거루 따위 유대류(有袋類)의) 낭상부(囊狀部). ¶ *A kangaroo carries its young in a ~.* 캥거루는 육아낭에 새끼를 넣고 다닌다. ― *vt.* (P6) **1** put (something) into a pouch. …을 주머니에 넣다. ¶ *~ money* 돈을 지갑에 넣다. **2** make (something) into the form of a pouch. …을 주머니처럼 만들다. ― *vi.* (P1) form a pouch. 자루〔주머니〕처럼 되다. [→pocket]

poul·ter·er [póultərər] *n.* Ⓒ《chiefly Brit.》 a person who deals in poultry for food. 가금상(家禽商); 새장수. [→pullet]

poul·tice [póultis] *n.* Ⓒ a heated wet mass of a soft substance, spread on a thin cloth and laid against the skin to lessen pain, swelling, etc. 찜질약; 습포(濕布). ― *vt.* (P6) apply a poultice on a sore place. …에 습포를 하다. [L. *puls* pap]

·poul·try [póultri] *n.* Ⓤ 《*collectively,* used as *pl.*》 domestic fowls, such as chickens, turkeys and ducks. (병아리·칠면조 따위의) 가금류(家禽類)(cf. *game*). [→pullet]

pounce [pauns] *vi.* (P1,2A,3) 《*on, upon, at*》 **1** leap or dash suddenly to seize something. 달려들다; 갑자기 덤벼들다. ¶ *The cat was poised ready to ~ upon the mouse.* 고양이는 쥐를 덮칠 자세를 취했다. **2** 《*fig.*》 criticize or intervene suddenly. 별안간 비난〔참견〕하다. ¶ *~ upon someone's mistake* 느닷없이 아무의 잘못을 닦아세우다. ― *n.* Ⓒ a sudden leap or attack. 갑자기 덤벼듦; 급습. ¶ *make a ~ upon a rat* 쥐를 덮치다. [?]

:pound[1] [paund] *n.* Ⓒ **1** a unit of weight, equal to 16 ounces. 파운드. 參考 무게 단위로 lb.로 생략함. **2** a unit of money in United Kingdom, equal to a hundred pence. 파운드. 參考 영국의 화폐 단위로 £로 생략함. [L. *pondus* weight]

pound[2] [paund] *vt.* (P6,7) **1** beat or crush (something) into small pieces or powder. …을 잘게 부수다. ¶ *~ stones for road-making* 길에 깔려고 돌을 분쇄하다 / *She pounded the meat to make it tender.* 그녀는 고기를 연하게 하려고 잘게 다졌다. **2** 《*out, down*》 beat (something) with force repeatedly. (피아노 따위를) 쾅쾅 쳐서 소리내다[연주하다]. ¶ *~ a piano* 피아노를 치다 / *~ (out) a tune on the piano* 피아노로 곡을 치다 / *He pounded a nail into the wall.* 그는 벽에 못을 박았다.
― *vi.* **1** (P1,2A,3) 《*at, on*》 hit heavily or repeatedly; beat violently. 세게 두드리다; 연타하다; (심장이) 두근거리다. ¶ *~ on the door* 〔*a drum*〕 문〔북〕을 탕탕 치다 / *After a hard run my heart pounds.* 힘껏 달려 가슴이 뛴다. **2** (P2A) walk or run heavily or noisily. 쿵쿵 걷다〔뛰어가다〕. ¶ *~ along a road* 뚜벅뚜벅 길을 가다.
― *n.* a heavy blow, or its sound. 세게 침; 또 그 소리. [E.]

pound[3] [paund] *n.* Ⓒ **1** an enclosure for keeping stray animals. (임자 없는 짐승을 가두는) 울. **2** a prison. 유치장. [E.]

pound·age [páundidʒ] *n.* Ⓤ a fee, rate or tax of so much per pound of money or weight. (금액·무게 등의) 1 파운드에 대한 수수료〔세금〕. [→pound[1], -age]

pound-fool·ish [páundfúːliʃ] *adj.* foolish or careless in handling large sums of money. 한 푼 아끼다 백 냥 잃는. ¶ 《*prov.*》 *Penny-wise and ~.* 기와 한 장 아끼다 대들보

썩는 줄 모른다.

:pour [pɔːr] *vt.* (P6,7,13,14) **1** cause (a liquid, etc.) to flow or fall in a stream; shed. …을 붓다; 따르다; 쏟다. ¶ ~ *coffee into a cup from a pot* 포트에서 커피를 잔에 따르다 / ~ *someone a cup of tea* = ~ *a cup of tea for someone* 아무에게 차를 한 잔 따르다 / ~ *arrows* 화살을 퍼붓다. **2** ⓐ send forth (light, etc.). (빛 따위)를 발하다. ¶ *The sun poured forth its rays.* 태양이 빛을 발했다. ⓑ utter; express freely. 연해 입을 놀리다. ¶ ~ *out one's trouble* 자기의 고민을 늘어놓다. **3** give freely. 잔뜩 주다. ¶ ~ *gifts upon someone.* — *vi.* (P2A,3) **1** flow in a steady stream. 흐르다. ¶ *Tear poured from her eyes.* 그녀의 눈에서 눈물이 흘러내렸다. **2** rain or fall heavily. (비 따위가) 억수같이 퍼붓다. ¶ *The rain poured down during the storm.* 폭풍이 치는 동안 비가 억수같이 퍼부었다 / 《*prov.*》 *It never rains but it pours.* 왔다 하면 장대비다; 화불단행(禍不單行). **3** 《*into*》 rush in a crowd. 밀어닥치다; 쇄도하다. ¶ *People poured out of* 〔*into*〕 *the building.* 사람들이 건물에서 쏟아져 나왔다〔에 몰려 들어갔다〕.

pour cold water on, discourage. …의 기를 죽이다.

pour in, come one after another. 연이어 오다.

pour oil on troubled waters, settle trouble peacefully. 분쟁을 원만히 수습하다.

— *n.* Ⓒ a heavy rain. 억수; 호우. [F.]

pout [paut] *vt., vi.* (P6,7; 1) push out the lips to show contempt, displeasure, etc. (입을) 삐죽거리다; 토라지다. ¶ *a pouting child* 토라진 아이 / ~ (*out*) *the lips* 입을 삐죽거리다. — *n.* Ⓒ the act of pouting. 입을 삐죽거림; 실쭉거림. [? O.N.]

·pov·er·ty [pávərti / pɔ́v-] *n.* Ⓤ **1** the state of being poor. 가난. ¶ *be brought up in* ~ 가난하게 자라다 / *rise out of* ~ 입신하여 가난에서 벗어나다 / *Being out of work causes* ~. 직업을 잃으면 가난해진다. **2** 《*of, in*》 lack of something essential or necessary; poorness. 결핍; 부족. ¶ ~ *of thought* 〔*imagination*〕 사상〔상상력〕의 빈곤 / ~ *in vitamins* 비타민 결핍 / *The poor crops were due to the* ~ *of the soil.* 흉작은 지력(地力)이 약한 탓이었다. [→pauper]

pov·er·ty-strick·en [pávərtistrikən / pɔ́v-] *adj.* very poor. 가난에 시달린. ¶ *a* ~ *people* 가난에 찌든 사람들.

:pow·der [páudər] *n.* Ⓤ **1** any dry, solid, dustlike substance; fine dust. 가루; 분말. ¶ *soap* ~ 가루 비누 / *grind into* ~ 가루로 만들다; 산산이 부수다. **2** a drug in the form of powder. 가루약. ¶ *The doctor gave her powders to take after meals.* 의사는 그녀에게 식후에 먹을 가루약을 주었다. **3** any special kind of powder applied to hair, teeth, face, etc. as a cosmetic. 가루 치약; 분; (예전의) 머리분. ¶ *put* ~ *on one's cheeks* 볼에 분을 바르다. **4** gun powder. 화약. ¶ *a* ~ *factory.*

keep one's powder dry, prepare for trouble. 만일에 대비하다.

not worth the powder and shot, not worth the trouble. 애쓸 필요가 없는.

smell a powder, have the experience of war. 실전을 경험하다.

— *vt.* (P6,13) **1** make (something) into powder. …을 가루로 하다; 분쇄하다. **2** cover (something) with powder; sprinkle. …에 가루를 뿌리다; 분을 바르다. ¶ *The woman was thickly powdered.* 그 여자는 짙은 화장을 하고 있었다 / ~ *cake with sugar* 과자에 설탕을 뿌리다 / *The ground was lightly powdered with snow.* 땅엔 엷게 눈이 깔려 있었다.

— *vi.* **1** (P1) become powder. 가루가 되다. **2** use powder on the face, hair, etc. 화장하다; 분칠하다. [L. *pulvis*]

pow·dered [páudərd] *adj.* made into powder; covered with powder. 가루(모양)의; 분을 바른.

pow·der-flask [páudərflæ̀sk, -flɑ̀ːsk] *n.* a bottle or can for carrying gunpowder. (구식 총의 휴대용) 화약통〔병〕.

pow·der-horn [páudərhɔ̀ːrn] *n.* a powder-flask made of the horn of an animal. (뿔로 된) 화약통(cf. *powder-flask*).

pow·der-mag·a·zine [páudərmæ̀gəziːn] *n.* a place where gunpowder is stored. 화약고(庫).

powder mill [⌐-⌐] *n.* a factory where gunpowder is produced. 화약 공장.

powder puff [⌐-⌐] *n.* Ⓤ a small, soft pad for applying cosmetic powder to the skin. 분첩; 퍼프.

pow·der·y [páudəri] *adj.* **1** of or like powder. 가루의〔같은〕. ¶ ~ *snow* 가루눈. **2** covered with powder. 가루투성이의. **3** that can be easily made into powder. 무른; 푸석푸석한. ¶ *a* ~ *rock* 푸석돌.

:pow·er [páuər] *n.* **1** Ⓒ ability to do something. 능력; 힘. ¶ *the* ~ *of movement* 〔*thought*〕 활동〔사고(思考)〕력 / *put it out of someone's* ~ *to do* 아무를 …할 수 없게 만들다 / *It is not in my* ~ *to do it.* 그 일은 내 능력 밖이다 / *The fairy had* ~ *to change into different shapes.* 요정은 여러 다른 모습으로 변할 수 있었다. **2** Ⓤ strengh; force; energy. 힘; 체력; 정력; 동력(動力). ¶ *obtain* ~ *from water* 물에서 동력을 얻다 / *More* ~ *to your elbow!* 기운 내라 / *lose one's powers* 힘이 빠지다 / 《*colloq.*》 *More* ~ *to you.* 더욱 건강하시기를 / *His powers are failing.* 쇠약해지고 있다. **3** Ⓤ authority; influence; control. 권력; 지배력. ¶ *the party in* ~ 여당; 집권당 / *I have* ~ *over them.* 나는 그들을 내 마음대로 할 수 있다 / *a* ~ *of attorney* 위임장 / *They voted to give the police more* ~. 그들은 경찰에게 더 많은 권한을 주기로 표결했다. **4** Ⓒ a person of great authority or influence; 《usu. *pl.*》 a nation having authority or influence. 세력가; 유력〔권력〕자; 강대국.

¶ *the Great Powers* 열강 / *a sea* ~ 해군력(국(國)) / *The treaty was signed by five powers.* 조약은 5대 강국에 의하여 조인되었다. **5** Ⓤ 《math.》 the result gained by multiplying a number by itself. 거듭제곱; 멱(冪). ¶ *16 is the fourth* ~ *of 2.* 16은 2의 네제곱이다. **6** Ⓒ 《*colloq.*》 a large number or amount. 다수; 대량. ¶ *a* ~ *of work* (*people*) 많은 일(사람). **7** Ⓤ the magnifying capacity of a lens. 렌즈의 배율. ¶ *a telescope of high* ~ 배율이 큰 망원경. **8** Ⓤ 《phys.》 energy used to do work; the rate at which work is done. 동력; 효력; 공률(工率). ¶ *a fifty candle-power electric bulb* 50 촉짜리 전구.

the powers that be, 《*colloq.*》 the authorities; persons in authority. 당국(자); (당시의) 권력자; 요로(要路).

— *adj.* **1** producing or supplying power. 동력을 내는. ¶ *a* ~ *plant* 발전소. **2** operated by engines or motors. 동력으로 움직이는. ¶ ~ *tools* 전력으로 움직이는 기구. [L. *potis* able]

:pow·er·ful [páuərfəl] *adj.* having great force, authority or influence; full of power; having considerable effects on other bodies. 강력한; 유력한; (약 따위가) 효과가 있는. ¶ *a* ~ *nation* 강국 / *a* ~ *odor* 강한(독한) 냄새 / *a* ~ *politician* 유력한 정치가 / *a* ~ *medicine* 잘 듣는 약 / *a* ~ *speech* 호소력이 있는 연설.

pow·er·ful·ly [páuərfəli] *adv.* in a powerful manner; with great power or strength; strongly. 강하게; 유력하게.

pow·er·house [páuərhàus] *n.* Ⓒ **1** a building where electric power is produced. 발전소. **2** 《*colloq.*》 an energetic person. 정력가; 추진력이 있는 사람.

pow·er·less [páuərlis] *adj.* having no power, authority or ability; helpless. 무력한. ¶ *I am* ~ *to do anything.* 내겐 어떠한 것도 할 힘이 없다 / *The mouse was* ~ *in the cat's claws.* 고양이 발톱에 쥐는 죽은 거나 다름 없었다.

power politics [⌐– ⌐––] *n. pl.* international politics in which the actions of nations are based on armed forces. 무력 외교.

power shovel [⌐– ⌐–] *n.* a large digging machine operated by an electric motor. 동력(動力)삽《굴착 기계》.

power station [⌐–⌐––] *n.* a powerhouse. 발전소.

pox [paks / pɔks] *n.* Ⓤ any disease that covers the skin with spots or sores. 발진(發疹)하는 병《천연두·수두·두창(痘瘡) 따위》. [→pock]

pp. **1** pages. **2** past participle.

p.p. **1** past participle. **2** postpaid.

prac·ti·ca·bil·i·ty [prӕktikəbíləti] *n.* Ⓤ the state or quality of being practicable. 실행할 수 있음; 실용성. [↓]

prac·ti·ca·ble [prǽktikəbəl] *adj.* that can be done, practiced or used. 실행할 수 있는; 실용적인; 사용 가능한. ¶ *a* ~ *road* 다닐 수 있는 길 / ~ *idea* 실용적인 사고(생각). [→practice]

:prac·ti·cal [prǽktikəl] *adj.* **1** of action; obtained through practice rather than theory. 실지의; 실제의. ¶ ~ *difficulty* 사실상(현실상)의 어려움 / *a* ~ *nurse* (정규 훈련을 받지 않은) 준 간호사 / *adopt* ~ *measures* 실제적인 조처를 취하다 / ~ *joke* (말뿐이 아니라 실제적인) 짓궂은 장난. **2** able; experienced. 유능한; 경험이 많은. ¶ *a* ~ *engineer* 노련한 기사. **3** useful; that can be used; good at practical affairs. 쓸모 있는; 실용적인; 실제(실무)에 적합한. ¶ ~ *knowledge* 실용적인 지식 / *a* ~ *mind* 실제적인 사람 / *a very* ~ *young man* 실무에 아주 밝은 젊은이. **4** having an inclination to action rather than thinking. 실행적인. ¶ *a* ~ *scheme* 실천 계획. **5** being so in actual fact. (명목은 다르나) 실질(사실)상의. ¶ *the* ~ *ruler of the country* 그 나라의 사실상의 지배자. [→practice]

:prac·ti·cal·ly [prǽktikəli] *adv.* **1** in a practical manner (way); in practice; really. 실제로; 사실상. ¶ *Practically, it is impossible.* 사실이지 그건 불가능하다 / *know a language* ~ 어떤 언어를 실지로 알다 / *Practically speaking, there is no more to be done.* 사실상 더 이상은 할 일이 없다. **2** 《*colloq.*》 almost. 거의. ¶ *There was* ~ *nothing left in it.* 그 안에는 거의 아무것도 남아 있지 않았다 / *I have* ~ *finished.* 나는 거의 끝마쳤다.

:prac·tice, 《Brit.》 **-tise** [prǽktis] *n.* **1** Ⓤ the act of carrying out something; performance. 실행; 실시. ¶ *Theory is one thing and* ~ *is another.* 이론과 실천은 별개 문제다 / *put in* (*into*) ~ 실행하다 / *A good idea, but will it work in* ~*?* 좋은 생각이다. 그러나 실행이 될까. **2** Ⓒ a habit or custom. 습관; 풍습; 관례. ¶ *It's my* ~ *to get up early.* 일찍 기상하는 것이 내 습관이다 / *a matter of common* (*daily*) ~ 보통(일상)의 일; 다반사 / *make a* ~ *of daily exercise* 매일 운동하는 것을 습관으로 하다. **3** Ⓤ ⓐ the act of doing something over and over; exercise. 연습; 실습. ¶ 《*prov.*》 *Practice makes perfect.* 배우기보다 익혀라 / *two hours'* ~ *at the piano* 두 시간 피아노 연습. ⓑ the skill gained by experience or exercise. (연습으로 익힌) 기술; 기량. **4** Ⓤ the business of a doctor or a lawyer; the patients; clients dealt with by them. (의사·변호사 등의) 업무; 환자; 사건 의뢰인. ¶ *The doctor* (*lawyer*) *has a large* ~. 그 의사(변호사)는 환자가(사건 의뢰인이) 많다 / *give up* (*sell*) *one's* ~ (의사·변호사) 영업을 그만두다(남에게 양도하다).

in practice, **a**) not as a mere theory but based on actual experience. 사실상; 실제로. **b**) in the course of practice. 연습해서. **c**) at work. 개업해서. ¶ *He is in* ~ *as a physician* (*lawyer*). 그는 의사(변호사)로 개업하고 있다.

make a practice of, do (something) habitually. 늘 …하다; …을 습관으로 하다.

out of practice, poor at or unable to do (something) because of lack of exercise or training. 연습 부족으로 서툴러. ¶ *I was out of ~ at golfing.* 나는 (연습을 안 해) 골프가 서툴렀다.

— *vt.* **1** (P6,9) do (something) habitually or repeatedly. …을 늘〔되풀이〕 행하다. ¶ *~ early sleeping and early rising* 늘 일찍 자고 일찍 일어나다. **2** (P6,9) put (something) into actual use. …을 실행〔실시〕하다. ¶ *Practice what you preach.* 네 말을 실천에 옮겨라 / *~ kindness* 친절을 행하다. **3** (P6,9) do exercise in (something). …을 연습하다. ¶ *~ the piano = ~ playing the piano* 피아노 연습을 하다. **4** (P6,9) work at (something) as a profession, etc. …을 개업하다; …에 종사하다. ¶ *~ medicine* 〔*law*〕 의사〔변호사〕 개업을 하다. **5** (P6,13) train; accustom. …에게 가르치다; 버릇들게 하다. ¶ *~ children in habits of obedience* 아이들에게 순종하는 버릇을 가르치다.

— *vi.* **1** (P1,3) exercise oneself. 연습하다. ¶ *~ at the piano* 피아노 연습하다. **2** (P1) work at a profession. 개업하다. ¶ *~ at the bar* 변호사 개업을 하다. **3** try to take advantage. 약점을 이용하다. ¶ *~ on another's weakness* 남의 약점을 이용하다. **4** (P4) make a custom of doing. 습관적으로 하다. ¶ *~ to deceive* 상습적으로 속이다. [Gk. *prassō* do]

prac·ticed, 《Brit.》 **-tised** [prǽktist] *adj.* skilled through experience; learned through practice; expert. 숙달된; 노련한; 연습을 쌓은. ¶ *a ~ hand at tennis* 노련한 테니스 선수 / *a ~ liar* 직업적인 거짓말쟁이.

:prac·tise [prǽktis] *v.* 《Brit.》 =practice.

prac·ti·tion·er [præktíʃənər] *n.* Ⓒ a person who is engaged in a profession, esp. medicine or law. 개업자《특히 개업의·변호사 등》. ¶ *a medical ~* 개업의 / *a general ~* 일반 개업의《전문의에 대하여》. [→practice]

prae·tor [príːtər] *n.* Ⓒ a public officer of ancient Rome who managed civil justice. 집정관(執政官). [L.]

prag·mat·ic [prægmǽtik], **-i·cal** [-ikəl] *adj.* **1** judging by practical value or results; of pragmatism. 실용적인; 실용주의의. **2** dogmatic. 독단적〔독선적〕인. **3** active in affairs; meddlesome. 활동적인; 참견을 잘하는. ¶ *a ~ kind of person* 오지랖 넓은〔주제넘은〕 사람. [→practice]

prag·ma·tism [prǽgmətìzəm] *n.* Ⓤ **1** 《philos.》 the theory that the value of a conception depends upon its practical results or effects. 실용주의; 프래그머티즘. **2** dogmatism. 독단. **3** the act of interfering in the matters of others. 오지랖 넓은 짓.

prair·ie [prέəri] *n.* Ⓒ a large, treeless grassland, esp. in the central area of the United States. (특히 북아메리카 중앙부의) 대초원. [L. *pratum* meadow]

prairie schooner [⌐-⌐-] *n.* 《U.S.》 a large covered wagon used by pioneers to travel to the West. (서부 개척 시대의) 대형 포장 마차.

:praise [preiz] *n.* Ⓤ **1** the act of speaking well of a thing or person; the expression of approval. 칭찬; 칭송. ¶ *win high ~* 대단한 칭찬을 받다 / *His conduct deserves* 〔*is beyond*〕 *all ~.* 그의 행동은 극구 칭찬받을 만하다〔이루 다 칭찬할 길이 없다〕 / *speak* 〔*write*〕 *in ~ of a friend* 친구를 칭찬하는 말을 하다〔쓰다〕. **2** the act or words of worshipping God. (신에의) 찬미. — *vt.* (P6,7,13) **1** speak well of (someone or something). …을 칭찬하다. ¶ *~ someone to the skies* 아무를 극구 칭찬하다. **2** glorify and worship (God). (신을) 찬미하다. [→price]

praise·wor·thy [préizwə̀ːrði] *adj.* deserving praise; commendable. 칭찬할 만한.

pram [præm] *n.* Ⓒ 《Brit. *colloq.*》 a baby carriage. 유모차《perambulator의 약자》.

prance [præns, prɑːns] *vi.* (P1,2A) **1** 《*along*》 (of horses) spring or bound forward on the hind legs. (말이) 뒷발로 겅정겅정 뛰(어 다니)다. **2** (of persons) walk in a proud, arrogant manner; jump about gaily. (사람이) 거들먹거리며 걷다; 껑충껑충 뛰다. [? O.F.]

prank [præŋk] *n.* Ⓒ a mischievous or playful trick. (짓궂은) 장난. ¶ *play pranks on someone* 아무를 놀리다 / *The fairy Puck liked to play pranks on people.* 요정 퍽은 사람들에게 짓궂은 장난을 잘했다. — *vt.* (P6) **1** dress up for show. …을 차려입다; 성장(盛裝)하다. ¶ *~ oneself out with fine clothes* 한껏 성장하다. **2** ornament. …을 장식하다. ¶ *meadows pranked with flowers* 꽃이 만발한 목장. [? Du.]

prate [preit] *vi., vt.* (P1,2A; 6,7) talk much about (something) foolishly or idly. (쓸데없이) 지껄이다; 수다떨다. ¶ *~ the news all over the town* 그 일을 온 동네에 퍼뜨리고 다니다. — *n.* Ⓤ foolish talk. 수다. [M.E.]

prat·tle [prǽtl] *vt., vi.* (P6,7; 1,2A) **1** prate. 수다 떨다. **2** talk just like a child. 혀짤배기 소리를 하다; (물 흐르는 소리가) 졸졸거리다. — *n.* Ⓤ **1** foolish talk. 수다; 실없는 소리. **2** childish talk. 혀짤배기 소리. **3** a sound like it. 위와 유사한 소리. ¶ 《*fig.*》 *the ~ of the brook* 졸졸거리는 시냇물 소리. [→prate]

prawn [prɔːn] *n.* Ⓒ an edible shellfish like a shrimp. 참새우 무리. [M.E.]

:pray [prei] *vi., vt.* (P1,2A; 6,11,15,20) **1** 《*for*》 offer praise or an earnest appeal, esp. to God. (…을) 빌다; 기도하다. ¶ *I prayed that I might be forgiven.* 용서를 빌었다 / *We go to church to ~.* 교회에 기도하러 간다. **2** 《*for*》 ask or beg earnestly for (something). (…을) 간청〔기원〕하다. ¶ *~ God's forgiveness and mercy* 하느님의 용서와 자비를 기원하다 / *~ for pardon* 용서를 빌다. **3** 《the elliptical form of *'I pray you'*》 please. 바라건대; 아무쪼록. ¶ *Pray let me hear from you.* 아무쪼록 소식을 전해 주시오 / *Pray sit down.* 어서 앉으십시오 / *Tell me the reason,* ~*!* 어디, 까닭이나 말씀해 주시오. [L. *precor*]

*•**pray·er**[1] [préiər] *n.* Ⓒ a person who prays. 기도하는[비는] 사람.

:**prayer**[2] [prɛər] *n.* Ⓒ **1** the act of praying. 빌기; 기도. ¶ *kneel in* ~ 무릎 꿇고 기도하다. **2** the words used in praying. 기도문. ¶ *the Lord's Prayer* 주기도문. **3** an earnest request. 소원; 간청. ¶ *an unspoken* ~ 비원(祕願) / *a humble petition and* ~ 하잘것없는 기도. **4** 《often *pl.*》 a religious service consisting chiefly of prayers. 기도식(式). ¶ *family prayers* 가족 예배 / *the morning* [*evening*] ~ 아침[저녁] 예배. [*pray*]

prayer book [⌐- ⌐] *n.* **1** a book of religious prayer. 기도서. **2** 《*P- B-*》 the Book of Common Prayer used in services of the Church of England. (영국 국교의) 기도서.

pre- [pri:-, pri-, prə-] *pref.* **1** before in time. '이전'의 뜻. ¶ *prewar* 전전(戰前). **2** before in place. '(장소적으로) 앞'의 뜻. ¶ *prealtar* 제단 앞. **3** before in rank or order. '(순서 등이) 앞, 먼저'의 뜻. ¶ *prejudge* 미리 판단하다; 속단하다. [L. *prae*]

:**preach** [pri:tʃ] *vi.* (P1,3) **1** speak to people about religion. 전도하다. ¶ ~ *to the heathen* 이교도에 전도하다. **2** give advice on a moral or religious subject; lecture. 설교하다; 타이르다; 설유(說諭)하다; 잔소리하다. ¶ *Stop preaching!* 설교는 그만하시오 / *She is too fond of preaching.* 그 여잔 걸핏하면 잔소리다 / ~ *against smoking* 흡연의 해독을 설유하다.

— *vt.* (P6,11,13) **1** speak and teach (a sermon). …을 설교하다. **2** make (something) known by preaching; urge (something) strongly. …을 전도하다; 타일러 가르치다; 고취하다. ¶ ~ *the Gospel* 복음을 전도하다 / ~ *a good sermon* 훌륭한 설교를 하다 / ~ *economy* [*patience*] 절약을[인내를] 고취하다 / *He was always preaching exercise and fresh air.* 그는 항상 운동과 신선한 공기를 역설하였다. [→predicate]

*•**preach·er** [prí:tʃər] *n.* Ⓒ a person who preaches; a clergyman. 설교[전도]자.

preach·i·fy [prí:tʃəfài] *vi.* (P1) preach too much. 지루하게 설교하다.

preach·ment [prí:tʃmənt] *n.* Ⓒ a long, dull sermon or speech. 지루한 설교; 장광설.

pre·am·ble [prí:æmbəl, pri:ǽm-] *n.* Ⓒ an introduction to a book or speech; an introducing statement in a legal document. (책·말의) 머리말; 서문; (법률 등의) 전문(前文). ¶ *the* ~ *to the statutes* 법규 전문.
— *vi.* (P1) make a preamble; open with a few remarks. 서론을 말하다; 서두를 꺼내다. [→amble]

pre·ar·range [prì:əréindʒ] *vt.* (P6) arrange (something) beforehand. …을 미리 조정[타협]하다. [pre-]

pre·car·i·ous [prikɛ́əriəs] *adj.* **1** dependent on circumstances or the will of another; uncertain. 타인의 마음에 달린; 불확실한; 불안정한. ¶ *a* ~ *livelihood* 불안정한 생계 / *a* ~ *argument* 불확실한 의론 / ~ *tenure* (언제 빼앗길지 모르는) 불확실한 보유권. **2** dangerous. 위험한. ¶ *the* ~ *life of a fisherman* 위험한 어부 생활 / *a* ~ *state of health* 위태로운 건강 상태. ●**pre·car·i·ous·ly** [-li] *adv.* [→pray]

*•**pre·cau·tion** [prikɔ́:ʃən] *n.* **1** Ⓤ the care taken beforehand to avoid danger or harm. 경계; 조심. ¶ *A few simple precautions will prevent accidents.* 그저 조금만 조심하면 사고를 예방할 수 있다. **2** Ⓒ 《*against*》 something done beforehand to avoid possible danger. 예방책. ¶ *Precautions against fires.* 불조심. [pre-]

pre·cau·tion·ar·y [prikɔ́:ʃənèri / -əri] *adj.* for or using precaution. 예방의. ¶ ~ *measures against catching cold* 감기 예방책.

*•**pre·cede** [prisí:d] *vt., vi.* (P6; 1) **1** go before (something) in place or order. (장소·순서가) 앞서다. ¶ *The regiment was preceded by its band.* 연대 선두에는 군악대가 선도했다 / *The book is preceded by a short life of the writer.* 그 책에는 필자의 짧은 생에 대한 서문이 있다. **2** happen or come before (something) in time. (시간적으로) 먼저 일어나다; 선행하다. ¶ *Lightning precedes thunder.* 번개가 천둥보다 먼저 친다 / *January precedes February.* 1월은 2월에 앞서 있다. **3** be higher than (someone or something) in rank, position, etc. …보다 상위(上位)다. ¶ *Some people think money precedes everything else.* 돈이 다른 무엇보다 낫다고 생각하는 사람이 있다 / *A colonel precedes a lieutenant colonel.* 대령은 중령보다 높다. [pre-; L. *cedo* go]

prec·e·dence [présədəns, prisí:-], **-den·cy** [-dənsi] *n.* Ⓤ the state or right of preceding in time, place, position, importance, etc. 앞섬; 선행; 상위; 우위; 우선권. ¶ *the order of* ~ 석차 / *give someone the* ~ 아무의 우위를 인정하다 / *National defence must take* ~ *over all questions.* 국방이 다른 모든 문제에 우선해야 한다. [↑]

take precedence of, be superior to. …에 우선하다; 상석(上席)이다.

prec·e·dent [présədənt] *n.* Ⓒ something that serves as an example for the future. 선례; 판례(判例). ¶ *The Queen has broken with* ~ *by sending her children to ordinary schools.* 여왕은 자식들을 일반 학교에 보냄으로써 그 전례를 깨뜨렸다. [*precede*]

pre·ced·ing [prisí:diŋ] *adj.* going before; coming before. 앞서의; 전의. ¶ *the* ~ *years* 전년(前年) / *in the* ~ *chapter* 전장(前章)에.

pre·cept [prí:sept] *n.* ⓊⒸ a rule of action

as a guide or an example. 교훈; 격언. ¶ *Example is better than* ~. 모범은 교훈보다 낫다. [→captious] ⌈teacher. 선생; 교사.

pre·cep·tor [priséptər, prí:sep-] *n.* Ⓒ a

pre·cinct [prí:siŋkt] *n.* Ⓒ **1** a space enclosed by walls, esp. within a church. 경내(境內)《특히 교회의》; 구내. ¶ *the school precincts* 학교 구내 / *the sacred precincts* 성역. **2** 《*pl.*》 a neighborhood; environs. 부근; 주변. **3** 《U.S.》 a small area in a town or city marked off for voting or police purposes. 선거〔투표〕구; 경찰 관구. ¶ *police precincts* 경찰 관할 구역 / *There are over 300 election precincts in that city.* 그 시의 투표구는 300 군데가 넘는다. [→cincture]

:pre·cious [préʃəs] *adj.* **1** very valuable; very costly. 귀중한. ¶ ~ *metals* 귀금속 / ~ *stones* 보석. **2** very dear; highly valued; beloved. 소중한. ¶ *my* ~ *child* 내 소중한 자식 / *His kindness is very* ~ *to me.* 그의 친절이 내게는 값진 것이다 / *My* ~*!* 내 사랑《여성》. **3** too refined; affected. 유체스러운; …인 체하는. ¶ *a* ~ *style* 부자연한 문체 / *a* ~ *pronunciation* 점잔빼며 하는 발음. **4** 《*colloq.*》 complete. 전적인; 순전한. ¶ *a* ~ *liar* 순 거짓말쟁이 / *leave things in a* ~ *confusion* 일을 엉망으로 해놓다 / *a* ~ *rascal* 철저한 악당.

— *adv.* 《*colloq.*》 very; extremely. 매우; 대단히. ¶ ~ *little money* 푼돈 / *It's* ~ *cold.* 지독하게 춥다 / *They took* ~ *little notice.* 그들은 전혀 관심이 없었다. [→price]

prec·i·pice [présəpis] *n.* Ⓒ **1** a very steep surface of a cliff. 절벽; 낭떠러지. **2** 《*fig.*》 a dangerous situation; a threatening condition. 위기. ¶ *For years before 1914 Europe stood on the brink of a* ~. 1914년 이전의 수년간 유럽은 위기 일발의 상태에 있었다. [L. *caput* head]

pre·cip·i·tant [prisípətənt] *adj.* falling or rushing head first; acting in a hasty manner; very sudden. 곤두박이치는; 황급한; 느닷없는. ¶ *Our men put the enemy to* ~ *flight.* 아군은 적을 썰물처럼 밀어버렸다.

— *n.* 《chem.》 a substance that causes another substance in solution in a liquid to sink to the bottom in solid form. 침전제(沈澱劑). [↓]

pre·cip·i·tate [prisípətèit] *vt.* (P6) **1** throw (something) downward from a height. 거꾸로 떨어뜨리다. ¶ ~ *a rock down a cliff* 낭떠러지 밑으로 바위를 던지다 / ~ *oneself into a struggle* 싸움에 말려들다〔뛰어들다〕. **2** cause (something) to happen sooner than expected; bring about suddenly. …을 촉진시키다; 돌연 일으키다. ¶ ~ *a failure* 〔*war*〕 실패를〔싸움을〕 재촉하다. **3** ⓐ 《chem.》 separate (a solid part) from a liquid and cause (it) to fall to the bottom. …을 침전시키다. ⓑ 《phys.》 condense (steam) into a liquid. …을 응결(凝結)시키다.

— *vi.* (P1) **1** fall with the head first. 거꾸로 떨어지다. **2** hurry on. 허둥거리다. **3** ⓐ 《chem.》 be separated from a liquid and fall to the bottom. 침전하다. ⓑ 《phys.》 (of steam) be condensed into a liquid. 응결하다.

— [prisípətit, -tèit] *n.* Ⓒ **1** 《chem.》 a substance separated from a liquid. 침전(물). **2** 《phys.》 a liquid condensed from steam. 응결된 수분.

— [prisípətit, -tèit] *adj.* **1** falling with the head first. 거꾸로; 곤두박이로. **2** sudden; hasty. 황급한; 바쁜. ¶ ~ *movement* 다급한 움직임 / *a* ~ *action* 조급〔경솔〕한 행동. [*precipice*]

pre·cip·i·ta·tion [prisìpətéiʃən] *n.* Ⓤ **1** precipitating. 낙하; 투하. **2** violent or headlong rush; impetuous or unpremeditated action. 돌진; 충동적인 행동; 경솔. **3** 《chem.》 the depositing of solid matter from solution. 침전. **4** 《meteor.》 the falling of moisture in the form of rain or dew. 강수(降水); 강우. [↑]

pre·cip·i·tous [prisípətəs] *adj.* of or like a precipice; very steep. 절벽의; 가파른. ¶ ~ *cliff* 가파른 절벽.

pré·cis [preisí:, ⌐—] *n.* Ⓒ (*pl.* **pré·cis** [-z]) 《used as *sing.* and *pl.*》 something that describes the point of a book, etc. within a limited number of words; a summary. (서적 등의) 개략; 대의(大意); 발췌; 요약.

— *vt.* (P6) make a précis of. 요약하다; 발췌하다. [F.]

·pre·cise [prisáis] *adj.* **1** exact; correct. 정확한. ¶ ~ *boundaries* 정확한 경계 / *arrive at the* ~ *moment* 정각에 도착하다. **2** (of a person) strictly following rules; (of behavior) overcareful in details; (of speech) speaking clearly and definitely. 규칙대로의; 꼼꼼한; (말이) 명확한. ¶ *He is* ~ *in his manner.* 그는 매너가 꼼꼼〔딱딱〕하다. [L. *caedo* cut]

·pre·cise·ly [prisáisli] *adv.* **1** in a precise manner. 정확히. **2** (as an answer) just so; quite true; exactly. 꼭 그대로; 틀림없이. ¶ *Tell me* ~ *what you want.* 뭘 원하는지 분명하게 말해라.

pre·ci·sian [prisíʒən] *n.* Ⓒ a person who strictly observes rules, esp. of religion. 꼼꼼한 사람; (종교적) 형식주의자.

pre·ci·sion [prisíʒən] *n.* Ⓤ the quality of being precise; exactness. 정확; 정밀(도). ¶ *the* ~ *of a machine* 기계의 정밀도 / ~ *in movement* 〔*calculation*〕 동작〔계산〕의 정밀.

pre·clude [priklú:d] *vt.* (P6,13) **1** eliminate. …을 없애다. ¶ ~ *all doubts* 모든 의혹을 배제하다. **2** prevent; make (something) impossible in advance. …을 방해하다; 막다; 불가능하게 하다. ¶ *Her care precluded any chance of failure.* 그녀는 조심성이 있어 결코 실수가 없었다 / *I am precluded from coming.* 나는 갈 수가 없다. [→close[1]]

pre·clu·sion [priklú:ʒən] *n.* Ⓤ the act of

precluding; the state of being precluded. 배제; 방해; 방지.

pre·clu·sive [priklúːsiv] *adj.* tending to preclude; preventive. 배제〔제외〕하는; 예방적인.

pre·co·cious [prikóuʃəs] *adj.* showing skill or development earlier than usual. 조숙한. ¶ *a ~ child* 조숙한 아이 / *a ~ growth* 이른 성장 / *She had a ~ knowledge of diseases.* 그녀는 질병에 대한 지식이 유난했다. [pre-, L. *coquo* cook]

pre·coc·i·ty [prikásəti / -kɔ́s-] *n.* Ⓤ the state or quality of being precocious; precociousness. 조숙. [↑]

pre·con·ceive [prìːkənsíːv] *vt.* (P6) form an opinion of (something) beforehand. …을 예상하다. ¶ *a preconceived notion* 선입관 / *The beauty of the scenery surpassed all our preconceived ideas.* 그 아름다운 경치는 애초에 우리의 모든 상상을 초월한 것이었다. [pre-]

pre·con·cep·tion [prìːkənsépʃən] *n.* Ⓒ **1** an opinion formed beforehand. 예상; 선입관. **2** a prejudice. 편견.

pre·con·cert [prìːkənsə́ːrt] *vt.* (P6) settle or arrange (something) beforehand. …을 미리 협정하다; 짜놓다; 손을 쓰다. ¶ *At a preconcerted signal the policemen rushed in.* 미리 약속한 신호에 따라 경찰관들이 뛰어들었다. [pre-]

pre·con·di·tion [prìːkəndíʃən] *n.* the condition that must exist before something can be considered. 전제 조건. — *vt.* (P6) condition in advance. 미리 조정〔대비〕하다. [pre-]

pre·cur·sor [prikə́ːrsər, príːkəːr-] *n.* Ⓒ a forerunner; a presage. 선구〔선각〕자; 전조(前兆); 선구. ¶ *Greek mathematics was the ~ of modern mathematics.* 그리스 수학은 현대 수학의 선구였다. [→courier]

pre·cur·so·ry [prikə́ːrsəri, príːkəːr-] *adj.* indicative of something to follow. 선구의; 선봉의.

pre·da·cious [pridéiʃəs] *adj.* living by eating other animals; predatory. 육식(肉食)의. ¶ *Lions and tigers are ~ animals.* 사자와 호랑이는 육식 동물이다. [↓]

pred·a·to·ry [prédətɔ̀ːri / -təri] *adj.* **1** living by plundering or robbing. 약탈하는; 약탈성의. ¶ *a ~ ruffian* 강도 / *have a ~ nature* 약탈성이 있다 / *a ~ border war* 경계(境界) 약탈전. **2** =predacious. [→prey]

pred·e·ces·sor [prédisèsər / príːdisèsər] *n.* Ⓒ **1** an ancestor. 선조; 조상. **2** a person who comes before another in the same position; a thing that comes before another. 전임자; 먼저 (있던) 것(opp. successor). ¶ *Our new doctor is much younger than his ~.* 새 의사는 전에 있던 분보다 훨씬 더 젊다 / *My present car is much better than its ~.* 지금 차는 먼저 차보다 좋다. [pre-, de-, L. *cedo* go]

pre·des·ti·nate [pridéstənèit] *vt.* (P13,20) **1** 《theol.》 destine (a man's fate) beforehand. (신이) …의 운명을 예정하다. ¶ *We are predestinated to eternal death.* 우리는 영원한 죽음에서 벗어날 수 없게 예정되어 있다. **2** determine beforehand; predestine. …을 예정하다. — [-nit, -nèit] *adj.* **1** determined by God's will. 예정된 운명의. **2** determined beforehand. 예정된. [pre-]

pre·des·ti·na·tion [pridèstənéiʃən] *n.* Ⓤ **1** the act of God of deciding what shall happen. 신의 예정. **2** the act of predestinating; the state of being predestinated. 숙명.

pre·des·tine [pridéstin] *vt.* settle or determine (something) beforehand. …을 운명지우다. ¶ *~ someone to a certain fate* 아무를 어떤 운명으로 예정하다.

pre·de·ter·mi·na·tion [prìːditə̀ːrminéiʃən] *n.* Ⓤ the act of predetermining; the state of being predetermined. 미리 정함; 예정. [↓]

pre·de·ter·mine [prìːditə́ːrmin] *vt.* (P6,13,20) determine or settle (something) beforehand. …을 미리 정하다; 예정하다. ¶ *We met at the predetermined time.* 우리는 약속한 시간에 만났다. [pre-]

pre·dic·a·ment [pridíkəmənt] *n.* Ⓒ **1** a dangerous or unpleasant condition; any condition. 곤경; 궁지; (어떤) 상태. ¶ *Having missed the last train home, Mary was in a real ~.* 집에 가는 막차를 놓쳐 메리는 정말 난감했다. **2** 《log.》 a category. 범주. [↓]

*__pred·i·cate__ [prédikit] *n.* Ⓒ **1** 《gram.》 the part of a sentence expressing something about the subject. (서)술부〔어〕. **2** 《log.》 what is predicated. 빈사(賓辭). — *adj.* 《gram.》 of the predicate. 술어의. ¶ *In "She is young", 'young' is a ~ adjective.* *"She ……"*에서 *'young'*이 서술형용사다. — [-kèit] *vt.* (P6,11) **1** say (something) to be true with certainty; affirm. …을 단언〔단정〕하다. ¶ *We ~ rationality of man.* 우리는 인성이 합리적이라고 단언한다. **2** 《log.》 say something about a subject. …을 서술하다. **3** imply. 내포〔시사〕하다. **4** found or base (a statement, action, etc.) on something. …에 기초를 두다. ¶ *The decisions of the courts are predicated upon the Constitution.* 법정의 판결은 헌법에 기초를 둔다. [L. *dico* declare]

pred·i·ca·tive [prédikèitiv, -kə- / pridíkətiv] *adj.* **1** showing predication. 단정적인. **2** 《gram.》 serving as a predicate. 서술적인(cf. *attributive*).

*__pre·dict__ [pridíkt] *vt., vi.* (P6,11,12; 1) try to make (something) known before it happens; foretell. 예언〔예보〕하다. ¶ *~ a bad crop* 흉작을 예언하다 / *~ the future* 미래를 내다보다. ● **pre·dict·a·ble** [-əbəl] *adj.* **pre·dic·tor** [-ər] *n.* [L. *dico* say]

pre·dic·tion [pridíkʃən] *n.* **1** Ⓤ the act of

predicting; the state of being predicted. 예언; 예보. **2** Ⓒ a thing predicted. 예언한 것; 예보. ¶ *His predictions seldom come true.* 그의 예언은 좀처럼 들어맞지 않는다.

pre·dic·tive [pridíktiv] *adj.* predicting. 예언적인; 예보하는.

pre·di·gest [prì:didʒést, -dai-] *vt.* (P6) make (food) more digestible by a special process before it is eaten. (음식)을 소화가 잘되게 조리하다. [pre-, *digest*]

pre·di·lec·tion [prì:dəlékʃən, prèd-] *n.* Ⓒ a favor; a liking; partiality. 좋아함; 편애(偏愛). ¶ *He has a ~ for rich food.* 좋은 음식만 가려 먹는다. [L. *diligo* love]

pre·dis·pose [prì:dispóuz] *vt.* (P13) (of a disease) give influence on (someone) easily; cause (someone) to incline to something; cause someone to incline to (something). …을 (병에) 걸리기 쉽게 만들다; (남)을 …에 기울게〔좋아하게〕 만들다. ¶ *~ the mind to certain ideas* 마음을 어떤 사상으로 기울게 만들다 / *Exhaustion predisposes someone to illness.* 피로하면 병나기 쉽다 / *A cold predisposes someone to other diseases.* 감기는 만병의 근원이다. [pre-]

pre·dis·po·si·tion [prì:dispəzíʃən] *n.* Ⓒ **1** the quality of being predisposed. 병약한 체질. **2** propensity; tendency. 성질; 경향. ¶ *She has a ~ toward seeing the dark side of things.* 그녀는 사물의 어두운 면을 보려는 경향이 있다.

pre·dom·i·nance [pridámənəns / -dɔ́m-] *n.* Ⓤ the state or quality of being predominant. 우위; 우세; 지배. ¶ *There was a ~ of weeds in the deserted garden.* 황폐한 정원에 풀이 무성했다. [↓]

pre·dom·i·nant [pridámənənt / -dɔ́m-] *adj.* greater in power, number, etc. 우세한; 뛰어난. ● **pre·dom·i·nant·ly** [-li] *adv.* [pre-, L. *domino* rule]

pre·dom·i·nate [pridámənèit / -dɔ́m-] *vi.* (P1,3) be greater in power, number, influence, etc. 우세하다; 뛰어나다. ¶ *In northern areas the pine forests ~ (over deciduous woodland).* 북부 지방에는 (낙엽수림보다는) 소나무들이 잘 자란다.

pre-em·i·nence [priémənəns] *n.* Ⓤ the state or quality of being pre-eminent; excellence. 우위; 우월; 탁월. ¶ *the ~ of Edison among inventors* 발명가들 중에서도 뛰어난 에디슨. [↓]

pre-em·i·nent [priémənənt] *adj.* superior to others. 발군의; 뛰어난; 우수한; 굉장한. ¶ *a ~ position* 유리한 입장; 우위 / *He is ~ among modern poets.* 그는 현대 시인 중에서도 특출한 시인이다. ● **pre-em·i·nent·ly** [-li] *adv.* [pre-]

pre·empt [priémpt] *vt.* (P6) **1** secure before someone else can. …을 선취(先取)하다. ¶ *He came early and preempted a good parking space.* 그는 일찍 와서 좋은 자리에 주차했다. **2** 《U.S.》 occupy (the public land) so as to have the right of preemption. 선매권(先買權)을 얻기 위해 (공유지를) 점유하다. [L. *emo* buy]

pre·emp·tion [priémpʃən] *n.* Ⓤ the act or right of buying something before other people. 선매(권).

preen [pri:n] *vt.* (P6,13) **1** (of a bird) smooth or clean (the feathers) with its bill. (새가 날개)를 부리로 다듬다. **2** dress up (oneself). (자기)의 몸치장을 하다. ¶ *She preens herself in front of the mirror.* 그녀는 거울 앞에서 자기 차림새를 다듬는다. [*prune*]

pre·ex·ist [prì:igzíst] *vi.* (P1) exist before something else. 선재(先在)하다. [pre-]

pre·ex·ist·ence [prì:igzístəns] *n.* Ⓤ existence of the soul before birth. 영혼의 선재(先在); 전세(前世).

pre·ex·ist·ent [prì:igzístənt] *adj.* existing before something else. 선재(先在)하는.

pref. preface; preferred; prefix.

pre·fab [prí:fæ̀b] *n.* Ⓒ 《U.S. *colloq.*》 a prefabricated house. 조립식 주택; 프리패브. — *adj.* prefabricated. 조립식의. [pre-]

pre·fab·ri·cate [pri:fǽbrikèit] *vt.* (P6) **1** make up (something) beforehand. …을 미리 만들다. **2** make up the standard parts of (a house) in a factory. (조립식 주택)의 부분품을 만들다. ¶ *a prefabricated house* 조립식 주택.

***pref·ace** [préfis] *n.* Ⓒ an introduction at the beginning of a book or speech. 서문; 머리말(cf. *prolog*). ¶ *Has your history book a ~?* 당신 역사 책에 머리말이 있소. — *vt.* (P13) introduce (a book or speech) with some statement. …에 서문을 쓰다; (이야기)의 허두를 꺼내다. ¶ *~ one's remarks by an apology* 말하기 앞서 사과부터 하다 / *~ a book by* 〔*with*〕 *a life of the writer* 책의 첫머리에 저자의 약력으로 책의 머리말을 삼다. [pre-, L. *for* speak]

pref·a·to·ry [préfətɔ̀:ri / -təri] *adj.* of a preface; introductory. 머리말〔허두〕의. ¶ *~ remarks in a speech* 연설의 허두. [↑]

pre·fect [prí:fekt] *n.* Ⓒ **1** 《Rom. hist.》 a high official of military and civil affairs in ancient Rome. (고대 로마의) 장관; 제독. **2** a chief official of a department of France. (프랑스의) 지사(知事). **3** 《Brit.》 a student with authority over others in a school. (학교의) 반장. [→fact]

pre·fec·tur·al [priféktʃərəl] *adj.* of a prefecture. 시(市)의; 도(道)의.

***pre·fec·ture** [prí:fektʃər] *n.* **1** Ⓒ an administrative area in certain countries. 시; 도. **2** Ⓤ the office or the term of a prefect. 지사·장관의 직〔임기〕.

:pre·fer [prifə́:r] *vt.* (**-ferred, -fer·ring**) **1** (P6,8,9,11,13) 《*to*》 like (something) better than other things. 오히려 …을 좋아하다. ¶ *Which do you ~?* 어느 것이 좋으냐? / *I ~ autumn to spring.* 봄보다는 가을을 좋아한다 / *I should ~ not to do it.* 그 일은 하고 싶

지 않다 / *He preferred to wait here rather than to go at once.* 그는 곧 가느니보다 여기서 기다리고 싶었다 / *~ death to surrender* 항복하느니 죽음을 택하다 / *Please sit down.— No, thank you, I ~ to stand.* 앉으시오.—고맙습니다만, 서 있는 편이 좋습니다. **2** (P6,13) move (someone) up to a higher rank; promote. …을 승진시키다. ¶ *He was preferred to the position over his boss.* 그는 상사보다 높은 지위에 임명되었다 / *He was preferred to be a bishop.* 그는 주교로 승진됐다. **3** (P6,13) offer (something) for consideration; put forward. …을 제출하다; 제기하다. ¶ *He preferred a charge against me.* 그가 나를 고소했다 / *~ a claim* 〔*request*〕 요구를 내걸다. [L. *fero* carry]

pref·er·a·ble [préfərəbəl] *adj.* more liked; more desirable. 오히려 더 나은. ¶ *English is ~ to geography.* 지리보다는 영어가 좋다 / *Poverty is ~ to ill health.* 병골(病骨)보다는 가난이 낫다.

pref·er·a·bly [préfərəbli] *adv.* by preference; rather. 즐겨; 차라리; 오히려; 되도록이면. ¶ *We want an editor, ~ one who has experience in teaching English.* 편집자가 한 사람 필요한데 되도록이면 영어를 가르친 경력이 있는 사람이면 좋겠다.

***pref·er·ence** [préfərəns] *n.* **1** Ⓤ Ⓒ the act of liking one thing over another. 좋아함; 기호. ¶ *a matter of personal ~* (개개인의) 기호의 문제 / *His ~ is for brandy, rather than whisky.* 그는 위스키보다는 브랜디를 좋아한다. **2** Ⓒ something preferred. (더) 좋아하는 것. ¶ *Her ~ in reading is a fairy tale.* 그녀가 읽기 좋아하는 건 동화다 / *This is my ~.* 내가 좋아하는 건 이거다. **3** the favoring of one above another. 편애. ¶ *A teacher should not show ~ for anyone of his pupils.* 선생은 제자의 어느 누구를 편애해서는 안 된다. **4** Ⓤ the right to choose something first. 우선권. ¶ *offer* 〔*afford*〕 *a ~* 우선권을 주다 / *~ shares* 〔*stocks*〕 우선주(株). **5** 《econ.》 the favoring of one country by discrimination in tariffs, allowing its goods to enter under lower customs duties than those from other countries. (교역상의) 특혜. [→prefer, -ence]

have a preference for, like (something). …을 더 좋아하다.

have the preference, be preferred. 선호되다.

in preference to, rather than (something). …보다는 오히려.

pref·er·en·tial [prèfərénʃəl] *adj.* showing, giving or receiving preference. 우선하는; 차별적인. ¶ *a ~ right* 우선권; 특혜 / *~ treatment* 우대 / *~ duties* 특혜 관세.

pre·fer·ment [prifə́:rmənt] *n.* Ⓤ **1** the act of moving up to a higher rank or position; promotion. 승진. **2** a higher position, esp. in the church. (성직자의) 고위(高位). **3** an office, rank, or honor to which a person is advanced. (승진한) 지위; 계급 (등). [→prefer, -ment]

pre·fig·ure [pri:fígjər] *vt.* **1** (P6) suggest a figure or type of (something) beforehand. …의 모양을 미리 보이다; 예시하다. **2** (P6,11,12) imagine (something) beforehand. …을 예상하다. ● **pre·fig·ure·ment** [-mənt] *n.* [pre-]

pre·fix [prí:fiks] *n.* Ⓒ 《gram.》 a word or syllable put in front of a word. 접두사(cf. *suffix*). —[pri:fíks, ⌐⌐] *vt.* (P6,13) 《*to*》 **1** put at the beginning of (something). …의 앞에 두다. ¶ *~ Mr. to a man's name* 남자 이름 앞에 Mr. 를 붙이다. **2** put (something) as a prefix. …에 접두사를 붙이다. [pre-]

preg·nan·cy [prégnənsi] *n.* Ⓤ **1** the state of being pregnant. 임신. **2** the state of being filled with meaning. 함축성이 있음; 의미심장. [↓]

preg·nant [prégnənt] *adj.* **1** (of a woman) having a child growing in her body. 임신한. ¶ *How long has she been ~?* 그녀가 임신한 지 얼마나 됐소. **2** filled with meaning; full of ideas; significant. 함축성이 있는. ¶ *~ words* 의미심장한 말. **3** abounding; filled. …이 가득한. ¶ *an event ~ with grave consequences* 심각한 결과를 배태한 사건. [pre-, L. *nāsci* to be born]

pre·hen·sile [prihénsil / -sail] *adj.* (of an animal) adapted for holding or seizing. 잡는〔쥐는〕 데 알맞은. ¶ *a monkey's ~ tail* 잡기에 좋게 된 원숭이 꼬리. [L. *prehensus*]

pre·hen·sion [prihénʃən] *n.* grasping; mental apprehension. 이해; 파악; 터득.

pre·his·tor·ic [prì:histɔ́:rik, -tár- / -tɔ́r-] *adj.* **1** of the time before recorded history. 유사 이전의. ¶ *~ man* 선사시대인. **2** 《*colloq.*》 very old; old-fashioned. 아주 오래된; 구식의. ¶ *a ~ joke* 진부한 농담. [pre-]

pre·judge [pri:dʒʌ́dʒ] *vt.* (P6) judge (someone or something) beforehand or without evidence. …을 미리 판단하다; …을 제대로 심리하지 않고 판결하다. ¶ *Try not to ~ the issue.* 그 문제를 속단하지 않도록 해라. [→judge]

***prej·u·dice** [prédʒədis] *n.* **1** Ⓤ Ⓒ an opinion formed without any knowledge or fair judgment; an unreasonable opinion. 편견; 선입관. ¶ *a ~ against popular music* 팝뮤직에 대한 편견 / *race ~* 인종적 편견 / *He has a ~ in our favor* 〔*in favor of Miss White*〕. 그는 우리를〔화이트양을〕 편든다. **2** Ⓤ 《law》 injury; damage. 불이익; (권리) 침해.

in 〔***to the***〕 ***prejudice of,*** so as to injure or damage. …의 손해가 되게끔.

without prejudice, without injuring any claims or rights. 편견 없이; 권리를 침해하지 않고.

— *vt.* (P6,7,13) **1** 《*against, in favor of*》 cause (someone) to have a prejudice. …에게 편견〔선입관〕을 갖게 하다. ¶ *All of them are prejudiced on this subject.* 그들 모두

가 이 문제에 편견을 가지고 있다 / *His voice and manner prejudiced his audience against him.* 그의 음성이나 태도가 청중에게 편견을 갖게 했다. **2** injure or harm, esp. in a law case. (권리 등)을 침해하다. ¶ ~ *someone's reputation* 아무의 신망을 손상하다 / *His past record prejudiced his chances of promotion.* 그의 지난 경력이 승진 기회를 망쳤다. [↑]

prej·u·di·cial [prèdʒədíʃəl] *adj.* causing prejudice, harm or danger. 편견을 품게 하는; 손해를 주는. ¶ *a course of action ~ to someone's interests* 아무에게 불리한 소송.

prel·ate [prélit] *n.* Ⓒ a high-ranking priest or clergyman. 고위 성직자. [L. *latus* bought]

pre·lim [príːlim, prilím] *n.* Ⓒ 《*colloq.*》 = preliminary.

·**pre·lim·i·nar·y** [prilímənèri / -nəri] *adj.* coming before the main thing; introductory; preparatory. 예비의; 준비의. ¶ *a ~ examination* 예비 시험 / *a ~ negotiation* 예비 교섭 / 《*law*》 *a ~ hearing* 예심. —— *n.* Ⓒ (*pl.* **-nar·ies**) **1** a preliminary examination. 예비 시험. **2** 《usu. *pl.*》 introductory actions, steps, etc. 예비 행위; 준비. ¶ *an indispensable ~ to the plan* 계획에 빠질 수 없는 사전 준비 / *without preliminaries* 단도직입적으로 / *He did well in the preliminaries of the contest.* 그는 예선에서 잘 했다. [L. *limen* threshold]

prel·ude [préljuːd, préi-, príː-] *n.* Ⓒ **1** something that comes before and introduces a more important matter. 머리말; 서론; 서문. ¶ *A lie may be the ~ to a quarrel.* 거짓말이 싸움의 발단이 될 수도 있다. **2** 《mus.》 a piece of music that introduces another musical work. 전주곡. —— *vt.* (P6,13) use as a prelude to. …의 서곡이 되다; 허두를 놓다. —— *vi.* (P2) play a musical prelude. 전주곡을 연주하다. [→ludicrous]

pre·ma·ture [prìːmətjúər, ⌐–⌐] *adj.* happening or coming before the proper time; too early; untimely. 조숙한; 올된; 너무 이른. ¶ *a ~ birth* 조산 / *~ death* 요절 / *It is ~ to say now who will win the election next week.* 다음 주의 선거에서 누가 이길지를 지금 말한다는 건 시기상조다. [pre-]

pre·med·i·cal [priːmédikəl] *adj.* preparing for the study of medicine. 의대 예과의. ¶ *a ~ student* 의예과생. [pre-]

pre·med·i·tate [priːmédətèit] *vt.* (P6) 《chiefly in *pp.*》 think about, plan or consider beforehand. 미리 생각[계획]하다. ¶ *a premeditated insult* 계획적인 모욕 / *a premeditated murder* 모살(謀殺) / *a premeditated attack on my reputation.* 내 명성에 대한 계획적인 공격. [pre-]

pre·med·i·ta·tion [priːmèdətéiʃən] *n.* Ⓤ the act of premeditating. 미리 생각함[꾸밈]. ¶ *The jury had to decide if the act was committed with ~.* 배심은 그 행동이 계획적이었는지 여부를 결정해야 했다.

·**pre·mier** [primíər, príːmi-] *n.* Ⓒ the prime minister. 수상. —— *adj.* first in rank, importance, time, etc. 수위의; 최초의. ¶ *take* [*hold*] *the ~ place* 수석이 되다. [→prime]

pre·miere [primíər, -mjέər] *n.* Ⓒ **1** the first public performance of a play. (연극의) 초연(初演). **2** (in a play, etc.) the leading actress. 주연 여배우. [F.]

pre·mier·ship [primíərʃìp, príːmi-] *n.* Ⓤ the office or term of a prime minister. 수상의 직[임기]. [*premier*]

prem·ise [prémis] *n.* Ⓒ **1** 《log.》 a statement used as a foundation from which a conclusion is to be drawn. 전제(前提). ¶ *the major* [*minor*] *~* 대[소]전제. **2** 《*pl.*》 《law》 a fact or thing mentioned beforehand. 전술한 사항[것]. **3** 《*pl.*》 a house or building with its grounds. 집[건물]과 대지. —— *v.* [primáiz, prémis] *vt.* (P11) set forth or state (something) as a premise. …을 전제로 하다[말하다]. —— *vi.* (P1) give a premise. 허두를 놓다; 전제하다. [→missile]

pre·mi·um [príːmiəm] *n.* Ⓒ **1** a reward or prize. 상; 포상금. ¶ *offer a ~ to the man with the highest sales* 최고의 매상을 올린 사람에게 포상을 제공하다. **2** a sum of money above the ordinary amount paid or charged. 할증금; 프리미엄(opp. discount). ¶ *Mr. Brown has to pay six percent interest on his loan and also a ~ of two hundred dollars.* 브라운씨는 대부금에 대한 6%의 이자와 200 달러의 수수료를 내야 한다. **3** an amount of money paid for a contract of insurance. 보험료. **4** the fee paid for training in a trade or profession. (직업 지도 등에 대한) 사례금; 수업료. [pre-, L. *emo* take]

at a premium, a) at a price higher than normal. 액면가 이상으로; 프리미엄을 붙여. b) much in demand; very valuable. 아주 수요가 많은; 진귀한.

put a premium on, give importance to (something); tempt others to prefer (something). …을 중히 여기다; …을 부추기다. ¶ *put a ~ on honesty* 정직을 중히 여기다 / *Mere giving money may put a ~ on idleness.* 단순한 금품 수여는 게으름을 부추길 수 있다.

pre·mo·ni·tion [prìːməníʃən] *n.* Ⓒ **1** an act of warning in advance. 예고; 전조. ¶ *a ~ of flood* 홍수 예고. **2** a feeling that something, esp. harmful or pleasant, is going to happen; foreboding. (불길한) 예감. ¶ *have a ~ of disaster* 재난의 예감이 들다. [pre-]

pre·mon·i·to·ry [primánitɔ̀ːri / -mɔ́nitəri] *adj.* giving warning in advance; acting as a premonition. 예고의; 전조가 되는. ¶ *a ~ symptom* 전구증(前驅症).

pre·na·tal [priːnéitl] *adj.* occurring or existing before birth. 출생 전의. [pre-]

pren·tice [préntis] *n.* Ⓒ 《*arch.*》 =apprentice.

pre·oc·cu·pa·tion [priːɑ̀kjəpéiʃən / -ɔ̀k-] *n.* Ⓤ **1** the act of preoccupying; the state of being preoccupied. 선점(先占); 선취. ¶ *On the site of excavation there is no evidence of* ~. 그 발굴 현장에는 누가 먼저 손댄 흔적이 없다. **2** a state in which the mind is preoccupied; mental absorption. 몰두; 전심. [pre-]

pre·oc·cu·py [priːɑ́kjəpài / -ɔ́k-] *vt.* (**-pied**) (P6) **1** hold all the attention of (someone). (…의 마음)을 사로잡다; …에 몰두하게 하다. ¶ *My mind is preoccupied with private care.* 내 마음은 내 걱정거리로 꽉 차 있다. **2** take possession of (land, etc.) before others. (땅 따위)를 선점(先占)하다. ¶ *My favorite seat had been preoccupied.* 내가 좋아하는 자리는 누가 먼저 차지했었다. [pre-, *occupy*]

pre·or·dain [prìːɔːrdéin] *vt.* (P6,11) decide (a fate, etc.) beforehand. (운명)을 미리 정하다. ¶ *I sometimes think our failure was preordained.* 우리가 실패한 것도 운명이라는 생각이 가끔 든다. [pre-]

prep [prep] *adj.* 《*colloq.*》 preparatory. 예비〔준비〕의. —— *n.* **1** Ⓒ 《U.S. *colloq.*》 a preparatory school. 예과; 예비교. **2** = preparation.

prep. **1** preparation. **2** preparatory. **3** preposition.

pre·paid [priːpéid] *v.* p. and pp. of **prepay.** —— *adj., adv.* paid in advance; paid for beforehand. 선불한; 선불하여. ¶ *Send this shipment* ~. 요금 선불된 이 선적 화물을 보내시오. [*prepay*]

:prep·a·ra·tion [prèpəréiʃən] *n.* **1** ⓊⒸ the act of preparing; the state of being prepared. 준비; 예비. ¶ *The* ~ *of dinner took an hour.* 정찬 준비에 한 시간 걸렸다 / *make* ~ *for* …의 준비를 하다 / *He spent most of his time in* ~ *for journey.* 여행 준비에 거의 모든 시간을 보냈다. **2** Ⓒ things done to prepare for something; food, medicine, or other substances made for special use. 준비된 것; 조리된 음식; 조제된 약. **3** 《*pl.*》 things to get ready for something. 준비(물). ¶ *preparations for war* 〔*election*〕 전쟁〔선거〕의 사전 준비. **4** Ⓤ preparedness. 준비; 각오. [*prepare*]

pre·par·a·tive [pripǽrətiv] *adj.* preparatory. 준비의. —— *n.* Ⓤ something that serves to prepare. 예비; 준비.

pre·par·a·to·ry [pripǽrətɔ̀ːri / -təri] *adj.* **1** preparing. 준비의; 예비의. ¶ ~ *training* 준비 훈련 / *a* ~ *stage* 준비 단계. **2** undergoing preparation for entering college. 대학 입학 준비의. [↓]

preparatory to, **a**) previous to. …에 앞서. ¶ *He made his will* ~ *to his voyage round the world.* 세계 일주 항해에 앞서 그는 유서를 작성했다. **b**) in preparation for. …의 준비로.

preparatory school [-ˊ--- ˋ] *n.* **1** 《Brit.》 a private school for pupils up to the age of 13, where they are made ready to attend a school for older pupils, public school. 진학을 위한 사립 예비교. **2** 《U.S.》 a private school that makes pupils ready for college. 대학 진학을 위한 사립 학교.

:pre·pare [pripέər] *vt.* **1** (P6,13) 《*for*》 make (something) ready for a particular purpose or use; fit; train. …을 준비〔채비〕하다. ¶ ~ *a meal* 식사 준비를 하다 / ~ *a house for habitation* 살 집을 마련하다 / ~ *ground for crops* (갈거나 해서) 농사 지을 땅을 만들다. **2** (P6) get ready for (a lesson, etc.) by study, work, practice, etc. …을 예습하다; …을 미리 조사〔준비〕를 하다. ¶ ~ *one's lessons* 학과를 예습하다 / *He prepared a speech he intended to make.* 자기가 할 연설을 준비했다. **3** (P6,8,13) put (someone) in a desired state of mind; make (someone) ready. …에게 마음의 준비를 갖추게 하다; 준비하게 하다. ¶ ~ *a boy for college* 소년에게 대학진학 준비를 시키다 / *I prepared him for the bad news.* 나는 그에게 나쁜 소식에 대한 마음의 준비를 하게 했다 / *He prepares himself to die.* = *He prepares himself for death.* 그는 죽음에 대해 각오하고 있다 / ~ *the mind to receive new idea* 새로운 사고를 받아들일 마음의 준비를 하다. **4** (P6) make or form (chemical products, etc.). (약 따위)를 조제〔조합〕하다. ¶ ~ *a drug* / ~ *a doctor's prescription* 의사의 처방약을 조제하다. **5** (P6) supply (something) with what is needed. …에 필요한 것을 갖추다. ¶ *They prepared an expedition.* 그들은 탐험 준비를 갖추었다. —— *vi.* (P3,4) 《*for*》 make things ready; make oneself ready in one's mind. 준비하다; 대비하다; 마음의 준비를 하다. ¶ ~ *for a journey* / ~ *for an emergency* 만일에 대비하다 / *She prepares to go to school early.* 그녀는 일찍 등교할 준비를 한다 / ~ *to go a long way* 먼 길을 떠날 준비를 하다 / ~ *for the worst* 최악에 대비하다; 만일의 각오를 하다. [pre-, L. *paro* set in order, make ready]

pre·par·ed·ness [pripέəridnis, -pέərd-] *n.* Ⓤ **1** the state of being prepared. 준비; 대비; 각오. **2** the possession of enough military forces. 군비. ¶ *The country is lack of military* ~. 그 나라의 군비는 부족하다.

pre·pay [priːpéi] *vt.* (P6) (**-paid**) pay for (something) in advance. …을 선불하다. ¶ ~ *a reply to a telegram* 전보의 반신료를 선불하다 / *Send us a prepaid envelope.* 우표가 있는 (빈)봉투를 보내시오. [pre-]

pre·pay·ment [priːpéimənt] *n.* ⓊⒸ payment in advance. 선불.

pre·pon·der·ance [pripɑ́ndərəns / -pɔ́n-] *n.* Ⓤ the state of being greater in weight, amount, power, influence, etc. (무게·수·힘·영향 등에서의) 우세. ¶ *There was a* ~ *of female students in the music department.* 음악부에는 여학생이 압도적으로 많았다. [→ponder]

pre·pon·der·ant [pripándərənt / -pɔ́n-] *adj.* **1** great in weight. 무게에서 우세한. **2** superior in number, power, influence. (수·힘에서) 우세한. ¶ *a ~ influence* 강한 영향력. **3** chief; most important. 주된; 주요한. ¶ *a ~ characteristic* 주된 특징. ● **pre·pon·der·ant·ly** [-li] *adv.*

pre·pon·der·ate [pripándərèit / -pɔ́n-] *vi.* (P1,2A) **1** be heavier than something else. 무게가 더 나가다. **2** ⓐ exceed in power, number, amount, influence, etc. (힘·수·양 등에서) 우세하다. ¶ *In November cloudy weather preponderates over sunshine.* 11월에는 갠 날보다 흐린 날이 더 많다. ⓑ be chief; be most important. 주를 이루다; 주요하다. ¶ *Oaks and maples ~ in these woods.* 오크와 단풍나무가 이 숲의 주된 나무다.

:**prep·o·si·tion** [prèpəzíʃən] *n.* Ⓒ 《gram.》 a word that connects a noun or pronoun with other words to show a relation between them. 전치사. [pre-]

prep·o·si·tion·al [prèpəzíʃənəl] *adj.* of a preposition; serving as a preposition. 전치사적인. ¶ *a ~ phrase* 전치사구(句).

pre·pos·sess [prì:pəzés] *vt.* (P6,7) 《usu. in *passive*》 **1** fill (someone) with a favorable feeling or opinion; prejudice. …에 미리 (좋은 인상·호감)을 갖게 하다. ¶ *I was prepossessed by the boy's frank face and modest behavior from the moment he entered.* 나는 소년이 들어서자마자 그의 솔직한 인상과 얌전한 행동이 마음에 들었다. **2** imbue or inspire (someone) with a feeling, idea, etc. (감정·관념 등을) 미리 …에게 갖게 하다. ¶ *His early training prepossessed him toward religion.* 어릴 적의 그의 교육이 종교에 관심을 갖게 했다. [pre-]

pre·pos·sess·ing [prì:pəzésiŋ] *adj.* making a favorable impression; attractive. 호감이 가는. ¶ *~ manner.*

pre·pos·ses·sion [prì:pəzéʃən] *n.* Ⓒ an impression in a favorable sense formed beforehand; a favorable prejudice or a liking. 선입관; 편견; 편애. ¶ *foolish prepossessions against organized society* 조직 사회에 반발하는 어리석은 편견 / *A well-written letter applying for a position will creat a ~ in the writer's favor.* 잘 쓰인 구직(求職) 편지는 그 쓴 사람에게 호감이 가게 한다.

pre·pos·ter·ous [pripástərəs / -pɔ́s-] *adj.* contrary to reason, nature or common sense; ridiculous; absurd. 터무니 없는; 사리에 어긋나는; 어리석은. ¶ *It is ~ to imagine that unqualified people can run a company.* 무자격자가 회사를 꾸려갈 수 있을 것이라는 생각은 어불성설이다. [pre-]

pre·req·ui·site [pri:rékwəzit] *adj.* required beforehand. 미리〔사전에〕 필요한. —*n.* Ⓒ 《*for, to*》 something required beforehand. 전제 조건. ¶ *This course is a ~ to more advanced studies.* 이 과정은 그 이상의 고등 학문 연구의 필요〔선행〕 조건이다. [pre-]

pre·rog·a·tive [prirágətiv / -rɔ́g-] *n.* Ⓒ a right or privilege that belongs to a person, class, etc. according to rank or position. 특권; 특전. ¶ *the ~ of mercy* 사면권 / *the royal ~* 대권(大權) / *It is within my ~ to do….* …하는 것은 내 특권〔자유〕이다. [↑, →rogation]

Pres. President.

pres. president; presidency; presumptive.

pre·sage [présidʒ] *n.* Ⓒ **1** a sign foretelling that something is going to happen; an omen. 전조(前兆); 조짐. ¶ *a ~ of a storm* 폭풍의 전조. **2** a feeling that something is going to happen. 예감. —[présidʒ, priséidʒ] *vt.* (P6) **1** have a presentiment of (something). …을 예감하다. **2** give a sign of (something) to happen. …을 예시하다. **3** foretell; predict. …을 예고〔예언〕하다. ¶ *The black clouds ~ a storm.* 검은 구름은 폭풍을 예고한다. [L. *sagio* discern]

pres·by·ter [prézbitər] *n.* Ⓒ **1** an elder in the early Christian Church. (초기 교회의) 장로(長老). **2** an elder in authority in the Presbyterian Church. (장로 교회의) 장로. **3** a priest or minister in the Episcopal Church. (영국 국교의) 목사. [Gk. *presbuteros* older]

Pres·by·te·ri·an [prèzbitíəriən] *adj.* of church government by presbyters; of the Presbyterian Church. 장로제(制)의; 장로 교회의. —*n.* Ⓒ a member of the Presbyterian Church. 장로 교회 신도.

pres·by·ter·y [prézbitèri / -təri] *n.* Ⓒ (*pl.* **-ter·ies**) 《religion》 **1** a court consisting of all the ministers and a few elders from a district. 장로회. **2** the district under the control of such a court. 장로회 관할구. **3** the house of the parish priest. 사제관(司祭館).

pre·school [prí:skú:l] *adj.* before the age of entering an elementary school. 취학 전의; 학령(學齡) 미달의. [pre-]

pre·sci·ence [préʃiəns, prí:-] *n.* Ⓤ the knowledge of things before they happen; foreknowledge; foresight. 예지(豫知); 미리 앎; 선견(先見). ¶ *People used to believe that animals have an instinctive ~ of the approach of danger.* 사람들은 동물에겐 다가오는 위험을 미리 아는 본능이 있다고 믿었다. [→science]

pre·sci·ent [préʃiənt, prí:-] *adj.* knowing or seeing ahead of time. 미리 아는; 선견지명이 있는. [↑]

*__pre·scribe__ [priskráib] *vt.* **1** (P6,10,12,13) order; lay down with authority as a direction; command. …을 지시〔명령〕하다; 규정하다. ¶ *~ his duties to someone* 아무에게 할 일을 지시하다 / *The law prescribes what should be done.* 법률은 해야 할 바를 규정하고 있다. **2** (P6,13) give medical advice; order as medicine or treatment. (약·요법 등)을

권하다; 처방하다. ¶ *The doctor prescribed hot drinks and rest.* 의사는 뜨거운 것을 마시고 안정을 취하라고 했다 / *~ medicine for* 〔*to*〕 *one's patient* 환자에게 약을 처방하다.
— *vi.* (P1,3) **1** give rules, orders, etc. 지시하다; 명령을 내리다. ¶ *The law does not ~ for such offences.* 그러한 범죄에 대해 법률에는 규정이 없다. **2** 《law》 claim a right or title through long use or possession. 시효에 따른 소유권을 주장하다. **3** give medical advice or prescriptions. 요법을 지시하다; 처방을 내리다. ¶ *~ for someone* 아무에게 처방을 내리다 / *~ for gout* 통풍(痛風) 치료법을 지시하다. [pre-, →scribe]

pre·scrip·tion [priskrípʃən] *n.* **1** Ⓤ a direction; an order. 규정; 법규. **2** Ⓒ a written order for making or using medicine. 처방(전). ¶ *a ~ for medicine* 약의 처방전 / *a ~ for a cough* 기침 처방약. **3** Ⓒ the medicine directed by a doctor. 처방약. **4** 《law》 Ⓤ a right or title gained by long use or possession. (오랜 사용·점유에 따른) 취득 시효; 시효. ¶ *negative* 〔*positive*〕 *~* 소멸〔취득〕 시효.

pre·scrip·tive [priskríptiv] *adj.* **1** directing; providing for a direction. 규정〔지시〕하는. **2** based on a legal prescription; owned by prescription. 시효에 의한〔의해 얻은〕. ¶ *a ~ right* 시효에 의해 취득한 권리. **3** arising from, established by, long use or custom. 오랜 사용〔관행〕에 의한; 관례의. ¶ *a ~ method of teaching* 관례에 준거한 교수법.

:pres·ence [prézəns] *n.* Ⓤ **1** the state of being present; attendance. 존재; 출석 (opp. absence). ¶ *~ of a ghost* 유령의 존재 / *demand the ~ of a witness* 증인 출석을 요구하다 / *I knew of her ~ in the next room.* 그녀가 옆 방에 있는 것을 알았다. **2** the place where a person is; the nearness of another person. 사람이 있는 자리; 면전(面前). ¶ *saving your ~* 당신의 면전이지만; 실례지만 / *be admitted to someone's ~* 아무의 접견이 허락되다 / *be banished from someone's ~* 아무의 접견이 허락되지 않다 / *in the ~ of others* 남의 면전에서. **3** ⓊⒸ the appearance; general behavior. 풍채; 인품; 태도. ¶ *a man of dignified ~* 기품 있는 사람 / *a man of no ~* 볼품이 없는 사람. [L. *praesens*]
in the presence of, in the sight or company of. …의 면전에서. ¶ *in the ~ of ladies* 숙녀들이 있는 자리에서 / *He signed his name in the ~ of two witnesses.* 두 증인이 보는 데서 서명했다 / *He was calm in the ~ of danger.* 위험에 직면해서 그는 침착했다.
presence of mind, composure; coolness in sudden emergencies. (위급시의) 침착; 냉정(opp. absence of mind).

:pres·ent[1] [prézənt] *adj.* **1** ⓐ being in a certain place. (어떤 장소에) 있는; 나와 있는 (opp. absent). ¶ *I am ~, sir.* (호명에서) 예 / *those here ~* 여기 있는 사람들 / *the people ~ there* 거기 출석한 사람들 / *All ~ heard it.* 참석자 모두는 그것을 들었다 / *the ~ company* 참석자 일동 / *~ to one's mind* 기억에 (남아) 있는. ⓑ 《*be ~*》 be or exist. 있는; 존재하는. ¶ *Oxygen is ~ in the air.* 산소는 공기 중에 존재한다. **2** at this time; not of the past or future. 현재의; 오늘(날)의. ¶ *the ~ fashion* 지금의 유행 / *at the ~ day* 오늘날에 / *the ~ king* 현국왕 / *at the ~ moment* 지금 이 순간. **3** at hand or in sight; instant. 바로 가까이의; 보이는; 즉석의. ¶ *a ~ wit* 기지(機智). **4** being discussed, written, read, etc. now. 지금 논의되고〔쓰고; 읽고〕 있는. ¶ *the ~ volume* 본서(本書); 이 책 / *the ~ writer* 본(本)필자. **5** 《gram.》 expressing an event as happening now. 현재의; 지금의. ¶ *the ~ tense* 현재 시제.
— *n.* Ⓤ **1** 《usu. *the ~*》 the present time. 지금; 현재. ¶ *up to* 〔*until*〕 *the ~* 오늘에 이르기까지 / *There is no time like the ~.* 이처럼 좋은 때는 또 없다《기회는 지금이다》. **2** 《gram.》 the present tense. 현재 시제. [↑]
at present, at the present time; now. 현재; 지금.
for the present, for the moment; for the time being. 지금으로서는; 당분간은. ¶ *I am staying in country for the ~.* 지금은 시골에 머물고 있다 / *Let's leave them as they are for the ~.* 그들을 당분간은 현 상태로 두자.

:pre·sent[2] *v.* [prizént] *vt.* **1** (P13) 《*with*》 make a gift to (someone); give (something) as a gift. …에 선물하다; …을 주다. ¶ *~ a gold medal to a winner = ~ a winner with a gold medal* 승자에게 금메달을 주다 / *They presented flowers to their teacher.* 그들은 담임 선생에게 꽃을 선물했다 / *Our class presented the school with a picture.* 우리 반에서는 학교에 그림 하나를 증정했다. **2** (P6) bring (something) before the public; show or exhibit. (극)을 상연하다; …을 보이다; 공개하다. ¶ *~ a new play* 새 연극을 상연하다 / *~ a poor appearance* 초라한 모습을 보이다 / *~ an appearance of* …처럼 보이다; …한 느낌을 주다 / *The situation presents great difficulties.* 사태는 매우 어려운 양상을 보인다. **3** (P6,13) put (oneself) in another's presence; introduce. 모습을 보이다; 출두하다; …을 소개하다. ¶ *He presented himself before the principal.* 교장 앞에 나아갔다 / *~ oneself at the meeting* 모임에 나가다 / *He presented his brother to the teacher.* 그는 동생을 선생님께 인사시켰다 / *Miss Smith, may I ~ Mr. Brown to you?* 스미스양, 브라운 씨를 소개합니다. **4** (P6,13) 《*to*》 hand; deliver; offer. …을 내놓다; 제출하다. ¶ *~ a report* 보고서를 제출하다 / *~ an argument* 의론을 제기하다 / *~ one's bill* 어음을 제시하다 / *Several new ideas were presented.* 몇 가지 새로운 안이 나왔다. **5** (P13) turn, aim or point (one's face, arms, etc.). (얼굴·무기 등)을 돌리다; 겨누다. ¶ *~ a pistol at someone*

아무에게 권총을 겨누다 / *She presented her face to me.* 내게 얼굴을 돌렸다. **6** (P6,13) 《law》 accuse. …을 고발하다.
—[prézənt] *n.* Ⓒ **1** something given; a gift. 선물. ¶ *She received a ~ on her birthday.* 그녀는 생일 선물을 받았다. **2** a position of a weapon in a salute. 받들어총의 자세. ¶ *at the ~* 받들어총 자세로. [↑]

pre·sent·a·ble [prizéntəbəl] *adj.* **1** suitable to be seen; fit to be presented. 보기 괜찮은; 선물하기에 적합한. ¶ *a ~ gift* 부끄럽지 않은 선물 / *a ~ play* 상연해서 좋은 극. **2** suitable in appearance, dress, manners, etc., for being introduced into society. (외모·복장·태도 등이) 남앞에 내세울〔소개할〕 수 있는. ¶ *look quite ~* 썩 단정한 차림이다.

pres·en·ta·tion [prèzəntéiʃən] *n.* **1** Ⓤ the act of presenting; the state of being presented. 증정; 수여. ¶ *the ~ of a gift* 선물 증정. **2** Ⓒ a gift. 선물. ¶ *A handsome ~ was made to the retiring rector.* 은퇴하는 교구장에게 괜찮은 선물이 증정되었다. **3** Ⓤ a formal introduction; an audience. 소개; 배알. ¶ *the ~ of a lady to the queen* 귀부인의 여왕에의 배알(拜謁). **4** ⓊⒸ a public performance; production. 상연; 공연. ¶ *the ~ of a play.* **5** Ⓤ the act of offering or bringing forward. 제출; 표시. ¶ *the ~ of credentials* 신임장의 제출.

pres·ent-day [prézəntdéi] *adj.* of the present time; modern; current; of today. 현대의; 지금의.

pre·sent·er [prizéntər] *n.* Ⓒ **1** a giver. 증정자. **2** an introducer. 소개자; 추천자.

pre·sen·ti·ment [prizéntəmənt] *n.* Ⓒ a feeling that something, esp. of an evil nature, is going to happen. 육감; (불길한) 예감. ¶ *a ~ of danger.* [→sense]

:pres·ent·ly [prézəntli] *adv.* **1** in a little while; before long; soon. 머지않아; 곧. ¶ *She will be home ~.* 곧 돌아올 것이다. **2** 《U.S.》 at the present time. 현재. ¶ *Bob is ~ on vacation.* 보브는 지금 휴가다. [*presence*]

pre·sent·ment [prizéntmənt] *n.* **1** ⓊⒸ a statement; a description. 진술; 서술; 묘사. ¶ *a careful ~ of character* 면밀한 성격 묘사. **2** Ⓤ the act of showing or offering; a presentation. 제시; 제출; 증정. **3** Ⓤ the act of putting a play or other show on the stage; performance. 상연; 연출. **4** 《law》 a statement by a grand jury of a fact, based on their own knowledge. (대배심의) 고발; 고소(告訴). [↑]

pres·er·va·tion [prèzərvéiʃən] *n.* Ⓤ **1** the act of preserving; keeping safe. 보존; 유지; 저장; 보호. ¶ *be engaged in the ~ of ancient buildings* 고대 건물들을 보존하는 일을 하다. **2** the condition of being preserved. 보존 상태. ¶ *eggs in a good state of ~* 보존 상태가 좋은 달걀 / *books in good ~* 잘 보존된 책. [→preserve]

pre·serv·a·tive [prizə́ːrvətiv] *n.* Ⓒ any substance that prevents (foods, etc.) from decay. 방부제. ¶ *Salt and sugar are common food preservatives.* 소금과 설탕은 흔히 쓰이는 식품 보존제다. —*adj.* that prevents; having the nature of preserving. 보존의; 보존력이 있는; 예방적인.

:pre·serve [prizə́ːrv] *vt.* (P6,13) **1** 《*from*》 keep (something) from harm, damage, or being forgotten; protect or save. …을 보호하다; 지키다. ¶ *~ eggs from damage* 달걀이 상하지 않게 하다 / *~ the wild animals from being killed* 야생 동물이 포살되지 않게 보호하다 / *May God keep and ~ you.* 신의 가호가 있기를 / *His quick thinking preserved his friend's life.* 그의 재빠른 판단이 친구의 목숨을 구했다. **2** keep (foods) from being spoiled, as by canning, salting or smoking. (통조림·훈제 등으로 식품)의 부패를 막다. ¶ *~ fish in salt* 생선을 소금에 절이다 / *~ oranges in sugar* 오렌지를 설탕절임으로 하다. **3** keep (something) alive; maintain. …을 잃지 않도록 하다; …을 유지하다. ¶ *~ silence* 잠자코 있다 / *~ health* 건강을 유지하다 / *~ the scene in a motion picture* 그 광경을 영화에 담아두다 / *a well-preserved man* 젊게 보이는 노인 / *~ the memory of another* 다른 사람에 대한 기억을 간직하다 / *~ peace* 평화를 유지하다. **4** keep (birds or animals) from being hunted. (새·짐승을) 보호하다; (조수)의 사냥을 금하다. ¶ *~ game* 조수의 사냥을 금하다 / *These woods are preserved.* 이곳 숲에서는 사냥을 못한다.
—*n.* Ⓒ **1** 《usu. *pl.*》 fruit cooked with sugar; jam. 설탕절이한 과일; 잼. ¶ *apple preserves* 사과잼 / *Mother made some plum preserves.* 어머니는 플럼 설탕절이를 좀 만들었다. **2** a place where wild animals or birds are protected. 금렵지. ¶ *There are many deer in the ~.* 그 금렵지에는 사슴들이 많다. [pre-, L. *servo* keep]

pre·serv·er [prizə́ːrvər] *n.* Ⓒ a person or thing that saves, protects or defends; a person who preserves game. 보존〔보호〕자; 구조자; 금렵지 관리인.

***pre·side** [prizáid] *vi.* (P1,2A) **1** 《*at, over*》 act as chairman at a meeting. 의장 노릇을 하다; 사회를 보다. ¶ *The conference was presided over by Mr. A.* A씨가 회의의 사회를 봤다. **2** 《*at, over*》 have direction, authority or control. 관장하다; 지배하다. ¶ *The manager presides over the business of a firm.* 지배인이 회사 업무를 총괄한다. [L. *sedeo* sit]

pres·i·den·cy [prézidənsi] *n.* 《usu. *the ~*》 the office or term of a president. 대통령〔장관·학장 등〕의 직·임기. ¶ *Lucy was elected to the ~ of the Junior Club.* 루시가 주니어클럽의 회장으로 뽑혔다 / *during the ~ of Lincoln* 링컨 대통령의 임기중에. [↓]

:pres·i·dent [prézidənt] *n.* Ⓒ **1** 《*P-*》 the highest executive officer of a modern republic. 대통령. ¶ *President Lincoln.* **2** the chief officer of a company, college, club, etc. 총재; 장관; 의장; 총장; 학장; 사장; 회장; 은행장 (등). ¶ *a party* ~ 당수; 당총재 / *a steel company* ~ 철강 회사 사장 / *the President of the Royal Society* (영국) 학술원 회장. [L. *praesideo*]

*__pres·i·den·tial__ [prèzidénʃəl] *adj.* of a president. 대통령〔장관; 학장 (등)〕의. ¶ *a* ~ *election* 대통령 선거 / 《U.S.》 *a* ~ *year* 대통령 선거년 / *a* ~ *candidate* 대통령 후보.

:**press**[1] [pres] *vt.* **1** (P6,7,13) ⓐ push (something) with force; put a heavy weight on; compress; squeeze. …을 누르다; 내리누르다; 압착하다. ¶ ~ *clothes* 옷을 다림질하다 / ~ *flowers* 꽃을 책갈피 사이에 끼워 납작하게 하다 / ~ *the switch that turns on the light* 불을 켜는 스위치를 누르다 / ~ *one's hand against a door* 손으로 문을 밀다 / ~ *a thing with* 〔*under*〕 *a stone* …을 돌로 눌러 놓다 / ~ *stickers on a wall* 벽에 스티커를 붙이다. ⓑ take out (juice) by pressing. …을 눌러 (즙)을 짜다. ¶ ~ *orange juice out* 오렌지를 짜서 즙을 내다 / ~ *oil out of seeds* 씨에서 기름을 짜다. **2** (P6,13) hold (something) tightly; take (someone or something) into one's arms; clasp; embrace. …을 꽉 쥐다; 껴안다. ¶ ~ *someone's hand* 아무의 손을 움켜 잡다《애정의 표시로》/ ~ *a baby to one's breast* 아기를 품에 껴안다 / *He pressed her closely against him.* 그는 그녀를 꼭 끌어안았다. **3** (P6,7,13,20) insist strongly; make (someone) do something by force. …을 조르다; 강요하다. ¶ ~ *someone to come* 아무를 오라고 조르다 / ~ *someone for money* 아무에게 돈을 달라고 조르다 / ~ *someone for an answer* 〔*explanation*〕 아무에게 답변〔해명〕을 요구하다 / *They pressed me to stay (for) the night.* 그들은 자고 가라고 내게 졸랐다 / ~ *someone into confession* 아무에게 자백을 강요하다. **4** (P6) insist; lay stress on (something). …을 주장하다; 강조하다. ¶ ~ *the point* 〔*matter*〕 그 점〔사항〕을 강조하다 / ~ *one's advantages rudely* 염치 없이 자기 이익을 내세우다. **5** (P13) 《chiefly in *passive*》 get (someone) to be troubled with or about something; straiten; weigh heavily; oppress. …을 애먹이다; 괴롭히다; 고생시키다. ¶ *She pressed me with questions.* 질문 공세로 날 애먹였다 / *be pressed for money* 돈에 쪼들리다 / *He is pressed with poverty.* 그는 가난에 시달리고 있다. —*vi.* **1** (P1,3) 《*against, on*》 push with force; squeeze. 누르다; 압박하다; 밀다. ¶ ~ *on the button* 버튼을 누르다. **2** (P3) 《*on, forward*》 force one's way; hurry. 밀어 제치고 나아가다; 서두르다. ¶ ~ *through a crowd* 군중을 헤치고 전진하다. **3** (P1) be urgent. 절박하다. ¶ *Time presses.* 시간이 절박하다 / *The matter is pressing.* 사태가 절박해진다. **4** (P2A,3) 《*up, round*》 crowd. 몰려들다. ¶ ~ *around the car* 차 주위에 몰려들다.

hard pressed, in difficulty; at a loss. 어려워져; 궁해서.

press hard upon, cause (someone) to be troubled with arguments, questions, etc. …에 육박하다; …을 다그치다; 추궁하다.

press on, **a**) go on with a strong will. 굳세게 밀고 나가다. **b**) go in haste toward (some place). …으로 서둘러 가다.

press on one's way, go in haste. 길을 재촉하다.

—*n.* Ⓒ **1** the act of pushing with force. 누름; 압박; 압착; 세게 쥠. ¶ *a* ~ *of the hand.* **2** a machine used for pressing. 압착기. **3** a printing machine. 인쇄기. ¶ *a rotary* ~ 윤전기. **4** Ⓤ 《*the* ~, *collectively*》 newspapers and magazines. 신문; 잡지. ¶ *send* 〔*come*〕 *to* (*the*) ~ 인쇄에 붙이다〔붙여지다〕 / *in the* ~ 인쇄중인 / *the daily* ~ 일간 신문. **5** ⓐ a large number of people together; a crowd. 군중; 군집; 붐빔. ¶ *The child was lost in the* ~ *of people.* 많은 사람들 틈에서 아이를 잃었다 / *in the* ~ *of battle* 싸움의 와중에. ⓑ hurry of business; urgency; crowding condition of affairs. 분주함; 절박; 일에 몰림. ¶ *the* ~ *of modern life* 현대 생활의 번잡 / *The* ~ *of duties keeps her busy.* 일에 몰린 그녀는 늘 바쁘다. **6** a closet. 책장; 찬장. [L. *premo*]

have a good press, be highly spoken of in the newspapers. 신문에서 호평을 받다.

out of press, (of books, etc.) sold out and no copies remaining. 절판(絶版)된; 매진된.

press[2] [pres] *vt.* (P7,13) 《hist.》 force into service, usu. naval or military service. (해군·육군에) 강제 징발하다. ¶ ~ *into one's service* 강제 징발하다 / *Navy officers used to visit towns and merchant ships to* ~ *men for the fleet.* 해군 사관들이 함대에 필요한 인력을 징모(徵募)하러 도시와 상선들에 나타나곤 했다. —*n.* 《*the* ~》 forcing into service. 강제 징모. [↑]

press agent [∠ ∠] *n.* a person employed by a theater, actor, etc., to attend to advertising and publicity. (극장 등의) 선전원; 보도〔홍보〕 담당원.

press-box [présbɑ̀ks / -bɔ̀ks] *n.* a place reserved for reporters at sports events, etc. (경기장 등의) 기자석.

press campaign 〔**stunt**〕 [∠ -∠〔∠〕] *n.* prosecution of political or other aims by newspaper letters and articles. 신문에 의한 선전.

press-cut·ting, -clip·ping [préskʌ̀tiŋ], [-klìpiŋ] *n.* a paragraph or short notice cut from a newspaper or magazine. (신문·잡지의) 스크랩.

press gallery [∠ ∠--] *n.* a gallery reserved for reporters, esp. in the House of Commons. (영국 하원의) 기자석.

press gang [∠ ∠] *n.* 《hist.》 a group of men employed to seize others for the navy. 수병 강제 징발대(cf. *press*[2]).

·press·ing [présiŋ] *adj.* **1** demanding immediate attention; urgent. 절박한; 급한. ¶ *a ~ necessity* 절박한 필요 / *a ~ demand* 긴급한 수요 / *a ~ invitation* 간절한 초대 / *~ business duties* 급히 처리할 업무들. **2** (of persons) insistent. 졸라대는; 끈질긴.

press·man [présmən] *n.* Ⓒ (*pl.* **-men** [-mən]) **1** a person who operates a printing press. 인쇄공. **2** 《Brit.》 a journalist; a reporter. 신문 기자.

:pres·sure [préʃər] *n.* Ⓤ **1** a steady press by a force; the continued action of a weight or force. 누름; 밀기; 압박. ¶ *the gentle ~ of her hand* 가만히 누르는 그녀의 손 / *the ~ of a boot on one's foot* 발에의 신발의 압박 / *the ~ of a crowd* 군중의 붐빔. **2** the force of air, gas, etc. against a unit of area. 압력. ¶ *the ~ of water* 수압 / *high* [*low*] *blood ~* 고[저]혈압 / *atmospheric ~* 기압. **3** a burden on the mind; trouble; distress; 《often *pl.*》 hardships. (정신적) 고뇌; 걱정; 어려움; 곤경(困境). ¶ *financial pressures* 재정난 / *the ~ of poverty* 가난의 고통 / *mental ~* 정신적 고뇌 / *the ~ of old debts* 묵은 빚이 주는 고통. **4** the state of being compelled; oppression. 억압; 강제. ¶ *~ of public opinion* 여론의 압력 / *act under ~* 강제당하다 / *put ~ upon* …에 압력을 가하다. **5** urgent demand. 절박한 필요; 분망(奔忙). ¶ *the ~ of business* 업무의 분망 / *the ~ of city life* 도시 생활의 분주함. [*press*[1]]

at high pressure, as quickly as possible and with the utmost energy. 전력을 다하여; 맹렬히.

bring pressure to bear [***put pressure***] ***on*** [***upon***], oppress; force or try to force. (남)을 압박하다; 강제하다. ¶ *Pressure was brought to bear on John to make him change his mind about not doing his work.* 일을 하지 않는 것에 대해 마음을 바꾸도록 존에게 압력이 가해졌다.

pres·tige [prestí:dʒ, préstidʒ] *n.* Ⓤ the influence or reputation gained by one's achievement, abilities, position, etc. 위신; 신망; 명성. ¶ *national ~* 국위(國威) / *acquire* [*seek*] *~* 명성을 얻다[추구하다] / *loss of ~* 위신 손상[실추]. [L. *praestringo* dazzle]

pres·to [préstou] *adj., adv.* 《mus.》 quick(ly). 빠른; 빠르게. — *n.* Ⓒ (*pl.* **-tos**) a passage to be played quickly. 급속곡(急速曲). [L. *praesto* ready]

pre·sum·a·ble [prizú:məbəl] *adj.* that can be taken for granted or expected; probable. 있음직한; 그럴 수도 있는; 추측이 가능한. ¶ *the ~ results of an act* 어떤 행동이 가져올 수 있는 결과 / *the ~ time of their arrival* 그들의 도착 추정 시각. [→presume]

pre·sum·a·bly [prizú:məbli] *adv.* as may be presumed or taken for granted; probably. 아마도; 생각건대.

·pre·sume [prizú:m] *vt.* **1** (P6,11,21) take (something) for granted; suppose. …을 추정하다; …라고 생각하다; 가정하다. ¶ *I ~ that they have seen him.* 그들이 그를 만났으리라 생각한다 / *I ~ this decision to be final.* 아마도 이게 최종 결정일 게다 / *I am presuming what you say to be true.* 네 말이 옳다고 생각한다. **2** (P8) dare to do (something); venture. 감히[무엄하게도] …하다. ¶ *May I ~ to ask you where you are going?* 죄송하지만 어디에 가십니까.
— *vi.* (P1,3) **1** make suppositions; guess. 추측하다; 생각하다. ¶ *You'll play out of doors, I ~, if it is fair.* 날씨가 좋으면 너희들은 밖에 나가 노는 게 좋겠다. **2** ⓐ take liberties; act with unreasonable rudeness. 건방지게 굴다; 기어오르다. ¶ *You ~.* 건방지군. ⓑ 《*on, upon*》 take advantage of someone's weak point, etc. 남의 약점(등)을 이용하다. ¶ *~ upon someone's good nature* 아무의 사람 좋음을 기화로 삼다 / *~ on another's friendship* 남의 우정을 이용하다. [pre-, L. *sumo* take]

pre·sum·ing [prizú:miŋ] *adj.* impudent; arrogant; too forward. 건방진; 주제넘은. ¶ *It would be ~ to camp in a man's yard without his permission.* 허락도 없이 남의 땅에 천막을 치는 것은 무례한 짓이다.

pre·sump·tion [prizʌ́mpʃən] *n.* **1** ⓊⒸ the act of presuming; a reason for presuming; probability. 가정; 추측(의 이유); 가망. ¶ 《law》 *~ of fact* 사실상의 추정《기지(既知)의 사실에서의》 / *~ of death* 사망 추정 / *As his mouth was sticky, the ~ was that he had eaten the cake.* 입이 끈끈한 걸 보니 그놈이 과자를 먹은 것 같다. **2** Ⓤ unpleasant arrogance or boldness. 건방짐; 주제넘음. ¶ *How dare you have the ~ to tell me what to do?* 네가 뭔데 날 보고 이래라 저래라 하나.

pre·sump·tive [prizʌ́mptiv] *adj.* based on presumption; without direct proof; taking for granted. 추정[가정]의. ¶ *~ evidence* [*proof*] 추정 증거.

pre·sump·tu·ous [prizʌ́mptʃuəs] *adj.* too self-confident or bold; boasting too much. 주제넘은; 건방진. ¶ *It would be ~ to take success for granted.* 의당 성공할 것이란 생각은 주제넘은 생각이다.

pre·sup·pose [prì:səpóuz] *vt.* (P6,11) **1** assume or suppose beforehand. …을 미리 가정하다; 예상하다. ¶ *Let us ~ that he wins the game.* 그가 경기에 이긴다고 가정하자. **2** demand or require (something) as a prior condition. …을 전제로 하다. ¶ *A healthy body presupposes healthful living.* 건강한 신체는 건전한 생활을 전제로 한다 / *True kindness presupposes sympathy.* 참다운 친절은 동정이 앞서야 한다. [pre-]

pre·sup·po·si·tion [prì:sʌpəzíʃən] *n.* Ⓤ **1** the act of presupposing. 가정. **2** Ⓒ that which is assumed beforehand; a guess. 예정; 전제. ¶ *The detective acted upon the ~ that the thief knew the value of the jewels.* 그

형사는 도둑이 보석의 가치를 알고 있었다는 전제 아래 행동했다.

pret. preterit.

·**pre·tence** [priténs] *n.* 《Brit.》＝pretense.

:**pre·tend** [priténd] *vt.* **1** (P6,8,11) make believe. …을 가장하다; …인 체하다. ¶ ～ *illness* 꾀병을 앓다 / *She pretended that she was asleep.* 그녀는 자는 척했다 / *He pretended not to know the facts.* 그는 사실을 모르는 척했다. **2** (P6,8) suppose oneself (to be) as in a play. (놀이에서) …시늉을 하다. ¶ *The children are pretending to be policeman and robbers.* 아이들은 경찰관과 도둑 흉내를 내고 있다. **3** (P8,11) dare to do; attempt. 감히 …하려고 하다; …을 꾀하다. ¶ *I cannot* ～ *to ask him for money.* 나는 그에게 돈 얘기를 못 하겠다.

— *vi.* **1** (P3) 《*to*》 lay claim; claim falsely to have. 권리를 주장하다; 요구하다; (가지고 있다고) 자처하다. ¶ ～ *to the throne* 〔*Crown*〕 왕위 계승권을 주장하다 / ～ *to genius* 천재를 자처하다 / *I don't* ～ *to great learning.* 내가 많이 안다고 자처하지는 않는다. **2** (P1) make believe; make a false show of something. 가장하다; (…인) 체하다. [pre-, →tend[1]]

pre·tend·ed [priténdid] *adj.* not real; false. 거짓의.

pre·tend·er [priténdər] *n.* Ⓒ **1** a person who pretends. …인 체하는 사람; 사칭(詐稱)하는 사람. **2** a person who makes a claim, esp. to a throne, without a right. 요구자; (특히) 왕위 요구자.

·**pre·tense,** 《Brit.》 **-tence** [priténs] *n.* Ⓤ **1** the act of pretending; make-believe. 겉치레; 가장; 거짓. ¶ ～ *of illness* 꾀병 / *She made a* ～ *to faint.* 까무러치는 체했다 / *make a* ～ *of affection* 애정을 가장하다 / *You can't keep up the* ～ *any longer.* 넌 더 이상 시치미를 뗄 수 없다. **2** ⓊⒸ a false allegation or claim; an excuse. 구실; 변명. **3** a false show or appearance. 허식; 가장. ¶ *There are no pretenses about him.* 그에게 허식은 없다. **4** a right insisted on; a claim. 주장; 요구. ¶ *She had no* ～ *to beauty.* 그녀는 조금도 미인인 체하지 않았다. [→pretend]

make pretense to, pretend to. …을 가지고 있다고 주장하다; …가 있는 체하다. ¶ *We make no* ～ *to deep knowledge.* 우리는 학식이 깊은 체하지 않는다.

under the pretense of, using a false show of. …을 구실로; …을 빙자하여; …을 가장하여. ¶ *He deceived me under the* ～ *of kindness.* 친절을 가장해 나를 속여먹었다.

pre·ten·sion [priténʃən] *n.* **1** Ⓒ a claim; a right to claim. 주장; 요구; (요구할) 권리. ¶ *He had* ～ *to the throne.* 그에게 왕위 계승권이 있었다. **2** Ⓤ false show; outward appearance; display. 가장; 태깔부림; 허식. ¶ *without* ～ 수수하게; 평범하게. **3** Ⓒ 《often. *pl.*》 self-importance. 자부(自負). ¶ *He has no pretensions to great scholarship.* 그는 조금도 학식이 많은 체하지 않는다. **4** Ⓒ an excuse; a pretext. 구실. [*pretend*]

pre·ten·tious [priténʃəs] *adj.* assuming an appearance of great importance, worth, etc.; showy. 거드름 피우는; 우쭐대는; 과장된. ¶ *a* ～ *person* 허세부리는 사람.

pret·er·it, -ite [prétərit] *n.* Ⓒ 《gram.》 the past tense. 과거(시제). — *adj.* past. 과거의. [L. *praeter* beyond, *eo* go]

pre·ter·mis·sion [prìːtərmíʃən] *n.* omission. 무시; 생략.

pre·ter·mit [prìːtərmít] *vt.* (P6) pass over without mention. …을 불문(不問)에 부치다. [→missile]

pre·ter·nat·u·ral [prìːtərnǽtʃərəl] *adj.* beyond the regular course of nature; supernatural. 초자연적인; 불가사의한.

pre·text [príːtekst] *n.* Ⓒ an excuse. 구실; 변명. ¶ *find a* ～ *for absence* 결석할 구실을 찾다 / *on some* ～ *or other* 이 핑계 저 핑계로 / *He used his sore finger as a* ～ *for not going to school.* 그는 등교 못 하는 구실로 생인손이라 했다. [pre-]

pret·ti·ly [prítili] *adv.* in a pretty manner. 곱게; 얌전하게. ¶ *dress* 〔*speak, sing*〕 ～ 곱게 차려입다〔말하다, 노래하다〕 / *behave* ～ 얌전하게 처신하다. [*pretty*]

pret·ti·ness [prítinis] *n.* Ⓤ the state of being pretty. 고움; 아름다움.

:**pret·ty** [príti] *adj.* (**-ti·er, -ti·est**) **1** charming; lovely. 매력적인; 귀여운(cf. *beautiful, handsome*). ¶ *a* ～ *girl* / *A baby is* ～ *and innocent.* 갓난아이는 귀엽고 순진무구하다 / ～ *manners* 깍듯한 예절. **2** fine; good. 훌륭한; 나무랄 데 없는. ¶ ～ *ways* 호감이 가는 태도 / *It was a* ～ *speech.* 훌륭한 연설이었다. **3** 《*iron.*》 awful; surprising. 터무니없는; 말도 안 되는. ¶ *Here's a* ～ *mess!* 이거 어찌된 셈판이냐; 골치 아프게 됐군 / *a* ～ *state of affairs* 난장판; 뒤죽박죽. **4** 《*colloq.*》 large. 상당한; 엄청나게 큰. ¶ *a* ～ *sum of money* 꽤 많은 금액 / *make a* ～ *fortune* 한재산 벌다.

— *n.* Ⓒ 《used as *My pretty!*》 **1** a pretty child. 아가. **2** 《usu. *pl.*》 something pretty. 고운 옷; 예쁘장한 장신구 (등). ¶ *She has put on all her pretties.* 그녀는 온갖 장신구로 치장했다.

— *adv.* 《*colloq.*》 **1** to some extent; fairly. 상당히; 꽤. ¶ *I feel* ～ *well now.* 이제 기분이 상당히 좋다 / *feel* ～ *ill* 꽤 아프다 / *It is* ～ *late.* 어지간히 늦군〔더디군〕. **2** very; quite. 아주; 대단히. ¶ *I am* ～ *tired.* 아주 피곤하다 / *speak* ～ *strongly* 큰소리치다 / *be* ～ *sick about it* 넌더리나다 / *You are* ～ *well-known.* 너 아주 유명하더라. [E.]

pretty much the same thing, almost the same thing. 그저 그만그만한 것〔일〕.

sitting pretty, 《*colloq.*》 in favorable circumstances; well off. 괜찮은 환경에; 유복하여. ¶ *We are sitting* ～. 잘 살고 있다.

·**pre·vail** [privéil] *vi.* (P1,3) **1** be widespread or prevalent; be in general use.

유행하다; 널리 퍼지다; 번지다. ¶ *Bad cold prevails throughout the country.* 전국에 독감이 유행하고 있다 / *A belief in magic still prevails among some tribes.* 아직도 종족에 따라 주술(呪術) 신앙이 널리 행해지고 있다. **2** 《*against, over*》 be victorious; succeed; win. 우세하다; 잘 돼가다; 이기다. ¶ ～ *over the enemy* 적을 이기다 / *Truth is great and will* ～. 진리는 위대하며 승리한다. **3** be effective. 효과가 있다. **4** 《*on, upon, with*》 persuade. 설복〔설득〕하다. ¶ *I finally prevailed on her to go.* 끝내 그녀를 가도록 만들었다 / *I tried but could not* ～ *with her.* 시도해 보았으나 그녀를 설득하지 못했다. [L. *varus* crooked]

·**pre·vail·ing** [privéiliŋ] *adj.* having strong influence or superior force; widely and generally existing; common. 유력한; 우세한; 일반적인; 널리 보급되어 있는; 보통의. ¶ *Yellow is the* ～ *color in her room.* 그녀의 방은 거의가 노랑색이다 / *a* ～ *style* 일반적인 스타일.

prev·a·lence [prévələns] *n.* Ⓤ the state of being prevalent. 유행; 우세; 보급(률); 널리 행해짐. ¶ *the* ～ *of television* 텔레비전의 보급 / *the* ～ *of cholera* 콜레라의 유행 / *the* ～ *of short hair among women* 여성들 사이의 짧은 머리의 유행.

·**prev·a·lent** [prévələnt] *adj.* widely existing; widespread; superior. 널리 행해지는; 유행하는; 우세한. ¶ *Colds are* ～ *in winter.* 감기는 겨울에 많다 / ～ *habits* 널리 행해지는 관습 / *Cholera is* ～ *in India.* 콜레라는 인도에 많다. [→prevail]

pre·var·i·cate [privǽrəkèit] *vi.* (P1) avoid telling the truth; make untrue statements; lie. 말끝을 흐리다; 얼버무리다; 속이다; 거짓말하다. [→prevail]

pre·var·i·ca·tion [privæ̀rəkéiʃən] *n.* Ⓤ the act of prevaricating; Ⓒ a statement or reply that turns aside from the truth. 말을 얼버무려 넘김; 발뺌; 속임; 거짓말함.

pre·var·i·ca·tor [privǽrəkèitər] *n.* Ⓒ a person who prevaricates. 말을 얼버무리는〔변명하여 발뺌하는〕 사람.

:**pre·vent** [privént] *vt.* (P6,13) stop or keep (someone or something) from doing something or happening; hinder. …을 막다; 예방하다; 방해하다; 막아서 …못 하게 하다. ¶ ～ *disease* 〔*war*〕 질병〔전쟁〕을 막다 / *if nothing prevents you* 지장이 없다면 / *The heavy rain prevented me from going out.* = *The heavy rain prevented me* 〔*my*〕 *going out.* 폭우 때문에 나갈 수 없었다 / *A business affair prevented my coming earlier.* 사업상 일 때문에 더 일찍 오지 못했다 / *Nothing will* ～ *from doing our duty.* 어떤 일이 있어도 임무를 완수할 것이다. [L. *venio* come]

pre·vent·a·ble, -i·ble [privéntəbəl] *adj.* that can be prevented. 예방〔방지〕할 수 있는.

·**pre·ven·tion** [privénʃən] *n.* **1** Ⓤ the act of preventing; hindrance. 방지; 방해; 예방. ¶ *the* ～ *of juvenile crimes* 미성년 범죄의 예방 / *the Society for the Prevention of Cruelty to Animals* 동물 학대 방지 협회(abbr. S.P.C.A.) / 《*prov.*》 *Prevention is better than cure.* 예방은 치료보다 낫다. **2** ⓊⒸ the means taken to guard against danger, disease, etc. 예방법; 방지책. ¶ *by way of* ～ 예방법으로서.

pre·ven·tive [privéntiv] *adj.* serving to prevent. 예방의; 방지하는; 방해하는. ¶ ～ *medicine* 〔*measures*〕 예방약〔책〕 / *be* ～ *of accidents* 사고를 막다. — *n.* Ⓒ anything that prevents; a means or medicine for keeping off disease, etc. 예방〔방지〕하는 것; 방지법; 예방약.

pre·view [príːvjùː] *n.* Ⓒ **1** a performance or showing in advance of the regular performance or showing of a motion picture, play, etc. 시사회; 시연회(試演會). **2** a brief showing of scenes from a motion picture for advertisement. (영화〔텔레비전 프로〕의) 예고편. — *vt.* (P6) look at (a motion picture, play, etc.) beforehand. 시사(試寫)를〔시연을〕 보다. [pre-]

:**pre·vi·ous** [príːviəs] *adj.* **1** occurring earlier in time; preceding; former. 앞서의; 이전의. ¶ *a* ～ *engagement* 선약(先約) / *a* ～ *illness* 기왕증(旣往症) / *on the* ～ *day* 전날에 / ～ *to one's departure* 출발에 앞서 / *a year* ～ *to the time of war* 전쟁이 있기 한 해 전 / *He spoke of you in a* ～ *letter.* 그는 먼젓번 편지에서 네 말을 했더라. **2** 《*colloq.*》 too early; too hasty. 너무 이른; 조급한. ¶ *You have been a little too* ～. 너는 좀 너무 서둘렀다. [L. *via* road]

previous to, before; prior to. …의 전에; …에 앞서. ¶ *Previous to the conference we had discussed the matter among us.* 회의에 앞서 우리끼리 그 문제를 토의했다.

·**pre·vi·ous·ly** [príːviəsli] *adv.* at an earlier time; beforehand. 앞서서; 미리.

pre·vi·sion [privíʒən] *n.* Ⓤ foresight; forecast; foreknowledge. 선견(先見); 예지(豫知).

pre·war [príːwɔ́ːr] *adj.* before the war. 전전(戰前)의(opp. postwar). [pre-]

:**prey** [prei] *n.* Ⓒ **1** an animal caught or killed by another for food. 먹이. ¶ *catch one's* ～ 먹이를 잡다 / *Sheep are the* ～ *of wolves.* 양은 늑대의 먹이다. **2** Ⓤ a habit of catching and killing animals for food. 포식(捕食)하는 습성. ¶ *an animal* 〔*a beast*〕 *of* ～ 맹수 / *a bird of* ～ 육식조(肉食鳥); 맹금(猛禽). **3** a person or an animal sacrificed, injured, etc.; a victim. 희생(자). ¶ *become a* ～ *to a lion* 〔*vanity*〕 사자밥이 되다〔허영의 노예가 되다〕 / *be* 〔*fall*〕 *a* ～ *to disease* 〔*circumstances*〕 병으로 쓰러지다〔환경의 희생자가 되다〕.

— *vi.* (P3) **1** 《*on, upon*》 hunt or kill animals, birds, etc. for food; plunder. 잡아먹

다; 먹이로 하다; 약탈하다. ¶ *Cats ~ upon mice.* 고양이는 쥐를 잡아 먹는다 / *Bands of armed robbers preyed upon the villages.* 무장 강도들이 마을들을 노략질했다. **2** 《*on*》 have an exhausting effect or influence; do harm. 괴롭히다; 해치다. ¶ *Care preyed on her health.* 걱정으로 그녀는 건강을 해쳤다. [L. *praeda*]

:price [prais] *n.* Ⓒ **1** the amount of money for which a thing is bought, sold, etc.; the cost. 가격; 값. ¶ *the ~ asked* 부르는 값 / *sell at a fixed* 〔*reduced*〕 *~* 정가로〔할인해서〕 팔다 / *What is the ~ of it ?* =*What ~ is it ?* 값이 얼마요 / 《*prov.*》 *Every man has his ~.* 돈 싫다는 사람은 없다. **2** money offered for the capture of a person; reward. 상금; 현상금; 보수. **3** something given or done for getting a thing. 대가(代價); 희생. ¶ *A life of toil is generally the ~ of fame and success.* 명성과 성공을 위해선 땀을 흘려야 한다 / *A high ~ was paid for peace.* 평화를 위해서 값진 희생이 치러졌다. **4** Ⓤ value; worth. 가치; 귀중성.

above 〔***beyond, without***〕 ***price,*** priceless; invaluable. 값을 매길 수 없는; 아주 귀중한.

at any price, no matter what the cost. 어떤 희생을〔대가를〕 치르더라도. ¶ *This must be done at any ~.* 어떠한 희생을 치르더라도 이 일은 완수해야 한다.

at the price of (=*at the sacrifice of*) *something.* …을 희생으로; …을 걸고.

put 〔***set***〕 ***a price on the head of,*** offer a reward for the arrest or killing of (a criminal, etc.). …의 체포〔목〕에 현상금을 걸다.

What price ...? 《*colloq.*》 **a**) What chance is there for...? 승산이 있는가. **b**) What do you think of...? 어떻게 생각하나. ¶ *What ~ fine weather tomorrow ?* 내일 날씨가 맑을까.

— *vt.* (P6,7) **1** ask the price of. …의 값을 묻다. ¶ *~ goods at various shops* 여러 가게에 값을 묻고 다니다. **2** set a price on. …에 값을 매기다. ¶ *The book is priced at 16 shillings net.* 그 책은 정가가 16실링이다. **3** estimate the value of. …을 평가하다. [L. *pretium*]

·prick [prik] *n.* Ⓒ **1** a sharp point. 찌르는 것〔물건〕; 바늘; 가시. ¶ *Roses are full of pricks.* 장미는 가시투성이다. **2** a small hole made by a sharp pointed thing. 찔러서 생긴 구멍. **3** sharp pain like that made by a sharp point. (바늘로 찔린 듯한) 아픔; 쑤심. ¶ *the ~ of conscience* (심한) 양심의 가책. **4** the act of pricking; the state of being pricked. 찌름; 찔림.

kick against the pricks, hurt oneself in opposing others. 무익한 저항을 하다.

— *vt.* **1** (P6) make a hole in (something) with something pointed. …에 구멍을 내다. ¶ *I pricked the map with a pin to show our route.* 우리 행로를 표시하기 위해 나는 핀으로 지도에다 구멍을 냈다. **2** (P6) cause (someone) to feel pain. …을 아프게 하다; 자극하다. ¶ *~ one's finger with* 〔*on*〕 *a needle* 손가락을 바늘에 찔리다 / *My conscience pricks* (*me*). 양심의 가책을 받는다. **3** (P6,7) 《*up*》 erect; raise. (개 따위가 귀)를 세우다. — *vi.* **1** (P1,2A) feel a sharp pain. 고통〔통증〕을 느끼다; 콕콕 쑤시다. ¶ *My fingers are pricking.* 손가락이 쑤신다. **2** point upwards. (귀가) 서다. [E.]

prick a bladder 〔***bubble***〕***,*** discover a dishonest trick. 가면을 벗기다.

prick up (***one's***) ***ears,*** **a**) raise the ears upward. (개·말 따위가) 귀를 쫑긋 세우다. **b**) listen closely. 주의해서 듣다.

prick·er [príkər] *n.* Ⓒ a person or thing that pricks. 찌르는 사람〔물건〕.

prick·le [príkəl] *n.* Ⓒ **1** a small, sharp point on a plant; a thorn. 가시; 바늘. **2** a feeling of sharp pain. 찌르는 듯한 아픔. — *vt.* **1** (P6) prick (someone or something) with something sharp. …을 찌르다. **2** give a pricking sensation to (something). …에게 찌르는 듯한 아픔을 주다. — *vi.* (P1) feel a pain like pricking. 따끔거리다. ¶ *Her skin prickled.* 피부가 따끔거렸다.

prick·ly [príkli] *adj.* (**-li·er, -li·est**) **1** full of sharp points or thorns. (식물 등이) 가시투성이의. ¶ *a ~ rosebush* 가시 많은 장미 덩굴. **2** having a sharp pain caused by a sting. 따끔거리는; 따끔따끔 아픈. ¶ *a ~ rash on the skin* 따끔거리는 피부의 발진(發疹)〔뾰루지〕.

prickly heat [∸-∸] *n.* a condition caused by very hot weather, in which your skin becomes hot and itchy and is covered with lots of tiny bumps. 땀띠.

:pride [praid] *n.* Ⓤ **1** 《sometimes *a ~* 》 a high opinion of one's own ability or importance; conceit. 자만; 오만; 거만; 교만. ¶ 《*prov.*》 *Pride goes before a fall.* 교만한 자는 오래 못 간다《교만은 패망의 선봉》. **2** a sense of one's own dignity or worth; self-respect. 자부심; 자존심; 프라이드. ¶ *a man of ~* 자존심이 강한 사람 / *wound* 〔*hurt*〕 *someone's ~* 아무의 자존심을 해치다 / *put one's ~ in one's pocket* 자존심을 억누르다; 수치를 참다. **3** a feeling of pleasure or satisfaction in one's accomplishments or possessions. 만족. ¶ *feel a ~ at* 〔*in*〕 *one's achievements* 자기의 업적에 만족해 하다. **4** something that gives someone pleasure or satisfaction. 자랑거리. ¶ *Her son is her ~.* 그녀에게 아들은 자랑거리다. **5** the best part; the most flourishing state or period. 전성; 한창; 정화(精華). ¶ *in the ~ of one's youth* 한창 나이에; 청춘 시절에 / *a peacock in his ~* 날개를 활짝 편 공작. **6** a band or group of animals or birds. (짐승·새 들의) 한 무리; 떼. ¶ *a ~ of lions.*

— *vt.* 《*reflexively*》 take a pride in; claim credit for (something). …을 자랑하다; 뽐내다. ¶ *~ oneself on one's work* 〔*ability*〕 자기의 일〔능력〕을 뽐내다 / *He prides himself on being* *a member of a good family.* 그는 자신이 명문 집안 출신임을 내세운다. [→proud]

:priest [pri:st] *n.* Ⓒ **1** a person who serves gods to perform religious acts. 성직자. **2** a clergyman or minister of a Christian church. (기독교의) 목사; 사제. [→presbyter]

priest·hood [prí:sthùd] *n.* Ⓤ **1** the position or duties of a priest. 성직(聖職). **2** 《*collectively*》 all priests. 성직자.

priest·ly [prí:stli] *adj.* (**-li·er, -li·est**) of, for, or like a priest. 성직자의; 성직자다운.

prig [prig] *n.* Ⓒ a narrow-minded person who is unusually strict about speech or conduct. 딱딱한〔까다로운〕 사람; 잔소리꾼. [?]

prig·gish [prígiʃ] *adj.* like a prig. 딱딱한; 까다로운.

prim [prim] *adj.* (**prim·mer, prim·mest**) very stiff and not easy in appearance or conduct; extremely neat or precise. 까다로운; 깐깐한; 꼼꼼한.
—*vt., vi.* (**primmed, prim·ming**) (P6; 1) put (the face, lips, etc.) into a prim expression. 정색(正色)하다; 입을 꾹 다물다. [?]
prim out 〔***up***〕, decorate affectedly. …을 (그럴싸하게) 꾸미다.

pri·ma·cy [práiməsi] *n.* Ⓤ **1** the state of being at the top or first in time, order, importance, etc. 첫째; 제 1 위; 수위; 탁월. **2** the office, rank or dignity of a primate. 대주교(大主教)의 직〔지위〕. **3** the superior power of the Pope in the Roman Catholic Church. 교황의 지상권(至上權). [→prime]

pri·ma don·na [prì(:)mə dɑ́nə, prímə dɔ́nə] *n.* (**p- don·nas** or **pri·me don·ne**) the leading woman singer in an opera. 프리마돈나 《가극의 주연 여배우·가수》. [It.=first lady]

pri·mae·val [praimí:vəl] *adj.* =primeval.

pri·ma fa·ci·e [práimə féiʃii:, -ʃi:] *adv., adj.* at first sight; on the face of it. 얼핏 보기에는; 첫인상으로〔는〕; 첫인상의. [L.=at first face]

pri·mal [práiməl] *adj.* **1** of the first age of the world; very ancient; first. 최초의; 원시의. **2** highest in rank or authority; at the head; basic. 제일의; 주요한; 근본이 되는. [→prime]

pri·mar·i·ly [praimérəli, ∠−−− / práimərili] *adv.* **1** mainly; principally; chiefly. 주로. ¶ *The course is ~ intended for beginners.* 이 코스는 주로 초심자를 위해 마련된 것이다. **2** in the first instance; originally. 최초로; 근본적으로; 원래. ¶ *The custom started ~ among farmers.* 이 풍습은 농민들 사이에서 비롯되었다. [↓]

·pri·ma·ry [práimèri, -məri] *adj.* **1** first in time or order. 첫째의; 초기의; 최초의. ¶ *Little children go to the ~ school.* 어린아이들은 초등 학교에 간다 / *the ~ accent* 제 1 악센트. **2** first of the kind; of the beginning; existing from the first; basic; original. 원시의; 본래의; 근본의; 기본적인. ¶ *~ meaning of the word* 말의 원뜻 / *The ~ colors are red, blue and yellow.* 원색은 빨강, 파랑, 노랑이다. **3** of the first in importance; chief. 가장 중요한; 주요한. ¶ *a matter of ~ importance* 가장 중요한 문제 / *Good health and character are ~.* 건강과 인격이 가장 중요하다. **4** fundamental. 초보의; 기초적인. ¶ *~ education* 초등 교육.
—*n.* Ⓒ (*pl.* **-ries**) **1** something which comes first in importance. 주요한 사물. **2** one of the primary colors. 원색(原色). **3** 《U.S.》 an election to name the candidates for the main election. 예비 선거. [→prime]

pri·mate [práimit, -meit] *n.* Ⓒ **1** an archbishop or chief bishop of a country. 대주교. **2** 《zool.》 the highest rank of mammals, including human beings, apes and monkeys. 영장류(靈長類)의 동물. [→prime]

·prime[1] [praim] *adj.* **1** highest in rank; chief; most important. 수위(首位)의; 첫째의; 가장 중요한. ¶ *of ~ importance* 가장 중요한 / *the Prime Minister* 수상 / *His ~ concern is the welfare of his country.* 그의 가장 중요 관심사는 나라의 복지이다. **2** first in time; original. 제 1 의; 최초〔근본〕의. ¶ *the ~ cost* 원가 / 《astron.》 *the ~ meridian* 본초 자오선. **3** first in quality; best. 최상의. ¶ *~ pork* 상등 돼지고기 / *feel ~* 기운이 넘치다 / *in the ~ condition* 썩 좋은 컨디션으로. **4** that can be divided evenly only by 1 or itself. 소수(素數)의. ¶ *a ~ number* 소수.
—*n.* Ⓒ 《usu. *the ~, one's ~*》 **1** the time of a person's life in which he is best in health, mind, beauty, etc. 전성기. ¶ *during (one's) ~* 전성기에 / *He has passed his ~.* 그는 한창때가 지났다. **2** the best part of anything. 가장 좋은 부분. **3** the beginning; youth. 최초; 초기; 청춘. ¶ *the ~ of the year* 봄. [L. *primus* first]

prime[2] [praim] *vt.* (P6) **1** get (a gun) ready for firing by putting in gunpowder. (총)에 화약을 재다. ¶ *~ a mine with explosive charge* 광산에 폭약을 장치하다. **2** supply (someone) with information in advance. …에게 미리 알려〔귀띔해, 가르쳐〕 주다. ¶ *fully primed with the latest news* 최근의 뉴스에 정통한. **3** 《*colloq.*》 supply, fill up, with food or drink. (음식·술)을 실컷〔배불리〕 먹이다. ¶ *wellprimed with a hearty meal* 배불리 실컷 먹은. **4** cover (a surface) with first coast of paint, oil, etc. …에 초벌칠하다. [↑]

prime mover [∠∠−] *n.* **1** a natural source of power 〔wind, water pressure, etc.〕. 원동력(原動力). **2** any machine that converts this power to useful purposes. 원동기(原動機). **3** the principal human agent in forwarding some affair. 주도자. ¶ *He was a ~ in the plot to assassinate the king.* 그는 국왕 시해 음모의 주모자였다.

prim·er [prímər / práimər] *n.* Ⓒ **1** a book

containing the first lessons in reading. 초보 독본; 첫걸음책. **2** the first training book in any subject. 입문서. **3** [prímər] 《print.》 one of two sizes of type. 프리머(활자). ¶ *great* 〔*long*〕 ~, *18* 〔*10*〕 포인트 활자.

pri·me·val, -mae- [praimíːvəl] *adj.* of the earliest ages; very old. 원시 시대의; 태고의. ¶ *a* ~ *forest* 원시림. [→prime, L. *aevum* age]

prim·ing [práimiŋ] *n.* Ⓤ **1** gunpowder or other material used for setting fire to an explosive. 기폭제(起爆劑); 점화약. **2** an undercoat or first coat of paint, etc. 초벌칠. [→prime²]

:prim·i·tive [prímətiv] *adj.* **1** of the earliest time. 원시의; 태고의. ¶ *a* ~ *man* 원시인. **2** simple; rough. 단순한; 소박한. ¶ *The natives of that region still live in* ~ *straw huts.* 그 지역의 토착민은 아직도 짚으로 된 오두막에 살고 있다 / *He is very* ~ *in his ways.* 그가 하는 방식은 아주 단순하다. **3** original. 본디의. ¶ ~ *colors* 원색. **—*n.*** Ⓒ **1** a primitive person. 원시인. **2** a painter or sculptor, or his work, of a period before the Renaissance. 문예 부흥기 이전의 작가; 그 작품. [→prime¹]

pri·mo·gen·i·tor [pràimoudʒénətər] *n.* Ⓒ **1** an ancestor. 조상; 선조. **2** the earliest ancestor of a family, a race, etc. 시조(始祖). [L.]

pri·mo·gen·i·ture [pràimoudʒénətʃər] *n.* Ⓤ **1** the state of being the first-born child of the parents. 장자임. **2** 《law》 the right of the eldest son to get all the property after his father dies. 장자 상속(권). [→prime, L. *gigno* beget]

pri·mor·di·al [praimɔ́ːrdiəl] *adj.* **1** primitive. 원시의. ¶ *a* ~ *cell* 원시 세포 / ~ *customs* 원시 시대의 습관들. **2** original, elementary. 기본의; 근본적인. [→prime, L. *ordior* begin]

primp [primp] *vi., vt.* (P1; 6) 《U.S.》 **1** dress (oneself) for show. 멋부리다; 모양을 내다. **2** dress carefully. 차려 입다. [*prim*]

prim·rose [prímròuz] *n.* **1** Ⓒ a plant, usu. with pale yellow flowers. 앵초(櫻草). **2** Ⓤ the color of this flower. 담황색. **—*adj.*** **1** pale yellow. 담황색의. **2** like a primrose; merry; cheerful. 앵초 같은; 명랑한. [→prime, →rose]

:prince [prins] *n.* Ⓒ **1** a son of a king or queen. 왕자. ¶ *the manners of a* ~ 기품 있는 태도. **2** the son of a royal family. 왕족의 아들. **3** the ruler of a small country. (소국의) 통치자; 군주; 왕후. ¶ *the Prince of Monaco* 모나코공(公). **4** the greatest or the best person in a group. 제1인자; 대가(大家). ¶ *a merchant* ~ 호상(豪商) / *a* ~ *of artists* 〔*poets*〕 화단〔시단〕의 중진 / *the* ~ *of bankers* 은행 왕. [L. *princeps*]

as happy as a prince, extremely happy. 아주 행복한.

live like a prince, live luxuriously. 호화롭게 살다.

prince·ly [prínsli] *adj.* (**-li·er, -li·est**) **1** worthy of a prince. 왕후〔왕자〕다운. **2** of or like a prince; noble. 군주〔왕후〕 같은; 고귀한.

:prin·cess [prínsis, prinsés] *n.* Ⓒ **1** the daughter of a king or queen. 공주; 왕녀. **2** the wife or widow of a prince. 왕자비. **3** the daughter of a royal family. 왕족의 딸.

:prin·ci·pal [prínsəpəl] *adj.* most important; main; chief. 주요한; 첫째의; 중요한. ¶ *the* ~ *rivers of a country* 나라의 주요 하천들 / *the* ~ *articles of food* 식품의 주요 품목 / *the* ~ *clause* 주절(主節).

—*n.* Ⓒ **1** the principal person. 장(長); 우두머리. ¶ *the* ~ *of a business* 〔*school*〕 영업소장〔학교장〕. **2** a person who takes a leading part. 중심 인물; 주역. **3** the head or director of a school or college. 교장; 학장. **4** a person actually responsible for a crime. 주범(主犯)(cf. *accessory*). **5** Ⓤ the sum on which interest is paid. 원금. **6** Ⓒ a person who hires another to act for him. (대리인에 대한) 본인. ¶ *Smith does the business of renting the houses for Mr. Jones, his* ~. 스미스는 존스 씨를 대리하여 가옥 임대업을 한다. [L. *princeps*]

prin·ci·pal·i·ty [prìnsəpǽləti] *n.* Ⓒ (*pl.* **-ties**) **1** a country or territory ruled by a prince. 공국(公國). ¶ *the Principality* 웨일스(Wales)의 별칭. **2** the state, rank, or authority of a prince. 공국 군주의 지위·권력.

prin·ci·pal·ly [prínsəpəli] *adv.* chiefly; above all; mainly; for the most part. 주로; 대개.

:prin·ci·ple [prínsəpl] *n.* **1** Ⓒ a truth on which other truths are based. 원리; 원칙. ¶ *the principles of economics* 경제 원리 / *the principles of democratic government* 민주정치의 원리. **2** Ⓤ settled rules of action or conduct. 주의; 방침. ¶ *as a matter of* ~ 주의로서 / *I make it a* ~ *never to borrow or to lend money.* 돈을 빌리지도 빌려주지도 않는 것이 내 신조다 / *religious principles* 종교적 신념. **3** Ⓒ a standard of honesty or righteousness. 절조; 도의. ¶ *He is a man of* ~. 그는 지조 있는 사람이다. **4** Ⓒ a natural or scientific law by which something works. 자연의 법칙. [L. *princeps*]

in principle, with reference to general truth; generally. 원칙적으로; 대체로.

on principle, **a**) according to a principle. 원칙에 따라. **b**) by principle. 주의로서.

:print [print] *n.* Ⓒ **1** a mark made on a surface of paper, sand, etc. by pressing something against it. 자국; 흔적. ¶ *the* ~ *of a foot on the floor* 마루에 난 발자국 / *the* ~ *of one's fingers on a glass* 유리컵의 손가락 자국. **2** 《*fig.*》 a mark left on a person's face by sorrow, etc.; an impression. 인상. ¶ *sorrow's* ~ *upon his face* 그의 얼굴에 남은 슬픔의 자국 / *a character which bore the* ~ *of ear-*

ly hardships 초년에 고생한 흔적이 보이는 사람. **3** Ⓤ the act of pressing letters or words; pressed things. 인쇄; 인쇄물. ¶ *This newspaper has clear* ~. 이 신문은 인쇄가 깨끗하다. **4** 《chiefly U.S.》 a newspaper; special paper used for newspapers. 신문; 신문지. ¶ *see one's name in* ~ (자기 의견 등)을 신문에 발표하다. **5** a picture, design, etc. made of block or plate and used to press; a picture made from a photographic film. 판화(版畫); (사진의) 양화(陽畫). ¶ *a collection of prints* 판화집. **6** Ⓤ cotton cloth on which a picture, design, etc. is pressed. 날염포(捺染布); 사라사.

in print, published. 인쇄〔출판〕되어.

out of print, no longer published; out of press. (책이) 절판(絕版)되어.

— *vt.* **1** (P6) mark (something) by pressure; impress. …의 자국을 내다. ¶ ~ *the mark of one's foot on the sand* 모래 위에 발자국을 내다 / ~ *a kiss upon the cheek* 볼에 키스하다. **2** (P6) press or publish (books, etc.). …을 인쇄하다; 출판〔발행〕하다. ¶ ~ *a leaflet* 삐라를 찍다 / ~ *book* 〔*lectures*〕 책을〔강의 자료를〕 인쇄하다 / *Most newspapers are printed everyday.* 대부분의 신문들은 일간으로 발행된다. **3** (P6) impress (something) upon the mind. …을 마음에 새기다. ¶ *The scene is printed on my memory.* 그 광경은 내 기억에 새겨져 있다. **4** form (letters) in writing like printed character. (글씨)를 활자체로 쓰다. ¶ *Please* ~ *all proper name in block letters.* 모든 고유명(固有名)은 블록체로 쓰시오. **5** (P6) mark (cloth, paper, etc.) with patterns or designs. …을 날염(捺染)하다. ¶ ~ *calico* 〔*cloth, wall-paper*〕 옥양목〔천, 벽지〕에 날염하다. **6** (P7) produce (a photograph) by passing light through a negative. (사진)을 인화하다.

— *vi.* **1** (P1) practise the art or business of a printer. 인쇄를 업으로 하다. ¶ *Caxton printed from 1476 to 1491.* 캑스턴은 1476년부터 1491년까지 출판업을 했다. **2** (P1, 2A,2B) come out as the result of printing. (사진 따위가) 인화(印畫)되다; (인쇄가) 잘 나오다. ¶ *The photograph has printed well.* 사진이 잘 나왔다. **3** (P1,2A,2B) make a print; publish books. 인쇄하다; 출판하다. [→press]

print·er [príntər] *n.* Ⓒ a person or thing that prints; an owner of a printing business. 인쇄공; 인쇄기; 인쇄업자.

***print·ing** [príntiŋ] *n.* Ⓤ **1** printed letters, words, etc. 인쇄된 글자〔말〕. **2** all the copies (of a book, etc.) printed at one time. 인쇄물. **3** letters that resemble print; the style of printing. 활자체(의 글자).

***pri·or**[1] [práiər] *adj.* **1** earlier; previous. 전의; 앞(서)의 (opp. posterior; cf. *antecedent, anterior, previous*). ¶ *a* ~ *engagement* 선약(先約). **2** first in importance or order. 가장 중요한. — *adv.* 《*to*》 earlier than; before. …보다 먼저〔전에〕. ¶ *Prior to my arrival he left the village.* 내가 도착하기 전에 그는 마을을 떠나고 없었다. [L.=earlier]

pri·or[2] [práiər] *n.* Ⓒ the head of a priory for men or monastery. 소(小)수도원의 원장. [↑]

pri·or·ess [práiəris] *n.* Ⓒ the head of a priory for women. 소(小)수녀원의 원장. [↑]

pri·or·i·ty [praiɔ́(:)rəti, -ɑ́r-] *n.* Ⓤ **1** the state of being or coming first in time, order, importance, etc. 먼저임; 앞섬; 우선. ¶ ~ *of birth* 먼저 태어남 / *The proceeds of sale will be distributed according to* ~. 판매 수입은 우선 순위에 따라 분배될 것이다. **2** the right to precede. 우선권. ¶ *give* ~ *to* … 에게 우선권을 주다 / *take* ~ *over* …보다 우선권이 있다 / *You have* ~ *over him in your claim.* 네 요구가 그의 것보다 우선권이 있다. [→prior[1], -ity]

pri·o·ry [práiəri] *n.* Ⓒ (*pl.* **-ries**) a religious house ruled by a prior or prioress, usu. ranked under an abbey. 소(小)수도원. [*prior*[2]]

prism [prízəm] *n.* Ⓒ **1** a block of regular shape with three or more flat sides and with two flat ends that are the same in size and shape. 각기둥; 각주(角柱). **2** a glass body of this shape, usu. three-sided which breaks up a ray of sunlight into the colors of the rainbow. 프리즘; 분광기(分光器). ¶ ~ *glasses* 프리즘쌍안경. [Gk. *prizō* saw]

pris·mat·ic [prizmǽtik] *adj.* **1** of or like a prism. 각기둥의〔같은〕. **2** (of colors) formed or divided by a prism. 분광(分光)의. **3** of these colors. 무지개 빛의; 색색의; 다채로운.

prismatic colors [–´–´ ´–], **the** *n.* the colors of the visible spectrum. 스펙트럼의 일곱 가지 색깔.

:pris·on [prízn] *n.* **1** Ⓒ a building where law breakers are kept and punished; a jail. 감옥; 교도소. **2** Ⓤ any place where a person is held against his will. 가두는 데; 감금〔구치〕소. [→pregnable]

:pris·on·er [príznər] *n.* Ⓒ **1** a person who is shut up in a prison or a soldier taken by the enemy. 죄수; 포로. **2** a person who is not free to move. 자유를 빼앗긴 자. ¶ *My work will keep me a* ~ *all summer.* 나는 일 때문에 여름 내내 꼼짝 못 하는 신세가 될 것 같다 / *Gout kept me a* ~ *to my room.* 통풍(痛風)으로 방 안에 갇혀 있었다 / *a* ~ *of love* 사랑의 포로.

pris·tine [prísti:n, -tain] *adj.* of the earliest ages; original; unspoiled and pure. 초기의; 원시 시대의; 소박한. ¶ *The colors of the paintings inside the pyramid had kept their* ~ *freshness.* 피라미드 내부에 있는 그림들의 색깔은 초기의 생생함을 그대로 간직하고 있었다. [L.]

pri·va·cy [práivəsi / prí-] *n.* Ⓤ **1** the state of being away from other people.

남의 이목을 피하기; 은둔; 사생활. ¶ *live in* ~ 은둔 생활을 하다 / *disturb one's* ~ 조용한 사생활을 방해하다. **2** the state of being secret. 비밀; 은밀. ¶ *I tell you this in strict* ~. 이 일은 절대 비밀의 이야기입니다. [↓]
in privacy, secretly. 비밀히; 숨어서.
in the privacy of (*one's*) ***thoughts,*** deep down in the heart. 마음속으로〔에서〕.
:pri·vate [práivit] *adj.* **1** belonging to a single person; personal. 개인의; 사유(私有)의 (opp. public). ¶ *on* ~ *business* 사삿일로 / ~ *life* 사생활 / *a* ~ *school* 사립 학교 / ~ *property* 사유 재산 / ~ *right* 사권(私權). **2** not official; having no public office. 비공식의; (공인이 아닌) 개인〔민간〕의; 사적인. ¶ *as a* ~ *person* 개인적으로; 비공식으로 / ~ *clothes* 사복 / ~ *means* (봉급 이외의) 불로 소득《이자 등》/ *a* ~ *citizen* 평민 / ~ *information* 비공식 통지 / *speak* 〔*act*〕 *in one's* ~ *capacity* (공인이 아닌) 개인으로서 말하다〔행동하다〕. **3** not known to others; secret. 비밀의. ¶ *a* ~ *letter* 사신(私信) / *keep a matter* ~ …을 비밀로 하다. **4** 《Brit.》 holding the lowest rank as a soldier. 일개 병졸의.
— *n.* Ⓒ **1** 《Brit.》 a common soldier. 병졸; 사병. **2** 《*pl.*》 the secret parts of the body. 음부(陰部). [L. *privo* deprive]
in private, secretly. 비밀로; 몰래.
pri·va·teer [pràivətíər] *n.* Ⓒ **1** an armed private ship allowed by the government to attack enemy ships. 사(私)나포선《전시에 적의 상선에 대한 나포가 허가된 무장 민간선》. **2** the captain or one of the crew of such a ship. 사나포선의 선장〔승무원〕.
pri·vate·ly [práivitli] *adv.* in a private manner; not publicly; secretly. 개인적으로; 내밀히.
pri·va·tion [praivéiʃən] *n.* ⓊⒸ **1** the lack of the needs of life, esp. food and clothing. 결핍; 궁핍. ¶ *the privations of life* 생활의 궁핍; 가난한 생활 / *He died of* ~. 그는 가난 때문에 죽었다 / *suffer* (*many*) *privations* 온갖 고생을 하다. **2** the state of being taken away; loss; absence. 박탈; 상실(喪失). ¶ ~ *of property* 재산의 몰수 / *Privation of the company of all other human beings is a serious hardship.* 모든 다른 동료들과의 단절은 견디기 어려운 고통이다.
priv·et [prívit] *n.* Ⓒ a shrub with dark green leaves and small white flowers, much used for hedges. 쥐똥나무의 일종. [?]
:priv·i·lege [prívəlidʒ] *n.* ⓊⒸ a special advantage, right or favor given to a person or a body of persons; 《*the* ~》 prerogative 특권; 특전; (개인적인) 은전〔특혜〕; 대권(大權) ¶ *the* ~ *of birth* 나면서부터 갖고 있는 특권 / *a writ of* ~ 특사장(特赦狀) / *the special* ~ *of wealth* 〔*high rank*〕 부(富)가〔고위직이〕 가지는 특권 / *grant a* ~ *to...* …에게 특권을 주다 / *Mr. Hope has given us the* ~ *of using his garden.* 호프씨는 우리에게 그의 정원을 마음대로 이용할 수 있는 특전을 주었다.
bill of privilege, the petition of a peer to be tried by his peers. 귀족이 귀족에 의한 심리를 요구하는 청원서.
breach of privilege, infringement of the privilege of Parliament. (국회 의원의) 특권 침해.
— *vt.* (P6,20) give a special right to (someone). …에게 특권을 주다. ¶ *Employees are privileged to buy at a discount.* 종업원들은 할인가로 살 특전이 있다. [→privy, →legal]
privilege cab [∠-- ∠] *n.* 《Brit.》 one admitted to stand for hire in a private place, esp. the railway station. 특전 택시 《정거장 등에서 승객을 기다리도록 허가된》.
priv·i·leged [prívəlidʒd] *adj.* having or granted a special right or advantages. 특권·특전이 있는; 특허의. ¶ *the* ~ *classes* 특권 계급 / *a* ~ *few* 소수 특권층의 사람들 / *a* ~ *parking place* 전용 주차장.
priv·i·ly [prívəli] *adj.* not publicly; in a secret manner. 비밀히; 은밀히.
priv·y [prívi] *adj.* (**priv·i·er, priv·i·est**) **1** belonging to a single person. 개인의; 사유〔사용(私用)〕의. ¶ *the* ~ *purse* 내탕금(內帑金) / ~ *rooms* 사실(私室). **2** 《*to*》 having secret information or knowledge. 내밀하게 관여하고 있는. ¶ *be* ~ *to the plot* 음모에 내밀히 관여하고 있다. — *n.* Ⓒ (*pl.* **priv·ies**) an outdoor toilet. 옥외 변소. [L. *privus* private]
Privy Council [∠- ∠-], **the** *n.* 《Brit.》 a body of people of high rank in politics and public life who may advise the king or queen on certain state affairs. 추밀원(樞密院).
:prize[1] [praiz] *n.* Ⓒ **1** something given to honor a person who has won a race, etc. 상(賞); 상금; 상품. ¶ *He won the first* ~ *in the marathon race.* 마라톤에서 1등상을 탔다 / *a* ~ *for good conduct* 선행상 / *He was awarded the Nobel Peace Prize.* 그는 노벨 평화상을 탔다. **2** anything worth making efforts to get. 얻으려고 노력할 만한 가치가 있는 것. ¶ *the prizes of life* 인생의 목표물《부(富)·명예 등》. **3** something good or valuable. 귀중한 것; 진품(珍品). ¶ *She picked up a* ~ *at a bargain sale.* 할인 매장에서 진품을 찾아냈다.
— *adj.* **1** given as a prize; got as a prize. 상품으로 주어진〔탄〕; 현상의. ¶ *a* ~ *novel* 현상 소설 / *a* ~ *cup* 〔*medal*〕 우승컵〔메달〕. **2** ⓐ worth getting a prize; fine. 상을 받을 만한; 훌륭한. ⓑ 《*colloq.*》 deserving a prize. 상을 줄 만한《반어적》. ¶ *a* ~ *idiot* 1등〔큰〕 바보.
— *vt.* (P6,7) value highly. …을 존중하다. ¶ ~ *honor above life* 목숨보다 명예를 중히 여기다. [→price]
prize[2] [praiz] *n.* Ⓒ something taken from the enemy in war, etc. (전시의) 포획물《나포선 및 그 화물》; 전리품. [→pregnable]

become the prize of [***to***] (=*be captured by*) *someone or something.* …에게 나포되다.
make a prize of (=*capture*) *someone or something.* …을 나포하다.

prize³ [praiz] *vt.* (P7,18) force, lift up, by leverage. 지레로 움직이다[올리다]; 집어 열다. ¶ ~ *open a door* 문을 지레로 비집어 열다 / ~ *up the lid of a box* 지레로 상자 뚜껑을 열다. [↑]

prize fight [⌐⌐] *n.* a boxing match for money. 현상 권투 시합; 프로 권투. [→*prize*]

prize ring [⌐⌐] *n.* the square space enclosed by ropes where a boxing match takes place. 현상 권투 시합장; 프로 권투의 링; 프로 권투계.

prize winner [⌐⌐–] *n.* **1** a person who wins a prize. 수상자. **2** a novel, etc. which is given a prize. 수상 작품.

pro¹ [prou] *adv.* in favor of; for. 찬성하여. — *n.* Ⓒ (*pl.* **pros**) an argument or a reason in favor of something. 찬성(의견·론)(opp. con). [L. *prō* for]
pros and cons of (=*arguments for and against*) *a question.* 찬부 양론(贊否兩論).

pro² [prou] *n.* Ⓒ (*pl.* **pros**) 《*colloq.*》 a professional player of a sport, etc. 직업 선수; 프로. ¶ *a golf* [*cricket*] ~. — *adj.* 《*colloq.*》 professional. 직업의; 직업적인. ¶ *a* ~ *golfer* 프로 골프 선수. [→professional]

pro-¹ [prou-] *pref.* **1** to the front; forward. '앞에, 앞으로'의 뜻. ¶ *proceed* 앞으로 나아가다. **2** in favor of. '찬성의, 편드는'의 뜻. ¶ *pro-slavery* 노예 제도 지지의. **3** instead of; substituted for. '…의 대신에, 대용으로, 부(副)…'의 뜻. ¶ *pronoun* 대명사. **4** publicly. '공공연히'의 뜻. ¶ *proclaim* 공포하다. [L. *prō* for, to, before]

pro-² [prou-] *pref.* before; in front of. '앞, …의 앞에'의 뜻. ¶ *prolog* 머리말. [Gk.]

·**prob·a·bil·i·ty** [prɑ̀bəbíləti / prɔ̀b-] *n.* (*pl.* **-ties**) **1** Ⓤ the state or quality of being probable; likelihood. 있음직함; 가장 그럴 듯함; 가능성; 가망. ¶ *a high* ~ 높은 가능성 / *What are the probabilities?* 가망이 있는가 / *There is every* ~ [*no* ~] *of success.* 다분히 성공할 것 같다[성공할 가망은 전무다]. **2** Ⓒ something likely to happen; a probable event. 있을 수 있는 일. ¶ *The* ~ *is that he will win.* 아마 그는 이길 것이다 / *The probabilities are against us* [*in our favor*]. 우리에게 승산이 없다[있다]. [↓]
in all probability, most likely; probably; almost certainly. 다분히; 십중 팔구.

·**prob·a·ble** [prɑ́bəbəl / prɔ́b-] *adj.* **1** likely to happen. 있음직한; 개연성이 있는. ¶ *the* ~ *results of an action* 어떤 행동의 있음직한 결과 / *the* ~ *cost* 어림잡은 비용 / *Success is possible but hardly* ~. 성공할 수 없는 것은 아니나, 실제로 그 가능성은 희박하다. **2** likely to be true; giving reason for belief. 틀림없을 것 같은; 믿을 만한. ¶ ~ *evidence* (믿을 만한) 확실한 증거 / *the* ~ *cause of the fire* 믿을 만한 화재의 원인. [→prove]

:**prob·a·bly** [prɑ́bəbli / prɔ́b-] *adv.* very likely. 아마; 필시. ¶ *It will* ~ *rain tomorrow.* 아마 내일은 비가 올 것이다 / *Shall we win?* —*Probably.* 우리가 이길까—그럴 게다.

pro·bate [próubeit] *n.* **1** 《law》 the official proving of a will. 유언의 검인(檢認). ¶ *a* ~ *court* 유언 검인 재판소. **2** a verified copy of a will with a certificate of this. 검인필 유언장. — *vt.* (P6) prove by legal process the genuineness of (a will). (유언장)을 검인하다. [→prove]

pro·ba·tion [proubéiʃən] *n.* ⓊⒸ **1** a trial or test of a person's conduct, ability, character, etc. (자격·능력 등의) 검정(檢定); 시험(試驗). ¶ *take someone on* ~ 아무를 가(假)채용하다 / *pass* ~ 시험을 통과하다. **2** the period of such trying or testing. 견습[수습] 기간. ¶ *After a period of* ~ *a novice becomes a nun.* 예비 수녀는 수습 기간을 거쳐 수녀가 된다. **3** 《law》 the legal system of permitting law breakers to go free under police management. 보호 관찰; (형의) 집행 유예. ¶ *place* [*put*] *an offender on* ~ 범인을 집행 유예 중 보호 관찰 아래 두다.

pro·ba·tion·al [proubéiʃənəl] *adj.* =probationary.

pro·ba·tion·ar·y [proubéiʃənèri / -nəri] *adj.* **1** of probation. 시험적인. **2** on probation. 수습 중인; 보호 관찰 중의. ¶ *a* ~ *prisoner* 보호 관찰 중인 피고.

pro·ba·tion·er [proubéiʃənər] *n.* Ⓒ a person who is on probation. 수습[견습]생; 가(假)채용[입학]자; 집행 유예 중인 피고.

probe [proub] *n.* Ⓒ **1** 《surg.》 a long, thin instrument used by doctors in examining a wound. 소식자(消息子); 탐침(探針)《상처 따위를 살피는 기구(器具)》. **2** the careful examination into crime or wrongdoing. (범죄·비행 등의) 조사. — *vt.* (P6) **1** examine (a wound) with a probe. (상처)를 탐침으로 살피다. **2** search or examine closely. …을 조사하다. ¶ ~ *rumors to the bottom* 루머를 철저히 조사하다. — *vi.* 《*into*》 search or examine with a probe. 소식자를 써서 (면밀히) 조사하다. ¶ 《*fig.*》 ~ *into the causes of a crime* 범죄의 동기를 규명하다. [→prove]

pro·bi·ty [próubəti, prɑ́b-] *n.* Ⓤ honesty; righteousness; goodness; sincerity. 청렴; 정직; 성실. [L. *probus* good]

:**prob·lem** [prɑ́bləm / prɔ́b-] *n.* Ⓒ **1** a question hard to understand; a matter hard to settle or decide. 문제. ¶ *the basic problems of our times* 현대의 기본적 문제 / *the problems of existence* 생존의 문제 / *It is a* ~ *how to make both ends meet.* 어떻게 하면 빚을 안 지고 살아가느냐가 문제다. **2** 《math.》 something to be solved. 문제; 과제. ¶ *a mathematical* ~ 수학 문제. — *adj.* causing difficulty. 문제의; 골치 아픈. ¶ *a* ~ *child* 문

제아. [pro-, Gk. *ballo* throw]

prob·lem·at·ic, -i·cal [prɑ̀bləmǽtik / prɔ̀b-], [-əl] *adj.* having problems; doubtful; questionable. 문제의; 문제가 되는; 불확실한; 미심쩍은. ¶ *a* ~ *matter* 미해결[미정]의 문제 / *Its success is* ~. 그것의 성부(成否)는 의심스럽다.

pro·bos·ci·des [proubɑ́sidìːz / -bɔ́s-] *n.* pl. of **proboscis.**

pro·bos·cis [proubɑ́sis / -bɔ́s-] *n.* Ⓒ (*pl.* **-cis·es** or **-ci·des** [-sidìːz]) **1** an elephant's trunk. 코끼리의 코. **2** any long, easily bent nose of other animals. (코뿔소·맥(貘)의 비죽 나온) 코. **3** the stretched mouth part of certain insects used for sucking liquids, etc. (곤충 등의) 주둥이. ¶ *the* ~ *of a fly* [*mosquito*] 파리[모기]의 주둥이. **4** 《*colloq., joc.*》 the nose of a human being. (사람의) 코. [pro-, Gk. *bosko* feed]

·pro·ce·dure [prəsíːdʒər] *n.* ⓊⒸ **1** the act or manner of proceeding in a course of action; a method of doing thing. 진행; 진행 방식; (일의) 처리 방법. ¶ *What is your* ~ *in making such puddings?* 그런 푸딩은 어떤 식으로 만들지. **2** a particular course of action. 절차; 수순(手順). ¶ *follow the* ~ 수순대로 하다; (소정의) 절차를 밟다. **3** an established way of carrying on legal or parliamentary business. (소송·의사(議事) 등의) 절차. ¶ *legal* ~ 소송 절차 / *the code of civil* [*criminal*] ~ 민사[형사] 소송법 / *summary* ~ 약식 재판 절차. [→proceed]

:pro·ceed [prousíːd] *vi.* **1** (P1,2A) move or go on, esp. after stopping. 나아가다; 가다. ¶ ~ *on a journey* 여행을 떠나다 / ~ *to New York* 뉴욕으로 가다 / *The train proceeded at the same speed as before.* 기차는 전과 같은 속도로 나아갔다. **2** (P1,2A,3,4) 《*with, in*》 carry on or continue to do something; go on to say. (일·행동 따위를) 계속하다; 말을 계속하다. ¶ ~ *with work* [*the game, investigation*] 일을[경기를, 조사를] 계속하다 / *Let us* ~ *with our lesson.* 자, 수업을 계속하자. **3** (P1,2A,3,4) begin (to do). 시작[착수]하다. ¶ ~ *to eat one's dinner* 저녁을 먹기 시작하다 / ~ *to take off one's coat* 저고리를 벗기 시작하다. **4** (P3) 《*from, out of*》 take place; go or come forth; arise from. 일어나다; 생기다; 솟아오르다. ¶ *This proceeded from ignorance.* 이건 무지에서 생겼다 / *Clouds of smoke proceeded from the chimney.* 굴뚝에서 연기가 뭉게뭉게 솟아올랐다 / *Sounds proceeded from the house.* 그 집에서 시끄러운 소리가 일어났다. **5** (P1,2A,3,4) 《*against*》 begin and carry on a legal action. 절차를 밟다; 소송을 일으키다. ¶ *I advise you not to* ~ *against him.* 나는 네가 그 사람을 제소하지 않기를 바란다. **6** (P3) take degree. 학위를 얻다. [pro-, L. *cedo* go]

·pro·ceed·ing [prousíːdiŋ] *n.* Ⓒ **1** Ⓤ a line of action or a course of action. (일련의) 행동; 진행. ¶ *a strange* ~ *on his part* 그의 역할에서의 이상한 행동. **2** the mode of procedure. 방식; 절차. **3** 《*pl.*》 《law》 a law process. 소송 절차. ¶ *start* [*take*] *proceedings against someone* 아무에 대해 소송을 제기하다. **4** 《*pl.*》 a record of things done at a meeting. 의사록(議事錄).

pro·ceeds [próusiːdz] *n. pl.* the amount of money gained from a business, etc.; the results from a business, etc.; the profit. 매상고; 수익; 수입. ¶ *He sold his house and is now living on the* ~. 그는 집을 팔고 그 돈으로 지내고 있다.

:proc·ess [prɑ́ses / próu-] *n.* **1** Ⓤ the course of being done; moving forward; progress. 과정; 진행. ¶ *the* ~ *of development* 발전 과정 / *in* ~ *of completion* 완성 과정에 있는. **2** Ⓤ the course of time. (시간의) 경과. ¶ *in* ~ *of time* 시간의 경과에 따라. **3** Ⓤ a continuous action or series of actions which lead to some end. 순서; 방법. ¶ *invent a new dyeing* ~ 새로운 염색법을 발명하다. **4** Ⓒ a special method of manufacturing or treatment. 공정(工程); 제법(製法). ¶ *By what processes is the cloth made?* 직물은 어떤 공정으로 만들어지나. **5** Ⓒ 《biol.》 the part that grows out, esp. on bone. 돌기; 융기(隆起). **6** Ⓒ 《law》 a written order or summons to appear in a law court; the whole series of steps taken in legal proceedings. (법정으로의) 소환장; 소송 절차. **7** Ⓤ 《print.》 any of various photomechanical or photoengraving processes. 사진 제판법. ¶ *the three-color* ~, 3색판(色版).

in process, in the course of being done. 진행 중; …중(中).

in process of time, in the course of time; soon. 시간이 지남에 따라; 이윽고.

serve a process on, issue a written order for someone's arrest. …에 영장을 발부하다.

— *vt.* (P6) **1** start legal proceeding against (someone). …을 기소하다; 법정에 소환하다. **2** treat or prepare (something) in a certain way; reproduce. …을 (가공) 처리하다. ¶ ~ *meat* 고기를 가공 처리하다.

— *adj.* treated in a special way. 가공된. [→proceed]

·pro·ces·sion [prəséʃən] *n.* **1** Ⓒ a formal parade; persons marching. 행렬; 행진; 그 사람들. ¶ *The funeral* ~ *numbered fully 2,000.* 장례 행렬은 족히 2천 명이나 되었다. **2** Ⓤ the act of going forward. 진행; 전진.

pro·ces·sion·al [prəséʃənəl] *adj.* **1** of a procession. 행렬의; 행진의. ¶ *a* ~ *march* [*hymn*] 행렬 행진곡[성가]. **2** used in a procession. 행렬용의. ¶ *a* ~ *cross* 행렬용 십자가. — *n.* Ⓒ **1** a piece of music suitable for a religious procession. 행렬 성가. ¶ *The choir and clergy entered the church singing the* ~. 성가대와 목사님이 행렬 성가를 부르며 교회 안으로 들어왔다. **2** a book containing hymns and prayers for religious processions. 행렬 성가집.

:pro·claim [proukléim] *vt.* **1** (P6,19,21) announce formally and publicly. …을 선언하다; 포고하다. ¶ ~ *war against* …에 대해 선전 포고를 하다 / ~ *him (to be) a traitor* = ~ *that he is a traitor* 그를 반역자라고 선언하다 / *The new state was proclaimed a republic.* 신생 국가는 공화국이라고 선포되었다. **2** (P6, 19,21) make (something) known to the general public. …을 발표하다; 성명하다. ¶ ~ *one's opinion* 자기 의견을 발표하다 / ~ *the good news* 희소식을 발표하다. **3** (P11,21) show; reveal. …을 나타내다; 증명하다. ¶ *His accent proclaims him an Irish.* 말씨로 그가 아일랜드인임을 알 수 있다 / *His manners proclaimed him a gentleman.* 그의 태도는 그가 신사임을 말하고 있다. **4** (P6) prohibit by declaration. 금지하다. ¶ ~ *a district* 어떤 지역에 금지령을 내리다 / ~ *a meeting* 집회를 위법이라고 금지하다. [pro-]

proc·la·ma·tion [prὰkləméiʃən / prɔ̀k-] *n.* Ⓒ a formal and public announcement; Ⓤ the act of proclaiming. 성명; 선언; 포고.

pro·cliv·i·ty [prouklívəti] *n.* Ⓒ (*pl.* **-ties**) a tendency; a willingness; an inclination. 경향; 성벽(性癖); 기질(氣質). [pro-, L. *clivus* slope]

pro·con·sul [proukánsəl / -kɔ́n-] *n.* Ⓒ **1** 《Rom. hist.》 an ancient Roman provincial governor. 고대 로마의 지방 총독. **2** a governing official in a colony. 식민지 총독. [pro-]

pro·cras·ti·nate [proukrǽstənèit] *vi.* (P1) put off action from day to day; go slowly; delay. 질질 끌다; 지연(遲延)하다; 꾸물거리다. — *vt.* (P6) put off; postpone. …을 연기하다. [pro-, L. *cras* tomorrow]

pro·cras·ti·na·tion [proukrӕstənéiʃən] *n.* Ⓤ the act or habit of putting something off till later. 지연; 연기. ¶ 《*prov.*》 *Procrastination is the thief of time.* 지연은 (남의) 시간의 도둑.

pro·cre·ate [próukrièit] *vt.* (P6) **1** become the father of (someone); beget. (아버지가) 자식을 보다; …을 낳다. ¶ ~ *children* 〔*offspring*〕 아이들〔자식〕을 낳다. **2** bring into being; produce. (신종(新種) 등)을 만들다. ¶ ~ *a new breed* 새 품종을 만들다. [pro-]

pro·cre·a·tion [pròukriéiʃən] *n.* Ⓤ the act of procreating. 자식 보기; 생식(生殖).

pro·cre·a·tive [próukrièitiv] *adj.* of or having the power of procreating or producing. 생식(生殖)의; 생산의; 생식력〔생산력〕이 있는.

proc·tor [práktər / prɔ́k-] *n.* Ⓒ **1** an official who keeps order in a university or school. 학생감(監). **2** a person who acts for another in a law court. 대리인; 소송 대리인. [pro-]

pro·cum·bent [proukʌ́mbənt] *adj.* prostrate; prone; 《bot.》 trailing. (납작) 엎드린; 땅 위를 기는. [pro-, L. *cumbo* lie]

pro·cur·a·ble [proukjúərəbəl, prə-] *adj.* that can be obtained or acquired. 손에 넣을 수 있는; 획득할 수 있는. [pro-]

proc·u·ra·tion [prὰkjəréiʃən / prɔ̀k-] *n.* Ⓤ authority for acting for another. 대리권(代理權).

proc·u·ra·tor [prákjərèitər / prɔ́-] *n.* Ⓒ a person who acts or has power to act for another. 소송 대리인; 대리인.

·pro·cure [proukjúər, prə-] *vt.* **1** get; obtain by care or effort. …을 획득하다; 손에 넣다. ¶ ~ *evidence* 증거를 입수하다 / ~ *the earliest edition of a book* 어떤 책의 초판본을 입수하다 / *My uncle procured an employment for me.* 아저씨가 나에게 일자리를 하나 얻어주었다. **2** cause (something) to happen. …을 일으키다; 야기시키다. ● **pro·cure·ment** [-mənt] *n.* obtainment; accomplishment. 획득; 달성. [pro-]

prod [prad / prɔd] *n.* Ⓒ **1** a pointed instrument used to prick or urge. 찌르는 물건《바늘·막대·침 따위》. **2** a thrust; a poke. 찌르기; 찌름. ¶ *Give him a* ~ *in the ribs.* 놈의 갈빗대를 한번 질러라. **3** 《*fig.*》 the action of stirring up the attention, feelings, etc. (행동·감정 등에) 자극을 주는 것; 암시; 조언(助言).
— *vt.* (**prod·ded, prod·ding**) (P6,7) **1** punch or poke (cattle, etc.) with a pointed instrument. …을 뾰족한 것으로 찌르다. ¶ ~ *a pig with a stick* 돼지를 막대기로 찌르다. **2** 《*fig.*》 urge; rouse. …을 재촉하다; 자극하다. ¶ ~ *a lazy boy to action by threats and entreaties* 게으른 아이를 으르고 달래서 행동하게 하다 / ~ *someone's memory* 기억을 불러일으키다. [E.]

prod·i·gal [prádigəl / prɔ́d-] *adj.* **1** careless with money; wasteful; dissipated. 낭비하는; 방탕한. ¶ ~ *expenditure* 낭비 / *the* ~ *son* 방탕아. **2** 《*of*》 too free in giving or spending. 아끼지 않고 주는〔쓰는〕; 활수(滑手)한; 손이 큰. ¶ ~ *of good things* 좋은 일에 손이 큰 / *be* ~ *of benefactions* 마구 베풀다. — *n.* Ⓒ a person who wastes money. 낭비자; 방탕아. ¶ *The father welcomed the* ~ *back home.* 아버지는 돌아온 탕아를 반겼다. [L. *prodigus*]

prod·i·gal·i·ty [prὰdəgǽləti / prɔ̀də-] *n.* Ⓤ **1** the act of spending money in a careless or too generous manner. 낭비; 물건을 아낄 줄 모름. ¶ *a man ruined by his* ~ 방탕으로 거덜난 사람. **2** plentifulness; richness. 풍부.

pro·di·gious [prədídʒəs] *adj.* **1** extremely large; very great; huge. 거대한; 막대한. ¶ *a* ~ *building* 거대한 건물 / *a* ~ *noise* 굉장한 소음. **2** wonderful; beyond what is ordinary. 놀라운; 비상한. ¶ *a* ~ *display of learning* 놀라운 학문의 과시 / *a* ~ *memory* 놀라운 기억력 / *a man of* ~ *energy* 경이적인 정력의 소유자. [↓]

prod·i·gy [prádədʒi / prɔ́d-] *n.* Ⓒ (*pl.*

-gies) **1** a wonderful or surprising thing or event. 경이적인 일〔사건〕. ¶ *An eclipse of the sun seemed a ~ to early man.* 일식(日蝕)이 옛날 사람에게는 경이적인 일이었을 것이다. **2** a person, esp. a child, with wonderful talent or power. 천재; 신동. ¶ *a ~ of learning* 불세출의 학자 / *an infant ~* 신동. [L. *prodigium* portent]

:pro·duce [prədjúːs] *vt.* (P6) **1** bring (something) into existence; cause. …을 생기게 하다; 일으키다. ¶ *~ a reaction* 반작용을 일으키다 / *~ misery* 불행을 가져오다 / *Pleasures do not ~ happiness.* 쾌락이 행복을 가져오지 않는다 / *~ pollution* 오염에 의한 공해를 생기게 하다 / *The experiment is expected to ~ fine results.* 그 실험은 좋은 결과를 맺으리라 기대되고 있다. **2** write (a novel, etc.); draw (a painting, etc.). (소설 등)을 쓰다; (그림 등)을 그리다. ¶ *~ a poem* 시를 쓰다 / *~ a good painting* 훌륭한 그림을 그리다. **3** create; yield. …을 생산하다; 만들어 내다. ¶ *~ rice* 쌀을 생산하다 / *The soil produces corn.* 땅은 옥수수를 생산한다. **4** bring forth; bear. …을 낳다; (열매)를 맺다. ¶ *The tree produces fruit.* 나무는 열매를 맺는다. **5** provide; supply; yield. …을 공급하다; 산출하다. ¶ *The mine produces fine gold.* 그 광산은 양질의 금을 산출한다. **6** bring (something) to view; exhibit; take out. …을 제시〔전시〕하다; 꺼내다. ¶ *The driver produced his license for the policeman.* 운전사는 경찰관에게 면허증을 제시했다 / *~ two coins from one's pocket* 주머니에서 동전 두 개를 꺼내다 / *~ a letter from a briefcase* 가방에서 편지를 꺼내다. **7** bring (a play, a movie, etc.) before the public. (극·영화 등)을 상연하다. ¶ *~ a new play* 신극을 상연하다. **8** make (goods for sale); manufacture. …을 제조〔제작〕하다. ¶ *~ steel* 철강을 생산하다 / *~ films* 영화를 제작하다 / *~ on the line* (유동 작업으로) 대량 생산하다 / *two reactors that will ~ 2,000,000 kilowatts of electricity,* 200만킬로와트의 전력을 생산하는 원자로 2기(基). **9** 《geom.》 lengthen; extend. (선)을 연장하다. ¶ *~ a line from one point to another* 한 점에서 다른 점으로 직선을 긋다.

—*vi.* (P1) create or bring forth something. 생산하다; 산출하다; 나다. ¶ *The mines no longer ~.* 그 광산에서는 더는 광석이 나오지 않는다 / *The factory hasn't begun to ~ yet.* 공장은 아직 생산을 않고 있다.

—[prádjuːs, próu-] *n.* Ⓤ **1** 《*collectively*》 that which is produced; products. 생산물. ¶ *the ~ of the field* 〔*factories*〕 농산물〔공산품〕 / *mineral ~* 광산물 / *the market for home ~* 국산품 시장. **2** the amount of something produced. 생산고. [pro-, L. *duco* lead]

·pro·duc·er [prədjúːsər] *n.* Ⓒ **1** a person who produces. 생산자(opp. consumer). **2** a person who presents a drama, a motion picture, etc. (극·영화 등의) 연출자; 제작자. **3** a special form of furnace for the making of producer gas. 가스 발생로(發生爐).

producer gas [–⌒–⌒] *n.* a gas produced by passing air through red hot carbon. 발생로 가스《연료》.

:prod·uct [prádəkt / prɔ́d-] *n.* Ⓒ **1** 《usu. *pl.*》 a thing that is produced. 산출물; 생산품; 제작품. ¶ *natural products* 천연 산물 / *factory products* 공장 제품 / *farm products* 농산물 / *Restlessness and discontent are the among products of modern social conditions.* 불안과 불만은 현대의 각종 사회적 상황의 소산이다. **2** the result of action. 성과; 결과. **3** 《math.》 the result of multiplying two or more numbers. 곱; 적(積). ¶ *40 is the ~ of 5 and 8.* 40은 5와 8의 곱이다. **4** 《chem.》 a compound not previously existing in a body but formed during its decomposition. 생성물. [→produce]

:pro·duc·tion [prədʌ́kʃən] *n.* **1** Ⓤ ⓐ the act of producing. 생산; 제작(opp. consumption). ¶ *efficient ~ method* 능률적 생산 방식 / *the ~ of wheat* 밀 생산 / *Production is up* 〔*falling off*〕. 생산이 늘었다〔줄어들었다〕 / *Our business is the ~ of fountain-pens.* 우리가 하는 사업은 만년필 생산이다. ⓑ extension. 연장. ¶ *the ~ of a line* 선의 연장. **2** Ⓒ a thing that is produced. 생산물; 제작품; 작품. ¶ *a literary ~* 문예 작품 / *These are his early productions as a painter.* 이 그림들은 화가로서의 그의 초기 작품이다. **3** Ⓤ the amount of what is produced. 생산고; 생산량. ¶ *Production is up this week.* 금주에 생산량은 늘었다. **4** Ⓒ a work produced on the stage(e.g. a motion picture, a play). 상연 작품〔극〕.

·pro·duc·tive [prədʌ́ktiv] *adj.* **1** 《*of*》 producing; yielding; tending to cause or produce. …을 생기게 하는; …을 낳는. ¶ *social conditions ~ of crime and sin* 범죄와 죄악을 생기게 하는 사회 환경 / *a controversy ~ of misunderstanding* 오해를 낳게 하는 논쟁. **2** making something of value. 생산하는; 생산력이 있는; 생산적인. ¶ *a ~ effort* 생산(적) 노력 / *fields now ~ only of weeds* 잡초뿐인 밭. **3** producing much; rich; fruitful. 다산(多産)의; 풍부한. ¶ *a ~ writer* 다작가(多作家) / *a ~ farm* 비옥한 농장〔농지〕.

pro·duc·tiv·i·ty [pròudʌktívəti, pràd- / prɔ̀d-] *n.* Ⓤ **1** the state of being productive. 생산; 풍요. **2** the power to bring forth. 생산성; 생산력. ¶ *labor ~* 노동 생산성 / *~ movement* 생산성 향상 운동.

pro·em [próuem] *n.* Ⓒ a preface or an introduction to some writing, a speech, etc. 서문; 머리말. [Gk. *prooimion*]

prof. professor.

prof·a·na·tion [pràfənéiʃən / prɔ̀f-] *n.* Ⓤ the act of profaning; the state of being profaned; talking about God without piety. 신성 모독; 독신(瀆神). ¶ *the ~ of a* *temple* 신전〔사원〕의 모독 / *the* ~ *of the name of God* 신의 이름의 남용《신의 이름을 함부로 초듦》. [↓]

pro·fane [prəféin, prou-] *adj.* (**-fan·er, -fan·est**) **1** not belonging to God; of this world. 세속적인; 비속한. ¶ *a* ~ *person* 세속의 사람; 속인(俗人) / ~ *history* 〔*writers, art*〕 세속사(史)〔작가, 예술〕《정통 종교사〔작가, 예술〕에 대한》. **2** relating to things not in the Bible. 이단(異端)의; 이교의. ¶ ~ *rites and ceremonies* 이교의 의식과 예법. **3** paying no respect to God or holy things. 불경스러운; 독신(瀆神)의.
— *vt.* (P6) **1** treat (something sacred) with abuse or contempt. 신성을 모독하다〔더럽히다〕. ¶ ~ *the national flag* 국기를 모독하다 / *The enemy soldiers profaned our shrines.* 적군은 나라의 사당(祠堂)들을 유린했다. **2** put (something) to improper use. …을 남용하다. ¶ ~ *the precious time* 귀중한 시간을 허투루 쓰다. [pro-, L. *fanum* temple]

pro·fan·i·ty [prəfǽnəti, prou-] *n.* (*pl.* **-ties**) **1** Ⓒ disrespectful conduct or speech; impious talk about God; an impious word or remark. (신성(神聖)에 대한) 모독적인 행위〔말〕. **2** Ⓤ want of respect. 불경; 모독.

∙**pro·fess** [prəfés] *vt.* **1** ⓐ (P8,11,21) make a public declaration of (something). …을 공언하다; 성명하다. ¶ ~ *one's dislike of long speeches* 대놓고 긴 연설을 싫다고 하다 / ~ *to know the truth* 진실을 안다고 공언하다. ⓑ (P21) 《*reflexively*》 state that one is…; represent oneself as being…. …라고 주장〔말〕하다; 단언하다. ¶ ~ *oneself glad to be home again* 귀국하게 되어 기쁘다고 말하다 / ~ *oneself a Christian* 기독교도라고 공언하다. **2** (P6,8,11) claim falsely; pretend. …라고 지칭하다; …인 체하다. ¶ *I don't* ~ *to be a learned man.* 나는 유식한 체하지 않는다 / ~ *eagerness* 〔*regret*〕 열심〔유감〕인 체하다. **3** (P6) declare one's belief in (something). …에의 신앙을 고백하다. ¶ ~ *no religion* 종교가 없다고 하다 / ~ *Christianity* 기독교에 대한 신앙을 고백하다. **4** (P6) have (something) as one's profession. …을 직업으로 하다. ¶ ~ *law* 〔*medicine*〕 변호사〔의사〕를 업으로 하다.
— *vi.* (P1,3) make a public declaration. 공언(公言)하다. [pro-, L. *fateor* confess]

pro·fessed [prəfést] *adj.* **1** openly declared. 공언한; 밝힌. ¶ *a* ~ *opponent of free trade* 자유 무역의 분명한 반대자. **2** pretended. 거짓의. ¶ *a* ~ *sorrow* 거짓 슬픔 / *their* ~ *neutrality* 그들의 위장된 중립. **3** having taken an oath and entered into a religious order. 서약하고 수도회에 들어간.

pro·fess·ed·ly [prəfésidli] *adv.* **1** by admission; openly. 허가〔승인〕되어; 공공연히. **2** so far as appearances go. 표면상(으로).

:**pro·fes·sion** [prəféʃən] *n.* Ⓒ **1** an occupation requiring special education or training. 직업; 전문직. ¶ *adopt some* ~ 어떤 직업을 택하다 / *He is a lawyer by* ~. 그의 직업은 변호사다 / *the learned profession* 학문적 직업《변호사·의사 등》. **2** Ⓤ 《*the* ~》 the group of persons engaged in an occupation. 동업자들. ¶ *the legal* ~ 법조계 / *The medical* ~ *favors this law.* 의학계에서는 이 법을 지지하고 있다. **3** an open declaration; a confession of faith. 공언; 고백. ¶ *a* ~ *of faith* 신앙 고백. [→profess, -sion]

:**pro·fes·sion·al** [prəféʃənəl] *adj.* **1** of a profession; suitable for a profession. 직업의; 직업에 적당한. ¶ ~ *knowledge* 〔*skill*〕 전문적 지식〔기술〕 / ~ *education* 전문 교육 / ~ *etiquette* 동종 업자들간의 예의 / *a* ~ *man* 전문가. **2** engaged in an occupation. 직업에 종사하고 있는. ¶ *the* ~ *classes* 전문적〔기능적〕 직업 계급. **3** making a trade of something which others practice for pleasure. 전문인; 직업적인; 프로의(opp. amateur). ¶ ~ *ballplayers* 프로 야구 선수.
— *n.* Ⓒ **1** a person who is engaged in an occupation requiring special education. 직업인; 전문가. **2** a person who plays sport as an occupation. 직업 선수; 프로 선수(opp. amateur).

pro·fes·sion·al·ism [prəféʃənəlìzəm] *n.* Ⓤ professional habits of mind, qualities, etc. 전문가적 기질; 장인 기질.

pro·fes·sion·al·ly [prəféʃənəli] *adv.* in a professional manner. 직업적〔전문적〕으로. ¶ *consult a doctor* 〔*lawyer*〕 ~ 의사〔변호사〕와 전문적인 입장에서 상의하다.

:**pro·fes·sor** [prəfésər] *n.* Ⓒ **1** a teacher of the highest rank in a college or university. 대학 교수. **2** 《*colloq.*》 an instructor in some popular art. (무용·권투 등의) 교사; 선생. ¶ *a* ~ *of dancing* 무용 교사; 춤선생. **3** 《*arch.*》 a person who publicly declares a religious belief. 신앙 고백자.

pro·fes·so·ri·al [pròufəsɔ́ːriəl, pràf- / prɔ̀f-] *adj.* of or characteristic of a professor. 교수의; 교수다운; 학자티를 내는. ¶ *a* ~ *manner* 교수다운 태도.

pro·fes·sor·ship [prəfésərʃìp] *n.* Ⓒ a professor's post or rank at a university. 교수의 직〔지위〕.

prof·fer [práfər / prɔ́fər] *vt.* (P6,8) present (something) for acceptance; tender; offer. …을 제공〔제출〕하다; 제의하다. ¶ ~ *one's services* 도움〔조력〕을 (자진해서) 제의하다 / *take the proffered hand* 내민 손을 잡다 / *refuse someone's proffered help* 남이 주겠다는 도움을 거절하다. — *n.* Ⓒ an offer. 제출; 제공(물); 제의. ¶ *proffers of peace* 평화의 제안. [pro-, →offer]

pro·fi·cien·cy [prəfíʃənsi] *n.* Ⓤ the state of being proficient; ability gained by practice. 숙달; (기술 등의) 향상. ¶ *her* ~ *at teaching* 〔*in music*〕 그녀의 교수법〔음악〕의 숙달〔향상〕 / *attain great* ~ *in English* 영어가 크게 향상하다. [↓]

pro·fi·cient [prəfíʃənt] *adj.* skilled; having much knowledge. 숙달된; 능숙한. ¶ *He is ~ in mathematics.* 수학이 숙달돼 있다 / *a ~ swimmer* 수영에 능한 사람. ― *n.* Ⓒ a person who has skill in some special thing; an expert. 대가(大家). [pro-, →fact]

pro·file [próufail] *n.* Ⓒ **1** a side view of a human face. 얼굴의 옆모습. ¶ *He has a fine ~, but is not so good looking full face.* 옆모습은 근사한데 정면으로는 그렇지도 않다. **2** an outline. 윤곽. ¶ *the ~ of the trees against the sky* 하늘을 배경으로 한 수목의 윤곽. **3** a short, vivid description of someone's life, abilities, etc. (신문·방송 따위에 의한) 인물의 짧은 소개〔단평〕. **4** a picture of a side view. 측면도.

in profile, sideward. 옆모습으로; 옆모습의; 측면에서 보아.

― *vt.* (P6) draw a profile or an outline of (someone or something). …의 옆모습〔윤곽〕을 그리다. [pro-, L. *filum* thread]

:prof·it [práfit / prɔ́f-] *n.* **1** Ⓤ gain, advantage, or benefit to someone's character, etc.; valuable result of an action, work, etc. (인격 따위에 의한) 이익; 득. ¶ *What's the ~ of doing so?* 그렇게 해서 무슨 득이 있는가 / *do something with ~ to one's health* 건강을 위해 득이 되는 …을 하다 / *I have read it to my ~.* 그걸 읽어 도움이 되었다. **2** Ⓒ 《often *pl.*》 money gained in business. 이득; 이윤; 소득. ¶ *a net ~* 순익 / *gross profits* 총수익 / *make a ~ on the sale of* 〔*by selling*〕 *a house* 집을팔아 이윤을 얻다 / *The profits in this business are not large.* 이 장사는 별로 남지 않는다.

make a profit on, earn much money by selling (something). …으로 벌다; 이익이 남다.

small profits and quick returns, sell large quantities in a short period at small profits. 박리 다매.

― *vt.* (P6,7) bring profit to or serve (someone or something). …의 이익이 되다; …의 도움이 되다. ¶ *This course of conduct won't ~ you.* 이런 행동 방식은 네게 좋을 것 없다 / *All his wealth did not ~ him.* 그의 모든 재산이 그에게는 아무 소용 없었다.

― *vi.* (P1,3) gain profit. 이익을 보다; 벌다. ¶ *~ by* 〔*over*〕 *a transaction* 거래에서 이득을 보다 / *My health has profited greatly from my stay abroad.* 외국에 체류해서 건강이 아주 좋아졌다. [→proficiency]

·prof·it·a·ble [práfitəbəl / prɔ́f-] *adj.* bringing profit; giving advantage; useful. 유리한; 이익이 남는; 유익한. ¶ *~ advice* 유익한 충고 / *a ~ business* 이익이 남는 장사.

prof·it·eer [pràfitíər / prɔ̀f-] *vi.* (P1) make great profits unfairly. (특히 전시(戰時) 등에) 부당 이득을〔폭리를〕 취하다. ― *n.* Ⓒ a person who makes big profits unfairly during a period of scarcity. 부당 이득자; 모리배. ¶ *a war ~* 전시 모리배 / *Profiteers made a great deal of money during the First World War.* 간상(奸商)들은 제1차 세계대전 중에 엄청난 돈을 벌었다.

prof·it·less [práfitlis / prɔ́f-] *adj.* bringing no profit; of no advantage; useless. 이익이 없는; 무익한; 헛된. ¶ *make ~ efforts* 헛수고하다 / *a ~ business* 밑지는 장사.

prof·li·ga·cy [práfligəsi / prɔ́f-] *n.* Ⓤ the state of being profligate; careless extravagance. 방탕; 낭비. [↓]

prof·li·gate [práfligit / prɔ́f-] *adj.* **1** living in an evil way; wicked. 품행이 나쁜. **2** carelessly spending much money. 낭비하는. ― *n.* Ⓒ a profligate person. 행실이 나쁜 사람; 낭비가. [pro-, L. *fligo* strike down]

·pro·found [prəfáund] *adj.* (**-found·er, -found·est**) **1** very deep. (아주) 깊은. ¶ *a ~ sleep* 〔*sigh*〕 깊은 잠〔한숨〕 / *a ~ interest* 깊은 관심 / *the profoundest depths of the ocean* 해양의 가장 깊은 곳. **2** deep in meaning. 뜻 깊은; 의미심장한. **3** deeply felt. 마음으로부터의; 충심에서의. ¶ *have ~ respect for* (*someone*) (아무)를 충심으로 존경하다 / *make a ~ curtsy* 〔*reverence*〕 정중하게 인사하다. **4** having or marked by great knowledge or thoughts. 조예가 깊은; 박식한. ¶ *~ knowledge* 깊은 학문 / *a ~ thinker* 〔*thought*〕 심오한 사색가〔사상〕. **5** humble; bent low. 겸손한. [pro-, →fund]

pro·found·ly [prəfáundli] *adv.* in a profound manner; sincerely. 깊이; 심심하게; 공손하게.

pro·fun·di·ty [prəfʌ́ndəti] *n.* (*pl.* **-ties**) **1** Ⓤ the state of being deep; depth. 깊음; 깊이; 심원(深遠). ¶ *the ~ of his feeling* 〔*sorrow, thought*〕 그의 감정〔슬픔, 생각〕의 깊이 / *No eye could fathom the ~ of its depths.* 아무도 그 깊이를 헤아릴 수 없었다. **2** Ⓒ a thing or place that is very deep. 심연(深淵). [→profound]

pro·fuse [prəfjúːs] *adj.* **1** very plentiful; abundant. 풍부한; 많은. ¶ *He was ~ in his apologies* 〔*thanks*〕. 그는 거듭 사죄했다〔고맙다고 인사했다〕. **2** spending freely; giving generously; wasteful. 아낄 줄 모르는; 손이 큰. ¶ *be ~ with* 〔*of*〕 *money* 돈 씀씀이가 헤프다. [pro-, L. *fundo* pour]

pro·fuse·ly [prəfjúːsli] *adv.* in a profuse manner; generously. 다량으로; 아낌없이; 풍부하게.

pro·fu·sion [prəfjúːʒən] *n.* Ⓤ **1** being profuse. 풍부. ¶ *in ~* 풍부하게 / *a ~ of gifts* 많은 선물. **2** the act of spending money in a careless or too generous manner; wastefulness. 사치; 낭비. ¶ *a house furnished with ~* 세간 치장이 심한 집.

pro·gen·i·tor [proudʒénətər] *n.* Ⓒ **1** an earlier member of the family; an ancestor; a forefather. 선조; 조상. **2** an originator of an idea, theory, etc. (학문 등의) 원조(元祖); 선각자. [↓]

prog·e·ny [prádʒəni / prɔ́dʒ-] *n.* Ⓒ (*pl.*

-nies) 《*collectively*》 children; descendants. 자손. [pro-, L. *gigno* beget]

prog·no·ses [pragnóusi:z / prɔg-] *n.* pl. of **prognosis.**

prog·no·sis [pragnóusis / prɔg-] *n.* (*pl.* **-ses**) Ⓒ **1** 《med.》 a forecast or an expectation, esp. of the probable course of a disease. 예후(豫後)(cf. *diagnosis*). **2** an estimate of what will probably happen. 예측; 예상. [pro-, Gk. *gignōskō* know]

prog·nos·tic [pragnástik / prɔgnɔ́s-] *adj.* telling something of the future. 전조(前兆)가 되는. ¶ ~ *symptoms* 징후《예후(豫後)를 나타내는》. — *n.* Ⓒ **1** a sign or an indication of what will happen. 전조. ¶ *a* ~ *of success* 〔*failure*〕 성공〔실패〕할 전조. **2** a forecast. 예측; 예지(豫知).

prog·nos·ti·cate [pragnástikèit / prɔgnɔ́s-] *vt.* (P6,11) show a sign of (something); declare (something) from facts beforehand; foretell; predict. …의 전조를 보이다; …을 예언하다; 예지(豫知)하다. ¶ ~ *success* 〔*failure*〕 성공을〔실패를〕 예언하다 / *The clouds* ~ *a storm.* 구름은 폭풍의 전조다.

prog·nos·ti·ca·tion [pragnàstikéiʃən / prɔgnɔ̀s-] *n.* **1** Ⓤ the act of foretelling or warning. 예언; 예지(豫知). **2** Ⓒ something which shows what is to come; an omen; a sign. 전조(前兆); 징후.

:**pro·gram,** 《Brit.》 **-gramme** [próugræm] *n.* Ⓒ **1** a list of events in a public show, etc. 차례표; 프로그램. ¶ *the first item on the* ~ 프로그램의 제1 종목 / *concert programs* 연주회 프로그램. **2** a group of things or events for a radio or television broadcast. 상연 종목; 연주 곡목. ¶ *appear on the T.V.* ~ 텔레비전 프로에 나오다 / *What is the next* ~ *?* 다음 프로그램은 뭐냐. **3** a plan to be done. 계획(표); 예정(표). ¶ *What is the* ~ *for next Sunday ?* 다음 일요일의 예정은 뭐냐 / *a school* ~ 학교 행사 예정표 / *a government* ~ 정부 행사 일정 / *draw up a* ~ *of work for next term* 다음 학기의 예정표를 짜다. **4** the precise sequence of instructions enabling a computer to solve a problem. 프로그램《컴퓨터에 작업 절차를 정밀하게 지시한 것》.
— *vt.* (**-grammed, -gram·ming**) (P6) **1** make a program of (something); plan for (something). …의 프로그램을 짜다; 예정을 세우다. **2** enter (something) in a program. …을 계획에 짜넣다; 프로그램에 넣다. [pro-, →graph]

:**pro·gress** [prágres / próu-] *n.* Ⓤ **1** the act of moving or going forward; advance. 전진; 진행. ¶ *in the* ~ *of time* 때가 감에 따라 / *Further* ~ *was delayed by deep snow.* 깊은 눈으로 해서 더 이상의 전진이 지지 부진했다. **2** growth; development; upward tendency. 진보; 발달; 향상. ¶ *the* ~ *of science* 과학의 진보 / ~ *in the art of agriculture* 농업 기술의 발달 / *the* ~ *of mankind* 〔*medicine*〕 인류〔의학〕의 진보. **3** a natural course; a forward movement. 추이; 경과; 진전. ¶ *the* ~ *of events* 사건의 추이 / *The war seems to make no* ~. 전쟁은 소강 상태로 들어서는 모양이다. **4** Ⓒ 《*arch.*》 an official journey of a king, etc. (왕후 등의) 행차; 순행. ¶ *a royal* ~ 왕의 거둥 / *'The Pilgrim's Progress'* '천로역정(天路歷程)'.
in progress, happening; going on. 진행중. ¶ *Building is now in* ~. 건축이 진행 중이다.
make progress, **a**) develop; improve. 진보하다; 진척되다. **b**) go forward. 전진하다.
move to report progress, (in Brit. Parliament) propose that debating should be ended. 토론 종결을 동의(動議)하다《흔히 방해가 목적》.
— [prəgrés] *vi.* (P1,2A) **1** move or go forward. 전진하다. ¶ *Our work is progressing.* 우리 일은 진척되고 있다 / *In three hours we hardly progressed at all.* 세 시간 동안 우리는 거의 나아가지 못했다. **2** ⓐ develop. 발전하다. ¶ *Science progresses.* 과학은 발전한다. ⓑ improve. 좋아지다. ¶ *Is your health progressing ?* 건강은 좋아지고 있느냐. [pro-, L. *gradior,* walk]

pro·gres·sion [prəgréʃən] *n.* Ⓤ the act of progressing. 전진; 진행. ¶ *Creeping is a slow method of* ~. 기는 것은 전진의 느린 방식의 하나다.

·**pro·gres·sive** [prəgrésiv] *adj.* **1** ⓐ going forward; making better. 전진적인. ¶ *a* ~ *movement* 전진 운동. ⓑ going on step by step or continuously. 점진적인; 누진적인. ¶ *a* ~ *change* 〔*reform*〕 점진적 변화〔개혁〕 / *a* ~ *taxation* 누진 과세. **2** ready to agree to new ideas. 진보적〔진취적〕인; 진보주의의. ¶ ~ *ideas* 진보 사상 / *a* ~ *organization* 진보적인 단체. **3** 《gram.》 indicating an action which is going on. 진행을 나타내는; 진행형의. ¶ *a* ~ *form* 〔*aspect*〕 진행형〔상〕. **4** favoring progress in government. 진보당의 (cf. *conservative*). ¶ *the Progressive Party* 진보당. **5** 《med.》 (of disease) continuously increasing. (병이) 진행성의.
— *n.* Ⓒ a person who favors political progress or reforms. 진보론자; 혁신주의자; 진보당원.

·**pro·hib·it** [prouhíbit] *vt.* (P6,13) **1** forbid (something) by law or authority. …을 금(지)하다. ¶ *Smoking is strictly prohibited.* 흡연 엄금 / ~ *the sale of liquor* 주류 판매를 금하다 / ~ *people from driving on a particular road* 특정 도로상의 차량 운행을 금하다. **2** prevent someone from (doing something). …을 방해하다. ¶ *Prohibit him from coming.* =*Prohibit his coming.* 그자가 못 오게 해라 / *His state of weakness prohibits much exercise.* 그는 몸이 약해서 운동을 많이는 못 한다. [pro-, →habit]

:**pro·hi·bi·tion** [pròuhəbíʃən] *n.* **1** Ⓤ the act of prohibiting. 금지. **2** Ⓒ a law or an order which forbids. 금지령. **3** 《U.S.》 Ⓤ the act of forbidding by law the making and selling of alcoholic drinks. 주류 양조 판매 금지. ¶ *the ~ law* 금주법.

pro·hi·bi·tion·ist [pròuhəbíʃənist] *n.* Ⓒ a person who favors prohibiting by law the making and selling of alcoholic drinks. (주류 양조 판매) 금지론자.

pro·hib·i·tive [prouhíbətiv] *adj.* tending to prohibit; (of a price, etc.) so high as to prevent buying, using, etc. 금지의; 너무 비싸 살 엄두를 내지 못하는. ¶ *a ~ price* (구매) 금지적 가격 / *I would like to buy a Picasso, but the price is ~.* 피카소 그림을 하나 샀으면 하는데 너무 비싸 엄두도 못 낸다.

pro·hib·i·to·ry [prouhíbətɔ̀:ri / -təri] *adj.* prohibitive. 금지의.

:proj·ect [prádʒekt / prɔ́dʒ-] *n.* Ⓒ **1** a plan; a design. 계획; 안(案). ¶ *an impossible ~* 실현 불가능한 계획. **2** an enterprise. 사업; 기업. — *v.* [prədʒékt] *vt.* **1** (P6) plan; contrive. …을 계획하다; 궁리하다. ¶ *~ a new plan of campaign* 새로운 작전 계획을 생각하다. **2** (P6) make (something) stand out. …을 돌출시키다; 툭 튀어나오게 하다. ¶ *a projected forehead* 앞짱구 / *a signpost projecting from the wall* 담 밖으로 나온 간판 기둥. **3** (P6,7) throw out; cast forward. …을 내던지다; 발사하다. ¶ *Big guns can now ~ shells for many miles.* 지금 대포는 포탄을 수마일 발사할 수 있다. **4** (P6,7) make (a beam of light) fall on a surface; make (a shadow) fall on a surface. (빛)을 투사하다; …을 투영〔영사〕하다. ¶ *~ a motion picture on the screen* 스크린에 화면을 비추다 / *The clouds projected their shadows on the grass.* 구름이 초원에 그림자를 드리웠다. **5** (P6) cause (idea, etc.) to take shape. …을 구체화시키다.

— *vi.* (P1) stand out; stretch out. 돌출하다; 삐죽 나오다. ¶ *projecting eyebrows* 숱 많은 눈썹 / *The rocky point projects far into the water.* 바위너설이 물속 깊이 삐죽 나와 있다. [pro-, L. *jacio* throw]

pro·jec·tile [prədʒéktil, -tail] *adj.* **1** shooting forward; that can be projected. 발사하는; 투사될 수 있는. ¶ *a ~ weapon* 발사 화기. **2** projecting; forcing forward. 밀고 나아가는; 추진하는. ¶ *a ~ movement* 〔*force*〕 추진 운동〔력〕. — *n.* Ⓒ an object thrown or shot; a cannon ball; a bullet. 발사물; 포탄; 총탄.

pro·jec·tion [prədʒékʃən] *n.* **1** Ⓒ a part that stands out; Ⓤ the state of standing out. 돌출부; 돌기. ¶ *small projections from the wall of the cave* 동굴 벽의 작은 돌기들 / *a ~ of rock* 바위의 돌출부. **2** Ⓤ the state of being shot. 발사. ¶ *the ~ of a cannon ball* 포탄의 발사. **3** Ⓤ the act of casting an image or a film on a screen. 영사(映寫). **4** Ⓤ planning. 계획. **5** 《geom.》 representing by a geometrical process. 투영법(投影法). **6** 《psych.》 the act of ascribing to someone else one's own attitude. 주관의 객관화.

pro·jec·tor [prədʒéktər] *n.* Ⓒ **1** an instrument for throwing a picture on a screen. 영사기. **2** a person who makes plans. 계획〔입안〕자.

pro·le·tar·i·an [pròulitέəriən] *adj.* of or belonging to the proletariat. 프롤레타리아의; 노동 계급의. — *n.* Ⓒ a member of the proletariat. 프롤레타리아; 무산자; 노동자 (opp. bourgeois). [L. *proles* offspring]

pro·le·tar·i·at(e) [pròulitέəriət] *n.* Ⓒ (*pl.* **-at**) **1** the very poor; the lowest class of society. 프롤레타리아〔무산〕 계급. ¶ *the dictatorship of the ~* 프롤레타리아 독재. **2** (in Europe) the working classes. 노동자 계급 (opp. bourgeoisie).

pro·lif·er·ate [proulífərèit] *vt., vi.* 《biol.》 (P6; 1) (cause to) grow rapidly by multiplication of parts, as in budding or cell division. (급속히) 증식시키다〔하다〕. [→prolific]

pro·lif·er·a·tion [proulìfəréiʃən] *n.* growth by active divisions of cells; production of a new part. (세포의) 증식.

pro·lif·ic [proulífik] *adj.* **1** producing many children. 다산(多産)의. ¶ *Rabbits are very ~.* 토끼는 새끼를 아주 많이 낳는다. **2** producing much; productive. 많이 내는; 풍부한; 생산적인. ¶ *a ~ writer* 다작 작가 / *a ~ tree* 열매가 많은 나무 / *a ~ imagination* 풍부한 상상력. [L. *proles* offspring]

pro·lix [proulíks] *adj.* using too many words; long and tiring; tedious. 말이 많은; 장황한; 지루한. ¶ *a ~ speech* 장황한 연설. [pro-, L. *liqueo* flow]

pro·lix·i·ty [proulíksəti] *n.* Ⓤ the state of being prolix. 장황; 용장(冗長).

pro·logue, 《U.S.》 **pro·log** [próulɔ:g, -lɑg / -lɔg] *n.* Ⓒ **1** an introduction spoken by an actor at the beginning of a play. (연극의) 개막사. **2** an introduction to a novel, a poem, etc. 머리말(cf. *epilog(ue)*, *preface*). ¶ *the Prologue to Chaucer's 'Canterbury Tales'* 초서의 '캔터베리 이야기'의 서시(序詩). **3** 《*fig.*》 any event or act serving as an introduction. 서막이 되는 사건. ¶ *The murder at Sarajevo was the ~ to World War 1.* 사라예보의 암살은 제1차 세계 대전의 서막적 사건이었다. [pro-, →logos]

·pro·long [proulɔ́:ŋ, -lɑŋ] *vt.* (P6) **1** make (something) longer; lengthen in space. (공간적으로) …을 길게 하다; 연장하다. ¶ *~ a line* 〔*road*〕 선〔길〕을 연장하다. **2** lengthen in time; put off. (시간적으로) …을 늘이다; 오래 끌다; 연기하다. ¶ *~ a party* 파티 시간을 끌다 / *~ one's stay in Germany* 독일 체류 기간을 연장하다. [pro-, L. *longus* long]

pro·lon·ga·tion [pròulɔ:ŋgéiʃən] *n.* **1** Ⓤ the state of being prolonged in time. 연기. **2** Ⓒ the part added to make something longer; an added part. 연장된 부분.

prom [prɑm / prɔm] *n.* **1** Ⓒ 《U.S. *colloq.*》 a ball or dance held by a college or high-school class. (대학·고교 등의) 무도회. **2** 《Brit. *colloq.*》 =promenade concert. [→promenade]

prom·e·nade [prɑ̀mənéid / prɔ̀m-] *n.* Ⓒ **1** a walk for joy or show. 산책; 산보. **2** a public place, esp. fit for walking. 산책길. **3** 《U.S.》 ⓐ a (student's) ball or formal dance. (학생들의) 무도회. ⓑ the march of all guests at the beginning of a ball or formal dance. (공식 무도회 개시 때의) 전체 내객의 행진.
— *vi.* (P1,2A) walk for joy. 산책하다. ¶ ~ *on the seafront* 해안길을 산책하다.
— *vt.* (P6) **1** walk in, on or through. …을 산책하다. ¶ ~ *the streets* 〔*deck*〕. **2** lead (someone) about a place, esp. for display. …을 자랑삼아 데리고 다니다. [pro-, L. *mino* drive]

promenade concert [--´- ´--] *n.* a concert at which audience is not seated and can move about freely. 프롬나드 콘서트 《앉지 않고 산책하거나 댄스를 하면서 듣는 (야외) 음악회》.

promenade deck [--´- ´] *n.* an upper deck on a liner, where passengers may promenade. 산책〔유보(遊步)〕 갑판(甲板).

Pro·me·the·us [prəmíːθiəs, -θjuːs] *n.* 《Gk. myth.》 the god who stole fire from Mt. Olympus and taught men its use. 프로메테우스. [Gk.]

prom·i·nence [prɑ́mənəns / prɔ́m-] *n.* **1** Ⓤ the state or quality of being prominent. 우수; 탁월. ¶ *a man of* ~ 유명 인사 / *come into* ~ 유명해지다. **2** Ⓒ something that stands out; a high place. 돌출물〔부〕. ¶ *the* ~ *of a man's nose* 코의 융기 / *a* ~ *in the middle of a plain* 들판 한 가운데의 고지. [↓]

***prom·i·nent** [prɑ́mənənt / prɔ́m-] *adj.* **1** famous, important. 유명〔저명〕한. ¶ *a* ~ *citizen* 〔*writer, politician*〕 저명한 시민〔작가, 정치가〕. **2** clearly seen; noticeable; conspicuous. 잘 보이는; 두드러진. ¶ *a* ~ *place in the newspaper* 신문의 잘 보이는 데. **3** standing out beyond a surface. 튀어나온. ¶ ~ *eyes* 통방울눈. ● **prom·i·nent·ly** [-li] *adv.* [L. *promineo* project]

prom·is·cu·i·ty [prɑ̀məskjúːəti / prɔ̀m-] *n.* Ⓤ the state of being promiscuous. 혼란; 어지러운 상태; 뒤범벅. [↓]

pro·mis·cu·ous [prəmískjuəs] *adj.* **1** confused; mixed. 난잡한; 어지러운. ¶ *a* ~ *heap of clothing* 어지럽게 쌓인 옷더미. **2** making no distinction; not limited to any particular person or class. 차별〔제한〕이 없는. ¶ ~ *sexual relation* 난잡한 성관계. **3** casual; random; without any plan or purpose. 그때 그때의; 되는 대로의. ¶ *take a* ~ *stroll* 어정어정 거닐다. [pro-, →mix]

:prom·ise [prɑ́mis / prɔ́mis] *n.* **1** Ⓒ an agreement given to another to do or not to do something; an informal contract. 약속; 계약. ¶ *a false* ~ 말뿐인 약속 / *a breach of* ~ 파약 / *make a* ~ 약속하다 / *He gave me a* ~ *of help.* 그는 날 돕겠다고 약속했다 / *fulfill* 〔*carry out*〕 *a* ~ 약속을 지키다〔이행하다〕. **2** Ⓒ something that a person agrees to do or not to do. 약속한 것. ¶ *Dont' you forget your* ~. 네가 약속한 것을 잊지 마라. **3** Ⓤ something which shows hope of success in the future. (전도의) 희망; 기대. ¶ *a boy that shows* ~ 유망해 보이는 소년.

give* 〔*afford*〕 *promise of, have a bright prospect of. …의 가망이 있다; 유망하다. ¶ *The sky gives* ~ *of fine weather.* 하늘을 보니 날씨가 좋아질 모양이다.

keep* 〔*break*〕 *one's promise, fulfill 〔do not fulfill〕 one's promise. 약속을 지키다〔어기다〕.

of great promise, very promising; full of promise. 아주 유망한.

the Land of Promise, Canaan. 가나안. 參考 신이 이스라엘 사람에게 약속한 땅.

— *vt.* **1** (P6,8,11,13,14,15,20) make a promise to (someone). …에게 약속하다. ¶ *He promised us the money.* =*He promised the money to us.* 우리에게 돈을 준다고 약속했다 / *You've promised me to marry me.* 너는 내게 나와 결혼한다고 약속했었잖아 / ~ *a friend a present* 친구에게 선물을 약속하다 / *Promise me that you'll stand by me.* 나를 지지하겠다는 약속을 해라 / *I promised him to go.* =*I promised him that I would go.* 그에게 가겠노라 약속했다 / *He promised to tell the truth.* 그는 진실을 말하겠다고 했다 / *He promised that he would never come here.* 그는 절대로 여기에 오지 않겠다고 말했다. **2** (P6,11) assure. …을 보증하다. ¶ *"I'll let you know if anything new happens," he promised.* "무슨 새로운 일이 생기면 네게 알려주마."라고 그는 다짐했다 / *I* ~ *you I don't know.* 나는 정말 모른다. **3** (P6) give hope of (something); be likely to do (something). …의 가망이 있다; …일 것 같다. ¶ *The weather promises heavy snow.* 날씨가 큰눈이 올 것 같다 / *Early mist promises fair weather.* 아침 안개는 날씨가 좋아질 전조이다.

— *vi.* **1** (P1) make a promise. 약속하다. ¶ *I can't* ~ *yet.* 아직 약속은 못 하겠다. **2** (P2A) 《often with *well* or *fair*》 give hope of something. 유망하다; 가망이 있다. ¶ *The weather promises well.* 날씨가 좋아질 모양이다 / *He promises highly.* 그는 유망한 사람이다 / *The crops* ~ *well.* 풍작일 것 같다. [pro-, →missile]

:prom·is·ing [prɑ́məsiŋ / prɔ́m-] *adj.* giving hope of success; hopeful. 유망한; 기대되는. ¶ *a* ~ *student* 유망한 학생 / *The wheat crop looks* ~. 밀 농사는 수확이 좋겠다.

prom·is·so·ry [prɑ́məsɔ̀ːri / prɔ́-] *adj.* containing a promise. 약속의.

promissory note [ˊ---- ˊ] *n.* a written promise to pay a certain sum of money at a fixed date. 약속 어음. [↑]

prom·on·to·ry [prámәntɔ̀:ri / prɔ́mәntәri] *n.* Ⓒ (*pl.* **-ries**) a point of land which extends into the sea; a cape. 곶; 갑(岬). [L. *promuntrium*]

·**pro·mote** [prәmóut] *vt.* (P6,7,13) **1** give (someone) a higher position or rank. …을 승진〔진급〕시키다(opp. demote). ¶ *be promoted to* …로 승진되다 / ~ *an officer* (*to the rank of*) *general* 장교를 장군으로 승진시키다 / *He was promoted over me.* 그는 나를 앞질러 승진했다. **2** help the growth or development of (something). …을 촉진하다; 발전시키다; 장려하다. ¶ ~ *digestion* 소화를 촉진시키다 / ~ *the love of learning* 학문에의 애정을 진작시키다. **3** start to organize (something). …을 조직화하다; 일으키다. ¶ ~ *a business* 〔*undertaking*〕 사업을 시작하다 / ~ *disorder* 혼란을 야기하다. **4** help to sell (something) by advertising it. 선전해서 …의 판매를 촉진하다. ¶ *a big advertising campaign to* ~ *new toothpaste* 새 치약의 판촉을 위한 대대적 광고전. [pro-, →move]

pro·mot·er [prәmóutәr] *n.* Ⓒ **1** a person or thing that promotes. 촉진자〔물〕. ¶ *a* ~ *of crime* 〔*disorder*〕 범죄〔혼란〕의 장본인 / *Good humor is a* ~ *of friendship.* 밝은 성품은 교우 관계의 촉매다. **2** a person who organizes a new company. 발기인; 창립자.

*__pro·mo·tion__ [prәmóuʃәn] *n.* **1** ⓊⒸ advance in rank or importance. 승진; 진급. ¶ *obtain* 〔*win, get*〕 ~ 승진하다 / *He was given a* ~. 그는 승진했다. **2** Ⓤ the act of helping the growth. 증진; 촉진; 장려. ¶ *the* ~ *of health* 건강 증진. **3** Ⓒ the act of starting to organize a company, etc. 주창; 발기. ¶ *the* ~ *of a company* 회사 창립〔발기〕 / *the* ~ *of learning* 학문의 진흥.

*__prompt__ [prɑmpt / prɔmpt] *adj.* **1** ready and quick in action. 신속한; 기민한. ¶ *a* ~ *and punctual supporter* 신속 정확한 지지자 / ~ *action* 즉각적인 행동 / *come to a* ~ *decision* 곧 결정이 나다〔결론에 이르다〕. **2** done at once or instantly. 즉시 …하는. ¶ *a* ~ *assistance* 빠른 원조 / *make a* ~ *answer* 즉각 대답하다 / *She's always* ~ *to criticize other people's ideas.* 남의 생각을 꼬집는 데는 늘 잽싸다. **3** 《comm.》 paid, delivered, at once. 즉시불의. ¶ ~ *cash* 즉시불; 맞돈 / ~ *delivery* 즉시 인도 / *be* ~ *in one's payment* 지불이 신속하다.
— *vt.* (P6,20) **1** cause (someone) to do something; move (someone) to action. …을 자극하다; 고무하다. ¶ *prompted by instinct* 본능에 이끌린 / *The weather prompted us to go out.* 날씨가 좋아서 외출하게 됐다 / *Conscience prompts us to do what is right.* 양심이 우리로 하여금 옳은 일을 하게 한다. **2** remind (someone) of something; suggest; inspire. (…에게) …이 생각나게 하다; (사상·감정)을 불어넣다. ¶ *Gay music prompts happy thoughts.* 밝은 음악은 행복한 생각이 들게 한다. **3** help (an actor) by telling him words which he has forgotten. (배우)에게 뒤에서 대사를 일러주다. ¶ *Do you know your part in the play or shall I* ~ *you?* 그 극에서 네 대사를 모른다면 내가 일러줄까.
— *n.* Ⓒ an act or words for prompting an actor, etc. 뒤에서 대사를 일러주기.
— *adv.* 《*colloq.*》 just; sharp. 정확히; 꼭. ¶ *at five* ~ 정각 다섯 시에. [L.]

prompt·er [prɑ́mptәr / prɔ́m-] *n.* Ⓒ a person who tells actors their speeches when they forget them on the stage. 대사를 일러주는 사람; 프롬프터.

promp·ti·tude [prɑ́mptәtjù:d / prɔ́m-] *n.* Ⓤ the state of being prompt. 신속; 기민.

:**prompt·ly** [prɑ́mptli / prɔ́mpt-] *adv.* in a prompt manner; readily; quickly; at once. 신속히; 즉시.

prom·ul·gate [prɑ́mәlgèit, proumʌ́lgeit / prɔ́mәlgèit] *vt.* (P6) **1** make (something) known formally and officially. …을 발표〔공포〕하다. ¶ ~ *news* 뉴스를 발표하다 / ~ *a law* 법령을 공포하다. **2** spread (something) widely; make (something) widely known. …을 널리 펴다; 보급하다. ¶ ~ *official secrets* 〔*a new form of religion*〕 직무상의 비밀을 퍼뜨리다〔새 종교를 보급시키다〕. [L.]

prom·ul·ga·tion [prɑ̀mәlgéiʃәn, pròum- / prɔ̀mәl-] *n.* Ⓤ the act of promulgating; the state of being promulgated. 공포; 발표; 보급. ¶ *the* ~ *of the law* 〔*news*〕.

pron. **1** pronoun; pronominal. **2** pronunciation.

prone [proun] *adj.* **1** having a tendency; likely; liable to. …한 경향의; …하기 쉬운. ¶ *be* ~ *to anger* 화를 잘 내다 / *He is* ~ *to act without thinking.* 그는 무턱대고 행동하는 경향이 있다. **2** lying with the face downward. 엎드린. ¶ *lie* ~ 엎드리다 / *fall* ~ 엎어지다. **3** sloping downward steeply; not level. 심한 내리받이의. ¶ *a* ~ *stretch of ground* 아래로 비탈진 땅. [L.]

prong [prɔ:ŋ / prɔŋ] *n.* Ⓒ **1** one of the pointed parts of a fork. (포크 따위의) 뾰족한 끝. **2** a rake; hay-fork. 갈퀴; 쇠스랑.
— *vt.* (P6,7) stick (something) with a pointed instrument. …을 찌르다; 꿰찌르다. [?]

pronged [prɔ:ŋd / prɔŋd] *adj.* divided into branches. 갈래진. ¶ *a four* ~ *fork* 네 갈래진 포크.

pro·nom·i·nal [prounɑ́mәnәl / -nɔ́m-] *adj.* of or having the nature of function of a pronoun. 대명사의; 대명사 구실을 하는. ¶ *a* ~ *adjective* 대명사적 형용사. [↓]

pro·nom·i·nal·ly [prounɑ́mәnәli / -nɔ́m-] *adv.* as a pronoun. 대명사적으로.

:**pro·noun** [próunàun] *n.* Ⓒ 《gram.》 a word used instead of a noun. 대명사.

[pro-, →nomen]

:pro·nounce [prənáuns] *vt.* **1** (P6) make the sounds of (words) clearly. …을 발음하다. ¶ ~ *every word clearly and correctly* 모든 단어를 분명하고 정확하게 발음하다 / ~ *English badly* 영어 발음이 좋지 않다. **2** (P6,11,20) say (something) with a decision; declare or state as one's opinion. …을 단언하다; 언명하다. ¶ ~ *judgment on* …에 판단을 내리다 / *The expert pronounced the picture to be a forgery.* 전문가는 그 그림이 가짜라고 잘라 말했다. **3** (P6) announce (something) formally. …을 선고하다. ¶ ~ *a man guilty* 아무에게 유죄를 선고하다 / *The judge pronounced sentence of death on the prisoner.* 판사는 피고에게 사형을 선고했다.

— *vi.* (P1) **1** make sounds. 발음하다. **2** give one's opinion. 의견을 말하다. ¶ ~ *on a subject* 어떤 문제에 대해 의견을 말하다 / ~ *for* 〔*in favor of*〕 …을 찬성하는 의견을 말하다 / ~ *against* …에 반대 의견을 말하다. **3** give a judgment. 판단을 내리다. ¶ *The committee will ~ upon the matter.* 위원회가 그 문제에 판단을 내릴 것이다. **4** make sounds utter. 발음하다. ¶ ~ *clearly* 〔*badly*〕. [pro-, L. *nuntio* announce]

·pro·nounced [prənáunst] *adj.* exact; clear; strongly marked. 단호한; 분명한; 두드러진. ¶ *a ~ Yorkshire accent* 두드러진 요크셔 악센트 / *a ~ smell of onion* 강한 양파 냄새 / *Age has made a ~ change in his appearance.* 나이가 들어 외모가 눈에 띄게 변했다.

pro·nounce·ment [prənáunsmənt] *n.* Ⓒ **1** a public statement; a declaration. 공고. **2** an opinion; a judgment. 의견; 결정; 판결.

·pro·nun·ci·a·tion [prənʌ̀nsiéiʃən] *n.* **1** Ⓤ Ⓒ the way of pronouncing sounds. 발음법. ¶ *teach English ~* 영어 발음(법)을 가르치다 / *What is the ~ of Czech?* Czech 를 어떻게 읽느냐. **2** Ⓤ the act of pronouncing. 발음 [→pronounce]

:proof [pru:f] *n.* (*pl.* **proofs**) **1** Ⓤ the act of showing that something is true or beyond doubt. 증명; 입증. ¶ *in ~ of his innocence* 그의 결백을 입증하기 위해 / *We must wait for better ~ before we believe.* 우리는 믿기에 앞서 더 입증될 때까지 기다려야 한다 / *I will give a ~ of my loyalty.* 내 성실성을 보여주겠다. **2** Ⓒ a fact that proves the truth of something; an evidence. 증거. ¶ *produce a ~* 증거를 제출하다 / *Is what you say a guess or do you have ~ ?* 네 말은 추측이냐, 아니면 증거라도 있느냐. **3** Ⓒ a test or an examination. 음미; 시험. ¶ 《*prov.*》 *The ~ of the pudding is in the eating.* 푸딩의 맛은 먹어봐야 안다《백문(百聞)이 불여일견(不如一見)》 / *That box looks big enough; but let us put it to the ~.* 그 상자는 크기가 그만하면 됐다. 그러나 한번 시험해 보자. **4** Ⓤ the tested strength of arms, etc.; the standard strength of alcohol. (무기 등의) 시험필의 강도; (술의) 표준 도수. ¶ *above* 〔*under*〕 ~ 표준 도수 이상〔이하〕의. **5** 《*pl.*》 《law》 documents used to prove something; testimony. 증거 서류; 증언. **6** Ⓒ ⓐ 《print.》 an impression taken from type as a way to correct mistakes. 교정쇄(校正刷). ¶ *make corrections in ~* 교정쇄에 교정하다. ⓑ 《photog.》 the first print taken from a negative. 시험 인화.

— *adj.* **1** strong or hard enough to resist something. …에 견디는; …이 관통하지 않는. ¶ *This watch is ~ against water.* 이 시계는 방수가 돼 있다 / ~ *against all temptations* 어떤 유혹에도 견디는. **2** tested. 검사필의; 보증이 붙은. [→prove]

-proof [-pru:f] *suf.* against. '…이 통하지 않는, 내(耐)…, 방(防)…' 의 뜻. ¶ *waterproof.*

proof·read [prú:frì:d] *vt.* (P6) read and correct (printers' proofs, etc.). …을 교정하다. [→prove]

proof·read·er [prú:frì:dər] *n.* Ⓒ a person who reads and corrects printed matter. 교정원(員).

prop [prɑp / prɔp] *vt.* (**propped** [prɑpt / prɔpt], **prop·ping**) (P6,7,13,18) **1** 《*up*》 support (something) by placing other thing against it; support a leaning or resting position; prevent from falling. …을 받치다; 괴다. ¶ ~ *up a drunken man* 술취한 사람을 부축하다 / ~ *a door open with a chair* 의자를 받쳐 문을 열어 두다 / *He propped his bicycle (up) against the fence.* 자전거를 담에다 기대 놓았다. **2** support; back up. …을 지지〔지원〕하다. — *n.* Ⓒ a person or thing that supports another one. 지지자; 지주(支柱). ¶ *A good son is a ~ for one's old age.* 착한 아들은 늘그막에 의지가 된다. [Du.]

·prop·a·gan·da [prɑ̀pəgǽndə / prɔ̀p-] *n.* Ⓤ **1** systematic efforts to spread some opinion. 선전; 선전 활동. ¶ *make ~ for a cause* 주의〔주장〕을 선전하다 / ~ *films* 선전 영화. **2** 《usu. *contempt.*》 an opinion or belief thus spread in a planned or official way, esp. by a government. (계획적으로 선전하는) 주의; 주장. ¶ *It is only ~.* 그건 선전일 뿐이다. **3** (*the P-*) Ⓤ 《Cath.》 a committee of in charge cardinals of foreign missions. (해외) 포교성성(布教聖省). [L. *propago* layer]

prop·a·gan·dist [prɑ̀pəgǽndist / prɔ̀p-] *n.* Ⓒ a person who spreads some opinion or belief by means of a plan or method. 선전자; 전도자; 선교자.

prop·a·gan·dize [prɑ̀pəgǽndaiz / prɔ̀p-] *vt.* (P6) spread a principle, belief of (something). …을 선전〔포교〕하다. — *vi.* (P1) spread propaganda. 포교하다.

prop·a·gate [prɑ́pəgèit / prɔ́pə-] *vt.* (P6) **1** increase the number of (plants or animals). …을 번식〔증식〕시키다. ¶ *Some trees cannot ~ themselves in new region.* 어떤 나무는 새 토양에서 번식을 하지 못한다 / ~ *a*

new variety of plant 식물의 새 품종을 증식시키다. **2** send further; carry forward through a medium. (매체를 통해) …을 전파하다; 전하다. ¶ ~ *sound* 〔*light*〕 소리를〔빛을〕 전(파)하다 / ~ *disease* 병을 옮기다. **3** spread (news, etc.). …을 보급시키다. ¶ ~ *doctrine* 교리를 널리 펴다.
— *vi.* (P1) **1** reproduce one's species. 번식〔증식〕하다. ¶ *Animal and vegetable pests* ~ *with extreme rapidity.* 동식물 해충은 굉장한 속도로 번져간다. **2** (of news) go in all direction. 퍼지다; 보급되다. [L. *propago* layer (of a plant), offspring]

prop·a·ga·tion [pràpəgéiʃən / prɔ̀p-] *n.* Ⓤ **1** the act of propagating; the state of being propagated. 증식; 번식. ¶ *the* ~ *of roses by cuttings* 꺾꽂이에 의한 장미 증식. **2** (of news) the act of spreading abroad. 보급. ¶ *the* ~ *of the principles of science* 과학 원리의 보급 / *the* ~ *of new ideas* 새로운 사상의 보급. **3** (of disease, heat, etc.) the state of being carried further; passing on; sending further. 전염; 전파; 전달. ¶ *the* ~ *of disease* / *the* ~ *of sound waves* 음파의 전달 / *the* ~ *of the shock of an earthquake* 지진 충격의 파급.

pro·pel [prəpél] *vt.* (**-pelled, -pel·ling**) (P6,7) push forward; drive forward; urge. …을 밀다; 추진하다; 몰아대다. ¶ ~ *a boat by rowing* 배를 저어 전진시키다 / *a person propelled by ambition* 야망에 사로잡힌 사람. [pro-, L. *pello* drive]

pro·pel·ler [prəpélər] *n.* Ⓒ **1** a device with turning round blades for propelling an airplane. (항공기의) 프로펠러. **2** a person who propels. 추진하는 사람; 추진자.

pro·pen·si·ty [prəpénsəti] *n.* Ⓒ (*pl.* **-ties**) 《*to, for*》 the way in which a person naturally feels and acts; a tendency. 경향; 성향; 성벽. ¶ *a* ~ *for gambling* 도박벽 / *a* ~ *to extravagance* 낭비벽 / *He has a* ~ *for saving things.* 물건을 아끼는 편이다. [pro-, L. *pendeo* hang]

:**prop·er** [prápər / prɔ́p-] *adj.* **1** fit; suitable. 적당한; 상응하는. ¶ *Do it in the* ~ *way.* 적절히 해라 / *as you think* ~ 적당히 / *with the dignity* ~ *to his high rank* 그의 고위직에 걸맞은 위엄을 갖추고 / *The* ~ *place to put books is in the library.* 책을 둘 적당한 자리가 도서관에 있다. **2** right; correct. 바른. ¶ *a* ~ *way of making a sound* 소리를 바르게 내는 법 / *What is the* ~ *dress to wear at a dinner?* 정찬회에 입는 정식 복장은 뭐냐. **3** 《*to*》 belonging to one thing and not to others; peculiar. 고유의; 독특한. ¶ *instincts* 〔*feelings*〕 ~ *to mankind* 인간 고유의 본능〔감정〕 / *a temperature* ~ *to August* 8월 특유의 기온 / *Ferocity is* ~ *to tigers.* 사나운 것이 호랑이의 특성이다 / *a climate* ~ *to this country* 이 나라 특유의 기후. **4** 《usu. placed after a *noun*》 rightly so called; real. 엄밀한 의미로서; 본래의. ¶ *England* ~ 영국 본토 / *literature* ~ 순문학 / *in the* ~ *sense of the word* 그 말의 엄밀한 의미에서. **5** modest; following etiquette; decent. 예의바른; 품위 있는. ¶ ~ *behavior* 예의바른 행동 / *The stories he told at the table were not quite* ~. 그가 식탁에서 한 말은 좀 점잖지 못했다. **6** 《Brit. *colloq.*》 complete. 완전한. ¶ *a* ~ *rascal* 순악당 / *in* ~ *rage* 격노해서. [L. *proprius*]

:**prop·er·ly** [prápərli / prɔ́p-] *adv.* **1** in a proper manner; suitably. 적당히; 알맞게. ¶ *He* ~ *refused.* 그가 거절한 것도 당연하다 / *She was* ~ *dressed.* 그녀는 옷차림이 단정했다. **2** correctly; fairly. 정확히; 바르게. ¶ *behave* ~ 바르게 행동하다 / ~ *speaking*= *speaking* ~ =*to speak* ~ 정확히 말하면. **3** 《*colloq.*》 thoroughly; completely. 철저히; 아주; 몹시. ¶ *I thrashed him* ~. 놈을 흠씬 패줬다.

prop·er·tied [prápərtid / prɔ́p-] *adj.* possessing a great deal of money, land, etc. 재산이 있는. ¶ *the* ~ *classes* 유산〔지주〕 계급. [↓]

:**prop·er·ty** [prápərti / prɔ́p-] *n.* (*pl.* **-ties**) **1** ⓊⒸ 《*collectively*》 a thing or things possessed. 재산; 소유물. ¶ *own a large* ~ 큰 재산이 있다 / *lose one's* ~ 재산을 잃다 / *a man of* ~ 자산가 / *The news is common* ~. 그 소식은 모르는 사람이 없다. **2** Ⓤ the right of possession. 소유권. ¶ *literary* ~ 저작권 / ~ *in copyright* 판권 소유 / *the rights and duties of* ~ 소유의 권리와 의무 / *There is no* ~ *in wild animals.* 야생 동물에 임자는 없다. **3** ⓊⒸ property consisting of land and a house. 소유지; 부동산. ¶ *a* ~ *owner* 지주 / *He bought a small* ~ *near the river.* 그는 강 부근에 땅을 좀 샀다 / *personal* 〔*real*〕 ~ 동산〔부동산〕. **4** Ⓒ a clear quality of a thing. 고유성; 특성. ¶ *a* ~ *of salt* 소금의 특성 / *One* ~ *of steel is its hardness.* 강철의 특성의 하나는 단단함에 있다. **5** 《*pl.*》 a piece of furniture or an item of dress used on the stage. (무대의) 소도구; 소품. ¶ *a* ~ *man* 소품 담당자. [→proper, -ty]

***proph·e·cy** [práfəsi / prɔ́-] *n.* Ⓒ (*pl.* **-cies**) the act of telling future events; something said about the future. 예언하기; 예언. ¶ *have the gift of* ~ 예언의 능력이 있다. [pro-, Gk. *phēmi* speak]

proph·e·sy [práfəsài / prɔ́-] *vt., vi.* (**-sied, -sy·ing**) (P6,11,12; 1,3) predict (something that will happen in the future); foretell (something) by means of help from God. …을 예언하다; 영감에 의해 예언하다. ¶ ~ *a severe storm* 대폭풍을 예언하다 / ~ *a fall in prices* 가격 하락을 예언하다.

***proph·et** [práfit / prɔ́-] *n.* **1** Ⓒ a person who prophesies. 예언자. ¶ *a weather* ~ 일기 예보자 / *Don't be a bad-luck* ~. 재수 없는 소리 마라. **2** a holy person who preaches what he claims has been revealed to him. 선지자(先知者). ¶ *Every religion has its prophets.* 종교마다 선지자가 있다. **3** 《*the P-*》

Mohammed. 마호메트. **4** 《*the Prophets*》 the books in the Old Testament written by prophets. 예언서.

proph·et·ess [prάfitis / prɔ́f-] *n.* Ⓒ a woman prophet. 여자 예언자.

pro·phet·ic [prəfétik] *adj.* **1** of a prophet; containing a prophecy; such as a prophet has. 예언(자)의. ¶ ~ *power* 예언의 능력 / *a* ~ *writing* 예언서. **2** telling something beforehand. 예언하는; 전조(前兆)의. ¶ *a* ~ *dream* 예언적인 꿈 / ~ *warnings* 불길한 전조.

pro·phy·lac·tic [pròufəlǽktik / prɔ̀f-] *adj.* serving to prevent disease. 질병 예방의. ¶ ~ *treatment* 예방 조치 / *a* ~ *medicine* 예방약. — *n.* Ⓒ a medicine or treatment which prevents disease. 예방약; 예방법; 예방 조치. ¶ *take cold baths as a* ~ *against colds* 감기 예방으로 냉수욕을 하다. [pro-, Gk. *phulassō* guard]

pro·pin·qui·ty [prəpíŋkwəti] *n.* Ⓤ **1** nearness in time and place. 가까움; 근접. **2** nearness of blood; likeness. 근친; 유사. ¶ *degrees of* ~ 촌수. [L. *prope* near]

pro·pi·ti·ate [prəpíʃièit] *vt.* (P6) gain the good will of (someone); make (some angry person) quiet or calm. …의 비위를 맞추다; …을 달래다. [L. *propitius* propitious]

pro·pit·i·a·tion [prəpìʃiéiʃən] *n.* Ⓤ the act of propitiating. 달래기; 비위 맞추기.

pro·pi·ti·a·to·ry [prəpíʃiətɔ̀ːri / -təri] *adj.* serving to calm someone or make him friendly. 비위 맞추는; 달래는; 화해의. ¶ *a* ~ *gift of flowers* 화해의 꽃선물.

pro·pi·tious [prəpíʃəs] *adj.* **1** (esp. of gods) kind; favorable. (신이) 호의적인; 자비로운. ¶ ~ *deity* 자비로운 신 / *May the gods be* ~ ! 신들이여 자비를 베푸소서. **2** favorably inclined; fortunate. 상서로운; 재수좋은. ¶ *a* ~ *sign* 길조 / *We were lucky in having* ~ *weather for our trip.* 운좋게 날씨는 여행에 그만이었다.

:pro·por·tion [prəpɔ́ːrʃən] *n.* **1** ⓊⒸ the amount of one thing measured in relation to another. 비(比); 비율. ¶ *a* ~ *of five to one* 1대 5의 비율 / *the* ~ *of births to the population* 인구에 대한 출생률 / *The door is narrow in* ~ *to its height.* 문이 높이에 비해 좁다. **2** Ⓤ the well-balanced arrangement of parts. 균형; 조화. ¶ *in perfect* ~ 완전히 조화되어 / *The large glasses which he wears are not in* 〔*are out of*〕 ~ *with his small face.* 쓰고 있는 큰 안경이 그의 작은 얼굴과 어울리지 않는다. **3** 《*pl.*》 the space that a thing occupies; length, width or thickness. 크기; 넓이; 치수; 용적. ¶ *a desert of vast proportions* 끝없이 넓은 사막 / *a building of magnificent proportions* 굉장히 큰 건물. **4** Ⓒ the part belonging to each one. (일정 비율의) 부분; 몫; 배당분. ¶ *The workmen receive a* ~ *of the profits.* 노동자는 이익의 일부를 받는다 / *take a large* ~ *of the space available* 이용할 수 있는 공간의 대부분을 차지하다 / *a small* ~ *of the profits* 수익의 적은 부분.

in proportion to 〔***as***〕, in proper relation to; in balance with. …에 비례하여.

out of proportion to, too great to correspond with. …와 균형이 맞지 않는; 불균형의.

— *vt.* **1** (P6,13) make (something) in proper proportion; set (something) just right. …을 균형잡히게 하다; 조화시키다. ¶ ~ *the various parts of a building* 건물의 각 부분이 균형을 이루게 하다 / *She is rather small but well-proportioned.* 그녀가 몸집은 작은 편이지만 몸매는 좋다. **2** (P6,7,13) divide and give out (something) in fair shares; apportion. …을 배당〔할당〕하다. [pro-, → portion]

pro·por·tion·al [prəpɔ́ːrʃənəl] *adj.* in proportion. 균형 잡힌; 조화된; 비례하는. ¶ *be directly* 〔*inversely*〕 ~ *to* …에 정〔반〕비례하다 / *a* ~ *amount* 적정량 / *The chimpanzee's long arms were not* ~ *to its height.* 침팬지의 긴 팔은 키와 어울리지 않았다.

pro·por·tion·ate [prəpɔ́ːrʃənit] *adj.* in proper proportion; proportional. 균형 잡힌; 비례를 이룬; 적응한. ¶ *success* ~ *to effort* 노력에 걸맞는 성공. — [-ʃənèit] *vt.* (P6,13) make (something) proportional. …을 균형잡히게 하다; 비례시키다. ● **pro·por·tion·ate·ly** [-li] *adv.*

·pro·pos·al [prəpóuzəl] *n.* **1** ⓊⒸ the act of offering something; a proposed method or scheme. 제의; 제안; 신청. ¶ *make* 〔*offer*〕 *proposals of* 〔*for*〕 *peace* 화평을 제의하다 / *a compromise* ~ 타협안. **2** Ⓒ an offer of marriage. 청혼. [↓]

:pro·pose [prəpóuz] *vt.* **1** (P6,7,8,9,11) offer (a plan) for consideration or acceptance. …을 제안하다. ¶ *I* ~ *that we* (*should*) *go at once.* 곧 출발하는 게 어떻겠소 / ~ *some measures* 몇 가지 방책을 제의하다 / ~ *marriage* 청혼하다 / ~ *a toast* 〔*someone's health*〕 아무의 건강을 위해 축배를 제창하다. **2** (P6,7,13) name (someone) as a candidate for an office, for membership in a club, etc.; recommend. …을 지명〔추천〕하다. ¶ ~ *someone for membership* 아무를 회원으로 추천하다 / *I* ~ *John for president.* 나는 존을 회장으로 추천한다. **3** (P8,9) intend; plan. 꾀하다; 기도하다. ¶ ~ *to dine out* 밖에서 식사하려고 하다 / *What do you* ~ *doing now?* 지금 뭘 하려고 하니.

— *vi.* (P1,3) **1** make an offer of marriage. 청혼하다. **2** suggest a plan. 제안하다. **3** form a plan. 꾀하다; 계획하다. ¶ 《*prov.*》 *Man proposes, God disposes.* 일을 꾀함은 인간이요, 일을 이룸은 신이다. [pro-, →pose]

·prop·o·si·tion [prὰpəzíʃən / prɔ̀p-] *n.* Ⓒ **1** something that is proposed. 제안. ¶ *He made a* ~ *about extending the railway.* 그는 철도를 연장할 것을 제의했다 / *I have a* ~

to put to you. 네게 제안할 것이 하나 있다. **2** something stated. 진술; 주장. **3** 《math.》 a rule that can be proved to be true. 정리(定理). **4** 《log.》 a problem to be solved. 명제(命題). **5** 《*colloq.*》 a task undertaken. 일; 사업. [pro-]

pro·pound [prəpáund] *vt.* (P6) offer (something) for consideration. …을 제안〔제출, 제기〕하다. ¶ ~ *a question* 문제를 제기하다. [pro-, L. *pono* place]

pro·pri·e·tar·y [prəpráiətèri / -təri] *adj.* **1** possessing. 소유의. **2** having much money, land, etc. 재산이 있는. ¶ ~ *class* 유산 계급. **3** possessed by a certain private person or company. 독점의. ¶ *a* ~ *medicine* 특허 매약(賣藥) / ~ *articles* 전매품 / ~ *rights* 소유권. — *n.* **1** Ⓒ a person who owns; a group of such persons. 소유자; 소유자 단체. **2** Ⓤ the right of possession. 소유권. [→proper]

*__pro·pri·e·tor__ [prəpráiətər] *n.* Ⓒ an owner; a person who possesses a shop, factory, etc. 소유자; 경영자. ¶ *a landed* ~ 지주 / *the* ~ *of a farm* 농장주.

pro·pri·e·tress [prəpráiətris] *n.* Ⓒ a woman proprietor. 여자 소유자.

pro·pri·e·ty [prəpráiəti] *n.* (*pl.* **-ties**) **1** Ⓤ the state or quality of being proper or fitting. 적당; 타당. ¶ ~ *of style* 〔*language*〕 문체〔용어〕의 적절함 / *I question the* ~ *of letting her go alone.* 그녀를 혼자 보내도 괜찮은지 모르겠다. **2** 《*pl.*》 proper manners and customs kept by polite people. 예절; 예모(禮貌). ¶ *observe the proprieties* 예의 범절을 지키다. [→proper]

pro·pul·sion [prəpʌ́lʃən] *n.* Ⓤ **1** the act of pushing forward. 추진. **2** a pushing force. 추진력. ¶ *This aircraft works by jet* ~ . 이 비행기는 분사 추진력으로 움직인다. [→propel]

pro·pul·sive [prəpʌ́lsiv] *adj.* pushing (something) more forward by force. 추진력이 있는. ¶ ~ *force.* [↑]

pro·ro·ga·tion [pròurəgéiʃən] *n.* ⓊⒸ the act of proroguing a meeting. 정회(停會); 폐회. [pro-, *rogation*]

pro·rogue [prouróug] *vt., vi.* (P6; 1) to discontinue or end a session of (a legislative assembly, as the British Parliament). (의회를) 휴회〔폐회〕하다. [pro-, L. *rogo* ask]

pro·sa·ic [prouzéiik] *adj.* (of sentences) ordinary; not fanciful; dull; common; like prose. 산문(체)의; 산문적(散文的)인; 따분한; 단조로운. ¶ ~ *details of everyday life* 일상생활의 단조로운 세부 묘사 / *a very* ~ *speaker* 아주 지루하게 말하는 사람. [→prose]

pro·sa·i·cal·ly [prouzéiikəli] *adv.* in a prosaic manner. 산문적으로; 평범하게.

pro·sce·ni·a [prousí:niə] *n.* pl. of **proscenium.**

pro·sce·ni·um [prousí:niəm] *n.* Ⓒ (*pl.* **-ums** or **-ni·a**) the part of a stage in front of the curtain. 앞무대《무대와 객석 사이》. [pro-, →scene]

pro·scribe [prouskráib] *vt.* (P6) **1** forbid (someone) to do something; forbid someone (to do something). …에게 하지 못하게 하다; …을 금하다. ¶ *The government proscribed the author's works.* 정부는 그 작가의 창작 활동을 금지시켰다. **2** put (someone) outside the protection of the law. …을 법률의 보호 밖에 두다. ¶ *In olden times, a proscribed person's property belonged to the state and anyone might kill him.* 예전엔 법익(法益)을 박탈당한 사람의 재산은 나라에 몰수되고 누구든 그를 살해해도 괜찮았다. **3** force (someone) to go away. …을 추방하다. **4** forbid to enter a certain place. …에의 출입을 금하다. [pro-]

*__prose__ [prouz] *n.* Ⓤ **1** the usual style of spoken or written language. 산문(散文); 산문체. **2** a dull or uninteresting talk or style. 단조로운 이야기〔문체〕. — *adj.* **1** belonging to prose; like prose. 산문의; 산문적인. **2** common; not fanciful. 평범한; 단조로운; 상상력이 없는. — *vi., vt.* speak or write (something) in a long and tiring manner. 무미건조하게 이야기하다〔쓰다〕. [L. *prosa* straightforward]

pros·e·cute [prásəkjù:t / prɔ́s-] *vt.* (P6, 13) **1** 《law》 ⓐ bring (someone) before a court of law. …을 기소〔고발〕하다. ¶ ~ *someone for theft* 아무를 절도죄로 기소하다. ⓑ try to obtain or enforce (a right, claim) at law. (법에 호소하여 권리)를 요구하다. ¶ ~ *a claim for damages* 손해 배상을 청구하다. **2** complete (a task). …을 수행하다; 해내다. ¶ ~ *war* 전쟁을 수행하다. **3** continue (a business, a task, etc.); follow; pursue. …을 계속하다. ¶ ~ *one's studies* 〔*business*〕 공부〔장사〕를 계속하다.
— *vi.* (P1) blame someone for a crime; start and carry on a suit. 기소하다. ¶ *the right to* ~ 기소권. [pro-, →second]

pros·e·cu·tion [pràsəkjú:ʃən / prɔ̀s-] *n.* **1** ⓊⒸ the act of prosecuting someone. 기소. ¶ *start a* ~ *against someone* 아무를 기소하다 / 《Brit.》 *the Director of Public Prosecution* 검찰 총장. **2** Ⓤ 《*the* ~ 》 the group of persons that begins a legal prosecution against someone. 기소자측; 검찰측(opp. defence). ¶ *the lawyers appearing for the* ~ 검찰측에 출두한 변호인단. **3** Ⓤ the act of carrying on. 실행; 수행.

pros·e·cu·tor [prásəkjù:tər / prɔ́-] *n.* Ⓒ **1** a law official who works against a prosecuted person. 검찰관; 검사. ¶ *the Public Prosecutor* 검사. **2** a person who prosecutes someone. 기소자. ¶ *Who is the* ~ *in this case?* 이 사건의 기소자는 누구냐.

pros·e·lyte [prásəlàit / prɔ́-] *n.* Ⓒ a person who has changed from one belief or opinion to another. 개종자; 전향자(轉向者). — *vt., vi.* (P6; 1) change or make (someone) change his opinions or belief. 개종〔전향〕시키다〔하다〕. [Gk. *pros* to, *eluth* come]

pros·e·lyt·ize [prάsələtàiz / prɔ́s-] *vt., vi.* = proselyte.

pro·sit [próusit] *interj.* 《L.》 《used in drinking health or wishing success》 good luck to you. 건강을 빕니다; 축하합니다 《축배를 들 때의 말》.

pros·o·dy [prάsədi / prɔ́s-] *n.* Ⓤ the science or study of the style of poetry. 작시법(作詩法); 운율학(韻律學). [Gk. *pros* to, → ode]

:pros·pect [prάspekt / prɔ́s-] *n.* **1** ⓊⒸ something looked forward to or expected; the act of expecting. 예상; 기대. ¶ *The ~ of a voyage excited him.* 항해에 대한 기대로 그는 흥분했다. **2** ⓊⒸ 《often *pl.*》 an outlook for the future. (장래의) 가망; 전망. ¶ *I see no ~ of his success.* 그가 성공할 가망은 없다 / *The ~ is gloomy.* 전망은 비관적이다 / *His prospects at present are poor.* 현재로선 그의 앞날은 시원치 않다 / *a man of no prospects* 아무 가망도 없는 사람. **3** Ⓒ 《U.S.》 a possible customer. 단골이 될 성싶은 손님. **4** Ⓒ a view or scene that is seen. 조망(眺望); 전망. ¶ *The window has a southern ~.* 그 창문은 남향이다 / *There is a fine ~ from this window.* 이 창문에서의 전망은 아주 좋다. **5** Ⓒ a spot giving prospects of mineral deposit. 채광(採鑛) 유망지.
— *vt., vi.* (P6; 1,3) have a look; search or examine (a place) for minerals. 답사〔시굴〕하다. ¶ *go round the farm and ~* 농장을 두루 답사하다 / *~ for gold* 〔*oil*〕 금을〔석유를〕 시굴하다 / *~ one's new property* 새로 산 땅을 답사하다. [pro-, L. *specio* see]

pro·spec·tive [prəspéktiv] *adj.* **1** likely to happen; expected. 예상되는(opp. retrospective). ¶ *~ benefits* 예상 이익. **2** concerned with the future. 미래의; 장래에 관한. ¶ *my ~ son-in-law* 내 사윗감 / *The measure* 〔*law*〕 *is purely ~.* 그 조치는〔법은〕 순전히 장래를 위한 것이다.

pros·pec·tor [prάspektər / prəspék-] *n.* Ⓒ a person who searches or examines a place, for minerals. 탐광자(探鑛者); 시굴자.

pro·spec·tus [prəspéktəs] *n.* Ⓒ a short printed account giving information about the activities of an enterprise, a school, etc. 취지서; (사업 등의) 설명서; (학교 등의) 안내.

·pros·per [prάspər / prɔ́spər] *vi.* (P1) succeed; flourish; be prosperous. 성공하다; 번영하다. ¶ *The country is prospering under a strong government.* 그 나라는 강력한 정부 주도 아래 번영하고 있다 / *The eldest brother went abroad and prospered.* 맏형은 해외에 나가서 성공했다. — *vt.* (P6) make (something) successful or prosperous. …을 성공시키다; 번영하게 하다. ¶ *a prospering breeze* 순풍 / *May Heaven ~ you.* 하늘이 도와서 성공하기를. [L. *prosperus* prosperous]

:pros·per·i·ty [prɑspérəti / prɔs-] *n.* Ⓤ the state of being prosperous; good luck; success. 번영; 성공; 행운(opp. adversity). ¶ *I wish you all ~.* 여러분 모두에게 행운이 있기를.

·pros·per·ous [prάspərəs / prɔ́s-] *adj.* successful; fortunate; flourishing; favorable; helpful. 성공한; 행운의; 번영하는; 운이 좋은; 순조로운; 도움이 되는. ¶ *in a ~ hour* 운좋게; 좋은 때에 / *a ~ person* 행운아 / *~ weather for growing wheat* 밀 농사에 좋은 기후 / *await a more ~ moment* 더 좋은 때를 기다리다.

pros·tate [prάsteit / prɔ́s-] *n.* Ⓒ the large gland accessory to male generative organs in mammals. 전립샘(前立-). [Gk.]

pros·ti·tute [prάstətjù:t / prɔ́s-] *n.* Ⓒ **1** an immoral woman who offers her body for money. 매춘부(cf. *whore*). **2** a person who does base things for money. 돈 때문에 치사〔비열〕한 짓을 하는 사람. — *vt.* (P6) **1** 《*reflexively*》 (of a woman) sell herself for an immoral purpose. 몸을 팔다; 매춘하다. **2** 《*fig.*》 put to a low and unworthy purpose for the sake of money. (명예·재능 등을)이익을 위해 악용하다〔팔다〕. ¶ *~ one's honor* 〔*talents*〕 이익을 위해 명예를〔재능을〕 팔다. [pro-, L. *statuo* set]

pros·ti·tu·tion [prὰstətjú:ʃən / prɔ̀s-] *n.* Ⓤ the act of prostituting; the state of being prostituted; a base or wrong use, as of one's abilities. 매춘; 매절(賣節); (재능 등의) 악용. ¶ *the ~ of one's genius* 자기 재능의 악용.

pros·trate [prάstreit / prɔstréit] *vt.* (P6) **1** lay (something) flat on the ground. …을 쓰러뜨리다. ¶ *~ oneself* 엎드리다; 굴복하다 / *trees prostrated by the gust* 강풍에 쓰러진 나무들 / *They prostrated themselves before the altar.* 그들은 제단 앞에 엎드렸다 / 《*fig.*》 *~ oneself before rank and wealth* 지위와 부(富)에 굴복하다. **2** 《usu. in *passive*》 make (someone) tired; exhaust; overcome. …을 지치게 하다. ¶ *He was prostrated by the heat.* 그는 더위에 지쳐버렸다 / *He was prostrated by the loss of wife.* 아내를 잃고 그는 넋나간 사람 같았다.
— [prάstreit / prɔ́s-] *adj.* 《Brit.》 **1** lying face down. 엎드린. ¶ *He was humbly ~ in prayer.* 그는 겸허하게 엎드려 기도했다. **2** lying flat on one's back. 벌렁 누운. ¶ *lie ~* 벌렁 눕다. **3** utterly exhausted; powerless; helpless. 지쳐버린; 기운을 잃은. ¶ *~ with illness* 병으로 탈진한. **4** completely crushed or conquered. 굴복한; 항복한. ¶ *lie ~ before the victor* 승자에게 굴복하다. [pro-, →stratum]

pros·tra·tion [prɑstréiʃən / prɔs-] *n.* ⓊⒸ

the act of prostrating; the state of being prostrated; Ⓤ great weariness. 엎드림; 굴복; 피로; 쇠약; 의기 소침. ¶ ~ *before the altar* 제단 앞에 부복(俯伏)함 / *a condition of complete ~ of mind and spirit* 심신의 탈진 상태.

pros·y [próuzi] *adj.* (**pros·i·er, pros·i·est**) of or like prose; not interesting or pleasant; long and dull. 산문(散文)의; 산문적인; 흥미 없는; 평범한; 따분한; 지루한. ¶ *a ~ speaker* 〔*style*〕 지루한 연사〔문체〕 / *a ~ book* 재미 없는 책. [→prose]

pro·tag·o·nist [proutǽgənist] *n.* Ⓒ **1** the most important character in a novel, play, etc. (극·소설 등의) 주역; 주인공. **2** a person taking a leading part in any movement. 주창자(主唱者); 선도자. [proto-, Gk. *agōnistes* actor]

pro·te·an [próutiən, proutí:ən] *adj.* changeable like Proteus; able to assume many shapes and forms. (Proteus 신처럼) 변화무쌍한. ¶ *the ~ changes of nature* 천변 만화(千變萬化)하는 자연 / *a ~ performer* 1인 다역의 연기자. [→Proteus]

:pro·tect [prətékt] *vt.* (P6,13) **1** 《*from, against*》 defend (someone or something) from danger, injury, etc.; guard. …을 (위험 등에서) 보호하다; 지키다. ¶ ~ *one's friend from* 〔*against*〕 *temptation* 친구를 유혹에서 지켜주다 / *Protect yourself from danger.* 위험하니까 조심해라 / *This book is protected by copyright.* 이 책은 저작권의 보호를 받고 있다. **2** 《econ.》 《*from, against*》 give or try to give an advantage to (home manufactures) against imported goods. (관세 등에 의해 국내 산업·제조업)을 보호하다. ¶ ~ *home industries* 국내 산업을 보호하다. [pro-, L. *tego* cover]

:pro·tec·tion [prətékʃən] *n.* **1** Ⓤ the act of protecting; the state of being protected. 보호; 방어; 방위. ¶ *put oneself under someone's ~* 아무의 보호를 받다 / *take someone under one's ~* 아무를 비호해주다 / *She went there under the ~ of policemen.* 그녀는 경찰의 보호 아래 거기로 갔다. **2** Ⓤ 《econ.》 the system of protecting home industries by laying taxes on imported goods. 보호 무역 제도(cf. *free trade*). **3** Ⓒ 《*from, against*》 a person or thing that protects. 보호자〔물〕. ¶ *a ~ against the sun* 볕가리개 / *Locks are ~ against theft.* 자물쇠는 도둑을 방지한다.

pro·tec·tion·ism [prətékʃənìzəm] *n.* Ⓤ the economic principle of protection; the system protecting domestic industries by laying taxes on imported goods. 보호 무역주의〔정책〕.

pro·tec·tion·ist [prətékʃənist] *n.* Ⓒ a person who supports protectionism. 보호 무역주의자. — *adj.* of or favoring protectionism; of a protectionist. 보호 무역주의(자)의.

pro·tec·tive [prətéktiv] *adj.* **1** giving protection; guarding; defensive. 보호하는; 지키는. ¶ ~ *custody* 보호 감금 / ~ *trade* 보호 무역 / ~ *armor* 보호 갑주(甲冑) / *the hard ~ covering of a turtle* 보호 구실을 하는 거북의 단단한 등딱지 / ~ *instinct* (부모 등의) 보호 본능 / ~ *coloring* 보호색. **2** 《econ.》 guarding against foreign-made goods by imposing a high tax or duty on them. 보호 무역 (정책)의. ¶ ~ *duties on goods from abroad* 수입품에 대한 보호 관세.

·pro·tec·tor [prətéktər] *n.* Ⓒ **1** a person or thing that protects; a guardian. 보호자〔물〕. ¶ *the ~ of the house* 〔*his wife's honor*〕 가정을〔아내의 명예를〕 보호하는 사람 / *a chest ~* (야구의) 가슴받이. **2** 《Brit. hist.》 a person who rules the kingdom in place of a king or queen; a regent. 섭정(攝政).

pro·tec·tor·ate [prətéktərit] *n.* **1** Ⓒ the country which is governed or controlled by a strong nation. 보호국; 보호령. **2** Ⓤ 《Brit. hist.》 government by a protector. 섭정 정치. ¶ *during the ~ of Cromwell* 크롬웰이 섭정하던 동안.

pro·tec·tress [prətéktris] *n.* Ⓒ a woman who protects. protector 의 여성형.

pro·té·gé [próutəʒèi] *n.* Ⓒ a person who is under the protection of another. 피(被)보호자. 參考 여성형은 protégée. [F.]

pro·teid [próuti:id] *n.* =protein.

pro·tein [próuti:in] *n.* ⒸⓊ 《chem.》 an important compound essential to all living animals and plants, found in all foods. 단백질. [proto-]

:pro·test [prətést] *vt.* (P6,11) **1** express an objection against (something); object to. …에 항의하다; …에 이의를 제기하다. ¶ ~ *the heavy taxes* 중세(重稅)에 항의하다 / *To appeal to a higher court is to ~ the judgment of the lower.* 상급 법원에의 항소(抗訴)는 하급 법원의 판결에 대한 이의 제기이다. **2** declare or affirm solemnly. …을 단언하다; 주장하다. ¶ ~ *someone's innocence* = ~ *that someone is innocent* 아무의 결백을 주장하다. **3** make a formal statement of refusal to honor or pay. (어음의) 지불을 거절하다. ¶ ~ *a check.*

— *vi.* (P1,3) **1** 《*against*》 express an objection. 항의하다. ¶ ~ *against a decision* 결정에 항의하다 / *I can't listen to such a false statement without protesting.* 그 따위 거짓 성명을 잠자코 듣고 있을 수는 없다 / *Tom protested against going to bed early.* 톰은 일찍 자라는 말에 항의했다. **2** say positively; declare. 단언하다.

— [próutest] *n.* **1** ⓊⒸ the act of protesting; an expression of objection. 항의; 단언. ¶ *He made a ~ against the judgment.* 그는 판결에 이의를 제기했다. **2** Ⓒ a document formally objecting to something. 항의서. ¶ *The premier sent a ~ to that country.* 수상은 그 나라에 항의서를 보냈다. [pro-, L. *testis* witness]

Prot·es·tant [prátəstənt / prɔ́t-] *n.* Ⓒ **1** a member of any of the Christian churches divided from the Roman Catholic church in the 16th century. 신교도. **2** ((*p-*)) a person making a protest. 항의자; 이의 제기자. — *adj.* of Protestants or Protestantism. 신교(도)의. [→protest, -ant]

Prot·es·tant·ism [prátəstəntìzəm / prɔ́t-] *n.* Ⓤ the religion or principles of Protestants. 신교(의 교리).

prot·es·ta·tion [pròutestéiʃən / prɔ̀t-] *n.* ⓊⒸ the act of protesting; a formal expression of disagreement; a strong or solemn statement. 항의; 주장; 단언. ¶ *make a ~ of one's innocence* 〔*love*〕 자기의 결백〔사랑〕을 주장〔단언〕하다.

Pro·teus [próutjuːs, -tiəs] *n.* **1** ((Gk. myth.)) a sea god who can change his appearance very easily. 프로테우스. **2** ((*p-*)) a person who can change his opinions, principles, character, etc. very rapidly. (주의·생각 등을) 걸핏하면 바꾸는 사람; 변덕쟁이.

pro·to- [proutə-] *pref.* first; principal; prehistoric; original. '제1, 주요한, 원시적, 최초의' 의 뜻. [Gk. *prōtos*]

pro·to·col [próutəkɑ̀l / -kɔ̀l] *n.* **1** Ⓒ an original draft of a treaty, negotiation, etc. (조약 따위의) 원안; 의정서(議定書); 프로토콜. **2** Ⓤ the rules of etiquette, esp. in diplomacy. (외교상의) 의례(儀禮). — *vt., vi.* (P6; 1) draw up protocols; record in a protocol. 의정서를 작성하다. [Gk. *kolla* glue]

pro·ton [próutɑn / -tɔn] *n.* Ⓒ ((phys., chem.)) the tiny positive unit of electricity forming a part of an atom. 프로톤; 양성자(陽性子). [proto-]

pro·to·plasm [próutouplæ̀zəm] *n.* Ⓤ ((biol.)) the jelly-like, essential material of living animal and plant cells; the living substance in such cells. 원형질(原形質). [→plasma]

pro·to·type [próutoutàip] *n.* Ⓒ the original form of anything; a fine example; a pattern; a model. 원형; 모범; 본. ¶ *It has been modeled on the European ~.* 그것은 유럽의 원형을 본떠 왔다. [proto-]

pro·to·zo·an [pròutəzóuən / -ɔn] *n.* Ⓒ any of a number of animals composed of a single cell. 원생(原生) 동물. — *adj.* of a protozoan. 원생 동물의. [proto-]

pro·tract [proutræ̀kt] *vt.* (P6) **1** make (something) longer in time; prolong; lengthen. …을 오래 끌게 하다; 연장하다. ¶ *~ an argument* 논의를 질질 끌다 / *a protracted stay* 〔*visit*〕 지연된 체류〔방문〕. **2** ((zool.)) stretch or thrust out; extend. (기관(器官)을) 내밀다; 뻗다. **3** draw (something) with a scale and protractor. (비례자·각도기로) …을 제도(製圖)하다; 도면을 뜨다. [pro-, →trace]

pro·trac·tion [proutræ̀kʃən] *n.* ⓊⒸ **1** the act of protracting; the state of being protracted. 오래 끌게 하기; 연장. **2** the act of drawing a figure, plan, etc. with a scale and protractor. 제도; 도면뜨기.

pro·trac·tor [proutræ̀ktər] *n.* Ⓒ **1** a person or thing that protracts. 오래 끄는 사람〔물건〕. **2** an instrument for measuring angles. 각도기.

pro·trude [proutrúːd] *vt., vi.* (P6; 1) stick out; thrust forth; extend forward; jut out. 내밀(게 하)다; 비어져 나오(게 하)다; 돌출시키다〔하다〕. ¶ *The baby often protrudes its tongue.* 그 아기는 가끔 혀를 내민다 / *Helen's teeth ~ too far.* 헬렌의 치아는 너무 삐드렁니다. [pro-, L. *trudo* push]

pro·tru·sion [proutrúːʒən] *n.* **1** Ⓤ the act of protruding; the state of being protruded. 돌출; 내밂. ¶ *Starvation caused the ~ of the poor cat's bones.* 굶주려서 불쌍한 고양이의 뼈가 불거져 나왔다. **2** Ⓒ a protruding part. 돌출부. ¶ *A ~ of rock gave us shelter from the storm.* 비어져 나온 바위로 우린 폭풍우를 피할 수 있었다.

pro·tru·sive [proutrúːsiv] *adj.* thrusting forward; projecting. 비쭉 나온; 돌출한; 내민; 주제 넘게 나서는.

pro·tu·ber·ance [proutjúːbərəns] *n.* **1** Ⓤ the state of being protuberant. 돌기(突起); 불거져 나옴. **2** Ⓒ a thing which sticks out; a knob. 돌기물; 융기물; 혹; 결절(結節). ¶ *The ~ on his neck is fortunately not malignant.* 목의 결절이 다행히 악성은 아니다. [pro-, →tuber]

pro·tu·ber·ant [proutjúːbərənt] *adj.* sticking out; swelling outward; projecting. 돌출〔돌기(突起)〕한; 불거져 나온. ¶ *~ eyes* 튀어나온 눈.

proud [praud] *adj.* **1** ((*of, to do*)) feeling or showing proper pleasure or satisfaction; highly pleased. 뽐내는; 자랑하는; 명예로 생각하는. ¶ *The father was ~ of his son's success.* 아버지는 아들의 성공을 자랑하고 있었다 / *We are ~ to fight for our country.* 우리는 나라를 위해 싸우는 것이 자랑스럽다 / *I am ~ of knowing him* 〔*to know him*〕. 나는 그와의 지면을 명예로 여긴다. **2** thinking well or making much of oneself. 거만한; 난 체하는. ¶ *~ ladies* 도도하게 구는 여인들. **3** making much of one's honor; self-respecting. 명예를 중히 여기는; 자존심이 있는. ¶ *~ poverty* 청빈(清貧) / *be too ~ to beg* 구걸을 하기는 자존심이 허락지 않다. **4** giving reason to be praised. 영광으로 여기는. ¶ *the proudest moment of my life* 내 생애에서 가장 영광으로 여기는 순간. **5** (of things) looking splendid or magnificent. 훌륭한; 당당한. ¶ *The ~ building towered over the huts.* 훌륭한 건물이 오두막집들 위로 우뚝 솟아 있었다. [F. *prud* good]

(**as**) ***proud as Punch*** 〔***a peacock, a turkey***〕, very vain or proud. 의기 양양하여; 우쭐해서.

do someone proud, ((colloq.)) do something

which causes someone else to feel proud or honored. …을 기쁘게 하다; 만족시키다. ¶ *You do me* ~. 더 없는 영광입니다 / *It does* 〔*will do*〕 *me* ~. 대단히 만족스럽습니다.

proud flesh [ˊ ˊ] *n.* overgrown flesh round a healing wound. (아문 상처에 생기는) 궂은살.

*****proud·ly** [práudli] *adv.* in a proud manner; with pride. 거만하게; 자랑스러운 듯이; 의기 양양해서.

prov·a·ble [prú:vəbəl] *adj.* that can be proved. 입증할 수 있는. ¶ *a* ~ *alibi* 입증할 수 있는 알리바이. [↓]

:prove [pru:v] *v.* (**proved, proved** or **prov·en**) *vt.* **1** (P6,11,21) show (something) to be true; make (something) sure. …을 증명〔입증〕하다. ¶ ~ *someone's innocence* 아무의 결백을 입증하다 / *I can* ~ *that what he says is true.* 그의 말이 사실임을 나는 입증할 수 있다 / *He has been proved* (*to be*) *wrong.* 그의 잘못이 입증됐다 / *He proved himself* (*to be*) *worthy of confidence.* 그는 자신이 신뢰할 만한 사람임을 증명했다 / *I can* ~ *that the painting is not genuine.* 나는 그 그림이 가짜임을 증명할 수 있다. **2** (P6) test (something) by experiment. …을 시험〔실험〕하다. ¶ ~ *a man's honesty* 그의 성실성을 시험하다 / ~ *a new tool* 〔*the purity of copper*〕 새 도구〔구리의 순도(純度)〕를 시험하다. **3** (P6) establish genuineness and validity of (a will). (유언장)을 검증하다; (유언장)의 검인을 받다. **4** (P6) 《print.》 take a proof impression of. …의 교정쇄를 찍다. **5** (P6) 《*arch.*》 learn by experience; suffer. 체험하다; 겪다. ¶ *I proved the extreme depths of poverty and sorrow.* 나는 극도의 가난과 슬픔이 어떤 것인가를 체험했다.
— *vi.* (P4) turn out to be; be found to be. …이 되다; …임을 알다. ¶ *The rumor proved* (*to be*) *true.* 소문은 사실이었다 / *The treatment proved successful.* 치료는 성공적이었다. [L. *probo* test]

prov·en [prú:vən] *v.* 《*arch.*, U.S.》 pp. of **prove.**

prov·en·der [právindər / prɔ́v-] *n.* Ⓤ **1** coarse dried food, esp. for horses, cattle, etc. 여물; 꼴. **2** 《*colloq.*》 food. 양식; 음식물. [L. *praebeo* grant]

*****prov·erb** [právə:rb / prɔ́v-] *n.* Ⓒ **1** a short, wise and usu. traditional saying that expresses a truth. 속담; 격언. ¶ *the* (*Books of*) *Proverbs* (구약 성서의) 잠언(箴言) / *as the* ~ *says* 〔*goes*〕 속담에 있듯이〔이르기를〕. **2** a person or thing well-known to be typical of a certain character; a byword. (어떤 특징 따위로 인해) 널리 알려진〔소문이 난〕 사람〔사물〕; 웃음거리. ¶ *to a* ~ 모르는 사람이 없을 정도로; 정평이 날 만큼 / *His ignorance is a* ~. 그의 무지는 세상이 다 안다 / *He is a* ~ *for inefficiency.* 무능하기로 소문이 나 있다. [pro-]

pro·ver·bi·al [prəvə́:rbiəl] *adj.* **1** of or like a proverb. 속담의〔같은〕. ¶ ~ *wisdom* 금언 / *a* ~ *brevity* 속담 같은 간결(함) / *a* ~ *saying* 속담. **2** widely or generally known; famous. 주지(周知)의; 유명한. ¶ *the* ~ *London fog* 유명한 런던의 안개 / *the* ~ *loyalty of dogs* 천하가 아는 개의 충직성.

pro·ver·bi·al·ly [prəvə́:rbiəli] *adv.* by means of a proverb; as known in a proverb; notoriously. 속담대로; 널리 알려져서.

:pro·vide [prəváid] *vt.* **1** (P6,13) 《*for*》 get ready or make preparations for (something); prepare. …을 준비하다; 마련하다. ¶ ~ *a meal* 식사 준비를 하다 / ~ *food for a voyage* 항해에 대비하여 식량을 마련하다 / ~ *a reason* 〔*an excuse, a means of escape*〕 이유를〔핑계를, 도망갈 방법을〕 마련하다. **2** (P6,13) 《*with, for, to*》 give (food, etc. needed); supply. (필요한 음식 등)을 공급하다; 주다. ¶ ~ *one's child with clothes* 아이들에게 옷을 주다 / *This house is not provided with a veranda.* 이 집에는 베란다가 없다 / *Can you* ~ *me with a room the night?* 하룻밤 방 하나 제공해 줄 수 있겠소 / *They* ~ *themselves with food and weapons.* 그들은 식량과 무기를 스스로 조달하고 있다. **3** (P11) (of a rule, etc.) declare (a matter) to be necessary; stipulate. (규칙 등이) …을 규정하다. ¶ *The club's rules* ~ *that dues must be paid monthly.* 클럽의 규칙은 매달 회비를 내도록 규정하고 있다 / *Our law provides that….* 우리 법에는 …라는 규정이 있다.
— *vi.* **1** (P3) 《*for, against*》 make preparations. 준비〔대비〕하다. ¶ ~ *against danger* 위험에 대비하다 / ~ *for old age* 노후에 대비하다. **2** (P1,3) 《*for*》 give what is necessary. 필요한 것을 공급하다〔주다〕; 부양하다. ¶ ~ *for one's family* 가족을 부양하다 / *The Lord will* ~. 주님께서 필요한 것을 주실 것이다. **3** (P3) 《law》 make impossible; forbid. 금지하다. ¶ ~ *against absence without leave* 무단결근을 금하다. [pro-, L. *video* see]

pro·vid·ed [prəváidid] *conj.* 《*that*》 on the condition that…; if. …이라는 조건으로; 만일 …이라면. ¶ *Provided* (*that*) *it is true, you may go.* 만일 그것이 사실이라면 가도 좋다.

*****prov·i·dence** [právədəns / prɔ́v-] *n.* Ⓤ **1** 《often *P-*》 the care or guidance of God; God. 섭리; 신의 뜻; 신조(神助); 신. ¶ *the plans of Providence* 신의 섭리 / *Her recovery was a special* ~ *of God.* 그녀의 회복은 신의 각별한 은총이었다. **2** prudent care or preparation for the future; foresight. 장래에 대한 배려; 선견지명. ¶ *lessons of* ~ *and thrift* 장래에 대한 배려와 검약의 가르침.

prov·i·dent [právədənt / prɔ́v-] *adj.* **1** having foresight. 선견지명이 있는. ¶ ~ *scheme* 앞을 내다본 계획. **2** cautious. 신중한; 조심성 있는. **3** economical; saving. 검소한. ¶ *He is* ~ *of his money.* 그는 돈의 씀씀이가 검소한 사람이다.

prov·i·den·tial [prὰvədénʃəl / prɔ̀v-] *adj.*

1 having good fortune; lucky; fortunate. 행운의; 운 좋은. ¶ *a ~ escape* 행운의 탈출. 2 of or by God's will. 신의 뜻에 의한. ¶ *~ help* 천우(天佑).

pro·vid·ing [prəváidiŋ] *conj.* =provided.

:prov·ince [právins / prɔ́v-] *n.* Ⓒ 1 a large division of certain countries. 주(州); 성(省). 2 《*pl.*》 ⓐ an area remote from the capital or largest cities. 지방; 시골. ¶ *in the provinces* 시골에서. ⓑ 《Brit.》 the whole country outside London. 런던을 제외한 전국. ¶ *London and the provinces* 런던과 전국 여러 지방. 3 a sphere or field of action, knowledge, business, etc.; a section; a department. 범위; 영역; 분야. ¶ *It is not* (*in, within*) *my ~.* 그것은 내 전문 분야가 아니다 / *the ~ of science* 〔*literature*〕 과학〔문학〕 분야. [L. *provincia*]

pro·vin·cial [prəvínʃəl] *adj.* 1 of or belonging to a province. 주(州)의; 도(道)의; 지방〔시골〕의. ¶ *a ~ tour* 지방 순회 / *~ government* 지방 정부. 2 having or showing the manners, viewpoints, etc. of people living in the country; rustic. 시골티가 나는. ¶ *~ accents* 시골 사투리 / *~ custom* 시골 풍습 / *her narrow-minded ~ attitude* 그녀의 속좁은 시골티 나는 태도. 3 not polished; rude; narrow. 세련되지 않은; 투박한; 편협한. ¶ *a ~ point of view* 옹졸한 견해.
— *n.* Ⓒ 1 a person living in a province or the provinces. 지방민; 촌사람. 2 an uncultivated, rude person. 세련되지 않은〔지적이 아닌〕 사람; 시골뜨기.

pro·vin·cial·ism [prəvínʃəlìzəm] *n.* ⒸⓊ 1 the state of being provincial. 지방성; 시골티. 2 a provincial manner, idea, way of speech, etc. 시골티 나는 태도〔생각·말투 따위〕; 촌스러움. 3 an example of narrowness of viewpoint or outlook. 편협; 옹졸. 4 a word, an accent, or a phrase, etc. peculiar to a certain province. 사투리; 방언.

:pro·vi·sion [prəvíʒən] *n.* 1 ⓊⒸ 《*for, against*》 careful preparation; arrangement made, esp. for the future. 예비; 준비; 대비. ¶ *make ~ against* 〔*for*〕 *a rainy day* 만일의 경우에 대비하다 / *Mr. Archer made ~ for his children's education.* 아처씨는 아이들의 교육을 위한 대비를 했다. 2 Ⓒ 《often *pl.*》 something prepared or provided; food. 저장〔비축〕품; 양식; 식량. ¶ *run out* 〔*short*〕 *of provisions* 양식이 떨어지다 / *Their ~ of oil is plentiful.* 그들의 석유 비축량은 풍부하다 / *They took plenty of provisions on their trip.* 여행을 위해 충분한 식량을 마련했다. 3 Ⓒ a condition or clause in a law. (법률의) 조항; 규정. ¶ *According to the provisions of the agreement the interest on the loan must be paid monthly.* 협약 조항에 따라 대부 이자는 매달 지불되어야 한다. [pro-]

pro·vi·sion·al [prəvíʒənəl] *adj.* of temporary arrangement; lasting for only a short time. 일시적인; 임시의; 가(假)…. ¶ *a ~ agreement* 〔*treaty*〕 가(假)조약 / *a ~ government* 임시 정부 / *a ~ order* 잠정 명령.

pro·vi·so [prəváizou] *n.* (*pl.* **-sos** or **-soes**) Ⓒ a sentence that states a condition in a legal document or other agreement; a condition. 단서(但書); 조건. ¶ *with* (*a*) *~* 조건부로 / *I make it a ~ that….* …이라는 것을 조건으로 한다 / *He was permitted to go abroad with the ~ that he should return at the end of two years.* 그는 만 2년이 되면 귀국한다는 조건으로 외국에 가는 것이 허락되었다. [L.=it being provided]

prov·o·ca·tion [pràvəkéiʃən / prɔ̀v-] *n.* 1 Ⓤ the act of provoking; the state of being provoked. 성나게 함; 성남; 도발(挑發). ¶ *commit a crime under ~* 홧김에 범죄를 저지르다 / *be guilty of grave ~* 중대한 도발의 죄가 있다 / *feel ~* 화나다 / *give ~* 성나게 하다. 2 Ⓒ something that stirs up anger, resentment, etc. 화나게 하는 것. [pro-, *vocation*]

pro·voc·a·tive [prəvákətiv / -vɔ́k-] *adj.* exciting to anger; stirring up action, feeling, etc.; stimulating. (남을) 성나게 하는; 도발적인; 자극〔유발〕하는. ¶ *be ~ of curiosity* 호기심을 자극하다 / *~ language* 〔*laughter*〕 남을 성나게 하는 언사〔웃음〕 / *behave in a ~ manner* 아니꼽게 굴다. — *n.* Ⓒ something that provokes. 화나게 하는 것; 자극〔도발〕물.

·pro·voke [prəvóuk] *vt.* (P6,7,13,20) make (someone) angry; stir up (someone's actions, feelings, etc.); irritate; excite. …을 성나게 하다; (행동·감정 등)을 불러일으키다; 유발시키다; …을 신경질나게 하다; 흥분시키다. ¶ *~ a storm* 큰 소동을 일으키다 / *~ someone to anger* 아무를 성나게 하다 / *be provoked by someone's impudence* 아무의 뻔뻔스러움에 분개하다 / *His haughty manner provoked me into discharging him at once.* 그자의 오만한 행동에 화가 나서 그를 당장 해고해 버렸다 / *She was provoked at his remark.* 그의 비평에 그녀는 발끈했다 / *~ people to revolt* 사람들이 반란을 일으키게 하다 / *~ a strong protest* 강한 반발을 사다 / *He was provoked to put forth more effort.* 그는 자극을 받아 가일층 분발했다. [pro-, L. *voco* call]

pro·vok·ing [prəvóukiŋ] *adj.* that provokes; exciting to anger; annoying; irritating. 화나는; 짜증나는; 괘씸한; 성가신; 귀찮은. ¶ *~ children* 성가신 아이들 / *~ words* 괘씸한 소리 / *with ~ coolness* 밉살스러울 정도로 냉정하게.

prov·ost [próuvoust, právəst] *n.* Ⓒ 1 the head of certain colleges, universities or churches. 대학의 학장; 주임 사제(司祭). 2 the chief magistrate in certain towns of Scotland; a mayor. (스코틀랜드의) 시장. [pro-, L. *pono* place]

prow [prau] *n.* Ⓒ 1 the front part of a boat or ship; something like it. 이물; 뱃머리(모양의 물건). 2 the forward part of an airplane. 기수(機首). [Gk. *prōira*]

prow·ess [práuis] *n.* Ⓤ **1** courage; bravery; brave or valorous actions. 무용(武勇); 용감(한 행위). **2** great ability or skill. 대단한 솜씨. ¶ *a football player of great* ~ 기량이 뛰어난 축구 선수. [→proud]

prowl [praul] *vi., vt.* (P1,2A; 6) 《*about, around*》 walk about slowly or cautiously looking for something to eat or steal; wander; roam. (먹이나 훔칠 것을) 찾아 헤매다; 배회하다; 어슬렁거리다. ¶ *Wolves are prowling* (*the forest*). 이리들이 먹이를 찾아 (숲을) 헤매고 있다 / ~ *around a building* 건물 주위를 배회하다 / *He prowled the streets for hours.* 그는 몇 시간 동안 거리를 돌아다녔다. — *n.* Ⓒ the act of prowling. 찾아 헤매기; 배회. ¶ *take a* ~ 배회하다. [E.]

prox. proximo.

prox·i·mate [práksəmit / prɔ́k-] *adj.* **1** nearest in time, place, etc. …에 가장 가까운. ¶ *the house* ~ *to the river* 강에 인접한 집. **2** almost the same; nearly correct; approximate. 근사한. [L. *proximus* next]

prox·im·i·ty [praksíməti / prɔk-] *n.* Ⓤ closeness; nearness. 근접; 가까움. ¶ ~ *of blood* 근친(近親) / *I rested in close* ~ *to the fire.* 나는 불 곁에서 쉬었다.

prox·i·mo [práksəmòu / prɔ́k-] *adj.* of or in the next month. 내달의(cf. *instant, ultimo*). 參考 prox.로 생략함. ¶ *on the 6th* ~ 내달 6일에.

prox·y [práksi / prɔ́ksi] *n.* (*pl.* **prox·ies**) **1** Ⓤ the act or authority of taking the place of another. 대리; 대리권. ¶ *vote by* ~ 대리[위임] 투표하다 / *be* [*stand*] ~ *for* …의 대리 노릇하다. **2** Ⓒ a person or company that acts for another. 대리인; 대리점. **3** Ⓒ a document giving the authority to act or vote for another. 위임장. [Abbr. procuracy]

prude [pru:d] *n.* 《*contempt.*》 Ⓒ a person who makes a show of being easily shocked and does not do or say anything supposed to be impure. 고상한 체하는 사람; 요조 숙녀인 체하는 여자. [F. *prud* good]

pru·dence [prú:dəns] *n.* Ⓤ **1** knowledge and good judgment. 사려 분별(이 있음); 신중. **2** wisdom in a keen, practical sense. 빈틈 없음. [↑]

***pru·dent** [prú:dənt] *adj.* taking careful thought for the future; thoughtful; careful in speech and action. 신중한; 사려 분별이 있는; 조심성 있는; 빈틈 없는. ¶ *a* ~ *businessman* 용의 주도한 상인 / ~ *in action* [*speech*] 행동[말]에 신중한.

pru·den·tial [pru:dénʃəl] *adj.* careful in speech and action; cautious; thoughtful. 신중한; 조심스러운; 분별 있는. ¶ ~ *motives* 타산적인 동기 / *a* ~ *student* 사려 깊은 학생.

pru·dent·ly [prú:dəntli] *adv.* in a prudent manner. 조심스럽게; 빈틈 없이.

prud·er·y [prú:dəri] *n.* Ⓤ the behavior of a prude. 고상한 체하는 행위; 요조 숙녀인 체하기. [→prude]

prud·ish [prú:diʃ] *adj.* like or characteristic of a prude; too modest or proper. 얌전[고상]한 체하는; 지나치게 얌전빼는. [↑]

***prune**[1] [pru:n] *n.* **1** Ⓒ a kind of dried plum. 말린 자두. **2** Ⓤ a deep purple color like that of prunes. 짙은 적자색(赤紫色). [Gk. *proumnon* plum]

***prunes and prism*(*s*),** an affected way of speaking. 점잔빼는 말씨.

prune[2] [pru:n] *vt.* (P6,7) **1** 《*away, down*》 cut off or cut away needless parts; reduce the length of (a speech, article, etc.). 쓸데 없는 부분을 삭제[제거]하다; (말·문장 등을) 간결하게 하다[줄이다]. ¶ ~ *the slang from a speech* 연설에서 속어를 빼버리다. **2** cut unnecessary twigs or branches from (a tree, etc.). (나무)의 쓸데 없는 가지를 치다; 전지하다. ¶ ~ *dead branches from a tree* 말라버린 나뭇가지를 치다. [F.]

prun·ers [prú:nərz] *n. pl.* pruning scissors; a tool used for pruning. 전정(剪定) 가위. [↑]

pru·ri·ent [prúəriənt] *adj.* full of lustful desire; not pure; indecent. 호색(好色)의; 색을 밝히는; 음란한. [L. *prurio* itch]

Prus·sia [prʌ́ʃə] *n.* a former state of Germany, in the northern part. 프로이센《독일의 북부에 있었던 왕국》.

Prus·sian [prʌ́ʃən] *n.* Ⓒ a person of Prussia. 프로이센 사람. — *adj.* of Prussia or Prussians. 프로이센(사람)의. [*Prussia*]

prus·sic acid [prʌ́sik ǽsid] *n.* 《chem.》 a deadly poisonous acid. 청산(青酸). [↑]

pry[1] [prai] *vi.* (**pried**) (P1,2A,3) **1** look with curiosity; peep. 엿보다; 훔쳐보다. ¶ ~ *about* [*into*] *a house* 어떤 집[집안]을 엿보다. **2** try to find out (someone's affair); inquire curiously. (남의 일에) 파고들다; 꼬치꼬치 캐다. ¶ ~ *into other people's affairs* 남의 일을 꼬치꼬치 캐다. — *n.* (*pl.* **pries**) **1** Ⓤ the act of prying. 엿보기; 꼬치꼬치 캐기. **2** Ⓒ a person who attempts to gain information by questions. 남의 일을 꼬치꼬치 캐는 사람. [E.]

pry[2] [prai] *vt.* (**pried**) **1** (P7,18) lift up (something) with a lever. …을 지레로 들어 올리다. ¶ ~ *open a door* 문을 지레로 비집어 열다 / ~ *up the lid of a box* 상자 뚜껑을 지레로 비집어 열다. **2** (P13) gain (something) by making a hard try. …을 가까스로 손에 넣다. — *n.* Ⓒ (*pl.* **pries**) a lever. 지레; 쇠지렛대. [prize[3]]

P.S., p.s. postscript.

***psalm** [sa:m] *n.* Ⓒ **1** a sacred song or poem; hymn. 찬송가; 성시; 성가. **2** 《*a P-*》 one of the sacred songs in the Old Testament. 시편(詩篇) 중의 한 편. **3** 《*the P-s*》 the book of the Old Testament consisting of 150 psalms. (구약 성서의) 시편(詩篇). [Gk.

psallō twang]

psalm·ist [sá:mist] *n.* Ⓒ **1** a person who writes psalms. 찬송가 작자. **2** 《*the P-*》 David, as the author of the Psalms. (시편 작자인) 다윗왕.

psal·mo·dy [sá:mədi, sǽlmə-] *n.* (*pl.* **-dies**) **1** Ⓤ the act of singing psalms. 성가 영창(詠唱). **2** 《*collectively*》 a book of psalms. 찬송가집(集).

psal·ter [sɔ́:ltər] *n.* **1** 《*the P-*》 the Book of Psalms. 시편(詩篇). **2** Ⓒ a prayer book containing any special version of the Psalms. (기도용의) 시편.

pseu·d(o)- [sú:d(ou)-] *pref.* false; pretended; not real. '가짜의, 모조의'의 뜻. ¶ *pseudo-religion* 사이비 종교. [Gk. *pseudēs* false]

pseu·do·nym [sú:dənim] *n.* Ⓒ a name used by a writer in place of his real name; a pen name. 필명; 펜네임. ¶ *write poems under a* ~ 시를 필명으로 쓰다. [pseudo-, Gk. *onuma* name]

Psy·che [sáiki] *n.* **1** 《Gk. myth.》 the soul, represented as a beautiful girl loved by Cupid. 사이키; 프시케. **2** Ⓒ 《*p-*》 the soul or mind of a human. 영혼; 정신. [Gk. *psukhē* breath, life]

psy·chi·a·trist [saikáiətrist, si-] *n.* Ⓒ a doctor treating mental diseases. 정신과 의사; 정신병 학자. [→psychic]

psy·chi·a·try [saikáiətri, si-] *n.* Ⓤ the treatment and healing of mental diseases. 정신병학; 정신병 치료법.

psy·chic [sáikik] *adj.* **1** of the soul or spirit. 정신의; 영혼의. ¶ *a* ~ *influence* 정신적 영향 / *a* ~ *trauma* 심적 외상(外傷); 정신적 쇼크. **2** beyond recognized laws of physics. 심령(心靈)의. ¶ ~ *force* 심령력 / ~ *research* 심령 연구. **3** easily influenced by psychic effect. 심령 작용을 받기 쉬운. —*n.* Ⓒ **1** a person who is easily influenced by supernatural forces. 심령 현상을 느끼기 쉬운 사람. **2** a person able to receive messages from the spirits of the dead. 영매(靈媒); 무당. [Gk. *psukhē* soul]

psy·chi·cal [sáikikəl] *adj.* =psychic.

psy·cho- [sáikou-] *pref.* breath; spirit; soul. '정신, 영혼'의 뜻. [Gk.]

psy·cho·a·nal·y·sis [sàikouənǽləsis] *n.* Ⓤ a method for treating certain mental disorders; a branch of psychology which studies the unconscious. 정신 분석(학, 법). [psycho-]

psy·cho·an·a·lyst [sàikouǽnəlist] *n.* Ⓒ a person who practices psychoanalysis. 정신분석가[학자].

psy·cho·log·i·cal [sàikəlɑ́dʒikəl / -lɔ́dʒ-] *adj.* of the mind; of psychology. 심리(학)의; 심리(학)적인. ¶ *Memories and dreams are* ~ *facts.* 기억과 꿈은 심리적 사실이다 / ~ *problem* [*explanation*] 심리학적인 문제[해석].

psy·chol·o·gist [saikɑ́lədʒist / -kɔ́l-] *n.* Ⓒ a person who studies psychology. 심리학자.

·psy·chol·o·gy [saikɑ́lədʒi / -kɔ́l-] *n.* Ⓤ **1** the science that studies the human mind and its activities. 심리학. **2** a person's mental processes, emotions, thoughts, etc. 심리.

psy·cho·ther·a·py [sàikouθérəpi] *n.* Ⓤ the medical treatment of disease by psychological methods. 정신 요법.

P.T.A. Parent-Teacher Association.

P.T.O., p.t.o. please turn over. 뒷면[이면] 참조; 다음 페이지에 계속.

Ptol·e·ma·ic system [tɑ̀ləméiik sístəm / tɔ̀l-], **the** *n.* the system or theory taught by Ptolemy that the sun, moon, and planets moved around the earth. 천동설(天動說). [Person]

pto·main(e) [tóumein, toumέin] *n.* Ⓤ 《chem.》 a substance, often poisonous, produced in decaying matter. 프토마인 《유기체의 부패로 생기는 독》. ¶ ~ *poisoning* 프토마인 중독. [Gk. *ptōma* corpse]

pub [pʌb] *n.* Ⓒ 《Brit. *sl.*》 a public house. 선술집. [abbr.]

pu·ber·ty [pjú:bərti] *n.* Ⓤ the physical beginning of manhood or womanhood. 사춘기. ¶ *arrive at* ~ 사춘기가 되다 / *the age of* ~ 결혼 적령기. [L. *pubes* genitals, hair on them]

:pub·lic [pʌ́blik] *adj.* (opp. private) **1** of or belonging to a nation and its people. 공중의; 공공(公共)의; 사회의; 국민의. ¶ ~ *opinion* 여론 / *a* ~ *holiday* 국경일; 공휴일 / ~ *interests* 공익 / ~ *health* 공중 위생 / *a* ~ *document* 공문서 / *the* ~ *debt* 공채 / *public works* 공공 토목 사업 / *declare someone a* ~ *enemy* 아무를 공적(公敵)이라고 선언하다. **2** for the use of all people; open to all people. 공중용[공공용]의; 공개의. ¶ *a* ~ *building* 공공 건물 / *a* ~ *library* 공공 도서관 / *a* ~ *bath* 공중 욕탕 / *in a* ~ *place* 공개적인 자리에서 / *a* ~ *meeting* [*debate*] 공개 회합[토론회]. **3** working for a nation and its people. 국가 및 국민을 위해 일하는. ¶ *a* ~ *servant* 공무원 / *a* ~ *office* 관청 / ~ *life* 공(公)생활. **4** known to people in general; open. 공공연한; 모르는 사람이 없는. ¶ *make* ~ 공표[발표]하다 / *a* ~ *scandal* 누구나 다 아는 추문 / *make something* ~ …을 공개하다 / *It is a matter of* ~ *knowledge.* 그것은 천하가 다 아는 일이다.

go public, become a public company. (회사가) 주식을 공개하다.

in the public eye, (of a person) often seen in public or on television, or mentioned in newspapers. 사회[세상]의 이목을 끌어.

—*n.* Ⓤ 《*the* ~, used as *sing.* and *pl.*》 **1** people in general; the members of a nation. 일반 대중; 국민; 사회. ¶ *the* ~ *at large* 일반 대중 / *the Korean* ~ (일반) 한국

인; 한국 국민 / *appeal to the* ~ 여론에 호소하다 / *The* ~ *is* 〔*are*〕 *not allowed to enter the place.* 일반인은 그 곳에 들어가지 못한다. **2** a special class of people. …계(界); …사회; …동아리. ¶ *the reading* ~ 독서계 / *the musical* 〔*sporting*〕 ~ 음악〔스포츠〕계 / *have a large* ~ 팬이 많다. **3** 《Brit. *colloq.*》 =public house. [L. *populus*]

in public, openly; not in private. 공공연히.

pub·li·can [pʌ́blikən] *n.* **1** 《Rom.》 a tax-collector of ancient Rome. 수세리(收稅吏). **2** 《Brit.》 the keeper of a public house, who is allowed to sell alcoholic drinks. 선술집 주인.

·**pub·li·ca·tion** [pʌ̀bləkéiʃən] *n.* **1** Ⓤ the act of making something known to the public. 발표; 공표. ¶ *the* ~ *of a death* 사망 공표. **2** Ⓤ the act of printing and offering books, newspapers, etc. to the public. 출판; 발행. **3** Ⓒ a thing which is published, as a newspaper, a magazine, a book, etc. 출판물. ¶ *a monthly* ~ 월간지.

public company [ㄹ– ㄹ––] *n.* a business company that offers its shares for sale on the stock exchange. 주식 공모 회사; 상장 회사.

public house [ㄹ– ㄹ] *n.* **1** 《Brit.》 a small house where alcoholic drinks are sold to be drunk there. 선술집(cf. *pub*). **2** an inn. 여관; 여인숙.

pub·li·cist [pʌ́blisist] *n.* Ⓒ **1** a specialist in international law. 국제법 학자. **2** a writer on current public or political topics; a journalist who deals with political matters. 정치 평론가; 정치부 기자.

·**pub·lic·i·ty** [pʌblísəti] *n.* Ⓤ **1** the state of being widely known. 주지(周知)(의 상태); 널리 알려짐. ¶ *The fact is in wide* ~. 그건 주지의 사실이다. **2** printed or spoken matter used to get public attention; public notice gained by advertising. 공표; 공개; 선전; 광고; 평판; 명성. ¶ *avoid* ~ *in the papers* 지상에 공표되는 것을 피하다 / *newspaper* ~ 신문 광고〔선전〕 / *a* ~ *campaign* 광고 활동 / *the* ~ *which actors desire* 배우들이 바라는 명성 / *a* ~ *agent* 광고 대리인.

pub·li·cize [pʌ́bləsàiz] *vt.* (P6) 《U.S.》 make (something) known to the public. …을 공표〔광고, 선전〕하다. ¶ ~ *a new policy* 신정책을 공표하다.

pub·lic·ly [pʌ́blikli] *adv.* in a public manner; in the presence of people; openly. 공적으로; 공공연히; 공개적으로.

pub·lic-mind·ed [pʌ́blikmáindid] *adj.* public-spirited. 공공심(公共心)이 있는.

public relations [ㄹ– –ㄹ–] *n. pl.* 《used as *sing.*》 the activities of improving the relations of an organization with the public. 섭외 (사무); 광고 (활동). 參考 P.R.로 생략함.

public school [ㄹ– ㄹ] *n.* **1** 《Brit.》 a private boarding school. (기숙사 제도의) 사립 중·고등 학교. **2** 《U.S.》 a free school supported by taxes. 초·중등 공립 학교.

pub·lic-spir·it·ed [pʌ́blikspíritid] *adj.* having or showing a desire for the public welfare. 공공심이 있는.

:**pub·lish** [pʌ́bliʃ] *vt.* (P6) **1** make (something) known publicly. …을 발표〔공표〕하다. ¶ ~ *the news* 뉴스를 발표하다 / ~ *the secrets* 비밀을 공개하다. **2** make (a law, etc.) known formally. (법률·명령 따위)를 공포하다. **3** print and offer (a book, a magazine, etc.) for sale. (책 등)을 발행〔간행〕하다. ¶ ~ *a new edition* 신판(新版)을 내다 / *He has published nothing of importance.* 그는 변변한 책을 낸 적이 없다. [→public]

·**pub·lish·er** [pʌ́bliʃər] *n.* Ⓒ a person or company that publishes a book, a magazine, etc. 출판자〔사〕; 발행자〔소〕.

puck[1] [pʌk] *n.* Ⓒ 《often *P-*》 the name of a mischievous elf in English folk tales. 개구쟁이 꼬마 요정. [E.]

puck[2] [pʌk] *n.* Ⓒ a hard rubber disk used in playing ice hockey. 퍽《아이스하키용의 고무 원반》. [?]

puck·er [pʌ́kər] *vt.* (P6,7) gather (the skin, lips, etc.) into small wrinkles. (입 따위)를 오므리다; (얼굴)을 찌푸리다; …에 주름을 잡다. ¶ ~ (*up*) *one's brows* 〔*forehead*〕 미간을 찌푸리다 / ~ *a piece of cloth* 천에 주름을 잡다. — *vi.* (P1,2A) wrinkle. 주름이 가다. ¶ *The cloth puckered badly after being wet.* 젖은 천에 보기 흉한 주름이 생겼다. — *n.* Ⓒ a wrinkle or a group of wrinkles. 주름(살). ¶ *folds and puckers in a cloth* 천의 주름살 / *in puckers* 주름이 져; 구겨져. [E.]

·**pud·ding** [púdiŋ] *n.* ⓊⒸ **1** a soft, boiled, sweet food. 푸딩. **2** a kind of sausage. 소시지〔순대〕의 일종. [E.]

pudding face [ㄹ– ㄹ] *n.* a round, flat, expressionless face. 둥글넓적하고 무표정한 얼굴.

pud·ding·head [púdiŋhèd] *n.* 《*colloq.*》 a dull, stupid person. 얼간이.

pud·dle [pʌ́dl] *n.* **1** Ⓒ a small pool of dirty water. (더러운) 물웅덩이. ¶ *a* ~ *of rainwater* 빗물 웅덩이. **2** Ⓤ a mixture of clay, sand, and water. 이긴 흙.

— *vt.* (P6,7) **1** make (something) muddy. …을 더럽히다; 흙투성이가 되게 하다. **2** ⓐ work (clay) with water. (진흙)을 이기다; 흙반죽을 만들다. ⓑ 《*up*》 use a mixture of wet clay and sand to stop water from running through. (물이 새는 구멍을 메우려고) 진흙을 바르다. ¶ ~ *up a hole* 〔*leak*〕 진흙으로 구멍〔새는 것〕을 메우다. **3** turn (melted iron) into wrought iron by melting and stirring. (정련(精鍊)하기 위해 쇳물)을 휘젓다.

— *vi.* (P2) poke about in muddy or dirty water. 흙탕물을 휘젓다〔철벅거리며 걸어다니다〕. [E.]

pudg·y [pʌ́dʒi] *adj.* (**pudg·i·er, pudg·i·est**) 《*colloq.*》 short, thick, and fat. 땅딸막한.

¶ *a child's ~ hand* 아기의 통통한 손 / *a ~ little man* 땅딸막한 사람. [?]

pueb·lo [pwéblou, puéb-] *n.* Ⓒ (*pl.* **-los** [-z]) **1** an Indian village or settlement built of adobe. 푸에블로《어도비 벽돌로 지은 인디언의 부락》. **2** an Indian living in such a village. 거기에 사는 인디언 원주민. [Sp.]

pu·er·ile [pjúːəril, -ràil] *adj.* childish; silly. 어린애 같은; 철없는. ¶ *a very ~ remark* 철없는 소리. [L. *puer* boy, *pario* bear]

pu·er·il·i·ty [pjùːəríləti] *n.* Ⓤ the state of being puerile; childishness; foolishness. 어린애 같음; 유치함.

Puer·to Ri·co [pwɛ́əːrtə ríːkou / pwə́ːrtə-] *n.* an island of the West Indies, belonging to the United States. 푸에르토리코. 參考 수도는 San Juan.

:puff [pʌf] *n.* Ⓒ **1** the act of sending out breath, smoke, etc. in a short, quick way; the sound of such an act; a bit of vapor, smoke, etc. sent out by this act; a sudden rush of wind. 훅 불기; 훅 부는 소리; 훅 내뿜기; 한 번 휙 부는 바람. ¶ *a ~ of smoke* 훅 내뿜은 (담배) 연기 / *a ~ of wind* 일진의 바람 / *take a ~ at one's pipe* 파이프 담배를 한 모금 빨다 / *the ~ of a locomotive* 기관차의 치익하는 소리. **2** anything light, soft and round. 가볍고 부드럽고 둥그스름한 것《옷의 불룩한 부분; 슈크림; 만두; 부풀린 머리 따위》. ¶ *a ~ of hair* 부풀린 머리 / *a cream ~* 슈크림. **3** a small pad used for putting powder on the skin. 퍼프; 분첩. **4** the act of giving exaggerated praise. 과장된 칭찬. ¶ *The critic gave the new play quite a ~.* 평론가는 그 신극(新劇)에 대해 꽤 과장된 칭찬을 하였다.

— *vi.* (P1,2A) **1** send out air, steam, etc. in puffs or blasts. 훅 불다; 내뿜다. **2** breathe quick and hard, esp. after extreme physical effort. 숨차하다; 헐떡이다. ¶ *pant and ~* 헐떡이다 / *She puffed hard as she climbed the stairs.* 그녀는 계단을 오르면서 몹시 헐떡거렸다. **3** 《*up, out*》 swell up with wind, pride, etc.; stick out. (바람·자만심 등으로) 부풀어 오르다; 부풀다. ¶ *~ out one's cheeks* 양볼을 불룩하게 내밀다. **4** (P3) move or go with puffs. 칙칙폭폭하며 움직이다. ¶ *The train puffed out of the station.* 기차는 칙칙거리며 역 밖으로 나왔다.

— *vt.* **1** (P6,7,13) send out (smoke, etc.) in a short and quick way. (연기 등)을 푹푹 내뿜다. ¶ *~ smoke in someone's face* 아무의 얼굴에 연기를 내뿜다 / *The engine puffed clouds of steam.* 기관차는 칙칙하며 흰 증기를 내뿜었다. **2** (P6) smoke. (담배)를 뻐끔뻐끔 피우다. ¶ *~ a cigar* 여송연을 뻐끔뻐끔 피우다. **3** (P6) 《*colloq.*》 make (someone) breathe quick and hard. …을 숨차게 하다. ¶ *I was frightfully puffed by the run.* 뛰어서 숨이 턱에 닿을 지경이었다. **4** (P6) swell (something) by puffing; swell (someone) with pride. …을 부풀리다; …을 우쭐하게 하다. ¶ *be puffed up with pride* 자만심으로 으쓱해지다. **5** (P6) praise or advertise too much. 마구 치켜 세우다; 과대 선전하다. ¶ *~ a book* 어떤 책을 과대 선전하다. [Imit.]

puff away, **a**) drive away by blowing in puffs. 훅 내뿜다. **b**) continue to take a puff. 뻐끔거리다. ¶ *He was puffing away at his pipe.* 파이프를 뻐끔뻐끔 피우고 있었다.

puff out, **a**) put out by puffing. 훅 불어 끄다. ¶ *~ out a candle* 촛불을 훅 불어 끄다. **b**) cause to swell out. 부풀리다. ¶ *~ out one's cheeks* 양볼을 불룩하게 하다 / *sails puffed out with wind* 바람을 받아 팽팽해진 돛 / 《*fig.*》 *He is puffed out with pride.* 우쭐해 있다. **c**) cause to become short of breath. 숨차게 만들다.

puff·y [pʌ́fi] *adj.* (**puff·i·er, puff·i·est**) **1** swollen; fat. 부푼; 비만한. ¶ *~ eyelids* 두툼한 눈꺼풀. **2** blowing in puffs. 훅 부는. **3** breathing hard. 숨이 찬. [↑]

pug [pʌg] *n.* Ⓒ **1** a small dog with an upturned nose and a curly tail. 퍼그《들창코인 발바리의 일종》. **2** a short upturned nose. 들창코. [? *puck*]

pug·nosed [pʌ́gnòuzd] *adj.* having an upturned nose. 들창코의.

:pull [pul] *vt.* **1** (P6,7,13,18) cause (someone or something) to move toward oneself; draw. …을 끌다〔당기다〕(opp. push). ¶ *~ a door open forcibly* 문을 세게 잡아당겨 열다 / *~ someone by the sleeve* (주의를 끌려고) 아무의 소매를 당기다 / *Pull the handle toward you in an emergency.* 비상시엔 핸들을 앞으로 당기시오 / *~ a cart* 수레를 끌다 / *~ one's hat over one's eyes* 모자를 눈 앞으로 내려 쓰다. **2** (P6,7) ⓐ draw (something) apart from another; extract (teeth). …을 떼어 놓다; (이 따위)를 뽑다. ¶ *~ weeds* 잡초를 뽑다 / *I have had my tooth pulled.* 나는 이를 뽑았다 / *~ the cork out of a bottle* 병마개를 뽑다. ⓑ tear; break into pieces. …을 (갈기갈기) 찢다; 조각조각 망그러뜨리다. ¶ *~ the cloth into shreds* 헝겊을 갈기갈기 찢다 / *~ a toy into bits* 장난감을 조각조각 망그러뜨리다. **3** remove (feathers) from the skin; pick up (flowers). (털)을 뽑다; (꽃)을 따다. ¶ *~ fruit* 〔*flowers*〕 열매를〔꽃을〕 따다. **4** 《U.S. *colloq.*》 attract; win. (고객을·인기를) 끌다; (투표를) 모으다; (지지를) 얻다. ¶ *~ someone's support* 아무의 후원을 얻다 / *~ many votes* 많은 표를 모으다. **5** ⓐ row (a boat). (배)를 젓다. ¶ *~ a boat* / *He pulls a good oar.* 그는 노를 잘 젓는다. ⓑ be rowed by (a certain number of oars). (배에 …개의 노가) 달려 있다. ¶ *The boat pulls six oars.* 이 배는 노 여섯으로 젓는다. **6** draw or take out (a knife, etc.). (칼 따위)를 꺼내다. ¶ *He pulled a dollar from his pocket.* 그는 주머니에서 달러 지폐를 꺼냈다 / *~ out a bottle of whisky* 술병 하나를 끄집어내다 / *~ (out) a gun* 권총을 뽑다 / *~ a knife* 칼을 빼다. **7** 《U.S. *colloq.*》 carry

out or do (a plan, etc.). (계획 등)을 해내다; …을 하다. ¶ ~ *a trick on someone* 아무에게 장난치다; 아무를 속여먹다 / *What are you trying to ~?* 이번엔 무슨 짓을 하려나.
— *vi.* **1** (P2A,3) 《*at*》 draw. 끌다; 당기다. ¶ ~ *at a rope* 줄을 당기다. **2** (P3) have a drink or smoke. (병에서 술 따위를) 꿀꺽 마시다[들이켜다]; (담배를) 피우다. ¶ ~ *at a jug* 한 조끼 들이켜다 / ~ *on a cigar* 여송연을 피우다. **3** (P2A,3) row a boat; be rowed. 배를 젓다; (배가) 저어지다. **4** (P1,2A,3) 《*through*》 manage to do something with difficulty. 가까스로 헤쳐나가다.
pull about, treat roughly. …을 거칠게 다루다.
pull a face, make the face look ugly; frown. (얼굴을) 찡그리다.
pull down, **a**) destroy (a house, etc.). …을 무너뜨리다; 파괴하다. ¶ ~ *down an old house* 낡은 집을 허물다. **b**) make (someone) weak. …을 허약하게 만들다. ¶ *He is pulled down by illness.* 그는 병으로 허약해졌다. **c**) humble. …의 콧대를 꺾다. ¶ ~ *down someone's pride* 아무의 자만심을 꺾다.
pull in, **a**) draw (one's head, etc.) in. (목 따위)를 움츠리다. **b**) (of a train) arrive at a station. (기차가) 역에 닿다. **c**) save. 절약하다. ¶ *You must ~ in (your expenses).* (비용을) 절약해야 한다.
pull someone's leg, make fun of someone; make a fool of someone. …을 놀리다; 바보 취급하다.
pull off, **a**) take off (one's coat, etc.). …을 벗다. ¶ ~ *off one's coat* [*boots*] 저고리[구두]를 벗다. **b**) win (a prize, etc.); succeed in gaining something. (상)을 받다; 잘 해내다. ¶ ~ *off a large undertaking* 큰 일을 해내다.
pull on, put on clothes. 옷을 입다.
pull out, **a**) make (a story, etc.) longer. (이야기 등)을 길게 늘이다; 오래 끌다. ¶ ~ *out a story.* **b**) draw out (a cork, a tooth, etc.). …을 뽑다. **c**) (of a train) begin to leave a station. (기차가) 역을 출발하다.
pull round, cause (someone) to recover from illness. …의 건강을 회복시키다. ¶ *The doctor tried to ~ him round.* 의사는 그의 건강을 회복시키려 노력했다.
pull through, (cause to) get through (an illness, danger, etc.); (help to) overcome (병·위험)을 헤쳐나가(게 하)다; 극복하(게 하)다. ¶ *Good nursing pulled him through.* 극진한 간호로 그는 위험한 고비를 넘겼다 / *We'll have to ~ through somehow.* 어떻게 하든 헤쳐나가지 않으면 안된다.
pull together, **a**) work together. 협력해서 일하다. ¶ *If we all ~ together we may succeed.* 우리 모두가 협력한다면 성공할 수도 있다. **b**) =pull oneself together.
pull oneself together, make an effort to recover one's self-control; recover one's courage. 자제심을 되찾으려고 애쓰다; 용기를 되찾다.

pull something to pieces, tear something to pieces. …을 갈기갈기 찢다.
pull up, **a**) stop; make (something) stop. 멈추(게 하)다. **b**) pull out by the roots; uproot. 뿌리째 뽑다; 근절하다. ¶ ~ *up a tree* 나무를 뿌리째 뽑다.
pull up to [***with***], come up level with (someone) from behind; overtake. …을 따라잡다; 추월하다.
— *n.* Ⓒ **1** the act of pulling, drawing or rowing. 끌기; 당기기; 노젓기. ¶ *He gave my arm a ~.* = *He gave a ~ at my arm.* 내 팔을 잡아당겼다 / *The pull of the moon on the sea causes the tides.* 바다에 미치는 달의 인력은 조수의 간만을 일으킨다. **2** 《*colloq.*》 an attraction; something attractive; an influence. 매력(있는 것); 세력; 영향력. ¶ *advance through someone's ~* 연줄을 타고 승진하다. **3** an act of drinking or smoking. 술 한 잔 하기; 담배 한대 피우기. ¶ *have* [*take*] *a ~ at a bottle* 병에서 술을 한 모금 들이켜다. **4** an advantage. 이점; 유리. ¶ *His wealth gives him a great ~.* 재력은 그에게 큰 이점이 된다. [E.]
pull·er [púlər] *n.* Ⓒ **1** a person or thing that pulls. 끄는 물건; 당기는 사람. **2** an instrument or a machine for pulling. (잡아) 뽑는 도구[기계]. **3** a person who rows a boat. 노 젓는 사람.
pul·ley [púli] *n.* Ⓒ a wheel which is grooved to receive a rope, used for changing the direction of power. 도르래; 활차. [Gk. *polos*]
pull·o·ver [púlòuvər] *n.* Ⓒ a sweater which is put on from the head. 머리로부터 입는 스웨터; 풀오버. [*pull*]
pul·mo·nar·y [pʌ́lmənèri / -nəri] *adj.* of the lungs. 폐의. ¶ ~ *disease* 폐병 / ~ *artery* 폐동맥. [L. *pulmo* lung]
***pulp** [pʌlp] *n.* Ⓤ **1** the soft part of fruit. 과육(果肉). **2** a soft, wet mass. 걸쭉한 것. ¶ *wood ~* 목재 펄프. **3** the soft inner part of a tooth. 치수(齒髓).
beat someone to a pulp, beat thoroughly. …을 늘씬하게 패주다.
be reduced to (***a***) ***pulp,*** be completely melted; be tired out. 흐늘흐늘해지다; 기진맥진하다.
— *vt.* (P6) reduce (something) to (a) pulp. …을 펄프로 만들다; 걸쭉하게 하다. [L. *pulpa*]
pul·pit [púlpit, pʌ́l-] *n.* Ⓒ **1** a raised desk for a preacher in a church. 설교단. ¶ *occupy the ~* 설교하다. **2** 《*the ~, collectively*》 the preachers; the work of preaching. 설교자; 설교. ¶ *the influence of the ~* 설교의 힘. [L. *pulpitum* platform]
pulp·y [pʌ́lpi] *adj.* (**pulp·i·er, pulp·i·est**) **1** of pulp; like the soft part of fruit. 펄프의; 과육(果肉) 같은. **2** soft; juicy. 부드러운; 즙이 많은. [→pulp]
pul·sate [pʌ́lseit / -ˊ] *vi.* **1** (P1) (of the

heart) beat. (심장이) 뛰다; 두근거리다. ¶ *His heart pulsated with excitement.* 흥분해서 가슴이 두근거렸다. **2** (P1,2A) (of a voice in singing) quiver. (음성이) 떨(리)다. [L. *pello* drive]

pul·sa·tion [pʌlséiʃən] *n.* **1** Ⓤ Ⓒ (of the heart) the beat. 맥박; 동계(動悸). **2** Ⓒ (of a sound) the quiver. (음의) 진동; 파동.

***pulse**[1] [pʌls] *n.* Ⓒ **1** the beat of the heart; the beat felt in the wrist. 고동; 동계; 맥박. ¶ *take* 〔*feel*〕 *a patient's* ~ 환자의 맥을 짚다. **2** the wave or quiver of sound or light. (소리·빛의) 파동; 진동. **3** intentions; feelings. 의향; 기분.

feel someone's pulse, **a**) try to feel the pulse of someone in the wrist. (아무)의 맥을 짚다. **b**) try to discover the intentions or feelings of someone. (아무)의 의향을 살피다.

stir someone's pulses, excite someone. (아무)를 흥분시키다.

— *vi.* (P2A) beat; throb. 맥이 뛰다; 두근거리다; 고동하다. ¶ *My heart pulsed fast with joy.* 기쁨으로 가슴이 마구 뛰었다. [L. *pello* drive]

pulse[2] [pʌls] *n.* 《*collectively*, often used as *pl.*》 peas; beans. 콩류(類); 콩. [L. *puls*]

pul·ver·ize [pʌ́lvəràiz] *vt.* (P6) grind (something) into powder. …을 가루로 만들다; 부수다. ¶ *pulverized coal* 분탄(粉炭). — *vi.* (P1) become powder or dust. 가루가 되다; 부서지다. ¶ *Even rocks* ~ *in the course of centuries.* 바위도 여러 세기를 지나는 동안 잘게 부서진다. [L. *pulvis* dust]

pu·ma [pjúːmə] *n.* Ⓒ 《zool.》 a large American wildcat. 퓨마(cf. *cougar*). [Peruv.]

pum·ice [pʌ́mis] *n.* Ⓤ a light, spongy stone, used for cleaning or polishing. 속돌; 경석(輕石). [L. *pumex*]

pum·mel [pʌ́məl] *vt.* (**-meled, -mel·ing** or 《Brit.》 **-melled, -mel·ling**) (P6,7) strike (something) with the fists; pommel. …을 주먹으로 치다. [→pommel]

:pump[1] [pʌmp] *n.* Ⓒ **1** a machine used for raising water or for forcing air in and out. 펌프. ¶ *a bicycle* ~ 자전거용 펌프 / *a feed* 〔*feeding*〕 ~ 급수 펌프 / *fetch a* ~ 펌프에 마중물을 붓다. **2** 《*colloq.*》 a stupid, dull, pompous fellow. 어리석으면서도 거들먹거리는 자.

— *vt.* **1** (P6,7,13) 《*up, out*》 raise (water, etc.) by means of a pump. (물 따위)를 펌프로 자아올리다. ¶ *Pump some water from the well into a bucket.* 우물물을 양동이에 퍼올려라 / ~ *a well dry* 펌프로 우물물을 모두 퍼내다. **2** (P7,13) fill something with (air, etc.) by means of a pump. (공기 등)을 펌프로 넣다; (지식·영양 따위)를 주입하다. ¶ ~ *air into a tire* 타이어에 공기를 넣다 / ~ *a tire hard* 〔*tight*〕 타이어에 공기를 잔뜩 넣다 / ~ *nourishment into someone* 아무에게 영양제를 주입하다 / 《*fig.*》 ~ *Latin grammar into a boy.* 소년 머리에 라틴 문법을 주입하다. **3** (P6) ask (someone) closely; get (information, etc.) by asking closely. …에게 꼬치꼬치 질문하다; 꼬치꼬치 캐물어 …을 알아내다. ¶ ~ *information out of someone* 유도 신문으로 …에게서 정보를 캐내다 / *She pumped me about my mother.* 그녀는 내게 어머니에 대한 것을 꼬치꼬치 캐물었다 / ~ *a secret out of someone* 아무에게서 비밀을 캐내다. **4** (P6) 《*out*》 cause (someone) to get tired or to be out of breath. (아무)를 지치게〔헐떡이게〕 하다. ¶ *He was fairly pumped out.* 그는 아주 지쳐 버렸다.

— *vi.* (P1) **1** use a pump; raise water by means of a pump. 펌프질하다; 펌프로 물을 퍼올리다. **2** get information by repeatedly asking question. 꼬치꼬치 물어 알아내다. **3** act like a pump. 펌프같이 작동하다. ¶ *The heart goes on pumping as long as life last.* 살아 있는 한 심장은 펌프 작용을 계속한다. [G.]

be pumped out, **a**) be tired out. 지치다. **b**) empty by pumping. 펌프로 다 퍼내다.

pump up, raise water; fill with air. 물을 퍼올리다; 공기를 넣다.

pump[2] [pʌmp] *n.* Ⓒ 《usu. *pl.*》 light low shoes without laces. 펌프스《끈 없는 굽 낮은 가벼운 신》. [? F.]

***pump·kin** [pʌ́mpkin, pʌ́ŋkin] *n.* Ⓒ a large, round, yellow fruit of a plant with heart-shaped leaves, used for pies, etc. (서양) 호박. [Gk. *pepōn* melon]

pumpkin head [´–`] *n.* a stupid fellow. 멍텅구리; 돌대가리.

pun [pʌn] *n.* Ⓒ a witty use of one word in two senses; a play on words that have the same sound but different meanings. 곁말; 신소리; 동음 이의(同音異義)의 익살. — *vi.* (**punned, pun·ning**) (P1,3) make a play on words. 신소리를 하다. [?]

***punch**[1] [pʌntʃ] *n.* Ⓒ **1** a tool or machine for cutting holes. 펀치; 천공기. **2** a tool or machine for stamping a design on some material. 타인기(打印器). — *vt.* (P6) make a hole in, by means of a punch. (천공기로) …에 구멍을 내다. ¶ *I had my ticket punched.* 펀치로 티켓을 개찰했다 / ~ *a hole* 구멍을 내다. [*puncheon*]

punch[2] [pʌntʃ] *vt.* (P6,13) **1** strike heavily, esp. with the fists. (주먹으로) 세게 때리다; 펀치를 먹이다. ¶ ~ *someone's head* = ~ *someone on the head* 주먹으로 아무의 머리를 때리다. **2** strike or hit. …을 치다〔두드리다〕. ¶ ~ *(the keys of) a typewriter* 타자기를 치다.

— *n.* **1** Ⓒ a sharp, sudden, blow with the fist. 펀치; 타격. ¶ *get a* ~ *on the nose* 코를 한대 얻어맞다. **2** Ⓤ 《*colloq.*》 vigor. 힘; 박력. ¶ *There was not much* ~ *in his remarks.* 그의 말엔 별로 힘이 없었다. [?]

pull one's punches **a**) 《boxing》 strike or attack less heavily than one could. 일부러 효과가 없는 펀치를 가하다. **b**) restrain one's full power. (비평 등에서) 사정을 봐주다.

punch³ [pʌntʃ] *n.* UC a drink made of wine or other liquor mixed with water, sugar, lemons, etc. 펀치《포도주·레몬즙·설탕 등의 혼합 음료》. [?]

pun·cheon [pʌ́ntʃən] *n.* C a large cask for holding liquor. 큰 술통. [F. *poinçon*]

punch·er [pʌ́ntʃər] *n.* C a person or tool that makes holes. 구멍 뚫는 사람[기구]. [→punch¹]

·punc·tu·al [pʌ́ŋktʃuəl] *adj.* arriving or appearing exactly at the fixed time; not late; on time. 시간을 엄수하는; 늦지 않는. ¶ *He is as ~ as a clock.* 그는 시계처럼 정확한 사람이다 / *~ to the minute* 1분도 틀리지 않는 / *~ payment* 기한대로의 지급 / *be ~ in paying rents* 집세를 기한 내에 꼬박꼬박 내다. [→punctuate]

punc·tu·al·i·ty [pʌ̀ŋktʃuǽləti] *n.* U the state of being punctual; the habit of being in good time. 시간 엄수; 정확함. ¶ *Our schoolteacher insists on ~.* 선생님은 시간 엄수를 주장하신다.

punc·tu·al·ly [pʌ́ŋktʃuəli] *adv.* in a punctual manner. 시간대로; 정확히; 꼼꼼하게.

punc·tu·ate [pʌ́ŋktʃuèit] *vt.* **1** (P6) mark (a sentence) with periods, commas, etc. (문장)에 구두점을 찍다. **2** (P6,13) interrupt (a speech, etc.). (박수·야유 등으로 연설)을 중단시키다. ¶ *a speech punctuated with cheers* 박수 갈채로 중단된 연설. **3** (P13) give point to (something); emphasize. …을 강조하다. ¶ *He punctuated each word by a blow.* 한 마디 한 마디를 주먹으로 탁자를 치며 강조했다. — *vi.* use punctuation marks. 구두점을 찍다. [L. *pungo* prick]

punc·tu·a·tion [pʌ̀ŋktʃuéiʃən] *n.* U **1** the use of certain marks, such as commas and periods, to make the sense clear in writing and printing. 구두(법). **2** a punctuation mark. 구두점.

punctuation marks [–––´–] *n.* marks such as colons, semicolons, commas and periods. 구두점《(:), (;), (,), (.)》.

punc·ture [pʌ́ŋktʃər] *n.* C **1** a small hole made by something pointed. (찔려서 난) 구멍; 펑크《타이어 따위의》. ¶ *a ~ in the tire of a motorcar* 자동차 타이어에 난 펑크. **2** the act of puncturing. 찌르기; 구멍을 내기. — *vt.* (P6) **1** make a small hole in (something) with a needle or something pointed. (바늘 따위로) …을 찌르다; …에 구멍을 내다. **2** 《*colloq.*》 make (a tire) flat with a nail, etc. (타이어)를 펑크내다. — *vi.* (P1) (of a tire) be punctured. (타이어)가 펑크나다. ¶ *The tire punctured a mile from home.* 집에서 1마일 되는 곳에서 타이어에 펑크가 났다. [→punctuate]

pun·gen·cy [pʌ́ndʒənsi] *n.* U **1** the quality of having a sharp smell or taste. 자극성《냄새·맛 등의》; 얼얼함; 매움. ¶ *the ~ of pepper* 고추의 매운 맛. **2** sharpness; severity. 신랄함; 매서움. ¶ *the ~ of someone's remarks* 아무의 비평의 신랄함. [L. *pungo* prick]

pun·gent [pʌ́ndʒənt] *adj.* **1** exciting to the organs of taste and smell. (맛·냄새가) 자극성이 있는. ¶ *~ sauce* 매운 소스 / *the ~ smell of burning leaves* 나뭇잎이 타는 매캐한 냄새. **2** sharp. 신랄한; 날카로운. ¶ *~ criticism* 신랄한 비판. ● **pun·gent·ly** [-li] *adv.*

:pun·ish [pʌ́niʃ] *vt.* (P6) **1** cause (someone) to suffer for a fault or crime; inflict a penalty for (an offense). (사람·죄)를 (처)벌하다. ¶ *He punished me for neglecting my work.* 일을 게을리했다고 나를 처벌했다 / *Murder is punished by death.* 살인하면 사형이다. **2** 《*colloq.*》 handle severely. …을 심하게 다루다; 혼내주다. ¶ *The enemy was severely punished by our machine guns.* 적은 아군의 기관총 사격에 혼쭐이 났다. ● **pun·ish·er** [-ər] *n.* [Gk. *poinē* penalty]

pun·ish·a·ble [pʌ́niʃəbəl] *adj.* deserving to be punished. 벌받아 마땅한; 처벌해야 할. ¶ *a ~ offense* 처벌해야 할 죄 / *The boy is ~.* 그 녀석은 벌받아야 한다.

:pun·ish·ment [pʌ́niʃmənt] *n.* UC **1** the act of punishing; the state of being punished. 벌주기; 벌받기. **2** a penalty imposed for an offense. 형벌; 벌. ¶ *inflict ~ upon* …을 벌하다[벌주다] / *capital ~* 극형; 사형 / *corporal ~* 체벌(體罰) / *The ~ which she received for stealing was a year in prison.* 절도에 대해 그녀가 받은 형은 1년 징역이었다. **3** 《*colloq.*》 severe handling; pain or damage. 가혹한 취급; 징벌; 혼내주기.

pu·ni·tive [pjú:nətiv] *adj.* of or inflicting punishment. 형벌의. ¶ *a ~ expedition* (반란 등의) 토벌 / *~ justice* 인과 응보 / *~ taxes* 벌금. [→punish]

punk [pʌŋk] *n.* 《U.S.》 **1** U decayed wood used as tinder. 불쏘시개감《썩은 나무》. **2** C 《*colloq.*》 anything worthless. 쓸모 없는 물건. — *adj.* 《U.S. *sl.*》 rotten; worthless; no good at all. 타락한; 아무짝에도 못 쓸; 하치의. [? Amer-Ind.]

pun·ster [pʌ́nstər] *n.* C a person who habitually makes puns. 신소리를 잘 하는 사람; 익살꾼. [*pun*]

punt¹ [pʌnt] *n.* C a flat-bottomed boat moved by pushing with a pole. 너벅선. — *vt.* (P6) advance (a boat) with a pole. …을 삿대로 젓다. [L. *ponto*]

〈punt¹〉

punt² [pʌnt] *vt.* (P6) 《football》 kick (a football), after dropping it from the hands and before it touches the ground. 손에서 떨어진 공이 땅에 닿기 전에 (그 공을) 차다; 펀트하다. — *n.* such a kick. 펀트하기. [? →bunt]

pu·ny [pjú:ni] *adj.* (**-ni·er, -ni·est**) **1** smaller, weaker, etc., than usual; undersized. 자그마한; 약하디 약한. ¶ *a ~ body* 작고 허약한 몸. **2** of no importance. 시시한; 하잘것 없는. [F. *puisne*= later born]

pup [pʌp] *n.* =puppy.

pu·pa [pjú:pə] *n.* Ⓒ (*pl.* **-pas** or **-pae**) a stage of an insect's life when it rests in a case; an insect in this stage. 번데기(cf. *larva*). [L.=doll, girl]

pu·pae [pjú:pi:] *n.* pl. of **pupa.**

pu·pal [pjú:pəl] *adj.* of or in a pupa. 번데기의. [*pupa*]

:pu·pil[1] [pjú:pəl] *n.* Ⓒ a boy or girl who is taught by a teacher. 학생; 제자. 参考 student에 대하여 초등학생·중학생을 이름. ¶ *a ~ teacher* 교생(教生) / *All these students* 〔*children*〕 *are pupils of mine.* 이 학생들〔아이들〕은 모두 내 제자다. [L. *pupillus, -la*]

pu·pil[2] [pjú:pəl] *n.* Ⓒ the black opening in the eye through which light enters. 눈동자. [↑]

pup·pet [pʌ́pit] *n.* Ⓒ **1** a doll worked by wires, strings, or the hands. (끈으로 동작이 조종되는) 작은 인형; 꼭두각시. ¶ *a ~ play* 〔*show*〕 인형극. **2** a person who obeys others blindly; a tool. 앞잡이; 괴뢰. ¶ *use someone as a ~* 아무를 앞잡이로 쓰다 / *a ~ government* 괴뢰 정부. [→pupa]

·pup·py [pʌ́pi] *n.* Ⓒ (*pl.* **-pies**) **1** a young dog. 강아지. **2** a vain, silly young man. 건방진 애송이 청년. [↑]

pur·blind [pə́:rblàind] *adj.* **1** partly blind. 반(半)소경의. **2** stupid; dull. 어리석은. [M.E. *pur* quite]

pur·chas·a·ble [pə́:rtʃəsəbəl] *adj.* that can be bought with money. 돈으로 살 수 있는. [↓]

:pur·chase [pə́:rtʃəs] *vt.* (P6) **1** get (something) by paying money; buy. …을 사다; 구입하다. ¶ *~ a car for 5,000,000 won,* 5백만 원에 차 한 대를 사다 / *~ a ticket for a concert* 음악회 입장권을 한 장 사다 / *He purchased her silence about what he had done.* 돈으로 그가 저지른 일을 그녀가 발설하지 않도록 했다. **2** get (something) at the cost of labor, etc. (희생을 치르고) …을 얻다. ¶ *~ victory with blood* 피로 승리를 획득하다 / *His success was dearly purchased at the cost of years of hard work.* 그의 성공은 여러 해의 힘든 노력의 대가다. **3** move or raise (something) by means of some mechanical power. (기계의 힘으로) …을 움직이다; 들어올리다. ¶ *~ an anchor* 닻을 감아 올리다. — *n.* **1** Ⓤ the act of purchasing. 구입; 구매; 획득. ¶ *make a ~* 물건을 사다 / *the ~ of food* 〔*coal*〕 식량〔석탄〕 구입. **2** Ⓒ a thing purchased. 산 물건; 구입품. ¶ *leave the shop with one's purchases* 산 물건을 들고 가게를 나오다 / *That hat was a good ~.* 그 모자는 싸게 산 것이다. **3** Ⓤ a yearly income obtained from land as rent; value or worth. (토지에서의) 연수(年收); 가격; 가치. ¶ *His life is not worth a day's ~.* 살아도 하루를 넘길까 말까다 / *twenty years' ~,* 20년간의 수익에 맞먹는 가격〔값〕. **4** ⓊⒸ 《mech.》 a firm hold to help in moving or raising something. 기중(起重) 장치; 지레; 도르래. ¶ *get a ~ an anchor* 도르래로 닻을 올리다 / *get a ~ with one's feet or hands when climbing* 등반에서 발붙일 데나 손잡을 데를 확보하다. [pro-, →chase]

pur·chas·er [pə́:rtʃəsər] *n.* Ⓒ a person who buys something. 구매자.

purchase tax [∠-∠] *n.* 《Brit.》 a tax included in the retail prices of certain articles. 구매세; 물품세(cf. *sales tax*).

:pure [pjuər] *adj.* **1** not mixed with anything else; clean; clear. 깨끗한; 순수한. ¶ *~ air* 맑은 공기 / *~ gold* 순금. **2** not mixed with foreign elements or blood. (언어; 피가) 외래 요소가 없는; 순수한. ¶ *~ English* 순정(純正) 영어 / *a ~ language* 순수어 / *a ~ Englishman* 토박이 영국인. **3** free from sins; innocent. 결백한; 순결한. ¶ *a ~ mind* 〔*character*〕 고결하고 정직한 마음〔인격〕. **4** mere; absolute. 순전〔단순〕한; 전적인. ¶ *I did it out of ~ necessity.* 정말 필요해서 그랬다 / *It was a ~ accident.* 그건 그저 우연한 사고였다. **5** dealing simply with the theory of a subject. 순정(純正)의; 순이론적인 (opp. applied). ¶ *~ science* 순수과학 / *~ literature* 순(수)문학. [L. *purus*]

pure and simple, and nothing else; nothing but. 섞인 것이 없는; 순전한.

pu·rée [pjúrei] *n.* ⓊⒸ **1** any soft food boiled and pushed through a sieve. 퓌레 《야채·고기 등을 삶아서 체에 거른 것》. **2** the thick soup made from this. 퓌레로 만든 진한 수프. [F.]

·pure·ly [pjúərli] *adv.* **1** in a pure manner; entirely; wholly. 순수하게; 깨끗하게. ¶ *be ~ English* 토박이 영국인이다. **2** merely; simply. 단순히. ¶ *~ accidental* 전혀 우연한 / *~ by chance* 전혀 우연히. [*pure*]

pure·ness [pjúərnis] *n.* Ⓤ the state of being pure. 순수; 결백; 청결.

pur·ga·tion [pə:rgéiʃən] *n.* Ⓤ the act of purging. 정화(淨化); 깨끗이 하기; (하제를 써서) 변이 잘 나오게 함. [→purge]

pur·ga·tive [pə́:rgətiv] *adj.* having the power of cleansing the bowels. 변을 통하게 하는; 하제(下劑)의. ¶ *a ~ medicine* 하제. — *n.* Ⓒ a medicine used to empty the bowels. 하제.

pur·ga·to·ry [pə́:rgətɔ̀:ri / -təri] *n.* Ⓒ (*pl.* **-ries**) **1** 《Cath.》 a place where the souls of those who have died are purified from sin by temporary suffering. 연옥(煉獄). **2** any place or state of temporary suffering. 일시적인 고난(의 자리). ¶ *During this period of his life he passed through a regular* ~. 그의 생애에서 이 동안에 그는 단단히 고초를 겪었다.

·**purge** [pəːrdʒ] *vt.* **1** (P6) make (something) free from impurities; cleanse. …을 깨끗이하다; 순수하게 하다. ¶ ~ *one's soul from sin* 죄악에서 벗어나 영혼을 깨끗이하다. **2** (P6,13) eliminate (an undesirable person) from a party, a government, etc. …을 숙청[추방]하다. ¶ ~ *dissidents from the party* 불평 분자를 당에서 추방하다. **3** (P6,7,13) empty the bowels of (someone) with medicine. …에게 하제(下劑)를 쓰다.
— *n.* Ⓒ **1** the act of purging. 정화; 순화; 숙청. **2** a medicine which empties the bowels. 하제. ¶ *A proper amount of castor oil will make a good* ~. 적당량의 아주까리 기름은 하제로 쓰면 좋다. [L. *purgo* cleanse]

pu·ri·fi·ca·tion [pjùərəfikéiʃən] *n.* Ⓤ the act of purifying or making someone clear of guilt or sin. 깨끗이 하기; 세정(洗淨); 정화; 속죄. [→purify]

pu·ri·fi·er [pjúərəfàiər] *n.* Ⓒ **1** a person who purifies. 깨끗이 하는 사람. **2** a kind of instrument for purifying gas or water. 정화기; 정화 장치.

pu·ri·fy [pjúərəfài] *v.* (**-fied**) *vt.* (P6,13) make (something) pure. …을 깨끗이 하다; 정화하다. ¶ *Filters are used to* ~ *water.* 여과기는 물을 정화하는 데 쓰인다 / *Gold is purified by fire.* 금은 불로 정련(精鍊)된다.
— *vi.* (P1,2A) become pure. 깨끗해지다. [L. *purus* pure, *facio* make]

pur·ism [pjúərizəm] *n.* Ⓤ avoidance of foreign words or slang words in order to purify a language. 언어 순화. [→pure]

pur·ist [pjúərist] *n.* Ⓒ a person who insists on purism. 언어 순화주의자.

Pu·ri·tan [pjúərətən] *n.* Ⓒ **1** a member of a group of English Protestants who wanted a simpler form of worship and stricter morals. 퓨리턴; 청교도. **2** 《*p-*》 a person who is very strict in religion and morals. (종교·도덕적인 면에서) 엄격한 사람.
— *adj.* **1** of the Puritans. 청교도의. **2** 《*p-*》 of a puritan. 청교도적인; 엄격한. [→purity]

pu·ri·tan·ic [pjùərətǽnik], **-i·cal** [-ikəl] *adj.* of or like a Puritan; very strict. 청교도의; 청교도적인; 엄격한.

Pu·ri·tan·ism [pjúərətənìzəm] *n.* Ⓤ the principles and beliefs of the Puritans. 청교(주의).

pu·ri·ty [pjúərəti] *n.* Ⓤ **1** the state of being pure; cleanness. 청정; 순수. ¶ ~ *of air* [*water*]. 청정 공기[수(水)] / ~ *of gold* 순금. **2** moral cleanness; innocence; virtue. 청렴; 결백. **3** correctness. (문체·국어 등의) 순정(純正). [→pure, -ity]

purl[1] [pəːrl] *vi.* (P1) flow with a gentle sound, as a small stream among stones. 물이 졸졸거리며 흐르다. ¶ *He often sat to see the brook* ~ *along.* 그는 때때로 졸졸거리며 흐르는 시냇물을 앉아 구경했다. — *n.* Ⓒ the gentle murmur of a stream. 졸졸 흐르는 물소리. [? Imit.]

purl[2] [pəːrl] *n.* ⓊⒸ **1** a chain of small loops used to edge lace, ribbon, or the like. 고리 모양의 가장자리 장식. **2** an inverted stitch in knitting. (편물의) 뒤집어뜨기. **3** a cord of twisted gold or silver wire. (가두리 장식·자수용의) 금[은]실. — *vt.* (P6) **1** edge (something) with small loops. …에 고리 모양의 가두리 장식을 달다. **2** invert (stitches) in knitting. …을 뒤집어뜨다. [?]

pur·loin [pəːrlɔ́in, ⌐–] *vt.* (P6) steal. …을 훔치다. [pro-, L. *longe* far]

:**pur·ple** [pə́ːrpəl] *n.* Ⓤ **1** a color made by mixing red and blue. 자줏빛. **2** crimson. 진홍색. **3** clothing worn by someone of imperial or royal rank. (왕·고관들이 입던) 자주색 의상. **4** royal power or dignity. 왕권.

be born in the purple, be born in a royal, or in a very high rank of life. 왕가[귀족 집안]에 태어나다.

be raised to the purple, be made emperor; be made a cardinal. 황제가 되다; 추기경이 되다.

— *adj.* **1** of the color of purple. 자줏빛[진홍색]의. ¶ ~ *cheeks* 추위로 자줏빛이 된 볼 / *turn* ~ *with rage* 불같이 성내다. **2** of royal power or dignity; imperial; royal. 왕권의; 제왕의.
— *vt., vi.* (P6; 1) make or become purple. 자줏빛이 되(게 하)다. [Gk. *porphura* shellfish yielding dye]

pur·plish [pə́ːrpliʃ] *adj.* somewhat purple. 자주색의; 자줏빛을 띤.

pur·port [pə́ːrpɔːrt] *n.* Ⓤ **1** meaning; intended meaning. (문서·연설 등의) 취지; 요지. ¶ *the* ~ *of his speech* 그의 연설 요지 / *The* ~ *of her letter was that she would not pay.* 그녀 편지의 요지는 돈을 안 내겠다는 거였다. **2** 《rare》 the purpose; object. 목적; 의도. ¶ *What is the* ~ *of his visit here ?* 그가 여기 온 목적은 뭐야.
— [pərpɔ́ːrt, pə́ːrpɔːrt] *vt.* **1** (P6,11) mean; imply. …을 의미하다; …의 뜻이다. ¶ *His answer purports his sickness* [*that he was sick*]. 그의 대답은 그가 아프다[아팠다]는 것을 의미한다. **2** (P8) claim (to be); give an impression of (something). …라고 칭하다; …을 뜻하다. ¶ *the law that purports to be in the interest of peace* 치안을 위한 것이라고 칭하는 법률 / *His speech may* ~ *his early resignation.* 그의 연설은 그의 조기 사임(辭任)을 시사하는 것 같다. [pro-, L. *porto* carry]

:**pur·pose** [pə́ːrpəs] *n.* **1** Ⓒ something which a person eagerly wants to get; an object or intention. 목적; 의도. ¶ *pursue a* ~ *steadily* 꾸준히 목적을 추구하다 / *the* ~ *of his visit* 그의 방문 목적 / *What is your* ~ *in doing this ?* 이걸 하는 의도는 뭐냐. **2** Ⓤ

will; resolution. 의지; 결심. ¶ *be firm of* ~ 의지가 강하다; 결단력이 있다 / *He is wanting in* ~. 그는 결단력이 부족하다 / *stick to one's* ~ 뜻을 굽히지 않다. **3** Ⓒ a matter under discussion. 논점.

of set purpose, with intention, intentionally. 계획적으로; 고의로.

on purpose, not by accident; intentionally. 고의로; 일부러; 의도적으로.

to little purpose, almost uselessly or in vain. 거의 쓸데 없이(헛되이).

to no purpose, not at all usefully. 전혀 쓸모 없이.

to some purpose, with a rather good result. 상당히 효과적으로.

to the purpose, serving one's purpose. 적절히.

— *vt.* (P6,8,9,11) intend; plan; aim. …하려고 하다; 의도하다. ¶ *I* ~ *finishing* (*to finish*) *my work in a week.* 나는 일을 1 주일 내에 끝내고자 한다 / *I* ~ *to go on with my studies.* 나는 연구를 계속할 생각이다. [pro-, →pose]

pur·pose·ful [pə́ːrpəsfəl] *adj.* **1** having a purpose; doing or done with an intention. 목적이 있는; 고의적인. **2** full of meaning. 의미 심장한.

pur·pose·ly [pə́ːrpəsli] *adv.* on purpose; intentionally. 고의로; 일부러.

purr [pəːr] *vi.* (P1,2A,3) make a low murmuring sound, as a cat does when it is satisfied. (고양이 따위가 기분이 좋아) 목을 가르랑거리다. ¶ ~ *with pleasure* (*satisfaction*). — *n.* Ⓒ a murmuring sound. 가르랑거리는 소리. [Imit.]

:purse [pəːrs] *n.* Ⓒ **1** a small bag or case for carrying money. 돈지갑. **2** money; wealth. 돈; 자력(資力). ¶ *the public* ~ 국고 / *the power of the* ~ 돈의 힘; 금력 / *a long* (*fat, heavy*) ~ 부(富); 부유 / *a cold* (*light, lean, slender*) ~ 가난 / *the privy* ~ ⇨privy. **3** a sum of money collected for a certain purpose or given as a prize. 현상금; 기부(증여)금. ¶ *collect a* ~ *for the retiring teacher.* 퇴직하는 선생의 전별금을 모으다. **4** anything like purse; a bag. 돈지갑 모양의 것; 낭(囊). ¶ *purses under the eyes* 양 눈밑의 처진 살. **5** 《U.S.》 a handbag. 핸드백; 손가방.

give (***put up***) ***a purse,*** offer money as a prize. 상금을 주다.

have a common purse, possess wealth in common. 공동 기금을 갖고 있다.

make up a purse for (=*collect money for*) *something* or *someone*. …을 위해 모금하다.

open one's purse, give or spend one's money. 돈을 내다(쓰다).

— *vt.* (P6,7) draw together (the lips) in folds. (입)을 다물다(오므리다). ¶ ~ *up one's lips.*

— *vi.* (P1) become wrinkled. 주름이 가다; 오므라들다. [Gk. *bursa* a hide]

purs·er [pə́ːrsər] *n.* Ⓒ an officer having charge of the accounts, tickets, etc. of a ship. (선박의) 사무장.

purse strings [ㅅㅅ] *n. pl.* a string for closing certain purses; the power or right to control the money. 주머니 끈; (돈의 출납을 관장하는) 재정상의 권한.

hold the purse strings, control the spending of money. 금전 출납을 맡다.

loosen (***tighten***) ***the*** (*one's*) ***purse strings,*** be generous (economical) in spending money. 돈을 헤프게(알뜰하게) 쓰다.

pur·su·ance [pərsúːəns / -sjúː-] *n.* Ⓤ **1** the act of pursuing. 추구; 추적. **2** the act of carrying out. 이행; 수행. [→prosecute]

in pursuance of, **a**) in accordance with. …에 따라. ¶ *in* ~ *of your orders* 당신의 지시에 따라. **b**) in the carrying out of. …을 이행하여. ¶ *in* ~ *of one's duties* (*intention*) 자기의 임무(의지)를 수행함에 있어. [*pursue*]

pur·su·ant [pərsúːənt / -sjúː-] *adj.* in accordance with; following ; carrying out. …에 따른; …에 준한. ¶ ~ *to one's intentions.* 뜻대로의 / ~ *to the rules* 규칙에 따라; 규칙대로의. — *adv.* in a way that is pursuant; in accordance. (…에) 의하여; 따라서; 준하여.

:pur·sue [pərsúː / -sjúː] *vt.* (P6) **1** ⓐ follow to catch or kill (something). …을 추적(추격)하다; 뒤쫓다. ¶ *The policeman pursued the robbers.* 경찰관은 도둑들을 추적했다. ⓑ follow closely and annoy. 따라다니며 괴롭히다. ¶ ~ *someone with questions* 자꾸 물어 아무를 귀찮게 하다 / *Ill luck persued him till his death.* 죽을 때까지 불행은 그에게 따라붙었다. **2** seek or aim at (something); strive for; try to get. …을 추구하다; 취하려(얻으려) 하다. ¶ ~ *pleasure* 쾌락을 추구하다 / ~ *the proper legal remedies* 적절한 법적 수단(방법)을 취하려고 하다. **3** continue or follow. …을 계속하다; 속행하다. ¶ ~ *one's studies* 연구를 계속하다 / ~ *one's business* 사업을 계속하다. **4** follow (a path, a way, a course of action, etc.). (길·방침 등)을 가다; 따르다.

— *vi.* (P1) follow to catch; follow; continue. 추적하다; 따르다; 계속하다. ¶ *He ran away, and he was not pursued.* 그는 도망쳤는데 아무도 그를 뒤쫓지 않았다. [→prosecute]

pur·su·er [pərsúːər / -sjúː-] *n.* Ⓒ **1** a person who follows after something. 추적자. **2** a person who pursues some object or aim. (목적 등의) 추구자. **3** a person who continues, follows, engages in, or studies something. (조사·연구 따위의) 속행자; 종사(연구)자. **4** (in English Civil Law) a prosecutor. 기소자; 고발자.

·pur·suit [pərsúːt / -sjúːt] *n.* **1** Ⓤ the act of pursuing; the act of following to catch or kill something. 추적; 추격. ¶ ~ *of the enemy* (*fox*) 적(여우)의 추격(추적) / *The dog is in* ~ *of the cat.* 개가 고양이를 쫓고 있다. **2** Ⓤ the act of following, performing or engaging in something. 속행; 수행; 종사. ¶ *the ~ of plan* 계획의 수행. **3** Ⓒ a profession; a business; recreation. 업무; 일; 오락. ¶ *agricultural* 〔*commercial*〕 *pursuits* 농업〔상업〕/ *daily pursuits* 일상의 일 / *Fishing is his favorite ~ ; reading is mine.* 그가 좋아하는 일은 낚시이고 내가 좋아하는 일은 독서다. **4** Ⓒ《U.S.》=pursuit plane. [*pursue*]

in hot pursuit, pursuing in earnest. 맹렬히 추구〔추적; 추격〕하여.

in pursuit of (=*following after or aiming at*) *something.* …을 추적하여; 추구하여.

pursuit plane [–´ ˋ] *n.* an airplane used for fighting. 추격기; 전투기.

pur·sy [pə́:rsi] *adj.* (**-si·er, -si·est**) **1** (esp. from fatness) easily becoming out of breath. (살이 쪄서) 숨이 가쁜〔찬〕. **2** fat. 살찐. [*pulse*[1]]

pu·ru·lence [pjúərələns] *n.* Ⓤ **1** the formation of yellowish-white matter in wounds. 화농(化膿). **2** the yellowish-white matter produced by wounds. 고름. [↓]

pu·ru·lent [pjúərələnt] *adj.* full of or forming yellowish-white matter in wounds; like pus. 고름의; 화농한; 화농성의; 고름 같은. ¶ *a ~ sore* 화농상(化膿傷) / *a ~ discharge from the nose* 고름같이 진한 콧물. [→pus]

pur·vey [pərvéi] *vt.* (P6) provide; supply (esp. food). …을 공급하다; 조달하다. ¶ *~ meat for the army* 군에 고기를 조달〔납품〕하다. [→provide]

pur·vey·ance [pərvéiəns] *n.* Ⓤ **1** the act of supplying food, etc. (식료품의) 조달; 공급; 납품. **2** the food, etc. supplied. (공급된) 식료품. ¶ *~ for the army* 군을 위한 (식료품의) 조달. **3** 《Brit. hist.》 the royal rights of preemption and requisition. (국왕의) 징발권.

pur·vey·or [pərvéiər] *n.* Ⓒ a person who supplies a large amount of food and other materials for an army, a city, etc. 식료품 공급자; 조달자; 조달업자.

pur·view [pə́:rvju:] *n.* Ⓒ the extent or range of operation, authority, activity or concern. 범위; 권한; 한계. ¶ *outside the ~ of practical politics* 실제 정치의 범위 밖에 / *within the ~ of one's studies* 자기의 연구 영역 안에. [→purvey]

pus [pʌs] *n.* Ⓤ the yellowish-white matter formed in wounds. 고름. [L.]

:push [puʃ] *vt.* **1** (P6,7,18) ⓐ press (someone or something) to move. …을 밀다; 누르다(opp. pull). ¶ *~ a baby carriage* 유모차를 밀다 / *Push him outdoors.* 그 자를 밖으로 밀어내라 / *~ a bell button* 초인종을 누르다 / *~ a door open* 문을 밀어서 열다. ⓑ cause to move by using force; shove; drive. …을 밀어 움직이다; 밀치다; 떼밀다. ¶ *~ a wineglass aside* 술잔을 옆으로 밀어놓다 / *~ a boat into the water* 배를 물로 밀어넣다 / 《*fig.*》 *~ aside all difficulties* 모든 곤란을 배제하다 / *~ back* 뒤로 밀치다. **2** (P6,7,20) put forth (buds, etc.); cause (something) to go forward. (싹)을 내다; (뿌리)를 뻗다; 내밀다. ¶ *The tree pushes its roots deep into the soil.* 나무는 땅속 깊이 뿌리를 뻗는다 / *A plant pushes out new shoots in spring.* 식물은 봄이 되면 새싹을 내민다. **3** press or urge (someone); emphasize; compel; drive. …에게 권〔재촉〕하다; 강요하다; 조르다. ¶ *~ someone to make a speech* 아무에게 연설하라고 강요하다 / *The store is pushing dry goods.* 그 가게는 의류 판매에 온갖 애를 다 쓰고 있다 / *~ someone to complete his task* 아무에게 일을 완성하라고 다그치다 / *~ a horse to greater speed* 더 빨리 달리라고 말을 몰아대다. **4** (P6,13) force (one's way, etc.); advance. …을 밀어제치며 나아가다; 밀고 나아가다. ¶ *~ one's way through the crowd* 군중을 헤집고 나아가다 / *They pushed their way into the room.* 그들은 방 안으로 억지로 밀고 들어갔다. **5** (P6,13) extend; expand. …을 확장하다; 증대시키다. ¶ *He pushes his business.* 그는 사업을 확장시켰다 / *~ the production of steel* 철강 생산을 늘리다 / *~ the frontier* 변경을 확대하다.

—*vi.* **1** (P1,3) press or thrust. 밀다; 밀치다; 떼밀다; 누르다. ¶ *You ~ while I pull.* 나는 당길 테니 너는 밀어라 / *He pushed on her shoulder.* 그는 그녀의 어깨를 눌렀다. **2** (P1,2A) go forward by force. 밀고 나아가다; 전진하다. ¶ *The party pushed on through the jungle.* 일행은 정글을 헤치며 전진했다. **3** (P2B) be pushed or move. 밀리다; 밀려 움직이다. ¶ *The door pushed open.* 밀었더니 문이 열렸다.

be pushed for time 〔***money***〕, be short of time 〔money〕. 시간〔돈〕에 쪼들리다.

push around, treat roughly or mercilessly. …을 거칠게 다루다; 들볶다. ¶ *I don't like to be pushed around by him.* 나는 그한테서 들볶임을 당하고 싶지 않다.

push in, **a**) move in to shore. 배가 기슭에 다가가다. **b**) press oneself in; enter with force. 끼어들다; 비집고 들어가다.

push off, **a**) move off from the shore. 배를 (기슭에서) 밀어 내보내다. **b**) 《*colloq.*》 go away; depart. 가버리다; 떠나다. ¶ *It's time for us to ~ off.* 이젠 갈〔떠날〕 시간이다.

push on, hurry on; hasten forward. 서둘러 가다; 몰아대다.

push over, cause to fall; overturn. 넘어뜨리다; 뒤집다.

push through, **a**) make one's way by pushing. 밀고 나아가다. ⇨*vt.* **4.** **b**) get (something) done; accomplish. (일을) 밀어붙여 해내다〔완수하다〕. ¶ *~ the matter* 〔*reform*〕 *through* 일〔개혁〕을 강행시켜 해내다. **c**) make an appearance. (싹 등이) 나다; 내밀다. ⇨*vt.* **2.**

—*n.* **1** Ⓒ the act of pushing; thrust or

shove. 밀기; 밀어내기; 찌르기. ¶ *He gave the car a ~ to see if he could start it.* 시동이 걸릴까 하여 차를 한 번 밀어봤다 / *give a hard ~* 힘껏 밀다. **2** ⓊⒸ 《*colloq.*》 ⓐ energy; force. 정력; 기운; 힘. ¶ *She has a plenty of ~.* 정력이 대단한 여자다 / *a man* (*full*) *of ~ and go* (아주) 정력적인 사람. ⓑ a vigorous effort. 분발. ¶ *make a ~* 분발하다 / *at one ~* 단숨에; 대번에. **3** Ⓒ a situation which requires that one do something necessary without losing any time; an emergency. 절박한 상태; 긴급; 위기. ¶ *come to the ~* 위급해지다 / *at a ~* 위기에 처하여. [L. *pello* drive]

get the push, 《*sl.*》 be dismissed from employment. 해고당하다.

give the push, 《*sl.*》 dismiss (a person). …을 해고하다.

push·cart [púʃkὰːrt] *n.* Ⓒ a cart which is pushed by the hand. 미는 손수레.

push·er [púʃər] *n.* Ⓒ a person or thing that pushes, esp. a person who pushes himself forward in the hope of rising in the world. 미는 사람(것); 출세에 열 내는 사람.

push·ful [púʃfəl] *adj.* =pushing.

push·ing [púʃiŋ] *adj.* **1** active. 활동적인; 활발한. **2** being busy with what is not one's concern. 중뿔나게 나서는; 주제넘은.

pu·sil·la·nim·i·ty [pjùːsələnímәti] *n.* Ⓤ the state of being pusillanimous. 무기력; 비겁; 겁많음. [L. *pusillus* petty, →animus]

pu·sil·lan·i·mous [pjùːsəlǽnəməs] *adj.* lacking strength of mind or courage. 기개가 없는; 무기력한; 겁많은; 비겁한. ¶ *The ~ man would not defend his own family.* 무기력한 사람은 제 식구도 지키지 못 한다.

puss [pus] *n.* Ⓒ **1** a cat. 고양이. **2** a merry, mischievous young girl. (명랑하고 장난기 있는) 소녀. [?]

***puss·y** [púsi] *n.* Ⓒ (*pl.* **puss·ies**) a cat. 고양이. [↑]

pus·tule [pʌ́stʃuːl] *n.* Ⓒ a spot on the skin containing pus. 부스럼; 종기. [→pus]

:put[1] [put] *v.* (**put, put·ting**) *vt.* **1** (P6,7,13, 18) move (something or someone) into a certain place; set; place; lay; throw. (어떤 상태에) …을 놓다; 앉히다; 얹다; 넣다; 두다. ¶ *~ a vase on the table* 꽃병을 탁자에 놓다 / *~ some water in a glass* 컵에 물을 붓다 / *~ someone in prison* 아무를 감옥에 넣다 / *What ~ that into your head?* 어떻게 그런 생각을 하게 되었나 / *~ one's car in a garage* 차를 차고에 넣다 / *~ money where no one can find it* 돈을 아무도 못 찾는 곳에 두다 / *~ one's mouth to someone's ear* 아무의 귓전에 입을 대다 / *~ sugar in one's tea* 차에 설탕을 넣다 / *~ a notebook in one's pocket* 수첩을 주머니에 넣다 / *She ~ her hand to his shoulder.* 그녀는 그의 어깨에 손을 얹었다. **2** (P7,13,18) cause (something or someone) to be in a certain state or relation. …을 어떤 상태로 하다; …을 어떤 상태(관계)에 놓다. ¶ *~ someone in rage* 아무를 성나게 하다 / *~ someone at his ease* 아무를 편하게 해주다; 안심시키다 / *~ someone out of temper* 아무를 화나게 하다 / *~ someone out of countenance* 아무를 당황케 하다 / *~ a room in order* 방을 정돈하다 / *~ one's ideas into shape* 생각을 구체화시키다 / *~ a watch right* 시간을 맞춰놓다 / *~ it good use* …을 활용하다 / *~ a machine in* (*into*) *motion* 기계를 가동시키다 / *~ oneself in another's place* 남의 입장이 되어보다 / *~ someone in a fix* (*hole*) 아무를 궁지에 몰아넣다(빠뜨리다) / *~ names in alphabetical order* 이름을 알파벳 순으로 하다. **3** (P7,13) turn (something) in a certain direction; apply; attach. (어떤 방향으로) …을 돌리다; 향하게 하다; (자금 따위를) …에 투입하다(쓰다); …에 대다(붙이다). ¶ *~ one's mind to a problem* 어떤 문제에 정신을 집중하다 / *~ a glass to one's lips* 컵을 입술에 대다 / *~ all one's energies into an enterprise* 기업에 온갖 정력을 다 기울이다 / *I'll ~ some money toward the campaign funds.* 나도 운동자금에 얼마간의 돈을 기부하겠다 / *~ horse's head toward home* 말머리를 집으로 돌리다. **4** (P6, 7,13) present or propose (something) for attention or consideration; suggest; ask. (주의·고려 등을 끌거나 얻기 위해) …을 내다; (문제·제안 등을) 제출(제안)하다. ¶ *~ a question before a committee* 위원회에 질의를 내다 / *~ a resolution to the meeting* 결의안을 모임에 내놓다 / *They ~ the problem before the mayor.* 그 문제를 시장에게 진정하였다. **5** (P7,13) state or express; lay before; translate; write. …을 말하다; 설명하다; 번역하다; 쓰다. ¶ *~ it in French* …을 불어로 쓰다 / *~ a phrase into French* 어떤 구를 불어로 번역하다 / *~ an idea in written words* 어떤 생각을 글로 나타내다 / *~ one's feelings in* (*into*) *words* 감정을 말로 표현하다 / *~ one's name to a document* 문서에 서명하다 / *~ ideas clearly* 생각을 분명히 말하다 / *~ down someone's speech in shorthand* 아무의 연설을 속기하다 / *Put down your address here.* 여기에 주소를 쓰시오 / *I don't know how to ~ it.* 그것을 어떻게 표현해야 할지 모르겠다. **6** (P6,13,20) force; drive; subject. (아무)에게 …하지 않을 수 없게 하다; …에게 (고통 따위를) 받게 하다. ¶ *~ someone to expense* 아무에게 돈을 쓰게 하다 / *~ the enemy to flight* 적을 패주시키다 / *~ someone to shame* 아무를 망신 주다 / *~ someone to death* 아무를 죽게 만들다(죽이다) / *~ someone through a lot of pain* 아무에게 큰 고통을 겪게 하다 / *The criminal will be ~ on trial.* 범인은 공판에 회부될 것이다. **7** (P13) 《*on, upon*》 lay (blame, a duty, etc.); impose. (책임·의무 따위)를 지우다; (벌을) 과(課)하다. ¶ *~ a tax on beer* 맥주에 과세하다 / *~ blame on others* 죄를 남에게 씌우다 / *~ a heavy load one's shoulder* 어깨에 무거운 짐을 지우다. **8** (P6,13) fix (a limit, etc.). (한도)를 정하다; (제한 따위)를 가하다

〔주다〕. ¶ ～ *an end* 〔*a period*〕 *to something* …을 끝(장)내다 / ～ *an end to a practice* 하나의 관행을 중단하다 / ～ *a limit to one's outlay* 지출에 제한을 가하다. **9** ⓐ (P6,7,13) form an opinion or judgment about (value, price, size, etc.). (가치 등)을 어림잡다; 평가하다. ¶ *I* ～ *the price at ten dollars.* 나는 그 값을 10달러로 보았다 / ～ *someone's age down at thirty* 아무의 나이를 30세 미만으로 보다 / *I* ～ *his income at* £*5,000 a year.* 나는 그의 수입을 연봉 5,000 파운드로 어림했다. ⓑ consider someone likely to (do); think someone not above (doing). 아무를 (능히) …할 사람이라고 생각하다. ¶ *I wouldn't* ～ *it past him to take a bribe.* 나는 그가 뇌물을 마다하지 않고 받을 것이라 생각한다. ⓒ 《*to*》 suggest. 추측하다. ¶ *I* ～ *it to you that you have done it.* 내 생각에는 네가 그 일을 한 것 같다. **10** (P6,13) lay out (money) to profitable use; bet. …에 투자하다; (돈)을 걸다. ¶ ～ *one's money in real estate* 돈을 부동산에 투자하다 / ～ *ten dollars on a horse* 경마에 10 달러 걸다. **11** (P6) throw; cast; hurl. …을 던지다. ¶ *putting the shot* 포환 던지기.

— *vi.* (P2A,3) (of a ship) take a certain course. (배가) 나아가다; 진로를 잡다. ¶ ～ *out to sea* 바다로 나아가다; 출범하다. [E.]

put about, **a**) change the course of (a boat). (배)의 진로를 바꾸다. ¶ ～ *a sailing ship about* 범선의 진로를 바꾸다 / *We* ～ *about at this point.* 우리는 이 지점에서 방향을 돌렸다. **b**) spread (gossip, etc.); circulate. (소문 등)을 퍼뜨리다. ¶ ～ *about a rumor* 소문을 퍼뜨리다. **c**) 《*colloq.*》 worry; distress; vex. 괴롭히다; 애먹이다. ¶ *He is much* ～ *about by this.* 그는 이 일로 인해서 고민이 대단하다.

put across, **a**) take over (someone or something) in a boat. …을 배로 건네다. ¶ ～ *a man across a river* 어떤 이를 배로 강을 건네주다. **b**) express or explain effectively. …을 효과적으로 나타내다. ¶ *I didn't know how to* ～ *myself across.* 어떻게 하면 내 생각을 이해시킬 수 있을지 (그 방법을) 몰랐다. **c**) 《*sl.*》 lie to (someone) successfully; deceive. (…을) 감쪽같이 속이다. ¶ *You can't* ～ *that across the teacher again.* 너도 그 수법으로 선생님을 또다시 속일 수는 없다.

put aside, **a**) place (something) to one side. …을 옆으로 치우다. ¶ *She* ～ *aside her sewing and looked at me.* 그녀는 재봉일감을 옆으로 치우고 나를 보았다. **b**) save (money, etc.) for later use. (후일을 위해) …을 저축해 두다. **c**) dismiss from the mind; throw aside. (생각 등)을 지워버리다; 무시하다. ¶ ～ *aside one's work* 〔*duty*〕 일〔책임〕을 팽개치다.

put away, **a**) put (something) in its proper place; lay aside. …을 제자리에 (치워)두다. ¶ ～ *away the tools* 연장을 제자리에 챙겨 넣다. **b**) save (money, etc.) for later use. …을 저축〔비축〕하다. ¶ *He has a nice sum of money* ～ *away.* 그는 모아 놓은 돈이 꽤 있다. **c**) 《*colloq.*》 eat or drink. …을 먹다〔마시다〕. ¶ ～ *away a gallon of beer* 맥주를 한 갤런이나 마시다. **d**) 《*colloq.*》 put in prison; confine. …을 투옥〔감금〕하다. **e**) kill. …을 죽이다.

put back, **a**) (of a boat) return to the shore. (배를〔배가〕 해안으로) 되돌아가게 하다〔되돌아가다〕. ¶ ～ *a ship back to port for repairs* 배를 수리하기 위해 항구로 되돌아가게 하다. **b**) put (something) where it was before. (…을) 제자리에 되돌려 놓다. ¶ *Put back the book where you found it.* 책을 제자리에 갖다 놓아라. **c**) move backward. (시계 바늘)을 뒤로 돌리다. ¶ ～ *back* (*the hands of*) *the clock three minutes* (바늘을 돌려) 시계를 3분 늦추다.

put by, keep (something) in order to make use of it later; set aside; lay up. …을 저축해 두다. ¶ ～ *money by* 저금하다.

put down, **a**) place down (something). …을 내려놓다. ¶ ～ *down the book one is reading* 읽던 책을 내려놓다. **b**) record; write down. …을 기록하다. ¶ *Please* ～ *down your telephone number.* 전화 번호를 기록해 주십시오. **c**) stop (a riot, etc.) by force. (폭동 등)을 진압하다. ¶ ～ *down a rebellion* 반도(叛徒)를 진압하다. **d**) cut down; lower. …을 축소하다; 줄이다; 내리다. ¶ ～ *the price down ten shillings* 값을 10실링 내리다.

put forth, **a**) grow (leaves, shoots, etc.). (잎·싹 따위)를 내(밀)다. **b**) propose; offer. …을 제안〔제출〕하다. **c**) bring into action; exercise; exert. (힘 따위)를 발휘하다. ¶ ～ *forth all one's energies* 온 정력을 쏟다 / ～ *forth one's best effort* 최선을 다하다.

put forward, **a**) suggest; propose. …을 제안〔제출〕하다. ¶ ～ *forward a new plan.* **b**) cause (something) to go forward; advance. …을 촉진〔진척; 발전〕시키다. ¶ ～ *the business forward* 사업을 발전시키다.

put in, **a**) place in (something); insert. …을 넣다; (말)을 삽입〔첨가〕하다. ¶ *He opened his purse and* ～ *in some money.* 그는 지갑을 열고 얼마간의 돈을 넣었다 / ～ *in a good word for one's friend* 친구를 위해 변호를 해주다. **b**) name or choose (someone) for a position. …을 지명〔임명〕하다. ¶ ～ *in a board of directors* 이사회에 앉히다. **c**) set forward (something); present. …을 제출하다. ¶ ～ *in a claim* 클레임을 제기하다 / ～ *in a document as evidence* 증거 서류를 제출하다. **d**) 《naut.》 enter a harbor; visit (some place). 입항하다; …에 들르다. **e**) 《*colloq.*》 spend (time) in a certain manner. (시간)을 보내다. ¶ ～ *in a lot of time playing golf* 장시간 골프를 치며 지내다.

put in for, 《*colloq.*》 ask or apply for (something); be a candidate for. …에 출원하다; 신청〔청구〕하다; …에 입후보하다. ¶ ～ *in for a 20 percent pay increase,* 20%의 임금인상

을 요구하다 / ~ *in for membership of a club* 클럽의 입회를 신청하다 / ~ *in for the position of president* 회장에 입후보하다.

put off, **a**) take off (a coat, etc.); remove. (옷)을 벗다; …을 치우다. ¶ ~ *off one's hat* 〔*coat*〕 모자〔코트〕를 벗다 / ~ *off doubt* 의심을 떨어버리다. **b**) postpone; delay. …을 연기하다; 미루다. ¶ ~ *off one's departure* 출발을 연기하다. **c**) keep (someone) from doing something; stop. (아무)를 단념하게 하다; (아무를) 방해하다. ¶ *They ~ me off everytime I was going to speak.* 내가 말하려고 할 때마다 그들은 방해를 했다. **d**) start away; set out. …을 출발하다; 떠나다. ¶ ~ *off on a journey* 여행을 떠나다. **e**) avoid with some excuse; evade. (핑계 따위로) 피하다〔모면하다; 발뺌하다〕. ¶ ~ *off a child's question with lies* 아이의 질문을 거짓말로 어물쩍 넘기다 / *He tried to ~ me off with a false promise.* 그는 거짓 약속으로 나를 피하려 들었다.

put on, **a**) clothe oneself in (something); wear. (옷)을 입다; (안경)을 쓰다; (연지)를 바르다; (반지)를 끼다. ¶ ~ *on one's coat* 코트를 입다 / ~ *on glasses* 안경을 쓰다 / ~ *on lipstick* 립스틱을 바르다. **b**) assume the appearance of (something). …을 가장하다; …하는 체하다. ¶ ~ *on a show* 〔*an act*〕 *of innocence* 모르는 척하다; 순진한 척 굴다 / *His modesty is all but ~ on.* 그의 겸손은 순전한 겉치레다. **c**) add to (something); gather (speed, etc.). (속력 등)을 늘리다. ¶ ~ *on speed* 속도를 늘리다 / ~ *on weight* 〔*flesh*〕 체중이 늘다. **d**) bring (a play) on the stage. (극)을 상연하다. ¶ ~ *on a new play* 새로운 연극을 상연하다. **e**) move forward (the hands of a clock, etc.). (시계 등)을 빠르게 하다. ¶ ~ *on* (*the hands of*) *a clock* 시계 바늘을 앞으로 돌려 놓다.

put out, **a**) hold out one's hand; put forth (something). (손)을 내밀다; …을 제출하다. ¶ ~ *one's hand* 〔*tongue*〕 손을〔혀를〕 내밀다 / ~ *one's head out* (*of the window*) 머리를 (창 밖으로) 내밀다. **b**) stop (fire from burning); extinguish. (불)을 끄다. ¶ ~ *out a fire with water* 물로 불을 끄다 / ~ *out a lamp* 등불을 끄다. **c**) put money into (a business, etc.); place or lend money at interest. …에 투자하다; (이자를 붙여) 대출하다. ¶ ~ *out money on a profitable business* 유리한 사업에 돈을 투자하다 / ~ *out money at six percent* 돈을 6푼 이자로 빌려주다. **d**) make (someone) angry. …을 성나게 하다. ¶ *He is not easily ~ out.* 그는 좀처럼 화를 내지 않는다.

put through, **a**) carry out; accomplish; perform. …을 수행하다; 해내다. ¶ ~ *a plan through* 계획을 제대로 수행하다. **b**) connect (someone) by telephone with another. …에게 전화를 연결하다. ¶ ~ *through a call to London* 런던에 전화를 걸다. **c**) make to go or pass through. (로프 따위를) 구멍에 꿰다; 관통시키다. ¶ ~ *a rope through a hole* 구멍에 끈을 꿰다 / ~ *a bullet through someone's head* …의 머리에 총탄을 관통시키다. **d**) cause to do or undergo. (시련, 검사)를 받게 하다. ¶ ~ *someone through a test* …을 검사받게 하다.

put together, form (a whole) out of parts; construct. …을 조립하다. ¶ ~ *together a good dinner* (갖가지 것들을 모아) 진수성찬을 만들다 / *His share is more than all the others' ~ together.* 그의 몫은 다른 사람의 것 모두를 합친 것보다 많다.

put to it, worry; press hard; distress. 애먹이다; 괴롭히다. ¶ *He is hard ~ to it.* 그는 고생이 막심하다.

put up, **a**) hold up (a flag, etc.); raise. (…)을 올리다. ¶ ~ *up the sails* 돛을 올리다 / ~ *up one's hand* 〔*hands*〕 손을 들다〔두 손을 들다《항복하다》〕 / ~ *up posters* 벽보를 붙이다. **b**) build (a house). (집)을 짓다. **c**) propose (someone) for election; offer (something) for sale. (선거에) 입후보시키다; 후보자로 지명하다; …을 매물(賣物)로 내놓다. ¶ *He has been ~ up for Parliament.* 그는 의회 후보자로 지명되었다 / ~ *up goods at an auction* 물건을 경매에 내놓다. **d**) return to it's proper place; put away. 제자리에 되돌려 놓다; 거두다; 치우다. ¶ ~ *up a sword* 칼을 칼집에 꽂다 / ~ *up a car in the garage* 차고에 자동차를 넣어 두다. **e**) preserve (food) in a vessel. (소금에 절여 음식)을 그릇에 저장하다. ¶ ~ *up pork* 〔*beef*〕 *in barrels* 돼지〔쇠〕고기를 절여 통에 저장하다. **f**) show; exhibit; display. …을 상연〔전시〕하다; (용감한 태도 따위)를 보이다. ¶ ~ *up a play* 연극을공연하다 / ~ *up a good fight* 멋지게 싸우다; 선전(善戰)하다. **g**) stay at a hotel, etc.; lodge. 숙박하다. ¶ ~ *up someone for a night* 아무를 하룻밤 재우다. **h**) cause (a wild bird or animal) to drive out of its hiding place. (사냥감)을 숨은 데에서 몰아내다. **i**) offer (a prayer). (기도)를 드리다.

put upon, take advantage of; take in; deceive. …을 이용하다; 속이다. ¶ *I won't be ~ upon.* 나는 속지 않을 것이다.

put someone up to (=*talk someone into doing*) *something.* …하도록 아무를 설득하다.

put up with, bear or endure. …을 참다〔견디다〕. ¶ ~ *up with simple food* 조식(粗食)으로 참고 지내다.

put² [pʌt] *vt.* =putt.

pu·tre·fac·tion [pjùːtrəfǽkʃən] *n.* Ⓤ (of food) the act or process of putrefying. (음식의) 부패(작용). [↓]

pu·tre·fy [pjúːtrəfài] *vt.* (**-fied**) (P6) make (some part in a living body, food, etc.) go bad. …을 화농〔부패〕시키다. —— *vi.* (P1) become bad or worse. 화농하다; 썩다. ¶ *Putrefying meat has a bad smell.* 썩은 고기는 냄새가 고약하다. [L. *putreo* rot]

pu·trid [pjúːtrid] *adj.* **1** being putrefied; dirty; producing a strong, bad smell. 썩은;

더러운; 구린. 2 《*colloq.*》 extremely unpleasant; bad. 아주 불쾌한; 고약한. ¶ *a perfectly ~ book* 〔*dinner*〕 아주 고약한 책〔식사〕. [↑]

putt [pʌt] *n.* Ⓒ 《golf》 a gentle stroke used to drive the ball into the hole. 가볍게 치기; 퍼트. — *vt., vi.* (P6; 1) 《golf》 drive (the ball) into the hole with a gentle stroke. 퍼트하다. [*put*]

put·tee [pʌ́ti] *n.* Ⓒ a long strip of cloth wound from the ankle to the knee. 각반(脚絆). [Hind.=bandage]

put·ter[1] [pʌ́tər] *n.* Ⓒ 《golf》 **1** a person who putts. 퍼트하는 사람. **2** a golf club used in putting. 퍼트하는 데 쓰는 채〔클럽〕.

put·ter[2] [pʌ́tər] *vi.* (P1,2A) work in an idle way; walk without purpose. 꾸물거리며 일하다; 어정거리다; 빈둥거리다. ¶ *~ about the house* 집에서 빈들거리다. — *vt.* (P7) waste (time). (시간)을 허비하다. ¶ *~ away one's time.* 허송 세월하다.

put·ty [pʌ́ti] *n.* Ⓤ soft cement used for filling cracks or for fastening glass in a window frame. 퍼티《유리와 창살의 접합제》. — *vt.* (**-tied**) (P6,7) fill with putty; fix glass with putty. 퍼티로 메우다〔접합하다〕. [→pot]

:puz·zle [pʌ́zl] *n.* Ⓒ **1** a difficult problem; a very hard question. 난문제; 수수께끼. ¶ *the great ~ of human existence* 인간 생존의 커다란 수수께끼〔난제〕 / *How to get all my things into one trunk is a ~.* 트렁크 하나에 내 물건 전부를 어떻게 넣느냐 하는 것이 어려운 문제로다. **2** a state of being unable to answer or decide; a state of being confused. 곤혹; 당혹. ¶ *in a ~* 당황〔난처〕해서. **3** a problem or task to be done for fun. 퍼즐. ¶ *a crossword ~* 글자 맞추기 퍼즐. — *vt.* (P6,7) **1** make (someone) unable to answer or understand; confuse. …을 당황하게 하다. ¶ *I'm puzzled what to do.* 어찌해야 좋을지 난감하다 / *~ one's brains* 골치를 썩이다 / *The question puzzles me.* 그 문제는 알다가도 모르겠다. **2** 《*out*》 think out; try to solve. …을 생각해내다; 헤아리다. ¶ *~ out a riddle* 수수께끼를 풀다. — *vi.* (P3) be confused; be unable to answer or decide. 당황하다; 난감해하다. ¶ *They puzzled over their arithmetic for an hour.* 그들은 한 시간 동안 산수와 씨름했다. [E.]

puzzle out, find the answer of (something) by thinking hard. …을 풀다; …의 해답을 내다.

puz·zle·ment [pʌ́zlmənt] *n.* Ⓤ the state of being puzzled. 당황. [E.]

P.X. [pí:éks] (*pl.* **PXs** [-éksiz]) (in the Army of U.S.A.) post exchange. 피 엑스; 군매점(軍賣店).

pyg·my [pígmi] *n.* Ⓒ (*pl.* **-mies**) **1** a very small person. 난쟁이. **2** 《*P-*》 a member of an African race of very small people. 피그미족의 사람. — *adj.* of a pygmy; very small. 난쟁이의; 아주 작은. ¶ *a ~ mind* 소인 / *one's ~ effort* 아주 작은 노력; 미력(微力). [Gk. *pugmē* cubit]

py·ja·mas [pədʒɑ́:məz, -dʒǽm-] *n. pl.* 《Brit.》 =pajamas.

py·lon [páilɑn / -lɔn] *n.* Ⓒ **1** a gate of an Egyptian temple. (고대 이집트의) 탑문(塔門); 필론. **2** a tower marking the course for an airplane. (비행장의) 지시탑; 관제탑. **3** 《electr.》 one of a series of towers supporting electric wires. (고압선용의) 철탑. [↓]

py·lo·rus [pailɔ́:rəs, pi-] *n.* Ⓒ (*pl.* **-ri** [-rai]) 《anat.》 the opening from the stomach into bowels. 유문(幽門). [Gk. *pulē* gate, *ouros* warder]

·pyr·a·mid [pírəmìd] *n.* Ⓒ **1** 《geom.》 a solid body with a flat base and triangular sides meeting at the top; something shaped like such a body. 각뿔; 각뿔 모양의 것. **2** 《often *P-*》 one of the ancient Egyptian royal tombs shaped like a pyramid. 피라미드. [Gk. *puramis*]

py·ram·i·dal [pirǽmədəl] *adj.* having the shape of a pyramid. 각뿔 모양의; 피라미드형의. ¶ *a ~ roof* 방추형(方錐形) 지붕.

pyre [páiər] *n.* Ⓒ a heap of wood for burning a dead body. 화장용 장작더미. [Gk. *pur* fire]

py·ri·tes [paiəráiti:z] *n.* Ⓤ a mineral compound of sulfur, iron, copper, etc. 황철광; 황동광. [↑]

py·ro·tech·nic [pàiəroutéknik], **-ni·cal** [-nikəl] *adj.* of fireworks. 꽃불의. ¶ *a ~ display* 꽃불놀이. [↑; →technical]

py·ro·tech·nics [pàiəroutékniks] *n. pl.* 《usu. as *sing.* and *pl.*》 the art of making fireworks; the showing of fireworks. 꽃불 제작술; 꽃불 올리기.

Pyr·rhic [pírik] *adj.* of King of Epirus. 피로스 왕의. [Person]

Pyrrhic victory [⌒ ⌒⌒] *n.* one obtained at too great cost. 피루스의 승리《막대한 희생을 치른; 보람없는 승리》.

Py·thag·o·ras [piθǽgərəs] *n.* (582?-500? B.C.) a Greek philosopher and mathematician. 피타고라스《그리스의 철학자·수학자》.

Py·thag·o·re·an [piθæ̀gərí:ən] *adj.* of Pythagoras. 피타고라스의. ¶ *the ~ proposition* 〔*theorem*〕 피타고라스의 정리. [Person]

py·thon [páiθɑn, -θən] *n.* Ⓒ **1** a very large snake with no poison. 비단뱀; 이무기. **2** 《*P-*》 《Gk. myth.》 the large snake which Apollo killed at Delphi. (아폴로가 죽인) 거대한 뱀; 피톤. [Gk. *puthōn*]

q Q

Q, q [kjuː] *n.* Ⓒ (*pl.* **Q's, Qs, q's, qs** [kjuːz]) the 17th letter of the English alphabet. 영어 알파벳의 17째 글자.

***qt.** **1** quantity. **2** quart(s).

quack[1] [kwæk] *n.* Ⓒ the cry of a duck. 꽥꽥《오리 우는 소리》. — *vi.* (P1) **1** make a sound like a duck's cry. 꽥꽥거리다. **2** 《*fig.*》 talk idly and loudly. 시끄럽게 수다떨다. [Imit.]

quack[2] [kwæk] *n.* Ⓒ a person who pretends to be skilled in a particular field, esp. in medicine. 돌팔이 의사; 협잡꾼 (cf. *charlatan*). — *adj.* false; sham. 가짜의. ¶ *a ~ doctor* 돌팔이 의사 / *~ medicines* 〔*remedies*〕 가짜 약〔엉터리 요법〕. [Imit.]

quack·er·y [kwǽkəri] *n.* ⓊⒸ (*pl.* **-er·ies**) the practice or method of a quack. 엉터리 치료(법). [↑]

quad [kwɑd / kwɔd] *n.* 《*colloq.*》 =quadrangle.

quad·ran·gle [kwɑ́dræ̀ŋgəl / kwɔ́d-] *n.* Ⓒ **1** 《math.》 a figure having four angles and four sides. 4각형; 4변형. **2** 《Brit.》 the four-sided courtyard surrounded by buildings, esp. in colleges and universities. (건물에 둘러 싸인) 네모난 안뜰《특히 대학의》. [→quadri-, angle]

quad·ran·gu·lar [kwɑdrǽŋgjələr / kwɔd-] *adj.* having four sides and four angles. 4각[4변]형의. [↑]

quad·rant [kwɑ́drənt / kwɔ́d-] *n.* Ⓒ **1** 《math.》 one fourth of a circle. 사분원(四分圓). **2** 《astron., naut.》 an instrument formerly used for measuring altitudes or angles. 사분의(四分儀); 상한의(象限儀)(cf. *sextant*). [L. *quadrans*]

quad·rate [kwɑ́drit / kwɔ́d-] *adj.* square; rectangular. 정사각형의; 방형(方形)의. — *n.* Ⓒ something square or rectangular. 정4각형; 방형. — [kwɑ́dreit / kwɔdréit] *vt., vi.* (P6; 1) conform; cause to correspond. 일치시키다〔하다〕. [L. *quadro* square]

quad·rat·ic [kwɑdrǽtik / kwɔd-] *adj.* 《math.》 involving the square of an unknown quantity but no higher powers. 2차의. ¶ *a ~ equation* 2차 방정식 / *~ paper* 그래프 용지; 모눈종이.

quad·ren·ni·al [kwɑdréniəl / kwɔd-] *adj.* lasting for four years; occurring every four years. 4년마다의; 4년마다 일어나는. [↑, →annual]

quad·ri- [kwɑ́drə- / kwɔ́drə-], **quad·ru-** [kwɑ́dru- / kwɔ́dru-] *pref.* four. '4'의 뜻. [L.]

quad·ri·lat·er·al [kwɑ̀drəlǽtərəl / kwɔ̀d-] *n., adj.* (a figure) having four sides. 4변형(의). [quadri, →lateral]

qua·drille [kwɑdríl, kwə-] *n.* Ⓒ a square dance for four couples; music for this. 카드리유《네 사람이 한 조로 추는 춤》; 그 곡(曲). [↑]

quad·ril·lion [kwɑdríljən / kwɔd-] *n.* **1** 《Brit.》 a cardinal number represented by one followed by 24 zeros. 백만의 4제곱 (10^{24}). **2** 《U.S.》 a cardinal number represented by one followed by 15 zeros. 천의 5제곱(10^{15}). [quadri-, →million]

quad·roon [kwɑdrúːn / kwɔd-] *n.* a person having one-fourth negro blood. 4분의 1흑인. [Sp. *cuarteron* a fourth; →mulato]

quad·ru·ped [kwɑ́drupèd / kwɔ́d-] *n.* Ⓒ an animal that has four feet. 네발짐승. — *adj.* having four feet. 네발을 가진. [quadru-, →pedal]

quad·ru·ple [kwɑdrúːpəl, kwɑ́dru- / kwɔ́drupəl] *adj.* **1** having or composed of four parts. 네 부분으로 된. **2** four times as much or as many; fourfold. 네 배의; 네 겹의. ¶ *a size ~ to that of the moon* 달의 네 배의 크기 / *have a ~ share* 몫이 네 배다 / *a rate ~ of* 〔*to*〕 *that of another* 다른 사람의 네 배의 비율 / *a ~ alliance* 4국 동맹. **3** 《mus.》 having four beats in a bar. 4박자의.

— *n.* 《*the ~*》 a number or quantity four times as much or as many. 4배수(倍數); 4배량(倍量). ¶ *80 is the ~ of 20.* 80은 20의 4배수다.

— *vt., vi.* (P6; 1) make (something) or become four times as much or as many. …을 4배하다; 4배가 되다. [L. *quadr-* four, *-plex* fold]

quad·ru·pli·cate [kwɑdrúːplikit / kwɔd-] *adj.* fourfold; quadruple. 4배의. — *n.* Ⓒ one of four things. (서류 따위가) 4통 중의 하나. ¶ *in ~* (같은 문서를) 4통으로 하여. — [-plikèit] *vt.* (P6) make fourfold. 네 배로〔네 겹으로〕 하다. [→quadruple]

quaff [kwɑːf, kwæf] *vt., vi.* (P6,7; 1) 《*lit.*》 《*off, up*》 drink in large quantities. 꿀떡꿀떡 마시다. ¶ *sit quaffing all day* 종일 술만 퍼마시다 / *~ off a glass of beer* 맥주 한 잔을 단숨에 들이켜다. — *n.* Ⓒ the act of drinking deeply. 꿀꺽꿀꺽 들이켜기; 통음(痛飮). [L., G. =overindulge]

quag·mire [kwǽgmàiər] *n.* Ⓒ **1** a soft, muddy piece of land; a marsh. 늪; 습지. **2** 《*fig.*》 a dangerous position. 곤경(困境); 궁지. [→quag, -mire]

quail[1] [kweil] *n.* Ⓒ (*pl.* **quails** or *collec-*

tively **quail**) a game bird like a partridge. 메추라기. [F. *quaille*]

quail[2] [kweil] *vi.* (P1,3) 《*at, before*》 shrink back from fear of pain; lose courage. 기가 죽다; 주눅들다. ¶ *His heart quailed at the sight.* 그 광경에 그는 기가 죽었다 / *They quailed before the enemy's attack.* 적의 공세에 그들은 사기가 죽었다. [M.E.]

*__quaint__ [kweint] *adj.* odd but attractive; curious, esp. in an old-fashioned way. 별난; 기묘한; (특히) 예스러운 멋이 있는. ¶ ~, *old-fashioned customs* 묘한 예스러운 풍습 / *a ~ old house* 풍치 있는 고택(古宅). [L. *cognosco* learn]

quaint·ly [kwéintli] *adv.* in a quaint manner. 별나게; 기묘하게.

quake [kweik] *vi.* (P1,2A) **1** 《*with, for*》 (of a person) shake; tremble. (무서워) 떨다. ¶ *He was quaking with fear.* 그는 무서워 떨고 있었다. **2** (of inanimate things) shake; tremble; move to and fro. (무생물이) 진동하다; (앞뒤로) 흔들리다. ¶ *The earth quaked.* 땅이 흔들렸다. — *n.* Ⓒ **1** the act of shaking or trembling. 떨기; 떪; 진동; 흔들림. **2** 《*colloq.*》 an earthquake. 지진. [E.]

Quak·er [kwéikər] *n.* Ⓒ 《orig. *contempt.*》 **1** a member of a Christian sect formally called the 'Society of Friends'. 퀘이커 교도. **2** 《U.S.》 a dummy gun in a ship or a fort. (선박이나 요새의) 위포(僞砲)《가짜 대포》; 목포(木砲). [↑]

Quak·er·ism [kwéikərìzəm] *n.* Ⓤ the principles, customs or ways of the Quakers. 퀘이커주의〔교리, 관습〕.

qual·i·fi·ca·tion [kwɑ̀ləfəkéiʃən / kwɔ̀l-] *n.* ⓊⒸ **1** the act of qualifying; the state of being qualified. 자격 부여; 자격. ¶ *have the qualifications of a teacher* 교사 자격증을 가지다 / *He has no qualifications for his office.* 그는 그 직을 맡을 자격이 없다. **2** a restriction; a modification; a limiting condition. 제한; 수정; 조건. ¶ *We can praise the play, but with certain qualifications.* 우리는 그 극을 칭찬할 수 있다, 단 어떤 조건 아래에서 / *(a statement) without any ~* 어떤 (유보) 조건도 없는 (성명). [→qualify]

qual·i·fied [kwɑ́ləfàid / kwɔ́l-] *adj.* **1** having the required qualifications. 자격이〔면허가〕 있는. ¶ *a ~ medical practitioner* 면허 개업의(醫) / *a man well ~ for his position* 그 지위에 아주 적임인 사람. **2** limited; modified. 제한된; 수정〔조정〕된. ¶ *~ consent* 조건부 승인 / *a ~ statement.*

*__qual·i·fy__ [kwɑ́ləfài / kwɔ́l-] *v.* (**-fied**) *vt.* **1** (P6,7,13,20) make (someone) fit for a job, an office, etc. …에 필요한 실력을 주다; 적격으로 하다. ¶ *The training qualified him for the job.* 그 훈련으로 그는 그 일을 할 수 있는 적격자가 되었다 / *~ someone as a voter* 아무에게 선거권을 주다 / *~ oneself for one's lifework* 필생의 사업에 알맞은 실력을 갖추다. **2** (P6,7,13) give (someone) legal power or authorization. (아무에게) 자격〔권한〕을 주다. ¶ *be qualified to teach* 가르칠 자격을 얻다. **3** (P6,13,19) 《*as, for*》 call; name. …을 (…이라고) 보다; …라고 부르다. ¶ *He may be qualified as a villain.* 그 자는 악당이라 해도 좋다. **4** (P6) make (something) less strong, positive; make weaker. …을 누그러뜨리다; 완화시키다. ¶ *~ the whisky with water* 물을 타서 위스키를 순하게 하다 / *~ a statement by adding 'perhaps'* '경우에 따라'라는 말을 첨가해 성명의 강도(強度)를 줄이다. **5** (P6) 《gram.》 modify; limit the meaning of. …을 수식하다; …의 뜻을 제한하다. ¶ *Adverbs ~ verbs, adjectives, or other adverbs.* 부사는 동사, 형용사, 혹은 다른 부사를 수식한다.

— *vi.* (P1,3) become fit or competent for something; get a license. 자격을 얻다; 면허를〔검정을〕 따다. ¶ *~ as a doctor* 의사 자격을 얻다 / *I didn't ~ for the finals.* 나는 결승전에 나갈 자격을 얻지 못했다. [L. *qualis* of what sort]

qual·i·ta·tive [kwɑ́lətèitiv / kwɔ́lətə-] *adj.* of or concerned with quality or qualities. 성질상의; 질적(質的)인(opp. quantitative). ¶ *~ limitation* (군비(軍備) 등의) 질적 제한. [→quality]

qualitative analysis [´---- -´--] *n.* 《chem.》 a chemical analysis of a substance in order to determine its nature or element. 정성 분석(定性分析)(cf. *quntative analysis*).

*__qual·i·ty__ [kwɑ́ləti / kwɔ́l-] *n.* ⓊⒸ (*pl.* **-ties**) **1** something which makes someone or something different from others; the essential nature; a characteristic. 특징; 특성; 질(質); 성질. ¶ *Hardness is one ~ of iron.* 굳은 것이 쇠의 한 특질이다 / *the ~ of mercy* 자비의 본질. **2** value; worth; a degree of goodness. 가치; 품질의 양부(良否); 품질. ¶ *Quality matters more than quantity.* 양보다 질 / *a thing of good* 〔*high, poor*〕 *~* 품질이 좋은〔고급의, 나쁜〕 물건 / *aim at ~ rather than quantity* 양보다 질을 목표로 하다 / *We only sell things of the best ~.* 우리 가게에서는 극상품만을 판다. **3** kinds of worth; excellence. 양질(良質); 우수성. ¶ *goods of ~* 고급품 / *They proclaimed the ~ of their products.* 그들은 그들 제품의 우수성을 내세웠다 **4** Ⓤ ⓐ 《*arch.*》 high social rank. 높은 신분. ¶ *a lady of ~* 귀부인. ⓑ 《*the ~*》 people of high rank or good birth. 상류 사회의 사람들. [→qualify]

qualm [kwɑːm, kwɔːm] *n.* ⒸⓊ **1** a sudden feeling of faintness or sickness. 현기증; 구역질. ¶ *qualms of seasickness* 뱃멀미. **2** uneasiness or disturbance of conscience. (양심의) 가책. ¶ *He had no qualms about cheating the tax inspector.* 그는 세무 조사원을 속여 먹는 걸 예사로 안다. **3** a misgiving; a doubt; uneasiness. 불안; 걱정; 의구심. [L.]

quan·da·ry [kwándəri / kwɔ́n-] *n.* Ⓒ (*pl.* **-ries**) a state of uncertainty, difficulty or being puzzled; a dilemma. 곤혹; 곤경; 당혹. [? L. *quando* when]
be in a* (*great*) *quandary, be at one's wit's end; be very puzzled what to do. (완전히) 진퇴 양난에 빠져 있다.

quan·ta [kwántə / kwɔ́n-] *n.* pl. of **quantum.**

quan·ti·ta·tive [kwántətèitiv / kwɔ́ntə-] *adj.* **1** of or concerned with quantity. 분량상의; 양에 관한; 정량(定量)의(opp. qualitative). ¶ *in a ~ respect* 양적(量的)인 면에 있어서는; 양적으로는. **2** that can be measured. 분량상으로; 양적으로. [L. quantity]

quantitative analysis [∸∸∸∸ ∸∸∸∸] *n.* 《chem.》 a chemical analysis of a substance to determine the amounts of its elements. 정량 분석(定量分析)(cf. *qualitative analysis*).

:quan·ti·ty [kwántəti / kwɔ́n-] *n.* (*pl.* **-ties**) **1** ⓊⒸ an amount; the property of a thing which can be measured. 양(量)(opp. quality). ¶ *a large ~ of milk* 대량의 우유 / *prefer ~ to quality* 질보다 양. **2** 《often *pl.*》 a large amount; a large number. 다량; 다수. ¶ *We've had quantities of rain this fall.* 올 가을엔 비가 많았다 / *He collected a ~* 〔*quantities*〕 *of old pictures.* 그는 다수의 고화(古畫)를 수집했다 / *flowers in* (*large*) *quantities* 많은 꽃. **3** an amount, sum, or number. 수(량); 액. ¶ *What ~ can be supplied?* 얼마나 주려나 / *a certain ~ of material* 〔*books*〕 일정량의 재료〔서적〕. **4** Ⓤ 《mus.》 the length of a note or a sound. 음표의 길이; 음량. **5** Ⓒ 《math.》 something that can be measured. 수량으로 표시되는 것. ¶ *a known ~* 기지수(既知數). [L. *quantus* how much]
a negligible quantity, an unimportant person or thing. 하찮은 사람〔물건〕.

quan·tum [kwántəm / kwɔ́n-] *n.* Ⓒ (*pl.* **-ta**) **1** an amount; a quantity; a share. 액(額); 양; 몫. ¶ *Each man received his proper ~.* 각자 응분의 몫을 받았다. **2** 《phys.》 an elemental unit of energy. 양자(量子). ¶ *~ mechanics* 양자 역학. [↑]
have one's quantum of, have a sufficient quantity of; do sufficiently. …을 충분히 얻다〔행하다〕.

quantum suf·fi·cit [kwántəm sʌ́fisit / kwɔ́n-] *adv.* 《L.》 as much as suffices. 충분히.

quantum theory [∸∸ ∸∸∸] *n.* 《phys.》 양자론(量子論).

quar·an·tine [kwɔ́:rəntì:n, kwár-] *n.* Ⓤ **1** the time during which incoming ships are kept in order to be examined for disease. 검역 정선(檢疫停船) 기간. **2** the act of keeping a person who has a contagious disease away from others; the state of being kept away. 격리; 고립. ¶ *be in ~* 격리되어 있다. **3** Ⓒ a place where people or animals are kept away from others. 격리소; 격리 병원. ── *vt.* (P6) keep (a person or an animal) away from others. …을 격리하다. [L. *quadraginta* forty days]

:quar·rel [kwɔ́:rəl, kwár-] *n.* Ⓒ **1** an angry argument; a fight with words. 언쟁; 말다툼; 입씨름. ¶ *have a ~ with someone* 아무와 언쟁하다 / *take up another's ~* 남의 싸움을 맡고 나서다 / *fasten* 〔*fix*〕 *a ~ on* 〔*upon*〕 *someone = seek* 〔*pick*〕 *a ~ with someone* 아무에게 싸움걸다 / *make up one's* 〔*a*〕 *~* 화해하다. **2** a cause of dispute; a complaint. 싸움〔언쟁〕의 원인; 불평; 불만. ¶ *fight in a good ~* 이유가 정당한〔정의의〕 싸움을 하다 / *find ~ in a straw* 사소한 일에도 트집을 잡다 / *I have no ~ against* 〔*with*〕 *you.* 나는 너에게 아무런 불만이 없다. **3** the lack of harmony or agreement; the act of breaking friendly relations. 불화; 반목.
── *vi.* (**-reled, -rel·ing** or 《Brit.》 **-relled, -rel·ling**) **1** (P1,3) ⓐ have a quarrel; fight with words; dispute. 싸우다; 다투다; 언쟁하다. ¶ *~ with someone about* 〔*for, over*〕 *something* 어떤 일로 아무와 싸우다 / *They always ~ over trifles.* 그들은 늘 사소한 일로 다툰다. ⓑ stop being friend. 티격나다; 불화하게 되다. **2** (P3) 《*with*》 find fault; complain. 나무라다; 트집을 잡다; 불평을 하다. ¶ 《*prov.*》 *A bad workman quarrels with his tools.* 서투른 목수가 연장을 나무란다 / *She quarrels with everything I do.* 그녀는 내게 사사건건 트집이다 / *One can't ~ with destiny.* 사람은 운명을 감수(甘受)하지 않을 수 없다. [L. *queror* complain]
quarrel with one's bread and butter, give up or leave one's employment. 생업(生業)을 버리다.

quar·rel·some [kwɔ́:rəlsəm, kwár-] *adj.* fond of disputing or fighting. 싸우기〔언쟁하기〕 좋아하는; 툭하면 다투는.

quar·ry[1] [kwɔ́:ri, kwári] *n.* Ⓒ (*pl.* **-ries**) **1** a place where stone is obtained by cutting or blasting. 채석장. **2** 《*fig.*》 some source from which information can be gotten. (지식·자료 등의) 원천; 출처; (인용 등의) 전거. ¶ *a ~ of information* 지식의 원천. ── *vt., vi.* (P6,7,13;1,3) **1** get (stone) from the earth. (채석장 따위에서) (돌)을 잘라 내다〔떠내다〕. **2** 《*fig.*》 dig out information from (books, records, etc.). (지식·정보 따위)를 찾다; 캐내다. ¶ *~ in the old manuscript* 고문서 중에서 자료를 발굴하다. [→quadrate]

quar·ry[2] [kwɔ́:ri, kwári] *n.* Ⓒ (*pl.* **-ries**) **1** an animal that is hunted; game. 사냥감. ¶ *The ~ was in sight.* 사냥감이 나타났다. **2** 《*fig.*》 an object which is eagerly searched for or followed. 추구물(追求物). [L. *corium* skin]

·quart [kwɔ:rt] *n.* Ⓒ **1** a measure for liquids, equal to one fourth of a gallon. 쿼트 《액량의 단위, 1/4 갤런》. **2** a measure for dry things, equal to one eighth of a peck or 67.201 cubic inches. 건량(乾量)의 단위《1/8 peck》. **3** a container holding a quart. 1 쿼트들이의 그릇. [L. *quartus* fourth]

try to put a quart into a pint pot, try to do something impossible. 불가능한 일을 하려들다.

:quar·ter [kwɔ́ːrtər] *n.* Ⓒ **1** one of four equal parts; one fourth part. 4분의 1 ¶ *a ~ of a mile,* 1/4 마일 / *a mile and three quarters,* 1 3/4 마일 / *three less a ~,* 2 3/4 / *divide an apple into quarters* 사과를 네 쪽으로 가르다 / *The bottle is only a ~ full.* 병은 4분의 1밖에 차지 않았다. **2** a fourth of a year or a school year; a three month period for the payment of rent, etc. 1년의 4분의 1; (4학기제의) 1학기; (4분기 지불의) 1기(期). ¶ *the first ~* 제1·4분기(分期) / *pay one's rent at the end of each ~* 매분기의 마지막 날에 집세를 내다 / *the rent for this ~* 이번 분기의 집세 / *The first ~ begins in September.* 첫 학기는 9월에 시작한다. **3** a fourth of an hour; 15 minutes. 1시간의 1/4; 15분. ¶ *at a ~ past*〔*to*〕*two.* 2시 15분〔15분 전〕에. **4** 《U.S. or Can.》 a fourth of a dollar; 25 cents; a silver coin having this value. 25센트; 25센트 은화. **5** one of four parts of an animal, including one leg. 네발 짐승의 4반분(半分)《다리 하나를 포함함》. **6** any one of four main directions of the compass. (동서 남북의) 한 방위. ¶ *From which ~ is the wind blowing?* 어느 방위에서 바람이 불어 오느냐 / *They arrived from every ~*〔*all quarters.*〕. 그들은 사방 팔방으로부터 왔다. **7** 《often *pl.*》 a region; a district; a particular section of a city or town. 지방; 지역; 구역; 지구; …가(街). ¶ *the Jewish ~* 유태인가〔지구〕 / *the residental ~* 주거〔주택〕지역 / *the business quarters* 상업 지구 / *from all quarters* 사방에서. **8** a person or persons serving as a source of information. (정보 등의) 출처; 소식통. ¶ *from a reliable ~* 믿을 만한 소식통에서 / *The news came in from several quarters.* 그 뉴스는 여러 방면에서〔소식통을 통해서〕 들어왔다. **9** 《often *pl.*》 a place, house or room to stay in or lodge at; lodgings. 숙소; 거처; 주거; (군대의) 병영(兵營). ¶ *the servants' quarters* 하인 방 / *excellent quarters at a hotel* 호텔의 특실 / *take up one's quarters* (*at, in, with*) …에 숙소를 잡다. **10** Ⓤ mercy granted to an enemy; permission to live. (투항자 등에 베푸는) 관용; 용서; 구명(救命). ¶ *ask for*〔*cry*〕 *~* (포로 등이) 구명을 호소하다 / *give ~ to someone* 아무의 목숨을 살려 주다 / *receive ~* 용서 받다; 구명되다 / *Give no ~* (*to him*). 가차없이 처치해라. **11** 《astron.》 a fourth of the moon's monthly revolution around the earth. (달이 차고 기우는 주기의) 4분의 1; 현(弦). ¶ *the first*〔*last*〕 *~* 상현(上弦)〔하현〕. **12** 《naut.》 the back part of a ship's side; the post or position appointed to a crew on a ship. (선박의) 선미측(船尾側); (함선 내의) 부서. ¶ *on the ~* 선미에서 / *be at quarters* (자기) 부서에 자리잡다〔위치하다〕. **13** 《her.》 one of four parts into which a shield is divided by lines. (방패의) 4분의 1.

a bad quarter of an hour, a short, unpleasant experience. (짧으나) 불쾌한 한때.

at close quarters, near and in the small space. 바짝 접근하여.

beat to quarters, 《naut.》 summon the crew to appointed stations. 승무원을 부서에 배치하다.

not a quarter, not nearly; nothing like. 조금도 …않다. ¶ *It is not a ~ as good as it should be.* 그건 도무지 돼먹지 않았다《본래의 바람직한 상태와는 거리가 멀다》.

— *vt.* **1** (P6) divide (something) into four equal parts. …을 4(등)분하다. ¶ *~ a cake* 케이크를 4등분하다 / *The traitor was condemned to be quartered.* 역적은 사지(四肢)를 찢어 죽이는 형이 선고됐다. **2** (P6,7) provide lodgings for (soldiers); place (troops) in lodgings. (병사)를 숙영(宿營)시키다. ¶ *Soldiers were quartered in the houses on the hill.* 병사들은 언덕에 있는 집들에 숙영되었다 / *~ oneself on*〔*with*〕 …에 숙소를 잡다; …와 동숙하다. **3** (of hounds) range (the ground) in every direction. (사냥개가) 사냥감을 찾아 자귀를 짚으며 이리저리 돌아다니다. **4** (P6,7) 《naut.》 assign to a quarter for service on a battle ship. (전함에서) …을 부서에 배치하다.

— *vi.* (P1) 《*at, with*》 (of soldiers) lodge; stay. 숙영하다. [L. *quartarius* fourth part]

quarter day [∠-∠] *n.* one of the four days of the year on which quarterly payments are due. 사계(四季) 지불일.

quar·ter·deck [kwɔ́ːrtərdèk] *n.* **1** Ⓒ the part of the upper deck of a ship restricted to officers. 후갑판. **2** 《*the ~, collectively*》 the officers of a ship. 고급 선원.

quar·ter·ly [kwɔ́ːrtərli] *adj.* occurring four times a year. 연(年) 4회의. ¶ *a ~ meeting* 한 해 네 번의 집회 / *a ~ issue* 계간(季刊). — *adv.* once every three months. 연 4회로. ¶ *The rent is paid ~.* 집세는 한 해 네 번 낸다. — *n.* Ⓒ (*pl.* **-lies**) a magazine issued every three months. 계간지(誌); 연(年) 4회 간행물.

quar·ter·mas·ter [kwɔ́ːtərmæ̀stər, -mɑ̀ːs-] *n.* Ⓒ **1** 《*naut.*》 an officer on a ship having charge of steering, signals, etc. 조타수(操舵手). **2** 《army》 an officer in charge of supplies for the soldiers. 병참 장교. 參考 Q.M.으로 생략함.

quar·ter·staff [kwɔ́ːrtərstæ̀f, -stɑ̀ːf] *n.* Ⓒ (*pl.* **-staves**) a strong wooden stick 6 to 8 feet long which was formerly used as a weapon in fighting and in country sport. 옛날 농민이 무기나 경기용에 쓰던 장대.

quar·ter·staves [kwɔ́ːrtərstèivz] *n.* pl. of **quarterstaff.**

quar·tet, 《Brit.》 **-tette** [kwɔːrtét] *n.* Ⓒ **1** 《mus.》 a group of four musicians; a piece of music to be performed by such a group. 4중창〔중주〕단; 4중주〔중창〕곡. **2** anything consisting of four parts; a group of four persons or things. 4인조; 넷 한 짝; 네 개 한 벌이 되는 것. [→quarter]

quar·to [kwɔ́ːrtou] *n.* (*pl.* **-tos**) ⒸⓊ a book size, usu. about 9 by 12 inches; Ⓒ a book of this size. 4절판(의 책). 參考 4to 또는 4°로 생략함. [↑]

***quartz** [kwɔːrts] *n.* Ⓤ a hard, common mineral. 석영(石英). [G. *qarz*]

quash [kwɑʃ/kwɔʃ] *vt.* (P6) **1** 《*colloq.*》 put down; crush; subdue. …을 분쇄하다; 진압하다. ¶ ~ *a rebellion* 반란을 진압하다 / ~ *a row at a meeting* 모임에서 언쟁을 가라앉히다. **2** 《law》 bring to nothing; reject as invalid. …을 무효로 하다; 파기하다. ¶ *The judge quashed the indictment against the statesman.* 판사는 그 정치가에 대한 기소를 기각했다. [L. *quatio* shake]

qua·si [kwéisai, -zai, kwɑ́ːsi, -zi] *adv., adj.* in a sense; almost. 어떤 의미에서(의); 거의; 준(準)…. [L.]

Q

quat·rain [kwɑ́trein/kwɔ́t-] *n.* Ⓒ a stanza of four lines. 사행시(四行詩). [L. *quattuor* four]

quat·re·foil [kǽtərfɔ̀il, kǽtrə-] *n.* Ⓒ **1** a leaf or flower with four leaflets or petals. (클로버 등의) 네 잎; 사판화(四瓣花). **2** 《archit.》 an ornament in this shape. 네 잎〔꽃잎〕 장식. [F. *quatrefeuille*]

qua·ver [kwéivər] *vi., vt.* **1** (P1) (of a voice) shake; tremble. (목소리가) 떨리다. **2** (P6) speak or sing in a trembling voice. 떨리는 소리로 말〔노래〕하다. — *n.* Ⓒ **1** a quivering sound. 떨리는 음성. **2** 《Brit. mus.》 an eighth note. 8분 음표. [E. (→quake)]

quay [kiː] *n.* Ⓒ a landing place for ships to load and unload; a wharf. 부두; 선창. [F. *quai*]

quea·sy [kwíːzi] *adj.* (**-si·er, -si·est**) **1** sick at the stomach. (속이) 메슥거리는; 구역질나는. **2** hard to please; uncomfortable. (성미가) 까다로운; 불쾌한. [? O.N. *kveis* a ulcer]

⁝**queen** [kwiːn] *n.* Ⓒ **1** the wife of a king. 왕비. ¶ ~ *mother* 황태후. **2** a woman ruler. 여왕. **3** a goddess. 여신. **4** a girl or woman who is very important, beautiful, etc. 여왕 같은 여자. ¶ *the* ~ *of society* 사교계의 여왕 / *a* ~ *of beauty* 미의 여왕 / *the rose,* ~ *of flowers* 꽃의 여왕, 장미. **5** the only female in a group of bees, ants, etc., that lays eggs. 여왕벌〔개미〕. **6** a playing card bearing a picture of a queen. 퀸《카드 놀이에서》. ¶ *the* ~ *of hearts* 하트의 퀸; 미인. — *vt.* (P6) reign over (a country) as queen. …에 여왕으로서 군림하다. 參考 queen it (over)처럼 별 뜻이 없는 it을 첨가해서 쓰는 경우가 많음. [E.; A.S. *cwen*]

queen·ly [kwíːnli] *adj.* (**-li·er, -li·est**) like or proper to a queen. 여왕 같은; 여왕다운. ¶ *a* ~ *mother* 여왕 같은 어머니. — *adv.* in a queenly manner. 여왕답게.

Queen's Counsel [⌐⌐] *n.* 《Brit.》 ⇨ King's Counsel.

Queen's English [⌐⌐−] the *n.* ⇨ King's English.

⁝**queer** [kwiər] *adj.* **1** different from what is normal in some way; strange; odd; peculiar. 별난; 기묘한; 괴상한. ¶ *a* ~ *fish* 괴짜 / *a* ~ *sort of fellow* 괴상한 놈 / *speak a* ~ *language* 이상한 말을 쓰다. **2** not well; slightly ill; giddy. 기분이 좋지 않은; 현기증 나는. ¶ *a feel a little* ~ 기분이 별로 안 좋다. **3** ⓐ probably bad; doubtful. 수상한; 의심스러운. ¶ *a* ~ *sort of story* 미덥지 못한 이야기 / *a* ~ *transaction* 수상한 거래. ⓑ slightly mad. 머리가 좀 돈. ¶ *become* 〔*go*〕 ~ 머리가 좀 이상해지다 / ~ *in the head* 제정신이 아닌. **4** not genuine; counterfeit. 가짜의. ¶ ~ *money* 위폐.

in Queer Street, (of a business man, etc.) in money difficulties. (사업가 등이) 돈에 쪼들려.

— *vt.* (P6) 《*sl.*》 cause to wrong; spoil. …을 망쳐 놓다. ¶ *Bad weather queered our plan.* 나쁜 날씨로 계획이 엉망이 됐다. [? G. *quer* crosswise]

queer someone's pitch, 《Brit.》 spoil his chances of success (by doubtful means). (수를 써서) …의 성공할 기회를 망쳐 놓다.

queer·ly [kwíərli] *adv.* in a queer manner. 기묘하게.

queer·ness [kwíərnis] *n.* Ⓤ **1** the state of being queer; singularity; discomfort. 기묘; 불쾌. **2** something strange or odd. 기묘한〔불쾌한〕 것.

quell [kwel] *vt.* (P6) 《*lit.*》 put down, cause to die down, crush (a rebellion, fears, etc.). …을 억누르다; 가라앉히다; 소멸시키다; 분쇄〔진압〕하다. [E.]

***quench** [kwentʃ] *vt.* (P6) **1** put out (a fire, light, one's desire). …을 끄다. ¶ ~ *a fire with water* 물로 불을 끄다. **2** put an end to (something); cease. …을 없어지게 하다; 멎게 하다. ¶ ~ *thirst* 갈증을 풀다. **3** cool suddenly. …을 급히 냉각하다. ¶ ~ *steel* 강철을 급랭하다. [E.]

quer·u·lous [kwérjələs] *adj.* complaining; fretful. 투덜거리는; 짜증내는. [→quarrel[1]]

que·ry [kwíəri] *n.* Ⓒ (*pl.* **-ries**) **1** a question, esp. containing a doubt or objection. (의혹을 품은) 질문. ¶ *raise a* ~ 질문〔질의〕하다. **2** a doubt. 의문. **3** the question mark. 물음표(?). — *vt.* (**-ried**) **1** (P12) 《*about*》 ask about; express doubt about (something). …에게 (…인지 어떤지) 묻다; …을 의아해하다. ¶ *I* ~ *whether his word can be relied upon.* 그의 말을 믿어도 되는지 의심스럽다 / *I* ~ *very much whether* 〔*if*〕 *it is wise to act so hastily.* 그렇게 성급하

게 구는 게 현명한지 어떤지 매우 의심스럽다. **2** (P6) place the sign (?) after. …에 물음표를 찍다. [L. *quaere* inquire]

*__quest__ [kwest] *n.* Ⓒ **1** a search; a hunt. 탐색; 탐구. ¶ *the ~ of the Holy Grail* 성배(聖杯)의 탐색. **2** an adventurous expedition made by knights. (중세 기사의) 원정. **3** object sought for. 탐구의 목적물.

crowner's quest, 《*sl.*》 a coroners inquest. 검시(檢屍).

in quest of, trying to find. …을 찾아. ¶ *He left home in ~ of adventure.* 그는 모험을 찾아 집을 떠났다.

— *vi.* (P2A,3) (of a dog, etc.) make a search. (사냥개 등이 짐승의) 자귀를 짚다; 찾다. ¶ *~ (about) for game* 사냥감의 발자국을 짚어 찾아다니다. [↑]

:**ques·tion** [kwéstʃən] *n.* Ⓒ **1** the act of asking; an inquiry; something asked. 질문; 질의. ¶ *May I ask a ~ ?* 한가지 질문해도 괜찮겠습니까 / *ask (someone) a ~* (…에게) 질문하다 / *Please answer my ~.* 내 질문에 대답해 주시오. **2** something doubtful or uncertain; a doubt. 의심; 의문; 미심쩍은 일. ¶ *raise a ~ about the matter* 그 문제에 대하여 질문을 하다 / *His honesty is beyond ~.* 그가 정직하다는 것은 의심할 여지가 없다. **3** a matter to be discussed or inquired into; a problem. 문제; 논점; 현안(懸案). ¶ *a ~ of housing* 주택 문제 / *What is the ~ you have raised ?* 네가 제기한 문제가 뭐지 / *It is a ~ of acting at once or not at all.* 당장 실행하느냐 아니면 아예 마느냐의 문제다 / *The ~ is whether we can arrive in time.* 우리가 제시간에 도착하느냐 못 하느냐가 문제다 / *It is only a ~ of time.* 그건 단지 시간의 문제다. **4** a sentence in the interrogative form. 의문문. ¶ *"Who did this ?" is a ~.* "누가 했느냐"는 의문문이다.

beside the question, off the subject. 문제[주제]를 벗어난; 논외의.

beyond question, undoubtedly; certainly. 의심할 여지 없이; 확실히; 물론.

call in question, raise objection to. …에 이의(異議)를 제기하다.

in question, in dispute; in doubt. 문제가 되고 있는; 문제의.

make no question of, have no doubts in one's mind about (something). …을 의심하지 않다; 문제 삼지 않다.

out of the question, not to be considered; impossible. 생각할 수 없는; 불가능한.

put the question, take vote; decide the matter by voting. …을 표결하다.

— *vt.* **1** (P6) 《*about, on*》 ask question of; put question to; interrogate. …에게 묻다; 심문하다. ¶ *~ a prisoner* 포로를 심문하다. **2** (P6,12) call in question; doubt. 문제시하다; 의문시하다; 의심하다. ¶ *~ whether he will succeed* 그가 성공할지 어떨지 의문시하다 / *~ someone's honesty* 아무의 성실성을 의심하다. **3** (P6) study (stars, books, etc.) in order to get information. …을 탐구[연구]하다. ¶ *~ the stars [the Scriptures]* 별을[성서를] 연구하다. — *vi.* (P1) ask question. 질문하다. [*quest*]

ques·tion·a·ble [kwéstʃənəbəl] *adj.* doubtful; uncertain. 의심스러운; 애매한. ¶ *a ~ statement* 의심스러운 진술 / *~ conduct* 수상한 행위.

question mark [ˊ–ˋ] *n.* a mark (?) placed at the end of a sentence asking a question. 의문부; 물음표.

ques·tion·naire [kwèstʃənɛ́ər] *n.* Ⓒ a list of questions with spaces to write answers in. 질문서; 앙케트. [F.]

queue [kju(:)] *n.* Ⓒ **1** a braid of hair hanging down the back. 땋아 늘인 머리; 변발(辮髮). **2** a line of persons waiting their turn. 차례를 기다리는 사람[차량]의 행렬; 줄. ¶ *form a ~* 줄을 서다 / *in a ~* 줄을 지어 / *a bus ~* 버스를 기다리는 사람들의 줄. — *vi., vt.* (P3; P6) **1** 《*up*》 form a line; join or stand in queue. 줄을 짓다. ¶ *Queue here.* 여기에 줄을 서시오 / *~ up for a movie* 영화 구경하려고 줄서다. **2** dress hair in queue. 머리를 땋아 늘이다[변발로 하다]. [L. *cauda* tail]

quib·ble [kwíbl] *n.* Ⓒ **1** the use of skillful but unfair words to avoid talking about the subject under discussion. 둔사(遁辭); 궤변; 핑계. ¶ *a mere ~* 순전한 핑계. **2** a witty joke; a pun. 익살; 신소리; 곁말. — *vi.* (P1) use a quibble. 익살부리다; 애매하게 말하다. [*quip*]

:**quick** [kwik] *adj.* **1** coming soon; immediate. 즉석의; 당장의. ¶ *a ~ answer* 즉답. **2** fast; rapid. 빠른; 날랜. ¶ *a ~ sports car* 빠른 스포츠 카 / *in ~ motion* 재빨리 / *A gallop is the quickest gait of a horse.* 갤럽은 말의 가장 빠른 보조다 / *Be ~ (about it)!* 빨리 해라; 서둘러라. **3** done in a short time. 단시간에 행해지는; 서두르는. ¶ *a ~ meal* 빠른 식사 / *a ~ note* 급히 쓴 메모 / *Quick at meat, ~ at work.* 식사가 빠른 사람은 일도 빠르다. **4** (of work, study, etc.) acting swiftly or rapidly. 민첩한; 일이 빠른. ¶ *~ writing* 속필 / *a ~ worker* 일이 빠른 사람. **5** easily excited. 성마른; 성미가 급한. ¶ *a ~ temper* 급한 성미 / *be ~ of temper* 걸핏하면 화내다. **6** (of the senses) keen and lively. 민감한. ¶ *a ~ sense of hearing* 예민한 청각 / *He is very ~ at smelling cookies.* 그는 쿠키 냄새에 아주 민감하다. **7** understanding or learning rapidly; clever. 이해가 빠른; 머리가 좋은. ¶ *He is a ~ learner.* 그는 이해가 빠른 사람이다 / *He is ~ at figures.* 그는 계산이 빠르다 / *Some children are very ~.* 어떤 아이는 아주 영리하다. **8** 《arch.》 living. 살아 있는. ¶ *go down ~ into hell* 살아서 지옥에 떨어지다.

— *n.* Ⓤ 《usu. *the ~*》 **1** a very tender part of the body, esp. the skin under the fingernail. 생살; (특히) 손톱 밑의 속살. **2** 《*the ~*》 living persons. 생자(生者). ¶ *the ~*

Q

and the dead 산 자와 죽은 자. **3** the most important part. 급소. **4** the center of feeling. (감정의) 중추. ¶ *He cut me to the* ~ *with unkind words.* 그는 매정한 말로 나의 마음을 아프게 했다.
— *adv.* in a quick manner; rapidly; soon. 즉시; 빨리; 신속히. ¶ *Come as* ~ *as you can.* 당장 오너라. [E.]

·**quick·en** [kwíkən] *vt.* (P6) **1** hasten; hurry; increase the speed of. …을 서두르게 하다; …을 빠르게 하다. ¶ *Quicken your step.* 빨리 걸어라. **2** bring (someone) to life; make (someone) live; arouse. …을 되살아나게 하다; …을 자극하다. ¶ ~ *the imagination* 상상의 날개를 펴다 / *The walk quickened our appetites.* 걸었더니 식욕이 났다.
— *vi.* (P1) become more alive or rapid. 기운이 나다; 활기 띠다; 빨라지다. ¶ *His anger quickened.* 성이 더 났다 / *His pace quickened.* 걸음이 빨라졌다.

quick-freeze [kwíkfrìːz] *vt.* (P6) (**-froze, -fro·zen**) freeze (food) rapidly in order to store it. (보존용 식품)을 급속 냉동시키다.

quick-froze [kwíkfròuz] *v.* p. of **quick-freeze.**

quick-fro·zen [kwíkfròuzən] *v.* pp. of **quick-freeze.**

quick·lime [kwíklàim] *n.* Ⓤ a white substance obtained by burning limestone and used for making mortar. 생석회.

:**quick·ly** [kwíkli] *adv.* in a quick manner. 빠르게; 신속히. ¶ *Can't you work more* ~? 더 빨리 일할 수 없겠니.

quick·ness [kwíknis] *n.* Ⓤ the state or quality of being quick. 기민(機敏); 신속; 성급.

quick·sand [kwíksæ̀nd] *n.* ⓊⒸ **1** a dangerous, deep mass of loose and wet sand which will not support a person's weight. 유사(流砂). **2** anything treacherous. 믿을〔방심할〕 수 없는 것.

quick·set [kwíksèt] *n.* Ⓒ a hedge formed of living plants, esp. of hawthorn. 산울타리.

quick·sil·ver [kwíksìlvər] *n.* Ⓤ mercury. 수은.

quick·step [kwíkstèp] *n.* Ⓒ the rapid step used in marching; music in a march rhythm of quick time. 속보; 빠른 행진곡.

quick-tem·pered [kwíktémpərd] *adj.* quick to lose one's temper; short-tempered; easily angered. 성마른; 성미가 급한; 걸핏하면 화내는.

quick time [∠∠] *n.* 《mil.》 an ordinary rate of marching, 120 paces a minute. 속보(速步).

quick-wit·ted [kwíkwítid] *adj.* alert or clever in action, speech, or mind. 기지에 찬; 재치 있는; 약삭빠른. ¶ *a* ~ *reply* 재치 있는 대답.

quid [kwid] *n.* Ⓒ a piece of hard, compressed tobacco leaf used for chewing. (1회분의) 씹는 담배. [→cud]

quid pro quo [kwíd prou kwóu] *n.* 《L.》 a thing given as compensation. 대상물(代償物). [L.=something for something]

qui·es·cence [kwaiésns] *n.* Ⓤ the state of being quiescent. 정지(靜止); 침묵. [↓]

qui·es·cent [kwaiésnt] *adj.* motionless; calm; still. 정지한; 고요한.

:**qui·et** [kwáiət] *adj.* **1** still; moving very little. 고요한; 움직이지 않는. ¶ *The sea was* ~. 바다는 고요했다 / *I want to be* ~ *for a few days after my journey.* 여행후에는 조용히 며칠 쉬고 싶다 / *Keep* ~ *for a time after dinner.* 식후에는 잠시 움직이지 마라. **2** with no or little noise; free from disturbance; silent. 소음이 없는〔적은〕; 조용한. ¶ *a* ~ *machine* 소음이 거의 없는 기계 / *Everybody, be* ~ *for a moment.* 여러분, 잠시 조용해 주세오 / *a* ~ *street* 〔*night*〕 조용한 거리〔밤〕. **3** making no disturbance or trouble; gentle; mild. 말썽을 부리지 않는; 얌전한. ¶ *She is a* ~ *girl at school.* 그녀는 학교에서 얌전한 아이이다 / *nice* ~ *people* 얌전한 사람들 / *a* ~ *horse* 순한 말. **4** with the usual or natural condition not disturbed by sudden happenings; peaceful; calm. 평온한; 평화로운. ¶ *a* ~ *place in the country* 시골의 조용한 곳 / *a* ~ *dinner party* 몇 사람만의 조용한 비공식 만찬회 / *a* ~ *life in the country* 시골에서의 평화로운〔단조로운〕 생활. **5** not showy or bright. 수수한; 점잖은(opp. loud). ¶ *Beige is a* ~ *color.* 베이지는 수수한 색깔이다 / *a* ~ *(style of) dress* 수수한 옷차림. **6** secret; private. 비밀의; 은밀한. ¶ *I kept it* ~. 나는 그것을 겉으로 드러내지 않았다 / *a* ~ *reproach* 에둘러〔빗대어〕하는 비난. **7** (of business) not busy or active. (장사가) 잘 안 되는; 한산한. ¶ *a* ~ *market* 거래가 한산한 시장.
— *n.* Ⓤ the state of being quiet; stillness; calmness; peace. 정지; 고요; 평온; 평화.
— *vt.* (P6) make (someone or something) quiet. …을 가라앉히다; 진정시키다; 달래다. ¶ *She quieted the crying baby.* 그녀는 우는 아기를 달랬다 / *The evening light has a quieting effect on us.* 저녁 불빛은 우리들 마음을 차분히 가라앉힌다 / *He quieted their fears.* 그는 그들을 안심시켰다.
— *vi.* (P2A) become quiet; die down. 조용해지다; 가라앉다. [L. *quies* quiet]

qui·et·ly [kwáiətli] *adv.* in a quiet manner; silently; peacefully; in a modest way. 조용히; 평온하게; 수수하게.

qui·et·ness [kwáiətnis] *n.* Ⓤ the state of being quiet; stillness; peacefulness. 고요; 평온.

qui·e·tude [kwáiət*j*ùːd] *n.* Ⓤ the state of being quiet; stillness; calmness; repose. 고요; 평온; 휴식.

qui·e·tus [kwaiíːtəs] *n.* Ⓒ **1** the final

release of someone from debt, duty, or life. 인생의 총결산; 죽음. **2** a finishing stroke. 최후의 일격; 결정타.
get one's quietus, die. 죽다.
give someone his quietus, kill. …을 죽이다.

quill [kwil] *n.* Ⓒ **1** a long, strong feather. 큰 깃축. **2** a pen made from such a feather. 깃촉펜. ¶ *a ~ driver* (하급) 서기; 문필가《경멸적으로》. [M.E.; ? O.F. *quille*]

quilt [kwilt] *n.* Ⓒ a soft bedcover made of two pieces of cloth with a layer of cotton or wool between and stitched in an ornamental pattern. 누비 이불; 누비 침대 커버. — *vt.* (P6) **1** make (a quilt); stitch (a piece of cloth, etc.) in an ornamental pattern or design. (누비 이불)을 만들다; …에 수를 놓다. **2** sew up (coin, letters, etc.) between two layers of garment, etc. (화폐, 글자 등)을 옷 (따위) 사이에 꿰매 넣다. [L. *culcita* cushion]

quilt·ing [kwíltiŋ] *n.* Ⓤ **1** something made by quilting. 누비 자수 제품. **2** material for making quilts. 누비 이불 재료.

quince [kwins] *n.* Ⓒ a hard, yellow, pear-like fruit; its tree. 마르멜로(나무). [L. *Cydonia* Place]

qui·nine [kwáinain / kwiní:n], **quin·i·a** [kwíniə] *n.* Ⓤ a medicine used for preventing or curing malaria. 퀴닌; 키니네; 금계랍. [Peru. *kina* bark]

quin·sy [kwínzi] *n.* Ⓤ a disease of the throat with an abscess in the tonsils. 편도선염(炎). [Gk. *kunagkhē*]

quin·tal [kwíntl] *n.* Ⓒ a unit of weight; a hundredweight. 퀸틀《무게의 단위; 미국에서는 100kg》. [Arab.]

quin·tes·sence [kwintésns] *n.* Ⓤ **1** the purest form of something. 정수(精髓); 진수. **2** the most typical example of something. 전형(典型). [L. *quinta essentia* fifth substance (underlying the four elements)]

quin·tet, -tette [kwintét] *n.* Ⓒ **1** a group of five musicians. 5중주〔중창〕단. **2** a piece of music for this group. 5중주〔중창〕곡. **3** a group of five persons or things. 5인조; 5개 한 벌. [↑]

quin·tu·ple [kwint*j*ú(:)pl] *adj.* **1** fivefold; consisting of five parts. 다섯 겹의; 5개 부분으로 되는. **2** five times as great. 5배의. — *vi., vt.* (P1; 6) become or make five times as great. 5배로 되다〔하다〕. — *n.* number, amount, etc. five times as great as another. 5배. [↑, →quadruple]

quip [kwip] *n.* Ⓒ **1** a witty or ironic saying. 경구; 명언; 빈정대는 말. **2** a quibble. 핑계. **3** something queer. 기묘한 것. — *vi.* (P1) (**quipped, quip·ping**) make a quip. 빈정거리다; 비꼬다. [L. *quippe* indeed]

quire[1] [kwáiə*r*] *n.* Ⓒ a set of 24 or 25 uniform sheets of paper. 한 첩(帖)《종이 24-25장》. [L. *quatuor* four]
in quires, unbound. 미제본(未製本)의.

quire[2] [kwáiə*r*] *n.* Ⓒ《*arch.*》a choir. 성가대. [→chorus]

quirk [kwə:*r*k] *n.* Ⓒ **1** a peculiar manner; a quick turn of mind. 기벽(奇癖); 괴벽; 변덕. **2** a clever or witty evasion of the truth in speaking. 궤변; 핑계; 발뺌. **3** a flourish in writing. (글씨, 그림의) 멋부려 꾸며 쓰기〔그리기〕. [O.N.]

quirt [kwə:*r*t] *n.* 《U.S.》a riding whip of twisted hide with a short handle. 엮어 꼰 가죽 말 채찍. [Sp.]

quis·ling [kwízliŋ] *n.* Ⓒ a traitor, esp. one who betrays his own country by helping an invading enemy. 매국노; 배반자. [Person]

:quit [kwit] *v.* (**quit·ted** or **quit, quit·ting**) *vt.* (P6) **1** 《U.S.》stop. …을 그만두다; 그치다. ¶ *Quit gambling.* 노름을 그만해라 / *Quit teasing me.* 사람 그만 좀 놀려라 / *~ work* 일을 집어치우다 / *~ smoking* 담배를 끊다. **2** leave; go away from (some place); give up. …을 저버리다; …와 헤어지다; …을 물러나다. ¶ *~ the army* 제대〔예편〕하다 / *~ school* 퇴학하다; 졸업하다 / *I have to ~ him.* 그와 헤어져야겠다 / *~ a house* 집을 떠나다 / *~ an office* 사임하다. **3** pay back; pay off (a debt). …에 대갚음하다; (빚)을 갚다. ¶ *~ love with hate* 사랑을 미움으로 갚다. **4** 《*arch.*》《*reflexively*》behave oneself. 처신하다. ¶ *Quit you like men.* 남자답게 굴어라.
— *vi.* (P1) **1** 《U.S. *colloq.*》stop doing something. 그만두다; 중지하다. ¶ *~ at noon* 정오에 중지하다. **2** go away; leave. 떠나다; 물러가다. ¶ *We have received notice to ~.* 우리는 나가라는 통지를 받았다. **3** give up one's job. 사직하다.
— *adj.* 《*of*》free; clear. 자유로운. ¶ *He was ~ of his debts.* 그는 빚을 청산했다 / *be ~ of a bad friend* 나쁜 친구와 손을 끊다. [→quiet]

quit·claim [kwítklèim] *n.* **1** Ⓤ the giving up of a claim or right (to land, etc.). (토지 등에 대한) 요구〔권리〕의 포기. **2** Ⓒ a written paper stating that somebody gives up a claim (to land, etc.). (토지 등에 대한) 권리 포기〔양도〕 증서. — *vt.* (P6) give up a claim to. …을 포기하다. [↑]

:quite [kwait] *adv.* **1** completely; entirely; absolutely. 완전히; 전혀; 절대적으로. ¶ *I'm ~ sure.* 나는 확신하고 있다 / *She is not ~ well.* 그녀는 아직 완쾌되지 않았다 / *I was ~ pleased with it.* 나는 그것으로 아주 기뻤다 / *I ~ agree with you.* 나는 너와 전적으로 동감이다. **2** actually; really. 사실상; 정말로. ¶ *It is ~ a picture.* 그거 정말 그림 같다 / *He is ~ an artist.* 그는 이제(제 몫을 하는) 한 사람의 예술가이다. **3** to a considerable degree; rather. 상당히; 꽤. ¶ *~ a pretty girl* 꽤 아름다운 소녀 / *It's ~ cold.* 날씨가 꽤 춥다 / *You are getting ~ a big boy now.* 이제 (실업계의) 거물이 다 돼 가는군요 / *Their new house is ~ nice.* 그들의 새 집은

상당히 좋다. **4** 《Brit.》 《as *an answer* to a question》 true; yes. (대답에서) 예, 그럼은요. [→quiet]

quite a few, many; a lot. 상당수의; 꽤 많은.

quits [kwits] *adj.* even or on equal terms by having given back or paid back something. 대차(貸借) 없는; 피장파장인. ¶ *If you pay me another ten dollars, we shall be* ~. 나에게 10달러 더 주면 우린 셈이 끝난다. [→quit]

call* 〔*cry*〕 *quits, agree to settle all differences, not to go on quarreling. 비긴 것으로 하다; 무승부로 하다.

quit·tance [kwítəns] *n.* **1** Ⓤ a discharge from a debt or an obligation; a document certifying this; Ⓒ a receipt. 면제; 사면; 영수증. **2** Ⓤ a repayment; a return. 변제; 보답. [↑]

·**quiv·er**[1] [kwívər] *vi.* (P1,2A) tremble. 떨다. ¶ ~ *with fear* 무서워 떨다 / *The leaves quivered in the breeze.* 나뭇잎이 산들바람에 흔들렸다. — *vt.* (P6) cause to quiver. 떨게 하다. ¶ *The butterfly quivered its wings.* 나비가 날개를 떨었다. — *n.* Ⓒ a shudder; a trembling movement or sound. 떨림; 떪; 떨리는 소리. [Imit.]

quiv·er[2] [kwívər] *n.* Ⓒ a case for carrying arrows. 화살통; 전동(箭筒). [Teut.]

Qui·xo·te [kihóuti, kwíksət / kihɔ́:te], **Don** *n.* the absurdly chivalrous title character of a famous Spanish novel. 돈키호테《Cervantes 작의 주인공》. [*Don Q.,* a book written by Cervantes]

quix·ot·ic [kwiksátik / -sɔ́t-] *adj.* **1** like Don Quixote; absurdly chivalrous or romantic. 돈키호테 같은; 기사 행세를 하는. **2** not practical. 환상적인.

quiz [kwiz] *vt.* (**quizzed, quiz·zing**) (P6) **1** 《U.S.》 examine (someone) by questions; give (a pupil) an informal examination. …에게 질문하다; (선생이) 테스트하다. **2** make fun of (someone). …을 놀리다. **3** look at closely. 뚫어지게〔빤히〕 보다. — *n.* Ⓒ (*pl.* **quiz·zes**) **1** 《U.S.》 an informal test. (선생의) 간단한 테스트; 시험. **2** an absurd or puzzling question. 퀴즈. **3** a person who makes fun of others; a practial joke. 남을 놀리는 사람; 짓궂은 장난. [U.S.]

quiz·mas·ter [kwízmæ̀stər, -mɑ̀:s-] *n.* Ⓒ a person who asks questions in a game of a radio or television program. 퀴즈 프로그램의 사회자.

quiz·zi·cal [kwízikəl] *adj.* **1** odd; funny; comic. 별난; 우스운. **2** fond of teasing. 짓궂은. **3** looking closely. 빤히 보는. ¶ *She gave him a* ~ *glance.* 그녀는 그를 빤히 쳐다봤다.

quoin [kwɔin] *n.* Ⓒ **1** an exterior angle or corner of a building; one of the stones forming such an angle or corner; a cornerstone. (건물의) 외각(外角); (외각의) 귀돌. **2** a wedge-shaped stone or piece of metal. 쐐기《석제·철제》. [→coin]

quoit [kwait / kɔit] *n.* **1** Ⓒ a flat iron, rope, or rubber ring meant to be thrown at a peg. (고리던지기에 쓰는) 고리. **2** 《*pl.* used as *sing.*》 a kind of game played with such rings. 고리던지기 놀이(cf. *discus*). [? O.F. *coite*]

quon·dam [kwándəm / kwɔ́n-] *adj.* former. 원래의; 이전의. [L.=formerly]

quo·rum [kwɔ́:rəm] *n.* Ⓤ the number of members of a society or body, generally more than half, needed at a legal meeting. (회의 성립에 필요한) 정족수(定足數). [L. =of whom]

quo·ta [kwóutə] *n.* Ⓒ a share. 몫; 할당. ¶ *production quotas* 생산 기준량 / *the* ~ *system* 할당제 / ~ *restrictions* 할당제한. [L. *quotus* how many]

quot·a·ble [kwóutəbəl] *adj.* that can be quoted; worth quoting. 인용할 수 있는; 인용 가치가 있는. ¶ *His language was not* ~. 그의 말은 인용할 만한 것이 못 됐다. [→quote]

:**quo·ta·tion** [kwoutéiʃən] *n.* **1** Ⓤ the act of quoting. 인용. **2** Ⓒ words or a passage from a speech, a book, a poem, etc. of another. 인용문〔구, 어〕. ¶ *His speech was full of quotations from the Bible.* 그의 연설에는 성경에서의 인용문이 많았다 / *From which writer does this* ~ *come?* 이 인용문은 어느 작가의 것이냐. **3** Ⓒ 《comm.》 ⓐ the current market price. 시세; 시가. ¶ *the daily market* ~ 일일 시장 시세. ⓑ the calculated cost of a price of work. 견적가(見積價). ¶ *His* ~ *for painting my house was too high.* 우리집 페인트 칠에 대한 그의 견적가는 너무 비쌌다. **4** 《print.》 quadrat used for filling up blanks. 공목(空木). [→quote, -ation]

quotation marks [–⁻– ⁻] *n. pl.* a mark of punctuation (“ ” or ‘ ’) used at the beginning or end of a quotation. 인용부; 따옴표.

:**quote** [kwout] *vt.* (P6,13,14) **1** repeat a passage from (a book, a poem, etc.); repeat (words, etc.). (남의 말·글)을〔에서〕 인용하다. ¶ *He quoted* (*it*) *from the Bible.* 그는 그것을 성서에서 인용했다. **2** 《comm.》 state the current market price of (something). 시세를〔가격을〕 부르다. **3** tell some fact or event which serves as an example. (예증, 전거로) 예시(例示)하다. — *n.* Ⓒ 《*colloq.*》 **1** a quotation. 인용문. **2** 《usu. *pl.*》 quotation marks. 따옴표; 인용부. [L. *quoto* mark with numbers]

·**quoth** [kwouθ] *vt.* 《*arch., poet.*》 said. 말했다. 參考 제 1·3인칭 직설법 과거를 나타냄. ¶ *"Very true,"* ~ *I* 〔*he, she*〕. "옳습니다"라고 나〔그, 그녀〕는 말했다. [E.]

quo·tient [kwóuʃənt] *n.* Ⓒ 《math.》 the result obtained when one number is divided by another. 나눗셈의 답; 몫; 상(商). ¶ *If you divide 20 by 2, the* ~ *is 10.* 20을 2로 나누면 몫은 10이다. [L. *quot* how many]

r R

R, r [ɑːr] *n.* (*pl.* **R's, Rs, r's, rs** [ɑːrz]) Ⓒ **1** the eighteenth letter of the English alphabet. 영어 알파벳의 열여덟째 글자. **2** something shaped like the letter R. R 자 모양의 것.
the three R's, reading, writing and arithmetic as the basis of an elementary education. (기초 교육으로서의) 읽기·쓰기·셈.
rab·bi [rǽbai] *n.* (*pl.* **-bis** or **-bies**) a Jewish doctor of law. 랍비《유태의 율법사(律法師)》. [Heb. =master]
rab·bies [rǽbiːz] *n.* pl of **rabbi.**
:rab·bit [rǽbit] *n.* Ⓒ **1** a small, short-tailed animal with long ears and soft fur. 토끼(cf. *hare*). ¶ *run like a* ~ 쏜살같이 달아나다 / (*as*) *frightened as a* ~ 토끼처럼 잔뜩 겁을 먹고. **2** 《*fig.*》 a weak person. 나약한 사람. **3** 《Brit. *colloq.*》 a poor, weak, but eager player of a game. 못 하면서도 경기엔 열심인 선수. [E.]
rab·ble [rǽbəl] *n.* Ⓒ **1** a disorderly crowd; a mob. 오합지졸; 어중이떠중이. **2** 《*the* ~》 《*contempt.*》 the rude lower class. 하층민. [? Du.]
rab·id [rǽbid] *adj.* **1** furious; violent. 광포(狂暴)한; 사나운; 맹렬한. ¶ ~ *hate* 격렬한 증오 / *a* ~ *reformer* 과격한 혁신자. **2** affected with rabies; mad. 광견병에 걸린. ¶ *a* ~ *dog* 미친 개. ● **rab·id·ly** [-li] *adv.* [L. *rabio* rave]
ra·bies [réibiːz] *n.* Ⓤ a disease of dogs and other animals causing madness. 광견병; 공수병(恐水病). [↑]
rac·coon [rækúːn, rə-] *n.* Ⓒ a small grayish animal with a ringed tail, which lives in trees. 미국너구리. 參考 racoon이라고도 씀. [Amer-Ind.]
:race[1] [reis] *n.* Ⓒ **1** a contest of speed in running, skating, swimming, etc. 경주; 레이스. ¶ *a boat* 〔*horse, dog*〕 ~ / *run a* ~ 경주하다 / *He has won the* ~. 그는 경주에서 우승했다. **2** 《*the* ~*s*》 a series of horse-racing events on a regular course. 경마. ¶ *go to the races* 경마에 가다 / *play the races* 경마에 걸다. **3** a contest for a prize, an office, etc. (일반적으로) 경쟁. ¶ *a* ~ *for wealth* 치부(致富) 경쟁 / 《*fig.*》 *Two candidates entered the* ~ *for mayor.* 두 후보가 시장 선거에 입후보했다. **4** a swift current of water; a channel for a current of water. 급류; 수로(水路). **5** the course of life. 인생 행로. ¶ *His* ~ *is nearly run.* 그의 생애도 거의 끝나 간다.
— *vi.* **1** (P1,3) 《*with*》 run a race. 경주하다. ¶ *He raced along the road.* 그는 길을 따라 달렸다 / ~ *with a competitor.* **2** (P1,2A,3) go swiftly; hurry. 질주하다; 서두르다. **3** (P1) attend horse-racing regularly. 경마에 빠지다. — *vt.* (P6,13) **1** compete against (someone or something) in speed. …와 경주〔경쟁〕하다. ¶ *I'll* ~ *you to the corner* 〔*home*〕. 모퉁이〔집〕까지 경주하자. **2** cause (a horse, etc.) to compete in a race. …을 경주〔경쟁〕시키다. ¶ ~ *a yacht* 요트 경주를 하다. **3** cause (something or someone) to go swiftly. …을 서두르게 하다. ¶ ~ *the bill through the House* 서둘러 의안을 통과시키다 / *They raced the patient to the hospital.* 그들은 서둘러 환자를 병원에 실어 갔다. [N.]
race one's fortune away, lose one's fortune by horse-racing. 경마로 가산을 탕진하다.
:race[2] [reis] *n.* **1** ⓊⒸ a group of people having a common origin; a family. 일족; 자손; 가계; 혈통. ¶ *a man of noble* ~ 명문 출신. **2** a group of animals or plants belonging to the same kind. 종족; 품종; 종류. ¶ *the winged* 〔*feathered*〕 ~ 조류 / *the human* ~ 인류 / *the white* ~ 백인종. **3** ⓐ a group of people with a common language, religion, culture and other background factors. 인종; 민족. ¶ *the Teutonic* ~ 튜턴 민족. ⓑ a class or group of persons with distinguish quality in common. (어떤 특출한) 부류; 동아리; 패거리. ¶ *the* ~ *of artists* 예술가 부류 / *the* ~ *of gamblers* 도박 패거리. **4** a special or characteristic flavor. 특성; 풍미(風味). [It. *razza*]
ra·ceme [reisíːm, rə-] *n.* 《bot.》 an inflorescence with separate flowers attached by short equal and equidistant stalks along central stem. 총상 화서(總狀花序). [L. =bunch of grapes]
rac·er [réisər] *n.* Ⓒ **1** a person, horse, bicycle, car, etc. that takes part in races. 경주하는 사람; 경주에 쓰이는 것들《말, 자전거 등》. **2** a black American snake. 미국산의 검은 뱀. [→race[1]]
race·track [réistræ̀k] *n.* a field or course for races. 경주로; 경마장.
ra·cial [réiʃəl] *adj.* of or about a race. 민족의; 인종〔종족〕의. ¶ ~ *characteristics* 인종적 특성 / ~ *dislike* 〔*prejudice*〕 인종적 반감〔편견〕. [→race[2]]
ra·cial·ism [réiʃəlìzəm] *n.* Ⓤ ill feeling between different races; racial prejudice. 인종주의; 인종적 차별〔편견〕.
ra·cial·ly [réiʃəli] *adv.* in respect to a

R

race. 인종적으로; 인종상.

rac·ing [réisiŋ] *n.* **1** the act of running in races. 경주. ¶ *horses used for* ~ 경주마. **2** the act of attending horse- or motorcar-races, or of running horses or motorcars in races. 경주 경기《경마, 자동차 경주 등》. — *adj.* suitable for or used in races. 경주용의. ¶ *a* ~ *car* 〔*boat*〕/ ~ *colors* 기수(騎手)의 재킷과 모자의 빛깔《등록이 돼 있음》/ *a* ~ *man* 경마광(狂); 경마팬. [→race[1]]

rac·ism [réisizəm] *n.* Ⓤ the belief or doctrine that certain races are by nature superior or inferior to others; racial prejudice. 인종적 편견; 인종 차별. [→race[2]]

:rack[1] [ræk] *n.* Ⓒ **1** 《usu. in *compounds*》 a framework of bars, pegs, shelves, etc. on or in which articles may be hung, held, or displayed. (물건을 얹는) 선반; …걸이; (기차 등의) 그물 선반. ¶ *a hat* ~ 모자걸이 / *a clothes* ~ 옷걸이 / *a baggage* 〔*luggage*〕 ~ (기차 등의) 그물 선반. **2** a framework for holding hay and other food for cattle. (마소의) 건초〔꼴〕 시렁. ¶ *a hay* ~. **3** 《*the* ~》 an old instrument of torture; torment; strain. 고문대; 고문; 긴장. ¶ *put someone on* 〔*to*〕 *the* ~ …을 고문하다. **4** 《mech.》 a bar with teeth into which the teeth on a wheel fit. 래크《톱니바퀴의 톱니받이》.

⟨rack[1] 4⟩

be on the rack, be in a very painful situation. 몹시 고통스러워하다〔고민하다〕.

— *vt.* (P6) **1** torture; hurt very much; strain. …을 고문하다; 괴롭히다. ¶ *be racked with a cough* 기침으로 몹시 괴로워하다 / 《*fig.*》 *Doubt and despair racked him.* 그는 의혹과 절망으로 괴로워했다. **2** put (something) on a rack. …을 선반〔걸이〕에 얹다〔걸다〕. **3** (of a landlord) oppress (a tenant) by demanding too much rent. (소작인)을 착취하다. ¶ *a racking landlord* 착취 지주 / ~ *rent from tenants* 소작인에게서 소작료를 착취하다. [Du. *recken* stretch]

rack one's brains, think very hard. 머리를 짜다; 골머리를 앓다.

rack[2] [ræk] *n.* Ⓤ 《*lit.*》 a flying mass of broken clouds driven by the wind. 조각 구름. [→wreck]

rack[3] [ræk] *n.* Ⓤ destruction or wreck. 파괴; 황폐(cf. *wrack*). [↑]

go 〔***bring***〕 ***to rack and ruin,*** (of a person, house) become decayed. 파멸하다〔시키다〕; 황폐해지다.

:rack·et[1] [rǽkit] *n.* **1** ⓊⒸ loud noise; Ⓤ noisy talk and play. 시끄러운 소리; 소음; 떠들썩한 소란. ¶ *kick up* 〔*cause*〕 *a* ~ 큰 소란을 일으키다 / *What a* ~*!* 왜들 이러나, 시끄럽다 / *Don't make a* ~. 떠들지 마라. **2** Ⓒ 《*colloq.*》 a dishonest way of getting money from others; an illegal business. 사기; 협잡; 부정. ¶ *a drugs* ~ 마약 밀매. **3** 《*sl.*》 Ⓒ a business. 장사; 직업. **4** 《*arch.*》 a time of gay parties and social excitement. 흥겨운 놀이; 유흥. ¶ *She lives in a* ~ *of enjoyment.* 그녀는 흥청망청 지내고 있다. **5** 《*the* ~》 trying experience. 쓰라린 시련〔경험〕.

stand the racket of, **a**) come successfully through the test of; accept the consequences of. …의 시련을 이겨 내다; 책임을 지다. **b**) pay the expenses of. 비용을 대다; 돈을 내다.

— *vi.* (P1,2A) **1** move about noisily. 소란 떨다. ¶ ~ *about* 떠들고 다니다. **2** live gaily; lead a gay life. 흥청거리며 지내다. [? Imit.]

rack·et[2] [rǽkit] *n.* Ⓒ **1** a light, wide bat with a network stretched in a frame, used in games such as tennis and badminton. (테니스 등의) 라켓. **2** a paddle with a handle, used in table tennis. (탁구의) 라켓. **3** 《*pl.* used as *sing*》 a game of the tennis type for two or four players, played in a closed four-walled court. 라켓구기(球技). 參考 racquet이라고도 씀. [F. *raquette*]

rack·et·eer [rӕkitíər] *n.* Ⓒ a person who gets money by threatening or by violence. 공갈치는〔등쳐먹는〕 사람. [→racket[1]]

rack·e·ty [rǽkiti] *adj.* **1** noisy. 시끄러운; 소란스러운. **2** leading a gay, exciting life; dissipated. 흥청거리는; 방탕하는. [↑]

rack railway [´-´-] *n.* a railway designed to operate on steep slopes which connects with a cogwheel attached to the engine. 아프트(Abt)식 철도. [*rack*[1]]

rack-rent [rǽkrènt] *n.* an excessively high rent; esp. one (almost) equal to the full annual value of the land. 엄청난 지대〔소작료〕. — *vt.* exact rack-rent from. 엄청난 지대〔소작료〕를 거둬들이다. [*rack*[1]]

rac·on·teur [rӕkɑntə́ːr / -kɔn-] *n.* a person skilled in telling anecdotes or stories. 만담가; 이야기꾼. ¶ *a good* 〔*skillful*〕 ~. [F.]

ra·coon [rækúːn, rə-] *n.* =raccoon.

rac·y [réisi] *adj.* (**rac·i·er, rac·i·est**) **1** (of speech, writing, etc.) vigorous; full of life; lively. (말·글이) 생동하는; 기운찬. ¶ *He writes in a* ~ *style.* 그의 글은 생동감이 있다. **2** with a peculiar taste. 독특한 풍미가 있는. ¶ *a* ~ *apple.* ●**rac·i·ly** [-li] *adv.* [→race[2]]

racy of the soil, having a simplicity and flavor peculiar to the country; rural. 그 고장 특유의 맛이 나는.

·ra·dar [réidɑːr] *n.* ⒸⓊ an instrument for finding the direction and distance of unseen objects by the reflection of radio waves. 전파 탐지기; 레이더. [abbr.]

ra·di·al [réidiəl] *adj.* **1** arranged like rays. 방사상(放射狀)의. ¶ ~ *roads* 방사상 도로 / *a* ~

axle 방사축(軸). **2** of a ray; of or in rays. 광선의; 방사[복사]의. [→radius]

ra·di·ance [réidiəns] *n.* Ⓤ **1** brightness. 빛남. ¶ *the ~ of the sun* 태양의 (찬연한) 빛남 / 《*fig.*》 *the ~ of someone's smile* 아무의 밝은 미소. **2** radiation. 방사(放射); 복사(輻射). [↓]

***ra·di·ant** [réidiənt] *adj.* **1** 《phys.》 sending out rays of light or heat. (빛·열을) 방사(放射)하는. ¶ *We get ~ energy from the sun.* 우리는 태양에서 방사 에너지를 얻는다 / *~ heat* 방사열. **2** shining; brilliant. 빛나는; 번쩍이는. ¶ *the ~ sun* 빛나는 태양 / *the ~ morning.* **3** full of joy, delight, etc. (기쁨·즐거움 등으로) 빛나는; 밝은. ¶ *a ~ face* 희색이 가득한 얼굴 / *a ~ smile* 밝은 미소 / *a ~ intelligence* 번득이는 지성 / *be ~ with hope* 희망으로 빛나다. [→ radiate]

ra·di·ant·ly [réidiəntli] *adv.* brightly. 빛나서; 번쩍번쩍.

ra·di·ate *v.* [réidièit] *vi.* **1** (P1,3) give out rays of light or heat. (빛·열이) 발하다; 방사(放射)하다. ¶ *Heat radiates from hot steam-pipes.* 뜨거운 증기 기관에서 열이 방사한다. **2** (P1,2A) come out from a center. 중심에서 뻗치다. ¶ *Roads ~ from the city in every direction.* 도로가 시에서 팔방으로 뻗어 있다. **3** (P1) spread joy, happiness, etc. (기쁨·행복 등이) 발산되다.

— *vt.* (P6) **1** send out (light, heat, etc.) in rays. …을 방사하다. **2** spread (happiness, etc.) in every direction. …을 발산하다. ¶ *He radiates happiness around him.* 그는 주변에 행복을 발산한다.

— [réidiit, -èit] *adj.* radiating from a center. 방사하는; 방사상의. ¶ *A daisy is a ~ flower.* 데이지는 방사상 꽃이다. [→radius]

ra·di·a·tion [rèidiéiʃən] *n.* **1** Ⓤ the act or process of radiating; giving out (light, heat, etc.). (방사능, 빛, 열 등의) 발산; 복사(輻射). ¶ *the ~ of heat from a stove* 난로의 열 발산 / 《*fig.*》 *the ~ of happiness* 행복의 발산. **2** Ⓒ something radiated from a center. 방사물. ¶ *~ sickness* 방사능증(症) / *~ treatment* 방사능 치료(법). **3** Ⓒ radiant energy. 방사능.

ra·di·a·tor [réidièitər] *n.* Ⓒ **1** a device for heating a room or building consisting of a set of pipes through which hot water or steam passes. 방열기; 라디에이터. **2** a device for cooling a motor. (모터의) 냉각 장치.

***rad·i·cal** [rǽdikəl] *adj.* **1** of or from a root or roots; basic; fundamental; thorough. 근본의; 근본적인; 철저한. ¶ *~ errors* 근본적인 잘못 / *a ~ difference* 근본적인 상위[차이] / *a ~ change* 근본적인 변화. **2** 《often *R-*》 (of a political party or view) favoring an extreme change; extreme. (정당 등이) 급진적인; 과격한. ¶ *a ~ program* 과격한 정책 / *a ~ speech* 과격한 연설 / *His ideas are too ~ for most of us to accept.* 그의 생각은 우리들 대부분이 받아들이기에 너무 과격하다. **3** 《math.》 relating to the root of a number. 근(根)의. ¶ *the ~ sign* 근호(√).

— *n.* Ⓒ **1** a person with an extreme opinion; a person belonging to a radical party. 과격론자; 급진당원. **2** 《math.》 a root. 근(根). **3** 《chem.》 an atom or a group of atoms acting as a unit. 기(基). [L.=root]

rad·i·cal·ism [rǽdikəlìzəm] *n.* Ⓤ the principles of radicals; radical views. 급진주의; 과격론.

rad·i·cal·ly [rǽdikəli] *adv.* fundamentally; completely. 근본적으로; 전적으로.

rad·i·cle [rǽdikəl] *n.* Ⓒ **1** a little root. 작은 뿌리. **2** the part of a seed that grows into the main root. 유근(幼根). [L. *rādix* root]

ra·di·i [réidiài] *n.* pl. of **radius.**

:**ra·di·o** [réidiòu] *n.* (*pl.* **-os**) **1** Ⓤ 《often *the ~*》 the way of sending or receiving messages, music, etc. by means of electric waves; broadcasting. 라디오 방송; 무선 전신. ¶ *send a message by ~* 무전으로 통신하다 / *talk over the ~* 무전기로 얘기하다 / *receive a ~* 무전을 수신하다 / *listen to the news on the ~* 라디오로 뉴스를 듣다 / *Please turn the ~ up* 〔*down, off*〕. *It is too soft* 〔*loud, noisy*〕. 라디오를 크게 해라〔낮춰라, 꺼라〕. 소리가 너무 작다〔크다, 시끄럽다〕. **2** Ⓒ an instrument for receiving broadcasting; a radio set. 라디오 수신기. **3** Ⓒ a message sent by radio. 무선에 의한 통신(문). ¶ *listen to the ~* 무전을 듣다.

— *adj.* on or of radio. 라디오의. ¶ *a ~ set.*

— *vt.* (P6) send (a message, etc.) by radio. …을 라디오로〔무선으로〕 방송하다.

— *vi.* (P1) send a message, music, etc. by radio. 무선으로〔라디오로〕 방송하다. [L.]

ra·di·o·ac·tive [rèidiouǽktiv] *adj.* 《phys.》 giving off rays of energy by breaking down atoms. 방사능〔성〕의. ¶ *Radium is ~.* 라듐은 방사능이다 / *~ contamination* 방사능 오염 / *~ waste* 방사능〔성〕 폐기물.

ra·di·o·ac·tiv·i·ty [rèidiouæktívəti] *n.* Ⓤ the condition of being radioactive. 방사능〔성〕.

radio frequency [⌐–– ⌐––] *n.* the frequency of electrical vibrations. 무선 주파수.

ra·di·o·gram [réidiougræ̀m] *n.* Ⓒ **1** a telegram sent by radio. 무선 전보. **2** an X-ray photograph; a radiograph. 방사선〔뢴트겐〕 사진. **3** 《Brit.》 a combined radio-receiver set and record player; a radio-gramophone. 라디오 겸용 전축.

ra·di·o·graph [réidiougræ̀f, -grɑ̀ːf] *n.* Ⓒ an X-ray photograph. 방사선〔뢴트겐〕 사진.

— *vt.* (P6) make a radiograph of (something). …을 뢴트겐 사진〔엑스선〕으로 찍다.

ra·di·og·ra·phy [rèidiágrəfi / -ɔ́g-] *n.* Ⓤ

the art of making radiographs. 방사선〔뢴트겐〕 사진술.

ra·di·o·i·so·tope [rèidiouáisətòup] *n.* Ⓒ a radioactive isotope, used in medical or biological research. 라디오아이소토프; 방사성 동위 원소.

ra·di·om·e·ter [rèidiámitər / -ɔ́m-] *n.* 《phys.》 an instrument for measuring the degree of radiation. 방사〔복사(輻射)〕계(計).

ra·di·o·phone [réidiouf òun] *n.* =radiotelephone.

ra·di·o·sonde [réidiousànd / -sɔ̀nd] *n.* a radio transmitter sent into the air by a balloon and dropped by a parachute to broadcast the pressure, temperature, and humidity at various altitudes every few seconds. 라디오존데《대기 상층의 기상 관측 기계》.

ra·di·o·tel·e·graph [rèidioutéləgræ̀f, -grɑ̀:f] *n.* Ⓒ a telegraph sent by radio. 무선 전신; 무전.

ra·di·o·tel·e·phone [rèidioutéləfòun] *n.* Ⓒ a telephone in which sound is sent by radio waves. 무선 전화; 무전.

ra·di·o·ther·a·py [rèidiouθérəpi] *n.* Ⓤ the treatment of disease by means of radioactive substances or X-rays. 라듐〔방사선〕 요법.

R

radio tube [´-- `] *n.* a vacuum tube for a radio set. 라디오 진공관.

rad·ish [rǽdiʃ] *n.* Ⓒ 《bot.》 a garden plant whose red or white root is used in salads. 무. [L.=root]

***ra·di·um** [réidiəm] *n.* Ⓤ 《chem.》 a metallic chemical element, which gives off rays which are used in treating cancer. 라듐《방사성 원소》. [↓]

ra·di·us [réidiəs] *n.* Ⓒ (*pl.* **-di·i** or **-us·es**) **1** 《geom.》 a straight line from the center of a circle or sphere to its edge. 반지름. **2** the area bounded by a circle of a given radius. 일정 반경의 권내(圈內); 반지름내의 범위. ¶ *They searched within a* ~ *of one mile from the school.* 그들은 학교에서 반경 1마일의 지역을 조사했다. **3** a range; a scope. 범위. ¶ *within the* ~ *of one's capacity* 자기의 능력 범위 내에서. [L. =spoke, ray]

RAF, R.A.F. [ræf] Royal Air Force. 영국 공군.

raff·ish [rǽfiʃ] *adj.* disreputable; vulgar; showy. 평판이 나쁜; 속된; 야비한. [O.N. *rafs* rubbish]

raf·fle [rǽfəl] *n.* Ⓒ a sale in which people have chances to win a prize for a small sum of money. 복권식 판매《당첨이 되면 상품을 줌》. — *vt.* (P6,7) 《*off*》 sell (something) by means of a raffle. …을 복권식으로 팔다. ¶ ~ *off a watch* 시계를 복권식으로 팔다. — *vi.* (P3) 《*for*》 take part in a raffle. 복권식 판매에 참가하다. ¶ ~ *for a color television set* 컬러 텔레비전의 복권식 판매에 참가하다. [M.E. *rafle* dice game]

raft [ræft, rɑ:ft] *n.* Ⓒ a number of logs tied together to make a flat boat. 뗏목. ¶ *cross the river on a* ~. — *vt.* (P6,7) send (something) by raft; make (logs) into a raft. …을 뗏목으로 나르다; 뗏목으로 엮다. ¶ ~ *goods from one place to another* 물건을 뗏목에 실어 다른 곳으로 옮기다. — *vi.* (P3) go on a raft; use a raft. 뗏목으로 건너다; 뗏목을 이용하다. [N.]

raft·er[1] [rǽftər, rɑ́:ftər] *n.* Ⓒ a sloping beam to support a roof. 서까래. [E.]

from cellar to rafter, everywhere in a house. 집안 샅샅이.

raft·er[2] [rǽftər, rɑ́:ftər] *n.* Ⓒ a person who is employed on a raft; a raftsman. 뗏목을 만드는〔타는〕 사람. [→raft]

rafts·man [rǽftsmən, rɑ́:fts-] *n.* (*pl.* **-men** [-mən]) =rafter². [↑]

***rag**[1] [ræg] *n.* Ⓒ **1** a piece of old cloth torn from a larger piece. 넝마; 걸레. ¶ *Use some clean rags to rub this mirror bright.* 깨끗한 걸레로 이 거울을 닦아라 / *His clothes were in rags.* 그의 옷이 넝마처럼 되어 있었다. **2** 《*pl.*》 worn-out, shabby clothes. 누더기(옷). ¶ *a man in rags* 누더기를 걸친 남자 / 《*sl., iron.*》 *glad rags* 나들이옷 / *I have nothing but my old rags to wear.* 입을 것이라곤 누더기 같은 헌 옷뿐이다. **3** anything that resembles a rag; 《*contempt.*》 a cheap, valueless newspaper or magazine. 넝마 비슷한 것; 삼류 신문〔잡지〕. **4** a small piece of anything; a small amount. 단편; 소량. ¶ *a* ~ *of cloud* 조각 구름 / *He has still a few rags of reputation left.* 그에게 아직 다소의 신망은 남아 있다. **5** 《used as *adj.*》 made of rags. 넝마로 만든. ¶ *a* ~ *doll* 봉제(縫製) 인형 / *a* ~ *rug* 넝마로 만든 깔개. [N.]

chew the rag ⇨chew.

have not a rag to one's back, have no clothes fit to wear (and want some new ones). 입을 만한 옷이 없다.

like a red rag to a bull, acting as a cause of extreme anger. (소에 붉은 천을 보인 것처럼) 격분〔흥분〕시키는.

not a rag of, no... at all. 조금도 …않다. ¶ *There is not a* ~ *of evidence.* 아무 증거도 없다.

rag[2] [ræg] *vt.* (**-ged**) 《*sl.*》 **1** (P6) scold. …을 꾸짖다. **2** (P6,7,13) 《Brit. *colloq.*》 tease. …을 놀리다. ¶ *They ragged him about his big ears.* 그들은 그의 귀가 크다고 놀렸다. — *n.* 《Brit.》 a joke. 농담. ¶ *I only said it for a* ~. 그 말은 그저 농담이었다. [Sc.]

rag·a·muf·fin [rǽgəmʌ̀fin] *n.* Ⓒ a ragged, dirty child or fellow. 누더기를 걸친 아이〔사람〕. [*rag*[1]]

***rage** [reidʒ] *n.* **1** ⒸⓊ violent anger; fury. 격노; 분격. ¶ *in a* ~ 불끈해서 / *fly into a* ~ 벌컥 화내다 / *His arms quivered with* ~. 그는 화가 나서 팔이 부르르 떨렸다 / *Mad* *with* ~, *he dashed into the fight.* 미칠 듯이 화가 나서 그는 대들어 싸웠다. **2** Ⓤ uncontrolled violence. 격렬; 맹위. ¶ *the* ~ *of the wind* 맹렬한 바람. **3** Ⓒ ⓐ a strong desire. 열망. ¶ *have a* ~ *for fishing* 낚시에 미치다 / *He had a* ~ *to live.* 그는 생에 대한 강한 욕구가 있었다. ⓑ《*the* ~》 what many people are eager to get or do (for a short time). 일시적인 대유행. ¶ *Red ties are* (*all*) *the* ~ *this season.* 붉은 넥타이가 요즘 대유행이다. **4** Ⓒ a fit of emotion. 감동; 격동. ¶ *burst into a* ~ *of tears* 와락 울음을 터뜨리다.

— *vi.* (P1,2A,3) **1** be violently angry. 격노하다. ¶ *Keep your temper; don't* ~. 화내지 말고 참아라. **2** act or speak violently. 격하게 행동〔말〕하다. ¶ *He raged about the room in his agony.* 그는 고통을 못 이겨 방에서 몸부림쳤다 / ~ *against* 〔*at*〕 *fate* 운명을 저주하다. **3** ⓐ (of a storm, etc.) be violent. (폭풍 등이) 거칠어지다. ¶ *A storm is raging.* ⓑ (of a disease, etc.) be widely prevalent and severe. (질병 등이) 창궐하다. ¶ *Smallpox is raging.* [L. *rabio* mad]

rage itself out, (of violence, etc.) come to an end. 잠잠해지다. ¶ *The storm raged itself out.* 폭풍이 그쳤다.

***rag·ged** [rǽgid] *adj.* **1** torn into rags; dressed in worn-out clothing. 누덕누덕한; 누더기를 입은. ¶ ~ *clothing* 누더기옷 / *a* ~ *boy* 누더기를 입은 아이. **2** uneven; rough; neglected; imperfect. 들쭉날쭉한; 거친; 손질을 하지 않은; 불완전한. ¶ *a sleeve* ~ *at the edge* 해진 소매 끝 / *a* ~ *garden* 손질하지 않은 정원 / ~ *rocks* 울퉁불퉁한 바위들 / *His essay is too* ~. 그의 평론은 너무 엉성하다. **3** harsh. 귀에 거슬리는. ¶ *a* ~ *sound.* ● **rag·ged·ness** [-nis] *n.* [*rag*[1]]

rag·ged·ly [rǽgidli] *adv.* in rags; unevenly; roughly; harshly. 누더기를 입고; 거칠게; 귀에 거슬리게.

rag·lan [rǽglən] *n.* Ⓒ a kind of overcoat with sleeves continuing from the collar without shoulder seams. 래글런 (외투). [Person]

〈raglan〉

rag·man [rǽgmæ̀n, -mən] *n.* Ⓒ (*pl.* **-men** [-mèn, -mən]) a person who gathers, buys or sells rags. 넝마주이; 넝마장수. [*rag*[1]]

rag·tag [rǽgtæ̀g] *n.* 《also ~ *and bobtail*》 all sorts of low or worthless people; the riffraff. 사회의 찌꺼기; 하층민. [↓]

rag·time [rǽgtàim] *n.* Ⓤ rhythm in which the accents fall at unusual places; an early type of jazz. 래그타임《절분음(切分音)이 많은 음악》; (초기의) 재즈. — *adj.* not serious; comic. 익살스러운; 우스꽝스러운. [*rag*[1]]

raid [reid] *n.* Ⓒ **1** a sudden attack. 급습; 기습. ¶ *an air* ~ 공습 / *make a* ~ *on* 〔*upon*〕 *someone* 〔*something*〕 …을 기습하다; 덮치다. **2** 《*on, upon, into*》 an unexpected, sudden visit by the police to search for illegal goods or a suspect. (경찰의) 불시 단속. ¶ *a* ~ *on a gambling house* 경찰의 도박장 불시 검색. — *vt.* (P6) attack suddenly. …을 기습하다. ¶ *be* ~ *by the police* 경찰의 불시 검색을 받다. — *vi.* (P1) engage in a raid. 급습〔기습〕하다. [→ride]

raid·er [réidər] *n.* Ⓒ a person or thing that makes a raid. 급습자; 습격물《배·비행기 등》.

:**rail**[1] [reil] *n.* Ⓒ **1** any level bar of wood or metal. 가로장; 난간. ¶ *a* ~ *fence* 가로장 울타리 / *a towel* ~ (욕실 등의) 수건 걸이 / *a stair-rail* 계단《난간을 포함한 한 줄의》. **2** a railroad. 철도; 레일. **3** one of the two metal lines on which trains run. 선로; 궤조(軌條).

by rail, by train. 기차로. ¶ *travel by* ~ *and by boat* 기차와 배로 여행하다.

off the rails, **a**) (of trains, etc.) derailed. (기차가) 탈선해서. **b**) 《*fig.*》 off the proper course; insane. 혼란하여; 미쳐서. ¶ *go* 〔*run*〕 *off the rails* 탈선하다; 이상하게 되다.

— *vt.* (P6,7,13) **1** enclose (something) with bars. …을 가로장으로 둘러막다. ¶ ~ *off a space for the horses* 말들을 가로장 울로 가둬 놓다. **2** lay rails on (something). …에 레일을 부설하다. **3** send (a parcel, etc.) by railway. …을 철도편으로 보내다. [→rule]

rail[2] [reil] *vi.* (P1,3) 《*against, at*》 reproach or complain bitterly; speak angrily. 욕지거리하다; 악담하다. ¶ *He railed at his hard luck.* 그는 자기의 악운을 저주했다 / *The angry master railed against his servants.* 성난 주인은 하인들에게 욕을 퍼부었다. [F. *railler*]

rail[3] [reil] *n.* Ⓒ 《bird》 any of several kinds of wading birds with a short tail and wings but long legs. 흰눈썹뜸부기류(類). [F. *râle*]

rail·ing[1] [réiliŋ] *n.* Ⓒ **1** 《often *pl.*》 a fence or barrier made of rails and supports. 울타리; 난간. **2** 《*collectively*》 material for making rails. (위의) 재료. [*rail*[1]]

rail·ing[2] [réiliŋ] *n.* Ⓤ bitter reproach or complaint; abuse. 욕설; 매도. [*rail*[2]]

rail·ler·y [réiləri] *n.* (*pl.* **-ler·ies**) **1** Ⓤ good-natured satire or ridicule; banter. (선의의) 야유; 조롱. **2** Ⓒ a playful, teasing act or remark. 놀리는 짓〔말〕. [↑]

:**rail·road** [réilròud] *n.* Ⓒ 《chiefly U.S.》 **1** a track laid with two parallel rails on which trains run. 철도 선로; 궤도. **2** a whole railroad system, including tracks, trains, etc. 철도 (시설).

— *vt.* **1** (P6) send (something) by railroad; lay a railroad on (a place). …을 철도로 수송하다; …에 철도를 부설하다. ¶ ~ *a plain* 평원에 철도를 부설하다. **2** (P13)

R

《*colloq.*》 put through quickly usu. without following the proper form. …을 무리하게 통과시키다. ¶ ~ *an urgent motion through the committee.* 위원회에서 긴급 동의를 단숨에 통과시키다.
— *vi.* (P1) work on a railroad; travel by train. 철도에서 일하다; 철도로 여행하다. [*rail*¹]

:rail·way [réilwèi] *n.* 《Brit.》 =railroad.

rai·ment [réimənt] *n.* Ⓤ 《*poet.*》 clothing; dress. 옷; 의상. [→array]

:rain [rein] *n.* **1** ⓊⒸ the water falling to earth in small drops; the fall of such drops; Ⓤ rainy weather. 비; 강우(降雨); 우천(雨天). 語法 형용사가 따를 때는 흔히 부정관사 a를 붙임. ¶ *a heavy* 〔*light, fine*〕 ~ 호우〔보슬비, 가랑비〕 / *in the* ~ 비를 무릅쓰고 / *a driving* 〔*pelting, pouring*〕 ~ 장대비 / *a cold, drizzling* ~ 찬 부슬비 / *It looks like* ~. 비가 올 듯하다 / *large drops of* ~ 굵은 빗방울 / *The* ~ *has stopped* 〔*cleared up*〕. 비가 그쳤다〔개었다〕 / *The* ~ *was coming down in sheets* 〔*torrents*〕. 비가 억수로 내리고 있었다. **2** 《*the* ~*s*》 the rainy season in a tropical country. (열대 지방의) 우기. **3** Ⓤ 《*a* ~》 something falling rapidly or thickly like rain. (…의) 비. ¶ *a* ~ *of ashes* 쏟아져 내리는 재 / *a* ~ *of tears* 비 오듯 흐르는 눈물 / *a* ~ *of kisses* 〔*blows*〕 키스〔주먹〕 세례 / *a* ~ *of letters* 〔*presents*〕 쇄도하는 편지〔선물〕.
rain or shine, in any event. 청우(晴雨)에 관계 없이; 비가 오건 안 오건.
— *vi.* (P1,2A,3) **1** (of rain) fall; fall in drops of water. 비가 내리다. 語法 주어는 흔히 it. ¶ *It has stopped raining.* 비가 그쳤다 / *It is raining cats and dogs.* 비가 억수로 쏟아지고 있다 / *It rains in.* 비가 들이친다. **2** fall like rain; come in abundance. 비 오듯 하다. ¶ *Shells and bullets rained upon us.* 우리들 위로 총탄이 비 오듯 쏟아졌다 / *Letters rained upon her.* 그녀에게 편지가 쇄도했다.
— *vt.* (P6,7,13) pour down in rain or like rain. 비를 내리다; 비 오듯 퍼붓다. ¶ *It rained blood.* 피가 비 오듯 흘렀다 / *I rained blows upon him.* 나는 그에게 주먹 세례를 퍼부었다 / *It has rained itself out.* 비가 그쳤다 / *They rained presents on the bride and groom.* 그들은 신랑 신부에게 선물을 한아름씩 안겼다. [E.]
It never rains but it pours. 《*prov.*》 Troubles never come singly. 왔다 하면 장대비; 화불단행(禍不單行).

·rain·bow [réinbòu] *n.* Ⓒ an arch of light in seven colors which appears in the sky soon after rain. 무지개.
all the colors of the rainbow, many different colors. 가지가지의 빛깔.

rain·coat [réinkòut] *n.* Ⓒ a coat worn to protect oneself against the rain. 레인코트; 비옷.

rain·drop [réindrɑ̀p / -drɔ̀p] *n.* Ⓒ a drop of rain. 빗방울.

rain·fall [réinfɔ̀ːl] *n.* Ⓒ a shower of rain; Ⓤ the amount of rain falling within a given time and area. 강우; 강우량. ¶ *the yearly* ~ 연중 강우량.

rain gauge [ㅅㅡ] *n.* an instrument for measuring rainfall. 우량계.

rain·less [réinlis] *adj.* without rain. 비가 오지 않는.

rain·proof [réinprùːf] *adj.* keeping from rain. 방수(防水)의. ¶ *a* ~ *coat.* — *vt.* keep (something) from being damaged or made wet by rain. …에 방수 처리를 하다.

rain·storm [réinstɔ̀ːrm] *n.* Ⓒ a storm with heavy rain. 폭풍우.

rain water [ㅅㅡㅡ] *n.* water coming down as rain. 빗물.

:rain·y [réini] *adj.* (**rain·i·er, rain·i·est**) **1** having much rain; wet with rain. 비가 많은〔잦은〕; 비에 젖은. ¶ *The* ~ *season has set in.* 장마철에 들어섰다 / *a* ~ *day* 〔*district*〕 비오는 날〔비가 많은 지역〕. **2** bringing rain. 비를 가져오는. ¶ ~ *clouds* 〔*winds*〕 비구름〔비를 몰고 오는 바람〕. **3** wet with rain. 비에 젖은. ¶ ~ *streets* 〔*pavements*〕.

rainy day [ㅅㅡㅅ] *n.* a time of need or misfortune in the future. 만일의 경우; 궁할 때. ¶ *provide for* 〔*against*〕 *a* ~ *day* 만일의 경우에 대비하다.

:raise [reiz] *vt.* (P6,7,13) **1** ⓐ cause (someone or something) to rise; hold up; lift up(cf. *lift*, which now usu. refers to heavy objects). …을 일으키다; 세우다; 들어올리다. ¶ ~ *a flag* 기를 올리다 / ~ *one's eyebrows* 눈썹을 치켜올리다《놀라거나 해서》 / ~ *a sunken ship* 침몰선을 인양하다 / ~ *one's glass to someone* 아무를 위해 축배를 들다 / ~ *one's hand to someone* 아무를 향해 손을 들다 / ~ *one's hand against someone* 아무를 치려고 손을 치켜들다 / ~ *one's hat to someone* 아무에게 모자를 들어 인사하다 / ~ *the window* 창을 밀어올려 열다 / ~ *one's eyes* 눈을 치켜뜨다. ⓑ cause to stand upright; place erect. 곧추〔똑바로〕 세우다. ¶ ~ *a mast* 돛대〔장대〕를 세우다 / ~ *a fallen pillar* 쓰러진 기둥을 곧추 세우다. **2** build; construct; set upright. (집 따위)를 세우다; 건축〔건립〕하다. ¶ ~ *a monument* 〔*building*〕 기념탑〔건물〕을 세우다. **3** cause (the dust, etc.) to be or appear. (먼지 등)을 일으키다. ¶ ~ *a cloud of dust* 자욱한 먼지를 일으키다 / *His long absence raised doubts about his safty.* 장기 결석으로 그의 안위를 염려하게 되었다. **4** stir up (someone) to some action; incite. …을 분기시키다; (소동 등)을 일으키다. ¶ ~ *a rebellion* 반란을 일으키다 / ~ *the country against the enemy* 적에 대항해 국민을 분기시키다 / ~ *someone's spirit* 〔*courage*〕 아무의 용기를 불러일으키다. **5** 《often *reflexively*》 cause (someone) to rise in the world; promote. …을 출세〔승진〕시키다. ¶ ~ *one-*

self 입신 출세하다 / *He was raised to the rank of captain.* 그는 대위로 진급됐다 / ~ *a salesman to be a manager* 판매원을 지배인으로 승진시키다. **6** increase (something) in value, amount, degree, strength, etc.; advance (fame, etc.). (가격·양·정도 등)을 올리다; 명성 등을 높이다. ¶ ~ *the rent* 세를 올리다 / ~ *a salary* 급료를 인상하다 / ~ *one's reputation* 신망을 높이다 / ~ *the temperature of a room* 실내의 온도를 높이다 / ~ *the volume of a radio* 라디오의 음량을 높이다. **7** bring back (someone) from death; give life to; rouse; call up; summon. (죽은 자)를 소생시키다; …을 불러일으키다. ¶ ~ *old memories* 옛 기억을 되살리다 / ~ *someone from the dead* 아무를 되살아나게 하다 / ~ *a ghost* 〔*an evil spirit*〕 망령〔악령〕을 불러내다. **8** collect; gather. (돈·군사 등)을 모으다. ¶ ~ *funds* 기금을 모으다 / ~ *armies* 모병하다. **9** utter (a cry, etc.) loudly; bring up (an objection, etc.) for consideration; mention. (함성 등)을 지르다; (이의 등)을 제기하다. ¶ ~ *a cheer* 환성을 올리다 / ~ *a question* 이론을 제기하다. **10** grow; rear; breed; bring up. …을 기르다; 재배하다; 키우다. ¶ ~ *cattle* 가축을 기르다 / ~ *a family* 가족을 부양하다 / ~ *wheat* 밀을 재배하다. **11** make (dough) rise or lighten. (빵)을 부풀리다. ¶ ~ *bread.* **12** 《mil.》 end; give up (a siege, etc.). (포위 등)을 풀다. ¶ ~ *a siege.*

raise a dust, 《*sl.*》 make a fuss. 소동을 일으키다.

raise Cain 〔***hell, the devil***〕***,*** cause a great disturbance. 대소동을 일으키다. ¶ *He will ~ merry hell if he hears it.* 그걸 들으면 그 사람은 펄펄 뛸 거다.

raise the wind, procure money for some purpose. 돈〔자금〕을 조달하다.

raise one's voice against, protest. …에 항의하다.

— *n.* Ⓤ Ⓒ **1** the act of raising. 올림; 올리기. **2** 《U.S.》 an increase in salary, etc. 증가; (특히) 임금 인상. ¶ *give someone a raise* …의 월급을 올려 주다 / *get* 〔*have*〕 *a ~ in salary* 월급이 오르다. [N.]

rais·er [réizər] *n.* Ⓒ a person who grows plants or animals. 재배자; 사육자. ¶ *a ~ of fine vegetables* 양질 채소의 재배자 / *a cattle ~* 가축 사육자.

rai·sin [réizən] *n.* 《usu. *pl.*》 a small dried grape. 건포도 [→raceme]

rai·son d'ê·tre [réizoun détrə] *n.* (*pl.* **rai·sons ~**) 《F.》 reason for existence. 존재이유.

ra·jah, ra·ja [rɑ́:dʒə] *n.* Ⓒ 《Ind.》 a king; a nobleman. 왕; 귀족. [Hind.]

***rake**[1] [reik] *n.* Ⓒ a farm or garden tool having a bar with a row of teeth at the end of a long handle, used for smoothing the soil or gathering together leaves, hay, etc. 갈퀴; 고무래; 쇠스랑. ¶ *thin as a ~* (말라서) 피골이 상접한.

— *vt.* **1** (P6,7,18) ⓐ use a rake upon. …에 갈퀴질하다. ¶ ~ *a field* 고무래로 밭을 고르다. ⓑ move with a rake; collect or gather together with a rake. …을 갈퀴로 긁다〔모으다〕. ¶ ~ *leaves off the lawn* 갈퀴로 잔디에서 낙엽을 긁어 치우다 / ~ *out the fire* 불을 긁어 내다 / *They were raking the paths clean.* 그들은 갈퀴로 길을 깨끗이 청소하고 있었다. **2** (P6,7,13) gather together; collect. …을 모으다. ¶ ~ *recruits from every class* 모든 계층에서 신병을 모집하다 / ~ *up the money* 돈을 그러모으다. **3** (P6,7,13) ⓐ search carefully. …을 수색하다; 샅샅이 뒤지다. ¶ ~ *the library for a special book* 전문 서적을 찾아 도서관을 샅샅이 뒤지다. ⓑ 《*out*》 search out. …을 찾아내다. ¶ ~ *out information* 정보를 찾아내다. ⓒ 《*up*》 stir up; revive. …을 (쑤셔) 일으키다; 되살리다. ¶ ~ *up old scandals* 해묵은 추문을 들추다. **4** (P6,7) ⓐ sweep with shot. …을 소사(掃射)하다. ¶ ~ *a ship with fire.* 함선에 기총 소사를 하다. ⓑ sweep with the eyes, etc. (죽) 훑어보다. ¶ ~ *the sky with a search light* 탐조등으로 하늘을 죽 비추다.

— *vi.* **1** (P1,2A) use a rake. 갈퀴를 쓰다. **2** (P2A,3) 《*fig.*》 make a close search. 샅샅이 뒤지다. ¶ *He raked* (*around*) *among his old papers.* 그는 그의 묵은 서류들을 샅샅이 뒤졌다. [E.]

rake[2] [reik] *n.* Ⓒ a slope. 경사(傾斜). ¶ *the ~ of a ship's funnel* 배의 굴뚝의 경사.

— *vi.* (P1) incline; slant. 기울다; 경사지다.

— *vt.* (P6) cause (something) to incline. …을 기울게 하다. [?]

rake[3] [reik] *n.* Ⓒ a man of bad character; a person who wastes his life in foolish pleasures. 방탕자; 난봉꾼. [E.]

rak·ish[1] [réikiʃ] *adj.* **1** extremely smart 아주 멋진. ¶ *a hat set at a ~ angle* 멋을 부려 삐딱하게 쓴 모자. **2** (of a ship, etc.) suggesting dash and speedy. 경쾌한. ¶ *a ~ boat.* [*rake*[2]]

rak·ish[2] [réikiʃ] *adj.* like a rake; immoral. 방탕한. [*rake*[3]]

***ral·ly**[1] [rǽli] *v.* (**-lied**) (P6,7) *vt.* **1** bring (men, troops, animals, etc.) together again. …을 다시 모으다. ¶ *The general was able to ~ the scattered soldiers of his army.* 장군은 흩어진 휘하의 장병들을 재집결시킬 수 있었다. **2** collect. …을 규합하다. ¶ ~ *one's supporters* 지지자를 규합하다. **3** revive; recover. …을 회복하다. ¶ ~ *one's spirits* 기력을 되찾다.

— *vi.* (P1,3) **1** come together again for a purpose or an action. (목적·행위를 위해) 다시 모이다. ¶ ~ *round the flag* 깃발 주위에 다시 집결하다 / *The villages are ralling for battle.* 마을 사람들은 전투에 대비해 재집결하고 있다. **2** come to help someone; come together for common

R

action. 도우러 오다; (공동의 목적을 위해) 모이다. ¶ *They rallied for the election campaign.* 그들은 선거 운동을 위해 모여들었다. **3** recover strength. 원기를 되찾다. ¶ *He seemed to be dying but he suddenly rallied.* 그는 곧 죽을 것 같더니 갑자기 기운을 추슬렀다. **4** (in tennis) hit a ball rapidly back and forth. 공을 연달아 서로 쳐 넘기다; 랠리하다.

— *n.* Ⓒ (*pl.* **-lies**) **1** ⓐ the act of rallying; coming together again. 재집결. ¶ *a ~ of men for battle.* ⓑ a mass meeting in support of something; an assembly. (어떤 목적을 위한) 대회; 집회. ¶ *a political ~* 정치 집회. **2** a recovery from an illness. 병후의 회복. **3** (in tennis) a series of action of hitting a ball rapidly back and forth. 랠리. [re-, →ally]

ral·ly2 [rǽli] *vt.* (**-lied**) (P6,13) laugh at; ridicule. …을 놀리다; 조롱하다. ¶ *The boys rallied John on his haircut.* 아이들은 존의 이발 모양을 놀려 댔다. — *n.* banter. 조롱. [→rail2]

Ralph [rælf / reif] *n.* a man's name. 남자 이름.

***ram** [ræm] *n.* Ⓒ **1** a male sheep. 숫양 (cf. *ewe*). **2** (formerly) a device used for battering the walls of forts. (예전의) 공성퇴(攻城槌).

R

— *vt.* (**rammed, ram·ming**) (P6,7,13) **1** strike against (something) violently. …에 세게 부딪다. ¶ *A car rammed the pole.* 차가 기둥을 들이받았다 / *~ one's head against the door in the dark* 어둠 속에서 머리를 문에 세게 부딪다. **2** pack (something) roughly or forcibly; stuff. …을 쑤셔 넣다. ¶ *~ earth into a hole* 흙을 구멍에 다져 넣다 / *~ a stake into the ground* 말뚝을 땅에 때려 박다 / *~ the clothes into a trunk* 트렁크 속에 옷을 쑤셔 넣다. **3** force (knowledge, ideas, etc.) into the mind of another; cram. (지식 등)을 주입시키다. ¶ *I had the list rammed into me by repetition.* 몇 번이고 반복해서 나는 그 일람표를 머릿속에 집어넣었다. [E.]

ram down** someone's* ***throat ⇨throat.

ram·ble [rǽmbəl] *vi.* (P1,2A,3) **1** wander about without purpose. (지향 없이) 거닐다. ¶ *They rambled here and there in the woods.* 그들은 숲속을 이리저리 돌아다녔다. **2** talk or write about first on thing and then another without useful connections. 두서없이 말하다[쓰다]. ¶ *~ in one's speech* 두서없이 말하다. **3** (of a plant) grow and spread in various directions. 만연하다; 퍼지다.

ramble on, continue to speak in a wandering way. 장황하게 두서없이 지껄이다.

— *n.* Ⓒ **1** an aimless walk. 이리저리 거닐기; 소요; 산책. ¶ *go for a country ~* 시골에 바람 쐬러 가다. **2** aimless talking or writing. 만담(漫談); 만필(漫筆). [?, →roam]

ram·bler [rǽmblər] *n.* Ⓒ **1** a person who rambles. ramble하는 사람. **2** a climbing rose. 덩굴장미.

ram·bling [rǽmbliŋ] *adj.* **1** wandering about. 이리저리 거니는. **2** lacking plan or unity. 두서[종작]없는. ¶ *a long very ~ letter* 장황하고 도무지 두서없는 편지. **3** spread out in an irregular way. 무질서하게 뻗은. ¶ *a ~ house* [*street*].

ram·i·fi·ca·tion [ræ̀məfikéiʃən] *n.* ⓊⒸ **1** the act of ramifying; the state of being ramified. 분지(分枝). **2** a branch; a part. 분파; 지파(支派); 소구분. ¶ *the ~ of a nerve* 신경의 지맥(支脈). [↓]

ram·i·fy [rǽməfài] *v.* (**-fied**) *vi.* (P1) divide or spread out into branches. 분지(分枝)하다. — *vt.* (P6) 《in *passive*》 divide (something) into branches. …을 분지하다; 소구분하다. [L. *ramus* branch]

ram·jet [rǽmdʒèt] *n.* **1** a jet engine in which the stream of air used for the burning of the fuel is compressed by the force of the forward motion rather than by a compressor. 램제트 (엔진)《유입 공기의 에너지로 공기를 압축하여 추진력을 얻는 분사(噴射) 추진 엔진》(cf. *turbojet*). **2** an airplane driven by such engines. 램제트기. [*ram*]

ram·mer [rǽmər] *n.* **1** a block of wood used for ramming soil. 땅 다지는 메; 달구. **2** a machine for driving home piles. 래머《토목 공사용 파일 박는 기구》. **3** a means for driving home the charge in a gun. (총포의) 탄알 장전구(裝塡具). [→ram]

ramp [ræmp] *n.* Ⓒ **1** a short, sloping way connecting two different levels of a building or road. 램프《높이가 다른 두 건물·도로를 잇는 경사로》. **2** a movable stairway by which passengers enter or leave an aircraft. (항공기의 타고 내리는) 이동식 계단; 트랩. ¶ *a boarding ~* (항공기의) 트랩.

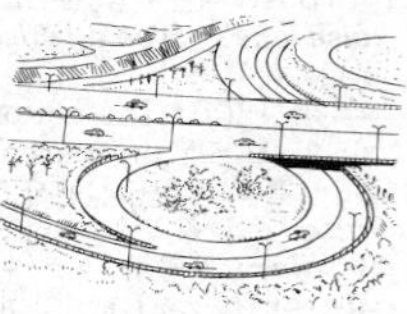
〈ramp 1〉

— *vi.* (P1,2A) **1** (esp. of a lion in her.) stand or rise on the hind legs. (문장(紋章)에서 사자가) 뒷다리로 서다. **2** 《*joc.*》 move violently or excitedly; leap or dash with anger. 사납게 날뛰다[덤벼들다]. ¶ *The lion ramped about the circus tent.* 사자가 곡마단 천막 안을 날뛰며 다녔다. [F. *ramper* creep, climb]

ram·page [rǽmpeidʒ / –⌐] *n.* Ⓒ a violent and noisy behavior. 사납게 날뛰기. ¶ *The horse went on the ~ and kicked it's driver.* 말이 광포(狂暴)해지더니 마부를 발로 걷어찼다. — [ræmpéidʒ] *vi.* (P1) run about violently. 사납게 날뛰다. [→ramp]

ramp·ant [rǽmpənt] *adj.* **1** violent; threatening. 광포한; 사나운; 위협적인. ¶ *He is a ~ radical.* 그자는 과격한 급진 당원이다. **2** growing widely; unchecked. 무성하게 번지는; 만연하는; 어거할 수 없는. ¶ *The weeds grew ~ in the garden.* 잡초가 정원에 무성했다 / *Disease is ~ in that part of town.* 질병이 도시의 그 지역에 만연하고 있다. **3** 《her.》 standing on the hind legs. 뒷발로 선. ¶ *a lion ~* 뒷발로 선 사자. [→ramp]

ram·part [rǽmpɑːrt, -pərt] *n.* Ⓒ **1** a wide wall of earth placed around a fort for protection. 성벽; 누벽(壘壁). **2** 《*fig.*》 anything that defends; a defence. 방어물. — *vt.* (P6) make a wall around (a fort, etc.); defend with a rampart. …에 성벽을 두르다; 방어하다. [ante-, L. *paro* prepare]

ram·rod [rǽmrɑ̀d / -rɔ̀d] *n.* Ⓒ a rod for pushing gunpowders, etc. into firearms. 탄약 재는 쇠꼬챙이. 參考 지금은 꽂을대로 쓰임. [→ram]

(as) *stiff as a ramrod,* very stiff in appearance, manner, etc. (외양; 태도 등이) 아주 딱딱한; 부자연스러운.

ram·shack·le [rǽmʃæ̀kəl] *adj.* loosely made; shaky; likely to come apart. 흔들〔덜컥〕거리는; 무너질 것 같은. ¶ *a ~ old car* 덜컥거리는 고물차 / *a ~ cottage* 쓰러져 가는 오두막. [?]

:ran [ræn] *v.* p. of **run.**

***ranch** [ræntʃ] *n.* Ⓒ **1** 《U.S., Can.》 a large farm for raising cattle. 큰 목장. **2** a farm for a special crop. 농장. ¶ *a fruit ~* 과수원 / *a chicken ~* 양계장. **3** 《*the ~, collectively*》 persons working on a ranch. 목장〔농장〕에서 일하는 사람들. — *vi.* (P1) manage a ranch; work on a ranch. 목장을 경영하다; 목장〔농장〕에서 일하다. [Sp. *rancho* common meal]

ranch·er [rǽntʃər] *n.* Ⓒ a person who owns or works on a ranch. 목장주; 목장 노동자.

ranch·man [rǽntʃmən] *n.* (*pl.* **-men** [-mən]) =rancher.

ran·cid [rǽnsid] *adj.* **1** having an unpleasant, smell or taste, like stale fat or butter. (비계 썩은) 구린내가 나는; 맛이 고약한. ¶ *~ butter* 구린 버터. **2** not fresh. 신선하지 않은. [L. *rancidus* stinking]

ran·cor, 《Brit.》 **-cour** [rǽŋkər] *n.* Ⓤ deep-rooted hatred; ill will. 뿌리 깊은 증오〔원한〕; 적의. ¶ *attack a man with ~* 깊은 증오심으로 남을 공격하다 / *bear* 〔*have*〕 *no ~ against someone* …에게 아무 원한도 없다. [↑]

ran·cor·ous [rǽŋkərəs] *adj.* full of rancor; spiteful. 원한에 사무친; 악의 있는.

***ran·dom** [rǽndəm] *adj.* 《as *attributive*》 occurring without definite aim or reason; guided by chance. 되는 대로의; 멋대로의. ¶ *a ~ shot* 난사(亂射) / *a ~ guess* 억측 / *a ~ remark* 되는 대로 하는 말. [F. *randir* gallop]

at random, aimlessly; with no purpose. 아무렇게나; 무작위로. ¶ *read at ~* 되는 대로 읽다 / *The people for the experiment were chosen completely at ~.* 그 실험의 대상자들은 전혀 무작위로 선정되었다.

:rang [ræŋ] *v.* p. of **ring.**

:range [reindʒ] *n.* Ⓒ **1** Ⓤ the extent or scope; the area; the distance at which someone can see or hear. 범위; 지력(知力)의 범위; 넓이; 시계(視界); 음역(音域). ¶ *within* 〔*out of*〕 *one's ~* 자기 힘이 미치는〔못 미치는〕 / *outside the ~ of human understanding* 인간의 이해 영역을 넘어 / *a wide ~ of meadows* 광활한 목장 / *It is in the ~ of my influence.* 그것은 내 영향권 안에 있다 / *the ~ of hearing* 가청(可聽) 범위 / *He has a wide ~ of knowledge.* 그는 해박한 지식을 갖고 있다 / *I am afraid that high note is beyond my ~.* 나는 저런 고음을 내지 못할 것 같아요 / *Several cars are available within this price ~.* 이 값으로 살 수 있는 차가 몇 대 있습니다. **2** the distance between limits. 변동의 범위. ¶ *a wide ~ of prices* 상품의 너른 시세폭 / *the ~ of a thermometer* 온도계의 승강의 한도. **3** ⒸⓊ the distance to which a gun will shoot. 사정(射程); 착탄 거리. ¶ *within* 〔*out of*〕 *~* 사정내〔외〕에 / *at long* 〔*short*〕 *~* 원〔근〕거리에서 / *an effective ~* 유효 사거리. **4** ⒸⓊ a row, line, or series; a chain of mountains; a rank. 줄; 열; 잇닿음; 산맥; 계급. ¶ *a ~ of mountains* 산맥; 연산(連山) / *a ~ of pictures* 일련의 그림들. **5** a place to practise shooting. 사격장. ¶ *a rifle ~* 소총 사격장. **6** 《U.S.》 an unfenced land where cattle eat grass. (가축의) 방목(放牧) 구역; 방목지. **7** the area over which a plant or animal may be found. (동식물의) 분포〔서식〕 구역. ¶ *the ~ of the violet* 제비꽃 서식지. **8** a large cooking stove. (요리용) 레인지.

— *vt.* **1** (P6,7) arrange (someone or something) in order or in a row or rows; classify. …을 나란히 놓다; 정렬시키다; 분류하다. ¶ *~ books on a shelf* 선반의 책을 가지런히 하다 / *He ranged his soldiers in order of size.* 그는 병사들을 키순대로 정렬시켰다 / *~ plants according to genus* 식물을 종류에 따라 분류하다. **2** (P6) 《*arch., poet.*》 travel or wander over. 걸어다니다; 거닐다. ¶ *~ the woods* 숲속을 거닐다 / *~ the country side* 시골을 돌아다니다. **3** (P6) 《U.S.》 pasture (cattle, etc.) on a range. (가축)을 방목 구역에 방목하다. **4** (P6,13) 《*reflexively* or in *passive*》 take sides; put oneself in a certain line, class, group, etc. …을 편들다; 동아리에 넣다. ¶ *be ranged against* …의 반대측에 가담하다 / *be ranged among* …의 속에 끼이다 / *be ranged with* 〔*on the side of*〕 =*~ oneself with.* …을 편들다 / 《*lit.*》 *He ranged himself by marring.* 장가들어 가정을 이루었다. **5**

R

(P6,7,13) aim or point (a gun, telescope, etc.) at someone or something. (총 따위)를 돌려대다; 조준하다. ¶ ~ *a pistol on someone* 아무에게 권총을 들이대다 / ~ *a telescope on an object* 망원경을 목표물에 맞추다.

— *vi.* **1** (P2A,3) ⓐ stretch; extend; lie in a line. 연잇다; 뻗다; (…와) 병행하다. ¶ *The forest ranges for five miles.* 그 삼림(森林)은 5마일을 뻗어 있다. ⓑ be distributed. 분포되어 있다. ¶ *Camels ~ from North Africa to Central Asia.* 낙타는 북아프리카에서 중앙 아시아에 걸쳐 분포되어 있다. **2** (P2A,3) vary within limits. (일정 범위 내에서) 변하다; 변동하다. ¶ ~ *between A and B,* A와 B 사이를 움직이다 / *The temperature ranges from over 100 degrees to less than 60 degrees in the course of the day.* 기온은 하루 동안 100도 이상에서 60도 이하까지 오르내린다. **3** (P3) wander about; move freely. 방황하다; 돌아다니다. ¶ ~ *through the woods in search of game* 사냥감을 찾아 숲속을 돌아다니다. [F. *rang* rank]

range finder [⌐⌐] *n.* an instrument used for determining the distance from an observer to an object. 거리 측정기; 거리계.

rang·er [réindʒər] *n.* Ⓒ **1** a person employed to guard a tract of forest. 삼림 경비원. **2** a member of a body of mounted men patrolling a large area. 기마 경찰대원. **3** a wanderer. 돌아다니는 사람; 부랑자(浮浪者). **4** 《*R-s*》《U.S.》 soldiers esp. trained for surprise attacks. 기습 부대원; 유격병. **5** 《Brit.》 a keeper (of a royal park, etc). (왕실 소유림 등의) 감시원.

R

:rank[1] [ræŋk] *n.* **1** Ⓒ a line or row. 열. ¶ *a ~ of taxis* 한 줄로 선 택시 / *mountains in ranks* 중첩한 산들. **2** ⒸⓊ a distinct grade in the army, navy, etc.; a social class or division. (군대의) 계급; 신분; 사회적 계층. ¶ *a man of high* (*no*) ~ 신분이 높은(낮은) 사람 / *men of all rankes and classes* 각계 각층의 사람들. **3** Ⓤ high social position; eminence, honor, or dignity. 높은 신분; 고관(高官); 귀현(貴顯). ¶ *a man of ~* 지체 높은 사람; 고관 / *a lady of ~* 귀부인 / *the ~ and fashion* 상류사회 / *a writer of the first ~* 일류 작가. **4** Ⓒ 《mil.》 a row of soldiers ranged side by side. 횡렬; 횡대(opp. file[1]). ¶ *the front* (*rear*) ~ (2열 횡대의) 전(후)열. **5** 《*the ranks*》 the common soldiers; the common people. 사병; 졸병; 신분이 낮은 사람. ¶ *rise* (*come up*) *from the ranks* 일개 사병에서 장교가 되다; 낮은 신분에서 출세하다 / *He was reduced to the ranks.* 그는 사병으로 강등되었다.

break rank, fall out of line; be thrown into confusion. 낙오하다; 열을 흐트러뜨리다(opp. keep rank).

fall into rank, fall into line or orderly arrangement. 정렬하다.

keep rank, remain in line; keep order. 낙오하지 않다; 질서를 지키다(opp. break rank).

take rank of, be above in position. …의 윗자리를 지키다; 상석을 차지하다.

take rank with, take one's place among; be consideres equal to. …와 어깨를 나란히 하다.

— *vt.* (P6,7) **1** place (someone or something) in a rank or ranks. …을 나란히 하다; 정렬시키다. ¶ ~ *books on a shelf* 선반의 책을 가지런히 하다. **2** assign a rank or class to (someone or something); classify; estimate; make much of. …에 등급을 매기다; …을 분류하다; 평가하다; 중시하다. ¶ *I ~ her abilities very high.* 나는 그녀의 능력을 높이 평가한다 / *His name will be ranked with the great names of history.* 그의 이름은 역사에 위대한 이름으로 남을 것이다. **3** 《U.S.》 have a higher rank than (someone). …보다 위다(낫다). ¶ *Ambassadors ~ ministers.* 대사는 공사의 윗자리다.

— *vi.* **1** (P2A) hold a rank or position; equal. 지위를 차지하다; 어깨를 겨루다. ¶ *The King ranks above the lords.* 왕은 영주의 윗자리다 / *John ranked low in his class.* 존은 반에서 하위였다 / *He ranks next to me.* 그의 석차는 나 다음이다. **2** (P1) have the highest rank. 제1위를 차지하다. ¶ *He ranks.* 그가 일등이다. [*range*]

rank[2] [ræŋk] *adj.* **1** (of plants, grass, etc.) growing too thickly. 매우 무성한. ¶ ~ *grass* 무성한 풀 / *a garden ~ with weeds* 잡초가 무성한 정원. **2** bad-smelling; disagreeable to the taste or sense of smell. 악취가 나는; 맛이 고약한. ¶ ~ *butter* 썩어서 구린내가 나는 버터 / ~ *tobacco* 저질 담배. **3** (in a bad sense) excessive; extreme. 지나친; 과도한. ¶ *a ~ mistake* 지나친 착오 / ~ *nonsense* 터무니없는 난센스 / ~ *poison* 맹독(猛毒) / ~ *treason* 대역(죄). [E.]

rank and file [⌐⌐⌐] *n.* **1** common soldiers. 사병; 졸병. **2** general membership of an organization; common people. 평사원; 평민; 대중. [→rank[1]]

rank·er [rǽŋkər] *n.* Ⓒ an officer risen from the ranks. 사병 출신의 장교. [→rank[1]]

rank·ing [rǽŋkiŋ] *n.* Ⓤ relative position. 순위; 서열; 랭킹. — *adj.* of the first class. 일류의; 뛰어난; 발군의. ¶ *a ~ player* 일류 선수. [↑]

ran·kle [rǽŋkəl] *vi.* 《*poet.*》 (P1) **1** continue to be painful; be sore. (계속) 수시다; 아프다. ¶ *The wound rankled.* 상처가 자꾸 수셨다. **2** be the source of mental pain or irritation. 마음을 아프게 하다. ¶ *Her harsh words rankled long in his mind.* 그녀의 매정한 말이 오랫동안 그의 마음을 아프게 했다. [L. *dracunculus* little serpent]

ran·sack [rǽnsæk] *vt.* (P6) **1** ⓐ search

thoroughly. …을 샅샅이 찾다. ¶ ~ *a dictionary to find just the right word* 딱 들어 맞는 말을 찾아 사전을 뒤지다. ⓑ 《*fig.*》 search (the mind) thoroughly. (기억)을 더듬다. ¶ ~ *one's memory for forgotten things* 잊은 일에 대한 기억을 더듬다. **2** take (something) by force; rob. …을 약탈하다. ¶ *The enemy ransacked the town.* 적이 마을을 노략질했다. [N. *rann* house, →seek]

***ran·som** [rǽnsəm] *n.* **1** Ⓒ a price paid or demanded for the release of a captive, etc. 몸값. ¶ *hold someone for* ~ …을 잡아놓고 몸값을 요구하다 / *The robber chief demanded a ~ of a thousand pounds.* 도둑의 괴수는 몸값으로 천 파운드를 요구했다. **2** Ⓤ the redemption of a prisoner or kidnapped person for a price. 몸값을 치르고 …을 되찾기.

a king's ransom, a very large sum demanded to set free a king captured in war; 《*fig.*》 a very large sum of money. 왕의 몸값; 엄청난 돈.

— *vt.* (P6) **1** pay a price for (a captive) to be set free. (몸값을 치르고) …을 되찾다. **2** set (a captive) free by obtaining a price. …을 몸값을 받고 풀어주다. [→redemption]

rant [rænt] *n.* **1** Ⓤ wild, loud and meaningless speech. 호언 장담. **2** Ⓒ a spree. 야단법석. — *vt.* (P6,7) speak in a wild, loud meaningless manner; utter (something) in a violent manner. 큰소리치다; …을 격렬하게 말하다. ¶ ~ *out a speech* 열변을 토하다 / ~ *a scene on the stage* 무대에서 한 장면을 고함치며 연기하다. ●**rant·er** [-ər] *n.* [Du. *randten* rave]

***rap**[1] [ræp] *v.* (**rapped, rap·ping**) *vt.* **1** (P6,13) ⓐ strike (something) quickly or lightly; tap. …을 (톡톡) 두드리다. ¶ *The chairman rapped the table to call the meeting to order.* 의장은 탁자를 치며 회중(會衆)에게 질서를 지킬 것을 요구했다. ⓑ 《*fig.*》 blame. …을 꾸짖다; 처벌하다. **2** (P6,7) 《*out*》 ⓐ say sharply. …을 쏘아붙이다. ¶ ~ *out an answer* 쏘아붙이듯이 대답하다. ⓑ (of a spirit etc.) express by means of raps. (혼령 등)이 두드려서 뜻을 말하다. ¶ ~ *out a message* 똑똑 두드리며 말을 전하다. ⓒ express by rapping. 표현하다. ¶ ~ *out a tune on the piano* 피아노 곡을 치다.

— *vi.* (P1,2A,3) 《*at, on*》 knock something smartly so as to make a noise. 톡톡 두드리다. ¶ ~ *on a door.*

— *n.* Ⓒ **1** a quick and light blow; a knock. 톡톡 두드림; 노크. ¶ *I hear a ~ on the door.* 문을 노크하는 소리가 들린다. **2** 《*sl.*》 blame; punishment. 비난; 처벌. ¶ *take the* ~ 책망 듣다; 벌받다. [E.]

get* 〔*give someone*〕 *a rap over the knuckles, 《*fig.*》 get 〔give〕 a rebuke. 꾸중듣다〔꾸짖다〕.

rap[2] [ræp] *n.* **1** a worthless thing. 쓸모 없는 것. **2** the least bit. (아주) 조금. ¶ *I don't care a* ~. 조금도 관심이 없다 / *I wouldn't give a ~ for it.* 그 따위는 서푼어치도 안 된다. [E.]

ra·pa·cious [rəpéiʃəs] *adj.* **1** seizing by force or violence; extortionate. 강탈하는. ¶ *a ~ band of robbers* 한 무리의 강도들. **2** greedy. 탐욕스러운. ¶ *a ~ miser* 탐욕스러운 구두쇠. **3** (of an animal or bird) living on prey. (새·짐승이) 육식(肉食)하는. [↓]

rape[1] [reip] *n.* ⓊⒸ **1** 《*arch., poet.*》 the act of seizing or carrying off by force. 강탈; 약탈. **2** the act of forcing a woman to have sexual intercourse against her will. (부녀자에 대한) 성폭행; 능욕. — *vt.* (P6) **1** 《*arch., poet.*》 seize or take (something) by force. …을 강탈〔약탈〕하다. **2** violate (a woman). (부녀자)를 성폭행하다. [L. *rapio* seize]

rape[2] [reip] *n.* ⓊⒸ 《bot.》 a plant used as food for sheep, etc. 평지. [L. *rapum* turnip]

rape·seed [réipsìːd] *n.* ⒸⓊ **1** the seed of the rape, from which oil is obtained. 유채〔평지〕씨. **2** the plant itself. 유채; 평지.

:rap·id [rǽpid] *adj.* (sometimes **-er, -est**) **1** occurring or happening in a short time; very quick; swift. 빠른; 날랜. ¶ *a ~ stream* 급류; 여울 / *a ~ journey* 황망한 여행 / *a ~ thinker* 〔*speaker, worker*〕 머리 회전〔말, 일〕이 빠른 사람 / *take a ~ glance* 흘끔 보다. **2** (of a slope, etc.) steep. 가파른. ¶ *a ~ descent in a road* 길의 가파른 내리받이. — *n.* 《usu. *pl.*》 a part of a stream where the water runs very fast. 급류; 여울. [→rape[1]]

rapid fire [∠-∠] *n.* 《mil.》 a rate of firing small arms that is intermediate between slow fire and quick fire. 속사(速射).

rap·id-fire [rǽpidfáiər] *adj.* **1** (of a gun) firing or occurring in rapid succession. 속사의. **2** (of a question, etc.) spoken quickly one after the other. 잇따른. ¶ ~ *questions* 잇따른 질문; 질문 공세.

ra·pid·i·ty [rəpídəti] *n.* Ⓤ quickness; swiftness; speed. 빠름; 신속; 속도.

:rap·id·ly [rǽpidli] *adv.* with great speed; swiftly. 빠르게; 민첩하게.

rap·ine [rǽpin, -pain] *n.* Ⓤ 《*poet., lit.*》 the act of robbing by force; violent seizure. 강탈; 약탈. ¶ *The soldiers in the enemy's land procured their food by* ~. 적지의 병사들은 약탈에 의해 식량을 마련했다. [→rape[1]]

rap·port [ræpɔ́ːr] *n.* Ⓤ **1** harmonious relation or connection. 친교(親交). **2** communication. (강신술(降神術)의) 영교(靈交). [F.]

rap·proche·ment [ræ̀prouʃmáːŋ / ræprɔ́ʃmɑːŋ] *n.* Ⓤ establishment or re-establishment of friendly relations between states. 화해; 친선〔국교〕 회복. [F.]

rapt [ræpt] *adj.* deeply absorbed; lost in delight. 열중한; 정신이 팔린; 더없이 기쁜. ¶ *He was ~ in his reading.* 독서에 열중하고 있었다 / *He listened with ~ attention to the lecture.* 그는 강의를 듣는데 온 정신을 쏟았다 / *a ~ smile* 기쁨에 찬 미소. [→rape[1]]

·rap·ture [rǽptʃər] *n.* CU 《often *pl.*》 **1** very great joy or delight. 환희; 큰 기쁨. ¶ *The children greeted him with raptures of delight.* 아이들은 뛸 듯이 기뻐하며 그를 맞았다. **2** the expression of great joy. 기쁨의 표현. [↑]

rap·tur·ous [rǽptʃərəs] *adj.* full of rapture or delight; delighted. 미칠 듯이 기뻐하는; 열광적인. ●**rap·tur·ous·ly** [-li] *adv.*

:rare[1] [rɛər] *adj.* **1** scarce; not often found; unusual. 드문; 진기한; 희귀한. ¶ *a ~ book* 희귀본 / *on ~ occasions* 드물게 / *~ earths* 희토류(稀土類) / *a ~ event* 드문 일 / *It is ~ for him to be late.* 여간해서 그는 지각을 않는다 / *a ~ beauty* (보기) 드문 미인. **2** unusually great or excellent. 아주 뛰어난〔우수한〕. ¶ *wine of ~ quality* 고급 포도주 / *have a ~ time of it* 아주 즐겁게 지내다 / *I had ~ fun with him.* 나는 그와 아주 즐겁게 지냈다. **3** thin; not dense; scattered. 희박한; 드문드문한. ¶ *the ~ air* 희박한 공기 / *a few ~ houses here and there* 여기저기 띄엄띄엄 있는 집 몇 채.

rare and ..., 《*colloq.*》 very. 대단히; 몹시. ¶ *I'm ~ and happy.* 아주 행복하다.

●**rare·ness** [-nis] *n.* [L. *rarus*]

rare[2] [rɛər] *adj.* 《orig. U.S.》 underdone; not thoroughly cooked. 덜 구운; 설익은(cf. *underdone, well-done*). ¶ *a ~ steak.* [O.E. *hrēre*]

rar·e·fac·tion [rɛ̀ərəfǽkʃən] *n.* U the act of rarefying; the state of being rarefied. 희박해짐; 희박(opp. condensation). [*rare*[1], *-faction*]

rar·e·fy [rɛ́ərəfài] *v.* (**-fied**) *vt.* (P6) **1** make (air, gas, etc.) rarer or thinner. (기체 따위)를 희박하게 하다. ¶ *The air is rarefied at this great height.* 이렇게 높은 곳에서는 공기가 희박하다. **2** 《*fig.*》 refine; purify. …을 순화〔정화〕하다. ¶ *~ one's earthly desires* 세속적인 욕망을 정화하다. — *vi.* (P1) become rarefied. 희박해지다. [*rare*[1]]

:rare·ly [rɛ́ərli] *adv.* **1** seldom; not often. 드물게. ¶ *These stamps are ~ seen.* 이 우표들은 보기 드물다 / *I come here very ~.* 내가 여기 오는 일은 좀처럼 없다. **2** unusually well. 매우; 대단히. ¶ *He is ~ honest.* 그는 아주 정직하다 / *We dined ~.* 아주 잘 먹었다. [*rare*[1]]

rarely, if ever, 《*colloq.*》 seldom. 좀처럼; 드물게. ¶ *He ~, if ever, goes out.* 여간해서 외출을 안한다.

rar·i·ty [rɛ́ərəti] *n.* (*pl.* **-ties**) **1** U the state or quality of being rare. 드묾; 희귀; 희박. ¶ *the ~ of the air high in the mountains* 고산에서의 공기의 희박성 / *a thing of great ~* 대단한 진품(珍品). **2** C something rare or uncommon. 진품. ¶ *an expensive ~* 고가의 진품 / *Such a fine day is a ~ here.* 여기선 이런 좋은 날씨가 드물다 / *A man over a hundred years old is a ~.* 백 살 넘은 사람은 드물다. [*rare*[1]]

·ras·cal [rǽskəl / rɑ́:s-] *n.* C **1** a bad or dishonest person. 악당; 깡패. **2** 《*joc.*》 a mischievous or playful child. 개구쟁이. ¶ *You young ~!* 요 못된 개구쟁이야.

— *adj.* 《*arch.*》 of the rabble. 오합지졸(烏合之卒)의. ¶ *the ~ crowd* 잡배(雜輩)들의 무리. [F. *rascaille* rabble]

ras·cal·i·ty [ræskǽləti / rɑ:s-] *n.* CU (*pl.* **-ties**) a bad, dishonest act, conduct or character. 나쁜 짓; 악당 근성. ¶ *He is up to some new ~.* 뭔가 또 못된 일을 꾸미고 있다.

ras·cal·ly [rǽskəli / rɑ́:s-] *adj.* mean; base; dishonest. 치사한; 못된. ¶ *a ~ fellow* 치사한 친구 / *To steal the poor boy's lunch was a ~ trick.* 그 불쌍한 아이의 도시락을 훔친 일은 못된 장난이었다. — *adv.* in a rascally manner. 야비〔악랄〕하게.

rase [reiz] *vt.* =raze.

rash[1] [ræʃ] *n.* C a skin eruption with many small red spots. 뾰루지; 발진. ¶ *Some illnesses cause a ~.* 발진이 생기는 병이 있다. [F.]

·rash[2] [ræʃ] *adj.* hasty; careless. 경솔한; 조심성 없는. ¶ *a ~ general* 〔*act*〕 경솔한 장군〔행동〕 / *It was ~ of you to cross the street without looking both ways.* 좌우를 살피지 않고 길을 건너려 한 것은 경솔했다. ●**rashness** [-nis] *n.* [E.]

rash·er [rǽʃər] *n.* C a thin slice of bacon or ham for cooking; a group of such thin slices. (요리용의) 얇은 베이컨〔햄〕 조각. [E.]

rash·ly [rǽʃli] *adv.* too hastily; without due consideration; recklessly. 경솔하게; 무턱대고. [→rash[2]]

rasp [ræsp, rɑ:sp] *vt.* **1** (P6,7,18) 《*off, away*》 rub with a rasp; rub; scrape. …을 줄질하다; 비벼 닦다; 문질러 반반하게 하다. ¶ *The water rasps away the rocks.* 물이 바위들을 마모(摩耗)시킨다. **2** (P6) irritate. …을 짜증나게 하다. ¶ *Her singing rasps my nerves.* 그녀 노랫소리가 신경을 건드린다 / *Her rasped feeling exploded into anger.* 짜증스러워하더니 그녀는 그만 화를 냈다. **3** (P6,7) utter (something) in a rasping voice. …을 귀에 거슬리는 소리로 말하다. ¶ *~ out an order* 신경을 거스르는 소리로 명령을 내리다.

— *vi.* (P1) **1** grate roughly. 쓸리다; 갈리다. **2** make a grating, harsh voice. 귀에 거슬리는 소리를 내다.

— *n.* C **1** a metal tool for smoothing surfaces. 줄. **2** a rough, grating sound. 삐걱삐걱하는 소리. **3** irritation of mind. 초조; 신경질. [F. *rasper*]

rasp·ber·ry [rǽzbèri, -bəri, rá:z-] *n.* Ⓒ (*pl.* **-ries**) **1** a small berry, usu. red or black, which grows on a bush. 나무 딸기. **2** a plant which bears this berry. 그 나무. [E.]

:rat [ræt] *n.* Ⓒ **1** a long-tailed animal like a mouse, usu. gray, brown or white. 쥐(cf. *mouse*). **2** a mean person; a person who abandons his fellows esp. in trouble. 비열한 놈; (특히 어려울 때) 동료를 저버리는 배반자. **3** a worker who will not support a strike. 파업 불참자.

die like a rat, be killed by poison. 독살되다.

like a drowned rat, wet through; wet and miserable. 온몸이 젖어; 후줄근해져; 풀이 죽어.

Oh, rats! 《*sl.*》 Nonsense! I don't believe it. 허튼 소리 마라.

smell a rat, 《*fig.*》 think that some secret plan is being made; feel suspicious. 어떤 낌새를 채다.

— *vi.* (P1) **1** hunt or catch rats. 쥐를 잡다. **2** behave like a mean or disloyal person. 비열한 짓을 하다; 변절하다. [E.]

rat·a·ble [réitəbəl] *adj.* **1** that can be rated or appraised. 평가할 수 있는. **2** 《Brit.》 liable to pay local taxes. 지방세를 물어야 할. **3** proportional. 비례상의. ¶ ~ *share* 비례 배분. [→rate[1]]

ra·tan [rætǽn, rə-] *n.* =rattan.

ratch·et [rǽtʃət] *n.* Ⓒ **1** a hinged piece which stops a gearwheel from turning backward. (톱니바퀴 역회전 방지용) 미늘; 래칫. **2** a gearwheel which is controlled by a ratchet. 깔쭉톱니바퀴. **3** a device consisting of a gearwheel and a ratchet. 톱니바퀴 역회전 방지 장치. — *vt.* fit (a wheel) with ratchets. (바퀴)에 래칫을 장치하다. [F. *rochet* lance head]

:rate[1] [reit] *n.* Ⓒ **1** the amount or degree of something in relation to something else. 비율. ¶ *the birth* 〔*death*〕 ~ 출생〔사망〕률 / *the* ~ *of interest* 이율 / *at the* ~ *of* … 의 비율로 / *The drug has a high success* ~ *in curing the disease.* 그 약은 그 병을 치료하는데 성공률이 높다. **2** speed. 속도. ¶ *at a dangerous* ~ 위험한 속도로 / *at the* ~ *of 30 miles an hour* 시속 30마일로 / *His heart was beating at a rapid* ~. 그의 심장은 빠른 속도로 뛰고 있었다. **3** a fixed relation between two things. 시세. ¶ *the* ~ *of exchange* 환시세. **4** a set price or wage; a charge. 값; 요금. ¶ *at a high* 〔*low*〕 ~ 비싸게〔싸게〕 / *at any easy* ~ 헐값으로; 쉽게 / *buy at a cheap* ~ 싸게 사다 / *postal rates* 우편 요금 / *railroad rates* 철도 요금 / *They cut the rates on all household items.* 그들은 모든 가계비(家計費)를 줄였다. **5** a class or grade. 등급. ¶ *a ship of the first-rate* 제1급 선박 / *first* 〔*second*〕 ~ 일류〔이류〕 / *second-rate ability* 시원찮은 능력 / *This fruit is very second-rate.* 이건 형편 없는 과일이다. **6** 《*pl.*》 《Brit.》 a local property tax. 지방세. ¶ *rates and taxes* 지방세와 국세.

at any rate, **a**) in any case; whatever happens. 어쨌든. ¶ *At any* ~ *I will do nothing without further directions.* 어쨌든 추후 지시가 없는 한 나는 아무 일도 하지 않겠다. **b**) at least. 적어도. ¶ *We won the first match at any* ~. 적어도 우린 첫 게임에는 이겼다.

at that rate, **a**) in that case; if what you say is true. 그렇다면. ¶ *At that* ~ *we shan't get any dinner today.* 그렇다면 오늘 저녁을 굶어야 하는구나. **b**) in that way. 그런 식으로는. ¶ *If you go on at that* ~ *you will lose your health.* 그래가지고는 건강을 해칠 것이다.

at this rate, in this way; if the present situation continues. 이 상태로는; 이래서는. ¶ *At this* ~ *we shan't get home tonight.* 이래서는 오늘 밤 집에 도착하지 못할 것이다.

— *vt.* **1** (P6,7,18) estimate or judge the value of (something); regard as; consider. …을 평가하다; …이라 간주하다. ¶ ~ *someone's merit high* 아무의 공적을 높이 평가하다 / *The dealer rated the picture at* 〔*as worth*〕 *$5,000.* 상인은 그 그림을 5천 달러로 평가했다 / *He is rated* (*as*) *one of the richest men of this city.* 그는 이 시의 최고 갑부의 한 사람으로 간주되고 있다. **2** (P6) 《U.S.》 deserve. …을 할 만하다. ¶ *The essay rates a high grade.* 그 평론은 높은 점수를 받을 만하다. **3** (P6,7,13) 《Brit.》 《usu. *passive*》 fix the rate on (property) for local taxes. …을 과세의 목적으로 평가하다; …에 지방세를 과하다. ¶ *Houses are rated at a sum smaller than the rent.* 가옥의 과세액은 임대료보다 적게 매긴다.

— *vi.* (P1) 《*as*》 be ranked or valued. 평가되다. ¶ *England rates highest in the cotton industry.* 영국은 면공업(綿工業)에서 최고로 평가받고 있다 / *He rated very high in his class.* 그는 반에서 성적이 아주 상위권이었다. [L. *reor* reckon]

rate[2] [reit] *vt., vi.* (P6; 1,3) scold angrily. (…을) 꾸짖다; 매도하다; 욕설하다. ¶ ~ (*at*) *someone for his dishonesty* 아무의 불성실을 타박하다 / *He was soundly rated by his teacher.* 선생한테 심한 꾸중을 들었다. [E.]

:rath·er [rǽðər, rá:ð-] *adv.* **1** more willingly; preferably; sooner. 오히려; 어느 쪽이냐 하면. ¶ *I will go to meet him* ~ *than wait for him.* 그를 기다리느니 차라리 찾아가서 만나겠다 / *I should* ~ *think so.* 그렇고 말고. **2** more accurately; more properly. 더 정확히 말하면. ¶ *We got home late last night, or* ~, *early this morning.* 우리는 어젯밤 늦게, 아니 정확히는 오늘 아침 일찍 귀가했다 / *The color seems green* ~ *than blue.* 그 색은 청색이라기보다는 초록빛 같다 / *This is* ~ *for father to decide than for you.* 이건 너보다도 아버지가 결정할 일이다. **3** somewhat; to some extent. 다소; 어느

정도. ¶ *That is a ~ clever book.* 그 책은 꽤 잘된 책이다 / *I feel ~ better today.* 오늘은 좀 괜찮다 / *It is ~ cold today.* 오늘은 좀 추운 편이다 / *This book is ~ too easy for me.* 이 책은 내게 좀 너무 쉽다 / *I ~ think you know him.* 네가 그 사람을 알 것 같은데. [語法] 형용사를 수식할 경우 부정 관사의 위치는 영국에서는 rather a cold day, 미국에서는 a rather cold day와 같이 됨. **4** on the contrary. 도리어. ¶ *He is no worse; ~ , he is better.* 그는 병이 더치지 않았다. 아니 도리어 호전됐다. **5** 《Brit. *colloq.*》 [rǽðə́ːr, rɑ́ːð-] (in answering a question) certainly. 그렇고 말고. ¶ *Do you think so? Rather!* 그렇게 생각하나. 물론이지 / *Do you know her? —Rather!* 그 여자를 아니. —알다 뿐인가. [E.]

had* 〔*would*〕 *rather, would prefer. 오히려 … 한 편이 좋다. ¶ *He had ~ drink tea than coffee.* 그는 커피보다는 홍차를 즐겨 마신다 / *You'd ~ not do a thing at all than do it badly.* 시원찮게 하려거든 아예 하지를 마라 / *I had ~ have never been born than have seen this day of shame.* 이런 치욕을 당하느니 차라리 태어나지나 말았을 걸 / *Rather than get rich in such a way, I would beg in street.* 그렇게 돈을 버느니 길에서 비럭질하는 것이 낫겠다 / *I would ~ you came tomorrow.* 내일 와 주었으면 싶다.

the rather that, so much the more because. …하므로 더〔더욱〕.

rat·i·fi·ca·tion [rætəfikéiʃən] *n.* Ⓤ Ⓒ the act of ratifying; the state of being ratified; confirmation. 비준; 승인. ¶ *the ~ of a treaty* 조약의 비준. [↓]

rat·i·fy [rǽtəfài] *vt.* (**-fied**) (P6) make (a treaty, etc.) valid by signing; approve; confirm. (조약 따위)를 비준〔승인〕하다. ¶ *~ the treaty* 조약을 비준하다. [→rate[1]]

rat·ing [réitiŋ] *n.* **1** Ⓤ the act of valuing according to relative value. 평가. **2** Ⓤ Ⓒ classification according to relative value. 등급; 격(格)매김. **3** 《*pl.*》 all the members of a ship's crew of the same rank. 동일 계급의 전체 선원. **4** 《Brit.》 an amount fixed as a municipal rate. 지방세 부과액. [→rate[1]]

·ra·tio [réiʃou, -ʃiòu] *n.* Ⓤ Ⓒ (*pl.* **-tios**) the relation between two things in number, degree or quantity; a proportion. 비; 비율. ¶ *the ~ of births to deaths* 출생과 사망의 비율 / *The boys and girls of our school are in the ~ of 3 to 2.* 우리 학교의 남녀 학생 비율은 3대 2다 / *The audience contains a very high ~ of young people.* 청중에서 젊은 층이 차지하는 비율이 매우 높다. [→rate[1]]

ra·ti·oc·i·nate [ræʃiɑ́sənèit, ræ̀ti-, -óus-] *vi.* (P1) reason or deduce logically; use syllogisms. 추리〔추론〕하다; 삼단 논법으로 추리하다. [↑]

ra·tion [rǽʃən, réi-] *n.* Ⓤ **1** a fixed allowance or portion of food or supplies in a time of shortage, esp. during a war. (전시 등의) 정량(定量); 배급(량). ¶ *rations of sugar* 〔*bread*〕 설탕〔빵〕 배급 / *We have used up our ~ of coal for the week.* (배급된) 1주일분의 석탄을 다 써버렸다. **2** 《usu. *pl.*》 the daily allowance of food for a soldier or sailor. (군인의) 하루치 식량. ¶ *an iron ~* (휴대용) 비상 식량. **3** 《*pl.*》 food; provisions. 식량; 양식.

be put on rations, be rationed; be put on an allowance. 배급제로 되다.

on short rations, on a limited allowance of food. 식량(배급)이 제한되어.

— *vt.* (P6) **1** supply (someone) with rations; distribute (food, supplies, etc.) in limited amounts. …에 정량〔정액〕을 지급하다; (식량 등)을 제한하다. ¶ *~ citizens when supplies are scarce* 공급이 달릴 때 시민에게 정량을 배급하다 / *~ sugar* 설탕을 제한하다. **2** supply with the daily ration of food, etc. …에게 (식량 따위)를 배급하다. ¶ *The army is well rationed.* 군에는 급식이 잘 되고 있다. [L. *ratiō* a reckoning]

·ra·tion·al [rǽʃənl] *adj.* **1** of reason; based on reasoning; able to reason clearly. 이성의; 이성적인. ¶ *Man is a ~ animal.* 인간은 이성이 있는 동물이다. **2** reasonable; sensible; moderate. 분별 있는; 사리를 아는. ¶ *a ~ man* 사리를 아는〔양식 있는〕 사람 / *a ~ act* 합리적인 행동. **3** based on reason only. 순이론적인. ¶ *a ~ explanation* 순이론적인 설명 / *a ~ belief* 이론적인 확신. **4** 《math.》 expressible by finite terms. 유리(有理)의(opp. irrational). ¶ *a ~ number* 유리수. [↑]

ra·tion·ale [ræ̀ʃənǽl, -nɑ́ːl] *n.* Ⓒ **1** a reasoned explanation. 이론적 해석. **2** the fundamental principle or reason. 근본적 이유; (사물의) 논리적 근거.

ra·tion·al·ism [rǽʃənlìzəm] *n.* Ⓤ the theory that reason is the supreme source of knowledge. 이성론(理性論); 합리주의(cf. *empiricism*).

ra·tion·al·ist [rǽʃənlist] *n.* Ⓒ a person who believes in rationalism. 이성론자; 합리론자.

ra·tion·al·is·tic [ræ̀ʃənlístik] *adj.* of rationalism. 이성〔합리〕주의의.

ra·tion·al·i·ty [ræ̀ʃənǽləti] *n.* Ⓤ (*pl.* **-ties**) the quality of being rational; reasonableness; 《usu. *pl.*》 a reasonable practice, view or belief. 합리성; 이성적 행동〔견해, 생각〕.

ra·tion·al·i·za·tion [ræ̀ʃənlizéiʃən] *n.* Ⓤ the act of rationalizing; the state of being rationalized. 합리화.

ra·tion·al·ize [rǽʃənlàiz] *vt.* (P6) **1** make (something) rational or more efficient. …을 합리화하다. ¶ *~ an industry* 산업을 합리화하다. **2** treat or explain (something) entirely by reason. …을 이론적으로 생각하

다[설명하다]. ¶ ～ *myths* 신화를 합리적으로 설명하다. **3** justify (one's behavior, etc.) to oneself; find excuses for (a fault, etc.). …에 이유를 붙이다; 구실을 만들다. ¶ *She rationalized her prejudice.* 그녀는 자기의 선입관을 그럴 듯하게 정당화했다 / ～ *one's failure* 실패한 이유를 내세우다. **4** 《econ.》 make (the process of production) more efficient. (산업)을 합리화하다.

— *vi.* think or act in a rational manner; practice rationalism. 이론적으로 생각하다; 합리화시키다.

rat·line, -lin [rǽtlin] *n.* Ⓒ 《naut.》 《usu. *pl.*》 steps of rope across the shrouds of a ship, used as a ladder. (줄사닥다리의) 디딤줄. [E.]

rat race [∠∸] *n.* a fierce competition to obtain wealth, power, etc., esp. in one's career. 격심한 경쟁《부·출세를 위한》. [↓]

rats·bane [rǽtsbèin] *n.* Ⓤ any poison to kill rats. 쥐약. [→rat]

rat·tan [rætǽn, rə-] *n.* **1** Ⓤ a palm tree with long, tough stems. 등나무. **2** Ⓒ a walking stick made of the wood of this tree. 등나무 지팡이. [Malay]

rat·ter [rǽtər] *n.* Ⓒ **1** a person, an animal or a device that catches rats. 쥐 잡는 사람 [짐승, 도구]. ¶ *Our cat is a good* ～. 우리집 고양이는 쥐를 잘 잡는다. **2** a person who betrays his associates or party in a crisis; a deserter. (어려울 때의) 변절자; 탈당자; 배신자. [→rat]

·**rat·tle** [rǽtl] *vi.* **1** (P1,2A,3) make short, sharp sounds in rapid succession. 덜걱덜걱 소리나다. ¶ *The window rattled in the wind.* 유리창이 바람에 덜컹거렸다 / *Someone rattled at the door.* 누군가가 문을 덜거덕거렸다 / *The beggar rattled the coins in his tin.* 거지는 깡통 속의 동전을 딸랑거렸다. **2** (P1,2A,3) go, move or fall with a rattling noise. 덜걱[덜컹·덜거덕·후두둑]거리며 가다 [움직이다, 떨어지다]. ¶ *The old car rattled along the road.* 고물차는 덜커덩거리며 길을 굴러갔다 / *A shower of stones rattled down on his head.* 돌멩이들이 그의 머리 위로 우르르 떨어졌다 / *The hailstones rattled on the tin roof.* 후두둑거리며 우박이 양철 지붕에 쏟아졌다. **3** (P2A) talk rapidly and thoughtlessly. 재잘거리다; 빠른 말로 지껄이다. ¶ ～ *on* [*away*] *for hours* 몇 시간이고 떠들다 / *She rattled on gaily about her dress.* 그녀는 자기 옷을 가지고 수다를 늘어놓았다 / *He rattled through his speech.* 그는 빠른 말로 연설했다.

— *vt.* **1** (P6,7) cause (something) to make a rattling noise. …을 덜걱[덜컹]거리게 하다[울리다]. ¶ *The wind rattled the window.* 바람이 창문을 덜컹거렸다 / ～ *the dishes* 접시를 달가닥거리다 / *The train rattled us about.* 우리가 탄 열차는 덜커덩거리며 달렸다. **2** (P6,7) 《*off*》 say, utter rapidly. 빠른 말로 지껄이다. ¶ *The girl rattled off the poem.* 소녀는 그 시를 줄줄 외웠다. **3** (P6,7) perform some action rapidly. …을 빠르게 처리하다. ¶ ～ *the bills through the House* 의안을 의회에서 신속히 처리하다 / ～ *a piece of business through* 일을 데꺽 해치우다. **4** (P6) 《*colloq.*》 confuse; cause (someone) to be nervous. …을 혼란시키다; 당황케 하다. ¶ *She was badly rattled by her failure in her exam.* 그녀는 시험에 떨어져 마음의 갈피를 잡을 수 없었다 / *The constant interruptions rather rattled the speaker.* 계속 방해하는 바람에 연사는 상당히 당황했다.

— *n.* Ⓒ **1** a rattling sound; a number of short, sharp sounds. 덜걱[덜컹]거리는 소리; 짧은 단속적인 소리. ¶ *the* ～ *of milk bottles* 우유병의 달그락거리는 소리 / *a* ～ *in the throat* (특히 임종 때의) 가르랑거리는 소리. **2** loud trivial chatter; a person who rattles. 시끄럽게 지껄임; 그 소리; 떠버리. **3** ⓐ a baby's toy which makes a rattling sound. 딸랑이. ¶ *The baby shakes his* ～. 아기가 딸랑이를 흔든다. ⓑ the part of a rattlesnake's tail which makes a noise. 방울뱀의 소리내는 기관《꼬리》. [Du. *ratelen*]

rat·tle·brain [rǽtlbrèin] *n.* Ⓒ an empty-headed, noisy person. 골빈 떠버리.

rat·tle-brained [rǽtlbrèind] *adj.* having an empty brain; thoughtless; careless. 머리가 빈; 지각이 없는.

rat·tler [rǽtlər] *n.* Ⓒ **1** anything that makes a clattering sound. 덜걱[덜커덕]거리는 것. **2** 《*colloq.*》 =rattlesnake. **3** a chatterer. 떠버리; 수다쟁이. **4** 《*sl.*》 a first-rate person or thing. 일류의 사람[물건].

rat·tle·snake [rǽtlsnèik] *n.* Ⓒ a poisonous American snake whose tail rattles sharply when disturbed. 방울뱀.

rat·tling [rǽtliŋ] *adj.* **1** making a rattling noise. 덜거덕[덜컹]거리는. ¶ *a* ～ *window.* **2** 《*colloq.*》 vigorous; brisk; quick. 기운찬; 활발한; 빠른. ¶ *at a* ～ *pace* 쾌속으로. **3** 《*colloq.*》 splendid; excellent. 훌륭한; 멋진. ¶ *have a* ～ *time* 아주 즐겁게 지내다 / *a* ～ *good story* 아주 재미있는 이야기.

rau·cous [rɔ́:kəs] *adj.* harsh-sounding; hoarse. (듣기 나쁜) 쉰 목소리의. ¶ *a* ～ *voice* / *the* ～ *caw of a crow* 까마귀의 까옥까옥 소리. [L.]

rav·age [rǽvidʒ] *vt.* (P6) **1** rob (something) with violence; plunder and lay waste. …을 약탈하다; 황폐시키다. ¶ *The enemy ravaged the city.* 적은 그 시를 약탈했다 / *The victors ravaged the countryside.* 정복자들이 시골 지방을 노략질했다. **2** ruin; destroy; spoil. …을 파괴하다; (병 따위가) 못쓰게 만들다; 손상하다. ¶ *Her face is ravaged by time* [*grief*]. 그녀 얼굴은 세월로[비탄으로] 못쓰게 됐다.

— *vi.* (P1) do ruinous damage; commit ravages. 약탈하다; 쑥밭을 만들다.

— *n.* **1** Ⓤ destruction by violence; ruin. 파괴; 황폐. ¶ *They tried to secure themselves*

R

from ~ by fire. 그들은 화재로 인한 피해를 막으려고 애썼다. **2** 《usu. *pl.*》 destructive effects; havoc. 파괴의 흔적. ¶ *the ravages of war* 전화(戰禍) / *the ravages of time* 세월이 지남으로 생긴 황폐한 흔적. [→rape[1]]

rave [reiv] *vi., vt.* (P1,2A,3;7,18) **1** talk wildly or irrationally like a mad man. (미친 사람처럼) 소리소리 지르다; 종작 없이 지껄이다. ¶ *An excited, angry man raves; so does a madman.* 미친 사람이 그렇듯이, 흥분하고 성난 사람은 고함을 지른다 / *He must be raving to talk like that.* 저렇듯 지껄이는 걸 보니 그는 미쳤나 보다. **2** 《*colloq.*》《*about, of*》 talk in an extreme manner, usu. enthusiastically. 열광적으로〔열심히〕 이야기하다. ¶ *The critics raved over the play.* 비평가들은 그 극에 대해 열변을 토했다 / *~ at* 〔*about, of*〕 *one's misfortunes* 자기의 불운한 이야기를 늘어놓다. **3** (of the sea, wind, etc.) howl; roar. (바람·바다가) 노호(怒號)하다. ¶ *The sea raves against the cliff.* 파도가 미친 듯이 벼랑에 부딪치며 물보라를 날린다 / *The wind raved through the mountains.* 바람이 사납게 산속을 휘몰아쳤다 / 《*reflexively*》 *The storm has raved itself out.* 폭풍이 몰아치다가 그쳤다. [L. *rabio*]

rave about, say that someone or something is wonderful. …을 격찬하다. ¶ *~ about a new author* 신진 작가를 격찬하다 / *Everyone is raving about the latest fashion.* 모두가 최신 유행에 대해 극구 칭찬하고 있다.

rave oneself hoarse, cry so much as to become hoarse in voice. 목이 쉬도록 소리를 지르다.

rav·el [rǽvəl] *v.* (**-eled, -el·ing** or 《Brit.》 **-elled, -el·ling**) *vt.* **1** (P6,7) draw out the threads of (something); untwist. …의 얽힌 것을 풀다. ¶ *~ rope's end* 밧줄 끝을 풀다. **2** (P6) ⓐ tangle; throw into a confused mass. …을 꼬이게 하다; 엉키게 하다. ¶ *raveled wool* 뒤얽힌 양털. ⓑ 《*fig.*》 make confused. …을 혼란시키다. ¶ *the raveled skein of life* 복잡하게 얽힌 인생. **3** (P7) 《*out*》 disentangle. …을 풀다; 해결하다. ¶ 《*fig.*》 *~ all the matter out* 모든 문제를 해결하다.
— *vi.* **1** (P1,2A) become unwoven. (실·피륙 따위가) 풀리다. ¶ *The sweater began to ~ at the elbow.* 스웨터의 팔꿈치가 풀리기 시작했다 / *The rope has raveled at the end.* 밧줄 끝이 풀어졌다. **2** (P1) become tangled or confused. 얽히다; 혼란해지다. **3** (P2A) 《*out*》 be disentangled. (얽힌 것이) 풀리다. ¶ 《*fig.*》 *The difficulty will soon ~ out.* 어려움은 쉬이 해결될 것이다.
— *n.* Ⓒ **1** an unraveled thread; a confused condition. 실의 얽힘; 혼란. ¶ *a ~ of rope* 밧줄의 꼬임 / 《*fig.*》 *the ~ of life* 복잡한 인생. **2** a loose end. (밧줄 등) 풀어진 끝. [Du. *ravelen*]

ra·ven[1] [réivən] *n.* Ⓒ a large, black bird like a crow. 갈가마귀. — *adj.* deep, shining black. 새까맣고 윤나는. ¶ *~ hair* 윤기나는 검은 머리. [E.]

ra·ven[2] [rǽvən] *vi.* (P1,2A,3) **1** 《*about, after*》 seek for prey. 먹이를 찾다. ¶ *Lions are ravening after their prey.* 사자들이 먹이를 찾아다니고 있다. **2** 《*for*》 have a ravenous appetite for. 기갈이 들다. ¶ *He ravens for ice-cream.* 아이스크림 생각이 굴뚝 같다 / *~ for blood* 피에 굶주리다. — *vt.* devour; eat very hungrily. 게걸스레 먹다. [→rape[1]]

rav·en·ing [rǽvəniŋ] *adj.* extremely hungry; rapacious. 굶주린; 탐욕스러운. ¶ *~ wolves* 굶주린 이리떼. [↑]

rav·en·ous [rǽvənəs] *adj.* very hungry; starving; greedy. 굶주린. ¶ *~ for food* 밥에 주리다. ● **rav·en·ous·ly** [-li] *adv.*

ra·vine [rəvíːn] *n.* Ⓒ a long, deep valley, usu. worn by running water; a gorge. 협곡; 깊은 계곡. [→rape[1]]

rav·ing [réiviŋ] *adj.* **1** talking wildly. 함부로 떠드는. ¶ *a ~ lunatic* 날뛰는 미치광이. **2** raging; frenzied. 광란하는. ¶ *a ~ storm* 휘몰아치는 폭풍우. **3** 《U.S. *colloq.*》 remarkable; notable. 훌륭한; 유명한. ¶ *a ~ beauty* 굉장한 미인. — *n.* 《often *pl.*》 wild, irrational talk. 난폭하고 종잡을 수 없는 말. ¶ *the ravings of a mad man* 광인의 헛소리. [*rave*]

rav·ish [rǽviʃ] *vt.* (P6) **1** fill (someone) with strong emotion or delight; enchant. …을 몹시 기쁘게 하다; 황홀하게 하다. ¶ *The prince was ravished by Cinderella's beauty.* 왕자는 신데렐라의 미모에 넋을 잃었다 / *Our ears were ravished by the sweet music.* 감미로운 선율에 우리는 황홀해졌다. **2** 《*arch.*》 take away (something) by force; violate (a woman). …을 강탈하다; (부녀자)를 폭행〔강간〕하다. ¶ *~ a kiss* 강제로 키스하다 / *Death has ravished her baby from her.* 죽음이 그녀에게서 아기를 앗아갔다. [→rape[1]]

rav·ish·ing [rǽviʃiŋ] *adj.* very delightful; charming. 매혹적인; 황홀한. ¶ *a ~ voice* 매혹적인 목소리 / *jewels of ~ beauty* 보석의 황홀한 아름다움.

rav·ish·ment [rǽviʃmənt] *n.* **1** the act of carrying off by force. 강탈. **2** 《*arch.*》 the act of violating a woman or girl. 부녀자에 대한 폭행. **3** delight. 환희; 기쁨.

:raw [rɔː] *adj.* **1** not cooked. 날 것의. ¶ *~ meat* 날고기 / *eat fish ~* 생선을 날로 먹다 / *Don't eat your food ~.* 음식을 날로 먹지 마라. **2** in the natural state; unprocessed; unrefined. 원료 그대로의; 가공하지 않은. ¶ *~ cotton* 원면 / *~ material* 원료 / *~ rubber* 생고무 / *~ silk* 생사 / *~ oil* 원유 / *~ sugar* 원당. **3** not trained; not experienced. 미숙한; 경험이 없는. ¶ *a ~ recruit* 신병 / *He is ~ to the work.* 그는 그 일에 서투르다. **4** (of the weather) damp and cold. 습하고 추운. ¶ *a ~ morning* 으스스한 아침 / *a ~ wind* 습기 찬 바람 / *~ weather* 으스스한 날씨. **5** (of wounds) with the skin rubbed off; painful. 살이 까진; 얼얼한; 쓰린. ¶ *a ~ cut* 생채기 / *My throat is ~ from shouting.* 소리를 질렀더니 목이 아프다. **6** recently finished; fresh. 갓 …한. ¶ *~ paint* 갓 칠한 페인트 / *~ plaster* 굳지 않은 회반죽. **7** 《U.S. *colloq.*》 harsh; unjust; indecent. 사정 없는; 부당한; 상스러운. ¶ *a ~ deal* 매정한 처사.

— *n.* 《*the ~*》 an exposed sore spot on the body. 살가죽이 까진 데. ¶ *a ~ on a horse's back* (마찰로 인한) 말 등의 벗겨진 데; 찰과상(擦過傷). [E.]

in the raw, **a**) 《U.S.》 in the natural state. 자연 그대로의. **b**) 《*sl.*》 naked. 알몸의.

touch someone on the raw, wound someone in a very sensitive spot. 남의 아픈 데를 건드리다; 약점을 찌르다.

raw·boned [rɔ́:bóund] *adj.* having little flesh covering the bones; very thin; bony. 삐삐 마른; 뼈가 앙상한. ¶ *a ~ horse* 비쩍 마른 말. [↑]

Ray [rei] *n.* a nickname for Raymond. Raymond의 애칭.

:ray[1] [rei] *n.* Ⓒ **1** a line or beam of light; a line or stream of heat, electrons, etc. 광선; 사선(射線); 열선(熱線); 방사선. ¶ *X rays* 뢴트겐선; 엑스레이 / *the rays of the sun* 태양 광선 / *infra-red* 〔*ultra-violet*〕 *rays* 적외〔자외〕선. **2** one of several parts coming out from a common center. 사출형(射出形)〔방사꼴〕의 것. ¶ *the rays of a daisy* 데이지의 방사꼴 꽃잎 / *a starfish's rays* 불가사리의 팔. **3** 《*fig.*》 a beam of mental light. (광명·희망 등의) 빛. ¶ *a ~ of truth* 진리의 빛 / *There isn't a ~ of hope left for us.* 이제 우리에게 한가닥의 희망도 없다.

— *vi., vt.* (P1;6) issue in rays; send out rays. (빛 따위가) 나다; (빛 따위)를 내다; 발하다; 방사하다. [→radius]

ray[2] [rei] *n.* Ⓒ a flat, fan-shaped fish with a thin, whip-like tail. 가오리. [L. *raia*]

Ray·mond [réimənd] *n.* a man's name. 남자 이름.

ray·on [réiɑn / -ɔn] *n.* Ⓤ a silklike fiber or fabric made from wood pulp; artificial silk. 레이온; 인조 견사. [→ray[1]]

raze [reiz] *vt.* (P6,7) **1** 《usu. *fig.*》 scratch away; erase. …을 지우다; 없애다. ¶ *I razed his name from my memory.* 나는 그의 이름을 내 기억에서 지워버렸다. **2** destroy utterly; bring (something) down to the ground. …을 완전히 파괴하다; 무너뜨리다. 參考 rase로도 씀. ¶ *The whole town was razed by the earthquake.* 마을 전체가 지진으로 파괴되었다 / *Fire razed the city to the ground.* 화재로 그 시는 완전히 파괴되었다. [L. *rado* scrape]

·ra·zor [réizər] *n.* Ⓒ a sharp-edged tool, used esp. for shaving hair off the skin. 면도칼. ¶ *a safety ~* 안전 면도칼 / *a ~ strap* 혁지(革砥). [↑]

as sharp as a razor, very sharp. 아주 날카로운; 빈틈 없는.

be on the 〔*a*〕 ***razor's edge,*** 《*fig.*》 be in a very dangerous situation. 아주 위험한 처지에 있다.

ra·zor·back [réizərbæ̀k] *n.* Ⓒ **1** 《zool.》 a kind of whale. 큰고래. **2** a half-wild hog with a sharp ridge-like back, living in the southern United States. 반(半)야생의 돼지. **3** a sharp, narrow back like a razor. 뾰족한 산등 (따위).

razor·edge [réizərèdʒ] *n.* Ⓒ **1** the sharp edge of a razor; a sharp ridge of a hill. 면도날; 뾰족한 산등. **2** a critical point. 위기.

be on a razoredge, be in extreme difficulty or danger. 위기에 처해 있다. ¶ *His life was on a ~ for days.* 그는 며칠 동안 위기에 처해 있었다.

R.C. **1** Red Cross. **2** Reserve Corps. **3** Roman Catholic.

Rd., rd Road.

Re 《*chem.*》 rhenium.

re[1] [rei, ri:] *n.* 《mus.》 the second note of the scale. 레《장음계의 둘째음》. [It.]

re[2] [rei, ri:] *prep.* 《chiefly law, comm.》 《*colloq.*》 in the matter of; concerning. …에 관하여; …의 건에 대하여. ¶ *I'd like to have a talk with you ~ your plan.* 네 계획에 대해 이야기하고 싶다 / *~ estate of Robinson* 로빈슨씨의 재산 건에 관하여. [L.]

re- [ri:-, ri-, rə-] *pref.* **1** again; anew. '다시, 되풀이, 새로'의 뜻. ¶ *rearrange* 재정리하다 / *rebuild* 재건하다. **2** back. 되돌리다. ¶ *reclaim* 교정〔교화〕하다 / *repay* 갚다; 보답하다. [L.]

:reach [ri:tʃ] *vt.* **1** (P6) arrive at; get or come to; attain to. …에 도착하다; 이르다; 닿다. ¶ *~ Seoul* 서울에 도착하다 / *~ a conclusion* 결론에 이르다 / *~ a good age* 지긋한 나이가 되다; 고령에 달하다 / *~ one's destination* 목적지에 이르다 / *The letter did not ~ me.* 편지가 내게 오지 않았다 / *~ the top of the mountain* 산꼭대기에 다다르다. **2** (P6) ⓐ extend to; extend as far as. …에 미치다; …까지 뻗다. ¶ *The path reaches the sea.* 그 길은 바다까지 뻗어 있다. ⓑ amount to. (수량이) …에 이르다. ¶ *The cost has reached millions.* 비용은 수백만 달러에 달한다. **3** (P6) communicate with; get in touch with. …와 연락하다. ¶ *You can ~ them by cable.* 그들과 전화로 연락이 된다 / *Where can I ~ you?* 너와 어디서 접촉이 되나 / *He can't be reached.* 그와는 연락이 안 된다. **4** (P6,7) stretch out (the hand, etc.). (손 따위)를 뻗다; 내밀다. ¶ *~ one's hand across a table* 탁자 너머로 손을 뻗다 / *A tree reaches out its branches toward the light.* 나무는 햇빛을 향해서 가지를 뻗는다. **5** (P7,14) touch or seize (something) by stretching out the hand; get and pass (something) to someone else. 손을 내밀어 …을 집다; 집어 건네주다. ¶ *~ a book on the top shelf* 팔을 뻗어 꼭대기 선반에서 책을 집다 / *Please ~ me the* *salt.* 그 소금 좀 집어주세요 / *Can you ~ that book for me?* 그 책을 집어주게나 / *Will you kindly ~ me the sugar?* 그 설탕 좀 집어주시겠소. **6** (P6) influence; affect. (남의 마음)을 움직이다. ¶ ~ *someone's conscience* 아무의 양심을 움직이다.

— *vi.* **1** (P2A,3) stretch out the hand, foot, etc. 손〔발〕을 뻗다. ¶ ~ *for a flower* 손을 뻗어 꽃을 따다 / ~ *out for a pen* 펜을 집으려고 팔을 뻗다 / *He reached out to open the door.* 그는 문을 열려고 손을 내밀었다 / *She reached in her bag and pulled out a letter.* 그녀는 가방에 손을 집어넣어 편지 한 통을 꺼냈다. **2** (P3) 《*after*》 try to obtain. 얻으려고 노력하다. ¶ ~ *after happiness* 행복을 추구하다. **3** (P2A,3) extend in space, time, etc. 퍼지다; 이르다; 도달하다. ¶ *The park reaches down to the sea.* 그 공원은 바다까지 다다른다. **4** (P2A,3) (of the eye, voice, etc.) go as far as. (시력·소리가) 미치다; 닿다. ¶ *as far as the eye can ~* 눈길이 미치는 한 / *His voice reached to the end of the hall.* 그의 음성은 홀의 끝까지 들렸다.

— *n.* Ⓒ 《usu. *a ~*》 **1** the act of reaching or stretching out (the hand, etc.). 잡으려고 손을 뻗음. ¶ *get a book by a long ~* 팔을 길게 뻗어 책을 집다 / *make a ~ for a thing* 물건을 집으려고 손을 뻗다. **2** ⓐ the distance someone or something can stretch; range. (손·발이) 미치는 거리. ¶ *above* 〔*beyond, out of*〕 *one's ~* 손이 못 미치는 데에 / *She jumped beyond* 〔*out of*〕 *his ~.* 그가 잡지 못하게 그녀는 껑충 뛰었다 / *The village is within easy ~ of the station.* 마을은 역에서 쉽게 갈 수 있는 데에 있다. ⓑ Ⓤ range of action or power. (행동·힘이) 미치는 범위. ¶ *The problem is beyond my ~.* 그 문제는 나로서는 감당 못 한다 / *He has a wonderful ~ of imagination.* 그의 상상력은 놀랍다. **3** the power of grasping with the mind. 이해력. ¶ *This arithmetic problem is beyond my ~.* 이 산수 문제는 모르겠다. **4** Ⓒ 《usu. *pl.*》 a continuous stretch or extent; an expanse; a straight part of a river. (넓게) 퍼짐; (강의) 바라볼 수 있는 구역. ¶ *a ~ of woodland* 넓은 산림 지대 / *the upper* 〔*lower*〕 *reaches of a river* 강의 상〔하〕류 / *a ~ of grassland* 일대의 초원. [E.]

reach-me-down [rí:tʃmidàun] *n.* 《usu. *pl.*》 《Brit. *colloq.*》 a ready-made piece of clothes. 기성복. — *adj.* 《Brit. *colloq.*》 hand-me-down; ready-made; cheap. 기성품의; 싸구려의.

re·act [ri:ǽkt] *vi.* (P1,2A,3) **1** 《*on, upon*》 act in return; have a reverse effect upon each other. 반작용하다; 서로 작용하다. ¶ *The wheel and the drag ~ upon each other.* 바퀴와 브레이크는 상호 작용을 한다 / *Tyranny reacts upon the tyrant.* 폭정(暴政)이 폭군에 반역한다; 악은 악에 의해 보복된다. **2** 《*to*》 act in response. 감응하다; 반응을 나타내다. ¶ ~ *to a mother's affection* 어머니의 애정에 반응을 보인다 / *Dogs ~ to human kindness.* 개는 인간의 친절에 반응을 나타낸다 / *The eye reacts to light.* 눈은 빛에 반응한다. **3** act in opposition; return to a previous state. 반발〔반대〕하다. ¶ ~ *against a plan* 계획에 반발하다 / *The people reacted against the despotism.* 국민들은 전제 정치에 반항했다. [re-]

re-act [ri:ǽkt] *vt.* (P6) act or perform again. …을 되풀이하다. ¶ ~ *a play* 재연(再演)하다. [re-]

***re·ac·tion** [ri:ǽkʃən] *n.* ⓊⒸ **1** an opposing action. 반동; 반발. ¶ *action and ~* 작용과 반작용; 작동과 반동 / ~ *against militarism* 군국주의에 대한 반발. **2** a response to some force. 반응. ¶ *A common ~ to jokes is to laugh.* 농담에 대한 일반적인 반응은 웃음이다 / *What was his ~ to it?* 그걸 보고〔듣고〕 그가 어찌하든. **3** a political movement back to a former condition; dislike of new ideas. 복고 운동; 보수 반동. ¶ *a ~ against new ideas* 신사조에 대한 반발 / *The forces of ~ are often stronger than those of progress and reform.* 보수 반동 세력이 진보 개혁 세력보다 강할 수가 흔히 있다. **4** 《chem.》 a chemical change. 화학 반응.

re·ac·tion·ar·y [ri:ǽkʃənèri / -ʃənəri] *adj.* of political reaction. 보수 반동의. ¶ *The bad results of the revolution brought about a ~ feeling.* 혁명의 나쁜 결과가 그에 대한 반감을 조성했다. — *n.* Ⓒ a person who opposes political progress. 반동〔보수〕주의자.

re·ac·tor [ri:ǽktər] *n.* Ⓒ **1** a person or thing that reacts. 반동〔반응·반발〕하는 사람〔물건〕. **2** 《phys.》 a large tank in which atomic energy is produced. 원자로.

:read [ri:d] *v.* (**read** [red]) *vt.* **1** (P6,7) get the meaning of (something written or printed). …을 읽다. ¶ ~ *a book* 〔*newspaper*〕 책〔신문〕을 읽다 / *take up a letter and ~ it* 편지를 집어들고 읽다 / ~ *a novel through* 〔*over*〕 소설을 통독(通讀)하다 / *You should not ~ in the bright sunlight.* 밝은 햇빛에서 읽어서는 안 된다. **2** (P6,7,11,13) ⓐ learn the true meaning of (something); understand the meaning of; solve. …을 해석하다; 알다; 이해하다. ¶ *be read as…* …라고 해석되다 / ~ *someone's hand* 아무의 손금을 보다 / ~ *a flag signal* 수기(手旗) 신호를 해독하다 / ~ *the riddle* 수수께끼를 풀다 / ~ *a dream* 해몽하다 / *We can ~ Chinese but we cannot speak it.* 중국어를 읽을 수는 있으나 말은 못 한다. ⓑ understand the nature of by observation; learn the character of. (표정 등에서 마음·생각)을 이해하다; 간파하다. ¶ ~ *a girl's mind* 〔*sentiment*〕 소녀의 마음〔기분〕을 이해하다 / *She ~ his thoughts in his face.* 그의 표정을 보고 그녀는 그의 생각을 간파했다. ⓒ get knowledge of by reading; learn from a book, newspaper, etc. …을 읽고 알다. ¶ ~ *an account of the murder in the*

R

papers 신문에서 그 살인 기사를 읽다 / *She ~ in the papers that her friend had met with an accident.* 그녀는 신문에서 친구가 사고를 당했다는 것을 알았다. **3** (P6) foresee; foretell. …을 예견하다; 예언하다. ¶ *~ the future* 미래를 예언하다 / *~ someone's fortune* 아무의 운세를 봐주다 / *~ the sky* 점성(占星)을 보다; 천기(天氣)를 살펴보다. **4** (P6,7,14) say aloud (something written or printed). …을 소리내서 읽다; 음독(音讀)하다. ¶ *~ out a letter to someone* 아무에게 편지를 읽어주다 / *Read me (off) the list.* 그 명단을 읽어다오. **5** (P6) show; point out; indicate. (온도계 등이) …을 가리키다; 나타내다. ¶ *The thermometer reads 20°.* 온도계는 20°이다. **6** (P6,7) study in order to obtain. …을 위해 연구하다. ¶ *~ law* 법률을 공부하다 / *~ medicine for a degree* 학위를 얻기 위해 의학을 공부하다. **7** (P13) bring (someone) into a certain state by reading. …에게 읽어주어 —하게 하다. ¶ *~ a child to sleep* 아이에게 책을 읽어주어 재우다 / *~ oneself to sleep* 책을 읽다가 잠들다. **8** (P6,7) 《polit.》 lay before the House and discuss. …을 의회에 상정하다; 회부하다. ¶ *The bill was ~ a third times.* 의안은 제3 독회에 회부되었다.

—*vi.* **1** (P1,2A,3) get the meaning of something written or printed; say aloud something written or printed. 읽다; 소리내어 읽다; 낭독하다. ¶ *~ aloud* 소리내어 읽다 / *~ from* 〔*out of*〕 *a book* 책의 어느 한 구절을 골라서 읽다 / *~ in a book* 독서에 골몰하다; 탐독하다 / *~ for someone* 아무에게 읽어주다. **2** (P3) 《*of, about*》 learn by reading; learn from a book, newspaper, etc. 읽고 알〔게 되〕다. ¶ *I have ~ about* 〔*of*〕 *the accident in the paper.* 나는 그 사고 사실을 신문에서 읽고 알았다. **3** (P3) study. 연구하다. ¶ *~ for a degree* 〔*the Bar*〕 학위를 따려고〔변호사가 되려고〕 공부하다. **4** (P2A) give a certain meaning. …라고 씌어 있다. ¶ *The passage reads as follows.* 그 구절은 다음과 같다 / *The sentence reads oddly.* 그 글엔 이상한 것이 씌어져 있다.

read between the lines, find a meaning which is not actually expressed. 말〔글〕의 숨은 뜻을 알아내다.

read into (=*give a certain explanation to; find a certain meaning in*) *something.* …라는 뜻으로 해석하다.

read to *oneself,* read silently. 묵독하다.

read up (=*make a special study of*) *something.* (어떤 학문)을 연구〔전공〕하다.

read with *someone,* go to someone as a tutor. …의 가정 교사 노릇을 해주다.

—*n.* Ⓒ the act of reading; a period of time given to reading. 독서; (1회의) 독서 시간. ¶ *I have no time for a long ~.* 오래 읽을 시간이 없다 / *enjoy a ~ before the fire* 난로 앞에서 독서를 즐기다 / *take a quick ~ at a book* 책을 부리나케 읽다. [E.]

read·a·ble [ríːdəbəl] *adj.* **1** easy and pleasant to read; interesting. 읽기 쉬운; 읽어 재미있는. ¶ *a ~ book* 재미있는 책. **2** easy to read. 판독이 쉬운(cf. *legible*). ¶ *a ~ handwriting* 읽기 쉬운 필적.

re·ad·dress [rìːədrés] *vt.* **1** write a new address on (a letter, etc.). (편지 따위)에 주소를 고쳐쓰다; 바꿔쓰다; 전송(轉送)하다. ¶ *I asked them to ~ my letters (to the new house).* 내 편지들을 (새 집으로) 전송해 달라고 했다. **2** speak to (someone) again. …에게 다시 말을 걸다. [re-]

:read·er [ríːdər] *n.* **1** a person who reads. 책 읽는 사람; 독자; 독서가. ¶ *He is a great ~.* 그는 대단한 독서가이다. **2** a printer's (proof)reader. 교정원. **3** a publisher's reader. 출판사의 고문《원고 채택 여부를 결정함》. **4** a book for learning to read. 독본; 리더. **5** ⓐ 《Brit.》 an official lecturer of high rank at a university. (대학의) 강사. ⓑ 《U.S.》 an assistant. 조수. [*read*]

:read·i·ly [rédəli] *adv.* **1** quickly. 즉각; 재빨리. ¶ *He ~ agreed to their suggestion.* 그는 즉각 그들의 제의에 응했다. **2** easily. 쉽게. ¶ *It can ~ be understood.* 그건 쉽게 이해할 수 있다. **3** willingly; without hesitation. 기꺼이; 쾌히. ¶ *A bright boy answers ~ when called on.* 부탁이 있자 한 영리한 소년이 기꺼이 응하고 나섰다. [→ready]

·read·i·ness [rédinis] *n.* Ⓤ **1** the state of being ready; preparation. 준비(가 된 상태). **2** quickness. 신속. ¶ *~ of wit* 기지(機智). **3** ease. 용이. **4** willingness; cheerful consent. 쾌락; 자진해서 함. ¶ *~ to undertake a difficult task* 어려운 일을 자진해서 맡음. [↑]

in readiness, ready. 준비를 갖추고. ¶ *Hold yourself in ~ for the start.* 출발 준비를 하고 있어라 / *get* 〔*put*〕 *everything in ~ for …* …을 위한 만반의 준비를 갖추다 / *All is in ~.* 준비 완료.

with readiness, willingly; easily. 기꺼이; 「자진해서; 쉽게.

:read·ing [ríːdiŋ] *n.* **1** Ⓤ the study of books; knowledge got by the study of books. 서책의 연구; (독서에 의한) 지식. ¶ *He is a man of wide ~.* 그는 박식한 사람이다. **2** Ⓤ ability to read. 읽기; 독서(력). ¶ *teach ~, writing, and arithmetic* 읽기, 쓰기, 계산을 가르치다. **3** ⓊⒸ a written or printed thing to be read. 읽을거리; 기사. ¶ *This book is good ~.* 이건 유익한 책이다 / *There is not much ~ in today's paper.* 오늘 신문에 볼만한 기사가 별로 없다. **4** Ⓒ a record of an instrument shown by letters, figures, or signs. 기록; 표시 도수. ¶ *The ~ of the thermometer was 45 degrees.* 온도계 도수는 45도였다. **5** Ⓒ the form of a given word or passage in a particular copy of a book. (판에 따라) 다른 어구; 이본(異本)에 나오는 글〔본문〕. ¶ *compare the different readings in the folios and quartos of Shakespeare* 이절판(二

R

切判)과 4절판에 나오는 셰익스피어 글의 다른 어구를 비교하다. **6** Ⓒ (in Parliament) the presentation of a bill. 독회(讀會). ¶ *the first* 〔*second, third*〕 ~ 제1〔2, 3〕 독회. — *adj.* fond of reading a book. 독서를 즐기는. [→read]

re·ad·just [riːədʒʌ́st] *vt.* (P6) arrange or put (something) in order again. …을 다시 정리〔조정〕하다. [re-]

re·ad·just·ment [riːədʒʌ́stmənt] *n.* ⓊⒸ the act of readjusting; the state of being readjusted. 재정리; 재조정.

:read·y [rédi] *adj.* (**read·i·er, read·i·est**) **1** 《as *predicative*》 《*for, to do*》 (of a person or thing) prepared and fit. 준비된. ¶ *Dinner is* ~. 식사 준비가 되었습니다 / *Everything is* ~ *for work.* 일할 준비가 됐다 / *I am* ~ *to go.* 갈 준비가 됐다 / *Ready! Set! Go!* 준비, 땅《경주에서》 / *Are you* ~? 준비됐니 / *I am* ~ *when you are.* 너만 되면 나는 언제라도 떠날 수 있다. **2** 《as *predicative*》 《*for, to do*》 prepared (in mind) for or to do; willing to do. 언제라도 (기꺼이) …하는. ¶ *I am* ~ *for death.* (언제라도) 죽을 각오가 돼 있다 / *I am* ~ *to forgive you.* 기꺼이 널 용서하련다 / *She gave* ~ *agreement.* 그녀는 기꺼이 동의했다. **3** 《as *predicative*》 《*to do*》 about to; likely; apt. 막 …할 것 같은; …하기 쉬운. ¶ *The ship was* ~ *to sink any time.* 배는 당장이라도 침몰할 것 같았다 / *The bud is just* ~ *to burst.* 봉오리가 곧 필 것 같다 / *Don't be so* ~ *to find fault.* 그렇게 남의 허물만 들추려 하지 마라. **4** quick; prompt. 재빠른; 신속한; 즉시의. ¶ *a* ~ *answer* 즉답 / ~ *wit* 기지 / *be* ~ *at excuses* 핑계를 잘 대다 / *pay* ~ *money* 맞돈을 치르다 / *find* ~ *acceptance* 곧 허락을 받다 / *be a* ~ *reckoning* 계산이 빠르다. **5** easy to get at; easy to reach; handy. 쉽게 얻을 수 있는; 가까이에 있는; 편리한. ¶ *be* ~ *at* 〔*to*〕 *hand* 바로 곁에 있다 / *Help is* ~ *at hand.* 거들 사람은 구하기 쉽다 / *The prisoner hit upon the readiest way of escape.* 그 포로는 도망하기 가장 쉬운 방법이 떠올랐다.

get* 〔*make*〕 *ready (=*prepare*) ***for something.*** …의 준비를 하다. ¶ *get the children* ~ *for a walk* 아이들에게 산책나갈 준비를 시키다 / *Get* ~ *quickly and we'll start at once.* 빨리 준비해라, 우린 곧 떠난다.

— *adv.* **1** 《followed by *pp.*》 in a state of preparation. 미리 준비하여. ¶ *The boxes are packed* ~ 〔 ~ *packed*〕. 상자들은 포장돼 있다 / *food* ~ *cooked* 미리 조리된 식사. **2** 《usu. in *comparative* and *superlative*》 promptly. 즉시. ¶ *He answered readiest.* 그는 곧 대답했다. [E.]

·read·y-made [rédiméid] *adj.* **1** already made for immediate use or for general sale. 기성품의(opp. custom-made, made-to-order, made-to-measure, bespoke). ¶ *a* ~ *suit* 〔*clothes*〕 기성복. **2** 《*fig.*》 not original; taken over from others. 제것이 아닌; 빌려온. ¶ *a* ~ *opinion* 진부한 의견.

ready reckoner [´- ´--] *n.* a book of tables of various calculations for quick use in commerce. 계산 조견표(早見表).

read·y-to-wear [réditəwέər] *adj.* 《U.S.》 (of clothes) ready-made. 기성품인.

read·y-wit·ted [rédiwítid] *adj.* quick in thought or understanding. 기민한; 재치있는.

re·a·gent [riːéidʒənt] *n.* Ⓒ a substance used to produce a chemical change. 시약(試藥). [→react]

:re·al [ríːəl, ríəl] *adj.* (sometimes **-al·er, -al·est**) **1** exsisting in fact; true; not imagined. 실제의; 현실의(opp. imginary). ¶ ~ *image* 실상(實像) / ~ *life* 실생활 / *have* ~ *existence* 실재하다 / *It was a* ~ *man I saw, not a ghost.* 내가 본 것은 유령이 아니고 실제 사람이었다. **2** genuine; not man-made. 진짜의; 진정한(opp. artificial). ¶ ~ *silk* 본견(本絹) / *a* ~ *friend* 진정한 친구 / *a* ~ *man* 거짓말을 모르는 사람 / *the* ~ *thing* 진짜; 최상품 / ~ *money* 경화(硬貨) / *effect a* ~ *cure* 근치하다 / *The actor drank* ~ *wine on the stage.* 그 배우는 무대에서 진짜 술을 마셨다. **3** having to do with land or buildings; 《law》 not movable. 부동산의(cf. *personal*). ¶ ~ *estate* 〔*property*〕 부동산. **4** 《philos.》 having an existence. 실재적〔현실적〕인(opp. ideal). **5** not invented or fictitious; actual. 사실의; 실재의. ¶ *the* ~ *state of affairs* 일의 실상(實相) / *What is the man's* ~ *name?* 그 사람 본명이 뭐냐. **6** true in fact. 실질적인; 사실상의(opp. formal, nominal). ¶ *the* ~ *ruler of the country* 그 나라의 사실상의 지배자 / *the* ~ *reason* 진짜 이유. **7** sincere; not put on. 진심의; 참된. ¶ *I feel* ~ *sympathy with you.* 진심으로 동정합니다 / *She is a very* ~ *person.* 그녀는 참으로 성실한 여인이다.

— *adv.* 《*colloq.*》 really. 정말로. ¶ *We have a* ~ *good time.* 우리는 정말 즐겁게 지낸다 / *I am* ~ *pleased to see you.* 만나서 정말 기쁘다.

— *n.* 《*the* ~》 something that actually exists; reality. 현실; 실체. [L. *res* thing]

re·al·ism [ríːəlìzəm] *n.* Ⓤ **1** a tendency to be practical. 현실주의. **2** 《literature, art》 the attempt to describe people and things as they really are. 사실주의(opp. romanticism). **3** 《philos.》 ⓐ the theory that material objects exist in themselves, independent of the mind. 실재론(opp. idealism). ⓑ the belief that general ideas exist objectively. 실념론(實念論)(opp. nominalism). [→real, -ism]

re·al·ist [ríːəlist] *n.* Ⓒ **1** a person who is interested in practical matters. 현실주의자. **2** a writer or an artist who tries to describe or paint things exactly as they really are. 사실주의자. **3** 《philos.》 a believer in realism. 실재론자.

re·al·is·tic [rì:əlístik] *adj.* **1** with a tendency to face facts; practical. 현실적. **2** 《literature, art》 describing life as it really is; true to life. 사실적인; 사실파의; 진실감이 나는. ¶ *a ~ novel* 사실파 소설. **3** of realism. 실재론(實在論)의.

:re·al·i·ty [ri:ǽləti] *n.* (*pl.* **-ties**) **1** ⓊⒸ real existence. 실재; 현실. **2** Ⓒ a person or thing that is real. 실물《사람·물건》. **3** Ⓤ close resemblance to the original. 실물 그대로임; 현실감.

in reality, really; in fact. 실은; 실제는.

***re·al·i·za·tion** [rì:ələzéiʃən / -lai-] *n.* Ⓤ **1** the act of realizing; the state of being realized. 충분한 이해; 실감. ¶ *The hunters had a full ~ of the dangers they would face.* 사냥꾼들은 그들이 겪을 수 있는 위기들을 잘 알고 있었다 / *The ~ that she was now alone filled her with terror.* 그녀는 이제 자기 혼자라는 것을 깨닫고 공포에 휩싸였다. **2** the act of bringing something imagined into real existence. 실현. ¶ *The ~ of one's hopes.* 희망의 실현 / *be brought to ~* 실현되다. **3** change of property into money. (재산의) 현금화. [↓]

:re·al·ize [rí:əlàiz] *vt.* **1** (P6,11,12) understand fully; become fully aware of (something). …을 충분히 이해하다; 실감하다. ¶ *~ one's own danger* 신변의 위험을 깨닫다 / *I could not ~ my situation—it had happened so suddenly.* 너무 갑작스러운 일이라서 내 처지를 깨달을 수 없었다. **2** (P6) ⓐ make (something) real; bring (something) into being. …을 실현하다. ¶ *His plan was fully realized.* 그의 계획은 완전히 실현되었다 / *My wildest wishes have been realized.* 나의 절실한 소망이 이루어졌다. ⓑ 《rare》 give reality to; cause to appear as real. …에 현실감을 주다; 생생히 나타내다. ¶ *Scott can ~ the events and personages of history for us.* 스콧은 역사적인 사건과 인물들을 생생하게 기술해 준다. **3** (P6) change (property) into money. (재산)을 현금화하다. ¶ *Before going to England to live, he realized all his property.* 영국으로 이주하기 전에 그는 모든 재산을 현금화했다. **4** (P6, 13) bring as a return or profit; be sold for. (대가나 이익)을 가져오다; (얼마)에 팔리다. ¶ *(The sale of) his pictures realized £10,000.* 그의 그림은 만 파운드 어치가 팔렸다. **5** (P6) gain; get (something) as a profit. …을 벌다. ¶ *We realized a profit on the sale of the house.* 집을 팔아 이익을 보았다. [→real, -ize]

:re·al·ly [rí:əli] *adv.* **1** in fact; actually; truly; indeed. 정말; 참으로; 실은. ¶ *Do you ~ mean it?* 그게 정말이냐 / *Has he ~ gone?* 그는 정말 갔나 / *I ~ do mean what I say.* 나는 진지하게 말하고 있다 / *But it was not ~ his fault.* 그러나 실은 그게 그의 잘못이 아니다. **2** 《expressing surprise or mild protest》 참; 뭐야; 정말. ¶ *Well, ~! what a stupid thing to do.* 원참, 무슨 짓을 하고 있는 거냐 / *Oh, ~?* 뭐야, 정말이냐; 어머, 그래. [*real*]

:realm [relm] *n.* Ⓒ **1** a kingdom. 왕국. ¶ *the laws of the ~* 왕국의 법률; 국법. **2** a region or field; a sphere. 범위; 영역. ¶ *the ~ of science* 과학 분야 / *the ~ of Nature* 자연계 / *in the ~ of fancy* 공상의 세계에. [→rex]

re·al·ty [rí:əlti] *n.* Ⓤ real estate; one's land or house. 부동산(opp. personalty). [→real]

ream[1] [ri:m] *n.* Ⓒ 480 or 500 sheets of paper. 연(連)《480 매 내지 500매, 현재는 500매》. [Arab.=bundle]

ream[2] [ri:m] *vt.* (P6,7) enlarge or shape a hole in metal. (금속의 구멍)을 넓히다. [E.]

ream·er [rí:mər] *n.* Ⓒ **1** a tool for enlarging holes. 리머; 확공기(擴孔器). **2** a device for making juice by squeezing lemons, oranges, etc. 과즙기(果汁器). [↑]

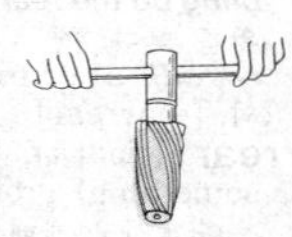
〈reamer 1〉

re·an·i·mate [rì:ǽnəmèit] *vt.* (P6) **1** restore (something or someone) to life; give (something or someone) fresh spirit to. …을 소생시키다. ¶ *~ the apparently drowned* 물에 빠져 죽은 사람을 소생시키다. **2** 《*fig.*》 encourage again. …을 고무하다. ¶ *with reanimated courage* 분발하여 / *He reanimated his discouraged friends.* 그는 실망한 친구들을 격려했다. [re-]

***reap** [ri:p] *vt., vi.* (P6;1) **1** cut and gather in a crop. …을 거둬들이다; 수확하다 (opp. sow). ¶ *~ a field* 밭의 작물을 거둬들이다 / *~ a splendid harvest of corn* 풍작을 이룬 곡식을 거둬들이다. **2** 《*fig.*》 gain (something) as a reward. (보답으로 …을) 받다. ¶ *~ the benefits of kindness* 친절에 대한 보답을 받다 / *~ a harvest of trouble* 고생한 보람을 찾다 / 《*prov.*》 *As you sow, so shall you ~.* 자업 자득이다; 인과 응보다. [E.]

***reap as* [*what*] *one has sown* = *reap the fruits of one's action* [*labors*],** receive the result of what one has done; suffer for what one has done. 뿌린 씨를 거두다; 인과 응보.

reap where one has not sown, make a profit from what others have done. 남의 공을 가로채다.

sow the wind and reap the whirlwind ⇨ whirlwind.

reap·er [rí:pər] *n.* Ⓒ a person who reaps; a reaping machine. 수확하는 사람; (자동) 수확기.

re·ap·pear [rì:əpíər] *vi.* (P1) appear again; come into sight again. 다시 나타나다.

[re-]

re·ap·pear·ance [rìːəpíərəns] *n.* Ⓤ the act of appearing again. 재현; 재발.

re·ap·point [rìːəpɔ́int] *vt.* (P6) appoint (someone) again; place (someone) again in a former position. …을 재임명하다; 복직시키다. [re-]

:rear[1] [riər] *n.* Ⓒ **1** the back part of something. 뒤; 후부. ¶ *the ~ door of the car* 차의 뒷문 / *They followed in the ~.* 그들은 뒤에서 따라갔다. **2** 《mil.》 the back part of an army or a fleet. 후위(後衛); 후미; 후위대. ¶ *take* 〔*attack*〕 *the enemy in* (*the*) ~ 적의 배후를 치다. **3** 《*colloq.*》 a watercloset. 변소. **4** 《*colloq.*》 buttocks. 엉덩이.

at* 〔*in, on*〕 *the rear of, behind. …의 뒤〔배후〕에(opp. in front of). ¶ *The kitchen is at the ~ of the house.* 부엌은 집 뒤쪽에 있다.

bring up the rear, march last; come last. 후위를 맡다; 맨 뒤에서 오다.

— *adj.* at or in the back. 뒤의; 후부〔후미〕의. [→arrear]

rear[2] [riər] *vt.* **1** (P6) make (someone or something) grow; bring up. …을 기르다; 키우다; 사육〔재배〕하다. ¶ *~ a child* / *~ crops* / *~ cattle* 〔*pigs*〕 / *A delicate child is very difficult to ~.* 예민〔허약〕한 아이는 키우기 힘들다 / *~ one's family* 가족을 돌보다〔부양하다〕. **2** (P6) 《*lit.*》 set up; build. …을 세우다. ¶ *~ a monument* 기념비를 세우다 / *~ a temple* 절을 짓다. **3** (P6,7) 《*lit.*》 raise; lift up. …을 올리다; 들다; 솟게 하다. ¶ *~ one's head* 고개를 들다 / 《*fig.*》 *Vice could not ~ its head.* 악덕은 대두될 수가 없었다 / *The mountain reared its top above the clouds.* 산봉우리가 구름 위로 우뚝 솟아 올라 있다.

— *vi.* (P1,2A) 《*up*》 **1** stand on the hind legs, as a horse. (말 따위가) 뒷발로 곧추 서다. ¶ *The horse reared up at the strange sound.* 이상한 소리에 말은 뒷발로 곧추 섰다. **2** start up in angry excitement. 자리를 박차고 일어서다. **3** raise high or tower aloft, as a building. 우뚝 솟다. [E.]

rear admiral [´ ´––] *n.* a naval officer who ranks above a captain. 해군 소장. [→rear[1]]

rear guard [´ ´] *n.* 《mil.》 a group of soldiers guarding the rear of an army. 후위; 후진(後陣).

re·arm [ríːɑ́ːrm] *vt., vi.* (P6;1) **1** arm again; arm oneself again. (…에게) 재무장시키다〔하다〕. **2** supply (someone) with new weapons. (…에게) 신형 무기를 갖게 하다〔갖추다〕. [re-]

re·ar·ma·ment [riːɑ́ːrməmənt] *n.* Ⓤ the act of rearming; the state of being rearmed. 재군비; 재무장.

rear·most [ríərmòust] *adj.* farthest back; coming last of all. 최후미의; 맨 뒤의. ¶ *the ~ carriage of the train* 기차의 맨 뒤의 칸. [→rear[1]]

re·ar·range [rìːəréindʒ] *vt.* (P6) arrange (something) in a different way; arrange again. …을 다시 배치〔배열〕하다; 재정리하다. [re-]

re·ar·range·ment [rìːəréindʒmənt] *n.* Ⓤ the act of rearranging; the state of being rearranged. 재배치; 재정리.

rear·ward [ríərwərd] *adj.* at, in or toward the rear. 뒤쪽에 있는; 후방의. — *adv.* backward; toward the rear. 배후에〔로〕; 후방에〔으로〕. [→rear[1]]

rear·wards [ríərwərdz] *adv.* =rearward.

:rea·son [ríːzən] *n.* **1** Ⓤ the ability or power to think, judge, etc.; sanity. 이성; 판단력; 제정신. ¶ *Man has ~; animals do not.* 사람에게는 이성이 있고, 짐승에겐 없다 / *on ~* 이성으로 판단하여 / *lose one's ~* 제정신을 잃다; 미치다 / *come* 〔*be restored*〕 *to ~* 제정신이 들다 / *Man alone of living creatures possesses ~.* 살아 있는 동물 중에서 사람만이 이성을 가지고 있다. **2** Ⓤ what is right or generally agreed; common sense. 도리(道理); 건전한 판단; 분별; 상식. ¶ *disregard ~* 도리를 무시하다; 사리에 어긋나다 / *bring someone to ~* 아무에게 도리〔사리〕를 깨우치다 / *There is ~ in what he says.* 그의 말에는 일리가 있다 / *He refuses to listen to ~.* 그는 사리를 따르려하지 않고 억지만 부린다. **3** ⓊⒸ a cause for action or thought; a motive. 이유; 까닭; 동기. ¶ *the woman's ~* 여자의 이유《'그저 좋으니까 좋다는' 식의 이유가 되지 않는 이유》 / *The ~ for his absence was illness.* 그가 결석한 까닭은 병 때문이었다 / *Give me your reasons for doing it.* 왜 그것을 하는지 이유를 말해봐라 / *He complains, and with* (*good*) *~.* 그가 불평을 하는데, 그럴 만한 이유가 있다 / *He has every ~ to hope that he will be elected.* 그에게는 당선을 기대할 만한 충분한 이유가 있다 / *I see no ~ to go* 〔*for going*〕 *to such trouble.* 내가 그런 골치 아픈 일에 끼어들 이유가 없다.

by reason of, because of. …때문에.

for no other reason than that* 〔*but this*〕*, only because that 〔of this〕. 단지 …라는 것〔이것〕만의 이유로.

for this* 〔*what, etc.*〕 *reason, for this 〔what, etc.〕 cause; on this 〔what, etc.〕 account or ground. 이런 〔무슨〕 까닭으로. ¶ *For some ~ she didn't come.* 어떤 까닭으로 해서 그녀는 오지 못했다 / *For what ~ do you wish to go?* 무슨 까닭으로 너는 가려고 하는가.

hear* 〔*listen to*〕 *reason, pay attention to reasonable advice. 이치를 알아듣다.

in reason, reasonable. 합당한; 사리에 닿는. ¶ *It is not in ~ to expect me to do so.* 내게 그러기를 바라는 것은 도리에 맞지 않는다 / *I will do anything in ~.* 사리에 닿는 일이라면 무엇이든 하겠다.

neither ryhme nor reason =without rhyme or reason.

out of reason, unreasonable. 도리가 아닌;

터무니 없는.

stand to reason, be reasonable. 이치에 닿다; 도리에 맞다. ¶ *It stands to ~ that I should decline the offer.* 내가 그 제의를 사양한 것은 당연하다.

without rhyme or reason, lacking common sense; without meaning. 분별이 없는; 까닭을 모르는.

— *vi.* **1** (P1,2A,3) think logically; draw conclusions from data. 추론(推論)하다; 결론을 내리다. ¶ ~ *from experience* 경험으로 추론하다. **2** (P3) 《*with*》 urge reasons which should determine belief or action; talk in a logical way. (도리를 따져) 설득하다〔말하다〕. ¶ ~ *with someone on* 〔*about*〕 *his folly* 아무에게 그의 어리석음을 깨닫게 하다 / *It's no use trying to ~ with her.* 그녀를 설득하려 해도 소용없다.

— *vt.* **1** (P7,11,12) think (out) logically about (something); discuss; conclude or infer. (논리적으로) …에 대해 생각하다〔생각해 내다〕; …을 논하다; 추론(推論)하다. ¶ ~ *out a conclusion* 논구(論究)해서 결론을 얻다 / ~ *why it is wrong* 그것이 왜 잘못되어 있는가를 논하다 / ~ *what is meant by it* 그것이 무엇을 뜻하는지를 논하다 / *He reasoned that they were guilty.* 그는 그들이 유죄라고 판단했다. **2** (P13) 《*into, out of*》 give one's reason to (someone) and make him accept one's wishes, ideas, etc.; persuade. 이치〔도리〕를 설명하여 …하게 하다; …을 설득하다. ¶ ~ *oneself into a conviction* 제멋대로 생각하고 확신하다 / ~ *someone out of his fears* 아무를 설득해서 공포심을 없애다 / ~ *someone down* 아무를 설득하다. [→rate¹]

rea·son·a·ble [rí:zənəbəl] *adj.* **1** having the power to think clearly or logically; sensible. 이치〔사리〕에 맞는; 사려 분별이 있는. ¶ *a ~ excuse* 그럴 듯한 핑계 / *a ~ employer* 사리를 아는 고용주 / *You must really be ~, and prepared to cooperate.* 당찮은 말 그만하고 협력하도록 해라. **2** (of a price, etc.) not very high; not excessive; moderate; fair. (가격 등이) 알맞은; 온당한. ¶ *a ~ price* 알맞은 값 / *a ~ demand* 무리가 없는 요구 / *on ~ terms* 온당한 조건으로.

rea·son·ing [rí:zəniŋ] *n.* Ⓤ **1** the act of using the power of reason. 추론(推論); 추리. **2** proofs, arguments, etc., used in such reasoning. 논의; 논증; 논거. ¶ *The pupils understood the teacher's ~.* 학생들은 선생이 하는 논증을 알아들었다. — *adj.* **1** able to reason. 이성이 있는. ¶ *Man is a ~ creature.* 인간은 이성이 있는 동물이다. **2** connected with reason. 추리의. ¶ *the ~ faculties.* 추리력.

re·as·sem·ble [rì:əsémbəl] *vt., vi.* (P6;1) gather (things) again; put (machines, etc.) together again; come to together again. 다시 모으다〔모이다〕; (기계 따위를) 재조립하다. ¶ ~ *a motor* 모터를 재조립하다. [re-]

re·as·sert [rì:əsə́:rt] *vt.* (P6) say positively again. …을 재차 단언하다. [re-]

re·as·sume [rì:əsú:m] *vt.* (P6) take or seize (something) again. …을 다시 취하다; 되찾다. [↑]

re·as·sur·ance [rì:əʃúərəns] *n.* Ⓤ the act of reassuring; the state of being reassured; new assurance. 안심(시키는 것) 《격려의 말 따위》; 재보증; 새로운 자신; 재보험. [↓]

re·as·sure [rì:əʃúər] *vt.* (P6) **1** set (someone's mind) at ease; give fresh confidence to (someone); give back courage to. …을 안심시키다; …에 자신을 주다; 기운을 되찾게 하다. ¶ *His words did much to ~ her.* 그의 말에 그녀는 많은 자신을 얻었다 / *She was quite reassured.* 그녀는 아주 안심이 되었다. **2** assure (someone or something) again. …을 재보증하다. **3** 《rare》 reinsure. …에 재보험을 들다. [re-, →assure]

re·as·sur·ing [rì:əʃúəriŋ] *adj.* setting someone's mind at ease; giving fresh confidence to; encouraging. 안심시키는; 자신을 주는; 용기를 주는.

re·bate [rí:beit, ribéit] *n.* Ⓒ a return of part of a payment; a discount; a reduction. 리베이트; 환불; (어음 등의) 할인. ¶ *a ~ for prompt payment* 즉시불(卽時拂)에 대한 할인. — *vt.* (P6) give a rebate to (someone); reduce; deduct. …에게 환불하다; 할인하다; 리베이트하다. [re-, →abate]

Re·bec·ca [ribékə] *n.* a girl's name. 여자 이름.

***re·bel** [rébəl] *n.* Ⓒ a person who resists authority or government. 반역자; 반항자. ¶ *The rebels rose against the ruler.* 반항자들은 통치자에 대하여 봉기했다 / *a ~ army* 반란군.

— *adj.* resisting authority; rebellious. 반역의.

— [ribél] *vi.* (**-elled, -el·ling**) (P1,3) 《*against*》 **1** resist authority or government by force; revolt. 반역하다; 배반하다. ¶ ~ *against the Establishment* 체제에 반항하다 / *Such treatment would make anybody ~.* 그런 처우엔 누구든 반항할 것이다 / *They rebelled against the government.* 그들은 정부에 반항했다. **2** feel or show a great dislike; react. 몹시 싫어하다; 혐오하다. ¶ *His whole temper rebelled against the conditions in which he lived.* 그는 자기가 처한 생활 환경이 넌덜나게 싫었다 / *The stomach rebels against too much food.* 과식하면 위가 받아들이지 않는다. [re-, L. *bellum* war]

***re·bel·lion** [ribéljən] *n.* ⓊⒸ the act of rebelling; armed resistance to authority or government. 반란; 폭동; 반항. ¶ *rise in ~* 폭동을 일으키다.

re·bel·lious [ribéljəs] *adj.* **1** resisting government or control; acting like a rebel; taking part in a rebellion. 반역하

는; 반역에 가담하는. ¶ ~ *subjects* 역신(逆臣); 역도(逆徒). **2** of the nature of a rebellion. (성격이) 반항적인. ¶ ~ *acts* 반항적 행위 / *a ~ temperament* 반항적인 기질 / *The ~ boy would not obey the school rules.* 반항적인 아이는 학교 규칙을 지키려 들지 않는다. **3** hard to manage; 《med.》 difficult to treat. 다루기 힘든; 치료하기 힘든. ¶ ~ *curls* (곧 풀려서) 다루기 힘든 곱슬머리 / *a ~ disease* 난치병.
● **re·bel·lious·ly** [-li] *adv.* **re·bel·lious·ness** [-nis] *n.*

re·birth [riːbə́ːrθ] *n.* ⓊⒸ new birth; revival. 신생; 부활; 재생. [re-]

re·born [riːbɔ́ːrn] *adj.* born again; having a new life. 다시 태어난; 갱생(更生)한. [re-]

re·bound [ribáund] *vi.* (P1,3) **1** spring back; bounce back. 되튀다. ¶ *A ball rebounds from a wall.* 공이 벽에 맞아 되튄다. **2** return; react. (행동이 본인에게) 되돌아오다; 반발(반동)하다. ¶ *His lies rebounded on him in the end.* 그의 거짓말이 결국에는 그에게 다시 돌아왔다. **3** 《*fig.*》 spring back into life or strength. (좌절 따위에서) 다시 일어서다; 만회하다. ¶ *His spirits rebounded after his long illness.* 긴 병을 앓고 난 후 기운이 회복됐다.
— [ríːbàund, ribáund] *n.* Ⓒ the action of springing back. 되튐; 반동. [re-]
on the rebound, **a**) after (a ball) has sprung back from the ground, wall, etc. 되튀어나온 것을. ¶ *hit a ball on the ~* 공이 되튀어나온 것을 치다. **b**) after (someone) has been disappointed by someone. (실망 등의) 반발로; 반동으로. ¶ *She married him on the ~ after an unhappy love-affair.* (다른 남자와의) 불행한 애정 관계의 반발심으로 그와 결혼했다. [re-]

re·broad·cast [riːbrɔ́ːdkæ̀st, -kɑ̀ːst] *vt., vi.* (**-cast** or **-cast·ed**) (P6;1) **1** broadcast again. 재방송하다. **2** broadcast (a program, etc. received from another station); relay. 중계 방송하다. — *n.* Ⓒ **1** the act of rebroadcasting. 중계(재)방송. **2** a program that is rebroadcast. 중계(재)방송 프로그램. ¶ *listen to a ~ of a drama* 드라마의 재방송을 듣다.

re·buff [ribʌ́f] *n.* Ⓒ a flat refusal of another's advice, help, etc. 퇴짜; 단호한 거절. ¶ *get a ~* 퇴짜를 맞다 / *He proposed to a girl only to be given a flat ~.* 한 소녀에게 구애했지만 보기좋게 거절당했다. — *vt.* (P6) give a rebuff to (someone). …을 퇴짜놓다; 저지하다. ¶ *The friendly dog was rebuffed by a kick.* 꼬리치던 개가 발길질로 쫓김을 당했다. [It. *ribuffo*]

re·build [riːbíld] *vt.* (**-built** [-bílt]) (P6) build (something) again or in a new way. …을 다시 짓다; 재건하다. ¶ *The house has been entirely rebuilt.* 집은 완전히 개축되었다. [re-]

•**re·buke** [ribjúːk] *vt.* (P6,7,13) find fault with (someone); blame; scold. …을 꾸짖다; 비난(견책)하다. ¶ *The teacher rebuked the boy for neglecting his duties.* 선생은 자기 일에 태만한 아이를 꾸짖었다. — *n.* ⒸⓊ a severe criticism. 비난; 견책; 책망. ¶ *receive a ~* 책망을 듣다 / *give a rough ~* 몹시 꾸짖다 / *without ~* 나무랄데 없이; 대과없이. [re-, F. *bucher* beat]

re·bus [ríːbəs] *n.* Ⓒ a riddle composed of pictures that suggest syllables or words. 수수께끼 그림(e.g. A picture of an *ox on a ford* is a rebus for *Oxford*). [L. =by things]

re·but [ribʌ́t] *vt.* (**-but·ted, -but·ting**) (P6) **1** push back; prove (what has been said, etc.) to be wrong. …을 물리치다; 반박하다. ¶ ~ *someone's theory* 아무의 이론을 반박하다. **2** 《law》 oppose by argument or proof. 반박(항변)하다; …의 반증을 들다. ¶ *rebutting evidence* 반증(反證). [re-, F. *bouter* push]

re·but·tal [ribʌ́tl] *n.* Ⓒ **1** the act of rebutting. 반박; 논박. **2** 《law》 the production of rebutting evidence. 반증; 반증의 제출. ¶ *draw prompt rebuttals from all neighboring nations* 모든 인접국의 즉각적인 반박을 초래하다.

rec. receipt; recipe; record.

re·cal·ci·trance [rikǽlsətrəns] *n.* Ⓤ refusal to obey authority, etc.; disobedience. 반항; 고집. [↓]

re·cal·ci·trant [rikǽlsətrənt] *adj.* 《*at, against*》 refusing to obey authority, etc.; disobedient. (권위에) 반항하는; 고집이 센. ¶ ~ *children* 고집 불통의 아이들. — *n.* Ⓒ a disobedient person. 고집센 사람; 반항자. [re-, L. *calx* heel]

:**re·call** [rikɔ́ːl] *vt.* (P6,13) **1** call back; bid (someone) to return. …을 소환하다; 리콜하다. ¶ ~ *the ambassador* 대사를 소환하다 / *He was recalled from abroad by urgent private affairs.* 그는 급한 사적인 일로 본국으로 소환되었다 / *The captain was recalled from the front line.* 대위는 전선에서 소환당했다. **2** take back; withdraw (an order, etc.). (명령 따위를) 철회(취소)하다. ¶ ~ *one's words* 한 말을 취소하다 / ~ *one's order* 명령을 철회하다. **3** call (something) back to mind; remember. …을 상기하다; 기억해 내다. ¶ ~ *old faces* 옛 지기(知己)들의 면면을 회상하다 / *He frowned as though trying to ~ something to his mind.* 그는 무언가를 생각해 내려는 듯 미간을 찌푸렸다. **4** 《*fig.*》 bring back; remind. …을 상기시키다. ¶ ~ *someone to a sense of his duties* 아무에게 책임감을 상기시키다. **5** call back from death to life. …을 소생(부활)시키다. ¶ *We would not, if we could, ~ him from the grave to such a life of pain.* 그것이 설령 가능할지라도 그 고생을 또 하라고 그를 무덤에서 살아나게 하고 싶지는 않다.
— [rikɔ́ːl, ríːkɔ̀ːl] *n.* ⓊⒸ **1** the act of calling back; an order or signal to return. 소

환; 리콜; (해군의) 소환 신호. ¶ *the ~ of a general* 〔*an ambassador*〕 장군〔대사〕의 소환. **2** 《U.S.》 the right or procedure of removing an official by popular vote. (일반 투표에 의한 관리의) 해임(권); 리콜. **3** Ⓤ the act of remembering. 회상. ¶ *John has total ~ and never forgets anything.* 존은 기억력이 비상해서 무엇 하나 잊는 일이 없다. [re-]

beyond 〔***past***〕 ***recall,*** unable to be brought back or remembered; forgotten. 돌이킬 수 없는; 기억이 나지 않는. ¶ *a matter past ~* 돌이킬 수 없는 일.

re·cant [rikǽnt] *vt., vi.* (P6;1) take back (a statement, an opinion, etc.) publicly. (진술·의견 등을) 취소하다; 철회하다. ¶ *~ one's belief in a religion* 종교에 대한 자기 신념을 철회하다. [re-, →chant]

re·can·ta·tion [rìːkæntéiʃən] *n.* ⓊⒸ the act of recanting. 취소; 철회.

re·ca·pit·u·late [rìːkəpítʃəlèit] *vt., vi.* (P6;1) sum up; tell (the contents, etc.) briefly or in outline; repeat the chief points of (arguments, etc.). (…을) 요약하다; 요점을 되풀이 말하다. ¶ *After listening to the speakers, he recapitulated their main argument.* 연사들의 발언을 듣고 난 후 그는 그들의 논의 요지를 요약했다. [re-, →capital]

re·ca·pit·u·la·tion [rìːkəpìtʃəléiʃən] *n.* ⒸⓊ **1** repetition of main points. 요점의 반복. **2** a summary. 요약. **3** 《mus.》 (esp. of sonata form) repetition of a theme in a final form. (소나타 형식의) 재현부.

re·cap·ture [riːkǽptʃər] *vt.* (P6) capture again; recover. …을 되찾다. ¶ *He recaptured the spirit of his youth.* 젊었을 적의 기백을 되찾았다. —*n.* Ⓤ the act of taking again; Ⓒ a thing which is recaptured. 탈환; 탈환물. [re-]

re·cast [riːkǽst, -kάːst] *vt.* (**-cast**) (P6) **1** cast or mold again. …을 다시 주조(鑄造)하다. ¶ *~ bells into guns* 종을 대포로 개주(改鑄)하다. **2** reconstruct; remodel. …을 개조하다. ¶ *~ one's plan* 계획을 다시 짜다 / *~ a book* 책을 다시 쓰다. **3** change the cast (of a play, etc.). (극 따위의 배역)을 바꾸다. **4** count a second time. …을 다시 계산하다. ¶ *~ the accounts.* —[⌐⌐] *n.* Ⓒ the act of recasting; a thing which is recast. 개주물(改鑄物); 개작(改作); 개작품. [re-]

re·cede [risíːd] *vi.* (P1,3) **1** 《*from*》 go or move backward; retire. 물러나다; 퇴각하다. ¶ *I heard footsteps receding in the distance.* 발소리가 멀어지는 것이 들렸다 / *The shore receded as our ship left the harbor.* 배가 항구를 떠남에 따라 해안은 뒤로 멀어졌다. **2** incline backward; slope backward. 뒤쪽으로 기울다. ¶ *a receding chin* 주걱턱 / *The cliff recedes abruptly from its base upwards.* 벼랑은 기단에서부터 가파르게 뒤쪽으로 기울어 있다. **3** 《*from*》 withdraw. (계약 따위에서) 손을 떼다; 몸을 빼다. ¶ *~ from a contract* 계약에서 손을 떼다 / *An army recedes from a position.* 군대가 진지에서 빠져나오다. **4** become lower or less. (가치 등이) 떨어지다; 하락하다. ¶ *Its value has receded.* 그것의 가치는 떨어졌다 / *His powers seem to have receded.* 그의 체력도 쇠퇴한 모양이다. **5** become more distant and less clear (in the memory). (기억 속에서) 희미해지다. ¶ *The faces of the friends of our childhood ~ in the dim past.* 어릴 적 벗들의 얼굴이 아득한 과거로 흐려진다. [re-. L. *cedo* go]

recede into the background, **a**) (of a person) lose influence. 세력을 잃다. **b**) (of a question, right, etc.) become less important. (문제 등이) 중요성을 잃어가다. ¶ *It has receded in importance.* 그것은 중요성이 감소됐다.

·re·ceipt [risíːt] *n.* **1** Ⓒ a piece of paper showing that money or goods have been received. 영수증. ¶ *write* 〔*make*〕 *out a ~* 영수증을 쓰다〔발행하다〕 / *a ~ stamp* 수입인지 / *Please send a ~ by return.* 받는 즉시 영수증을 보내주시오. **2** 《*pl.*》 money or goods received. 수령액; 수익. ¶ *Our expenses were less than our receipts.* 비용이 수익보다 적었다. **3** Ⓤ the act of receiving. 수령; 수취. ¶ *the ~ of books* 책의 수령 / *I* (*beg to*) *acknowledge* (*the*) *~ of your letter.* 귀한(貴翰)은 이상 없이 배수(拜受)하였습니다《상용문》. **4** 《rare》 a recipe. 처방(전); 제조법.

be in (***the***) ***receipt of,*** receive. …을 받다. ¶ *We are in ~ of your letter.* 귀하의 편지를 받았습니다.

on (***the***) ***receipt of,*** as soon as a person receives. 받는 대로〔즉시〕. ¶ *pay the money on* (*the*) *~ of goods* 물건을 받는 즉시 돈을 내주다.

—*vt.* (P6) **1** give a receipt for. …에게 영수증을 끊다〔발행하다〕. **2** write 'Received' on, as a sign that payment has been made. '영수필(領收畢)'이라고 쓰다. ¶ *~ a bill* 계산서에 영수필(Received)이라고 표시하다. [re-, receive]

re·ceiv·a·ble [risíːvəbəl] *adj.* **1** that can be received; suitable for acceptance. 받을 수 있는. ¶ *goods not in a ~ condition* 수령할 수 있는 상태가 아닌 상품 / *The broadcast is not ~ here.* 여기서 그 방송은 청취 불능이다. **2** 《comm.》 requiring payment. 지급을 요구하는. ¶ *bills ~* 받을 어음.

:re·ceive [risíːv] *vt.* (P6) **1** take; get; be given. …을 받다. ¶ *~ a letter* / *~ X-mas presents* 크리스마스 선물을 받다 / *~ money* 〔*twenty dollars as a fee*〕 돈을〔수수료로 20 달러를〕 받다 / *~ much help from someone* 아무에게서 많은 도움을 받다 / *~ a good education* 좋은 교육을 받다 / *I received a telegram from my mother.* 어머니에게서 전보를 한 장 받았다. **2** undergo; suffer; meet with; experience. …을 입다; 겪다; 당하다; 경험하다. ¶ *~ a mortal wound* 치명상을 입다 / *~ a* *hearty welcome* 뜨거운 환영을 받다 / ~ *punishment* 처벌받다 / ~ *a heavy sentence* 중형(重刑)을 선고받다 / ~ *a heavy blow on the head* 머리를 되게 얻어 맞다 / ~ *a shock* 〔*jolt*〕 충격을 받다 / ~ *fair treatment* 환대 받다. **3** accept. …을 받아들이다; 수리〔응〕하다. ¶ ~ *a proposal* 제안을 받아들이다 / ~ *someone's confession* 아무의 참회를 듣다. **4** ⓐ admit; entertain; welcome. …을 맞아들이다; 접대하다; 환영하다. ¶ ~ *a guest* 손님을 맞아들이다 / *I cannot ~ him this morning.* 오늘 아침은 그를 맞이할 수 없다 / *She is not receiving* (*visitors*) *today.* 오늘은 (손님을) 맞을 예정이 없다. ⓑ let into one's family, a club, society, etc.; admit. …을 가족으로〔회원으로〕 받아들이다; 입회시키다. ¶ ~ *someone into one's family as a son* 아무를 양자로 받아들이다 / ~ *him as partner* 그를 동업자로 삼다 / ~ *someone into a club* 아무를 클럽에 입회시키다. **5** bear the load or burden of; hold; sustain; resist (an attack). (무게 등)을 지탱하다; 버티다; (공격)을 받아 저지하다. ¶ *The columns ~ the weight of the building.* 여러 개의 기둥이 건물의 무게를 지탱하고 있다 / *They prepared to ~ the enemy.* 그들은 적을 맞을 준비를 갖추었다. **6** take in; have room for; contain; absorb. …을 수용하다; 흡수하다. ¶ *a hole large enough to ~ two men* 두 사람이 들어갈 만큼의 구멍 / *The lungs ~ air.* 폐는 공기를 흡입한다. **7** recognize (something) as true. …을 용인하다.

— *vi.* (P1) **1** get something. (물건을) 받다. **2** be at home to guests or visitors. 방문을 받다. ¶ *She receives on Wednesday.* 그녀는 수요일을 면회일로 잡고 있다. **3** 《radio, TV》 change electric waves into sound signals. 수신하다. [re-, L. *capio* take, seize]

re·ceived [risíːvd] *adj.* generally accepted as correct. 용인〔인정〕된.

·re·ceiv·er [risíːvər] *n.* Ⓒ **1** a person who receives. 수취인; 접대자. **2** the part of a telephone which is held to the ear. (전화의) 수화기. ¶ *speak into the ~* 수화기를 들고 이야기하다. **3** the part of a receiving set for a radio, etc. 수신기; 수상기. **4** 《law》 a person appointed by a court to take charge of another's property or money. 재산 관리인. ¶ *an official ~ in bankruptcies* 파산 관재인(管財人). **5** a person who receives or buys stolen goods. 장물아비.

re·cen·cy [ríːsənsi] *n.* the state or quality of being recent; recentness; 새로움; 최신. ¶ *the ~ of the news* 〔*events*〕 최근의 뉴스〔사건들〕. [→recent]

re·cen·sion [risénʃən] *n.* the critical examination and correction of the text of a book; a text so corrected. 교정(校訂); 교정본. [re-, →censor]

:re·cent [ríːsənt] *adj.* not long past; done or made lately; modern; new; fresh. 최근의; 근대의; 새로운. ¶ *a ~ event* 최근의 사건 / *in ~ years* 근년; 요 몇해. [L. *recens*]

:re·cent·ly [ríːsəntli] *adv.* not long ago; lately. 최근; 바로 얼마 전. 語法 lately 나 of late 처럼, 완료형과 과거형에 두루 쓰임. 현재시제로는 쓰이지 않음. ¶ *until ~* 최근까지 / *He has ~ been to France.* 그는 최근에 프랑스에 다녀 왔다 / *It was only ~ that I get well.* 내가 완쾌한 것은 아주 최근의 일이었다.

re·cep·ta·cle [riséptəkəl] *n.* Ⓒ **1** anything used to contain or hold something, such as a bag or a cup; a container. 용기; 그릇. ¶ *a ~ for butter* 버터 그릇. **2** 《bot.》 a basis of flower. 화탁(花托); 꽃턱. [→receive]

·re·cep·tion [risépʃən] *n.* **1** Ⓤ the act of receiving; the state of being received. 받아들임; 수령; 수취. ¶ *the ~ of air into the lungs* 폐로 공기를 들이마시는 일 / *the ~ of wireless signals* 무선 신호의 수취 / *Reception* (*i.e. by wireless*) *was good.* 수신 상태는 양호했다. **2** Ⓒ the way of receiving. 대우; 응대. ¶ *a favorable ~* 호평 / *The play had* 〔*met with*〕 *a cold ~.* 그 극에 대한 반응은 냉담했다 / *The enemy were given a hot ~.* 적은 격렬한 저항을 받았다 **3** Ⓒ a gathering to welcome or honor guests. 환영회; 리셉션. ¶ *A ~ was held in honor of the ambassador.* 대사를 위하여 환영회가 열렸다 / *hold a wedding ~* 결혼 피로연을 열다. **4** Ⓤ the act of allowing; admission. 수리; 용인. ¶ *the ~ of evidence by a court of law* 법원의 증거 수리. [→receive]

re·cep·tion·ist [risépʃənist] *n.* Ⓒ a person employed to receive visitors. 접수계원.

re·cep·tive [riséptiv] *adj.* able or quick to receive new ideas, impressions, etc. 수용력〔이해력〕이 있는; 감수성이 풍부한. ¶ *a ~ mind* 이해가 빠른 머리 / *a mind ~ of new ideas* 새로운 사상을 받아들이는 머리 / *The audience were not ~.* 청중의 반응은 무뎠다.

re·cep·tive·ness [riséptivnis] *n.* Ⓤ ability or willingness to receive. 감수〔수용〕성.

·re·cess [ríːses, risés] *n.* **1** Ⓤ a brief stop of work, study, business, etc.; 《U.S.》 a vacation. (잠시의) 휴식; 휴가. ¶ *Our school has an hour's ~ at noon.* 학교에서는 정오에 1 시간의 휴식이 있다 / *Parliament is now in ~.* 의회는 지금 휴회중이다. **2** Ⓒ a part set back from the rest; an alcove. (벽 따위의) 오목하게 들어간 곳; 벽감(壁龕). ¶ *This long seat will fit nicely into that ~.* 이 긴 의자는 저 벽감 속에 꼭 들어맞겠다. **3** 《usu. *pl.*》 a remote, quiet or secret place; an inner part. 멀리 외진 곳; 후미진 곳; 구석; 안쪽. ¶ *the deepest recesses of the country* 그 나라의 가장 외진 곳 / *the recesses of a cave* 굴의 맨 안쪽 / 《*fig.*》 *the secret recesses of the heart* 마음의 아주 깊은 곳.

— *vt.* (P6) **1** make a recess in (some-

thing). …을 우묵하게 하다. ¶ ~ *a wall* 벽감을 만들다. **2** set back from a line; set in a recess. …을 (쑥) 들어가게 하다. ¶ ~ *a house from the line of a road* 집을 도로 변에서 들어가게 하다.
— *vi.* (P1) (of a meeting, etc.) take a recess. 휴회〔휴교〕하다. ¶ *The court will ~ for lunch.* 법정은 점심 시간 동안 휴정한다. [→recede]

re·ces·sion [risé∫ən] *n.* **1** Ⓤ the act of going back; withdrawal. 후퇴; 물러남. ¶ *the ~ of objects as seen from a moving train* 달리는 열차에서 보이는 멀어져가는 물체들. **2** Ⓒ a part which recedes. 우묵 들어간 곳. **3** Ⓒ 《econ.》 a period of reduced economic activity; a slump. 경기 후퇴(기).

re·ces·sion·al [risé∫ənəl] *adj.* **1** of the recession of the clergy and choir. (목사·성가대의) 퇴장시의. ¶ *a ~ hymn* 목사가 퇴장할 때 부르는 찬송가. **2** 《Brit.》 of a parliamentary recess. (의회가) 휴회의. — *n.* Ⓒ a recessional hymn or music sung or played while the clergy and choir leave the chancel. (목사·성가대가) 퇴장할 때 부르는 찬송가.

re·ces·sive [risésiv] *adj.* **1** tending to go back. 퇴행의; 역행(逆行)의. **2** 《biol.》 taking after an ancestor. 열성(劣性)의.

***rec·i·pe** [résəpìː] *n.* Ⓒ **1** a list of directions for preparing or mixing medicine, foods, drinks, etc.; a prescription. (약의) 처방; (요리의) 조리법. ¶ *Give me your ~ for cookies.* 댁의 쿠키 요리법을 알려주시오. **2** any means or method to do or make something; a remedy or cure. 수단; 비법; 조처. ¶ *a ~ for success in life* 인생 성공의 비결 / *the latest ~ for our social failures* 지금의 사회적 낙오자들을 치유하는 최신의 방법. [L.=take thou]

re·cip·i·ent [risípiənt] *n.* Ⓒ a person or thing that receives. 수납자; 용기; 그릇. ¶ *the ~ of the prize* 상금 수상자 / *the ~ of the letter* 〔*grant*〕 편지 수신인〔보조금 수령자〕. — *adj.* receiving; ready to receive. 받는; 받아들이는; 감수성이 있는. ¶ *He has a ~ mind.* 그는 감수성이 있는 사람이다. [→receive]

re·cip·ro·cal [risíprəkəl] *adj.* done or given in return; mutual. 서로의; 상호적인; 답례의. ¶ ~ *help* 상호 원조 / *a ~ treaty* 호혜 조약 / ~ *affection* 상사(相思) / ~ *visits* 〔*gifts*〕 답례 방문〔선물〕 / *a ~ benefit* 답례로서 받는 이익 / ~ *trust* 상호 신뢰 / *a ~ ratio* 〔*proportion*〕 반비례 / *They have a ~ loathing for* 〔*of*〕 *each other.* 서로 앙숙이다.
— *n.* **1** a thing that is reciprocal to something else. 상호적〔상관적〕인 것; 상대되는 것. **2** 《math.》 number so related to another that their product is 1. 역수(逆數). [L. *reciprocus*]

re·cip·ro·cal·ly [risíprəkəli] *adv.* in a reciprocal manner; mutually. 서로; 상호적으로; 호혜적으로.

re·cip·ro·cate [risíprəkèit] *vt.* (P6) **1** give or get (something) in exchange; interchange; repay; give (something) in return. …을 교환하다; 답례하다; 보답으로 …을 주다. ¶ *She loves me and I ~ her love.* 그녀가 나를 사랑하기에 나도 그녀를 사랑한다 / ~ *favors* 서로 친절을〔호의를〕 베풀다 / *His dislike of me is entirely reciprocated.* 그가 나를 싫어하는 것만큼 나도 그를 싫어한다. **2** make (something) move back and forth. …에 왕복 운동을 시키다.
— *vi.* (P1,3) **1** interchange; give and receive mutually. 교환하다; 서로 주고 받다. ¶ *To every attack he reciprocated with a blow.* 공격을 받을 때마다 그는 반격을 가했다. **2** move back and forth. 왕복 운동을 하다. ¶ *a reciprocating engine* 왕복 기관 / *reciprocating motion* 왕복 운동.

re·cip·ro·ca·tion [risìprəkéi∫ən] *n.* Ⓤ the act of reciprocating. 교환; 주고받기; 보답; 왕복 운동. ¶ *the ~ of a favor received* 받은 은혜에 대한 답례 / *the ~ of favors* 〔*ideas*〕 호의〔사상〕의 교환.

rec·i·proc·i·ty [rèsəprásəti / -prɔ́s-] *n.* Ⓤ **1** a reciprocal state; mutual action. 상호 관계〔작용〕. **2** mutual exchange of privileges. 호혜; 상호의 이익.

***re·cit·al** [risáitl] *n.* **1** Ⓒ a program of music given by a single singer or player. 독창〔독주〕회; 리사이틀. ¶ *My music teacher will give a ~ on Tuesday evening.* 화요일 저녁에 음악 선생님의 독주회가 있을 예정이다. **2** Ⓤ the act of reciting; narration. 낭독; 음송(吟誦). **3** Ⓒ a story; an account. 이야기; 설명. ¶ *We heard her long ~ of her troubles.* 우리는 장황한 그녀의 고생담을 들었다. [→recite]

rec·i·ta·tion [rèsətéi∫ən] *n.* ⓊⒸ **1** the act of reciting prose or poetry in public. 낭독; 음송. **2** 《U.S.》 the act of reciting a lesson prepared in advance by pupils before a teacher in a classroom. (선생님 앞에서의) 암송; 복창. ¶ *a ~ in history* 역사(과)의 암송. [→recite]

rec·i·ta·tive [rèsətətíːv] *n.* 《mus.》 **1** Ⓤ a style of music halfway between speaking and singing, used in opera. (오페라의) 서창조(敍唱調). **2** Ⓒ a passage in this style. 서창부(部).

***re·cite** [risáit] *vt.* (P6) **1** repeat (a poem, prose, etc.) from memory. (시 따위)를 읊다; 암송〔음송〕하다. ¶ ~ *a poem.* **2** give an account of (something) in detail. …을 상세히 이야기하다. ¶ *He recited the history of his adventure.* 그는 자기의 모험담을 세세하게 이야기했다. **3** tell one by one. …을 열거하다. ¶ *Will you ~ the names of the pupils who have not been absent this term?* 이번 학기에 개근한 학생들 이름을 열거해 봐라. **4** 《U.S.》 repeat (a lesson) in the classroom. (과제)를 암송하다.

¶ *Pupils ~ their lessons.*
— *vi.* (P1) **1** repeat something learnt by heart. 암송하다. **2** 《U.S.》 reply to a teacher's question on a lesson or assignment. (숙제 따위에 관해) 선생님 질문에 대답하다. [re-. L. *cito* cite]

reck [rek] 《*arch., poet.*》 *vi.* (P1,2A,3) care. 마음쓰다; 개의하다. ¶ *The brave soldiers recked little of danger.* 용감한 병정들은 위험을 전혀 개의치 않았다 / *It recks little whether he should marry.* 그가 결혼을 하든 아니 하든 아무래도 좋다 / *What ~ they whether they live or die?* 그들이 죽건 살건 알 바가 아니다. — *vt.* (P6,7,17) care about; matter to. …에 개의하다; 신경쓰다. ¶ *~ nothing of* 전혀 개의치 않다 / *What recks it whether we win or lose?* 우리가 지든 이기든 그게 무슨 대수냐 / *It recks him not what others think or say.* 남이야 뭐라건 그는 오불관언이다. [E.]

:**reck·less** [réklis] *adj.* without care; careless about results; rash. 부주의한; 무모한; 개의치 않는. ¶ *~ driving* 난폭 운전 / *~ expenditure* 무모한 지출 / *be ~ of danger* 위험을 개의치 않다.

reck·less·ly [réklisli] *adv.* in a reckless manner; carelessly. 무모하게.

•**reck·on** [rékən] *vt.* **1** (P6,7) count; calculate; count up. …을 세다; 합계〔계산〕하다. ¶ *~ up the bill* 계산서를 합산하다 / *My child is reckoning the days till Christmas.* 우리 집 아이는 성탄절까지의 날짜를 손꼽고 있다. **2** (P7,13,21) judge; consider; regard; conclude. …을 평가하다; …라고 간주하다; …라고 단정하다〔결론짓다〕. ¶ *~ someone an enemy* 아무를 적으로 치부하다 / *I ~ him as* 〔*for, to be*〕 *a wise man.* 나는 그를 현명한 사람으로 본다 / *We ~ him among our supporters.* 우리는 그를 지지자의 한 사람으로 생각하고 있다. **3** (P11) 《*colloq.*》 think; suppose. …라고 생각하다. ¶ *I ~ that it is going to rain.* 내 생각엔 비가 올 듯하다 / *He will come soon, I ~.* 그가 곧 오리라 생각한다. — *vi.* **1** (P1) count; calculate. 세다; 계산하다. ¶ *~ from 10 to 100,* 10 에서 100 까지 세다. **2** (P1,3) 《*on, upon*》 rely; depend. 기대하다; 의지하다. ¶ *~ on someone's help* 아무의 도움을 기대하다. **3** (P1,2A) 《*colloq.*》 consider; suppose; guess. 생각하다; 추측하다. ¶ *Can you do it? —I ~ so.* 할 수 있겠나 —그럴 거라 생각한다. [E.]

reckon in (=*include*) *something.* …을 계산에 넣다.

reckon with, **a**) settle accounts with (someone). …을 청산〔처리〕하다. ¶ *We will ~ with these defaulters later.* 이들 채무 불이행자들을 나중에 처리하겠다. **b**) take (something) into account. …을 고려에 넣다. ¶ *~ with the possibility of rain* 비 올 경우를 생각해보다.

reckon without, leave out of consideration; not count; not depend on. …을 고려에 넣지 않다〔무시하다〕. ¶ *You had better ~ without me, as I am not sure whether I shall be able to be present.* 내가 참석할 수 있을지는 미정이니 나를 고려에 넣지 않는 게 좋겠다.

reckon without one's host ⇨host[1].

reck·on·er [rékənər] *n.* Ⓒ **1** a person who reckons. 계산하는 사람. **2** a book of mathematical tables. 계산 조견표.

reck·on·ing [rékəniŋ] *n.* **1** Ⓤ the act of counting; calculation. 계산; 셈. ¶ *He is good at ~.* 그는 계산을 잘 한다 / *By my ~ we are halfway there* 〔*home*〕. 내 셈으론 거기〔집〕까지 반은 왔다. **2** Ⓤ settling an account; 《*fig.*》 paying for one's sins. 청산; 결산; 속죄. **3** Ⓒ a bill, esp. at an inn. (술집 따위의) 계산서. ¶ *pay the ~* 셈을 치르다 / 《*fig.*》 *There will be a heavy ~ to pay for his crimes.* 그의 죄값은 무거울 것이다. **4** Ⓤ 《naut.》 the act of determining the position, esp. of a ship. 선박의 위치 측정. ¶ *dead ~* (선박의) 추측 항법(航法).

be out in one's reckoning, miscalculate one's position; be mistaken in one's judgment. 잘못 생각하다; 헛짚다.

the day of reckoning, the day when the final accounts must be settled with God; the Day of Judgment. 최후의 심판일.

re·claim [rikléim] *vt.* (P6,13) **1** lead (someone) into better ways; reform. …을 개심하게 하다; 교화하다. ¶ *Her mission was to ~ former criminals.* 그녀의 임무는 죄지은 사람들을 교화하는 일이었다. **2** bring (something) into use; bring (land) under cultivation. …을 이용하다; 농지로 만들다. ¶ *~ the desert* 황무지를 개간하다 / *This land was reclaimed from the sea.* 이 땅은 바다를 매립한 것이다. **3** =re-claim. — *n.* Ⓤ reformation; restoration. 개심; 교화; 회복. [re-, L. *clamo* call out]

re-claim [rikléim] *vt.* ask for the return of (something); get back. …의 반환을 요구하다; 회수하다. ¶ *~ lost property* 상실한 재산의 반환을 요구하다 / *You may be entitled to ~ some of the tax you paid last year.* 당신은 작년에 낸 세금의 일부를 반환 청구할 권리가 있다.

rec·la·ma·tion [rèkləméiʃən] *n.* ⓊⒸ the act of reclaiming; the state of being reclaimed. 개심; 개간; 반환 요구. ¶ *the ~ of land* 토지 개간.

re·cline [rikláin] *vt.* (P13) 《*on*》 cause to lean or lie back or down. …을 기대다; 의지하다; (몸)을 눕히다. ¶ *~ one's head on the pillow* 베개에 머리를 얹다 / *with his head reclined on his hand* 머리를 손으로 받쳐 괴고 / *They lay reclined upon the grass.* 그들은 풀 위에 드러누워 있었다. — *vi.* (P1,2A,3) **1** 《*against*》 lean back; lie down. 기대다; 눕다. ¶ *~ against a wall* 벽에 기대다 / *The tired woman reclined in the armchair.* 지친 부인은

안락 의자에 기대어 앉았다. **2** 《*fig.*》 depend on. …에 기대다; 의지하다. ¶ *He reclines too much on doubtful supporters.* 그는 미덥지 못한 지지자들에게 너무 의지한다. [L. *reclino*]

rec·luse [riklúːs, rékluːs] *n.* Ⓒ a person who lives shut up or apart from the world; a hermit. 속세를 떠난 사람; 은둔자. — *adj.* withdrawn from the world; solitary. 쓸쓸한; 적적한; 속세를 떠난〔등진〕. ¶ *a ~ monk* 세속을 떠난 수도사 / *He is living a ~ life.* 그는 은둔 생활을 하고 있다. [re-, L. *claudo* shut]

*__rec·og·ni·tion__ [rèkəgníʃən] *n.* Ⓤ **1** ⓐ the act of recognizing; the state of being recognized; notice; salutation. 알아봄; 인식; 인사. ¶ *He gave no sign of ~.* 그는 아는 체하지 않았다 / *He only gave me a passing smile of ~.* 나를 지나치면서 그저 미소로 눈인사를 했을 뿐이다. ⓑ the act or possibility of identifying. 보고 앎; 식별. ¶ *My ~ of him was immediate.* 나는 그를 보자마자 곧 알아보았다 / *He had changed beyond ~.* 그는 몰라보게 달라져 있었다. **2** acknowledgment; the state of being recognized. 승인; 인지; 인가. ¶ *the ~ of a child as the lawful heir* 아이에 대한 법적 상속인으로의 승인 / *the ~ of a new state* 신국가의 인정〔승인〕/ *gain official ~* 공인받다. **3** favorable 〔special〕 notice; attention; gratitude. (공적 등을) 인정하기; 치하; 감사. ¶ *deserve ~ for…* …에 대하여 치하를 받을 가치가 있다 / *in ~ of the service* 봉사의 공로를 인정하여 / *receive* 〔*meet with*〕 *~ in return for services* 노고를 인정 받다 / *They gave him a gold watch in ~ of his long service to the school.* 그들은 학교에 대한 그의 오랜 봉사를 치하하여 금시계를 주었다. [→recognize]

rec·og·niz·a·ble [rékəgnàizəbəl] *adj.* that can be recognized. 인식〔인지, 승인〕할 수 있는; 알아볼 수 있는.

rec·og·niz·a·bly [rékəgnàizəbəli] *adv.* **1** in a recognizable manner. 뚜렷이 눈에 띄게. **2** to a recognizable extent or degree. 꽤; 상당히.

re·cog·ni·zance [rikágnəzəns / -kɔ́g-] *n.* Ⓒ **1** 《law》 the recorded promise binding someone to do some particular act. 서약(서). ¶ *enter into recognizances* 서약서에 서명하다. **2** the money to be forfeited if the act in question is not performed. 서약 보증금; 보석금. ¶ *forfeit one's ~* 서약 보증금을 몰수당하다.

:**rec·og·nize** [rékəgnàiz] *vt.* **1** (P6,7,11, 21) acknowledge; take notice of (something); accept; admit. …을 인정(認定)하다; 승인하다; 인지하다. ¶ *~ the new government* 새로운 정부를 인정하다 / *~ a baby as one's son* 아기를 친자로 인정하다 / *I ~ that I have been wrong.* 나는 나의 과오를 인정한다 / *You must ~ the difficult position the company is in.* 회사가 지금 어려운 처지에 있는 것을 인정해야 한다. **2** (P6,11) realize to have seen (something) before; identify. …을 알아보다. ¶ *~ an old friend* 옛 친구를 알아보다 / *You have grown so much that I scarcely recognized you.* 네가 얼마나 자랐던지 나는 겨우 알아봤다. **3** (P6) show appreciation of; acknowledge. (공로·수고 따위)를 알아주다; 인정하다. ¶ *~ someone's services* 아무의 공로를 인정하다 / *~ a man for what he is* 그의 진가를 알아주다 / *His great learning has at last been recognized.* 그의 박학다식이 마침내 인정되었다. **4** (P6) 《U.S.》 acknowledge as having the right to speak, as in a meeting. …의 발언권을 인정하다. [re-, L. *cognosco* learn]

re·coil [rikɔ́il] *vi.* (P1,3) **1** spring back; come back. 되튀다; 뒤로 물러나다; 반동하다. ¶ *A gun recoils after being fired.* 총은 발사 후 후퇴한다. **2** retreat; retire. 퇴각하다. ¶ *The enemy recoiled.* 적군은 퇴각했다. **3** 《*at, before, from*》 shrink back. 움찔하다; 움츠리다. ¶ *The boy recoiled at the sight of blood.* 소년은 피를 보고는 움찔했다. **4** 《*fig.*》 react upon. 되돌아오다. ¶ *His cruelty to others recoiled in the end upon himself.* 남에 대한 그의 잔인한 행위는 결국 그에게로 돌아왔다.

— [rikɔ́il, ríːkɔ̀il] *n.* **1** Ⓒ sudden backward, esp. of a gun when it is fired. 되튐; (총포의) 반동. ¶ *the ~ of a gun.* **2** Ⓤ shrinking. 위축; 움츠림. **3** Ⓤ repugnance. 혐오; 반감. [re-, L. *culus* rump]

*__rec·ol·lect__ [rèkəlékt] *vt., vi.* (P6,10,11, 12;1) call (something) back to mind; remember. (…을) 회상하다; 생각해 내다. ¶ *I cannot ~ his name* 〔*the exact words*〕. 그의 이름이〔그 정확한 말이〕 생각나지 않는다 / *As you no doubt ~,….* 네가 똑똑히 기억하듯이… / *I cannot ~ how to get there.* 어떻게 거기 갔는지 기억이 나지 않는다. [re-]

re-col·lect [rìːkəlékt] *vt.* (P6) **1** gather or collect again. …을 다시 모으다. **2** compose (one's thoughts, etc.); recover (oneself). (마음 따위를) 가라앉히다; (용기 등)을 불러일으키다. ¶ *be re-collected* 침착해지다 / *~ oneself* 마음을 가라앉히다. [re-]

*__rec·ol·lec·tion__ [rèkəlékʃən] *n.* **1** Ⓤ the act or power of calling back to the mind. 생각해내기; 회상; 기억(력). ¶ *be in* 〔*within*〕 *one's ~* 기억에 남아 있다 / *be past* 〔*beyond*〕 *~* 생각나지 않다; 기억에 없다 / *have no ~ of …* …의 기억이 없다. **2** Ⓒ 《often *pl.*》 a memory; something that is recollected. 추억(되는 일). ¶ *That evening together is my happiest recollections.* 함께 한 그날 저녁이 나의 가장 행복한 추억이다.

re·com·mence [rìːkəméns] *vt., vi.* (P6;1) start or begin again. 다시 시작하다; 다시 하다. [re-]

*__rec·om·mend__ [rèkəménd] *vt.* **1** (P6,7, 13,14) speak or write well of (someone or something). …을 추천〔천거〕하다. ¶ ~ *a good doctor* 용한 의사를 천거하다 / *He was recommended for the position* 〔*as the most suitable person*〕. 그 자리에〔가장 적합한 사람으로〕 그가 추천됐다. **2** (P6,11,20) advise; suggest to. …을 권(고)하다; 충고하다. ¶ ~ *someone to try a new medicine* …에게 다른 약을 써보라고 권하다 / *I ~ you to take a holiday.* 자네 휴가를 얻어 좀 쉬는 것이 좋겠어. **3** (P6) make (someone) attractive; make pleasing or acceptable. (행위·성질 따위가) …의 호감을 사게끔하다. ¶ *Her honesty recommends her.* 그녀는 성실해서 남의 호감을 산다 / *Your plan has very little to ~ it.* 네 계획에 취할 데라고는 없다. **4** (P13) give in charge or trust. …에 맡기다; 위탁하다. ¶ ~ *one's soul to God* 자신의 혼을 신에게 맡기다. [re-]

***rec·om·men·da·tion** [rèkəmendéiʃən] *n.* **1** Ⓤ the act of recommending. 추천; 천거; 충고; 권고. **2** Ⓒ a letter recommending someone to another. 추천장. **3** Ⓒ a strong point. 취할 점; 장점. ¶ *He has no recommendations but honesty.* 그의 장점이라면 성실뿐이다. [re-]

re·com·mit [rìːkəmít] *vt.* (**-mit·ted, -mit·ting**) (P6) **1** send or order back. …에게 다시 보내다. ¶ *He was recommitted to prison.* 그는 재수감됐다. **2** refer again to a committee. …을 다시 위원회에 회부하다. **3** commit (an offense, error) again. (죄·과오 따위)를 다시 저지르다; 재범하다. [re-]

rec·om·pense [rékəmpèns] *vt.* (P6,13) **1** pay back; reward. …에게 갚다; 보답하다. ¶ ~ *someone for his labor* 수고에 대하여 아무에게 보답하다 / ~ *good with evil* 선을 악으로 갚다; 배은 망덕하다. **2** make amends; make a fair return for. …의 보상을 하다; …을 깨끗이 변상하다. ¶ *We agreed to ~ for all losses.* 우린 모든 손실을 변상하기로 합의했다. — *n.* ⓊⒸ a reward; amends. 보수; 보상. ¶ *in ~ for one's injury* 상해에 대한 보상으로 / *without ~* 무보수로 / *Kindness brings its own ~.* 친절을 베풀면 저절로 그 보답이 온다. [re-, →compensate]

re·con·cil·a·ble [rékənsàiləbəl] *adj.* that can be reconciled. 화해〔조정〕할 수 있는; 조화〔일치〕시킬 수 있는. [↓]

***rec·on·cile** [rékənsàil] *vt.* **1** (P6,13) make (persons) friends again after a quarrel. …을 화해시키다. ¶ ~ *Tom and Jack with each other* 톰과 잭을 화해시키다 / *They became reconciled.* 그들은 다시 사이가 좋아졌다. **2** (P6) settle (a quarrel, etc.). (분쟁 등)을 조정(調停)하다. ¶ ~ *a quarrel* 다툼을 조정〔중재〕하다. **3** (P6,13) harmonize; make consistent with. …을 조화〔일치〕시키다. ¶ ~ *rights and duties* 권리와 의무를 조화〔양립〕시키다 / ~ *words with actions* 언행을 일치시키다 / *the problem of reconciling all the different versions of this event* 이 사건에 대한 모든 각기 다른 견해를 조화시키는 문제. **4** (P13) 《usu. *reflexively*》 persuade oneself to accept; be contented with. …을 (스스로 체념하고) 감수하다; …으로 만족하다. ¶ *He reconciled himself to his misfortune.* 그는 자기의 불행을 감수했다 / *He is reconciled to living in the country.* 그는 시골 생활에 만족하고 있다. [re-]

rec·on·cil·i·a·tion [rèkənsìliéiʃən] *n.* ⓊⒸ **1** the act of reconciling; the state of being reconciled. 화해; 사화(私和). ¶ *There was no hope of a ~ between the two families.* 그 두 집안이 화해할 가망은 없었다. **2** the act of settling a quarrel or dispute; the settlement of disagreements; differences, etc. 조정; 조화. ¶ *the ~ of religion and science* 종교와 과학의 조화.

rec·on·dite [rékəndàit, rikán- / rikɔ́n-] *adj.* **1** profound; difficult to understand. 심원(深遠)한; 난해한. ¶ *the ~ motives of human action* 인간 행위의 심원한 동기 / *a ~ expression* 난해한 표현. **2** little known; obscure. 모호한; 애매한. ¶ *a ~ fact* 〔*subject*〕 애매한 사실〔문제〕. [re-, L. *condo* hide]

re·con·di·tion [rìːkəndíʃən] *vt.* (P6) put (something) to a good condition again; repair. …을 수리하다; 고치다. [re-]

re·con·nais·sance [rikánəsəns, -zəns / -kɔ́n-] *n.* ⓊⒸ an investigation for military or scientific purposes. 정찰; 수색; 답사. ¶ *a ~ plane* 정찰기. [→recognize]

rec·on·noi·ter, 《Brit.》 **-tre** [rèkənɔ́itər, rìːk-] *vt., vi.* (P6;1) examine or explore for military or scientific purposes. 정찰하다; 답사하다. ¶ *It seemed wise to ~ the town before entering.* 마을에 들어가기 전에 정찰을 하는 것이 좋을 듯싶었다. [↑]

re·con·sid·er [rìːkənsídər] *vt.* (P6) consider again. …을 재고하다; 다시 생각하다. ¶ ~ *one's decision* 결정을 재고하다. ●**re·con·sid·er·a·tion** [-sidəréiʃən] *n.* [re-]

re·con·sti·tute [rìːkánstətjùːt / -kɔ́n-] *vt.* (P6) set up or form again; give a new constitution to. …을 재구성〔재편성〕하다. ¶ *decide to ~ the committee under a new chairman* 새 위원장 밑에 위원회를 재구성하기로 결정하다. [re-]

re·con·struct [rìːkənstrʌ́kt] *vt.* (P6) **1** construct again; build again. …을 재건〔개축, 개조〕하다. **2** recreate in the mind from given or available information. (주어진 또는 이용이 가능한 자료로) …을 재구성〔재현〕하다. ¶ *The police are trying to ~ the crime from the clues they have.* 경찰은 그들이 가진 단서들을 이용하여 그 범죄의 재구성을 시도하고 있다. [re-, →construct]

re·con·struc·tion [rìːkənstrʌ́kʃən] *n.* Ⓤ the act of rebuilding, remodeling or restoring. 재건; 개조; 부흥.

re·con·struc·tive [rìːkənstrʌ́ktiv] *adj.* of reconstruction; tending to rebuild or restore. 재건〔개조〕의; 부흥의.

:re·cord [rikɔ́:rd] *vt.* (P6) **1** set down in writing to keep the memory of (something); write down officially; register. …을 기록하다; 기록에 남기다; 등기[등록]하다. ¶ ~ *daily events in a diary* 매일의 사건들을 일기에 적어두다 / *Her busy pencil was recording his words.* 그녀의 연필을 잡은 손은 바쁘게 그의 말을 기록하고 있었다 / *She recorded the pupils' grades.* 그녀는 생도들의 성적을 기장(記帳)했다. **2** put (sounds, etc.) on a phonograph disk, tape, etc. …을 녹음[녹화]하다. ¶ ~ *Bach's cantatas* 바흐의 칸타타를 녹음하다 / *The conversation was secretly recorded.* 그 대화는 몰래 녹음되었다. **3** (of an instrument) show; indicate. (한란계 따위가) …을 나타내다. ¶ *The thermometer records 20°C.* 온도계는 섭씨(攝氏) 20도를 가리키고 있다 / *A seismograph records earthquakes.* 지진계는 지진을 기록한다.
— [rékərd / -kɔ:rd] *n.* Ⓒ **1** the act of recording; Ⓤ the state or fact of being recorded. 기록; 기록해 두기; 등록. ¶ *a matter of* ~ 기록된 사항 / *write a* ~ *of one's journey* 여행기를 쓰다 / *put on* ~ 기록[기재]하다. **2** a written account of events, facts, etc.; an official document containing an account of events, etc. 기록된 것; 기록 문서; 공문서. ¶ *a court of* ~ 등록 법원 / *a congressional* ~ 의사록; 의회 기록 / *the records of the Foreign office* 외무부 기록 / *keep to* [*travel out of*] *the* ~ 본제(本題)를 벗어나지 않다[벗어나다]. **3** the facts known about one's career, conduct, etc. 경력; 이력; 성적. ¶ *have a good* [*bad*] ~ 이력이 좋다[좋지 않다] / *His* ~ *is against him.* 그의 이력은 그에게 불리하다 / *He has a criminal* ~. 그에겐 전과가 있다 / *a man with a clean* ~ 전력이 깨끗한 사람 / *has a fine* ~ *at school* 학교 성적이 좋다. **4** the best achievement, esp. in sports. (스포츠 따위의) 최고 기록. ¶ *beat* [*break, cut*] *the* ~ 기록을 깨다 / *set* (*up*) *a new* ~ 신기록을 세우다 / *hold the world's* ~ 세계 기록을 보유하다. **5** a disk used on a phonograph. 음반; 레코드; 테이프.
***bear record to** something,* prove the truth of. …의 증언을 하다.
go on record, 《orig. U.S.》 express one's opinion publicly. 자기 의견을 공표하다.
off the record, 《*colloq.*》 not for publication. 비공식의; 공표해서는 안 되는.
on record, **a**) written in a document. (문서에) 기록된. ¶ *The case is on* ~. 그 사건은 기록에 남아 있다. **b**) known or remembered as a fact. 널리 알려진; 기록적인. ¶ *Last summer was the wettest one on* ~. 지난 여름의 비는 기록적이었다.
— *adj.* making a record; quite different from others. 기록적인; 공전(空前)의. [re-, L. *cor* heart]

re·cord·er [rikɔ́:rdər] *n.* Ⓒ **1** a person who makes and keeps official records. 기록자; 등록계. **2** a machine which keeps records. 녹음기. **3** a musical instrument like a flute. 플루트의 일종.

record holder [⌐-⌐-] *n.* a person who officially holds the best record. 최고 기록 보유자.

re·cord·ing [rikɔ́:rdiŋ] *n.* Ⓤ the act of a person who records; Ⓒ the act of registering sound on a record. 기록; 녹음.
— *adj.* that records. 기록[녹음]하는.

recording angel [-⌐-⌐-] *n.* an angel who makes records of a man's good and evil deeds. (사람의 선악의 행동을 기록하는) 기록 천사.

record player [⌐-⌐-] *n.* an instrument for producing the sounds on phonograph records. 전축; 레코드 플레이어.

re·count [rikáunt] *vt.* (P6) tell (something) in detail. …을 세세히 이야기하다. ¶ *He recounted the events of the day.* 그는 그날의 사건들을 자세하게 설명했다. [re-]

re-count [ri:káunt] *vt.* (P6) count again. …을 다시 세다[계산하다]. — [rí:kàunt] *n.* a second counting, esp. of votes at an election. (선거에서) 투표의 재계표(再計票). [re-]

re·coup [rikú:p] *vt.* (P6,13) **1** make up for (a loss, etc.); make good. (손실 등)을 메우다; 벌충하다. ¶ *I recouped my loss.* 손해를 벌충했다 / *He will* ~ *you for what you spent.* 네가 쓴 비용을 그가 메워줄 것이다 / ~ *one's health* 건강을 회복하다. **2** 《law》 deduct. 공제하다. [re-]

re·course [rí:kɔ:rs, rikɔ́:rs] *n.* **1** Ⓤ an appeal for help or protection; an appeal. 의지; 의뢰; 간원; 호소. ¶ *His last* ~ *was to return to his native home.* 그의 마지막 소원은 옛집에 돌아가는 것이었다 / *As a last* ~ *he called the police.* 마지막 의지(依支)로서 그는 경찰을 불렀다. **2** Ⓒ a person or thing turned to for help. 의지가 되는 사람[물건]. ¶ *He is our last* ~. 마지막으로 의지가 되는 사람은 그다. [re-]
have recourse to, turn to … for help. …에 호소[의지]하다. ¶ *have* ~ *to violence* 폭력에 호소하다.
without recourse to, without turning to … for help. …에 의지하지 않고.

:re·cov·er [rikʌ́vər] *vt.* (P6) **1** ⓐ get back (something lost or stolen). …을 되찾다; 회복하다. ¶ ~ *stolen property* [*a lost umbrella*] 빼앗긴 재산[잃어버린 우산]을 되찾다 / *He has recovered his reputation as an artist.* 그는 예술가로서의 명성을 되찾았다. ⓑ regain (lost physical powers). (건강·의식 따위)를 되찾다; 회복하다. ¶ ~ *consciousness* [*one's senses*] 의식을 되찾다 / ~ *one's health* 건강을 회복하다 / *He is very ill and unlikely to* ~. 병이 매우 깊어 회복될 것 같지 않다 / ~ *one's balance* 마음의 평정을 되찾다. **2** 《*reflexively*》 regain control,

balance, etc. of (oneself). 제정신이 들다; 평정을 되찾다. ¶ ~ *oneself* 제정신이 들다; 침착해지다; 정상을 되찾다. **3** make up for (a loss). (손실)을 벌충하다; 메우다. ¶ ~ *one's losses* 손실을 메우다 / ~ *time wasted or lost* 허비된〔잃은〕 시간을 벌충하다 / *He recovered his losses by hard work.* 열심히 일해서 손실을 만회했다. **4** 《law》 obtain (payment for a loss or for damage) by a legal process. (손해 배상)을 받다.
— *vi.* (P1,3) **1** 《*from*》 get well again; regain health, prosperity, etc. 회복되다; 원상으로 되다. ¶ ~ *from a disaster* 재해에서 복구되다 / ~ *from* 〔*of*〕 *an illness* 병이 낫다 / *I have quite recovered from my cold.* 감기가 다 나았다 / *The patient has recovered very quickly.* 환자는 매우 빨리 회복되었다. **2** obtain a favorable judgment in a suit. 소송에 이기다. **3** regain one's balance, etc. 냉정을 되찾다. [→recuperate]
recover one's feet 〔***legs***〕, get up after a fall. 쓰러졌다가 일어서다.

re·cov·er [ri:kʌ́vər] *vt.* (P6) put a new cover on (something). …을 다시 바르다; 갈아대다. ¶ *I got my old umbrella re-covered.* 우산천을 갈았다. [re-]

***re·cov·er·y** [rikʌ́vəri] *n.* Ⓤ **1** the act of getting back to a proper position or condition. 회복; 복귀; 복구. ¶ *He stumbled, but made a good* ~. 그는 쓰러졌으나 곧 일어섰다. **2** the state of being healthy or normal again. (병에서의) 회복. ¶ *I heard of your* ~ *from your illness.* 병이 나으셨다구요. **3** the act of recovering; recovering something lost. (잃은 것을) 되찾음. ¶ *the* ~ *of stolen property* 빼앗긴 재산의 회수. [→recover[1]]

rec·re·ant [rékriənt] *adj.* 《*poet.*》 **1** cowardly. 겁이 많은; 소심한. **2** faithless to one's duty or cause. 성실하지 못한. — *n.* Ⓒ a coward; an unfaithful person. 겁쟁이; 배신자. [re-, →creed]

rec·re·ate [rékrièit] *vt.* (P6) 《rare》 refresh physically or mentally; relax. …에게 기운을 되찾게 하다; 기분 전환을 시키다; 쉬게 하다. ¶ *Change of work recreates us.* 일을 바꾸면 기분 전환이 된다 / *In summer I* ~ *myself with swimming.* 여름에는 수영을 하며 몸을 푼다. — *vi.* (P1) take relaxation. 기분 전환을 하다. [re-]

re-cre·ate [rì:kriéit] *vt.* create (something) anew. 개조하다; 고쳐〔다시〕 만들다.

***rec·re·a·tion** [rèkriéiʃən] *n.* ⓊⒸ refreshment of mind or body after work; any form of relaxation or amusement. 휴양; 기분 전환; 레크리에이션. ¶ *a* ~ *ground* 유원지. [→recreate]

rec·re·a·tive [rékrièitiv] *adj.* serving as recreation; refreshing. 기분 전환이 되는; 기운을 되찾는.

re·crim·i·nate [rikrímənèit] *vi.* (P1) accuse or blame in return. 서로 비난하다. [re-, L. *crimen* crime]

re·crim·i·na·tion [rikrìmənéiʃən] *n.* ⓊⒸ the act of expressing mutual reproach; accusation in return. 서로 헐뜯기. ¶ *The warring nations made many recriminations against each other.* 교전국은 지지 않고 서로 비난을 했다.

re·cru·des·cence [rì:kru:désns] *n.* Ⓤ (of disease, evil, etc.) the act of breaking out anew. (병·범죄 따위의) 재발. [re-, →crude]

***re·cruit** [rikrú:t] *n.* Ⓒ a man who has just entered military service; a person who has just joined a group, class, etc.; a rookie. 신병(新兵); 신입 회원; 초심자. ¶ *Fifty recruits have joined the police force.* 경찰대에 새로 50명이 투입되었다 / *We gained only a few recruits to our party.* 우리 당에 신당원은 소수에 불과했다.
— *vt.* (P6) **1** enlist (new soldiers, members); get (someone) to join the military forces, a club, etc.; enroll. (신병·신회원)을 모집하다; …을 신병〔신회원〕으로 하다. ¶ ~ *men for the army* 신병을 모집하다 / ~ *a party* 당에 새 당원을 영입하다. **2** restore (health or strength). (건강·체력)을 회복하다. ¶ ~ *oneself* 정양하다 / ~ *one's health* 건강을 회복하다. **3** make full or complete again by providing a new supply. (여축)을 보충하다; 채우다. ¶ *Before sailing, we recruited our food supplies.* 출항 전에 식량 공급을 보충했다.
— *vi.* (P1) **1** get new men or fresh supplies. 신병〔신회원〕을 모집하다; 보충하다. **2** recover health or strength. 건강을 회복하다. ¶ *You must take a holiday and try to* ~ . 휴가를 얻어서 몸을 좀 추스리게. [re-, L. *cresco* grow]

rec. sec. recording secretary.

rect. receipt; rector; rectory.

rect- [rekt-], **rec·ti-** [rekti-] *pref.* straight; right. '곧은, 직각'의 뜻. [L. *rego* rule, *rēctus* straight]

rec·ta [réktə] *n.* pl. of **rectum.**

rec·tan·gle [réktæ̀ŋgəl] *n.* Ⓒ a four-sided figure having four right angles. 직사각형 (cf. *square*). [rect-, →angle]

rec·tan·gu·lar [rektǽŋgjələr] *adj.* shaped like a rectangle. 직사각형의.

rec·ti·fi·ca·tion [rèktəfikéiʃən] *n.* Ⓤ the act of rectifying; the state of being rectified. 개정; 수정; 조정; 정류(精溜); 정류(整流). [↓]

rec·ti·fy [réktəfài] *vt.* (**-fied**) (P6) **1** amend; correct; make right. …을 개정〔수정〕하다. ¶ ~ *mistakes.* **2** 《chem.》 refine; purify. …을 정류(精溜)하다. ¶ ~ *wine.* **3** 《electr.》 change (an alternating current) to a direct current. …을 정류(整流)하다. [rect-, fy]

rec·ti·lin·e·al [rèktəlíniəl] *adj.* =rectilinear.

rec·ti·lin·e·ar [rèktəlíniər] *adj.* formed

by straight lines; in a straight line. 직선의. [recti-]

rec·ti·tude [réktətjùːd] *n.* Ⓤ righteousness; correctness; honesty. 공정; 정직; 정확. [↑]

rec·to [réktou] *n.* (*pl.* **-tos**) the right-hand page of an open book. (펼쳐 놓은 책의) 오른쪽 페이지(opp. verso). [L. *réctus* right]

rec·tor [réktər] *n.* Ⓒ **1** a clergyman in charge of a parish in the Protestant Episcopal Church or the Church of England. (신교 감독 교회의) 교구 목사; (영국 국교의) 교구장(cf. *vicar*). **2** the head of a unversity, school, esp. in Scotland and Germany. (대학·학교 등의) 총장; 학장; 교장.

rec·to·ry [réktəri] *n.* Ⓒ (*pl.* **-ries**) a rector's house or income. rector 의 주택〔수입〕.

rec·tum [réktəm] *n.* Ⓒ (*pl.* **-ta**) 《anat.》 the lower end of the intestine. 직장(直腸). [L. =straight]

re·cum·bent [rikʌ́mbənt] *adj.* leaning; reclining. 기댄; 가로누운. [re-, L. *cumbo* lie]

re·cu·per·ate [rikjúːpərèit] *vt.* (P6) **1** bring back (to health, etc.); restore. (병·손실(損失) 등으로부터) 회복시키다. ¶ *The men paused to ~ their horses.* 그들은 말을 쉬게 하려고 잠시 멈췄다 / *~ someone* …의 건강을 회복시키다. **2** recover (a financial loss). (재정 손실)을 만회하다. —*vi.* (P1) get well after an illness; recover one's health. 건강을 회복하다. ¶ *It took him several weeks to ~ after his illness.* 그는 앓고 나서 건강을 되찾는 데 여러 주일이 걸렸다. [L. *recupero*]

re·cu·per·a·tion [rikjùːpəréiʃən] *n.* Ⓤ the act of recuperating; recovery from illness, losses, etc. (병·손실 등으로부터의) 회복; 만회.

re·cu·per·a·tive [rikjúːpərèitiv, -rət-] *adj.* of recovery; helping or promoting recuperation. 회복하는; 기운을 돋우는; 회복에 도움이 되는.

re·cur [rikə́ːr] *vi.* (**-curred, -cur·ring**) (P1,3) **1** (of thoughts, memories, etc.) come back to mind; be remembered; (of subjects, etc.) go back; return. (생각·기억 등이) 마음에 다시 떠오르다; (화제 등이) 처음으로 되돌아가다. ¶ *~ to* 〔*in, on*〕 *one's mind* ~ 마음에 떠오르다 / *~ to the former subject* 처음의 화제로 되돌아가다 / *Past experiences often ~ to me.* 지난 경험들이 가끔 생각난다. **2** (of problems, etc.) come up or occur again; repeat. (문제 따위가) 재발하다; 반복되다. ¶ *If the pain recurs, take these tablets.* 통증이 재발하거든 이 알약을 드시오. **3** 《math.》 be repeated indefinitely. 순환하다. ¶ *a recurring decimal* 순환 소수. **4** resort. (…에) 호소〔의지〕하다. [re-, →current]

re·cur·rence [rikə́ːrəns, -kʌ́r-] *n.* ⓊⒸ the act of recurring; recollection. 재기; 재발; 회상. ¶ *the ~ of a fever.*

re·cur·rent [rikə́ːrənt, -kʌ́r-] *adj.* **1** coming back at intervals; occurring periodically; recurring. 재발하는. ¶ *a ~ fever* 회귀열(熱). **2** 《anat.》 turning back in the opposite direction. 회귀성의. ¶ *a ~ nerve* 회귀신경. [→recur, -ent]

re·cy·cle [riːsáikl] *vt.* treat (substances already used for industry, etc) so that further use is possible 재처리하다, 재생하다.

:red [red] *adj.* (**red·der, red·dest**) **1** of the color of fresh blood. 붉은; 빨간. ¶ *be ~ with anger* 성이 나서 뻘게진 / (*as*) *~ as a rose* 장미처럼 붉은 / *a ~ rag* (*to a bull*) 화나게 하는 것 / *become ~ with shame* 부끄러워 (얼굴이) 새빨개지다. **2** inflamed; blood-stained; fierce. 핏발이 선; 피에 물든; 격렬한. ¶ *~ eyes* 핏발이 선〔충혈된〕 눈 / *with ~ hands* 살인을 하고 / *a ~ battle* 혈전. **3** politically radical or revolutionary; Communist. (정치적으로) 과격한; 혁명적인; 공산주의의(opp. white). ¶ *~ ideas* 과격 사상.

paint the map red, extend the British Empire. 영국 영토를 넓히다.

paint the town red, celebrate boisterously, esp. by making a round of stops at bars and nightclubs. 떠들썩하게 술집을 돌아다니다.

—*n.* **1** ⓊⒸ the color of red; a pigment producing this color. 빨강; 적색. **2** Ⓤ red clothes. 붉은 옷. ¶ *a woman in ~* 붉은 옷을 입은 부인. **3** a red pigment. 붉은 그림물감. **4** 《*the ~*》 a net loss. 적자; 손실. **5** Ⓒ 《often *R-*》 a communist. 공산주의자. [E.]

be in the red, 《*colloq.*》 become bankrupt; be in debt. 거덜나다; 빚지다(opp. be in the black).

come out of the red, 《*colloq.*》 begin to gain. 적자에서 헤어나다; 흑자로 돌아서다.

see red, 《*colloq.*》 become very angry. 격노하다.

re·dact [ridǽkt] *vt.* (P6) edit. …을 편찬하다. [re-, L. *ago* bring]

red·breast [rédbrèst] *n.* Ⓒ 《U.S.》 《bird》 a robin. 울새. [*red*]

red·cap [rédkæ̀p] *n.* Ⓒ **1** 《U.S.》 a porter who works at a railroad station. (역의) 짐꾼. **2** 《Brit. *colloq.*》 a military policeman. 육군 헌병.

red cent [∠∠] *n.* 《U.S. *colloq.*》 a cent; a bit. 1센트 동전; 조금. ¶ *I don't care a ~.* 내 관심 밖이다.

red·coat [rédkòut] *n.* Ⓒ 《*colloq.*》 a British soldier, esp. during the American Revolution. (미국 독립 전쟁 때의) 영국군.

Red Cross [∠∠], **the** *n.* an international or a national society for helping those who have been sick and wounded in a war, in a flood, etc. 적십자사. 參考 정식으로는 the Red Cross Society.

red·den [rédn] *vt., vi.* (P6;1) make (something) red; become red; blush. (…을) 붉히

다; 붉어지다; 낯을 붉히다. [*red*]

red·dish [rédiʃ] *adj.* tinged with red; somewhat red. 불그레한; 불그스름한.

***re·deem** [ridíːm] *vt.* (P6,13) **1** buy (something) back; regain (something) by paying a price. …을 되사다; 되찾다. ¶ ~ *mortgaged property* 저당물을 찾다. **2** restore; recover. …을 (노력해서) 회복하다; 다시 찾다. ¶ ~ *one's right* 〔*position, honor*〕 권리〔지위, 명예〕를 회복하다 / *He redeemed his* (*good*) *name.* 그는 명성을 되찾았다. **3** fulfill; perform; carry out. …을 이행하다. ¶ ~ *a promise* 약속을 이행하다 / *Has the government redeemed all its election promises?* 정부는 모든 선거 공약을 이행했는가. **4** pay off. …을 상환하다. ¶ ~ *the national debt* 국채(國債)를 상환하다. **5** make up for (a fault, mistake, etc.). (결점·과실 등)을 메우다; 벌충하다. ¶ ~ *a fault* 결점을 메우다. **6** ⓐ set free, esp. by payment; ransom. (속전(贖錢)을 치르고) …을 구해내다. ¶ ~ *a prisoner.* ⓑ (of God or Christ) save from sin and hell. (신이) …을 죄악과 지옥에서 구하다. [re-, L. *emo* buy]

re·deem·er [ridíːmər] *n.* **1** Ⓒ a person who redeems. 되사는〔되찾는〕 사람; 구조자. **2** 《*the R-*》 Jesus Christ. 구세주; 그리스도.

re·demp·tion [ridémpʃən] *n.* Ⓤ the act of redeeming; the state of being redeemed; rescue; ransom; salvation. 환매; 되찾음; (약속의) 이행; 속전(贖錢)으로 죄인을 구함; 구출; (기독교에 의한) 구제. ¶ *the* ~ *of one's promise* 약속의 이행 / *Christ died for the* ~ *of mankind.* 그리스도는 인류의 구속(求贖)을 위해 죽었다. [→redeem]

beyond* 〔*past*〕 *redemption, impossible to save or recover. 구제〔회복〕 불능의.

re·demp·tive [ridémptiv] *adj.* of redemption; tending or serving to redeem. 되사는; 되찾는; 속량(贖良)〔구제〕의; 속죄의.

red-hand·ed [rédhǽndid] *adj.* **1** having hands red with blood. 손이 피투성이가 된. **2** in the very act of committing a crime. 현행범의. ¶ *He was caught* ~ *in the act of robbery.* 그는 강도 현장에서 붙잡혔다. **3** (of actions) bloody; violent. 피비린내 나는; 광포한. [*red*]

red·head [rédhèd] *n.* Ⓒ a person with red hair. 머리가 붉은 사람.

red-hot [rédhát / -hɔ́t] *adj.* **1** red from high heat; very hot. 적열(赤熱)의; 혹서(酷暑)의. ¶ ~ *iron.* **2** 《*fig.*》 greatly excited; furious. 몹시 흥분한; 격노한. ¶ ~ *anger* 격노. **3** 《*sl.*》 very fresh from the source. 최신의. ¶ ~ *news* 최신 뉴스.

Red Indian [∠-∠-] *n.* a North American Indian. 북아메리카 원주민.

re·dis·cov·er [riːdiskʌ́vər] *vt.* (P6) discover (something) again. …을 재발견하다. [re-]

red-let·ter [rédlétər] *adj.* **1** marked by a red letter. 붉은 글자의. **2** worthy to be remembered. 기념할 만한. [*red*]

red-letter day [∠-- ∠] *n.* a festival day; a day of some joyful event. 축제일 《달력에 붉은 글자로 표시한 데서》.

red meat [∠ ∠] *n.* beef, mutton, etc. 빨간 고기《쇠고기·양고기 따위》(cf. *white meat*).

red·ness [rédnis] *n.* Ⓤ the state of being red. 붉음; 적색.

red·o·lent [rédələnt] *adj.* **1** fragrant; scented; smelling. 향기로운; …한 냄새가 나는. ¶ *be* ~ *of roses* 장미 향기가 나다 / *flowers* ~ *of springtime* 봄의 향기를 풍기는 꽃들 / *a house* ~ *of fresh paint* 갓 칠한 페인트 냄새가 나는 집. **2** 《*fig.*》 《*of*》 suggestive. …을 생각나게 하는; 암시적인. ¶ *tales* ~ *of ancient memories* 옛 생각이 나게 하는 이야기. [re-, L. *oleo* smell]

re·dou·ble [riːdʌ́bəl] *vt., vi.* (P6; 1) **1** double again. (…을) 배가(倍加)하다. **2** increase greatly. (…을) 강화하다; 강화되다. ¶ ~ *one's effort* 더욱 노력하다 / *The noise redoubled.* 소리는 더 커졌다. **3** echo; resound. 반향하다. [re-]

re·doubt·a·ble [ridáutəbəl] *adj.* awaking fear or respect. 무서운; 경외(敬畏)할. ¶ *a* ~ *enemy.* [re-, →doubt]

re·dound [ridáund] *vi.* (P3) **1** 《*to*》 have an effect; contribute. (…에) 미치다; 돌아가다. ¶ *The sins of the fathers do not* ~ *to the children.* 아비의 죄가 자식들에게는 미치지 않는다. **2** 《*upon*》 come back upon someone; react upon. (…에) 되돌아오다. ¶ *His praises* ~ *upon himself.* 남을 칭찬한 말은 그 자신에게 되돌아온다. **3** 《*to*》 increase. 늘다; 증가하다. ¶ ~ *to one's advantage* …에게 이익을 더하다 / *Any help you can give us will* ~ *to your credit.* 우리를 도와주신다면 사람들은 당신을 칭송할 것이오. [re-, L. *unda* wave]

re·dress [ridrés] *vt.* **1** (P6) make (something wrong or out of order) right; repair; compensate. …을 고치다; 교정하다; 배상하다. ¶ ~ *the balance of...* …의 불균형을 시정하다 / 《*fig.*》 *The king tried to* ~ *the wrongs in his kingdom.* 왕은 나라의 그릇된 점을 바로 잡으려고 애썼다 / ~ *social evils* 사회악을 시정하다. **2** (P6) relieve. …을 구제하다.

— [ríːdres, ridrés] *n.* Ⓤ the act of making right; compensation for a wrong or loss. 교정; 배상; 구제. ¶ *There can be no* ~ *for the loss of his honor.* 그의 실추된 명예를 돌이킬 방도는 없다 / *The pollution victims seek* ~ *for their sufferings.* 오염의 피해자들은 그들이 입은 피해 보상을 요구하고 있다. [re-]

re-dress [ridrés] *vt.* (P6) dress again. 다시 입히다; 다시 붕대를 감다. [re-]

red·skin [rédskìn] *n.* =Red Indian.

red tape [∠ ∠] *n.* **1** a tape of a red color used for tying official documents. 공문서를 매는 붉은 끈. **2** excessive or rigid formality. 관료적 형식주의; 관청식; 번문 욕례(繁文縟禮). ¶ *There is a lot of* ~ *in some school sys-*

tems. 학교 제도중에는 형식적인 것이 많다. [*red*]

:re·duce [ridjú:s] *vt.* (P6,13) **1** make (something) smaller or less in size, number, weight, price, etc. (수량·무게·값 따위)를 줄이다; 축소하다. ¶ ~ *the price* 값을 내리다 / ~ *the speed* 속력을 줄이다 / ~ *one's weight* 체중을 줄이다 / ~ *one's expenditure* 경비를 줄이다 / ~ *supplies* 〔*production*〕 공급〔생산량〕을 줄이다 / *He won't* ~ *the rent of our house.* 그는 집세를 깎아주지 않을 것이다. **2** 《*to*》 lower (someone) in rank or grade. (지위 등)을 내리다; 강등시키다. ¶ ~ *an officer in rank* 장교를 강등시키다 / *The officer was reduced to the ranks.* 그 장교는 사병으로 강등당했다. **3** make (someone) weak physically; weaken. (체력)을 떨어뜨리다; 쇠약하게 하다. ¶ ~ *one's sight* 시력을 떨어뜨리다 / *be greatly reduced by illness* 병으로 몹시 쇠약해지다 / *be reduced to nothing* 〔*a skeleton*〕 말라서 피골이 상접해지다. **4** 《*to*》 change (something) into another form. …을 바꾸다; 변형시키다. ¶ ~ *wood to pulp* 나무를 펄프로 만들다 / ~ *a compound to its elements* 화합물을 원소들로 분해하다 / *a reducing agent* 환원제(還元劑) / ~ *dollars to cents* 달러를 센트로 바꾸다 / ~ *a rule to practice* 규칙을 시행에 옮기다. **5** 《*to*》 bring (someone) to a certain condition; bring (someone or something) under control; conquer. …을 (강제로) …하게 하다; 복종〔항복〕시키다. ¶ ~ *an enemy* / ~ *someone to tears* 〔*silence*〕 아무를 울게 만들다〔침묵시키다〕 / ~ *someone to submission* 아무를 굴복시키다 / *The teacher soon reduced the noisy class to order.* 선생님은 곧 시끄러운 교실을 조용하게 만들었다 / *The soldiers reduced the castle by fire.* 병사들은 화공(火攻)으로 성을 점령했다. **6** 《usu. used in *passive*》 compel by force of circumstances to do (something). (환경 따위가) …에 몰아넣다. ¶ *be reduced to stealing* 부득이 도둑질하게 되다 / *He was reduced to begging in the street.* 그는 거리에서 구걸할 수밖에 없었다. **7** 《*to*》 bring (something) into order, groups, classes, etc. …을 정리하다; 종합하다; 분류하다. ¶ ~ *language to rules* 말을 정리해 어법에 맞게 하다 / ~ *a statement to its simplest form* 진술을 가장 간단한 형태로 바꾸다 / ~ *one's ideas to writing* 생각을 글로 정리하다. **8** restore (a broken or displaced bone, etc.) to its the normal position. (탈구(脫臼) 등)을 복원(復元)하다. — *vi.* **1** become reduced. 줄다. **2** 《*colloq.*》 become thinner by dieting. (다이어트로) 체중을 줄이다. [re-, →duct]

re·duc·i·ble [ridjú:səbl] *adj.* that can be reduced. 변형〔축소〕할 수 있는; 약분할 수 있는.

·re·duc·tion [ridʌ́kʃən] *n.* Ⓤ Ⓒ **1** the act of reducing; the state of being reduced. 변형; 축소; 감소. ¶ ~ *of armaments* 군비 축소 / *make a* ~ *in price* 값을 할인하다. **2** a reduced copy. 축사(縮寫); 축도. ¶ *a* ~ *of a photograph* 〔*map*〕. **3** the amount by which something is reduced. 감소된 수량; 할인고(高). ¶ *No* ~ *is made.* 할인 없음 / *a* ~ *of two pounds in weight,* 2파운드의 체중 감소 / *a* ~ *in cost of* £ *300,* 3백 파운드의 비용 절감.

re·dun·dance [ridʌ́ndəns] *n.* =redundancy.

re·dun·dan·cy [ridʌ́ndənsi] *n.* (*pl.* **-cies**) **1** Ⓤ the quality or state of being more than enough. 과다(함); 여분; 용장(冗長). ¶ *There is much* ~ *in his writing.* 그의 글에는 군말이 많다. **2** Ⓒ something or a part of something that is redundant. 여분의 물건; 과잉 부분. **3** the condition or fact of being unemployed; unemployment. 실업 상태. ¶ *The slump caused widespread* ~. 불황은 광범한 실업 사태를 가져왔다. [↓]

re·dun·dant [ridʌ́ndənt] *adj.* **1** more than enough; excessive. 여분의; 너무 많은. ¶ ~ *food* 남아 도는 음식 / *Because of the slump they fired 500* ~ *workers.* 불경기로 5백명의 과잉 노동력을 해고했다 / ~ *words* 군더더기말《e.g. 'an *annual* income of £2,000 *a year*'의 *a year*》. **2** plentiful. 풍부한. **3** using more words than are needed. 장황한. ¶ ~ *style* 용장(冗長)한 문체. ●**re·dun·dant·ly** [-li] *adv.* [→redound]

re·du·pli·cate [ridjú:plikèit] *vt.* (P6) double; repeat; copy. …을 이중으로 하다; 되풀이하다. [re-]

re·du·pli·ca·tion [ridjù:plikéiʃən] *n.* **1** Ⓤ the act of reduplicating; repetition. 이중으로 함; 반복. **2** Ⓒ a copy. 사본; 카피. ¶ *On the desert island each day seemed to me a* ~ *of the day before.* 고도에서의 생활은 매일 매일이 전날의 복사판 같았다.

red·wood [rédwùd] *n.* Ⓒ a very large Californian tree. 미국삼나무. [*red*]

re-ech·o [ri(:)ékou] *vt., vi.* (P6;1) echo back; resound. 되울리다; 울려 퍼지다. ¶ *The house re-echoed with the voices of children.* 아이들 소리가 집안에 울려 퍼졌다 / *The walls* ~. 벽은 소리를 반향시킨다. — *n.* Ⓒ (*pl.* **-oes**) an echo; an echo of an echo. 반향; 되울림. [re-]

·reed [ri:d] *n.* Ⓒ **1** 《bot.》 a kind of tall grass growing near water. 갈대. **2** ⓐ a musical pipe made of the stem of this grass. 갈대 피리. ⓑ 《poet.》 an arrow. 화살. **3** a thin, vibrating tongue in a musical instrument; 《usu. *pl.*》 such musical instruments. (악기의) 혀; (관현악의) 리드 악기. [E.]

lean on a reed, trust in an unreliable person or thing. 못 믿을 사람〔것〕에 의지하다.

reed·y [rí:di] *adj.* (**reed·i·er, reed·i·est**) **1** full of reeds. 갈대가 무성한. ¶ *a* ~ *pond.* **2** 《*poet.*》 made of reeds. 갈대로 만든. ¶ *the* *shepherd's ~ pipe* 목동의 갈대 피리. **3** like a reed; long; weak. 갈대 같은; 갈대처럼 호리호리한. ¶ ~ *grass* 갈대 같은 풀 / 《*fig.*》 *a ~ youth* 연약한 청년. **4** sounding like a reed instrument. 리드 악기 소리 같은. ●**reed·i·ness** [-nis] *n.*

reef[1] [ri:f] *n.* Ⓒ a sand bar or a shelf of rock or coral at or near the surface of the water. 모래톱; 암초; 산호초. ¶ *The ship struck a ~.* 배가 좌초했다. [N.]

reef[2] [ri:f] *n.* Ⓒ 《naut.》 a part of a sail which can be folded or rolled to shorten the sail. 축범부(縮帆部). — *vt.* (P6) reduce (a sail) by folding or rolling up a part of it. (돛)을 말아 줄이다; 축범하다. [N.]
take in a reef, shorten a sail; cut down expenses; proceed carefully. 돛을 줄이다; 비용을 줄이다; 조심스럽게 전진하다.

reek [ri:k] *n.* Ⓤ steam; a disagreeable smell. 뜨거운 김; 증기; 악취.
— *vi.* (P1,3) **1** send out vapor, smoke or a strong unpleasant smell. 연기를 내다; 김을 내다; 악취를 풍기다; 냄새가 나다. ¶ *His clothes ~ of tobacco.* 그의 옷에서 담배 냄새가 난다 / *reeking chimneys* 연기가 오르는 굴뚝 / 《*fig.*》 *The story reeks with mystery.* 그 이야기에는 신비적인 데가 있다 / *That whole transaction reeks of* 〔*with*〕 *dishonesty.* 그 모든 거래에서 구린내가 난다. **2** be wet and steaming with sweat or blood. (땀·피에) 젖어 있다. ¶ *Workers return reeking from their factory.* 노동자들이 땀투성이가 되어 공장에서 돌아온다 / *The murderers' hands reeked with blood.* 살인자들의 손은 피투성이었다. [N.]

•**reel**[1] [ri:l] *n.* Ⓒ **1** a device with a frame turning on an axis, for winding thread, wire, rope, etc. 릴; 얼레. **2** a spool. 실패; (낚싯대의) 릴. **3** something held in a reel, esp. a strip of film. 릴에 감은 것; (특히) 필름 한 통. ¶ *two reels of cinema film* 영화 필름 2권.
off the reel, 《*colloq.*》 quickly and easily; without pause. 술술; 거침 없이. ¶ *He tells a story off the ~.* 그는 막힘없이 얘기를 한다.
— *vt.* (P6,7,13) **1** wind (thread, etc.) on or off a reel. (실 따위)를 얼레에 감다; …에서 풀다. **2** draw in (a fish, etc.) by winding a line on a reel. (물고기 등)을 릴로 감아 당기다. **3** say or write without pause. 계속 말하다〔쓰다〕. ¶ *He reeled off one story after another.* 그는 이야기가 하나 끝나면 계속 다음 이야기를 했다. [E.]

reel[2] [ri:l] *vi.* (P1,2A,3) **1** stagger from side to side in walking. 비틀거리다; 갈지자 걸음을 하다. ¶ *~ along the street.* **2** ⓐ feel dizzy. 현기증을 느끼다. ¶ *My brain reels.* 머리가 어지럽다. ⓑ seem to rock or whirl. (물체가) 흔들리듯이 보이다. ¶ *Everything reeled before his eyes.* 눈 앞의 모든 물체들이 빙빙 도는 듯했다. **3** be overwhelmed by a shock of sudden emotion. (충격 등으로) 아찔해지다. ¶ *His mind reeled at the news.* 그 소식을 듣고 그는 마음이 어지러웠다. [E.]

reel[3] [ri:l] *n.* Ⓒ a lively Scottish dance; the music for this dance. 릴 춤; 그 곡. [↑]

re·e·lect [rí:ilékt] *vt.* (P6) elect again. …을 재선하다. [re-]

re·em·bark [rì:embá:rk] *vt., vi.* (P6;1) put (something) or go on board a ship again; set sail again. 다시 승선시키다〔하다〕; 재출범하다. [re-]

re·en·force [rì:infɔ́:rs] *vt.* =reinforce.

re·en·ter [ri:éntər] *vt., vi.* (P6;1) enter again. 다시 들어가다〔들이다〕. ¶ *~ the country* 재입국하다. [re-]

re·en·try [ri:éntri] *n.* Ⓒ (*pl.* **-tries**) **1** the act of entering again. 다시 들어가기. **2** the act of coming back to the Earth's atmosphere. (대기권에의) 재돌입. ¶ *The spacecraft made a successful ~ into Earth's atmosphere.* 우주선은 성공적으로 대기권에 재돌입했다. [re-]

re·es·tab·lish [rì:estǽbliʃ] *vt.* (P6) establish again. …을 재건〔부흥〕하다. ¶ *Peace has now been re-established.* 평화가 회복되었다. [re-]

ref. referee; reference; referred; reformation; reformed; refunding

Ref. Ch. Reformed Church.

re·fec·tion [rifékʃən] *n.* **1** Ⓤ the act of recovering one's vigor by eating or drinking. (음식에 의한) 원기 회복. ¶ *Milk and eggs were offered for our ~.* 우유와 달걀을 먹었더니 원기가 회복됐다. **2** Ⓒ a light meal. (간단한) 식사. ¶ *She served a light ~ to her guest.* 그녀는 손님들에게 가벼운 식사를 대접했다. [re-, →fact]

re·fec·to·ry [riféktəri] *n.* Ⓒ (*pl.* **-ries**) a dining room in a monastery, school, etc. (수도원·학교 등의) 구내 식당. [↑]

:**re·fer** [rifə́:r] *v.* (**-ferred, -fer·ring**) *vt.* (P13) **1** 《*to*》 tell (someone) to ask or consult in order to know a certain fact. …을 조회시키다; 참조시키다. ¶ *I beg to ~ you to Mr. Smith for my character.* 내 사람됨에 대해서는 스미스씨에게 알아보시오 / *I ~ you to the dictionary for the correct meaning.* 그 정확한 뜻은 사전을 참조해 봐라. **2** 《*to*》 cause (someone) to consult. …의 주의를 돌리게 하다. ¶ *This mark refers readers to a footnote.* 이 표시는 각주(脚註)를 보라는 지시다. **3** 《*to*》 leave (something) to others' decision. (문제 등)을 맡기다. ¶ *~ a bill to a committee* 의안을 위원회에 위임하다 / *~ a dispute to the law court* 분쟁을 법정에 가져가다 / *I ~ myself to your generosity.* 당신의 관대한 처분에 맡깁니다 / *They referred the question to experts.* 그들은 문제를 전문가에 일임했다. **4** 《*to*》 regard (something) as the cause. …을 —(의 탓)으로 돌리다. ¶ *~ one's success to Providence* 성공을 하늘의 뜻으로 돌리다 / *He referred his wealth to his own hard work.* 그는 부자가 된 것은

노력 덕분이라고 했다 / *Some people ~ all their troubles to bad luck instead of to lack of ability.* 어떤 사람은 고생을 제 능력이 없어서가 아니라 팔자 탓이라고 한다.
— *vi.* (P3) **1** 《*to*》 seek information from something. 참조〔참고〕하다; 조회하다; 알아보다. ¶ *~ to the Bible / ~ to a former employer for someone's character* 아무의 인물됨을 전 고용주에게 조회하다 / *~ to one's notes for assisting one's memory* 기억을 살리려고 메모를 보다. **2** 《*to*》 speak of something; mention. 언급하다; 인용하다. ¶ *He referred to his past experience.* 그는 자기의 지난날 체험을 이야기했다 / *He often referred to me in his speech.* 그는 이야기 도중 가끔 내게 대해 언급했다. **3** 《*to*》 apply to something; concern. 적용되다; 관계〔관련〕되다. ¶ *The rule refers only to special cases.* 그 규칙은 특별한 경우에만 적용된다 / *This rule does not ~ to girls.* 이 규칙은 여직원들에게는 예외(例外)다. **4** pay attention to something. 주목하다. **5** resort for aid or information. 호소하다; 참고로 하다. [re-, L. *fero* bring]

re·fer·a·ble [réfərəbəl, rifə́:r-] *adj.* 《*to*》 that can be considered as a result of something else. 돌릴〔탓이라 할〕 수 있는.

ref·er·ee [rèfərí:] *n.* Ⓒ **1** a judge or an umpire in a game. 심판원; 레퍼리. **2** an arbitrator. 중재인. — *vt., vi.* (P6;1) judge as referee; act as referee. (…을) 심판하다; 중재하다.

•**ref·er·ence** [réfərəns] *n.* **1** ⓊⒸ the act of consulting something for information or help. 참조〔참고〕하기. ¶ *a ~ to a dictionary for ...* …을 사전에서 찾아보기 / *make ~ to the guide-book* 안내서를 참고하다 / *Reference to a map will make the position clear.* 지도를 보면 위치를 정확히 알 수 있다. **2** Ⓤ the act of speaking of something; Ⓒ a matter spoken of. 언급; 논급(論及). ¶ *You make no ~ to your plans in your letter.* 네 편지에는 네 계획에 대한 말이 없다 / *Don't make any ~ to his lameness.* 그가 다리를 저느니어쩌니 하는 말은 아예 마라. **3** Ⓒ a letter or person that tells of another person's character or ability. 신원 보증인; 신원 조회처; 신원 증명서. ¶ *an excellent ~* 훌륭한 신원 증명서 / *Who is your ~?* 신원 보증인이 누구입니까 / *John gave his principal as a ~.* 존은 교장 선생님이 자기 신원 보증인이라고 했다 / *The new worker had good references.* 신입 사원의 신원 조회서는 훌륭했다. **4** Ⓒ a book or note used for information; a source of information. 인용문; 참고 자료. ¶ *a book of ~ =a ~ book* 참고 서적. **5** Ⓤ 《*to*》 relation; connection. 관계; 관련. ¶ *These views have ~ to the war.* 이 그림들은 전쟁과 관계된 것이다 / *The parts of a machine all have ~ to each other.* 기계의 각 부품은 서로가 연관이 있다. [*refer*]
in* 〔*with*〕 *reference to, about; in regard to. …에 관하여.
make reference to, refer to; mention; speak of. …을 참조하다; …에 언급하다.
without reference to, having no relation to. …에 관계 없이. ¶ *The test is given without ~ to age.* 그 테스트는 나이와는 상관이 없다.

ref·er·en·da [rèfəréndə] *n.* pl. of **referendum.**

ref·er·en·dum [rèfəréndəm] *n.* Ⓒ (*pl.* **-da** or **-dums**) the process of submitting a law to all the people of a country, state, etc. asking for their opinion of the law. (의회를 통과한 정책 등에 대한 찬부를 전국민에게 묻는) 국민 투표. [*refer*]

re·fill [ri:fíl] *vt., vi.* (P6;1) fill again; become filled again. 다시 채우다〔채워지다〕. ¶ *~ a pipe* 파이프에 담배를 다시 채우다. — *n.* [rí:fìl] Ⓒ **1** a replacement. 재보충(물). ¶ *I need a new ~ for my ball-point pen.* 볼펜 심을 갈아야 하겠다. **2** a second serving of food or drink. (음식물의) 두 그릇〔잔〕째. ¶ *Your glass is empty; would you like a ~?* 잔이 비었소. 한잔 더 하시려오. [re-]

•**re·fine** [rifáin] *vt.* (P6) **1** make (something) pure or fine. …을 정련〔정제〕하다. ¶ *~ metal / ~ one's thought* 자기 사상을 순화시키다 / *Sugar, oil, and metal are refined before being used.* 설탕, 기름, 금속은 사용전에 정제된다. **2** 《*fig.*》 make (something) polished or cultivated. …을 품위 있게 하다; 세련되게 하다; (문장 등)을 다듬다. ¶ *~ one's taste, manner, and language.* 취미, 태도 및 말씨를 품위 있게 하다.
— *vi.* (P1,3) **1** become pure or fine. 순수해지다; 점잖아지다. **2** 《*on, upon*》 improve. 개량되다; 좋아지다. **3** become more polished, as in language, etc. (말씨 등이) 세련되다; 품위 있게 되다. **4** employ subtlety. 교묘하게 하다. **5** discourse with subtlety; make fine distinction. 자세히 이야기하다; 세세히 구별하다. [re-, →fine]

re·fined [rifáind] *adj.* **1** made pure. 정제된. ¶ *~ sugar* 정당(精糖). **2** 《*fig.*》 having good manners, taste, etc.; polished. 점잖은; 품위 있는; 세련된. ¶ *He is a man of ~ tastes and manners.* 취미나 태도가 세련된 사람이다 / *~ society* 상류 사회.

•**re·fine·ment** [rifáinmənt] *n.* Ⓤ **1** the act of refining; the state of being refined. 정제; 정련. **2** elegance; good manners and taste. 세련; 우아; 고상. ¶ *a person of ~* 점잖은 사람. **3** subtlety; fine distinction. 정교; 세밀한 구분. ¶ *the refinements of metaphysical thought* 형이상학적 사고의 정치(精緻).

re·fin·er [rifáinər] *n.* Ⓒ a person or thing that makes something pure, polished or fine. 정제〔정련〕하는 사람〔기계〕.

re·fin·er·y [rifáinəri] *n.* Ⓒ (*pl.* **-er·ies**) a factory for making pure sugar, metal, etc. 정제소; 제련소.

re·fit [riːfít] *v.* (**-fit·ted, -fit·ting**) *vt.* (P6) prepare (something) for use again; repair. …을 수리하다; (선박 등)을 개장(改裝)하다. ¶ *~ a ship for a voyage.* —*vi.* (P1) be made ready for use again. (특히 배가) 수리를 받다. ¶ *The ship had to ~ in a week.* 배는 1주일 내에 수리돼야 한다. —[ríːfit] *n.* Ⓤ the act of refitting. (특히 선박의) 수리. [re-]

:**re·flect** [riflékt] *vt.* **1** (P6) throw back (light, heat, sound, etc.). …을 반사하다. ¶ *A mirror reflects light.* 거울은 빛을 반사한다 / *The moon reflects the lights of the sun.* 달은 태양 빛을 반사한다 / *The pavement reflects heat on a hot day.* 더운 날에 포장 도로는 열을 반사한다. **2** (P6,13) give back an image of (something) as a mirror does. …을 비추다; 반영(反映)하다. ¶ *Mountains were reflected in the lake.* 산들이 호수에 비치고 있었다. **3** (P6) express. …을 나타내다. ¶ *His face reflected his emotions.* 그의 표정이 감정을 말해주고 있었다 / *Your suit reflects your good taste.* 옷이 네 고상한 취미를 말하고 있다. **4** (P6, 13)《*on, upon*》 bring back (something) as a result. …을 초래하다; 가져오다. ¶ *His conduct reflected great credit on him.* 그의 행위는 그에게 대단한 신망을 가져왔다. **5** (P10,11,12) think carefully; consider. …을 곰곰이 생각하다. ¶ *He reflected how to get out of the difficulty.* 그는 어떻게 하면 난관을 넘길까를 궁리했다 / *She reflected that this was her last chance.* 그녀는 이것이 마지막 기회라고 생각했다.

—*vi.* **1** (P1) throw back light, sound, etc.; give back an image. 반사[반향]하다; 반영하다; 비치다. ¶ *Change your seat if the light reflects in your eyes.* 눈이 부시면 자리를 바꾸어라. **2** (P1,3) 《*on, upon*》 think deeply about; meditate on. 곰곰이 생각하다. ¶ *After reflecting for a time (on the problem) he decided not to go.* (문제를) 한동안 생각하다가 그는 가지 않기로 했다 / *I want time to ~.* 생각할 시간이 필요하다 / *Reflect upon all I have said to you.* 내가 네게 한 말을 모두 곰곰이 생각해 봐라. **3** (P1,3) 《*on, upon*》 cast blame upon. 비난하다. ¶ *He reflected on my veracity.* 그는 나의 성실성에 관해 트집을 잡았다. **4** (P1,3) 《*on, upon*》 have a bad effect. 나쁜 영향을 주다[미치다]. ¶ *This decision will ~ seriously upon his future career.* 이 결정이 그의 장래에 큰 화근이 될 거다. [re-, L. *flecto* bend]

•**re·flec·tion** [riflékʃən] *n.* **1** Ⓤ the act of reflecting; the state of being reflected. 반사; 반향. ¶ *The moon looks bright because of the ~ of light.* 달은 빛의 반사 때문에 밝게 보인다. **2** ⓊⒸ a sound, light, etc. which is reflected. 반향음; 반사광[열]. **3** Ⓒ something reflected; an image. 영상; 그림자. ¶ *We could see the ~ of the mountain in the lake.* 호수에 비치는 산을 볼 수 있었다 / 《*fig.*》 *He is simply a ~ of his father.* 그는 아버지를 빼쏘았다. **4** 《*on, upon*》 careful thinking; meditation. 숙고; 심사. ¶ *After much ~ I decided not to accept the proposal.* 오래 생각한 끝에 그 제의를 거절하기로 했다. **5** 《usu. *pl.*》 an idea, a remark or thought which is the result of careful thinking. 감상; 평(評); 견해; 의견. ¶ *Emerson's reflections on the universe* 우주에 관한 에머슨의 고찰 / *I leave you to your reflections.* 이 일은 네 생각에 맡기겠다 / *I have just a few reflections to offer on what you have said.* 네가 한 말에 대해 몇 가지 견해를 말하고 싶다. **6** Ⓒ an unfavorable remark; something which throws blame or dishonor. 비난; 꾸중; 불명예. ¶ *throw* [*cast*] *a ~ on someone's honor or ability* 아무의 명예나 능력을 나쁘게 말하다 / *His behavior in this matter is a grave ~ upon his honesty.* 이 일에 있어 그의 처신은 그의 성실을 크게 훼손한다.

re·flec·tive [rifléktiv] *adj.* **1** throwing back light, an image, etc. (빛·형체를) 반사[반영]하는. ¶ *the ~ surface of a polished table* 윤나는 탁자의 반사면. **2** thoughtful. 사려 깊은. ¶ *a ~ mind* 내성적인 사람.

re·flec·tor [rifléktər] *n.* Ⓒ **1** anything which sends back heat, light, sound, etc. 반사물[기]; 반사경. **2** 《*fig.*》 a person, book, etc. that reflects mental impressions, feelings, etc. (느낌 등을) 반영하는 사람[것]. ¶ *Where can one find a true ~ of public opinion?* 여론의 진정한 대변자는 어디에서 찾을 수 있을까.

re·flex [ríːfleks] *adj.* **1** 《physiol.》 showing an automatic or unconscious response. 반사적인. ¶ *a ~ action* 반사 작용. **2** introspective. 내성적인. **3** reactive; retroactive. 반동적인; 되돌아오는. **4** recurved. 뒤로 젖혀진.

—*n.* Ⓒ **1** a reflection of light, sound, etc.; a mirrored image. (빛·소리 등의) 반사; 반영; 영상; 그림자. **2** something reflected; a reflection. 반영. ¶ *A law should be a ~ of the will of the people.* 법률은 국민의 뜻을 반영한 것이라야 한다. **3** 《physiol.》 an unconscious movement. 반사 작용. ¶ *The doctor tested the patient's reflexes by hitting his knee.* 의사는 환자의 무릎을 쳐서 반사 작용을 테스트했다 / *a conditional ~* 조건 반사. [→reflect]

re·flex·ion [riflékʃən] *n.* =reflection.

re·flex·ive [rifléksiv] *adj.* 《gram.》 (of a verb or pronoun) indicating an action that turns back on the subject. 재귀(再歸)의. ¶ *a ~ verb* [*pronoun*]. —*n.* Ⓒ a reflexive verb or pronoun. 재귀동사[대명사]. 參考 He killed himself. 의 kill 은 재귀동사; himself 는 재귀대명사. ● **re·flex·ive·ly** [-li] *adv.* [↑]

ref·lu·ent [réfluənt] *adj.* flowing back.

역류하는; 썰물의. [re-]

re·flux [rí:flʌ̀ks] *n.* Ⓤ the act of flowing back; the ebb tide. 역류(逆流); 썰물. ¶ *the flux and* ~ 조수의 간만; 밀물과 썰물; 흥망 성쇠. [re-]

re·for·est [ri:fɔ́(:)rist, -fár-] *vt.* (P6) re-plant trees on (land). …에 다시 나무를 심다; 재식림(再植林)하다. ● **re·for·est·a·tion** [rì:fɔ(:)ristéiʃən, -fɑr-] *n.* [re-]

:re·form [rifɔ́:rm] *vt.* (P6) make or change (something) better by removing its faults; improve. …을 개심시키다; 교정하다; (제도·사태)를 개혁〔개량〕하다; 개정하다. ¶ ~ *the system of society* 〔*education*〕 사회〔교육〕 제도를 개혁하다 / ~ *oneself* 마음을 고쳐먹다; 개심하다.

— *vi.* (P1) become better. 개심하다; 면목을 일신하다. ¶ *The criminal promised to* ~ *if given another chance.* 범인은 다시 기회를 준다면 개심하겠다고 약속했다.

— *n.* ⓊⒸ **1** a change for a better state. 개혁; 개량; 혁신. ¶ 《Brit.》 *the Reform Bill* 선거법 개정안《1832년의》. **2** a change from a bad to a good character. 개심; 회개. ¶ 《U.S.》 *a* ~ *school* =refomatory. ● **re·form·a·ble** [-əbl] *adj.* [re-]

re-form [ri:fɔ́:rm] *vt., vi.* (P6;1) make or form again. 고쳐 만들다; 다시 만들다. ¶ *The army re-formed, ready to attack again.* 육군은 다시 공격하려고 진용을 재편성했다.

ref·or·ma·tion [rèfərméiʃən] *n.* **1** ⓊⒸ the act of reforming; the state of being reformed; a change for the better in social or political conditions. 개혁; 쇄신; 개량. ¶ *the* ~ *of social life* / *a* ~ *of* 〔*in*〕 *manners* 풍습〔예절〕의 개혁. **2** 《*the R-*》 the religious movement in Europe, begun by Martin Luther in the 16th century. 종교 개혁. [*reform*]

re·form·a·tive [rifɔ́:rmətiv] *adj.* able to reform; tending to reform. 개혁할 수 있는; 개량하는.

re·form·a·to·ry [rifɔ́:rmətɔ̀:ri / -təri] *adj.* tending to correct. 감화〔교정〕하는. — *n.* Ⓒ (*pl.* **-ries**) a school for the special training of young offenders against the law. 소년원.

re·form·er [rifɔ́:rmər] *n.* Ⓒ a person who carries out a change for the better. 개혁자.

re·fract [rifræ̃kt] *vt.* (P6) bend (a ray of light) from a straight line as it enters or leaves water. (광선)을 굴절시키다. ¶ *Water refracts light.* 물은 광선을 굴절시킨다. [re-, L. *frango* break]

re·frac·tion [rifræ̃kʃən] *n.* Ⓤ the act of re-fracting; the state of being refracted. (빛·음파 등의) 굴절 (작용). ¶ *index of* ~ 굴절률. [→refract, -tion]

re·frac·tive [rifræ̃ktiv] *adj.* having the power of refraction. 굴절하는; 굴절력이 있는.

re·frac·to·ry [rifræ̃ktəri] *adj.* **1** fixed in one's opinion; unmanageable. 완고한; 말을 듣지 않는. ¶ *a* ~ *child* 말썽꾸러기 / *Horses are* ~ *for beginners.* 말은 초심자에게 거칠게 군다. **2** (of illness) hard to cure. (병이) 난치의; 고질의. ¶ *She had a very* ~ *cough.* 고질의 해수(咳嗽)를 앓고 있다. **3** (of metals) hard to melt. (금속이) 녹기 어려운. ● **re·frac·to·ri·ly** [-li] *adv.*

***re·frain**[1] [rifréin] *vi.* (P1,3) 《*from*》 stop oneself from doing something; abstain oneself; check oneself from; keep oneself aloof. 그만두다; 참다; 삼가다; 자제하다. ¶ ~ *from one's tears* 눈물을 참다 / *She could not* ~ *from laughing.* 그녀는 웃지 않을 수 없었다 / *He refrained from saying what he thought.* 그는 생각한 것을 말하려다 참았다. [re-, L. *frenum* bridle]

re·frain[2] [rifréin] *n.* Ⓒ a phrase or verse repeated in a poem or song. 반복구; 후렴. [*refract*]

***re·fresh** [rifréʃ] *vt.* **1** (P6) make (something or someone) fresh again; give (someone or something) new energy with food, drink or rest. …을 상쾌하게 하다; 생기를 돋우다; 다시 성하게 하다. ¶ ~ *oneself with a cup of coffee* 커피 한 잔으로 기분 전환을 하다 / *I feel refreshed.* (심신이) 상쾌하구나 / *I was able to* ~ *my memory by a look at the notebook.* 수첩을 보고 기억을 되살릴 수 있었다. **2** (P6,13) give a fresh supply to. …에 새로 공급하다. ¶ ~ *a ship with stores and water* 선박에 식량과 물을 싣다〔재보급하다〕 / ~ *a fire with more fuel* 〔*wood*〕 연료를〔장작을〕 더 넣어 불을 세게 하다.

— *vi.* (P1) **1** become fresh again; take refreshment. 원기를 회복하다; 상쾌해지다; 음식을 먹다. **2** (of a ship) take in food or water. (배가) 양식〔물〕을 보충하다. [re-, L. *fresche* fresh]

re·fresh·er [rifréʃər] *n.* Ⓒ a person or thing that refreshes. 원기를 회복시키는 사람〔것〕.

refresher course [-⌐-⌐] *n.* **1** a study course serving as a review of previous education. 재교육 과정. **2** a training course given to bring someone's knowledge up to date, esp. knowledge needed for a job. (특히 취업을 위한) 최신 기술 이수 과정.

re·fresh·ing [rifréʃiŋ] *adj.* making fresh again; pleasant to the senses. 기분을 상쾌하게 하는. ¶ *a* ~ *breeze* 시원한 바람 / ~ *drinks* 청량 음료.

***re·fresh·ment** [rifréʃmənt] *n.* **1** Ⓤ the act of refreshing; the state of being refreshed. 기분을 상쾌하게 함; 원기 회복. ¶ *feel* ~ *of mind and body* 심신이 상쾌해지다. **2** 《often *pl.*》 something that refreshes; food and drink served to guests at a party, meeting, etc. 기분을 회복시키는 것; (모임 등에서의) 음식; 다과. ¶ *Let me offer you some* ~. 뭣 좀 드시지요 / *The sight was* *a* ~ *to me.* 그 경치에 기분이 좋았다 / *You can get refreshments at the station.* 정거장에 가면 먹을 것들이 있다.

refreshment car [–⌒– ⌒] *n.* 《Brit.》 a dining coach or car; a diner. 식당차.

refreshment room [–⌒– ⌒] *n.* 《Brit.》 a dining room at a station or on a train. (역·열차의) 식당.

re·frig·er·ant [rifrídʒərənt] *adj.* cooling; 《med.》 reducing fever. 차게 하는; 해열의. — *n.* Ⓒ any substance that makes cool. 냉각제; 해열제. [↓]

re·frig·er·ate [rifrídʒərèit] *vt.* (P6) make or keep (something) cool; freeze. …을 차게 하다; 냉장하다; 냉동시키다. — *vi.* (P1) become cool, cold or frozen. 차게 되다; 얼다. [re-, L. *frigus* cold]

re·frig·er·a·tion [rifrìdʒəréiʃən] *n.* Ⓤ the act of refrigerating; the state of being refrigerated. 냉각; 냉장.

***re·frig·er·a·tor** [rifrídʒərèitər] *n.* Ⓒ a cabinet, box, room, etc. in which food, drink, etc. are kept cool. 냉장고; 아이스박스; 냉각기.

reft [reft] 《*arch., poet.*》 p. and pp. of **reave.** — *adj.* 《*poet.*》 robbed. 빼앗긴; 잃은. ¶ ~ *of one's power* 힘을 잃은; 실권한. [E.]

re·fu·el [riːfjúːəl] *v.* (**-eled, -el·ing;** 《Brit.》 **-elled, -el·ling**) *vt.* (P6) provide (something) with fuel again. …에 연료를 재보급하다. — *vi.* (P1) take on a fresh supply of fuel. 연료를 재보급받다. ¶ *The plane refueled at Anchorage.* [re-]

***ref·uge** [réfjuːdʒ] *n.* Ⓒ **1** a place of safety from danger or trouble; a shelter. 피난처; 은신처. ¶ *a mountain* ~ *for climbers* 등산객을 위한 산장 / *a harbor of* ~ 피난항. **2** 《*fig.*》 a person or thing to which one has recourse for aid, relief, or escape. 의지가 되는 사람〔물건〕; 위안이 되는 것. ¶ *He found a* ~ *in books* 〔*movies*〕. 그는 독서〔영화〕에서 위안을 찾았다. **3** a raised halting place for passengers crossing a road; an traffic island. (도로의) 교통섬《도로 횡단자를 위해 차선 사이에 마련한 안전 지대》. **4** Ⓤ the act of keeping off from danger, distress, etc. 피난; 도피. ¶ *a house of* ~ 양육원 / *give* ~ *to someone* 아무를 보호해 주다 / *seek* 〔*take*〕 ~ *from a storm* 폭풍우를 피하다. [re-, →fugitive]

ref·u·gee [rèfjudʒíː, ⌒–⌒] *n.* Ⓒ a person who flees for safety, esp. to another country for political reasons. 피난자; (특히) 망명자.

re·ful·gent [rifʌ́ldʒənt] *adj.* shining radiantly; splendid. 빛나는; 번쩍이는; 찬란한. ¶ ~ *armor* 번쩍이는 갑옷. [re-]

re·fund [rifʌ́nd, ríːfʌnd] *vt., vi.* (P6;1) give or pay back (money). 갚다; 돌려주다. ¶ ~ *what has been borrowed* 빌린 것을 돌려주다〔갚다〕 / *If you give me the money now I will* ~ *it later.* 지금 돈을 꾸어주면 나중에 갚으마. — [ríːfʌnd] *n.* =refundment. [re-, L. *fundo* pour]

re·fund·ment [rifʌ́ndmənt] *n.* Ⓤ return of money paid; repayment. 변제; 반환.

***re·fus·al** [rifjúːzəl] *n.* **1** ⓊⒸ the act of refusing; rejection; denial. 거절; 거부. ¶ *receive a* ~ 거절당하다 / *a* ~ *to answer a question* 질문에 대한 답변 거부 / *I will take no* ~. 싫다고는 못하게 할 거다 / *My offer met with a flat* ~. 내 제의는 일언지하에 거절당했다. **2** 《*the* ~》 the right to refuse or accept a thing before it is offered to others. 취사 선택권; 우선권. ¶ *give the* ~ *of a proposal* 제안의 선택권을 주다 / *When the property is offered for sale, I have first* ~. 그 부동산을 팔려고 내놓으면 내게 선매권(先買權)이 있다 / *Please give me the* ~ *of the car till the end of the month.* 그 차를 내가 살지 안 살지 월말까지 말씀드리지요. [↓]

:re·fuse[1] [rifjúːz] *vt.* **1** (P6,8,14) decline to accept (an invitation, a request, etc.); reject or deny (a demand, etc.). …을 거절하다. ¶ ~ *admittance* 입장을 거절하다 / *He refused to obey my orders.* 그는 내 명령을 거부했다 / *He can* ~ *her nothing.* = *He can* ~ *nothing to her.* 그는 그녀 말이라면 무엇이건 거절을 못 한다 / *I have never been refused before.* 나는 부탁을 거절당한 적이 없다 / *We refused to accept his resignation.* 우리는 그의 사임을 수락하지 않았다 / *I asked him to leave, but he refused.* 떠나 달라고 했으나 그는 거부했다 / ~ *leave of absence* 휴가를 거절하다. **2** (P6) (of a horse) decline to leap over. (말이) 뛰지 않고 버티다. ¶ ~ *a fence* (말이) 장애물 앞에서 버티고 서다.
— *vi.* (P1) **1** decline. 거절하다. **2** (of a horse) decline to jump. (말이 장애물 앞에서) 딱 멈추다. ¶ *The horse refused at the first fence.* [L. *recuso*]

ref·use[2] [réfjːs, -fjuːz] *n.* Ⓤ useless material; rubbish; garbage. 쓰레기; 폐물; 찌꺼기. ¶ *take away all* ~ *from the streets* 거리의 쓰레기들을 모두 치우다. — *adj.* useless; worthless. 쓸데 없는. ¶ ~ *matter* 폐물.

ref·u·ta·tion [rèfjutéiʃən] *n.* Ⓤ the act of refuting; Ⓒ something that proves something else to be false. 논박; 반박; 논파(論破)하는 의론〔의견〕. [↓]

re·fute [rifjúːt] *vt.* (P6) prove (an opinion, etc.) to be false; defeat (an opinion, etc.) by argument. …을 논박하다; 논파(論破)하다. [re-, →futile]

***re·gain** [rigéin] *vt.* (P6) **1** get back; recover. …을 되찾다; 회복하다. ¶ ~ *health* / ~ *consciousness* 의식을 회복하다 / ~ *one's feet* 〔*footing*〕 넘어졌다가 일어서다 / ~ *someone's affections* …의 애정을 되찾다. **2** reach again; return to (a place, a state, etc.). …에 복귀하다; 돌아가다. ¶ ~ *one's native country* 고국에 돌아가다 / ~ *the shore* 해변

에 돌아오다. [re-]

re·gal [ríːgəl] *adj.* **1** kinglike; fit for a king. 제왕다운. ¶ *a ~ banquet* 굉장한 향연 / *live in ~ splendor* 제왕처럼 떵떵거리며 살다. **2** belonging to a king; royal. (제)왕의. ¶ *~ power* 왕권 / *~ government* 왕정. [L. *rex*]

re·gale[1] [rigéil] *vt.* (P6,13) ⟪*on, with*⟫ delight; entertain; feast. …을 크게 대접하다; 즐겁게 해 주다. ¶ *~ oneself with a glass of wine* 술을 한잔하다 / *~ the guest with choice food* 손을 진수 성찬으로 대접하다 / ⟪*fig.*⟫ *Delightful music regaled my ears.* 즐거운 음악은 아주 듣기 좋았다. — *vi.* (P1,3) ⟪*on*⟫ feast; eat a rich meal. 성찬을 먹다; 잘 먹다. ●**re·gale·ment** [-mənt] *n.* [It. *regalo* gift]

re·ga·le[2] [rigéili] *n.* sing. of **regalia.**

re·ga·li·a [rigéiliə, -ljə] *n. pl.* (*sing.* **-ga·le**) **1** the symbol of royalty, such as the crown, scepters, etc. 왕위를 상징하는 것. ¶ *Crowns, scepters, etc. are ~.* 왕관, 홀(笏) 등은 왕위의 상징이다. **2** any ornaments to show a person's position of authority. (관위(官位) 등의) 기장(記章). [↓]

re·gal·i·ty [rigǽləti] *n.* **1** Ⓤ royalty. 왕위; 왕의 신분. **2** ⟪*pl.*⟫ sovereign powers. 왕권. **3** a kingdom. 왕국. [→regal]

:re·gard [rigɑ́ːrd] *vt.* **1** (P6,13) look at (something) attentively; watch. …을 주시하다; 주목해 보다. ¶ *She regarded him with a strong stare.* 그녀는 그를 뚫어지게 보았다 / *He regards her with favor* 〔*dislike*〕. 그는 호의적인〔혐오스런〕 눈으로 그녀를 본다 / *She regarded him with suspicion.* 그는 그녀를 의심스럽게 보았다. **2** (P6,7) ⟪*as*⟫ think of (something); consider. …을 —하게 보다〔여기다〕. ¶ *~ the situation as serious* 사태를 심각하게 보다 / *They regarded him as a great artist.* 그들은 그를 위대한 예술가로 생각했다. **3** (P6) ⟪usu. *negative*⟫ pay attention to (something). …에 주의하다; 신경을 쓰다. ¶ *None regarded her absence.* 그녀가 없는 것에 아무도 관심을 두지 않았다 / *If you fail to ~ my warning, you may be sorry.* 내 경고를 우습게 알았다간 후회할 거다 / *He does not ~ my advice.* 그는 내 충고에 아랑곳하지 않는다. **4** (P6) respect. …을 존중하다; 존경하다. ¶ *She regards honesty highly.* 그녀는 성실성을 중시한다. **5** (P6) relate to; concern. …와 관계되다. ¶ *This does not ~ me at all.* 이건 나와 전혀 무관하다 / *The question does not ~ the matter.* 그 문제는 이 일과 별개다.

as regards (= *as to; concerning*) *something.* …에 관해서는. ¶ *As regards money, I have enough.* 돈이라면 내게 충분히 있다.

— *n.* Ⓤ **1** care; attention; consideration. 주의; 관심; 고려. ¶ *He has no ~ for the feelings of others.* 그는 남의 기분엔 관심이 없다 / *He paid no ~ to his studies.* 공부는 거들떠보지도 않았다. **2** respect; esteem. 존경; 존중; 호의. ¶ *a high ~ for courage* 용기에 대한 높은 평가 / *hold someone in high* 〔*low*〕 *~* …을 존경〔경멸〕하다 / *The teacher has a proper ~ for his ability.* 선생님은 그의 능력을 제대로 보고 있다 / *have little ~ for other people's opinions* 남의 의견을 거의 무시하다. **3** ⟪*pl.*⟫ compliments; best wishes. 인사. ¶ *Please give my kindest* 〔*best, cordial*〕 *regards to your mother.* 어머니에게 안부 전해 주시오 / *With kind regards.* (편지 끝에 적어) 재배(再拜). **4** relation; point; reference. 관계; 사항; 관련. ¶ *in this* 〔*his*〕 *~* 이에〔그에〕 관해서는 / *His remarks have special ~ to the question.* 그의 말은 그 문제와 특별한 관련이〔관계가〕 있다. [re-, →guard]

without regard to, not taking into account. …에 개의치 않고. ¶ *act without ~ to other people's feelings* 다른 사람들 기분은 아랑곳없이 행동하다.

with 〔***in***〕 ***regard to,*** in relation to; concerning. …에 관해서. ¶ *The teacher wishes to speak to you in ~ to your being late.* 선생님은 네가 지각한 데 대해 할 말씀이 계시단다.

re·gard·ful [rigɑ́ːrdfəl] *adj.* mindful; showing respect. 주의 깊은; 경의를 표(表)하는. ¶ *He is ~ of his appearance.* 그는 자기 외관에 신경을 쓴다 / *~ manner* 공손한 태도.

***re·gard·ing** [rigɑ́ːrdiŋ] *prep.* concerning; about; in respect of. …에 관해서(는); …의 점에서(는). ¶ *He said nothing ~ the lost book.* 잃어버린 책에 대해 아무 말이 없었다 / *A letter ~ the boy's rudeness was sent to his father.* 아이가 버릇 없는 데에 대한 선생님의 편지가 아버지에게 보내졌다.

***re·gard·less** [rigɑ́ːrdlis] *adj.* ⟪*of*⟫ careless; indifferent. 부주의한; 무관심한. ¶ *~ of expense* 비용을 개의치 않고 / *~ of life* 목숨을 걸고 / *~ of age or sex* 연령·성별을 불문하고. ●**re·gard·less·ly** [-li] *adv.*

re·gat·ta [rigǽtə] *n.* Ⓒ a boat or yacht race. 레가타⟪보트·요트 경주 대회⟫. [It. *regata*]

re·gen·cy [ríːdʒənsi] *n.* ⒸⓊ (*pl.* **-cies**) government by a regent; the office, position or period of a regent. 섭정 정치; 그 직〔지위, 기간〕. [→regent]

re·gen·er·ate [ridʒénərèit] *vt.* (P6) **1** ⟪biol.⟫ produce (something) anew. …을 재생시키다. ¶ *Certain animals are able to ~ lost parts of the body.* 어떤 동물은 신체의 떨어져 나간 부분을 재생시킬 수도 있다. **2** improve or reform morally. …을 갱생시키다. **3** cause (someone) to be reborn spiritually. …을 거듭나게 하다.

— *vi.* (P1) **1** be produced anew. 재생하다. ¶ *Nails and hair are constantly regenerating.* 손톱과 머리는 잘라도 계속 자란다. **2** be improved morally. (도덕적으로) 갱생하다. **3** be filled with new life or power. 새로운 생명을 얻다.

— [ridʒénərit] *adj.* spiritually reborn; reformed. 새로 난; 거듭난; 개량된.

● **re·gen·er·a·tor** [-ər] *n.* [re-]

re·gen·er·a·tive [ridʒénərèitiv, -rətiv] *adj.* tending to regenerate. 갱생(신생·재생)시키는.

re·gent [ríːdʒənt] *n.* Ⓒ **1** a person who rules in the name and place of another. 섭정(攝政). **2** 《U.S.》 a member of the governing board of certain universities or other institutions. (대학 등의) 평의원; 이사. — *adj.* ruling in place of another. 섭정의. 語法 명사 뒤에 둠. ¶ *the Prince Regent* 섭정궁(宮). [L. *rego* rule]

reg·i·cide [rédʒəsàid] *n.* Ⓤ the act or crime of killing a king; Ⓒ a murderer of a king. 국왕 시해(죄); 국왕 시해범. [→rex, L. *caedo* kill]

re·gime, ré·gime [reiʒíːm, ri-] *n.* Ⓒ **1** a social or political system. 사회 제도; 정체(政體). ¶ *Under the old ~ women enjoyed fewer rights.* 구(舊)정치 체제에서 여권(女權)은 제한적이었다. **2** =regimen. [→regent]

reg·i·men [rédʒəmən / -mèn] *n.* Ⓤ **1** a system of diet, exercise, etc. to improve health. 식이 요법; 양생법. ¶ *be put on a strict ~* 엄격한 식이 요법에 들어가다 / *He follows a daily ~.* 매일의 다이어트에 충실하다. **2** 《*arch.*》 =regime 1. [↑]

·**reg·i·ment** [rédʒəmənt] *n.* Ⓒ **1** 《mil.》 an organized body of soldiers. 연대. **2** 《often *pl.*》 a large number. 다수(多數). ¶ *whole regiments of grasshoppers* 큰 메뚜기떼. — [rédʒəmènt] *vt.* (P6) **1** organize. …을 조직화하다. **2** form into a regiment or group. …을 연대로 편성하다. [↑]

reg·i·men·tal [rèdʒəméntl] *adj.* of a regiment. 연대의. ¶ *the ~ color* 연대기(旗). — *n.* 《*pl.*》 a regimental, military uniform. 연대복; 군복.

reg·i·men·ta·tion [rèdʒəmentéiʃən] *n.* Ⓤ **1** the act of forming into organized groups of soldiers. 연대 편성. **2** organization; systematization. 조직화.

:**re·gion** [ríːdʒən] *n.* Ⓒ **1** 《often *pl.*》 an area; a large part of a country; a district. 지방; 지역; 지대. ¶ *forest regions* 산림 지대. **2** a sphere; a realm. (천지를 상하로 구분한) 부분; 역(域); 영역; 분야. ¶ *the lower (upper) regions* 지옥(천국) / *the upper regions of the air* 대기의 상층권 / *the ~ of science* 과학 분야. **3** a part of the body. (신체의) 부위. ¶ *the ~ of the heart* 흉부. [→regent]

airy region, heaven. 하늘.

in the region of, in the neighborhood of; about. …의 부근에; 약. ¶ *in the ~ of 100 won* 백 원 안팎.

the region beyond the grave, lower world. 저승; 황천.

re·gion·al [ríːdʒənəl] *adj.* of an area, a country, etc.; local. 지방(지역)의. ¶ *the ~ authorities* 지방 당국 / *a ~ accent* 지방 사투리 / *~ planning* 지역(지방) 계획.

:**reg·is·ter** [rédʒəstər] *n.* Ⓒ **1** an official written record; a written list. 등록; 기록. **2** a book in which such records or lists are written. 등록(등기)부. ¶ *a hotel ~* 숙박부 / *a ~ of attendance* 출석부 / *a ship's ~* 선적 증명서 / *a ~ of births, marriages, and deaths* 출생·결혼·사망 등록부. **3** a machine for recording speed, numbers, etc.; an automatic recorder. 자동 등록기. ¶ *a cash ~* 금전 등록기. **4** (in a stove, furnace, etc.) a device for regulating the passage of air. (난로 등의) 통풍 장치. **5** the range of the human voice or of a musical instrument. 성역(聲域); 음역(音域). ¶ *the ~ of the voice.*

— *vt.* (P6) **1** record officially; enroll. …을 등기(등록)하다. ¶ *a registered trademark* 등록 상표 / *My father was registered as a doctor.* 아버지는 의사로 등록되어 있었다 / *a registered design* 등록 의장. **2** protect (a letter or parcel) from loss or damage by payment of a special fee. …을 등기 우편으로 부치다. ¶ *registered mail* 등기 우편 / *I want to have (get) this letter registered.* 이 편지를 등기로 해 주시오. **3** record in one's mind; remember. …을 명심(銘心)하다; 마음에 새기다. ¶ *I registered the event in my memory.* 나는 그 사건을 마음에 새겼다 / *His face was registered in my memory.* 그의 얼굴은 내 마음에 새겨져 있다. **4** (of instruments) indicate; record. (온도계 등이) …을 나타내다. ¶ *The thermometer registers five degrees of frost.* 온도계는 영하 5도를 가리키고 있다.

— *vi.* (P1) **1** write one's name in a register. (숙박부 등에) 기록(등록)하다. ¶ *~ at a hotel* 호텔에 투숙하다 / *You must ~ if you want to take part in this group.* 이 단체에 들려면 등록을 해야 한다. **2** show surprise, joy, etc. (놀람·기쁨 등을) 표정(동작)으로 나타내다. [re-, L. *gero* carry]

reg·is·trar [rédʒəstràːr, ⌐—⌐] *n.* Ⓒ an official whose task is to keep records. 기록계; 등기소 관리. [↑]

reg·is·tra·tion [rèdʒəstréiʃən] *n.* **1** Ⓤ the act of registering; the state of being registered. 기록; 등록; 기장. ¶ *~ of voters* 선거인 등록. **2** Ⓒ the total number of persons registered. 등록자 총수.

reg·is·try [rédʒəstri] *n.* (*pl.* **-tries**) **1** Ⓤ the act of registering. 기재; 등기; 등록. ¶ 《U.S.》 *the ~ fee* 등기 우편료. **2** Ⓒ a book in which a list is kept. 등록부. **3** Ⓒ a place where records are kept. 등기소. ¶ *a ~ office* 호적 등기소.

registry office [⌐—⌐—] *n.* **1** an office where records of births, marriages, and deaths are kept. 호적 등기소. **2** an employment office through which domestic servants are supplied. 직업 안내소.

reg·nant [régnənt] *adj.* **1** ruling; reigning. 통치(지배)하는. ¶ *the Queen Regnant* (주권자로서의) 여왕. **2** 《*fig.*》 prevailing; having more power than others. 우세한; 유력한. ¶ *the ~ fashion* 지금 한창의 유행 / *the ~ quality in his character* 그의 성격에서의 돋보이는 장점. [L. *regnum* reign]

re·gress [rí:gres] *n.* Ⓤ 《*in, into*》 backward a movement. 후퇴; 역행; 퇴보. ¶ *the right of free egress and ~* 출입의 자유권. —[rigrés] *vi.* (P1) go back; move backward. 후퇴하다; 역행하다. [re-, L. *gradior* tread]

re·gres·sion [rigréʃən] *n.* Ⓤ the act of going back; a movement which is opposite to the usual direction. 역행; 퇴보; 복귀.

:re·gret [rigrét] *vt.* (**-gret·ted, -gret·ting**) **1** (P6,8) feel sorrow for or grieve for (something); deplore. …을 애석해하다; 애도하다. ¶ *~ someone's death* …의 죽음을 애석해하다 / *I ~ to hear of his loss.* 그가 실패했다니 안타까운 일이다 / *I ~ to say that Mr. Smith has died.* 애통하게도 스미스 씨가 작고하셨답니다. **2** (P6) remember (something lost) with sorrow; miss. …이 없음을 아쉬워하다; 그리워하다. ¶ *~ one's happy youth* 행복했던 청춘을 아쉬워하다 / *~ the old home* 옛집을 그리워하다. **3** (P6,8,9, 11) feel sorry for (one's own act, word, etc.); repent of (something). …을 후회하다; 유감으로 여기다. ¶ *~ the foolish behaviors of one's youth* 젊어서의 어리석은 짓을 뉘우치다 / *I ~ being unable to help you.* =*I ~ that I cannot help you.* 너를 돕지 못하는 것이 유감이다 / *I ~ to have done such a thing.* =*I ~ having done such a thing.* 내가 왜 그런 짓을 했을까 / *He regretted his mistake all his life.* 그는 자기 실수를 평생 후회하며 지냈다.

—*n.* ⓊⒸ **1** sorrow; grief; disappointment. 슬픔; 비탄; 실망; 유감. ¶ *hear with ~ of* 〔*that …*〕 …을 듣고 애통해하다 / *He expressed ~ for his faults.* 그는 자기 잘못을 사과했다 / *I feel no ~ at her absence.* 그녀가 없어도 아무렇지 않다. **2** painful feeling for one's own wrong act; repentance; remorse. 후회; 회한. ¶ *to one's ~* 유감스럽게도 / *feel ~ for past misdeeds* 지난날의 비행을 뉘우치다 / *It is a matter of ~ that I could not help him at that time.* 그 때 그를 돕지 못한 것이 후회스럽다 / *She felt ~ for having lost her temper.* 그녀는 화를 냈던 것을 후회했다 / *waste time in useless regrets* 쓸데없이 후회만 하고 지내다 / *I should have no ~ if I were to die tomorrow.* 내일 죽어도 여한이 없다. **3** 《often *pl.*》 a polite expression or letter of refusal. 정중한 사절; 그 편지. ¶ *refuse with many regrets* 매우 미안하지만 사절하다 / *Please accept my regrets.* 애석하게도 받아들일 수 없습니다 / *She could not come but sent her regrets.* 갈 수 없어서 그녀는 사절장을 보냈다. [F. *regret*]

re·gret·ful [rigrétfəl] *adj.* feeling sorry for a loss; remembering with sorrow or disappointment. 유감으로 여기는; 뉘우치는; 슬퍼하는. ¶ *I am most ~ for my mistake.* 내 실수에 대하여 크게 뉘우치고 있다 / *a ~ apology* 심심한 사과 / *a ~ look* 미안한〔뉘우치는〕 표정.

re·gret·ful·ly [rigrétfəli] *adv.* in a regretful manner. 안타까운 듯이; 슬픈 듯이.

re·gret·ta·ble [rigrétəbəl] *adj.* causing a wish that it had been otherwise; to be regretted. 유감스러운; 섭섭한; 안된. 語法 I am regrettable 이라고는 하지 않음. ¶ *It is ~ that….* …은 유감이다 / *a ~ error* 〔*mistake*〕 안타까운 실수 / *It is ~ that the government has found it necessary to use such secretive methods.* 불가피했다고는 하나 정부의 그런 음성적인 수법은 유감스럽다.

:reg·u·lar [régjələr] *adj.* (opp. irregular) **1** ⓐ according to a rule, principle, etc.; orderly; systematic. 규칙이나 원칙에 맞는; 정연한; 계통이 선. ¶ *~ work* 정직(定職) / *~ features* 단정한 용모 / *lead a ~ life* 규칙적인 생활을 하다 / *~ teeth* 고른 잇바디 / *a ~ plan for streets* 정연한 도로 계획. ⓑ properly fitted; in agreement with a generally accepted standard or rule of conduct. 격식에 맞는; 법도에 어긋나지 않는. ¶ *The procedures were ~.* 절차는 정상이었다 / *What is the ~ dress for such occasions?* 그런 경우 어떤 옷이 좋을까. **2** not changing; usual; habitual. 불변의; 늘 하는; 일상적인. ¶ *a ~ customer* 단골 손님 / *a ~ member* 정(正)회원 / *~ breathing* 고른 호흡 / *He keeps ~ hours.* 그는 규칙적인 생활을 한다. **3** happening at fixed times or at the same interval of time; constant. 정기적인; 규칙적인. ¶ *a ~ beating of the heart* 심장의 규칙적인 박동 / *~ meals* 규칙적인 식사 / *a ~ meeting* 정기적인 모임 / *Sunday is a ~ holiday.* 일요일은 정규 휴일이다. **4** formally admitted; recognized. 면허 있는; 정규(正規)의. ¶ *a ~ doctor* 정식 의사 / *a ~ cook* 전문 요리사 / *the ~ army* 정규군 / *~ soldiers* 정규병. **5** 《gram.》 having normal changes of the form. 규칙 변화를 하는. ¶ *a ~ verb* 규칙 동사. **6** 《geom.》 having all the sides and angles equal. 등각 등변(等角等邊)의. ¶ *a ~ polygon* 정다각형(正多角形). **7** 《*colloq.*》 thorough; complete. 순; 진짜의. ¶ *a ~ hero* 진정한 영웅 / *a ~ rascal* 순 악당. **8** 《U.S. *colloq.*》 pleasant; amiable. 기분이 좋은; 호감이 가는. ¶ *a ~ fellow* 좋은 친구.

—*n.* Ⓒ **1** 《usu. *pl.*》 a regular soldier. 정규병. ¶ *The army was composed of regulars and volunteers.* 군은 정규병과 지원병으로 구성되어 있었다. **2** 《*colloq.*》 a person who is regular; a regular customer. 상시(常時) 고용인; 단골. [L. *regula* rule]

reg·u·lar·ize [régjələràiz] *vt.* (P6) make (something) regular. …을 규칙 바르게 하다; 질서를 세우다.

·reg·u·lar·ly [régjələrli] *adv.* **1** in a regular manner; at regular intervals. 규칙

바르게; 정기적으로. ¶ *The streets are arranged* ~. 가로는 질서 정연하였다 / *behave* ~ 바르게 행동하다 / *dress* ~ 정장하다 / *He calls here* ~ *every week.* 그는 매주 정기적으로 여기를 방문한다. **2** 《*colloq.*》 thoroughly; completely. 철저히; 완벽하게. ¶ *I was* ~ *taken in over that business.* 나는 그 일에서 감쪽같이 속았다.

·**reg·u·late** [régjəlèit] *vt.* (P6) **1** control (something) by a rule, an established custom, etc. …을 (규칙 따위로) 단속하다; 통제하다. ¶ *Accidents sometimes happen even in the best regulated families.* 아주 규모 있는 집안에서도 사고는 때로 생긴다 / ~ *one's expenditure* 지출을 억제하다. **2** keep (something) in proper order; put (something) in a desirable or proper condition. …을 규칙 바르게 하다; 조절하다. ¶ *The clock is regulated every week.* 시계는 매주 시간을 조정한다 / *The prices are regulated by demand and supply.* 가격은 수요와 공급으로 조절된다 / ~ *the speed of a machine* 기계의 속도를 조절하다. [*regular*]

·**reg·u·la·tion** [règjəléiʃən] *n.* **1** Ⓤ control or adjustment; being regulated. 단속; 조정; 조절. ¶ *the* ~ *of temperatures* 온도 조절 / ~ *of conduct* 행동 규제. **2** Ⓒ a rule or law. 규칙; 규정. ¶ *the school regulations* 교칙 / *the regulations of a club* 회칙 / *a* ~ *against smoking* 금연법. —*adj.* standard; ordinary. 정규〔표준〕의. ¶ *a* ~ *uniform* 정복 / *of the* ~ *size* 표준 크기의 / *at a* ~ *rate* 〔*speed*〕 규정 비율〔속도〕로.

reg·u·la·tor [régjəlèitər] *n.* Ⓒ **1** a person or thing that regulates. 규정자; 단속인; 조정자; 조정기(器). **2** a device in a clock or watch to control its speed. 시간 조절 장치. ¶ *the* ~ *of a clock.* **3** a correct clock used as a standard of time. 표준 시계. **4** a regulating principle. 표준.

re·gur·gi·tate [rigə́:rdʒətèit] *vt.* (P6) **1** pour or throw back. …을 역류시키다; 되내뿜다. **2** vomit up. …을 토하다. —*vi.* (P1) flow back. 역류하다. [re-, →gurgitation]

re·ha·bil·i·tate [ri:həbílətèit] *vt.* (P6) **1** restore (someone or something) to a former state or to a good condition. …을 원상태로 돌리다; 복원〔복구〕시키다; 복위〔복권; 복직〕시키다. ¶ ~ *an army officer who has been stripped of his rank* 계급을 박탈당한 장교를 원계급으로 복권시키다 / ~ *oneself* 〔*one's character*〕 명예를 회복하다. **2** restore (*e.g.* old buildings) to a good condition. …을 수리〔수선〕하다. ¶ ~ *an old house.* **3** restore someone to health through training, etc. (훈련을 거쳐 장애자 등)을 사회 복귀시키다. [re-, →habilitate]

re·ha·bil·i·ta·tion [ri:həbìlətéiʃən] *n.* Ⓤ the act of rehabilitating; the state of being rehabilitated. 복구; 복원; 복권; 복직; 사회 복귀. ¶ *a* ~ *center* (장애인) 사회 복귀 시설.

re·hash [ri:hǽʃ] *vt.* (P6) deal with again; arrange (something already used) and use again in a new form. …을 재처리하다; 개작(改作)하다. ¶ *The plan was rehashed again and again.* 그 계획은 수정에 수정을 거듭했다 / ~ *an old story* 옛 이야기를 재탕하다 / *a politician who keeps rehashing the same old speech* 연설을 조금만 개작해서 자꾸 써먹는 정치가. —*n.* Ⓒ something old put in a new form. 재탕; 개작. [re-]

re·hears·al [rihə́:rsəl] *n.* **1** Ⓤ the act of rehearsing. 연습. **2** Ⓒ a practice in preparation for a public performance. 예행 연습; 시연(試演); 리허설. ¶ *a* (*full*) *dress* ~ (의상을 갖추고 하는) 리허설 / *a public* ~ 공개 시연. [↓]

re·hearse [rihə́:rs] *vt.* **1** (P6) practice (a play, a ceremony, etc.) in preparation for a public performance. …을 예행 연습하다; 시연(試演)하다. ¶ *We rehearsed our parts for the school play.* 학예회에서 우리가 맡은 역을 연습했다. **2** repeat; tell in full. 되풀이하여〔자세히〕 얘기하다. ¶ *The child rehearsed the happenings of the day to his father in the evening.* 아이는 저녁때 그 날 있었던 일들을 아버지에게 자세히 이야기했다. —*vi.* (P1) practice in a rehearsal. 예행 연습〔시연〕을 하다. [re-, L. *hercer* harrow]

Reich [raik: 《G.》 raiç] *n.* Germany. 독일.

:**reign** [rein] *n.* **1** Ⓤ sovereignty; supreme rule; royal power. (제왕 등의) 통치; 군림; 통치권. ¶ *They were under the* ~ *of a wise king.* 그들은 총명한 군주 밑에 살았다. **2** Ⓒ the period of a ruler. 치세. ¶ *a long and splendid* ~ 길고 영광된 성대(聖代) / *After a* ~ *of seventy years the king died.* 70 년 동안의 치세를 끝으로 왕은 죽었다. **3** Ⓤ prevailing influence. 우세; 지배(력). ¶ *Night resumes her* ~. 다시 밤의 세계가 되다 / *the* ~ *of fashion* 〔*law, peace*〕 유행〔법, 평화〕의 지배.
—*vi.* (P1) rule; prevail. 지배하다. ¶ *Silence reigned in the wood.* 정적(靜寂)이 숲을 지배하고 있었다 / *The Queen reigned over a vast dominion.* 여왕은 광대한 영토를 지배했다. [L. *rego* rule]

re·im·burse [rì:imbə́:rs] *vt.* (P6,13) pay back; compensate. 갚다; 변제하다. ¶ ~ *someone for his expenses* 비용을 아무에게 물어주다 / 《*fig.*》 *Eager to* ~ *themselves for this dishonor, they at last rose against the enemy.* 그들은 이 치욕을 씻으려고 마침내 적에 대항하여 궐기했다. [re-, in²-, →bourse]

re·im·burse·ment [rì:imbə́:rsmənt] *n.* ⓊⒸ the act of reimbursing; the state of being reimbursed. 보상; 환불.

·**rein** [rein] *n.* Ⓒ **1** 《often *pl.*》 one of the two long straps used to control or guide a horse. 고삐(cf. *harness*). ¶ *adjust the reins* 고삐를 뜻대로 다루다 / *a loose* ~ 느슨한 고삐 / *Pull on the reins.* 고삐를 당기고 있어라. **2** 《usu. *pl.*》 《*fig.*》 a means of control. 통어〔제어〕법. ¶ *assume the reins of* *government* 정권을 잡다 / *drop the reins of power* 정권을 내놓다; 하야하다 / *The queen kept in her own hand the reins of power.* 여왕은 국권을 한손에 쥐고 있었다.

give rein to, allow to act without any control. …에게 자유를 주다; …가 좋을 대로 내버려 두다.

hold a rein on, restrain. …을 억제하다. ¶ *hold a ~ on one's appetite* 욕구를 자제하다.

keep a tight rein on, train severely; keep under one's strict control. …을 엄격히 훈련시키다〔제어하다〕; 다잡아 죄다.

— *vt.* (P6,7) guide; control; restrain. …을 지배하다; 억제하다. ¶ *He reins his horse well.* 말을 잘 다룬다 / 《*fig.*》 *~ in one's temper* 화를 억누르다 / *Rein your tongue.* 입을 다물어라. [F. *resne*]

re·in·car·nate [rìːinkáːrneit] *vt.* (P6) give a new body to (a soul). …을 다시 태어나게 하다; 환생(還生)시키다. ¶ *He believed that he would be reincarnated.* 그는 자기가 사후 다시 태어나리라고 믿었다. — [rìːinkáːrnit] *adj.* taking a new body. 환생한; 딴 몸으로 태어난. [→incarnate]

re·in·car·na·tion [rìːinkaːrnéiʃən] *n.* Ⓤⓒ rebirth in a new bodily form; a new embodiment. 환생; 화신.

rein·deer [réindìər] *n.* Ⓒ (*pl.* **-deer** or **-deers**) a kind of deer with large horns, found in northern regions. 순록(馴鹿). [N. *hreinn, deer*]

re·in·force [rìːinfɔ́ːrs] *vt.* (P6) **1** make (something) stronger with additional material or support. …을 보강하다; 강화하다. ¶ *reinforced concrete* 철근 콘크리트 / *~ a bridge* 다리를 보강하다. **2** make (an army) stronger by adding new forces. …에 원병을 보내다; 증원하다. ¶ *~ an army* 군을 증원하다 / *~ a fleet* 함선을 늘리다. **3** strengthen. …을 강화하다. ¶ *~ an effect* 〔*a stock, a supply*〕 효과를〔재고를, 공급을〕 증대시키다. [re-, →enforce]

re·in·force·ment [rìːinfɔ́ːrsmənt] *n.* **1** Ⓤ the act of reinforcing; the state of being reinforced. 보강; 증원. **2** Ⓒ 《often *pl.*》 additional troops or warships to reinforce an army or a fleet. 증원군; 증파 함대. ¶ *Reinforcements were sent to the battlefront.* 증원군이 전선에 투입되었다.

re·in·state [rìːinstéit] *vt.* put (someone) back into a former position or condition. …을 본디의 지위〔상태〕로 돌리다; 복직시키다. ¶ *He was dismissed, but was later reinstated when his innocence was proved.* 그는 해직되었으나 나중에 결백이 밝혀져 복직됐다 / *~ someone to his lost right* 아무를 복권시키다. [re-, in-[2]]

re·in·state·ment [rìːinstéitmənt] *n.* Ⓤ the act of reinstating; the state of being reinstated. 복직; 복권; 회복.

re·in·vig·or·ate [rìːinvígərèit] *vt.* (P6) give life or energy again to (someone or an animal); refresh; invigorate again. …을 소생시키다; 다시 활기 띠게 하다. [re-, →invigorate]

re·is·sue [riːíʃuː / -ísjuː] *vt.* (P6) publish again. …을 다시 발행하다. — *n.* Ⓒ something issued again. 재발행물; 재판. [re-]

re·it·er·ate [riːítərèit] *vt.* (P6) say or do again and again; repeat. (말·행동)을 반복하다. ¶ *~ requests* 요구를 되풀이하다 / *reiterated cries of disagreement* 연호(連呼)하는 이의(異議)의 함성. [re-]

re·it·er·a·tion [riːìtəréiʃən] *n.* Ⓤ the act of repeating several times; Ⓒ a repetition. 되풀이; 반복.

***re·ject** [ridʒékt] *vt.* (P6) **1** refuse to take, believe or use (something). …을 거절하다. ¶ *~ an offer* 제의를 거절하다 / *He rejected our help.* 그는 우리 도움을 거절했다 / *~ a bill in Parliament* 의회에서 의안을 부결하다 / *He rejected the accusation as patently absurd.* 그는 명백히 터무니없는 비난이라고 일축했다. **2** throw (something) away as worthless or useless. (쓸데없는 것이라고) 버리다; 퇴짜놓다(opp. accept). ¶ *~ a candidate* 지원자를 퇴짜놓다 / *~ all spotted apples* 흠 있는 사과는 모조리 버리다 / *~ a poorly written article* 잘 쓰지 못한 기사를 제외하다. **3** throw up (food); vomit. (음식)을 토하다.

— *n.* a rejected person or thing. 퇴짜맞은 사람〔것〕.

● **re·ject·er** [-ər] *n.* [re-, L. *jacio* throw]

re·jec·tion [ridʒékʃən] *n.* **1** Ⓤ the act of rejecting; the state of being rejected. 거절; 퇴짜; 구토. **2** Ⓒ something rejected. 거부된 것; 구토물.

***re·joice** [ridʒɔ́is] *vi.* (P1,3,4) 《*at, in, over*》 feel joy; be glad. 기뻐하다. ¶ *~ at one's success* 성공을 기뻐하다 / *Let's ~ together on this great occasion.* 이 경사스러운 날을 우리 다 함께 즐깁시다 / *I ~ in your happiness.* 행복하시니 제가 기쁩니다 / *I ~ to see you here.* 너를 여기서 만나니 기쁘다.

— *vt.* (P6) **1** give joy to (someone); make (someone) glad. …을 기쁘게 하다. ¶ *The news rejoiced him.* 그 소식에 그는 기뻤다 / *~ a father's heart* 아버지를 기쁘게 하다 / *a sight to ~ one's eyes* 보아서 즐거워지는 광경. **2** 《in *passive*》 《*at, by*》 be glad or happy. …을 즐겁게 하다. ¶ *I am rejoiced to hear* 〔*at hearing, by hearing*〕 *the news.* 그 소식에 나는 기쁘다. [re-, →joy]

re·joic·ing [ridʒɔ́isiŋ] *n.* Ⓤ **1** gladness; happiness. 기쁨; 행복. **2** 《usu. *pl.*》 celebration. 축하; 기쁜 일.

re·join[1] [riːdʒɔ́in] *vt.* (P6) **1** meet (someone) again. …와 다시 만나다; 재회하다. ¶ *~ one's regiment* 자신의 연대를 만나다 / *You go on and I will ~ you later.* 계속 가거라, 뒤에 만나게 된다. **2** unite to or with (someone) again. …와 재결합하다. — *vi.* (P1) become joined together again. 재결합하

다. [re-]

re·join² [ridʒɔ́in] *vi., vt.* (P1;6) answer; reply. 대답하다. [re-]

re·join·der [ridʒɔ́indər] *n.* Ⓒ an answer; a reply; a retort. 응답; 대답; 반박; 말대꾸. [↑]

in rejoinder, in reply. 대답으로.

re·ju·ve·nate [ridʒúːvənèit] *vt., vi.* (P6;1) make or become young again. 다시 젊어지(게 하)다. ¶ *The long rest and new clothes had rejuvenated her.* 푹 쉬고 새 옷으로 갈아입은 그녀는 젊어진 듯했다. [re-, →juvenile]

re·ju·ve·na·tion [ridʒùːvənéiʃən] *n.* Ⓤ the act of rejuvenating. 회춘; 원기 회복. ¶ ~ *in old age* 회춘.

re·kin·dle [riːkíndl] *vt.* (P6) **1** set (something) on fire again. …에 다시 불을 붙이다. ¶ ~ *a dying fire* 꺼져 가는 불을 일구다. **2** 《*fig.*》 rouse again; excite (someone) again. 다시 기운을 돋우다. ¶ ~ *hope* 〔*interest*〕 다시 희망을〔관심을〕 가지게 하다 / *The king's anger was rekindled against the enemy.* 적에 대한 왕의 분노가 다시 일었다.

— *vi.* (P1) **1** catch fire again. 다시 불타다. ¶ *The fire rekindled and completely destroyed the building.* 다시 불길이 일어 건물을 완전히 태워 버렸다. **2** 《*fig.*》 become excited again. 다시 흥분하다. ¶ *All his anger rekindled at the sight.* 그 광경에 그는 온 분노가 다시 치밀었다. [re-]

re·lapse [rilǽps] *vi.* (P1,3) **1** fall or slip back into a former state. 다시 본디 상태로 되다; 되돌아가다. ¶ *After one cry of surprise she relapsed into silence.* 그녀는 놀라서 한 번 소리치더니 다시 조용해졌다 / ~ *into melancholia* 〔*coma*〕 다시 우울증〔혼수 상태〕에 빠지다. **2** fall back into a former bad habit after reform. 다시 악화되다〔나쁜 길로 빠지다〕. ¶ ~ *into vice* 〔*crime, drunkenness*〕 다시 악〔범죄, 술〕에 빠지다. — *n.* Ⓒ the state of relapsing. 되돌아감; 재발. ¶ *have a* ~ 재발하다 / *He seemed to be getting over his illness but had a* ~. 그는 병이 회복되는 듯싶더니 재발했다. [re-]

:re·late [riléit] *vt.* **1** (P6) tell; give an account of (something). …에 관하여 이야기하다. ¶ *The explorer related his adventures.* 그 탐험가는 자신의 모험담을 얘기하였다 / ~ *one's grievances*〔*experiences*〕 자기의 불만〔체험〕을 얘기하다 / *Strange to* ~, *they never met again.* 이상한 말이지만 그들은 다시는 만나지 않았다. **2** (P13) bring (something) into connection with or association to another thing. …을 관련시키다. ¶ ~ *A with* 〔*to*〕 *B,* A를 B에 연관시키다 / ~ *theory and practice* 이론과 실제를 연관시키다 / *The police are still trying to* ~ *these two pieces of evidence.* 경찰은 계속 이 두 증거물을 연결시키려 하고 있다. **3** (P13) 《usu. in *passive*》 《*to*》 be connected by birth or marriage. …와 친척〔혈연〕 관계가 있다. ¶ *He is relateded to her.* 그는 그녀의 친척이다 / *The cat is distantly related to the tiger.* 고양이와 호랑이는 먼 친척 사이이다 / *They are related to each other.* 그들은 서로 친척간이다.

— *vi.* (P1,3) 《*to*》 have a connection; refer. 관계가 있다; 관계하다. ¶ *Your information does not* ~ *well with the facts.* 네 보고는 그 사실들과 그다지 관계가 없다 / *This account relates to my father.* 이건 아버지와 관계된 이야기이다 / *To what events did your remarks* ~ *?* 네가 하는 말은 무슨 사건을 가리키는 거냐. [re-, L. *latus* pp. of *fero* bear]

·re·lat·ed [riléitid] *adj.* **1** connected. 관계된. ¶ *The program deals with drug addiction, juvenile crime, and* ~ *issue.* 그 프로그램은 마약 중독, 청소년 범죄 및 그와 관계된 문제를 다룬다. **2** connected by origin, marriage, etc.; of the same kind. 혈연의; 동류의. ¶ *She and I are* ~. 그녀와 나는 인척간이다.

:re·la·tion [riléiʃən] *n.* **1** Ⓤ connection in thought or meaning. (추상적인) 관계. ¶ *the* ~ *between cause and effect* 원인과 결과의 관계 / *The* ~ *of mother and child is the closest in the world.* 어머니와 아이의 관계가 세상에서 제일 가깝다 / *the* ~ *of the weather to the quality of the crops* 기후와 농작물 품질과의 관계 / *I don't see any* ~ *between the two.* 그 둘 사이에 무슨 관계가 있는지 모르겠다. **2** Ⓒ 《often *pl.*》 connection between persons, groups, states, etc. (단체·국민·국가 간의) 관계. ¶ *keep close relations with the neighboring countries* 이웃 나라와의 긴밀한 관계를 유지하다. **3** Ⓒ a member or the same family; a person connected by birth or marriage. 가족; 친척. 參考 후자의 뜻으로는 relative 가 보통임. ¶ *One's parents and one's children are one's nearest relations.* 부모와 자식 간이 자기와 가장 가까운 혈연 관계이다. **4** Ⓤ consideration; the act of looking in a book, etc. for consideration. 고려; 참고. **5** Ⓤ the act of telling; an account. 이야기하기; 언급; 이야기. ¶ *the* ~ *of a story* 진술; 언급 / *We were interested in his* ~ *of his adventures.* 그의 모험담이 재미있었다.

bear no relation to (=*have nothing to do with*) *something.* …와 무관하다.

in 〔***with***〕 ***relation to,*** as regards; in reference to. …에 관련하여. ¶ *in* ~ *to this matter* 이 문제에 관하여 / *You must judge his work in* ~ *to the circumstances.* 주위 사정과 관련해서 그의 일을 판단해야 한다.

make relation to (=*tell about*) *something.* …에 대해 언급하다.

·re·la·tion·ship [riléiʃənʃìp] *n.* **1** Ⓤ connection by birth or marriage. 친척〔인척〕(관계). ¶ *claim* ~ *to* 〔*with*〕 *someone* 아무와 인척임을 내세우다. **2** Ⓒ connection. 관계. ¶ *Time could not change our* ~. 세월은 우리의 관계를 갈라 놓지 못했다.

:rel·a·tive [rélətiv] *adj.* **1** 《*to*》 relating to; considered in connection with something else. 관계된; 관련 있는. ¶ *a newspaper ~ to the matter* 그 일에 관련된 신문 / *'Hot' and 'cold' are ~ terms.* '덥다'와 '차다'는 관련어다 / *evidence hardly ~ to what has to be proved* 입증되어야 할 것과는 거의 관계 없는 증거. **2** comparative; not absolute. 비교상의; 상대적인. ¶ *~ merits* 우열 / *the ~ advantages of gas and electricity* 가스와 전기의 비교상의 이점 / *the ~ speed of two moving bodies* 움직이는 두 물체의 상대 속도 / *the ~ values of the dollar and won* 달러와 원화의 비교 가치. **3** having proportion. 비례한. ¶ *Supply is ~ to demand.* 공급은 수요에 비례한다. **4** having mutual relations. 상호의. ¶ *the ~ responsibilities of a ruler and his people* 통치자와 국민의 상호 의무. **5** 《gram.》 relating to a word which goes before in a sentence. 관계를 나타낸. ¶ *~ adjectives* 관계 형용사 / *a ~ pronoun* 관계 대명사.

— *n.* Ⓒ **1** a person connected by blood or marriage; a family relation. 친척〔인척〕; 일가. ¶ *Cousins and nieces are relatives.* 사촌과 조카딸은 친척이다. **2** 《gram.》 a relative word, esp. a relative pronoun. 관계사《특히 관계 대명사》. ¶ *'Who', 'which', 'what', and 'that' are relatives.*

·rel·a·tive·ly [rélətivli] *adv.* **1** in relation to something else; compared with something else. 상대적으로; 비교적. ¶ *He is ~ a wealthy man.* 비교적 유복한 사람이다. **2** in proportion to. …에 비례하여.

rel·a·tiv·i·ty [rèlətívəti] *n.* Ⓤ **1** the state of being relative. 상관〔관련〕성; 관계 있음. **2** 《phys.》 Einstein's theory of the universe. 아인슈타인의 상대성 원리. ¶ *the (special 〔general〕) principle of ~* (특수〔일반〕) 상대성 원리.

·re·lax [rilǽks] *vt.* **1** make (something) loose; stop the strain on (one's nerves). …을 늦추다; …의 힘을 빼다; 긴장을 풀다. ¶ *~ one's hold* 잡은 손을 늦추다 / *~ one's features* 낯을 펴다 / *The heat relaxed my muscles.* 더워서 몸이 나른하다. **2** ⓐ 《*fig.*》 make (something) less strict. …을 관대히 하다; 완화하다. ¶ *I hope this college will ~ its regulations.* 이 대학이 교칙을 좀 완화했으면 좋으련만. ⓑ ease; give rest to. 편안하게 하다; 쉬게 하다. ¶ *Seeing a good comedy relaxes one's mind.* 좋은 코미디를 보면 마음이 편안해진다. **3** reduce; weaken. …을 경감하다. ¶ *~ one's efforts* 노력을 아끼다.

— *vi.* (P1, 3) become loose; become less strict. 풀어지다; 느슨해지다. ¶ *Muscles ~ in sleep.* 자는 동안에 근육이 풀린다 / *~ in manner* 태도를 부드럽게 하다. [re-]

re·lax·a·tion [rìːlækséiʃən] *n.* Ⓤ **1** the act of loosening or making less strict. 풀림; 느슨해짐; 경감; 완화. ¶ *the ~ of the muscles* 근육의 이완 / 《*fig.*》 *the ~ of a rule* 규칙의 완화. **2** rest from effort or work; Ⓒ something providing amusement; recreation. 쉼; 휴양; 기분 전환(이 되는 것). ¶ *My chief relaxations are hunting and swimming.* 나의 주된 기분 전환거리는 사냥과 수영이다.

re·lay [ríːlei] *n.* Ⓒ **1** a fresh supply of men or horses to take over work from tired ones. 교대자; 교대마(馬). ¶ *New relays of troops were sent to the battlefront.* 새로운 병력이 전선에 투입되었다. **2** a relay race. 릴레이 경기. **3** 《Brit.》 an electric device to control a current. 계전기(繼電器). **4** (of radio or television) a program or broadcast sent from another station and rebroadcasted to the listeners. 중계 방송. ¶ *We listened to a ~ of the concert.* 콘서트 중계를 들었다.

work in* 〔*by*〕 *relays, work in turns. 교대로 일하다.

— [ríːlei, riléi] *vt.* (P6) **1** supply (new men, horses, etc.). …을 새로이 공급하다. **2** receive and then pass on (something). …을 중계하다. ¶ *~ a message.* **3** rebroadcast. 중계 방송하다. [F. *relaise*]

re-lay [riːléi] *vt.* (**-laid**) (P6,13) lay again. …을 다시 놓다. ¶ *That floor must be relaid.* 저 마루는 널을 다시 깔아야겠다. [re-]

relay race [⌐-⌐] *n.* a race between teams in which each member runs only one part of the course. 계주; 릴레이 경주. [→relay]

:re·lease [rilíːs] *vt.* (P6,13) **1** 《*from*》 set (someone) free; free (someone) from duties, suffering, a tax, etc. …을 해방〔석방〕하다; 면제하다. ¶ *~ someone from pain* 아무의 통증을 없애 주다 / *~ a prisoner* 죄수를 석방하다 / *~ someone from prison* 아무를 감옥에서 방면(放免)하다 / *The nurse is released from duty at seven o'clock.* 간호사는 일곱 시에 근무를 마친다 / *~ someone from his debt* 아무의 빚을 탕감해 주다 / *be released from cares* 시름이 가시다. **2** let (someone or something) go; unfasten. …을 놓다; 풀다. ¶ *The man released an arrow from his bow.* 그 사람은 활에서 화살을 날려 보냈다 / *Release the catch, and the box will open.* 고리를 풀면 상자가 열릴 거다. **3** allow (movies, books, news, etc.) to be shown, known, issued, etc. for the first time. …을 발표하다; 개봉(開封)하다. **4** 《law》 give (a claim, right, estate, etc.) to someone; surrender. (권리 등)을 양보하다.

— *n.* Ⓤ **1** ⓊⒸ the act of setting free; an order to set free; relief. 해방 (명령); 면제. ¶ *apply for ~ from duty* 의무의 면제를 신청하다 / *Lincoln proclaimed the ~ of the slaves.* 링컨은 노예 해방을 선언했다 / *After my examination I had a feeling of ~.* 시험이 끝나서 해방감을 느꼈다. **2** the act of letting go. 놓아 줌. **3** (of books, movies, news, etc.) the state of being released to the public; Ⓒ a book, film, etc. which has been releasd. (서적·영화 등의) 발표; 발간; 개봉; 발간된 서적; 개봉된 영화. **4** 《law》 the act of giving up (a claim or right); a document by which this is done. 기권; 양도 (증서). **5** 《mech.》 a device for holding or releasing a mechanism. 이완〔방기(放氣)〕 장치. [→relax]

rel·e·gate [réləgèit] *vt.* (P13) **1** 《*to*》 send (someone) to a lower position or grade; send (someone) into exile. …을 좌천하다; 추방하다. ¶ ~ *a battleship to the second class* 전함을 2급함으로 만들다 / ~ *one's old clothes to a bazar* 헌옷들을 시장에 내다 팔다 / ~ *an agitator beyond the city limits* 선동자를 시계(市界) 밖으로 몰아내다. **2** 《*to*》 hand over (a matter) for decision or carrying out. (처리·결정을 위해) …을 이관하다; …을 위임하다. ¶ ~ *a question to another authority* 문제를 다른 관할 당국에 넘기다 / ~ *a book to an upper shelf* 책을 윗 선반에 옮기다. [re-]

rel·e·ga·tion [rèləgéiʃən] *n.* Ⓤ the act of relegating; the state of being relegated. 좌천; 추방; (일 따위의) 위탁. [↑]

re·lent [rilént] *vi.* (P1) 《*at, toward*》 be more tender; become less harsh or cruel; yield to pity. (마음이) 누그러지다; 측은하게 여기다. ¶ *After hours of cruel treatment of the prisoners, the soldiers relented.* 포로들을 몇 시간 닥달하고 나서야 병사들은 직성이 풀렸다 / ~ *at the sight of misery* 참혹한 모양을 보고 측은해하다. [re-, L. *lentus* soft]

re·lent·less [riléntlis] *adj.* **1** without pity; cruel; harsh. 매정한; 잔혹한. ¶ *a* ~ *master* 인정머리없는 주인 / *a man with a* ~ *mind* 냉혹한 사람 / *Death is* ~. 죽음은 가차없다. **2** steady and persistent; continuous. 집요한; 지속적인. ¶ *a* ~ *noise* 신경질나는 소음.

re·lent·less·ly [riléntlisli] *adv.* cruelly; harshly. 가차없이; 잔혹하게.

rel·e·vance [réləvəns] *n.* Ⓤ the state of being relevant; being to the point. 관련; 적절. ¶ *His answer would thus come with more* ~ *and effect.* 따라서 그의 답변은 더욱 적절하고 효과적일 수 있다 / *It is of no* ~ *to the history of literature.* 그것은 문학사와는 아무 관련이 없다. [↓]

rel·e·van·cy [réləvənsi] *n.* =relevance.

rel·e·vant [réləvənt] *adj.* 《*to*》 **1** related; connected; proper. 관련된; 적절한(opp. irrelevant). ¶ *be* ~ *to the matter in hand* 지금의 이 문제와 관련되다 / *not* ~ *to the present question* 당면 문제와 무관하다. **2** to the point; pertinent. 적절한. [→relieve]

rel·e·vant·ly [réləvəntli] *adv.* in a relevant manner. 관련되어; 적절히.

re·li·a·bil·i·ty [rilàiəbíləti] *n.* Ⓤ the state or quality of being reliable; trustworthiness. 신뢰할 수 있음; 신빙〔확실〕성. ¶ *A machine has* ~ *when it can be counted on always to do what is expected of it.* 기계란 항상 소기의 구실을 할 수 있는 상태일 때 신뢰하게 된다 / *We want doctors to bear a stamp of* ~. 우리에겐 믿어도 된다는 정평이 나 있는 의사가 필요하다. [↓]

***re·li·a·ble** [riláiəbəl] *adj.* fit to be trusted or relied on; trustworthy; dependable. 의지가 되는; 믿을 수 있는; 확실한. ¶ *a* ~ *man* 믿음직한 남자 / *a* ~ *source of information* 믿을 수 있는 소식통 / *She may forgot to come. — She is not very* ~. 그녀는 온다는 걸 잊었을 거다 —별로 미덥지 못한 여자니까. [→rely]

re·li·a·bly [riláiəbəli] *adv.* in a reliable manner; to a reliable degree. 믿을 수 있도록; 확실하게〔히〕.

re·li·ance [riláiəns] *n.* **1** Ⓤ trust; confidence; dependence. 신뢰; 신용; 의지. ¶ *put* 〔*place*〕 ~ *in* 〔*on*〕 *another person* 엉뚱한 사람을 믿다 / *No* ~ *is to be placed on his word.* 그 사람 말은 믿을 게 못 된다. **2** Ⓒ something or someone relied on. 믿을 수 있는 사람〔것〕. ¶ *His chief* ~ *was his own courage.* 그가 믿는 것이란 자신의 용기뿐이었다. [→rely]

in reliance on 〔***upon***〕, trusting. …을 믿고. ¶ *wait in* ~ *on someone's promise* 아무의 약속을 믿고 기다리다.

re·li·ant [riláiənt] *adj.* **1** 《*on, upon*》 having trust, confidence, or dependence. 믿는; 의지하는. **2** relying on oneself. 자신을 믿는; 독립 독행의.

***rel·ic** [rélik] *n.* Ⓒ **1** 《*pl.*》 a thing or a custom that remains from the past. 유물; 유풍(遺風). ¶ *This ruined bridge is a* ~ *that reminds us of the war.* 이 부서진 다리가 그 전쟁을 생각나게 하는 유물이다 / *In the laws of modern peoples we can often trace the relics of ancient custom.* 현대인들의 관행에서 우리는 옛 풍속의 흔적들을 찾아볼 수 있다. **2** ruins remaining from the past. 유적. **3** 《*religion*》 a part of the body or an object kept as a sacred memorial of a saint, etc. (성인(聖人) 등의) 유골; 유품. ¶ *the pilgrimage to the relics of St. Thomas at Canterbury* 켄터베리에 있는 성(聖)토마스의 유품 순례. [re-, L. *linguo* leave]

:re·lief[1] [rilí:f] *n.* Ⓤ **1** ⓐ freedom from previous pain, trouble, difficulty, etc. (고통·어려움 등의) 제거; 경감; 안심. ¶ *draw a breath of* ~ 한숨 돌리다 / *give a patient* ~ *from pain* 환자의 고통을 덜어 주다 / *give a sigh of* ~ 안도의 한숨을 쉬다 / *feel a sense of* ~ 마음이 놓이다; 안심하다. ⓑ ⓊⒸ a thing, circumstance, etc. which affords relief from pain, trouble, etc. (고통·근심 등을) 덜어 주는 것; 안심〔위안〕을 주는 것. ¶ *A hot bath is a* ~ *after a long journey.* 긴 여행 후의 뜨거운 목욕은 여독을 풀어 준다 / *It was a great* ~ *to find that my family were all safe.* 식구 모두가 무사한 것을 알고 크게 안심했다. **2** help given to poor, aged or handicapped people. (빈민·장애자 등의) 구제; 원조. ¶ *a* ~ *fund* 구제 기금 / ~

works 취로 사업 / *Relief was quickly sent to the sufferers from the fire.* 화재 이재민에게 급히 원조 물자가 보내졌다. **3** help given or sent in time of need or danger. 구원; 구조. ¶ *Reinforcements were sent to the ~ of the garrison.* 수비대의 구원에 증원군이 파견되었다. **4** ⓐ release from work, duty, etc. 휴식. ¶ *He worked from noon untill dark with no ~.* 낮부터 어두워질 때까지 그는 쉬지도 않고 일했다. ⓑ remission. 면제. ¶ *A court may grant ~ from a fine.* 법원이 벌금 면제를 승인할 수도 있다. **5** the exchange of persons on duty; Ⓒ a person who replaces someone else in his work. 교대; 교체; 교대인. ¶ *the ~ of the workers* 노동자의 교체. [↓]

re·lief² [rilíːf] *n.* Ⓤ **1** (in sculpture) the projection of a figure from the flat surface; Ⓒ a piece of work so made. 돋을새김; 부조(浮彫); 양각 세공물(cf. *round*). ¶ *a ~ map* 입체 모형 지도 / *work carved in ~* 양각 세공품. **2** 《*fig.*》 distinctness. 두드러짐; 돋보임; 선명. ¶ *a figure* 〔*object*〕 *seen in ~ against the sky* 하늘을 배경으로 선명하게 보이는 사람 모습〔물체〕 / *His deeds stand out in bold ~.* 그의 행위는 돋보이는 바 있다.

:re·lieve [rilíːv] *vt.* (P6,13) **1** remove or reduce (pain or trouble); make easier. (고통·근심 등)을 제거하다; 경감하다; 덜다. ¶ *A cup of coffee relieved my tiredness.* 커피 한 잔 했더니 피곤한 게 풀렸다 / *We telephoned to ~ our mother's uneasiness.* 어머니가 걱정을 안 하시게 전화를 해 드렸다. **2** 《*of, from*》 set (someone) free from a burden or duty. …을 (무거운 짐·고통에서) 해방시키다. ¶ *~ someone from anxiety* …의 걱정을 없애 주다 / *I feel relieved to hear that.* 그 말 들으니 안심이다 / *Your coming relieves me of the bother of writing a long letter.* 네가 와서 긴 편지 쓰는 내 수고를 덜어 주는구나 / *Let me ~ you of that heavy parcel.* 그 무거운 보따리를 내가 들어 드리지요. **3** bring aid to; give help to (someone). …을 도와 주다; 구원하다. ¶ *~ the poor and needy* 가난하고 어려운 자를 돕다 / *Soldiers were sent to ~ the besieged city.* 포위된 도시를 구원하기 위해 군인들이 파견되었다. **4** make (someone) free from duty; take the place of (someone on duty). …와 교대하다. ¶ *~ a sentry* 보초를 교대하다 / *I will ~ you for the afternoon.* 오후에는 내가 교대해 주겠다. **5** send (someone) away from his position; send (someone) out of his own country as a punishment. …을 해임하다; 추방하다. ¶ *~ someone of his rank* 〔*office, position*〕 아무의 계급을〔직위를, 지위를〕 박탈하다 / *I have been relieved of my post at my own request.* 내 자의(自意)로 직장을 그만두었다 / *~ someone of his property* 아무의 재산을 빼앗다. **6** 《*against*》 make (something) sharply distinct; make (something) less monotonous. …을 돋보이게 하다; …에 변화를 주다. ¶ *His lectures were relieved by wit.* 그의 강의는 위트가 섞여 지루하지 않다 / *The black dress was relieved by white trimming.* 검은 드레스에 흰 트리밍으로 변화를 주었다 / *The white building is clearly relieved against the dark woods behind.* 흰 건물이 검은 숲을 배경으로 선명하게 돋보인다. [re-, L. *levo* lift]

relieve** one's **feelings, express one's feelings in some way, e.g. by weeping, and so make them easier to bear. (울거나 해서) 기분 전환을 하다; 감정을 풀다.

relieve nature 〔***the bowels, oneself***〕**,** evacuate bowels or bladder. 대소변을 보다.

:re·li·gion [rilídʒən] *n.* Ⓤ **1** belief in and worship of some superhuman power as the creator or ruler of the universe. 종교. **2** Ⓒ a particular system of worship, etc. 종파; …교. ¶ *the Buddhist ~* 불교. **3** Ⓤ devotion to a religious faith; a way of life based on this. 신앙(생활). ¶ *the life of ~* 신앙 생활 / *enter* (*into*) *~* 신앙 생활에 들어가다. **4** 《*fig.*》 an object of great devotion (=worship). 신조(信條). ¶ *The pursuit of success became a ~ to him.* 성공한다는 것이 그의 신조가 되었다. [L. *religio*]

make (***a***) ***religion of** doing something,* do something very seriously and without fail. 반드시 …하다. ¶ *He makes a ~ of making money.* 돈벌이가 그의 신조다.

:re·li·gious [rilídʒəs] *adj.* **1** of religion. 종교의; 종교상의. ¶ *a ~ ceremony* 종교 의식 / *~ duties* 성무(聖務); 종교적 의무 / *a ~ order* 수도회 / *~ books* 〔*wars*〕 종교 서적〔전쟁〕 / *~ ecstasy* 법열(法悅) / *a ~ house* 수도〔수녀〕원 / *She is very ~ and goes to church four times a week.* 신앙심이 대단해서 주에 네 번씩 교회에 간다. **2** 《*fig.*》 strict; done with great care. 엄격한; 세심한. ¶ *He keeps his promise with ~ care.* 그는 자기 약속에 엄격하다. **3** devoted to a religious faith. 신앙심이 깊은. — *n.* (*pl.* **religious**) **1** 《*a ~*》 a monk or nun; a member of a religious order. 수사(修士); 수녀. **2** 《*the ~, some ~, several ~;* used as *pl.*》 religious persons. 종교인.

re·li·gious·ly [rilídʒəsli] *adv.* in a religious manner; strictly. 종교적으로; 독실하게; 양심적으로.

re·lin·quish [rilíŋkwiʃ] *vt.* (P6) **1** give up (a plan, policy, habit, etc.). (계획 등)을 포기하다; 버리다. ¶ *She has relinquished all hope of going to Europe this year.* 그녀는 올해 유럽에 갈 희망은 아예 포기해 버렸다. **2** give (one's right, claim, etc.) to someone else; retire from. (권리 등)을 양도하다; 물러나다; 내놓다. ¶ *~ a position to the enemy* 진지를 적에게 내주다 / *lands relinquished by their former owners* 전 소유주로부터 양도된 땅. **3** stop holding or grasping (something). …을 놓다. ¶ *~ one's hold of a rope*

잡은 밧줄을 놓다. [→relic]

re·lish [réliʃ] *n.* **1** Ⓤ 《sometimes *a* ~》 a good flavor; a pleasant taste. 맛; 풍미(風味); 방향(芳香); 향기. ¶ *There is a ~ of the sea in the air.* 대기 중에 바다 냄새가 감돈다 / *a ~ of garlic* 마늘의 맛. **2** Ⓤ ⓐ a liking; enjoyment; pleasure. 기호; 즐거움. ¶ *He ate his meal with ~.* 그는 맛있게 식사를 했다. ⓑ 《*fig.*》 an attractive quality. 흥미; 의욕. ¶ *Danger gives ~ to an adventure.* 모험은 위험하기 때문에 의욕이 생긴다 / *Without betting, racing would lack its ~ for many.* 돈을 걸지 않고선 경마를 재미있어하는 사람은 별로 없을 게다. **3** ⒸⓊ anything served with food to give a pleasant taste. 조미료; 양념.

give relish to, make (something) taste better or enjoyable. …에 풍미를 더하다.

have no relish for, do not like at all. …에 흥미가 없다. ¶ *I have no ~ for poetry.* 난 시에는 흥미가 없다.

— *vt.* (P6) **1** enjoy; like; be pleased with; eat with pleasure. …을 즐기다; 맛있어하다. ¶ *~ gossip* 가십을 즐기다 / *~ one's food* 맛있게 먹다 / *I don't much ~ the prospect of a long journey.* 여행이 길어진다면 난 별로 생각이 없다. **2** give flavor to (something). …에 풍미를 더하다; 맛을 내다.

— *vi.* (P3) **1** 《*of*》 taste; have the flavor. …한 맛이 나다. ¶ *It relishes well.* 맛이 괜찮다 / *Greek wine relishes of resin.* 그리스 포도주는 송진 맛이 난다. **2** have a trace or suggestion. …한 기미가 있다. ¶ 《*fig.*》 *conversation which relishes of wit* 위트 있는 대화. [F. *reles* aftertaste]

re·load [riːlóud] *vt.* (P6) **1** put a load on (a cart, etc.) again. …에 다시 짐을 싣다. **2** charge (a gun) again. (총)에 다시 장전하다. ¶ *They were ordered to fire and ~.* 그들은 발포와 (동시에) 재장전 명령을 받았다. [re-, →load]

re·luc·tance [rilʌ́ktəns] *n.* Ⓤ **1** a feeling of not wanting to do something; unwillingness. 마음이 내키지 않음. ¶ *show ~ to make a reply* 대답하기 싫어하다. **2** 《electr.》 magnetic resistance. 자기(磁氣) 저항(抵抗). [↓]

without reluctance, willingly. 기꺼이.

with reluctance, unwillingly. 마지못해. ¶ *She agreed with ~ to take part in the game.* 마지못해 그녀는 경기에 참가했다.

·**re·luc·tant** [rilʌ́ktənt] *adj.* unwilling; disinclined. 마음 내키지 않는; 꺼리는. ¶ *She was ~ to marry.* 그녀는 결혼에 그다지 마음이 없었다 / *a ~ consent* 〔*answer*〕 마지못해 하는 동의〔답변〕 / *The policeman led the ~ boy to the principal.* 경찰은 싫어하는 아이를 데리고 교장에게 갔다. [re-, L. *luctor* struggle]

re·luc·tant·ly [rilʌ́ktəntli] *adv.* unwillingly. 마지못해.

·**re·ly** [rilái] *vi.* (**-lied**) (P3) 《*on, upon*》 depend; trust; have confidence. 의지하다; 믿다. ¶ *You can always ~ on me to do my best.* 내가 항상 너를 위해 최선을 다한다는 것을 믿어도 된다 / *He is not to be relied upon.* 그는 믿을 사람이 못된다 / *You may ~ upon it that he will be here early.* 그가 일찍 이리 올 것임을 믿어도 된다. [re-, →ligament]

re·made [riːméid] *v.* p. and pp. of **remake.**

:**re·main** [riméin] *vi.* **1** (P2A) stay; continue in the same place. (가지 않고) 있다; 체류하다. ¶ *~ abroad* 해외에 체류하다 / *~ at home* (외출하지 않고) 집에 있다 / *Only he remained in the room.* 그만이 방 안에 남아 있었다 / *The car remained where it was parked.* 차는 세워 둔 데에 그냥 있었다 / *He remained at his post.* 그는 현직에 그냥 있었다. **2** ⓐ (P1,3) be left after a part has been taken away. 남다; 잔존하다. ¶ *the years of life that ~* 여생 / *If you take 2 from 6, 4 remains.* 6에서 2를 빼면 4가 남는다 / *A few apples ~ on the table.* 탁자 위에 사과 몇 개가 남아 있다 / *The wall of the house still remains.* 가옥의 벽은 아직 남아 있다 / *with one's last remaining strength* 마지막 힘을 다해. ⓑ (P2,5) continue to exist; endure. 계속 있다; 지속하다. ¶ *Of the crew only three remained to tell the story.* 그 얘기를 할 선원은 셋밖에 남아 있지 않다 / *The fact remains that he has done his best.* 그가 최선을 다했다는 사실에는 변함이 없다. **3** (P4) be left to be done, told, etc. (…하지〔되지〕 않고) 그대로 있다. ¶ *Nothing remains but to wait for him.* 이젠 그를 기다리는 일뿐이다 / *Much remains to be done.* 할 일이 많이 남아 있다 / *That remains to be seen.* 두고 볼 일이다 / *The work remains to be finished.* 일이 덜 끝났다 / *There remains nothing to be said.* 할 말은 다했다. **4** (P1,3,5) continue to be; continue in the same state; go on being; keep. …한 대로이다; 여전히 …이다. ¶ *~ silent* 침묵을 지키다 / *The weather remained unsettled.* 날씨가 여전히 변화무쌍했다 / *Let it ~ as it is.* 그대로 둬라 / *I ~, yours truly* 〔*sincerely*〕. 경구(敬具)《편지 끝맺음 말》.

— *n.* Ⓒ 《usu. *pl.*》 **1** what is left; a person who is left. 남은 것〔사람〕. ¶ *the remains of a fortune* 남은 재산 / *The remains of the meal were fed to the dog.* 남은 음식을 개먹이로 주었다. **2** a dead body. 유해. ¶ *His remains are buried here.* 그는 여기 묻혀 있다. **3** 《*fig.*》 ancient ruins. 유적; 유물. ¶ *the remains of ancient Rome* 옛 로마의 유적 / *the remains of a country's glory* 〔*history*〕 한 나라의 영광〔역사〕의 자취. **4** the writings collected after the author's death. 유고(遺稿). [re-, →manor]

·**re·main·der** [riméindər] *n.* Ⓒ **1** 《usu. *the* ~》 the remaining people or things; the rest. 남은 사람들〔물건〕; 나머지. ¶ *He ate the ~ of the candy.* 그는 남은 과자를 먹

었다 / *The ~ of the company was lost.* 일행의 다른 사람은 행방 불명이 되었다 / *the ~ of the feast* 잔치의 남은 음식들 / *for the ~ of his life* 그의 여생을 위하여. **2** a book sold at a reduced price after sales have slowed. 떨이책; 덤핑책. **3** 《math.》 the number left after subtraction or division. 나머지; 잉여.

re·make [riːméik] *vt.* (**-made**) (P6) make again; make differently. …을 다시 만들다; 개작(改作)하다. [re-]

re·mand [rimǽnd, -máːnd] *vt.* (P6) **1** send (something) back. …을 돌려보내다. **2** 《law》 send (a prisoner) back to jail. …을 재(再)수감하다. — *n.* **1** Ⓤ the act of remanding; the state of being remanded. 반송; 재수감. **2** Ⓒ a person remanded. 재수감자. [re-, →mandate]

:re·mark [rimáːrk] *vt.* **1** (P6,11,12) 《rare》 notice; perceive; observe. …을 알아차리다; 인지하다; 주목하다. ¶ *We remarked his sad face.* 우리는 그의 슬픈 표정을 보았다 / *I remarked the heat as soon as I entered the room.* 방에 들자마자 후끈했다. **2** (P6,11) say or write (something) as a comment. (의견)을 말하다. ¶ *He remarked that I had better see the doctor.* 의사의 진찰을 받는 게 좋다고 그는 말했다 / *I should like to ~ that ....* 나는 …라고 말하고 싶다 / *Many writers have remarked that ....* 많은 필자들이 …에 언급해 왔다.

— *vi.* (P3) 《*on, upon*》 make a comment. 말하다; 언급〔논평〕하다. ¶ *He remarked upon the subjects.* 그는 그 문제에 대해 언급했다.

— *n.* **1** Ⓤ act of remarking; observation; notice. 주의; 관찰. ¶ *buildings, pictures, worthy of ~ by visitors* 방문객들이 주목할 만한 건물, 그림들 / *a matter of general ~* 세간의 이야깃거리. **2** Ⓒ a comment; what is said briefly. 논평; 촌평. ¶ *We laughed at his remarks.* 우리는 그의 말을 일소에 부쳤다 / *Did you make 〔pass〕 a ~ on the subject?* 그 문제에 대해 뭐라고 말했나 / *Let it pass without ~.* 묵인해라; 덮어 둬라. [re-]

the theme of general remark, the topic talked about by everybody. 항간의 화젯거리.

***re·mark·a·ble** [rimáːrkəbəl] *adj.* worthy of notice; extraordinary; unusual. 주목할 만한. ¶ *He has a ~ memory.* 기억력이 대단한 사람이다 / *a ~ event* 놀라운 사건 / *make oneself too ~* 너무 유별나게 굴다 / *It is ~ that I should not have been told.* 내게 얘기가 없었던 것은 이상한 일이다 / *He is ~ for his cleverness.* 그는 매우 영리하다.

re·mark·a·bly [rimáːrkəbəli] *adv.* in a remarkable way; to a remarkable degree. 두드러지게; 매우; 상당히.

re·mar·riage [riːmǽridʒ] *n.* ⓊⒸ the act of marrying again. 재혼. [↓]

re·mar·ry [riːmǽri] *vt., vi.* (P6;1) marry again. 재혼하다. ¶ *Widows might ~, if they like.* 과부도 제가 좋다면 재혼할 수 있다. [re-]

re·me·di·a·ble [rimíːdiəbəl] *adj.* that can be remedied; curable. 치료할 수 있는; 구제〔교정〕 가능한. [→remedy]

re·me·di·al [rimíːdiəl] *adj.* intending or helping to cure; of a remedy; providing a remedy. 치료의〔를 위한〕; 치료〔교정〕용의. ¶ *~ laws 〔punishment〕* 수정적 법률〔교정적 처벌〕 / *~ treatment* 치료. [↓]

:rem·e·dy [rémədi] *n.* ⓊⒸ (*pl.* **-dies**) **1** a medicine or a treatment that cures a disease. 의약; 치료; 의료. ¶ *a ~ for a cold* 감기약 / *home remedies* 민간 요법. **2** a method of removing any bad condition. 교정법; 구제책. ¶ *There is no ~ but to....* …할 밖에 다른 도리가 없다 / *There is no wrong without a ~.* 못 고칠 잘못은 없다 / *beyond 〔past〕 ~* 고칠 방법이 없는; 구제 불능의 / *The law provides no ~ for this injustice.* 법이 이런 부정을 바로잡지 못한다.

— *vt.* (P6) **1** cure. …을 치료하다. ¶ *~ a cough.* **2** repair; correct. …을 수리〔보수〕하다; 교정하다. ¶ *~ a leak in a pipe* 관의 새는 구멍을 막다 / *~ social evils* 사회악을 시정하다. [re-, →medicine]

:re·mem·ber [rimémbər] *vt.* **1** (P6,9,10,11,12) keep (someone or something) in the memory. …을 기억하고 있다(opp. forget). ¶ *~ what is told* 들은 말을 기억하고 있다 / *I ~ seeing him once.* =*I ~ that I saw him once.* 그를 한번 만난 기억이 있다. 語法 ~ having seen이 정확하나 ~ seeing이 보통임 / *I don't ~ how to open the safe.* 이 금고를 어떻게 여는지 잊었다 / *I ~ her as a girl.* 그녀를 소녀로 기억하고 있다 / *I remembered suddenly that I had an appointment.* 갑자기 나는 약속이 생각났다. **2** (P8) be careful not to forget. 잊지 않고 …하다(opp. forget). ¶ *Remember to write to him.* 그에게 편지 내는 것을 잊지 마라. 語法 ~ to do는 미래, ~ doing은 과거일 때 씀 / *Remember to call me if anything happens.* 무슨 일이 생기거든 내게 꼭 전화해라. **3** (P6,9,10,11,12) call back (something or someone) to mind by an effort of will; have (something) come into one's memory again. …을 생각해 내다; …을 상기하다. ¶ *~ oneself* 퍼뜩 생각나다 / *I just can't ~ him 〔his〕 saying so.* 그가 그런 말을 했는지 좀처럼 생각이 나질 않는다 / *I can't ~ anything that happened on the day.* 그 날 무슨 일이 있었는지 기억이 안 난다 / *I know your face, but cannot ~ your name.* 당신 얼굴은 알겠는데 이름이 기억나지 않아요 / *I can't ~ where 〔when〕 it was.* 그것이 어딘지〔언젠지〕 생각이 안 난다 / *Oh, yes, I ~.* 아, 그렇지, 생각난다 / *I ~ that she was wearing a large hat.* 그녀가 큰 모자를 쓰고 있었던 것이 기억납니다. **4** (P6,13) give (someone) a present or tip; leave (someone) some money or a piece of property. …에 선물하다; …에 유산을 남기다. ¶ ~ *someone in one's will* 유언으로 아무에게 유산을 주다 / *My dead uncle remembered me in his will.* 작고한 숙부가 유언장에 내 이름을 적으셨다 / ~ *a child on its birthday* 아이한테 생일 선물을 주다. **5** (P13) 《*to*》 mention (someone) to another as sending greetings. …로부터 안부를 전하다. ¶ *Remember me* (*kindly*) *to Mr. A.* A씨에게 안부 전해 주시오 / *He wished to be remembered to you.* 그가 당신의 안부를 물었습니다.

— *vi.* (P1) **1** possess the power of memory. 기억력이 있다. ¶ *As a person gets older he does not* ~ *as he used to.* 사람이 늙어 가면 기억이 전만 못해진다. **2** (P1,3) 《*of*》 have in mind; call back to mind. 기억하다; 생각나다. ¶ *as I* ~ 내 기억으로는 / *She remembered of her aged mother.* 그녀는 노모의 생각이 났다. [re-, →memory]

*__re·mem·brance__ [rimémbrəns] *n.* **1** Ⓤ Ⓒ the act of remembering; the state of being remembered; memory. 기억; 추상; 추억. ¶ *a sad* ~ 슬픈 추억 / *That has long passed from my* ~. 그 일은 잊은 지 오래다. **2** Ⓤ the power to remember. 기억력. **3** Ⓒ a thing which reminds someone of a person, an event, etc.; a souvenir; a memento. 기억나게 하는 것; 기념품. ¶ *I sent a small* ~. 작은 기념품을 하나 보냈다. **4** 《*pl.*》 《used in a letter》 greetings. 전언(傳言); 안부. ¶ *Give my kind remembrances to your mother.* 어머님께 안부 여쭈어 주십시오 / *send remembrances to all* 모두에게 안부 전하다. [→remember, -ance]

bear* 〔*have, keep*〕 *something in remembrance, keep something in mind; remember. …을 기억하다.

bring something to remembrance, cause someone to remember something. …을 생각나게 하다.

call to remembrance, call back to mind. …을 생각해 내다; 회상하다.

come to remembrance, come into one's mind. …이 기억나다.

escape one's remembrance, cannot be remembered. …을 잊다.

have no remembrance of, do not remember (something) at all. …이 전혀 기억에 없다.

in remembrance of (=*in memory of*) *something.* …의 기념으로.

It comes to my remembrance that …. I remember that …. …기억이 난다.

:**re·mind** [rimáind] *vt.* (P6,13,15,16,17,20) 《*of*》 make (someone) think of (something); cause (someone) to remember. …을 생각나게 하다. ¶ *You* ~ *me of your father.* 너를 보니 네 아버지 생각이 난다 / *That reminds me.* 그래서 생각났다 / *Please* ~ *me to write tomorrow.* 내일 편지 쓰도록 내게 일러 다오 / *This picture reminds me of a story I heard.* 이 그림을 보니 내가 들은 이야기가 생각난다. [re-]

re·mind·er [rimáindər] *n.* Ⓒ a person or thing that reminds. 생각나게 하는 사람〔것〕. ¶ *My note will serve as a* ~ *of our appointment.* 내 메모를 보면 우리가 약속한 일을 알게 될 것이다 / *He hadn't paid the bill, so the shop sent him a* ~. 그가 셈을 치르지 않아서 상점은 그에게 청구서를 보냈다.

rem·i·nis·cence [rèmənísns] *n.* **1** Ⓤ the act of recalling past experience; recollection. 회상. **2** Ⓒ something remembered; a memory. 기억; 추억. ¶ *a faint* ~ *of what happened* 무슨 일이 있었는지의 희미한 기억. **3** 《*pl.*》 a story of interesting events in one's life remembered. 회고담. ¶ *an old man's* ~ 한 늙은이의 회고담 / *We listened his* ~ *of the war.* 우리는 그 전쟁에 대한 그의 회고담을 들었다. **4** Ⓒ a thing that suggests something else; a reminder. 생각나게 하는 것〔일〕. [L. *reminiscor* remember]

rem·i·nis·cent [rèmənísnt] *adj.* **1** talking of or recalling past events. 추억의; 추억에 잠기는. ¶ ~ *talk* 회고담. **2** having the habit of recalling the past. 회고적인. ¶ *Old men are likely to become* ~. 노인들은 회고적이 되기 쉽다. **3** 《*of*》 bringing to mind something else; suggestive. 생각나게 하는; 시사하는. ¶ *a villa built in a style* ~ *of an ancient castle* 옛 성곽을 방불케 지은 별장 / *a taste* ~ *of chicken* 닭고기 같은 맛.

re·miss [rimís] *adj.* 《as *predicative*》 **1** 《*in*》 careless in duty; neglectful. 부주의한; 게으른; 굼뜬. ¶ *be* ~ *in one's duty* 직무에 태만하다 / ~ *in one's payment* 셈이 흐린 / *He has been* ~ *in his work.* 늘 일에 굼뜨다. **2** lacking force or energy. 나약한; 무기력한. [→remit]

re·mis·si·ble [rimísəbəl] *adj.* that can be remitted. 용서할 수 있는; 면제해도 좋은.

re·mis·sion [rimíʃən] *n.* **1** Ⓤ Ⓒ the act of remitting; discharge of debt, punishment, etc. (빚·벌 따위의) 면제; 용서. ¶ *gain* ~ 용서받다 / *the* ~ *of sins* 사죄(赦罪) / *the* ~ *of a debt* 빚의 탕감 / ~ *of taxation* 〔*a penalty, punishment*〕 세금〔벌금, 처벌〕 면제. **2** Ⓤ Ⓒ forgiveness of sins or crimes; pardon. (죄 따위의) 사면. **3** Ⓤ the act of lessening pain or a disease. (고통·병 등의) 경감; 차도. ¶ *The disease went into* ~ *last month.* 지난 달 병에 차도를 보였다.

re·miss·ness [rimísnis] *n.* Ⓤ the state of being remiss. 부주의; 태만.

re·mit [rimít] *v.* (**-mit·ted, -mit·ting**) *vt.* **1** (P6) forgive or pardon (sins). (죄)를 용서하다. **2** (P6) cancel (a penalty, a tax, etc.); refrain from exacting. (벌·세금 등)을 면제하다. ¶ *The judge remitted the prison sentence.* 판사는 금고형을 면제했다 / ~ *a fine* 벌금을 면제하다. **3** (P6) make (something) less; lessen; decrease. …을 경감하다; 완화하다. ¶ ~ *one's anger* 부아를 누그러

뜨리다 / ~ *one's efforts* 노력을 아끼다. **4** (P6,13) send (money). (돈을) 보내다; 송금하다. ¶ ~ *money by post* 우편으로 송금하다 / ~ *goods by railway* 철도편으로 물건을 보내다. **5** (P6) put off; postpone. …을 연기하다. ¶ ~ *a matter to* 〔*till*〕 *a certain date* 어떤 일을 어느 날로〔날까지〕 미루다. **6** (P6,13) ⓐ take or send (a question to be decided) to some authority. (결정)을 당국에 위탁〔위임〕하다; 넘기다. ⓑ 《law》 send (a case) to a lower court for further consideration. (송사)를 하급 법원에 환송하다.

— *vi.* (P1,2A) **1** send money (as in payment). 송금하다. ¶ *Enclosed is our bill; please remit.* 계산서를 동봉하오니 송금을 부탁합니다. **2** become less. 누그러지다. ¶ *The fever has remitted.* 열이 내렸다 / *His anger remitted a little.* 그의 화가 좀 풀렸다. [re-, →missile]

re·mit·tance [rimítəns] *n.* Ⓤ the act of sending money; Ⓒ the sum of money sent. 송금; 송금한 돈; 송금액. ¶ *make* (*a*) ~ 송금하다 / *He sends her a small* ~ *each month.* 그녀에게 매달 조금씩 송금한다 / *We will forward the goods on* ~ *of* £*20.* 20 파운드 송금하시면 물건을 보내 드리겠습니다.

remittance man [–⌐– ⌐] *n.* 《esp. Brit.》 a man living in a distant country on money sent to him from home. 본국에서의 송금으로 사는 사람《게으른 자의 표본》.

*__rem·nant__ [rémnənt] *n.* Ⓒ **1** 《often *pl.*》 ⓐ something left over after use; food, etc. left. 먹다 남은 것. ¶ *the remnants of a feast* 잔치에서 남은 음식. ⓑ odds and ends, short pieces of cloth, etc. left over after the greater part has been sold. 자투리. ¶ *a* ~ *sale* 떨이 판매. **2** 《*fig.*》 a small part left. 자취; 흔적. ¶ *the last remnants of courage* 〔*strength*〕 마지막 남은 용기〔힘〕 / *a* ~ *of ancient custom* 〔*belief*〕 고대 풍습〔신앙〕의 자취. [→remain]

re·mod·el [riːmádl / -mɔ́dl] *vt.* (**-eled, -el·ing** or 《Brit.》 **-elled, -el·ling**) (P6,13) make (something) again; remold. …을 고쳐 만들다; 개조하다; 본〔형〕을 고치다. ¶ ~ *a dress* 드레스를 개조하다 / ~ *an old barn into a house* 낡은 헛간을 집으로 개조하다 / ~ *the party program* 〔*a play, a novel*〕 파티 진행표를〔극·소설의 내용을〕 바꾸다. [re-]

re·mold [riːmóuld] *vt.* (P6) make or shape again. …을 개조하다; …의 형〔본〕을 고치다. [re-]

re·mon·strance [rimánstrəns / -mɔ́n-] *n.* ⓊⒸ protest; complaint; a strong objection; advice. (강한) 항의; 항변; 충고. ¶ *say in* ~ *that …* …라고 항의하다 / *loud cries of* ~ 요란한 항의 / *make remonstrances with someone against his conduct* 아무의 행위에 관해 충고하다. [→remonstrate]

re·mon·strant [rimánstrənt / -mɔ́n-] *adj.* remonstrating; objecting; protesting. 항의하는; 충고의. — *n.* Ⓒ a person who remonstrates. 항의〔충고〕자. [↓]

re·mon·strate [rimánstreit / -mɔ́n-] *vi.* (P3) 《*with, against, on*》 urge reasons in opposition; protest; complain. 항의하다; 나무라다; 충고하다. ¶ ~ *against someone's behavior* 아무의 (잘못된) 태도를 고치도록 충고하다 / *I remonstrated with him about his treatment of his friends.* 그의 친구를 대하는 태도를 나무랐다. — *vt.* (P6,11) say in protest, objection, etc. …을 항의하다; …에 항의하여 말하다. [re-, L. *monstro* show]

*__re·morse__ [rimɔ́ːrs] *n.* Ⓤ the deep regret for one's past wrong-doing; a sense of guilt. 후회; 자책; 양심의 가책(cf. *repentance*). ¶ *feel a twinge of* ~ *for one's past* 자신의 과거에 대하여 심한 양심의 가책을 느끼다 / *The child felt* ~ *for having stolen the money.* 그 아이는 돈 훔친 것을 뉘우쳤다 / *He was filled with* ~ *after hitting the child.* 그는 아이를 때리고 나서 몹시 후회했다. [re-, →mordant]

without remorse, pitilessly. 가차〔사정〕 없이.

re·morse·ful [rimɔ́ːrsfəl] *adj.* feeling or showing remorse. 뉘우치는; 후회하는.

re·morse·less [rimɔ́ːrslis] *adj.* having no pity; merciless; cruel. 무자비〔무정〕한; 잔인한.

*__re·mote__ [rimóut] *adj.* (**-mot·er, -mot·est**) **1** (of a place or space) distant; far away; set apart. 먼; 멀리 떨어진; 외진. ¶ *a* ~ *place* 먼 곳; 멀리 떨어져 있는 곳 / *a house* ~ *from the village* 마을에서 멀리 떨어진 외따로 있는 집 / *live* ~ *from the town* 읍에서 멀리 떨어진 곳에서 살다 / *a* ~ *village* 벽촌. **2** (of time) far from the present. (시간적으로) 현재(現在)에서 떨어진; 먼. ¶ *in the* ~ *past* 〔*future*〕 아득한 과거에〔미래〕에 / *a custom of* ~ *antiquity* 먼 옛날의 풍습. **3** distant in relation, connection, etc. 관계가 먼; 간접적인. ¶ *a* ~ *relative* 먼 친척 / *a* ~ *cause* 원인(遠因) / *a* ~ *effect* 간접적인 영향 / *The connection between these two ideas is very* ~. 두 가지 이념은 관련성이 별로 없다. **4** (of an intention, idea, etc.) slight; faint. 근소한; 미미한. ¶ *a* ~ *possibility* 만에 하나의 가능성 / *I haven't the remotest* 〔*have only a* ~ 〕 *idea* (*of*) *what you mean.* 네가 무엇을 말하려는 것인지 도무지 모르겠다 / *There's not the remotest chance of success.* 성공은 어림도 없다. **5** (of behavior, etc.) not showing interest in others. 무관심한; 쌀쌀〔냉담〕한. ¶ *a* ~ *air* 쌀쌀맞은 태도 / *Her manner was polite but* ~. 그녀는 정중했으나 쌀쌀맞은 태도였다. [→remove]

remote control [–⌐ –⌐] *n.* **1** the control of a machine, weapon, etc. from a distance, esp. by radio waves. (기계·무기 따위의) 원격 제어〔조정〕. **2** a hand-held device used to control the operation of a television set, etc. (TV 따위의) 리모컨.

re·mote·ness [rimóutnis] *n.* Ⓤ the

state of being remote. 멂; 원격; 무관계.

re·mould [rimóuld] *vt.* 《Brit.》 =remold.

re·mount [ri:máunt] *vt.* (P6) **1** mount again. (말)에 다시 타다; …에 다시 오르다. ¶ *The fallen rider remounted his horse.* 낙마한 기수는 다시 말에 올라탔다 / *The soldiers remounted the hill.* 병사들은 다시 산을 올라갔다. **2** 《mil.》 furnish with fresh horses. 새로 말을 공급하다. **3** put (a precious stone) in a new metal setting. (보석)을 갈아끼우다.
— *vi.* (P1,3) **1** mount again. 다시 올라타다. **2** go back to. 거슬러 올라가다. ¶ *The origin of these customs remounts to a primitive state of society.* 이들 관습의 기원은 원시사회에로 소급된다 / *Royal pedigrees often ~ to the remotest antiquity.* 왕통(王統)은 흔히 태고에까지로 거슬러 올라간다.
— [rí:màunt] *n.* Ⓒ 《mil.》 a fresh horse to replace another. (갈아 탈) 새 말; 보충[예비]마. [re-]

re·mov·a·ble [rimú:vəbəl] *adj.* that can be removed (from a place or office). 옮길 수 있는; 제거[면직]할 수 있는. ¶ *~ faults* 없앨 수 있는 결함. [re-]

***re·mov·al** [rimú:vəl] *n.* **1** ⓊⒸ the act of removing; the state of being removed; change of place. 이동; 이전. ¶ *the ~ of furniture* 가구의 이전[이동] / *a ~ to a new house* 새 집으로의 이사. **2** Ⓤ dismissal. 면직; 해임. ¶ *the ~ of a judge* 판사의 해임. **3** ⓊⒸ taking away; getting rid of. 제거; 배제. ¶ *snow ~* 제설 / *~ of grievance* 불만의 제거[해소] / *demand the ~ of the U.N. troops* 유엔군의 철수를 요구하다. [↓]

:re·move [rimú:v] *vt.* **1** (P6,13) 《*from*》 move (something) from a place; take away; withdraw. …을 옮기다; 이전하다; 치우다. ¶ *~ oneself* 물러가다 / *~ one's hand* 손을 치우다[떼다] / *~ the dishes from the table* 식탁에서 접시들을 치우다 / *~ one's eyes from the book* 책에서 눈을 떼다. **2** (P6) take off. …을 벗다. ¶ *Remove your hat.* 모자를 벗으시오 / *~ one's coat* [*boots, spectacles*] 코트를[신발을, 안경을] 벗다 / *~ one's hat* (*as in greeting*) 모자를 들어 인사하다. **3** (P6,13) wipe out; get rid of; kill. …을 닦아 내다; 제거하다; …을 죽이다. ¶ *~ stains* 얼룩을 닦아 내다 / *~ a name from a list* 명단에서 이름을 지우다 / *~ the cause of a doubt* 의혹의 원인을 제거하다 / *He was removed by poison.* 그는 독살당했다 / *an operation to ~ the tumor* 종양 제거 수술 / *~ all grounds of complaint* 불평의 소지(素地)를 없애다. **4** (P6,13) 《*from, for*》 dismiss (someone) from an official position; transfer (someone) to another post. …을 물러나게 하다; 면직시키다. ¶ *~ one's son from school on account of ill health* 건강이 나빠서 아들을 퇴학시키다 / *The governor removed the mayor for failing to do his duty.* 지사는 시장을 직무 태만으로 면직시켰다. — *vi.* (P1,2A,3) go from one place to another; change residence. 옮기다; 이사하다. ¶ *~ to London* 런던으로 이사하다 / *~ into the country* 시골로 이사하다.
remove mountains, perform a miracle. 기적을 행하다.
— *n.* Ⓒ **1** a degree of distance; one step in a scale of distances; a specified distance in relationship. 거리; 간격(의 단계); 촌수. ¶ *at a certain ~* 좀 떨어져서 보면 / *a cousin at first ~* 사촌의 아들; 친조카 / *see a painting at a ~* 조금 거리를 두고 그림을 보다 / *Genius is only one ~ from insanity.* 천재와 광인은 백지 한 장의 차이다 / *He is many removes from the wild days of his youth.* 그는 젊어서의 거칠었던 생활에 비하면 지금은 달라도 많이 다르다. **2** 《rare》 a move; a change of residence. 이전(移轉); 이사. ¶ 《*prov.*》 *Three removes are as bad as a fire.* 이사 세 번이면 살림은 거덜난다. **3** 《Brit.》 a promotion to a higher class. 진급. ¶ *He has not got his ~.* 그는 진급을 못 했다. [re-, →move]

re·moved [rimú:vd] *adj.* **1** 《*from*》 remote; distant; not connected. 떨어진; 무관계의. ¶ *motives entirely ~ from self-interest* 사욕(私慾)과는 아주 거리가 먼[무관계한] 동기 / *What you say is far ~ from what you said before.* 지금의 네 말은 전에 했던 것과는 사뭇 다르다. **2** separated by a specified number of degrees of relationship. (척분(戚分)이) …촌(寸)의. ¶ *a cousin once ~* 육촌.

re·mov·er [rimú:vər] *n.* Ⓒ a person or thing that removes. 제거하는[지우는] 사람[것]; 제거제; 이전자. ¶ *a stain ~* 얼룩 제거제 / *a paint ~* 페인트 제거제.

re·mu·ner·ate [rimjú:nərèit] *vt.* (P6,13) pay (someone) for work, service, loss, trouble, etc.; make up for (something); reward. …에 보수[수고비]를 주다; 배상[보답]하다. ¶ *~ someone for his trouble* [*work, labor*] …에게 수고비를[품삯을] 주다 / *The boy who returned the lost jewels was remunerated.* 잃어버린 보석을 돌려 준 아이에게 사례를 했다 / *The harvest will ~ the laborers for their toil.* 수고한 일꾼들에겐 추수가 보답할 것이다. [re-, L. *munus* reward]

re·mu·ner·a·tion [rimjù:nəréiʃən] *n.* Ⓤ the act of remunerating; reward; pay; compensation. 보수; 보상.

re·mu·ner·a·tive [rimjú:nərèitiv / -nərə-] *adj.* rewarding; profitable. 보수가 있는; 유리한. ¶ *a ~ position* [*salary*] 괜찮은 자리[보수] / *a ~ business* 수지맞는 장사 / *a ~ deal* 유리한 거래.

***ren·ais·sance** [rènəsá:ns, -zá:ns, ⌐–⌐ / rinéisəns] *n.* **1** Ⓒ cultural or artistic revival. (문화·예술의) 부흥; 부활. ¶ *a ~ of the theater* [*popular music*] 연극[대중 음악]의 부활. **2** 《*the R-*》 the great revival in art and literature in Europe in the 14th, 15th, and 16th centuries; the period when this revival occurred; the style of art, literature, etc. of this period. 문예 부흥(기(期)); 르네상스의 미술·문예의 양식. ¶ *Renaissance sculpture* 르네상스식 조각. [re-, →nascent]

re·nal [ríːnəl] *adj.* of the kidneys. 콩팥의; 신장의. [→reins]

re·name [riːnéim] *vt.* (P6) give a new name to (someone or something). …의 이름을 바꾸다. ¶ *The street has been renamed Silver Lane.* 거리의 이름은 Silver Lane 으로 바뀌었다. [re-]

re·nas·cence [rinǽsəns] *n.* Ⓒ **1** a new birth; revival. 신생; 부활. ¶ *the ~ of plants in spring* 봄의 초목의 신생 / *a ~ of religion* 종교 부흥. **2** 《*the R-*》 =the Renaissance. [→renaissance]

re·nas·cent [rinǽsənt] *adj.* showing new life; reviving. 재생한; 부활한. [↑]

rend [rend] *v.* (**rent**) *vt.* (P6,7,13) **1** break (cloth, etc.) by pulling apart violently; tear. …을 (잡아) 찢다. ¶ *~ one's garments* 옷을 잡아 찢다 / 《*fig.*》 *A terrible cry rent the air.* 끔찍한 비명 소리가 허공을 갈랐다. **2** split (something) violently. …을 쪼개다; 분열시키다. ¶ *a party rent by factions* 여러 당파로 분열된〔쪼개진〕 당. **3** 《*from, away, off*》 take (something or someone) away violently. …을 빼앗다〔강탈하다〕. ¶ *~ a child from his mother* 아이를 어머니로부터 빼앗다. **4** disturb violently. …을 헤집어 놓다. ¶ 《*fig.*》 *~ the feelings* 감정을 헤집어 놓다. — *vi.* (P1) tear or split apart. 찢어지다; 쪼개지다; 분열하다. [E.]

:ren·der [réndər] *vt.* **1** (P6,7,13) 《*to, for*》 give (something) in return; give (something due or owed); show (obedience, etc.). …을 돌려 주다; 갚다; …에 치르다; 바치다; (복종심 등)을 나타내다. ¶ *~ thanks to God* 하느님께 감사하다 / *~ good for evil* 악을 선으로 갚다 / *~ honor to someone* 아무에게 명예를 돌리다 / *~ a present to a conqueror* 정복자에게 공물을 바치다 / *~ blow for blow* 한 대 맞으면 한 대 치다; 주먹엔 주먹으로 / *He asked so much of his servants and rendered so little.* 그는 하인들을 잔뜩 부려먹기만 하고 그 대가는 거의 치르지 않았다 / *~ obedience to one's lawful superior* 법을 준수하는 상관에게 순종하다. **2** (P6,13,14) give; provide; do (a service, etc.). (남에게 원조 등)을 주다; …을 하다. ¶ *~ someone assistance* =*~ assistance to someone* 아무를 도와 주다〔원조하다〕 / *~ help in time of need* 필요할 때 도와 주다 / *Can I ~ any help?* 뭣 좀 도와 드릴까요 / *What service has he rendered to the school?* 그가 학교를 위해서 무슨 도움을 주었지. **3** (P6,13) present (an account for payment, a statement, etc.). (계산서·설명서 등)을 내다〔건네다〕; 제출하다. ¶ *~ an account* 〔*a bill*〕 *for payment to a customer* 손님에게 계산서를 건네다 / *an account rendered* 지불 청구서 / *The committee rendered a report.* 위원회는 보고서를 제출했다. **4** (P18,19) make; cause (someone or something) to be or become. …을 —이 되게 하다〔—로 하다〕. ¶ *Running render me tired.* 뛰니까 피곤하다 / *My efforts were rendered useless.* 애는 썼는데 헛수고가 되었다 / *An accident has rendered him very cautious* 사고를 한 번 당하자 그는 매우 조심스러워졌다 / *He was rendered speechless with anger.* 화가 나서 말이 제대로 나오지 않았다. **5** (P6,7,13) hand over; deliver; give up; surrender. …을 넘겨 주다; (말 따위)를 전하다; 명도〔양도〕하다; 포기하다. ¶ *~ a message* 말을 전하다; 전갈(傳喝)하다 / *They rendered up their city to the enemy.* 적군에게 도시를 내주었다. **6** (P6) play; perform; express artistically. …을 연기하다; 예술적으로 표현하다. ¶ *The piano solo was well rendered.* 피아노 독주는 훌륭하였다 / *~ the part of Hamlet* 햄릿역을 하다 / *A portrait renders a personality.* 개성을 표출한 초상화 / *She rendered the song beautifully.* 그 곡을 아름답게 불렀다. **7** (P6,13) 《*into*》 change from one language to another; translate. …을 번역하다. ¶ *Render that Korean proverb into English.* 그 우리 나라 속담을 영어로 옮겨라 / *~ the sense of the original in a translation* 번역에서 원문(原文)의 뜻을 제대로 나타내다. **8** (P6,7) make pure by melting; melt (fat, etc.). …을 녹여서 정제하다. ¶ *Fat from pigs is rendered into lard.* 돼지 비계는 녹여서 라드로 정제된다. **9** (P6) apply a coat of plaster directly to. 초벌〔초벽〕질을 하다. [re-, L. *do* give]

render an account of, give an account of; tell about; tell of. …을 설명하다; 이야기하다. ¶ *The committee rendered an account of all the money spent.* 위원회는 모든 지출 내역을 설명했다 / *~ an account of one's actions* 자기 행동의 연유를 말하다.

ren·der·ing [réndəriŋ] *n.* ⓊⒸ **1** submitting; presentation. 제출. **2** payment. 지불; 청산. **3** giving; giving in return. 반환; 보답. **4** depicting. 묘사; 표출(表出). **5** performance; presentation. 연출; 연주; 연기. **6** translation. 번역. **7** making. 작성. **8** melting. 용해(溶解). **9** coating with plaster. 초벌칠.

ren·dez·vous [rɑ́ːndivùː / rɔ́n-] *n.* Ⓒ (*pl.* **-vous** [-vuːz]) **1** a meeting by appointment. (약속에 의한) 만남; 랑데부; 데이트. ¶ *He made a ~ with his girlfriend.* 그는 애인과 데이트를 했다. **2** ⓐ an appointed place for meeting; an assembling place for troops or ships. (예정된) 회합 장소; (군대·함선의) 지정 집결지. ⓑ a popular or fixed place for meeting. 인기 있는〔정해진〕 만남의 장소. ¶ *The park was our favorite ~.* 그 공원은 우리가 즐겨 만나는 정해진 장소였다 / *This club is a ~ for writers.* 이 클럽은 작가들이 잘 모이는 곳이다. **3** an appointment to meet at a certain time or place. (회합의) 약속.

— *vi., vt.* (P1;6) meet at a certain time or place. (어떤 장소에) 모이다; (예정 장소에) 모으다《군대 등을》. [F.=betake yourselves]

ren·di·tion [rendíʃən] *n.* Ⓒ **1** performance of music; performance of a part in a drama, etc. 연주; 출연. **2** translation. 번역. [*render*]

ren·e·gade [rénigèid] *n.* Ⓒ a person who changes his religion or political beliefs; a deserter; a traitor. 배교자; 변절자; 탈당자; 배반자. [re-, →negation]

:re·new [rinjúː] *vt.* (P6) **1** make (something) new, fresh, or strong again. …을 다시 새롭게〔젊게, 강하게〕하다. ¶ *The moon renews itself.* 달은 다시 신월이 된다 / *His coat was renewed in places.* 그의 코트는 군데군데 기운 곳이 있었다. **2** put back (an original spirit, freshness, etc.) as it was. (원기·신선함 등)을 되찾다; 부흥하다. ¶ ~ *one's health* 건강을 되찾다 / ~ *one's youth* 되젊어지다. **3** begin (something) again; repeat. …을 재개하다; 되풀이하다. ¶ ~ *one's demands* 〔*complaint*〕 요구〔항의〕를 되풀이하다 / ~ *an attack* 공격을 재개하다 / ~ *an old quarrel* 묵은 분쟁(紛爭)을 다시 시작하다 / ~ *a former practice* 구습을 답습하다. **4** replace (something) by something new of the same kind; fill (something) again. …을 (똑같은 종류의) 새것과 대체하다; 다시 채우다. ¶ *She renews the sleeves of her dress.* 옷소매를 갈았다 / *The well renews itself no matter how much water is taken away.* 우물은 아무리 물을 퍼내도 다시 채워지곤 한다 / ~ *the water in a tank* 탱크의 물을 다시 (가득) 채우다. **5** extend (a contract, etc.). (계약 등)을 연장〔갱신〕하다. ¶ ~ *a magazine subscription* 잡지의 정기 구독을 계속하다 / ~ *an agreement* 계약 기간을 연장하다; 재계약하다. **6** bring back to existence. …을 부활시키다. ¶ ~ *ancient jealousies* 옛 질투심에 다시 불지르다 / ~ *long-forgotten disappointment* 잊은 지 오랜 실망감을 되새기다.

— *vi.* (P1) become new again; start again. 다시 새로워지다; 재개하다. [re-]

re·new·a·ble [rinjúːəbəl] *adj.* that can be renewed. 새롭게 할 수 있는; 갱신할 수 있는.

re·new·al [rinjúːəl] *n.* ⓊⒸ the act of renewing; the state of being renewed; restoration; revival. 일신(一新); 회복; 재개; 부활.

re·nounce [rináuns] *vt.* (P6) **1** give up (a claim, right, etc.) formally; abandon (a habit). (공식적으로) …을 포기하다; (습관)을 버리다. ¶ *She renounced her claim to the property.* 그녀는 그 재산권을 정식으로 포기했다 / ~ *one's former religion* 이전의 신앙을 버리다 / ~ *one's old bad habits* 오랜 악습을 버리다. **2** refuse to recognize (something); cast off. …을 거절하다; 부인하다; …와의 인연을 끊다. ¶ ~ *the authority of the law* 법의 권위를 부인하다 / ~ *a debt* 채무 변제를 거부하다 / ~ *friendship* 〔*a friend*〕 절교하다 / *How could you ~ your own son?* 어찌 자식과 의절한단 말이냐.

— *vi.* 《card》 follow with a card of other suit for want of right one. (같은 짝의 패가 없어) 다른 짝의 패를 내다. [re-, L. *nuntio* announce]

ren·o·vate [rénəvèit] *vt.* (P6) make (something) new again; put (something or someone) in good condition; refresh; repair; clean up. …을 새롭게 하다; …에게 기운을 차리게 하다; …을 수선하다; 깨끗이 하다. ¶ ~ *a garment* 옷을 수선하다 / *The old house is being renovated.* 그 헌집은 수리중이다. [re-, →novel]

ren·o·va·tion [rènəvéiʃən] *n.* ⓊⒸ the act of renovating; the state of being renovated; renewal; refreshment; repair. 혁신; 원기 회복; 수선.

ren·o·va·tor [rénəvèitər] *n.* Ⓒ a person who renovates. 수선하는 사람; 혁신자.

·re·nown [rináun] *n.* Ⓤ fame; reputation. 명성. ¶ *a man of ~* 명망가 / *have great ~ for...* …으로 매우 유명하다 / *He won ~ as a painter.* 화가로서 이름이 났다. [re-, →nomen]

be of* 〔*great, high*〕 *renown, be (very) famous. (매우) 유명하다.

re·nowned [rináund] *adj.* famous. 유명한. ¶ *be ~ for...* …로 유명하다 / *He is ~ for his learning.* 박식하기로 이름이 나 있다.

·rent¹ [rent] *n.* ⓊⒸ a sum of money for the use of a house, room, land, machinery, etc. 집세; 방세; 지대(地代); 사용료. ¶ *They paid a heavy ~ for the house.* 집세를 많이 물었다 / *a ~ collector* 임대료 수금자.

for rent, available to be rented. 세 주는; 임대하는. ¶ *a house for ~* 셋집 / *For ~.* 세놓음 《게시》.

— *vt.* (P6,13) **1** occupy (something) in return for paying rent. …을 세내다; 임차하다. ¶ *We ~ed a house from Mr. Smith.* 스미스씨의 집을 세냈다〔임차했다〕. **2** 《chiefly U.S.》 allow (someone) to occupy (a house, etc.) in return for paying rent. (집 따위)를 빌려주다; 세놓다. ¶ *He rents the house cheaply.* 집을 싸게 세놓는다〔임대한다〕 / *a house rented at $2,000 a year* 임대료가 연 2천 달러인 집 / *She rents (out) rooms to students.* 학생들에게 방들을 세놓고 있다.

— *vi.* (P3) be rented. 임대되다. ¶ *The house rents at a high sum.* 그 집은 임대료가 비싸다. [→render]

rent² [rent] *n.* Ⓒ **1** a split; a torn place. 갈라진〔째진〕 데〔틈〕. ¶ *a ~ in a hillside* 언덕의 갈라진 데 / *rents in one's clothes* 옷의 여기저기 찢어진 데. **2** 《*fig.*》 a division or difference in opinion. (의견의) 분열. ¶ *a ~ in a party* 당의 분열. [*rend*]

rent[3] [rent] *v.* p. and pp. of **rend.**

rent·al [réntl] *n.* Ⓤ **1** the amount paid or received as rent; an income from rents. 총 임대료(지대); 임대료 수입. **2** a house, apartment, car, etc. offered for rent. 임대물《집·아파트·차량 등》. [→rent[1]]

rental library [ˊ– ˋ–––] *n.* a collection of popular current books available for loan upon payment of a small fee. (유료) 대출 도서관; 대출 문고.

rent·er [réntər] *n.* Ⓒ a person who pays rent. 임차인《집·토지 등의》. [*rent*[1]]

rent-free [réntfríː] *adj., adv.* (occupied) without any rent-charge. 임대료가 없는(없이). ¶ *He lives there* ~. 거기에 세없이 살고 있다 / *a* ~ *house* 임대료 없는 집.

ren·tier [rɑ̃ːntjéi] *n.* a person whose income is derived from investments. (투자에 의한) 금리(이자) 생활자; 불로 소득 생활자《주주·지주·임대 가옥주 따위》. [F. *rente*]

re·nun·ci·a·tion [rinʌ̀nsiéiʃən, -ʃi-] *n.* Ⓤ the act of giving up a right, possession, title, etc. (권리 등의) 포기; 단념. [→renounce]

re·o·pen [riːóupən] *vi.* (P1) open again. 다시 열다(시작하다). ¶ *School will* ~ *in September.* 학교는 9월에 다시 시작된다(개학한다) / *Talks between the two countries have reopened.* 양국간의 회담이 재개되었다. —*vt.* (P6) **1** open again. …을 다시 열다. ¶ ~ *a theater* / ~ *a window* (*door*) 창(문)을 다시 열다. **2** begin again. 다시 시작하다. ¶ ~ *fire* 다시 총격을 가하다 / ~ *an attack* (*argument*) 공격(토론)을 재개하다. [re-]

re·or·gan·i·za·tion [riːɔ̀ːrgənizéiʃən] *n.* Ⓤ the act of reorganizing; the state of being reorganized. 재편성. [re-]

re·or·gan·ize [riːɔ́ːrgənàiz] *vt., vi.* (P6;1) arrange (something) in a new way; form (something) into a new system. 재편성하다. ¶ ~ *an army* 부대를 재편성하다 / ~ *a Ministry* 개각하다 / ~ *the staff of a business* 업무 진용을 개편하다 / ~ *the country's finances* 국가 재정을 재건하다. [re-]

Rep. Republication.

rep. report(er); representative; republic.

re·paid [riːpéid] *v.* p. and pp. of **repay.**

re·paint [riːpéint] *vt.* paint again. …에 페인트칠을 다시 하다. [re-]

:re·pair[1] [ripέər] *vt.* (P6) **1** mend; put (something broken or wrong) in good condition again. …을 수선(수리)하다. ¶ *She repaired her shoes.* 그녀는 구두를 수선했다 / *He had his shoes repaired.* 그는 그의 구두를 수선케 했다 / *I'm afraid this old piano is beyond* ~. 이 피아노는 너무 낡아서 수리하기가 어려울 것 같다. **2** cure (a wound). (상처를) 치료하다. **3** ⓐ correct (a mistake). …을 정정하다. ¶ ~ *a mistake* 잘못을 고치다. ⓑ make up for. …을 보상하다; 벌충하다. ¶ *How can I* ~ *the wrong I have done her?* 그녀에게 저지른 내 잘못을 어떻게 보상한다지.
—*n.* Ⓤ **1** the act of repairing; 《usu. *pl.*》 an instance of repairing. 수선; 수리; 수리 공사. ¶ *make repairs on a house* 집을 수리하다 / *a house in need of* ~ 수리를 요하는 가옥 / *a building under* ~ 수리 중인 빌딩 / *Repairs* (*will be*) *done while you wait.* 수리는 기다리시는 동안에 다 됩니다《광고문》. **2** the state of being repaired; the general state of needing repairs. 수리된 상태; 수리를 필요로 하는 상태. ¶ *keep the roads in* ~ 도로를 잘 수리해 두다 / *be in good* (*bad*) ~ =*be in* (*out of*) ~ 손질이(수리가) 잘 되어 있다(있지 않다). **3** a mended place. 수리한(고친) 데. ¶ *a neat* ~ *on the elbow of the coat* 코트 팔꿈치의 얌전히 기운 곳. [re-, →pare]

re·pair[2] [ripέər] *vi.* (P3) 《*lit.*》 go (to a place), esp. often or in numbers. (여럿이) 가다; 종종(자주) 가다. ¶ ~ *to one's home* 자기 집으로 가다 / *Many birds* ~ *to warmer places in winter.* 많은 새들이 겨울엔 따뜻한 곳으로 간다. —*n.* 《*arch.*》 a resort or haunt. 사람들이 모이는 곳; 출입이 잦은 곳. [re-, L. *patria* one's country]

re·pair·a·ble [ripέərəbəl] *adj.* that can be repaired. 수리할 수 있는. ¶ *The boats are not* ~. 그 배들은 수리가 불가능하다. [*repair*[1]]

re·pair·er [ripέərər] *n.* Ⓒ a person who repairs. 수리인; 수선공. ¶ *I sent the broken chair to an excellent* ~. 망가진 의자를 아주 잘 고치는 사람한테 보냈다. [*repair*[1]]

rep·a·ra·tion [rèpəréiʃən] *n.* **1** Ⓤ the act of repairing; the state of being repaired; restoration to a good condition. 수리; 수복; (원상) 회복. **2** the act of giving satisfaction to someone by repairing damage done at him. 보상; 배상. ¶ *make* ~ *for one's faults* 실수에 대한 보상을 하다 / *demand* ~ *for…* …의 보상을 요구하다. **3** 《*pl.*》 money paid for damages. 배상금. ¶ *the reparations for the war.* [↑]

rep·ar·tee [rèpɑːrtíː] *n.* **1** Ⓒ a quick, clever reply; conversation made up of such remarks. (임기 응변의) 재치 있는 즉답(대화). **2** Ⓤ skill in making quick, witty replies. 재치 있게 즉답하는 재간. ¶ *He is famous for* ~. 재치 있게 즉답하는 재간으로 이름이 나 있다. [re-, →part]

re·past [ripǽst, -pɑ́ːst] *n.* Ⓒ 《*lit.*》 a meal; food and drink for a meal. 식사; 음식물. ¶ *Breakfast at our house is a light* ~. 우리 집 아침 식사는 간단하게 한다 / *a generous* (*rich*) ~ 푸짐한 식사. [re-, →pasture]

re·pa·tri·ate [riːpéitrièit / -pǽt-] *vt.* (P6) send (someone) back to his native country. …을 본국에 송환하다. ¶ ~ *refugees.* —[riːpéitriit / -pǽt-] *n.* Ⓒ a person so sent back. 송환되는 사람. [→repair[2]]

re·pat·ri·a·tion [riːpèitriéiʃən / -pæ̀t-] *n.* Ⓤ the act of repatriating someone; the state of being repatriated. 본국 송환.

·re·pay [ri:péi] *v.* (**-paid**) *vt.* **1** (P6,14) pay back (money). (돈)을 돌려주다; 갚다. ¶ *I'll ~ the money you lent.* 네가 빌려 준 돈을 갚겠다 / *When will you ~ me? — I will ~ you as soon as possible.* 너 돈은 언제 갚겠느냐 —되도록이면 빨리 갚으마. **2** (P6,13) make return for (something); reward. …에 보답하다. ¶ *~ someone for his kindness* 아무의 친절에 보답하다. —*vi.* (P1) **1** pay back something. 갚다; 돌려주다. ¶ *You must ~ as soon as you can.* 되도록 빨리 갚아라. **2** give equal favor or injury in return; reward or punish. 대갚음하다; 보복하다. [re-]

re·pay·a·ble [ripéiəbəl] *adj.* that can be repaid. 돌려줄〔반제(返濟)할〕 수 있는.

re·pay·ment [ripéimənt] *n.* UC the act of repaying. 반제; 상환; 보답; 보복.

re·peal [ripí:l] *vt.* (P6) do away with; annul. (법률 등)을 무효로 하다; 폐지하다. ¶ *~ a resolution* 결의를 파기하다. —*n.* UC the act of repealing. 폐지; 폐기. ¶ *He voted against the ~ of that law.* 그 법률 폐지안에 그는 반대표를 던졌다. [re-, →appeal]

:re·peat [ripí:t] *vt.* **1** (P6,11) speak〔say〕 again. …을 되풀이하여 말하다; 반복하다. ¶ *She repeated the question.* 그녀는 질문을 반복했다 / *I repeated my words.* 나는 한 말을 되풀이했다 / *Let me ~ what I have just said.* 지금 내가 한 말을 다시 되풀이하겠다. **2** (P6) do again; make again. …을 되풀이하여 행하다; 반복하다. ¶ *History repeats itself.* 역사는 반복한다 / *He often repeats the same mistake.* 그 사람은 같은 잘못을 자주 되풀이한다 / *Such conduct must never be repeated.* 그런 짓을 다시는 되풀이하지 마라. **3** ⓐ (P6) say the same thing that someone else has already said; say the same words soon after another person. (남이 한 말을) 그대로 전하다; (남의 말을) 뒤를 따라 그대로 말하다; 복창(復唱)하다. ¶ *She said, "Repeat this sentence after me," to her pupils.* 그녀는 학생들에게 "나를 따라 이 글을 읽어라"고 말했다 / *~ an order* 명령을 복창하다. ⓑ (P6,13) tell (something heard) to another. (들은 비밀 따위)를 남에게 알리다〔털어 놓다〕. ¶ *Please don't ~ this to anybody.* 아무에게도 이것을 발설하지 마라 / *I will tell you the secret if you'll promise not to ~ it.* 남에게 말 않겠다고 약속하면 내 그 비밀을 알려주마. **4** (P6) say (a poem, etc.) over and over again to memorize it. (시 따위)를 암송(暗誦)하다. ¶ *Mary can ~ many poems from memory.* 메리는 암송하는 시가 많다. —*vi.* (P1) **1** happen again; say or do anything again. 다시 일어나다〔발생하다〕; 되풀이하여 말〔행〕하다. **2** (of something taken into the stomach) rise; belch. (먹은 것이 입으로) 되올라오다; 트림하다. **3** (of numbers) recur. (수가) 순환하다. ¶ *a repeating decimal* 순환 소수. **4** 《U.S.》 vote more than once. 두 번 이상 투표하다《부정 행위》. —*n.* C **1** an act of repeating; something repeated; repetition. 반복하기; 반복된 것; 반복. **2** 《mus.》 ⓐ a passage to be repeated. 반복절. ⓑ a sign calling for the repetition. 도돌이표(𝄇); 반복 기호. [re-, L. *peto* ask]

·re·peat·ed [ripí:tid] *adj.* done, said or made again. 반복되는; 종종 있는.

re·peat·ed·ly [ripí:tidli] *adv.* over and over again; frequently. 되풀이하여; 자주. ¶ *I've told you ~ not to do that.* 그러지 말라고 몇 번이나 말했는데.

re·peat·er [ripí:tər] *n.* C a rifle firing several shots without reloading. 연발총.

re·pel [ripél] *vt.* (**-pelled, -pel·ling**) (P6) **1** drive back; force away. …을 쫓아버리다; 물리치다(cf. *repulse*). ¶ *We repelled the enemy.* 우리는 적을 물리쳤다 / *~ an attack* 공격을 격퇴하다. **2** reject; refuse. …을 거절하다. ¶ *~ the offer*〔*request*〕 제의〔요구〕를 거절하다 / *a fabric that repels moisture* 습기 차지 않는 천; 방습포(布). **3** cause dislike; displease. …을 불쾌하게 하다. ¶ *Spiders and worms ~ me.* 거미와 연충(蠕蟲)은 질색이다 / *His manner repels me.* 그의 행동이 불쾌하다 / *He was repelled by the thought of the uninteresting work.* 그 따분한 일을 생각하니 그는 기분이 나빠졌다. [re-, →pulse]

re·pel·lent [ripélənt] *adj.* **1** driving back or away. 물리치는; 쫓아버리는. ¶ *a mosquito-repellent spray* 모기약 스프레이. **2** causing dislike; disagreeable. 싫은; 마음에 들지 않는. ¶ *a ~ fellow* 싫은 놈 / *He has cold, ~ manner.* 태도가 차고 거부감을 준다 / *To me he is the most ~ person I have ever met.* 저렇게 꼴보기 싫은 놈은 난생 처음이다. —*n.* **1** a medicine that serves to prevent swelling. (종기 따위를) 삭히는 약. ¶ *an insect ~* 구충제. **2** a kind of waterproof fabric. 방수포(布). [↑]

·re·pent [ripént] *vi.* (P1,3) feel sorry for one's own act, thought, etc. 뉘우치다; 후회하다. ¶ *He repented of what he had done.* 그는 자기가 한 일을 뉘우쳤다 / *She repented of her hasty marriage.* 그녀는 성급한 결혼을 후회했다 / *I have many things to ~ of.* 후회할 일이 많다. —*vt.* (P6,9) feel sorry for (something). …을 뉘우치다. ¶ *~ a fault*〔*one's misconduct*〕 과실〔자기 비행〕을 후회하다 / *You shall ~ this.* 언제고 반드시 이것을 후회하게 될 것이다 / *~ one's sins* 죄를 뉘우치다 / *They will soon bitterly ~ what they did.* 그들은 머지 않아 그들이 저지른 일에 대해서 크게 후회할 것이다. [re-, →penitent]

re·pent·ance [ripéntəns] *n.* U the act of repenting. 후회(cf. *remorse*).

re·pent·ant [ripéntənt] *adj.* feeling regret or sorrow. 뉘우치는; 후회의. ¶ ~

tears 회한의 눈물 / *If you are truly* ~ *you will be forgiven.* 참으로 뉘우친다면 용서받을 것이다.

re·per·cus·sion [rìːpərkʌ́ʃən] *n.* UC **1** 《usu. *pl.*》《*fig.*》 an indirect result of something done or said. (사건·행동 따위의) 영향; 반향. ¶ *An action of the British Cabinet may have repercussions all over Europe.* 영국 내각의 한 조처는 전유럽에 영향을 미칠 것이다. **2** a rebound; the act of springing back. 되튐; 반동. ¶ *the* ~ *of a cannon* (발사 후) 대포의 반동. **3** an echoing sound; echo. (소리의) 반향. [re-]

rep·er·toire [répərtwɑ̀ːr] *n.* C the list of plays, operas, musical pieces or parts that a company, an actor, or a musician is ready to play or sing. 상연 목록; 연주 곡목; 레퍼토리. [↓]

rep·er·to·ry [répərtɔ̀ːri / -təri] *n.* C (*pl.* **-ries**) **1** =repertoire. **2** a storehouse. 창고. **3** 《*fig.*》 a stock of things ready for use. 저장물. ¶ *a* ~ *of useful information* 유익한 지식의 보고(寶庫). [re-, →parent]

repertory company [⌐−−− ⌐−] *n.* a theatrical company preparing several plays and performing them alternately. 레퍼토리 극단.

repertory theater [⌐−−− ⌐−] *n.* one in which a permanent acting company presents a varied selection of plays. 레퍼토리〔실험〕 극장.

·rep·e·ti·tion [rèpətíʃən] *n.* **1** UC the act of repeating; something repeated. 반복; 되풀이(된 것). ¶ *the* ~ *of a word or a phrase* 단어나 구(句)의 반복 / *the* ~ *of a mistake* 실수의 반복 / *That is a mere* ~ *of what you said before.* 그건 네가 앞서 한 말의 반복(反復)일 뿐이다. **2** C a copy; an imitation. 사본; 복사; 모방(물). ¶ *Each of this author's books is but a* ~ *of the others with slight differences.* 이 작가의 책들은 남의 것을 조금 다르게 손질한 복사물에 지나지 않는다. **3** U the act of repeating what has been learnt. 복송(復誦); 암송(暗誦). ¶ *Repetition is a useful exercise for the memory.* 암송은 기억을 위한 유익한 연습이다. **4** C a piece so learnt for recitation. 암송문. ¶ *The* ~ *for tomorrow will be this passage.* 내일 암송할 대목은 이 구절이다. **5** 《mus.》 the repeating of a note rapidly by instrument. 복주(復奏). [→ repeat]

rep·e·ti·tious [rèpətíʃəs] *adj.* full of repetitions. 반복이 많은.

re·pet·i·tive [ripétətiv] *adj.* =repetitious.

re·pine [ripáin] *vi.* (P1,3) complain; be discontented. 불평하다; 투덜거리다. ¶ *Whatever misfortunes overtake him, he never repines.* 어떤 불행이 닥쳐도 그는 한마디의 불평도 않는다 / *It does no good to* ~ *at one's fate.* 자기 운명을 탓해서 좋을 것 없다. [re-]

:re·place [ripléis] *vt.* (P6,13) **1** put back; put in place again. …을 본디의 자리에 놓다. ¶ *He replaced the book on the shelf.* 책을 책장에 도로 끼웠다. **2** ⓐ fill or take the place of (something); get another in place of. …에 대신하다; …로 대체하다. ¶ ~ *an original picture with a copy* 원화(原畫)를 복사한 것과 바꾸다 / ~ *coal fires by gas* 석탄불을 가스로 대체하다 / *I will* ~ *the cup I broke.* 내가 깬 컵을 대체해 놓겠다. ⓑ take the place of. …을 승계하다; …의 후임자가 되다. ¶ *George has replaced Edward as captain of the team.* 조지가 에드워드 후임으로 팀 주장이 됐다. **3** repay. …을 갚다; 돌려주다. ¶ ~ *stolen or borrowed money* 훔쳤거나 빌린 돈을 돌려주다. ● **re·place·a·ble** [-əbəl] *adj.* [re-]

re·place·ment [ripléismənt] *n.* **1** U the act of replacing. 제자리에 되돌리기; 교체; 대치(代置). ¶ *the* ~ *of worn-out parts* 마모된 부품의 교체 / *The law required the* ~ *of all wooden carriages by steel carriages.* 법은 모든 목제 마차를 철제로 바꿀 것을 규정했다. **2** C a person or thing that takes the place of another. 교체자〔물〕. ¶ *We need a* ~ *for the secretary who left.* 나간 비서를 대신할 사람이 필요하다.

re·plant [riːplǽnt, -plɑ́ːnt] *vt.* (P6) plant again. …을 다시 심다. [re-]

re·play [riːpléi] *vt.* (P6,13) 《*with*》 play over again. 재시합하다. ¶ *The game ended in a draw, so they'll* ~ *it on Wednesday.* 경기는 비겼다. 그래서 수요일에 재시합을 할 것이다. [re-]

re·plen·ish [riplénis] *vt.* (P6,13) fill up (something) again; make (something) complete again. …을 다시 채우다. ¶ ~ *a fire* 장작을 더 지피다 / ~ *a glass with wine* 잔에 술을 다시 채우다 / ~ *the stock of goods* 물건의 재고를 보충하다. [re-, →plenary]

re·plen·ish·ment [riplénišmənt] *n.* U the act of replenishing. 보충.

re·plete [riplíːt] *adj.* **1** completely filled or furnished; well supplied. 가득 찬; 충만한; 충분히 갖춘. ¶ ~ *with every comfort and luxury* 안락과 호사(豪奢)를 극한 / *a mind* ~ *with learning* 박식한 사람. **2** stuffed or filled with food and drink. 포식한. ¶ *I am* ~ *(with food).* 잔뜩 먹었다. [re-, L. *pleo* fill]

re·ple·tion [riplíːʃən] *n.* UC **1** the state of being replete, completely full, or well supplied. 충실; 충만. ¶ *a vessel filled to* ~ 넘치도록 가득 찬 그릇〔용기(容器)〕. **2** the state of having eaten and drunk too much. 포식. ¶ *eat to* ~ 포식하다. **3** 《med.》 fullness of blood. 다혈(증).

rep·li·ca [réplikə] *n.* C an exact copy of a picture or statue. (회화·조각의) 복사; 모사; 모형. ¶ *This portrait is a* ~ *of the original.* 이 초상은 원화(原畫)의 복사이다. [↓]

:re·ply [riplái] *v.* (**-plied**) *vi.* (P1,3) 《*to*》 answer in words or by an action. 대답하다; 응답〔응수〕하다; 응전하다(opp. ask, inquire). ¶ ~ *to a question* 질문에 대답하다 / *The enemy did not ~ to our fire.* 적은 아군의 포화에 응전하지 않았다 / *When asked her age, she didn't ~.* 나이를 물었을 때 그녀는 대답하지 않았다 / ~ *to a letter* 답장을 보내다 / *I don't know how to ~.* 뭐라고 대답해야 할지 모르겠다 / *He replied with a violent blow.* 그는 격렬한 타격으로 응수해 왔다 / ~ *to a signal* 신호에 응하다. —*vt.* (P6,11) say or write (something) in answer. …라고 대답하다; 회신하다. ¶ *He replied not a word.* 그는 단 한마디도 대답하지 않았다 / *What did she ~?* 뭐라고 답하던가 / *I have nothing to ~.* 아무것도 대답할 것이 없다〔대답하고 싶지 않다〕.

reply for, answer instead of another. …의 대신 대답하다.

—*n.* Ⓒ (*pl.* **-plies**) the act of replying; an answer in words or by an action. 대답; 응답; 회신; 응전(opp. question, inquiry). ¶ *a ~ card* 왕복 엽서 / ~ *paid* 반신료 지불필(畢) / *in ~ to a question* 질문에 대답해서 / *make a ~* 대답〔회신〕하다 / *a ~ to the enemy's attack* 적에 대한 반격. [re-, →ply]

:re·port [ripɔ́ːrt] *vt.* **1** (P6,9,11,13) give an account of (what one has seen, heard, learned, etc.); communicate; tell; relate. …을 보고하다; 보도〔전〕하다; 이야기〔말〕하다. ¶ *He reported her disappearance to the police.* 그는 그녀의 실종을 경찰에 신고했다 / *It is reported that ….* …라는 이야기〔보도〕가 있다; …라고 전해진다 / *They reported having met her.* 그들은 그녀를 만났다고 보고했다 / *The war is reported to be over.* 전쟁은 끝났다고 한다 / *They reported that they had seen him in Brington.* 그들은 브링턴에서 그를 봤다고 말했다 / ~ *the results of an expedition* 탐험 결과를 보고하다 / ~ *a new discovery* 새로운 발견을 보고하다 / ~ *the train* 열차의 도착을 전하다 / *All variations are to be reported daily.* 모든 변동은 매일 보고되지 않으면 안 된다 / *They reported him much recovered.* 그들은 그가 많이 회복되었다고 전했다 / *He was reported killed in action.* 그는 전사했다고 전해졌다 / *His property is reported to be worth a million.* 그의 재산은 백만 달러어치가 된다고 한다 / *He is well reported of among his friends.* 그는 친구들 사이에서 평(評)이 좋다. **2** (P6,9, 11,13,15) announce officially; give an account of (something) regularly. …을 공표(公表)하다; 정기적으로 보고하다. ¶ *The Treasury reports the total receipt and expenditure for the year.* 재무부는 총세입 세출액을 공표한다. **3** (P6) write an account of (an event, etc.) for publication; esp. in a newspaper; write down. …의 (실황) 기사를 쓰다; 기록하다(cf. *reporter*). ¶ ~ *trial at a law court* 법정의 공판 실황 기사를 쓰다 / ~ *debates in Congress* 의회의 토론을 기록하다. **4** (P6,13) 《*to*》 complain about (someone) to the authorities. (상관 등에게) …에 관한 일을 고자질하다; 일러바치다. ¶ ~ *a salesgirl to the manager* 여점원 일을 지배인에게 고자질하다 / *He reported the boy to the teacher for smoking on the school premises.* 그는 그 아이가 학교 구내에서 담배를 피웠다고 선생님한테 일러바쳤다 / ~ *someone for misconduct* 아무의 비행을 일러바치다. **5** (P6,13) 《*oneself to*》 present (oneself) to someone in authority. …에 출두하게 하다. ¶ *Report (yourself) to the manager between 1 and 3 o'clock.* 1 시에서 3 시 사이에 지배인 앞으로 출두하시오 / ~ *oneself at a law court* 법정에 출두하다.

—*vi.* (P1,3) 《*on*》 **1** make a report. 보고하다; 보고서를 만들다. ¶ ~ *on the condition of the crops* 작황(作況)에 관해 보고하다 / *He reports well of the prospects.* 그는 전도가 유망하다고 보고한다. **2** 《*for*》 work as a reporter. 탐방 기자로 일하다. ¶ ~ *for the Times* 타임스지(紙) 기자로 근무하고 있다. **3** 《*to, for*》 present oneself at a given place or time. 출두하다; 나타나다. ¶ ~ *to the police* 경찰에 출두하다 / ~ *for duty* 〔*work*〕 출근하다 / *What time do you have to ~ at airport?* 공항에는 몇 시에 나가야 하느냐 / ~ *at* 〔*to*〕 *the office* 사무소에 출두하다.

—*n.* Ⓒ **1** a statement or an account of something seen, heard, done, etc.; an account published in the newspapers, through the radio, etc. 보고(서); 보도; 기사. ¶ *make a ~* 보고를 하다 / *make* 〔*give*〕 *a full detailed ~* 자초지종을 보고하다 / *make a favorable ~ on the plan* 그 계획에 유리한 보고서를 쓰다〔만들다〕 / *a medical ~ on a patience* 환자의 진료 보고 / *present* 〔*put in*〕 *a ~* 보고서를 제출하다 / *a weather ~* 기상 통보〔예보〕 / *according to the press* 〔*newspaper*〕 *reports* 신문 보도에 의하면. **2** an official statement; a statement as to a pupil's work and conduct issued by his teachers. 공보(公報); (학교의) 성적표. ¶ *The boy has had a bad ~ this term.* 그 아이는 이번 학기에 성적이 나빴다. **3** ⓊⒸ rumor; Ⓤ reputation. 소문; 평판. ¶ *be of good* 〔*ill*〕 ~ 평판이 좋다〔나쁘다〕 / *through good and evil ~* 평판이 좋든 나쁘든간에 / *as ~ has it* 소문에 의하면 / *Report goes* 〔*runs, has it*〕 *that….* …(이)라는 소문이다; 풍문에 의하면 …하다 / *things of good* 〔*ill*〕 ~ 평이 좋은〔나쁜〕 것 / *The ~ spread all over the town.* 소문은 온 마을에 퍼졌다. **4** the sound of an explosion. 폭음; 포성; 총성. ¶ *the ~ of a gun* 총소리 / *explode with a loud ~* 꽝 소리를 내며 폭발하다. **5** 《usu. *pl.*》 books containing a record of court cases, etc. 판례집; 의사록. ¶ *Law Reports* 판례집 / *Parliamentary Reports* 영국 국회 의사록. [re-, →port[3]]

re·port·ed·ly [ripɔ́ːrtidli] *adv.* according to the report. 전하는 바에 의하면; 소문으로는.

·re·port·er [ripɔ́ːrtər] *n.* Ⓒ **1** a person who reports. 보고자. **2** a person who collects news for a newspaper, magazine, etc. 취재 기자; 통신원. **3** a person who writes official accounts in a law court. (법원의) 서기.

·**re·pose**[1] [ripóuz] *vi.* **1** (P1,3) lie down to rest; take a rest by lying down. (누워서) 쉬다. ¶ *Kate reposed on the bench.* 케이트는 벤치에 누워 쉬었다 / ~ *in sleep* 잠자다. **2** (P1,3) be asleep; lie in a grave. 잠자다; 영면하다. ¶ *He reposes at Arlington Cemetery.* 그는 알링턴 국립 묘지에 안장되어 있다 / *She reposes in eternal peace.* 그녀는 영원한 평화 속에 잠들어 있다. **3** (P3) lie quiet; be peacefully calm. (땅 등이) 고요히 가로놓여 있다. ¶ *The land seemed to ~ in beauty.* 땅은 아름답게 누워 있는 듯이 보였다. **4** (P3) ((*on*)) be based on; depend on. …에 기초(근거)를 두다; 의지하다. ¶ *The plan reposes on a recovery of trade.* 그 계획은 경기 회복을 그 바탕으로 하고 있다. **5** (P1,3) ((*on*)) remain, dwell, or linger on. 머무르다; 떠나지 않다. ¶ *His mind reposed on the past.* 과거의 일이 언제까지나 그의 마음에서 떠나지 않았다.

— *vt.* (P6,13) lay or put to rest; give a rest to. 눕히다; 쉬게 하다. ¶ ~ *one's head on a pillow* 베개를 베고 쉬다 / *Repose yourself on a bed.* 침대에 누워 쉬어라.

— *n.* Ⓤ **1** rest; sleep. 휴식; 휴양; 수면. ¶ *disturb one's* ~ 수면을 방해하다 / *enjoy a short* ~ 잠시의 휴식을 즐기다. **2** calmness; quietness. 평정; 침착; 안정. ¶ ~ *of mind* 마음의 평정 / *lack of* ~ 침착성의 결여 / *She has ~ of manner.* 거동이 침착한 여인이다. [re-, →pose]

re·pose[2] [ripóuz] *vt.* (P13) put; place. (신용·희망·신뢰 따위)를 두다. ¶ ~ *hope in promises* 약속을 믿다 / *We ~ entire confidence in his honesty.* 우린 전적으로 그의 정직함을 믿는다. [re-, →posit]

re·pose·ful [ripóuzfəl] *adj.* quiet. 평온한; 침착한.

re·pos·i·tory [ripázitɔ̀:ri / -pɔ́zitəri] *n.* (*pl.* **-ries**) Ⓒ **1** a place or container where things are stored; a store-house. 저장소; 창고. ¶ *a ~ for old papers* 서류 보관소. **2** something that contains a large amount of anything. (지식 등의) 보고(cf. *depository*). ¶ *A library is a ~ of information.* 도서관은 지식의 보고다 / *He was a ~ of the learning of his time.* 그는 당대의 석학이었다. **3** a person to whom secrets, etc. are entrusted. (비밀을 털어 놓을) 믿을 수 있는 사람. ¶ *He was the only ~ of all her secrets.* 그 사람이야말로 그녀가 모든 비밀을 터놓고 말할 수 있는 유일한 사람이었다.

re·pos·sess [rì:pəzés] *vt.* (P6) possess again; esp. take back from a buyer who cannot make the proper payments. …을 되찾다; (상품을) 회수하다((특히 구매인의 대금 지불 불이행으로)). ¶ ~ *property one has lost* 잃은 재산을 되찾다 / *be repossessed in a title to land* 토지 소유권을 회복하다. [re-]

rep·re·hend [rèprihénd] *vt.* (P6,13) blame; scold. …을 꾸짖다; 질책하다. [re-, → pregnable]

rep·re·hen·si·ble [rèprihénsəbəl] *adj.* blamable; deserving blame. 비난할(나무랄) 만한.

rep·re·hen·sion [rèprihénʃən] *n.* Ⓤ blame; the act of scolding. 비난; 질책.

:**rep·re·sent** [rèprizént] *vt.* **1** (P6,13,17,23) portray (something or someone) by pictures, language, or in some other way. …을 묘사하다; 표현하다. ¶ *What does this picture ~?* 이건 무슨 그림이지 / *This picture represents the artist's home when he was a child.* 이 그림은 화가의 어릴 때 살던 집을 그린 것이다 / *The painter has represented him in his uniform.* 화가는 제복을 입은 자화상을 그렸다 / *a tall stone figure representing the god of war* 전쟁의 신을 표현한 높은 석상(石像). **2** (P6,7,11,13,21) describe; state; make clear; explain; point out. …이라고 말하다; 진술(주장)하다; …을 설명(지적)하다. ¶ *He represented the differences clearly.* 그는 차이점을 분명하게 말(지적)했다 / *They represented him as stern.* 그들은 그가 엄한 사람이라고 말했다 / *He represented that his salary was inadequate.* 그는 봉급이 적다고 단호히 말했다 / *The subject is so difficult that I do not know how to ~ it to you.* 그 문제를 너에게 설명해주기는 너무 어렵다 **3** (P6) mean; symbolize; stand for. …을 의미하다; 상징하다. ¶ *Such excuses ~ nothing at all to me.* 그런 핑계는 내게 전혀 안 통한다 / *The dove represents peace.* 비둘기는 평화의 상징이다 / *The scepter of a king represents his power and authority.* 왕홀(王笏)은 왕의 권한과 권위를 상징한다. **4** (P6) correspond to. …에 상당하다. ¶ *The llama of the New World represents the camel of the Old World.* 신세계의 야마는 구세계의 낙타에 상당한다. **5** (P6,13) act or speak in place of or as agent for (someone or a body of persons); appear as a fair sample of (something). …의 대리 노릇을 하다; …을 대표(대변)하다; …의 표본(일례)이다. ¶ ~ *a client* 소송 의뢰인을 대신하다 / *He represents this city.* 그는 이 시를 대표한다 / *We chose a committee to ~ us.* 우리는 우리를 대표하는 위원을 선출했다. **6** (P6) perform (a play); play the part of (someone). (극)을 상연하다; …의 역을 하다. ¶ ~ *Hamlet* 햄릿을 상연하다 / *He is somewhat old to ~ Romeo.* 그가 로미오역을 하기엔 나이가 좀 많다. [re-, →present]

represent oneself as [***to be***], describe oneself as. 자기는 …이라고 주장하다.

represent to oneself, imagine. 마음에 그리다; 상상하다.

·**rep·re·sen·ta·tion** [rèprizentéiʃən] *n.* ⓊⒸ **1** the act of representing or expressing in painting, etc.; the state of being represented. 표현; 묘사; 대표; 대리; 상연. ¶ *The ~ of movement is a question which painters are always trying to solve.* 그림에서 움직임의 묘사는 화가들이 늘 해결하려고 시도하고 있는 문제이다 / *A ~ of the story of Rip Van Winkle will be given at the school meeting today.* 오늘 학생회에서는 립 밴 윙클 이야기가 상연된다. **2** Ⓒ a picture portraying someone. 초상화. **3** a sign or symbol. 표; 기호; 상징. **4** ⓐ an account or statement. 설명; 진술. ⓑ 《usu. *pl.*》 a statement of facts, reasons, arguments, etc., esp. for polite protest. 주장; 진정; 항의. ¶ *make representations against* 〔*to*〕 *the government* 정부에 진정〔항의〕하다. **5** the act of representing a party, etc.; the fact or right of being represented. 대표〔대리〕를 하기; 대리; 대표; 대표권. ¶ *proportional ~* 비례 대표제 / *The ~ of persons of various opinions is no easy matter.* 여러 사람들의 각기 다른 의견을 대표하기란 쉬운 일이 아니다. **6** 《*collectively*》 a group of representatives, esp. in government. 대표단; 의원단. [re-]

:rep·re·sent·a·tive [rèprizéntətiv] *n.* Ⓒ **1** ⓐ a person who stands for a group of people. 대표자; 대리인. ¶ *a ~ of a trading firm* 상사의 대표자; 사장; 회장. ⓑ 《*R-*》 a member of the House of Representatives. 대의원; 하원 의원. ¶ *Who is your Representative in Congress?* 당신 선거구의 국회 의원은 누구요. **2** a characteristic example; a type. 견본; 표본; 전형. ¶ *a ~ of the national character* 국민성의 전형 / *This building is a ~ of modern architecture.* 이 건물은 현대 건축의 한 전형이다.
the House of Representatives, the lower house of the Congress of the United States. (미국의) 하원.
— *adj.* **1** typical; characteristic. 대표적인; 전형적인. ¶ *Balls, blocks, and trains are ~ toys.* 공, 집짓기 나무쪽, 기차는 장난감의 대표적인 것들이다. **2** having authority to stand for a group of people. 대표하는; 대리의. ¶ *He was sent in a ~ capacity.* 그가 대표 자격으로 파견되었다. **3** representing or serving to represent. 묘사〔표현〕하는. ¶ *The drawings are ~ of animals.* 이 그림들은 동물을 묘사한 것이다. **4** having its citizens represented by chosen persons. 대의제(代議制)의. ¶ *~ government* 대의 정치〔정체〕. [re-]

re·press [riprés] *vt.* (P6) keep (something or someone) under control; put down; suppress. …을 억누르다; 제지하다;진압하다. ¶ *~ one's emotion* 감정을 억누르다 / *~ tears* 눈물을 참다 / *~ a riot* 폭동을 진압하다 / *He repressed a sigh.* 한숨을 꾹 참았다. [re-]

re·press·i·ble [riprésəbəl] *adj.* that can be repressed. 억제〔제압〕할 수 있는.

re·pres·sion [ripréʃən] *n.* ⓊⒸ the act of repressing; the state of being repressed; suppression. 진압; 억제. ¶ *the ~ of rebellion* 반란 진압 / *the ~ of one's feeling* 자기 감정의 억제 / *political ~* 정치 탄압.

re·pres·sive [riprésiv] *adj.* tending to repress. 진압의; 억압적인. ¶ *~ acts* 〔*measures*〕 억압적인 행위〔수단〕 / *Under the general's ~ regime, thousands of people were imprisoned without trial.* 장군의 억압적인 정권 아래에서 수천명의 국민이 재판도 받지 않고 투옥되었다.

re·prieve [riprí:v] *vt.* (P6) **1** 《law》 delay the execution of (a prisoner sentenced to death). …의 사형 집행을 연기〔유예〕하다. ¶ *At the last moment the prisoner was reprieved for three weeks.* 마지막 순간에 죄수의 형집행이 3주 연기되었다. **2** give (someone) relief for a while from pain, trouble, etc. (…의 고통 등)을 잠시 덜어주다.
— *n.* Ⓒ **1** 《law》 temporary delay in carrying out the sentence of a judge. 집행 유예《사형의》. **2** the order giving authority for such a delay. 형 집행 유예 영장. **3** a temporary relief from any evil or trouble. 일시 모면; 유예. [*reprove*]

rep·ri·mand [réprəmænd, -mɑ̀:nd] *n.* ⓊⒸ a severe or formal reproof. 질책; 징계. — *vt.* (P6,13) give (someone) a severe scolding, esp. for a fault. …를 질책하다; 징계하다. ¶ *The principal reprimanded the boy for smoking.* 교장 선생님은 담배를 피운 아이를 호되게 꾸짖었다. [→repress]

re·print [ri:prínt] *vt.* (P6) print again. (책 따위를) 재판하다(cf. *republish*). — *n.* Ⓒ a reprinted book usu. without any change. 재판; 증쇄(增刷)《개정하지 않은》. [re-]

re·pris·al [ripráizəl] *n.* ⓊⒸ injury or revenge done in return for an injury, esp. by one country to another in a war. 앙갚음; 보복. ¶ *a ~ raid* 보복적인 습격 / *~ measures* 보복 조치 / *make reprisal(s)* 보복하다. [→reprehend]

·re·proach [ripróutʃ] *n.* **1** Ⓤ the act of reproaching; blame; Ⓒ an expression of blame. 질책; 비난; 비난의 말. ¶ *a look of ~* 나무라는 표정 / *Bad people bring ~ on their families.* 좋지 않은 사람은 그 집안을 욕되게 한다 / *a term of ~* 욕설; 비난의 소리. **2** ⓊⒸ a cause of blame or disgrace. 불명예; 치욕(거리). ¶ *The slums are a ~ to London.* 슬럼가는 런던의 치부(恥部)다.
beyond reproach, impeccably. 훌륭하게; 나무랄 데 없이.
bring 〔***draw***〕 ***reproach upon*** 〔***on***〕, bring shame upon. …의 치욕이〔불명예가〕 되다.
heap reproaches on, reprove severely. …을 훌닦다; 비난하다.
take away one's reproach, wipe away one's disgrace. 치욕을 씻다.
— *vt.* (P6,13) 《*for*》 **1** blame; scold; find

fault with; 《*with*》 charge (someone) with. …을 나무라다; …을 꾸짖다; 비난하다. ¶ ~ *someone with carelessness* 아무의 부주의를 꾸짖다 / *His mother reproached him for his bad manners.* 어머니는 그의 무례함을 꾸짖었다 / *It wasn't your fault, you have nothing to ~ yourself with.* 그건 네 잘못이 아니니, 자책할 것 없다. **2** 《rare》 bring shame or dishonor upon. …의 체면을 손상하다. ¶ ~ *someone's character* 아무의 인격을 손상시키다. [F. *reproche(r)*]

re·proach·a·ble [ripróutʃəbəl] *adj.* blamable. 꾸짖을 만한; 나무라야 할.

re·proach·ful [ripróutʃfəl] *adj.* **1** full of reproach; expressing reproach. 꾸짖는; 비난의. ¶ *a ~ speech* 〔*look, letter*〕 비난조의 말〔표정, 편지〕. **2** deserving of reproach; shameful. 욕먹을; 치욕의. ¶ *a ~ life* 부끄러운〔치욕의〕 생활.

re·proach·ful·ly [ripróutʃfəli] *adv.* in a reproachful manner. 꾸짖듯이; 비난조로.

rep·ro·bate [réprəbèit] *n.* Ⓒ a sinful or wicked person rejected by God. 타락자; 신에게서 버림 받은 사람. ¶ *He is an old ~ who spends all his money on beer.* 그는 재산을 술로 탕진하는 타락한 늙은이다. — *adj.* wicked; vicious. 타락한. ¶ *a ~ person* 〔*character*〕 타락한 사람. — *vt.* (P6,13) disapprove of (something) strongly. …을 비난〔반대〕하다. ¶ ~ *plans* 계획을 반대하다 / *They reprobated the cruelty and misdeeds of their countrymen.* 그들은 동족에 의한 잔학 행위와 악행을 비난했다. [re-, →prove]

rep·ro·ba·tion [rèprəbéiʃən] *n.* Ⓤ the act of reprobating; disapproval. 비난; 반대.

re·pro·duce [rìːprədjúːs] *vt.* (P6,13) **1** produce again; cause to appear again. …을 재생하다; 재현시키다. ¶ ~ *a scene from a play* 극의 어떤 장면을 재연하다 / *To ~ the social conditions of prewar days is impossible.* 전쟁 전의 사회 환경을 재현시키는 일은 불가능하다 / *Lobsters are able to ~ claws when they are torn off.* 바닷가재는 집게발이 떨어져나가도 재생시킬 수 있다. **2** make a copy of (something). …을 복사하다; 복제하다. ¶ ~ *a picture on canvas* 캔버스에 그림을 복제하다 / ~ *a movement on a film* 필름에 어떤 동작을 재현하다 / *artistic work which cannot be reproduced today* 오늘날 복제가 불가능한 예술 작품. **3** bear (something) as offspring; become the parent of. …을 낳다; 번식시키다. ¶ ~ *offspring* 자손을 번성시키다. [re-]

re·pro·duc·i·ble [rìːprədjúːsəbəl] *adj.* that can be reproduced. 재생〔복사〕할 수 있는; 번식시킬 수 있는.

re·pro·duc·tion [rìːprədʌ́kʃən] *n.* **1** Ⓤ the act of reproducing. 재생; 재현. **2** Ⓤ a copy. 복사; 복제. **3** Ⓒ something made by reproducing. 복사물; 복제품.

re·pro·duc·tive [rìːprədʌ́ktiv] *adj.* **1** of reproduction. 재현의; 재생의. ¶ ~ *industries* 재생 산업. **2** concerned with reproduction. 생식의. ¶ *the ~ organs* 〔*functions*〕 생식 기관〔기능〕 / *a ~ race* 다산족(多產族).

re·proof [riprúːf] *n.* Ⓤ blame; Ⓒ an expression or words of blame. 비난; 질책; 비난의 말. ¶ *I'll not stand ~ of any kind.* 어떤 비난에도 나는 가만있지 않겠다 / *a word of ~* 비난의 말 / *You can scarcely expect to escape ~ for such irresponsible behavior.* 네 그런 무책임한 행동은 도저히 비난을 면치 못할 것이다. [↓]

re·prove [riprúːv] *vt.* (P6,13) 《*for*》 reproach; scold; blame. …을 꾸짖다; 비난하다. ¶ ~ *someone* 아무를 비난하다 / ~ *someone's conduct* 아무의 행동을 꾸짖다 / *She reproved him for telling lies.* 그녀는 거짓말을 했다고 그를 비난했다. [→reprobate]

re·prov·ing·ly [riprúːviŋli] *adv.* in a blaming manner. 비난하듯이; 비난조로.

rep·tile [réptil, -tail / -tail] *n.* Ⓒ **1** any cold-blooded animal that creeps, such as a snake. 파충류. **2** a mean person. 비열한 인간. ¶ *What ~ hit the blind boy?* 비열한 인간이군, 눈먼 아이를 치다니. — *adj.* **1** of or like a reptile; creeping. 파충류의; 기어다니는. ¶ *a country teeming with ~ life* 파충류가 많은 지역 / *the ~ race* 파충류. **2** low; mean. 비열한; 야비한. ¶ *the ~ press* 어용 신문. [L. *repo* crawl]

rep·til·i·an [reptíliən] *adj.* **1** of reptiles. 파충류의. **2** mean. 비열한.

:re·pub·lic [ripʌ́blik] *n.* Ⓒ **1** a nation ruled by elected representatives of the people. 공화국. ¶ *the French Republic* 프랑스 공화국. **2** the form of such government. 공화 정체(政體). **3** a society whose members are equally engaged in the same activity. (공통의 목적을 가진) …사회; …계(界); 단(壇). ¶ *the ~ of letters* 문단; 문학계. [L. *res* concern, →public]

·re·pub·li·can [ripʌ́blikən] *adj.* **1** of a republic; like that of a republic. 공화국의; 공화 정체의. ¶ *a ~ system* 공화 제도 / *Many countries have a ~ form of government.* 많은 국가들이 공화 정체이다. **2** 《*R-*》 《U.S.》 of the Republican Party in the United States. 공화당의. **3** supporting the principles of a republic. 공화주의의. ¶ *hold ~ opinions* 공화주의를 신봉하다. — *n.* Ⓒ **1** a person who favors republican government. 공화주의자. **2** 《*R-*》 《U.S.》 a member of the Republican Party. 공화 당원(cf. *Democrat*).

re·pub·li·can·ism [ripʌ́blikənìzəm] *n.* Ⓤ **1** republican principles. 공화주의; 공화 정체. **2** 《*R-*》 《U.S.》 principles or policies of the Republican Party in the United States. 공화당의 주의〔정책〕.

Republican Party [-ˊ-- ˊ-], **the** *n.* one of the two major political parties in the United States. 미국 공화당.

re·pub·li·ca·tion [rìːpʌbləkéiʃən] *n.* Ⓤ the act of publishing again; Ⓒ something published again. 재판(再版); 재판물 (cf. *reprint*). [↓]

re·pub·lish [riːpʌ́bliʃ] *vt.* (P6) publish again. …을 재판(再版)하다. [re-]

re·pu·di·ate [ripjúːdièit] *vt.* (P6) **1** refuse to accept (something); reject. …을 거절(거부)하다. ¶ ~ *a gift* 선물을 거절하다 / ~ *a doctrine* (*someone's authority*) 교리(아무의 권위)를 거부하다 / *I* ~ *emphatically any suggestion that I may have acted dishonorably.* 내 행동이 떳떳하지 못했다는 어떤 시사도 나는 단호히 배격한다. **2** refuse to have anything to do with (someone). …와 의절(義絕)하다; 인연을 끊다. ¶ ~ *a son* 아들과 의절하다 / ~ *one's relations* 친척들과 인연을 끊다. **3** refuse to pay (a debt, etc.). (부채 등)의 청산을 거절하다. ¶ ~ *a debt* (*an obligation*) 채무(債務)(책임) 이행을 거부하다 / *The country has repudiated its foreign debts.* 그 나라는 외채 상환을 거부했다. [re-, →pudency]

re·pu·di·a·tion [ripjùːdiéiʃən] *n.* Ⓤ the act of repudiating; the state of being repudiated. 거부; 거절; 의절.

re·pug·nance [ripʌ́gnəns] *n.* ⓊⒸ **1** 《*to, against*》 strong dislike. 강한 혐오; 혐오감. ¶ *feel a* ~ *for someone* …에게 혐오감을 느끼다. **2** a contradiction; inconsistency. 모순; 불일치. ¶ *a* ~ *between two theories* 두 이론사이의 모순. [↓]

re·pug·nant [ripʌ́gnənt] *adj.* **1** 《*to*》 disagreeable; unpleasant. 싫은; 불쾌한. ¶ *This work is* ~ *to lazy men.* 게으른 자에게 이 일은 싫을 거다 / *All food is* ~ *to me just now.* 지금은 아무 것도 먹기 싫다 / *That man has a most* ~ *character.* 저 자는 아주 돼먹지 않은 놈이다. **2** contrary; inconsistent. 모순의; 앞뒤가 맞지 않는. **3** objecting; opposed. 반대하는. ¶ *George Washington was* ~ *to every sort of dishonesty.* 워싱턴은 모든 부정직을 혐오했다. [re-, →pugnacious]

re·pulse [ripʌ́ls] *vt.* (P6) **1** repel; drive back. (적을) 물리치다; 격퇴하다. ¶ *Our soldiers repulsed the enemy.* 아군은 적을 격퇴했다. **2** reject; refuse to accept. 퇴짜 놓다; (제의 등)을 거절하다. ¶ *She coldly repulsed him.* 그녀는 차갑게 그의 말을 거절했다. —*n.* ⓊⒸ **1** an act of driving back. 격퇴. ¶ *meet with* (*suffer*) (*a*) ~ 격퇴당하다 / *The quick* ~ *of the enemy by his army surprised the general.* 장군은 자기 군대가 적을 신속히 격퇴하자 놀랐다. **2** a refusal. 거부. ¶ *His request met with another* ~. 그의 요청은 재차 거절당했다. [re-]

re·pul·sion [ripʌ́lʃən] *n.* Ⓤ **1** strong dislike. 혐오. **2** the act of driving back. 격퇴. **3** 《phys.》 the force tending to drive two bodies further apart. 척력(斥力); 반발 작용 (opp. attraction). [↑]

re·pul·sive [ripʌ́lsiv] *adj.* **1** causing strong dislike. 싫은; 혐오감을 주는(opp. attractive). ¶ *Snakes are* ~ *to some people.* 사람에 따라 뱀은 심한 혐오감을 준다 / *a* ~ *sight* 끔찍한 광경 / *a* ~ *smell* (*taste*) 고약한 냄새(맛). **2** 《phys.》 having repulsion. 반발하는. ¶ ~ *forces* 척력(斥力).

rep·u·ta·ble [répjətəbəl] *adj.* having a good reputation; honorable. 평판이 좋은; 훌륭한. ¶ *He is a man of* ~ *character.* 그는 인격이 훌륭한 사람이다 / *He leads a* ~ *life.* 그는 남이 본받을 만한 생활을 하고 있다. ● **rep·u·ta·bly** [-i] *adv.* [→repute]

:rep·u·ta·tion [rèpjətéiʃən] *n.* ⓊⒸ **1** a good name; fame. 명성; 신망. ¶ *a man of* ~ 명망가 / *lose one's* ~ 신망을 잃다 / *He enjoys a high* ~ *as a writer.* 그는 작가로서의 명성이 높다 / *a man of world-wide* ~ 세계적으로 알려진 덕망가 / *a person of no* ~ 덕망이 없는 사람. **2** what people think and say about the character of a person or thing; one's character in the opinion of others. 세평(世評); 평판(評判). ¶ *He is in good* (*bad, poor*) ~. 그는 평판이 좋다(나쁘다) / *This store has an excellent* ~ *for fair dealing.* 이 가게는 정직하기로 평판이 나 있다 / *He has a* ~ *for being kind to the poor.* 그는 가난한 자에게 친절하기로 소문이 나 있다 / *live up to one's reputation* 명성에 부끄럽지 않게 살다 / *He has the* ~ *of being bright.* 머리가 좋다는 평이다 / *He has the* ~ *of being difficult to get on with.* 그는 사귀기 힘들다는 소문이다.

re·pute [ripjúːt] *n.* Ⓤ reputation; fame. 평판; 호평. ¶ *a man of good* ~ 평판이 좋은 사람 / *the author of* ~ 이름있는 작가 / *This is a district of bad* ~ *on account of many robberies.* 여기는 도둑이 많기로 이름이 난 지역이다 / *know someone by* ~ …을 소문을 듣고 알고 있다 / *wines of* ~ 맛 좋기로 이름난 포도주. —*vt.* (P21) 《usu. *passive*》 think; suppose. …라고 생각하다; 간주하다. ¶ *He is reputed to be stingy.* 그는 쩨쩨한 사람이라고 한다 / *He is reputed to be a perfect fool.* 그를 숙맥이라고들 한다 / *be well* (*ill*) *reputed* 평이 좋다(나쁘다). [re-, L. *puto* think]

re·put·ed [ripjúːtid] *adj.* supposed; considered to be. …라 일컬어지는(생각되는). [↑]

re·put·ed·ly [ripjúːtidli] *adv.* by reputation. 소문(평판)으로는.

:re·quest [rikwést] *n.* **1** ⓊⒸ the act of asking for something. 부탁; 요청; 요구; 소망. ¶ *yield to* ~ 부탁을 들어주다 / *I did it at his* ~. 그의 요청으로 한 일이다 / *I made a* ~ *for his help.* 나는 그의 도움을 요청했다 / *A catalog will be mailed free on* (*upon*) ~. 요청하시면 카탈로그를 무료로 우송해 드립니다 / *make many requests for assistance* 도와 달라고 많은 요청을 하다 / *Your* ~ *for a ticket was made too late.* 표 부탁을 너무 늦게 했다. **2** Ⓒ that which is asked for. 부탁(요구)한 것. ¶ *What is your* ~*?* 부탁이 뭔데 / *Your requests are granted.* 부탁을 들어드

리지요 / *The king granted his* ~. 왕은 그의 요구를 들어주었다. **3** Ⓤ demand. 수요(需要). ¶ *She is such a good dancer that she is in great* ~. 그녀는 춤을 잘 춰 대인기다.

by request, in answer to a request. 요청에 의해. ¶ *She sang again by* ~. 그녀는 요청에 의해 재창했다.

(***much***) ***in request,*** asked for by many people; in demand. 수요가 많은. ¶ *Is this book much in* ~? 이 책은 잘 팔리나.

— *vt.* (P6,8,11,13,15,20) 《*from, for, of*》 ask for (something); ask (someone) to do something. …을 —에게 청하다; 부탁하다. ¶ ~ *a loan from a friend* 친구에게 돈을 부탁하다 / *He requested his guests to sit down.* =*He requested that his guests* (*should*) *sit down.* 그는 손님들에게 앉으라고 권했다. 語法 미국에서는 that clause의 should는 생략됨 / *Your presence is requested immediately.* 즉시 와주십시오 / *The presence of all members is requested.* 모든 회원은 참석하기 바람 / ~ *leave* 〔*permission*〕 *to do* 〔*see, go*〕 하기〔보기, 가기〕를 허락해주길 바라다 / *We* ~ *the favor of a reply.* 답변해주시길 바랍니다 / *He requested me to write a letter of recommendation.* 그는 내게 추천장을 써달라고 부탁했다. [re-]

req·ui·em [rékwiəm, rí-] *n.* Ⓒ 《Cath.》 a mass for the dead; music for this mass. 죽은 이를 위한 미사; 레퀴엠; 그 곡. [L.= rest]

:re·quire [rikwáiər] *vt.* **1** (P6,11,13,20) demand; ask; order. …을 요구하다; 명하다. ¶ *The police required my appearance.* 경찰은 나의 출두를 요구해 왔다 / *He did all that was required of him.* 그에게 요구하면 무어든 다 했다 / *He required me to pay the money.* =*He required that I* (*should*) *pay the money.* 그는 내게 돈을 갚으라고 했다. 語法 미국에서는 that-clause 의 should 는 흔히 생략함 / *You are required to report to the police at once.* 경찰에 즉시 보고하라는 명령이다 / *The law requires strict observance in every detail.* 법률은 모든 세부 사항을 엄수할 것을 요구하고 있다. **2** (P6,8,9,11) need; want; call for. …을 필요로 하다. ¶ *We shall* ~ *more help.* 우리에겐 도움이 더 필요하다 / *We* ~ *to know it.* 우린 그것을 알아야 하겠다 / *These girls* ~ *looking after.* 이 소녀들을 돌봐줄 필요가 있다 / *This matter requires careful consideration.* 이 문제는 신중히 생각할 필요가 있다 / *Do not tie it more tightly than required.* 그걸 필요 이상으로 꽉 묶지 마라.

— *vi.* (P1) 《chiefly Brit.》 be necessary; demand. 필요로 하다. ¶ *if circumstances* ~ 사정이 어쩔 수 없다면; 부득이하다면. [re-, L. *quaero* seek, ask]

***re·quire·ment** [rikwáiərmənt] *n.* Ⓒ a need; something required. 요구(되는 것); 필요(물). ¶ *the requirements for entrance to college* 대학에 입학하기 위한 필요 조건 / *My requirements are few and reasonable.* 내 요구는 얼마 되지도 않고 경우에 틀리는 것도 아니다 / *You have not fulfilled the requirements of the law.* 너는 법적인 구비 요건을 갖추지 못했다.

req·ui·site [rékwəzit] *adj.* necessary; very much required. 필요한; 없어서는 안 될. ¶ *a* ~ *amount of food* 필요한 만큼의 식량 / *Do you have the* ~ *patience for such work?* 너 그런 일을 감당할 수 있겠니 / *the qualities* ~ *for a leader* 지도자가 갖춰야 할 자질 / *the number of votes* ~ *for election* 표결에 필요한 투표 수. — *n.* Ⓒ something required. 필수품. ¶ ~ *for life* 생필품 / *Hard work seems no longer a* ~ *for a living.* 이제는 살아가는 데 꼭 열심히 일해야 하는 것도 아닌 모양이다. [*require*]

req·ui·si·tion [rèkwəzíʃən] *n.* **1** ⓊⒸ the act of requiring. 요구. **2** Ⓒ a formal written demand. 청구서. ¶ *the* ~ *of supplies for troops* 증원군 요청서. **3** 《rare》 Ⓒ an essential condition. 필요 조건.

be in requisition, be in demand. 수요가 있다. ¶ *His new bicycle was in constant* ~ *for family errands.* 그의 새 자전거는 집안 심부름에 필요했다.

— *vt.* (P6,13) **1** make demands upon; demand supplies from; order. …에 요구하다; 징발을 명하다. ¶ ~ *a town for food* 마을에 식량 징발을 명하다. **2** demand or take by authority. …을 소집〔징발〕하다(cf. *embargo*). ¶ ~ *all the horses in a district* 어떤 지역의 모든 말을 징발하다. [↑]

re·quit·al [rikwáitl] *n.* Ⓤ **1** the act of requiting; a return for wrong; punishment. 앙갚음; 보복. ¶ *The wicked man got a severe* ~. 그 악한 자는 모진 보복을 당했다 / *I have made full* ~. 앙갚음을 충분히 했다. **2** the act of rewarding; payment. 보답; 보상. ¶ *What* ~ *can I make for all his help?* 그의 도움을 무엇으로 보답한다지 / *do something in* ~ *of* 〔*for*〕 *a service* 수고의 보답으로 …을 해주다. [re-, →quiet]

re·quite [rikwáit] *vt.* (P6,13) pay back; reward; make a return for (a service, an injury, etc.). …에게 보답하다; 앙갚음하다. ¶ ~ *evil with good* 악을 선으로 갚다 / ~ *someone for a kindness* 아무의 친절에 보답하다. [↑]

requite like for like, return good for good or evil to evil. 같은 수단으로 갚다; 은혜는 은혜로, 악은 악으로 갚다.

re·read [riːríːd] *vt.* (**-read** [-réd]) (P6) read again. …을 다시 읽다. [re-]

re·scind [risínd] *vt.* (P6) cancel; repeal; cut off by force. …을 취소하다; 무효로 하다. ¶ ~ *a law* 〔*resolution, judgment, contract*〕 법률〔결의, 판결, 계약〕을 무효화시키다. [re-, L. *scindo* cut]

re·scis·sion [risíʒən] *n.* Ⓤ the act of rescinding. 취소; 무효. [↑]

re·script [ríːskrìpt] *n.* Ⓒ **1** an official

announcement by a ruler, etc. 칙령; 칙유(勅諭). **2** a written reply to a question or petition. (청원 따위에 대한) 칙답서(勅答書). [re-]

:res·cue [réskju:] *vt.* (P6,13) 《*from*》 save; set free; deliver. …을 구하다; 놓아주다. ¶ ~ *a prisoner* 죄수를 석방시키다 / ~ *someone from a fire* 불길에서 아무를 구해내다 / ~ *an old building from decay* 낡은 건물의 황폐화를 막다. — *n.* UC the act of saving from danger or harm. 구조; 구출. ¶ *The fireman was praised for his brave ~ of the children in the burning house.* 소방수는 불타고 있는 집에서 아이들을 용감하게 구출하여 칭찬받았다 / *He went to her ~.* 그는 그녀를 구조하러 갔다. [re-, ex-, →quash]

res·cu·er [réskju:ər] *n.* C a person who rescues. 구조자.

·re·search [risə́:rtʃ, rí:sə:rtʃ] *n.* UC careful study or investigation for accurate or new information. 연구; 조사; 탐구. ¶ *Men of science are continuing ~ on peaceful uses of atomic energy.* 과학자들은 원자력의 평화적 이용을 위한 연구를 계속하고 있다 / *make researches into the causes of cancer* 암의 원인을 조사 연구하다. — *vi.* (P1,3) make researches; investigate; study. 조사하다; 연구하다. ¶ ~ *into a problem* 문제를 조사하다. [re-]

re·search·er [risə́:rtʃər, rí:sə:r-] *n.* C a person who does research; an investigator. 연구자; 조사원.

re·seat [ri:sí:t] *vt.* (P6) **1** seat again. …을 다시 앉히다. ¶ *The callers reseated themselves.* 방문객들은 다시 자리에 앉았다 / *He was reseated on the committee after he had been found innocent of all charges.* 그는 그에 대한 모든 비난이 사실 무근임이 밝혀져 위원회에 복귀되었다. **2** ⓐ supply (a theater, etc.) with new seats. …에 새 좌석을 마련하다. ¶ ~ *a church* 교회에 새 좌석을 마련하다. ⓑ put a new seat on. (의자의) 앉는 부분을 갈다. ¶ ~ *a chair* 의자 바닥을 갈아대다. [re-]

re·sem·blance [rizémbləns] *n.* UC the state of being similar; something which resembles; likeness; similarity. 유사(점). ¶ *He shows a great ~ to his mother.* 그는 자기 어머니를 빼쏘았다 / *There is a strong ~ between the two sisters.* 두 자매는 아주 닮았다 / *a certain ~ between the styles of the two writers* 두 작가의 문체의 어떤 유사점. [↓]

bear* 〔*have*〕 *a resemblance to (=*be very similar to*) *someone or something.* …와 닮다.

:re·sem·ble [rizémbəl] *vt.* (P6) be like; be very similar to (someone). …와 비슷하다; 닮다. ¶ *She resembles her sister.* 그녀는 언니를 닮았다 / *She resembles her sister in appearance but not in character.* 그녀는 외모는 언니를 닮았으나 성격은 그렇지 않다. [re-, →similar]

·re·sent [rizént] *vt.* (P6,9) feel angry at (doing) (something); be irritated by (someone or something). …에 화내다; 분개하다. ¶ *Grace resented being called a baby.* 그레이스는 아기라는 말에 화를 냈다 / *He resented her remarks about his driving.* 그는 자기 운전에 대한 그녀의 비평에 화를 냈다 / *He doesn't have the spirit to ~ an insult.* 그는 모욕을 당해도 화낼 줄 모른다. [re-, →sense]

re·sent·ful [rizéntfəl] *adj.* feeling anger or displeasure; angry. 불쾌한; 화가 난.

·re·sent·ment [rizéntmənt] *n.* U anger; displeasure. 분개; 분함; 원망.

·res·er·va·tion [rèzərvéiʃən] *n.* **1** ⓐ UC the act of holding back; reserving in part; something not expressed; a limiting condition. 보류; 유보; 조건. ¶ *I agree with the ~ that….* …라는 조건으로 동의한다 / *She accepted the invitation with mental reservations.* 그다지 마음내키지 않았으나 그녀는 초대에 응했다. ⓑ C 《often *pl.*》 an arrangement to keep a thing for someone; something reserved. 예약(된 것). ¶ *We have reservations for rooms at that hotel.* 그 호텔에 방을 몇 개 예약했다. **2** UC limitation. 제한. **3** C 《U.S.》 land set aside, esp. for American Indians. (미국에서 인디언을 위한) 보류지; 보호 지역. [↓]

make reservations, reserve. 예약하다.

without reservations, unconditionally. 조건 없이.

with reservations, conditionally. 조건부로. ¶ *I agree with you, but with some reservations.* 네게 동의는 하나 몇가지 조건이 있다.

:re·serve [rizə́:rv] *vt.* (P6,13) **1** keep back (something) for later use. …을 여축(餘蓄)〔비축〕하다. ¶ ~ *money for emergencies* 비상 사태를 위해 돈을 저축하다 / *Reserve your strength* 〔*yourself*〕 *for the climb.* 등산을 대비해 힘을 아껴 둬라. **2** keep (something) for a special person. …을 예약하다. ¶ *All seats reserved.* 전좌석 예약필 / ~ *a seat at a theater* 극장에 자리 하나를 예약하다. **3** put off (something) till a later time; postpone; delay. …을 연기하다. ¶ *I'll ~ my decision until I hear from him.* 그에게서 소식이 있을 때까지 결정을 미루겠다 / *This question must be reserved for further consideration.* 이 문제는 더 두고 생각해봐야 한다 / *The court will ~ judgement.* 법정은 판결을 연기한다. **4** keep (something) for oneself; retain. …을 보유하다. ¶ *He reserves all rights in this book.* 이 책의 저작권은 그에게 있다 / *All rights reserved.* 저작권 소유. **5** destine. …을 운명지우다. ¶ *A great future is reserved for this boy.* 이 아이의 앞날은 창창하다 / *The invention was reserved for Edison.* 이 발명은 에디슨에 의해서 처음으로 이루어졌다 / *Fate reserved a severe punishment for him.*

그에게는 가혹한 벌이 숙명적으로 기다리고 있었다.

— *n.* **1** Ⓤ the state of being reserved; Ⓒ something reserved. 비축; 예비; 예비품. ¶ *a ~ of food* 식량의 비축 / *the* 〔*a*〕 *gold ~* 금(金)준비 / *have* 〔*keep*〕 *a little food in ~* 식량을 좀 비축해 두다 / *The city's ~ of water is low.* 그 시의 급수 저장량은 많지 않다. **2** ⓐ《often *pl.*》 troops kept back in battle and held ready for support. 예비대(隊). ¶ *Reserve will be sent to help the men fighting at the front.* 지원군이 전방군의 지원을 위해 투입될 것이다. ⓑ forces outside regular army and navy liable to be called out in emergencies. 예비군. ¶ *call up the reserves* 예비군을 소집하다. **3** Ⓒ an area of land reserved for a special use. 특별 보류지. ¶ *a game ~* 금렵구(禁獵區) / *a ~ for wild animals* 야생 동물 보호구 / *a forest ~* 보안림. **4** ⓊⒸ limitation; exception; condition ; (of mental condition) the act of keeping back. 제한; 제외; 조건; (심리적인) 유보. ¶ *We publish this with all ~.* 발표는 하지만 그 진위(眞僞)를 보증하지 못함 / *accept a statement with* 〔*without*〕 *~* 성명을 조건부로〔조건 없이〕 수락하다 / *You may speak before her without ~.* 그녀 앞에선 꺼리낌없이 얘기해도 괜찮다 / *place* 〔*put*〕 *a ~ upon a house* 〔*picture*〕 가옥〔그림〕에 최저가를 매기다 / *be sold without ~* 값에 제한을 안 두고 팔리다. **5** Ⓤ self-control in speech and behavior. 자제(自制); 삼감. ¶ *break down* 〔*throw off*〕 *~* 터놓고 지내다 / *the traditional ~ of the Englishman.* 영국인의 전통적인 신중함 / *She told me all about it without ~.* 그녀는 내게 그것에 대해 터놓고 다 이야기했다. **6** a silent manner that keeps people from making friends easily. (거리를 둔) 말없고 쌀쌀한 태도; 냉담. ¶ *He received my advances with considerable ~.* 그는 나의 접근을 선뜻 받아들이지 않았다.

— *adj.* kept in reserve; forming a reserve. 예비의; 준비해 둔. ¶ *a ~ fund* 준비금. [L. *servo* keep]

re·served [rizə́ːrvd] *adj.* **1** kept in reserve; set apart. 보류된; 따로 둔; 예약된; 전세낸. ¶ *a ~ car* 전세차 / *a ~ seat* 예약〔지정〕석. **2** quiet in manner; self-restrained in action or speech. (태도가) 겸손한; 말수가 적은; 수줍어하는. ¶ *She is a very ~ girl.* 그녀는 아주 내성적인 소녀다 / *He has a very ~ manner.* 그는 태도가 아주 겸손하다.

re·serv·ist [rizə́ːrvist] *n.* Ⓒ a soldier or sailor not on active service. 예비군; 재향 군인.

res·er·voir [rézərvwàːr, -vwɔ̀ːr] *n.* Ⓒ **1** a place where water is collected and stored for use. 저수지. ¶ *Most of the city's water comes from this ~.* 도시가 쓰는 물은 대부분 이 저수지에서 온다. **2** anything to hold a liquid. 용기(容器). ¶ *the ~ of a lamp* 램프의 기름통 / *the ink ~ of a fountainpen* 만년필의 잉크통. **3** a place where anything is collected and stored 저장소. ¶ *His mind is a ~ of information.* 그의 머리는 지식의 저장소다. **4** a great supply. 축적. ¶ *a ~ of knowledge* 〔*wealth, strength*〕. 지식〔부, 힘〕의 축적. [→reserve]

re·set [riːsét] *vt.* (**-set, -set·ting**) (P6) **1** set or place again. …을 고쳐 놓다; 바꿔 놓다〔끼우다〕. ¶ *~ a diamond in platinum* 백금에 다이아몬드를 고쳐 박다 / *John's broken arm had to be ~.* 존의 부러진 팔은 접골을 해야 했다. **2** sharpen again. 다시 갈다. ¶ *~ a saw.* — [ríːsèt] *n.* Ⓤ the act of resetting. 다시 놓기; 고쳐 박기. [re-]

re·set·tle [riːsétl] *vt., vi.* (P6;1) settle again; settle in a new place or a new way of life. 다시 정주(定住)시키다〔하다〕. [re-]

re·shape [riːʃéip] *vt.* form (something) into a new shape. 고쳐 만들다; 새로운 모양으로 하다. [re-]

re·shuf·fle [riːʃʌ́fəl] *vt.* (P6) **1** mix (playing cards) again. (카드 패를) 다시 치다. ¶ *~ cards.* **2** organize or arrange again. …을 재편성하다. ¶ *~ the Cabinet* 개각하다. — *n.* Ⓤ the act of reshuffling; the state of being reshuffled. (카드 패의) 다시 치기; (내각 등의) 재편성; 개각. [re-]

·re·side [rizáid] *vi.* (P2A;2B) **1** 《*at, in*》 live; have one's home at; dwell. 살다; 거주〔거류〕하다. ¶ *He resides in New York, but is now staying in the country.* 그는 뉴욕에 거주하고 있으나 지금은 시골에 있다 / *They ~ abroad.* 그들은 해외에 거주하고 있다 / *In order to keep a term at Oxford, one must ~ for at least seven weeks.* 옥스퍼드 대학에 한 학기 다니려면 거기서 적어도 7주간을 살아야 한다. **2** 《*in*》 (of rights, etc.) exist; rest in. (권리 등이) …에 있다; 귀속하다. ¶ *In a democracy it is with the people that the real power resides.* 민주주의에서는 진정한 권리는 국민에게 있다 / *Authority resides for the most part in old people.* 권위는 대부분이 나이 많은 사람들 차지다 / *The power to change the law resides in Parliament.* 법률 개정권은 의회에 있다. **3** 《*in*》 be in; be found in. (성질 등이) …에 있다; 발견되다. ¶ *Happiness resides in having many friends.* 행복은 벗이 많은 데 있다 / *It is in such actions that true courage resides.* 그러한 행동에서 진정한 용기를 보게 된다. [re-, L. *sedeo* sit]

:res·i·dence [rézidəns] *n.* **1** Ⓒ a home; a large and fine house. 주거; 주택; (특히) 저택. ¶ *He will be found at his ~.* 그분은 지금 댁에 계실겁니다 / *a delightful French ~ for sale* 팔려고 내놓은 훌륭한 프랑스풍의 저택 / *an official ~* 관저. **2** Ⓤ the act of living; the act of dwelling; the period of residing somewhere. 거주; 거주 기간. ¶ *He took up ~ in Jamaica.* 그는 자메이카에 살러 갔다. [↑]

***res·i·dent** [rézidənt] *n.* Ⓒ **1** a permanent inhabitant in a place. 거주자; 정주자(opp. visitor). ¶ *summer residents* 피서객 / *foreign residents* 주재 외국인 / *He is a ~ of London.* 그는 런던 주민이다. **2** a non-migratory bird. 텃새; 유조(留鳥). — *adj.* **1** staying; dwelling. 거주하는; 주재하는. ¶ *Grandmother wants a resident companion.* 할머니는 동무 삼아 같이 살 사람을 원하신다 / *a ~ doctor at the hospital* 병원에서 숙식하는 수련의 / *a ~ tutor* 입주 가정 교사 / *the ~ population* 상주 인구. **2** existing; present; peculiar to. 내재하는; 고유의. ¶ *faculties ~ in a particular part of the brain.* 뇌의 특정 부위가 가지는 기능 / *powers which are ~ in the royal prerogative* 대권(大權) 고유의 권력.

res·i·den·tial [rèzidénʃəl] *adj.* **1** of or related to residence. 주거의. ¶ *a ~ hotel* 주거용 호텔 / *the ~ qualification for voters* 투표자에게 필요한 거주 자격. **2** suitable for, used for, or occupied by private houses. 주택의; 주택에 적합한. ¶ *He lives in a good ~ quarter.* 그는 좋은 주택 구역에 살고 있다 / *a ~ district* 주택 지구 / *There are no stores in ~ areas.* 주택지에는 가게가 없다.

re·sid·u·a [rizídʒuə] *n.* pl. of **residuum.**

re·sid·u·al [rizídʒuəl] *adj.* **1** left over. 나머지의. **2** (of an error in calculations) still unaccounted for. (계산의 오차를) 설명할 수 없는. [*reside*]

re·sid·u·ar·y [rizídʒuèri / -əri] *adj.* **1** remaining. 나머지의. **2** ⟪law⟫ of the residue of an estate. 잔여 재산의. ¶ *the ~ legatee* 잔여 재산 수유자(受遺者).

res·i·due [rézidjùː] *n.* Ⓒ **1** what remains after a part has been taken away; the rest. 나머지. ¶ *Ash is the ~ of coal.* 재는 탄이 타고 남은 찌꺼기다 / *The syrup had dried up, leaving a sticky ~.* 시럽이 말라버리고 끈끈한 찌꺼기가 남았다. **2** ⟪law⟫ the part of an estate remaining after payment of all debts, etc. (채무 등을 갚고 남은) 잔여 재산. [*reside*]

re·sid·u·um [rizídʒuəm] *n.* Ⓒ (*pl.* **-sid·u·a**) something that remains at the end of a process; a remainder. 찌꺼기; 나머지. [↑]

re-sign [riːsáin] *vt.* (P6) sign again. …에 다시 서명하다. [re-]

***re·sign** [rizáin] *vt.* **1** (P6) give up. …을 그만두다; 단념하다; 사직하다. ¶ *~ one's position on the school board* 교육 위원 자리를 내놓다 / *~ one's office* 사직하다 / *~ all hopes* 모든 희망을 버리다 / *~ one's expectations* 기대를 버리다 / *If Paul resigns, who will get the job ?* 폴이 그만둔다면 그 일을 누가 맡지. **2** (P13) ⟪*to*⟫ hand over to; yield to. …에 양도하다. ¶ *~ one's duties to more capable hands* 더 유능한 사람에게 직무를 넘겨주다. **3** (P13) ⟪*oneself* [*one's mind*] *to*⟫ ⓐ submit to; yield to. …에 따르다; 몸을 맡기다. ¶ *Resign yourselves to the will of God.* 하느님의 뜻에 따라라 / *He resigned himself to fate.* 그는 운명에 몸을 맡겼다. ⓑ reconcile oneself; accept and suffer calmly. …을 체념[단념]하다. ¶ *~ oneself to performing a disagreeable duty* 하기 싫은 일이지만 체념하고 수행하다. — *vi.* **1** (P1,3) ⟪*from, as*⟫ give up a position or an office. 사직[사임]하다. ¶ *He refused to ~ from his office.* 그는 사임하기를 거부했다 / *The manager of the football team resigned.* 축구 팀 감독은 사임했다. **2** accept something as inevitable; submit. 맡기다; 따르다. ⟪*to*⟫ ¶ *We must ~ to our fate.* 우리는 운명에 따라야 한다. [re-]

res·ig·na·tion [rèzignéiʃən] *n.* **1** Ⓤ the act of giving up; the act of giving up a position. 단념; 사직. ¶ *the ~ of the Ministry* [*Cabinet*] 내각의 총사직 / *There have been so many resignations from the committee that a new one must be formed.* 위원들의 사직이 너무 많아 위원회의 재구성이 불가피하다. **2** Ⓒ a formal statement showing that one gives up a position; an offer to resign. 사표; 사직원. ¶ *send* [*hand*] *in one's ~* 사표를 제출하다 / *His ~ was immediately accepted.* 그의 사직원은 즉각 수리되었다. **3** Ⓤ the state of being resigned to something. 체념. ¶ *She bore the pain with ~.* 체념하고 고통을 참았다 / *She accepted the misfortune with ~.* 그녀는 체념하고 불행을 받아들였다. [*resign*]

re·signed [rizáind] *adj.* accepting calmly and with patience. 체념한; 감수하고 있는. ¶ *She is ~ to her fate.* 그녀는 자기 운명을 감수하고 있다 / *We grow ~ to old age.* 우리는 어쩔 수 없이 늙어가고 있다.

re·sign·ed·ly [rizáinidli] *adv.* in a resigned manner. 체념하고.

re·sil·i·ence [rizíljəns, -liəns] *n.* Ⓤ the ability to spring back; the power of recovery; elasticity. 되튐; 탄력(성); 회복력. ¶ *Rubber and sponge have ~.* 고무와 스펀지에는 탄력이 있다 / *The Prime Minister lacked the ~ to survive the crisis.* 수상은 위기를 극복하고 헤어날 능력이 부족하였다. [re-, →sailent]

re·sil·i·ent [rizíljənt, -liənt] *adj.* **1** springing back; elastic. 되튀는; 탄력 있는. ¶ *the ~ bough of a young tree* 어린 나무의 탄력 있는 가지 / *~ steel* 탄력강(鋼). **2** cheerful; having the power of quick recovery. 쾌활한; 복원력이 강한. ¶ *a ~ nature* 쾌활한 성격 / *It's been a terrible shock, but she is very ~ and will get over it soon.* 그것은 엄청난 충격이었다. 그러나 그녀는 극히 낙천적이어서 곧 다시 일어설 것이다. [↑]

res·in [rézin] *n.* ⓊⒸ a sticky material found in certain trees, esp. the pine and the fir. 송진; 수지(cf. *gum*[1], *rosin*). ¶ *~ soap* (제지용) 수지(樹脂) 비누 / *Resin is used in medicine, varnishes, etc.* 수지는 약품, 니스 등에 쓰인다 / *Pine ~ is frequently* *used and is often called 'rosin'.* 송진은 많이 쓰이는데 이것을 흔히 '로진'이라 한다. [L. *resina*]

res·in·ous [rézənəs] *adj.* made of resin; containing resin. 수지(樹脂)로 만든; 수지성의. ¶ ~ *wood* 수지가 많은 나무.

:re·sist [rizíst] *vt.* (P6,9) **1** stand up against (someone or something). …에 저항하다; 반대하다. ¶ *The door resisted her efforts to open it.* 그녀가 문을 열려고 했으나 문은 열리지 않았다 / *The sea-wall cannot ~ the force of the waves.* 호안(護岸)은 파도의 힘에 견뎌낼 수 없다 / *The city resisted the enemy onslaught for two weeks.* 시는 2주간이나 적의 공격에 저항해 싸웠다. **2** drive back by force; hinder. …을 격퇴하다; 방해하다. ¶ *We resisted the attacks of the enemy.* 우린 적의 공격을 물리쳤다 / ~ *the police in the discharge of their duty* 경찰의 공무 집행을 방해하다. **3** remain uninjured by; be proof against. …에 견디다. ¶ ~ *disease* 병을 이겨내다 / *Her weak frame was unable to ~ the fatigues of the journey.* 약골인 그녀는 여행의 피로를 견딜 수 없었다. **4** try to prevent; keep from. …을 참다. ¶ *I couldn't ~ laughing.* 웃지 않을 수 없었다 / *He can never ~ making a joke.* 그는 농담을 안 하고는 못 배긴다 / *I cannot ~ your invitation to shoot.* 네가 사냥을 가자는데 안 갈 수야 없지 / *It was so ludicrous, she could scarcely ~ a smile.* 너무 익살맞아서 웃음을 참을 수 없었다. [re-, L. *sisto* stand]

·re·sist·ance [rizístəns] *n.* Ⓤ **1** the act of resisting or opposing. 저항; 반항. ¶ *He made no ~ to the robber.* 그는 도둑에게 저항하지 않았다 / *With a pistol pointed at him, the bank clerk could make no ~ to the robber.* 권총을 들이대자 은행원은 강도한테 저항할 수 없었다. **2** power to resist. 저항력. ¶ *He has little ~ to germ.* 그는 세균에 대한 저항력이 거의 없다 / *Alcohol lessens ~ to disease.* 술은 병에 대한 저항력을 약화시킨다 / *The aircraft is streamlined to cut down wind ~.* 비행기는 공기의 저항력을 줄이기 위해 유선형으로 되어 있다. **3** 《electr.》 ⓐ the property of a conductor by which the flow of an electric current is opposed. 저항. ¶ *Copper has less ~ than lead.* 구리는 납보다 저항이 약하다. ⓑ =resistor.

the line of least resistance, 《*fig.*》 the easiest mothod of course. 가장 손쉬운 방법.

re·sist·ant [rizístənt] *adj.* resisting. 저항하는. ¶ *This new type of infection is ~ to antibiotics.* 이 새 유형의 전염병은 항생물질에 저항력이 있다.

re·sist·less [rizístlis] *adj.* **1** that cannot be resisted. 저항할 수 없는. ¶ *A ~ impulse made him wander over the earth.* 참을 수 없는 충동이 그로 하여금 세상을 떠돌게 만들었다. **2** lacking power to resist. 저항력이 없는.

re·sis·tor [rizístər] *n.* Ⓒ 《electr.》 a conducting body used in an electric circuit. 저항기(器).

re·sol·u·ble [rizáljəbəl / -zɔ́l-] *adj.* capable of being resolved. 분해할 수 있는. [↓]

·res·o·lute [rézəlùːt] *adj.* firm; determined. 단호한; 결심이 굳은. ¶ *Despite the opposition to his plan, he remained ~.* 그의 계획에 대한 반대가 있었으나 그는 단호했다 / *a ~ optimist* 철저한 낙천가 / *a ~ will* 결연한 의지. [→resolve]

·res·o·lu·tion [rèzəlúːʃən] *n.* **1** ⓊⒸ fixed determination. 결의; 결심. ¶ *a man of ~* 의지가 굳은사람 / *He made a ~ to be kind to people.* 남에게 친절해야겠다고 결심했다 / *She's always making good resolutions but she seldom carries them out.* 그녀는 늘 행실을 고치겠다고 결심하지만 실행은 드물다. **2** Ⓤ the power of holding firmly to a purpose. 의지; 과단(성). ¶ *He is a man of little ~.* 우유부단한 사람이다. **3** ⓊⒸ the act of solving; solution. 해결; 해답. ¶ *the ~ of a doubt* 〔*problem*〕 의문〔문제〕의 해결. **4** the act or process of resolving into compoment parts. 분해; 분석.

re·solv·a·ble [rizálvəbəl / -zɔ́l-] *adj.* that can be resolved. 분해〔해결〕할 수 있는.

:re·solve [rizálv / -zɔ́lv] *vt.* **1** (P8,11) make up one's mind; determine. …을 결심하다. ¶ *I resolved to give up smoking.* 담배를 끊기로 결심했다 / *He resolved that no one should prevent him from going to America.* 그는 누가 뭐래도 미국에 가기로 결심했다. **2** (P8,11) decide (something) by vote. …을 의결(議決)하다. ¶ *Most of the problems were resolved at the last meeting.* 문제의 대부분은 마지막 집회에서 의결되었다. **3** (P6,11) find the answer to (a problem, etc.); solve; make (doubts, etc.) clear. (문제 등)을 풀다; 해결하다; (의혹 등)을 해소하다. ¶ *All doubts were resolved.* 모든 의혹은 해소됐다 / *The question resolves itself into this.* 문제는 이렇게 결말이 났다. **4** (P6,11) 《*into*》 separate (something) into part; analyze; transform. …을 분해〔용해·분석〕하다; (분해하여) 변형시키다. ¶ ~ *a substance into its elements* 물질을 원소로 분해하다. — *vi.* **1** (P3) 《*into, to*》 be resolved; change into a simpler form. 분해하다; 환원하다(opp combine). **2** (P1,3) 《*on, upon*》 determine; decide. 결심하다. ¶ *The government resolved on a bold policy.* 정부는 과감한 방침을 취하기로 했다 / *He resolved on going up to Seoul.* 그는 상경하기로 결심했다.

be resolved (=*have made up one's mind*) ***to do.*** …할 결심을 하고 있다.

— *n.* ⓊⒸ a fixed intention; something determined; a resolution; firmness of character or purpose. 결심; 결의; 의결; 결단. ¶ *a man of ~* 결의가 굳은 사람 / *He kept his ~ not to drink.* 그는 금주하겠다는 결심을 지켰다 / *Her encouragement and support strengthen our ~.* 그녀의 격려와 지지로 우리는 결심을 굳혔다. [re-, L. *solvo* solve]

re·solved [rizálvd / -zɔ́l-] *adj.* firm; determined; firmly decided. 단호한. ¶ *I am ~ to do this.* 이건 꼭 하고야 말겠다.

re·solv·ent [rizálvənt / -zɔ́l-] *adj.* resolving. 분해하는.

res·o·nance [rézənəns] *n.* Ⓤ **1** resounding quality; echo. 반향; 울림. ¶ *the ~ of an organ* 오르간 소리. **2** 《phys.》 reinforcing and prolonging of sound by reflection or by the vibration of other objects; a vibration caused in this way. 공명; 공진. [↓]

res·o·nant [rézənənt] *adj.* **1** resounding; vibrating; ringing. (소리가) 울리는. ¶ *a ~ voice* 울리는 음성. **2** tending to increase sound. 공명하는; 공명을 일으키는. ¶ *~ walls* 공명하는 벽들. [re-, →sound²]

:re·sort [rizɔ́ːrt] *vi.* (P3) **1** 《*to*》 go; visit; go often; go in large numbers. 가다; 자주〔잘〕 가다. ¶ *a place to which many tourists ~* 많은 관광객들이 잘 찾는 곳 / *~ to the sea-side.* 해변에 (자주) 가다. **2** 《*to*》 use something as a help or means; adopt as a means. 의지하다; 도움을 청하다; 호소하다. ¶ *~ to violence* 폭력에 호소하다; 폭력을 쓰다 / *He resorted to his friend for money.* 그는 친구에게 돈을 부탁했다 / *He resorted to stealing when he had no more money.* 돈이 떨어지면 그는 도둑질을 했다 / *When polite requests failed he resorted to threat.* 그는 좋은 말로 부탁해서 안 되면 협박으로 나갔다.

— *n.* **1** Ⓤ the act of resorting to a place. (자주) 다님; 감. ¶ *a place of popular ~* 사람들이 잘 가는 곳. **2** Ⓒ a place to which people often go for health or recreation. 유흥지; 휴양지. ¶ *a health ~* 보양지(保養地) / *a holiday ~* 휴일에 놀러가는 곳; 행락지 / *a summer* 〔*winter*〕 *~* 피서〔피한(避寒)〕지. **3** ⒸⓊ turning to for help; means. 의지하기; 호소; 수단. ¶ *have* 〔*make*〕 *~ to force* 폭력에 호소하다 / *Selling their house was their last ~.* 집을 파는 것이 그들의 최후 방법이었다 / *without ~ to force* 〔*arms*〕 폭력〔무력〕에 호소하지 않고. **4** a person or thing turned to for help. 의지가 되는 사람〔물건〕. ¶ *Books are her ~ when she is lonely.* 외로울 때는 책이 그녀의 의지가 된다 / *Friends are the best ~ in trouble.* 어려울 때는 벗들이 가장 의지가 된다. [re-, F. *sortier* come out]

as* (*in*) *the last resort, when everything else has failed; as a final attempt. 백계(百計)가 다하면; 마지막 수단으로.

re·sound [rizáund] *vi.* **1** (P1) give back sound; echo. 울리다; 반향하다. ¶ *The hall resounded with applause.* 홀은 박수 갈채로 가득 찼다. **2** (P1,2A) produce an echoing sound; sound loudly. 크게 울려퍼지다. ¶ *The horn resounded through the forest.* 뿔피리 소리가 온 숲에 울려 퍼졌다 / *His voice resounded far.* 그의 음성이 멀리까지 들렸다. **3** (P1,2A,3) 《*fig.*》 be much talked about; be widely known: 평판이 자자하다; 널리 알려지다. ¶ *The fame of Lindbergh's flight resounded all over the world.* 린드버그의 비행 소문은 전세계에 알려졌다.

— *vt.* (P6) **1** (of a place, etc.) give out an echo. …을 울려 퍼지게 하다. **2** 《*fig.*》 make widely know. …을 널리 알리다. ¶ *~ someone's fame* 아무의 명성을 널리 알리다. [re-]

·re·source [ríːsɔːrs, -zɔːrs, risɔ́ːrs] *n.* **1** 《usu. *pl.*》 any supply of anything useful(e.g. wealth, property, raw material, etc.). 자원(資源); 자재; 물자. ¶ *a country's natural resources* 한 나라의 천연(天然) 자원 / *The job called for all my resources of energy and patience.* 그 일엔 내 온 정력과 인내력이 필요했다. **2** any means of obtaining success or getting out of trouble. 수단; 방법. ¶ *Flight was his only ~.* 그는 달아날 수밖에 없었다 / *I am at the end of my resources.* 나는 이제 백계(百計)가 다했다. **3** Ⓒ knowledge of what to do in a difficulty or an emergency. 둘러맞춤; 임기응변의 재주; 기지. ¶ *a man of great* 〔*full of*〕 *~ in any emergency* 어떤 위기에서도 잘 대처하는 사람. [re-]

re·source·ful [risɔ́ːrsfəl, -zɔ́ːrs-] *adj.* **1** abounding in resources. 자력〔자원〕이 풍부한. **2** good at finding a way of doing things. 임기 응변의 재주가 많은; 기지에 뛰어난. ¶ *It was very ~ of her to make that shelter out of old packing cases.* 낡은 나무상자를 이용하여 저런 가옥(假屋)을 짓는 일에 그녀는 아주 뛰어났다. ●**re·source·ful·ly** [-fuli] *adv.* **re·source·ful·ness** [-nis] *n.*

re·source·less [risɔ́ːrslis] *adj.* lacking in resource or resources. 자력〔자원〕이 없는.

:re·spect [rispékt] *vt.* (P6) **1** feel or show esteem for (someone); look upon (someone) with respect. …을 존경하다. ¶ *~ oneself* 자존심이 있다 / *I ~ him for his bravery.* 그의 용기를 존경한다 / *~ one's parents* 부모를 존경하다 / *We ~ him as a great musician.* 우리는 그를 위대한 음악가로 존경한다. **2** pay attention to; take care of (something). …에 유의하다; …을 고려하다; 존중하다. ¶ *We must ~ his opinion.* 우리는 그의 의견을 존중해야 한다. **3** keep; obey. ¶ *We should ~ the laws of our country.* 나라의 법은 지켜야 마땅하다 / *I ~ his silence.* 나는 그의 침묵을 방해하지 않는다 / *I ~ your confidence* 〔*privacy*〕. 네 비밀〔사생활〕을 보장한다.

— *n.* **1** Ⓤ esteem; honor. 존경; 존중. ¶ *We should show ~ to our elders.* 우리는 윗사람을 공경해야 한다 / *have ~ for someone's opinion* 아무의 의견을 존중하다 / *be held in ~* 존경받다 / *They have great ~ for* *him.* 그들은 그를 몹시 존경한다. **2** 《*pl.*》 greetings. 인사. ¶ *Give* 〔*Send*〕 *them our best respects.* 여러분께 안부 전해 주십시오. **3** Ⓤ attention; regard. 주의; 관심. ¶ *pay* 〔*have*〕 ~ *to* …에 관심을 가지다 / *without* ~ *to another's feeling* 남의 기분은 아랑곳 없이 / *Respect should be paid to his wishes.* 그의 뜻에 관심을 가져야 한다. **4** Ⓤ relation; reference. 관계; 관련. ¶ *It has* ~ *to this event.* 그건 이 사건과 관련이 있다 **5** Ⓒ a point; a detail. 점; 세목. ¶ *in all* 〔*many, some*〕 *respects* 모든〔많은, 어떤〕 점에서 / *In certain respects the book is good.* 어떤 점에선 그 책은 좋다 / *I think you are wrong in this* ~. 이 점에서 네가 틀렸다고 생각한다. [re-, →special]

in respect of 〔***to***〕 (=*with regard to*) *something.* …의 점에서는. ¶ *In* ~ *of* 〔*to*〕 *that there is nothing to be said.* 그 점에 관해서는 아무 할 말이 없다.

in respect that ..., 《*arch.*》 considering; because of the fact that …. …을 생각하면; …이므로.

without respect (=*paying no attention*) ***to*** *something.* …을 고려하지 않고. ¶ *Anyone can join the club, without* ~ *to class, race, or sex.* 계층, 인종, 성별을 불문하고 누구든 이 클럽에 가입할 수 있다.

with respect to (=*concerning; as to*) *something.* …에 대해서는. ¶ *With* ~ *to your other proposals, I am not yet able to tell you our decision.* 당신의 그 밖의 제안에 대해서는 아직 우리의 결정을 말할 수 없습니다.

re·spect·a·bil·i·ty [rispèktəbíləti] *n.* **1** Ⓤ the quality of being respectable; good character. 존경할 만함; 훌륭한 인격. **2** Ⓒ a respectable person or persons; a person of good reputation and fair social standing. 존경할 만한 사람(들); 상당한 사회적 지위의 사람. **3** 《*pl.*》 social conventions, customs, etc. that are accepted as respectable. 인습적인 사회적 관례〔풍습〕.

***re·spect·a·ble** [rispéktəbəl] *adj.* **1** worthy of honor; considered right or good enough to be respected; of good character; having a good reputation. 존경할 만한. ¶ ~ *citizens* 훌륭한 시민들 / *He is a most* ~ *man.* 가장 존경할 만한 사람이다. **2** fairly large or good. (크기·품질이) 상당한; 우연만한. ¶ *His skill is* ~, *but no more.* 썩 대단치는 않으나 그런대로 기술이 상당하다 / *John's record in school was always* ~, *if never excellent.* 존의 학교 성적은 우수한 편은 아니나 늘 그만했다 / *a* ~ *sum of money* 꽤 많은 돈. **3** 《*iron.*》 far too observant of external propriety. 너무 점잖은. ¶ *He's altogether too* ~ *for my taste.* 그는 너무 점잖아서 내 비위엔 싫다. **4** good enough to use; fit to be seen; suitable for the occasion. 그만하면 괜찮은; 흉하지 않은. ¶ *I must put on some more* ~ *clothes.* 이것보다는 좀 괜찮은 옷을 입어야겠다 / *This hat is hardly* ~. 이 모자는 거의 쓸 수 없다.

— *n.* 《usu. *pl.*》 a respectable person. 존경할 만한〔훌륭한〕 사람.

● **re·spect·a·bly** [-i] *adv.*

re·spect·ful [rispéktfəl] *adj.* showing respect; showing honor to; polite. 경의를 표하는; 예의 바른. ¶ *He was always* ~ *to older people.* 그는 늘 어른들에게 공손(恭遜)했다 / *He made a* ~ *bow.* 그는 공손하게 인사를 했다. ● **re·spect·ful·ly** [-fəli] *adv.* **re·spect·ful·ness** [-nis] *n.*

re·spect·ing [rispéktiŋ] *prep.* concerning; regarding; about. …에 관하여.

***re·spec·tive** [rispéktiv] *adj.* belonging to each; individual. 각자의. ¶ *Go to your* ~ *rooms.* 각자의 방에 돌아가거라 / *Tell me your opinion of the* ~ *merits of the books.* 그 책마다의 장점에 대한 너의 의견을 말해봐라 / *The two friends said goodbye and went to their* ~ *home.* 두 친구는 작별 인사를 하고 제각기 집으로 돌아갔다.

re·spec·tive·ly [rispéktivli] *adv.* as relating to each; as regards each one in his turn. 각자; 따로따로. ¶ *Andy, Dick, and Helen are 6, 8, and 10 years old,* ~. 앤디, 딕, 그리고 헬렌은 각자 나이가 여섯 살, 여덟 살, 열 살이다 / *We discussed the virtues of both men* ~. 우리는 두 사람의 미덕에 대해 각자가 이야기했다.

res·pi·ra·tion [rèspəréiʃən] *n.* Ⓤ the act or process of breathing. 호흡. ¶ *artificial* ~ 인공 호흡 / *Respiration becomes difficult at great heights.* 아주 높은 산에서는 호흡하기가 어려워진다. [→respire]

res·pi·ra·tor [réspərèitər] *n.* Ⓒ **1** a device (usu. of gauze) worn over the nose and mouth to prevent inhaling harmful substances; a gasmask. (거즈로 된) 마스크; 가스 마스크. **2** a device used in or for giving artificial respiration. 인공 호흡 장치.

res·pi·ra·to·ry [résp*ə*rətɔ̀:ri, rispáiərə-/ rispáiərətəri] *adj.* of breathing. 호흡의. ¶ *The lungs are* ~ *organs.* 폐는 호흡 기관이다 / *a* ~ *disease* 호흡기 질환.

re·spire [rispáiər] *vt., vi.* (P6;1) **1** breathe. 호흡하다. **2** 《*fig.*》 enjoy relief; take rest; take hope or spirit again. 한숨 돌리다; 쉬다; (희망·기운)을 되찾다. [re-, →spirit]

res·pite [réspit] *n.* Ⓒ **1** a delay; the act of putting off; postpone, esp. putting off in the carrying out of a sentence of death. 연기; 유예; (특히 사형의) 집행 유예. **2** a rest from work; a short pause in work, pain, etc. (노동에서의) 휴식 시간; (고통 등의 일시적) 중지. ¶ *The farmer kept digging without* ~. 농부는 쉬지 않고 땅을 파고 있었다 / *take a short* ~ *from one's labor* 일을 잠시 쉬다. [→respect]

re·splend·ence [rispléndəns] *n.* Ⓤ the quality of being resplendent; great brightness. 광휘(光輝); 번쩍임; 찬란. [↓]

re·splend·ent [rispléndənt] *adj.* brilliant; very bright; splendid; shining. 번쩍이는; 눈부신; 빛나는. ¶ *The hall was ~ with chandeliers.* 홀은 샹들리에로 눈부시게 밝았다 / *The officers were ~ in full uniform.* 예장(禮裝)을 갖춘 장교들은 기라성 같았다. [re-, →splendid]

***re·spond** [rispánd / -spɔ́nd] *vi.* (P1,3) **1** 《*to*》 answer; reply. 대답하다. ¶ *Please ~ to my letter.* 편지에 회신을 바랍니다 / *He quickly responded to the question.* 질문에 즉각 대답했다. **2** 《*to*》 act as an answer to another person's deed. 응하다; 응답하다. ¶ *The boy responded to her kindness.* 그 소년은 그녀의 친절에 고마워했다 / *Mary responded quickly to the medicine and was well in a few days.* 메리는 약효가 빨라서 며칠 만에 회복했다. [re-, →sponsor]

***re·sponse** [rispáns / -spɔ́ns] *n.* **1** Ⓒ a reply; an answer by word or act. 대답. ¶ *Her ~ to my letter was quick.* 내 편지에 그녀는 곧 회신을 보내 왔다 / *I acted in ~ to the call of duty.* 나는 소집에 응했다 / *My letter to him brought no ~.* 그에게 보낸 내 편지에는 회답이 없었다. **2** Ⓤ an action as an answer to another person's action. 반응. ¶ *His speech called forth no ~ in his audience.* 그의 연설에 청중은 아무 반응이 없었다. [↑]

:re·spon·si·bil·i·ty [rispὰnsəbíləti / -spɔ̀n-] *n.* (*pl.* **-ties**) **1** Ⓤ the state of being responsible. 책임. ¶ *He does not feel much ~.* 그는 별로 책임을 느끼지 않고 있다 / *I take (full) ~ for losing the money.* 그 돈을 잃은 데에는 내가 (전적으로) 책임을 진다. **2** Ⓒ a matter for which a person must be responsible; a duty; a burden. 의무; 책임이 되는 것; 부담. ¶ *A child is a ~ to its parents.* 아이는 부모에게 책임이 있다 / *The master felt the responsibilities of his position.* 주인은 자기 위치에 부담을 느꼈다. **3** Ⓤ capability; reliability, esp. in meeting debts or payments. 지급능력. [↓]

on** *one's* **own responsibility, on one's own initiative. 독단으로; 자기 책임으로. ¶ *I did it on my own ~.* 내 책임으로 그 일을 했다; 내 독단으로 했다.

:re·spon·si·ble [rispánsəbəl / -spɔ́n-] *adj.* **1** expected to do something correctly; expected to make something go right; that can be trusted with important matters. 책임 있는. ¶ *a ~ job* 책임 있는 일 / *I am not ~ to you for my actions.* 내 행위에 관해 네게 해명할 의무가 없다 / *The caretaker is ~ for locking up the building.* 관리인은 건물의 문단속을 할 의무가 있다. **2** reliable; trustworthy. 믿을 수 있는. ¶ *He is a ~ person.* 그 사람은 믿을 수 있다 / *The class should choose a ~ pupil to take care of its money.* 학급은 학급의 돈을 맡을 믿을 만한 학생을 선출해야 한다. **3** having the cause of something. …의 원인이 되는; …의 책임(탓)인. ¶ *He is ~ for it.* 그가 그 일에 책임이 있다 / *The heavy rain was ~ for the landslide.* 산 사태는 폭우 탓이었다. [→respond, -ible]

re·spon·sive [rispánsiv / -spɔ́n-] *adj.* **1** making answer; responding. 대답하는; 응하는. **2** easily moved; responding readily. 감응(감동)하기 쉬운; 민감한. ¶ *a ~ audience* 민감한 청중 / *have a ~ nature* 감수성이 많다 / *I didn't find him very ~ when I talked to him.* 그에게 말해 보았으나 별 관심이 없는 듯 싶었다. ● **re·spon·sive·ly** [-li] *adv.* **re·spon·sive·ness** [-nis] *n.*

:rest[1] [rest] *n.* **1** ⒸⓊ a period of free time from work, activity, etc.; ease after work. 휴식 시간; 휴식. ¶ *a long ~* 긴 휴식 / *a temporary ~* 잠시의 휴식 / *take a ~* 잠시 쉬다 / *give a ~* 잠시 쉬게 하다 / *Let's have a ~.* 자, 좀 쉬자 / *absolute ~* 절대 안정 / *We need ~ after a long journey.* 오랜 여행 끝에는 휴식이 필요하다. **2** Ⓤ the condition of having free time; absence of motion. 휴식; 정지. ¶ *A car came to ~.* 차가 멎었다 / *bring a machine to ~* 기계를 세우다. **3** Ⓤ 《sometimes *a ~*》 ease; quiet; peace. 안락; 평안. ¶ *The medicine gave him a short ~ from pain.* 약으로 그의 고통은 조금 가라앉았다. **4** ⓊⒸ sleep. 수면. ¶ *I had eight hours of ~ last night.* 간밤에 여덟 시간 잤다 / *have a good night's ~* 잘 자다; 숙면하다 / *retire to ~* 잠자리에 들다; 자다. **5** Ⓒ a resting or lodging place; a hotel, motel, etc. 휴식처; 숙박소. ¶ *a seamen's ~* 선원 숙소 / *traveler's ~* 여인숙. **6** Ⓤ death; grave. 죽음; 무덤. ¶ *go to one's ~* 영면하다; 죽다 / *lay someone to ~* 아무를 매장하다 / *She was laid to ~ in the village churchyard.* 그녀는 죽어 마을의 교회 묘지에 묻혔다. **7** Ⓒ that on which something rests; a support. (물건을 놓는) 대(台); 받침대. ¶ *a ~ for a gun* 총가(銃架) / *a ~ for a violin* 바이올린의 턱받침. **8** Ⓒ 《mus.》 an interval of silence; a sign which marks this. 쉼표. ¶ *an eighth* (*a half*) *~* 8분(1/2) 쉼표.

at rest, **a**) still. 정지하여. **b**) free from activity; not active. 휴식하여. ¶ *a volcano at ~* 휴화산. **c**) free from care. 안심하여. ¶ *set someone's mind at ~* 아무의 마음을 편하게 해 주다; 안심시키다. **d**) settled. 해결하여. ¶ *set a question* (*matter*) *at ~.* 문제를 해결하다. **e**) dead. 죽어; 영면하여.

go* (*retire*) *to rest, go to bed. 자다.

— *vi.* **1** (P1,2A,2B,3) stop working; be still. 쉬다; 휴식하다. ¶ *~ a while* 잠시 쉬다 / *~ from toil* (*one's labors*) 일손을 쉬다 / *~ for an hour every afternoon* 오후에 한 시간씩 쉬다. **2** (P3) sleep; be dead. 잠자다; 영면하다. ¶ *~ in peace* 편히 자다 / *~ in the grave* 영면하다 / *He rests with his* *forefathers.* 조상들의 묘소에 묻혀 있다. **3** be at peace or ease. 안심하(고 있)다. ¶ *I can't ~ until I hear from my son.* 아들의 소식을 들을 때까지 마음을 놓을 수 없다. **4** (P3) 《*in*》 believe; trust. 믿다; 신뢰하다. ¶ *~ in God* 신을 믿다. **5** (P2A,3) lean; lie; sit. 기대다; 위치하다. ¶ *~ against a tree* 나무에 기대다 / *~ on a couch* 소파에 앉다 / *~ on one's arm* 팔베개를 베다 / *with one's head resting on* 〔*against*〕 *a cushion* 베개를 베고. **6** (P1,2A,3) 《*on*》 be placed; be fixed. (…에) 있다; (시선이 …에) 쏠리다; (…에게) 지우다. ¶ *The responsibility rested upon him.* 책임이 그에게 있었다 / *His eyes rested on the picture.* 그의 시선이 그림에 멈췄다 / *The duty rests heavily on me* 〔*my mind*〕. 그 임무 때문에 어깨가〔마음이〕 무겁다. **7** (P3) 《*on, upon*》 rely. 의지하다; 믿다. ¶ *Our hope rests on you.* 우리의 희망은 네게 있다 / *I cannot ~ on your pormise.* 네 약속은 못 믿겠다. **8** (P3) be present; remain, settle, or linger. 있다; 머무르다; 감돌다. ¶ *Clouds ~ upon the mountaintops.* 구름이 산 꼭대기에 머물러 있다 / *A smile rested on the girl's lips.* 미소가 소녀의 입술에 감돌았다. **9** (P3) 《*with, on*》 depend; have the base. …나름이다; …에 의거하다. ¶ *Government rests with the people.* 정치는 국민이 할 나름이다 / *Everything rests on his answer.* 모든 것이 그의 대답에 달려 있다 / *His fame rests mainly on this book.* 그의 명성은 주로 이 저서 때문이다.

— *vt.* **1** (P6) give rest to (someone). …을 쉬게 하다. ¶ *~ oneself* 쉬다; 휴식하다 / *~ one's eyes* 눈을 감다 / *May God ~ his soul!* 신이여, 그의 영혼을 고이 쉬게 하소서 / *I am* 〔*feel*〕 *quite rested.* 푹 쉬었다 / *~ a horse for an hour* 말을 한 시간 쉬게 하다. **2** (P13) cause (something) to be supported; put; place. …을 기대게 하다; 놓다; 얹다. ¶ *~ one's head on a pillow* 베개를 베다 / *~ a stick against the wall* 지팡이를 벽에 기대놓다 / *~ an elbow on a desk* 탁자 위에 팔을 괴다. **3** (P13) found or base; let depend. …에 의지〔의거〕하다. ¶ *We rest our hopes on him.* 우리 희망은 그에게 있다. [E.]

rest[2] [rest] *n.* 《*the ~*, *sing.* only》 **1** what is left. 남은 것; 나머지. ¶ *You know the ~.* 다음 말은 안 해도 알 것이다 / *Eat some and give the ~ away.* 좀 먹고 나머지는 버려라. **2** 《as *pl.*》 the others. 그 밖의 사람들. ¶ *The ~ of the guests were in the hall.* 여타의 손님들은 홀에 있었다

among the rest, above all. 그 중에서도 특히.

and (***all***) ***the rest*** (***of it***), and everthing else; much more besides. 그 밖의 모두. ¶ *She is young and beautiful and rich and all the ~ of it.* 그녀는 젊고 아름답고 부자고 다 좋은 것뿐이다.

(***as***) ***for the rest,*** as to other matters. 그 밖의 것에 대해서(는).

— *vi.* (P5) continue to be. 여전히 …이다; …한 채로 있다. ¶ *You may ~ assured that everything has been tried.* 다 시험해 보았으니 안심해도 된다 / *The meaning rests unknown.* 그 뜻은 알려지지 않은 채로 있다. [re-, L. *sto* stand]

re·state [riːstéit] *vt.* (P6) state again or in a new way. …을 다시 진술하다; 환언하다. [re-]

re·state·ment [riːstéitmənt] *n.* Ⓤ statement made again or in a new way. 재차 진술한 것; 환언.

***res·tau·rant** [réstərənt, -ràːnt / -rɔ̀nt, -rɔ̀ːŋ] *n.* Ⓒ a place where meals are served to customers; an eating house. 음식점; 요리점; 레스토랑. [→restore]

rest·ful [réstfəl] *adj.* giving rest; quiet. 편안한; 조용한. ¶ *a ~ life* 안락한 생활 / *Pale greens and yellows make a ~ color scheme for a room.* 연둣빛과 담황색은 방에 안정감을 주는 색조다. [→rest[1]]

res·ti·tu·tion [rèstətjúːʃən] *n.* Ⓤ **1** the act of giving back what has been taken away to its owner. 반환. ¶ *the ~ of anything to its proper owner* 무엇이건 정당한 소유주에의 반환. **2** payment for damage done. 손해 배상. ¶ *We should make ~ for the harm we have done.* 우리가 입힌 손해는 마땅히 배상해야 한다. [re-, L. *statuo* place]

res·tive [réstiv] *adj.* **1** (of a horse) refusing to go ahead. (말이) 앞으로 나아가기를 거부하는. ¶ *a ~ horse.* **2** (of a person) hard to manage; too impatient to be still. (사람이) 다루기 힘든; 침착하지 못한. ¶ *He is a very ~ child.* 아주 골치 아픈 아이다. [*rest*[1]]

***rest·less** [réstlis] *adj.* **1** always active; always moving. 늘 활동적인; 쉬지 않는. ¶ *a man of ~ energy* 활동가; 정력가. **2** uneasy; never still or quiet. 침착하지 못한; 불안정한. ¶ *That nervous boy is very ~.* 저 신경질적인 아이는 늘 좌불안석이다. **3** without rest or sleep. 쉴〔잠잘〕 수 없는. ¶ *a ~ night* 잠 못 이루는 밤 / *The patient was ~ from pain.* 환자는 아파서 잠을 못 잤다. [*rest*[1]]

rest·less·ly [réstlisli] *adv.* without rest; continuously; uneasily. 쉬지 않고; 부단히; 마음을 못 잡고; 들떠서.

rest·less·ness [réstlisnis] *n.* Ⓤ the state of being restless or uneasy. 불안정; 불안.

re·stock [riːstɑ́k / -stɔ́k] *vt.* (P6) supply (some place) with a new stock again. …에 새로 사들이다; 보충하다. [re-]

***res·to·ra·tion** [rèstəréiʃən] *n.* **1** Ⓤ the act of putting back as it was; the state of being restored. (건강의) 회복; 복구; 복고(復古); (그림·건조물 등의) 복원. ¶ *the ~ of one's health* / *the ~ of a king* 왕의 복위 / *the ~ of a Roman temple* 〔*of ancient works of art*〕 로마 신전〔고대 예술품〕의 복원.

2 《*the R-*》 (the period of) the English re-establishment of the monarchy in 1660. (영국의) 왕정 복고 (시대). [→restore]

re·stor·a·tive [ristɔ́:rətiv] *adj.* being able to restore; tending to restore health or strength. 회복시키는; 원기를 회복시키는. ¶ *a ~ medicine* 보약. — *n.* something that restores to consciousness. 각성제. ¶ *Ammonia is used as a ~ when a person has fainted.* 암모니아는 의식을 잃었을 때 각성제로 쓰인다.

:re·store [ristɔ́:r] *vt.* (P6) **1** ⓐ bring back; put (something or someone) back as it was or to a former condition. …을 본디 자리에 되돌리다. ¶ ~ *the book to the shelf* 책을 책꽂이에 도로 꽂다 / ~ *the color to someone's face, and brightness to his eyes* 아무의 얼굴에 핏기가 돌게 하고 눈에 생기를 되찾게 하다. ⓑ place (someone) once more in the position, rank, etc. which he formerly held. …을 복직시키다. ¶ *The captain was restored to his rank and honors.* 선장은 복직이 되고 명예도 되찾았다. **2** reconstruct (something) as it was; repair. …을 복구[복원]시키다. ¶ ~ *an old temple* 낡은 사원을 복원시키다 / *The old painting was damaged in the flood and had to be painstakingly restored.* 그 옛 그림은 침수로 손상되어 공들여 복원해야 했다 / *be restored out of all recognition* 몰라보게 복구되다. **3** 《*to*》 give back; bring back to the owner. …을 돌려주다; 반환하다. ¶ *You should ~ the borrowed books to the owner.* 빌린 책을 임자에게 돌려주어야 하지 않니 / *Who can ~ the lost years of our youth?* 누가 우리들의 잃어버린 청춘을 돌려줄 것인가. [L. *restauro*]

re·stor·er [ristɔ́:rər] *n.* Ⓒ a person or thing that restores. 본디로 돌려주는 사람[물건]. ¶ *a hair ~* 모발 재생약.

·re·strain [ristréin] *vt.* (P6,13) **1** 《*from*》 hold back; check; keep within limits. …을 억제하다; 억누르다. ¶ ~ *oneself* 자제하다; 참다 / *He could not ~ her from going.* 그는 그녀가 가는 것을 막을 수 없었다 / *I could not ~ my desire to laugh.* 우스워 견딜 수 없었다. **2** 《*from*》 prevent from doing something. …을 하지 못하게 하다; 제지하다. ¶ ~ *someone from wasting his money* 아무가 돈을 함부로 못 쓰게 하다. **3** keep (someone) in prison. …을 감금[구속]하다. ●**re·strain·a·ble** [-əbəl] *adj.* **re·strain·er** [-ər] *n.* [→restrict]

·re·straint [ristréint] *n.* ⓊⒸ **1** the act of holding back; self-control. 억제(력); 제지; 자제. ¶ *That poor man is not right in his mind and requires ~.* 저 불쌍한 사람은 지금 제정신이 아니다, 자제를 해야 하는데 / *The wise man exercises ~ in his behavior and enjoyments.* 현명한 사람은 (자기의) 행실과 향락에 신중을 기한다. **2** confinement. 구속; 감금. ¶ *put a mad man under ~* 미친 사람을 가두다. **3** a means of restraining. 억제 수단. ¶ *constitutional restraints on the power of president* 대통령 권한에 대한 합헌적인 제한 조치. [↓]

·re·strict [ristríkt] *vt.* (P6,13) 《*to, within*》 keep (something) within limits; confine. …을 제한[한정]하다. ¶ ~ *a meaning* 뜻을 한정하다 / *The use of the golf course* [*links*] *is restricted to members.* 골프장 사용은 회원으로 한정되어 있다 / ~ *a patient to a certain diet* 환자에게 규정식만을 먹게 하다. [re-, L. *stringo* tie]

re·strict·ed [ristríktid] *adj.* **1** limited; kept within limits. 한정[제한]된; 좁은. ¶ *She is on a very ~ diet, and can have no sweets.* 그녀는 엄격한 규정식을 먹게 돼 있어 단 것은 안 된다 / *It has a very ~ application.* 그 응용 범위는 매우 좁다. **2** having restriction or limiting rules. 규제된; (사용 따위가) 특정 사람들에게만 제한된. ¶ *a ~ club* 비개방적인 클럽 / *a ~ garden* 일반인 비공개 정원 / *Factories may not be built in this ~ residential section.* 이 주거 지역에 공장은 들어서지 못한다.

·re·stric·tion [ristríkʃən] *n.* ⓊⒸ the act of restricting; something that restricts. 제한(하는 것). ¶ *place restrictions on the use of the gymnasium* 체육관 사용을 규제[제한]하다 / *There are no restrictions on swimming here.* 여기선 수영을 마음대로 해도 좋다 / *restrictions imposed by law* 법률에 의해 과해진 제한 / *You are permitted to use these tools without ~.* 너는 이 연장들을 마음대로 써도 좋다.

re·stric·tive [ristríktiv] *adj.* **1** limiting; restricting. 제한[한정]하는. **2** 《gram.》 limiting the meaning of the modified element. 한정적인. ¶ *a ~ adjective* 한정 형용사. ●**re·stric·tive·ly** [-li] *adv.*

rest room [⊿⊿] *n.* 《U.S.》 a lavatory; a toilet. 화장실; 변소. [*rest*¹]

:re·sult [rizʌ́lt] *n.* ⓊⒸ that which is produced by a cause; effect. 결과; 결말; 성과. ¶ *a satisfactory ~* 만족스러운 결과 / *as a ~ of* …의 결과로서 / *in (the) ~* 결국 / *with the ~ that…* …라는 결과로; 그 결과 / *as a natural ~* 당연한 결과로서 / *The ~ was that….* 그 결과는 …이었다 / *I made every effort without ~.* 노력을 다했으나 허사였다 / *What was the ~ of the game?* 게임 결과는 어떻게 됐나.
— *vi.* (P1,3) 《usu. *from*》 **1** follow as a consequence. (결과로서) 일어나다; 생기다. ¶ *Nothing has resulted from my efforts.* 노력했으나 허탕이었다 / *His death resulted from an overdose of drugs.* 그의 죽음은 약물 과용 탓이었다 / *From what you say, it results that we have failed.* 네 말대로라면 우리는 실패했다는 것이로구나. **2** 《*in*》 end; have as a consequence. 결국 …로 끝나다. ¶ ~ *in good* 좋게 끝나다 / *The accident resulted in the death of two people.* 그 사고

로 해서 두 사람이 죽었다. [re-, →salient]

re·sult·ant [rizʌ́ltənt] *adj.* producing as a result; resulting. 결과로서 생기는; 합성적인. ¶ *the ~ damage to the crops* 결과적인 작물의 피해 / 《phys.》 *a ~ force* 합성력. — *n.* Ⓒ **1** that which results; a consequence. 결과. **2** 《phys.》 a resultant force. 합성력. [↑]

∗re·sume [rizúːm / -zjúːm] *vt.* (P6) **1** begin again; go on (doing something) after stopping. …을 다시 시작하다; 계속하다. ¶ ~ *conversation* 다시 대화를 시작하다 / *Let us ~ reading where we left off.* 아까 읽다가 만 곳에서부터 계속해 읽자 / *We resumed our discussion after a short rest.* 잠시 쉬었다가 우리는 토론을 계속했다. **2** take (something) again after once leaving or losing. …을 되찾다; 다시 차지하다; 회복하다. ¶ ~ *one's liberty* 〔*sway*〕 자유를〔세력을〕 회복하다〔되찾다〕 / *He resumed his health.* 그는 건강을 회복했다 / ~ *one's seat* 다시 자기 자리에 앉다〔돌아오다〕 / ~ *one's hat* (벗었던) 모자를 다시 쓰다 / *The vehicle resumed the speed.* 차는 속력을 되찾았다. **3** sum up. …을 요약하다; 개요를 말하다.

— *vi.* (P1,2A) (of a speaker) continue or go on after a pause; begin again. (말을 끊었다가) 계속하다; 다시 시작하다〔찾다〕. ¶ *Well, to ~ ...* 그런데, 얘기를 계속하자면.... [re-, L. *sumo* take]

ré·su·mé [rèzuméi, ⌐–⌐] *n.* Ⓒ 《F.》 **1** a summary; an outline. 대략; 개요. ¶ *make a ~ of a book* 책의 개요를 말하다. **2** 《U.S.》 a brief account of one's career, qualification, and employment record. 이력서. [F.]

re·sump·tion [rizʌ́mpʃən] *n.* ⓊⒸ the act of resuming. 재개시; 속행(續行); 회복. ¶ *the ~ of the meeting* 회의의 재개 / *the ~ of duties after a holiday* 휴일 후 업무의 속행. [→resume]

re·sur·face [riːsə́ːrfis] *vt.* (P6) put a new surface on (a road, etc.). (길)을 다시 포장하다; …의 겉면을 바꾸다〔꾸미다〕. — *vi.* (P1) (of a submarine) come to the surface again. (잠수함이) 다시 떠오르다. [re-]

re·sur·gence [risə́ːrdʒəns] *n.* Ⓤ the act of rising again. 재기(再起); 되살아남. [↓]

re·sur·gent [risə́ːrdʒənt] *adj.* rising again; reviving. 재기〔부활〕하는. [re-]

res·ur·rect [rèzərékt] *vt.* (P6) **1** bring (someone) back to life. …을 소생〔부활〕시키다. **2** bring (something) back into use, fashion, etc. (잊혀졌던 관습·유행 따위를) 다시 행해지게 하다; 부활시키다. ¶ *It's a mistake to ~ old quarrels.* 묵은 시비 거리를 또 끄집어내는 것은 잘못이다 / ~ *an old law* 구법을 부활시키다. — *vi.* (P1) rise from the dead. 소생〔부활〕하다. [re-, →surge]

res·ur·rec·tion [rèzərékʃən] *n.* **1** Ⓤ the act of resurrecting; revival. 소생; 재기; 부활. ¶ *the ~ of one's hopes* 희망의 소생 / *nature's ~ in the spring* 봄철의 자연의 소생. **2** 《*the R-*》 Christ's rising from the grave. 그리스도의 부활.

re·sus·ci·tate [risʌ́sətèit] *vt.* (P6) bring (something) back to life; bring back into activity or use. …을 소생〔부활〕시키다. — *vi.* come back to life or consciousness. 소생〔부활〕하다. [re-, sub-, →cite]

re·sus·ci·ta·tion [risʌ̀sətéiʃən] *n.* Ⓤ the act of resuscitating. 소생; 부활.

∗re·tail [ríːteil] *n.* Ⓤ the sale of goods in small quantities or amounts. 소매(opp. wholesale). ¶ *a ~ dealer* 소매상 / *A grocery store sells at* 〔*by*〕 ~. 식료품 가게는 소매로 판다.

— *adv.* by the sale of goods in small quantities. 소매로. ¶ *buy ~* 소매로 사다 / *Do you sell wholesale or ~?* 도매로 팝니까 소매로 팝니까.

— *adj.* **1** of or having to do with the selling of goods directly to consumers. 소매의; 소매상의. ¶ *The ~ price of this hat is $30.* 이 모자의 소매 가격은 30달러이다 / *the ~ trade* 소매업. **2** engaged in such selling. 소매를 하는. ¶ *a ~ merchant* 소매상 / *a ~ grocer* 식료품 소매업자.

— *vt.* (P6) **1** sell (goods) in small quantities directly to the consumer. …을 소매하다. **2** [ritéil] tell (gossip, rumor) to others; tell over again. (소문)을 퍼뜨리다. ¶ *She retails everything she hears about her acquaintances.* 그녀는 아는 사람의 얘기는 무엇이건 들은 대로 소문낸다.

— *vi.* (P3) 《*at, for*》 be sold in small quantities directly to consumers. (얼마로) 소매되다. ¶ *The pencil retails at* 〔*for*〕 *200 won.* 이 연필은 소매로 200 원이다 / *This cloth retails for five dollars a yard.* 이 천은 소매로 야드당 5 달러이다. [re, →tally]

re·tail·er *n.* Ⓒ **1** [ríːteilər] a merchant who sells at retail. 소매상. **2** [ritéilər] a person who repeats. 말전주꾼.

:re·tain [ritéin] *vt.* (P6) **1** keep; preserve; continue to hold; keep in one's possession. …을 보유〔유지〕하다; 계속 지니다. ¶ ~ *an old custom* 옛 관습을 유지하다 / ~ *one's rights* (자기) 권리를 보유하다 / ~ *a secret* 비밀을 지키다 / ~ *one's self-respect* 자존심을 잃지 않고 있다 / *China dishes ~ heat longer than metal pans.* 사기 접시는 철제보다 열을 더 오래 간직한다 / *He retains something of the professor in his features.* 그의 얼굴 모습에는 어딘가 대학 교수 노릇을 했던 사람의 모습이 남아 있다. **2** keep (something) in mind; remember. …을 기억하고 있다. ¶ *He retained the memory of that experience for years.* 그는 여러 해 동안 그 경험을 기억하고 있었다 / *She retained the tune but not the words of the song.* 그녀는 그 노래의 곡은 기억하나 가사는 생각나지 않았다. **3** employ (a lawyer, etc.) by payment of advance fee. (변호사 등)을 고용〔선임〕해 두다; 의뢰해 놓다. ¶ *The defendant retained the best lawyer in the town to* *defend his case.* 피고인은 자기 사건을 변호하기 위해 읍에서 최고의 변호사를 선임해 두었다. [re-, →tenable]

re·tain·er [ritéinər] *n.* Ⓒ **1** a person or thing that retains. 보유자〔물〕. **2** a fee paid to a lawyer. 변호료. **3** a person who serves someone of high rank; a servant. 가신(家臣); 종자(從者).

re·take [riːtéik] *vt.* (**-took, -tak·en**) (P6) take again. …을 다시 잡다; 되찾다; (사진)을 다시 찍다. —[ríːtèik] *n.* Ⓒ a second or subsequent photographing of a scene in a movie, etc. 재촬영. [re-]

re·tak·en [riːtéikən] *vt.* pp. of **retake.**

re·tal·i·ate [ritǽlièit] *vi., vt.* (P1,3; 6) return blow for blow, wrong for wrong; pay back (wrong, injury) in the same way. (상대와 같은 수단으로) 보복하다. ¶ ~ *in kind* 동일 수단으로 보복하다 / ~ *upon one's enemy* 적에게 보복하다 / ~ *for an injury upon someone* 아무에게 상해에 대한 보복을 하다. [re-, L. *talis* such]

re·tal·i·a·tion [ritæ̀liéiʃən] *n.* Ⓤ the act of retaliating. 보복.

re·tal·i·a·tive [ritǽlièitiv] *adj.* =retaliatory.

re·tal·i·a·to·ry [ritǽliətɔ̀ːri / -ətəri] *adj.* disposed to retaliate; returning evil for evil. 보복적인. ¶ *a ~ bombing raid* 보복 공습 / ~ *measures* 보복 조치.

re·tard [ritáːrd] *vt.* (P6) **1** make slow; keep back; delay. …을 늦어지게 하다; 지연시키다. ¶ *Lack of education retarded the progress of the country.* 교육의 빈곤이 그 나라의 발전을 지연시켰다 / *I was retarded by a visitor at the last moment.* 막 나가려는데 손님이 와서 늦어지고 말았다. **2** hinder; put off. (성장·진행 따위)를 방해〔저지〕하다; 연기하다. ¶ ~ *someone's arrival* 아무의 도착을 연기하다 / *His death was retarded by some years by the skill of the doctor.* 그의 생명은 의사가 용해서 몇 해 더 연장되었다.
— *vi.* (of tides, etc.) occur later than the normal or calculated time. (조수의 간만 등이) 늦어지다.
— *n.* **1** the state of being retarded; delay. 늦어짐; 지연. **2** [ríːtaːrd] 《U.S. *sl.*》 a retarded person. 정신 박약자; 바보. [re-, →tardy]

re·tar·da·tion [rìːtaːrdéiʃən] *n.* ⓊⒸ **1** the act of retarding; the state of being retarded. 지체; 지연. **2** something that retards; a hindrance. 방해물.

retch [retʃ] *vi.* (P1) try to vomit. 구역질나다. [E.]

re·tell [riːtél] *vt.* (**-told**) (P6) tell again. …을 다시 말하다. ¶ ~ *a story.* [re-]

re·ten·tion [riténʃən] *n.* Ⓤ **1** the act of retaining. 보유; 보존; 유지. ¶ *They advocate the ~ of our nuclear power plants.* 그들은 우리의 원자력 발전소의 보유를 주장하고 있다. **2** the ability to remember. 기억력. [→retain]

re·ten·tive [riténtiv] *adj.* **1** 《*of*》 able to keep. 보유하는; 보유력이 있는. ¶ *soils ~ of moisture* 습기를 유지시키는 토양. **2** able to remember. 기억력이 좋은. ¶ *a ~ mind* 기억력이 좋은 사람 / *She has a very ~ memory.* 그녀는 기억력이 아주 좋다.

ret·i·cence [rétəsəns] *n.* Ⓤ tendency to be silent; reserve in speech. 과묵; 말수가 적음. ¶ *He is a man of ~.* 그는 입이 무거운 사람이다. [↓]

ret·i·cent [rétəsənt] *adj.* tending to be silent; reserved in speech. 과묵한; 말수가 적은. ¶ ~ *about one's hopes and fears* 자기의 희망이라든가 두려움을 좀처럼 말하려 하지 않는 / *He was ~ on what happened.* 그는 무슨 일이 있었는지 좀처럼 말하려 하지 않았다. [re-, →tacit]

re·tic·u·late [ritíkjəlit, -lèit] *adj.* netlike; covered with something like a network. 그물 모양의. —[-lèit] *vt., vi.* (P6;1) make network of; form a network. 그물 모양으로 하다〔되다〕. [L. *rete* net]

ret·i·na [rétənə] *n.* Ⓒ (*pl.* **-nas** or **-nae**) 《anat.》 the back of the eye which reacts to light. (눈의) 망막(網膜). [L.]

ret·i·nae [rétəniː] *n.* pl. of **retina.**

ret·i·nue [rétənjùː] *n.* Ⓒ 《*collectively*》 the group of followers and servants of a prince or nobleman. 시종(侍從); 수행원. ¶ *Two whole floors of the hotel were booked for president's ~.* 호텔의 두층 전부가 대통령 수행원을 위해 예약되었다. [→retain]

:re·tire [ritáiər] *vi.* **1** (P1,2A,3) give up one's business, position, etc.; go away to a place kept apart from others. 퇴직하다; 퇴역하다; 은퇴하다. ¶ ~ *from business* 사업에서 손을 떼다 / ~ *from the service* 퇴직〔퇴역〕하다 / ~ *from public life* 공직 생활에서 은퇴하다 / ~ *from the world* 은퇴하다; 속세를 버리다 / ~ *into the country* 낙향하다 / ~ *under the age clause* 정년으로 퇴직하다 / ~ *from the army* 제대하다 / *He is 70 but refuses to ~.* 그는 나이가 70인데도 은퇴하지 않겠다고 한다. **2** (P1) go away; go back; withdraw; retreat. 가버리다; 물러가다; 퇴각하다. ¶ ~ *to one's room* 제방으로 물러가다 / *The moon retired behind the mountains.* 달이 산 뒤로 넘어갔다 / ~ *in good order* 질서 있게 물러가다〔후퇴하다〕/ *Heavy machine-gun fire caused the enemy to ~.* 중기관총 사격으로 적은 퇴각했다. **3** (P1,3) go to bed. 잠자리에 들다; 자다. ¶ ~ *at ten o'clock,* 10시에 잠자리에 들다 / ~ *for rest* 쉬다.
— *vt.* (P6) **1** cause (someone) to retire. …을 퇴직〔퇴역, 은퇴〕시키다. ¶ *It was found necessary to ~ several generals who were old and lacked energy.* 늙고 기력이 떨어진 몇몇 장군들을 퇴역시키는 것은 불가피한 일이었다. **2** take (bills, etc.) out of circulation. (어음·화폐 등)을 회수하다. **3** 《mil.》

cause to retreat. (군대)를 퇴각〔후퇴〕시키다.
— *n.* Ⓒ 《mil.》 a signal to troops to retire. 퇴각 신호. [re-, F. *tirer* draw]

re·tired [ritáiərd] *adj.* **1** withdrawn from activity. 은퇴한; 퇴직한. ¶ *a ~ officer* 〔*teacher*〕 퇴역 장교〔퇴직 교사〕/ *~ pay* 〔*allowance*〕 퇴직 급여 / *the ~ list* 퇴직자〔퇴역 군인〕 명부. **2** reserved; shy; hidden. 숫기가 적은; 내성적인; 궁벽한. ¶ *He is leading a ~ life.* 그는 은둔 생활을 하고 있다 / *a ~ spot* 궁벽한 곳.

re·tire·ment [ritáiərmənt] *n.* **1** Ⓤ retiring; being retired. 은퇴; 퇴직. ¶ *After his ~ the general went to live in the country.* 퇴역 후 장군은 시골로 내려갔다. **2** Ⓒ a quiet way or place of living. 은거; 벽촌. ¶ *She lives in ~, reading books and strolling in the countryside.* 그녀는 책을 읽거나 시골을 이곳저곳 돌아다니면서 은거 생활을 하고 있다.

go into* 〔*live in*〕 *retirement, lead a retired life. 은퇴 생활을 하다.

re·tir·ing [ritáiəriŋ] *adj.* shy; quiet; modest. 사교성이 없는; 내성적인. ¶ *He has a ~ nature.* 그는 내성적인 사람이다.

re·told [ri:tóuld] *v.* p. and pp. of **retell.**

re·took [ri:túk] *v.* p. of **retake.**

•**re·tort**[1] [ritɔ́:rt] *vt.* (P6,11,13) answer back sharply or quickly; pay back. …에게 말대꾸하다; 응수하다; 보복하다. ¶ *~ insult for insult* 모욕에는 모욕으로 응수하다. — *vi.* (P1) answer sharply or quickly. 반론하다; 말대꾸하다. ¶ *"It's none of your business", he retorted.* "네 알 바가 아니다" 라고 그는 응수했다 / *He will surely ~ with another question.* 필시 그는 다른 문제로 네게 반론할 것이다. — *n.* ⓊⒸ a sharp, angry, or ready reply. 반박; 말대꾸. [re-, →torment]

re·tort[2] [ritɔ́:rt] *n.* Ⓒ 《chem.》 a container for turning liquids to vapor. 레토르트; 증류기. [↑]

re·touch [ri:tʌ́tʃ] *vt.* (P6) touch up; improve (a painting, photograph, etc.) by adding a few touches. (그림·사진 따위)에 가필(加筆)하다; …을 수정하다. ¶ *The photograph should be retouched.* 그 사진은 수정해야겠다. [re-]

re·trace [ritréis] *vt.* (P6) **1** go over again. (길 따위)를 되돌아가다. ¶ *~ one's steps* (*to find one's lost thing*) (잃은 물건을 찾기 위해) 왔던 길을 되돌아가다. **2** repeat. …을 되풀이하다. ¶ *~ the story of someone's fall* 아무가 낙상(落傷)한 이야기를 되풀이하다. **3** go over again in memory; look back upon; recall to mind. …을 회고〔회상〕하다. ¶ *~ the events and experiences of one's youth* 젊었을 때에 있었던 일, 경험을 회상하다. [re-]

re·tract [ritrǽkt] *vt., vi.* (P6; 1) draw back; take back (one's opinion, promise, etc.). (혀 등을 입 안으로) 쏙 들이키다; (말 등을) 취소〔철회〕하다. ¶ *A cat can ~ its claws at pleasure.* 고양이는 발톱을 자유 자재로 들이킬 수 있다 / *He refused to ~ what he said about you.* 그는 너를 두고 한 말을 철회하지 않겠다더군. [re-, →trace]

re·trac·tion [ritrǽkʃən] *n.* ⓊⒸ the act of taking or drawing back. 이미 한 말의 취소; 철회; 오므림. ¶ *the ~ of a false statement* 허위 진술의 철회.

re·tread [ri:tréd] *vt.* (P6) furnish (an old tire) with a new tread. (낡은 타이어)를 재생하다. — [rí:trèd] *n.* a tire furnished with a new tread. (접지면을 갈아 댄) 재생 타이어. [re-]

:**re·treat** [ritrí:t] *vi.* (P1,3) go back; draw back from action; retire. 물러가다; 은퇴하다; 퇴각하다. ¶ *The defeated army had to ~ hastily from the battlefield.* 패전군은 서둘러 싸움터에서 퇴각해야 했다 / *Seeing the big cat, the rat retreated rapidly.* 커다란 고양이를 보자 쥐는 재빨리 도망갔다. — *vt.* (P6) 《chess》 move (a piece) backward. (말)을 뒤로 물리다.
— *n.* **1** ⓊⒸ the act of going back or drawing back. 퇴각〔퇴거〕; 은퇴. ¶ *The enemy was in full ~.* 적은 총퇴각을 했다. **2** a signal for a retreat. 퇴각 신호. ¶ *The drums beat* 〔*sounded*〕 *a* 〔*the*〕 *~.* 퇴각하라는 북이 울렸다. **3** Ⓒ a safe, quiet place. 은둔처; 피난처. ¶ *a summer ~* 피서지. [→retract]

beat* 〔*sound*〕 *a retreat, **a**) go back; run away. 퇴각하다. **b**) 《*fig.*》 give up an undertaking. 사업을 그만두다.

re·trench [ritréntʃ] *vt.* (P6) **1** cut down (payments, money used, etc.); reduce. (비용 등)을 줄이다; 절감하다. **2** shorten; cut out. 생략하다; 삭제하다. ¶ *Several passages of the book might be retrenched.* 그 책의 몇 구절은 삭제될지도 모른다. — *vi.* (P1) cut down expenses; economize. 절약〔검약〕하다. [re-]

re·tri·al [ri:tráiəl] *n.* Ⓒ a second examination; 《law》 a second trial. 재시험; (재판의) 재심(再審). [re-]

ret·ri·bu·tion [rètrəbjú:ʃən] *n.* Ⓤ reward or punishment which comes to oneself. 응보; 천벌. ¶ *the day of ~* 최후의 심판일. [re-, →tribute]

re·trib·u·tive [ritríbjətiv] *adj.* paying back; of retribution. 응보의. ¶ *~ justice* 인과 응보(因果應報).

re·triev·al [ritrí:vəl] *n.* Ⓤ the act of retrieving. 회복; 만회; 복구. ¶ *beyond* 〔*past*〕 *~* 회복할 가망이 없는; 구제 불능의. [↓]

re·trieve [ritrí:v] *vt.* (P6) **1** get (something lost) back again; recover. …을 되찾다; 만회하다. ¶ *He retrieved his spirits.* 그는 기운을 되찾았다 / *I should like to ~ the bag I left in the car.* 차에 두고 내린 가방을 가져 왔으면 좋겠는데. **2** bring back (something damaged) to a former condition. …을 보상〔벌충〕하다. **3** (of a hunting dog) find and bring back (a dead or wounded animal or bird) to a hunter. (사냥개가 잡은 사냥감)을 찾아서 가지고 오다. ¶ *The dog retrieved the wounded duck.* 사냥개가 부상당한 오리를 찾아서 물고 왔다. **4** set or put right; repair. …을 바로잡다; 고치다. ¶ ~ *a mistake* 잘못을 바로잡다. **5** (P6,13) save (from error, mistake, etc.). (잘못 등에서) …을 구해내다. ¶ ~ *someone from bad ways* 〔*ruin*〕 아무를 나쁜 길〔파멸〕에서 구해내다. ● **re·triev·a·ble** [-əbl] *adj.* [re-, F. *trouver* find]

re·triev·er [ritríːvər] *n.* Ⓒ a trained dog which finds and brings back shot animals or birds to its master. 리트리버《잡은 짐승을 찾아서 갖고 오도록 훈련된 사냥개》.

ret·ro- [rétrou-] *pref.* back; backward; in return. '뒤로, 거꾸로, 거슬러'의 뜻. [L.]

re·tro·ac·tive [rètrouǽktiv] *adj.* acting upon what is past; working backward. 소급(遡及)하는; 반동하는. ¶ *a* ~ *law* 소급법 / ~ *to April,* 4월로 소급하여 / *Your new salary will be* ~ *to last month.* 너의 새 봉급은 지난달로 소급하여 지급될 것이다. [retro-]

re·tro·cede [rètrəsíːd] *vt.* (P6) give (territory) back again. (영토 따위)를 돌려주다; 반환하다. —*vi.* (P1) **1** move back; draw back. 물러가다; 되돌아가다. **2** (of disease, etc.) pass to the inner part of the body; strike inward. (병이) 내공(內攻)하다. [retro-]

ret·ro·grade [rétrəgrèid] *vi.* (P1) move backward; become worse. 후퇴하다; 악화되다. ¶ *The civilization of this country is retrograding.* 이 나라의 문명은 퇴보하고 있다. —*adj.* moving backward; becoming worse. 후퇴하는; 더 나빠지는. ¶ *a* ~ *movement* 후퇴; 역행 / *in a* ~ *order* 역순(逆順)으로. [retro-]

ret·ro·gress [rétrəgrès] *vi.* move backward; become worse. 후퇴하다; 되돌아가다; 악화하다. [retro-]

ret·ro·gres·sion [rètrəgréʃən] *n.* Ⓤ backward movement; return to an inferior, worse state. 후퇴; 악화. ¶ *the* ~ *of a motorcar* 자동차의 후진 / *the* ~ *of civilization* 문명의 퇴보.

ret·ro·gres·sive [rètrəgrésiv] *adj.* **1** moving backward. 후퇴〔역행〕하는. ¶ ~ *motion* 역행 운동. **2** becoming worse. 퇴화〔퇴보〕하는. ¶ *a* ~ *change* 퇴행성 변이(變異).

ret·ro·rock·et [rétrourɑ̀kit / -rɔ̀k-] *n.* a rocket engine used to retard, arrest, or reverse the motion of an aircraft, spacecraft, missile, etc. 역추진 로켓. [retro-]

ret·ro·spect [rétrəspèkt] *n.* Ⓤ the act of thinking about past events. 회고; 회상. [→special]

in* (*the*) *retrospect, when looking back. 회고하건데. ¶ *Life is pleasant in* (*the*) ~. 생각해보니 사는 것이란 재미있다.

ret·ro·spec·tion [rètrəspékʃən] *n.* Ⓤ looking back on things past. 회상; 회고. ¶ *indulge in* ~ 추억에 잠기다 / *Old people often enjoy* ~. 노인들은 흔히 회상을 즐긴다.

ret·ro·spec·tive [rètrəspéktiv] *adj.* **1** looking back on things past. 회고하는; 회상의. ¶ *in a* ~ *mood* 회고조로 / *a* ~ *exhibition* 회고전. **2** (of laws, payments, etc.) applying to the past. 소급(遡及)하는. ¶ *a* ~ *law* 소급법. **3** lying behind one. (풍경 등이) 뒤쪽에 있는. ¶ *a* ~ *view* 배경.

⁑re·turn [ritə́ːrn] *vi.* **1** (P1,2A) go or come back to a former place. (본디의 자리로) 되돌아 가〔오〕다. ¶ ~ *home* 귀가하다 / ~ *from abroad* 귀국하다 / ~ *to one's seat* 제자리로 돌아가다. **2** (P3) 《*to*》 go back again in thought or treatment. (화제 등이 …로) 되돌아가다. ¶ *Let's* ~ *to the subject.* 본론으로 돌아가자 / *To* ~. 본론에 돌아가서; 여담은 그만두고 / ~ *from a digression* 여담을 끝내고 본론으로 돌아가다. **3** (P1,3) 《*to*》 go back to a former state; happen or appear again. (본디의 상태로) 되돌아가다; 재발하다. ¶ ~ *to one's work* 하던 일을 다시 하다 / ~ *to power* 다시 집권하다 / ~ *to oneself* 제정신이 들다; 정신차리다 / ~ *to dust* 흙으로 돌아가다; 죽다 / ~ *to life* 소생하다 / *Consciousness has not returned yet.* 아직 의식이 회복되지 않았다 / *The fine weather has returned.* 날씨가 좋아졌다 / ~ *to a bad habit* 못된 버릇이 돌아오다 / *Spring returns.* 봄이 돌아온다 / *He gave up drinking for a while, but* ~ *to his old ways.* 잠시 술을 끊더니 옛 상태로 되돌아 갔다. **4** (P1) pass back; go back to a former owner. (원소유주에) 돌아가다. ¶ *The property will* ~ *to the original owner.* 그 재산은 원소유주에 귀속될 것이다.

—*vt.* **1** (P6,13,14) bring or put back. …을 돌려주다; (제자리)에 되돌려 놓다. ¶ ~ *a book to the shelf* 책을 책꽂이에 도로 끼우다 / *Return my pen, please.* 내 펜을 돌려다오 / ~ *the borrowed money* 차용한 돈을 갚다 / *He returned the girl to her home.* 그는 소녀를 그녀의 집까지 데려다 주었다 / ~ *a ball* 공을 받아치다 / *Fortunately the hostages were returned unharmed.* 다행히 인질들은 무사히 돌아왔다. **2** (P6,13) give back (something) in the same manner. …에 답례하다; 갚다. ¶ ~ *a visit* 답례 방문을 하다 / ~ *a blow* 되갈기다 / ~ *good for evil* 악을 선으로 갚다. **3** (P6) reply; answer. …에 대답하다. **4** (P6,7,13) report officially. …을 보고하다; 복명(復命)하다. ¶ *The soldier is returned as killed.* 그 병사는 전사했다는 보고다 / *He returned his earnings as £9000 on the tax declaration.* 그는 세금 신고에 소득이 9천 파운드라고 보고했다. **5** (P6,13) 《*to*》 elect; choose formally. …을 선출하다. ¶ *a returning officer* 선거 관리인 / *He was returned* (*to Parliament*) *for Devonshire.* 그는 데번셔에서

(의원으로) 선출되었다. **6** (P6) yield; produce as profit. 이익을 내다. ¶ *~ a profit* / *~ good interest* 이자가 많이 생기다.

— *n.* **1** UC the act of going or coming back. 돌아감〔옴〕; 귀환; 반환. ¶ *a ~ home* 귀가 / *wait (for) his ~ from a journey* 여행에서 돌아오는 그를 기다리다. **2** UC the act of coming again; reappearance; repetition. 복귀; 회귀; 재발; 반복. ¶ *a ~ of illness* 병의 재발 / *Many happy returns (of the day)!* (생일을) 축하합니다 / *the ~ of spring* 회춘(回春) / *a ~ of the pain* 통증의 재발. **3** UC something returned; recompense; repayment. 답례; 보답; 반환; 반제(返濟). ¶ *the ~ of a salute* 답례 / *I asked him the ~ of the money.* 돈을 돌려 달라고 했다 / *make ~ for something* …에 보답하다 / *a ~ for the kindness received* 친절에 대한 보답 / *poor returns for one's labor* 수고에 대한 시원찮은 보수. **4** C a reply. 대답. **5** 《often *pl.*》 a profit; an increase. 수익; 이윤. ¶ *a poor ~ on one's investment* 투자에 대한 형편 없는 이익 / *give a ~* 이윤을 내다 / *small profits and quick returns* 박리 다매(薄利多賣) / *The goods bring in fair returns.* 이 물건은 수익이 괜찮다. **6** C an official report. 보고(서). ¶ *official returns* 공보(公報) / *make a ~ of the survey* 조사 결과를 보고하다 / *make a ~ of one's income* 소득 신고를 하다 / *prepare a ~ of the money spent* 지출 보고서를 작성하다. **7** UC an election. 선출. ¶ *secure a ~ for California* 캘리포니아에서 선출되다. **8** 《Brit.》 C a return ticket. 왕복표. **9** 《archit.》 a part of the surface of a building, forming an angle with the main surface. (돌출부 등의) 정면에서 측면으로의 꺾임; 곡벽(曲壁). **10** 《sports》 ⓐ the act or manner of returning the ball. 공을 되받아치기. ⓑ the ball which is returned. (정구 따위에서) 쳐넘긴 공.

by return (of mail [post]), by the next mail out. (서신을) 받는 대로 곧. ¶ *answer a letter by ~ (of mail)* 편지를 받는 즉시 회신하다.

in return, as a return. 답례로. ¶ *pay money in ~ for jewels* 보석의 대가로 돈을 지불하다 / *love and be loved in ~* 서로 사랑을 주고 받다.

in return for [to] (=*as repayment for*) *something.* …의 답례로〔보답으로〕. ¶ *gain nothing but blame in ~ for one's efforts* 애만 쓰고 그 보답으로 욕만 먹다

— *adj.* returning; returned; of a return. 돌아가는〔오는〕; 답례의; 왕복의. ¶《Brit.》 *a ~ ticket* 왕복표(=《U.S.》 round trip ticket). [re-]

re·un·ion [riːjúːnjən] *n.* **1** U ⓐ the state of coming together again. 재결합; 재회. ¶ *the ~ of parted friends* 헤어졌던 벗과의 재회 / *the ~ of a family* 가족의 재결합. ⓑ friendly relations after quarrels. 화해. ¶ *the ~ of a former enemy* 전날의 적과의 화해. **2** C a happy meeting of friends who have not met for a long time; a social gathering. 친목회; 모임; 회합. ¶ *We have a monthly ~ at this hotel.* 우린 이 호텔에서 매달 한 번씩 친목회를 가진다. [re-]

re·u·nite [rìːjuːnáit] *vt.* (P6) unite (persons) again after separation. …을 재결합〔재회〕시키다. ¶ *The States were reunited after the Civil War.* 남북 전쟁 후 각 주는 재결합했다. — *vi.* (P1) become joined again. 재결합하다; 화해하다. [↑]

Rev. Reverend; Revelation. 묵시록(默示錄).

rev. revenue; reverse; review(ed); revision; revolution; revolving.

re·val·u·a·tion [riːvæ̀ljuéiʃən] *n.* U value estimated or recognized again. 재평가; 평가 절상. [↓]

re·val·ue [riːvǽljuː] *vt.* estimate value of (something) again; (esp.) increase the value of a currency. …을 재평가하다; (특히) 평가 절상하다. ¶ *The dollar is being revalued.* 달러가 평가 절상(切上)되고 있다. [re-]

re·vamp [riːvǽmp] *vt.* (P6) 《U.S.》 **1** mend; patch up. …을 깁다; …에 덧대다. **2** 《*colloq.*》 revise and improve. …을 개정〔개작〕하다. ¶ *~ a play* 각본을 다시 쓰다 / *~ the cabinet* 개각하다. [re-]

:re·veal [rivíːl] *vt.* (P6,11,13) expose to view (what has been hidden); show; make known. …을 나타내다; 폭로하다; 보이다; 알리다. ¶ *~ a secret* 비밀을 폭로하다 / *~ oneself* 신분을 밝히다 / *Her laugh revealed her even teeth.* 웃으니 그녀의 고른 잇바디가 보였다 / *Promise never to ~ my secret.* 내 비밀을 지켜주겠다고 약속을 해라 / *She turned so that her face was revealed.* 얼굴이 보이도록 그녀는 돌아섰다. [re-, → veil]

rev·el [révəl] *v.* (**-eled, -el·ing** or 《Brit.》 **-elled, -el·ling**) *vi.* **1** (P1) make merry; feast. 주연을 베풀다; 마시며 흥청거리다. ¶ *They were reveling all night.* 그들은 밤새도록 술마시며 흥청거렸다. **2** (P3) 《*in*》 indulge freely in; take great pleasure in. …에 탐닉하다〔빠지다〕; 한껏 즐기다. ¶ *~ in excess of every kind* 아무것에나 지나치게 빠지다 / *He reveled in his freedom.* 자유를 만끽했다. — *vt.* (P7) 《rare》 spend in reveling. …을 낭비하다. ¶ *~ one's time away* 시간을 낭비하다. — *n.* 《often *pl.*》 a merrymaking; a noisy good time. 환락; 흥겹게 떠들고 놂. [→rebel]

rev·e·la·tion [rèvəléiʃən] *n.* **1** U the act of making known something previously secret. 발각; 폭로; (비밀의) 누설. ¶ *The ~ of the plot of the traitors caused their capture.* 음모가 발각되어 반역자들은 체포됐다. **2** C something that is made known; something unexpected. 폭로된 것; 뜻밖의 사실. ¶ *It was a ~ to me.* 그것은 내게 정말 뜻밖의 일이었다 / *The boy's great knowledge of astronomy was a ~ to us.* 소년의 천문학에 대한 해박한 지식은 우리들에게 하나의 경이였

다 / *What a* ~ *!* 정말 놀랍다 / *The* ~ *that he was her father astonished her.* 그가 그녀의 아버지였다는 사실에 그녀는 경악했다. [→reveal]

rev·el·er, 《Brit.》 **-el·ler** [révələr] *n.* Ⓒ a person who enjoys revels. 주연을 즐기는 사람; 난봉꾼. [→revel]

rev·el·ry [révəlri] *n.* Ⓤ a gay and noisy state, with much drinking. 술 마시고 흥겹게 떠들기. [↑]

:**re·venge** [rivéndʒ] *vt.* **1** (P6) do harm to (someone) in return for a wrong. …에 복수하다. ¶ ~ *wrong with wrong* 악에는 악으로 갚다 / *I will* ~ *that insult.* 나는 그 모욕을 앙갚음하고 말겠다. **2** (P6,13) take revenge on behalf of. …을 대신해 원수를 갚다. ¶ ~ *one's deceased father* 죽은 아버지의 원수를 갚다.

— *n.* Ⓤ **1** the act of paying back harm for harm. 복수; 보복. ¶ *They took* ~ *on the thieves by beating them.* 그들은 도둑들을 두들겨 패서 분풀이했다 / *This was done in* ~ *for a former wrong.* 이건 앞서의 악행에 대한 보복이다. **2** a desire to return evil for evil. 복수심. **3** 《sports, cards, etc.》 a return game. 설욕전. ¶ *After I'd beaten him at chess I gave him a chance to get his* ~. 그에게 장기를 이기고 나서 나는 그에게 설욕할 기회를 주었다. [re-, L. *vindico* claim]

re·venge·ful [rivéndʒfəl] *adj.* wanting to revenge always. 복수를 노리는; 앙심을 먹은. ¶ *a* ~ *person* 복수심에 불타는 사람.

***rev·e·nue** [révənjù] *n.* Ⓤ **1** income; the general income of a government. 소득; 수입; 세입. ¶ *the national revenues* 국가의 총수입 / *the Public* ~ 국고 세입 / *enjoy an immense* ~ 거액의 소득이 있다. **2** 《*pl.*》 the items of revenue. 수입 항목; 세입 명세 / *defraud the* ~ 탈세하다. **3** a governmental department collecting the state revenue. 국세청. ¶ *a* ~ *officer* 세무관 / *a* ~ *cutter* (세관의) 밀수 감시정. [re-]

revenue stamp [∠-- ∠] *n.* a stamp to show that a person has paid a tax to the government. 수입 인지.

re·ver·ber·ate [rivə́ːrbərèit] *vt., vi.* **1** (P6; 1) echo back; resound. …을 반향시키다[하다]; 울리[게 하]다. ¶ *The thunder reverberated throughout the house.* 우렛소리가 온 집안을 흔들었다 / *His voice reverberated in the cave.* 그의 목소리가 굴 속에 울려퍼졌다. **2** (P1) reflect (light, heat, etc.). (빛·열 따위를) 반사하다. [re-, L. *verbero* beat]

re·ver·ber·a·tion [rivə̀ːrbəréiʃən] *n.* Ⓤ **1** the act of echoing back; the state of being reverberated; a reechoed sound. 반향; 반향음; 여운. ¶ *The reverberation(s) of the shot died away slowly.* 총성의 여운은 서서히 사라졌다. **2** reflection. 반사.

re·vere [rivíər] *vt.* (P6) respect and love deeply; show reverence for. …을 존경하다. ¶ *a poet revered by all* 모든 사람에게 존경받는 시인. [re-, L. *vercor* fear]

***rev·er·ence** [révərəns] *n.* Ⓤ **1** a feeling of respect mixed with wonder, fear, and love. 존경; 경외(敬畏). ¶ *feel* ~ *for parents* 부모를 존경하다 / *The old queen was held in great* ~. 노여왕은 대단한 존경을 받고 있었다 / *pay* ~ *to the king* 국왕에 경의를 표하다. **2** Ⓒ 《*arch., joc.*》 a deep bow. 정중한 인사. ¶ *make a* ~.

Saving your reverence .... 《*arch., joc.*》 Excuse me when I say that .... 이런 말씀드려서 죄송하오나 ….

your* [*his*] *reverence, 《*arch., joc.*》 a mode of addressing or referring to clergymen. 신부[목사]님《성직자에 대한 존칭》.

— *vt.* (P6) revere. …을 존경하다. [↑]

***rev·er·end** [révərənd] *adj.* **1** worthy of deep respect. 존경해야 할. **2** 《*the R-*》 used as a title for a clergyman. …님《성직자의 존칭》. 參考 Rev.로 생략함. ¶ *The Reverend Thomas A. Johnson will preach to us.* 존슨 신부님께서 강론하시겠습니다.

— *n.* 《usu. *pl.*》 a clergyman. 성직자; 신부; 목사. [↑]

rev·er·ent [révərənt] *adj.* feeling reverence. 존경하는. ¶ *He gave* ~ *attention to the sermon.* 그는 경건한 마음으로 설교를 들었다.

rev·er·en·tial [rèvərénʃəl] *adj.* =reverent.

rev·er·ie [révəri] *n.* ⓊⒸ dreamy thoughts; a fantastic, unpractical idea. 환상; 몽상; 공상. ¶ *He was sank in* ~ *and did not hear me.* 그는 몽상에 빠져 있어 내 말을 못 들었다 / *Your plans are reveries that will never be realized.* 네 계획들은 절대로 실현되지 못할 공상이다. [F. *rêverie*]

re·ver·sal [rivə́ːrsəl] *n.* ⓊⒸ a change to the opposite; being reversed. 역전; 전도. ¶ *a* ~ *of the natural order of things* 사물의 자연스러운 질서의 전도(顚倒). [↓]

***re·verse** [rivə́ːrs] *vt.* (P6) **1** turn (something) inside out, upside down, or backward. …을 뒤집다; 거꾸로 하다; 반대로 하다. ¶ ~ *a cup* 컵을 엎어 놓다 / *They had to* ~ *their direction.* 그들은 방향을 반대로 바꿔야 했다. **2** put (things) in each other's place. …을 바꿔 놓다; 교환하다. ¶ *Their positions are now reversed.* 그들의 처지는 지금 서로 바뀌어 있다 / ~ *the normal order* 정상적인 순서를 역으로 바꿔 놓다. **3** cause (something) to move backward. (자동차 따위)를 후진시키다; (기계)를 역전[역회전]시키다. ¶ ~ *an engine* 엔진을 역전시키다 / *I reversed the car through the gate.* 나는 차를 후진시켜 대문을 나갔다. **4** 《law》 take away the value of (something); cancel. …을 파기하다; 취소하다. ¶ ~ *a sentence* 판결을 파기하다 / *The appeal court reversed the original verdict and set the prisoner free.* 항소 법원은 원심을 파기하고 피고를 석방시켰다.

— *vi.* (P1) move in the opposite direction. 역전하다; 거꾸로 돌다. ¶ *The dancers reversed.* 댄서는 역으로 돌았다.

Reverse arms! an order to carry arms pointing downward (at funerals, etc.). (장례식 등에서) 거꾸로 총.

— *n.* Ⓒ **1** 《*sing.* only, *the* ～》 the opposite or contrary of something. 역; 반대. ¶ *He did the ～ of what he was asked to do.* 그는 하라고 지시 받은 일과는 반대의 일을 했다 / *Is she pretty? — No, quite the ～.* 그 여자 예쁘냐 — 아니, 정반대야 / *'Slow' is the ～ of 'fast'.* 'slow'는 'fast'의 반대다. **2** Ⓒ the back of a coin or medal. (동전 따위의) 뒤; 뒷면(opp. obverse). ¶ *The British tenpence piece has a lion on the ～.* 영국의 10펜스짜리 뒷면에는 사자가 새겨져 있다. **3** Ⓒ a change from good to bad; a misfortune. 악화; 실패; 불운. ¶ *the ～ of fortune* 비운; 재난 / *have* 〔*suffer*〕 *a ～* 실패〔패배〕하다 / *under the stroke of unexpected reverses* 뜻밖의 불행을 당하여 / *express one's sympathy at someone's reverses* 아무의 불운에 대하여 동정의 인사말을 하다 / *The enemy met with a ～.* 적은 패퇴했다 / *experience reverses* 적자를 보다. **4** Ⓤ (of a machine) backward movement. 역전; 후진. ¶ *He drove his car in ～.* 그는 차를 후진시켰다.

— *adj.* opposite; contrary; upside-down; inside-out; inverted. 반대의; 거꾸로의. ¶ *～ circulation* 역류 / *a ～ gear* 후진 기어 / *by the ～ method* 반대되는 방법으로 / *Play the ～ side of that record.* 그 레코드판의 뒷면을 틀어라. [→revert]

re·verse·ly [rivə́ːrsli] *adv.* in an opposite direction; on the other hand. 거꾸로; 한편으로는; 이에 반하여.

re·vers·i·ble [rivə́ːrsəbəl] *adj.* **1** that can be reversed. 거꾸로 할 수 있는. **2** (of textile fabrics, clothes, etc.) finished on both sides so that either may be used as the right side. (피륙·옷 따위가) 안팎을 다 쓸 수 있는; 양면의. ¶ *～ cloth* 양면천 / *a ～ coat* 뒤집어서도 입는 코트; 리버서블 코트.

re·ver·sion [rivə́ːrʒən, -ʃən] *n.* ⓊⒸ **1** a return to a former condition or habit; the act of turning back. 역전; 되돌아가기; 복귀. **2** 《law》 the return of property to the grantor or his heirs after the end of the grant; the right of succession, future possession, or enjoyment. (양도 조건 기간 만료 후, 양도인 또는 상속인에게로의) 재산의 복귀; 계승〔상속〕권; 장래 소유권.

re·vert [rivə́ːrt] *vi., vt.* **1** (P1,3) go back. 되돌아가다. **2** (P1,3) 《law》 return to (the original owner or his heirs) 복귀〔귀속〕하다. ¶ *If a man dies without heirs, his property reverts to the State.* 상속인 없이 죽은 사람의 재산은 국가에 귀속된다. **3** (P3) direct one's attention back to; refer to again. (본래의 화제 따위로) 되돌아가다. ¶ *～ to the former topic of conversation* 앞서의 화제로 되돌아가다 / *My thoughts reverted to the last time that I had seen her.* 내 생각은 그녀를 마지막으로 만났던 때로 되돌아갔다. **4** (P6) turn (the eyes) back. 뒤돌아보다. **5** (P3) return to (a former state). (본디의 상태로) 되돌아가다. ¶ *After the settler left, the natives reverted to their savage customs.* 식민자가 가버리자 원주민들은 이전의 미개 습관으로 되돌아갔다. [re-, L. *verto* turn]

rev·er·y [révəri] *n.* (*pl.* **-ries**) =reverie.

:re·view [rivjúː] *vt.* (P6) **1** pass over (past events, etc.) again in one's mind; study (something previously learnt) again. …을 회고하다; (배운 것)을 복습하다. ¶ *She reviewed the day's happenings.* 그녀는 그 날 있었던 일을 회고해 보았다 / *He reviewed his lessons every day.* 그는 배운 것을 매일 복습했다. **2** inspect (troops, etc.) formally or officially. …을 검열하다. ¶ *～ soldiers* 〔*troops*〕 열병(閱兵)하다. **3** look at (something) again to examine it. …을 재조사하다. ¶ *A higher court may ～ the proceedings and judgments of a lower one.* 상급 법원은 하급 법원에서의 소송 절차와 판결을 재심할 수 있다. **4** write a criticism of (a new book, play, etc.) in a magazine or newspaper. (잡지 등에서) …을 비평하다; 평론하다. ¶ *This book has been reviewed favorably in several newspapers.* 이 책은 몇몇 신문에서 평이 좋았다 / *He reviews books by profession.* 그는 평론가다.

— *vi.* (P1) write reviews of books, plays, etc. 평론을 쓰다.

— *n.* **1** Ⓤ the act of looking over, studying, considering, etc. again. 회고; 복습. ¶ *pass one's life in ～* 살아 온 인생을 회고하다 / *Before the examination we have a ～ of the term's work.* 시험에 앞서 우리는 그 학기 동안 배운 것을 복습한다. **2** ⒸⓊ a formal, official inspection, esp. of naval or military forces. 검열; 열병. ¶ *a ～ of the army* 열병식 / *a naval ～* 관함식 / *A ～ of the troops will be held during the general's visit to camp.* 장군이 주둔지를 방문한 동안에 사열식이 있을 것이다. **3** Ⓤ the second exact view or examination. 재조사. **4** ⒸⓊ a criticism of a new book, play, etc. printed in a magazine or newspaper. (잡지 등에 실린) 서평; 비평; 극평; 평론. ¶ *The book received good reviews.* 그 책은 좋은 평을 받았다 / *I hope your new book gets good* 〔*favorable*〕 *reviews.* 당신이 새로 낸 책에 대한 평이 좋기를 바랍니다. **5** Ⓒ 《law》 examination by a higher court of the decision of a lower court. 재심. [re-]

re·view·er [rivjúːər] *n.* Ⓒ a person who writes a criticism of a book, play, etc. in a magazine or newspaper. 평론가.

re·vile [riváil] *vt., vi.* (P6; 1) use bad words to (someone); call (someone) bad names. (…을) 욕하다; 욕설하다. ¶ *The beggar reviled the man who drove him off.* 거지는 자기

를 쫓아낸 사람을 욕했다 / *Their much reviled system in fact works far better than many highly praised ones elsewhere.* 나쁘다고 많이도 욕 먹은 그들의 제도가 실은 높이 평가된 많은 다른 데의 것들보다 훨씬 잘 운영된다. [re-]

re·vise [riváiz] *vt.* (P6) **1** read again, esp. to discover and correct errors in (a text, etc.); correct. …을 교정하다; 개정〔정정〕하다. ¶ *revised and enlarged* 개정 증보의 / *~ a book* 책을 개정하다 / *a revised version* 개정판 / *He revised the manuscript of his book before sending it to the publisher.* 그는 책의 원고를 출판사에 넘기기 전에 교정을 봤다. **2** change. (의견 등)을 바꾸다. ¶ *~ one's opinion* 의견을 바꾸다. — *n.* UC 《print.》 **1** the process of revising. 교정; 개정. **2** a proof-sheet taken from earlier corrected proof. 재교쇄. [→review]

Re·vised Version [riváizd vǝ́:rʒǝn, -ʃǝn] *n.* the revised form of the Authorized Version of the Bible. 개역(改譯) 성서. 參考 Authorized Version 의 개정판이며 R.V.로 생략함.

re·vis·er [riváizǝr] *n.* C a person who revises. 교정〔교열〕자; 정정〔수정〕자.

re·vi·sion [rivíʒǝn] *n.* U **1** the act of revising. 교정; 개정. **2** something that has been revised; a revised copy. 개정판. ¶ *A ~ of this book will be published in June.* 이 책의 개정판이 6월에 출간된다. [→review]

re·vis·it [ri:vízit] *vt.* visit again. …을 다시 방문하다. [re-]

re·viv·al [riváivǝl] *n.* UC **1** the state of being brought back to life. 소생; 부활. ¶ *the ~ of a drowned man* 익사자의 소생 / *a ~ from death* 〔*unconsciousness*〕 죽음〔의식 불명〕에서의 회생. **2** the state of being brought back to health or vigor. (건강·기력 따위의) 회복. ¶ *the ~ of one's spirits* 기력의 회복. **3** the act of coming back to public use and attention; the state of being brought to public use and attention; restoration. (옛 습관·전통 따위의) 부흥; 재흥; (영화 등의) 재상영. ¶ *the ~ of an old style* 옛 스타일의 재(再)유행 / *the ~ of an old fashion* 옛 유행의 부활 / *the ~ of learning* 〔*letters*〕 문예 부흥 / *the ~ of old movies* 옛 영화의 재상영. **4** a meeting or series of meetings to arouse interest in religion. (신앙 부흥을 위한) 전도 집회. [↓]

***re·vive** [riváiv] *vi.* (P1) **1** come back to life or consciousness. 소생하다; 의식을 되찾다. ¶ *~ after fainting* 기절했다가 깨어나다 / *He revived with artificial respiration.* 그는 인공 호흡으로 의식을 되찾았다. **2** return to a healthy and lively state. 기운이 나다; 생기를 되찾다. ¶ *The faded flowers revived in water.* 물을 주니 시든 꽃들이 생기를 되찾았다 / *His spirits* 〔*hopes*〕 *revived.* 원기를〔희망을〕 되찾았다 / *I felt my courage ~ in me.* 나는 용기가 되살아나는 걸 느꼈다. **3** come back to public use and attention. 부흥하다; 재유행하다. ¶ *a fashion that has revived* 되살아난 유행.

— *vt.* (P6) **1** cause (someone) to come back to life or consciousness. …을 소생시키다; …의 의식을 되찾게 하다. ¶ *He felt rather faint but the fresh air soon revived him.* 의식이 혼미해지는 듯했으나 신선한 공기로 이내 제정신이 들었다. **2** refresh; give (someone) strength and energy again. …의 기운을 되찾게 하다. ¶ *Tea often revives a tired person.* 차를 마시면 피곤한 사람이 기운을 되찾는 일이 흔히 있다 / *A cool bath revived me after a tiring journey.* 냉수욕을 했더니 여독이 풀렸다 / *A run of success revived his hopes and spirits.* 한 차례 성공하자 그의 희망과 용기가 되살아났다. **3** bring back to the mind. (기억)을 되살아나게 하다. ¶ *~ a memory* 기억을 되살리다 / *~ interest in a subject* 문제에 다시 흥미를 불러일으키다. **4** bring back (something) to public use and attention. …을 부활시키다. ¶ *Many old movies are being revived now.* 많은 옛 영화들이 요즘 재상영되고 있다 / *~ an old law* 구법을 다시 시행하다 / *~ a play* 극을 재상연하다. [re-, L. *vivo* live]

rev·o·ca·ble [révǝkǝbǝl] *adj.* that can be canceled. 취소할 수 있는. [→revoke]

rev·o·ca·tion [rèvǝkéiʃǝn] *n.* UC the act of canceling. 폐지; 취소. ¶ *the ~ of a law* 법령의 폐지 / *the ~ of an order* 명령의 취소. [↓]

re·voke [rivóuk] *vt.* (P6) take back; cancel; withdraw; annul. …을 취소〔철회〕하다. ¶ *~ a license* 면허를 취소하다 / *~ a promise* 약속을 취소하다 / *The government revoked its permission for them to enter the country.* 정부는 그들에 대한 입국 허가를 취소하였다. [re-, →voice]

***re·volt** [rivóult] *n.* **1** C the people's act of rising up against authority. 반란; 폭동. ¶ *rise in ~* 반란을 일으키다 / *in ~ against* …에 반항하여; 반란을 일으켜서 / *The people were in ~ against the government.* 국민은 정부에 항거하는 반란을 일으키고 있었다. **2** U a feeling of disgust. 혐오; 반감. ¶ *I feel ~ at the sight of him.* 그 자를 보면 구역질이 난다.

— *vi.* (P1,3) **1** 《*from, against*》 rise up against authority. 반란을 일으키다. ¶ *The people revolted against the dictator.* 국민들은 독재자에 반기를 들었다 / *~ from one's allegiance* 충성을 저버리다 / *They revolted against their foreign ruler.* 외국 지배자에게 반란을 일으켰다. **2** 《*by*》 be disgusted by something bad or unpleasant. 메스꺼워지다. ¶ *~ at a bad smell* 악취에 속이 울렁거리다 / *My nature revolts against such treatment.* 나는 그러한 처우엔 못 견디는 사람이다.

— *vt.* (P6) cause to feel disgust. …을 구역질나게 하다; 불쾌하게 만들다. ¶ *Snake ~*

me. 뱀은 질색이다 / *Cruelty and meanness ~ decent people.* 잔학 행위와 비열한 행위는점잖은 사람들에게 반감을 갖게 한다. [re-, L. *volvo* toll]

:rev·o·lu·tion [rèvəlúːʃən] *n.* ⓒⓤ **1** a complete change in the government or political system; any complete change in habits of thought, methods of labor, etc. 혁명; 변혁. ¶ *the ~ in modern physics* 근대 물리학의 대변혁 / *The French Revolution* 프랑스 혁명 / *The invention of machines caused a ~ in the way we live.* 기계의 발명은우리들 생활 양식에 일대 변혁을 가져왔다. **2** one complete turn of a motor. (기계의) 회전. ¶ *a speed of 100 revolutions per minute* 분당 100 회전의 속도. **3** ⓤ the act of turning of a heavenly body around a central point; the time it takes to complete one such revolution. (천체의) 공전; (연·월·계절의) 순환; 주기(週期). ¶ *the ~ of the seasons* 4계절의 순환 / *The earth makes one ~ round the sun in about 365 days.* 지구는 약 365일에 태양의 주위를 한 번 공전한다. [↑]

·rev·o·lu·tion·ar·y [rèvəlúːʃənèri / -nəri] *adj.* **1** of or causing a revolution. 혁명의; 일대 변화를 가져오는. ¶ *~ ideas* 〔*speeches*〕 혁명적인 사고〔연설〕/ *a ~ new way of growing rice* 쌀의 획기적 재배법. **2** 《*R-*》 of or pertaining to the American Revolution. 미국 독립 전쟁(시대)의〔에 관한〕.

rev·o·lu·tion·ist [rèvəlúːʃənist] *n.* ⓒ a person who supports or takes part in a revolution. 혁명 당원.

rev·o·lu·tion·ize [rèvəlúːʃənàiz] *vt.* cause a complete change in (something). …에 혁명을 일으키다. ¶ *~ an industry* 산업에 혁명을 일으키다 / *The airplane revolutionized our lives.* 항공기는 우리 생활에 대변혁을 가져왔다 / *English philology has been revolutionized during the last half-century.* 영어학은지난 반 세기 동안 일대 혁신이 가해졌다.

·re·volve [rivɑ́lv / -vɔ́lv] *vi.* **1** (P1,3) turn around on the central point of itself. (지구·차바퀴 등이) 회전하다; 자전하다. ¶ *The earth revolves once in 24 hours.* 지구는 24 시간에 한 번 자전한다 / *The wheels of a train revolves when it runs.* 기차 바퀴는 기차가 달릴 때 회전한다 / *Wheels ~ on their axles.* 수레 바퀴는 축을 중심으로 돈다. **2** (P1,3) 《*around*》 move in a curved path around a center. (다른 것의 둘레를) 돌다; 회전하다. ¶ *The moon revolves around the earth.* 달은 지구 주위를 돈다 / *The hotel has revolving doors.* 그 호텔에는 여러 개의 회전문이 있다. **3** (P1) come round again and again; return periodically. 순환하다. ¶ *the revolving seasons* (주기적으로) 순환하는 계절.
— *vt.* (P6,13) **1** cause (something) to move around a center. …을 회전시키다〔돌리다〕. ¶ *He revolved the dial of the safe.* 금고(金庫)의 다이얼을 돌렸다. **2** consider (something) again and again from many points of view. …을 (여러 각도로) 곰곰이 생각하다. ¶ *~ a problem in one's mind* 어떤 문제를 여러 모로 곰곰이 생각하다 / *You need to ~ the problem before giving an answer.* 대답하기 전에 문제를 잘 생각해 봐야 한다 / *~ plans for revenge* 복수할 계획을 궁리하다. [*revolt*]

re·volv·er [rivɑ́lvər / -vɔ́lv-] *n.* ⓒ a pistol with a revolving cylinder so that several shots may be fired at one loading. 연발 권총. [↑]

re·vue [rivjúː] *n.* ⓒⓤ 《F.》 an amusing musical play with several changes of scene and many songs and dances. 르뷔; 해학적인 악극(樂劇).

re·vul·sion [rivʌ́lʃən] *n.* ⓤ a sudden and violent change of feeling. (감정·운명 등의) 격변. ¶ *My feelings towards George underwent a ~ when I learned of his cruelty and dishonesty.* 조지의 잔인함과 부정직함을 알고 그에 대한 나의 감정은 일대 격변을 겪었다. [re-, L. *vello* pull]

Rev. Ver. Revised Version (of the Bible). 개역(改譯) 성서.

:re·ward [riwɔ́ːrd] *n.* **1** ⓤ something given in return for service. 보수; 포상. ¶ *the ~ of courage* 용기에 대한 포상 / *He was promoted in ~ for his services.* 봉사에 대한 포상으로 그는 승진되었다 / *As a ~ for passing her exam she got a new bike from her parents.* 시험에 합격한 포상으로 그녀는 부모에게서 새 자전거를 받았다. **2** ⓒ the money given for the return of something lost, for information or for the capture of a criminal. 현상금; 사례금. ¶ *There is a ~ of $10,000 for the capture of this criminal.* 이 범인의 체포에 대한 현상금은 1만 달러다 / *offer a ~* 현상금을 걸다 / *Rewards are given for the return of lost property.* 분실물을 찾아 주면 사례금이 주어진다.
— *vt.* (P6,13) 《*for, with*》 give a reward to (someone); give a reward for (a service, etc.). …에 보답하다; 상을〔보수를〕 주다. ¶ *Success has rewarded my efforts.* =*My efforts have been rewarded success.* 노력은 성공으로 보답되었다 / *I rewarded him well for his services.* 그의 공로에 후히 포상했다. [→regard]

re·wire [riːwáiər] *vt.* **1** telegraph again. …에 재차 전보를 치다. **2** put new wires on or in (a house, etc.). (집 따위)에 배선(配線)을 갈다. [re-]

re·word [riːwə́ːrd] *vt.* (P6) put into other words; state again. …을 바꾸어 말하다; 되풀이해 말하다. ¶ *This section of the contract should be reworded to make its meaning clear.* 계약서의 이 부분은 그 뜻을 분명히 하기 위해 다른 말로 바꿔야 한다. [re-]

***re·write** [riːráit] *vt.* (**re·wrote, re·writ·ten**) (P6) write again; write in a different form. …을 다시 쓰다; 고쳐 쓰다. [re-]

re·writ·ten [riːrítn] *v.* pp. of **rewrite.**

re·wrote [riːróut] *v.* p. of **rewrite.**

rhap·so·dize [rǽpsədàiz] *vi.* write or talk with great enthusiasm. 열광적으로 쓰다〔말하다〕. [↓]

rhap·so·dy [rǽpsədi] *n.* (*pl.* **-so·dies**) **1** Ⓤⓒ an enthusiastic highflown utterance or composition. 열광적이고 과장된 말〔글〕. ¶ *Everyone went into rhapsodies over her lovely dress.* 그녀의 멋진 의상을 보고 모두가 열광적인 환성을 질렀다. **2** ⓒ an epic verse or a piece of such a verse of length for one recitation. 서사시(의 한 절). **3** ⓒ 《mus.》 emotional irregular piece of music. 광시곡; 랩소디. [Gk. *rhapō* stitch, →ode]

rhe·a [ríːə] *n.* ⓒ a small South American three-toed ostrich. 레아; 아메리카 타조.

Rhen·ish [réniʃ, ríːn-] *adj.* 《*arch.*》 of the river Rhine or the regions near it. 라인 강의; 라인 강 유역의. ── *n.* Ⓤ Rhine wine. 라인 백포도주. [L. *Rhenus* Rhine]

rhe·o·stat [ríːəstæ̀t] *n.* ⓒ 《electr.》 an instrument which regulates the strength of an electric current by varying the resistance to it. 가감 저항기. [Gk. *rheō* flow]

rhet·o·ric [rétərik] *n.* Ⓤ **1** the art of the correct, forceful and effective use of language; a book about this art. 수사(修辭)법; 작문법; 수사학서(書). **2** mere display of language. 미사 여구(美辭麗句). [Gk. *rhētōr* orator]

rhe·tor·i·cal [ritɔ́(ː)rikəl, -tɑ́r-] *adj.* **1** of rhetoric; using rhetoric. 수사법(修辭法)의; 수사적인. **2** oratorical. 웅변의. ¶ *a man of great ~ power* 대단한 웅변가. **3** intended, esp. for display. 수사적인; 과장된. ¶ *a ~ style* 수사적인 문체.

rhetorical question [-´-- ´-] *n.* a question asked only for effect and not requiring answer. 수사(修辭) 의문《*e.g. Who does not know ?* =Everyone knows》.

rhet·o·ri·cian [rètəríʃən] *n.* ⓒ **1** a person skilled in rhetoric. 수사학자(修辭學者). **2** a rhetorical speaker. 웅변가. **3** 《often. *contempt.*》 a person given to using flowery language. 미사 여구를 쓰는 사람.

rheum [ruːm] *n.* 《*arch.*》 **1** a watery discharge, such as tears, saliva, etc. 카타르성 분비물《눈물·콧물 따위》. **2** catarrh; a cold. 코카타르; 감기. **3** 《poet.》 tears. 눈물. [Gk. *rheō* flow]

rheu·mat·ic [rumǽtik] *adj.* of or having rheumatism. 류머티즘의〔에 걸린〕. ¶ *~ fever* 류머티즘열(熱). ── *n.* ⓒ a person suffering from rheumatism. 류머티즘 환자. [↑]

rheu·ma·tism [rúːmətìzəm] *n.* Ⓤ disease causing painful swelling of the muscles and joints. 류머티즘.

***Rhine** [rain], **the** *n.* a river flowing through Switzerland, Germany and the Netherlands into the North Sea. 라인 강.

Rhine·land [ráinlæ̀nd], **the** *n.* the region along the Rhine. 라인 강 유역 (지방).

rhine·stone [ráinstòun] *n.* ⓒ **1** an imitation diamond. 모조 다이아몬드. **2** a kind of crystal. 수정의 일종. [→Rhenish]

rhi·no[1] [ráinou] *n.* (*pl.* **-nos**) =rhinoceros.

rhi·no[2] [ráinou] *n.* 《*sl.*》 money. 돈.

rhi·noc·er·os [rainɑ́sərəs / -nɔ́s-] *n.* ⓒ (*pl.* **-os** or **-os·es**) a large, thick-skinned animal with one or two horns on its nose, found in Africa and south Asia. 코뿔소; 무소. [Gk. *rhsi* nose, *keras* horn]

rhi·zome [ráizoum] *n.* ⓒ a rootlike stem lying along or under the ground. 지하경(地下莖); 근경(根莖). [Gk.]

Rhode Island [ròud áilənd] *n.* a State in the northeastern part of the United States, which is the smallest State in the United States. 로드아일랜드. 參考 R.I.로 생략함. 주도는 Providence.

rho·do·den·dron [ròudədéndrən] *n.* ⓒ 《bot.》 an evergreen treelike plant with large pink or white flowers. 철쭉속(屬)의 식물. [Gk. *rhodon* rose, *dendron* tree]

rhu·barb [rúːbɑːrb] *n.* Ⓤ **1** a plant with large leaves and thick red stalks. 장군풀; 대황(大黃). **2** the stem of this plant, used as food. 그 잎자루. **3** the medicine made from the roots of a kind of rhubarb. 대황근(大黃根)《하제용》. [Gk. *rha* rhubarb, →barbarian]

***rhyme** [raim] *n.* **1** ⓒ a word ending with the same sound as another. 동운어(同韻語). **2** Ⓤ agreement or similarity in sound of a certain part, esp. the final part, of two or more words or lines of verse. 운; 운각(韻脚). **3** 《usu. *pl.*》 verse or poetry with agreement in the final sounds of the lines. 운문(韻文); 시.

neither rhyme nor reason =***without rhyme or reason*** ⇨reason *n.*

── *vi.* (P1) **1** sound alike in the final part. 운을 밟다; 운이 맞다. ¶ *'Night' rhymes with 'flight'.* Night는 flight와 운이 맞다. **2** make verse. 운문을 짓다; 시를 쓰다.

── *vt.* (P6) **1** compose (verse, etc.) in metrical form and with rhyme. 운문을〔시를〕 짓다. **2** use (a word or words) to rhyme with another. …에 운을 밟게 하다. [↓]

rhythm [ríðəm] *n.* Ⓤⓒ **1** a regular beat of poetry, music, or dancing. 리듬; 율동; 규칙적인 반복 운동. ¶ *the ~ of speech* 말의 리듬 / *the ~ of the heartbeat* 규칙적인 심장의 고동 / *the ~ of the tides* 조수의 규칙적인 밀물과 썰물. **2** arrangement of beats in a line of poetry. (시의) 운율(韻律). **3** 《mus.》 the pattern of regular or irregular pulse caused in music. 리듬. ¶ *a sense of ~* 리듬에 대한 감각; 리듬감. **4** the regular recurrence of events, etc. 주기적 변동. ¶ *the ~ of* *the seasons* 〔*nature*〕 계절〔자연계〕의 (주기적인) 순환 / *the* ~ *of histroy* 역사의 (주기적인) 반복. [→rheum]

rhyth·mic [ríðmik], **-mi·cal** [-mikəl] *adj.* of rhythm; having rhythm. 리듬의; 율동적인. ¶ ~ *movements* 율동적인 운동 / *the* ~ *courses of nature* 규칙적으로 순환하는 자연의 추이.

:rib [rib] *n.* Ⓒ **1** one of the curved bones of the breast. 늑골; 갈빗대. **2** any narrow curved piece of material. 늑골 모양의 것. ¶ *The curved timbers in a ship's frame are called ribs.* 선체의 만곡된 목재들을 일컬어 늑재(肋材)라고 한다. [E.]

rib·ald [ríbəld] *adj.* (of person, jokes, etc.) low; unpleasant; dirty. 입정 사나운; 입이 건; 상스러운. ¶ *the* ~ *laughter of the drunken men* 주정뱅이들의 상스러운 웃음소리. —*n.* Ⓒ a ribald person. 입정 사나운〔추잡한〕 사람. [F. *ribaut* a menial]

rib·ald·ry [ríbəldri] *n.* Ⓤ ribald language. 상스러운 말. [↑]

:rib·bon [ríbən] *n.* **1** ⓊⒸ a long, narrow band or strip of silk, satin, etc. 리본; 띠. **2** Ⓒ ⓐ anything like such a strip. 끈 모양의 것. ¶ *a typewriter* ~ 타자기의 리본. ⓑ 《*pl.*》 ragged strips. 갈기갈기 찢어진 조각. ¶ *The sails of the ship were torn to ribbons.* 배의 돛들이 갈기갈기 찢겨 있었다. **3** a band of ribbon used as a symbol of an order of knighthood, etc. (훈장의) 수(綬). **4** 《*pl.*》 《*colloq.*》 reins. 고삐. ¶ *handle* 〔*take*〕 *the ribbons well* 말을 잘 다루다〔몰다〕. [F. *riban*]

rib·boned [ríbənd] *adj.* with a ribbon or ribbons. 리본을 단.

ri·bo·fla·vin [ràibouflέivin] *n.* 《biol., chem.》 the principal growth-promoting factor in vitamin B_2 complex. 리보플라빈. [alteration of *arabinose*]

ri·bo·nu·cle·ic acid [ràibounju:klí:ik ǽsid] *n.* a universal polymeric constituent of all living cells. 리보 핵산(核酸). 參考 RNA로 생략함. [↑]

ri·bose [ráibous, -bouz] *n.* a pentose obtained esp. from RNA. 리보오스. [↑]

:rice [rais] *n.* Ⓤ **1** a kind of grass grown for its seed. 벼. ¶ *a* ~ *field* 논 / *a* ~ *plant* 벼. **2** the seed of this plant boiled for food. 쌀. ¶ *curried* ~ 카레라이스. [Gk. *oruza*]

:rich [ritʃ] *adj.* **1** having much money or property; wealthy. 부자의; 돈 많은; 부유한 (opp. poor). ¶ *a* ~ *man* 부자 / *He was born* ~. 그는 부잣집에 태어났다 / *The* ~ 〔*Rich people*〕 *are not always happy.* 돈 많은 사람들이 늘 행복한 것은 아니다 / *This invention made him* ~. 이 발명으로 그는 부자가 됐다 / (*as*) ~ *as Croesus* 〔*a Jew*〕 거만(巨萬)의 부를 가진; 아주 돈이 많은 / *The* ~ *get richer, the poor get poorer.* 돈이 돈을 벌고 가난이 가난을 낳는다. **2** having much; abundant. 풍부한; …이 많은. ¶ *words* ~ *in variety of meanings* 여러 가지 뜻을 가진 말 / *a hot spring* ~ *in minerals* 광물질이 풍부한 온천 / *He is* ~ *in knowledge.* 그는 아는 것이 많다. **3** (of land, etc.) producing much; fertile. 비옥한; 많이 산출하는. ¶ ~ *land* 비옥한 땅 / *a* ~ *mine* 산출이 많은 광산. **4** valuable; costly. 귀중한; 고가의. ¶ ~ *silk* 고가의 비단 / *the richest jewel* 최고급 보석 / ~ *suggestion* 귀중한 암시. **5** plentiful; ample. 풍부한. ¶ *a* ~ *harvest* 풍작 / ~ *experience* 풍부한 경험. **6** (of food) thick; nutritious; very tasty; very sweet. 영양이 많은; 맛있는. ¶ ~ *milk* 진한 우유 / ~ *dish* 맛있는 반찬. **7** (of sound, color, etc.) full; deep; vivid. (소리가) 낭랑한; (빛이) 진한; 선명한. ¶ ~ *red* 진홍 / *a* ~ *tone* 풍부한 음질 / *the* ~ *smell of roses* 짙은 장미 향기. **8** 《*colloq.*》 very amusing. 아주 재미있는〔우스운〕. ¶ *a* ~ *joke* 〔*scene, idea*〕 재미있는 농담〔장면, 생각〕 / *That's* ~. 그거 멋있다. **9** 《*colloq.*》 absurd. 터무니없는. ¶ *an* ~ *opinion.* [E.]

Rich·ard [rítʃərd] *n.* a man's name. 남자 이름.

·rich·es [rítʃiz] *n. pl.* wealth; abundance. 부(富); 재산; 풍부. ¶ *heap up* ~ 많은 부를 쌓다 / 《*prov.*》 *Riches have wings.* 돈은 날개가 있다; 돈은 헤픈 것 / *He is rolling in* ~. 그는 엄청난 부자다 / *the* ~ *of the harvest* 많은 수확 / *the* ~ *of the soil* 비옥한 땅. [E.]

rich·ly [rítʃli] *adv.* in a rich manner. 풍부하게; 부유하게. ¶ *He* ~ *deserves punishment* 〔*to be punished*〕. 그는 모름지기 벌을 받아야 한다.

Rich·mond [rítʃmənd] *n.* the capital of Virginia. 리치먼드(미국 버지니아주(州)의 주도).

rich·ness [rítʃnis] *n.* Ⓤ the state of being rich. 부유; 풍부. ¶ ~ *of material* 〔*color*〕 풍부한 물자〔다양한 색채〕 / *The* ~ *of this soil favored the growth of crops.* 이 땅의 기름진 토질이 곡식의 생장에 좋다. [*rich*]

rick [rik] *n.* Ⓒ a stack of hay, straw, etc. (건초·곡물 등의) 가리. —*vt.* (P6) make (hay, straw, etc.) into a rick. …을 가리로 쌓다; 가리다. [E.]

rick·ets [ríkits] *n. pl.* 《used as *sing.*》 a disease of children caused by lack of vitamin D, calcium, or sunshine and marked by curving of the bones. 구루병(佝僂病); 곱사병. [?]

rick·et·y [ríkiti] *adj.* **1** suffering from rickets. 구루병을 앓는. **2** feeble; shaky. 흔들거리는; 뒤뚱거리는. ¶ *a* ~ *chair.* [?]

ric·o·chet [ríkəʃèi / -ʃèt] *n.* Ⓒ the jumping or skipping motion of an object as it goes along a flat surface; the motion of rebounding from one surface to another. (물수제비뜨듯) 수면을 스치며 튀기. ¶ *the* ~ *of a stone thrown along the surface of a pond* 호수의 위로 물수제비뜬 돌. —*vi.*

(**-cheted, -chet·ing** or 《Brit.》 **-chet·ted, -chet·ting**) (P1) move with such a motion. 물 위를 스치면서 튀다. ¶ *The bullet ricocheted off the wall and killed a passerby.* 총알이 벽을 스치며 행인 한 사람을 죽였다. [F.]

:rid [rid] *vt.* (**rid** or **rid·ded, rid·ding**) (P6, 13) 《*of*》 make free. …에게 면하게 하다; …에서 제거하다. ¶ ~ *the house of the rats* 집에서 쥐를 퇴치하다 / ~ *oneself of debt* 빚을 갚아 버리다 / ~ *someone* 〔*a country*〕 *of something harmfull* 아무에게서〔나라에서〕 해로운 것을 제거하다. [E.]

be rid of (= *be freed from or relieved of*) *something undesirable.* (바람직하지 않은 것)을 면하다; 벗어나다. ¶ *We are well* ~ *of that troublesome fellow.* 저 성가신 놈을 잘 떨쳐 버렸다.

get rid of (= *get free from; do away with*) *something undesirable.* (바람직하지 않은 것)을 면하다; 제거하다; 쫓아 버리다. ¶ *I can't get* ~ *of this cold.* 도무지 감기가 안 떨어진다 / *I shall have to get* ~ *of my servant.* 하인을 내보내야겠다 / *We got* ~ *of the rats with poison.* 쥐약으로 쥐를 박멸했다.

rid·dance [rídəns] *n.* ⓊⒸ the act of ridding; the state of being rid. 면함; 벗어남; 제거. ¶ *make clean* ~ *of* …을 일소하다 / *So he's gone at last; that's a good* ~. 드디어 놈이 가 버렸다. 아주 시원하다. [*rid*]

:rid·den [rídn] *v.* pp. of **ride.** — *adj.* pressed down; under the control of; obsessed. 억눌린; 고통받은. 語法 주로 복합어로 쓰임. ¶ *bed-ridden* (환자로) 누워서만 지내는 / *fear-ridden people* 공포에 짓눌린 사람들 / ~ *by fears* 〔*prejudices*〕 공포〔편견〕에 사로잡혀 / *a country* ~ *by soldiers* 군(軍)이 지배하는 나라.

·rid·dle[1] [rídl] *n.* Ⓒ **1** a puzzling question. 수수께끼; 퍼즐. ¶ *You talk in riddles.* 무슨 말을 하는지 모르겠군 / *Robert's disappearance is a complete* ~. 로버트가 사라진 것은 정말 모를 일이다. **2** a person or thing difficult to understand. 수수께끼의 사람〔사물〕. ¶ *read a* ~ 수수께끼를 풀다 / *That painting is a* ~ *to us.* 저게 무슨 그림인지 모르겠다.

speak in riddles, speak with a doubtful meaning. 알 수 없는〔수수께끼 같은〕 말을 하다.

— *vi.* (P1) speak in riddles. 수수께끼를 내다. — *vt.* (P6,14) answer (a riddle). (수수께끼)를 풀다. [E.]

rid·dle[2] [rídl] *n.* Ⓒ a coarse sieve. 어레미. — *vt.* (P6,13) **1** sift. 체질하다. ¶ ~ *sand.* **2** make many holes in (something). …을 구멍투성이로 만들다. ¶ ~ *the target with bullets* 총알로 과녁을 구멍투성이로 만들다 / ~ *someone* 〔*ship*〕 *with shot* 아무〔배〕를 총격으로 벌집처럼 만들다 / *The pears were all riddled by worms.* 배는 온통 벌레 구멍투성이다. **3** 《*fig.*》 subject to severe criticism; show the weakness of. …을 혹평하다; 깎아내리다; …의 약점을 들춰내다. ¶ ~ *an argument* 〔*a theory*〕 어떤 논증〔이론〕을 깎아내리다. [E.]

:ride [raid] *v.* (**rode, rid·den**) *vi.* **1** (P1,2B, 3,4) 《*in, on*》 be carried in a car, train, boat, etc. (자동차·기차 등에) 타다. ¶ ~ *on a bicycle* 자전거를 타다 / ~ *in a bus* 버스를 타다 / ~ *60 miles,* 60마일을 달리다 / ~ *up* 〔*down*〕 *in a lift.* 승강기를 타고 오르다〔내리다〕. **2** (P1,2A,2B,3,4) sit on a horse or other animal and make it go. (말 따위에) 타다; 타고 가다. ¶ ~ *horseback* 말을 타다 / ~ *bareback* 안장 없는 말을 타다 / ~ *behind* (기수의) 뒤에 타다 / ~ *away* 〔*off*〕 말 타고 가 버리다 / ~ *at full gallop* 전속력으로 말을 몰다 / *She likes to* ~ *for pleasure.* 그녀는 재미로 말타기를 좋아한다. **3** (P3) 《*on*》 sit on as if on a horse, etc. 말 타듯이 올라타다. ¶ ~ *on someone's back* 〔*shoulders*〕 …의 등에 올라타다〔목말 타다〕. **4** (P2A,2B,3) (of a ship) lie at anchor; move or float on the water. (배가) 정박하다; 물에 뜨다. ¶ *The ship is riding at anchor.* 배가 정박 중이다. **5** (P2A,2B,3) (of the moon, the sun, etc.) seem to be floating through the sky. (달·태양 등이) 공중에 뜨다. ¶ *The moon is riding high* 〔*above the clouds*〕. 달이 하늘 높이〔구름 위에〕 떠 있다 / *The bird rides on the wind.* 새가 바람을 타고 날고 있다. **6** (P5) be in a specified condition for riding or being ridden. 타는 기분이 …하다. ¶ *This horse rides easy* 〔*hard*〕. 이 말은 타기가 좋다〔나쁘다〕 / *The ground rides soft.* 지면이 승마하기에는 무르다 / *The car rides comfortably.* 이 차는 승차감이 좋다. — *vt.* **1** (P6,13) sit on or in and cause (a horse, a vehicle, etc.) to move. (말·탈것 등)에 타다; 타고 가다. ¶ ~ *a horse* 말을 타다 / ~ *a car* 차를 타(고 가)다 / ~ *a horse over a fence* 말을 타고 담장〔장애물〕을 뛰어넘다 / ~ *shank's mare* 걸어가다 / ~ *a bicycle along a road* 자전거를 타고 길을 가다. **2** (P6,7) ride through or over. …을 말을 타고 가다〔건너다〕. ¶ ~ *the country* 〔*deserts*〕 말을 타고 교외를〔사막을〕 지나가다 / ~ *a ford* 말 타고 여울을 건너다. **3** (P6,7) be carried on; float on. …에 뜨다; …에 걸리다. ¶ *The ship rides* (*over*) *the waves.* 배가 파도를 타고 가다 / *Spectacles* ~ *his nose.* 안경이 코에 얹혀 있다. **4** (P6,7,13) carry (someone) on something as if riding on horseback. …을 태워 주다. ¶ ~ *a child on one's shoulder* 아이를 목말 태우다. **5** (P6) take part in. …에 가담하다. ¶ ~ *a race* 경마에 참여하다. **6** (P6) dominate; tyrannize over; torment. …을 지배하다; 탄압하다; 괴롭히다. ¶ *The nightmare rides the sleeper.* 자는 사람이 가위에 눌리다.

ride and tie, (of two persons with one horse) ride by turns; ride and walk in turn. 말 한 필을 둘이 번갈아 타고 가다.

ride at, turn or direct toward. …을 향해 달리게 하다. ¶ ~ *one's horse at a fence* 담장[장애물]을 넘으려고 말을 달리게 하다.

ride bodkin, squeeze oneself between two others. 두 사람 사이에 끼어 타고 가다.

ride down, **a**) overtake (someone) by riding. 말로 …에 따라붙다. **b**) overcome. …을 압도하다. **c**) exhaust (a horse) by riding it too hard. (말 따위를) 지치게 만들다. **d**) allow one's horse or vehicle to hit and knock down (someone or something). …에 말[탈것]을 부딪쳐 쓰러뜨리다. ¶ ~ *down a runaway slave* 달아나는 노예를 말로 받아 넘어뜨리다.

ride for a fall, **a**) ride recklessly 난폭하게 말을 몰다. **b**) act recklessly. 난폭한 짓을 하다.

ride *one's* ***horse to death,*** **a**) kill one's horse by exhausting it. 말을 혹사해서 죽게 만들다. **b**) be disliked for too much riding one's hobby. 한 가지 장기(長技)만 부려 남들이 싫어하다.

ride off on side issues, introduce side issues to cover evasion of the point. 지엽적인 문제를 끄집어 내 요점을 호도(糊塗)하다.

ride *someone* ***on rail,*** carry someone astride on a rail as punishment. (벌로) …을 가로장에 태워 회술레 돌리다.

ride out, **a**) (of a ship) come through safely. …을 잘 넘기다. ¶ ~ *out a storm* 폭풍우를 잘 견뎌 내다. **b**) endure successfully. …을 이겨 내다.

ride (***roughshod***) ***over,*** treat (something) without sympathy. …을 짓밟다.

ride rusty, become contumacious; oppose ill-naturedly. 외고집을 부리다.

ride the goat, 《*colloq.*》 join a secret society. 비밀 결사에 가입하다.

ride the whirlwind, take the occasion of a revolution. 혁명의 기운을 타다; 풍운을 타다.

ride to hounds, go fox-hunting. (사냥개로) 여우 사냥을 하다.

ride up, work, slide, upward out of its proper position. (넥타이 등이) 밀려 올라가다. ¶ *His collar has ridden up.* 칼라가 비어져 나왔다.

— *n.* Ⓒ **1** an act of riding; a journey on a horse, on or in a vehicle, etc. (말·탈것 등에) 타기; 태우기; 타고 가기. ¶ *a ~ on a bicyle* 자전거타기 / *take a ~ in a bus* [*train*] 버스[기차]에 타다 / *give someone a ~* 아무를 태워 주다 / *The hotel is situated within ten minutes' ~ of the station.* 호텔은 역에서 10분 타고 가면 있다. **2** a road for riding 승마용 도로. [E.]

rid·er [ráidər] *n.* Ⓒ **1** a person who rides, esp. a horse. 타는 사람; (특히) 기수. ¶ *He will never make a ~.* 그 사람 말타기는 글렀다 / *a good ~* 훌륭한 기수. **2** an addition to a bill, a document, etc. 추가 조항; 첨부 서류; 첨서(添書). ¶ *by way of ~ to…* …의 추가로. **3** a part of a machine, placed above, and working upon, another part. 다른 것에 얹혀[걸쳐서] 움직이는 부분; 라이더. **4** 《math.》 a problem testing students' mastery of principles on which its solution depends. 응용 문제. [↑]

:ridge [ridʒ] *n.* Ⓒ **1** the backbone of an animal. (짐승의) 등; 등줄기. ¶ *the ~ of a whale* 고래의 등. **2** a long and narrow range of hills or mountains. 산등성이; 능선. ¶ *We walked along the mountain ~.* 우리는 능선을 따라 걸었다. **3** the long, narrow top of something. 융기(隆起). **4** the raised part between furrows. 이랑; 두둑. ¶ *the ~ of a wave* 파도의 물마루 / *the ridges in ploughed ground* 쟁기로 간 땅의 이랑들 / *the ridges on corduroy cloth* 코르덴 천의 골. **5** a line where two sloping surfaces meet. 마루. ¶ *the ~ of a roof* 용마루 / *the ~ of the nose* 콧대.

— *vt.* (P6) make (something) into ridges; cover (something) with ridges. …을 이랑지게 하다; …에 두둑을 만들다.

— *vi.* (P1) be covered with ridges. 이랑이 지다; 물결치다. [E.]

ridge·pole [rídʒpòul] *n.* Ⓒ a horizontal timber along the top of a roof or tent. (집의) 마룻대; (천막의) 들보.

rid·i·cule [rídikjùːl] *n.* Ⓤ mocking laughter; words or actions that make fun of someone or something. 비웃기; 조롱; 조소. ¶ *bring someone into ~ =turn someone to* [*into*] *~* 아무를 비웃다 / *His curls made him an object of ~.* 고수머리 때문에 그는 놀림감이 됐다. — *vt.* (P6) laugh at; make fun of (someone). …을 비웃다; 놀리다. ¶ *They all ridiculed my suggestion.* 나의 제안을 그들은 모두 비웃었다. [L. *rideo* laugh]

hold *someone* ***up to ridicule,*** make fun of someone. …을 놀리다; 비웃다; 조롱하다.

·ri·dic·u·lous [ridíkjələs] *adj.* deserving or exciting ridicule; absurd. 웃기는; 바보 같은. ¶ *It would be ~ to walk backward all the time.* 사람이 노상 뒷걸음질만 한다면 우스울 게다.

ri·dic·u·lous·ly [ridíkjələsli] *adv.* in a ridiculous manner. 우습게.

rid·ing [ráidiŋ] *n.* **1** the action of riding. 승마. **2** a track for riding along on horseback. 승마길. [→ride]

riding habit [⌐-⌐-] *n.* clothes esp. a woman's dress, for riding on horseback. (특히) 여성용 승마복.

riding master [⌐-⌐-] *n.* a person who teaches horseback riding. 마술 교사.

rife [raif] *adj.* 《*with*》 **1** common; widespread. (질병·소문 등이) 유행하는; 돌고 도는; 널리 퍼진. ¶ *Reports became ~.* 소문이 퍼졌다 / *Superstition is ~ among uncivilized people.* 미개인들에게 미신이 만연돼 있다. **2** full; well supplied; numerous. 많은; 풍부한; 무수한. ¶ *a thesis ~ with error* 오류투성이의 논문 / *Modern society is ~ with various* *kinds of critics.* 현대 사회에는 각양 각색의 비평가들이 많다. [E.]

rif·fle [rífəl] *n.* **1** 《mine》 a channel or groove set in a long open vessel, etc. for catching particles of gold washed out of sand. (사금(砂金) 채집용 용기에 달린) 홈. **2** 《U.S.》 a rapid in a stream; a ripple on the surface of water. 여울; 잔물결. [*ri*pple, ru*ffle*]

riff·raff [rífræ̀f] *n.* 《*the* ~, *collectively*》 worthless people; the lowest class of people; the rabble. 하층민; 천민. ¶ *the ~ of society* 사회의 인간 쓰레기. [F. *rif et raf*]

:ri·fle[1] [ráifəl] *n.* Ⓒ **1** a gun with sprial grooves inside its barrel. 라이플총; 선조총(旋條銃). **2** 《*pl.*》 soldiers armed with rifles. 라이플총 부대. **3** one of the spiral grooves inside such a gun. (총신의) 선조(旋條); 강선(腔綫). — *vt.* (P6) **1** cut spiral grooves in (a gun barrel). (총신)에 강선을 파다. **2** shoot with rifle. 라이플로 쏘다. [F. *rifler* graze]

ri·fle[2] [ráifəl] *vt.* (P6) **1** search and rob. …을 샅샅이 뒤져 빼앗다(훔치다). ¶ ~ *a desk* (*house*) 책상(집)을 샅샅이 뒤져 훔쳐 가다. **2** steal; take away; plunder. …을 훔치다; 강탈하다; 약탈하다. [↑]

ri·fle·man [ráifəlmən] *n.* Ⓒ (*pl.* **-men** [-mən]) a soldier armed with a rifle; a man skilled in using a rifle. 라이플병(兵); 라이플의 명사수.

ri·fle-range [ráifəlrèindʒ] *n.* **1** a place for practicing rifle-shooting. 라이플 사격장. **2** the distance covered by a rifle bullet. 라이플 사정(射程).

ri·fle-shot [ráifəlʃɑ̀t / -ʃɔ̀t] *n.* **1** a person skilled in shooting with a rifle. 라이플 사수. **2** a bullet fired from a rifle. 라이플 탄환. **3** =rifle-range 2.

rift [rift] *n.* Ⓒ a cleft; a split; a crack; a break. 깨진(터진) 틈; 틈새기. ¶ *a ~ in the rock* (*clouds*) 바위(구름)의 갈라진 데 / *The ~ in the party is threatening to break up the government.* 당의 균열이 정부의 해산을 위협하고 있다. — *vt., vi.* (P6;1) split; crack. 가르다; 찢다; 갈라지다. [→rive]

rig [rig] *vt.* (**rigged, rig·ging**) **1** (P6,13) equip (a ship) with ropes, sails, masts, spars, etc. (배)에 돛·삭구(索具) 등을 갖추다; 장비하다. ¶ *a fully rigged vessel* 장비가 잘된 배. **2** (P7) provide (someone) with clothing, etc.; dress. …에게 옷을 입히다; 차려 입히다. ¶ *He was rigged out as a clown.* 그는 광대로 차려 입었다. **3** (P7) 《*colloq.*》 set up hastily or as makeshift; erect. …을 임시 방편으로 짓다(세우다). ¶ ~ *a tent by a river* 급한 대로 강가에 천막을 치다 / *The troops rigged up a shelter for the night.* 부대는 그 밤을 나기 위해 간단한 막사를 세웠다. **4** (P6) deal with (something) dishonestly. …을 부정하게 다루다. ¶ ~ *the prices* 값을 조작하다.

— *n.* **1** Ⓒ an arrangement of sails, masts, etc. on a ship. 의장(艤裝). **2** Ⓤ 《*colloq.*》 clothes, esp. those designed for a particular purpose. (어떤 특수한) 복장; 옷차림. ¶ *a cowboy's ~* 카우보이 옷차림 / *He looked rather out of place when he turned up in full ornamental ~.* 그가 한껏 차려 입고 나타났을 때 어쩐지 분위기에 어색하게 보였다. **3** a trick; cheating. 계교(計巧); 사기(詐欺); (못된) 장난. ¶ *run a ~ upon someone* 아무를 희롱하다. [O.N. *rigga* wrap]

rig·ging [rígiŋ] *n.* Ⓤ **1** the ropes, chains, etc. used to support and work the masts, sails, etc. on a ship. (선박의) 삭구(索具). **2** equipment. 채비; 준비. **3** 《*colloq.*》 clothing; dress. 복장; 의상. [↑]

:right [rait] *adj.* **1** obeying the moral law; just; good. (도덕적으로) 옳은; 올바른 (opp. wrong). ¶ *act a ~ part* 옳은 일을 하다 / *It was ~ to say so.* 그 말이 옳았다 / *Do what is ~.* 옳은 일을 행하라 / *He was quite ~ to refuse* (*in refusing*). 그가 거절한 것은 아주 당연했다 / *I'll try to do whatever is ~.* 옳은 일이라면 무엇이건 하겠다. **2** correct; true. 바른; 정확한; 틀림없는(opp. wrong). ¶ *the ~ answer* 정답 / *the ~ leather* 진짜 가죽 / *get it ~* 바르게 이해시키다(하다) / *the ~ way* 바른 길; 정도 / *~ or wrong* 옳건 그르건; 좋든 나쁘든 / *Is that the ~ address?* 그 주소가 맞느냐 / *Your opinions are ~ enough.* 네 의견은 지극히 당연하다 / *That's ~.* 맞다; 그대로다. **3** fit; suitable; proper 적절한; 어울리는; 제격인. ¶ *the ~ man for the position* 그 자리에 제격인 사람 / *Is this dress ~ to wear to a wedding?* 이 옷은 결혼식에 입어도 괜찮을까. **4** satisfactory; most convenient. 나무랄 데 없는; 안성 맞춤의. ¶ *All's ~* (*with the world*). 만사가 잘되고 있다 / *Right you are.* 좋다; 됐다 / *Things will probably be all ~.* 모든 게 잘될 것이다. **5** healthy; normal; sound. 건강한; 온전한. ¶ *I feel all ~.* 컨디션이 아주 좋다 / *Is he in his ~ mind?* 그 사람 지금 제정신인가 / *He isn't ~ in the* (*his*) *head.* 그는 제정신이 아니다; 머리가 이상한 모양이다. **6** on or toward the side opposite to the left side. 오른쪽의; 우측의 (opp. left). ¶ *one's ~ hand* 오른손 / *the ~ bank of a river* 강의 우안(右岸) / *make a ~ turn at the corner* 모퉁이에서 우회전하다 / 《mil.》 *the ~ flank* (*wing*) 우익(右翼). **7** front; upper; most finished or ornamental. 정면의; 겉의; 표면의(opp. wrong). ¶ *the ~ side of the medal* 메달의 앞면 / *the ~ side of cloth* 천의 거죽 / *the ~ side up* 거죽을 위로. **8** straight; of 90°. 곧은; 직각의. ¶ *a ~ line* 직선 / *a ~ angle* 직각. **9** 《often *the R-*》 (of political opinion, etc.) conservative. (정치상의) 우익의; 보수파의. (**as**) ***right as rain*** (***a trivet***), 《*colloq.*》 perfectly well, sound, or comfortable. 만사가 순조로운; 아주 건강하여.

***get on the right side of** someone,* ⟪*colloq.*⟫ win someone's favor. …의 환심을 사다; 마음에 들게 하다.

get** something **right, **a**) correct. …을 고치다. **b**) understand clearly. …을 분명하게 이해하다. ¶ *Just let's get this ~ before I go.* 내가 가기 전에 이것을 분명히 해 두자.

***on the right side of** fifty,* under. (50세) 전인; 미만인.

put* 〔*set*〕** *someone* or *something* ***right, put something in order; correct; restore. …을 정리하다; 바로잡다; 건강을 회복시키다. ¶ *I put my watch ~.* 시계를 바로 맞췄다 / *Good nursing will put him ~.* 그는 간호를 잘하면 회복될 것이다 / *Please put me ~ if I make a mistake.* 내가 틀리거든 고쳐 주시오.

put** one's **right hand to the work, work in earnest. 다잡아 일을 하다.

put* 〔*set*〕** *oneself* ***right with *someone,* get on good terms with someone; make up a disagreement with someone. …와 사이좋게 지내다; 화해하다.

— *adv.* **1** morally; justly; correctly. 바르게; 옳게. ¶ *act ~* 바르게 행하다 / *guess ~* 알아맞히다 / *if I remember ~* 내 기억이 틀림없다면 / *Nothing goes ~ with me.* 뭐 하나 제대로 되는 게 없다. **2** properly; in a satisfactory manner. 훌륭하게; 만족하게. ¶ *turn out ~* 잘 돼 가다; 제대로 되다 / *The dinner is served ~.* 저녁은 훌륭하다. **3** straight; directly; all the way. 똑바로; 내처. ¶ *come ~ back* 곧장 돌아오다 / *~ at a target* 적중하여 / *sink ~ to the bottom* 곧장 바닥으로 가라앉다 / *He went ~ to the place.* 그는 그 곳으로 직행했다 / *~ overhead* 머리 바로 위 / *go ~ on* 내처 가다. **4** exactly; precisely. 바로; 정확히. ¶ *~ here* 바로 여기. **5** completely. 완전히. ¶ *He turned ~ round.* 그는 빙 돌았다 / *go ~ to the end* 갈 데까지 가다. **6** to the right hand or side. 오른쪽에〔으로〕. ¶ *turn ~* 우회전하다 / *Then you should turn ~.* 그리고는 우회전해야 합니다 / *He looks neither ~ nor left.* 그는 좌우 어느 쪽도 보지 않는다. **7** (in time or position) immediately. (시간·장소가) 바로; 곧. ¶ *~ now* 바로 지금 / *~ after dinner* 저녁 먹고 곧 / *~ by the hospital* 병원 바로 옆 / *~ in the middle* 바로 중앙에. **8** ⟪*arch., dial.*⟫ in a high degree; very. 대단히; 몹시. ¶ *a ~ cunning fellow* 아주 교활한 놈 / *I know ~ well.* 난 훤히 알고 있다 / *Right sad we are.* 유감 천만이다.

come right, improve; turn out well. 좋아지다; 잘 돼 가다.

come right in, come straight in. 곧바로 들어오다.

right and left, in all directions. 사방으로. ¶ *The crowd divided ~ and left.* 군중은 사방으로 갈라졌다.

***right away* 〔*off*〕,** immediately. 곧; 즉시.

— *n.* **1** Ⓤ that which is morally or legally right; justice; truth; correctness. (도덕·법률적으로) 올바름; 정의; 정당. ¶ *be in the ~* 생각이 바르다 / *Might is ~.* 힘이 정의다 / *fight for the ~* 정의를 위해 싸우다. **2** ⓊⒸ privilege; a just claim; Ⓒ that to which a person has a just claim. 권리. ¶ *the ~ to vote* 투표권 / *defend one's ~* 권리를 지키다 / *civil rights* 시민권 / *I have no ~ to say such a thing to him.* 내가 그에게 그렇게 말할 권리는 없다. **3** ⟪*the ~* or *one's ~, sing.* only⟫ the right side or direction. 오른쪽(opp. left). ¶ *on one's ~* 오른쪽에 / *on the ~ of* …의 오른편에 / *go* 〔*turn*〕 *to the ~ about* 뒤로 돌다; 주의 등을 바꾸다 / *keep on one's ~* 오른쪽으로 나아가다; 정도를 걷다 / *Keep to the ~.* 우측 통행⟪게시⟫ / *You will find it on your* 〔*the*〕 *~.* 그건 네 오른쪽에 있다. **4** ⟪*pl.*⟫ a true fact. 진상. ¶ *the rights (and wrongs) of the matter* 일의 진상 / *I have never heard the rights of the story.* 그 이야기의 진상(眞相)을 나는 들은 바가 없다. **5** ⟪usu. *the R-*⟫ a conservative party; people who have conservative political ideas. 보수당; 우파; 보수파의 사람들.

***by* 〔*of*〕 *right* =*by* (*good*) *right*(*s*),** justly; properly; in justice. 올바르게; 당연히. ¶ *The land belongs to him by right*(*s*). 그 땅은 의당 그의 것이다.

by* 〔*in*〕 *right of, by virtue of; on account of; because of. …의 권한으로; …한 이유로. ¶ *He claimed the land by ~ of his uncle's will.* 그는 숙부의 유언에 따라 그 땅을 요구했다.

do** someone **right, treat someone rightly. …을 공평히 다루다〔대하다〕.

in** one's **own right, through one's own ability, authority, etc. 자기 능력〔권한〕으로. ¶ *She is a queen in her own ~.* 그녀는 (왕비로서 여왕이 된 것이 아니고) 승계에 의한 여왕이다.

put* 〔*set*〕** *something* ***to rights, put something in order; correct; repair. …을 정돈하다; 고치다. ¶ *The list was set to rights.* 목록은 바로잡혔다 / *A good sleep will put you to rights.* 한잠 푹 자면 좋아질 거다.

— *vt.* (P6) **1** correct. …을 고치다; 바로잡다. ¶ *~ a wrong* 잘못을 고치다 / *Such a fault will ~ itself.* 그런 과실은 저절로 고쳐진다. **2** put (something) in order; make (something) straight or upright. …을 정리하다; 바로 세우다. ¶ *~ oneself* 도로 일어서다; 회복하다 / *~ the room* 방을 정돈하다 / *~ a capsized boat* 뒤집힌 배를 바로 하다. **3** do justice to (someone); secure rights for (someone); relieve. …에게 권리를 회복시키다; 당연한 권리를 가지게 하다; …을 구제하다. ¶ *It is our duty to ~ the oppressed.* 억압받는 사람들을 구하는 것이 우리의 의무다.

— *vi.* (P1) (of a ship, etc.) get into a correct or upright position. (기울어진 배 따위가) 바로 서다. ¶ *The ship righted again.* [E.]

right·a·bout [ráitəbàut] *n.* ⟪*the ~* ⟫ the direction directly opposite. 반대(反對) 방향.

send someone to the rightabout, send packing; dismiss peremptorily. …을 내쫓다; 가차없이 해고하다. — *adj., adv.* in the opposite direction. 반대 방향의〔으로〕. [↑]

right angle [⌐⌐] *n.* an angle of 90 degrees. 직각.

right-down [ráitdáun] *adj.* thorough. 철저한. — *adv.* thoroughly. 철저히.

right·eous [ráitʃəs] *adj.* **1** (of a person, character, etc.) doing what is right; just. 올바른; 정의의. ¶ *a ~ act* 정의의 행동 / *the ~ and the wicked* 의인(義人)과 악인들 / *a ~ man* 의인(義人). **2** justifiable. 정당한; 당연한. ¶ *~ anger over injustice* 불의에 의한 의분.

right·eous·ly [ráitʃəsli] *adv.* in a righteous manner. 올바르게; 공정히; 당연히.

right·eous·ness [ráitʃəsnis] *n.* Ⓤ the state of being right; justice. 공정; 정의; 당연.

right·ful [ráitfəl] *adj.* right; just; according to law; lawful. 올바른; 합법의; 정당한. ¶ *one's ~ property* 정당한 자기 재산 / *the ~ heir to the throne* 정당한 왕위 계승자 / *a ~ cause* 정의 / *Who is the ~ owner of this car?* 이 차의 진짜 소유주는 누구냐.

right-hand [ráithǽnd] *adj.* **1** on or to the right; of, for, or with the right hand. 오른쪽의; 우측의; 오른손의. ¶ *the ~ side* 우측 / *a ~ glove* 오른쪽 장갑 / *the ~ page* 오른쪽 페이지. **2** most helpful or reliable. 믿을 수 있는; 의지가 되는. ¶ *one's ~ man* 보좌역; 심복.

right-hand·ed [ráithǽndid] *adj.* **1** using the right hand more skillfully than the left. 오른손잡이의(opp. left-handed). **2** done with the right hand. 오른손으로 한. ¶ *a ~ blow.* **3** made to be used with the right hand. 오른손용의. ¶ *a ~ golf club.* **4** turning from left to right. 오른쪽으로 도는. ¶ *a ~ screw.*

Right Honorable [⌐⌐——], **the** *n.* the title of nobles below the rank of Marquis. 후작 아래 귀족의 경칭.

right·ist [ráitist] *n.* a person who has conservative or reactionary ideals in politics. 보수파의 사람. — *adj.* having conservative or reactionary ideals in politics. 보수적〔반동적〕인.

right·ly [ráitli] *adv.* **1** justly; properly. 올바르게; 정당하게. ¶ *judge ~* 옳게 판단하다 / *a duty ~ performed* 정당하게 수행된 직무. **2** correctly. 정확히. ¶ *You are ~ informed.* 네 말이 맞다 / *He believed, ~ or wrongly, that she was guilty.* 진위가 어쨌든 그는 그녀의 잘못이라고 단정했다.

right-mind·ed [ráitmáindid] *adj.* having right opinions; honest. 정직한.

right·ness [ráitnis] *n.* Ⓤ the state or quality of being right. 올바름; 정직; 공정.

right-of-way [ráitəvwéi] *n.* (*pl.* **rights-or -ways**) **1** the right to pass over another's property. (사유지의) 통행권. ¶ *We have a ~ through this farm to the highway.* 우리는 이 농장을 지나 큰길로 나갈 권리가 있다. **2** the right to go first. 선행권(先行權). ¶ *It's our ~ at this road junction.* 이 교차로에선 우리가 먼저 갈 권리가 있다.

right·ward [ráitwərd] *adj.* toward the right; directed to the right. 우측으로 가는; 우측의. — *adv.* toward the right; in the direction of the right. 오른쪽 방향으로; 우측에(으로).

right·wards [ráitwərdz] *adv.* = rightward.

right wing [⌐⌐] *n.* **1** a conservative or reactionary political party or a group of such parties; the people who have conservative or reactionary ideas. 보수당; 보수적인 사람들. **2** the more conservative or reactionary section of a party. 우익; 우파; 보수파. ¶ *He is on the ~ of his party.* 그는 당에서 보수파다.

right-wing [ráitwíŋ] *adj.* of the right wing. 우익(수)의; 우파〔보수파〕의. ¶ *~ ideas* 보수적인 사상 / *She is very ~.* 그녀는 아주 보수적이다.

·rig·id [rídʒid] *adj.* **1** not bending; hard; stiff. 휘지 않는; 단단한. ¶ *a ~ stick* 단단한 막대기 / *Hold your arm ~.* 팔에 꽉 힘을 주어라 / *She was ~ with fear.* 무서워서 몸이 뻣뻣해졌다. **2** strict; severe. 엄격한. ¶ *~ discipline* 엄격한 규율〔훈육〕 / *In our home, it is a ~ rule to wash our hands before eating.* 우리 집에선 식사 전에 손 씻는 것이 철칙이다. **3** firmly fixed; not easily bent. 완고한; 융통성 없는. ¶ *~ in one's views* 생각이 고루한 / *~ adherence to the regulations* 규정에의 우직한 집착. [→rigorous]

ri·gid·i·ty [ridʒídəti] *n.* Ⓤ **1** stiffness; firmness. 딱딱함; 굳음. ¶ *They were lying dead, but still warm, and their limbs, as yet, devoid of ~.* 그들은 죽어서 누워 있었다. 그러나 아직 온기는 있었고 팔다리가 경직(硬直) 상태에 이르지는 않고 있었다. **2** strictness. 엄격.

rig·id·ly [rídʒidli] *adv.* in a rigid manner. 굳게; 엄격히; 완고하게.

rig·ma·role [rígmərὸul] *n.* Ⓒ a long confusing and foolish talk; nonsense. 장황하고 실없는 이야기. [E.]

rig·or, 《Brit.》 **-our** [rígər] *n.* Ⓤ **1** strictness; severity. 엄격. ¶ *moral ~* 도덕성의 엄격함 / *enforce a law with ~* 법을 엄격히 집행하다. **2** 《often *pl.*》 hardship; severity. 신고(辛苦); 고난; 매서움. ¶ *experience the rigors of pioneer life* 고된 개척 생활을 겪다 / *the rigors of a northern winter* 북부 지방 겨울의 혹독함. **3** preciseness; exactness. 엄밀; 정밀. **4** [rígər / ráigɔːr] 《med.》 the shivering and chill felt before fever. 오한(惡寒). [L. *rigeo* be stiff]

rig·or·ous [rígərəs] *adj.* **1** very severe;

strict; harsh. 준엄한; 매서운; 엄격한. ¶ ~ *discipline* 엄한 규율. **2** exact; precise. 정밀〔정확〕한. ¶ *a ~ scientific method* 정밀한 과학적 방법 / *The planes have to undergo ~ safety checks.* 항공기는 정밀한 안전 점검을 거쳐야 한다.

rig-out [rígàut] *n.* 《Brit. *colloq.*》 a person's clothes, etc.; costume. 의복; 의상; 옷가지.

rile [rail] *vt.* (P6) 《*colloq.*》 make angry; irritate. …을 화나게 하다; 신경질나게 하다. [var. of *roil*]

rill [ril] *n.* Ⓒ 《*poet.*》 a little brook. 작은 내; 시내; 개울(물). — *vi.* (P1,2A) flow in a small stream. 시내처럼 흐르다. [Du.]

•**rim** [rim] *n.* Ⓒ an edge; a margin; a border. 테; 가두리; 가장자리. ¶ *the ~ of an eyeglass* 안경테 / *the golden ~* 왕관 / *the ~ of a wheel* 바퀴테. — *vt.* (**rimmed, rimming**) (P6) put a rim around (something). …에 테를 달다. ¶ *Wild flowers rimmed the little pool.* 들꽃들이 작은 연못가에 피어 있었다. [E.]

rime[1] [raim] *n., v.* =rhyme.

rime[2] [raim] *n.* Ⓤ 《*poet.*》 white frost. 서리. — *vt.* (P6) cover (something) with rime. …을 서리로 덮다. [E.]

rind [raind] *n.* ⓊⒸ **1** the firm outer covering of a nut, a piece of fruit, etc. (과일 따위의) 껍데기; 껍질. **2** the bark of a tree. 나무 껍데기; 수피(樹皮). [E.]

:**ring**[1] [riŋ] *n.* Ⓒ **1** a circular band of metal, wood, etc. used for holding or fastening; a circular band, often of a precious metal set with gems, worn on as an ornament. 고리 (모양의 것); 반지; 귀걸이 (등). ¶ *a key ~* 열쇠 고리 / *a rubber ~* 고무 밴드 / *a nose ~* 코걸이 / *a wedding* 〔*an engagement*〕 *~* 결혼〔약혼〕 반지. **2** a circle; a circular line, mark or figure; anything circular. 원; 동그라미; 둥근 것. ¶ *rings in water* 파문(波紋) / *form a ~* 원을 이루다 / *sit in a ~* 둥글게 앉다; 둘러앉다 / *dance in a ~* 원무(圓舞)를 추다 / *draw a ~ on the ground* 땅에 원을 그리다 / *puff out rings of smoke* 담배 연기를 동글동글하게 내뿜다. **3** an annual layer in the trunk of a tree. (나무의) 나이테. **4** an enclosed place for contests, exhibitions, sports, etc. (원형의) 경기장; 경마장; 권투장 (등). ¶ *the ~ of a circus* 서커스장. **5** a group of persons working together, often for unlawful purposes. 도당(徒黨); 패거리; 일당. ¶ *a black market ~* 암시장패 / *a smuggler ~* 밀수단 / *a spy ~* 스파이단. **6** 《*the ~*》 the sport of boxing. 권투; 복싱.

make 〔***form***〕 ***a ring,*** combine to make a corner; combine to control the market. 동맹하여 시장을 장악하다〔좌우하다〕. ¶ *make a ~ on the stock market* 결탁하여 주식 시장을 좌우하다.

make 〔***run***〕 ***rings round*** *someone,* go or do things incomparably quicker than someone. …보다 훨씬 빨리 가다〔하다〕.

meet in the ring, play a game (of boxing or wrestling). (권투·레슬링) 시합을 하다.

— *vt.* **1** (P6,7) surround; encircle. …을 둘러싸다; 에워싸다. ¶ *~ (up) cattle* 말타고 주변을 돌면서 가축을 모으다 / *The pond is ringed with pine trees.* 그 연못은 소나무들로 빙 둘러싸여 있다 / *The old house was ringed (about) with trees.* 그 고옥(古屋) 둘레에는 나무들이 있었다 / *Indians ringed the camp.* 인디언들은 오두막 둘레에 모였다. **2** (P6) provide (something) with a ring. …에 고리를 끼우다. ¶ *~ a bull* 황소에 코뚜레를 하다 / *~ a pigeon* 비둘기 발에 고리를 끼우다. **3** (P6) toss a ring over (a pin, etc.). (놀이로) …에 고리를 던지다. **4** (P6) cut a circular groove in the bark of (a tree). …의 껍질을 고리 모양으로 벗기다.

— *vi.* **1** form into a ring. 둥글게 되다; 원을 이루다. **2** move in a ring. 빙글빙글 돌다. **3** (of a bird) fly in circles. (새가) 원을 그리며 날아 오르다. [E.]

:**ring**[2] [riŋ] *v.* (**rang, rung**) *vi.* **1** (P1,2A) (of a bell, a coin, etc.) sound musically or clearly when struck. (종 따위가) 울리다. ¶ *The doorbell rang loudly.* 현관 벨이 요란하게 울렸다 / *A shot rang out.* 한 방의 총성이 울렸다 / *The telephone is ringing noisily.* 전화 벨이 시끄럽게 울리고 있다. **2** (P5) produce a certain effect when heard; seem; appear to be. …처럼 들리다. ¶ *Her words rang true.* 그녀의 말이 사실인 것 같았다 / *The coin rings false* 〔*true*〕. 이 동전은 소리를 들어보니 가짜〔진짜〕 같다. **3** (P1,3) signal by sounding a bell or buzzer. 벨을 울리다〔울려서 부르다〕. ¶ *Did you ~?* 벨을 울렸느냐 / *We rang at the front door.* 현관에서 벨을 울렸다 / *She rang for the servant.* 그녀는 벨을 울려 하인을 불렀다. **4** (P1,2A,3) sound loudly and clearly; remain in one's mind. (소리·음성이) 울려 퍼지다; (소리가) 쟁쟁하다. ¶ *Her voice rings through the house.* 그녀 목소리가 온 집안에 울려 퍼진다 / *His words are still ringing in my ears.* 그의 말은 아직도 귀에 쟁쟁하다 / *The words were ringing in my mind all day.* 그 말이 온종일 마음에서 떠나지 않았다. **5** (P1,2A,3) 《*with*》 (of a place) be filled with sound; be famous. (장소가) 울리다; 평판이 자자하다. ¶ *The room rang with cheers.* 방안이 왁자지껄했다 / *The world rang with his fame.* 세계에 그의 명성이 자자했다. — *vt.* **1** (P6,7) cause (a bell, etc.) to sound. (종·벨 따위)를 울리다. ¶ *~ the bell* 벨을 울리다 / *I rang the doorbell but no one answerd.* 초인종을 눌렀으나 아무 응답이 없었다. **2** (P6,7) announce, summon, signal, warn, etc. (someone or something) by the sound of a bell; telephone. 벨을 울려서 …을 부르다〔알리다〕; …에게 전화를 걸다. ¶ *~ an* *alarm* 경종을 울리다 / ~ *a maidservant in* 〔*down, up*〕 벨을 울려서 하녀를 안〔아래층, 위층〕으로 부르다 / ~ *the hours* 종을 쳐 시간을 알리다 / *Will you ~ his office, please?* 그의 사무실에 전화 좀 해 주겠느냐.

ring a bell, 《*colloq.*》 call to mind; cause to think of something. 생각나게 하다; …을 상기시키다. ¶ *Her name rings a bell with me, but I can't remember whether I've ever met her.* 그녀 이름은 생각나지만 내가 그녀를 만난 일이 있는지 잘 모르겠다.

ring down 〔***up***〕 ***the curtain,*** lower 〔raise〕 a theater curtain; give a signal for lowering 〔raising〕 a theater curtain; end 〔begin〕. (벨을 울려) 막을 내리다〔올리다〕; 폐막〔개막〕 신호를 하다; 끝마치다〔시작하다〕. ¶ *His death rang down the curtain on an era of history.* 그의 죽음은 역사의 한 시대의 종언(終焉)을 고했다.

ring off, end a phone call. 전화를 끊다.

ring the bell, be successful. 잘 돼가다; 성공하다.

ring (***the***) ***changes on,*** repeat the same thing in slightly different words. 같은 말을 조금씩 다르게 되풀이하다.

ring the knell, indicate the downfall of. …의 조종을 울리다; 폐지를〔몰락을〕 알리다.

ring up, make a phone call. 전화 걸다. ¶ *I will ~ you up at six.* 여섯 시에 전화하마.

— *n.* Ⓒ **1** the sound of or like a bell; an act of ringing a bell. 종을 울림; 종 울리는 소리. ¶ *There is a ~ at the door.* 대문 벨이 울린다 / *The coin has the true* 〔*right*〕 *~.* 소리를 들으니 그 동전은 진짜다. **2** 《*sing.* only》 any loud, clear echoing sound. 울려퍼지는 소리. ¶ *the ~ of voices.* **3** a telephone call. 전화하기. ¶ *Give me a ~ tomorrow.* 내일 전화 주시오. **4** 《*sing.* only》 a sound or tone that suggests a particular quality. 가락; 느낌. ¶ *the ~ of truth* 진실인 것 같은 느낌 / *His excuse had a familiar ~.* 그의 변명은 귀에 익은 느낌이었다. [E.]

ringed [riŋd] *adj.* **1** marked with, or formed like a ring or rings. 고리가 있는; 고리 모양의. **2** wearing a ring or rings; married or engaged. 반지를 낀; 결혼〔약혼〕한. [*ring*[1]]

ring·er[1] [ríŋər] *n.* Ⓒ a person or thing that rings or encircles. 에워싸는 사람〔것〕. [*ring*[1]]

ring·er[2] [ríŋər] *n.* Ⓒ **1** a person or thing that rings a bell, chime, etc. 종〔방울〕 울리는 사람; 명종(鳴鐘)장치. **2** 《*sl.*》 a person who greatly resembles someone else. 흡사하게 닮은 사람〔것〕. ¶ *He is a dead ~ for his brother.* 그는 자기 형과 아주 닮았다. [*ring*[1]]

ring finger [⌐ ⌐] *n.* the third finger, esp. of the left hand, on which the wedding ring is worn. (왼손의) 약손가락.

ring·lead·er [ríŋlìːdər] *n.* Ⓒ a person who leads others in a riot, a crime, etc. (폭동 등의) 주모자; 수괴(首魁).

ring·let [ríŋlit] *n.* Ⓒ **1** a little ring. 작은 고리〔바퀴〕. **2** a long curl of hair. (긴) 고수머리. ¶ *Jane has golden ringlets.*

ring·side [ríŋsàid] *n.* Ⓒ **1** the place just outside the ring at a boxing match, etc. (권투장 등의) 링 주변(의 좌석). **2** a place giving a close view. (일반적으로) 아주 가까이(에서) 볼 수 있는 장소.

ring·worm [ríŋwə̀ːrm] *n.* a contagious skin disease causing ring-shaped patches. 백선(白癬); 도장부스럼.

rink [riŋk] *n.* Ⓒ a sheet of artificial ice for skating; a smooth floor used for roller skating. 스케이트장; 롤러스케이트장. [O.F. *renk* rank]

rinse [rins] *vt.* (P6,7,13) 《*away, off, out, out of*》 wash lightly; wash (something) in clean water. …을 헹구다; 씻어내다; 가시다. ¶ ~ *the soap out of one's hair* 머리에서 비눗물을 씻어내다 / ~ (*out*) *dishes* 설거지하다 / ~ *out the mouth* 입을 가시다 / ~ *one's hands* 손을 씻다. — *n.* Ⓒ the act of rinsing. 헹구기; 가시기. ¶ *Give it a last ~ in cold water.* 그걸 마지막에는 찬물로 헹궈라. [F. *rincer*]

ri·ot [ráiət] *n.* **1** Ⓒ a noisy, unlawful act by a crowd of people. 폭동; 소동. ¶ *raise a ~* 폭동을 일으키다 / *The police were called to control the ~.* 폭동을 진압하기 위해 경찰이 투입됐다. **2** Ⓤ loose living; disorderly conduct. 방탕. **3** 《*fig.*》 《*a ~*》 luxuriance; a great quantity; an unrestrained display. 화려함; 다채로움; 풍부; (감정 등의) 분출; 격발. ¶ *The garden is a ~ of color.* 정원엔 꽃이 흐드러지게 피어 있다 / *The sunset was a ~ of color.* 저녁놀이 진 하늘은 빛깔이 찬란했다 / *a ~ of emotion* 감정의 격발.

run riot, **a**) run wild; act without restraint. 함부로 날뛰다. **b**) 《*fig.*》 (of grass, etc.) grow wildly. (풀 따위가) 멋대로 자라다.

— *vi.* (P1,3) take part in a riot; live in a loose, wild manner; revel. 폭동에 가담하다; 방탕하다; 흥청거리다.

— *vt.* 《*away*》 waste (money, time, etc.) in loose, wild living. …을 방탕으로 낭비하다. [F. *riote*(*r*)]

Riot Act [⌐ ⌐], **the** *n.* an English statute of 1715 making it a felony for 12 or more persons to assemble unlawfully and riotously and to refuse to disperse upon proclamation. 소요 단속법.

read the Riot Act, 《*lit., joc.*》 give a warning to unruly persons or children. (행동을 삼가도록) …에게 경고하다.

ri·ot·er [ráiətər] *n.* Ⓒ a person who riots. 폭도; 방탕자.

ri·ot·ous [ráiətəs] *adj.* **1** taking part in a riot. 폭동에 가담하는. **2** behaving lawlessly; disorderly; running wild. 함부로 구는; 난폭한; 무질서한; 시끄러운. ¶ *Sounds of ~ glee* *came from the theater.* 극장에서 요란한 웃음소리가 들려왔다 / *Two students were expelled from school for ~ conduct.* 두 학생이 행동이 나빠 학교에서 쫓겨났다 / *a ~ fancy* 멋대로의 공상.

ri·ot·ous·ly [ráiətəsli] *adv.* in a riotous manner. 난폭하게; 소란스럽게.

***rip**[1] [rip] *v.* (**ripped, rip·ping**) *vt.* **1** (P6,7,18) cut or tear (something) with violence. …을 찢다. ¶ *~ a sack open* 봉지를 찢어 열다 / *~ one's coat on a nail* 못에 걸려 옷이 찢기다 / *~ off* 떼내다; 벗겨내다. **2** (P6) (of clothes) undo the seam of, by cutting or pulling out the stitches. (옷솔기)를 뜯다. **3** 《*colloq.*》《*out*》 speak with violence. 내뱉듯이 말하다. ¶ *~ out an oath* 저주하는 말을 내뱉다. — *vi.* (P1) **1** become torn apart. 찢기다; 쪼개지다. ¶ *the sort of cloth that rips at once* 잘 찢어지는 천 / *The sail ripped under the force of the wind.* 돛이 바람에 찢겼다. **2** 《*colloq.*》 move with speed and violence. 돌진하다.

Let her* 〔*it*〕 *rip. 《*colloq.*》 Let it go. Make it go. (차·엔진 등을) 멈추지 마라; 내버려 두어라.

let things rip, be careless of the result; allow events to follow their course without trying to guide them. (결과야 어떻든) 되는 대로 내버려 두다.

— *n.* Ⓒ a torn place; a long tear. 찢어진 데; 타진 데. [? (→reap)]

rip[2] [rip] *n.* **1** a stretch of rough water made by cross currents meeting. 두 조류가 만나서 되는 격랑. ¶ *Between these islands there is a ~.* 이들 섬 사이에 물살이 센 데가 있다. **2** a swift current made by the tide. 물살이 빠른 조류; 급류. [? →ripple]

rip[3] [rip] *n.* **1** a dissolute person. 불량배; 건달. **2** an old worthless horse. 늙어 쓸모없는 말. [? abbr. of *reprobate*]

R.I.P. 《L.》 *requiescat* 〔*requiescant*〕 *in pace* (=may he 〔she, they〕 rest in peace). 고이 잠드소서《비문》.

ri·par·i·an [ripέəriən, rai-] *adj.* of or on the bank of a river or lake. 강기슭의; 호숫가의. — *n.* a person who owns property on the bank(s) of a river or lake. 강기슭〔호반〕 토지 소유자. [L.]

rip-cord [rípkɔ̀ːrd] *n.* **1** a cord to be pulled to open a parachute for descent. 낙하산 펴는 줄. **2** a cord to open the gas bag of a balloon. (기구·비행선의) 가스 빼는 줄《급강하용》. [*rip*[1]]

:ripe [raip] *adj.* **1** ⓐ (of fruit, etc.) ready to be gathered and used for food; full-grown. 익은; 여문. ¶ *~ fruit* 〔*grain, vegetable*〕 익은 과일〔곡식, 채소〕. ⓑ 《*fig.*》 the color of ripe fruit. 익은 과일 빛깔의. ¶ *~ cheeks* 빨간 볼. **2** (of persons) fully developed; mature. 성숙한; 원숙한; 한창때의. ¶ *a person of ~ years* 원숙한 사람; 성인 / *~ beauty* 원숙미 / *die at a ~ age* 고령으로 죽다 / *~ knowledge* 〔*learning, experience*〕 원숙한 지식〔학문, 경험〕. **3** prepared; ready. 준비가 된; (기회가) 무르익은; 막 …하게 되어 있는. ¶ *~ for war* 전기(戰機)가 무르익은 / *a plan ~ for execution* 이제 곧 실행할 계획 / *The opportunity is ~ to be seized.* 절호의 기회다 / *This land is ~ for industrial development.* 이 곳은 산업 발전으로 발돋움하고 있다. [E.]

***rip·en** [ráipən] *vi.* (P1) become ripe. 익다; 원숙하다. ¶ *His thought ripened into action.* 그의 생각은 행동으로까지 발전했다. — *vt.* (P6) make (something) ripe. …을 익게 하다. ¶ *The bright sun ripened the orange.* 빛나는 햇살이 오렌지를 여물게 했다.

ri·poste [ripóust] *n.* **1** 《fencing》 quick return thrust in fencing. 되찌르기. **2** ready and witty reply, retort. 재치 있는 즉답〔대꾸〕; 응구 첩대(應口輒對). — *vi.* (P1) deliver riposte. 되찌르다; 잽싸게〔재치 있게〕 대답하다. [→respond]

rip·ping [rípiŋ] *adj.* 《Brit. *sl.*》 splendid; excellent. 멋있는; 훌륭한. [→ripe]

***rip·ple** [rípəl] *n.* Ⓒ **1** ⓐ a very little, gentle wave. 잔물결. ¶ *Ripples spread in rings on the water.* 수면에 잔물결이 둥글게 퍼졌다. ⓑ anything that seems like a tiny wave. 잔물결 모양의 것. ¶ *ripples in a field of grain* 들판의 곡식의 물결. **2** a slight curling. (머리털 등의) 자잘한 웨이브. ¶ *ripples in hair.* **3** a light, soft sound like that of rippling water. 잔물결이 이는 듯한 소리. ¶ *A ~ of laughter went through the audience.* 청중 속에 잔잔한 웃음소리가 번져갔다.

— *vt.* (P6) form (something) into ripples. …에 잔물결을 일으키다. ¶ *A breeze rippled the surface of the pond.* 산들바람이 연못에 잔물결을 일으켰다.

— *vi.* (P1) be formed into ripples; make a light, soft sound. 잔물결이 일다; 잔물결 같은 (살랑살랑·찰싹찰싹) 소리가 나다. [? *rip*[1]+*-le*]

rip·plet [ríplit] *n.* Ⓒ a little ripple. (아주 작은) 잔물결. [↑]

rip-saw [rípsɔ̀ː] *n.* a saw for cutting wood along the grain. 내릴톱. [*rip*[1]]

:rise [raiz] *v.* (**rose, ris·en**) *vi.* (P1,2A,2B,3) **1** 《*from, to*》 stand up. 일어서다; 일어나다. ¶ *~ from the table* (식사가 끝나) 식탁을 떠나다 / *~ to one's feet* 일어서다 / *~ from one's knees* 무릎을 꿇은 자세에서 일어나다 / *He rose to make a speech.* 그는 연설하려고 일어섰다. **2** ⓐ get up from bed. 기상하다. ¶ *He rises early.* 그는 일찍 일어난다 / *~ with the lark* 〔*sun*〕 아침 일찍 일어나다. ⓑ come to life after dying. 다시 살아나다. ¶ *~ from the dead* (죽음에서) 다시 살아나다. **3** ⓐ go or move up; move upward. 올라가다; (하늘에) 오르다; 상승하다(opp. fall). ¶ *A balloon rises.* 풍선이 올라간다 / *Smoke rises up* 〔*into*〕 *the air.* 연기

가 하늘로 올라간다 / *The curtain rises.* 막이 오른다 / *The mist rose up from the marsh.* 늪에서 안개가 일었다 / *Morning* 〔*Dawn*〕 *rises.* 아침〔새벽〕이 된다. ⓑ (of fish) come to the surface of the water, esp. attracted by a bait. (물고기가 미끼를 물려고) 수면에 떠오르다. ¶ *The fish rises.* / *Fish rose to my bait.* 물고기가 미끼를 보고 떠올랐다 / 《*fig.*》 *He rose to my bait and admitted everything.* 그는 내 뇌물을 받고는 무엇이나 들어줬다. ⓒ slope upward by degrees. (길 따위가) 오르막이 되다. ¶ *The road rises here.* 길은 여기서 오르막이다 / *rising ground* 대지(臺地). **4** (of the sun, the moon, etc.) appear above the horizon. (해·달 등이) 떠오르다; 솟다(opp. set). ¶ *The sun rises in the east.* 해는 동쪽에서 떠오른다. **5** grow taller or higher; stand high; tower up. 높아지다; 성장하다; 높이 솟다. ¶ *The tower rises high above the trees.* 탑은 수목들 위로 높이 솟아 있다 / *The new skyscraper rises higher each day.* 새로 짓는 고층 건물은 날마다 높아진다 / *The mountain rises 800 meters above the sea.* 이 산은 해발 800미터이다. **6** 《*against*》 revolt; rebel. 반항하다; 반항해 일어서다; 배반하다. ¶ ~ *in arms* 무장하여 일어나다 / ~ *against a king* 〔*the government*〕 왕〔정부〕에게 반기를 들다. **7** come into view or existence; appear; come to the mind. 보이다; 나타나다; (마음에) 떠오르다. ¶ *Land rose on the right.* 오른쪽에 육지가 나타났다 / *Thoughts* ~ *in the mind.* 생각들이 마음에 떠오른다. **8** increase in degree, amount, price, etc. (물가·양 따위가) 오르다; 늘다. ¶ *Prices are rising.* 물가가 오르고 있다 / *His spirit rises.* 그는 사기가 오르고 있다 / *His temper rose.* 그의 감정은 격해졌다 / *His voice rose in excitement.* 흥분해서 목소리가 높아졌다 / *The wind often rises to a wild fury.* 바람은 자주 사납게 몰아친다 / *Her color rose.* 그녀 얼굴이 홍조를 띠었다. **9** go to a higher position in society; become famous, successful, etc. 출세하다; 승진하다; 유명해지다. ¶ ~ *in the world* 출세하다 / ~ *to fame* 명성을 얻다 / ~ *from the ranks* 낮은 신분에서 출세하다 / *She eventually rose to an important position in the firm.* 마침내 그녀는 회사의 요직에 올랐다. **10** begin; happen; occur; have a source or origin. 시작하다; 일어나다; 발생하다; 근원을 이루다. ¶ *A rumor rose.* 소문이 났다 / *A wind rose suddenly.* 갑자기 바람이 일었다 / *This river rises in the mountains.* 이 강은 그 산에서 발원한다. **11** end a meeting. 끝나다; 폐회하다. ¶ *The parliament will* ~ *next month.* 의회는 다음 달에 폐회할 것이다. **12** increase in size; swell. 부풀다; (강의) 물이 붇다. ¶ *The bread is rising.* 빵이 부풀고 있다 / *The river is rising rapidly.* 강물이 급속히 불어나고 있다.

— *vt.* (P6) **1** cause (birds) to fly up from the ground. (새 따위)를 날아가게 하다. **2** cause (fish) to come to the surface of the water. (물고기를) 수면에 떠오르게 하다. **3** 《naut.》 cause (something) to rise above the visible horizon. 수평선상에 나타나게 하다.

— *n.* Ⓒ **1** ⓐ the act of rising or going up. 오름; 상승. ¶ *the* ~ *of a balloon* 풍선의 상승. ⓑ appearance of a fish at the water's surface for food or bait. (물고기가 미끼를 물려고) 떠오름. ¶ *I fished all day but hadn't a* ~. 종일 낚시를 했으나 한 마리도 낚지 못했다. **2** an increase in degree, amount, price, etc.; the rate or degree of this. 증가; 증대; 그 정도 또는 비율. ¶ *a sudden* ~ *in food prices* 식료품 값의 갑작스런 상승 / *The price is on the* ~. 물가가 오르고 있다 / *The* ~ *of the river was four meters.* 수위는 4미터나 높아졌다 / *a sudden* ~ *in temperature* 기온의 급상승. **3** advance in rank, power, position, influence, etc. 입신; 출세; 승진. ¶ *her* ~ *to fame* 그녀의 인기 상승 / *have* 〔*make*〕 *a* ~ 입신양명〔출세〕하다 / *his unforeseen* ~ *to power* 그의 예상 밖의 출세. **4** an upward slope; a small hill. 오르막; 언덕. ¶ *a* ~ *in the road* 오르막길 / *the* ~ *of a roof* 지붕의 물매 / *We sat at the top of a small* ~. 우리는 작은 언덕 마루에 앉았다 / *The laboratory stands on a* ~. 실험실은 언덕 위에 있다. **5** an origin or a source; a beginning. 기원; 발생; 시초; 시작. ¶ *the* ~ *of the stream* / *The river takes* 〔*has*〕 *its* ~ *in the mountains.* 이 강은 산에서 발원한다. **6** 《Brit.》 an increase in salary or wages. 급료 인상(cf. 《U.S.》 *raise*). ¶ *get a* ~ *of salary* 월급이 인상되다 / *a 15 percent* ~ *in wages* 임금의 15퍼센트 인상. **7** the process of beginning or developing. 융성; 번영. ¶ *the* ~ *and fall of Rome* 로마의 성쇠. [E.]

buy for the rise, buy anticipating higher prices. 값이 오를 것을 내다보고 사다.

get* 〔*take*〕 *a rise out of, make (someone) angry by good-natured teasing; get a desired reaction or response from. …을 지분거려 화나게 하다; …를 부추겨서 바라는 바를 이루다.

give rise to, cause to appear or take place; be the cause of. …을 일으키다. ¶ *Those words will give* ~ *to doubts* 〔*mistakes, much controversy*〕. 그 말들이 의혹〔오해, 많은 논쟁〕을 가져오게 될 것이다 / *give* ~ *to serious trouble* 심각한 불화를 낳다 / *The oil crisis is giving* ~ *to inflation all over the world.* 석유 파동이 전세계에 인플레를 야기하고 있다.

on the rise, going up. 오름세에. ¶ *Prices are on the* ~. 물가는 오름세에 있다.

:ris·en [rízən] *v.* pp. of **rise.**

ris·er [ráizər] *n.* Ⓒ **1** a person who rises. 기상자(起床者). ¶ *an early* ~ 일찍 일어나는 사람. **2** the upright part of a step, a stair, etc. (층계 등의) 층뒤판.

ris·i·bil·i·ty [rìzəbíləti] *n.* readiness to laugh; an inclination to laugh. 잘 웃음; 잘 웃는 성질. ¶ *A man running after his hat arouses the risibilities of many people.* 제 모자를 주우러 뛰어가는 그의 모습이 많은 사람들의 웃음을 자아낸다. [↓]

ris·i·ble [rízəbəl] *adj.* **1** of or connected with laughter. 웃음의; 웃음에 관계된. ¶ *the ~ muscles* 소근(笑筋). **2** able to laugh; inclined to laugh. 웃을 수 있는. ¶ *Man is the only ~ animal.* 사람만이 웃을 수 있는 동물이다. **3** causing laughter; laughable. 웃음을 자아내는; 우스운. [L. *rideo* laugh]

ris·ing [ráiziŋ] *n.* **1** Ⓤ upward movement. 오름; 상승. ¶ *the ~ of the sun* 해돋이 / *Seven o'clock is my hour for ~.* 일곱시가 내 기상 시간이다. **2** Ⓤ resurrection. 부활. **3** Ⓒ a revolt; a rebellion. 반란; 모반.
— *adj.* **1** going up; increasing in importance, value, power, etc. 오르는; 승진의; 신진의; 발전하는. ¶ *the ~ sun* 떠오르는 태양 / *a ~ singer* 〔*novelist*〕 신인 가수〔작가〕 / *a ~ man* 신진 인물. **2** ⓐ growing; maturing. 발달〔성장〕하고 있는. ¶ *the ~ generation* (다음 세대를 짊어질) 젊은이들. ⓑ approaching the age of; nearing. (나이가) …이 되어가는; …에 가까운. ¶ *He is ~ forty years.* 그는 곧 마흔이 된다 / *He is nine, ~ ten.* 그는 아홉 살인데 곧 열 살이 된다. **3** sloping upward. 올라가는; 오르막의. ¶ *a ~ hill* 오르막. [*rise*]

:risk [risk] *n.* ⓊⒸ a chance of damage, harm, or loss; danger. 위험; 리스크. ¶ *at all risks* 〔*any ~*〕 어떤 위험이 있더라도 / *at one's own ~* 자기 책임으로 / *at the ~ of* … 의 위험을 무릅쓰고 / *run* 〔*take*〕 *a ~* 모험을 하다 / *He rescued the boy at the ~ of his own life.* 그는 제 목숨을 걸고 소년을 구해 냈다 / *If you drive carefully, there is no ~ of being fined.* 조심해 운전한다면 과료(科料) 같은 걸 물 염려는 없다.
— *vt.* **1** (P6,13) expose (something) to risk. …을 위태롭게 하다. ¶ *~ one's fortune* 전재산을 걸다 / *You are risking your neck trying to climb that tree.* 저 나무에 오르다가 죽을지도 모른다. **2** (P6,9) take a chance of (something). 위험을 무릅쓰고 …을 하다; 감행하다. ¶ *They risked defeat in fighting the larger army.* 그들은 패전을 각오하고 우세한 적군과 싸웠다. [F. *risque(r)*]

risk·y [ríski] *adj.* (**risk·i·er, risk·i·est**) having danger; dangerous. 위험한; 아슬아슬한. ¶ *a ~ journey* 〔*business*〕 모험적인 여행〔사업〕.

ris·qué [riskéi] *adj.* 《F.》 (of a story, play, etc.) tending toward impropriety; immoral. (이야기 등이) 외설스러운; 부도덕한. [F. *risquer* risk]

rite [rait] *n.* **1** Ⓒ a solemn, formal ceremony. 의식(儀式). ¶ *burial* 〔*funeral*〕 *rites* 장례식 / *a ~ of baptism* 세례식. **2** general custom. 관습; 관례. [L. *ritus*]

rit·u·al [rítʃuəl] *adj.* of a rite or rites; done as a rite. 의식(儀式)의. ¶ *~ laws* 의례준칙 / *a ~ dance* 의식 무도. — *n.* Ⓒ **1** 《*collectively*》 a set form or system of rites. 의식; 예식. ¶ *The rites of baptism, marriage, and burial are parts of the ~ of the church.* 세례식, 결혼식 및 장례식은 교회 의식의 일부분이다. **2** a book of prescribed rites. 의식서(儀式書). [↑]

:ri·val [ráivəl] *n.* Ⓒ a competitor; an equal. 경쟁자; 적수; 라이벌. ¶ *without a ~* 무적으로 / *a ~ in love* 연적(戀敵) / *a ~ in trade* 사업상의 적수 / *He is jealous of his ~.* 그는 라이벌을 시기하고 있다 / *Who will be his main ~ in the election?* 이번 선거에서 누가 그의 주요한 적수일까.
— *adj.* acting as a rival; competing. 경쟁하는.
— *vt.* (**-valed, -val·ing** or 《Brit.》 **-valled, -val·ling**) (P6,13) try to equal or surpass; compete with (someone); be close (in some quality). …와 경쟁하다; …에 뒤지지 않다. ¶ *She rivals her sister in beauty.* 그녀는 언니 못지 않게 아름답다 / *Ships can't ~ aircraft for speed.* 배는 속도면에서 비행기를 당해낼 수 없다. [L. *rivus* stream]

ri·val·ry [ráivəlri] *n.* ⓊⒸ (*pl.* **-ries**) the state of being rivals; competiton. 경쟁; 대항; 적대. ¶ *the ~ among shops* 가게끼리의 경쟁 / *There was a friendly ~ between the two women.* 두 부인은 서로를 격려하는 경쟁 관계였다.

rive [raiv] *vt., vi* (**rived, riv·en,** or **rived**) (P6,7,13;1) 《*arch.*》 split; tear apart; cleave. 찢(기)다; 쪼개(지)다. ¶ *The lightning rived the oak.* 번개가 오크를 쪼개 놓았다 / *She used me in such a manner as has rived my heart.* 그녀는 내 가슴을 찢어놓는 그런 태도로 나를 대했다. [N.]

riv·en [rívən] *v.* pp. of **rive.** — *adj.* split; torn apart. 찢어진. [↑]

:riv·er [rívər] *n.* Ⓒ **1** a large stream of water. 강; 하천. ¶ *the River Nile.* **2** 《*fig.*》 any great stream or plentiful flow. 다량의 흐름. ¶ *a ~ of lava* 엄청난 용암의 유출 / *Rivers of blood flowed during the war.* 전쟁동안 피바다를 이루었다. [L. *ripa* bank]

river basin [´– ´–] *n.* the area drained by a river. (강의) 유역.

riv·er·bed [rívərbèd] *n.* Ⓒ the sandy bottom of a river. 하상(河床).

riv·er·head [rívərhèd] *n.* Ⓒ the source of a river. 강의 수원(지).

riv·er·side [rívərsàid] *n.* Ⓒ the bank of a river. 강가; 강변. — *adj.* on the bank of a river. 강가〔강변〕의.

riv·et [rívit] *n.* Ⓒ a short metal bolt with a head on one end, used to fasten together two or more pieces of wood, metal, etc. 리벳; 대갈못. ¶ *Rivets fasten steel beams together.* 리벳은 강철빔을 죄어 놓는 데 쓰인다 / 《*fig.*》 *the ~ of love* 사랑의 거멀쇠.

— *vt.* (P6,7,13) **1** fasten (plates, etc.) with a rivet or rivets. …을 리벳으로 고정시키다. **2** fasten firmly. …을 움직이지 못하게 하다. ¶ *Seize him and ~ him to the rock.* 그 놈을 붙잡아 바위에다 단단히 붙들어 매놔라 / *The shock riveted him to the spot.* 그 충격에 그는 그 자리에 못박힌 듯 서 버렸다. **3** fix (the eyes, the mind, etc.) firmly. (눈·마음 등)을 집중하다. ¶ *~ one's attention on* 〔*upon*〕 *something* …에 주의를 집중하다 / *He riveted his eyes on her.* 그는 그녀에게서 눈을 떼지 않았다. ● **riv·et·er** [-ər] *n.* [F.]

riv·u·let [rívjəlit] *n.* Ⓒ a very small stream. 개울; 시내. [→rival]

R.N. **1** Registered Nurse. 공인 간호사. **2** Royal Navy. 영국 해군.

roach[1] [routʃ] *n.* =cockroach.

roach[2] [routʃ] *n.* Ⓒ (*pl.* **roach·es** or *collectively* **roach**) a fresh-water fish of the carp family. 잉어과의 물고기. [F. *roche*]

as sound as a roach, thoroughly healthy. 아주 건강하여.

:road [roud] *n.* Ⓒ **1** a highway along which people can travel; a public way for travel. 도로; 길. ¶ *the beaten ~* 늘 다니는 길; 상도 / *make a ~* 길을 내다 / *This ~ goes to London.* 이 길로 가면 런던이다 / *Our ~ went through the woods.* 길이 숲으로 나 있었다 / *travel by ~* (걷건 타건) 육로로 여행하다. **2** 《*fig.*》 a way; a course; a means to approach. 수단; 방법. ¶ 《*prov.*》 *There is no royal ~ to learning.* 학문엔 왕도가 없다 / *the ~ to happiness* 〔*success, ruin*〕 행복으로〔성공으로, 파멸로〕 가는 길. **3** 《U.S.》 a railroad. 철도. **4** 《often *pl.*》 =roadstead. [→ride]

break a road, cut one's way through difficulties. 난관을 헤치고 나아가다.

burn up the road, 《*sl.*》 drive or move very fast. 전속력으로 달리다.

gentleman 〔***knight***〕 ***of the road*** = road agent.

get in someone's road, hinder; prevent someone from doing what he wishes to do. …을 방해하다.

get out of someone's 〔***the***〕 ***road,*** move out of the way. 방해가 되지 않도록 비켜서다.

go on 〔***take to***〕 ***the road,*** **a**) start traveling. 여행을 떠나다; 길을 나서다. **b**) 《*arch.*》 become a highwayman. 노상 강도가 되다.

hit the road, begin to travel on. 여행을 떠나다.

one for the road, 《*colloq.*》 a final drink of an alcoholic beverage in the way of bidding farewell. (떠나기에 앞서) 석별의 한 잔.

on the road, on tour; traveling, esp. as a salesman. 여행중인; 행상을 하는.

take the road of, take precedence of. …의 위에 서다; …보다 낫다.

road agent [⌐ ⌐–] *n.* 《U.S.》 a highwayman. 노상 강도.

road·bed [róudbèd] *n.* Ⓒ the foundation or bed for a road or railroad. 노상(路床); (철도의) 노반(路盤).

road·block [róudblɑ̀k / -blɔ̀k] *n.* a barricade set up by police to stop or slow down traffic. (검색·검문을 위한) 도로상의 방책; 바리케이드.

road·book [róudbùk] *n.* a guidebook for travelers by road. 도로 안내서.

road hog [⌐ ⌐] *n.* a driver who is reckless and inconsiderate of others. 난폭한 운전자; 폭주광.

road·house [róudhàus] *n.* Ⓒ a tavern, an inn, or a night club at the side of a road in the country. 도로변의 술집〔여인숙, 나이트클럽〕.

road·man [róudmən] *n.* Ⓒ (*pl.* **-men** [-mən]) a man who is employed to keep roads in repair. 도로 인부.

road-met·al [róudmètl] *n.* broken stone for road-making. 도로 포장용 자갈.

road-sense [róudsèns] *n.* the capacity for safe behavior or handling of vehicles on the road. 도로 감각《차량 운전자나 보행인의》.

road show [⌐ ⌐] *n.* **1** a show performed by a touring group of actors. (극단의) 지방 흥행. **2** a special show of a new motion picture, usu. at a special advanced price. (영화의) 특별 흥행; 로드 쇼.

road·side [róudsàid] *n.* Ⓒ 《usu. *the ~*》 the side of a road. 길가; 도로변. ¶ *by* 〔*on*〕 *the ~* 노변에. — *adj.* on or at the side of a road. 노변의. ¶ *a ~ inn* 노변의 여인숙 / *~ plants* 가로수.

road·stead [róudstèd] *n.* Ⓒ a stretch of water near the shore where ships can ride at anchor. (항구 밖의) 정박지.

road·ster [róudstər] *n.* Ⓒ **1** a horse used for driving or riding on the road. (도로상에 쓰이는) 승용마. **2** an open automobile with a single seat, usu. for two persons. (2·3인용) 무개(無蓋) 자동차; 로드스터. **3** a ship at anchor in a roadstead. (항구 밖 정박지에) 정박중인 배.

road·way [róudwèi] *n.* Ⓒ **1** a road. 도로. **2** the part of a road used by vehicles. 차도 (cf. *footpath*). ¶ *Walk on the path, not in the ~.* 차도로 걷지 말고 인도로 가시오.

·roam [roum] *vi., vt.* (P1,2A,3;6) 《*about*》 wander; go from place to place aimlessly. (…을) 거닐다; 배회〔방황〕하다. ¶ *~ about the forest* 숲을 거닐다 / *Crowds of youths roamed the streets looking for trouble.* 젊은 패거리들이 시빗거리를 찾아 길거리를 배회하고 다녔다 / *~ the countryside* 시골을 돌아다니다 / *~ over hill and dale* 산과 계곡을 헤매다. — *n.* Ⓒ a walk with no special aim. 배회; 방황. [E.]

roan [roun] *adj.* (of horses and cattle) deep reddish-brown or yellowish, thickly sprinkled with gray or white. 회색이나 흰색 바탕에 밤색과 노랑의 얼룩이 있는. — *n.* Ⓤ a roan color; Ⓒ a roan horse. 그러한 색깔;

또, 그런 말. [F.]

:roar [rɔːr] *vi.* (P1,2A,3) **1** utter a loud, deep sound. 으르렁거리다; 울리다. ¶ *A storm roars.* 폭풍우가 사납게 휘몰아친다 / *Cannons ~ far away.* 멀리서 대포 소리가 울린다 / *The lion roared with anger.* 사자는 성이 나서 으르렁거렸다 / *The fire roars up the chimney.* 불길이 요란한 소리를 내며 굴뚝으로 치솟았다. **2** cry out, or laugh loudly; speak in a loud, deep voice, esp. with anger. 고함치다; 소리지르다; 크게 웃다. ¶ *~ with laughter* 큰소리로 웃다 / *Don't ~ at me.* 내게 그렇게 언성을 높이지 마시오.
— *vt.* (P6,7,18) shout loudly at (someone); utter (something) with a loud, deep sound. 소리쳐 …하게 하다. ¶ *~ a speaker down* 큰 소리로 야유를 하여 연사가 말을 못 하게 하다 / *He roared out a song.* 그는 큰소리로 노래를 불렀다 / *He roared himself hoarse.* 그는 너무 소리를 질러 목이 쉬었다 / *~ a command* 큰 소리로 명령하다.
— *n.* Ⓒ a loud, deep sound; a loud cry or noise; a loud burst of laughter. 으르렁거리는 소리; 노호(怒號); 요란한 웃음소리. ¶ *a ~ of disapproval* 요란한 반대 소리 / *the ~ of an angry lion* 성난 사자의 포효 / *set the table in a ~* 좌중의 사람을 한바탕 웃기다. [E.]

roar·ing [rɔ́ːriŋ] *n.* Ⓤ the sound made by a person or thing that roars. 으르렁대는 소리; 포효; 노호(怒號). — *adj.* **1** noisy; stormy. 시끄러운; 노호하는; 폭풍우가 사나운. ¶ *a ~ night* 폭풍우의 밤; 진창 마시고 떠드는 밤 / *He came back ~ drunk.* 그는 억병으로 취해 집에 왔다. **2** brisk; active; healthy. 활발한; 활기찬. ¶ *a ~ trade* 크게 번창하는 장사 / *in ~ health* 기운이 넘쳐 / *The film was a ~ success.* 그 영화는 대성공이었다.

:roast [roust] *vt.* (P6) **1** cook (meat or other food) in an oven or before a fire. (고기 등)을 오븐[불]에 굽다; 볶다; 로스트하다. ¶ *We roasted meat and potatoes.* 우리는 고기와 감자를 번철에다 볶았다 / *The beef is roasting nicely on the spit.* 쇠고기 꼬치구이가 잘 익는다. **2** expose to great heat; dry by exposure to heat. 불에 쬐다[말리다]; 뜨겁게 하다. ¶ *~ one's feet* 발을 불에 쬐다 / *I roasted myself in the sun on the beach.* 해안에서 일광욕을 했다 / *~ coffee beans* 커피콩을 볶다 / *be roasted alive* 화형에 처해지다. **3** bring to the state of extreme heat for the purpose of removing impurities. (광석)을 배소(焙燒)하다. ¶ *~ a metal ore.*
— *vi.* (P1) **1** be cooked in an oven or before a fire. 구워지다; 볶아지다. ¶ *The joint will never ~ with such a small fire.* 큰 고깃덩어리는 이런 약한 불엔 굽지 못한다. **2** 《chiefly in *pres. p.*》 extremely hot. 찌는 듯이 덥다. ¶ *I'm simply roasting.* 지독하게 덥다.
— *n.* Ⓒ a piece of meat to be roasted. 로스트용 고기.
rule the roast, be a master. 좌지우지하다; 지배하다.
— *adj.* roasted. 구운; 로스트한. ¶ *~ beef* 불고기. [F. *rostir*]

roast·er [róustər] *n.* Ⓒ **1** a pan for roasting. 굽는 기구; 번철. **2** a young pig, chicken, etc. suitable to be roasted. (로스트용) 새끼돼지; 병아리 (등).

Rob [rɑb / rɔb] *n.* a nickname of Robert. Robert의 애칭.

:rob [rɑb / rɔb] *v.* (**robbed, rob·bing**) *vt.* (P6,13) 《*of*》 take something away from (someone) by force; deprive (someone) of his rights or property. …에서 빼았다; 강탈하다; 훔치다. ¶ *~ a lady of her handbag* 여자의 핸드백을 강탈하다 / *~ a bank* 은행을 털다 / *I've been robbed.* 도둑을 맞았다 / *The boys robbed the orchard.* 아이들이 과수원에서 서리를 했다 / *~ someone of his rights* 아무의 권리를 빼앗다 / *~ someone of his fair name* 아무의 명성을 잃게 하다. — *vi.* (P1) commit an act of robbing. 강도짓을 하다; 강탈하다. [F. *rober*]

***rob·ber** [rɑ́bər / rɔ́bər] *n.* Ⓒ a person who robs. 강도; 도둑. [→rob]

rob·ber·y [rɑ́bəri / rɔ́bəri] *n.* ⒸⓊ (*pl.* **-ber·ies**) the act of robbing. 강도(짓). ¶ *He had committed several robberies in the neighborhood.* 그는 이웃을 여러 번 털었다 / *To ask such prices is sheer ~.* 이 따위로 값을 부르면 날강도나 다름없다.

:robe [roub] *n.* Ⓒ **1** a long, loose indoor garment. 헐렁하고 긴 겉옷. ¶ *The Arabs wear robes.* 아랍 사람들은 로브를 입는다. **2** 《often *pl.*》 a ceremonial dress worn as a sign of rank, office, etc. 예복; 관복. ¶ *the judge's ~* 재판관의 법복 / *gentlemen of the long ~* 변호사들; 법조계 인사들. **3** ⓐ 《U.S.》 a wrap. (여행용) 무릎덮개. ⓑ 《chiefly *poet.*》 a covering or wrap. 덮개; 장막; 가리개. ¶ *the ~ of night* 밤의 장막 / *Nature wore a ~ of snow.* 천지 만물이 눈에 덮이어 있었다. — *vt.* (P6) dress (someone) with a robe. …에 예복[관복]을 입히다. — *vi.* (P1) put on a robe. 예복[관복]을 입다. [F.]

Rob·ert [rɑ́bərt / rɔ́b-] *n.* a man's name. 남자 이름.

Rob·in [rɑ́bin / rɔ́b-] *n.* a nickname of Robert. 로버트의 애칭.

:rob·in [rɑ́bin / rɔ́b-] *n.* Ⓒ **1** a small bird with a red breast. 울새. **2** 《U.S.》 a large American thrush with a red breast. 개똥지빠귀의 일종. [*Robert*]

Rob·in Good·fel·low [rɑ́bin gúdfelou / rɔ́b-] *n.* a merry, mischievous goblin. 장난꾸러기 작은 요정. [E.]

Rob·in·son Cru·soe [rɑ́binsən krúːsou / rɔ́b-] *n.* a novel by Daniel Defoe; the hero of this novel. 로빈슨 크루소《D. Defoe의 소설; 그 주인공》.

ro·bot [róubət, -bɑt / -bɔt] *n.* Ⓒ **1** a machine that acts or looks like a man. 로봇; 인조 인간. **2** a person who acts like a machine. 감정이 없고 기계적인 사람. **3** machine that performs mechanical functions, esp. in industry otherwise performed by men. 산업용 로봇. [Pol. *robota* work]

ro·bust [roubʌ́st, róubʌst] *adj.* **1** strong and healthy; hardy or vigorous. 튼튼한; 건강한. ¶ *He is in ~ health.* 그는 건강한 사람이다 / *a ~ intellect* 건전한 지성. **2** suited to or requiring bodily strength or endurance. 힘이 드는. ¶ *~ exercises* 힘이 드는 〔격렬한〕 운동. **3** rough; rude. 거친; 조잡한. ¶ *rather ~ criticism* 좀 거친 비평. ● **ro·bust·ly** [-li] *adv.* [L. *robur* strength]

roc [rɑk / rɔk] *n.* Ⓒ an enormous bird in old Arabian tales. 로크《아라비아 전설의 거대한 괴조(怪鳥)》. ¶ *The ~ comes and seizes Sindbad in his claws.* 로크가 날아오더니 발톱으로 신드바드를 잡는다. [Arab.]

a roc's egg an incredible thing. 믿을 수 없는 것.

:rock[1] [rɑk / rɔk] *n.* **1** ⓊⒸ a large mass of stone. 바위; 암석. ¶ *There is danger from falling rocks.* 바위가 굴러 떨어질 위험이 있다. **2** Ⓒ the mass of mineral matter forming the earth's crust. 암반(岩盤); 암상(岩床). ¶ *This building's foundations stand on ~.* 이 건물의 기초는 암반에 닿아 있다 / *We kept on digging until we struck the ~.* 우리는 암반이 나타날 때까지 파내려갔다. **3** a portion of rock in the sea. 암초. ¶ *The ship was wrecked on the rocks.* 배는 암초에 걸려 난파했다. **4** any circumstance causing failure, disagreement. 난관; 위험(물); 화근. ¶ *The division of the money was the ~ on which the thieves split.* 그 돈의 분배 때문에 도둑들은 사이가 틀어졌다. **5** Ⓤ something firm like a rock; a support. 견고한 지지물. ¶ *The Lord is my ~.* 주(主)는 나의 반석이시다. [F. *roche*]

(*as*) *firm as* (*a*) *rock,* very steady. 아주 단단한; 부동의.

go* 〔*run, be*〕 *on the rocks, 《*fig.*》 be in very serious trouble; be wrecked or ruined. 진퇴양난이 되다; 파멸되다. ¶ *Their marriage was on the rocks.* 그들의 결혼은 난관에 부딪쳤다.

on the rocks, **a**) in or into a state of disaster or ruin. 파멸되어; 결딴나서. **b**) 《*fig.*》 being in money-difficulties; penniless. 돈에 쪼들려; 파산하여. **c**) 《U.S.》 (of a drink, esp. whisky) served with ice cubes. (위스키 등) 얼음덩이 위에 따른.

:rock[2] [rɑk / rɔk] *vt.* (P6,7,13) **1** move (something) backward and forward. …을 앞뒤로 흔들다. ¶ *The waves rocked the ship.* 파도가 배를 앞뒤로 흔들었다 / *Rock it back and forth.* 그걸 앞뒤로 흔들어라. **2** move or swing in a cradle. (요람에 태워) 흔들다. ¶ *Mother rocked the baby to sleep.* 어머니는 아기를 흔들어 재웠다. **3** shake violently. 진동시키다. ¶ *The earthquake rocked the houses.* 지진이 가옥들을 크게 흔들었다.
— *vi.* (P1) move backward and forward. 앞뒤로 흔들리다. ¶ *The boat rocks on the water.* 보트가 물에서 뒷질하고 있다.
— *n.* Ⓤ a rocking movement. 흔들림; 동요. [E.]

rock bottom [´ ´–] *n.* Ⓤ **1** the lowest level. 최저. ¶ *Prices have reached ~.* 물가는 바닥 시세가 됐다. **2** solid fact underlying appearances. 진상. [*rock*[1]]

rock-bot·tom [rɑ́kbɑ́təm / rɔ́kbɔ́t-] *adj.* (of prices) down to the very bottom; very lowest. 최저의. ¶ *~ prices* 최저가.

rock-bound [rɑ́kbàund / rɔ́k-] *adj.* (of a coast) surrounded by rocks. 바위로 에워싸인.

rock candy [´ ´–] *n.* 《U.S.》 sugar in the form of rocks. 얼음 사탕.

rock crystal [´ ´–] *n.* a colorless, transparent quartz. 수정(水晶).

rock·er [rɑ́kər / rɔ́k-] *n.* Ⓒ **1** one of the curved pieces of wood on which a cradle or a rocking chair moves backward and forward. (요람·흔들 의자 밑의) 활 모양의 막대. **2** a rocking chair. 흔들 의자. [*rock*[2]]

off one's rocker, crazy. 미친; 정신이 돌아버린.

rock·er·y [rɑ́kəri / rɔ́k-] *n.* Ⓒ (*pl.* **-er·ies**) a heap of stones or small rocks with flowers among them, as part of a garden. 석가산(石假山) 정원. [*rock*[1]]

***rock·et** [rɑ́kit / rɔ́k-] *n.* Ⓒ **1** a machine propelled by means of self-contained gases. 로켓. ¶ *a ~ gun* 로켓포 / *a ~ launcher* 로켓 발사기〔장치〕. **2** a kind of firework shooting high into the air, used in displays or for signaling. 화전(火箭); 봉화. — *vi.* (P1) go up high and fast. 높이 빠르게 날아오르다. [F. *roquet*]

Rock·ies [rɑ́kiz / rɔ́k-], **the** *n. pl.* = the Rocky Mountains.

rock·ing chair [rɑ́kiŋ tʃɛ̀ər / rɔ́k-] *n.* a chair set on rockers for rocking back and forth. 흔들 의자. [*rock*[2]]

rocking horse [´– `] *n.* a toy horse on rockers for children. 흔들 목마.

rock salt [´ `] *n.* salt got from mines in solid form. 암염(岩塩). [*rock*[1]]

***rock·y**[1] [rɑ́ki / rɔ́ki] *adj.* (**rock·i·er, rock·i·est**) **1** full of rocks; made of rocks; like rock. 바위가 많은; 바위로 된. ¶ *a ~ road.* **2** 《*fig.*》 like a rock; hard and firm. 바위 같은; 부동의; 태연 자약한. [*rock*[1]]

***rock·y**[2] [rɑ́ki / rɔ́ki] *adj.* (**rock·i·er, rock·i·est**) 《*colloq.*》 **1** not firm; shaky; unsteady. 흔들거리는; 불안정한. ¶ *After the recent problems, the company faces a ~*

road ahead. 최근의 문제들로 인해 회사는 앞으로 걱정이 많다. **2** dizzy. 어지러운. [*rock²*]

Rocky Mountains [ˊ-ˊ-], **the** *n. pl.* the chief mountain range in North America, extending from New Mexico to Alaska. 로키 산맥.

ro·co·co [rəkóukou, ròukəkóu] *n.* Ⓤ a style of architecture or decoration with very much ornamentation. 로코코식(式)(cf. *baroque*). — *adj.* 《archit.》 of or on this style; much ornamented but ugly. 로코코식의. ¶ *a building of ~ style* 로코코 양식의 건물. [F.]

:rod [rɑd / rɔd] *n.* Ⓒ **1** a long, straight stick made of wood or metal. 장대; 막대; 지팡이. **2** a stick or whip used to punish. 몽둥이; 회초리. ¶ *kiss the ~* 달게 벌을 받다 / 《*prov.*》 *Spare the ~ and spoil the child.* 귀한 자식은 매로 키워라 / *give the ~* 매질하다. **3** a fishing rod. 낚싯대. **4** a measure of length, equal to 5 1/2 yards. 로드《길이의 단위; 약 5 1/2 야드》. **5** power; authority. 권력; 권위. **6** 《U.S. *sl.*》 a pistol or revolver. 권총. [E.]

have a rod in pickle for, have punishment waiting for. …을 벌주려고 벼르다.

make a rod for oneself [***for one's own back***], do things for which one will be punished. 화를 자초하다; 사서 고생하다.

:rode [roud] *v.* p. of **ride.**

ro·dent [róudənt] *n.* Ⓒ any animal that gnaws with its front teeth, which are constantly growing. 설치 동물. ¶ *Rats, mice, and rabbits are rodents.* 쥐, 생쥐, 토끼들이 설치 동물이다. — *adj.* **1** of or like a rodent. 설치류의[같은]. **2** gnawing; biting. 갉는; 갉아먹는. **3** (of waves) wearing away the shore. (파도가) 기슭을 침식하는. [L. *rodo* gnaw]

ro·de·o [róudiòu / roudéiou] *n.* Ⓒ (*pl.* **-de·os**) 《U.S.》 **1** a contest in which cowboys show skills in roping cattle or riding horses. 로데오《말을 타거나 올가미를 던져 소를 잡거나 하는 카우보이 경기》. **2** the act of driving cattle together for branding. (낙인을 찍기 위해) 가축을 한데 모으기. [Sp. =going round]

rod·o·mon·tade [rɑ̀dəmɑntéid, ròu-, -tɑ́:d] *n.* boastful speech; brag. 허풍; 호언장담; 뻥. — *vi.* (P1) talk rodomontade. 허풍떨다; 흰소리치다. [Person]

roe¹ [rou] *n.* Ⓤ fish eggs. 어란(魚卵); 곤이(鯤鮞). [N.]

roe² [rou] *n.* ⒸⓊ (*pl.* **roes** or *collectively* **roe**) a small kind of deer found in Europe and Asia. 노루. [E.]

roe·buck [róubʌ̀k] *n.* Ⓒ (*pl.* **-bucks** or *collectively* **-buck**) a male deer. 수노루.

Roent·gen rays [réntgən rèiz] *n.* X-rays. 뢴트겐선; 엑스선.

Rog·er [rɑ́dʒər / rɔ́dʒər] *n.* a man's name. 남자 이름.

·rogue [roug] *n.* Ⓒ **1** a dishonest person; a rascal. 불량배; 악당. **2** 《*joc.*》 a mischievous or playful person. 장난이 심한 사람. ¶ *The little ~ has his grandpapa's glasses on.* 저 개구쟁이가 제 할아버지 안경을 썼군. **3** an animal with a savage nature, living apart from the group. 무리를 떠나 사는 사나운 짐승. [? →rogation]

ro·guer·y [róugəri] *n.* (*pl.* **-guer·ies**) **1** ⒸⓊ a dishonest trick; the conduct of rogues. 못된 짓. ¶ *He tempted me to ~.* 그는 날보고 한탕치자고 했다. **2** Ⓤ playful mischief. 장난. ¶ *the ~ of children* 아이들의 장난. [↑]

ro·guish [róugiʃ] *adj.* **1** dishonest; rascally. 옳지 못한; 깡패 같은. **2** mischievous. 장난의. ¶ *a ~ trick.*

roi [rwa] *n.* 《F.》 a king. 왕.

le roi le veult [lə rwa lə vø], the King wills it. 짐이 재가(裁可)하노라.

le roi s'avisera [lə rwa savizəra], the King will consider. 짐이 생각해 보겠노라《재가하지 않음》.

Roi fai·né·ant [rwa fèineiɑ́:ŋ] *n.* King Do-nothing. 이름뿐인 왕. [F.]

roist·er [rɔ́istər] *vi.* (P1) **1** talk noisily and loudly; feast merrily. 술 마시며 큰소리로 떠들다. ¶ *They roistered in a wayside inn.* 그들은 길가의 여인숙에서 한바탕 마시고 놀았다. **2** swager; bluster. 뻐기다; 으스대다. [→rustic]

roist·er·er [rɔ́istərər] *n.* Ⓒ a person who roisters. 시끄럽게 떠드는 사람; 술 먹고 마구 떠들어 대는 사람.

Ro·land [róulənd] *n.* a man's name. 남자 이름.

·role, rôle [roul] *n.* Ⓒ **1** a part taken by an actor or an actress in a play. (극의) 배역. ¶ *Helen wished to play the leading ~.* 헬렌은 주연을 맡고 싶었다 / *Oliver played the ~ of Hamlet.* 올리버가 햄릿역을 했다. **2** a part in real life. (실생활에서의) 임무; 역할. ¶ *He played an important ~ in the conference.* 회의에서 그는 중요한 역할을 했다. [↓]

:roll [roul] *vi.* **1** (P1,2A,3) move along by turning over and over; move on wheels. 구르다; 회전하다. ¶ *~ down* 굴러 떨어지다 / *Rocks rolled down the hill.* 산에서 바위들이 굴러 떨어졌다 / *The horse fell and rolled on the ground.* 말이 넘어져 땅에서 뒹굴었다 / *He rolled over in his bed.* 그는 자면서 몸을 뒤치락거렸다 / *The ball rolled into a hole.* 공이 구멍에 굴러 들어갔다. **2** (P1,2A) 《*on, by, away*》 (of time) pass; move steadily. (시간·세월이) 지나다; 경과하다. ¶ *Two years rolled by.* 2년이 지나갔다. **3** (P1,3) ⓐ (of the eyes) move round. (눈이) 희번덕거리다. ¶ *His eyes ~ strangely.* 그의 눈이 이상하게 희번덕거린다. ⓑ 《*fig.*》 《*in*》 live in (a certain state); indulge in;

wallow in. …하게 지내다; 탐닉하다. **4** (P1,2A,3) (of a ship, etc.) swing from side to side. (배가) 옆질하다(cf. *pitch*[2]). ¶ *The boat rolled heavily* (*to right and left*). 배는 (좌우로) 심하게 옆질했다. **5** (P1,2A,3) (of surfaces) have gentle rising and falling slopes; gently rise and fall; advance with a rising and falling motion. 기복(起伏)하다; 굽이치다; 파동하다. ¶ *a rolling plain* 기복이 있는 평야 / *The hills ~ down to the sea.* 산들은 기복을 이루면서 바다에 이른다 / *The sea rolls.* 바다가 놀친다 / *The flood rolled down the valley.* 큰물이 소용돌이치면서 골짜기를 흘러내려갔다 / *The waves rolled against the ship.* 파도가 굽이치며 뱃전을 때렸다. **6** (P1,2A) float gently; drift slowly and heavily. 감돌다; 떠돌다. ¶ *a rolling mist* 자욱이 낀 안개 / *Smoke rolls up.* 연기가 뭉게뭉게 피어오른다. **7** (P1) make a loud and echoing sound. (우르르) 울리다. ¶ *The thunder rolls in the distance.* 멀리서 천둥이 울린다 / *Drums ~.* 북이 둥둥 울린다. **8** (P1,2A,3) ⓐ travel about; wander. 여행하다; 떠돌다; 헤매다. ⓑ walk heavily with a rocking motion. 몸을 흔들며 걷다. ¶ *An elderly man rolled in his gait.* 늙수그레한 남자가 몸을 흔들면서 걷고 있었다. **9** (P1,2A) move heavily on wheels. (차가) 굴러가다; 나아가다. ¶ *The howitzers rolled by on their way to the front.* 곡사포들이 전선을 향해 전진했다. **10** (P1) move in a cycle. (천체가) 순환〔운행〕하다. —*vt.* **1** (P6,7,13) cause (something) to move by turning over and over; cause (something) to move along on wheels. …을 굴리다; 회전시키다; 굴려 가다. ¶ *~ a ball along the ground* 땅에 공을 굴리다 / 《*sl.*》 *Roll your hoop.* 네 할일이나 해라 / *~ a wheelbarrow* 외바퀴 손수레를 밀고 가다. **2** (P6,7,13) wrap or wind (something) into the shape of a ball or cylinder; cause (something) to move round and round. …을 동그랗게 하다; 감싸다; 돌리다. ¶ *~ yarn into a ball* 실을 동그랗게 감다 / *She rolled her child in a blanket.* 그녀는 아이를 담요로 감쌌다 / 《*fig.*》 *~ a matter in one's mind* 일을 곰씹어 생각하다 / *~ a thing up in paper* 물건을 종이에 뭉쳐 싸다 / *chopped meat rolled in cabbage leaves* 양배추잎에 싼 다진 고기 / *The cat rolled itself into a ball.* 고양이는 동그랗게 몸을 오므렸다. **3** (P6,7,13) ⓐ turn (one's eyes) from side to side. (눈)을 희번덕거리다. ¶ *He rolled his eyes on us.* 우리에게 눈을 부라렸다. ⓑ cause (something) to turn over. …을 쓰러 뜨리다. ¶ *~ someone over* 아무를 때려 눕히다. **4** (P6) make (something) flat, smooth, or thin by using a roller. …을 롤러로 판판하게 하다; …로 밀어 늘리다; 얇게 펴다; (금속)을 압연(壓延)하다. ¶ *rolled steel* 압연강 / *~ the grass* (풀 깎는 기계를 밀며) 풀을 깎다 / *~ a road* 〔*tennis court*〕 길을〔테니스 코트를〕 고르다. **5** (P6) give a swinging motion to (a ship). (배)를 옆질하게 하다. ¶ *The sea rolled the ship to right and left.* 파도로 인해 배가 좌우로 옆질했다. **6** (P6) ⓐ speak, sing, or give off a sound in an easy flow or rising and falling easily. 낭랑하게 노래〔말〕하다. ¶ *The organ rolled forth solemn music.* 풍금에서는 장엄한 곡이 울려퍼졌다 / *~ out a song* 낭랑한 목소리로 노래하다. ⓑ say with vibrating or trembling voice. 떨리는 소리로 말하다. ¶ *~ one's r's,* r를 혀끝을 굴리며 발음하다. **7** (P6,7,13) move (something) in a rising and falling motion. …을 굽이치게 하다. ¶ *The sea rolls its waves against the rock.* 바다는 파도가 쳐 바위에 부딪친다.

be rolling in (=*have much*) *money, etc.* (돈 따위가) 지천이다.

roll in, **a**) come in large numbers. 밀려오다; 쇄도하다. ¶ *Offers of help are rolling in.* 구조 요청이 쇄도하고 있다. **b**) go to bed. 자다. ¶ *I usually ~ in at ten o'clock.* 나는 보통 열 시에 취침한다.

roll on, **a**) move forward steadily and continuously. (꾸준히) 나아가다. **b**) (of time) move steadily; pass. (시간이) 흘러가다; 지나다. ¶ *Time rolls on.* 시간이 간다; 세월이 흐른다.

roll out, make flat, as with a roller. 펴서 판판하게 하다. ¶ *roll out pastry* 〔*dough*〕 반죽을 판판하게 하다 / *roll out metal.*

roll over, cause to turn completely over; turn from one side to the other. 굴리다; 구르다.

roll up, **a**) wrap up (something) by turning over and over. …을 말(아올리)다; 싸다. ¶ *~ up the sleeves of one's shirt* 셔츠의 소매를 걷어올리다 / *~ up one's sleeves* 팔을 걷어붙이다; 일에 착수하다; 열심히 일하다. **b**) increase; collect. (돈 따위가) 모이다; 모으다. **c**) arrive. 나타나다.

—*n.* Ⓒ **1** the act of rolling; a rolling motion. 구르기; 회전. ¶ *have a ~ on the grass* 풀밭에서 한 번 뒹굴다 / *The ~ of the boat threw us into the water.* 배가 기우뚱하며 우리는 바다에 떨어졌다 / *The ship took a ~ to the right.* 배가 오른쪽으로 기우뚱했다. **2** a gentle rising and falling on the surface. (땅의) 굽이침; 기복. ¶ *the ~ of a plain* 〔*waves*〕 들판의 기복〔파도의 굽이침〕. **3** a loud and echoing sound. 울림. ¶ *a distant ~ of thunder* 멀리서 들려오는 천둥 소리 / *the ~ of drums* 북소리. **4** a list of names; an official record. 명부; 기록. ¶ *the ~ of honor* 전사자 명부 / *call a ~* 점호하다; 출석을 부르다 / *put on the rolls* 명부에 싣다. **5** anything made into the shape of a pipe or cylinder by being rolled. 두루마리. ¶ *a ~ of paper* 종이 한 두루마리 / *a ~ of film* 필름 한 통. **6** a small kind of bread. 롤빵. **7** 《U.S. *colloq.*》 a bundle of paper money; money in general. 지폐 뭉치; 돈; 자금. ¶ *It's quite a* ~. 상당한 금액이다. [L. *rota* wheel]

strike** someone **off the rolls, remove someone's name from the list; take from someone the right to practice as a lawyer. …을 명부에서 빼내다; (변호사 명부에서) 제명하다.

roll call [⸗⸗] *n.* the act of calling a list of names to find out who are present. 점호.

·roll·er [róulər] *n.* Ⓒ **1** ⓐ a heavy cylinder of stone, metal, or a wood for grinding, smoothing, crushing, etc. 롤러; 땅 고르는 기계; 압연기; 산륜(散輪). ¶ *A steamroller is used in making and repairing roads.* 증기 롤러는 도로 공사에 쓰인다. ⓑ a person who rolls something. 롤러를 쓰는 사람. **2** a long, swelling wave. (폭풍우 후의) 큰 놀. ¶ *Huge rollers broke on the rockey shore.* 거대한 파도가 바위 많은 해안에 밀려왔다. **3** a kind of canary. 롤러카나리아. [*roll*]

roller coaster [⸗⸗ ⸗⸗] *n.* a railroad for amusement with a train that runs along high, winding, often descending tracks. (유원지의) 롤러코스터; 제트코스터(=《Brit.》 switchback).

roller skate [⸗⸗ ⸗] *n.* a skate with small wheels used on a floor, etc. 롤러스케이트.

roll·er-skate [róulərskèit] *vi.* (P1) skate on roller skates. 롤러스케이트를 타다.

rol·lick [rálik / rɔ́l-] *vi.* (P1) act in a merry way. 까불다; 신이 나서 떠들다. — *n.* ⓊⒸ the state of being merry; a frolic. 신이 나서 까붊. [? *roll+frolic*]

rol·lick·ing [rálikiŋ / rɔ́l-] *adj.* merry; frolicking. 명랑〔쾌활〕한; 까부는.

roll·ing mill [róuliŋmìl] *n.* **1** a factory where metal is rolled into sheets and bars. 압연(壓延) 공장. **2** a machine used for doing this. 압연기. [*roll*]

rolling pin [⸗⸗ ⸗] *n.* a cylinder for rolling out dough. 밀방망이.

rolling stock [⸗⸗ ⸗] *n.* 《*collectively*》 the locomotives, carriages, and trucks of a railroad. (철도의) 차량.

rolling stone [⸗⸗ ⸗] *n.* a person of restless habits, esp. one who is always changing his occupation, situation, and place of abode. 진득하지 못한 사람; 직업을〔주거를〕 자주 바꾸는 사람.

roll·top desk [róultàp désk / -tɔ̀p-] *n.* a desk with a flexible, sliding cover. 접이식 뚜껑이 달린 책상; 롤톱데스크. [*roll*]

〈rolltop desk〉

ro·ly·po·ly [róulipóuli] *n.* Ⓒ (*pl.* **-lies**) **1** a pudding that is rolled up. 꽈배기 푸딩; 롤리폴리. **2** a short and fat person. 땅딸막한 사람. — *adj.* (esp. of a child) short and thick. 토실토실한. ¶ *a* ~ *child.* [*roll*]

Rom. Roman; Romance; Romans.

rom. roman type.

:Ro·man [róumən] *adj.* **1** of Rome or its people. 로마(인)의. ¶ *the* ~ *Empire* 로마제국 / ~ *numerals* 로마 숫자《i, ii, iii, etc.》/ *a* ~ *nose* 매부리코. **2** of the Roman Catholic Church. 카톨릭 교회. **3** 《usu. *r-*》 《print.》 of or in roman type, as distinguish from italic. 로마 글자체(體)의. ¶ ~ *letters.* — *n.* Ⓒ **1** a citizen of Rome. 로마인. **2** a Roman Catholic. 카톨릭 교도. **3** Ⓒ 《usu. *r-*》 《print.》 roman type used in printing. 로마자(字)(cf. *Gothic, italic*). **4** 《*pl.*》 one of books of the New Testament. 로마서. [L. *Roma* Rome]

Roman Catholic [⸗⸗ ⸗⸗] *n.* a member of the Church of Rome. (로마) 카톨릭 교도. — *adj.* of the Church of Rome. (로마) 카톨릭교의.

:ro·mance [roumǽns, róumæns] *n.* **1** Ⓒ the unreal; the fanciful; that which is far away in time or space. 가공의 일; 지어낸 일. **2** Ⓒ a fanciful story; a love story. 공상 같은 이야기; 연애담. **3** Ⓒ a real event that is like a story; a love affair. 소설 같은 사건; 정사(情事). **4** Ⓒ ⓐ a series of unusual adventures. (일련의) 모험. ¶ *His whole life is a* ~. 그의 생애는 일련의 모험이다. ⓑ a story of adventure. 모험담. ¶ *The Arabian Nights and Treasure Island are romances.* 아라비안 나이트나 보물섬은 모험담들이다. **5** Ⓤ 《*R-*》 a language which comes from Latin, such as French, Italian, and Spanish. 로망스어.

— *adj.* 《*R-*》 of Romance languages. 로망스어의.

— *vi.* (P1,3) make up a fanciful story; think or talk in a romantic way; exaggerate; tell a lie. 꾸며낸 이야기를 하다; 과장하다; 거짓말하다; 날조하다. [*Roman*]

ro·manc·er [roumǽnsər] *n.* Ⓒ **1** the writer of a romance; a person who makes up a fanciful story. 전기(傳奇) 소설 작가; 이야기를 꾸며내는 사람; 공상가. **2** a liar. 거짓말쟁이.

Ro·man·esque [ròumənésk] *n.* Ⓤ a style of building using round arches, popular in Europe in the early Middle Ages. 로마네스크 (건축) 양식. — *adj.* of this style. 로마네스크 양식의.

Ro·ma·ni·a [rouméiniə, -njə] *n.* =Rumania.

Ro·ma·ni·an [rouméiniən, -njən] *n.* = Rumanian.

Ro·man·ic [roumǽnik] *adj.* **1** of Romance languages. 로망스어의. **2** of Rome ; of a person of Rome. 로마(인)의.

Ro·man·ist [róumənist] *n.* Ⓒ **1** a member of the Roman Catholic Church. (로마) 카톨릭교도. **2** a student of Roman law. 로마법 연구자.

Ro·man·ize [róumənàiz] *vt., vi.* (P6;1) **1** make (something) or become Roman in character. 로마식으로 하다(되다); 로마화(化)하다. **2** make (someone) or become Roman Catholic. (로마) 카톨릭교(도)화하다.

·ro·man·tic [roumǽntik] *adj.* **1** full of romance; fanciful; appealing to fancy and the imagination. 공상 소설 같은; 로맨틱한; 공상에 잠기는. ¶ ~ *stories of love and adventure* 사랑과 모험의 소설 같은 이야기. **2** having ideas or feelings suited to romance. 낭만적인. ¶ *a* ~ *person* (*mind, imagination*) 로맨틱한 사람(마음, 공상) / *The young couple had a* ~ *idea of married life.* 젊은 부부는 결혼 생활에 대해 낭만적인 생각을 가지고 있었다. **3** fanciful and imaginative rather than real and correct in art or literature. 낭만주의의(cf. *classical*). ¶ *the* ~ *movement* 낭만주의 운동 / ~ *poets* 낭만파 시인.
— *n.* **1** Ⓒ a writer or an artist who believes in romanticism; a romantic person. 낭만파의 사람; 낭만적인 사람. **2** 《*pl.*》 a romantic characteristic, feeling, thought, etc. 공상적인(로맨틱한) 표현(정서·생각)(등). ¶ *indulge in romantics* 낭만적인 생각에 빠지다.
● **ro·man·ti·cal·ly** [-kəli] *adv.*

ro·man·ti·cism [roumǽntəsìzəm] *n.* Ⓤ the romantic movement or spirit in art and literature. 낭만주의; 로맨티시즘(cf. *classicism, realism*).

Ro·man·ti·cist [roumǽntəsist] *n.* Ⓒ a writer or an artist who believes in romanticism. 낭만주의자.

Rom. Cath. Roman Catholic.

:Rome [roum] *n.* **1** the capital of Italy. 로마《이탈리아의 수도》. **2** the ancient Roman Empire. (고대) 로마 제국. ¶《*prov.*》 *Do in* ~ *as the Romans do.* 입향순속(入鄕循俗) / ~ *was not built in a day.* 로마는 하루 아침에 이루어진 것이 아니다. [L. *Roma*]

romp [rɑmp / rɔmp] *vi.* (P1,2A,3) **1** play in a lively and rough way; run quickly and without effort. (아이가) 장난치며 놀다; 뛰어다니다. **2** (esp. in racing, of horses, etc.) move swiftly and easily. (경기·경마에서) 쾌주(快走)하다. ¶ ~ *home* (*in*) (크게 앞질러) 수월하게 이기다. — *n.* Ⓒ **1** a lively game or frolic; a child who likes to romp. 까불며 뛰놂; 그렇게 노는 아이. **2** a child, esp. a girl, who plays roughly and noisily. 말괄량이. [E.]

romp·ers [rάmpərz / rɔ́mp-] *n. pl.* a one-piece outer garment worn by small children at play. 롬퍼즈《아이들 놀이옷》.

Rom·u·lus [rάmjələs / rɔ́m-] *n.* 《Rom. myth.》 the founder and first king of Rome. 로물루스《로마 건설자로 초대왕》.

ron·deau [rάndou / rɔ́ndou] *n.* (*pl.* **-deaux**) artificial forms of short poem with thirteen or ten lines. 론도체(의 시). [→round]

ron·deaux [rάndouz / rɔ́ndouz] *n.* pl. of **rondeau.**

ron·do [rάndou / rɔ́n-] *n.* Ⓒ (*pl.* **-dos**) 《mus.》 a work in which the theme is repeated in a certain way. 론도. [It.]

Rönt·gen rays [réntgən rèiz, -dʒən-, rʌ́ntgən-] *n. pl.* X-rays. 뢴트겐선; 엑스선.

rood [ruːd] *n.* Ⓒ **1** 《*arch.*》 a cross with the figure of Christ on it. 예수 수난의 십자가. **2** 《Brit.》 a quarter of an acre. 루드《토지 면적의 단위. 1/4 에이커》. [E.]
by the rood, certainly; upon one's word. 십자가에 맹세코; 틀림없이.

:roof [ruːf, ruf] *n.* Ⓒ (*pl.* **roofs**) **1** the top covering of a building. 지붕. **2** something like a roof. 지붕 모양의 것. ¶ *the* ~ *of a cave* 동굴 천장 / *the* ~ *of the mouth* 입천장; 구개(口蓋) / *The trees met overhead to form a* ~. 나무들이 머리 위에서 만나 지붕을 이루었다.
be (***left***) ***without a roof,*** be without a house to live in. 거처할 집이 없다; 올데 갈데가 없다.
raise the roof, 《*colloq.*》 be very noisy; create a loud noise. 몹시 시끄럽다; 요란한 소리를 내다. ¶ *The applause raised the* ~. 박수 갈채가 터져나왔다.
the roof of heaven, the sky. 하늘.
the roof of the world, the Pamirs; a high mountain range. 세계의 지붕《파미르 고원; 높은 산맥》.
under someone's roof, staying at someone's house; being entertained by someone. …의 집에 묵어; …의 신세를 지고.
— *vt.* (P6,7,13) **1** cover with a roof. …을 지붕으로 덮다; 지붕을 달다. ¶ ~ *a house* 지붕을 이다. **2** form a roof over. …의 지붕이 되다. ¶ *a road roofed with overhanging branches* 나뭇가지들이 지붕처럼 드리워진 길. [E.]

roof garden [∸∸] *n.* **1** a garden on the flat roof of a building. 옥상 정원. **2** the roof or top story of a building, ornamented with plants, etc. (used for a restaurant, theater, etc.). (식당·극장 등으로 쓰이는) 옥상 정원.

roofing [rúːfiŋ] *n.* **1** material used for roofs. 지붕 재료; 루핑. ¶ *Shingles are a common* ~ *for houses.* 널판자가 흔히 쓰이는 지붕감이다. **2** the act of covering with a roof. 지붕이기.

roof·less [rúːflis, rúf-] *adj.* **1** without a roof. 지붕이 없는; 무개(無蓋)의. **2** having no shelter. 집이 없는. ¶ *After the storm* (*fire*) *many people were left* ~. 폭풍우(화재)로 많은 사람들이 거처를 잃었다.

roof·tree [rúːftrìː, rúf-] *n.* Ⓒ the large timber or piece of wood along the top the roof. 마룻대.

rook[1] [ruk] *n.* Ⓒ **1** a black bird like a crow. 떼까마귀. **2** 《*fig.*》 a person who get a money using a trick at dice, cards, etc. 사기 도박꾼. — *vt.* (P6) **1** cheat (someone) to get money by using a trick at cards; swindle. 도박에서 …을 사기치다. ¶ *He was rooked of his savings.* 저축한 돈을 노름에서 사기당했다. **2** charge (high prices). 바가지 씌우다. ¶ *I was rooked £10 for it.* 나는 그것을 10 파운드나 주고 샀다 / *Five pounds for that! You'v been rooked.* 그게 5 파운드라니, 너 바가지 썼다. [E.]

rook[2] [ruk] *n.* Ⓒ《chess》a chess piece, a castle. 성장(城將). [Pers.]

rook·er·y [rúkəri] *n.* Ⓒ (*pl.* **-er·ies**) **1** a colony of rooks or certain other birds such as penguins; a place where rooks, penguins, etc. breed. 떼까마귀나 펭귄 등의 무리; 그것들의 번식지. **2**《*fig.*》a group of dirty and poor houses. 빈민가. [rook[1]]

rook·ie [rúki] *n.*《*sl.*》**1** a newly-enlisted soldier. 신병(新兵); 신출내기. **2**《U.S.》an inexperienced person; a new member, as in a professional sport. 풋내기; (프로 스포츠의) 신인 선수. [*recruit*]

:room [ru(ː)m] *n.* **1** Ⓒ a part of a house or other building enclosed by walls. 방; 실(室). ¶ *a dining* ~ 식당 / *a living* ~ 거실 / *a* ~ *to let* 셋방 / *a school* ~ 교실 / *I could hear a telephone in the next* ~. 옆방의 전화 소리를 들을 수 있었다. **2** Ⓤ space. 자리; 공간. ¶ *This desk takes up too much* ~. 이 책상은 자리를 너무 많이 차지한다 / *There is* ~ *in the car for another person.* =*There is* ~ *for one more in the car.* 이 차에는 한 사람 더 탈 수 있다 / *The street was so crowded that the cars did not have* ~ *to move.* 거리가 어찌나 붐볐던지 차들이 움직일 틈이 없었다 / *have plenty of* ~ 자리가 많다〔넓다〕. **3** Ⓤ the space within which something may happen; chance; opportunity. 여지; 여유; 기회. ¶ *There is no* ~ *for doubt.* 의심할 여지가 없다 / *His work isn't bad but there's still plenty of* ~ *for improvement.* 그가 하는 일이 나쁘진 않지만 아직 더 개선의 여지가 많다. **4**《*collectively, the* ~》the people in a room. 한 방〔자리〕의 사람들. ¶ *The* ~ *became silent.* 좌중이 조용해졌다 / *keep the whole* ~ *laughing* 방 안 사람들을 모두 웃기다. **5**《*pl.*》a set of private rooms; an apartment; lodgings in another's house. (침실·거실·응접실 등의) 한 가구의 방; 하숙방; 셋방. ¶ *Rooms for rent.* 셋방 있음《게시》/ *rooms in a boarding house* 하숙집의 하숙방 / *Come along to my rooms.* 내 방에 놀러 오려무나.

in the room of, in place of; in stead of. …의 대신에. ¶ *Will you take goods in the* ~ *of money?* 돈 대신 물건을 받아 주겠소.

make room for, leave a space free for; open a passage for. …을 위해 자리를 비우다〔양보하다〕. ¶ *He made* ~ *for the old woman.* 그는 노파에게 자리를 양보하였다.

no room to swing a cat =***no room to turn in,*** very narrow space. 아주 비좁은.

prefer a someone's room to his company, prefer someone's absence. …가 (그 자리에) 없는 것을 더 좋아하다.

set the room in a roar, make the company laugh aloud. 좌중을 크게 웃기다.

— *vi.*《chiefly U.S.》《*with*》live in a room or rooms of another's house; lodge. 하숙하다; 셋방살이하다. ¶ *He rooms at Mr. Smith's house.* 그는 스미스 씨 집에 하숙하고 있다 / *He is rooming at our house.* 그는 우리 집에 세들어 살고 있다. [E.]

roomer [rú(ː)mər] *n.*《chiefly U.S.》a person who lives in a rented room or rooms in another's house; a lodger. 셋방든 사람; 하숙인. [↑]

room·ful [rú(ː)mful] *n.* Ⓒ enough in number or amount to fill a room;《*collectively*》the people in a room. 한 방 가득(한 사람·물건); 방 안의 사람들. ¶ *a* ~ *of furniture* 방 안에 가득한 가구.

room·i·ness [rú(ː)minis] *n.* Ⓤ the state of being spacious. 널찍함.

room·ing house [ˊ-ˊ] *n.*《U.S.》a house with rooms to rent; a boarding house. 하숙집.

room·mate [rú(ː)mmèit] *n.* Ⓒ《U.S.》a person who shares a room with one or more persons. 한방 사람; 동숙인. ¶ *My* ~ *is very untidy.* 내 방 사람은 도무지 깨끗하지 못하다.

room service [ˊ ˊ-] *n.* serving refreshments to a guest in his room, e.g. in a hotel; the department in a hotel or similar establishment responsible for providing such service. (호텔의) 룸서비스; 그 담당자〔부서〕.

room·y [rú(ː)mi] *adj.* (**room·i·er, room·i·est**) having plenty of space; spacious. 널찍한. ¶ *a* ~ *house* 〔*cupboard*〕 널찍한 집〔찬장〕.

roost [ruːst] *n.* Ⓒ **1** a branch, bar or perch on where a bird rests. 새가 앉는 나뭇가지; 홰. **2**《*fig.*》a place to rest; a resting place. 휴식처. ¶ *a robber's* ~ *in the mountain* 산 속의 도둑의 소굴 /《*prov.*》*Curses, like chickens, come home to* ~. 누워 침뱉기; 남잡이가 제잡이.

be at roost, be sitting on a perch; be sleeping. (새가) 홰에 앉다; (사람이) 자다; 잠들다.

go to roost,《*colloq.*》go to bed. 잠자리〔보금자리〕에 들다.

rule the roost, dominate; control. …을 지배하다; 좌지우지하다(cf. *rule the roast*).

— *vi.* (P1) sit on a perch; go to bed. 홰에 앉다; 잠자리에 들다. [E.]

roost·er [rúːstər] *n.* Ⓒ《U.S.》a male chicken; a cock. 수탉.

:root [ruːt] *n.* Ⓒ **1** a part of a plant usu. growing under the ground;《*pl.*》a plant with a root used as food; root crops. 뿌리; 근채류(根菜類). **2** 《*fig.*》 a part of anything like a root. 뿌리 모양의 것; 밑동; 밑뿌리; 기슭. ¶ *the ~ of the tongue* 혀뿌리 / *at the ~ of a hill* 산기슭에 / *the roots of the hair* 모근. **3** the essential part; the cause; the source; the origin. 근본; 근저; 원인; 근원. ¶ *go to* 〔*get at, get to*〕 *the ~ of a matter* 사물의 본질을 규명하다 / *the ~ of the trouble* 말썽의 원인 / *The love of fame is the ~ of his ruin.* 공명심이 그의 파멸의 원인이다 / *His illness has its roots in unhappiness.* 그의 병은 불행 탓이다. **4** 《math.》 a quantity that produces a given quantity when multiplied by itself. 근(根). ¶ *a cubic* 〔*square*〕 *~* 세곱〔세제곱〕근. **5** 《linguistics》 the essential form of a word. 어근; 원형. 參考 지금은 base를 많이 씀. ¶ *'Roll' is the ~ of 'roller' and 'enroll'.*

pull up by the roots, uproot. 뿌리째 뽑다.

root and branch, 《*fig.*》 entirely; thoroughly. 완전히; 철저히. ¶ *This evil system must be destroyed ~ and branch.* 이 사악한 조직은 철저하게 분쇄되어야 한다.

take 〔***strike***〕 ***root,*** **a**) send out roots. 뿌리박다. **b**) become established. 정착하다. ¶ *The idea gradually began to take ~.* 그 관념〔의식〕이 서서히 정착하기 시작했다.

— *vt.* **1** (P6,13) cause (a plant) to take roots; plant. …을 뿌리 내리게 하다; 심다. **2** (P6,13) (of nonmaterial things) fix; establish firmly. …을 정착시키다; 고정시키다. ¶ *Fear rooted him to the ground.* 그는 무서워 그 자리에서 움직이지 못했다 / *~ a principle in the mind* 주의를 마음에 심다 / *deeply rooted hate* 뿌리 깊은 증오심. **3** (P6,13) be the cause, base, principle, etc. of (something); establish deeply. …에 근거하다; 기인하다. ¶ *be rooted in the fact* 사실에 근거하다 / *The matter is rooted in his idleness.* 그 일은 그의 게으름이 원인이다. **4** (P7) remove completely. …을 뿌리 뽑다; 근절시키다. ¶ *~ out superstition* 미신을 타파하다 / *~ out crime* 범죄를 근절하다.

— *vi.* **1** (P1) send out roots; become established. 뿌리 박다; 정착하다. **2** (P2A,3) dig; turn up or over. 파다; 파헤치다. ¶ *A pig roots (about) for acorns with its snout.* 돼지가 주둥이로 도토리를 찾아 땅을 후빈다. **3** (P1) search for something by turning things over. …을 헤집어〔뒤적여〕 찾다. ¶ *~ about in a drawer* 서랍 속을 뒤적이다. **4** (P1,3) 《U.S. *sl.*》 encourage by cheering. 성원〔응원〕하다. ¶ *They rooted for our team.* 그들은 우리 팀을 응원했다. [E.]

root crop [ˊˋ] *n.* a crop grown for its root, which people eat, such as sweet potatoes. (고구마 등) 근채(根菜) 작물.

root·er [rúːtər] *n.* Ⓒ 《U.S. *sl.*》 a person who supports or cheers. (열광적인)응원〔지지〕자.

root hair [ˊˋ] *n.* 《bot.》 any of the hairlike tubular outgrowths from a growing root, which serve to absorb water and minerals from the soil. 근모(根毛); 뿌리털.

rootle [rúːtl] *vi.* (P2A,3) 《Brit.》 turn up or dig in the earth. (돼지 등이) 주둥이로 땅을 헤집다. ¶ *Pigs are rootling for food.* 돼지들이 먹이를 찾아 땅을 헤집고 있다. [*root*]

root·let [rúːtlit, rúːt-] *n.* Ⓒ a branch of a root. 지근(枝根); 잔뿌리.

root·stock [rúːtstɑ̀k / -stɔ̀k] *n.* Ⓒ a stem under the ground like a root. 근경(根莖).

:rope [roup] *n.* **1** ⒸⓊ a thick, strong cord. 새끼; (밧)줄; (노)끈; 로프. ¶ *coil up a ~* 밧줄을 둘둘 감다 / *They tied the prisoner up with ropes.* 포승으로 죄수를 단단히 묶었다. **2** 《*the ~*》 a cord used in hanging; punishment by hanging. 목매는 밧줄; 교수형. **3** 《*pl.*》 a box ring enclosed by the ropes. 권투장; 링. **4** Ⓒ a number of things linked together in the form of a cord. 한 꿰미; 한 두름 (등). ¶ *a ~ of pearls* 진주 한 꿰미 / *a ~ of hair* 머리 한 타래. **5** Ⓒ a sticky thread, esp. in wine, dough, etc. (포도주, 반죽 등의) 실모양의 끈끈한 물질; 진. **6** 《*the ~s*》 the hang. 요령.

a rope of sand, 《*fig.*》 a frail, useless bond or support. 믿을 수 없는 결합〔지지〕.

be at 〔***come to***〕 ***the end of*** *one's* ***rope,*** reach the limit of one's means or endurance. 백계무책이다; 진퇴유곡에 빠지다.

give *someone* (***plenty of***) ***rope,*** give someone freedom of action in the hope that they will cause their own ruin or failure in the end. (실패할 것을 기대하고) …을 멋대로 내버려두다.

know 〔***learn***〕 ***the ropes,*** 《*colloq.*》 know well about the details of a business, etc. 사정에 정통하다; 훤히 알다.

on the high ropes, in high spirits; strung up. 의기양양해서; 신이 나서.

on the rope (of mountain climbers) roped together. (등산자들이) 자일에 몸을 서로 이어매고.

on the ropes, **a**) against the ropes of a boxing ring and almost not able to stand up. (권투에서) 로프에 매달려. **b**) almost defeated; in a desperate condition. 궁지에 몰려.

put *someone* ***up to the ropes*** =***show*** *someone* ***the ropes,*** teach someone the arrangements, customs, etc. of a business, etc. …에게 요령을 일러주다.

— *vt.* (P6,7,13) **1** fasten or tie (something) with a rope. …을 밧줄로 묶다. ¶ *~ and tie someone's feet* 아무의 다리를 밧줄로 단단히 묶다 / *~ a box* 상자를 끈으로 묶다. **2** separate or enclose (a place) with a rope. …을 밧줄로 구획하다. ¶ *~ off a place from* …하지 않도록 어떤 장소에 줄을

쳐서 경계를 짓다.

— *vi.* (P1) form sticky thread. 밧줄이 되다; 끈적끈적한 실처럼 되다; 진을 내다. ¶ *Some kind of candy are cooked till they ~.* 캔디 중에는 끈적끈적해지도록 고아서 만든 것도 있다. [O.E. *rāp*]

rope·danc·er [róupdæ̀nsər / -dɑ̀:n-] *n.* Ⓒ a person who walks or dances on a rope high above the ground. 줄타기 광대.

rope·walk [róupwɔ̀:k] *n.* a long, low, narrow place used for making ropes. (길고 좁다란 통로가 있는) 밧줄 공장. [*rope*]

rope·walk·er [⌐wɔ̀:kər] *n.* =ropedancer.

rope·way [róupwèi] *n.* a means of carrying passengers or goods in vehicles suspended from an overhead cable or cables. 로프웨이; 공중 삭도; 공중 케이블.

rop·y [róupi] *adj.* (**rop·i·er, rop·i·est**) forming sticky threads. (액체 등이) 끈적끈적한; 끈끈한.

Ro·sa [róuzə] *n.* a woman's name. 여자 이름.

ro·sa·ry [róuzəri] *n.* Ⓒ (*pl.* **-ries**) **1** 《Cath.》 a string of beads for counting a series of prayers; a series of prayers thus counted on a rosary. 로사리오; 묵주(默珠); 로사리오의 기도. **2** a rose garden. 장미꽃밭. [↓]

:rose[1] [rouz] *n.* Ⓒ **1** a sweet-smelling flower growing on a bush with thorny stems. 장미(꽃). ¶ 《*prov.*》 *No ~ without a thorn.* 가시 없는 장미는 없다《완전한 행복이란 없다》. **2** Ⓤ a pink color. 장밋빛. ¶ *Her dress was ~.* **3** Ⓤ 《*pl.*》 rosy complex. 발그레한 얼굴빛. ¶ *She has roses in her cheeks.* 그녀의 볼은 발그레하다. **4** something shaped like a rose. 장미꽃 모양의 것. **5** 《her.》 the sign of England. 영국을 나타내는 휘장.

a bed of (life's) roses =***a path strewn with roses,*** very easy and pleasant conditions. 걱정없는 환경〔자리〕.

gather (life's) roses, seek the pleasures of life. 환락을 추구하다.

It is not all roses. It is not always easy. 꼭 편하지만은 않다.

under the rose, in secret; in strict confidence. 비밀히.

— *adj.* of a rose color; rosy. 장밋빛의.

— *vt.* (P6) make (something) rosy. …을 장밋빛으로 하다. [L. *rosa*]

:rose[2] [rouz] *v.* p. of **rise.**

ro·se·ate [róuziit, -èit] *adj.* **1** of a rose color; rosy. 장밋빛의. **2** hopeful: optimistic. 유망한; 낙관적인. [*rose*[1]]

rose·bud [róuzbʌ̀d] *n.* Ⓒ the bud of a rose. 장미 봉오리.

rose·bush [róuzbù∫] *n.* Ⓒ a bush bearing roses. 장미나무〔덩굴〕.

rose color [⌐ ⌐–] *n.* a pink color. 장밋빛.

rose·col·ored, 《Brit.》 **-col·oured** [róuzkʌ̀lərd] *adj.* **1** pink. 장밋빛의. **2** hopeful; optimistic. 유망한; 낙관적인.

rose·leaf [róuzlì:f] *n.* a leaf of a rose bush; a petal of a rase. 장미(나무)잎; 장미꽃잎.

rose·mar·y [róuzmɛ̀əri] *n.* Ⓒ (*pl.* **-maries**) 《bot.》 an evergreen and sweet-smelling bush, the leaves of which are used for making perfume. 로즈메리. [L. *ros* dew, →marine]

ro·sette [rouzét] *n.* Ⓒ **1** a ribbon in the shape of a rose used as an ornament. 장미꽃 매듭〔술〕. **2** a piece of stone or glass cut in the shape of a rose and used as an ornament. 장미꽃 (모양의) 장식. [→rose[1]]

rose water [⌐ ⌐–] *n.* **1** a sweet-smelling water made from roses. 장미 향수. **2** flattery. 아첨; 겉치레 말.

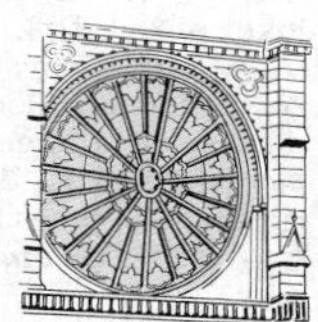
〈rose window〉

rose window [⌐ ⌐–] *n.* an ornamental round window chiefly used in churches. 장미창.

rose·wood [róuzwùd] *n.* Ⓤ a beautiful, hard, dark-red wood used for furniture. 자단(紫檀).

ros·i·ly [róuzili] *adv.* **1** in a rosy manner; with a rosy color. 장밋빛으로 **2** cheerfully; optimistically. 쾌활하게; 낙관적으로.

ros·in [rázən, rɔ́(:)zn] *n.* Ⓤ a solid substance obtained from the sticky juice of the pine tree. 로진《송진에서 테레빈유(油)를 채취하고 남은 물질》. — *vt.* (P6) rub (something) with rosin. …을 로진으로 문지르다. ¶ *~ a violin bow.* [→resin]

ros·i·ness [róuzinis] *n.* Ⓤ the state or quality of being rosy. 장밋빛임; 유망함; 낙관적임. ¶ *the ~ of the sky at the fall of day* 해질녘의 장밋빛 하늘. [→rose[1]]

Ross [rɑs / rɔs] *n.* a man's name. 남자 이름.

ros·ter [rástər / rɔ́s-] *n.* **1** 《mil.》 a list of officers and enlisted men available for duty. 근무〔당번〕표. **2** any list or roll of names. 명부; 명단. [Du. *rooster*]

ros·tra [rástrə / róstrə] *n.* pl. of **rostrum.**

ros·trum [rástrəm / rɔ́strəm] *n.* Ⓒ (*pl.* **-trums** or **-tra**) a platform for public speaking; a stage. 설교단; 연단. ¶ *take the ~* 등단(登壇)하다. [L. =beak & in *pl.* platform]

·ros·y [róuzi] *adj.* (**ros·i·er, ros·i·est**) **1** like a rose; rose-red; blushing. 장밋빛 같은; 장밋빛의; 홍안의. ¶ *~ cheeks.* **2** 《*fig.*》 bright; cheerful; promising; optimistic. 밝은; 쾌활한; 유망한; 낙관적인. ¶ *a ~ future* 밝은 미래 / *~ views* 낙관론 / *He painted a ~ picture of the company's prospects.* 그는 회사의 전망을 낙관적으로 내다봤다. [→rose[1]]

rot [rɑt / rɔt] *v.* (**rot·ted, rot·ting**) *vi.* **1** (P1) decay; go bad; spoil. 썩다; 상하다. ¶ *So much rain will make the fruit* ~. 이렇게 비가 많이 오면 과일이 상하겠다 / *Dampness rots wood.* 습기로 목재가 상한다. **2** (P1,2A) 《*fig.*》 become spoilt or useless. 못쓰게 되다; 타락하다. ¶ *Too much television rots your brain.* 텔레비전을 너무 보면 네 머리에 좋지 않다. **3** (P1) 《Brit. *sl.*》 talk nonsense; talk ironically. 허튼소리 하다; 빈정거리다. ¶ *He is only rotting.* 그저 괜한 소리다. —*vt.* (P6) **1** cause to rot. …을 썩이다. ¶ 《*fig.*》 *They left him to* ~ *in prison for twenty years.* 그를 20년이나 감옥에서 썩게 내버려두었다. **2** 《Brit. *sl.*》 make fun of; joke. …을 놀리다.
—*n.* Ⓤ **1** decay; rotten matter. 부패; 썩은 것. **2** certain diseases of plants; a liver disease of a sheep. (식물의) 부패증; (양의) 디스토마병. **3** 《Brit. *sl.*》 nonsense; rubbish. 허튼 소리. ¶ *What* ~*!* 무슨 말 같잖은 소리 / *Don't talk* ~*!* 바보같은 소리 그만 해라.
—*interj.* an exclamation expressing disgust, contempt, etc. 시시하게; 젠장 (등). ¶ *Rot!* 시시한〔당치도 않은〕 소리. [E.]

rota [róutə] *n.* **1** a list of persons who take turns at certain duties; a list of duties to be performed in turn. 당번 명단; 그 임무. **2** 《*R*-》 the supreme court in the Roman Catholic Church. 교황청 항소원(抗訴院). [→rotate]

Ro·tar·i·an [routέəriən] *n.* Ⓒ a member of a Rotary Club. 로터리 클럽 회원. —*adj.* of Rotary Clubs. 로터리 클럽의.

ro·ta·ry [róutəri] *adj.* turning around; rotating. 회전하는. ¶ *a* ~ *fan* 선풍기 / *a* ~ *machine* 〔*press*〕 윤전기 / *a* ~ *engine* 로터리엔진(cf. *reciprocating engine*). —*n.* (*pl.* **-ries**) **1** Ⓒ a rotary machine. 윤전기. **2** 《*R*-》 = Rotary Club. [→rotate]

Rotary Club [∠-- ∠] *n.* an association of business and professional men organized for social and charitable purposes. 로터리 클럽. [↓]

ro·tate [róuteit / -∠] *vi.* (P1) **1** turn on an axis; turn in a circle. 회전(回轉)하다; 돌다. ¶ *The earth rotates on its axis.* 지구는 그 축을 중심으로 자전한다. **2** follow in regular and repeated succession; take turns. 순환하다; 교대하다. ¶ *The seasons* ~. / *Ten men* ~ *at this job.* 열 사람이 이 일을 교대로 한다. —*vt.* (P6,13) cause (something) to turn on an axis; cause (something) to take turns or to happen in turns. …을 회전시키다; 교대하게 하다. ¶ ~ *crops* 작물을 윤작(輪作)하다 / ~ *men in office* 교대로 직무를 맡기다. [L.=wheel]

ro·ta·tion [routéiʃən] *n.* ⓊⒸ the act of rotation; the state of being rotated. 회전; 순환; 교대(cf. *revolution*). ¶ *the* ~ *of a top* 팽이의 회전 / *the daily* ~ *of the earth* 지구의 자전 / *the* ~ *of seasons* 사계의 순환.
by 〔*in*〕 ***rotation,*** in turn; in regular succession. 번갈아; 윤번으로. ¶ *hold office in* ~ 윤번제로 재직(在職)하다.
the rotation of crops, varying the crops grown in the same field. 윤작(輪作); 돌려짓기.

ro·ta·to·ry [róutətɔ̀ːri / -təri] *adj.* **1** rotating; rotary. 회전하는. ¶ ~ *motion* 회전 운동. **2** causing rotation. 순환하는. ¶ *a* ~ *organ* 순환 기관. **3** passing or following from one to another continuously. 윤번(제)의. ¶ *a* ~ *office in a club* 클럽의 임원 윤번제. [→rotate]

rote [rout] *n.* Ⓤ a set, mechanical way of doing something; repeated study using memory rather than understating. 기계적인 방법〔암기법〕. [E.]
by rote, by memory. 기계적으로. ¶ *learn by* ~ (기계적으로) 암기하다.

•**rot·ten** [rɑ́tn / rɔ́tn] *adj.* (**-er, -est**) **1** decayed; spoiled. 썩은. ¶ *a* ~ *egg* 썩은 달걀. **2** 《*fig.*》 corrupt; morally base. 타락〔부패〕한. ¶ ~ *to the core* 속속들이 부패한. **3** not in good condition; likly to break. 취약한; 부서지기 쉬운. ¶ *The* ~ *ice gave way, letting the skater fall into the water.* 얇게 언 얼음이 꺼져 내리며 스케이터는 물에 빠졌다. **4** 《*sl.*》 bad; disagreeable. 나쁜; 불쾌한. ¶ *a* ~ *voice* 듣기 싫은 목소리 / *a* ~ *luck* 불운 / ~ *weather* 궂은 날씨 / *I felt* ~ *about having to sack him, but I had no alternative.* 그를 해고하기가 꺼려졌지만 달리는 대안이 없었다. [*rot*]

rot·ten·ness [rɑ́tnnis / rɔ́t-] *n.* Ⓤ the state of being rotten; decay; corruption. 부패; 타락; 하등(下等).

ro·tund [routʌ́nd] *adj.* **1** round; plump. 둥근; 통통한. ¶ *a* ~ *face* 통통한 얼굴 / *a* ~ *figure* 통통한 몸매. **2** (of a voice, speech, etc.) full-sounding; (of an expression, a style, etc.) exaggerated; grandiloquent. 음성이 낭랑한; (문체 등이) 과장된. ¶ *a* ~ *voice* 낭랑한 음성 / 《*fig.*》 *a* ~ *style of writing* 과장된 문체. [→rota]

ro·tun·da [routʌ́ndə] *n.* a round building or room, esp. one with a dome. 둥근 지붕의 건물; 둥근 천정의 홀. [↑]

ro·tun·di·ty [routʌ́ndəti] *n.* **1** the condition or state of being round or plump. 통통함; 둥긂. ¶ *the* ~ *of a country girl* 시골 처녀의 오동통함. **2** something round. 둥근〔구형의〕 것. **3** rounded fullness of tone; (음성의) 낭랑함. ¶ *There is smoothness and* ~ *in his speech.* 그의 말씨에는 매끄러움과 낭랑함이 있다. [→rotund]

rou·ble [rúːbəl] *n.* =Ruble.

roué [ruːéi, ∠-] *n.* 《F.》 a man who leads a wild life; a rake. 난봉꾼; 탕아.

rouge [ruːʒ] *n.* Ⓤ red powder or paste used for coloring the cheeks and lips. 입술연지; 루주. —*vi., vt.* (P1;6) color (something) with rouge. …에 루주를 바르다. [L. *rubeus* red]

:**rough** [rʌf] *adj.* **1** not smooth; not level; coarse. 거친; 거칠거칠한; 울퉁불퉁한(opp. smooth). ¶ ~ *hands* 거친 손 / *feel* ~ (감촉이) 껄끄럽다 / *The road is* ~. 길이 울퉁불퉁하다 / ~ *country* 기복이 심한 지역. **2** violent; stormy. 악천후의; 폭풍우의. ¶ ~ *weather* 험악한 날씨 / *The sea is* ~. 바다가 거칠다 / *a* ~ *night* 폭풍우가 치는 밤 / *a* ~ *voyage* 난항. **3** not gentle; rude; vulgar. 난폭한; 거친; 버릇없는. ¶ *a* ~ *man* 난폭한 사람 / *a* ~ *usage of children* 아이들에 대한 난폭한 대우 / *a* ~ *gesture* 거친 몸짓 / *be* ~ *of* 〔*in*〕 *speech* 말씨가 사납다 / *a* ~ *welcome* 거칠지만 진심이 담긴 환영 / *He is* ~ *in manner.* 행동이 거칠다; 버릇이 없다. **4** (of sounds) harsh; (of tastes) harsh or sharp. (소리가) 귀에 거슬리는; (맛이) 떫은. ¶ ~ *music* 귀에 거슬리는 음악 / ~ *wine* 신 포도주 / *a* ~ *clanging of bells* 요란한 벨소리. **5** not refined; natural; raw. 미가공의; 손질이 안 된; 날림의. ¶ ~ *ruby* 루비 원석 / *a* ~ *oat* 쓿지 않은 귀리 / ~ *skin* 원피(原皮); 생가죽. **6** without polish or fine finish. 마무리가 덜 된; 다듬어지지 않은. ¶ *The work is still in a* ~ *state.* 작품은 아직 마무리가 안 된 상태이다 / *a* ~ *sketch* 밑그림. **7** not precise; not complete. 대강의; 어림한. ¶ *a* ~ *guess* 어림짐작 / *a* ~ *estimate* 어림셈 / *give someone a* ~ *outline* 아무에게 대략적인 윤곽을 설명하다. **8** 《*colloq.*》 difficult; severe. 괴로운; 엄한; 모진. ¶ *have a* ~ *time* 고된 시련을 겪다 / *You are* ~ *on him in saying so.* 그를 그렇게 말하는 것은 심하다.

rough and ready, made in a hurry to use for a short time. 날림이지만 그런대로 잠시 동안 쓸 만한.

— *adv.* roughly. 거칠게; 함부로; 대충. ¶ *treat someone* ~ 아무를 심하게 대하다 / *live* ~ 고생하다.

— *n.* **1** Ⓤ that which is rough; a rough part of something. 거친 것; 꺼칠꺼칠한 것. **2** Ⓤ a rough piece ground. 울퉁불퉁한 땅. **3** Ⓒ 《Brit.》 a rough person. 난폭한 사람; 망나니. **4** Ⓤ an unfinished or natural state; a rough sketch. 미완성; 미가공; 초벌그림. **5** Ⓤ a difficult state. 고생. ¶ *the* ~ *and the smooth* 인생의 부침(浮沈).

in the rough, **a**) in an unfinished or natural state. 미완성의; 미가공의. **b**) nearly. 대강; 대충. **c**) 《*colloq.*》 in a difficult situation. 곤경에; 난처해서.

take the rough with the smooth, accept facts as they are; be prepared to meet the hardships of life. 고락을 감수하다; 인생의 부침을 덤덤하게 맞이하다.

— *vt.* **1** (P6) make (something) rough. …을 거칠게 하다; 헝클어뜨리다. ¶ *The wind roughed up her hair.* 바람으로 그녀의 머리가 헝클어졌다 / *The bird roughed its feathers.* 새가 털을 부스스하게 곤두세웠다. **2** (P6,7) ⓐ 《*up*》 cut roughly. 건목치다; 대충 윤곽을 내다. ¶ ~ *a diamond.* ⓑ treat roughly. …을 학대하다. **3** 《*in, out*》 sketch roughly. …의 개략을 쓰다. — *vi.* become rough; behave roughly. 거칠게 되다; 난폭하게 굴다. [E.]

rough it, **a**) live without comforts or conveniences. 불편한 생활을 하다; 고생하다. ¶ ~ *it in the woods* 숲 속에서 고생하다. **b**) behave rudly. 난폭하게 굴다.

rough out, plan in outline. 대충 계획을 세우다.

rough·age [rʌ́fidʒ] *n.* Ⓤ **1** rough or coarse material. 조악한〔거친〕 재료. **2** the coarse parts or kinds of food. 조악한 음식물.

rough-and-read·y [rʌ́fənrédi] *adj.* rough or crude, but effective enough; hastily prepared. 졸속주의의; 임시 변통의; 날림의. [→rough]

rough-and-tum·ble [rʌ́fəntʌ́mbl] *adj.* violent and disorderly; disregarding all rules and formalities. 무질서한; 뒤죽박죽의; 멋대로의. — *n.* Ⓒ a fight or struggle of this kind. 난투; 난전.

rough·cast [rʌ́fkɑ̀:st] *n.* Ⓤ coarse plaster. 회반죽. — *a.* coated with this. 애벌칠의. — *vt.* (P6) **1** coat walls with rough-cast. 초벽을 치다; 애벌칠하다. **2** plan out in the rough ; arrange the general form of. 대충 계획을 세우다〔틀을 잡다〕.

rough diamond [´–´––] *n.* = diamond in the rough.

rough·dry [rʌ́fdrài] *vt.* (P6) dry (clothes) after washing without ironing them. …을 빨아서 다리지 않고 말리기만 하다.

rough·en [rʌ́fən] *vt., vi.* (P6;1) make (something) rough; become rough. …을 거칠게 하다; 거칠게 되다. ¶ *The wind roughens one's skin.* 바람에 피부가 거칠어진다.

rough-hew [rʌ́fhjú:] *vt.* (P6) (**-hewed, -hewn** or **-hewed**) cut or chop (stone, timber, etc.) roughly or without smoothing; shape or form roughly. (돌·재목 등)을 대충 깎다; 건목치다. ¶ ~ *a statue* 석상을 대강 다듬다 / 《*fig.*》 He rough-hewed his novels rapidly and then polishes slowly. 그는 소설을 빠르게 초잡은 다음 천천히 다듬는다.

rough-hewn [rʌ́fhjú:n] *v.* pp. of **rough-hew.** — *adj.* roughly shaped; rugged; unpolished. 대충 깎은; 건목친; 거친. ¶ *a wall of* ~ *blocks* 막벽돌로 쌓은 담.

rough-house [rʌ́fhàus] *n.* 《*colloq.*》 an unruly meeting; a fight, esp. indoors. (집·방 안에서의) 난장판; 싸움질.

***rough·ly** [rʌ́fli] *adv.* **1** in a rough manner. 거칠게; 함부로. **2** approximately. 대충; 대략. ¶ ~ *speaking* 대충 말하면.

rough·ness [rʌ́fnis] *n.* Ⓤ the state or

quality of being rough; harshness; coarseness. 거칢; 난폭; 조잡.

rough·rid·er [rʌ́fràidər] *n.* Ⓒ a person who is skilled in breaking in and riding rough wild horses. (사나운 말의) 조마사.

rough·shod [rʌ́fʃɑ́d / ⁻ʃɔ́d] *adj.* (of a horse) having horseshoes with projecting nails (미끄러지지 않게) 스파이크 편자를 박은.

ride roughshod over, follow one's own way without regard to others; treat roughly. (남이야 뭐라든) 제 고집대로 하다; 거칠게 다루다. ¶ *The chairman rode ~ over the committee's suggestion.* 의장은 위원회측의 제안을 뭉개 버렸다.

rough-spo·ken [rʌ́fspòukən] *adj.* using rough, coarse language. 말을 거칠게 하는.

rou·lette [ru:lét] *n.* **1** Ⓤ a gambling game played with a turning wheel and a ball. 룰렛. **2** Ⓒ a small, toothed wheel for making rows of marks or dots. (점선을 치는) 점선기; (재봉용) 룰렛. [F.]

〈roulette 1〉

Rou·ma·ni·a [ru(:)méiniə] *n.* =Rumania

Rou·ma·ni·an [ru(:)méiniən] *adj., n.* =Rumanian.

:round [raund] *adj.* **1** ⓐ shaped like a ball, ring, circle or cylinder; curved like part of a circle. 둥근; 구형(球形)의; 원통형의; 반원형의. ¶ *a ~ apple* / *a ~ face* 동그스름한 얼굴 / *a ~ window* / *a ~ arch* 반원형 아치. ⓑ curved; humped. 굽은; 곱사등의. ¶ *~ shoulders* 새우등 / *a ~ back* 곱사등. **2** nicely fat; plump. 포동포동 살찐; 토실토실한. ¶ *a ~ man* 포동포동 살찐 사람 / *~ cheeks* 〔*arms*〕 토실토실한 볼〔팔〕. **3** moving in a circle. 한 바퀴 도는; 일주하는. ¶ *a ~ trip* 주유〔왕복〕 여행 / *a ~ dance* 원무 / *a ~ game* (조를 짜지 않고) 각자 단독으로 하는 게임. **4** (of a voice) full, rich, and loud; sonorous; (of a style) flowing; (of a taste) rich and mellow. (음성이) 낭랑하게 울리는; (문체가) 유창〔원숙〕한; (맛이) 향긋한. ¶ *a ~ voice* / *a ~ style* 유창한 문체 / *a ~ wine* 향긋한 포도주. **5** full; complete. 완전한; 순전한. ¶ *a ~ dozen* 꼭 한 다스 / *a ~ trick* 순전한 사기 / *a ~ angle* 360도. **6** pretty much; ample. 상당한; 꽤 많은. ¶ *a good ~ sum of money* 꽤 많은 돈 / *at a ~ price* 비싸게. **7** nearly correct; approximate. 어림수의; 대략의. ¶ *in ~ numbers* 어림수로. **8** straight forward; frank; plain and blunt. 솔직한; 곧이곧대로의; 기탄 없는. ¶ *a ~ oath* 심한 욕설 / *be ~ with others* 남에게 솔직하게 말하다 / *He scolded me in good, ~ terms.* 그는 사정없이 마구 나를 몰아세우더군. **9** vigorous; brisk. 활발한; 씩씩한. **10** 《phon.》 pronounced with rounded lips. 원순음(圓脣音)의.

— *n.* Ⓒ **1** something round; anything shaped like a ball or circle or tree trunk. 원; 원형의 물건; 고리; 공(모양의 것); 원통형의 것. ¶ *this earthly ~* 지구 / *dance in a ~* 원무를 추다 / *the golden ~* 금빛 왕관. **2** 《often. *pl.*》 a circular course; a regular course. 한 바퀴 (돎); 순회 (구역). ¶ *go for a long ~* (먼 거리를) 한 바퀴 빙 돌아오다 / *a policeman on his rounds* 구역 순찰 중인 경찰관 / *The watchman makes his rounds every hour.* 경비원은 매시간 자기 구역을 순회한다 / *doctor's ~* 의사의 회진 / *make the rounds of nightclubs* 나이트클럽을 차례차례 마시며 순례하다. **3** a series of succession of actions, events, duties, etc. 연속; 순환. ¶ *a ~ of visits* 순방(巡訪) / *one's daily ~* 나날의 생활〔일〕 / *the ~ of the seasons* 계절의 순환. **4** a group of people. (사람의)한 무리. ¶ *a ~ of students* 일단의 학생들. **5** a part into which a fight or a game is divided. (승부의) 한 게임; 한 판 ¶ *a fight of fifteen rounds* 15회전 / *a ~ of card* 카드 놀이 한 판. **6** 《mus.》 a song sung by several persons beginning at different times; a dance which moves in a circle. 돌림노래; 원무. **7** a discharge of guns by a group of soldiers altogether; powder, bullets, etc. for one such discharge. 일제 사격; 그에 필요한 탄약; 탄알. ¶ *fire two rounds* 일제 사격을 두 번 계속하다 / *Only three rounds of amunition were left.* 탄알은 세 번의 일제 사격분만 남겨졌다. **8** an act which a number of people do together. (박수·함성 따위의) 한 차례. ¶ *a ~ of applause* 〔*cheers*〕 한 차례의 박수 갈채〔환성〕 / *three rounds of cheers* 만세 삼창; 세 차례 터져 나오는 환성. **9** 《sculp.》 a figure which is full and completely rounded. 환조(丸彫).

go the round*(*s*) *of (=*be passed around*) *a place.* (소문이) …에 퍼지다. ¶ *News goes the ~ of a village.* 소문이 온 마을에 돌았다.

— *adv.* =around.

round about, **a**) in every direction around. 둘레에; 사방에. **b**) in or to the opposite direction. 반대쪽에.

round and round, many times around; with repeated revolutions. 몇 번이고; 빙글빙글. ¶ *turn ~ and ~* 빙글빙글 계속 돌다.

show someone round, act as guide for someone. …을 안내하고 다니다.

sleep the clock round ⇨sleep.

taking something all round, considering it from every point of view. …을 여러 모로 생각하다.

— *prep.* =around.

— *vt.* **1** (P6,7) make (something) round ; pronounce with round lips. …을 둥글게 하다; …을 입술을 둥글게 하고 발음하다. ¶ ~

one's eyes 눈을 휘둥그레 뜨다 / ~ *the corners of a table* 탁자 모서리를 둥글리다 / *stones rounded by the action of water* 물의 작용으로 둥글게 된 돌들 / *We ~ our lips to say 'oo'.* 'oo'를 발음할 때 입술을 둥글게 한다. **2** (P6,7) 《*fig.*》 complete; finish. 완성하다. ¶ ~ *one's character* 인격을 도야하다. **3** (P6) go around. …을 일주하다; 돌다. ¶ ~ *a corner* 모퉁이를 돌다 / ~ *an island* 섬을 한 바퀴 돌다.

— *vi.* **1** (P1,2A) become round. 둥글게 되다. **2** (P1,2A,3) 《*into*》 develop to perfection. 발전하다; 원숙해지다. ¶ ~ *into womanhood* 여자다워지다; 숙녀가 되다. **3** (P1,2A) go around ; turn round. 순회하다; 돌다. ¶ ~ *on one's heals* 뒤돌아서다 / ~ *to the right* 우회전하다. [→rotund]

round off, **a**) make (something) round. …을 둥글게 하다. **b**) complete. …을 완성하다. ¶ ~ *off the evening with a dance* 그 날 밤을 춤으로 마무리짓다 / ~ *off a sentence* 문장을 완성하다.

round (= *make a sudden, usu. verbal attack*) ***on*** 〔***upon***〕 *someone.* …을 꾸짖다.

round out, **a**) make or become round. 둥글게 하다〔되다〕 ¶ *Her figure has rounded out.* 살이 올라 몸매가 통통해졌다. **b**) complete. …을 완성하다.

round up **a**) drive(cattle, etc.) together. (가축)을 몰아서 한데 모으다. **b**) gather. …을 모으다. **c**) make round; arrest. 검거〔체포〕하다.

round·a·bout [ráundəbàut] *adj.* **1** not following the direct way. 멀리 돌아서 가는; 에워 가는. ¶ *a ~ route* 멀리 돌아가는 길. **2** (speech etc.) indirect. 에두르는; 완곡한. ¶ *speak in a ~ way* 에둘러 말하다. **3** (of the figure) fat; round. 살찐; 통통한. — *n.* Ⓒ **1** an indirect way. 돌아가는 길; 우회로. **2** 《Brit.》 a merry-go-round. 회전 목마. **3** 《Brit.》 a place where all traffic follows a circular, indirect course. 환상 교차로; 로터리. **4** 《U.S.》 a short jacket for boys. (남아용) 짧은 자켓.

roun·del [ráundl] *n.* Ⓒ **1** something round; a small round ornament, shield, window, etc. (자그마한) 둥근 것; 원형 문장(紋章)〔방패〕; 작은 원창(圓窓). **2** a rondo. 론도. [*round*]

roun·de·lay [ráundilèi] *n.* Ⓒ **1** a short song in which one part is continually repeated. 후렴이 있는 짧은 노래. **2** a dance in a circle. 원무의 일종. [↑]

round·er [ráundər] *n.* Ⓒ **1** a person who makes a round of calls. 순회하는 사람. **2** a tool which rounds a thing. 둥글리는 연장. **3** a habitual drunkard or criminal. 주정뱅이; 상습범. **4** (*pl.,* used as *sing*) 《Brit.》 a game somewhat like baseball. 라운더스《야구 비슷한 구기》. [*round*]

Round·head [ráundhèd] *n.* Ⓒ a member of the Parliament side in the English Civil War of the 17th century, so called from his close-cut hair. 의회당원《머리를 짧게 둥글린 데서》.

round·house [ráundhàus] *n.* Ⓒ **1** 《naut.》 a cabin on the after part of a ship's deck. 후갑판의 선실. **2** 《U.S.》 a circular building in which locomotives are stored and repaired. (원형의) 기관차고(庫).

round·ish [ráundiʃ] *adj.* rather round. 둥그스름한.

round·ly [ráundli] *adv.* **1** in a round form. 둥글게. ¶ *swell ~* 둥글게 부풀다. **2** in plain or severe words. 솔직하게; 가차없이. ¶ *refuse someone ~* 아무를 딱 부러지게 거절하다 / *scold someone ~* 아무를 호되게 꾸짖다. **3** fully; completely. 완전하게. **4** roughly. 대충; 어림으로. ¶ *reckon ~* 개산(概算)하다; 어림잡다.

round-shoul·dered [ráundʃóuldərd] *adj.* having the shoulders bent forward. 어깨가 둥근; 새우등의.

rounds·man [ráundzmən] *n.* (*pl.* **-men** [-mən]) **1** 《Brit.》 a man employed to deliver milk, bread, etc. to customers. (우유·빵 따위의) 배달인. **2** 《U.S.》 a policeman on a round of inspection. 감독 경관《경찰의 근무 상황을 순시하는》.

round table [ˊ ˋ‒] *n.* a group of persons gathered together for an informal discussion; such a discussion. 원탁에 둘러 앉은 사람들; 원탁 회의.

round trip [ˊ ˊ] *n.* 《U.S.》 a trip to a place and back to the starting point. 왕복 여행(= 《Brit.》 return trip).

round·up [ráundʌ̀p] *n.* Ⓒ **1** 《U.S.》 the act of driving cattle, etc. together. (가축을) 몰아 한데 모으기. **2** any act of gathering persons together. 사람들을 모으기; 소집. ¶ *a ~ of old friends* 옛 벗들을 모으기《동창회 따위》. **3** a gathering. 모임; 집회. **4** the collection by the police of criminals or other persons for arrest. (범인 등의) 일제 검거.

***rouse** [rauz] *vt.* **1** (P6,7) waken; excite. …을 깨우다; …을 일으키다. ¶ ~ *oneself* 분기시키다 / ~ *someone to do a thing* 아무를 자극하여 …시키다 / ~ *someone from sleep* 아무를 잠에서 깨우다 / *I was roused by the telephone.* 전화 소리에 잠을 깼다 / *He was roused to anger by the insult.* 그는 모욕을 당하자 몹시 화가 났다 / *He wants rousing.* 그는 (게을러서) 좀 자극해 줄 필요가 있다. **2** (P6) stir up; mix well. …을 휘젓다; 교반하다. **3** (P6,13) cause (an animal or a bird) to leave a hiding place. (사냥감)을 몰아내다. ¶ *The dogs roused foxes from the woods.* 사냥개들이 숲에서 여우들을 몰아냈다.

— *vi.* (P1,2A) awake from sleep; become active. 잠에서 깨다; 분기〔분발〕하다. [Sw. *rusa* rush]

rout[1] [raut] *n.* **1** Ⓤ a noisy, disorderly

crowd. 폭도; 무질서한 군중. **2** Ⓤⓒ a disorderly flight of defeated army. 패주(敗走). ¶ *put to* ~ 패주시키다 / *the total* ~ *of the enemy forces* 적군의 전면적인 패주. — *vt.* (P6) make (an enemy) run away. (적)을 패주시키다. [→rupture]

rout[2] [raut] *vt., vi.* (P7,13;1,2A) **1** root up; dig up. (…을) 파내다. **2** drive or drag by force. 강제로 끌어내다. ¶ ~ *someone out of bed* …을 잠자리에서 끌어내다. [→root]

:route [ru:t, raut] *n.* **1** ⓒ a road; a way; a course. 길; 노선; 항로. ¶ *an air* ~ 항공로 / *take one's* ~ *to the destination* 목적지를 향해 나아가다 / *the shortest* ~ 가장 가까운 길 / *The school is on a bus* ~. 학교까지 버스 노선이 나 있다. **2** 《U.S.》 a specific area covered regularly by a specific person. (신문·우편 따위의) 집배 구역; 길. ¶ *postal* ~ 우편 집배로. **3** [raut] 《mil.》 marching order. 진군 명령.

get the route, receive marching orders. 행군[출발] 명령을 받다.

— *vt.* (P6,13) 《chiefly U.S.》 **1** arrange the route for (something). …의 노정[절차]을 마련[정]하다. ¶ *He routed the way for his followers.* 그는 사람들을 위해 노정을 정했다. **2** send by a certain route. (어떤 노선·경로를 통해) …을 발송하다. ¶ *They routed the goods through Chicago.* 그들은 그 물건을 시카고 경유로 발송했다. [F.]

route march [⌐ ⌐] *n.* long march of troops, when in training. 도보 행군《훈련》.

·rou·tine [ru:tí:n] *n.* **1** ⓒ a regular way of doing something. 판에 박힌 일; 정해진 일과. ¶ *the* ~ *of office work* 사무소의 판에 박힌 일 / *the daily* ~ *of classes and homework* 수업하고 숙제하는 일과 / *the day's* ~ 일과. **2** Ⓤ the ordinary course. 관례. — *adj.* of a routine; regular; habitual. 정해진; 판에 박힌. ¶ ~ *method* 정해진 방식 / ~ *workers* 매일 같은 일을 되풀이하는 근로자. [*route*]

·rove [rouv] *vi.* (P1,2A,3) **1** wander about; go from place to place. 헤매다; 방황하다. ¶ *He loved to* ~ *over the fields and woods.* 그는 들과 숲을 돌아다니길 좋아했다. **2** (of the eyes) look in changing directions. (눈이) 두리번거리다. ¶ *His eyes roved about the crowded room looking for his brother.* 그는 방 안의 많은 사람 중에서 동생을 찾기 위해 눈을 두리번거렸다. — *vt.* (P6) wander over. …을 배회하다. ¶ ~ *the woods* 숲 속을 배회하다. — *n.* ⓒ the act of roving. 배회; 돌아다님. [D. *roover* robber]

rov·er [róuvər] *n.* ⓒ **1** a wanderer. 돌아다니는 사람; 배회자. **2** 《*arch.*》 a pirate; a pirate ship. 해적; 해적선. [↑]

shoot at rovers, shoot aimlessly. 무턱대고 쏘다; 난사하다.

:row[1] [rou] *n.* **1** a number of objects arranged to form a single line. 줄; 열. ¶ *a row of soldiers* [*trees*] 한 줄로 늘어선 군인[가로수]들 / *The children stood in a row.* 아이들이 한 줄로 섰다 / *Corn is planted in rows.* 옥수수가 나란히 심어져 있다. **2** a line of houses on either side of a street; the street. (거리를 사이에 두고) 마주 보고 늘어선 집들; 거리. [E.]

a hard [***long***] ***row to hoe,*** 《U.S.》 a difficult task to perform. 성사하기 어려운 일.

:row[2] [rou] *vi.* (P1,2A) move a boat by means of oars. 배를 젓다; 노질하다. ¶ ~ *down* [*up*] *the stream* 노를 저어 강을 내려가다[올라가다]. — *vt.* (P6,7,13) **1** propel (a boat) by means of oars. (배)를 젓다. ¶ ~ *40 to the minute* 1분에 마흔 번 노질하다 / ~ *a fast stroke* 빠르게 노질하다 / ~ *across a river* 배를 저어 강을 건너다 / ~ *against the wind* 바람을 안고 노질하다. **2** carry (something) in a boat. …을 배를 저어[배로] 나르다. ¶ *He rowed her across* (*a stream*). 그는 배로 그녀를 건네 주었다. **3** perform (a race, etc.) by rowing. (보트 레이스에) 참가하다. ¶ ~ *a race* 보트 레이스에 출전하다. **4** be moved by (a certain number of roars). …자루의 노를 쓰다. ¶ *The boat rows 6 oars.* 그 배는 노 여섯으로 젓는다.

row down, overtake by rowing. 저어서 따라붙다.

— *n.* ⓒ **1** the act of using oars; a trip in a rowboat. 노젓기; 뱃놀이. ¶ *Let's have a* ~ *on the lake.* 그 호수에서 뱃놀이하자 / *go for a* ~ 뱃놀이 가다. **2** the distant rowed. 노 젓는 거리. ¶ *It is a long* ~ *across the lake.* 그 호수를 저어 건너려면 대단한 거리다. [E.]

row[3] [rau] *n.* 《*colloq.*》 **1** Ⓤ loud noise. 소동; 소란. ¶ *kick up a* ~ 시끄럽게 굴다; 시끄럽게 항의하다 / *What's all this* ~ *about.* 왜들 이 법석이냐. **2** ⓒ a noisy quarrel. 싸움질; 언쟁. ¶ *a street* ~ 거리에서의 난투 / *have a* ~ *with someone* 아무와 한바탕 싸우다. **3** the act of scolding; the state of being scolded. 꾸짖음; 질책. ¶ *make a* ~ *about* …일로 아무를 꾸짖다. — (P1,2A) 《*colloq.*》 quarrel noisily; make much noise. 소란 피우다; 싸우다. — *vt.* (P6,13) 《*colloq.*》 scold. …을 꾸짖다. [*rouse*]

row·an [róuən, ráu-] *n.* ⓒ 《bot.》 a shrub of the rose family; its red berry. 마가목의 일종; 그 빨간 열매. [Scand.]

row·boat [róubòut] *n.* ⓒ a boat moved by means of oars. (노로 젓는) 배. [*row*[2]]

row·dy [ráudi] *adj.* (**-di·er, -di·est**) rough; noisy and rude. 난폭한; (사람이) 시끄러운. — *n.* ⓒ (*pl.* **-dies**) a rowdy person. 난폭한 사람; 시끄러운 사람. [*row*[3]]

row·dy·ish [ráudiiʃ] *adj.* rowdy; rough and disorderly. 난폭한; 소란 떠는.

row·dy·ism [ráudiìzəm] *n.* Ⓤ rough, noisy behavior. 난폭; 소란.

row·el [ráuəl] *n.* a small wheel with

sharp points at the end of a spur. (박차 끝에 달린) 작은 톱니바퀴. [→rota]

row·ing boat [róuiŋ bòut] *n.* 《Brit.》 a rowboat. (노로 젓는) 배〔보트〕. [*row*[2]]

row·lock [rálək, rʌ́l- / rɔ́lək, rʌ́-] *n.* Ⓒ a wooden or metal part on a boat to hold the oar; an oarlock. 노받이(cf. *oarlock*). [*row*[2]]

Roy [rɔi] *n.* a man's name. 남자 이름.

:roy·al [rɔ́iəl] *adj.* **1** of a king or queen and their families. 왕〔여왕〕의; 왕실의. ¶ *a ~ palace* 왕궁 / *a ~ crown* 왕관 / *a ~ prince* 〔*princess*〕 왕자〔왕녀〕/ *the ~ family* 왕족 / *~ power* 왕권. **2** under the rule of a king or queen; having the rank of a king or queen. 왕립의; 칙허(勅許)의; 왕위의. ¶ *a ~ charter* 칙허장 / *the ~ forest* 왕실림. **3** fit for a king or queen; noble; majestic. 왕(자)다운; 고귀한; 위엄이 있는. ¶ *behave with ~ dignity* (왕자다운) 위엄 있게 처신하다 / *a ~ feast* 〔*welcome*〕 대단한 성찬〔환영〕/ *live in ~ state* (왕후처럼) 떵떵거리며 지내다. **4** 《*colloq.*》 splendid; fine; excellent. 멋들어진; 굉장한; 훌륭한. ¶ *be in ~ spirits* 원기 왕성하다.

— *n.* **1** 《*the Royals*》 the first British regiment of foot. 영국 보병 제1연대. 參考 지금은 Royal Scots Regiment라 함. **2** royal paper. 로열판(25×20 인치의 인쇄지). **3** 《naut.》 a royal sail. 로열마스트의 돛. [→rex]

roy·al·ist [rɔ́iəlist] *n.* Ⓒ a supporter of a king or a royal government. 왕당원.

roy·al·ly [rɔ́iəli] *adv.* in a royal or majestic manner. 왕답게; 당당하게.

roy·al·ty [rɔ́iəlti] *n.* (*pl.* **-ties**) **1** Ⓤ the rank or power of a king or queen. 왕위; 왕권. ¶ *The crown is the symbol of ~.* 왕관은 왕의 상징이다. **2** Ⓒ 《usu. *pl.*》 a royal person; 《*collectively*》 royal persons. 왕족. ¶ *There is a box in the theater reserved for ~.* 극장에는 왕족을 위한 특별 관람석이 하나씩 있다. **3** Ⓤ royal quality; kingliness. 왕의 존엄성; 왕의 위풍. **4** Ⓒ a payment to the owner of a copyright or patent. 인세; 특허권 사용료; 로열티. ¶ *An author receives royalties from the publishers of his books.* 저자는 출판사로부터 저서에 대한 인세를 받는다.

R.S.P.C.A. Royal Society for the Prevention of Cruelty to Animals. 영국 동물 애호 협회.

R.S.V. Revised Standard Version.

R.S.V.P. *Répondez s'il vous plaît* (=please answer). [F.]

:rub [rʌb] *v.* (**rubbed, rub·bing**) *vt.* **1** (P6,7,13,18) press (one thing) against another and move it back and forth, or up and down. …을 비비다; 마찰하다. ¶ *~ one's hands with soap* 손에 비누칠을 하다 / *~ lotion on one's skin* 피부에 로션을 바르다 / *The dog rubbed its head against his legs.* 개가 머리를 다리에 대고 비볐다 / *He rubbed his hands (together) to warm them.* 그는 따뜻하게 하기 위해 양손을 비볐다. **2** (P7,13,21) clean, smooth or polish (something) by rubbing; wipe thoroughly. …을 (문질러) 닦다〔지우다〕; 닦아내다. ¶ *I rubbed myself dry.* 나는 몸을 닦아 말렸다 / *Rub out your work with an eraser and do it over again.* 쓴 것을 지우개로 지우고 다시 써라 / *~ silver with a cloth* 헝겊으로 은그릇을 닦다. **3** (P6,7) make (something) sore by rubbing. …을 까지게 하다. ¶ *My shoe is rubbing my heel.* 구두에 발뒤꿈치가 까진다. **4** (P6) take an impression (of something engraved) by rubbing paper etc. placed above with black lead etc. …을 탁본(拓本)하다. **5** (P6) massage. …을 주무르다; 마사지하다. ¶ *Mother rubbed my sore ankle.* 어머니가 아픈 발목을 주물러 주셨다.

— *vi.* (P1,2A,3) **1** move with pressure against something. 마찰하다; 쓸리다; 삐걱거리다. ¶ *The door rubbed on the floor.* 문이 마루에 닿아 삐걱거렸다 / *Your coat has rubbed against the wet paint.* 코트에 페인트가 묻었구나. **2** 《*along, on, through*》 keep going with difficulty; manage to exist. 어렵게〔그럭저럭〕 해나가다. ¶ *~ on from hand to hand* 가까스로(그날그날)살아가다 / *~ through* 〔*along*〕 *the world* 그럭저럭 살아가다 / *You can ~ on somehow.* 어떻게 해나가게 되겠지.

rub down, **a**) give a massage to (someone). …을 마사지하다. **b**) rub thoroughly with a towel to clean and dry. …을 닦아내다. ¶ *~ a horse down* 말에 솔질하다. **c**) polish, smooth, or wear down (something) by rubbing. …을 문지르다; 문질러 닦다. ¶ *~ a box down with sandpaper* 사포로 상자를 문질러 광내다.

rub elbows 〔***shoulders***〕 ***with*** (=*meet and mix with*) *someone.* …와 교제하다; 사귀다.

rub one's hands, 《*fig.*》 express satisfaction. 만족해 하다. ¶ *He was rubbing his hands over the result of the election.* 그는 선거 결과를 흡족해 하고 있었다.

rub in, force in by rubbing. …을 문질러 바르다. ¶ *~ ointment in* 연고를 문질러 바르다.

rub it in, 《*colloq.*》 keep mentioning a failure, mistake, etc. in order to irritate someone. (잘못 따위를) 자꾸 초들어 말하다.

rub off, remove by friction; tend to come off. 문질러 없애다.

rub out, **a**) erase. …을 지워 없애다. **b**) 《*sl.*, orig. U.S.》 kill. …을 죽이다.

rub the wrong way, offend; hurt feelings of; make angry. …의 기분을 건드리다; 화나게 하다.

— *n.* Ⓒ **1** an act of rubbing. 마찰; 비빔; 문지름. ¶ *give something a ~* …을 닦다; 문지르다. **2** an obstacle; a difficulty. 곤란; 장애. ¶ *the rubs and worries of life* 인생의 갖은 어려움과 고초 / *There's the ~.* 그게 곤란한 점이다. **3** a thing that rubs or hurts the feelings. 싫은 소리; 기분 나쁘게 하는 것. ¶ *I got many severe rubs from them.* 그들 때문에 기분 나쁜 일이 많았다. [? G.]

rub-a-dub [rʌ́bədʌ̀b] *n.* Ⓒ the sound made by beating a drum; a loud noise. 둥둥《북소리》. [Imit.]

:rub·ber[1] [rʌ́bər] *n.* **1** Ⓤ an elastic substance produced from the milky juice of certain trees; Ⓒ something made of this substance. 고무; 고무 제품. ¶ *crude* ~ 생고무 / *natural* ~ 천연 고무 / *synthetic* ~ 인조 고무 / *Rub out* 〔*Erase*〕 *the pencil marks with a* ~. 고무로 연필 자국을 지워라. **2** 《*pl.*》 《U.S.》 overshoes made of rubber. 고무 덧신. **3** a person or thing that rubs. 문지르는〔닦는〕 사람〔것〕. — *adj.* made of rubber. 고무로 만든. — *vt.* (P6) cover or coat (something) with rubber. …에 고무를 입히다. [*rub, -er*]

rub·ber[2] [rʌ́bər] *n.* 《*the* ~》 Ⓒ the winning of a series of two games out of three or three out of five games in cards or bridge; the deciding game in such a series. 3판 양승 또는 5판 3승전; 결승전. ¶ *win the* ~. [? M.E.]

rub·ber·ize [rʌ́bəràiz] *vt.* (P6) cover or treat (something) with rubber. …에 고무를 입히다; 고무로 처리하다. [*rubber*[1]]

***rub·bish** [rʌ́biʃ] *n.* Ⓤ **1** waste material; trash. 쓰레기; 폐물. ¶ *Pick up the* ~ *and burn it.* 쓰레기를 주워 태워라. **2** anything useless or worthless. 쓸데없는 것; 무용지물. ¶ *The goods in this shop are just* ~. 이 가게 물건은 하나도 쓸 게 없다. **3** worthless ideas; nonsense. 실없는 생각; 난센스. ¶ *Don't talk* ~. 실없는 소리 그만해라 / *Oh,* ~*!* 무슨 소리 하는 거냐. [F.]

rub·bish·y [rʌ́biʃi] *adj.* like rubbish; worthless. 쓰레기의; 폐물의; 쓸데없는.

rub·ble [rʌ́bəl] *n.* Ⓤ rough broken pieces of stone, rock, brick, etc. 쇄석; 잡석. [F.]

Ru·bi·con [rú:bikɑ̀n / -kən] *n.* a small river in northern Italy. 루비콘 강.

cross* 〔*pass*〕 *the Rubicon, take a decisive step (by crossing the Rubicon, Caesar began a civil war). 단호한 조처를 취하다; 건곤 일척하다. [the boundary stream of ancient Italy]

ru·bi·cund [rú:bikʌ̀nd] *adj.* (of the face, etc.) reddish; ruddy. (얼굴 등이) 붉은; 발그레한. ¶ *a jolly* ~ *farmer* 거나해서 얼굴이 불그레한 농부. [L. *rubeo* be red.]

ru·ble, rou- [rú:bəl] *n.* Ⓒ the unit of money in the Russia. 루블《러시아의 화폐 단위》. [Russ.]

ru·bric [rú:brik] *n.* Ⓒ **1** the title of a chapter written or printed in red. 주서(朱書)《제목 등 붉게 인쇄한 것》. **2** a direction in a prayer book for conducting religious services. 예배 규정. [→rubicund]

Ru·by [rú:bi] *n.* a woman's name. 여자 이름.

ru·by [rú:bi] *n.* (*pl.* **ru·bies**) **1** Ⓒ a precious red stone. 루비; 홍옥. **2** Ⓤ a deep, glowing red color. 루비색; 진홍색(眞紅色). ***above rubies,*** invaluable. 매우 귀중〔중요〕한. — *adj.* deep, glowing red. 진홍의. ¶ ~ *lips* 〔*wine*〕. [*rubric*]

ruck·sack [rʌ́ksæ̀k, rúk-] *n.* Ⓒ a kind of knapsack carried on the back by the straps. 륙색; 배낭. [G. =back sack]

ruc·tion [rʌ́kʃən] *n.* Ⓒ 《usu. *pl.*》 《*colloq.*》 trouble; a quarrel; a protest. 소동; 싸움질; 항의. [*erruption*]

rud·der [rʌ́dər] *n.* Ⓒ **1** a flat piece at the back of a ship, boat, or an airplane used to change the course. (배의) 키; (비행기의) 방향타. **2** that which serves as a guide. 지침이 되는 것. **3** the tail of a fish or an animal. (물고기·짐승의) 꼬리; 꽁지. [E.]

rud·di·ness [rʌ́dinis] *n.* Ⓤ the state of being ruddy; a healthy redness of skin. 붉음; 홍안(紅顔). [↓]

rud·dy [rʌ́di] *adj.* (**-di·er, -di·est**) red; having the color of good health. 붉은; 혈색이 좋은. ¶ ~ *cheeks* 붉은 볼 / *a* ~ *sky* 붉게 타는 하늘 / ~ *health* 넘치는 건강. [E.]

:rude [ru:d] *adj.* **1** rough in manner; impolite. 무례한; 버릇없는; 실례의. ¶ ~ *remarks* 폭언 / ~ *bands* 막된 무리 / *be* ~ *to someone* 아무에게 무례한 짓을 하다; 아무를 모욕하다 / *It is* ~ *to stare at people or to point.* 사람을 빤히 보거나 손가락질 하는 것은 예의가 아니다. **2** violent; severe. 난폭한; 거친. **3** primitive; uncivilized. 미개한; 교양없는. ¶ *a* ~ *people* 미개인 / ~ *mountain tribes* 미개한 산악 부족. **4** roughly made or done; coarse; raw; without finish or polish. 조잡한; 미가공의; 건목친. ¶ ~ *cotton* 원목 / ~ *ore* 원석; 원광(原鑛) / ~ *produce* 천연 산물 / *He made a* ~ *bed from the branches of trees.* 그는 나뭇가지를 모아 엉성한 잠자리를 만들었다 / *a* ~ *drawing* 아무렇게나 그린 그림. **5** unskillful; rough. 미숙한; 대강의. ¶ *a* ~ *estimate* 대강의 견적. **6** (of health) robust; vigorous. 건강한; 튼튼한. ¶ *be in* ~ *health* 원기 왕성하다. [L. *rudies*]

ru·di·ment [rú:dəmənt] *n.* Ⓒ **1** 《usu. *pl.*》 one of the basic principles; the first or beginning of something. 기본; 기초 원리; 초보. ¶ *the rudiments of law* 법률 원론 / *learn the rudiments of radio* 라디오의 기본 원리를 배우다 / *the rudiments of grammar* 기초 문법 / *the rudiments of civilization* 문명의 시초. **2** 《biol.》 (of a plant or an animal) an imperfectly developed part or organ; vestige. (생물의) 퇴화된 기관; 흔적. [L. *rudimentum*]

ru·di·men·tal [rù:dəméntl], **-ta·ry** [-təri] *adj.* **1** elementary; beginning; basic. 기본〔근본〕의; 초보의. ¶ *a* ~ *knowledge of mathematics* 수학의 초보〔기초〕 지식. **2** undeveloped; vestigial. 미발달〔미발육〕의; 흔적

의. ¶ *a ~ organ* 흔적 기관(痕迹器官); 퇴화 기관.

rue[1] [ruː] *vt.* 《*arch.*》 (P6) regret; grieve; be sorry for. …을 후회하다; 유감으로 여기다. ¶ *She will ~ the day when she insulted your mother.* 그녀는 네 모친을 모욕하던 날을 뉘우칠 것이다 / *He will live to ~ it.* 언젠가는 그것을 후회할 날이 올 것이다. — *vi.* sorrow; feel sorrow; regret. 슬퍼하다; 후회하다. [E.]

rue[2] [ruː] *n.* Ⓤ 《bot.》 a small evergreen shrub with yellow flowers and bitter-tasting leaves. 루타《남유럽 원산의 상록 관목》. 參考 본시 흥분제〔자극제〕로 썼음. [Gk.]

rue·ful [rúːfəl] *adj.* filled with regret; mournful; causing pity. 뉘우치는; 슬퍼하는; 가엾은. ¶ *a ~ expression* 뉘우치는 표정 / *a ~ sight* 가엾은 광경. [*rue*[1]]

rue·ful·ly [rúːfəli] *adv.* in a rueful manner; mournfully. 후회하여; 슬픈듯이.

ruff [rʌf] *n.* Ⓒ **1** a high, frilled, stiff collar worn in the 16th and 17th centuries. (16-17 세기의) 높고 빳빳한 주름 칼라. **2** a ring of feathers or fur like a collar around the neck of a bird or an animal. (새·짐승의) 목둘레의 고리 모양의 깃털〔털〕. **3** 《bird》 a kind of sandpiper. 목도리도요류(類). [Du.]

〈ruff 1〉

ruf·fi·an [rʌ́fiən, -fjən] *n.* Ⓒ a brutal, cruel, lawless person. 악당; 무뢰한; 무법자. — *adj.* =ruffianly. [E.]

ruf·fi·an·ism [rʌ́fiənìzəm, -fjən-] *n.* Ⓤ brutality; violence. 악당 근성; 잔인한 행위.

ruf·fi·an·ly [rʌ́fiənli, -fjən-] *adj.* like a ruffian; brutal; violent. 악당 같은; 흉악한.

***ruf·fle** [rʌ́fəl] *vt.* (P6,7) **1** fold (cloth, etc.) into ruffles; put ruffles on. …에 주름을 잡다. **2** wrinkle; ripple. …에 주름살지게 하다; …을 물결일게 하다. ¶ *The wind ruffled the water.* 바람으로 수면이 물결쳤다. **3** make (feathers, etc.) stand up in a ruff. (깃털)을 곤두세우다. ¶ *The bird ruffled (up) its feathers at the sight of the dog.* 새는 개를 보자 깃털을 곤두세웠다. **4** disturb; irritate. …을 어지럽게 만들다; 신경질나게 하다. ¶ *~ someone's composure* 아무의 마음을 어지럽게 하다; 아무의 침착성을 잃게 하다 / *Nothing ever ruffled him.* 무엇에나 그는 화내는 일이 없었다 / *~ the feelings of* …의 감정을 건드리다.

— *vi.* (P1) **1** become wrinkled. 구겨지다. **2** become disturbed. 화나다; 짜증이 나다.

— *n.* Ⓒ **1** a piece of cloth gathered into folds and used for trimming. 프릴; 주름장식. **2** a ruff of feathers or fur. (새의) 목털. **3** a ripple. 잔물결. **4** irritation; a disturbance. 안달; 초조; 소동. ¶ *put someone in a ~* 아무를 안달나게〔성나게〕 하다. [Du.]

:**rug** [rʌg] *n.* Ⓒ **1** a heavy mat for covering the floor. (바닥의) 깔개; 융단. **2** 《chiefly Brit.》 ⓐ a piece of heavy cloth laid over the knees. 무릎 덮개. ¶ *a traveling ~* 여행용 무릎 덮개. ⓑ a thick warm cloth used as covering. 모포; 담요. ¶ *We wrapped our child in a ~.* 우리는 아이를 담요로 감쌌다. [Sw. *rugg* rough hair]

·**Rug·by** [rʌ́gbi] *n.* **1** a city in central England. 럭비시(市). **2** a famous boy's school in that city. 럭비교(校). **3** 《often *r-*》 a form of football; Rugby football; rugger. 럭비; 러거(cf. *association football*). [Place]

:**rug·ged** [rʌ́gid] *adj.* (sometimes **-ged·er, -ged·est**) **1** rough; uneven; steep and rocky. 울퉁불퉁한; 가파른; 바위 투성이의 (opp. smooth). ¶ *a ~ coast* 바위가 많은 들쭉날쭉한 해안 / *~ walls* 가파른 성벽. **2** wrinkled. 주름진. ¶ *a ~ face* 주름진 얼굴. **3** rude; unpolished. 세련미가 없는; 무무한. ¶ *~ manners* 버릇없는 거친 행동. **4** stern; harsh; severe. 엄한; 호된. ¶ *a ~ teacher* 엄격한 선생 / *a ~ winter* 엄동 / *his ~ looks* 그의 딱딱하고 위엄있는 표정. **5** strong; firm. 억센; 건장한; 단단한. ¶ *a ~ body* 튼튼한 몸 / *a ~ character* 억센〔강인한〕 성격. [E.]

rug·ger [rʌ́gər] *n.* Ⓤ 《Brit. *sl.*》 Rugby football. 럭비; 러거. [→Rugby]

:**ru·in** [rúːin] *n.* **1** Ⓤ ⓐ destruction; downfall; decay; bankruptcy. 파괴; 몰락; 멸망; 황폐; 파산. ¶ *the ~ of my hopes* 내 희망의 무너짐 / *The house is falling to ~.* 그 집은 황폐해 가고 있다 / *He is on the brink of ~.* 그는 파멸〔파산〕 직전에 있다 / *He brought his country to ~.* 그는 나라를 파멸시켰다 / *go* 〔*come, fall*〕 *to ~* 멸망하다. ⓑ a fallen or decayed condition. 파괴〔황폐〕된 상태. ¶ *be in ~* 황폐한 상태에 있다. **2** Ⓒ 《often *pl.*》 the remains of a building, a wall, etc. destroyed or fallen into decay. 폐허; 파괴된 옛 터〔잔해〕. ¶ *the ruins of Rome* 로마의 폐허 / *the ruins of a building* 파괴된 건물의 잔해. **3** Ⓒ 《usu. *sing.*》 a cause of ruin. 파멸의 원인; 화근. ¶ *Gambling* 〔*Drink*〕 *was his ~.* 그가 망한 까닭은 노름〔술〕 때문이었다.

— *vt.* (P6) **1** bring (someone or something) to ruin; destroy. …을 파멸시키다; 파괴하다. ¶ *~ someone's prospects* 아무의 장래를 망쳐버리다 / *~ oneself* 몸을 망치다 / *The rain has ruined my new dress.* 비가 내 새옷을 엉망으로 만들었다 / *~ one's career* 신세를 망치다 / *I was (financially) ruined by that lawsuit.* 나는 그 송사로 거덜이 났다. **2** seduce; deprive (a woman) of chastity. …을 유혹하다; (여자)를 타락시키다. ¶ *~ a woman* 여자를 버려놓다.

— *vi.* (P1) go or come to ruin. 파멸〔황폐〕하다; 몰락하다. [L. *ruo* fall]

ru·in·a·tion [rùːinéiʃən] *n.* **1** Ⓤ ruin;

downfall. 파괴; 파멸; 영락. **2** Ⓒ a cause of ruin. 파멸의 원인; 화근. [↑]

ru·in·ous [rúːinəs] *adj.* **1** bringing ruin; causing destruction. 파멸적(파괴적)인; 파멸을 초래하는. ¶ *a ~ war* 파괴적인 전쟁 / *~ inflation* 파멸적인 인플레이션 / *~ folly* 일신의 파멸을 초래하는 우행(愚行). **2** fallen into ruins. 황폐한. ¶ *a barn in a ~ state* 황폐한 상태의 헛간.

:rule [ruːl] *n.* **1** Ⓒ a principle that must be kept by all; a regulation; a law. 법칙; 규칙; 규정. ¶ *the rules of the game* 경기 규칙 / *the ~ of the air* 〔*road*〕 항공〔도로〕 규칙 / *apply a ~* 규정을 적용하다 / *break a ~* 규칙을 위반하다 / *follow* 〔*observe*〕 *the ~* 규칙을 준수하다 / *a ~ against smoking* 흡연 금지의 규정. **2** Ⓒ a usual way; a custom; a habit. 습관; 상습(常習). ¶ *I make it a ~* 〔*It is a ~ with me*〕 *to take a walk in the park every morning.* 나는 매일 아침 공원을 산책하기로 돼 있다 / *I make it a ~ not to give to beggars.* 나는 걸인에게 적선하지 않기로 하고 있다. **3** Ⓒ something common; a standard. 흔히 있는 일; 통칙; 표준. ¶ *Failure is the ~, success the exception.* 실패는 흔한 일이고, 성공은 예외이다 / *a hard and fast ~* (융통성이 없는) 딱딱한 규준. **4** Ⓤ control; government. 지배; 통치. ¶ *The islands are under direct ~ of the United States.* 그 섬들은 미국의 직접 통치하에 있다 / *Democracy means the ~ of the people.* 민주주의란 국민에 의한 통치를 말한다 / *during the ~ of Elizabeth* 엘리자베스 여왕 치세 중에. **5** a straight strip of wood, metal, etc. used to measure or as a guide in drawing; ruler. 자; 잣대. **6** 《law》 an order made by a court of justice. (법정의) 명령. **7** Ⓒ 《print.》 a thin line for dash in printing. 괘(罫); 괘선.

as a rule, usually. 대개; 일반적으로.

by rule, according to rules. 규정대로. ¶ *He does everything by ~.* 그는 무엇이건 규정대로 한다.

by rule and line, 《*fig.*》 accurately. 정확히; 엄밀하게.

work to rule, 《Brit.》 work following the regulations exactly in the knowledge that this will hinder operation. (노동 조합이) 준법 투쟁을 하다.

— *vt.* **1** (P6) govern; control. …을 지배〔통치〕하다. ¶ *~ one's country* 국가를 통치하다 / *~ someone's action* 아무의 행동을 규제하다 / *Don't be ruled by your passions.* 네 감정에 지배당하지 마라. **2** control (one's desires, etc.). …을 억제하다. ¶ *~ one's appetite* 식욕을 억제하다 / *~ one's passions* 〔*actions*〕 감정〔행동〕을 억제하다. **3** (P6,7, 11,21) give a formal decision; determine. …을 규정하다; 판결하다. ¶ *The judge ruled that he had no right to claim the property.* 판사는 그에게 그 재산을 요구할 권리가 없다고 판결했다. **4** (P6) 《usu. in *passive*》 《*arch.*》 guide; have an influence over. …을 이끌다; 좌우하다. ¶ *be ruled by* …의 충고에 따르다 / *Listen to me, and be ruled by me.* 잘 들어라, 그리고 내 말대로 하여라. **5** (P6,13) draw (a straight line) with a ruler; mark a straight line on (paper, etc.) with a ruler. (선)을 자로 긋다; …에 괘선을 치다. ¶ *~ lines on the sheet* = *~ the sheet* 종이에 선을 긋다.

— *vi.* (P1,3) **1** 《*over*》 govern. 통치하다; 지배하다. ¶ *King ought to ~ with justice, but with mildness.* 왕은 공정하게 다스리되 관대해야 한다. **2** make a formal decision. 판결〔판단〕하다. ¶ *The court has ruled in favor of the sacked employee.* 법원은 해고된 자에게 유리한 판결을 내렸다. **3** (P1,5) (of prices, etc.) have a certain general level; be current. (물가가) 보합을 이루다. ¶ *The prices ~ high* 〔*low*〕. 물가는 높은〔낮은〕 보합세를 지속하고 있다. [L. *regula*]

rule off, **a**) exclude. (선수 등)을 실격시키다; 제외하다. **b**) separate by ruling a line. 선을 그어 구획하다.

rule something out, decide that it cannot be admitted. (규정에 따라) …을 제외시키다; 금지하다.

rule of thumb [´-´] *n.* a rule based on experience. 주먹구구; 눈어림; 경험 법칙.

:rul·er [rúːlər] *n.* Ⓒ **1** a person who rules. 지배〔통치〕자. ¶ *a wise ~* 현명한 통치자. **2** a strip of wood, metal, etc. used in drawing lines or in measuring. 자; 괘선 긋는 기구.

rul·ing [rúːliŋ] *adj.* **1** governing. 지배〔통치〕하는. ¶ *the ~ classes* 지배 계급 / *a ~ race* 지배 민족. **2** chief. 주된; 유력한. **3** general. 일반적인; 평균의. ¶ *the ~ price* 시가 / *The ~ feeling of the students is in favor of their new teacher.* 새로 부임한 선생님에 대하여 학생들은 대체적으로 호의적이다. — *n.* Ⓒ 《law》 a decision by a judge; Ⓤ the act of drawing a line. 판결; 선을 긋기.

rum[1] [rʌm] *n.* Ⓤ **1** a strong alcoholic drink made from sugar cane, molasses. 럼주(酒). **2** 《U.S.》 any alcoholic drink. 술. [?]

rum[2] [rʌm] *adj.* 《Brit. *sl.*》 odd; queer. 기묘한; 별난. ¶ *a ~ start* 별난 사건 / *a ~ customer* 괴짜. [E.]

Ru·ma·ni·a [ruːméiniə, -njə] *n.* a country in south central Europe. 루마니아.

Ru·ma·ni·an [ruːméiniən] *adj.* of Rumania, its people or their language. 루마니아(사람·어)의. — *n.* Ⓒ a person of Rumania; Ⓤ the language of Rumania. 루마니아 사람; 루마니아 어.

rum·ba [rʌ́mbə, rú(ː)m-] *n.* Ⓒ a light and quick dance of Cuban Negro origin; a piece of music for this dance. 룸바; 그 곡. — *vi.* dance the rumba. 룸바를 추다. [Sp.]

rum·ble [rʌ́mbəl] *vi.* (P1,2A,3) **1** make a

deep rolling sound. 우르르 울리다. ¶ *The big guns rumbled in the distance.* 멀리서 대포 소리가 우르릉했다 / *I'm hungry —my stomach's rumbling.* 배가 고프다. 배에서 꾸르륵 소리가 난다. **2** move or go with such a sound. 덜거덕거리며 가다. ¶ *The train rumbled away.* 기차가 덜거덕거리며 지나갔다. — *vt.* (P7) **1** cause (something) to make such a sound. …을 우르르 소리나게 하다. **2** move (something) with such a sound. …을 덜거덕거리며 가게 하다.
— *n.* **1** Ⓤ a deep, heavy, rolling sound. 우르르하는 소리. ¶ *the distant ~ of thunder* 멀리서 천둥치는 소리 / *the ~ of guns* 쿵쾅거리는 대포 소리. **2** Ⓒ the rear part of a car or carriage containing an extra seat or a place for luggage. (자동차 따위, 차량 뒤쪽의) 여분의 좌석이나 화물칸. ¶ *the ~ seat.* [Sw.]

ru·mi·nant [rúːmənənt] *adj.* **1** (of some grass-eating animals) eating food and then bringing it back from the stomach to chew it again. (초식 동물이) 반추하는; 되새기는. **2** (of persons) often meditating; reflective. (사람이) 사색에 잠기는. — *n.* Ⓒ a grass-eating, ruminant animal. 반추 동물. ¶ *Cows, sheep and camels are ruminants.* [↓]

ru·mi·nate [rúːmənèit] *vi., vt.* (P1,3;6) **1** chew one's food and bring it back from the stomach to chew it again. 반추하다; 되새기다. ¶ *Cows ~.* **2** 《*about, over*》 think about (something) deeply; meditate. 곰곰이 생각하다. ¶ *He ruminated on* 〔*over*〕 *his failure.* 자기의 실패를 되씹어 생각했다. [L. *rumen* throat]

ru·mi·na·tion [rùːmənéiʃən] *n.* Ⓤ the act of ruminating. 반추; 되새김; 심사 숙고; 묵상.

ru·mi·na·tive [rúːmənèitiv / -nətiv] *adj.* meditating often. (곰곰이) 생각하는; 생각에 잠기는. ¶ *a ~ frown* 생각에 잠긴 우거지상.

rum·mage [rʌ́midʒ] *vt.* **1** (P6,13) search thoroughly by moving things about. (…을 찾아) 샅샅이 뒤지다〔찾다〕. ¶ *I rummaged my pockets for my passport.* 패스포트를 찾기 위해 주머니마다 샅샅이 뒤졌다. **2** (P6,7,13) 《*out, up*》 fish out or up; pull from among other things; fetch by searching. …을 찾아내다; 찾아서 가져오다. ¶ *~ up old clothes out of a cupboard* 벽장에서 헌 옷가지를 찾아내다.
— *vi.* (P1,2A,3) 《*about, for, among, in*》 search thoroughly. 샅샅이 찾다〔뒤지다〕. ¶ *I rummaged in my drawer for a pair of gloves.* 장갑 한 켤레를 찾아 서랍을 뒤졌다.
— *n.* **1** a rummaging search. 샅샅이 뒤지기. **2** things got by rummaging. 뒤져서 찾아낸 것. **3** odds and ends. 잡동사니. [F. *arrumer* stow cargo]

rummage sale [∠-∠] *n.* a sale of used articles as a way of collecting money for a good, charitable purpose. 잡동사니 시장; 자선시(慈善市).

rum·my [rʌ́mi] *adj.* (**-mi·er, -mi·est**) 《Brit. *sl.*》 =rum².

*__ru·mor,__ 《Brit.》 **-mour** [rúːmər] *n.* ⒸⓊ a story that passes from person to person without any proof that it is true; gossip. 소문; 풍문; 낭설. ¶ *start a ~* 소문을 내다 / *Rumor says* 〔*runs, has it*〕 *that war will break out.* 전쟁이 터진다는 소문이 돈다 / *a mere ~* 단순한 헛소문. — *vt.* (P6,11) 《usu. *passive*》 tell or spread (something) by rumor. …라는 소문을 내다. ¶ *It is rumored that….* …이라는 소문이다 / *the rumored disaster* 그 소문의 비극. [L. *rumor*]

rump [rʌmp] *n.* Ⓒ the back part of an animal; a cut of meat from this part. (짐승의) 엉덩이; 엉덩이살《특히 소의》. [Ice. *rumpr*]

rum·ple [rʌ́mpəl] *vt.* (P6) gather up (paper or cloth) in a disorderly way; make (hair) disorderly. (종이·옷 따위를) 구기다; (머리를) 헝클어뜨리다. ¶ *~ one's hair* 머리를 헝클어뜨리다 / *~ a sheet of paper* 한장의 종이를 구기다. — *n.* Ⓒ an uneven fold or crease; a state of being rumpled. 구김살; 주름(살). [Du.]

rum·pus [rʌ́mpəs] *n.* 《used as *sing.*》 《*colloq.*》 noise; uproar; a noisy quarrel. 소음; 소동; 싸움. ¶ *kick up* 〔*make*〕 *a ~* 소동을 일으키다. [G.]

:run [rʌn] *v.* (**ran, run, run·ning**) *vi.* **1** ⓐ (P1,2A,3,4) move with quick steps; move faster than in walking. 뛰다; 달리다. ¶ *She walked out rapidly; she was almost running.* 그녀는 잽싸게 걸어나갔다. 거의 뛰다시피 했다 / *The boys suddenly started to ~.* 아이들은 갑자기 뛰기 시작했다 / *~ out to call a taxi* 택시 잡으러 뛰쳐나가다 / *~ up* 〔*down*〕 *the stairs* 계단을 뛰어 올라가다〔내려가다〕. ⓑ (P1,2A,3,4) go away hastily; escape swiftly. (급하게) 달아나다; (재빠르게) 도망치다. ¶ *The enemy ran.* 적은 패주했다 / *~ for one's life* 걸음아 날 살려라 하고 달아나다. **2** (P1,2A,4) hasten; rush. 서둘러 가다; 서두르다; 돌진하다. ¶ *~ through one's work* 일을 서둘러 해버리다 / *~ to catch the train* 기차를 놓치지 않으려고 내달리다 / *We ran to her aid.* 그녀를 돕기 위해 서둘러 갔다 / *~ for a doctor* 급히 의사를 부르러 가다. **3** (P1,2A,2B,3) ⓐ take part in a race; run in a race. 경주에 나가다. ¶ *~ in a hurdle-race* 장애물 경주에 나가다 / *The horses ran neck and neck.* 말들은 호각지세로 달렸다. ⓑ 《*for*》 be a candidate for or in an election, contest, etc. 입후보〔출마〕하다. ¶ *~ for president* 대통령에 출마하다 / *~ for a beauty contest* 미인 콘테스트에 나가다. **4** (P1,2A,3,4) (of a train, a bus, a ship, etc.) start and arrive regularly. (기차 등이) 다니다; 운행하다. ¶ *The buses ~ every five minutes.* 버스는 5분마다 다닌

다 / *The bus runs between A and B* 〔*from A to B*〕. 버스는 A와 B간을 운행한다. **5** move at a certain speed. 일정 속도로 달리다. ¶ ~ *at 60 miles an hour* 한시간에 60마일의 속도로 달리다. **6** (P2A) (of time) pass; go by. (시간이) 경과하다; 흐르다. ¶ *How fast the years ~ by!* 세월의 흐름이 참 빠르기도 하구나. **7** (P1,2A,3) (of a stream, etc.) flow along; (of a liquid) flow; be covered with a flow of a liquid; overflow. (강 따위가) 흐르다; (액체가) 흐르다; 넘쳐 흐르다. ¶ *Rivers ~ into the sea.* 강은 바다로 흘러든다 / *A nose runs.* 콧물이 나온다 / *The floor ran with water.* 마룻바닥에 물이 질펀하게 흘렀다 / *Tears ran down from her eyes.* 그녀 눈에선 눈물이 흘렀다 / *The current is running high.* 물살이 거칠다 / *Blood ran from the cut.* 상처에서 피가 흘러나왔다. **8** (P1,2A,3) melt and spread to other parts. 녹아 흐르다〔번지다〕; 배어나오다. ¶ *The ink runs on this paper.* 이 종이에 잉크는 번진다 / *The butter ran.* 버터가 녹아 흘렀다. **9** (P1,2A,3) (of a machine) work; operate. (기계가) 돌아가다; 움직이다. ¶ *This machine runs by electricity.* 이 기계는 전동식이다 / *Things ~ smoothly.* 만사가 순조롭게 돌아간다 / *The machines ~ day and night.* 기계들은 밤낮으로 돌아간다 / *keep an engine running* 엔진을 계속 돌게 하다. **10** (P1,3) (of fire, news, etc.) spread rapidly. (불·소문 따위가) 빠르게〔급히, 확〕 번지다〔퍼지다〕. ¶ *Fire ran along the street.* 불길이 거리를 따라 확 퍼져 나갔다 / *The rumor runs that he is sick.* 그가 아프다는 소문이 쫙 퍼졌다. **11** (P2A,3) (of thoughts, eyes, etc.) pass quickly; come and go quickly; occur. (생각 등이) 퍼뜩〔문득〕 떠오르다; 홱 지나가다; 나타나다; 죽 훑어보다. ¶ *A thought ran through my mind.* 문득 어떤 생각이 머리를 스쳤다 / *His eyes ran over the room.* 그는 방안을 죽 둘러 봤다 / *A cold shiver ran down his spine.* 등골이 오싹 했다. **12** (P1,2A,3) extend; stretch out. 뻗다; 뻗어〔이어져〕 있다; 통하다. ¶ *The road runs some miles by the sea.* 길은 해안을 따라 수마일이나 뻗어 있다 / *The fence runs round the house.* 담은 집 주위를 빙 둘러싸고 있다 / *The road runs north.* 도로는 북쪽으로 뻗어 있다. **13** (P1,2A,2B) continue; be performed on the stage continuously; be continued or repeated. 계속하다; (연극 따위가) 계속 공연되다; (효력 따위가) 계속되다. ¶ *The play ran for a year.* 극은 1년 동안 속연됐다 / *The law runs for ten years.* 법은 10년간 유효하다. **14** (P5) become; get. …이 되다. ¶ ~ *mad* 미치다; 발광하다 / ~ *big* 커지다 / ~ *strong* 튼튼해지다 / ~ *dry* 말라버리다 / ~ *to seed* 종자〔씨〕가 되다 / ~ *to ruin* 황폐해지다 / *He ran short of money.* 돈이 궁해졌다. **15** (P5) be written or expressed. …라고 씌어〔말해지고〕 있다. ¶ *So the story runs.* 이야기가 그렇게 돼 있다 / *The letter runs as follows.* 편지는 다음과 같다 / *The rumor runs that he is going abroad.* 그가 해외로 나간다는 소문이다. **16** (P1,2A) (of cloth) become loosened; drop stitches. (옷의) 올이 풀리다. ¶ *Silk stockings often ~.* 비단 양말은 올이 잘 풀린다. **17** (P2A,3) appear continuously in print; be published. 판(版)을 거듭하다; 출판되다. ¶ *The book has ~ through* 〔*into*〕 *ten editions.* 그 책은 10판을 거듭했다 / *The story is now running in the newspapers.* 그 이야기는 지금 신문에 게재되고 있다.

— *vt.* **1** (P6,7,13) cause (someone or something) to run or move; work; operate. …을 달리게 하다; 움직이게 하다; 작동〔가동〕하다. ¶ ~ *a horse to death* 말을 너무 몰아서 죽게 만들다 / ~ *a steamer* 기선을 운항시키다 / ~ *a sewing machine* 재봉틀을 돌리다. **2** (P6) escape from (a place). …에서 도망치다. ¶ ~ *one's country* 망명하다. **3** (P6) drive (an animal); force to run out, and follow; hunt. (짐승)을 몰다; 쫓다; 사냥하다. ¶ ~ *a fox* 〔*hare*〕 여우〔토끼〕를 몰다 / ~ *a hare to earth* 토끼를 굴속에 몰아넣다 / ~ *someone out of town* 아무를 도시 밖으로 쫓아내다 / ~ *a deer* 사슴사냥을 하다. **4** (P6) do (something) by running or by moving. 달려서 …을 하다. ¶ ~ *a race* 경주하다 / ~ *errands* (줄달음쳐)심부름을 하다. **5** (P6) run along (a road, etc.); go over (a distance) by running. 뛰어 …을 지나가다; (어떤 거리)를 달리다. ¶ ~ *the streets* 거리를 달려가다 / ~ *bases* 주루(走壘)하다 / ~ *a hundred miles,* 100마일을 달리다. **6** (P6,13) support (someone) to be elected; put up as a candidate. …을 입후보〔출마〕시키다. ¶ ~ *someone for the Senate* 아무를 상원에 입후보시키다. **7** (P13) cause (one's eyes, etc.) to pass quickly; cause to move lightly or quickly. 대강 …을 훑어보다; 가볍게〔빠르게〕 살짝 움직이다. ¶ ~ *one's eyes over a letter* 편지를 죽 훑어보다 / ~ *one's fingers over the keys of a piano* 가볍게 피아노 건반을 두드리다 / ~ *one's eye over a map* 지도를 대충 한번 훑어 보다. **8** (P6,13) drive; thrust. …을 꿰찌르다; 찔러 넣다. ¶ ~ *a thread through a needle's eye* 바늘에 실을 꿰다 / ~ *one's hand into one's pocket* 주머니에 손을 찔러 넣다 / ~ *a knife into the body* 몸에 칼을 찌르다. **9** (P7,13) cause (water, etc.) to flow. …을 흘리다; 흐르게 하다. ¶ ~ *tears* 눈물을 흘리다 / ~ *water into a pool* 수영장에 물을 대다 / *Have you left the water running?* 네가 수돗물을 틀어 놓은 채로 두었느냐. **10** (P6) manage; conduct. …을 경영하다; 지휘하다. ¶ ~ *a hotel* 호텔을 경영하다 / ~ *a camera store* 카메라 가게를 운영하다 / ~ *a business* 사업을 경영하다 / ~ *a campaign* 정치 운동을 지휘하다. **11** (P6) expose oneself to (danger, adventure, etc.); undergo. (위험 등)을 초래하다; 무릅쓰다; 겪다. ¶ ~ *risks* 모험하다 / ~ *the risk of* …의 위험을 무릅쓰다 / ~ *the danger of losing all one's money* 전 재산을 날릴 수 있는 위험한 짓을 하다. **12** (P6) publish; print. …을 출판[인쇄]하다. **13** (P6,7,13) smuggle in. …을 밀수입하다.

run across, meet (someone) by chance; find; come across. …을 우연히 만나다[찾아내다]. ¶ *I ran across an old friend in the street.* 거리에서 우연히 옛 친구를 만났다.

run after, **a**) follow and try to catch; pursue. …의 뒤를 쫓다. ¶ ~ *after a thief* 도둑의 뒤를 쫓다. **b**) 《*colloq.*》 try to become friendly with. 사귀려고 …의 꽁무니를 쫓아다니다. ¶ ~ *after girls* 여자들 뒤꽁무니를 쫓아다니다.

run against, **a**) rush against; collide with (something). …에 충돌하다[부딪치다]. ¶ *The ship has ~ against a rock.* 배는 좌초됐다. **b**) meet (someone) by chance. 우연히 마주치다.

run around, run or go from place to place. 여기저기 (뛰어) 돌아다니다.

run around with, 《*colloq.*》 associate with. …와 교제하다; 사귀다.

run at, run towards; spring at; attack. …을 공격하다; 덮치다. ¶ *A dog ran at the boy.* 개 한 마리가 소년에게 덤벼들었다.

run away, **a**) escape; flee. 도망치다. **b**) go away; leave home and go elsewhere. 가출하다.

run away with, **a**) carry off; steal. …을 가지고 달아나다; 훔치다. **b**) go away with (someone). …을 데리고[…와 함께] 도망치다. ¶ ~ *away with a lover* 애인과 함께 도망치다. **c**) cause (someone) to lose self-control. …의 자제심을 잃게 하다. ¶ *Don't let your anger ~ away with you.* 화내지 말고 진정해라. **d**) carry off (a prize, honors, etc.); win. (상)을 차지하다; 이기다.

run counter to, go against; be opposed or contrary to; oppose. …에 반(反)하다; …에 위배되다; 반대하다.

run down, **a**) (of a machine) stop operating. (기계 등이) 서다; 멎다. ¶ *My watch has ~ down.* 시계가 멎었다. **b**) catch (someone) after a long pursuit. …을 뒤쫓아서 잡다. ¶ ~ *down a thief* 도둑을 뒤쫓아가 잡다. **c**) knock down; collide with (something). 부딪쳐[들이받아] 쓰러뜨리다; …와 충돌하다. ¶ *He was ~ down by a car.* 그는 자동차에 부딪쳐 쓰러졌다. **d**) speak ill of (someone); criticize severely. …을 헐뜯다; 비난[혹평]하다. **e**) 《in *passive*》 be in weak health. 쇠약하다[해지다]. ¶ *He is ~ [running] down.* 그는 쇠약해졌다[쇠약해지고 있다]. **f**) run along. 뛰어가다. ¶ ~ *down the street* 거리를 따라 뛰어가다 / 《*fig.*》 ~ *down the track [trail]* 코스[발자취]를 따라 뛰어가다. **g**) look through; examine: search out. 꿰뚫어 보다; 정사(精査)하다; 찾아내다. ¶ ~ *down the records* 기록을 조사하다.

run for it, 《*colloq.*》 run in order to escape or avoid something. 도망치다; 달아나다.

run in, **a**) 《*sl.*》 seize (someone) by authority of the law; arrest. …을 체포하다; 구금하다. **b**) visit casually. …을 불쑥 방문하다. ¶ *I just ran in to speak with you.* 말할 게 있어 잠깐 들렀다.

run into, **a**) strike against (another car, etc.). …와 충돌하다; 부딪히다. **b**) meet (someone) by chance. …와 우연히 만나다. **c**) pass into a certain condition. 어떤 상태에 빠지다. ¶ ~ *into danger [trouble]* 위험[고민]에 빠지다 / ~ *into debt* 빚지게 되다. **d**) amount to (a certain degree). …에 이르다. ¶ ~ *into a large sum of money* 큰 금액에 달하다. **e**) follow; succeed. …에 계속되다.

run off, **a**) run away. 달아나다; 도망치다. **b**) flow away; cause (water, etc.) to flow away. 흘러가다; …을 유출시키다. **c**) write or speak fluently. 막힘없이 써나가다[말하다].

run on, **a**) continue without a break or new paragraph. (인쇄물의 내용 따위가) 절(節)·행(行)을 바꾸지 않고 계속되다. **b**) continue. …을 계속하다. ¶ *The story ran on (and on).* 이야기는 계속 이어졌다.

run out, come to an end; become used up. 끝나다; 다하다; 동나다. ¶ *The coal has ~ out.* 석탄이 다 떨어졌다 / *Time is running out.* 시간이 다 끝나간다.

run out of (= *use up; have no more of*) *something.* …을 다 써버리다. ¶ *We have ~ out of food.* 우린 양식이 떨어졌다.

run over, **a**) do again; repeat. …을 복습하다; 되풀이하다. **b**) ride or drive over (someone). (특히 차가) …을 치다. ¶ *A child was ~ over by a car.* 어린아이 하나가 차에 치었다. **c**) overflow. …을 넘쳐 흐르다. ¶ *Water runs over the banks.* 물이 둑을 넘쳐 흐르고 있다.

run through, **a**) examine, review, read, etc. quickly. …을 대충 훑어보다. **b**) pierce; thrust. …을 꿰뚫다; 찌르다. **c**) use up (something) carelessly or recklessly. …을 마구 써 버리다[낭비하다]. ¶ ~ *through one's money* 돈을 흥청망청 쓰다.

run to, **a**) reach (an amount, a number, etc.). (수량이) …에 이르다; 달하다. ¶ *The cost runs to ten thousand dollars.* 비용은 1만 달러에 이른다. **b**) have money for (something); (of money) be enough for (something). …할 자력이 있다; (돈이) …하기에 충분하다. ¶ *My wages won't ~ to buying a car.* 내 벌이로는 차 살 형편이 안된다.

run up, **a**) increase continuously; cause (something) to increase; pile up. 계속 증가하다; …을 늘리다. ¶ ~ *up expenses* 비용을 늘리다 / ~ *up bills [accounts]* 계산서가 밀리다. **b**) raise; hoist. …을 게양하다; 올리다. ¶ ~ *up a flag* 기를 게양하다. **c**) add up (a column of figures). (숫자들을) 합계하다.

d) make or build rapidly; sew rapidly. (집·구조물 따위를) 서둘러 짓다〔만들다〕; 급히 꿰매다.

run upon, **a**) strike. …을 치다. **b**) (of thoughts, etc.) be concerned with (something). (생각이) …에 미치다. **c**) meet (someone) by chance. …을 우연히 만나다.

run wild, **a**) (of plants) grow in all directions. (식물이) 마구 퍼지다. **b**) live or act in a wild manner; be out of control. 멋대로 굴다; 날뛰다.

— *n.* Ⓒ **1** the act of running; a running pace. 달리기; 뛰기; 구보. ¶ *at a* ～ 뛰어서; 구보로 / *take a* ～ 한차례 뛰다 / *go out for a* ～ 한바탕 뛰기 위해 나가다 / *take a ten-minute* ～ *before breakfast* 아침 식사 전에 10분간 달리기 하다. **2** Ⓤ capacity for running. 달리는 힘; 주력. ¶ *There is no more* ～ *left in him.* 그는 더는 뛸 힘이 없다. **3** ⓐ a quick trip. (급한) 여행; 짧은〔단거리〕 여행. ¶ *a* ～ *on the Continent* 서둘러 하는 유럽 대륙 여행. ⓑ the regular trip of a ship, train, etc. between two places (선박·기차 등에 의한 두 지점간의) 규칙적인 운항; 운행; 항행. ¶ *the* ～ *from A to B* 〔*between A and B*〕 A지점과 B지점 사이의 운항〔운행〕 / *a nonstop* ～ *from A to B,* A 지점에서 B 지점까지의 직행(편). **4** the distance covered by running or in a trip. 주행 거리; 행정(行程). ¶ *a* ～ *of a mile* 1마일의 주정(走程) / *the train's* ～ *from Seoul to Pusan* 서울서 부산까지의 기차의 주행 거리. **5** continuation; succession. 계속; 연속. ¶ *a* ～ *of good weather* 연일 계속되는 쾌청한 날씨 / *The play had a long* ～. 그 연극은 장기 흥행을 했다 / *have a* ～ *of good* 〔*bad*〕 *luck* 행운〔불운〕의 연속이다 / *His new fiction has a good* ～. 그의 신작 소설은 연일 호평이다. **6** free use. 사용·출입의 자유. ¶ *I give you the* ～ *of my car.* 내 차를 마음대로 써도 좋다 / *give someone the free* ～ *of a place* 아무에게 출입의 자유를 주다. **7** the average sort. 보편적인 것; 보통의 종류〔형〕. ¶ *the common* ～ *of men* 보통〔평범한〕 사람 / *out of the usual* ～ 유별나게 / *the general* ～ *of modern fiction* 보통의 흔히 있는 현대 소설. **8** a number of animals moving together; a number of fish moving up a stream. 한 무리의 짐승 떼; (산란기의) 강을 거슬러 오르는 물고기 떼. ¶ *a* ～ *of salmon.* **9** an enclosed area for domestic animals or fowl; a feeding ground. (가축·가금의) 우리; 사육장; 방목장. ¶ *a sheep* 〔*cattle*〕 ～ / *a chicken* ～ 양계장. **10** 《U.S.》 a long, narrow hole or break in a stocking, cloth, etc.; 《Brit.》 ladder. (직물·스타킹 따위의) 올의 풀림. **11** 《baseball》 a scoring point. 득점; 1점《베이스의 일순(一巡)》. ¶ *score two runs* 두 점을 얻다. [E.]

a run for one's money, **a**) some satisfaction or enjoyment gained in return for one's money, time, efforts, etc. 돈 쓴〔애쓴〕 만큼의 보람. ¶ *I had quite a* ～ *for my money.* 돈도 썼지만 아주 즐거웠다. **b**) a fair chance; a chance of winning. 호기; 승기(勝機). ¶ *give someone a* ～ *for his money* 아무에게 좋은 기회를 한번 주다.

at a run, at a running pace. 구보로; 뛰어서. ¶ *She left at a* ～. 그녀는 뛰어서 갔다.

by the run, suddenly; with a run. 갑자기; 일제히.

come down with a run, fall rapidly. 급락하다. ¶ *Prices came down with a* ～. 물가가 폭락했다.

in the long run, in the course of things; in the end; eventually. 결국; 마침내. ¶ *The best is the cheapest, in the long* ～. 제일 좋은 물건(을 사는 것)이 결국은 제일 싸게 먹힌다.

on the run, **a**) running; while running. 뛰어서; 뛰면서. **b**) active; busy. 부산한; 바쁜. ¶ *He is always on the* ～. 그 사람은 늘 바쁘다. **c**) running away from an enemy, the police, etc.; in flight or hiding. 쫓기는; 도망다니는.

run·a·bout [rʌ́nəbàut] *n.* Ⓒ **1** a person who runs about from one place to another. (공연히) 돌아다니는 사람; 부랑〔방랑〕자. **2** a light, open automobile; a light motorboat. 소형 자동차〔모터보트〕. [*run*]

run·a·way [rʌ́nəwèi] *n.* **1** Ⓒ a person, horse, etc. that runs away or escapes. 도망자; 탈주자; 고삐 풀린 말. **2** Ⓤ the act of running away. 도망; 탈주. — *adj.* **1** escaping; out of control. 도망 간; 다루기 힘든. ¶ *a* ～ *horse* 고삐 풀린 말 / *a* ～ *car* 폭주하는 차. **2** eloping. 눈맞아 달아난. ¶ *a* ～ *marriage* 사랑의 도피 결혼. **3** (of a race, victory, etc.) easily won. 쉽게 이긴; 낙승한. [*run*]

run-down [rʌ́ndàun] *adj.* **1** tired; sick. 피곤한; 병약한. ¶ *You look a bit* ～. 약간 피곤해 보인다. **2** that has stopped working. (기계 따위가)정지한; 서버린. **3** falling to pieces; dilapidated. 결딴난; 황폐한. ¶ *an old* ～ *hotel* 낡고 황폐한 호텔. [↑]

rune [ru:n] *n.* Ⓒ **1** any letter of an ancient alphabet which originated in North Europe. 룬 문자. **2** a magic sign. 신비로운 기호. [N.]

:rung[1] [rʌŋ] *v.* p. and pp. of **ring**[2].

rung[2] [rʌŋ] *n.* Ⓒ **1** one of the steps of a ladder; a crosspiece set between the legs of a chair. (사다리·의자 따위의) 가로대; 횡목. **2** a spoke of a wheel. (수레의) 바퀴살. **3** 《Scot.》 a cudgel. 곤봉; 몽둥이. [E.]

ru·nic [rú:nik] *adj.* of or written in runes. 룬 문자의; 룬 문자로 쓰여진. [*rune*]

run·let [rʌ́nlit] *n.* Ⓒ =runnel.

run·nel [rʌ́nl] *n.* Ⓒ **1** a small stream. 시내. **2** a small channel for water. 작은 수로(水路). [*run*]

***run·ner** [rʌ́nər] *n.* Ⓒ **1** a person who runs or is running; a racer. 뛰는 사람; 경주자〔마〕. ¶ *a poor* 〔*fast*〕 ～ / *The* ～ *arrived* *out of breath.* 주자는 숨을 헐떡이며 도착했다. **2** a messenger. 메신저; 사자(使者); 심부름꾼. **3** one of the long narrow pieces on which a sleigh slides; the blade of a skate. (썰매·스케이트의) 활주부(滑走部); 날. **4** 《bot.》 a creeping stem that issues from main stem and takes root. 덩굴; 포복지(匍匐枝). **5** a smuggler. 밀수업자.

run·ner-up [rʌ́nərʌ́p] *n.* a player or team that takes second place in a contest. (경기의) 차점자; 차위 팀.

:run·ning [rʌ́niŋ] *adj.* **1** that runs; moving rapidly; flowing. 뛰는; 달리는; 흐르는. ¶ *at the ~ pace* 구보로 / *These fishes prefer to live in ~ water.* 이 물고기 종류들은 흐르는 물에서 잘 산다. **2** going or carried on continuously; repeated continuously. 연속적인; 계속하는. ¶ *five times ~* 5회 연속 / *~ fire* 연속 속사 / *a ~ commentary* 실황 방송 / *for three nights ~* 사흘 밤 계속. **3** (of plants) creeping. (식물이) 땅을 기는; 포복을 하는; 덩굴로 감는. **4** current. 목하의; 지금의. ¶ *the ~ month* 이달; 금월. **5** discharging pus. 고름을 내는. ¶ *a ~ sore* 고름이 나오는 상처.

— *n.* Ⓤ something that runs or flows; the amount that runs or flows. 유출물; 유출량. [*run*]

in* 〔*out of*〕 *the running, in 〔out of〕 the competition; having a chance 〔no chance〕 to win. 경기에 참가하여〔참가하지 않고〕; 승산이 있어〔없어〕.

make the running, set the pace. (말이 선두에 서서 다른 말의) 보조를 정하다.

take up the running, set a standard or be a leader. 솔선하다; 앞장서다.

running board [∠– ∠] *n.* a board along the side of an automobile on which a person steps to get in or out. (자동차의) 발판.

running hand [∠– ∠] *n.* rapid handwriting. 초서체. ¶ *Running hand joins all letters of a word together.* 초서체로 쓸 때에는 한 단어의 글자는 모두 붙인다.

run-off [rʌ́nɔ̀(ː)f, -ɑ̀f] *n.* **1** Ⓒ a final, deciding race, game, etc. (동점자의) 결승전. **2** Ⓤ something that flows out. (빗물 등) 흘러가는 것.

runt [rʌnt] *n.* Ⓒ **1** a small-sized animal, person or plant. 작은 짐승〔사람·식물〕. **2** an ox or cow of a small breed. 품종이 작은 소. [E.]

run·way [rʌ́nwèi] *n.* Ⓒ **1** a way, track, or the like, along which something moves, slides, etc. 주로(走路); 통로. **2** the part of an airport made for airplanes to land on and take off from. 활주로. **3** the beaten track of deer or other animals. 짐승들이 다니는 길. [*run*]

rup·ture [rʌ́ptʃər] *n.* **1** ⓊⒸ the act of bursting or breaking apart. 파열. ¶ *the ~ of a blood vessel* 혈관 파열. **2** ⓊⒸ an interruption of friendly relations. 불화; 사이가 틀어짐. ¶ *come to a ~* (교섭이) 결렬되다; 사이가 틀어지다 / *a ~ between friends* 친구간의 불화 / *~ of friendly relations* 우호 관계의 결렬. **3** Ⓒ 《med.》 a hernia. 헤르니아; 탈장.

— *vt.* (P6) **1** break apart; burst. …을 터뜨리다; 파열시키다. **2** interrupt (a connection, a relation, etc.). …의 사이를 갈라놓다. **3** 《med.》 cause a hernia in (someone). …을 헤르니아에 걸리게 하다.

— *vi.* (P1) **1** break. 파열되다; 터지다. **2** suffer or develop a hernia. 헤르니아에 걸리다. [L. *rumpo* break]

***ru·ral** [rúərəl] *adj.* of the countryside. 전원의; 시골의; 농촌의(opp. urban). ¶ *a ~ area* 농촌 지역 / *a ~ life* 농촌 생활 / *in ~ seclusion* 인가에서 떨어져 / *~ scenes* 시골 풍경 / *~ economy* 농촌 경제. [L. *rus* the country]

ruse [ruːz] *n.* Ⓒ a trick; a deceitful way of acting; Ⓤ fraud. 계략; 책략; 사기. [E.]

:rush[1] [rʌʃ] *vi.* **1** (P1,2A,3,4) move with speed; hurry; dash. 돌진하다; 돌격하다. ¶ *~ at the enemy* 적을 향해 돌격하다 / *~ for a good seat* 좋은 자리를 잡으려고 들입다 뛰다 / *Policemen rushed to the spot of murder.* 경찰이 살인 현장으로 달려 갔다 / *He came rushing into the room.* 그는 방으로 뛰어 들어 왔다 / *~ back from one's trip* 여행에서 급히 돌아오다 / *The stream rushes over the rocks.* 격류가 바위를 덮치며 흐른다. **2** (P3) 《*into*》 act swiftly without thinking enough; act hastily. 성급하게 굴다; 덤비다. ¶ *~ into debt* 닥치는 대로 돈을 꾸다 / *~ to a conclusion* 성급히 결론을 내리다 / *The nation rushed into a war.* 그 나라는 무모하게 전쟁을 시작했다. **3** (P3) go, appear, pass, or come rapidly or suddenly and swiftly. 갑자기 나타나다; (생각 등이) 문득 떠오르다. ¶ *~ into one's mind* 갑자기 마음에 떠오르다 / *Blood rushed to her face.* 그녀는 확 얼굴이 상기됐다 / *Words rushed to his lips.* 그의 입에서 말이 튀어나왔다 / *Tears rushed to her eyes.* 그녀의 눈에서 눈물이 쏟아져 나왔다. **4** pass rapidly. 빠르게 지나다. ¶ *The years rushed by us.* 세월은 빠르게 흘렀다.

— *vt.* **1** (P6,7,13) cause (someone or something) to go or move swiftly; hurry. …을 다그치다; 몰아세우다. ¶ *The teacher rushed the boy out of the room.* 선생님은 그 아이를 교실 밖으로 내쫓았다. **2** (P6,13,20) force (someone) to act hastily; hurry; urge. …을 서두르게 하다; 재촉하다. ¶ *~ someone to decide* 아무에게 결심을 재촉하다 / *I don't like to be rushed.* 나는 재촉받는 건 싫다. **3** (P6) do swiftly. …을 급히 〔서둘러〕 하다. ¶ *~ one's work* 일을 서둘러 진행하다. **4** (P6,7,13) send or carry swiftly. …을 급히 보내다〔나르다〕. ¶ *~ a wounded child to a hospital* 다친 아이를 서둘러 병원에 보내다 / *~ an ambulance to the* *scene* 구급차를 급히 현장에 보내다 / ~ *a message* 지급 전보를 치다 / ~ *a letter to the post office* 우체국으로 급히 편지를 가져가다. **5** (P6) attack suddenly; get (something) by a sudden attack. …을 급습하다. ¶ ~ *a fort* 〔*bridge*〕 요새를〔교량을〕 급습하다 / *They rushed him and knocked him down.* 그들은 그에게 달려들어 때려 눕혔다. **6** (P6) pass or get over by riding at high speed. 빠르게 뛰어넘다; 돌파하다. ¶ ~ *a fence* (말을 몰아) 울타리를 뛰어넘다. **7** (P6,13,14) 《*colloq.*》 charge exorbitant prices. …에게 터무니없는 값을 부르다. ¶ *They rushed me shockingly.* 내게 엄청난 바가지를 씌웠다.

— *n.* Ⓒ **1** the act of rushing; a dash. 돌진; 돌격. ¶ *a ~ of wind* 일진(一陣)의 돌풍 / *He made a ~ for the door.* 그는 급히 문으로 달려 갔다 / *They were swept away by the ~ of the river.* 그들은 세찬 물살에 휩쓸려 내려갔다. **2** a state of being unusually busy or crowded; a hurry. 붐빔; 서두름. ¶ *a ~ of work* 밀어닥치는 일거리 / *come home during the evening ~* 저녁의 한창 붐빌 때 귀가하다 / *What's the ~? —Wait a minute.* 뭐가 바쁘냐. —잠깐 기다려 / *send someone in a ~* 아무를 서둘러 보내다 / *There is no great ~ about it.* 그것은 급히 서두를 것 없다. **3** ⓐ 《*on, for*》 a great or sudden demand. 대단한 수요; (주문의) 쇄도. ¶ *a ~ for uranium* 우라늄의 수요 급증 / *a ~ on mining stocks* 광산주(鑛山株)로의 주문의 쇄도. ⓑ a sudden increase; a sudden, rapid development. 급격한 증가; 급속한 발달. ¶ *a ~ of business* 사업 번창 / *a great ~ of parcels at a post office* 우체국으로의 소포의 쇄도 / *a ~ of buds* 꽃봉오리의 신속한 성장.

with a rush, suddenly and forcefully. 일제히; 갑자기. ¶ *The flowers came out with a ~.* 일제히 꽃이 피어났다.

— *adj.* 《*colloq.*》 that must be done in a hurry; requiring haste; busy; crowded. 시급한; 지급을 요구하는; 쇄도하는. ¶ *a ~ act* 지급을 요하는 행동 / *a ~ work* 급한 일. [F. *rehusser*]

rush² [rʌʃ] *n.* **1** Ⓒ a plant with tall leaves that grows in or near water; Ⓤ slender long stems of this plant, used for making chair seats, etc. 등심초속(屬)의 식물; (의자 등 세공용의) 골풀줄기. **2** Ⓒ 《usu. in *negative*》 《*fig.*》 something of little or no value. 하찮은 것. ¶ *do not care a ~* 조금도 개의치 않다; 무시하다. [E.]

rush·y [rʌ́ʃi] *adj.* (**rush·i·er, rush·i·est**) full or made of rushes; covered with rushes. 등심초가 많은; 골풀로 만든. [↑]

rusk [rʌsk] *n.* Ⓒ a slice of sweet raised bread dried and baked again in the oven. 러스크《딱딱한 빵의 일종》. [Sp. *rosca* twist]

rus·set [rʌ́sət] *adj.* of reddish brown or yellowish brown. 황갈색의. ¶ *The leaves in the autumn are scarlet, yellow, and ~.* 가을철 나뭇잎은 주홍에다 노랑 그리고 고동색이다. — *n.* **1** Ⓤ reddish brown; yellowish brown. 황갈색; 고동색. **2** Ⓤ a rough, russet-colored cloth. 황갈색 수직(手織)천. **3** Ⓒ a winter apple with a rough, brownish skin. 황갈색의 겨울 사과. [L. *russus*]

:Rus·sia [rʌ́ʃə] *n.* **1** a former empire in eastern Europe and western nothern Asia, 1547-1917. 러시아 제국. **2** a country in eastern Europe and Northern Asia, established in 1991 upon the breakup of the U.S.S.R. (소련 붕괴후의) 러시아《수도는 모스크바》. [Place]

:Rus·sian [rʌ́ʃən] *adj.* of Russia, its people or their language. 러시아의; 러시아어〔인〕의. — *n.* Ⓒ a native of Russia; Ⓤ the language of Russian people. 러시아인; 러시아어.

·rust [rʌst] *n.* Ⓤ **1** the reddish-brown coating that forms on iron or steel when exposed to air or dampness. 녹. ¶ *gather ~* 녹이 슬다. **2** 《bot.》 a fungus which causes a plant disease with colored spots. 녹병(病). **3** 《*fig.*》 a weakened state of mind. (정신의) 무딘 상태; 생기를 잃음. ¶ *Don't leave your talents to ~.* 네 재능을 녹슬게 두지 마라.

— *vi.* (P1,2A) become covered with rust; 《*fig.*》 grow worthless because of idleness. 녹슬다; 무디게 되다. ¶ *Stainless steel does not ~.* 스테인리스강(鋼)은 녹슬지 않는다.

— *vt.* (P6) cause (something) to rust. …을 녹슬게 하다. ¶ *The rain will ~ the iron.* 쇠는 비를 맞으면 녹이 슨다. [E.]

·rus·tic [rʌ́stik] *adj.* **1** of the countryside; rural. 시골의(opp. urban). ¶ *~ dwelling* 시골집 / *The village has a certain ~ charm.* 그 마을은 어떤 시골다운 멋이 있다. **2** simple; plain; rough; lacking refinement. 단순한; 소박한. ¶ *~ furniture* 소박한 가구 / *~ simplicity* 소박한 단순(미) / *~ speech* 가식 없는 말. **3** made of rough, bark-covered branches or roots. 거칠게 만든; 통나무로 된. ¶ *a ~ bridge* 통나무 다리. — *n.* Ⓒ a country person. 시골 사람. ● **rus·ti·cal·ly** [-kəli] *adv.* [→ rural]

rus·ti·cate [rʌ́stəkèit] *vi.* (P1) go to the country; live in the country. 시골에 가다; 시골에 살다. — *vt.* (P6) **1** send (something) to the country; make (someone) rustic; make (something) in the rustic style. …을 시골로 보내다; 시골티가 나게 하다. **2** 《Brit.》 send (a student) away from the university for a while as a punishment. …에게 정학을 명하다.

rus·tic·i·ty [rʌstísəti] *n.* Ⓤ **1** the quality or state of being rustic; Ⓒ rustic life. 시골풍; 시골〔전원〕 생활. **2** simplicity; ignorance. 소박; 단순; 무교양.

rust·i·ness [rʌ́stinis] *n.* Ⓤ the state of being rusty. 녹이 슮.

·**rus·tle** [rʌ́səl] *vi.* (P1,2A) **1** (of silk clothes, leaves, etc.) make a soft light sound. (옷·나뭇잎 등이) 바삭거리다; 바스락거리다. ¶ *The leaves rustled in the night breeze.* 나뭇잎들이 밤바람에 바스락거렸다 / *~ in silk* 비단옷을 입다. **2** 《U.S. *colloq.*》 《*up*》 act or do with energy. 정력적으로 움직이다[하다].
— *vt.* (P6) **1** 《U.S. *colloq.*》 steal (cattle, etc.). (가축 등)을 훔치다. **2** move or stir (something) so that it makes a soft light sound. …을 바삭거리게 하다; 바스락 소리가 나게 하다. ¶ *~ papers.*
— *n.* ⒸⓊ a soft sound made by the wind, clothes, etc. 살랑살랑[바스락바스락] 하는 소리; 옷 스치는 소리. [Imit.]

rus·tler [rʌ́sələr] *n.* Ⓒ **1** 《U.S. *colloq.*》 an energetic person. 정력가; 활동가. **2** 《U.S. *colloq.*》 a person who steals cattle, etc. 가축 도둑.

rust·proof [rʌ́stprù:f] *adj.* resisting rust. 녹슬지 않는. [↓]

·**rust·y** [rʌ́sti] *adj.* (**rust·i·er, rust·i·est**) **1** covered with rust. 녹슨. ¶ *~ iron* 녹슨 쇠 / *a ~ knife* 녹슨 칼. **2** not working perfectly because of lack of use. (쓰지 않아서) 무디어진; 둔해진. ¶ *He is a bit ~ in shooting.* 사격 솜씨가 서툴러졌다 / *My French has got rather ~.* (안했더니) 프랑스어가 서툴러졌다 / *I am ~ on that subject.* 그 문제는 생각이 안 난다. **3** colored like rust; faded. 녹빛의; 색이 바랜. ¶ *a ~ old coat* 색이 바랜 헌 코트. [→rust]
turn rusty, take offence; get rather angry. 화를 내다; 기분이 나빠지다.

rut[1] [rʌt] *n.* Ⓒ **1** a hollow track made by a wheel. 바퀴 자국. **2** a fixed way of acting or thinking. 관례; 상습. ¶ *move in a ~* 판에 박힌 일을 하다 / *fall into a ~* 틀에 박히다.
— *vt.* (P6) (**rut·ted, rut·ting**) 《usu. in *passive*》 make a rut or ruts in (something). …에 바퀴 자국을 내다. ¶ *the rutted surface of the road* 바퀴 자국이 있는 길. [*route*]

rut[2] [rʌt] *n.* sexual excitement of deer, goats, sheep, etc., occurring at regular intervals. (사슴·양 등의) 발정(cf. *heat*).
— *vi.* (P1) be in rut. 발정하다; 암내내다. [L. *rugio* roar]

Ruth [ru:θ] *n.* a woman's name. 여자 이름.

ruth·less [rú:θlis] *adj.* having no pity; merciless; cruel. 무정한; 사정 없는; 잔인한. [*ruth, less*]

rye [rai] *n.* Ⓤ **1** a plant producing a grain which can be made into a coarse dark bread; the grain of this plant. 호밀(cf. *barley, wheat*). **2** 《U.S.》 =rye whisky. [E.]

rye whisky [⌐ ⌐—] *n.* 《U.S.》 whisky made from rye. 라이 위스키《미국·캐나다 주산》.

s S

S[1], **s** [es] *n.* Ⓒ (*pl.* **S's, Ss, s's, ss** [ésiz]) **1** the 19th letter of the English alphabet. 영어 알파벳의 열아홉째 글자. **2** anything having the shape of an S. S자 모양(의 것).

S[2] **1** south; southern. **2** 《chem.》 sulfur. **3** Saint. **4** School. **5** Saturday; Sunday. **6** September. **7** soprano.

s. (*pl.* **ss**) shilling(s); second(s); singular.

's **1** 《*colloq.*》 《contr. of *has, is, does,* or *us*》 has, is 등의 간약형. ¶ *He's done it.* / *She's a student.* / *What's he want?* / *Let's go.* **2** possessive s. 명사의 소유격 어미. ¶ *Jame's* / *man's* / *baby's* / *babies'* / *King of England's.*

Sab·bath [sǽbəθ] *n.* **1** 《usu. *the* ~》 a day of the week for rest and services in honor of God, Saturday for Jews, Sunday for most Christians. 안식일(安息日) 《유대교는 토요일, 기독교는 일요일》. ¶ *keep* 〔*break*〕 *the* ~ 안식일을 지키다〔어기다〕. **2** Ⓒ 《*s-*》 a period of rest, peace, quiet, etc. 휴식 기간; 안식(安息). [Heb. =rest]

Sabbath day's journey, the distance a Jew was allowed to travel on the Sabbath. (유대인의) 안식일의 행정(行程).

sab·bat·i·cal [səbǽtikəl] *adj.* **1** of or like the Sabbath. 안식일의; 안식일 같은. **2** of or for a rest from work. 안식의. [↑]

sabbatical leave [–∸–– ∸] *n.* =Sabbatical year.

sabbatical year [–∸–– ∸] *n.* a year off from duties, allowed once every seven years to teachers. (학교·대학 따위의) 안식년; 안식 휴가; 휴가 연도.

sa·ber, 《Brit.》 **-bre** [séibər] *n.* Ⓒ a heavy sword with a curved blade used by cavalry soldiers. 사브르; 기병도(騎兵刀). — *vt.* strike or kill (someone) with a saber. …을 사브르로 베다〔죽이다〕. [G. *sabel*]

sa·ble [séibəl] *n.* (*pl.* **-bles** or *collectively* **-ble**) **1** Ⓒ a small flesheating animal covered with beautiful dark fur. 검은담비. **2** Ⓤ the fur of this animal. 검은담비의 모피. **3** 《*poet.*》 ⓐ 《*pl.*》 black mourning garments. 상복(喪服). ⓑ the color black. 흑색. — *adj.* **1** made of sable. 검은담비 가죽의. **2** 《*poet.*》 black; dark; gloomy. 검은; 암흑의; 음침〔음울〕한. ¶ ~ *night* 깜깜한 밤. [Slav.]

sab·ot [sǽbou] *n.* Ⓒ **1** a shoe made out of a piece of wood. 목화(木靴); 나막신. **2** a shoe with a wooden sole. 나무창의 가죽신. [F.]

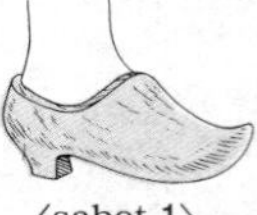
〈sabot 1〉

sab·o·tage [sǽbətɑ̀ːʒ, -tidʒ] *n.* Ⓤ **1** the act of breaking the machinery by workmen as an attack on or a threat against an employer. (노동 쟁의에 있어서의) 기계류의 파괴 행위; 사보타주; 태업(怠業). **2** damage to a nation's property by persons who act for the enemy. (전시에 적의 앞잡이에 의한) 파괴. — *vt.* (P6) damage or destroy (something) by sabotage. …에 대해 파괴〔방해〕 행위를 하다; 사보타주〔태업〕하다. [↑]

sab·o·teur [sæ̀bətə́ːr] *n.* a person who takes part in sabotage. 파괴〔방해〕 행위를 하는 사람; 태업자(怠業者). [F.]

sa·bre [séibər] *n., v.* 《Brit.》 =saber.

sac [sæk] *n.* Ⓒ 《biol.》 a baglike part of a plant or an animal, usu. for holding liquids. 낭(囊); 액낭(液囊). [→sack[1]]

sac·cha·rin [sǽkərin] *n.* Ⓤ a very sweet, white substance made from coal tar. 사카린. [Gk. =sugar]

sac·cha·rine [sǽkəràin, -rin, -rìːn] *adj.* **1** of, containing saccharin. 사카린의; 사카린을 함유한. **2** like sugar; very sweet. 당(糖)과 같은; 매우 단. **3** 《*fig.*》 too sweet. (태도·말 따위가) 달콤한. ¶ *a ~ smile* 아첨의 미소 / ~ *sympathies* 달콤한 동정. — [-rin, -rìːn] *n.* =saccharin. [↑]

sac·er·do·tal [sæ̀sərdóutl] *adj.* of or having to do with priests or the work of priests. 성직자〔사제〕의; 성직자다운; 성직(제)의. [L. *sacerdos* priest]

sac·er·do·tal·ism [sæ̀sərdóutəlìzəm] *n.* the system of priests. 성직〔사제〕 제도; 성직자의 관행. [↑]

sac·er·do·tal·ize [sæ̀sərdóutəlaiz] *vt.* (P6) rule by the priests. 성직자에 의해 지배하다.

sa·chem [séitʃəm] *n.* Ⓒ **1** a chief among American Indians. (북아메리카 인디언 종족의) 추장. **2** a very important person. 거물; 지도자. [Native]

sach·et [sæʃéi / ∸∸] *n.* Ⓒ **1** a small bag or pad containing perfumed powder. 향낭(香囊). **2** sweet-smelling powder. (향낭에 넣는) 향분(香粉). [F.]

:sack[1] [sæk] *n.* Ⓒ **1** a bag made of coarse cloth used for holding corn coal, etc. (곡물 따위의) 자루; 마대; 부대. **2** any bag. 봉지. **3** the amount a bag holds. 한 부대의 양. **4** 《U.S. *sl.*》 《*the* ~》 a sleeping bag; a bed. 침낭(寢囊); 침상(寢床). ¶ *be still in the* ~ 아직도 잠자리에 있다. **5** a loose jacket or dress for a woman or

child. (여성·어린이의) 낙낙한 상의(上衣)·드레스; 색. **6** 《Brit. *colloq.*》 dismissal from employment. 해고. ¶ *give someone the* ~ 아무를 해고하다; 퇴짜[딱지]를 놓다.
get [***have***] ***the sack,*** be dismissed. 해고되다.
hit the sack, 《U.S. *sl.*》 go to bed. 잠자리에 들다; 자다.
hold the sack, 《U.S. *colloq.*》 take the consequences (=results) of a bad situation. (나쁜 결과에 대한) 전책임을 혼자 지다. — *vt.* (P6) **1** put (something) into a sack. …을 부대[자루, 봉지]에 담다. ¶ ~ *potatoes.* **2** 《Brit. *colloq.*》 dismiss (someone) from his occupation. …를 해고하다. ¶ *He was sacked for being lazy.* 게을러서 해고되었다. [Heb.]

sack[2] [sæk] *n.* 《*the* ~》 the act of robbing violently in a town seized in war. (점령지 따위에서의) 약탈. — *vt.* (P6) rob violently after the capture of (a town, etc.). (도시 따위)를 약탈하다. [L. *saccum* sack[1]]

sack·cloth [sǽkklɔ̀ːθ, -klɑ̀θ] *n.* Ⓤ the coarse cloth used for making sacks. 부대용 거친 마포(麻布); 즈크. [*sack*[1]]
in sackcloth and ashes, 《Bible》 in a state of penitence or sorrow. 깊이 뉘우치고; 비탄에 젖어.

sack coat [ㄴㅅ] *n.* a man's short, loose-fitting coat usu. a part of a business suit. 신사복의 상의. 參考 신사복 한 벌은 sack suit.

sack·ful [sǽkfùl] *n.* Ⓒ the amount that a sack can contain. 한 부대[포대] 분의 양(量). ¶ *a* ~ *of sugar* 설탕 한 포대.

sack·ing [sǽkiŋ] *n.* Ⓤ the coarse cloth used for making sacks; sackcloth. (부대용) 거친 마포(麻布); 즈크(=sackcloth).

sac·ra·ment [sǽkrəmənt] *n.* Ⓒ **1** a solemn, religious act or ceremony of the Christian church. 성예전(聖禮典); 성사(聖事). **2** 《often *the S-*》 the Lord's supper communion. 성찬; 성체. ¶ *go to the* ~ 성찬식에 참여하다 / *take* [*receive*] *the* ~ …하기를 맹세하고 영성체하다. [→sacred]

sac·ra·men·tal [sæ̀krəméntl] *adj.* **1** of or used in a sacrament. 성예전(聖禮典)의; 성찬(식)의. ¶ ~ *wine* 성찬식용 포도주. **2** sacred or holy. 신성한. — *n.* Ⓒ the act of crossing or of using holy water, oil, etc. 준성사(準聖事). ● **sac·ra·men·tal·ism** [-təlìzəm] *n.* Ⓤ ascription of great importance to the sacraments. 성찬 중시론(重視論). **sac·ra·men·tal·ist** [-təlist] *n.*

:sa·cred [séikrid] *adj.* **1** holy; belonging to God. 신성한; 신의. ¶ ~ *history* 성사(聖史) / *a* ~ *edifice* 신성한 건물 / *hold* ~ 신성시하다; 존중하다. **2** associated with the religion of a people; of religion; religious. 종교와 관련 있는; 종교의; 종교적인(opp. profane; secular). ¶ ~ *music* 종교 음악 / ~ *books* [*writings*] 성전(聖典)《성경·코란 따위》. **3** not to be violated. 침범할 수 없는. ¶ ~ *oaths* 극히 신성한 맹세 / ~ *rights* 침범받지 않는 권리. **4** worthy of reverence; treated with great respect. 존경할 만한; 존중되는. ¶ *Nothing is* ~ *to young people.* 청년들에게 있어 존경할 만한 것은 아무것도 없다. **5** 《*to*》 dedicated to (some purpose or person). (어떤 목적·사람)에(게) 바쳐진. ¶ *a bird* ~ *to Jupiter* 주피터 신에게 바쳐진 새 / *a fund* ~ *to charity* 자선을 위한 기금 / *the monument* ~ *to the memory of the Unknown Soldier* 무명 용사를 기리기 위해 바쳐진 기념비. [L. *sacer* holy]
be sacred from, be protected against. …을 면하다. ¶ *No place was* ~ *from outrage.* 난동을 면한 곳은 한 군데도 없었다.
hold sacred, respect. …을 존중하다. ¶ *hold a promise* ~ 약속을 존중하다.

sacred cow [ㄴㄴ] *n.* 《*iron.*》 something too holy to be criticized. 비판할 수 없는 신성한 것.

:sac·ri·fice [sǽkrəfàis] *n.* **1** ⓊⒸ the act of offering something to God. 희생(犧牲)·제물을 바치기. **2** Ⓒ a thing offered to God. 희생; 제물. ¶ *kill an ox as a* ~ *to Jupiter* 주피터 신에게 바치는 제물로서 수소를 죽이다. **3** ⓊⒸ the act of giving up something valuable to gain something else. (보다 중요한 것을) 희생으로 하기; 희생적 행위. ¶ *a* ~ *hit* (야구에서) 희생타 / *at any* ~ 어떠한 희생을 치르더라도 / *He would make any* ~ *to save me.* 그는 나를 구하기 위해 어떤 희생도 마다하지 않을 것이다. **4** Ⓒ the thing made a sacrifice to something else. 희생(되는 것). ¶ *make a* ~ *of* …을 희생하다. **5** Ⓒ damage; loss. 손실. ¶ *sell at a large* ~ 덤핑 판매하다 / *make a* ~ 투매(投賣)하다.
at [***by***] ***the sacrifice of,*** at the cost of. …을 희생으로 하여.
fall a sacrifice (=*fall a victim*) ***to*** *someone.* …의 희생이 되다.
make a sacrifice to (=*pay sacrifice to*) *someone.* …을 위해 희생을 치르다.
— *vt.* **1** (P6,13) offer (something) go God. …을 희생으로[제물로] 바치다. ¶ *They sacrificed sheep to their gods.* 그들은 신에게 양을 제물로 바쳤다. **2** (P6,7,13) give up (something) as a sacrifice. …을 희생시키다; 포기하다; 버리다; 바치다. ¶ ~ *one's life for the country* 나라를 위해 목숨을 바치다 / ~ *one's personal interest to public good* 공익을 위해 자기 개인의 이익을 희생시키다 / *You must not* ~ *studies for pleasure.* 쾌락을 위해 공부를 희생으로 해서는 안 된다. **3** sell (something) at a loss. …을 투매하다.
— *vi.* (P3) **1** 《*for, to*》 make a sacrifice. 희생[제물]을 바치다. **2** 《baseball》 advance a runner by means of a sacrifice hit. 희생 번트를 치다. [→sacred, -fic]

·sac·ri·fi·cial [sæ̀krəfíʃəl] *adj.* **1** of a sacrifice. 희생의; 제물의. **2** devoted to God as a sacrifice. 신(神)에게 바쳐진. **3** selling at a loss. 투매의; 덤핑 판매의.

S

sac·ri·lege [sǽkrəlidʒ] *n.* Ⓤ an intended violence or disrespect toward anyone or anything holy. 신성(神聖)을 더럽힘; 신성 모독(행위). [→sacred, L. *lēgo* pick]

sac·ri·le·gious [sæ̀krəlídʒəs, -lí:-] *adj.* of sacrilege; showing contempt or disregard for God or holy things. 신성을 모독하는; 신성 모독의.

sa·cring [séikriŋ] *n.* 《*arch.*》 **1** consecration of elements in the mass. (미사의) 축성(祝聖); (성체용의 빵과 포도주의) 청정(淸淨). **2** consecration of bishop, sovereign, etc. 취임식; 축성식. [→sacred]

sac·ris·tan [sǽkrəstən] *n.* an official keeping sacred vessels and vestments of church, etc. (성당의) 성물(聖物) 보관계원. [→sacred]

sac·ro·sanct [sǽkrousæ̀ŋkt] *adj.* very sacred; set apart for a holy purpose. 더없이 신성한; 신성하여 범할 수 없는. [→sacred, →saint]

:sad [sæd] *adj.* (**sad·der, sad·dest**) **1** (of a person, the mind, etc.) not happy; sorrowful. 슬퍼하는; 슬픈; 서글픈. ¶ *a ~ heart* 슬픈 마음 / *a ~ expression in one's eyes* 눈 속의 슬픈 표정 / *be ~ at parting from one's friend* 친구와의 헤어짐을 슬퍼하다. **2** (of an event, etc.) causing sorrow or grief. 슬프게 하는; 슬퍼할 만한. ¶ *~ news* 비보(悲報) / *a ~ story* 슬픈 이야기 / *a ~ disappointment in love* 사랑에서의 애처로운 좌절. **3** (of color) dull in color; sober; dark. (색이) 칙칙한; 충충한; 어두운. **4** 《*colloq.*, usu. *joc.*》 very bad; shocking; shameful. 지독한; 통탄할; 어이없는; 비참[한심]한. ¶ *a ~ rouge* 지독한 악당 / *a ~ attempt* 어처구니없는 시도 / *be in a ~ plight* 비참한 처지[상태]에 있다. **5** (of bread, etc.) (빵 따위가) 말랑말랑하게 부풀지 않은; 설구운. [E.]

in sad earnest, in all soberness; seriously. 진정으로; 진지하게.

make sad work of (=*be a failure in*) *something.* …에 실패하다; 못쓰게 만들다.

write sad stuff, write a bad sentence. 형편없는 문장을 쓰다.

sad·den [sǽdn] *vt.* (P6) make (someone) mournful, melancholy, gloomy, etc. …을 슬프게[우울하게] 하다. — *vi.* (P1) become sad. 슬퍼[우울해]지다; 어두워지다. ¶ *The sky saddened.* 하늘이 컴컴해졌다.

:sad·dle [sǽdl] *n.* Ⓒ **1** a seat for a rider on horseback or on a bicycle. (말·자전거 따위의) 안장. **2** anything like a saddle. 안장 모양의 것. **3** a ridge between two mountain peaks. 산등성이; 능선. **4** a piece of meat including the backbone and ribs. 등심 고기.

at home in the saddle, skilled in the art of riding. 승마술에 능숙한.

be in the saddle, **a**) ride on horseback. 말을 타다. **b**) have a job. 취직해 있다; 직장이 있다. **c**) have power. 권력을 쥐고 있다.

cast out of the saddle, dismiss from office. 면직(免職)하다.

get into the saddle, get a job. 취직하다.

lose the saddle, fall from a horse's back. 낙마(落馬)하다.

put [***lay, set***] ***the saddle on*** [***upon***] ***the right*** [***wrong***] ***horse.*** 《Brit. *colloq.*》 blame a blameworthy [blameless] person. 책해야 할 [엉뚱한] 사람을 책하다.

take [***get into***] ***the saddle,*** begin to ride on horseback. 말을 타다.

— *vt.* **1** (P6) place a saddle on (a horse's back). …에 안장을 얹다. **2** (P13) 《usu. *with*》 place (someone) a burden or responsibility on. …에게 책임[부담]을 짊어지우다. ¶ *~ someone with a heavy task* 아무에게 무거운 임무를 과하다 / *~ heavy taxes upon the nation* 국민에게 중세를 과하다. [E.]

sad·dle·bag [sǽdlbæ̀g] *n.* Ⓒ one of a pair of bags laid over a horse's back. 안낭(鞍囊)《안장 뒤에 붙이는》.

saddle horse [⌐–⌐] *n.* a horse fit for riding. 승용마(乘用馬).

sad·dler [sǽdlər] *n.* Ⓒ a person who makes and mends saddles, reins, etc. 마구(馬具) 제조[수선]인.

sad·dler·y [sǽdləri] *n.* **1** the work of a saddler; the shop of a saddler. 마구(馬具) 제조[판매]업; 마구전(廛). **2** 《*collectively*》 saddles, harness, etc. for horses. 마구류(類).

sad·ism [sǽdizəm, séid-] *n.* Ⓤ abnormal sexual satisfaction gained by causing or watching cruelty. 사디즘; 가학성(加虐性) 변태 성욕증(cf. *masochism*). [F. *sadisme* (count de *Sade*)]

sa·dis·tic [sədístik, sei-] *adj.* of or having to do with sadism. 사디즘의; 가학성(加虐性)의; 변태 성욕의. [↑]

:sad·ly [sǽdli] *adv.* **1** in a sad manner; sorrowfully; mournfully. 슬프게; 슬픈 듯이. ¶ *She stood ~ beside the grave.* 그녀는 슬픈 듯이 무덤 곁에 서 있었다. **2** badly. 지독히; 몹시; 비참히; 어이없게. ¶ *be ~ wounded* 몹시 다치다 / *You are ~ changed since we last met.* 지난 번 만나본 이후 몹시도 변했군 그래. [*sad*]

·sad·ness [sǽdnis] *n.* Ⓤ the state of being sad; great sorrow. 슬픔. ¶ *She had an air of ~ about her.* 그녀는 어딘가 슬픈 기색을 띠고 있었다.

sa·fa·ri [səfá:ri] *n.* a hunting trip or expedition, esp. in East Africa. (특히 동아프리카에서의) 사냥 여행. [Arab.]

:safe [seif] *adj.* **1** free from danger; secure from harm. 안전한; 무해(無害)한. ¶ *be ~ from attack* 공격을 받을 걱정이 없다 / *put money in a ~ place* 돈을 안전한 곳에 두다. **2** not causing harm or danger; not injured. 위험하지 않은; 부상하지 않은; 무사한. ¶ *arrive ~ and sound* 무사히 도착하다 / *Is your dog ~ ?* 자네 집 개는 안전한가[물 염려가 없는가] / *The car crashed but he was ~.*

차가 충돌했으나 그는 무사했다 / *The patient is now* ~. 병자는 이제 고비를 넘겼다 / *I saw her ~ home.* 그녀를 무사히 집에까지 바래다 주었다. **3** ⓐ sure; reliable. 확실한; 믿을〔신뢰할〕 수 있는. ¶ *a ~ investment* 확실〔안전〕한 투자 / *a ~ guide* 신뢰할 수 있는 안내인 / *a ~ first,* 1등이 확실한 사람 / *from a ~ quarter* 틀림없는 소식통에서. ⓑ《*to do*》 certain to do. …할 것이 확실한; 틀림없이 …하는. ¶ *The President is ~ to be re-elected.* 대통령이 재당선될 것이 틀림없다 / *We are ~ to win.* 우리 측의 승리는 확실하다. **4** no longer dangerous; securely held. (잡혀서) 위험이 없는; 도망할 염려가 없는. ¶ *The murderer is ~ in prison.* 살인범이 감옥에 갇혀 안심이다. **5** cautious in avoiding danger. 신중한〔을 기하는〕; 조심스러운. ¶ *~ driving* 안전 운전 / *a ~ player* 신중한 선수; 신중을 기하는 사람 / *We decided to play it ~.* 우리는 안전을 기하기로 했다. **6** 《baseball》 successful in reaching base. (야구에서) 타자〔주자〕가 죽지 않고 산; 세이프의.

be on the safe side, do not take any risks. 신중〔안전〕을 기하다. ¶ *I took an umbrella to be on the ~ side.* 안전을 기하기 위해 우산을 휴대했다.

It is safe to say that ..., It may be said without risk of exaggeration. …이라고 (말) 해도 과언은 아니다.

play safe, be prudent or cautious. 신중히 행동하다.

safe and sure, certain. 확실한.

— *n.* Ⓒ **1** a strong steel or iron box for money, jewels, etc. 금고. **2** an air-cooled cupboard for food. 냉장고. ¶ *a meat ~.* [L. *salvus*]

safe-con·duct [séifkándʌkt / -kɔ́n-] *n.* **1** Ⓤ a permission or accepted right to pass safely through a dangerous district, esp. in time of war. (특히 전시의) 안전 통행권(權). **2** Ⓒ a document granting this right; a pass. (안전을 보장하는) 통행권(通行券).

safe-de·pos·it [séifdipàzit / -pɔ̀z-] *adj.* providing safekeeping for valuables. 귀중품을 안전하게 보관하는.

safe·guard [séifgɑ̀ːrd] *vt.* (P6,13) **1** guard (someone); protect (someone or something). …을 보호〔방호〕하다; 지키다. ¶ *~ children against traffic accidents* 교통사고를 당하지 않게 어린이들을 보호하다. **2** accompany (someone) in order to guard them; escort. …에게 호위로서 동반하다.

— *n.* ⓊⒸ **1** ⓐ the act of defending or guarding. 보호. ⓑ something that serves as a protection. 보호하는 것; 보호물. **2** the act of escorting. 호위하기.

safe·keep·ing [séifkìːpiŋ] *n.* Ⓤ the act of keeping safe or defending; care. 보관; 보호. ¶ *be in ~ with* …에 보관해 있다.

***safe·ly** [séifli] *adv.* in a safe manner; securely. 안전히; 확실히.

:**safe·ty** [séifti] *n.* (*pl.* **-ties**) **1** Ⓤ the state of being safe and sound. 안전; 무사. ¶ *Safety first.* 안전 제일 / *~ zone* 안전 지대 / *flee for ~* 피난하다 / *be anxious about someone's ~* 아무의 안부를 걱정하다 / *There is ~ in numbers.* 수효가 많은 편이 안전하다. **2** Ⓒ an apparatus or a device protecting from danger. (총 따위의) 안전 장치. [L. *salvus*]

play for safely, be careful. 신중〔안전〕을 기하다.

with safety, safely. 안전히.

safety belt [∠– ∸] *n.* **1** a belt holding a person to the seat of a car or aircraft. (차·비행기의) 안전 벨트(=seat belt). **2** a belt worn by a person working at great heights to prevent falling. (고소(高所) 작업 중 떨어지는 것을 막는) 안전 벨트.

safety catch [∠– ∸] *n.* a device to prevent the accidental firing of a gun. (총의 오발을 막기 위한) 안전 장치.

safety curtain [∠– ∸–] *n.* a fireproof curtain in a theater to be lowered in case of fire. (극장의) 방화막(防火幕)《화재시에 내려뜨리는 석면이나 금속제의 막》.

safety glass [∠– ∸] *n.* two sheets of glass with a plastic layer between to prevent shattering. 안전 유리.

safety lamp [∠– ∸] *n.* a miner's lamp in which the flame is protected from setting fire to explosive gases by a piece of wire gauze. (광산용의) 안전등.

safety lock [∠– ∸] *n.* **1** a lock that can be opened only by its own key. (도난 방지용) 안전 자물쇠. **2** =safety catch.

safety match [∠– ∸] *n.* a match which lights only when rubbed on the special surface of a match box. 안전 성냥.

safety pin [∠– ∸] *n.* a bent pin with a guard covering its point. 안전핀.

***safety razor** [∠– ∸–] *n.* a razor with a guard that prevents it from cutting the skin. 안전 면도(칼).

safety valve [∠– ∸] *n.* **1** a valve to control the pressure in a steam boiler. (보일러의) 안전판(瓣). **2** something that serves as an outlet for the release of strong emotion. (감정·정신력 따위의) 배출구. ¶ *Golf is his safety valve.* 골프는 그의 억압된 감정의 배출구이다.

safety zone [∠– ∸] *n.* 《U.S.》 an area in the street made to guard passengers getting on and off the streetcars, buses, etc. 안전 지대(=safety island).

saf·fron [sǽfrən] *n.* **1** Ⓒ 《bot.》 a kind of plant with purple flowers. 사프란. **2** Ⓤ bright yellow. 사프란색; 샛노랑. — *adj.* bright yellow colored. 사프란 색의; 샛노랑의. [Arab.]

sag [sæg] *vi.* (**sagged, sag·ging**) (P1,2A,3) **1** ⓐ sink or curve downward under weight or pressure, esp. in the middle. (무게·압력 따위를 받아 가운데가) 아래로 내려앉다; 처지

다; 휘다. ¶ ~ *under the weight* 무게로 휘다〔처지다〕/ *The ceiling is sagging.* 천장이 축 처져 있다. ⓑ hang down loosely or unevenly. (느스러지게 또는 불규칙하게) 늘어지다; 축 처지다. ¶ *the sagging branches of the willows* 축 늘어져 있는 버들가지 / *Your skirt is sagging at the back.* 치마가 뒤에서 늘어져 있다 / *His shoulders sagged slovenly from fatigue.* 피곤으로 그의 양 어깨가 축 처져 있었다. **2** (of a price, etc.) fall; decline. (가격 따위가) 떨어지다; 하락하다. **3** (of the mind, spirits, etc.) weaken; become less firm. (기운 따위가) 약해지다; 의기 소침해지다.
— *n.* Ⓒ **1** the act of sagging. 휨; 처짐; 늘어짐. **2** the place of such sagging or sinking; a sunken place. 휜 곳; 처진〔늘어진〕 곳; (땅 따위의) 꺼진 곳. [Sw. *sacka* settle]

sa·ga [sɑ́:gə] *n.* Ⓒ **1** an old Norse legend or history of heroic deeds. 북유럽 중세의 전설; 무용담(武勇談). **2** a long novel or series of novels about the members of one family or group through several generations. 대하(大河) 소설. [N.(→say)]

sa·ga·cious [səgéiʃəs] *adj.* having a sharp intelligence; showing sound judgment. 총명〔현명〕한; 기민한; 민감한; 영리한. [L. *sagio* discern]

sa·gac·i·ty [səgǽsəti] *n.* Ⓤ good judgment; sharpness of intellect; keenness of insight. 현명; 총명; 영리함; 기민.

SAGE [seidʒ] Semi-Automatic Ground Environment. (반자동식 방공(防空) 관제 지상 시설) (cf. *BADGE*).

S

·**sage**[1] [seidʒ] *adj.* wise. 현명한; 사려 깊은. ¶ *a ~ reply* 현명한 대답. — *n.* Ⓒ a very wise man. 현인(賢人). [→sapient]

sage[2] [seidʒ] *n.* Ⓒ **1** a plant with dull green leaves used for giving flavor in cooking, etc. 세이지; 샐비어. **2** =sagebrush. [L. *salvia*]

sage·brush [séidʒbrʌ̀ʃ] *n.* Ⓒ a weed or bushy plant common on the plains of the western United States. 쑥의 일종《미국 서부 평원에 흔함》. [↑]

Sag·it·ta·ri·us [sæ̀dʒətɛ́əriəs] *n.* 《astron.》 the Archer, a zodical constellation. 궁수(弓手)자리(=the Archer). [L.]

sa·go [séigou] *n.* (*pl.* **-gos**) **1** Ⓤ a powdered starch used in making pudding, etc. (사고야자 나무 심에서 뽑은) 전분; 녹말. **2** Ⓒ 《bot.》 a kind of palm tree from which this starch is made. 사고야자(=sago palm). [Malay]

Sa·har·a [səhɛ́rə, -hɑ́:rə, -hɛ́ərə] *n.* the great desert in North Africa. 사하라 사막.

sa·hib [sɑ́:*h*ib] *n.* 《without *an article*》 sir; master. (used by people of India when they address European people.) 각하; 나으리; …님《식민지 시대의 인도인이 유럽인에게 쓴 존칭》. [Arab. =friend]

:**said** [sed] *v.* p. and pp. of **say.**
— *adj.* 《law》 named or spoken of before. 앞서 말한; 전기(前記)의; 상술(上述)의. ¶ *the ~ person* 본인 / *the ~ witness* 전술한 증인 / *the ~ sum* 우(右)〔상기(上記)의〕 금액.

:**sail** [seil] *n.* **1** Ⓒ a large sheet of heavy cloth spread to catch the wind and make a ship move; Ⓤ 《*collectively*》 some or all of a ship's sails. 돛; 배의 돛의 일부 또는 전부. ¶ *with all sails set* 돛을 전부 올리고〔피고, 달고〕/ *hoist* 〔*put up*〕 *a ~* 돛을 올리다 / *lower* 〔*haul down*〕 *a ~* 돛을 내리다 / *shorten a ~* 돛을 줄이다. **2** Ⓒ a ship, esp. a sailing ship; 《*collectively*》 ships. (특히) 돛배; 범선; 배. ¶ *a fleet of 10 ~,* 10척 편성의 선대(船隊). **3** Ⓤ a voyage on a boat with sails. (돛배로의) 항해; 범주(帆走). ¶ *go for a ~* 범선 여행에 나서다 / *a ~ around the world* 범선으로의 세계 순항. **4** Ⓒ something like a sail in shape or purpose; an arm of a windmill. 돛 모양의 것; 풍차의 날개.

clap on 〔***crowd***〕 ***sail,*** set every sail possible. 돛을 전부 펴다.

in full sail, with all sails spread. 돛을 전부 펴고〔달고〕.

make sail, **a**) spread out the sails. 돛을 펴다. **b**) set out on a voyage. 출범〔출항〕하다.

Sail ho! 《naut.》 A ship is in sight! 배가 보인다.

set sail, start a voyage; hoist a boat's sails. 출범하다; (떠나기 위해) 돛을 올리다. ¶ *We set ~ for Hawaii tomorrow.* 내일 배가 하와이로 떠난다.

strike sail, **a**) lower a sail. 돛을 내리다. **b**) 《*arch.*》 be modest; submit. 주제넘게 나서지 않다; 항복하다.

take in sail, **a**) lower or reduce the amount of sail spread. 돛을 내리다; 돛을 줄이다. **b**) lower one's ambitions, etc. (욕망·야심 따위를) 억제하다.

take the wind out of *someone's* ***sails,*** frustrate someone, e.g. by saying what he was about to say, etc. 아무를 꼭뒤지르다; 아무의 의표를 찌르다.

under sail, with sails spread on one's way; sailing. 돛을 올리고; 항해중에. ¶ *get under ~* 출범〔출항〕하다.
— *vi.* (P1,2A,2B,3) **1** (of a ship.) move along the surface of the sea, etc. by the use of sails or engine power. (배가 바람·엔진으로) 범주(帆走)하다; 항행하다. ¶ *a ship sailing along the coast* 연안을 따라 항해하는 배 / *~ in = ~ into harbor* 입항하다 / *~ out to sea* 출항하다 / *~ with a fair wind* 순풍을 받아 항해하다 / *Many ships are sailing on the sea.* 많은 배가 바다 위를 항행하고 있다. **2** ⓐ (of a person) travel in a ship. 배로 가다; 배로 여행하다. ¶ *~ in a steamer* 기선으로 여행하다 / *~ across the Pacific Ocean on a small yacht.* 작은 요트로 태평양을 횡단하다. ⓑ (of cargo) be sent off by sea. (화물이) 배로 탁송되다. ¶ *The goods sailed yesterday from Inchon.* 화물은 어제 배에 실려 인천을 떠났다. **3** (of a ship or a person) start on a

sea voyage. 출범〔출항〕하다; 배가 떠나다. ¶ *Our ship sails at noon.* 우리 배는 정오에 떠난다 / *He sailed yesterday for London.* 그는 어제 런던을 향해 출항했다. **4** (of a person) handle a sailing ship or yacht. 배·요트를 조종하다. **5** ⓐ (of a bird, etc.) pass or fly smoothly through the air as if sailing. 미끄러지듯〔스치듯〕 날다〔지나가다〕. ¶ *a swan sailing on the lake* 호수 위를 미끄러지듯 헤엄치는 고니 / *A flock of gulls sailed over our head.* 한떼의 갈매기가 머리 위를 스치듯이 날아갔다. ⓑ (of a person) move in an important manner like a ship in full sail. 당당히〔유연히〕 나아가다; 가만가만 걷다. ¶ ~ *into a room* 유연한 태도로 방안에 들어오다. — *vt.* (P6) **1** pass over or travel (a body of water) on a ship. (바다 등)을 항해하다; 항행하다. ¶ ~ *the Pacific on a raft* 뗏목을 타고 태평양을 횡단하다. **2** manage or direct (a ship or boat with sails, etc.). (배 따위)를 조종하다. ¶ ~ *a yacht* 요트를 조종하다. [E.]

sail against the wind, **a**) sail in a direction other than that of the wind. 바람을 거슬러 나아가다. **b**) work under difficulties or against opposition. 곤란을〔반대를〕 무릅쓰고 강행하다.

sail in, **a**) enter port. 입항하다(=sail into). **b**) intervene with confidence and effect. …에 적극적으로 개입하다〔나서다〕. ¶ ~ *in and settle the dispute* 분쟁 해결에 적극 나서다. **c**) =sail into **b**).

sail into, **a**) =sail in **a**). **b**) begin (a task, etc.) with energy. (일 따위를) 정력적으로 시작하다. **c**) 《*colloq.*》 attack (someone) with words. …을 말로 공격하다; 욕하다; 꾸짖다.

sail near 〔***close to***〕 ***the wind,*** 《*fig.*》 come close to breaking a law or rule. (법률·도덕 따위에) 저촉될까 말까의 아슬아슬한 짓을 하다; 위태로운 처세를 하다.

sail·boat [séilbòut] *n.* Ⓒ 《U.S.》 a boat moved forward by the wind blowing on sails. 돛배; 범선(cf. 《Brit.》 *sailing boat*).

sail·cloth [séilklɔ̀(:)θ, -klɑ̀θ] *n.* Ⓤ canvas or other material for making sails. 범포(帆布); 즈크.

sail·er [séilər] *n.* Ⓒ a sailboat; any kind of fast ship. 범선(帆船); 배(cf. *steamer*). ¶ *a fast* 〔*swift*〕 ~ 빠른 배.

sail·ing [séiliŋ] *n.* Ⓤ **1** the act of sailing. 범주(帆走); 항해; 항행; 배 여행. **2** (the time of) a ship's scheduled departure. (정기선의) 출항(시간). ¶ *The next ~ is at 2:00 p.m.* 다음 출항은 오후 2시에 있다. — *adj.* (of a sailboat) that sails; that moves or starts by the action of wind on sails. 범주하는; 출범〔출항〕의; 항해의. [*sail*]

sailing boat [ㅅ-ㅅ] *n.* 《Brit.》 =sailboat.

sailing ship [ㅅ-ㅅ] *n.* a large ship moved by sails. (대형) 범선(帆船); 돛배.

sailing vessel [ㅅ- ㅅ-] *n.* a sailboat; a sailing ship. 범선(帆船); 돛배.

:**sail·or** [séilər] *n.* Ⓒ **1** ⓐ a person who sails; esp. one who works on a boat; one of the crew. 뱃사람; 선원. ¶ *a ~ before the mast* 평선원 / *a good* 〔*bad*〕 ~ 뱃멀미를 안하는〔하는〕 사람. ⓑ a seaman below the rank of officer. 하급 선원. **2** a member of seaman who is not an officer. 수병.

sailor hat [ㅅ-ㅅ] *n.* kinds of women's and children's straw hat. 납작한 밀짚 모자.

sail·or·ly [séilərli] *adj.* **1** like a sailor; fit for a sailor. 뱃사람 같은; 뱃사람에 적합한. **2** smart; capable. 빈틈 없는; 유능한.

:**saint** [seint] *n.* Ⓒ **1** a holy and godly person. 성인; 성자; 성도(聖徒). ¶ *Young saints, old devils* 〔*sinners*〕. 젊은 때의 신심(信心)은 믿을 수가 없다. **2** 《usu. *pl.*》 a dead man; a person who has gone to heaven. 타계한〔죽은〕 사람; 천국에 간 사람. ¶ *the departed ~* 고인(故人). **3** a person who is recognized as a saint by the Roman Catholic Church. 사도(使徒); 교부(教父). **4** a person who lives a pure life. 깨끗한 사람; 덕이 높은 사람; 성인; 군자. ¶ *play the ~* 신앙이 돈독한 체하다.

It would provoke 〔***try the patience of***〕 ***a saint.*** be exceedingly annoying. 성인이라도 노하겠다.

the (***blessed***) ***saints,*** **a**) God's chosen people. 천상의 성도들. **b**) members of the Christian Church. 기독교도.

— *adj.* [seint, sənt] 《*S-*》 holy; sacred. 신성한; 성(聖)…. 參考 흔히 St., St의 간약형을 씀. ¶ *St. Paul* 성(聖)바울.

— *vt.* (P6) make a saint of; canonize. 성도 반열(班列)에 올리다. [L. *sancio* consecrate]

Saint Bernard [ㅅ ㅅ-, ㅅ-ㅅ] *n.* Ⓒ a large, powerful, intelligent dog, often trained to search for and rescue travelers lost in the snow. 세인트 버나드견(犬). 參考 본디 알프스 산중의 St. Bernard에 있는 수도원에서 눈에 갇힌 사람을 구해 내기 위해 기른 개.

saint·ed [séintid] *adj.* **1** regarded as a saint. 성인이 된; 시성(諡聖)한. **2** in heaven; dead. 천국에 있는; 죽은. ¶ *my ~ father* 나의 돌아가신 아버지. **3** pious; holy; sacred. 독신(篤信)의; 신성한; 성스러운. ¶ *a ~ place* 신성한 곳. **4** looking a saint; saintly. 성도 같은.

saint·li·ness [séintlinis] *n.* Ⓤ the state or quality of being saintly. 성자다움; 거룩함.

saint·ly [séintli] *adj.* (**-li·er, -li·est**) like a saint; very sacred. 성인 같은; 거룩한.

saith [seθ] *v.* 《*arch.*》 third person singular, present of **say**; says.

:**sake** [seik] *n.* Ⓤ cause; object; end; purpose; interest. 원인; 목적; 이익. 語法 흔히 for the sake of; for …'s sake '…을 위해, …을 보아서'의 형태로 쓰임. ¶ *for the ~ of peace* 평화를 위해 / *art for art's ~* 예술을 위한 예술 / *for your mother's ~* 자네 어머니를

위해 / *for convenience'(s)* ~ 편의상 / *He didn't do it for his own* ~. 자신을 위해서 하지는 않았다 / *It is foolish to work only for the* ~ *of making money.* 돈만을 위해 일하는 것은 어리석다. [E. =cause]

for any sake, anyhow. 어쨌든; 하여튼.

for heaven's* [*goodness', God's, mercy's, pity's*] *sake, an exclamation making appeal for pity or expressing great surprise or dismay. 부탁이니까; 제발(이지). ¶ *For goodness'* ~, *stop fighting.* 제발 싸움 좀 그만해라.

for old sake's* [*time's*] *sake, for the sake of old friendship. 옛 정을 생각해서; 옛 정으로 보아서.

Sakes* (*alive*) *! 《U.S. *sl.*》 an exclamation of surprise or dismay. 이거 놀랐는걸; 어렵쇼.

Sak·ha·lin [sǽkəli:n, 《Russ.》 sὰ:xɑ:lí:n] *n.* a Russian island north of Japan, east of Siberia 사할린.

sal [sæl] *n.* 《chem.》 salt. 소금; 염(塩).

sa·laam [səlɑ́:m] *n.* Ⓒ an Oriental, esp. Mohammedan, greeting which means 'peace', made by placing the right hand on the forehead; a low bow. (이슬람 교도의) 이마에 오른손을 대고 하는 인사; 경례; 경의. ¶ *send salaams* 경의를 표하다. — *vi.* (P1) make a salaam; bow and say the word 'salaam'. 절을 하며 '살람'이라 하다; 인사를 하다. [Arab.]

sal·a·ble [séiləbəl] *adj.* suitable or easy to be sold; marketable. 팔기에 알맞은; 팔리는; 시장성이 있는. ¶ *a* ~ *price* 알맞은 값. [*sale*]

sa·la·cious [səléiʃəs] *adj.* **1** full of physical desire. 호색(好色)의. **2** (of a writing, etc.) not decent; obscene. 외설[추잡]한. [→salient.]

:sal·ad [sǽləd] *n.* **1** ⓊⒸ a cold dish of raw vegetables or fruit, usu. served with dressing, sometimes mixed with chopped cold meat, fish, etc. 샐러드; 생채 요리. ¶ *a vegetable* ~. **2** Ⓤ any plant used for such a dish or eaten raw. 샐러드용 야채. [→saline]

salad days [⌐–⌐] *n.* one's inexperienced youth. (경험이 적은) 풋내기 시절.

salad dressing [⌐–⌐–] *n.* a sauce of oil, vinegar, mustard, etc. for salad. 샐러드 드레싱《샐러드용 소스》.

salad oil [⌐–⌐] *n.* refined olive-oil. (드레싱용) 샐러드 기름.

sal·a·man·der [sǽləmæ̀ndər] *n.* Ⓒ **1** a lizard-like animal belonging to the frog family that lives either in water or on land. 도롱뇽; 영원(蠑螈). **2** a reptile or lizard which supposedly lived in fire. 불도마뱀《불 속에 산다는 전설의 괴물》. **3** a person who can stand great heat. 화열(火熱)에 견디는 사람. **4** one of the genii fabled to live in fire. 불의 정(精)(cf. *nymph, sylph*). **5** a cook's implement for scorching things brown. (요리용의) 구이철판. [Gk.]

sa·la·mi [səlɑ́:mi] *n.* Ⓒ a highly spiced, salted sausage, orig. Italian, of (pork and) beef. 살라미《마늘로 맛을 낸 이탈리아 소시지》. [L. *sal* salt]

sal·a·ried [sǽlərid] *adj.* **1** accepting a salary; paid by salary. 봉급을 받는. ¶ *a* ~ *man* 봉급[월급]쟁이. **2** (of employment) having a salary attached to it. (지위·관직 등이) 유급(有給)의. ¶ *a* ~ *post* 유급직(職). [↓]

:sal·a·ry [sǽləri] *n.* Ⓒ (*pl.* **-ries**) a regular payment, usu. paid monthly. 봉급; 급료(cf. *wages*). ¶ *a* ~ *of $ 30,000 per annum* 연봉 3만 달러 / *get* [*draw*] *a high* ~ 높은 급료를 받다. [→saline]

:sale [seil] *n.* **1** Ⓤ the act of selling; ⓊⒸ the exchange of goods for an agreed price. 판매; 매각; 매매; 거래. ¶ *a* ~ *for cash* 현금 거래 / *a* ~ *on credit* 외상 판매 / *offer for* ~ 팔려고 내놓다 / *dispose of something by* ~ 팔아버리다; 매각하다. **2** Ⓤ the demand for goods; 《often *pl.*》 the amount sold. 팔림새; 수요; 매상(고). ¶ *a sales slip* 매상 전표 / *be dull of* ~ 팔림새가 좋지 않다 / *Sales of tobacco have gone down.* 담배의 매상고가 떨어졌다 / *These articles have a good* ~. 이 물건들은 잘 팔린다. **3** Ⓒ the act of selling at reduced prices; a discounted sale; a clearing sale. 특매; 염가[할인] 판매; 재고 정리 판매. ¶ *a bargain* ~ 염가 대매출. **4** Ⓒ a public sale or auction. 공매(公賣); 경매. [E.]

for* [*on*] *sale, available; that can be bought. 팔려고 내놓은; 파는 물건의. ¶ *That car is for* ~. 저 차는 매물(賣物)로 나온 거다 / *These are on* ~ *at the supermarket.* 이것들은 슈퍼마켓에서 판다.

not for sale, not to be sold. 팔지 않는; 비매(非賣)의. ¶ *an article not for* ~ 비매품.

put up something for sale, offer something to sell. …을 팔려고 내놓다; 경매에 부치다.

sale·a·ble [séiləbəl] *adj.* =salable.

sales·clerk [séilzklə̀:rk] *n.* Ⓒ 《U.S.》 a person employed to sell goods in a store. 점원; 판매원.

sales·girl [séilzgə̀:rl] *n.* Ⓒ a girl whose work is to sell goods in a store. 여점원; 여자 판매원.

sales·la·dy [séilzlèidi] *n.* =saleswoman.

***sales·man** [séilzmən] *n.* Ⓒ (*pl.* **-men** [-mən]) a man who sells goods, esp. by traveling around. 세일즈맨; 외판원.

sales·man·ship [séilzmənʃip] *n.* Ⓤ skill in selling goods. 판매술(術); 판매[외교] 수완.

sales tax [⌐⌐] *n.* 《U.S.》 a tax added to the prices of goods sold in a shop. 판매세《판매 가격에 포함됨》(cf. *purchase tax*).

sales·wom·an [séilzwùmən] *n.* Ⓒ (*pl.* **-wom·en** [-wìmin]) a woman who sells goods or services, esp. in a store. 여점원;

여자 판매원.

sa·li·ent [séiliənt, -ljənt] *adj.* **1** outstanding; prominent; striking. 현저한; 두드러진. ¶ *a ~ feature of a face* 〔*landscape*〕 얼굴〔풍경〕의 특징 / *the ~ points in a speech* 연설의 (가장 중요한) 요점. **2** projecting. 돌출한; 튀어나온. **3** jumping; leaping; jetting. 뛰(어오르)는; 튀는; 분출하는. ¶ *a ~ fountain* 용솟음쳐 나오는 샘. — *n.* Ⓒ **1** a projecting angle. 철각(凸角). **2** the part of a battle line projecting toward the enemy. (전선(戰線) 따위의) 돌출부. [L. *salio* leap]

sa·line [séili:n, -lain] *adj.* **1** containing salt; salty. 염분이〔소금기가〕 있는; 짠. ¶ *a ~ lake* 염수호(塩水湖); 함호(鹹湖) / *This water has a ~ taste.* 이 물은 짠맛이 난다. **2** of or like salt. 염류(塩類)의; 염성(塩性)의. — *n.* **1** Ⓒ a salt lake, marsh, etc. 염수호; 염소(塩沼). **2** Ⓒ anything that contains salt; Ⓤ a salty substance. 함염물(含塩物); 염류(塩類). [L. *sal* salt]

sa·li·va [səláivə] *n.* Ⓤ the liquid in the mouth; spit; spittle. 침; 타액. [L.]

sal·i·var·y [sǽləvèri / -vər-] *adj.* of saliva; producing saliva. 침의; 타액의; 타액을 분비하는. ¶ *the ~ glands* 침샘; 타액선.

sal·low[1] [sǽlou] *adj.* (**-low·er, -low·est**) (of skin) of a pale, sickly yellow color. (피부가 병적으로) 누런; 혈색이 나쁜; 창백한. ¶ *a ~ face.* — *vt.,vi.* (P6;1) make (something) yellowish; become yellowish. …을 누렇게 하다; 누레지다. [E.]

sal·low[2] [sǽlou] *n.* 《bot.》 low-growing kinds of willow. 갯버들. [E.]

Sal·ly [sǽli] *n.* a woman's name. 여자 이름.

*__sal·ly__ [sǽli] *n.* Ⓒ (*pl.* **-lies**) **1** a surprise attack by besieged troops. (농성군에 의한) 반격; 출격. ¶ *make a brave ~ against the besieging force* 포위군에 대해 용감한 반격전을 벌이다. **2** the act of going to the outskirts or suburbs; an excursion. (교외로의) 소풍; 가벼운 여행. ¶ *make a ~ into* …로 소풍을 가다. **3** an outburst of activity, feeling, etc. 돌연한 행동; (감정 따위의) 격발. ¶ *a ~ of anger* 노여움의 폭발. **4** a witty remark; a satirical remark. (재치가 넘치는) 말; 익살; 경구; 비꼼.

— *vi.* (**-lied**) (P1,2) **1** 《mil.》 make a surprise attack from a defensive position. (방어 자세에서) 기습 공격을 하다; 반격하다. **2** 《*forth, out*》 ⓐ go out suddenly. 갑자기 나가다. ¶ *She opened the door and sallied forth to face the waiting crowd of journalists.* 그녀는 문을 열고는 기다리는 보도진을 향해 뛰쳐나갔다. ⓑ go forth for an excursion, etc. (소풍 등을) 떠나다. ¶ *~ forth* 〔*out*〕 *on a picnic.* 소풍을 떠나다. [→salient]

*__salm·on__ [sǽmən] *n.* Ⓒ (*pl.* **-ons** or *collectively* **-on**) a large, edible fish with silvery scales and pink flesh. 연어. — *adj.* orange-pink; like the color of salmon flesh. 연어살빛의. [L.]

sa·lon [səlán / -lɔ́n] *n.* Ⓒ **1** a large room for receiving guests; a reception room. 큰 응접실; 살롱. **2** a reception held by a lady in Parisian society; a fashionable assembly of distinguished persons in such a room. (파리 상류층 부인의) 사교 초대회; 명사들의 모임. **3** ⓐ (a large hall used for) exhibitions of works of art; an art gallery. 미술 전람회장. ⓑ 《*the S-*》 the annual exhibition of works by living artists, held in Paris. 살롱《파리의 미술 전람회》. **4** 《U.S.》 a small stylish shop. (양장점·미용원 따위의) 가게; …실. ¶ *a beauty ~* 미용실. [F. =hall, room]

*__sa·loon__ [səlú:n] *n.* Ⓒ **1** ⓐ a large room for social use in a hotel, ship, or train. (호텔·기선·열차의) 큰 방; 홀. ⓑ a public room for some special purpose. (특별 목적의) 공개된 방. ¶ *a dining ~* 식당 / *a dancing ~* 댄스홀 / *a billiard ~* 당구장. **2** ⓐ a first-class cabin in a passenger ship. (여객선의) 1등 선실. ⓑ a cabin for passengers in a large aircraft. (여객기의) 객실. ⓒ 《Brit.》 a large luxurious railway carriage. 특별 우등 열차. **3** ⓐ 《U.S.》 a bar. 술집; 바. ⓑ 《Brit.》 a salon bar. 술집의 특실. 參考 public house 에서 일반 주석(酒席)과 분리된 방. **4** 《Brit.》 a large motorcar with a hard roof and no partition behind the driver. 설룬형 자동차(=《U.S.》 sedan). [*salon*]

sal·si·fy [sǽlsəfi, 《U.S.》 -fài] *n.* (*pl.* **-fies**) 《bot.》 a plant with long fleshy roots cooked as vegetable. 선모(仙茅)(=oysterplant). [? It.]

SALT Strategic Arms Limitation Talks (전략 무기 제한 회담).

:**salt** [sɔ:lt] *n.* Ⓤ **1** a white powder used in cooking, usu. found in sea water, etc.; anything like salt. 소금; 식염; 소금 비슷한 것. ¶ *Salt is used to flavor and preserve food.* 소금은 양념과 식품 보존에 쓰인다 / *Please pass me the ~.* 소금(통) 좀 건네주시오. **2** Ⓒ a chemical compound of any alkali with any acid; 《*pl.*》 any of various salts used as medicines. (화학상의) 염(塩); (각종의) 약용염(塩). **3** 《often *a ~*》 dry wit; that which gives liveliness or interest to anything. 기지; 재치; 자극. ¶ *Adventure is the ~ of life.* 모험은 인생의 자극제다.

above 〔***below***〕 ***the salt,*** at the upper 〔lower〕 seat. 상석(上席)〔말석〕에; 귀족〔하층 계급〕에 속하여.

***eat** someone's **salt** =**eat salt with** someone.* be his guest. (아무)의 손님〔식객〕이 되다.

in salt, sprinkled with salt. 소금을 뿌린〔친〕; 소금에 절인.

not 〔***hardly***〕 ***worth** one's **salt,*** not 〔hardly〕 deserving the salary one gets; good for nothing. 받는 급료만큼 일을 하지 못하는; 밥만 축내는; 쓸모 없는.

S

rub salt in someone's wound(s), make someone's sorrow, pain, etc., even worse. …의 슬픔〔고통 등〕을 더하게 하다; 사태를 악화시키다.
take* 〔*receive*〕** a story, etc. ***with a grain* 〔*pinch*〕 *of salt, be doubtful in believing a story, etc. (이야기 따위)를 에누리해서 듣다.
the salt of the earth, those who help to make society good and wholesome; the really good people. 이 땅의 소금《사회의 부패를 방지하는 사람들》.
— *adj.* **1** containing salt; tasting of salt. 소금기가 있는; 짠. ¶ ~ *breezes* 바닷바람 / ~ *water* 염수(塩水); 바닷물 / *a* ~ *spring* 염천(塩泉) / *This soup is too* ~. 이 수프는 너무 짜다. **2** treated with salt. 소금에 절인. ¶ ~ *pork* 절임 돼지 고기.
— *vt.* **1** (P6,7) season, treat, or preserve (something) with salt. …에 소금을 치다; …을 소금에 절이다. ¶ *salted meat* 소금절이한 고기. **2** (P6) make (a story, etc.) keen or biting. (이야기 따위)를 흥미를 돋우다; 재미있게 하다. ¶ *He salts his conversation with wit.* 그는 대화를 재치로써 재미있게 이끈다. [O.E.,M.E. *sealt;* O.N., Goth. *salt;* L. *sal;* Gk. *háls*]
salt a mine, introduce rich ore fraudulently into a mine to create a false impression of value. 다른 광산의 질 좋은 광석을 갱 속에 넣어 속이다.
salt an account, 《comm., *vulg.*》 ask a fancy price. 값을 더 부르다〔에누리하다〕.
salt away* 〔*down*〕*, **a**) preserve with salt. (고기 따위를) 소금에 절여두다. **b**) 《*colloq.*》 save (money, etc.), esp. secretly. (돈 따위를 몰래) 챙겨두다; 저축하다.

sal·ta·tion [sæltéiʃən] *n.* Ⓤ **1** leaping; dancing; a jump. (껑충) 뜀; 춤을 춤; 도약. **2** sudden transition. 급격한 변동; 격변. [→falient]

salt·cel·lar [sɔ́:ltsèlər] *n.* Ⓒ a small pot or dish containing salt, used on the table. (식탁용) 소금 그릇. [*salt*]

salt lick [⌐⌐] *n.* a place, as a dried salt pond, where animals go to lick salt. 야생 동물이 소금을 핥으러 가는 곳《말라붙은 함택(鹹澤) 따위》.

salt·pan [sɔ́:ltpæ̀n] *n.* a depression (natural or artificial) near the sea in which salt water gathers and from which salt is obtained by evaporation. (바다 근처의) 천연 또는 인공 염전.

salt·pe·ter, 《Brit.》 **-tre** [sɔ̀:ltpí:tər / ⌐⌐—] *n.* Ⓤ a white salty mineral used to make gunpowder and matches and to preserve meat. 초석(硝石); 칠레 초석. [*salt*]

salt-shak·er [sɔ́:lt-ʃèikər] *n.* 《U.S.》 a container with a perforated top which allows the salt to be shaken out. (윗 부분에 구멍이 뚫린) 식탁용 소금 그릇.

salt-wa·ter [sɔ́:ltwɔ́:tər, -wɑ́t-] *adj.* of or living in the sea. 바닷물의; 바닷물에 사는 (cf. *freshwater*). ¶ *a* ~ *fish* 바닷물고기.

salt·y [sɔ́:lti] *adj.* (**salt·i·er, salt·i·est**) **1** containing or tasting of salt. 소금기가 있는; (맛이) 짠. ¶ *This salad is too* ~. 이 샐러드는 너무 짜다. **2** keen; witty; sharp; biting. 기지〔재치〕 있는; 신랄한. ¶ *a* ~ *remark* 신랄한 말. **3** suggesting the sea. 바다의; 항해〔해상 생활〕의. ¶ *a* ~ *smell* 바다 냄새.

sa·lu·bri·ous [səlú:briəs] *adj.* (of air, climate, etc.) giving health; good for the health; healthful. 건강에 좋은. ¶ *a* ~ *climate* 건강에 좋은 기후 / *the* ~ *mountain air.* [L. *salus* health]

sa·lu·bri·ty [səlú:brəti] *n.* Ⓤ the state of being salubrious. 위생적임; 건강에 좋음.

sal·u·tar·y [sǽljətèri / -təri] *adj.* **1** helpful; useful. 유익한; 도움이 되는. ¶ *a* ~ *lesson* 유익한 교훈 / *have a* ~ *effect on someone* 아무에게 좋은 영향을 주다 / *He gave me some* ~ *advice.* 그는 나에게 유익한 충고를 주었다. **2** good for the health. 건강에 좋은. ¶ *a* ~ *exercise* 건강에 좋은 운동. [↓]

sal·u·ta·tion [sæ̀ljətéiʃən] *n.* **1** ⓐ Ⓤ the act of saluting or greeting. 인사. ¶ *He waved his hand in* ~. 인사로 그는 손을 흔들었다. ⓑ Ⓒ an expression of greeting, goodwill, or welcome. 인사의 말〔동작〕. ¶ *raise one's hat in* ~ 모자를 들어 인사를 하다 / *utter a cordial* ~ 정중한 인사말을 하다 / *give a perfunctory* ~ 형식적인 인사를 하다. **2** the formal opening words of a letter or speech such as 'Dear Sir', 'Ladies and Gentlemen.' (편지나 연설 서두의 틀에 박힌) 인사의 말. [→salute]

sa·lu·ta·to·ry [səlú:tətɔ̀:ri / -təri] *adj.* of or expressing a welcome. 인사〔환영〕의.
— *n.* 《U.S.》 an opening address at the commencement exercises in high schools or colleges. 고등 학교나 대학 졸업식에서의 개회식사(式辭)(cf. *valedictory*). [↓]

·sa·lute [səlú:t] *n.* Ⓒ **1** a gesture of respect, made esp. at meeting or parting; a greeting. 절; 인사. ¶ *give a* ~ 인사하다 / *wave a* ~ 손을 흔들어 인사하다. **2** 《mil.》 an act of military, naval, or other official respect, done by raising a hand, lowering a flag or firing guns. (군대 따위의) 경례; 받들어총; 예포(禮砲). ¶ *a return* ~ 답례 / *a* ~ *of 21 guns,* 21발의 예포 / *stand at (the)* ~ 경례의 자세로 서다; 거수 경례하다 / *take the* ~ (사열식 등에서 사열관이) 일동의 경례를 받다.
at the salute, at the present arms. 받들어 총을 하고.
fire a salute, discharge guns in sign of respect. 예포를 쏘다.
— *vt.* (P6) **1** ⓐ greet (someone) with kind wishes, words, a kiss, a bow, etc.; greet. …을 따뜻이 맞이하다; …에게 인사하다. ¶ *They saluted each other by shaking hands.* 그들은 서로 악수를 하며 인사를 나누었다. ⓑ receive or meet in a certain way. (어떤 식으로) 맞이하다. ¶ ~ *someone with a smile* 아무를 미

소로 맞이하다 / ~ *the enemy with a volley* 적에게 일제 사격을 퍼붓다. **2** 《mil.》 honor (someone) by raising a hand, lowering a flag, etc. …에게 (거수 따위로) 경례하다; (기(旗) 를 숙여) 경의를 표하다. ¶ *The soldiers saluted the general.* 병사들은 장군에게 경례를 했다 / *They ~ the national flag every day at school.* 그들은 매일 학교에서 국기에 대해 경례를 한다.

— *vi.* (P1) make a salute. 인사[경례]하다. [L. *salus* health, safety, greeting]

sal·vage [sǽlvidʒ] *n.* Ⓤ **1** the act of saving cargo or a ship after a wreck. 해난(海難) 구조; 샐비지. ¶ *a ~ boat* 해난 구조선 / *in the ~ operation* (침몰선의) 인양 작업 중. **2** the money or payment for rescuing a ship or cargo. 해난 구조료(料). **3** the act of saving goods or property from fire, etc. (화재 때의) 구조. ¶ *a ~ corps* 화재 구조대. **4** the goods, cargo, or ship rescued in case of shipwreck, fire, etc. 건져낸 재화(財貨) [선박].

— *vt.* (P6,13) rescue (goods or property) from fire or shipwreck. (해난·화재 때) …을 구출하다; 건지다. ¶ *They salvaged the ship and its cargo.* 그들은 해난을 당한 배와 화물을 건져냈다 / *He salvaged a few clothes from the fire.* 그는 옷가지 몇 점을 불에서 건졌다. [→safe]

***sal·va·tion** [sælvéiʃən] *n.* **1** Ⓤ the act of saving; the state of being saved. 구조; 구제; 구조[구제]된 상태. ¶ *~ of a ship* 조난선의 구조 / *The ~ of his country was his only aim.* 조국을 구하는 것이 그의 유일한 목표였다. **2** Ⓒ that which makes safe or saves; a person or thing that saves. 구제 수단; 구제자[물]. ¶ *Christ is the ~ of the world.* 그리스도는 세상의 구세주다. **3** Ⓤ 《*religion*》 the act of rescuing the spirit or soul; freedom from sin. (죄·벌로부터의) 구제; 구세(救世). ¶ *the ~ of souls* 영혼의 구제.

be the salvation (=*become the rescuer*) ***of*** *someone* or *something.* …의 구제가 되다.

find salvation, be converted. 개종(改宗)하다.

work out *one's* ***own salvation,*** find how to save oneself by one's own efforts. 자력으로 자기 영혼의 구제책을 강구하다.

Salvation Army [–⏑– ⏑–], **the** *n.* a Christian organization which engages in mission work and helps the poor. 구세군.

salve[1] [sæ(:)v, sɑ:v / sælv] *n.* **1** Ⓤ 《chiefly *poet.*》 a substance made from oil, rubbed on the skin to heal pain. 연고; 고약. ¶ *a ~ good for burns* 화상에 잘 듣는 연고 / *apply ~ to a wound* 상처에 연고를 바르다. **2** ⓊⒸ anything that makes less a pain of the spirit. (마음의 아픔을) 덜어주는 것; 위안물. ¶ *a ~ to wounded feelings* 상처받은 마음을 달래주는 것.

— *vt.* (P6) **1** put or rub salve on (wounds, etc.). …에 고약을 바르다. **2** 《*fig.*》 calm; soothe. (고통)을 가라앉히다; 완화[진정]시키다. ¶ ~ *one's conscience* 양심의 가책을 달래다 / *Nothing could ~ his wounded pride.* 아무것도 그의 상처받은 자존심을 달래줄 수 없었다. [E.=ointment, anoint; some senses from, or due to confusion with, 《*arch.*》 *salve* =save]

salve[2] [sælv] *vt.* (P6,13) salvage. (해난·화재 등에서) …을 구출하다; 건지다. [↑]

sal·ver [sǽlvər] *n.* Ⓒ a tray of silver or other metal, used for carrying small things. (금속제의) 쟁반. [Sp. *salva* assaying of food (→safe)]

sal·vi·a [sǽlviə] *n.* Ⓒ 《bot.》 a garden plant with bright red flowers of the mint family. 샐비어. [? L. *salvus* healthy]

sal·vo[1] [sǽlvou] *n.* Ⓒ (*pl.* **-voes** or **-vos**) **1** the act of firing guns all at the same time as a salute or in a fight. 일제 연속 사격. **2** loud cheers or shouts from a crowd. 요란한 박수 갈채[환호]. [It. *salva*]

sal·vo[2] [sǽlvou] *n.* a reservation or proviso. 유보 조항; 단서. [L. =(so-and-so being) safe]

Sam [sæm] *n.* a man's name. 남자 이름 《Samuel 의 애칭》. [*Samuel*]

Upon my Sam, a form of asseveration. 맹세코; 기필코.

Sa·mar·i·tan [səmǽrətn] *n.* Ⓒ **1** a person of Samaria. 사마리아 사람. **2** a kind person who gives practical help to other persons in trouble. 곤란에 처해 있는 사람을 동정해 돕는 사람. ¶ *a good ~* 친절한 사마리아 사람; 인정 많은 사람. — *adj.* of Samaria or its people. 사마리아(사람)의. [*Samaria*]

sam·ba [sǽmbə, sɑ́:m-] *n.* an African dance adapted and modified in Brazil. 삼바 춤. [Afr.]

⁝**same** [seim] *adj.* **1** 《*the, this, that ~*》 not another; not different; identical. 같은; 동일한. ¶ *in the ~ place as yesterday* 어제와 같은 곳에서 / *attend the ~ school that* [*as*] *he does* 그와 같은 학교에 다니다 / *This is the ~ watch that I lost.* 이건 내가 잃었던 바로 그 시계다. **2** 《*the ~*》 exactly alike in kind, amount, degree, quality, etc.; similar; corresponding. (종류·수량 등이) 같은; 동등한; 똑같은; …상당의. ¶ *the ~ sort* [*kind*] *of thing* 같은 종류의 것 / *at the ~ price* 같은 값으로 / *be of the ~ mind* 같은 마음이다; 찬성이다 / *These are the ~ rules, though differently worded.* 이것들은 비록 말[표현]은 다르지만 같은 규칙이다 / *Several women have on the ~ dress as you.* 몇몇 여자들은 당신과 같은 옷을 입고 있다 / *This is the ~ watch as I lost.* 이건 내가 잃어버린 것과 같은 형의 시계다. 語法 흔히 the same… as 는 '동종의 것'을, the same … that 는 '동일한 것'을 말함. 다만 생략형에선 항상 as임 / *It was colder at the ~ time last year.* 작년 이때에는 더 추웠었다. **3** 《*the ~*》 not changed in character, condition, etc. (이전과) 같은; 변치 않는. ¶ *He is the ~ kind*

S

gentleman. 그는 여전히 친절한 신사다 / *The patient is much the* ~ (*as yesterday*). 환자의 병세는 어제와 거의 같다 / *It is the* ~ *town after all these years.* 이만큼의 세월이 흘렀는데도 마을은 전과 다름 없다. **4** 《*the, this, that* ~》 just mentioned before. 앞서 말한; 전술(前述)의; 예의; 바로 그. ¶ *On that* ~ *day, the office was wrecked by a bomb.* 바로 그날 회사는 폭격으로 파괴되었다.

all the same, **a**) yet; nevertheless. 그래도 역시. ¶ *I shall go all the* ~. 그래도 역시 나는 간다 / *He is often rude, but I like him all the* ~. 그는 종종 버릇없이 굴지만 그래도 나는 그를 좋아한다. **b**) of no difference. 차이가 없는; 아무래도 좋은. ¶ *If it is all the* ~ *to you,* .... 만일 괜찮으시다면, … / *It is all the* ~ *to me whether our team loses or wins.* 우리 팀이 지건 이기건 아무래도 좋다.

come 〔***amount***〕 ***to the same thing,*** have the same result. 결국 마찬가지가 되다; 결국 같다.

just the same, **a**) nevertheless. 그래도 역시. **b**) in the same way. 같은 방식으로.

much 〔***about***〕 ***the same,*** not very different. 거의 같은.

one and the same, absolutely the same. 완전히 같은〔동일한〕. ¶ *The two parts were played by one and the* ~ *actor.* 그 두 역(役)을 같은 배우가 연기했다.

the very same, exactly the same. 완전히 같은; 바로 그. ¶ *You have made the very* ~ *mistake again!* 다시 똑같은 잘못을 저질렀군.

— *pron.* 《*the* ~》 the same thing. 같은 것; 동일물. ¶ *Please give me some more of the* ~. 같은 것을 더 주시오 / *They all said the* ~. 그들은 모두 같은 말을 했다 / *I experienced the* ~. 같은 일을 경험했다 / *Merry Christmas!* — (*The*) ~ *to you!*

— *adv.* 《*the* ~》 in the same way. 같게; 마찬가지로. ¶ *feel the* ~ *toward someone* 아무에 대한 마음에 변함이 없다. [E.]

S

same·ness [séimnis] *n.* Ⓤ the state of being the same; absence of variety or change. 동일; 무변화; 단조로움. ¶ *Don't you ever get tired of the* ~ *of the work in this office.* 이 사무실의 단조로운 일이 지겹지도 않더냐.

sam·o·var [sǽmouvɑ̀ːr, ⌐—⌐] *n.* Ⓒ a metal pot used for boiling water to make tea in Russia. 사모바르. [Russ.]

sam·pan [sǽmpæn] *n.* Ⓒ a small, flat-bottomed boat used in China which has one sail and one or more oars. 삼판선(船)《중국의 작은 평저선(平底船)》. [Chin.]

〈sampan〉

***sam·ple** [sǽmpəl, sɑ́ːm-] *n.* Ⓒ **1** a part of something taken to show the kind or quality of the whole; an example; a specimen. 견본; 표본; 샘플; 실례. ¶ *a* ~ *fair* 견본시(市) / *come up to* ~ 견본에 맞다 / *be* 〔*be not*〕 *up to* ~ 견본대로다〔견본과 틀리다〕 / *give* 〔*show*〕 *a* ~ *of one's knowledge* 지식의 일단을 보이다 / *The salesman showed some samples of dress material.* 외판원은 몇 가지 옷감의 샘플을 보였다. **2** 《*fig.*》 a representative example; an illustration. 실례; 표본. ¶ *That is a fair* ~ *of his manners.* 저게 그 사람의 행동거지란다.

— *vt.* (P6) take (something) as a sample; test the quality of (something) by a sample. …을 견본으로 뽑다; 견본으로 시험해 보다; …의 맛을 보다. ¶ *She sampled the stew and found it very good.* 그녀는 스튜를 시식(試食)해 보았는데 매우 맛있었다 / *I sampled the wine before giving it to the others.* 다른 사람들에게 권하기 전에 포도주를 시음해 봤다. [→example]

sam·pler [sǽmplər, sɑ́ːm-] *n.* Ⓒ **1** a person who tests samples. 견본 검사인. **2** a piece of cloth that shows one's skill in needlework. 자수 시작품(試作品).

Sam·son [sǽmsən] *n.* **1** 《Bible》 a powerful hero and judge in Israel. 삼손. **2** a very strong man. 아주 힘센 사람; 장사. [Heb.]

san·a·to·ri·a [sæ̀nətɔ́ːriə] *n.* pl. of **sanatorium.**

san·a·to·ri·um [sæ̀nətɔ́ːriəm] *n.* Ⓒ (*pl.* **-ri·ums** or **-ri·a**) **1** a hospital, esp. one for people suffering from diseases of the lungs. 새너토리엄; 요양소. **2** a health resort. 보양지; 휴양지. [→sane]

san·a·to·ry [sǽnətɔ̀ːri / -təri] *adj.* helpful to the health. 건강에 좋은; 치유력이 있는. [↑]

sanc·ta [sǽŋktə] *n.* pl. of **sanctum.**

sanc·ti·fi·ca·tion [sæ̀ŋktəfikéiʃən] *n.* Ⓤ the act of making something or someone holy; the state of being sanctified. 신성하게 함〔됨〕; 신성화. [↓]

sanc·ti·fy [sǽŋktəfài] *vt.* (**-fied**) (P6) **1** make (someone or something) holy. …을 신성하게 하다; 청정하게 하다. **2** set (someone or something) apart for some holy use. …을 성별(聖別)〔축성〕하다. **3** make (human beings) free from sin. (인류)의 죄를 씻다. ¶ ~ *one's heart* 마음을 깨끗이 하다. **4** justify; make right. 정당화하다; 시인하다. ¶ ~ *a marriage* 결혼을 정당한 것으로 인정하다 / *The end sanctifies the means.* 목적은 수단을 정당화시킨다. [→saint]

sanc·ti·mo·ni·ous [sæ̀ŋktəmóuniəs] *adj.* pretending to love serving God and the church; hypocritical. 신앙이 깊은 체하는; 위선적인. [↑]

***sanc·tion** [sǽŋkʃən] *n.* Ⓤ **1** formal permission or approval from the authorities; support. 비준; 허가; 인가(認可); 찬성. ¶ *give* ~ *to* …을 인가〔재가〕하다 / *obtain the* ~ *of the proper authorities* 당국의 허가를 얻다. **2** 《*usu. pl.*》 punishment of the country

after it has broken an international law. (국제법 위반국에 대한) 제재. **3** punishment imposed for law-breaking. (법률 위반에 대한) 처벌. ¶ *the ~ against theft* 절도에 대한 형(벌) / *suffer the last ~ of the law* 사형을 받다. **4** Ⓒ something that forces the keeping of a rule or standard. (행동 규범 따위에) 구속력을 주는 것. ¶ *the ~ of conscience* 양심의 구속.
— *vt.* (P6) permit (someone); approve (something). …을 허가〔인가, 시인〕하다; 재가하다. [L. *sancio* consecrate]

sanc·ti·ty [sǽŋktəti] *n.* (*pl.* **-ties**) **1** Ⓤ the state of being very holy; holiness; sacredness. 신성〔거룩〕함; 고결함; 존엄성. ¶ *the ~ of one's life* 생활의 고결함 / *the ~ of a temple* 사원의 신성함. **2** 《*pl.*》 holy duties or feelings. 신성한 의무〔감정〕. ¶ *the sanctities of the home* 가정의 신성한 의무.

sanc·tu·ar·y [sǽŋktʃuèri / -əri] *n.* Ⓒ (*pl.* **-ries**) **1** a holy place; a temple; a church. 성스러운 곳; 신전; 사원. ¶ *the ~ of sciences* 학문의 성지(聖地). **2** the holiest part of a temple or church. (성당·교회의) 지성소(至聖所). **3** a special temple or church in which a person is protected from the power of the law; a place of protection. 성역《중세에 법률의 힘이 미치지 못한 교회》; 피난처. ¶ *The escaped criminals found ~ in the church where no arrest could be made.* 도망 범죄자들은 아무도 체포할 수 없는 교회를 피신처로 삼았다. **4** a place protecting birds or animals from hunters. 사냥 금지 구역.
break sanctuary, violate it. 성역을 침범하다.
take* 〔*seek*〕 *sanctuary, avail oneself of it for refuge or protection. 보호를 받기 위해 성역으로 도망쳐 들어가다.

sanc·tum [sǽŋktəm] *n.* Ⓒ (*pl.* **-tums** or **-ta**) **1** a sacred place. 신성한 곳; 성지. **2** 《*colloq.*》 a private room or study where a person can be undisturbed. (무엇에도 방해받지 않는) 사실(私室); 서재. [→saint]

sanctum sanc·to·rum [sǽŋktəm sæŋktɔ́:rəm] *n.* **1** the holy of Holies. 지성소(至聖所). **2** the most private part of a house, etc. 밀실. **3** esoteric doctrine of a faith, etc. 오의(奧義).

⁑**sand** [sænd] *n.* Ⓤ **1** tiny grains of crushed or worn-down rocks. 모래(알). ¶ *~ on the seashore* 해변의 모래. **2** 《*pl.*》 large area of sandy land; a seaside area composed mostly of sand; the desert. 모래땅〔밭〕; (해변의) 모래펄; 사막. ¶ *play on the sands* (해변) 모래펄에서 놀다 / *travel on the sands* 사막을 걷다 / *footprints on the sands of time* 이 세상에서 생활한 (사람의) 발자취. **3** 《usu. *pl.*》 ⓐ the sand of an hourglass. 모래 시계의 모래. ⓑ 《*fig.*》 the moments of alloted time or of one's life. 시각; 시간; 수명; 명수(命數). ¶ *The sands are running out.* 시간이 다 되어 간다; 명수가 끝나 간다.
build on* (*the*) *sand, do meaningless or useless things. 헛된 짓을 하다; 불안전한 일을 하다.
make ropes of sand, try to do something impossible. 불가능한 일을 시도하다.
***numberless* 〔*numerous*〕 *as the sand*(*s*),** numberless. 무수한.
plow* 〔*sow*〕 *the sands, do something in vain; do useless things. 헛수고를 하다; 무익한 짓을 하다.
***put* 〔*throw*〕 *sand in the wheels* 〔*machine*〕,** hinder. 일을 방해하다; 파괴하다.
— *vt.* (P6) scatter sand on (something); cover (something) with sand; mix (something) with sand; polish (something) with sand or sandpaper. …에 모래를 뿌리다; …을 모래로 덮다; …에 모래를 섞다; …을 모래〔사포(砂布)〕로 닦다. [E.]

san·dal [sǽndl] *n.* Ⓒ **1** a kind of shoe held to the foot by leather cords or straps, used by the ancient Greeks and Romans. (고대 그리스·로마 사람이 신던) 샌들(신). **2** in modern times, a light, topless shoe for children and women. (현대의 여성·어린이용) 샌들신(발). **3** a rubber overshoe with no heel. (굽이 없는) 덧신의 일종. [Gk.]

san·dal·wood [sǽndlwùd] *n.* Ⓤ sweet-smelling wood used for making fans, etc. 백단향재(材). ¶ *red ~* 자단(紫檀).

sand·bag [sǽn*d*bæ̀g] *n.* Ⓒ a bag filled with sand. 모래 부대; 사낭(砂囊). — *vt.* (**-bagged, -bag·ging**) (P6) protect (something) with sandbags; hit (someone) down with a sandbag. …을 모래 부대로 쌓아 막다; 모래 부대로 때려 눕히다. [*sand*]

sand·bank [sǽn*d*bæ̀ŋk] *n.* Ⓒ a bank of sand rising from the sea bed. 모래톱; 사구(砂丘).

sand bar [⌐⌐] *n.* a shallow sandy ridge formed by the action of water currents. 모래톱《강어귀나 항구의 얕은 여울》.

sand·blast [sǽn*d*blæ̀st, -blɑ̀:st] *n.* **1** Ⓤ a blast of air or steam containing sand, used to clean, grind, or cut hard surfaces. 모래뿜이. **2** Ⓒ an apparatus used to apply such a blast. 분사기(噴砂機).

sand-blind [sǽn*d*blàind] *adj.* 《*arch.*》 dim-sighted. 눈이 침침한.

sand·boy [sǽn*d*bɔ̀i] *n.* a peddler of sand at a seashore resort. 모래 팔이 소년. 語法 주로 다음 성구로 쓰임.
(*as*) *happy* 〔*jolly*〕 *as a sandboy,* very happy 〔jolly〕. 아주 즐거운〔명랑한〕.

sand·glass [sǽn*d*glæ̀s, -glɑ̀:s] *n.* Ⓒ an hourglass filled with sand, used to measure time. 모래 시계.

sand hill [⌐⌐] *n.* a hill of sand formed by the wind. 모래 언덕; 사구(砂丘).

sand·man [sǽn*d*mæ̀n] *n.* Ⓒ (*pl.* **-men** [-mèn]) a fairy supposed to make children sleep by dropping sand into their eyes. 잠귀신; 수마(睡魔)《동화에서 어린이

눈에 모래를 넣어 잠들게 한다는》.

sand martin [ㅅ-ㅅ] *n.* 《bird》 a kind of swallow nesting in sandy banks. 개천제비 (=bank swallow).

sand·pa·per [sǽndpèipər] *n.* Ⓤ strong paper coated with sand, used for smoothing or polishing the surfaces of things. 사포(砂布). ¶ (*as*) *rough as* ~ 몹시 까칠까칠한. —*vt.* (P6) smooth or polish (something) with sandpaper. 사포로 (문질러) 닦다.

sand·pip·er [sǽndpàipər] *n.* Ⓒ a small bird living on sandy shores. 삑삑도요·깝작도요의 무리.

sand·pit [sǽndpìt] *n.* a hole from which sand can be taken; a place filled with sand for children to play in. 모래 채취장; 사갱(砂坑); (어린이를 위한) 모래터.

sand·stone [sǽndstòun] *n.* Ⓤ a kind of rock made mostly of sand. 사암(砂岩).

sand·storm [sǽndstɔ̀ːrm] *n.* Ⓒ a storm with clouds of sand blown by the wind in a desert or wasteland. (사막의) 모래 폭풍.

sand·wich [sǽndwitʃ / sǽnwidʒ, -witʃ] *n.* Ⓒ **1** the two slices of bread between which meat, etc. is inserted. 샌드위치. ¶ *ham* 〔*cheese*〕 *sandwiches.* **2** anything formed like sandwich. 샌드위치 형태의 것. ¶ *ride* 〔*sit*〕 ~ 둘 사이에 끼어 앉다. —*vt.* (P6,13) 《*in*》 put (something) in between two things. …을 삽입하다; 사이에 끼우다. [Person]

sandwich man [ㅅ-ㅅ] *n.* (*pl.* **s- men**) a person carrying two advertising boards, one hanging before him and one behind his back. 샌드위치 맨《앞뒤에 광고판을 걸치고 다니는 사람》.

***sand·y** [sǽndi] *adj.* (**sand·i·er, sand·i·est**) **1** of sand; covered with sand. 모래의; 모래투성이의. ¶ ~ *soil* 모래땅〔흙〕. **2** (of hair, etc.) rather yellow-red. (두발 따위가) 모래빛의; 엷은 갈색의. **3** not stable. 불안정한. [*sand*]

***sane** [sein] *adj.* **1** in a sound condition of mind. 정신이 건전한; 제정신의(opp. insane). ¶ *He is not quite* ~. 그는 머리가 좀 이상하다. **2** having good sense and judgment; moderate. (사상 따위가) 온건한; 양식〔분별〕 있는. ¶ *a* ~ *policy* 온건한 정책 / *a* ~ *proposal* 분별 있는 제의. ● **sane·ly** [-li] *adv.* **sane·ness** [-nis] *n.* [L. *sanus* healthy]

San·for·ize [sǽnfəràiz] *vt.* (P6) 《U.S.》 shrink (cotton or linen cloth) by a patented process before it is tailored. 방축(防縮)하다. [*Sanford Cluett,* the inventor]

San Fran·cis·co [sǽn frənsískou / -fræn-] *n.* a large seaport in California. 샌프란시스코《California 주의 항구 도시》.

sang [sæŋ] *v.* p. of **sing.**

sang-froid [sɑːŋfrwɑ́] *n.* 《F.》 Ⓤ coolness of mind. 냉정; 침착. [F. =cold blood]

San·graal [sæŋgréil], **-greal** [-grìəl] *n.* Holy Grail. 성배(聖杯). [→grail]

san·gui·nar·y [sǽŋgwənèri / -nəri] *adj.* **1** with the shedding of blood; covered with blood. 유혈의; 피투성이의; 피비린내 나는. ¶ ~ *hands* 피투성이의 손 / *a* ~ *struggle* 유혈의 투쟁 / *a* ~ *battle* 피비린내 나는 싸움. **2** taking great pleasure in the shedding of blood; cruel. 유혈〔살육〕을 좋아하는; 피에 굶주린; 잔인한. ¶ *a* ~ *tyrant* 잔인한 폭군 / *a* ~ *villain* 피에 굶주린 악한 / *with* ~ *purposes* 〔*thoughts*〕 살벌한 목적을 품고. **3** 《Brit. *euphem.*》 bloody. 굉장한; 지독한. ¶ *a* ~ *fool* 지독한 바보 / *She told him not to talk such* ~ *nonsense.* 그녀는 그에게 그런 허튼 소리는 하지 말라고 말했다. [L. *sanguis* blood]

san·guine [sǽŋgwin] *adj.* **1** hopeful; confident. 쾌활한; 자신에 찬. ¶ *a man of* ~ *disposition* 성질이 명랑한 사람; 낙천가. **2** of a healthy red color. 혈색이 좋은. ¶ *a* ~ *complexion* 혈색 좋은 안색. **3** having a passionate temperament. 다혈질의. **4** cruel. 잔인한; 흉포한.

be sanguine of, be optimistic about. …을 낙관하고 있다. ¶ *He was* ~ *of success.* =*He was* ~ *that he would succeed.* 그는 성공할 자신에 차 있었다.

● **san·guine·ly** [-li] *adv.* [↑]

san·i·tar·i·a [sæ̀nətɛ́əriə] *n.* pl. of **sanitarium.**

san·i·tar·i·an [sæ̀nətɛ́əriən] *n.* Ⓒ a person who is well acquainted with or who takes part in sanitary work. 위생학자; 공중위생 개량가. —*adj.* relating to health or preventing disease; sanitary. 위생의; 공중 위생의. [→sanitary]

san·i·tar·i·um [sæ̀nətɛ́əriəm] *n.* (*pl.* **-i·ums** or **-i·a**) 《U.S.》 =sanatorium

***san·i·tar·y** [sǽnətèri / -təri] *adj.* **1** of or for health. (공중) 위생의; 위생에 관한. ¶ *a* ~ *inspector* 위생 감사관 / ~ *science* 공중 위생학 / *The Sanitary Office* 검역소. **2** favorable to health; clean. 건강에 좋은; 위생적인; 청결한. ¶ *a* ~ *kitchen* 청결한 주방. —*n.* Ⓒ a public toilet; a water closet. 공중 변소. [L. *sānitās* health]

San·i·tas [sǽnitæs] *n.* an anticeptic and disinfectant. 방부제(防腐劑). [Trade name]

san·i·ta·tion [sæ̀nətéiʃən] *n.* Ⓤ the act of protecting health; the public facilities that protect health, such as drainage. 공중위생; 위생 시설《하수 설비 따위》. [→sanitary]

san·i·ty [sǽnəti] *n.* Ⓤ (opp. insanity) **1** health of the mind. 정신의 멀쩡함; 제정신. ¶ *lose one's* ~ 정신이 돌다; 미치다. **2** the soundness of judgment; moderateness. (사상·판단 등의) 건전함; 온건함. ¶ ~ *of thoughts* 〔*outlook*〕 사고〔견해〕의 건전함. [L. *sanus* sane]

:sank [sæŋk] *v.* p. of **sink.**

sans [sænz, sɑ̃] *prep.* 《*arch.*, F.》 without. …없이. [L. *sine*]

sans ce·re·mo·nie [sɑ̃ séremɔni] *adv.* 《F.》 without ceremony; in a friendly way. 스스럼 없이.

sans doute [sɑ̃ dut] *adv.* 《F.》 without doubt; certainly. 의심의 여지없이; 확실히.

san·ser·if [sænsérif] *n.* a printing type without serifs. 산세리프체의 활자《보기: ABC abc》. [*sans*]

San·skrit, -scrit [sǽnskrit] *n.* the ancient literary language of India. 산스크리트; 범어(梵語). [Skr.]

sans phrase [sɑ̃ frɑ́:z] *adv.* 《F.》 without circumlocution. 단도 직입적으로.

***San·ta Claus** [sǽntə klɔ̀:z] *n.* an old man with a white beard who visits houses giving children presents on Christmas Eve. 산타클로스《어린이의 수호신 St. Nicholas의 일컬음》. [Du. =St. Nicholas]

San·ti·a·go [sæ̀ntiɑ́:gou] *n.* the capital of Chile. 산티아고《Chile 의 수도》.

***sap**[1] [sæp] *n.* Ⓤ **1** the liquid in a plant. 수액(樹液). ¶ *Sap does for trees what blood does for us.* 수액이 나무에 하는 일은 혈액이 우리에게 하는 일과 같다. **2** 《*fig.*》 vigor; vitality. 기운; 생기; 활력. ¶ *the ~ of life* 활력; 정력 / *the ~ of youth* 청년기의 생기 / *lack ~* 활력이 없다. **3** the white part just inside the skin of a tree; sapwood. (수피(樹皮) 밑의) 백목질(白木質). [E.]

sap[2] [sæp] *v.* (**sapped, sap·ping**) *vt.* (P6) **1** 《mil.》 attack or get near by means of saps. 대호(對壕)를 파들어가 (적 진지를) 공격하다((적 진지에) 접근하다). **2** dig under or wear away the foundation of. 토대의 밑을 파서 약화시키다. ¶ *The boat-house had been sapped by the waves.* 보트 셋집은 물결에 의해 그 토대가 잠식당해 왔었다. **3** 《*fig.*》 make slow destruction of. …을 서서히 파괴하다(약화시키다). ¶ *Science was sapping old beliefs.* 과학은 낡은 신앙심을 서서히 쇠퇴시키고 있었다.

— *vi.* dig a covered, protected saps; approach an enemy in this way. 대호를 파다; 대호를 파서 적에 접근하다.

— *n.* Ⓒ a covered sap; the act of digging a sap. 대호(를 파기). [F. *sappe* spade]

sap[3] [sæp] *n.* 《*sl.*》 a fool. 바보. ¶ *You ~ !* 바보 같은 새끼. [E.]

sa·pi·ence [séipiəns] *n.* 《often *iron.*》 wisdom. 지혜; 슬기. [↓]

sa·pi·ent [séipiənt] *adj.* **1** 《now rare》 wise. 현명한; 약은. **2** pretending to be wise. 현명한(약은) 체하는. ● **sa·pi·ent·ly** [-li] *adv.* [L. *sapio* have savor, be wise]

sap·less [sǽplis] *adj.* **1** (of a plant) without its natural juice; dry. 수액(樹液)이 없는; 시든. ¶ *~ plants* 시든(말라 죽은) 식물. **2** 《*fig.*》 without any active energy. 활기(생기) 없는; 김빠진. [→sap[1]]

sap·ling [sǽpliŋ] *n.* Ⓒ **1** a young tree. 어린(애)나무. **2** a young man; a youth. 젊은이; 풋내기. [↑]

sap·o·na·ceous [sæ̀pənéiʃəs] *adj.* soapy. 비누 같은. [L. *sapo* soap]

sa·pon·i·fy [səpɑ́nəfài / -pɔ́n-] *vt., vi.* make (a fat or oil) into soap by treating with an alkali. 비누화(化)하다《지방·기름을 알칼리로 처리하여 비누로 바꾸다》. [↑]

sap·per [sǽpər] *n.* 《Brit.》 a soldier who digs saps, makes field fortifications, lays and detects land mines, etc. 공병(工兵). [sap[2]]

Sap·phic [sǽfik] *adj.* having to do with Sappho. 사포의; 사포풍의; 사포 시체(詩體)의; 《*s-*》 of homosexuality among women; lesbian. (여성의) 동성애의. — *n.* **1** 《*pl.*》 a Sapphic verse. 사포풍의 시. **2** a lesbian. (여성의) 동성 연애자. [*Sappho*]

sap·phire [sǽfaiər] *n.* **1** Ⓒ a deep blue, hard and clear jewel. 사파이어; 청옥(青玉). ¶ *a ~ ring* 사파이어 반지. **2** Ⓤ the color of this jewel. 사파이어 빛; 짙은 하늘색. — *adj* deep blue. 사파이어 빛(짙은 하늘색)의. ¶ *a ~ sky.* [Gk.]

Sap·pho [sǽfou] *n.* (620?-565? B.C.) Greek lyric poetess whose works survive only in fragments. 사포《고대 그리스의 여류 시인》. [Gk.]

sap·py [sǽpi] *adj.* (**-pi·er, -pi·est**) **1** having much sap; juicy. 수액(樹液)이 많은. **2** 《*fig.*》 full of vigor; lively. 활기에 찬. **3** 《*sl.*》 silly; foolish. 어리석은; 바보 같은. ● **sap·pi·ness** [-nis] *n.* [→ sap[1]]

sap·ro·phyte [sǽprəfàit] *n.* a vegetable organism living on decayed organic matter. 부생(腐生) 식물; 사물(死物) 기생 식물《균류 따위》. [Gk. *sapros* rotten, *phuō* grow]

sap·wood [sǽpwùd] *n.* Ⓤ the soft, living part of wood just beneath the bark of a tree. (나무 껍질 밑의) 백목질(白木質); (목재의) 변재(邊材)(cf. *heartwood*). [E.]

Sar·a·cen [sǽrəsən] *n.* Ⓒ **1** an old name for an Arab. 사라센 사람. **2** a Mohammedan at the time of the Crusades. 십자군 시대의 이슬람 교도. — *adj.* of the Saracens; relating to the Saracens. 사라센(사람)의; 사라센풍의. [Gk.]

Sar·ah [sέərə] *n.* a woman's name. 여자 이름.

sar·casm [sɑ́:rkæzəm] *n.* **1** Ⓒ bitter, ironical words. 비꼬는(빈정거리는) 말; 빗대는 말. **2** Ⓤ the act of using such words. 빈정댐; 비꼼; 풍자. ¶ *in bitter ~* 신랄하게 비꼬아 / *squelch someone with biting ~* 통렬히 비꼬아 아무를 끽소리 못 하게 하다. [Gk.]

sar·cas·tic [sɑ:rkǽstik] *adj.* expressing sarcasm; mocking; ironical. 빈정(비아냥)대는; 빗대는; 풍자적인. ¶ *have a ~ tongue* 늘 빈정거리다. [↑]

sar·cas·ti·cal·ly [sɑ:rkǽstikəli] *adv.* in a sarcastic manner. 비꼬아(서); 빈정거리며; 빗대어.

sar·co·ma [sɑ:rkóumə] *n.* (*pl.* **-ma·ta**) 《med.》 any of various harmful tumours of connective tissue. 육종(肉腫). [Gk. *sarkōma* flesh]

sar·co·ma·ta [sɑːrkóumətə] *n.* pl. of **sarcoma.**

sar·coph·a·gi [sɑːrkáfədʒài, -gài / -kɔ́f-] *n.* pl. of **sarcophagus.**

sar·coph·a·gus [sɑːrkáfəgəs / -kɔ́f-] *n.* (*pl.* **-a·gi** or **-gus·es**) a stone coffin, esp. an ornamental one. 석관(石棺). [Gk. = flesh-consumer]

sar·dine [sɑːrdíːn] *n.* Ⓒ (*pl.* **-dines** or esp. *collectively* **-dine**) a small fish, usu. preserved in oil for use as food. 정어리. [Gk.] ***packed like sardines,*** so closely crowded that it is almost impossible to move. 꽉 (들어) 차; 콩나물 시루가 되어.

sar·don·ic [sɑːrdánik / -dɔ́n-] *adj.* sneering; mocking; scornful; cynical. 냉소적인; 빈정대는; 비웃는. ¶ *a* ~ *laugh* 〔*smile*〕 냉소적인 웃음. [Gk.]

sar·don·i·cal·ly [sɑːrdánikəli / -dɔ́n-] *adv.* in a sardonic manner; sneeringly. 냉소적으로; 빈정대는 투로.

sa·ri, sa·ree [sáːri(ː)] *n.* a robe worn by Indian women wrapped round the body with one end thrown over the shoulder. (인도의) 사리《여성이 천으로 몸을 휘감고 한쪽 끝은 어깨에 올림》. [Hind.]

sa·rong [sərɔ́(ː)ŋ, -ráŋ] *n.* a type of skirt worn by men and women in Malaya. 사롱 《말레이 반도 등지의 남녀가 허리에 두르는 치마 같은 옷》. [Malay]

sar·sa·pa·ril·la [sɑ̀ːrsəpərílə] *n.* **1** 《bot.》 a tropical American plant or its root. 청미래덩굴속(屬)의 식물; 그 뿌리. **2** a medicine or a cooling drink made from the root. (그 뿌리로 만든) 약; 탄산수. [Gk.]

sar·to·ri·al [sɑːrtɔ́ːriəl] *adj.* 《usu. *joc.*》 of tailors or their work. 재봉(사)의; 양복장이의; 바느질의; 옷의. ¶ *the finest* ~ *workmanship* 최고의 양복 제조 솜씨 / *His suit is a* ~ *triumph.* 그의 양복은 아주 잘 지어진 것이다. [L. *sarcio* patch]

***sash**[1] [sæʃ] *n.* Ⓒ an ornamental, long, wide piece of ribbon worn around the waist or over one shoulder. (여성·어린이용의) 띠; (어깨에서 내려뜨리는) 현장(懸章); 장식띠. [Arab. =muslin]

sash[2] [sæʃ] *n.* Ⓒ the frame that holds the glass in a window or door. 창틀; 새시. —*vt.* furnish (windows) with sashes. (창문)에 창틀을 달다. [→chassis]

sash window [⌐ ⌐–] *n.* a window that opens by sliding sashes up and down. 내리닫이 창.

sas·sa·fras [sǽsəfræ̀s] *n.* **1** a tree of the laurel family in North America. 사사프라스《북아메리카산의 녹나뭇과의 나무》. **2** the sweet-smelling bark of its root, used in medicine and to flavor candy, soft drinks, etc. 사사프라스의 뿌리 껍질《방향성으로 약·청량 음료·향료 따위로 쓰임》. [Sp.]

:**sat** [sæt] *v.* p. and pp. of **sit.**

Sat. Saturday.

***sa·tan** [séitən] *n.* Ⓒ a wicked spirit; the spirit of evil; 《*S-*》 the Devil. 악령(惡靈); 악마; 사탄. [Heb. =enemy.]

sa·tan·ic [seitǽnik, sət-], **-i·cal** [-ikəl] *adj.* of or like Satan; wicked; evil. 사탄〔악마〕의; 악마 같은; 흉악한. ¶ *a* ~ *smile* 악마 같은 웃음 / ~ *cruelties* 극악 무도한 잔학 행위. ***His Satanic Majesty,*** 《*joc.*》 Satan. 악마 대왕. ***satanic energy,*** energy so great as to be abnormal. 초인적 힘.

satch·el [sǽtʃəl] *n.* Ⓒ a small cloth or leather bag for carrying books, clothes, etc. 작은〔학교〕 가방; 손가방. [*sack*[1]]

sate[1] [seit] *vt.* (P6) satisfy (something) completely; weary (someone) with an excessive supply of something. …을 만끽시키다; 물리게〔넌더리나게〕 하다. ¶ *be sated with food* 음식에 물리다; 물리도록 먹다. [*sad*] ***sate oneself with,*** satisfy completely or beyond measure. …을 만끽하다.

sate[2] [seit, sæt] *v.* 《*arch.*》 p. and pp. of **sit.**

sa·teen [sætíːn] *n.* cotton or woollen cloth made to imitate satin. 면수자(綿繻子); 모(毛)수자. [*satin*]

sat·el·lite [sǽtəlàit] *n.* Ⓒ **1** a heavenly body that moves around a planet. 위성(衛星). ¶ *an artificial* 〔*earth*〕 ~ 인공 위성 / *a* ~ *station* 인공 위성〔우주선〕 기지 / *Sputnik was the first artificial* ~ *launched by man.* 스푸트니크는 사람에 의해 쏘아올린 최초의 인공 위성이었다. **2** a follower of an important person; a steady attendant. 붙어다니는 사람; 종자(從者). [L. *satelles* guard]

sa·ti·a·ble [séiʃiəbəl / -ʃə-] *adj.* that can be supplied with something too much; that can be satisfied. 물리게 할 수 있는; 만족시킬 수 있는. [↓]

sa·ti·ate [séiʃièit] *vt.* (P6) **1** 《usu. in *passive*》 satisfy (the appetite, etc.) fully. …을 만족시키다. **2** make (someone) weary too much. …에 물리게〔넌더리나게〕 하다. ¶ *be satiated with cake* 과자에 싫증이 나 있다 / *He is satiated with pleasures.* 그는 쾌락에 넌더리를 내고 있다. ● **sa·ti·a·tion** [sèiʃiéiʃən] *n.* [→satis]

sa·ti·e·ty [sətáiəti] *n.* Ⓤ the state of being satiated; a strong feeling of dislike because of overfullness. 포식; 만끽; 물림. ¶ *to* ~ 물릴 정도로. [↑]

sat·in [sǽtən] *n.* Ⓤ silk or rayon cloth with glossy surface. 새틴; 견수자(絹繻子); 공단. —*adj.* **1** of satin; made of satin. 새틴〔수자〕의. **2** like satin; smooth and glossy. 새틴〔수자〕 같은; 매끄러운; 광택 있는. [F.]

sat·in·wood [sǽtənwùd] *n.* **1** Ⓒ 《bot.》 an East-Indian tree of the mahogany family. 마호가니류의 나무《동인도산》. **2** Ⓤ the satin-surfaced wood of this tree, used in making furniture. 위의 재목《가구재》. [↑]

·**sat·ire** [sǽtaiər] **1** Ⓤ the use of bitter irony to attack an evil or foolish thing. 풍자; 비꼼; 싫은 소리. ¶ ~ *on life* 인생에 대한 비꼼 / *a ~ on the politics of the day* 당시의 정치에 대한 풍자 / *Satire is wasted on him.* 그에게는 비꼬는 소리를 해도 효과가 없다. **2** Ⓒ a poem, essay, story, etc. used to attack in this manner. 풍자시(문). **3** Ⓤ a sarcastic piece of writing. 풍자 문학. [L. *satura* medley]

sa·tir·ic [sətírik], **-i·cal** [-ikəl] *adj.* of or like satire; ironical; sarcastic; cutting. 풍자의; 비꼬는; 빈정대는; 풍자적인; 신랄한. ¶ *a ~ man* 풍자가; 잘 비꼬는 사람 / *with a ~ smile* 빈정거리는 웃음을 띄우고 / *a ~ poem* 〔*poet*〕 풍자시〔시인〕. [↑]

sa·tir·i·cal·ly [sətírikəli] *adv.* in a satirical manner; sarcastically. 비꼬는〔빈정거리는〕 투로; 풍자적으로.

sat·i·rist [sǽtərist] *n.* Ⓒ a person who is fond of indulging in satire; a person who writes satires. 비꼬기〔빈정거리기〕 좋아하는 사람; 풍자 작가.

sat·i·rize [sǽtəràiz] *vt.* (P6) denounce (someone) by means of satire; criticize (someone) satirically. …을 빗대어 공격〔비난〕하다; 풍자하다; 비꼬다; 비꼬아 비판하다. ¶ *~ a hypocrite* 위선자를 비꼬다.

sat·is [sǽtis] *n., adv.* 《L.》 enough. 충분(히). [L.]

:**sat·is·fac·tion** [sæ̀tisfǽkʃən] *n.* Ⓤ **1** the act of satisfying; the state of being satisfied; contentment. 만족시킴〔만족함〕; 만족; 충족. ¶ *a feeling of ~* 만족감 / *for the ~ of one's curiosity* 〔*desires*〕 호기심〔욕망〕을 채우기 위해 / *for your ~* 당신이 만족하도록 / *express one's ~ at* 〔*with*〕 *the result* 결과에 만족의 뜻을 표하다 / *I heard the news with great* 〔*much*〕 *~.* 그 소식을 듣고 매우 만족했다. **2** Ⓒ 《*a ~*》 anything that makes persons feel satisfied. 만족의 원인; 만족시키는 것〔일〕. ¶ *The news was a great ~ to all of them.* 그 소식은 그들 모두에게 크게 만족스러운 것이었다 / *It will be a ~ to know that….* …을 알게 되면 만족스러울 것이다. **3** the payment of a debt; making up for damage. (빚의) 변제; (손해의) 배상; 보상. ¶ *demand* 〔*refuse*〕 *~* 배상을 요구〔거절〕하다 / *make ~ for* …의 배상을 하다. [→satis]

demand satisfaction, **a**) demand an apology. 사죄를 요구하다. **b**) claim damages. 손해 배상을 요구하다.

find satisfaction in (=*be contented with*) *something.* …에 만족하다. ¶ *find ~ in doing one's work well* 일을 잘 하는 것에 만족하다.

give satisfaction to, **a**) satisfy. …을 만족시키다. **b**) accept a challenge to duel. 결투 신청에 응하다.

in satisfaction of (=*in compensation for*) *something.* …의 보상으로서.

to one's satisfaction = ***to the satisfaction of,*** so that one is contented, pleased or convinced. 만족스럽게도; 만족할 수 있도록. ¶ *She proved it to my ~.* 그는 나를 충분히 납득시켰다 / *It is difficult to settle the matter to the ~ of everyone.* 모든 사람을 만족시킬 수 있도록 문제를 해결하기는 어렵다.

sat·is·fac·to·ri·ly [sæ̀tisfǽktərəli] *adv.* in a satisfactory manner. 만족하게〔하여〕; 더없이; 생각대로. ¶ *The engine works ~.* 엔진이 만족스럽게 작동하고 있다.

:**sat·is·fac·to·ry** [sæ̀tisfǽktəri] *adj.* giving contentment; fulfilling all needs or wishes; satisfying. 만족을 주는; 만족스러운〔할 만한〕; 더할 나위 없는; 충분한. ¶ *a ~ answer* 〔*result*〕 만족스러운 대답〔결과〕 / *a ~ explanation* 납득할 만한 설명 / *The student's progress is ~.* 그 학생의 진척도는 만족할 만하다 / *His reply to my questions was not ~.* 내 질문에 대한 그의 대답은 충분치가 못했다 / *The cooking here is very ~.* 이곳의 요리는 매우 훌륭하군요.

:**sat·is·fy** [sǽtisfài] *v.* (**-fied**) *vt.* **1** (P6,13) give (someone) what he desires, needs, or demands; fulfill (desires, needs, etc.); content. …을 만족시키다; (욕구·필요·요구 따위)를 충족시키다; 채우다. ¶ *~ one's thirst* 〔*curiosity*〕 갈망〔호기심〕을 만족시키다 / *~ one's lust for power* 권력욕을 채우다 / *I satisfied my hunger with a sandwich and milk.* 허기진 배를 샌드위치와 우유로 채웠다 / *Nothing else won't ~ me.* 그 외의 것으로는 만족하지 않는다 / *They are satisfied with the new house.* 그들은 새 집에 만족하고 있다. **2** (P6,13,15) 《*of*》 remove (a doubt, an anxiety, etc.); make (someone) believe; convince; persuade. (의심)을 없애다〔풀다〕; (걱정 따위)를 가라앉히다; …을 납득〔확신〕시키다. ¶ *~ one's doubts* 의심을 풀다 / *~ one's fears* 불안을 가라앉히다 / *I had doubts, but your explanation satisfies me.* 의혹이 있었는데 당신의 설명을 들으니 의심이 풀립니다 / *He satisfied her that he was innocent.* 그는 자신이 결백하다는 것을 그녀에게 확신시켰다 / *I easily satisfied him that there was no danger.* 나는 위험이 없음을 그에게 쉽게 납득시켰다. **3** (P6,13) pay off; discharge; make reparation to or for. …을 변제하다; …을 이행하다; …을 배상〔보상〕하다. ¶ *~ an obligation* 의무를 다하다 / *~ an offended person* 마음에 상처를 준 사람에게 보상을 하다 / *~ one's creditors* 채권자에게 변제하다 / *He had to ~ all claims for the damage he had caused.* 그는 자기가 입힌 손해에 대한 모든 배상 청구에 응해야만 했다.

— *vi.* (P1) give satisfaction. 만족을 주다. ¶ *Riches do not always ~.* 부(富)가 반드시 만족을 주지는 않는다. [→satis]

be satisfied that ..., no longer doubt that…. …을 확신하다.

rest satisfied with, be contented with. …에 만족하다.

S

***satisfy** oneself,* attain to conviction. 확인하다. ¶ *She satisfied herself of the truth of my report.* 그녀는 내 보고의 진실성을 확인했다.

satisfy the examiners, reach the passing mark. 합격점에 달하다.

sat·u·rate [sǽtʃərèit] *vt.* (P6,13) **1** soak fully; make (something) very wet; fill completely. (액체에) …을 잠〔담〕그다; 흠뻑 적시다; 깊이 스며들게 하다. ¶ *The rain saturated the earth* 〔*my clothes*〕. 비가 땅을〔내 옷을〕 흠뻑 적셨다 / *The mountain air was saturated with moisture.* 산 공기는 습기를 머금고 있었다. **2** 《chem.》 cause (one substance) to combine with the greatest possible amount of another substance. …을 포화(飽和)시키다. ¶ *a saturated solution* 포화용액 / ~ *water with salt* 물을 소금으로 포화시키다. [L. *satur* full]

be saturated with, be soaked thoroughly with; be filled with. 깊이 …이 스며들어 있다; 포화되어 있다.

saturate** oneself in* =be saturated in,*** study deeply. …에 몰두하다. ¶ *He is saturated in English literature.* 그는 영문학에 열중해 있다.

sat·u·ra·tion [sæ̀tʃəréiʃən] *n.* Ⓤ the act of saturating; the state of being saturated. 침투; 포화. ¶ ~ *point* 포화점 / ~ *bombing* 집중〔융단〕 폭격.

:Sat·ur·day [sǽtərdi, -dèi] *n.* the seventh day of the week. 토요일. 參考 Sat.로 생략함. [L. *Sāturni diēs* day of Saturn]

S

Sat·urn [sǽtərn] *n.* **1** 《Rom. myth.》 the god of agriculture. 농경의 신. 參考 그리스 신화의 Cronus에 해당함. **2** 《astron.》 the large planet, sixth from the sun, with a ring around it. 토성(土星). ¶ *Saturn's rings* 토성환(環). [L.]

Sat·ur·na·li·a [sæ̀tərnéiliə] *n.* (*pl.* **-li·a**) **1** the ancient Roman festival of Saturn, held in December with wild noisy feasting. (옛 로마의) 농신제(農神祭). **2** 《*s-*》 Ⓒ a scene or period of unrestrained merry-making. 법석; 야단 법석(의 기간). [L.]

saturnalia of crime, an unrestrained evil-doing. (제재받지 않고) 하고 싶은 대로 구는 못된 짓.

Sa·tur·ni·an [sætə́ːrniən] *adj.* **1** of the Roman god Saturn. (로마의) 농경신(農耕神)의. **2** of the golden age when he reigned. 황금 시대의. **3** successful; peaceful; happy. 번영하는; 평화로운; 행복한. **4** of the planet Saturn. 토성(土星)의. [L.]

sat·ur·nine [sǽtərnàin] *adj.* dark; saddened; not gay. 음침한; 음울한; 무뚝뚝한; 뚱한. ¶ *a person of* ~ *temper* 기질이 무뚝뚝한 사람. [L.]

sat·ya·gra·ha [sʌ́tjəgrʌ̀hə] *n.* the policy of passive resistance inaugurated by Gandhi. (간디가 주창한) 불복종 저항 정책. [Skr. *satya* truth, *graha* grasping]

sa·tyr [séitər, sǽt-] *n.* Ⓒ **1** 《Gk. myth.》 a forest god, part man and part beast; a follower of Bacchus. 사티로스; 숲의 신(神)《반인 반수(半人半獸) 괴물》의. **2** a man who has uncontrolled sexual desires. 호색한(好色漢). [Gk.]

***sauce** [sɔːs] *n.* **1** ⓊⒸ a liquid served with food to improve the taste of the food. 소스. ¶ *spaghetti and tomato* ~ 토마토 소스를 친 스파게티 / *put* ~ *on cold roast* 냉(冷)불고기에 소스를 치다 / *Hunger is the best* ~. 시장이 반찬이다. **2** 《U.S.》 stewed and sweetened fruit. 과일의 설탕 조림. **3** Ⓒ 《*fig.*》 something that adds interest or excitement. 재미를 더해주는 것; 자극을 주는 것. ¶ *the* ~ *of danger* 위험이라는 자극물 / *It is a* ~ *to the monotony of a quiet life.* 그것은 조용하고 단조로운 생활에 흥미를 더해주는 것이다. **4** Ⓤ 《*colloq.*》 impoliteness; impertinence; impudence. 무례; 건방짐; 뻔뻔함. ¶ *give* ~ *to* …에게 건방진 짓을 하다 / *I don't want any of your* ~ ! 건방진 소리 하지 마라.

None of your sauce! Don't speak such a saucy thing! 건방진 수작 마라.

poor man's sauce, hunger; appetite. 시장함; 식욕.

Sauce for the goose is sauce for the gander. 《*prov.*》 Aggressors must not complain of retaliation. 남 잡이가 제 잡이.

serve with the same sauce, retaliate. 앙〔대〕갚음하다; 보복하다.

— *vt.* (P6) **1** flavor or season (food) with sauce. …에 소스로 맛을 내다. **2** 《*colloq.*》 be saucy to (someone). …에게 건방진 소리를 하다. ¶ *Don't* ~ *me!* 내게 건방진 소리 마라. [→ saline]

sauce·boat [sɔ́ːsbòut] *n.* Ⓒ a boatshaped bowl in which sauce is served. 배 모양의 소스 그릇.

〈sauceboat〉

sauce·box [sɔ́ːsbɑ̀ks / -bɔ̀ks] *n.* 《*colloq.*》 a saucy child, etc. 건방진 아이.

sauce·pan [sɔ́ːspæ̀n] *n.* Ⓒ a small metal cooking pan with a handle. (손잡이가 달린) 스튜 냄비.

:sau·cer [sɔ́ːsər] *n.* Ⓒ **1** a shallow dish to hold a cup. (커피 잔 따위의) 받침 접시; (화분 따위의) 받침. ¶ *a cup and* ~ 받침 접시가 달린 컵 / ~ *eyes* 접시처럼 크고 둥그스름한 눈; (놀란 것같이) 휘둥그렇게 뜬 눈. **2** a small, round dish with a curved edge. 전이 있는 둥근 접시. **3** something shallow and round like a saucer. 운두가 낮고 둥근 접시 모양의 것. ¶ *a flying* ~ 비행 접시.

sau·cer-eyed [sɔ́ːsəràid] *adj.* having large, round, wide-open eyes, usu. as a result of surprise. 눈이 휘둥그런; 눈을 크게 뜬.

sau·ci·ly [sɔ́ːsili] *adv.* in a saucy manner. 건방지게; 뻔뻔스럽게; 무례하게.

sau·cy [sɔ́ːsi] *adj.* (**-ci·er, -ci·est**) **1** impudent; rude. 건방진; 뻔뻔스런; 무례한. ¶ *a ~ remark* 〔*manner*〕 건방진 말〔태도〕 / *get ~* 건방져지다. **2** smart; a stylish. 멋진. ¶ *a ~ little hat* 멋지고 귀여운 모자.

Sa·u·di Arabia [sáudi əréibiə] *n.* a country occupying most of Arabia. 사우디 아라비아.

sau·er·kraut [sáuərkràut] *n.* 《G.》 Ⓤ finely-sliced cabbage, salted and allowed to get sour. 소금 절임한 양배추.

saun·ter [sɔ́ːntər, sáːn-] *vi.* (P1,2A,3) walk slowly and idly; stroll. 산책하다; 어슬렁어슬렁 걷다. ¶ *~ through the park* 공원을 어슬렁어슬렁 빠져나가다 / *~ through life* 일생을 빈둥거리며 보내다. — *n.* Ⓒ a leisurely walk. 만보(漫步); 산책. ¶ *take a morning ~* 아침 산책을 하다 / *come at a ~* 어슬렁어슬렁 오다. [Rom.]

***sau·sage** [sɔ́ːsidʒ / sɔ́s-] *n.* ⓊⒸ ground pork, beef, or other meat cut small and put in a thin, tubelike skin. 소시지. ¶ *I don't pay a ~ for that.* 그런 것에는 돈 한 푼도 안 낸다. [→saline]

sau·té [soutéi, sɔː-] *adj.* 《F.》 fried quickly and lightly. 소량의 기름에 가볍게 튀긴. — *n.* a dish cooked in this way. 이같이 한 요리.

sauve qui peut [sóuv kìː pə́ː] *n.* 《F.》 flight in which every man looks to his own safety. 앞을 다투어 달아나는 대궤주(大潰走).

:sav·age [sǽvidʒ] *adj.* (usu. **-ag·er, -ag·est**) **1** wild; rugged. (토지·풍경 따위가) 황량한; 쓸쓸한. ¶ *~ wilderness* 황야 / *a ~ scene* 황량한 풍경. **2** not civilized; barbarous. 미개한; 야만의. ¶ *~ tribes* 미개 종족; 야만족 / *~ customs* 야만 풍습 / *~ beliefs* 미개한 신앙 / *explore ~ countries* 미개한 나라들을 답사하다. **3** fierce; cruel; untamed. 사나운; 흉포한; 잔인〔잔혹〕한; 야성의; 길들지 않은. ¶ *~ beasts* 맹수 / *a ~ person* 잔인한 사람 / *The ~ tiger attacked the hunter.* 사나운 호랑이가 사냥꾼을 덮쳤다. **4** 《*colloq.*》 out of temper; angry. (사람이) 격노한; 성난. ¶ *get ~ with someone* 아무에게 몹시 노하다〔화를 내다〕 / *make someone ~* 아무를 격노시키다.
— *n.* Ⓒ **1** a person of an uncivilized country. 미개인; 야만인. ¶ *the savages of Central Africa* 중앙 아프리카의 야만족. **2** a brutal and cruel person. 잔인한 사람. [→silvan]

sav·age·ly [sǽvidʒli] *adv.* in a savage manner. 야만스럽게; 사납게; 잔인하게.

sav·age·ry [sǽvidʒəri] *n.* (*pl.* **-ries**) Ⓤ **1** the state of being wild or uncivilized. 야만의〔미개한〕 상태. ¶ *live in ~* 야만적인〔원시〕 생활을 하다 / *a gradual change from ~ to civilization* 야만 상태에서 문명으로의 점진적인 변화. **2** the quality of being brutal; Ⓒ a brutal fierce act. 잔인성; 야만(스런 행위).

sa·van·na, -nah [səvǽnə] *n.* Ⓒ a flat, treeless stretch of land, esp. in the parts of America. (열대 지방의) 대초원; 사바나《특히, 아메리카의 남부의 대초원》. [Sp.]

sa·vant [səvɑ́ːnt / sǽvənt] *n.* Ⓒ 《F.》 a great scholar. 대학자.

:save [seiv] *vt.* **1** (P6,9,13,14) ⓐ 《*from*》 bring or keep (someone or something) out of danger, harm, disaster, etc.; rescue; protect. (위험·재난·손상·손실 따위로부터) …을 구하다; 구조하다; 지키다; 보호하다. ¶ *~ one's life* 목숨을 건지다 / *~ one's country* 나라를 구하다 / *~ someone from drowning* 아무를 익사로부터 구조하다 / *The woman saved her jewels from the fire.* 그 여자는 화재로부터 자신의 귀중품을 건졌다. ⓑ set free from sin and its result. (죄에서) …을 구원하다. ¶ *~ souls* 영혼을 구원하다 / *Christ came to ~ the world.* 그리스도는 세상을 건지기 위해 오셨다. **2** (P6,7,13) 《sometimes *for, up*》 store up for future use, enjoyment, etc.; reserve. (장차에 대비해서) 저축하다; (…을 위해 무엇)을 따로 떼어〔남겨〕 두다; 간직해 두다. ¶ *~ (up) money for one's old age* 노년을 위해 저축하다 / *~ the weekend for his yacht* 주말을 요트 놀이를 위해 (다른 약속 없이) 비워 두다 / *~ one's strength for tomorrow's work* 내일의 일을 위해 힘을 남겨두다. **3** (P6,13) ⓐ avoid losing time or spending money, etc.; economize. (시간·돈 따위)를 절약하다; 경제하다. ¶ *~ time by taking a short cut* 지름길을 택하여 시간을 절약하다 / *We can ~ three hours if we take the express.* 급행을 타면 3시간을 절약할 수 있다 / *He saved his bus fares and walked.* 그는 버스비를 절약해서 걸었다. ⓑ prevent or spare. (필요·수고 따위)를 덜(어 주)다; …을 면하게 하다. ¶ *~ one's pains* 수고를 덜다 / *~ oneself* 수고를 아끼다; 체력을 소모하지 않게 하다. ¶ *Your going saves me from having to go.* 네가 가면 나는 가지 않아도 된다 / *Machines ~ us much time and trouble.* 기계는 많은 시간과 수고를 덜어준다 / 《*prov.*》 *A stitch in time saves nine.* 제 때의 한 땀 아홉 수고 던다; 적시의 조치는 후환을 막는다. **4** (P6) keep from being tired, hurt, etc. (피로·손상이 적게) 소중히 하다; 보호하다. ¶ *Large print saves one's eyes.* 큰 활자는 눈의 피로를 막는다. **5** (P6,13) keep safe; intact, or unhurt; protect. 안전하게 하다; 손상을 입지 않게 하다. ¶ *~ one's honor* 〔*credit*〕 명예를〔신용을〕 지키다 / *~ appearances* 체면을 유지하다 / *God ~ the Queen* 〔*King*〕*!* 여왕〔국왕〕 폐하 만세.
— *vi.* (P1) **1** 《sometimes *up*》 keep money for future use. 저축하다. ¶ *I have never saved.* 저축을 해본 적이 없다 / *One should ~ (up) for a rainy day.* 사람은 만일의 경우에 대비해서 저축을 해야 한다. **2** avoid waste; be economical. 낭비를 막다; 절약하다. **3** ⓐ keep someone or something from danger, harm, evil, etc. 구(조)하다. ⓑ deliver from sin. 죄에서 구원하다. ¶ *Christ*

S

alone can ~. 오직 그리스도만이 구원할 수 있다. **4** (of food) keep or be preserved. (음식이) 상하지 않다; 오래 가다. ¶ *Fish saves best in a cold place.* 생선은 냉한 곳에서 (상하지 않고) 가장 오래 간다.
save** one's **bacon, 《*colloq.*》 escape death or injury. 목숨을 건지다; (간신히) 위해(危害)를 모면하다.
save** one's **breath, keep silence. 침묵을 지키다; 쓸데 없는 말을 않다.
save** one's **face, keep one's good name; escape shame. 체면을 유지하다〔손상시키지 않다〕; 창피를 면하다.
***save** someone **from** oneself,* protect someone from the results of his own folly. 아무를 …에서 구하다; 아무에게 …을 면하게 하다.
save** one's (**own**) **skin, (위험·죽음 따위의) 위난(危難)을 면하다; 부상을 면하다; 명성의 손상을 면하다.
save** one's **pocket, relieve him of spending money. 출비(出費)를 면하게 하다; 돈을 쓰지 않(게 하)다.
save the day, do something that prevents disaster. 재난을 막을 일을 하다; 재난에서 구하다.
Save the mark! I beg your pardon for saying that. 이거 실례했습니다《실언(失言)했을 때》.
save the situation, deal successfully with a situation which seems hopeless. 시국을〔사태를〕 수습하다.
save up, keep money, etc. for future use. (장래에 대비해서) 저축을 하다.
— *prep.* 《*arch., poet.*》 except; but. …을 제외하고(는); …이외에는. ¶ *All the guests have left ~ one.* 한 사람을 제외한 모든 손님들이 떠났다.
save and except, except. …을 제외하고는; …이외는; …인 것을 제외하고(는).
save for, except. …을 제외하고.
— *conj.* 《*arch.*》《*that*》 except. …을 제외하고(는). ¶ *She knew nothing about him ~ that he was from Scotland.* 그녀는 그에 대해 스코틀랜드에서 왔다는 사실 이외에는 아무것도 몰랐다. [→safe]

sav·er [séivər] *n.* Ⓒ a person or thing that saves. 구제〔구조, 구원〕자; 구조물; 절약가; 절약하는 것〔물건〕. ¶ *A vacuum cleaner is a ~ of time and labor.* 진공 청소기는 시간과 노력을 덜어 주는 물건이다.

:sav·ing [séiviŋ] *adj.* **1** rescuing. 구원의; 구제〔구조〕의. ¶ *a ~ faith* 구원의 신앙. **2** economical; not wasteful. 절약하는; 알뜰한. ¶ *a ~ housekeeper* 알뜰한 주부 / *Americans are not a ~ race.* 미국인은 절약하는 민족이 아니다. **3** in reserve. 보류하는; 유보의. ¶ *a ~ clause* 보류 조항. **4** redeeming. 메우는; 벌충하는. ¶ *His only ~ grace is a sense of humor.* 그의 결점을 메우는 유일한 장점은 유머 감각이다.
— *n.* Ⓤ **1** the act of saving or rescuing. 구제; 구조. **2** the act or way of saving money, time, etc.; economy. 절약; 절감. ¶ *a ~ of work and time* 노력과 시간의 절약 / *a ~ of over 10 percent,* 10% 이상의 절감. **3** 《*pl.*》 money saved. 저금. ¶ *draw one's savings from a bank* 은행에서 예금을 찾다 / *lose all one's savings* 저금한 돈을 몽땅 잃어버리다.
— *prep.* **1** except; excepting. …외에는; …을 제외하고(는). ¶ *Saving a few stones, nothing remains of the building.* 돌 몇 개를 제외하고는 건물은 아무 것도 남아 있지 않다. **2** in honor of someone; as a mark of respect for someone. …에게 충분한 경의를 표하면서도; 실례입니다만. ¶ ~ *your presence* (이렇게 말씀드리는 것은) 실례입니다만.
— *conj.* except. …을 제외하고는.

sav·ings bank [´-- ˋ] *n.* a bank which receives small amounts of money and pays interest on them. 저축 은행.

sav·ior, 《Brit.》 **-iour** [séivjər] *n.* **1** Ⓒ a person who rescues. 구제자; 구조자. **2** 《*the S-*》 Christ. 구(세)주; 그리스도. ¶ *the* 〔*our*〕 *Savior, Jesus Christ* 구세주 예수 그리스도. [→safe]

sa·vor, 《Brit.》 **-vour** [séivər] *n.* **1** Ⓤ the quality of something that affects the sense of taste or smell. 맛; 향; 냄새. ¶ *a fishy ~* 비린내 / *food with a pleasant ~* 맛좋은 음식. **2** Ⓒ a particular taste or smell; a flavor. 독특한 맛; 풍미; 향기. ¶ *the ~ of a rose* 장미의 향기 / *the ~ of the durian* 두리안의 독특한 맛. **3** ⓊⒸ 《*fig.*》 anything that adds interest or excitement. 흥미; 재미; 자극. ¶ *a book without ~* 재미 없는 책 / *Danger adds a ~ to adventures.* 위험은 모험에 흥미를 더해 준다. **4** Ⓒ a distinctive quality. 특징; 특성. ¶ *the ~ of local life* 지방 생활의 취향. **5** 《*of*》 a slight suggestion or touch of. 낌새. ¶ *There was a ~ of insolence in his manner.* 그의 태도에는 무례한 데가 있었다.
— *vi.* (P1,3) 《*of*》 **1** have a particular taste or smell. 풍미〔향기, 냄새〕가 있다〔나다〕. ¶ *This soup savors of onions.* 이 수프는 양파 맛이 난다 / *The kitchen savored of fresh bread.* 주방에서 갓 구운 빵 냄새가 풍겼다. **2** have a characteristic quality. …의 성질〔특징〕이 있다. ¶ *That savors of the crime.* 다소 범죄의 냄새를 풍긴다. **3** having a touch of something. …의 낌새가 있다. ¶ *His talk savors of self-conceit.* 그의 말엔 우쭐대는 데가 있다.
— *vt.* (P6) **1** give a flavor to (something). …에 맛을〔풍미를〕 내다. **2** 《*lit.*》 taste; smell; appreciate. …을 (즐겁게) 맛보다; 즐기다; 음미〔상미(賞味)〕하다. ¶ ~ *the garden's odors* 정원의 향기를 즐기다 / *He savored the wine with pleasure.* 그는 포도주를 즐기며 음미했다. [→sapid]

sa·vor·y, 《Brit.》 **-vour·y** [séivəri] *adj.* (**-vor·i·er, -vor·i·est,** 《Brit.》 **-vour·i·er, -vour·i·est**) **1** pleasing in taste or smell; of a fine flavor. 맛이 좋은; 풍미가 있는; 향기로

운. ¶ *a ~ dish* 맛있는 요리. **2** salty; sharp. 짭짤한; 짠; 톡 쏘는(opp. sweet). — *n.* Ⓒ (**-vor·ies** or 《Brit.》 **-vour·ies**) a highly seasoned dish served at the beginning or end of a dinner. 정식 전〔후〕에 나오는 조미료의 맛을 잘 살린 요리; 입가심(으로 먹는 음식). [L.]

:saw[1] [sɔː] *n.* Ⓒ a cutting tool made of a thin, steel blade with a row of sharp teeth along or around the edge. 톱. ¶ *set a ~* 톱니의 날을 세우다.

— *v.* (**saw·ed, sawn** or **saw·ed**) *vt.* (P6,7,13) **1** cut (something) with a saw. …을 톱으로 썰다〔자르다〕; 톱질하다. ¶ *~ a log in half* 〔*two*〕 통나무를 톱질하여 반으로〔둘로〕 자르다 / *~ off a branch* 톱으로 나뭇가지를 잘라내다. **2** make (something) with a saw. 톱으로 …을 만들다. ¶ *~ a log into boards* = *~ planks out of a log* 통나무를 켜서 널빤지로 하다. **3** make motions as if using a saw. 톱질하는 것 같은 동작〔손짓〕을 하다.

— *vi.* (P1,2A) **1** use a saw. 톱을 사용하다. ¶ *He saws well.* 그는 톱질을 잘 한다. **2** (of the saw itself) cut. 톱(날)이 잘 썰리다. ¶ *This saw won't ~ at all.* 이 톱은 도무지 안 썰린다. **3** (of material to be sawn) be cut with a saw. 톱으로 썰어지다〔켜지다〕. ¶ *This kind of wood saws easily* 〔*badly*〕. 이런 종류의 나무는 톱이 잘 먹힌다〔먹히지 않는다〕. [E.]

saw the air, move the arms as if sawing. 톱질하듯 팔을 앞뒤로 움직이다. ¶ *~ the air with the hands* (톱질하듯) 손을 앞뒤로 움직이다.

saw up, cut into pieces with a saw. 톱으로 잘게〔몇 토막으로〕 켜다.

saw[2] [sɔː] *n.* Ⓒ 《*arch.*》 a short, wise saying used for a long time by many people; a proverb; a saying. 속담; 격언.

:saw[3] [sɔː] *v.* p. of **see**. └[→say]

saw·bones [sɔ́ːbounz] *n.* (*pl.* **-bones** or **-bones·es**) 《*sl.*》 a surgeon. 외과의(醫). [*saw*[1]]

saw·dust [sɔ́ːdʌ̀st] *n.* Ⓤ the small powdered pieces of wood which result from sawing. 톱밥.

saw·fish [sɔ́ːfìʃ] *n.* 《fish》 a kind of fish armed with toothed snout. 톱상어.

saw·horse [sɔ́ːhɔ̀ːrs] *n.* Ⓒ a frame for holding wood which is being sawn. 톱질 모탕(cf. *bucksaw*).

saw·mill [sɔ́ːmìl] *n.* a factory where timber is sawn up by machines. 제재소.

sawn [sɔːn] *v.* pp. of **saw.**

saw·yer [sɔ́ːjər] *n.* Ⓒ a person whose work is sawing wood. 톱장이. [*saw*[1]]

sax·horn [sǽkshɔ̀ːrn] *n.* a kind of trumpet. 색스혼. [Person *Sax*]

sax·i·frage [sǽksəfridʒ] *n.* Ⓤ 《bot.》 kinds of Alpine or rock plant. 범의귀류(類). [L. *saxum* rock, *frango* break]

Sax·on [sǽksən] *n.* **1** Ⓒ a member of any of several German tribes in what is now northwestern Germany. 색슨 사람. **2** =Anglo-Saxon. **3** Ⓤ the language of the Saxons. 색슨 말. — *adj.* of the Saxons. 색슨 사람〔말〕의. [Teut.]

sax·o·ny [sǽksəni] *n.* Ⓤ a kind of fine wool produced in Saxony; a fine woolen cloth made from this. 색스니(독일의 동부 지방)산의 메리노 양털; 이것으로 쫀쫀하게 짠 순모직. [Teut.]

sax·o·phone [sǽksəfòun] *n.* Ⓒ a musical instrument consisting of a metal body with many keys and a reed mouthpiece. 색소폰. [Person]

:say [sei] *v.* (**said**) *vt.* (P6,11,13) **1** 《*to*》 utter; speak. …을 말하다. ¶ *~ yes to* …에게 '네'라고 하다; …을 승낙〔승인〕하다 / *~ no* 〔*nay*〕 *to* …에게 '아니'라고 하다; …을 거절〔부인〕하다 / *What did you ~ ?* 뭐라고 말했나 / *Say what you mean in clear, simple language.* 말하고자 하는 바를 분명하고도 간단한 말로 말해라 / *He said to me, 'Good night'.* 그는 내게 '잘 자라'고 말했다 / *He said* (*that*) *he was hungry.* 그는 배가 고프다고 말했다 / *He said that it was raining outside.* 밖에 비가 내리고 있다고 그는 말했다. **2** 《*to*》 express (something) in words; declare (something) as one's opinion or decision. …을 말로 나타내다〔하다〕; 표명하다; 주장하다; 판단하다; 결정하다. ¶ *Say what you mean.* 무슨 말인지 해보아라 / *He says it is true.* 그는 이것이 사실이라고 말한다 / *I cannot ~ who will win.* 누가 이길지 모르겠다. **3** 《often in *passive*》 report; state as a common opinion or belief. (세상 사람들이) …라고 전하다; 평판하다; …라고(들) 하다. ¶ *People* 〔*They*〕 *~ that….* …라는〔하다는〕 소문이다 / *They say* 〔*It is said*〕 *that he is a great scholar.* 그는 대학자라는 소문이다 / *People* 〔*They*〕 *~ he will resign.* 그가 사직하리란 소문이다 / *It is said to be so.* 그렇다고들 한다 / *Don't believe everything people ~.* 사람들이 말하는 것을 모두 믿지는 마시오 / *It says in the Bible that….* = *The Bible says that….* 성경에는 …라고 씌어져 있다. **4** 《with *to-infinitive*》 order. 명령하다. ¶ *He said to get off.* 그는 내리라고 했다 / *Do as he says you are to do.* 그가 하라는 대로 하시오. **5** recite in words; repeat by heart. (기도문·시 따위)를 외다; 암송하다. ¶ *~ one's part* 대사를 외다 / *He said his prayers.* 그는 기도문을 외었다. **6** indicate; show. 가리키다; 나타내다. ¶ *The church clock says half past two.* 교회의 시계가 2시 반을 가리키고 있다 / *These tracks ~ that a rabbit has passed by here.* 이 발자국들은 토끼가 이곳을 지나갔다는 것을 말해주고 있다. **7** 《*imperatively;* abbr. of *let us say*》 assume (something) as true; suppose. …라고 가정하자; 예컨대; 말하자면. ¶ *He will probably come here in, ~, five minutes.* 그는 이곳에, 그렇지, 아마 5분이면 도착할 게다.

— *vi.* (P1) make a statement; express

an opinion or ideas in words. 말하다; 이야기하다; 주장〔단언〕하다; 의견을 말하다. ¶ *just as you* ~ 자네의 말대로 / *I cannot* ~. 뭐라고 말할 수가 없다; 나는 모른다 / *Say on!* 말을〔이야기를〕 계속하세요 / *You don't* ~ *so!* 설마 / *You may well* ~ *like that.* 자네가 그렇게 말하는 것도 당연하다.

***have** something **to say for** oneself,* be able to make an excuse. 변명하고 싶은 것이 있다.

I say! =《U.S.》 ***Say!*** an expression used to draw attention, open conversation, or express surprise. 이봐; 여보(세요); 저(기); 어이; 이거 놀랍군.

It goes without saying that.... It is so obvious that.... …임은 말할 것도 없다.

let us say, a) about; approximately. 약; 대략. ¶ *The car was running, let us* ~, *80 km an hour.* 차는 시속 약 80킬로의 속도로 달리고 있었다. b) for example. 예를 들면; 예컨대. ¶ *Anyone, let us* ~ *yourself, might have done it.* 누군가, 예컨대 너라도, 했을지도 모른다.

No sooner said than done. The act followed at once. 말이 끝나기가 무섭게 곧 실행했다.

not to say, and almost; or perhaps even. …은 아니더라도; …라고는 할 수 없어도. ¶ *It would be foolish, not to* ~ *mad, to sell your car.* 너의 차를 판다는 것은, 미쳤다고는 할 수 없으나, 바보 같은 짓이다.

Say (*he has ten houses*), Assume that (*he has ten houses*). (그에게 집 열 채가 있다)고 치자〔하자〕.

***say for** oneself,* excuse oneself or offer as something in favor or defense. 변명을 하다; 변호하다.

say out, utter frankly. 숨김 없이〔솔직히〕 말하다; 털어놓다.

say over, a) say by heart. 암송하다; 외다. b) say again. 다시〔되풀이해〕 말하다.

***say to** oneself,* think; talk to oneself. (마음속으로) 생각하다; 혼잣말하다.

so to say, so to speak; as it were. 말하자면. ¶ *She is, so to* ~, *a bird in a cage.* 그녀는, 말하자면, 새장 속에 갇힌 새다.

that is to say, that is; in other words. 즉; 바꿔 말하면.

There is no saying .... It is impossible to say.... …라고 말할 수는 없다.

to say nothing of, without mentioning; not to mention. …은 제쳐놓고; …은 말할 것도 없고. ¶ *Six people badly hurt, to* ~ *nothing of damage to the building.* 건물에 대한 피해는 말할 것도 없고 여섯 사람이 크게 다쳤다.

What do you say to...? What is your opinion of...?; How would you like...? …하지 않겠습니까; …하는 게 어떤가. ¶ *What do you* ~ *to a short walk?* 잠깐 산책하지 않겠나.

When all is said (***and done***), after all. 뭐라고 하든지; 결국(은).

You don't say so! formula of surprise. 설마; 정말인가.

You may well say so. What you say is perfectly correct. 네가 그렇게 말하는 것도 당연하다.

—— *n.* Ⓒ 《*sing.* only》 **1** what one wants to say or has to say. 하고 싶은 말; (해야) 할 말; 말해야 할 일〔것〕. ¶ *I have a* ~ *in the matter.* 이 일에 할 말이 있다. **2** the chance or right to express an opinion, etc. 발언의 기회〔권리〕. ¶ *Let her have her* ~. 그녀로 하여금 하고 싶은 말을 하게 하자. **3** 《*the* ~》 the power to decide. 결정권. ¶ *have the* ~ 최종 결정권을 가지다; 마음대로 하다 / *It is now your* ~. 이번엔 자네가 말할 차례다. [E.]

be** one's **say, =be one's turn to express one's opinion. 말할 차례이다.

have a say in (*a matter*), have some influence or weight in the decision of. (문제의) 결정에 영향력이 있다; 발언권이 세다.

have no say in (*a matter*), have no right to express an opinion about. (문제)에 발언권이 없다.

have** one's **say =***say** one's **say,*** (be allowed to) say what one has to say. (기회를 얻어) 할 말을 하다; 발언권을 가지다.

:say·ing [séiiŋ] *n.* Ⓒ **1** something which is said; a statement. 말하기; 말; 진술. **2** a proverb; a maxim. 속담; 격언. ¶ *"Haste makes waste" is a* ~ "급하면 돌아가라"는 (말은) 격언이다. [*say*]

as the saying is 〔***goes***〕, to quote the proverb, etc. 흔히 사람들이 말하듯이; 속담에서 이르듯이; 이른바.

go without saying, be needless to say; be evident. …은 말할 것〔필요〕도 없다.

saying and doing, speech and action. 언행.

There is no saying that .... It is impossible to say that .... …을 말할〔알〕 수는 없다.

scab [skæb] *n.* Ⓒ **1** a dry cover formed over a wound. (부스럼·상처의) 딱지. ¶ *The* ~ *from his vaccination has just dropped off.* 우두 맞은 딱지가 이제 막 떨어졌다. **2** Ⓤ a skin disease of animals, esp. sheep. (양 따위의) 옴. **3** 《*colloq.*》 a worker who will not join a strike; a strikebreaker. 파업 불참자; 파업을 깨뜨리는 노동자. —*vi.* (**scabbed, scab·bing**) (P1,3) **1** become covered with a scab. (상처에) 딱지가 앉다. **2** 《*colloq.*》 act or work as a scab. 파업을 깨뜨리다. [N. (→shabby)]

scab·bard [skǽbərd] *n.* Ⓒ a case for a sword. (칼 따위의) 집. [↑]

throw 〔***fling***〕 ***away the scabbard,*** commit oneself to fighting out. 끝까지 싸우다.

scab·by [skǽbi] *adj.* (**-bi·er, -bi·est**) covered with many scabs. 많은 딱지로 덮인; 딱지투성이의.

sca·bies [skéibi:z / -bii:z] *n.* any of several infectious skin diseases. 옴; 개선(疥癬). [L.]

scab·rous [skǽbrəs / skéib-] *adj.* **1** (of animals, plants, etc.) having a rough surface. (표면이) 까칠까칠한; 울퉁불퉁한. **2** (of subjects) difficult to write in a delicate way; indecent. 다루기 어려운; 외설한; 음란한. ¶ *~ books* 음란 서적. **3** full of difficulties. 곤란한. [↑]

scaf·fold [skǽfəld, -fould] *n.* Ⓒ **1** a framework for holding workmen or materials during building, painting, repairing, etc. (건축용의) 비계. ¶ *a flying ~* 매단 비계. **2** 《*the ~*》 a wooden platform for putting criminals to death by hanging. 교수대; 처형대.

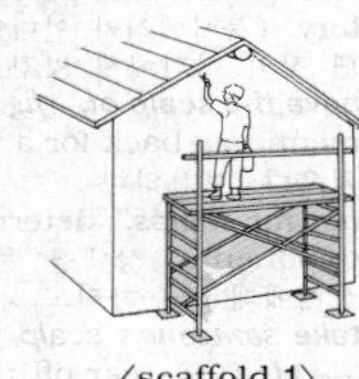
〈scaffold 1〉

go to* 〔*mount*〕 *the scaffold, be put to death; be killed. 사형을 당하다.

send* 〔*bring*〕 *someone to the scaffold, put someone to death. …을 사형에 처하다.

— *vt.* (P6) provide (a building) with a scaffold. …에 비계를 만들다. [ex-, → catafalque]

scaf·fold·ing [skǽfəldiŋ, -ould-] *n.* **1** Ⓒ a scaffold; a system of scaffolds. (건축용) 비계; 비계의 구조. **2** Ⓤ materials for making a scaffold. 비계 재료.

scal·a·wag, 《Brit.》 **Scal·la-** [skǽləwæ̀g] *n.* 《usu. *joc.*》 a scamp (=an idle, lazy, useless fellow) 건달; 무뢰한; 깡패. [Place]

scald [skɔːld] *vt.* (P6) **1** burn (the hand, etc.) with boiling water, oil, steam, etc. (뜨거운 물·김에) …을 데게 하다; 화상을 입히다. ¶ *~ oneself with boiling water* 끓는 물에 데다. **2** ⓐ pour boiling water over (something). …에 끓는 물을 붓다. ⓑ put (something) into boiling water. …을 끓는 물에 담그다. ⓒ clean (dishes, etc.) with boiling water or steam. (접시 따위)를 뜨거운 물·김으로 씻다〔소독하다〕 ¶ *~ (out) dishes* 접시를 뜨거운 물에 소독하다. **3** heat (water, oil, etc.) almost to the boiling point. (비등점 가까이까지) 끓이다. ¶ *~ milk* 우유를 끓이다.

— *vi.* have a burn. …에 데다; 화상을 입다.

scalded cream, cream from scalded milk. 우유를 끓여 만든 크림.

scalding tears, tears of bitter sorrow, etc. 뜨거운 눈물.

— *n.* Ⓒ a burn caused by boiling water, oil, steam, etc. (끓는 물·김 따위에 의한) 화상. [ex-, L. *calidus* hot]

:scale¹ [skeil] *n.* Ⓒ **1** a regular series of marks on a stick, dial, etc. used for measuring. 눈금; 저울눈; 척도. ¶ *the ~ on a tape measure* 줄자의 눈금 / *A thermometer has a ~.* 온도계는 눈금이 있다. **2** ⓐ an instrument with marks at regular distances for measuring, etc. 자. ¶ *a folding ~* 접자. ⓑ 《math.》 a system of numbering. 진법(進法). ¶ *the decimal ~* 십진법. **3** an arrangement in steps or degrees; any graded system. 등급; 계급; 단계. ¶ *a ~ of wages* 임금률 / *the ~ of taxation* (누진세의) 세율의 단계 / *a person who is high in the social ~* 사회 계급이 높은 사람 / *sink in the ~* 사회적 지위가 떨어지다 / *be low in the ~ of civilization* 문명의 도가 낮다. **4** the size of a picture, plan, model, etc. compared with the size of the thing itself. (실물에 대한 크기의) 비율; 축소비(比); 축척. ¶ *a map drawn to a ~ of ten miles to the inch* 10마일을 1인치로 축척한 지도 / *a map drawn to a ~ of 1/50,000,* 5만분의 1 지도 / *a model on a ~ of one inch to one foot* 1피트 대 1인치의 비율에 의한 모형. **5** a relative size or degree. 규모; 정도; 스케일. ¶ *a building of a large ~* 규모가 큰 대형 건물 / *do business on a large* 〔*small*〕 *~* 대〔소〕규모로 사업을 하다. **6** 《mus.》 a series of tones going up or down in pitch. 음계. ¶ *the major* 〔*minor*〕 *~* 장〔단〕음계.

out of scale, too large or too small for its surroundings. 주변에 비해 너무 큰〔작은〕.

to scale, with a uniform reduction or enlargement. 일정 비율로 축소〔확대〕된.

— *vt.* (P6) **1** climb, esp. by means of a ladder. …을 (사닥다리)로 기어오르다; (산 따위에) 등반하다. ¶ *~ a cliff* 절벽을 기어오르다 / *They scaled the mountain in three days.* 그들은 사흘 걸려서 산에 올랐다. **2** ⓐ make a copy of (something) according to a scale. …을 비율로 나타내다; 축척으로 제도〔설계〕하다. ¶ *~ a map* 축척 지도를 그리다 / *~ a building* 축척으로 건물을 설계하다. ⓑ adjust or control with respect to something else. (다른 것과) 비율에 따라 정〔조절〕하다. ¶ *Our work is scaled to our individual capacities.* 일은 개인의 능력에 따라 정해진다. [L. *scala* ladder]

***scale down* 〔*up*〕,** reduce 〔increase〕 (something) by a certain proportion. …의 비율로 —을 감소〔증가〕시키다. ¶ *~ down wages* 임금을 일정률로 낮추다.

:scale² [skeil] *n.* Ⓒ **1** one of the two pans or dishes of a balance. 천칭의 접시. **2** 《*the ~s, a pair of ~s*》 a balance for weighing; any form of weighing machine. 천칭; 저울. ¶ *weigh in the scales* 저울에 (무게를) 달다.

***hold the scales true* 〔*even*〕,** be fair in one's judgment. …을 공정하게 판가름하다.

***turn* 〔《also U.S.》 *tip*〕 *the scale*(*s*),** **a)** cause one of two sides to outweigh the other. 저울이 한쪽으로 기울게 하다. **b)** decide in favor of one side; reverse a situation. (한쪽에 유리하게) 사태를〔국면을〕 결정하다; 형세를 역전시키다.

turn* 〔《also U.S.》 *tip*〕 *the scale*(*s*) *at, weight. …의 무게가〔중량이〕 있다. ¶ *The jockey turned the scales at 40 kg.* 그 기수(騎

手)의 몸무게는 40킬로그램이었다.
— *vt.* (P6) **1** weigh (something) with scales. …을 저울에 달다. **2** amount to (a certain weight). …의 무게가 나가다. ¶ *It scales 150 pounds.* 무게가 150파운드다. [N. = bowl]

•**scale**³ [skeil] *n.* Ⓒ **1** ⓐ one of the small, thin, hard plates covering the bodies of some fish, snakes and insects. (물고기·뱀 따위의) 비늘; 인편(鱗片). ⓑ any thin, dry flake like fish scales. (생선) 비늘 모양의 얇은 조각; 박편(薄片). ¶ *The paint came off in scales.* 칠이 박편이 되어 벗겨져 떨어졌다. **2** one of the small, thin flakes of dry, dead skin. 피부의 박편; 비듬; 딱지. **3** 《without *an article*》 a coat of hard matter which forms inside boilers, etc.; tartar. (보일러 속 따위에 끼는) 물때; 버캐; 치석(齒石). **4** one of the tiny leaves covering a flower bud. (식물의) 아린(芽鱗). **5** 《*pl.*》 《*fig.*》 something that causes blindness to the true nature of things, etc. (사람의 판단력을) 흐리게 하는 것.
remove the scales from someone's eyes, 《*fig.*》 enable someone who has been deceived to realize the true state of affairs. 이제까지 흐리게 했던 것을 눈에서 떼다; 아무의 눈을 뜨게 하다; 일의 진상을 깨닫게 하다.
The scales fall from one's eyes. 《Bible》 One's eyes are opened to something. 무엇에 눈을 뜨다; 잘못을 깨닫다.
— *vt.* (P6,7,13) **1** remove scales or a scale from (something). …의 비늘을〔물때를, 버캐를〕 벗기다; 치석을 제거하다. ¶ ~ *a fish* / ~ *a boiler* 보일러에 낀 물때를 벗기다 / *I had my teeth scaled.* 이의 치석 제거를 해 받았다. **2** cover (something) with scales. …을 비늘로 덮다; 물때〔버캐〕로 덮다. ¶ *Water scales a boiler.* 물은 보일러에 물때가 끼게 한다. **3** 《U.S.》 throw (a flat stone) so that it skips along the surface of water. (납작한 돌을) 던져 물수제비를 뜨다.
— *vi.* (P1,2A,3) **1** 《*off*》 come off in scales or flakes. (비늘·칠 따위가) 벗겨져 떨어지다. ¶ ~ *off* 벗겨지다; 떨어지다 / *The paint is scaling off (the house).* (집의) 페인트 칠이 벗겨지고 있다. **2** (of a boiler, skin, etc.) form scales. 물때〔버캐〕가 끼다; 딱지가 앉다. [Teut.]

sca·lene [skeilíːn] *adj.* having unequal sides. 부등변의. ¶ *a ~ triangle* 부등변 삼각형. [Gk.]

scal·la·wag [skǽləwæ̀g] *n.* =scalawag.

scal·lion [skǽljən] *n.* 《bot.》 a kind of onion. 부추; 골파. [→shallot]

scal·lop [skάləp, skǽl- / skɔ́l-], **scol-** [skάl- / skɔ́l-] *n.* Ⓒ **1** a shellfish with two fan-shaped shells. 가리비. **2** the muscle of this shellfish, valued as food. 조개관자. **3** 《usu. *pl.*》 a curving ornamental edging of a dress. (옷의) 물결 모양의 선두름. — *vt.* (P6) **1** bake (fish, oysters, etc.) with sauce, bread crumbs, etc. in a scallop shell or dish. …을 조가비 속〔작은 접시〕에 넣어 굽다. ¶ *scalloped oysters.* **2** decorate (the edge of dress, etc.) with scallops. …에 물결 모양으로 선두르다. [Teut.]

scal·ly·wag [skǽliwæ̀g] *n.* =scalawag.

scalp [skælp] *n.* Ⓒ **1** the skin and hair on the top of the head. (머리카락이 붙어 있는) 머릿가죽. **2** this part as cut off by American Indians and preserved as a sign of victory. (북아메리카 인디언이 전리품으로서 잘라낸 적의 머리에서 벗긴) 머릿가죽의 일부.
have the scalp of, 《*fig.*》 defeat in an argument; pay back for a wrong. 패배시키다; 해치우다; 보복하다.
out for scalps, determined to beat one's opponents. 상대를 무찌르려고〔해치우려고〕; 상대에게 복수하려고. 「…에게 이기다.
take someone's scalp, 《*fig.*》 have a victory.
— *vt.* (P6) tear off the scalp of (an enemy, etc.). (적 따위의) 머릿가죽을 벗기다. [E.]

scal·pel [skǽlpəl] *n.* Ⓒ a small knife used by surgeons. (작고 가벼운) 외과용 메스. [L. *scalpo* scrape]

scal·y [skéili] *adj.* (**scal·i·er, scal·i·est**) **1** covered with scales. 비늘로 덮인; 비늘이 있는. ¶ *This iron pipe is ~ with rust.* 이 쇠파이프는 녹이 슬어 있다. **2** like scales. 비늘 모양의. **3** coming off in flakes. 벗겨져 떨어지는. [*scale*³]

scamp [skæmp] *n.* Ⓒ a rascal; a worthless fellow. 무뢰한; 건달; 깡패. — *vt.* (P6) **1** do (work, etc.) carelessly and hastily; skimp. (일 따위를) 되는 대로 하다; 겉날리다; 노력을 아끼다. **2** make from inferior (= poor) materials. 저질의 재료를 써서 만들다. [O.F.]

scam·per [skǽmpər] *vi.* (P1,2A,3) **1** run away quickly; go hurriedly. (동물·어린이가) 허둥지둥 달아나다; 급히 가다; 대충 훑어보다. ¶ ~ *off in all directions* 사방으로 달려가다 / ~ *through a book* 책을 통독하다 / *The squirrels scampered away when the boys came.* 아이들이 오자 다람쥐는 급히 달아났다. **2** run about playfully. 뛰어놀다; 뛰어다니다. ¶ *The children were scampering about the garden.* 애들이 정원에서 뛰어놀고 있었다.
— *n.* Ⓒ **1** a quick run. 급주(急走). **2** a hurried trip. 급한 여행. ¶ *a ~ through Europe* 유럽에의 급한 여행. [↑]

scan [skæn] *v.* (**scanned, scan·ning**) *vt.* (P6) **1** watch (something) closely; examine with care. …을 자세히 (쳐다)보다; 세밀히 조사하다. ¶ ~ *the distance* 거리를 정사(精査)하다 / ~ *someone from head to foot* 아무를 머리끝에서 발끝까지 세밀히 보다 / *The detective scanned every bit of evidence.* 형사는 모든 증거 하나하나를 세밀히 살폈다. **2** glance at (something) quickly. …을 급히 훑어보다. ¶ *He scanned the newspaper while having his breakfast.* 그는 아침 식사를

하는 동안 신문을 대충 훑어보았다. 3 ⓐ divide (a line of poetry) into metrical feet. (시)를 운각(韻脚)으로 나누다. ⓑ read or recite (a line of poetry) so as to show its rhythmic structure. (시)를 운율을 붙여 읽다. 4 《TV》 traverse (a surface) with a beam of light or electrons in order to reproduce or transmit a picture. (화면)을 주사(走査)하다.
— *vi.* (P2A) 1 examine the rhythmic structure of poetry. (시의) 운율을 살피다. 2 accord with the rules of meter. 운율의 규칙에 따르다. 3 《TV》 scan a surface. 주사(走査)하다. [L. *scando* climb]

***scan·dal** [skǽndl] *n.* Ⓤ 1 ⒸⓊ a shameful action or state that brings dishonor. 부끄러운 행위; 추문; 부정 사건. ¶ *be fired on a charge of the* ~ 예의 추문으로 파직되다. 2 the feeling of indignation so caused. (세상의) 분격; 물의; 반감. ¶ *give rise to* 〔*cause*〕 ~ 세상에 물의를 일으키다; 세상을 떠들썩하게 하다; 세인을 분격시키다. 3 disgrace. 치욕; 불명예. ¶ *Her conduct is a* ~ *to us.* 그녀의 행동은 우리들의 수치다. 4 careless or wicked public talk about someone. 중상(적인 이야기); 악의에 찬 평판. ¶ *talk* ~ 뒷전에서 험담하다 / *be interested in* ~ 뒷공론을 좋아하다. [Gk. *skandalon* snare]

scan·dal·ize, 《Brit.》 **-ise** [skǽndəlàiz] *vt.* (P6) shock or offend (someone) by actions or opinions considered wrong or immoral. …을 분개시키다; 괘씸히 여기게 하다; 어처구니없게 하다. ¶ *Amy scandalized her mother by smoking.* 에이미는 담배를 피워 그녀 어머니를 어이없게 했다.

scan·dal·mon·ger [skǽndlmʌ̀ŋgər] *n.* Ⓒ a person who spreads scandal. 추문을 퍼뜨리는 사람; 뒤에서 험담하는 사람.

scan·dal·ous [skǽndələs] *adj.* 1 shameful; shocking. 명예롭지 못한; 수치스러운; 괘씸한. ¶ ~ *behavior in public* 대중 앞에서의 수치스런 행동 / *It is* ~ *that* …. …하다니 괘씸하다. 2 fond of spreading scandal; tending to damage someone's reputation; speaking or spreading slander. 명예를 손상하는; 중상적인; 험담하는. ¶ *a* ~ *rumor* 중상적인 소문 / *a* ~ *tongue* 비방을 좋아하는 사람.

scan·dal·ous·ly [skǽndələsli] *adv.* in a scandalous manner; shamefully; terribly; blamably. 괘씸할 정도로; 명예롭지 못하게도; 수치스럽게; 몹시 비난하여.

Scan·di·na·vi·a [skæ̀ndənéiviə] *n.* 1 Norway, Sweden, Denmark and Iceland. 스칸디나비아. 2 the peninsula that consists of Norway and Sweden. 스칸디나비아 반도.

Scan·di·na·vi·an [skæ̀ndənéiviən] *adj.* of Scandinavia; of Scandinavian people or languages. 스칸디나비아의; 스칸디나비아 사람〔말〕의. ¶ *the* ~ *Peninsula* 스칸디나비아 반도. — *n.* 1 Ⓒ a person of the Scandinavian countries. 스칸디나비아 사람. 2 Ⓤ one or all of the languages of Scandinavia, including Norwegian, Swedish and Danish. 스칸디나비아어. [Teut.]

scan·sion [skǽnʃən] *n.* Ⓤ the act of dividing lines of poetry according to the rhythm or meter. 시를 운율(韻律)에 따라 구획짓기. [*scan*]

scant [skænt] *adj.* 1 not enough in size or amount. 부족한; 적은. ¶ *a* ~ *amount* 적은 수량 / *a* ~ *supply of provisions* 부족한 식량 공급 / *with* ~ *attention* 충분한 주의를 기울이지 않고 / *be* ~ *of breath* 숨이 차다; 헐떡이다. 2 《U.S.》 less than full; barely enough. 빠듯한; 채 안 되는 / *Add a* ~ *teaspoon of salt.* 한 찻숟갈이 채 안 되는 양의 소금을 넣으시오.

scant of, not having enough; be lacking in. …이 충분하지 않은; 부족한.

with scant courtesy, rather rudely. (예절에) 좀 소홀하게.

— *vt.* (P6) 《chiefly U.S.》 make scant; cut down. (공급·수량)을 줄이다; 깎다. ¶ *Don't* ~ *the family's food.* 가족의 양식을 줄이지 마시오. [N.]

scant·i·ly [skǽntili] *adv.* in a scanty manner; not sufficiently. 불충분하게; 부족하게. ¶ *a* ~ *lighted street* 가로등이 부족한 어두운 거리.

scant·i·ness [skǽntinis] *n.* Ⓤ the state of being scanty; shortage. 불충분; 부족; 적음.

scant·ling [skǽntliŋ] *n.* 1 a small beam or piece of timber. (두께 5인치 이하의) 각재(角材); 오리목. 2 ⓐ 《*collectively*》 small beams or timbers. (두께 5인치 이하의) 각재류(類) ⓑ a size to which stone or timber is to be cut. (목재·석재의) 치수. 3 《*a* ~ 》 a small quantity or amount. 소량; 소수. [F. *escantillon* pattern.]

***scant·y** [skǽnti] *adj.* (**scant·i·er, scant·i·est**) 1 not quite enough in amount or size. (필요한 양·크기·정도)가 부족한; 불충분한 (opp. ample). ¶ ~ *provisions* 부족한 식량 / ~ *evidence* 불충분한 증거 / *a* ~ *bathing dress* 꼭 끼는 수영복 / *The* ~ *rainfall is causing water shortages.* 비가 충분하게 오지 않아서 물이 부족하다. 2 barely enough. 빠듯한. 3 thin; poor. 빈약한. ¶ ~ *knowledge of Latin* 빈약한 라틴어 지식. 4 poor; not plentiful. 적은; 얼마 안 되는. ¶ *a* ~ *income* 얼마 안 되는 수입 / *a* ~ *crop of rice* 쌀의 흉작. [*scant*]

be scanty of praise, spare praise. 좀처럼 칭찬을 하지 않는.

be scanty of words, be not given to tongue. 말수가 적다.

scape[1] [skeip] *n.* Ⓒ 1 《bot.》 the stem of a flower. 꽃줄기. 2 《archit.》 the shaft of a column 기둥몸. 3 《zool.》 the shaft of a feather. 날갯깃의 중축(中軸). [Gk.]

scape[2], **'scape** [skeip] *vi., vt., n.* 《*poet.*》 = escape.

scape·goat [skéipgòut] *n.* Ⓒ 1 《Bible》 a goat selected to bear the sins of the people and driven out into the wilderness. 속죄양

《고대 유대에서 사람의 죄를 대신 지고 황야로 쫓겨난 양》. **2** 《*fig.*》 a person who bears all the blame for others who are guilty. 남을 대신해서 비난〔죄책〕을 짊어지는 사람; 희생양. [*escape*]

scape·grace [skéipgrèis] *n.* Ⓒ a worthless fellow; a rascal. (말썽만 부리는) 귀찮은 존재; 애물; 깡패. [↑]

scap·u·la [skǽpjələ] *n.* (*pl.* **-lae** or **-las**) 《anat.》 either of the two flat bones of the shoulder. 견갑골; 어깨뼈(= shoulder blade). [L.]

scap·u·lae [skǽpjəlìː, -lài] *n.* pl of **scapula.**

scap·u·lar [skǽpjələr] *adj.* of the scapula. 어깨뼈의. — *n.* Ⓒ kinds of monastic vestment. (수사가) 어깨에 걸치는 (소매 없는) 옷. [L.]

∗**scar**[1] [skɑːr] *n.* Ⓒ **1** a mark left on the skin after a wound, burn, etc. has become well. 흉터; 상처 자국. ¶ *heal to a* ~ 상처가 아물어 흉터가 남다. **2** ⓐ any mark like a scar. 흉터 같은 자국; 흔적. ¶ *knife scars on a table* 식탁 위의 칼자국. ⓑ 《*fig.*》 an effect left on the mind by past suffering. 마음에 남긴 상처. ¶ *It made a* ~ *on my mind.* 그 일로 마음에 상처를 입었다.
— *v.* (**scarred, scar·ring**) *vt.* (P6,13) mark (something) with a scar. …에 상처 자국을〔흉터를〕 남기다. ¶ *His cheek was scarred by a cut.* 베인 상처가 뺨에 흉터를 남겼다 / 《*fig.*》 *a face scarred with sorrow* 슬픔의 상처를 간직하고 있는 얼굴.
— *vi.* (P1,2A) 《usu. *over*》 become well, forming a scar. 나아서 상처 자국이 남다. ¶ *The cut on her cheek scarred over.* 뺨의 베인 상처가 나아서 흉터가 남았다. [Gk. *eskhara* health]

scar[2] [skɑːr] *n.* a precipice; a cliff. 벼랑; 절벽(=scaur). [N. =reef]

scar·ab [skǽrəb] *n.* **1** a beetle, esp. the sacred beetle of the ancient Egyptians. 풍뎅이; (특히) 고대 이집트 사람이 신성시한 왕쇠똥구리. **2** an image of this beetle. 왕쇠똥구리상(像). 參考 《고대 이집트인이 부적이나 장식품으로 썼음》. [L. *scarabaeus* beetle]

∗**scarce** [skɛərs] *adj.* **1** not sufficient; not plentiful. 불충분한; 부족한; 결핍한. ¶ *Fruit is* ~ *and dear this season.* 이 계절에는 과일이 부족해 값이 비싸다 / *Food is still* ~ *in the region.* 그 지역은 아직도 식량이 부족하다. **2** difficult to get; not easily found; uncommon; rare. 입수하기 어려운; 좀처럼 없는; 드문; 희귀한. ¶ *a* ~ *book* 진서(珍書); 희귀본(本) / *Good cooks are* ~. 훌륭한 요리사는 구하기 어렵다.
make oneself scarce, 《*colloq.*》 go away; keep out of the way. (갑자기) 떠나다; 물러나 있다; 피하다.
— *adv.* 《*poet.*》 =scarcely. [L. *excerpo* excerpt]

:**scarce·ly** [skɛ́ərsli] *adv.* **1** with difficulty; barely. 가까스로; 간신히; 겨우. ¶ *There were* ~ *fifty people present.* 겨우 50명이 될까 말까한 사람들이 출석해 있었다. **2** hardly. 거의 …아니다〔않다〕. ¶ *I can* ~ *see.* 거의 안 보인다 / *I* ~ *know him.* 나는 그를 거의 모른다 / *There is* ~ *anytime left.* 시간은 이제 거의 남아 있지 않다. **3** certainly not; probably not. 설마 …아닐〔않을〕 테지. ¶ *He can* ~ *have done that.* 설마 그가 그 일을 했을 리는 없다 / *She can* ~ *have said so.* 아무려면 그녀가 그렇게 말했을까 / *You can* ~ *expect me to do that.* 설마 나보고 그 일을 하라는 건 아니겠지.
scarcely any, hardly any. 거의 없다.
scarcely ... but, hardly any ... that — not. —하지 않는 …은 드물다〔거의 없다〕.
scarcely ever, rarely. 좀처럼 …없다〔아니다, 않다〕. ¶ *Scarcely ever was he without a book.* 그가 책을 지니고 있지 않는 때가 거의 없었다.
scarcely less, hardly less. 거의 같게.
scarcely ... when 〔***before***〕**,** as soon as .... …하자마자; …하기가 무섭게. ¶ *He had* ~ 〔《*lit.*》 *Scarcely had he*〕 *rung the bell when the door flew open.* 벨을 울리자마자 문이 핵 열렸다.

scar·ci·ty [skɛ́ərsəti] *n.* Ⓤ **1** 《sometimes *a* ~》 too small a supply; lack; dearth. 부족; 결핍; 기근. ¶ *a* ~ *of food* 〔*rain*〕 식량〔비의〕 부족 / *The war was followed by a period of* ~. 전쟁이 지나가고 기근이 뒤따랐다. **2** rareness. 드묾. [→scare, -ity]

:**scare** [skɛər] *vt.* (P6,7,13) **1** strike (someone) with sudden fear; make (someone) afraid. …을 놀라게〔겁나게〕 하다; 협박하다. ¶ *His idea scared me.* 그의 생각은 나를 놀라게 했다 / *He was scared by a* 〔*at the*〕 *sudden noise.* 그는 갑작스런 소리에 겁이 났다. **2** 《*away, off*》 drive (someone or something) away by fear. …을 위협하여〔에게 겁을 주어〕 쫓아 버리다. ¶ *The boy scared the dogs away.* 그 아이는 을러대어 개들을 쫓아 버렸다. — *vi.* (P1,3) be frightened; fill with fear. 깜짝 놀라다; 겁내다.
scare up, 《U.S. *colloq.*》 drive out by fright; raise (money, etc.). 몰아내다; 몰이하다; (돈 따위를) 그러모으다.
— *n.* Ⓒ **1** a sudden fear. 겁; 놀람; 공포. ¶ *a war* ~ 전쟁의 불안. **2** an ill-founded alarm. 놀라게 함; 소동. **3** commercial panic. 공황. [N.]

scare·crow [skɛ́ərkròu] *n.* Ⓒ **1** a figure of a man set up in a field to frighten birds away from crops. 허수아비. **2** a person dressed in ragged clothes. (허수아비처럼) 누더기를 걸친 사람; 초라한 사람. **3** a statement which fills people with needless fear. 엄포; 공갈.

scared [skɛərd] *adj.* very frightened. 몹시 놀란; 겁먹은.

scare·mon·ger [skɛ́ərmʌ̀ŋgər] *n.* a

person who produces and spreads news that fills people with needless fear. (쓸데없는 공포감을 조성하여) 세상을 시끄럽게 하는 사람; 유언비어를 퍼뜨리는 사람.

*__scarf__[1] [skɑːrf] *n.* Ⓒ (*pl.* **scarfs** or **scarves**) **1** a long or broad piece of silk, wool, etc. worn about the neck or shoulders or over the head. 목도리; 스카프. **2** 《U.S.》 a long strip of cloth used as a cover for furniture. (테이블·피아노 따위의) 덮개; 커버. [Teut. →(scrip)]

scarf[2] [skɑːrf] *n.* (pl. **scarfs**) a joint in which the ends of beams are cut so that they lap over. (목재의) 엇턱[엇걸이]이음; 사모턱이음. — *vt.* (P6) join with a scarf. 엇턱[엇걸이]이음하다; 끼워 맞추다. [Sw.]

scar·i·fy [skǽrəfài] *vt.* **1** make scratches or cuts in the surface of (the skin, etc.). (수술 따위에서 피부 표면에) 긁힌 상처를[칼자국을] 내다; 난절(亂切)하다. **2** 《*fig.*》 criticize without mercy. …을 혹평하다. ● **scar·i·fi·ca·tion** [skæ̀rəfəkéiʃən / skὲərifi-] *n.* [Gk. *skariphos* a style]

*__scar·let__ [skɑ́ːrlit] *n.* Ⓤ **1** a very bright red. 주홍; 진[다]홍색. **2** cloth or clothing of this color. 진홍색의 옷. ¶ *wear* ~ 주홍색 옷을 입다. — *adj.* of a bright red color. 주홍[다홍·진홍](색)의. ¶ *turn* ~ *with anger* 성이 나서 얼굴이 시뻘게지다. [Pers. =rich cloth]

scarlet fever [´-´-] *n.* **1** a disease marked by a scarlet rash, a sore throat, and fever. 성홍열. **2** 《*joc.*》 a tendency to fall in love with soldier. 여성의 군인(과 사랑에 빠지는) 열(熱).

scarlet woman [´-´-] *n.* 《*euphem., joc.*》 a sexually promiscuous woman, esp. a prostitute. 음부(淫婦); 매춘부.

scarp [skɑːrp] *n.* Ⓒ **1** a sharp slope. 급한 비탈; 급경사(면). **2** 《fortif.》 the inner side of the ditch in fortification. (해자(垓字)의) 안쪽 경사면. — *vt.* (P6) **1** cut in a deep slope or face. …에 가파른 비탈을 만들다. **2** provide (a rampart, etc.) with a scarp. (성루(城壘) 따위를) 급경사면으로 하다. **3** 《*sl.*》 steal. …을 훔치다. [It.]

scarves [skɑːrvz] *n.* pl. of **scarf**[1].

scar·y [skέəri] *adj.* 《*colloq.*》 **1** causing fear. 무서운. ¶ *a* ~ *threat* 무서운 협박 / *push these* ~ *thoughts out of one's mind* 이러한 무서운 생각들을 물리치다 / *watch a* ~ *scene in a movie* 영화에서 무서운 장면을 보다. **2** easily frightened; timid. 놀라기 잘하는; 흠칫흠칫 놀라는; 겁 많은. ¶ *a* ~ *girl* 겁 많은 소녀. [*scare*]

scat [skæt] *vi.* (**scat·ted, scat·ting**) (P1) 《usu. *imperative*》 《*colloq.*》 go off in a great hurry. 부리나케 떠나다. ¶ *Say, You kids,* ~ *!* 야, 이놈들 꺼져. [*hiss, cat*]

scathe [skeið] *n.* 《now chiefly *dial.*》 Ⓤ injury. 해; 손해; 손상. ¶ *do* ~ 손해를 주다 / *keep from* ~ 손상을 면하다. [N.]

without scathe, not harmed. 무사히.

scath·ing [skéiðiŋ] *adj.* (of criticism. etc.) bitter; severe. 격렬한; 통렬한. ¶ ~ *criticism* 신랄한 비평. [↑]

*__scat·ter__ [skǽtər] *vt.* **1** (P6,7,13) ⓐ 《*over, about*》 throw (something) here and there. …을 (흩)뿌리다. ¶ ~ *seeds over the fields* 밭에 씨를 뿌리다 / *Rubbish was scattered all over the lawn.* 잔디 위에는 온통 쓰레기가 흩뿌려져 있었다. ⓑ spread over (with something). 여기저기 흩뜨리다; 산재시키다. ¶ *He scattered his articles with French words.* 그는 논문의 여기저기에 프랑스어를 썼다 / *The ground was scattered with fallen leaves.* 땅에는 낙엽들이 어지러이 흩뜨러져 있었다. **2** (P6,13) separate and drive (a mob, etc.) off in different directions. (군중 등을) 뿔뿔이 흩어 버리다; 쫓아 버리다. ¶ *The police scattered the disorderly crowd.* 경찰은 무질서한 군중을 흩어 버렸다. **3** (P6) waste. (금전)을 낭비하다. ¶ *He is scattering his money about.* 그는 여기저기 돈을 낭비하고 있다. — *vi.* (P1,2A,3) separate and go off in different directions. (뿔뿔이) 사방으로 흩어지다. ¶ *The hens scattered when they saw the cat.* 암탉들은 고양이를 보자 뿔뿔이 흩어져 달아났다. [E.]

scat·ter·brain [skǽtərbrèin] *n.* a person who cannot keep his thoughts on one subject for long. 정신이 산만한 사람; 침착하지 못한 사람.

scat·ter·brained [skǽtərbrèind] *adj.* not able to think steadily or clearly. 생각[정신]이 산만한; 침착지 못한.

scat·tered [skǽtərd] *adj.* lacking a proper relation; lying in all different directions. 통일이 없는; 뿔뿔이 흩뜨러진; 산만한. ¶ *a few* ~ *fishing villages* 몇 개의 산재한 어촌 마을.

scat·ter·ing [skǽtəriŋ] *adj.* distributed widely; spread out here and there. 뿔뿔이 흩어진; 산재한; 드문드문 있는.

scaur [skɑːr, skɔːr] *n.* **1** a precipitous rock or cliff. 단애(斷崖); 절벽. **2** a low-lying rock or reef in the sea. 암초. [→scar[2]]

scav·enge [skǽvəndʒ] *vt., vi.* clean up (a street, etc.). …을 청소하다. [↓]

scav·en·ger [skǽvindʒər] *n.* Ⓒ **1** 《Brit.》 ⓐ a person who cleans streets, taking away dirty things. 거리의 청소부; 환경 미화원. ⓑ a junkman. 넝마주이. **2** an animal that feeds on decaying flesh. 부육(腐肉)을 먹는 동물. ¶ *Vultures are scavengers.* 독수리는 썩은 고기를 먹어 치우는 동물이다. [Teut. →(show)]

sce·nar·i·o [sinέəriòu, -nɑ́ːr-] *n.* Ⓒ (*pl.* **-os**) 《It.》 **1** an outline of a motion picture, giving the story of the scenes, direction for the actors, etc. (영화의) 극본; 각본; 시나리오. **2** an outline of any play. 연극[영화·가극]의 줄거리. [L. *sēna* scene]

sce·nar·ist [sinέərist, -nɑ́ːr-] *n.* Ⓒ a person who writes scenarios for motion pictures. (영화의) 극본〔시나리오〕 작가.

:scene [siːn] *n.* Ⓒ **1** the place where some event occurs. (어떤 행위·사건이 일어나는) 장소; 현장. ¶ *the ~ of a famous battle* 유명한 싸움이 있었던 곳 / *the ~ of the murder* 살인 현장 / *The policeman soon appeared on the ~ of the crime.* 경찰관이 곧 범행 현장에 나타났다. **2** one of the parts into which an act of a play is divided. (연극의) 장(場). ¶ *The ghost of the dead king appears in the castle in Hamlet, Act I, Scene 1.* 햄릿 제1막 제1장에 죽은 왕의 유령이 성 안에 나타난다. **3** a painted background on the stage, showing the place of action. (무대의) 배경. ¶ *change* 〔*shift*〕 *the scenes* (무대) 배경을 바꾸다〔옮기다〕. **4** the place or circumstances in which action of a play or story takes place. 무대(로서 설정된 곳); 장소. ¶ *The ~ is laid in London after World War I.* 무대는 제1차 대전 후의 런던으로 설정되어 있다. **5** a particular incident in a story, play or novel. (극·영화·소설 따위의) 특정 장면〔신〕. ¶ *the ghost ~ in Hamlet* 햄릿에서 유령이 나오는 장면 / *The trial ~ is the most exciting one in 'The Merchant of Venice.'* '베니스의 상인'에서 재판 장면은 가장 재미있는 신이다. **6** an action or incident occurring in reality or represented in literature or art. (현실 생활·문학·미술에 나타나는) 사건; 생긴 일; 행위. **7** what is seen by the eye; a view; a landscape. 광경; 경치; 풍경(cf. *scenery*). ¶ *a desolate ~* 황량한 풍경 / *country scenes* 전원 풍경 / *The happy ~ still lurks in my memory.* 그 즐거웠던 광경이 아직도 내 기억에 남아 있다. **8** 《*colloq.*》 a show of strong emotion, esp. of anger. (감정·노여움 따위를 드러내는) 추태. ¶ *Please don't make a ~!* 제발 볼썽 사나운 짓은 하지 마라. [Gk. *skēnē* tent, stage]

a change of scene, getting out of one's usual surroundings. 환경의 변화; 전지(轉地).

behind the scenes, behind the curtains; secretly. 무대 뒤에서; 막후에서; 내밀히.

come on the scene, appear; come into notice. 나타나다; 눈을 끌다.

make a scene, have a nice scene. 활극을 벌이다; 한바탕 소란〔법석〕을 떨다.

quit the scene, die. 죽다.

***scen·er·y** [síːnəri] *n.* Ⓤ 《*collectively*》 **1** the general view of a landscape. 풍경; 경치; 경관(cf. *scene*). ¶ *picturesque ~* 그림 같은 풍경 / *stop to admire the ~* 경치에 취해 멈추다 / *enjoy mountain ~* 산의 경치를 즐기다. **2** the painted hangings, screens, etc. used on a stage to show the location. (무대의) 배경. ¶ *The ~ represents a city street.* 배경은 시가를 나타내고 있다.

sce·nic [síːnik, sén-] *adj.* **1** having natural beauty; of natural scenery. 경치〔풍경〕의; 경치가 좋은. ¶ *a ~ painter* 풍경 화가 / *the ~ beauty of Naples* 나폴리의 풍경미(美) / *a ~ highway* 경치 좋은 고속 도로 / *such ~ attractions as Ch'unch'ŏn and Tanyang* 춘천, 단양 같은 경승지. **2** of the stage or a play. 무대의; 극의. ¶ *a ~ writer* 극작가 / *~ performances* 〔*effects*〕 무대 상연〔효과〕.

***scent** [sent] *n.* **1** ⒸⓊ smell; a sweet smell. 냄새; 향기. ¶ *the ~ of flowers* 꽃향기 / *a nasty ~* 고약한〔지독한〕 냄새. **2** Ⓒ the sense of smell; the power to smell. 후각. ¶ *Hounds have a keen ~.* 사냥개는 예민한 후각을 갖고 있다. **3** 《*the ~*, used as *sing.*》 the smell left by an animal. (짐승의) 유취(遺臭). ¶ *a hot ~* 강한 유취 / *follow up the ~* (사냥개가 짐승의) 냄새 자취를 따라 추적하다 / *Our dogs lost* 〔*picked up*〕 *the fox's ~.* 우리 개들은 여우의 냄새 자취를 놓쳤다〔찾아냈다〕. **4** Ⓒ a clue aiding investigation. (뒤쫓을) 단서; 실마리. ¶ *a false ~* 그릇된 단서. **5** Ⓤ perfume; liquid having a sweet smell. 향수. ¶ *a bottle of ~* 향수병(하나) / *put ~ on one's handkerchief* 손수건에 향수를 묻히다.

off the scent, = ***on a wrong*** 〔***false***〕 ***scent.*** searching along mistaken lines; unlikely to succeed. (지나간) 냄새 자취를 놓쳐; 단서〔실마리〕를 못 찾아.

on the scent, successful in following someone in trying to discover a secret, etc. 단서를 잡아; 추적하여. ¶ *The police are on the ~ of the robber.* 경찰은 강도를 뒤쫓고 있다.

put** someone **off the scent, mislead someone. …를 따돌리다; 자취를 감추다.

— *vt.* (P6) **1** smell at (something). …을 냄새맡다. **2** get a slight suggestion of (something); try to catch (something) by using the sense of smell. (사냥감 따위의) 냄새를 맡아 내다. **3** spread the sweet smell of (something) around oneself; spray perfume on (something). 향기 따위를 풍기다; …에 향수를 뿌리다. ¶ *~ one's handkerchief* 손수건에 향수를 뿌리다 / *Roses scented the air.* 장미가 향기를 풍기고 있었다. **4** suspect the presence of; be aware of (a secret, etc.). (비밀 등을) 알아채다; 눈치〔낌새〕 채다. ¶ *~ danger* 위험을 깨닫다 / *~ a plot* 음모를 알아채다.

— *vi.* (P1) hunt by the sense of smell. (사냥개가) 냄새를 맡고 추적하다. [→sense]

scent·less [séntlis] *adj.* having no smell. 냄새 없는; 무취(無臭)의.

scep·ter, 《Brit.》 **-tre** [séptər] *n.* Ⓒ **1** a stick held by a king as a sign of royal power. (왕권의 상징으로서의) 홀(笏). **2** 《*the ~*》 royal power; royal rank. 왕권; 왕위. ¶ *assume the ~ of the country* 국왕의 자리에 앉다. [Gk.]

lay down the scepter, cease to be a ruler. 왕위를 물러나다.

sway 〔***wield***〕 ***the scepter,*** be a ruler. 군림하다; 지배하다.

scep·tered, 《Brit.》 **-tred** [séptərd] *adj.*

having a scepter; having royal power or rank. 홀(笏)을 가진; 왕권을 가진.

scep·tic [sképtik] *n., adj.* =skeptic.

scep·ti·cal [sképtikəl] *adj.* =skeptical.

scep·ti·cism [sképtəsìzəm] *n.* =skepticism.

***sched·ule** [skédʒu(:)l / ʃédju:l] *n.* Ⓒ **1** a list; a catalog; a detailed statement. 표; 일람표; 목록; 세목표; 명세서. ¶ *a ~ of prices* 가격표 / *the ~ of games* (경기의) 대진표(對陣表). **2** a list of the times for the comings and goings of trains; a timetable; a program. 시간표; 예정표. ¶ *a train ~* 열차 시간표 / *behind* (*the*) *~* 예정보다 늦게〔더디게〕/ *make out a ~* 예정표를 만들다 / *leave for London on ~* 예정대로 런던을 향해 떠나다. **3** a plan. 계획; 예정. ¶ *a hard ~* 꽉 찬〔빡빡한〕 예정 / *according to* (*the*) *~* 계획〔예정〕대로.
on the schedule 〔***time***〕***,*** according to the timetable or the program. 예정〔시간표〕대로.
— *vt.* (P6,13) **1** make a list of (something). …의 표〔예정표·시간표·일람표〕를 만들다. **2** 《chiefly U.S.》 make a plan of (something to be done at a certain time). …을 예정하다. ¶ *I'm scheduled to meet him next Sunday.* 다음 일요일에 그를 만날 예정이다 / *The prime minister is scheduled to visit Kwangju tomorrow.* 국무 총리는 내일 광주를 방문할 예정이다. [L. *sceda*]

sche·mat·ic [ski(:)mǽtik] *adj.* of a plan; shown in a figure drawn with lines. 개요의; 도해〔도표〕의. ● **sche·mat·i·cal·ly** [-əli] *adv.* [↑]

:**scheme** [ski:m] *n.* Ⓒ **1** a plan. 계획; 안(案). ¶ *a ~ for building a new highway* 새 고속 도로 건설 계획 / *lay down a ~* 계획을 세우다 / *carry out a ~* 계획을 실행하다 / *hit on a ~* (문득) 어떤 안이 생각나다. **2** a secret and cunning plan to cheat someone; a plot. 흉계; 음모. ¶ *schemes to evade taxes* 납세 회피의 흉계 / *a ~ to get control of the government* 정부를 지배하려는 음모. **3** a system; a carefully constructed arrangement. 조직; 체계; 구성; 배합; 배열. ¶ *an educational ~* 교육 제도 / *a ~ of philosophy* 철학 체계 / *the present ~ of society* 현재의 사회 조직 / *the color ~ of a painting* 그림의 색 배합. **4** an outline. 대요; 대강. ¶ *the ~ of the novel* 소설의 대요(大要).
— *vi., vt.* (P1,2A,3,4;6,7) **1** make a plan of (something). (…을) 계획〔안출〕하다. ¶ *be well schemed* 잘 계획돼 있다 /~ (*out*) *a system of water supply* 물 공급 방식을 계획하다. **2** make a secret and cunning plan to cheat someone; plot. 음모〔흉계〕를 꾸미다. ¶ *~ the robbery of a bank* 은행을 털 흉계를 꾸미다 / *~ to kill someone* 아무를 죽일 음모를 꾸미다. [Gk. =shape]

schem·ing [skí:miŋ] *adj.* full of tricks; cunning. 계획적인; 책동적인; 교활한.

scher·zi [skέərtsi:] *n.* pl. of **scherzo.**

scher·zo [skέərtsou] *n.* Ⓒ 《It.》 (*pl.* **-zos** or **-zi**) a light, playful passage in music. 스케르초; 해학곡(諧謔曲).

schism [sízəm, skíz-] *n.* ⓊⒸ **1** a divided state resulting from a difference of opinion in a church. (종교적 견해가 다름으로써 생기는) 분열; 종파 분립. **2** the sin of causing such a division. 종파 분립죄. [Gk. *skhizo* split]

schis·mat·ic [sizmǽtik, skiz-], **-i·cal** [-əl] *adj.* of or causing a schism. 분리〔분열〕의; 교회 분립을 꾀하는. — *n.* a member of a shism. 종파 분립론자. [↑]

schiz·o·phre·ni·a [skìzəfrí:niə, -tsə-] *n.* Ⓤ a mental disorder; splitting of the personality. 정신 분열증. [Gk. *schizo* split, *phrēn* soul]

schiz·o·phren·ic [skìzəfrénik, -tsə-] *adj.* of or suffering from schizophrenia. 정신 분열증의. — *n.* a person having schizophrenia. 정신 분열증 환자.

***schol·ar** [skɑ́lər / skɔ́l-] *n.* Ⓒ **1** ⓐ a person who has much expert knowledge, esp. in the humanities. (특히 인문과학에 깊은 지식을 가진) 학자(cf. *scientist*). ¶ *a distinguished Shakespearean ~* 저명한 셰익스피어 연구 학자. ⓑ 《*colloq.*》 an educated man. 교육을 받은 사람; 배운 사람. ¶ *I am not much of a ~.* 나는 그리 대단한 지식인은 못 된다. **2** a clever student receiving money from a school to help him continue his studies. 장학생. ¶ *a King's ~* (영국의) 국비 장학생. **3** ⓐ 《*arch.*》 a student. 학생. ¶ *an apt* 〔*a bright*〕 *~* 머리 좋은 학생 / *a dull ~* 머리 나쁜 학생. ⓑ a person who learns. 배우는 사람; 학습자. ¶ *At 80 he is still a ~.* 나이 80에 그는 아직도 학습자이다. [L. *schola* school[1]]

schol·ar·ly [skɑ́lərli / skɔ́l-] *adj.* **1** of a scholar; fit for a scholar; having much knowledge. 학자의; 학자다운; 학자로서의 자질이 있는; 박학한. **2** fond of learning. 학문을 좋아하는. ¶ *a ~ young woman* 학문을 좋아하는 젊은 여성.

***schol·ar·ship** [skɑ́lərʃìp / skɔ́l-] *n.* **1** Ⓤ the knowledge gained by long study; much knowledge. 학식; 학문; 박학. **2** Ⓒ the special money given to a clever student to help him continue his studies. 장학금. ¶ *a ~ association* 〔*society*〕 육영회 / *receive* 〔*win*〕 *a ~* 장학금을 받다 / *study on a Fulbright ~* 풀브라이트 장학금으로 공부하다.

scho·las·tic [skəlǽstik] *adj.* **1** relating to a school, student or teacher; of education. 학교의; 교육의. ¶ *a ~ year* 학년(도) /~ *attainments* 학업 성적 /~ *achievements* 학문적 업적 / *the ~ profession* 교직(敎職). **2** like academic life. 학자풍의; 학자연하는. ¶ *with a ~ air* 학자인 체하여.

scho·las·ti·cism [skəlǽstəsìzəm] *n.* Ⓤ 《sometimes *S-*》 scholastic philosophy. 스콜라 철학.

:school[1] [sku:l] *n.* Ⓒ **1** a place for teaching and learning; a schoolhouse or schoolroom. 학교; 교사(校舍); 교실. ¶ *a primary* 〔*an elementary*〕 ~ 초등학교 / *a junior* 〔*senior*〕 *high* ~ 중〔고등〕 학교 / *enter a* ~ 학교에 입학하다 / *keep a* ~ (사립) 학교를 경영하다 / *Our* ~ *is opposite the church.* 우리 학교는 교회의 맞은편에 있다. **2** 《*the* ~, *collectively*》 the complete group of pupils or teachers. 전교 학생; 교사와 학생 전체. ¶ *the entire* ~ / *before the* ~ 전교생을 앞에 두고 / *speak to the whole* ~ 전교생에게 훈화하다 / *The* ~ *is happy over the victory.* 전교생이 승리를 기뻐하고 있다. **3** Ⓤ 《usu. without *an article*》 the time of lessons; a boy's or girl's school period or state. 수업(시간); 재학 기간. ¶ ~ *age* 취학 연령 / ~ *days* 학창 시절 / ~ *hours* 수업 시간 / *after* ~ 방과 후(에) / *be at* ~ 수업중이다; 취학중이다 / *be in* ~ 재학중이다 / *go to* ~ 학교에 다니다 / *attend* ~ 등교하다 / *leave* ~ 졸업하다; 퇴학하다 / *be late for* ~ 학교에 지각하다 / *send* 〔*put*〕 *one's son to* ~ 아들을 학교에 보내다 / *stay away from* ~ 학교를 쉬다 / *School is over.* 학교가 끝났다 / *School begins at 9 o'clock.* 학교는 9시에 시작한다 / *There is* 〔*We have*〕 *no* ~ *today.* 오늘은 수업이 없다. **4** a division of a university occupied with one branch of learning. (대학의) 학부. ¶ *a medical* ~ 의학부 / *a graduate* ~ 대학원 / *the school of dentistry* 치과부. **5** ⓐ the place or condition where a special sort of training is given. 시련(試練)〔단련〕장; 수양의 도장(道場); 환경. ¶ *the hard* ~ *of experience* 경험이라는 모진 시련장 / *brought up in a hard* ~ 고된 시련의 환경에서 자란. ⓑ a special institution for teaching, instruction or research in some special subject. (특수한 기능을 가르치는) 교습소; 훈련소; 연구소; (대학의) 교실. ¶ *the physics* ~ 물리학 교실 / *a dancing* ~ 댄스 교습소 / *a trade* 〔*vocational*〕 ~ 직업 훈련소 / *a cooking* ~ 요리 학교. **6** a group of thinkers or artists who have the same ideas; the principles, methods or characteristics of a group of thinkers or artists. 파(派); 학파; 유파. ¶ *the* ~ *of Plato* 플라톤파 / *the Stoic* ~ 스토아 학파 / *found the* ~ *of positivism* 실증주의 학파를 창시하다.

go to school to, be taught or trained by. …에게서〔…의〕 가르침을 받다.

in the schools =***in for one's schools.*** undergoing university examination at Oxford. 학위 시험을 치르는 중인.

teach school, 《U.S.》 be a schoolmaster. 교편을 잡다.

tell tales out of school, 《*fig.*》 tell others what a person wishes to keep secret. 안의 비밀을 외부에 누설하다.

the old 〔***new***〕 ***school,*** the body of old 〔new〕 opinions, customs, manners, etc. held by people in common. 구〔신〕파; 구〔신〕식; 구사상〔신사상〕.

— *vt.* (P6,7,13) educate (someone) at school; give training to; bring under control. …을 교육시키다; 가르치다; 훈련하다; 누르다; 억제〔통제〕하다. ¶ ~ *a horse* 〔*dog*〕 말을〔개를〕 훈련시키다 / ~ *one's temper* 화를 내지 않도록 훈련을 쌓다 / *School yourself to patience.* 인내심을 길러라. [Gk. *skholē* leisure, lecture]

school[2] [sku:l] *n.* Ⓒ a large group of the same kind of fish or sea animals swimming together. (물고기·고래 따위의) 떼. ¶ *a* ~ *of mackerel* 〔*whales*〕 고등어〔고래〕 떼. — *vi.* (P1) (of fish, whales, etc.) swim in large numbers. (물고기·고래 따위가) 떼를 짓다; 떼지어 유영(游泳)하다. ¶ ~ *up* (물고기 따위가) 수면 가까이 몰려들다. [Du.]

school board [⌐⌐] *n.* **1** 《U.S.》 a committee managing the public schools. 교육 위원회. **2** 《Brit.》 a local education authority. (지방의) 학무 위원회.

school·book [skú:lbùk] *n.* Ⓒ a book used in schools; a textbook. 교과서.

·school·boy [skú:lbɔ̀i] *n.* Ⓒ a boy studying in school. 남학생.

school·child [skú:ltʃàild] *n.* (*pl.* **-chil·dren** [-tʃìldrən]) a child attending school. 학동.

school days [⌐⌐] *n. pl.* the time of being at school. 학창〔학생〕 시절.

school·fel·low [skú:lfèlou] *n.* Ⓒ a companion at school. 학교 친구; 학우.

·school·girl [skú:lgə̀:*r*l] *n.* Ⓒ a girl studying in school. 여학생.

·school·house [skú:lhàus] *n.* Ⓒ **1** a building used for school. 교사(校舍). **2** 《Brit.》 the headmaster's house at some of the public schools. (국민 학교 부속의) 교장 사택.

school·ing [skú:liŋ] *n.* Ⓤ the education in school. 학교 교육; (통신 교육에서의) 교실 교육; 스쿨링. ¶ *lack formal* ~ 정식 교육을 받지 못하다 / *He didn't get much* ~. 그는 학교 교육을 많이 못 받았다. [↑]

school·ma'am [skú:lmàm, -mæ̀m], **-marm** [-mà:*r*m] *n.* 《*colloq.*》 =schoolmistress.

·school·mas·ter [skú:lmæ̀stə*r*, -mà:s-] *n.* Ⓒ a man teaching in school; a school principal. (남자) 교사〔선생〕; (남자) 교장.

school·mate [skú:lmèit] *n.* Ⓒ a fellow at school. 학교 친구; 학우(=schoolfellow).

school·mis·tress [skú:lmìstris] *n.* Ⓒ a woman teaching in school; a woman school principal. 여교사; 여교장.

school·room [skú:lrù(:)m] *n.* Ⓒ a classroom. 교실.

school·teach·er [skú:ltì:tʃə*r*] *n.* Ⓒ a teacher in school. 교사; 교원.

school·time [skú:ltàim] *n.* Ⓒ **1** the hours of teaching in school. 수업 시간. **2** school days. 학교〔학창, 학생〕 시절.

school·work [skú:lwə̀:rk] *n.* Ⓤ the studies; the lessons. 학업; (학교에서의) 수업; 숙제.

school·yard [skú:ljɑ̀:rd] *n.* Ⓒ a ground of a school. (학교의) 운동장; 교정(校庭).

schoon·er [skú:nər] *n.* Ⓒ **1** a small sailing boat with two or more masts. 스쿠너선(船) 《둘 내지 네 개의 돛대를 가진 돛배》. **2** 《U.S.》 a large beer glass. (맥주용의) 큰 컵. **3** 《U.S.》 =prairie schooner. [→skim]

〈schooner 1〉

Schu·bert [ʃú:bərt], **Franz** *n.* (1797-1828) an Austrian composer. 슈베르트《오스트리아의 작곡가》.

Schu·mann [ʃú:mɑ:n], **Robert** *n.* (1810-56) a German composer. 슈만《독일의 작곡가》.

sci. science; scientific.

sci·at·ic [saiǽtik] *adj.* of, in, or belonging to the hip. 엉덩이의; 좌골(坐骨)의. ¶ *the ~ foramen* 좌골공(孔). [L.]

sci·at·i·ca [saiǽtikə] *n.* Ⓤ pain along the course of a sciatic nerve, esp. in the back of the thigh. 좌골(坐骨) 신경통.

:sci·ence [sáiəns] *n.* **1** Ⓤ the study of all material things, observing and arranging them in a systematic law; the subjects relating to this study, such as biology, chemistry, and physics; Ⓒ a branch of such knowledge. 과학; 자연 과학; (그러한) 학문(의 한 분야); …학(學). ¶ *a man of ~* 과학자 / *the ~ of language* 언어학 / *the ~ of history* 역사학 / *cultural ~* 인문 과학 / *(the) applied ~* 응용 과학 / *Politics and economics are social sciences.* 정치학과 경제학은 사회 과학이다. **2** Ⓤ skill; technique. 기(技); 술(術); 기술. ¶ *the ~ of fencing* 검술 / *In judo, ~ is more important than strength.* 유도에서는 힘보다 기술이 더 중요하다. [L. *scio* know]

the seven liberal sciences, grammar, rhetoric, logic, arithmetic, geometry, music, astronomy. 문법, 수사학, 논리학, 산수, 기하학, 음악, 천문학의 7가지 고등 학예(學藝).

science fiction [∠-∠-] *n.* a work of fiction based on some actual or fanciful elements of science. 과학 소설.

:sci·en·tif·ic [sàiəntífik] *adj.* **1** of science. 과학의〔에 관한〕. ¶ *a ~ book* 과학서 / *~ studies* 과학의 연구 / *~ knowledge* 과학 지식. **2** using or based on the methods and principles of science; accurate; systematic; skillful. 과학상의; 과학적인; 정확(精確)한; 체계적인; 기량 있는. ¶ *a ~ method* 과학적인 방법 / *~ farming* 과학적 영농(營農) / *a ~ boxer* 기량이 뛰어난 권투 선수 / *a meticulous and ~ precision* 조금의 어김도 없는 과학적인 정밀함 / *under new rational and ~ management* 새로운 합리적이고도 과학적인 경영으로 / *consider the matter in a ~ way* 사물을 과학적으로 생각하다.

sci·en·tif·i·cal·ly [sàiəntífikəli] *adv.* in a scientific manner; skillfully. 과학적으로; 교묘히.

:sci·en·tist [sáiəntist] *n.* Ⓒ a person who is learned in science, esp. natural science. 과학자; (특히) 자연 과학자(cf. *scholar*).

scim·i·tar, -ter [símətər] *n.* Ⓒ a short curved sword, used by Arabs and other Oriental people. (아랍인 등이 쓰는) 언월도(偃月刀). [It. *scimitarra*]

scin·til·la [sintílə] *n.* Ⓒ **1** a spark; a glimmer. 불꽃; 번쩍임. **2** 《usu. in *negative*》 《*fig.*》 a small piece. 미량(微量); 약간의 흔적; 편린(片鱗). ¶ *There is not a ~ of evidence.* 아무런 증거도 없다. [↓]

scin·til·late [síntəlèit] *vi.* **1** send out little sparks; shine suddenly. 불꽃〔불똥〕을 튀기다; 번쩍하다. ¶ *eyes scintillating with bliss* 행복에 빛나는 눈. **2** 《*fig.*》 (of wit, intelligence, etc.) flash. (재치·지성 따위가) 번뜩이다. ¶ *a scintillating satire* 재치 있는 풍자. [L. =spark]

scin·til·la·tion [sìntəléiʃən] *n.* Ⓤ **1** the act of scintillating; a spark. 불꽃을 발하기; 불꽃; 섬광(閃光). **2** Ⓒ a flash (of wit). (재치의) 번득임. **3** 《astron.》 the twinkling of stars. 별의 반짝임.

sci·o·lism [sáiəlìzəm] *n.* superficial knowledge. 수박 겉 핥기식 학문; 천박한 지식. ● **sci·o·lis·tic** [sàiəlístik] *adj.* [→science]

sci·on [sáiən] *n.* Ⓒ **1** a slender shoot of a plant, used for attaching to another or for planting. (접붙이에 쓰이는) 애가지; 접지(椄枝). **2** a descendant, esp. of a noble or rich family. (특히 명문의) 자손. [F.]

scis·sor [sízər] *vt.* (P6,13) 《*colloq.*》 cut with scissors; cut from anything. 가위로 자르다; 잘라〔오려〕 내다. ¶ *~ off a piece of cloth* 천조각을 잘라 내다 / *~ an article from a newspaper* 신문에서 한 기사를 오려 내다. [→chisel]

·scis·sors [sízərz] *n. pl.* a cutting tool with two sharp blades which work towards each other. 가위. ¶ *a pair of* 〔*three pairs of*〕 *~* 가위 한〔세〕 자루 / *Where are my ~?* 내 가위가 어디 있나.

scissors and paste, the compiling of books out of cuttings or excerpts from others. (풀과 가위로) 따붙이기식의 편찬. ¶ *There's nothing new in the book; it's just a ~ and paste job.* 그 책엔 아무 새로운 내용이 없다. 그저 따붙이기식의 독창성 없는 제품이다.

scoff [skɔ:f, skɑf] *n.* Ⓒ the act of laughing at someone; an expression of contempt or scorn; an object of contempt or scorn. 냉소; 조소; 조소의 대상. ¶ *aim scoffs at someone* 아무를 비웃다 / *be the ~ of the world* 세상의 웃음거리가 되다. —*vi., vt.* (P1,3; 6) 《*at*》 mock; sneer. (…을) 조소하다; 비웃다. ¶ *~ someone in one's heart* 아무를 속으로 비웃다 / *~ at a speaker* 연설자를 조롱하

다 / ~ *at the plan as utopian* 그 계획을 공상적이라고 비웃다. [E.]

scof·fing·ly [skɔ́ːfiŋli, skɑ́f-] *adv.* scornfully. 냉소하여.

*__scold__ [skould] *vi., vt.* (P1,2A; 6,13) blame (someone) with angry words; speak sharply and angrily to (someone). (…을) 꾸짖다; (…에게) 잔소리를 하다. ¶ ~ *at each other* 서로 비난하다 / ~ *one's child out of dropping things* 아이가 물건을 떨어뜨린다고 야단치다 / *be scolded about one's extravagance* 방종하다고 야단맞다 / *His mother scolded him for being naughty.* 말을 듣지 않는다고 어머니는 그를 꾸짖었다 / *My father is always scolding at me.* 아버지는 내게 노상 잔소리다.
— *n.* Ⓒ a person who constantly finds fault with others; esp. a sharp-tongued, noisy woman. 잔소리가 심한 사람; (특히) 앙알[쨍쨍]거리는 여자(cf. *virago*). [→scald]

scold·ing [skóuldiŋ] *n.* Ⓒ a sharp or severe rebuke. 질책; 잔소리. ¶ *give a child a* ~ 아이에게 잔소리를 하다; 아이를 야단치다.
— *adj.* (esp. of a woman) faultfinding; scolding constantly. (특히 여자가) 잔소리가 심한; 시끄러운; 앙알거리는.

scol·lop [skɑ́ləp / skɔ́l-] *n., v.* =scallop.

scon [skɔn] *n.* =scone.

sconce[1] [skɑns / skɔns] *n.* Ⓒ a candlestick with a handle or an ornamental bracket fixed to a wall. (벽에 붙박이한) 돌출 촛대. [→abscond]

sconce[2] [skɑns / skɔns] *n.* 《colloq.》 the head. 머리; 두개(頭蓋)(=skull). ¶ *get a crack on the* ~ 머리를 한대 얻어맞다. [Du.]

scone [skoun, skɑn / skɔn] *n.* Ⓒ a soft, round, flat cake, usu. cooked quickly in a hot oven. 스콘《핫 케이크 같은 둥근 빵》. [Sc.]

scoop [skuːp] *n.* Ⓒ **1** a tool like a shovel, used for taking up or moving coal, grain, etc. (석탄·곡물 따위를 퍼내는) 삽. **2** ⓐ any of several kitchen utensils to take out sugar, salt, flour, etc.; a large spoon. (주방용) 국자; (밀가루·설탕·소금 따위를 퍼내는) 스콥; 작은 삽; 큰 숟갈; (아이스크림 퍼내는) 주걱. ¶ *a flour* ~ 밀가루 푸는 삽. ⓑ the bucket of a dredge, an earth-moving machine, etc. (준설기·토목용의) 흙 퍼내는 버킷. **3** the amount obtained at one time by a scoop. 한번 퍼내는 양. ¶ *a* ~ *of sugar* 한 스콥의 설탕. **4** the act of skimming. 퍼내기; 떠내기. ¶ *drink from one's hand with quick scoops* 한 손으로 잽싸게 몇 번이고 떠마시다 / *earn a lot of money in one* ~ 단번에 큰 돈을 벌다. **5** 《colloq.》 the act of obtaining striking news before any rival newspaper does; beat; the news thus obtained. (신문의) 스쿠프; 특종 기사. ¶ *make a* ~ 특종 기사를 내다. **6** 《colloq.》 a large profit obtained by good luck. 큰 횡재; 대성공. ¶ *make a fine* ~ 대성공을 거두다.
— *vt.* **1** (P6,7,13) 《out, up》 take up (something) with a scoop; dig up. …을 퍼내다; 퍼[떠]올리다; 파(내)다; (퍼올리듯) 집(어올리)다; 꺼내다. ¶ ~ (*out*) *a hole in the sand* 모래에 구멍을 파다 / ~ *water out of a boat* 보트에서 물을 퍼내다 / ~ *up spilled grains* 엎지른 곡식을 줍다. **2** (P6) 《colloq.》 gather in (profits, etc.), as if by a scoop. (돈·이익 따위)를 긁어[쓸어] 모으다; 크게 벌다. **3** (P6) 《colloq.》 get and publish (striking news) before a rival newspaper does. (신문이) 특종을 내다. ¶ *The New York Times scooped some wonderful news yesterday.* 뉴욕 타임스는 어제 놀라운 뉴스를 특종으로 실었다. [Teut.]

scoop·ful [skúːpfùl] *n.* Ⓒ (*pl.* **-fuls**) the amount a scoop contains. 한 국자[삽](의 양).

scoot [skuːt] *vi.* (P1,2A,3) 《colloq.》 run away swiftly; hurry off. 빨리 뛰다; 급히 (달려) 가다. ¶ ~ *for a party* 파티에 달려가다 / *When he saw me, he scooted round the corner.* 나를 보자 그는 잽싸게 골목을 돌아 달아났다. [N.]

scoot·er [skúːtər] *n.* Ⓒ **1** a child's toy vehicle with two wheels which a rider drives by pushing against the ground with one foot. (어린이의) 스쿠터. **2** 《U.S.》 a small bicycle that moves by means of a motor. 모터스쿠터; 스쿠터 자전거. — *vi.* move by scooter. 스쿠터로 달리다[가다]. ¶ ~ *to school.*

*__scope__ [skoup] *n.* Ⓤ **1** the extent of understanding or knowledge. (지력(知力) 등의) 범위; 지식의 한계. ¶ *a man of wide* [*limited*] ~ 시야가 넓은[좁은] 사람 / *a book beyond the* ~ *of such a small child* 그런 어린 아이의 이해 능력을 넘어선 책. **2** the area covered or reached by a study, plan, activity, etc.; extent. (연구·활동 등의) 범위. ¶ *an investigation of wide* ~ 광범위한 수사 / *a work beyond the originally planned* ~ 당초 예정됐던 한도를 넘어선 일 / *enlarge one's* ~ 활동 범위를 넓히다 / *It is beyond the* ~ *of science.* 그것은 과학의 범위를 벗어나 있다《과학의 힘이 미치지 않는다》. **3** room for free activity; opportunity; freedom. (활동 등의) 여지; 기회; 자유. ¶ *seek* ~ *for* …의 기회를 찾다 / *give full* [*ample*] ~ *for* [*to*] …을 발휘할 충분한 기회를 주다 / *give* ~ *to ability* 능력[수완]을 발휘하다 / *work that gives plenty of* ~ *for courage and new ideas* 용기와 새 아이디어를 발휘할 기회가 많은 일 / *He needs more* ~ *for displaying his abilities.* 그에겐 능력을 발휘할 보다 많은 기회가 필요하다. [Gk. *skopos* aim, object]

scor·bu·tic [skɔːrbjúːtik] *adj.* 《med.》 of, like, affected with scurvy. 괴혈병의[에 걸린].
— *n.* a scorbutic person. 괴혈병 환자. [F. *scorbut* scurvy]

*__scorch__ [skɔːrtʃ] *vt.* (P6) **1** burn slightly the surface of (something). …을 눋게 하다; (표면을) 약간 태우다. ¶ *a scorching day* 불볕

더위의 날 / *a scorched-earth policy* 초토 전술 / *a sun-scorched girl* 볕에 그을은 소녀 / *The maid scorched the shirt in ironing it.* 가정부가 다림질할 때 셔츠를 태웠다. **2** wither (grass, etc.); dry up (something) by heat. (햇볕으로) …을 시들게 하다; 말라붙게 하다. ¶ *The grass is scorched by the summer sun.* 잔디가 여름 불볕에 시들었다. **3** laugh at (someone) bitterly; abuse. …을 매도하다; 혹평하다. **4** 《*colloq.*》 (of cyclists, motorists, etc.) drive at high speed. …을 질주시키다.

— *vi.* (P1) **1** burn slightly; wither by heat. (표면이) 약간 눋다; 타다; (열 때문에) 시들다; 말라죽다. **2** 《*colloq.*》 run at full speed. 전속력으로 달리다. ¶ *The car scorched down the road at 90 miles an hour.* 차는 시속 90 마일로 쏜살같이 길을 내리달렸다.

— *n.* Ⓒ **1** a mark made by burning. 탄(눌은) 자국. **2** 《*colloq.*》 (a period of) driving at very high speed. 질주. [E.]

scorch·er [skɔ́ːrtʃər] *n.* Ⓒ **1** a person or thing that scorches. 태우는(눋게 하는) 사람·것. **2** 《*colloq.*》 a very hot day. 찌는 듯이 더운 날. **3** 《*colloq.*》 a person who drives very fast. (자동차 따위를) 질주시키는 사람; 폭주족.

:score [skɔːr] *n.* Ⓒ **1** a cut, mark, or line made with a sharp point. 새긴 금(표); 칼(긁힌) 자국; 베인 상처. ¶ *scores on rock* 바위에 새겨진 금 / *the scores of the whip on the boy's back* 소년의 등에 난 회초리 자국 / *He had deep scores of sorrow and suffering on his face.* 그의 얼굴에는 슬픔과 고난의 자국이 깊이 새겨져 있었다. **2** the record of points made in a game, a contest, a test, etc. (경기·시험 따위의) 득점; 점수; 성적. ¶ *make a good* ~ 대량 득점을 하다; 성적이 좋다 / *make a perfect* (*poor*) ~ *on the science test* 과학 시험에서 만점을(나쁜 점수를) 받다 / *win* (*lose*) *by a* ~ *of 5 to 2,* 5대 2로 이기다(지다) / *The* ~ *was 9 to 6 in our favor.* 득점은 9대 6으로 우리가 이겼다. **3** a debt; an amount or a sum owed; an account. 빚; 부채; 계산(청구)서. ¶ *pay one's* ~ 빚을 갚다 / *run up a* ~ (*scores*) *to someone* 아무에게 빚을 지다 / 《*prov.*》 *Death pays all scores.* 죽으면 셈은 끝난다; 죽은 자를 원망치 않는다. **4** ⓐ 《*pl.* score》 twenty (persons or things). 20; 20명; 20개. ¶ *a* ~ *of people* 스무 사람 / 《Bible》 *three* ~ *and ten* (인간의 평균 수명으로서) 70년 / *by the* ~, 20개 단위로 / *about a* ~ *of years ago* 약 20년 전. ⓑ 《*pl.*》 a great number (many). 다수. ¶ *scores of people* 많은 사람 / *scores of times* 몇 번이나; 여러 차례 / *People came in* (*by*) *scores.* 사람들이 무척 많이 왔다. **5** a point; a reason; an excuse. 점; 이유; 원인. ¶ *I have no regrets on that* ~. 그 점에서는 후회하지 않는다. **6** 《mus.》 a copy of work of music showing separate parts for different instruments or voices. 악보(樂譜); 모음악보. ¶ *in* ~ 모음악보로. **7** any successful act, remark, etc.; an advantage gained for oneself by such an act, etc. (상대를 골리는) 멋진 수법(방식, 말, 동작); 성공; 행운. ¶ *a* ~ *against someone* 남을 해치우는 수법 / *a great* ~ 매우 잘 됨; 대성공 / *He is always making cheap scores.* 그는 늘 하찮은 일로 남을 애먹인다.

go* (*set, start*) *off at* (*full*) *score, start vigorously. 갑자기 돌진하다; 기운차게 하기 시작하다.

keep the score, record runs, points, etc. (경기 등에서) 득점을 기록하다.

know the score, 《U.S. *colloq.*》 be aware of the true facts of situation. …의 진상(실상)을 알다.

make a score off *one's* ***own bat,*** do single-handed. (남의 힘을 빌리지 않고) 혼자 힘으로 하다.

on more scores than one, for more than one reason. 한 가지 이상의 이유로.

on the score of, on account of. …때문에. ¶ *be absent on the* ~ *of illness* 병 때문에 결석(결근)하다 / *complain on the* ~ *of low pay* 낮은 임금 때문에 불평하다.

pay off* (*full*) (*settle, clear, quit*) *old scores, **a**) get equal with (someone) for past wrongs or injuries. 묵은 셈을 갚다; …에게 쌓인 원한을 풀다. **b**) pay out. 변제하다; 갚다.

— *vt.* **1** (P6,7,13) mark with cuts, lines, scratches. …에 칼자국을(진집을, 긁힌 상처를) 내다; 표시를 하다; 선을 긋다(그어 지우다). ¶ ~ *mistakes in red ink* 틀린 곳을 붉은 잉크로 지우다 / ~ *the surface of a board* 널빤지에 칼자국(흠집)을 내다 / *be scored with underlining* 밑줄이 그어지다 / *Her face was scored with sorrow.* 그녀 얼굴에는 슬픔이 어려 있었다. **2** (P6) get (a specified number of points) in a game or test; gain; achieve (a) success. …을 득점하다(얻다); 이기다; 거두다; 획득하다. ¶ ~ *a knockout in the 5th round.* 5라운드에서 케이오승(勝)을 거두다 / *Tom scored two runs for our team.* 톰은 우리 팀에게 2득점을 올려 주었다 / *The play scored a great success.* 연극은 대성공을 거두었다. **3** (P6,7,13) ⓐ keep a record of(the number of points in a game or the amount owed). (득점 따위)를 기록하다; …빚을 셈(계산)하다. ¶ *He was appointed to* ~ *the basketball game.* 농구 시합의 득점을 기록하도록 명령받았다 / ~ *up $ 20 against him* 빚으로서 그의 앞으로 20 달러를 달아두다. ⓑ 《U.S.》 grade or mark (an examination, a candidate, etc.). (시험 따위)를 채점하다; 점수를 매기다. ¶ ~ *a test.* **4** (P6) 《mus.》 arrange (music) for different instruments or voices. 모음악보에 기입하다; 작곡하다. **5** 《U.S.》 criticize severely. 호되게 비난하다(까다); 혹평하다. — *vi.* (P1) **1** make a point; achieve a success; gain an advantage. 득점하다; 성공하다; 이익을 얻다. ¶ *an actor who scores every time* 출연할 때마다 성공을 거두는 배우 / *Neither team scored.* (두 팀 중) 어느 팀

도 득점을 못했다. **2** keep a score in a game. 득점을 기록하다. **3** 《*with*》《*sl.*》 (of a man) have sex with a woman. (여자와) 관계하다. [Scand. *skor* notch]

score off, 《Brit. *colloq.*》 get an advantage over (someone); get the better of (someone) in an argument, etc. (상대)를 해치우다; (의론 따위에서) …을 이기다; 찍소리하지 못하게 하다.

score out, cancel (written words, etc.) by drawing lines through or under. (글자 등)에 선을 그어 지우다; 말소하다.

score up, make a score or record. (득점·셈 따위)를 기록하다. ¶ ~ *up runs as they are made* 득점할 때마다 기록하다 / *Score the bill up against me.* 계산서는 내 앞으로 달아 두시오.

score·board [skɔ́:rbɔ̀:rd] *n.* Ⓒ a board that shows the score in a game. 득점 게시판.

score·book [skɔ́:rbùk] *n.* Ⓒ a book in which the scores of the game are written and kept for reference. 득점표; 스코어 북.

scor·er [skɔ́:rər] *n.* Ⓒ a person who keeps the score. 채점 계원; 득점 기록 계원.

:scorn [skɔ:rn] *n.* **1** Ⓤ a feeling of strong dislike; contempt; disdain. 경멸; 멸시. ¶ *have* 〔*feel*〕 ~ *for someone* 아무에게 경멸감을 품다 / *He poured* ~ *on my suggestion.* 그는 내 제안을 비웃고 거들떠보지도 않았다. **2** Ⓒ a person or thing that is despised; an object of contempt. 경멸〔비웃음〕당하는 사람〔것〕; 웃음거리; 조롱가마리. ¶ *become* 〔*be*〕 *the* ~ *of all the village* 온 마을의 조롱가마리가 되다 / *He is a* ~ *to his neighbors.* 그는 이웃의 웃음거리이다.

hold in scorn, hold in contempt; despise. …을 경멸하다; 멸시하다.

laugh** someone **to scorn, mock. 비웃다; 조소하다.

think 〔***hold***〕 ***it scorn to*** (*do*)***,*** be too proud to (do). …하는 것을 떳떳하게 여기지 않다.

think scorn of =hold in scorn.

— *vt.* (P6,8,9) **1** show contempt for(someone); despise. …을 경멸하다; 멸시하다. **2** reject (something) as mean or low. (경멸하며) 거부〔거절〕하다; 퇴짜놓다; 물리치다. ¶ ~ *the advice of one's friend* 친구의 충고를 물리치다 / *The judge scorned to take a bribe.* 판사는 뇌물을 거절했다 / *I would* ~ *to do it.* 나는 그런 일을 하는 것을 떳떳치 않게 여긴다 / ~ *lying* 〔*to lie*〕 = ~ *to tell* 〔*telling*〕 *a lie* 거짓말 하는 것을 수치로 여기다. [Teut.]

·scorn·ful [skɔ́:rnfəl] *adj.* showing disdain openly; full of contempt. 경멸하는; 조소적인. ¶ *a* ~ *smile* 경멸조의 미소 / *He is* ~ *of our old car.* 그는 우리 집 낡은 차를 비웃고 있다.

·scorn·ful·ly [skɔ́:rnfəli] *adv.* in a scornful manner; disrespectfully. 경멸〔멸시〕하여.

Scor·pi·o [skɔ́:rpiòu] *n.* 《astron.》 the name given to a group of stars that were thought of as arranged in the shape of a scorpion. 전갈자리. [Gk.]

scor·pi·on [skɔ́:rpiən] *n.* Ⓒ **1** a small animal having eight legs, two large claws and a tail with a poisonous sting. 전갈. **2** an evil person. 음흉한 사나이. **3** 《*the S-*》 = Scorpio.

·Scot [skɑt / skɔt] *n.* Ⓒ a person of Scotland; a Scotchman. 스코틀랜드 사람. ¶ *Great* ~*!* 아뿔싸; 아차. [L. *Scottus*]

scot [skɑt / skɔt] *n.* tax or rate. 세금; 부담액. [E.]

pay scot and lot, contribute one's share to municipal expenses. 응분의 할당 몫〔세금〕을 내다.

·Scotch [skɑtʃ / skɔtʃ] *adj.* of Scotland, its people or their language. 스코틀랜드(사람·말)의. ¶ ~ *whisky* 스카치 위스키.

— *n.* **1** 《*the* ~*, collectively*》 the people of Scotland. 스코틀랜드 사람. **2** the language of Scotland. 스코틀랜드 말. **3** Ⓤ a fine kind of whisky made in Scotland. 스카치 위스키. ¶ *"Scotch on the rocks, please."* 스카치 위스키에 얼음을 얹어 주시오. [→Scot.]

Scotch and soda, whisky and soda. 위스키 소다.

scotch [skɑtʃ / skɔtʃ] *vt.* (P6) 《*arch.*》 **1** make temporarily powerless. (…에) 죽지 않을 만큼의 상처를 입히다; 반죽음만 시키다. ¶ ~ *a snake without killing it* 뱀을 죽이지는 않고 반죽음시키다. **2** put down; stop. 진압〔박멸·탄압〕하다; 중지시키다. ¶ ~ *a mutiny* 폭동을 진압하다 / ~ *a plan* 계획을 중지시키다. [M.E. *scocche*]

Scotch broth [∠∠] *n.* soup or stew with meal, bareley and vegetables. 양고기·보리·야채로 만든 수프.

Scotch cousin [∠∠–] *n.* distant relative. 먼 친척.

Scotch·man [skɑ́tʃmən / skɔ́tʃ-] *n.* Ⓒ (*pl.* **-men** [-mən]) a person of Scotland; a Scotsman. 스코틀랜드 사람.

Scotch mist [∠∠] *n.* mist resembling fine rain. 안개비; 짙은 안개.

Scotch·wom·an [skɑ́tʃwùmən / skɔ́tʃ-] *n.* Ⓒ (*pl.* **-wom·en** [-wìmin]) a woman of Scotland. 스코틀랜드 여자.

scot·free [skɑ́tfrí: / skɔ́t-] *adj.* completely free from harm, punishment, payment, etc.; unpunished; unharmed; safe. 해를 입지 않고; 벌을 면하고; 무사히; 지불 면제의. ¶ *go* 〔*get off*〕 ~ 무사히 달아나다; 무죄 석방되다 / *He got off* ~ *from the murder charge.* 살인 혐의를 면(免)했다. [*scot*]

·Scot·land [skɑ́tlənd / skɔ́t-] *n.* the northern part of Great Britain. 스코틀랜드. [*Scot*]

Scotland Yard [∠–∠] *n.* the headquarters of the London Police, esp. the department of criminal investigation. 런던시 경찰청. 參考 구(舊)소재지 이름에서 따온 것. ¶ *call in* ~ (지방 경찰이 어려운 사건을) 런던 시경에 수사를 의뢰하다.

Scots [skɑts / skɔts] *adj.* of Scotland; Scottish. 스코틀랜드의. — *n. pl.* **1** 《*the* ~, *collectively*》 the people of Scotland. 스코틀랜드 사람. **2** Ⓤ the language or dialect of Scotland. 스코틀랜드 말〔사투리〕.

Scots·man [skɑ́tsmən / skɔ́ts-] *n.* (*pl.* **-men** [-mən]) =Scotchman.

Scots·wom·an [skɑ́tswùmən / skɔ́ts-] *n.* (*pl.* **-wom·en** [-wìmin]) =Scotchwoman.

***Scot·tish** [skɑ́tiʃ / skɔ́t-] *adj., n.* =Scotch.

scoun·drel [skáundrəl] *n.* Ⓒ an evil man; a wicked man; a rascal. 무뢰한; 악당. ¶ *The scoundrels who set fire to the barn have been caught.* 헛간에 방화한 악당들이 체포되었다. [?]

scour[1] [skáuər] *vt., vi.* **1** (P6,7,13; 1) polish (something) by hard rubbing; burnish. (…을) 문질러 닦다; 윤〔광〕내다. ¶ ~ *a rusty pot with emery paper* 녹슨 냄비를 사포로 닦아 윤을 내다. **2** (P6,7,13; 1) 《*away, off, out*》 remove or wash off (dirt, grease, etc.) by hard rubbing or with water. (…을) 세게 문질러 떼어내다〔없애다〕; 물로〔물을 흘려〕 씻어내다. ¶ ~ *rust off a knife* 칼의 녹을 문질러 없애다 / ~ *stain away* 얼룩을 지우다 / ~ *(out) a ditch* 물을 흘려 도랑을 깨끗이 쳐내다.
— *n.* **1** Ⓤ the act of scouring. 문질러〔비벼〕 닦기; 물로〔물을 흘려〕 깨끗이 하기. ¶ *give a dirty frying pan a good* ~ 더러운 프라이팬을 깨끗이 닦다. **2** an apparatus or material used in scouring. 연마재(材); 연마기. ¶ *Sand is a good* ~. 모래는 좋은 연마재다. [L. *ex-* completely, *cura* care]

scour[2] [skáuər] *vt.* (P6,13) search for (someone or something) quickly and thoroughly; pursue thoroughly. …을 급히 찾아다니다; 샅샅이 찾다. ¶ *The police scoured the city for the thief.* 경찰은 도둑을 잡으려고 시내를 구석구석 뒤졌다 / *We scoured the woods for the lost child.* 길 잃은 아이를 찾아 숲속을 샅샅이 뒤졌다. — *vi.* (P2A,3) move swiftly, as if searching. 재빨리 움직이다; 뛰어다니다; 질주하다. ¶ *We scoured over the hillside for firewood.* 땔나무를 하러 산허리를 부지런히 돌아다녔다. [L.]

***scourge** [skəːrdʒ] *n.* Ⓒ **1** the act of whipping; a whip. 매(질); 채찍. **2** a person or thing that causes great trouble or misfortune. 큰 불행이나 재난의 씨〔원인〕. ¶ *In olden times, an outbreak of disease was called a* ~. 예전에는 질병이 발생하면 천벌이라고 했다.
the scourge of Heaven, the punishment of Heaven. 천벌; 벌력.
— *vt.* (P6) strike or hit (someone) with a whip; punish severely; torment very much. …를 매질하다; 엄하게 벌하다; …을 몹시 괴롭히다. ¶ *He was scourged by the memory of his sins.* 자신이 지은 죄를 생각하고 몹시 괴로워했다. [→excoriate]

scour·ings [skáuəriŋz] *n. pl.* **1** dust or material rubbed off. (문지르거나 긁어 떨어뜨린) 흙먼지; 오물. **2** the rubbish removed from grain. 곡물의 찌꺼기. [*scour*[1]]

:scout[1] [skaut] *n.* Ⓒ **1** a person, a ship, an airplane, etc. sent or used to obtain information about the enemy. 척후(병); 정찰함〔기〕. **2** the act of obtaining information about the enemy. 정찰; 척후. ¶ *be in* 〔*on*〕 *the* ~ 정찰중이다 / *go on the* ~ 정찰 나가다. **3** a member of the Boy Scouts or Girl Scouts. 보이〔걸〕스카우트의 일원. **4** 《*colloq.*》 a fellow. 놈; 녀석. **5** 《Brit.》 a road patrolman to help motorists. 도로 순찰자. **6** 《Brit.》 a male servant in an Oxford college. (옥스퍼드 대학에서) 학생 시중을 드는 사환; 용원(傭員). **7** 《U.S.》 a person whose work is to discover and employ persons with talent, as in sports or entertainments. (스포츠나 연예에 재능이 있는 자를) 발굴하는 사람.
— *vi.* (P1,2A,3) perform as a scout; search for something. 척후〔정탐·정찰〕하다; 찾아다니다. ¶ *He is out scouting.* 그는 정찰을 나가 있다. [L. *ausculto* listen]
***scout about* 〔*around*〕,** go from place to place, searching for (something); search about for (something). 여기저기 찾아다니다. ¶ ~ *about for a building site* 건축 부지를 구하러 다니다.

scout[2] [skaut] *vt.* (P6) reject (a proposal, idea) with scorn or as absurd. (제의·의견 등을) 뿌리치다; 물리치다. ¶ *She scouted all objections to her plan.* 그녀는 그녀 계획에 대한 모든 반대를 물리쳤다. [Scand. *skuta* taunt]

scout·mas·ter [skáutmæ̀stər, -mɑ̀ːs-] *n.* Ⓒ a leader of a band of Boy Scouts. 보이스카우트 단장. [*scout*[1]]

scow [skau] *n.* a large, flat-bottomed boat used to carry sand, rock, etc. (모래·돌을 실어나르는) 대형 평저선(平底船). [Du.]

scowl [skaul] *vi.* (P1,3) 《*at, on*》 look displeased or angry; frown at someone heavily. 얼굴을 찡그리다; 눈살을 찌푸리다; 쏘아〔노려〕보다. ¶ *The man scowled at me.* 사나이는 나를 쏘아 보았다 / *He made no reply, but simply scowled.* 그는 대답은 하지 않고 그저 못마땅한 얼굴을 했다.
— *vt.* (P7) **1** 《*down, away, into*》 make (someone) do something by scowling. …에게 얼굴을 찌푸려〔못마땅한 얼굴을 하여〕 —시키다. ¶ ~ *her into silence* 불쾌한 얼굴을 지어 그녀를 침묵시키다. **2** express (angry feelings, etc.) with a scowl. 눈살을 찌푸려 (노여움 따위)를 나타내다. ¶ ~ *one's disappointment at* … 상을 찡그려 …에게 실망을 나타내다.
— *n.* Ⓒ a frowning face; a sulky face. 찌푸린 얼굴; 불쾌한 표정. [Scand.]

scrab·ble [skrǽbəl] *vi., vt.* (P1; 6) **1** 《usu. *about*》 scratch about with the hands or paws. 긁다; 휘젓다; 뒤져서 찾다. ¶ ~ *about in the mud for coins* 진흙 속을 뒤져 동전을 찾다. **2** write carelessly or hastily; scribble. (급히) 휘갈겨 쓰다. ¶ *She scrabbled a note to* *the milkman.* 그녀는 우유 배달원에게 쪽지 하나를 급히 적어 주었다. [Du.]

scrag [skræg] *n.* Ⓒ **1** a thin, skinny person or animal. 앙상하게 말라빠진 사람〔동물〕. **2** Ⓤ a lean, bony part of a sheep's neck, used for making soup. (뼈가 많은) 양의 목고기. **3** 《*colloq.*》 a neck. 목; 모가지. — *vt.* (**scragged, scrag·ging**) (P6) 《*colloq.*》 twist or wring the neck of (someone); put (someone) to death by hanging or strangling. …의 목을 비틀다〔조르다〕; 목 졸라 죽이다. [→crag]

scrag·gy [skrǽgi] *adj.* (**-gi·er, -gi·est**) **1** thin; skinny; bony. 말라빠진; 비쩍 마른 (cf. *scrawny*). **2** (of rocks, etc.) ragged; rough. (바위 따위가) 우툴두툴한; 삐죽삐죽한.

∗**scram·ble** [skrǽmbəl] *vi.* (P1,2A,3,4) **1** 《*up, along*》 climb or move along with the hands and feet. 기어오르다; 기다. ¶ ~ *up a cliff* 절벽을 기어오르다 / ~ *down the steep canyons* 험한 협곡을 기어 내려가다 / ~ *out of the blazing bus* 불타는 버스에서 기어나오다 / ~ *over the fence* 울타리를 기어넘다. **2** struggle or fight with others for something. 서로 빼앗다; 쟁탈하다; 다투다. ¶ *They scrambled for the coins.* 동전을 차지하려고 서로 다투었다 / *They scrambled to get the best seats.* 그들은 앞을 다투어 좋은 자리를 차지하려 했다. **3** 《mil.》 take off quickly to intercept enemy aircraft. (적기를 요격하기 위해) 긴급 발진하다. — *vt.* (P6) **1** collect (something) in a hurry; mix (something) together. …을 그러모으다; (휘저어) 뒤섞다. ¶ ~ *the cards.* **2** mix the whites and yolks of (eggs) together. (달걀)을 익히면서 휘젓다. ¶ *scrambled eggs* 풀어서 지진 달걀. **3** alter the frequency of transmission on a telephone line to prevent someone who is tapping the line from understanding the conversation. 전화의 주파수를 계획적으로 바꿔 도청을 못 하게 조작하다.

***scramble along* 〔*on*〕*,* a**) climb on. 기어 나아가다. **b**) make one's way. 이럭저럭 해나가다〔지내다〕.

— *n.* Ⓒ **1** the act of climbing a steep hill, etc. 기어 오르기; 빠른 등반. **2** a hard or disorderly struggle. 쟁탈. [?]

∗**scrap**[1] [skræp] *n.* Ⓒ **1** ⓐ a small or broken piece. (작은) 조각; 파편; 단편; 부스러기; 지스러기. ¶ *a* ~ *of paper* 종잇조각 / *a house with a* ~ *of garden* 손바닥만한 마당이 있는 집 / *put the scraps of paper in the wastepaper basket* 종잇조각들을 휴지통에 넣다 / *I have a few scraps of news.* 몇 가지 단편적인 소식이 있다. ⓑ 《*fig.*》 a very small portion of anything. 조금. ¶ *I haven't eaten a* ~ *all day.* 온종일 조금도 먹지 못했다. **2** 《*pl.*》 pieces of paper, etc. that are cut from books, newspapers, etc. (책·신문 따위에서) 오려낸 것; 발췌; 스크랩. **3** ⓐ 《*collectively*》 wasted metal, such as pieces of iron. 쇠부스러기; 파쇠; 고철. ¶ ~ *iron* 파쇠; 고철. ⓑ 《*pl.*》 useless remains, esp. bits of uneaten food. 불필요하게 남은 것; 음식 찌꺼기; (특히) 먹다 남은 음식. ¶ *The maid gave the scraps to her cat.* 가정부는 먹다 남은 음식을 고양이에게 주었다. **4** 《*pl.*》 the fat of an animal remaining after the oil has been taken away. 지방의 찌끼. [Scand.(→scrape)]

do not care a scrap, do not care or mind at all. 조금도 개의치〔상관〕 않다.

not a scrap, not at all. 조금도 …않다.

— *vt.* (**scrapped, scrap·ping**) (P6) make (something) into scraps; throw (something) away as useless. …을 휴지 조각으로 만들다; 무용지물로서 버리다; 폐기하다. ¶ ~ *a battleship* 전함을 폐선(廢船)으로 하다 / *You had better* ~ *that worn-out machine.* 닳아빠진〔노후한〕 그 기계를 버리는 게 좋겠다. [Scand. (→scrape)]

scrap[2] [skræp] *n.* 《*colloq.*》 a fight; a quarrel. 싸움; 다툼; 드잡이. ¶ *He had a bit of a* ~ *with the police.* 그는 경찰과 약간 다퉜다. — *vi.* (**scrapped**) (P1,3) fight; quarrel. 싸움을 하다; 말다툼을 하다. [var. of *scrape*]

scrap·book [skrǽpbùk] *n.* Ⓒ a book of blank pages for pasting and keeping clipping from newspapers, etc. 스크랩북 《신문 따위에서 오려붙인 책》. [→scrap[1]]

∗**scrape** [skreip] *vt.* **1** (P6,7,13,18) ⓐ rub the surface of (something) with a rough or sharp tool, so as to make clean, smooth, or level. 비비(어 없애)다; 문질러 깨끗이〔반반하게, 반드럽게〕 하다. ¶ ~ *a wall* (부착된 칠·종이를 떼기 위해) 벽을 박박 긁다 / ~ *potatoes* 감자 껍질을 비벼 벗기다 / ~ *one's chin* (면도로) 수염을 깎다 / ~ *a ship's bottom* (붙어 있는 굴 등을 떼려고) 선저(船底)를 닦다 / *Scrape your shoes before you come in!* 들어오기 전에 신발에 묻은 (진)흙을 문질러 터시오. ⓑ 《*off, out, from*》 remove (mud, grease, paint, paper, etc.) in this way. …을 비벼〔문질러〕 벗기다〔떼다〕; 긁어 없애다. ¶ ~ *old paint from a door* 문의 낡은 칠을 긁어 벗기다 / ~ *mud off one's shoes* 신발의 흙을 비벼 떼다 / ~ *scales off a fish* 생선의 비늘을 긁어 벗기다 / ~ *out a stain* 얼룩을 비벼 없애다. **2** (P7,13) 《*on, against*》 injure or scratch (something) by scraping. …을 긁히게 하다; 긁혀 까지게〔상처를 입게〕 하다. ¶ *I scraped my knee on a stone.* 돌에 무릎이 까졌다 / *The car scraped its side against the wall.* 차가 벽에 받쳐 옆 부분이 긁혔다. **3** (P6,7) ⓐ make by scraping. 긁어〔비벼〕 만들다; 파다. ¶ ~ (*out*) *a hole in the sand* 모래에 구멍을 파다 / ~ *the way through* 몸을 비비대며 빠져나가다. ⓑ 《*away, off, out*》 clear by scraping. 긁어〔비벼〕 깨끗이 하다; 긁어내다. ¶ ~ *out the ashes from a grate* 난로 쇠살대에서 재를 긁어내다. **4** (P6,7,13) rub with a harsh sound. 비벼 소리를 내다; 마찰음을 내다. ¶ ~ *a pen over paper* 펜이 긁히는 소리를 내며 종이 위에 써나가다 / ~ *a violin* 바이올린을 켜다. **5** (P6,7) 《usu. *up, together*》 collect in small

amounts or with difficulty. 그러모으다; 애를 써서〔푼푼이〕 모으다. ¶ ~ *up a sum for the trip* 여행에 필요한 금액을 어렵게 마련하다 / *The hungry boy scraped up the last crumbs from his plate.* 그 굶주린 아이는 접시의 마지막 빵부스러기까지 깨끗이 비웠다.
— *vi.* (P1,2A,3) **1** rub anything with a hard object. 문지르다; 비비다. ¶ *He scraped at his face.* 그는 얼굴을 문질렀다. **2** produce a rough sound. 비비며〔긁혀〕 소리를 내다. ¶ *the rain scraping on the roof* 지붕을 때리는 비 / ~ *on a violin* 낑낑(거슬리는 소리로) 바이올린을 켜다 / *His chalk scraped on the blackboard.* 그의 백묵이 칠판에서 긁히는 소리를 냈다. **3** 《often *by, along, through*》 ⓐ go or pass along touching or almost touching. 스치며〔비벼대며〕 가다; 스칠 듯이 지나가다. ¶ *The two buses scraped past each other.* 두 버스는 서로 스칠 듯이 지나갔다. ⓑ succeed barely or manage with difficulty. 간신히〔가까스로〕 …하다. ¶ ~ *along* 간신히 지나가다; 그럭저럭 지내다 / ~ *through the muddy ground* 진창을 가까스로 빠져나가다 / *He barely scraped through on the test.* 간신히 시험에 합격〔통과〕했다. **4** make money slowly and with difficulty. 푼푼이〔고생하며〕 돈을 모으다. ¶ ~ *together out of one's earnings* 벌이 중에서 어렵게 돈을 푼푼이 모으다. **5** draw back the foot when bowing. (절을 할 때) 한 쪽 발을 뒤로 빼다.

bow and scrape, draw back the foot in making a bow; flatter. (절을 할 때) 한 쪽 발을 뒤로 빼다; 아첨하다; 알랑거리다.

scrape along, rub harshly on or across as in passing; manage or get by with difficulty. 스칠 듯이 지나가다; 그럭저럭〔근근이〕 지내다.

scrape and screw, practice laborious economy or saving. 푼푼이 어렵게 저축하다.

scrape down, **a**) foot down by moving one's feet noisily on floor. 발을 구르며 야유하다. **b**) level with a road grader. 길을 평평하게 고르다.

scrape out, play (music) on a violin, etc. with rough sounds. 바이올린 따위로 (귀에 거슬리는) 긁히는 소리를 내다.

scrape one's plate, leave nothing on it. 접시의 음식을 비우다.

scrape the mug, 《U.S. *colloq.*》 shave. 면도하다.

scrape through, get, pass through with difficulty. 간신히 해내다〔통과하다·지내다〕.

***scrape up* 〔*together*〕,** gather or save (something) with difficulty. (어렵게) …을 모으다.

scrape* (*up*) *an acquaintance with, meet (someone) by making advances; get a chance to meet (someone) by pushing oneself into his company. …에게 환심을 사려고 (남의 소개도 없이) 무리하게 접근하다.
— *n.* **1** Ⓤⓒ the act or sound of scraping. 비빔; 긁음; 스침; 비비는〔긁히는〕 소리. ¶ *the ~ of the bow on a viloin* 활로 바이올린을 켜는 귀에 거슬리는 소리. **2** Ⓒ a scraped place. 긁힌〔스친〕 상처. ¶ *a ~ on the shin* 정강이의 찰과상. **3** Ⓒ a difficult or unpleasant situation caused by one's bad behavior. 어려움; 궁지; 곤경. ¶ *He got into a ~.* 그는 궁지에 빠졌다. [E.]

be in a scrape, be in difficulties. 곤경에 처해 있다. ¶ *If he had obeyed his mother, he would not be in his present ~.* 어머니 말을 따랐다면 현재의 곤경에 처하지는 않았을텐데.

scrap·er [skréipər] *n.* Ⓒ **1** a tool for scraping. 긁어내는〔문지르는, 벗겨 떼는〕 도구. **2** a door mat. (신발의) 흙떨이. ¶ *wipe shoes on the ~* 신발의 흙을 흙떨이에 문질러 떨다. **3** a tool for leveling the ground. 땅을 고르는 기계; (도로 공사용) 스크레이퍼.

scrap heap [⌐⌐] *n.* a pile of useless articles; a pile of iron scraps. 쓰레기더미; 파쇠더미.

scrap·ing [skréipiŋ] *n.* 《usu. *pl.*》 something scraped. 긁어〔비벼〕 뗀 부스러기; 쓰레기. [→scrape]

scrap·py [skrǽpi] *adj.* (**-pi·er, -pi·est**) **1** made up of scraps. 부스러기의; 지스러기의. **2** consisting of fragments; disconnected. 단편적인; 지리멸렬한. ¶ *a ~ speech* 갈피를 잡을 수 없는 연설.

:scratch [skrætʃ] *vt.* **1** (P6,7) ⓐ mark or cut the surface of (something) slightly with something sharp or rough; break, cut, or mark (something) lightly by doing this.… …의 표면을 (날카로운 것·거친 것으로) 긁(히게 하)다; …에 긁힌 상처를〔흠집을〕 내다. ¶ ~ *one's hand on a nail* 손을 못에 긁히다 / *Don't ~ the table.* 테이블에 긁힌 자국〔흠집〕을 내지 마라 / *I've scratched my hands with the thorns.* 나뭇가시에 손을 긁혔다. ⓑ tear or dig with the nails or claws. (손톱·발톱으로) 할퀴다; 긁어 파다. ¶ *The cat scratched him.* 고양이가 그를 할퀴었다. **2** (P6) rub or scrape with the fingernails to relieve an itch. (가려운 데)를 긁다. ¶ ~ *oneself* 가려운 곳을 긁다 / ~ *one's head* (난처하여) 머리를 긁적이다 / *Don't ~ your mosquito bite.* 모기에 물린 곳을 긁지 마라 / 《*prov.*》 *Scratch my back, and I will ~ yours.* 오는 정이 있어야 가는 정이 있다. **3** (P6,7) make (a hole, etc.) by scratching. (구멍 따위)를 파다; 긁어〔후벼〕 내다. ¶ ~ (*out*) *a hole in the ground* 땅을 후벼 구멍을 내다. **4** (P6,7,13) rub, esp. with a harsh noise. 비벼〔긁어〕 귀에 거슬리는 소리를 내다. ¶ *Don't ~ matches on the desk.* 책상에 성냥을 긋지 마라. **5** (P6) blot out or erase (writing, etc.); withdraw (a horse, a candidate, etc.) from a race or contest. …을 지우다; 삭제〔말소〕하다; (경마의 출장, 후보자의 이름)을 취소하다. ¶ ~ *a horse.* **6** (P6,7) write in a hurry and carelessly. (휘)갈겨 쓰다. ¶ *He scratched off a letter.* 그는 편지를 휘갈겨 썼다.
— *vi.* (P1,2A,3) **1** perform the action of

scratching (in various senses). (여러 의미로) 긁다; 할퀴다. ¶ *Cats ~, dogs bite.* 고양이는 할퀴고 개는 문다 / *Itching makes one want to ~.* 가려움은 사람들로 하여금 긁고 싶어하게 한다 / *This pen scratches badly.* 이 펜은 몹시 긁힌다 / *The dog scratched at* 〔*on*〕 *the door.* 개가 문을 박박 긁었다. **2** scratch the ground (to find something). (무엇을 찾으려고) 땅을 긁어 파다. ¶ *The dog is scratching about for the buried bone.* 개가 묻힌 뼈다귀를 찾으려고 땅을 긁어 파헤치고 있다. **3** ⓐ withdraw from a competition. (경기·경쟁 따위에서) 손을 떼다; 물러나다; 취소하다. ⓑ 《*fig.*》 give up an undertaking. 사업을 그만두다〔포기하다〕.

scratch about for, try to collect (evidence, etc.). (증거 따위)를 찾아 헤매다; 수집하다.

scratch along, 《*colloq.*》 make a living by hard work; get along somehow. 간신히 살아가다; 그럭저럭〔근근이〕 지내다.

scratch one's head over, wonder what to do about. 어찌할 바를 모르다; 망연자실하다.

scratch out 〔***off, through***〕***,*** strike out words, etc. by drawing a line through. 선을 그어 지우다〔말소하다〕.

scratch the surface of, 《*fig.*》 deal with or treat of (a problem) in a superficial way. (문제)의 거죽만을 감죽거리다; …을 피상적으로〔소홀히〕 다루다; …의 초보를 해보다. ¶ *You have so far only scratched the surface of the subject, there is still much more to learn.* 너희들은 이제까지 문제를 피상적으로만 다루었는데 아직 더 배워야 할 것이 많다.

scratch up 〔***together***〕***,*** gather (something) with difficulty. 어렵게 모으다; 그러모으다.

scratch (*someone*) ***where he itches,*** cater to someone's wishes. …의 가려운 데를 긁어주다; …의 뜻에 영합〔아첨〕하다.

— *n.* Ⓒ **1** a mark, cut, wound, or sound made by scratching. 긁힌〔할퀸〕 상처〔자국〕; 찰상(擦傷); 긁(히)는 소리. ¶ *a ~ on fresh paint* 새로 칠한 것에 난 긁힌 자국 / *the ~ of a match* 성냥 긋는〔켜는〕 소리 / *feel the ~ on one's cheek* 뺨의 찰과상을 만져 보다 / *His face was covered with scratches.* 그의 얼굴은 온통 할퀸 상처투성이였다 / *Not badly hurt; it's only a ~.* 큰 부상은 아니고 가벼운 상처에 불과하다. **2** Ⓤ the act of scratching. 긁기; 할퀴기. ¶ *Dogs enjoy a good ~.* 개는 마음껏 몸을 긁는 것을 좋아한다. **3** 《only *sing.* no *article*》 the starting-place of a race. (경주의) 출발선〔점〕. **4** a hurried piece of handwriting. 휘갈겨 쓰기; 일필(一筆).

a scratch of the pen, a few words quickly and hastily written; a signature. (펜으로) 몇 자 휘갈겨 쓴 것; 서명; 사인.

come (***up***) ***to the scratch,*** not back out of something. 용감히 맞서다.

from 〔***on***〕 ***scratch,*** **a**) from the very beginning. 처음부터; 출발점부터. ¶ *redo one's work from ~* 처음부터 다시 시작하다. **b**) from nothing. 영(零)〔무(無)〕에서; 아무것도 없이. ¶ *the business built up from ~* 빈손으로 이룩한 사업.

up to scratch, **a**) ready to start a race. (경기자가) 스타트라인〔출발선〕에 서서. **b**) 《*colloq.*》 ready to meet difficulties. (어려움에 부닥칠) 각오가 되어. **c**) 《*colloq.*》 as good as expected; in proper or fit condition. 일정 표준에 달하여; 더할 나위 없이; 만족할 만한; 적절한. ¶ *His performance was not up to ~.* 그의 연기는 만족스럽지 못했다.

— *adj.* 《as *attributive*》 **1** made up of people hurriedly got together; made with anything that is available. (사람들을) 서둘러 끌어모은; 급히 만든〔편성한〕; (마침) 있는 것으로 차린. ¶ *a ~ team* 급조(急造)팀 / *a ~ meal* (집에) 있는 것으로 차린 식사. **2** used for hasty writing, notes, etc. 휘갈겨 쓰기용의. [E.]

scratch pad [스스] *n.* 《U.S.》 a pad of paper used for hurried or casual writing. 갈겨 쓰기용 종이; 메모장(=scribbling pad).

scratch·y [skrǽtʃi] *adj.* (**scratch·i·er, scratch·i·est**) **1** (of writing, drawing, etc.) written or drawn hastily or carelessly. 갈겨쓴; 아무렇게나 쓴〔그린〕. ¶ *~ handwriting* 갈겨쓴 글씨. **2** making the sound of scratching. (펜이) 긁히는; 직직 소리가 나는. ¶ *a ~ pen* 잘 긁히는 펜. **3** irritating; itchy. (입은 옷이) 따끔거리는; 스멀거리는. ¶ *a ~ sweater* (살갗에 닿아) 스멀거리는 스웨터. ●**scratch·i·ly** [-li] *adv.* **scratch·i·ness** [-nis] *n.*

scrawl [skrɔːl] *vi., vt.* (P1,3; 6,13,14) write or draw carelessly or hastily; make meaningless writing. (…을) 아무렇게나 쓰다〔그리다〕; 갈겨쓰다; 낙서하다. ¶ *~ all over the door* 문에 온통 낙서를 하다 / *He scrawled his name hastily across the blackboard.* 그는 흑판에 급히 이름을 갈겨썼다.

— *n.* Ⓒ a bad, careless or meaningless handwriting; a letter written quickly and badly. 서투른 필적; 갈겨쓰기; 갈겨쓴 글씨; 낙서; 휘갈겨쓴 편지. [*scribble, sprawl*]

scraw·ny [skrɔ́ːni] *adj.* (**-ni·er, -ni·est**) 《U.S.》 lean and bony. 비쩍 마른; 앙상한(cf. *scraggy*). ¶ *a long ~ neck* 비쩍 마른 긴 목. [Scand.]

***scream** [skriːm] *vi.* (P2A,3) **1** make a loud, sharp cry from pain, strong emotion, etc. 날카로운 비명을〔새된 소리를〕 지르다. ¶ *~ in pain* 〔*fright, fear*〕 고통으로〔놀라서, 공포로〕 날카롭게 소리치다 / *The baby screamed.* 아기가 자지러지게 울었다. **2** (of a bird, etc.) give a loud, sharp cry; (of wind, etc.) make a loud noise; give a whistle. (새 따위가) 날카로운 소리로 울다; (바람 따위가) 윙윙거리다. **3** 《usu. *with*》 laugh heartily and noisily. (큰 소리로) 자지러지게 웃다. ¶ *He was so funny, he made us ~ with laughter.* 그는 매우 익살맞아서 우리를 자지러지게 웃겼

다 / *Everybody screamed at his jokes.* 그의 농담에 모두 깔깔대었다.
— *vt.* (P6,7) **1** 《usu. *out*》 say (something) with a loud sharp cry. …을 (비명을 지르며) 말하다; 소리쳐 말하다; 절규하여 알리다. ¶ ~ (*out*) *curses* 소리쳐 저주의 말을 하다 / *She screamed* (*out*) *that there was a ghost by the window.* 그녀는 창가에 유령이 있다고 비명을 질렀다. **2** 《*reflexively*》 bring oneself to a specified state by screaming. 소리를 질러 …하게 하다. ¶ ~ *oneself hoarse* 크게 소리 질러 목이 쉬게 하다.
— *n.* Ⓒ **1** a loud, sharp cry; a shriek. 날카로운〔새된〕 목소리; 비명; 절규. ¶ *give a little* ~ *of indignation* 짧은 분노의 소리를 지르다 / *I thought I heard a* ~. 비명 소리를 들었다고 생각했다. **2** 《*colloq.*》 a person or thing that is very funny. 우습기 짝이 없는 사람〔일〕. ¶ *It was a perfect* ~. 그건 정말 우스운 일이었다. [E.]

scream·ing [skríːmiŋ] *adj.* **1** uttering screams. (날카롭게) 소리치는; 새된〔날카로운〕 소리를 내는. **2** extremely funny. 몹시 우스운; 배를 움켜 쥐게 하는. ¶ *a* ~ *farce* 요절할 소극(笑劇). **3** sensational; startling. 선풍적인; 깜짝 놀라게 하는; 요란한; 야단스러운. ¶ ~ *headlines* (신문 따위의) 요란한 표제.

scream·ing·ly [skríːmiŋli] *adv.* in a screaming manner. 포복 절도할 정도로 우습게. ¶ ~ *funny* 포복 절도할 만큼 우스운.

scree [skriː] *n.* 《Brit.》 《often *pl.*》 (a slope covered with) small loose fragments of rock. 석(石)비레(로 덮인 가파른 비탈). [N. =landslip]

screech [skriːtʃ] *n.* Ⓒ a sharp, loud cry. 날카롭게 외치는 소리; 새된 (목)소리. ¶ *The woman's screeches brought the police.* 여자의 날카로운 비명 소리에 경찰이 달려왔다.
— *vi., vt.* (P1,3;6,7,13) 《often *out*》 cry out (something) in a sharp, loud voice; make a harsh or shrill noise. 날카로운 소리를 내다〔소리로 외치다〕; 새된 (목)소리로 말하다; 비명을 지르다. ¶ ~ *a reply* 소리쳐 대답하다 / *'Help! help!' she screeched.* '사람 살려, 사람 살려'하고 그녀는 비명을 질렀다 / *The breakes screeched as the bus stopped.* 버스가 멈추면서 브레이크가 끼익 소리를 냈다 / *The captain screeched out orders.* 선장은 새된 소리로 명령했다. ●**screech·er** [⌐ər] *n.* [Imit.]

screech owl [⌐ ⌐] *n.* **1** 《Brit.》 a sort of owl that cries out sharply in a high voice. (새된 울음 소리의) 올빼미. **2** 《U.S.》 a small owl with hornlike ear tufts of feathers. 작은 부엉이의 일종.

screed [skriːd] *n.* a long (and usu. tiresome) speech or writing. 장황하고 따분한 연설〔이야기·논문〕. [→shred]

***screen** [skriːn] *n.* Ⓒ **1** a covered frame or panels used to hide or protect. 칸막이; 병풍. ¶ *a folding* ~ 병풍 / *a sliding* ~ 장지; 미닫이. **2** a window made of wire. (창문에 끼우는) 망창(網窓); 방충망창. ¶ *We have screens at the windows to keep out insects.* (모기·파리 따위) 벌레를 막기 위한 그물 창을 치고 있다. **3** a thing that divides or separates a room into parts, esp. in a church. (방의, 특히 교회 내의) 칸막이. **4** anything like a screen; a shelter. 가리는〔감추는〕 것; 차폐물. ¶ *under* ~ *of darkness* 야음을 틈타 / *a smoke* ~ 연막 / *a* ~ *of secrecy* 비밀의 장막 / *A* ~ *of trees hides our house from the road.* 나무에 가려져 우리 집은 길에서 안 보인다. **5** ⓐ the white surface on which a motion picture is projected. 영사막(映寫幕); 은막. ⓑ the surface of a TV set or radar apparatus upon which images appear. 텔레비전·레이더의 영상 스크린. **6** 《*the* ~, *collectively*》 the movies. 영화. ¶ *a play adapted for the* ~ 영화에 맞게 각색한 극본. **7** a tool made of wire net and used to separate sand, coal, seeds, etc. (모래·석탄·자갈 따위를 걸러내는) 어레미.
— *vt.* **1** (P6,7,13) ⓐ 《*from*》 shelter, protect, or hide with a screen. …을 가리다〔가로막다〕; 감추다; 막다. ¶ ~ *oneself from all external influence* 모든 외적인 영향에 물들지 않도록 하다 / *a valuable preventive medicine screening procedure* 병의 진행을 막는 효능이 있는 예방약 / *I screened my face with a handkerchief.* 손수건으로 얼굴을 가렸다 / *We have screened our windows against* 〔*to keep out*〕 *flies.* 파리의 침입을 막기 위해 창문에 방충망을 달았다 / *Creepers* ~ *the window from view.* 덩굴식물이 창문을 가려 밖이 안 보인다. ⓑ 《*fig.*》 protect from discovery, punishment, etc. 감싸다; 비호하다. ¶ *The mother tried to* ~ *her son.* 어머니는 아들을 비호하려고 애썼다 / *I won't* ~ *you from blame.* 당신에 대한 비난을 막아 주지 않을 테다. **2** (P6) project (a motion picture) on a screen. …을 영사(映寫)하다. **3** (P6) photograph (a scene, etc.) by using a camera. (장면 등)을 카메라로 촬영하다. **4** (P6) adapt (a novel, story, etc.) in making a motion picture. (소설 따위)를 영화화하다. **5** 《*off*》 divide, shut off, with a screen, curtain, etc. (칸막이, 커튼 따위로) 칸막이하다. ¶ ~ *off a corner of a room* 방의 일각을 칸막이로 막다. **6** (P6) ⓐ sift by using a sieve. (모래·자갈·석탄 따위)를 체질하여 가려내다; 체질하다. ⓑ 《*fig.*》 examine (people) so as to select those who are trusted. …을 심사하다; 선발하다; 선별하다; 가려〔추려〕내다. ¶ *screening test* 적격 심사 / ~ *the applicants* 응모자를 선발하다.
— *vi.* be suitable for (being made into) a motion-picture. 영화에 적합하다; 사진이 잘 받다. ¶ ~ *well* 〔*badly*〕 (배우 등이) 사진이 잘 받다〔받지 않다〕. [E.]

screen out, **a**) stop coming through by a covering or screen. 씌우개·차폐물로 차단하다; 가리다; 막다. ¶ *The curtains* ~ *out the sunlight.* 커튼은 햇빛이 들어오는 것을 막는다.

b) get rid of (an unsuitable person, request, etc.) by screening. (심사·시험 따위로 부적격자, 부당한 요구 따위)를 제외하다; 배제하다.

•**screw** [skru:] *n.* Ⓒ **1** a nail of metal driven into wood, etc. by being turned around or twisted. 나사(못). ¶ *Turn the ~ to the right to tighten it.* 죄기 위해 나사를 오른쪽으로 틀어라. **2** anything like a screw; a propeller of a ship or an airplane. 나사 모양의 것; (선박·비행기의) 나선 추진기〔프로펠러〕. **3** a turn or motion of a screw. 한 번 틀기〔돌리기〕. ¶ *give a ~ to a cork* 코르크 마개를 한 번 틀다 / *Give the nut a good ~.* 너트를 충분히 돌리시오. **4** 《Brit. *colloq.*》 (the amount of) a salary or wages. 급료; 봉급; 임금. ¶ *have a good* 〔*poor*〕 *~* 좋은〔낮은〕 급료를 받다. **5** 《Brit.》 a small, twisted-up piece of paper and its contents. 종이의 양끝을 틀어서 만든 봉지; 그 봉지에 든 것. ¶ *a ~ of tea* 〔*tobacco*〕. **6** 《*colloq.*》 a very stingy person; a miser. 몹시 인색한 사람; 구두쇠.

have a screw loose, 《*colloq.*》 something wrong or not working properly (esp. in one's mind); be slightly mad. 머리가 좀 이상하다〔돌다〕.

put 〔***apply, turn***〕 ***the screw*** 〔***screws***〕 ***on,*** use one's power to force (someone) to do something. 아무를 강제〔압박〕하여 …하게 하다; …하도록 압력을 넣다.

There is a screw loose somewhere. Something is wrong with a machine, an organization, etc. 무언가 잘못된 데가 있다; 어딘가 고장이 있다.

— *vt.* (P6,7,13) **1** press, force, fasten, or tighten (something) with a screw; apply a screw to (something). …을 나사로 죄다; …에 나사못을 박(아 고정시키)다. ¶ *~ on a knob* (문)손잡이를 나사로 고정시키다 / *~ down a lid* 뚜껑에 나사를 박다 / *~ a lock on a door* 문에 자물쇠를 달다 / *~ a bracket to the wall* 까치발을 나사로 벽에 달다. **2** ⓐ turn as a screw; twist. (비)틀다; 꼬다. ¶ *~ someone's arm* 아무의 팔을 비틀다 / *~ up a piece of paper into a ball* 종잇조각을 비비 뭉쳐 둥글리다 / *~ a lid on* 〔*off*〕 *the jar* 병 마개를 틀어 죄다〔열다〕. ⓑ turn round as far as possible. 돌리다. ¶ *He screwed his head round to see me.* 그는 나를 보기 위해 고개를 돌렸다. **3** 《often *up, into*》 twist; contort. 뒤틀다; (얼굴)을 찡그리다; 일그러뜨리다. ¶ *~ up one's face* 얼굴을 찡그리다 / *~ up one's mouth* 〔*lips*〕 입〔입술〕을 비쭉 내밀다 / *~ one's face* 얼굴을 찡그리다 / *~ one's face into wrinkles* 얼굴을 찌푸려 주름지게 하다. **4** 《*out, out of*》 ⓐ press out by twisting; squeeze out. (물기 따위)를 비틀어 짜다 / *~ water out of a sponge* 스폰지에서 물기를 짜내다. ⓑ compel to give or tell. (금품·정보·자백 따위)를 강요하다; 억지로 받아내다. ¶ *~ money out of someone = ~ someone out of money* 아무에게서 돈을 우려내다 / *~ the information out of someone* 아무로부터 무리하게 정보를 캐〔언어〕내다. ⓒ pay or give money with reluctance. 마지못해 돈을 내주다. ¶ *At last he screwed out 50 dollars.* 마침내 50달러를 (빼앗기다시피) 내주었다. **5** 《often in *passive*》 《*sl.*》 cheat; take something unfairly from; take advantage of. …을 속이다; 이용하다. ¶ *I've often been screwed.* 나는 늘 속아 왔다 / *I'm afraid you got screwed, friend.* 이 친구야, 안 됐지만 자넨 속았다고 생각하네. **6** force as if by the action of a screw. (용기)를 불러일으키다; (심신)을 다잡다. ¶ *~ oneself up* 용기를 불러일으키다 / *He needs screwing up.* 정신 좀 차리게 할 필요가 있다.

— *vi.* **1** (P1,2A) turn in the manner of a screw; move with twisting movements. 나사 모양으로 돌(아 가)다; 틀리다. ¶ *This handle won't ~.* 이 핸들은 도무지 돌지를 않는다 / *The lid ~ off* 〔*on to*〕 *the jar.* 마개를 돌려서 병뚜껑을 열다〔병뚜껑을 닫다〕. **2** be fitted for being put together or taken apart by a screw. 나사로 한데 붙박아지다; 나사로 떼어지다. ¶ *The hatrack screwed on to the wall.* 모자걸이가 벽에 달렸다. **3** (P1) (of a person) be very stingy. 몹시 인색하다; 절약하다. ¶ *He has been screwing all his life.* 그는 전생애를 절약하며 살아오고 있다. [F. *escroue*]

be screwed, 《chiefly Brit. *sl.*》 be drunk. 술에 취하다.

have one's head screwed on the right way, be clever and wise; have good judgment. 빈틈이 없다; 분별이 있다.

have one's head well screwed on = have one's head screwed on the right way.

screw up, **a**) twist (something) out of its natural shape. (얼굴 따위)를 찡그리다; 일그러뜨리다. ¶ *~ up one's mouth* 입을 비쭉 내밀다. **b**) tighten by a screwing movement. 죄어 팽팽히 켕기다. ¶ *~ up the string of a violin* 바이올린 줄을 죄어 켕기다 / *~ up discipline* 규율을 엄격히 하다.

screw up one's courage, overcome one's fear; strengthen one's courage 〔oneself〕. 두려움을 이겨내다; 용기를 불러일으키다.

screw·driv·er [skrúːdràivər] *n.* Ⓒ a tool used to turn a screw. 나사 돌리개.

scrib·ble [skríbl] *vt., vi.* (P6;1) write hastily or carelessly; make meaningless or hard-to-read handwriting. (…을) 급히 아무렇게나 쓰다; 휘갈겨 쓰다; 낙서하다. ¶ *~ away* 휘갈겨 쓰다 / *~ a letter* 편지를 갈겨 쓰다 / *~ a wall* 벽에 낙서하다. — *n.* Ⓒ something written carelessly and hastily; a handwriting, esp. when illegible; the meaningless or hard-to-read marks that are so written. 갈겨쓴 것; 난필; 낙서. ¶ *I can not read my own scribbles.* 내 자신이 쓴 글씨를 읽을 수가 없다. [L. *scribo* write]

scrib·bler [skríblər] *n.* Ⓒ **1** a person

who writes carelessly or hastily. 난필가; 악필가. **2** 《*colloq.*, often *joc.*》 an author who writes poor books. 시시한 문사(文士).

scrib·bling pad 〔**block**〕 [⌐— ⌐〔⌐〕] *n.* 《Brit.》 =scratch pad.

scribe [skraib] *n.* Ⓒ **1** ⓐ in former times, a person who copied writings as a professional; a person who writes letters, etc. for another as a job. (주로 인쇄술이 없던 시대의) 필사자(筆寫者); 대서인; 필기자. ⓑ 《U.S.》 a journalist. 신문 기자. **2** 《Bible》 in ancient times, a person who studied and taught Jewish Law. (고대 유대인의) 율법학자. [→scribble]

scrim [skrim] *n.* loosely woven cotton or linen material, used for window curtains. 스크림《성기게 짠 무명 또는 린네르 직물; 주로 커튼감으로 쓰임》. [G.]

scrim·mage [skrímidʒ] *n.* Ⓒ **1** a confused struggle or fight. 난투; 격투; 드잡이. ¶ *be caught in the whirl of a* ~ 난투의 와중(渦中)에 말려들다. **2** 《rugby》 =scrummage. — *vi., vt.* (P1; 6) **1** take part in a confused struggle. 격투〔난투〕를 벌이다. **2** 《rugby》 =scrummage. [var. of *skirmish*]

scrimp [skrimp] *vt.* (P6) cut down (expenses, etc.); use (something) less than enough. (경비 따위)를 바싹 줄이다〔조리차하다〕. — *vi.* (P1) **1** avoid useless expenses. 절약하다. **2** be too economical in spending money or in the use of thing. 몹시 인색하게 굴다; 지나치게 경제를 하다(=skimp). [Teut.]

scrimp·y [skrímpi] *adj.* (**scrimp·i·er, scrimp·i·est**) scanty; meager. 얼마 안 되는; 부족한; 빈약한(=skimpy).

scrip [skrip] *n.* Ⓒ **1** a provisional receipt showing a right to something. 가(假)증서; 가(假)증권. **2** paper money of denominations less than a dollar, formerly issued in the United States. (옛 1달러 미만의) 소액 지폐. [var. of *script*]

script [skript] *n.* **1** Ⓤ handwriting as distinguished from print. 손으로 쓴 글자; 필적. ¶ ~ *style* 필기체. **2** Ⓤ a kind of printing type imitating handwriting. 스크립트《초서체 활자》. **3** Ⓒ a manuscript of a play, an actor's part, etc.; a text used in broadcasting. (영화의) 대본; 극본; (라디오 방송용의) 원고. ¶ *a film* ~ 영화 대본. [↓]

scrip·tur·al [skríptʃərəl] *adj.* 《also *S*-》 of the Bible; based on the Bible. 성서〔성경〕의; 성서의 가르침에 의거한. ● **scrip·tur·al·ly** [-əli] *adv.* [→scribble]

scrip·ture [skríptʃər] *n.* Ⓒ **1** 《*S-, Holy S-, the S-s*》 the Bible. 성서; 성경. **2** the religious writings of any other religion. (기독교 이외의) 경전; 성전(聖典). [↑]

scrive·ner [skrívnər] *n.* 《*arch.*》 **1** a clerk. 서기. **2** =scribe 1 ⓐ. [L. *scribo* write]

scrof·u·la [skrɔ́:fjulə, skrɑ́f- / skrɔ́f-] *n.* Ⓤ 《med.》 a tuberculous disease with glandular swellings. 나력(瘰癧). [L.]

scroll [skroul] *n.* **1** Ⓒ a roll of paper or the skin of goats or sheep, used as a writing material, etc.; a book written on such a roll. (종이나 양피지의) 두루마리. **2** ⓊⒸ an ornamental design based on curving or coiled form. 소용돌이 무늬〔문양〕; 소용돌이형(型). [Teut. (→shred)]

scroop [skru:p] *n., vi.* (P1) (make) grating noise. 삐걱〔끼익〕 소리(를 내다). [Imit.]

scrounge [skraundʒ] *vi., vt.* (P2,2A,3;6) **1** 《often *contempt.*》 collect or get unofficially, without spending money or by persuading others; 찾아 모으다; 찾아내다; 감언으로 손에 넣다 **2** 《*around*》 go looking for things. …을 찾아다니다. **3** 《*colloq.*》 pilfer. 가만히〔몰래, 슬쩍〕 훔치다. [? *scrunge* wander about idly]

***scrub**[1] [skrʌb] *v.* (**scrubbed, scrub·bing**) *vt.* (P6,7,18) clean by rubbing hard with a brush, soap and water. …을 박박 문지르다; 문질러 빨다〔닦다, 훔치다〕; 비비다. ¶ ~ *the windowpane clean* 창유리를 박박 긁어 깨끗이 하다 / ~ *paint off one's hands* 손에 묻은 페인트를 문질러 없애다 / *He scrubbed the boat with a brush.* 솔로 배를 박박 문질러 닦아냈다. — *vi.* (P1) clean by rubbing hard. 박박 문질러〔긁어〕 깨끗이 하다. — *n.* Ⓒ the act of cleaning by hard rubbing. 박박 문질러〔긁어〕 닦기. ¶ *Give your face and hands a good* ~. 얼굴과 손을 잘 문질러 닦아라. [Teut.]

scrub[2] [skrʌb] *n.* **1** Ⓤ 《*collectively*》 a shrub; (land covered with) trees or bushes that are of poor quality and small. 관목; 잡목숲(이 우거진 토지). **2** Ⓒ anything that is inferior or small in size. 지질한〔왜소한〕 사람〔것〕; 하찮은 사람〔것〕. **3** Ⓒ a player of a second team as opposed to a regular team. 2군 팀의 선수. [→shrub]

scrub·bing brush [skrʌ́biŋbrʌ̀ʃ] *n.* a brush used for washing, or heavy cleaning jobs. (박박 문지르는) 빳빳한 세탁솔; 솔솔; 수세미(=《U.S.》 scrub brush). [*scrub*[1]]

scrub·by [skrʌ́bi] *adj.* (**-bi·er, -bi·est**) **1** ⓐ (of trees, animals, etc.) small or checked in growth. (나무·동물 등이) 잘 자라지 못한; 주접이 든. ¶ ~ *trees* 주접든 나무. ⓑ covered with scrub. 관목으로 덮인. ¶ *ride through* ~ *country* 말을 타고 관목 지대를 빠져나가다. **2** (of a person) poor; shabby. (사람이) 왜소한; 초라한. **3** inferior; insignificant. 하등〔열등〕의; 시시한. [*scrub*[2]]

scruff [skrʌf] *n.* Ⓒ 《usu. *the* ~ *of the neck*》 the back of the neck. 목덜미. ¶ *He took* 〔*seized*〕 *the cat by the* ~ *of the neck.* 그는 고양이의 목덜미를 잡았다. [N.]

scruff·y [skrʌ́fi] *adj.* (**scruff·i·er, scruff·i·est**) 《*colloq.*》 untidy; dirty. 단정치〔깨끗하지〕 못한; 더러운.

scrum [skrʌm] *n.* 《Brit. *colloq.*》 =scrummage.

scrum·mage [skrʌ́midʒ] *n.* Ⓒ 《Rugby》 a

play in which the forward of the two teams make a compact mass around the ball. 스크럼. — *vi.* (P1) take part in a scrummage. 스크럼을 짜다(=scrum). [*scrimmage*]

scru·ple [skrú:pəl] *n.* **1** Ⓒ a unit of weight that equals 20 grains. 스크루플《약량(藥量)의 단위》. **2** Ⓤ《often *pl.*》a feeling of uneasiness, suspicion or hesitation in deciding; uneasiness of conscience. 의혹; 망설임; 양심의 가책. ¶ *a man of no scruples* 양심이 없는 사람 / *do a thing without* ~ 태연히 …을 하다 / *I have scruples* 〔*no scruples*〕 *about accepting the money.* 돈을 받는 것에 대해 망설인다〔아무 망설임없이 돈을 받는다〕 / *He makes no scruples to tell a lie.* 거짓말하는 것을 예사로 여긴다.

stand on scruple, hesitate. 주저하다; 망설이다; 거리끼다.

— *vi.* (P3,4) 《*at, about*》 hesitate because of conscience or a feeling. 망설이다; 양심〔마음〕에 거리끼다. ¶ *He doesn't* ~ *at* 〔*about*〕 *lying.* 그는 거짓말하는 데 양심의 가책을 느끼지 않는다. [L. *scrupulus*]

scru·pu·los·i·ty [skrù:pjəlásəti / -lɔ́s-] *n.* Ⓤ being scrupulous. 신중함; 면밀함. [↑]

scru·pu·lous [skrú:pjələs] *adj.* **1** cautious to follow one's sense of right or duty. 양심적인; 견실한; 정직한. ¶ *with* ~ *honesty* 양심적인 성실한 태도로. **2** paying attention to details; very careful. 면밀(주도)한; 빈틈 없는; 정확한; 세심〔신중〕한. ¶ *a* ~ *investigation* 면밀한 조사 / *be* ~ *in one's attire* 복장에 빈틈이 없다; 복장이 단정하다. [↑]

be scrupulous about, be precise about. …에 까다롭다.

pay scrupulous attention to, …에 세심한 주의를 기울이다.

scru·ti·nize [skrú:tənàiz] *vt.* **1** (P6) examine closely; inspect carefully. 정밀 조사하다. ¶ *Holmes scrutinized the knob for fingerprints.* 홈즈는 지문을 찾기 위해 문손잡이를 정밀 조사했다. **2** look at very carefully. 자세히〔유심히〕 보다. [L. *scrutor* examine]

scru·ti·ny [skrú:təni] *n.* (*pl.* **-nies**) **1** Ⓤ the act of staring at someone's face. (얼굴을) 뚫어지게 보기; 응시. **2** ⓊⒸ a close examination; a careful inspection. 정밀 조사〔음미, 검사〕; 정사(精査); 자세히 보는 일. ¶ *make a* ~ *into* ... …을 정사하다 / *as* ~ *of the results will confirm* 결과를 자세히 조사해보면 알겠지만 / *prove on closer* ~ *to be a diary* 더 정밀 조사로 일기임이 판명되다. [↑]

not bear scrutiny, be suspicious. 의심쩍은〔구린〕 데가 있다.

scu·ba [skú:bə] *n.* self-contained underwater breathing apparatus. 스쿠버; 잠수용 수중 호흡기구. ¶ ~ *diving* 스쿠버 다이빙. [Abbr.]

scud [skʌd] *vi.* (**scud·ded, scud·ding**) (P1,2A,3) run swiftly; move lightly over. 질주하다; (특히 구름·배가) 빨리 움직이다. ¶ *Clouds are scudding across the sky.* 구름이 하늘을 가로질러 휙 지나갔다 / *Our yacht scudded along driven by the strong wind.* 우리 요트는 강한 바람을 받고 달렸다. — *n.* **1** Ⓒ the act of moving swiftly. 휙 달림〔날아감〕; 질주. **2** Ⓤ clouds driven by the wind. (바람에 불리어) 날아가는 구름; 비운(飛雲); Ⓒ a shower. 소나기; 지나가는 비; 한동안의 소낙비. [Norw.]

scuff [skʌf] *vi.* (P1,2A,3) **1** walk without lifting the feet from the ground. 발을 질질 끌며 걷다; 지척거리다. **2** become scraped or worn in patches on the surface. 문지르다; (구두·마루 등이) 닳다. — *vt.* **1** (P6) scrape (the ground, floor, etc.) with the feet. (땅바닥·마루 등을) 발로 문지르다. **2** wear a rough place or places on the surface of (a shoe, etc.). (구두 따위를) 닳도록 신다. **3** move (the feet) with a dragging motion. (발을) 질질 끌다. [↓]

scuf·fle [skʌ́fəl] *vi.* **1** (P1,2A) struggle in a confused manner. 격투〔드잡이〕하다; 난투하다. **2** drag the feet. 발을 질질 끌며 걷다. — *n.* **1** Ⓒ a confused fight or struggle. 격투; 드잡이; 맞붙어 싸움. **2** the act or sound of feet shuffling. 발을 질질 끄는 걸음〔소리〕. [Scand. *skuffa* push]

scull [skʌl] *n.* Ⓒ **1** an oar rowed from side to side at the end of a boat. 스컬《작은 배 후미에 붙여 좌우로 움직여 젓는 노》. **2** one of a pair of oars rowed with each oar in one hand. 한 쌍의 노의 하나. **3** a racing boat with two sculls. 2개의 노로 젓는 경조(競漕)용 배.

〈scull 3〉

— *vt., vi.* (P6;1) row (a boat) with an oar or oars. (보트를) 스컬로 젓다. [E.]

scul·ler·y [skʌ́ləri] *n.* Ⓒ (*pl.* **-ler·ies**) 《chiefly Brit.》 a small room near a kitchen where dirty kettles, pots, etc. are cleaned. (주방의) 설거지하는 곳; 식기 세척실. [→scuttle]

sculp [skʌlp] *vt., vi.* 《*colloq.*》 =sculpture.

***sculp·tor** [skʌ́lptər] *n.* Ⓒ an artist who carves or models figures in stone, wood, etc. 조각가. ¶ *Sculptors make statues of marble or bronze and models in clay.* 조각가는 대리석상(像)이나 동상 및 찰흙으로 모형을 만든다. [→sculpture]

sculp·tress [skʌ́lptris] *n.* a woman sculptor. 여류〔여성〕 조각가.

sculp·tur·al [skʌ́lptʃərəl] *adj.* of sculpture. 조각의. ● **sculp·tur·al·ly** [-i] *adv.*

***sculp·ture** [skʌ́lptʃər] *n.* **1** Ⓤ the art of making figures in stone, wood, clay, etc. 조각(술). **2** Ⓒ a piece of such work; a figure formed by this art. 조각품〔물〕; 조각상

(像). ¶ *There are many famous sculptures in Italy.* 이탈리아에는 유명한 조각물들이 많이 있다.

—*vt.* (P6,13) **1** cut (stone, wood, etc.) into figures. (돌·나무 따위를) 조각하다. ¶ ~ *a bust in stone* 돌로 흉상(胸像)을 조각하다 / ~ *a statue out of bronze* 청동으로 상(像)을 조각하다. **2** cover or ornament with sculpture. …에 조각을 하다; …을 조각으로 장식하다. ¶ *a sculptured pillar* 조각물로 장식된 기둥.

—*vi.* (P1) be a sculptor; do sculpture. 조각가가 되다; 조각을 하다. [L. *sculpo* carve]

sculp·tur·esque [skʌ̀lptʃərésk] *adj.* (of attitude, figure, etc.) fit for or suggesting a sculpture. (몸가짐·모양 따위가) 조각(물과) 같은; 조각적인; 반듯한; 당당한.

scum [skʌm] *n.* Ⓤ **1** 《*of*》 the thin layer of foam or dirt on the top of some liquids. (발효 때 등의) 뜬 찌끼; 거품; 더껑이. **2** 《*fig.*》 《*collectively*》 refuse or offscourings; low worthless people. 찌꺼기; 인간 쓰레기. ¶ *The place is always filled with the ~ of the town.* 그곳엔 언제나 마을의 인간 쓰레기들로 득시글거린다 / *You filthy ~!* 이 변변찮은 밥벌레 같은 놈아. —*v.* (**scummed, scum·ming**) *vt.* remove scum from; skim. …에서 뜬 찌꺼기를 걷어내다. —*vi.* form scum; become covered with scum. 뜬 찌끼〔더껑이〕가 생기다: 뜬 찌끼〔더껑이〕로 덮이다. [Teut.]

scum·ble [skʌ́mbəl] *vt.* (P6) soften by overlaying with thin coat of opaque color. 색을〔색조를〕 부드럽게 하다; 바림하다. —*n.* scumbled effect or part; coat of color used. 바림(부분); 바림칠. [↑]

scup·per [skʌ́pər] *n.* Ⓒ an opening in the side of a ship to let water run off the deck. (갑판의) 배수구. —*vt.* (P6) **1** 《*colloq.*》 wreck; ruin. (계획 따위를) 좌절시키다. **2** 《Brit.》 sink one's own ship deliberately. (배를) 고의적으로 침몰시키다. [E.]

scurf [skəːrf] *n.* Ⓤ the small bits of dead skin on the surface of the head. 비듬. [E.]

scurf·y [skə́ːrfi] *adj.* (**scurf·i·er, surf·i·est**) covered with scurf. 비듬 투성이의.

scur·ril·i·ty [skəríləti, skʌr-] *n.* (*pl.* **-ties**) **1** Ⓤ the quality of being scurrilous. 상스러움; 비열(함). **2** Ⓒ a coarse, abusive remark. 상스러운〔거친〕 말; 독설. ¶ *use* ~ 상소리 하다. [↓]

scur·ri·lous [skə́ːrələs, skʌ́r-] *adj.* (of a person and language) using rough and vulgar abuse or jokes; vulgar in using language. 입정 사나운; (사람·말 따위가) 천한; 상스러운. ¶ *The newspaper made a ~ attack on* 〔*upon*〕 *the new mayor.* 신문은 신임 시장에 대해 독설적인 공격을 해댔다. [L. *scurra* buffoon]

scur·ry [skə́ːri, skʌ́ri] *vi.* (**-ried**) (P1,2A,3) run with quick, short steps. 급히 가다〔움직이다〕; 종종걸음으로 달리다. ¶ ~ *off* 〔*away*〕 종종 걸음으로 사라지다 / *We saw the mice ~ into the hole.* 우리는 그 생쥐가 조르르 구멍으로 들어가는 것을 보았다 / *The shower sent us scurrying for shelter.* 소나기는 우리로 하여금 비 그을 만한 데를 찾아 종종 걸음치게 했다. —*n.* (*pl.* **-ries**) **1** Ⓒ a hurried movement; Ⓤ the act or state of walking in such way. 급한 발걸음〔움직임〕; 어수선함; 부산함. ¶ *With much fuss and ~, Aunt Merry at last go started.* 법석을 떨며 메리 아줌마는 마침내 떠났다. **2** Ⓒ a very light fall of snow. (바람과 함께) 갑자기 쏟아지는 눈. [*hurry-scurry*]

scur·vy [skə́ːrvi] *n.* Ⓤ a disease caused by the lack of fresh fruits and vegetables. 괴혈병. —*adj.* (**-vi·er, -vi·est**) low and bad; mean. 천한; 비열한; 야비한. ¶ *a ~ trick* 〔*fellow*〕 비열한 수단〔놈〕. ● **scur·vi·ly** [-li] *adv.* [*scurf*]

scut [skʌt] *n.* Ⓒ the short tail of a rabbit, etc. (토끼 따위의) 짧은 꼬리. [Scand.]

scutch·eon [skʌ́tʃən] *n.* =escutcheon.

scut·ter [skʌ́tər] *vi.* (P1,2) run in a fussy or startled way. 허둥지둥 달리다. [→scuttle²]

scut·tle¹ [skʌ́tl] *n.* Ⓒ **1** a bucket used to carry coal. (담아 나르는) 석탄통. **2** an amount of coal that fills this. 석탄통 하나의 양(量). [L. *scutella* dish]

scut·tle² [skʌ́tl] *n.* Ⓒ the act of running away at a quick pace. 급히〔허둥지둥〕 달아나기〔떠나기, 가기〕. —*vi.* (P2A,3) 《*away, off*》 run away quickly with short steps; hurry off. 급히〔허둥지둥〕 달리다; 천방지축 달아나다(cf. *scurry*). ¶ ~ *out of someone's way* 허둥지둥 아무를 피하다 / *The dogs scuttled off into the woods.* 개들은 급히 숲 속으로 달아났다. [*scud*]

scut·tle³ [skʌ́tl] *n.* Ⓒ a small opening or window in a roof of a house, or in a deck or side of a ship. (지붕·벽 따위의) 뚜껑 달린 채광창(窓); 천창(天窓); (배의) 현창(舷窓); 배의 갑판의 승강구 입구. —*vt.* (P6) make a hole through (the bottom or sides) of a ship to sink it. (배에) 구멍을 내어 가라앉히다. [Du.]

Scyl·la [sílə] *n.* 《Gk. myth.》 (a six-headed monster living on) a dangerous rock opposite the whirlpool called Charybdis [kəríbdis] (between Sicily and Italy). 스킬라《선원을 잡아먹는 여자 괴물》. [Homer, *Od.* xii]

between Scylla and Charybdis, between two dangers, one of which must be met. 진퇴양난에 빠져.

scythe [saið] *n.* Ⓒ a cutting tool with a long, curved

〈scythe〉

handle, used for mowing grass or grain. (자루가 긴) 풀베는 큰 낫.
— *vt., vi.* (P6,7;1) cut with a scythe. 큰 낫으로 베다. [E.]

'sdeath [zdeθ] *interj.* 《*arch.*》 expressing anger, determination, etc. (가벼운 저주를 나타내어) 에이; 지겨워; 빌어먹을. [=God's death]

SDR Special Drawing Rights. (국제 통화 기금의) 특별 인출권.

Se 《chem.》 selenium.

S.E. southeast; southeastern.

se- [si, sə, se] *pref.* apart; without. '떨어져, …없이'의 뜻. ¶ *seclude.* [L.]

:sea [siː] *n.* Ⓒ **1** 《*the* ~》 ⓐ a large body of salt water covering the earth; the ocean. 바다; 대양(大洋)(opp. land). ¶ *an arm of the* ~ 내포(內浦); 후미 / *across* 〔*beyond, over*〕 *the* ~〔*seas*〕 바다를 건너; 해외로. ⓑ any large body of salt water, smaller than an ocean. 육지에 둘러싸인 해양; …해〔바다〕. ¶ *the North Sea* 북해 / *the Mediterranean Sea* 지중해 / *the Black Sea* 흑해 / *the closed* ~ 영해. **2** the state of the sea. 바다의 상태. ¶ *a calm* ~ 잔잔한 바다. **3** a large, high wave. 놀; 큰 파도〔물결〕. ¶ *a heavy* ~ 격랑(激浪) / *a rough* 〔*high*〕 ~ 거친 바다 / *ship a* ~ (배가) 큰 물결을 뒤집어 쓰다. **4** anything like the sea in its greatness or depth; a large quantity. 바다처럼 넓고 깊은 것; 매우 많음; …의 바다. ¶ *a* ~ *of flame* 불바다 / *a* ~ *of faces* 수많은 얼굴들 / *the* ~ *of air* 광대 무한의 대기. [E.]

above the sea, above the sea level. 해발; 표고.

at sea, a) in a ship on the sea. 해상에(서의); 항해중에. ¶ *be away at* ~ 항해에 나가 있다. b) 《*fig.*》《usu. *all at sea*》 not knowing what or how to do; bewildered. 어찌할 바를 몰라; 안개 속에. ¶ *find oneself at* ~ 완전히 오리무중이다 / *I can't understand this problem; I'm all at* ~. 이 문제는 알 수가 없다; 아주 캄캄하다.

by sea, through sea. 해로(海路)〔물길〕로; 배로(opp. by land).

by the sea, on the coast. 해변〔바닷가〕에서.

command of the sea, mastery of the sea. 제해권.

follow the sea, become a sailor. 뱃사람〔선원〕이 되다.

go (***down***) ***to the sea,*** go to the coast, or the seaside. 해안으로 가다; 해변으로 가다.

go to sea =follow the sea.

half seas over, drunk; intoxicated. 얼큰히 취하여.

keep the sea, keep an offing; keep command of the sea. 앞바다에 나와 있다; 제해권을 유지하(고 있)다.

on the sea, a) in ship, etc. 해상에; 배를 타고. b) situated on seashore. 바다에 면하여.

put (***out***) ***to sea,*** begin a voyage. 출범〔출항〕하다.

stand to sea, leave land to the open sea. 뭍을 떠나 난바다〔공해〕로 나아가다.

sea anemone [⌐ -⌐--] *n.* an animal shaped like a flower which has a tubelike body and lives in the sea. 말미잘.

sea bathing [⌐ ⌐-] *n.* the enjoyment of bathing in the sea. 해수욕.

sea·beach [síːbiːtʃ] *n.* Ⓒ a beach beside the sea. 해변; 바닷가.

sea·board [síːbɔ̀ːrd] *n.* Ⓒ the land along the sea; the seacoast. 해안(선); 연안 지방. ¶ *the Pacific* ~ 아메리카의 태평양 연안.

sea boat [⌐⌐] *n.* a ship having the power to go out to the ocean. 외양선(外洋船).

sea·borne [síːbɔ̀ːrn] *adj.* carried by ships. 배로 운반된; 해상 수송의. [*sea*]

sea breeze [⌐⌐] *n.* a wind blowing toward the land from the sea. (육지로 부는) 바닷바람; 해연풍(海軟風)(cf. *land breeze*).

sea calf [⌐⌐] *n.* a large animal living in the sea, hunted for its skin. 바다표범.

sea chart [⌐⌐] *n.* a map relating to the sea, used by sailors on a voyage. 해도(海圖).

sea·coast [síːkòust] *n.* Ⓒ the seashore. 해안; 연안. [↑]

sea cow [⌐⌐] *n.* 《zool.》 **1** =walrus. **2** dugong; manatee. 바다소《매너티 듀공 따위》.

sea cucumber [⌐ ⌐--] *n.* a trepang; a sea slug. 해삼.

sea dog [⌐⌐] *n.* **1** an old, experienced sailor. (특히 노련한) 뱃사람〔선원〕. **2** =sea calf. **3** a dogfish. 돔발상어류의 일종.

sea elephant [⌐ ⌐--] *n.* an elephant seal. 해마(海馬).

sea·far·er [síːfɛ̀ərər] *n.* Ⓒ 《*poet.*》 a sailor; a person who travels by sea. 뱃사람; 선원; 항해자. [*sea*]

sea·far·ing [síːfɛ̀əriŋ] *adj.* living on the sea as a sailor; traveling by sea. 바다에 사는; 항해의; 뱃사람〔선원〕을 직업으로 하는.
— *n.* Ⓤ the business of a sailor. 배를 타는 직업; 항해.

sea forces [⌐⌐] *n.* navy. 해군.

sea·front [síːfrʌ̀nt] *n.* the street of a town facing the sea. (도시의) 해안 거리.

sea·girt [síːgə̀ːrt] *adj.* 《*poet.*》 enclosed by the sea. 바다에 둘러싸인. ¶ *this* ~ *isle.* [*sea*]

sea·go·ing [síːgòuiŋ] *adj.* **1** (of a ship) made for crossing the ocean. (배가) 원양(遠洋) 항해의〔에 알맞은〕. ¶ *a* ~ *vessel* 항해선. **2** (of a person) living as a sailor. (사람이) 항해를 업으로 하는. ¶ *a* ~ *job* 뱃사람〔선원〕 일.

sea green [⌐⌐] *n.* the color of light bluish green. 해록색(海綠色).

sea gull [⌐⌐] *n.* a large bird that lives near the sea and feeds on fish. 갈매기.

sea horse [⌐⌐] *n.* **1** 《myth.》 a sea animal, half horse and half fish. (전설에 나오는) 반어반마(半魚半馬). **2** 《fish》 a kind of small fish with a head like that of a horse. 해마. **3** =walrus.

:seal[1] [siːl] *n.* Ⓒ **1** a design impressed on a piece of wax or other soft material to show ownership; a paper stamped with such a design. 인장(印章); 도장; 날인된 서류. ¶ *The government papers are stamped with the ~ of the United States.* 그 정부의 서류에는 합중국의 인장이 찍혀 있다. **2** a piece of wax, metal, etc. stamped with a design and placed on a letter or package to close it. 봉인(封印). ¶ *put under ~* 봉인하다 / *take off* 〔*break*〕 *the ~* 봉인을 뜯다; 개봉하다. **3** ⓐ something that closes another thing tightly. 밀봉(密封). ⓑ something for keeping a thing secret. (…의) 입을 봉하는 것; 입막음. ¶ *Her promise sealed her lips.* 그녀는 약속을 지켜 비밀을 말하지 않았다. **4** a decorative stamp, such as a Christmas seal. 장식 우표; (크리스마스) 실. **5** something that makes safe. 보증의 표시; 확증. ¶ *the ~ of love* 사랑의 표시 / *a handshake as a ~ of friendship* 우정의 표시로서의 악수.

affix** one's **seal to, stamp one's seal to. …에 도장을 찍다.

break the seal, unseal. 개봉하다.

put 〔***set***〕 ***one's seal to,*** stamp one's seal to; authorize or confirm. …에 도장을 찍다; …을 시인하다; …을 보증하다.

receive 〔***return***〕 ***the seals,*** take 〔leave〕 office as Lord Chancellor or Secretary of State. 대법관〔장관〕 직에〔을〕 취임〔사임〕하다.

the Lord 〔***Keeper of the***〕 ***Privy Seal,*** the high official who keeps the seal of state. 옥새 상서(玉璽尙書).

the seal of love, pledge of love. 사랑의 보증; 사랑의 표시《키스·결혼·출산 따위》.

under 〔***with***〕 ***a flying seal,*** with the seal open. 봉인을 뜯어; 개봉하여.

under the seal of secrecy, on the promise to keep the secret. 비밀을 지킬 것을 약속하여.

— *vt.* (P6,7,13) **1** put a seal on (papers, etc.). (문서 등에) 도장〔인〕을 찍다. **2** fasten (a letter, etc.) with a seal. (편지 따위)를 봉하다. **3** ⓐ close tightly; shut; fasten. …을 단단히 봉하다〔닫다〕; 밀봉하다. ¶ *~ a leak* 새는 곳을 막다 / *She sealed* (*up*) *the letter.* 편지를 (꼭) 봉했다 / *Our ship was sealed in the ice.* 우리의 배가 얼음에 갇혔다. ⓑ make air-tight or water-tight. 공기나 물이 통하지 않게 하다; 밀폐하다. ¶ *The windows were sealed up.* 창문들은 밀폐되었다. **4** give a mark to (something) to show that it is true. …을 확실한 것으로 하다; …을 증명하다. ¶ *They sealed their bargain by shaking hands.* 그들은 악수를 함으로써 그들의 계약〔협약〕을 확인했다. **5** settle; determine. …을 결정〔확정〕하다. ¶ *His love sealed her fate.* 그의 사랑이 그녀의 운명을 결정했다. [→sign]

seal up, **a**) close tightly. 밀봉하다. **b**) determine. 결정하다.

***seal**[2] [siːl] *n.* Ⓒ (*pl.* **seals** or 《*collectively*》 **seal**) a large animal living in the sea in cold regions, hunted for its skin and oil; Ⓤ the fur of this animal. 바다표범; 물개; 강치; 그 모피. — *vi.* (P1) hunt seals. 바다표범을 〔물개·강치를〕 잡다. ¶ *go sealing.* [E.]

sealed [siːld] *adj.* closed up tightly with a seal. 밀봉한〔된〕. [*seal*[1]]

sealed book [ˊˊ] *n.* something beyond understanding and therefore unknown. 내용을 알 수 없는 책; 비밀; 신비; 수수께끼.

sealed pattern [ˊ ˊ–] *n.* 《Brit.》 standard pattern (of British army and navy equipment). (군용 장구의) 표준형.

sea legs [ˊ ˋ] *n. pl.* 《*colloq.*》 **1** the ability to adjust one's sense of balance to the motion of a ship at sea. 흔들리는 배 안을 잘 걷는 능력; 배에 익숙해짐. **2** the ability to remain free of seasickness. 뱃멀미 안 하기. [*sea*]

find 〔***get***〕 ***one's sea legs*** (***on***), get used to the motion of a ship so that a person no longer feels sick. (뱃멀미하지 않고) 배의 흔들림에 익숙해지다.

seal·er[1] [síːlər] *n.* Ⓒ **1** a person who seals. 날인자. **2** an official who checks weights and measures. 도량형 검사관. [*seal*[1]]

seal·er[2] [síːlər] *n.* Ⓒ a man or ship that hunts seals. 바다표범 잡이(배). [*seal*[2]]

sea level [ˊ ˋ–] *n.* the surface of the sea. 해수면; 평균 해면. ¶ *The heights of mountains are measured as being so many feet above ~.* 산의 높이는 해발 얼마로 측정된다. [*sea*]

seal·ing wax [síːliŋ wæ̀ks] *n.* a kind of wax used to seal letters, packages, etc. 봉랍(封蠟). [*seal*[1]]

sea lion [ˊ ˋ–] *n.* 《zool.》 a large animal with a long body and flippers instead of feet, living in the North Pacific. 강치. [*sea*]

seal ring [ˊ ˋ] *n.* a kind of finger ring engraved with a picture, initials, etc. 인발이 새겨진 반지. [*seal*[1]]

seal·skin [síːlskìn] *n.* Ⓤ the skin of a seal; Ⓒ a garment made of this skin. 바다표범〔물개〕 가죽; 그것으로 만든 옷. [*seal*[2]]

***seam** [siːm] *n.* Ⓒ **1** the line formed by sewing two pieces of cloth together; any line made by joining two edges of material. 솔기; 이어맞춘 곳; 이음매. ¶ *the seams of a coat* / *The seams of the boat must be caulked.* 배의 이음매는 뱃밥으로 틀어막아야 한다. **2** a mark like a seam, but made by cutting. 벤 상처〔자국〕; 봉합선. ¶ *the ~ of an old cut* 오래된 벤 상처 / *An old sword cut had left a ~ in his face.* 그의 얼굴엔 오래된 칼 자국이 남아 있었다. **3** a layer of a mineral in the earth. 광물의 층(層). ¶ *a ~ of coal.*

— *vt.* (P6,7) **1** sew (two pieces of cloth) together; join (two things) together. …을 한데 이어맞추다[꿰매다]; …에 솔기를 대다. **2** mark (a face, etc.) with wrinkles, scars, etc. …에 상처 자국을 내다[남기다]; 주름을 내다. [E.]

sea·man [síːmən] *n.* Ⓒ (*pl.* **-men** [-mən]) **1** a sailor. 뱃사람; 선원. ¶ *a good* [*poor*] ~. **2** 《nav.》 a sailor who is below the rank of an officer. 해군 병사; 수병. [*sea*]

sea·man·ship [síːmənʃip] *n.* Ⓤ skill in controlling a ship. 선박 조종술; 항해술.

sea·mark [síːmàːrk] *n.* Ⓒ **1** a landmark on shore, such as a lighthouse, used as a guide for a ship's course. 항로 표지. **2** a line on the shore showing the limit of the tide. 해안선.

sea mew [∸∸] *n.* a large sea bird; a sea gull. 갈매기.

seam·less [síːmlis] *adj.* (of clothes) having no seam. 솔기가 없는. [*seam*]

seam·stress [síːmstris / sém-] *n.* Ⓒ a woman who earns her living by sewing. 여자 재봉사; 침모(針母).

seam·y [síːmi] *adj.* (**seam·i·er, seam·i·est**) **1** having seams. 솔기[이음매]가 있는; 상처 자국이 있는. **2** worse; unpleasant. 이면의; 어두운. ¶ *the ~ side of life* 인생의 이면; 사회의 암흑면. [*seam*]

se·ance [séiɑːns] *n.* 《F.》 **1** a sitting; session. (공공·학회·단체 따위의) 회의; 모임. **2** a meeting of people seeking messages from spirits of the dead. 강신술자(降神術者)의 모임; 교령회(交靈會).

sea·plane [síːplèin] *n.* Ⓒ an airplane designed to come down on and rise from water. 수상 비행기. [*sea*]

sea·port [síːpɔ̀ːrt] *n.* Ⓒ a port for seagoing ships; a town with such a port. 해항(海港); 항구 도시.

sea power [∸∸] *n.* **1** naval strength. 해군력. **2** a nation that has great naval strength. 해군국.

sear [siər] *vt.* (P6) **1** burn the outside of (something). …의 거죽을 태우다; 화상을 입히다. ¶ *He seared his hand on a hot steam pipe.* 뜨거운 스팀 파이프에 손을 데었다. **2** make (something) dry up. …을 시들게 하다; 마르게 하다. ¶ *The wind seared the leaves.* 바람이 잎을 시들게 했다. **3** make (a mind, etc.) hard and insensible. (양심 따위를) 마비시키다; 무감각하게 하다. ¶ *one's soul seared by injustice* 부정으로 마비된 마음. — *vi.* 《*arch.*》 dry up; wither. 시들다; 말라 죽다. — *adj.* dried up; withered. 말라 비틀어진; 시든. [E.]

:search [səːrtʃ] *vt.* **1** (P6,7) look for; try to find something hidden by looking over or going through (a place, etc.) carefully; carefully look in the clothing of (a prisoner, etc.) for something stolen. …을 찾다; (장소를) 수색하여 찾다; (죄인 따위)를 문초[심문]하다; 탐색[수색]하다. ¶ ~ *a house* 집을 수색하다 / ~ *a drawer* [*one's pockets*] 서랍을[주머니를] 뒤지다 / *The police searched the prisoner for* [*to see if he had*] *weapons.* 경찰은 죄수가 무기를 지니고 있나 몸수색을 했다. **2** (P6,7,13) ⓐ examine. 자세히 조사하다[살피다]; (기억 따위)를 더듬다. ¶ ~ *one's memory* 기억을 더듬다. ⓑ go into every part of. 구석구석까지 스며들다. ¶ *The sunshine searched the room.* 햇볕이 방안 구석구석까지 환하게 비쳤다. — *vi.* (P1,2A,3) look for or try to find something. 찾다; 수색[심문]하다; 조사하다. ¶ *You will find your purse if you ~ properly.* 철저히 찾으면 돈지갑을 찾을 게다 / *I searched through the telephone directory for his telephone number.* 그의 전화 번호를 찾기 위해 번호부를 뒤졌다.

search after, seek; try to find or obtain what is lacking or lost. …을 찾다.

search a wound, probe into a wound. (외과 기구 등으로) 상처를 살피다.

search for, seek; look for. …을 찾다. ¶ *We searched all day for the lost child.* 우리는 잃어버린 아이를 온종일 찾았다.

search into, examine. …을 조사하다. ¶ *We must ~ into the matter.* 우리는 그 문제를 조사해봐야 한다.

Search me! 《U.S. *colloq.*》 I have no idea. (질문·심문에 대해) 나는 모른다; 난 결백하다.

search out, find (something) by searching. …을 찾아내다. ¶ ~ *out an old friend* 옛 친구를 찾아내다.

— *n.* ⓊⒸ **1** the act of searching; an examination. 찾기; 수색(하기); 조사; 음미. ¶ *make a careful ~ for* [*after*] *a lost ring* 잃어버린 반지를 찾다. **2** an attempt to gain. 추구. ¶ *the ~ for truth* [*wealth*] 진리[부(富)]의 추구. [→circle]

in search of, looking for; trying to find. …을 찾아.

search·er [sə́ːrtʃər] *n.* one who searches. 찾는[조사하는] 사람; 추구자.

***search·ing** [sə́ːrtʃiŋ] *adj.* **1** examining carefully or keenly; piercing. 날카로운; 면밀한; 수색[탐색]하는. ¶ *a ~ investigation* 면밀한 조사 / *a ~ glance* [*look*] 날카로운 시선[일별] / *a ~ mind* 마음을 꿰뚫어보는 마음[사람]. **2** (of a test, etc.) thorough; sharp. 철저한; 날카로운. ¶ *a ~ examination* 철저한 시험 / ~ *questions* 날카로운 질문. **3** severe. (바람·추위 따위가) 사무치는; 혹심한. ¶ ~ *cold* 심한 추위. — *n.* the act of examining, esp. one's conscience. 수색; 탐색; 검사; 가책. ¶ *searchings of heart* 양심의 가책.

search·light [sə́ːrtʃlàit] *n.* Ⓒ a large, powerful, movable electric light used for seeking out airplanes or ships in time of war, etc. 탐조등(探照燈).

search party [∸∸] *n.* a body of persons sent out to look for a lost person or thing. 수색대.

search warrant [∸∸] *n.* a paper authorizing the searching of a house or building for stolen goods, etc. 가택 수색 영장.

sea rover [⌐⌐─] *n.* **1** a pirate; a searobber. 해적. **2** a pirate ship; a ship used by a pirate. 해적선. [*sea*]

sea·scape [síːskèip] *n.* **1** Ⓒ a picture of a scene on the sea. 바다 그림. **2** Ⓤ the scenery on the sea. 바다 경치(opp. landscape).

sea serpent [⌐⌐─] *n.* an imaginary sea monster. (뱀 모양의 상상의) 바다 괴물.

sea shell [⌐⌐] *n.* a shell of any shell-bearing animal living in the sea. 바닷조개; 조가비.

***sea·shore** [síːʃɔ́ːr] *n.* Ⓒ a seacoast; the land at the edge of the sea; a beach. 해안; 해변; 바닷가.

sea·sick [síːsik] *adj.* suffering from sickness caused by the pitching and rolling of a boat. 뱃멀미하는. ¶ *He easily gets* ~. 그는 뱃멀미를 잘한다.

sea·sick·ness [síːsiknis] *n.* Ⓤ sickness caused by the motion of a ship at sea. 뱃멀미.

***sea·side** [síːsàid] *n.* Ⓒ 《usu. *the* ~》 the land close to the sea. 해안; 해변; 바닷가. ¶ *go to the* ~ *for the summer holidays* 해변으로 여름 휴가를 떠나다. — *adj.* on or of the seashore. 해안의; 해변에 면한; 바닷가의. ¶ *a* ~ *hotel* 해변 호텔.

:**sea·son** [síːzən] *n.* Ⓒ **1** one of the four parts of a year, such as spring and autumn. 계절. ¶ *at any* ~ (*of the year*) (일년 중) 어느 때고 / *in all seasons* 사계절을 통하여 / *Autumn is the best* ~ *for traveling.* 가을(철)은 여행하기에 가장 좋은 계절이다. **2** ⓐ any period of time marked by something special. (기후·활동·행사 따위로 특징지어진) 계절; 시절; 시기〔시즌〕; …철. ¶ *the Christmas* ~ 크리스마스 철〔시즌〕/ *the holiday* ~ 휴가기(期)〔철〕/ *the dry* 〔*rainy*〕 ~ 건기(乾期)〔우기〕/ *the baseball* ~ 야구 시즌 / *a closed* ~ 금렵기 / *an open* ~ *on deer* 사슴 사냥철. ⓑ a period when certain crops are most plentiful or in their prime harvest. (작물 따위의) 한창 (쏟아져 나올) 때. ¶ *the* ~ *of harvest* 수확기 / *the strawberry* ~ 딸기철. **3** a suitable or fit time. …에 적합한 시기; 좋은 시기. **4** a period.(일반적으로) 시기. ¶ *a* ~ *of inaction* 불활동기. **5** 《Brit.》 =season ticket.

at all seasons, throughout the year. 일년(중) 내내; 사철을 통하여.

for a* (*passing*) *season, for a while. 잠시 동안.

in season, **a**) at the right time; timely. 때맞춘; 시의(時宜) 적절한. **b**) (of fresh foods) at the time when they are usually ready for eating. (과일 따위가) 제철 때에. **c**) at the busiest time of year. 한창 때인. **d**) permitted to be hunted at the time. 사냥철로서.

in season and out of season, at any time; all the time. 철을 가리지 않고; 언제나.

out of season, not in season. 한창 때를 지난; 철 지난; 금렵기에.

— *vt.* **1** (P6,13) ⓐ give a good taste to (food) with salt, sugar, etc. (양념 따위로) …에 맛을 내다; 간을 맞추다. ¶ *highly seasoned dishes* 강하게 맛을 낸 요리 / *She seasoned the soup with salt.* 수프에 소금으로 간을 맞췄다. ⓑ 《*fig.*》 give interest to. …에 재미〔흥미·정취〕를 곁들이다. ¶ ~ *one's speech with wit* 이야기에 재치로 흥미를 곁들이다. **2** (P6,13) 《*lit.*》 make (something) less severe; soften. …을 누그러뜨리다; 완화하다. ¶ ~ *anger* 노여움을 누그러뜨리다 / ~ *justice with mercy* 자비로써 법을 완화하다. **3** (P6) ⓐ dry and harden (lumber) for use by exposure to the air, etc. (뒤틀리거나 오그라들지 않게) (재목 따위)를 말리다. ¶ ~ *lumber well in the open air* 목재를 한데에서 잘 말리다. ⓑ mature. (술 따위를) 숙성(熟成)시키다. ¶ ~ *wine in a cask* 통 속의 포도주를 숙성시키다. ⓒ accustom. 익숙해지게 하다; 단련시키다. ¶ *troops seasoned to* 〔*by, in*〕 *battle* 역전의 부대 / *a seasoned veteran* 노련한 베테랑 / ~ *oneself to cold* 추위에 익숙해지다.

— *vi.* (P1) become mature; come into good condition. 익다; 숙성하다; 쓸 수 있는 상태로 되다. [L. *satio* sowing]

sea·son·a·ble [síːzənəbəl] *adj.* **1** suitable to the season. 계절의; 계절에 맞는. **2** occurring at the correct or proper time; timely. 때맞춘; 시기에 적절한. ¶ *a* ~ *gift* 때맞춘 선물 / ~ *weather* 계절에 맞는 날씨.

sea·son·a·bly [síːzənəbəli] *adv.* on a seasonable occasion; at the right time. 시후(時候)에 맞게; 호기에; 때맞춰.

sea·son·al [síːzənəl] *adj.* of the seasons; occurring only at a certain period of the year; periodical. 계절의; 어떤 계절에 한정된; 주기적(인). ¶ ~ *disease* 계절병 / ~ *changes of climate* 기후의 계절적 변화 / *a* ~ *phenomenon* 주기적 현상.

sea·soned [síːzənd] *adj.* ripe; dried; familiar. 익은; (잘) 말린; 익숙한.

sea·son·ing [síːzəniŋ] *n.* Ⓒ **1** something that gives food a better taste. 조미료; 양념. **2** 《*fig.*》 anything that increases enjoyment. 재미〔흥취〕를 더해 주는 것. ¶ *a* ~ *of humor* 유머의 맛.

season ticket [⌐─ ⌐─] *n.* **1** a ticket which allows its holder to attend a series of games, concerts. (극장 따위에서) 기간중 내내 입장할 수 있는 입장권. **2** 《Brit.》 a ticket which allows its holder to travel between two stated stations for a certain period. 정기 승차권(=《U.S.》 commutation ticket).

:**seat** [siːt] *n.* Ⓒ **1** a thing used to sit on. 자리; 좌석; 걸상. ¶ *have* 〔*take*〕 *a* ~ 앉다; 착석하다 / *give one's* ~ *to someone* …에게 자리를 양보하다 / *rise from one's* ~ 자리에서 일어

서다〔기립하다〕/ *find a vacant* ～ 빈 자리를 발견하다 / *Take a* ～, *please.* 앉으십시오 / *Please keep your seats.* 그대로 앉아 계십시오. **2** a place in which one has a right to sit; the right to sit in that place. 의석; 의석권. ¶ *win* 〔*lose*〕 *one's* ～ *in a parliament* 의회에 의석을 얻다〔잃다〕; 의원 선거에 당선〔낙선〕하다. **3** the part of a chair, stool, bench, etc. on which someone sits. (의자 따위의) 앉는 부분. ¶ *This chair has a broken* ～. 이 의자는 앉는 자리가 부서져 있다. **4** the part of the body on which one sits; the part of the clothes covering it. (몸의) 엉덩이; (바지 따위의) 엉덩이. ¶ *the* ～ *of his trousers.* **5** the manner of sitting on a horse's back. 말탄 자세; 말타기; 앉음새. ¶ *He has a good* 〔*poor*〕 ～ *on a horse.* 그는 말을 잘 탄다〔타지 못한다〕. **6** something on which anything rests; a base. (기계 따위의) 대(臺); 대좌. **7** a large house in the country; home. 시골의 저택; 영지. **8** a place where something usu. is. 장소; 소재지; 중심지. ¶ *the* ～ *of learning* 〔*commerce*〕 학문〔상업〕의 중심지 / *the* ～ *of a disease* 병의 부위 / *The* ～ *of our government is in Seoul.* 우리 정부의 소재지는 서울이다.

seat of honor, 《*joc.*》 the buttocks. 엉덩이.
the seat of war, the theater of war. 전장.

— *vt.* (P6) **1** set or place (someone) on a seat. …을 착석시키다; (자리·의석에) 앉히다. ¶ ～ *someone in a chair* 아무를 의자에 앉히다 / *keep* 〔*remain*〕 *seated* 앉은 채로 있다 / *They succeeded in seating their candidate in Parliament.* 그들의 후보를 의석에 앉히는 데 성공했다. **2** have seats for (a fixed number of people). …을 수용하다; …만큼의 좌석을 가지다. ¶ *Our school auditorium seats one thousand pupils.* 우리 학교 강당은 천 명의 학생을 수용한다 / *The theater is seated for about 700 people.* 이 극장은 약 7백 개의 좌석이 있다. **3** repair or place seats on (something). …에 자리를 (갈아) 대다. ¶ ～ *an old chair* 낡은 의자의 자리를 갈다. **4** fix firmly. (받침·대 따위에) 붙박다; 고정시키다. ¶ ～ *a machine.* [N. (→sit)]

be seated, **a**) sit down. 앉다; 착석하다. ¶ *Please be seated, gentlemen.* 신사 여러분, 앉아 주십시오. **b**) be sitting. 앉아 있다. ¶ *Three old men were seated at the table.* 세 분의 노인이 식탁에 앉아 있었다. **c**) be situated. 위치해 있다.

***seat** oneself,* sit down. 착석하다; 앉다.

seat belt [ˊ ˋ] *n.* a safety belt. 안전 띠〔벨트〕.

SEATO, Seato [síːtou] Southeast Asia Treaty Organization. 동남아 조약 기구.

sea urchin [ˊ ˋˊ] *n.* a small, round-shaped sea animal that has a thin shell covered with sharp spines. 성게. [*sea*]

sea wall [ˊ ˋ] *n.* a wall or sea bank built to protect the shore against the damage of waves. 호안(護岸) 제방; 방파제.

sea·ward [síːwərd] *adj.* **1** facing or directed toward the sea. 바다로 향한; 바다쪽의. **2** (of wind) from the sea. 바다로부터의. — *n.* Ⓤ 《*the* ～》 the direction toward the sea. 바다쪽. ¶ *look to the* ～ 바다쪽을 보다. — *adv.* toward the sea. 바다쪽으로; 바다를 향해.

sea·wards [síːwərdz] *adv.* =seaward.

sea·way [síːwèi] *n.* Ⓒ **1** a route over the sea. 뱃길; 해로; 항로. **2** a rough sea. 거친 바다; 물결. ¶ *in a* ～ 거친 물결에 시달려. **3** Ⓤ the forward motion of a ship through the waves. (배의) 전진; 항진(航進). **4** an inland waterway that is deep enough for large ships. 내륙 수로.

sea·weed [síːwìːd] *n.* ⓊⒸ any plant growing in the sea. 해초(海草); 바닷말.

sea·wor·thy [síːwə̀ːrði] *adj.* (of a ship) fit to sail on the sea; good for a sea trip. 항해에 적합한〔견디는〕. ¶ *a stout* ～ *ship* 내항성(耐航性)이 좋은 튼튼한 배.

se·ba·ceous [sibéiʃəs] *adj.* 《physiol.》 having to do with fat; fatty, greasy. 지방(脂肪)의; 피지(皮脂)의. ¶ *the* ～ *glands* 기름샘; 피지선(皮脂腺). [L. *sebum* tallow]

SEC Securities and Exchange Commission. 증권 거래 위원회.

sec. secretary; second; section.

se·cede [sisíːd] *vi.* (P1,3) 《*from*》 withdraw from a political party, a church, etc. (정당·교회 따위로부터) 탈퇴〔분리〕하다. ¶ ～ *from the union* 조합을 탈퇴하다 / *The Southern States seceded from the Union.* 남부의 주(州)들은 연방에서 탈퇴했다. [se-, L. *cedo* go]

se·ces·sion [siséʃən] *n.* ⓊⒸ the act of seceding from a political party, etc. (정당·교회 따위로부터의) 탈퇴; 탈당; 탈회; 분리. [↑]

se·clude [siklúːd] *vt.* (P6,13) separate (someone) from others; keep (someone) away from others. …을 떼어놓다; 분리〔격리〕하다. ¶ ～ *oneself from society* 〔*the world*〕 사회에서 은퇴하다. [se-, L. *cloudo* shut]

se·clud·ed [siklúːdid] *adj.* set apart from others; isolated. (사회 활동·사람들로부터) 격리된; 차단된; 은둔한. ¶ *a* ～ *life* 은둔 생활 / *a* ～ *spot* 마을에서 멀리 떨어진 곳.

se·clu·sion [siklúːʒən] *n.* **1** Ⓤ the act of secluding; the state of being secluded; retirement. 격리; 차단; 은퇴; 은둔. ¶ *a policy of* ～ 쇄국 정책 / *live in* ～ 은둔 생활을 하다 / *in the* ～ *of one's own home* 자신의 집에 틀어박혀. **2** Ⓒ a secluded place. 마을에서 떨어진 (후미진) 곳.

:sec·ond[1] [sékənd] *adj.* **1** coming just after the first. 두 번째의; 제 2 의. ¶ *the* ～ *runner* 제 2 주자 / *the* ～ *house from the corner* 모퉁이에서 2번째의 집 / *James* Ⅱ 제임스 2세 / *the* ～ *row from the front* 앞에서 두 번째줄 / *every* ～ *day* 하루 걸러. **2** next to the first in rank, quality, etc.; sub-. 2 위의; 2 등의; 부(副)의; (질 따위가) 떨어지는. ¶ *a*

~ *cabin*, 2 등선실 / *the* ~ *prize*, 2 등상 / *the* ~ *city in England* 영국에서 둘째 가는 도시 / *the* ~ *officer on a ship*, 2 등 항해사 / *goods of* ~ *quality*, 2 류품. **3** another; like the first one. (또) 다른; 또 하나의; 제2의. ¶ *a* ~ *time* 또〔다시〕 한 번 / *He has been called a* ~ *Nero.* 그는 제2의 네로로 불리어 왔다.

at second hand, through, from, another. 간접(적)으로; 중개자를 통하여; 중고품으로.

in the second place, secondly. 둘째로; 두 번째로; 다음으로.

on second thoughts, after thinking it over again. 다시 생각해 본 후에; 생각을 고치어.

play second fiddle (***to…***) ⇨ fiddle.

second to none, without a superior. 누구〔무엇〕에도 못하지〔뒤지지〕 않는. ¶ *He is* ~ *to none in playing golf.* 그는 누구 못지 않게 골프를 잘 친다.

— *n.* Ⓒ **1** 《usu. *the* ~》 a person or thing next after the first in place, rank, etc. 제 2 위(의 사람, 것); 둘째. ¶ *the* ~ *of March*, 3 월 2 일 / *He got a* ~. 2 등으로 졸업했다. **2** 《often *pl.*》 goods of the second grade. 2 등〔2 급〕품. ¶ *These stockings are seconds and have some slight defects.* 이 양말은 2 등품이어서 약간의 흠집들이 있다. **3** an assistant, esp. as in a boxing match. (권투 따위의) 조수; 세컨드.

— *vt.* (P6) **1** act as an assistant to (someone). …의 조수〔세컨드〕를 보다. **2** support; back up. …을 후원〔보좌〕하다; 지지〔찬성〕하다. ¶ *He seconded our motion.* 그는 우리의 동의에 찬성했다. **3** [sikάnd, sékənd / -kɔ́nd] transfer (an official) to another post. 임시 전근〔전속〕시키다.

— *adv.* in the second place; second in order, importance, etc. 제 2 로; 둘째로; 두 번째로. ¶ *Bill spoke* ~. 빌은 2 번째로 말을 했다 / *travel* ~ (열차 따위의) 2 등칸으로 여행하다. [L. *sequor* follow]

come in 〔***finish, place***〕 ***second,*** be second in a race. (경주에서) 2 위〔2 등〕하다. ¶ *He finished* ~ *in the race.*

:sec·ond[2] [sékənd] *n.* Ⓒ (of time or degree) 1/60 part of a minute; a moment; a short time. 초; 매우 짧은 시간; 잠깐. ¶ *Sixty seconds make one minute.* 60 초는 1 분이다 / *Just wait a* ~. 잠깐만 기다리시오. [↑]

Second Advent 〔**Coming**〕 [⌐– ⌐–〔⌐–〕], ***the*** *n.* the prophesied return of Christ to the earth at the end of the world. 예수의 재림. [*second*]

***sec·ond·ar·y** [sékəndèri / -dəri] *adj.* **1** second in order, rank, value, place, time, etc. 제 2(위)의; 둘째〔두 번째〕의; 이류의(cf. *primary*). ¶ ~ *education* 중등 교육 / *a* ~ *accent* 제 2 악센트. **2** coming after the original; having less importance. 제 이차적인; 부(副)…. ¶ *a matter of* ~ *importance* 이차적인 문제; 덜 중요한 일.

be of secondary importance, be of minor importance. 그리 중요하지 않다.

— *n.* Ⓒ (*pl.* **-ar·ies**) something that is secondary. 이류의〔이차적인〕 것.

secondary school [⌐––– ⌐] *n.* a school ranking between a primary school and a college or university. 중등 학교《한국의 중학교와 고등 학교를 합친 것에 해당함》.

sec·ond-best [sékəndbést] *adj.* next to the best. 두 번째로 좋은; 둘째의; 차선의. ¶ *one's* ~ *clothes* 두 번째로 좋은 나들이옷.

come off second-best, get the worst of it. 지다.

second childhood [⌐– ⌐–] *n.* a foolish or childish condition caused by old age. 도망; 망령.

sec·ond-class [sékəndklǽs, -klάːs] *adj.* **1** of the class or grade next to the first. 2 등〔급, 류〕의. ¶ *a* ~ *passenger*, 2 등 승객 / *a* ~ *hotel*, 2 류 호텔. **2** lower in quality; of inferior quality of grade. (질이) 떨어지는; 그다지 좋지 않은. — *adv.* on a second-class ticket. 2 등으로; 2 등표로〔승객으로〕. ¶ *travel* 〔*go*〕 ~, 2 등석으로 여행하다.

second hand [⌐– ⌐] *n.* **1** the hand of a clock which points to the seconds. (시계의) 초침. **2** a thing which has already been used. 고물; 중고품.

:sec·ond-hand [sékəndhǽnd] *adj.* **1** not new; used by someone else. 써서 낡은; 고물의; 중고(품)의. ¶ *a* ~ *car* 중고차 / ~ *clothes* 헌옷. **2** learned or heard from someone else; not original. 전해 들은; 간접의; 받아 옮기는. ¶ ~ *information* 간접〔얻어들은〕 정보. **3** of a store buying and selling used goods. 고물상의; 중고품상의. ¶ *a* ~ *bookshop* 헌책 가게. — *adv.* **1** after being used by someone else. 헌것〔중고품〕으로. ¶ *Did you buy it new or* ~? 그것을 새것으로 샀느냐 중고품으로 샀느냐. **2** indirectly. 간접적으로; 전문(傳聞)으로. ¶ *get news* ~ 소식을 전해 듣다.

sec·ond·ly [sékəndli] *adv.* in the second place; in the place next to the best. 제 2 로; 두 번〔둘〕째로; 다음으로. [*second*]

second nature [⌐– ⌐–] *n.* a habit, etc. so long practiced as to be almost instinctive. 제 2 의 천성. ¶ *Habit is* ~ *nature.* 습관은 제 2 의 천성이다.

sec·ond-rate [sékəndréit] *adj.* **1** of the second rank. 이류의; 2 등(급)의. ¶ *a* ~ *hotel* 〔*poet*〕 이류 호텔〔시인〕. **2** inferior. 열등한; 평범한. ¶ *a man with* ~ *brains* 머리가 좋지 않은 사람.

second sight [⌐– ⌐] *n.* the ability to look into the future. 천리안; 투시력.

second string [⌐– ⌐] *n.* an alternative course of action, kept in reserve. (행동·계획 따위의) 차선책.

second teeth [⌐– ⌐] *n.* those which grow after a child's first teeth (i.e. milk-teeth) are out. 영구치(齒).

***se·cre·cy** [síːkrəsi] *n.* Ⓤ **1** the state of being secret. 비밀; 내밀. ¶ *done with* 〔*in*〕 *ab-*

solute ~ 극비리에 이루어진. **2** the act or ability of keeping things secret. 비밀을 지키는 힘; 비밀주의. ¶ *rely on* 〔*upon*〕 *someone's* ~ 아무가 비밀을 지켜줄 것을 믿다. [*secret*]

in secrecy, secretly. 비밀히.

in the secrecy of** one's* ***heart, deep down in one's heart; truly; sincerely. 마음 속 깊이; 마음 속으로.

with the utmost secrecy, in profound secrecy. 극비로.

:se·cret [síːkrit] *adj.* **1** kept from the sight or knowledge of others; not known. 숨겨진; 알려지지 않은; 비밀의; 기밀의. ¶ ~ *diplomacy* 비밀 외교 / *a* ~ *door in the wall* 벽의 비밀문 / *a* ~ *society* 비밀 결사 / *be in* ~ *agreement with someone* 아무와 비밀 협정을 맺고 있다 / *He kept the matter* ~ *from his family.* 그는 그 일을 가족에겐 숨겨두었다. **2** hard to understand or discover. 이해가〔발견이〕 곤란한; 알 수 없는. ¶ *the* ~ *ways of God* 하느님의 불가사의한 섭리.

—*n.* **1** Ⓒ something hidden or unknown; a mystery. 비밀; 신비. ¶ *the secrets of nature* 자연의 신비 / *an entire* 〔*a dead*〕 ~ 극비 사항 / *keep a* ~ 비밀을 지키다 / *break* 〔*let out, betray*〕 *a* ~ 비밀을 누설하다 / *cease to be a* ~ 사람들에게 알려지다 / *let someone in* 〔*into*〕 *a* 〔*the*〕 ~ 아무에게 비밀을 밝히다 / *have no secrets from someone* 아무에게 숨기는 일은 아무것도 없다. **2** Ⓤ a true way of doing something. 비결. ¶ *The* ~ *of health is moderation in all things.* 건강의 비결은 만사에 중용을〔절제를〕 지키는 일이다. [se-, L. *cerno* separate]

an open secret, something supposed to be confidential, but which is widely known. 공공연한 비밀.

in secret, not openly; secretly. 비밀히; 몰래.

in the secret, sharing a secret. 비밀에 관여하여 알고.

secret agent [ˊ–ˊ–] *n.* an agent of the government secret service. 첩보부원; (특히 외국에서 활동하는) 군사 첩보원.

sec·re·tar·i·al [sèkrətέəriəl] *adj.* of a secretary. 서기의; 비서의; 장관의. [*secretary*]

sec·re·tar·i·at, -i·ate [sèkrətέəriət] *n.* **1** Ⓤ the position of a secretary. 서기〔비서〕의 직. **2** Ⓒ《*the* ~, often *collectively*》ⓐ the office or place where the secretarial staff works. 비서과〔실〕; 사무국; 서기국. ⓑ a group of secretaries. 사무국 직원.

:sec·re·tar·y [sékrətèri / -təri] *n.* Ⓒ (*pl.* **-tar·ies**) **1** a person employed to write letters, keep written records, etc. for a person or an organization. 서기(관); 사무관; 비서. ¶ *a private* ~ 개인 비서 / *work as a* ~ *to*... …의 비서로 일하다 / *She is the president's* ~. = *She is the* ~ *of the president.* 그녀는 사장의 비서다. **2** 《*S-*》 a government official in charge of a department. 각료; 각부의 장관(cf. *minister*). ¶ *the Secretary of State* 《U.S.》 국무 장관 / *the Secretary of the Treasury* 《U.S.》 재무 장관 / *the Home* 〔*Foreign*〕 *Secretary* = *the Secretary of State for Home* 〔*Foreign*〕 *Affairs* 《Brit.》 내무〔외무〕 장관. [→secret, -ary]

secretary bird [ˊ–––ˋ] *n.* a long-legged, large African bird of prey. (뱀을 잡아먹는) 독수리의 일종.

se·crete [sikríːt] *vt.* (P6) **1** keep (a matter) secret; hide (something) from someone. …을 숨기다; 감추다; 비밀로 하다. ¶ ~ *oneself* 숨다 / *The spy secreted the stolen microfilms.* 스파이는 훔친 마이크로필름을 숨겼다. **2** 《physiol.》 produce (a substance) in the body. 분비하다 (cf. *excrete*). ¶ *Glands in the mouth* ~ *saliva.* 입안의 샘은 침을 분비한다. [*secret*]

se·cre·tion [sikríːʃən] *n.* Ⓤ **1** Ⓒ the substance that is produced by an animal, etc. 분비물. ¶ *Bile is the* ~ *of the liver.* 담즙은 간장의 분비물이다. **2** the act of producing a substance in the body. 분비작용. **3** the act of hiding. 숨기기.

se·cre·tive [síːkrətiv, sikríː-] *adj.* **1** tending to keep things secret; of the principle of secrecy. 숨기는; 솔직하지 않은; 비밀주의의. **2** causing secretion. 분비를 촉진하는.

se·cret·ly [síkritːli] *adv.* in a secret manner. 몰래; 비밀로.

se·cre·to·ry [sikríːtəri] *adj.* of the action of secreting. 분비의〔하는〕. —*n.* Ⓒ (*pl.* **-ries**) a secreting organ of the body. 분비기관. [*secret*]

secret service [ˊ–ˊ–] *n.* **1** the branch of a government that makes secret investigations. (정부의) 비밀 정보 기관; 첩보부. **2** an official service of a secret nature. (정부를 위한) 비밀 활동; 첩보 활동.

sect [sekt] *n.* Ⓒ a group of people having the same opinions, esp. about religion. 종파; 교파; 분파; 당파. ¶ *religious* ~ 종파. [→ second]

sec·tar·i·an [sektέəriən] *adj.* **1** of a sect. 분파〔종파〕의; 학파의. ¶ ~ *politics* 파벌정치. **2** strongly devoted to a particular sect. 당파심이 강한; 파벌적인. —*n.* Ⓒ a person strongly devoted to a sect. 종파심이 강한 사람; 파벌적인 사람. [*sect*]

:sec·tion [sékʃən] *n.* Ⓒ **1** the act of cutting off. 절개; 절단. **2** a part divided or cut off. 절단〔분리〕된 부분; 단편. ¶ *divide a cake into three sections* 케이크를 셋으로 자르다. **3** one of several parts that can be put together to make a complete structure. (전체를 하나로 짜맞추기 위한) 부(분)품. ¶ *a boat built in sections* 조립식 보트 / *fit together the sections of a machine* 기계를 조립하다. **4** a division of a book. (책의) 절(節); 항(項). ¶ *Chapter II has six sections.* 제2장은 6절로 되어 있다. **5** a district; an area distinctly limited. 지역; 구역; 지구. ¶ *the farming* ~ 경작 구역 / *the poor* ~ *of* *town* 시의 빈민 구역 / *a residential* ~ 주택 지역. **6** a picture or diagram of an object as it would appear if cut through. 단면(도). — *vt.* (P6) **1** cut into sections; arrange in sections. 해체하다; 구분하다. **2** show by a section. 단면도를 만들다. [L. *seco* cut]

sec·tion·al [sékʃənəl] *adj.* **1** of or like a section. 구분의; 부문의; 부분의; 지역〔지방〕적인. ¶ ~ *interests* 지역의 이해(利害). **2** composed of parts joined together; made of sections. 몇 개의 부분으로 된; 조립식의. ¶ *a* ~ *boat* 조립식 보트 / *a* ~ *plan of a building* 건물의 단면도.

sec·tion·al·ism [sékʃənəlìzəm] *n.* too great regard for sectional interests; sectional prejudice or hatred. 지역〔파벌〕주의; 지방적 편견.

sec·tor [séktər] *n.* **1** Ⓒ 《geom.》 the part of a circle between two radii. 부채꼴. **2** 《mil.》 a section of a battle-line. 선형(扇形) 전투 지구. [*section*]

sec·u·lar [sékjələr] *adj.* **1** of this world's life; not religious or sacred. 세속의; 속인의; 정신적이 아닌; 비종교적인. ¶ ~ *affairs* 세속의 일 / ~ *music* 세속〔일반〕 음악 / ~ *interests* 세속에의 관심. **2** lasting for a long period of time; immortal. 오랜 세월에 걸친; 불후의. ¶ *the* ~ *fame* 불후의 명성 / *the* ~ *bird* 불사조. **3** living in the world; not shut up in monasteries. (성직자가) 수도회에 소속되지 않은; 수도원에 얽매이지 않는(cf. *ecclesiastical*). — *n.* Ⓒ a parish priest. 교구 목사. [L. *saeculum* an age]

sec·u·lar·ize [sékjələràiz] *vt.* (P6) **1** make (something) worldly. …을 세속화하다; 현세적으로 하다. ¶ ~ *education* 교육을 종교에서 분리하다. **2** remove (property, etc.) from the ownership of a church to that of the government. …을 교회 소유에서 정부 소유로 옮기다; 속용(俗用)으로 제공하다.

se·cun·do [sikʌ́ndou] *adv.* 《L.》 secondly. 제 2 로; 둘째로.

se·cun·dum [sekúndəm] *prep.* 《L.》 according to. …에 의하여; …에 따라. [→second]

secundum ar·tem [sekúndəm ɑ́:rtem] *adv.* according to the rules of the art, in skillful fashion. 기술적으로; 교묘히.

secundum na·tu·ram [sekúndəm nətjúərəm] *adv.* 《L.》 in the natural way. 자연히; 천연으로.

:se·cure [sikjúər] *adj.* (**-cur·er, -cur·est**) **1** free from fear or danger; safe; protected. 안전한; 걱정이 없는; 위험이 없는. ¶ *a* ~ *hiding-place* 안전한 은신처 / *be* ~ *from* 〔*against*〕 *attack* 공격당해도 안전하다 / *The building is* ~ *from any earthquake.* 이 건물은 어떠한 지진에도 안전하다. **2** kept so as not to escape; safe against loss; in good keeping. 도망칠 염려 없는; 엄중히 감금되어 있는; 안전히 보관된. ¶ *keep* 〔*hold*〕 *the prisoners* ~ 죄수를 엄중히 감금해 두다 / *Land in a growing city is a* ~ *investment.* 성장하는 도시의 토지는 안전한 투자이다. **3** certain; sure. 확실한; 확신하고 있는. ¶ *We are* ~ *of victory.* 우리는 승리를 확신하고 있다 / *We know in advance that his success is* ~. 그의 성공이 확실하다는 것을 우리는 이미 알고 있다. **4** 《as *attributive*》 firmly fastened; not likely to move away. 단단히 고정된; 견고한; 튼튼한. ¶ *Is the door* ~ ? 그 문은 튼튼히 달렸느냐 / *He made the boat* ~. 배를 견고하게 만들었다.

be secure (=*sure*) ***of something.*** …을 확신하다.

— *vt.* (P6,13) **1** 《*against, from*》 make (something) safe or secure from danger; protect. …을 안전하게 하다; 보호하다. ¶ ~ *oneself against the cold* 〔*loss*〕 방한의 준비를 하다〔손해를 보지 않도록 하다〕 / *We must* ~ *our house against* 〔*from*〕 *the coming storm.* 닥쳐올 폭풍우로부터 집을 보호할 대책을 세우지 않으면 안 된다. **2** keep (someone) so that he can not escape. …을 달아나지 못하게 하다. **3** succeed in getting; gain; obtain. 획득〔확보〕하다; 얻다; 손에 넣다. ¶ *She has at last secured a good maid.* 그녀는 마침내 좋은 가정부를 구했다 / *Can you* ~ *me two good seats for the play?* 그 연극에 좋은 좌석 2개만 확보해 주실 수 있습니까. **4** make (something) sure. …을 보증하다. **5** ⓐ fix firmly; fasten. …을 움직이지 않게 하다; 고정시키다. ¶ ~ *a rope* 밧줄을 팽팽히 고정시키다. ⓑ make firm or fast. 단단히 닫다〔잠그다〕. ¶ *Don't forget to* ~ *the doors and windows before leaving the house.* 집을 떠나기 전에 문과 창문을 꼭 잠그는 것을 잊지 마라. [se-, L. *cura* care]

se·cure·ly [sikjúərli] *adv.* in a secure manner; firmly; tightly. 확실히; 단단히.

:se·cu·ri·ty [sikjúəriti] *n.* (*pl.* **-ties**) **1** Ⓤ the state of being safe; freedom from danger or fear. 안전; 안심; 무사. ¶ *personal* ~ 신체의 안전 / 《*prov.*》 *Security is the greatest enemy.* 방심은 금물이다. **2** Ⓒ a thing which secures; a kind of protection. 방어〔보호〕물; 방위〔보호〕 수단. ¶ *A fire alarm is a* ~ *against a fire.* 화재 경보기는 화재의 방위 수단이다. **3** Ⓒ something given as a pledge, esp. for the payment of a debt. 담보물. ¶ *give something as* (*a*) ~ 무엇을 담보에 넣다 / *borrow money on the* ~ *of one's house* 집을 담보로 돈을 빌리다. **4** Ⓒ a person who gives security for another. 보증인. ¶ *go* 〔*stand*〕 ~ *for someone* 아무의 보증인이 되다〔아무의 보증을 서다〕. **5** 《usu. *pl.*》 stocks and bonds. (유가) 증권. ¶ *government securities* 국채; 공채(公債) / *a* ~ *firm* 〔*market*〕 증권 회사〔시장〕. [→secure, -ity]

in security, safely. 안전하게.

in security for, in pledge for. …의 담보로.

secy., sec'y secretary.

se·dan [sidǽn] *n.* Ⓒ **1** an automobile for four or more persons. 세단(형 자동차). **2** =sedan chair. [L. *sedeo* sit]

sedan chair [-ˊ ˋ] *n.* a covered chair carried on poles by two men. 의자 가마.

se·date [sidéit] *adj.* serious in mind or manner; calm; quiet. 진지한; 침착한; 조용한; 차분한. ¶ *a ~ dinner party* 조용한 만찬회 / *He is very ~ for a child.* 그는 어린애치고는 매우 침착하다. [L. *sedeo* sit]

se·date·ly [sidéitli] *adv.* in a sedate manner; quietly; calmly. 진지하게; 조용히; 침착하게; 수수하게.

sed·a·tive [sédətiv] *n.* Ⓒ a medicine that lessens pain or excitement. 진정제. ¶ *The ~ helped me to get to sleep.* 이 진정제가 잠자는 데 도움이 되었다. — *adj.* lessening pain or excitement; calming down. 진정시키는; 가라앉히는. ¶ *~ pills* 진정제.

sed·en·tar·y [sédəntèri / -təri] *adj.* **1** (of a person) being in the habit of sitting for a long time. 앉은 채 있는; 앉아 있기를 좋아해 운동을 하지 않는. **2** (of work) required much sitting. 앉아서 하는. ¶ *~ work* 앉아 하는 일; 좌업(坐業). **3** motionless. 정지한; 움직임이 없는. **4** 《zool.》 settled at one spot; not moving from one place to another. 정착성〔정주성〕의; 이주하지 않는. ¶ *~ birds* 정착성 조류; 텃새. [*sedate*]

sedge [sedʒ] *n.* Ⓒ a grasslike plant growing in wet places. 사초속의 각종 식물. ●**sedg·y** [sédʒi] *adj.* [E.]

sed·i·ment [sédəmənt] *n.* Ⓒ the matter setting at the bottom of a liquid. 침전물; 앙금(cf. *deposit*). ¶ *When the river Nile over-flows, it leaves ~ on the surrounding fields.* 나일 강이 홍수로 범람할 때면 주변 평야에 침전물을 남긴다. [→sedate]

sed·i·men·ta·ry [sèdəméntəri] *adj.* **1** of sediment. 침전물의; 퇴적성의. **2** formed from sediment. 침전 작용에 의한. ¶ *~ rocks* 퇴적암.

se·di·tion [sidíʃən] *n.* Ⓤ an action, speech, or piece of writing which arouses resistance against lawful authority. 선동 (행위). ¶ *stir up* 〔*quell*〕 *~* 반란을 선동하다〔가라앉히다〕. [se-, L. *es* go]

se·di·tious [sidíʃəs] *adj.* **1** of sedition; likely to cause sedition. 치안 방해의; 선동의; 반란적인. **2** taking part in sedition. 선동〔폭동〕에 가담한.

se·duce [sidjúːs] *vt.* (P6,13) **1** persuade (someone) to do wrong; tempt to do wrong. …을 꼬드기다〔부추기다〕; 유혹하다. ¶ *~ a girl in some way or other* 어떻게 해서든지 여자의 정조를 빼앗다 / *He was seduced by the offer of a large bribe.* 그는 많은 뇌물 제공에 유혹되었다. **2** lead (someone) away from the right way. …을 타락시키다. ¶ *~ someone from* 〔*out of*〕 *the right way in* 〔*into*〕 *a wrong one* 아무를 바른길에서 잘못된 길로 빠뜨리다. **3** charm; attract. 매혹하다; 끌(어들이)다. ¶ *The store is seducing customers with a special sale.* 가게는 특별 세일로 고객을 끌고 있다. [L. *sē-* apart, *dūco* lead]

se·duc·er [sidjúːsər] *n.* Ⓒ a person who seduces, esp. a man who seduces a woman. 유혹자; 여자 농락꾼; 색마.

se·duc·tion [sidʌ́kʃən] *n.* **1** Ⓤ the act of seducing; the state of being seduced. 유혹; 꾐; 꼬드김; 부추김. ¶ *~ to vice* 악에의 유혹. **2** 《usu. *pl.*》 a quality or nature of someone or something that seduces or attracts. 매력; 꾀는〔꼬드기는〕 것; 끄는 것; 유혹물. ¶ *the seductions of the country life* 전원 생활의 매력.

se·duc·tive [sidʌ́ktiv] *adj.* very attractive; charming; tending to tempt. 사람을 끄는; 유혹〔매혹〕적인; 유혹하는. ¶ *a ~ smile* 매혹적인 미소 / *woo new subscribers by the most ~ advertising* 가장 마음을 끄는 선전으로 새로운 구독자를 권유하다.

se·du·li·ty [sidjúːləti] *n.* diligence; assiduity. 근면; 정려(精勵). [↓]

sed·u·lous [sédʒuləs] *adj.* diligent; hard-working; painstaking. 부지런한; 정성을 다한. ¶ *a ~ student* 부지런한 학생 / *with ~ care* 주도(周到)한 주의를 기울여. ●**sed·u·lous·ly** [-li] *adv.* [L. *sedulus*]

⁑**see**[1] [siː] *v.* (**saw, seen**) *vt.* **1** (P6,13, 22,23,24) perceive (something) by the eye; look at (something). …이 보이다; …을 보다; 눈을 돌리다. ¶ *What do you ~ above the hill?* 산 위에 무엇이 보입니까 / *I saw Tom get off a bus.* 톰이 버스에서 내리는 것을 보았다 / *I saw her dancing last night.* 간밤에 그녀가 춤추는 것을 보았다 / *She was seen to enter the house.* 그녀가 집으로 들어가는 것이 보였다 / 《*prov.*》 *Seeing is believing.* 백문이 불여일견이다. **2** (P6,10,11,12) perceive with the mind; understand. …을 알다; 깨닫다; 이해하다. ¶ *~ the meaning of* …의 의미를 이해하다〔알다〕 / *I ~ what you mean.* 자네가 하고자 하는 말을 알고 있다 / *Now you ~ why I did it.* 내가 왜 그 일을 했는지 이제 아실 테죠 / *I don't ~ how to refuse his offer.* 그의 제의를 어떻게 거절해야 할지 모르겠다 / *He can't ~ a joke.* 그는 농담을 이해하지 못한다. **3** (P6) have experience of; live through. …을 경험〔체험〕하다; …을 알다. ¶ *~ life* 세상을 알다 / *I have never seen such rudeness.* 이러한 무례는 처음이다 / *~ service in the foreign corps* 외국의 군대 생활을 경험하다 / *She has seen a lot of life.* 그녀는 많은 인생을 경험했다 / *He has seen better days.* (지금은 영락했지만) 한때는 좋은 때도 있었다; 그에게도 전성기가 한번은 있었다 / *This coat has seen hard wear.* 이 코트는 거칠게 입어 낡았다. **4** ⓐ (P6) visualize; have the illusion. 눈앞에 떠올려 보다; 마음에 그리다; (꿈 따위에) 보다. ¶ *~ a vision* 몽상하다 / *~ things* 환각을 일으키다 / *I saw my dead father in a dream last might.* 간밤 꿈에 돌아가신 아버지를 보았다. ⓑ (P6,7,18,23) perceive by the imagination; imagine; consider; think. …을 상상하다; 생각하다. ¶ *I ~ things differently now.* 지금은 생각이 다르다 / *He saw it right to do so.* 그는 그렇게 하는 것이 옳다고 생각했

다 / *I can't quite ~ myself doing that.* 내가 그 것을 한다는 것은 상상도 할 수 없다. **5** (P6) ⓐ look at; attend as a spectator. …을 구경〔관람, 시청〕하다. ¶ *~ a play* 관극하다 / *~ a baseball game* 야구 경기를 구경하다. ⓑ visit. 방문하다; 가다. ¶ *~ the sights* 관광하다 / *I am seeing her tomorrow.* 내일 그녀를 찾아 볼 예정이다 / *Have you ever seen New York?* 뉴욕에 가 본 적이 있습니까. **6** (P6) ⓐ meet; come across. 만나다; 보다. ¶ *Very glad to ~ you.* 만나 뵈어 반갑습니다 / *I haven't seen you for ages.* 오랫동안 만나 뵙지 못했습니다 / *I hope to ~ him for a few minutes tomorrow.* 내일 그를 잠시 만났으면 한다. ⓑ come upon; have under one's notice; set eyes on. …을 보다〔만나다, 발견하다〕; 눈에 띄다. **7** (P6) give an interview with; have an interview with; consult. 만나(보)다; 회견〔면담, 면접〕하다; (의사의) 진찰을 받다. ¶ *I'm too busy to ~ you now.* 너무 바빠서 너를 만날 수가 없다 / *Mr. Smith can't ~ anyone today.* 스미스 씨는 오늘 아무도 만날 수가 없다 / *You had better ~ a doctor at once.* 곧 의사의 진찰을 받는 것이 낫겠다. **8** (P7,13) go with; accompany; escort. …을 바래다 주다; 배웅하다. ¶ *He saw her home* 〔*to the bus stop*〕. 그녀를 집〔버스 정류장〕까지 바래다 주었다 / *May I ~ you home?* 댁까지 모시고 갈까요. **9** (P11) take care (that); make sure (that); examine. …하도록 주의〔조처〕하다; …하도록 하다; 잘 조사〔확인〕하다. ¶ *See that the work is done.* 일이 꼭 완성되도록 하시오 / *See* (*that*) *you don't catch your foot.* 돌부리에 채여 넘어지지 않도록 조심해라 / *See* (*that*) *you come home early.* 일찍 귀가하도록 해라 / *Stay and ~ the door locked.* 뒤에 남아 문을 꼭 잠그고 오너라 / *You had better ~ the house before taking it.* 집에 세들기 전에 집을 잘 보아 두는 것이 좋겠다.

— *vi.* **1** (P1,2A) have the power of sight. 보(이)다; 볼 수 있다. ¶ *I tried hard to ~.* 보려고 눈을 집중시켰다 / *Owls can ~ in the dark.* 올빼미는 어둠 속에서 볼 수 있다. **2** (P1) perceive with the mind; understand; become aware. 이해〔납득〕하다; 알다; 깨닫다. ¶ *The whole thing was a mistake, don't you ~?* 모든 것이 잘못이었다네, 안 그런가 / *Oh, I ~ now, he was only joking.* 아 이제 알겠다, 그 사람 그저 농담을 하고 있었던 거야. **3** (P1) take care; find out; learn. 주의〔유의, 조처, 주선〕하다; 알아보다; 조사〔확인〕하다. **4** (P1,3) consider; think things over. 생각하다; 숙고하다. ¶ *Let me ~ —how does that song go.* 가만 있자, 그 노래 가사가 어떻게 나가더라 / *Will you come tomorrow? — Well, I'll ~.* 내일 오겠나. —글쎄, 생각해 보지. [E.]

as I see it, as it seems to me. 내가 보는 바로는.

Do you see? Do you understand? 알겠나.

see about, a) take (something) into consideration; think over. …을 고려하다; 숙고하다. ¶ *I can't give you a decision now, but I will ~ about it.* 지금은 결정할 수 없지만 생각해 보죠. b) take steps to do (something). …의 조처를 취하다; 수단을 강구하다. c) investigate; inquire about. …을 조사하다; 묻다.

see after (=*take care of; look after*) *something.* …을 돌보다; 보살피다.

see *someone* **blowed** 〔**damned**〕 **first,** 《*colloq.*》 absolutely refuse to do what he asks, etc. …의 요구 따위를 딱 잘라 거절하다; 자빡대다.

see eye to eye, be in agreement; agree with each other. 의견이 일치하다.

see fit to *do,* think it right to do. …하는 것이 좋다고 생각하다.

see for *oneself,* find out by oneself. 자신이 직접(알아)보다; 자신이 조사하다. ¶ *If you don't believe me, go and ~ for yourself.* 저를 믿지 못하신다면 직접 가서 알아보시죠.

see into, a) examine; make inquiries into. …을 조사하다. b) have an insight into. …을 꿰뚫어보다.

see much of, meet very often. 자주 만나다.

see nothing of, never meet. 전혀 만나 보지 못하다.

see *something* **of,** meet sometimes. 가끔 만나다.

see *someone* **off,** accompany him until he goes away. …을 바래다 주다; 배웅〔전송〕하다. ¶ *I have been to the airport to ~ my friend off.* 친구를 배웅하기 위해 공항까지 갔다 왔다.

see *someone* **out,** accompany someone to the door. …를 문〔현관〕까지 전송하다.

see *something* **out,** live, stay or wait until the end of something; persist to the end with. …까지 살다; (끝까지) 해내다; 지켜보다. ¶ *~ out a long play* 긴 연극을 끝까지 지켜보다.

see over 〔**around**〕 (=*look over; inspect*) *something.* …을 둘러보다; 시찰하다; 검사하다. ¶ *Let's ~ over the house that we wish to buy.* 사고자 하는 집을 가서 둘러보도록 하자.

see red, 《*colloq.*》 be violently angry; be filled homicidal fury. 격렬히 노하다; 살기 등등하다.

see through, a) understand the real nature or purpose of (something); detect. …의 본질·목적을 꿰뚫어보다; 간파하다; 이해〔파악〕하다. ¶ *~ through someone's motives* 아무의 동기를 간파하다. b) carry out (something) to the end; finish. …을 끝까지 해내다; 끝내다. ¶ *Once you start, you must ~ the task through.* 일단 시작했으면 그 일을 끝까지 해내야 한다.

see *someone* **through,** help (someone) to overcome a difficulty. …을 도와서 어려움을 극복하게 하다. ¶ *I'll ~ you through* (*your troubles*). 어려움에서 헤어나도록 너를 돕겠다.

see to (=*attend to; take care of*) *something.* …에 주의하다; …을 처리하다; 돌보다. ¶ *You go and play, I'll ~ to the dishes.* 설거지는 내가 할 테니 나가 놀아라.

see (to it) that ..., take care that ...; make sure that .... …하도록 주의[유의, 조처, 주선]하다. ¶ *I'll ~ to it that you ~ her at the party.* 파티 석상에서 그녀를 만날 수 있도록 해 주겠네.

see visions, **a**) be a seer. 예언자가 되다. **b**) be an enthusiast. 열광하다.

***see one's way* (*clear*) *to do* (*doing*),** feel disposed to do; manage to do. …하고 싶은 마음이 되다; 어떻게든 하여[그럭저럭] …하다. ¶ *He doesn't ~ his way to giving assistance to them.* 그들을 도와줄 마음이 내키지 않는다.

you see, you know, isn't it? here! 어때, 알겠지[알았지]; 봐라.

You shall see. I will tell it to you afterward.; You will understand someday. 나중에 이야기하지; 곧 알게 돼.

see² [siː] *n.* Ⓒ the position or authority of a bishop; the district over which a bishop has authority. bishop의 지위[권력, 관구] (cf. *diocese, bishopric*). [L. *sedes* seat]

:seed [siːd] *n.* Ⓒ (*pl.* **seed** or **seeds**) **1** ⒸⓊ a small object produced in a plant which itself grows into a young plant. 씨; 종자. ¶ *sow* (*plant*) *~* 씨를 뿌리다[심다] / *Part of every crop is saved for* (*as*) *~.* 모든 곡물의 일부는 종자용으로 따로 떼어둔다. **2** 《Bible》 descendants. 자손. ¶ *the ~ of Abraham* 아브라함의 자손; 유대인. **3** 《*pl.*》 a source or an origin of anything. (사물의) 근원; 발생원; 원인; 불씨. ¶ *the seeds of disease* 질병의 발생원 / *sow the seeds of discontent* 불만의 불씨가 되다. **4** sperm. 정액; 정자.

go* (*run*) *to seed, come to the end of usefulness, prosperity, etc.; become careless of one's appearance. 전성기[한창때]가 지나다; 외양에 무심해지게 되다.

sow the good seed, preach the gospel. 복음을 전하다; 포교하다.

— *vi.* (P1) produce seeds; shed seeds. 씨를 맺다; 씨앗이 생기다; 씨를 떨어뜨리다.

— *vt.* **1** (P6,13) 《*down, with*》 sow seeds over (a garden, etc.). …에 씨를 뿌리다. ¶ *The farmer seeded the ricefield with rice.* 농부는 논에 볍씨를 뿌렸다 / *Dandelions ~ themselves.* 민들레는 스스로 씨를 뿌린다. **2** (P6) remove the seeds from (fruit, etc.). …에서 씨를 제거하다[없애다]. ¶ *~ a melon.* **3** (esp. in tennis) separate good players from poor players to make a tournament more interesting. (테니스 경기 등에서) 강자끼리 초반에 맞붙지 않도록 대진표를 짜다. [E.]

seed·bed [síːdbèd] *n.* Ⓒ **1** a bed of fine soil where seeds are sown. 모판; 묘상(苗床). **2** 《*fig.*》 favorable environment for development. 온상. ¶ *a ~ of revolution* 혁명의 온상.

seed·cake [síːdkèik] *n.* a cake containing caraway seeds. (캐러웨이 씨가 들어 있는) 짙은 향기의 맛이 단 케이크.

seed·er [síːdər] *n.* Ⓒ **1** a person or thing that sows seeds. 씨 뿌리는 사람; 파종기. **2** a device or machine that takes seeds out of fruit, etc. (씨 빼는) 채종기(採種機).

seed·i·ness [síːdinis] *n.* **1** having many seeds. 씨가 많음. **2** 《*colloq.*》 shabbiness of appearance. 외양의 초라함. **3** 《Brit. *colloq.*》 ill health. 불건강.

seed·ing [síːdiŋ] *n.* Ⓤ **1** the act or fact of distributing seeds. 씨뿌림; 파종. **2** 《sports》 the distributing of players in a tournament. 선수 대진표 짜기.

seed·less [síːdlis] *adj.* having no seeds. 씨 없는.

seed·ling [síːdliŋ] *n.* Ⓒ a young plant or tree which has grown from a seed; a tree which is not yet three feet high. 실생(實生); 어린[애] 나무; 묘목.

seed pearl [∠∠] *n.* a very small pearl. 매우 작은 진주(1/4 grain 이하).

seeds·man [síːdzmən] *n.* Ⓒ (*pl.* **-men** [-mən]) a dealer in seed. 씨앗 장수.

seed·time [síːdtàim] *n.* the season for sowing seeds. 씨 뿌릴 때; 파종기.

seed·y [síːdi] *adj.* (**seed·i·er, seed·i·est**) **1** full of seed. 씨가 많은. **2** 《*colloq.*》 shabby; of shabby appearance. 초라한; 초라한 모습의. ¶ *~ clothes* 초라한 옷 / *a ~ old tramp* 초라한 차림의 늙은 부랑자. **3** 《Brit. *colloq.*》 feeling ill; out of sorts. 기분이 언짢은. ¶ *look ~* 기분이 좋지 않아 보이다 / *feel ~* 기분이 언짢다. [E.]

·see·ing [síːiŋ] *n.* **1** Ⓤ the sense of sight. 시각; 시력. **2** ⓊⒸ the act of seeing. 봄. ¶ *record one's seeings and doings* 자신이 보고 들은 것을 기록하다.

Seeing is believing. 《*prov.*》 The best proof of anything is one's own sight or direct knowledge of it. 백문이 불여일견.

— *adj.* able to see. 눈에 보이는; 시각을 가진. ¶ *a ~ man* 분별이 있는 사람.

— *conj.* 《*that*》 since; considering (that). …이므로[하므로]; …을 고려에 넣으면; …한 것을 보면; …한 견지에서. ¶ *Seeing* (*that*) *he is still young, the salary is not a bad one.* 그는 아직 어리므로, 월급이 적은 것은 아니다. [→see¹]

:seek [siːk] *v.* (**sought**) *vt.* **1** (P6,7) 《*out*》 look or search for (something). …을 찾다; (얻으려고) 구하다. ¶ *~ a gold mine* 금광을 찾아다니다 / *~ one's fortune* 행복을 찾다 / *~ the causes of a disease* 병의 원인을 찾다. **2** (P6) get or gain (help, advice, etc.); ask for. (도움·충고 따위)를 구하다; 청하다; 추구하다. ¶ *He seeks your advice.* 그는 자네의 충고를 청하고 있다. **3** (P8) try to do (something); attempt. …하려고 애쓰다[노력하다]. ¶ *For many years they sought to overcome the difficulty.* 여러 해에 걸쳐 그들은 그 곤란을 이겨 내려고 노력했다. **4** (P6) 《*poet.*》 go to (a place, etc.); visit. …로 가다. ¶ *~ a place to rest* 쉴 수 있는 곳으로 가다.

— *vi.* (P1,3) 《*after, for*》 make a search; try to find or obtain. 찾다; 구하다; 수색하다.

¶ *He is seeking after wealth and power.* 그는 부와 권력을 추구하고 있다. [E.]

be much to seek, be very rarely found. 극히 드물다.

be not far to seek, 《*lit.*》 be easy to find; be obvious. 가까운 곳에 있다; 명백하다.

be sought after, be desired or in demand. 요망〔요구〕되고 있다; 수요가 있다.

be to seek, 《*arch.*》 be lacking (in). 결여되어 있다; 없다. ¶ *be yet to* ～ 아직 안 보이다; 결여되어 있다.

seek** someone's **life, plot to kill someone. …을 죽이려고 꾀하다.

seek out, find out; look for carefully. 찾아내다; 열심히 찾다.

***seek through** a place, etc.,* examine a place, etc. thoroughly. …을 샅샅이 찾다.

seek·er [síːkər] *n.* Ⓒ a person who tries to find something or to learn something; a person who tries to obtain something. 찾는 사람; 수색자; 추구〔탐구〕자. ¶ *a scientific* ～ *of the truth* 진리를 과학적으로 추구하는 사람 / *a* ～ *after pleasure* 쾌락을 추구하는 사람.

:seem [siːm] *vi.* (P4,5) **1** appear to be; look like. …처럼 보이다; …하게 생각되다; …(인 것) 같다. ¶ *He seems (to be) deaf.* 그는 귀가 먹은 것 같다 / *It seems good to me to do so.* 그렇게 하는 것이 내게 좋을 것 같다 / *She seems to have been ill.* 그녀는 병을 앓고 있었던 것 같다 / *I* ～ *to hear someone calling.* 누가 부르는 소리가 들리는 것 같다. **2** appear to be true 〔probable〕; it appears. 진실〔사실〕인 것 같다; 일어날〔있을〕 것 같다. ¶ *It seems to me that you told a lie.* 아무래도 네가 거짓말을 한 것 같다 / *It seems that the weather is improving.* 날씨가 좋아질 것 같다 / *It seems likely to rain.* 아무래도 비가 올 것 같다. [N. → (same)]

it should 〔would〕 seem, it seems; probably it is. 아무래도 …인 것 같다. ¶ *It would* ～ *that he has stolen a large sum of money.* 아무래도 그가 큰 돈을 훔친 것 같습니다만.

seem·ing [síːmiŋ] *adj.* appearing to be; apparent. 외견상〔표면상〕의; 겉으로만의; 그럴듯한. ¶ *her* ～ *friendship* 그녀의 가장된 우정. — *n.* the outward appearance. 외견; 겉모양; 표면; 가장.

seem·ing·ly [síːmiŋli] *adv.* in outward appearance; apparently. 일견한 바로는; 외관으로; 표면상. ¶ ～ *insoluble problems* 일견 해결할 수 있을 것 같지 않은 문제 / *He was* ～ *satisfied with the result.* 그는 표면적으로는 결과에 만족했다 / *The house was* ～ *empty.* 그 집은 언뜻 보기에는 비어 있었다.

seem·li·ness [síːmlinis] *n.* Ⓤ the quality of being seemly; fitness; suitability; propriety. 예의에 맞음; 점잖음; 어울림; 적당함.

seem·ly [síːmli] *adj.* (**-li·er, -li·est**) suitable; becoming; proper; decent. 적당한; 어울리는; 점잖은. ¶ ～ *behavior.*

:seen [siːn] *v.* pp. of **see**[1].

seep [siːp] *vi.* (P2A,3) (of liquid) leak through small holes slowly and gradually; ooze. 새다; 스며나오다. ¶ *Water seeped into the basement.* 물이 지하실로 스며들었다. [O.E. *sipian* soak]

seep·age [síːpidʒ] *n.* Ⓤ the act or process of seeping. (물·기름 따위의) 스며나옴; 삼출; 누출.

se·er [síːər] *n.* Ⓒ a person who foretells the future; a prophet. 예언자; 선각자. [→ see[1]]

seer·suck·er [síərsʌ̀kər] *n.* Ⓤ a fabric, usu. striped cotton with alternate stripes crinkled in the weaving. 시어서커《무명 날실로 번갈아 줄무늬를 넣은 따위 직물》.

see·saw [síːsɔ̀ː] *n.* Ⓒ a board balanced at the middle, while the ends move up and down; Ⓤ a game of children played on such a board; ⓊⒸ any up-and-down movement. 시소판; 시소(놀이); 상하동(上下動). — *vi.* (P1) ride on a seesaw; move up and down. 시소를 타다; 아래위로 움직이다; 동요하다. — *adj.* moving up and down or back and forth. 아래위로 움직이는; 올라갔다 내려갔다 하는; 동요하는. — *adv.* up and down. 아래위로; 상하로. [saw[1]]

seethe [siːð] *vi., vt.* (P1,2A,3;6) **1** boil; stew. 끓다; 끓어오르다; …을 끓이다. **2** surge or foam as if boiling. 소용돌이치다; 들끓다. ¶ *The seething waters carried the light boat down the falls.* 소용돌이치는 물결이 작은 보트를 폭포 아래로 떨어뜨렸다. **3** 《*with*》 get violently agitated or excited. 법석이다; 떠들썩해지다. ¶ *The streets were seething with demonstrators.* 거리는 시위대로 시끄러웠다. [E.]

seg·ment [ségmənt] *n.* Ⓒ **1** a piece or part cut off, marked off, or broken off; a division; a section. (분할·구분되어 있는) 부분; 구분; 층; 조각. ¶ *a* ～ *of an orange* 귤한 조각〔쪽〕 / *large segments of the people* 넓은 계층에 걸친 사람들. **2** 《geom.》 the part of a circle included between an arc and its chord. (원·구에서 절단된) 한 부분; 궁형; 활꼴. — [*also* segmént] *vt., vi.* divide or be divided into segments. 부분으로 가르다〔갈라지다〕; 분할하다〔되다〕. ● **seg·men·tal** [segméntəl] *adj.* [→section]

seg·men·ta·tion [sègməntéiʃən] *n.* Ⓤ **1** the act of dividing into segments; the state of being divided into segments. 분열; 절단; 구분; 분할. **2** 《biol.》 the act of forming many cells from a single cell. 세포 분열.

seg·re·gate [ségrigèit] *vt., vi.* (P6;1) separate (someone) from others; keep apart; become separated; isolate. (…을) 분리하다; 격리하다〔되다〕. ¶ ～ *patients with infectious diseases* 전염병 환자를 격리시키다 / ～ *hardened criminals* 상습범을 (사회로부터) 격리하다. [se-, L. *grex* flock]

seg·re·ga·tion [sègrigéiʃən] *n.* Ⓤ the

act of segregating; the state of being segregated; isolation; a separation of one race from other races. 분리; 격리; 인종적 구별; 인종 차별. ¶ ~ *between races* 인종 간 (특히 백인과 흑인)의 분리 / *racial* ~ 인종 차별(opp. integration).

sei·gneur, -gnior [seinjə́ːr] *n.* Ⓒ《hist.》a feudal lord or landowner. 봉건 영주〔군주〕. [→senior]

Seine [sein], **the** *n.* a river which flows through Paris and into the English Channel. 센 강.

seine [sein] *n.* Ⓒ a large fishingnet which hangs straight down in the water. 후릿그물; 트롤망. — *vi., vt.* (P1;6) fish with a seine; catch (fish) with a seine. 후릿그물로〔저인망으로〕 고기를 잡다. [Gk. *sagēnē*]

seis·mic [sáizmik] *adj.* of or caused by an earthquake. 지진의; 지진에 의해 생기는. ¶ *the ~ area* 〔*region*〕 지진대(帶)〔지역〕 / *the ~ center* 〔*focus*〕 진원지. [Gk. *sēio* shake]

seis·mo·gram [sáizməgræ̀m] *n.* Ⓒ a record which is made by a seismograph. (지진계가 그린) 진동도(震動圖). [↑]

seis·mo·graph [sáizməgræ̀f, -grɑ̀ːf] *n.* Ⓒ an instrument which registers the vibrations of earthquakes. 진동계; 지진계.

seis·mo·log·i·cal [sàizməládʒikəl / -lɔ́dʒ-] *adj.* of seismology. 지진학의.

seis·mol·o·gist [saizmálədʒist / saizmɔ́l-] *n.* Ⓒ a person who is especially trained in the science of earthquakes. 지진학자.

seis·mol·o·gy [saizmálədʒi / -mɔ́l-] *n.* Ⓤ the science or study of earthquakes. 지진학.

:seize [siːz] *vt.* (P6,13) **1** ⓐ take hold of suddenly; grasp. …을 (붙)잡다; 붙들다; 꽉〔움켜〕 쥐다. ¶ ~ *a rope* 밧줄을 꼭 붙들다 / ~ *someone by the arm* 〔*throat*〕 아무의 팔을 잡다〔멱살을 움켜쥐다〕 / 《*fig.*》 ~ *an opportunity* 기회를 잡다 / *In terror she seized his arm.* 공포로 그녀는 그의 팔을 꽉 잡았다. ⓑ catch (something) by force; capture. (힘으로) 붙잡다; 체포하다. ¶ *The robbers were seized by the police.* 강도들은 경찰에 잡혔다. **2** grasp with the mind; understand; see. (속으로) 파악하다; 이해하다; 알다. ¶ *I can't quite ~ your meaning.* 무슨 말인지 도무지 모르겠네. **3** take possession of (something) by force or by authority. …을 빼앗다; 강탈하다; 압수〔몰수〕하다. ¶ ~ *the enemy's castle* 적의 성채를 빼앗다 / ~ *enemy ships* 적선을 나포하다.

— *vi.* (P3) 《*on, upon*》 grasp; hold; catch. (붙)잡다. [F. *saisir*]

be seized with, be suddenly attacked by (a disease, terror, pity, etc.). …에 사로잡히다; (병에) 걸리다.

seize hold of (=*grasp*) *something.* …을 (붙)잡다; 꽉〔움켜〕 쥐다.

seize on 〔***upon***〕, catch hold of (something) suddenly; take possession of. …을 꽉(붙) 잡다; …을 손에 넣다.

seize up 《of a machine》 stop (e.g. when overheated). (기계가 과열되었을 때 따위) 멈추다; 서우다.

sei·zure [síːʒər] *n.* **1** ⓊⒸ the act of seizing; the state of being seized; capture. (붙)잡기; 강탈; 포착; 강점; 압류; 압수. ¶ *the student ~ of campus buildings* 학생에 의한 대학 교사의 점거. **2** Ⓒ a sudden attack of a disease, esp. a stroke. (병 따위의) 발작; (특히) 뇌일혈. ¶ *You had a kind of ~.* 일종의 발작이었네. [↑]

:sel·dom [séldəm] *adv.* not often; rarely. 드물게; 좀처럼 …않다. ¶ *She is ~ ill.* 좀처럼 병이 나지 않는다 / *He ~ complains.* 그는 좀처럼 불평하지 않는다 / *I ~ go to the movies.* 좀처럼 영화 구경을 가지 않는다. [E.]

not seldom, often. 자주; 종종; 왕왕. ¶ *It not ~ happens that ....* …은 자주 일어나는〔있는〕 일이다.

seldom or never =***seldom if ever*** =***very seldom,*** hardly ever. 좀처럼 …않다〔없다〕. ¶ *She ~ or never expresses her opinion.* 그녀가 의견을 말하는 일은 좀처럼 없다 / *He ~ if ever smokes.* 그는 좀처럼 담배를 피우지 않는다 / *She attends our meeting very ~.* 그녀는 좀처럼 우리 모임에 출석하지 않는다.

:se·lect [silékt] *vt.* (P6) pick out or choose carefully. …을 고르다; 뽑다; 선택〔선발〕하다. ¶ ~ *a hat to wear in the sun* 햇볕막이로 쓸 모자를 고르다 / *You must ~ good books for your children.* 당신 아이들에게 좋은 책을 골라주어야 한다.

— *adj.* **1** especially or carefully chosen as the best; choicest; of best quality. 가려〔추려〕낸; 정선한; 극상의; 일류의. ¶ ~ *musicians* 일류의 음악가들 / *a few ~ friends* 몇몇 훌륭한 친구들 / *The captain needs a ~ crew for this dangerous job.* 선장은 이 위험한 일에 선정된 선원들을 필요로 하고 있다. **2** (of a society, club, etc.) not easy to join; exclusive. (조건 따위가) 까다로운; 몹시 가리는; 비개방적인. ¶ *a ~ club* 입회 조건이 까다로운 클럽 / *be ~ in one's books* 책의 선택이 까다롭다 / *She is very ~ in the people she invites.* 그녀는 초청 손님에게 몹시 까다롭다. [se-, L. *lego* pick]

select committee [⌐–⌐–] *n.* a small parliamentary committee for a special inquiry. (국회의) 특별 위원회(=special committee).

se·lect·ed [siléktid] *adj.* chosen or picked out as best. 가려〔추려〕낸; 뽑힌; 선택된; 선발된. [*select*]

***se·lec·tion** [silékʃən] *n.* **1** Ⓤ the act of selecting; the state of being selected; choice. 뽑음; 뽑힘; 선택; 선발; 선정. ¶ *a ~ of friends* 친구의 선택 / *vocational ~* 직업의 선택 / *make a ~* 〔*selections*〕 …에서 선택하다 / *Her ~ of a hat took a long time.* 그녀의 모자 고르기에 오랜 시간이 걸렸다. **2** Ⓒ a person, thing or group selected. 가려낸

〔골라낸, 뽑아낸〕 것; 선택물; 정선품; 발췌. ¶ *read selections from Shakespeare* 셰익스피어 선집을 읽다. **3** Ⓤ 《biol.》 the process of selecting for the purpose of survival which is seen in animals and plants. 선택. ¶ *natural* ~ 자연 선택〔도태〕.

se·lec·tive [siléktiv] *adj.* of selection; having the power to choose; selecting. 선택의〔하는〕; 도태하는. ¶ *a* ~ *reader* 좋은 읽을거리를 골라 읽는 사람 / *a* ~ *translation* 초역(抄譯) / ~ *service* 의무 병역.

se·lect·man [siléktmən] *n.* Ⓒ (*pl.* **-men** [-mən]) 《U.S.》 a member of a board of town officials in New England, chosen each year to manage public affairs. (미국 New England 각 주의) 도시 행정 위원.

:self [self] *n.* (*pl.* **selves**) **1** Ⓒ ⓐ one's own personality. 자기; 자신; 자아. ¶ *one's own* ~ 자기〔나〕 자신 / *his former* ~ 이전의 그(사람) / *my humble* ~ 소생; 불초《겸손의 말》/ *a second* 〔*other*〕 ~ 제2의 나; 또 하나의 자기; 둘도 없는 친구 / *a clear recognition of the* ~ 명확한 자기 인식. ⓑ individuality; nature; character. 개성; 특질; 본성; 성격의 일면. ¶ *my better* ~ 나의 좋은 면; 나의 양심 / *one's own frank* ~ 본디 가지고 있는 솔직한 성격 / *show* 〔*reveal*〕 *one's real* 〔*true*〕 ~ 본성을 드러내다. **2** Ⓤ personal interest or advantage. 사리; 이기심. ¶ *control the* ~ 자제하다 / *put* ~ *first* 사리를 앞세우다; 자기 본위로 하다 / *put public service before* ~ 사익보다 공익을 우선하다. **3** Ⓒ the essential quality or nature of anything. 본질. **4** ⓊⒸ 《comm.; *vulg.*》 myself; yourself; himself; herself. 본인. ¶ *a check drawn to* ~ 본인 앞으로 발행한 수표 / *your good selves* 귀사 / *pay to* ~ 서명인지급《수표의 문구》. [E.]

self- [self-] *pref.* of, by, to, in or for oneself. '자기, 스스로'의 뜻. [E.]

self-a·ban·doned [sélfəbǽndənd] *adj.* giving oneself up to bad ways. 자포 자기의. [*self-*]

self-a·ban·don·ment [sélfəbǽndənmənt] *n.* Ⓤ the state or condition of being self-abandoned. 자포 자기.

self-a·base·ment [sélfəbéismənt] *n.* Ⓤ the act of degrading or humbling oneself, as in rank, position, etc. 겸손; 자기를 낮춤.

self-ab·sorbed [sélfəbsɔ́ːrbd, -æb-, -zɔ́ːrbd] *adj.* giving one's whole mind, attention, etc. to oneself or to one's interests. 자기 생각에 잠긴; 자기 일에 몰두〔열중〕해 있는.

self-ab·sorp·tion [sélfəbsɔ́ːrpʃən, -zɔ́ːrp-] *n.* Ⓤ the state of being self-absorbed. 자기 몰두; 열중.

self-a·buse [sélfəbjúːs] *n.* Ⓤ **1** abuse of oneself. 자기 비난. **2** masturbation. 수음.

self-ac·cu·sa·tion [sélfækjuzéiʃən] *n.* Ⓤ the act of accusing oneself. 자책.

self-act·ing [séifǽktiŋ] *adj.* acting by itself; automatic. 자동(식)의.

self-ad·just·ing [séifədʒʌ́stiŋ] *adj.* able to adjust itself automatically. 자동 조절〔조정〕의.

self-as·sert·ing [sélfəsə́ːrtiŋ] *adj.* insisting on one's own claims, opinions, importance, etc. 자기를 주장하는; 주제넘은; 오만한.

self-as·ser·tion [sélfəsə́ːrʃən] *n.* Ⓤ the act of insisting on one's own claims, opinions, importance, etc. 자기 주장; 주제넘게 나서기.

self-as·ser·tive [sélfəsə́ːrtiv] *adj.* =self-asserting.

self-as·sur·ance [sélfəʃúərəns] *n.* Ⓤ confidence in oneself; self-confidence. 자신(自信); 자기 과신.

self-cen·tered, 《Brit.》 **-tred** [sélfséntərd] *adj.* interested only in one's own affairs; selfish. 자기 본위〔중심〕의; 이기적인. ¶ ~ *people* 자기 중심적인 사람들.

self-col·ored, 《Brit.》 **-oured** [sélfkʌ́lərd] *adj.* **1** of a single color. 단색의. **2** of the natural color. 자연색의.

self-com·mand [sélfkəmǽnd, -mɑ́ːnd] *n.* Ⓤ control of one's own emotions and actions; self-control. 극기; 자제; 침착.

self-com·pla·cence [sélfkəmpléisns], **-cen·cy** [-snsi] *n.* Ⓤ the state of being satisfied with oneself. 자기 만족.

self-com·pla·cent [sélfkəmpléisnt] *adj.* satisfied or excessively pleased with oneself. 자기 만족의; 독선적인.

self-con·ceit [sélfkənsíːt] *n.* Ⓤ too much pride in one's own abilities; vanity. 자부〔자만〕심; 허영심.

self-con·ceit·ed [sélfkənsíːtid] *adj.* having too much self-conceit; vain. 자부심이 강한; 허영의.

***self-con·fi·dence** [sélfkɑ́nfədəns / -kɔ́n-] *n.* Ⓤ belief in one's own self and ability. 자신; 자기 과신. ¶ *gain* ~ 자신을 얻다.

self-con·fi·dent [sélfkɑ́nfədənt / -kɔ́n-] *adj.* believing in oneself and one's own ability. 자신이 강한; 자기를 과신하는.

self-con·scious [sélfkɑ́nʃəs / -kɔ́n-] *adj.* too much aware of one's appearance, manners, actions, etc. esp. in the presence of others; shy. 자의식이 강한; 내성적인; 남을 의식하는; 수줍어하는. ● **self-con·scious·ness** [-nis] *n.*

self-con·sis·tent [sélfkənsístənt] *adj.* consistent with oneself. 시종(始終) 일관한; 조리가 서는; (앞뒤가) 동이 닿는.

self-con·tained [sélfkəntéind] *adj.* **1** ⓐ (of a person) hardly ever talking; reserved. 말수가 적은; 말이 없는; 마음을 터놓지 않는. ⓑ having or showing self-control. 자제하고〔자제력이〕 있는. **2** (of a thing) having all that is necessary; independent of others; complete in itself. 필요한 것이 모두 갖춰진; 자급 자족적인; 독립된; 그것만으로

(도) 완비된. ¶ *a ~ apartment* 독립식의 아파트 / *a ~ community* (진료소·식당·각종 가게 따위가) 모두 완비된 공동체 / *a ~ and sufficient economy* 자급 자족의 경제.

self-con·tra·dic·tion [sélfkɑ̀ntrədíkʃən / -kɔ̀n-] *n.* ⓊⒸ the act or fact of contradicting oneself or itself. 자기 모순; 자가 당착.

self-con·tra·dic·to·ry [sélfkɑ̀ntrədíktəri / -kɔ̀n-] *adj.* contradicting oneself or itself; not consistent. 자기 모순의.

self-con·trol [sélfkəntróul] *n.* Ⓤ control of one's own acts, desires, emotions, feelings, etc. 극기; 자제(심). ¶ *lose one's ~* 자제심을 잃다.

self-de·fense, 《Brit.》 **-de·fence** [sélfdiféns] *n.* Ⓤ the act of protecting one's own person, property, reputation, rights, etc. 자위; 정당 방위.

in self-defense, (not by way of attack but) in order to defend oneself. 정당 방위를 위해. ¶ *fire in ~* 자위를 위해 발포하다.

the (***manly***) ***art of self-defense,*** boxing. 남자다운 호신술; 권투.

***self-de·ni·al** [sélfdináiəl] *n.* Ⓤ refusal to enjoy oneself, often for the benefit of others; self-sacrifice. 자기 부정; 극기; 무사(無私); 자기 희생.

self-de·ny·ing [sélfdináiiŋ] *adj.* of self-denial; sacrificing oneself; unselfish. 극기의; 무사(無私)의; 헌신적인.

self-de·struc·tion [sélfdistrʌ́kʃən] *n.* Ⓤ the destruction of oneself or itself; self-ruin; suicide. 자멸; 자살.

self-de·ter·mi·na·tion [sélfditə̀ːrminéiʃən] *n.* Ⓤ **1** the act of making decisions by oneself. 자기 결정〔결단〕. **2** (of a nation) the act of people making decisions on the form of government without being influenced by other nations. 민족 자결.

self-de·vo·tion [sélfdivóuʃən] *n.* Ⓤ self-sacrifice; the act of giving up oneself to another person or other people. 자기 희생; 헌신.

self-dis·ci·pline [sélfdísəplin] *n.* Ⓤ the act of training oneself for the purpose of improving of one's abilities. 자기 훈련〔수양〕.

self-ed·u·cat·ed [sélfédʒukèitid] *adj.* educated by one's own efforts without going to school or being taught by a teacher; self-taught. 독학의. ¶ *a ~ man* 독학한 사람.

self-es·teem [sélfestíːm] *n.* Ⓤ self-respect; too high an opinion of oneself. 자존(自尊); 자부심. ¶ *bruise someone's ~ rudely* 아무의 자존심을 몹시 상하게 하다.

self-ev·i·dent [sélfévədənt] *adj.* clear without any additional proof. 자명한; 뻔한. ¶ *a ~ axiom* 자명한 원리.

self-ex·am·i·na·tion [sélfigzæ̀minéiʃən] *n.* Ⓤ examination into one's own conduct, manners, motives, etc. 자기 검토; 반성; 자성(自省).

self-ex·ist·ent [sélfigzístənt] *adj.* having an independent existence. 독립적으로 존재하는; 독립〔자립〕의.

self-ex·plan·a·to·ry [sélfiksplǽnətɔ̀ːri / -təri] *adj.* clear in itself; self-evident. 자명한; 설명을 필요로 하지 않는.

self-ex·pres·sion [sélfikspréʃən] *n.* Ⓤ the expression of one's personality. 자기 표현〔표출〕.

self-fill·ing [sélffíliŋ] *adj.* able to fill itself. 자동 주입식의.

self-gov·ern·ing [sélfgʌ́vərniŋ] *adj.* **1** governing itself; independent. 자치의; 자립의. **2** having self-control. 자제의; 극기의.

self-gov·ern·ment [sélfgʌ́vərnmənt, -ərmənt] *n.* Ⓤ **1** government of a nation by its own people. 자치(cf. *autonomy*). **2** self-control. 자제; 극기.

self-help [sélfhélp] *n.* Ⓤ the act of doing something without help or guidance from others. 자조(自助); 자립; 자구(自救)(행위); 독립 독행(獨立獨行).

self-im·por·tance [sélfimpɔ́ːrtəns] *n.* Ⓤ the state of having or showing too much pride in oneself. 자존; 자부(심); 젠 체함.

self-im·por·tant [sélfimpɔ́ːrtənt] *adj.* having or showing too much pride in oneself. 자존의 마음이 강한; 젠 체하는.

self-im·posed [sélfimpóuzd] *adj.* (of a task, etc.) imposed on oneself by oneself; self-chosen. 스스로 과한; 자진해서 하는.

self-im·prove·ment [sélfimprúːvmənt] *n.* Ⓤ improvement of one's mind, etc. by one's own efforts. (스스로의 노력에 의한) 자기 개선; 수양; 도야.

self-in·dul·gence [sélfindʌ́ldʒəns] *n.* Ⓤ the act of giving way to one's own desires, passions, etc.; the act of paying little attention to others' happiness, interests, etc. 제멋대로 굴기; 방종.

self-in·dul·gent [sélfindʌ́ldʒənt] *adj.* characterized by self-indulgence. 제멋대로 구는; 방종한.

self-in·ter·est [sélfíntərist] *n.* Ⓤ one's own interest or welfare; the act of thinking of one's own welfare; selfishness. 사리(私利); 사욕; 이기주의.

***self·ish** [sélfiʃ] *adj.* chiefly thinking of one's own interests, wishes, etc. 저밖에 모르는; 자기 본위의; 이기주의의. ¶ *A ~ person always puts his own interests first.* 이기주의의 사람은 언제나 제 이익만을 앞세운다.

self·ish·ly [sélfiʃli] *adv.* in a selfish manner. 이기적으로.

self·ish·ness [sélfiʃnis] *n.* Ⓤ the state or quality of being selfish; too great care for oneself; too little care for others. 이기주의; 저만 생각함.

self·less [sélflis] *adj.* not thinking of one's own profits; sacrificing one's own interests; unselfish. 사리(私利)를 생각지 않는;

무사 무욕(無私無慾)의.

self-love [sélflʌ́v] *n.* Ⓤ instinctive love of oneself; selfishness. (본능적인) 자애(自愛); 이기심〔주의〕.

self-made [sélfméid] *adj.* having succeeded without others' help; made by one's own ability or efforts. 자력으로 입신한; 제힘으로 만든. ¶ *a ~ man* 자력으로 성공한 사람; 자수 성가한 사람.

self-mas·ter·y [sèlfmǽstəri, -mɑ́ːs-] *n.* Ⓤ self-control; self-command; self-possession. 극기; 자제; 침착.

self-mur·der [sélfmə́ːrdər] *n.* Ⓤ the act of killing oneself; suicide. 자살.

self-o·pin·ion·at·ed [sèlfəpínjənèitid] *adj.* thinking or insisting too much that one is right. 자부심이 강한; 고집이 센; 완고한.

self-pit·y [sélfpíti] *n.* Ⓤ pity for oneself. 자기 연민.

self-por·trait [sélfpɔ́ːrtrit, sèlfpɔ́ːrtreit] *n.* Ⓒ a portrait of oneself painted, etc. by oneself. 자화상.

self-pos·sessed [sélfpəzést] *adj.* (of the mind or behavior) being or showing calm; not excited. (감정·행동을) 억제하는; 냉정한; 침착한.

self-pos·ses·sion [sélfpəzéʃən] *n.* Ⓤ the act or state of controlling one's mind, feelings, behavior, etc. 감정〔행동〕의 억제; 냉정; 침착. ¶ *a woman of great ~* 매우 침착한 여자.

self-pres·er·va·tion [sélfprèzərvéiʃən] *n.* Ⓤ the act of keeping oneself from danger, harm, destruction, etc.; the instinctive desire to do so. 자기 보존; 자위 (본능).

self-re·al·i·za·tion [sélfrìːəlizéiʃən] *n.* Ⓤ realization or development of one's abilities. 자기 (능력의) 실현; 자기 계발.

self-re·cord·ing [sélfrikɔ́ːrdiŋ] *adj.* making a record automatically. 자동 기록(식)의.

self-re·gard [sélfrigɑ́ːrd] *n.* Ⓤ **1** love of oneself; the act of paying attention to one's own interests. 자애(自愛); 이기(심). **2** self-respect; respect for oneself. 자존(심).

self-re·li·ance [sélfriláiəns] *n.* Ⓤ dependence on one's own abilities, etc. 자력〔자기〕 의존; 자신.

self-re·li·ant [sélfriláiənt] *adj.* having or showing self-reliance. 자기 힘을 믿는; 독립 독행(獨行)의.

self-re·proach [sélfripróutʃ] *n.* Ⓤ blame of oneself by one's conscience. 자책(自責); 양심의 가책; 후회.

self-re·spect [sélfrispékt] *n.* Ⓤ pride in oneself; proper respect for oneself. 자존(심). ¶ *lose one's ~* 자존심을 잃다.

self-re·spect·ing [sélfrispéktiŋ] *adj.* having or showing self-respect. 자존심이 있는.

self-re·straint [sélfristréint] *n.* Ⓤ self-control; the act of controlling one's desires or passions by one's own will. 자제; 극기. ¶ *the spirit of ~* 극기심.

self-right·eous [sélfráitʃəs] *adj.* thinking that one's own opinion or thought is superior to others'. 독선적인.

self-sac·ri·fice [sélfsǽkrəfàis] *n.* Ⓤ sacrifice of one's personal desires, life, etc. for the sake of others or one's duty. 자기 희생; 헌신.

self·same [sélfsèim] *adj.* 《*emph.*》 the very same; identical. 아주 (똑)같은; 동일한. ¶ *She is dressed in the ~ clothes as yesterday.* 그녀는 어제와 똑같은 옷을 입고 있다.

self-sat·is·fac·tion [sélfsæ̀tisfǽkʃən] *n.* Ⓤ satisfaction or contentment with oneself. 자기 만족; 독선.

self-sat·is·fied [sélfsǽtisfàid] *adj.* satisfied or contented with oneself; complacent; vain. 자기 만족의; 독선의.

self-seek·er [sélfsíːkər] *n.* Ⓒ a selfish person; a person who always thinks about his own interests. 자기 본위의 사람; 이기주의인 사람.

self-seek·ing [sélfsíːkiŋ] *adj.* selfish. 이기주의의; 자기 본위의. —*n.* Ⓤ selfishness. 이기주의; 자기 본위.

self-serv·ice [sélfsə́ːrvis] *n.* Ⓤ the act of serving oneself in a restaurant, a store, etc. (식당·가게 등에서의) 셀프서비스; 자급식(自給式).

self-start·er [sélfstɑ́ːrtər] *n.* Ⓒ an electric motor to start an engine automatically. (자동차·기계 따위의) 셀프스타터; 자동 시동기.

self-styled [sélfstáild] *adj.* using a name which one has given oneself; named by oneself. 자칭의; 자임의. ¶ *a ~ patriot* 자칭 애국자.

self-suf·fi·cien·cy [sélfsəfíʃənsi] *n.* Ⓤ the state of being self-sufficient. 자급 자족; 자부; 지나친 자신. ¶ *foodstuff ~* 식량의 자급 자족.

self-suf·fi·cient [sélfsəfíʃənt] *adj.* **1** able to supply one's needs by oneself. 자족할 수 있는; 자급 자족의. **2** too proud of oneself; overconfident. 자부심이 강한; 자신이 지나치게 강한.

self-sup·port·ing [sélfsəpɔ́ːrtiŋ] *adj.* earning money for one's own living expenses, etc.; getting along without help from others. 자활하는; 자급하는; 자립하는.

self-sus·tain·ing [sélfsəstéiniŋ] *adj.* self-supporting; needing no outside help. 자활〔자급〕의; 독립의.

self-taught [sélftɔ́ːt] *adj.* taught by one's own efforts and without any help from others; self-educated. 독학의; 독습의. ¶ *~ typing* 혼자 배운 타자 기술.

self-will [sélfwíl] *n.* Ⓤ insistence that one should have one's own way; the state of not being obedient. 제멋대로임; 완고; 외고집.

self-willed [sélfwíld] *adj.* being inclined to have one's own way; showing self-will;

stubborn. 제멋대로 구는; 외고집의.

self-wind·ing [sélfwáindiŋ] *adj.* (of a clock, a watch, etc.) winding itself by a mechanism; wound automatically. (시계 태엽이) 자동적으로 감기는.

:sell [sel] *v.* (**sold**) *vt.* **1** (P6,7,13,14) give (something) in exchange for money. (돈을 받고) 팔다; 처분〔매도, 매각〕하다(opp. buy). ¶ ~ *something at a loss* 〔*discount*〕 …을 손해를 보고〔할인하여〕 팔다 / *He sold the watch at a good price.* 시계를 좋은 값에 팔았다 / *He sold the book for 3,000 won.* 그는 책을 3천 원에 팔았다 / *Will you ~ me your car?* 자네 차를 내게 팔지 않으려나. **2** (P6) deal in; be engaged in the sale of. 팔(고 있)다; …장사를 하고 있다. ¶ *They ~ shoes at the store.* 저 가게에서는 구두를 팔고 있다 / *Do you ~ postage stamps?* 우표를 파십니까 / *Do you ~ monthly magazines?* (점원에게) 월간 잡지 있습니까. **3** (P6) help in the sale of; cause to be sold. 팔리게 하다. ¶ *Good advertising will ~ goods.* 훌륭한 광고는 상품이 잘 팔리게 한다. **4** (P6) 《*fig.*》 give up in return for a bribe; be a traitor; break one's faith with. (사리·사욕 따위를 위해) 양심·명예를 팔다; 배반〔배신〕하다. ¶ ~ *one's honor* 〔*self-respect*〕 명예를〔자존심을〕 팔다 / ~ *one's country* 조국을 팔다 / ~ *a match* 짬짜미 시합을 하다 / ~ *one's back* (레슬링에서) 뇌물을 받고 일부러 져주다 / ~ *her body cheaply* 육체를 싸게 팔다. **5** (P6) 《usu. in *passive*》 《*sl.*》 play a trick upon; cheat. 속이다. ¶ *be sold over a bargain* 흥정에서 감쪽같이 속아 넘어가다. **6** (P6) 《*sl.*》 convince (someone) of; advertise the merits of. (아무에게) 납득시키다; 받아들이게 하다; 선전하다. ¶ ~ *an idea to the public* 생각을 대중에게 선전하다 / *To succeed you have to ~ yourself.* 성공하기 위해서는 자신을 선전해야 한다.
— *vi.* (P1) find buyers; be sold. 팔리다. ¶ ~ *like wildfire* 날개 돋친 듯이 팔리다 / *This dictionary sells well.* 이 사전은 잘 팔린다 / *Oranges ~ at a high price this year.* 올해엔 귤이 비싸다.

be sold on, 《U.S.》 be absorbed in; be enthusiastic about. …에 열중해 있다.

sell someone a pup, 《*sl.*》 cheat him; give him a bad bargain. 아무를 속이다; 거래에서 아무를 속이다.

sell one's life dear(ly), die after having inflicted a great loss on the enemy. 될 수 있는 한 많은 적을 죽이고 죽다.

sell off, sell all the stock of (goods, etc.) cheaply. 싼 값에 …을 다 팔아〔처분해〕 버리다.

sell out, **a**) sell all the stock of (goods, etc.). …을 모두 팔아치우다. **b**) 《U.S.》 betray by a secret bargain. 몰래 배반하다.

sell up, 《Brit.》 sell all a debtor's property in order to pay his creditor. …을 경매하다.
— *n.* **1** 《*colloq.*》 a disappointment. 실망; 기대 밖. ¶ *an awful ~* 아주 실망하기. **2** 《*sl.*》 a trick; a cheat. 속임; 사기. ¶ *What a ~!* 속았다. [E.]

·sell·er [sélər] *n.* Ⓒ **1** a person who sells. 파는 사람; 판매인(opp. buyer). **2** a thing that sells. 팔리는 것. ¶ *a good* 〔*bad*〕 ~ 잘〔안〕 팔리는 것 / *a best ~* 베스트 셀러.

sellers' market [´-- ´-] *n.* a market at which a seller is at advantage because of scarcity of supply. 판매자 시장《공급이 달리고 수요가 많음》(opp. buyers' market).

sel·vage, -vedge [sélvidʒ] *n.* Ⓒ an edge of cloth woven so as to prevent it from separating into thread. (직물의) 변폭(邊幅). [*self, edge*]

selves [selvz] *n.* pl. of **self.**

se·man·tic [simǽntik] *adj.* having to do with the meanings of words. (언어의) 의미의; 어의(語義)의. [Gk.]

se·man·tics [simǽntiks] *n. pl.* 《used as *sing.*》 the study of the meanings of words and their changes of meaning. 의미론; 어의학(語義學).

sem·a·phore [séməfɔ̀ːr] *n.* Ⓒ **1** an apparatus for sending signals by mechanical arms, flags, lanterns, etc. used in railroad signaling. (철도의) 까치발 신호기; 시그널. **2** a system of signaling by means of a flag held in each hand, used in the army. (군대의) 수기(手旗) 신호. — *vt.* (P6) signal (messages, commands, etc.) by (a) semaphore. …을 신호(기)로 알리다. [Gk. *sēma* sign, *pherō* bear]

sem·blance [sémbləns] *n.* ⒸⓊ **1** an outward appearance; pretense. 외형; 외관; 가장. ¶ *in ~* 외견〔외관〕은 / *under the ~ of friendship* 우정을 가장하여 / *put on a ~ of shyness* 부끄러운 듯한 태도를 가장하다; 부끄러운 체하다. **2** likeness; resemblance. 비슷한 것; 유사; 닮음. ¶ *have the ~ of...* …다운〔비슷한〕 데가 있다. [→similar]

se·men [síːmən] *n.* Ⓤ generative fluid of males. 정액. [L. *sero* sow]

se·mes·ter [siméstər] *n.* Ⓒ one of two terms of a school year. (연 2학기제의) 1학기. [L. *sex* 6, *mensis* month]

sem·i- [semi-] *pref.* half, twice or partly. '반, 두번, 얼마쯤' 의 뜻. [L.]

sem·i·an·nu·al [sèmiǽnjuəl, sèmai-] *adj.* happening every half year; lasting for half a year. 연 2회의; 반년간의. [↑]

sem·i·breve [sémibrìːv, sémai-] *n.* Ⓒ 《Brit. mus.》 a note having half the length of a breve. 온음표(=《U.S.》 whole-note).

sem·i·cir·cle [sémisə̀ːrkəl] *n.* Ⓒ half a circle. 반원; 반원형.

sem·i·cir·cu·lar [sèmisə́ːrkjələr] *adj.* of a semicircle; having the form of a semicircle. 반원(형)의. ¶ ~ *canal* (귀의) 반(半)고리관(管).

sem·i·civ·i·lized [sèmisívəlàizd, sèmai-] *adj.* partly or somewhat civilized. 반문명〔반미개〕의.

·sem·i·co·lon [sémikòulən] *n.* Ⓒ a mark

of punctuation(;) showing a more distinct separation than a comma, but not so distinctly as a period. 세미콜론; 포갤꽁지점.

sem·i·con·scious [sèmikánʃəs, sèmai-/sèmikɔ́n-] *adj.* partially conscious. 반(半)의식이 있는; 부분적으로 의식하는.

sem·i·de·tached [sèmiditǽtʃt, sèmai-] *adj.* partly detached; (of a house) joined to other buildings by a common wall on one side. 반쯤 떨어진; (집이 이웃채에) 한쪽 벽이 붙어 이어진.

sem·i·fi·nal [sèmifáinəl, sèmai-] *n.* Ⓒ a match, round or contest just before the final one. 준결승(전). — *adj.* of such a match, round, contest, etc. 준결승(전)의. ● **sem·i·fi·nal·ist** [-fáinəlist] *n.*

sem·i·flu·id [sèmiflú:id, sèmai-] *adj.* not completely fluid. 반(半)유동체의. — *n.* ⓊⒸ a substance which is neither completely solid nor fluid. 반유동체.

sem·i·month·ly [sèmimʌ́nθli, sèmai-] *adj.* occurring or done twice a month. 반달마다의; 월 2회〔두 번〕의. — *n.* Ⓒ (*pl.* **-lies**) anything that is published twice a month. 월 2회의 출판물. — *adv.* twice a month. 한 달에 2번〔회〕; 반달〔보름〕마다.

sem·i·nar [sémənà:r] *n.* Ⓒ **1** a group of students in a university doing research or advanced study under the direction of the teacher. (대학의) 세미나《교수의 지도에 의한 학생 공동 연구 그룹》. **2** a course or subject of study for such a group. 연구 과정〔과제〕; 연습. [*semen*]

sem·i·nary [sémənèri/-nəri] *n.* Ⓒ (*pl.* **-nar·ies**) **1** a school, esp. one beyond a high school. (특히 고교 이상의) 학교. **2** an academy or boarding school, esp. for young women. 여학교; 기숙 학교. ¶ *a ~ for young ladies* 여자 전문 학교. **3** a school which prepares or trains students to be priests. 신학교.

sem·i·of·fi·cial [sèmiəfíʃəl, sèmai-] *adj.* partly official; not entirely official. 반관적(半官的)인. [semi-]

Sem·ite [sémait/sí:m-] *n.* Ⓒ a member of one of the groups of people, including the Hebrews, Arabs, Phoenicians, and Assyrians who speak Semitic languages. (유태인을 포함한) 셈인(人); 셈족; 셈어(語)를 쓰는 종족. [*Shem,* see *Gen.* X.21]

Se·mit·ic [simítik] *adj.* of the Semites or their languages. 셈족(族)의; 유태인의; 셈어(語)의. — *n.* Ⓤ a group of languages which include Hebrew, Arabic, Phoenician, and Assyrian. 셈어. [↑]

sem·i·tone [sémitòun] *n.* Ⓒ **1** 《mus.》 a tone which is half a tone different from another. 반음. **2** an interval between these two tones. 반음정. [semi-]

sem·i·trans·par·ent [sèmitrænspɛ́ərənt, sèmai-] *adj.* imperfectly transparent; translucent. 반투명의.

sem·i·trop·i·cal [sèmitrápikəl, sèmai-/-trɔ́p-] *adj.* half tropical; subtropical. 아열대의(=subtropical).

sem·i·vow·el [sémivàuəl, sèmai-] *n.* a vowel sound which does not form the center of syllable, as *w, y,* in *win, yet.* 반모음(半母音).

semp·stress [sémpstris] *n.* =seamstress.

Sen. Senate; Senator.

sen. senior.

:sen·ate [sénət] *n.* Ⓒ **1** 《*the S-*》 the upper house of Congress in the United States, France, etc. 상원. **2** the supreme legislative and governing body in ancient Rome. (고대 로마의) 원로원. [L. *senex* old man]

:sen·a·tor [sénətər] *n.* Ⓒ a member of a senate. 상원 의원; 원로원 의원(cf. *Congressman*).

sen·a·to·ri·al [sènətɔ́:riəl] *adj.* **1** of senators or a senate. 상원(의원)의; 원로원(의원)의. ¶ *~ rank* 상원 의원의 지위 / *~ powers* 상원의 권능. **2** 《U.S.》 entitled to elect a senator. 상원 의원 선거권을 가진. ¶ *~ district* 상원 의원 선거구.

:send [send] *v.* (**sent**) *vt.* **1** (P6,7,13,14) cause (something or someone) to go from one place to another. …을 보내다; 가게 하다; 파견하다. ¶ *~ a letter* 〔*parcel*〕 *by mail* 우편으로 편지〔소포〕를 보내다 / *~ goods by train* 철도편으로 물건을 보내다 / *~ help at once* 곧 원조를 보내다 / *~ someone to school* 아무를 학교에 보내다 / *~ a boy on an errand* 아이를 심부름보내다 / *I will ~ a man around tomorrow.* 내일쯤에는 누군가를 심부름 보내도록 하겠습니다 / *They sent me a letter of appreciation.* 그들은 나에게 감사장(感謝狀)을 보내왔다. **2** (P6,13) ⓐ cause (an object) to move in a certain direction or manner, by throwing, striking, etc. (… 방향으로) …을 던지다. ¶ *~ a ball* 공을 던지다 / *~ a blow home* 세게 일격을 가하다 / *~ a punch to the jaw* 턱에 주먹을 먹이다 / *~ a stone through the window* 창문으로 돌을 던지다. ⓑ hand; pass 건네〔넘겨〕 주다; 돌리다. ¶ *~ the wine round again* 포도주 잔을 다시 돌리다. **3** (P6,11,13,14,21) (of God) give; grant. (신이) …을 주다. ¶ *God ~ him success!* 하느님 그를 성공하게 하소서 / *May God ~ us rain.* 신이여 우리에게 비를 내려 주시옵기를. **4** (P7,18) cause to become; drive. (어떤 상태로) 빠뜨리다〔몰다〕; …하게〔되게〕 하다. ¶ *~ the enemy flying* 적을 패주시키다 / *The noise sent him mad.* 소음이 그를 미치게 했다. — *vi.* (P1,3,4) send a message. 사자를〔전언을〕 보내다. ¶ *We sent to him at once.* 곧 그에게 사자를 보냈다. [E.]

send** someone **about his business, dismiss; send away. 아무를 해고하다; 내쫓다.

send away, **a**) dismiss (one's cook, servant, etc.). 내쫓다; 해고하다. **b**) send to a distance. 멀리 보내다; 발송하다. ¶ *~ a present away by mail* 선물을 우송하다. **c**)

send a message or order to another place. 주문하다; 시키다. ¶ *We have to ~ away for our groceries.* 식료 잡화를 주문해야 한다.
send back, return. (되)돌려 주다〔보내다〕.
send down, **a**) lower; cause to fall. 떨어뜨리다; 하락시키다. ¶ ~ *the temperature down* 기온을 떨어뜨리다 / 《*fig.*》 ~ *prices down* 물가를 하락시키다. **b**) 《Brit.》 expel from a college or university. (대학에서) 정학〔퇴학〕시키다.
send for, **a**) send a messenger asking (someone) to come; call. …을 부르러 보내다; 불러 오게 하다. ¶ ~ *for a doctor* 의사를 부르러 보내다. **b**) send a request or order for something. …을 주문하다. ¶ ~ *for book* 책을 주문하다. **c**) send a message to request the dispatch of. …을 (요)청하다. ¶ ~ *for help* 도움을 청하다.
send forth, give out; produce. …을 내다; 방출〔발산〕하다. ¶ *The sun sends forth light and heat.* 태양은 빛과 열을 방출한다.
send in, **a**) hand in through a messenger. (전갈 나온 사람에게) 명함을 내놓다. ¶ ~ *in one's card* 아무의 명함을 내놓다. **b**) enter (one's name, work, etc.) by post. (참가) 신청을 하다; 제출하다; 출품하다. ¶ ~ *in one's name as a candidate* 후보자로 참가 신청을 하다.
send off, **a**) dispatch. 보내다; 발송하다. ¶ ~ *off one's baggage* 짐을 발송하다. **b**) see (someone) start or leave. …을 배웅〔전송〕하다. ¶ *I went to the station to ~ him off.* 그를 배웅하기 위해 역에 갔다. **c**) drive away (persons); dismiss. 쫓아 버리다〔내다〕; 내쫓다.
send on, dispatch (something) in advance; forward. …을 미리 보내다; (편지 따위)를 회송〔전송(轉送)〕하다.
send out, **a**) dispatch. 보내다; 파견하다. ¶ ~ *out young men as missionaries* 젊은이들을 선교사로 파견하다. **b**) give out by post, etc.; cause to be received. (주문품·초대장 따위를) 발송하다. ¶ ~ *out invitations* 초청장을 발송하다. **c**) give off or out; put forth. 발(산)하다; 방출하다; 내다. ¶ *A stove sends out heat.* 난로는 열을 발산한다 / *A plant sends out new shoots.* 식물은 새싹을 낸다.
send *someone* **packing,** dismiss someone abruptly. 그 자리에서 내쫓다; 당장 해고하다. ¶ *We sent our maid packing for stealing the money.* 돈을 훔쳤기에 우리 가정부를 당장 내보냈다.
send up, **a**) cause to go up. 올리다. ¶ ~ *up a spacecraft* 우주선을 쏴 올리다 / ~ *up smoke* 연기를 내다 / ~ *prices up* 물가를 올리다. **b**) =send in b). ¶ ~ *up a painting* 그림을 출품하다. **c**) 《U.S. *colloq.*》 imprison. 감옥에 처넣다. ¶ *He was convicted and sent up for life.* 유죄를 선고받고 종신형을 살았다. **d**) 《*sl.*》 satirize; parody. 풍자하다; 비웃다; 놀리다.
send word, have a message conveyed by any method. 전(언)하다; 알리다. ¶ *Send me word of your arrival.* 도착을 알려 주시오.

send·er [séndər] *n.* Ⓒ **1** a person who sends. 발송인; 보내는 사람. ¶ *the ~ of a letter* 편지 발송인. **2** a device that sends, such as a transmitter in telegraphy. 발신기; 송신〔송화〕기.

send-off [séndɔ̀(:)f, -ɑ̀f] *n.* Ⓒ a friendly demonstration for someone starting out on a journey. 배웅; 송별. ¶ *a ~ party* 송별회 / *give someone a good ~* 아무를 성대히 송별하다.

Sen·e·gal [sènigɔ́:l] *n.* a republic of western Africa. 세네갈. 參考 수도는 Dakar.

se·nes·cent [sinésənt] *adj.* growing old. 노경에 접어든; 노쇠한. ●**se·nes·cence** [sinésəns] *n.* [→senate]

sen·e·schal [sénəʃəl] *n.* Ⓒ a steward of a prince or great noble in the Middle Ages. (중세의 왕족·귀족의) 집사. [Teut. =old servant]

se·nile [síːnail, sén-] *adj.* of old age; suffering from weakness caused by old age. 고령〔노인〕의; 노쇠한; 노령에 의한. [→senate]

se·nil·i·ty [siníləti] *n.* Ⓤ **1** old age. 고령; 노년. **2** bodily or mental weakness caused by old age. 노쇠; 망령.

·**sen·ior** [síːnjər] *adj.* **1** older in years. 연상의; 연장의. **2** the older used after the name of a father when his son has the same name. (같은 이름의 부자·형제들 중에서) 아버지의; 연장의; 나이가 많은 (쪽의) 《abbr. *Sr*(.), *sr., sen.*》. ¶ *John Parker, Senior* 아버지인 존 파커 / 《Brit.》 *Smith Sen.* (한 반의 같은 이름의 두 학생 중) 나이 많은 쪽의 스미스 (cf. *major, junior*). **3** higher in rank, standing, position, etc. 상위〔상급〕의; 윗사람의; 선임의; 선배의. ¶ *a ~ officer* 상급 사관 / *the ~ delegate* 수석 대표 / *a ~ partner* 고참 사원〔동료〕/ *the ~ members of a club* 클럽의 고참 회원. **4** 《U.S.》 of the final year of high school or college. (대학 등의) 최상급의; 최고 학년의.
be (*three*) **years senior to** =be one's senior by (three) years.
—*n.* Ⓒ **1** a person who is older. 연장자; 어른. ¶ *have respect for one's seniors* 연장자를 공경하다. **2** a person who is higher in rank or position. 선배; 선임(자); 윗사람; 상관. ¶ *He is my ~ in office.* 그는 나의 상사이다. **3** 《U.S.》 a student in his final year of high school or college. 최상급생 (cf. *freshman, sopomore, junior*). [→senate]
be one's senior by (*three*) **years,** be (three) years older than. …보다 3살이 위다. ¶ *Paul is my ~ by three years*〔*three years my ~* 〕. 폴은 나보다 3살이 위다 / *He was my ~ at Oxford by two years.* 그는 옥스퍼드 대학에서 2년 선배였다.

senior citizen [´– ´––] *n.* 《U.S.》 a person of or over the age of retirement. (특히) 은퇴한 연금 생활자; 고령자.

sen·ior·i·ty [siːnjɔ́ːriti, -njár-] *n.* Ⓤ the state or condition of being senior in age, rank, standing, etc. 연상; 연장; 고참〔선배〕(임); 선임(자). ¶ *Promotion should not go by ~ but by merit.* 승진은 연공보다 실력에 따른 것이어야 한다. [→senior, -ty]

senior man [⌐–⌐] *n.* an upper-class student. 상급생.

senior service [⌐– ⌐–], **the** *n.* 《Brit.》 the Navy. 해군.

sen·na [sénə] *n.* **1** 《bot.》 the cassia plant; any of various similar plants. 센나《석결명류》. **2** a laxative made from the dried leaves of this plant. (말린) 센나잎《완하제》. [Arab.]

se·ñor [senjɔ́ːr] *n.* 《Sp.》 a title used in speaking to or of a Spanish gentleman. …씨; …님; 나리. [→senior]

se·ño·ra [senjɔ́ːrə] *n.* 《Sp.》 a title used in speaking to or of a married Spanish lady. …부인; …마님; …아씨.

se·ño·ri·ta [sèinjɔríːtə, siː-] *n.* 《Sp.》 a title used in speaking to or of an unmarried Spanish lady. …양; 아가씨.

senr. senior.

•**sen·sa·tion** [senséiʃən] *n.* ⒸⓊ **1** a feeling in one's body or mind. 느낌; 기분; 감각; 지각. ¶ *a ~ of cold* 차가운 느낌 / *a ~ of freedom* 해방감 / *lose all ~ of feeling* 모든 감각을 잃다 / *Tom has a ~ of dizziness when he walks along cliffs.* 톰은 절벽을 끼고 걸을 때면 현기증을 느낀다 / *Blindness is the loss of the ~ of sight.* 실명은 시각의 상실을 말한다. **2** the state of being in great excitement. 흥분; 감동; 대인기. ¶ *the ~ of victory* 승리의 흥분〔감동〕 / *create* 〔*cause, make, produce*〕 *a great ~* 대단한 센세이션을 일으키다. **3** Ⓒ a cause of such excitement. 감동을 주는 것〔사람·사건〕. ¶ *He was a ~ as Hamlet.* 그는 햄릿역으로 선풍적인 인기였다. [→sense]

the latest sensation, a subject of eager discussion. 최근 화제에 오른 것《사건·사람 등》.

sen·sa·tion·al [senséiʃənəl] *adj.* **1** causing excitement; arousing excited feeling. 세상을 떠들썩하게 하는. ¶ *~ news* / *a ~ crime* 세상을 떠들썩하게 하는 범죄. **2** giving news in such a way as to arouse great excitement; startling. 선정적인; 충동〔충격〕을 주는. **3** of the senses. 감각의; 지각의.

:**sense** [sens] *n.* **1** Ⓤ the power to feel, see, hear, taste, etc. 감각; 지각. ¶ *the five senses* 오감 / *He has a keen ~ of smell.* 그는 후각이 예민하다. **2** Ⓤ 《sometimes *a ~*》 the power to understand or judge; judgment. 분별(력); 사려; 관념. ¶ *a man of ~* 분별 있는 사람 / *a ~ of guilt* 죄의식 / *the moral ~* 도덕 관념 / *sound ~* 양식 / *You should have had more ~ than to do that.* 그런 짓을 할 만큼 무분별하지는 않았어야 했다. **3** 《*pl.*》 the normal condition of mind; sanity. (정상적인) 제정신; 건전한 의식〔정신〕. ¶ *out of one's senses* 정신이 돌아 / *collect one's senses* 정신을 수습하다; 마음을 가라앉히다 / *lose one's senses* 머리가 돌다; 미치다; 의식을 잃다; 기절하다 / *recover* 〔*come round*〕 *one's senses* 제정신을 되찾다〔으로 돌아오다〕. **4** ⓊⒸ ⓐ a meaning 의미. ¶ *in a ~* 어떤 의미로는 / *in a narrow* 〔*broad, wide*〕 *~* (*of the word*) (그 말의) 좁은〔넓은〕 의미로; 협의〔광의〕로 / *in the strict ~* 엄밀한 의미에서 / *This word has several senses.* 이 낱말은 몇 가지 뜻이 있다 / *Mr. Johnson is a gentleman in the true ~.* 존슨 씨는 참된 의미의 신사다. ⓑ the tendency, purport of what is said, done, etc. 의의; 의도; 취지. ¶ *You mistake the ~ in which I spoke.* 내가 말한 취지를 잘못 이해하고 있네 / *What is the ~ of speaking to her like that?* 그녀에게 그렇게 말한 의도가 뭐냐. **5** the general feeling or opinion. (특히 집회·집단의) 의견; 의향. ¶ *the ~ of a meeting* 회중(會衆)의 의향.

bring someone to his senses, bring someone to himself. …를 제정신으로 돌아오게 하다.

come to one's senses, come round to oneself. 제정신으로 돌아오다.

have the sense to do, be wise enough to do. …할 만한 분별은 있다.

make sense, can be understood easily. …의 뜻이 되다; 이해할 수 있다. ¶ *His attitude doesn't make ~.* 그의 태도는 이해가 안 간다.

make sense of, find a meaning in. …의 의미를 알다; 이해하다. ¶ *I can make no ~ of it.* 그건 이해할 수가 없다 / *Can you make ~ of what he says?* 그의 하는 말을 알겠나.

take sense, talk in a sensible manner. 사리에 맞는 소리를 하다.

take the sense of someone, make sure of someone's opinion. …의 의향을 확인하다.

talk the sense, speak sense. 이치에 맞는 말을 하다.

— *vt.* (P6,11) feel; be vaguely aware of; understand. …을 느끼다; 막연히 깨닫다; 이해하다. ¶ *~ danger* 위험을 느끼다 / *I sensed that she was tired.* 그녀가 피곤하다는 것을 알았다. [L. *sentio* feel]

sense·less [sénslis] *adj.* **1** without feeling; unconscious. 무감각의; 무의식의; 인사불성의. ¶ *He was made ~ by a blow on the head.* 머리를 한 대 맞고 의식을 잃었다. **2** stupid; foolish. 무분별한; 어리석은. ¶ *a ~ action* 어리석은 행동 / *Stop such a ~ argument.* 그 따위 바보 같은 논의는 집어치워라. **3** meaningless. 무의미한.

fall senseless, become unconscious. 기절하다; 의식을 잃다. ¶ *He fell ~ to the ground.* 의식을 잃고 땅에 쓰러졌다.

knock senseless, knock someone so as to make him unconscious. …을 때려 기절시키다. ¶ *A hard blow knock him ~.*

sense organ [⌐ ⌐–] *n.* any part of the body which receives sensations of heat, sound, color, smell, pain, etc. 감각 기관(=

receptor).

sen·si·bil·i·ty [sènsəbíləti] *n.* (*pl.* **-ties**) **1** Ⓤ capacity to feel. 감각 (능력); 감도. ¶ *the ~ of the skin* 피부의 감각 / *the ~ of a thermometer* 온도계의 감도. **2** Ⓤ sensitiveness; delicacy in the capacity for emotion. 감수성; 민감(함); 섬세한 감정. ¶ *~ to pain* 고통에 대해 민감함 / *She has a fine ~ for colors.* 그녀는 색채 감각이 아주 예민하다[훌륭하다]. **3** ((*pl.*)) a tendency to feel hurt or offended too easily. 감정의 상하기 쉬움; 손상되기 쉬운 감정. ¶ *Their jokes offended his sensibilities.* 그들의 농담은 그의 감정을 상하게 했다.

*·**sen·si·ble** [sénsəbəl] *adj.* **1** that can be perceived by the senses. 느낄 수 있는; 지각할 수 있는. ¶ *the ~ world around us* 감지할 수 있는 주변의 세계. **2** great enough to be noticed. 상당한; 두드러진. ¶ *a ~ difference in the temperature* 온도의 두드러진 차이 / *a ~ change for the better* [*worse*] 두드러지게 좋아짐[나빠짐]. **3** having possession of one's senses; conscious. 의식이 있는. ¶ *The wounded man was still ~ when picked up.* 부상자는 발견됐을 때 아직 의식은 있었다. **4** ((*of*)) conscious of; aware of. …을 의식하고 있는; 깨닫고[알고] 있는. ¶ *be ~ of someone's suffering* 아무의 괴로움을 잘 알고 있다 / *He is ~ of his own shortcomings.* 그는 자기의 결점을 알고 있다. **5** ⓐ (for a person) possessing good sense and judgment. 분별 있는; 사려[양식] 있는. ¶ *a ~ young man* 양식 있는 청년 / *be ~ about the matter* 그 일에 양식 있는 태도를 취하다 / *He's not brilliant, but he's very ~.* 그는 재기 발랄하지는 않지만 매우 분별이 있다. ⓑ (of actions ideas, etc.) based on or showing good sense. 현명한. ¶ *It's a very ~ thing to keep your money in a purse.* 돈을 지갑에 간수하는 것은 매우 현명한 일이다.

sen·si·bly [sénsəbəli] *adv.* **1** in a sensible manner; remarkably. 지각할 수 있을 만큼; 두드러지게. **2** wisely. 현명하게; 분별 있게.

*·**sen·si·tive** [sénsətiv] *adj.* **1** quick to receive impressions from external conditions. 느끼기 쉬운; 민감한. ¶ *have a ~ ear* 귀가 밝다; 청력이 좋다. **2** easily influenced 과민한; 영향을 받기 쉬운; 반응이 빠른. ¶ *a ~ market* 변동하기 쉬운[불안정한] 시장 / *The photographic film is ~ to light.* 사진 필름은 빛에 민감하다. **3** easily hurt or damaged. (정신적·감정적으로) 민감한; 신경질인; 마음에 두는; 걱정하는; 상처받기 쉬운. ¶ *~ to blame* 비난에 민감한 / *be ~ about one's appearance* 외관에 신경을 쓰다 / *Alice is a ~ child.* 앨리스는 신경질적인 아이다. **4** of senses or sensations. 감각의; 감수성의. **5** ((photog.)) affected by light. 빛에 민감한; 감광하는. ¶ *~ paper* 감광지(感光紙). ●**sen·si·tive·ness** [-nis] *n.* [*sense*]

sen·si·tiv·i·ty [sènsətívəti] *n.* Ⓤ the state or quality of being sensitive. 민감함; 감수성; 감도.

sen·si·tize [sénsətàiz] *vt.* (P6) ((photog.)) make (a film) sensitive to light. …에 감광성을 주다.

sen·so·ri·a [sensɔ́ːriə] *n.* pl. of **sensorium.**

sen·so·ri·um [sensɔ́ːriəm] *n.* (*pl.* **ri·ums** or **-ri·a**) the seat of sensation in the brain. 감각[지각] 중추; 감관(感官). [↓]

sen·so·ry [sénsəri] *adj.* of senses or sensations. 감각의; 지각의; 지각 기관의. ¶ *~ nerves* 지각 신경 / *The eyes and ears are ~ organs.* 눈과 귀는 지각 기관이다. [*sense*]

sen·su·al [sénʃuəl] *adj.* **1** of the pleasure of the bodily senses; not mental or spiritual. 육체의; 육감적인. ¶ *~ pleasures* 관능적[육체적] 쾌락 / *a ~ delight in eating* 먹는 것의 즐거움. **2** given up to the pleasures of the body; lustful. 육욕에 빠진; 호색적인. ¶ *a ~ young woman* 성적으로 방종한 젊은 여자. [*sense*]

sen·su·al·ism [sénʃuəlìzəm] *n.* Ⓤ **1** sensuality. 육욕에 빠짐; 호색. **2** ((eth.)) the theory that the highest good consists in sensual gratification. 쾌락주의. **3** ((art)) emphasis on objective sensuality. 관능주의. **4** the doctrine of sensationalism. 감각주의.

sen·su·al·i·ty [sènʃuǽləti] *n.* Ⓤ the state of being too sensual. 육욕에 빠짐; 호색.

sen·su·al·ize [sénʃuəlàiz] *vt.* (P6) make sensual. 육욕적으로 하다; 관능에 빠지게 하다.

sen·su·ous [sénʃuəs] *adj.* appealing to the senses. 감각에 호소하는; 감각적인. ¶ *~ impressions* 감각적 인상 / *~ qualities of music* 음악의 감각적 성질.

:**sent** [sent] *v.* p. and pp. of **send.**

:**sen·tence** [séntəns] *n.* Ⓒ **1** ((gram.)) a group of words that expresses a complete thought. 문장; 글. ¶ *a simple* [*compound, complex*] *~* 단(單)[중(重), 복(複)]문. **2** ((law)) judgment given on a prisoner by a court; punishment. 선고; 판결(cf. *verdict*); 형벌. ¶ *be under ~ of death* 사형 판결을 받고 있다 / *pass ~ of death upon ...* …에게 사형을 선고하다 / *receive a heavy ~* 무거운 형을 받다 / *His ~ was ten years in prison.* 그에게 금고 10년의 형이 선고되었다. **3** ((*arch.*)) saying; proverb. 금언; 속담.
— *vt.* (P6,13) pronounce a judgment on or decide a punishment for (a prisoner). …에게 판결을 내리다; 형(刑)을 선고하다. ¶ *The judge sentenced the thief to five years in prison.* 판사는 도둑에게 금고 5년을 선고했다. [L.]

sen·ten·tious [senténʃəs] *adj.* **1** full of proverbs. 금언적인; 교훈적인. **2** expressing much in few words. 간결하고도 함축성 있는; 의미 심장한. **3** speaking self-importantly; too proud of one's own opinion. 교훈조[설교조]의. ¶ *a ~ speaker* [*speech*] 설교조의 연사[연설].

sen·tient [sénʃənt] *adj.* having the ability of feeling. 지각력[감각]이 있는. ¶ *a ~ being*

감각이 있는 생물. — *n.* Ⓒ a person or thing that is sentient. 감각이 있는 사람[것]. [L.]

:**sen·ti·ment** [séntəmənt] *n.* ⓊⒸ **1** an opinion based on one's feeling or emotion. 감정; (심)정; 정서. ¶ *religious sentiments* 종교심 / *have friendly* [*hostile*] *sentiments toward...* …에게 호의[적의]를 품다. **2** a feeling, esp. of pity or affection. 정에 무름; 다감; 감상(感傷). ¶ *a man of* ~ 감정가; 다감한 사람 / *free from* ~ 감정을 섞지 않은; 감상적이 아닌 / *appeal to his* ~ 그의 감정에 호소하다. **3** 《often *pl.*》 the thought which expresses one's feeling; one's personal opinion. 의견; 감상(感想); 소감. ¶ *public sentiments* 여론 / *express one's* ~ *about* [*on*] *the subject* 그 문제에 관한 소감을 말하다 / *What are your sentiments in regard to this matter?* 이 문제에 관해 당신의 의견은 어떻습니까. [L. *sentio* feel]

sen·ti·men·tal [sèntəméntl] *adj.* **1** easily moved to pity, love, sympathy, etc. 감정에 움직이기 쉬운; 감상적인. ¶ ~ *poetry* 감상적인 시 / ~ *motives* 감정적인 동기 / *for* ~ *reasons* 감정상의 이유로 / *a* ~ *young girl* 감상적인 소녀. **2** appealing to one's emotions. 감정에 호소하는; 정서적인. **3** of sentiment. 감정의; 정서의.

sen·ti·men·tal·ism [sèntəméntəlìzəm] *n.* Ⓤ **1** the tendency or characteristic of being easily moved by emotion. 감정에 움직이기 쉬움; 감상벽; 감상주의. **2** sentimental speech or behavior. 감정적[감상적] 언동.

sen·ti·men·tal·ist [sèntəméntəlist] *n.* Ⓒ a sentimental person; a person who is given to sentimentality. 감상가; 감상적[감정적]인 사람.

sen·ti·men·tal·i·ty [sèntəmentǽləti] *n.* (*pl.* **-ties**) **1** Ⓤ the quality of being sentimental. 감상적임; 감상성. **2** Ⓒ a sentimental characteristic, manner, way of behavior, expression, etc. 감상적 특징[언동, 표현].

sen·ti·men·tal·ize [sèntəméntəlàiz] *vt., vi.* (P6;1,3) make sentimental; behave sentimentally. 감상적으로 하다; 감상적이 되다; 감상에 젖다.

sen·ti·men·tal·ly [sèntəméntəli] *adv.* in a sentimental manner. 감상적[감정적]으로.

sen·ti·nel [séntənl] *n.* Ⓒ a person who keeps watch and guards. 보초; 파수(把守). ¶ *stand* ~ (*over*) 망을 보다; 보초를 서다.
— *vt.* guard or watch over (an enemy, etc.). …을 망보다; 보초를 서다. [It. *sentinella*]

sen·try [séntri] *n.* Ⓒ (*pl.* **-tries**) a soldier who keeps watch and guards. 보초; 초병. ¶ *be* [*stand*] *on* ~ 보초를 서다. [↑]

Seoul [soul] *n.* the capital of the Republic of Korea. 서울.

Sep. September.

se·pal [síːpəl] *n.* Ⓒ 《bot.》 one of the little leaflike parts at the base of a flower which protect the bud. 꽃받침. [*separate* (with ending to match *petal*)]

sep·a·ra·ble [sépərəbəl] *adj.* that can be separated. 분리할[뗄] 수 있는. [↓]

:**sep·a·rate** [sépərèit] *vt.* (P6,13) **1** ⓐ sever by cutting, etc. …을 가르다; 분리시키다. ¶ ~ *a bough from the trunk* 가지를 줄기에서 떼어 내다. ⓑ remove by sifting, etc.; extract. (걸러서) 분리하다; 가려[추려, 골라]내다; 추출[제거]하다. ¶ ~ *the chaff from the grain* 곡물에서 겉겨를 제거하다. ⓒ put apart; take away. 따로 놓다[두다]. ¶ *Please* ~ *the pens from the pencils.* 펜과 연필을 따로 갈라 놓아라 / *Separate your things from mine.* 네 물건은 내 것과 따로 두어라. **2** ⓐ remove (a person) from the society or nearness of another (person, place, etc.). (사이, 관계를) 떼어[갈라] 놓다. ¶ ~ *a mother from her child* 엄마를 아이로부터 떼어 놓다 / ~ *two fighting boys* 싸우는 두 아이를 떼어 놓다 / ~ *oneself from one's friends* 친구와 헤어지다. ⓑ cause disagreement between; divide in feelings, opinions, etc. 사이가 틀어지게[불화하게] 하다. ¶ *He is separated from his wife.* 아내와 별거하고 있다. **3** ⓐ divide up; place dividing lines, boundaries, etc. …을 가르다; 분리[분할]하다. ¶ ~ *a tract of land* (*up*) *into small plots* 일대의 토지를 작은 구획으로 분할하다 / *have the two lines of traffic separated.* 2차선으로 가르다. ⓑ be between; keep apart. 사이에 들다; 갈라 놓다. ¶ *The river separates the two states.* 그 강은 두 주를 갈라 놓는다 / *A channel separates the island from the mainland.* 해협이 섬을 본토와 갈라 놓고 있다. **4** ⓐ distinguish between; see the difference between (things). …의 차이를 식별[구별, 분간]하다. ¶ ~ *butterflies from moth* 나방과 나비를 구별하다 / *I cannot* ~ *the two arguments.* 두 논점의 차이를 모르겠다. ⓑ put (things) in different groups. …을 분류하다. ¶ ~ *the flock* 가축을 (무리로) 분류하다.
— *vi.* (P1,3) **1** be or become divided; come apart. (하나이던 것이) 갈라지다; 떨어[끊어]지다. ¶ *The rope separated.* 밧줄이 끊어졌다. **2** go apart. 헤어지다. ¶ *The children separated at the station.* 어린이들은 정거장에서 헤어졌다.
— [sépərit] *adj.* divided from others; not connected; alone. 분리된; 개개의. ¶ *two* ~ *houses* 떨어져 있는 두 집 / *The prisoners are kept* ~ *from one another.* 죄수들은 서로 따로따로 수감돼 있다 / *The girls have* ~ *bedrooms.* 소녀들은 제각기 침실이 있다. [se-, L. *paro* get, prepare]

sep·a·rate·ly [sépəritli] *adv.* in a separate manner; one by one. 따로; 개개로; 하나하나; 분리하여. ¶ *Do we go together or* ~ *?* 우리 함께 가나요 따로따로 가나요.

·**sep·a·ra·tion** [sèpəréiʃən] *n.* ⓊⒸ **1** the act of separating; the state of being separated. 분리; 분할; 이별; 떨어짐. ¶ *Old friends got together after extended* ~. 옛 친구들이 오

랜만에 만났다. **2** the act or state of a husband and wife living apart by order of a court of law or by agreement. (부부의) 별거. ¶ *Separation from her husband made her sad.* 남편과의 별거는 그녀를 슬프게 했다.

sep·a·ra·tist [sépərèitist, -rə-] *n.* Ⓒ a member of a group, esp. a political or religious group, who wants separation and independence. 분리주의자; 독립주의자(opp. unionist).

sep·a·ra·tive [sépərèitiv, -rə-] *adj.* inclined to separate; causing separation. 분리성의〔적인〕; 독립적인.

sep·a·ra·tor [sépərèitər] *n.* Ⓒ **1** a person or thing that separates. 분리하는 사람〔것〕. **2** a device used for separating the cream from milk, etc. 분리기(器); 선별기; 분할기.

se·pi·a [sí:piə] *n.* Ⓤ **1** a dark brown paint made from the inky fluid of a cuttlefish. 세피아《오징어의 먹물(로 만든 갈색 안료)》. **2** a dark-brown color. 세피아색; 암갈색. — *adj.* of a dark-brown color. 세피아(색)의; 암갈색의. [Gk. =cuttle fish]

sep·sis [sépsis] *n.* Ⓤ《med.》a disease caused by poisonous matter spreading in the blood vessels. 패혈증. [→septic]

sept [sept] *n.* a clan. 씨족. [→sect]

Sept. September.

sep·tan [séptən] *adj.* occurring every seven days. 7일마다 일어나는. ¶ *a* ~ *fever*, 7일열(熱). [↓]

:Sep·tem·ber [septémbər] *n.* the ninth month of the year. 9월. [L. *septem* seven]

sep·tic [séptik] *adj.* **1** infected. 병독이 있는; 감염성의. ¶ *a* ~ *wound* 병독이 있는 상처. **2** caused by germs such as those that cause blood-poisoning. 패혈증〔성〕의. ¶ ~ *fever* 부패열. — *n.* a substance tending to bring about a septic condition. 패혈증 병원체. [Gk. *sēpō* rot]

sep·ti·ce·mi·a [sèptəsí:miə] *n.*《med.》a blood-poisoning disease. 패혈증.

sep·tu·a·ge·nar·i·an [sèptʃu:ədʒənέəriən, -tju:-] *adj.* of the age of 70 years, or between 70 and 80 years old. 70세〔대〕의. — *n.* Ⓒ a person of this age. 70세〔대〕의 사람. [↓]

Sep·tu·a·gint [séptjuədʒint, -tju:-] *n.* 《*the* ~》the Greek translation of the Old Testament. 70인역 그리스어 성서. [→septan]

sep·ul·cher, 《Brit.》**-chre** [sépəlkər] *n.* Ⓒ a tomb; a grave; a place of burial. 무덤; 매장지. — *vt.* (P6) bury (a dead body) in a sepulcher. 매장하다. [L. *sepelio* bury]

se·pul·chral [səpʌ́lkrəl] *adj.* **1** of or connected with a sepulcher or tomb. 무덤의. **2** of burial. 매장의. ¶ ~ *ceremonies* 장례식. **3** gloomy; dismal. 음울〔음침〕한. ¶ *a* ~ *look* 〔*visage*〕 음울한 표정〔얼굴〕. [↑]

sep·ul·ture [sépəltʃər] *n.* Ⓤ burial. 매장.

seq. *sequentia* (L. =the following).

se·quel [sí:kwəl] *n.* Ⓒ **1** something that follows or comes after; a continuation. 후속(의 사건); 속편. ¶ *the* ~ *to* 〔*of*〕 *a novel* 소설의 속편 / *Famine was the* ~ *to* 〔*of*〕 *the war.* 전쟁에 뒤따라 기근이 왔다. **2** a result; an effect. 결과; 귀결. ¶ *The* ~ *to* 〔*of*〕 *such a speech can be foreseen.* 그런 말의 결과는 예견할 수 있다. [→second]

in the sequel, later on; after all. 나중에; 「결국.

se·que·la [sikwí:lə] *n.* (*pl.* **-lae**)《med.》a consequential disease. 후유증.

se·que·lae [sikwí:li:] *n.* pl. of **sequela.**

se·quence [sí:kwəns] *n.* **1** Ⓤ the act of following; the coming of one thing after another. 잇따라 일어남; 속발; 연속. ¶ *follow the* ~ *of events* 사건을 발생 순서대로 더듬다〔조사하다〕. **2** the order of sequence. 순서; 차례. ¶ *alphabetical* ~ 알파벳순 / *The* ~ *of events on the night of the murder isn't known.* 그 날 밤의 살인 사건 경위는 아직 미상이다. **3** Ⓒ ⓐ a connected series. 연속적으로 일어나는 일〔것〕; 연속물. ¶ *a* ~ *of misfortunes* 일련의 불행한 일들. ⓑ《cinema》a series of shots together forming a main division of a film. (영화에서) 한 연속의 장면. **4** something that follows; a result. 후속해서〔수반되어〕 일어나는 사건; 여파; 결과; 귀결. ¶ *the natural* ~ *of folly* 어리석은 짓을 한 당연한 응보. [↓]

in regular sequence, in good order. 정연히; 순서 바르게.

in sequence, one after another. 다음에서 다음으로; 차례차례.

sequence of tenses, 《gram.》principles by which the tenses of subordinate clauses are made to suit those of principal clauses. 시제(時制)의 일치.

se·quent [sí:kwənt] *adj.* **1** comming after; following. 다음에〔잇따라〕 오는; 잇따라 일어나는. **2** following or happening as a result. 결과로서 일어나는〔따르는〕. [*sequel*]

se·quen·tial [sikwénʃəl] *adj.* sequent. 잇딴; 결과로서 일어나는.

se·ques·ter [sikwéstər] *vt.* (P6) **1** set apart; separate; withdraw (someone) from public view. …을 격리시키다; 은퇴시키다. ¶ ~ *oneself from society* 〔*the world*〕 사회〔세상〕에서 은퇴하다; 은둔하다. **2** take away (property) for a time till legal claims are satisfied. …을 압류하다; 압수하다. **3** take and control (the property of an enemy). …을 몰수하다; 징발하다. [L. *sequester* trustee]

se·ques·tered [sikwéstərd] *adj.* **1** isolated; quiet. 으슥한; 후미진; 고립된. ¶ *a* ~ *cottage* 〔*place*〕 후미진 오두막〔곳〕. **2** withdrawn from society. 은퇴한; 은둔한. ¶ *live a* ~ *life* 은거 생활을 보내다.

se·ques·trate [sikwéstreit] *vt.* (P6) =sequester 2, 3. ¶ *The soldiers sequestrated horses and food from the people they conquered.* 군인들은 정복한 인민들로부터 말과 식량을 징발했다.

se·quin [sí:kwin] *n.* Ⓒ **1** a small ornamental spangle. 세퀸; 스팽글. **2** a former Italian gold coin. 옛날 이탈리아의 금화. [Arab.]

se·quoi·a [sikwɔ́iə] *n.* Ⓒ a very tall evergeen tree of California. 세쿼이어.

se·ra [síərə] *n.* pl. of **serum.**

se·rac [séræk] *n.* 《*pl.*》 castle-shaped masses formed in glacier ice. (빙하에 생기는) 탑상 빙괴(塔狀氷塊). [F.]

se·ra·gli·o [siræ̃ljou, sirɑ́:liòu] *n.* (*pl.* **-os**) the women's quarters of a Mohammedan house or palace; a harem. (이슬람 교도의) 처첩용의 방; 후궁; 도장방. [L. *sera* bolt]

se·rang [səræ̃ŋ] *n.* a petty officer of Indian seamen. (동인도 사람의) 갑판장. [Pers.]

ser·aph [sérəf] *n.* Ⓒ (*pl.* **ser·aphs** or **-a·phim**) an angel of the highest rank. 최고 천사. [Heb.]

se·raph·ic [siræ̃fik] *adj.* of or like a seraph. 천사와 같은.

ser·a·phim [sérəfìm] *n.* pl. of **seraph.**

Serb [sə:rb] *n., adj.* =Serbian.

Ser·bi·a [sə́:rbiə] *n.* a region and former kingdom of the central Balkan Peninsula; a major component of the Kingdom of the Serbs, Croats, and Slovenes and a constituent republic of Yugoslavia after 1946; Serbia and Montenegro formed a new Yugoslavian country in 1992. 세르비아 《발칸 반도에 있던 옛 왕국》. [↓]

Ser·bi·an [sə́:rbiən] *n.* **1** Ⓒ a person of Serbia. 세르비아 사람. **2** Ⓤ the language of Serbia. 세르비아 어. — *adj.* of the serbia or Serbian. 세르비아(사람·어)의. [Native]

Ser·bo·ni·an bog [sə:rbóuniən bɑg, -bɔ(:)g] *n.* **1** a marsh in Egypt. 세르보니스의 늪. **2** a great confusion. 대혼란. [↑]

sere [siər] *adj.* 《*poet.*》 dried up; withered. 바짝 말라붙은; 시든(=sear). [E.]

ser·e·nade [sèrənéid] *n.* Ⓒ a piece of music played or sung at night, esp. under a lady's window by someone who loves her; a piece of music suitable for this. 세레나데; 소야곡. — *vt., vi.* (P6;1) sing or play a serenade (for a lady). (…에게) 세레나데를 연주하다[부르다]. [↓]

:**se·rene** [sirí:n] *adj.* (**-ren·er, -ren·est**) **1** clear; bright. 청명한; 맑게 갠. ¶ *The sky is ~ and bright.* 하늘이 맑게 갰다 / *In the clear sky the moon shines ~.* 맑은 하늘에는 달빛이 교교히 비치고 있다. **2** calm; peaceful. 조용[평온]한; 평화로운. ¶ *a ~ smile* 잔잔한 미소 / *~ happiness* 조용한 행복 / *~ old age* 편안히 보내는 노후 / *a ~ life* 평온한 생활. [L. *serenus*] ***His* [*Your, etc.*] *Serene Highness,*** princely titles in certain royal family. 전하(殿下).

se·rene·ly [sirí:nli] *adv.* in a serene manner; calmly. 맑게; 청명하게; 조용[평온]히; 평화롭게.

se·ren·i·ty [sirénəti] *n.* ⓊⒸ (*pl.* **-ties**) **1** clearness; brightness. 청명; 맑음; 화창함. **2** calmness; peacefulness. 평정; 평온; 침착.

serf [sə:rf] *n.* Ⓒ (*pl.* **serfs**) **1** in the Middle Ages, a person who belonged to the land and was usually sold with it. 농노(農奴). **2** 《*fig.*》 a person treated almost like a serf. 농노처럼 취급되는 사람; 노예. [L. *servus* slave]

serf·dom [sə́:rfdəm] *n.* Ⓤ the condition or quality of being a serf. 농노(農奴)의 처지[신분](=serfage, serfhood). [↑]

Serg., Sergt. sergeant.

serge [sə:rdʒ] *n.* Ⓤ a woolen material used for dresses, suits, etc. 서지; 세루. [Gk. *Sēres* the Chinees]

·**ser·geant** [sɑ́:rdʒənt] *n.* Ⓒ **1** a noncommissioned officer in the army or marines ranking next above a corporal. 병장; 하사관. **2** a police officer of a minor rank. 경사(警査). [→serf]

sergeant at arms [⌐–⌐] *n.* (*pl.* **sergeants at a-**) 《Brit.》 an officer who keeps order in a law court, Parliament, etc. (법정·의회 따위의) 수위.

sergeant major [⌐–⌐] *n.* (*pl.* **s- majors** or **sergeants m-**) 《Brit.》 an army officer who ranks next above a sergeant. 특무 상사.

se·ri·al [síəriəl] *n.* Ⓒ a story told in successive parts or numbers in a magazine or thus broadcast on television. etc. 연속물; 연재 소설; 정기 출판물; 시리즈. ¶ *a ~ novelist* 연재 소설가 / *watch the television ~* 텔레비전의 연속극을 보다. — *adj.* **1** arranged in a series. 연속의. ¶ *~ numbers* 일련 번호 / *in ~ order* 번호순으로. **2** published, broadcast, televised, etc. one following one another. 연속물의; 연재물의. ¶ *a new ~ story* 새로운 연재 소설. [L. *sero* join]

se·ri·al·ly [síəriəli] *adv.* in a series. 연속적으로; 연속물로서.

se·ri·a·tim [sìəriéitim] *adv.* 《L.》 one after another in regular order. 연속하여; 잇따라; 차례로.

se·ri·ceous [siríʃəs, sə-] *adj.* like silk. 비단 같은; 비단의. [F.]

ser·i·cul·tur·al [sèrəkʌ́ltʃərəl] *adj.* of sericulture. 양잠의. [→sericeous]

ser·i·cul·ture [sérəkʌ̀ltʃər] *n.* Ⓤ the art or process of growing silkworms for the production of silk. 양잠업.

ser·i·cul·tur·ist [sèrəkʌ́ltʃərist] *n.* Ⓒ a person who is engaged in sericulture. 양잠가; 양잠업자.

:**se·ries** [síəri:z] *n.* Ⓒ (*pl.* **-ries**) **1** a number of similar things or events following one after another. 연속돼 있는 것; 연속물; 일련; 연속. ¶ *the first ~* (총서 등의) 제1집 / *a ~ of experiments* 일련의 실험 / *a ~ of victories* [*defeats*] 연승[연패] / *a ~ of misfortunes* 잇딴 불행 / *a ~ of lectures* 연속 강연. **2** a number of similar events planned to take place one after the other. (같은 참

가자에 의한) 일련의 게임(경기). ¶ *a* ~ *of baseball games* 일련의 야구 경기. **3** a number of similar things forming a set. (동종의 화폐·우표 따위의) 한 조(組)(세트). ¶ *a* ~ *of six stamps* 6매 1세트의 우표. **4** 《math.》 the sum of the terms of a sequence of entities. 급수. [→serial]

in series, **a**) arranged in the order of a series. 연속하여; 순차로; 총서로서. **b**) 《electr.》 with the positive pole joined to the negative of the next. 직렬로.

ser·if [sérif] *n.* 《print.》 a thin or smaller crossline used to finish off a main stroke of a letter, as at the top and bottom of M, I, H. 세리프《M, I, H 따위 활자에서 볼 수 있는 상하의 가는 선》. [→scribe]

se·ri·o·com·ic [sìərioukámik / -kɔ́m-] *adj.* partly serious and partly comic. 진지하기도 하고 우습기도 한. ¶ *a* ~ *novel* 진지하고도 익살맞은 소설. [↓, +*comic*]

:se·ri·ous [síəriəs] *adj.* **1** grave; thoughtful; sincere; not joking. 진지한; 진정인; 생각이 깊은. ¶ *a* ~ *face* 진지한 얼굴 / *Are you* ~*?* 자네 진정인가 / *She was quite* ~ *about the matter.* 그녀는 그 문제에 관해 아주 진지했다. **2** requiring thought and attention. 사고를 요하는; 심각한. ¶ *a* ~ *book* 집중력을 요하는 책. **3** important because it is dangerous. 중대한; 위험한; 중요한. ¶ *a* ~ *illness* 중병 / *a* ~ *accident* 중대 사건. [L.]

:se·ri·ous·ly [síəriəsli] *adv.* in a serious manner. 진지하게; 심각하게; 중하게; 곧이곧대로. ¶ *Don't take it so* ~. 그걸 그리 심각하게 생각하지 마라 / *He is* ~ *injured.* 그는 중상이다.

be seriously ill, be in a critical condition. 위독하다; 중태이다.

se·ri·ous·ness [síəriəsnis] *n.* Ⓤ the state of being serious. 진지함; 중대함; 심각함; 위독. ¶ *The* ~ *of the matter made us anxious.* 문제의 심각성이 우리를 불안하게 했다.

in all seriousness, very seriously. 몹시 진지하게.

ser·jeant [sá:rdʒənt] *n.* =sergeant.

·ser·mon [sə́:rmən] *n.* Ⓒ **1** a public speech on religion or religious matters, usu. given in a church. 설교. ¶ *the Sermon on the Mount* 산상 수훈(山上垂訓). **2** any serious talk on morals, conduct, etc. (도덕적인) 설교; 훈화. ¶ *a* ~ *against adultery* 간통을 훈계하는 설교 / *give* (*deliver*) *the sermons* 잔소리를 하다. **3** a long, dull speech. 길고 따분한 이야기. [L. *sermo* speech]

ser·mon·ize [sə́:rmənàiz] *vi., vt.* (P1;6,18) preach, lecture; preach at. 설교하다; …에게 훈계를 주다; 잔소리하다.

·ser·pent [sə́:rpənt] *n.* Ⓒ **1** 《*lit.*》 a snake, esp. a big one. 뱀《특히 큰 것》. **2** 《*fig.*》 a sly, deceitful person. 음험(교활)한 사람. **3** 《Bible》 《*the* (*old*) *S-*》 the Devil; Satan. 악마. [L. *serpo* creep]

ser·pen·tine [sə́:rpəntàin, -tì:n] *adj.* **1** snakelike; winding; twisting. 뱀의; 뱀 같은; 꾸불꾸불한; 나사 모양의. ¶ *the* ~ *course of a stream* 꾸불꾸불한 강의 흐름. **2** 《*fig.*》 deceitful; treacherous; sly. 음험한; 교활한. ¶ *a* ~ *suggestion* 교활한 제안. — *n.* Ⓤ a kind of rock, usu. green and sometimes spotted like a serpent's skin. 사문암(蛇紋岩).

ser·rate [sérət, səréit] *adj.* having a toothed edge like a saw. 톱니 모양의. ¶ *a* ~ *leaf* 톱니 모양의 잎. [L. *serra* saw]

ser·rat·ed [séreitid / -ˊ-] *adj.* =serrate.

ser·ried [sérid] *adj.* crowded closely together. 꽉 찬; 빽빽한; 밀집한. [→seraglio]

se·rum [síərəm] *n.* ⓊⒸ (*pl.* **-ra** or **-rums**) **1** the pale yellow, watery part of the blood. 혈청(血清); 혈장(血漿). **2** such a fluid, taken from an animal that has been given a certain disease and then injected into a human body to help in fighting the same disease. 면역 혈청. [L.=whey]

:serv·ant [sə́:rvənt] *n.* Ⓒ **1** a person employed to carry out household or personal duties. 고용인; 하인; 하녀(cf. *master*). ¶ *engage* (*dismiss*) *a* ~ 사용인을 고용(해고)하다. **2** a person who works for the public. 관리; 공무원; 공복. ¶ *a civil* ~ 문관 / *Policemen and firemen are public servants.* 경찰관과 소방사는 공복이다. **3** a person who is devoted to a certain belief. (신앙·예술 따위에) 일신을 바친 사람; 봉사자. ¶ *a* ~ *of art* 예술에 일신을 바친 사람 / *Ministers are called the servants of God.* 성직자는 신의 봉사자로 일컬어진다. [→serf]

Your obedient servant. 《Brit.》 a form of ending to an official letter, whether to a superior or not. (공문서·편지의 맺음말로서) 여불비례(餘不備禮).

serv·ant-girl [sə́:rvəntgə̀:rl], **-maid** [-mèid] *n.* a girl employed as a domestic servant. 가정부; 하녀.

:serve [sə:rv] *vt.* **1** (P6) work or do good for (someone or something); do one's duty for (someone). …을 위해 일(봉사·근무)하다; (의무)를 다하다; 진력하다; 섬기다. ¶ ~ *one's master* 주인을 섬기다 / *He serves me well.* 그는 나에게 잘해 준다 / *He served his country as a diplomat.* 그는 조국을 위해 외교관으로 근무했다. **2** (P6,7,13) ⓐ bring (food or drink) to someone; prepare and present (food) at table. (식사·음식)을 내다; 담다; 대접하다. ¶ ~ *someone* (*with*) *a meal* 아무에게 식사를 내다(대접하다) / ~ *up the plates* 식탁에 접시를 늘어놓다 / *May I* ~ *you some tea and cake?* 다과를 드릴까요. ⓑ hand round; distribute. 차례로 도르다(분배하다); (식탁에) 나르다. ¶ ~ *coffee in Ich'ŏn cups* 이천요(利川窯)의 찻잔에 커피를 내오다. ⓒ take care of (someone) at table or in a shop. …을 시중들다; 심부름을 하다; (가게에서 손님 주문)을 응대하다. ¶ ~ *someone with tea* 아무에게 차를 따라 주다 / *Is there no one to* ~ *me?* 내

시중을 들[내 주문에 응대할] 사람은 아무도 없는가. **3** (P7) treat. (어떤 방식으로) 대(우)하다; 취급하다. ¶ ~ *someone a bad turn* 아무에게 심한 처사를 하다 / *He served me very badly.* 그는 내게 못되게 굴었다. **4** (P6,7) be adequate to; fulfill. (목적)에 맞다; (요구·바람 따위)를 만족시키다. ¶ ~ *its purpose* 목적에 맞다; 충분하다 / *That will ~ me* [*my purpose*]. 그것이면 된다. **5** (P6,7) be of service to; be of use to; help. …의 도움이 되다; 쓸모가 있다. ¶ *I am only too glad if I can ~ you in any way.* 어쨌든 내가 도움이 될 수 있다면 그저 기쁠 따름입니다 / *The sofa served him as* [*for*] *a bed.* 소파는 그에게 침대 대용으로 쓸모가 있었다. **6** (P6,7) supply (someone) with goods or services; satisfy the wants of. (…에게 계속적으로) 공급하다; 필요를 만족시키다. ¶ ~ *customers* 손님의 요구를 충족시키다; 장사를 하다 / *What can we ~ you with?* (가게에서) 무엇을 보여 드릴까요; 무엇을 찾으십니까 / *The company serves our town with gas.* 그 회사는 우리 시(市)에 가스를 공급하고 있다 / *This elevator serves all the floors.* 이 승강기는 각층마다 섭니다. **7** (P6) go through; pass time in. 임기를 채우다[마치다]; 복역하다. ¶ ~ *one's apprenticeship* 도제(徒弟) 연한을 마치다 / ~ *one's full term* [*time*] *in office* 임기를 채우다. **8** (P6,13) 《law》 deliver (to). (영장 따위)를 송달하다; 교부하다. ¶ ~ *someone with a summons* = ~ *a summons on someone* …에게 소환장을 내다. **9** (P6) 《tennis, etc.》 put (the ball) into play. (공을) 서브하다. — *vi.* **1** (P1,3) work for another; do one's duties. 봉사하다; 섬기다; 근무[복무]하다. ¶ ~ *as a soldier* 군인으로 복무하다 / ~ *in the kitchen* 주방에서 일하다 / *He serves as a clerk in a bank.* 그는 은행원으로 근무하고 있다. **2** (P3) wait at table. (식사에) 시중들다; 심부름하다. ¶ *The daughter served at* (*the*) *table.* 딸이 식탁의 시중을 들었다. **3** (P1,2A,4) ⓐ be what is needed or useful. 목적에 맞다; 도움이 되다; 어떤 용도를 가지다; 유용하다. ¶ *A single example will ~ to illustrate the point.* 단 하나의 본보기는 요점을 설명하는 데 도움이 될 것이다. ⓑ 《*as*》 act as a substitute for. …의 대용이 되다. ¶ *This box can ~ as a table.* 이 궤짝은 식탁 대용을 할 수 있다. **4** (P1,2A,4) be convenient or favorable. (날씨·시간 따위가) 형편이 좋다; 적당하다. ¶ *come when* [*as*] *occasion serves* (아무 때고) 형편이 닿을[편리한] 때 오다 / *The tide serves for setting sail.* 조수 상태가 배를 출범시키기에 알맞다. **5** (P1) 《tennis, etc.》 put the ball into play. 서브를 하다.

as memory serves, whenever one thinks of it. 생각나는 대로.

as occasion serves, when an opportunity presents itself. 기회가 닿는 대로.

serve a gun, continue bombarding. 포격을 계속하다.

serve for (=*be used as*) *something.* …로서 쓸모가 있다[쓰이다]. ¶ *This tool serves for many purposes.* 이 도구는 여러 용도에 쓰인다 / *He serves for nothing.* 그는 아무짝에도 쓸모가 없다.

serve out, **a**) dish out; distribute. (음식을) 별러 담다; 분배하다. **b**) get avenge on …에게 복수[대갚음]하다. ¶ *She finally served him out.* 그녀는 마침내 그에게 복수했다.

serve** someone **right, be the right punishment for his behavior. 당연한 벌[보답]이다. ¶ *It serves you* [*him*] *right!* 꼴 좋다; 고것 고소하다; 그것 봐라.

serve round, **a**) hand (food, etc.) to each in turn. (음식 따위)를 차례로 도르다. **b**) tie to. …에 동여매다.

serve the devil, do evil. 못된 짓을 하다.

serve** one's **time [***a sentence***]*,* be in prison for a certain time as a punishment. (교도소에서) 복역하다; 형을 살다.

serve** someone's **turn [***need***]*,* be of use to him; answer his purpose. (아무)에게 소용이 되다; 목적에 맞다.

serve two masters, 《*fig.*》 be divided between two opposite principles. 둘 사이에 끼여 난처해지다.

***serve under** someone,* serve someone. …밑에서 일하다.

serve up, bring (food, drink, etc.) to a table; wait upon. …을 식탁에 나르다; (음식) 시중을 들다.

— *n.* 《tennis, etc.》 the act of serving; the turn to serve. (테니스 등에서) 서브; 서브할 차례; 서브권(權). [→serf]

serv·er [sə́:rvər] *n.* Ⓒ **1** a person who serves. 섬기는[일하는] 사람; 봉사자; 급사; 근무자. **2** 《tennis, etc.》 the player who puts the ball in play. 서브하는 사람. **3** a tray for dishes. (식사 때 쓰이는) 접시.

:serv·ice [sə́:rvis] *n.* **1** ⓊⒸ the work or kindness done for others; the duty required in one's business. 봉사; 근무; 복무; 업무; 진력(盡力). ¶ *sea ~* 해상 근무 / *the diplomatic ~* 외교관근무 / *public ~* 공무 / *thirty years' ~ with the company* 그 회사에서의 30년의 근무 / *be in ~* 근무하고 있다 / *be in the ~ to mankind* 인류에 봉사하다 / *do someone a ~* 아무를 위해 진력하다 / *He was of great ~ to me.* 그는 나에게 잘 봉사해 주었다. **2** ⒸⓊ a system or means for public use. 공공의 편(便); 사업; 시설; 운행. ¶ *the telephone ~* 전화 사업 / *air ~* = *aerial flight ~* 항공 사업[편] / *There is good train ~.* 열차편이 좋다. **3** Ⓒ supply; arrangements for supplying. 공급. ¶ *water ~* 급수(사업). **4** 《often *pl.*》 an act performed for the benefit or advantage of another. (타인에 대한) 진력(盡力); 공헌; 봉사 (사업). ¶ *medical services* 의료 활동[봉사] / *render great services to one's country* 나라에 크게 이바지하다. **5** Ⓤ advantage; benefit; use. 도움이 됨; 이익; 유익; 유용. ¶ *be of* (*great*) *~ to* …을 위해 (크게) 도움이 되다 / *Can I be of any ~*

to you? 무언가 도와드릴 일이 있습니까. **6** [C][U] a religious meeting, ceremony, etc. (종교상의) 의식; 예배(식); 근행. ¶ *a marriage* 〔*funeral*〕 ~ 결혼〔장례〕식. **7** [U] the manner of serving food and drink (as at a restaurant, hotel, etc.). (레스토랑·호텔 등의) 손님 접대; 대접; 서비스. ¶ *The food was good, but the ~ was bad.* 음식은 좋았으나 서비스가 나빴다 / *The ~ in this hotel is excellent.* 이 호텔의 서비스는 훌륭하다. **8** [U][C] the act of supplying a customer's needs after the sale of an article. (필요한 편의를 제공하는) 서비스(업); (시설 유지·수리 등의) (애프터) 서비스. ¶ *a television repair ~*, TV 수리업. **9** [U] 《law》 the serving of a summons. 영장의 송달. ¶ *personal ~* 본인 직접 송달. **10** [C] a set of dishes. 식기 1습〔벌〕. ¶ *a silver tea ~ for six,* 6인분의 은제(銀製) 다구(茶具) 한 세트. **11** [C][U] 《tennis, etc.》 the act of serving a ball to begin the play. 서브.

***at someone's* service,** ready to do what someone wants. 언제라도 …의 도움이 되는; …의 마음〔뜻〕대로. ¶ *place* 〔*put*〕 *something at someone's ~* 아무에게 무엇을 마음대로 사용케 하다 / *I am at your ~.* 무엇이건 말씀해 주십시오 / *You will have my car at your ~ at all times.* 언제든지 마음대로 제 차를 이용하십시오.

be of service to, be useful to. …에게 도움이 되다; 유익하다.

have seen service, have been in the field. 실전(實戰)의 경험이 있다.

in* 〔*on*〕 *active service, actually at work; be in a branch of the armed forces. 현역의; 재직중에〔의〕.

take someone into one's service, employ someone as one's servant or employee. …을 사용인으로서 고용하다.

take service with (=*be employed; work for*) *someone.* …을 섬기다; …에 근무하다.

— *vt.* (P6) repair or maintain after sale. 사용할 수 있도록 하다; 수리하다; 손을 보다. ¶ *I have my car serviced regularly.* 정기적으로 내 차를 수리해 받고 있다. [→serve]

serv·ice·a·ble [sə́:rvisəbəl] *adj.* **1** that can give good service; useful. 도움이 되는; 편리한. ¶ *the book which will be ~ for our study* 우리들의 연구에 도움이 되는 책. **2** that can stand long use; useful for a long time; durable. 오래 가는; 마딘; 내구력이 있는. ¶ *~ cloth* 튼튼한 천.

service flat [∠-∠] *n.* 《Brit》 a flat where daily cleaning and other services are supplied by the landlord, and meals will sometimes be sent if ordered. 식사·청소 따위의 서비스가 있는 아파트《완전 호텔식 아파트》.

serv·ice·man [sə́:rvismæ̀n] *n.* (*pl.* **-men** [-mèn]) **1** a member of the armed forces. 군인. **2** 《U.S.》 a man who repairs or maintains machinery, equipment, etc. 수리인. ¶ *He is a television ~.* 그는 텔레비전 수리공이다.

service station [∠-∠-] *n.* a place selling gasoline, oil, etc. for cars. 급유소; 주유소.

ser·vi·ette [sə̀:rviét] *n.* [C] a napkin. 냅킨.

ser·vile [sə́:rvil, -vail] *adj.* like a slave; humble like a slave; lacking a spirit of self-respect. 노예의; 노예 근성의; 비굴한; 굴욕적인. ¶ *a ~ flatterer* 비열한 아첨꾼 / *be ~ to public opinion* 여론에 추종(追從)하다. [→serf]

ser·vil·i·ty [sə:rvíləti] *n.* [U] manners like a slave; lack of self-respect; the state of being a slave. 노예 근성; 비굴; 노예 상태.

ser·vi·tor [sə́:rvətər] *n.* 《*arch.*》 a servant; an attendant. 종복; 머슴; 종자(從者).

ser·vi·tude [sə́:rvətjù:d] *n.* [U] the state of being a slave; forced labor as a punishment. 노예 상태; 예속; (형벌로서의) 강제 노동; 고역(苦役). ¶ *penal ~* 중(重)징역.

ses·a·me [sésəmi] *n.* **1** [C] a plant whose seeds have much oil and are used for food. 참깨. **2** [U] 《*collectively*》 the seeds. 참깨씨. [Gk.]

open sesame, **a**) magic words used, in the tale of 'Ali Baba and the Forty Thieves' in the 'Arabian Nights', to get the door to the cave open. 열려라 참깨 《'아라비안 나이트'에서 도둑의 동굴 문을 열게 하는 주문》. **b**) 《*fig.*》 a key to a mystery; a way out of a difficulty. 신비를 푸는 열쇠; 어려움을 벗어나는 수단.

·ses·sion [séʃən] *n.* **1** [U] a meeting of a law court, a council, a parliament, etc.; [C] a series of such meetings. (법원의) 개정(開廷); (회의·의회 따위의) 개회; 일련의 그러한 회의. ¶ *a full* 〔*plenary*〕 *~* 총회 / *an ordinary* 〔*a regular*〕 *~ of the National Assembly* 정기 국회 / *in full ~* 총회에서; 정식 회의에서; 전원 출석으로. **2** [C] a period of such meetings. (국회·의회 따위의) 회기. **3** [C] 《U.S.》 a period of lessons and study; the hours of lessons. 학기《보통 7개월》; 수업 시간. ¶ *the summer ~* 여름학기 / *Our school has no afternoon sessions on Saturday.* 우리 학교는 토요일엔 오후 수업이 없다. **4** 《*colloq.*》 a meeting or period devoted to some activity. (특수한 활동을 위해 모이는) 모임; 활동기간. ¶ *a ~ for tourists* 여행자를 위한 설명기간. [→sedate]

in session, holding a meeting. 회의중(에, 의); 개회중; 개정중. ¶ *The doctors were in ~ all Friday afternoon.* 의사들은 금요일 오후 내내 회의중이었다 / *Parliament is now in* 〔*out of*〕 *~.* 의회는 지금 개회〔폐회〕중이다.

the Court of Session, the Supreme Civil Court in Scotland. 고등 민사 재판소.

:set [set] *v.* (**set, set·ting**) *vt.* **1** (P6,7,13) 《*on, in*》 put (something) in a specified position; place. …을 두다; 놓다. ¶ ~ *a vase on a table* 탁자 위에 꽃병을 놓다 / ~ *one's foot on a step* 발로 계단을 밟다 / ~ *one's foot on* (*a worm, etc.*) 발로 (벌레 따위)를 짓밟다 / ~ *a stake in the ground* 땅에 말뚝을 박다 / ~ *a vase upside down on the table* 꽃병을 테이블 위에 거꾸로 놓다 / *He ~ his hand on my shoulder.* 그의 손을 내 어깨에 올려놓았다. **2** (P13) ⓐ《*to, on*》 move (something) into contact with something else. …을 (갖다) 대다; (불)을 붙이다〔놓다〕; 지르다. ¶ ~ *a glass to one's lips* 〔*one's lips to a glass*〕 술잔을 입에 대다 / ~ *a match to the fallen leaves* 낙엽에 성냥불을 긋다 / ~ *fire to a house;* ~ *a house on fire* 집에 불을 지르다〔방화하다〕 / ~ *pen to paper* 쓰다. ⓑ move or cause (something) to turn in a certain direction. (얼굴 따위)를 돌리다; 향하다; …쪽으로 돌리다〔가다〕. ¶ ~ *one's face to*(*ward*) *the sun* 얼굴을 태양쪽으로 돌리다 / ~ *one's horse toward home* 말머리를 집으로 돌리다 / ~ *one's face against* (*a proposal, etc.*) …에 강력히 반대하다. **3** (P6,7,13,18) ⓐ put (something) in the proper condition or place; regulate; make (something) ready for use. (기계·기구 따위)를 조정〔조절〕하다; 바른 위치에 두다; 사용할 수 있게 하다; 준비하다. ¶ ~ *a watch* 시계를 맞추다 / ~ *sails* 돛을 달다 / ~ *a trap* 덫을 놓다 / ~ *a chair back on its feet* 의자를 원위치대로 놓다 / ~ *the table for dinner* 식사를 위해 식탁을 차리다 / ~ *men up on a chess board* 말을 장기판에 늘어놓다 / ~ *the alarm-clock for* 〔*at*〕 *5 o'clock* 자명종이 5시에 울리도록 맞추어 놓다 / ~ *one's watch by the radio* 라디오 시보로 시계 바늘을 맞추다. ⓑ put together (the ends of a broken bone) for healing. (부러진 뼈)를 정골(整骨)하다; 접골(接骨)하다. ¶ *The doctor ~ his broken leg.* 의사는 그의 부러진 다리를 접골했다. **4** (P6,13,14,20) ⓐ appoint (someone) for certain duties. …에게 임무를 주다; (임무 수행을 위해) 배치하다; 임명하다. ¶ ~ *spies on someone* 아무에게 감시를 붙이다 / ~ *a guard at the gate* 문에 위병을 배치하다. ⓑ bid or make (someone) do something. …에게 —하게 하다; 명하다. ¶ ~ *someone to dig a well* 아무에게 우물을 파게 하다 / ~ *someone a sum* 아무에게 계산을 시키다 / *I ~ my children to rake the fallen leaves.* 아이들에게 낙엽을 긁어 모으게 했다. ⓒ give a lesson, task, etc. to (a learner, etc.) to do; give (an example, a pattern, a lesson, etc.) to someone. (문제·일 등)을 과(課)하다; (모범·보기 따위)를 보이다. ¶ ~ *someone an example* 아무에게 모범을 보이다 / ~ *someone a problem* 아무에게 문제를 과하다 / ~ *easy questions in an examination* 쉬운 시험 문제를 과하다 / ~ *a precedent for* …의 선례가 되다. **5** (P13) fix (a gem, etc.) in gold, etc.; fix (something) firmly in a frame. (보석 따위)를 박아넣다; 틀에 끼우다. ¶ ~ *diamonds in a crown* 왕관에 다이아몬드를 박아넣다 / ~ *the glass in the window* 창문에 유리를 끼우다. **6** (P6) sow or plant (seeds or plants). (씨)를 뿌리다; (식물)을 심다. ¶ ~ *young plants* 묘목을 심다. **7** (P7,13,18) put (someone or something) into some condition or relation. …을 —상태로 하다; …하게 하다. ¶ ~ *things right* 일을 잘 정돈하다 / ~ *someone right* 아무의 잘못을 바로잡다 / ~ *a room* 〔*one's affairs*〕 *in order* 방을〔문제를〕 정돈하다 / ~ *a prisoner free* 죄수를 석방하다 / ~ *someone thinking* 아무로 하여금 생각하게 하다 / ~ *an engine going* 엔진을 작동시키다 / ~ *someone's mind at rest* 〔*ease*〕 아무를 안심시키다 / *Set your hat straight.* 모자를 똑바로 써라. **8** (P6) ⓐ direct (the thoughts or feelings) with serious attention; keep (one's hopes, heart, etc.) firmly on something. (희망·정신 따위)를 집중하다; 쏟다; (마음에) 정하다. ¶ ~ *one's mind* 〔*brain*〕 (*on*) *to a particular subject* 마음을 특정 문제에 쏟다〔집중하다〕 / ~ *one's heart on a dress* 새옷을 사려고 정하다 / ~ *one's mind on going to church* 교회에 나가기로 마음을 정하다. ⓑ《*reflexively*》 make up one's mind; begin to apply (oneself) to a job, etc.; undertake. 결심하다; (일 따위에) 전념하기 시작하다; 착수하다. ¶ *He ~ himself to finish his homework.* 그는 숙제를 끝내기로 결심했다 / *She ~ herself to study it.* 열심히 그것을 연구하려고 했다. **9** (P6) cause (something) to become firm or hard. …을 굳히다; 응고시키다; 단단하게 하다; 고정하다. ¶ ~ *milk for cheese* 치즈를 만들기 위해 우유를 굳히다 / ~ *the white of an egg by boiling it* 달걀을 삶아서 흰자위를 굳히다 / ~ *a color in dying* 염색에서 물이 잘 들게 하다 / *have one's hair ~* 머리를 세트하다 / *with his mouth ~ in a sunken line* 입을 한일자로 굳게 다물고 / *The mortar is not yet ~.* 회반죽이 아직 굳어 있지 않다. **10** (P13) fix (the price or value) of something; estimate. …에 값을 매기다〔치다〕; 평가하다. ¶ ~ *a price on an article* 상품에 값을 붙이다 / ~ *the value at $200,* 2백 달러로 값을 매기다 / ~ *store by* 높이 평가하다 / *He ~ $2,000 as the right amount for the car.* 그는 그 차의 적정 가격으로 2천 달러를 매겼다. **11** (P6) fix (a time, date, etc.) for something; fix (boundaries or limits). (시간·날짜 따위)를 정하다; (경계·제한 따위)를 정하다. ¶ ~ *a time* 〔*speed*〕 *limit* 시간〔속도〕 제한을 정하다 / ~ *a wedding date* 결혼식 날짜를 정하다 / ~ *bounds to* …을 제한하다 / ~ *the date* 〔*hour*〕 *for an interview* 면회 날짜를〔시간을〕 정하다. **12** (P6) place (a hen) on eggs; place (eggs) under hen. (닭이·닭에게) 알을 품게 하다. **13** (P6,13) ⓐ《mus.》 write (words) to music; write (music) to words. (곡)에 가사를 붙이다; (가사)에 곡을 붙이다; 작곡〔편곡〕하다. ⓑ compose (type); put (copy) into type. (활자)를 짜다; (원고)를 활자로 짜다. — *vi.* **1** (P1) (of the sun, moon, etc.)

sink below the horizon. (해·달이) 지다. ¶ *The sun sets in the west.* 해는 서쪽으로 진다. **2** (P1) (of a liquid, any soft substance, etc.) become hard or solid. (부드러운 것·액체 따위가) 굳어지다; 응고하다. ¶ *The glue* [*jelly*] *has* ~. 아교[젤리]가 굳어졌다. **3** (P1,2A,3) (of a current, opinion, custom) have a definite motion, direction, or tendency. (흐름·바람 따위가) 일정 방향으로 흐르다; (여론 따위가) …경향이 있다. ¶ *The wind sets to the north.* 바람은 북쪽으로 불고 있다 / *The tide sets in his favor.* 형세는 그에게 유리하게 돌아가고 있다. **4** (P2A) 《U.S.》 (of clothes) fit. (옷 따위가 몸에) 꼭 맞다. **5** (P2A) (of a hen) sit on eggs. (암탉이) 알을 품다. **6** (P1) (of flowers or plants) develop fruit. (꽃·식물이) 열매를 맺다; 결실하다. ¶ *The apples won't* ~ *this year.* 사과는 올해엔 잘 열리지 않을 것이다. **7** (P2A) (of a sporting dog) take a stiff attitude as a sign that birds, etc. are present. (사냥개가) 부동의 자세로 사냥감의 위치를 가리키다.

set about, **a**) begin; start; take steps toward doing. …을 시작[착수]하다. ¶ ~ *about one's task* 일에 착수하다. **b**) assault; attack. …을 공격하다. **c**) spread abroad. 퍼뜨리다. ¶ ~ *about a scandal* 추문을 퍼뜨리다.

set a case, suppose. 가정하다.

set against, **a**) balance; compare. …와 균형을 맞추다; …을 비교하다. **b**) make (someone) unfriendly with someone else; fill with dislike for. …와 사이가 틀어지게 하다; …에 반감을 품게 하다.

set (***a***) ***going,*** move; drive. 움직이게 하다; 운전[진행]시키다.

set apart, **a**) =set aside a). ¶ ~ *some food apart for later on* 나중을 위해 얼마의 식량을 따로 떼어두다. **b**) reject; dismiss; disregard. 물리치다; 버리다; 무시하다. **c**) separate. 떼다; 갈라놓다. ¶ ~ *the dogs apart* (*from each other*) 개를 서로 떼어놓다.

set aside, **a**) reserve; put on one side; keep for special use. (특별 목적·용도를 위해) 따로 떼어두다; (따로) 모아 두다. ¶ ~ *money aside for one's children's education* 아이들 교육을 위해 돈을 따로 떼어두다. **b**) make (something) of no effect. …을 무효로 하다. **c**) reject. 물리치다. ¶ *He* ~ *all their offers aside.* 그들의 모든 제의를 물리쳤다. **d**) disregard. 무시하다. ¶ *Let's* ~ *aside all formalities.* 모든 딱딱한 격식은 집어치웁시다.

set at, attack; make (a dog, etc.) attack something. …을 공격하다[덮치다]; (개 따위)를 부추기다.

set at variance, cause to quarrel. 불화하게 하다; 이간하다.

set back, **a**) stop the advance or progress of. …을 방해[저지]하다. ¶ *All their efforts have been* ~ *back.* 그들의 모든 노력은 저지되었다. **b**) move back; turn backward. (시계 바늘)을 뒤로 돌리다; 늦게 가게 하다. ¶ *Hearing the time-signal, she* ~ *the clock back two minutes.* 시보(時報)를 듣고 그녀는 시계 바늘을 2분 늦췄다. **c**) 《U.S. *sl.*》 cost (someone) so much. 비용이 들다. ¶ *This book* ~ *me back 7 dollars.* 이 책은 7달러나 들었다.

set before, **a**) present to (someone); offer to. …앞에 내(밀)다; 제출[제공]하다. ¶ ~ *a cup of coffee before a guest* 손님 앞에 커피 한 잔을 내다. **b**) explain (facts) to someone. …에게 설명하다. ¶ ~ *a plan before the boss* 사장에게 기획을 설명하다.

set by, reserve or save. …을 따로 떼어두다; 따로 저축해 두다.

set down, **a**) put (something) in writing or print. …을 써넣다; 적어두다; (인쇄하여) 남겨두다; 기록하다. ¶ *It is all* ~ *down in the book.* 그건 모두 책에 쓰여져 있다. **b**) put out of one's hand; put down. 밑에 (내려)놓다. ¶ ~ *down a load* 짐을 내려놓다. **c**) let (passengers) get off. (승객)을 내리다. ¶ *I* ~ *her down at her door.* 그녀 집 문 앞에서 그녀를 내려주었다. **d**) 《*as*》 reckon; consider. …로 생각하다: …로 보다. ¶ ~ *someone down as a fool* 아무를 바보로 보다. **e**) 《*to*》 attribute to. …의 탓으로 돌리다. ¶ ~ *down one's success to luck* 성공을 행운의 탓으로 돌리다. **f**) establish; fix. (원칙·규칙 따위)를 정하다; 규정하다. ¶ *Rules have been* ~ *down and must be obeyed.* 규칙이 정해졌으므로 지켜야만 한다.

set eyes on, see. …을 보다; 발견하다.

set forth, **a**) start on a journey; set out. 여행을 떠나다; 출발하다. ¶ ~ *forth on one's travels.* **b**) explain or state. 설명하다; 말하다; 공포하다. ¶ ~ *forth one's views* 의견을 말하다. **c**) exhibit; lay out. 진열[전시]하다; 늘어놓다.

set forward, **a**) move forward. (시계) 바늘을 앞으로 돌리다; (시간이) 빠르게[더가게] 하다(opp. set back b)). **b**) promote. …을 촉진[조성]하다. ¶ ~ *forward the cause of better housing* 보다 좋은 주택이라는 목표를 촉진하다. **c**) present. …을 제출하다. **d**) start; set out. 출발하다; 떠나다.

set in, **a**) begin; start. 시작되다. ¶ *Winter has* ~ *in early this year.* 올해엔 겨울철이 일찍 시작되었다. **b**) move; flow. (바람이) 육지를 향하여 불다; (조수가) 밀려오다. ¶ *The current sets in to the shore.* 조수가 해변으로 밀려오고 있다. **c**) become settled in a particular state. (계절·유행 따위가) 정착되다. ¶ *The rainy season has* ~ *in.* 장마철이 되었다.

set off, **a**) explode. 폭발시키다; 점화하다. ¶ ~ *off a gun* 총을 발사하다; 발포하다 / ~ *off fireworks* 불꽃을 쏘아 올리다. **b**) cause to start doing. …하기 시작하게 하다; 계속 …하게 하다. ¶ *That* ~ *us all off laughing.* 그것을 듣고우리 모두는 웃음을 터뜨렸다. **c**) begin a journey; start off. 여행을 시작하다; 떠나다. ¶ ~ *off on a journey round the world*

세계 일주 여행을 떠나다. **d**) make more striking by contrast. (대조적으로) 돋보이게 하다; 눈에 띄게 하다. ¶ *The red scarf ~ off her beautiful face.* 빨간 목도리는 그녀의 예쁜 얼굴을 돋보이게 했다.

set on 〔***upon***〕, **a**) cause to attack or pursue; urge on; incite. 공격시키다; …을 추적하게 하다; 부추기다; 선동하다. ¶ *~ one's dog on a stranger* 개를 부추겨 낯선 사람을 공격하게 하다 / *~ a crew on to mutiny* 승무원을 꼬드겨 반란을 일으키다. **b**) attack suddenly. (갑자기) 공격하다; 덮치다. ¶ *The dog ~ on me savagely.* 개는 내게 맹렬히 덤벼들었다.

set out, **a**) start to go. 출발하다; 떠나다. ¶ *~ out for home* 귀로(歸路)에 오르다. **b**) spread or arrange (something) for display, sale, etc. (판매·전시 따위를 위해) 펼쳐〔늘어〕 놓다; 진열하다; 정리〔정돈〕하다. ¶ *~ out all the goods on the shelves* 상품을 전부 진열대에 늘어놓다. **c**) state; explain. 설명〔진술〕하다; 말하다. ¶ *~ out one's ideas clearly* 자신의 생각을 분명하게 말하다. **d**) have the intention to do; undertake. …하려고 하다; (…에) 착수하다. ¶ *He ~ out to write a history of Korea.* 그는 한국사 저술에 착수했다.

set over, **a**) place in authority over. 윗자리에 앉히다; 감독자로 정하다. **b**) hand over. 양도하다.

set the axe to, **a**) cut down. …을 베다〔자르다〕. **b**) 《*fig.*》 destroy. …을 파괴하다.

set to, **a**) apply oneself vigorously; begin a piece of work in earnest. 일에 전념하다; 일에 열심히 달라붙다. **b**) start doing something (esp. fighting or eating). …하기 시작하다; 싸우기〔먹기〕 시작하다. ¶ *If you are hungry, you'd better ~ to at once.* 시장하면 곧 식사를 시작하는 게 좋겠다.

set to work, start working. 일을 시작하다. ¶ *She ~ to work to clean the room.* 그녀는 방 청소하는 일을 시작했다.

set up, **a**) start in (business, etc.). (사업 따위)를 시작하다. ¶ *~ up for oneself* 독립하여 사업을 시작하다. **b**) erect or place in position or view. 세우다; 일으키다; 올리다; 내걸다; 붙이다. ¶ *~ up the fallen tree* 쓰러진 나무를 일으켜 세우다 / *~ up a notice* 게시를 붙이다. **c**) build; establish; assemble. 건설하다; 창설〔창립, 수립〕하다; 세우다; 조립하다. ¶ *~ up a new school* 새 학교를 세우다 / *~ up a machine* 기계를 조립하다 / *~ up a government* 정부를 수립하다. **d**) get (someone) established or started. …을 입신〔독립〕시키다; 생업을 갖게 하다. ¶ *He ~ up his son in business.* 그는 아들을 사업으로 입신시켰다. **e**) put forward. 발의(發議)하다; 제언〔제기〕하다. ¶ *~ up a protest* 항의를 제기하다. **f**) utter loudly; raise. 큰 소리를 내다〔지르다〕. ¶ *~ up a shout* 큰 소리를 지르다 / *~ up a clamor* 와자지껄 떠들다. **g**) raise (someone) in place, power, etc. (…을) 높은 지위〔권력〕의 자리에 올리다. **h**) 《*passive*》 furnish with; provide; equip. 공급하다; 갖추게 하다. ¶ *be well ~ up with* 〔*in, for*〕 *clothes* 의복이 충분히 지급되다. **i**) train or develop (the body). (몸)을 단련하다; 훈련하다; 발달시키다. ¶ *~ up soldiers* 병사들을 훈련하다 / *He has a well set-up figure.* 훌륭한 체격을 갖고 있다. **j**) restore to health. 건강을〔원기를〕 되찾게 하다. ¶ *A holiday will ~ you up.* 하루 쉬면 기운을 회복할 게다. **k**) 《in form of *oneself up as* 〔*to be*〕》 pretend to be. …인 체하다; (스스로) …라고 주장〔자처〕하다. ¶ *He ~ himself up as a great artist.* 그는 위대한 예술가로 자처했다 / *I don't ~ myself up to be better than you.* 나는 나 자신이 당신보다 낫다고 주장하지는 않는다. **l**) arrange type; put into type. (활자를) 짜다; (원고를) 활자로 짜다. ¶ *~ up type* / *~ an article* 논문을 활자로 짜다.

set up for, 《*colloq.*》 pretend to be. …인 체하다; …을 자임〔자처〕하다. ¶ *~ up for a prophet* 예언자라고 공언하다.

— *adj.* **1** (of a smile, the eyes, a look, etc.) fixed; unmoving. (미소·눈·표정 따위가) 고정된; 움직이지 않는; 경직된. ¶ *~ eyes* 까딱도 않는 눈 / *a ~ smile* 억지웃음 / *with ~ teeth* 이를 악물고; 큰 결심을 하고. **2** (of a purpose) intentional. 고의의; 일부러의. **3** (of a time or date) arranged in advance. (시간·날짜 따위) 미리 정한; 예정된; 정해진. ¶ *at a ~ time* 예정〔규정〕된 시간에. **4** formed; made; built. 붙박아 고정된; 설치〔장치〕된. ¶ *a ~ machine* 고정 설치된 기계 / *a ~ scene* 영화 촬영용 장치의 장면. **5** (of a speech, prayer, etc.) formal; regular; customary. (연설·문구 따위) 틀에 박힌; 정규의; 관례상의. ¶ *a ~ speech* (미리 준비된) 틀에 박힌 연설 / *a ~ phrase* 관용구 / *a ~ form of prayer* 일정한 양식의 기도 / *in ~ terms* 틀에 박힌 문구로. **6** 《*on, upon*》 (of a person, one's mind, etc.) determind; obstinate. 단호한; 완고한. ¶ *~ defiance* 완강한 반항 / *be ~ in one's opinions* 의견이 완고하다 / *He is ~ on going today.* 오늘 가기로 결심이 되어 있다 / *with a ~ purpose* 단호히. **7** (of eggs, jelly, etc.) having set; solid. (달걀 따위) 굳은; 단단한. **8** (of the weather) good and giving no sign of change. (날씨 따위가) 불변의; 지속적인. **9** (of the sun, etc.) below the horizon. (태양 따위가) 지평선〔수평선〕 아래로 진.

— *n.* **1** Ⓒ a group of similar or related things meant to be used as a whole. 한 벌; 일습; 한 세트. ¶ *a ~ of tools* 도구 1습 / *a ~ of golf clubs* 한 벌의 골프 채 / *a ~ of lectures* 일련의 강의 / *a ~ of false teeth* 의치(義齒) 한 벌 / *a complete ~ of Sakespeare* 셰익스피어 전집. **2** Ⓒ a group of persons joined by common interests, etc. (공통의 이익 따위로 결집된) 일단; 일당; 동아리. ¶ *a literary ~* 문인 동아리 / *a ~ of murderous thieves* 살인 강도의 일당 / *the best ~* 상류 사회 / *the smart*

~(사교계의) 하이칼라들 / *He is not one of my ~.* 그는 나와는 파(派)가 다르다. **3** Ⓒ a radio or television receiver. (라디오·TV 의) 수신기(세트). **4** 《*the* ~》 form; shape. 형태; 모양; 자세. ¶ *the ~ of one's shoulders* 어깨의 모양 / *the ~ of one's features* 얼굴의 생김새; 이목구비. **5** Ⓒ a group of games which count as unit. (테니스 따위의) 승부의 1회; 세트. ¶ *a ~ of tennis.* **6** Ⓤ 《*poet.*》 the setting of the sun. 해의 짐; 일몰(日沒)(opp. rise). ¶ *at ~ of sun* 해질녘에; 일몰에. **7** Ⓒ the place or stage of an action in a play, a movie, etc. 무대 장치; (영화 따위의) 세트《장치를 한 옥내 또는 야외 촬영 장면》. **8** Ⓤ 《*the* ~》 the direction of the wind or current; the tendency of opinion. (흐름이나 바람의) 방향; (여론의) 경향. ¶ *the ~ of public opinion* 여론의 경향 / *the ~ of the wind* 바람의 방향. **9** 《*the* ~》 (of clothing) the way clothing fits or hangs. (옷 따위의) 맞음새; 입음새. ¶ *the ~ of a hat* 모자의 맞음새. **10** Ⓒ a young shoot for planting. 모종. **11** a cutting. 꺾꽂이. **12** the hardening of a liquid or a semi-liquid substance. 굳어짐; 응고(凝固). **13** an arrangement of the hair. (머리의) 세트; 세트한 머리형(型). **14** 《math.》 aggregate. 집합. [E.]

make a dead set at, **a**) attack strongly and violently. …을 맹공격[필사적으로 공격]하다. **b**) (of a girl) try hard to attract the notice or love of (a man). (여성이) 남성의 환심을 사려고 하다.

set·back [sétbæ̀k] *n.* Ⓒ a stop or check to any progress or advancement. 진보의 방해; 역행; 후퇴; 좌절. ¶ *He had a ~ in his business.* 그의 사업에 좌절이 있었다.

set·down [sétdàun] *n.* bitter blame. 질책; 견책.

Seth [seθ] *n.* **1** a man's name. 남자 이름. **2** 《Bible》 a son of Adam. Adam 의 셋째 아들.

set·off [sétɔ̀:f, -ɑ̀f / -ɔ̀f] *n.* Ⓒ **1** something used to make someone or something look better; a decoration. 돋보이게 하는 것; 장식. **2** a start. 출발. [*set*]

set·out [sétàut] *n.* Ⓤ start; beginning. 출발; 개시.

set square [∠∠] *n.* a triangle with angles of 90°, 60° and 30°, or of 45°, 45°, and 90° used to draw lines. 삼각자.

set·tee [setí:] *n.* Ⓒ a sofa or a long seat with a back and arms. 팔걸이·등받이가 달린 긴 의자[소파]. [→settle[2]]

set·ter [sétər] *n.* Ⓒ **1** a long-haired hunting dog. (사냥개의) 세터종(種). **2** 《print.》 a person who sets. 활자를 짜는 사람; 식자공(工). [*set*]

set·ting [sétiŋ] *n.* **1** the act of a person or thing that sets. 붙박아 놓기; 고정시킴; (해·달의) 짐. ¶ *the ~ of the sun* 해의 짐; 일몰. **2** Ⓒ a frame or other thing in which something is set or fastened; a framework in which jewels are fixed. 끼워넣는 틀; 붙박아 두는 받침; 보석 받침; 거미발. ¶ *My pearl ring has a gold ~.* 내 진주 반지는 금제 거미발이 있다. **3** Ⓒ the background of a story; the stage furniture, etc. of a play. 이야기의 배경; 무대 장치. **4** Ⓤ music composed esp. to accompany a story or poem. (이야기·시 따위에 붙인) 곡; 작곡; 편곡. **5** Ⓒ the eggs that a hen sits on for hatching. (닭의) 한 배에 깐 알. [*set*]

:set·tle[1] [sétl] *vi.* **1** (P3) 《*on*》 come to rest; stop. (새 따위가) 앉다; 내려앉다. ¶ *A bird settled on the branch.* 새가 나뭇가지에 내려앉았다. **2** (P1,3) make one's home in a new country or place; build up colonies. (새로운 나라·장소에) 자리를 잡다; 이주[정착]하다; 식민하다. ¶ *~ in Paris* 파리에 자리잡다 / *Many Frenchmen settled along the Mississippi.* 많은 프랑스인들은 미시시피강 연안에 식민했다. **3** (P1,2A) ⓐ sink to the bottom; (of dust, etc.) sink. (찌끼가) 가라앉다; (먼지 따위가) 앉다; 쌓이다. ¶ *The dust has settled on the desk.* 책상 위에 먼지가 쌓여 있다. ⓑ (of a liquid) become clear. (액체가) 맑아지다. **4** (P1,2A) (of a ship, a building, an earth, etc.) sink down to a lower level. (서서히) 가라앉다; 내려앉다; 침하(沈下)하다; 기울다. ¶ *The ship was settling.* 배가 가라앉고 있었다. **5** (P1) become calm; pass into a lasting, stable condition, position, etc. (날씨 따위가) 조용[잠잠]해지다; 안정되다; 고정되다. ¶ *The weather has settled at last.* 날씨가 마침내 안정되었다. **6** (P3) 《*to*》 apply oneself or one's mind to; occupy oneself continuously with. (일 등에) 본격적으로 착수[전념]하다; 자리잡고 지속적으로 하다. ¶ *I can't ~ to anything today.* 오늘은 아무것도 마음잡고 할 마음이 안 든다. **7** (P3) decide; determine. (…로) 정하다; 결심[결정]하다. ¶ *Have you settled on a date for your departure?* 출발할 날짜를 정했느냐 / *I can't ~ finally till I know more details.* 좀더 자세한 내용을 알기까지는 최종 결정을 할 수가 없다. **8** (P3) pay a bill, debt, etc. 셈을 지불하다; 빚을 갚다; 청산하다. ¶ *~ for one's meals* 식대를 지불하다 / *Will you ~ for me?* 내게 빚을 갚지 않으려나.

— *vt.* **1** (P6,7,13) place or set (someone or something) in a fixed state, occupation, etc. …을 움직이지 않게 놓다; …을 안치[정치(定置)], 설치]하다; 자리잡히게 하다; 직업[가정]을 가져 안정시키다. ¶ *~ oneself (down) in an easy chair* 안락 의자에 앉다 / *~ one's daughter by marriage* 딸을 결혼시켜 가정을 갖게 하다 / *~ one's son in business* 아들에게 사업을 하게 하다 / *~ oneself in life* 생활이 안정되다. **2** (P6) ⓐ put (something) in order; arrange. (…을 정연히) 처리[정리]하다; 결말을 내다. ¶ *~ one's affairs* 가사(家事)를[재산을] 정리하다; 유언서를 만들다 / *~ one's problem* 문제를 잘 처리하다. ⓑ bring (an argument, a doubt, etc.) to an end; adjust. (분쟁·의혹 따위)를 해결하다; 조정하

다. ¶ ~ *a dispute* 〔*difficulties*〕 분쟁〔어려움〕을 해결하다 / ~ *someone's doubts* 아무의 의혹을 풀다 / *That settles the whole thing.* 그것으로 만사 해결이다. **3** (P6,13) provide (a place) with settlers; bring (people) to live in a country. …을 이주〔이민〕시키다; …에 식민하다. ¶ *Groups of Puritans from England settled New England.* 영국으로부터 청교도 집단은 뉴잉글랜드에 이주했다. **4** make (the nerves, etc.) calm or quiet; pacify; compose. (신경 따위)를 안정시키다; 가라앉히다. ¶ ~ *a heated imagination* 흥분한 상상력을 가라앉히다 / *The medicine settled her nerves.* 약은 그녀의 신경을 안정시켰다. **5** (P6,7,8,10,11,12) make up one's mind about. …로 (결)정하다; 결심하다. ¶ ~ *conditions* 〔*a price*〕 조건〔가격〕을 정하다 / ~ *the date of one's return* 귀환 날짜를 정하다 / ~ *which way to take* 〔*what to do*〕 어느 길을 택해야〔무엇을 해야〕 할지 결정하다. **6** (P6,7,13) pay (a bill, debt, etc.); fulfill. 셈을 지불하다〔치르다〕; 빚을 갚다; 청산〔결산〕하다. ¶ ~ (*up*) *with a waiter* 웨이터에게 계산을 지불하다 / ~ *a bill with a desk clerk* (호텔에서 나갈 때) 프런트에 요금을 지불하다 / ~ (*up*) *a claim* 채무를 청산하다. **7** (P6) ⓐ cause (something) to sink to the bottom; make (a liquid) pure and clear. …을 침전시키다; (액체)를 맑게 하다. ¶ ~ *the dregs* 찌끼를 침전시키다. ⓑ cause (dust, etc.) to sink. (먼지 따위가) 앉게 하다; 쌓이게 하다. [→sit]

settle down, **a**) live a more regular, stable way of life. (결혼 따위로) 가정을 갖다; 자리를 잡다; (직업 따위로) 안정된 생활을 하다. ¶ *marry and ~ down* 결혼해서 가정을 갖다. **b**) fix one's home somewhere permanently. 자리를 잡고 살다; 정착하다. **c**) become quiet and peaceful. (흥분 따위가) 가라앉다; 조용〔평온〕해지다. ¶ *The excitement will soon ~ down.* 흥분은 곧 가라앉을 게다. **d**) (of a ship, foundations, etc.) sink to the lowest point. (배·지반(地盤) 따위가) 가라〔내려〕앉다; 침하하다. **e**) (of a liquid) become clear. (액체가) 맑아지다. **f**) apply one to. …에 전념〔몰두〕하다; 본격적으로 하다.

settle down to, begin to work steadily at. 본격적으로 착수하다; …에 전념하다. ¶ *be unable to ~ down to studying* 차분히 공부할 수가 없다 / *He settled down to correcting examination papers.* 그는 시험 답안지를 수정하기 시작했다.

settle for, decide in favor of; agree to have or accept. (불만이지만) 좋다고 하다; …에 만족해 하다.

settle in, **a**) start living in a new house. 새집에 자리잡다; 거처를 정하다. **b**) help (a person) to settle in. 자리잡고 살게 하다; 이주시키다; 식민하다.

settle on 〔***upon***〕, **a**) decide to do; make up one's mind to have. …으로 (결)정하다; …로 마음을 정하다. ¶ ~ *upon a plan* 계획을 정하다 / *Which shoes have you settled on* 〔*upon*〕*?* 어떤 구두로 마음을 정하셨습니까. **b**) bestow (property, etc.) legally on. …에게 물려주다〔양도하다〕.

settle up, complete one's transactions; pay up. 결말을 짓다; 셈을 치르다〔지불하다〕; 빚을 갚다. ¶ ~ *up one's debts* 빚을 청산하다.

settle (***up***) ***with,*** **a**) come to an understanding with. …와 해결을 보다; …와 화해하다. **b**) pay one's debts to. …에게 빚을 갚다; 지불하다. ¶ *have an account to ~ with someone* 아무에게 갚아야 할 셈이 있다《좋지 않은 성질의 해결할 일이 있다》.

set·tle[2] [sétl] *n.* Ⓒ a long, wooden bench with arms and a high, straight back. (등받이가 높고 팔걸이가 있는) 긴 의자.

set·tled [sétld] *adj.* **1** fastened or fixed firmly; permanent. 고정된; 영구적인. **2** placed on a sure basis. 단단한; 뿌리 깊은.

:set·tle·ment [sétlmənt] *n.* **1** ⓊⒸ the act of settling; the state of being settled; the act of bringing a quarrel to an end. 해결; 화해; 처리; 정리. ¶ *come to a ~* 해결하다. **2** Ⓤ the establishment of one's life by marriage. (결혼 따위에 의한) 생활의 안정; 자리잡기. **3** ⓐ Ⓤ the process of colonizing. 식민; 이민. ¶ *The ~ of Canada was begun by the French.* 캐나다의 식민은 프랑스인들에 의해 시작되었다. ⓑ Ⓒ a place where a number of people have gone to live; a colony. 식민지; 개척〔이주〕지. ¶ *establish a ~ in South Africa* 남아프리카에 식민지를 만들다. **4** ⓊⒸ decision; the complete payment of a bill. 결정; 지불; 청산. ¶ *the ~ of a debt* 빚의 청산 / *the ~ of the date* 날짜의 결정. **5** ⓊⒸ arrangement; putting in order. 정돈; 조절; 조정. ¶ *No ~ of the dispute is possible unless each side yields some points.* 양쪽이 약간씩 양보하지 않는 한 분쟁의 조정은 불가능하다. **6** Ⓒ a small, isolated group of houses and the people living in them; a hamlet. (인구가 드문 지대의) 촌락; 부락. ¶ *a ~ in the woods* 숲지대의 부락. **7** Ⓤ the settling of property upon a person or persons. (재산 등의) 양도; 처분; (특히 가족을 위한) 계승적 부동산 처분. **8** Ⓒ a group of persons living in a poor and crowded section of a large city for giving educational or recreational service to the people in that section; a building used for this purpose. 인보(隣保) 사업단《빈민가에서 그곳의 생활 향상을 꾀하는 복지 단체》; 인보 회관. ¶ *a ~ house* 인보관. [→settle, -ment]

settlement day [∠–– ∠] *n.* the date on which accounts are settled. 청산일.

·set·tler [sétlə*r*] *n.* Ⓒ a person who settles in a new country; a colonist. 이주자; 식민자. [*settle*[1]]

set·tling [sétliŋ] *n.* Ⓤ **1** the state of being fixed; the state of living in one place for a long time. 고정; 정주; 정착. **2** the settlement of accounts; a decision. 결산; 결정. **3** ⟪*pl.*⟫ things which sink to the bottom of liquid. 침전물; 찌끼.

set-to [séttù] *n.* Ⓒ (*pl.* **-tos**) ⟪*colloq.*⟫ a fight; a vigorous argument. 싸움; 격렬한 언쟁. [*set*]

set-up [sétʌ̀p] *n.* Ⓒ **1** organization; the way in which something is begun or done. 조직; 기구; 구성. ¶ *a democratic* ~ 민주적 조직〔기구〕 / *a power* ~ 권력 기구. **2** an arrangement. 장비; 배치. **3** bearing. 태도. **4** a game that has been fixed. 짬짜미 시합.

:sev·en [sévən] *n.* **1** Ⓤ the number between six and eight; 7. 일곱; 7. **2** Ⓒ any group or set of seven persons or things. 7인; 7개. **3** Ⓒ anything shaped like 7. 7자(字) 형의 것. — *adj.* of 7. 일곱의; 7의. [E.]

sev·en·fold [sévənfòuld] *adv., adj.* **1** seven times as much or as many. 7배로〔인〕; 7겹으로; 일곱 겹인. **2** having seven parts. 7 부분으로 된.

:sev·en·teen [sévəntíːn] *n.* **1** Ⓤ the number between sixteen and eighteen; 17. 열일곱; 17. **2** Ⓒ any group or set of seventeen persons or things. 17인; 17개. — *adj.* of 17. 17의; 열일곱의.

:sev·en·teenth [sévəntíːnθ] *n.* **1** ⟪usu. *the* ~⟫ the number 17; 17th. 제17; 열일곱(번)째. **2** Ⓒ one of 17 equal parts of anything. 17분의 1. — *adj.* of the 17th. 제17의; 열일곱(번)째의; 17분의 1의.

:sev·enth [sévənθ] *n.* **1** ⟪usu. *the* ~⟫ the number 7; 7th. 제7; 일곱(번)째. **2** Ⓒ one of 7 equal parts of anything. 7분의 1. — *adj.* of the 7th. 제7의; 일곱(번)째의; 7분의 1의.

seventh heaven [⸗–⸗–], **the** *n.* the highest part of heaven; a very happy condition. 제7천국; 최고천(最高天); 의기양양. ¶ *the* ~ *of delight* 기쁨의 극치〔절정〕 / *be in the* ~ 더없는 행복에 젖어 있다.

sev·enth·ly [sévənθli] *adv.* in the seventh place. 제7에; 일곱(번)째에. [E.]

:sev·en·ti·eth [sévəntiiθ] *n.* **1** ⟪usu. *the* ~⟫ the number 70; 70th. 제70; 70번째. **2** Ⓒ one of 70 equal parts of anything. 70분의 1. — *adj.* of 70th. 제70의; 70(번)째의.

:sev·en·ty [sévənti] *n.* Ⓤ **1** seven times ten; 70. 일흔; 70. **2** ⓐ ⟪*the seventies*⟫ the years 70 to 79 of a particular century. (세기의) 70년대. ⓑ ⟪*one's seventies*⟫ the years from the age of 70 to the age of 79. (나이의) 70(세)대. — *adj.* of 70. 70의.

sev·er [sévər] *vt.* (P6,13) **1** cut apart; cut off; separate. …을 절단하다; 떼다; 분리시키다. ¶ *His arm was severed from his body in the accident.* 그 사고로 그는 한쪽 팔이 절단됐다 / *The sailor severed the rope with a knife.* 뱃사람은 나이프로 밧줄을 끊었다. **2** break off (friendly relations). …을 불화하게 하다; 이간시키다. ¶ ~ *one's connection with* …와의 관계를 끊다 / *The two countries severed friendly relations.* 두 나라는 우호 관계를 단절했다. **3** divide; lie between. 갈라놓다. ¶ *The Channel severs England from France.* 영국 해협이 영국과 프랑스를 떼어놓고 있다. — *vi.* (P1) become divided. 끊어지다; 떨어〔갈라〕지다. ¶ *The rope severed and the swing fell down.* 줄이 끊어져서 그네는 땅에 떨어졌다. [→separate]

:sev·er·al [sévərəl] *adj.* **1** some; three or more, but not many. 몇 개의; 몇몇의. ¶ ~ *ways of doing it* 그것을 행하는 몇 가지 방법 / *I have said so* ~ *times.* 몇 번이나 그렇게 말해 왔다. **2** separate; individual. 따로따로의; 각자의; 제각기의. ¶ *They went their* ~ *ways.* 그들은 제각기의 길을 갔다 / *Each has his* ~ *ideal.* 모두 각자의 이상을 갖고 있다. — *pron.* several persons or things. 몇 사람; 몇 개. ¶ *I already have* ~. 이미 몇 개 갖고 있다 / *Several of them failed.* 그들 중 몇은 실패했다. [L. *separ* distinct]

Several men, several minds. ⟪*prov.*⟫ So many men, so many minds. 각인각색.

sev·er·al·ly [sévərəli] *adv.* separately; individually. 각각; 따로따로; 개별적으로.

sev·er·al·ty [sévərəlti] *n.* separate character. 개별; 별개; 개별성; (재산, 특히 토지의) 단독 보유.

in severalty, ⟪law⟫ in one's own right. 단독 보유의.

sev·er·ance [sévərəns] *n.* Ⓤ the act of severing; the state of being severed; division; separation. 절단; 분리; 단절. ¶ ~ *of the leg below the knee* 무릎 아랫부분의 절단 / *the* ~ *of diplomatic relations between two countries* 양국간의 국교 단절. [→sever]

:se·vere [sivíər] *adj.* **1** strict; stern. 엄(격)한; 단호한; 가차 없는; 가혹한. ¶ ~ *laws* 가혹한 법률 / *a* ~ *punishment* 엄벌 / *act as a* ~ *judge* 엄격한 판단을 내리다 / *He is* ~ *with his children.* 그는 자식들에게 엄하다. **2** serious; grave. 심각한; 엄숙한; 중대한. ¶ *a* ~ *look* 엄숙한 얼굴 / *a* ~ *illness* 중병 / *be in a* ~ *position* 중대한 입장에 있다. **3** violent; sharp. (격)심한; 맹렬한. ¶ *a* ~ *cold* 혹한 / *a* ~ *winter* 엄동 / *a* ~ *pain* 격통 / *That was a* ~ *storm.* 그것은 대단한 폭풍이었다. **4** extremely plain or simple. 간소한; 꾸밈이 없는. ¶ *a dress of* ~ *style* 수수한 스타일의 옷. **5** difficult. 힘겨운; 어려운. ¶ *a* ~ *test of his powers* 그에게는 힘겨운 시련〔시험〕. [L. *severus*]

be severe on 〔***upon***〕***,*** be hard on; treat badly. …에게 모질게 대하다. ¶ *Don't be too* ~ *on him. —He couldn't help it.* 그에게 너무 심하게 말아라—그로서는 어쩔 수 없었다.

·se·vere·ly [sivíərli] *adv.* in a severe manner; violently; plainly; simply. 호되게; 격심하게; 맹렬히; 간소하게.

se·ver·i·ty [sivérəti] *n.* Ⓤ **1** strictness; sternness; harshness. 호됨; 엄격; 가혹; 통렬. **2** seriousness. 진지함; 중후. **3** violence; sharpness. 격렬; 날카로움. ¶ *the* ~ *of* *pain* 격통 / *the ~ of grief* 격심한 슬픔. **4** simplicity or plainness of style or taste. (문체·취미 따위의) 간소; 순수함. ¶ *the ~ of her dress* 그녀 옷의 수수함. **5** ⟪*pl.*⟫ severe treatment or experiences. 가혹한 처사〔경험〕.

:sew [sou] *v.* (**sewed, sewed** or **sewn**) *vt.* (P6,7,13) **1** make (clothes) by means of making stitches. (옷)을 꿰매다; 재봉하다; 박다. **2** join or attach (something) to another thing by making stitches. …을 꿰매어 달다〔붙이다〕. ¶ *~ a button on a coat* 상의에 단추를 달다. **3** close or repair (a wound, a tear, etc.) by means of making stitches. (상처·터진 데 따위)를 꿰매다; 봉합하다. —*vi.* (P1) work with needle and thread. 바느질하다; 꿰매다; 박다. [E.]

sew in, tuck in. 꿰매다; 박다.

sew on, fasten by sewing on. (꿰매어) 달다; 붙이다.

sew up, stitch together; sew in; shut up by sewing. 꿰매(어 잇)다; 꿰매어 박다.

sew·age [sú:idʒ] *n.* Ⓤ waste water or matter carried (away) through a sewer. 하수(下水); 하수 오물; 구정물. [ex-, L. *aqua* water]

sew·er[1] [sjú:ər] *n.* Ⓒ an underground pipe to carry off waste water, waste matter, etc. 하수관(管); 하수구(溝)〔도〕. [↑]

sew·er[2] [sóuər] *n.* Ⓒ a person or thing that sews. 바느질하는〔꿰매는〕 사람; 재봉사; 재봉틀. [*sew*]

sew·er·age [sjú:əridʒ] *n.* Ⓤ **1** the system of sewers. 하수 시설; 하수도. **2** removal of waste by sewers. 하수 처리. **3** sewage. 하수 오물; 하수. [sewer[1]]

•sew·ing [sóuiŋ] *n.* **1** Ⓤ work with needle and thread. 바느질; 재봉. **2** ⟪*pl.*⟫ thread for sewing. 바느질〔박는, 꿰매는〕 실. —*adj.* to be used for sewing. 재봉용〔바느질용〕의. [*sew*]

sewing machine [⌐— —⌐] *n.* a machine for making stitches, etc. 재봉틀; 미싱.

sewn [soun] *v.* pp. of **sew**.

•sex [seks] *n.* **1** ⟪*collectively*⟫ one of the two groups into which creatures or plants are divided; male or female. 남〔여〕; 암〔수〕. ¶ *Which ~ is the chick?* 그 병아리는 수컷인가 암컷인가. **2** ⓊⒸ the characteristics which distinguish any creature or plant as either male or female. 성(性); 성별. ¶ *the fair* 〔*gentle, softer, weaker*〕 *~* 여성 / *the rough* 〔*sterner, stronger*〕 *~* 남성 / *the equality of the sexes* 남녀의 평등. **3** Ⓤ anything connected with sexual matters, esp. the instinct or attraction drawing one sex toward another. 성(性)과 관계 있는 일; (특히) 성욕. [L. *sexus*]

sex·a·ge·nar·i·an [sèksədʒənέəriən] *adj.* of the age of 60 years, or between 60 and 70 years old. 60세의; 60대의. —*n.* Ⓒ a person in this age. 60세〔대〕의 사람. [L. *sex* six]

sex·a·ges·i·mal [sèksədʒésəməl] *adj.* of the number sixty. 60의.

sex·cen·te·na·ry [seksséntənèri / sèks-sentí:nəri] *adj.* of six hundred years. 6백년의. —*n.* a 600th anniversary or its celebration. 육백년제.

sex·less [sékslis] *adj.* **1** having no sex. 남녀〔암수〕의 구별이 없는; 무성(無性)의. **2** lacking in a sense of sex. 성(性)감각이 없는.

sex·pot [sékspɑ̀t, -pɔ̀t] *n.* a sexy woman. 성적 매력이 넘치는 여자.

sex·tant [sékstənt] *n.* Ⓒ **1** an instrument used by sailors for measuring the height of the sun or a star above the horizon in order to determine their positions at sea. 육분의(六分儀). **2** one sixth of a circle. 원의 6분의 1. [L. *sex* six]

⟨sextant 1⟩

sex·tet, -tette [sekstét] *n.* Ⓒ **1** a piece of music for six voices or instruments. 6중창〔주〕. **2** six singers or players. 6중창단; 6중주단. **3** any group of six. 6인조(組). [↑]

sex·to·dec·i·mo [sèkstoudésəmòu] *n.* **1** a sheet of paper folded in 16 leaves. 16절판의 종이. **2** a book made by folding thus. 16절판의 책. 參考 16 mo로 생략. [↑]

sex·ton [sékstən] *n.* Ⓒ a man who takes care of a church and churchyard and who attends to burials. (교회의) 관리인; 교회지기. [→sacristan]

sex·u·al [sékʃuəl] *adj.* **1** of sex. 성(性)의. ¶ *~ morality* 성도덕. **2** having sex; either male or female. 유성(有性)의; 남녀의; 자웅의. **3** of the sexual appetite. 성욕의. ¶ *a ~ appetite* 〔*desire*〕 성욕 / *~ perversion* 성적 도착. **4** of the sexual organs. 생식기의.

sex·y [séksi] *adj.* (**sex·i·er, sex·i·est**) arousing sexual desire. 성욕을 불러 일으키는.

sez [sez] *v.* ⟪*colloq.*⟫ =says.

sez you, as you say (, but I doubt it, or I don't believe it). 말씀은 그렇지만 글쎄요〔어떨는지요〕. [*says you*]

SF, sf science fiction.

sf., sfz. ⟪mus.⟫ sforzando.

sfor·zan·do [sfɔ:rtsá:ndou / -tsǽn-] *adj., adv.* ⟪It.⟫ with sudden emphasis. 갑자기 힘주어; 스포르찬도.

sg, s.g. senior grade.

sgd signed.

Sgt. Sergeant.

SHA ⟪naut.⟫ sidereal hour angle. 항성〔(恒星) 시각.

shab·bi·ly [ʃǽbili] *adv.* in a shabby manner. 초라하게. [*shabby*]

shab·bi·ness [ʃǽbinis] *n.* Ⓤ the state or quality of being shabby. 초라함; 비열(함); 인색함.

•shab·by [ʃǽbi] *adj.* (**-bi·er, -bi·est**) **1** much worn; used too much. 오래 입어 낡은. ¶ *~ clothes* / *a ~ old hat* (오래 써) 찌든

모자. **2** wearing worn clothes. 누더기 옷을 걸친; 초라한. ¶ *She is always* ~. 그녀는 늘 초라한 차림을 하고 있다. **3** mean; not generous; unfair. 야비한; 비열한; 인색한. ¶ ~ *behavior* 비열한 행동 / *It is* ~ *not to speak to an old friend because he is poor.* 그가 가난하다고 해서 옛 친구에게 말을 하지 않는다는 것은 야비한 짓이다. [E. =scabby]

shack [ʃæk] *n.* Ⓒ 《U.S., Can.》 a very small, poor house; a hut. (초라한) 오두막집; 판잣집. [N -Amer.]

shack·le [ʃǽkəl] *n.* Ⓒ **1** 《usu. *pl.*》 iron rings to be fastened around a prisoner's ankle or wrist so as to stop him from escaping. 족쇄; 쇠고랑; 수갑. **2** any device used to fasten or couple. 연결시키는 것; (열차의) 연결 고리 (따위). **3** anything that prevents freedom; restraint. 구속하는 것; 속박; 굴레; 방해. ¶ *shackles of debt* 빚의 속박 / *break through the shackles of convention* 인습의 굴레를 벗어나다.

— *vt.* (P6) **1** put shackles on (someone). …에게 쇠고랑을〔족쇄를〕 채우다. **2** fasten or couple (two things) together with a shackle. …을 연결 고리로 잇다; 연결하다. **3** 《*fig.*》 prevent; restrain. …을 방해하다; 구속〔속박〕하다. [E.]

:shade [ʃeid] *n.* **1** Ⓤ a slight darkness or coolness made by something blocking the light; Ⓒ a partly dark place. 응달; 그늘 (cf. *shadow*). ¶ *light and* ~ 명암(明暗) / *under the* ~ *of a tree* 나무 그늘에서 / *sit in the* ~ 그늘에 앉다 / *The tree makes a pleasant* ~. 그 나무는 시원한 그늘을 만들어 준다. **2** 《*the* ~*s*》 the darkness of the evening or night. 땅거미; 어스름; 야음(夜陰). ¶ *the shades of evening* 〔*night*〕 땅거미〔야음〕. **3** Ⓒ something that shuts out light or brightness. 차양; 차일; 커튼; 전등의 갓. ¶ *Pull down the shades of the windows.* 창문의 블라인드를 내려라. **4** Ⓒ ⓐ a degree of color. 명암〔농담(濃淡)〕의 정도; 색조. ¶ *all shades of blue* 여러가지 색조의 청색. ⓑ the darker parts of a picture. 음영(陰影); (그림의) 어두운 부분(opp. light). **5** ⓐ 《*a* ~》 a slight degree or amount. 극히 조금〔약간〕; 낌새. ¶ *a* ~ *to the right* 약간 오른쪽으로 / *There is not a* ~ *of doubt.* 한점의 의혹도 없다 / *The coffee is a* ~ *too bitter.* 커피가 좀 쓰다. ⓑ a slight difference. 미묘한 차이. ¶ *Many English words have delicate shades of meaning.* 많은 영어 낱말들은 미묘한 의미의 차이가 있다. **6** Ⓒ 《*poet.*》 ⓐ a ghost; a spirit. 망령; 영혼. ¶ *He saw the shades of his former companions.* 이전 친구들의 망령을 보았다. ⓑ 《*the* ~ *s*》 the world of the dead. 저승; 황천.

cast 〔***throw, put***〕 *someone* or *something* ***into the shade,*** make someone or something obscure. …로 하여금 빛을 잃게〔무색하게〕 하다; …을 눈에 띄지 않게 하다.

fall into the shade, be obscured. 희미해지다; 세상에서 잊혀지다.

the shadow of a shade, an illusion. 환영(幻影); 곡두.

without light and shade, monotonous. 명암이 없는; 단조로운.

— *vt.* **1** (P6,13) ⓐ keep (something) from light or heat; cover; darken. …을 (빛·열 따위로부터) 가로막다; 덮어 가리다; …을 어둡게 하다. ¶ ~ *one's face with one's hand* 손으로 얼굴을 가려 햇볕을 피하다. ⓑ cast shade upon. …을 그늘지게 하다; 그림자를 드리우다. ¶ *The tree* ~ *the house.* 나무가 집을 그늘지게 한다. **2** (P6) make (parts of a picture, etc.) darker to give differences of brightness, etc. (그림에) 음영(陰影)을 만들다.

— *vi.* (P2A,3) 《*into, off*》 change little by little, esp. in color. 점차〔조금씩〕 변화하다. ¶ *blue shading off into green* 점차 녹색으로 변하는 파랑 / *This scarf shades from deep rose to pale pink.* 이 목도리는 짙은 장밋빛에서 엷은 핑크빛으로 조금씩 바래고 있다. [E.]

shad·ing [ʃéidiŋ] *n.* **1** Ⓒ a slight difference in color or tone. (색·음조의) 약간의 변화; 차이. **2** Ⓤ 《*paint.*》 the representation of light or shade in a painting or drawing. 명암법; 음영(陰影).

:shad·ow [ʃǽdou] *n.* Ⓒ **1** a dark form made on the ground, etc. by a thing that cuts off light. (일정한 모양의) 그림자; 투영(投影). ¶ *be afraid of one's* ~ 자신의 그림자를 무서워하다; 흠칫흠칫 놀라다 / *follow someone about like a* ~ 그림자처럼 아무를 붙어다니다 / *May your* ~ *never grow less!* 오래오래 건재하시기를 빕니다. **2** ⓐ Ⓤ shade; darkness; the dark part of a place or picture. 그늘; 어둠; (그림의) 음영부(陰影部). ¶ *the* ~ *of a tree* 나뭇그늘 / *Don't turn on the light; we like to sit in the* ~. 불을 켜지 마라, 우린 어둠 속에 앉아 있는 게 좋으니까. ⓑ 《*the* ~ *s*》 the darkness after sunset. (일몰 후의) 어스름; 땅거미. ¶ *The shadows of evening are falling.* 땅거미가 지고 있다. **3** sadness; gloom. (마음의) 어두운 그림자; 슬픔; 우울. ¶ *the* ~ *of death* 죽음의 어두운 그림자 / *cast a* ~ *on his reputation* 그의 명성에 먹칠을 하다. **4** 《*a* ~, usu. in *negative*》 a small degree; a very slight sign. (극히) 조금; 미량; 기색. ¶ *beyond the* ~ *of a doubt* 추호의 의심도 없이 / *He has no* ~ *of pity.* 눈꼽만큼의 동정심도 없다. **5** a person who follows another about everywhere; a person who watches another. (그림자처럼) 붙어다니는 사람; 미행자. ¶ *put a* ~ *on him* 그에게 미행을 붙이다 / *Nancy is Mary's* ~. 낸시는 항상 메리와 붙어다닌다 / *Trouble is a* ~ *to life.* 말썽은 인생에 붙어다니는 것이다. **6** a poor likeness of a former condition; an unreal thing. 희미한 옛 모습〔자취〕; 환영; 이름뿐인 것. ¶ *run after a* ~ 환영을 좇다 / *a* ~ *of one's former life* 지난 날의 옛모습 / *have only the* ~ *of freedom* 이름만의 자유를 가지다. **7** a ghost. 유령; 망령. **8** Ⓤ protection. 비호; 보호. ¶ *sanctuary in the* ~ *of the*

church 교회의 비호를 받는 은신처〔피난처〕.
under* 〔*in*〕 *the shadow of something, **a)** very near to something. …의 바로 가까이; …에 인접하여. **b)** protected by. …의 보호하에. ¶ *under the ~ of an angel's wings* 천사의 날개에 수호되어.

— *vt.* (P6) **1** send a shade or shadow upon (something or someone); protect (something) from light, heat, etc. …에 그림자를 드리우다〔던지다〕; …을 그늘지게〔어둡게〕 하다; 가로막다. ¶ *Her face is shadowed from the light.* 그녀의 얼굴은 빛으로부터 가려져 있다. **2** follow and watch closely. …을 미행하다; 뒤를 밟다. ¶ *He felt he was being shadowed.* 그는 미행당하고 있음을 느꼈다. **3** 《*forth, out*》 represent vaguely. …을 어렴풋이 나타내다. [E.]

shad·ow·y [ʃǽdoui] *adj.* (**-ow·i·er, -ow·i·est**) **1** filled with shadows. 그림자로 싸인〔덮인〕; 그늘진. ¶ *~ woods* 그늘진 숲. **2** like a shadow; faint; dim. 그림자 같은; 희미한; 어두운. ¶ *He saw a ~ outline on the window curtain.* 창문 커튼에 비친 희미한 윤곽을 보았다. **3** unreal, like a ghost. 환영(幻影)의; 곡두의.

***shad·y** [ʃéidi] *adj.* (**shad·i·er, shad·i·est**) **1** sheltered from the light; shaded. 그늘이 져 있는. ¶ *walk along a ~ road* 그늘진 길을 걷다. **2** giving shade. 그늘을 이루는; 그늘지게 하는. ¶ *a ~ tree* 그늘을 이루고 있는 나무. **3** 《*colloq.*》 of doubtful character; questionable. 수상쩍은; 의심스러운; 뒤가 구린. ¶ *a ~ conduct* 〔*character*〕 수상한 행위〔인물〕 / *~ dealings* 뒤가 구린 거래; 암거래. [→shade]
keep something shady, keep something out of sight. …을 비밀로 하다; 남의 눈을 피하다.
on the shady side of, older than; beyond the age of. (어떤 나이를) 넘어선; …이상의. ¶ *He is on the ~ side of forty.* 그는 40의 고개를 넘어서 있다.

***shaft** [ʃæft, ʃɑːft] *n.* Ⓒ **1** the long stem or handle of an arrow or spear. (화)살대; (창·도끼 따위의) 자루. **2** an arrow; a spear. 화살; 창. ¶ 《*fig.*》 *shafts of envy* (공격적인) 질투의 화살《질투의 표현》. **3** a beam of light; a ray. 전광(電光); 광선. **4** a bar supporting the part that turns in a machine or engine. 샤프트; 굴대; 축. **5** 《*archit.*》 the main part of a column. 주신(柱身); 기둥몸. **6** 《*pl.*》 the pole of a carriage or wagon. (수레의) 채. **7** ⓐ a passage by which to enter an underground mine. 수갱(竪坑); 곧은바닥. ⓑ a well-like passage. (우물처럼) 위아래로 뚫린 공간; 샤프트; 수직 공간. ¶ *a lift* 〔*an elevator*〕 *~* 승강기 샤프트. [E.]

shag [ʃæg] *n.* Ⓤ **1** rough, matted hair. 거친〔텁수룩한〕 털; 조모(粗毛). **2** a kind of coarse tobacco. 거친 살담배의 일종. **3** a long, rough nap of cloth. 보풀; 괴깔. **4** cloth having a long, rough nap. 거친 보풀이 있는 직물. [E.]

shag·gy [ʃǽgi] *adj.* (**-gi·er, -gi·est**) covered with rough, uneven hair. 털이 텁수룩한; 털북숭이의; 털이 많은. ¶ *a ~ dog* 삽사리 / *a ~ beard* 텁수룩한 턱수염.

sha·green [ʃəgríːn, ʃæ-] *n.* Ⓤ a kind of untanned leather made from the skin of horses or asses. (말·당나귀 따위의) 무두질하지 않은 우툴두툴한 가죽. [Turk.]

shah [ʃɑː] *n.* (a title of) the ruler of Iran. 이란 국왕(의 칭호). [Pers.]

:shake [ʃeik] *v.* (**shook, shak·en**) *vt.* **1** (P6,7) ⓐ move (something or someone) rapidly from side to side or up and down. …을 잡아 흔들다; 뒤흔들다. ¶ *~ a closed door* 닫힌 문을 흔들다 / *His heavy steps shook the room.* 그의 육중한 발걸음이 방을 진동시켰다. ⓑ bring, throw, or scatter (something) by a shaking movement. …을 (뒤)흔들어 —하게 하다. ¶ *~ a tree and bring the fruit down* 나무를 흔들어 열매를 떨어뜨리다 / *~ the sand from* 〔*out of*〕 *one's shoes* 신발을 흔들어 모래를 떨어버리다. **2** (P6,13) make (someone) afraid; give a shock to (someone); weaken; disturb. …을 두려워하게 하다; 놀라게〔흔들리게〕 하다; 불안하게 하다; 충격을 주다. ¶ *~ one's decision* 결심이 흔들리게 하다 / *be shaken by* 〔*with, at*〕 *the news* 그 소식을 듣고 충격을 받다〔놀라다〕 / *Her lying shook my faith in her.* 그녀의 거짓말은 그녀에 대한 나의 믿음을 흔들어 놓았다. **3** (P6,13) take grip of (someone's hand); take grip of the hand of (someone) in greeting. (인사로서 상대의 손)을 꼭 쥐다; …와 악수하다. ¶ *~ hands with someone = ~ someone's hand= ~ someone by the hand.* 아무와 악수하다. **4** (P6,13) wave about. …을 흔들다; 휘두르다. ¶ *~ a handkerchief* 손수건을 흔들다 / *~ one's fist* 〔*stick*〕 *at someone* 아무에게 주먹〔단장〕을 휘두르다. **5** (P6,7) cause to tremble. 떨리게 하다. ¶ *Chills shook his body.* 냉기가 그의 몸을 떨게 했다. **6** mix; blend. …을 섞다. ¶ *~ milk before pouring it* 우유를 따르기 전에 흔들어 섞다. **7** 《*U.S. colloq.*》 get rid of (someone or something). …을 뿌리치다〔없애다〕; (추적자)를 따돌리다. ¶ *He could not ~ his pursuers.* 추격자들을 따돌릴 수가 없었다.

— *vi.* (P1,2A) **1** be shaken; tremble. 흔들리다; 진동하다; 덜덜 떨리다. ¶ *The earth shook violently.* 땅이 몹시 흔들렸다 / *He was shaking with cold* 〔*fear*〕. 그는 추위〔공포〕로 떨고 있었다 / *Her voice shook with anger.* 그녀의 목소리는 노여움으로 떨렸다. **2** become unsteady. (결심 따위가) 흔들리다; 비틀거리다. **3** 《often *imperative*》 shake hands. 악수하다.
shake a foot* 〔*leg*〕*, **a)** dance. 춤추다. **b)** hurry. 서두르다.
shake down, **a)** cause (fruit, etc.) to fall by shaking a tree, etc. (나무에서 과실 따위)를 흔들어 떨어뜨리다. **b)** settle or become compact by shaking. 흔들어〔추슬러〕 꽉 채우다. **c)** make a bed on the sofa, floor, etc.

(소파 따위에) 임시 잠자리를 만들(어 자)다. **d**) become accustomed to new surroundings. 새로운 환경에 익숙해지다. ¶ *The boy will soon ~ down at his new school.* 그 아이는 곧 새 학교에 적응할 게다.
shake** one's **head, move it from side to side to indicate 'no', or doubt, hesitation, disapproval. (부정·의심 등을 나타내어) 고개를 가로젓다.
shake in** one's **shoes, be in a fright. 부들부들 떨다; 흠칫거리다.
shake off, get rid of (someone or something unwelcome). …을 떨어버리다; 없애다; 따돌리다. ¶ *~ the snow off one's coat* 코트의 눈을 떨어버리다. / *~ off one's headache* 〔*a bad habit*〕 두통〔못된 버릇〕을 없애다 / *We managed to ~ off him in the crowd.* 우린 그럭저럭 사람들 틈에서 그를 따돌렸다.
shake** one's **sides, hold one's sides with laughter. 배를 움켜쥐고 웃다; 포복절도하다.
shake the elbow, 《*colloq.*》 play with dice. 주사위 놀이를 하다; 도박하다.
shake** oneself **together, be stir oneself. 분발하다.
shake together up, fit in together. 사이좋게 하다.
shake up, **a**) mix by shaking. (액체 따위)를 흔들어 섞다. ¶ *~ up a bottle of medicine* 약병을 흔들어 섞다. **b**) restore to shape by shaking 흔들어 본디 모양으로 하다. ¶ *~ up a pillow* 흔들어 베개 모양을 바로잡다. **c**) stir up; make awake. 일으키다; 분기시키다; 각성시키다. **d**) upset; disturb. (정신적·육체적으로) 흥분〔동요〕시키다.
— *n.* Ⓒ **1** the act of shaking. 흔듦; 흔들기; 한번 흔듦. ¶ *with a ~ of the head* 고개를 가로저어(《'no'라는 몸짓》). **2** 《*colloq.*》 a moment. 일순; 순간. ¶ *for a ~* 잠깐 동안 / *in two shakes* 〔*half a ~* 〕 곧; 즉시. **3** 《mus.》 a trill. 전음(顫音); 떤꾸밈음. **4** a drink mixed by shaking quickly; a milk shake. 흔들어 만든 음료수; 밀크 셰이크. [E.]
a brace of shake, very short time; moment. 극히 단시간; 순시(瞬時).
all of a shake, trembling. 벌벌 떨며.
give a shake, shake; dismiss. 한번 흔들다; 내쫓다.
no great shakes, of no great ability; unimportant; common. 특별한 능력이 없는; 그저 그런; 평범한.

:shak·en [ʃéikən] *v.* pp. of **shake.**

shak·er [ʃéikər] *n.* Ⓒ **1** a person who shakes. 흔드는 사람. **2** a container for pepper, salt, etc. from the top of which the contents are shaken out. (후추·소금 등을) 흔들어 뿌리는 용기. **3** a shaking device used in mixing or blending something. 교반기(攪拌器). **4** 《*S-*》 a member of a certain religious sect in the United States. 셰이커 교도. [*shake*]

·Shake·speare, Shak- [ʃéikspiər], **William** *n.* (1564-1616) England's greatest poet and dramatist. 셰익스피어.

Shake·spear·i·an, Shake·sper-, -spear·e·an, -sper·e·an [ʃeikspíəriən] *adj.* of or suggestive of Shakespeare or the style of his works. 셰익스피어(풍(風))의.
— *n.* Ⓒ a scholar who studies Shakespeare's works. 셰익스피어 학자〔연구가〕.

shake-up [ʃéikʌ̀p] *n.* Ⓒ **1** a complete change in business, a department, etc. 대이동; 대정리; 대개조; 쇄신. ¶ *There's been a government ~.* 대폭적인 개각이 있었다. **2** unrest; uproar. 동요; 소동. [*shake*]

shak·o [ʃǽkou, ʃéik-] *n.* (*pl.* **-os**) a kind of high military cap with a plume. 샤코(《깃털 장식이 있는 군모(軍帽)의 일종》). [Hang.]

Shak(s). Shakespeare.

shak·y [ʃéiki] *adj.* (**shak·i·er, shak·i·est**) **1** ⓐ shaking; not secure. 떨리는; 흔들리는; 비틀거리는; 불안정한. ¶ *a ~ hand* 떨리는 손〔필적〕 / *speak in a ~ voice* 떨리는 목소리로 이야기하다 / *be ~ on one's legs* 다리가 비틀거리다. ⓑ likely to break down. 무너질 것 같은; 위험한. ¶ *a ~ bridge* 위험한 다리. **2** uncertain; not to be relied on. 불확실한; 믿을 수 없는; (어쩐지) 불안한. ¶ *~ loyalty* 믿을 수 없는 충성 / *~ evidence* 불확실한 증거 / *a bit ~ in one's grammar* 문법이 약간 불안한. **3** not well; weak. (건강이) 시원치 않은; (허)약한; 병든 몸의. [*shake*]

shale [ʃeil] *n.* Ⓤ a kind of rock formed from clay or mud and easily split into thin sheets. 셰일; 혈암(頁岩); 이판암(泥板岩). [→scale[3]]

:shall [ʃæl, ʃəl] *auxil. v.* (**should**) **1** ⓐ 《used with the first person to express *simple future time*》 …일〔할〕 것이다. ¶ *I ~ be twenty years old next year.* 내년이면 20살이 된다 / *We ~ hear about it tomorrow.* 내일 그 일에 관해 들을 게다 / *Shall I be in time for the train?* 나는 열차 시간에 댈 수 있을까요 / *Shan't I know before tomorrow?* 내일 전에 알 수 없을까요 / *He said he should be back by five.* 그는 5시까지는 돌아온다고 했다. ⓑ 《replacing will in questions in the second person which expect the answer 'I shall'》 …을〔할〕까요; 합〔입〕니까. ¶ *Shall you be at home tomorrow?* 내일 댁에 계실 겁니까. **2** ⓐ 《esp. U.S.》 《expressing intention to do something in the future》 be to; be determined to. …할 작정〔예정〕이다. ¶ *I ~ come back home every day.* 나는 매일 귀가할 예정이다 / *We ~ not go.* 우린 가지 않을 작정이다. ⓑ 《questions in the second person》 …하시렵니까; …할 예정입니까. ¶ *Shall you go abroad this summer?* 이번 여름에 해외에 나가십니까. **3** ⓐ 《used with the second and third person to exrpess the speaker's will》 have to; must; may. …하게 하겠다; …하여야 하다. ¶ *They ~ not pass.* 그들을 통과시키지 않겠다 / *He ~ die.* 그는 죽어야 한다 《그를 죽이겠다》 / *You ~ have this book.* 이 책을 너에게 주겠다. ⓑ 《*negative*; expressing a prohibition》 must not. …해서는 안 된다. ¶ *You ~ not do so.* 그렇게 해서는 안된다 / *You shan't have your own way in everything.* 만사 네 멋대로 하게 내버려 두지는 않을 테다 / *Thou shalt not kill.* 살인하지 말지어다. **4** 《used to ask the intention of the second person》 …할까요; …하게 할까요. ¶ *Shall I open the window?* 창문을 열까요 / *Shall the man wait?* 그 사람을 기다리게 할까요 / *Shall I remain till four o'clock?* 4시까지 여기 있을까요 / *Shall we go for a walk?* (우리) 산책 나갈까요 / *When ~ he call on you?* 그를 언제 오라고 할까요 / *Let's go to see a movie, ~ we?* 영화 보러 가지 않으려나. **5** ⓐ 《used in the clauses of a contract》 …해야 하다; …할 것. ¶ *Each party ~ respect the conditions of this contract.* (각 당사자) 양쪽은 이 계약 조건들을 존중해야 한다. ⓑ 《*lit.*》 《used in laws with all persons》 …일〔할〕 것이다; …이어야 하다. ¶ *Article 1. The President ~ be the symbol of the State.* 제1조. 대통령은 국가의 상징이어야 한다. **6** 《questions in the first person, when the speaker is trying to decide》 ¶ *What ~ I do?* 어떻게 해야 좋을까(요); 무엇을 할까요 / *What ~ we do next?* 다음엔 무엇을 할까요. [E.]

shal·loon [ʃəlúːn, ʃæl-] *n.* Ⓤ light cloth for linings and dresses. 섈룬직(織). [*Chalons*, Place]

shal·lop [ʃǽləp] *n.* Ⓒ 《*arch.*》 a small, light boat. 소형 보트의 일종; 조각배. [F. *chaloupe*]

•**shal·low** [ʃǽlou] *adj.* **1** not deep. 얕은; 깊지 않은. ¶ *~ water* 얕은 물 / *a ~ dish* 운두가 낮은 접시 / *a ~ grave* 나지막한 묘. **2** not earnest or serious; superficial; lacking thought. 천박한; 표면적인; 생각이 모자라는. ¶ *a ~ mind* 천박한 생각 / *~ sympathy* 겉으로만의 동정. — *n.* Ⓒ 《sometimes *the ~ s*》 a shallow place in the water. 얕은 여울; (토사(土砂)가 쌓여) 얕은 곳. — *vt., vi.* (P6;1) make or become shallow. 얕게 하다; 얕아지다. [E.]

shal·low-brained [ʃǽloubréind] *adj.* shallow; foolish. 천박한; 어리석은.

shal·low-head·ed [ʃǽlouhédid] *adj.* = shallow-brained.

shal·low-pat·ed [ʃǽloupéitid] *adj.* = shallow-brained.

shalt [ʃælt, ʃəlt] *auxil. v.* 《*arch.*》 shall. ¶ *Thou ~ not kill.* 살인하지 말지어다.

sham [ʃæm] *n.* Ⓒ **1** fraud; pretence; imitation. 속임(수); 거짓; 협잡; 가짜. ¶ *The news was all ~.* 그 소식은 모두 거짓이었다 / *These pearls are all shams.* 이 진주는 모두 가짜다 / *His illness was only a ~.* 그의 병은 꾀병에 불과했다. **2** a person who pretends to be what he is not. …인 체 속이는 사람; (겉을) 가장하는 사람; 사기〔협잡〕꾼.

— *v.* (**shammed, sham·ming**) *vt.* (P6) **1** make an imitation of (something). …의 가짜를 만들다. **2** pretend to be (ill, etc.). …인 체하다; …을 가장하다. ¶ *~ death* 〔*dead*〕 죽은 체하다.

— *vi.* (P1) arrange a false appearance of something. 가장을 하다; (겉을 꾸며) 속이다. ¶ *Tom is not really sick but only shamming.* 톰은 정말 병난 것이 아니고 꾀병을 부리고 있을 뿐이다.

— *adj.* pretended; not real. 가장된; 거짓의; 가짜의. ¶ *a ~ jewel* 모조 보석 / *a ~ doctor* 가짜 의사 / *The soldiers had a ~ battle.* 병사들은 모의전을 했다. [corrupt of *shame*]

sham·ble [ʃǽmbəl] *vi.* (P1,2A) walk unsteadily. 비틀비틀〔비실비실〕 걷다; 지척거리며 걷다. — *n.* Ⓒ unsteady walking. 비틀 걸음. [?]

sham·bles [ʃǽmbəlz] *n. pl.* 《often used as *sing.*》 **1** a house where animals are killed for food. 도살장. **2** 《*colloq.*》 a scene of great disorder or bloodshed. 수라장; 유혈의 장면. ¶ *turn cities into ~* 도시를 수라장으로 만들다 / *The sightseers left the place a ~.* 유람객들이 그 자리를 엉망으로 해놨다. [L. *scamnum* bench]

:**shame** [ʃeim] *n.* **1** Ⓤ a painful feeling which attacks a person when he has done something wrong. 부끄러움; 부끄러운 마음〔기분〕; 수치심. ¶ *suffer ~* 부끄럽게 생각하다 / *feel ~ at having told a lie* 거짓말한 것을 부끄러워하다 / *She hid her face in ~.* 그녀는 부끄러워 얼굴을 가렸다 / *He is past ~.* 그는 수치심을 모른다. **2** Ⓤ disgrace; dishonor. 불명예; 치욕; 창피. ¶ *His foolish actions brought ~ on* 〔*upon*〕 *his fine family.* 그의 어리석은 행동은 그의 훌륭한 가문에 치욕을 가져왔다. **3** 《*a ~*》 a person or thing to be ashamed of. 부끄러운 사람〔일〕. ¶ *I think it a ~ to behave like that.* 그처럼 행동하는 것은 부끄러운 일이라고 생각한다. **4** 《*a ~*》 ⓐ 《*colloq.*》 something regrettable. 유감스러운 일; 안 된 일(cf. *a pity*). ¶ *It was a ~ that the rain spoiled your holiday.* 비 때문에 휴일을 망쳐서 안 됐다 / *What a ~ you can't come to the party!* 파티에 네가 올 수 없다니 정말 안 됐구나. ⓑ something unfair. 심한〔너무한〕 일. ¶ *What a ~ to treat you like that!* 너를 그같이 대하다니 정말이지 지독하기도 하다.

a life of shame, prostitution. 매음; 추업(醜業); 더러운 생업.

be lost to shame, have no sense of shame. 부끄럼을〔창피를, 수치를〕 모르다.

cannot do it for very shame, too ashamed to do it. (너무나) 부끄러워 …할 수 없다.

cry shame on 〔***upon***〕 ***someone,*** say that he ought to be ashamed of himself. 마땅히 창피함을 알라고 …를 비난하다.

dead to 〔***past***〕 ***shame,*** without a sense of shame. 부끄럼을〔창피를〕 모르는.

For shame! You should feel ashamed! (마땅히) 부끄러운 줄을 알아라.

from 〔***for, out of***〕 ***shame,*** because of shame. 부끄러워(서); 부끄러운 나머지.

put* [*bring*] *someone to shame, **a**) cause someone to be ashamed. …을 부끄럽게 만들다; 창피를 주다. **b**) surpass someone. …을 능가하다; 압도하다.
Shame* (*on you*) *! =For shame !.
— *vt.* **1** (P6) cause (someone) to feel shame. …을 부끄러워 하게 하다; …에게 창피를 주다. **2** bring disgrace on (someone). …의 면목을 잃게 하다; 이름을 더럽히다; 먹칠을 하다. ¶ ~ *one's father* 아버지를 부끄럽게 만들다〔욕되게 하다〕. **3** (P13) 《*into, out of*》 drive or force (someone) to do or not to do something because of his sense of shame. 부끄러워 …하도록〔하지 않도록〕 만들다. ¶ *He was shamed into working* 〔*out of his bad habits*〕. 그는 부끄러워 일을 하게〔못된 버릇을 버리게〕 되었다. [E.]

shame·faced [ʃéimfèist] *adj.* shy; showing shame or embarrassment. 부끄러운 듯한; 부끄러운; 수줍어하는. ¶ ~ *apologies* 수줍은 듯한 사과.

***shame·ful** [ʃéimfəl] *adj.* causing shame; disgraceful. 부끄러운; 창피스러운; 괘씸한. ¶ ~ *conduct* 부끄러운 행동 / *a* ~ *sight* 창피스러운 광경.

shame·ful·ly [ʃéimfəli] *adv.* in a shameful manner; disgracefully. 부끄럽게도; 창피하게(도); 발칙하게(도).

shame·less [ʃéimlis] *adj.* without any sense of shame. 부끄럼을 모르는; 조신하지 않은; 뻔뻔한; 외설한. ¶ *a* ~ *liar* 뻔뻔스러운 거짓말쟁이 / *a* ~ *picture* 춘화(春畫).

shame·less·ly [ʃéimlisli] *adv.* in a shameless manner. 뻔뻔스럽게; 파렴치하게.

sham·poo [ʃæmpúː] *vt.* **1** wash (the hair) with shampoo. (머리털)을 샴푸로 감다. **2** 《*arch.*》 massage. 마사지를 하다. — *n.* **1** Ⓒ the act of washing the hair. 머리 감기; 세발(洗髮). ¶ *give someone a* ~ 샴푸로 아무의 머리를 감아주다. **2** ⓊⒸ something used to wash the hair. (머리털) 세척제; 세발제〔분〕; 샴푸. [Hind.]

sham·rock [ʃǽmrɑk / -rɔk] *n.* Ⓒ a kind of three-leaved plant of the clover family. 클로버; 토끼풀. [Ir.]

shan·dy·gaff [ʃǽndigæ̀f] *n.* 《Brit.》 a mixture of beer and ginger-beer. 맥주와 진저비어와의 혼합 음료. [?]

shang·hai [ʃǽŋhai, ─ˊ] *vt.* (P6) 《naut. *sl.*》 make (a man) unconscious by drugs, liquor, etc., and put him on a ship to serve as a sailor. (마약·술 따위를 먹여) 배로 강제 납치해 불법으로 선원을 만들다. [Place]

shank [ʃæŋk] *n.* Ⓒ **1** the part of a leg between the ankle and the knee in man and some animals. 정강이; 다리; 경골(脛骨). **2** the straight part of a tool, a plant, etc. (도구·식물 따위의) 직선 부분; 손잡이; 축(軸); 굴대; 줄기; 잎자루. [E.]
go on* [*ride*] *shank's* [*Shanks's*] *mare, use one's own legs, instead of riding, driving, etc.; walk. 자기발〔도보〕로 걷다〔가다〕; 정강말을 타다.

shan't [ʃænt, ʃɑːnt] shall not.

shan·ty[1] [ʃǽnti] *n.* Ⓒ (*pl.* **-ties**) a hut; a rude cabin. (초라한) 오두막; 판자집. [F.]

shan·ty[2] [ʃǽnti] *n.* =chanty.

:shape [ʃeip] *n.* **1** ⓊⒸ the form or figure of a thing; an outward form or appearance; outline. (외면적인) 모양; 외형; 윤곽; 모습. ¶ *clouds of different shapes* 각기 다른 모양의 구름 / *a monster of human* ~ 인간의 모양을 한 괴물 / *the* ~ *of my head* 〔*a tree*〕 내 머리〔나무〕의 모양 / *An apple is different in* ~ *from a banana.* 사과는 모양이 바나나와는 다르다. **2** Ⓤ definite form or pattern; orderly arrangement. (구체적인) 모양; 형태; 또렷이〔하나로〕 정리; 정돈. ¶ *put one's plan* 〔*thoughts*〕 *into* ~ 계획〔생각〕을 구체화하다 / *Give* ~ *to your ideas.* 네 생각을 구체적으로 정리해라 / *The new boat gradually took* ~. 새 배는 점차 모양이 잡혔다. **3** Ⓤ 《U.S.》 condition; state. 상태. ¶ *precarious financial* ~ 불안정한 재정 상태 / *Everything was in bad* ~. 모든 것이 상태가 좋지 않았다. **4** Ⓒ a dimly-perceived form; ghost. 어렴풋한 모습; 유령. ¶ *A vague* ~ *stood at the door.* 희미한 그림자가 문 앞에 서 있었다. **5** ⓊⒸ false appearance. 가장된 모습. ¶ *a devil in human* ~ 인간의 모습을 한 악마. **6** Ⓒ something used to give form. (모양을 만들기 위한) 틀; 형(켈). ¶ *a hat* ~ 모자꼴.
a shape of fear, a phantom. 유령
in any shape or form, in any way; at all. 방법은 어떻든; 어떠한 형태로라도.
in good* [*bad*] *shape, in good 〔bad〕 condition. (몸의) 상태가 좋은〔나쁜〕.
in no shape =not in any shape or form.
in the shape of, in the form of. …모양〔형식〕으로(의). ¶ *a prince in the* ~ *of a beast* 짐승 모습의 왕자 / 《*fig.*》 *a reward in the* ~ *of an extra holiday* 특별 휴가로서의 보답.
lick into shape, train; drill; make (something) perfect. (훈련을 통해) …을 어연번듯하게〔상당한 것으로〕 만들다.
not in any shape or form, in no way whatever; not at all. 어떤 형태든 …않다; 조금도 … 않다〔아니다〕.
out of shape, **a**) having lost its original shape or form. 모양이 엉망이 되어. **b**) in poor physical condition. 몸 상태가 좋지 않아.
take shape, become clearer or more definite; 모양이 잡히다; 명확해지다; 구체화하다. ¶ *The new building gradually took* ~. 새 건물이 점차 모양이 잡혔다 / *My intention took* ~ *in action.* 나의 의도는 행동으로 실현되었다.
— *vt.* (P6,13) **1** give a definite form or character to (something or someone). …을 모양짓다; 형체를 이루다; 구체화하다. ¶ ~ *a piece of wood into a statue* 나뭇조각을 깎아 상(像)을 만들다 / ~ *the habit* 습관을 들이다 / ~ *a plan* 계획을 구체화하다. **2** direct

(one's course). (진로·미래)를 결정하다; 방향 지우다. ¶ *This event shaped his life.* 이 사건은 그의 인생을 결정지었다. **3** adapt (something) in shape; make (something) suitable. …을 적합〔적응〕시키다; 맞추다. ¶ *a dress shaped to one's figure* 몸에 맞춘 양복.
— *vi.* (P1) **1** take shape. 모양을 이루다〔취하다〕. **2** develop; turn out. (…하게) 되다; 잘 되어가다; 발달하다. ¶ *The crops are shaping well.* 작황은 더할 나위 없이 좋다 / *The boy is shaping satisfactorily.* 남자 아이는 만족스럽게 발육되고 있다. [E.]
shape up, 《U.S. *colloq.*》 **a**) take on a certain form or appearance; develop. 구체적인 모양을 취하다; 어떤 모양으로 낙착되다; 좋은 방향으로 나아가다. **b**) show a certain tendency. 어떤 경향을 보이다.

shaped [ʃeipt] *adj.* having a given shape. …모양의; 모양이 …한. ¶ *boat-shaped* 배 모양의 / *The earth is shaped like an orange.* 지구는 모양이 귤과 같다.

shape·less [ʃéiplis] *adj.* **1** without definite form or shape. 정형(定形)이 없는. **2** ill-formed. 모양〔볼품〕 없는. ¶ *He wore a ~ old hat.* 그는 모양 없는 낡은 모자를 쓰고 있었다.

shape·ly [ʃéipli] *adj.* well-shaped; well-balanced. 모양이 좋은; 균형이 잡힌. ¶ *She has a ~ pair of legs.* 그녀는 다리가 미끈하다.
●**shape·li·ness** [-nis] *n.*

:share[1] [ʃɛər] *n.* **1** Ⓒ a part of something belonging to one individual. (배당)몫. ¶ *cry shares* 몫을 요구하다 / *do one's ~ of work* 자신에게 할당된 일을 하다 / *have a ~ in the profits* 이익 배당에 참여하다 / *go ~ and ~ alike* 평등하게 나누다; 등분하다. **2** Ⓤ a part of something given or belonging to one of a group of persons who own or undertake it together. 역할; 공헌; 분담. ¶ *What ~ had he in our success?* 우리들 성공에 그는 무슨 역할을 했나 / *He had a large ~ in building up the company.* 회사를 일으키는데 그는 큰 몫을 했다. **3** one of the equal proportions into which a company's capital stock is divided. 주식; 주(株). ¶ *have 10,000 shares in a business firm* 상사(商社)에 1만 주를 갖고 있다.
bear 〔***take***〕 ***one's share of,*** pay or do what one should. …의 할당 몫을 지불하다; 분담하다.
go shares with *someone,* share equally with someone. …와 똑같이 나누다; 분담하다. ¶ *Let me go shares with you in the expenses.* 비용을 분담케 해주시오.
on 〔***upon***〕 ***shares,*** sharing in the risks and profits. 기업의 손익을 똑같이 분담하여; 공동 책임으로. ¶ *We agreed to work on shares.* 우리는 공동 책임으로 일할 것에 의견 일치를 보았다.
take 〔***have***〕 ***a*** 〔***one's***〕 ***share in,*** share. 분담하다; …에 참여〔관여〕하다.
take the lion's share, take the largest amount of profits, etc. 최대의 몫을 차지하다; 단물을 빨다.
— *vt.* **1** (P6,7,13) divide (something) into parts and distribute them. …을 나누다; 분배하다. ¶ *The profits are shared among us all.* 이익은 우리들 모두 사이에 분배된다 / *He shared his cake with his sister.* 그의 케이크를 누이동생과 나누었다. **2** (P6) 《*with*》 have a share of (something); have (something) in common. …의 (배당)몫을 취하다; …을 분담하다; …을 함께 쓰다; …을 공용(共用)하다. ¶ *~ joys and sorrows in life* 인생의 고락을 함께 하다 / *I don't ~ their opinions.* 그들 의견에 동감하지 않는다 / *He shared the room with his brother.* 그는 방을 동생과 함께 썼다. — *vi.* (P3) 《*in*》 give or receive a share; take part in. (배당)몫을 받다〔주다〕; 참여〔관여〕하다. [*shear*]
share and share alike, make an equal division. 등분하다; 평등하게 나누다.
share out, hand out in shares. 몫으로 나눠주다. ¶ *~ out food and clothing to the poor* 가난한 사람들에게 식량과 의류를 나눠주다.

share[2] [ʃɛər] *n.* the blade of a plough. 보습의 날. [↑]

share·crop·per [ʃɛ́ərkràpər / -krɔ̀pər] *n.* 《U.S.》 a tenant farmer who pays his rent with a part of his crop. 소작인.

share·hold·er [ʃɛ́ərhòuldər] *n.* Ⓒ 《Brit.》 a person who owns shares of stock; a stockholder. 주주(株主).

shark [ʃɑːrk] *n.* Ⓒ **1** a large sharp-toothed fish found in warm seas. 상어. **2** 《*fig.*》 a dishonest person who preys on others; a swindler 탐욕스러워 남을 봉으로 삼는 사람; 사기〔협잡〕꾼; 야바위꾼. [L. *carcharus*]

:sharp [ʃɑːrp] *adj.* **1** having a thin, cutting, keen edge or point. 날카로운 (날을 가진); 끝이 날카로운; 예리한(opp. blunt, dull). ¶ *a ~ knife* 잘 드는 나이프. **2** having a point; not rounded. (끝이) 뾰족한; 날카로운; 모가 진. ¶ *a ~ nose* 〔*peak*〕 뾰족한 코〔산봉우리〕 / *a ~ corner in a box* 상자의 모가 진 모서리. **3** ⓐ with a sudden change of direction. (방향·진로가) 갑자기 바뀌는; 갑자기 꺾이는; 급한. ¶ *a ~ turn* 〔*bend, curve*〕 *in the road* 도로의 급커브. ⓑ (of a slope, etc.) steep. (경사 따위가) 급한; 험한; 깎아지른. ¶ *a ~ slope* 〔*drop*〕 급한 경사〔내리받이〕. **4** (of an angle) narrow. (각도가) 예각의. **5** (of a sound or voice) high; seeming to go through the head. ((목)소리가) 날카로운; 귀청을 찢는; 새된. ¶ *a ~ cry* 날카로운 외침 / *a ~ noise* 귀청을 찢는 소리. **6** (of an outline, etc.) distinct; clear. (윤곽 따위가) 또렷한; 분명〔명확〕한; 선명한. ¶ *a ~ outline* 〔*contrast*〕 뚜렷한 윤곽〔대조〕 / *I could see everything ~ and clear.* 모든 것이 명확하게 보였다. **7** (of the senses, intelligence, etc.) quickly aware of things; keen; clever. (감각·머리 따위가) 예민한; 총명한; 날카로운.

¶ ~ *ears* 예민한 귀〔청력〕/ *a* ~ *boy* 총명한 아이 / *a secretary* (*as*) ~ *as a needle* 머리가 기막히게 돌아가는 비서. **8** ⓐ intensely painful; intense; eager. (고통·욕망 따위가) 격심한; 강렬〔치열〕한. ¶ *a* ~ *pain* 격통 / *a* ~ *desire* 강렬한 욕망. ⓑ (of air, etc.) very cold. (공기 따위가) 매우 차가운; 몹시 추운; 살을 에는 것 같은. ¶ ~ *weather* 몹시 추운 날씨 / *a* ~, *biting wind* 살을 에는 듯싶은 바람. **9** (of a taste or smell) affecting the senses keenly; acid; biting. (맛·냄새 따위가) 톡 쏘는; 자극성의; 얼얼한; 신. ¶ *a* ~ *smell* 톡 쏘는 냄새 / *a* ~ *taste* 얼얼한 맛. **10** violent; severe; fierce; bitter. 격렬한; 격심한; 신랄한; 통렬한. ¶ *a* ~ *remark* 신랄한 말 / *a* ~ *contest* 격심한 경쟁 / *be* ~ *on* 〔*upon*〕 …을 가혹하게 대하다. **11** dishonest; quick to look after one's own advantage. 부정한; 교활한; (자신의 이해에) 빈틈없는. ¶ *a* ~ *merchant* 빈틈없는 상인 / ~ *at making a bargain* 거래를 빈틈없이 하는 / *be* (*as*) ~ *a fox* 여우처럼 교활하다 / *He was much too* ~ *for me.* 그는 나로선 너무나 버거운 상대였다. **12** (of a fight, a walk, etc.) quick; brisk; energetic. (행동이) 기민〔민첩〕한; 활발한; 기운찬. ¶ *a* ~ *walk* 활발〔급〕한 발걸음 / ~ *work* 재빠른 일솜씨. **13** watchful; wide-awake. 방심하지 않는; 빈틈없는. ¶ *keep a* ~ *watch on someone* 아무를 빈틈없이 감시하다. **14** 《mus.》 raised half a step in pitch. 반음 높은(opp. flat).

have a sharp tongue, make cutting, biting remarks. 독설을 퍼붓다.

Sharp is the word! Hurry up! 서둘러라.

sharp practices, swindling. 협잡; 야바위.

— *adv.* **1** ⓐ promptly; keenly; abruptly. 돌연; 갑자기; 날카롭게. ¶ *turn* ~ *right* 갑자기 오른쪽으로 돌다 / *pull up a car* ~ 갑자기 차를 멈춰 세우다. ⓑ briskly; quickly. 재빨리; 신속히. **2** punctually; exactly. (시간이) 정각; 딱; 꼭; 정확히. ¶ *Come at 5 o'clock* ~. 5시 정각에 오너라.

Look sharp! Be quick! Hurry up! 빨리 해라; 서둘러라.

— *n.* Ⓒ 《mus.》 a tone one half step above a given tone; the symbol (♯) indicating this. 샤프; 올림표. [E.]

sharp-cut [ʃáːrpkʌ́t] *adj.* having a clear outline. (윤곽이) 뚜렷한; 선명한.

·**sharp·en** [ʃáːrpən] *vt.* (P6) **1** make (something) sharp. (날)을 예리하게 하다; 갈다; 뾰족하게 하다. ¶ ~ *a pencil* 연필을 깎다 / *This knife needs sharpening.* 이 칼은 갈아야 겠다. **2** 《*fig.*》 ⓐ make quick and ready. 활발하게 하다. ¶ *Sharpen your wits.* 재치를 활발히 발휘시켜라. ⓑ intensify. 강하게 하다; 격화시키다. ¶ ~ *the controversy* 논쟁을 격화시키다 / *The wine has sharpened my appetite.* 포도주는 나의 식욕을 돋구었다. [*sharp*]

sharp·en·er [ʃáːrpənər] *n.* Ⓒ a person or thing that sharpens. (날붙이를) 가는 사람〔것〕; 깎는 사람〔것〕. ¶ *a pencil* ~ 연필 깎이.

sharp·er [ʃáːrpər] *n.* Ⓒ a cheater; a gambler, esp. at cards. 사기꾼; 전문 도박꾼.

sharp-eyed [ʃáːrpáid] *adj.* having keen sight; sharp-sighted; quick to notice. 눈이 날카로운〔잘 보이는〕; 눈치 빠른; 관찰력이 예리한.

:**sharp·ly** [ʃáːrpli] *adv.* in a sharp manner. 날카롭게; 호되게; 세게; 빈틈없이; 뚜렷이.

sharp·ness [ʃáːrpnis] *n.* Ⓤ the state of being sharp. 날카로움; 예리; 통렬; 영리(함); 교활함.

sharp-set [ʃáːrpsèt] *adj.* keen; very hungry; eager to dominate. 날카로운; 배고픈; 굶주린; 갈망하는; 열렬한.

sharp·shoot·er [ʃáːrpʃùːtər] *n.* Ⓒ **1** a person who is very good at shooting, esp. with a rifle. 사격의 명수; 명사수. **2** a sniper. 저격병(狙擊兵).

sharp-sight·ed [ʃáːrpsáitid] *adj.* having keen sight; sharp-eyed. 눈이 날카로운; 눈이 잘 보이는; 시력이 좋은.

sharp-wit·ted [ʃáːrpwítid] *adj.* having a quick, sharp mind. 재치 있는; 머리 회전이 빠른; 총명한; 잽싼.

·**shat·ter** [ʃǽtər] *vt.* (P6) **1** break or smash (something) into pieces. …을 부수다〔분쇄하다〕; 산산이 부수다. ¶ ~ *window-panes* 유리창을 깨뜨리다. **2** destroy; ruin; disturb greatly. …을 파괴하다; 망치다; 못 쓰게 만들다. ¶ ~ *someone's hopes* 아무의 희망을 꺾다 / *His health was shattered by the war.* 그의 건강은 전쟁으로 망가졌다. — *vi.* (P1) be broken into pieces; be damaged. 산산 조각이 되다; 부서지다; 손상되다. [→ scatter]

shat·ter·proof glass [ʃǽtərprùːf glǽs] *n.* unsplinterable glass used in motor-cars, etc. with a transparent sheet of plastic between two sheets of glass. (자동차 따위의) 잘게 바스러지지 않는 안전 유리 (=triplex glass). [*shatter, proof*]

∗**shave** [ʃeiv] *v.* (**shaved, shaved** or **shav·en**) *vt.* **1** (P6,7) cut off (hair, etc.) with a razor. (머리털·수염 따위)를 깎다; 밀어 없애다; 면도하다. ¶ ~ *one's face* 얼굴을 면도하다 / ~ *one's legs* 다리의 털을 밀어 없애다 / ~ *a customer* (이발소에서) 손님의 수염을 면도하다 / *He has shaved* (*off*) *his moustache.* 그는 콧수염을 깎았다. **2** (P6,7) cut off in thin slices. …을 얇은 조각으로 베다〔썰다〕; 얇게 깎다. ¶ *shaved beef* 얇게 썬 쇠고기. **3** (P6) come very close to; graze. …을 스칠 듯이 지나다; 스치다. ¶ *The car shaved the gatepost.* 차는 문 기둥을 스칠 듯이 지나갔다. — *vi.* (P1) cut off hair or a beard with a razor. 머리·수염을 깎다; 면도하다. ¶ *He looks as though he hadn't shaved for a week.* 그는 마치 1주일 동안 면도를 안한 것같이 보인다.

— *n.* Ⓒ **1** the act of cutting off with a razor. (면도로) 깎기; 면도하기. ¶ *He needs a* ~ *badly.* 그는 면도하는 일이 몹시 필요하다.

2 a thin slice. 얇은 조각; 박편. ¶ *take a ~ off the surface of a piece of wood* 나뭇조각의 표면을 한번 (대패로) 밀다. **3** a device for shaving, scraping, etc. 깎는 기구; 면도기구. **4** a narrow escape. 간신히 모면하기. ¶ *I had a close* 〔*narrow*〕*~.* 아슬아슬하게〔간발의 차로〕 모면했다. [E.]

shav·en [ʃéivən] *v.* pp. of **shave.**

shav·er [ʃéivər] *n.* Ⓒ **1** a person who shaves. 깎는 사람; 면도사; 이발사. **2** an instrument for shaving. 깎는 도구; 면도기(구).

shav·ing [ʃéiviŋ] *n.* Ⓤ **1** the act of shaving. 깎음; 면도질; 깎아냄; 대패질. **2** 《often *pl.*》 thin slices of wood cut off by a plane or knife. 깎아낸 부스러기; 대팻밥. ¶ *Shavings of wood are cut off by a plane or similar tool.* 대패밥은 대패 또는 비슷한 도구로 깎아낸다.

shawl [ʃɔːl] *n.* Ⓒ a square or oblong piece of cloth worn over the shoulders by women. 숄; (여성용) 어깨걸이. [Pers.]

shay [ʃei] *n.* 《*arch.*》 =chaise. [*chaise*]

:she [ʃiː, ʃi] *pron.* (*pl.* **they**) a girl, woman, or anything imagined as a female mentioned before. 그녀는; 그녀가. 語法 인간 이외에도 여성으로 취급되는 것, 예컨대 배·달·국가 따위에도 쓰임. —*n.* Ⓒ a girl; a woman; a female animal. 여자 아이; 여자; 암컷〔놈〕. ¶ *Is the baby a he or a ~?* 아기는 사내아인가요 계집앤가요. [E.]

she- [ʃiː] *pref.* female. '여성, 암컷'의 뜻. ¶ *a she-cat* 〔*wolf*〕 암고양이〔늑대〕. [E.]

sheaf [ʃiːf] *n.* Ⓒ (*pl.* **sheaves**) a bundle of things of the same kind tied together. 묶음; 뭉치; 단. ¶ *a ~ of wheat* 밀 한 다발 / *a ~ of arrows* 한 묶음의 화살 / *a ~ of papers* 한 묶음의 서류. —*vt.* (P6) make sheaves of; sheave. 묶다; 다발짓다. [E.]

·shear [ʃiər] *n.* Ⓒ 《usu. *pl.*》 a large double-bladed instrument for cutting, such as scissors. 큰 가위. ¶ *a pair of shears* (한 자루의) 큰 가위.

—*v.* (**sheared, sheared** or **shorn**) *vt.* (P6,7) **1** cut off (hair, wool, etc.) with shears or scissors. (머리털·양털 따위)를 큰 가위로 깎아〔잘라〕내다. ¶ *~ the sheep* 양털을 깎다 / *~ off the long hair* 긴 머리털을 깎아〔잘라〕내다. **2** 《usu. in *passive*》 deprive. …을 빼앗다. ¶ *be shorn of* (*something*) …을 빼앗기다. —*vi.* (P1) cut with shears or scissors; cut off wool from sheep with shears or clippers. 가위로 베다〔깎다〕; 양털을 깎다. [E.]

come home shorn, return stripped and naked. 빈털터리가 되어 돌아오다.

shear off, remove by shearing. 베어〔잘라, 깎아〕내다.

sheath [ʃiːθ] *n.* Ⓒ (*pl.* **sheaths** [ʃiːðz, ʃiːθs]) **1** a case or covering for a sword blade or knife. 칼집. **2** any similar protective covering, esp. as a part of an animal or plant. (위와 비슷한) 덮개; 시초(翅鞘); 엽초(葉鞘). [E.]

sheathe [ʃiːð] *vt.* (P6) **1** ⓐ put (a sword, etc.) into a sheath. (칼 따위)를 칼집에 넣다〔꽂다〕. ¶ *~ a sword.* ⓑ 《*fig.*》 make peace. 싸움을 그만두다; 화해하다. **2** protect (something) with a covering. (보호물)로 …을 덮다. ¶ *~ a ship's bottom with copper* 뱃바닥에 구리판을 입히다. [E.]

sheath·ing [ʃíːðiŋ] *n.* **1** Ⓤ the act of covering (something) with a sheath. 칼집에 넣음〔꽂기〕. ¶ *the ~ of the sword* 칼을 칼집에 꽂기; 화해하기. **2** a cover; a thing that protects something. (보호하기 위한) 덮개; 씌우개. ¶ *~ copper* 피복용 구리판.

sheave [ʃiːv] *vt.* (P6) gather (grain) into a sheaf or sheaves. 단〔다발〕을 짓다; 묶음으로 하다. —*n.* a wheel with a grooved edge as in a pulley. 도르래. [E.]

sheaves [ʃiːvz] *n.* pl. of **sheaf.**

:shed[1] [ʃed] *v.* (**shed, shed·ding**) *vt.* (P6) **1** cause (blood, tears, etc.) to flow or drop. (피·눈물 따위)를 흘리다. ¶ *I can't read such a story without shedding tears.* 그와 같은 소설은 눈물 없이는 읽을수가 없다. **2** ⓐ throw off; cast or take off (leaves, hair, skin, etc.) by a natural process. (잎 따위)를 떨어뜨리다; (털 따위)를 갈다; (옷 따위)를 벗어버리다. ¶ *Trees ~ their leaves in fall.* 나무는 가을에 잎이 떨어진다 / *A snake sheds its skin.* 뱀은 허물을 벗는다 / *Birds ~ their feathers.* 새는 털갈이를 한다. ⓑ cause to flow off. (천 따위가) 물이 스며들지 않다; 겉돌다. ¶ *This cloth sheds water.* 이 천은 물이 겉돈다. **3** ⓐ give off (light, sound, etc.); send out. (빛·소리 따위)를 발(산)하다; 내다; 쏟다. ¶ *~ love* 애정을 쏟다 / *~ light on* …을 비추다; …을 밝히다 / *The sun sheds light.* 태양은 빛을 발한다. ⓑ (of non-material things) give forth; spread. (영향 따위)를 끼치다; 주다. ¶ *~ a good influence* (*around*) (주변)에 좋은 영향을 미치다. —*vi.* **1** take off hair, skin, etc. by a natural process. 탈모〔탈피〕하다; 허물을 벗다; 털갈이하다. **2** (of leaves, seeds, etc.) drop off; fall out. (잎·씨 따위가) 떨어지다. [E. =sever]

shed one's blood, sacrifice oneself; die. 희생이 되다; 죽다. ¶ *He ~ his blood for his country.* 그는 나라를 위해 피를 흘렸다.

shed the blood of, kill or wound. 죽이다; 상처를 입히다.

·shed[2] [ʃed] *n.* Ⓒ a small one-floor building for storing tools or supplies, for sheltering animals, etc.; an out-house. 작고 허술한 집; 곳간; 헛간; 광; 가축 우리. ¶ *a bicycle ~* 자전거 두는 곳 / *a cattle ~* 소우리; 외양간 / *a wagon ~* 차고. [shade]

she'd [ʃiːd, ʃid] **1** she had. **2** she would.

sheen [ʃiːn] *n.* Ⓤ brightness, esp. that caused by a shining surface that reflects light; gloss. 번쩍임; 광택. [E. =beautiful]

sheen·y [ʃíːni] *adj.* (**sheen·i·er, sheen·i·est**)

having a sheen; bright; glossy. 광택있는; 번쩍이는; 윤나는.

:sheep [ʃi:p] *n.* Ⓒ (*pl.* **sheep**) **1** a weak, cowardly animal with a thick coat of wool. 양(cf. *ram*). ¶ *a flock of* ~ 한떼의 양 / *keep five* ~ 양 5마리를 치다. **2** a weak, cowardly person. 겁쟁이. **3** 《*collectively*》 members of a church or religious community. 신자; 교구민(教區民). **4** Ⓤ sheepskin. 양가죽; 양피. [E.]

follow like sheep, follow a leader blindly or without thinking. (지도자를) 맹종하다; 순순히〔얌전히〕 따르다.

make 〔***cast***〕 ***sheep's eyes at,*** give a longing, loving look at. …에게 추파를 던지다.

separate the sheep and 〔***from***〕 ***the goats,*** distinguish the good from the bad. 선인(善人)과 악인을 구별하다.

sheep that have no 〔***without a***〕 ***shepherd,*** helpless people; people without a leader. 의지할 데 없는 사람들; 지도자 없는 사람들.

the black sheep of a family, a person who is different, in a bad sense, from the rest of his family. (가족 중의) 말썽꾸러기.

sheep·cote [ʃí:pkòut], **-cot** [⌐kàt / ⌐kɔ̀t] *n.* Ⓒ 《chiefly Brit.》 an enclosure where sheep are kept. 양우리(=sheepfold).

sheep dog [ʃí:p dɔ̀(:)g, -dàg] *n.* a dog trained to look after or protect sheep along with a shepherd. 양지기 개; 목양견(牧羊犬).

sheep·fold [ʃí:pfòuld] *n.* Ⓒ a small enclosure or yard for sheep; a sheepcote. 양우리; 양사(羊舍).

sheep·ish [ʃí:piʃ] *adj.* **1** like a sheep; weak and cowardly shy. 양과 같은; 마음 약한; 수줍어〔부끄러워〕하는. ¶ *a* ~ *smile* 수줍은 미소. **2** somewhat silly. 어리석은.

sheep run [⌐⌐] *n.* a large tract of land on which sheep are pastured. 큰 목양장.

sheep·skin [ʃí:pskin] *n.* **1** Ⓤ the skin of a sheep, usu. with the wool still on it, used for garments. 양피(羊皮). **2** Ⓤ leather or parchment made from the skin of sheep. 양피지(羊皮紙). ¶ *a book bound in* ~ 양피지 장정의 책. **3** Ⓒ 《U.S. *colloq.*》 a graduation diploma. 졸업 증서.

***sheer**[1] [ʃiər] *adj.* **1** pure; unmixed. 순수한; 섞이지 않은. **2** absolute; complete. 순전한; 완전한. ¶ *a* ~ *waste of time* 순전한 시간 낭비 / ~ *nonsense* 순전한 난센스. **3** (of cloth) very thin; that can be seen through. 아주 얇은; 비치는. ¶ ~ *curtain* 얇은 커튼 / *She wore a* ~ *white dress.* 그녀는 비치는 하얀 옷을 입고 있었다. **4** (of a slope) straight up and down; steep. 수직의; 깎아지른. ¶ *a* ~ *cliff* 깎아지른 절벽. — *adv.* **1** steeply; straight. 수직으로; 직립하여. ¶ *a tower rising up* ~ *into the sky* 하늘 높이 치솟은 탑. **2** completely. 완전히; 순전히. [E.]

sheer[2] [ʃiər] *vi.* (P1,2A) 《naut.》 swerve; turn from a course. 방향을 바꾸다; 옆으로〔침로에서〕 벗어나다. ¶ *The ship sheered to the north.* 그 배는 홱 북쪽으로 침로를 바꾸었다. — *n.* swerving. 침로에서 벗어나기; 나아가는 방향을 바꾸기. [D. *scheren* shear]

:sheet [ʃi:t] *n.* Ⓒ **1** a large, thin piece of anything. 판상(板狀)〔종이 모양〕의 것; …장〔매〕. ¶ *a* ~ *of paper* 〔*glass*〕 종이〔유리〕 한 장. **2** a piece of cloth to cover a bed. 시트; 커버; 홑이불. **3** a single piece of paper; a letter; a newspaper. 1장〔매〕; 편지; 신문. ¶ *sell sheets hot from the press* 갓 나온 신문을 팔다. **4** a wide space or surface. (물·불따위의) 넓게 퍼진 면; 온통…. ¶ *a* ~ *of flame* 〔*blood*〕 불〔피〕바다. **5** a rope attached to a sail. (돛의) 마룻줄; 아딧줄.

a blank sheet, the mind or character of a young person, to be easily influenced by education, surroundings, etc. (교육·주위의) 영향을 받기 쉬운 마음〔사람〕.

a clean sheet, a clean record of conduct; a good character. 아무런 오점이나 잘못이 없는 경력; 훌륭한 인물.

be 〔***have***〕 ***a sheet in the wind*** 〔***wind's eye***〕***,*** be a little drunk. 약간 취해 있다.

be 〔***get***〕 ***between the sheets,*** be in bed. 잠자리에 들어 있다.

in sheets, **a**) heavily. 억수같이. ¶ *The rain fell in sheets.* 비가 억수같이 퍼부었다. **b**) (of a book) printed but not bound. (인쇄는 했으나) 제책이 안 된.

— *vt.* (P6) cover (a bed) with a sheet. 시트를 깔다; 시트〔홑이불〕로 덮다. [E.]

sheet anchor [⌐⌐–] *n.* **1** a large emergency anchor. 비상용 큰 닻; 예비 닻. **2** 《*fig.*》 chief support. 마지막 믿을〔의지할〕 데.

sheet·ing [ʃí:tiŋ] *n.* Ⓤ **1** 《*collectively*》 cotton or linen material for sheets. 시트(감). **2** the act of making (something) into sheets. 판(板) 모양으로 하기.

sheet iron [⌐⌐–] *n.* iron rolled in the form of a sheet or plate. (얇은) 철판.

sheik, sheikh [ʃi:k, ʃeik] *n.* Ⓒ **1** the chief of an Arab family, tribe, or village, used as a title of respect. (아라비아의) 가장(家長); 족장. **2** a leader in Mohammedan countries. (이슬람의) 교주(教主). [Arab.]

shek·el [ʃékəl] *n.* **1** an ancient silver coin of the Hebrews; the basic monetary unit of Israel. 히브리 사람의 옛 은화; 이스라엘의 통화 단위. **2** 《*pl.*》 《*colloq.*》 money; riches. 돈; 현금; 부(富). ¶ *rake in the shekels* 돈을 많이 모으다〔벌다〕. [Heb.]

she·ki·nah [ʃikáinə, -kí:-] *n.* a visible glory of Jehovah. 여호아의 광운(光雲); 하느님의 시현(示顯). [Heb.]

shel·drake [ʃéldrèik] *n.* 《bird》 a bright plumaged wild duck. 혹부리오리. [Du. *schillede* pied, drake]

***shelf** [ʃelf] *n.* Ⓒ (*pl.* **shelves**) **1** a thin, flat piece placed on a wall for holding things. 선반; 서가(書架). **2** anything like a shelf. 선반 모양의 것《모래톱·바위 따위》. [Teut.]

on the shelf, out of use; undesirable; out of duty or active service. 쓰이지〔사용되지〕 않아; 유보〔묵살〕되어; 해고되어. ¶ *He was laid* 〔*put*〕 *on the* ～. 그는 해고되었다.

*__shell__ [ʃel] *n.* Ⓒ **1** a hard outside covering on some animals, vegetables, or kinds of fruit. (딱딱한) 껍질; 껍데기; 깍지; 꼬투리. **2** the skeleton of a building, a ship, etc.; a framework.(건물·선박 따위의) 골조(骨組). **3** a very light racing boat. 레이스 보트. **4** a case holding gunpowder to be fired from a rifle, pistol, cannon, etc. 약협(藥莢); 포탄. ¶ *a gas* ～ 가스탄 / *an illuminating* ～ 조명탄 / *a tear* ～ 최루탄.

come out of** one's **shell, become sociable and less shy; talk in a familiar manner. 허물 없이 친해지다; 마음을 터놓다.

go 〔***retire***〕 ***into** one's **shell,*** become shy and less sociable. 마음을 터놓지 않다; 스스러워하다.

— *vt.* (P6) **1** remove a shell from (something); take out (something) from a shell. …에서 껍데기〔깍지〕를 벗기다; 껍데기〔깍지〕에서 …을 끄집어 내다. ¶ ～ *nuts* 호두를 까다 / ～ *peas* 콩깍지를 까다. **2** fire shells at (something); fire at with artillery; fire a cannon at. …을 포격하다. ¶ *The enemy shelled our trenches.* 적군은 우리의 참호 진지를 포격했다. — *vi.* (P2A) come out of a shell; (of a shell, etc.) fall; peel off. (열매 따위가) 깍지〔꼬투리〕에서 나오다; (껍질·껍데기 따위가) 벗겨지다. [E.]

shell out, 《*colloq.*》 pay out; hand over. …을 남김없이 지불하다; 건네주다. ● **shell·like** [ʃéllàik] *adj.*

:**she'll** [ʃiːl] **1** she will. **2** she shall.

shel·lac [ʃəlǽk] *n.* Ⓤ a sticky substance used in making varnish. 셸락《lac을 정제한 니스, 절연재(材) 따위의 원료》. — *vt.* (**-lacked, -lack·ing**) **1** coat or cover (something) with shellac; put shellac on. …에 셸락을 바르다. **2** 《U.S. *sl.*》 defeat decisively. 완전히 쳐부수다. [*shell, lac*]

Shel·ley [ʃéli], **Percy Bysshe** *n.* (1792-1822) an English poet. 셸리《영국의 낭만파 시인》.

•**shell·fish** [ʃélfiʃ] *n.* Ⓒ (*pl.* **-fish·es** or *collectively* **-fish**) a water animal with a shell, such as a lobster, a crab, or an oyster. 갑각류(甲殼類)《조개·게·새우 따위》의 총칭. [*shell*]

shell shock [⌐⌐] *n.* 《med.》 a nervous or mental disorder resulting from the noise or strain of war. (폭탄 파열 따위에 의한) 기억력·시각의 상실증; 전투〔전쟁〕 치매증(癡呆症). [*shell*]

shell·y [ʃéli] *adj.* (**shell·i·er, shell·i·est**) **1** full of shells; abounding in shells. (조개) 껍질이 많은. ¶ *a* ～ *beach* 조개 껍질이 많은 바닷가. **2** consisting of a shell or shells. 조개 껍질로 된. **3** like a shell. 조개 껍질 같은. [*shell*]

:**shel·ter** [ʃéltər] *n.* **1** Ⓒ something that covers or protects from any danger; a safe place. (위험으로부터) 보호해 주는 것; 피난 장소. ¶ *an air-raid* ～ 방공호. **2** Ⓤ the state of being protected or covered; protection; refuge. 보호; 피난. ¶ *find* 〔*take*〕 ～ *from a storm* 폭풍우로부터 대피하다 / *give* 〔*provide*〕 ～ *to* (*someone*) (아무)를 보호하다 / *provide food, clothing, and* ～ *for one's family* 자기 가족의 의식주를 돌보다.

— *vt.* (P6,13) protect; shield; cover. …을 보호〔비호〕하다; 숨기다. ¶ ～ *someone for the night* 아무를 하룻밤 재워주다 / *The wood shelters the house from the north wind.* 그 숲은 북풍으로부터 그 집을 보호한다. — *vi.* (P1,3) find shelter. 피난하다. ¶ *Let us* ～ *till the storm is over.* 폭풍우가 멎을 때까지 피난토록 하자. [E.]

shelter oneself, take refuge; seek safety. 피난하다; 안전을 구하다. ¶ ～ *oneself under* 〔*behind*〕 *someone* 아무의 밑〔그늘〕에 몸을 숨기다; 아무에게 책임을 전가하다.

shelve[1] [ʃelv] *vt.* (P6) **1** put (something) on a shelf. …을 선반 위에 얹다. ¶ ～ *boxes* 상자들을 선반 위에 얹다. **2** put off (problems, etc.) indefinitely; lay side. (문제 따위의 해결)을 미루다; 제쳐놓다. ¶ ～ *the question* 문제의 해결을 미루다. **3** remove someone from active service; force to retire; dismiss. 해고하다; 퇴직시키다. ¶ ～ *an official* 공무원을 퇴직시키다. **4** furnish with shelves. 선반을 달다. [*shelf*]

shelve[2] [ʃelv] *vi.* (P1) slope gradually. 완만하게 경사를 이루다. [Teut.]

shelves [ʃelvz] *n.* pl. of **shelf.**

shelv·ing [ʃélviŋ] *n.* Ⓤ **1** material for shelves. 선반〔시렁〕의 재료. **2** 《*collectively*》 shelves. 선반; 시렁. [*shelf*]

:**shep·herd** [ʃépərd] *n.* Ⓒ **1** a person who looks after sheep. 양치는 사람. ¶ *a shepherd's dog* 양치기 개. **2** 《*fig.*》 a minister; a priest. 목사. ¶ *the Good Shepherd* 예수 그리스도. — *vt.* (P6,13) **1** look after (sheep); take care of (someone). (양을) 지키다; …을 돌보다〔보살피다〕. **2** guide or direct. …을 이끌다; 인도하다. ¶ ～ *a group into a train* 여럿을 이끌어 기차에 태우다. [*sheep, herd*]

shep·herd·ess [ʃépərdis] *n.* Ⓒ a female shepherd. 여자 양치기.

sher·bet [ʃə́ːrbit] *n.* Ⓤ a frozen dessert made of fruit juice, milk, whites of eggs, gelatin, etc.; an ice water with a fruit flavor. 셔벗《과즙에 달걀 흰자·우유·설탕 따위를 첨가하여 얼린 것》; 찬 과즙 음료. [Arab.]

*__sher·iff__ [ʃérif] *n.* **1** 《U.S.》 the chief law officer in a county, elected by the people. (민선의) 군(郡) 보안관. **2** 《Brit.》 an honorary official of a county or shire in England, usu. called High Sheriff. (임기 1년의 명예직) 주(州) 장관. [*shire, reeve*[1]]

sher·ry [ʃéri] *n.* Ⓤ a strong wine, its

color varies from light brown to dark brown, originally made in Spain. 셰리《스페인산의 독한 호박색 포도주》. [Place]

***she's** [ʃiːz] **1** she is. **2** she has.

shew [ʃou] *vt., vi.* (**shewed, shewn**) 《Brit. *arch.*》 =show.

shib·bo·leth [ʃíbəliθ, -lèθ] *n.* Ⓒ a test word; a catch word. (음의 발음 여부를) 시험해 보는 물음 말; (특수 계급이나 단체의) 변말; 표어. [→*Judg.* xii. 6]

:**shield** [ʃiːld] *n.* Ⓒ **1** a piece of metal, wood, etc. carried on the arm by soldiers to protect the body in fighting. 방패. **2** 《*fig.*》 a person or thing that protects; a protector. 보호물〔자〕. **3** something shaped like a shield, such as a trophy. 방패 모양의 것; 실드. — *vt.* (P6,13) 《*from*》 protect; defend. …을 보호하다; 지키다. ¶ *The fence shields the cattle from the wind.* 그 담은 가축을 바람으로부터 막아준다 / ~ *one's child from punishment* 〔*blame*〕 자식을 처벌〔책망〕받지 않도록 지켜 주다. [E.]

:**shift** [ʃift] *vt.* (P6,7,13) **1** move (something) from one place to another; change the position of. …의 위치를 바꾸다; 이동시키다; 옮기다. ¶ ~ *a suitcase from one hand to another* 여행 가방을 이 손에서 저 손으로 옮겨들다 / ~ *responsibility on to someone else* 책임을 누군가 딴 사람에게 돌리다〔전가하다〕 / *He tried to ~ the blame on to me.* 그는 잘못〔비난〕을 나에게 떠넘기려고〔돌리게 하려고〕 하였다. **2** change. …을 바꾸다; 갈아치우다. ¶ ~ *friends* 친구를 갈다 / ~ *one's partner* 파트너를 바꾸다 / ~ *one's lodgings* 하숙을 옮기다. **3** get rid of (something); remove. …을 제거하다. ¶ *Shift this rubbish out of the way.* 이 쓰레기를 외딴 곳으로 치워버려라. — *vi.* **1** (P1,2A,3) (of a person) move from one place, position, etc. to another. (위치·장소 따위를) 옮기다; 바꾸다. **2** (P2A,3) ⓐ (of a something) move out of the original position; slip or slide away from a given place. (본래의 위치·장소에서) 이동하다; 움직이다; 옮겨지다. ¶ *Cargo shifts in a ship's hold.* 뱃짐은 선창에서 이리저리 움직인다. ⓑ (of the wind) change direction. (풍향이) 바뀌다. ¶ *The wind has shifted to the east.* 바람이 동풍으로 바뀌었다. ⓒ 《U.S.》 change gears in driving. (자동차의) 기어를 바꿔 넣다; 변속하다. ¶ ~ *into second gear* 기어를 2단으로 변속하다 / *The car shifts automatically.* 그 자동차는 자동으로 변속한다. **3** (P2A) manage somehow 〔to get along〕; do with difficulty. 그럭저럭 꾸려나가다; 겨우겨우 힘들게 해내다. ¶ ~ *with a small income* 적은 수입으로 그럭저럭 꾸려가다 / *I must ~ as I can.* 나는 할 수 있는 만큼은 해야 한다.

shift for oneself, do the best one can; manage without help from others. 자기의 최선을 다하다; 자기 힘으로 꾸려나가다.

shift one's ground, change one's point of view in an argument. 논거(論據)를 바꾸다.

— *n.* Ⓒ **1** the act of shifting; change. 변화; 전환; 변천. ¶ *a ~ of the tide* 조류의 변화 / *shifts in fashion* 유행의 변천. **2** the period during which work is regularly done. (교대제의) 근무 시간. ¶ *an eight-hour* ~ 8시간 근무제 / *They work in three eight-hour shifts.* 그들은 3교대 8시간 근무제로 일한다 / *The working day is divided into three shifts.* 하루의 근무일은 3교대제로 나뉜다. **3** a group of people working at one time. 일교대 시간내에서 일하는 근로자들; 교대조(組). ¶ *a night* 〔*a day*〕 ~ 야간〔주간〕 근무조 / *The night ~ leaves at 8 a.m.* 야간 근무조는 오전 8시에 떠난다. **4** 《often *pl.*》 plot; trick. 계획; 궁리; 묘안. ¶ *the last shifts* 최후의 수단. [E.]

make a shift, manage somehow. 그럭저럭 꾸려나가다.

shift·less [ʃíftlis] *adj.* lacking the will to accomplish something; lazy; incapable. 하고 싶은 마음이 없는; 게으른; 무력한.

shift·y [ʃífti] *adj.* (**shift·i·er, shift·i·est**) **1** deceitful; tricky. 술책이 많은; 교묘한. **2** not to be trusted; unreliable. 미덥지 못한; 부정직한.

:**shil·ling** [ʃíliŋ] *n.* Ⓒ a former British silver coin once equal to twelve pence. 실링《영국의 화폐 단위; 1971년 2월 15일 폐지됨》. 參考 1 파운드의 20분의 1이며, s.로 생략함. [E.]

cut off with a shilling ⇨cut.

take the King's 〔***Queen's***〕 ***shilling,*** 《Brit.》 enlist as a soldier; enter the army. (응모하여) 군인이 되다; 입대하다.

shil·ly-shal·ly [ʃíliʃæ̀li] *n.* Ⓤ indecision in trifling things; hesitation. 우유부단; 주저. — *vi.* (P1) be slow to decide; hesitate. 망설이다; 주저하다. — *adj.* undecided; irresolute; hesitating; vacillating. 우유부단한; 결단을 못 내리는; 동요하는. — *adv.* in a hesitating 〔vacillating〕 manner. 주저하여; 망설여. [*shall I?*]

shim·mer [ʃímər] *vi.* (P1) shine with a wavering light; glimmer; gleam faintly. 희미하게 반짝이다; (빛이) 가물거리다. ¶ *The moonlight is shimmering on the sea.* 달빛이 해수면 위에서 너울거리고 있다. — *n.* Ⓒ 《*sing.* only》 a faint, wavering light or gleam. 희미한〔가물거리는〕 빛; 미광(微光). ¶ *Pearls have a beautiful* ~. 진주에는 아름다운 은은한 빛이 있다. [E.]

shin [ʃin] *n.* Ⓒ the front part of the leg between the ankle and the knee. 정강이(뼈). — *vt., vi.* (**shinned, shin·ning**) **1** (P3) 《*up*》 climb (a rope, tree, etc.) with hands and legs. 기어오르다. ¶ ~ *up a tree* 〔*pole*〕 나무〔돛대〕에 기어오르다. **2** (P6) kick (someone) in the shins. (아무의) 정강이를 차다. ¶ ~ *oneself against a chair* 의자에 정강이를 부딪치다. **3** (P1,2A) 《U.S.》 run; walk fast. 달리다; 빠르게 걷다. [E.]

shin·dy [ʃíndi] *n.* Ⓒ (*pl.* **-dies**) 《*colloq.*》 a disturbance; an uproar. 소동. [*shinny*]

:shine [ʃain] *v.* (**shone**) *vi.* (P1,2A) **1** give out or reflect light. 빛나다; 빛을 반사하다; 비치다. ¶ *The sun shines bright in the sky.* 태양이 하늘에서 밝게 빛나고 있다 / *A light shone in the window.* 창문에 등불 하나가 밝게 빛났다 / *Her eyes* ~. 그녀의 눈이 빛난다. **2** 《*fig.*》 appear very bright; be bright. (기쁨·흥분으로 표정이) 밝다; 빛나다. ¶ *Her face shone with joy.* 그녀의 얼굴은 기쁨에 빛나고 있었다. **3** be best; be excellent; do very well; excel or be conspicuous. 가장 우수하다; 빼어나다; 탁월하다; 이채를 띠다. ¶ ~ *as a teacher* 교사로서 가장 뛰어나다 / ~ *at baseball* 야구를 매우 잘한다 / *He shines in mathematics.* 그는 수학에서 타의 추종을 불허한다 / *He does not* ~ *in society.* 그는 사교계에서 별로 두드러져 있지 않다. — *vt.* (P6) **1** cause (something) to reflect light; cause to shine. …을 빛나게 하다; 비추다. ¶ *The policeman shone his flashlight on the thief.* 경찰관은 그의 회중 전등을 도둑에게 비추었다. **2** (**shined**) 《*colloq.*》 make bright; polish. 광을 내다; 닦다. ¶ *I must have my shoes shined.* 나는 내 구두를 닦아야 한다.

shine up to, 《U.S. *sl.*》 try to please. …의 환심을 사려 들다.

— *n.* **1** Ⓤ sunshine. 햇빛; 일광. **2** Ⓤ bright (fair) weather. 맑은 날씨; (날씨의) 맑음. ¶ *rain or* ~ 날씨에 상관 없이. **3** Ⓤ brightness; light; glow. 빛남; 빛; 광휘. **4** 《*sing.* only》 《*colloq.*》 polish; gloss. 윤; 광택. ¶ *get a* ~ *on one's shoes* 구두에 광을 내다 / *Silk has a* ~. 비단에는 광택이 있다. [E.]

make no end of a shine, make a fuss. 대소동을 일으키다; 법석을 떨다.

put a good shine on, polish. 광(光)을 내다.

take a shine to, 《U.S. *colloq.*》 take a liking to; become fond of. …가 좋아지다; …에 반하다.

take the shine off (***out of***) ***someone,*** make someone appear to be inferior; make someone's efforts seem unimportant. …의 광택을 없애다; …을 볼품없게 만들다; (노력 따위를) 무색하게 하다.

shin·er [ʃáinər] *n.* **1** a person or thing that shines. 빛나는 물건; 번쩍 띄는 인물. **2** 《Brit. *sl.*》 a new coin. 새 동전. [↑]

shin·gle[1] [ʃíŋgəl] *n.* Ⓒ **1** a thin piece of wood, slate, etc. used in making roofs. 지붕널; 지붕 이는 판자. **2** 《U.S. *colloq.*》 a small signboard, esp. for a doctor's or lawyer's office. (의사·변호사 사무실 등의) 작은 간판. **3** a kind of haircut for women. (여성 뒷머리의) 싱글 커트; 짧게 치켜 깎기. — *vt.* (P6) **1** cover (a roof) with shingles. (지붕을) 지붕널로 이다. **2** cut (a woman's hair) short. (여성의 머리를) 싱글 커트로 하다. [L. *scandula*]

shin·gle[2] [ʃíŋgəl] *n.* Ⓒ (*pl.* **-gle**) 《chiefly Brit.》 small pebbles on a beach; a beach covered with shingle. (강가·해변의) 조약돌; 조약돌이 깔린 해변. [Imit.]

shin·gles [ʃíŋgəlz] *n. pl.* 《*sing.* in use》 a disease of the skin marked by a band of inflamed spots. 대상 포진. [L. *cingo* gird]

shin·gly [ʃíŋgli] *adj.* covered with small pebbles. 자갈(조약돌)이 많은. [*shingle*[2]]

shin guard [∠ ⊿] *n.* (in football, hockey, etc.) a heavy guard worn to protect the shins. (축구·하키용의) 정강이받이. [*shin*]

shin·ing [ʃáiniŋ] *adj.* **1** bright; reflecting light. 빛나는; 번쩍이는. **2** remarkable; distinguished; brilliant. 뛰어난. ¶ *a* ~ *player* 뛰어난 선수 / *a* ~ *example* 모범; 두드러진 훌륭한 보기. ● **shin·ing·ly** [-li] *adv.* [*shine*]

Shin·to [ʃíntou] *n.* the native religion of Japan. (일본의) 신도(神道). [Chin. =way of the Gods]

shin·ty [ʃínti], **shin·ny** [ʃíni] *n.* a simple kind of hockey. 하키 비슷한 간단한 경기. [*shin ye* cry]

shin·y [ʃáini] *adj.* (**shin·i·er, shin·i·est**) **1** bright; shining. 빛나는; 번쩍이는. **2** polished. 윤나는; 광택이 있는. ¶ ~ *shoes* 광택이 나는 구두 / *My nose is* ~. 나의 코는 번들번들 윤이 난다. **3** glossy because of long wear. 오래 입어 반들반들한. ¶ *a* ~ *coat* 오래 입어 반들반들한 코트. [*shine*]

:ship [ʃip] *n.* Ⓒ **1** a large sea-going boat. 배. ¶ *go to America by* ~ 배로 미국에 가다 / *leave a* ~ *at Inch'ŏn* 인천에서 배로 떠나다 / *be in a* ~ 배 안에 있다 / *a* ~ *of the desert* 낙타《사막의 배란 뜻》. **2** something like a ship in use or shape. 배 모양의 것. ¶ *an airship* 비행선 / *a spaceship* 우주선. **3** 《*collectively*》 officers and crew of a vessel. 승무원.

on board a ship, into a ship; in a ship. 배 안으로; 배 안에서.

take ship, go on board a ship. 배를 타다; 배로 가다.

when one's ship comes home, when one gets money; when one's hopes have been realized. 부자가 되면; 운이 트이면.

— *vt.* **1** (P6,7) carry (something) by ship; 《U.S.》 carry (something) by a ship, train, truck, etc.; send. …을 배로 나르다(수송하다); 보내다. ¶ *Did he* ~ *it by express or by rail?* 그는 그것을 급행편으로 보냈느냐 또는 철도편으로 보냈느냐. **2** (P6) employ (someone) for service on a ship. (선원)을 고용하다. ¶ ~ *a new crew* 새 선원 하나를 고용하다. **3** (P6) put or take (goods) on board a ship. 배에 물품을 싣다; 선적하다. ¶ ~ *coal for France* 프랑스행의 석탄을 선적하다. **4** (P6) fix (a mast, rudder, etc.) in its proper place in a ship. (돛·키 따위를) 정해진 자리에 설치하다(두다). ¶ ~ *a mast* 돛을 제자리에 설치하다 / ~ *oars* 노를 거두어 제자리에 두다. **5** (P6) 《naut.》 take in (water) over the side. (배가 파도를) 뒤집어 쓰다. ¶ *A boat ships water* (*a wave, a sea*) *on a stormy* *sea.* 폭풍우의 바다에서 배는 파도를 뒤집어 쓴다. — *vi.* (P1,2A) **1** go on board a ship; sail. 배에 타다; 승선하다; 항해하다. ¶ *We ~ at Pusan tomorrow.* 우리는 내일 부산에서 배를 탄다. **2** take a job on a ship; be a sailor. 선원이 되다. ¶ *He shipped as a sailor.* 그는 선원으로 취업하였다. [E.]

ship off, **a)** send (someone) to another country by ship. (아무를) 배로 외국에 보내다. ¶ *~ a young man off to the colonies* 한 청년을 선편으로 해외 식민지에 보내다. **b)** send away; get rid of. 좇아버리다; …을 면하다〔벗어나다〕.

-ship [-ʃip] *suf.* **1** state or quality. '지위, 성질, 상태'의 뜻. ¶ *friendship* 우정. **2** office, dignity, or profession. '직, 직업'의 뜻. ¶ *kingship* 왕위. **3** art or skill. '기량, 수완'의 뜻. ¶ *penmanship* 서법. [E.]

ship·board [ʃípbɔ̀ːrd] *n.* Ⓤ a ship. 배.

on shipboard, on a ship. 선상에. ¶ *go on ~* 승선하다.

ship-breaker [ʃípbrèikər] *n.* a contractor who breaks up old ships for scrap. 폐선 해체업자.

ship-broker [ʃípbròukər] *n.* an agent who buys and sells ships, cargoes etc. 선박 중개업자.

ship·build·er [ʃípbìldər] *n.* Ⓒ a person who designs or builds ships. 조선업자; 조선 기사.

ship·build·ing [ʃípbìldiŋ] *n.* Ⓤ the construction of ships; the art of constructing ships. 조선; 조선 기술. — *adj.* of shipbuilding. 조선의; 조선술의.

ship canal [ㅗ-ㅅ] *n.* a canal through which a ship can pass. (큰 배가 지나갈 수 있는) 운하.

ship chandler [ㅗㅅ-] *n.* 《chiefly Brit.》 a person who deals in supplies for ships. 선구상(船具商).

ship·load [ʃíplòud] *n.* Ⓒ a full load or cargo for a ship. 배 한 척 분의 적하량.

ship·mas·ter [ʃípmæ̀stər, -mɑ̀ːs-] *n.* Ⓒ the master, commander, or captain of a merchant ship. 선장.

ship·mate [ʃípmèit] *n.* Ⓒ a fellow sailor on a ship. (같은 배의) 동료 선원.

·**ship·ment** [ʃípmənt] *n.* **1** Ⓤ the act of loading goods into a ship. 출하(出荷); 선적. ¶ *the ~ of coal* 석탄의 선적. **2** Ⓒ goods transported at one time by a ship or by any means of transportation. 적하(積荷); (배나 기타 수송 수단에 의해) 발송된 짐. ¶ *The ~ of boxes from the factory has not reached us.* 그 공장에서 발송한 상자들은 아직 우리에게 도착하지 않았다.

ship·own·er [ʃípòunər] *n.* Ⓒ an owner of a ship or ships. 선주.

ship·per [ʃípər] *n.* Ⓒ a person who sends goods by ship or any means of transportation. 하주(荷主).

·**ship·ping** [ʃípiŋ] *n.* Ⓤ **1** 《*collectively*》 all the ships of a port, a nation, a company, etc. 선박. ¶ *merchant ~* 상선. **2** the act or business of transporting goods. 선적; 운송〔해운〕업.

ship·shape [ʃípʃèip] *adj.* having everything in good order; neat. 잘 정돈되어 있는; 정연한. — *adv.* in a shipshape manner. 정연히.

ship·worm [ʃípwə̀ːrm] *n.* Ⓒ a small animal with a soft and wormlike body which makes holes in the timbers of ships under the water. 좀조개.

ship·wreck [ʃíprèk] *n.* **1** Ⓤ the destruction or loss of a ship by an accident at sea. 난파. **2** Ⓒ a wrecked ship; the scattered pieces of a wrecked ship. 난파선(의 잔해). ¶ *Only two people were saved from the ~.* 겨우 두 사람이 난파선에서 구조되었다. **3** 《*fig.*》 Ⓤ destruction; failure. 파괴; 실패. ¶ *The ~ of his plans discouraged him.* 그의 계획의 실패는 그를 실망시켰다.

make a shipwreck of (= *destroy or ruin*) *something.* …을 파멸시키다.

— *vt.* (P6) **1** destroy (a ship) by shipwreck. …을 난파시키다. ¶ *be shipwrecked* 난파〔조난〕하다. **2** destroy (something like a hope, happiness, etc.). …을 파괴하다. ¶ *shipwrecked hopes* 좌절된 희망.

— *vi.* (P1) **1** suffer shipwreck. 배가 난파하다. **2** come to ruin. 파멸하다.

ship·wright [ʃípràit] *n.* Ⓒ a person who builds or repairs ships. 배목수; 조선공.

ship·yard [ʃípjɑ̀ːrd] *n.* Ⓒ a yard or place where ships are built or repaired. 조선소.

shire [ʃáiər] *n.* Ⓒ a county in Great Britain. (영국의) 주(州). [E.]

shirk [ʃəːrk] *vi., vt.* (P1,2A,3; 6,9) avoid or evade (work, duty, etc.) purposely; escape. (일·의무 따위를) 회피〔기피〕하다; 도망치다. ¶ *~ one's work* 〔*duty*〕 자기의 일〔책임〕을 회피하다 / *~ from one's duty* 의무를 회피하다. [G. *schurke* sharper]

shirk·er [ʃə́ːrkər] *n.* Ⓒ a person who escapes doing works, etc. (일·책임 따위를) 회피하는 사람; 게으름부리는 사람.

shirr [ʃəːr] *n.* Ⓒ 《U.S.》 a gathered arrangement of cloth, etc. 주름. — *vt.* (P6) **1** gather (cloth) on three or more parallel threads. (세가닥 이상의 바늘땀을 내서) …에 주름을 잡다. ¶ *a shirred skirt* 주름을 잡은 스커트. **2** bake (eggs) in a shallow dish with butter, etc. (달걀을) 버터 바른 얇은 접시에 고르게 담아 굽다. [?]

:**shirt** [ʃəːrt] *n.* Ⓒ **1** ⓐ a man's thin garment with sleeves and a collar, worn under a coat or jacket. 와이셔츠; 셔츠. ⓑ 《U.S.》 the undergarment for the upper part of the body; an undershirt. 속셔츠; 속내의. **2** a woman's blouse. (여성용의) 블라우스. [E.]

get someone's shirt off, make someone angry. …을 화나게 하다.

***have** one's **shirt out** [**off**],* 《*sl.*》 be angry. 화나다; 불끈하다.
in** one's **shirt-sleeves, not wearing a coat or waistcoat. 셔츠 바람으로; 상의를 벗고.
keep** one's **shirt on, 《*sl.*》 not get angry; remain calm. 침착[냉정]을 유지하다.
lose** one's **shirt, 《*sl.*》 lose everything; become penniless. 무일푼이 되다.
put** one's **shirt on (*a horse*), bet all one has on. (한 경마에다) 있는 돈을 몽땅 걸다.
stripped to the shirt, reduced to the barest necessities. 몸에 걸친 것을 몽땅 털려.
without [***not***] ***a shirt to** one's **back,*** extremely poor; in great poverty. 몹시 가난하여.

shirt front [∠∠] *n.* the front of a man's shirt. 와이셔츠의 앞가슴.

shirt·ing [ʃə́:rtiŋ] *n.* Ⓤ material for making shirts. 셔츠[와이셔츠] 감.

shirt sleeve [∠∠] *n.* the sleeve of a shirt. 와이셔츠의 소매.

shirt-sleeve [ʃə́:rtslì:v] *adj.* 《*colloq.*》 informal; plain; rude. 비공식의; 솔직한; 거친; 세련되지 않은.

shirt·waist [ʃə́:rtwèist] *n.* Ⓒ 《U.S.》 a woman's blouse with a collar and cuffs worn under a skirt. (여성용의 와이셔츠식) 블라우스.

shirt·y [ʃə́:rti] *adj.* (**shirt·i·er, shirt·i·est**) 《chiefly Brit. *sl.*》 angry. 성난. [E.] ● **shirt·i·ness** [-nis] *n.*

shit [ʃit] *n.* 《*vulg.*》 **1** excrement. 똥. **2** defecating. 배변. **3** heroin. 헤로인; 마약. **4** an objectionable person. 빌어먹을 놈. — *vi., vt.* (P1; 6) defecate. 똥누다. [E.]

•**shiv·er**[1] [ʃívər] *vi.* (P1,2A,3) tremble with fear or cold. (추위·공포 따위로) 와들와들 떨다. ¶ *stand shivering in the snow* 눈을 맞으며 와들와들 떨고 서 있다. — *n.* Ⓒ **1** the act of trembling from cold or fear. 떨림; 전율. **2** 《*the* ~*s*》 《*colloq.*》 ⓐ an attack of shivering. 한기(寒氣); 오한. ⓑ a feeling of horror. (공포로 인한) 섬뜩함; 전율. ¶ *give someone the shivers* 아무를 전율케[섬뜩하게] 하다. ● **shiv·er·er** [-rər] *n.* [E.]

shiv·er[2] [ʃívər] *n.* Ⓒ 《usu. *pl.*》 a small piece. 작은 조각; 파편. ¶ *break into* [*in*] *shivers.* 산산조각이 나다; 분쇄하다. — *vt., vi.* (P6,13; 2A) break (something) into many small pieces. 산산조각이 나게 부수다[부서지다]. ¶ ~ *glass with a hammer* 해머로 유리를 산산조각이 나게 부수다. [E.]

shiv·er·y [ʃívəri] *adj.* inclined to shiver; causing shivers from cold or fear. 떨리는; (추위·공포 따위로) 덜덜 떠는; 오싹[섬뜩]하는. [shiver[1]]

shoal[1] [ʃoul] *n.* Ⓒ **1** a shallow place in the water; a sandbank in a river or the sea. (강·바다의) 얕은 여울[곳]; 사주(砂洲). ¶ *the deeps and shoals* 깊은 곳과 얕은 곳 / *The ship was wrecked on the shoals.* 그 배는 사주에서 난파했다. **2** 《usu. *pl.*》 a hidden or unexpected danger. 숨은 위험. — *adj.* shallow. 얕은. — *vi.* (P1) 《*of*》 become shallow. 얕아지다. — *vt.* **1** make shallow. 얕아지게 하다. **2** sail into a shallow. (배를) 얕은 곳으로 가게 하다. [E.]

shoal[2] [ʃoul] *n.* Ⓒ **1** a large number or mass, esp. of fish. (물고기 따위의) 큰 떼. ¶ *a* ~ *of flying fish* 날치의 떼. **2** 《*colloq.*》 a large crowd. 다수; 다량. ¶ *shoals of students* 많은 수의 학생들 / *He gets letters in shoals.* 그는 많은 수의 편지를 받는다. — *vi.* (P1) (of fish) crowd and swim together. (물고기가) 떼지어 모여들다; 떼지어 유영(游泳)하다. [→school[2]]

:shock[1] [ʃak / ʃɔk] *n.* **1** Ⓒ a sudden blow or shake. (폭발·타격 등에 의한) 충격; 진동. ¶ *the* ~ *of an explosion* 폭발의 충격 / *the severe* ~ *of an earthquake* 지진의 격심한 진동. **2** Ⓒ a sudden great sorrow or surprise; Ⓤ a condition of physical or mental weakness caused by a shock. (정신적인) 쇼크[충격]; 쇼크(증). ¶ *The news gave a great* ~ *to me.* 그 뉴스는 나에게 큰 쇼크를 주었다 / *He died of* ~. 그는 쇼크사 하였다 / *His death was a* ~ *to us all.* 그의 죽음은 우리 모두에게 하나의 충격이었다 / *The bad news left us all speechless from* ~. 그 좋지 않은 뉴스는 우리 모두를 충격으로 말을 잊게 하였다. **3** a disturbance produced by an electric current passing through the body. 전기 쇼크; 감전. ¶ *an electric* ~ 전기 쇼크; 전격. — *vt.* (P6) cause (someone) to feel horror, anger, disgust, etc. …에 충격을 주다; …을 깜짝 놀라게 하다; 분개시키다. ¶ *I was shocked to see the scene.* 나는 그 광경을 보고 충격을 받았다 / *I hope you won't be shocked by* [*at, to hear*] *his coarse stories.* 나는 그의 추잡한 이야기에 네가 깜짝 놀라지 않았으면 한다. [F. *choquer* collide]

shock[2] [ʃak / ʃɔk] *n.* Ⓒ a pile of corn or a group of bundles of grain set up in a field to dry after the harvest. 볏가리; 옥수수의 단[다발]. — *vt.* (P6) make into shocks. (벼·옥수수 따위의 단을) 가리다. [E.]

shock[3] [ʃak / ʃɔk] *n.* Ⓒ 《usu. *a* ~ *of hair*》 a thick, untidy mass of hair. 헝클어진 머리. ¶ *He has a* ~ *of red hair.* 그는 붉은 색의 헝클어진 머리를 하고 있다. — *adj.* bushy or shaggy, as hair. (머리(카락) 따위가) 헝클어진; 난발의. [→shag]

shock absorber [∠-∠-] *n.* a device that absorbs or lessens shocks. 완충기. [*shock*[1]]

shock·er [ʃákər / ʃɔ́k-] *n.* Ⓒ a person or thing that gives a shock. 오싹 놀라게 하는 사람[것]; 싫은 놈. [*shock*[1]]

shock·head·ed [ʃákhèdid / ʃɔ́k-] *adj.* having a thick, untidy mass of hair. 머리털이 부스스한; 난발의. [*shock*[3]]

shock·ing [ʃákiŋ / ʃɔ́k-] *adj.* **1** disgusting; unpleasant. 괘씸한; 불유쾌한. ¶ ~ *conduct* 괘씸한 행동. **2** causing horror or surprise. 소름끼치는; 쇼킹한. ¶ ~ *cruelty* 오

싹 소름을 끼치게 하는 잔학성 / *a ~ accident* 소름끼치는 사건 / *His conduct was ~ .* 그의 행동은 쇼킹한 것이었다. **3** 《*colloq.*》 very bad. 조잡(粗雜)한; 형편 없는. ¶ *a ~ dinner* 형편 없는 식사 / *a ~ coward* 지독한 겁쟁이. — *adv.* 《*colloq.*》 very. 매우; 아주. ¶ *It was a ~ bad speech.* 그것은 아주 형편 없는 연설이었다. [*shock*[1]]

shock·ing·ly [ʃákiŋli / ʃɔ́k-] *adv.* as if giving a shock; extremely. 깜짝 놀랄 만큼; 지독하게; 몹시.

shod [ʃad / ʃɔd] *v.* p. and pp. of **shoe.** — *adj.* furnished with shoes. 신을 신은. ¶ *a well-shod horse* 제대로 편자를 박은 말. [*shoe*]

shod·dy [ʃádi / ʃɔ́di] *n.* (*pl.* **-dies**) **1** Ⓤ Ⓒ cloth of wool of poor quality made from woolen waste, old rags, yarn, etc. 재생 모직(물)〔털실〕. **2** Ⓒ anything of poor quality which looks better than it really is. 가짜; 위조품. — *adj.* (**-di·er, -di·est**) **1** made of shoddy. 재생 털실의. ¶ *~ clothes* 재생 털실로 짠 옷. **2** of poor quality; of poorer quality than it looks. 질이 나쁜; 가짜의. ¶ *~ buildings* 조잡하게 지은 빌딩들 / *a ~ character* 비열한 사람. ● **shod·di·ness** [-nis] *n.* [?]

:shoe [ʃuː] *n.* Ⓒ **1** 《usu. *pl.*》 an outer covering for the foot usu. made of leather and having a thick or stiff sole at the heel. 구두. 參考 영국에서는 구두의 목이 없거나 짧은 단화를 말하며, 미국에서는 단화보다 목이 긴 편상화도 포함시켜 말함. ¶ *a pair of shoes* 한 켤레의 구두 / *put on* 〔*take off*〕 *one's shoes* 구두를 신다〔벗다〕 / *I have bought a new pair of shoes.* 나는 한 켤레의 새 구두를 샀다. **2** something in the shape of a shoe or used like a shoe; a U-shaped metal band fastened to a horse's hoof. 구두 모양의 것; 편자. **3** the part of a brake pressing on a wheel to stop a car. (자동차의) 브레이크슈. **4** a metal ring or cap for the protection of the end of a pole, stick, etc. (지팡이·깃대 따위의 끝에 박은) 물미; 마구리(쇠).

another pair of shoes, quite a different thing or matter. 전혀 별개의 일〔문제〕.

die in one's shoes, be hanged; die an unnatural death. 변사하다.

know where the shoe pinches, know the meaning of trouble or sorrow from one's own experience. 곤란〔슬픔, 재난 따위〕의 원인을 알다.

put the shoe on the right foot, blame or praise the right person. 나무랄 사람을 나무라다; 칭찬해야 할 사람을 칭찬하다.

shake in one's shoes, shiver; be afraid. 몸을 떨다; 두려워하다.

stand 〔***be***〕 ***in someone's shoes,*** take the place of someone. …을 대신하다; …의 입장이 되다.

wait for dead men's shoes, wait for a man's death in the expectation of his property or position. 남의 유산을〔지위를〕 노리다.

— *vt.* (**shod**) (P6) **1** fasten shoes on to (a horse). (말)에 편자를 박다. ¶ *A blacksmith shoes horses.* 편자공이 말에 편자를 박는다. **2** protect (the edge of a stick, etc. with metal). (지팡이 따위)의 끝에 물미〔마구리〕를 달다. [E.]

shoe·black [ʃúːblæ̀k] *n.* Ⓒ 《Brit.》 a person who cleans and polishes the shoes of passers-by to earn money. 구두닦이 (=《U.S.》 bootblack).

shoe·horn [ʃúːhɔ̀ːrn] *n.* Ⓒ a piece of metal, horn, or other material to get a foot into a shoe easily by making the shoe easier to slip on. 구둣주걱.

shoe·lace [ʃúːlèis] *n.* Ⓒ a string, cord, or leather strip used to fasten a shoe; a shoe string. 구두끈.

·shoe·mak·er [ʃúːmèikər] *n.* Ⓒ a person who makes or repairs shoes. 구두 만드는〔고치는〕 사람; 제화공.

shoe·mak·ing [ʃúːmèikiŋ] *n.* Ⓤ the act of making or mending shoes. 구두 만들기.

shoe·string [ʃúːstrìŋ] *n.* **1** Ⓒ 《esp. U.S.》 a shoelace. 구두끈. **2** 《*colloq.*》 a small amount of money. 소액의 돈. ¶ *start a business on a ~* 적은 자본으로 사업을 시작하다 / *live on a ~* 적은 돈으로 살다.

:shone [ʃoun / ʃɔn] *v.* p. and pp. of **shine.**

shoo [ʃuː] *interj.* a word used for driving or scaring away animals or birds. 쉬이; 쉿 《새 따위를 쫓는 소리》. — *vi., vt.* drive away (animals or birds) by crying 'Shoo!' (새 따위를) '쉬이' 하며 쫓다. [Imit.]

:shook [ʃuk] *v.* p. of **shake.**

:shoot [ʃuːt] *v.* (**shot**) *vt.* **1** (P6,7,13) fire (a gun); let fly (an arrow). (총·화살)을 쏘다; 발사하다. ¶ *~ an arrow* 화살을 쏘다 / *~ a gun at a target* 표적을 향해서 총을 쏘다. **2** (P6,7) ⓐ send (something) off quickly; throw forward with a sudden, quick movement. …을 홱 내던지다. ¶ *be shot out of a car* 자동차 밖으로 홱 내던져지다 / *~ rubbish* 쓰레기를 왈칵 (쏟아) 버리다. ⓑ 《*out, forth*》 thrust forward; stick out; put forth in growth. (팔·손 따위)를 쑥 내밀다; (초목이 새싹·가지)를 내밀다. ¶ *~ out one's hand* 손을 쑥 내밀다 / *~ out buds* 〔*leaves*〕 (초목이) 싹〔잎〕을 내밀다 / *The snake shot out its tongue.* 뱀이 혀를 날름 내밀었다. ⓒ 《*out, forth*》 send forth 〔swiftly〕. (질문 따위)를 잇따라 퍼붓다; 연발하다. ¶ *~ out a stream of witty words* 기지에 찬 말을 연발하다 / *He shot question after question.* 그는 연거푸 질문을 퍼부었다. **3** hit or kill (something) with a bullet or an arrow. …을 쏘아 맞히다〔떨어뜨리다〕. ¶ *~ a bird* 새를 쏘아 맞히다 / *~ a man through the head* 사람을 쏘아 머리를 관통시키다 / *~ down an enemy airplane* 적기를 쏘아 떨어뜨리다. **4** send (something) forth with sudden force. …

을 돌진시키다. ¶ ~ *a ball at the goal* 골을 향해 공을 쏜살같이 던지다〔차다〕. **5** flash out; direct or send forth suddenly. (빛 따위를) 발하다; (시선·미소 등)을 던지다; 보내다. ¶ *The sun shoots its beams through the mist.* 태양은 안개 사이로 그 햇살을 비친다 / ~ *a glance* 〔*smile*〕 *at a girl* 소녀를 향해 시선을〔미소를〕 보내다. **6** go over (an area) in hunting game. (어느 지역)에서 사냥하다. ¶ ~ *a country* 시골에서 사냥을 하다. **7** pass rapidly through or over. (여울 따위)를 쏜살같이 건너다; 타고 넘다. ¶ ~ *a rapid* 급류를 거침없이 건너다.

— *vi.* **1** (P1,2A) fire a gun; let fly an arrow 〔missile〕; send forth a bullet. 쏘다; 사격하다; 발사되다. ¶ *Hands up ! or I'll* ~ *!* 손들어, 그렇지 않으면 쏜다 / *He hunts and shoots, but doesn't fish.* 그는 사냥도 하고 사격도 하지만 낚시는 하지 않는다 / *My old rifle doesn't* ~ *well.* 내 낡은 소총은 잘 발사되지 않는다. **2** (P1,2A,3) move very fast; dash; rush. 쏜살같이 움직이다〔지나가다〕. ¶ *A bird shot across the sky.* 새 한 마리가 하늘을 쏜살같이 지나갔다 / *A car shot past us.* 차 한 대가 우리 옆을 휙 지나갔다 / *The pain shoots up the back of the leg.* 통증이 찌릿찌릿하고 다리의 뒤쪽을 지난다. **3** grow a fresh branch rapidly; grow up rapidly. (초목이) 싹트다; 싹이 나오다; 빠르게 성장하다. ¶ *The plants are beginning to* ~. 식물이 싹트기 시작하였다 / *The child has shot up wonderfully.* 그 아이는 놀랄 만큼 빠르게 성장했다. **4** feel a sharp pain. 욱신욱신 쑤시다; 통증이 심하다. ¶ *A decayed tooth shoots.* 썩은 이가 욱신욱신 쑤신다.

I'll be shot if ..., I will never .... 절대로 …은 아니다.

shoot ahead, outstrip. 추월하다.

shoot down, bring down; kill; defeat. (쏘아) 떨어뜨리다; 죽이다; 패배시키다.

shoot straight, shoot with good aim; be a good shot. 명중시키다.

— *n.* Ⓒ **1** the act of shooting. 사격. **2** a new growth; a young branch. 새싹; 어린 가지. ¶ *bean shoots* 콩나물. **3** a shooting match; a hunt. 사격 시합; 사냥. **4** a shooting distance or range. 사정 거리. **5** a sudden swift flow of water. 급류; 여울. [E.]

shoot·er [ʃúːtər] *n.* Ⓒ a person who shoots. 사수.

shoot·ing [ʃúːtiŋ] *n.* **1** Ⓤ the act of shooting. 사격. **2** Ⓒ 《chiefly Brit.》 a particular area rented in order to shoot game there; Ⓤ the right of shooting in a particular area. 총사냥 지역; 총렵권.

shooting box [⌐-⌐] *n.* 《chiefly Brit.》 a small house or lodge used during the shooting season. 사냥막.

shooting range [⌐-⌐] *n.* a place used to practice shooting with rifles; a rifle range. 사격장.

shooting star [⌐-⌐] *n.* a falling star; a meteor. 유성(流星).

shooting stick [⌐-⌐] *n.* a walking stick with a pike at one end and a small, folding seat at the other, used by spectators at sporting events, etc. (윗부분을 펴서 걸터앉게 된) 수렵용〔경기 관전용〕 단장(短杖).

:shop [ʃɑp / ʃɔp] *n.* Ⓒ **1** a small store. 가게; 소매점. ¶ *a fancy* ~ (여자의) 장신구 가게. **2** a place where things are made or repaired; a workshop. 수리 공장; 제작소. ¶ *a shoemaker's* ~ 구둣방 / *a carpenter's* ~ 목공소 / *an automobile repair* ~ 자동차 수리 공장.

all over the shop, 《*sl.*》 scattered everywhere; in disorder; in every place. 어수선하게; 난잡하게; 도처에.

keep a shop, be engaged in retail trade. 가게를 차리다〔내고 있다〕.

set up shop, start a business or work. 사업〔일〕을 시작하다.

shut up shop, **1**) close the shop for the night. (밤새) 폐점하다. **2**) retire from business. 사업을〔장사를〕 그만두다. **3**) 《*colloq.*》 stop doing something. 하던 일을 중단하다.

talk shop, talk about one's own business. (때와 장소를 안 가리고) 자기의 장사 이야기만 하다.

— *vi.* (P1) (**shopped, shop·ping**) visit shops or stores to look at and buy goods. (가게에 가서) 물건을 사다. ¶ *go shopping* 쇼핑 가다 / ~ *for groceries* 〔*new clothes*〕 식료품〔새 옷〕을 사러 가다. [E.]

shop assistant [⌐-⌐-] *n.* 《Brit.》 a person employed in a shop or store. 점원.

shop·boy [ʃápbɔ̀i / ʃɔ́p-] *n.* Ⓒ 《Brit.》 a young clerk in a shop or store. 어린 점원; 판매원.

shop·girl [ʃápgə̀ːrl / ʃɔ́p-] *n.* Ⓒ 《Brit.》 a young girl who works in a shop or store. 여점원(cf. 《U.S.》 *saleswoman, salesgirl*).

shop·hours [ʃápàuərz / ʃɔ́p-] *n. pl.* the hours during which a store is open for business. (상점의) 영업 시간.

shop·keep·er [ʃápkìːpər / ʃɔ́p-] *n.* Ⓒ 《Brit.》 an owner of a shop or store, usu. one that is not very big. 가게 주인; 소매 상인.

shop·keep·ing [ʃápkìːpiŋ / ʃɔ́p-] *n.* Ⓤ 《Brit.》 the business of a shopkeeper. 가게의 경영; 소매업.

shop·lift·er [ʃáplìftər / ʃɔ́p-] *n.* Ⓒ a person who steals goods displayed in a shop or store. (가게 물건을) 슬쩍하는 좀도둑; 들치기.

shop·lift·ing [ʃáplìftiŋ / ʃɔ́p-] *n.* Ⓤ the act of stealing from a shop while pretending to buy. (가게 물건을) 슬쩍하기; 들치기 행위.

shop·man [ʃápmən / ʃɔ́p-] *n.* Ⓒ (*pl.* **-men** [-mən]) **1** 《chiefly Brit.》 a salesman in a shop or store; a clerk. 상점원. **2** a shopkeeper. 소매 상인.

shop·per [ʃápər / ʃɔ́p-] *n.* Ⓒ a person

who goes to shops to buy things. (물건) 사는 손님.

shop·ping [ʃápiŋ/ʃɔ́p-] *n.* the act of buying things at the shops. 쇼핑; 물건사기. ¶ *I have a lot of ~ to do today.* 나는 오늘 쇼핑할 것이 많다.

shopping center [⌐-⌐-] *n.* a group of shops of different kinds, usu. outside the center of a town and planned and built as a whole. 쇼핑 센터; (변두리의) 상점가.

shop-soiled [ʃápsɔ̀ild/ʃɔ́p-] *adj.* =shopworn.

shop·walk·er [ʃápwɔ̀:kər/ʃɔ́p-] *n.* Ⓒ 《Brit.》 a person hired by a large store or shop to direct the customers or to control the shop assistants. (백화점 등에서) (판)매장 감독(=《U.S.》 floorwalker).

shop·win·dow [ʃápwìndou/ʃɔ́p-] *n.* Ⓒ a show window; a window used for showing goods sold at a shop. (점포의) 진열창(窓).

have* [*put*] *everything in the shopwindow, be superficial; make a great show of all one's knowledge, etc. 천박하다; 겉만 번드르르하다.

shop·worn [ʃápwɔ̀:rn/ʃɔ́p-] *adj.* (of goods) slightly dirty or damaged from having been displayed in a store. 상품이 오래 진열되어 찌든.

sho·ran [ʃɔ́:ræn] *n.* 《also *S*-》 a short-range navigation system by which a ship or an aircraft can determine its position by measuring the times required for a radar signal to reach and return from each of two ground stations. 단거리 무선 항법 장치; 쇼랜《두 송신국에 항공기나 배에서 전파를 주고 받아 그 시각의 차로 자기 위치를 구하는 항법(航法)》. [abbr.]

:shore[1] [ʃɔ:r] *n.* **1** Ⓒ the land on the edge of a sea, a lake, etc. (바다·호수·강의) 기슭. ¶ *go on ~* 상륙하다 / *live on the ~* 해안에 살다. **2** Ⓤ land. 육지. [→shear]

in shore, near or nearer the shore [on the water]. 해안 가까이에; (물이) 얕은 곳에.

off shore, away from the shore. 해안에서 떨어져서; 난바다에.

on shore, on land; landward; ashore. 육지에(서); 육지쪽의[쪽으로]; 육지에 가까운. ¶ *come* [*go*] *on ~* 상륙하다.

shore[2] [ʃɔ:r] *n.* Ⓒ a support which is placed against or beneath something like a ship, a building, a tree, etc. to hold it up. 지주(支柱). — *vt.* 《*up*》 support (something) with a shore or shores. …을 버팀대로 버티다[받치다]. [E.]

shore leave [⌐⌐] *n.* **1** permission to spend time ashore. 상륙 허가. **2** time allowed to sailor [officer] to spend on shore. 상륙 허가 시간.

shore·less [ʃɔ́:rlis] *adj.* 《*poet.*》 boundless. 끝없는. [*shore*[1]]

shore·line [ʃɔ́:rlàin] *n.* the line where shore and water meet. 해안선(線); 물가. [*shore*[1]]

shore·ward [ʃɔ́:rwərd] *adv., adj.* toward the shore. 해안 쪽으로[의].

shor·ing [ʃɔ́:riŋ] *n.* **1** 《*collectively*》 shores for supporting a wall, ship, etc. 버팀목. **2** the act of setting up shores. 버팀목으로 받치기. [*shore*[2]]

shorn [ʃɔ:rn] *v.* pp. of **shear.**

:short [ʃɔ:rt] *adj.* **1** ⓐ not long; not tall; lasting only a little time. 짧은; 키가 작은; 단기간의. ¶ *~ legs* 짧은 다리 / *a ~ journey* [*war*] 단기 여행[전(戰)] / *a ~ story* 짧은 이야기 / *a ~ life* 짧은 생애; 단명(短命) / *a ~ winter* 짧은 겨울 / *a ~ visit* 짧은[단기간의] 방문 / *a ~ walk* 단거리의 보행 / *a ~ man* 키가 작은 사람 / *The nights are getting shorter.* 밤이 점점 짧아지고 있다. ⓑ of no great distance; little in distance. 멀리 떨어지지 않은; 가까운. ¶ *a ~ way off* 조금 떨어진; 가까이에 / *a ~ cut* 지름길 / *at a ~ distance* 근거리에. **2** not enough; less than the right amount; not reaching a required standard. 불충분한; 부족한; 기준 미달의. ¶ *~ weight* [*measure*] 중량 부족 / *~ rations* [*commons*] 불충분한 식사 / *The change was five cents ~.* 거스름돈은 5센트가 부족했다 / *be ~ in experience* 경험이 부족하다 / *I'm rather ~ today.* 오늘은 주머니 사정이 좀 쓸쓸하다. **3** rudely brief; so brief as to be almost rude. 쌀쌀맞은; 퉁명스러운. ¶ *a ~ answer* 쌀쌀맞은 대답 / *a ~ temper* 성마른 기질. **4** brief; concise. 간결한; 간단한. ¶ *a ~ speech* 간결한 이야기 / *be ~ and to the point* 간결하면서 요점이 분명하다. **5** ⓐ 《phon.》 (of vowels, etc.) relatively brief in pronunciation. 단음의. ¶ *The vowels in 'fed' and 'foot' are short compared with those in 'fare' and 'food'.* 'fed'와 'foot'에 있는 모음은 'fare'와 'food'의 모음과 비교하면 단음이다. ⓑ 《prosody》 unaccented. 약음의. **6** (of clay, metal, pastry, etc.) not tough; easily broken; brittle. 차지지 않은; 부서지기 쉬운; 파삭파삭한. **7** (of drink) strong; undiluted. (술 따위가) 독한; 물을 타지 않은.

be short for, be an abbreviation of. …의 단축형[약어]이다.

be short of (=*have not enough of*) *something.* …이 부족하다. ¶ *We are ~ of money* [*food, hands*]. 우리는 돈[식량, 일손]이 모자란다.

be short with, show annoyance. …에게 쌀쌀맞게 굴다.

little short of, almost; near. 거의 …한; …에 가까운.

make short work of, dispatch. …을 재빨리 해치우다.

nothing short of, no less than; complete. 아주 …한. ¶ *nothing ~ of marvelous* 참으로 놀라운 / *His conduct was nothing ~ of madness.* 그의 행동은 아주 광적인 것이었다.

to make a long story short, briefly speaking; in a few words. 간단히 말하면; 요컨대.

— *adv.* **1** suddenly; quickly; briefly. 갑자기; 재빨리; 무뚝뚝하게; 간결히. ¶ *stop* ~ 갑자기 서다 / *bring* 〔*pull*〕 *up* ~ 급히 멈추다〔멈추게 하다〕 / *The rider pulled his horse up* ~. 말탄 사람은 그의 말을 갑자기 멈추게 했다 / *take someone up* ~ 아무의 말을 재빨리 가로막다. **2** not to reach. 미치지 않아; (목표 따위의) 바로 앞〔문턱〕에서. ¶ *jump* ~ 점프에 실패하다 / *park* ~ *of the gates* 대문 가까이에 자동차를 주차하다.

come 〔***fall***〕 ***short*** (***of ...***), **a**) fail to reach (as far as). (…에) 미치지〔달하지〕 못하다. ¶ *The arrow fell* ~ *of the mark.* 화살이 표적에 미치지 못했다. **b**) fail to reach, as a required or expected standard. (기대·예상 따위에) 어긋나다; 이르지 못하다. ¶ *The results fell* ~ *of our expectations.* 결과는 우리들의 기대에 어긋났다.

cut short, **a**) cause (someone) to stop speaking. (아무의) 이야기를 가로막다. ¶ *cut the speaker* ~ 연사의 이야기를 가로막다. **b**) cause (something) to end at once; stop suddenly before the end. …을 정지시키다; 갑자기 끝내다. ¶ *cut* ~ *someone's life* 아무의 생애를 중도에서 끝내게 하다 / *The accident forced them to cut their holiday* ~. 그 사고로 그들은 부득이 휴가를 중도에서 끝내야 했다.

run short (***of ...***), use up; be used up. 없어지다; 바닥나다. ¶ *We have run* ~ *of money* 〔*tea and sugar*〕. 우리는 돈〔차와 설탕〕이 다 떨어졌다 / *The gasoline is running* ~. 휘발유가 바닥이 나고 있다.

short of, except for; apart from. …을 별문제로 하고; …을 제외하고. ¶ *Short of murder, he will do anything.* 살인을 제외하고는, 그는 어떤 것이라도 할 것이다.

— *n.* **1** Ⓤ briefness; shortness. 짧음; 간결. **2** Ⓒ anything short or brief. 짧은〔간결한〕 것. **3** Ⓤ 《*the* ~》 the essential point. 요점; 적요. **4** 《usu. *pl.*》 shortage. 부족. **5** 《*pl.*》 ⇨shorts. **6** Ⓒ 《baseball》 a shortstop. 유격수. [E.]

for short, by way of making a name, etc. short. 약하여; 줄여서. ¶ *Samuel is called Sam for* ~. Samuel을 생략하여 Sam이라고 한다.

in short, briefly speaking; in a few words. 간결하게 말하면; 요컨대.

***short·age** [ʃɔ́ːrtidʒ] *n.* ⓊⒸ the state of being short or not enough; Ⓒ the amount of lack or by which something is short. 부족; 부족량〔액〕. ¶ *There is a* ~ *of food in this country.* 이 나라에는 식량이 부족하다.

short·bread [ʃɔ́ːrtbrèd] *n.* a flat, dry cake made with flour, sugar and much butter. (부서지기 쉬운) 카스텔라식의 과자.

short·cake [ʃɔ́ːrtkèik] *n.* ⓊⒸ 《U.S.》 a kind of sweetened sponge cake with fruit and cream on it. 쇼트케이크.

short circuit [ˊ ˊ–] *n.* 《electr.》 an abnormal circuit of electricity caused by the touching of two electric wires. 단락(短絡); 누전; 쇼트.

short·com·ing [ʃɔ́ːrtkʌ̀miŋ] *n.* Ⓒ 《often *pl.*》 a fault; a defect. 결점; 단점. ¶ *We all have some shortcomings.* 우리는 누구나 몇 가지 결점들을 가지고 있다 / *a comfortable house in spite of its shortcomings* 몇몇 결함에도 불구하고 살기에 편안한 집.

short cut [ˊ ˋ] *n.* a shorter way; a quicker method to do something. 지름길; 손쉬운 방법. ¶ *take a* ~ 지름길로 가다.

***short·en** [ʃɔ́ːrtn] *vt.* **1** make (something) short; cut off. …을 짧게 하다; (…의 치수 등을) 줄이다(opp. lengthen). ¶ *The new highway shortened the trip.* 새로 난 도로는 여행을 단축시켰다 / *She has had all her dresses shortened.* 그녀는 그녀의 모든 드레스를 짧게 줄였다 / ~ *a speech* 이야기를 줄이다. **2** make (a cake, etc.) crisp and flaky by adding butter, lard, etc. (케이크·과자 따위를 버터·라드 등을 가미하여) 부드럽게〔파삭파삭하게〕 하다. ¶ *use butter to* ~ *cakes* 케이크를 부드럽게 하기 위해 버터를 사용하다.

— *vi.* become short or less. 짧아지다; 줄다; 감소하다. ¶ *The days* ~ *in the fall.* 가을에는 낮이 짧아진다.

short·hand [ʃɔ́ːrthæ̀nd] *n.* Ⓤ a method of rapid writing in which symbols are used for words, phrases, etc.; stenography. 속기(법). ¶ *write* (*in*) ~ 속기하다. — *adj.* of or by shorthand. 속기(법)의; 속기에 의한. ¶ *a* ~ *writer* 속기자.

short-hand·ed [ʃɔ̀ːrthǽndid] *adj.* not having enough workmen. 일손〔사람〕 부족의.

short·horn [ʃɔ́ːrthɔ̀ːrn] *n.* Ⓒ a kind of cattle with short horns, raised for beef. 뿔이 짧은 소《낙농·식육용》.

short·ish [ʃɔ́ːrtiʃ] *adj.* rather short. 좀 「짧은.

short-lived [ʃɔ́ːrtlívd, -láivd] *adj.* living or lasting only a short time. 단명의; 오래 가지 못하는. ¶ *A butterfly is* ~. 나비는 단명하다 / ~ *happiness* 일시적인 행복.

:short·ly [ʃɔ́ːrtli] *adv.* **1** very soon. 곧; 이내. ¶ *The plane leaves* ~. 비행기는 이내 출발한다 / *The guests will arrive* ~. 손님들은 곧 도착할 것이다. **2** briefly; in a few words. 간략하게; 간단히. ¶ *to put it* ~ 간단히 말하면; 요컨대. **3** abruptly and rudely. 무뚝뚝하게; 퉁명스럽게. ¶ *He answered me very* ~. 그는 매우 퉁명스럽게 나에게 대답했다.

short·ness [ʃɔ́ːrtnis] *n.* Ⓤ the state of being short. 짧음.

shorts [ʃɔːrts] *n. pl.* short trousers cut above the knee; short pants. 짧은〔반〕 바지.

short-sight·ed [ʃɔ́ːrtsáitid] *adj.* **1** that cannot see things in the distance. 근시(안)의. **2** lacking in foresight; not thinking clearly of the future. 선견지명이 없는; 근시안적인. ¶ *a* ~ *policy* 근시안적인 정책 / *It's* *very* ~ *not to spend money on repairing your house.* 집 수리에 돈을 쓰지 않는 것은 너무나 근시안적이다.

short·stop [ʃɔ́ːrtstɑ̀p / -stɔ̀p] *n.* Ⓒ 《baseball》 a player between second and third base. 유격수.

short-tem·pered [ʃɔ́ːrttémpərd] *adj.* easily becoming angry; having a quick temper. 성마른.

short-term [ʃɔ́ːrttə́ːrm] *adj.* 《as *attributive*》 requiring payment of falling due in a short time (usu. less than a year). 단기의; 단기 만기의. ¶ *a* ~ *loan* 단기 융자.

short wave [∠∠] *n.* 《electr.》 a radio wave that is 60 meters or less in length. 단파(短波).

short-wind·ed [ʃɔ́ːrtwíndid] *adj.* becoming breathless very quickly; very easily out of breath. 숨이 찬; 숨이 쉬이 가빠지는.

:shot[1] [ʃɑt / ʃɔt] *n.* Ⓒ **1** a ball for a gun or cannon; 《*collectively*》 small balls for a shotgun. 탄환; 포탄. ¶ *a solid* ~ (구식의 둥근) 실탄 / *a cannon* ~ 포탄 / *fire a* ~ 포탄을 쏘다 / *A* ~ *passed through the wall.* 탄환은 벽을 관통했다. **2** the act of firing a gun or cannon; the sound of this. 발포; 사격; 총(포)성. ¶ *a flying* ~ 비행 물체 사격 / *take* (*have, make*) *a* ~ *at* …을 저격하다; 겨냥하여 사격하다 / *Was that a* ~ *I heard?* 들린 것은 총성(포성)이었나 / *That was a good* ~. 그것은 멋진 사격이었다 / *He fired five shots in rapid succession.* 그는 잇달아 다섯 발을 쏘았다. **3** Ⓤ the distance over which a shot can travel; a range. 사정(射程); 착탄 거리. ¶ *out of* (*in, within*) ~ 사정 밖(안)에 / *be within rifle* ~ 소총의 사정 거리 안에 있다. **4** an attempt to hit or do anything; a guess. 시도; 추측; 어림짐작. ¶ *make a bad* (*good*) ~ *at* …을 잘못(옳게) 어림짐작하다 / *have a* ~ *at winning the prize* 입상을 시도해 보다 / *I'll have a* ~ *at catching the train.* 열차를 탈 수 있을지 없을지 서둘러 보겠다. **5** a person who shoots. 사수(射手). ¶ *He's a good* (*poor*) ~. 그는 훌륭한(신통치 못한) 사수이다 / *He is not much of a* ~. 그는 사격 솜씨가 대단치 않다. **6** ⓐ a photograph, esp. a snapshot. (스냅) 사진. ¶ *a* ~ *of one's family* 가족의 스냅 사진. ⓑ a single series of motion-pictures or a television program taken by a camera without a break. (영화·TV 따위의) 한 화면(장면). **7** 《*colloq.*》 an injection of medicine into the body. 주사. ¶ *have one's polio* ~ 소아마비 주사를 맞다. [*shoot*]

a shot in the dark, a wild guess. 막연한 짐작.

have a shot for (=*try to catch*) *something.* …을 기도하다; 시도하다.

like a shot, at once. 즉시; 곧.

make a shot at (=*guess*) *something.* …을 어림짐작으로 말하다.

not a shot in the locker, with no money available. 수중에 무일푼으로.

not by a long shot, not at all. 조금도 …아니다.

pay one's shot, 《*colloq.*》 pay the bill. 셈을 치르다.

shot[2] [ʃɑt / ʃɔt] *v.* p. and pp. of **shoot.**
— *adj.* woven so as to change color when moved or seen from different angles. (직물을) 보는 각도에 따라 색깔이 달리 보이게 짠; 양색(兩色) 직물의. ¶ ~ *silk* 양색의 비단(실크). [↑]

shot·gun [ʃɑ́tgʌ̀n / ʃɔ́t-] *n.* Ⓒ a gun for shooting many small shots at one time at short range. 산탄총.

shotgun wedding (**marriage**) [∠— ∠—(∠—)] *n.* a wedding hastened or forced by the pregnancy of the bride. (처녀의 임신으로) 마지못해 하는 결혼.

shot put [∠∠] *n.* a contest in which a heavy metal ball is thrown a long distance. 투포환.

:should [ʃud, ʃəd] *auxil. v.* p. of **shall.** (P25) **1** 《used to express something uncertain in an *if-clause*》 만일 …이라면. ¶ *If it* ~ *rain, what should I do?* 만일 비가 온다면 어떻게 할까 / *If any one* ~ *call, say I'm out.* 전화가 오면 외출중이라고 말해다오 / *If I* ~ (*Should I*) *be free tomorrow, I will come.* 만일 내일 여가가 있다면, 가겠다. **2** ought to; must. …하여야 하다; …하는 것이 당연하다. ¶ *You* ~ *brush your teeth after each meal.* 식후마다 이를 닦아야 한다 / *Why* ~ *I obey his orders?* 왜 그의 명령에 복종하여야 하는가 / *You* ~ *be more careful.* 너는 좀 더 주의하여야 한다 / *He shouldn't do things like that.* 그는 그렇게 일을 하는 것이 아니다 / *You are not behaving as you* ~. 너는 네가 행하여야 할 바를 제대로 행하지 않고 있다. **3** 《used to express something that might have happened but did not》 …했어야 했는데; …하여야 했다《그런데 하지 않았다》. ¶ *You* ~ *not have said so.* 그렇게 말을 하지 않았어야 했다 / *If I had been you, I* ~ *have done it.* 만일 내가 너였더라면 그것을 했을 텐데 / *I* ~ *have done so if he had asked me.* 만일 그가 요청을 했더라면, 나는 그렇게 했을 텐데. **4** 《used to express a matter of course with verbs such as surprise, regret, and dislike》 …하다니; …이라니; …하는 것은. ¶ *It is natural that she* ~ *refuse it.* 그녀가 그것을 거절하는 것은 당연한 일이다 / *I'm surprised that you* ~ *have been so lazy.* 자네가 그렇게 게으르다니 난 놀라고 있네 / *It is a pity that he* ~ *miss such a golden opportunity.* 그가 이러한 절호의 기회를 놓치다니 안타까운 일이다. **5** 《used after what, who, how, etc. expressing surprise, etc.》 …하게 되다니; …하였다는 말인가. ¶ *Whom* ~ *I see but you?* 자네를 만나게 되다니 / *How* ~ *I know it?* 그것을 어찌 내가 안단 말인가 / *Why* ~ *he have done a thing like that?* 어찌해서 그는 그러한 일을 저질렀단 말인가. **6** 《used after *the past tense* of a verb expressing proposal, decision, or command》 must. …하여야 하다. ¶ *He insisted that the prisoners ~ be set free at once.* 그는 죄수들을 즉시 석방하여야 된다고 주장하였다. **7** 《used to express strong probability or expectation》 must; can. …임에 틀림없다; 반드시 …할 수 있다. ¶ *With an early start, they ~ be here by noon.* 일찍 출발하면, 그들은 오전에 이곳에 도착할 수 있다 / *If the farmer can get continuous sunshine, they ~ have a satisfactory harvest.* 만일 좋은 날씨가 계속된다면, 만족스러운 수확을 얻을 수 있을 것이다. **8** 《used to make a statement less direct or harsh》 …하고 싶지만; …합니다만. ¶ *I ~ think....* 내 생각으로는 …라고 여겨지는데 / *I ~ hardly say that.* 나로서는 그렇게까지 말하고 싶지 않습니다만 / *He is over sixty, I ~ think.* 그는 60세가 넘었으리라고 여겨지는데. **9** 《in giving advice》 (만일 내가 너의 입장이라면) …할 텐데. ¶ *I ~ take an umbrella* (*if I were you*). (내가 너라면) 우산을 가지고 가겠다《우산을 가지고 가는 것이 좋겠다》. [M.E. *scholde*]

lest one should do, (so) that one may not do; so as not to do. …하지 않도록. ¶ *Study hard lest you ~ fail.* 실패하지 않도록 열심히 공부하여라.

should like (=*want*) ***to do.*** …하고 싶다.

:shoul·der [ʃóuldər] *n.* Ⓒ **1** the part of a human or an animal body where an arm or a foreleg joins the trunk. 어깨. ¶ *over one's ~* 어깨 너머로 / *carry a bag over one's ~* 가방을 한 쪽 어깨에 메고 나르다 / *put one's ~ out* 어깨의 뼈를 삐다[겹질리다] / *I patted him on the ~.* 나는 그의 어깨를 가볍게 두드렸다. **2** 《*pl.*》 the upper part of the back. 등; 양 어깨의 상부; 견부(肩部). ¶ *a man with broad shoulders* 양어깨가 딱 벌어진 사람; 중책을 맡을 수 있는 사람 / *carry a burden on one's shoulders* 등에 짐을 지고 운반하다. **3** anything shaped like a shoulder. (어깨에 해당하는) 돌출한 부분. ¶ *the ~ of a mountain* 산의 등성이《정상 부근의 낮게 경사진 슬롭》. **4** either of the edges along a road, esp. that part upon which a vehicle can be parked in an emergency. (도로의) 갓길.

get the cold shoulder, be treated with contempt; have a cold reception. 멸시를 당하다; 냉대받다.

give [***turn***] ***the cold shoulder to*** (=*show dislike for; avoid*) *someone.* …을 냉대하다; …을 퇴짜놓다.

head and shoulders above ⇨head.

put [***set***] *one's* ***shoulder to the wheel,*** set to work with a great effort. 전력을 기울이다.

rub shoulders (=*associate*) ***with*** *someone.* …와 교제하다; 친해지다.

shift the blame [***responsibility***] ***on to other shoulders,*** make others take the blame. 남에게 책임을 전가하다.

shoulder to shoulder, side by side and close together; helping one another; with united effort. 어깨를 나란히 하며; 서로 도우면서; 협력하여.

stand head and shoulders above (=*be very much superior to*) *something.* …보다 한 단계 뛰어나다.

straight from the shoulder, directly; frankly. 단도직입적으로; 솔직히.

— *vt.* **1** (P6) take (something) upon a shoulder. …을 (어깨에) 짊어지다; 메다. ¶ *~ arms* 총을 메다. **2** (P6) assume (something) as a responsibility. …을 떠맡다; …의 책임을 지다. ¶ *I'll ~ the expense.* 그 비용을 책임지겠다. **3** (P7,13) push (something) aside with a shoulder. …을 어깨로 밀어젖히다. ¶ *~ someone aside* 아무를 어깨로 밀어젖히다 / *~ (one's way) through the crowd* 군중 속을 어깨로 밀어젖히며 뚫고 나아가다. — *vi.* push with a shoulder. 어깨로 밀어젖히며 나아가다. [E.]

shoulder *someone* ***out of the way,*** push someone aside with a shoulder. 어깨로 …을 밀어젖히다.

shoulder blade [⌐-⌐] *n.* one of the pair of flat bones of the shoulder. 어깨뼈; 견갑골.

shoulder strap [⌐-⌐] *n.* **1** a narrow strap worn over the shoulder to support a garment. 멜빵. **2** a strip at the shoulder of an officer's uniform to show his rank. (군인의) 견장(肩章).

***should·n't** [ʃúdnt] should not.

shouldst [ʃudst] *auxil. v.* 《*arch.*》 =should. ¶ *Thou ~.*

:shout [ʃaut] *vi.* (P1,2A) call out loudly; speak loudly. 외치다; 고함[소리]지르다; 큰 소리로 말하다. ¶ *~ with* [*for*] *joy* 환호하다 / *~ for a waiter* 큰 소리로 웨이터를 부르다 / *~ with a laugh* 큰 소리로 웃다 / *~ to a man to come* 어떤 사람에게 오라고 큰 소리로 부르다 / *Don't ~ at me.* 내게 고함지르지 마라. — *vt.* **1** (P6,7,11) say (something) loudly. …을 외치다; 고함치다. ¶ *~ one's orders* 큰 소리로 명령하다 / *~ someone's name* 아무의 이름을 큰 소리로 부르다. **2** (P18) bring into some state by shouting. 소리를 질러 …상태가 되게 하다. ¶ *~ oneself hoarse* 고함을 쳐서 목이 쉬다.

shout down, prevent (someone) from speaking by shouting. 고함쳐서 …을 못하게 하다. ¶ *The audience shouted the speaker down.* 청중들은 야유를 퍼부어 연사를 침묵하게 하였다.

— *n.* Ⓒ a loud and sudden cry or call. 외침; 큰 소리. ¶ *a ~ of joy* 기쁨의 외침. [E.]

shout·ing [ʃáutiŋ] *n.* Ⓤ loud crying or cheering; shouts. 외침; 환성.

***shove** [ʃʌv] *vt.* (P6,7,13) **1** push roughly. …을 (떠)밀다; 냅다 밀(치)다. ¶ *~ a book across the table to her* 테이블 위로 책을 냅다 밀어 그녀 쪽으로 보내다 / *~ someone off the pavement* 아무를 포장 도로 밖으로 냅다 밀어내다 / *~ a boat into the water* 보트를 물 속으

로 밀다 / ~ *one's way through the crowd* 군중 속을 밀치며 나아가다. **2** 《*colloq.*》 place; put. …을 넣다; 놓다. ¶ ~ *a book back in the shelves* 책꽂이에 책을 도로 꽂다. — *vi.* (P1) push a person or thing roughly; press. (거칠게) 밀(치)다. ¶ *Don't* ~, *wait your turn.* 밀지 말고 네 차례를 기다려라 / *If you pull, I'll* ~. 네가 당기면 나는 밀겠다.

shove** one's **clothes on, put one's clothes on. 옷을 (서둘러) 입다.

shove off, **a**) push (a boat) away from the shore. (배)를 밀어내다; 저어 나가다. **b**) 《*colloq.*》 go away; depart. 가버리다; 떠나다.

— *n.* Ⓒ a push. 밂; 떠밂. ¶ *give a boat a* ~ 보트를 한 번 냅다 밀다. [E.]

***shov·el** [ʃʌ́vəl] *n.* Ⓒ **1** a tool with a broad blade for digging, lifting or throwing coal, snow, grain, etc. 삽; 부삽. **2** =shovelful. — *vt.* (**-eled, -el·ing** or 《Brit.》 **-elled, -el·ling**) (P6,7,13) **1** take up, gather, or throw (something) with a shovel. …을 삽으로 푸다[모으다, 퍼서 던지다]. ¶ ~ *sand into a cart* 삽으로 모래를 손수레에 퍼담다. **2** make (a way, etc.) with a shovel. …을 삽으로 만들다. ¶ ~ *a path* 삽으로 길을 만들다. **3** put, throw, or gather in large quantities. …을 많이 퍼담다[모으다, 던지다]. ¶ ~ *sugar into coffee* 커피에 설탕을 많이 퍼넣다 / ~ *up* [*in*] *money* 돈을 긁어 모으다; 큰 돈을 벌다. [E.]

shov·el·ful [ʃʌ́vəlfùl] *n.* Ⓒ the amount a shovel can hold. 한 삽 가득(한 양).

:show [ʃou] *v.* (**showed, shown** or **showed**) *vt.* **1** (P6,7,13,14) cause (something) to be seen; cause (someone) to see; bring before sight; present to views. …을 (—에게) 보이다; 보여주다; 나타내다; 제시하다. ¶ ~ *one's passport* 여권을 제시하다 / ~ *the contents of one's pockets* 주머니에 있는 것들을 보여주다 / *He showed me his photos.* =*He showed his photos to me.* 그는 나에게 그의 사진들을 보여주었다 / *She never shows her feelings.* 그녀는 절대로 자기 감정을 겉으로 나타내지 않는다 / *The weather is showing signs of spring.* 날씨는 봄의 징후들을 보이고 있다 / *Show* (*me*) *your ticket, please.* 표를 좀 보여 주십시오. **2** (P6,7,13) ⓐ enter (animals, paintings, etc.) in a show or exhibition; exhibit. 출품하다; 전시[진열]하다. ¶ ~ *roses* [*paintings*] 장미[그림]들을 (전시회에) 출품하다 / ~ *a house* [*an apartment*] 집을[아파트를] (일반에게) 전시하다 / *Stores are showing new bathing suits.* 상점들이 새로 나온 수영복들을 진열해 놓고 있다. ⓑ present as a public entertainment. (영화·연극 등)을 상영[상연]하다. ¶ ~ *a film* [*movie*] 영화를 상영하다. **3** (P7,13) guide; lead. …을 안내하다; 인도하다. ¶ *He has shown me upstairs.* 그는 나를 2층으로 안내했다 / *Show him into this room.* 그를 이 방으로 안내해라 / ~ *a guest out* [*to the door*] 손님을 밖으로[문으로] 전송하다 / ~ *someone around the city* 아무에게 시내를 두루 안내하다. **4** (P6,7,10,11,12,13,14,15,16,17) ⓐ make (something) clear to someone; explain; teach. …을 분명히 하다; 설명하다; 가르치다. ¶ *Will you please* ~ *me the way to the station ?* 정거장으로 가는 길을 가르쳐 주시겠습니까 / *The fact shows that he is clever.* 그 사실로 그가 영리하다는 것을 알 수 있다 / *Show me how you have done it.* 그것을 어떻게 했는지 가르쳐다오 / ~ *the difference between them* 그들 사이의 차이점을 분명히 하다. ⓑ point out; indicate; prove. 가리키다; 나타내다; 증명하다. ¶ ~ *a noble spirit* 마음이 고상함을 나타내다 / *The speedometer shows 80.* 속도계는 80을 가리키고 있다 / *I can* ~ *that the man is innocent.* 나는 그가 결백하다는 것을 증명할 수 있다. **5** (P6,13,14) give; bestow; grant. …을 주다; 베풀다. ¶ *He has shown me much kindness.* 그는 나에게 매우 친절하게 해주었다 / ~ *mercy to one's enemy* 적에게 자비를 베풀다 / ~ *favor* [*kindness*] 호의를[친절을] 베풀다. — *vi.* (P1,2A) appear; be in sight; be visible. 나타나다; 보이다. ¶ *The light showed dimly through the fog.* 안개에 가려 빛은 희미하게 보였다 / *The oil painting shows best at a distance.* 유화는 거리를 두고 보아야 제대로 보인다 / *Luckily the stain on my dress doesn't* ~. 다행히 옷의 얼룩은 보이지 않았다.

***show** oneself,* be seen in public. (회합 따위에) 모습[얼굴]을 나타내다.

show** one's **face, appear. 얼굴을 내밀다.

show off, **a**) display. …을 진열하다. **b**) try to attract other's attention. 남의 주의를 끌려고 하다.

show** someone **the door, 《*colloq.*》 order someone to get out of the house. …에게 집 밖으로 나가라고 하다.

show up, **a**) cause (something) to be seen more clearly. …을 똑똑히 보이게 하다. **b**) stand out clearly. 두드러지다; 돋보이다. **c**) make (a secret, etc.) known to the public. …을 폭로하다. **d**) appear. (모임 따위에) 모습을 나타내다.

— *n.* **1** Ⓤ the act of showing. 보이기. **2** Ⓒ a display; an exhibition; any public performance. 전시; 전람회; 구경거리. ¶ *a flower* ~ 화초 전시회 / *a charity* ~ 자선 쇼. **3** Ⓤ 《sometimes *a* ~》 false appearance. 겉치레; 외관. ¶ *by a* ~ *of honesty* 정직을 가장하여. **4** Ⓒ a chance, esp. one to show one's ability. 기회. [E.]

by (***a***) ***show of hands,*** by raising hands to be counted. (찬부를) 거수(擧手)로.

for show, for effect; trying to attract others' attention. 효과를 노려; 자랑으로.

give a fair show, give a chance. 기회를 주다.

give away the show, betray its inadequacy. 마각을 드러내다.

Good show ! 《Brit.》 Well done ! 잘 했다.

in show, outwardly. 겉으로는.

make a good show, be showy; look pretty.

보기에 좋다.
make a show of, display. 전시하다.
make a show of oneself, become a laughing stock. 웃음거리가 되다.

show bill [∠ ∠] *n.* an advertising poster, placard, etc. 광고 쪽지; 포스터.

show·boat [ʃóubòut] *n.* Ⓒ a steamboat with a theater and carrying its own actors, dancers, etc. 연예선(船); 쇼보트.

show·case [ʃóukèis] *n.* Ⓒ a case with glass sides to show and protect articles in stores, museums, etc. (유리) 진열장; 진열 선반.

show·down [ʃóudàun] *n.* Ⓒ **1** 《*colloq.*》 a full disclosure of facts, purposes, plans, etc. (진상 따위의) 공개; 폭로. **2** 《orig. U.S.》 the laying down of the cards face up. (포커에서) 손에 든 패 전부를 보이기. **3** a final challenge. 대결.

:show·er[1] [ʃáuər] *n.* Ⓒ **1** a brief fall of rain, sometimes of hail or snow. 소나기; 갑자기 쏟아지는 우박[눈]. **2** something like a shower; a fall of many objects. (탄알·눈물·불꽃 따위가) 소나기처럼 쏟아짐; 빗발치듯 함. ¶ *a ~ of tears* 비오듯 흐르는 눈물 / *a ~ of sparks from an engine* 엔진에서 빗발치듯 발하는 불꽃[스파크] / *a ~ of questions* [*invitations*] 질문[초대]의 홍수 / *Letters came in showers.* 편지들이 쏟아져 들어왔다. **3** = shower party. **4** =shower bath.
— *vi.* (P1,2A) **1** fall or pour in a shower. 소나기가 오다. **2** take a shower bath. 샤워를 하다. ¶ *I'm going to ~ now.* 나는 지금 샤워를 할까 한다.
— *vt.* (P6,13) **1** make (something) wet with a shower. …을 소나기로 적시다. **2** give (something) in a large amount; pour down. …을 아낌없이 주다; 소나기처럼 퍼붓다. ¶ *~ stones on a dog* 개에게 돌멩이를 마구 던지다 / *She was showered with gifts.* 그녀는 아주 많은 선물을 받았다 / *~ someone with presents* 아무에게 선물 공세를 하다. [E.]

show·er[2] [ʃóuər] *n.* Ⓒ a person who shows or demonstrates. 보이는 사람. [*show*]

shower bath [∠– ∠] *n.* a bath in which water pours down on the body like a shower; an apparatus for such a bath. 샤워; 샤워 설비.

shower party [∠– ∠–] *n.* a party for giving presents to a future bride, etc. (신부감 따위에게) 축하 선물을 주는 파티.

show·er·y [ʃáuəri] *adj.* **1** falling in showers. 소나기처럼 쏟아지는. **2** abundant with showers. 소나기가 잦은. **3** of or like a shower. 소나기의[같은]. [E.]

show girl [∠ ∠] *n.* a chorus girl, esp. one who poses in showy costumes. 쇼걸《뮤지컬 등의 가수 겸 무용수》; 연기보다 용모로 한몫 보는 여배우. [*show*]

show·i·ly [ʃóuili] *adv.* in a showy manner. 화려하게; 야하게.

show·i·ness [ʃóuinis] *n.* Ⓤ the state of being showy. 화려함; 현란함.

show·ing [ʃóuiŋ] *n.* Ⓒ **1** 《*sing.* only》 the impression made by a person's appearance or actions, or by facts. 외관(外觀). **2** the act of showing; an exhibition. 전시; 전시회. ¶ *a ~ of new fashion* 뉴 패션의 전시회 / *the first ~ of a film before the public* 영화의 개봉.

show·man [ʃóumən] *n.* Ⓒ (*pl.* **-men** [-mən]) a person who presents shows or other entertainment. 흥행사.

show·man·ship [ʃóumənʃìp] *n.* Ⓤ the skill or ability of a showman. 흥행사의 수완[재능]; 예인 근성.

:shown [ʃoun] *v.* pp. of **show**.

show-off [ʃóuɔ̀(:)f, -ɑ̀f] *n.* **1** the act of showing off; a vain or showy display. 자랑스레 내보이기; 과시. **2** 《*colloq.*》 a person who shows off. 자랑꾼.

show·place [ʃóuplèis] *n.* a sightseeing place. 명승지.

show·room [ʃóurù(:)m] *n.* Ⓒ a room where things for sale are displayed. 전시실.

show window [∠ ∠–] *n.* a window in front of a store where things are displayed. (상품의) 진열창.

show·y [ʃóui] *adj.* (**show·i·er, show·i·est**) **1** making a striking display. 눈에 번쩍 띄는; 돋보이는. ¶ *A rose is a ~ flower.* 장미는 돋보이는 꽃이다. **2** too bright and not in good taste. 야한. ¶ *a ~ dress* 야한 옷. **3** intended to attract attention. 허세부리는. [*show*]

shpt. shipment.

shr. share(s).

shrank [ʃræŋk] *v.* p. of **shrink**.

shrap·nel [ʃrǽpnəl] *n.* Ⓒ (*pl.* **-nel**) a shell filled with bullets and powder, designed to burst in the air and scatter the bullets all over. 유산탄(榴散彈). ¶ *a piece of ~* 유산탄의 파편. [Person]

shred [ʃred] *n.* Ⓒ **1** a long, narrow piece torn or cut off; a fragment. (가느다란) 조각; 세편(細片). **2** a bit; a very small amount. 아주 조금; 약간. ¶ *There's not a ~ of truth in what he said.* 그가 말한 것 중에는 단 한 마디의 진실도 없다.
tear into [*in, to*] ***shreds,*** tear into pieces. 조각조각[갈기갈기] 자르다[찢다]. ¶ *The wind torn the sail to shreds.* 바람은 돛을 조각조각 찢어놓았다.
— *vt., vi.* (P6;1) tear or cut (something) into pieces. 갈기갈기[조각조각] 찢다[자르다, 끊어지다]. [E.]

shrew [ʃru:] *n.* Ⓒ **1** a bad-tempered woman who constantly quarrels. 앙알대는[잔소리 심한] 여자. **2** a small animal like a mouse with a long nose and small eyes. 뾰족뒤쥐. [↓]

·shrewd [ʃru:d] *adj.* **1** clever; sharp-witted; keen. 영리한; 빈틈 없는; 약빠른. ¶ *a ~ guess* (실제와 일치하는) 정확한 추측 / *He is a*

～ *businessman.* 그는 빈틈 없는 사업가이다. **2** 《*of*》 severe; sharp; biting. 격심한; 모진. ¶ *a ～ wind* 모진 바람. [E.]

shrewd·ly [ʃrú:dli] *adv.* in a shrewd manner; cleverly or wisely. 빈틈 없이; 기민하게.

shrew·ish [ʃrú:iʃ] *adj.* sharp-tongued; bad-tempered. 잔소리가 심한; 앙알대는; 심술궂은. ¶ *a ～ wife* 잔소리가 심한 아내.

***shriek** [ʃri:k] *vi.* (P1,2A,3) cry out in a loud and shrill voice; scream; utter a loud, sharp cry. 날카로운〔새된〕 소리를 지르다; 비명을 지르다. ¶ *～ with laughter* 깔깔거리며 웃다 / *～ with pain* 고통으로 비명을 지르다. —*vt.* (P6,7) utter (something) with a shriek. …을 새된 소리로 말하다. ¶ *～ curses at someone* 아무에게 새된〔날카로운〕 소리로 욕을 하다. —*n.* Ⓒ a sharp scream; an outcry; a loud, shrill sound. 비명; (귀를 째는 듯한) 날카로운 소리. [Imit.]

***shrill** [ʃril] *adj.* having a high-pitched tone; uttered in a shrill tone. (소리·목소리가) 날카로운; 새된〔높은〕 소리의. ¶ *a ～ note* 새된〔높은〕 음조 / *the ～ cry of a hyena* 하이에나의 날카로운 울음소리 / *make a ～ metallic sound* 날카로운 금속성의 소리를 내다. —*adv.* in a shrill tone. 새된〔날카로운〕 소리로. —*vt.* (P6) utter (something) in a sharp, shrill tone. …을 새된 소리로 말하다. —*vi.* (P1) cry in a sharp tone. 날카로운〔새된〕 소리를 내다. [E.]

shrimp [ʃrimp] *n.* Ⓒ **1** a small shellfish with a long tail, used for food. 작은 새우. **2** a small person; a person of little importance. 왜소한 사람; 하찮은 사람. —*vi.* (P1) catch shrimps; go catching shrimps. 작은 새우를 잡다〔잡으러 가다〕. [E.]

***shrine** [ʃrain] *n.* Ⓒ **1** a case or box to place holy things in. 성체 용기(聖體容器); 성골〔물〕함. **2** any sacred place of worship with a tomb or statue. 묘(廟); 사당(祠堂); 성당(聖堂). **3** a place made sacred for historic reasons. 전당; 성지(聖地). ¶ *Mecca is a Moslem ～.* 메카는 이슬람의 성지이다 / *a literary* 〔*historic*〕 *～* 문학〔역사〕의 전당. —*vt.* enshrine. …을 안치하다; 모시다. [L. *scrinium* case for books]

***shrink** [ʃriŋk] *v.* (**shrank** or **shrunk, shrunk** or **shrunk·en**) *vi.* **1** (P1) (of cloth, etc.) become smaller, shorter or less. (옷 따위가) 오그라들다; 줄다; 작아〔적어〕지다. ¶ *The sweater shrank when it was washed.* 스웨터를 세탁했더니 오그라들었다 / *She shrank with fear.* 그녀는 두려움으로 온몸이 움츠러들었다 / *The stream have shrunk for lack of water.* 시냇물은 물의 부족으로 줄어들었다 / *Our resources are gradually shrinking.* 우리의 자원은 점점 줄어들고 있다. **2** (P2A,3) start back suddenly; draw back; 《*from*》 try to avoid; fear; withdraw. 뒷걸음질치다; 움츠리다; 피하다. ¶ *～ back from a snake* 뱀에게서 뒷걸음질치다 / *～ back from the heat of the fire* 난로의 열을 피하여 뒷걸음질치다 / *～ from danger* 〔*responsibility*〕 위험〔책임〕을 피하다〔겁내다〕 / *～ away from someone* 아무로부터 피하다 / *He shrank from the task.* 그는 맡겨진 일을 피했다〔겁냈다〕. —*vt.* (P6) make (something) smaller, shorter or less. …을 오그라뜨리다; 줄어들게 하다. ¶ *The laundry has shrunk all my shirts.* 세탁을 했더니 셔츠가 모두 줄어들었다. [E.]

shrink·age [ʃríŋkidʒ] *n.* **1** Ⓤ the act of shrinking in size or amount. 수축; 감소. ¶ *There has been a lot of ～ of clothes in the wash.* 세탁 과정에서 옷이 많이 줄었다. **2** Ⓒ the amount or degree of shrinking. 수축량; 감소량. ¶ *a ～ of an inch in the length of a skirt* 스커트 길이의 1인치의 수축.

shrive [ʃraiv] *vt.* (**shrove** or **shrived; shriv·en** or **shrived**) 《*arch.*》 hear the confession of and give absolution to. 참회〔고해〕를 듣다; 참회〔고해〕를 듣고 용서하다. [→scribble]

shriv·el [ʃrívəl] *v.* (**-eled, -el·ing** or 《Brit.》 **-elled, -el·ling**) *vi.* (P1,2A) shrink and wrinkle; dry up. 주름(살)지다; 줄어들다; 시들다; 쭈그러들다. ¶ *His skin shriveled.* 그의 피부에는 주름살이 생겼다. —*vt.* (P6,7) curl up (something) with heat, cold, age, etc. …을 주름(살)지게 하다; 줄어들게 하다; 수축시키다. ¶ *The leaves are all shriveled up by the frost* 〔*hot sunshine*〕. 나뭇잎은 서리〔뜨거운 햇볕〕 때문에 완전히 시들었다〔오그라들었다〕. [Sw. *skryvla* wrinkle]

shriv·en [ʃrívən] *vt.* pp. of **shrive**.

shroud [ʃraud] *n.* Ⓒ **1** a cloth sheet or dress used to wrap a dead body for burial. 수의(壽衣). **2** something that covers or conceals. 덮개; 장막. ¶ *wrapped in a ～ of mystery* 〔*secrecy*〕 신비〔비밀〕의 장막에 싸여(있는). **3** 《usu. *pl.*》 a set of ropes from a mast to the sides of a ship for supporting the masts. (돛대 꼭대기에서 양쪽으로 뻗은) 돛대줄. —*vt.* (P6,13) **1** wrap (a dead body) in a shroud for burial. (시체)에 수의를 입히다. **2** cover or conceal. …을 싸다. ¶ *The earth is shrouded in darkness.* 지구는 어둠에 감싸였다. [E. =fittings]

shrove [ʃrouv] *vt.* p. of **shrive**.

Shrove Tuesday [⌐ ⌐—] *n.* the day immediately before Ash-Wednesday. 고해(告解) 화요일《성회(聖灰) 수요일 바로 전날》.

***shrub** [ʃrʌb] *n.* Ⓒ a woody plant smaller than a tree. 떨기나무; 관목. [E.]

shrub·ber·y [ʃrʌ́bəri] *n.* (*pl.* **-ber·ies**) **1** Ⓤ 《*collectively*》 a group of shrubs. 관목(숲). **2** Ⓒ a place planted with shrubs. 관목을 심은 곳.

shrub·by [ʃrʌ́bi] *adj.* (**-bi·er, -bi·est**) **1** abounding in shrubs. 관목이 많은. **2** like a shrub. 관목 같은.

***shrug** [ʃrʌg] *vt., vi.* (**shrugged, shrug·ging**) (P6;1) raise (one's shoulders) to show dislike, doubt, contempt, etc. (어깨를) 으쓱하다《싫음·의심·경멸 등을 나타냄》. ¶ *He* *just shrugged his shoulders in answer to our request for help.* 도움을 청하는 우리의 요구에 그는 단지 어깨를 으쓱했다. — *n.* Ⓒ the act of shrugging. 어깨를 으쓱하기. [E.]

shrunk [ʃrʌŋk] *v.* p. and pp. of **shrink.**

shrunk·en [ʃrʌ́ŋkən] *v.* pp. of **shrink.** — *adj.* grown smaller, thinner or withered. 쪼그라든; 시든. ¶ *a ~ face* 쪼그라든〔주름투성이의〕 얼굴 / *a ~ income* 줄어든 수입.

shtg. shortage.

shuck [ʃʌk] *n.* the outer covering of corn, nuts, etc.; a husk or pod. (옥수수·땅콩 따위의) 껍질; 깍지. — *vt.* (P6) remove the shucks from. 껍질을 벗기다. [?]

shucks [ʃʌks] *interj.* 《U.S. *colloq.*》 a mild exclamation of disgust or regret. 쳇; 아뿔싸.

•**shud·der** [ʃʌ́dər] *vi.* (P1,3,4) 《*at*》 tremble with fear, cold, horror, etc. (추위·공포 따위로) 떨다; 전율하다. ¶ *I shuddered at the mere thought of it.* 그것을 생각만 해도 몸서리가 났다 / *She shuddered when she saw the snake.* 그녀는 뱀을 보자 두려움에 떨었다. — *n.* Ⓒ a violent and sudden shake of the body. (몸을) 떪; 전율. ¶ *The sight gave me the shudders.* 그 광경을 보고 나는 몸서리쳤다 / *A ~ ran through me.* 온몸에 찌르르 하는 전율을 느꼈다. [E.]

shud·der·ing [ʃʌ́dəriŋ] *adj.* **1** trembling with fear, cold, horror, etc. (몸을) 떠는. **2** causing a shudder. 오싹하는; 몸서리치게 하는.

shuf·fle [ʃʌ́fl] *vt.* **1** (P6) drag (the feet) in walking or dancing. (발)을 질질 끌다. **2** (P6,7) mix together; mix (the cards in a pack) to change the order. 섞다; (카드)를 뒤섞다. ¶ *~ the* (*pack of*) *cards* 카드를 뒤섞다〔치다〕. **3** (P7) do (something) in a careless, clumsy or tricky manner. …을 얼버무리다; 속여서〔교묘히〕 …하다. ¶ *~ the money out of sight* 그 돈을 교묘히 감춰버리다. — *vi.* (P1,2) **1** walk with dragging feet. 발을 질질 끌며 걷다. ¶ *The old man shuffled along* 〔*into a room*〕. 그 노인은 발을 질질 끌며 걸었다〔방안으로 들어왔다〕. **2** mix the cards in a pack. 카드를 뒤섞다. **3** act in a tricky 〔careless〕 way. 속이다; 그럭저럭 해내다. ¶ *~ through one's work* 일을 그럭저럭 해내다.

shuffle into 〔***out of***〕, **a**) put on 〔take off〕 (one's clothes) carelessly. (옷을) 아무렇게나 걸치다〔벗어버리다〕. **b**) get into 〔out of〕 a situation by lies, etc. (속임수·거짓말 따위로) 교묘히〔용케〕 끼어들다〔빠져나가다〕. ¶ *~ out of the responsibility* 용케 책임을 면하다.

shuffle off, **a**) take off in a careless way. 벗어버리다. ¶ *~ off one's coat* 코트를 벗어버리다. **b**) get rid of. 면하다; 벗어나다. ¶ *~ off the responsibility* 책임에서 벗어나다.

shuffle on, put on in a careless way. 아무렇게나 입다.

— *n.* Ⓒ **1** the act of dragging the feet. 발을 질질 끌며 걷기. **2** the act of mixing cards. 카드를 뒤섞기. **3** a trick. 술책; 속임수.

● **shuf·fler** [-ər] *n.* [Teut. (→shove)]

•**shun**[1] [ʃʌn] *vt.* (**shunned, shun·ning**) (P6) keep away from (something); avoid. …을 피하다. ¶ *~ danger* 〔*work*〕 위험〔일〕을 피하다 / *a person to be shunned* 멀리해야 할 사람 / *He shuns society.* 그는 사교를 피한다.

● **shun·ner** [-ər] *n.* [E.]

shun[2] [ʃʌn] *interj.* attention! 차려. [abbr.]

shunt [ʃʌnt] *vt.* (P6,7) **1** turn (something) aside. …을 빗나가게 하다. **2** get rid of (something). …을 피하다. **3** switch (a train, etc.) from one track to another. (열차 따위를) 전철(轉轍)하다; 대피시키다. ¶ *~ a train on to a side track* 열차를 측선(側線)에 넣다. — *vi.* (P1) **1** move out of the way. 한 쪽으로 비키다. **2** (of a train, etc.) move from one track to another. (열차가) 대피하다. — *n.* Ⓒ **1** the act of turning aside. 한 옆으로 비키게 함. **2** a railroad switch. 전철기(轉轍器). [*shun*[1]]

⁝**shut** [ʃʌt] *v.* (**shut, shut·ting**) *vt.* (P6,7) **1** close. …을 닫다. ¶ *~ a window* 〔*gate*〕 창문〔대문〕을 닫다 / *~ the lid of a box* 상자의 뚜껑을 덮다 / *~ a drawer* 서랍을 닫다 / *~* (*up*) *a house* 〔*shop, school*〕 집〔상점, 학교〕의 문을 닫다《일시적인 폐쇄·휴업·휴교 따위로》 / *~ one's eyes* 〔*ears*〕 *to* …에 눈을 감다〔귀를 막다〕; …을 못 본〔들은〕 체하다 / *~ one's mind* 〔*heart*〕 *to* …을 받아들이지 않다; 승낙하지 않다 / *~ one's mouth* 입을 다물다; 침묵을 지키다 / *~ the door in someone's face* 아무의 면전에서 문을 닫다; 아무를 안으로 들이지 않다 / *He ~ the door with a loud bang.* 그는 문을 쾅 닫았다 / *Keep your eyes ~.* 눈을 감아라. **2** fold up. …을 접다; 덮다. ¶ *~ a book* 〔*an umbrella*〕 책을 덮다〔우산을 접다〕. **3** keep out. …을 들이지 않다; 내쫓다. ¶ *Do not ~ the new boy out of your games.* 새로 온 소년을 게임에서 빼지 마라 / *~ someone out from society* 아무를 사교 모임에 들이지 않다. **4** close in. …을 가두다. ¶ *She ~ her cat in the box.* 그녀는 고양이를 상자 안에 가두었다. — *vi.* (P1,2A) become closed. 닫히다. ¶ *The door won't ~.* 문이 닫히지 않는다 / *It shuts of itself.* 그것은 저절로 닫힌다 / *The door ~ with a bang.* 문이 쾅 하고 닫혔다.

shut down, **a**) close by lowering. (내려서) 닫다. ¶ *~ down a window* 창문을 내려서 닫다. **b**) repress. 억압〔금지〕하다. ¶ *~ down on the press* 신문의 발행을 금지시키다. **c**) stop working for a time. 휴업하다.

shut in, keep (someone or something) from going out; encircle, confine. …을 가두다; 에워싸다. ¶ *The house is much ~ in by trees.* 집은 나무들로 빽빽이 에워싸여 있다.

shut off, cut 〔stop〕 the flow of(gas, water, etc.). …을 막다. ¶ *~ off the gas* 〔*water*〕 가스〔물〕의 공급〔흐름〕을 막다; 가스를〔물을〕 잠그다.

shut out, **a**) keep (someone) from coming in. …를 들이지 않다; 내쫓다. **b**) 《baseball》 prevent an opposing team from scoring. 셧아웃〔영패〕시키다.
shut the door upon, refuse to permit or consider. 들이지 않다; 고려하지 않다.
shut to, close; fasten. 닫다.
shut together, interlock; glue together. 밀착시키다.
shut up, **a**) close completely. (집 따위를) 잠가 두다. **b**) shut in. …을 감금하다. **c**) 《*colloq.*》 stop talking. 이야기를 멈추다. ¶ *Shut up!* 입닥쳐 / *I wish he would ~ up.* 그가 말을 좀 안 했으면 좋으련만.
— *adj.* closed. 닫은. [E.]

shut-down [ʃʌ́tdàun] *n.* a closing of a factory, etc. for a time. (공장 따위의) 일시 휴업.

shut-in [ʃʌ́tìn] *adj., n.* 《U.S.》 (a person who is) kept indoors by sickness, weakness, etc. (병 따위로) 집 안에 갇힌.

shut-out [ʃʌ́tàut] *n.* **1** =lock-out. **2** 《U.S., sports》 a game in which one team is not allowed to score a point. 셧아웃; 영봉(零封); 완봉.

***shut·ter** [ʃʌ́tər] *n.* Ⓒ **1** a person or thing that shuts. 닫는 사람〔물건〕. **2** a movable cover or screen for a window. 덧문; 겉문. **3** 《*photog.*》 the part of a camera that covers the lens. (사진기의) 셔터.
— *vt.* close or furnish (a window) with a shutter. …의 덧문을 닫다; (창문에) 덧문을 달다. [E.]

shut·tle [ʃʌ́tl] *n.* Ⓒ **1** an instrument used to carry the thread from side to side in weaving. (직조기(織造機)의) 북. **2** a part of a sewing machine that holds and carries the lower thread. (재봉틀의) 밑실이 든 북. **3** anything that moves back and forth regularly between two places; 《U.S.》 a shuttle train. 두 지점 사이를 왕복하는 것; 근거리 왕복 열차. ¶ *a ~ bus* 근거리 왕복 버스; 셔틀 버스 / *~ service* (근거리) 왕복 운행.
— *vt., vi.* (P6,7;1,2A) move back and forth between two places. (북처럼) 좌우로 움직이게 하다〔움직이다〕; 왕복시키다〔왕복하다〕. [*shoot*]

shut·tle·cock [ʃʌ́tlkàk / -kɔ̀k] *n.* Ⓒ a cork stuck with feathers, used in the game of battledore and shuttlecock or in badminton. (배드민턴의) 셔틀콕; 깃털공. ¶ *play battledore and ~* 깃털 공치기를 하다.

shuttle train [∠-∠] *n.* a train that runs regularly back and forth over a short distance. 근거리 왕복 열차.

•**shy**[1] [ʃai] *adj.* (**shy·er, shy·est** or **shi·er, shi·est**) **1** 《*of, with*》 uneasy in the presence of other people; bashful. (성질이) 내향적인; 수줍어하는. ¶ *John is ~ and dislikes parties.* 존은 내향적인 성격이라 파티를 좋아하지 않는다 / *a ~ smile* 수줍은 미소. **2** easily frightened; timid. 잘 놀라는; 겁 많은.
fight shy of, avoid. …을 피하다. ¶ *He fights ~ of women* 〔*hard work*〕. 그는 여성〔힘든 일〕을 피한다.
shy of, **a**) cautious of; desiring to avoid; hesitating to; unwilling to. (…하기를) 조심스러워하는; 피하려 하는; 꺼리는; 싫어하는. ¶ *be ~ of* (*meeting*) *stranger* 낯선 사람 만나기를 싫어하다 / *~ of telling the truth* 진실을 말하기를 꺼리는. **b**) 《*sl.*》 short of; lacking in. (…이) 부족한. ¶ *~ of money* 〔*funds*〕 돈〔자금〕이 부족한.
— *vi.* (**shied**) (P1,3) 《*at*》 start back suddenly. 뒷걸음질치다. ¶ *The horse shied at the passing car.* 말은 지나가는 자동차에 겁을 먹고 뒷걸음질쳤다. [E.]

shy[2] [ʃai] *vt., vi.* (**shied**) (P13;1) throw. (…을) 던지다. ¶ *~ a stone at a tree* 나무를 향해 돌을 던지다. — *n.* Ⓒ (*pl.* **shies**) **1** a throw. 던지기. ¶ *a good ~* 멋진 던지기〔투구〕. **2** 《*colloq.*》 a try; a trial. 시도. [↑]
have a shy at, try to do (something). …을 시도하다.

Shy·lock [ʃáilɑk / -lɔk] *n.* **1** the cruel Jewish moneylender in Shakespeare's play 'The Merchant of Venice'. 샤일록. **2** a greedy moneylender; a cold-hearted person (in business matters). 욕심 많은 고리대금 업자; (사업에서) 냉혹한 사람.

shy·ly [ʃáili] *adv.* in a shy manner. 수줍어서; 소심해서. [*shy*[1]]

shy·ness [ʃáinis] *n.* the quality or state of being shy. 수줍음; 소심.

si [siː] *n.* 《mus.》 the 7th note of the scale. 시; 나《장음계의 제 7 음》. [It.]

Si·am [saiǽm, ∠-] *n.* the former name of Thailand. 샴《타이의 구칭》.

Si·a·mese [sàiəmíːz, -míːs] *adj.* of Siam, its people, or their language. 샴(사람, 말)의. ¶ *a ~ cat* 샴 고양이 / *a ~ twins* 샴 쌍둥이. — *n.* **1** Ⓒ the people of Siam. 샴 사람. **2** Ⓤ the language of Siam. 샴 어(語).

Si·be·ri·a [saibíəriə] *n.* a region of central and east Russia, in northern Asia, extending from the Ural Mountains to the Pacific. 시베리아.

Si·be·ri·an [saibíəriən] *adj.* of Siberia. 시베리아의. ¶ *the ~ Railway* 시베리아 철도. — *n.* Ⓒ a person of Siberia. 시베리아 사람.

sib·i·lant [síbələnt] *adj.* having a sound like that of steam in a radiator; of a hissing sound which is made by drawing out the sound of 's'. 쉬쉬 소리를 내는; 치찰음(齒擦音)의. ¶ *~ sounds* 치찰음. — *n.* Ⓒ 《phon.》 a sibilant sound. 치찰음《s, z, ʃ, ʒ》. [E.]

sib·yl [síbil] *n.* Ⓒ (in Greek and Roman mythology) one of several women who were believed to have powers of foretelling; a fortuneteller. (고대 그리스·로마의) 무당; 예언자. [Gk.]

sic [sik] *adv.* 《L.》 (used after a doubtful word in a quotation to show that it is quoted accurately) so; thus. 원문 그대로.

Si·cil·i·an [sisíliən] *adj.* of or belonging to Sicily or its people. 시칠리아 섬〔사람〕의. — *n.* a native of Sicily. 시칠리아 사람.

Sic·i·ly [sísəli] *n.* a largest island in the Mediterranean, consisting of a region of Italy. 시칠리아(섬).

:sick [sik] *adj.* **1** ill; in ill-health; 《as *predicative*》 being ill. 병의; 병든; 병에 걸린. ¶ *a ~ man* 병자; 병약자 / *a ~ child* 아픈 아이 / *~ people* = *the ~* 아픈 사람들; 환자들 / *be* 〔*feel, look*〕 *~* 〔《Brit.》 *ill*〕 아프다〔아파 보이다〕 / *He was taken ~.* 그는 병에 걸렸다 / *be ~ with a cold* 감기에 걸려 있다. **2** 《as *predicative*》 《esp. Brit.》 about to throw up food from the stomach. 메스꺼운; 느글거리는. ¶ *I feel ~ in the stomach.* = *I'm going to be ~.* 아무래도 토할 것만 같다 / *make someone ~* (아무를) 욕지기나게 하다 / *be ~ at* 〔*to, in, on*〕 *one's stomach* 메스껍다; 토할 것 같다. **3** 《*for*》 longing for. 열망하여. ¶ *~ for home* 〔*one's friend*〕 고향을〔친구를〕 몹시 그리워하다 / *He was ~ for a sight of home.* 그는 고향을 한번 보았으면 하고 간절히 바랐다. **4** 《*of*》 tired; bored; much troubled or annoyed. 신물이〔진저리가〕 나는; 시달리게 하는. ¶ *be ~ of doing nothing* 무위도식에 신물이 나다 / *be ~ and tired of life* 인생살이에 시달려 진력이 나다 / *I am ~ of his talk.* 그의 이야기는 이제 지긋지긋하다 / *I am ~ to death of politics.* 정치에 신물이 난다 / *It makes me ~ to think of it.* 그것을 생각만 해도 진저리가 쳐진다. [E.]

be sick at heart, be sad; become utterly disgusted; be disappointed. 슬퍼하다; 비관하고 있다; 넌더리가 나다; 실망하다.

fall 〔***get***〕 ***sick,*** become ill. 병이 나다.

feel 〔***turn***〕 ***sick,*** feel nausea. 메스껍다; 구역질나다.

go sick, give a sick-report. 병결 신고를 내다.

sick·bed [síkbèd] *n.* Ⓒ a bed on which a sick person lies. 병상. ¶ *lie on one's ~* 병상에 누워 있다.

sick·en [síkən] *vi.* **1** (P1,3) become ill. 병이 나다. ¶ *He sickened and died.* 그는 병이 나서 죽었다 / *The child is sickening for measles.* 그 아이는 홍역 증세를 보이고 있다. **2** (P3,4) 《*of*》 become tired of. 싫증이 나다; 물리다. ¶ *He soon sickened of his new wife.* 그는 이내 그의 새 아내에게 싫증이 났다. **3** (P3,4) feel sick or disgusted. 구역질이 나다. ¶ *~ at the sight of blood* 피를 보고 구역질이 나다.

— *vt.* (P6) **1** make (someone) ill. …를 병나게 하다. **2** make (someone) feel sick or disgusted. …에게 구역질나게 하다. ¶ *The sight of blood sickens him.* 피의 광경은 그를 구역질나게 한다. **3** make (someone) tired of something. 싫증〔넌더리〕나게 하다. [*sick*]

sick·en·ing [síkəniŋ] *adj.* making someone feel sick; disgusting. 구역질나게 하는; 싫증나게 하는. ● **sick·en·ing·ly** [-li] *adv.*

sick·ish [síkiʃ] *adj.* somewhat sick; somewhat sickening. (몸이) 지뿌드드한; 메스꺼운. ¶ *feel ~* 지뿌드드하다; 메스껍다 / *a ~ smell* 〔*taste*〕 메스꺼운〔역겨운〕 냄새〔맛〕. ● **sick·ish·ly** [-li] *adv.* **sick·ish·ness** [-nis] *n.*

sick·le [síkəl] *n.* Ⓒ a small tool consisting of a curved steel blade and a short handle for cutting grass, etc. 낫. [E.]

sick-list [síklìst] *n.* a list of sick persons. 환자 명부. ¶ *be on the ~* 병으로 결근 중이다; 건강이 나쁘다. [*sick*]

sick·ly [síkli] *adj.* (**-li·er, -li·est**) **1** weak in health; often sick. 병약한; 골골하는. ¶ *a ~ child* 병약한 아이 / *He has been ~ from birth.* 그는 태어날 때부터 병약하다. **2** harmful to health. 건강에 나쁜. ¶ *a ~ climate* 건강에 나쁜 기후. **3** making someone feel sick; causing disgust. 구역질나는; 넌더리나는. ¶ *a ~ smell* 구역질나는 냄새. **4** caused by illness; of sickness; faint, pale. 아픈; 병자 같은; 창백한. ¶ *a ~ smile* 연약한〔그늘진〕 미소 / *Her face has a ~ color.* 그녀의 얼굴은 창백하다.

·sick·ness [síknis] *n.* Ⓤ **1** the state of being sick. 병. **2** the state of feeling sick. 구역질.

sick·room [síkrù(:)m] *n.* Ⓒ a room where a sick person lies. 병실.

:side [said] *n.* Ⓒ **1** one of the surfaces of an object. 쪽; 측; 면. ¶ *the bright ~ of life* 인생의 밝은 면 / *Put down your name on both sides of the paper.* 용지의 양 면에 성명을 기입하시오 / *A box has a top, a bottom, and four sides.* 상자에는 윗면, 바닥과 네 개의 면이 있다. **2** an edge; one of the lines bounding an object. 가장자리; 테두리; 가; 변. ¶ *the ~ of a mouth* 〔*table*〕 입〔테이블〕의 가장자리 / *by the ~ of the road* 〔*river*〕 길가〔강가〕에. **3** the position right or left of the center. 우〔좌〕측. ¶ *on one ~ of the head* 머리의 우〔좌〕측에 / *at* 〔*by*〕 *the ~ of the bed* 침대의 우〔좌〕측에서. **4** a family line from the mother or the father. (혈통의) 계(系); 쪽. ¶ *the maternal* 〔*paternal*〕 *~* 모계(母系)〔부계(父系)〕 / *on the father's* 〔*mother's*〕 *~* 부계〔모계〕의〔에〕. **5** a group of people who hold the same opinion. 당(파); …편. ¶ *our ~* 우리 편〔쪽〕 / *I'm always on your ~.* 나는 항상 너의 편이다 / *Neither ~ has strong leaders.* (양쪽) 어느 편도 강력한 지도자를 갖고 있지 않다. **6** a right or left part of the body between the shoulder and the hip. 옆구리. ¶ *have a pain in one's ~* 옆구리에 통증이 있다 / *at* 〔*by*〕 *someone's ~* 아무의 곁〔옆〕에서. **7** a slope, sloping shoulder of a mountain, etc. (산의) 사면; 산허리. ¶ *on the ~ of a hill* 산중턱에. **8** either of the two surfaces of a flat, thin object. (종이·피륙 따위의) 한쪽 면; 페이지. ¶ *the right and wrong sides of a piece of cloth* 피륙의 앞면과 뒷면 / *six sides of argument,* 6페이지에 걸친 논증. **9** an aspect, viewed as partial only.

(문제 따위의) 한 면(面). ¶ *the educational ~ of a film* 영화의 교육적인 면 / *study all sides of a question* 문제의 모든 면을 연구하다.
at* [*by*] *the side of, **a**) beside; near to. …의 옆에; 곁에. **b**) compared with. …와 비교하여.
from all sides, from all directions; everywhere. 모든 곳으로부터; 모든 곳에서.
have* [*put on*] *too much side, be too swagger. 너무 젠체하다.
hold* [*shake*] *one's sides with laughter, laugh heartily. 포복 절도하다.
look on all sides, have a good look in every direction. 각 방면을 세밀히 관찰하다.
on the side, in addition to one's regular work; as a side-line. 부업으로. ¶ *He is a writer, but on the ~ he buys and sells works of art.* 그는 작가이지만 부업으로 예술품을 사고 판다.
on the ... side, tending toward being .... …한 낌새[기세]인. ¶ *Prices are on the high ~.* 물가는 오름세를 보이고 있다.
on the wrong* [*shady, other*] *side of, older than. (나이가) …을 넘은. ¶ *She looks on the wrong ~ of 50.* 그녀는 나이가 쉰은 넘어 보인다.
put something on* [*to*] *one side, set something apart or aside. …을 따로 두다; 치우다.
side by side, close together; beside each other. 나란히; 병행하여.
stand by someone's side, support someone. 아무를 지원하다.
take sides with (=*give support to*) *someone.* …에 편들다.
— *adj.* **1** of, to, or from one side. 옆[곁]의 [으로, 으로부터]; 측면의. ¶ *a ~ step* 옆걸음/*a ~ entrance* 통용문. **2** not so important; secondary. 종(從)의; 부(副)의. ¶ *~ job* 부업.
— *vi.* (P3) 《*with*》 have the same opinion as someone; support someone. (…에) 편들다; 찬성하다.
— *vt.* (P6) turn into siding; shunt; postpone the treatment or consideration of. 정리[처리]하다; 옆으로 치우다; 미루다. [E.]

side·board [sáidbɔ̀ːrd] *n.* Ⓒ a piece of furniture in a dining room for holding food, plates, etc. 찬장; 식기대; 살강.

side·car [sáidkɑ̀ːr] *n.* Ⓒ a small car for a passenger or baggage attached to the side of a motorcycle. (오토바이의) 사이드카.

side-dish [sáiddìʃ] *n.* an extra dish served at a dinner. 곁들여 내는 요리.

side·light [sáidlàit] *n.* Ⓒ **1** a light that comes from the side. 측면광(光). **2** Ⓤ information or knowledge about something that is interesting but not vital, and that is given by chance. 우연[간접]의 설명; 정보. **3** a lamp or light on the side of a ship or car. (배·자동차의) 차폭등.

side·line [sáidlàin] *n.* Ⓒ **1** a line limiting the area of the field in football, tennis, etc. (구기(球技) 따위의) 사이드 라인. **2** one's second trade in addition to a main trade. 부업.

side·long [sáidlɔ̀ːŋ / -lɔ̀ŋ] *adj.* to the side. 옆으로의; 비스듬한. ¶ *cast a ~ glance upon someone* 아무를 곁눈질로 힐끔 보다. — *adv.* sideways. 옆으로; 비스듬히. ¶ *look ~ at someone* 아무를 곁눈질로 보다 / *move ~* 옆으로 움직이다.

si·de·re·al [saidíəriəl] *adj.* of the stars; measured by the apparent motion of fixed stars. 별의; 항성(恒星)의; 항성의 운동을 바탕으로 측정한. ¶ *a ~ revolution* 항성 주기(週期) / *a ~ year* 항성년(年). [L. *sidus* star]

side-sad·dle [sáidsǽdl] *n.* a saddle for a woman, with both legs of the rider on the same side of the horse. 여성용 곁안장《양발을 나란히 한 옆으로 모으고 앉음》. [*side*]

side·show [sáidʃòu] *n.* **1** a small show or entertainment as part of a larger one. 곁들이 쇼; 여흥. **2** an event or activity of less importance. (부수되는) 소사건.

side·slip [sáidslìp] *n.* Ⓒ (of an airplane, a motorcar, etc.) a slip to one side. (자동차·비행기의) 옆으로 미끄러짐; 횡전(横轉). — *vt., vi.* (P6; 1) slip to one side. 옆으로 미끄러지(게 하)다.

sides·man [sáidzmən] *n.* an assistant to the church-warden. 교구 위원보(教區委員補).

side·split·ting [sáidsplìtiŋ] *adj.* causing laughter; extremely funny. 우스워 견딜 수 없는; 포복 절도할.

side-step [sáidstèp] *v.* (**-ped**) *vi.* step aside. 옆으로 (한 걸음) 비켜서다. — *vt.* avoid by stepping aside. 옆걸음으로 …을 피하다. — *n.* **1** a step to one side to avoid something. 옆으로 (한 걸음) 비켜서기. **2** a step or stair attached to the side of a horse carriage; a footboard. (마차 따위에 붙은) 발판; 옆 디딤판.

side·stroke [sáidstròuk] *n.* a swimming stroke in which the body is turned on its side in the water. 횡영(横泳).

side·track [sáidtræ̀k] *n.* Ⓒ 《chiefly U.S.》 a railroad track by the side of a main track. (철도의) 대피선; 측선. — *vt.* (P6) **1** send (a train, etc.) from a main track to a sidetrack. …을 대피선에 넣다. **2** set (something) aside; divert. …을 옆으로 돌리다; …을 회피하다. ¶ *The teacher sidetracked the pupils' conversation.* 선생님은 학생들의 대화를 옆길로 새게 했다 / *a sidetracking device of argument* 의론을 옆으로 슬쩍 돌리는 수단.

side view [⌐⌐] *n.* a view from one side; a profile. 측면도; 옆얼굴.

***side·walk** [sáidwɔ̀ːk] *n.* Ⓒ 《U.S.》 a path beside a street or road for foot passengers. 인도; 보도.

side·ward [sáidwərd] *adj., adv.* on or

toward one side. 옆의[에].

side·ways [sáidwèiz] *adv.* **1** toward or from the side. 옆으로(부터). ¶ *viewed* ~ 옆에서 본 / *look* ~ *at* …을 곁눈으로 보다. **2** with one side foremost. 비스듬하게. ¶ *Hold it* ~. 비스듬히 잡아라. — *adj.* directed toward or from the side. 옆의; 옆으로부터의. ¶ *a* ~ *glance* 곁눈질 / *a* ~ *walk* 옆걸음(질).

side-whisk·ers [sáid*h*wìskərz] *n. pl.* long whiskers on the sides of the cheeks. 긴 구레나룻.

side·wise [sáidwaiz] *adv.* & *adj.* =sideways.

sid·ing [sáidiŋ] *n.* Ⓒ a short railroad track by the side of a main track where a slow train can wait for a fast train to pass, etc. (철도의) 대피선; 측선. [*side*]

si·dle [sáidl] *vi.* (P2A) 《*along, up to*》 move sideways towards someone in a shy or stealthy manner. (가만가만) 다가들다; 옆걸음질하다. — *n.* Ⓒ an act of sidling. (가만가만) 다가섬; 옆걸음질. [→sidelong]

***siege** [si:dʒ] *n.* ⓊⒸ **1** the act of surrounding a place by an army to force it to surrender. 포위; 공성(攻城). ¶ *lay* ~ *to a town* 도시를 포위하다 / *raise the* ~ *of the capital* 수도의 포위를 풀다 / *withstand a long* ~ 오랜 포위 공격에 견디다. **2** a steady effort to win something. (애정·호의 따위를 얻으려는) 불굴의 노력. [L. *sedes* seat]

lay siege to, **a**) subject to a siege. …을 포위(공격)하다. ¶ *The Greeks laid* ~ *to Troy for ten years.* 그리스는 10 년간이나 트로이를 포위 공격했다. **b**) 《*fig.*》 attempt to win or overcome. …을 끈질기게 노력하다. ¶ *lay* ~ *to a lady's heart* 여인의 애정을 얻기 위해 끈질기게 노력하다.

si·en·na [siénə] *n.* Ⓤ a rich reddish-brown pigment or its color. 시에나토(土); 황갈색. [Place]

burnt sienna, color with reference to its preparation by heat. 대자색(代赭色)《황갈색과 적황색에 가까운 빛깔》.

si·er·ra [siέərə] *n.* Ⓒ a chain of mountains rising in jagged peaks like a saw. (톱날 모양의) 산맥. [→serrate]

si·es·ta [siéstə] *n.* Ⓒ a short sleep or rest taken at noon or in the afternoon, esp. in hot countries. (특히 더운 나라의) 점심 후의 낮잠. [L. *sextus* sixth (i.e. hour)]

sieve [siv] *n.* Ⓒ a frame with a wire net at the bottom, used for separating smaller pieces from larger ones.. 체. [E.]

have a head like a sieve, be very forgetful. 기억력이 아주 나쁘다.

— *vt.* (P6) separate with or make pass through a sieve. 체질하다. [E.]

***sift** [sift] *vt.* (P6,7,13) **1** 《*from*》 separate (smaller pieces) from larger ones with a sieve. …을 체로 치다. ¶ *Sift flour* [*the ashes*]. 밀가루[재]를· 체로 치다. **2** scatter (something) through a sieve. …을 체로 가려[걸러]내다. ¶ ~ *sugar over a cake* 케이크에 설탕을 체로 걸러 뿌리다 / ~ *sand through the fingers* 손가락 사이로 모래를 걸러내다. **3** examine [distinguish] (something) very carefully. …을 정밀히 조사하다[가려내다]. ¶ ~ (*out*) *the true from the false* 거짓으로부터 진실을 가려내다 / ~ *the evidence* 증거를 정선하다 / *Let us* ~ *the facts before we make a decision.* 결론을 내리기 전에 사실을 규명하자.

— *vi.* (P1,2A,3) come through a sieve. 체를 통과하다. ¶ *Sand sifts through one's clothes* [*into one's shoes*]. 모래가 옷[신발] 속으로 들어오다. [→sieve]

:sigh [sai] *vi.* **1** (P1) let out a long, deep breath to show sorrow, relief, fatigue, etc. 한숨 짓다[쉬다]; 탄식하다. ¶ ~ *with fatigue* [*relief*] 피로에 지쳐[안도의] 한숨을 짓다 / *We heard Mary* ~ *deeply.* 메리가 깊이 한숨짓는 소리를 들었다 / *She sighed for grief in spite of herself.* 그녀는 자신도 모르는 사이에 한숨을 내쉬었다. **2** (P3) 《*for*》 **a**) desire very earnestly. 간절히 바라다; 동경하다. ¶ *She sighed for the cool air of the country.* 그녀는 시골의 서늘한 공기를 간절히 바랐다[그리워했다]. **b**) regret. …을 애석하게 여기다. ¶ ~ *for lost friends* [*one's misspent youth*] 행방 불명된 친구들을[허송 세월한 젊은 시절을] 애석하게 생각하다.

— *vt.* (P6,7) **1** 《*out*》 express (sorrow, relief, etc.) by a sigh. …을 한숨으로 표현하다. ¶ ~ *out one's grief* 한탄하다 / *He sighed a long sigh.* 그는 길게 한숨을 내쉬었다. **2** lament (something) sighing. …을 탄식하며 말하다.

— *n.* Ⓒ a deep, audible breath from sorrow, relief, etc. 한숨; 탄식. ¶ *draw a* ~ 한숨짓다 / *sigh a deep* ~ 긴 한숨을 쉬다 / *breathe a* ~ *of relief* 안도의 한숨을 짓다.

● **sigh·er** [ˊ-ər] *n.* [E.]

:sight [sait] *n.* Ⓤ **1** the power of seeing. 시력; 시각. ¶ *lose one's* ~ 시력을 잃다 / *recover one's* ~ 시력을 회복하다 / *He has good* ~. 그는 시력이 대단히 좋다. **2** 《sometimes *a* ~》 the act of seeing; the state of seeing or being seen. 봄; 보임. ¶ *He ran away at the* ~ *of me.* 그는 나를 보자마자 곧 도망쳤다 / *I know him only by* ~. 나는 그와 안면이 있을 뿐이다 / *I hate the* ~ *of her.* 나는 그녀를 보기조차 싫다. **3** the range or field that one can see. 시야(視野); 시계(視界). ¶ *The hill came in* ~. 산이 시야에 들어왔다 / 《*prov.*》 *Out of* ~, *out of mind.* 헤어지면[안 보면] 정도 멀어진다 / *Peace is now in* ~. 평화가 눈앞에 다가왔다. **4** Ⓒ something worth seeing; a spectacle; 《*pl.*》 places worth seeing. 광경; 경치; 구경거리; 명승지. ¶ *The sunrise is a wonderful* ~. 일출은 놀라운 [멋진] 광경이다 / *see* [*do*] *the sights of Kyŏngju.* 경주 관광을 하다. **5** appearance. 모습. ¶ *I lost* ~ *of him in the crowd.* 군중들 속에서 그의 모습을 놓쳤다. **6** Ⓒ an instrument to help in aiming with a gun, etc. 조준(照準)(기). **7** judgment; opinion. 판단; 견해. ¶ *Do what's right in your own* ~. 너의 판단으로 옳다고 여겨지는 것을 행하라 / *All human beings are equal in the* ~ *of God.* 신의 눈으로 보면 사람은 모두 평등하다.

a* (*long*) *sight better, much better. 훨씬 좋은.

a sight, 《*adverbial*》 a good deal; much 훨씬; 많이. ¶ *He's a* ~ *too clever for you.* 그는 네가 상대하기에는 너무 영리하다.

a sight of, many; much. 다수(다량의). ¶ *a* ~ *of people* 〔*money*〕 많은 사람들〔돈〕.

at first sight, when first seen. 첫눈에.

at* 〔*on*〕 *sight, as soon as seen; at once. 보자마자; 곧. ¶ *a bill payable at* ~ 일람 출급 어음 / *play music at* ~ 연습 없이 연주하다.

catch* 〔*get, take*〕 *sight of (=*see*) *something.* …을 보다; 찾아내다.

know *someone* ***by sight,*** recognize someone, though not fully acquainted. 안면이 있다.

lose sight of, **a**) see no longer; fail to keep in sight. …을 (시야에서) 놓치다. **b**) forget; omit to take regard of. (…을) 잊다; 간과하다. ¶ *Such points must not be lost* ~ *of.* 그러한 점들이 간과되어서는 안된다.

make a sight of *oneself,* dress in a bizarre fashion. 야릇한 몸차림을 하다.

not by a long sight, definitely not. 결코 … 아니다.

out of sight, not to be seen; beyond the range of vision. 보이지 않는; 보이지 않는 곳에. ¶ *Get out of my* ~*!* 내 눈 앞에서 꺼져라 / *put something out of* ~ 어떤 것을 감추다.

see* 〔*do*〕 *the sights, visit the notable things in a town, etc. 명소를 구경하다.

take a sight of, cock a snook. 경멸하다.

take sight, aim. 겨냥〔조준〕하다.

within sight, near at hand. 가까이에; 보이는 곳에. ¶ *Victory is within sight.* 승리는 눈앞에 있다.

— *vt.* (P6) **1** see. …을 보다. **2** aim at (something) …을 조준〔겨냥〕하다. **3** look at (something) carefully; examine. …을 관찰하다.

— *vi.* (P1) aim at something with a gun, etc. 겨냥〔조준〕하다. [*see*]

sight·less [sáitlis] *adj.* blind; invisible; unseen. 맹목의; 눈에 보이지 않는.

sight·ly [sáitli] *adj.* (**-li·er, -li·est**) **1** pleasant to look at. 보기 좋은; 아름다운. **2** 《U.S.》 commanding or giving a fine view. 전망이 좋은.

sight·see·ing [sáitsìːiŋ] *n.* Ⓤ the act of going around to see places and things of interest. 관광; 구경. ¶ *go* ~ 관광하러 가다.

— *adj.* of sightseeing. 관광의. ¶ *a* ~ *bus* 〔*party*〕 관광 버스〔단〕 / *a* ~ *trip* 관광 여행. [var. of *see the sights*]

sight·se·er [sáitsìːər] *n.* Ⓒ a person who goes sight-seeing. 관광객; 유람객.

sigill. 《L.》 signet; seal. 도장; 봉인. [L. *sigillum*]

sig·ma [sígmə] *n.* a Greek letter corresponding to English S. 시그마《그리스 자모의 18번째 글자; Σ, σ, s; 영어의 s》. [Gk.]

:sign [sain] *n.* Ⓒ **1** a mark or letter that expresses some idea; a symbol. 부호; 기호. ¶ *the plus* ~ 덧셈 부호 / *the phonetic signs* 발음기호 / *Letters are signs used to represent sounds.* 문자는 소리를 나타내기 위해 사용된 부호이다. **2** anything that tells some fact; a proof; a token. 증거; 표지; 표상(表象). ¶ *a* ~ *of love* 사랑의 표시 / *a flag as a* ~ *of one's nation* 국가의 표상으로서의 국기 / *a black arm-band as a* ~ *of mourning* 상장(喪章)으로서의 검은 완장 / *Yawning is a* ~ *of sleepiness.* 하품은 졸음이 온다는 증거이다. **3** anything that tells of the future; an omen. 징후; 조짐; 전조. ¶ *the signs of the times* 시대의 추세 / *show signs of spring* 봄 기운이 나다 / *Black clouds are signs of a storm.* 검은 구름은 폭풍의 전조이다. **4** a gesture or signal used instead of words. 몸짓; 표시; 신호. ¶ *A nod of the head is a* ~ *of approval.* 머리를 끄덕이는 것은 찬성의 표시이다 / *He made a* ~ *to me to leave the room.* 그는 방을 나가라는 신호를 나에게 했다 / *The deaf and dumb talk by signs.* 귀머거리와 벙어리는 신호로써 말을 한다. **5** an indication or evidence of something coming or present; a trace or mark. 흔적; 자취. ¶ *Smoke is a sign of fire.* 연기는 불의 흔적이다 / *There were no signs of life anywhere.* 어느 곳에도 생명이 있다는 흔적이 없었다 / *The hunters found no signs of deer.* 사냥꾼은 사슴의 자취를 찾을 수 없었다.

in sign of, as a token of. …의 표시로.

make* 〔*give*〕 *a sign to, sign. …에 신호하다.

make no sign, be unaware. (기절하여) 꼼짝 않다.

make the sign of the cross, trace the cross with the hand as a religious act. 손가락으로 십자를 긋다.

seek a sign, seek a miracle. 기적을 찾다.

sign and countersign, a password. 변말; 암호.

signs and wonders, miracles. 기적(奇蹟).

— *vt.* **1** (P6,20) show (some idea, etc.) with a sign; signify. …을 기호로 나타내다; 신호하다. ¶ ~ *one's assent with a nod* 머리를 끄덕이며 동의를 나타내다 / *The teacher signed me to enter.* 선생님께서 나에게 들어오라고 신호했다. **2** (P6,7) write one's name on (a paper, etc.) to show one's consent, etc. …에 서명하다; 기명(날인)하다. ¶ ~ *a letter* 〔*cheque*〕 편지〔수표〕에 기명(날인)〔서명〕하다 / ~ *a note promissing to pay a debt* 채무 변제를 약속하는 각서에 기명(날인)하다 / *Please* ~ *your name here.* 여기에 서명하십시오. **3** (P13) mark. …에 표시를 하다. ¶ ~ *an infant with a sign of the cross* 어린애의 이마에 십자가를 그어 표시하다.

— *vi.* **1** (P1,2A) make a sign or signal. 서명하다; 신호하다. ¶ *He refused to* ~. 서명을 거절하였다 / *He signed for silence.* 그는 조용히 하라고 신호하였다 / *I signed to him to come.* 그에게 오라고 신호했다. **2** (P1,2A,3) engage oneself for service by affixing one's signature to a contract. 계약하다. ¶ ~ *for three years,* 3년 계약으로 고용되다 / *She signed up for a new film.* 새로운 영화에 출연 계약을 맺었다. [L. *signum.*]

sign assent, signify consent by gesture. 승낙을 몸짓으로 나타내다.

sign away, relinquish (right, property); write one's name to give up (a right, etc.). (증서에) 서명하여 …을 양도하다.

sign off, 《radio》 announce the end of a broadcast, mentioning the name of the station. 방송〔방영〕 종료 신호를 하다.

sign on, employ or be employed by signing one's name. (계약서에 서명하고) 고용하다〔되다〕. ¶ *He signed on as a bus-driver.* 그는 버스 기사로 고용되었다.

sign up, **a**) apply for; enlist in military service. 응모하다; 입대하다. **b**) =sign on.

:sig·nal [sígnl] *n.* Ⓒ **1** a gesture, look or sign giving information, notice of danger, etc.; a mechanical device for giving such a message. 신호; 신호기. ¶ *The traffic* ~ *turned red.* 교통 신호가 붉은 색으로 바뀌었다 / *give the* ~ *for departure* 출발 신호를 하다 / *a danger* 〔*storm*〕 ~ 위험〔폭풍〕 신호. **2** 《*for*》 anything which causes some other action. 동기. ¶ *the* ~ *for revolt* 폭동의 도화선 / *His remark was the* ~ *for the fight.* 그의 말이 싸움의 동기였다. **3** a token; an indication. 전조; 징후. ¶ *a* ~ *fire* 봉화 / *a* ~ *of danger* 위험 신호 / *make a* ~ 신호하다 / *Fainting is a* ~ *of ill-health.* 어지럼증은 병의 징후이다.

— *vt., vi.* (**-naled, -nal·ing** or 《Brit.》 **-nalled, -nal·ling**) (P6,7,20;1) make (something) known by a signal; communicate by means of a signal. 신호하다; (…을) 신호로 알리다. ¶ *He signaled the car to stop by raising his hand.* 그는 손을 들어 차에게 멈추라는 신호를 보냈다 / *He signaled the advance.* 그는 진격을 신호로 알렸다 / *He signaled to us to stop.* 그는 우리에게 정지하라고 신호했다.

— *adj.* **1** used as a signal or in signaling. 신호의. ¶ *a* ~ *lamp* 신호등. **2** remarkable; noteworthy. 현저한; 뛰어난. ¶ *a* ~ *success* 괄목할 만한 성공. [→sign]

sig·nal·er, 《Brit.》 **-nal·ler** [sígnələr] *n.* Ⓒ a person or thing that gives a signal. 신호수; 신호기.

sig·nal·ize [sígnlàiz] *vt.* make (someone or something) remarkable or notable; indicate (something) particularly. …을 돋보이게 하다; 특별히 지적하다.

sig·nal·ly [sígnəli] *adv.* in a signal manner; remarkably. 현저하게; 두드러지게.

sig·nal·man [sígnəlmən, -mæ̀n] *n.* Ⓒ (*pl.* **-men** [-mən, -mèn]) a person who signals or works with signals. 신호수.

sig·na·to·ry [sígnətɔ̀:ri / -təri] *n.* Ⓒ (*pl.* **-ries**) a person who has signed a document, esp. as a representative of a nation. 서명자 — *adj.* having signed a document. 서명한; 조인한. [*sign*]

***sig·na·ture** [sígnətʃər] *n.* Ⓒ **1** the name of a person written by himself; the act of writing one's name. 서명. **2** a mark at the beginning of a staff to show the key, time and pitch of music. (음조·박자의) 기호. [*sign*]

***sign·board** [sáinbɔ̀:rd] *n.* Ⓒ a board displaying a name, a notice, etc. esp. a painted one to show the name of an inn or a shop. 간판.

sig·net [sígnət] *n.* Ⓒ a small seal; an official seal. (막)도장; 인장; 인감; 직인.

***sig·nif·i·cance** [signífikəns] *n.* Ⓤ the state or quality of being significant; meaning; importance. 의미(가 있음); 의의; 중요. ¶ *a word of great* ~ 의미 심장한 말 / *a matter of* ~ 중요한 사항 / *understand the* ~ *of someone's words* 아무의 말의 뜻을 이해하다 / *be of no* ~ 별로 중요하지 않다 / *He gave the boy a look of deep* ~. 그는 소년에게 매우 의미 심장한 표정을 보였다 / *I could grasp the real* ~ *of his remark.* 나는 그의 말의 진의를 파악할 수 있었다. [→signify]

***sig·nif·i·cant** [signífikənt] *adj.* **1** full or expressive of meaning. 의미 있는; 의미를 나타내는. ¶ *a* ~ *look* 의미있는 듯한 표정 / *a smile* ~ *of pleasure* 기쁨을 나타내는 미소 / *the* ~ *of her smile* 그녀의 의미 있는 미소 / *Her gesture is* ~ *of consent.* 그녀의 몸짓은 승낙을 뜻한다. **2** important. 중요한.

● **sig·nif·i·cant·ly** [-li] *adv.*

sig·ni·fi·ca·tion [sìgnəfikéiʃən] *n.* ⒸⓊ the act of signifying; a meaning or sense. 의미; 의의. ¶ *give a new* ~ *to a word* 한 낱말에 새로운 어의를 부여하다.

sig·nif·i·ca·tive [signífəkèitiv / -kətiv] *adj.* 《*of*》 offering indication of. 표시하는; 뜻〔의미〕 있는.

***sig·ni·fy** [sígnəfài] *vt.* (**-fied**) (P6,11) **1** 《*with*》 show (something) by a sign, a gesture, etc.; indicate. (말·몸짓 등으로) …을 나타내다; 표시하다; 가리키다. ¶ ~ *one's consent with a nod* 고개를 끄덕여 승낙의 뜻을 표시하다 / ~ *one's satisfaction* 만족의 뜻을 표하다 / *He signified that he could not agree.* 그는 동의할 수 없다고 했다 / *He signified that we might go out.* 그는 우리가 밖에 나가도 좋다고 하였다. **2** become a sign of (something). …의 전조가〔조짐이〕 되다. ¶ *A red sunset signifies fine weather.* 저녁놀은 좋은 날씨의 조짐이 된다. **3** mean. …을 뜻하다; 의미하다. ¶ *Do you know what P.R. signifies?* 너는 P.R.이 무엇을 뜻하는지 아느냐 / *What does it* ~*?* 그것은 무엇이냐〔무슨 뜻이냐〕.

— *vi.* (P1) 《usu. in *negative*》 be of importance. 중요하다. ¶ *It does not* ~. 대단한 일이 아니다 / *What a fool says does not* ~. 어리석은 자의 말은 별로 중요할 게 없다. [L. *signum* sign]

sign manual [ˊ-ˊ--] *n.* signature. 서명.

si·gnor [síːnjɔːr] *n.* 《It.》 (*pl.* **si·gno·ri**) **1** 《a form of address to an Italian gentleman》 Mr.; sir. 씨; 님; 각하. **2** an Italian gentleman. (이탈리아의) 신사. [→senior]

si·gno·ra [siːnjɔ́ːrə] *n.* 《It.》 (*pl.* **si·gno·re**) **1** 《a form of address to an Italian lady》 Mrs.; madam. …부인; 아씨; 여사. **2** an Italian lady. (이탈리아의) 귀부인.

si·gno·re [siːnjɔ́ːrei] *n.* 《It.》 pl. of **signora**.

si·gno·ri [síːnjɔːri] *n.* 《It.》 pl. of **signor**.

si·gno·ri·na [sìːnjɔːríːnə] *n.* 《It.》 (*pl.* **si·gno·ri·ne**) **1** 《a form of address to an Italian young lady》 Miss. …양. **2** an Italian young lady. (이탈리아의) 아가씨.

si·gno·ri·ne [sìːnjoːríːnei] *n.* 《It.》 pl. of **signorina**.

sign·post [sáinpòust] *n.* Ⓒ a post having a sign, notice or direction on it for guidance or information. 광고〔간판〕 기둥; 도표(道標). [*sign*]

Sikh [siːk] *n.* a member of a religious sect of northern India, famous as fighters. 시크 교도. [Hind. =disciple]

Sik·kim [síkəm, síkiːm] *n.* a state, formerly protectorate, of India. 시킴《인도의 한 주(州)》.

si·lage [sáilidʒ] *n.* Ⓤ green food for farm animals, preserved in a silo. 사일로에 저장한 꼴. [→silo, -age]

:si·lence [sáiləns] *n.* Ⓤ **1** ⓐ absence of sound or noise; stillness. 정적; 고요함. ¶ *the* ~ *of the desert* 사막의 고요 / *There was* ~ *in the court-room.* 법정 안에는 정적이 감돌았다 / *The sirens broke the* ~ *of the night.* 사이렌 소리가 밤의 정적을 깨뜨렸다 / *the* ~ *of deathlike* 죽음과 같은 고요. ⓑ the state of being silent; not talking; not speaking about a matter. 침묵. ¶ 《*prov.*》 *Silence gives consent.* 침묵은 승낙의 표시 / *Mother passed over Tom's foolish remarks in* ~. 어머니는 톰의 어리석은 소견을 침묵으로 너그럽게 봐 주었다 / *There was* ~ *between them.* 그들은 둘 다 침묵하고 있었다 / 《*prov.*》 *Speech is silver,* ~ *is golden.* 웅변은 은, 침묵은 금. **2** the state of being forgotten; absence of mention. 망각; 묵살. ¶ *pass into* ~ (기억에서) 잊혀지다.

put 〔***reduce***〕 ***someone to silence,*** make someone silence; confute. …을 윽박 질러 아무 소리 못하게 하다.

— *vt.* (P6) **1** cause (someone) to be still. …을 침묵시키다. ¶ *The nurse silenced the baby's crying.* 유모는 애기의 울음을 그치게 했다. **2** put down; crush; confute. (적의 포화 등)을 침묵시키다; 진압하다; 끽소리 못하게 하다. ¶ ~ *criticism* 비난을 못하게 만들다 / ~ *the enemy's guns* 적의 포화를 침묵시키다.

— *interj.* be silent! 조용히; 쉿. [→silent]

si·lenc·er [sáilənsər] *n.* Ⓒ **1** a person or thing that silences. 침묵시키는 사람〔것〕. **2** a device that deadens the sound of an engine, a gun, etc. 소음기; 방음 장치.

:si·lent [sáilənt] *adj.* **1** saying little or nothing; mute. 침묵의; 말없는. ¶ *a* ~ *man* 말없는 사람 / *remain* 〔*keep*〕 ~ 침묵을 지키다 / *I'll be* ~ *about her conduct.* 그녀의 행실에 관해서 말하지 않겠다. **2** not mentioned or spoken. 언급하지 않는; 공표하지 않는. ¶ *His speech is* ~ *on the subject.* 그의 연설은 그 문제에는 언급하지 않고 있다. **3** making no noise; quiet; not active. 조용한; 쉬고 있는. ¶ ~ *as the grave* (무덤처럼) 매우 조용한; 정적에 싸인 / *a* ~ *picture* 〔*film*〕 무성 영화 / *a* ~ *volcano* 휴화산. **4** 《*phon.*》 written but not pronounced. 발음하지 않는; 묵음의. ¶ *The 'l' in 'palm' is* ~. palm의 *l*은 묵음이다. **5** taking no open or active part. 익명의. ¶ *a* ~ *partner* 익명 사원(=《Brit.》 sleeping partner). [L. *sileo* be silent]

si·lent·ly [sáiləntli] *adv.* in a silent manner; without making a sound; quietly. 조용히.

Si·le·nus [sailíːnəs] *n.* 《Gk. myth.》 Dionysus's foster-father. 실레노스《주신(酒神) 디오니소스의 양부》. [Gk. *Seilēmós* inflated with wine]

sil·hou·ette [sìluːét] *n.* Ⓒ a black outline portrait, esp. a profile; a dark figure of a person or thing against a light; a shadow. 그림자 그림; 실루엣; (사람·사물의) 검은 그림자.

in silhouette, shown in silhouette; shown in outline. 실루엣으로; 윤곽만으로.

— *vt.* (P6) 《usu. *pp.*》 show (something) in outline. …을 실루엣으로 그리다; …의 그림자를 비추다. ¶ *The tower was silhouetted against the sunset.* 탑은 일몰을 배경으로 윤곽이 뚜렷한 검은 모습을 보였다 / *a figure silhouetted against the evening sky* 저녁 하늘을 배경으로 검게 나타난 사람의 모습. [Person]

sil·i·ca [sílikə] *n.* ⓊⒸ 《chem.》 a hard white or colorless substance used in making glass, etc. 이산화규소; 실리카. [L. *silex* flint]

sil·i·cate [síləkèit] *n.* Ⓤ 《chem.》 one of the compound containing silica. 규산염.

si·li·ceous [silíʃəs] *adj.* of silica. 규산의.

sil·i·con [sílikən] *n.* Ⓤ a brown, nonmetallic element found in a combined state in mineral and rocks. 규소(珪素); 실리콘. [→silica]

:silk [silk] *n.* Ⓤ **1** a fine thread obtained from silkworms. 비단; 명주실; 견사(絹絲). ¶ *raw* ~ 생사(生絲) / *artificial* ~ 인조견(絹). **2** a cloth made from this thread. 견직물. **3** 《*pl.*》 garments made of silk. 비단옷.

¶ *be dressed in silks* 비단옷을 입고 있다. —*adj.* of or like silk. 견(絹)의; 견사〔견직〕 모양의. [Gk. *Sēres* the Chinese]

silk·en [sílkən] *adj.* **1** 《*arch., poet.*》 made of silk. 견(絹)의; 비단으로 만든. ¶ *a ~ dress* 비단옷. **2** like silk; soft and smooth; silky; glossy. 비단 같은; 부드럽고 매끄러운; 광택 있는. ¶ *She has ~ hair.* 그녀의 머리는 비단결 같다 / *a ~ manner* 우아하고 상냥스런 태도.

silk·worm [sílkwə̀ːrm] *n.* Ⓒ a moth caterpillar that produces a strong silk fiber to form its cocoon. 누에.

silk·y [sílki] *adj.* (**silk·i·er, silk·i·est**) of or like silk; fine and soft; glossy. 비단의; 비단 같은; 부드럽고 매끄러운; 광택 있는. ¶ *A cat has ~ fur.* 고양이 털은 비단 같다.

sill [sil] *n.* Ⓒ a piece of wood or stone forming the bottom of a window or door. 문지방; 문턱. [E.]

sil·la·bub [síləbʌ̀b] *n.* a dish of cream or milk curdled with wine, etc. 와인밀크〔크림〕. [E.=happy stomach]

sil·li·ness [sílinis] *n.* **1** Ⓤ the quality of being silly. 어리석음. **2** Ⓒ something silly; a silly act. 어리석은 것; 바보짓. [↓]

:sil·ly [síli] *adj.* (**-li·er, -li·est**) **1** foolish; having little sense or judgment. 어리석은; 지각〔분별〕 없는. ¶ *a ~ fellow* 바보; 멍청이 / *a ~ joke* 〔*question*〕 바보 같은 농담〔질문〕 / *You were very ~ to trust him.* 그를 믿다니 너는 참으로 어리석었다 / *Don't be ~!* 바보같은 소리〔짓〕 하지 마라 / *It would be ~ to die now.* 지금 죽는다는 것은 어리석은 짓이다. **2** 《*arch.*》 innocent; simple. 순진한. —*n.* Ⓒ (*pl.* **-lies**) 《*colloq.*》 a silly person. 바보; 멍텅구리. [E.=happy > innocent > unworldly > foolish]

si·lo [sáilou] *n.* Ⓒ (*pl.* **-los**) an airtight building or tower in which green food for animals is preserved. 사일로. [Gk.]

silt [silt] *n.* Ⓤ mud or sand carried by moving water and left behind. (강바닥 따위의) 침니(沈泥)《모래보다 곱고 진흙보다 거친 침적토》. —*vt., vi.* (P7;2A) 《*up*》 fill (something) or become filled with silt. 침니로 막다〔막히다〕. [Teut. (→salt)]

Si·lu·ri·an [silúriən, sai-] *adj.* **1** of the Silures; a people of ancient Britain 실루리아 사람의. **2** 《geol.》 of an early period in the earth development. 실루리아기(紀)의. —*n.* the Silurian Period. 실루리아기(紀). [*Silures*, British tribe]

sil·van [sílvən] *adj.* =sylvan.

:sil·ver [sílvər] *n.* Ⓤ **1** a soft, white, shining metal, used for making coins, dishes, etc. 은(銀). **2** 《*collectively*》 things made of this metal; coins made of silver. 은식기; 은세공품; 은화. ¶ *table ~* 식탁용 은식기《스푼·나이프·포크·접시 등》 / *200 dollars in ~* 은화로 200달러. **3** the color of silver. 은빛.

—*adj.* **1** made of silver 은의; 은제(製)의. ¶ *a ~ knife* 은제(銀製) 나이프 / *~ coins* 은화. **2** having the color of silver. 은빛〔은백색〕의. ¶ *~ hair* 은발 / *~ sand* 은백색의 모래 / *the ~ waves* 은파(銀波) / *the ~ rays of the moon* 은색의 달빛. **3** soft and clear in tune or voice. (목소리 따위가) 낭랑한; 곱고 맑은. ¶ *~ sounds* 은방울 굴리는 듯한 맑은 소리 / *~ tones* 낭랑한 어조. **4** eloquent; persuasive 유창한; 설득력이 있는. ¶ *a ~ tongue* 능변(能辯).

—*vt.* (P6) **1** coat or cover (something) with silver or something like silver. …에 은도금을 하다; 은을 칠하다. **2** make the color of silver. …을 은빛으로 하다. ¶ *The water of the lake was silvered by the moon.* 호수의 물은 달빛으로 은색이었다.

—*vi.* (P1,2A) become silver in color. 은백색이 되다. ¶ *The old man's hair had silvered.* 노인의 머리는 은발이 되어 있었다. [E.]

silver age [⌐– ⌐], **the** *n.* the period of Latin literature that followed the Augustan. 백은 시대. 參考 라틴 문학의 융성 시대; 14 - 138년경.

sil·ver·fish [sílvərfìʃ] *n.* **1** 《insect》 a silver insect found in books and moldy places. 반대좀. **2** a colorless variety of gold-fish. 은빛 물고기

sil·ver·gilt [sílvərgílt] *adj.* coated with silver or silverleaf. 은도금한; 은박을 입힌.

sil·ver-haired [sílvərhέərd] *adj.* having silvery-white or grey hair. 은발〔백발〕의.

Silver Jubilee [⌐– ⌐––], **the** *n.* a twenty-fifth anniversary. 25주년 기념(식).

silver lining [⌐– ⌐–] *n.* the brighter side of an unfortunate situation. 불행중 다행. ¶ 《*prov.*》 *Every cloud has a ~.* 어떤 구름도 뒤는 은빛으로 빛난다《어떤 불행에도 다행한 면이 있다》.

sil·vern [sílvərn] *adj.* 《*arch.*》 of or like silver. 은의; 은 같은.

sil·ver-pa·per [sílvərpéipər] *n.* **1** a fine white tissue-paper. 고급 박엽지(薄葉紙); 티슈페이퍼. **2** tinfoil. 은박지.

silver plate [⌐– ⌐] *n.* 《*collectively*》 tableware made of silver or coated with silver. 은제〔은도금한〕 식기류.

sil·ver-plat·ed [sílvərpléitid] *adj.* covered or coated with silver or a silverlike material. 은도금한; 은박을 입힌.

silver screen [⌐– ⌐] *n.* **1** a screen on which motion pictures are shown. 은막. **2** 《*the ~, collectively*》 motion pictures. 영화.

sil·ver·side [sílvərsàid] *n.* the best side of a round of beef. (소의) 허벅지 살.

sil·ver·smith [sílvərsmìθ] *n.* Ⓒ a person who makes silver articles. 은세공사(銀細工師); 은장이.

silver standard [⌐– ⌐–], **the** *n.* use of silver money alone as full legal tender. 은본위제.

sil·ver·tongued [sílvərtʌ́ŋd] *adj.* eloquent; persuasive. 웅변의; 설득력 있는.

sil·ver·ware [sílvərwὲər] *n.* Ⓤ 《*collectively*》 《U.S.》 articles made of or plated with silver. 은제〔은도금한〕 식기; 은식기.

silver wedding [⌐–⌐–] *n.* the 25th anniversary of a wedding. 은혼식.

sil·ver·weed [sílvərwìːd] *n.* 《bot.》 a silver-leaved wayside plant. 뱀딸기류(類).

sil·ver·y [sílvəri] *adj.* **1** like silver in color or appearance. 은과 같은; 은빛의. ¶ ~ *moonlight* 은빛으로 빛나는 달빛 / ~ *hair* 은발 / *a* ~ *light* 은색의 빛. **2** (of a sound, a voice, etc.) soft and clear. 낭랑한; 곱고 맑은; 은방울 같은 ¶ *The bell has a* ~ *sound.* 그 종은 은방울 같은 소리를 낸다. [E.]

:sim·i·lar [símələr] *adj.* **1** 《*to*》 almost alike; resembling. 유사한; 닮은. ¶ *in a* ~ *way* 비슷한 방식으로 / *Yours are very* ~ *to mine.* 당신의 것은 내 것과 아주 비슷하다 / *Pink and rose are* ~ *colors.* 분홍색과 장미색은 유사한 색깔이다 / *They are* ~ *in every point.* 그들은 모든 점에서 서로 닮았다 / *A is* ~ *to B in apperance* 〔*form*〕. A는 B와 외관이〔형식에서〕 유사하다. **2** 《*math.*》 having the same shape, but not the same size. 닮은꼴〔상사(相似)〕의. ¶ ~ *figures* 닮은꼴. [L. *similis*]

sim·i·lar·i·ty [sìməlǽrəti] *n.* (*pl.* **-ties**) **1** Ⓤ the state or quality of being similar; likeness. 유사(성). ¶ *There is a wonderful* ~ *between the twins.* 그 쌍둥이는 놀랄 정도로 닮았다 / ~ *of tastes* 취미의 유사성. **2** Ⓒ a point or feature in which things are similar. 유사점〔물〕.

sim·i·lar·ly [símələrli] *adv.* in the same way; likewise. 유사〔비슷〕하게.

sim·i·le [símәliː] *n.* Ⓒ an expression in which two different things or ideas are compared. 직유(直喩)(cf. *metaphor*). 參考 as brave as a lion; a face like marble 따위의 표현을 말함. [→similar]

si·mil·i·tude [similətjùːd] *n.* **1** Ⓤ the state or quality of being similar; similarity; resemblance. 유사(類似). ¶ *assume the* ~ *of* ... …의 모습을 취하다. **2** Ⓒ a comparison. 비교; 비유. ¶ *speak in* 〔*by*〕 ~ 비유로 말하다. **3** a person or thing that resembles another; a counterpart. 닮은 사람〔물건〕. [↑]

sim·mer [símər] *vt.* (P6) boil (water, food, etc.) gently. (물·음식 따위)를 뭉근히 끓이다. ¶ *She simmered the stew for two hours.* 그녀는 스튜 요리를 두 시간 동안 뭉근히 끓였다. —*vi.* (P1,2A) **1** make a low, humming sound while boiling gently. (약한 불에) 부글부글 끓다. ¶ *The kettle simmered on the gas range.* 주전자는 가스 레인지 위에서 부글부글 끓었다. **2** cook or keep at or just below the boiling point. 막 끓으려고 하다. **3** (of anger, or laughter) be about to burst out. (분노·웃음 따위가) 당장에라도 터질 듯하다. ¶ ~ *with laughter* 〔*anger*〕 당장에라도 웃음이〔분노가〕 터지려고 하다 / *simmering rebellion* 발발(勃發) 직전의 반란.

simmer down, **a**) become calm or cool. 냉정해지다; 식어지다. **b**) boil until the volume is reduced; boil down. 졸아들다.

—*n.* Ⓒ 《*sing.* only》 the state of boiling gently or being near the point of bursting out. 서서히 끓어오르는 상태; 폭발〔끓기〕 직전의 상태. ¶ *bring water to a* ~ 물을 서서히 끓어오르게 하다 / *keep the soup at a* ~ 국을 약한 불에 천천히 계속 끓이다. [Imit.]

Si·mon [sáimən] *n.* a man's name. 남자 이름.

Simon Pure [⌐–⌐] *n.* 《usu. *the real* ~》 the genuine person or thing; no counterfeit. 진짜; 본인《영국 작가 Centlivre 의 희극 중의 인물명에서》. [Person in a play]

si·mo·ni·ac [simóuniæ̀k, sai-] *n.* a person guilty of simony. 성직 매매자. [↑]

sim·o·ny [sáiməni, sím-] *n.* Ⓤ trafficking in church preferment. 성직 매매.

si·moom [simúːm, sai-], **-moon** [-múːn] *n.* Ⓒ a hot, dry, desert wind with sand in Arabia, Syria, etc. 열풍《아랍 지방의 사막에서 붊》. [Arab.]

sim·per [símpər] *vi.* (P1) smile in a silly, self-conscious way. 억지 웃음을 웃다; 선웃음치다. —*n.* Ⓒ a silly, self-conscious smile. 억지 웃음; 선웃음. [?]

sim·per·ing·ly [símpəriŋli] *adv.* with a simper. 선웃음치며; 히쭉거리며.

:sim·ple [símpəl] *adj.* (**-pler, -plest**) **1** easy to do or understand. 간단한; 용이한. ¶ *a* ~ *question* 간단한〔쉬운〕 질문 / *a* ~ *design* 〔*explanation*〕 간단한 디자인〔설명〕 / *This book is written in simple lauguage.* 이 책은 쉬운 말로 쓰여졌다. **2** plain; not decorated; not showy. 검소한; 꾸밈이 없는. ¶ *a* ~ *style* 간소한 문체〔양식〕 / *He eats* ~ *food and wears* ~ *clothing.* 그는 검소한 식사를 하며 수수한 옷을 입는다. **3** innocent; not affected. 순진〔천진〕한. ¶ *a* ~, *honest answer* 순진하고 정직한 대답 / *a pleasant and* ~ *smile* 붙임성 있는 순진한 미소 / *in a* ~ *manner* 순박한 태도로. **4** honest; sincere. 정직한; 성실한. ¶ *a* ~ *heart* 정직한 마음. **5** easily deceived; foolish. (바보스럽게) 사람 좋은; 잘 속는; 어리석은. ¶ *a* ~ *soul* 호인; 어수룩한 사람 / *I am not quite so* ~ *as to believe that.* 나는 그것을 믿을 정도로 어리석지는 않다. **6** humble; common. (신분이) 천한; 대단찮은. ¶ *His parents were* ~ *people.* 그의 부모들은 신분이 미천했다. **7** not mixed; mere. 순연한; 순전한. ¶ *a* ~ *fact* (본디 그대로의) 순연한 사실 / *fraud pure and* ~ 순전한 사기 / *Such an act is* ~ *madness.* 그러한 행동은 순전한 광기다.

simple diet, coarse food. 조식(粗食).

simple life, a practice of doing without servants and luxuries; an attempt to return to more primitive conditions. 검소

한 생활.
—*n.* Ⓒ **1** a foolish person. 바보. **2** something simple. 단순한 것. **3** any plant for medical use; the medicine made from such a plant. 약초(로 만든 약).
● **sim·ple·ness** [-nis] *n.* [L. *simplex*]
simple equation [ˊ- -ˊ-] *n.* 《alg.》 not involving the second or any higher power of unknown quantity. 일차 방정식 (cf. *quadratic*).
sim·ple-heart·ed [símpəlhá:rtid] *adj.* having a simple heart; sincere; frank. 순진한; 정직한.
sim·ple-mind·ed [símpəlmáindid] *adj.* easily deceived; stupid. 속기 쉬운; 어리석은.
simple sentence [ˊ- ˊ-] *n.* 《gram.》 a sentence without subordinate clauses. 단문.
sim·ple·ton [símpəltən] *n.* Ⓒ a silly, stupid person who is easily deceived. 바보.
·**sim·plic·i·ty** [simplísəti] *n.* Ⓤ **1** the quality or state of being simple. 단순. **2** freedom from difficulty or complexity; clearness or easiness. 간단; 간이. ¶ *the ~ of a machine* 〔*problem*〕 기계〔문제〕의 간단함. **3** absence of ornament; plainness; 검소. ¶ *Everybody admired the neat ~ of her dress.* 모두가 그녀의 깔끔하고 검소한 복장을 칭찬했다. **4** absence of show or pretence; naturalness; sincerity. 천진; 성실. ¶ *a man of childlike ~* 어린애처럼 순진한 사람. **5** lack of shrewdness; dullness. 우둔; 우직.
sim·pli·fi·ca·tion [sìmpləfikéiʃən] *n.* **1** Ⓤ the act of simplifying; the state of being simplified. 간이화; 단순〔간소〕화. ¶ *the ~ of a problem* 문제의 단순화. **2** Ⓒ something made simpler. 단순화된 것. [↓]
sim·pli·fy [símpləfài] *vt.* (**-fied**) (P6) make (something) simpler or easier. …을 간단〔단순〕하게 하다. ¶ *Try to ~ your explanation for the children.* 설명을 아이들이 알아듣게 간단히 해라. [→simple,-fy]
:**sim·ply** [símpli] *adv.* **1** in a simple, plain manner. 간단히. ¶ *a question answered quite ~* 매우 간단히 대답된 질문. **2** without ornament; plainly. 꾸밈없이; 검소하게. ¶ *live ~* 검소하게 살다 / *a woman ~ dressed* 검소한 옷차림의 여성. **3** foolishly. 우직스럽게. ¶ *smile ~* 우직하게 웃다. **4** merely; only. 단지; 단순히. ¶ *believe someone ~ on his word* 이야기만으로 아무를 신용하다 / *It is ~ a question of money.* 그것은 단지 돈의 문제다. **5** 《colloq.》 absolutely. 전혀; 정말로; 아주. ¶ *The cold was ~ awful.* 추위는 정말 지독했다 / *~ perfect* 아주 완벽한. [*simple*]
sim·u·la·cra [sìmjəléikrə] *n.* pl. of **simulacrum.**
sim·u·la·crum [sìmjəléikrəm] *n.* Ⓒ (*pl.* **-cra** or **-crums**) **1** an image. 상(像). **2** something made in resemblance to a thing; a slight likeness. 가짜; 환영(幻影). [↓]
sim·u·late [símjəlèit] *vt.* (P6) **1** pretend …을 가장하다. ¶ *~ illness* 꾀병부리다 / *~ interest* 〔*affection*〕 흥미를〔애정을〕 가장하다. **2** look or act like (something) …인 체하다; …을 흉내내다. ¶ *Some moths ~ dead leaves.* 나방 중에는 마른 잎처럼 보이게 하는 것이 있다. [L. *simulo* copy]
sim·u·la·tion [sìmjəléiʃən] *n.* Ⓤ the act of simulating; an imitation. (짐짓) …처럼 보이기; 의태(擬態).
sim·u·la·tor [símjəlèitər] *n.* one that simulates; a device that generates conditions approximating actual or operational conditions for the purpose of training or experimentation. 흉내를 내는 사람〔것〕; 모의 조종〔실험〕 장치.
si·mul·ta·ne·i·ty [sàiməltəní:əti, sìm-] *n.* Ⓤ the quality of being simultaneous. 동시 발생; 동시성. [↓]
si·mul·ta·ne·ous [sàiməltéiniəs, sìm-] *adj.* 《*with*》 existing or occurring at the same time. 동시의; 동시에 일어나는. ¶ *~ translation* 〔*interpretation*〕 동시 통역 / *~ acts* 〔*movements*〕 동시의 행동〔동작〕 / *~ broadcast* (동일 프로의) 라디오〔TV〕 동시 방송 / *All the people in the audience burst into ~ applause.* 청중의 모든 사람들은 일제히 박수 갈채를 터뜨렸다 / *The explosion was almost ~ with the announcement.* 폭발은 통고와 거의 동시였다. [→similar]
si·mul·ta·ne·ous·ly [sàiməltéiniəsli, sìm-] *adv.* at the same time; all at once. 동시에; 일제히.
:**sin** [sin] *n.* **1** ⓊⒸ the act of breaking God's laws; an immoral act. (종교상·도덕상의) 죄; 죄악. ¶ *live in ~* 불의〔불륜〕의 생활을 하다 / *commit* 〔*forgive*〕 *a ~* 죄를 범하다〔용서하다〕 / *the original ~* 원죄 / *Lying, dishonesty, and cruelty are sins.* 거짓말, 부정직 그리고 잔인함은 죄악이다. **2** Ⓒ something which is not reasonable; an offence against good manners. 죄가 될 수 있을 만한 일; 과실; 위반. ¶ *It is a ~ to waste time.* 시간을 낭비하는 것은 죄반을 일이다 / *a social ~* 사교상의 과실.
— *v.* (**sinned, sin·ning**) *vi.* (P1,3) 《*against*》 break one of God's laws; do wrong or evil. (종교상의) 죄를 범하다; 거역하다 — *vt.* (P6) commit (a wrong deed) (죄)를 범하다. [E.]
sin one's mercies, be ungrateful for good luck. 신의 은혜에 감사하지 않다.
Si·nai [sáinai, -niài] *n.* **1** 《*Mount* or *Mt.* ~》 (in the Bible) the mountain where the law was given to Moses from God. 시내산(山) 《모세가 십계명을 받은 산》. **2** a peninsula at the northern end of the Red Sea. 시나이 반도.
:**since** [sins] *prep.* from the time of; from (a past time) till now continuously; after (a past time) till now; during the time following. …때부터 (지금까지); …이후〔이

래]. ¶ ~ *then* 그 때부터 / *It has been raining ~ dawn.* 새벽부터 계속 비가 오고 있다 / *He has worked hard ~ leaving school.* 그는 학교를 떠난 이후 열심히 공부했다 / *Many things have happened ~ then.* 그 때부터 많은 일들이 일어났다 / *I've not seen her ~ Monday.* 그녀를 월요일부터 보지 못했다.
— *conj.* **1** from the time when ... till now. …(한) 때부터; …(한) 이후[이래]. ¶ *What have you been doing ~ I saw you last ?* 지난번 자네를 만난 이후 무엇을 하며 지내 왔는가 / *Ten years have passed ~ he died.* 그가 죽은 지 10 년이 됐다. **2** because; seeing that. …이므로; …인 까닭에. ¶ *Since you say so, it must be true.* 네가 그렇게 말하니까, 그것은 사실이겠지 / *It is useless to ask him, ~ he doesn't intend to do it.* 그는 할 의향이 없으므로, 요청해 봤자 소용없는 일이다.
— *adv.* **1** 《often *ever ~*》 from that time until now. 그 이후 (지금까지). ¶ *ever ~* 그 후 내내 / *I have not heard from him ~.* 그 후에 그에게서 소식이 없다 / *He left six years ago and has not been seen ~.* 그는 6년 전에 떠났는데, 그 이후 보지 못했다 / *John came on Saturday and has been here ever ~.* 존은 토요일에 왔는데, 그 이후 내내 여기에 있다. **2** before now; ago. 이전에. ¶ *It happened many years ~.* 그것은 여러 해 전에 일어났다 / *The word has long ~ been out of use.* 그 말은 안 쓰인 지 오래 됐다. **3** sometime after. 그 후[뒤]. ¶ *He lived in Pusan at that time but has ~ moved away.* 그는 그 때 부산에 살고 있었으나 그 후 이사하였다 / *Mr. Cole was ill last week but has ~ recovered.* 콜씨는 지난 주 앓고 있었으나 그 후 회복되었다. [E. =after that]

•**sin·cere** [sinsíər] *adj.* (usu. **-cer·er, -cer·est**) honest; faithful. 진실한; 성실한; 순수한. ¶ *a ~ friend* 진실한 친구 / *He is ~ in his promises* [*in what he says*]. 그는 그의 약속[그의 말]에 성실하다 / *His grief is quite ~.* 그의 슬픔은 매우 순수한 것이다. [L.]

:**sin·cere·ly** [sinsíərli] *adv.* in a sincere manner; heartily. 진심으로; 진정으로. ¶ *I ~ hope you are right.* 나는 네가 옳기를 진심으로 바란다 / *Yours ~.* 경구(敬具); 불비(不備) 《편지의 맺음말》.

•**sin·cer·i·ty** [sinsérəti] *n.* Ⓤ the state of being sincere; honesty. 정직; 성실; 순수. ¶ *No one doubts the ~ of Abraham Lincoln.* 링컨의 성실성을 의심하는 사람은 아무도 없다.

sin·ci·put [sínsəpʌt] *n.* a head from the forehead to the crown. 전두부(前頭部). [semi-, →capital]

si·ne [sáini] *prep.* 《L.》 without. …없이.

si·ne·cure [sáinikjùər, síni-] *n.* Ⓒ an office or position that is paid well and does not require much work or responsibility. 한직; 일[책임]이 별로 없는 (유급(有給)의) 지위. ¶ *His job is hardly* [*not*] *a ~.* 그의 직무는 대단히 바쁜 직무이다. [→sine, →cure]

sine die [sáini dáii:], indefinitely. 《L.》 무기한으로.

sine qua non [sáini kwei nɔ́n] *n.* indispensable condition or qualification. 필수 조건[자격]. [L.]

sin·ew [sínju:] *n.* Ⓒ **1** a tough piece of tissue that joins muscle to a bone. 건(腱). **2** 《often *pl.*》 muscular strength; energy. 완력; 원기. ¶ *a man of mighty sinews* 대단한 완력[정력]가. **3** 《*pl.*》 source of strength. 원동력. ¶ *the sinews of war* 군자금; 운용 자금.
— *vt.* strengthen; give (someone) power. …을 힘나게 하다; …의 힘을 북돋우다. [E.]

sin·ew·y [sínju:i] *adj.* **1** having many sinews that join muscle to a bone. 근육질의; 근골이 늠름한. ¶ *a ~ piece of beef* 근육질의 쇠고기. **2** strong and vigorous. 건장한; 튼튼한. ¶ *~ arms* [*shoulders*] 건장한 팔[어깨].

sin·ful [sínfəl] *adj.* full of sin; immoral; wrong. 죄 있는. ¶ *a ~ man* [*life*] 죄 많은 사람[인생] / *a ~ act* [*thought*] 죄가 되는 행동[생각]. ● **sin·ful·ly** [-fəli] *adv.* **sin·ful·ness** [-nis] *n.* [*sin*]

:**sing** [siŋ] *v.* (**sang, sung**) *vi.* **1** (P1,2A,3) make musical sounds with the voice. 노래하다. ¶ *~ in tune* 가락에 맞춰 노래하다 / *~ in a low voice* 저음으로 노래하다 / *learn to ~* 노래를 배우다 / *~ to the piano* 피아노에 맞추어 노래하다 / *People ~ in church.* 사람들이 교회에서 노래한다. **2** (P1) make musical sounds, as do birds, the wind, etc. (새 따위가) 울다; 지저귀다; 윙윙[부글부글, 졸졸]거리다. ¶ *Birds are singing.* 새가 지저귀고 있다 / *The kettle sang.* 주전자가 부글거렸다 / *The wind sang in the trees.* 바람이 나무 사이를 윙윙거리며 불었다. **3** (P3) 《*of*》 say words with musical tones; tell or praise in verse or poetry. (운에 맞춰) 읊다; 음송하다; (시·노래로) 읊조리다[예찬하다]. ¶ *Homer sang of Troy in his 'Iliad'.* 호머는 '일리어드'에서 트로이를 시로 읊었다.
— *vt.* **1** (P6,7,13,14) praise or tell of (someone or something) in song; chant. …을 노래로 읊다[예찬하다]; 노래하다; 음송하다. ¶ *~ a song* 노래를 부르다. **2** bring (someone) into a certain state by singing. 노래하여 (아무를) …하게 하다. ¶ *~ a child to sleep* 노래해서 아이를 잠들게 하다 / *~ the Old Year out and the New Year in* 노래하여 묵은 해를 보내고 새해를 맞이하다. [E.]

sing another song [***tune***], become humbler. 겸손해지다.

sing small, be crestfallen; cease boasting. 나약한 소리를 하다; 풀이 죽다.

sing. singular.

Sin·ga·pore [sìŋgəpɔ́:r] *n.* **1** an island off the southern tip of the Malay Peninsula. 싱가포르 섬. **2** a country comprising this island and near islets. 싱가포르.

singe [sindʒ] *v.* (**singed, singe·ing**) *vt.* (P6) burn slightly; remove or take off (feathers, the feathery part of cloth, etc.) by slight burning. …을 그스르다; (새·천 따위의) 털〔보풀〕을 태워〔그슬러〕 없애다. ¶ *The hot iron has slightly singed the cloth.* 다리미가 헝겊의 보풀을 그슬렀다 / *have one's hair singed* 머리털을 인두로 지져 다듬(게 하)다 / ~ *someone's hair* 아무의 머리털을 (고데로) 지지다〔그스르다〕 / ~ *a chicken* 병아리의 털을 불에 그슬러 없애다. — *vi.* burn a little. (거죽이) 타다; 눋다.

singe one's feathers 〔***wings***〕, take harm in an ambitious attempt. 명성을 떨어뜨리다; 평판을 나쁘게 하다.

— *n.* Ⓒ a slight burn or scorch on the surface of something. 그스름; 탐. [E.]

:sin·ger [síŋər] *n.* Ⓒ **1** a person or bird that sings. 가수; 우는 새. ¶ *Enrico Caruso was a famous* ~. 엔리코 카루소는 유명한 가수였다 / *I fear I'm not a* ~. 나는 노래를 잘하지 못한다 / *Our canary is a fine* ~. 우리 집 카나리아는 고운 목소리로 멋지게 잘 운다. **2** 《*lit.*》 a poet. 시인. ¶ *the singers of the past* 과거의 시인. [*sing*]

Sin·gha·lese [sìŋgəlíːz] *adj.* =Sinhalese.

sing·ing [síŋiŋ] *n.* Ⓤ **1** the sound made by a person who sings; the act of the singer. 노래; 노래하기. **2** the whistling sound of a bullet, etc. (화살·탄환 따위의) 울리는 소리. [*sing*]

:sin·gle [síŋgəl] *adj.* **1** only one; one and no more. 단 하나의; 단독의. ¶ *a* ~ *piece of chalk* 단 한 개의 분필 / *answer in a* ~ *word* 단 한 마디로 응답하다 / *the* ~ *piece of evidence* 유일한 증거 / *He would not move a* ~ *step from the place.* 그는 그 장소로부터 단 한 걸음도 움직이려 하지 않았다 / *There's not a* ~ *one left.* 단 한 사람도 남아 있지 않다 / *Hardly a* ~ *man was to be seen on the street.* 거리에는 단 한 사람도 눈에 띄지 않았다. **2** 《bot.》 having only one ring of petals. (꽃 따위가) 홑〔외〕겹의; 단판(單瓣)의(opp. double). ¶ *a* ~ *flower* 단판화 / *Some roses are double; others are* ~. 장미에는 겹꽃 장미도 있고 홑겹 장미도 있다. **3** unmarried; for one person. 독신의; 일인용의. ¶ *a* ~ *bed* 1인용 침대 / *a* ~ *man* 독신자 / a ~ *room at a hotel* 호텔에 있는 1인용 방 / *There are two* ~ *beds in the room.* 방 안에는 두 개의 1인용 침대가 있다. **4** having only one on each side in a fight. (시합 등에서) 1대 1의; 단식(單式)의. ¶ (*a*) ~ *combat* 1대1의 시합. **5** 《Brit.》 for only one course on a railway. 편도의. ¶ *a* ~ *ticket* 편도 승차권. **6** sincere; honest. 성실한; 정직한. ¶ *a* ~ *heart* 〔*mind*〕 성심 / *a* ~ *devotion* 헌신 / *a man of* ~ *meaning* 외곬으로 성실〔고지식〕한 사람 / *with a* ~ *eye* 성심 성의로.

— *n.* Ⓒ **1** 《*pl.*》 (in tennis) a game played with one person on each side. (테니스의) 단식 경기. **2** 《baseball》 a base hit. 단타(單打). **3** a one-way ticket. 편도 승차권.

— *vt.* (P7) 《*out*》 choose (someone or something) from others. …을 뽑아내다; 선발〔발탁〕하다. ¶ *The teacher singled Harry out for punishment.* 선생님께서는 벌을 주기 위해 해리를 뽑았다. [L. *singuli* individual]

sin·gle-breast·ed [síŋgəlbréstid] *adj.* (of a coat, etc.) having one line of buttons in the center of the breast. (신사복의 상의가) 외줄 단추의; 싱글의.

sin·gle-eyed [síŋgəláid] *adj.* **1** having only one eye. 홑눈의; 단안의. **2** devoted to only one purpose; earnest. 한눈 팔지 않는; 외곬의.

sin·gle-hand·ed [síŋgəlhǽndid] *adj., adv.* **1** of or by only one hand. 한쪽 손의〔으로〕. **2** of or by only one person without any help from others. 단독의; 혼자 힘으로. ¶ ~ *sailing* 단독 항해 / *He did the job* ~. 그는 혼자 힘으로 그 일을 했다.

● **sin·gle-hand·ed·ly** [-li] *adv.*

sin·gle-heart·ed [síŋgəlháːrtid] *adj.* having an honest, simple heart; free from deceit, faithful. 성실한; 성의 있는.

● **sin·gle-heart·ed·ly** [-li] *adv.*

sin·gle-mind·ed [síŋgəlmáindid] *adj.* devoted to one purpose; single-hearted; sincere. 외곬의; 성실한.

sin·gle·ness [síŋgəlnis] *n.* Ⓤ **1** the state of being single. 단일. **2** sincerity; honesty. 성실. ¶ *with* ~ *of purpose* 한 가지 목적에 일심 불란하여. **3** the state of unmarried life; a single life. 독신.

sin·gle·stick [síŋgəlstìk] *n.* Ⓒ a sword-like, wooden stick held in one hand, used in fencing; Ⓤ fencing with such a stick. 목검; 목검술.

sin·glet [síŋglit] *n.* Ⓒ an undershirt or jersey. 내의.

sin·gle·ton [síŋgəltən] *n.* Ⓒ **1** 《cards》 a player's only card of a suit. 한 장(패). **2** a lone person. 외톨이.

sin·gle·track [siŋgəltræ̀k] *adj.* **1** 《railway》 having only a single track. 단선(單線)의. **2** =one-track.

sin·gly [síŋgli] *adv.* **1** one by one; individually; separately. 하나하나씩; 한 사람씩; 따로따로. ¶ *Misfortunes never come* ~. 불행은 절대로 홀로 오지 않는다《화불단행(禍不單行)》 / *Let us deal with the questions* ~. 우리 문제들을 개별적으로 다루도록 하자. **2** by oneself; without others' help. 홀로; 혼자 힘으로.

sing·song [síŋsɔ̀ːŋ / -sɔ̀ŋ] *n.* Ⓒ **1** a monotonous rising and falling tone. 단조로운 가락〔음조〕. **2** 《Brit.》 a meeting of amateurs to sing well-known song. 즉흥 합창회.

— *adj.* monotonous in tone or sound. 단조로운 (어조의); 억양이 없는. ¶ *a* ~ *recitation of a poem* 단조로운 어조로 하는 시의 낭송. [*sing*]

·sin·gu·lar [síŋgjələr] *adj.* **1** extraordinary; uncommon, unusual. 보통이 아닌; 비범

한. ¶ *a story of ~ interest* 대단히 흥미 있는 이야기. **2** strange; queer; not in accordance with general customs. 기묘한; 기이한. ¶ *a most ~ story* 〔*phenomenon*〕 매우 기이한 이야기〔현상〕 / *~ habits* 기벽(奇癖) / *She is ~ in her looks.* 그녀의 옷차림은 완전히 색다르다. **3** 《gram.》 of one person or thing. 단수의(opp. plural). ¶ *the first person ~* 제1인칭 단수 / *the ~ number* 단수.

—*n.* Ⓒ 《usu. *the ~* 》 the singular number; the form of a word of the singular number. 단수(형). ¶ *The ~ of 'mice' is 'mouse'.* 'mice'의 단수형은 'mouse'이다. [L. *singulus* single]

all and singular, 《law》 all whether taken together or separately. 전부.

sin·gu·lar·i·ty [sìŋgjəlǽrəti] *n.* (*pl.* **-ties**) **1** Ⓤ the state of being singular; strangeness; a special quality. 단독; 기이(奇異). ¶ *The ~ of his appearance attracted our attention.* 그의 특이한 모습은 우리의 주목을 끌었다. **2** Ⓒ something singular or peculiar. 기묘〔진귀〕한 것; 특(이)성. ¶ *One of singularities of this strange beast is that its horn grows out of its nose.* 이 이상한 동물의 특이성 중의 하나는 코 바깥쪽으로 뿔이 자란다는 것이다.

sin·gu·lar·ly [síŋgjələrli] *adv.* strangely; particularly. 기묘하게.

Sin·ha·lese [sìnhəlíz, -s] *adj.* of Sri Lanka, its native people, or their language. 신할리즈(족, 어)의. —*n.* (*pl.* **Sin·ha·lese**) Ⓒ a person of Sri Lanka; Ⓤ the language of Sri Lanka. 신할리즈족〔인, 어〕. [Skr.]

sin·is·ter [sínistər] *adj.* **1** suggesting the possibility of misfortune, disaster, etc. 불길한. ¶ *~ symptoms* 〔*expression*〕 불길한 조짐〔표정〕 / *a ~ remark* 불길한 말. **2** showing ill will or evil intentions. 악의가 있는. ¶ *a ~ look* 인상이 나쁜 얼굴 / *a ~ rumor* 악의가 있는 소문 / *a ~ character* 속이 검은〔음험한〕 사람. **3** not fortunate; unfavorable. 불행한. ¶ *He met with a ~ fate.* 그는 불운을 만났다. [L.]

:sink [siŋk] *v.* (**sank** or **sunk, sunk** or **sunk·en**) *vi.* **1** (P1,3) go downward little by little. (조금씩) 하강하다; (해·달 따위가) 지다. ¶ *The sun is sinking in the west.* 해가 서쪽으로 지고 있다 / *The road sinks toward the lake.* 도로는 호수 쪽으로 내리막이다 / *The heavy clouds began to ~ lower and lower.* 짙은 검은 구름이 점점 낮게 내려오기 시작했다 / *The moon sank behind the mountain.* 달이 산 너머로 졌다. **2** (P1,3) fall under water, snow, etc. 가라앉다. ¶ *~ in mud* (*up*) *to one's knees* 무릎까지 흙탕 속에 빠지다 / *The ship sank to the bottom of the sea.* 그 배는 바다 밑으로 가라앉았다 / *Wood floats on water but metal sinks.* 나무는 물에서 뜨지만 쇠는 가라앉는다. **3** (P1,2A) become lower than the usual level. 내려앉다. ¶ *~ into the ground* 땅 속으로 꺼지다 / *The building sank under its weight.* 그 건물은 자체의 무게로 내려앉았다 / *The district is sinking.* 그 지방의 지반은 내려앉고 있다. **4** (P1,3) become less in value, degree, etc. 저하〔감소〕하다; 약해지다; 줄다; 떨어지다. ¶ *~ in price* 값이 떨어지다 / *The wind has sunk down.* 바람이 약해졌다 / *The storm is beginning to sink.* 폭풍우가 가라앉기 시작하고 있다 / *His voice sank to a whisper.* 그의 목소리는 속삭임으로 약해졌다 / *Have the figures of unemployment sunk since last year?* 지난해 이래로 실업자 수가 줄어들었느냐 / *My heart sunk.* 낙심하였다. **5** (P1,3) 《of the body or a part of the body》 fall or slide down gradually; drop down; bend downward. 쓰러지다; 풀썩 주저앉다; 수그러지다. ¶ *~ into a chair* 의자에 털썩 주저앉다 / *She sank into his arms.* 그녀는 그의 팔에 몸을 내던졌다 / *His head sank on his breast.* 그는 고개를 가슴에 푹 수그렸다 / *He let his arms ~ from weariness.* 그는 맥이 빠져서 두 팔을 축 늘어뜨렸다. **6** (P1,3) become or seem deep or hollow. 우묵해지다; 쑥 들어가다. ¶ *His eyes* 〔*cheeks*〕 *sank in.* 그의 두 눈〔양 볼〕이 쑥 들어갔다. **7** (P1,3) pass or fall into some state. (…한 상태에) 빠지다. ¶ *~ into deep sleep* 깊은 잠에 빠지다. **8** soak; enter gradually into; be absorbed by. 침투하다. ¶ *The dye sinks into the cloth.* 염료는 옷감에 스며든다 / *Let the lesson ~ into your mind.* 그 교훈이 네 마음 속에 새겨지도록 하여라.

—*vt.* **1** (P6) cause (something) to sink; send below the surface. …을 가라앉히다; 침몰시키다. ¶ *The ship was sunk by the storm.* 그 배는 폭풍우로 침몰되었다. **2** make (value, degree, etc.) lower; lower the level of. …을 저하〔감소〕시키다; 줄이다. ¶ *~ the reservoirs* 저수지의 수위를 저하시키다 / *~ a national debt* 국채를 상환하다. **3** (P6,13) dig. …을 파다. ¶ *~ a well* 〔*hole*〕 우물〔구멍〕을 파다. **4** fix or bury (a pole, etc.) firmly into the ground. …을 (땅 속에) 묻다〔세우다〕. ¶ *~ a pipe* 파이프를 땅에 묻다 / *~ a post ten feet into the ground* 기둥을 땅 속에 10피트 깊이로 묻어 세우다. **5** (P6) let fall to a lower position. 수그리다. ¶ *~ one's head on someone's arms* 아무의 팔에 머리를 수그려 기대다. **6** (P6) lower in tone or pitch. (가락·음조를) 낮추다. ¶ *~ one's voice* 목소리를 낮추다. **7** (P6,13) invest in some business. 투자하다. ¶ *He sank all his capital in house-building.* 그는 그의 모든 자본을 주택 건축에 투자했다.

One's ***heart sinks within*** *one.* One despairs (of). 실망하다.

sink in *someone's* ***estimation,*** lose credit with him. 아무의 신용을 잃다.

sink *oneself* 〔*one's* ***own interest***〕***,*** be altruistic. 사리(私利)를 버리고 남을 위하다.

sink or swim, risk and take chances. 흥하든 망하든.

sink the shop, be silent about one's oc-

cupation. 직업을 숨기다.
sink under, give way to. (몸을) …에 내맡기다.
— *n.* **1** Ⓒ a kitchen basin with a pipe to carry away water, used for washing dishes, pots, etc. (부엌의) 수채; 물 버리는 곳; 싱크대. **2** a place of vice or corruption. 소굴. [E.]

sink·er [síŋkər] *n.* Ⓒ **1** a person or thing that sinks. 가라앉(히)는 사람[물건]. **2** a weight to sink a fishing line or net. (낚싯줄의) 봉돌; 추. **3** 《baseball》《U.S. *colloq.*》 a ball that drops sharply downward when it reaches the batter. 싱커《공을 드롭시키는 투구의 일종》.

sink·ing [síŋkiŋ] *n.* ⓊⒸ a feeling of collapse from weakness, fear, etc. 의기 소침. — *adj.* that sinks; dying. 가라앉는; 쇠하는.

sinking fund [⌐-⌐] *n.* a fund which is set aside periodically by a government, a corporation, etc. to pay a debt. 감채(減債) 기금; 상각(償却) 적립금.

sin·less [sínlis] *adj.* free from sin; innocent. 죄 없는; 순결한. [*sin*]

sin·ner [sínər] *n.* Ⓒ a person who commits sin or does wrong. 죄인; 나쁜 사람; 위반자.

Si·no- [sáinou-, sínou-] *pref.* Chinese. '중국의'의 뜻. ¶ *Sino-Korean* 한중(韓中)의. [Chin. *Ch'in* 秦]

Si·nol·o·gist [sainálədʒist, si- / -nɔ́l-] *n.* an expert in sinology. 중국학 학자. [↓]

Si·nol·o·gy [sainálədʒi, sin- / -nɔ́l-] *n.* Ⓤ the study of Chinese literature, history, art, etc. 중국학. [Gk. *Sinai* the Chinese]

sin·u·os·i·ty [sìnjuásəti / -ɔ́s-] *n.* **1** 《often *pl.*》 a bend, esp. in a river or road. (강·도로의) 굽이진 곳. **2** the state of being sinuous; a sinuous form or character. 굴곡; 만곡(彎曲); (성격의) 비뚤어짐. ¶ *The road is marked by* ~. 그 도로의 특징은 굴곡이 심한 것이다. [→sinus]

sin·u·ous [sínjuəs] *adj.* **1** having many curves; winding. 꾸불꾸불한; 굽이진. ¶ *The path takes a* ~ *course up the hill.* 그 길은 꾸불꾸불한 코스로 산에 오른다. **2** not straight; not honest. 곧지 않은; 부정직한. ¶ *a* ~ *question* 에두르는 질문 / *a* ~ *character* 빙퉁그러진 성질. ● **sin·u·ous·ly** [-li] *adv.* [↓]

si·nus [sáinəs] *n.* Ⓒ (*pl.* **sin·us·es** or **sinus** [sáinju:s]) **1** a cavity in a bone or the skull. 공동(空洞); 두(竇). **2** a long narrow abscess with a small opening. 누(瘻). **3** a curve, bend. 만곡(부). **4** an inlet. 후미; 만(灣). [L. *sinus* recess, hollow]

Si·on [sáiən] *n.* =Zion.

•**sip** [sip] *vt., vi.* (**sipped, sip·ping**) drink (tea, coffee, etc.) slowly and only a very little at a time. (…을) 홀짝이다. ¶ ~ *at the wine* 포도주를 홀짝이다 / *She sipped her tea.* 그녀는 차를 홀짝홀짝 마셨다. — *n.* Ⓒ a very small mouthful of a drink. 한 번 홀짝임. ¶ *take a* ~ 홀짝홀짝 마시다. [E.]

si·phon [sáifən] *n.* Ⓒ **1** a tube or pipe in the shape of U which carries liquid from one level to a lower level by air pressure. 사이펀. **2** a bottle with a tube through which the liquid, such as soda water, is forced by the pressure of the gas in it; a siphon bottle. (탄산수 따위를 넣는) 사이펀 병. — *vt., vi.* (P7;1,2) draw off or pass through a siphon. 사이펀으로 빨아올리다[옮기다]; 사이펀에서 흘러나오다. ¶ ~ *water out of a tank* 탱크에서 사이펀으로 물을 빨아내다. [Gk. =tube]

sip·pet [sípit] *n.* one of the pieces of toast or fried bread served with soup, mince, etc. (구운) 빵조각. [→sop]

!sir [sə:r, sər] *n.* Ⓒ **1** a polite form of address used to a man. 님; 선생님; 귀하; 각하 《손윗사람에 대한 호칭》. ¶ *A boy calls an older man 'Sir'.* 소년은 손위의 남자분에게 'Sir'하고 부른다 / *No,* ~. 그렇지 않습니다 / *Dear Sir* 근계(謹啓)《*Dear Sirs*가 되면 '근계·귀중(貴中)·제위(諸位)'의 뜻, 미국에서는 *Gentlemen*을 대신 쓴다; 보통 상용문의 서두에 씀》. **2** an ironic title. 이봐; 이놈아. **3** 《*S-*》 a title of a knight or baronet. 서; 경(卿) 《영국에서 나이트 작, 준남작의 이름·호칭에 붙임》. ¶ *Sir Walter* (*Scott*) 월터 (스코트) 경 《*Sir Scott*라고는 하지 않음》. [→sire]

sire [sáiər] *n.* Ⓒ **1** a title of respect formerly used in addressing a king or a great noble. 폐하. **2** 《poet.》 a father; an ancestor. 아버지; 조상. **3** (of animals) the male parent. (말 따위의) 아비; 종마 (opp. dam). — *vt.* (P6) be the father of. …을 낳게 하다. [→senior]

si·ren [sáiərən] *n.* Ⓒ **1** a sea nymph, part woman and part bird, who attracted sailors to destruction on the rocks by her singing. 바다의 요정; 반인 반수의 마녀. **2** a beautiful or charming woman who deceives men. 요부(妖婦); 마녀. **3** a device for producing a loud, shrill sound. 사이렌; 경적. ¶ *We heard the sirens of a police car.* 우리는 경찰차의 사이렌 소리를 들었다. — *adj.* of a siren; tempting; charming. 매혹적인. ¶ *a* ~ *song* (*voice*) 매혹적인 노래[목소리]. [Gk.]

si·re·ni·an [saiərí:niən] *n., adj.* 《zool.》 (of) a fish-like aquatic mammal. 해우(海牛)(의).

Sir·i·us [síriəs] *n.* the brightest star in the sky; the Dog Star. 시리우스; 천랑성. [Gk.]

sir·loin [sə́:rlɔin] *n.* ⓊⒸ the part of beef taken from the upper loin. 소의 허리 고기의 윗부분. ¶ *a* ~ *steak* 서로인 스테이크. [sur-[2]]

si·roc·co [sirákou / -rɔ́k-] *n.* Ⓒ (*pl.* **-cos**) **1** a hot, unpleasant wind which blows from Africa to south European countries. 열풍; 시로코 바람《아프리카에서 남유럽

으로 몰아치는 더운 바람》. **2** any hot unpleasant wind. 강열풍. [Arab.]

sir·rah [sírə] *n.* 《*arch.*》《used as a term of address to inferiors》 fellow. 어이; 이놈; 이 자식. ¶ *'Silence, ～!' said the prince to the stable boy.* 왕자는 '조용해라, 이놈!' 하고 어린 마부에게 말했다. [→sir]

sir·up [sírəp, sə́ːr-] *n.* ＝syrup.

sis [sis] *n.* Ⓒ 《U.S. *colloq.*》＝sister.

sis·al [sáisəl, sís-] *n.* Ⓤ a strong, white fiber of a kind of hemp used for making rope; sisal hemp. 사이잘 삼의 섬유; 사이잘 삼. [Place]

sis·sy [sísi] *n.* Ⓒ (*pl.* **-sies**) **1** a sister. 자(姉); 매(妹). **2** a man whose behavior, interests, etc. are like those of a woman. 여자 같은 사내. [↓]

⁝**sis·ter** [sístər] *n.* Ⓒ **1** a girl or woman who has the same parents as another person. 자매; 언니; 누이동생. ¶ *my elder* 〔*younger*〕 ～ 나의 누이〔누이동생〕 / *brother and* ～ 형제와 자매 / *be like sisters* 자매처럼 친밀하다 / *the three* 〔*Fatal*〕 *Sisters* 운명의 3여신. **2** a girl or woman who is a very close friend to another. 자매 같은 사람; 여자 친구. **3** a woman who belongs to the same class, society, church, etc. 여자 동급생; 동지의 여성; 여성 회원. **4** a member of a religious community of women; a nun. 수(도)녀. **5** a nurse, esp. a head nurse in a ward of a hospital. (수)간호사. [E.]

sis·ter·hood [sístərhùd] *n.* **1** Ⓤ the state of being sisters. 자매임. **2** Ⓒ an association of women with a common aim. 여성 단체; 부인회.

sis·ter-in-law [sístərinlɔ̀ː] *n.* Ⓒ (*pl.* **sis·ters-**) a sister of one's husband or wife; the wife of one's brother; the wife of the brother of one's husband or wife. 형수; 계수; 동서; 시누이; 올케; 처형; 처제《따위》.

sis·ter·ly [sístərli] *adj.* like a sister; suitable for a sister; (of women) very kind or intimate. 자매 같은〔다운〕. [E.]

Sis·y·phe·an [sìsəfíːən] *adj.* endless and fruitless. 헛수고의. [Gk.]

⁝**sit** [sit] *v.* (**sat, sit·ting**) *vi.* **1** (P1,2A,3) rest on the lower part of the body; be seated; use a seat. 앉다; 착석하다. ¶ ～ *on* 〔*in*〕 *a chair* 의자에 앉다 / ～ *at table* 식탁에 앉다 / ～ *on the throne* 왕위〔왕좌〕에 오르다. **2** (P1,2A) 《*on*》 (of a bird) come to rest on a branch, etc.; (of some animals) rest on the haunches. (새가) 나뭇가지에 앉다; (개가) 쭈그리고 앉다. ¶ ～ *on a branch* (새가) 나뭇가지에 앉다 / *The dog was sitting on his back legs.* 개가 뒷다리를 쭈그리고 앉아 있었다. **3** (P3) be situated; lie. 위치하다; 가로놓이다. ¶ *The village sits in a hollow.* 그 마을은 분지에 가로놓여 있다 / *The house sits back from the road.* 집은 도로에서 쑥 들어간 곳에 위치하고 있다. **4** (P3) hold a special position of the body for an artist, a photographer, etc.; 《esp. Brit.》 attempt to pass an examination. (초상화·촬영을 위해) 자세를 취하다; 앉다; (시험을) 치르다. ¶ ～ *for a painter* 화가의 모델이 되다 / ～ *for one's portrait* (포즈 따위를 취해서) 초상화를 그리게 하다 / ～ *to a photographer* (사진사로 하여금) 사진을 찍게 하다 / ～ *for one's degree* 학위 시험을 치르다. **5** (P1,2A,3) press or weigh. 압박하다; 고통이 되다. ¶ ～ *heavy on the stomach* 속이 거북하다; 위에 큰 부담이 되다 / *Food at night is likely to* ～ *heavy on one's stomach.* 밤에 먹는 음식은 위에 큰 부담을 주기 쉽다. **6** (P1) (of a committee, Parliament, etc.) be at work; be in session; meet. (의회 따위가) 개회하다. ¶ ～ *on the question of...* …의 문제로 개회하다〔의사를 행하다〕 / *Parliament will* ～ *in the autumn.* 의회는 가을에 개회될 예정이다. **7** (P1,2) have a position as a member; have a seat officially; take a seat in an official assembly. (의회 따위의) 일원이 되다; 벼슬〔직위〕에 앉다. ¶ ～ *in Congress* 국회 의원이 되다 / ～ *as a member of the committee* 위원회의 일원이 되다 / *The judge will not* ～ *on Saturday.* 판사는 토요일엔 재판하지 않는다. **8** (P2A) (of clothes) fit; suit. (옷 따위가) 어울리다; 맞다. ¶ *Your coat does not* ～ *in the shoulders.* 네 코트는 어깨가 맞지 않는다 / *The dress does not* ～ *well on her.* 그 옷은 그녀에게 잘 어울리지 않는다. **9** (of a bird) cover eggs so as to make young come out. (새가) 알을 품다. ¶ *The hens are sitting* (*on eggs*) *now.* 암탉들은 지금 알을 품고 있다.

— *vt.* (P6,7) **1** cause (someone) to sit; seat. …을 앉히다; 착석시키다. ¶ *He sat her on his right.* 그는 그녀를 그의 오른쪽에 앉혔다. **2** ride (a horse). (말·보트 따위를) 타다. ¶ *She sits her horse well.* 그녀는 말을 잘 탄다. [E.]

make one sit up, 《*colloq.*》 subject him to hard work, pain, surprise, etc. 아무를 깜짝 놀라게 하다; 혹사하다.

sit around, stay at home doing nothing. (집에서) 빈둥거리다.

sit at home, be inactive. 한거(閑居)하다.

sit back, remain inactive; relax. (수수)방관하다; (일을 끝낸 후) 긴장을 풀다.

sit down, take a seat. 앉다; 자리잡다.

sit down under, accept (an insult, etc.) without complaint. (모욕 따위)를 감수하다.

sit for, **a**) 《esp. Brit.》 take (an examination); take a formal examination for. 시험을 치르다. ¶ ～ *for an examination* 시험을 치르다. **b**) be a member of Parliament for (a district); represent. 의회 의원이 되다; (선거구를) 대표하다.

sit in, 《*colloq.*》 take part in (a conference, etc.). (회의 따위에) 참가하다. ¶ *be invited to* ～ *in on a rehearsal* 리허설에 참가하도록 초대받다.

sit in judgment, assume the right of

judging others, be censorious. …을 제멋대로 비판하다.

sit on* 〔*upon*〕*, **a**) meet in judgment on (a case, etc.); investigate. …에 관하여 협의하다; …을 조사하다. ¶ *~ on a case* 위원으로서 사건을 조사하다 / *~ on a jury* 배심원으로 있다. **b**) 《*colloq.*》 rebuke; check. 꾸짖다; 제지하다. ¶ *~ on a rude person* 무례한 사람을 나무라다.

sit out, **a**) stay later than (another); stay until the end of (something). (다른 방문객보다) 오래 머물다; …의 끝까지 있다. ¶ *~ out a play* 연극을 마지막까지 보다 / *Which of the visitors will ~ out the other?* 방문객들 중 어느 방문객이 가장 오래 남아 있겠느냐. **b**) remain seated during (a dance); refuse to participate in (something). (댄스 파티 따위에서) 춤을 추지 않다; (일에) 참가〔관여〕하지 않다. ¶ *~ out a rumba* 〔*waltz*〕 룸바〔왈츠〕를 추지 않고 빼먹다 / *~ out any war* 어떤 전쟁에도 참전하지 않다.

sit through, stay to the end of. …의 끝까지 있다. ¶ *It is painful to ~ through a long sermon.* 기나긴 설교를 끝까지 듣기란 고통스럽다.

sit under, attend the sermons of (someone); study under (a teacher). …의 설교를 듣다.

sit up, **a**) not go to bed till late. (늦게까지) 잠자지 않고 일어나 있다. ¶ *~ up all night playing cards* 카드놀이하느라 밤을 새다. **b**) raise the body to an erect sitting position. 똑바로〔단정히〕 앉다. ¶ *~ up in bed* (환자 따위가) 침대에서 일어나 앉다 / *All the pupils sat up when the teacher came in.* 선생님께서 들어오셨을 때 학생들은 단정히 앉았다. **c**) 《*colloq.*》 be surprised or startled. 깜짝 놀라다. ¶ *Her dress made us all ~ up.* 그녀의 옷은 우리 모두를 깜짝 놀라게 하였다.

sit well on, suit; fit. …에 잘 맞다〔어울리다〕.

sit-down strike [sítdaun stràik] *n.* a strike in which the workers do not work at all but instead remain idle until their demands are satisfied. 연좌 파업〔스트라이크〕. [*sit*]

***site** [sait] *n.* Ⓒ **1** a piece of land to build a house on; the place where something is located. 부지(敷地); 용지(用地). ¶ *buy a ~ for building* 건물용 부지를 매입하다. **2** the place where something has happened. 유적; 장소; 위치. ¶ *the ~ of the battle of Waterloo* 워털루 전투의 유적 / *the ~ of recent fire* 최근의 화재가 있었던 장소. [L. *situs* position]

sit·ter [sítər] *n.* Ⓒ **1** a person who sits. 착석자(着席者). **2** a person who is hired to take care of a child or children while the parents are away, esp. in the evening; a baby sitter. 어린애 돌보는 사람. **3** a bird that sits on eggs in order to hatch them. 알을 품고 앉아 있는 새〔닭〕. [*sit*]

sit·ting [sítiŋ] *n.* Ⓒ **1 a**) the act of one who sits. 착석; 앉음. **b**) the act of posing for one's portrait, etc. 초상화의 모델이 됨. ¶ *give a ~ to a photographer* 사진 작가의 모델로 한 번 앉다 / *finish a portrait in three sittings* 세 번의 모델 앉기로 초상화를 끝내다. **c**) the time of remaining seated, as in posing, in reading, or in doing some work. (작업·독서 따위를) 앉은 채로〔일정한 상태대로〕 계속하는 시간. ¶ *finish a job at a* 〔*one*〕 *~* 일을 단번에 끝내다. **2** a session or meeting of a court, legislature, etc. 개회; 개정(開廷); 회기. **3** a group of eggs on which a bird is sitting in order to hatch them. 포란(抱卵); 포란수(數). [*sit*]

at a* 〔*one*〕 *sitting, without rest; all at once. 단번에; 단숨에. [*sit*]

***sitting room** [⌐-⌐] *n.* **1** a living room. 거실. **2** space sufficient to sit in. 들어가 앉기에 충분한 공간. ¶ *~ for two persons only* 겨우 두 사람이 들어가 앉을 수 있는 공간.

***sit·u·at·ed** [sítʃuèitid] *adj.* located; placed. …에 위치하고 있는; …에 있는. ¶ *Seoul is situated in the center of Korea.* 서울은 한국의 중앙에 위치하고 있다 / *be awkwardly ~* 난처한 입장에 있다 / *His family were well ~.* 그의 가족들은 유복하였다. [↓]

:**sit·u·a·tion** [sìtʃuéiʃən] *n.* Ⓒ **1** a place or position; a site; a locality. 장소; 위치. ¶ *the ~ of a hospital* 병원의 위치 / *a delightful ~ for a house* 집을 짓기에 좋은 장소. **2** a condition of being situated; a place or position of an object in relation to its environment. 상태; 위치; 입장. ¶ *I am in a dangerous ~.* 나는 위험한 상태에 처해 있다 / *He found himself in an embarrassing ~.* 그는 난처한 입장에 처하게 되었다 / *come out of a difficult ~ with credit* 어려운 처지에서 훌륭하게 빠져 나오다. **3** a condition; a case. 경우. **4** a combination of circumstances; the state of affairs. 사태; 국면; 상황. ¶ *the political ~* 정국 / *the international ~* 국제 정세 / *save the ~* 사태를 수습하다. **5** a place to work; a job. 일자리; 일. ¶ *find a ~ as a maid* 가정부로서의 일자리를 구하다 / *be in* 〔*out of*〕 *a ~* 취직〔실직〕해 있다. [→site]

:**six** [siks] *n.* **1** Ⓤ the number between five and seven; 6. 여섯. ¶ *half-past ~* (*o'clock*), 6시 30분 / *a child of ~* 여섯 살의 아이. **2** Ⓒ (in volleyball, etc.) any group or set of six persons or things. 6인〔6개〕 일조의 것. ¶ *a party of ~* 6인조. **3** Ⓒ anything shaped like 6. 6자 모양의 것.

at sixes and sevens, in great confusion; in disagreement. 혼란하여; 의견이 일치되지 않아.

It is six of one and half a dozen of the other. There is no real difference. 오십보 백보; 비슷비슷하다.

— *adj.* of 6; amounting to six. 여섯의; 여섯 개의; 6인의. ¶ *~ feet high* 6피트 높이 / ~

years old 여섯 살. [E.]

six-fold [síksfòuld] *adj.* **1** six times as much or as many. 여섯 배의. **2** having six parts. 여섯 겹의. — *adv.* six times as much or as many. 여섯 배로(겹으로).

six·foot·er [síksfútər] *n.* Ⓒ a person or thing that is six feet tall. 신장 6피트의 사람; 높이 6피트의 것.

six·pence [síkspəns] *n.* **1** Ⓒ a small silver coin of Great Britain worth half a shilling. 6펜스의 은화. ¶ *He put two sixpences in the slot.* 그는 자동 판매기에 두 개의 6펜스 은화를 넣었다. **2** Ⓤ six British pennies. 6 펜스. ¶ *It costs* ~. 그것은 6펜스이다. **3** 《*negative*》 a bit. 아주 적은 값; 조금. ¶ *It doesn't matter* ~. 그것은 별것 아니다; 그런 일은 아무래도 좋다 / *I don't care* ~ *about it.* 조금도 상관(개의치) 않는다.

six·pen·ny [síkspəni, -pèni] *adj.* **1** worth or costing sixpence. 6 펜스의. **2** of little value. 하찮은; 값싼.

six-shoot·er [síksʃúːtər] *n.* Ⓒ a revolver which can fire six shots without reloading. 6 연발 권총.

:six·teen [sìkstíːn] *n.* Ⓤ the number between fifteen and seventeen; 16. 열여섯. — *adj.* of 16. 열여섯의.

:six·teenth [sìkstíːnθ] *n.* **1** 《usu. *the* ~ 》 the number 16; 16th. 제16; 열여섯 번째. **2** Ⓒ one of the 16 equal parts of anything. 16분의 1. ¶ *An ounce is one* ~ *of a pound.* 1온스는 1 파운드의 16분의 1이다. — *adj.* of the 16th. 제16의; 열여섯 번째의; 16분의 1의.

:sixth [siksθ] *n.* **1** 《usu. *the* ~ 》 the number 6; 6th. 제 6; 여섯 번째. **2** Ⓒ one of six equal parts of anything. 6분의 1. — *adj.* of the 6th. 제6의; 여섯 번째의; 6분의 1의. ¶ *Friday is the* ~ *day of the week.* 금요일은 1주일 중 여섯 번째의 날이다.

:six·ti·eth [síkstiiθ] *n.* **1** 《usu. *the* ~ 》 the number 60; 60th. 제 60; 육십 번째. **2** Ⓒ one of 60 equal parts of anythings. 60분의 1. — *adj.* of the 60th. 제 60 의; 육십 번째의; 60 분의 1 의.

six·ty [síksti] *n.* Ⓤ six times ten; 60. 육십. ¶ *Not more than* ~ *(persons) were present.* 기껏 60명 정도가 참석했다 / *I'll give you* ~ *won for it.* 그것 값으로 60원을 주겠다. — *adj.* of 60. 60 의.

a sixty four (thousand) dollar question, 《*colloq.*》 a question whose correct answer brings a big prize; a very important question. 중요한 문제《큰 상을 주는 TV·라디오의 퀴즈 프로에서》.

siz·a·ble [sáizəbəl] *adj.* rather large; of a considerable size. 꽤 큰. [*size*]

:size[1] [saiz] *n.* **1** Ⓤ the bigness or amount of a thing; scale; bulk. (물건의) 크기; 양; 규모; 부피. ¶ *of natural* ~ …의 실물 크기 / *a medium* ~ 중간 크기 / *the* ~ *of an industry* 사업의 규모 / *of some* ~ 꽤 큰 / *take the* ~ *of* …의 치수를 재다 / *the* ~ *of an apple* 사과 하나의 크기 / *a crowd of considerable* ~ 상당한 규모의 군중 / *This book is the same* ~ *as that.* 이 책은 그것과 같은 크기이다 / *Size matters less than quality.* 크기보다는 질이 중요하다. **2** Ⓒ one of a series of measures for articles. 치수; 사이즈. ¶ *children's* ~ 아동용 치수(사이즈) / *shoes of* ~ *5,* 사이즈 5의 구두 / *a hat two sizes larger* 두 치수만큼 큰 모자 / *What* ~ *is it?* 그것의 치수는 얼마지 / *What* ~ *do you take (want) in gloves?* 원하시는 장갑의 치수는 얼마인가요 / *The* ~ *of card I want is 3 by 5 inches.* 내가 원하는 카드의 치수는 3×5 인치입니다. **3** Ⓤ intellectual ability or force of character. 역량; 수완. ¶ *a man of considerable* ~ 상당한 역량의 사람. **4** 《*colloq.*》 the actual condition; the truth. 실상; 진상. ¶ *That's about the* ~ *of it.* 대체로 그것이 진상이다.

be of a size (all sizes), be of the same size (various sizes). 모두 같은(갖가지의) 크기이다.

life size(d), a full-size. 실물(등신)대의.

of a size, equal in size. 같은 크기의.

of some size, fairly large. 상당히 큰.

take the size up, take one's measure. 치수를 재다.

— *vt.* (P7) **1** arrange or separate (things) according to size. …을 크기에 따라 분류하다. **2** make (something) in a certain size. …을 어떤 크기로 만들다. [→assize]

size up, **a**) measure the size of (something). …의 치수를 재다. **b**) form an opinion or a judgment of (someone) conclude. (인물·상황 따위)를 평가(판단)하다. ¶ ~ *up the situation* 상황을 판단하다.

size[2] [saiz] *n.* Ⓤ special material made from glue, starch, etc., used for coating paper, cloth, etc. 반수(礬水); 아교 포수. — *vt.* (P6) coat or treat (something) with size. …에 반수를 먹이다. [↑]

siz·zle [sízəl] *vi.* make a hissing sound such as oil in a very hot frying pan does. (튀김 따위를 할 때 기름이) 지글지글 소리를 내다; 지글거리다. — *n.* 《*sing.* only》 a hissing sound. 지글지글하는 소리. [Imit.]

skald, scald [skɔːld] *n.* an ancient Scandinavian poet and singer of long ago. (옛 스칸디나비아의) 음송(吟誦) 시인. [N.]

:skate[1] [skeit] *n.* Ⓒ 《usu. *pl.*》 **1** a frame with a steel blade fixed to a shoe so that a person wearing it can glide over ice. 스케이트. ¶ *go for a* ~ 스케이트를 타러 가다. **2** a plate with wheels for gliding over any smooth surface; a roller skate. 롤러 스케이트(구두). — *vi.* (P1,2A) 《*over*》 glide on skates. 스케이트를 타다. ¶ *Let's* ~ *to the corner.* 저 코너까지 스케이트를 타고 가자. [F.=stilt]

skate over thin ice, deal with a problem which is very hard to solve. 어려운 문제를 다루다.

skate[2] [skeit] *n.* 《fish》 a kind of broad, flat fish. 홍어의 일종 [N.]

skat·er [skéitər] *n.* Ⓒ a person who skates. 스케이트를 타는 사람. [*skate*[1]]

skat·ing [skéitiŋ] *n.* the art or sport of moving on skates. 얼음지치기; 스케이트 타기.

skat·ing rink [⌐— ⌐] *n.* Ⓒ **1** a floor for roller skating. 롤러 스케이트장(場). **2** a smooth stretch of ice for skating. 아이스 스케이트장.

ske·dad·dle [skidǽdl] *vi.* (P1) flee; make off. 도망치다. — *n.* flight. 도주. [?]

skein [skein] *n.* Ⓒ a small bundle of yarn or thread. 실타래. [F.]

skel·e·tal [skélətl] *adj.* of forming, or related to a skeleton; like a skeleton. 골격〔해골〕의. [↓]

skel·e·ton [skélətn] *n.* Ⓒ **1** the bony framework of a man or an animal. 골격; 해골. ¶ *Of the body nothing was left but the* ~. 몸체는 아무것도 없고 남은 것이라곤 해골뿐이었다. **2** a very thin person or animal. 뼈만 앙상한 사람〔동물〕. ¶ *be reduced to a* ~ 매우 수척해지다 / *a mere living* ~ 피골이 상접한 사람. **3** the supporting framework of a building, a ship, etc. (배·가옥 따위의) 골조; 뼈대. ¶ *the steel* ~ *of a building* 건물의 (앙상한) 철골. **4** an outline or general idea for anything. 골자; 윤곽; 개략. [Gk. *skellō* parch]

***a skeleton in the cupboard* 〔*closet*〕,** something that a family tries to keep secret because of shame. (밖에 알려지기를 꺼리는) 한 집안의 비밀.

***skeleton at the feast* 〔*banquet*〕,** a thing that alloys pleasure. 흥을 깨뜨리는 것.

***skeleton crew* 〔*regiment*〕,** staff with few men. 기간 요원〔승무원〕; 연대의 간부.

skel·e·ton·ize [skélətənàiz] *vt.* (P6) **1** reduce to a skeleton. 해골로 만들다. **2** abstract by destroying the flesh. 개요를 적다; 요약하다.

skeleton key [⌐—— ⌐] *n.* a key which is made to open many locks. (여러 자물쇠에 맞는) 곁쇠.

skep·tic [sképtik] *n.* Ⓒ a person who cannot help questioning any fact or theory; a person who doubts the truth of a religious belief. 회의론자; 종교적 회의론자. — *adj.* =skeptical. [Gk. *skeptomai* examine]

skep·ti·cal [sképtikəl] *adj.* inclined to doubt the truth of any facts or theories; not believing anything easily. 의심 많은; 회의적인.

skep·ti·cism [sképtəsìzəm] *n.* Ⓤ **1** skeptical attitude. 회의적인 태도. **2** doubt or unbelief with regard to a religion. 종교적 회의.

•**sketch** [sketʃ] *n.* Ⓒ **1** a drawing made simply and quickly. 스케치; 사생화; 밑그림. **2** a rough draft; an outline. 초고; 초안; 소묘(素描); 개략. **3** a short description, story, stage play, etc. 소품문(小品文); 단편 각본. — *vt.* (P6) **1** make a sketch of (something). …을 스케치하다. ¶ ~ *someone's head* 아무의 머리를 스케치하다. **2** explain (something) briefly and quickly. …을 개설〔개략〕하다. ¶ ~ *out a plan* 계획의 개요를 작성하다. — *vi.* (P1,3) make a sketch. 스케치하다. ¶ ~ *from nature* 사생하다 / *go sketching* 사생하러 가다. [It. *schizzo*]

sketch·book [skétʃbùk] *n.* Ⓒ **1** a book of drawing paper for sketches. 사생화첩; 스케치북. **2** a book of short stories, essays, etc. 소품집(小品集); 단편집; 수필집.

sketch·y [skétʃi] *adj.* (**sketch·i·er, sketch·i·est**) **1** like a sketch. 스케치 같은〔모양의〕. **2** showing only outlines; imperfect; done incompletely. 대략만의; 피상적인; 미완성의. ¶ *a* ~ *meal* 빈약한 식사 / *only a* ~ *knowledge of philology* 언어학의 피상적인 얕은 지식.

skew [skju:] *adj.* **1** slanting; twisted. 비스듬한; 비뚤어진. **2** not symmetrical. 대칭적이 아닌. — *n.* Ⓒ a slant; a twist. 비뚤어짐; 비스듬함. — *vt., vi.* give a slanting form to (something); twist; turn aside. 비뚤어지게 하다〔비뚤어지다〕; 구부리다〔굽다〕. [F.]

skew·er [skjú:ər] *n.* Ⓒ a wooden or metal pin to hold meat together while cooking. 꼬치; 구이용 꼬챙이. — *vt.* (P6) fasten (meat, fish, etc.) with or as if with a skewer. …을 꼬챙이에 꿰다. [E.]

:ski [ski:] *n.* Ⓒ (*pl.* **skis** or **ski**) one of a pair of long, narrow pieces of wood, metal or plastic, to be fastened to the shoes for gliding over snow. 스키; 스키 용구(用具). — *vi.* (P1) move over snow on skis. 스키로 활주하다; 스키를 타다. [N.]

skid [skid] *n.* Ⓒ **1** a frame, a rail, etc. on which heavy objects roll or slide. (트럭 따위에서 무거운 짐을 하역할 때 걸치는) 활재(滑材); 침목(枕木). **2** a piece of wood or metal used to prevent a wheel from going around. 제륜〔제동〕기; 미끄럼막이; 제동용 쐐기.

— *v.* (**skid·ded, skid·ding**) *vi.* (P1) slip or slide sideways suddenly. 옆으로 미끄러지다. ¶ *The car skidded on the wet road.* 자동차가 젖은 도로 위에서 옆으로 미끄러졌다.

— *vt.* (P6,7) **1** pull (something heavy) on a rail, a timber, etc. …을 굴림대 위에서 끌다. **2** prevent (a wheel, etc.) from turning around by means of a skid. …에 미끄럼 방지용 쐐기를 끼우다. [Scand.]

ski·er [skí:ər] *n.* Ⓒ a person who skis. 스키를 타는 사람. [*ski*]

skiff [skif] *n.* Ⓒ a small light rowboat. 소형의 노로 젓는 보트. [Teut. (ship)]

ski·ing [skí:iŋ] *n.* the art or sport of traveling on skis. 스키 타기; 스키술(術)〔경기〕. [*ski*]

ski jump [ㅅㄴ] *n.* **1** a jump that is made by a skier. 스키 점프. **2** a place for jumping with skis. 스키 점프 경기장.

***skil·ful** [skílfəl] *adj.* 《Brit.》 =skillful.

skil·ful·ly [skílfəli] *adv.* 《Brit.》 =skillfully.

skil·ful·ness [skílfəlnis] *n.* 《Brit.》 =skillfulness.

:skill [skil] *n.* Ⓤ the ability to do something very well as a result of long practice; cleverness. 숙련; 노련; 교묘; 능숙; 솜씨. ¶ *the skills of swimming and driving* 수영과 운전의 솜씨 / *a man of* ~ 노련한 사람 / *He plays the violin with* ~. 그는 바이올린을 능숙하게 연주한다 / *She has great* ~ *in painting.* 그녀는 미술에 뛰어난 솜씨가 있다 / *have no* ~ *to manage* 관리가 서투르다. [N. =distinction, difference]

have no skill in (=*be unable to do*) *something.* …을 할 수 없다; …이 서투르다.

***skilled** [skíld] *adj.* **1** able to do something well; trained; expert; skillful. 숙련된; 교묘한; 노련한. ¶ *a* ~ *workman* 숙련된 일꾼 / *a* ~ *politician* 노련한 정치가 / *be* ~ *in business* 〔*drawing*〕 사업을〔그림 그리기를〕 잘하다. **2** requiring skill. 숙련〔기술〕을 요하는. ¶ ~ *labor* 숙련 노동 / ~ *hands* 숙련공.

skil·let [skílit] *n.* Ⓒ **1** a small, shallow pan for frying; a frying pan. 프라이팬. **2** a long-handled saucepan. (손잡이가 긴) 스튜 냄비. [→scuttle[1]]

***skill·ful,** 《Brit.》 **skil-** [skílfəl] *adj.* having expert training; clever; experienced. 능숙〔능란〕한; 교묘한; 숙련된; 솜씨 좋은. ¶ *a* ~ *carpenter* 솜씨 좋은 목공 / *be* ~ *in teaching* 가르치는 요령이〔솜씨가〕 좋다 / *be* ~ *at dancing* 춤의 솜씨가 훌륭하다 / *a* ~ *production* 교묘한 제품 / *a* ~ *piece of work* 숙련된 솜씨로 만들어진 하나의 작품. [*skill*]

skill·ful·ly, 《Brit.》 **skil-** [skílfəli] *adv.* with skill. 능숙하게; 교묘히; 솜씨 있게.

skill·ful·ness 《Brit.》 **skil-** [skílfəlnis] *n.* Ⓤ the state of being skillful. 교묘; 숙련; 훌륭한 솜씨.

***skim** [skim] *v.* (**skimmed, skim·ming**) *vt.* **1** (P6,7,13) take off floating substances from the surface of (liquid); take up (something) from the surface of liquid. (액체의) 표면에 뜬 것을 걷어내다; …을 액체의 표면에서 취하다. ¶ ~ *the cream from* 〔*off*〕 (*the*) *milk* 우유 표면에 뜬 크림을 걷어내다 / ~ *milk to get cream* 크림을 우유의 표면에서 걷어내다. **2** (P6) move or glide over or along (the surface). (…의 표면을) 스쳐 지나가다; 미끄러지듯 가다. ¶ *A bird skimmed the water.* 새가 수면 위를 스치듯 날아갔다 / *A skater skims the ice.* 스케이트 타는 사람이 얼음 위를 미끄러지듯 지나간다. **3** (P6) read (a book, etc.) quickly or carelessly. (책을) 대충 훑어 읽다. ¶ ~ *one's report* 보고서를 대충 훑어보다 / *I skimmed the book.* 나는 그 책을 대충 훑어보았다.

— *vi.* **1** (P2A,3) pass or glide quickly over a surface. 표면을 스쳐〔미끄러지듯〕 지나가다. ¶ *The skater were skimming over the ice.* 스키 타는 사람이 얼음 위를 미끄러지듯 지나갔다 / *The swallows went skimming by.* 제비가 스치듯 지나갔다. **2** (P3) read quickly or carelessly. 대강 훑어 읽다〔보다〕. ¶ ~ *through a book* 책을 대강 훑어 읽다 / ~ *over a newspaper* 신문을 대강 훑어보다. **3** 《U.S.》 become covered with a thin film. 피막이 생기다.

skim the cream (***off milk***), take the best part off a thing. 우유로부터 크림을 취하다; 가장 좋은 것을 취하다.

skim the surface, deal with a thing superficially. 표면적〔피상적〕으로 다루다.

— *n.* Ⓒ floating substances. 웃더껑이(를 걷어내기). [→scum]

skim·mer [skímər] *n.* Ⓒ **1** a person who skims liquids; a thing used in skimming liquids. 더껑이를 걷어내는 사람〔도구〕. **2** a long-handled shallow ladle, full of holes, used in skimming liquids. 그물 국자; 석자. **3** a kind of sea bird with long wings. 제비갈매기류. [↑]

skim milk [ㅅㅅ] *n.* milk from which the cream has already been taken away. 탈지유(脫脂乳).

skim·ming [skímiŋ] *n.* **1** Ⓤ the act of skimming milk. etc. 더껑이를 걷어냄. **2** Ⓒ the cream obtained by skimming milk. 걷어낸 크림.

skimp [skimp] *vi.* (P1) be very economical; be thrifty. 매우 절약〔검약〕하다. ¶ ~ *and screw* 인색하게 굴다 / *We had to* ~ *to save for a new house.* 새로운 집을 마련하기 위한 저축을 하기 위해 절약하지 않으면 안 되었다. — *vt.* (P6) **1** do not supply (something) enough of. …을 인색하게 굴다〔아끼다〕. ¶ ~ *the butter in making a cake* 케이크를 만드는 데 버터를 인색하게 아끼다. **2** do poorly or carelessly. (일 따위를) 날림으로 하다; 겉날리다. [→scrimp]

skimp·y [skímpi] *adj.* (**skimp·i·er, skimp·i·est**) not rich or large enough; narrow. 불충분한; 빈약한; 좁은; 인색한. ¶ *a* ~ *skirt* (몸에) 꽉 끼는 스커트.

:skin [skin] *n.* ⓊⒸ **1** the outer cover of the body in persons and animals. (인간·동물의) 피부; 가죽; 껍질. ¶ *have a clear* 〔*fair*〕 ~ 피부가 아름답다〔희다〕 / *the inner* 〔*outer*〕 ~ 진〔외〕피 / *cast the* ~ (뱀 따위가) 허물을 벗다 / *be wet to the* ~ (옷 속까지) 흠뻑 젖다 / *Cows have thick skins.* 소는 가죽이 두껍다. **2** a cover of an animal after it has been removed from the body. (동물의) 생피(生皮); 피혁; (깔개로 쓰는) 수피(獸皮). **3** anything like a skin; the outer cover of a piece of fruit; bark. (과일 따위의) 껍질; (곡물 따위의) 겉껍질; (선체의) 외판(外板). ¶ *the* ~ *of an apple* 사과 껍질 / *He slipped on a banana* ~. 그는 바나나 껍질을 벗겼다.

4 Ⓒ a bag made of skin in which water, wine, etc. is kept. 가죽으로 만든 것; 가죽 부대《물·술통 따위》.

be in one's skin, be in one's stead. 아무의 입장이 되다.

be only skin and bone, be very thin. 몹시 마르다; 피골이 상접하다.

by 〔***with***〕 ***the skin of one's teeth,*** just barely; very narrowly; only just. 겨우; 가까스로; 간신히. ¶ *He escaped death by the ~ of his teeth.* 그는 간신히 죽음을 모면했다.

change one's skin, be metamorphosed. 성격을 바꾸다.

get under someone's skin, 《*sl.*》 **a**) anger or irritate someone. 아무를 성나게〔애타게〕 하다. **b**) take hold of someone's mind; affect someone deeply. 아무의 마음을 사로잡다.

have a thin 〔***thick***〕 ***skin,*** be easily 〔not easily〕 hurt or offended; be sensitive 〔not sensitive〕 to criticism, etc. 민감〔둔감〕하다.

jump 〔***fly***〕 ***out of one's skin,*** forget oneself because of joy, etc. (기쁨 따위로) 자신을 잊다.

save one's skin, save one's life; avoid injury. 무사히 도망하다; 위험을 피하다.

with 〔***in***〕 ***a whole skin,*** without harm; safely. 무사히.

— *v.* (**skinned, skin·ning**) *vt.* **1** (P6) remove or strip the skin from (something). …의 가죽〔껍질〕을 벗기다. ¶ ~ *a rabbit* 토끼의 가죽을 벗기다 / ~ *a banana* 바나나의 껍질을 벗기다. **2** (P6) cover (something) with skin. (상처 따위를) 살갗〔피막〕으로 덮다. ¶ *My wound is skinned* (*over*). 나의 상처는 새살이 나와 아물었다 / *be skinned with steel* 강철로 덮여 있다. **3** (P6,7) rub off a small piece of skin from (something). (피부를) 까지게〔벗어지게〕 하다; (표면·외피·얇은 막 따위를) 떼어〔벗겨〕내다. ¶ ~ *a stamp* 우표를 떼어내다. **4** (P6,13) 《*colloq.*》《*of, out of*》 take something from (someone) by a dishonest act. …로부터 빼앗다〔사취하다〕.

— *vi.* (P2A) become covered with skin. 피부로〔가죽으로, 껍질로〕 덮이다. ¶ *The wound has skinned over too quickly.* 상처는 (피부가) 너무나 빨리 아물었다. [N.]

keep one's eyes skinned, 《*sl.*》 be watchful or cautious. 눈을 부릅뜨고 지켜 보다.

skin-deep [skíndíːp] *adj.* **1** on the surface of the skin. (상처 따위가) 깊지 않은; 피부의 겉면만의. **2** shallow; slight. 얕은; 피상적인.

skin diver [´ ´–] *n.* an under water swimmer equipped with an aqualung, etc. 스킨 다이버.

skin diving [´ ´–] *n.* the sport of diving into the water with an aqualung. 스킨 다이빙.

skin·flint [skínflìnt] *n.* a mean, stingy person; a miser. 구두쇠; 인색한 사람.

skin·ful [skínfùl] *n.* (*pl.* **-s**) **1** contents of a wine-skinful. 가죽 부대〔주머니〕 가득. **2** as much liquor as one can hold. 배불리 잔뜩; 과음.

skin·ner [skínər] *n.* Ⓒ a person who deals in skins, furs, etc. 피혁상(皮革商).

skin·ny [skíni] *adj.* (**-ni·er, -ni·est**) **1** very thin; very lean. 바싹 여윈〔마른〕; 뼈와 가죽만 남은. **2** of or like skin. 가죽 모양의; 피질(皮質)의. ● **skin·ni·ness** [-nis] *n.*

·**skip** [skip] *v.* (**skipped, skip·ping**) *vi.* **1** (P1,2A,3) jump or spring lightly and quickly, as children do. (어린아이 따위가) 뛰어다니다; 깡충깡충 뛰(놀)다; 까불다. ¶ *Lambs are skipping in the fields.* 어린 양들이 들판에서 깡충깡충 뛰놀고 있다. **2** (P1,2A) hurry along in reading, omitting some parts of a book. 여기저기 빼먹고〔건너뛰어〕 읽다. ¶ *He skips as he reads.* 여기저기 빼먹고 읽는다. **3** jump lightly over a rope. 줄넘기를 하다. **4** (P2A,3) 《*out of*》 《*colloq.*》 run away rapidly and secretly. 도망치다. ¶ ~ *out of town* 마을에서 도망치다. **5** (P3) 《*over*》 pass along rapidly; travel quickly. 서둘러 통과〔여행〕하다. ¶ ~ *over to France for a week* 1주일 동안 서둘러서 프랑스를 여행하다.

— *vt.* (P6) **1** jump lightly over (something). …을 (살짝) 뛰어넘다. ¶ ~ *a fence* 담장을 살짝 뛰어넘다. **2** omit (some parts of a book). …을 건너뛰다; 빼먹다. ¶ *She skipped difficult words in reading.* 그녀는 어려운 낱말들을 건너뛰고 읽었다 / *I shall ~ the events of the next few days.* 다음 2, 3일간의 사건들은 생략하겠다. **3** fail to notice (something). …을 (못 보고) 빠뜨리다; 놓치다; …을 눈치채지 못하다. **4** 《*colloq.*》 leave (a place) rapidly and secretly. …을 (몰래) 빠져 나가다; …에서 도망치다. ¶ *He skipped his home town one night.* 그는 그의 고향을 야간 도주하였다.

— *n.* Ⓒ a light, quick, gay and dancing jump. (가볍게) 뜀; 도약. [E.]

skip·jack [skípdʒæ̀k] *n.* a jumping toy. 오뚝이류의 장난감.

skip·per[1] [skípər] *n.* Ⓒ **1** a captain of a small ship. (작은 상선·어선의) 선장. **2** a captain or leader of a cricket team, etc. (크리켓 따위에서) 한 팀의 주장. [Du. (ship)]

skip·per[2] [skípər] *n.* Ⓒ **1** a person or an insect that skips. 뛰는 사람〔벌레〕. **2** a butterfly that makes short, swift flights. 팔랑나비. [*skip*]

skipper's daughters [´– ´–] *n.* 《*fig.*》 tall white-crested waves. 높은 흰 파도.

skirl [skəːrl] *n.* Ⓒ a sound of bagpipes. 풍적(風笛)의 소리; 백파이프의 소리. [O.N.]

skir·mish [skə́ːrmiʃ] *n.* Ⓒ a slight and brief fight between small groups of soldier; any slight conflict or argument. (소부대간의) 작은 전투〔충돌〕; 승강이. — *vi.* (P1) (of small groups of soldiers) quarrel and fight; take part in a skirmish. 작은 전투를〔충돌을, 승강이를〕 하다. [It. *scaramuccia*]

:skirt [skə:rt] *n.* Ⓒ **1** a woman's or girl's outer garment hanging from the waist; the lower part of a coat, dress, etc. (여성의) 스커트; (일반적으로) 코트 따위의 아랫부분. **2** an edge; a border. 가장자리; 가; 테두리. **3** 《*pl.*》 the suburbs; the outer part of a place. 교외; 변두리. ¶ *Mr. Smith lives on the skirts of the town.* 스미스 씨는 도시 교외에 살고 있다.

— *vt.* (P6) **1** form the border or edge of; surround. …와 접경하다; …을 둘러싸다. ¶ *The road skirts the wood.* 도로가 숲을 둘러싸고 있다. **2** pass along the edge of (a place or a group of people); pass around instead of crossing. …의 가장자리를 지나다. ¶ *~ a forest* 숲의 가장자리를 지나다 / *~ a town to avoid heavy traffic* 교통 체증을 피하기 위해 도시 가장자리를 지나다 / *~ the issue* 논쟁이 될 문제를 피하다. [N. (shirt)]

skirt·ing [skə́:rtiŋ] *n.* material for making skirts. 스커트 감.

skirt·ing-board [skə́:rtiŋbɔ:rd] *n.* the board along the bottom of the wall of a room. 굽도리널; 걸레받이.

skit [skit] *n.* Ⓒ a short humorous sketch, esp. used or performed on a stage. 가벼운 풍자; 짧은 희극; 촌극. [↓]

skit·tish [skítiʃ] *adj.* **1** (of a horse, etc.) easily frightened. (말 따위가) 놀라기 잘하는. ¶ *a ~ horse* 잘 놀라는 말. **2** shy; coy. 암띤; 수줍어하는. **3** fickle; changeable. 변덕스런. [Scand.]

skit·tle [skítl] *vt.* (P7) **1** 《*away*》 waste. 낭비하다. **2** 《*out*》 get the batsman out quickly. (크리켓에서) 타자를 잇달아 아웃시키다. [?]

skit·tles [skítlz] *n. pl.* 《used as *sing.*》 a game in which a ball or disk is used to knock down ninepins. (영국식) 구주희(九柱戲). [Scand.]

beer and skittles, fun; pleasure; amusement; idle enjoyment. 즐거움; 재미; 무사 태평한 삶. ¶ *Life is not all beer and ~.* 인생은 즐겁기만 한 것이 아니다.

Skittles ! Nonsense ! 덜된 소리; 시시하다.

Skr., Skt. Sanskrit.

sku·a [skjú:ə] *n.* 《bird》 a large gull. 도둑갈매기. [N.]

skulk [skʌlk] *vi.* (P1) hide to avoid duties, dangers, etc. in a cowardly way; move stealthily with an evil purpose. 슬그머니 숨다; 살금살금〔몰래〕 하다. ¶ *The wolf was skulking in the woods.* 이리는 숲에서 살금살금 움직이고 있었다. [Scand.]

•skull [skʌl] *n.* Ⓒ the bones of the head; the head; the brain. 두개골; 머리; (두)뇌. [Norw.]

have a thick skull, be stupid; be a dullard. 우둔〔둔감〕하다.

skull and crossbones [⌐－⌐⌐] *n.* a picture of a skull and two crossed thigh bones which was formerly used as a symbol of death on a pirate's flag. 두개골 밑에 두 개의 대퇴골을 교차시킨 그림《예전에는 해적의 깃발로 쓰였으나, 현재는 독극물 용기 따위에 위험 표지로 쓰임》.

skull·cap [skʌ́lkæ̀p] *n.* Ⓒ a close-fitting cap, usu. used by an old man indoors. 챙이 없는 실내용 모자《노인용》.

〈skullcap〉

•skunk [skʌŋk] *n.* **1** Ⓒ a small black animal which gives off a very strong, unpleasant smell when frightened or attacked. 스컹크. **2** Ⓤ the fur of this animal. 스컹크의 모피. **3** Ⓒ a mean rascal. 비열한 녀석〔놈〕. [Amer-Ind.]

:sky [skai] *n.* Ⓒ (*pl.* **skies**) **1** the space over the world where the clouds are. 하늘; 천공. ¶ *a blue* 〔*cloudy*〕 *~* 푸른〔흐린〕 하늘 / *in the ~* 하늘에(서) / *under the open ~* 야외〔옥외〕에서 / *to the ~* 〔*skies*〕 하늘까지; 매우 높이; 크게 / *We did not see the ~ for weeks.* 몇 주 동안 푸른하늘을 보지 못했다. **2** 《*the ~* or *the skies*》 the place in heaven where God and His angels live. 천국; 천당. ¶ *be raised to the skies* 승천하다; 죽다. **3** 《often *pl.*》 weather; a climate. 날씨; 기후; 풍토. ¶ *from* 〔*judging by*〕 *the look of the ~* 날씨 모양새〔상태〕로 보아서〔판단해서〕 / *under a foreign ~* 이국의 하늘 밑에서.

If the sky fall, we shall catch larks. You need not be too pessimistic. 하늘이 무너지면 종달새라도 잡게 되겠지《앞일에 너무 비관적이지 마라》.

laud 〔***praise***〕 ***someone to the skies,*** praise highly. …를 극구 칭찬하다.

out of a clear sky, suddenly; unexpectedly. 갑자기; 느닷없이.

— *vt.* (**skied**) (P6) hit (a ball) high into the air. (공을) 하늘 높이 쳐 올리다. [N. =cloud]

sky blue [⌐⌐] *n.* a light clear blue. 하늘색.

sky-blue [skáiblú:] *adj.* of a clear soft blue. 하늘색의.

Skye [skai] *n.* **1** a breed of dog. 테리어개의 일종. **2** the largest island of the Inner Hebrides, Scotland. 스카이《스코틀랜드 서부의 섬》. [Place]

sky·er [skáiər] *n.* (크리켓의) 비구(飛球).

sky·ey [skáii] *adj.* 《*lit.*》 **1** of or from the sky. 하늘의; 하늘로부터의. **2** very high. 매우 높은. **3** sky-blue. 하늘빛의.

sky-high [skáihái] *adj., adv.* very high. 매우 높은〔높이〕.

sky·lark [skáilɑ̀:rk] *n.* Ⓒ a small bird known for its sweet song in early spring. 종달새. — *vi.* (P1) frolic; play pranks. 법석을 떨다; 장난치다.

sky·light [skáilàit] *n.* Ⓒ a window in a roof or ceiling. (지붕·천장에 낸) 채광창.
sky·line [skáilàin] *n.* Ⓒ **1** the line at which the sky seems to meet the earth; the horizon. 지평선. **2** the outline of mountains, trees, buildings, etc. against the sky. (산 따위의) 하늘을 배경으로 하는 윤곽.
sky pilot [ˊ ˋ–] *n.* 《*sl.*》 **1** a clergyman. 목사. **2** an aviator. 비행사.
sky·rock·et [skáiràkit / -rɔ̀k-] *n.* Ⓒ a firework that rises rapidly high in the air. 유성(流星) 불꽃. — *vi.* (P1) rise suddenly and rapidly. 급격히 상승하다.
sky·scape [skáiskèip] *n.* a picture with the sky as chief feature. 하늘 경치의 그림.
sky·scrap·er [skáiskrèipər] *n.* Ⓒ a very tall building. 마천루; 고층 빌딩.
sky·ward [skáiwərd] *adj., adv.* toward the sky. 하늘 쪽의[쪽으로].
sky·wards [skáiwərdz] *adv.* =skyward.
sky·writ·ing [skáiràitiŋ] *n.* the forming of written signals in the air by smoke emitted from an airplane. (비행기가 연막 따위로) 공중에 그린 글씨[그림].
slab [slæb] *n.* Ⓒ a flat and thick piece of wood, stone, etc.; a thick slice of bread, meat, etc. (재목·돌 따위의) 두꺼운 평평한 판; 슬래브; (빵·고기 따위를 판판하게 썬) 두꺼운 조각. ¶ *The terrace is paved with slabs of stone.* 테라스 바닥은 석판으로 깔려져 있다 / *He ate a* ~ *of cheese as big as my hand.* 그는 내 손바닥만한 크기의 두꺼운 치즈 조각을 먹었다. [E.]
slack[1] [slæk] *adj.* **1** loose; not tight. (옷 따위가) 느슨한; 늘어진. ¶ *The tennis net hung* ~. 테니스 네트가 늘어진 상태로 걸려 있었다 / *a* ~ *wire* 느슨한 철사(줄). **2** slow; moving very slowly. 느린; 꾸물거리는. ¶ *at a* ~ *pace* 느린 걸음걸이로 / *Their pace was* ~. 그들의 걸음걸이는 느렸다 / ~ *water* 정지 상태의 조수; 게조(憩潮). **3** not careful; lazy. 부주의한; 태만한; 게으른. ¶ ~ *discipline* 해이해진 규율 / *be* ~ *in one's work* [*duties*] 일에 빈틈이 없다 / *She is a* ~ *housekeeper.* 그녀는 알뜰하지 못한 가정 주부이다. **4** not busy; not active; dull. 침체된; 한산한; 활기 없는. ¶ *a* ~ *time* [*season*] (장사의) 불황기 / ~ *trade* 부진한 무역 / *Business is* ~ *at this season.* 이 계절에는 장사가 불경기이다.
keep a slack hand [***rein***], ride [govern] carelessly. 고삐를 늦추다; 관대히 다루다.
slack in stays, 《naut.》 slow in going about. (배가) 도는 것이 느린.
slack weather, unsettled weather. 끄물거리는 날씨.
— *n.* Ⓒ **1** a part of a rope, a wire, etc. that is not stretched tight. 느슨함; 느스러짐. **2** a dull season in business; a time of little activity; a dull period; a lazy time. 불황기; 한가한 시간. ¶ *I'm going to have a good* ~ *this afternoon.* 나는 오늘 오후에 충분한 휴식 시간을 가지려고 한다. **3** a turn of tide. 게조(憩潮).
— *vi.* (P1,2A) 《*off*》 be slack; work slackly; be idle; be lazy. 느슨해지다; 게을리하다; 느려지다. ¶ ~ *at one's job* 일을 게을리하다 / ~ *the whole afternoon* 오후 내내 일을 안하고 쉬다. — *vt.* (P6,7) **1** 《*off, up*》 to reduce in speed, effort, or tightness. 늦추다; 완화하다. **2** =slacken. [E.]
slack[2] [slæk] *n.* Ⓤ small pieces of coal; coal dust. 분탄(粉炭); 지스러기 탄. [Du. *slacke* slag]
slack·en [slǽkən] *vi.* (P1,2A) **1** become less firm; become loose. 느슨해지다; 느즈러지다. ¶ *His muscles slackened.* 그의 근육은 느슨해졌다. **2** become less active; become slower. 불황이 되다; 약해지다; 느려지다. ¶ *His energy slackens on a hot day.* 더운 날엔 그의 정력은 떨어진다 / ~ *in one's efforts* 노력을 늦추다. **3** 《*colloq.*》 take a rest; be lazy. 잠시 쉬다; 게으름 피우다.
— *vt.* (P6) **1** make (a rope, a wire, etc.) less firm. (로프 따위의 팽팽함)을 늦추다; 느즈러뜨리다. ¶ *Slacken the rope.* 로프를 늦추어라. **2** make (the speed, the pace, etc.) slower. (속도 따위를) 줄이다; 늦추다. ¶ *You must* ~ *speed at a crossroads.* 교차로에서는 속도를 줄여라 / ~ *one's pace* 걸음을 늦추다. [*slack*[1]]
slack·er [slǽkər] *n.* Ⓒ a person who tries to avoid work or duty; a lazy person. (일·임무에) 태만한 사람; 게으름뱅이.
slack·ly [slǽkli] *adv.* in a slack manner; loosely. 느슨하게; 엉성하게.
slack·ness [slǽknis] *n.* Ⓤ the state or quality of being slack; carelessness; inactivity. 느슨함; 태만; 침체.
slacks [slæks] *n. pl.* trousers; loose trousers for informal wear. 슬랙스《헐거운 스포티한 바지》.
slag [slæg] *n.* Ⓤ waste matter remaining when metal has been taken from a natural combination of minerals by melting. (광석을 용해할 때 생기는) 용재(鎔滓); 광재; 슬래그. — *vt., vi.* (**slagged, slag·ging**) (P6;1) form slag; be formed into slag. 용재로 하다; 용재를 형성하다. [Teut.]
slain [slein] *v.* pp. of **slay.**
slake [sleik] *vt.* (P6,13) **1** put out (a fire). (불을) 끄다 **2** satisfy (thirst or a desire). (갈증을)풀다; (욕망을) 채우다. **3** add water to (lime) in order to change its chemical nature. (석회를) 소화(消和)[비화(沸化)]하다. ¶ *slaked lime* 소석회 (cf. *quicklime*). [*slack*]
slam [slæm] *v.* (**slammed, slam·ming**) *vt.* **1** (P6,7,18) close or shut violently and noisily. …을 쾅[탕] 닫다. ¶ ~ *the door in someone's face* 들어오는 것을 (난폭하게) 막다; 문전 퇴짜를 놓다 / ~ *the box shut* 상자를 쾅 닫다 / ~ *a door* [*window*] 문[창]을 탕 닫

다 / *He slammed the door in anger.* 그는 화가 나서 문을 탕 닫았다 / *He slammed the window down.* 그는 창문을 쾅 내렸다. **2** (P6,7,13) 《*on*》 put or throw (something) with force and a loud noise. …을 털썩〔쿵, 탁〕 놓다〔던지다〕. ¶ ~ *a book down on a table* 테이블 위에 털썩 책을 내려 놓다 / *He slammed down the cap on the table.* 그는 모자를 테이블 위에 턱 내던졌다.

— *vi.* (P1,2A) (of a door, a window, etc.) shut with a bang. (문·창문 따위가) 쾅〔탕〕 닫히다. ¶ *hear a door* ~ 문이 쾅 닫히는 소리를 듣다 / *In the strong wind, the door slammed* (*to*) *behind me.* 강풍으로 문이 쾅하고 내 등 뒤에서 닫혔다.

— *n.* Ⓒ **1** the noise of a door shutting violently; a bang. (문 따위가) 쾅〔탕〕하고 닫히는 소리. ¶ *with a* ~ 쾅〔탕〕하고 / *John put the box down with a* ~. 존은 쾅하고 상자를 내려놨다. **2** the winning of 12 or 13 tricks in the game of bridge. (브리지 게임에서) 전승. [Norw.]

slan·der [slǽndər / slɑ́:n-] *n.* ⓊⒸ a false report or statement about someone in order to harm him. 중상; 비방. — *vt.* (P6) talk falsely about (someone) in order to hurt his character. …을 중상〔비방〕하다. [→scandal]

slan·der·er [slǽndərər / slɑ́:n-] *n.* Ⓒ a person who slanders. 중상자.

slan·der·ous [slǽndərəs / slɑ́:n-] *adj.* speaking or spreading slander. 중상적인; 헐뜯는. ¶ *a* ~ *tongue* 독설 / ~ *rumors* 중상적인 루머〔풍설〕.

● **slan·der·ous·ly** [-li] *adv.*

***slang** [slæŋ] *n.* Ⓤ **1** words or phrases used in popular speech, but not regarded as formal language. 속어. ¶ *'Cop' is* ~ *for 'policeman'.* 'Cop'은 경찰관을 뜻하는 속어이다. **2** the special language of a particular group of people. (어떤 사회의) 통용어; (도적·죄인 따위의) 은어(隱語). ¶ *thieves'* ~ 도적의 은어. — *vt.* (P6) use abusive language to. …에게 욕하다. [? Norw.]

slang·y [slǽŋi] *adj.* (**slang·i·er, slang·i·est**) of slang; full of slang; using slang. 속어의; 속어가 많은; 속어를 사용하는.

***slant** [slænt / slɑ:nt] *adj.* sloping. 비스듬한; 경사진. ¶ *a* ~ *edge* 사릉(斜稜) / ~ *eyes* 눈꼬리가 치켜올라간 눈. — *n.* Ⓒ **1** a slope. 경사; 비탈. ¶ *The mountain has a sharp* ~. 그 산은 경사가〔비탈이〕 심하다 / *Our roof has a slight* ~. 우리집 지붕은 완만한 경사를 이루고 있다. **2** a way of looking at something; an opinion; a point of view. (사물을 보는) 관점; 경향; 의견. ¶ *He has a new* ~ *on the novel.* 그는 소설에 대해 새로운 관점을 가지고 있다.

a slant of wind, a favorable breeze. 일진의 순풍.

on the 〔***a***〕 ***slant,*** aslant. 경사지게; 비스듬히. ¶ *The table is on the* ~. 테이블이 비스듬히 놓여 있다.

— *vt.* (P6) give a slope to (something). …을 기울이다; 경사지게 하다. ¶ ~ *a line* 선을 기울게 긋다. — *vi.* (P1,2A,3) be on a slope. 기울다; 경사지다. ¶ *The roof slants a bit.* 지붕은 조금 경사져 있다 / ~ *to the right* 우로 기울다. [Scand.]

slant·ing [slǽntiŋ / slɑ́:n-] *adj.* with a sloping direction. 경사진; 기운.

slant·ing·ly [slǽntiŋli / slɑ́:n-] *adv.* in a slanting direction or position. 경사지게; 기울게.

slant·wise [slǽntwàiz / slɑ́:nt-] *adv.* in a slanting manner. 비스듬히; 기울게.

— *adj.* slanting. 기운.

***slap** [slæp] *n.* Ⓒ a blow with the open hand or with something flat. 손바닥〔넓적한 것〕으로 철썩 때리기. ¶ *He gave me a* ~ *on the cheek.* 그는 철썩하고 나의 따귀를 때렸다 / *a* ~ *on the shoulder* 어깨를 철썩 때림.

a slap in 〔***across***〕 ***the face,*** **a**) a blow on the face with the open hand; insult. (손바닥으로) 철썩 빰〔얼굴〕을 때림; 모욕. **b**) a refusal. 거절.

— *vt.* (**slapped, slap·ping**) **1** (P6) hit (someone) with the open hand; strike with something flat. …을 손바닥〔넓적한 것〕으로 철썩 때리다. **2** (P7) throw (something) down with a noise; put down with force. …을 털썩〔탁〕 내려놓다〔던지다〕. ¶ *She slapped her notebook down on the desk.* 그녀는 노트를 책상 위에 털썩 내던졌다.

slap on, put (something) on quickly. 날쌔게〔덥석〕 입다〔쓰다〕. ¶ *He slapped his hat on* 〔*onto*〕 *his head.* 그는 모자를 집어 덥석 썼다.

slap someone on the back, pat someone on the back in a friendly manner. (다정하게 아무의) 등을 가볍게 치다.

— *adv.* **1** with a bang; straight; directly. 철썩; 곧바로; 정면으로. ¶ *I hit him* ~ *in the eye.* 나는 그의 눈을 철썩〔정통으로〕 때렸다 / *He ran* ~ *into me.* 그는 정면으로 나와 충돌하였다. **2** suddenly; unexpectedly. 갑자기; 불시에. ¶ *The handle came* ~ *off.* 자루가 갑자기 쑥 빠져 나왔다. [Teut.]

slap·dash [slǽpdæ̀ʃ] *adj.* impetuous; happy-go-lucky. 성급한; 무모한. — *adv.* hastily and carelessly. 무턱대고; 함부로.

slap·ping [slǽpiŋ] *adj.* 《*sl.*》 very fast or good. 무척 빠른〔좋은〕.

slap·stick [slǽpstìk] *n.* Ⓤ low comedy of the roughest kind. 익살극.

slap-up [slǽpʌ̀p] *adj.* 《*sl.*》 wonderful; first-class. 아주 훌륭한; 일류〔최고급〕의. ¶ *a* ~ *dinner* 일류의 식사.

slash [slæʃ] *vt.* **1** (P6,7,13) cut (something) violently and aimlessly. …을 깊이〔썩〕 베다; 난폭하게 마구 베다. ¶ ~ *one's face with a razor-blade* 면도날로 얼굴을 깊이 베다 / *Don't* ~ *the bark off the tree with your knife.* 칼로 나무 껍질을 벗겨내지 마라. **2** (P6) cut slits in (a dress) in order to

show the different material beneath. (옷의 일부분을) 터놓다《속 부분을 드러내기 위해》. ¶ *a slashed sleeve* 소매끝을 터놓은 소매. **3** (P6) whip repeatedly. …을 채찍질하다. **4** (P6) reduce (a budget, a salary, etc.) very much; cut down sharply. …을 큰 폭으로 삭감하다. ¶ ~ *costs* [*budgets, someone's salary*] 비용[예산, 아무의 월급]을 큰 폭으로 깎아내리다[삭감하다]. **5** (P6) criticize severely or unkindly. …을 혹평하다.
— *n.* Ⓒ a long cut; a sweeping stroke. 깊은 상처; 일격. [O.F.]

slat [slæt] *n.* Ⓒ a thin, narrow strip of wood, metal, etc. (나무·금속 따위의) 좁고 긴 얇은 판. [↓]

***slate** [sleit] *n.* **1** Ⓤ hard, blue-gray rock that easily splits into thin layers; Ⓒ a thin plate of this rock, used for coating a roof. 석판(石板); (지붕을 이는 한 장의) 슬레이트. **2** Ⓤ dark, bluish gray. 암청회색; 쥐색. **3** Ⓒ 《U.S.》 a list of candidates for election. 후보자 명단.
a clean slate, a record showing no marks of bad conduct; a good record. 깨끗한[훌륭한] 경력[기록].
clean the slate, rid oneself of obligations 의무를 다하다.
— *vt.* **1** (P6) cover (something) with slate. …를 슬레이트로 덮다[이다]. **2** (P6) list (candidates) for election. …을 후보자로 등록하다. **3** (P6) criticize severely. 혹평하다. **4** (P13) 《U.S. *sl.*》 schedule. 예정하다. [F. *esclater* burst, splinter]

slate club [⌐⌐] *n.* a mutual benefit society with small weekly contributions. 공제회.

slate pencil [⌐ ⌐–] *n.* a pencil used for writing on a slate. 석필.

slat·tern [slǽtərn] *n.* Ⓒ a woman who is careless and lazy; an untidy woman. 단정치 못한 여자. [E.]

slat·tern·ly [slǽtərnli] *adj.* (of a woman) careless and untidy; morally loose. 단정[칠칠]치 못한; 몸가짐이 헤픈.

slat·y [sléiti] *adj.* (**slat·i·er, slat·i·est**) of slate; slate-colored. 슬레이트(질(質))의; 석판 모양의; 암회색의. [*slate*]

***slaugh·ter** [slɔ́:tər] *n.* Ⓤ **1** the act of killing in great numbers; a massacre. 살육; 학살. **2** the act of killing animals for food. 도살. — *vt.* (P6) kill (people) in great numbers cruelly; kill (animals) for food. …을 살육하다; 도살하다. [N.(slay)]

slaugh·ter·er [slɔ́:tərər] *n.* Ⓒ a person who slaughters. 살육자; 도살자.

slaugh·ter·house [slɔ́:tərhàus] *n.* Ⓒ a place where animals are killed for food; a place or scene of cruel fighting. 도살장; 수라장.

slaugh·ter·ous [slɔ́:tərəs] *adj.* 《*lit.*》 murderous; destructive. 살벌한; 파괴적인.

Slav [slɑ:v, slæv] *n.* Ⓒ a member of one of the races living in eastern Europe, such as Russians, Poles, Czechs, Slovaks, Bulgarians and Yugoslavs. 슬라브 민족. — *adj.* of the Slavs and their languages. 슬라브 민족[어]의. [Native]

Slav. Slavic; Slavonian.

:slave [sleiv] *n.* Ⓒ **1** a person who has no freedom because of being the property of another. 노예. ¶ *work like a* ~ 뼈빠지게 일하다 / *Slaves could be bought and sold like horses.* 노예는 말처럼 사고 팔 수 있었다. **2** a person who works very hard like a slave. 노예처럼 일하는 사람. **3** a person who is given to some bad habit, desire, etc.; 《*to, of*》 a person completely devoted. (욕망·악습 따위의) 탐닉자; …에 빠진[헌신하는] 사람. ¶ *a* ~ *of* [*to*] *drink* [*to the bottle*] 술의 노예 / *a* ~ *to one's passions* 정욕의 노예 / *a* ~ *to duty* 의무를 위해 헌신적으로 일하는 사람 / *He is the* ~ *of tobacco.* 그는 대단한 골초이다.
— *vi.* (P1,2A) work very hard like a slave. (노예처럼) 뼈빠지게[고되게] 일하다. ¶ ~ *for one's family* 가족을 위해 뼈빠지게 일하다.
— *adj.* of slaves; done by slaves. 노예의; 노예제의. ¶ ~ *labor* 노예[강제] 노동. [Slav. (w. ref.) to servile state of medieval Slavs]

slave driver [⌐ ⌐–] *n.* **1** an overseer of slaves. 노예 감시인. **2** an employer who is unkind to his employees. 혹사자.

slave·hold·er [sléivhòuldər] *n.* Ⓒ a person who owns slaves. 노예 소유자.

slave·hold·ing [sléivhòuldiŋ] *n.* Ⓤ the act of owning slaves. 노예(奴隸)의 소유. — *adj.* having slaves. 노예 소유의.

slav·er[1] [sléivər] *n.* Ⓒ **1** a dealer in slaves. 노예 상인. **2** a ship used in the slave trade. 노예 무역선. [*slave*]

slav·er[2] [slǽvər, sléivər] *n.* Ⓤ the liquid that runs from the mouth. 침; 군침. — *vi.* (P1) let slaver flow from the mouth. 침을 흘리다. — *vt.* (P6) wet (something) with slaver. …을 침으로 더럽히다. [Scand.]

***slav·er·y** [sléivəri] *n.* Ⓤ **1** the custom of owning slaves. 노예 제도. **2** the state of being a slave. 노예의 신분; 예속. ¶ *They were sold into* ~. 그들은 노예로 팔렸다. **3** very hard work; severe toil. 혹심한 노동[일]; 고역(苦役). **4** the condition of being given to some bad habit or influence. (욕망·악습 따위의) 노예; 사로잡힌 사람; 심취. ¶ ~ *to habit* [*fashion*] 습관[유행]의 포로. [*slave*]

slave trade [⌐⌐] *n.* the business of selling and buying slaves. 노예 매매.

Slav·ic [slǽvik, slɑ́:v-] *adj., n.* =Slavonic.

slav·ish [sléiviʃ] *adj.* of a slave; base; mean. 노예의; 노예 근성의; 천한. [*slave*]

Sla·von·ic [sləvɑ́nik / -vɔ́n-] *adj.* of the Slavs and their languages. 슬라브족[말]의.
— *n.* Ⓤ the Slavic languages. 슬라브 말[어]. [*Slav.*]

slaw [slɔː] *n.* Ⓤ sliced cabbage served as salad. 양배추 샐러드. [F. →salad]

•**slay** [slei] *vt.* (**slew, slain**) (P6) kill violently. …을 죽이다; 살해하다. [E. =strike]

slay·er [sléiər] *n.* Ⓒ a person who kills or has killed a person. 살해자. [↑]

SLBM satellite-launched ballistic missile. 인공 위성 발사 탄도 미사일.

slea·zy [slíːzi] *adj.* (**-zi·er, -zi·est**) **1** (of cloth) thin or poor in texture. (직물이) 얄팍한; 흐르르한; 허울만의. **2** 《*colloq.*》 low, mean, or contemptible. 질이 낮은; 하잘것없는. [Place]

sled [sled] *n.* Ⓒ a flat, low, wooden framework for carrying loads on snow or ice. 썰매; (놀이용) 소형 썰매. — *vi., vt.* (**sled·ded, sled·ding**) (P1,6) ride on a sled; carry (something) on a sled. 썰매로 가다; …을 썰매로 운반하다. [Du. (slide)]

hard sledding, unfavorable conditions. 난국.

sledge[1] [sledʒ] *n.* Ⓒ a sled; a sleigh. 썰매 (cf. *sleigh*). — *vt., vi.* (P7; 2A) ride or carry (something) on a sledge. 썰매로 가다; …을 썰매로 운반하다. [↑]

sledge[2] [sledʒ] *n.* =sledgehammer.

sledge·ham·mer [slédʒhæ̀mər] *n.* Ⓒ a heavy hammer usu. used with both hands. 큰 쇠망치《두 손으로 사용하는 큰 해머》. — *vt.* (P6) **1** hit (something) with a sledgehammer. …을 큰 쇠망치로 치다. **2** do great damage to (the enemy, etc.). …에게 큰 타격을 주다. — *adj.* powerful; crushing. 강력한; 파괴적인. ¶ *a ~ blow* 대타격. [→slay]

sleek [sliːk] *adj.* **1** smooth; glossy; neat. 매끄러운; 윤기 있는. ¶ *~ hair* 〔*cat*〕 매끄러운〔윤기 흐르는〕 머리칼〔고양이〕. **2** flattering in speech; smooth in manners. 말주변이 좋은; 동작이 세련된. — *vt.* (P6,7) make (something) smooth and glossy. …을 매끄럽게〔단정하게〕 하다. ¶ *He sleeked down his hair.* 머리를 매만져 단정히 하다. [→slick]

:**sleep** [sliːp] *n.* Ⓤ **1** the state of being not awake; 《*a* ~》 a period of sleeping. 수면; 수면 시간. ¶ *a sound ~* 숙면 / *fall* (*into*) *~* 잠들다 / *go to ~* 잠자리에 들다 / *put someone to ~* 아무를 잠들게 하다 / *in one's ~* 잠들어 있는 동안 / *have a good night's ~* 하룻밤 푹 잘 자다 / *get eight hours' ~,* 8시간을 자다 / *talk in one's ~* 잠꼬대하다 / *a brief ~* 짧은 수면 시간. **2** a state like sleep; death. 활동하지 않음; 죽음. ¶ *the ~ of death* 죽음의 잠 / *the last ~* 영면 / *winter ~* 동면.

— *v.* (**slept**) *vi.* **1** (P1,2A,2B) ⓐ be in a state of sleep; go to bed. 잠자다. ¶ *~ well* 〔*badly*〕 잘 자다〔못 자다〕 / *She slept twelve hours.* 그녀는 12시간을 잤다 / *All animals ~.* 모든 짐승은 잠을 잔다 / *~ with one eye open* (경계·기다림 따위로) 제대로 잠을 못 자다; 자면서도 경계를 하다. ⓑ pass the night. 묵다; 머무르다; 자다. ¶ *I shall ~ in London tonight.* 오늘 밤은 런던에서 묵을 생각이다. **2** (P1) be motionless; be dead; be in a state like sleep. 꼼짝하지 않다; 죽어 있다; 동면하다. ¶ *~ in the grave* 무덤에 잠들어〔묻혀〕 있다 / *The town slept.* 도시는 쥐 죽은 듯 조용했다 / *His faculties* 〔*talents*〕 *are sleeping.* 그의 재능은 잠들어 있다.

— *vt.* (P6) **1** rest in (a kind of sleep). 잠자다. 語法 동족 목적어를 수반한다. ¶ *~ a sound sleep* 숙면하다 / *~ one's last sleep* 죽다. **2** (of a hotel, etc.) have beds enough for (persons); provide sleeping space for. (호텔 따위가) …을 숙박시키다. ¶ *This boat sleeps six persons.* 이 보트는 여섯 사람이 묵을 수 있다 / *This hut can ~ ten people.* 이 오두막은 10명을 수용할 수 있다. [E.]

sleep away, **a**) spend in one's sleep. 잠을 자며 보내다. ¶ *He slept away the whole morning.* 그는 오전 내내 잠을 자며 보냈다. **b**) get rid of (a headache, etc.) by sleeping. (두통 따위를) 잠을 자서 낫게 하다〔없애다〕. ¶ *~ away one's cares* 걱정을 잠으로 달래다.

sleep in, (of a domestic servant) sleep at the place where he works. (가정부 따위가) 일하는 집에 입주하다.

sleep like a top 〔*log*〕, sleep peacefully and deeply. 푹 잘 자다.

sleep off, recover from (a headache, etc.) by sleeping. (두통 따위를) 잠을 자서 낫게 하다〔없애다〕

sleep on 〔*upon*〕 ***a question,*** leave a decision until the next day. (문제 따위를) 하룻밤 자고 생각하다. ¶ *~ on the matter* 〔*a question*〕 일을〔문제를〕 하룻밤 자고 생각하다.

sleep the clock round, sleep for twelve hours continuously. 12시간을 내리 자다.

sleep with, 《*euphem.*》 have sexual intercourse with. 동침하다.

sleep·er [slíːpər] *n.* Ⓒ **1** a person who sleeps. 잠자는〔자고 있는〕 사람. ¶ *The noise woke the sleepers.* 소음이 자고 있는 사람들을 깨웠다 / *a good* 〔*bad, heavy, light*〕 *~* 잘 자는〔잠을 못 이루는, 잠이 들면 좀처럼 깨우기 힘든, 깊은 잠을 못 이루는〕 사람. **2** a horizontal beam. 침목(枕木) (=《U.S.》 tie). **3** = sleeping car. **4** a thing or a person that has or might become important or successful after a period of being unknown or ignored. 뜻밖에 성공한〔진가를 발휘한〕 사람〔것〕.

sleep·i·ly [slíːpili] *adv.* in a sleepy manner. 졸립게; 졸린 듯이.

sleep·i·ness [slíːpinis] *n.* Ⓤ the condition of being sleepy. 졸음.

:**sleep·ing** [slíːpiŋ] *n.* Ⓤ **1** sleep. 잠; 수면. **2** rest. 휴지(休止). — *adj.* **1** asleep. 자고 있는. **2** of or for sleep. 수면(용)의. ¶ *a ~ bag* 침낭; 슬리핑 백.

:**sleeping car** [⌐-⌐] *n.* a railway car with beds for passengers. 침대차.

sleeping sickness [⌐-⌐-] *n.* a disease of tropical Africa, causing fever, sleepiness, and usu. death. (열대 아프리카의) 수면병; 기면성(嗜眠性) 뇌염.

sleep·less [slíːplis] *adj.* **1** unable to sleep; not sleeping. 잠 못 이루는; 깨어 있는. ¶ *spend a ~ night* 눈 한번 붙이지 못하고 하룻밤을 새다. **2** restless; watchful. 쉬지 않는; 방심하지 않는. ¶ *the ~ ocean* 쉼 없는 대양 / *~ care* 방심치 않는 조심.

sleep·walk·er [slíːpwɔ̀ːkər] *n.* Ⓒ a person who walks about while sleeping. 몽유병 환자.

sleep·walk·ing [slíːpwɔ̀ːkiŋ] *n.* Ⓤ the act of walking while asleep. 몽유병. — *adj.* that walks about while asleep. 몽유병의.

•**sleep·y** [slíːpi] *adj.* (**sleep·i·er, sleep·i·est**) **1** ready or inclined to sleep; overcome by sleepiness. 졸린; 졸음이 오는; 졸린 듯한. ¶ *a ~ face* 졸린 얼굴. **2** (of a place, etc.) inactive; quiet. 활기가 없는; 조용한. ¶ *a ~ town* 조용한 마을. **3** causing or inducing sleep. 졸음이 오게 하는.

sleep·y·head [slíːpihèd] *n.* Ⓒ a person who looks half asleep; a sleepy person. 잠꾸러기; 멍청이.

sleet [sliːt] *n.* Ⓤ snow or hail mixed with rain; frozen or partly-frozen rain. 진눈깨비. — *vi.* (P1) shower half-frozen rain. 진눈깨비가 오다〔내리다〕. [E.]

sleet·y [slíːti] *adj.* (**sleet·i·er, sleet·i·est**) of sleet; with sleet falling. 진눈깨비의; 진눈깨비가 오는.

:**sleeve** [sliːv] *n.* Ⓒ **1** the part of a dress, coat, etc. that covers all or a part of the arm. 소매. **2** a tube into which a rod or another tub fits. 슬리브관; 투관(套管). **3** the cover of a record. (레코드의) 재킷; 커버. [E.]

hang on someone's sleeve, agree with someone in everything he says or does. 아무가 하라는 대로 다 하다.

have something up one's sleeve, keep something secretly ready for use when needed. …을 필요할 때 쓸 수 있도록 항상 준비하고 있다; 무슨 일을 꾸미고 있다.

laugh in 〔***up***〕 ***one's sleeve,*** be secretly amused. 조용히 득의의 미소를 짓다.

roll 〔***turn***〕 ***up one's sleeves,*** 《*fig.*》 prepare to work, fight, etc. 소매를 걷어 붙이다《일할〔싸울〕 준비를 하다》.

wear one's heart on one's sleeve, show one's feeling openly. 감정을 노골적으로 나타내다.

sleeve·less [slíːvlis] *adj.* without sleeves. 소매 없는. ¶ *a ~ dress* 소매 없는 드레스〔옷〕.

sleigh [slei] *n.* Ⓒ a carriage for use on snow or ice. (말이 끄는) 썰매. — *vi.* (P1,2A) travel or ride in a sleigh. 썰매로 가다; 썰매를 타다. — *vt.* (P7) carry by sleigh. 썰매로 나르다. [*sled*]

〈sleigh〉

sleigh·ing [sléiiŋ] *n.* Ⓤ the act or riding in a sleigh. 썰매를 타기〔사용하기〕.

sleight [slait] *n.* Ⓤ skill; dexterity; a skillful trick. 날랜〔숙련된〕 솜씨; 교묘한 속임수. [N. (sly)]

sleight of hand, skill with the hands, esp. in performing tricks, as in magic; a trick thus performed; a magic trick. (요술 따위의) 날랜 솜씨; 요술.

:**slen·der** [sléndər] *adj.* **1** long and thin; slim. 홀쭉한; 호리호리한; 날씬한. ¶ *He is ~ in build.* 그는 체격이 호리호리하다 / *A pencil is a ~ piece of wood.* 연필은 가느다란 나무의 한 토막이다. **2** not hopeful; weak; poor; small in amount, value, etc. 미덥지 못한; 약한; 빈약한; 얼마 안 되는. ¶ *a ~ income* 얼마 안 되는 수입 / *a ~ meal* 빈약한 식사 / *~ prospects* 희박한 전망 / *a man of ~ means* 자력(資力)이 빈약한 사람. [E.]

slen·der·ize [sléndəràiz] 《U.S.》 *vt.* (P6) **1** make slender or more slender. (더) 가늘게 하다. **2** cause to look slender. 가늘게 뵈도록 하다. — *vi.* (P1) become slender. 가늘어지다.

:**slept** [slept] *v.* p. and pp. of **sleep.**

sleuth [sluːθ] *n.* **1** =sleuthhound. **2** a detective. 탐정. [N. *slōð* track, trail]

sleuth·hound [slúːθhàund] *n.* Ⓒ a large dog used for hunting escaped prisoners; a bloodhound; 《*colloq.*》 a detective. 경찰견; 사냥개; 탐정.

•**slew**[1] [sluː] *v.* p. of **slay.**

slew[2] [sluː] *v., n.* =slue[2].

slew[3] [sluː] *n.*《U.S. *colloq.*》 a large number; a lot. 다수; 대량; 많음. ¶ *a ~ of people* 많은 사람들. [It.]

:**slice** [slais] *n.* Ⓒ **1** a thin, flat piece cut from something. (빵·햄 따위의) 얇게 썬 조각; 한 조각. ¶ *a ~ of bread* 〔*meat, cake*〕 얇게 자른 빵〔고기, 케이크〕 한 조각. **2** 《*of*》 a part; a portion; a share. 일부분; 몫. ¶ *demand a ~ of the profits* 이익의 한 몫을 요구하다 / *a ~ of the work* 일의 일부분 / *a ~ of territory* 영토의 일부분 / *a ~ of life* 인생의 한 단면. **3** a knife with a thin, broad blade. 날이 얇은 식칼; 생선 써는 칼〔나이프〕. **4** 《sports》 a slicing stroke, kick, hit, etc. (골프 따위의) 슬라이스.

— *vt.* **1** (P6,7,13,18) cut (something) into slices. …을 얇게 베다〔썰다〕. ¶ *~ (up) a loaf of bread* 한 덩어리의 빵을 얇게 썰다 / *eat sliced peaches* 얇게 썬 복숭아를 먹다. **2** (P6,7) 《*off*》 cut off; remove. 베어〔잘라〕내다. ¶ *~ off a piece of meat* 고기 한 조각을 베어내다. **3** (P6) go through (the air) with a cutting motion; hit with such a motion. 가르듯이〔헤치듯〕 나아가다; (골프 등에서) 곡타(曲打)하다; 깎아치다. [Teut.]

slick [slik] *adj.* **1** smooth; glossy; sleek. 매끄러운; 광택이 나는. ¶ *~ hair* 매끄러운 머리

털. **2** clever; smart; cunning; sly; tricky. 능란한; 교활한. ¶ *a ~ customer* 교활한 녀석〔놈〕. **3** too smooth in speech, manners, etc. 말솜씨가 좋은; (태도가) 빈틈 없는. **4** very slippery; easy to slip on. 미끄러운. ¶ *a street ~ with ice* 얼음으로 미끄러운 거리.
— *adv.* **1** directly; straight. 곧장; 정통으로. ¶ *His car ran ~ into mine.* 그의 차는 내 차와 정면으로 충돌했다. **2** smoothly. 매끄럽게. ¶ *go ~* 매끄럽게 운전하다〔나아가다〕. **3** cleverly. 능란하게.
— *n.* Ⓒ a smooth part of a road, etc. (길 따위의) 미끄러운 데.
— *vt.* (P6) make smooth. 매끄럽게 하다. [E.]

slick·er [slíkər] *n.* Ⓒ 《U.S.》 **1** a long, loose, waterproof coat. (길고 헐거운) 비옷; 레인코트. **2** 《*colloq.*》 a tricky person; a cheat; a swindler. 교활한 사람; 사기꾼.

•**slid** [slid] *v.* p. and pp. of **slide.**

•**slid·den** [slídn] *v.* pp. of **slide.**

:**slide** [slaid] *v.* (**slid, slid** or **slid·den**) *vi.* **1** (P1,2A,3) move smoothly, as over ice; glide. (얼음 위 따위를) 미끄러지다; 활주하다. ¶ *~ on the ice* 얼음 위를 미끄러지다 / *~ along* 〔*down, off*〕 미끄러지다〔내려가다; 떨어지다〕 / *~ into first base,* 1루로 슬라이딩하다 / *The book ~ off my knee.* 책이 내 무릎에서 미끄러져 떨어졌다. **2** (P2A,3) 《*into*》 move quietly and secretly. 조용히〔남모르게〕 움직이다; 잠입하다. ¶ *The cat slid back into the garden.* 고양이는 정원 안으로 살그머니 돌아왔다. **3** (P2A,3) 《*into*》 fall gradually or unconsciously into a certain condition. (어떤 상태로) 부지중에〔점차로〕 빠지다. ¶ *~ into bad habits* 부지중에 나쁜 습관에 빠지다. **4** (P2A,3) (of time, etc.) pass quietly or gradually; slip away. (시간 따위가) 어느새〔덧〕 지나가다; 경과하다. ¶ *Time slid by.* 시간은 어느새 지나가버렸다.
— *vt.* **1** (P7,13) cause (something) to move smoothly. …을 미끄러지게 하다; 활주시키다. ¶ *They slid the boat into the water.* 그들은 보트를 물에 밀어 넣었다. **2** 《*in, into*》 (P7,13) put (something) in quietly. …을 살그머니 넣다. ¶ *He slid his hand* 〔*purse*〕 *into his pocket.* 그는 살그머니 그의 손〔지갑〕을 주머니 속에 넣었다.
let** something **slide, leave something as it is. (…을) 돼가는 대로 내버려 두다; 상관하지 않다. ¶ *Let it ~!* 내버려 둬라.
slide away, leave or go away quietly and secretly; pass away gradually. 슬그머니 떠나가다; (시간이) 어느새 지나가다. ¶ *Her marriage life slid away to nothing.* 그녀의 생활은 어느새 허무하게 지나가 버렸다.
slide over, pass over quickly. …을 간단히〔시원스럽게〕 처리하다. ¶ *~ over a difficult problem* 어려운 문제를 간단히〔시원스럽게〕 처리하다.
— *n.* Ⓒ **1** the act of sliding. 미끄러짐; 활주. **2** any smooth, slippery road or surface. 미끄럼길; 활주장; 미끄럼틀. ¶ *a ski ~* 스키 활주장 / *a play ground ~* 유원지의 미끄럼틀 / *A frozen brook makes a good ~.* 얼어붙은 개울은 미끄럼 타기에 좋다. **3** a mass of earth, snow, etc. sliding down a steep slope; a landslide. (눈)사태; 산사태. **4** a thin sheet of glass used for examining specimens under a microscope; slides with pictures used in magic lanterns. (현미경의) 검경판(檢鏡板); (환등기의) 슬라이드. [E.]

slide fastener [ㅅ ㅡㅡ] *n.* a zipper. 지퍼.

slide projector [ㅅ ㅡㅅㅡ] *n.* a device for projecting magnified images from slides on to a wall or screen. 슬라이드 영사기.

slid·er [sláidər] *n.* Ⓒ **1** a person who slides. 미끄러지는 사람. **2** 《Baseball》 a sharp ball that curves slightly in front of a batter. 슬라이더.

slide rule [ㅅ ㅅ] *n.* a device consisting of a ruler with a sliding scale, used for making rapid calculations. 계산척〔자〕.

sliding scale [ㅅㅡ ㅅ] *n.* a scale of wages, prices, taxes, etc. that can be adjusted according to certain conditions. 슬라이딩 시스템; 종가(從價) 임금제.

:**slight** [slait] *adj.* **1** not much; not important; small. 약간의; 사소한; 얼마 안 되는. ¶ *a ~ rainfall* 약간의 비 / *a ~ increase* 얼마 안 되는 증가 / *a ~ difference of opinion* 의견의 사소한 차이. **2** slender; thin; not big. 가는; 홀쭉한; 날씬한. ¶ *a ~ girl* 날씬한 소녀. **3** frail; not strong. 경미한; (연)약한. ¶ *a ~ cold* 가벼운 감기 / *a ~ fabric* 연약한 조직 / *a ~ temporary construction* 견고하지 못한 가건물.
— *n.* Ⓒ an act of neglecting; an insult. 경시; 경멸.
put a slight upon (=*despise*) *someone.* …을 경시하다.
— *vt.* (P6) pay too little attention to; neglect; despise; have contempt for. …을 경시하다; 모욕〔멸시〕하다. ¶ *~ someone's request over…* …에 대한 아무의 요구를 무시하다 / *His argument cannot be slighted.* 그의 논리는 경시할 수 없다. [Scand.]

:**slight·ly** [sláitli] *adv.* **1** in a slight manner. 약하게; 가냘프게. **2** to a slight degree. 약간; 조금.

•**slim** [slim] *adj.* (**slim·mer, slim·mest**) **1** slender; thin. 가느다란; 가냘픈; 얇은. ¶ *a ~ person* 호리호리한 사람 / *a ~ volume* 얇은 책. **2** not much; scant; small. 약간의; 얼마 안 되는. ¶ *very ~ chances of success* 매우 희박한 성공의 가망. **3** sly; tricky. 간사한; 교활한. — *vi.* become thin; lose weight, as by dieting or exercise. 가늘어 지다; (감식(減食)·운동 등으로) 체중이 줄다. — *vt.* make (something) thin. (…을) 가늘게〔마르게〕 하다. [Du.]

slime [slaim] *n.* Ⓤ **1** soft, sticky mud. 점토; 진흙. ¶ *Your shoes are covered with ~.*

너의 구두는 진흙투성이다. **2** a sticky substance given off by the skin of snails, snakes, etc. (달팽이·뱀 따위의) 점액; 진액(津液). [E.]

slim·ly [slímli] *adv.* in a slim manner. 가느다랗게; 날씬하게; 불충분하게; 조금. [*slim*]

slim·y [sláimi] *adj.* (**slim·i·er, slim·i·est**) **1** covered with slime. 점토로 뒤덮인; 진흙투성이의. ¶ *a ~ road* 흙탕길. **2** of or like slime. 끈적끈적한; 점착(粘着)하는. ¶ *a ~ liquid* 끈적끈적한 액체. **3** flattering; mean; unpleasant. 굽신거리는; 비열한; 치사한. ¶ *a ~ manner* 치사한 태도 / *a ~ traitor* 비열한 배신자. ● **slim·i·ly** [-li] *adv.* [*slime*]

sling [sliŋ] *n.* Ⓒ **1** a strip of leather used for throwing a stone. 투석기(投石器); 새총. **2** a hanging loop of cloth fastened around the neck for supporting a wounded arm. 목에 걸어 늘어뜨린 붕대; 삼각건. ¶ *He had to carry his arm in a ~.* 그는 팔을 삼각건에 걸며 메야 했다. **3** any of several devices composed of ropes, chains, etc. for lifting or carrying heavy objects. 와이어 로프; 계삭(繫索); 슬링.

— *v.* (**slung**) *vt.* **1** (P6,7,13) throw (a stone) by means of a sling; cast; hurl; fling. 투석기로 (돌을) 날리다〔던지다〕; (내)던지다. ¶ *~ stones at a cat* 고양이에게 돌을 던지다 / *~ someone out of the room* 아무를 방 밖으로 내던지다. **2** lift or carry (something) in a sling. …을 달아올리다. **3** (P6,7) hang in a sling; hang (something) so that it swings. …을 매달다〔걸머메다〕; (축) 늘어뜨리다. ¶ *The soldier slung the rifle over his shoulder.* 병사는 소총을 어깨에 걸머메었다.

— *vi.* (P1) throw. 내던지다. [E.]

sling ink, 《*colloq.*》 write controversially. (마구) 갈겨쓰다.

slink [sliŋk] *vi.* (**slunk**) (P2A) move, walk or go in a secret or guilty manner. 살금살금〔조용조용〕 걷다; 은밀하게 움직이다. ¶ *~ into a corner* 살금살금 구석진 곳으로 가서 틀어박히다. [E.]

:slip[1] [slip] *v.* (**slipped, slip·ping**) *vi.* **1** (P1,2A) move out of position; slide accidentally and fall. (물건이) 미끄러지다; 미끄러져 떨어지다. ¶ *The knife slipped and cut my hand.* 칼이 미끄러져 손을 베었다 / *The napkin slipped off his lap.* 냅킨이 무릎에서 미끄러져 떨어졌다 / *Her shawl slipped down.* 그녀의 숄이 어깨에서 흘러내렸다 / *The drawer slipped out easily.* 서랍은 쉽게 열렸다. **2** (P1,2A) slide suddenly on a smooth surface; miss one's footing; fall down. (발이) 미끄러지다; 발을 헛디디다; 넘어지다. ¶ *~ on the ice* 얼음 위에서 미끄러져 넘어지다 / *My foot slipped on the stairs.* 계단에서 발을 헛디뎠다〔발이 미끄러졌다〕 / *Mind you don't ~.* 미끄러지지 않도록 조심해라. **3** (P1,2A) move or pass secretly and quickly; move quietly; move without attracting notice. 살그머니 떠나다〔들어가다; 움직이다〕; (때가) 어느덧 지나가다. ¶ *He slipped away without a sound.* 그는 소리 없이 떠나버렸다 / *He slipped into* 〔*out of*〕 *the room.* 그는 살그머니 방으로 들어왔다〔방 밖으로 나갔다〕 / *Time slips by* 〔*away*〕. 시간이 덧없이 흐른다 / *~ up behind someone* 아무의 뒤로 살그머니 다가가다 / *Don't let this chance ~ by.* 이 기회를 놓치지 마라. **4** (P1,2A,3) go or move smoothly, quietly, or quickly. 미끄러지듯 나아가다〔달리다; 움직이다〕. ¶ *~ along over the snow* 눈 위를 미끄러지듯 달리다 / *~ through the waves* (배가) 파도를 가르며 미끄러지듯 나아가다 / *~ into one's chair* 의자에 살짝 앉다. **5** (P1,2A) 《often *up*》 make a mistake or an error. 실수〔잘못〕하다. ¶ *~ in one's grammar* 문법상의 잘못을 저지르다 / *He often slips in his speech.* 그는 자주 말실수를 한다 / *Sometimes our judgment slips.* 때때로 우리의 판단은 실수를 한다. **6** 《*from*》 (P1,3) escape from one's memory. 잊다; 기억에서 사라지다. ¶ *Her name slipped from my mind.* 그녀의 이름이 생각나지 않는다 / *The details had slipped from my mind.* 자세한 내용들이 기억나지 않았다. **7** (P1,3) put a garment on or off easily. (옷을) 아무렇게나 입다〔벗다〕. ¶ *~ into* 〔*out of*〕 *a jacket.* **8** (P3) pass gradually into or out of some condition, habit, etc. (어느 틈엔가) …상태에 빠지다〔빠져들다〕. ¶ *~ into an intimacy* 어느 사이엔가 친숙해지다 / *~ into a peaceful life* 〔*new way of life*〕 평화로운 생활에〔새로운 생활 양식에〕 들어가다. **9** (P1,3) become worse or weaker. 나빠지다; 약해지다. ¶ *My memory is slipping.* 나의 기억력이 약해지고 있다 / *Prices have slipped during the past year.* 물가는 작년 한 해 동안 하락했다.

— *vt.* **1** (P6,13) cause (something) to slip, pass, or move quickly or easily. …을 쑥 끼우다〔밀어 넣다〕; 미끄러뜨리다. ¶ *~ a ring on* (*to*) *one's finger* 손가락에 반지를 쑥 끼우다 / *~ one's coat off* 코트를 훌훌 벗다. **2** (P7,13) put or take quickly or secretly. …을 살짝 넣다〔꺼내다〕. ¶ *~ a letter into one's pocket* 얼른 편지를 주머니에 넣다 / *She slipped a coin into the porter's hand.* 그녀는 동전 한 닢을 운반인의 손에 살짝 놓았다. **3** (P6) escape from (someone or something). …에서 도망치다〔빠져나가다〕; (기억·주의에서) 사라지다; 벗어나다. ¶ *The prisoner slipped his pursuers.* 그 죄수는 추적자들을 따돌리고 도망쳤다 / *The appointment slipped my memory* 〔*mind*〕. 그 약속을 깜빡 잊고 있었다 / *The dog slipped his collar and ran away.* 개는 목걸이에서 빠져나와 도망갔다. **4** (P6) let (something) loose, go, or pass; miss. …을 풀어〔놓아〕 주다; …을 놓치다; 잃다. ¶ *~ a hound* 사냥개를 풀어놓다 / *Don't ~ the chance.* 기회를 놓치지 마라.

slip along, 《*sl.*》 go at great speed. 굉장한 속도로 가다.

slip from one's memory, be forgotten. 잊다.

slip into, 《*sl.*》 pummel; belabor; eat heartily of. 계속해서 치다; 비난하다; …을 실컷 먹다.
slip off, **a**) depart without leave-taking. 인사도 없이 가버리다. **b**) get rid of. …을 버리다.
slip on, pull (a garment) hastily. …을 서둘러 입다.
slip through the fingers, slide down by being slippery through the fingers. 손가락 사이로 미끄러져 떨어지다.
slip up, **a**) trip; stumble. 헛디디다. **b**) 《U.S. *colloq.*》 make a mistake. 실패〔실수〕하다; 틀리다.
— *n.* Ⓒ **1** an act of slipping; a sudden slide. 미끄러짐; (발 따위를) 헛디딤. ¶ *a ~ on the ice* 얼음위에 미끄러져 넘어짐 / *take a ~ on the ice* 얼음을 지치다. **2** a small, unintentional mistake or error. 못보고 빠뜨림; 잘못; 실수. ¶ *a ~ of the tongue* 말의 실수; 실언 / 《*prov.*》 *There's many a ~ between the cup and the lip.* 입에 든 떡도 넘어가야 제것이다《끝까지 방심은 금물》 / *It is one of the slips a wise man sometimes makes.* 그것은 현명한 사람이 때때로 범하는 종류의 잘못이다. **3** a woman's underdress; a loose cover for a cushion, a bed, etc. 슬립《여성용 속옷》; 베갯잇. **4** a smooth slope on which a ship is built or repaired; 《U.S.》 a place for a ship between two piers. 조선대; (잔교(棧橋)와 잔교 사이의) 정박소. [Teut.]
give someone the slip, escape from someone. (추적자 따위)를 따돌리다.

slip² [slip] *n.* Ⓒ **1** a long, thin piece of paper, wood, etc. (종이·나무 따위의) 가늘고 기다란 조각; 종잇조각. **2** a small branch, stem, or twig cut from a plant, used for planting. 접지(椄枝); 꺾꽂이용 가지. **3** a young, thin person. 야윈〔몸집이 가냘픈〕 젊은이. [G. & Du. =split, slit]

slip·cov·er [slípkʌ̀vər] *n.* Ⓒ a cloth cover for a chair, a sofa, etc. (의자 따위의) 덮개; 커버. [*slip*¹]

slip·knot [slípnɑ̀t / -nɔ̀t] *n.* **1** a knot made to slip along the string around which it is formed. 나비매듭. **2** a knot which can be undone by a pull. 풀매듭.

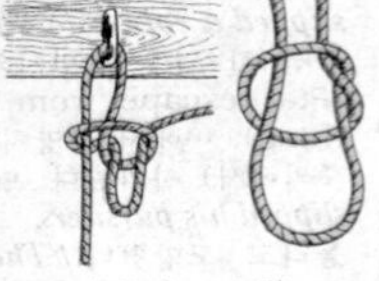
〈slipknot 2〉

slip-on [slípɑ̀n, -ɔ̀ːn / -ɔ̀n] *n.* an article of clothing, such as a shoe or sweater, that is easily put on or taken off. 손쉽게 입고 벗을 수 있는 옷〔스웨터·구두〕.

:slip·per [slípər] *n.* Ⓒ a light, low shoe for house wear. 슬리퍼.

·slip·per·y [slípəri] *adj.* (**-per·i·er, -per·i·est**) **1** (of a road) likely to cause slipping because of slime or smoothness. (길 따위가) 미끄러운. ¶ *a wet ~ road* 젖어 미끄러운 길 / *The steps are ~ with ice.* 계단은 얼음이 깔려 있어 미끄럽다. **2** that cannot be caught easily. 미끄러워 붙잡기 힘든. ¶ *a ~ bar of soap* 잡기에 미끈거리는 비누 / *as ~ as an eel* 미꾸라지같이 붙잡기 어려운. **3** not trustworthy; not to be depended on; unreliable; deceitful. 믿을〔의지할〕 수 없는; 속이는. ¶ *a ~ customer* 믿을 수 없는 사람 / *a clever but ~ fellow* 영리하지만 간교한 녀석 / *We know him to be ~.* 우리는 그가 믿을 수 없는 사람임을 안다. [*slip*¹]

slip·shod [slípʃɑ̀d / -ʃɔ̀d] *adj.* **1** wearing shoes worn down at the heels. 뒤축이 닳아빠진 구두를 신은. **2** rubbing the feet along the ground when walking. (걸을 때) 발을 질질 끄는. **3** careless; untidy. 홀게늦은; 단정치 못한. ¶ *~ work* 아무렇게나 하는 일.

slit [slit] *vt.* (**slit, slit·ting**) (P6,13,18) **1** make a long cut or opening in (something). …을 절개하다; …에 길게 째진 자리를 〔슬릿을〕 내다. ¶ *~ a skirt to make a pocket* 주머니를 내기 위해서 슬릿을 내다 / *~ an envelop open* 봉투를 개봉하다. **2** cut or tear (something) into long strips. …을 가늘고 길게 자르다〔베다, 째다, 찢다〕. ¶ *~ a hide into thongs* 짐승 가죽을 가늘고 길게 찢어서 가죽끈을 만들다. — *n.* Ⓒ a long, straight cut or opening. 가늘고 길게 째진〔베어진〕 자국〔상처〕. [E.]

slith·er [slíðər] *vi.* (P1,2A) move with a sliding motion. 주르르〔줄줄〕 미끄러지다. ¶ *~ over icy streets* 얼음이 덮인 거리를 미끄러지며 나아가다 / *The car began to ~ down the hill.* 자동차는 언덕을 주르르 내리닫기 시작했다. [A.S. *sliddérian*]

sliv·er [slívər] *n.* Ⓒ **1** a long, thin piece of wood, glass, etc.; a splinter. (재목 따위의) 쪼개진 조각; 가느다란 조각. **2** a loose fiber of wool, cotton, etc. 올이 굵은 섬유; 소모〔면〕(梳毛〔綿〕). — *vt., vi.* (P6,7;1) split or break (something) into slender fragments. (…을) 가늘고 길게〔세로로〕 베다〔찢다, 쪼개다〕; 찢어지다; 쪼개지다. [E.]

slob·ber [slɑ́bər / slɔ́b-] *vi.* (P1,3) **1** let saliva flow out of the mouth; soil with saliva. 침을 흘리다; 침으로 더럽혀지다. **2** 《*over*》 talk sentimentally or emotionally; show sentimental affection for. 우는 소리를 하다; 매우 감상적이 되다. ¶ *His aunts slobbered all over him when he fell ill.* 그가 병이 나자 숙모들은 무턱대고 걱정들만 했다. — *vt.* (P6,13) wet (something) with saliva; let fall (liquid); spill. …을 침으로 더럽히다; (우유 따위를) 흘리다. ¶ *~ a dress* 옷을 침으로 더럽히다 / *~ milk over a dress* 옷에 우유를 흘리다.
— *n.* Ⓤ **1** saliva. (군)침. **2** sentimental talk. 감상적인 이야기; 우는 소리. [E.]

sloe [slou] *n.* Ⓒ 《bot.》 a shrub with a small, plumlike fruit; the fruit. 자두류(의 열매). [E.]

slog [slɑg / slɔg] *vt., vi.* (**slogged, slog·ging**) **1** (P1; 6) (in boxing, cricket, etc.) hit hard. (권투·크리켓에서) 강타하다. **2** (P1,2A) work or walk doggedly. 꾸준히 일하다〔걷다〕. — *n.* Ⓒ a hard hit. 강타. [E.]

slo·gan [slóugən] *n.* Ⓒ **1** a word or phrase used by a party or group as a motto. 슬로건; 표어; 주의; 주장. ¶ *'Safety First' is our slogan.* '안전 제일'은 우리의 표어이다. **2** a war cry; a battle cry. 외침; 함성. [Gael.]

sloop [slu:p] *n.* Ⓒ a sailboat with a single mast. 외대박이 돛 배; 슬루프형의 배. [Du.]

slop [slɑp / slɔp] *n.* **1** Ⓒ water or other liquid carelessly spilled or splashed about. 엎지른 물〔액체〕; 튀기는 물. **2** 《often *pl.*》 dirty water from a kitchen. 구정물; 개숫물. **3** 《often *pl.*》 waste matter from a kitchen used as food for animals. 음식 찌꺼기; 먹다 남은 부엌찌끼《돼지먹이》. **4** 《often *pl.*》 weak, thin or poor liquid food. 반(半)유동식《죽·미음 등》. ¶ *live on slops* 죽〔미음〕을 먹고 살다.

— *vt.* (P6) **1** soil (something) by letting liquid fall upon it. (물 따위를 엎질러서) …을 더럽히다. **2** spill or splash (water). (물)을 엎지르다〔튀기다〕. ¶ ~ *water on the floor* 마루에 물을 엎지르다.

— *vi.* (P1) **1** spill or splash water. 물을 엎지르다〔튀기다〕. **2** 《*over, out*》 (of water) spill or splash out; run out in spilling; overflow. (물이) 엎질러지다; 넘치다; 넘쳐 흐르다. ¶ *The soup slopped over.* 국이 넘쳐 흘렀다. **3** walk or go through muddy water. (진)흙탕물 속을 걷다〔가다〕. [E.]

slop basin [⌐ ⌐–] *n.* a basin used to empty waste matter from teacups, etc. at table; a slop bowl. 차찌끼 버리는 그릇《찻잔 가신 물 따위를 쏟는 그릇》; 개수통.

:slope [sloup] *n.* **1** Ⓒ a slanting line or surface which goes upwards or downwards; rising and falling ground (as the side of a hill). 경사(면); 사면(斜面); 비탈. ¶ *go up* 〔*down*〕 *a* ~ 비탈을 오르다〔내려가다〕 / *the grassy slopes of a mountain* 산의 풀이 난 사면. **2** ⓊⒸ the amount or degree of a slope. 경사도; 물매. ¶ *a steep* 〔*gentle*〕 ~ 물매가 싼〔뜬〕 비탈 / *give a* ~ *to something* …에 물매를 주다; 경사지게 하다 / *the* ~ *of a roof* 지붕의 경사도.

— *vt.* (P6) cause (something) to go up or down at an angle. …을 기울이다; 경사지게 하다. ¶ *I sloped the ground so that the water could run away.* 나는 물이 잘 흘러나갈 수 있도록 지면을 경사지게 했다. — *vi.* (P1,2A) go up and down at an angle; slant; incline. 기울다; 비탈〔경사〕지다. ¶ *The path slopes down to the river.* 작은 길은 강쪽으로 비탈져 있다 / *The house has a sloping roof.* 그 집은 지붕이 경사져 있다. [E.]

slope about, saunter, walk about. 배회하다.

Slope arms! Place rifles sloping on shoulders! 어깨 총《구령》.

slop·py [slɑ́pi / slɔ́pi] *adj.* (**-pi·er, -pi·est**) **1** wet; muddy. 물기가〔수분이〕 많은; (진흙 따위로) 질척거리는. ¶ ~ *ground* 〔*roads*〕 질척거리는 지면〔도로〕 / ~ *weather* 구중중한 날씨. **2** splashed or soiled with liquid. 엎지른 물로 젖은〔더러워진〕. ¶ *a* ~ *table* 물·국물 따위로 더러워진 식탁. **3** careless; untidy; loose. 칠칠치 못한; 단정치 못한; 엉성한. ¶ *use* ~ *English* (어법상) 정확치 않은 영어를 사용하다 / *do* ~ *work* 일을 날림으로 하다. **4** 《*colloq.*》 (of sentiment or talk) stupidly sentimental; too emotional; silly. (감정·말이) 지나치게 감상적인; 어리석은. ¶ ~ *sentiment* 연약한 계집애 같은 감정〔감상〕 / ~ *talk* 푸념. [*slope*]

slot [slɑt / slɔt] *n.* Ⓒ a straight, narrow opening. 홈; 가늘고 긴 구멍. ¶ *a mail* ~ *in the door* 문의 편지 넣는 구멍 / *a* ~ *for a penny* (자동 판매기의) 요금 넣는 구멍 / *put* 〔*drop*〕 *a penny in a* ~ 자동 판매기에 동전을 넣다. — *vt.* (**slot·ted, slot·ting**) (P6) make a slot or slots in (something). …에 홈을 파다; (갸름한) 구멍을 내다. [F.]

sloth [slouθ, slɔ:θ] *n.* **1** Ⓤ laziness; idleness. 태만; 나태. **2** Ⓒ a South American animal which is very slow in moving and which lives in trees, hanging upside down from the branches. 나무늘보. [*slow*]

sloth·ful [slóuθfəl, slɔ́:θ-] *adj.* lazy; idle; indolent. 나태한; 게으른.

slot machine [⌐ –⌐] *n.* **1** 《Brit.》 a machine which sells peanuts, gum, etc., automatically when a coin is dropped into a slot. 자동 판매기; 슬롯머신. **2** 《U.S.》 a device for gambling. 자동 도박기.

slouch [slautʃ] *vi.* (P1,2A) **1** walk, stand or sit with the head or shoulders bent forward. 구부정한 자세로 걷다〔서다, 앉다〕. **2** droop or bend downward, like a halfdead plant. 몸을 앞으로 축 꾸부리다〔늘어뜨리다〕; (고개·머리를) 기운 없이 수그리다. — *vt.* (P6) cause (something) to bend downward. …을 수그러지게〔구부러지게〕 하다.

— *n.* Ⓒ **1** an act or state of bending the head or shoulders downward. 꾸부정함; 꾸부정한 자세. **2** a lazy person. 게으른 사람. [→slack]

slouch hat [⌐ ⌐] *n.* a hat with a broad brim which hangs over the face. 넓은 챙이 늘어진 중절모.

slouch·y [sláutʃi] *adj.* (**slouch·i·er, slouch·i·est**) slouching in an awkward manner; untidy. 앞으로 구부정한; 단정치 못한.

slough[1] [slau] *n.* Ⓒ **1** 《U.S.》 [slu:] a deep, muddy place; a marsh. 진구렁; 늪지대. **2** a condition of helplessness; a hopeless situation. 절망의 구렁텅이. [E.]

slough[2] [slʌf] *n.* Ⓒ **1** the old skin cast off by snakes and certain other animals. (뱀 따위의) 벗은 허물. **2** a layer of dead skin that drops off as a wound gets well. (상처가 아문 곳의) 딱지. — *vi.* (P2A) 《*off*》 be shed. 탈피하다; 허물벗다. — *vt.* (P6,7) **1** shed or cast off; throw off. …을 벗다; 벗어 버리다. ¶ *A snake sloughs its skin.* 뱀은 허물을 벗는다. **2** 《often *off*》 get rid of; throw off; discard. …을 버리다. ¶ ~ *off old customs* [*bad habits*] 묵은 관습[나쁜 습관]을 버리다. [E.]

Slo·vak [slóuvæk] *n.* **1** Ⓒ one of a Slavic people. 슬로바키아 사람. **2** Ⓤ their language. 슬로바키아 말. — *adj.* of Slovakia, its people or their language. 슬로바키아 민족[말]의. [*Slav*]

slov·en [slʌ́vən] *n.* Ⓒ a person who is careless in his appearance, habits, etc. (옷차림·습관 따위가) 단정치 못한 사람; 게으른 사람. [Du.]

slov·en·li·ness [slʌ́vənlinis] *n.* Ⓤ the state of being slovenly. 단정치 못함; 소홀함.

slov·en·ly [slʌ́vənli] *adj.* (**-li·er, -li·est**) untidy; careless in appearance, etc. 단정치 못한; 게으른; 소홀한. — *adv.* in a slovenly manner. 단정치 못하게; 소홀하게.

:slow [slou] *adj.* **1** not quick in motion; not rapid; moving at a low rate of speed. (속도가) 느린; 느릿느릿한. ¶ *a* ~ *walker* [*runner*] 속도가 느린 보행자[주자] / *a* ~ *horse* 느린 말 / *a* ~ *train* 완행 열차 / *a* ~ *march* 느릿느릿한 행진 / *by* ~ *steps* 느릿느릿한 발걸음으로. **2** taking a relatively long time to do [to complete]; taking much time; not hurrying. 시간이 좀 걸리는; 서서히 하는; 더딘; 서두르지 않는. ¶ *a* ~ *journey* 시간이 걸리는 여행 / *a* ~ *worker* 일이 더딘 일꾼 / *a* ~ *process* 시간이 좀 걸리는 과정 / ~ *progress* [*convalescence*] 더딘 진척[건강의 회복] / *The guests are* ~ *in arriving.* 손님의 도착이 늦다 / 《*prov.*》 *Slow and steady wins the race.* 느려도 착실하면 이긴다. **3** later than the correct time. (시계가) 늦은; 더디 가는(opp. fast). ¶ *My watch is* ~. 내 시계는 더디 간다 / *This watch is two minutes* ~. 이 시계는 2분 늦다. **4** dull in mind; not clever; not quick in understanding; stupid. (머리가) 둔한; 아둔한; 이해가 느린. ¶ *a* ~ *child* 지진아(遲進兒) / *a rather* ~ *girl* 좀 아둔한 소녀 / *a* ~ *pupil* 머리가 둔한[이해가 느린] 학생 / ~ *at arithmetic* 산수를 잘 못 하는 / ~ *in learning* [*understanding*] 공부를 잘 못 하는[이해가 더딘] / *a* ~ *learner* 이해가[습득이] 더딘 사람 / *He is* ~ *to learn* [*in learning his lessons*]. 그는 배우는 게 더디다[공부를 잘 못 한다] / *He is naturally so* ~. 그는 천성이 아둔한 사람이다. **5** not interesting; dull; not active. 재미 없는; 지루한; 활기가 없는. ¶ *a* ~ *game* 재미 없는[시시한] 게임 / *a* ~ *town* 활기 없는[침체된] 소도시 / *a* ~ *month* [*season*] 불경기의 달[계절] / ~ *trading* 부진한 무역 / *The market was* ~ *today.* 오늘의 시황은 활기가 없었다 / *I found the book rather* ~. 그 책은 (재미는커녕) 오히려 지루했다. **6** not quickly or easily moved. 좀처럼 …않는. ¶ ~ *to anger* 화를 잘 안 내는 / ~ *to take offense* 좀처럼 성을 내지 않는 / *The nation was not* ~ *to take up arms.* 그 나라는 무장 궐기하는 데 별로 시간이 걸리지 않았다 / *He is not* ~ *to grasp an opportunity.* 그는 기회 포착에 기민하다.

slow and steady, slow but steady. 천천히 착실하게.

slow of speech, tongue-tied. 입이 무거운.

slow of wit, dull-witted, stupid. 아둔한.

— *adv.* in a slow manner. 느리게; 천천히. ¶ *How* ~ *you read!* 너 참 더디 읽는구나 / *Do speak slower.* 좀더 천천히 말하시오 / *How* ~ *the time passes!* 시간이 참으로 더디 가는군 / *My watch goes* [*runs*] ~. 내 시계는 더디 간다.

go slow, **a**) neglect; be less active. 태만하다. **b**) be watchful against. …에 조심[유념]하다.

— *vt.* (P7) make (something) slow or slower. …의 속도를 떨어뜨리다. ¶ ~ *down an engine* [*a motorcar*] 엔진[자동차]의 속도를 떨어뜨리다. — *vi.* (P2A) become slow or slower. 속도를 늦추다; 속도가 떨어지다. ¶ *The car slowed down* [*up*] *over the bridge.* 자동차는 다리 위에서 속도를 낮추었다. [E.]

:slow·ly [slóuli] *adv.* not quickly. 느리게; 천천히. ¶ *Speak more* ~. 더 천천히 말하시오.

slow match [⌐ ⌐] *n.* a match of fuse that burns slowly, used for setting fire to gunpowder, dynamite, etc. 도화선(導火線).

slow-mo·tion [slóumóuʃən] *adj.* **1** moving at less than normal speed. (정상 속도보다) 느린. **2** showing action at much less than its actual speed. 고속도 촬영의; 슬로모션의.

slow·ness [slóunis] *n.* Ⓤ the state or quality of being slow. 느림; 더딤.

sludge [slʌdʒ] *n.* Ⓤ **1** soft mud. 진흙. **2** solid matter that sinks to the bottom of water. 침전물. **3** ⓐ a mass of melting snow; slush. 질척한 눈; 진창눈. ⓑ broken ice floating on the sea. (바다 위의) 부빙(浮氷). [→slut]

sludg·y [slʌ́dʒi] *adj.* (**sludg·i·er, sludg·i·est**) of soft mud; full of mud; muddy. 진창의; 질척거리는; 진흙투성이의.

slue[1] [slu:] *n.* =slough[1].

slue[2] [slu:] *vi., vt.* (P2;7) 《*around*》 turn; twist. (수평으로) 돌(리)다; (…을) 돌다; (…을) 비틀다. ¶ ~ *oneself round in one's chair* 의자에 앉아 빙글빙글 돌다. — *n.* Ⓒ the act of turning or twisting. (수평의) 회전; 선회; 비틀림. [?]

slug[1] [slʌg] *n.* Ⓒ **1** an animal like a snail, but without a shell. 민달팽이. **2** a person or thing that moves slowly. 느릿느릿 움직이는 것[사람·동물·차]. **3** a lump of metal. 금속의 덩어리. **4** a small piece of lead or other metal for firing from a gun. (공기총 따위의) 산탄; 작은 총알. **5** 《print.》 a thick piece of metal used in spacing (행간용의) 공목; 인테르. [Scand.]

slug[2] [slʌg] *n.* Ⓒ a hard hit or blow with a fist so as to make unconscious. 강타. — *vt.* (**slugged, slug·ging**) (P6) strike or hit (something) hard with a fist. …을 강타하다. [E.]

slug·gard [slʌ́gərd] *n.* Ⓒ a person who is idle or lazy. 게으름뱅이. ¶ *You ~!* 이 굼벵이 같은 놈아. — *adj.* idle; lazy. 게으른; 나태한. [*slug*[1]]

slug·gish [slʌ́giʃ] *adj.* **1** slow-moving. 느린. ¶ *a ~ stream* 흐름이 완만한 개울. **2** not active. (기능 따위가) 둔한; 활발치 못한. ¶ *a ~ liver* 기능 부전의 간장. **3** idle; lazy. 게으른. ¶ *a ~ market* 불황; 활기 없는 시황 / *a ~ disposition* 게으른 기질. ●**slug·gish·ly** [-li] *adv.* **slug·gish·ness** [-nis] *n.*

sluice [slu:s] *n.* Ⓒ **1** an artificial channel for controlling the water of a river, a lake, etc. 수로; 방수로. **2** a gate or valve for opening and closing such a channel; a sluice gate. 수문. **3** a device through which water is run for washing gold ore, etc. (채금용의) 세광통(洗鑛桶); 사금 채취통. — *vt.* (P6) **1** let out (water) by opening a sluice. 수문을 열어 (물)을 방출하다. **2** wash (gold ore) with water flowing in a sluice 세광통에 물을 흘려 (금광석)을 씻어 내다. **3** carry (something) in a sluice. …을 수로로 운반하다.

— *vi.* (P1,2A) run or flow in a sluice; rush out. (물이 수로를) 흐르다; 세차게 흘러나오다. [*exclude*]

sluice gate [ㅅ-ㅅ] *n.* a gate in an artificial passage for water, used to control its flow. 수문.

slum [slʌm] *n.* Ⓒ 《often *pl.*》 a crowded part of a city or town where the houses are dirty and unhealthy. 빈민가; 빈민굴. — *vi.* (**slummed, slum·ming**). (P1) visit slums for charitable or social purposes. (자선 등의 목적으로) 빈민굴을 방문하다. ¶ *go slumming* 빈민굴에서 자선(사업)을 하다; (호기심으로) 빈민가를 찾다. [? =room]

***slum·ber** [slʌ́mbər] *vi.* (P1) **1** 《chiefly *poet.*》 sleep. 잠자다; 졸다. **2** be in a state of rest, inactivity or sleeping; be not active. 잠자는 것 같은 휴식 상태에 있다; 활동하지 않다. ¶ *The volcano had slumbered for several years.* 그 화산은 수 년간 활동을 중지하고 있었다 / *His talents have slumbered for years.* 그의 재능은 여러 해 동안 잠자고 있다.

— *vt.* (P7) 《*away*》 spend; (time) in sleep; pass in sleep. 잠자며[하는 일 없이] (시간)을 보내다. ¶ *~ one's life away* 무위한 일생을 보내다 / *~ the afternoon away* 꾸벅꾸벅 졸면서 오후를 보내다.

— *n.* ⓊⒸ **1** 《often *pl.*》 sleep. 잠; 수면. ¶ *a deep ~* 깊은 잠 / *fall into (a) ~* 잠들어 버리다 / *break one's ~* 잠을 깨다 / *His slumbers were interrupted.* 그는 수면이 방해되었다. **2** the state of rest or inactivity. 잠든 것 같은 휴식 상태. [E.]

slum·ber·er [slʌ́mbərər] *n.* Ⓒ a person who slumbers. 잠자는 사람.

slum·ber·ous [slʌ́mbərəs] *adj.* **1** causing sleep; sleepy. 졸음이 오게 하는; 졸린. ¶ *~ heat* 졸음이 오게 하는 더위. **2** sleepy; drowsy. 졸리는.

slum·brous [slʌ́mbrəs] *adj.* =slumberous.

slump [slʌmp] *vi.* **1** (P2A) drop or sink down suddenly and heavily. 푹[쿵] 떨어지다; 쑥 빠지다. ¶ *~ into a chair* 의자에 털석 앉다 / *~ to the floor* 마루에 푹 쓰러지다. **2** (P1) (of price etc.) fall suddenly. 폭락하다. ¶ *Sales have slumped badly in the last month.* 지난 달 매상이 형편없이 뚝 떨어졌다.

— *n.* Ⓒ **1** the act of sinking down. 쿵[쑥] 떨어짐[빠짐]. ¶ *a ~ into mud* 진흙 속으로 쑥 빠짐. **2** a sudden drop in prices or trade. (주가 등의) 폭락; (사업 등의) 부진. ¶ *a ~ in prices* 가격의 폭락 / *Business is a ~ in Feb. and Aug.* 2월과 8월에는 사업이 부진하다. **3** a period of time when a Player or team does not play well; a period of depression in a person's activity etc. 슬럼프. [G. *schlumpen*]

slung [slʌŋ] *v.* p. and pp. of **sling.**

slunk [slʌŋk] *v.* p. and pp. of **slink.**

slur [slə:r] *vt.* (**slurred, slur·ring**) **1** (P6,7) 《*over*》 go through in a hurried or careless way; pass over without mention or consideration; refrain from mentioning. (일 따위를) 적당히[되는 대로, 아무렇게나] 처리하다[다루다]; 못 본 체하다; 간과하다; 언급을 삼가다. ¶ *He never slurs over his work.* 그는 절대로 일을 아무렇게나 하지 않는다 / *~ over someone's faults* 아무의 과실을 못 본 체 넘어가다. **2** (P6) pronounce (a word) hastily and indistinctly when speaking. …을 분명치 않게 발음하다. ¶ *If you ~ 'won't you', it sounds like 'wancha'.* 'won't you'를 단락없이 분명찮게 발음하면 'wancha'로 들린다. **3** (P6) 《mus.》 sing or play (two tones) in a smooth or connected way. (두 개의 음표를) 잇대어 노래[연주]하다. **4** (P6) mark with a slur; stain. …을 더럽히다. **5** (P6) speak badly of; slight; reproach. …을 중상[비방]하다; 헐뜯다.

— *vi.* (P1) pronounce or speak hurriedly and carelessly. 잰 말로 분명치 않게 말하다.

— *n.* Ⓒ **1** a hasty and indistinct pronunciation or way of pronunciation. 분명치 않은 발음. ¶ *talk with a ~.* **2** 《mus.》 a mark for two or more notes to be sung or played smoothly; a curved mark. 슬러; 연결선. **3** anything harmful to a person's reputation; a blot; an insulting or slighting remark. 오명(汚名); 오욕(汚辱); 중상. ¶ *There is no ~ on his good name.* 그의 명성에는 흠이 없다. [? *slut*]

put a slur upon =***cast slurs at,*** blame;

blot. …을 비난하다; 헐뜯다; (명성을) 더럽히다.

slur·ry [slə́:ri] *n.* a thin mixture of water and insoluble matter, e.g. clay, lime or cement. 슬러리; 현탁액(懸濁液)《진흙·석회 따위와 물의 혼합물》. [E.]

slush [slʌʃ] *n.* Ⓤ **1** soft mud; melted snow; snow melted with mud. 진창; (녹기 시작한) 진창눈. **2** 《*colloq.*》 silly sentiment; emotional talk or writing. 푸념. [? Dan. *slus*]

slush·y [slʌ́ʃi] *adj.* (**slush·i·er, shush·i·est**) of slush; full of slush. 진창의; 진창눈의.

slut [slʌt] *n.* Ⓒ a dirty, careless, or morally loose woman. 단정치 못한 〔허튼〕 계집. [E.]

slut·tish [slʌ́tiʃ] *adj.* (usu. of woman) careless; untidy. 단정치 못한; 허튼.

***sly** [slai] *adj.* (**sli·er** or **sly·er, sli·est** or **sly·est**) **1** cunning; full of tricks; apt to behave secretly. 교활한; 간사스러운; 남의 눈을 기이는. ¶ *as ~ as a fox* 여우처럼 교활한 / *a ~ dog* 교활한 녀석 / *a ~ trick* 〔*plot*〕 간교한 책략〔음모〕. **2** playful in an annoying way. 장난기 있는; 익살맞은. ¶ *a ~ humor* 〔*wink*〕 장난기 있는 익살〔윙크〕. [N. (*slay*)]

on* 〔*upon*〕 *the sly, secretly. 은밀히; 몰래.

sly·ly [sláili] *adv.* in a sly manner; secretly. 교활하게; 은밀히.

SM Service Man. 군인.

SMA Surplus Marketing Administration. 과잉 출하 관리국.

smack[1] [smæk] *n.* Ⓒ **1** a slight taste or flavor. 맛; 향; 풍미. ¶ *have a ~ of pepper* 〔*ginger*〕 후추〔생강〕의 맛이 나다 / *a tea with a smoky ~* 매캐한 냄새가 나는 홍차 / *a ~ of the cask in wine* 포도주에 남아 있는 술통의 향기. **2** a trace; a touch; a slight appearance; a suggestion. 조금 …한〔다운〕 데; 기미; 낌새. ¶ *add a ~ of papper to a dish* 요리에 후추를 조금 치다 / *a ~ of Europe* 유럽다운 점 / *The old sailor had a ~ of recklessness in his character.* 그 나이 든 선원은 성격에 좀 무모한 데가 있었다.

— *vi.* (P1) have a taste, trace, or touch of; suggest. …의 맛이 나다; …한 데〔기미〕가 있다. ¶ *This meat smacks of garlic.* 이 고기는 마늘 냄새가 난다 / *His speech smacked of arrogance.* 그의 말에는 오만한 데가 있었다. [E.]

smack[2] [smæk] *n.* Ⓒ **1** a quick, sharp noise made with the lips as a sign of enjoying food. 입맛 다시기. ¶ *a smack of the lips* 쩍쩍 입맛 다시기 / *eat it with a ~* 입맛을 다시며 먹다. **2** a quick blow with a whip; the sound of hitting by the flat of the hand. (찰싹하는) 채찍 소리; (철석 때리는) 손바닥 소리. ¶ *He gave* 〔*hit*〕 *me a ~ on the shoulder.* 그는 나의 어깨를 철석 때렸다 / *He brought his hand down with a ~ on the table.* 그는 손바닥으로 테이블을 철썩 내리쳤다. **3** a loud kiss. 쪽 소리 나는 키스. ¶ *He gave her a ~ on the cheek.* 그는 그녀의 뺨에 쪽 하고 키스했다.

— *vt.* (P6) **1** make a sharp sound with (the lips) as a sign of enjoying food. (쩍쩍) 입맛을 다시다. ¶ *~ one's lips over a favorite dish* 좋아하는 요리에 입맛을 다시다. **2** hit (someone or something) loudly with the flat of the hand. …을 손바닥으로 철썩 때리다. ¶ *~ a naughty child* 말썽꾸러기 아이를 손바닥으로 철썩 때리다 / *~ someone's face* 〔*cheek*〕 *with one's hand* 손바닥으로 아무의 따귀를 철썩 때리다. [? Du.; Imit.]

smack[3] [smæk] *n.* Ⓒ a small sailing boat with only one sail. (외대박이의) 소형 어선. [Du.]

smack·ing [smǽkiŋ] *adj.* lively; sharp. 활기 있는; 격렬한. ¶ *a ~ kiss* 열렬한 키스 / *a ~ blow* 일격 / *a ~ breeze* 세찬 바람. [Imit.]

:small [smɔ:l] *adj.* **1** ⓐ little in size; of less than usual or average size. (통상의 크기보다) 작은; 소형의(opp. big, large). ¶ *a ~ child* 작은 어린애 / *a ~ dog* 〔*desk, town, garden*〕 작은 개〔책상, 도시, 정원〕 / *a breed of ~ sheep* 작은 양의 품종; 혈통〔품종〕적으로 작은 양 / *~ letters* 소문자. ⓑ not great in number, amount, quality, degree, scale, etc. (양·수·정도·질·규모 등이) 얼마 안 되는; 적은; 소규모의. ¶ *a ~ business* 소기업 / *on a ~ scale* 소규모의〔로〕 / *~ hope of success* 적은 성공률 / *a ~ eater* 소식가 / *a ~ audience* 소수의 청중 / *a ~ number of people* 소수의 사람들 / *a ~ voice* 〔*sound*〕 작은〔가는〕 목소리〔소리〕 / *a ~ income* 〔*salary*〕 얼마 안 되는 수입〔급료〕 / *a man of ~ education* 별로 배우지 못한 사람 / *have ~ cause for gratitude* 감사해야 할 이유가 별로 없다 / *Small blame to him.* 그는 책망을 들어야 할 이유가 없다 / *The loss is ~.* 손실은 얼마 안 된다 / *I find my house rather ~.* 나의 집은 좀 작은 편이다. **2** of little worth or value; unimportant; of low social position; humble; petty. 중요치 않은; 하찮은. ¶ *a ~ mistake* 사소한 잘못 / *~ people* 보통〔하찮은〕 사람들 / *all the people, both great and ~* 모든 계층의 사람들 / *a ~ criminal* 경범죄인 / *~ cares and worries* 대단찮은 걱정거리 / *Don't bother me with such ~ matters.* 그런 자질구레한 일로 나를 번거롭게 하지 말게나. **3** narrow-minded; selfish; mean. 도량이 좁은; 비열한. ¶ *a ~ nature* 인색한 성질 / *a person of ~ mind* 도량이 좁은 소인 / *It's ~ of you not to forgive him.* 그를 용서치 않다니 너는 소인배다. **4** weak; light; diluted. (알코올 농도가) 약한; 싱거운. ¶ *~ ale* 〔*beer*〕 약한 맥주 / *This wine is very ~.* 이 포도주는 매우 싱겁다. [E.]

a small and early, a party with few guests and not kept up late. 일찍 끝나는 소인원수의 만찬.

feel small, be humiliated; feel ashamed or embarrassed 부끄럽게 여기다; 주눅이 들다.

great and small, all classes. 상하 귀천.
in a small way, on a small scale; unpretentiously. 소규모로; 검소히. ¶ *live in a ~ way* 검소하게〔조촐하게〕 살다.
It is small wonder that.... …을 이상하게 여길 것 없다; 매우 자연스럽다.
no small, a great. 대단한; 적지 않은.
of no small consequence, serious. 중대한.

small arms [ˊ ˊ] *n. pl.* weapons that can be easily carried by a man, such as a rifle or a pistol. 휴대용 병기; 소(小)화기《소총·권총 따위》.

small beer [ˊ ˊ] *n.* **1** very thin beer. 약한 맥주. **2** anything unimportant. 시시한 일〔것〕.

small capital 〔**cap**〕 [ˊ ˊ–– 〔ˊ〕] *n.* a letter of less height than the fount's regular capitals. 보통의 소문자 크기의 대문자.

small change [ˊ ˊ] *n.* **1** coins which have little value. 잔돈. **2** a person or thing that is not important. 하찮은 사람〔물건〕.

small fry [ˊ ˊ] *n.* **1** young fish in a shoal. 어린〔잔〕 물고기. **2** persons of no importance. 시시한 패거리; 송사리들. **3** 《*joc*》 young children. 어린애들.

small holder [ˊ ˊ–] *n.* 《Brit.》 a farmer who owns or rents small piece of land for farm. 소(小)자작농.

small holding [ˊ ˊ–] *n.* 《Brit.》 a small farm. 소 자작 농지.

small hours [ˊ ˊ], **the** *n.* the early hours of the morning just after midnight. 심야; 오밤중《새벽 1시에서 3시 사이》.

small·ish [smɔ́:liʃ] *adj.* rather small. 좀 작은(듯 싶은).

small letter [ˊ ˊ–] *n.* an ordinary letter; a letter which is not capital. 소문자.

small-mind·ed [smɔ́:lmáindid] *adj.* narrow-minded; limited in one's view of life; mean. 도량이 좁은; 인색한.

small·ness [smɔ́:lnis] *n.* Ⓤ the state or quality of being small in size, quantity, etc.; small-mindedness. (크기·양·수 따위가) 작음; 적음; 얼마 안 됨; 옹졸.

small·pox [smɔ́:lpɑ̀ks / -pɔ̀ks] *n.* Ⓤ a dangerous, easily spreading disease that causes spots on the skin. 천연두.

small talk [ˊ ˊ] *n.* easy, light conversation on general subjects of little importance. 잡담.

small-time [smɔ́:ltáim] *adj.* insignificant; unimportant. 중요치 않은; 시시한.

:smart [smɑ:rt] *adj.* **1** (of a blow or pain) severe; sharp. 날카로운; (격)심한; 쿡쿡 쑤시는. ¶ *a ~ blow* 강타 / *a ~ pain in the side* 옆구리의 심한 통증. **2** quick; lively; rapid and vigorous; quick and prompt in action; active. 재빠른; 민첩한; 활발한. ¶ *a ~ walk* 빠른 걸음걸이; 속보 / *walk with a ~ step* 빠른 걸음걸이로 걷다 / *You'd better be pretty ~ about the job.* 그 일을 하는 데는 좀 민첩한〔활발한〕 게 좋다. **3** skillful; quick and clever; capable; intelligent. 솜씨 있는〔좋은〕; 기민한; 재치 있는; 영리한. ¶ *a ~ carpenter* 솜씨 좋은 목수 / *be ~ at* 〔*in*〕 *one's work* 일이 재빠르고 솜씨가 있다 / *make a ~ job of it* 재치있게 일을 해치우다 / *a ~ student* 영리한 학생 / *He is ~ enough to do such thing easily.* 그는 영리하므로 그런 일은 간단히 할 수 있다. **4** pointed but superficial; clever and dishonest; unscrupulously clever; sharp in dealings; shrewd. 건방진; 교활한; 약아빠진; 빈틈없는. ¶ *a ~ attitude* 건방진 태도 / *She is given to saying ~ things.* 그녀는 건방진 소리를 하는 버릇이 있다 / *a ~ businessman* 약삭빠른〔빈틈이 없는〕 사업가 / *He is ~ in his dealings* 그는 거래에 빈틈이 없다. **5** neat; well dressed; fashionable. (옷차림이) 말쑥한〔단정한〕; 멋있는; 유행의. ¶ *a ~ dress* 멋있는 옷 / *a ~ appearance* 스마트한 외모 / *His clothes were not new, but they still looked ~.* 그의 옷이 새 것은 아니나, 아직도 멋있어 보였다. **6** 《*colloq*, but old-fashioned》 fairly large; considerable. 꽤 많은; 상당한. ¶ *a ~ number of people* 상당수의 사람들 / *a ~ few* 꽤 많은 수(의).

— *vi.* **1** (P1,3) feel a sharp pain on the surface of the skin. (피부가) 따끔따끔하다; 아리다; 욱신거리다. ¶ *The wound smarts.* 상처가 쑤신다 / *My face smarts with the cold wind.* 얼굴이 찬바람을 맞아 얼얼하다. **2** suffer mental pain; feel hurt; feel angry at. 괴로워하다; 상심하다; 분개하다. ¶ *He was still smarting from the insult.* 모욕당한 것을 아직도 분개하고 있었다.

— *n.* Ⓒ **1** a lively, sharp pain. (쿡쿡) 쑤시는 아픔; 쑤심. ¶ *the ~ of a cut* 〔*wound*〕 (벤) 상처의 쑤시는 아픔. **2** severe suffering and sorrow. 고뇌; 비통. ¶ *feel the ~ of one's folly* 자신의 어리석은 짓을 슬퍼하다〔분해하다〕. [E.]

smart-alec(**k**) [smá:rtæ̀lik] *n.* 《*colloq.*》 a person who tries to appear clever. 잘난〔똑똑한〕 체하는 사람.

smart·en [smá:rtn] *vt.* (P6,7) make (something) smart. …을 말쑥하게〔멋있게〕하다. ¶ *~ oneself up* 몸차림을 말쑥하게 하다 / *~ (up) one's clothes* 〔*house*〕 옷〔집〕을 산뜻하게〔깨끗하게〕 하다. — *vi.* (P1,2A) become smart. 깨끗해지다; 산뜻해지다.

smart·ish [smá:rtiʃ] *adj.* rather smart. 꽤 스마트한.

smart·ly [smá:rtli] *adv.* in a smart way. 말쑥하게; 기민하게.

smart·ness [smá:rtnis] *n.* the quality or condition of being smart. 세련됨; 멋있음; 빈틈없음.

·smash [smæʃ] *vt.* (P6,7) **1** break (something) into pieces with violence; shatter. …을 산산조각 내다; 때려부수다. ¶ *She dropped the plate and smashed it.* 그녀는 접시를 떨어뜨려 산산조각을 냈다 / *~ a window*

창유리를 부수다 / ~ *in a door* (밖에서) 문을 때려 부수다 / ~ *up the furniture* 가구를 때려 부수다 / ~ *a window open* 창문을 부수고 열다. **2** hit hard; give a blow to (something or someone); strike with a sudden blow. …을 세게 때리다[치다]. ¶ ~ *someone with the fist* 아무를 주먹으로 때리다 / ~ *a man on the nose.* 아무의 코에 한방 먹이다. **3** defeat completely; bring to nothing; destroy; crush. …을 참패[패배]시키다; 분쇄하다. ¶ ~ *an enemy* 적군을 격파하다 / ~ *an argument* 의론을 분쇄하다 / *His hopes were smashed.* 그의 희망은 산산조각이 났다. **4** ruin financially; make bankrupt. 파산시키다. **5** 《tennis》 hit (the ball) with a hard, fast, overhand stroke. (공)을 스매시하다.

— *vi.* **1** (P1,2A) be broken into many pieces; fall to pieces. 박살[산산조각]이 나다. ¶ *The cup fell and smashed to pieces.* 컵이 떨어져 산산조각이 났다. **2** (P3) ⓐ 《*into*》 rush against or into something violently; come into violent contact; dash or collide. 충돌하다. ¶ *The car smashed into the bridge.* 자동차는 다리에 충돌했다. ⓑ break away with force. 돌진하다; 튀어나가다. ¶ *A bullet smashed through the windscreen.* 총알이 (자동차의) 바람막이 유리창을 뚫고 날아갔다. **3** (P3) become ruined; be financially ruined. 파산하다.

— *n.* Ⓒ **1** an act or a sound of breaking to pieces. 분쇄(하는 소리); 부서지는 소리. ¶ *the ~ of glasses breaking on the floor.* 마룻바닥에서 컵들의 깨지는 소리. **2** a violent collision; a crash; a wreck. 대충돌. ¶ *a railway ~* 열차의 충돌. **3** a fall; a complete ruin in business; failure. 몰락; 파산; 실패. ¶ *the ~ of a great business* 대사업의 파산. **4** 《tennis》 a hard, fast, overhand stroke. 스매시.

go* [*come*] *to smash, be ruined; fail completely. 무너지다; (완전히) 찌부러지다; 파산하다.

— *adv.* with a smash. 철썩; 쿵; 쟁그렁; 정통으로. ¶ *The cars ran ~ into each other.* 두 자동차는 정면 충돌하였다. [Imit.]

smash·ing [smǽʃiŋ] *adj.* **1** so strong and powerful as to shatter or destroy something extraordinary; crushing; disastrous. 분쇄적[파괴적]인; 맹렬한. ¶ *a ~ blow* [*defect*] 대타격[대참패] / *a ~ victory* 대승리. **2** 《*colloq.*》 terribly good. 매우 좋은. ¶ *a ~ success* 굉장한 성공 / *We had a ~ time.* 참으로 재미있었다.

smash-up [smǽʃʌ̀p] *n.* Ⓒ a violent accident between motor vehicles; a failure in business; a great misfortune. (자동차 따위의) 대충돌; (사업의) 실패; 파산; 재난. ¶ *a head-on ~* 정면 충돌.

smat·ter·er [smǽtərər] *n.* Ⓒ a person with little knowledge of something. (지식·학문 등이) 어설픈 사람; 반거들충이. [↓]

smat·ter·ing [smǽtəriŋ] *n.* 《*a ~* 》 little knowledge of something. 수박 겉핥기식의 지식; 어설픈[데아는] 지식. ¶ *have a ~ of physics* 물리학을 데알고 있다. [Swed.]

smear [smiər] *vt.* (P13) **1** cover or spoil (something) with anything dirty, sticky, or greasy. (기름 따위)를 …에 처바르다[칠하다]; …을 (기름으로) 더럽히다. ¶ ~ *one's fingers with milk* =~ *milk on one's fingers* 손가락을 우유로 더럽히다 / ~ *one's face with jam* 잼으로 얼굴을 더럽히다 / *Mary smeared the table with black sauce.* 메리는 식탁을 검은 소스로 더럽혔다. **2** rub or spread. 문질러 더럽히다. ¶ ~ *the address on letter* 편지에 쓰여 있는 주소를 문질러 읽을 수 없게 만들다. **3** harm or injure the good reputation of (someone), esp. falsely. (명성 따위)를 더럽히다; 훼손하다.

— *vi.* (P1) cause a smear; be or become smeared. 더러워지다. ¶ *Anything written with a soft pencil smears easily.* 무른 연필로 쓰여진 것은 쉽게 더러워진다.

— *n.* Ⓒ **1** a dirty mark made by smearing. 얼룩; 오점. **2** an act of harming a reputation. (명예 따위)를 더럽힘; 명예 훼손; 중상; 비방. ¶ *The newspapers ran a ~ campaign against him.* 신문들이 그에 대한 비방 운동을 벌였다. [E.]

smear·y [smíəri] *adj.* (**smear·i·er, smear·i·est**) **1** smeared; full of dirty spots. 더러워진; 얼룩투성이의. ¶ *a woman's face ~ with paint and powder* 진한 화장으로 얼룩이 진 여인의 얼굴. **2** tending to smear; sticky; greasy. 끈적이는; 기름이 밴. ¶ ~ *paint* 끈적이는 페인트. [↑]

:smell [smel] *v.* (**smelled** or **smelt**) *vt.* **1** (P6,23) get the odor of (something) through the nose; perceive an odor by the sense of smell. …의 냄새를 맡다. ¶ *Do you ~ something burning?* 무언가 타는 냄새가 나지 / *I ~ something burning.* 무언가 타는 냄새가 난다 / ~ *a powder* ⇨powder / ~ *a rat* ⇨rat. **2** (P6) test by the sense of smell; test by the scent or odor; sniff. (…을 알기 위해) …의 냄새를 맡아 보다. ¶ ~ *each perfume* 향수를 하나씩 냄새 맡아 보다 / ~ *the milk to see if it is sour* 시어지지 않았나 해서 우유의 냄새를 맡아 보다 / *Just ~ this rose.* 이 장미의 냄새를 좀 맡아 보게. **3** 《*out*》 track, discover, by means of the sense of smell; discover. 알아채다; 찾아내다. ¶ ~ *danger* 위험을 감지하다 / ~ *trouble brewing* 문제거리가 일어날 낌새를 알아채다 / ~ *treason* 모반을 알아채다. — *vi.* **1** (P3) 《*at*》 try to get an odor through the nose; sniff the odor at; use the sense of smell at. 냄새를 맡다. ¶ ~ *at a flower* 꽃의 냄새를 맡다. **2** (P1) have the sense of smell. 후각이 있다. ¶ *One cannot ~ with a cold in the nose.* 코감기가 걸리면 냄새를 못 맡는다. **3** (P1,3) 《*of*》 have an odor; give out an odor, good or bad. 냄새가 나다. ¶ ~ *good* [*bad*] 좋은[나쁜] 냄새가 나다 / *The meal smells good.* 식사는 맛있는 냄새가 난다 / *He smells of fish.*

그에게서 생선 냄새가 난다 / *In hot weather meat soon begins to smell.* 날씨가 더울 때는 고기에서 이내 상한 냄새가 난다 / *The house smells of paint.* 집에서 페인트 냄새가 난다. **4** (P3) suggest; have a trace of. …의 낌새가 있다. ¶ *the dead leaves smelling of autumn* 가을을 느끼게 하는 낙엽 / *His offer smells of shady dealing.* 그의 제의는 뭔가 수상쩍은 데가 있는 거래란 느낌이 든다.

smell out, find out another's secret, etc. (비밀 따위)를 알아 내다.

— *n.* **1** Ⓤ the sense of smell. 후각. ¶ *A dog has keen* ~. 개는 후각이 예민하다 / *Taste and* ~ *are closely concerned.* 맛과 냄새는 밀접한 관계가 있다. **2** ⓊⒸ odor; scent. 냄새; 향기. ¶ *the* ~ *of a rose* 장미꽃 향기 / *a* ~ *of gas* 가스 냄새 / *a pleasing* 〔*disgusting*〕 ~ 기분 좋은〔구역질나는〕 냄새. [E.]

take a smell at 〔***of***〕, inhale in order to ascertain …의 냄새를 맡아 보다.

smelling salts [ㅅ-ㅅ] *n. pl.* a preparation for smelling, used to relieve faintness, headaches, etc. 각성제.

smell·less [sméllis] *adj.* having no smell. 무취의; 냄새가 없는.

smell·y [sméli] *adj.* (**smell·i·er, smell·i·est**) 《*colloq.*》 having or giving out a strong or unpleasant smell. 불쾌한〔코를 찌르는〕 냄새가 나는.

smelt[1] [smelt] *vt.* (P6) melt (ore or metal) so as to separate the metal out of it; refine (impure metal) by melting. (금속을) 용해하다; 제련〔정련〕하다. [Teut. (*melt*)]

:**smelt**[2] [smelt] *v.* p. and pp. of **smell.**

smelt·er [sméltər] *n.* Ⓒ **1** a person who smelts ores or metals. 제련업자. **2** a place where ores or metals are smelted. 제련소. **3** a furnace for melting ores. 용광로.

:**smile** [smail] *vi.* (P1,3,4) **1** show pleasure or happiness in the face; indicate mild amusement by means of the expression of one's face; give a smile. 미소짓다; 생긋 웃다. ¶ *He smiled to see the children play.* 어린애들이 노는 것을 보고 그는 미소지었다 / ~ *through one's tears* 눈물이 글썽한 눈으로 웃다 / *She smiled at him.* 그녀는 그를 보고 웃었다. **2** present a cheerful aspect; show a pleasant aspect or look. (경치 따위가) 환하다; 밝고 산뜻하다. ¶ *a smiling landscape* 밝고 산뜻한 경치 / *All nature smiled.* 천지는 희색에 차 있었다. **3** look 〔regard〕 with favor; look pleasant. (운·기회 등이) 트이다; 열리다. ¶ *Fortune smiled on her.* 그녀에게 운이 트였다; 운명이 미소지었다 / *The weather smiled on us.* 날씨는 우리에게 알맞았다.

— *vt.* (P6,7) **1** express (something) by smiling. …을 미소로써 나타내다. ¶ ~ *farewell* 미소로 작별을 고하다 / *She smiled a pleased welcome.* 그녀는 미소지으며 기쁜 듯 환영했다. **2** 《*into, out of*》 change or affect (someone) by smiling. 미소로써 …하게 하다. ¶ *She smiled me out of my anger.* 그녀는 미소로써 나의 노여움을 풀어 주었다 / ~ *one's tears* 〔*grief*〕 *away* 웃음으로 눈물〔슬픔〕을 거두게〔잊게〕 하다. **3** give (a smile). …한 웃음을 웃다. ¶ ~ *a hearty* 〔*sad, bitter*〕 ~ 진심에서 우러나오는〔슬픈, 쓰디쓴〕 웃음을 웃다. 語法 동족 목적어를 수반함.

smile at, **a**) look at with pleasure or amusement. …을 보고 미소짓다. **b**) regard (something) with slight scorn. …을 일소에 부치다. ¶ *I can* ~ *at your threats.* 나는 너의 위협을 웃으며 넘겨 버릴 수 있다.

smile away, drive or put away (tears, etc.) by smiling. (눈물 따위)를 웃어 지우다.

smile on 〔***upon***〕***,*** show favor to (someone); look on (someone) with approval. …에 호의를 표시하다; (운 따위가) …에게 향하다〔열리다〕.

— *n.* Ⓒ **1** an act of smiling; an ironical smile. 미소; 빈정대는 웃음. ¶ *greet someone with a* ~ 미소로 아무를 맞이하다 / *raise a* ~ *on someone's face* 아무의 얼굴에 미소를 자아내게 하다. **2** a smiling face; a pleasant or agreeable aspect or look. 웃는 얼굴; (경치 따위의) 맑고 환한 모습. ¶ *the* ~ *of spring* 봄의 미소. **3** 《usu. *pl.*》 가호(加護); 은총. ¶ *the smiles of fortune* 운명〔행운〕의 미소. [Teut.]

smil·ing [smáiliŋ] *adj.* showing smiles; looking pleasant; looking favorable. 웃는; 명랑한; 밝은; 호의적인. ● **smil·ing·ly** [-li] *adv.*

smirch [smə:rtʃ] *vt.* (P6) **1** make (something) dirty; soil with dirt, dust, etc. …을 더럽히다. **2** dishonor (someone, reputation); disgrace. (아무의 명성·명예 따위)를 더럽히다; 중상하다. — *n.* Ⓒ a dirty mark; a blot or stain (on a good name, etc.). (명성 따위의) 오점; 더럼. ¶ *It has left a* ~ *on his reputation.* 그것은 그의 명성에 오점을 남겼다. [? O.F.]

smirk [smə:rk] *n.* Ⓒ an affected smile; a self-satisfied smile. 억지 웃음; (자기 만족의) 싱글거리는 웃음. — *vi.* (P1) smile in this way. 억지 웃음을〔능글맞게〕 웃다. [→smile]

smit [smit] *v.* pp. of **smite.**

***smite** [smait] *v.* (**smote, smit·ten** or **smit**) *vt.* (P6,7) **1** 《chiefly *arch., joc.*》 strike or hit hard with the hand, a stick, etc. …을 세게 치다〔때리다〕. ¶ ~ *someone on the back with a stick* 몽둥이로 아무의 등을 세차게 때리다 / ~ *someone dead* 아무를 때려 죽이다. **2** 《*lit.*》 defeat, punish, or destroy; kill. …을 멸망〔대패〕시키다; 징벌하다; 죽이다. ¶ ~ *the enemy* 적을 쳐부수다. **3** attack (someone or something) with force. (병·재난 따위가) …을 덮치다. ¶ *The plague smote the entire country.* 페스트가 전국을 휩쓸었다. **4** move the feelings of (someone) with a strong feeling such as love, fear or grief. …의 마음을 찌르다〔사로잡다〕; 괴롭히다. ¶ *be smitten with fear* 공포에 사로잡히다 / *His conscience*

smote him. 그는 양심의 가책을 받았다 / *He was smitten with her at first sight.* 그는 첫눈에 그녀에게 반했다.
— *vi.* (P2A,3) 《*upon*》 come with force. 세게 치다; 부딪다. ¶ ~ *on the door* 문을 쾅쾅 두드리다 / ~ *at someone* 아무를 세게 때리다 / *His knees smote together.* (두려움 따위로) 그는 오금이 저려 꼼짝 못 했다.
— *n.* Ⓒ a heavy blow; trial. 강타; 시도. [E.]

smith [smiθ] *n.* Ⓒ a person who makes things of metal with a hammer and an anvil. 대장장이; 금속 세공인. [G. *schmied*]

smith·y [smíθi, smíði] *n.* Ⓒ (*pl.* **smith·ies**) a blacksmith's workshop. 대장간. [E.]

smit·ten [smítn] *v.* pp. of **smite.**

smock [smak / smɔk] *n.* Ⓒ a long loose outer garment for protecting clothing. (옷 위에 걸치는) 긴 겉옷; 스목.
— *vt.* (P6) trim or ornament (a dress, a blouse, etc.) with smocking. …에 장식 주름을 달다[붙이다]. [E.] 〈smock〉

smock·ing [smákiŋ / smɔ́k-] *n.* Ⓤ an ornamental gather for smocks, dresses, etc. (다이아몬드형 따위의) 장식 주름.

smog [smag, smɔ(:)g] *n.* Ⓤ smoky fog; a mixture of smoke and fog in the air, esp. over a city. 스모그; 연무(煙霧). [*smoke*+*fog*]

:smoke [smouk] *n.* **1** Ⓤ cloud-like gas that rises when something burns. 연기. ¶ *a cloud of* ~ 뭉게뭉게 올라가는 연기. **2** anything like smoke, such as vapor, fog, etc. 연기 비슷한 것《증기·안개·물보라 따위》. ¶ *the* ~ *of a waterfall* 폭포의 물안개. **3** 《*sing.* only》 the act of smoking. (담배) 한 대 피우기. ¶ *have a* ~ 담배 한 대 피우다 / *Will you have a* ~*?* 담배 한 대 피우겠습니까. **4** Ⓒ a cigar; a cigarette. 엽궐련; 궐련.

end in smoke, end in failure; have no solid result. 실패로 끝나다.

from smoke into smother, from one evil to another or a worse. 갈수록 태산.

like smoke, 《*sl.*》 rapidly; easily. 잽싸게; 쉽게.

There is no smoke without fire. 《*prov.*》 Every story has some foundation. 아니 땐 굴뚝에 연기 날까.

— *vt.* **1** (P6) cure by exposure to smoke; treat (meat, fish, etc.) with smoke in order to flavor or preserve it. 훈제(燻製)하다. ¶ ~ *a ham* [*salmon*] 햄을[연어를] 훈제하다. **2** (P6) breathe in and out the smoke of (tobacco). (담배를) 피우다. ¶ ~ *a cigarette* 궐련을 한 대 피우다. **3** (P6) ⓐ make black with smoke; color or darken by smoke. 그을리게 하다. ¶ *The lamp smokes the ceiling.* 등잔불이 천장을 검게 그을린다 / *smoked glass* 검게 그을린 유리《태양 관찰용》. ⓑ spoil the taste of (food) by allowing smoke to reach it when cooking. (요리할 때 음식에) 연기 냄새[단내]가 나게 하다. ¶ *The milk has been smoked.* 우유가 눌어 버렸다. **4** (P6,7) 《usu. *out*》 ⓐ drive or force out with smoke or chemical fumes; make (someone) free from harmful insects, animals, etc. by forcing in smoke. 훈증하다; (벌레 따위를) 연기를 피워 쫓아내다. ¶ ~ *rats out of a barn* 연기를 피워 창고에서 쥐를 몰아내다 / ~ *out a sickroom* 병실을 연기로 소독하다 / ~ *plants* 식물을 훈증하다. ⓑ force (someone) out of hiding; bring into the open. (은신처에서 범죄자 따위를) 나오게 하다; 폭로하다. ¶ ~ *out a criminal* 범인을 찾아내다. **5** (P18) bring into a certain state by smoking. 흡연으로 …한 상태가 되게 하다. ¶ ~ *oneself sick* 흡연으로 어질어질해지다.
— *vi.* (P1,2A) **1** give out smoke. 연기를 내다. ¶ *On every hill a bonfire smoked.* 모든 산마다 화톳불이 하나씩 연기를 냈다. **2** give off offensive or too much smoke; give out smoke in the wrong direction, esp. into a room. 연기가 많이 나다; (연기가 잘 빠지지 않고) 내다. ¶ *The lamp* [*wood*] *smokes.* 등잔내[나무내]가 난다 / *The fireplace smokes.* 그 아궁이는 불이 잘 들이지 않는다. **3** give off something like smoke. 김이 무럭무럭 나다; 땀을 줄줄 흘리다; 먼지를 피우다. ¶ *The horses were smoking after the gallop.* 말들은 전속력으로 달린 뒤라 몸에서 김이 무럭무럭 나고 있었다. **4** breathe in and out the smoke of tobacco. 담배를 피우다. ¶ *Woman* ~ *these days.* 요즘은 여성들도 담배를 피운다 / *He smokes like a chimney.* 그는 화통처럼 계속 담배를 피운다 / *No smoking.* 금연《게시》. [E.]

smoke-dried [smóukdràid] *adj.* dried in smoke. 훈제(燻製)의.

smoke·house [smóukhàus] *n.* Ⓒ a place where meat, fish, etc., are smoked. (육류의) 훈제실(燻製室).

smoke·less [smóuklis] *adj.* producing or having no smoke. 무연(無煙)의; 연기 없는.

smok·er [smóukər] *n.* Ⓒ **1** a person who smokes tobacco. 흡연자. ¶ *a heavy* ~ 골초; 애연가. **2** a railway car, or a part of one, where a person may smoke. (열차의) 흡연 찻간; 흡연칸[실]. **3** 《Brit.》 = smoking-concert. **4** 《U.S.》 an informal social gathering for men only. 남자들만의 사교모임.

smoke screen [ㅅㅅ] *n.* **1** a cloud of thick smoke for hiding ships, airplanes, etc. from the enemy. 연막. **2** something used to cover up or hide; a veil. (의도·활동 따위를 숨기기 위한) 베일; 위장.

smoke·stack [smóukstæ̀k] *n.* Ⓒ a tall chimney of a factory, a ship, etc. (기선·공장 따위의) 높은 굴뚝.

smok·ing-car [smóukiŋkɑ̀:r], 《Brit.》

-car·riage [-kæ̀ridʒ] *n.* a car 〔carriage, compartment〕 where smoking is allowed. (열차의) 흡연칸〔실〕.

smok·ing-com·part·ment [smóukiŋ-kəmpɑ̀:rtmənt] *n.* = smoking-car.

smok·ing-con·cert [smóukiŋkɑ̀nsə:rt / -kɔ̀n-] *n.* 《Brit.》 a concert at which smoking and drinking are allowed. (흡연·음주가 허락된) 음악회.

smoking room [∠-∠] *n.* a room for smoking or in which smoking is permitted. 흡연실.

smok·y [smóuki] *adj.* (**smok·i·er, smok·i·est**) **1** giving off much smoke. 연기가 많이 나는; 내운. ¶ *a ~ fire* 내운 불. **2** full of smoke; covered by smoke. 연기가 많은〔자욱한〕. ¶ *a ~ room* 〔*town*〕 연기가 자욱한 방〔도시〕. **3** darkened or stained with smoke. (연기로) 검게 그을은. ¶ *a ~ ceiling* 연기로 검게 그을은 천장. **4** like smoke in color, smell, etc. (색깔·냄새·맛·모양 따위가) 연기와 같은; 매캐한; 거무칙칙한. ¶ *She has eyes of a ~ grey.* 그녀의 눈빛은 짙은 회색이다 / *the ~ flavor of ham* 햄의 훈연(燻煙) 맛.

smol·der, 《Brit.》 **smoul-** [smóuldər] *vi.* (P1) **1** burn or give out smoke slowly without any flame. (불꽃 없이) 내다; 연기나다; (불이 잘 타지 않고) 연기만 내다. ¶ *the smoldering ashes of a cigar* 모락모락 연기나는 엽궐련의 재. **2** (of feelings, etc.) exist in one's heart, though showing little outward sign; exist or continue in a suppressed condition. (분노·불만 등의 감정이) 속에서 끓다; 마음에 서리다. ¶ *smoldering anger* 가슴에 서린 분노 / *Hatred smoldered in him.* 증오가 그의 가슴 속에 서렸다. **3** show a suppressed emotion. (억압된 감정을) 겉으로 나타내다. ¶ *His eyes were smoldered with anger.* 그의 두 눈은 분노를 억제하고 있는 듯했다.

— *n.* **1** Ⓒ the state of burning slowly without any flame. 연기; 냄. **2** Ⓤ a smoldering fire. 내는 뭉근한 불. [A.S. *smoca*]

:smooth [smu:ð] *adj.* **1** not rough (to the touch); polished, silky; having an even surface. 매끄러운; 평탄한. ¶ *a ~ paper* 표면이 매끈매끈한 종이 / *a ~ piece of wood* 매끄러운 표면의 나뭇조각 / *a ~ floor* 〔*skin, stone*〕 매끈매끈한 마루〔피부, 돌〕 / (*as*) *~ as marble* 대리석처럼 표면이 매끄러운 / *a ~ road* 〔*lawn*〕 평탄한 도로〔잔디밭〕 / *the ~ slope of a hill* 언덕의 평탄한 경사. **2** (of edges) with no points sticking out; even. 모가 나지 않은; 둥그스름한. ¶ *The ~ edge of a table.* 모서리가 둥그스름한 테이블. **3** gently and easily moving; not interrupted; without trouble 〔difficulties〕. 원활히〔막힘 없이〕 움직이는; 순조로운; (사물이) 순조롭게 진행되는. ¶ *a ~ drive* 〔*voyage*〕 순조로운 노정(路程)〔항해〕 / *the ~ running of an engine* 엔진의 원활한 작동 / *~ motion* 유연한 움직임〔운동〕 / *make things ~ for* …(일의) 장애를 제거하다; …을 순조롭게 하다. **4** ⓐ (of water) mild, calm, not broken by waves. 잔잔한. ¶ *a ~ sea* 〔*stream*〕 잔잔한 바다〔물의 흐름〕 / *The sea is ~.* 바다는 잔잔하다. ⓑ (of feelings) not easily disturbed; calm. 차분한. ¶ *a ~ temper* 차분한 성질. **5** (of speech) flowing; fluent; flattering. (말이) 유창한; 발림말하는. ¶ *a ~ tongued man* 말이 유창한 사람 / *~ things* 발림말; 듣기 좋은 말 / *a ~ manner* 나긋나긋한 태도. **6** ⓐ (of the skin) not hairy; free from hair, beard, etc.; not wrinkled or rough. 털〔수염·주름〕이 없는; 민숭민숭한. ¶ *a ~ face* 수염이 없는 얼굴 / *the ~ cheeks of youth* 젊은이의 주름 없는 양볼. ⓑ (of the hair) well brushed; glossy. (머리칼이) 잘 손질된; 함치르르한. **7** (of a liquid mixture) well mixed; without lumps; not coarse. (반죽·풀 따위가) 고루 잘 섞인; 응어리지지 않은. ¶ *a ~ paste* 고르게 잘 쑨 풀. **8** (of taste) not harsh, sharp, or bitter; soft; mellow. (음식물 따위가) 부드러운; 감미로운. ¶ *a ~ cocktail* 감칠맛 나는 칵테일 / *Good wine should be silky and ~.* 좋은 포도주는 보드랍고 감미로워야 한다.

get to* 〔*reach*〕 *smooth water, come safely through difficulties. 난관을 뚫고 무사히 도착하다; 어려움을 극복하다.

in smooth water, passed obstacles or difficulties. 난관을 통과하여.

— *vt.* (P6,7) **1** make even or level on the surface; polish. (땅을) 고르다; 평탄하게 하다; 매끄럽게 하다. ¶ *~ rough ground* 울퉁불퉁한 지면을 고르다. **2** arrange neatly and evenly by brushing or pressing down; make smooth by brushing, pressing down. (주름·구김살 따위를) 펴다; 다리다; 고르게 매만지다. ¶ *~ down one's hair* 머리칼을 고르게 매만지다 / *~ out wrinkles from a shirt* 와이셔츠의 주름을 펴다 / *~ a crumpled piece of paper out* 구겨진 종이를 펴다. **3** make (something) easy by removing difficulties, etc.; make calm, sooth; regulate. …을 용이하게 하다; 원활하게 하다; 진정시키다. ¶ *~ one's way* (장애·곤란 따위를) 제거하여) 앞길을 순탄하게 만들다 / *~ the way* 〔*path*〕 가는 길의 장애를 제거하다 / *~ one's feelings* 기분을 가라앉히다. **4** 《*over*》 make (something) seem less wrong or unpleasant. (잘못 따위를) 감싸 주다. ¶ *~ over faults* 잘못들을 감싸 주다.

— *vi.* (P2A) 《*down*》 become smooth, calm or quiet. 매끈해〔반드러워〕지다; 평온해지다.

smooth away (=*get rid of*) *difficulties, etc.* (어려움 따위를) 제거하다.

smooth down, make or become calm. 가라앉히다; 가라앉다. ¶ *The sea gradually smoothed down.* 바다는 점차로 잔잔해졌다 / *Affairs have smoothed down since the cause of the trouble was removed.* 사태는 그 원인이 제거되자 진정되었다 / *~ down a quarrels* 싸움을 진정시키다.

• **smooth·ness** [-nis] *n.* [E.]

smooth-bore [smúːðbɔ̀ːr] *adj.* having no grooves or ridges on the inner surface of the barrel; not rifled. (총신 내부에) 강선(腔線)이 없는. — *n.* a smooth-bore gun. 활강총(滑腔銃).

smoothe [smuːð] *vt., vi.* =smooth.

smooth-faced [smúːðféist] *adj.* **1** (of a face) having a smooth surface; beardless; clean-shaven. (얼굴이) 매끈매끈한; (얼굴에) 수염이 없는. ¶ *a ~ tile* 표면이 매끈한 타일. **2** agreeable in speech and manners, but with little sincerity. (겉보기에) 사람이 부드러운; 본성을 숨긴; 위선의. ¶ *a ~ hypocrite* 가면을 쓴 위선자.

***smooth·ly** [smúːðli] *adv.* in a smooth manner; fluently. 매끄럽게; 온화하게; 유창하게.

smooth-spo·ken [smúːðspóukən] *adj.* speaking agreeably and pleasantly, but not sincerely. 구변이 좋은; 감언이설의.

smooth-tongued [smúːðtʌ́ŋd] *adj.* = smooth-spoken.

***smote** [smout] *v.* p. of **smite.**

smoth·er [smʌ́ðər] *vt.* **1** (P6) make it difficult for (someone) to breathe; kill (someone) by stopping or preventing the breath. …을 숨막히게 하다; 질식시키다; 질식시켜서 죽이다. ¶ *be smothered by thick smoke* 짙은 연기로 숨이 막히다 / *He was smothered to death.* 그는 질식사했다 / *The stupid mother smothered her baby.* 미련한 어미는 아기를 질식사시켰다. **2** (P6) put out (a fire) by covering it thickly. (불을) 덮어 끄다. ¶ *~ a fire with a blanket* (불을) 담요를 덮어 끄다. **3** (P6,7,13) conceal; (of feelings, etc.) suppress. …을 감추다[은폐하다]; (감정 따위를) 억제하다. ¶ *~ a yawn* 하품을 삼키다 / *~ a scandal* 추문(醜聞)[스캔들]을 은폐하다 / *~ one's grief* 슬픔을 억제하다. **4** cover thickly; heap on. 푹 덮다[감싸다]; 마구 베풀다[주다]. ¶ *Snow smothered the road.* 눈이 길을 온통 덮어 버렸다 / *London smothered in fog.* 안개로 감싸인 런던 / *She smothered the child with kisses.* 그녀는 아이에게 마구 키스를 퍼부었다. — *vi.* (P1) have difficulty in breathing. 질식하다.

smother up, keep from notice or publicity. 쉬쉬하며 얼버무려 치우다.

— *n.* 《*a ~* 》 a thick cloud of dust or smoke. 짙은 연기[먼지]. [E.]

smoul·der [smóuldər] *v., n.* 《Brit.》 = smolder.

smudge [smʌdʒ] *n.* Ⓒ **1** a dirty mark; a spot; a stain; a smear. 때; 더러움; 얼룩; 오점. **2** 《chiefly U.S.》 a smoldering fire for driving away insects, etc. 모깃불. — *vt.* **1** (P6) make dirty marks on (something). …을 더럽히다[얼룩지게 하다]. ¶ *a face smudged with soot* 검댕으로 얼룩진 얼굴 / *The painting was smudged.* 그림이 더러워졌다. **2** 《chiefly U.S.》 give out smoke to drive away insects from (a place). 모깃불을 피우다. — *vi.* (P1) become dirty. 더러워지다. ¶ *This paper smudges easily.* 이 종이는 쉬이 더러워진다. [→sludge]

smudg·y [smʌ́dʒi] *adj.* (**smudg·i·er, smudg·i·est**) marked with smudges. 더러워진; 얼룩투성이의.

smug [smʌg] *adj.* (**smug·ger, smug·gest**) very pleased with oneself; narrow-minded; self-satisfied. 점잔빼는; 잘난 체하는. ¶ *a ~ smile* 점잔빼는 너털웃음. [? G.]

smug·gle [smʌ́gəl] *vt.* (P6,7,13) bring (goods) into or take (goods) out of a country secretly, without paying custom duties; carry secretly. …을 밀수출[밀수입]하다; 밀수하다; 몰래 들여오다. ¶ *~ opium into the country* 아편을 밀수입하다 / *~ a letter into* [*out of*] *a prison* 교도소 안[밖]으로 편지를 몰래 들여오다[가져 나오다] / *He tried to ~ his puppy into his bedroom.* 그는 몰래 그의 강아지를 침실로 들여오고자 시도했다. — *vi.* (P1) import or export secretly. 밀수입[밀수출]하다. [Du.]

smug·gler [smʌ́glər] *n.* Ⓒ **1** a person who smuggles. 밀수출[밀수입]자. **2** a ship used for smuggling. 밀수선.

smut [smʌt] *n.* **1** Ⓒ a small bit of soot, coal, or dirt; a dirty spot; a black or dirty mark. (검댕·석탄·먼지 따위의) 작은 덩어리; 얼룩; 더럼. **2** Ⓤ words or talk that cause a person to feel shame. 음탕한[외설된] 말[이야기]. ¶ *talk ~* 외설된 말을 하다. **3** Ⓤ a disease of wheat in which the ears of grain are ruined. (밀의) 깜부기병(病).

— *v.* (**smut·ted, smut·ting**) *vt.* (P6) make (something) dirty or black. …을 더럽히다. — *vi.* (P1) become dirty or black; be attacked by the disease of smut. 더러워지다; 흑수병에 걸리다. [→smudge]

smut·ty [smʌ́ti] *adj.* (**-ti·er, -ti·est**) **1** soiled with soot, dirt, etc. 더러워진; 그을은. **2** foul; nasty; indecent; 음란한; 외설된. ¶ *~ stories* 외설된 이야기. **3** attacked by the plant disease of smut. 깜부기병(病)에 걸린. [→smudge]

snack [snæk] *n.* Ⓒ **1** a light meal taken in a hurry. 가벼운 식사. ¶ *He takes* [*eats*] *a ~ of soup and salad before going to bed.* 그는 잠자리에 들기 전에 수프와 샐러드의 가벼운 식사를 한다. **2** something which is divided for a person; a share. 몫. ¶ *Snacks!* 몫을 나누자. [Du.]

go snack, take each a share. 몫으로 나누다.

snack-bar [snǽkbɑ̀ːr], 《Brit.》 **-count·er** [-kàuntər] *n.* a public eating place where snacks are served usu. at a counter. 간이 식당; 스낵바.

snaf·fle[1] [snǽfəl] *n.* a jointed bit used on a bridle. (말에 물리는) 작은 재갈. — *vt.* (P6) control or manage by a snaffle. 작은 재갈을 물리다. [Du.]

snaf·fle[2] [snǽfəl] *vt.* 《Brit. *sl.*》 **1** steal. 훔

치다. **2** take away quickly before anyone else. (남보다 빨리) 낚아[가로]채다. [↑]

snag [snæg] *n.* Ⓒ **1** a tree or branch held fast in a river or lake, etc. and sticking upward; a tree hidden in a river. (배의 통행을 방해하는) 수중에 잠긴 나무. **2** any sharp projecting point; a piece, part, or point that sticks out sharply, as the broken end of a branch. 돌기물; (나무의) 꺾어진 가지. **3** a broken or irregular tooth. 뻐드렁니; 부러진 치근. **4** unexpected difficulties; something that prevents progress. 뜻하지 않은 장해. ¶ *run* [*come up*] *against a* ~ *in an undertaking* 맡은 일에서 뜻하지 않은 장해[암초]에 부딪치다.
— *vt.* (**snagged, snag·ging**) (P6) **1** run or ~. 물속의 나무에 걸리다. **2** hinder. 방해하다. **3** clear of snags. (물속에) 잠긴 나무를 제거하다. [Scand.]

snail [sneil] *n.* Ⓒ **1** a small animal with a spiral shell on its back that crawls very slowly. 달팽이. ¶ *at a snail's pace* 매우 느리게 / *an edible* ~ 식용 달팽이. **2** a slow-moving person. 늘보. [E.]

∙**snake** [sneik] *n.* Ⓒ **1** a long, crawling animal without legs. 뱀. ¶ *have snakes in one's boots* 곤드레만드레가 되도록 취하다 / *raise* [*wake*] *snakes* 소동을 일으키다. **2** an unsincere or double-faced person. 음험한 사람.
a snake in one's bosom, a person who repays one's kindness with treachery. 은혜를 원수로 갚는 사람.
snake in the grass, a hidden danger or enemy. 숨은 적[위험].
Snakes! an exclamation of anger. 제기랄.
— *vi.* move or wind like a snake. (뱀처럼) 꿈틀꿈틀 움직이다. [E.]

snake charmer [´-`-] *n.* a person who controls snakes by music. 뱀 부리는 사람.

snak·y [snéiki] *adj.* (**snak·i·er, snak·i·est**) **1** of or like a snake. 뱀의; 뱀 같은. **2** twisting; winding. 꾸불꾸불한. ¶ *a* ~ *river* 꾸불꾸불한 강. **3** untrustworthy. 음험한. [*snake*]

:snap [snæp] *v.* (**snapped, snap·ping**) *vi.* **1** (P1) break suddenly with a sharp sound. 딱[뚝]하고 부러지다[망가지다]. ¶ *The branch snapped under the heavy snows.* 나뭇가지는 쌓인 눈의 무게에 못 이겨 뚝하고 부러졌다 / *A rope snaps at its weakest point.* 밧줄은 가장 약한 곳에서 뚝하고 끊어진다. **2** (P1) make a sharp, sudden sound. 찰깍[딱]하고 소리를 내다. ¶ *The wood snapped as it burned.* 그 나무는 탈 때 따다닥 소리를 냈다 / *A whip snapped.* 채찍이 찰싹했다. **3** (P2) be shut or opened with a sharp sound. (문 따위가) 덜컹[탕, 찰깍]하고 닫히다[열리다]. ¶ *The door snapped behind me.* 내 등 뒤에서 문이 탕하고 닫혔다 / *The door snapped to* (*shut*). 문이 덜컥하고 닫혔다. **4** (P3) say sharply or angrily. 딱딱거리다. ¶ *He is always snapping at people.* 그는 항상 사람들에게 딱딱거린다. **5** (P3) move quickly. 민첩하게 움직이다. ¶ ~ *to attention* 민첩하게 차려 자세를 취하다. **6** (P1,3) 《often *at*》 make a hasty, sudden bite at; try to bite. 덥석 물다[물려고 하다]. ¶ ~ *at meat* 고기를 덥석 물다 / *I hate a dog that snaps at a visitor.* 나는 방문객에게 물려고 달려드는 개를 싫어한다. **7** (P3) 《often *at*》 seek eagerly to seize or secure; accept eagerly. (기꺼이) 달려들다; 두말 않고 받아들이다. ¶ ~ *at a bargain* [*an offer*] 두말 않고 계약[제안]에 응하다 / ~ *at a chance* 기회를 재빨리 잡다.
— *vt.* **1** (P6,7,13,18) break (something) suddenly and with a sharp sound. …을 뚝[딱]하고 부러뜨리다[꺾다, 쪼개다]. ¶ ~ *a stick in two* 작대기를 뚝하고 부러뜨리다 / ~ *off a twig* 나무의 잔가지를 딱하고 꺾다. **2** (P6) cause (something) to make a short, sharp sound. (…을) 딱[찰깍] 소리나게 하다. ¶ ~ *a whip* 채찍을 휘둘러 찰싹[딱] 소리내다 / ~ *one's fingers* 손가락으로 딱 소리를 내다. ¶ ~ *on* [*off*] *the switch* 스위치를 딱하고 켜다[끄다]. **3** (P6,7) bite or seize suddenly with teeth or beak. (갑자기 달려들어) …을 덥석 물다; 물어뜯다. ¶ *The dog snapped a piece out of my trousers.* 개는 내 바지를 물어 천 조각을 뜯어냈다 / *The shark snapped his leg off.* 상어가 그의 다리 하나를 물어뜯었다. **4** (P7) ⓐ 《*up*》 pick up hastily, greedily, or eagerly; seize, or snatch suddenly. …을 덥석 낚아채다. ¶ *The dog snapped up the piece of meat.* 개는 고깃점을 덥석 낚아챘다. ⓑ take, buy, or obtain hastily and eagerly. 서둘러[앞다투어] 취하다[사다, 획득하다]. ¶ *All the best houses have already been snapped up.* 최상의 좋은 집들은 이미 모두 팔렸다. **5** (P6) take a photograph of (something) instantly. …의 스냅 사진을 찍다. ¶ *He was snapped falling off his horse.* 그는 낙마하는 장면을 스냅 사진으로 찍혔다. **6** (P6) close with a short, sharp noise. (문·뚜껑 따위를) 탕[쾅, 찰깍]하고 닫다. ¶ ~ *down the lid of a box* 상자의 뚜껑을 탕하고 닫다 / ~ *open a watch* (회중) 시계를 찰깍하고 열다.
snap at the chance, accept eagerly. 기회를 재빨리 붙잡다.
snap one's fingers at, make a stroke smartly on the ball of the thumb as a gesture of derision. 경멸하다.
snap into it, 《U.S. *colloq.*》 move quickly, hurry. 서둘다.
snap off one's nose, cut his words short with a retort. 짓궂게 남의 말을 방해하다.
snap short, break with a sharp crack. 뚝 꺾다; 부러뜨리다.
snap someone up, interrupt someone rudely. 버릇없이 …의 말을 가로막다.
— *n.* Ⓒ **1** an act of snapping. 딱[뚝] 부러뜨림. **2** a sharp, short sound. 찰깍[딱, 쾅]하는 소리. ¶ *shut a window with a* ~ 창문을 철

껵하고 닫다. **3** a sudden bite. 덥석 물. **4** a fastener that closes with a snapping sound. (찰깍 채워지는) 죔쇠; 걸쇠. **5** a photograph taken instantly; a snapshot. 스냅 사진. **6** weather which has suddenly changed. 날씨의 급변. ¶ *a cold* ~ 갑작스런 추위.

— *adj.* sudden; unexpected. 불의의; 예기치 않은. ¶ *a* ~ *decision* 황급한 결정.

— *adv.* with a sharp and sudden sound. 딱; 뚝; 찰깍. [Teut.]

snap·drag·on [snǽpdrӕ̀gən] *n.* a garden plant with spikes of white, yellow, red, or purple flowers. 금어초(金魚草).

snap fastener [∸ ∸--] *n.* a fastener for clothes consisting of two parts, male and female, which fit together when pressed. 스냅; 똑딱단추.

snap·pish [snǽpiʃ] *adj.* **1** tending [apt] to snap or bite; likely to bite. (개 따위가) 무는 버릇이 있는; 잘 무는. ¶ *a* ~ *dog.* **2** sharp in speech or manner; apt to be irritated. 딱딱거리는; 성마른. ¶ *a* ~ *old man* 성마른 노인 / *a* ~ *answer* 퉁명스러운 대답.

snap·py [snǽpi] *adj.* (**-pi·er, -pi·est**) **1** =snappish. **2** 《*colloq.*》 lively; bright. 기운 찬; 쾌활한. ¶ *a* ~ *conversation* 활기에 찬 대화. **3** irritable. 성미가 급한; 성마른.

Look* [*Make in*] *snappy! 《*colloq.*》 Hurry up! Be quick! 서둘러라; 빨리 해라.

snap·shot [snǽpʃɑ̀t / -ʃɔ̀t] *n.* Ⓒ **1** a photograph taken quickly. 스냅 사진. **2** a quick shot. 속사(速射). — *vt., vi.* (**-ted**) take a photograph quickly and informally. 스냅 사진을 찍다.

•**snare** [snɛər] *n.* Ⓒ **1** a trap, often made with a loop of cord or wire, for catching a small animal or bird. 덫; 올가미. ¶ *catch a rabbit in a* ~ 덫으로 토끼를 잡다 / *a rabbit caught by a* ~ 덫에 의해 잡힌 토끼. **2** a thing which attracts or tempts; anything which brings one into difficulties, trouble or disgrace. 유혹; 함정. ¶ *lay* [*set*] *a* ~ *for innocent person* 순진한 사람에게 함정을 파놓다. — *vt.* (P6) catch (a bird or an animal) with a snare. …을 덫으로 잡다. [N.]

•**snarl**[1] [snɑːrl] *vi.* (P1) **1** (of a dog, etc.) make a low noise in the throat; show the teeth (with anger). (개가) 으르렁거리다; (노여움 따위로) 이를 드러내다. ¶ *The dog snarled at me.* 개는 나에게 (이를 드러내고) 으르렁거렸다. **2** 《*at*》 speak in a harsh, angry tone. 고함[호통]치다. **3** (P6,7) 《*out*》 say or utter with a snarl. 딱딱거리며 이빨을 드러내며 말하다.

— *vt.* utter or say (something) in a rough, harsh voice. …을 호통치다; 버럭 소리지르며 말하다.

— *n.* Ⓒ a sharp growl; the act or sound of snarling. 으르렁거림; 서로 으르렁거리기. ¶ *A* ~ *was his only reply.* 한 번의 호통이 그의 유일한 대답이었다. [Imit.]

snarl[2] [snɑːrl] *n.* Ⓒ a knot; a tangle; a confused state. 뒤얽힘; 혼란. ¶ *comb the snarls out of one's hair* 엉클어진 머리카락을 빗질하여 풀다 / *The traffic is all in a* ~. 교통은 대혼란이다. — *vt.* (P6,7) make (something) tangled or confused. 엉클어지게 하다; (교통·통신 등을) 혼란케 하다. — *vi.* (P1) become confused. 엉클어지다; 혼란해지다. [M.E. *snarle*]

•**snatch** [snætʃ] *vt.* (P6,7,13) **1** seize suddenly or without warning; take (something) suddenly by force. …을 잡아채다[낚아채다]; 빼앗다. ¶ ~ *a thing from someone's hand* 아무의 손에서 어떤 물건을 잡아채다 / *The fox snatched the chicken and ran away.* 여우는 병아리를 낚아채더니 도망갔다 / ~ *a kiss from a girl* (낚아채듯) 갑자기 소녀에게 키스하다 / *He snatched off his hat.* 그는 급히 그의 모자를 벗었다. **2** take, get, or secure hastily or while there is a chance; secure with difficulty. 급히[서둘러] 취하다[먹다, 얻다]; 간신히 구해 내다. ¶ ~ *a hurried* [*hasty*] *meal* 급히 식사를 하다 / ~ *a few hours of sleep* [*repose*] 몇 시간 동안의 수면[휴식]을 서둘러 취하다 / ~ *a child from the fire* 불 속에서 아이를 간신히 구해 내다.

— *vi.* (P1,3) 《*at*》 try to snatch; try to grasp or seize. 잡아[낚아]채려 하다; (잡으려고) 달려들다. ¶ ~ *at the purse* 지갑을 낚아채려 하다 / ~ *at an offer* 제안에 달려들다 / ~ *at the chance of ....* …의 좋은 기회를 놓칠세라 달려들다.

snatch a kiss, kiss unexpectedly. 불의에 키스하다.

snatch at an offer, take it eagerly. 기꺼이 응하다.

— *n.* Ⓒ **1** an act of snatching. 잡아[낚아]챔. **2** 《often *pl.*》 a short time; a small amount; a small piece; a bit. 잠시; 짧은 시간; 소량[액]; 한 조각; 단편. ¶ *eat a* ~ 한 입 먹다 / *work in* [*by*] *snatches* (생각난 듯이) 이따금 일하다 / *sleep in snatches* 짬짬이 조금씩 자다 / *He had a* ~ *of sleep sitting in his chair.* 그는 의자에 앉아서 잠시 동안 잠을 잤다. **3** a short song or tune. (노래·시 따위의) 짧은 하나의 구절. [E.]

by snatches, by fits and starts. 이따금.

make a snatch at, try to snatch. …을 낚아채려고 하다; …에 달려들다.

snatchy [snǽtʃi] *adj.* irregular; disconnected. 단속적인; 불규칙한.

SNCC [snik] 《U.S.》 Student Nonviolent Coordinating Committee. 학생 비폭력 조정 위원회(cf. *CORE*).

sneak [sniːk] *vi.* **1** (P2A) come into or go out of a place; in a secret manner; move quietly so as to avoid being seen or heard. 몰래 들어오다[나가다]; 살금살금[몰래] 움직이다. ¶ ~ *into* [*out of*] *a room* 몰래 방 안으로 들어오다[방에서 나가다] / ~ *about for a chance to steal* 도둑질할 기회를 노리고 여기저기 기웃거리다 / ~ *off* [*away*] 슬그머니

〔몰래〕 떠나가다. **2** (P3) act in a sly way. 비열하게 행동하다. ¶ ~ *out of duty*〔*danger*〕 임무〔위험〕에서 슬그머니 도망치다〔벗어나다〕. **3** (P1) tell tales; inform. 고자질하다. — *vt.* **1** (P6) move, carry, put, pass, do, etc. in a stealthy manner. …을 몰래〔살금살금〕 움직이다〔소지하고 다니다, 두다, 지나다, 행하다〕. ¶ ~ *a smoke* 몰래 담배를 피우다 / ~ *a pistol into one's pocket* 주머니에 권총을 몰래 집어넣다. **2** (P6) 《*colloq.*》 steal. …을 훔치다.
sneak out of, avoid or escape (one's duty, task) by slyness. (임무·책임 따위를) 슬쩍 피하다〔빠지다〕.

— *n.* Ⓒ **1** a cowardly, mean person. 몰래 살금살금하는 사람; 비열한 사람. **2** a person who tells about others' faults. 고자질하는 사람. [O.E. *snican*]

sneak·er [sní:kər] *n.* Ⓒ **1** a person who sneaks. 몰래〔살금살금〕 행동하는 사람; 비열한 사람. **2** 《*pl.*》 canvas shoes with soles of rubber or another light material. 고무창이 달린 운동화.

sneak·ing [sní:kiŋ] *adj.* **1** walking stealthily. 살금살금 걷는. **2** mean; not open or frank. 비열한; 비밀의. ¶ ~ *excuses* 비열한 핑계 / *a* ~ *ambition* 마음 속에 품고 있는 야심 / *have a* ~ *fondness for jazz* 재즈에 대한 남에게 알려지지 않은 취미.

sneak-thief [sní:kθì:f] *n.* a person who steals small things, by sneaking in through open doors, windows, etc. 좀도둑; 빈집털이.

·sneer [sniər] *vi.* (P1,3) 《*at*》 show scorn or contempt; laugh in scorn; speak ironical words. 비웃다; 냉소하다; 비꼬다. ¶ ~ *at someone's reputation* 아무의 명성을 비웃다. — *vt.* (P7,13) 《*into, out of*》 speak to (someone) by sneering; affect (someone) in a certain condition by sneering. …을 비웃으며 말하다; 조소하여 …하게 하다. ¶ ~ *someone into silence* 아무를 냉소하여 침묵시키다 / ~ *one's contempt for*… …를 경멸하다 / ~ *someone down* 아무에게 냉소를 퍼붓다. — *n.* Ⓒ a scornful smile or remark. 냉소; 경멸; 비웃는 말. [Imit.]

sneer·ing·ly [sníəriŋli] *adv.* in a sneering way. 냉소하여.

sneeze [sni:z] *n.* Ⓒ a sudden burst of breath through the nose and mouth; the sound produced by this. 재채기 (소리). — *vi.* (P1) make a sneeze. 재채기하다. [E.]
not to be sneezed at, not to be despised; worth having or considering. 깔볼 수 없는; 고려할 가치가 있는. ¶ *The offer isn't to be sneezed at.* 그 제안은 고려할 만한 가치가 있다.

snick [snik] *vt.* (P6) make a slight cut in. …에 가는 눈금〔새김금〕을 내다. — *n.* a slight cut. 가는 칼자국; 새김눈. [→snickersnee]

snick·er [snikər] *vi.* laugh in a half-suppressed way. 킬킬 웃다; 킬킬거리다. — *n.* Ⓒ such a laugh. 킬킬거리는 웃음. [Imit.]

snick·er·snee [eníkərsnì:] *n.* a knife, usable as a weapon. 단도. [Du.=thrust or cut]

snide [snaid] *a.* counterfeit. 가짜의. — *n.* Ⓤ a snide jewelery or money. 인조 보석; 위조 화폐. [?]

Sni·der [snáidər] *n.* a breech-loading rifle of an early pattern. 스나이더식 총《후장총(後裝銃)》. [Person]

·sniff [snif] *vi.* (P1,3) **1** 《*at*》 draw air or breathe through the nose (to smell). (냄새를 맡기 위해) 코를 킁킁거리다; (소리를 내며) 코로 숨쉬다. ¶ ~ *at the bottle of perfume* 향수병의 냄새를 맡다 / *Sniff at this milk and see if it is fresh.* 이 우유가 신선한 것인지, 냄새를 맡아보아라. **2** 《*at*》 show a feeling of contempt. 코방귀 뀌다; 경멸하다. ¶ *She sniffed at my plan.* 그녀는 나의 계획에 대해 코방귀를 뀌었다.

— *vt.* (P6,7) **1** make a sound while smelling (something); draw in through the nose in breathing. …을 (킁킁거리며) 냄새 맡다; (코로) 들이마시다. ¶ ~ *the sea air* 바다 공기를 들이마시다 / *He sniffed the cold mountain air.* 그는 차가운 산 속의 공기를 들이마셨다. **2** notice (danger, a trick, etc.); detect. (위험 따위를) 낌새 채다〔알아차리다〕. ¶ ~ *danger* 위험을 눈치채다 / *I can* ~ *something burning.* 무언가 타는 냄새가 난다.
— *n.* Ⓒ the act or sound of sniffing. (킁킁거리며) 냄새 맡음〔맡는 소리〕. [Imit.]

snif·fle [snífəl] *vi.* (P1) make a sniffing sound again and again. (코를) 킁킁거리다. — *n.* Ⓒ 《*the* ~*s*》 a loud sniffing sound; a slight cold in the nose. (감기 따위로) 코를 킁킁거림; 코감기.

snig·ger [snígər] *vi., n.* =snicker.

snip[1] [snip] *vt., vi.* (**snipped, snip·ping**) (P6,7;3) cut (something) by scissors with a short, quick motion. (…을) 가위로 싹독 자르다. ¶ *She snipped the thread.* 그녀는 실을 싹독 잘랐다. — *n.* Ⓒ **1** a single cut with scissors; the act of snipping; a small piece (cut off). 싹독 자름; 가위질; 잘린 작은 조각. **2** 《*pl.*》 scissors for cutting sheets of metal. 쇠 자르는 가위. [Du.]

snip[2] [snip] *n.* 《Brit.》 a profitable bargain; certainty of success or profit. 의외로 싸게 산 물건; 성공〔이익〕의 확실한 전망.

snipe [snaip] *n.* Ⓒ (*pl.* **snipe**) a bird with a long bill that lives in marshes. 도요새. — *vi.* **1** hunt this bird. 도요새잡이를 하다. **2** shoot enemies from a hidden place. (적을 숨어서) 저격하다. — *vt.* shoot (soldiers, etc.) in this way. …을 저격하다. [E.]

snip·er [snáipər] *n.* a person who snipes at enemy soldiers. 저격병.

snip·pet [snípit] *n.* a small piece cut off; a snip; a bit. (가위로 잘라낸) 작은 조각;

단편. ¶ *snippets of news* 단편적인 뉴스〔보도〕. [*snip*[1], *-et* small]

sniv·el [snívəl] *vi.* (**-eled, -el·ing** or 《Brit.》 **-elled, -el·ling**) (P1) **1** have liquid coming〔have mucus running〕 from the nose. 콧물을 흘리다; 코를 훌쩍이다. **2** cry with sniffling; complain in a tearful manner. 코를 훌쩍이며〔흐느껴〕 울다; 우는소리를 하다. **3** whine; put on a show of grief. 슬픈 체하다. — *n.* Ⓒ **1** running liquid from the nose. 콧물. **2** a pretended grief. 슬픈 체하는 태도. **3** 《the ~*s*》 a slight cold in the head. 가벼운 코감기. [E.]

snob [snɑb / snɔb] *n.* Ⓒ **1** a person who too much admires persons of wealth or in a high position, and looks down on those below him. 신사연하는 속물《지위·재산만을 존중하며, 윗사람에게 아첨하고 아랫사람에게 교만한 사람》. **2** a person who regards himself as better than others in intellectual and artistic taste. 사이비 인텔리. ¶ *a literary* ~ 사이비 문학가 / *an intellectual* ~ (잘 알지도 못하면서) 아는 체하는 속인. [N.]

snob·ber·y [snɑ́bəri / snɔ́b-] *n.* Ⓤ the character or state of being snobbish. 속물근성. [↑]

snob·bish [snɑ́biʃ / snɔ́b-] *adj.* of or like a snob. 윗사람에게 아첨하고 아랫사람에게는 교만한; 속물 근성의.

snob·bish·ness [snɔ́biʃnis] *n.* the character or conduct of a snob; the state or quality of being snobbish. 속물 근성.

snood [snù:d] *n.* **1** 《Sc. *arch.*》 a band or ribbon formerly worn round the hair by young unmarried women. 머리를 동이는 리본《미혼 여성의 표시》. **2** a hairnet worn at the back of a woman's head. 헤어네트《여성의 뒷머리를 감싸 주는 자루 모양의 것》.
— *vt.* bind or hold up (the hair) with a snood. snood 를 두르다〔로 동여매다〕. [E.]

snook [snu(:)k] *n.* Ⓒ a derisive gesture of putting a thumb to the nose and spreading fingers. 경멸의 동작《엄지손가락을 코끝에 대고 다른 네 손가락을 펴보이는 동작》. ¶ *cock a* ~ 〔*snooks*〕 바보 취급 하다; 놀리다. [Norw.]

snoop [snu:p] *vi.* 《*colloq.*》 move about secretly; search curiously; look into other's things in a secret, sneaking way. 수상하게 배회하다; 기웃거리며 (캐고) 돌아다니다.
— *n.* Ⓒ a person who snoops. 기웃거리며 (캐고) 다니는 사람. [Du.]

snooze [snu:z] *vi.* (P1) have a short nap but not in bed; take a nap. 수잠 자다; 꾸벅꾸벅 졸다. — *n.* Ⓒ a short nap not taken in bed. 수잠; 꾸벅꾸벅 졺. [Dan.]

snore [snɔ:r] *vi.* (P1) breathe noisily through the nose, or nose and mouth, while sleeping. 코를 골다. — *vt.* (P7) 《*away*》 pass or spend time in snoring. 코를 골며 (시간을) 보내다. ¶ *The lazy boy snored away the whole afternoon.* 그 게으른 소년은 오후를 몽땅 코를 골며 시간을 보냈다.
— *n.* Ⓒ the act or noisy sound of snoring. 코골기; 코 고는 소리. [Imit.]

snor·er [snɔ́:rər] *n.* Ⓒ a person who habitually snores. 코 고는 사람.

snort [snɔ:rt] *vi.* (P1) **1** (of a horse) force the air out through the nose violently. (말이) 콧김을 내뿜다. ¶ *The horse snorted at me.* 말은 나를 보자 으흐흥하고 콧김을 뿜었다. **2** make a sound like this. (기관차 따위가) 칙칙거리는 소리를 내다. ¶ *The engine snorted once and stopped.* 기관차는 한번 칙칙거리더니 멈춰 섰다. **3** express anger or contempt by making a harsh, noisy sound. (노여움·경멸 따위를 나타내어) 코를 씨근거리다; 코방귀 뀌다.
— *vt.* (P6) talk or express (something) by a harsh, noisy sound. …을 씩씩거리며 말하다. ¶ *"You are late again!" snorted the teacher.* "너 또 늦었구나!" 선생님은 거칠게 말씀하셨다.
— *n.* Ⓒ a harsh, noisy sound which results from breathing through the nose violently; the act or sound of snorting. 거센 콧바람〔콧김〕; 그 소리. [*snore*]

snort·er [snɔ́:rtər] *n.* Ⓒ a violent gale. 폭풍. [Imit.]

snot [snɑt / snɔt] *n.* Ⓤ the liquid of the nose. 콧물. [E.]

snot·ty [snɑ́ti / snɔ́ti] *a.* **1** running with snot. 콧물을 흘리는. **2** despicable. 천한.

snout [snaut] *n.* Ⓒ **1** (of a pig, a dog, etc.) the projecting part around nose. (돼지·개 따위의) 코. **2** anything pointed like an animal's snout. (동물의 코처럼) 삐죽하게 튀어나온 것. [E.]

:snow [snou] *n.* **1** Ⓤ small flakes of frozen water falling from the sky; ⓊⒸ a fall of snow. 눈; 강설(降雪). ¶ *a heavy (fall of)* ~ 대설 / *Snow is falling thick and fast.* 눈이 쉴 사이 없이 계속 내리고 있다 / *Snow is expected tomorrow.* 내일은 눈이 내릴 것이 예상된다 / *be buried under deep* ~ 눈 속 깊이 파묻히다. **2** 《often *pl.*》 a mass of snow on the ground. 적설. ¶ *the snows of the Himalaya* 〔*the mountainous country*〕 히말라야〔산악국〕의 눈〔적설〕 지대. **3** Ⓤ something like snow in its whiteness, etc.; Ⓤ 《*poet.*》 pure whiteness. 눈처럼 흰 것; 설백. ¶ *the snows of venerable age* 노인의 백발 / *the* ~ *of a maiden's breast* 눈처럼 흰 처녀의 가슴 / *peach* ~ (순백의) 복숭아 푸딩《달걀 흰자위를 원료로 한 죽 모양의 디저트용 요리》.
— *vi.* **1** (P1) drop from the sky in the form of snow. 눈이 내리다. ¶ *It is snowing.* 눈이 내리고 있다 / *It will* ~ *tonight.* 오늘밤은 눈이 내릴 것이다. **2** (P2A) fall like snow; come in heavy showers or large numbers. 눈처럼 내리다; 쇄도하다; 마구 퍼붓다. ¶ *Letters came snowing in.* 편지가 쇄

도했다.
— *vt.* (P6) cover (something) with snow. …을 눈으로 덮다. ¶ *be snowed in* 〔*up, over*〕 눈에 갇히다 / *The train was snowed up* 〔*under*〕. 열차는 눈에 갇혔다〔파묻혔다〕 / *We were snowed in.* 우리는 눈에 발이 묶여 나다닐 수 없었다. [E.]

snow·ball [snóubɔ̀ːl] *n.* Ⓒ a ball of snow packed for throwing. 눈뭉치; 눈덩이. ¶ *The children rolled a big* ~. 아이들은 큰 눈덩이를 만들었다. — *vt., vi.* (P6;1) **1** throw balls of snow. 눈뭉치를 던지다; 눈싸움하다. **2** grow rapidly (like a snowball). (눈덩이처럼) 빠르게 커지다.

snow·bank [snóubæ̀ŋk] *n.* a large mass or drift of snow. (산허리·계곡 등에) 휘몰아쳐 쌓인 큰 눈더미.

snow·bird [snóubə̀ːrd] *n.* an American small, grey bird seen in flocks during the winter. 흰멧새.

snow·blind [snóublàind] *adj.* blinded for a short time by the glare of the sunlight reflected from snow or ice. 설맹(雪盲)의.

snow-bound [snóubàund] *adj.* shut in by a heavy fall of snow. 눈에 갇힌〔발이 묶인〕.

snow bunting [´-´-] *n.* =snowbird.

snow-capped [snóukæ̀pt] *adj.* covered with snow on the top. (산꼭대기가) 눈으로 덮인.

snow·drift [snóudrìft] *n.* **1** Ⓒ a heap of snow piled up by the wind. (바람이) 휘몰아쳐 쌓인 눈더미. **2** snow carried along with the wind. 바람에 휘날리는 눈.

snow·drop [snóudrɑ̀p / -drɔ̀p] *n.* Ⓒ a small plant with snow-white flowers which bloom in early spring. 갈란투스《이른 봄에 조그마한 흰꽃이 피는 풀》.

snow·fall [snóufɔ̀ːl] *n.* ⒸⓊ **1** a fall of snow. 강설. ¶ *There has been a* ~ *of two feet.* 2피트의 강설이 있었다. **2** the amount of snow which falls in a certain period. 강설량. ¶ *a 10cm* ~, 10cm 의 강설량 / *a* ~ *of 16 cm,* 16cm 의 강설량.

snow·field [snóufìːld] *n.* Ⓒ a region always covered with snow. 설원(雪原).

snow·flake [snóuflèik] *n.* Ⓒ a small, white, featherlike crystal of snow. 눈송이.

snow line [´-´] *n.* the line on mountains above which snow never melts. 설선(雪線)《만년설의 최저 경계선》.

snow·man [snóumæ̀n] *n.* Ⓒ (*pl.* **-men** [-mèn]) a human figure made of snow. 눈사람. ¶ *the Abominable Snowman* 설인(雪人)《히말라야의》.

snow·plow, 《Brit.》 **-plough** [snóuplàu] *n.* Ⓒ a machine for clearing away snow from railway tracks or roads. 제설기〔차〕.

snow·shoes [snóuʃùːz] *n. pl.* a pair of wooden frames with nets of leather, etc. for walking on deep and soft snow. 눈신.

snow·slide [snóuslàid] *n.* Ⓒ a slide of snow down a steep slope (of a mountain). 눈사태.

snow·storm [snóustɔ̀ːrm] *n.* Ⓒ a heavy fall of snow with strong winds. 눈보라.

snow·white [snóuhwáit] *adj.* white as snow. 눈같이 흰; 새하얀.

snow·y [snóui] *adj.* (**snow·i·er, snow·i·est**) **1** having much snow; covered with snow. 눈이 많은; 눈이 내리는; 눈으로 덮인. ¶ *a* ~ *day* 눈이 내리는 날 / ~ *mountain* 눈으로 덮인 산. **2** like snow; white as snow. 눈처럼 흰. ¶ ~ *hair* 백발 / *The girl has* ~ *skin.* 소녀는 눈처럼 흰 피부를 가지고 있다. **3** pure and clean. 깨끗한; 더럽혀지지 않은. [E.]

snub [snʌb] *vt.* (**snubbed, snub·bing**) (P6) **1** treat (someone) coldly or scornfully, or with contempt. …을 냉대하다; (무시하여) 윽박지르다. ¶ ~ *someone down* 아무를 윽박지르다 / ~ *someone into silence* 윽박질러서 침묵하게 하다. **2** stop or check (a boat, a horse, etc.) suddenly. …을 급히 멈추게 하다〔중지시키다〕. ¶ ~ *a vibration* 진동을 급히 멈추게 하다. — *adj.* (of the nose) short and turned up at the tip. 들창코〔사자코〕의. — *n.* Ⓒ **1** an example of cold scornful or contemptuous treatment. 냉대; 윽박지름. **2** a sudden check or stop. 급정지; 갑작스런 중지. [E.]

snub-nosed [snʌ́bnóuzd] *adj.* with a snub nose. 들창코의.

snuff[1] [snʌf] *n.* Ⓤ powdered tobacco to be taken into the nose by sniffing. 코담배《코에 갖다대고 냄새를 맡는 가루 담배》.
— *vt.* (P6,7) draw in (something) through the nose; perceive through the nose; sniff. …을 코로 들이쉬다; (흥흥거리며) 냄새를 맡다. ¶ ~ *the sea air* 바닷공기를 코로 들이마시다 / ~ *tobacco* 코담배의 냄새를 맡다.
— *vi.* (P1) smell (powdered tobacco). 냄새맡다; 코담배를 맡다. ¶ *The dog was snuffing at the foot of the post.* 개는 기둥 밑에서 냄새를 맡고 있었다. [Du.]

beat to snuff, knock (someone) down. 때려 눕히다.

give someone snuff, deal sharply with someone. …를 냉대하다.

take it in snuff, take offence at it. 화를 내다.

up to snuff, **a**) 《Brit. *colloq.*》 clever; shrewd. 영리한; 빈틈없는. **b**) 《U.S.》 normal in health, usual in quality. (건강·품질 따위가) 양호한; 좋은.

snuff[2] [snʌf] *n.* Ⓒ the burnt part of a candlewick. 양초 심지의 검게 탄 부분.
— *vt.* **1** (P6) cut off the snuff of (a candle). (양초의) 탄 심지를 자르다《밝게 하기 위해》. **2** put out (a candle); extinguish. (양초 따위의) 불을 끄다.

snuff out, **a**) put out (a candle). (양초 따위를) 끄다. ¶ ~ *out a candle* 촛불을 끄다. **b**) bring (something) to an end suddenly; destroy. …을 갑자기 끝장내다; 멸하다. ¶ ~ *out a potential talent* 숨은 재능을 망치

다 / *His hopes were snuffed out.* 그의 희망은 끝장이 나고 말았다. **c**) suppress; kill. 억압하다. ¶ ~ *out opposition* 반대를 눌러 없애다. **d**) 《*colloq.*》 die. 죽다. [E.]

snuff·box [snʌ́fbɑ̀ks / -bɔ̀ks] *n.* Ⓒ a box for holding snuff. 코담뱃갑.

snuff·er [snʌ́fər] *n.* **1** a habitual snuff-taker. 코담배를 냄새 맡는 사람. **2** a tool used for snuffing out candles, consisting of a hollow cone attached to a handle. 촛불끄개《자루 끝에 종 모양의 쇠붙이가 달린》.

snuff·ers [snʌ́fərz] *n. pl.* small tongs used for taking off burned wicks. (양초의) 심지 자르는 가위.

snuf·fle [snʌ́fəl] *vi.* **1** (P1) breathe noisily and with difficulty through the nose like a person with a cold in the head; breathe noisily through the nose. (감기 따위로) 코를 킁킁거리다. **2** speak or sing through the nose. 콧소리를 내다. — *vt.* utter (something) in a nasal tone. …을 콧소리로 말하다. — *n.* Ⓒ **1** a noisy breathing through the nose. 코를 킁킁거림. **2** 《*the* ~*s*》 a nasal tone of voice; (of the nose) the state of being stuffed up; a cold in the head. 콧소리; (코를) 킁킁거리는 소리; 코가 막힘(멤); 코감기. [*snuff*[1]]

snuff·y [snʌ́fi] *a.* discolored with snuff-taking. 코담배로 더러워진. [*snuff*[1]]

*__snug__ [snʌg] *adj.* (**snug·ger, snug·gest**) **1** comfortable; warm and sheltered; cosy. 아늑한; 포근하고 따스한; 안락한. ¶ *a* ~ *seat by the fire* 난로 곁의 따스한 자리 / *lie* ~ *in bed* 편안하게 침대에 눕다 / *The baby is* ~ *in its cradle.* 갓난아기는 요람에서 따뜻하고 편안하다. **2** neat; compact; fitting closely, tight. 아담한; 단정한; (옷 따위가) 꼭 맞는. ¶ *a* ~ *little house* 아담하고 조그마한 집 / *a* ~ *gentleman* 단정한 신사 / *a* ~ *coat* 몸에 꼭 맞는 코트 / *Her dress is a little too* ~. 그녀의 드레스는 몸에 너무 꼭 낀다. **3** (of a ship) well-built; trim. (배가 훌륭하게) 잘 건조(정비, 정돈)된. ¶ *a* ~ *ship* 튼튼히 건조된(잘 정비된) 배 / *make ropes* ~ 로프를 잘 정돈하다. **4** (of an income, post, etc.) not very much but enough; good enough to give ease and comfort; of comfortable size. (아주 많지는 않으나) 충분한; 불편이 없을정도의; 넉넉한. ¶ *a* ~ *income* 넉넉한 수입. ***as snug as a bug in a rug,*** very comfortable. 매우 편안하게.

— *adv.* in a snug manner; snugly. 편안하게; 아늑(포근)하게.

— *v.* (**snug·ged, snug·ging**) *vt.* (P6) make (something) comfortable and neat. …을 단정하게 하다; …을 편안하게(기분 좋게)하다. — *vi.* (P1) lie comfortably. 편안하게 눕다. [Scand.]

snug·gery [snʌ́gəri] *n.* **1** someone's private room arranged for comfort. (개인용의) 아늑한 방(장소). **2** the bar-parlor of an inn. (여관의) 술 파는 곳. [*snug*]

snug·gle [snʌ́gəl] *vi.* (P2A) 《*in*》 come closer for warmth or from affection; nestle close and snug to; lie comfortable. (따뜻함을 느끼거나 애정의 표시 등으로) 다가들다; 다가붙다; 기분 좋게 뒹굴다. ¶ ~ *against* (*up to*) *someone* 아무에게 다가붙다 / ~ *down in bed* 기분 좋게 침대에서 뒹굴다. — *vt.* (P7,13) draw or hold (someone) closely. …을 끌어안다; 끌어당기다. ¶ *She snuggled the baby in her arms.* 그녀는 어린애를 두 팔로 끌어안았다. [*snug*]

snug·ly [snʌ́gli] *adv.* in a snug manner. 포근하게; 아늑하게.

:so [sou] *adv.* **1** ⓐ in the way or manner shown or understood; in that (this) way; in such a manner; as stated or reported; just as said; in the condition shown. 그(이)와 같이; 그런(이런) 식으로; 그(이)렇게; 그런 상태로; 그러하게. ¶ *Do it just* ~. (꼭) 이와 같이(이런 식으로) 하여라 / *You must not behave* ~. 그렇게 행동해서는 안 된다 / *if* ~ 만약 그렇다면 / *Is that* ~? 아, 그렇습니까 / *I don't think* ~. 그렇게 생각하지 않는다 / *I told you* ~. 내가 그렇게 말했잖아 / *He* (*It*) *is better* ~. 그는(그것은) (현재의) 그대로가 좋다 / *You will never do it* ~. 너는 결코 그것을 그리 하지 않을 것이다 / *Do you say* ~? =*You don't say* ~? 《an expression of surprise》 설마; 정말로 그래요《놀람》. ⓑ 《*as … so*》 in like manner; in the same way. …와 마찬가지로; …하는 것처럼. ¶ *As you treat me,* ~ *I will treat you.* 네가 나를 대(우)하는 것처럼 나도 너를 대(우)하겠다 / *As it rained harder,* ~ *the sea grew rougher.* 비가 심하게 쏟아짐에 따라 바다도 더욱 거칠어졌다 / *He is brave and* ~ *am I.* 그는 용감하다, 그런데 나도 그 못지않게 용감하다. **2** 《often used after *a negative*》 to that extent in that degree; to the same extent or degree. 그(이) 정도로; 그렇게; 그리. ¶ *He did not live* ~ *long.* 그는 그리 오래 살지 못하였다 / *He is not* ~ *great a man as you.* 그는 너처럼 그리 위대한 사람이 아니다 / *Don't talk* ~ *fast.* 그렇게 빠르게 말하지 마라 / *He could not speak, he was* ~ *angry.* 그는 말을 할 수 없었다, 그 정도로 그는 화가 나 있었다 / *How are you* ?—*Not* ~ *bad.* 어떻게 지내니—응, 그저 그래 / *He is not* ~ *stupid as he looks.* 그는 보기처럼 그렇게 바보는 아니다. **3** very; very much; extremely; indeed; truly. 대단히; 매우; 실로; 참으로. ¶ *I am* ~ *sleepy.* 나는 매우 졸리다 / *My teeth ache* ~. 이가 몹시 아프다 / *So kind of you.* 매우 친절하십니다 / *I am* ~ *glad.* 나는 참으로 기쁘다 / *You said it was good, and* ~ *it is.* 너는 그것이 좋다고 했는데 참으로 좋군 / *She* ~ *wants to go.* 그녀는 가기를 간절히 원한다. **4** also; too; likewise. …도 또한(역시); 마찬가지로. ¶ *We were wrong, and* ~ *were you.* 우리는 틀렸었는데, 너희들도 마찬가지였다 / *Mary enjoys music, and* ~ *does her father.* 메리는 음악을 즐기는데, 그녀의 아버지도 음

악을 즐긴다 / *I saw it, and ~ did he.* 나는 그것을 보았고 그도 보았다. **5** as a result; therefore. 그 때문에; 따라서; 그러므로. ¶ *It was stormy, and ~ he did not come.* 폭풍우 때문에 그는 오지 않았다 / *I was ill(and) ~ I could not go to the party.* 나는 아파서 파티에 갈 수 없었다 / *It is now late, ~ we had better go to bed.* 이제 늦었으니 잠자리에 드는 것이 좋겠다. **6** in a manner previously mentioned; in the state or condition mentioned above. 앞서 말한 상태로. ¶ *The board fence is brown and has been ~ for some time.* 그 널담장은 갈색인데 얼마 동안 갈색 그대로 있었다 / *The glass is broken, and has long been ~.* 유리는 깨졌는데 오랫동안 깨진 채로 있었다.

— *conj.* **1** therefore. 그러므로; 그래서. ¶ *It was late, ~ we went home.* 늦었다, 그래서 우리는 집으로 갔다 / *She told me to go, ~ I went.* 그녀가 내게 가라고 해서 갔다. **2** 《U.S.》 in order that. …하도록; …하기 위하여. ¶ *Go away ~ I can rest.* 내가 쉴 수 있도록 저리 가거라. **3** provided that. …이기만 하다면; …하는 이상은. ¶ *So that it is true, what matters who said it?* 진실이기만 하다면 누가 말했든 무슨 문제냐.

— *pron.* **1** 《used after *or*》 more or less. 대체로; 그 정도로. ¶ *a pound or ~,* 1 파운드 가량[정도]. **2** what has been said or described. 그렇게; 그처럼. ¶ *He is a poor writer and will remain ~.* 그는 가난한 작가이고 앞으로도 그 상태가 계속될 것이다.

— *interj.* well; all right; Is that true?; How can that be. 저런; 됐어; 참말인가; 그럴 수가《놀람·의문·시인 등을 나타내어》. ¶ *So! Late again!* 이런, 또 늦었어 / *"The train is late!" "So?"* "기차가 늦는데." "정말이야." / *So, that's who did it.* 아니, 그렇다면 역시 그 사람 짓이었느냐. [E.]

and so, after which. 그 뒤에; 그로부터.

and so on [***forth***], and more of the same sort; et cetera. 따위; 등등. ¶ *He told me his name, age, occupation, and ~ on.* 그는 나에게 그의 이름·나이·직업 따위를 말했다.

if so, if that is the case. 만일 그렇다면.

not [***without***] ***so much as,*** not [without] even. …조차[까지]도 …않다. ¶ *He cannot ~ much as write his own name.* 그는 그의 이름조차도 쓸 줄 모른다.

not so much ... as, not ... but rather. …이라기보다는 오히려. ¶ *He is not ~ much a scholar as a writer.* 그는 학자라기보다는 오히려 작가이다.

or so, about many or as much as stated; more or less; approximately. …내외; …쯤; …정도. ¶ *He must be forty or ~.* 그는 40세 정도임에 틀림없다 / *It happened a day or ~ ago.* 그것은 하루이틀 전에 일어났다.

so and so ⇨so-and-so.

so as to, in order to; in such a way as to. …하도록; …할 수 있도록. ¶ *Walk fast ~ as to be in time.* 시간 안에 도착할 수 있도록 빨리 걸어라 / *Come early ~ as to have plenty of time.* 충분한 시간을 가질 수 있도록 일찍 오너라.

so ... as to, to such a degree that; in such a way that. …할 만큼[정도로] —한[하게]. ¶ *He was ~ angry as to be unable to speak.* 그는 말을 할 수 없을 만큼 화가 나 있었다 / *Don't play ~ hard as to become tired.* 지칠 정도로 심하게 놀지 마라.

so be it, a formula of acceptance, resignation. 그렇다면 좋다[할 수 없지]《승낙·체념 등의 상투어》.

so called, what is called. 이른바; 흔히 말하는.

so far, up to that point; to that extent. 여기[지금, 이점]까지(는).

so far as, to the extent to which. …하는 한에서는; …만으로는.

so far from, far from. …은커녕 도리어.

so long, 《*colloq.*》 goodbye. 안녕.

so long as, provided that; on the understanding that. …이기만 하다면; …이라면. ¶ *You may stay here ~ long as you keep quiet.* 네가 조용히 해 주기만 한다면 얼마든지 오래 있어도 괜찮다.

so much, **a**) (of) such a quantity not particulary stated or determined. 얼마 정도의; 얼마쯤의. ¶ *~ much brandy and ~ much water* 브랜디 얼마에 물 얼마 / *earn ~ much a week* 일주일에 얼마쯤의 돈을 번다. **b**) of equal amount. 그만큼의; 같은 양의. ¶ *The house burnt like ~ much paper.* 그 집은 마치 종이 더미처럼 타 버렸다.

so much for, no more need to be said about. …의 이야기는[…에 관하여는] 이제 그만. ¶ *So much for today.* 오늘은 이제 그만.

so much the better, the better for it. 그만큼 더욱 좋다.

so so, not very well or good; fair. 좋지도 나쁘지도 않다; 그저 그렇다.

so that, **a**) in order that. …하도록; …할 수 있도록. ¶ *We got up early ~ that we might catch the first train.* 우리는 첫 기차를 탈 수 있도록 일찍 일어났다 / *I stayed on ~ that he might not feel lonely.* 나는 그가 외로움을 느끼지 않도록 남아 있었다. **b**) therefore; with the result that. 그러므로; 그래서; 그 때문에. ¶ *The dog ran slowly, ~ that he was easily caught.* 그 개는 느리게 달렸다, 그래서 쉽게 잡혔다 / *The bridge had been destroyed, ~ that they could not return.* 그 다리는 파괴되었기 때문에 그들은 돌아올 수 없었다. **c**) in such a way that. …한 방식으로.

so ... (***that***), **a**) to such a degree that. 대단히 …해서 —하다; …할 만큼 그렇게 —하다. **b**) in order that. …할 수 있도록 —하다. ¶ *He studied ~ hard that he passed the entrance examination.* 그는 입학 시험에 합격할 수 있도록 열심히 공부했다. **c**) in such a way that. …할 형편으로 —이다. ¶ *It ~ happened that he was not at home.* 그는 마침 집에 없었다.

·**soak** [souk] *vi.* (P1,2A,3) **1** become wet throughout; become thoroughly wet; remain in liquid. 흠뻑 젖다; 잠기다; 담그다. ¶ *Put the clothes in water and let them ~ for several hours.* 옷을 물 속에 넣고 여러 시간 동안 담가 두어라. **2** 《*in, through, out*》 pass through pores, holes, etc; pass into from elsewhere by soaking; penetrate; percolate. 스며들다; 스미다; 스며나오다; 여과되다. ¶ *Water soaked into the cellar.* 물이 지하실에 스며들었다 / *The rain has soaked through his coat.* 비가 그의 코트로 스며들었다. **3** 《*fig.*》 sink into the mind; be impressed on the mind. 마음 속에 스며들다; 서서히 알게 되다. ¶ *The reason began to ~ into her mind.* 그녀는 이유를 점차로 알게 되었다 / *His advice soaked in.* 그의 충고를 서서히 알게 되었다. **4** 《*colloq.*》 drink excessively and habitually. 술을 많이〔습관적으로〕 마시다. ¶ *~ at the pub* 술집에서 많이 마시다.

— *vt.* **1** (P6) make (something) very wet. 흠뻑 젖게 하다; 적시다. ¶ *be soaked to the skin* 흠뻑 젖다 / *The heavy rain soaked the whole village.* 폭우로 온 마을이 흠뻑 젖었다 / *The coat was soaked with blood.* 코트는 피로 흥건히 젖어 있었다. **2** (P6) make (something) soft or wet by leaving it in water. …을 물에 담그다〔불리다〕; 물에 불려 연하게 하다. ¶ *~ clothes before washing* 세탁하기 전에 옷을 물에 담그다 / *~ bread in milk* 빵을 우유에 담그다. **3** (P7) suck up; absorb; take in. …을 흡수하다; 빨아들이다. ¶ *The sponge soaks up water.* 스펀지는 물을 빨아들인다 / *Blotting-paper soaks up ink.* 압지는 잉크를 빨아들인다 / *~ a stain out* 얼룩을 빼다. **4** (P6,7) 《*fig.*》 learn so as to become thoroughly familiar with (a subject); devote oneself to; be absorbed in (지식 따위를) 흡수하다〔익히다〕; 전심〔몰두〕하다. ¶ *~ up information* 지식을 흡수하다 / *be soaked in literature* 문학에 전심하다 / *~ oneself in music* 음악에 몰두하다. **5** (P6) 《*sl.*》 overcharge; tax very heavily; extract money from by an extortionate charge, taxation, etc. 바가지 씌우다; …에 엄청난 값을 부르다. ¶ *~ the rich* 부자에게 바가지를 씌우다. [E.]

soak *oneself* **to** (=*devote oneself*) **in** *something.* …에 몰두하다.

— *n.* Ⓒ **1** the act of soaking; the state of being soaked. 담그기; 적시기; 침투; 흡수; 흠뻑 젖음. ¶ *Give the clothes a long ~.* 옷을 푹 담가 두어라. **2** the act of heavy drinking; a drunkard; a heavy drinker. 통음; 주정뱅이; 술고래. **3** a heavy rainfall. 큰비; 호우. [E.]

soak·er [sóukər] *n.* **1** a person or thing that soaks. 담그는〔적시는〕 사람〔것〕. **2** a drenching fall of rain. 억수. **3** a habitual heavy drinker. 술고래.

so-and-so [sóuənsòu] *n.* Ⓒ (*pl.* **-sos**) someone; such-and-such a person; a person whose name is forgotten or not known; a person whose name is concealed. 아무개; 모. ¶ *Mr. ~* 모〔아무개〕씨 / *Never mind what ~ will say.* 누가 무엇이라 말을 하든 걱정하지 말게 / *I'll never speak to that crazy ~.* 난 그런 정신나간 사람과는 말을 않겠다. [*so*]

:**soap** [soup] *n.* Ⓤ a substance made of fat and an alkali, used for washing. 비누. ¶ *a bar*〔*cake*〕 *of ~* 비누 한 개 / *wash with ~ and water* 물과 비누로 씻다 / *toilet*〔*washing*〕 *~* 세숫〔세탁〕비누. — *vt.* (P6,7) rub or wash with soap. 비누로 문지르다〔씻다〕. ¶ *~ one's hand* 비누로 손을 씻다. [E.]

soap·box [sóupbɑ̀ks / -bɔ̀ks] *n.* Ⓒ **1** a large wooden box for soap. 비누 운반용의 상자. **2** a box used as a platform by agitators or street speakers. (가두 연설용 연단으로 쓰이는) 빈 상자.

soap-bub·ble [sóupbʌ̀bəl] *n.* a filmy ball of soap and water. 비눗방울.

soap opera [⌐ ⌐–] *n.* 《U.S. *colloq.*》 a radio or television serial of a melodrama. 연속 라디오〔텔레비전〕 드라마.

soap·stone [sóupstòun] *n.* a kind of stone which feels somewhat like soap. (비누 비슷한 부드러운) 동석(凍石).

soap·suds [sóupsʌ̀dz] *n. pl.* foam made with soap and water. 비누 거품; (거품이 인) 비눗물.

soap·y [sóupi] *adj.* (**soap·i·er, soap·i·est**) **1** of or like soap. 비누의; 비누 같은; 비누질(質)의. **2** covered with soap; full of soap. 비누투성이의. ¶ *~ water* 비눗물. **3** flattering. 아첨하는.

·**soar** [sɔːr] *vi.* (P1,2A) **1** ⓐ fly high; rise far above. 높이 날다〔오르다〕; 치솟다. ¶ *A lark soared into the sky.* 종달새 한 마리가 하늘 높이 날아 올랐다 / *The church spire soared above the houses.* 교회의 뾰족탑이 집들 위로 높이 솟아 있었다. ⓑ fly or glide high in the air. (기류를 타고 높이 미끄러지듯) 하늘을 날다; 활공하다. ¶ *An eagle*〔*airplane*〕 *soars through the air.* 독수리 한 마리〔비행기 한 대〕가 높은 하늘을 날아가고 있다. **2** (of one's spirit, hope, etc.) rise beyond what is usual. (의기·희망 따위가) 고양되다; 솟구치다. ¶ *Her hopes soared at the news.* 그녀의 희망은 그 뉴스로 고양되었다 / *His ambition soared high.* 그의 야망은 솟구쳐 올랐다. **3** (of prices, etc.) rise higher rapidly. (물가가) 급등하다. ¶ *Prices have soared.* 물가가 급등했다. [ex-, L. *aura* air]

:**sob** [sɑb / sɔb] *v.* (**sobbed, sob·bing**) *vi.* (P1) **1** cry or weep with gasping short breaths. 흐느껴 울다; 흐느끼다. **2** make such noises. 흐느끼는 듯한〔흑흑, 쉭쉭하는〕 소리를 내다. ¶ *The wind sobbed in the trees.* 바람이 나무숲에서 윙윙거렸다. — *vt.* (P7) **1** speak (something) with tears and sobs. …을 흐느끼며〔울면서〕 말하다. ¶ *"I have lost my doll," the child sobbed.* "내 인형을 잃어버렸어." 라고 아이는 울면서 말하였

다 / ~ *one's grief* 자기의 슬픔을 울면서 말하다. **2** 《*reflexively*》 bring to a condition by sobbing. 흐느껴 울면서 (…한 상태로) 이르게 하다. ¶ *Jane sobbed herself to sleep.* 제인은 흐느껴 울다가 잠이 들었다.

sob** one's **heart out, express one's grief convulsively and noisily 〔violently in sobbing〕. 울부짖으며 자기의 슬픔을 털어놓다.

— *n.* Ⓒ **1** a tearful cry or word. 오열; 흐느낌. **2** a sound like that of the wind. (바람 따위의) 흐느끼는 듯 울리는 소리. [Imit.]

S.O.B., SOB [èsòubí:] *n.* 《*vulg.*》 son of a bitch. 개새끼.

sob·bing [sábiŋ / sɔ́b-] *adj.* weeping with short, quick breaths. 흐느껴 울고 있는.

sob·bing·ly [sábiŋli / sɔ́b-] *adv.* in a sobbing manner; with tears. 목메어〔흐느껴〕 울며.

:so·ber [sóubər] *adj.* (usu. **-ber·er, -ber·est**) **1** not drunk. 술 취하지 않은. ¶ *He was not ~ at the time of the car accident.* 자동차 사고가 났을 때, 그는 맑은 정신이 아니었다《술 먹은 상태였다》. **2** temperate by habit; habitually temperate in the use of liquor. 절주하고 있는; 금주의. **3** ⓐ not extreme in action or thought; moderate. (행동·사고 등이) 과장이 없는; 있는 그대로의; 온건한. ¶ *~ facts* 있는 그대로의 사실 / *in ~ fact* (상상이 아닌) 실제에 / *tell the ~ truth* 사실 그대로의 진상을 말하다 / *a ~ solution to the problem* 그 문제에 대한 온건한 해결. ⓑ quiet; serious; solemn. (흥분하지〔덤벙대지〕 않고) 조용한; 진실된; 근엄한. ¶ *a ~ occasion* 엄숙한 경우 / *a girl too ~ for her age* 나이에 비해 지나치게 침착한 소녀 / *He looks ~.* 그는 진실되게〔근엄하게〕 보인다 / *lead a ~, hard-working life* 진실되고 근면하게 세상을 살아가다. ⓒ characterized by reason or self-control; sane or reasonable. 이성적인; 자제심이 있는; 이치에 맞는. ¶ *~ restraint* 냉정한 자제 / *a person of ~ judgment* 냉정하게 사물을 판단하는 사람 / *a ~ opinion* 이치에 맞는 의견. **4** (of color, clothes, etc.) not bright 〔gay〕; quiet; modest. (옷·색깔 따위가) 수수한; 칙칙한; 소박한. ¶ *be painted in ~ colors* 수수〔침착〕한 색으로 도색되었다 / *She clothed herself in a ~ suit.* 그녀는 수수한 복장을 하고 있었다.

as sober as a judge, completely sober. 매우 진지한.

— *vt.* (P6,7) **1** make (someone) sober. (아무의) 술을 깨게 하다. ¶ *~ oneself by thinking about the bill* (술값의) 계산서에 관해 생각하며 정신을 차리다《술에서 깨다》. **2** make (something) calm or quiet. (…을) 진정시키다.

— *vi.* (P2A) 《*up, off, down*》 become sober. 술이 깨다; 진정되다. ¶ *She seemed to have sobered up completely.* 그녀는 완전히 취기가 가신 것처럼 보였다 / *The excited people sobered down.* 흥분한 사람들은 진정되었다. [L.]

so·ber·ly [sóubərli] *adv.* in a sober manner. 취하지 않고; 제정신으로.

so·ber-mind·ed [sóubərmáindid] *adj.* calm and quiet in mind; self-controlled; reasonable. 침착한; 자제심이 있는; 분별 있는.

so·ber·sides [sóubərsàidz] *n.* (*pl.* **-sides**) 《used as *sing.*》 《*colloq.*》 a serious, solemn person. 진실〔근엄〕한 사람.

so·bri·e·ty [soubráiəti] *n.* Ⓤ **1** the state of being sober; temperance. 술 취해 있지 않음; 금주; 절주. **2** seriousness; quietness; calmness. 진지함; 냉정; 침착. [*sober*]

so·bri·quet, sou- [sóubrikèi] *n.* Ⓒ a nickname. 별명. [F.]

Soc., soc. society.

·so-called [sóukɔ́:ld] *adj.* named or called so, but not truly so; called thus. 소위; 이른바. 語法 보통 불신·경멸의 뜻을 포함함. ¶ *the ~ authority* 소위 (말하는) 권위.

soc·cer [sákər / sɔ́k-] *n.* Ⓤ a form of football played between two teams of 11 players each with a ball that must not be touched with the hands. 사커; 축구. [*association*]

so·cia·bil·i·ty [sòuʃəbíləti] *n.* Ⓤ the quality of being sociable; social disposition; friendliness. 사교를 좋아함; 사교성; 붙임성이 있음. [*social*]

so·cia·ble [sóuʃəbəl] *adj.* fond of company; companionable; friendly; not formal. 사교적인; 사교를 좋아하는; 붙임성이 있는; 친목적인. ¶ *a ~ person* 사교적인 사람 / *We had a ~ afternoon together.* 우리는 함께 화기애애한 오후를 보냈다. — *n.* Ⓤ 《U.S.》 an informal social gathering. 비공식의 친목회.

●so·cia·bly [-bli] *adv.*

:so·cial [sóuʃəl] *adj.* **1** of human beings living together in a group; concerned with human beings as a group; of the happiness and welfare of people. 사회의; 사회 생활을 하는; 사회적인; 사회 복지의. ¶ *the ~ problem* 사회 문제 / *~ good* 사회 복지 / *Man is a ~ animal* 〔*being*〕. 인간은 사회적 동물이다 / *~ progress* 〔*reform*〕 사회 진보〔개혁〕 / *~ environment* 사회 환경 / *~ justice* 사회 정의 / *~ morality* 사회 도덕 / *~ work* 〔*service*〕 사회 사업 / *~ security* 사회 보장. **2** fond of company; friendly; of, for, or having to do with companionship or friendliness; connected with fashionable society. 사교적인; 사교〔교제〕를 좋아하는; 교제상〔친목〕의; 사교계의. ¶ *~ life* 사교 생활 / *a ~ club* 사교 클럽 / *a ~ evening* 친목을 위한 저녁 / *a ~ party* 친목회 / *She has a ~ nature.* 그녀는 사교적인 성질을 가지고 있다 / *Walker is the ~ leader in our town.* 워커씨는 우리 읍에서 사교계의 지도자이다. **3** having to do with ranks or grades of society. 사회적 지위의〔에 의한〕. ¶ *one's ~ equals* 〔*inferiors, superiors*〕 사회적 동일층〔하위층·우위층〕 / *long for ~ advancement* (자기의) 사회적 지위 향상을 바라다. **4** (of animals) living in organized communities. 군거(群居)〔군생(群生)〕

하는[의]. ¶ ~ *birds* [*plants*] 군거[군생]하는 새[식물]들. **5** of socialism. 사회주의의. [L. *socius* comrade]

so·cial·ism [sóuʃəlìzəm] *n.* Ⓤ the theory of social organization in which the means of production and distribution are owned, managed and controlled by the government. 사회주의.

·so·cial·ist [sóuʃəlist] *n.* Ⓒ a person who believes in socialism. 사회주의자. ¶ *the Socialist party* 사회당 / *a ~ organization* 사회주의 단체.

so·cial·is·tic [ʃòuʃəlístik] *adj.* of socialism or socialists. 사회주의(자)의.

so·cial·ite [sóuʃəlàit] *n.* 《U.S. *colloq.*》 a leading person in high society. 사교계의 명사.

so·cial·i·za·tion [sòuʃəlizéiʃən] *n.* Ⓤ the act of socializing; the state of being socialized. 사회에의 적응; 사회화; 사회주의화.

so·cial·ize [sóuʃəlàiz] *vt.* (P6) **1** make (someone) social; make fit for living with others. …을 사교적으로 하다; 사회[공동] 생활에 적응케 하다. **2** change or regulate (a country) according to socialism. …을 사회주의화하다.

socialized medicine [⌐−−⌐−⌐] *n.* a system for providing the entire population with medical care through public funds. 의료 사회화 제도.

so·cial·ly [sóuʃəli] *adv.* in a social or friendly manner. 사회적으로; 사교상.

:so·ci·e·ty [səsáiəti] *n.* (*pl.* **-ties**) **1** Ⓤ ⓐ the system by which people live together in an organized community. 사회 (제도). ¶ *a primitive ~* 원시 사회 / *the progress of ~* 사회의 발달[진보]. ⓑ 《without *an article*》 persons living together, as a whole; all the people, regarded collectively as forming a community; the people of any particular time or place. (사회) 집단; 인간 사회; 세상 사람들. ¶ *work for the benefit* [*good*] *of ~* 인간 사회의 이익을 위하여 일하다 / *as a member of ~* 사회의 일원으로서 / *The habits of ~ have changed greatly since World War II.* 세상 사람들의 습관은 세계 제2차 세계 대전 이래로 크게 달라졌다. **2** Ⓤ the upper class; people of high rank; the fashionable class; its doings. 상류 계층[사회]; 사교계(의 사람들). ¶ *high ~* 상류 사회 / *go* [*get*] *into ~* 사교계에 나가다 / *She is anxious to get into ~.* 그녀는 사교계에 나가고 싶어 안달이다 / *be received* [*admitted*] *~* 사교계에 수용되다. **3** Ⓤ companionship. 교제; 사교. ¶ *I enjoy the ~ of young people.* 나는 젊은 사람들과의 교제를 즐긴다. **4** Ⓒ ⓐ a group of persons joined together for a common purpose or interest. (공통의 목적·취미 등에 의해 결성된) …회; 단체; 조합. ¶ *a medical ~* 의사회 / *a learned ~* 학회 / *a philanthropic ~* 자선 단체 / *a building ~* 건축 조합. ⓑ some particular class of society. …계(界). ¶ *a literary ~* 문학계. [→social]

so·ci·o·log·i·cal [sòusiəlɑ́dʒikəl, -ʃi- / -lɔ́dʒ-] *adj.* of sociology. 사회학(상)의. ¶ *a ~ problem* 사회학의 문제.

so·ci·ol·o·gist [sòusiɑ́lədʒist, -ʃi- / -ɔ́l-] *n.* Ⓒ a scholar of sociology. 사회학자.

so·ci·ol·o·gy [sòusiɑ́lədʒi, -ʃi / -ɔ́l-] *n.* Ⓤ the science which studies the nature, development, and origin of human society; the science of the forms, institutions and functions of society. 사회학.

:sock[1] [sɑk / sɔk] *n.* Ⓒ (*pl.* **socks** or **sox**) **1** 《usu. *pl.*》 a short stocking reaching halfway to the knee. 짧은 양말. ¶ *a pair of baby socks* 어린애 양말 한 켤레 / *skating socks* 스케이트용 양말. **2** a removable inner sole of a shoe. (구두의) 안창. [L.]

Pull up one's socks, 《Brit. *colloq.*》 make greater efforts. 크게 노력하다.

sock[2] [sɑk / sɔk] *vt.* (P6) hit hard. 세게 치다[때리다]. — *n.* a hard blow; a blow of the fist or missile. 세게 때림; 강타. ¶ *give someone a ~* 아무를 세게 한 차례 때리다. — *adv.* plump; square. 퍽; 쿵; 정통으로. ¶ *He hit me ~ in the eye.* 그는 내 눈을 정통으로 한 방 먹였다. [15c. cant]

sock·er [sɑ́kər / sɔ́k-] *n.* =soccer.

sock·et [sɑ́kit / sɔ́k-] *n.* Ⓒ a hollow or hole into which something fits. (뻥 뚫린) 구멍; (꽂거나 끼우는) 구멍; (전기 따위의) 소켓. ¶ *the ~ of the eye* 눈구멍; 안와 / *an electric light ~* 전등의 소켓 / *His eyes nearly jumped from their sockets in surprise.* 그는 너무나 놀라서 눈알이 튀어나올 것 같았다. [F.]

soc·le [sɑ́kəl, sóukəl / sɔ́kəl] *n.* a plinth, esp. as a pedestal of a statue or column. (기둥 따위의) 받침돌; 주춧돌. [→sock[1]]

SOCONY [sɔ́kɔni] *n.* Standard Oil Company of New York.

Soc·ra·tes [sɑ́krətìːz / sɔ́k-] *n.* (469-399 B.C.) a philosopher of Athens. 소크라테스.

So·crat·ic [səkrǽtik / sɔ-] *adj.* of Socrates and his philosophy. 소크라테스(철학)의. — *n.* Ⓒ a followers of Socrates. 소크라테스 문하생[학도]. 「대화법.

Socratic method [−⌐− ⌐−] *n.* dialetics.

sod [sɑd / sɔd] *n.* **1** Ⓤ ground covered with grass; turf. 잔디(밭); 떼. ¶ *be under the ~* 땅속[무덤]에 묻히다. **2** Ⓒ a piece of turf, usu. cut square. (네모진) 뗏장. — *vt.* (**sod·ded, sod·ding**) (P6) cover (a piece of ground, etc.) with sod. 떼를 입히다; …을 잔디로 덮다. [Du.]

·so·da [sóudə] *n.* ⓊⒸ **1** a substance containing sodium. 소다; (중)탄산 소다; 중조(重曹). ¶ *Soda is used in manufacture of soap and glass.* 소다는 비누와 유리 제조에 사용된다. **2** =soda water. ¶ *a whisky and ~* 하이볼. [L. *solidus*]

soda fountain [⌐− ⌐−] *n.* **1** an apparatus for soda water, syrups, etc. 소다수 용기[통, 추출기]. **2** 《U.S.》 a counter where soda water, soft drinks, ice cream, etc. are sold. 소다수 코너《소다수·청량 음료·아이스크림 따위를 판매함》.

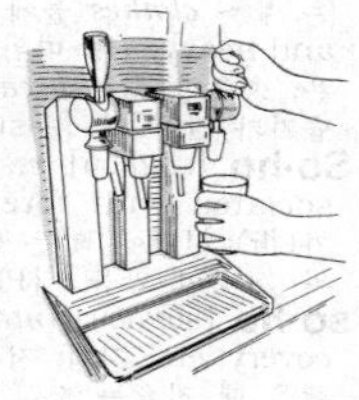
〈soda fountain 1〉

:soda water [⌐–⌐–] *n.* water containing gas to make it bubble and fizz. 소다수; 탄산수.

sod·den [sádn / sɔ́dn] *adj.* **1** soaked and wet through. 흠뻑 젖은; 물에 불은. ¶ *The lawn was ~ with rain.* 잔디밭은 비로 흠뻑 젖었다. **2** (of bread) half-burnt; heavy and moist. (빵이) 설 구워진; 눅진눅진한. ¶ *This bread is ~ because it was not baked enough.* 이 빵은 설 구워져서 눅진눅진하다. **3** stupid or dull-looking because of drunkenness or fatigue. (술이나 피로 때문에) 모습이 멍청한; 후줄근한. [→seeth]

so·di·um [sóudiəm] *n.* Ⓤ a silver-white, metallic substance found in salt, soda, etc. 소듐; 나트륨. [*soda*]

sod·om·ite [sádəmàit / sɔ́d-] *n.* a person guilty of sodomy. 남색자(男色者). [*Sodom* (*Gen.* xix)]

sod·om·y [sádəmi / sɔ́d-] *n.* an unnatural sexual intercourse between males. 남색(男色); 비역. [↓]

so·ev·er [souévər] *adv.* at all; in any case; of any kind; in any way. 아무리 …이라도; 조금도 …(않다). ¶ *how fast ~ he may run* 아무리 그가 빨리 달릴지라도 / *He gave no information ~.* 그는 전혀 정보를 주지 않았다. [*so, ever*]

·so·fa [sóufə] *n.* Ⓒ a long padded couch with a back and two arms. 소파; 긴 의자. [Arab.]

SOFAR [sóufɑːr] *n.* a system of Sound Fixing and Ranging. 조난자 구조용의 수중 측음(測音) 장치(cf. *sonar*).

sof·fit [sáfit / sɔ́-] *n.* 《archit.》 a downward surface of the top of a doorway, window aperture. (인방·보·아치 따위의) 밑면. [→suffix]

S. of Sol. Song of Solomon. (구약의) 아가.

:soft [sɔ(ː)ft, sɑft] *adj.* **1** not hard; easily cut or shaped; lacking in hardness. 부드러운; 유연한; 세공하기 쉬운(opp. hard, tough). ¶ *a ~ bed* 푹신한 침대 / *~ clay* 부드러운 찰흙 / *(as) ~ as butter* 매우 부드러운〔유연한〕/ *~ ground* 부드러운〔무른〕 땅 / *~ goods* 《Brit.》 직물(textiles) / *~ metal* 연질의 금속 / *Pure gold is ~.* 순금은 단단하지 않다. **2** (of cloth, etc.) smooth to the touch; not rough or coarse. (피부·천 따위의 표면이) 매끄러운; 보들보들한; 촉감이 좋은(opp. rough). ¶ *~ hair* (윤이 나는) 매끄러운 머리칼 / *a skin as ~ as silk* 비단결같이 매끄러운 피부 / *a ~ hand* 보드라운 손. **3** (of light, color, etc.) not bright or hard 〔intense〕; subdued. (색·빛이) 부드러운; 차분한. ¶ *a ~ color* 차분〔수수〕한 색깔 / *~ shades of green and blue* 녹색과 청색의 부드러운 색의 조화. **4** (of an outline; of lines in a picture, etc.) not sharp or clear; not clearly outlined. (윤곽·그림의 선 따위가) 부드러운; 아련한; 또렷하지 않은. ¶ *the ~ contours of distant hills* 멀리 보이는 산들의 부드러운〔아련한〕 윤곽. **5** (of sound, etc.) not loud or harsh; gentle; low. (소리가) 낮은; 조용한; 부드러운. ¶ *a ~ voice* 조용한 목소리 / *speak in ~ tones* 부드러운 어조로 이야기하다. **6** (of the weather, air, etc.) mild; gentle; warm; not excessively cold or hot. (날씨 등이) 온화한; 따스한; 상쾌한. ¶ *~ air* 상쾌한 공기 / *a ~ climate* 온화한 기후 / *a ~ breeze from the west* 서쪽에서 불어오는 산들바람 / *a ~ rain* 가랑비. **7** (of a disposition) gentle; kind; tender; kind-hearted. (성질 따위가) 온화〔관대〕한; 친절한; 상냥한; 다정한. ¶ *a ~ heart* 다정한 마음 / *~ words* 친절한 말 / *a ~ smile* 온화한 미소 / *a ~ manner* 온화〔조용〕한 태도 / *~ terms* 관대한 조건 / *a ~ sentence* 관대한 판결 / *be ~ with children* 어린이들에게 엄하지 않다 / *It is a mistake to be ~ with criminals.* 범죄자들에 대해 관대하게 대하는 것은 잘못이다. **8** ⓐ (of a person or character) weak; not fit to endure hardships; not strong or energetic. 연약한; 어려움에 견디지 못하는; 강하지 않은. ¶ *~ muscles* 연약한 근육 / *He was too ~ for the Marines.* 그는 몸이 약해서 해병대에는 알맞지 않았다 / *He is too ~ for such a responsible position.* 그는 그러한 책임있는 자리에 앉을 정도로 강하지 않다. ⓑ 《colloq.》 (of mental capacity) of weak intellect; silly. (머리가) 좀 모자라는; 어리석은. ¶ *I think he is a bit ~ (in the head).* 나는 그가 좀 모자란다고 생각한다. **9** ⓐ 《U.S.》 having no alcohol. 알코올 성분을 포함하지 않은. ¶ *a ~ drink* 청량 음료. ⓑ (of water) free from mineral salts; easily lathered. (물에) 염분〔무기물〕이 없는; 쉬이 거품이 이는. ¶ *~ water* 연수. **10** 《phon.》 (of *c* and *g*) pronounced as in *cent* and *gentle* instead of as in *cake* or *get.* 연음(軟音)의《cent 의 c, gentle 의 g 따위》. **11** 《comm.》 (of markets and prices) subject to a steady decline. (시세 따위가) 약세의; 연조의(opp. hard).

be soft on* 〔*upon*〕 *someone, have a tender feeling toward someone. …을 사랑하고 있다.

— *n.* Ⓒ **1** a soft part; something soft. 부드러운 부분. **2** a silly or weak person. 얼빠진 사람.

— *adv.* in a soft manner; softly. 부드럽게; 조용히. ¶ *fall ~* (소리없이) 부드럽게 떨어지다 / *lie ~* (부드러운 마루 따위에) 편안하게 조용히 눕다. [E.]

:soft·ball [sɔ́(ː)ftbɔ̀ːl, sɑ́ft-] *n.* Ⓤ a game similar to baseball but played with a larger and softer ball; Ⓒ the ball used in

this game. 소프트볼; 소프트볼 경기용의 공.
soft-boiled [sɔ́(:)ftbɔ́ild, sáft-] *adj.* (of eggs, etc.) boiled only a short time so that the yolk does not become hard. (달걀이) 반숙의.
soft corn [ˊˋ] *n.* moist thickening of skin between toes. (발가락 사이의) 물집.
*__sof·ten__ [sɔ́(:)fən, sáfən] *vt., vi.* (P6;1) make (something) soft or softer; become soft or softer. (…을) 부드럽게 하다[되다]; 누그러뜨리다; 누그러지다. ¶ *Her gentle face softened his hard heart.* 그녀의 온화한 얼굴은 그의 굳어진 마음을 누그러뜨렸다 / *Lard softens in heat.* 라드는[반고체의 돼지 기름은] 열에 누그러진다[녹는다]. [*soft*]
soft glances [ˊˊ–] *n.* amorous glances. 추파; 윙크.
soft-heart·ed [sɔ́(:)fthá:*r*tid, sáft-] *adj.* gentle; tender-hearted. 정이 많은; 정에 약한; 동정심이 많은.
soft landing [ˊˊ–] *n.* the landing of a space vehicle on a celestial body preventing damage. 연착륙(軟着陸).
:**soft·ly** [sɔ́(:)ftli, sáft-] *adv.* in a soft manner; kindly; quietly and calmly. 부드럽게; 상냥하게; 관대히; 조용히.
soft money [ˊˊ–] *n.* paper money. 지폐; 어음.
soft·ness [sɔ́(:)ftnis, sáft-] *n.* Ⓤ the state or quality of being soft; comfort; gentleness; mildness. 부드러움; 온화함; 연약; 온순; 관대.
soft nothings [ˊˊ–] *n.* amorous talk. (남녀간의) 달콤한 속삭임.
soft palate [ˊˊ–] *n.* the back of the palate. 연구개(軟口蓋).
soft sell [ˊˊ] *n.* 《*colloq.*》 a subtly persuasive and low-pressure method of selling. 유연한 설득에 의한 판매 방법(cf. *hard sell*).
soft 〔**softer**〕 **sex** [ˊ〔ˊ–〕ˊ] *n.* women. 여성.
soft solder [ˊˊ–] *n.* kinds of it used for easily fusible metal. 가용성 금속용의 땜납.
soft-spo·ken [sɔ́(:)ftspóukən, sáft-] *adj.* talking or spoken in a gentle voice. 말씨가 상냥한; 표현이 부드러운.
soft thing 〔**job**〕 [ˊˊ] *n.* a transaction in which money can be easily earned. 편하고 수입이 많은 일.
soft·ware [sɔ́(:)ftwὲə*r*, sáft-] *n.* Ⓤ any programs or data used for operating a computer. 소프트웨어(cf. *hardware*).
soft·wood [sɔ́(:)ftwùd, sáft-] *n.* **1** Ⓤ wood that is easy to cut. 연한 나무; 연재(軟材). ¶ *Pine is a ~, oak is a hardwood.* 소나무는 연한 나무고 오크는 단단한 나무다. **2** Ⓒ any cone-bearing tree, such as the pine and spruce; Ⓤ the wood of such a tree. 침엽수(의 재목).
sog·gy [sɔ́(:)gi, sági] *adj.* (**-gi·er, -gi·est**) **1** completely 〔thoroughly〕 wet; filled with water; soaked. 물에 흠뻑 젖은[잠긴]; 물에 불은. ¶ *~ clothes* 물에 흠뻑 젖은 옷. **2** damp and heavy. (빵 따위가) 설구워진; 습기가 많은; 축축한. ¶ *~ bread* 설구워진 빵 / *~ land* 습기가 많은 땅. [→suck]
So·ho [sou*h*óu] *n.* a London district associated with foreign restaurants. 소호가(街)《런던에 있는 한 지역으로 외국인 경영의 식당이 많음》. [Place]
so·ho [sou*h*óu] *interj.* announcing a discovery, etc. 저기; 저것 (봐)《사냥감 등을 발견했을 때 지르는 소리》. [F.]
soi-di·sant [swὰ:di:zá:ŋ] *adj.* 《F.》 self-styled; pretended. 자칭의.
:**soil**[1] [sɔil] *n.* **1** the part of the earth's surface consisting of crumbled rock and decayed matter of plants and animals; the ground in which plants grow; earth; dirt. 흙; 토양; 땅. ¶ *Most plants grow best in rich ~.* 대부분의 식물들은 비옥한 토양에서 잘 자란다. **2** the ground in general; a land or country. 토지; 국토. ¶ *one's native ~* 고국; 고향 / *on foreign ~* 이국에서. [L. *solium* seat]
*__soil__[2] [sɔil] *n.* Ⓤ **1** a soiled mark; (a) stain; dirt. 오점; 더럼; 오물. **2** manure used to enriching the earth. 분뇨; 거름. — *vt., vi.* (P6;1) **1** make (something) dirty; put dirty marks upon; become dirty. 더럽히다; …에 얼룩을 묻히다; 더러워지다. ¶ *Nancy soiled her dress.* 낸시는 옷을 더럽혔다 / *White shirts ~ easily.* 흰 셔츠는 쉬이 더러워진다. **2** disgrace; dishonor; bring shame upon; corrupt morally. (명예·가문 등을) 욕되게 하다; 더럽히다; 타락하다. ¶ *~ the family name* 가문을 욕되게 하다 / *George's good reputation was soiled by his son's unlawful act.* 조지의 좋은 평판은 그의 아들의 불법 행위로 손상되었다. [L. *sus* pig]
soiled [sɔild] *adj.* not clean; dirty. 깨끗하지 않은; 더러워진.
soi·ree, soi·rée [swɑ:réi / ˊ–] *n.* Ⓒ an evening party. 야회(夜會). [L. *serus* late]
so·journ [sóudʒə:*r*n, –ˊ / sɔ́dʒ-] *vi.* (P2A) stay for a time. (일시적으로) 머무르다; 체재[기류]하다. ¶ *~ in Paris* 파리에 머무르다. — [sóudʒə:*r*n / sɔ́dʒ-] *n.* Ⓒ a short or temporary stay. (일시적) 체재; 기류. ¶ *make a ~ in a mountain* 산에 일시 머무르다 / *during one's ~ in Africa* 아프리카에 체재하고 있는 동안. [sub-, →diurnal]
so·journ·er [sóudʒə:*r*nə*r*, –ˊ– / sɔ́dʒ-] *n.* Ⓒ a person who sojourns. 체재자; 기류인.
Sol [sɑl / sɔl] *n.* **1** the sun. 태양. **2** the Roman god of the sun. 태양신. [L.]
sol [soul, sɑl / sɔl] *n.* 《mus.》 the fifth tone of the scale. 솔《장음계의 다섯째 음》. [→do[1]]
Sol. Solicitor; Solomon.
sol. solicitor; soluble; solution.
sol·ace [sáləs / sɔ́l-] *n.* ⓊⒸ comfort in trouble or sorrow; consolation. 위안; 위로. ¶ *find ~ in music* 음악에서 위안을 찾다 /

seek ~ *from grief* 슬픔으로부터의 위안을 찾다. — *vt., vi.* (P6,13;1) give relief, comfort, etc. to (someone); console; cheer. 위안하다; 위안이 되다. ¶ *She solaced herself with reading the Bible.* 그녀는 성경을 읽으면서 스스로를 위로했다 / *Great literature solaces.* 위대한 문학 작품은 위안이 된다. [L. *solatium*]

so·lar [sóulər] *adj.* **1** of or having to do with the sun. 태양의; 태양에 관한. ¶ *a* ~ *eclipse* 일식 / *the* ~ *system* 태양계. **2** coming from or produced by the sun; measured by the sun. 태양에서 나오는; 태양을 이용한; 태양에 의해 측정된. ¶ ~ *energy* 태양 에너지 / *the* ~ *rays* 태양 광선 / *the* ~ *calendar* 태양력 / ~ *time* 태양시 / *a* ~ *battery* 태양 전지. [→Sol]

solar day [´-´] *n.* 《astron.》 an astronomical day. 천문일(天文日).

solar fever [´-´-] *n.* dengue. 뎅기열《모기에 의한 바이러스성 열대 전염병》.

solar flowers [´-´-] *n.* flowers which remain open only for some hours in the day. 낮에만 일정 시간 동안 피는 꽃.

so·lar·i·a [souléəriə] *n.* pl. of **solarium.**

so·lar·i·um [souléəriəm] *n.* Ⓒ (*pl.* **-ums** or **-lar·i·a**) a room to enjoy the warmth and heat of the sun; a sunroom. 일광욕실.

solar month [´-´] *n.* an exact twelfth of the year. 태양 월(月)《1년이 12개월임》.

solar plexus [´-´-] *n.* 《anat.》 the complex of nerves at the pit of the stomach. 태양 신경총(叢).

solar spot [´-´] *n.* a spot on the sun. 태양 흑점.

:sold [sould] *v.* p. and pp. of **sell.**

sol·der [sádər / sɔ́ldər] *n.* **1** Ⓤ a metal or an alloy used to join or mend metal surfaces. 땜납. **2** Ⓒ anything that unites or joins firmly; a bond. 결합시키는 것; 결합물; 유대. — *vt.* (P6,7) join or fasten (something) with solder; unite; join. …을 납으로 땜질하다; 결합하다. [→solid]

sol·der·ing iron [sádəriŋ àiərn / sɔ́l-] *n.* a tool for joining or fastening (metal plates, etc.) together with solder. 납땜인두.

·sol·dier [sóuldʒər] *n.* Ⓒ **1** a man who serves in an army; an enlisted man as distinguished from an officer. (육군) 군인; 병사; 하사관. ¶ *officers and soldiers* 장병 / *serve as a* ~ 사병으로 복무하다 / *a militia* ~ 국민병 / *go for a* ~ 병역을 지원하다; 군인이 되다. **2** a man who is skilled and experienced in war. (우수한) 무인〔지휘관〕; 명장. **3** a great leader in any cause. (주의(主義)의) 투사.

***a soldier of Christ* 〔*the cross*〕,** a missionary of Christianity. 열성적인 기독교 전도사.

a soldier of fortune, a person who is willing to serve in any army for money or adventure; an adventurer. (급료와 모험이 목적인) 용병; 모험가.

— *vi.* (P1) **1** become a soldier. 군인이 되다. **2** 《*colloq.*》 do not work hard; pretend to work. 일을 게을리 하다; 일하는 척만 하다. [L. *solidus* a coin]

sol·dier·like [sóuldʒərlàik] *adj.* = soldierly.

sol·dier·ly [sóuldʒərli] *adj.* like a soldier; suitable for a soldier. 군인다운; 군인 기질의. ¶ *a* ~ *appearance* 〔*mind, character*〕 군인다운 모습〔마음가짐, 성격〕.

sol·dier·ship [sóuldʒərʃip] *n.* Ⓤ military skill. 군사상의 수완〔기량〕.

sol·dier·y [sóuldʒəri] *n.* 《*collectively,* often *a* ~ 》 soldiers. 군인; 군대. ¶ *a wild undisciplined* ~ 난폭하고 규율이 없는 병사들.

·sole[1] [soul] *adj.* **1** one and only; unique. 유일한; 단 하나의; 독특한. ¶ *the* ~ *survivor* 유일한 생존자 / *the* ~ *brilliance of the diamond* 다이아몬드 특유의 광택. **2** of or for only one person; exclusive. 독점적인; 단독의. ¶ *the* ~ *right* 독점권 / *the* ~ *agent* 총대리인 / (*the*) ~ *manager* 총지배인. **3** not married; single. 미혼의; 독신의. [L. *solus*]

sole[2] [soul] *n.* Ⓒ **1** the bottom of the foot, shoes, boots, etc. 발바닥; 신발〔구두〕의 창〔바닥〕. **2** the lower part. (물건의) 밑면; 토대. — *vt.* (P6) put a sole on (shoes, etc.). (구두 따위)에 창을 대다〔갈다〕. ¶ *I must have my shoes soled.* 나는 내 구두창을 갈아야 한다. [L. *solea*]

sol·e·cism [sáləsìzəm / sɔ́l-] *n.* Ⓒ **1** incorrect grammar or usage of a language. 문법〔어법〕 위반; 파격. ¶ *'Between you and I' is a* ~. 'Between you and I'는 어법 위반이다. **2** a breach of etiquette; bad manners. 예법에 어긋남; 버릇없음; 부적당. [Gk.]

·sole·ly [sóulli] *adv.* in a sole manner; singly; only. 단독으로; 오로지; 전혀. ¶ *I am* ~ *responsible.* 나의 단독 책임이다 / *The plants grow outdoors* ~ *in the tropics.* 그 식물은 오로지 열대 지방의 옥외에서만 자란다 / *read* ~ *for enjoyment* 오로지 즐기기 위해 읽다 / *a* ~ *fictitious story* 전혀 허구의 이야기. [*sole*[1]]

·sol·emn [sáləm / sɔ́l-] *adj.* (**-emn·er, -emn·est**) **1** serious; grave; sacred. 엄숙〔장중〕한; 신성한. ¶ *a* ~ *hymn* 성가 / *a* ~ *oath* 엄숙한 서약 / ~ *truth* 엄숙한 진실 / ~ *music* 장중한 음악. **2** dignified; formal; ceremonial; pompous. 위엄을 지닌; 격식 차린; 의식을 갖춘; 성대한. ¶ *a* ~ *state dinner* 성대한 공식 만찬회. **3** valuable; important. 귀중한; 중대〔엄중〕한. ¶ *on a* ~ *occasion* 중대한 시기에 / *give a* ~ *warning* 엄중한 경고를 발하다. [L.]

so·lem·ni·ty [səlémnəti] *n.* Ⓤ (*pl.* **-ties**) **1** the state of being solemn; great seriousness. 장엄; 엄숙. ¶ *the* ~ *of a state funeral* 국장의 장엄함 / *the* ~ *of his speech* 그의 연설의 엄숙함. **2** 《often *pl.*》 a formal ceremony. (종교적) 의식; 제전. ¶ *Easter is observed* *with* ～. 부활절은 의식에 따라 지켜진다.

sol·em·ni·za·tion [sὰləmnizéiʃən / sɔ̀ləm-] *n.* UC the act of solemnizing; the state of being solemnized. 장엄화(化); 식을 올림.

sol·em·nize [sάləmnàiz / sɔ́l-] *vt.* (P6) perform (something) with religious ceremonies; celebrate or perform (a marriage, etc.) in a proper manner. …을 장중〔장엄〕하게 행하다; (결혼식 따위)를 (엄숙히) 거행하다; 식을 올려 축하하다. ¶ ～ *a wedding* 결혼식을 거행하다 / *The coronation was solemnized in the Abbey.* 대관식은 웨스트민스터 사원에서 장중하게 거행되었다.

sol·emn·ly [sάləmli / sɔ́l-] *adv.* in a solemn manner; gravely; seriously; formally. 엄숙하게; 장엄하게; 딱딱하고 점잖게; 정식으로.

sol·fa [sòulfά: / sɔ̀l-] *n.* U a system or way of singing using syllables corresponding to the notes of the scale. 계명(階名)〔도레미파〕 창법. —— *vi., vt.* (P1;6) sing thus and not with words. 계명으로〔도레미파로〕 노래하다. [→do[1]]

so·li [sóuli:] *n.* pl. of **solo.**

***so·lic·it** [səlísit] *vt., vi.* (P6,13;1) 《*for, of, from*》 ask for (something) earnestly; entreat and beg repeatedly; make appeals. (…을) 간청하다; 졸라대다. ¶ ～ *someone for money* 아무에게 돈을 달라고 졸라대다 / ～ *advice* 〔*contribution*〕 조언을〔기고를〕 간청하다 / *We* ～ *favors from* 〔*of*〕 *you.* 부디 애호해 주시기 바랍니다《관용적인 상용문》. [L. *sollicitus* anxious]

so·lic·i·ta·tion [səlìsətéiʃən] *n.* UC **1** the act of soliciting; earnest request and appeal. 간원(懇願); 간청; 권유. **2** the temptation of a street girl. (매춘부의) 손님 끌기; 유혹.

so·lic·i·tor [səlísətər] *n.* C **1** ⓐ 《Brit.》 a lawyer; a member of the legal profession who prepares cases for barristers. 변호사. 參考 주로 재판〔소송〕 사무를 취급함. ⓑ 《U.S.》 an officer having charge of the legal business of a city, town, etc. (시·읍 따위의) 법무관. ¶ *a city* ～ 시(市) 법무관 / *a Solicitor of the Treasury* 재무부 법무관. **2** a person who entreats and appeals repeatedly; a person who seeks trade. 간청자; 권유원; 주문받는 사람. [↑]

solicitor general [–∸–– ∸––] *n.* (*pl.* **solicitors g-**) **1** 《Brit.》 a law officer who assists the attorney general. 법무 차관. **2** 《U.S.》《*S- G-*》 the chief law officer. 수석 검사(cf. *attorney general*).

so·lic·it·ous [səlísətəs] *adj.* **1** 《*about, for*》 anxious; concerned; full of care or concern; troubled. 마음을 쓰는; 걱정〔염려〕하는; 근심스러운. ¶ *be* ～ *about the future of one's family* 가족의 장래를 염려하다 / *be* ～ *about someone's health* 아무의 건강에 대해 마음을 쓰다 / *I am* ～ *for his future.* 나는 그의 장래를 걱정한다. **2** 《*of, to do*》 eagerly looking for (something); desirous; full of anxious desire. 간절히 바라는; 갈망하는; 열심인. ¶ *be* ～ *for his daughter's happiness* 그의 딸의 행복을 간절히 바라다 / *be* ～ *of honor* 명예를 갈망하다 / *be* ～ *to please* (…의) 마음에 들려고 애쓰다.

so·lic·i·tude [səlísətjù:d] *n.* U anxiety; uneasiness of mind; anxious care; concern. 우려; 근심; 걱정.

:sol·id [sάlid / sɔ́l-] *adj.* (**-id·er, -id·est**) **1** not a liquid or a gas; firm; hard. 고체의; 고형(固形)의; 단단한. ¶ *When water becomes* ～, *we call it ice.* 물이 고체가 되었을 때, 이것을 얼음이라고 한다 / ～ *bodies* 고체 / ～ *food* 고형식(固形食) / *the* ～ *ground* 단단한〔굳은〕 땅. **2** without holes or spaces inside; filled with matter; thick. 속이 비지 않은; 충실한; 옹골진; 짙은. ¶ *a* ～ *iron bar* 속이 찬 금속봉 / *a* ～ *tire* 통 타이어 / ～ *masses of clouds* 짙은 뭉게구름의 덩어리. **3** all of one material, color, or kind; consisting of the same material or color throughout; pure. 속까지 동질의; 동일 색조의; 순수한. ¶ *a* ～ *color* 동일 색조의〔농담이 한결 같은〕 빛깔 / *a fork of* ～ *silver* 〔*gold*〕 순은〔순금〕의 포크 / *a* ～ *blue dress* 무지의 푸른색 드레스. **4** (of structures, furniture, etc.) strongly built; (of reasons, etc.) sound; with a sound financial position. (건물·구조 따위가) 견고한; 튼실〔튼튼〕한; (이유·근거 따위가) 합리적인; (재정적으로) 신용 있는; 견실한. ¶ *a man of* ～ *built* 튼튼〔튼실〕한 체격의 사람 / *a* ～ *building* 견고한 빌딩 / *Some of these new houses don't look very* ～. 이 몇몇 새로 지은 집들은 별로 견고해 보이지 않는다 / *a* ～ *basis* 확실한 근거 / ～ *reasons* 근거가 확실한 이유 / *a* ～ *business* 〔*firm*〕 (재정적으로) 견실한 사업〔회사〕 / *a* ～ *merchant* 신용 있는〔견실한〕 상인 / *He has no* ～ *ground for his actions.* 그는 그의 행동에 대한 합리적인 근거가 없다. **5** reliable; of sound character; firm in views or opinions. 신뢰할 수 있는; (생각·의견 등이) 견실〔확실, 온건〕한. ¶ *a man of* ～ *character* 신뢰할 수 있는 사람 / *a* ～ *citizen* 온건한 시민 / *a man of* ～ *sense* 분별 있는 사람. **6** firmly united in support of something; united in a single opinion. 단결된; 만장 일치의. ¶ *a* ～ *vote of approval* 만장 일치의 찬성 투표 / *a* ～ *combination* 일치 단결. **7** real; true; complete. 진실된; 진짜의; 완전한. ¶ ～ *comfort* 진정한 위안 / ～ *satisfaction* 진심으로 느끼는 만족. **8** 《U.S. *colloq.*》 very friendly. 사이가 좋은. ¶ *be* ～ *with someone* 아무와 사이가 좋다. **9** having no breaks or openings; undivided; continuous. 잘리거나 터진 곳이 없는; 연속된. ¶ *a* ～ *wall* 끊기거나 터진 곳이 없는 벽 / *a* ～ *row of buildings* 끊긴 곳 없이 연속(連續)된 건물들 / *Don't cross the* ～ *white line.* 연속된 흰 줄을 가로 넘지 마라. **10** (of food) full and rich; substantial. (식사가) 실속 있는; 실질적인. ¶ *a* ～ *meal* 실속 있는 식사. **11** full;

whole; entire. 결여됨이 없는; 완전한; 온. ¶ *a ~ hour* 꼬박 한 시간 / *for three ~ days* 온 3일 동안 / *He talked for two ~ hours.* 그는 두 시간 내내 이야기하였다.
be* 〔*go*〕 *solid for, be united or act together in favor of. …을 위해 일치 협력하다; 단결하여 …을 지지하다.
be solid with, 《U.S. *colloq.*》 be on good terms with. …와 사이가 좋다.
— *n.* Ⓒ **1** a body or substance that is not a liquid or a gas. 고체; 고형물. **2** a body that has length, breadth, and thickness. 입체.
— *adv.* in complete agreement. 만장 일치로. ¶ *vote ~* 만장 일치로 투표하다. [L. solidus]

sol·i·dar·i·ty [sàlədǽrəti / sɔ̀l-] *n.* Ⓤ **1** unity and cooperation arising from common feelings and interests; holding together. 단결; 일치; 결속. ¶ *the ~ of a party* 당의 단결 / *the ~ of the working class* 근로계급의 결속. **2** mutual responsibility. 연대책임. [*solid*]

so·lid·i·fi·ca·tion [səlìdəfikéiʃən] *n.* Ⓤ the act of solidifying; the state of being solidified; unity. 응고; 고체화; 결속; 단결.

so·lid·i·fy [səlídəfài] *vt., vi.* (**-fied**) (P6;1) **1** make (something) solid; become solid. …을 단단하게〔굳게〕 하다; 단단해〔굳어〕지다; 응고시키다〔되다〕. ¶ *the solidifying point* 응고점 / *Freezing solidifies water into ice.* 동결은 물을 얼음으로 응고시킨다. **2** make (people) unite; become firmly united. (…을) 결속시키다〔하다〕. ¶ *~ people into a party* 하나의 당으로 사람들을 결속시키다.

so·lid·i·ty [səlídəti] *n.* Ⓤ the state of being solid; firmness; sureness. 고체성; 충실; 확실함.

solid science [⌐– ⌐–] *n.* the study of the uppermost stratum of the earth's surface. 토양 과학.

sol·id-state [sálidstéit / sɔ́l-] *adj.* 《electronics》 of semi-conducting materials, components and related devices. (트랜지스터 따위의) 반도체를 이용한; 솔리드 스테이트의.

solid waste [⌐– ⌐] *n.* waste matters difficult to be discomposed by natural process. 자연 분해가 안되는 폐기물.

so·lil·o·quize [səlíləkwàiz] *vi.* (P1) talk to oneself; utter a dramatic monologue on stage, etc. 혼잣말하다; 독백하다. [→sole[1], locution]

so·lil·o·quy [səlíləkwi] *n.* (*pl.* **-quies**) **1** Ⓤ the act of speaking to oneself. 혼잣말. **2** Ⓒ an act of speaking to the audience in a drama. 독백. ¶ *Hamlet's ~* 햄릿의 독백.

sol·i·taire [sálitɛ̀ər / sɔ́l-] *n.* Ⓒ **1** a single gem, esp. a diamond, set by itself. (반지 따위에) 한 개 박은 보석〔다이아몬드〕. **2** Ⓤ a game of cards played by one person alone. 혼자서 하는 카드놀이. [→sole[1]]

•**sol·i·tar·y** [sálitèri / sɔ́litəri] *adj.* **1** ⓐ alone; living alone; single. 혼자의; 혼자 사는. ¶ *a ~ cell* 독방 / *~ confinement* 〔*imprisonment*〕 독방 감금 / *a ~ task* 혼자서 하는 일. ⓑ without companions; lonely; lonesome. 친구가 없는; 외로운. ¶ *He leads a ~ life in the woods.* 그는 숲 속에서 외로운 삶을 살고 있다 / *feel ~* 외롭게〔쓸쓸하게〕 느끼다. **2** seldom visited; remote. 외진; 외딴. ¶ *a ~ village* 외진 마을 / *The house is in a ~ place.* 그 집은 외딴 곳에 있다. **3** not having anything similar; only one; single. 단 하나의; 유일한. ¶ *a ~ instance* 〔*exception*〕 유일한 예〔예외〕.
— *n.* Ⓒ (*pl.* **-tar·ies**) a person who lives alone. 혼자 사는 사람; 은둔자.

•**sol·i·tude** [sálitjù:d / sɔ́li-] *n.* **1** Ⓤ the state of being alone. 고독; 홀로 삶. ¶ *live in ~* 홀로〔고독하게〕 살다. **2** Ⓒ a lonely place. 외진〔쓸쓸한〕 곳; 벽지. ¶ *spend three years in these solitudes* 이런 외진 곳들에서 3년을 보내다.

so·lo [sóulou] *n.* Ⓒ (*pl.* **-los** or **-li**) **1** a piece of music played or sung by one person. 독창〔독주〕(곡). ¶ *a piano ~* 피아노 독주. **2** anything done by one person. (무용·비행 따위의) 단독으로 (행)하기; 단독비행; 독무(獨舞).
— *adj.* done by one person alone. 혼자서 하는; 단독의. ¶ *a ~ flight* 단독 비행 / *a ~ dance* 혼자서 추는 춤; 독무.
— *adv.* alone; by oneself. 혼자서; 단독으로. ¶ *After ten lessons, he flew ~.* 열 학과를 마치고 그는 단독으로 비행하였다.
— *vi.* (**-loed, -lo·ing**) perform by oneself; make a solo flight in an airplane. 혼자서 하다; 단독 비행하다. [→sole[1]; the series from L. numerals]

so·lo·ist [sóulouist] *n.* Ⓒ 《mus.》 a person who performs a solo. 독주〔독창〕자.

Sol·o·mon [sáləmən / sɔ́l-] *n.* **1** 《Bible》 a king of Israel in the 10th century B.C. who was famous for his wisdom and the great temple he built. 솔로몬 왕. **2** Ⓒ a very wise man like Solomon. 현인. [Heb.]
be no Solomon, be stupid. 바보이다.

So·lon [sóulən] *n.* **1** (638?-559? B.C.) a wise Athenian law-giver. 솔론《고대 그리스의 입법가》. **2** a sage; a wise legislator. 현인(賢人); 명(名)입법가. [Gk.]

so long, so-long [sòu lɔ́:ŋ] *interj.* goodbye. 안녕.

sol·stice [sálstis / sɔ́l-] *n.* Ⓒ either of the two points in the sun's path at which the sun is at its greatest distance from the celestial equator. (태양의) 지점(至點). ¶ *the summer ~* 하지 / *the winter ~* 동지. [→Sol, sation]

sol·u·bil·i·ty [sàljəbíləti / sɔ̀l-] *n.* Ⓤ the quality of being soluble. 용해성〔도〕; 해결 가능성. ¶ *the ~ of sugar in water* 물에서의 설탕의 용해성. [→solve]

sol·u·ble [sáljəbəl / sɔ́l-] *adj.* **1** that can be dissolved in a liquid. 녹는; 용해할 수 있는. ¶ *Sugar is readily ~ in water.* 설탕은 물에 잘 녹는다. **2** that can be solved or explained. (문제 따위가) 해결할 수 있는. ¶ *~ puzzles* 풀 수 있는 수수께끼들. [↑]

sol·ute [sálju:t, sóulu:t / sɔ́lju:t] *n.* 《chem.》 the substance dissolved in a solution. 용질(溶質)(cf. *solvent*). [↓]

:so·lu·tion [səlú:ʃən] *n.* **1** Ⓤ the act of solving a problem; Ⓒ an answer to a problem. (문제 따위의) 해결; 해답. ¶ *They cannot find a ~ of* [*for, to*] *the difficulty.* 그들은 그 난문제에 대한 해결책으로 고심하고 있다. **2** Ⓤ the act of dissolving a substance into a liquid; the state of being dissolved. 용해(상태). ¶ *chemical ~* 화학적 용해 / *salt in ~* 용해된 소금 / *difficult* [*easy*] *of ~* 용해하기 어려운[쉬운]. **3** ⓊⒸ a liquid or some other mixture formed by dissolving. 용액. ¶ *a ~ of salt* 식염 용액 / *a strong* [*weak*] *~* 진한[묽은]용액 / *make a ~ of ammonia* 암모니아 용액을 만들다. **4** Ⓤ the action of separating or breaking up into parts; dissolution. 분해. [→solve]

solv·a·ble [sálvəbəl / sɔ́l-] *adj.* that can be solved or dissolved. 풀[해결할] 수 있는; 분해할 수 있는. [↓]

:solve [salv / sɔlv] *vt.* (P6) find the answer to or explanation of (a problem, a puzzle, etc.); clear up; explain. (문제 따위)를 풀다; 해결하다. ¶ *He solved all the problems in the examination.* 그는 시험에 나온 모든 문제들을 풀었다. [L. *solvo* loosen]

sol·ven·cy [sálvənsi / sɔ́l-] *n.* Ⓤ the ability to pay one's debts. 지불 능력; 자력(資力). [↑]

sol·vent [sálvənt / sɔ́l-] *adj.* **1** able to pay one's debts. 지불[변제] 능력이 있는. ¶ *That firm* [*company*] *is ~.* 저 회사는 지불 능력이 있다 / *a ~ firm* 지불 능력이 있는 회사. **2** able to dissolve some other substance. 용해력이 있는. ¶ *~ fluids* [*liquids*] 용액 / *the ~ action of water* 물의 용해 작용. **3** able to weaken a feeling, emotion, etc. (마음·감정 따위를) 누그러뜨리는. ¶ *the ~ power of laughter* 사람의 마음을 누그러뜨리는 웃음의 힘. —*n.* Ⓒ a substance that can dissolve some other substance. 용제; 용매. ¶ *Water is a ~ for sugar and salt.* 물은 설탕과 소금의 용제이다. [↑]

som·ber, 《Brit.》 **-bre** [sámbər / sɔ́m-] *adj.* **1** dark and dull; dimly lighted; shadowy; dark-colored. 어둠침침한; 거무스름한. ¶ *a ~ sky* 어둠침침한 하늘 / *a ~ room* 어두컴컴한 방 / *a ~ color* [*dress*] 거무스름한 색깔[옷]. **2** tending to make someone feel sad and gloomy; melancholy. 우울한; 음울한. ¶ *a ~ expression* 음울한 표정 / *The outlook is ~ indeed.* 전도는 참으로 암담하다 / *My life just now is rather ~.* 지금의 내 삶은 오히려 우울한 편이다. [L.]

som·bre·ro [sambréərou / sɔm-] *n.* Ⓒ (*pl.* **-ros**) a hat, usu. made of felt and with a broad brim, worn esp. in Spain, Latin America, etc. 솜브레로《양태가 넓은 스페인·라틴 아메리카 등의 중절모》. [Sp.]

:some [sʌm, səm, sm] *adj.* **1** a certain amount or number of; a few. 다소[약간]의; 얼마간의. ¶ *~ money* 약간의 돈 / *for ~ time* 얼마 동안 / *Will you have ~ tea?* 차를 좀 드시겠습니까 / *drink ~ milk* 우유를 약간 마시다 / *Won't you have ~ sandwiches?* 샌드위치를 조금 드시지 않겠습니까 / *I saw ~ people that I knew.* 나는 내가 아는 몇몇 사람들을 보았다. **2** not known; a certain. 어떤; 누군가의; 무언가의. ¶ *Some boy did it.* 어떤 소년이 그것을 했다 / *There is ~ man at the door.* 누군가가 현관에 와 있다 / *Some car or other broke down our fence.* 어떤 차가 우리 집 울타리를 부셨다 / *Pick out ~ one card.* 어떤 것이든 카드 한 장을 뽑으시오 / *He went to ~ place in Africa.* 그는 아프리카 어딘가로 갔다. **3** [sʌm] 《*colloq.*》 ⓐ of considerable worth; rather important; remarkable; striking. 대단한; 상당한; 굉장한. ¶ *It was ~ party.* 그것은 대단한 파티였다 / *He is ~ scholar.* 그는 대단한[꽤 중시되는] 학자이다 / *It took ~ patience to persuade him to give up the plan.* 그에게 그 계획을 단념시키는데 굉장한 인내를 필요로 하였다. ⓑ to a certain extent. 어느 정도의. ¶ *have ~ reading knowledge of France* 어느 정도 프랑스어의 독해 능력이 있다. **4** [sʌm] a considerable number or quantity; pretty large amount of. 상당한[꽤 많은] 수[수량]의. ¶ *He left ~ time ago.* 그는 꽤 오래 전에 떠났다 / *I stayed there for ~ days.* 나는 여러 날 거기에 머물렀다. **5** 《with *numerals*》 about. 약 …. ¶ *~ 20 miles off* 약 20마일 떨어진.

after some time, after a while. 얼마 후.

for some time, for a while. 잠시 동안.

in some degree, in some measure. 다소.

in some way, somehow. 어떻게든 해서.

some day, on a certain future day. 언젠가; 훗날; 일간.

some days ago, a few days ago. 얼마 전(에).

some few [***little***]***,*** a small number. 소수.

some girl, a pretty girl. 미인.

some more, a little more. 조금 더.

some other day, another day. 후일.

some time, at a certain future time. 언젠가; 가까운 시일 안에.

some time ago, a little while ago. 아까; 조금 전.

—*pron.* **1** persons or things whose names are not known. 어떤 사람들; 어떤 것. ¶ *Some say one thing and others another.* 사람에 따라 말하는 것이 다르다 / *Some are silver and ~ (are) gold.* 은제(銀製)의 것이 있는가 하면 금제(金製)의 것도 있다 / *There is no agreement; ~ say yes, ~ say no.* 합의란 없다. 어떤 사람은 찬성이고 어떤 사람은 반대

이다. **2** a certain amount or number. 약간; 다소; 얼마. ¶ *I have just drunk* ~. 조금 마셨다 / *He took away* ~ *of it.* 그가 그것을 얼마 가져 갔다.

— *adv.* **1** 《*colloq.*》 somewhat; to some extent; rather. 얼마쯤; 다소. ¶ *He is* ~ *better today.* 그는 오늘 상태가 다소 좋다. **2** 《U.S. *colloq.*》 good deal; to a great extent. 상당히; 꽤. ¶ *He seemed tired* ~. 그는 꽤 피곤해 보인다. [E.]

:some·body [sʌ́mbɑ̀di, -bʌ̀di, -bədi / -bɔ̀di] *pron.* a person unknown; someone. 누군가; 어떤 사람. ¶ *Somebody will find it.* 누군가가 그것을 발견할 것이다 / *I want* ~ *to help me.* 나를 누군가가 도와주면 좋겠다 / *Somebody has taken my pen.* 누군가가 나의 펜을 가져 갔다. — *n.* Ⓒ (*pl.* **-bod·ies**) a person of importance. 잘난(뛰어난, 대단한) 사람. ¶ *He thinks himself to be* (*a*) ~. 그는 자신을 꽤 잘난 사람이라고 생각하고 있다.

somebody else, someone else. 누군가 다른 사람.

:some·how [sʌ́mhàu] *adv.* in one way or another; in some way not known or stated. 어떻게든지 하여; 웬일인지. ¶ *I must finish this work* ~. 나는 어떻게든 이 일을 끝내지 않으면 안된다 / *Somehow I don't like him.* 웬일인지 나는 그가 싫다 / *He never trusted me,* ~. 무슨 영문인지 그는 결코 나를 신뢰하지 않았다.

somehow or other, in one way or another. 이럭저럭; 어떻게든지 하여; 웬일인지《somehow 의 강조형》.

:some·one [sʌ́mwʌ̀n, -wən] *pron.* somebody. 누군가; 어떤 사람. ¶ *Someone has to lock up the house.* 누군가가 그 집을 잠가야 한다.

som·er·sault [sʌ́mərsɔ̀:lt] *n.* Ⓒ **1** an acrobatic leap or dive in which one turns the heels over the head while in the air. 공중제비; 재주넘기. ¶ *a double* ~ 계속해서 두 번 재주넘기 / *He turned* 〔*performed*〕 *a* ~ *in the air.* 그는 공중에서 재주넘기를 하였다. **2** a complete change of opinion, attitude, etc. (의견·태도 따위의) 전환. — *vi.* (P1) perform a somersault. 재주넘다; 공중제비하다. [↓]

som·er·set [sʌ́mərsèt] *n., v.* =somersault. [L. *supra* above, salient]

:some·thing [sʌ́mθiŋ] *pron.* **1** a thing not clearly pointed out; some thing. 무언가; 어떤 것(일). ¶ ~ *important* 무언가 중요한 것 / *Give me* ~ *else.* 무언가 다른 것을 주십시오 / *There is* ~ *on the table.* 테이블 위에 무언가가 놓여 있다 / *I must get* ~ *to eat.* 뭐 좀 먹을 것을 구해야 한다 / *Here is* ~ *for you.* 여기 네게 줄 뭐가 있다 / *There is* ~ *in it.* 그것에도 일리가 있다 / *There is* ~ *about her I don't like.* 그녀에게는 무언가 호감이 안 가는 데가 있다 / *You can't get* ~ *for nothing.* 노력 없이 손에 들어오는 것은 없다. **2** a certain amount; a portion; a part. 다소; 얼마간; 부분. ¶ *He has* ~ *of the painter in him.* 그에게는 화가의 소질이 다소 있다 / *There is* ~ *of uncertainty in it.* 그것에는 다소 불확실한 데가 있다.

or something, (expressing the lack of definite information) or something of that sort; of some kind. 무언가; …인지 뭔지《불확실한 일·말 등에 대하여 이야기할 때》. ¶ *He is a doctor or* ~. 그는 의사이거나 뭐 그런 거다 / *She's got a cold or* ~. 그녀는 감기인지 뭔지 그 비슷한 것에 걸렸다.

— *n.* Ⓒ an important thing or person. 중요한 것(사람). ¶ *He thinks* ~ *of himself.* =*He thinks himself* ~. 그는 자신을 상당히 잘난 사람이라고 생각하고 있다 / *He is really* ~ *!* 그는 참으로 대단한(훌륭한) 사람이다.

— *adv.* **1** in some degree; to some extent; more or less; somewhat; rather. 어느 정도; 다소; 어딘가; 꽤. ¶ *He is* ~ *troubled today.* 그는 오늘 좀 난처해 하고 있다. **2** 《*sl.*》 to a high degree; very. 매우; 참으로. ¶ *He swore* ~ *shocking.* 그는 참으로 충격적인 욕설을 했다. [*some*]

something like, **a**) something approaching or resembling; somewhat like. 다소 …같은(닮은); 어딘가 …같은. ¶ *It was* ~ *like this.* 그것은 대체로 이것과 비슷하다. **b**) nearly; almost. 약 …; 거의. ¶ *It must be* ~ *like six o'clock.* 6시쯤 됐을 것이다. **c**) 《*colloq.*》 《with the accent on *like*》 very good; excellent. 굉장한; 매우 훌륭한. ¶ *Edmond Kean was* ~ *like an actor!* 에드먼드 킨은 참으로 훌륭한 연기자였다 / *Now, that's* ~ *like a dinner!* 야, 이것 참 굉장한 정찬이로군 그래.

:some·time [sʌ́mtàim] *adv.* **1** at a time not exactly known or decided; at an indefinite future time. 언젠가; 조만간. ¶ ~ *during the night* 언제일지 확실치는 않으나 밤에 / ~ *or other* 언젠가; 조만간. **2** 《*arch.*》 formerly. 이전에. ¶ *He was* ~ *Mayor of Seoul.* 그는 이전에 서울 시장이었다. — *adj.* former. 이전의. ¶ *the* ~ *professor at Harvard University* 이전의 하버드 대학 교수.

:some·times [sʌ́mtàimz, səmtáimz] *adv.* now and then; from time to time; at times. 때때로; 때로는. ¶ ~ *rich,* ~ *poor* 때로는 부유하게, 때로는 가난하게 / *I* ~ *see him.* 나는 때때로 그를 본다 / *He has* ~ *visited us.* 그는 가끔 우리를 방문했다 / *Sometimes I wonder if he is honest.* 나는 이따금 그가 정말로 정직한가 하고 생각한다 / *He is* ~ *in Paris,* ~ *in London.* 그는 때로는 파리에, 때로는 런던에 있다.

some·way [sʌ́mwèi] *adv.* in some way; somehow. 어떻게든 하여; 어찌 된 일인지.

:some·what [sʌ́m*h*wɑ̀t, -*h*wʌ̀t / -*h*wɔ̀t] *adv.* to a certain extent or degree; a little. 얼마간(쯤); 좀. ¶ *He was* ~ *puzzled.* 그는 좀 당혹했다 / *My hat is* ~ *like yours.* 내 모자는 네 것과 좀 닮았다 / *I am* ~ *tired.* 나는 좀 피곤하다. — *pron.* some part or amount. 어느 정

도; 다소. ¶ *He is ~ of a musician.* 그는 다소 음악가다운 데가 있다.

some·when [sʌ́mhwèn] *adj.* 《rare》 at some time. 언젠가는.

:some·where [sʌ́mhwɛ̀ər] *adv.* **1** in or to one place or another. 어딘가에(서); 어디론가. ¶ *He lives ~ about here.* 그는 여기 어딘가에 살고 있다 / *You'll find the quotation ~ in Shakespeare.* 셰익스피어 작품의 어딘가에 그 인용문이 있다. **2** at some point in time, amount, degree, etc. (때·양·정도 따위가) 가량; 쯤; 대략; 정도. ¶ *It happened ~ about three.* 그것은 대략 3시경에 일어났다.

som·nam·bu·lism [sɑmnǽmbjəlìzəm / sɔm-] *n.* Ⓤ sleepwalking; the act or state of walking while one sleeps. 몽유병. [L. *somnus* sleep, *ambulo* walk] 「술.

artificial somnambulism, hypnotism. 최면

som·nam·bu·list [sɑmnǽmbjəlist / sɔm-] *n.* Ⓒ a sleepwalker. 몽유병자.

som·no·lence [sɑ́mnələns / sɔ́m-] *n.* Ⓤ sleepiness; drowsiness. 졸림. [↓]

som·no·lent [sɑ́mnələnt / sɔ́m-] *adj.* **1** sleepy or drowsy. 졸린. **2** causing someone to sleep. 졸리게 하는; 졸음을 오게 하는. [L. *somnus* sleep]

:son [sʌn] *n.* Ⓒ **1** a male child in relation to his parent or parents. 아들(opp. daughter). ¶ *the eldest ~* 장남 / *an adopted ~* 양자 / *He is a true ~ of his father.* 그는 과연 그 아버지의 아들이다. **2** a male descendent. (남자) 자손. ¶ *the sons of Adam* 아담의 자손 《인류를 말함》 / *the sons of Abraham* 유대인 (=the Jews). **3** ⓐ a native of a country; a member of a particular nation. … 나라 사람; … 국민. ¶ *a faithful ~ of England* 충성스런 영국인. ⓑ an inhabitant. 주민(住民). **4** anything regarded as the product of a particular nation, age, civilization, etc.; a person viewed as inheriting an occupation, quality, influence, cause, etc. …의 아들; …자; (학교·학회 따위의) 일원; 회원. ¶ *sons of liberty* 〔*freedom*〕 자유의 아들들 / *a ~ of toil* 노동자 / *a ~ of the ocean* 뱃사람 / *sons of Oxford* 옥스퍼드의 자제들. **5** a friendly term of address to a boy. 자네; 젊은이; 군. ¶ *my ~* 젊은이《친근한 호칭》/ *old ~* 자네《친근한 호칭》. **6** 《*the S-*》 Jesus Christ. 예수 그리스도. [E.]

a son of a bitch 〔***gun***〕, 《*vulg.*》 a despicable man; a rascal; a hard task. 개자식; 경칠 놈.

a son of earth, a man of low origin. 태생이 천한 사람.

a son of the soil, a dweller in the country. 토착민; 농부.

a son of war, a soldier. 군인.

one's son and heir, the eldest son. 장남.

the Son of Man, Christ. 예수.

the sons of men, mankind. 인류.

son. sonata.

so·nant [sóunənt] *adj.* 《phon.》 involving voice. 유성음의. ── *n.* **1** a voiced sound. 유성음. **2** a syllabic sound. 음절 주음(主音). [→sound[1]]

sonar, SONAR [sóunɑːr] *n.* Sound Navigation Ranging. 수중 음파 탐지기(cf. *sofar*).

so·na·ta [sənɑ́ːtə] *n.* Ⓒ a type of musical composition in three or four movements, usu. for the piano. 소나타; 주명곡(奏鳴曲). [→sound[2]]

sonde [sɑnd / sɔnd] *n.* 《rocket》 a rocket used as a probe for observation. 존데《고공 기상 측정기》. [*sound*[3]]

:song [sɔ(ː)ŋ, sɑŋ] *n.* **1** Ⓒ a piece of music composed to be sung. 가곡; 노래. ¶ *sing a ~* 노래를 부르다 / *a popular ~* 유행가. **2** Ⓤ the act of singing; music produced by the human voice. 노래하기; 가창(歌唱). ¶ *burst into ~* 노래하기 시작하다. **3** Ⓤ the sounds like singing produced by a bird. 새의 지저귀는 소리. ¶ *a bird's ~* 새의 지저귐. **4** Ⓒ a piece of poetry suitable to be set to music. 시가(詩歌); 단가(短歌). **5** Ⓒ 《*colloq.*》 a trifle; a low price. 하찮은〔사소한〕 것; 싸구려. [*sing*]

a song and dance, 《U.S. *colloq.*》 talk or explanation that is pointless. (재미는 있어도) 앞뒤가 안 맞는 이야기〔설명〕《주로 관객들을 꾀어들이기 위한 것》.

for a song, for very little money. 헐값으로.

nothing to make a song about, 《*colloq.*》 a thing of no importance. 하찮은〔시시한〕 것.

song·bird [sɔ́(ː)ŋbə̀ːrd, sɑ́ŋ-] *n.* Ⓒ a singing bird such as a canary, nightingale, or lark. 우는 새; 명금(鳴禽).

song·book [sɔ́(ː)ŋbùk, sɑ́ŋ-] *n.* Ⓒ a book containing a number of songs. 가요집; 노래책.

song·ful [sɔ́(ː)ŋfəl, sɑ́ŋ-] *adj.* **1** melodious. 가락이 좋은. **2** full of song. 노래가 많은; 노래 잘하는.

song·ster [sɔ́(ː)ŋstər, sɑ́ŋ-] *n.* Ⓒ **1** a person who sings; a singer. 가수. **2** a songbird. 명금; 우는 새. **3** a person who writes songs or poems. 시인.

song·stress [sɔ́(ː)ŋstris, sɑ́ŋ-] *n.* Ⓒ **1** a female singer. 여자 가수. **2** a female writer of songs or poems. 여성 노래 작가〔시인〕.

song thrush [ˊˋ] *n.* a European songbird. (유럽산) 지빠귀의 일종.

son·ic [sɑ́nik / sɔ́n-] *adj.* **1** of sound. 소리의. **2** having the speed of sound in air (about 1,087 feet per second or 738 m.p.h. at sea level). 음속의. [L. *sonus* sound]

son-in-law [sʌ́ninlɔ̀ː] *n.* Ⓒ (*pl.* **sons-**) the husband of one's daughter. 사위. [*son*]

son·net [sɑ́nət / sɔ́n-] *n.* Ⓒ a poem of fourteen lines expressing a single theme or idea. 14행시; 소네트. [→sound[2]]

son·net·eer [sɑ̀nətíər / sɔ̀n-] *n.* a composer of sonnets. 14행 시인. ── *vi., vt.* (P1; 6) write sonnets; address sonnets to.

(…을 위해) 14행시를 짓다.

son·ny [sʌ́ni] *n.* Ⓒ (*pl.* **-nies**) a pet name or a familiar way to call a little boy; a young son. 아가야; 애야《소년에 대한 친근한 호칭》. [*son*]

so·nor·i·ty [sənɔ́ːrəti, -nár-] *n.* Ⓤ the state of being sonorous. 울려 퍼짐. [↓]

so·no·rous [sənɔ́ːrəs, sánə-] *adj.* **1** giving a full, deep or loud sound. 울려 퍼지는; 깊고 우렁찬 소리의. ¶ *a* ~ *voice* 낭랑한 목소리 / *a* ~ *bell* (소리가) 울려 퍼지는 종. **2** (of speech or writing) making a deep impression. (연설·문체 등이) 깊은 감명을 주는; 격조 높은. [→sound²]

:soon [suːn] *adv.* **1** in a short time; before long; in the near future. 곧; 이내; 이윽고. ¶ *He will* ~ *be back.* 그는 곧 돌아올 것이다 / *Summer will* ~ *be here.* 여름이 곧 온다 / *You'll be better* ~. 곧 좋아질 것이다 / *They arrived* ~ *after sunset.* 그들은 해가 지자 이윽고 도착했다. **2** early; before time. 빨리; 이르게. ¶ *Winter has come rather* ~ *this year.* 금년은 겨울이 조금 빠르게 왔다 / *If we arrive too* ~, *we shall have to wait.* 너무 일찍 도착하면 기다려야 할 것이다 / *You spoke too* ~. 너무 일찍 입을 열었다. **3** quickly; promptly; at once; easily. 재빠르게; 신속하게; 쉽게. ¶ 《*prov.*》 *The sooner the better.* 빠르면 빠를수록 좋다 / *He came as* ~ *as possible.* 그는 가능한 한 빨리 왔다 / 《*prov.*》 *Least said, soonest mended.* 말은 적을수록 좋다 / 《*prov.*》 *Soon got,* ~ *gone.* 쉽게 얻은 돈은 쉽게 없어진다. **4** readily; willingly. 기꺼이. ¶ *Will you come?* — *I would just as* ~ *not.* 함께 가겠느냐 — 별로 가고 싶지 않습니다 參考 not 뒤에 come as come 이 관용적으로 생략된 것임 / *I would as* ~ *walk as ride.* 타느니 걷는 게 좋겠다. [E.]

as soon as, at once; immediately. …하자마자; …하자 곧. ¶ *Be ready to start as* ~ *as I give the signal.* 내가 신호하자마자 떠날 수 있게 준비해라.

at the soonest, at the earliest. 아무리 빨라도.

none too soon, in good time. 알맞은 때에.

no sooner ... than, hardly ... when; scarcely ... before. …하자마자; …하자 곧. ¶ *He had no sooner seen me than he ran away.* 그는 나를 보자마자 도망갔다 / *No sooner said than done.* 말 떨어지기가 무섭게 실행됐다.

sooner or later, some day; at some unknown time. 조만간; 머지않아. ¶ *You will be sorry for it sooner or later.* 머지않아 너는 그것을 후회하게 될 것이다.

would sooner ... than —, would rather ...than —. —하기보다는 차라리 …하고 싶다. ¶ *I would sooner sleep than do it.* 그것을 하느니 차라리 잠을 자겠다.

soot [su(ː)t] *n.* Ⓤ a soft, black substance produced as part of the smoke when coal, wood, oil, etc. are burned. 검댕; 매연; 유연(油煙). ¶ *sweep the* ~ *out of chimneys* 연통의 검댕을 쓸어내다. — *vt.* (P6,7) cover with soot. …을 검댕으로 더럽히다. ● **soot·less** [-lis] *adj.* [E.]

sooth [suːθ] *n.* 《*arch.*》 truth; fact. 진실; 사실. ¶ *He speaks* ~. 그는 사실을 말하고 있다. [E.]

sooth to say, if truth must be told. 사실을 말하면.

·soothe [suːð] *vt.* (**soothed, sooth·ing**) (P6) **1** make (someone) calm or quiet. …을 달래다; 진정시키다. ¶ *The babysitter soothed the crying child.* 아이 보는 사람은 우는 아이를 달랬다. **2** make (pain) less severe; soften; relieve. (고통 따위)를 누그러뜨리다; 완화하다. ¶ ~ *the pain of (a) toothache* 치통을 누그러뜨리다. ● **sooth·er** [-ər] *n.* [E.]

sooth·ing·ly [súːðiŋli] *adv.* in a soothing manner. 달래어; 위로하여.

sooth·say·er [súːθsèiər] *n.* Ⓒ a person who tells what will happen. 예언자; 점쟁이.

sooth·say·ing [súːθsèiiŋ] *n.* Ⓤ the act of foretelling future events. 예언; 점.

soot·y [sú(ː)ti] *adj.* (**soot·i·er, soot·i·est**) **1** covered or stained with soot. 그을은. ¶ ~ *smoke* 매연. **2** of or like soot; soiled by soot. 검댕의; 검댕 같은; 검댕투성이의. ¶ *a* ~ *face* 검댕투성이의 얼굴. **3** dark-brown. 거무스름한. [*soot*]

sop [sap / sɔp] *n.* Ⓒ **1** a piece of bread dipped or soaked in milk, soup, etc. (우유·수프 따위에 적셔 먹는) 빵 조각. **2** something given to someone to soothe him. 뇌물. **3** a person or thing thoroughly soaked. 물에 흠뻑 젖은 사람(것). ¶ *The ground is a mere* ~. 땅은 온통 물웅덩이다. — *v.* (**sopped, sop·ping**) *vt.* **1** (P6) dip; soak. …을 담그다; 적시다. ¶ ~ *bread in milk* 빵을 우유에 적시다. **2** (P7) take up (water) by absorbing; wipe. …을 빨아들이다; 훔치다. ¶ *Please* ~ *up the water on the floor with old rags.* 헌 걸레로 마루의 물을 훔쳐 주시오. **3** (P6) wet (something) thoroughly; drench. …을 흠뻑 젖게 하다. ¶ *He was sopped to the skin.* 그는 흠뻑 젖었다. — *vi.* (P1) soak; become drenched. 흠뻑 젖다. [E.]

sop. soprano.

soph·ism [sáfizəm / sɔ́f-] *n.* Ⓤ a clever but misleading argument or form of reasoning; Ⓒ a false argument. 궤변. [Gk. *sophos* wise]

soph·ist [sáfist / sɔ́f-] *n.* Ⓒ **1** one of a group of teachers in ancient Greece who taught rhetoric, politics, philosophy, etc. and used sophisms. 소피스트《고대 그리스의 철학, 수사학의 교사》. **2** a person who uses sophisms. 궤변가. [Gk. *sophistés* expert, deviser]

so·phis·ti·cal [səfístikəl] *adj.* **1** clever but unsound and misleading. 궤변의. **2** using a false argument. 궤변을 부리는.

so·phis·ti·cate [səfístəkèit] *vt.* (P6) **1** use sophistical arguments about (something); mislead (someone). …에게 궤변을 부리다; …을 궤변으로 속이다. **2** spoil the natural simplicity of (someone); change (a text) without authority. …을 세파에 물들게〔닳고 닳게〕 하다; (원작)을 제멋대로 바꾸다. **3** make (wine, tobacco, etc.) impure by mixture. (술·담배 따위)에 섞음질을 하다. ― *vi.* (P1) use sophistry. 궤변을 부리다. ―[səfístəkit, -kèit] *n.* Ⓒ a sophisticated person. 세파에 물든〔닳고 닳은〕 사람. [Gk. *sophistikós*]

so·phis·ti·cat·ed [səfístəkèitid] *adj.* **1** ⓐ lacking in natural simplicity; artificial. 순진한 데가 없는. ⓑ wise in worldly ways; having or showing worldly experience, education, culture, etc. (세상사에) 닳고 닳은; 세련된. ¶ *a ~ person* 세련된 사람. **2** misleading. 속이는; 헷갈리게 하는. ¶ *the politician's ~ arguments* 사람을 현혹시키는 정치가의 의론. **3** not in a natural state. 섞음질을 한; 불순한. ¶ *a ~ oil* 불순한 기름. **4** suited to the taste of sophisticated persons. 고상한. ¶ *~ music* 고상한 음악. **5** highly developed; complex. 고성능의; 정교〔복잡〕한. ¶ *a ~ machine* 정교한 기계. **6** (of a motorcar) with the latest equipment. (자동차 따위가) 최신 부품을 갖춘.

so·phis·ti·ca·tion [səfìstəkéiʃən] *n.* Ⓤ **1** the act of sophisticating; the state or quality of being sophisticated. 궤변을 농함; 가짜; 세정(世情)에 물듦; 세속화. **2** sophisticated character, ideas, ways, etc. 세련된 성질〔생각, 양식〕. ¶ *the ~ of the wealthy* 유산 계급들의 세련된 생활 양식.

soph·ist·ry [sáfistri / sɔ́f-] *n.* (*pl.* **-ries**) **1** ⓐ Ⓤ clever and unsound reasoning. 궤변. ⓑ Ⓒ a particular argument on false reasoning. 억지 이론. **2** Ⓤ the art, skill, or learning of the sophists of ancient Greece. (고대 그리스의) 궤변법. [*sophist*]

soph·o·more [sáfəmɔ̀ːr / sɔ́f-] *n.* Ⓒ 《U.S.》 a second year student of a university, college or high school. (대학·고교의) 2년생 (cf. *freshman, junior, senior*). [*sophism*]

soph·o·mo·ric [sàfəmɔ́ːrik / sɔ̀f-] *adj.* 《U.S.》 **1** of a sophomore. (고교·대학의) 2년생의. **2** making a show of one's learning though it is shallow; satisfied with oneself though knowing little. 잘난 체하나 미숙한; 건방진. [↑]

so·po·rif·ic [sàpəríﬁk, sòupə-] *adj.* **1** causing sleep. 잠이 오게 하는; 최면의. **2** sleepy. 졸린. ― *n.* Ⓒ something, esp. a drug, that causes sleep. 최면제. [L. *sopor* sleep]

sop·py [sápi / sɔ́p-] *adj.* (**-pi·er, -pi·est**) **1** very wet; rainy. 흠뻑 젖은; 우천(雨天)의. ¶ *~ ground* 흠뻑 젖은 지면 / *~ weather* 비오는 날. **2** 《Brit. *colloq.*》 too sentimental. 너무〔몹시〕 감상적인. [*sop*]

so·pran·o [səprǽnou, -prάːn-] *n.* (*pl.* **-pran·os**) **1** Ⓤ the highest singing voice of a woman or boy. 소프라노; 최고음. **2** Ⓒ a singer with this voice. 소프라노 가수. **3** Ⓤ a part of music for such a voice. 소프라노; 최고음부. ― *adj.* of the soprano. 소프라노의. [→super]

sor·cer·er [sɔ́ːrsərər] *n.* Ⓒ a person who practices magic through the aid of evil spirits; a magician. 마술사; 마법사. [→sort]

sor·cer·ess [sɔ́ːrsəris] *n.* Ⓒ a woman sorcerer. 여자 마술사.

sor·cer·y [sɔ́ːrsəri] *n.* Ⓤ magic performed through the aid of evil spirits; witchcraft. 마법; 마술. ¶ *charm someone by ~* 아무를 마법에 걸다.

sor·did [sɔ́ːrdid] *adj.* **1** dirty; filthy; foul. (환경 등이) 더러운; 지저분한. ¶ *live in a place with ~ surroundings* 더러운 환경에서 살다 / *The poor family lived in a ~ slum.* 그 가난한 가족은 지저분한 빈민굴에서 살았다. **2** morally mean or low; degraded; meanly selfish. 비열한; 천한; 치사한. ¶ *a ~ quarrel* 비열한 싸움 / *~ desires* 치사한 욕심. [L. = dirty]

:sore [sɔːr] *adj.* (**sor·er, sor·est**) **1** painful when touched; feeling pain from a wound, a bruise, etc. (상처 등이) 살짝 닿아도 아픈〔쑤시는〕. ¶ *a ~ finger* 쑤시는 손가락 / *Mary has a bad cold and a ~ throat.* 메리는 심한 감기로 목이 아프다. **2** filled with sadness or sorrow; distressed. 비탄에 잠긴; 슬픈. ¶ *a ~ heart* 슬픈 마음 / *a ~ bereavement* 가슴 아픈 사별(死別) / *There are many ~ hearts at home after the war.* 전후 국내에는 슬픔으로 가슴 아픈 사람들이 많이 있다. **3** 《*colloq.*》《*about, over*》 easily offended; inclined to feel injured or hurt. 성마른; 민감한; 상처받기 쉬운. ¶ *feel ~ about something* …에 성내다; …에 화가 나다 / *get ~ on* 〔*over, at*〕 *it* 그것에 대해 화를 내다 / *He is ~ at* 〔*about*〕 *losing the game.* 시합에 패배해 화를 내고 있다 / *He got ~ over such an innocent remark.* 그는 그러한 악의 없는 비평에 대해서도 화를 냈다. **4** severe; intense. 심한; 격렬한. ¶ *in ~ need* 몹시 궁핍하여.

a sight for sore eyes, something pleasant to see; a pleasant sight. 보기만 해도 즐거운 것〔경치〕.

be sore about, worry about. …을 괴로워하다.

get sore, 《*sl.*》 get angry. 화를 내다. ¶ *Don't get ~; I didn't mean it.* 화내지 말게. 나는 그런 뜻이 아니었다.

like a bear with a sore head, bad-tempered; irritable; touchy. 기분이 매우 나쁜; 심통이 난.

touch** someone **on 〔***in***〕 ***a sore place*** 〔***spot***〕, say something which will hurt or annoy someone. 아무의 아픈 곳을 찔러 말하다.

― *n.* Ⓒ **1** a painful or diseased spot on one's skin. 건드리면 아픈 곳; 상처; 헌데. ¶ *a*

~ *on a foot.* **2** a cause of pain, grief, irritation, etc.; a painful memory. 고통의 원인; 옛 상처. ¶ *Time does not always cure old sores.* 시간이 반드시 옛 상처를 아물게 하지는 않는다.
— *adv.* severely; sorely. 심하게; 격렬히. ¶ *be ~ afflicted* 〔*oppressed*〕 심하게 괴로움〔압박〕을 당하다. [E.]

sore·ly [sɔ́ːrli] *adv.* **1** painfully; severely. 아파서; 쓰려; 심하게. **2** extremely; very much. 대단히. ¶ *I feel ~ inclined to go.* 가고 싶어 못견딜 지경이다.

sore·ness [sɔ́ːrnis] *n.* Ⓤ the state of being sore; painfulness; offense. 쓰림; 아픔; 분개; 불화. ¶ *cause ~* 아프다 / *feel ~ at* …에 화가 나다; …을 나쁘게 생각하다 / *There was some ~ between them.* 그들 사이는 좋지가 않았다.

so·ror·i·ty [sərɔ́ːrəti, sərɑ́rəti] *n.* Ⓒ (*pl.* **-ties**) 《U.S.》 a club or society of women at many colleges. 대학내의 여학생 사교 클럽 (cf. *fraternity*). [L. *soror* sister]

sor·rel[1] [sɔ́ːrəl, sɑ́r-] *n.* Ⓒ any of several plants with sour-tasting leaves used in salads. 수영속(屬)의 식물. [Teut. =sour]

sor·rel[2] [sɔ́ːrəl, sɑ́r-] *adj.* reddish-brown. 밤색의. — *n.* Ⓒ a reddish-brown horse. 밤색의 말. [F.]

:sor·row [sɑ́rou, sɔ́ːr-] *n.* Ⓤ **1** sadness; grief. 슬픔; 비애. ¶ *feel ~ for someone's dishonor* 아무의 불명예를 슬퍼하다 / *be in great ~* 매우 슬퍼하고 있다 / *yield to ~* 비탄에 잠기다 / *cause much ~ to …* …을 매우 슬프게 만들다 / *to one's ~* 슬프게도 / 《*prov.*》 *When ~ is asleep, wake it not.* 쓸데없는 걱정은 안하는 게 좋다. **2** 《*at, for, over*》 regret for what one has done. 후회; 유감. ¶ *She expressed ~ at her mistake.* 그녀는 잘못을 후회했다 / *the conventional expression of ~ and sympathy* 유감과 동정의 형식적 표시. **3** ⓊⒸ 《often *pl.*》 a cause of grief, disappointment, regret, etc.; a misfortune. 불행; 고통; 고생. ¶ *the Man of Sorrows* 예수 그리스도 / *I have had many sorrows.* 나는 여러 가지 불행을 체험했다.
— *vi.* (P1,3) feel or show sadness. 슬퍼하다. ¶ *~ at* 〔*for, over*〕 *a misfortune* 불행을 한탄하다.
● **sor·row·er** [-ər] *n.* **sor·row·less** [-lis] *adj.* [E.]

·sor·row·ful [sɑ́roufəl, sɔ́ːr-] *adj.* **1** full of sadness; showing sadness; sad; unhappy. 슬픈; 비탄에 잠긴. ¶ *My soul is ~.* 나의 마음은 슬픔에 잠겨 있다 / *His death left us all very ~.* 그의 죽음은 우리 모두를 비탄에 잠기게 했다. **2** causing or feeling sadness. 슬프게 하는; 가슴 아프게 하는. ¶ *a ~ sight* 가슴 아픈 광경.

sor·row·ful·ly [sɑ́roufəli, sɔ́ːr-] *adv.* in a sorrowful manner; with sorrow. 슬퍼서; 슬퍼하여. [↑]

:sor·ry [sɑ́ri, sɔ́ː-] *adj.* (**-ri·er, -ri·est**) **1** 《as *predicative*》 feeling regret for something. 유감스러운; 후회하는; 미안하게 생각하는. ¶ *I'm ~ to trouble you.* 폐를 끼쳐 미안합니다 / *Aren't you ~ for what you've done?* 네가 한 일을 미안하다고 생각지 않느냐 / *Say you are ~ and I'll forgive you.* 미안하다고 말하면 용서해 주겠다 / *We are* (*so*) *~* (*that*) *we cannot come to the party.* 파티에 갈 수 없어서 매우 유감스럽습니다 / *You will be ~ for this some day.* 너는 언젠가 이 일을 후회하게 될 것이다. **2** 《as *predicative*》 feeling pity or sad for someone; sympathy or regret; distressed in mind. 가엾게〔딱하게〕 생각하는. ¶ *We were ~ to hear of your father's death.* 춘부장의 별세를 애도합니다 / *I'm ~ you are ill.* 아프시다니 안됐습니다 / *I'm ~ for him, but it's his own fault.* 그에겐 참 안됐지만, 그건 자기 탓이다 / *Poor fellow! I feel ~ for him.* 못난 녀석, 안됐구나. **3** poor; worthless; useless. 서투른; 가치〔쓸모〕가 없는. ¶ *a ~ excuse* 서툰 변명 / *a ~ horse* 쓸모 없는 말 / *a ~ performance* 서투른 연기. **4** sad; miserable; wretched. 지독한; 비참한; 형편 없는. ¶ *A slum is a ~ place.* 빈민굴은 비참한 곳이다 / *He was in ~ clothes.* 그는 형편 없는 옷을 입고 있었다 / *She lived in a ~ place.* 그녀는 형편 없는 곳에서 살았다.

I am sorry. = ***I am so sorry.*** = ***So sorry.*** = ***Sorry.*** apologies for slight offence. 미안합니다.

sorry for oneself, dejected. 낙심〔낙담〕하여.

● **sor·ri·ly** [sɑ́rili, sɔ́ːri-] *ad.* **sor·ri·ness** [sɑ́rinis / sɔ́ːri-] *n.* [→sore]

:sort [sɔːrt] *n.* Ⓒ **1** a kind; a class; a type. 종류; 부류; 타이프. ¶ *this ~ of* (*a*) *person* 이런 부류의 사람 / *the latest ~ of music* 최신의 음악 / *things of a different ~* 다른 종류의 물건 / *chocolates of several sorts* 몇 가지 종류의 초콜릿 / *all sorts and conditions of men* 온갖 종류〔계급〕의 사람들 / *people of their ~* 그러한 부류의 사람들 / *What ~ of friends do you have?* 네겐 어떤 부류의 친구들이 있느냐 / *We have every ~ of boot* 〔*boots of every ~*〕 *in stock.* 우리는 여러 가지 종류의 구두를 재고로 가지고 있다 / *There are many sorts of roses.* 많은 종류의 장미가 있다 / *What ~ of trees are these?* 이것들은 무슨 종류의 나무들인가 / *I like this ~ of candy best.* 나는 이런 종류의 사탕을 가장 좋아한다 / *He is not the ~* (*of man*) *to do a mean thing.* 그는 비열한 짓을 할 그런 부류의 사람이 아니다. **2** a quality; a character; a nature. 품질; 성격; 기질. ¶ *girls of a nice ~* 마음씨가 고운 소녀들 / *He is a quiet ~ of man.* 그는 조용한 성격의 사람이다 / *He is a good* 〔*not a bad*〕 *sort* (*of man*). 그는 성질이 괜찮은 사람이다 / *The coffee is of an inferior ~.* 그 커피는 품질이 좋지 않은 것이다 / *He isn't* (*of*) *my ~.* 그는 나와는 성질이 다르다.

after a sort, in a sort. 약간; 어느 정도.

a sort of, a kind of. …의 일종; 일종의 …. ¶ *a ~ of invention* 일종의 발명.

in any sort, at any cost. 어떻게든.
in some sort, to a certain extent. 어느 정도(까지).
of a sort =***of sorts,*** of a poor or unsatisfactory kind; not deserving the name. (그 종류로서는) 신통치 않은; 엉터리의. ¶ *a lawyer of a* ~ 신통치 않은 변호사 / *an actor of sorts* 엉터리 연기자 / *whisky of sorts* 믿고 마실 수 없는 위스키 / *He can speak English of a* ~. 그는 신통치 않은 영어나 말할 수 있다.
of the sort, like that; such. 그러한 (식, 종류의). ¶ *something of the* ~ 그러한 식[종류]의 것 / *I don't believe anything of the* ~. 그러한 일은 믿을 수 없다 / *nothing of the* ~ 천만에; 당치도 않다(=not at all).
out of sorts, 《*colloq.*》 not feeling well; uncomfortable; slightly ill. 기분이 언짢은; 편치 않은. ¶ *I am a little out of sorts today.* 오늘 기분이 좀 안좋다[컨디션이 나쁘다].
sort of, 《*colloq.*》 《as *adv.*》 to some extent; more or less; somewhat; rather. 다소; 얼마간; 오히려. ¶ *I* ~ *of expected it.* 얼마간 예기하고 있었다 / *I* ~ *of hoped you would come.* 네가 와주기를 오히려 바라고 있었다.
— *vt.* (P6,7) 《*over, out*》 arrange (things) according to the class of each; classify; arrange in order; select. …을 분류[정돈]하다; 가려내다. ¶ *Sort these eggs by size.* 이 달걀들을 크기에 따라 분류하라 / ~ *(out) the good from the bad* 나쁜 것과 좋은 것을 가려내다. [L. *sors* lot]

sor·tie [sɔ́ːrti] *n.* Ⓒ **1** a sudden attack by troops who are themselves surrounded. (포위군에 대한) 출격. **2** a single flight of an aircraft to attack the enemy. 단기(單機) 출격. [F.]

sor·ti·tion [sɔːrtíʃən] *n.* lot-casting. 제비뽑기; 추첨. [→sort]

SOS [ésòués] *n.* Ⓒ (*pl.* **SOS's** [-iz]) **1** a call for help, usu. sent by radio in an emergency. 조난 (무전) 신호. ¶ *send out* 〔*pick up*〕 *an* ~ 조난 신호를 보내다[받다]. **2** any call for help. 구원 요청. ¶ *send an* ~ *home for more cash* 돈을 더 보내라는 구원 요청을 집으로 보내다. [arbitrary]

sos., sost, sosten. 《It.》 《mus.》 sostenuto. (음을) 연장하여; 계속해서.

so-so [sóusòu] *adj., adv.* 《*colloq.*》 neither very good nor very bad; not so good; passable. 그저 그런 (정도의); 좋지도 나쁘지도 않은. ¶ *His play was only* ~. 그의 연주는 겨우 그저 그런 정도였다 / *How do you feel ? —Oh,* ~. 기분이 어때. —응, 그저 그래. [*so*]

sot [sɑt / sɔt] *n.* Ⓒ a person in the habit of heavy drinking; a habitual drunkard. 주정뱅이; 술고래. [F. =fool]

sot·tish [sɑ́tiʃ / sɔ́t-] *adj.* of or like a sot; given to heavy drinking. 주정뱅이의[같은].

sot·to vo·ce [sɑ́touvóutʃi / sɔ́t-] *adv.* 《It.》 in a low voice which cannot be overheard. 작은 목소리로.

sou [suː] *n.* Ⓒ **1** a former French coin worth 5 centimes. 프랑스의 옛 동화; 5 상팀 동화. **2** the least little bit of money. 푼돈. ¶ *He hasn't a* ~. 그에겐 피천 한 잎도 없다. [→solid]

sou·bri·quet [súːbrikèi] *n.* 《F.》 Ⓒ =sobriquet.

sou·chong [suːʃɑ́ŋ, -tʃɑ́ŋ] *n.* a kind of black tea made from youngest leaves. 고급 홍차. [Chin.]

souf·fle [suːfléi] *n.* 《F.》 Ⓒ kinds of dish containing beaten white of eggs and baked till it forms a brown puffy top. 수프레《달걀 흰자위를 거품이 일게 하여 구운 요리》.

sough [sau, sʌf] *vi.* (P1) make a low, murmuring sound. (바람이) 윙윙거리다. — *n.* Ⓒ a low, murmuring sound, made by the wind. 윙윙거리는 소리. [E.]

:**sought** [sɔːt] *v.* p. and pp. of **seek.**

:**soul** [soul] *n.* **1** Ⓒ ⓐ the immaterial part of man; the part of the human being that thinks, feels, and makes the body act (distinguished from body). 영혼; 혼. ¶ *the immortality of the* ~ 영혼의 불멸 / *sell one's* ~ *for money* 돈을 위해 영혼을 팔다 / *the transmigration of souls* 윤회(輪廻) / *not able to call* 〔*cannot call*〕 *one's* ~ *one's own* 완전히 남에게 지배[좌지우지]당하고 있다 / *commend one's* ~ *to God* (임종의 사람이) 영혼을 신에게 맡기다; 사후의 행복을 빌고 죽다 / *The* ~ *is believed to exist forever.* 영혼은 영원히 존재한다고 믿어지고 있다. ⓑ man's spirit; the moral and emotional part of man; energy of mind or feelings. 정신. ¶ *She put her heart and* ~ *into the work.* 그녀는 그 일에 그녀의 마음과 정신을 쏟아 넣었다. **2** Ⓤ the emotional or intellectual energy; spiritual or emotional warmth, force, etc.; emotional part of man's nature. 기백; 감정; 정. ¶ *His music lacks* ~. 그의 음악엔 기백[열정]이 없다 / *a man with more* ~ *than brains* 이지적이라기보다는 정이 많은 사람 / *art* 〔*artist*〕 *without* ~ 정열[박력]이 없는 예술(가). **3** Ⓤ essential part. 정수; 원리. ¶ *Brevity is the* ~ *of wit.* 간결은 기지의 정수; 말은 간결해야 한다 / *The* ~ *of commerce is upright dealing.* 상업의 원리는 정직한 거래이다. **4** a human being; a man. 인간. ¶ *every* ~ 누구든지 / *a kind* 〔*an honest*〕 ~ 친절한[정직한] 사람 / *Not a* ~ *was to be seen.* 사람이라곤 그림자 하나 보이지 않았다 / *Poor* ~, *she has had a lot of trouble.* 가엾은 사람, 그녀는 어찌 그리 많은 어려움을 겪는고. **5** Ⓒ 《*the* ~》 a leader; a person who is the example of some quality; personification. 지도자; (어떤 특성의) 화신(化身); 전형(典型). ¶ *the* ~ *of a boycott movement* 불매 운동의 지도자 / *He is the* ~ *of honor.* 그는 명예의 전형이다. **6** the spirit of a dead person. 영혼; 망령. [E.]
by my soul, for my soul. 진심으로.
have no soul, lack passion. 정열[기백]이

없다.
keep soul and body together, manage to live. 살림을 겨우겨우 해나가다.
upon my soul, by God; surely. 맹세코; 확실히.

soul·ful [sóulfəl] *adj.* full of or showing deep feeling or emotion. 영혼〔정신〕이 담긴; 정열적인.

soul kiss [ㅅㅅ] *n.* a long passionate, open-mouthed kiss. 긴 열정적인 키스.

soul·less [sóullis] *adj.* having no soul; without deep feeling or emotion; cruel. (영)혼이 없는; 감정이 없는; 무정한. ● **soul·less·ly** [-li] *adv.*

:sound[1] [saund] *adj.* **1** healthy; without any bad point. 건전한; 완전한. ¶ *a man of ~ body and mind* 심신이 모두 건전한 사람 / 《*prov.*》 *A ~ mind in a ~ body.* 건전한 정신은 건전한 신체에 깃들인다 / *His heart is not ~.* 그의 심장은 튼튼하지 않다 / *~ fruit* 〔*timber*〕 썩지 않은 과일〔재목〕. **2** correct; right; reasonable. 올바른; 정당한. ¶ *a ~ judgment* 올바른 판단 / *~ advice* 이치에 맞는 충고 / *a man of ~ understanding* 이해력이 확실한 사람 / *~ reasoning* 정확한 추론. **3** complete; deep. 완전한; 깊은. ¶ *a ~ recovery* 완쾌 / *a ~ sleep* 숙면. **4** safe; reliable. 안전한; 견실한. ¶ *a ~ business firm* 견실한 재정의 회사 / *a ~ investment* 안전한 투자 / *~ finance* 건전 재정 / *The bank is ~.* 그 은행은 견실하다. **5** legal; lawful. 합법의; 공식의. ¶ *a ~ title to land* 합법적인 토지 소유권. **6** laid on with force; heavy; severe. 힘껏 친; 격렬한; 호된. ¶ *give someone a ~ beating* 아무를 흠씬 패주다.
— *adv.* soundly. 깊이. ¶ *sleep ~* 깊이 잠들다. [E.]

:sound[2] [saund] *n.* **1** ⓊⒸ what is heard. 음; 음향. ¶ *the ~ of music* 음악 소리 / *the ~ of gun* 〔*drum*〕 총〔북〕소리 / *the ~ of voices* 사람의 목소리 / *What made that ~?* 그거 무슨 소리였지 / *Not a ~ was heard.* 아무 소리도 들리지 않았다. **2** Ⓒ a tone; a note. 음조. **3** Ⓤ noise. 소음. ¶ *~ and fury* 소음과 분노. **4** Ⓒ a meaning; an impression. 의미; 느낌; 인상. ¶ *This sentence has a strange ~.* 이 문장은 묘한 느낌을 준다 / *That has no inviting ~.* 들을만한 이야기도 아니다. **5** Ⓤ the distance something can be heard. 들리는 범위〔거리〕. ¶ *within the ~ of the whistle* 호루라기 소리가 들리는 거리에(서) / *beyond* 〔*out of*〕 *~ of* …이 들리지 않는 곳에(서).
— *vi.* (P1) **1** make sounds. 소리가 나다; 울리다. ¶ *The buzzer sounds.* 버저가 울린다. **2** give a certain impression to someone's ear. …에 …하게 들리다. ¶ *~ alike* 〔*loud*〕 …처럼〔크게〕 들리다 / *The music sounds well.* 그 음악은 듣기에 매우 좋다. **3** (P2,5) appear; seem. (…하게) 보이다; 생각되다. ¶ *His story sounds like fiction.* 그의 이야기는 꾸며낸 것 같다 / *The plans ~ promising.* 그 계획은 유망할 것 같다 / *His voice sounds as if he had a cold.* 감기들린 목소리 같다.
— *vt.* (P6) **1** cause (something) to make a noise. …을 울리다; …을 소리나게 하다. ¶ *~ a trumpet* 〔*bell*〕 나팔을 불다〔벨을 울리다〕 / *~ a horn* 경적을 울리다. **2** utter; express. (소리를 내어) 말하다; 발음하다. ¶ *~ each letter* 글자마다 발음하다 / *He sounds the 't' in 'often'.* 그는 often의 t를 발음한다. **3** order or direct by a sound, signal; make known; spread abroad. (종·나팔 따위로) 신호하다; 알리다; (평판 따위를) 퍼뜨리다. ¶ *~ the charge* 〔*retreat*〕 돌격〔퇴각〕 나팔을 불다 / *The clock sounded twelve.* 시계가 12 시를 알렸다 / *~ someone's praise* 아무의 칭찬을 하다. **4** examine (something) by hitting and making it sound. …을 타진〔진찰〕하다. ¶ *~ someone's breast* 아무의 가슴을 진찰하다. [L. *sonus*]

sound[3] [saund] *vt.* **1** (P6) measure the depth of (water) by lowering a weight attached to the end of a line. (추를 사용하여) …의 깊이를 재다〔측량하다〕. **2** (P6,7) try to find someone's feelings, opinion, etc.; examine with a surgical probe. …의 의중을 살피다; (소식자(消息子) 등으로) …을 진찰하다. ¶ *~ someone's opinion* 아무의 의중을 살피다 / *~ out public opinion* 여론을 조사하다 / *~ the bladder* 방광을 소식자로 진찰하다.
— *vi.* (P1) **1** measure the depth of water. 수심을 재다. **2** go to the bottom; dive deeply into water. 바닥에 닿다; 물속 깊이 잠입하다. ¶ *The whale sounded.* 고래는 물속 깊이 들어갔다.
— *n.* 《med.》 a long, solid, slender instrument used for sounding or exploring body cavities or canals. 소식자; 존데. [E. =swimming]

sound[4] [saund] *n.* Ⓒ **1** a long stretch of water joining two large areas of water or lying between the mainland and an island. 해협. **2** an air bag of a fish. (물고기의) 부레. [↑]

sound-box [sáundbɑ̀ks, -bɔ̀ks] *n.* **1** a chamber in a musical instrument, e.g. the body of a guitar or violin, intended to increase its sonority. (악기의) 공명(共鳴) 상자. **2** the part of a gramophone which contains the diaphragm. (구식 축음기의) 사운드 박스. [*sound*[2]]

sound film [ㅅㅅ] *n.* a motion picture film with a sound track on one edge. 발성 영화(opp. silent film).

sound·ing[1] [sáundiŋ] *adj.* **1** making a sound; noisy. 울리는. **2** high-sounding but meaningless. 과장된. ¶ *~ oratory* 과장된 요란한 웅변 / *a ~ promise* 실속 없는 약속.

sound·ing[2] [sáundiŋ] *n.* Ⓒ **1** 《often *pl.*》 the act of measuring the depth of water by lowering a weight attached to a line. 수심 측량. **2** 《*pl.*》 the depth of water measured in this way. 수심. [*sound*[3]]

sound·less [sáundlis] *adj.* **1** having no sound; perfectly quiet. 소리가 나지 않는. **2** (of the depth of water) that cannot be measured. (수심(水深)이) 잴 수 없을 만큼 깊은. [*sound*[2, 3]] ● **sound·less·ly** [-li] *adv.* [*sound*[2, 3]]

sound·ly [sáundli] *adv.* **1** in a sound manner; healthily; reasonably. 건전하게; 합리적으로. **2** without being awakened; deeply. (잠을 깨지 않고) 깊이; 푹. ¶ *sleep* ~ 숙면하다; 푹 자다. **3** completely; thoroughly. 완전히; 전혀. ¶ ~ *defeated* 완패당한 / *beat someone* ~ 아무를 완패시키다. [*sound*[1]]

sound·ness [sáundnis] *n.* Ⓤ the state or quality of being sound. 건전; 건강.

sound·proof [sáundprúːf] *adj.* not allowing sound to pass through. 방음의. ¶ *a* ~ *door* 〔*studio*〕 방음 장치가 된 문〔스튜디오〕.
— *vt.* make (something) soundproof. …에 방음 장치를 하다. [*sound*[2]]

sound track [∠∠] *n.* a sound record along one side of a motion picture film. (발성 영화 필름 가장자리에 있는) 녹음대(帶).

sound waves [∠∠] *n.* 《phys.》 vibrating waves which produce sounds when they strike the hearing organs. 음파(音波).

:soup [suːp] *n.* Ⓤ a liquid food made by boiling meat, bones, vegetables, fish, etc. in water, milk, etc. 수프; 고깃국물. ¶ *eat* ~ 국을 먹다〔마시다〕. [F.]
in the soup, 《*sl.*》 in trouble; in a fix. 곤경에 처하여. ¶ *He left many persons in the* ~. 그는 많은 사람들을 곤경에 빠뜨렸다.

soup-and-fish [súːpənfíʃ] *n.* 《U.S. *colloq.*》 a swallow-tailed coat. 연미복.

soup·çon [suːpsɔ́ːŋ, ∠–] *n.* 《F.》 very small quantity. 소량. [F.=suspicion]

soup·y [súːpi] *adj.* (**soup·i·er, soup·i·est**) **1** of or like soup. 수프 같은. **2** 《*colloq.*》 (of a song) sentimental. 감상적인. [*soup*]

***sour** [sáuər] *adj.* **1** having a taste like vinegar or green fruit; (of milk, etc.) spoiled. 시큼한; 신; (우유 따위가) 산패(酸敗)한. ¶ ~ *milk* 신 우유 / *Green fruit is* ~. 익지 않은 과일은 시다. **2** bad-tempered; disagreeable. 심술궂은; 불쾌한. ¶ *make a* ~ *face* 불쾌한 얼굴을 하다 / *a* ~ *job* 불쾌한 일 / *a* ~ *old maid* 심술궂은 노처녀 / *a* ~ *temper* 몹시 까다로운 기질. **3** (of soil) sterile; unproductive. (땅이) 불모(不毛)의. ¶ ~ *soil* 메마른 땅.
be sour on, 《U.S. *colloq.*》 dislike (something), esp. after one has previously liked it. (좋아하던) …을 싫어하다; …이 싫어지다.
— *vt., vi.* (P6;1) **1** make (something) sour; become sour. (…을) 시게 하다; 시어지다. ¶ *Milk sours quickly in warm weather.* 우유는 더운 날씨에 쉽게 시어진다 / *Thunder will* ~ *beer* 〔*milk*〕. 천둥이 울리면 맥주〔우유〕가 시어진다. **2** make (someone) bad-tempered; become bad-tempered. (아무를) 화나게〔비뚤어지게〕 하다; 불쾌해지다; 비뚤어지다. ¶ *a temper soured by disappointment* 실망으로 비뚤어진 성질.
— *n.* something sour. 시큼한 것. ¶ *the sweet and* ~ *of life* 인생의 고락. [E.]

:source [sɔːrs] *n.* Ⓒ **1** the beginning of a stream or river. 원천; 수원(지). ¶ *the sources of the Thames* 템스 강의 수원 / *The river takes its* ~ *from the lake.* 그 강은 수원이 호수에서 시작되고 있다. **2** a place from which something comes; a cause. 출처; 원인. ¶ *historical sources* 사료(史料) / *a* ~ *of light* 광원 / *the* ~ *of political unrest* 정치적 불안의 원인 / *It has its* ~ *in envy.* 그 원인은 질투에 있다 / *the* ~ *of revenue* 〔*wealth*〕 세입〔재〕원(源) / *an informed* ~ 소식통 / *I have heard it from a reliable* ~. 나는 그것을 믿을 만한 곳에서 들었다. [→surge]

sour grapes [∠∠] *n.* the act of pretending to scorn something one cannot have but would like to. 오기(傲氣); (사실 따위를) 인정하기 싫어함《이솝 우화에서》.

sour·ly [sáuərli] *adv.* in a sour manner; with bad temper. 시큼하게; 꾀까다롭게; 불쾌하게; 심술궂게. [*sour*]

sour·ness [sáuərnis] *n.* Ⓤ the state or quality of being sour. 시큼함; 심; 꾀까다로움.

souse [saus] *n.* Ⓤ **1** liquid used for pickling. 간국; (절이는 데 쓰는) 소금물. **2** Ⓤ something preserved in salt pickle. 소금에 절인 것. **3** Ⓒ the act of plunging into water. 물에 담금; 흠뻑 젖음. ¶ *give someone a* ~ 아무를 물에 푹 잠기게 하다 / *I get a thorough* ~ *in the thunderstorm.* 나는 심한 뇌우로 흠뻑 젖었다.
— *vt., vi.* (P6,13;1) **1** pickle; put in salt water 〔vinegar〕. (…을) 소금에 절이다〔절여지다〕; 식초에 담그다. ¶ ~ *a mackerel in vinegar* 고등어를 식초에 담그다. **2** make (someone) or become wet to the skin. (…을) 흠뻑 젖게 하다; (…이) 흠뻑 젖다. ¶ *We were soused to the skin.* 우리는 흠뻑 젖었다.
— *adv.* with a souse. 첨벙; 풍덩; 거꾸로. ¶ *fall* ~ *into the water.* [→salt]

sou·tane [suːtáːn] *n.* 《Rom. Cath.》 a priest's cassock. (신부가 입는 검은) 평상복; 수단. [L. *subtus* under]

sou·te·neur [sùːtənə́ːr] *n.* 《F.》 a man living on a prostitute's earnings. (매춘굴의) 포주; 뚜쟁이(=pimp).

:south [sauθ] *n.* **1** 《*the* ~》 one of the four points of the compass; the direction opposite to the north. 남(쪽). ¶ *a wind from the* ~ 남쪽에서 부는 바람 / *We traveled toward the* ~. 우리는 남쪽을 향해 여행했다. **2** 《*the S-*》 the area or part to the south. 남부(지방); 남쪽 나라. ¶ *in* 〔*on*〕 *the* ~ *of* …의 남부에〔남쪽에 접하여〕 / *to the* ~ *of* …의 남쪽을 향해 / *the* ~ *of London* 〔*England*〕 런던〔잉글랜드〕의 남부. **3** 《*the S-*》 《U.S.》 the Southern

States. 남부의 여러 주(州).
— *adj.* situated in or at the south; southern; facing south; coming from the south. 남쪽의; 남쪽을 향한; (바람 등이) 남쪽에서 부는. ¶ *a* ~ *window* 남쪽을 향한 창문 / *the South Pole* 남극 / *the* ~ *coast* 남부 연안 / *the* ~ *wind* 남풍.
— *adv.* toward, in or from the south. 남쪽에〔으로, 으로부터〕. ¶ *sail* ~ 남쪽을 향해 항해하다 / *The wind is blowing* ~. 바람은 남쪽으로부터 불어오고 있다 / *New York is* ~ *of Boston.* 뉴욕은 보스턴 남쪽에 있다. [E.]

South America [ㅗㅡㅗㅡㅡ] *n.* a continent southeast of North America. 남아메리카; 남미.

South American [ㅗㅡㅗㅡㅡ] *adj.* of South America or its people. 남아메리카의; 남아메리카인의. — *n.* a person of South America. 남아메리카인.

South Carolina [ㅗㅡㅡㅗㅡ] *n.* a state in the southeastern part of the United States, on the Atlantic coast. 사우스캐롤라이나 주(州). 參考 생략 : S.C.임. 주도: Columbia.

***south·east** [sàuθíːst; 《naut.》 sauíːst] *n.* 《*the* ~》 the point of compass halfway between south and east; a place situated in this direction. 남동; 남동 지방. ¶ *in the* ~ *of London* 런던의 남동 지방에서. — *adj.* of, in, at, from, or toward the southeast. 남동의〔으로부터의, 으로의〕. ¶ *a* ~ *wind* 남동풍 / ~ *London* 런던의 남동부. — *adv.* in, from, or toward the southeast. 남동에〔으로부터, 으로〕.

south·east·er [sàuθíːstər; 《naut.》 sàuíː-] *n.* Ⓒ a wind or storm coming from the southeast. 남동풍; 남동의 강풍〔폭풍〕.

south·east·er·ly [sàuθíːstərli; 《naut.》 sàuíː-] *adv., adj.* toward or from the southeast. 남동으로(의); 남동으로부터(의).

south·east·ern [sàuθíːstərn; 《naut.》 sàuíː-] *adj.* of the southeast; from, toward or situated in the southeast. 남동의; 남동으로부터의〔으로의〕; 남동에 있는.

south·er·ly [sʌ́ðərli] *adv., adj.* in, toward or from the south. 남의〔으로(의)〕.

:**south·ern** [sʌ́ðərn] *adj.* of, in, toward, from or situated in the south. 남의; 남으로의〔으로부터의〕; 남쪽에 있는. ¶ *the* ~ *aspect* 남향 / *the Southern States* 남부 제주(諸州).

south·ern·er [sʌ́ðərnər] *n.* Ⓒ **1** a person who lives in or comes from the south. 남부 사람. **2** 《*S-*》 a person of the south part of the United States. 남부 여러 주(州)의 사람.

Southern Hemisphere [ㅗㅡ ㅗㅡㅡ] *n.* the half of the earth that is south of the equator. 남반구.

south·ern·most [sʌ́ðərnmòust / -məst] *adj.* most southern; situated farthest to the south. 최남쪽의.

South Pole [ㅗㅗ] *n.* the southernmost end of the earth, in the Antarctic region. 남극.

***south·ward** [sáuθwərd] *adj., adv.* toward the south. 남쪽으로(의). ¶ *sail* ~ 남쪽으로 항행하다. — *n.* 《*the* ~》 the south. 남방; 남부 (지방).

***south·wards** [sáuθwərdz] *adv.* =southward.

***south·west** [sàuθwést; 《naut.》 sàuwést] *n.* 《*the* ~》 the point of the compass halfway between south and west; 《*the S-*》 a place in this direction. 남서(쪽); 남서지방. ¶ *in the* ~ *of London* 런던의 남서쪽에 / ~ *by south* 남서미(微)남 / ~ *by west* 남서미(微)서. — *adj.* of, in, at, from, or toward the southwest. 남서의〔로부터의, 쪽으로의〕. ¶ *a* ~ *wind* 남서풍 / *a* ~ *aspect* 남서향(向). — *adv.* in, from or toward the southwest. 남서쪽에〔에서, 으로〕.

south·west·er [sàuθwéstər; 《naut.》 sàuwéstər] *n.* Ⓒ **1** a strong wind or storm from the southwest. 남서의 강풍. **2** a waterproof hat with a broad brim, worn by seamen. (뱃사람 등이 폭우 때 쓰는) 방수모.

south·west·er·ly [sàuθwéstərli; 《naut.》 sàuw-] *adv., adj.* from or toward the southwest. 남서로부터(의); 남서쪽으로(의).

sou·ve·nir [sùːvəníər, ㅗㅡㅗ] *n.* Ⓒ something that reminds a person of some person, place, event, etc. 수버니어; 기념품; 선물. [F.]

***sov·er·eign** [sɑ́vərin, sʌ́v-] *n.* Ⓒ **1** a ruler; a monarch; a king or queen. 통치자; 원수(元首); 군주. ¶ *King George, the late* ~ *of England* 붕어하신 영국의 통치자 조지 왕. **2** a state having independent power. 독립국. **3** a British gold coin equal to one pound. 영국의 1 파운드 금화.
— *adj.* **1** having absolute power. 주권을 가진. ¶ *a* ~ *prince* 군주 / ~ *power* 〔*authority*〕 주권. **2** having independent power. 독립의; 자주의. ¶ *a* ~ *state* 독립국. **3** best; greatest. 최상의; 최고의. ¶ *the* ~ *good* 지고선(至高善) / *a matter of* ~ *importance* 더할 나위 없이 중요한 일 / *Character is of* ~ *importance.* 인격은 가장 중요한 것이다. **4** very effective; excellent. 특효가 있는; 매우 뛰어난. ¶ *a* ~ *remedy* 특효약 / *their* ~ *sense of humor* 그들의 매우 뛰어난 유머 감각. [→super]

sov·er·eign·ty [sɑ́vərinti, sʌ́v-] *n.* (*pl.* **-ties**) **1** Ⓤ the chief ruling power or authority; 《*over*》 the power that a state holds over other states. 주권; 통치권. ¶ *popular* ~ 재민 주권 / *the U.S.* ~ *over Puerto Rico* 미국의 푸에르토리코에 대한 통치권. **2** Ⓒ a sovereign state. 독립국.

***so·vi·et** [sóuvièt, sóuviit] *n.* **1** Ⓒ a council in the Soviet Union, and now in Russia and Uzbekistan. (구 소련과 현재의 러시아·우즈베키스탄의) 회의; 평의회. **2** 《*the S-*》 a former country in both eastern Europe and western Asia. 소련. 參考 정식명은 The

Union of Soviet Socialist Republics《U.S.S.R.》. 1991년 12월 소련은 붕괴되고 독립 국가 연합(CIS; Commonwealth of Independent States)이 탄생하였음. — *adj.* **1** of a soviet. 회의의. **2**《*S-*》of the Soviet Union. 소련의. [Russ.]

so·vi·et·ize [sóuvietàiz] *vt.* (P6) make soviet or like soviet. …을 소비에트화하다.

:sow[1] [sou] *vt., vi.* (**sowed, sown** or **sowed**) **1** (P6,13;1) throw and spread (seed) on the earth; plant (seed) in the earth. (씨를) 뿌리다. ¶ ~ *the field with barley* = ~ *barley in the field* 밭에 보리를 뿌리다 / ~ *seed in spring* 봄에 씨를 뿌리다 / ~ *the seeds of hatred* 〔*revolution*〕 증오〔혁명〕의 씨를 뿌리다. **2** spread; 《in *pp.*》 stud. (소문·원인·해악 따위를) 퍼뜨리다; 유포하다; 흩뿌리다. ¶ ~ *distrust* 〔*dissension*〕 불신〔불화〕의 씨를 퍼뜨리다 / *a sky sown with stars* 별들이 흩뿌려진 하늘. [E.] 「[E.]

sow[2] [sau] *n.* Ⓒ a female pig. 암퇘지.

sow·bread [sáubrèd] *n.* 《bot.》 kinds of cyclamen. 시클라멘《앵초과의 다년초》. [↑]

sow·er [sóuər] *n.* Ⓒ **1** a person or thing that sows. 씨를 뿌리는 사람〔기계·파종기〕. **2** 《*fig.*》 a person who spreads news, gossip, etc. among people. 유포자. [*sow*[1]]

:sown [soun] *v.* pp. of **sow**.

sow thistle [sáuθìsl] *n.* 《bot.》 a plant with small yellow flowers and milky juice. 방가지똥. [E.]

sox [sɑks / sɔks] *n.* pl. of **sock**.

soy [sɔi] *n.* Ⓤ a salty sauce made from soybeans used in the Orient, for fish and other dishes. 간장. [Jap.]

soy·bean [sɔ́ibìːn] *n.* Ⓒ a plant grown, esp. in China, Korea and Japan; its seed, used in making flour, soy, or oil. 대두(大豆); 콩. 「자손 없이.

s.p. 《law》 *sine prole* (L. =without issue).

spa [spɑː] *n.* Ⓒ **1** a mineral spring. 광천(鑛泉). **2** a place which has such a mineral spring. 온천지. [Place]

:space [speis] *n.* **1** Ⓤ the unlimited room extending in all directions. 공간. ¶ *time and* ~ 시간과 공간 / ~ *occupied by a body* 물체가 점하는 공간 / *celestial* ~ 천공; 천계(天界) / *vanish into* ~ 허공 속으로 사라지다. **2** Ⓤ the region outside the earth's atmosphere in which are the moon, sun, and stars. 우주 (공간). ¶ *launch a spaceship into* ~ 우주로 우주선을 발사하다 / *The earth moves through* ~. 지구는 우주 공간 속을 움직인다. **3** ⓊⒸ a limited area or distance; room. (일정한) 공간; 장소; 거리; 간격. ¶ *an open* ~ 빈터 / *take up too much* ~ 너무 많은 장소를 차지하다 / *for the* ~ *of a mile* 1마일 거리에 걸쳐 / *Plant the trees at equal spaces apart.* 나무들을 일정한 간격으로 심어라 / *a parking* ~ 주차 공간 / *There isn't enough* ~ *in this room for two sofas.* 이 방에는 두 개의 소파를 놓을만한 충분한 공간이 없다. **4** Ⓒ a length of time. (시간의) 동안; 기간. ¶ *for the* ~ *of one year* 1년 동안 / *in so short a* ~ *of time* 그렇게 짧은 시간에 / *by the* ~ *of two years,* 2년이라는 기간 중에 / *in the short* ~ *of human life* 짧은 인생에 있어서. **5** Ⓒ 《mus.》 a degree or open place between the lines of the staff. (악보의) 선간(線間). **6** Ⓒ 《print.》 a blank interval between words; a thin piece of metal used to make this. 어간의 공백; 행간(行間); 스페이스. ¶ *a blank* ~ 여백. [L. *spatium*]

in space, after a while. 잠시〔얼마〕 후에.

— *vt.* (P6) **1** arrange (something) at intervals. …을 사이를〔간격을〕 두고 배치하다. **2** 《print.》 separate (words, lines, etc.) by spaces. (어간·행간)에 사이를〔간격을〕 두다. [L. *spatium*]

space biology [⌐-⌐--] *n.* a branch of biology studying extraterrestrial living organisms; exobiology or astrobiology. 우주 생물학.

space capsule [⌐⌐-] *n.* a container for space travel in which a man rides. 우주 캡슐.

space charge [⌐⌐] *n.* an electric charge in a vacuum carried by a stream of electrons and ions. 공간 전하(電荷).

space·craft [spéiskræ̀ft, -krɑ̀ːft] *n.* something driven by rockets to carry men and things from the earth through space to the moon or planets. 우주선.

spaced-out [spéistáut] *adj.* 《*sl.*》 not fully conscious of what is happening around one, e.g. because of the effect of drugs. 마약에 취한; 정신이 몽롱한.

space flight [⌐⌐] *n.* a flight of a manned or unmanned vehicle through space. 우주 비행.

space·man [spéismæ̀n, -mən] *n.* (*pl.* **-men** [-mèn, -mən]) **1** an astronaut. 우주 비행사. **2** (of a term in science fiction) a visitor to the earth from outer space. 우주인.

space medicine [⌐⌐--] *n.* a branch of medicine dealing with the effects on man during space flight. 우주 의학.

space probe [⌐⌐] *n.* a spacecraft used to investigate conditions in outer space. 우주 탐사기.

space science [⌐⌐-] *n.* a branch of study dealing with the facts or truths of space travel. 우주 과학.

space·ship [spéisʃìp] *n.* =spacecraft.

space sickness [⌐⌐-] *n.* one of various ailments resulting from manned space flight. 우주 멀미; 우주병.

space station [⌐⌐-] *n.* a manned artificial satellite used as base for operations in space. 우주 스테이션.

space·suit [spéissùːt] *n.* a sealed suit worn by a spaceman. 우주복.

space-time [spéistáim] *n.* the four-dimensional continuum of one temporal and three spatial coordinates in which any physical object or event can be located. 시공 연속체(時空連續體)《3차원의 공간에 1차원의 시간을 합친 4차원의 연속체》.

spac·ing [spéisiŋ] *n.* Ⓤ the act of arranging spaces; Ⓒ the spaces thus arranged. 간격을 띄우기; 어간; 행간; 자간; 간격.

*__spa·cious__ [spéiʃəs] *adj.* **1** having much space; vast. 넓디넓은; 광대한. ¶ *a ~ plain* 광대한 평야 / *a ~ hall* 〔*church*〕 넓은 홀〔교회당〕. **2** broad in view, etc. 견해〔시야〕가 넓은; 스케일이 큰. ¶ *the ~ times of Queen Elizabeth* 스케일이 큰 엘리자베스 여왕의 시대 / *a ~ approach to a problem* 문제에 대한 폭넓은 접근법 / *a man of ~ intellect* 광범위한 지식을 가진 사람. [*space*]

:**spade**[1] [speid] *n.* Ⓒ a tool which has a broad blade of iron and a long handle used for turning over the earth. 가래; 삽. ***call a spade a spade,*** speak plainly. …을 솔직하게〔사실 그대로〕 말하다.
— *vt.* (P6,7) dig (a garden, etc.) with a spade. (정원 따위)를 삽으로 파다. [E.]

spade[2] [speid] *n.* Ⓒ a black figure like a pointed spade; 《*pl.*》 one of the four suits of playing cards marked with such figures. (카드의) 스페이드; (카드 놀이에서) 스페이드 한 벌. [↑]

spade·ful [spéidfùl] *n.* Ⓒ the amount that a spade can hold. 한 삽〔가래〕; 한 삽〔가래〕의 가득한 분량.

spade·work [spéidwə̀ːrk] *n.* Ⓤ hard necessary work on which more advanced work is to be based. 면밀한 주의를 요하는 예비 공작; (힘드는 일의) 기초 작업.

spa·ghet·ti [spəgéti] *n.* Ⓤ food made from flour in long, slender pieces. 스파게티. [It.]

*__Spain__ [spein] *n.* a country in southwest Europe. 스페인. 參考 수도는 Madrid.

spal·peen [spælpíːn, ⌐⌐] *n.* 《Ir.》 a mean fellow; a rascal. 불한당; 악당. [Ir.]

*__span__[1] [spæn] *n.* Ⓒ **1** the distance between the tips of a man's little finger and thumb when extended (usu. nine inches). 한 뼘《엄지와 새끼손가락을 잔뜩 벌린 거리; 통상 9인치》. **2** a short period of time; a short distance. 짧은 기간〔거리〕. ¶ *Our life is but a short ~.* 인생이란 덧없는 것 / *How brief is the ~ of human life!* 인간의 일생이란 얼마나 짧은 것인가. **3** the full extent in space or time. 전장(全長); 전체의 기간. ¶ *the ~ of one's arms* 양팔을 벌린 길이 / *the ~ of a bridge* 다리의 전장 / *the ~ of memory* 기억이 미치는 범위 / *the average live ~* 평균 수명 / *the whole ~ of Roman history* 로마사(史)의 전기간. **4** the distance between the supports of an arch, a bridge, etc.; the full length of the wings of an airplane. 경간(徑間); (아치·교량 따위) 지주(支柱) 사이의 길이; 비행기의 날개 길이. ¶ *a bridge of four spans,* 4경간의 교량.
— *vt.* (**spanned, span·ning**) (P6) **1** measure (something) by the spread of a hand. 손가락〔뼘〕으로 재다; (거리 등을) 목측하다. ¶ *~ a distance* 거리를 재다 / *~ one's wrist* 손목을 뼘으로 재다 / *His eye spanned the intervening space.* 그는 간격을 목측했다. **2** (of a bridge, etc.) extend or stretch over or across (something). (다리 따위가) …에 걸리다〔걸치다〕. ¶ *~ a river with a bridge* 강에 다리를 놓다 / *A bridge spans the river.* 강에 다리가 걸려 있다. **3** extend over (a period of time). (시간적으로) …에 걸치다〔미치다〕. ¶ *a memory that spans 90 years,* 90년이란 기간에 걸친 기억 / *in a career that spans four decades,* 40년에 걸친 생애에서. **4** make fast. 묶다. ¶ *~ a boom* 활대를 잡아매다. [E.]

span[2] [spæn] *n.* Ⓒ 《U.S.》 a pair of horses or other animals harnessed together to pull a cart. 한 멍에에 매인 한 쌍의 말〔소〕. [E.]

span[3] [spæn] *v.* 《*arch.*》 p. of **spin.**

span·gle [spǽŋgəl] *n.* Ⓒ a small metal disk sewn on a dress for ornament; any small piece of shining metal used for decoration. 스팽글《번쩍이는 장식용 쇳조각》. ¶ *a gold ~* (크리스마스의) 황금색 장식.
— *vt.* decorate (something) with spangles. …에 번쩍이는 장식을 달다. ¶ *the Star-Spangled Banner* 성조기 / *The sky is spangled with stars.* 하늘엔 별들이 수놓은 듯 반짝이고 있다. [Du.]

*__Span·iard__ [spǽnjərd] *n.* Ⓒ a person of Spain. 스페인 사람. [*Spain*]

span·iel [spǽnjəl] *n.* Ⓒ a medium-sized dog with long, silky hair and hanging ears. 스패니엘《털이 길고 귀가 축 늘어진 개》. [↑]

*__Span·ish__ [spǽniʃ] *adj.* of Spain, its people or their language. 스페인(사람·어)의.
— *n.* Ⓤ the language of Spain; 《*the ~, collectively*》 the people of Spain. 스페인어; 스페인 사람. ¶ *~ America* 스페인어를 사용하는 중남미 / *~ American* 스페인어를 사용하는 중남미의 주민; (미국에 사는) 스페인계 미국인 / *the ~ Armada* 스페인의 무적 함대. [↑]

spank [spæŋk] *vt.* (P6) punish (someone) by striking him with the open hand, a slipper, etc. (손바닥·슬리퍼 따위로) 벌로 …을 찰싹 때리다. ¶ *The nurse spanked the naughty child.* 간호사는 말을 듣지 않는 아이의 볼기짝을 찰싹 때렸다. — *n.* Ⓒ a blow with the open hand, a slipper, etc. 찰싹 때리기. [Imit.]

spank·er [spǽŋkər] *n.* **1** a fast-going horse. 준마(駿馬). **2** 《*sl.*》 ⓐ a stunner. 훌륭〔근사〕한 것. ⓑ a whopper. 허풍.

spank·ing [spǽŋkiŋ] *adj.* **1** moving rapidly and smartly; quick and vigorous; blowing strongly. 기민하게〔빠르게〕 움직이는; 활발한; (바람이) 강한. ¶ *a ~ trot* 활발한 속

보 / *a ~ breeze* 세차게 부는 바람 / *go at a ~ pace* 성큼성큼 빠르게 걷다. **2** 《*colloq.*》 unusually fine, large, strong, vigorous, etc. 멋진; 근사한; 훌륭한. ¶ *have a ~ time* 대단히 재미있는 시간을 보내다.

span·ner [spǽnər] *n.* 《Brit.》 a tool for tightening or turning a nut, a bolt, etc. 스패너《너트를 조이거나 푸는 공구》. [G.]

throw a spanner in the works, 《Brit. *colloq.*》 cause confusion; upset a person's plans. (남의 계획을) 방해놓다; 망치다.

spar[1] [spɑːr] *n.* Ⓒ **1** a pole of a ship, used to support and stretch the sails of a ship. 원재(圓材)《돛대·활대 따위》. **2** a main part of the framework of an airplane wing. 익형(翼桁)《비행기 날개의 골조(骨組) 중의 주요부》. — *vt.* (**sparred, spar·ring**) (P6) provide (a ship) with spars. (배)에 원재를 대다〔설치하다〕. [Teut.]

spar[2] [spɑːr] *vi.* (**sparred, spar·ring**) (P1,3) **1** fight with the arms and fists, esp. as a part of training. 스파링하다. ¶ *a sparring partner* 스파링 파트너《시합전 권투 선수의 연습 시합 상대》 / *~ at someone* 아무에게 때리며 달려 들다. **2** 《*fig.*》 talk to someone violently in trying to prove something. 말다툼하다. — *n.* Ⓒ the act of sparring. 권투 (연습) 시합; 말다툼. [?]

spar[3] [spɑːr] *n.* a shiny mineral that splits into flakes easily. 섬광 광석. [Teut.]

:spare [spɛər] *vt.* **1** (P6) use (something) in an economical way. …을 절약하다; 아껴 쓰다. ¶ *~ oneself* 수고를 아끼다 / *Don't ~ your efforts.* 노력을 아끼지 마라 / *~ no trouble* 〔*expense*〕 수고를〔비용을〕 아끼지 않다 / 《*prov.*》 *Spare the rod and spoil the child.* 매를 아끼면 자식을 버린다《귀한 자식은 고생을 시켜라》. **2** (P6,13,14) do without (something); afford to give. …없이 지내다; …을 나누어 주다. ¶ *I can't ~ him today.* 오늘은 그가 꼭 필요하다 / *My office can't ~ me.* 내가 없으면 사무실은 큰일 난다 / *I have no time to ~ today.* 나는 오늘 여가가 조금도 없다 / *Can you ~ me a pencil? = Can you ~ a pencil for me?* 나에게 연필 한 자루 나누어 주지 않겠니 / *Can you ~ me a few minutes?* 나에게 잠깐 시간을 내줄 수 있겠니 / *He would not ~ a thought for her.* 그는 그녀에 대해 생각조차 해주려고 하지 않았다. **3** (P6,13,14) save (someone) from killing, punishing, etc.; show mercy to (someone); avoid harming or destroying (something). …의 목숨을 살려주다; …에게 인정을 베풀다; 위해(危害)를 가하지 않다. ¶ *~ one's enemy* 적을 살려 주다〔놓아 주다〕 / *The prisoner was spared.* 그 죄수는 목숨을 구했다〔용서를 받았다〕 / *if I am spared* (신의 가호로) 목숨이 이어진다면… / *Spare (me) my life.* 목숨만은 살려 주십시오 / *His sharp tongue spares nobody.* 그의 신랄한 말은 아무도 용납하지 않는다 / *He spared her feelings.* 그는 그녀의 기분을 상하게 하지 않았다 / *Spare my blushes.* 나를 낯뜨겁게 하지 마시오《지나치게 칭찬하지 마라》. **4** (P6,13,14) save or protect (someone) from strain, discomfort, etc. (아무에게 수고·불편 등을) 끼치지 않다; 덜다. ¶ *This machine will ~ you a lot of trouble.* 이 기계로 너는 크게 수고를 덜 것이다 / *~ someone worry* 아무에게 염려를 끼치지 않다. — *vi.* (P1,3) **1** live economically. 절약하다; 검약하다. **2** show mercy; forgive. 인정을 베풀다; 용서하다.

and to spare, plenty of. 충분한; 많은 (양의). ¶ *time and to ~* 충분한 시간.

enough and to spare, more than is needed. 남아 돌아갈 만큼의. ¶ *Ten pounds will be enough and to ~.* 10 파운드면 남아 돌만큼 충분할 것이다 / *He has bread enough and to ~.* 그에게는 남아 돌아갈 만큼의 식빵이 있다.

— *adj.* **1** free for other uses; extra. 여분의; 예비의. ¶ *~ time* 여가 / *a ~ room* 객실; (손님용) 예비 침실 / *a ~ tire* 예비 타이어 / *a ~ hand* 예비 요원 / *~ cash* 여분의 현금. **2** (of a person) thin. 마른. ¶ *a ~ man* 마른 사람 / *a man of ~ frame* 마른 형의 사람 / *a tall, ~ man* 키가 크고 홀쭉한 사람. **3** (of a meal, etc.) poor; small. 빈약한; 적은. ¶ *a ~ diet* 시원찮은 식사 / *a ~ moustache* 빈약한 수염.

— *n.* Ⓒ something which is spare or extra. 예비품; 여분의 것. [E.]

spare·ribs [spɛ́ərrìbs] *n.* ribs of pork with little meat. (살을 발라낸) 돼지 갈비.

spar·ing [spɛ́əriŋ] *adj.* economical in money. 삼가는; 아끼는. ¶ *a ~ use of…* …의 절약 / *be ~ in speech* 말수가 적다 / *a ~ use of sugar* 설탕의 절약. [*spare*]

spar·ing·ly [spɛ́əriŋli] *adv.* in sparing manner; economically. 삼가서; 절약하여.

·spark [spɑːrk] *n.* Ⓒ **1** a small particle of burning matter thrown off by something burning; any flash or gleam. 불꽃; 섬광; 광채; (재기 등의) 번득임. ¶ *a ~ of light* 섬광 / *a ~ of genius* 〔*wit*〕 천재성〔재치〕의 번득임 / *strike sparks out of someone* 아무의 재기를〔재능을〕 발휘하게 하다 / *Burning wood throws off sparks.* 타고 있는 나무는 불꽃을 낸다. **2** a sign of life. 생기. ¶ *the ~ of life* 활기; 생기. **3** 《*a ~*, chiefly in *negative*》 a small amount; a slight trace. 아주 조금; 흔적. ¶ *She hasn't a ~ of interest in the plan.* 그녀는 그 계획에는 털끝 만큼의 흥미도 갖고 있지 않다. **4** a flash of light produced by an electrical discharge. (전기 방전에 의한) 스파크; 불꽃. **5** a gay and showy young man; a gallant. 멋쟁이; 미남자.

as the sparks fly upward, with the certainty of a law of nature. 순리에 따라서; 틀림없이.

spark telegraphy, wireless. (불꽃식) 무선 전신.

strike sparks out of, elicit something enlightening from. …의 재기를 발휘시키다.

— *vi.* (P1) give off sparks. 불꽃이 튀다; 스

파크하다. ¶ *Her eyes sparked with indignation.* 그녀의 두 눈은 분노로 불꽃이 튀었다.
—*vt.* (P6) 《*off*》 ignite; stimulate. …에 발화시키다; 자극하여 …시키다; 야기시키다. ¶ ~ *off a quarrel* 말다툼을 야기시키다 / *The event sparked the great war.* 그 사건이 대전의 도화선이 되었다. [E.]

spark·ing-plug [spɑ́ːrkiŋplʌ̀g] *n.* 《Brit.》 = spark plug.

∗**spar·kle** [spɑ́ːrkəl] *n.* Ⓒ a little spark; a flash of light. 불똥; 불꽃; 번쩍임. ¶ *the ~ of a diamond* 다이아몬드의 번쩍임 / *There was a ~ in her eyes.* 그녀의 두 눈에는 번쩍이는 광채가 있었다. —*vi.* **1** give off little sparks; flash. 불꽃을 내다; 번쩍[번득]이다. ¶ *The diamond sparkled.* 다이아몬드가 번쩍였다 / *The woman's eyes sparkled with delight.* 그 여인의 두 눈은 기쁨으로 빛났다. **2** produce bubbles. 거품이 일다. ¶ *The beer sparkles.* 맥주는 거품이 인다. [*spark*]

spark plug [⌐ ⌐] *n.* a piece fitted into the cylinder of a petrol engine by which the mixture of petrol and air is exploded. 점화 플러그.

⁝**spar·row** [spǽrou] *n.* Ⓒ a small, common, brownish-grey bird found in most parts of the world. 참새. [E.]

spar·row-hawk [spǽrouhɔ̀ːk] *n.* a small hawk which feeds on sparrows. 새매. [↑]

sparse [spɑːrs] *adj.* thinly spread or scattered. 드문드문한; 성긴; 희박한. ¶ *a ~ population* 희박한 인구 / *~ hair* 머리숱이 적은 두발(opp. dense). [L. *spargo* scatter]

sparse·ly [spɑ́ːrsli] *adv.* in a sparse manner. 드문드문; 성기게; 희박하게. ¶ *be ~ populated* 인구가 희박하다.

sparse·ness [spɑ́ːrsnis] *n.* Ⓤ the state of being sparse. 드문드문함; 성김; 희박.

Spar·ta [spɑ́ːrtə] *n.* an ancient city in Greece, famous for its strict and hard training. 스파르타. [*Spartocus,* leader in ancient Roman servile wars]

Spar·tan [spɑ́ːrtən] *adj.* **1** of Sparta or its people. 스파르타 (사람)의. **2** like the Spartans; brave; highly-trained. 스파르타식의; 용감한; 엄격한. ¶ *~ training* 스파르타식 교육. —*n.* Ⓒ **1** a person of Sparta. 스파르타 사람. **2** a person who has Spartan characteristics. 굳세고 용맹스런 사람.

spasm [spǽzəm] *n.* Ⓒ a sudden, abnormal tightening of a muscle; a sudden, violent feeling or shock. 경련; 발작. ¶ *a ~ of the stomach* 위경련 / *He was in a ~.* 그는 경련을 일으키고 있었다 / *The ~ passed off.* 경련이 가라앉았다 / *I had a ~ of laughing at his words.* 그의 이야기에 웃음을 터뜨렸다. [Gk. *spaō* draw]

spas·mod·ic(al) [spæzmɑ́dik(əl) / -mɔ́d-] *adj.* characterized by spasms; happening suddenly and violently. 경련의; 발작적인. ¶ *a ~ cough* 〔*asthma*〕 경련성 기침〔천식〕 / *~ efforts* 〔*attempts*〕 발작적〔돌발적〕인 노력〔시도〕. [↑]

spas·mod·i·cal·ly [spæzmɑ́dikəli / -mɔ́d-] *adv.* in a spasmodic manner. 경련적으로; 발작적으로.

∗**spat**[1] [spæt] *v.* p. and pp. of **spit.**[1]

〈spat[2]〉

spat[2] [spæt] *n.* Ⓒ 《usu. *pl.*》 a short cloth covering for the upper part of the boot or shoe and the ankle. 스패츠《발등과 발목을 덮는 짧은 각반》. [short for spatterdash]

spat[3] [spæt] 《U.S.》 *n.* **1** a slight quarrel. 승강이; 말다툼. **2** a light blow; a slap. 손바닥으로 가볍게 때리기. —*vi., vt.* (**-ted**) (P1;6) **1** have a slight quarrel. 승강이하다. **2** slap lightly. 가볍게 손바닥으로 때리다. [? Imit.]

spat[4] [spæt] *n.* the spawn of shellfish, esp. an oyster; a young oyster. 굴〔조개〕의 알; 새끼 굴. —*vi., vt.* (**-ted**) (P1;6) (of oysters) lay eggs; spawn. (굴이) 알을 슬다. [?]

spatch·cock [spǽtʃkɑ̀k / -kɔ̀k] *n.* a fowl killed and cooked in a hurry. 즉석 새요리. [*dispatch*]

spate [speit] *n.* Ⓒ 《Brit.》 a sudden downpour of rain; a flood; a sudden river-flood. 큰비; 홍수; (하천의) 급작스러운 범람. [E.]

spa·tial [spéiʃəl] *adj.* of space; existing in space. 공간의. [→space]

spat·ter [spǽtər] *vt.* (P6,13) **1** splash (water, mud, etc.) in all directions. (물·진흙 따위)를 튀기다; 흩뿌리다. ¶ *~ ink on one's dress* 옷에 잉크를 튀기다 / *The car spattered us with mud.* 자동차가 우리들에게 진흙을 튀겼다. **2** ⓐ soil or spot with such drops. (물·진창 따위를) 튀겨 묻히다; 더럽히다. ¶ *~ the tablecloth with grease* 기름을 튀겨 식탁보를 얼룩지게 하다. ⓑ hurt the good name of; defame. 명성을 훼손하다; 중상하다.
—*vi.* (P2A,3) fall in drops. 후두둑 떨어지다. ¶ *Rain is spattering on the zinc roof.* 비가 양철 지붕 위에 후두둑 소리를 내며 떨어지고 있다.
—*n.* Ⓒ **1** a light splash. 튐; 튄 것. ¶ *a ~ of mud* 튀긴 진흙. **2** the act or sound of spattering. 후두둑거리는 소리; 후두둑거림. ¶ *a ~ of rain on one's umbrella* 우산 위에 후두둑 떨어지는 빗소리. [Du. & G. *spatten* burst, spout]

spawn [spɔːn] *n.* Ⓤ **1** the eggs of fish, frogs or other water creatures. (물고기·개구리 따위의) 알. **2** offspring. 자손. **3** result; product. 산물. **4** the threadlike thing from which mushroom grows. 균사

(菌絲). — *vi., vt.* (P1;6) **1** lay or produce (eggs) in large numbers. (물고기 따위가) 알을 낳다. ¶ *Salmon go up rivers to* ~. 연어는 알을 낳기 위해 강을 거슬러 올라간다. **2** bring forth; give rise to; generate. 낳다. [→expand]

S.P.C.A. Society for the Prevention of Cruelty to Animals. 동물 학대 방지회《지금은 R.S.P.C.A. (Royal Society for the Prevention of Cruelty to Animals 영국 동물 애호 협회)》.

:speak [spi:k] *v.* (**spoke, spok·en** or 《*arch.*》 **spake, spoke**) *vi.* **1** (P1,2A) say words; talk. 말하다; 이야기하다. ¶ ~ *more slowly* 〔*clearly*〕 좀더 천천히〔똑똑하게〕 말하다 / *The child cannot* ~ *yet.* 그 어린이는 아직 말을 할 줄 모른다 / *generally speaking* 일반적으로〔대충〕 말하면 / ~ *under one's breath* 소곤소곤 이야기하다 / ~ *a good deal* 〔*very little*〕 말을 많이 하다〔거의 하지 않다〕. **2** make a speech. 연설하다. ¶ ~ *in public* 공중 앞에서 연설하다 / ~ *at a meeting* 모임〔회〕에서 연설하다 / ~ *about half an hour and then answer questions,* 30분 정도 연설하고 질의 응답으로 넘어가다. **3** 《*about*》 talk together; converse; discuss. 담화하다; 상담하다; (…에 관해) 이야기를 나누다〔하다〕. ¶ ~ *to someone about one's travel* 자기 여행에 관해 아무에게 이야기를 하다 / *I spoke to him about it.* 그것에 관해 그와 이야기를 나눴다 / *Is this the book you spoke of yesterday?* 이것이 네가 어제 이야기한 책이냐 / ~ *about one's war experience* 전쟁의 체험담을 이야기하다 / *The book speaks of modern art.* 그 책에는 근대(近代) 미술에 관한 것이 씌어져 있다. **4** express an idea, a feeling, etc.; tell. 사상·의견 따위를 전(달)하다; 표현하다. ¶ *Actions speak louder than words.* 행동은 말보다 더 분명히 뜻을 전달한다 / *Her eyes spoke for her.* 그녀의 눈이 그녀의 기분을 대변하고 있었다. **5** (of guns, musical instruments, etc.) sound. (총·악기 따위가) 소리를 내다; 울리다. ¶ *The trumpets* 〔*guns*〕 *spoke.* 나팔〔총〕이 울렸다 / *When the guns* ~, *it is too late to argue.* 대포가 울리면 말로 어떻게 하기에는 이미 늦다.

— *vt.* **1** (P6) use (a language) in speaking. (어느 국어를) 말하다; 쓰다. ¶ *She can* ~ *French.* 그녀는 프랑스어를 말한다 / *English spoken.* 영어가 통합니다《상점의 게시문 따위》 / *He speaks several languages.* 그는 여러 나라 말을 한다. **2** make (something) known; express. …을 말하다; 전하다; 나타내다. ¶ ~ *words of praise* 칭찬의 말을 하다 / ~ *a word* 한 마디 하다 / *Her smile spoke a warm welcome.* 그녀의 미소는 마음으로부터의 환영을 말하고 있었다. [E.]

nothing to speak of, nothing worth mentioning. 별로 이렇다 할 만한 것이 못되다.
so to speak, speaking in general terms; as it were. 말하자면.
speak about, talk of. …에 관해 말하다.
speak against, speak ill of. …의 욕을 하다.
speak at, talk at. …에 빗대어 말하다.
speak by the book, make accurate statements. 정확히 말하다.
speak for, **a**) represent; speak in behalf of (someone). …을 대변하다. **b**) recommend. …을 권하다. **c**) 《U.S.》 reserve. …을 예약하다.
speak for oneself, express one's own view only. 자기 설(說)〔의견〕을 말하다.
speak for itself, be clear. 자명하다.
speak highly of, praise highly. …을 칭찬하다.
speak one's mind, say frankly what one thinks. 의중을 털어놓다.
speak of, mention. …에 관하여 말하다.
speak out 〔***up***〕, **a**) say openly. (큰맘 먹고) 털어놓다; 털어놓고 이야기하다. **b**) speak loudly and clearly. 큰 소리로 말하다.
speak well 〔***ill***〕 ***of*** (=*praise* 〔*blame*〕) *something or someone.* …에 관해 좋게〔나쁘게〕 말하다.
speak with, talk with. …와 상담하다.
speak without book, give facts from memory. 기억에 의존하여 이야기하다.

speak·eas·y [spí:kì:zi] *n.* Ⓒ 《U.S. *sl.*》 a place where alcoholic liquors are sold contrary to law. 무허가 술집《금주법 철폐 이전의》.

·speak·er [spí:kər] *n.* Ⓒ **1** a person who speaks. 말하는〔이야기하는〕 사람. **2** a person who makes effective speeches in public. 연설자. ¶ *He is no* ~. 그는 연설이 서툴다. **3** 《*the S-*》 the chairman of a lawmaking body, such as the House of Commons. (하원) 의장. ¶ *the Speaker of the House* = *the Speaker of Parliament* 하원 의장.

speak·ing [spí:kiŋ] *adj.* **1** having the power of speech; allowing speech. 말할 수 있는; 말을 (서로) 나눌 수 있는 관계〔정도〕의. ¶ *a good* ~ *voice* (듣기에 좋은) 말하는 목소리. **2** seem to speak; very expressive; vivid; lifelike. 말이라도 할 것 같은; 표정이 풍부한; 생생한. ¶ *a* ~ *proof* 자명한 증거 / *a* ~ *look* 말을 하고 있는 듯한 눈초리 / ~ *eyes* 표정이 풍부한 눈 / *a* ~ *portrait* 살아 있는 듯한 생생한 초상화.

speaking trumpet [∠-∠-] *n.* an instrument like a trumpet used to make louder the sound of the human voice. 확성기; 메가폰.

speaking tube [∠-∠] *n.* a tube or pipe through which a voice can be sent from one part of a building to another. (빌딩 따위의) 통화관(通話管).

·spear [spiər] *n.* Ⓒ a weapon consisting of a long, slender stick with a sharp-pointed metal head. 창; 작살. ¶ *catch a fish with a* ~ 작살로 물고기를 잡다. — *vt.* strike (something) with a spear. …을 창으로 찌르다. ¶ *He speared a potato with his fork.* 그는 포크로 감자를 쿡 찔렀다. [E.]
the spear side, the male line. 부계(父

系)(opp. distaff side).

spear·head [spíərhèd] *n.* Ⓒ **1** the point of a spear. 창 끝. **2** a person or thing that comes first in an attack, an undertaking, etc. (공격·사업·개발 따위의) 선봉; 선두에 서는 사람.

spear·man [spíərmən] *n.* Ⓒ (*pl.* **-men** [-mən]) a man, esp. a soldier, armed with a spear. 창병(槍兵).

spec. special; specification.

:spe·cial [spéʃəl] *adj.* **1** distinct from others; particular in kind. 특별한; 특수한; 독특한. ¶ *receive ~ care* 각별한 보살핌을 받다 / *~ circumstances* 특수 사정 / *for a ~ purpose* 특별한 목적을 위하여 / *a ~ kind of key* 특수한 열쇠 / *a ~ talent* 독특한 재능 / *Speech is a ~ attribute of man.* 말은 인간에게 특유한 재능이다. **2** made for a particular purpose; specialized extra. 특별한 목적을 위한; 전문의; 전공의; 임시로 마련된. ¶ *a ~ tool* 특수 공구 / *a ~ train* 임시 열차 / *a ~ correspondent* 특파원 / *a ~ hospital* 전문 병원 / *make a ~ study of* …를 전공하다 / *a ~ holiday flight* (비행기의) 휴가용 특별〔임시〕편. **3** private. 개인의. ¶ *my ~ chair* 나의 개인용 의자 / *It is her ~ business.* 그것은 그녀 개인의 일이다. **4** unusual; distinguished; exceptional; (of friends) close; intimate. 예외적인; 유다른; 유별난; (친구가) 아주 가까운〔친한〕. ¶ *a ~ brand* 매우 우수한 품질의 유명 상품 / *a ~ occasion* 특별히 중요한 경우〔기회〕/ *a ~ friend* 대단히 친한 친구 / *Today is a ~ holiday.* 오늘은 예외적인 특수한 휴일이다.
— *n.* Ⓒ **1** a special thing or person. 특별한 사람〔것〕. **2** a special train. 특별〔임시〕 열차. ¶ *a commuter ~* 통근자용 특별 열차. **3** a special edition of a newspaper. (신문의) 호외; 특별판; 임시 증간(增刊). [L. *specio* look]

special delivery [⌐–⌐––] *n.* 《U.S.》 a kind of mail delivered, for an extra fee, sooner than regular mail. 속달; 속달 우편(물)(=《Brit.》 express delivery).

spe·cial·ism [spéʃəlìzəm] *n.* ⓊⒸ a devotion to a particular branch of study or work. 전문; 전공.

·spe·cial·ist [spéʃəlist] *n.* Ⓒ a person who is devoted in a particular field of study, business, medicine, etc. 전문가; 전문의. ¶ *an eye ~* 안과 전문의 / *a ~ in diseases of the heart* 심장병 전문의.

spe·ci·al·i·ty [spèʃiǽləti] *n.* Ⓒ (*pl.* **-ties**) **1** a special quality or characteristic of a person or thing. 특색. **2** a special point; a particular; a detail. 특별 사항; 명세. **3** a special or particular field of study, business, etc. 전문; 전공. **4** a special product. 특제품; 특산품. ¶ *Jam is our ~.* 잼은 폐점의 전문입니다.

spe·cial·i·za·tion [spèʃəlizéiʃən] *n.* Ⓤ the act of specializing; the state of being specialized. 특수화; 전문화.

·spe·cial·ize [spéʃəlàiz] *vi., vt.* (P1,3;6) **1** make (something) special; direct (something) to a particular object. (…을) 특수화하다; (…을) 전문화하다(opp. generalize). ¶ *The business is now highly specialized.* 그 사업은 지금 매우 전문화되어 있다. **2** state or consider separately; go into details. (…을) 상세히 말하다. ¶ *First give a general outline, then ~.* 먼저 전반적인 개요를 설명하고, 그 다음에 상세히 말하라. **3** limit in scope or interest; make fit a special purpose or condition. (범위·관심 등을) 한정〔국한〕하다; (특수 상황에) 적합시키다. ¶ *~ a course of study* 학습 과정의 범위를 한정하다. **4** 《*in*》 follow or pursue some particular branch of work, study, etc. 전공하다. ¶ *~ in English literature* 영문학을 전공하다 / *He specializes in chemistry.* 그는 화학 전공이다.

·spe·cial·ly [spéʃəli] *adv.* especially; particularly; for a special purpose. 특히; 일부러. ¶ *a meeting ~ called* 임시 소집의 회의 / *~ appointed* 특별 임명의 / *I came here ~ to see you.* 너를 만나기 위해 일부러 왔다.

spe·cial·ty [spéʃəlti] *n.* Ⓒ (*pl.* **-ties**) **1** a special branch of work or study. 전문; 전공. ¶ *His ~ is music.* 그의 전공은 음악이다. **2** a special quality or characteristic. 특성; 특질. **3** an article to which special attention is given. 특제품. ¶ *The ~ of this restaurant is seafood.* 이 요리점의 일품 요리는 해산물 요리다. **4** 《law》 a deed. 날인 증서. ¶ *debts of ~* 날인 증서 채무.

spe·cie [spíːʃi(ː)] *n.* Ⓤ money in coins; metal money. 정금(正金); 정화(正貨)(opp. paper money). ¶ *a ~ bank* 정금(正金) 은행 / *~ money* 정화(正貨). [↓]

·spe·cies [spíːʃi(ː)z] *n.* (*pl.* **-cies**) **1** a group of animals or plants of the same general kind with important, common characteristics; a kind. 종(種); 종류. ¶ *butterflies of many ~* 각종의 나비 / *the (human) ~* 인류 / *The Origin of Species* 종(種)의 기원 / *The ~ are very numerous.* 그 종류는 대단히 많이 있다. **2** bread and wine used in the Mass. 미사용의 빵과 포도주. [→special]

·spe·cif·ic [spisífik] *adj.* **1** particular. 특정한〔의〕; 특수의. ¶ *a ~ sum of money* 특정 금액 / *The money was lent for a ~ purpose.* 그 돈은 특정한 목적으로 대부되었다. **2** of species. 종(種)의; 종에 관한. ¶ *the ~ name of an animal* 한 동물의 종(種)의 이름 / *a ~ fig* 특종의 무화과. **3** having a special effect in curing a certain disease. 특효가 있는. ¶ *a ~ medicine* 특효약. **4** clear and exact; definite; precise. 명확한; 상세한. ¶ *a ~ statement* 명확한 진술 / *with no ~ aim* 이렇다 할 뚜렷한 목적 없이. **5** characteristic of; peculiar to. 독특한; 특유의. ¶ *the ~ qualities of a drug* 어떤 약의 특성 / *a way of living ~ to Korea* 한국 고유의 생활 양식.
— *n.* Ⓒ **1** any specific quality. 특성. **2** a cure for a certain disease. 특효약. ¶ *Qui-*

nine is a ~ for malaria. 키니네는 말라리아의 특효약이다. [→special]

spe·cif·i·cal·ly [spisífikəli] *adv.* definitely; particularly. 명확히; 특별히. ¶ *The doctor warned him ~ not to eat eggs.* 의사는 그에게 달걀을 먹지 말라고 특별히 주의하였다.

spec·i·fi·ca·tion [spèsəfikéiʃən] *n.* Ⓤ **1** the act of stating in detail. 상술; 상기(詳記). **2** 《*pl.*》 a detailed description of requirements to carry out some work or plan. (건물 따위의) 시방서(示方書); (설계) 명세서; 명세; 내역. ¶ *the architect's specifications for a new building* 새 빌딩에 대한 건축사의 시방서.

specific gravity [-ˊ- ˊ--] *n.* 《phys.》 the ratio between the weight of a certain substance and that of another substance, esp. water in the same volume. 비중.

spec·i·fy [spésəfài] *vt.* (**-fied**) (P6,11) **1** mention or describe (something) in detail; state fully and clearly. …을 상세하게 말하다〔기록하다〕; (하나하나) 명시〔명기〕하다. ¶ *~ the persons concerned* 관계자의 이름을 자세히 쓰다 / *~ reasons for one's failure* 실패의 이유를 명기하다 / *~ those to whom invitations are to be sent* 초청장을 받을 사람들의 이름을 하나하나 명기하다 / *~ a time and a place for a meeting* 회의할 시간과 장소를 명시하다. **2** include in a specification; require. 시방서에 기입〔지정〕하다. ¶ *The architect specified oak for the floor.* 건축사는 시방서에 마루재(材)로 오크를 지정하였다. [→special]

***spec·i·men** [spésəmən] *n.* Ⓒ **1** a part of something, or one of a group of something which represents the whole; a typical example; a sample. 견본; 표본; 실례. ¶ *~ pages* (책의 내용을 보기 위한) 견본쇄(刷) / *a rare ~ of the earliest English postage stamps* 초기 영국 우표의 희귀한 견본 / *a ~ of the 14th century handwriting,* 14세기 서법의 견본 / *He is a fair ~ of manhood.* 그는 남성의 전형(典型)이다. **2** an example of a natural thing preserved, classified, and exhibited as a sample of its kind. 표본. ¶ *an insect ~* 곤충의 표본 / *a stuffed ~* 박제 / *specimens of rocks and minerals* 암석과 광물의 표본 / *a museum ~* 진열용 표본. **3** 《*colloq., contempt.*》 an odd or peculiar kind of person. 괴짜. ¶ *What a ~!* 참 별난 녀석이군 / *He's a nasty ~.* 그 녀석은 고약스런 괴짜야. [→species]

spe·cious [spíːʃəs] *adj.* seeming good or correct, but not really so. 허울〔외양〕만 좋은; 그럴 듯한. ¶ *a ~ argument* 〔*plea, excuse*〕 그럴듯한 의론〔구실, 변명〕 / *a ~ appearance of prosperity* 겉모양만 번드르르한 번영 / *~ reasoning* 그럴 듯한 추리. [↑]

spe·cious·ly [spíːʃəsli] *adv.* in a specious manner; plausibly. 그럴 듯하게.

spe·cious·ness [spíːʃəsnis] *n.* Ⓤ the state or quality of being specious. 그럴듯함; 겉모양만 번드르르함.

***speck** [spek] *n.* Ⓒ **1** a small spot on something; a stain. 작은 오점〔반점〕; 얼룩. ¶ *specks on paper* 종이 위의 반점〔얼룩〕 / *a ~ of decay in fruit* 과일의 썩은 흠〔반점〕. **2** a very tiny thing; a bit. 작은 알갱이〔조각〕; 조금. ¶ *I don't like it a ~.* 나는 그것이 전혀 마음에 안 든다 / *I have not a ~ of interest in it.* 나는 그것에 대해 조금도 흥미가 없다 / *The ship became a mere ~ in the distance.* 배는 저 멀리 단지 하나의 작은 점이 되었다. — *vt.* 《usu. in *passive*》 (P6) mark (something) with spots. …에 반점을 찍다. [E.]

speck·le [spékəl] *n.* Ⓒ a small spot or mark on something. 작은 반점; 얼룩. ¶ *a gray dog with white speckles* 흰 반점이 있는 회색의 개. — *vt.* 《usu. in *passive*》 (P6) mark (something) with speckles. …에 작은 반점을 찍다; 얼룩지게 하다. ¶ *the land speckled with houses* 집들이 점재하는 시골.

speck·less [spéklis] *adj.* having no spot; without a speck; clean. 반점〔오점〕이 없는.

specs [speks] *n. pl.* 《*colloq.*》 a pair of spectacles. 안경. [Abbr.]

***spec·ta·cle** [spéktəkəl] *n.* Ⓒ **1** something impressive to look at; a public show. 광경; 구경거리. ¶ *a charming ~* 아름다운 광경 / *a lamentable* 〔*moving*〕 *~* 비참한〔사람의 마음을 움직이는〕 광경 / *He was a sad ~ in his rags.* 그는 다 떨어진 옷을 입은 형편없는 몰골이었다 / *The opening ceremony was a fine ~.* 개회식은 멋진 광경이었다 / *The sunrise was a splendid ~.* 해뜨는 모습은 하나의 장관이었다. **2** 《*pl.*》 a pair of eyeglasses to help a person to see. 안경. ¶ *a man in spectacles* 안경을 낀 남자. [L. *specio* look]

make a spectacle of oneself, behave or dress ridiculously. 남의 웃음거리가 될 행동〔복장〕을 하다.

see everything* 〔*life*〕 *through rose-colored spectacles, take a cheerful view of life. 사물〔인생〕을 낙관적으로 보다.

spec·ta·cled [spéktəkəld] *adj.* **1** wearing spectacles. 안경을 낀. **2** having markings like spectacles in form. 안경 모양의 무늬가 있는. ¶ *a ~ bear* 안경곰《남아메리카산》.

spec·tac·u·lar [spektǽkjələr] *adj.* **1** of a spectacle or show. 볼 만한; 구경거리의. ¶ *a ~ play* 볼 만한 경기. **2** making a wonderful show. 장관의. ¶ *in a ~ fashion* 눈부시게 / *do ~ things* 눈부신 일을 하다 / *~ scenes in a moving picture* 어떤 영화의 장엄한 장면.

***spec·ta·tor** [spékteitər, -ˊ-] *n.* Ⓒ a person who looks on at some event; an observer. 구경꾼; 방관자. ¶ *a crowd of spectators at a game* 시합의 대관중 / *remain a ~* 방관자로 있다〔남다〕 / *sit as a ~* 방관하다 / *He remained a mere ~ of the great war.* 그는 대전(大戰)의 단순한 방관자로 있었다.

spec·ter, 《Brit.》 **-tre** [spéktər] *n.* Ⓒ a ghost. 유령. [L. *spectrum* apparition]

spec·tra [spéktrə] *n.* pl. of **spectrum.**

spec·tral [spéktrəl] *adj.* **1** of or like a ghost. 유령의〔같은〕. **2** of the spectrum. 스펙트럼의. ¶ ~ *colors* 분광색《무지개의 일곱 가지 색》/ ~ *analysis* 스펙트럼 분석.

spec·tre [spéktər] *n.* 《Brit.》 =specter.

spec·tro·gram [spéktrəgræ̀m] *n.* Ⓒ a photograph of a spectrum. 분광 사진; 스펙트럼 사진. [→spectrum]

spec·tro·graph [spéktrəgræ̀f, -grɑ̀:f] *n.* Ⓒ an instrument for photographing spectra. 분광 사진기.

spec·tro·scope [spéktrəskòup] *n.* Ⓒ an instrument for making spectra from any source. 분광기. [→spectacle]

spec·trum [spéktrəm] *n.* Ⓒ (*pl.* **-tra** or **-trums**) **1** the band of colors formed when light passes through a prism, a water drop, etc. 스펙트럼; 분광(分光). ¶ ~ *analysis* 스펙트럼 분석 / *a solar* ~ 태양 스펙트럼. **2** a continuous range or entire extent. 영역; 전체의 범위. ¶ *a wide* ~ *of interests* 광범위한 흥미 / *the* ~ *of political beliefs* 각인 각색의 정치적 신념. [L. =image, apparition, →species]

spec·u·la [spékjələ] *n.* pl. of **speculum**.

spec·u·late [spékjəlèit] *vi.* (P1,3) **1** 《*about, on*》 consider a subject carefully; meditate. 사색하다; 깊이 생각하다. ¶ ~ *about the meaning of life* 인생의 의의에 대하여 깊이 생각하다 / ~ *on the origin of the universe* 우주의 기원에 관하여 사색하다. **2** buy or sell stock, land, etc. with the hope of profiting by a change in the price. 투기하다. ¶ ~ *in stocks* 〔*shares*〕 주식에 손을 대다 / ~ *on a fall* 〔*rise*〕 (값의) 하락을〔등귀를〕 예상하고 투기를 하다 / ~ *in land* 땅 투기를 하다. [L. *specio* look]

***spec·u·la·tion** [spèkjəléiʃən] *n.* **1** Ⓤ meditation; consideration. 사색. ¶ *be much given to* ~ 사색에 잠겨 있다. **2** Ⓒ an opinion or a conclusion reached by such meditation. 추론(推論). **3** Ⓤ the act of buying or selling stocks, land, etc. when there is a large risk, but with the hope of making large profits. 투기; 사행(射倖). ¶ *on* ~ 투기로; 요행을 걸고 / *engage in* ~ 투기를 하다 / *buy land as a* ~ 투기 목적으로 땅을 사다 / ~ *in stocks* 증권 투기.

spec·u·la·tive [spékjəlèitiv, -lə-] *adj.* **1** thoughtful; theoretical; not practical. 사색적인; 이론상의; 공론(空論)의. ¶ ~ *geometry* 순정 기하학 / ~ *philosophy* 사변(思辨) 철학. **2** of commercial or financial speculation. 투기적인. ¶ *a* ~ *venture* 투기적인 모험 사업 / ~ *purchase* 투기 구매《값이 오를 것을 예상하고 하는 매입》/ ~ *market* 투기 시장.
● **spec·u·la·tive·ly** [-li] *adv.*

spec·u·la·tor [spékjəlèitər] *n.* Ⓒ **1** (in business) a person who is engaged in financial speculation. 투기업자; 투기꾼. **2** a person who buys tickets in advance to sell them later at a higher price; a ticket speculator. 입장권 매점자; 암표상. **3** a person who devotes himself to mental speculation. 사색가; 이론가.

spec·u·lum [spékjələm] *n.* (*pl.* **-la**) an instrument for dilating cavities of human body for inspection. 자궁경(子宮鏡).

:sped [sped] *v.* p. and pp. of **speed.**

:speech [spi:tʃ] *n.* **1** Ⓤ language. 언어. **2** Ⓤ the act of speaking. 말하기; 발언. ¶ *freedom of* ~ 언론의 자유 / *express oneself in writing not in* ~ 말이 아니라 글로 자신을 표현하다 / *Speech is silvern, silence is golden.* 웅변은 은이요, 침묵은 금이다. **3** Ⓤ the manner of speaking. 말씨; 말투. ¶ *His* ~ *is not clear.* 그의 말투는 똑똑하지가 않다 / *a man of rapid* 〔*slow, thick*〕 ~ 말씨가 빠른〔더듬거리는, 답답한〕 사람 / *He is slow of* ~. 그는 말을 더듬거린다. **4** Ⓤ the power of speaking. 언어 능력. ¶ *lose one's* ~ 언어 능력을 잃다 / *an impediment in* ~ 언어 장애 / *Man alone has the gift of* ~. 인간만이 언어 능력을 가지고 있다. **5** Ⓒ a talk given in public; an address. 연설. ¶ *an opening* ~ 개회사 / *make* 〔*deliver, give*〕 *a* ~ 연설하다 / *an after-dinner* ~ 테이블 스피치 / *a set* ~ 준비된 연설 / *a* ~ *of thanks* 감사의 인사말 / *a debating* ~ 토론 연설. **6** 《gram.》 narration. 화법. ¶ *direct* 〔*indirect*〕 ~ 간접〔직접〕 화법. **7** the particular form of language used by a certain group of people; a language or dialect. 한 지방〔나라〕의 말; 국어; 방언. ¶ (*the*) *English* ~ 영어 / *the native* ~ *of Ireland* 아일랜드의 토착어. [*speak*]

speech day [∠∠] *n.* 《Brit.》 the last day of the school year, when prizes and oral exercises are given. 졸업식; 종업(終業)식 날. (cf. 《U.S.》 *commencement*)

speech·i·fy [spí:tʃəfài] *vi.* (**-fied**) make a long, dull speech. 연설하다; 연설조로 말하다.

speech·less [spí:tʃlis] *adj.* **1** unable to speak; silent. 말을 하지 못하는; 입을 열지 않는. ¶ *a* ~ *person* 말이 없는 사람 / *He was* ~ *with surprise.* 그는 놀라서 아무 말도 못했다 / *I stood* ~ *with fear.* 나는 겁에 질려 멍하니 서있었다. **2** that cannot be expressed in words. 형언할 수 없는. ¶ *a* ~ *grief* 말로 다 할 수 없는 슬픔.

:speed [spi:d] *n.* **1** Ⓤ swift or quick movement. 빠른 움직임; 신속한 동작. ¶ *with* ~ 신속하게 / *make* ~ 서두르다 / *More haste, less* ~. 서둘수록 속도는 늦어진다《급할수록 천천히 돌아 가라》. **2** ⓊⒸ the rate of motion or progress. 속도; 속력. ¶ *at a* ~ *of fifty miles an hour* 시속 50 마일로 / (*at*) *full* ~ = 《U.S.》 *at top* ~ =*at the top of one's* ~ 전속력으로 / *the* ~ *of sound* 음속 / *landing* ~ 착륙 속도 / *make a* ~ *of 18 knots,* 18 노트의 속력을 내다. **3** 《*arch.*》 success; good luck. 성공; 행운. ¶ *God send* 〔*give*〕 *you good* ~. 너의 성공을 빈다.

—*v.* (**sped** or **speed·ed**) *vi.* (P1,2A) **1** go

fast; move quickly. 급히〔빠르게〕 가다; 나는 듯이 달리다. ¶ *He sped along the street.* 그는 거리를 질주했다 / *A boat sped across the waves.* 보트는 파도를 가르며 빠르게 나아갔다. **2** drive a car more rapidly than is safe or allowed by law. (자동차가) 위반 속도를 내다; 스피드를 내다. **3** 《*arch.*》 live; get on. 살아가다; 지내다; (일이) 진행되어 가다. ¶ ~ *ill* 〔*well*〕 (일이) 잘 되어가지 않다〔되어 가다〕 / *How have you sped?* 어떻게 지내고 계십니까.

— *vt.* (P6) **1** cause (something) to move, go, or pass quickly. …을 서두르게 하다; 촉진하다; …의 속력을 빠르게 하다. ¶ ~ (*up*) *an engine* 엔진의 회전을 빠르게 하다. **2** cause (something) to succeed or prosper; wish good luck or success to. …을 성공〔번영〕시키다; …의 성공을 빌다. [E.]

God speed you! 《said at *parting*》 It is my hope that God will take care of you. 행운〔성공〕을 비네.

speed up, accelerate; go faster; cause (something) to go more quickly. 빠르게 하다; 빨라지다; …의 속도를 빠르게 하다. ¶ *Speed up the work.* 일의 속도를 빠르게 하라.

speed·boat [spíːdbòut] *n.* a motorboat built to go at a high speed. 고속 모터 보트.

speed·er [spíːdər] *n.* **1** a person who drives too fast or at a higher speed than is legal or safe. 속도 위반자. **2** a device for regulating speed. 속도 조절 장치.

speed·i·ly [spíːdili] *adv.* with speed; soon. 빠르게; 즉시.

speed·ing [spíːdiŋ] *n.* the act of driving motorcars faster than is allowed by law. (자동차의) 속도 위반. ¶ *He was arrested for* ~. 그는 속도 위반으로 체포되었다.

speed limit [∠ ∠–] *n.* the fastest speed permitted by law. (허용된) 최고 속도.

speed·om·e·ter [spiːdɑ́mitər / -dɔ́-] *n.* Ⓒ an instrument attached to an automobile or other vehicle to measure its speed. 속도계.

speed-up [spíːdʌ̀p] *n.* **1** an increase in speed. 속도 증진; 고속도화. **2** an increase in the rate of production. (기계 따위의) 생산 촉진.

speed·way [spíːdwèi] *n.* Ⓒ 《U.S.》 **1** a road or highway for high-speed traffic. 고속 도로. **2** a track for automobile races. 자동차 경주장.

***speed·y** [spíːdi] *adj.* (**speed·i·er, speed·i·est**) **1** fast; rapid. 빠른; 신속한. ¶ *a* ~ *flight* 재빠른 도주 / ~ *progress* 장족(長足)의 진보 / *a* ~ *recovery* 급속한 회복. **2** without delay; prompt. 즉시의; 지체 없는. ¶ *a* ~ *answer* 즉답 / *a* ~ *retribution* (재빠른) 즉각적인 보복. ● **speed·i·ness** [-nis] *n.*

:spell[1] [spel] *v.* (**spelled** or **spelt**) *vt.* **1** (P6) write or say the letters of (a word) in correct order. (낱말을 정확하게) 철자하다; …의 철자를 말하다〔쓰다〕. ¶ ~ *a word* 낱말을 철자하다 / *How do you* ~ *your name?* 너의 이름은 어떻게 철자하지. **2** make up or form (a word). (낱말이) …라고 철자되다; (…로 철자하여) —라고 읽다. ¶ *O-n-e spells 'one.'* o-n-e로 철자(綴字)하면 'one'이 된다. **3** mean; result in. …을 의미하다; …한 결과가 되다. ¶ *Delay spells danger.* 늦어지면 위험하다 / *Such an error spells our ruin.* 그러한 과오는 우리의 파멸을 뜻한다 / *These changes* ~ *ruin to the farmer.* 이 변혁들은 농부에게 파멸(破滅)을 가져온다. — *vi.* (P1) form words with letters. 낱말을 철자하다. ¶ *We learn to* ~ *in school.* 학교에서 철자법을 배운다 / ~ *correctly* 정확하게 철자하다. [Teut.]

spell backward, write the letters of word in reverse order; pervert the meaning of. 거꾸로 철자하다; 곡해(曲解)하다.

spell out, **a**) read each word with difficulty. 한 자 한 자 힘들여 읽다. **b**) spell correctly and perfectly. (생략하지 않고) 완전하게 철자하다. **c**) make out; find out. 똑똑히 설명하다. ¶ ~ *out the meaning* 뜻을 명확히 설명하다.

***spell**[2] [spel] *n.* Ⓒ **1** a word or words which are supposed to have magic power. 주문(呪文); 진언(眞言). ¶ *be bound by a* ~ 주문에 걸려 있다 / *cast a* ~ *on someone* 아무에게 마술을 걸다. **2** charm; fascination. 마력; 매력. ¶ *be under the* ~ *of her beauty* 그녀의 아름다움에 매료되어 있다. [Teut.]

***spell**[3] [spel] *n.* Ⓒ **1** a period of work. (교대로 하는) 한차례〔한바탕〕의 일. ¶ *a* ~ *of work* 한 차례의 일 / *have* 〔*take*〕 *a* ~ *at the oars* (아무와) 교대하여 한 차례 노를 젓다. **2** a turn at work in place of another. (일의) 교대. ¶ *a* ~ *of eight hours,* 8시간 근무(교대) / *have a* ~ 교대하다 / *keep* ~ (아무와) 교대를 하고 있다 / *take* ~ (아무와) 교대하다. **3** a period of a specified sort of weather; a short period; a little while. (날씨의) 한동안의 계속; 잠시 동안. ¶ *a long* ~ *of fine weather* 한동안 계속되는 좋은 날씨 / *a hot* ~ 더위의 계속 / *sleep for a* ~ 잠시 동안 잠자다 / *a* ~ *ago* 얼마 전. **4** 《U.S.》 a period of some illness. 기분〔건강〕이 나쁠 때. ¶ *old spells* 지병(持病) / *a* ~ *of coughing* 기침의 발작.

by spells, alternately. 교대로.

for a spell, for a while. 잠시 동안.

give someone a spell, take turns. …와 교대해 주다.

spell and spell, spell for spell. 윤번으로.

— *vt.* (P6) work in place of (another). …와 교대하다. ¶ *I'll* ~ *you at driving.* 내가 운전을 교대할게. [E.=substitution]

spell·bound [spélbàund] *adj.* held by a spell; too attracted to move; fascinated. 주문(呪文)에 걸린〔얽어 매인〕; 홀린; 매혹된. ¶ *listen* ~ 넋을 잃고 듣다 / ~ *listeners* 매료된 청중들. [→spell[2]]

spell·er [spélər] *n.* Ⓒ **1** a person who spells words. 철자하는 사람. ¶ *a good* ~ 철

자가 정확한 사람. **2** 《U.S.》 a spelling book. 철자 교본. [→spell[1]]

*__spell·ing__ [spéliŋ] *n.* Ⓒ the way in which a word is spelled. 철자법. ¶ *He is poor at* ~. 그는 철자(법)에 약하다 / *the right* 〔*correct*〕 ~ 바른 철자법 / *English* ~ *is very irregular.* 영어의 철자법은 매우 불규칙하다.

spell·ing-bee [spéliŋbì:] *n.* a spelling competition. 철자 시합.

spell·ing-book [spéliŋbùk] *n.* an exercise book to teach spelling. 철자 교본.

spelt[1] [spelt] *v.* p. and pp. of **spell**[1].

spelt[2] [spelt] *n.* a kind of wheat. 밀의 일종 《가축 사료》. [L.]

:**spend** [spend] *v.* (**spent**) *vt.* (P6) **1** pay out (money, etc.). (돈 따위를) 쓰다; 소비하다. ¶ *I spent ten dollars today.* 나는 오늘 10달러를 썼다 / *How much have you spent?* 얼마만큼의 돈을 썼느냐. **2** (P6) give (labor, time, etc.) for some purpose. (어떤 목적에 노력·시간 따위)를 들이다; 소비하다. ¶ *Don't* ~ *much time on that lesson.* 그 과목에 너무 많은 시간을 들이지 마라 / ~ *all one's efforts* 모든 노력을 다 기울이다. **3** (P6) use up; exhaust; wear out (oneself or itself). …을 다 써 없애다; (세력)을 약화시키다. ¶ ~ *one's energy on work* 정력을 일에 모두 써버리다 / *Our food was all spent.* 식량이 다 떨어졌다 / *The storm has spent itself.* 폭풍은 (세력이 약해져서) 잠잠해졌다. **4** (P6) pass (time, days, etc.) in a particular manner, place, etc. (시간)을 보내다. ¶ ~ *a sleepless night* 잠 못 이루는 하룻밤을 보내다 / ~ *the summer at the beach* 해변에서 여름을 보내다 / ~ *an evening* 〔*two hours*〕 *with friends* 친구들과 하루 저녁〔두 시간〕을 보내다 / ~ *one's life in a small town* 조그마한 도시에서 일생을 보내다. **5** (P6) 《naut.》 lose. 잃다. ¶ ~ a mast 돛대를 잃다. — *vi.* (P1) pay out money. 돈을 쓰다. ¶ *They* ~ *freely.* 그들은 돈을 마구 쓴다. [*expend*]

spend one's breath, talk to no purpose. 부질없는 말을 지껄이다.

Spen·der [spéndər], **Stephen** *n.* (1909-) an English poet and critic. 스펜더《영국의 시인·비평가》.

spen·der [spéndər] *n.* Ⓒ **1** a person who spends. 쓰는〔소비하는〕 사람. **2** a person who wastes money. 낭비하는 사람. [*spend*]

spend·thrift [spéndθrìft] *n.* Ⓒ a person who spends money carelessly and foolishly. 돈 씀씀이가 헤픈 사람; 낭비가. — *adj.* wasteful; extravagant. 돈을 헤프게 쓰는; 사치스러운. [→spend]

Spen·ser [spénsər], **Edmund** *n.* (1552?-99) a British poet. 스펜서《영국의 시인》.

:**spent** [spent] *v.* p. and pp. of **spend.** — *adj.* tired out; used up; without any more power or energy. 지쳐 버린; 오래 써서 낡은; 다 써 버린; 기진한. ¶ *a well-spent life* 유익하게 지내온 일생 / *a* ~ *battery* 다 쓴 전지 / *a* ~ *swimmer* 기진한 수영 선수 / *The storm is* ~. 폭풍은 잠잠해졌다 / *a* ~ *herring* 산란을 끝낸 청어. [*spend*]

sperm [spə:rm] *n.* Ⓤ the generative fluid of a male animal. 정액. [Gk.=seed]

sper·ma·cet·i [spə̀:rməséti, -sí:ti] *n.* Ⓤ substance got from the head of a sperm-whale. 경랍(鯨蠟). [*sperm,* Gk. *kētos* whale]

sper·mat·ic [spə:rmǽtik] *adj.* of sperm. 정액의. [→sperm, *rheum,* zoology]

sper·ma·tor·rhoe·a, -rhe·a [spə̀:rmətərí:ə, spə:rmǽtə-] *n.* 《med.》 involuntary seminal discharge. 유정(遺精). [↑]

sper·ma·to·zo·a [spə̀:rmətəzóuə, spə:rmǽtə-] *n.* pl. of **spermatozoon.**

sper·ma·to·zo·on [spə̀:rmətəzóuən, spə:rmǽtə-] *n.* (*pl.* **-zo·a**) 《physiol.》 the male fertilizing element in semen. 정자. [↑]

sperm oil [∠∠] *n.* a yellowish oil taken from the sperm whale. 고래 기름; 경유(鯨油). [*sperm*]

sperm whale [∠∠] *n.* a large square-headed whale. 향유고래.

spew [spju:] *vt., vi* (P6,7; 1,2A) 《*up, out*》 throw out through the mouth; vomit. 토해내다; 뿜어 내다. — *n.* something spewed. 토해 낸〔뿜어 낸〕 것. [E.]

*__sphere__ [sfiər] *n.* Ⓒ **1** a round body like a ball; a globe. 구(球). **2** one of the stars or planets; a heavenly body. 천체. **3** a globe representing the earth or its surface. 지구의(地球儀). **4** the extent of knowledge, influence, activity, etc.; a scope; a range. (세력) 범위; (활동) 영역. ¶ *a* ~ *of influence* 세력권 / *remain in one's* ~ 자기의 본분을 지키다 / *the* ~ *of light* 빛이 미치는 범위 / *the* ~ *of the act* 그 법령의 적용 범위 / *be out of one's professional* ~ 자기의 전문 영역 밖에 있다 / *Women are entering into the spheres of men.* 여성이 남성의 활동 영역 안으로 들어가고 있다. **5** social order or rank. 지위. **6** 《*pl., collectively*》 《*poet.*》 all the stars in the sky; the sky; the heavens. 하늘; 창공. ¶ *a celestial* ~ 천구(天球). [Gk. *sphaira* ball]

the music of the spheres, the music supposed to be produced by the movements of the spheres or heavenly bodies. 천체의 음악.

spher·i·cal [sférikəl] *adj.* of a sphere; having a form like a sphere. 구(球)의; 구형(球形)〔구면(球面)〕의. ¶ *a* ~ *body* 구면체(球面體) / ~ *geometry* 구면(球面) 기하학.

sphe·roid [sfíərɔid] *n.* a body shaped somewhat like a sphere. 구상체(球狀體). [*sphere*]

sphe·roi·dal [sfiərɔ́idl] *adj.* of or like a spheroid. 구상체의.

sphinc·ter [sfíŋktər] *n.* 《anat.》 a ringlike muscle closing and opening an orifice. 괄약근(括約筋). [Gk.]

sphin·ges [sfíndʒi:z] *n.* pl. of **sphinx.**

sphinx [sfiŋks] *n.* (*pl.* **sphinx·es** or

sphin·ges). **1** 《*the S-*》《Gk. myth.》 a monster with the head of a woman and the body of a winged lion. 스핑크스. **2** 《*the S-*》 a huge statue in Egypt with a human head and a lion's body. (이집트에 있는) 스핑크스 상(像). **3** Ⓒ a mysterious person. 수수께끼의 인물. [Gk.]

sp. ht. specific heat. 비열(比熱).

·**spice** [spais] *n.* Ⓤ **1** a substance with a strong flavor added to food, such as pepper, nutmeg, cloves, and ginger; 《*collectively*》 such substances. 양념; 향(신)료. **2** 《often *a* ～》 ⓐ something that gives flavor or interest. 멋; 정취. ¶ *a* ～ *of humor* 유머의 멋 / *Humor is the* ～ *of life.* 유머는 인생의 정취이다. ⓑ a slight trace or suggestion. …한 낌새〔자취〕. ¶ *There is a* ～ *of madness in his character.* 그의 성격에는 광기의 기미가 있다.
— *vi.* **1** 《*with*》 put spice in (something). …에 양념을〔향료를〕 넣다〔치다〕. ¶ ～ *with ginger* 생강으로 맛을 내다〔조미하다〕/ *food spiced with pepper* 후추를 친 식품. **2** give interest or flavor to (something). …에 멋을〔정취를, 재미를〕 곁들이다. ¶ ～ *one's speech with humorous anecdotes* 재미있는 일화를 곁들여 이야기를 재미있게 하다. [→species]

spic·i·ness [spáisinis] *n.* the state or quality of being spicy; a spicy flavor or smell. (맛·냄새 등이) 향긋〔짜릿, 매콤, 싸〕함; 풍미가〔양념 맛이〕 있음. [↑]

spick-and-span [spíkənspǽn] *adj.* entirely new; neat and clean; fresh; smart. 아주 새로운; 깔끔한; 말쑥한. ¶ *a* ～ *uniform* 새로 맞춘 제복 / *He looks very* ～. 그는 매우 말쑥해 보인다 / *a* ～ *kitchen* 잘 정돈된 깨끗한 부엌 / *She keeps her home* ～. 그녀는 항상 집을 깔끔하게 정리한다. [*span-new* (N. =new as a chip)]

spic·y [spáisi] *adj.* (**spic·i·er, spic·i·est**) **1** flavored with spice; having the flavor of a spice. 향신료를〔양념을〕 넣은; 향신료의 맛이 〔냄새가〕 나는. ¶ ～ *foods* 〔*dishes*〕 양념으로 맛을 낸 음식〔요리〕. **2** ⓐ witty; pungent; lively; smart. 재치 있는; 자극성의; 풍미가 있는. ¶ ～ *criticism* 통렬한 비평. ⓑ a little improper; somewhat sexy. 좀 외설적인. ¶ *a* ～ *story* 외설적인 이야기. [→spice]

·**spi·der** [spáidər] *n.* Ⓒ **1** one of a number of small eight-legged animals, many of which spin webs to catch insects for food. 거미. **2** something like a spider in appearance, character, etc.; a kind of three-legged gridiron. 거미 비슷한 기구; 삼발이. [*spin*]

spi·der·y [spáidəri] *adj.* **1** like a spider or a spider's web. 거미의〔같은〕; 거미집의〔같은〕. **2** long and thin like the legs of a spider. 거미 다리 모양의. **3** full of spiders. 거미가 많은.

spig·ot [spígət] *n.* Ⓒ **1** a small plug or peg used to stop the flow of liquid through the hole of a cask, a barrel, etc. (통 따위의) 마개. **2** 《U.S.》 a faucet. 수도꼭지; (액체를 따르는) 주둥이. [↓]

spike [spaik] *n.* Ⓒ **1** a large, heavy nail; a sharp-pointed rod, bar, etc. at the top of a wall. 대못; 담장못. **2** sharp-pointed metal pieces on the sole of a shoe. (경기용 신발 바닥의) 스파이크. ¶ *Runners wear shoes with spikes to prevent slipping.* 주자(走者)는 미끄럼 방지를 위해 스파이크가 박힌 신발을 신는다. **3** an ear of corn; a long, pointed flower cluster on a stem. (밀 따위의) 이삭; 수상 화서(穗狀花序).
— *vt.* **1** fasten (something) with spikes; pierce (something) with a spike. …을 대못으로 박다; …에 대못을 박다. ¶ *spiked shoes* 스파이크 구두. **2** make (a cannon, a gun, etc.) useless by driving a spike into its opening. (사용 할 수 없도록 총·대포의) 화문(火門)을 막다. ¶ ～ *someone's gun* 총포의 화문을 막다('아무의 계획을 망쳐 놓다'). **3** make (a plan, etc.) useless or ineffective. …을 방해하다; 좌절시키다. ¶ ～ *an attempt* 하나의 시도를 좌절시키다. [L. *spica* corn-ear]

spike·let [spáiklit] *n.* a very small spike. 작은 이삭.

spike·nard [spáiknɑːrd, -nərd] *n.* Ⓤ **1** fragrant oil obtained from a tree. 감송향(甘松香). **2** 《bot.》 an East Indian aromatic plant. 감송(甘松).

spik·y [spáiki] *adj.* (**spik·i·er, spik·i·est**) **1** shaped like a spike; having spikes. 끝이 뾰족한; (큰)못투성이의. ¶ ～ *thorns* 끝이 뾰족한 가시. **2** (of a person, etc.) difficult to handle. (사람이) 다루기 힘든. [*spike*]

·**spill**[1] [spil] *v.* (**spilt** or **spilled**) *vt.* (P6) **1** cause (liquid, powder, etc.) to fall or flow out. …을 엎지르다; 흘리다. ¶ ～ *water* 〔*milk*〕 물을〔우유를〕 엎지르다 / *Don't* ～ *a drop.* 한 방울도 흘리지 마라 / ～ *sand* 모래를 흩뜨리다 / ～ *someone's blood* 아무를 죽이다 / 《*prov.*》 *It is no use crying over spilt milk.* 엎지른 물은 주워 담을 수 없다. **2** 《*from*》《*colloq.*》 throw out (someone or something) from a horse or vehicle. (말·차 따위에서) 내던지다; 팽개치다; 내동댕이치다. ¶ *The horse spilled the boy.* 말은 소년을 내동댕이쳤다 / *He was spilt from a vehicle.* 그는 자동차에서 내동댕이쳐졌다. **3** 《naut.》 let wind out of (a sail). (돛에서) 바람이 빠지게 하다. ¶ ～ *a sail* 돛의 바람을 빼다.
— *vi.* (P1,2A) overflow; flow out. 엎질러지다; 넘치다. ¶ *The water spilt from the bucket.* 물이 양동이에서 넘쳐 흘렀다.
— *n.* Ⓒ a fall from a horse or vehicle. (말·차 따위에서) 내던져짐. ¶ *get* 〔*have*〕 *a bad* ～ 심하게 내던져지다. [E.]

spill[2] [spil] *n.* Ⓒ a thin piece of wood or paper to light candles, pipes, etc. 나무의 얇은 조각; (점화용의) 쏘시개; 심지. [Du.]

spilt [spilt] *v.* p. and pp. of **spill**[1].

·**spin** [spin] *v.* (**spun** or 《*arch.*》 **span, spun,**

spin·ning) *vt.* (P6) **1** 《*into, out of*》 draw out and twist (cotton, wool, etc.) into threads. (실을) 잣다; (솜·털 따위로) 실을 만들다〔뽑다〕. ¶ ~ *cotton into yarn* 솜을 자아 실을 만들다〔뽑다〕/ ~ *thread out of cotton* 솜에서 실을 잣다. **2** make (a web, a cocoon, etc.) by giving out thread from the body. (거미·누에 따위가) 실을 내다; 치다. ¶ *A spider spins a web.* 거미가 거미줄을 친다 / ~ *a cocoon* (누에가) 고치를 짓다. **3** ⓐ tell〔compose〕(a story, etc.). …을 (장황하게) 이야기하다; (이야기 따위를) 꾸며대다. ¶ ~ *a (long) tale* 긴 이야기를 늘어놓다 / *He spun a tale of bygone days.* 그는 지난 일을 장황하게 이야기하였다. ⓑ 《*out*》 prolong; make long. 오래〔질질〕 끌다. ¶ ~ *out a story tediously* 이야기를 지루하게 질질 끌다 / ~ *out the time by talking* 이야기로 시간을 오래 끌다. **4** cause (something) to turn around swiftly. (팽이 따위를) 돌리다; 회전시키다. ¶ ~ *a top* 팽이를 돌리다 / ~ *a coin on the table* 동전을 테이블 위에서 빙글빙글 돌리다《앞면이냐 뒷면이냐로 승부 따위를 결정짓기 위해》. — *vi.* (P1) **1** spin thread; turn around swiftly. 실을 잣다; 빙글빙글 돌다. ¶ *The wheel began spinning round.* 수레 바퀴가 빙글빙글 돌기 시작했다. **2** move along swiftly. 질주하다. ¶ ~ *along the road* 도로를 질주하다. **3** feel dizzy. 어지럽다; 눈이 핑 돌다. ¶ *My head is spinning.* 머리가 어질어질하다.

spin a yarn, tell a story at full length. 길게 이야기를 늘어놓다.

spin out, make (something) long. …을 오래 끌다; 길게 늘리다.

— *n.* **1** ⒸⓊ swift turning motion. 회전. ¶ *fall in* ~ 빙글빙글 돌며 떨어지다 / *the* ~ *of a wheel* 수레바퀴의 회전. **2** Ⓒ a swift movement; a short drive or ride. 질주; 한바탕 달리기. ¶ *go for a* ~ *in a car* 자동차로 드라이브하러 가다. **3** 《aeron.》 a circling, nose-down fall of an aeroplane; a tail-spin. 나선식 급강하. [E.]

get into a flat spin, 《*colloq.*》 get into confusion; lose one's self-control. 혼란에 빠지다; 자제심을 잃다.

spin·ach [spínitʃ/-nidʒ] *n.* Ⓤ a common vegetable with green leaves which can be cooked and eaten. 시금치. [F.]

spi·nal [spáinl] *adj.* of the spine or backbone. 등뼈〔척추〕의. ¶ *the* ~ *column* 척추 / *the* ~ *cord* 척수. [→spine]

spin·dle [spíndl] *n.* Ⓒ **1** a long, thin rod or pin used in spinning to twist and wind the thread. 물레가락; 방추(紡錘). **2** a rod or pin about which something turns; an axle. 축(軸); 굴대. — *vi.* (P1) grow long and thin. 가늘고 길게 되다. [→spin]

spin·dle-leg·ged [spíndllègid] *adj.* having long, slender legs. 가늘고 긴 다리의. ¶ *a* ~ *table* 다리가 가늘고 긴 테이블.

spin·dle·legs [spíndllègz] *n. pl.* **1** long, slender legs. 가늘고 긴 다리. **2** 《used as sing.》 《*colloq.*》 a person who has long, slender legs. 다리가 가늘고 긴 사람.

spin·dle-shanked [spíndlʃæ̀ŋkt] *adj.* = spindle-legged.

spin·dle-shanks [spíndlʃæ̀ŋks] *n. pl.* = spindlelegs 2.

spin·dling [spíndliŋ] *adj.* 《U.S.》 long and thin; too tall and thin. 가늘고 긴; 껑충한.

spin·dly [spíndli] *adj.* (**-dli·er, -dli·est**) = spindling.

spin·drift [spíndrìft] *n.* Ⓤ spray blown and dashed up from the waves. 물보라. [→spin]

spindrift clouds [⌐-⌐] *n.* light, feathery clouds. 권운(卷雲); 새털구름.

spine [spain] *n.* Ⓒ **1** the backbone. 등뼈; 척추. **2** the back of a book, with the title and the author's name on it. 책의 등《책명·저자명 등을 씀》. **3** a sharp-pointed part sticking out from a plant, an animal, etc.; a thorn. (동물·식물 따위의) 바늘; 가시; 가시 모양의 돌기. [L. *spina*]

spi·nel(le) [spinél, spínəl] *n.* kinds of mineral of various colors occurring in regular crystals. 첨정석(尖晶石). [F.]

spine·less [spáinlis] *adj.* **1** having no spine. 등뼈〔척추〕가 없는. **2** having no courage, energy or determination; irresolute. 우유 부단한; 결단력이 없는. [→spine]

spin·et [spínit, spinét] *n.* Ⓒ an old-fashioned musical instrument like a small harpsichord. 스피넷《harpsichord 비슷한 옛날의 악기명》. 參考 16-18세기 경에 사용했던 피아노의 전신. [Person]

spin·na·ker [spínikər, 《naut.》 spǽŋkər] *n.* a large sail, triangular in shape, used chiefly on a racing yacht when running before the wind. 큰 삼각돛《경조용 요트에 쓰임》. [*Sphinx* =a yacht in which it was used]

spin·ner [spínər] *n.* Ⓒ a person who spins; a machine for spinning cotton, wool, etc. 방적공〔기〕. [→spin]

spin·ner·et [spínərèt] *n.* 《zool.》 the spinning-organ in spiders, silkworms, etc. (거미·누에 등의) 방적 돌기《실이 나오는 구멍》. [*spin*]

spin·ning [spíniŋ] *n.* Ⓤ drawing and twisting of cotton, flax, or wool. 방적. [*spin*]

spin·ning-jen·ny [spíniŋdʒèni] *n.* an early form of spinning machine. 다축(多軸) 방적기.

spinning wheel [⌐-⌐] *n.* a machine with a spindle driven by a

〈spinning wheel〉

large wheel, once used for spinning yarn. 물레.

spin·ster [spínstər] *n.* Ⓒ **1** a woman who spins yarn. 실 잣는 여자. **2** an unmarried woman; esp. an elderly woman who has not married. 미혼 여자; 노처녀. [→spin]

spin·y [spáini] *adj.* (**spin·i·er, spin·i·est**) **1** covered with or full of spines. 가시투성이의. **2** full of difficulties. 어려운; 곤란한. [→spine]

spi·ra·cle [spáiərəkəl, spír-] *n.* a breathing-hole in insects and some fishes; an air-hole; a blow-hole. 숨구멍; 기공(氣孔); 분수공(噴水孔). [*spirit*]

spi·ral [spáiərəl] *adj.* winding around a point in a widening coil; coiled. 소용돌이 모양의; 나선형의. ¶ *a ~ staircase* 나선형 계단 / *a ~ spring* 나선형 용수철. — *n.* Ⓒ a winding coil around a point in increasingly larger circles; anything that has a spiral shape. 와선(渦線); 나선형. — *vt., vi.* (**-raled, -ral·ing** or 《Brit.》 **-ralled, -ral·ling**) (P6;1,2) move in a spiral course; form into a spiral. (…을) 나선형으로 움직이게 하다〔움직이다〕; 나선형으로 하다〔나선형이 되다〕. ¶ *The aeroplane spiraled.* 비행기는 나선형으로 비행했다. ● **spi·ral·ly** [-rəli] *adv.* [Gk. *speira* coil]

spir·ant [spáiərənt] *n.* 《phon.》 fricative. 마찰음. — *adj.* of the nature of a spirant. 마찰음의. [→spirit]

spire[1] [spaiər] *n.* Ⓒ **1** the pointed top of a steeple. 뾰족탑; 첨탑(尖塔). **2** something shaped like a spire. 뾰족탑 모양의 것. ¶ *the rocky spires of a mountain* 산의 뾰족한 바위 / *a ~ of grass* 끝이 뾰족한 가는 풀잎. — *vi.* (P1) **1** point upward. 돌출하다. **2** shoot up. 싹트다. — *vt.* (P6) **1** furnish (something) with a spire. …에 뾰족탑을 달다. **2** cause (a plant, etc.) to shoot up. …을 싹트게 하다; 발아(發芽)시키다. [E.]

spire[2] [spaiər] *n.* Ⓒ a spiral; a single coil or turn in a spiral. 나선; 소용돌이. [Gk. *speira* coil]

:spir·it [spírit] *n.* **1** Ⓤ soul; mind; intelligence. 정신; 마음(opp. body). ¶ *body and ~* 육체와 정신 / *develop the ~* 정신을 도야하다 / *the poor in ~* 마음이 가난한 자 / *in the ~* 마음 속에서; 내심 / *the world of ~* 정신 세계 / *the ~ of reform* 개혁의 정신. **2** 《*the S-*》 God; Holy Ghost; Ⓤ the part of man that lasts forever. 신; 성령; 혼; 영(혼). ¶ *They believe that his ~ lives on.* 그의 영혼이 살아 있다고 믿는다 / *the immortality of the ~* 영혼의 불멸 / *the (Holy) Spirit* 성령 / *the life of the ~* 영적 생활 / *God is a Spirit.* 신은 영(靈)이시다. **3** Ⓒ a ghost; a fairy. 유령; 요정. ¶ *good* 〔*evil*〕 *spirits* 선한〔악한〕 귀신. **4** Ⓤ courage; energy of mind and character; firmness. 용기; 활기; 기백; 기운. ¶ *a man of ~* 용기 있는〔활기가 넘치는〕 사람 / *He has no ~ to complete the task.* 그는 그 과업을 완수할 만한 기백을 갖고 있지 않다 / *face the enemy with ~* 용기를 가지고 적과 맞서다 / *have a high ~* 활기가 넘치다. **5** 《usu. *pl.*》 feelings or mood; state of mind; way of feeling. 기분; 마음의 상태. ¶ *in good spirits* 기분이 좋아서; 기운차게 / *out of spirits* 풀이〔기가〕 죽어서 / *give someone spirits* 아무의 기분을 북돋아 주다. **6** 《often *a ~*》 nature; mood; temper; disposition; inclination. 성품; 마음가짐; 기질. ¶ *public ~* 공공심 / *fighting ~* 투지 / *the frontier ~* 개척자 정신 / *say something in a kind ~* …을 친절심에서 말하다 / *meek in ~* 마음씨가 고운 / *He is a poet in ~.* 그는 시인 기질이 있다. **7** 《usu. *pl.*》 alcohol; strong alcoholic drinks. 알코올; 독한 술.

be full of animal spirits, be full of youthful vigor. 혈기 왕성하다.

break someone's spirits, despirit. 아무의 기운을 꺾다.

catch someone's spirit, be impressed by another's appreciation of oneself. 아무의 의기에 감동하다.

give up the spirit, die. 죽다.

good 〔***high, great***〕 ***spirits,*** cheerfulness and buoyancy. 매우 좋은 기분.

in (***the***) ***spirit,*** mentally or spiritually or imaginatively even if not in body. 상상(想像)상의.

in spirits, vividly. 생기 발랄하게.

keep up one's spirits, be animated. 정신을 바짝 차리고 있다.

lose one's spirit, be dejected. 사기를 잃다; 낙심하다.

low 〔***poor***〕 ***spirits,*** depression. 의기 소침.

recover one's spirits, pick up one's spirits. 기운을 내다.

spirits of salt, hydrochloric acid. 염산.

spirits of wine, alcohol. 알코올.

the poor in spirit, the meek. 겸손한 사람들.

to one's spirit, to one's heart of hearts. 마음 속까지.

— *vt.* (P7) **1** 《*away, off*》 take away (someone) in secret, as if by magic; kidnap. …을 유괴하다; 감쪽같이 가져가다〔채가다〕. ¶ *The child has been spirited away.* 그 아이는 유괴당했다 / *~ someone to* 〔*out of*〕 *a place* 아무를 어떤 장소로〔에서〕 감쪽같이 데려가다〔채가다〕. **2** give spirit or life to (someone); cheer; encourage. …의 기운을 돋우다; 활기를 주다. ¶ *~ up someone with alcohol* = *~ someone with alcohol* 아무를 술을 먹여 기운을 북돋우다 / *~ someone up* 〔*on*〕 아무를 고무〔격려〕하다. [L. *spiro* breathe]

spir·it·ed [spíritid] *adj.* **1** full of life or energy; lively. 원기〔생기〕 있는; 활발한. ¶ *a ~ old man* 원기 있는 노인 / *a ~ attack* 맹렬한 공격 / *a ~ girl* 활발한 소녀. **2** 《in *compounds*》 having a particular character or mood. …의 정신을 가진; …한 기분〔기질〕의. ¶ *evil-spirited* 악랄한 / *jealous-spirited* 질투심

이 많은 기질의 / *mean-spirited* 비열한 / *high* 〔*low*〕*-spirited* 기백이 있는〔없는〕.

spir·it·ed·ly [spíritidli] *adv.* in a spirited manner. 생기〔원기〕 있게; 활발하게.

spir·it·ism [spíritìzəm] *n.* =spiritualism.

spirit lamp [⌐─⌐] *n.* a lamp in which alcohol is burnt. 알코올 램프.

spir·it·less [spíritlis] *adj.* lacking spirit or courage; not lively; not eager. 원기〔생기, 용기〕가 없는. ¶ *a ~ talk* 〔*answer*〕 생기〔열의〕가 없는 이야기〔대답〕.

spirit level [⌐─ ⌐─] *n.* a glass tube containing alcohol used to find out whether a surface is level shown by an air-bubble. 기포 수준기.

***spir·i·tu·al** [spíritʃuəl] *adj.* **1** of the spirit or mind. 정신의; 영적인(opp. material). ¶ *~ awakening* 깨달음 / *one's ~ welfare* 정신적 행복 / *~ growth* (종교적) 정신의 발달. **2** of religion or sacred things; of the church or religion; holy; sacred. 신앙의; 교회〔종교〕의; 신성한. ¶ *the ~ life* 신앙 생활; 영적(靈的)생명 / *~ songs* 성가 / *~ authority* 교회의 권위 / *a ~ corporation* 종교단체 / *~ gifts* 신의 선물 / *a ~ court* 종교 재판소 / *Lords Spiritual* 《Brit.》 성직(聖職) 상원 의원. **3** not worldly minded; absorbed in high thought. 고상〔숭고〕한. ¶ *a ~ mind* 〔*face, expression*〕 숭고한 정신〔얼굴, 표정〕.
— *n.* Ⓒ 《U.S.》 a religious song or hymn sung by the Negroes of the South. 흑인 영가. [→spirit]

spir·i·tu·al·ism [spíritʃuəlìzəm] *n.* Ⓤ **1** the belief that spirits of the dead can talk with living people through a special person. 심령주의; 심령론. **2** the philosophical doctrine that spirit alone is real. 유심론(唯心論); 관념론(opp. materialism).

spir·i·tu·al·ist [spíritʃuəlist] *n.* Ⓒ a person who believes in spiritualism. 심령론자; 유심론자.

spir·i·tu·al·i·ty [spìritʃuǽləti] *n.* (*pl.* **-ties**) **1** Ⓤ the state or quality of being spiritual. 정신적임; 영성(靈性). **2** 《usu. *pl.*》 the right, income, or property of a church or a clergyman. 교회〔성직자〕의 권리〔수입, 재산〕.

spir·i·tu·al·ize [spíritʃuəlàiz] *vt.* (P6) **1** make (something) spiritual or pure. …을 정신적으로 하다; 고상하게 하다. **2** interpret or understand spiritually. …을 정신적 의미로 해석하다(opp. literalize).

spir·it·u·al·ly [spíritʃuəli] *adv.* in a spiritual manner. 정신적으로.

spir·i·tu·ous [spíritʃuəs] *adj.* **1** containing much alcohol. 알코올 분(分)을 함유한. **2** distilled. 증류한. ¶ *~ liquors* 증류주류(類) (opp. fermented).

spi·rom·e·ter [spàiərámitər / -rɔ́m-] *n.* Ⓒ an instrument for measuring the breathing capacity of the lungs. 폐활량계. [L. *spiro* breathe, →mater]

spirt [spəːrt] *v., n.* =spurt.

spir·y [spáiəri] *adj.* shaped like a spire; abounding in spires. 첨탑〔뾰족탑〕 모양의; 첨탑이 많은. [*spire*]

***spit**[1] [spit] *v.* (**spat** 《*arch.*》 **spit, spit·ting**) *vt.* **1** (P6,7) 《*forth, out, up*》 throw out (saliva, blood, etc.) from the mouth; eject. (침·피 따위를) 뱉다; 토하다; 내뿜다. ¶ *~ blood* 피를 토하다 / *~ out a bit of broken tooth* 부러진 이빨 조각을 내뱉다 / *The guns spat fire.* 대포들이 불을 토했다. **2** (P6) throw out or utter (an oath, etc.) violently. (욕 따위를) 내뱉다; 내뱉듯이 말하다. ¶ *She angrily spat out her answer.* 그녀는 화가 나서 내뱉듯이 대답했다 / *~ one's words at* …에게 내뱉듯이 말하다 / *~ out curses at…* …에게 욕설을 퍼붓다. — *vi.* **1** (P1) 《*in, on, upon*》 throw out saliva from the mouth. 침을 뱉다. ¶ *~ in someone's face* 아무의 얼굴에 침을 뱉다. **2** 《*at, up, upon*》 treat or regard with contempt. 멸시하다; 모욕하다. ¶ *~ at* 〔*on*〕 *someone* 〔*his idea*〕 아무를〔아무의 생각을〕 업신여기다〔모욕하다, 미워하다〕 / *No spitting.* 침뱉지 마시오《게시》. **3** (P1,3) (of a cat, etc.) make an angry, hissing sound. (성난 고양이 따위가) 으르렁거리다. **4** (P1) rain slightly or briefly. (비가) 잠시 후두두 내리다.
spit it out, 《*sl.*》 speak out. …을 모욕하다.
— *n.* Ⓤ **1** saliva. 침. **2** Ⓒ the act or sound of spitting. 침뱉기; 침뱉는 소리. **3** Ⓒ a light or brief rain. 잠시 후두두 뿌리는 비. [E.]
be the very spit of, be exactly alike. …을 빼쏘다. ¶ *He is the very ~ of his father.* 그는 그의 부친을 꼭 닮았다.
spit and polish, furbishing work of a soldier. (군인들이 총기 따위를 번쩍번쩍 빛나게) 닦는 일.

spit[2] [spit] *n.* Ⓒ **1** a long, pointed rod or bar to hold meat for roasting. (고기 굽는) 쇠꼬챙이; 꼬치. **2** a narrow point of land extending into the water. 곶; 갑(岬); (바다에 길게 돌출한) 모래톱. — *vt.* (**spit·ted, spit·ting**) (P6) pierce (something) with a spit. …을 꼬치구이로 하다. [E.]

:spite [spait] *n.* Ⓤ ill-will; 《*a ~*》 hatred toward someone. 악의; 원한. ¶ *from* 〔*out of, in*〕 *~* 분풀이로 / *He did it from* 〔*out of*〕 *~.* 그는 그것을 분풀이로 했다 / *bear someone a ~* =*have a ~ against someone* …에 대해 원한을 품다 / *vent one's ~ upon someone* 아무에게 분풀이를 하다.
in spite of, notwithstanding; although. …에도 불구하고; …을 무릅쓰고. ¶ *In ~ of his misfortune, he is quite cheerful.* 불운에도 불구하고 그는 명랑하다 / *She arrived at school on time in ~ of the bad weather.* 그녀는 나쁜 날씨에도 불구하고 제시간에 학교에 도착하였다.
in spite of oneself, unconsciously. 저도 모르게; 무심코. ¶ *I laughed in ~ of myself.* 무심코〔나도 모르게〕 웃음을 터뜨렸다.

in spite of** one's **nose, in spite of one's teeth. 반대에도 불구하고.
— *vt.* (P6) show ill-will to (someone); injure. …에 심술부리다; 괴롭히다. ¶ *The bad children left the room dirty to ~ their maid.* 못된 아이들은 하녀에게 심술을 부리느라고 방을 어지럽혀 놓았다. [→despite]

spite·ful [spáitfəl] *adj.* full of ill-will; desiring to annoy or injure. 짓궂은; 악의에 찬. ¶ *~ words* 짓궂은(악의에 찬) 말.

spit·fire [spítfàiər] *n.* Ⓒ **1** a quick-tempered person, esp. a woman. 성마른 사람 《특히 여자》; 불뚱이. **2** a cannon. 대포. [→spit[1]]

spit·tle [spítl] *n.* Ⓤ saliva, esp. when spit out. (특히 내뱉은) 침. [→spit[1]]

spit·toon [spitú:n] *n.* Ⓒ a container like a jar to spit into. 타구(唾具). [↑]

spitz [spits] *n.* 《zool.》 a Pomeranian dog; a kind of small dog with long, silky hair and a narrow pointed nose. 스피츠. [G.]

·**splash** [splæʃ] *vt.* **1** (P6,7,13) cause (water, mud, etc.) to fly about; wet or soil by splashing; make (something) wet with mud, water, etc. (물·진흙 따위를) 튀기다; (물 따위를) 튀겨 더럽히다(적시다); (진흙·물 따위를) …에 튀기다. ¶ *~ a dress with mud* = *~ mud on a dress* 옷에 진흙을 튀기다 / *~ water about* 주위에 물을 튀기다 / *~ ink on one's fingers* 손가락에 잉크를 튀겨 더럽히다 / *~ a page with ink* (*ink on a page*) 페이지에 잉크를 튀기다 / *The car splashed me with mud.* 자동차가 내게 흙탕물을 튀겼다. **2** (of a liquid) fall in drops upon (something). (물 따위가) …에 튀다. ¶ *The mud has splashed my car.* 흙탕물이 내 차에 튀었다. **3** (P13) make (one's way, etc.) by splashing. 철벅거리며 …하다. ¶ *~ one's way across a stream* 철벅철벅거리며 개울을 건너가다. **4** (P6) adorn with scattered ornaments irregularly placed. 불규칙한 얼룩 무늬로 꾸미다. ¶ *The wallpaper is splashed with bright colors.* 벽지는 밝은 색깔의 불규칙한 얼룩 무늬이다.
— *vi.* (P1,2A) **1** ⓐ (of a liquid) fly about. (물 따위가) 튀다. ¶ *The paint splashed over the floor.* 페인트가 마루에 튀었다 / *The waves splashed on the beach.* 파도가 해변에 철썩철썩 들이쳤다. ⓑ cause liquid to fly about; scatter in drops. (사람이) 물을 튀기다. ¶ *The baby likes to ~ in the bath.* 어린애는 목욕통에서 물을 첨벙첨벙 튀기기를 좋아한다 / *Don't ~ !* 물을 튀기지 마라. **2** 《*across, along, with, into*》 fall or move with splashes or splashing noises. 풍덩(텀벙) 떨어지다(빠지다); 철벅철벅 소리를 내며 가다. ¶ *~ through a stream* 개울을 첨벙첨벙 소리내며 건너가다 / *He splashed into the dirty water.* 그는 더러운 물 속으로 텀벙 빠졌다.
— *n.* Ⓒ **1** the act or sound of splashing. 튀김; (물)튀기는 소리. ¶ *with a ~* 텀벙하고 / *fall into the water with a ~* 텀벙하고 물에 빠지다(떨어지다) / *The boat upset with a loud ~.* 보트는 첨벙하는 요란한 소리를 내며 뒤집혔다. **2** a spot or mark of liquid splashed. (흙탕물·잉크 따위가) 튄 것; (튀어서 생긴) 얼룩; 반점. ¶ *a mud ~ on the wall* 벽에 붙은 진흙 튄 것 / *She has a ~ of ink on her dress.* 그녀는 옷에 잉크의 얼룩이 있다. **3** an irregular spot of color. (짐승의) 불규칙한 반점. ¶ *a white dog with black splashes* 바둑이. **4** 《colloq.》 a striking show; a prominent display. 화려한(인상적인, 두드러진) 겉치레(전시). ¶ *a ~ headline* 사람의 눈길을 끄는 큰 표제. [→plash]
make a splash, **a**) make a sound of splashing. 텀벙(철벅)하고 소리를 내다. **b**) attract the attention of others. 큰 평판을 얻다; 주의를 끌다. ¶ *make a ~ with a best seller* 베스트셀러로 대호평을 얻다.

splash·board [splǽʃbɔ̀:rd] *n.* Ⓒ a screen or guard on a vehicle for protecting from splashes made by the turning wheels. (자동차의) 흙받기.

splash·down [splǽʃdàun] *n.* the landing of a missile or spacecraft on a body of water or its moment of impact. 착수 (시각).

splash·y [splǽʃi] *adj.* (**splash·i·er, splash·i·est**) **1** making a splash; liable to splash; wet and muddy. 튀기는; 튀기 쉬운; 질척한. **2** full of splashes or spots. 튄 흙(얼룩)투성이의. **3** 《colloq.》 attracting much attention; sensational. 남의 이목을 끄는; 대평판의.

splat·ter [splǽtər] *vt., vi.* **1** (P6) make continuous splashing sound. (계속해서) 절벅절벅 소리를 내다. **2** (P1) speak unintelligibly. 입 속에서 중얼거리다. [*spatter, splash*]

splay [splei] *vt.* (P6) **1** 《archit.》 slope outward. (문설주·창틀 따위를) 바깥쪽으로 벌어지게 하다. **2** dislocate. 탈구(脫臼)시키다. ¶ *a splayed shoulder-bone* 탈구된 어깨뼈.
— *n.* Ⓒ a surface making oblique angle with another. 사면(斜面). — *adj.* wide and flat; turned outward; awkward. 넓고 평평한; 모양 없는. ¶ *a ~ feet* 편평족. [*display*]

spleen [spli:n] *n.* **1** Ⓒ an organ at the left of the stomach which changes the structure of the blood. 비장; 지라. **2** Ⓤ ill nature; bad temper; melancholy. 기분이 언짢음; 심술; 우울. [Gk.]

:**splen·did** [spléndid] *adj.* **1** magnificent; glorious. 훌륭한; 화려한. ¶ *a ~ sunset glow* 장려한 석양의 놀 / *a ~ palace* (*scene*) 화려한 궁전(광경) / *a room ~ with chandeliers* 샹들리에를 장식한 화려한 방. **2** worthy of praise; fine. 칭찬할 만한; 장한. ¶ *a ~ achievement* 위대한 업적 / *a ~ victory* 장한 승리. **3** 《colloq.》 very good; excellent. 매우 멋진; 극상의. ¶ *a ~ idea* 아주 멋진 생각 / *We had a ~ time.* 아주 멋진 시간을 보냈

다. [L. *splendeo* shine]

splen·did·ly [spléndidli] *adv.* in a splendid manner. 화려하게; 훌륭히.

splen·dif·er·ous [splendífərəs] *a.* 《*colloq.*》 extremely good. 대단히 좋은.

•**splen·dor,** 《Brit.》 **-dour** [spléndər] *n.* Ⓤ **1** brilliance; brightness. 빛남; 광채. ¶ *the ~ of the jewel* 보석의 광채 / *the ~ of the sun* 태양의 광휘. **2** magnificence; impressiveness. 장려; 훌륭함. ¶ *the ~ of the building* 건물의 장려함 / *live in ~* 호사스런 생활을 하다. **3** 《*pl.*》 illustriousness; preeminence. 현저; 탁월. ¶ *the ~ of his art as a pianist* 피아니스트로서 그의 예술의 탁월함.

sple·net·ic [splinétik] *adj.* **1** of the spleen. 비장(脾臟)〔지라〕의. **2** bad-tempered; impatient. 기분이 언짢은; 성마른. — *n.* Ⓒ a person who gets angry easily. 성마른 사람. [→spleen]

splen·ic [splí:nik, splé-] *adj.* of (the) spleen. 비장〔지라〕의. [↑]

splice [splais] *vt.* (P6) **1** join (ropes, etc.) together by weaving the untwisted ends into each other. (두 밧줄 끝의 가닥을) 풀어 꼬아 잇다. **2** join (pieces of wood or metal) together by fastening in an overlapping position. (재목·금속·테이프 따위를) 겹쳐 잇다. ¶ *~ timbers* 재목을 잇다 / *~ a film* 〔*tape-recording*〕 필름을〔녹음 테이프를〕 잇다. **3** 《*colloq.*》 marry. …을 결혼시키다. — *n.* Ⓒ a union of ropes or pieces of wood, etc. made by splicing. 가닥을 꼬아 잇기; 겹쳐 잇기. [Du.]

splint [splint] *n.* Ⓒ **1** a piece of wood, metal, etc. for holding a broken bones etc. in the right position. (접골 치료용의) 부목(副木). **2** a thin strip of wood used to make a basket, a chair, etc. (바구니 따위를 엮을 때 쓰는) 얇은 나무 오리. **3** a fibula. 비골(腓骨)《종아리뼈》. [Du.]

splin·ter [splíntər] *n.* Ⓒ a thin, sharp piece of broken glass, wood, metal, etc.; a fragment. (나무·유리 따위의) 부서진〔쪼개진〕 조각; 파편. ¶ *a ~ of a bullet* 포탄의 파편 / *in* 〔*into*〕 *splinters* 산산조각으로 / *The floor was covered with splinters of glass.* 마루는 깨진 유리 조각으로 덮여 있었다 / *I got a ~ in my finger.* 손가락에 가시가 박혔다. — *vt., vi.* (P6;1) break (something) into splinters. 쪼개(지)다; 찢(어지)다. ¶ *A shot splintered the window.* 탄환이 유리창을 박살냈다. [↑]

splin·ter·bar [splíntərbɑ̀:r] *n.* a swingletree. (마차 따위의) 스프링을 받치는 가로장.

splin·ter·y [splíntəri] *adj.* **1** of or like a splinter. 부서진〔쪼개진〕 조각의〔같은〕; 파편의. **2** apt to break into splinters. 쪼개〔찢어〕지기 쉬운. **3** full of splinters; sharpedged. (가장자리 따위가) 톱니 모양의; 날이 날카로운. [*splinter*]

•**split** [split] *v.* (**split, split·ting**) *vt.* **1** (P6) break (something) from top to bottom; tear violently. …을 쪼개다; 찢다; 째다. ¶ *~ a stick into two* 막대기를 둘로 쪼개다 / *~ logs* 통나무를 쪼개다 / *~ a cake open and fill it with jam* 케이크를 쪼개 벌리고 그 안에 잼을 채우다. **2** (P6,7) cause (a group, a party, etc.) to separate; cause disagreement between; break the union of. …을 분열시키다; 이간시키다. ¶ *~ a party into three factions* 당을 세 파벌로 분열시키다 / *Such a proposal would ~ a class in two.* 그러한 제안은 클래스를 둘로 분열시킬 것이다. **3** (P6) divide (something) into parts; share. …을 나누다; 분배하다. ¶ *~ the cake with him* 〔*among ourselves*〕 그와〔우리끼리〕 케이크를 나누다 / *~ a farm into several plots* 한 농장을 여러 소구획으로 분할하다 / *~ a bottle of wine with someone* 아무와 한 병의 포도주를 나눠 마시다 / *~* (*up*) *the profits* 〔*job, cost*〕 이익〔일, 비용〕을 나누다.

— *vi.* **1** (P1,2A) be broken in parts; separate. 쪼개지다; 찢어지다; 갈라지다; 분열하다. ¶ *~ in half* 〔*two*〕 반으로〔둘로〕 쪼개지다 / *~ equal* 똑같이 나누다 / *The party ~ into two groups.* 당은 두 집단으로 분열되었다 / *Wood splits easily.* 나무는 쉽게 쪼개진다 / *The judges ~ on the decision.* 심사원은 그 결정에 대해 의견이 엇갈렸다. **2** (P1) ache violently. 심하게 아프다〔쑤시다〕. ¶ *My head is splitting.* 머리가 빠개지는 것처럼 아프다.

— *n.* Ⓒ **1** an act or a result of splitting. 쪼개〔갈라〕짐; 쪼갬; 쪼개진〔갈라진〕 틈〔금〕. ¶ *a ~ in a board* 판자의 갈라진 틈 / *mend a ~ in one's coat* 코트의 찢어진 곳을 수선하다. **2** a piece split off; a crack. 쪼개진 조각; 파편. **3** a special group in a party; a division; separation into parties; schism. 분파; 당파; 분열; 불화. ¶ *Do you belong to the ~?* 너는 그 당파에 소속되어 있느냐 / *the internal ~ on political ideology* 정치 이데올로기에 관한 내부의 불일치.

— *adj.* broken from top to bottom. 쪼개진; 갈라진. ¶ *a ~ opinion* 갈라진 의견. [Du.]

split infinitive [ˊ-ˊ--] *n.* 《gram.》 infinitive with an adverb inserted between to and the verb. 분리부정사.

split personality [ˊ-ˊ---] *n.* 《psych.》 a schizophrenic condition in which a person appears to have two or more irreconcilable characters. 이중〔다중〕 인격.

split·ting [splítiŋ] *adj.* (of a headache) very severe. 빠개지는 듯한; 심한. ¶ *a ~ headache* 심한 두통.

splodge [splɑdʒ / splɔdʒ] *n.* 《Brit.》 ｢=splotch.

splotch [splɑtʃ / splɔtʃ] *n.* Ⓒ a large, irregular spot; a dirty mark. 반점; 얼룩; 오점. — *vt.* (P6) make splotches on. 오점을 내다; 얼룩지게 하다. [*spot,* blotch]

splurge [splə:rdʒ] *n.* 《*colloq.*》 a noisy display. 과시. — *vi.* (P1) show off. 과시하다. [Imit.]

splut·ter [splʌ́tər] *vi.* (P1,2A) **1** speak in a hasty, confused way; sputter. 빠르

게 중얼중얼 지껄이다. ¶ *He often splutters when excited.* 그는 흥분하면 종종 말을 빠르게 지껄인다. **2** make hissing or spitting sounds; throw off small particles or bits with spitting sounds (as an oyster frying in oil). 탁탁〔쉬쉬, 지글지글〕 소리를 내다. — *vt.* (P7) say (something) in a spluttering manner. …을 빠르게 중얼거리다. — *n.* a spluttering sound; a confused talk. 탁탁〔쉬쉬, 지글지글〕하는 소리; 중얼중얼 거림. [Imit.]

:spoil [spɔil] *v.* (**spoiled** or **spoilt**) *vt.* (P6) **1** make (something) bad and useless; destroy; damage. …을 못 쓰게 만들다; 망쳐놓다; 손상하다. ¶ *a watch spoilt by the dampness* 습기 때문에 못 쓰게 된 시계 / *A spot of ink spoiled her clothes.* 잉크의 반점은 그녀의 옷을 망쳐 놓았다 / *The rain has spoilt the fresh paint.* 비는 갓 칠한 페인트를 망가뜨렸다 / *She spoiled three sheets of paper to write a letter.* 그녀는 편지 한 장을 쓰기 위해 석장의 종이를 못 쓰게 만들었다 / *~ eggs* 달걀을 (오래 보관하여) 못 먹게 만들다〔곯게 하다〕 / *~ one's appetite* (식전에 무엇을 먹든지 해서) 식욕을 떨어뜨리다. **2** make (something) less valuable, interesting, etc. …의 가치를 떨어뜨리다; …의 흥미를 깨다. ¶ *The rain spoiled the picnic.* 비로 인해 소풍이 엉망이 되었다 / *The sad news spoiled my dinner* [*sleep*]. 슬픈 소식은 밥맛을 가시게 했다〔잠을 제대로 못 이루게 했다〕 / *~ someone's pleasure* 아무의 흥을 깨다. **3** cause (someone) to be lazy or weak in his character by too much kindness. …을 성격적으로 나쁘게 만들다; (아이)를 버릇 없게 기르다. ¶ 《*prov.*》 *Spare the rod and ~ the child.* 매를 아끼면 아이를 버린다《귀한 자식은 엄하게 기르라》 / *~ someone with praise* 아무를 칭찬하여 우쭐거리게 하다. **4** 《*arch.*》 deprive by force; rob. …을 강탈〔약탈〕하다. — *vi.* (P1) become useless; decay; rot. 못 쓰게 되다; 썩다. ¶ *Meat easily spoils if not kept cold.* 고기는 냉동해서 보관하지 않으면 쉬 상한다.

be spoiling for (***a fight***), be eager for (a fight). 싸움을 하고 싶어 못 견디다.

spoil the Egyptians, make profit of one's enemies without scruple. 적의 물건을 가차없이 빼앗다.

— *n.* Ⓤ **1** 《often *pl.*》 a thing which is taken from other by violence; stolen goods. 약탈품; 전리품; 훔친 물건. ¶ *the spoils of war* 전리품 / *The thieves escaped with their spoils.* 도둑들은 그들이 훔친 물건들을 가지고 도망쳤다. **2** 《usu. *pl.*》 profits got by means of one's political power; 《U.S.》 public offices given to the supporters of a political party. 직책으로 인한 이득〔이권〕; (정권을 잡은 정당이 정치적 권리로서 지지자들에게 주는) 관직. ¶ 《U.S.》 *spoils system* 엽관 제도. [L. *spolium*]

spoil·er [spɔ́ilər] *n.* a plunderer. 약탈자.

spoil-sport [spɔ́ilspɔ̀ːrt] *n.* one who spoils sport. 즐거움을 방해하는 사람.

spoilt [spɔilt] *v.* p. and pp. of **spoil.**

spoke[1] [spouk] *n.* Ⓒ **1** one of the bars extending from the center of a wheel to the rim. (수레바퀴의) 살; 스포크. **2** a stick or bar to stop the wheels from turning. 자동차의 바퀴멈춤대. **3** a step of a ladder. 사다리의 디딤대. **4** 《naut.》 one of the handles sticking out from the rim of a steering-wheel. (조타륜(操舵輪) 둘레의) 손잡이. [E.]

put a spoke in someone's wheel, obstruct someone's designs. 아무의 계획을 방해하다.

:spoke[2] [spouk] *v.* p. of **speak.**

:spo·ken [spóukən] *v.* pp. of **speak.**
— *adj.* **1** oral; told. 구두(口頭)의. ¶ *a ~ message* 구두(口頭) 전언 / *the ~ language* 구어; 음성 언어 / *in ~ English* 구어 영어에서(는)(opp. written). **2** speaking in a certain way. 말솜씨가 …한. ¶ *smooth-spoken* 말을 잘 하는. [*speak*]

spokes·man [spóuksmən] *n.* Ⓒ (*pl.* **-men** [-mən]) a person who speaks for others; a representative. 대변인; 대표자. ¶ *act as ~ for the family* 가족의 대변인 노릇을 하다 / *the ~ of the factory workers* 공장 근로자의 대변인〔대표자〕.

spo·li·a·tion [spòuliéiʃən] *n.* Ⓤ **1** robbery of neutral ships at sea in wartime. (전시에, 교전국의 중립국 선박에 대한) 약탈. **2** extortion. 강탈. **3** 《law》 destruction of document to prevent its being used as evidence. 문서 파기. [→spoil]

spon·dee [spɑ́ndiː / spɔ́n-] *n.* Ⓒ 《*poet.*》 a metrical foot consisting of two long syllables. 강강격(強強格)《스스》. [Gk.]

·sponge [spʌndʒ] *n.* **1** Ⓒ a kind of sea animal having a soft, yellow, fiberlike skeleton; ⓊⒸ (a piece of) its light skeleton used for washing and cleaning. 해면동물; 해면. **2** ⓊⒸ something like this soft skeleton. 해면 모양의 것. **3** Ⓒ 《*colloq.*》 a person who lives at the expense of others. 기식자; 식객. **4** 《*colloq.*》 a drunkard. 술고래.

have a sponge down, take a bath with sponge. 스펀지로 몸을 닦다.

pass the sponge over, agree to forget (offences). …을 깨끗이 잊다.

throw [***chuck***] ***up the sponge,*** (of boxers) throw it into the air as a token of defeat; admit defeat. 패배를 인정하다.

— *vt.* wipe or absorb (something) with a sponge; wipe out with a sponge; remove. …을 해면으로 닦다〔빨아들이다〕; (해면으로) 닦아내다; 지우다. ¶ *~ down dust* 먼지를 해면으로 닦다 / *~ one's body* 해면으로 몸을 닦다 / *~ out a stain* 얼룩을 해면으로 지우다 / *~ up water* 해면으로 물을 빨아들이다 / *~ away the blood* 피를 스펀지로 닦아내다.
— *vi.* (P1,3) **1** gather sponges. 해면을 채집하다. **2** 《*on, upon*》 live at the expense of others. 기식(寄食)하다; …의 식객이

되다; (돈 따위를) 우려내다. ¶ ~ *on someone for money* 아무에게서 돈을 우려내다 / *He sponges on his brother.* 그는 그의 형〔동생〕의 식객이다 / ~ *off one's family* 가족의 신세를 지다. **3** be absorbent. (액체를) 흡수하다. ¶ *This cloth sponges well.* 이 천은 흡수를 잘 한다. [Gk.]

sponge cake [ˊ ˋ] *n.* a soft, light cake made of flour, sugar, eggs, etc. 스펀지 케이크; 카스텔라.

sponge-cu·cum·ber [spʌ́ndʒkjù:kəmbər], **-gourd** [-gùərd] *n.* 《bot.》 a kind of gourd used in Turkish baths as a towel. 수세미외.

spong·er [spʌ́ndʒər] *n.* Ⓒ **1** a person or ship that gathers sponges. 해면 채집선(船)〔자〕. **2** 《*colloq.*》 a person who lives at the expense of others. 기식자(寄食者); 식객.

spong·ing-house [spʌ́ndʒiŋhàus] *n.* 《Brit. hist.》 a bailiff's house for a temporary lodging of an arrested debtor. 채무자 구류소.

spon·gy [spʌ́ndʒi] *adj.* (**-gi·er, -gi·est**) **1** of or like a sponge. 해면 모양의; 해면질의. **2** hard and full of holes. 작은 구멍이 많고 단단한. ¶ *a* ~ *rock* 다공성(多孔性)의 암석.

spon·son [spɑ́nsən / spɔ́n-] *n.* 《naut.》 a platform projecting from a ship's side. 뱃전 밖으로 쑥 내민 부분《포좌(砲座) 따위를 설치함》. [*expansion*]

spon·sor [spɑ́nsər / spɔ́n-] *n.* Ⓒ **1** 《*for*》 a person who is responsible for another. 보증인. **2** a person who answers for a child at his baptism; a godparent. 대부모(代父母). ¶ *stand* ~ *to someone* …의 대부모가 되다. **3** a promoter; a person who supports another. 발기인; 후원자. ¶ *the* ~ *of a law* 법률의 기초자. **4** a person, a company, etc. that pays the cost of radio or television programs as an advertisement. 광고주; 스폰서.
— *vt.* (P6) act as sponsor for (something). …을 보증하다; 후원하다; …의 스폰서가 되다. ¶ ~ *a television program* 텔레비전 프로를 제공하다. [L. *spondeo* pledge]

spon·so·ri·al [spɑnsɔ́:riəl / spɔn-] *adj.* of a sponsor. 보증인〔후원자〕의.

spon·sor·ship [spɑ́nsərʃìp / spɔ́n-] *n.* being a sponsor. 대부모(代父母)〔보증인·후원자〕임; 후원; 발기.

spon·ta·ne·i·ty [spɑ̀ntəní:əti / spɔ̀n-] *n.* Ⓤ the state or quality of being spontaneous; a spontaneous nature. 자발성; 자연 발생. [↓]

spon·ta·ne·ous [spɑntéiniəs / spɔn-] *adj.* happening naturally; arising from a natural impulse; not planned; self acting; natural. 자발적인; 무의식적인; 자연의. ¶ *a* ~ *action* 〔*remark, offer*〕 자발적인 행동〔말, 제안〕 / *a* ~ *burst of applause* 뜻밖에 갑자기 터져나온 박수 갈채 / *a* ~ *expression of joy* 〔*admiration*〕 저절로 터져나온 기쁨〔칭찬〕의 목소리〔말〕 / *a* ~ *thought* 〔*feeling*〕 자연히 떠오르는 사상〔감정〕 / ~ *movement* 무의식적인 동작; 자동성의 운동 / *a* ~ *growth of wood* 자연 발생의 숲. [L. *sponte* of one's own accord]

spontaneous combustion [ˊ—ˊ— —ˊ—] *n.* fire which begins of itself. 자연발화.

spon·ta·ne·ous·ly [spɑntéiniəsli / spɔn-] *adv.* in a spontaneous manner; naturally. 자발적으로; 자연히. ¶ *act* ~ 자발적으로 행동하다.

spoof [spu:f] *n.* ⓊⒸ 《*colloq.*》 a mischievous trick or joke. 장난으로 속이기. — *vt.* (P6) trick jokingly. …을 (장난으로) 속이다. [fancy word]

spook [spu:k] *n.* Ⓒ 《*colloq.*》 a ghost. 유령. [Du.]

spook·y [spú:ki] *adj.* (**spook·i·er, spook·i·est**) 《*colloq.*》 of, like, or suggesting the presence of a spook or spooks; ghostly; haunted. 유령 같은; 유령이 나올 것 같은.

spool [spu:l] *n.* Ⓒ a hollow reel of wood or metal on which thread, wire, tape, etc. is wound. 실패; (테이프·전선 따위를 감는) 릴; 감개. — *vt.* (P6) wind (thread, wire, etc.) on a spool. …을 실패〔릴(reel)〕에 감다. [Teut.]

:spoon [spu:n] *n.* Ⓒ **1** a small, shallow bowl with a long handle, used in lifting, serving or eating food. 숟가락. **2** something like a spoon in its shape. 숟가락 모양의 것. **3** a simpleton. 바보. **4** a silly fond lover. 바람둥이.

be born with a silver spoon in one's mouth, be born rich. 부유한 집안에 태어나다.
— *vt.* (P6,7) take up (something) with a spoon. …을 숟가락으로 떠내다〔푸다〕. ¶ ~ *up soup* 수프를 숟가락으로 뜨다.
— *vi.* (P1) 《*colloq.*》 make love; behave amorously. 애무하다. [E.]

spoon-bill [spú:nbìl] *n.* any of various wading birds with a spoon-shaped bill. 노랑부리저어새.

spoon·drift [spú:ndrìft] *n.* =spindrift.

spoon-fed [spú:nfèd] *adj.* **1** (of a child, a patient, etc.) fed with a spoon. 숟가락으로 떠먹이는. **2** given too much care or protection. 지나치게 보호를 받는; 과보호의.

spoon·ful [spú:nfùl] *n.* Ⓒ the amount that a spoon can hold. 한 숟갈 가득(한 양). ¶ *two spoonfuls of sugar* 두 숟갈 가득한 양의 설탕.

spoon-meat [spú:nmì:t] *n.* soft or liquid food, esp. baby's food. (특히 어린애용의) 유동식(流動食).

spoon·y [spú:ni] *adj.* (**spoon·i·er, spoon·i·est**) 《*colloq.*》 foolish; silly; foolishly in love; amorous. 어리석은; 바보 같은; 정에 여린; 여자에게 무른.

spoor [spuər] *n.* the track or footprints of a wild animal; an animal's scent. (야수의) 자취; 발자국; 취적(臭跡). ¶ *follow a* ~ 야수의 뒤를 밟다. — *vt., vi.* (P6;1) track.

자귀 짚다; 뒤를 밟다. [Du.]

spo·rad·ic [spərǽdik] *adj.* **1** happening occasionally; seen apart or widely separated from others. 때때로〔간헐적으로〕 일어나는; 산재하는. ¶ *~ outbreak of riot* 산발적인 폭동 / *a ~ growth of fern* 양치류가 드문드문 산재해서 자라고 있는 일. **2** (of a disease) appearing or occurring in single cases. (병 따위가) 산발성의. ¶ *a ~ case of cholera* 〔*a disease*〕 콜레라〔질병〕의 산발예(散發例). [Gk. *speirō* sow]

spo·rad·i·cal·ly [spərǽdikəli] *adv.* in a sporadic manner; separately. 산발적으로; 이따금.

spore [spɔːr] *n.* Ⓒ a very small cell that grows into a new plant or animal. (식물의) 포자(胞子); 아포(芽胞); 생식 세포(生殖細胞). [Gk. *sporá* seed]

:**sport** [spɔːrt] *n.* Ⓒ **1** a form of game or way of playing, esp. outdoor. 스포츠; 운동. ¶ *athletic sports* 운동 경기 / *take part in a ~* 운동을 하다 / *Baseball is a favorite ~ for those boys.* 야구는 소년들이 좋아하는 운동이다. **2** 《*pl.*》 a meeting for athletic contests. 운동회; 경기회. ¶ *hold the school sports* 운동회를 개최하다 / *intercollegiate sports* 대학간(間)의 운동 경기. **3** Ⓤ fun; amusement. 오락; 농담. ¶ *It is great ~ to drive.* 자동차 운전은 매우 재미있는 오락이다 / *The children thought it was great ~ to pretend to be asleep.* 아이들은 잠든 체하는 것을 매우 재미있는 일로 생각하였다 / *a ~ of terms* 신소리. **4** a thing played with; the object of a joke; a plaything. 장난〔놀림〕감; 웃음거리. ¶ *be the ~ of circumstances* 환경에 농락당하다 / *The ship was the ~ of the wind.* 배는 작은 장난감처럼 바람에 이리저리 까불림을 당했다. **5** 《biol.》 an animal or a plant that shows a sudden variation from the normal type. 돌연 변이. **6** 《*colloq.*》 a sportsman. 운동가. ¶ *a good* 〔*bad*〕 *~* 훌륭한〔나쁜〕 스포츠맨. **7** 《*colloq.*》 a gambler. 노름꾼. **8** 《U.S. *colloq.*》 a gay, showy, good-humored person. 멋쟁이; 바람둥이.

in 〔***for***〕 ***sport,*** as a joke. 농담으로. ¶ *He said* 〔*did*〕 *it in ~.* 그는 그것을 농담으로 말했다.

make sport of (=*laugh at*) *something* or *someone.* …를 놀리다〔조롱하다〕.

— *adj.* 《often *~s*》 **1** suitable for outdoor or informal wear. (옷 따위가) 야외용의; 평상시에 스포티하게 입을 수 있는. ¶ *a sport(s) coat* 〔*shirt*〕 평시에 스포티하게 입을 수 있는 코트〔셔츠〕. **2** of or for sports. 스포츠용의. ¶ *a sports car* 스포츠 카.

— *vi.* **1** (P1,2A) engage in a sport. 운동을 하다. **2** (P1,3) play; make a joke or jest. 놀다; 장난치다; 농하다. ¶ *The little cat sported with its tail.* 새끼 고양이는 자기 꼬리를 가지고 놀았다. **3** become suddenly different from the normal type. 돌연 변이를 일으키다.

— *vt.* (P6,7) show off; display. …을 과시하다; 자랑해 보이다. ¶ *~ a fur coat* 모피 코트를 자랑해 보이다. [→disport]

sport one's oak, 《Brit.》 (of a university student) fasten one's outer door. 바깥문을 잠그고 면회를 사절하다.

sport·ing [spɔ́ːrtiŋ] *adj.* **1** of or interested in sports. 스포츠〔운동 경기〕의; 스포츠〔운동 경기〕를 좋아하는. ¶ *a ~ magazine* 스포츠 잡지 / *~ goods* 운동 용품 / *a ~ coat* 운동복 / *a ~ man* 운동가. **2** having the characteristics of a sportsman; fair. 운동가다운; 정정 당당한. ¶ *~ conduct* 훌륭한〔정정 당당한〕 행위 / *~ spirit* 〔*manner*〕 운동가다운 정신〔태도〕. **3** interested in gambling; willing to take risks. 도박적(賭博的)인; 모험적인. ¶ *a ~ chance* 승산이 반반인 기회; 모험 / *a ~ thing to do* 위험한〔모험적인〕 일.

spor·tive [spɔ́ːrtiv] *adj.* playful; merry. 놀기 좋아하는; 명랑한. ¶ *The old man was as ~ as a young boy.* 그 노인은 어린 소년처럼 명랑하셨다.

spor·tive·ly [spɔ́ːrtivli] *adv.* playfully; merrily. 신명나게 까불며; 명랑하게.

sports [spɔːrts] *adj.* of sport or sports. 스포츠의; 운동의. ¶ *~ clothes* 운동복 / *~ shoes* 운동화 / *a ~ fan* 스포츠 팬.

:**sports·man** [spɔ́ːrtsmən] *n.* Ⓒ (*pl.* **-men** [-mən]) **1** a person who takes part in sports. 스포츠맨; 운동가. **2** a person who plays fair and does not complain even if he loses. 스포츠맨다운 사람; (운동가답게) 정정당당히 행동하는 사람.

sports·man·like [spɔ́ːrtsmənlàik] *adj.* like a sportsman. 스포츠맨〔운동가〕다운; 정정당당한.

sports·man·ship [spɔ́ːrtsmənʃip] *n.* Ⓤ **1** qualities and behavior of a sportsman; fair play. 운동(가) 정신; 정정 당당한 (경기) 태도. **2** skill in sports. 운동 경기의 기량.

sports·wom·an [spɔ́ːrtswùmən] *n.* Ⓒ (*pl.* **-wom·en** [-wìmin]) a woman who takes part in sports. 여자 운동가.

sport·y [spɔ́ːrti] *adj.* (**sport·i·er, sport·i·est**) 《*colloq.*》 **1** sportsmanlike. 운동가다운. **2** smart, gay and showy in dress, appearance, manner, etc. (복장 따위가) 화려한; 야한; (태도·외양(外樣) 따위가) 경쾌한; 발랄한. ● **sport·i·ness** [-nis] *n.*

:**spot** [spɑt / spɔt] *n.* Ⓒ **1** a dirty mark; a stain; a small 〔round〕 mark, differing in color, etc. from the rest. 얼룩(점); 더러운 점; 반점. ¶ *a ~ of ink* 잉크의 얼룩(점) / *a ~ on the sun* 태양의 흑점 / *His tie is red with white spots.* 그는 붉은 바탕에 흰 얼룩 무늬가 있는 넥타이를 하고 있다 / *a black dog with white spots* 바둑이. **2** a moral stain on a good character, reputation or name. (도덕상의) 오점; 결점; (인격상의) 흠. ¶ *a ~ on one's character* 〔*reputation, honor*〕 인격〔명성, 명예〕의 오점 / *His character is without a ~.* 그의 인격에는 한 점의 흠도 없다. **3** a place; a location. 지점; 장소; 현장. ¶ *a* *convenient* 〔*dangerous*〕 ~ 편리한〔위험한〕 지점 / *the* (*very*) ~ *where the accident took place* 사고(事故)가 일어난 (바로) 그 장소 / *I found a nice* ~ *to play.* 놀기에 아주 좋은 장소를 발견했다. **4** 《Brit. *colloq.*》《*of*》 a small amount. 소량; 조금. ¶ *a* ~ *of leave* 〔*rest*〕 아주 잠시 동안의 휴가〔휴식〕 / *a* ~ *of whisky* 한 잔의 위스키 / *How about a* ~ *of lunch?* 간단하게 점심 식사하지 않겠나. **5** a spotlight. 스포트라이트. **6** 《*colloq.*》 a spot advertisement or announcement. (프로와 프로 사이의) 짧은 삽입 (광고) 방송.

hit the high spots, 《*colloq.*》 mention only the main points of a topic being reported or discussed. (보고·토의된 논제의) 중요한 점만 언급하다.

hit the spot, 《*colloq.*》 please; satisfy; be satisfactory. (음식물 따위가) 더할 나위 없다; 만족스럽다. ¶ *This drink exactly hits the spot.* 이 음료는 아주 더할 나위 없다.

in a spot, 《*sl.*》 in trouble; in a difficult situation. 곤란하여; 어려운 입장에 처하여. ¶ *be in a bad* 〔*tight*〕 ~ 매우 곤란〔위험〕한 처지에 있다.

knock the spots off 〔***out of***〕***,*** defeat. …을 완패시키다.

on the spot, **a**) at once; immediately. 즉석에서. ¶ *decide on the* ~ 즉석에서 결정하다 / *He was killed on the* ~. 그는 즉시 살해되었다. **b**) at the very place; there. 현장에서. ¶ *the people on the* ~ 현장에 있는〔있던〕 사람들 / *The doctor was on the* ~ *a few minutes later.* 의사는 수 분 후에 현장에 도착해 있었다. **c**) 《*sl.*》 =in a spot.

price on the spot, a price for spot cash. 현금 판매 가격.

— *v.* (**spot·ted, spot·ting**) *vt.* (P6,13) **1** make spots on (something); stain. …에 반점〔오점〕을 찍다; …을 더럽히다〔얼룩지게 하다〕. ¶ ~ *a dress* 옷을 더럽히다 / ~ *the wall with green paint* 녹색 페인트로 벽을 얼룩덜룩하게 하다 / ~ *one's fingers with ink* 손가락을 잉크로 더럽히다. **2** stain (one's character or reputation); injure. (명성 따위)를 더럽히다; …을 손상시키다. ¶ ~ *someone's character* 〔*reputation*〕 아무의 인격〔명성〕에 상처를 내다. **3** see; recognize; discover (an exact position). …을 찾아내다; 발견하다; 인정하다; 간파하다; (소재)를 알아내다. ¶ ~ *a friend in a crowd* 군중 속에서 친구를 찾아내다 / ~ *the cause of the trouble* 분쟁의 원인을 찾아내다 / *I spotted him at once for* 〔*as*〕 *an American.* 나는 그가 미국인이라는 것을 곧 간파했다. **4** place (someone or something) in a certain spot. …을 (어느 위치에) 두다; 배치하다. ¶ *Guards were spotted along the shore.* 해변을 따라 보초가 배치되어 있었다.

— *vi.* (P1) become spotted; make a spot. 더럽혀지다; 얼룩〔오점〕이 생기다. ¶ *fabrics which* ~ *readily* 더럽혀지기 쉬운 직물류.

— *adj.* **1** paid or delivered at once; on hand; ready. 현금 지불의; 즉석의. ¶ *a* ~ *answer* 즉답 / ~ *questions* 임의 선택의 질문 / ~ *cash* 맞돈 / *a* ~ *sale* 현금 판매 / ~ *delivery* 현장 인도(引渡) / *a* ~ *transaction* 현금 거래 / ~ *goods* 현물. **2** (of advertisements or announcements) made between regular radio or television programs. (광고 따위가) 정규 프로 사이에 삽입된. [E.]

spot·less [spátlis / spɔ́t-] *adj.* having no spot; without a spot or stain; perfectly clean; pure. 오점이 없는; 무구(無垢)의; 청정한. ¶ *a* ~ *white apron* 순백의 앞치마 / *a* ~ *mind* 깨끗한〔결백한〕 마음 / *a* ~ *reputation* 더럽혀지지 않은 명성.

spot·light [spátlàit / spɔ́t-] *n.* Ⓒ **1** a strong beam of light focused upon a person or thing on the stage. (무대에 투사되는) 스포트라이트. **2** public attention. 세인의 주시〔주목〕. ¶ *be in the* ~ 세인의 주시를〔주목을〕 받고 있다.

spot·ted [spátid / spɔ́t-] *adj.* **1** marked or covered with spots. 얼룩진; 얼룩덜룩한; 반점이 있는. ¶ *a* ~ *dog* 반점이 있는 개《바둑이》. **2** stained. 더럽혀진.

spotted fever [⌐– ⌐–] *n.* **1** cerebrospinal meningitis. 뇌척수막염. **2** any of various febrile diseases accompanied by skin eruptions. 발진 티푸스.

spot·ty [spáti / spɔ́ti] *adj.* (**-ti·er, -ti·est**) **1** having spots; spotted. 반점〔얼룩〕이 있는. **2** irregular or uneven in quality. 한결같지 않은. ¶ *a* ~ *piece of work* (내용이) 한결같지 않은 작품 / ~ *attendance* (나왔다 안 나왔다 하는) 한결같지 않은 출석 (상태). **3** pimply. 여드름이 난〔여드름투성이의〕.

spous·al [spáuzəl] *n.* 《*arch.*》《often *pl.*》 marriage. 결혼(식). — *adj.* nuptial. 결혼(식)의. [↓]

spouse [spaus, spauz] *n.* Ⓒ a partner in marriage; a husband or wife. 배우자. ¶ *meet one's beloved* ~ 사랑하는 배우자를 만나다. [→sponsor]

spout [spaut] *vt.* (P6,7) **1** throw out (a liquid) in a jet or stream with force. (액체 따위)를 내뿜다; 분출시키다. ¶ *A whale* 〔*fountain*〕 *spouts water* (*into the air*). 고래〔분수〕는 물을 (하늘로) 내뿜는다 / *The chimney spouted smoke.* 연통은 연기를 내뿜었다. **2** 《*colloq.*》 say (something) in a self-important way; utter in declamatory manner. …을 도도히〔막힘 없이〕 말하다; (말)을 줄줄 퍼붓다; 낭독하다. ¶ ~ *one's own verses* 자작시를 줄줄 읊다 / *Don't* ~ *off big talk.* 호언 장담을 늘어놓지 마라.

— *vi.* (P1,2A) **1** 《*from, out of*》 come out in a jet or stream. 분출하다; 뿜어 나오다. ¶ *A fountain spouts.* 샘이 분출한다 / *Blood spouted from the wound.* 피가 상처에서 뿜어 나왔다. **2** speak in a self-important manner; speak long or loudly. 막힘〔거침〕 없이 말하다; 입심좋게 지껄여대다. ¶ *He is too fond of spouting.* 그는 지나칠 정도로 지껄이기를 좋아한다.

— *n.* Ⓒ **1** a projecting tube, nozzle, pipe, etc. through which a liquid flows out. (주전자 따위의) 주둥이; 물꼭지. ¶ *the ~ of a teapot* 〔*pump*〕 찻주전자〔펌프〕의 주둥이. **2** a stream or jet of liquid. 분수; 분출. **3** a pipe for carrying off water from a roof. (물받이) 홈통. **4** a blow-hole of a whale. (고래의) 분수공(孔). **5** a water-spout. 바다 회오리. **6** a shoot. 급류. **7** 《Brit. *sl.*》 a pawnbroker's shop. 전당포. [E.]

up the spout, **a**) 《*sl.*》 in pawn. 전당 잡혀. **b**) 《*colloq.*》 hard up; in trouble. 곤경에 빠져.

sprain [sprein] *vt.* (P6) injure (a joint or muscle) by a sudden twist. (근육·관절 따위)를 삐다; 접질리다. ¶ *~ one's ankle* 발목을 삐다. — *n.* Ⓒ an injury to a muscle or joint caused by a bad twist or wrench. 삠; 접질림; 염좌(捻挫). [L. *exprimo* extort]

:sprang [spræŋ] *v.* p. of **spring.**

sprat [spræt] *n.* (*pl.* **sprats** or *collectively* **sprat**) **1** 《fish》 a small European herringlike fish. 청어속(屬)의 작은 물고기. **2** 《*joc., contempt.*》 a small or inconsequential person or thing. 꼬마; 하찮은 놈〔것〕. [E.]

***set* 〔*throw*〕 *a sprat to catch a herring* 〔*a whale*〕,** offer something small so as to get something big. 새우로 대어를 낚다《대리(大利)를 얻기 위해 소리(小利)를 버리다》. [E.]

sprawl [sprɔːl] *vi.* (P1,2A) **1** lie or sit with the limbs spread out. (큰대자로) 드러눕다; 팔다리를 쭉 뻗다. ¶ *~ on the bed* 침대 위에 큰대자로 드러눕다. **2** crawl along. (엎드려) 기어가다. ¶ *go sprawling* 엎드려 기어가다 / *Two figures sprawled out.* 두 사람이 기어 나왔다. **3** (P3) (of writing, plant, town, etc.) spread out irregularly. 불규칙하게 퍼지다; 마구 뻗다. ¶ *The city sprawls without plan.* 도시는 무계획적으로 마구 뻗어나가고 있다. — *vt.* (P6) spread out (something) in an ungraceful manner. …을 큰대자로〔보기 흉하게〕 뻗다〔뻗게 하다〕. ¶ *be sprawled dead* (축) 늘어지다.

send someone sprawling, knock someone down. 때려 눕히다.

— *n.* Ⓤ the act of sprawling. 큰대자로 드러눕기; 허우적거림. ¶ *lie in a ~* 큰대자로 드러눕다. [E.]

•spray[1] [sprei] *n.* **1** ⓐ Ⓤ fine waterdrops going through the air. 물보라; 물안개. ¶ *the ~ of a water fall* 폭포의 물안개 / *wet with the ~ of the sea* 바다의 물보라에 의해 젖다. ⓑ Ⓒ a quantity of small objects flying through the air. 공중에 빗발 치는 것. ¶ *a ~ of bullets* 빗발 치는 탄환; 탄우(彈雨). **2** ⓊⒸ a liquid, esp. a medicine, used in a spray machine. (향수·소독약 등의) 분무액; 스프레이. **3** Ⓒ an instrument for scattering fine waterdrops or vapor. 분무기. ¶ *a perfume ~* 향수 분무기.

— *vt.* (P6) **1** apply fine drops of liquid to (something); shoot out liquid in a spray. …에 물보라를 일으키다; …에 (액을) 분무하다〔뿌리다〕. ¶ *~ mosquitoes with insecticide* 모기에게 살충제를 뿌리다 / *~ an insecticide on apple-trees* 사과나무에 살충제를 분무하다. **2** scatter (a liquid) in fine drops. …을 안개 모양으로 하여 분무시키다〔뿜다〕. ¶ *~ a sore throat* 아픈 목에 스프레이를 뿜다. — *vi.* form spray. 물보라가 일다〔되다〕. [E.]

spray[2] [sprei] *n.* Ⓒ **1** a small branch or piece of a plant with its leaves, flowers or berries. (잎·꽃·열매 따위가 붙어 있는) 작은 가지. **2** an ornament like this. 작은 가지 모양의 무늬〔장식〕. [E.]

:spread [spred] *v.* (**spread**) *vt.* **1** (P6,13) 《*on, with*》 cover the surface of (something) with a thin substance; put (a thin substance) so as to cover. …의 표면에 얇게 바르다〔칠하다〕; …을 —으로 덮다. ¶ *~ butter on toast = ~ toast with butter* 토스트에 버터를 바르다 / *~ paint evenly on a floor board* 마루에 페인트를 고르게 칠하다 / *~ varnish on the exposed part* 노출된 부분에 니스를 칠하다. **2** (P6,7,13) 《*with, on, out*》 open (something rolled or folded); open out; extend or stretch (the limbs, etc.). (감은 것·접힌 것 따위)를 펴다; 펼치다; 늘리다; (손가락·팔 따위를) 벌리다; 뻗다. ¶ *~ a tablecloth on the table = ~ the table with a tablecloth* 식탁에 식탁보를 깔다 / *~ out one's arms* 팔을 벌리다; 팔을 뻗고 두 손을 벌리다 / *the view ~ out before us* 우리들 눈앞에 펼쳐진 경치 / *~ out a map* 지도를 펼치다 / *The eagle ~ its wings.* 독수리는 날개를 폈다 / *She ~ the wet blanket to dry.* 그녀는 젖은 담요를 말리기 위해 널어놓았다. **3** (P6) make (news, etc.) widely known to many people; communicate; extend (something) in all directions; scatter. (뉴스·질병 따위)를 퍼뜨리다; 보급시키다; 발산하다. ¶ *~ a disease* 병을 퍼뜨리다 / *~ knowledge* 지식을 보급하다 / *roses spreading their fragrance* 향기를 풍기고 있는 장미꽃들 / *~ news* 뉴스를 퍼뜨리다 **4** (P6,13) 《*on, with*》 set (a table, etc.) for a meal. (식탁)을 준비하다〔차리다〕; (요리)를 차려놓다. ¶ *~ the table* (*with dishes*) *= ~ dishes on the table* 식탁에 요리를 차려놓다. **5** 《*on*》 record (in full). …을 (자세히) 기록하다.

— *vi.* (P1,2A,3) **1** extend over an area; expand. (공간적으로) 퍼지다; 펼쳐지다; 멀리 미치다; 전개되다. ¶ *The desert spreads for miles and miles.* 사막은 몇 마일이고 광활하게 전개되어 있다 / *The floods have ~ over the valley.* 홍수는 유역 전체로 널리 퍼졌다 / *The farm spreads out like an open fan.* 농장은 부채처럼 넓게 펼쳐져 있다. **2** (of news, disease, etc.) become widely known, suffered, etc.; go in all directions; scatter. (뉴스·질병 따위가) 퍼지다; 만연하다; 흩어지다. ¶ *The disease is spreading.* 질병이 만연되고 있다 / *The story ~ all over the* *country.* 그 이야기는 전국으로 퍼져 나간다 / *Buddhism has ~ over the countries of the East.* 불교(佛敎)는 동양 여러 나라에 퍼져 있다 / *Rumors ~ quickly.* 소문은 빨리 퍼진다. **3** be placed as a thin substance. 얇게 늘어나다[퍼지다]. ¶ *~ like butter* 버터처럼 얇게 퍼진다. **4** extend in time. (시간적으로) 걸치다; 계속되다. ¶ *The course of study spreads over three years.* 그 연구 과정은 3년간에 걸친다 / *The lectures ~ over into the second semester.* 그 강의는 2학기까지 이어지고 있다.

spread oneself, 《*colloq.*》 talk bumptiously. 허풍떨다; 자랑하다.

spread oneself thin, try to do too many things at once. 한번에 너무 많이 하려고 하다.

spread to, be circulated to. …에 전해지다.

— *n.* Ⓒ **1** the act of spreading; growth; expansion. 퍼짐; 펼침; 보급; 분포. ¶ *the ~ of the city* 도시의 확장 / *the ~ of education* 교육의 보급 / *the ~ of cancer* 암의 전이(轉移) / *the alarming ~ of the floods* 놀랄만한 홍수의 확산(擴散) / *the ~ of rumor* [*scientific knowledge*] 소문의 퍼짐[과학 지식의 보급] / *a wide ~ of country* 넓게 전개된 전원 지방. **2** width; extent. 범위; 넓이. ¶ *measure the ~ of the branches* [*wings*] 가지[날개]의 벌어진 넓이를 재다 / *The sail has a ~ of 60 feet.* 돛의 폭은 60피트다. **3** a cloth covering for a bed, table, etc. 식탁보; 침대 시트. **4** 《*colloq.*》 a meal; a feast. 요리; 잔치; 연회. ¶ *give someone a regular ~* 아무에게 멋진 성찬을 베풀다 / *What a ~!* 대단한 성찬이군. **5** 《U.S.》 a soft food for spreading on bread, etc. such as jam. 빵에 바르는 것《버터·잼 따위》. [E.]

spread eagle [ㅅ ㅅ] *n.* the figure of an eagle with the legs and wings spread. 날개를 편 독수리《미국의 문장(紋章)》.

spread·er [sprédər] *n.* **1** one who spreads. 퍼뜨리는 사람; 전파자. ¶ *a ~ of bad news* 나쁜 소식의 전파자. **2** a thing that spreads(e.g. a butter knife). 퍼뜨리는 것; 버터 바르는 나이프.

spree [spri:] *n.* Ⓒ **1** merry-making; a gay time. 흥청거림; 법석댐. ¶ *have a ~* 법석대다 / *a spending* [*shopping*] *~* (충동적으로) 낭비하며[물건을 마구 사며] 흥청거리기. **2** a period of drinking. 주연(酒宴).

on the spree, allowing oneself a spree. 흥겹게 마시고 떠들며. ¶ *be* [*go*] *on the ~* 통음하다; 흥겹게 마시고 떠들다.

— *vi.* (P1) carouse. 흥겹게 마시고 떠들다. [Ir. *spre* spark]

•**sprig** [sprig] *n.* Ⓒ **1** a small branch. 작은 가지. **2** an ornament or design in the form of a spray. 작은 가지 모양의 무늬. **3** ⓐ a young man. 젊은이. ⓑ an offshoot of a family. 자손. **4** a small, headless brad. (대가리 없는 작은) 못; 징. — *vt.* (**sprigged**) (P6) **1** remove sprigs from. …에서[의] 잔가지를 치다. **2** decorate with sprigs. 잔가지로 꾸미다. **3** 《*down, on*》 fasten with small, headless brads. 못[징]을 박다. [E.]

spright·ly [spráitli] *adj.* (**-li·er, -li·est**) lively; gay. 쾌활한; 명랑한. ¶ *a ~ old gentleman* 쾌활한 노신사. — *adv.* in a sprightly manner. 기운차게; 쾌활[명랑]하게. [→ spirit]

:spring [spriŋ] *v.* (**sprang** or **sprung, sprung**) *vi.* **1** (P1,2A,3) leap; jump; rise up suddenly. 껑충 뛰다; 튀다; 뛰어오르다; 벌떡 일어서다. ¶ *~ out of bed* 잠자리에서 벌떡 일어나다 / *~ into the air* 공중으로 뛰어오르다 / *~ over a fence* 울타리를 뛰어 넘다 / *~ to the aid of someone* 아무를 도우려고 뛰어가다 / *Boys on bicycles sprang off.* 자전거를 타고 있던 소년들이 훌쩍 뛰어내렸다. **2** (P3) 《*from*》 arise; grow; come from some source. (물 따위가) 솟아오르다; (식물이) 싹트다; 돋아나다; (원인·근거로 인해) 생기다; (아무가) … 출신이다. ¶ *~ from seeds* 씨에서 싹이 트다 / *The water springs from the ground.* 물은 땅에서 솟아오른다 / *The river springs from a lake.* 그 강은 호수에서 발원(發源)한다 / *courage springing from conviction* 확신에서 생기는 용기 / *All our errors have sprung from carelessness.* 우리들의 잘못은 다 부주의에서 생겨났다 / *~ from a noble family* 명문 출신이다 / *~ from the people* 서민 출신이다 / *The family springs from* [*out of*] *ancient kings.* 그의 집안은 옛날 왕가의 후예이다. **3** (P1,2A,3) arise, come, or appear suddenly. (갑자기) 생기다; 일어나다; 출현하다. ¶ *~ out of the darkness* 어둠 속에서 불쑥 나타나다 / *~ into fame* 갑자기 유명해지다 / *A light breeze has sprung up.* 산들바람이 불기 시작했다 / *A strange thought sprang in my mind.* 이상스런 생각이 갑자기 마음 속에 떠올랐다. **4** (P1,2A) move suddenly and rapidly by the action of a spring; move back as a reaction. (용수철·탄력성 있는 것이) 튀기다; 되튀다; 튀어서 되돌아오다. ¶ *The branch sprang back.* 나뭇가지가 (휘었다가) 되튀었다 / *The doors sprang open.* 문이 홱 열렸다 / *The lid sprang to.* 뚜껑이 쾅하고 닫혔다. **5** (P1) (of wood) become bent or cracked. (재목 따위가) 휘다; 뒤틀리다; 갈라지다. ¶ *The door has sprung.* 문이 뒤틀렸다.

— *vt.* **1** (P6,13,21) cause (something) to spring; jump over or across (something). …을 뛰게[뛰어오르게] 하다; 뛰어 넘다. ¶ *~ a fence* 울타리를 뛰어 넘다 / *~ a horse* 말을 달리게 하다 / *~ a pheasant from the covert* 숨은 곳으로부터 꿩을 날아오르게 하다. **2** (P6) release the spring of (something). …의 용수철을 되튀게 하다. ¶ *~ a trap* 덫을 덜컥 튀게 하다 / *~ a watchcase open* (회중) 시계의 뚜껑을 찰칵하고 열다. **3** (P6,13) explode. …을 폭발시키다. ¶ *~ a mine* 지뢰를 폭발시키다. **4** (P6,13) 《*on*》 produce or do unexpectedly and suddenly. …을 갑자기 꺼내다[제출하다]. ¶ *~ a surprise on someone* 갑자기 아무를 놀라게 하다 / *~ a new proposal upon someone* 갑자기

아무에게 새로운 제안을 내놓다 / ～ *a motion upon an assembly* 느닷없이 회의에 동의를 내놓다 / *He sprang this information on me soon after I got home.* 집에 도착하자마자 느닷없이 그는 나에게 이 정보를 전해줬다. **5** cause (wood) to bend or crack. (재목 따위)를 휘게 하다; 구부리다. ¶ ～ *a beam* 들보를 휘게 하다〔구부리다〕.

spring a leak, develop a hole through which water leaks. 구멍이 생겨 물이 새기 시작하다. ¶ *The boat* 〔*roof*〕 *sprang a leak.* 보트〔지붕〕에 구멍이 생겨 물이 새기 시작했다.

spring a somersault, turn a somersault. 공중제비하다.

spring at, jump at; attack suddenly. …에 달려〔덤벼〕들다; 급습하다.

spring forth, spring forward; sprout. 뛰어나오다; 싹트다.

spring off, burst open. 튀기다.

spring on =spring at.

spring over, jump over. 뛰어넘다.

spring to one's feet, rise suddenly and rapidly from a sitting posture. 벌떡 일어서다.

— *n.* Ⓒ **1** the act of springing; a leap or jump. 튀어오름; 뜀; 도약. ¶ *rise with a* ～ 뛰어올라 서다; 벌떡 일어서다 / *The rabbit gave a* ～. 토끼가 껑충 뛰었다 / *He made a* ～ *at me.* 그는 나에게 와락 덤벼들었다. **2** a coil of wire that returns to its first shape after being pulled or bent. 용수철; 스프링; 태엽. ¶ *the* ～ *of a watch* 〔*clock*〕 시계의 태엽 / *the* ～ *of a carriage* 마차의 (완충용) 스프링 / *Beds have many wire springs.* 침대에는 많은 철제 스프링이 있다 / *It works by* (*means of*) *a* ～. 그것은 태엽으로〔용수철로〕 움직인다. **3** Ⓤ ⓐ elastic quality or energy; a bouncing or leaping movement; backward movement from constrained position. 되튀기; 탄력(성); 반동. ¶ *the* ～ *of a bow* 활의 탄력성 / *There is no* ～ *left in this old piece of rubber.* 이 오래된 고무 조각에는 아무런 탄력도 남아 있지 않다 / *The young man has a fine* ～ *in his step.* 그 청년의 걸음걸이에는 멋진 탄력이 있다. ⓑ power of the mind; spirit. (마음의) 탄력; 활력. ¶ *His mind has lost its* ～. 그의 정신에 활력〔탄력〕이 없어졌다. **4** a place where water or natural oil comes to the surface of the ground; a natural well; a fountain. 샘; 광천; 원천. ¶ *a hot* 〔*mineral*〕 ～ 온〔광〕천 / *a* ～ *of pity* (샘처럼) 솟구치는 연민의 정. **5** a source or origin; a cause of action. 근원; 동기. ¶ *the* ～ *of mankind* 인류의 근원 / *The custom has its* ～ *in another country.* 그 풍습의 기원은 다른 나라에 있다 / *the springs of one's conduct* 행위의 동기. **6** ⓊⒸ the first season of the year; the season between winter and summer; the period of beginning; 《*fig.*》 the first stage of growth; youth. 봄; 초기; 젊음. ¶ *the* ～ *of life* 인생의 봄《청춘 시대》/ *in the* ～ *of 1994,* 1994년의 봄에 / *the* ～ *of the year* 연초. **7** ⓐ a warp or crack in timber. (목재 따위의) 뒤틀림; 갈라진 틈. ⓑ 《naut.》 a leak caused by warping or cracking. (배의) 누수구(漏水口).

— *adj.* of or in spring; of a spring. 봄의; 용수철의. ¶ *a* ～ *rain* 봄비 / *a* ～ *bed* 스프링 침대. [E.]

spring-balance [spríŋbǽləns] *n.* a balance that measures weight by the action of a spring. 용수철 저울.

spring-bed [spríŋbéd] *n.* a bed with metal springs in the mattress. 스프링 침대.

spring·board [spríŋbɔ̀ːrd] *n.* Ⓒ **1** a springy board used in jumping, etc. to get added height or spring. 뜀판; 도약판. **2** a diving board. (수영의) 스프링보드; 도약대.

spring·bok, [spríŋbɑ̀k / -bɔ̀k], **-buck** [-bʌ̀k] *n,* a South African antelope. 영양(羚羊)의 일종《남아프리카산》.

springe [sprindʒ] *n.* a snare. (새·쥐 따위의 작은 동물용) 덫. [*spring*]

spring-gun [spríŋgʌ̀n] *n.* a concealed gun arranged to go off when struck by a person who has broken in. 용수철〔스프링〕총.

spring·halt [spríŋhɔ̀ːlt] *n.* a horse-disease with convulsive movement in lifting hind legs. (말의) 절름증(症).

spring·tide [spríŋtàid] *n.* =springtime.

spring tide [ㅅㅅ] *n.* the tide at its greatest height, occurring at each new moon and full moon. 한사리; 대조(大潮).

spring·time [spríŋtàim] *n.* Ⓤ the season of spring. 봄. ¶ *Flowers bloom in the* ～. 꽃들은 봄에 핀다.

spring-wa·ter [spríŋwɔ̀ːtər, -wɑ̀t-] *n.* water flowing or obtained from a spring. 샘물; 용수(湧水).

spring·y [spríŋi] *adj.* (**spring·i·er, spring·i·est**) **1** capable of springing back to the former shape; that springs; elastic; flexible. 탄력이 있는〔많은〕; 유연한. ¶ *a* ～ *board* 탄력이 있는 판(板) / *walk with a* ～ *step* 경쾌한〔빠른〕 걸음걸이로 걷다. **2** full of springs of water. 샘이 많은.

·**sprin·kle** [spríŋkəl] *vt.* **1** (P6,7,13) scatter (water, powder, etc.) in small drops or tiny bits. …을 뿌리다; 흩뿌리다. ¶ ～ *salt on meat* 고기에 소금을 뿌리다 / ～ *water on flowers* 꽃에 물을 뿌려 주다. **2** (P6,13) scatter small drops or tiny bits on or over (something). …에 (흩)뿌리다; 끼얹다. ¶ ～ *the dusty street with water* 먼지나는 가로에 물을 끼얹다 / *The sky was sprinkled with stars.* 하늘은 별들을 뿌려놓은 듯했다.

— *vi.* (P1) **1** scatter in drops or tiny bits. 흩어지다. **2** rain lightly. 비가 부슬부슬 내리다. ¶ *It began to* ～. 비가 부슬부슬 내리기 시작했다.

— *n.* Ⓒ **1** the act of sprinkling. (흩)뿌리

기. **2** a light shower of liquid. 가랑비. ¶ *It was just a* ~. 가랑비에 지나지 않았다. **3** a small quantity or number. 소량; 소수; 조금. ¶ *a* ~ *of snow* 〔*students*〕 소량〔소수〕의 눈〔학생들〕. [E.]

sprin·kler [spríŋklər] *n.* Ⓒ **1** a person who sprinkles. (물·분말 따위를) 뿌리는 사람. **2** a device or a vehicle for sprinkling water, etc. 살수차; 살수기; 스프링클러.

sprin·kling [spríŋkliŋ] *n.* Ⓒ **1** a small quantity of liquid, etc. that falls in scattered drops. (비 따위가) 부슬부슬 내림; 소량. ¶ *a* ~ *of snow* 조금 내린 눈. **2** a small number of people. 소수(의 사람). ¶ *a* ~ *of students in the audience* 청중 속에 드문드문 보이는 학생.

sprint [sprint] *n.* Ⓒ a short race at full speed. 단거리 경주(=《U.S.》 dash). ¶ *a* ~ *race* 단거리 경주. — *vi.* (P1,2A) run a short distance at full speed. (단거리를) 전속력으로 달리다. ¶ *He sprinted out for* 〔*to call*〕 *a taxi.* 그는 택시를 잡기〔부르기〕 위해 냅다 달려 나갔다. [N.=dart]

sprint·er [spríntər] *n.* Ⓒ a person who takes part in a sprint race. 단거리 경주 선수; 스프린터. [↑]

sprit [sprit] *n.* 《naut.》 a small spar extending diagonally upward from a mast. (돛의) 사형(斜桁). [E.]

sprite [sprait] *n.* Ⓒ a fairy; an elf. 요정(妖精). [→*spirit*]

sprit·sail [sprítsèil, 《naut.》 -səl] *n.* a triangular sail extended by a sprit. 사형범(斜桁帆). [E.]

sprock·et [sprákit / sprɔ́k-] *n.* Ⓒ **1** a tooth-like projection on the outer rim of a wheel arranged so as to fit into the links of a chain. 사슬톱니. **2** a wheel with such teeth. 사슬톱니바퀴. [?]

sprout [spraut] *n.* Ⓒ **1** a bud. 싹. **2** 《*pl.*》 =Brussels sprouts. — *vi.* (P1,2A) start to grow; send out new shoots. 싹이 트다; 자라기〔나기〕 시작하다. ¶ *The weeds* 〔*seeds, buds*〕 ~ *in spring.* 잡초〔씨, 싹〕들은 봄에 나기 시작한다. — *vt.* (P6) cause (a bud) to grow. …의 싹을 트게〔나게〕 하다. ¶ *The rain and warm weather sprouted the flowers.* 비와 따뜻한 날씨가 꽃들을 싹트게 했다 / *The trees sprouted leaves.* 나뭇잎들이 싹텄다. [E.]

spruce[1] [spru:s] *n.* **1** Ⓒ an evergreen tree with cones and short, needle-shaped leaves. 가문비나무속의 일종《갯솔·전나무·종비나무 따위》. **2** Ⓤ the wood of this tree. 그 목재. [↓]

spruce[2] [spru:s] *adj.* (**spruc·er, spruc·est**) neat and tidy in appearance; smart. (외모가) 단정〔말쑥〕한; 스마트한. ¶ *How* ~ *he looks in his new coat!* 새 코트를 입으니 아주 말쑥해 보이는군. — *vt.* (P6,7) make something spruce. …을 맵시 있게〔말쑥하게〕 하다. ¶ ~ *up the room* 방을 깨끗하고 단정하게 하다. — *vi.* (P2A) 《*colloq.*》 make oneself neat. 몸단장을 하다. ¶ ~ *oneself up for dinner* 만찬을 위해 몸 단장을 하다. [*Prussia*]

spruce beer [⌐ ⌐] *n.* a medicinal infusion from spruce. 가문비나무 술《괴혈병 치료제》.

:sprung [sprʌŋ] *v.* p. and pp. of **spring.**

spry [sprai] *adj.* (**spry·er** or **spri·er, spry·est** or **spri·est**) full of life; quick and active; nimble. 기운찬; 활발한; 민첩한. ¶ *A mouse is a* ~ *animal.* 쥐는 매우 민첩한 동물이다. [Sw. =active]

look spry, hurry up; look sharp. 서두르다; 민첩히 굴다.

spud [spʌd] *n.* **1** a short narrow spade for digging up or cutting off the roots of weeds. (제초용) 작은 가래. **2** 《*colloq.*》 a potato. 감자. — *vt.* (**spudded, spud·ding**) (P6) dig up or remove with a spud. …을 작은 가래로 파내다. [Da.]

spue [spju:] *vi., vt., n.* =spew.

spume [spju:m] *n.* Ⓤ foam; froth. 거품. — *vi., vt.* (P1;6) foam; froth. 거품이 일다; …을 거품일게 하다. [L.]

:spun [spʌn] *v.* p. and pp. of **spin.** — *adj.* formed by or as if by spinning. (물레 따위로) 자아서 만들어진; 자은. ¶ ~ *glass* 실유리; 유리 섬유 / ~ *gold* 금실 / ~ *silk* 방적 견사(絹絲) / 《naut.》 ~ *yarn* 꼰 밧줄. [*spin*]

spunk [spʌŋk] *n.* Ⓤ **1** touchwood; tinder. 부싯깃. **2** 《*colloq.*》 courage; mettle; hot temper. 용기; 기개; 뻣성; 화증. [L. *spongia*]

spunk·y [spʌ́ŋki] *adj.* (**spunk·i·er, spunk·i·est**) **1** of or like touchwood. 부싯깃의〔같은〕. **2** courageous; spirited; touchy. 용감한; 활기 있는; 성마른; 걸핏하면 화내는.

·spur [spəːr] *n.* Ⓒ **1** a pointed metal instrument fitted to a rider's boot heel for urging on a horse. 박차. ¶ *set* 〔*put*〕 *spurs to one's horse* 말에 박차를 가하다. **2** anything that urges on; a stimulus. 자극; 격려. ¶ *Ambition is an excellent* ~ *for the young.* 야망은 청년들에게 훌륭한 자극이다 / *offer a prize as a* ~ *to good work* 훌륭한 작업 성과에 대한 격려로서 포상을 제의하다 / *need the* ~ 박차를 가할〔자극을 줄〕 필요가 있다. **3** anything like a spur, as a sharp spine on a rooster's leg, etc. 박차 모양의 것《수탉의 며느리발톱 따위》. **4** something sticking out like a spur. 박차처럼 비죽이 나온 것. ¶ *a* ~ *of rock sticking out from the mountain* 산에서 삐죽 내민 바위. **5** a short branch railroad track. (철도의) 지선(支線).

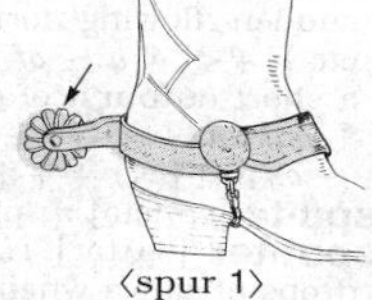
〈spur 1〉

on the spur, at full speed. 전속력으로.

on the spur of the moment, impromptu; on a momentary impulse; without pause for thought; impulsively; suddenly. 즉흥적〔충동적〕으로; 느닷없이. ¶ *act on the ~ of the moment* 앞뒤 생각 없이 행동하다.

put* 〔*set*〕 *spurs to, prick with spurs; incite. …에 박차를 가하다; 격려하다.

win one's spurs, **a**) 《hist.》 gain knighthood. 나이트 작위를 받다. **b**) win honor and fame; make a name. 이름을 떨치다.

with whip and spur =***with spur and yard,*** at once. 즉석에서.

— *v.* (**spurred, spur·ring**) *vt.* **1** (P6,7) prick (a horse) with a spur or spurs. 박차를 가하여 (말)을 달리게 하다. ¶ *The rider spurred his horse* (*on*). 기수는 말에 박차를 가했다〔가해 달리게 했다〕. **2** (P6,7,20) urge on; excite; stimulate. …을 자극하다; 격려하다. ¶ *Ambition spurred him to succeed.* 야심에 자극되어 그는 성공했다. **3** (P6) provide (a boot) with a spur. …에 박차를 달다.

— *vi.* (P2A) spur a horse; ride quickly. 말에 박차를 가하다; 말을 달리다; 질주하다. [E.]

spu·ri·ous [spjúəriəs] *adj.* **1** not genuine; false. 가짜의; 위조의(opp. genuine). ¶ *a ~ banknote* 위조 지폐 / *a ~ pedigree* 가짜 족보 / *~ pregnancy* 상상 임신. **2** 《rare》 of a child whose parents were not married; illegitimate. 사생(아)의. ¶ *the ~ stock* 사생(私生)의 가문. [L.]

spurn [spəːrn] *vt.* (P6,7,13) **1** 《*arch.*》 kick away. …을 차다. ¶ *~ the ground* (펄쩍) 뛰다; 뛰어오르다. **2** drive (something) away roughly. …을 쫓아버리다; 내쫓다. ¶ *He spurned the beggar from his door.* 그는 거지를 문전에서 쫓아 버렸다. **3** reject or treat (someone) with contempt. …을 퇴짜놓다; …을 거절〔일축〕하다; 코방귀 뀌다. ¶ *~ someone's offer* 아무의 제의를 일축하다 / *~ a bribe* 뇌물을 사절하다. [E.]

spurred [spəːrd] *adj.* wearing or fitted with spurs. 박차를 단. ¶ *a ~ horseman* (구두에) 박차를 단 기수. [*spur*]

spurt [spəːrt] *vi.* (P1,2A,3) **1** flow forth suddenly in a stream or jet. 분출하다; 뿜어나오다. ¶ *~ out in streams* 분출해〔솟구쳐〕 흐르다 / *Blood spurted from the wound.* 상처에서 피가 솟아나왔다. **2** show a sudden burst of energy. 일시에 전력을 다하다. ¶ *~ to the finishing-line* 결승 라인을 향해 스퍼트하다. — *vt.* (P6) cause (something) to flow forth. …을 분출시키다. — *n.* Ⓒ **1** a sudden flowing forth of (liquid, fire, etc.). 분출. ¶ *a ~ of flames* 화염의 분출. **2** a short outburst of energy. 역주; 스퍼트. ¶ *make a ~* 역주하다; 스퍼트를 내다 / *put a ~ on* (최후의) 분투를 하다. [Ice]

spu·ta [spjúːtə] *n.* pl. of **sputum.**

sput·ter [spʌ́tər] *vi.* (P1,2A) **1** spit out drops of saliva when speaking angrily or excitedly. (입에서) 침을 튀기다. **2** make a noise like sputtering. 푸푸〔탁탁〕 소리를 내다. ¶ *A wet candle sputters.* 젖은 초는 (불을 켜면) 지글지글 소리를 낸다. **3** talk in an excited manner. 흥분하여 빠르게〔웅얼웅얼〕 지껄이다. — *vt.* (P6) throw out (bits or drops) suddenly. …을 내뱉다; 튀기다; 분출하다. — *n.* Ⓤ **1** Ⓒ the act of sputtering. 침 따위를 튀김; 웅얼거림; 탁탁 소리를 냄. **2** a sputtering noise. 푸푸〔지글지글, 탁탁〕하는 소리. **3** an excited and hasty remark, etc. 흥분하여 빠르게 지껄임; 빠른 말. [Imit.]

spu·tum [spjúːtəm] *n.* (*pl.* **spu·ta**) Ⓤ **1** spit; saliva. 타액; 침. **2** 《*pl.*》 what is coughed up from the lungs. 담; 가래. [L.]

:spy [spai] *n.* Ⓒ (*pl.* **spies**) **1** a person who is employed to keep a secret watch on others. 탐정. ¶ *a ~ on someone's conduct* 아무의 행위를 몰래 살피는 사람 / *be a ~ on ...* …을 탐정〔정찰〕하다 / *set spies after* 〔*upon*〕 …에 탐정을 붙이다. **2** a person who secretly enters an enemy's land to get information about it. 스파이; 간첩. ¶ *a ~ ring* 간첩단 / *on a ~ mission* 스파이 임무를 띠고 / *an industrial ~* 산업 스파이.

— *v.* (**spied, spy·ing**) *vt.* (P6,7) **1** watch (someone or something) secretly and carefully. …을 탐정〔정찰·감시〕하다. ¶ *~ the enemy* 적을 정찰하다 / *~ a ship in the distance* 멀리서 배를 몰래 살피다 / *He sat with his glass, spying the movements across the water.* 그는 망원경을 지니고 앉아서, 강 건너의 움직임을 감시했다. **2** catch sight of (someone or something); discover (someone or something) by careful and secret examination. …을 찾아〔알아〕내다; 발견하다. ¶ *~ out a secret* 비밀을 알아내다 / *~ a rare bird overhead* 머리 위에서 희귀한 새를 발견하다 / *He is quick at spying his neighbors' faults.* 그는 이웃들의 결점을 찾아내는데 재빠르다. — *vi.* (P1,3) **1** watch secretly and carefully. 몰래 살피다; 탐정하다. ¶ *~ into someone's actions* 아무의 행동을 몰래 살피다. **2** act as a spy. 스파이 노릇을 하다. ¶ *~ for the enemy* 적을 위해 간첩 노릇을 하다. [→espy]

I spy strangers. 《Brit.》 I wish to have the galleries cleared. 방청 금지를 원합니다《영국 하원의 의회 용어》.

spy into, examine carefully and secretly. 은밀히 조사하다.

spy out, make secret investigations in; explore secretly. 탐색하다.

spy upon, keep a secret watch upon. …을 탐정〔정찰〕하다.

spy·glass [spáiglæ̀s, -glɑ̀ːs] *n.* Ⓒ a small telescope. 소형 망원경.

Sq. Squadron.

sq. square; sequence; 《L.》 *sequens* (= the following).

sq. ft. square foot 〔feet〕.

sq. in. square inch(es).

sqq. 《L.》 *sequentia* (=the following).

squab [skwɑb / skwɔb] *n.* Ⓒ **1** a very young bird, esp. a young pigeon. 새새끼;

(특히) 비둘기 새끼. **2** a short, fat person. 똥똥한 사람; 땅딸보. **3** a soft, stuffed cushion; a sofa. 폭신한 쿠션; 소파. — *adj.* **1** (of a bird) unfledged or newly hatched. (새가) 털이 아직 안 난; 갓 부화된. **2** fat and short; plump. 땅딸막한; 살찐. — *adv.* with a heavy fall. 쿵하고; 털썩. [Scand.]

squab·ble [skwɑ́bəl / skwɔ́b-] *n.* Ⓒ a noisy quarrel about some unimportant matter. 하찮은 언쟁〔말다툼〕. — *vi.* (P1, 2A,3) quarrel noisily about some unimportant matter. 하찮은 일로 말다툼하다. [Imit.]

squad [skwɑd / skwɔd] *n.* Ⓒ **1** a small number of soldiers grouped for drill or work. 분대; 반(班). ¶ *an awkward* ~ 신병반; 미숙한 사람들 / *a* ~ *drill* 분대 교련. **2** a small group of people working together. 한 조(組)〔팀〕; 일단(의 사람들). ¶ 《U.S.》 *a* ~ *car* 경찰 순찰차 / *a* ~ *of police* =*a police* ~ 일대(一隊)의 경관 / *a relief* ~ 구조대 / *a football* ~ 풋볼팀. [→square]

squad·ron [skwɑ́drən / skwɔ́d-] *n.* Ⓒ **1** a body of soldiers on horses, usu. containing from 120 to 200 men. 기병 중대. **2** a unit of airplanes under one command. 비행(대)대. **3** a group of warships. 소함대. **4** any organized group. 단체.

squail [skweil] *n.* **1** 《*pl.*》《used as *sing.*》 a table game like bowls and curling. 과녁맞히기 놀이《작은 원반을 튀겨서 판의 복판 과녁에 맞히는 놀이》. **2** a disk used in the game. (과녁 맞히기 놀이용의)원반. [? E.]

squal·id [skwɑ́lid / skwɔ́l-] *adj.* **1** very dirty, poor and neglected; filthy. 더러운; 지저분한. ¶ *a* ~ *house* 누추한 집 / ~ *slums* 지저분한 빈민가 / *a woman* ~ *in attire* 초라한 옷차림의 여자. **2** base; mean. 비열〔야비〕한. ¶ *a* ~ *quarrel* 비열한 싸움. [L.]

squal·id·ly [skwɑ́lidli / skwɔ́l-] *adv.* in a squalid manner; dirtily; meanly. 지저분하게; 더럽게; 상스럽게.

squall[1] [skwɔːl] *n.* Ⓒ **1** a sudden, violent windstorm with rain or snow. 돌풍; 스콜. **2** 《*colloq.*》 a piece of trouble; a disturbance. 소동. [Imit.]

look out for squalls, be on one's guard against trouble or danger. 위험을 경계〔대비〕하다.

squall[2] [skwɔːl] *vi., vt.* (P1;6) cry out loudly; scream violently. 울부짖다; 비명〔고함〕을 지르다. ¶ *The baby began to* ~. — *n.* Ⓤ a loud cry or scream. 비명; 고함; 울부짖는 소리. ¶ *the* ~ *of a parrot* 앵무새의 비명(소리). [Imit.]

squall·y [skwɔ́ːli] *adj.* (**squall·i·er, squall·i·est**) **1** of a squall; having many squalls. 질풍의; 폭풍이 일 것 같은. ¶ *It looks* ~. 폭풍이 일 것 같다. **2** threatening. (형세가) 험악한; 심상치 않은. [↑]

squal·or [skwɑ́lər, skwɔ́(ː)lər] *n.* Ⓤ the state of being squalid; miserable and dirty conditions. 더러움; 비참함; 치사함. [L.]

squan·der [skwɑ́ndər / skwɔ́n-] *vt.* (P6) spend (money, time, etc.) wastefully and foolishly. …을 낭비하다; 헛되이 쓰다. ¶ ~ *money* 〔*time*〕. [→mania]

squan·der·ma·ni·a [skwɑ̀ndərméiniə / skwɔ̀n-] *n.* a craze for extravagant expenditure. 낭비광. [↑]

:square [skwɛər] *n.* Ⓒ **1** a figure having 4 equal sides and 4 right angles; anything having this form. 정사각형; 네모진 것. ¶ *a tiny* ~ *of mirror* 사각형의 작은 거울 / *a neat white* ~ *of folded handkerchief* 네모지게 접은 산뜻한 흰 손수건. **2** an area in a city bounded by four streets; 《U.S.》 the length of the side of such an area. (사면이 가로로 둘러 싸인) 한 구획; 그 한 변의 거리; 가구(街區); 블록(block). ¶ *This* ~ *is full of shops.* 이 가구는 상점들로 꽉 차 있다 / *Go two squares north.* 북쪽으로 두 구획〔블록〕을 가시오. **3** a large open place, often a park, in a city. (도시의) 광장. ¶ *Times Square* 타임스 스퀘어 / *Red Square* 붉은 광장. **4** an instrument, L-shaped or T-shaped, used for drawing or measuring right angles. (L자·T자 모양의) 직각자; 곱자. **5** the answer when a number is multiplied by itself. 제곱; 평방. ¶ *bring to a* ~ 제곱하다 / *36 is the* ~ *of 6.* 36은 6의 제곱이다. **6** a body of troops drawn up in a square form. (옛 군대의) 방진(方陣). **7** a unit of measurement for flooring, roofing, etc. equal to 100 square feet. 스퀘어《면적의 단위; 100 제곱〔평방〕 피트》.

by the square, exactly. 정확히.

on the square, honest; trustworthy. 정직하게; 공정히.

out of square, **a**) not at right angles. 직각이 아닌. **b**) not in harmony or agreement; irregular(ly); incorrect(ly). 조화가 안 되어; 일치하지 않고; 불규칙〔부정확〕한〔하게〕.

— *adj.* **1** having 4 equal sides and 4 equal angles. 정사각형의; 사각(四角)의. ¶ *a* ~ *box* 네모진 상자 / *a* ~ *house* 상자형의 집 / *a* ~ *farm* 네모 반듯한 농지. **2** of the form of a right angle. 직각의. ¶ *a* ~ *corner* 직각의 모서리 / *make a line* ~ *with another* 한 선을 다른 선과 직각으로 하다. **3** like a square; of a shape suggesting a square. (어깨 따위가) 네모진; 모가 난. ¶ *a* ~ *jaw* 모가 진 턱 / ~ *shoulders* 딱 벌어진 어깨. **4** even; balanced; having all accounts settled. 평등〔동등〕의; 서로 같은; 셈이 끝난. ¶ *get* 〔*make*〕 *one's accounts* ~ (대차를) 결제〔청산〕하다 / *Is the account* ~*?* 셈이 끝났나 / *be* ~ *with one's landlord* 집 주인과 셈이 끝나다. **5** fair or honest; clear; direct; in good order. 공정한; 정직한; 단호한; 정돈된. ¶ *a* ~ *deal* 공정한 처리〔거래〕 / *a* ~ *refusal* 단호한 거절 / *get things* ~ 물건들을 정돈하

다 / *He was the squarest man I ever knew.* 그 사람이야 말로 가장 공명 정대한 인물이었다 / *keep ~ with one's conscience* 양심에 조금도 부끄러울 것이 없다. **6** 《*colloq.*》 satisfying; full. 충실한; 실속 있는; 충분한. ¶ *a ~ meal* 실속 있는〔푸짐한〕 식사 / *make a ~ meal* 충분한 식사를 하다. **7** multiplied by itself. 평방의; 제곱의. ¶ *a ~ mile* 한 평방 마일 / *3 ~ yards,* 3제곱〔평방〕야드 / *In British, there are 567 people to the ~ mile.* 영국에서는 1제곱〔평방〕 마일당 인구가 567명이다.

— *adv.* **1** so as to be in a square form. 4각으로; 직각으로. ¶ *fold a towel ~* 타월을 네모지게 접다 / *The street turns ~ to the right.* 거리는 오른쪽으로 직각으로 구부러져 있다. **2** frankly; honestly. 솔직히; 정직하게. ¶ *treat someone fair and ~* 아무를 공명정대하게 대하다. **3** directly; firmly. 정면〔정통〕으로; (시선을 돌리지 않고) 똑바로. ¶ *I hit him ~ between the eyes.* 나는 그의 미간을 정통으로 때렸다 / *Stand ~ to him.* 그와 정면으로 마주 서라 / *look him ~ in the face* 그의 얼굴을 똑바로 보다.

— *vt.* **1** (P6) make (something) square; form (something) into a right angle. …을 정사각형으로〔네모지게〕 하다; 직각으로 하다. ¶ *~ the edge of a board* 판자의 모서리를 네모지게 깎다 / *~ off the log* 통나무를 각재(角材)로 하다 / *The children squared off the footpath to play hopscotch.* 아이들은 돌차기 놀이를 하기 위해 보도를 (여러 개의) 네모진 칸으로 구획했다. **2** (P6) bring (something) near the form of a right angle or straight line. …을 모지게 하다; …을 바르게〔쭉〕 펴다. ¶ *~ one's shoulders* 〔*elbows*〕 어깨〔팔꿈치〕를 쭉 펴다 / *He squared himself in his chair.* 그는 의자에서 자세를 바르게 했다. **3** (P6) make (something) even; settle; pay (a bill). …을 서로 같게 하다; …을 청산〔결제〕하다. ¶ *~ a debt* 빚을 청산하다 / *~ accounts with someone* 아무에게 빚을 갚다〔앙갚음하다〕 / *~ oneself for someone* 아무와 화해하다 / *~ someone by paying him money* 돈을 지불하여 아무와의 사이를 원만히 하다 / *~ the score* 스코어를 동점으로 하다. **4** (P13) 《*by, with*》 adapt; fit; accomodate. …을 적합하게〔알맞게〕 하다; 일치〔적응〕시키다. ¶ *~ one's theory with ascertained facts* 확정된 사실에 자기 이론을 적응시키다 / *~ one's actions with one's words* 말과 행동을 일치시키다 / *~ one's opinion to the prevailing tendencies* 자기의 의견을 시대적 경향에 적합토록 하다. **5** (P6) multiply (a number or quantity) by itself. …을 제곱하다. ¶ *5 squared is 25,* 5의 제곱은 25다. **6** (P6) bribe. 매수하다. — *vi.* **1** (P1) make square; form a right angle. 직각〔사각〕을 이루다. **2** (P1,3) 《*with*》 fit; agree. 일치하다. ¶ *His statement does not ~ with the facts.* 그의 성명은 사실과 다르다 / *Your ideas and mine do not ~.* 너와 나의 의견은 일치하지 않는다. [→ex-, quadrate]

square off, take up a position for attack or defense, as in boxing. (복싱 따위에서) 싸울 자세를 취하다.

square the circle, **a**) try to construct a square exactly equal in area to a given circle. 원을 네모지게 하다. **b**) try to do something impossible. 불가능한 일을 하려 들다.

square up, **a**) prepare to fight. (싸울) 태세를 취하다. **b**) pay debts or bills; pay off. …을 청산하다. ¶ *~ up one's accounts* …을 청산하다; 셈을 끝내다 / *~ up with someone* 아무에게 앙갚음하다.

square dance [⌐ ⌐] *n.* a dance consisting of a series of set steps for a group of couples. 스퀘어 댄스.

square·ly [skwέərli] *adv.* **1** in a square form; in a right angle. 네모꼴로; 네모지게. ¶ *The house is built ~.* 그 집은 네모꼴로 세워졌다. **2** directly. 정면으로; 똑바로. ¶ *She looked him ~ in the eyes.* 그녀는 그의 눈을 정면으로 마주 보았다 / *face a difficult situation ~* 어려운 입장을 피하지 않고 정면으로 맞서다 / *face someone ~* 아무와 정면으로 마주 대하다. **3** honestly. 정직하게.

square·ness [skwέərnis] *n.* Ⓤ **1** the state of being square. 네모짐; 사각(四角). **2** sincerity; honesty. 정직.

square-rigged [skwέərrígd] *adj.* 《naut.》 having the principal sails set square across the masts. 횡범(橫帆)〔가로돛〕 장치의. ¶ *a ~ vessel* 〔*ship*〕 횡범선.

squash[1] [skwɑʃ / skwɔʃ] *vt.* **1** (P6,13) ⓐ crush (something) into pulp. …을 으깨다; 눌러서 찌부러뜨리다. ¶ *~ a fly* 파리를 (파리채 따위로) 쳐죽이다 / *~ strawberries for a sauce* 소스용으로 딸기를 으깨다 / *The package was squashed.* 그 소포는 눌려서 납작해졌다. ⓑ cram; pack tight. 쑤셔넣다. ¶ *~ too many people into a bus* 버스에 승객을 마구 밀어넣다. **2** (P6) stop (something) by force; suppress. …을 진압하다. ¶ *The police quickly squashed the riot.* 경관은 신속하게 폭동을 진압했다. **3** (P6) 《*colloq.*》 make (someone) silent with a crushing argument. …을 (윽박질러) 끽소리 치지 못하게 하다.

— *vi.* (P2A,3) **1** crush. 으스러〔찌부러〕지다. ¶ *The fruit will ~ if it is badly packed.* 과일은 포장을 잘못하면 찌부러진다. **2** fall or move with a squashing sound; make a sound of squashing. 철썩 떨어지다; 철썩거리다. ¶ *fall squashing to the ground* 땅에 털썩 떨어지다 / *~ through the mud* 진창 속을 철썩거리며 가다. **3** 《*into*》 force one's way. 비집고〔헤치고〕 들어가다〔나아가다〕. ¶ *~ into a crowded bus* 만원 버스를 비집고 들어가 타다.

— *n.* Ⓒ **1** something crushed; a crushed mass; something soft and easily squashed. 으스러진〔찌부러진〕 것; (으스러져) 흐물흐물한 덩어리; 으스러지기 쉬운 것. ¶ *go to ~* 으스러지다〔흐물흐물해지다〕. **2** a squashing sound. 철썩〔털썩〕(하는 소리).

¶ *A tomato fell with a* ～. 토마토 한 개가 털썩 떨어졌다. **3** a crowd; a crowded state. 군중; (사람들의) 붐빔. **4** Ⓤ 《Brit.》 a drink made from the juice of crushed fruit and soda water. 스쿼시; 과즙에 소다수를 넣은 음료. ¶ *orange* 〔*lemon*〕 ～ 오렌지〔레몬〕 스쿼시. **5** Ⓤ a game somewhat like tennis. 테니스 비슷한 구기. [→ex-, quash]

squash[2] [skwɑʃ / skwɔʃ] *n.* Ⓒ (*pl.* **squash**) a large fruit which is green outside and yellow inside, used as a vegetable. 호박. [Algonquian]

squash hat [⌐ ⌐] *n.* a soft felt hat with a broad brim. 챙이 넓은 소프트 모자《접을 수 있음》. [*squash*[1]]

squash·y [skwɑ́ʃi / skwɔ́ʃi] *adj.* (**squash·i·er, squash·i·est**) **1** easily crushed. 찌부러지기 쉬운. **2** soft and wet; muddy. 질퍽〔질척〕거리는. ¶ ～ *ground* 질퍽질퍽한 땅. [↑]

squat [skwɑt / skwɔt] *vi.* (**squat·ted** or **squat, squat·ting**) (P1,2A) **1** ⓐ (of a person) sit on one's heels; sit with the legs drawn up closely beneath the body. 웅크리다; 쭈그리고 앉다. ¶ ～ *down on one's hams* (궁둥이를 붙이고) 쭈그리고 앉다. ⓑ (of an animal) sit close to the ground, esp. to avoid being seen; crouch close to the ground. (짐승이) 납작하게 땅에 엎드리다; 숨다. ¶ *A cat squats before jumping.* 고양이는 점프하기 전에 몸을 웅크린다. **2** settle on another's land without permission; settle on a piece of public land to get possession of it. 공유지 또는 남의 땅에 무단으로 정주하다; 불법 점거하다.

— *adj.* **1** sitting; bending down. 쭈그린; 웅크린. **2** short and thick; low and broad. 땅딸막한; 낮고 폭이 넓은. ¶ *a* ～ *dark man* 땅딸막하고 거무스름한 사람 / *a* ～ *teapot* 낮고 몸통이 굵은 찻주전자.

— *n.* Ⓒ the act of squatting. 웅크리기〔쭈그리기〕. [→ex-. L. *cogo* force]

squat·ter [skwɑ́tər / skwɔ́tər] *n.* Ⓒ **1** a person or animal that sits or bends down. 웅크리는 사람〔동물〕. **2** a person who settles on land without permission; a person who settles on a piece of public land to get possession of it. (남의 땅, 공유지의) 무단 거주자. **3** 《Australia》 a sheep-farmer. 목양업자(牧羊業者).

squaw [skwɔː] *n.* Ⓒ **1** an American Indian woman or wife. (북아메리카 원주민의) 여자; 아내. **2** 《*colloq.*》 a woman or wife. 여자; 아내. [Native]

squawk [skwɔːk] *vi.* (P1) (of a hen or duck) make a short, loud cry. (암탉·오리 따위가) 꼬꼬꾝〔꽉꽉〕 울다. — *n.* Ⓒ a short, loud cry. 꽉꽉〔꼬꼬꾝〕 우는 소리. [↓]

squeak [skwiːk] *vi.* (P1) **1** make a short, high sound. (쥐 따위가) 찍찍〔끽끽〕 울다; (구두·바퀴 따위가) 삐걱거리다. ¶ *A mouse squeaks.* 생쥐 한 마리가 찍찍 울다 / *Shoes* ～. 구두가 삐걱거린다. **2** 《*sl.*》 turn informer; let out information. 밀고하다; 고자질하다. — *n.* Ⓒ **1** the short, high cry of a mouse, etc. 쥐 따위의 울음소리; 삐걱거리는 소리. **2** 《always with *narrow*》 a narrow escape. 위기 일발. ¶ *have a narrow* ～ 가까스로〔간신히〕 살아나다〔시간에 대다, 이기다, 해내다 따위〕. ● **squek·er** [-ər] *n.* [Imit.]

squeak·y [skwíːki] *adj.* (**squeak·i·er, squeak·i·est**) making short, high sounds. 찍찍〔끽끽〕거리는; 삐걱거리는. ¶ *a* ～ *door* 〔*shoe*〕 삐걱거리는 문〔구두〕.

squeal [skwiːl] *vi.* **1** (P1) make a long, high cry or sound. 찌익찌익〔끼익끼익〕 울다; 비명을 지르다. ¶ *The pig squealed in pain.* 돼지는 고통으로 끼익끼익 울었다 / *She squealed with delight.* 그녀는 기뻐서 환성(歡聲)을 질렀다. **2** (P1) 《*colloq.*》 ⓐ act as an informer, esp. to the police to betray someone. 밀고하다. ⓑ complain; protest excitedly. 불평〔항의〕하다. — *vt.* (P6) say with a squeal. 길게 새된 소리로 말하다.

make someone squeal, blackmail him. 아무를 협박하다.

— *n.* Ⓒ a long, sharp, shrill cry. 비명. [Imit.]

squeam·ish [skwíːmiʃ] *adj.* **1** easily shocked; very sensitive; fastidious. 신경질의; 꾀까다로운. **2** easily nauseated 〔turned sick〕, e.g. on a ship. (승선할 때 따위에) 쉬이 잘 토하는. ¶ *I feel* ～. 토할 것 같다. [F.]

squee·gee [skwíːdʒiː, ⌐⌐] *n.* Ⓒ **1** a substitute for a broom, with a rubber edge instead of bristles. 고무 걸레〔빗자루〕. **2** 《photog.》 a small rubber roller for drying photographic prints. (습기 제거용의) 고무 롤러. [↓]

·**squeeze** [skwiːz] *vt.* **1** (P6,7,18) get (juice, water, etc.) by pressure. …을 압착하다; 짜(내)다. ¶ ～ *a lemon* 레몬을 짜다 / ～ *juice from a lemon* 레몬에서 즙을 짜내다 / ～ *water from a wet towel* 젖은 타월에서 물을 짜내다 / ～ *toothpaste out of a tube* 튜브에서 치약을 짜내다. **2** (P6,7,18) press (something) hard; hold (someone or something) tightly. …을 짓눌러 찌부러뜨리다; 꼭〔꽉〕 쥐다〔껴안다〕. ¶ *be squeezed to death* 압사하다 / ～ *someone's hand* 아무의 손을 꽉 쥐다 《우정·애정의 표시》 / ～ *one's child* 아이를 꼭 껴안다. **3** (P6,7,18) ⓐ get or extract (something) by force or unfair means. …을 강제로 빼앗다〔우려 내다〕; (자백·허가 등을) …로부터 강제로 받아내다. ¶ ～ *a confession from someone* 아무로부터 억지로 자백을 받아내다 / ～ *money from someone* 아무에게서 돈을 우려내다. ⓑ put pressure on (someone) to do or obtain something; threaten; oppress. …을 압박〔강제〕하다; 위협〔착취〕하다. ¶ ～ *a victim for more money* 돈을 더 내라고 피해자를 강요하다 / ～ *the peasants* 소작인을 착취하다 / *Heavy taxes squeezed the people.* 중세(重稅)는 국민들의 고혈(膏血)을 짜냈다. **4** (P7,13) pack (something)

tightly. …을 쑤셔[밀어] 넣다. ¶ ～ *oneself into* …에 억지로 끼어들다 / ～ *things into a box* 상자 속에 물건을 마구 쑤셔넣다. — *vi.* **1** (P1,2A) produce the result of pressure; be pressed. 짜지다; 압착되다. ¶ *Oranges ～ easily.* 오렌지는 쉬이 짜진다[압착된다]. **2** 《*through, in, out*》 move or force one's way. 비집고[헤치고] 나아가다. ¶ ～ *through a crowd* 군중을 비집고 나아가다.
squeeze out a tear, weep perfunctorily. 거짓 눈물을 짜내다.
— *n.* Ⓒ 《usu. *sing.*》 **1** the act of squeezing. 압착; 짜기. **2** a firm friendly pressure of another's hand; a tight hold in the arms. 굳은 악수; 꼭 껴안기. **3** the crowded state; a crowd. 붐빔; 혼잡. ¶ *I got in, but it was a tight ～*. 어떻게 들어가기는 했으나, 대단한 혼잡이었다. [E.]

squeezed orange [⌐ ⌐—] *n.* a person or thing whence no more can be got. (즙을 다 짜낸 오렌지처럼) 이용 가치가 없어진 사람[것].

squeeze play [⌐ ⌐] *n.* 《baseball》 a play to get one score while the batter tries to bunt. 스퀴즈 플레이《3루의 주자를 번트로 생환시키는 공격법》.

squeez·er [skwíːzər] *n.* Ⓒ **1** a person who squeezes. 압착[착취]자. **2** an instrument to squeeze fruit for juice. 압착기. ¶ *a lemon-squeezer* 레몬을 짜는 기구[압착기]. **3** 《*pl.*》 playing-cards with the value indicated in the top right-hand corner. 오른쪽 윗 구석에 점수가 기입된 포커용 카드.

squelch [skweltʃ] *vt.* **1** (P6) crush (something) by stamping upon it. …을 눌러[밟아] 찌부러뜨리다; 진압하다. ¶ ～ *a riot* 폭동을 진압하다. **2** cause (someone) to become silent by criticizing him. …를 (윽박질러) 입 다물게[아무 말 못하게] 하다. — *vi.* (P1,2A) make a splashing sound when walking in mud. (진창 따위를) 철벅거리며 걷다. — *n.* Ⓒ **1** a crushing sound. 철벅철벅하는 소리. **2** the act of crushing. 눌러 찌부러뜨리기. **3** a crushing answer or argument. 꺽소리 못하게 하는 말. [Imit.]

squib [skwib] *n.* Ⓒ **1** a small firework that gives off sparks white burning and explodes with a loud noise. 폭죽. **2** a tube of gunpowder used to fire a charge. 도화폭관(導火爆管). **3** a short, witty attack in speech or writing. 풍자. — *vi., vt.* (P1;6) **1** shoot off (a squib). (폭죽 등을) 터뜨리다. **2** write or utter squibs. 풍자하다; 풍자문을 쓰다. [Imit.]

squid [skwid] *n.* Ⓒ (*pl.* **squids** or *collectively* **squid**) **1** a kind of small cuttlefish. 오징어. **2** a kind of artificial bait. (오징어 모양의) 가짜 낚시 미끼. [*squirt*]

squif·fer [skwífər] *n.* Ⓒ 《Brit. *sl.*》 a concertina. 손풍금. [?]

squif·fy [skwífi] *adj.* 《*colloq.*》 drunk. 술 취한. [?]

squill [skwil] *n.* Ⓒ a crustacean. 해총(海葱)《갑각류》. [Gk.]

squint [skwint] *adj.* with each eye looking in a different direction. 사시(斜視)의; 사팔눈의; 곁눈질하는.
— *n.* Ⓒ **1** the state of being squint. 사시; 사팔눈; 사팔뜨기. ¶ *She has a bad ～*. 그녀는 지독한 사팔눈이다. **2** a sidelong glance. 곁눈질. **3** 《*colloq.*》 a quick glance. 일별; 힐끗봄. ¶ *Let me have a ～ at it.* 어디 한 번 잠깐 보자.
— *vi.* **1** (P1) be squint. 사팔눈이다. ¶ *She squints.* 그녀는 사팔눈이다. **2** (P3) 《*at, through*》 look with eyes half closed; look hastily and sideways. 눈을 가늘게 뜨고 보다; 곁눈질로 보다. **3** (P3)《*at*》 take a glance. 힐끗[잠깐] 보다; 일별하다. **4** (P3) incline; have a tendency. 기울다; 경향이 있다.
— *vt.* (P6) **1** cause to squint. 사팔뜨기가 되게 하다. **2** close (the eyes) partly; keep (one's eyes) half closed. 눈을 가늘게 뜨다. ¶ *He squinted his eyes to concentrate his thoughts.* 그는 생각을 집중하느라고 눈을 반쯤 감았다. ● **squint·er** [-ər] *n.* [E.]

squint-eyed [skwíntàid] *adj.* **1** with each eye looking in a different direction. 사팔눈의; 사시의. **2** malicious. 악의 있는.

·**squire** [skwaiər] *n.* Ⓒ **1** 《Brit.》 the chief landowner of some district. 지주. **2** 《U.S.》 a justice of the peace. 치안 판사. **3** 《hist.》 a young person who attended a knight. 기사의 종자(從者). **4** a woman's escort; a gallant. 여성을 에스코트하는 사람; 멋쟁이. — *vt.* (P6,7) act as a squire to; accompany or attend on (a lady). (여성을) 에스코트하다. [*esquire*]

squire·arch·y [skwáiərɑːrki] *n.* **1** Ⓤ the government by landed proprietors. 지주 정치. **2** Ⓒ 《*the ～*》 the class of landed proprietors. 지주 계급; 지주들.

squirm [skwəːrm] *vi.* (P1,2A) **1** writhe; wriggle. 꿈틀거리다. **2** 《*fig.*》 show or feel humiliation or embarrassment. 머뭇거리다; 어색해하다. [Imit.]

·**squir·rel** [skwə́ːrəl / skwír-] *n.* Ⓒ (*pl.* **-rels** or *collectively* **-rel**) a small leaping animal with a large bushy tail, usu. gray or brown, which lives in trees. 다람쥐. [Gk.]

squirt [skwəːrt] *vi.* (P1,3) flow forth in a stream out of a tube, etc. 분출하다; 뿜어나오다. ¶ *water squirting into the air* 하늘로 솟아오르는 물. — *vt.* (P6,7) force out (liquid) out of a small opening. (액체를) 분출시키다; 뿜어나오게 하다. ¶ ～ *water from a water pistol* 물딱총으로 물을 내쏘다. — *n.* Ⓒ **1** a stream or jet of liquid. 분출. **2** any device for squirting a liquid. 액체를 분출시키는 장치. **3** 《*sl.*》 an insignificant self-assertive fellow. 같잖은 어정뱅이; 소인. [E.]

sq. yd. square yard(s).

Sr strontium.

Sr. **1** Senior. **2** Sir.

Sra. *Señora.*

Sri Lan·ka [srì:lɑ́:ŋkə, -lǽŋkə] *n.* **the Republic of ~** an island republic in the Indian Ocean, South of India. 스리랑카.

S.R.O. Standing Room Only. 입석뿐임.

Srta. *Señorita.*

SS, S.S. *Schutzstaffel*(G. =Protective Rank or Force). 나치스 친위대.

SS. *Sancti*(L. =Saints); Saints.

S.S. steamship; Sunday School; *supra scriptum*(L. =written above).

ss. sections; shortstop.

SSB Social Security Board.

SSR Soviet Socialist Republic.

SST supersonic transport.

SSW south-southwest.

***St.** Saint; Strait; Stratus; Street.

St., st. statute(s).

s.t. short ton.

Sta. Santa; Station.

sta. stationary.

***stab** [stæb] *v.* (**stabbed, stab·bing**) *vt.* **1** (P6,13) wound (someone) with a sharp pointed weapon. …를 찌르다. ¶ ~ *someone with a dagger* =~ *a dagger into someone* 아무를 단검으로 찌르다 / ~ *someone in the arm* 아무의 팔을 찌르다 / ~ *someone to death* 아무를 찔러 죽이다. **2** (P6) ⓐ hurt (the feelings, etc.) sharply and deeply. (감정·명성 따위를) 심하게 해치다[상처를 내다]. ¶ ~ *someone's name* 명성에 상처를 내다[입히다]. ⓑ 《*fig.*》 inflict sharp pain on; injure maliciously. 몹시 아프게[쓰라리게] 하다; 중상(中傷)하다. ¶ *He was stabbed to the heart by the girl's jeer.* 그 여자의 조소로 그는 가슴을 에는 듯한 괴로움을 느꼈다. — *vi.* **1** (P3) 《*at*》 wound with a stab. 찌르다. ¶ ~ *at her with a knife* 나이프로 그녀를 찌르다. **2** (P1) (of pain) give a sensation as if stabbed by a sharp weapon. 찌르듯이 아프다.

stab someone in the back, 《*fig.*》 speak ill of an absent person; slander [betray] someone. 아무의 험담을 하다; (아무를) 중상[배신]하다.

— *n.* Ⓒ **1** a thrust or blow with a sharp weapon; a wound made by such a way. 찌르기; 찔린 상처. **2** a painful sensation. 정신적인 고통; 양심의 가책. **3** a sudden sharp throb of pain. 찌르는 듯한 아픔; (갑작스런) 격통. ¶ *She felt a ~ of pain in her temple.* 그녀는 관자놀이에 격심한 통증을 느꼈다. **4** 《*colloq.*》 an attempt; a try. 기도(企圖); 시도(試圖). [E.]

make* [*have*] *a stab at, 《U.S. *colloq.*》 try at. …을 해보다. ¶ *make* [*have*] *a ~ at solving the problem* 문제를 해결하려고 시도하다.

stab·ber [stǽbər] *n.* Ⓒ **1** a person who stabs someone else. 자객. **2** an instrument used for stabbing. 찌르는 것; 송곳.

***sta·bil·i·ty** [stəbíləti] *n.* Ⓤ the state of being stable; firmness. 안정(도); 착실(성). ¶ *economic* ~ 경제적 안정. [→stable[1]]

sta·bi·li·za·tion [stèibəlizéiʃən] *n.* Ⓤ the act of stabilizing; the state of being stabilized. 안정(화(化)). ¶ *the ~ of the currency* 통화의 안정.

sta·bi·lize [stéibəlàiz] *vt.* (P6) **1** make (something) firm, steady or dependable. …을 안정시키다. ¶ ~ *prices* 물가를 안정시키다 / ~ *one's life* [*income*] 생활[수입]을 안정시키다 / ~ *the cost of living* 생계비를 안정시키다. **2** keep the balance of (an airplane, etc.) by automatic devices. (비행기 따위)의 안정을 유지하다.

sta·bi·liz·er [stéibəlàizər] *n.* Ⓒ **1** a person or thing that stabilizes something. 안정시키는 사람[것]. **2** a device for keeping the balance of an airplane, a ship, etc. (비행기·선박 따위의) 안정 장치.

:sta·ble[1] [stéibl] *adj.* **1** fixed; firm; not easily moved. 견고[튼튼]한; 안정된. ¶ ~ *foundations* 견고한 토대 / *a ~ government* 안정된 정부 / (*a*) ~ *currency* 안정된 통화. **2** firm in character; unwavering. 착실한; 견실한. ¶ ~ *opinions* 착실[견실]한 의견 / *a ~ character* 착실한 사람. [L. *sto* stand]

***sta·ble**[2] [stéibl] *n.* Ⓒ **1** a house in which horses are kept. 마구간. **2** a group of horses kept in such a building. (한 마구간에 소속된 전체의) 말. — *vt., vi.* (P6;1) put (horses) in a stable. (말을) 마구간에 넣다. [L. *stabulum*]

sta·ble·boy [stéiblbɔ̀i] *n.* Ⓒ a boy who works in a stable. 마구간을 담당한 젊은이[소년].

sta·ble·man [stéiblmən, -mæ̀n] *n.* Ⓒ (*pl.* **-men** [-mèn, -mən]) a man who works in a stable. 마부; 마구간을 담당한 사람.

sta·bly [stéibli] *adv.* in a stable manner, firmly. 안정[고정]되어; 단단히. [*stable*[1]]

stac·ca·to [stəkɑ́:tou] *adj.* 《mus.》 disconnected; with breaks between successive tones. 끊음음의; 스타카토의. ¶ *a ~ mark* 끊음음표. — *adv.* in a staccato manner. 끊음음으로. [It.]

stack [stæk] *n.* Ⓒ **1** a large pile of hay, straw, etc. (건초·밀짚 따위의) 쌓아 올린 더미; 낟가리. **2** an orderly pile of anything. …의 (차곡차곡 쌓인) 더미; 퇴적. ¶ *a ~ of books* 차곡차곡 쌓인 책 더미. **3** 《usu. *pl.*》 a set of bookcases in a library. 서가; 서고. ¶ *books in the stacks* 서가에 있는 책들 / *go into the stacks* 서고에 들어가다. **4** a chimney of a steamer. (기선 따위의) 굴뚝. **5** rifles arranged with their openings together in the form of a pyramid. 걸어총.

— *vt.* (P6,7,13) arrange (something) in a stack; heap or pile up. …을 쌓아올리다; 퇴적하다. ¶ ~ *a desk with papers* 책상 위에 서류를 쌓아 올리다 / ~ *hay* 건초를 쌓아 올리다. — *vi.* (P1,2A) 《*up*》 form a stack. (산더미같이) 쌓이다. [N.]

sta·di·a [stéidiə] *n.* pl. of **stadium.**

***sta·di·um** [stéidiəm] *n.* Ⓒ (*pl.* **-di·ums** or **-di·a**) **1** a running track for foot races in ancient Greece with seats for spectators all around it. (고대 그리스의) 도보 경주장. **2** a similar modern sports field. (현재의) 육상 경기장; 스타디움. [Gk.]

:staff [stæf, stɑːf] *n.* Ⓒ (*pl.* **staffs** or **staves**) **1** 《*collectively*》 (in the army) a group of officers as advisers. 참모; 막료. ¶ *the general and his* ~ 장군과 그의 참모 / *a* ~ *officer* 참모 장교 / *the General Staff* 참모 본부 / *the joint* ~ 합동 참모 / *the chief of the general* ~ 참모(參謀) 총장 / *a naval* ~ *college* 해군 대학 / *a* ~ *college* 육군 대학 / ~ *work* 참모의 일. **2** 《*collectively*》 a group of persons working as one unit. 직원; 간부 요원; 부원. ¶ *the editorial* ~ 편집 부원 / *the teaching* ~ *of a college* 대학의 교수진 / *the medical* ~ *of a hospital* 병원의 의료 요원 / *the member of the* ~ 사원; 부원 / *He is on the* ~ *of a railroad company.* 그는 철도 회사의 간부 직원이다. **3** a stick; a rod; a pole. 지팡이; 막대기; 장대. ¶ *a flag* ~ 깃대 / *lean on one's* ~ 지팡이에 의지하다. **4** 《*fig.*》 a support. 의지; 지주. ¶ 《*prov.*》 *Bread is the* ~ *of life.* 빵은 생명의 지주이다. **5** 《mus.》 the five lines with the spaces between them on which music is written. 오선(五線); 보표(譜表).

— *vt.* (P6) provide a staff for (an office). …에 직원〔사원〕을 두다. ¶ *a well-staffed college* 교수진이 잘 갖추어진 대학 / *His office is not sufficiently staffed.* 그의 사무실에는 직원이 충분하지 않다. [E.]

stag [stæg] *n.* Ⓒ (*pl.* **stags** or *collectively* **stag**) **1** a grown-up male deer. (성숙한) 수사슴. **2** a male of various kind of animals. (동물의) 수컷. **3** 《U.S. *colloq.*》 a man who goes to a social gathering unaccompanied by a lady. (무도회 따위에) 여성을 동반하지 않고 가는 사람. **4** 《stock》 a person who applies for allotments in new concerns with a view to selling at once at a profit. 권리주 매매 투기자. [E.]

:stage [steidʒ] *n.* Ⓒ **1** a high platform in a theater on which a play is acted, etc. (극장의) 무대. ¶ *a* ~ *set* 무대 장치 / *put on the* ~ 상연하다 / *a revolving* ~ 회전 무대 / *bring* 〔*put, present*〕 *a comedy on the* ~ 희극을 상연하다. **2** 《*the* ~》 the profession of an actor. 배우업; 연극계. ¶ *give up the law for the* ~ 변호사를 그만두고 배우가 되다. **3** 《*the* ~》 the drama. 연극. ¶ *the medieval* ~ 중세의 연극 / *the French* ~ 프랑스 연극. **4** a scene or place of action. (활동의) 무대; (전쟁 따위가 있었던) 장소. ¶ *the* ~ *of one's operation* 활동 무대 / *Europe was the* ~ *for war.* 유럽은 전쟁의 무대였다 / *Waterloo was the* ~ *of a famous battle.* 워털루는 유명한 전투가 있었던 장소이다 / *leave the* ~ *of politics* 정계를 떠나다. **5** a period in a development. (발달 따위의) 단계; 기(期); 시기. ¶ *an early* ~ *of civilization* 문명의 초기 / *in stages* 단계적으로 / *at this* ~ 현 단계에 있어서(는) / *in the earlier* 〔*later*〕 *stages of one's life* 인생의 초기〔후기〕에 / *the earlier* 〔*advanced, final*〕 *stages of cancer* 암의 초기〔중기, 말기〕 단계 / *The dispute approached its final* ~. 분쟁은 최종 단계에 이르렀다. **6** a stopping-place on a journey; the distance between two stoppingplaces. (옛날 역마차·버스 따위의) 역; 역참; 여정. ¶ *travel to the last* ~ 최종역까지 가다. **7** a stagecoach. 역마차. **8** a wooden frame put up around a building which is being built. (건축용의) 비계; 작업용 발판.

come on* 〔*upon*〕 *the stage, appear on the stage. 무대에 오르다.

go on* 〔*take to*〕 *the stage, become an actor. 배우가 되다.

travel by stages, travel at one's ease. 천천히 〔마음 편히〕 여행하다.

— *vt.* (P6) **1** ⓐ put (a play) on the stage. (연극을) 상연하다. ¶ *His play was first staged in London.* 그의 연극은 최초로 런던에서 상연되었다. ⓑ dramatize. 각색하다. **2** plan, arrange, and carry out. 계획〔준비, 실시〕하다. ¶ ~ *a demonstration* 데모를 하다 / ~ *the coup* 쿠데타를 계획하다.

— *vi.* (P2A) **1** be suitable for staging. 상연에 알맞다. ¶ *a play that stages well* 〔*badly*〕 흥행거리가 좋은〔나쁜〕 연극. **2** travel by stagecoach. 역마차로 여행하다.

• **stage·like** [-làik] *adj.* [→stable[2]]

stage·coach [stéidʒkòutʃ] *n.* Ⓒ a large coach, drawn by horses, formerly used for carrying passengers over a regular route. 역마차.

〈stagecoach〉

stage·craft [stéidʒkræ̀ft, -krɑ̀ːft] *n.* Ⓤ the art of writing, adapting, or presenting plays. 극작〔연출, 연기〕 기술〔기법〕.

stage direction [´-`-] *n.* a direction written or printed on the text of a play telling the actors how they should act on the stage. 무대 지시(서).

stage effect [´-`] *n.* any means or device used on the stage for creating a certain effect. 무대 효과.

stage fright [´`] *n.* the nervous fear felt by an actor or speaker when appearing before an audience. 무대 공포증.

stage manager [´`--] *n.* a person who has general control of the stage during the performance or rehearsals of a play. 무대 감독.

stag·er [stéidʒər] *n.* Ⓒ a person who has long experience. 노련가.

stage whisper [ㅅ ㅅ] *n.* 《theatr.》 a loud whisper meant to be heard by others than the person addressed. (말하는 대상자보다는) 제 3자에게 일부러 들으라고 하는 큰 속삭임.

***stag·ger** [stǽgər] *vi.* **1** (P1,2A) walk back and forth or weave from side to side unsteadily. 비틀거리다; 비틀거리며 나아가다. ¶ ~ *down the street* 거리를 비틀거리며 가다 / ~ *to one's feet* 비틀거리며 일어서다 / ~ *across the road* 비틀비틀 길을 건너다. **2** (P3) show signs of giving way or losing confidence; waver in purpose; hesitate. (자신감을 잃고) 멈칫〔주춤〕하다; 동요하다; 망설이다; 주저하다. ¶ *The soldiers staggered under the severe gunfire.* 병사들은 격렬한 포화에 주춤하기 시작했다 / ~ *at the news* 그 소식으로 마음이 흔들리다.
— *vt.* (P6,13) **1** cause (someone) to move back and forth or from side to side. 비틀거리게 하다. ¶ *The boxer was staggered by the blow.* 그 권투 선수는 일격에 비틀거렸다 / *The heavy kick staggered him for a moment.* 강력한 발의 일격으로 그는 잠시 동안 휘청거리었다. **2** make (someone) hesitate. …을 흔들리게 하다. ¶ ~ *someone's resolution* 결심을 흔들리게 하다. **3** shock or surprise very much. …을 깜짝 놀라게 하다. ¶ *The price staggered him.* 가격은 그를 깜짝 놀라게 했다 / *I was staggered by the news.* 그 뉴스에 깜짝 놀랐다. **4** arrange (something) so that it does not happen at the same time as (another thing); put in a zigzag order; arrange at different times. (동시에 행해지거나 겹쳐지지 않도록) …을 서로 엇갈리게〔교체적으로〕 하다; …을 시차를 두다. ¶ ~ *lunch* 〔*office*〕 *hours* 점심〔근무〕 시간을 시차제로 하다 / *The captain staggered his troops along the road.* 대장은 그의 부대를 도로를 따라 지그재그 대형으로 배치하였다.
— *n.* Ⓒ **1** an unsteady movement. 비틀거림. **2** 《*the* ~*s*》 ⓐ 《used as *sing.*》 a nervous disease of horses, cattle, etc. that causes them to stagger or fall suddenly. (말·소 따위의) 훈도병(暈倒病). ⓑ 《*pl.*》 a feeling of giddiness. 현기증. [N.]

stag·ger·er [stǽgərər] *n.* **1** a person who staggers or hesitates. 비틀거리는 사람. **2** a thing that staggers a person; a difficult question. 비틀거리게〔깜짝 놀라게〕 하는 것; 난문제.

stag·hound [stǽghàund] *n.* Ⓒ a kind of large dog once used for hunting stags or other animals. 스태그하운드《원래 사슴을 사냥하던 큰 사냥개》. [*stag*]

stag·ing [stéidʒiŋ] *n.* **1** Ⓤ a platform of boards for support; scaffolding. 발판; 비계. **2** ⒸⓊ the act or manner of putting a play on the stage. (극 따위의) 각색; 상연. **3** Ⓤ driving the stage-coach. 역마차 여행. [*stage*]

stag·nan·cy [stǽgnənsi] *n.* Ⓤ the state of being stagnant. 침체; 불경기. [↓]

stag·nant [stǽgnənt] *adj.* **1** (of water, air, etc.) motionless; not flowing; foul or stale from standing still. 괴어 있는; 흐르지 않는; (정체되어) 썩은. ¶ ~ *air* (흐르지 않는) 탁한 공기 / *a* ~ *pool* 물이 괴어 있는 더러운 웅덩이. **2** not active; dull. 활발하지 못한; 침체된. ¶ *a* ~ *economy* 침체된 경제 / *a* ~ *brain* 둔한 머리 / *Trade is* ~. 상황(商況)은 불경기이다. [L. *stagnum* pond]

stag·nant·ly [stǽgnəntli] *adv.* in a stagnant manner. 정체되어; 부진하여.

stag·nate [stǽgneit] *vi.* (P1) be or become stagnant. (물 따위가) 흐르지 않다; 괴다; 침체되다; 부진하게〔불경기가〕 되다. — *vt.* (P6) make (something) stagnant. …을 괴게 하다; 부진하게 하다.

stag·na·tion [stægnéiʃən] *n.* Ⓤ the act of stagnating; the state of being stagnant. 정체; 침체; 부진; 불황. ¶ *fall into* ~ 정체〔불황〕에 빠지다 / *the* ~ *of commerce* 〔*in the market*〕 무역〔시장〕의 침체〔부진〕 / *face* ~ 불황에 직면하다 / *threaten the nation with economic* ~ 나라를 경제 불황의 위기로 몰아넣다.

stag·y [stéidʒi] *adj.* (**stag·i·er, stag·i·est**) **1** of the stage. 무대의. **2** theatrical or artificial in speech, manner, etc.; not real or natural; affected. 연극조의; 꾸민 티가 나는; 과장된; …체 하는. ¶ *a* ~ *person* 젠체하는 사람 / *a* ~ *tone* 연극조의〔부자연스런〕 어조. [*stage*]

staid [steid] *adj.* settled and steady; sober; quiet. 침착한; 착실한; 성실한. ¶ ~ *behavior* 침착(沈着)한 태도 / ~ *colors* 침착한 색깔. ● **staid·ness** [-nis] *n.* **staid·ly** [-li] *adv.* [*stay*]

***stain** [stein] *vt.* **1** (P6,13) make a blot on (something). …을 더럽히다; …을 얼룩이 지게 하다. ¶ *a stained shirt* 때로 얼룩이 진 셔츠 / ~ *one's fingers with ink* 잉크로 손가락을 더럽히다 / *hands stained with blood* 피로 얼룩진 손. **2** (P6) 《*fig.*》 spoil (one's reputation, character, etc.) by disgrace. (명성 등을) 더럽히다; 훼손하다. ¶ ~ *one's name* 이름을 더럽히다 / *a character stained by vice* 악에 물든 성격. **3** (P6,18) put color on or in (something). …에 착색하다. ¶ ~ *wood* 〔*walls*〕 나무를〔벽을〕 채색하다 / *She stained the table black to match her new chairs.* 그녀는 새 의자에 어울리도록 식탁을 검은 색으로 칠하였다.
— *vi.* **1** (P1) take a stain; become stained. 더러워지다; 얼룩지다. ¶ *The cloth will not* ~. 그 천은 얼룩이 지지 않는다. **2** (P2A) produce a stain. 얼룩이 되다; 얼룩이 지게 하다. ¶ *Ink stains worse than almost anything.* 잉크는 다른 어떤 것보다 더 고약하게 얼룩이 진다.
— *n.* Ⓒ **1** a dirty spot. 얼룩; 더럼. ¶ *an ink* ~ 잉크 얼룩 / *a* ~ *on* 〔*upon*〕 *the table-*

cloth 식탁보에 저있는 얼룩 / *He has blood stains on his shirt.* 그의 셔츠에는 핏자국이 있다. **2** a moral defect; dishonor. 오점; 흠. ¶ *without a ~ on one's character* 인격에 조그만 흠 하나 없는 / *a ~ on one's reputation* 명성의 흠〔오점〕. **3** Ⓤ a color given to wood, glass, wall paper, etc.; the coloring matter for this. 착색; 염료; 안료. [dis-, tinge]

stained glass [stéind ㅅ] *n.* glass that has been stained or colored by various methods, used widely for decorative windows, esp. in churches. (착)색 유리; 스테인드 글라스.

*__stain·less__ [stéinlis] *adj.* **1** without a stain. 얼룩지지 않은; 더럼이 없는. **2** free from guilt or sin; blameless. 무구(無垢)한; 결백한. **3** not easily stained or discolored; resisting rust. 더럼이 잘 타지 않는; 변색하지 않는; 녹슬지 않는. ¶ *~ steel* 스테인리스 강(鋼).

:**stair** [stɛər] *n.* Ⓒ **1** any one of a set of steps for going from one level to another. 계단의 한 단. ¶ *a short passage and then three stairs* 짧은 통로 그리고 다음에는 세 단의 계단 / *the top ~ but one* 위에서 두 번째의 계단 / *He tripped on the top ~.* 그는 최상단에서 발을 헛디뎠다. **2** 《usu. *pl.*》 a set of such steps. 계단. ¶ *a winding* 〔*screw, spiral*〕 *stairs* 회전식〔나선형〕 계단 / *A short ~ leads to the first floor.* 짧은 계단을 올라가면 1층〔2층〕으로 나간다. [E.]

a flight of stairs, a set of stairs in a straight line. 한 줄로 이어진 계단.

below stairs, in the lower floor or basement of a house; in the kitchen or servants' quarters. 아래층〔지하실〕 에서〔으로〕; 부엌〔하인방〕 에서〔으로〕.

up stairs, on or to the upper floor(s). 위층에서〔으로〕. ¶ *go up the stairs* 계단을 올라가다.

stair carpet [ㅅ ㅅ-] *n.* a carpet woven in a narrow strip for laying on stairs. 계단용 융단.

*__stair·case__ [stɛ́ərkèis] *n.* Ⓒ a set of stairs with a supporting framework and a handrail. (난간 등을 포함한 한 줄의) 계단.

stair rod [ㅅ ㅅ] *n.* a metal or wooden bar for holding a stair carpet in position. 계단의 융단 누르개.

stair·way [stɛ́ərwèi] *n.* Ⓒ 《chiefly U.S.》 a staircase. 계단; 층계.

:**stake**[1] [steik] *n.* Ⓒ **1** a stick or post sharpened at one end for driving into the ground. 말뚝; 막대기. ¶ *drive in a ~* 말뚝을 박다 / *tie a plant* 〔*an animal*〕 *to a ~* 묘목〔동물〕을 말뚝에 잡아 매다. **2** ⓐ the post to which people were tied and burned to death in olden times. 화형주(火刑柱). ¶ *be burnt at the ~* 화형에 처해지다. ⓑ 《*the ~*》 death by burning. 화형. ¶ *be condemned to the ~* 화형의 선고를 받다. **3** a small anvil used by a tinsmith. 생철장이의 작은 쇠모루.

pull up stakes, 《U.S.》 move away. 떠나가다; 이사가다.

— *vt.* (P6,7) **1** fasten (something) to a stake; support, secure with a stake. …을 말뚝에 (잡아)매다; 말뚝으로 …을 받치다〔고정하다〕. ¶ *~ a horse* 말을 말뚝에 매다 / *~ rose vines* 덩굴장미를 막대기로 반쳐주다. **2** 《U.S.》 《*off, out*》 mark (the ground) with stakes. …을 말뚝으로 구획하다. ¶ *~ off* 〔*out*〕 *a boundary* 말뚝을 박아 경계를 구획하다 / *~ in* 〔*up*〕 *the site* 부지를 말뚝을 박아 에두르다. [E.]

stake[2] [steik] *n.* Ⓒ **1** 《usu. *pl.*》 money risked; something which is staked. 내기; 내기에 건 돈〔것〕. ¶ *play for high* 〔*big*〕 *stakes* 큰 내기를〔도박을〕 하다 / *play at cards for small stakes* 돈을 조금 걸고 카드 놀이를 하다 / *The ~ is our life.* 우리는 생명을 걸고 있다. **2** 《often *pl.*》 the prize or reward in a contest or race. 배당; 상금. ¶ *play for some stakes* 상금을 노리고 게임을 하다 / *win the stakes* 상금을 타다. **3** a share or interest in property. 이해 관계. ¶ *have a ~ in an undertaking* 사업에 이해 관계를 가지다 / *He has a big ~ in the success of the firm.* 회사의 성공에 그는 큰 이해 관계를 갖고 있다.

at stake, risked; in question; in danger of being lost; depending on the result of some event. (돈·목숨·운명 등이) 걸리어; 문제가 되어; 위태로워져서. ¶ *Life itself is at ~.* 생명 그 자체가 걸려 있다 / *My honor is at ~.* 나의 명예가 걸려 있는 문제이다 / *The safety of mankind was at ~.* 인류의 안전이 위기에 처해 있었다.

— *vt.* (P6,13) risk (money, one's life, etc.) on some event. …을 걸다. ¶ *~ one's life* 목숨을 걸다 / *~ a fortune on a single race* 단 한 번의 경주에 재산을 걸다 / *I ~ my reputation on his honesty.* 명예를 걸고 그가 정직하다는 것을 보증한다. [E.]

sta·lac·tite [stǽləktàit, stəlǽktait] *n.* Ⓒ a formation of limestone shaped like an icicle, hanging from the roof of a cave. 종유석(鍾乳石). [Gk. *stalassō* drip]

sta·lag·mite [stəlǽgmait, stǽləgmàit] *n.* Ⓒ a formation of limestone shaped like a cone, forming on the floor of a cave. 석순(石筍). [Gk. *stalassō* drip]

*__stale__[1] [steil] *adj.* **1** not fresh any longer; having lost freshness; not new; having no taste; dried out. 신선미가 없는; 김이 빠진; (시들어) 말라 빠진; (딱딱하게) 마른. ¶ *~ beer* 김빠진 맥주 / *~ bread* 딱딱하게 굳어진 빵 / *~ air* 탁한 공기 / *~ food* 신선미가 없는 식품. **2** not interesting because of constant use. 진부한; 케케묵은. ¶ *a ~ joke* 진부한 농담 / *~ news* 케케묵은 뉴스. **3** out of condition because of too much activity. (과로 따위로) 생기가 없는; 컨디션이 나쁜; 몹시 지친. ¶ *The horse has gone ~.* 말

은 기진맥진했다 / *He has become ~ through overtraining.* 그는 과도한 연습으로 몸의 컨디션이 나빠졌다.
— *vt., vi.* (P6;1) make or become stale. 신선미를 잃다[가 없어지다]; 김빠지(게 하)다. [Teut.]

stale[2] [steil] *n.* Ⓤ urine of horses and cattle. (소·말의) 오줌. — *vi.* (P1) make water. (소·말이) 오줌을 누다. [F.]

stale·mate [stéilmèit] *n.* Ⓒ **1** (in chess) a position in which no move can be made without placing the king in check. (체스에서) 수의 막힘《쌍방이 다 둘 만한 수가 없어 비기게 되는 상태》. **2** a position in which any further action is impossible; a deadlock. 막다름; 궁지; 교착 상태. ¶ *nuclear ~* 핵무장 경쟁의 막다름 / *be at a ~* 교착 상태에 빠져 있다; 막다른 상태에 있다. — *vt.* (P6) put (something) in such a position. …의 수를 막히게 하다; …을 궁지에 몰아넣다[막다르게 하다]. [F. *estale* standstill]

***stalk**[1] [stɔːk] *n.* Ⓒ **1** the stem of a plant, a leaf, a flower or a piece of fruit. 줄기; 대; 잎자루. **2** any support like a stem. 가늘고 긴 버팀대. **3** a stem of a wineglass. 술잔의 길쭉한 굽. **4** 《archit.》 an ornament like a stalk of plant. 줄기 모양의 장식. **5** a tall chimney. 높은 굴뚝. [E.]

***stalk**[2] [stɔːk] *vt.* (P6) **1** follow or approach (an animal or person) secretly. 살그머니 (짐승·사람)의 뒤를 밟다; …에 몰래 접근하다. ¶ *The hunter stalked the deer.* 사냥꾼이 사슴에게 살그머니 다가갔다. **2** walk or spread through silently and threateningly. (질병·재앙 따위가) …에 퍼지다; …을 휩쓸다. ¶ *Famine stalked the land.* 기근이 나라를 휩쓸었다. — *vi.* (P1,2A) **1** walk in a stiff, proud manner. 당당하게 걷다; 활보하다. ¶ *~ along the street* 거리를 활보하다. **2** approach silently and secretly. 몰래 다가가다. — *n.* Ⓤ the act of stalking. (짐승에게) 살그머니 다가감; 활보. [E.]

stalk·ing-horse [stɔ́ːkiŋhɔ̀ːrs] *n.* Ⓒ **1** a horse or figure of a horse behind which a hunter hides in approaching game. 은신마(隱身馬)《사냥꾼이 몸을 숨기고 사냥감에 다가가는 말 또는 말 모양의 것》. **2** 《*fig.*》 anything put forward to hide one's plans, etc.; a pretext. 위장; 구실. [E.]

***stall**[1] [stɔːl] *n.* Ⓒ **1** a place for an animal in a stable. 마구간; 마구간[외양간]의 한 칸[구획]. **2** a table or booth on which things are displayed for sale. 매점; 상품 진열대. ¶ *a street ~* 노점 / *a ~ at a bazaar* 바자의 매점 / *a flower ~* 꽃가게. **3** 《Brit.》 a seat near the stage or screen, esp. one separated from others. (영화관·극장 따위의) 1층 특등석. **4** a fixed seat in the choir of a church for the clergy. (교회의) 성가대석.
— *vt.* **1** (P6) keep (an animal) in a stall, esp. for fattening. …을 마구간[외양간]에 넣(어 두)다. ¶ *The horses were safely stalled.* 말들은 안전하게 마구간에 수용되었다. **2** (P6) cause (a vehicle, etc.) to stick fast in mud, snow, etc.; unintentionally cause (a vehicle's engine) to come to a standstill. (말·마차 따위)를 눈이나 진흙 속에 빠지게 하다; …을 오도가도 못 하게 하다. ¶ *a train stalled by snow* 눈으로 꼼짝 못 하게 된 열차 / *get stalled in the mud* 진흙 속에 빠져 오도가도 못 하게 되다 / *We were stalled in the car for an hour.* 차 속에서 1시간 동안 꼼짝 못했다.
— *vi.* (P1) **1** stick fast in mud; come to a standstill; (of a motor engine) stop working. 진흙에 빠지다; 오도가도 못 하다; (엔진이) 정지하다. ¶ *The car stalled on the hill.* 자동차는 언덕에서 엔진이 멎었다. **2** (of an airplane) lose flying speed and fall. (비행기가) 실속(失速)하다. **3** (of an animal) live in a stall. (소·말이) 축사에 들어가 있다[살다]. [E.]

stall[2] [stɔːl] *n.* Ⓒ a pickpocket's confederate. 소매치기의 바람잡이. — *vi., vt.* (P1;6) fence conversationally; avoid giving a clear answer to a question. 교묘하게 둘러대어 빠져나가다[피하다]. [E.]

stal·lion [stǽljən] *n.* Ⓒ a male horse kept for breeding. 종마(種馬). [E.]

stal·wart [stɔ́ːlwərt] *adj.* **1** strongly built; brave. 튼튼한; 용감한. ¶ *a ~ soldier* 용감한 병사 / *a man of ~ build* 건장한 체격의 남자. **2** firm and reliable; very loyal to someone or a cause. (지조·정치적 신념 따위가) 확고한; 신뢰할 수 있는. ¶ *a ~ supporter* 지조 있는 확고한 지지자 / *They are always my ~ friends.* 그들은 언제나 신뢰할 수 있는 친구들이다. — *n.* Ⓒ a brave, reliable person. 신뢰할 수 있는 사람. [E.=place-worthy]

sta·men [stéimən / -men] *n.* Ⓒ 《bot.》 the part of a flower bearing pollen. 수술; 웅예. [L.=warpthread]

stam·i·na [stǽmənə] *n.* Ⓤ the physical strength to work hard and long. 정력; 지구력; 스태미나. ¶ *It requires great ~ to run a marathon race.* 마라톤 경주에는 굉장한 지구력이 요구된다. [↑]

***stam·mer** [stǽmər] *vi.* (P1,3) repeat the same sound several times before uttering a word; hesitate in speaking. 말을 더듬다; 말을 머뭇거리다. ¶ *~ over words* 말을 머뭇[더듬]거리며 말하다. — *vt.* (P6,7) 《*out*》 utter (something) in this manner. …을 더듬[머뭇]거리며 말하다. ¶ *~ out an excuse* 더듬거리며 변명을 늘어놓다. — *n.* Ⓒ the act of stammering. 말더듬기. [E.]

stam·mer·er [stǽmərər] *n.* Ⓒ a person who stammers. 말더듬이.

stam·mer·ing·ly [stǽməriŋli] *adv.* in a stammering manner. (말을) 더듬거리며.

***stamp** [stæmp] *n.* Ⓒ **1** an instrument for pressing some mark on paper, etc.; a mark pressed by this. 도장; 스탬프; (각(刻))인(印). ¶ *a rubber ~* 고무 도장 / *a ~ of* *payment* 지불필의 도장 / *an official* ~ 공인(公印) / *These articles bear the* ~ *of the maker.* 이들 제품에는 제조자의 각인이 찍혀 있다. **2** a small piece of printed paper, put on letters or documents to show that a fee has been paid; a postage stamp. 인지(印紙); 우표. ¶ *a postage* ~ 우표 / *a trading* ~ 경품 교환권 / *a revenue* ~ 수입 인지 / *stick a* ~ *on an envelope* 봉투에 우표를 붙이다 / *cancel a* ~ 우표에 소인을 찍다. **3** anything that shows the truth; an impression; a sign; a characteristic. 표적; 자국; 흔적; 특징. ¶ *bear the* ~ *of learning* 학문을 한 표시가 난다 / *It bears the* ~ *of breeding* 〔*genius*〕. 가정 교육〔천재〕의 특징을 나타내고 있다 / *His face bears the* ~ *of suffering.* 그의 얼굴에는 고생한 자국이 남아 있다. **4** 《used as *sing.*》 a kind; a form. 종류; 형(型). ¶ *men of the same* ~ 같은 타입의 사람들 / *a man of serious* ~ 고지식한 사람 / *men of that* 〔*his*〕 ~ 그런〔그와 같은〕 타입의 사람들. **5** the act of stamping one's foot. 발구르기; 짓밟기. **6** a machine or a part of a machine for crushing rock, etc. 쇄광기(碎鑛機).

— *vt.* **1** (P6,7,13) press a mark on (something); impress (a mark) on something 〔a surface〕. …에 도장을 찍다〔날인하다〕; (도장)을 누르다〔찍다〕. ¶ ~ *a document with the address and date* 서류에 주소 성명과 날짜를 도장으로 찍다 / *goods stamped with the maker's name* 제조자 이름이 각인되어 있는 상품 / ~ *a plan 'top secret'* 계획에 '일급 비밀'이란 도장을 찍다 / ~ *'paid' on the bill* 청구서에 '영수필'의 도장을 찍다 / ~ *one's name on the title page* 속표지에 이름을 도장으로 찍다 / ~ *patterns on cloth* 옷감에 무늬를 찍다 / *This document is stamped with his seal.* 이 서류에는 그의 도장이 찍혀 있다. **2** (P6) put a stamp on (a letter, etc.). …에 우표〔인지〕를 붙이다. ¶ ~ *a letter* 편지에 우표를 붙이다 / ~ *a document* 서류에 인지를 붙이다. **3** (P6,7,18) put (one's foot) down with force. (발)을 구르다; 쿵쿵거리다. ¶ ~ *one's foot in anger* 화가 나서 발을 쿵쿵거리다 / *The audience stamped the floor with impatience.* 청중들은 안달이 나서 마루를 쿵쿵 굴렀다. **4** (P6,7) destroy or crush (something) by stamping one's foot; tread. …을 짓밟다; 밟아 뭉개다. ¶ ~ *the flower bed* 꽃밭을 짓밟다 / ~ *the grass flat* 잔디를 밟아 뭉개다 / ~ *out a fire* 불을 밟아 끄다. **5** (P6,13) make a deep impression on (someone). …에 깊은 인상을 주다. ¶ *The deed is stamped on my memory.* 그 행위는 나의 기억에 깊은 인상을 남겼다. **6** (P7) show to be of a certain quality or character; indicate; mark. …의 본성을 나타내다; …을 —라고 나타내다〔드러내다〕. ¶ *His manners* ~ *him as a gentleman.* 그의 태도를 보니 그는 신사임이 확실하다. **7** (P7) 《*out*》 cut out; give shape to (a piece of metal, dough, etc.) by means of a die, cutter, etc. 틀로 찍어내다; 타출(打出)하다. ¶ ~ *out rings from metal sheets* 금속판에서 고리형(型)을 찍어내다. **8** (P6) crush (ore, etc.) by pressure. (광석 등을) 분쇄하다.

— *vi.* (P1,2A) put one's foot down with force. 발을 구르다; 짓밟다. ¶ ~ *on a worm* 벌레를 밟아 뭉개다 / ~ *on the accelerator* 액셀러레이터를 밟다. [E.]

stam·pede [stæmpí:d] *n.* Ⓒ **1** a sudden, wild running away of a herd of frightened animals. (가축의 떼 따위가) 놀라서 우르르 달아남; 대폭주. **2** any sudden, wild running away of a large group; a general rush. (많은 사람들이) 앞을 다투어 도망감; 몰려듦; 쇄도. ¶ *the* ~ *of panic-stricken crowd from a burning building* 불타고 있는 건물로부터 앞을 다투어 도망쳐 나온 공포에 질린 군중 / *a* ~ *for the exit* 출구로 와락 몰려듦 / *a* ~ *to newly discovered gold mines* 새로 발견된 금광으로의 쇄도.

— *vi.* (P1) move together in panic. 우르르 도망치다.

— *vt.* (P6) cause (something) to run away suddenly and wildly. …을 우르르 도망치게 하다. ¶ *Thunderstorms often* ~ *cattle.* 심한 뇌우는 자주 가축들을 폭주하게 한다. [↑]

stamp·er [stǽmpər] *n.* Ⓒ a person or thing that stamps. 도장〔소인〕을 찍는 사람〔것〕.

stamp·ing ground [stǽmpiŋ gràund] *n.* 《*colloq.*》 a place that a person frequents; a favorite haunt. 늘〔잘〕 다니는 곳.

stance [stæns] *n.* Ⓒ a position of a player's feet in a golf, baseball, etc. when hitting a ball. (골프·야구 등에서) 타자의 발 위치; 스탠스. [→state]

stanch[1] [stɑ:ntʃ, stɔ:ntʃ] *vt.* (P6) stop or check the flow of (blood, etc.); stop the flow of blood from (a wound). (피의 흐름을) 멈추게 하다; (출혈·상처를) 지혈하다.

— *vi.* (P1) (of blood, etc.) stop flowing. 피가 멎다. [→stagnant]

stanch[2] [stɑ:ntʃ, stɔ:ntʃ] *adj.* =staunch[2].

stan·chion [stǽnʃən, -tʃən / stɑ́:nʃən] *n.* Ⓒ an upright bar, post, beam or support in a window, a wall, etc. 지주(支柱); 칸막이 나무. [↑]

:stand [stænd] *v.* (**stood**) *vi.* (P1,2A,3,4) **1** rise to one's feet; take or keep an erect position on the feet. 서다; 일어서다; 선 자세로 있다. ¶ ~ *straight* 똑바로 서다 / ~ *at ease* 쉬어 자세로 서다 / *Please* ~. 일어서시오 / *Will volunteers please* ~ ? 지원자들께서는 일어서 주십시오 / *Everyone stood* (*up*) *when the band played the national anthem.* 밴드가 국가를 연주하였을 때 모든 사람은 일어섰다 / ~ *on one's head* 〔*hands*〕 물구나무서다 / *Stand straight, don't stoop.* 똑바로 서라, 구부려서는 안 된다 / *He stood still, looking at the picture.* 그는 그 그림을 보면서 가만히 서 있었다 / *It is more tiring to* ~ *for a long time than to walk a long distance.* 먼 거리를

걷는 것보다 오랜 시간 서 있는 것이 더 피로하다. **2** (of a person or thing) be in an erect position. (사람·물건이) 서 있다. ¶ ~ *still* 그대로 서 있다 / *The building still stood after the earthquake.* 지진 뒤에도 그 건물은 그대로 서 있었다 / *The table will not ~ without support.* 그 테이블은 지지물 없이는 바로 놓여 있지 못한다 / *I cannot get this to ~.* 이것을 서 있게 할 수 없다. **3** be placed; be situated. 위치하다; (…에) 있다. ¶ *The vase stands over there.* 화분은 저기 있다 / *My house stands on a hill.* 나의 집은 언덕 위에 있다 / *The clock stands on the table.* 괘종 시계는 테이블 위에 놓여 있다 / *The post office stands at 17th Street and 6th Avenue.* 우체국은 17번가(街)와 6번가(街)가 교차하는 지점에 위치해 있다《미국에서는 Avenue는 남북, Street는 동서로 뻗어 있는 큰 도로에 붙여 씀》. **4** be kept in a certain position or condition. (…한) 상태〔입장〕에 있다. ¶ ~ *fast* 〔*firm*〕 견지〔고수〕하다 / ~ *alone* 고립하다〔해 있다〕; 비길 데〔자〕가 없다 / ~ *amazed* 놀라워하고 있다 / *The door stood open.* 문이 열린 채로 있었다 / *He stands ready for anything.* 그는 어떤 일에도 끄떡도 안할 태세가 돼 있다 / *He stood accused* 〔*convicted*〕 *of murder.* 살인죄로 고소를 당했다〔의 선고를 받았다〕 / *They ~ in need of help.* 그들은 원조를 필요로 하고 있다 / *Jim stood in awe of his teacher.* 짐은 선생님에게 경외스런 마음을 품고 있었다 / *He stands well with his boss.* 그는 상관에게 좋은 평가를 받고 있다. **5** remain valid; be still in force; be unchanged. 유효하다; 그대로의 상태에 있다. ¶ *The rule still stands.* 그 규칙은 아직까지 유효하다 / *This contract will ~ good for another year.* 이 계약은 앞으로 1년 더 유효하다. **6** be of a certain height; be at a certain point on a scale; occupy a certain place in a series of things. (높이가) …이다; (온도가) …도이다; (등급이) …이다. ¶ ~ *five feet (tall) in one's socks* 신장은 신발을 벗고 5피트이다 / *The thermometer stands at 37°.* 온도계는 37°를 나타내고 있다 / *She stands second in her class.* 그녀는 그의 반에서 2등이다. **7** (of a person, etc.) stop (movement); remain motionless; gather and stay. 멈춰 서다; 움직이지 않다; 괴어 있다. ¶ *Stand where you are.* 그 자리에 서라〔움직이지 마라〕 / *Stand and be identified!* 정지, 누구냐 / *The tears stood in her eyes.* 그녀의 눈에는 눈물이 괴어 있었다. **8** 《chiefly Brit.》 become a political candidate. 입후보하다. ¶ *He is standing for Parliament.* 국회 의원으로 입후보하고 있다. **9** 《naut.》 hold a course at sea. 어떤 방향으로 나아가다. ¶ *They stood into harbor.* 그들은 항구를 향해 침로(針路)를 잡았다. — *vt.* **1** (P7) place (something or someone) in an upright position or in a certain position. …을 세우다; 세워 놓다; 어떤 위치에 놓다. ¶ ~ *a dictionary on end* 사전을 똑바로 세워 놓다 / ~ *a desk in the corner* 구석에 책상을 놓다 / ~ *a boy in front of a blackboard* 흑판 앞에 소년을 서게 하다 / ~ *a candle on a table* 식탁 위에 양초를 세워 놓다 / *I shall ~ you in the corner.* (벌로서) 구석에 세워 놓겠다 / ~ *a ladder against a wall* 벽에 사다리를 세워 놓다. **2** (P6) endure; bear. …을 참다; …에 견디다. ¶ ~ *great heat* 굉장한 더위에 견디다 / *Can you ~ the pain of a toothache?* 너 치통을 참고 견딜 수 있느냐 / *I cannot ~ any nonsense.* 난 허튼 수작에는 가만히 있을 수가 없다 / *I never can ~ that woman.* 저런 여자는 얼굴을 대하는 것조차도 역겹다 / *He could not ~ being kept waiting so long.* 그는 그렇게 오래도록 기다리게 하는 데에는 참을 수가 없었다 / *This book will ~ the test of time.* 이 책은 시간이란 시련을 견뎌내고 후세까지 남을 것이다 / *Will this ramshackle staircase ~ my weight?* 이 흔들거리는 계단이 나의 무게에 견딜수 있을까. **3** (P6) be subjected to; pass through. …을 받다〔겪다〕. ¶ ~ *one's trial* 재판을 받다. **4** (P6,13,14) 《*colloq.*》 pay for or bear the cost of something; pay for (food, drink, etc.) for another person. …의 대가를 치르다; …에게 한턱 내다. ¶ *I will ~ you a drink* 〔*dinner*〕. 술 한 잔〔저녁 식사를〕 대접하겠네 / *Who's going to ~ treat?* 누가 한턱 낼거냐; 누가 (술값·식대 따위) 비용을 낼거냐.

stand a chance, have a chance. 가능성이〔기회가〕 있다.

stand aside, **a**) move to one side. 비켜 서다. ¶ *He stood aside to let me pass.* 그는 내가 지나가도록 비켜 섰다. **b**) do nothing. 아무 일도 않다. ¶ *She never stands aside when there is something that needs to be done.* 그녀는 해야 할 일을 놔두고 가만히 있지 못한다. **c**) take no part. 관여〔가담〕하지 않다.

stand back, **a**) move back. 뒤로 물러서다. ¶ *They were ordered to ~ back.* 그들은 뒤로 물러나도록 명령을 받았다. **b**) be situated away (from). 떨어진 곳에 있다. ¶ *My house stands back from the road.* 나의 집은 도로에서 떨어진 곳에 있다.

stand by, **a**) help; support. …을 원조하다; …에게 편들다. ¶ *I'll ~ by you whatever happen.* 무슨 일이 일어나든 너를 지지하겠다. **b**) be ready to act; wait for a broadcast or TV to resume. 대기하다; (방송·TV 출연자가) 방송〔방영〕 개시에 대비하다. ¶ ~ *by in case of trouble* (돌발) 사건에 대비하다. **c**) keep (a promise, etc.). (약속 따위를) 지키다. ¶ ~ *by one's promise* 약속을 지키다. **d**) remain as an onlooker. 방관하다.

stand clear, move away. 멀리하다〔떨어지다〕. ¶ *Stand clear from* 〔*of*〕 *the gates.* 게이트로부터 (멀리) 떨어지시오.

stand down, withdraw from a contest, election, etc. (선거·경연 따위에서) 물러나다.

stand for, **a**) mean; represent. …을 나타내다; 의미하다. ¶ *The olive branch stands for peace.* 올리브의 가지는 평화의 표상이다 / *What do these initials ~ for?* 이 머리글자들

은 무엇을 뜻합니까. **b**) take the place of (something). …의 대표〔대리〕가 되다. **c**) take the side of (something). …을 지지하다; …의 편이 되다. ¶ *I ~ for liberty.* 나는 자유를 지지한다 / *~ firmly for women's liberation* 여성 해방 운동을 굳게 지지하다. **d**) 《*colloq.*》 endure; suffer willingly. …을 참고 견디다. ¶ *That was more than she could ~ for.* 그건 그녀에게 매우 참기 어려운 것이었다.
stand in, **a**) cost; cause the expense of. 비용〔돈〕이 들다. ¶ *This coat stood me in $20.* 이 코트는 돈이 20달러 들었다. **b**) act as a substitute. (영화 따위에서) …의 대역을〔대리를〕 하다. ¶ *~ in for a sick actress* 아픈 여배우의 대역을 하다. **c**) take part in; give help. …에 참가〔가세〕하다.
stand in with, **a**) be in agreement with; be friendly to; support. …와 일치하다; …을 지지〔지원〕하다. ¶ *~ in with the progressive party* 진보적인 정당을 지지하다. **b**) take a share with. (비용 따위를) …와 함께 나누다〔부담하다〕. ¶ *I'll ~ in with you in this expense.* 나는 이 비용을 너와 함께 부담하겠다.
stand off, **a**) keep one's distance; be apart. 멀리하다. **b**) dismiss temporarily from employment. 임시 해고하다.
stand off and on, 《naut.》 sail alternately away from and toward the shore so as to keep a point in sight. 육지에서 떨어졌다 다가갔다 하면서 (한 목표를 놓치지 않도록) 항해하다.
stand on 〔***upon***〕, **a**) insist on 〔upon〕. …을 주장하다; …을 굳게 지키다. ¶ *~ on one's rights* 자기 권리를 주장하다. **b**) depend on. …에 근거하다. **c**) 《naut.》 continue on the same course. 일정 침로(針路)를 계속 유지하다.
stand out, **a**) be noticeable; attract special attention. 두드러지다; 걸출하다. **b**) continue to endure. 끝까지 버티다.
stand over, be postponed. 연기하다〔되다〕.
stand up, **a**) get to one's feet. 일어서다. **b**) endure; last. 견디다; 지속하다.
stand up for, defend; support; take the side of (something). …을 옹호하다; …에 편들다.
stand up to, **a**) resist boldly and bravely. …에 용감하게 맞서다. **b**) (of a thing) remain in good condition in spite of (long wear, hard, use, etc.). (물건이) …에 견디다. ¶ *This car will ~ up to all kinds of strain.* 이 차는 어떤 험한 쓰임에도 견딜 수 있을거다.
— *n.* Ⓒ **1** a stop 〔halt〕; the act of stopping. 섬; 정지(停止); 정지(靜止). ¶ *come to a ~* 멈춰 서다; 막다르다 / *bring (something) to a ~* …을 멈춰 서게 하다. **2** an attitude; a position supported with regard to something. 태도; 입장; 견해. ¶ *one's ~ toward the matter* 그 일〔문제〕에 대한 자기의 견해〔생각〕 / *take one's ~ on something* …에 대하여 자기의 입장을 주장하다 / *On racial issues they don't usually take strong stands.* 인종문제에 관해서 그들은 통상 강경한 태도를 취하지 않는다. **3** a place where a person or thing stands. 위치; 장소. ¶ *take one's ~ near the window* 창문 가까이에 자리잡다 / *an ideal ~ for a shop* 〔*bank*〕 상점〔은행〕으로서의 이상적인 위치 / *The guard took his ~ near the door.* 수위는 문 가까이에 서 있었다. **4** an outdoor counter where things are sold. 매점; 노점. ¶ *a newsstand* 신문 판매대 / *a popcorn ~* 튀김 옥수수 판매점 / *a hot-dog ~* 핫도그 판매점. **5** a small table or frame to put things on or in. (물건을 올려놓는) 대(臺); …걸이; …꽂이. ¶ *a music ~* 악보대 / *a hat ~* 모자걸이 / *an umbrella ~* 우산꽂이. **6** a raised platform, as for a speaker. 연단. **7** a set of sloping outdoor seats on which people sit to see games, etc. 관람석; 스탠드. ¶ *the grand ~* 정면의 특별 관람석. **8** a place where taxis or public vehicles may wait. (택시 따위의) 주차〔정류, 승차〕장. ¶ *a taxi* 〔*cab*〕 *~* 택시 정류장〔승차장〕 / *a bus ~* 버스 정류소. **9** (of an army, etc.) a stop made in defending one's territory; resistance. 저항; 방어. ¶ *make a ~ for independence* 독립을 위해 저항하다. **10** 《U.S.》 a witness box. (법정의) 증인석. ¶ *take the ~* 증인석에 앉다; 증인대에 서다. **11** 《U.S.》 ⓐ a group of growing trees. 입목(立木). ⓑ a growth on the field. 수확; 작물. [E.]
be at a stand, 《*arch.*》 halt; be at a loss. 멈춰 있다; 어찌 할 바를 모르다.
make a stand against 〔***for***〕, fight against. …에 〔…을 위해〕 저항하다. ¶ *make a last ~ against the enemy* 적에 대항하여 마지막 저항을 하다.
put to a stand, bring to a halt. 멈추게 하다.
take a 〔*one's*〕 ***stand,*** **a**) base; rely (on). 논거로 하다. **b**) adopt a positive opinion and position. 태도를 정하다.

:stand·ard [stǽndərd] *n.* Ⓒ **1** a flag; a banner. 기(旗). ¶ *the regimental ~* 연대기 / *join the ~ of* …의 기치하에 들어가다 / *under a ~ of* …의 기치 아래에(서) / *raise the ~ of revolt* 반기(反旗)를 들다. **2** any state, degree or level taken as a desirable one or as a basis of comparison; a model. 표준; 기준; 규격. ¶ *the ~ of living* 생활 수준 / *safety standards* 안전 기준 / *the ~ of length* 〔*weight*〕 길이〔중량〕의 단위 / *below ~* 표준 이하의 / *come up to the ~* 표준에 달하다 / *set (up) a high moral ~* 높은 도덕적 기준을 설정하다 / *Each generation has its own ~ of judgment.* 각 세대는 그들 자신의 판단 기준을 가지고 있다 / *Your work is below* 〔*not up to*〕 *our standards.* 네가 한 일은 우리들의 기준 이하이다. **3** an authorized measure of weight, length, quality, etc. 도량형 원기(原器). **4** 《Brit.》 a grade in an elementary school. (국민 학교의) 학년. **5** anything upright used as a support. 곧바른 지주(支柱). **6** a tree with one tall straight stem. 입목(立木).

— *adj.* **1** used or generally recognized as a model; used as a standard. 표준의. ¶ ~ *English* 표준 영어 / *the* ~ *time* 표준시 / ~ *language* 표준어 / *the* ~ *weights and measures* 표준 도량형 / *the* ~ *size* 표준 사이즈. **2** having recognized excellence or authority. 권위 있는; 탁월(우수)한. ¶ *the* ~ *books on history* 정평이 나 있는 역사에 관한 책들 / *a* ~ *author* (*writer*) 일류 작가. **3** of the ordinary type; usual; common. 일반(보통)형의; 보통의; 평범한. ¶ *the* ~ *model of a washing machine* 일반적인 모델의 세탁기. **4** standing; upright. 서 있는; 곧바른. [→extend, -ard; *stand*]

stand·ard-bear·er [stǽndərdbὲərər] *n.* Ⓒ **1** a soldier who carries a standard or flag. 기수(旗手). **2** the leader of a movement, political party, etc. 지도자; 주창자(主唱者).

stand·ard·i·za·tion [stæ̀ndərdizéiʃən / -dai-] *n.* Ⓤ the act of standardizing; the state of being standardized. 표준(규격)화; 통일.

stand·ard·ize [stǽndərdàiz] *vt.* (P6) **1** make (something) standard in size, weight, quality, etc. …을 표준에 맞추다; 규격화하다. ¶ ~ *the parts of an automobile* 자동차 부품을 규격화하다 / *standardized wares* 규격 상품 / *These parts are standardized by KS.* 이들 부품은 한국 공업 규격에 맞는다. **2** 《chem.》 test by a standard. …을 표준에 따라 시험하다.

stand·by [stǽndbài] *n.* Ⓒ (*pl.* **-bys**) **1** a person or thing that can always be relied upon. (급할 때) 의지가 되는 사람(것). ¶ *a* ~ *for a possible rainy day* 만일의 경우에 의지가 되는 것 / *Religion is a great* ~. 종교는 만일의 경우에 큰 의지가 된다. **2** a signal for a boat or ship to wait nearby. 대기 신호. **3** a traveler who is waiting to board a plane, etc. as a result of a cancelation. (비행기 등 좌석의) 예약 취소로 인한 공석을 대기하는 손님. ¶ *a* ~ *passenger.* [*stand*]

stand·ee [stændíː] *n.* 《U.S.》 a person who has to stand in a theater or bus. 입석 손님(승객).

stand-in [stǽndìn] *n.* Ⓒ **1** 《U.S. *colloq.*》 a position of favor; good standing. 유리(유력)한 입장. **2** 《U.S.》 a person who works as a substitute for a motion picture actor or actress in dangerous scenes, etc. 대역 배우. **3** any substitute. 대리(代理).

***stand·ing** [stǽndiŋ] *adj.* **1** remaining in an upright position. 서 있는. ¶ ~ *corn* 베어 들이지 않은 밀(옥수수). **2** done from an upright position. 선 자세로 행하는. ¶ *a* ~ *jump* 제자리 멀리뛰기 / *a* ~ *ovation* 기립한 자세에서의 환영. **3** not moving or flowing. 멈춰 있는; 움직이지 않는; 괴어 있는. ¶ ~ *water* 괴어 있는 물 / *a* ~ *engine* (*factory*) 운전을 정지한 엔진(조업 정지 중의 공장). **4** not movable; established; permanent; lasting. 고정된; 상비(常備)의; 영구적(지속적)인. ¶ *a* ~ *bed* 붙박이 침대 / *a* ~ *prohibition* 항구적 금지령 / *a* ~ *joke* 판에 박은 정해진 농담; 언제나 웃음거리가 되는 사람(것) / *a* ~ *army* 상비군 / ~ *orders* 의사(議事) 규정 / ~ *customers* 단골 손님.

— *n.* **1** ⓊⒸ position; rank; reputation. 지위; 입장; 신분; 평판. ¶ *people of high* ~ 고위직에 있는 사람 / *a member in good* ~ 정식 회원 / *men of good* ~ 평판이 좋은 사람들 / *He is in good* ~. 그는 인기가 좋다. **2** Ⓤ duration; period of existence. 계속; 지속. ¶ *a custom of long* ~ 오래 지속되어 온 습관 / *a dispute of long* ~ *between two countries* 두 나라 사이의 오랜 분쟁.

stand-off [stǽndɔ̀(ː)f, -ɑ̀f] *adj.* holding aloof. 쌀쌀한; 서먹서먹한. — *n.* **1** aloofness. 쌀쌀함. **2** a tie or draw. 무승부.

stand-off·ish [stæ̀ndɔ́(ː)fiʃ, -ɑ́f-] *adj.* **1** standing apart. 떨어져 있는. **2** not friendly. 쌀쌀(서먹서먹)한.

stand-pipe [stǽndpàip] *n.* a large vertical tower for water, etc. 급수탑; 수조(水槽).

stand·point [stǽndpɔ̀int] *n.* Ⓒ a position or point at which one stands to consider or judge something; a point of view. 견지; 관점. ¶ *from an educational* ~ 교육상의 견지에서 / *From the* ~ *of justice, the man should be given a fair trial.* 공정을 기한다는 관점에서 그 사람은 공정한 재판을 받아야 한다.

stand·still [stǽndstìl] *n.* ⒸⓊ a complete stop; state of deadlock. 정지; 정체; 정돈(停頓). ¶ *be at a* ~ 정돈 상태에 있다 / *come* (*be brought*) *to a* ~ 멈추다; 멎다; 콱 막히다; 정돈 상태에 빠지다 / *The car came to a* ~. 자동차는 정지했다 / *The experiment is at a* ~. 실험은 정체 상태에 있다.

stand-up [stǽndʌ̀p] *adj.* **1** standing upright. 서 있는; 곧추 선(opp. turndown). ¶ *a* ~ *collar* 선 깃; 스탠드 칼라. **2** done or taken while standing. 선 채로 하는(행해지는). ¶ *a* ~ *meal* 선 채로 먹는 식사 / *a* ~ *bar* 입식형(立食型)의 바(술집); 스탠드바. **3** (of a fight) thoroughgoing. (권투 따위의) 격렬하게 치고 받는. ¶ *a* ~ *fight.*

***stan·za** [stǽnzə] *n.* Ⓒ a group of four or more lines forming a unit or a section of a poem. (시의) 절; 연(聯). ¶ *He recited the first and last stanzas of the poem.* 그는 시의 첫째와 마지막 연을 암송했다. [L. *sto* stand]

sta·ple[1] [stéipəl] *n.* Ⓒ **1** a U-shaped piece of metal used to hold hooks. U자형 못. **2** a similar piece of thin wire used to hold papers together. (호치키스의) 철침; 바늘. — *vt.* (P6) fasten (something) with a staple. …에 U자 못을 박다; …을 호치키스로

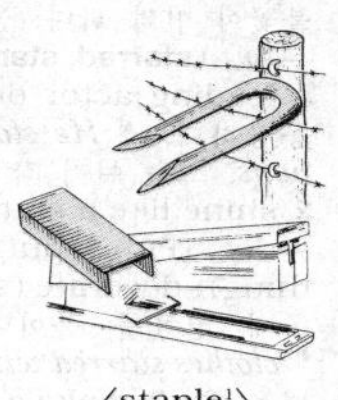
〈staple[1]〉

철하다. ¶ ~ *the papers together* 서류를 (호치키스로) 철하다. [Teut. =prop]

sta·ple² [stéipəl] *n.* **1** Ⓒ the chief or most important product of a place. 주요 산물. ¶ *the staples of Korea* 한국의 주요 산물 / *Rice is the ~ of Thailand.* 쌀은 타이의 주요 산물이다. **2** Ⓒ the chief element or part. 주요소. ¶ *the ~ of diet* 식품의 주요소 / *Cowboy dramas are a ~ on television.* 서부극은 텔레비전의 주요 프로이다. **3** Ⓤ raw material; stuff ready for manufacture. 원료. **4** Ⓤ the fiber of wool, cotton, etc. 섬유. ¶ *wool of fine ~* 상질(上質)의 양모(羊毛).
— *adj.* principal; chief. 주요한. ¶ *~ food* 주식 / *the ~ industries of our country* 우리 나라의 주요 산업 / *~ topics* 주요한 화제들.
— *vt.* (P6) classify (wool, etc.) according to the quality of its fiber. (양모 따위)를 분류하다. [↑]

staple fiber, 《Brit.》 **-bre** [⌐-⌐-] *n.* fiber produced by artificial means. 인조 섬유; 스프.

sta·pler [stéiplər] *n.* Ⓒ a device for fastening together papers with wire staples. 종이를 철하는 도구; 호치키스. [*staple*¹]

:star [stɑːr] *n.* Ⓒ **1** any of the heavenly bodies, which is seen in the night sky, esp. a self-luminous one. 별; 항성(恒星). ¶ *the morning ~* (새벽녘의) 샛별 / *the evening ~* 태백성; 개밥바라기 / *this ~* 지구 / *the ~ of day* 〔*noon*〕 태양 / *a falling ~* 유성; 별똥별 / *Stars are twinkling like diamonds in the sky.* 하늘에는 별들이 보석처럼 반짝이고 있다. **2** a figure with five or six points. 별 모양의 것; 별표. ¶ *the Stars and Stripes* (미국의) 성조기 / *a five-star hotel* 일류급 호텔. **3** a leading player or actor. (영화·연극 따위의) 스타; 인기인〔배우〕. ¶ *a ~ player* 최고 인기의 운동 선수 / *a movie ~* 영화 배우 / *an all-star cast* 인기 배우 총출연. **4** fate; fortune. 운명; 운세. ¶ *He was born under a lucky ~.* 그는 행운(의 별)을 타고 났다 / *thank* 〔*bless*〕 *one's lucky ~* 행운을 감사하다 / *trust one's ~* 자기의 운세를〔성공을〕 믿다 / *The Stars were against it.* 운세가 나빴다; 실패할 운명이었다 / *It's not my ~ to be wealthy.* 부자가 되는 것은 나의 운명이 아니다.

see stars, have a feeling of seeing flashes of light (e.g. as the result of a severe blow on the eye, back of the head, etc.). 눈에서 불꽃이 번쩍 튀다; 눈앞이 아찔해지다.
— *v.* (**starred, star·ring**) *vi.* (P1) **1** act as a leading actor or player. 주연〔주역〕으로 등장하다. ¶ *He starred in several productions.* 그는 여러 작품에서 주연으로 등장했다. **2** shine like a star. 별처럼 빛나다.
— *vt.* (P6) **1** put a starmark on (something); decorate (something) with stars. …에 별표를 붙이다; …을 별로 장식하다. ¶ *clothes starred with gems* 온통 보석을 박아 넣은 옷. **2** make a star of (someone); act as a star in (a movie, etc.). …을 스타로〔주역으로〕 하다; …에 주연하다. ¶ *a film starring a famous actor* 유명한 배우가 주연하는 영화 / *The movie stars a famous actress.* 그 영화는 유명한 여배우가 주연하고 있다. [E.]

star·board [stɑ́ːrbɔ̀ːrd] *n.* Ⓤ the right side of a ship as one faces the bow. 우현(右舷)(opp. port). ¶ *I sighted a steamer to ~.* 우전방에 한 척의 기선(汽船)을 발견했다.
— *adj.* on the right side of a ship. 우현의〔에 있는〕. ¶ *a ~ side* 〔*cabin*〕 우현측〔선실〕.
— *vt., vi.* (P6;1) turn (the helm) to the right side. (배의 키를) 우현으로 돌리다〔잡다〕. [*steer*¹]

starch [stɑːrtʃ] *n.* Ⓤ **1** a white, tasteless food substance found in nearly all plants, but esp. in grain and potatoes. 전분; 녹말. **2** ⓐ a powdered form of this substance used for stiffening cloth, etc. when mixed with water. (풀감용의) 전분. ⓑ a preparation of this used to stiffen clothes. 풀. **3** 《*fig.*》 stiffness; a stiff, formal manner. 거북살스러움; (태도 따위가) 딱딱하고 융통성이 없음; 형식주의. — *vt.* (P6) stiffen (cloth, etc.) with starch. (옷)에 풀을 먹이다. ¶ *a starched white shirt* 풀 먹인 흰 와이셔츠 / 《*fig.*》 *a starched manner* 거북스럽고 딱딱한 태도. [→stark]

starch·y [stɑ́ːrtʃi] *adj.* (**starch·i·er, starch·i·est**) **1** of or like starch; containing starch. 전분의; 전분질의; 풀 같은. ¶ *~ food* 전분질의 식품. **2** stiffened with starch. 풀을 먹인. **3** 《*colloq.*》 stiff and formal in manner. (태도 등이) 딱딱한; 격식〔형식〕을 차리는. [↑]

star·dom [stɑ́ːrdəm] *n.* Ⓤ **1** the status or position of a star. 스타의 신분〔지위〕. **2** 《*collectively*》 a body of professional stars. 스타들; 스타계(界). [*star*]

:stare [stɛər] *vi.* **1** (P1,3) look with the eyes wide open. 눈을 동그랗게 뜨고 보다; 노려〔뚫어지게〕 보다. ¶ *~ with surprise* 놀라서 눈을 크게 뜨다 / *~ straight in front of one* 자신의 전방을 응시하다 / *It is very rude to ~ (at others).* (남을) 빤히 보는 것은 큰 실례다. **2** (P1) be very striking 〔evident〕. 눈에 잘 띄다. ¶ *This misprint stares.* 이 오식은 유달리 눈에 잘 띈다.
— *vt.* (P7) **1** look at (someone or something) steadily or fixedly. …을 응시하다; 빤히〔뚫어지게〕 보다. ¶ *~ someone up and down* 아무를 위아래로 훑어보다 / *He stared me in the face.* 그는 뚫어져라 나의 얼굴을 보았다. **2** cause (someone) to be in a specified condition by staring. 노려보아 (아무를) …하게 하다. ¶ *She stared him dumb* 〔*into silence*〕. 그녀는 노려보아 그를 침묵하게 했다.
— *n.* Ⓒ a long fixed look or gaze. 응시. ¶ *give someone a rude ~* 아무를 무례한 시선으로 응시하다 / *with a cold* 〔*glassy*〕 *~* 냉담한

〔흐리멍덩한〕 눈초리로. [E.]

star·fish [stɑ́ːrfìʃ] *n.* Ⓒ (*pl.* **-fish** or **-fishes**) a sea animal with a star-shaped body. 불가사리. [*star*]

star·gaz·er [stɑ́ːrgèizər] *n.* Ⓒ an astronomer; an idealist. 천문학자; 공론가(空論家).

star·ing [stέəriŋ] *adj.* striking or too bright in colors. (빛깔 따위가) 야한; 현란한. ¶ *a* ~ *red tie* 야한 붉은 색깔의 넥타이. [M.E.]

stark [stɑːrk] *adj.* **1** stiff; rigid. 굳어진; 경직된. ¶ *a* ~ *and cold corpse* 경직된 차가운 시체 / *lie* ~ *in death* 죽어서 경직되어 있다. **2** complete; absolute. 완전한; 순전한. ¶ ~ *madness* 완전한 미치광이 / ~ *terror* 피가 얼어 붙을 듯한 공포 / *He stared with* ~ *terror.* 그는 공포에 질려 눈을 동그랗게 떴다. **3** harsh; stern. (법률·훈련 따위가) 가차 없는; 엄한. **4** bare; bleak. 드러낸; 황량한. ¶ *a* ~ *electric bulb* 나전구(裸電球) / *a* ~ *landscape* 황량한 경치.
— *adv.* completely. 완전히.
stark naked, having no clothes on at all. 전라의; 홀랑 벗은.
●**stark·ly** [-li] *adv.* [E.]

star·less [stɑ́ːrlis] *adj.* without stars or starlight. 별(빛)이 없는. [*star*]

star·let [stɑ́ːrlit] *n.* **1** a little star. 작은 별. **2** a young actress who is being coached for leading roles. 신진〔신출내기〕 여배우. [*star*]

star·light [stɑ́ːrlàit] *n.* Ⓤ light given by the stars. 별빛. — *adj.* lighted by the stars. 별빛의. ¶ *a* ~ *night* 별 밝은 밤.

star·like [stɑ́ːrlàik] *adj.* like a star in shape or brilliance; shining like stars. 별 모양의; 별처럼 빛나는.

star·ling [stɑ́ːrliŋ] *n.* Ⓒ a bird about the size of a robin which makes its nest near buildings. 찌르레기. [E.]

star·lit [stɑ́ːrlìt] *adj.* lighted by the stars. 별빛의. ¶ *a* ~ *night.* [*star*]

starred [stɑːrd] *adj.* **1** decorated or marked with stars. 별로 장식한; 별표가 있는. **2** considered to be influenced by the stars. …의 별을 타고 난; … 운명의. ¶ *ill-starred* 운이 나쁜.

star·ry [stɑ́ːri] *adj.* (**-ri·er, -ri·est**) **1** of stars; star-shaped. 별의; 별 모양을 한. ¶ ~ *light* 별의 빛 / ~ *worlds* 별의 세계. **2** containing many stars. 별이 많은. ¶ *a* ~ *sky* 별이 많은 하늘. **3** shining bright like stars. 반짝반짝 빛나는. ¶ ~ *eyes* 반짝이는 눈동자.

star-span·gled [stɑ́ːrspæ̀ŋgəld] *adj.* with many stars here and there. 별을 점점이 박은. ¶ *the Star-Spangled Banner* 성조기.

:start [stɑːrt] *vi.* **1** (P1,3) begin. 시작하다; 착수하다. ¶ ~ *in life* 인생을 시작하다 / ~ *on an enterprise* 사업을 시작하다 / ~ *off at one's work* 일에 착수하다 / *The performance started at last.* 이윽고 연주가 시작되었다 / *The quarrel started over a trifle.* 싸움은 사소한 일에서 시작되었다 / *They started on cleaning the yard.* 그들은 마당을 청소하기 시작했다. **2** (P1) begin to move; set out. (기계가) 움직이기 시작하다; 시동하다. ¶ *I can't get the engine to* ~. = *The engine won't* ~. 도무지 엔진이 시동되지 않는다. **3** (P1,3) begin to go somewhere. 출발하다; 떠나다. ¶ *He started today for London.* 그는 오늘 런던으로 떠났다 / *Let's* ~ *at nine.* 아홉시에 출발하자 / *He started on a journey.* 그는 여행을 떠났다 / ~ *from Seoul to Pusan* 서울에서 부산으로 떠나다. **4** (P1,3) arise; come into existence; have its origin. 일어나다; 발생하다. ¶ *The fire started in the kitchen.* 화재는 부엌에서 일어났다 / *How did the war* ~*?* 왜 전쟁이 일어났느냐. **5** (P1,2A,3) jump with a sudden fear; be amazed. (놀람·공포 따위로) 움찔하다; 뛰어 오르다; 깜짝 놀라다. ¶ ~ *in terror* 공포로 움찔하다 / ~ *from one's seat* 벌떡 자리에서 일어나다 / ~ *to one's feet* 깜짝 놀라 일어서다 / *He started aside* 〔*back*〕. 그는 홀짝 옆으로〔뒤로〕 비켜 섰다 / *They started at the sound of a rifle shot.* 그들은 총성을 듣고 깜짝 놀랐다. — *vt.* **1** (P6,8,9) begin. …을 시작하다. ¶ ~ *dinner* 식사를 시작하다 / *It started to rain.* = *It started raining.* 비가 내리기 시작했다 / ~ *a conversation* 대화를 시작하다 / ~ *school* 취학하다 / ~ *college* 대학생이 되다 / *He started to study Russian.* 그는 러시아어를 공부하기 시작했다 / *She started crying* 〔*to cry*〕. 그녀는 울기 시작했다. **2** (P6,9) cause (something) to begin, to arise, to move, etc. …을 시작하게 하다; 일으키다; 움직이다. ¶ ~ *a fire* 화재를 일으키다 / ~ *an engine* 엔진을 작동시키다 / *He started a newspaper.* 그는 신문사를 차렸다 / ~ *an idea* 어떤 사상을 주창하다 / ~ *a company* 회사를 설립하다. **3** (P13,23) make (someone) begin; cause. (아무)를 …하게 하다; …에게 시키다. ¶ *The news started her crying.* 그 소식을 듣고 그녀는 울기 시작했다 / *This started me thinking.* 이 때문에 나는 생각하기 시작했다 / *The heavy smoke started me coughing.* 짙은 연기로 나는 기침을 하기 시작했다. **4** (P13,23) help (someone) to begin his career. …을 세상에 내어 보내다; (장사 따위를) 시작하게 하다. ¶ ~ *someone in business* 아무를 사업에 종사시키다.
start after, begin to pursue or seek. …을 뒤쫓다.
start against, enter into competition with. …와 겨루다; …의 상대 후보로 나서다.
start back, shrink back; recoil. 뒷걸음질 치다.
start for, **a**) set out for. …으로 향해 떠나다. **b**) offer oneself as a candidate for. …의 후보로 나서다.
start in, begin; set to work. (일을) 시작하다.
start off, start; begin to move. (움직이기) 시작하다.
start out, **a**) begin a journey. (여행을) 떠나

다; 출발하다. **b**) begin a career. (직업상의) 생애를 시작하다. ¶ ~ *out as a messenger* 사자(使者)로서의 생애를 시작하다. **c**) 《*colloq.*》 begin to act with the intention of doing. (의욕적으로) 착수하다; 나서다. ¶ *He started out to reform the society.* 그는 사회의 개혁에 의욕적으로 덤벼들었다.
start up, **a**) jump up. (껑충) 뛰어오르다. **b**) appear suddenly. 갑자기 나타나다〔떠오르다〕. ¶ *A new idea started up.* 새로운 아이디어가 떠올랐다. **c**) put into motion. 작동시키다. ¶ ~ *up an engine* 엔진을 작동시키다〔걸다〕. **d**) begin to function. 활동〔기능을〕하기 시작하다. ¶ *The English course starts up next week.* 영어 코스는 내주에 시작한다.
to start with, in the first place; firstly. 우선 첫번째로. ¶ *To ~ with, we must do our best.* 우선 첫째로, 우리는 최선을 다해야 한다.
— *n.* Ⓒ **1** an act of starting; a starting point. 출발; 스타트; 출발점. ¶ *make an early ~* 일찍 출발하다 / *prepare for the ~* 출발을 위해 준비하다 / *a ~ in life* 인생의 첫 출발 / *have a lucky ~ in one's career* 행운이 깃든 인생의 출발을 하다 / *at the ~ of winter* 초겨울에 / *walk to the ~* 출발점을 향해 걸어가다 / *give someone a ~ in life* 아무를 (취업시켜) 세상에 내보내다 / *make a ~ on a job* 일을 시작하다 / *line up for the ~* 출발점에 나란히 서다. **2** a sudden movement or shock. 급작스런 움직임; (깜짝) 놀람. ¶ *jump up with a ~* 깜짝 놀라서 펄쩍 뛰다 / *On seeing the snake, Mary sprang up with a ~.* 뱀을 보자, 메리는 놀라 펄쩍 뛰었다 / *I awoke with a ~.* 흠칫 놀라 잠에서 깨어났다 / *What a ~ you gave me!* 정말로 사람 놀라게 하는군 그래. **3** an advantage at the beginning of a race, etc. 선발권(先發權). ¶ *have* 〔*give*〕 *a few yards ~* 몇 야드 앞에 나와 있다〔내보내다〕 / *I gave her seven meter's ~.* 나는 그녀를 7미터 앞서 출발하도록 했다 / *You must give me a ~ if I am to race you.* 내가 너와 경주를 한다면 나에게 선발권을 주어야 한다. [E.]
from start to finish, from beginning to end. 처음부터 끝까지; 시종 일관.
get a start, be surprised. (흠칫) 놀라다.
get the start of, forestall. 기선(機先)을 제(制)하다.
give someone a start, help someone to begin; startle someone. 아무의 시작을 도와주다; 아무를 깜짝 놀라게 하다.

start·er [stɑ́ːrtər] *n.* **1** a person who gives a signal for a race to start. 출발 신호원(員). **2** a person, horse, etc. that takes part in a race even if he doesn't finish. 경주에 나가는 사람〔말〕. **3** a device for causing an engine to start working. (엔진의) 시동 장치.

start·ing-point [stɑ́ːrtiŋpɔ̀int] *n.* the place or point from which a start or beginning is made. 출발점; 기점.

:star·tle [stɑ́ːrtl] *vt.* (P6,13) cause (someone or something) to start or move suddenly; frighten. (깜짝) 놀라게 하다; 펄쩍 뛰게 하다. ¶ *We were very much startled by the news.* 우리들은 그 소식을 듣고 깜짝 놀랐다 / *You startled me!* 깜짝 놀랐잖아; 놀래지 마라 / *The noises startled me out of my sleep.* 시끄러운 소음 때문에 퍼뜩 잠에서 깨었다. — *n.* **1** Ⓤ a shock or surprise. 놀람. **2** Ⓒ something which gives a shock or surprise. 놀라게 하는 것. [E.]

·star·tling [stɑ́ːrtliŋ] *adj.* surprising; alarming. 놀라운; 깜짝 놀라게 하는. ¶ ~ *news* 〔*events*〕 놀라운 소식〔사건〕.

star·tling·ly [stɑ́ːrtliŋli] *adv.* in a startling manner. 놀랍도록; 놀랍게도.

star·va·tion [stɑːrvéiʃən] *n.* Ⓤ the state of being starved; death caused by lack of food. 굶주림; 기아(飢餓); 아사(餓死). ¶ ~ *wages* 기아 임금《최저 생활도 불가능할 정도의 저임금》 / ~ *diet* 기아〔단식〕 요법 / *die of ~* 굶어 죽다. [↓]

:starve [stɑːrv] *vi.* **1** (P1,4) suffer or die from a lack of food. 굶주리다; 굶어 죽다. ¶ ~ *to death* 아사하다 / *leave one's family to ~* 가족을 굶어 죽도록 방치하다 / *The poor dog starved to death.* 가엾은 개는 굶어 죽었다. **2** (P1,2A) 《*colloq.*》 feel very hungry. 배고프다. ¶ *You must be starving.* 너 배가 고프겠구나 / *I'm simply starving.* 나는 배가 무지하게 고프다. **3** (P3) 《*for*》 have a strong desire or need. 갈망〔열망〕하다. ¶ ~ *for friendship* 우정을 간절히 바라다 / *They are starving for affection.* 그들은 애정에 굶주려 있다. — *vt.* **1** (P6,13) cause (a person or an animal) to suffer or die from lack of food or something needed. …을 굶기다; 굶겨 죽이다. ¶ ~ *oneself* 아사〔단식〕하다 / *The cruel man half starved his horses.* 그 잔인한 사람은 그의 말들을 죽지 않을 정도로 굶주리게 했다 / ~ *a castle into surrender* 보급 차단으로 성을 함락시키다. **2** (P7,13) deprive. (필요한 것)을 빼앗다. ¶ *The engine was starved of fuel.* 엔진은 연료가 다 떨어졌다. [E. =die]

starve·ling [stɑ́ːrvliŋ] *adj.* starving; hungry-looking. 굶주린; 허기진. — *n.* Ⓒ a thin, weak person or animal suffering from lack of food. 굶주려서 여윈 사람〔동물〕. [↑]

:state [steit] *n.* Ⓒ **1** 《usu. *sing.*》 the condition in which a person or thing is. 상태; 형세; 사정. ¶ *the ~ of affairs* 〔*things*〕 상황; 형세 / *one's ~ of health* 자기의 건강 상태 / *in a ~ of confusion* 혼란 상태에서 / *a house in a ~ of disrepair* 황폐한 상태의 가옥 / *the ~ of the case* 실정; 진상 / *the patient ~* 환자의 용태 / *the married* 〔*single*〕 *~* 결혼〔독신〕 상태 / *He is in a poor* 〔*precarious*〕 *~ of health.* 그는 건강이 나쁜〔위험한〕 상태에 있다 / *The world is in a terrible ~.* 세계는 가공할 상황에 처해 있다. **2** 《usu. *sing.*》 a particular mental condition; a condition of anxiety, distress, etc. 정신 상태; 흥분〔불안·슬픈〕 상태. ¶ *be in a agitated* ~ 흥분 상태에 있다 / *in quite a* ~ 매우 자제를〔평정을〕 잃은 상태에서 / *I told him not to get into a* ~. 나는 그에게 흥분하지〔화내지〕 말라고 이야기하였다 / *What a* ~ *you are in!* 그게 무슨 꼴이냐, 너 굉장히 흥분하고 있구나. **3** 《often *the S-*》 the whole body of people under one government; a nation. 국가; 나라. ¶ *affairs of* ~ 국사(國事) / *the Department of State* =*the State Department* (미국의) 국무부 / *fight for the State* 국가를 위해 싸우다 / *the Arab oil States* 아랍 산유국 / *Railways in Great Britain are owned by the State.* 영국의 철도는 국가 소유다 / *That country is now an independent* ~. 그 나라는 이제 하나의 독립 국가이다 / *a welfare* ~ 복지 국가. **4** ⓐ 《often *S-*》 one of the main political and geographical units that are joined to form a nation; one of the United States. (특히 미국 등지의) 주(州). ¶ *the fifty States of the United States* 미국의 50개 주 / *the State of California* 캘리포니아 주(州) / *a federal State* 연방 구성주 / *Hawaii became the 50th* ~ *of the U.S.A. in 1959.* 하와이는 1959년에 미국의 제 50번째의 주가 되었다. ⓑ 《*the States*》 《*colloq.*》 the United States of America. 미합중국. 參考 미국인이 외국에서 자기 나라를 일컫는 말. ¶ *go back to the States* 미국〔본국〕으로 돌아가다. **5** one's position in life; rank; social status. 지위; 신분. ¶ *persons of every* ~ *of life* 온갖 계층의 사람들 / *live in a style befitting one's* ~ 자기 신분에 상응한 살림살이를 하다. **6** Ⓤ style of living, esp. of a high-placed person; luxury and splendor; dignity. (특히 높은 신분의) 생활 양식; 호사 (생활); 위엄. ¶ *live in* ~ 호화 생활을 하다 / *keep one's* ~ 위엄을 지키다; 거드름 피우다 / *a visit of* ~ 공식 방문 / *the chair of* ~ 왕좌.

in a state of nature, **a**) in a condition of man before society is organized. 미개하여. **b**) in a state of bodily nakedness. 벌거벗고.

in state, with all due ceremony. 당당히; 정식으로. ¶ *The Queen drove in* ~ *through London.* 여왕은 위풍 당당하게 런던을 통과했다.

keep one's state, stand upon one's dignity. 젠체하다; 점잔빼다.

lie in state, (of a corpse) be placed on view in a public place with honor. (국왕 등의 유해가 공중 앞에) 안치되다.

— *adj.* **1** used for occasions of ceremony; formal; intended for persons of high rank. 의식용의; 공식의; 내빈용의. ¶ *a* ~ *call* 공식 방문. **2** 《often *S-*》 of a country; belonging to the nation. 국가의; 국사에 관한; 국가에 속하는. ¶ *a* ~ *prisoner* 〔*criminal*〕 국사범(國事犯) / ~ *papers* 공문서 / *a* ~ *trial* 국사범 재판 / ~ *control* 국가 관리 / ~ *service* 국무 / *a State forest* 국유림 / *the* ~ *railways* 국유 철도 / *a* ~ *guest* 국빈 / *State police* 국립 경찰 / *bring under* ~ *ownership* 국유로 하다. **3** 《usu. *S-*》 of a State; belonging to one of the states which together form a nation. 주(州)의. ¶ *a State Bank* 주립 은행 / *State University* 주립 대학 / *a State highway* 주도(州道) / *a State government* 주정부.

— *vt.* **1** (P6,11) express (a fact, an opinion, etc.) in words; say. (사실·의견 따위)를 말하다; 진술하다. ¶ ~ *one's views* 〔*reasons*〕 자기 견해를〔의견을〕 말하다 / ~ *one's case* 자기 입장을 진술하다 / *It is stated that....* …이라는 이야기다 / *Would you please* ~ *your frank opinion of the plan?* 그 계획에 대한 너의 솔직한 의견을 말해 주겠나. **2** place in a certain position; settle; fix. (날짜 따위를) 정하다. ¶ *at a stated date* 정해진 날에. [L. *sto* stand]

state·craft [stéitkræ̀ft, -krɑ̀:ft] *n.* Ⓤ the art or skill of managing public affairs; statesmanship. 정치; 치국책(治國策).

stat·ed [stéitid] *adj.* fixed or settled beforehand. 정해진; 규정된. ¶ *at a* ~ *time* 소정의〔정해진〕 시간에 / *for a* ~ *fee* 규정된 요금으로 / *at* ~ *intervals* 정기적으로 / *Meetings are held at* ~ *intervals* 〔*times*〕. 회합은 정기적으로〔정해진 시간에〕 개최된다.

state·house [stéithàus] *n.* 《U.S.》 《sometimes S-》 the capitol of a State. 주(州)의사당.

state·less [stéitlis] *adj.* without a state or nationality. 국적이〔나라가〕 없는.

state·li·ness [stéitlinis] *n.* the quality of being stately; stately appearance or behavior. 당당함; 위엄.

***state·ly** [stéitli] *adj.* (**-li·er, -li·est**) having a grand or dignified manner or appearance; majestic. 위엄있는; 당당한. ¶ *a* ~ *manner* 〔*walk*〕 위엄 있는 태도〔걸음걸이〕.

state medicine [⌐ ⌐−−] *n.* socialized medicine. 의료의 국가 관리.

:state·ment [stéitmənt] *n.* ⓊⒸ **1** the act of expressing an opinion, a fact, a belief, etc. in words; something stated. 진술; 성명. ¶ *a written* ~ 성명서 / *an official* ~ 공식 성명서 / *a random* ~ 엉터리 진술 / *issue a* ~ 성명서를 내다 / *make a* ~ 진술하다 / *We think some of his statements are highly questionable.* 그의 진술의 어떤 부분은 매우 의심스럽다고 생각한다. **2** a report of a financial condition. 결산서; 영업 보고서. ¶ *a financial* ~ 재무 제표.

state·room [stéitrù:m] *n.* Ⓒ **1** a private room or cabin on a ship. (배의) 특등실. **2** 《U.S.》 a private compartment on a railroad train. (기차의) 특별실. **3** a room for ceremonies in a palace. (궁중 따위의) 대접견실; 의전실.

·states·man [stéitsmən] *n.* Ⓒ (*pl.* **-men** [-mən]) a person with experience in the management of public affairs and the art of government. 정치가. ¶ *A politician* *thinks of the next election; a ~, of the next generation.* 정치꾼은 다음 선거를 생각하지만, 정치가는 다음 세대를 생각한다.

states·man·like [stéitsmənlàik] *adj.* having the qualities of a good statesman. 정치가다운; 정치가에 어울리는.

states·man·ship [stéitsmənʃip] *n.* Ⓤ the qualities or methods of a statesman; skill in managing public or national affairs. 정치가적 성격; 정치적 수완.

stat·ic [stǽtik] *adj.* **1** standing still; at rest; not moving. 정적(靜的)인. ¶ *a ~ installation* 고정 설비 / *a ~ concept* 불변의 개념 / *a ~ feudal society* 변화가 없는 봉건 사회. **2** of static or atmospheric electricity. 정전기(靜電氣)의. — *n.* Ⓤ static or atmospheric electricity. 정전기; 공전(空電). [→state]

stat·ics [stǽtiks] *n. pl.* 《used as *sing.*》 the branch of mechanics dealing with bodies at rest or with forces that balance one another. 정역학(靜力學).

:sta·tion [stéiʃən] *n.* Ⓒ **1** a place where trains, buses, etc. stop to pick up or set down passengers; the building connected with this place. 정거장; 역; 역사(驛舍). ¶ *a bus ~* 버스 정거장 / *a railway ~* 철도역 / *I met him at the ~.* 나는 그를 정거장에서 만났다 / *This train stops at every ~.* 이 열차는 정거장마다 다 선다. **2** a building or place used for some particular official work; a military post; a naval base. (관청 따위의) 서(署); 국(局); 소(所); (군대 따위의) 주둔지. ¶ *a police ~* 경찰서 / *a gas [filling] ~* 주유소 / *a military ~ abroad* 해외의 군 주둔지 / *a naval ~* 군항 / *a fire-station* 소방서 / *a power ~* 발전소 / *a broadcasting ~* 방송국. **3** an assigned location or place. (지정 또는 임명된) 위치; 부서. ¶ *a lifeboat ~* (인명) 구조선 두는 곳 / *a sentinel's ~* 보초의 초소 / *take up one's appointed ~* 지정된 부서에 자리잡다 / *keep one's ~* 부서를 떠나지 않다. **4** ⓊⒸ one's social position; rank; a high position. 신분; 지위; 고위(직). ¶ *a man of high [humble] ~* 높은[낮은] 지위의 사람 / *a ~ in life* 신분 / *people in all stations of life* 각계각층의 사람들 / *a woman of high ~* 지체 높은 여성 / *have ideas above one's ~* 신분에 어울리지 않는 생각을 가지다. **5** a place for sending out or receiving programs, etc. by radio or television. 방송국. ¶ *tune in a ~* (수신기를) 어떤 방송국에 맞추다.
— *vt.* (P6,13) 《*at*》 place (someone) in a certain post, position, rank or situation. …을 배치하다; 부서에 앉히다. ¶ *~ a guard at the gate* 대문에 경비원을 세우다 / *~ oneself at the porch* 현관에 서다 / *He was stationed in China.* 그는 중국에 보직되었다. [L. *sto* stand]

station agent [⌐– ⌐–] *n.* 《U.S.》 a stationmaster. 역장(驛長).

sta·tion·ar·y [stéiʃənèri / -nəri] *adj.* **1** not moving; standing still. 움직이지 않는; 부동(不動)의; 정지(靜止)된. ¶ *The shadow remained ~.* 그림자가 움직이지 않고 가만히 있었다 / *a row of ~ vehicles* 멈춰 서 있는 차량의 행렬. **2** settled; fixed in a certain position. 정주(定住)하고 있는; 움직일 수 없는; 고정된. ¶ *a ~ crane* 정치(定置)된 기중기 / *a ~ bicycle* (건강 체조·미용용의) 고정 자전거 / *a ~ engine* (움직일 수 없게) 장치된 엔진 / *~ disease* 한 지역에 수년간 유행하고 있는 전염병 / *~ troops* 주둔군. **3** unchanging in condition, number, etc. 변동이 없는. ¶ *a ~ population* 변동이 없는 인구 / *The temperature was ~.* 온도는 변동 없이 일정했다. [→station, -ary]

stationary front [⌐––– ⌐] *n.* 《meteor.》 a transition zone between two nearly stationary air masses of different density. 정체 전선(停滯前線).

sta·tion·er [stéiʃənər] *n.* Ⓒ a person who sells writing goods. 문방구상.

sta·tion·er·y [stéiʃənèri / -əri] *n.* Ⓤ 《*collectively*》 writing goods, such as papers, pens, pencils, inks, envelopes, etc. 문방구. ¶ *hotel ~* 호텔의 (봉투가 딸린) 편지지.

sta·tion·mas·ter [stéiʃənmæ̀stər, -mɑ̀ːs-] *n.* Ⓒ a person in charge of the operation of a railroad station; a station agent. (큰 역의) 역장.

station wagon [⌐– ⌐–] *n.* 《U.S.》 a passenger car designed also to carry goods, with a rear door for loading. 스테이션 왜건《뒤 끝에 문이 있고 짐도 실을 수 있는 세단 승용차》(=《Brit.》 estate car).

stat·ist [stéitist] *n.* =statistician.

sta·tis·ti·cal [stətístikəl] *adj.* of or based on statistics. 통계(상)의. ¶ *a ~ table* 통계표. [→statistics]

stat·is·ti·cian [stæ̀tistíʃən] *n.* Ⓒ an expert or a specialist in statistics. 통계가; 통계학자. [↓]

***sta·tis·tics** [stətístiks] *n. pl.* **1** facts or data shown by numbers. 통계. ¶ *~ of population* 인구 통계 / *cite ~* 통계를 인용하다[예로 들다] / *collect ~* 통계를 잡다. **2** 《used as *sing.*》 the science of gathering and classifying such facts and data. 통계학. [L. *status* state]

stat·u·ar·y [stǽtʃuèri / -əri] *n.* Ⓤ **1** 《*collectively*》 statues. 조상(彫像). **2** the art of making statues. 조상술(術). — *adj.* of or suitable for statues. 조상(彫像)의; 조상용(用)의. [↓]

:stat·ue [stǽtʃuː] *n.* Ⓒ the image of a person or an animal carved in stone, etc. or cast in metal. 상(像); 조상(彫像). ¶ *the Statue of Liberty* 자유의 여신상. [L. *sto* stand]

stat·u·esque [stæ̀tʃuésk] *adj.* like a statue in dignity, formal grace or beauty. 조상(彫像) 같은; 조상처럼 위엄이 있는[우아한, 아름다운].

stat·u·ette [stæ̀tʃuét] *n.* Ⓒ a small statue. 작은 조상(彫像).

·**stat·ure** [stǽtʃər] *n.* Ⓤ **1** the height of a person or an animal. 신장; (사람·동물의) 키. ¶ *small in* ~ 몸집이 작은 / *be short of* ~ 키가 작다 / *of imposing* 〔*mean*〕 ~ 훤칠한〔보통〕 키의 / *grow in* ~ 키가 자라다 / *He is above average* ~. 그는 평균 신장 이상이다. **2** spiritual or moral worth or development. (정신적·도덕적) 능력; 성장; 발달. ¶ *a writer of* ~ 재능이 있는 작가. [*statue*]

sta·tus [stéitəs, stǽt-] *n.* Ⓤ **1** the position, state, or rank of a person in relation to others. 지위(地位). ¶ *his* ~ *among novelists* 소설가들 중에서의 그의 지위 / *a man's* ~ *as a scholar* 학자로서의 지위 / *raise the* ~ *of woman* 여성의 지위를 높이다 / *a rise in* ~ 지위의 향상 / *live in a big house as a symbol of one's* ~ 지위의 상징으로서 큰 집에서 살다. **2** 《law》 legal position. (법률상의) 신분. **3** condition; situation. 상태; 사정. ¶ *the economic* 〔*social*〕 ~ 경제〔사회〕 사정〔상태〕. [L. = state]

·**stat·ute** [stǽtʃuːt] *n.* Ⓒ **1** a law passed by a legislative body. 성문법(成文法); 성문율; 법령. **2** an established rule. 규칙.

statute law [⌐-⌐] *n.* a law established by a legislative body. 성문법.

stat·u·to·ry [stǽtʃutɔ̀ːri / -təri] *adj.* of a statute; fixed or established by statute. 법정의; 법령의〔에 의거한〕. ¶ *a* ~ *offense* 법에 규정된 범죄 / *a* ~ *provision* 법령의 조항.

staunch[1] [stɔːntʃ, stɑːntʃ] *v.* =stanch[1].

staunch[2] [stɑːntʃ, stɔːntʃ] *adj.* **1** reliable; firm; loyal. 믿을 수 있는; (신념·주장이) 변치 않는; 충실한. ¶ *a* ~ *friend* 〔*supporter*〕 충실한 친구〔지지자〕. **2** watertight; seaworthy. 내수(耐水)의; 항해에 견디는. ¶ *a* ~ *ship.* **3** solidly made. 견고한; 튼튼한. [L. *sto* stand, →stanch]

stave [steiv] *n.* Ⓒ **1** one of the curved, narrow pieces of wood which form the sides of a tub, a barrel, etc. 통널. **2** a heavy stick or staff. 막대기. **3** 《mus.》 five lines with spaces between them for writing music. 보표(譜表); 5선보(譜). **4** a verse or stanza of a poem. 시의 일절.

— *v.* (**staved** or **stove**) *vt.* (P7) **1** break a hole through the side of (a barrel, a boat, etc.); break (something). (통 따위)에 구멍을 뚫다; 부수다. ¶ ~ *to pieces* …을 산산이 부수다 / ~ *in a cask* 통에 구멍을 내다 / *The side of the boat was staved in by the collision.* 그 배의 옆구리는 충돌로 인해 구멍이 뚫렸다〔크게 부서졌다〕. **2** furnish (something) with staves. …에 통널을 붙이다. — *vi.* (P2A) become smashed or broken. 부서지다. [→staff]

staves [steivz] *n.* **1** pl. of **staff. 2** pl. of **stave.**

⁑**stay**[1] [stei] *vi.* **1** (P1,2A,4) remain in one place; wait. (장소에) 머무르다; 기다리다. ¶ ~ (*at*) *home* (외출하지 않고) 집에 있다 / ~ *in hospital* 입원해 있다 / *Stay where you are.* (움직이지 말고) 거기 그대로 있어라 / *Stay here until I return.* 내가 돌아올 때까지 여기서 기다려라 / *I cannot* ~ *for you.* 나는 너를 기다릴 수 없다 / *Get him to* ~ *a minute.* 잠시 그를 기다리도록 해라. **2** (P2A,3) live for a while as a guest or visitor. 체재하다; (손님으로) 묵다; 숙박하다. ¶ ~ *overnight* 일박하다 / ~ *at* 〔*in*〕 *a hotel* 호텔에 숙박하다 / *I stayed at my uncle's.* 나는 숙부댁에 묵었다 / *Stay with us.* 저희 집에 묵으세요 / *Won't you* ~ *for* 〔*to*〕 *supper?* 좀더 있다가 저녁 식사하고 가시지요. **3** (P5) remain; continue to be. …인 채로 있다; (어떤 상태에) 머물러 있다. ¶ *Prices* ~ *high.* 값이 비싼 채로 있다 / ~ *single* 독신을 지키다 / ~ *still* 꼼짝 않고 가만히 있다 / ~ *in power* 권력의 자리를 유지하다 / *The door stayed closed.* 문이 닫힌 상태로 있었다 / *The weather stayed fine.* 날씨가 계속 좋았다 / *This won't* ~ *clean.* 이것은 곧 더러워질 거다 / *These clothes won't* ~ *white.* 이 옷들은 흰색인 채로 있지 못할 거다. **4** (P1,2A,3) endure; last. 견디다; 지탱하다. ¶ ~ *to the last* 마지막까지 지탱하다〔버티다〕 / ~ *well* 잘 견뎌 내다. — *vt.* (P6) **1** stop the progress of (something); check. …을 멈추다〔멈추게 하다〕; 막다; 가로막다. ¶ ~ *one's steps* 멈춰 서다 / ~ *the spread of disease* 질병의 만연을 멈추게 하다 / ~ *bloodshed* 유혈의 사태를 막다〔저지하다〕 / ~ *someone's hand* 치려는 아무의 손을 막다. **2** satisfy (hunger, thirst, etc.) for a time. (허기·목마름 따위를) 일시적으로 만족시키다〔채우다〕. ¶ ~ *one's hunger* 공복을 채우다 / *He ate some bread and butter to* ~ *his hunger till dinner time.* 저녁 식사 때까지 허기를 때우기 위해 약간의 버터 바른 빵을 먹었다. **3** put off; delay. …을 연기하다; 유예하다. ¶ ~ *judgment* 〔*decision, punishment*〕 판결〔결정, 처벌〕을 연기하다 / *I'll* ~ *judgment till I hear the other side.* 나는 다른 편의 진술을 들을 때까지 판단을 보류하겠다. **4** remain in the same place or condition through or during (a period of time). …의 끝까지 머무르다〔지속하다〕; 버티다. ¶ ~ *the course in a mile race,* 1 마일 경주의 전 코스를 끝까지 달리다 / *She decided to* ~ *the week out.* 그녀는 1 주일 내내 머무르기로 결심하였다.

come to stay, be regarded as permanent. 《*colloq.*》 오래 계속되다; 영구화하다; 정착하다. ¶ *The fine weather seems to have come to* ~. 좋은 날씨가 오래 계속될 것 같다.

stay away, be absent (from). 결석하다.

stay one's hand, refrain from action. 행동을 억제하다〔삼가다〕.

stay one's hunger, satisfy one's hunger. 굶주림을 채우다.

stay in, stay at home. 집안에 있다. ¶ *The cold made me* ~ *in for three days.* 추위로 3일 동안 집안에 있었다.

stay out, **a**) remain outdoors; do not

come home. 집밖에 머무르다; 외출해 있다. ¶ *You mustn't ~ out after dark.* 어두워진 다음에 집밖에 있어서는 안 된다. **b**) outstay. 오래 머무르다.
stay put, 《*colloq.*》 remain in place; be firmly fixed or established. 놓인 채로(한 장소에) 그대로 있다; 끄떡도 하지 않다. ¶ *His fame will ~ put.* 그의 명성은 요지 부동일 것이다.
stay up, sit up. 밤샘하다.
— *n.* **1** Ⓒ the act or time of staying; a visit. 체재; 체재 기간. ¶ *a short ~ in* (*the*) *hospital* 단기간의 입원 / *make a long ~ in London* 런던에 장기간 체재하다 / *I have very much enjoyed my ~ here.* 이곳에 체재하는 동안 매우 즐거웠습니다. **2** ⓊⒸ a delay; a stop. 연기; 중지. ¶ *a two year's ~ of execution* 형의 집행 유예 2년 / *a ~ of execution* 형의 집행 정지. [E. (→state)]

stay² [stei] *n.* Ⓒ **1** a support or prop to steady something. 지주(支柱); 버팀. **2** a strong rope or wire to support a mast of a ship. (돛대를 버텨주는) 지삭(支索). **3** someone that supports. 의지(지주)가 되는 것. ¶ *He is the chief ~ of his family.* 그는 집안의 대들보이다. **4** 《*pl.*》《Brit.》 a corset. 코르셋. — *vt.* support (something) with a rope, wire, etc. …을 지삭으로 버티다. [↑]

stay-at-home [stéiəthòum] *adj.* 《*colloq.*》 staying mostly at home. 집에만 틀어박혀 있는. — *n.* Ⓒ a person who stays at home and will not go out or travel. 집에만 틀어박혀 있는 사람; 외출을 싫어하는 사람.

staying power [⌐–⌐–] *n.* the ability or strength to last or endure. 지구력; 내구성.

stay-in strike [stéiìn stràik] *n.* a strike in which the employees stay at their place of work but refuse to perform their duties. 연좌 파업.

stead [sted] *n.* Ⓤ **1** the place or position which another person or thing has or might have. 대신; 대리. ¶ *He died in my ~.* 그는 나 대신(에) 죽었다. **2** advantage; use. 도움; 이익. [E. =place]
stand someone in good stead, be useful or advantageous to someone. 크게 …에게 도움이 되다(유익하다). ¶ *His ability to swim stood him in good ~ when the boat upset.* 그의 수영 실력은 배가 뒤집혔을 때 그에게 큰 도움이 되었다.

·stead·fast [stédfæ̀st, -fəst] *adj.* steady; fixed firmly; unchanging. 확고 부동한; 부동의; 변치 않는. ¶ *a ~ faith* 확고한 신념 / *a ~ gaze* 응시 / *a ~ man* 의지가 굳은(신념이 강한) 사람 / *He was ~ to his principles.* 그는 그의 주의를 굽히지 않았다.

stead·fast·ly [stédfæ̀stli, -fəst-] *adv.* in a steadfast manner. 확고히; 굳건히.

:stead·i·ly [stédili] *adv.* in a steady manner; firmly; continuously. 견실(착실)하게; 끊임없이.

stead·i·ness [stédinis] *n.* Ⓤ the state of being steady. 착실; 부동; 한결같음.

:stead·y [stédi] *adj.* (**stead·i·er, stead·i·est**) **1** fixed; firm. 확고한; 안정된; 흔들리지 않는. ¶ *a ~ chair* (흔들리지 않는) 안정된 의자 / *a ~ gaze* 응시 / *a ~ step* 안정된 걸음걸이 / *hold the ladder ~* 흔들리지 않도록 사다리를 붙들고 있다 / *This post is as ~ as a rock.* 이 기둥은 큰 바위처럼 끄떡도 하지 않는다. **2** not changing in mind; constant. (마음이) 굳건한; 불변의. ¶ *~ friendship* (*love*) 변치 않는 우정(사랑). **3** regular; uniform. 규칙 바른; 착실한; 한결같은. ¶ *a ~ wind* 한결같이 고르게 부는 바람 / 《*prov.*》 *Slow and ~ wins the race.* 서둘지 않고 꾸준히 노력하면 성공한다. **4** having good habits; serious. 진실된; 진지한.
— *v.* (**stead·ied, stead·y·ing**) *vt.* **1** (P6) make or keep (something) steady. …을 견고(확고)하게 하다; 흔들리지 않게 하다. ¶ *~ a table leg* 테이블 다리를 흔들리지 않게 고정시키다. **2** make (something) constant. …을 일정하게(한결 같게) 하다; 견실하게 하다.
— *vi.* (P1,2A) become steady. 견고(침착)해지다; 안정되다. ¶ *The boat soon steadied again.* 배는 곧 다시 안정되었다.

·steak [steik] *n.* ⓊⒸ **1** a thick slice of meat or fish cut for broiling or frying. (쇠고기·생선 따위를 굽거나 튀기기 위해) 두껍고 넓적하게 썬 고기(저민 생선살). **2** beefsteak. 비프스테이크. [N.]

:steal [sti:l] *v.* (**stole, stol·en**) *vt.* (P6,13) **1** 《*from*》 take (another's property) without permission or right; take away unlawfully. …을 훔치다; 절취(도둑질)하다. ¶ *~ money from a safe* 금고에서 돈을 훔치다 / *Someone has stolen my money.* 누군가가 나의 돈을 훔쳤다 / *A thief stole jewels from that shop.* 도둑이 저 가게에서 보석을 도둑질했다 / *He has his watch stolen.* 그는 시계를 도둑맞았다. **2** gain or do (something) secretly. …을 교묘히 손에 넣다; 살며시(몰래) 하다. ¶ *~ a kiss from a girl* 한 소녀에게 살며시 도둑 키스를 하다 / *~ a ride on a train* 기차에 무임 승차하다 / *~ a glance at someone* 아무를 몰래 훔쳐 보다 / *~ someone's heart* 아무의 마음을 본인도 모르게 사로잡다. **3** 《baseball》 gain (a base) without the aid of a hit. 도루(盜壘)하다. ¶ *~ a base* 도루하다.
— *vi.* **1** (P1) commit an act of stealing. 도둑질하다. ¶ 《Bible》 *Thou shalt not ~.* 도둑질하지 말라. **2** move quietly or secretly; come or go without notice. 살며시(몰래·조용히) 움직이다; 몰래 가다(오다). ¶ *She stole softly out of* (*into*) *the room.* 그녀는 살며시 방밖(안)으로 나갔다(들어왔다) / *The years stole by.* 세월은 어느덧 지나갔다 / *The winter has stolen upon us.* 어느새 겨울이 다가왔다.
steal a march on, get the start of unnoticed. …을 앞지르다; 꼭뒤 지르다.
steal away, go away secretly. 몰래 가버리다.

steal in, slip in secretly; smuggle. 살그머니 들어가다〔침입하다〕; 밀수입하다.
— *n.* **1** 《*colloq.*》 an act of stealing. 훔침; 절도. **2** something stolen. 훔친 물건. **3** 《baseball》 the act of stealing a base; an instance of this. 도루; 스틸. [E.]

stealth [stelθ] *n.* Ⓤ secret or sly means of doing something. 은밀히〔아무도 눈치 못 채게〕 하기. ¶ *do good by* ~ 음덕을 베풀다 / *He obtained the letter by* ~. 그는 은밀히 그 서신을 손에 넣었다. [→steal, -th]

stealth·i·ly [stélθili] *adv.* secretly; slyly. 비밀리에; 은밀히.

stealth·y [stélθi] *adj.* (**stealth·i·er, stealth·i·est**) done secretly or cautiously. 남의 눈을 피하는; 몰래 하는. ¶ *a* ~ *glance* 훔쳐보기 / *I heard* ~ *footsteps in the dark.* 어둠 속에서 살금살금 걸어오는 발자국 소리를 들었다.

:steam [sti:m] *n.* Ⓤ **1** the vapor that rises from boiling water. (수)증기; 김. ¶ *give off* ~ 증기를 방출하다 / *a building heated by* ~ 증기로 난방되는 건물 / *Boiling water gives off* ~. 끓는 물은 증기를 방출한다 / *These engines are driven by* ~. 이 기관〔엔진〕들은 증기로 작동된다. **2** 《*colloq.*》 energy. 원기; 기운.

at full steam, at full speed. 전속력으로.

get up steam, **a**) begin to put forth one's strength or energy. 정력을 다 쏟다; 분발하다. **b**) get excited. 흥분하다.

let 〔***blow***〕 ***off steam,*** 《*colloq.*》 express strong feelings. 울분을 터뜨리다〔풀다〕.

put on steam, brace oneself up. 힘〔기운〕을 내다.

under steam, worked by steam; 《*colloq.*》 being vigorous. 증기의 힘으로; 기운〔힘〕을 내서.

— *vt.* (P6) expose (something) to steam; soften (something) by steam. …을 (증기로) 찌다. ¶ ~ *potatoes* 감자를 찌다. — *vi.* (P1,2A) **1** give off steam. 김을 내다; 증기를 내뿜다. ¶ *The kettle is steaming.* 주전자가 증기를 내뿜고 있다 / *A horse steams after a hard gallop.* 말은 질주 후에 김을 내뿜으며 땀을 흘린다. **2** move by the power of steam. 증기의 힘으로 달리다. ¶ *The train steamed into the station.* 기차는 칙칙거리며 정거장으로 들어왔다 / *The ship can* ~ *20 knots an hour.* 배는 시속 20노트로 항행할 수 있다. **3** rise in the form of vapor or steam. 증발하다. [E.]

steam along 〔***ahead***〕, make great progress. 큰 진전을 이루다.

steam away, **a**) become exhausted in the form of steam. 증발해 버리다. **b**) =steam along.

steam up, **a**) become covered with vapor. 증기로 뿌옇게 되다〔흐려지다〕. **b**) use one's energy. 기운을 내다. **c**) make (someone) excited or angry. …을 흥분시키다〔화나게 하다〕.

***steam·boat** [stí:mbòut] *n.* Ⓒ a boat driven by steam. (소형) 기선; 증기선.

steam boiler [⌐ ⌐–] *n.* a boiler in which water is boiled to make steam. 증기 보일러.

steam engine [⌐ ⌐–] *n.* an engine operated by the pressure of steam. 증기 기관.

:steam·er [stí:mər] *n.* Ⓒ **1** a steamship or steamboat. 기선. **2** an engine operated by steam. 증기 기관. **3** a container in which food is steamed. (요리용) 찜통.

steam hammer [⌐ ⌐–] *n.* a powerful machine hammer worked by steam. 증기 해머.

steam heat [⌐ ⌐] *n.* heat given off by steam. 증기열.

steam-heated [stí:mhìtid] *adj.* kept warm by steam heat. 증기〔스팀〕 난방의. ¶ *a* ~ *building* 스팀 난방의 건물.

steam·ing [stí:miŋ] *adj.* giving off steam; very hot. 증기를〔김을〕 내뿜는; 매우 뜨거운. ¶ ~ *coffee* 김이 나는 따끈한 커피. — *adv.* to a steaming degree. 증기를〔김을〕 내뿜을 만큼. ¶ *be* ~ *hot* 김이 날 만큼 뜨겁다; 매우 뜨겁다〔덥다〕.

steam iron [⌐ ⌐–] *n.* an electric iron which gives off steam as it presses the fabric. 증기 다리미.

steam-power [stí:mpàuər] *n.* force applied to machinery driven by steam. 증기 동력.

steam·roll·er [stí:mròulər] *n.* **1** a heavy roller driven by steam, used for leveling roads. 증기 롤러. **2** 《*fig.*》 an overwhelming power or influence. 강압적인 힘; 압력.

:steam·ship [stí:mʃìp] *n.* Ⓒ a ship driven by steam power. (증)기선. 參考 S.S. 또는 SS로 생략함. ¶ *the S.S. Titanic* 타이타닉호 / *a* ~ *company* 기선〔상선〕 회사.

steam·y [stí:mi] *adj.* (**steam·i·er, steam·i·est**) **1** of or like steam. 증기의; 증기 모양의. **2** covered or filled with steam. 증기가〔김이〕 자욱한. ¶ ~ *fields* 안개가 자욱한 들판 / ~ *windows* 김이 뿌옇게 낀 창문. **3** giving off steam. 증기를 내는. **4** 《*sl.*》 erotic. 에로틱한.

***steed** [sti:d] *n.* Ⓒ 《*arch., lit.*》 a horse, esp. a riding horse or a spirited horse. 말《특히 승용마(乘用馬)》; 기운찬 말. [E.]

:steel [sti:l] *n.* Ⓤ **1** a compound of iron with carbon and other elements. 강철; 강(鋼). ¶ *hard* ~ 경강(硬鋼). **2** something made from steel. 강철 제품. ¶ *a cold* ~ 도검(刀劍) / *an enemy worthy of one's* ~ 상대로서 부족함이 없는 적; 호적수. **3** great, steel-like hardness. (강철 같이) 단단함; 견고함. ¶ *a grip of* ~ (강철 같은) 억센 악력(握力); 꽉 잡아쥠 / *a heart of* ~ 냉혹한 마음 / *have nerves of* ~ 강철 같은 신경〔심장〕을 가지고 있다 / *muscles of* ~ 강철 같은 강인한 근육.
— *adj.* made of or like steel. 강철의; 강철제의. ¶ *a* ~ *pen* 강철 펜 / *a* ~ *mill* 제철

소 / *the ~ industry* 제강업; 제철 산업.
— *vt.* (P6) **1** cover (something) with steel. …에 강철을 입히다. **2** make (something) hard, strong or firm. …을 단단하게 〔견고하게〕 하다. ¶ ~ *one's heart against someone* 아무에 대하여 마음을 모질게〔단단히〕 먹다. [E.]

steel-clad [stíːlklæ̀d] *adj.* covered with armor. 장갑의; 갑옷으로 무장한.

steel wool [´ ´] *n.* fine shavings of steel used for scouring and polishing. 철면(鐵綿)《연마용》.

steel·work [stíːlwə̀ːrk] *n.* **1** steel parts or articles. 강철 부품〔제품〕. **2** the steel frame or superstructure of a building, bridge, etc. (고층 건물·교량 따위의) 강철 구조물〔골조(骨組)〕.

steel·works [stíːlwə̀ːrks] *n. pl.* 《used as *pl.* and *sing.*》 a place where steel is manufactured; a steel mill. 제철소.

steel·y [stíːli] *adj.* (**steel·i·er, steel·i·est**) **1** of or made of steel. 강철의; 강철제의. **2** like or suggesting steel; hard and strong; merciless. 강철 같은; 단단한; 무정한. ¶ *a ~ glance* 아주 차가운 시선〔눈초리〕 / *a ~ composure* (강철같이) 냉랭한 평정〔침착〕.
● **steel·i·ness** [-inis] *n.*

steel·yard [stíːljɑ̀ːrd, stíljəd] *n.* Ⓒ a scale for weighing with arms or unequal length. 대저울.

:steep[1] [stiːp] *adj.* **1** having a sharp slope or incline. 가파른; 급경사진. ¶ *a ~ hill* 가파른 언덕 / *a ~ flight of stairs* 가파른 계단 / *a ~ decline* 급격한 하강. **2** 《*colloq.*》 (of prices) unreasonable; very high. (가격 등이) 터무니없는; 엄청난. ¶ *a ~ tax* 〔*price*〕 터무니없이 높은 세금〔가격〕 / *His demand is a bit ~.* 그의 요구는 좀 엄청나다 / *That story is rather ~.* 그 이야기는 좀 황당 무계해서, 믿기가 힘들다. — *n.* Ⓒ a steep slope; a precipice. 가파른 언덕; 가풀막; 벼랑. ¶ *the rugged steeps of the mountain* 산의 험한 벼랑〔낭떠러지〕. [E.]

steep[2] [stiːp] *vt.* (P6,13) 《*in*》 **1** soak (something) in a liquid. (물·액체 따위에) …을 담그다. ¶ ~ *the vegetables in water* 야채를 물에 담그다 / ~ *tea in boiling water* 끓는 물에 찻잎을 넣다 / *a sword steeped in blood* 피로 물든 칼. **2** wet or fill thoroughly; imbue. …을 깊이 스며〔배어〕들게 하다; 몰두하다. ¶ *be steeped in crime* 악에 깊이 물들어 있다 / ~ *oneself in reading books* 독서에 몰두하다 / *He is steeped in French literature.* 그는 프랑스 문학에 깊이 빠져 있다. — *n.* Ⓤ the act of steeping; Ⓒ a liquid to soak something in. 담그기; 담그는 액체. ¶ *in ~* 담가서; 잠기어. [E.]

steep·en [stíːpən] *vt., vi.* (P6;1) make (something) steep or steeper or become so. 가파르게〔험준하게〕 하다〔되다〕.

·stee·ple [stíːpəl] *n.* Ⓒ a high tower above the roof of a church, usu. capped with a spire. 뾰족탑; 첨탑(尖塔). [*steep*[1]]

stee·ple·chase [stíːpəltʃèis] *n.* Ⓒ a horse race across country obstructed with ditches, hedges, walls, etc. (야외 횡단) 장애물 경마.

stee·pled [stíːpəld] *adj.* having a steeple. 뾰족탑이 있는.

stee·ple·jack [stíːpəldʒæ̀k] *n.* a man employed to climb up steeples, chimneys, etc. for purposes of repair. (뾰족탑·높은 굴뚝 따위의) 수리공.

steep·ly [stíːpli] *adv.* in a steep manner; with a steep slope. 가파르게; 험준하게. ¶ *The road rose ~ in front of us.* 도로는 우리 앞에서 가파르게 솟아올라 있었다.

steep·ness [stíːpnis] *n.* Ⓤ the state or quality of being steep. 가파름; 험준함.

:steer[1] [stiər] *vt.* (P6,7,13) **1** direct or guide the course of (a ship, an automobile, etc.). (배·자동차 따위)를 조종하다; 몰다; 운전하다. ¶ ~ *a ship* 배를 조종하다〔몰다〕 / ~ *an automobile toward the beach* 자동차를 해변 쪽으로 운전하다. **2** direct; control. …을 이끌다〔인도하다〕; 나아가게 하다. ¶ ~ *one's country to peace and prosperity* 자기 나라를 평화와 번영으로 인도하다 / ~ *a team to victory* 팀을 승리로 이끌다 / ~ *a steady course* 한걸음한걸음 나아가다 / ~ *one's way to…* …으로 나아가다〔향하다〕 / ~ *the conversation into one's favorite topic* 대화를 흥미있는 화제로 이끌다 / *He steered our efforts to success.* 그는 우리의 노력을 성공으로 이끌었다.
— *vi.* (P1,2A,3) direct a ship, an automobile, etc.; follow a course. (배·자동차의) 키를〔핸들을〕 잡다; 나아가다. ¶ ~ *toward* 〔*for*〕 *harbor* 항구를 향해 키를 잡다. [E.]
steer clear of (=*avoid*) *someone or something.* …을 피하다.

steer[2] [stiər] *n.* Ⓒ **1** ⓐ any castrated male cattle. 거세한 황소. ⓑ a young ox. 수송아지. **2** a male beef cattle. 식용우. [E.]

steer·age [stíəridʒ] *n.* **1** the section of a ship occupied by passengers traveling at the lowest fare. (상선의) 최저 요금의 객실; 3등 선실. ¶ *a ~ passenger* (배의) 3등 선실의 승객 / *travel ~* 3등 선실로 여행하다. **2** ⓊⒸ the act of steering. 조타(操舵); 조종. [*steer*[1]]

steer·ing gear [stíəriŋ gìər] *n.* Ⓤ the mechanism controlling the steering of a ship, etc. (배의) 조타(操舵) 장치; (자동차의) 조향(操向) 장치; 스티어링 기어.

steering wheel [´‐ ´] *n.* a wheel to turn a ship's rudder or to guide a motorcar. 조타륜(操舵輪); (자동차의) 핸들.

steers·man [stíərzmən] *n.* Ⓒ (*pl.* **-men** [-mən]) a person who steers a vessel. 조타수(操舵手).

stel·lar [stélər] *adj.* **1** of or like a star. 별의; 별 같은 (모양의). ¶ ~ *light* 별빛 / *a ~ night* 별이 총총한 밤. **2** 《U.S.》 principal. 주요한. ¶ *a ~ role* 주역(主役). [L.]

:stem[1] [stem] *n.* Ⓒ **1** the main part of a plant that holds a flower, a leaf, a branch, etc. (초목의) 줄기; 대; 잎〔꽃〕자루. ¶ *terrestrial* 〔*subterranean*〕 ~ 지상〔지하〕경(莖) / *the* ~ *of an apple* 사과 꼭지. **2** something like a stem of a plant. 줄기〔대〕 모양의 것. ¶ *the* ~ *of a wine-glass* 술잔의 높다란 굽 / *the* ~ *of a tobacco-pipe* 담배 설대. **3** the bow or front end of a boat. 선수(船首); 이물. **4** a branch of a family. 가계(家系); 혈통. ¶ *be descended from an ancient* ~ 구가(舊家)의 혈통〔출신〕이다. **5** 《gram.》 the part of a word to which endings are added. 어간(語幹).

from stem to stern, from end to end. 선수에서 선미까지; 모조리.

— *vt.* (P6) pluck the stem from (a leaf, etc.). (잎 따위에서) 줄기를 떼어 내다.

— *vi.* (P1) 《*from, out of*》 《U.S.》 spring or develop; originate in. 생기다; 일어나다. ¶ *Our friendship stems from a chance meeting.* 우리들의 우정은 우연한 만남에서 생겨났다 / ~ *from a noble family* 명문가의 출신이다. [E.]

:stem[2] [stem] *vt.* (**stemmed, stem·ming**) (P6) **1** make progress or headway against (the wind, etc.). (바람 따위)에 거슬러 나아가다. ¶ ~ *the tide* 조류에 거슬러 나아가다 / ~ *the tide of opposition* 〔*public opinion*〕 반대(세력)에 저항하다〔여론에 역행하다〕. **2** stop or check. 저지하다; 막다. ¶ ~ *the flow of water* 물의 흐름을 막다. [N.]

stem cell *n.* 줄기세포.

stench [stentʃ] *n.* Ⓤ a very bad smell or odor. 악취. [*stink*]

sten·cil [sténsil] *n.* Ⓒ a thin sheet of metal, paper, etc. with letters or designs cut through it. 스텐실; 형판(型板); (등사용) 원지(原紙). ¶ ~ *paper* 등사 원지 / *a* ~ *pen* (등사판용) 철필. — *vt.* (**-ciled, -cil·ing** or 《Brit.》 **-cilled, -cil·ling**) (P6) make copies of (something) by using a stencil. …에 스텐실을 대고 찍다; 등사하다. [→tinsel]

sten·o·graph [sténəgræ̀f, -grɑ̀:f] *n.* Ⓒ **1** a keyboard instrument used for printing shorthand symbols. 속기용 타이프라이터. **2** a symbol for shorthand. 속기 문자. — *vt.* write (something) in shorthand. …을 속기하다. [Gk. *stenos* narrow]

ste·nog·ra·pher [stənágrəfər / -nɔ́g-] *n.* Ⓒ a person who is a specialist in stenography. 속기사(速記士).

sten·o·graph·ic [stènəgrǽfik] *adj.* of stenography; written in shorthand. 속기(술)의; 속기에 의한. ¶ *take* ~ *notes of* … …을 속기하다.

ste·nog·ra·phy [stənágrəfi / -nɔ́g-] *n.* Ⓤ a method of writing rapidly using simplified symbols; the act of writing in such symbols; the art of rapid writing; shorthand. 속기(술).

ste·no·sis [stənóusis] *n.* (*pl.* **ste·no·ses** [-si:z]) 《med.》 a narrowing or stricture of a passage or vessel. 협착(증).

sten·to·ri·an [stentɔ́:riən] *adj.* (of a voice) very loud. 큰 목소리의. [Person]

:step [step] *n.* Ⓒ **1** one movement of the leg in walking or running. 걸음; 한 걸음. ¶ *take two steps forward,* 2 보 전진하다 / *miss one's* ~ =*make* 〔*take*〕 *a false* ~ 발을 헛디디다 / *at every* ~ 한 걸음마다 / *put one's best* ~ *forward* 가능한 한 길을 서두르다 / *retrace one's steps* 되돌아가다〔오다〕 / *Watch* 〔*Mind*〕 *your* ~*!* 발밑을 조심해라 / *He took a* ~ *back.* 그는 한 걸음 물러섰다. **2** the distance covered by one such movement; a short distance. 1 보의 간격; 보폭(步幅)《통상 3 피트》; 한 발짝; 가까운 거리. ¶ *be unable to walk a* ~ 단 한 발짝도 걸을 수 없다 / *If you move a* ~*, I'll shoot!* 한 발짝이라도 움직이면 쏘겠다 / *His house is only a few steps from the station.* 그의 집은 정거장에서 불과 몇 발짝 안 떨어져 있다 / *I'm too tired to walk a* ~ *farther.* 너무 피곤해서 한 발짝도 걸을 수가 없다. **3** a sound or mark made by the foot in walking, etc. 발소리; 발자국. ¶ *know someone's* ~ 아무의 발소리를 알다 / *steps in the ground* 지면에 있는 발자국들 / 《*fig.*》 *tread in the steps of* …을 본뜨다 / *Steps were heard approaching.* 다가오는 발소리가 들렸다 / *The police found the burglar's steps in the snow.* 경찰은 눈 위에서 도둑의 발자국을 발견했다. **4** ⓊⒸ the manner of walking; pace, esp. in marching; a regular movement of the feet in dancing. 걸음걸이; 걸음새; 보조(步調); (댄스의) 스텝. ¶ *a light* 〔*heavy*〕 ~ 가벼운〔무거운〕 걸음걸이 / *double-quick steps* 구보 / ~ *for* ~ 동일 보조로; 보조를 맞추어 / *dance with fancy steps* 멋진〔환상적인〕 스텝으로 춤추다 / *walk with quick* 〔*slow*〕 *steps* 빠른〔느린〕 걸음걸이로 걷다. **5** one of the parts of a stair or ladder; 《*pl.*》 a flight of stairs. 단(段); 디딤판; 계단; 계급. ¶ *a doorstep* 현관의 층대 / *run down* 〔*up*〕 *the steps* 계단을 뛰어내리다〔오르다〕 / *cut steps in the rock* 바위에 발 디딜 자리를 파다 / *a staircase of 30 steps,* 30 계단의 층층대 / *Each flight of stairs has 12 steps.* 각 계단에는 12 개의 층계가〔단(段)이〕 있다. **6** a degree in grade or rank; an advance that forms one of a series. 단계; 계급; 승진; 승급. ¶ *get one's* ~ 승진하다 / *give someone a* ~ 아무를 승진시키다 / *He got his* ~. 그는 승진했다 / *A sergeant is one* ~ *above a corporal.* 병장은 상등병의 윗 계급이다. **7** an act or a measure done for some purpose. 수단; 처치. ¶ *a bold* ~ 대담한 처치 / *the first* ~ *in our work* 우리 일에서의 첫번째 조치 / *We must take steps to prevent it.* 그것을 방지하는 방법을 강구하지 않으면 안 된다. **8** an interval in music; a tone. 음정(音程).

break step, get out of step. (일부러) 보조를 흩뜨리다〔그치다〕.

in step, at the same pace with another

person or thing. 보조를 맞추어; 조화하여. ¶ *keep in* ~ 보조를 맞추다.

in one's steps, following his example. 전례에 따라서.

keep step with (=*move at the same pace as*) *someone.* …와 보조를 맞추다.

out of step, having a different pace with another person or thing. 보조를 흩뜨려; 조화되지 않아.

step by step, gradually; slowly. 한걸음 한걸음; 조금씩 착실하게.

— *vi.* (P1,2A,3) **1** go, come or move by one or more steps; walk a short distance. 걷다; 가다. ¶ ~ *forward* 〔*backward*〕 전진하다〔물러서다, 후진하다〕 / ~ *inside* 〔*outside*〕 안으로 들어가다〔밖으로 나가다〕/ ~ *across* …을 가로지르다 / ~ *on to the platform* 승강장에 내려서다 / *Step this way, please.* 어서, 이쪽으로 오십시오. **2** 《*on, upon*》 press the foot on something. (짓)밟다; 디디다. ¶ ~ *on a worm* 벌레를 밟다 / ~ *on the brake* 브레이크를 밟다 / *Did I* ~ *on your foot?* 내가 네 발을 밟았느냐. — *vt.* (P6,7) **1** take (a step, a stride, etc.). (걸음)을 걷다; (발)을 내딛다. ¶ ~ *two paces* 2보 전진하다 / ~ *foot in a place* 〔*on the moon*〕 어떤 장소〔월면〕에 (처음으로) 발을 내딛다. **2** measure (a distance) by steps. …을 보측(步測)하다. **3** perform the steps of (a dance). (댄스의) 스텝을 밟다. [E.]

step aside, make way for others. 옆으로 비키다.

step down, **a**) retire from (a position of authority). (직책)을 사직하다. **b**) reduce (an electric current, etc.). (전압)을 낮추다.

step in, **a**) enter. …에 들어가다. ¶ ~ *in a house* 집 안으로 들어가다. **b**) come or be between. …에 끼어들다.

step off, 《U.S.》 measure (a distance) by steps. …을 보측하다.

step out, **a**) start to walk with long strides. 성큼성큼 걷다. **b**) leave a house, room, etc. for a short time. 잠시 집 밖으로 나가다. ¶ *I stepped out to get a newspaper.* 신문을 구하기 위해 잠시 집 밖으로 나갔다. **c**) 《U.S.》 《*colloq.*》 go out to have a good time. 놀러 나가다.

step up, increase; speed up. …을 올리다; 촉진하다. ¶ ~ *up sales* 판매를 촉진하다.

step- [step-] *pref.* made nominally so by the death of one and the remarriage of the other of a wedded pair. '의붓…', 계(繼)…'의 뜻. [E. =orphaned]

step·broth·er [stépbrʌ̀ðər] *n.* Ⓒ a son of one's stepfather or stepmother by a former marriage. 이복〔배다른〕 형제. [↑]

step·child [stéptʃàild] *n.* Ⓒ (*pl.* **-chil·dren**) a child of one's husband or wife by a former marriage. 의붓자식.

step·chil·dren [stéptʃìldrən] *n.* pl. of **stepchild.**

step·daugh·ter [stépdɔ̀ːtər] *n.* Ⓒ a daughter of one's husband or wife by a former marriage. 의붓딸.

step-down [stépdàun] *adj.* converting an electric current from a higher to a lower voltage. 전압을 내리는〔낮추는〕. [*step*]

step·fa·ther [stépfɑ̀ːðər] *n.* Ⓒ a man married to one's mother after the death or divorce of one's own father. 의붓아버지; 계부. [step-]

Ste·phen [stíːvən] *n.* a man's name. 남자 이름.

step·lad·der [stéplæ̀dər] *n.* Ⓒ a short portable ladder with flat steps and, often, folding legs. 발판 사닥다리; 접사다리. [*step*]

step·moth·er [stépmʌ̀ðər] *n.* Ⓒ a woman married to one's father after the death or divorce of one's own mother. 의붓어머니; 계모. [step-]

step·par·ent [stéppὲərənt] *n.* Ⓒ a stepfather or stepmother. 의붓어버이; 계부모.

steppe [step] *n.* Ⓒ a vast, grassy plain without trees; 《*the S-*》 the vast, treeless Russian grasslands. 대초원; 스텝《시베리아의 대초원》. [Russ.]

step·ping·stone [stépiŋstòun] *n.* **1** one of a line of stones placed in a shallow stream, soft turf, etc. 디딤돌. **2** 《*fig.*》 《*to*》 something used as a means of advancing or rising. (어떤 목적을 달성하기 위한) 수단. ¶ *a* ~ *to victory* 승리를 위한 수단. [*step*]

step·sis·ter [stépsìstər] *n.* Ⓒ a daughter of one's stepfather or stepmother by a former marriage. 배다른〔이복〕 자매. [step-]

step·son [stépsʌ̀n] *n.* Ⓒ a son of one's husband or wife by a former marriage. 의붓아들〔자식〕.

ster·e·o·graph [stériəgræ̀f, stíər-, -grɑ̀ːf] *n.* one of a pair of photographs for use in a stereoscope. 입체 사진. [Gk. *stereós* solid, *hard*]

ster·e·o·phon·ic [stèriəfɑ́nik, stìər-/ -fɔ́n-] *adj.* of or giving sound reproduction through two or more channels at the same time. 스테레오의; 입체 음향의.

ster·e·o·scope [stériəskòup, stíər-] *n.* Ⓒ an instrument through which two pictures of the same scene appear to be one which has depth. 입체〔실체〕경(鏡).

ster·e·o·type [stériətàip, stíər-] *n.* Ⓒ **1** a printing metal plate made by casting composed type in a mold; the process of making such metal plates. 스테로판(版); 연판(鉛版); 연판 제조. **2** 《*fig.*》 a fixed expression. 상투적인 문구. — *vt.* **1** (P6) print (something) from a stereotype. …을 연판〔스테로판〕으로 하다. **2** conventionalize; give a settled form to (something). …을 판에 박다; 정형화(定型化)하다.

ster·e·o·typed [stériətàipt, stíər-] *adj.* 《*fig.*》 fixed once for all; fixed or settled in form. 판에 박은; 진부한; 정형화된. ¶ ~ *ideas* 〔*phrases*〕 진부한 생각〔문구〕.

ster·ile [stéril / stérail] *adj.* **1** unable to produce offsprings. 자식을〔새끼를〕 못 낳는. ¶ *a ~ cow* 새끼를 못 낳는 암소 / *a ~ marriage* 자식이 없는 결혼 (생활). **2** not fertile; barren. 불모의(opp. fertile). ¶ *a wild stretch of ~ land* 광막한 불모의 땅 / *a ~ year* 흉년. **3** free from any living germs. 살균한; 무균의. ¶ *a ~ bandage* 살균한 붕대 / *~ culture* 무균 배양 / *Surgical knives are always kept ~.* 메스는〔수술칼은〕 항상 살균되어 보관된다. **4** unsuccessful; useless. 효과가 없는; 소용〔쓸모〕 없는. ¶ *~ hopes* 헛된 희망 / *~ negotiations* 헛된〔소용 없는〕 교섭. **5** lacking interest, emotion, imagination, etc. 흥미〔감정, 독창성, 사상 따위〕가 없는; 단조로운. ¶ *a ~ lecture* 내용이 빈약한 강의. [L.]

ste·ril·i·ty [stəríləti] *n.* Ⓤ the state or quality of being sterile; barrenness. 불임; 불모; 무미 건조.

ster·i·li·za·tion [stèrəlizéiʃən] *n.* Ⓤ the act of sterilizing; the state of being sterilized. 살균 소독; 불임케 함. ¶ *~ of the unfit* 부적자(不適者) 단종(斷種).

ster·i·lize [stérəlàiz] *vt.* (P6) **1** free (something) from living germs. …을 살균하다; 소독하다. ¶ *~ water by boiling* 물을 끓여서 살균하다 / *sterilized milk* 멸균 우유 / *Surgical instruments must be sterilized before they are used.* 수술용 도구는 사용하기 전에 반드시 소독되어져야 한다. **2** deprive (an animal) of reproductive power. …을 불임케 하다; 단종(斷種)하다.

ster·ling [stə́:rliŋ] *adj.* **1** of British money. 영국 화폐의; 영화(英貨)의. 參考 s., stg. 로 생략하며, 파운드 뒤에 부기함. ¶ *£500s. = £500 stg.* 영화(英貨) 500 파운드 / *a ~ loan* 영화(英貨) 공채(公債) / *the ~ area* 파운드 지역. **2** of real value; excellent. 진정의; 진짜의. ¶ *~ worth* 진가 / *a ~ spoon* 순은제의 숟가락 / *a man of ~ character* 훌륭한 품성의 사람 / *a ~ article* 진짜 물건. — *n.* Ⓤ British money. 영국 화폐; 영화(英貨). [E. = penny]

:**stern**[1] [stə:rn] *adj.* **1** severe; strict. 엄격한. ¶ *a ~ teacher* 엄격한 교사 / *a ~ command* 엄명 / *a ~ parent* 〔*master*〕 엄격한 부모〔주인〕 / *~ discipline* 엄격한 훈육〔훈련〕. **2** firm; hard. 단호한; 엄숙한. ¶ *a ~ resolve* 단호한 결심 / *a ~ face* 엄숙〔준엄〕한 얼굴. [E.]

stern[2] [stə:rn] *n.* Ⓒ the back part of a ship. 선미(船尾)(opp. bow). ¶ *from stem to ~* 이물에서 고물까지; 선내(船內) 구석구석(까지). [N. (→steer)]

ster·na [stə́:rnə] *n.* pl. of **sternum.**

stern·ly [stə́:rnli] *adv.* in a stern manner; severely; strictly. 엄하게; 엄격히.

ster·num [stə́:rnəm] *n.* (*pl.* **ster·na** or **ster·nums**) the breastbone. 흉골(胸骨). [Gk.]

stet [stet] *n.* a word written on a proof sheet directing the printer to print as before. (교정지에) 지운 것을 다시 살림《교정 용어》. [L. = let it stand]

steth·o·scope [stéθəskòup] *n.* Ⓒ an instrument used by doctors for listening to heartbeats. 청진기. [Gk. *stēthos* breast]

ste·ve·dore [stí:vədɔ̀:r] *n.* Ⓒ a person who carries packages onto or off a ship. (부두의) 하역 인부. [L. *stipo* pack]

***stew** [stju:] *vt., vi.* (P6,7; 1,2A) **1** boil slowly. …을 뭉근한 불로 끓이다〔불에 끓다〕. ¶ *~ meat and vegetables* 육류와 채소를 뭉근한 불에 끓이다. **2** 《*colloq.*》 worry. 속타게〔애타게〕 하다; 마음을 졸이게 하다〔졸이다〕; 속을〔애를〕 태우다. ¶ *be stewed up with anxiety* 걱정으로 애를 태우다 / *~ oneself into an illness* 안달복달하다가 병이 나다.

***let someone* stew *in someone's* own juice,** do not help someone out of difficulty. (아무를) 멋대로 어리석은 짓을 하게 내버려 두다.

— *n.* **1** ⒸⓊ a stewed dish made of meat and vegetables. 스튜 (요리)《고기와 각종 채소를 뭉근한 불로 오래 끓여 익힌 걸쭉한 요리》. ¶ *We had beef ~ for supper.* 우리는 저녁 식사로 쇠고기 스튜를 먹었다. **2** Ⓒ 《*colloq.*》 a state of worry; a difficulty. 근심; 걱정. ¶ *She is all in a ~ over her lost trunk.* 그녀는 잃어버린 가방으로 근심 걱정에 잠겨 있다. [Rom. →stove]

***stew·ard** [stjú:ərd] *n.* Ⓒ **1** a man to manage the household affairs of his master's family. 집사; 간사(幹事). **2** a waiter on a ship or train, at a club, etc. (객선·여객기·열차 따위의) 웨이터; 여객 계원; 스튜어드; 급사. [E. = housewarden]

stew·ard·ess [stjú:ərdis] *n.* Ⓒ a waitress on a ship, an airplane, etc. (여객기 따위의) 여자 안내원; 스튜어디스; 여성의 steward.

stew·ard·ship [stjú:ərdʃip] *n.* the rank, office, or work of a steward. 스튜어드의 직〔지위〕. ¶ *give an account of one's ~* 사무 보고를 하다.

stew·pan [stjú:pæ̀n] *n.* Ⓒ a pan used for making stew. 스튜 요리용 냄비. [→stew]

:**stick**[1] [stik] *n.* Ⓒ **1** a piece of wood cut or broken from a tree; a long, narrow piece of wood. 막대기; (마른) 나뭇가지; 몽둥이. ¶ *gather dry sticks for the fire* 땔 나뭇가지를 주워 모으다 / *Put some sticks on the fire.* 불에 나뭇가지를 좀 지펴라〔올려놓아라〕. **2** something like a stick in shape or use; a walking stick; a hockey stick. 막대기 모양의 것; 단장; 지팡이; (하키의) 스틱. ¶ *walk with a ~* 지팡이를 짚고 걷다 / *a ~ of candy* 막대 모양의 캔디 / *a cosmetic ~* 막대 모양의 화장품. **3** 《*colloq.*》 a dull or stupid person. 바보; 멍청이. ¶ *He is a ~.* 그는 멍청한 바보이다.

***cut one's* stick,** 《*sl.*》 go away. 달아나다.

get hold of the wrong end of the stick, misunderstand a situation; form a wrong idea concerning a matter. (상황을) 잘못 판

단하다; (사물을) 오해하다.

in a cleft stick, in a dilemma. 진퇴 양난에 빠져.

— *vt.* (P6) support with a stick or sticks. (식물 따위)를 막대기로 버티다〔받치다〕. ¶ ~ *a plant* 식물을 막대기로 받치다. [↓]

:stick² [stik] *v.* (**stuck**) *vt.* (P6,7,13) **1** 《*into, through, with*》 push (a pointed thing) into someone or something; thrust or pierce (something or someone) with a pointed thing. …에 (바늘 따위 뾰족한 것)을 찌르다; (예리한 것으로) …을 (꽤)찌르다; 꿰뚫다; 찔러 죽이다. ¶ ~ *a fork into a potato* 포크로 감자를 푹 찌르다 / ~ *a knife into one's belly* 아무의 배를 칼로 찌르다 / ~ *one's finger with a needle* 바늘로 손가락을 찌르다. **2** 《*on, in*》 fix or fasten (something) by or on a point. …을 찔러 달다〔고정하다, 꽂다, 끼우다, 꾸미다〕. ¶ ~ *a flower in a buttonhole* 꽃을 단춧구멍에 꽂다 / ~ *a piece of meat on a spit* 고깃조각을 꼬치에 꽂다 / ~ *candles in a birthday cake* 생일 케이크에 초를 꽂다 / ~ *one's hands into one's pockets* 주머니에 손을 질러 넣다. **3** 《*on, to*》 fix or attach (something) with paste glue, etc. …을 붙이다; 들러붙게 하다; 고착시키다. ¶ ~ *a stamp on a letter* 편지에 우표를 붙이다 / ~ *a notice to a door* 문에 게시문을 붙이다 / *Stick no bills.* 삐라를 붙이지 마시오 / *Stick this picture in your book.* 너의 책에 이 그림을 붙여라 / *He stuck the broken pieces together with glue.* 그는 접착제로 깨진 파편들을 모아 붙였다. **4** 《*into, out of, in*》 put or thrust (something) in a place or position. (어떤 장소·위치에) …을 놓다〔두다〕; 내밀다; 끼워 넣다. ¶ ~ *a letter in one's pocket* 주머니에 편지를 집어넣다 / ~ *papers in a drawer* 서류를 서랍 속에 넣어 두다 / ~ *a book on the shelf* 책을 선반 위에 두다 / *Don't* ~ *your head out of the train window.* 기차의 창 밖으로 머리를 내밀지 마라 / *Just* ~ *it down there.* 그냥 거기에 내려 놓아라. **5** 《usu. in *passive*》 《*in*》 bring (something) to a stop. …을 꼼짝하지 못하게 하다. ¶ *The car was stuck in the mud.* 자동차는 진흙에 빠져 꼼짝 못 했다 / *We have been stuck here for three days by a heavy snowstorm.* 심한 눈보라로 인해 3일간이나 이 곳에 꼼짝 못 하고 있다. — *vi.* (P1,2A,3) **1** 《*in*》 be thrust; become infixed by means of a pointed end. 찔리다; 꽂히다. ¶ *A splinter stuck in his leg.* 파편 하나가 그의 다리에 박혔다 / *A fishbone stuck in my throat.* 생선 가시 하나가 내 목에 걸렸다 / *The needle stuck in her finger.* 바늘이 그녀 손가락을 찔렀다 / *I found a nail sticking in the tire.* 타이어에 못이 박혀 있었다. **2** 《*to*》 become attached or fastened; adhere. 들러붙다; 접착하다; 붙여져 있다. ¶ *This envelope will not* ~. 이 봉투는 달라붙지 않는다 / ~ *close* 〔*fast*〕 철썩 들러붙다 / *The mud has stuck to my shoes.* 구두에 진흙이 붙어 떨어지지 않는다 / *Several pages have stuck together.* 여러 페이지가 하나로 들러붙어 있다. **3** 《*to*》 keep close; hold fast. 달라붙어 있다. ¶ *an event that sticks in one's mind* 마음 속에 집착되어 있어 잊혀지지 않는 사건 / *The nickname has stuck to him.* 그 별명은 그에게서 떨어져 나가지 않고 있다 / *The boy stuck to his mother's heels.* 그 소년은 어머니 뒤에 바싹 붙었다 / *Whatever may happen, we must* ~ *together.* 무슨 일이 일어나든, 우리는 서로 단결해야 한다. **4** become motionless; stay; remain. 행동을 하지 않다; 머무르다. ¶ ~ *at home* 집 안에 들어박혀 있다 / *Stick where you are!* 지금 있는 곳에서 꼼짝 말고 그대로 있어라. **5** be fixed; become jammed; be unable to go farther; be at a standstill. (움직일 수 없도록) 꽉 막히다〔끼이다〕; 옴짝달싹 못 하다; 움직일 수 없게 되다. ¶ *This door always sticks.* 이 문은 항상 꽉 끼어서 열리지 않는다 / *Our car stuck in the mud.* 자동차는 진흙에 빠져 꼼짝 못 하게 되었다 / *The key stuck in the lock.* 열쇠가 자물통 안에 꽉 끼어 꼼짝 않았다. **6** be in trouble; be puzzled. 난처해지다; 당혹스러워하다; 망설이다. ¶ *I* ~ *at mathematics.* 나는 수학이라면 두 손을 든다. **7** keep on; hold fast; persevere. 고집하다; 끝까지 고수하다〔견뎌 내다〕. ¶ ~ *to what one said* 자기가 말한 것을 고집하다 / *He never sticks to anything for very long.* 그는 어떤 일에도 오래도록 지속하는 경우가 없다 / *You will surely succeed if you* ~ *at your work.* 하는 일을 끝까지 착실히 해낸다면 틀림없이 너는 성공할 것이다. [E.]

stick around, 《*colloq.*》 stay in or near a place; linger. 옆〔가까이〕에 (대기하고) 있다; 머물러 있다.

stick at, **a**) keep hard at (one's job, etc.). …을 고집하다. **b**) hesitate or stop for (something). …에 대해 주저하다〔망설이다〕. ¶ *She'll* ~ *at nothing* (*to gain her ends*). 그녀는 (목적 달성을 위해서라면) 무슨 일이라도 주저하지 않을 것이다.

stick by, 《*colloq.*》 remain loyal or faithful to. …에 충실하다; 고수하다.

stick down, **a**) 《*colloq.*》 put down. 내려놓다. **b**) 《*colloq.*》 write down. (주소 등을) 적어 두다. **c**) fasten with paste, etc. (풀 따위로) 붙이다. ¶ ~ *down the flap of an envelope* 봉투의 접어 젖힌 부분을 붙이다.

stick in one's throat ⇨throat.

stick it (**out**), 《*colloq.*》 put up with it; bear to the end. 끝까지 버티다〔계속하다〕.

stick on, **a**) remain on. 떨어지지 않다; 단단히 말에 타고 있다. ¶ ~ *on a horse* 말에서 떨어지지 않고 올라 타 있다. **b**) fasten on with paste, etc. 붙이다. ¶ ~ *on a stamp* 우표를 붙이다.

stick out, **a**) thrust out; stand out. 튀어나오다; 내밀다. ¶ ~ *out one's tongue* 혓바닥을 내밀다. **b**) be plainly apparent. 명료하다; 두드러지다. ¶ 《*colloq.*》 ~ *out like a sore thumb* 일목 요연하다. **c**) be insistent and not give in; persist. 끝까지 버티다〔요구하다〕;

완강히 주장하다. ¶ ~ *out for higher wages* 임금 인상을 악착같이 요구하다.

stick to, **a**) keep on with; continue with (one's work, etc.). …에 집착하다; …을 고수하다; 계속하다. ¶ ~ *to one's task* 자기 과업을 고수하다. **b**) be faithful to; be true to; keep. …에 충실하다; 지키다. ¶ ~ *to one's agreement* 약속을 지키다.

stick up, **a**) be or make (something) upright. 곧추서다; …을 곧추세우다. ¶ ~ *up a post* 기둥을 곧추세우다. **b**) 《*sl.*》 enter and rob. (은행 따위에) 침입하여 털다. ¶ ~ *up a bank* 은행을 털다.

stick up for, support (someone) in an argument; defend. …을 지지하다; 변호하다; 지키다. ¶ ~ *up for a friend* 〔*one's right*〕 친구를〔자기의 권리를〕 옹호하다.

stick·er [stíkər] *n.* Ⓒ **1** a person or thing that sticks. 붙이는 사람〔것〕. **2** 《U.S.》 a gummed label. 스티커. [*stick*[2]]

stick·ing-plas·ter [stíkiŋplæ̀stər/-plɑ̀ːs-] *n.* a sticky tape of cloth for covering and closing slight wounds. 반창고.

stick-in-the-mud [stíkinðəmʌ̀d] *n.* Ⓒ 《*colloq.*》 a person who resists progress or change. 고루한〔구식〕 사람.

stick·le [stíkəl] *vi.* (P1,3) 《*at*》 insist or hesitate for petty reasons. 하찮은 일에 까다롭다〔구애되다〕. [E.]

stick·ler [stíklər] *n.* Ⓒ 《*for*》 a person who worries or is concerned about small matters. 하찮고 사소한 일에 까다로운 사람; 잔소리꾼. ¶ *a* ~ *for etiquette* 〔*time*〕 에티켓〔시간〕에 관해 잔소리가 많은 사람.

stick·y [stíki] *adj.* (**stick·i·er, stick·i·est**) **1** that sticks. 끈적끈적한. ¶ *The paste left my fingers* ~. 풀이 손가락에 남아 끈적거렸다. **2** 《*colloq.*》 (of weather) unpleasantly hot and wet. (날씨 따위가) 무덥고 끈끈한. ¶ ~ *weather* 무덥고 끈끈한 날씨. ● **stick·i·ly** [-li] *adv.* **stick·i·ness** [-nis] *n.* [*stick*[2]]

:stiff [stif] *adj.* **1** not easily bent; firm; rigid. 빳빳한; 딱딱한; 경직된; 굳은. ¶ *a* ~ *collar* 빳빳한 칼라 / *stand straight and* ~ 부동 자세로 서 있다. **2** not able to move without pain; hard to move or operate. (관절 따위가) 아파서 잘 움직일 수 없는; 잘 움직이지 않는. ¶ ~ *hinges* (잘 움직이지 않는) 뻑뻑한 경첩 / *have a* ~ *neck* 목이 뻣뻣하다 / *An old man's joints are* ~. 노인의 관절은 굳어서 움직일 때 아프다. **3** formal; cold in one's manner. (태도·행위 등이) 형식적인; 딱딱한; 쌀쌀한. ¶ *a* ~ *manner* 쌀쌀한〔딱딱한〕 태도 / *He made a* ~ *bow.* 그는 딱딱하게 절을 했다 / *He writes in a* ~ *style.* 그는 딱딱한 문체로 글을 쓴다. **4** difficult; hard. 어려운; 힘든. ¶ *a* ~ *examination* 어려운 시험 / *a* ~ *climb* 힘든 등반 / *This book is* ~ *reading.* 이 책은 읽기가 힘이 든다. **5** not yielding or giving way; obstinate. 양보하지 않는; 고집스러운; 완고한. ¶ *a* ~ *opposition* 완고한 반대 / *He is very* ~ *about it.* 그는 그것에 대해 매우 완고하다. **6** (of winds, currents, etc.) strong; (of alcoholic drinks) very strong; more than seems suitable or reasonable; excessive; (of a penalty, etc.) severe. (바람·조류가) 거센; 맹렬한; (술이) 독한; (물가 따위가) 비싼; 엄청난; (형벌이) 엄한. ¶ *a* ~ *gale* 강풍 / *a* ~ *fine* 엄청난 벌금 / *a* ~ *drink* 독한 술 / *a* ~ *price* 〔*tax*〕 (엄청나게) 비싼 값〔높은 세금〕 / *a* ~ *punishment* 엄한 처벌 / *He asked me a* ~ *price for his house.* 그는 엄청나게 비싼 그의 집값을 나에게 요구하였다. **7** not flowing easily; thick and heavy. (반죽 따위가) 된; 걸쭉한. ¶ *a* ~ *varnish* 걸쭉한 니스. [E.]

feel stiff, suffer from stiffness of muscles or limbs. (근육·수족이) 뻐근〔뻑적지근〕하다.

keep a stiff lip, remain grave; remain unmoved. 점잔빼다; 동하지 않다.

take a stiff line, take a firm attitude. 강경하게 나오다.

— *adv.* 《*colloq.*》 completely; extremely. 완전히; 극도로; 몹시.

stiff·en [stífən] *vt., vi.* (P6;1) make (something) stiff; become stiff. 빳빳〔딱딱〕하게 하다; 빳빳〔딱딱〕해지다. ¶ *She stiffened the sheets with starch.* 그녀는 시트에 풀을 먹여 빳빳하게 하였다 / *He stiffened his attitude.* 그는 그의 태도를 딱딱하게 하였다 / ~ *one's resolve* 결의를 굳히다 / *His will stiffened with years.* 그의 의지는 해가 갈수록 완고해졌다. [*stiff*]

***stiff·ly** [stífli] *adv.* in a stiff manner. 딱딱하게; 완고하게.

stiff neck [ˊˊ] *n.* a person who is hard to control; a stubborn person. 완고한 사람.

stiff·ness [stífnis] *n.* Ⓤ the state or quality of being stiff. 굳음; 강도.

sti·fle [stáifəl] *vt.* (P6) **1** prevent (someone) from breathing; smother. …을 질식시키다; 숨막히게 하다. ¶ ~ *someone with smoke* 〔*by gas*〕 연기〔가스〕로 아무를 질식시키다 / *The smoke almost stifled the firemen.* 연기는 소방관을 거의 질식시킬 뻔했다 / *The large crowds in the train stifled me.* 기차에는 너무나 사람들이 많아서 숨이 막힐 것 같았다. **2** put out; cause to die down. (불 따위를) 끄다; 꺼지게 하다. ¶ ~ *a fire* 불을 끄다. **3** hold back or stop. …을 억〔짓〕누르다; 억제하다. ¶ ~ *tears* 눈물을 억누르다 / ~ *a yawn* 하품을 참다 / ~ *a complain* 〔*rebellion*〕 불평〔반란〕을 억누르다〔진압하다〕.

— *vi.* (P1) become unable to breathe freely. 숨막히다; 질식하다. [?]

sti·fling [stáifliŋ] *adj.* in a condition where it is difficult to breathe. 질식할 것 같은; 숨이 막힐 듯한. ¶ *be* ~ *hot* 숨막힐 듯이 덥다 / *He was* ~ *in that little room.* 그는 그 작은 방에서 숨이 막힐 지경이었다 / *This room is* ~. 이 방은 (너무 덥거나 공기가 나빠서) 질식할 것 같다. [?]

stig·ma [stígmə] *n.* Ⓒ (*pl.* **-mas** or **-ma·ta**) **1** a mark of shame or dishonor. 오명(汚名).

¶ *the ~ of illegitimacy* 사생아라는 오명 / *affix a ~ to* …에 오명을 씌우다. **2** a burnt sign on a slave or criminal in olden days. 낙인. **3** the upper part of a flower. (꽃의) 주두(柱頭); 암술머리. [Gk. *stizō* prick]

stig·ma·ta [stígmətə] *n.* pl. of **stigma.**

stig·mat·ic [stigmǽtik] *adj.* of the nature of a stigma. 불명예스러운; 낙인이 찍힌; 추한.

stig·ma·tize [stígmətàiz] *vt.* (P7) **1** mark (someone) as shameful. …에 오명을 씌우다. ¶ *~ someone as a coward* 아무를 겁쟁이라고 부르다. **2** put a burnt sign on (a slave, etc.). …에 낙인을 찍다. [→stigma]

stile [stail] *n.* Ⓒ a step or steps for getting over a fence. (가축 우리의 울타리를 사람이) 넘어다니기 위한 층계(발판). [E.]

〈stile〉

sti·let·to [stilétou] *n.* Ⓒ (*pl.* **-tos** or **-toes**) **1** a small weapon shaped like a knife. (송곳 모양의) 단검. **2** a tool for making small holes in cloth. (자수용의) 구멍 뚫는 바늘(송곳). [L. *stilus*]

:still[1] [stil] *adj.* **1** quiet; making no sound; silent. 조용한; 소리가 없는; 말이 없는. ¶ *a ~ evening* 조용한 저녁 / *in ~ meditation* 심사(숙고)하여 / *The air is perfectly ~.* 바람 한 점 없는 조용한 날씨이다 / *The room was so ~ that you could have heard a pin drop.* 방안은 바늘 떨어지는 소리라도 들릴 만큼 매우 조용했다. **2** having no motion; without movement; (of water) calm. 움직이지 않는; 정지(靜止)한; (수면이) 잔잔한. ¶ *Please stand ~.* 조용히 서 있으시오 / 《*prov.*》 *Still waters run deep.* 잔잔한 물이 깊다. **3** (of sounds) soft; low. (소리가) 조용한; 부드러운; (음성이) 낮은. ¶ 《Bible》 *a* (*the*) *~ small voice* 조용하고 작은 목소리《신·양심의 속삭임》. **4** (of wine, etc.) not sparkling. 거품이 일지 않는.

— *adv.* **1** up to this or that time; now, as before; as yet. 아직(도); 지금도; 여전히. ¶ *The baby is ~ asleep.* 아기는 아직도 잠자고 있다 / *She will ~ be here tomorrow.* 그녀는 내일도 여기에 있을 것이다 / *He ~ works there.* 그는 (여전히) 지금도 거기서 일하고 있다 / *Was the shop ~ open?* 그 상점은 아직도 열려 있었느냐. **2** 《used with *a comparative*》 even; 《used *intensively*》 yet. 더욱(더); 더 한층《비교급과 더불어》. ¶ *~ greater efforts* 더 한층의 노력 / *That's ~ better.* 그것이 한층 더 좋다. **3** 《used *conjunctively*》 however; in spite of that. 그러나; 역시; 그럼에도 불구하고《접속적으로 쓰여》. ¶ *He is a good man, ~ I don't like him.* 그는 좋은 사람이지만, (그러나) 나는 싫다 / *He is rich,* (*and*) *~ he craves more.* 그는 부자임에도 불구하고 더 많은 부를 원한다. **4** in addition; besides. 그 위에; 추가해서. ¶ *give ~ another example* 추가로 예문을 하나 더 들다.

— *vt.* (P6) make (something) quiet, silent, or calm. …을 가라앉히다(조용하게 하다); 진정시키다; 달래다. ¶ *~ a crying baby* 우는 아기를 달래다 / *~ waves* (*winds*) 파도를(바람을) 잔잔하게 하다 / *~ one's desire* 욕망을 가라앉히다 / *The people prayed that the storm might be stilled.* 사람들은 폭풍이 잔잔해지기를 기도하였다.

— *vi.* (P1) become still. 조용해지다; 가라앉다.

— *n.* Ⓒ **1** 《*poet.*》 silence. 고요; 침묵. ¶ *in the ~ of night* 밤의 고요(정적) 속에서. **2** a single photograph from the series that form a motion picture film. 스틸 사진. [E.]

still[2] [stil] *n.* Ⓒ an apparatus used for making whisky or brandy. (알코올류의) 증류기. [L. *stillo* drip]

still·born [stílbɔ̀ːrn] *adj.* dead when born. 사산(死産)의. [*still*[1]]

still life [ㅅㅅ] *n.* inanimate objects as flowers, pottery, etc. shown in a picture; a picture containing such things. 정물(화)(靜物(畫)).

•still·ness [stílnis] *n.* Ⓤ silence. 조용함.

still-room [stílrù(ː)m] *n.* 《Brit.》 **1** a room in a large house where liquor and preserves are kept. (대저택의) 식료품 저장실. **2** a distilling room. (화주(火酒) 제조용의) 증류실. [*still*[2]]

still·y [stíli] *adj.* (**still·i·er, still·i·est**) 《*poet.*》 quiet; still. 고요한; 소리 없는. [*still*[1]]

stilt·ed [stíltid] *adj.* **1** raised on stilts. 죽마(竹馬)를 탄. **2** too formal; not natural. 과장된. [↓]

stilts [stilts] *n. pl.* a pair of wooden poles for walking above the ground. 죽마(竹馬). ¶ *walk on ~* 죽마를 타고 걷다. [E.]

stim·u·lant [stímjələnt] *n.* Ⓒ some drink or medicine that gives power and excitement to the body. 흥분성 음식물《커피·술 따위》; 자극물. ¶ *Alcoholic drinks and coffee are stimulants.* 알코올 음료와 커피는 흥분성 음식물이다. [→stimulus]

•stim·u·late [stímjəlèit] *vt.* (P6,13,20) excite or encourage (someone) to action; quicken the activity of (some bodily function). …을 자극하다; 기운을 북돋우다. ¶ *~ someone's interest* (*curiosity*) 아무의 흥미를(호기심을) 자극하다 / *~ production* 생산을 자극하다 / *~ someone into activity* 아무를 자극하여 활동케 하다 / *Wine stimulates a sick person.* 포도주는 환자의 기운을 북돋았다 / *Praise stimulates students to work hard.* 칭찬은 학생에게 격려가 되어 열심히 공부하게 한다 / *Success will ~ a man to further efforts.* 성공은 사람을 자극하여 더 한층 노력하게 한다.

stim·u·lat·ing [stímjəlèitiŋ] *adj.* exciting mental or physical activity. 자극하는; 기운을 북돋우는.

stim·u·la·tion [stìmjəléiʃən] *n.* Ⓤ the act of stimulating; the state of being stimulated. 자극; 격려; 흥분.

stim·u·la·tive [stímjəlèitiv] *adj.* having power to stimulate someone. 자극하는; 자극적인; 격려하는.

stim·u·lat·or [stímjəlèitər] *n.* Ⓒ a person or thing that stimulates. 자극자〔물〕.

stim·u·li [stímjəlài] *n.* pl. of **stimulus.**

stim·u·lus [stímjələs] *n.* Ⓒ (*pl.* **-li**) **1** something that urges someone to action. (정신에 작용하는) 자극; 자극물. **2** =stimulant. [L. =goad, spur]

:sting [stiŋ] *n.* Ⓒ **1** a sharp, pointed organ in some insects, animals, and plants which often contains poison. (곤충 따위의) 침; 독아(毒牙); 독침; (식물의) 가시. **2** the wound or pain caused by a sting. 찔린 상처; 자통(刺痛). ¶ *a face covered with stings* 찔린 상처투성이의 얼굴 / *feel a sharp* ~ 격렬한 자통을 느끼다. **3** the act of stinging. 찌르기; 쏘기. ¶ *be hurt by a* ~ 찔리어 상처를 입다. **4** ⒸⓊ any sharp, sudden pain of mind or body. (일반적으로) 찌르는 듯한 아픔; 격통; (정신적인) 심한 고통; 괴로움. ¶ *the* ~ *of the wind* 바늘로 찌르는 듯한 매서운 바람 / *the sting(s) of hunger* 기아〔배고픔〕의 고통 / *the sting(s) of conscience* 양심의 가책 / *the stings of remorse* 깊은 회한(悔恨). **5** wounding quality or capacity; the power to rouse or excite. 자극(력〔성〕); 신랄함; 빈정댐. ¶ *a jest with a* ~ *in it* 신랄한 농담 / *The breeze has a* ~ *in it.* 산들바람은 상쾌하다.

— *v.* (**stung**) *vt.* (P6,13) **1** wound or pierce (someone or something) with a sting; prick the skin and drive in position. (바늘·침으로) …을 찌르다. ¶ *A bee stung her cheek.* 벌이 그녀의 뺨을 쏘았다 / *I was stung by a bee.* 나는 벌에 쏘였다. **2** give a sharp physical pain to (someone); cause sharp pain to. …을 찌르듯 아프게 하다; 따끔거리게〔얼얼하게〕 하다. ¶ *The hail stung my face.* 우박은 내 얼굴을 사정없이 내리갈겼다 / *Pepper stings one's tongue.* 후추는 혀를 얼얼하게 자극한다. **3** give sharp emotional pain to (someone); give keen mental pain to. 아무에게 정신적인 고통을 주다; 괴롭히다; (마음을) 상하게 하다. ¶ *His conscience stung him.* 그는 양심의 가책을 받았다 / *She was stung by the insult.* 그녀는 그 무례한 짓에 감정을 상했다 / *His remark stung my pride.* 그의 이야기는 나의 자존심을 상하게 했다. **4** 《*into, to*》 stimulate; excite (someone) to act. …을 자극하여 —하게 하다. ¶ *He was stung into action.* 그는 행동을 하도록 자극을 받았다 / *The insult stung him into an angry reply.* 그 모욕적인 말은 그로 하여금 거친 응수를 하게 하였다 / *Anger stung him to* 〔*into*〕 *action.* 홧김에 그는 행동을 개시했다.

— *vi.* (P1) **1** prick with a sting; have a sting. 찌르다; 침이〔가시가〕 있다. ¶ *Some bees do not* ~. 어떤 벌들은 쏘지 않는다 / *The rosebush stings.* 장미 덩굴에는 가시가 있다. **2** feel a sharp physical pain. 따끔따끔〔얼얼〕하다; 쿡쿡 쑤시다. ¶ *My tooth stings.* 이가 쿡쿡 쑤신다 / *The blow made his hand* ~. 일격을 맞아 그의 손은 얼얼하였다. **3** give keen mental pain. 심적 고통을 주다; 괴롭히다. ¶ *Reproach* 〔*Blame*〕 *stings.* 질책〔비난〕은 상대에게 심적 고통을 준다. [E.]

stin·gi·ness [stíndʒinis] *n.* the state or quality of being stingy. 인색; 단작스러움.

sting·ing [stíŋiŋ] *adj.* **1** (of a plant, insect, etc.) having a sting. 침이〔가시가〕 있는. **2** causing sharp pain. 쿡쿡 쑤시는; 몹시 아픈. ¶ *a* ~ *blow* 날카로운 일격. **3** exciting anger in a person. 신랄한; (말에) 가시가 있는. ¶ ~ *words* 신랄한 언사.

sting·ray [stíŋrèi] *n.* a broad flat fish which can give severe wounds with the sharp spines on its tail. 노랑가오리.

stin·gy [stíndʒi] *adj.* (**-gi·er, -gi·est**) mean in giving or spending money. 인색한; 너무 아끼는. ¶ *She is so* ~ *that she never tips.* 그녀는 팁을 주는 일이 절대로 없을 만큼 인색하다 / *Don't be so* ~ *with the butter!* 버터 사용에 너무 인색하지 마라. ● **stin·gi·ly** [-li] *adv.*

stink [stiŋk] *v.* (**stank** or **stunk, stunk**) *vi.* (P1) 《*of*》 give off a bad smell. 악취가 나다. ¶ *Rotten fish stinks.* 상한 생선은 악취가 난다 / *Your breath stinks of garlic.* 너의 입에서는 고약한 마늘 냄새가 난다. — *vt.* (P7) 《*out*》 drive or force (someone) out by means of a bad smell. …을 악취를 풍겨 내쫓다. ¶ ~ *out a fox* 연기를 피워 여우를 내몰다.

— *n.* Ⓒ **1** a very bad smell. 악취. **2** 《*pl.* used as *sing.*》 《Brit. *sl.*》 chemistry. 화학. [E.]

***stink in someone's* nostril,** be highly offensive to someone. 아무에게 심한 미움을 사다.

***stink of* money,** be very rich. 주체 못할 만큼 돈이 많다.

stint [stint] *vt.* (P6,13) **1** spend or give not enough of (something); keep someone without enough food, etc. (비용·식사 따위를) 바싹 줄이다; 긴축하다. ¶ ~ *one's children in* 〔*of*〕 *food* 자식들의 먹을 것을 바싹 줄이다 / *He stinted himself to buy books.* 그는 책의 구매를 바싹 줄였다. **2** limit (something) within a certain amount or number; give (food, material, help) in a small amount or unwillingly. (식사·물건·도움 따위를) 내기 아까워하다; 아끼다. ¶ *Don't* ~ *the sugar.* 설탕의 씀씀이를 아까워 마라 / *He does not* ~ *his praise.* 그는 칭찬의 말을 아끼지 않는다.

— *n.* **1** Ⓤ a limit. 제한. ¶ *give* 〔*spend*〕 *without* ~, *freely* 아낌없이〔무제한으로〕 주다〔소비하다〕. **2** Ⓒ a limited 〔fixed, assigned〕 amount of work. 할당된〔일정한〕 일. ¶ *do one's daily* ~ 하루에 할당된 일을 하다. [E.]

sti·pend [stáipend] *n.* Ⓒ a fixed payment for work; a salary, esp. of a clergyman or a teacher. (목사·교사 등의) 봉급. [L.]

sti·pen·di·ar·y [staipéndièri / -diəri] *adj.*

receiving a stipend; serving for salary. 봉급을 받는; 유급의. —*n.* Ⓒ (*pl.* **-ar·ies**) a person who receives a stipend. 유급자; 봉급쟁이.

stip·u·late [stípjəlèit] *vt.* (P6,11) fix [arrange] definitely as part of an agreement; demand as a condition of agreement. …을 규정[약정]하다; 계약의 조건으로서 요구하다. ¶ *An increase in the working hours was not stipulated.* 근무 시간의 증가는 규정되어 있지 않았다 / *The witness, before telling his story, stipulated that his name should be kept secret.* 그 증인은 진술을 하기 전에 그의 이름을 비밀에 부쳐 줄 것을 조건으로 요구하였다. —*vi.* (P3) 《*for*》 insist upon (as essential part of an agreement. etc.) (계약의 중요 사항으로) 규정[명기]하다. ¶ ~ *for the use of marble* [*for marble to be used*] 대리석의 사용을 명기[규정]하다. [L.]

stip·u·la·tion [stìpjəléiʃən] *n.* **1** ⓊⒸ the act of stipulating. 약정; 규정; 계약. **2** Ⓒ something that is stipulated. 조항; 조건; (계약의) 명기 사항.

stip·ule [stípju:l] *n.* 《bot.》 one of the pair of little leaf-like parts at the base of a leaf-stem. 턱잎; 탁엽(托葉). [L.]

:stir [stə:*r*] *v.* (**stirred, stir·ring**) *vt.* (P6,7) **1** move; shake. …을 (조금) 움직이다; 흔들다. ¶ *The tide stirs the boat.* 조수가 배를 아주 조금씩 움직인다 / *A light breeze stirred the leaves.* 남실바람은 나뭇잎을 살랑거리게 했다 / *He stirred neither hand nor foot.* 그는 손도 발도 움직이지 않았다 / *Stir yourself!* 빨리 해라; 기운을 내라. **2** mix (a liquid, etc.) by moving it around with a spoon, etc. 휘젓다; (액체 따위를) 뒤섞다. ¶ ~ *coffee with a spoon* 스푼으로 커피를 젓다 / ~ *sugar into one's coffee* 커피에 설탕을 넣고 휘젓다. **3** 《*to*》 cause (someone or something) to act, feel, or think; excite. (아무의 감정·상상 따위를) 움직이다; …을 선동하다. ¶ ~ *one's interest* (아무의) 흥미를 돋우다 / ~ *one's imagination* 상상력을 자극하다 / ~ *someone's blood* 아무의 피를 끓게 하다 / ~ *someone to pity* 동정심을 일으키게 하다 / *He was deeply stirred by the news.* 그는 그 소식에 깊은 감명을 받았다 / *Tom stirred* (*up*) *the other children to* [*to do*] *mischief.* 톰은 다른 아이들을 부추겨 나쁜 짓을 시켰다.

—*vi.* (P1,2A) **1** be active; be in motion; move little. 활동하고 있다; 일어나 있다; (조금) 움직이다. ¶ *Something stirred in the wood.* 숲 속에서 무엇인가가 움직였다 / *Not a wind was stirring.* 바람 한 점 일지 않았다 / *Nobody is stirring in the house.* 그 집 안에는 아무도 일어나 있지 않다 / *As it was wet all day, I didn't ~ out of the house.* 하루 종일 비가 왔기 때문에 나는 집 밖에 나가지 않았다. **2** be mixed. 뒤섞이다. ¶ *This dough stirs hard.* 이 반죽은 잘 이겨지지 않는다. **3** become excited; begin to develop. (감정 따위가) 일어나다. ¶ *Pity stirred in her heart.* 동정심이 그녀의 마음에 일었다.

not stir a finger, make no effort. 노력하지 않다.

not stir an eyelid, remain perfectly motionless. 전혀 움직이지 않다.

stir one's stumps ⇨stump.

stir up, **a**) mix. …을 잘 섞다[젓다]. **b**) stir thoroughly 고루 잘 젓다. **c**) cause to rise by stirring. …을 마구 저어대다[들춰내다]. ¶ *Don't ~ up the mud.* 진창을 저어대지 마라 《불유쾌한 사실을 들춰내지 마라》. **d**) excite; bring into existence. 돋우다; 일으키다. ¶ ~ *up trouble* 골치 아픈 문제를 일으키다.

—*n.* **1** Ⓒ a very small motion. 아주 작은 움직임. ¶ *There was not a ~ in the audience.* 청중 가운데서는 아주 작은 움직임도 없었다 / *Not a ~ was heard.* 바스락 소리 하나 없었다. **2** ⓊⒸ the state of excitement; general or public interest. 흥분; 큰 소동[평판·물의]; 법석. ¶ *make a ~* 큰 소동[평판]이 나다 / *His behavior caused a great ~.* 그의 행동은 아주 큰 물의를 일으켰다 / *The scandal created* [*made*] *a big ~ in the country.* 그 스캔들은 온 나라에 큰 센세이션을 일으켰다. **3** ⓊⒸ the act of stirring a liquid, etc. 휘젓기. ¶ *give the soup a ~* 국물을 젓다. [E.]

stir·rer [stə́:rə*r*] *n.* an implement or device for stirring something. 교반기(攪拌器).

stir·ring [stə́:riŋ] *adj.* **1** moving; exciting. 감동시키는; 고무하는. ¶ *a ~ speech* 사람의 마음을 감동시키는 연설 / *a ~ event* 세상을 떠들썩하게 하는 사건. **2** full of action. 활발한. ¶ ~ *times* 시끄러운 세상 / *a ~ city* 활기찬 도시.

stir·rup [stə́:rəp, stír-, stʌ́r-] *n.* Ⓒ one of a pair of supports for a horse rider's feet. 등자(鐙子). [E.=climb-rope]

·stitch [stitʃ] *n.* Ⓒ **1** a complete movement of the threaded needle in sewing or knitting. 한 바늘[시침]; 한 땀; 한 코. ¶ *make small* [*long*] *stitches* 바느질을 촘촘하게[성글게] 하다 / 《*prov.*》 *A ~ in time saves nine.* 제때의 한 바늘이 나중의 아홉 바늘을 던다. **2** a loop or knot made by a stitch. 바늘 땀[코]; 솔기; 바느질 자리. **3** a method of taking stitches. 꿰매는[뜨는] 법. ¶ *a cross-stitch* 십자 뜨기 / *a buttonhole ~* (단춧구멍의) 사뜨기. **4** 《*sing.* only》 a sudden, sharp pain. (옆구리 따위의) 격통. ¶ *I got a ~ from running after dinner.* 식후의 달음질로 옆구리에 심한 고통을 느꼈다. **5** 《surg.》 one movement of a needle through the edges of a wound; a piece of thread to close a wound. (상처를 꿰매는) 한 바늘. **6** 《*colloq.*》 《*negative*》 ⓐ even the smallest article of clothing. 조그마한 헝겊[천] 조각. ¶ *I haven't a ~ to wear.* 입을 만한 것이 아무것도 없다 / *I haven't a ~ on.* 나는 실오라기 하나 걸치지 않았다. ⓑ 《*of*》 a bit; even the least bit. 조금; 약간. ¶ *He won't do a ~ of work.* 그는 조금도 일을 하려 들지 않았다.

have not a dry stitch on, be wet to the

skin. 함빡 젖어 있다.
— *vt.* join, mend or fasten (something) with stitches. …을 꿰매다; 감치다; 호다.
— *vi.* make stitches; sew. 바느질하다; 꿰매다. [E.=prick]

sti·ver [stáivər] *n.* 《*sl.*》 the most trifling coin; anything of little worth. 가장 소액의 동전; 하찮은 것. [Du.]
not a stiver, not a bit, nothing. 조금도〔아무것도〕 없다.

St. Lou·is [seint lú:is, sənt-] *n.* a city in eastern Missouri. 세인트루이스《미주리 주 동부의 도시》.

stoat [stout] *n.* 《zool.》 the ermine in its summer coat of brown. 담비. [E.]

:stock [stɑk / stɔk] *n.* **1** ⓊⒸ a store of things for use or sale. 저장; 재고; (지식 등의) 축적; 재고품. ¶ *dispose of a* ~ 재고품을 처분하다 / *have a small* ~ *on hand* 재고품이 조금 있다 / *lay*〔*get*〕 *in a large* ~ *of sugar* 많은 양의 설탕을 사들이다 / *have a great* ~ *of knowledge* 풍부한 지식을 가지고 있다 / *His store has a large* ~ *of goods.* 그의 상점에는 다량의 재고품이 있다 / *The book is in*〔*out of*〕 ~. 그 책은 재고가 있다〔매진되었다〕. **2** Ⓤ cattle or other farm animals. 가축. ¶ *fat* ~ 식육용 가축. **3** Ⓒ a trunk or stem of a tree or plant; the lower part of a tree trunk. (나무·풀 따위의) 줄기; 나무 줄기의 밑동. **4** ⓐ Ⓤ family line as having certain qualities; birth; race; a group of related languages. 가계(家系); 혈통; (언어의) 어계(語系). ¶ *the languages of German* ~ 독일어계(系) / *He comes of a noble* ~. 그는 고귀한 가계(家系)의 출신이다. ⓑ 《biol.》 a colony or related group of organisms. 군락(群落); 군체(群體). **5** Ⓒ a part of a thing used as its support, handle, or base. (도구의) 자루; 받침 나무. ¶ *the* ~ *of a rifle* 총의 개머리판 / *the* ~ *of a plough* 쟁기의 자루. **6** Ⓤ raw material; liquid in which bones, meat, etc. have been cooked, used for making soup, etc. 원료; (수프·소스 등을 만드는) 곰국; (뼈·고기·생선 따위를) 삶은 국물〔진국〕. ¶ *paper* ~ 제지 원료 / *soup* ~ 수프의 진국. **7** ⒸⓊ capital or shares of a business company; 《*the* ~*s*》 《Brit.》 money lent to the government at fixed interest. 주식; 주; 영업 자본; 공채(公債). ¶ *bank stocks* 은행 주식 / *a* ~ *and share broker* 공채〔주식〕 중매인 / *She has money in stocks.* 그녀는 돈을 공채화해서 가지고 있다 / *The profits of a company are divided among the owners of* ~. 회사의 이익은 주식의 소유주들에게 분배된다. **8** Ⓒ a sweet-smelling garden flower. 자라난화(紫羅欄花)《관상용 식물》. **9** 《*pl.*》 the frame on which a ship is built. 조선대(造船臺). ¶ *off the stocks* 진수하여; 완성하여 / *on the stocks* (배가) 건조중인. **10** 《*pl.*》 a frame used for punishment. 차꼬; 족가(足枷). **11** the stem into which a graft is put. 접본(椄本); 대목(臺木). **12** 《*arch.*》 a band of cloth worn round the neck. (여자 옷의) 세운 깃; (옛날, 남성용 셔츠의) 목닫이.

〈stock 10〉

on the stocks, (of a plan, etc.) in progress. (계획 따위가) 진행중인〔의〕.
stocks and stones, lifeless objects. 목석(木石); 무정한 인간.
take stock, check the quantity of goods on hand. 재고를 조사하다.
take 〔***put***〕 ***stock in,*** **a**) trust 〔have faith〕 in something; attach importance to. …을 신용하다; …을 중히 여기다. ¶ *I take little* ~ *in what she says.* 그녀가 말하는 것에 대하여 나는 전연 믿지를 않는다. **b**) invest money by buying shares in. …의 주(株)를 사다.
take stock of, 《*fig.*》 observe and estimate the value, character, etc. of. 평가하다; 품평(品評)하다.
— *vt.* (P6,13) 《*with*》 **1** supply; store up. …에 사들이다; 비축하다. ¶ ~ *a store with goods* 상품을 가게에 사들이다 / ~ *the lake with fish* 호수에 물고기를 방류하다 / ~ *a refrigerator with tinned foods* 냉장고에 통조림 식품을 채워 넣다 / *He has a memory well stocked with information.* 그에게는 풍부한 여러 가지 사항에 관한 기억이 있다. **2** keep (something) regularly for use or for sale; have in stock. …을 (늘) 비축하다〔간직해 놓다〕. ¶ *a shop well stocked with goods* 재고품이 풍부한 상점 / *He does not* ~ *that kind of food.* 그런 종류의 식품은 비축해 놓지 않는다 / *The shop only stocks cheap goods.* 저 상점은 싸구려 물건만 갖춰 놓고 있다 / *Do you* ~ *men's socks?* 남자용 양말을 비축하고 있느냐. **3** furnish (a farm) with cattle, etc.; sow (land) with seed, etc. (농장에) 가축을 넣다; (밭·토지에) …씨를 뿌리다. 「움이 나다〔트다〕.
— *vi.* (P1) (of a plant) produce suckers.
— *adj.* **1** kept on hand regularly; standard. 늘 재고로 있는; 표준의. ¶ ~ *articles* 재고품 / ~ *sizes in shoes* 표준 사이즈의 신발. **2** 《*fig.*》 in common use; ordinary. 흔히 있는; 고리타분한; 진부한. ¶ *a* ~ *joke* 진부한 농담 / *a* ~ *phrase* 흔해 빠진 문구. [E.]

stock·ade [stɑkéid / stɔk-] *n.* Ⓒ a strong fence used as a defense or enclosure for cattle, etc. 방책(防柵). — *vt.* (P6) surround with a stockade. 방책을 두르다. [→stake]

stock-breed·er [stɑ́kbrì:dər / stɔ́k-] *n.* a person who rears cattle. 축산〔목축〕업자. [*stock*]

stock·bro·ker [stɑ́kbròukər / stɔ́k-] *n.* a person who buys and sells stocks and shares for others for a commission. 증권〔주식〕 중개인(cf. *stockjobber*).

stock·bro·king [stákbròukiŋ / stɔ́k-] *n.* Ⓤ the business or work of a stockbroker. 주식〔증권〕 매매.

stock-car [stákkɑ̀ːr / stɔ́k-] *n.* 《U.S.》 a railway car for carrying livestock. (철도의) 가축 운반용 화물차.

stock exchange [⌐–⌐] *n.* a place where stocks and shares are bought and sold. 증권 거래소.

stock-farm [stákfɑ̀ːrm / stɔ́k-] *n.* a farm for raising animals for sale. 목축장.

stock-farm·er [stákfɑ̀ːrmər / stɔ́k-] *n.* =stock-breeder.

stock·hold·er [stákhòuldər / stɔ́k-] *n.* Ⓒ 《U.S.》 a person who holds stocks or shares in a company(cf. 《Brit.》 *shareholder*). 주주(株主).

:stock·ing [stákiŋ / stɔ́k-] *n.* Ⓒ 《usu. *pl.*》 a close-fitting covering for the foot and leg. 긴 양말; 스타킹. ¶ *a pair of stockings* 양말 한 켤레 / *in one's stockings* 양말만 신고; 신을 신지 않고 / *stand six feet in one's stockings* (신을 신지 않고) 양말만 신고 키가 6 피트이다.

stock-in-trade [stákintréid / stɔ́k-] *n.* **1** a stock of goods for sale at a store. 재고품. **2** a workman's tools or materials for carrying on a trade. 장사 밑천〔도구〕. ¶ *Books are a scholar's* ~. 책은 학자의 장사 밑천이다. **3** one's means for any purpose. 상투 수단. [*stock*]

stock·job·ber [stákdʒɑ̀bər / stɔ́kdʒɔ̀b-] *n.* **1** 《Brit.》 a member of a stock-exchange who buys 〔sells〕 stocks and shares from 〔to〕 a stockbroker, often on speculation. 증권 거래인. **2** 《U.S.》 =stockbroker.

stock·man [stákmən, -mæ̀n / stɔ́k-] *n.* (*pl.* **-men** [-mən]) **1** 《chiefly Australian》 a man in charge of livestock. 목축〔축산〕업자. **2** 《U.S.》 a person in charge of a stock of goods. 재고품 관리원 .

stock market [⌐–⌐] *n.* **1** a stock exchange. 증권 거래소. **2** the business in such a place. 주식〔증권〕 거래. **3** the prices of stocks and bonds. 주식〔증권〕 시세.

stock·pile [stákpàil / stɔ́k-] *n.* Ⓒ a supply of raw material, goods, etc. held in reserve for use when needed. (원료의) 비축. — *vt., vi.* (P6;1) keep a stockpile. (원료를) 비축하다.

stock·pot [stákpɑ̀t / stɔ́kpɔ̀t] *n.* a pot in which stock for soup, etc. is made and kept. 수프〔곰국용〕 냄비.

stock raising [⌐–⌐] *n.* the act or business of raising livestock. 목축〔축산〕(업).

stock-still [stákstíl / stɔ́k-] *adj.* entirely motionless. 전혀 움직이지 않는; 꼼짝하지 않는. ¶ *stand* ~ 꼼짝 않고 (서)있다.

stock·tak·ing [stáktèikiŋ / stɔ́k-] *n.* Ⓤ periodical check of the quantity of goods in a store. 재고 조사.

stock-whip [stákhwìp / stɔ́k-] *n.* a short-handled and long-lashed whip for cattle-herding. 목장용 말채찍.

stock·y [stáki / stɔ́ki] *adj.* (**stock·i·er, stock·i·est**) short, stout and strong. 땅딸막한. ¶ *He is* ~ *in build.* 그는 체격이 땅딸막하다. [*stock*]

stock·yard [stákjɑ̀ːrd / stɔ́k-] *n.* Ⓒ a place where cattle are kept before being sent to market or killed. 임시 가축 수용장.

stodge [stɑdʒ / stɔdʒ] *n.* 《*colloq.*》 dull, heavy, filling food. 소화가 잘 안 되는 진한 음식. [?]

stodg·y [stádʒi / stɔ́dʒi] *adj.* (**stodg·i·er, stodg·i·est**) **1** (of food) heavy. 소화가 잘 안 되는. ¶ *a* ~ *meal* 소화가 잘 안 되는 식사. **2** (of a book, talk, etc.) dull and uninteresting. 지루하고 재미 없는. ¶ *a* ~ *book* 재미없는 책. **3** short and fat. 땅딸막한. ¶ *a* ~ *person* 땅딸막한 사람. [?]

Sto·ic [stóuik] *adj.* **1** of the philosophy of the Stoics or their philosophy. 스토아 철학(파)의. **2** 《*s-*》 stoical. 금욕주의의. — *n.* Ⓒ **1** a member of a school of philosophy founded by Zeno, who believed that man should be free from all passion. 스토아 철학자. **2** 《*s-*》 a person who is always calm and shows indifference to his passion, etc. 금욕주의자. [Gk.]

sto·i·cal [stóuikəl] *adj.* self-controlled; indifferent to joy, pleasure, passion, etc. 금욕〔극기〕의; 냉정한.

sto·i·cal·ly [stóuikəli] *adv.* in a stoic manner. 금욕적으로; 냉정히.

Sto·i·cism [stóuəsìzəm] *n.* Ⓤ **1** the philosophy of the Stoics. 스토아 철학. **2** 《*s-*》 self-control; indifference to pleasure and pain. 극기(克己); 냉정. [Gk.]

stoke [stouk] *vt., vi.* (P6;1,2A) 《often *up*》 **1** put (fuel) on a fire; attend to (a fire). 불을 때다〔지피다〕; 화부일을 하다. **2** 《*colloq.*》 《*up*》 eat. …을 먹다. [Du.]

stoke·hold [stóukhòuld] *n.* a place in a steamer where the boilers are. (배의) 기관실; 보일러실.

stoke·hole [stóukhòul] *n.* **1** = stokehold. **2** a hole through which fuel is put into a furnace. (노·보일러의) 아궁이.

stok·er [stóukər] *n.* **1** a man who puts fuel into a furnace, esp. on a steamer or steamengine. 화부; 보일러공. **2** a mechanical device for putting fuel into a furnace. (자동) 급탄기(給炭機).

STOL [stoul, stɔ́ːl] *n.* 《aeron.》 short takeoff and landing. 단거리 이착륙.

:stole[1] [stoul] *v.* p. of **steal**.

stole[2] [stoul] *n.* Ⓒ **1** a long strip of silk, etc. worn around the neck by a priest. (성직자가 양어깨에 걸치는) 영대(領帶). **2** a woman's scarf of cloth or fur worn over the shoulders. (견직물·모피 따위로 만든 여성용) 어깨걸이; 스톨. [Gk.=robe]

:sto·len [stóulən] *v.* pp. of **steal.** — *adj.* obtained by theft. 훔친. ¶ ~ *goods* 장물; 도둑 맞은 물건.

stol·id [stálid / stɔ́l-] *adj.* not easily excited; dull; showing no emotion or feeling. 둔감한; 신경이 무딘. [L.]

sto·lid·i·ty [stɑlídəti / stɔl-] *n.* Ⓤ the state or quality of being stolid. 둔감; 무신경.

stol·id·ly [stálidli / stɔ́l-] *adv.* in a stolid manner; dully; impassively. 멍청하게; 무신경하게.

stol·id·ness [stálidnis / stɔ́l-] *n.* Ⓤ =stolidity.

:stom·ach [stʌ́mək] *n.* **1** Ⓒ a baglike part of the body where food is swallowed and digested. 위(胃). ¶ *put the ~ out of order* 배탈이 나다 / *My ~ rises at it.* 그것을 보면 역겨워진다 / *We cannot work on an empty ~.* 공복으로 일을 할 수는 없다 / *You had better not swim on a full ~.* 배가 부를 때는 수영하지 않는 것이 좋다. **2** Ⓒ the part of the body containing the stomach; the belly. 배; 복부(cf. *abdomen*). ¶ *lie down flat on one's ~* 배를 깔고 납작 엎드리다 / *He hit Dick in the ~.* 그는 딕의 복부를 쳤다. **3** Ⓤ appetite; desire to eat. 식욕. ¶ *I've no ~ for this heavy food.* 나는 이런 느끼한 음식은 먹고 싶지 않다. **4** Ⓤ 《usu. *negative*》 desire; liking; inclination. 욕망; 좋아함; 기분; …하고 싶은 마음. ¶ *He has no ~ for fighting.* 그에게는 싸우고 싶은 마음이 없다.

— *vt.* (P6) **1** be able to eat (food); digest (food). …을 먹을 수 있다; 소화하다. **2** 《mostly in *negative* or *interrogative*》 bear. (모욕 따위를) 참다; 견디다. ¶ *He could not ~ her constant nagging.* 그는 그녀의 끊임없이 계속되는 잔소리에 참을 수가 없었다 / *Who can ~ such insult?* 그러한 모욕에 견딜 수 있는 사람이 누가 있겠나. [Gk.]

stom·ach·ache [stʌ́məkèik] *n.* ⓊⒸ pain in the stomach. 복통. ¶ *have a ~* 위[배]가 아프다.

stom·ach·er [stʌ́məkər] *n.* 《hist.》 a part of a woman's dress covering the stomach and chest. 가슴받이《15-16 세기에 유행》.

sto·mach·ic [stəmǽkik] *adj.* **1** of the stomach. 위(胃)의. **2** good for the stomach or appetite. 위에 좋은; 식욕을 돋구는. — *n.* Ⓒ medicine for the stomach. 건위제; 소화제.

:stone [stoun] *n.* **1** ⓊⒸ a small piece of rock larger than a grain sand; a hard mineral material found in the earth. 돌; 돌멩이; 잔돌. ¶ *throw a ~ at a dog* 개에게 돌을 던지다 / *road covered with stones* 잔돌로 뒤덮인 도로 / *a heart of ~* 돌덩이 같은 무정한 마음 / *I have a ~ in my shoe.* 구두 안에 잔돌이 하나 들어 있다 / 《*prov.*》 *A rolling ~ gathers no moss.* 구르는 돌에는 이끼가 끼지 않는다. **2** Ⓤ a piece of rock shaped and used for a particular purpose. 석재(石材). ¶ *a paving ~* 포장용 돌[석재] / *a wall (made) of ~* 돌담 / *a ~ house* 돌로 지은 집. **3** Ⓒ a precious stone; a jewel. 보석. ¶ *The ring is set with five stones.* 그 가락지에는 다섯 개의 보석이 박혀 있다. **4** Ⓒ a hard seed of a piece of fruit. (과실의 단단한) 씨; 핵(核). ¶ *a peach-stone* 복숭아씨 / *take the stones out of the fruit* 과실의 씨를 뽑아내다. **5** Ⓒ a hard mass formed inside the body in certain diseases; a gall-stone. 결석; 담석(膽石). **6** (*pl.* **stone**) an English unit of weight, usu. 14 pounds. 스톤《통상, 14 파운드의 중량 단위》. ¶ *He weighs as much as 18 ~.* 그는 자그만치 무게가 18 스톤이나 된다.

(as) cold 〔**hard**〕 **as a stone,** very cold 〔hard〕. 돌처럼 차가운〔단단한〕.

break stones, be reduced to extremities. 매우 곤궁하다; 최저 생활을 하다.

cast 〔**throw**〕 **a stone at,** 《*fig.*》 blame; make an attack on *someone's* character. …을 비난하다.

cast the first stone, be the first to criticize. 맨 첫번째로 비난하다.

give *someone* **a stone for bread,** 《Bible》 offer a mockery of help. 우롱하다.

heart of stone, a hard, unfeeling nature. 냉혹; 무정.

kill two birds with one stone, 《*prov.*》 accomplish two purposes with one action. 일거 양득(一擧兩得)의 효과를 얻다.

leave no stone unturned, try every means. 모든 수단을 다 쓰다.

mark (*a day*) **with a white stone,** record as happy or fortunate. …을 행운의 날로 특기하다.

squeeze 〔**wring**〕 **blood out of a stone** ⇨ blood.

— *vt.* **1** (P6,7) throw stones at (someone or something). …에(게) 돌을 던지다. ¶ *~ someone to death* 아무에게 돌을 던져 죽이다 / *The cruel boys stoned the dog.* 잔인한 소년들이 개에 돌을 던졌다. **2** (P6) take seeds out of (fruit). (과일에서) 씨를 빼내다 〔바르다〕. ¶ *~ cherries* 버찌의 씨를 바르다. **3** (P6) pave 〔face, line〕 (something) with stone. …에 돌을 깔다〔덮다, 쌓다〕. ¶ *~ a wall* 돌로 담을 쌓다.

— *adj.* made of stone. 석조의; 돌의. ¶ *a ~ bridge* 돌다리. [E.]

Stone Age [ˊˋ], **the** *n.* a prehistoric period when stone was used for tools and weapons. 석기 시대.

stone·blind [stóunbláind] *adj.* completely blind. 눈이 아주 먼.

stone·cut·ter [stóunkʌ̀tər] *n.* Ⓒ **1** a person who is engaged in cutting or carving stone. 석공; 석수(石手). **2** a machine for cutting stone. 돌 절단기.

stone-dead [stóundéd] *adj.* completely dead. 완전히 죽은.

stone-deaf [stóundéf] *adj.* completely deaf. 전혀 듣지 못하는.

stone fruit [ㅅㅅ] *n.* 《bot.》 any fruit containing a hard core inside a soft layer of pulp. (매실·복숭아 따위의) 핵과(核果).

Stone·henge [stóunhèndʒ / ㅅㅅ] *n.* a prehistoric, ruined stone structure on Salisbury Plain in England. 환열 석주(環列石柱) 《석기 시대 후기의 이중 원진(圓陣) 거석주(巨石柱)의 군(群)》.

stone·less [stóunlis] *adj.* **1** without stones. 돌이 없는. **2** without hard seeds. 씨〔핵과〕가 없는.

stone·ma·son [stóunmèisn] *n.* Ⓒ a person who cuts stone for use in making walls, buildings, etc. 석공; 석수(石手).

stone pit [ㅅㅅ] *n.* a place where stone is got out by cutting or blasting; a quarry. 채석장.

stone's cast 〔**throw**〕 [ㅅㅅ〔ㅅ〕] *n.* a short distance. 가까운 거리. ¶ *It is only a stone's throw away.* 그것은 아주 가까운 거리에 있다 / *live within a stone's throw of the staition* 정거장 가까이에서 산다.

stone·ware [stóunwὲər] *n.* Ⓤ a kind of pottery used for earthen pipes, jars, etc. which is rough and hard, but covered with a shining surface. 도자기.

stone·work [stóunwə̀ːrk] *n.* Ⓤ **1** the art of working in stone. 돌 세공. **2** the part of a building made or built in stone. 석조(건축)물.

***ston·y** [stóuni] *adj.* (**ston·i·er, ston·i·est**) **1** covered with stones; full of stones. 돌을 깐; 돌이 많은. ¶ *a ~ path* 돌이 많은〔돌을 깐〕 길 / *~ ground* 석질(石質)의 땅. **2** hard like stone; cold or cruel. (돌처럼) 단단한; 냉혹한. ¶ *a ~ heart* 냉혹〔무정〕한 마음 / *a ~ mass* 돌처럼 단단한 덩어리. **3** having hard seeds. 단단한 씨가 있는; 핵(核)이 있는. ¶ *a ~ fruit* 핵과(核果). **4** showing no feeling. 무표정한. ¶ *a ~ face* 무표정한 얼굴. **5** fixed; motionless as a stone. 움직이지 않는. ¶ *a ~ stare* 〔*gaze, look*〕 응시 / *with ~ patience* 끄떡하지 않는 인내로. [→stone]

stony broke, 《*sl.*》 with no money or credit left. 돈도 신용도 없이. [*stone*]

ston·y-heart·ed [stóunihɑ́ːrtid] *adj.* showing no feeling; having no pity. 돌처럼 차가운 마음의; 무정한.

:stood [stud] *v.* p. and pp. of **stand.**

:stool [stuːl] *n.* Ⓒ **1** a seat without back or arms. (등받이가 없는) 걸상. **2** a rest for the feet or knees. (발 올려놓는) 발판; 무릎을 기대는 대(臺). **3** an article or a place used as a toilet. 변기; 변소. **4** the waste matter from the bowels. 대변. ¶ *send a specimen of one's ~ to the doctor* 의사에게 검사용의 대변을 보내다. **5** a pole to which a bird is fastened as a trick. 미끼새를 매어둔 홰. **6** a root of a tree that sends out shoots. (싹이 나는) 뿌리. [E.]

fall between two stools, lose an opportunity by hesitating between two courses. 토끼 두 마리를 쫓다가 한 마리도 잡지 못한다 《"한번에 여러 가지 욕심을 부리면 하나도 얻지 못한다"란 뜻》.

:stoop[1] [stuːp] *vi.* **1** (P1,2A,4) bend the upper part of the body down and forward. (몸을) 구부리다; 굽히다. ¶ *~ to pick up a stone* 돌을 줍기 위해 몸을 굽히다 / *~ over a desk* 책상 위에 몸을 웅크리다 / *He stooped down and picked up the pencil.* 그는 몸을 굽혀 연필을 주워 들었다. **2** (P1,2A) carry the head and shoulders habitually bent forward. 새우등이다; 허리가 구부정하다. ¶ *~ from age* 나이를 먹어 허리가 구부정해지다〔하다〕 / *Sit up straight and don't ~.* 허리를 꼿꼿이 하고 앉아라, 그리고 앞으로 굽히지 마라. **3** (P2A,3,4) lower or disgrace oneself. 자기〔품위〕를 낮추어 …하다; 수치를 무릅쓰고 …하다. ¶ *~ to meanness* 비열한 짓도 하다 / *~ to conquer* 〔*win*〕 굴욕을 참고 목적을 이루다 / *He'd never ~ to murder.* 그는 사람을 죽일 그런 사람이 아니다.

— *vt.* (P6) bend (the head, the shoulders, etc.) forward. (머리·어깨 등을) 구부리다; 굽히다; 웅크리다. ¶ *~ oneself* 몸을 굽히다 / *He stooped his head and got into the car.* 그는 고개를 숙이고 차 안으로 들어갔다.

— *n.* Ⓒ 《usu. *sing.*》 **1** the act or position of stooping. 앞으로 몸을 굽힘; 새우등. **2** the act of lowering oneself. 굴종(屈從); 품위를 떨어뜨림. [E.]

stoop[2] [stuːp] *n.* Ⓒ 《U.S.》 an uncovered porch or platform in front of a house. 현관 입구의 계단. [Du. *stoep*]

:stop [stɑp / stɔp] *v.* (**stopped, stop·ping**) *vt.* **1** (P6) cause (something or someone) to cease to move or act. (움직이고 있는 것)을 멈추다; 정지시키다; 세우다. ¶ *~ the press* 윤전기를 멈추다 / *~ a factory* 공장의 조업을 정지시키다 / *The accident stopped the traffic.* 사고는 교통을〔왕래를〕 정지시켰다 / *She stopped her car at the red light.* 그녀는 붉은 신호등에서 차를 멈췄다 / *The earthquake stopped the clock.* 지진은 괘종 시계를 멈추게 했다 / *He was running too fast to ~ himself.* 그는 너무 빨리 달리고 있어서 스스로 멈출 수가 없었다. **2** (P6,13) 《*from*》 prevent; check. …을 방해하다〔막다〕; 억지〔제지〕하다. ¶ *~ a speaker* 연사의 말을 중지시키다 / *~ a fight* 싸움을 말리다 / *~ a passage* 〔*the way*〕 통로(通路)를〔길을〕 (가로)막다 / *Nothing will ~ me from going.* 내가 가는 것을 막을 일은 아무것도 없다 / *She stopped the water from running by turning off the faucet.* 그녀는 수도꼭지를 돌려서 흘러나오는 물을 멎게 했다 / *He stopped the boys from teasing the dog.* 그는 개를 괴롭히는 소년들을 그러지 못하도록 제지했다 / *She could not ~ a smile from flickering.* 그녀는 웃음을 억제할 수가 없

었다. **3** (P6) bring (doing something) to an end; cease. …을 그만두다; 그치다; 하지 않게 되다. ¶ ~ *running* 달리기를 그만두다 / ~ *work* 〔*talking*〕 일을〔이야기를〕 그치다 / ~ *smoking* 금연하다 / *Stop that nonsense!* 그런 시시한 소리 그만두어라 / *Do ~ grumbling.* 투덜대지 마라 / *The phone stopped ringing.* 전화의 벨 소리가 멈췄다 / *It has stopped rainning.* 비가 그쳤다. **4** (P6) 《*up, in, with*》 fill (a hole, a crack, etc.); close or obstruct (a passageway, etc.); block. (구멍·통로 따위를) 막다; 메우다; (흐르는 것을) 막다; 차단하다. ¶ ~ *a wound* 상처의 피를 멎게 하다 / ~ *one's ears* 귀를 틀어막다 / ~ (*up*) *a leak in a dike* 제방의 물 새는 곳을 틀어막다 / ~ *the way* 통로를〔진행을〕 막다 / ~ *a bottle with a cork* 병을 코르크 마개로 막다 / *I had my decayed tooth stopped.* 나는 충치의 구멍을 충전(充塡)시켰다 / *A big box is stopping up the doorway.* 큰 상자 하나가 출입구를 막고 있다 / *Dead leaves stopped* (*up*) *the drain.* 낙엽들로 배수도랑이 막혔다. **5** (P6) cut off; hold back (some regular payment). (지불·공급 따위를) 중단〔정지〕하다. ¶ ~ *supplies* 공급을 중단하다 / ~ *someone's allowance* 〔*wages*〕 아무의 수당〔급료〕 지급을 정지하다 / ~ *a check* 은행에 수표의 지급을 정지시키다 / *Some of the banks have stopped payment.* 몇몇 은행들은 지급을 정지하였다. — *vi.* (P1,2A,4) **1** cease from moving or from doing something; come to rest; pause; cease to function. (움직이고 있는 것이) 멈추다; 멎다; 멈춰 서다; 정지하다. ¶ ~ *to smoke* 담배를 피우기 위해 멈춰 서다 / ~ *for a moment in one's walk* 산책 도중 잠시 멈춰 서다 / ~ *at a port* 기항하다 / ~ *to* 〔*for*〕 *rest* 멈춰서〔그만두고〕 쉬다 / *The train stops at all stations.* 열차는 역마다 다 정차한다 / *This must ~ at once.* 이것은 즉시 그만두지 않으면 안 된다 / *The clock* 〔*His heart*〕 *has stopped.* 시계가〔그의 심장이〕 섰다〔멎었다〕. **2** come to an end; cease. 그치다; 끝이 나다; 그만두다. ¶ *The music stopped suddenly.* 음악이 갑자기 그쳤다 / *The rain has stopped.* 비가 그쳤다 / *The paved way stops here.* 포장 도로는 여기서 끝이 나 있다. **3** 《*at*》 stay; visit. 묵다; 체재하다. ¶ ~ *at a hotel* 호텔에 묵다 / *She is stopping with her aunt.* 그녀는 숙모 댁에 묵고 있다 / *We stopped at a bar.* 잠시 술집에 들렀다.

stop a bullet 〔**shell**〕**,** be shot to death. 총알에 맞아 죽다.

stop a gap, 《*fig.*》 act as a substitute in an emergency, etc.; take someone's place. 대리인으로 행동하다; 아무의 지위를 차지하다.

stop *someone's* **breath,** kill someone by smothering or otherwise. 목졸라 죽이다.

stop by, drop in. (…에) 잠시 들르다.

stop down, 《photog.》 reduce the exposed part of a lens by partly covering with a diaphragm. (렌즈의) 조리개를 조르다.

stop off, make a brief stay at a place while on a journey. (여행 도중에) 잠시 머무르다; 도중 하차하다.

stop out, cut off. (바람·햇빛 등을) 가로막다.

stop over, 《U.S.》 stop for a short period at a certain place in the course of a longer trip. (여행 중) 도중 하차하다; 잠시 머무르다.

stop short 〔**dead**〕**,** stop suddenly. 갑자기 멈춰 서다.

stop up, block; close. …을 막다; 메우다; 채우다. ¶ *He stopped up the rat-holes.* 그는 쥐구멍들을 모두 막았다.

stop *someone's* **way,** be or act as obstruction, prevent someone's progress. …의 가는 길을 방해하다.

— *n.* Ⓒ **1** the act of stopping; the state of being stopped. 정지; 휴지; 중지. ¶ *be at a ~* 정지해〔쉬고〕 있다. **2** a place where a bus, a train, etc. stops. 정거장; 정류소. ¶ *the bus ~* 버스 정류장 / *How many stops is it* 〔*are there*〕 *from here to Chicago?* 여기서 시카고까지 정류소가 몇 군데나 있느냐. **3** a short visit; a stay. 체재; 숙박. ¶ *Above all, he enjoyed his ~ in Naples* 특히 나폴리에서의 체류를 즐겼다. **4** a thing that stops, such as a plug, a stopper, etc. 마개; 쐐기. **5** 《chiefly Brit.》 any of the marks of punctuation which act to conclude a sentence or an independent part of a sentence, such as a semicolon (;), a question mark (?), etc. but esp. a period. 구두점; 마침표; 종지부. ¶ *a full ~* 단락점; 종지부. **6** a key or device that controls the pitch of a musical instrument, esp. an organ. (오르간 따위의) 음전(音栓). **7** 《photog.》 a means of controlling the amount of light. 조리개. **8** 《phon.》 폐쇄음《e.g. [b, p, g, k, d, t]》(cf. *spirant*). [Gk. *stuppē* oakum]

at a stop, not proceeding or unable to proceed. 정지 중; 전진하지 않고.

come to a stop, come to an end; be unable to continue. 끝나다; 막다르다.

make a stop, stop. 멈추다; 머무르다. ¶ *We made a three-day ~ in Seoul.* 우리는 서울에서 3일간 체류했다.

put a stop to, stop; end. …을 그만두게 하다; 끝내다. ¶ *We must find some way of putting a ~ to that noise.* 저 소음을 멈추게 하는 방법을 찾아 내야 한다.

without a stop, continually. 계속해서. ¶ *The train goes through without a ~.* 그 열차는 계속 직행한다.

stop·cock [stápkàk / stɔ́pkɔ̀k] *n.* Ⓒ a valve that opens and closes a pipe carrying a liquid or gas; a faucet. (수도 따위의) 꼭지; 고동; 조절판. [↑]

stop·gap [stápgæ̀p / stɔ́p-] *n.* Ⓒ a temporary substitute; a thing for taking the place of something else, usu. temporarily. 임시 변통의 것〔사람〕; 일시적인 대체물; 미봉책. — *adj.* serving as a stopgap. 임시 변

통의. ¶ *a ~ budget* 〔*cabinet*〕 잠정 예산〔내각〕.

stop·o·ver [stápòuvər / stɔ́p-] *n.* Ⓒ 《U.S.》 **1** a brief stop or stay in the course of a journey. (여행 중의) 일시 체재〔체류〕; 도중 하차. **2** a train ticket permitting such a trip. 도중 하차 차표.

stop·page [stápidʒ / stɔ́p-] *n.* ⓊⒸ the act of stopping; the state of being stopped. 정지; 두절; 멈추기; 멎기.

stop·per [stápər / stɔ́p-] *n.* Ⓒ a plug or cork to close a bottle, a pipe, etc. (병)마개. — *vt.* close (a bottle, pipe, etc.) with a stopper. …에 마개를 하다.

stop watch [스스] *n.* a watch that can be stopped or started to measure the exact duration of an event. 스톱 워치.

·**stor·age** [stɔ́:ridʒ] *n.* **1** Ⓤ the act of storing goods; the state of being stored; method of doing this. 저장; 저장법. ¶ *put the fish in cold ~* 생선을 냉장 보관하다. **2** Ⓒ a place for storing goods. 저장소; 창고. ¶ *put one's furniture in ~* 가구를 창고에 넣다. **3** Ⓤ the price for storing goods. (창고의) 보관료. [↓]

:**store** [stɔ:r] *n.* Ⓒ **1** a supply for future use; a reserve. 저축; 저장; 비축. ¶ *a ~ of food* 〔*fuel*〕 식료품〔연료〕의 저장 / *lay in stores of coal for the winter* 겨울에 대비하여 석탄을 비축하다. **2** 《usu. *a ~*》 a large amount; an accumulation of knowledge in the mind. 다량; (지식 따위의) 축적. ¶ *a great stores of apples* 다량의 사과 / *a ~ of learning* 〔*information, wisdom*〕 학식〔정보·지혜〕의 축적 / *have a ~* 〔*stores*〕 *of knowledge* 박식하다 / *have a ~ of energy* 많은 힘〔정력〕을 지니다. **3** 《*pl.*》 a supply of goods needed for some special purpose. (선박 따위의) 비품; 필수품. ¶ *ship's stores* 선박용품 / *household stores* 가정용품 / *military stores* 군수품. **4** 《chiefly U.S.》 a shop. 가게; 상점. ¶ *a candy* 〔*furniture*〕 *~* 과자 가게〔가구점〕 / *a clothing ~* 옷가게 / *a general ~* (마을의) 잡화점 / *buy candy at a ~* 가게에서 사탕을 사다 / *keep ~* 상점을 경영하다. **5** 《*pl.* or *S-s*》 《Brit.》 a large shop which sells all kinds of things(cf. 《U.S.》 *department store*). 백화점. ¶ *I get most things at the stores.* 나는 대부분의 물품들을 백화점에서 산다. **6** 《Brit.》 a place where goods are kept; a warehouse or storing-place. 창고; 저장소.

in store, **a**) kept for future use. 저축〔준비〕하여. ¶ *be in ~* 저축〔준비〕되어 있다 / *have* 〔*keep, hold*〕 *a thing in ~* 물건을 비축해 놓다 / *There is sufficient food in ~ for next year.* 내년에 쓸 식량이 충분히 준비되어 있다. **b**) waiting; reserved by fate. 기다리고 있는; (운명 등에 의해) 마련〔준비〕되어 있는. ¶ *Who knows what is in ~ for us?* 장차 무엇이 일어날는지 아무도 모른다 / *You can never tell what the future has in ~.* 장래가 어떻게 될지 알 수 없다 / *I little thought of the calamity which was in ~ for us.* 우리에게 닥치게 될 재난에 관해서는 전혀 생각하지 않았다.

set store by, value highly. …을 중히 여기다. ¶ *set no* 〔*little*〕 *~ by* …을 경시하다.

— *vt.* (P6,7) **1** keep (something) for future use; lay up. …을 저축〔저장〕하다; 축적하다. ¶ *The Aswan Dam was built to ~ the water of the Nile.* 아스완 댐은 나일 강의 물을 저장하기 위해 만들어졌다 / *All these facts were stored in his memory.* 이런 사실들은 모두 그의 기억에 축적되었다. **2** 《esp. in *passive*》 supply; fill (something) with supplies. …에 공급하다; 준비〔비축〕하다. ¶ *~ the ship with fresh water* 배에 신선한 물을 공급하다 / *~ the mind with knowledge* 머리에 지식을 집어넣다 / *The cellar was stored with apples.* 지하 저장실에 사과가 비축되었다. **3** put (something) in a place used for preserving; hold. …을 창고 따위에 보관하다; (창고 따위가) 저장할 여지가 있다. ¶ *~ goods in the cellar* 지하실에 물품을 보관하다 / *The harvest has been stored.* 수확물의 창고 보관 작업은 끝났다 / *The shed will ~ 20 tons of coal.* 이 헛간에는 석탄 20 톤이 들어간다. **4** 《electr.》 accumulate. 축전(蓄電)하다. [L. *instauro* renew]

store up, keep (something) for future use. …을 저장〔축적〕하다. ¶ *~ up fuel for the winter* 겨울에 대비하여 연료를 많이 저장하다 / *~ up knowledge* 지식을 축적하다.

store·house [stɔ́:rhàus] *n.* Ⓒ (*pl.* **-houses**) a place for keeping goods; anything similar to such a place. 창고; 보관소. ¶ *a ~ for food* 식료품 저장소 / *He* 〔*The book*〕 *is a ~ of information.* 그는 만물 박사이다〔그 책은 지식의 보고이다〕.

store·keep·er [stɔ́:rkì:pər] *n.* Ⓒ **1** 《U.S.》 a person who is in charge of a store(cf. 《Brit.》 *shopkeeper*). 소매 상인; 상점 주인. **2** an official in charge of stores. 창고 관리인.

store·room [stɔ́:rrù(:)m] *n.* Ⓒ a room for keeping goods. 저장실.

·**sto·rey** [stɔ́:ri] *n.* Ⓒ 《Brit.》 =story.

sto·ried[1] [stɔ́:rid] *adj.* **1** famouse in story or history. 이야기〔역사〕에서 유명한. ¶ *a ~ place* (역사·전설 등에서) 잘 알려진 곳. **2** decorated with designs showing happenings in history or story. 역사화(畫) 따위로 장식한〔된〕. [*story*[1]]

sto·ried[2] [stɔ́:rid] *adj.* having stories or floors. …층으로 지은. ¶ *a two-storied house* 이층집 / *a five-storied pagoda,* 5층탑. [*story*[2]]

stork [stɔ:rk] *n.* Ⓒ a large bird with long legs and a long bill. 황새. [E.]

:**storm** [stɔ:rm] *n.* Ⓒ **1** a strong wind with heavy rain, snow, etc. 폭풍(우). ¶ *A ~ is gathering.* 폭풍우가 다가오고 있다 / *The ~ has broken out.* 폭풍우가 멎었다 / *The ~ did a lot of harm.* 폭풍은 많은 피해를 남겼다 / *A ~ caught us.* 폭풍우를 만났다 /

After a ~ *(comes) a calm.* 《*prov.*》 고진감래. **2** anything like a storm; a violent outburst. …의 빗발; (감정의) 격발〔발작〕. ¶ *a* ~ *of bullets* 빗발처럼 쏟아지는 탄환 / *a* ~ *of cheers* 우레와 같은 박수 갈채 / *a* ~ *of jealousy* 〔*indignation*〕 질투〔분노〕의 발작〔격발〕. **3** a violent disturbance or excitement. (사회·가정에서) 소동; 동요. ¶ *the social* ~ *of the 1930s.* 1930년대의 사회적 동요 / *The* ~ *of revolution swept over the country.* 혁명의 소용돌이가 전국을 휩쓸었다. **4** Ⓤ a violent attack. 강습(強襲); 급습. ¶ *storm-troops* (나치스의) 돌격대 / *the castle taken by* ~ 급습으로 함락된 성.

a storm in a teacup, great excitement over something unimportant. 헛소동; 집안 싸움. —*vi.* **1** (P1) blow, rain, snow, etc. violently. (날씨가) 사나워지다. ¶ *It stormed all day.* 하루 종일 폭풍이 일었다. **2** (P2A) shout loudly and angrily. 호통 치다; 마구 고함 지르다. ¶ ~ *at someone* 아무에게 호통을 치다 / ~ *in reply* 고함지르며 대답하다. **3** rush angrily and violently. 돌격〔돌진〕하다. ¶ ~ *out of room* 방 밖으로 달려나가다 / *The mob stormed through the streets.* 폭도들은 거리를 돌진해서 지나갔다. [E.]

storm·beat·en [stɔ́ːrmbìːtn] *adj.* damaged by a storm. 폭풍우에 휩쓸린〔피해를 입은〕.

storm·bound [stɔ́ːrmbàund] *adj.* separated from others, stopped or delayed by storms. 폭풍우에 의해 고립된〔발이 묶인〕. ¶ ~ *travelers* 폭풍으로 발이 묶인 여행자들.

storm center [⌐⌐–] *n.* **1** the center of a storm. 폭풍우의 중심. **2** the center of trouble. 소동〔난동〕의 중심.

storm cloud [⌐⌐] *n.* **1** a heavy cloud showing the coming of a storm. 폭풍우를 실은 구름. **2** a sign of some coming trouble. 동란의 전조(前兆).

·**storm·y** [stɔ́ːrmi] *adj.* (**storm·i·er, storm·i·est**) **1** of a storm; likely to have storms indicating the presence or approach of a storm. 폭풍우의; 폭풍우가 일 듯한; 폭풍우를 동반한. ¶ ~ *weather* (폭풍이 일 듯한) 험악한 날씨 / *a* ~ *sea* 〔*night*〕 폭풍이 이는 사나운 바다〔밤〕 / *The sky looks* ~. 하늘을 보니 폭풍이 일 것 같다. **2** showing violent emotion. 격정적인. ¶ *a* ~ *debate* 격론 / ~ *passions* 격렬한 정열 / *a* ~ *temper* 성마른 성질 / *The meeting was* ~. 그 모임은 격정적이었다 / *a* ~ *life* 파란 많은 인생.

:**sto·ry**[1] [stɔ́ːri] *n.* Ⓒ (*pl.* **-ries**) **1** anything told or written of an event; a report. (사실의) 이야기〔전말〕; 보고; 보도. ¶ *a newspaper* ~ *of a traffic accident* 교통 사고에 대한 신문의 보도 / *according to his own* ~ 그의 이야기로는 / *the* ~ *of one's life* 자기 신상의 이야기 / *Tell me the* ~ *of how he got such a large sum of money.* 그가 어떻게 그런 큰 돈을 손에 넣었는지 이야기해 주시오 / *They all tell the same* ~. 그들이 하는 이야기는 모두 일치한다 / *It is quite another* ~ *now.* 지금은 전혀 다른 이야기가 되었다《지금은 사정이 달라졌다》. **2** a tale of fiction; rumor. 가공의 이야기; 소문. ¶ *the* ~ *of Cinderella* 신데렐라의 이야기 / *a ghost* ~ 유령 이야기 / *The* ~ *goes that….* …하다는 소문이다 / *as the* ~ *goes* 〔*runs*〕 소문에 의하면. **3** anything acted or said by someone during his life; an anecdote. 이력; 신상 이야기; 일화(逸話). ¶ *a woman with a* ~ (내놓고 말 못할) 사연이 있는 여자 / *His* ~ *was an eventful one.* 그의 이력은 파란 만장했다 / *I know her* ~. 나는 그녀의 신상에 관해 안다. **4** an outline 〔the plot〕 of a novel or play. (소설·연극 등의) 줄거리; 꾸밈새. ¶ *read only for the* ~ 단지 줄거리를 알기 위해 읽다 / *The* ~ *of the opera was printed in the program.* 그 오페라의 줄거리는 프로그램에 인쇄되어 있었다. **5** 《*colloq.*》 a lie. 거짓말. ¶ *tell stories* 거짓말을 하다. [→history]

the whole story, full particulars. 일의 자초지종.

to make a long story short, if I may omit details; in short. 한 마디로 말하면; 요약하면.

·**sto·ry**[2], 《Brit.》 **-rey** [stɔ́ːri] *n.* Ⓒ (*pl.* **-ries** or 《Brit.》 **-reys**) any level of a building; a floor. 층. ¶ *a one-story house* 단층집 / *a two-story house* 이층집 / *the first-story* 1층. [↑]

sto·ry·tell·er [stɔ́ːritèlər] *n.* Ⓒ **1** a person who tells or writes stories. 이야기를 하는〔쓰는〕 사람; 설화 작가. **2** 《*colloq.*》 a person who tells a lie. 거짓말쟁이. [*story*[1]]

stoup [stuːp] *n.* **1** a drinking-vessel of various sizes. 음료 용기; 잔. ¶ *a* ~ *of wine* 술잔. **2** the amount it holds. 그 한 잔의 분량. **3** 《arch.》 a basin for holy water. 성수반(聖水盤). [N.]

:**stout** [staut] *adj.* **1** strong; tough. 튼튼한. ¶ *a* ~ *ship* 튼튼한 배 / ~ *cords* 튼튼한 밧줄 / *a* ~ *man* 건강한〔튼튼한〕 사람. **2** brave; stubborn. 용감한; 완강한. ¶ *a* ~ *heart* 용기 / *a* ~ *fighter* 〔*opponent*〕 용감한 투사〔적수〕 / *make a* ~ *resistance* 완강히 저항하다. **3** bulky; fat. 뚱뚱한; 살찐. ¶ *a* ~ *old gentleman* 뚱뚱한 노신사. —*n.* Ⓤ a dark, strong beer. 흑맥주. [Teut.]

stout-heart·ed [stáuthάːrtid] *adj.* brave; fearless. 용감한; 대담한.

stout·ly [stáutli] *adv.* bravely; firmly. 용감히; 완강하게.

stout·ness [stáutnis] *n.* Ⓤ the state or quality of being stout. 튼튼함; 용감; 비만.

:**stove**[1] [stouv] *n.* Ⓒ a device for heating and cooking, which uses coal, wood, gas, etc. 스토브; 요리용 화덕. [E. =bath]

stove[2] [stouv] *v.* p. and pp. of **stave.**

stow [stou] *vt.* (P6,7,13) 《*with*》 pack (something) carefully or closely. …을 챙겨 넣다; 가득 채워 넣다. [E. =place]

stow away, hide on a ship or airplane, etc. without paying or secretly. 밀항하다.

stow·a·way [stóuəwèi] *n.* Ⓒ a person

who hides on a ship, a airplane, etc. secretly. 밀항자. [↑]

strad·dle [strǽdl] *vi.* **1** stand, sit, or walk with the legs wide apart. 다리를 벌리고 서다〔앉다, 걷다〕. **2** 《*colloq.*》 support both sides of a question; not stand on a certain side decisively. 애매한 태도를 취하다. —*vt.* (P6) stand or sit with the legs wide apart on or across (something). …에 두 다리를 벌리고 올라 타다〔서다, 앉다〕. ¶ ~ *a horse* 말에 올라 타다. —*n.* Ⓒ the act of straddling. 양 다리를 벌리고 힘껏 버팀; 양다리를 걸치고 앉음. [→stride]

strafe [streif, strɑːf] *vt.* (P6) 《*sl.*》 machine-gun and bomb; shell or bombard heavily. 맹공격하다. [G.]

strag·gle [strǽgəl] *vi.* (P1,2A) **1** wander away from the main group; stray; wander in a scattered way. (본대에서 이탈하여) 헤매다; 낙오하다; 뿔뿔이〔흩어져〕 가다. ¶ *The crowd straggled along.* 군중은 뿔뿔이 〔하나씩 흩어져〕 가 버렸다 / *They straggled in one by one.* 한 사람씩 뿔뿔이 흩어졌다. **2** ⓐ (of hair, etc.) hang down in an irregular manner. (모발 따위가) 헝클어지다; 흐트러지다. ⓑ spread or extend in an irregular manner. 무질서하게 퍼지다. ¶ *Rambler roses straggled over the porch.* 덩굴장미가 베란다 위로 제멋대로 뻗어 나갔다. **3** occur here and there. 산재하다; 흩어져 있다. ¶ *The houses* ~ *along the road.* 인가들이 도로를 따라 산재되어 있다. [E.]

strag·gler [strǽglər] *n.* Ⓒ a person or thing that straggles. 동료에게서 처진 사람; 낙오자; 길 잃은 철새.

strag·gling [strǽgliŋ] *adj.* **1** wandered away from the main group. 동료에게서 떨어진; 낙오한. ¶ *a* ~ *soldier* 낙오병 / *a* ~ *procession* 제멋대로 흐트러진 행렬. **2** hanging down irregularly. (모발 따위가) 헝클어진; 흐트러진. ¶ *a* ~ *wisp of hair* 헝클어진 머리다발. **3** occurring or existing here and there. 여기저기 흩어진; 산재하는. ¶ *a* ~ *village* 집이 불규칙하게 산재해 있는 마을.

:straight [streit] *adj.* **1** not bent or curved; not twisted; direct. 곧은; 일직선의. ¶ *a* ~ *line* 직선 / *a* ~ *back* 곧은 등 / ~ *hair* 곱슬거리지 않는 머리칼 / *a* ~ *road* 직선 도로. **2** level; upright; vertical. 수평의; 곧추 선; 수직의. ¶ *put a picture* ~ 그림을 똑바르게 걸다 / *Is the picture* ~*?* 그림이 똑바르게 걸려 있느냐. **3** honest; sincere; frank. 정직한; 진지한; 솔직한. ¶ *a* ~ *answer* 솔직한 대답 / ~ *talk* 〔*speech*〕 직언 / *I'll be* ~ *with you.* 솔직하게 말씀드리겠습니다. **4** in good order or condition; right or correct. 잘 정돈〔정리〕된; 올바른. ¶ *a* ~ *thinker* 올바르게〔정확히〕 생각하는 사람 / ~ *thinking* 논리 정연한 사고(思考) / *keep* 〔*put, set*〕 *a room* ~ 방을 정돈하다 / *put one's hat* ~ 모자를 바르게 쓰다 / *The accounts are* ~. 계산은 깨끗이 결제됐다 / *I'm* ~ *with the world.* 난 누구에게도 빚이 없다. **5** reliable. 신뢰할 수 있는; 믿을 만한. ¶ *a* ~ *piece of information* 신뢰할 수 있는 하나의 정보. **6** not mixed with anything else; not changed. 섞인 것이 없는; 순수한. ¶ ~ *whisky* 물을 타지 않은 위스키 / *drink gin* ~ 진을 스트레이트로 마시다. **7** continuous. 연속된. ¶ *win five* ~ *victories,* 5연승하다 / *the* ~ *sequence of events* 연속된 사건 / *for seven* ~ *days,* 7일간 계속하여 / *in* ~ *succession* 끊임 없이; 연속하여.

keep straight, live a moral life. 행실을 바르게 하다; 정조를 지키다.

make straight, straighten; put in order. 곧게 하다; 정돈하다. ¶ *make* 〔*get*〕 *one's affairs* ~ 신변의 일들을 정리하다.

—*adv.* **1** in a straight line; directly. 곧장; 똑바로; 일직선으로. ¶ *fly* ~ *as an arrow* 화살처럼 (일직선으로) 날다 / *walk* ~ 곧장 걷다 / *shoot* 〔*hit*〕 ~ 명중시키다 / *The smoke rose* ~ *upward.* 연기가 곧장 위로 올라갔다. **2** upright. 곧추 서서; 수직으로. ¶ *stand* ~ 곧추 서다 / *hang pictures* ~ 그림을 똑바로 걸다. **3** in the shortest way. 곧장; 바로; 빗나가지 않고. ¶ *go* ~ *home* 집으로 곧장 가다 / *drink liquor* ~ *from the bottle* 술을 병째로 마시다 / *She looked* ~ *into his eyes.* 그녀는 그의 눈을 똑바로 보았다 / *He will go* ~ *to Paris.* 그는 파리로 직행한다. **4** at once; without loss of time. 곧; 즉각. **5** frankly; honestly. 솔직하게; 정직하게. ¶ *Tell me* ~ *what you think.* 네가 생각하는 바를 솔직히 말해라 / *I told it* ~. 나는 그것을 모조리 털어 놓았다. **6** continuously. 계속해서. ¶ *keep* ~ *on* 순조롭게 계속되다 / *for three years* ~, 3년 연속으로.

come straight to the point, explain clearly and directly. 바로 요점을 말하다. ¶ *Let's come* ~ *to the point.* 자, 어서 요점을 말하시오 / *He came* ~ *to the point.* 그는 바로 요점을 말했다.

go 〔***run***〕 ***straight,*** 《*fig.*》 behave as an honest man. (출감후) 착실한 생활을 하다.

straight away 〔***off***〕, at once. 곧; 즉시.

—*n.* 《*the* ~》 a straight line; a straight part of a race track just before the goal. 직선; 직선 코스. ¶ *on the* ~ 곧장; 일직선으로 / *be out of the* ~ 구부러져 있다 / *shoulders off the* ~ 수평이 아닌 양 어깨. [→stretch]

straight angle [스스] *n.* 《math.》 an angle of one hundred and eighty degrees. 평각(平角)《180°》.

straight·a·way [stréitəwèi] *n.* Ⓒ a straight course. 직선 코스. —*adj.* in a straight course. 일직선의.

·straight·en [stréitn] *vt.* (P6,7) **1** make (something) straight; become straight. 똑바르게〔곧게〕 하다. ¶ ~ *a path* 길을 곧게 하다 / ~ *an iron bar* 철봉을 곧게 펴다. **2** put (something) in order. …을 정돈하다; 바르게 고치다. ¶ ~ *the kitchen* 부엌을 정돈하다 / ~ *one's tie* 넥타이를 바르게 고쳐매다.

straighten out, a) make (something)

straight. …을 똑바로 하다. ¶ ~ *out the world* 세상을 바로잡다. **b**) make (something) clear; put (something) in order. …을 청산하다; 단정히 하다.

straight fight 〔**race, game**〕 [ˊ ˊ] *n.* a fight 〔race, game〕 between parties doing their best to win. 전력을 다하는 싸움〔경기, 게임〕.

straight·for·ward [strèitfɔ́ːrwərd] *adj.* **1** going in a direct course or manner. 똑바른; 곧은. ¶ *a ~ glance* 직시(直視). **2** honest; simple. 정직한; 간단한. ¶ *a ~ answer* 〔*person*〕 솔직한 대답〔사람〕 / *a ~ piece of work* 간단한 일 / *a ~ style* 읽기 쉬운 문체 / *He is ~ in his dealings.* 정직하게 거래한다.

straigh·for·ward·ly [strèitfɔ́ːrwərdli] *adv.* in a straightforward manner. 똑바르게; 솔직히.

straight jet [ˊ ˊ] *n.* a jet plane. 제트기.

straight·ness [stréitnis] *n.* Ⓤ the state or quality of being straight. 곧음; 정직함.

straight ticket [ˊ ˊ–] *n.* 《U.S.》 the party program without modification. (각종 의원 등에 대한 동시 선거에서, 모든 투표가 동일 정당의 후보자에게 던져지는) 연기(連記) 투표 용지.

***straight·way** [stréitwèi] *adv.* at once; without delay. 곧; 지체 없이.

:strain[1] [strein] *vt.* **1** (P6) pull or stretch (something) as much as possible. …을 (팽팽하게) 펴다〔치다〕; (힘껏) 잡아당기다. ¶ *~ a rope to the breaking point* 밧줄을 끊어질 정도로 팽팽하게 당기다 / *The weight of the rock strained the rope almost to breaking.* 바위의 무게로 밧줄은 거의 끊어질 정도로 팽팽해졌다. **2** (P6) put (one's powers, etc.) to the fullest possible use. …을 긴장시키다; 최대한으로 작용시키다〔쓰다〕. ¶ *~ one's ears* 귀를 기울이다 / *~ one's voice* 〔*wit*〕 목소리〔지혜〕를 짜내다 / *~ oneself* 가능한 한 노력하다. **3** (P6) hurt or weaken (a muscle or another part of the body) by using it too much or wrongly. (근육·신체 기관 따위를) 너무 써서 손상〔약화〕시키다; 접질리다; 삐다. ¶ *~ the wrist* 손목을 삐다 / *~ a tendon* 근육을 접질리다 / *~ one's eyes by reading small print* 작은 활자의 책을 읽느라고 눈을 손상시키다 / *~ oneself by overwork* 과로로 몸을 해치다 / *He slipped and strained his ankle.* 그는 미끄러져 넘어지면서 발목을 삐었다. **4** (P6) stretch (the meaning, etc.) beyond the proper limit; pervert the meaning of. (의미 따위를) 곡해〔왜곡〕하다; 억지로 갖다 붙이다. ¶ *~ the meaning of a passage* 글의 뜻을 왜곡하다 / *~ the truth* 진실을 왜곡하다 / *~ the law* 법을 억지 해석하다 / *He strained the rule to his advantage.* 그는 자기 이익을 위해 규칙을 억지 적용했다. **5** (P6) make excessive demands on (someone's patience, friendship, etc.). 강요하다; 기화로 삼다. ¶ *~ someone's generousity* 〔*good temper*〕 사람이 활수한〔좋은〕 점을 기화로 삼다 / *The quality of mercy is not strained.* 자비는 강요될 성질의 것이 아니다. **6** (P6;7) make (liquid) pure or get (solids) from liquid matter by using a cloth or wire net. …을 거르다; 걸러 내다. ¶ *~ coffee* 커피를 거르다 / *~ seeds from lemon juice* 레몬즙에서 씨를 걸러 내다 / *~ the soup before serving it* 식탁에 올리기 전에 수프를 거르다 / *~ the lumps out of the soup* 수프에서 (풀리지 않은) 덩어리를 걸러 내다. **7** (P7) hold tightly. …을 껴안다. ¶ *~ a child to one's breast* 가슴에 아이를 꼭 껴안다.

— *vi.* **1** (P1,3) 《*at*》 pull hard. 잡아당기다. ¶ *~ at a rope* 밧줄을 잡아당기다 / *a dog straining at a leash* (매인) 가죽끈을 팽팽히 당기고 있는 개. **2** (P1,3,4) make a great physical or mental effort. 긴장하다; 몹시 애쓰다〔노력하다〕. ¶ *The swimmer strained to reach the shore.* 그 수영자는 해변에 닿으려고 필사적이었다 / *eyes straining through the mist* 안개 속을 꿰뚫어 보려고 애쓰는 눈. **3** (P1,2A) make liquid pure by using a cloth or net. 거르다; 여과하다.

strain after, make great efforts to obtain. …을 얻으려고 노력하다. ¶ *~ after effects* 무리하게 효과를 얻으려고 하다.

strain a point, go further than could be required. 월권 행위를 하다.

strain at, be too scrupulous about. …에 지나치게 까다롭다〔세심하다〕.

strain at a gnat, be scrupulous in trifles. 하찮은 일에 까다롭게 굴다.

strain at the oar, make great efforts to row. 열심히 노를 젓다.

strain courtesy, omit some degree of ceremony; exceed or insist on the requirements of courtesy. 의례를 약식으로 하다; 지나치게 의례〔예의〕를 따지다.

strain every nerve, make every endeavour. 전력을 다하다〔기울이다〕. ¶ *He strained every nerve to get the work finished in time.* 그는 그 일을 제시간에 끝내기 위하여 전력을 기울였다.

strain off, remove (impurities, etc.) from a liquid by passing it through a strainer. 거르다; 여과하다.

strain under pressure, strive hard under pressure. 악착같이 참고 견디다.

— *n.* **1** ⓊⒸ the act of straining; the state of being strained. 잡아당김; 긴장; 팽팽함. ¶ *keep a ~ on a rope* 밧줄을 팽팽하게 당겨 놓다 / *The rope broke under the ~.* 밧줄이 지나치게 당겨져서 끊어졌다 / *The rope will bear the ~.* 밧줄은 당기는 힘에 견딜 수 있을 것이다. **2** ⓊⒸ any severe or violent, trying effort; tiredness caused by such effort; its effect on the body or mind. 각고의 노력; 과로; (심신의) 긴장. ¶ *the ~ of sleepless nights* 여러 밤을 지새운 과로 / *the ~ of worry* 심로(心勞) / *suffer from the ~ of modern life* 현대 생활의 긴장에 시달리다 / *give a great ~* 크게 노력하다 / *The work* *was a ~ on him.* 그 일은 그에게는 무거운 부담이 되었다. **3** Ⓒ an injury or a damage caused by straining. (근육 따위의) 접질림; 삠. ¶ *a ~ in the arm* 팔의 접질림 / *have a ~ in a leg* 다리의 근육을 접질리다. [L. *stringo* draw or bind tight]

be on the strain, be strained. 긴장하고 있다.

stand the strain, withstand an overwork. 억지로 견디다.

under the strain, owing to the strain; being overworked. 과로로. ¶ *He became ill under the ~ of overwork.* 그는 과로로 병이 났다.

strain[2] [strein] *n.* **1** ⓊⒸ family line; race; breed. 가계(家系); 종족. ¶ *come of (a) noble* 〔*good*〕 *~* 명문〔양가〕의 출신이다. **2** ⒸⓊ a marked quality that runs through personality, a family or a race. (선천적) 기질; 유전적 성질. ¶ *a weak ~* 허약 체질 / *There is a ~ of insanity in the family.* 그 집안에는 정신 이상의 유전적 소인이 있다 / *He has a ~ of cruelty in his character.* 그의 성격에는 선천적으로 잔인한 기질이 있다. **3** Ⓒ 《often *pl.*》 a part of a piece of music; a melody; a song. 가곡; 선율; 가락. ¶ *martial* 〔*pathetic*〕 *strains* 씩씩한〔감상적인〕 곡. **4** Ⓒ the manner or style of writing or speaking. 문체; 말투; 어조. ¶ *a ~ of humor* 익살스러운 말투 / *He spoke in a dismal ~.* 그는 우울한 말투로 말했다 / *in the same ~* 동일한 말투로. **5** ⓊⒸ 《phys.》 condition of a body subjected to stress; molecular displacement. 왜곡(歪曲); 변형; 스트레인. [E.]

strained [streind] *adj.* **1** (of a rope, etc.) drawn tightly; being in a high state of tension. 팽팽한; 긴장한. ¶ *~ ropes* 팽팽히 당겨진 밧줄 / *Relations between the two countries have become ~.* 두 나라 사이의 관계가 긴장되었다. **2** not natural. 부자연스런. ¶ *a ~ laugh* 〔*smile*〕 억지〔거짓〕 웃음〔미소〕 / *a ~ manner* (꾸며 하는) 부자연스런 태도. [*strain*[1]]

strain·er [stréinər] *n.* Ⓒ **1** a person or thing that strains. 잡아당기는 사람〔물건〕. **2** (in making coffee, tea, etc.) a kitchen instrument with a net for separating the liquid. 여과기; 체. ¶ *a coffee-* 〔*tea-*〕 *~* 커피〔차〕 여과기. [↑]

·**strait** [streit] *n.* Ⓒ **1** a narrow channel joining two large bodies of water. 해협. 語法 지명에 붙이는 경우는 단수·복수 두 가지 형이 있으나 단수 취급임. ¶ *the Bering Strait* 베링 해협 / *the Straits of Dover* 도버 해협. **2** 《often *pl.*》 difficulties; need. 곤란; 궁핍. ¶ *drive someone into* 〔*to*〕 *straits* 아무를 매우 곤란하게 하다; 아무를 괴롭히다 / *He was in great straits for money.* 그는 돈에 크게 쪼들리고 있었다. — *adj.* 《*arch.*》 narrow. 좁은. ¶ *Enter ye in at the ~ gate.* 《Bible》 좁은 문으로 들어가라. [→*strain*[1]]

strait·en [stréitn] *vt.* (P6) 《chiefly used as *pp.*》 put (someone) into financial difficulties. …을 궁핍〔곤궁〕하게 하다. ¶ *be in straitened circumstances* 궁핍한 상태에 있다 / *be straitened for moeny* 〔*time*〕 돈〔시간〕이 없어서 애를 먹고 있다.

strait-jacket [stréitdʒǽkit] *n.* Ⓒ a special coat that holds the arms close to the sides, for restricting the movements of a mad person. (미친 사람 등에게 입히는) 구속복.

strait-laced [stréitléist] *adj.* very strict in matters of conduct. (행동·사람이) 엄격〔딱딱〕한.

strait·ness [stréitnis] *n.* 《*arch.*》 **1** narrowness. 좁음; 편협. **2** strictness. 엄격.

strait-waist·coat [stréitwéistkòut / ⌐wéskət] *n.* =strait-jacket.

strand[1] [strænd] *n.* Ⓒ 《*poet.*》 a shore. 바닷가; 해안. — *vi., vt.* (P1; 6) **1** drive or run ashore. 좌초하다〔시키다〕. ¶ *The storm stranded the ship on the rocks.* 폭풍으로 배는 바위에 좌초했다. **2** bring or be left in a difficult state because of lack of moeny, etc. 궁지에 빠지(게 하)다. ¶ *be stranded penniless* 무일푼이 되어 어찌할 바를 모르다 / *He was stranded in a strange city without money.* 그는 돈이 한푼도 없어서 낯선 도시에서 꼼짝 못 하게 되었다. [E.]

strand[2] [strænd] *n.* Ⓒ **1** one of the threads, wires, etc. forming a rope. (여러 가닥으로 꼬인 밧줄·케이블 따위에서) 한 가닥; 한 가닥의 섬유〔실, 철사〕. **2** one of the elements in character, etc. 하나의 요소. [E.]

:**strange** [streindʒ] *adj.* **1** not familiar; not known, seen, or heard of before. 낯선; 알지 못하는; 본 적이 없는; 들어보지 못한. ¶ *a ~ man* 〔*face, name*〕 낯선 사람〔얼굴, 이름〕 / *It feels ~.* 이런 느낌은 처음이다 / *This handwriting is ~ to me.* 이 필적은 누구의 것인지 모르겠다 / *She is moving to a ~ place.* 그녀는 낯선 곳으로 이사를 간다 / *The language is quite ~ to me.* 그 언어는 나에게는 전혀 새로운 것이다. **2** odd; unusual; queer. 이상한; 별난; 기묘한. ¶ *a ~ occurrence* 이상한 사건 / *~ clothes* 별난 옷 / *see ~ sights* 이상한 것을 보다 / *~ to say* 이상한 이야기지만 / *~ as it may sound* 이상하게 들리겠지만 / *It's very ~ that you haven't heard from him.* 네가 그의 소식을 모른다니 거참 이상하다 / *It is ~ that you should think so.* 네가 그렇게 생각하다니 이상스런 일이군 / *He is ~ in his manner.* 그는 행동이 좀 이상하다 / *What a ~ experience!* 참으로 별난 경험이군 그래. **3** not at home; out of place; not accustomed. 생무지의; 익숙지 않은; 생소한; 미숙한. ¶ *He is still ~ to his job.* 그는 아직 그의 일에 익숙지 않다 / *The poor girl felt ~ in my house.* 그 가엾은 소녀는 우리 집에서 서먹서먹함을 느꼈다 / *I'm quite ~ here.* 나는 이곳이 전혀 생소한 곳이다. **4** 《*arch.*》 foreign. 타국〔이국〕의. ¶ *in a ~ land* 이국 땅에서 / *follow ~ gods* 이국의 신을 좇다 / *visit ~ lands* 외국을 방문하다. [→extra]

·**strange·ly** [stréindʒli] *adv.* in a strange manner. 이상하게(도). ¶ ~ *enough* 이상한 일이지만; 묘하게도 / *He is ~ silent about it.* 그는 이상하게도 그것에 관해 아무 말이 없다.

strange·ness [stréindʒnis] *n.* Ⓤ the state or quality of being strange; unfamiliarity. 기묘; 이상함; 미지(未知).

:**stran·ger** [stréindʒər] *n.* Ⓒ **1** a person whom one does not know; a person from another place or another country. 알지 못하는 사람; 외국인. ¶ *an utter* 〔*a perfect*〕 ~ 생판 모르는 사람 / *be shy in the presence of strangers* 모르는 사람 앞에서 수줍어하다 / *make a* 〔*no*〕 ~ *of* …을 쌀쌀하게〔따뜻하게〕 대하다 / 《*colloq.*》 *You are quite a* ~. 참으로 오래간만일세 / *He is a* ~ *to us.* 그는 우리가 모르는 사람이다. **2** 《*to*》 a person or thing new to a place; a person not used to something. 문외한; 미숙한〔생소한〕 사람. ¶ *I am a complete* ~ *to country life.* 나는 시골 생활에는 아주 생소하다 / *I am a* ~ *to New York.* 나는 뉴욕을 모른다 / *I am a* ~ *here* 〔*in these parts*〕. 나는 이 곳〔이 지방〕이 낯설다.

stran·gle [strǽŋgəl] *vt.* (P6) **1** kill (a living thing) by pressing the throat. …을 목졸라 죽이다; 교살하다. ¶ ~ *someone to death* 아무를 교살하다. **2** (of a collar etc.) cause (someone or something) difficulty in breathing; squeeze. (깃 따위가) 목을 답답하게 하다; 죄다. **3** 《*fig.*》 suppress; keep under control. …을 억압〔억제〕하다; 억누르다. ¶ ~ *a bill* 의안을 묵살하다 / ~ *a sob* 〔*sigh*〕 울음〔한숨〕을 꾹 눌러 참다. ● **stran·gler** [-ər] *n.* [Gk. *straggos* twisted]

stran·gle·hold [strǽŋgəlhòuld] *n.* **1** a hold in wrestling which prevents free breathing. 목조르기. **2** 《*fig.*》 any force or influence which prevents freedom of action. (행동 등을) 억누르는〔저해하는〕 힘; 속박.

stran·gu·late [strǽŋgjəlèit] *vt.* (P6) **1** kill (someone or something) by pressing the throat. …을 교살하다. **2** 《med.》 press (a tube of a body) to stop the circulation of air, liquid, etc. (혈관·식도 따위의 순환)을 압박하여 멈추게 하다. [*strangle*]

stran·gu·la·tion [strӕ̀ŋgjəléiʃən] *n.* Ⓤ the act of strangulating; the state of being strangulated. 교살.

·**strap** [stræp] *n.* Ⓒ **1** a narrow strip of leather, etc. to hold things together; a strip of leather, etc. for a standing person to hold for support. (가죽)끈; 띠; (전철 따위의) 가죽 손잡이. ¶ *hold on to a* ~ 가죽 손잡이를 잡다 / *Put a* ~ *round the trunk.* 끈으로 트렁크를 묶어라 / *a watch* ~ *of metal* 금속의 시곗줄. **2** a strip of leather for sharpening razors. 가죽 숫돌.
—*vt.* (**strapped, strap·ping**) (P6,7) **1** fasten (something) with a strap …을 가죽끈으로 묶다〔매다〕. ¶ *She strapped the bag onto her back.* 백을 끈으로 매서 등에 둘러 멨다 / ~ *on a wristwatch* 손목 시계를 차다 / ~ *books together* 책들을 (가죽)끈으로 한데 묶다. **2** beat (someone) with a strap. …을 가죽끈으로 때리다. **3** sharpen (a razor) on a strap. …을 가죽 숫돌에 갈다. [L. *struppus*]

strap·hang·er [strǽphæ̀ŋər] *n.* a passenger on a bus, train, etc. who holds onto a strap; a commuter. (버스·전철 등에서) 가죽 손잡이를 잡고 있는 승객; 통근자.

strap·ping [strǽpiŋ] *adj.* 《*colloq.*》 tall, strong and healthy 키가 크고 몸이 건장한. ¶ *a* ~ *girl.* —*n.* Ⓤ **1** an adhesive plaster in strips. 반창고. **2** a flogging. 채찍질.

stra·ta [stréitə, -rǽt-] *n.* pl. of **stratum.**

strat·a·gem [strǽtədʒəm] *n.* ⓊⒸ **1** a trick or scheme to deceive an enemy in war. 전략; 군략. **2** any trick. 계략. ¶ *devise a* ~ 계략을 꾸미다. [Gk. *stratēgos* general]

stra·te·gic [strətíːdʒik], **-gi·cal** [-dʒikəl] *adj.* **1** of or based on strategy. 전략(상)의; 계략의. ¶ *a* ~ *retreat* 전략적인 퇴각〔후퇴〕 / *a* ~ *point* 〔*target*〕 전략 요점〔목표〕. **2** important in strategy. 전략상 중요한. ¶ ~ *materials* 전략(상 중요한) 물자〔자재〕. [↑]

stra·te·gi·cal·ly [strətíːdʒikəli] *adv.* in a strategic manner. 전략상; 전략적으로.

strat·e·gist [strǽtədʒist] *n.* Ⓒ a person who is skilled in strategy. 전략가.

strat·e·gy [strǽtədʒi] *n.* Ⓤ **1** the art or science of military movement in war. 용병학; 병법(cf. *tactics*). **2** skill in managing or planning. 전략.

stra·ti [stréitai] *n.* pl. of **stratus.**

strat·i·fi·ca·tion [strӕ̀təfikéiʃən] *n.* 《geol.》 arrangement in layers. 성층(成層). [↓]

strat·i·fy [strǽtəfài] *vt., vi.* (**-fied**) (P6;1) form into layers. 층을 이루게 하다; 층을 이루다. ¶ *stratified rock* 성층암. [→stratum]

strat·o·sphere [strǽtəsfìər] *n.* Ⓒ the highest part of the atmosphere above the earth. 성층권. [↓]

stra·tum [stréitəm, -rǽt-] *n.* Ⓒ (*pl.* **-ta** or **-tums**) **1** a layer of rock or earth. 지층(地層). **2** a rank in society. 계급; 계층. ¶ *a* ~ *of society* 사회의 계층 / *a lower* 〔*upper*〕 *social* ~ 하층〔상층〕 사회. [L. *strātus* (↓)]

stra·tus [stréitəs] *n.* Ⓒ (*pl.* **stra·ti**) a low layer of gray clouds spreading widely. 층운(層雲). [L. *sterno* strew, stretch out]

:**straw** [strɔː] *n.* **1** ⓊⒸ the stalk of grain; cut and dried stalks of grain used for making hats, etc. 짚; 밀짚. ¶ *made of* ~ 밀짚으로 만든 / *a* ~ *hat* 밀짚 모자 / *a house thatched with* ~ 초가집. **2** Ⓒ trifle; anything practically worthless. 하찮은 것. ¶ *not worth a* ~ 지푸라기 만큼의 값어치도 없는. **3** Ⓒ a hollow stalk, or something like this. 빨대. ¶ *She drank her soda through a* ~. [E.]

a man of straw, a) a person who looks important, but actually has little power and acts in obedience to others. 실권이 없는 사람. **b**) a weak, unreliable person. 믿을 수 없는 힘 없는 사람. **c**) a puppet. 앞잡이.

a straw in the wind, a small thing that is a sign of coming events. 바람의 방향〔여론의 동향〕을 나타내는 것; 조짐.

catch 〔***snatch***〕 ***at a straw*** 〔***straws***〕***,*** try anything in desperation. 지푸라기라도 잡으려 하다. ¶《*prov.*》 *A drowning man will catch at a* ~. 물에 빠진 사람은 지푸라기라도 잡으려 한다.

draw straws, draw lots with straws of different lengths. 제비뽑기를 하다.

not care a straw 〔***two straws***〕***,*** not care a bit. 조금도 개의치 않다. ¶ *He doesn't care a* ~ *what happen.* 그는 무슨 일이 일어나든 개의치 않는다.

throw straws against the wind, attempt an impossibility. 불가능한 일을 꾀하다.

***straw·ber·ry** [strɔ́:bèri / -bəri] *n.* Ⓒ (*pl.* **-ries**) a small red fruit of a low-growing plant; this plant; a red color of or like that of this fruit. 딸기; 딸깃빛. [*straw, berry,* the plant's runners being likened to straw]

straw·board [strɔ́:bɔ̀:rd] *n.* Ⓤ a thick, stiff paper made from straw and used for boxes, etc. 마분지. [*straw*]

straw color [스스–] *n.* the color of straw; pale yellow. 담황색.

:**straw·hat** [strɔ́:hæ̀t] *n.* Ⓒ a hat made of straw. 밀집 모자.

straw man [스스] *n.* a bundle of straw made into the likeness of a man (often used as a scarecrow). (허수아비로 쓰는) 짚 인형.

straw vote [스스] *n.* 《U.S.》 an unofficial vote taken to find out the general opinion. 비공식〔모의〕 투표《여론 조사용》.

straw·y [strɔ́:i] *adj.* (**straw·i·er, straw·i·est**) of or like straw; made of straw. 짚의; 짚 같은; 짚으로 만든.

***stray** [strei] *vi.* (P1,2A,3) **1** lose one's way; go astray; wander; get separated from the flock. 길을 잃다; 헤매다; 무리에서 떨어지다. ¶ *His dog has strayed off somewhere.* 그의 개는 길을 잃고 어디론가 가 버렸다 / ~ *aimlessly through the woods* 숲속을 방향을 잃고 헤매다 / *We strayed off the main road and were soon lost.* 간선 도로를 벗어나자 우리는 곧 길을 잃었다. **2** 《*fig.*》 turn aside from strict morality; fall into sin. 정도(正道)에서 벗어나다; 죄를 범하다. **3** depart temporarily from the main subject in talking or thinking about something. (이야기·생각 등이) 빗나가다; 탈선하다. ¶ *Her thoughts strayed from the subject.* 그녀의 의견은 본제에서 벗어나 있었다.

— *n.* Ⓒ **1** a person or domestic animal that has strayed. 길 잃은 사람〔가축〕; 미아(迷兒). **2** a wanderer. 떠돌이; 부랑자.

— *adj.* **1** wandering; lost; homeless. 길을 잃은; 헤매는; 이탈한. ¶ *a* ~ *dog* 〔*sheep*〕 길 잃은 개〔양〕 / *a* ~ *child* 미아 / *a* ~ *bullet* 유탄 / *A* ~ *cat is crying at the door.* 집 없는 고양이가 현관에서 울고 있다. **2** happening occasionally; sporadic; not frequently; occasional; scattered. 이따금의; 뿔뿔이 흩어진. ¶ *a few* ~ *pedestrians* 이따금 눈에 띄는 두세 명의 보행자 / ~ *hairs* 흐트러진 머리 / *pick up* ~ *cigarettes* 흩어진 담배를 줍다 / *A few* ~ *shots were heard.* 산발적인 몇 발의 총성이 들렸다 / *A* ~ *customer or two came in.* 한두 명의 뜨내기 손님이 들어왔다. [→astray]

***streak** [stri:k] *n.* Ⓒ **1** a long, narrow mark or line; a stripe. 줄무늬; 줄; 선. ¶ *a* ~ *of lightning* 〔*moonlight*〕 한 줄기의 번개〔달빛〕 / *like a* ~ *of lightning* 전광 석화처럼; 전속력으로 / *He has a* ~ *of paint on his arm.* 그의 팔에는 한 가닥의 줄이 칠해져 있다 / *He has streaks of gray in his hair.* 그의 머리에는 몇 가닥의 흰 머리가 섞여 있다. **2** a layer of something. 층. ¶ *streaks of fat in meat* 고기의 비계층 / *Bacon has streaks of fat and lean.* 베이컨에는 지방층과 살코기층이 있다. **3** a tendency in behavior, etc.; a trace. 경향; 낌새; …한 데〔점〕. ¶ *He does not have a* ~ *of humor.* 그는 전연 유머를 모른다 / *He has a* ~ *of humor, though he looks very serious.* 비록 엄숙하게 생겼지만, 유머러스한 데가 있다.

— *vt.* (P6,13) mark (something) with streaks. …에 줄을〔줄무늬를〕 긋다〔넣다〕. ¶ *be streaked with color* 색깔 있는 줄무늬가 들어 있다 / *Her hair was streaked with gray.* 그녀의 머리에는 흰 머리가 섞여 있었다 / *The Indians used to* ~ *their faces with paint.* 인디언들은 그림물감으로 얼굴에 줄무늬를 그리는 습관이 있었다.

— *vi.* (P2A) **1** become streaked. 줄이〔줄무늬가〕 되다. **2** 《*colloq.*》 move at a high speed; go fast. 전속력으로 달리다; 질주하다. [E.]

streak·y [strí:ki] *adj.* (**streak·i·er, streak·i·est**) marked with streaks; occurring in or as streaks. 줄이〔줄무늬가〕 있는; 줄(무늬)로 된. ¶ ~ *bacon* (고기와 지방이) 줄 모양의 층을 이룬 베이컨. [↑]

:**stream** [stri:m] *n.* Ⓒ **1** a flow or current of water; running water; a brook. (물의) 흐름; 흐름의 방향; 개울. ¶ *flow in a great* ~ 큰 흐름을 이루고〔도도히〕 흐르다. **2** a flow of liquid, gas, etc. (액체나 유동체의) 흐름; 유출. ¶ *a* ~ *air* 공기의 흐름 / *a* ~ *of tears* 〔*blood*〕 흐르는 눈물〔피〕. **3** a continuous flow; a succession; any steady flow. 끊임없는 흐름; 연속. ¶ *a* ~ *of cars* 차량의 물결 / *a* ~ *of people* 사람의 물결〔행렬〕 / *a* ~ *of traffic* 교통의 흐름 / *a* ~ *of words* 계속 쏟아지는 말; 말의 홍수 / *come out* 〔*go by*〕 *in a* ~ 〔*streams*〕 계속해 나오다〔지나가다〕. **4** 《usu. *the* ~》 a general direction; a tendency; a current (of the times). 경향; 풍조; 형세.

¶ *the ~ of time* 〔*times*〕 시간의 흐름; 시세 / *the ~ of popular opinion* 세론의 경향 / *the ~ of thought* 사조(思潮) / *the main ~ of English literature* 영문학의 주류 / *The ~ of public opinion is tending toward greater personal freedom.* 여론의 방향은 더 많은 개인의 자유를 추구하는 경향이다.

down* (*the*) *stream, with the current. 흐름을 따라; 하류에.

go with* 〔*against*〕 *the stream, fall in with 〔oppose〕 the general tendency; do 〔do not do〕 as others do. 흐름을〔시류를〕 따라〔거슬러〕 가다.

in a stream* 〔*streams*〕*, successively. 연속하여; 계속; 잇달아.

up* (*the*) *stream, against the current of water. 흐름을 거슬러; 상류에.

— *vi.* **1** (P1,2A,3) flow like a stream; flow in a stream. 흐르다; 흘러나오다; 흘러들다. ¶ *eyes that ~ with tears* 눈물이 흘러나오는 눈 / *Light streamed through the window.* 빛이 창문을 통해 흘러들어 왔다 / *Her face was streaming with perspiration.* 그녀의 얼굴에 땀이 흐르고 있었다 / *Tears ~ down her cheeks.* 눈물이 그녀의 뺨을 흘러내렸다. **2** (P2A) move continuously like a stream. 잇달아〔쉴새없이〕 계속되다. ¶ *People streamed out of the building.* 사람들이 건물에서 쏟아져 나왔다. **3** (P3) (of a flag, etc.) move up and down; (of hair) wave. (깃발 따위가) 펄럭이다; (머리카락이) 나부끼다. ¶ *The flags streamed in the wind.* 깃발들이 바람에 펄럭였다 / *hair streaming in the wind* 바람에 나부끼는 머리칼.

— *vt.* (P6) **1** cause (liquid, gas, etc.) to flow. …을 흘리다; 흘러나오게 하다. ¶ *Her eyes streamed tears.* 그녀의 눈에서 눈물이 흘러나왔다 / *The wounds streamed blood.* 상처에서 피가 흘렀다. **2** cause (a flag, hair, etc.) to wave. …을 펄럭이다; 나부끼게 하다. [E.]

stream·er [strí:mər] *n.* Ⓒ **1** a long, narrow flag. 기(旗)드림. **2** any long, narrow, flowing strip. 가늘고 긴 장식 리본(헝겊). ¶ *Streamers of colored paper hung from the ceiling.* 색종이로 만든 기다란 장식 리본들이 천장에 매달려 있었다. **3** 《U.S.》 a newspaper headline that extends across the full page. (신문 상단의) 전단(全段) 표제.

stream·let [strí:mlit] *n.* a small stream; a brook. 작은 시내; 실개천.

stream·line [strí:mlàin] *n.* Ⓒ **1** a course of water, air, etc. that finds the least resistance in flowing. 유선(流線). **2** a shape offering the least resistance to a current of air, etc. 유선형.

— *adj.* having a shape or an outline designed to offer the least resistance to air or water. 유선형의. ¶ *a ~ form* 〔*shape*〕 유선형(型) / *a ~ car* 유선형 자동차.

— *vt.* (P6) **1** make (something) into a streamline form. …을 유선형으로 하다. ¶ *~ a motorcar* 자동차를 유선형으로 하다. **2** change (a process of work, etc.) to make it more efficient. (일 따위를) 합리화하다; 능률적으로 하다. ¶ *~ the municipal bureaucracy* 시의 관료식 절차를 간소화하다 / *Customs procedures must be streamlined.* 세관 절차는 합리화되어야 한다. [E.]

stream·lined [strí:mlàind] *adj.* **1** having a streamline form. 유선형의. ¶ *a ~ train* 유선형 열차. **2** arranged or designed to gain the greatest efficiency. (근대적으로) 능률화된. ¶ *a ~ office* 능률화된 사무실. **3** up-to-date; modernized. 최신식의.

:street [stri:t] *n.* Ⓒ a public road in a city, a town, or a village, usu. with buildings on one or on both sides. 거리; 가로; …가(街). ¶ *a main* 〔*broad*〕 *~* 큰〔넓은〕 거리; 대로 / *a side ~* 옆골목 / *live in a quiet ~* 조용한 거리에 살다 / *run out into the ~* 길로 뛰어나오다 / *The hospital is located on Lincoln Street.* 병원은 링컨가(街)에 위치하고 있다 / *I met her on* 〔《Brit.》 *in*〕 *the ~.* 나는 그녀를 거리에서 만났다 / *Be careful when you cross the streets.* 길을 건널 때는 조심하여라. [→stratum]

live in the street, be constantly outside one's house. 자주 외출하다.

not in the same street with, not able to be compared with; being no match for. …와 비교가 안 되는.

on the streets, earning money by prostitution. 매춘부가 되어.

streets ahead of, very far in advance of. (학식·능력 등이) 훨씬 앞서 있는.

the man in* 〔《U.S.》 *on*〕 *the street, the typical citizen. (도시의) 평민; 보통 사람.

street Arab [∠ ∠–] *n.* a homeless or neglected child who roams in the streets. 집 없는 아이; 부랑아.

:street·car [strí:tkɑ̀:r] *n.* Ⓒ 《U.S.》 a public vehicle that runs regularly along rails in a street. 전차(cf. 《Brit.》 *tramcar*).

street cries [∠ ∠] *n.* cries of hawkers. (행상인의) 외치는 소리.

street-door [strí:tdɔ̀:r] *n.* the main door of a building. (가로에 면한) 대문.

street·light [strí:tlàit] *n.* Ⓒ a light for illuminating a street, usu. supported by a post. 가로등.

street railway [∠ ∠–] *n.* a company operating streetcars or buses. 시내 전차〔버스〕 회사.

street smarts [∠ ∠] *n.* cunning or shrewdness needed to live in, or to deal with people living in, an urban environment characterized by poverty, crime, etc. 어려운 도시 생활에 필요한 지혜〔처세술〕.

:strength [streŋkθ] *n.* Ⓤ **1** the quality or state of being physically strong; power; force. 세기; 힘; 체력. ¶ *a man of ~* 힘이 센

사람 / *a task beyond human* ~ 인력으로는 어쩔 수 없는 일 / *get back one's health and strength after an illness* 병후에 건강과 체력을 회복하다 / *That is too much for my* ~. 그것은 내 힘에 겨운 일이다 / *He has not the* ~ *to walk.* 그는 걸을 힘도 없다. **2** mental, intellectual or moral power. (의지·성격 따위의) 강함; 정신력; 지력. ¶ *the* ~ *of one's mind* 〔*will*〕 정신〔결단〕력 / ~ *to surmount difficulties* 어려움을 이겨 내는 불굴의 정신 / *He didn't have enough* ~ *of mind to refuse.* 그에게는 거절할 수 있을 만한 정신력이 없었다. **3** strong point. 장점; 이점. ¶ *His* ~ *lies in his honesty.* 그의 장점은 정직함에 있다 / *French is her* ~. 프랑스 말을 할 수 있는 것이 그녀의 강점이다. **4** power to resist or endure; toughness. (물건의) 내구도〔력〕; 튼튼함. ¶ *the* ~ *of a rope* 밧줄의 강도 / *the* ~ *of a beam* 〔*bridge, building*〕 빔〔교량, 건물〕의 내구력 / *the* ~ *of a fortified place* 요새의 저항력. **5** force as measured by the number of soldiers, warships, etc. 병력; 군세; 인원수. ¶ *military* ~ 병력 / *peace* 〔*war*〕 ~ 평시〔전시〕 병력 / *The enemy were* 〔*was*〕 *in great* ~. 적의 병력은 막강했다 / *an employed* ~ *of 5000,* 오천 명의 종업원 / *in full* ~ 전원 모여서. **6** degree of concentration or intensity. 강도; 농도. ¶ *the* ~ *of poison gas* 독가스의 농도 / *the* ~ *of tea* 〔*alcoholic liquor*〕 차〔주정 음료〕의 농도. 〔*strong*〕

on the strength of, relying on; influenced or encouraged by. …에 의지하여; …에 영향〔격려〕되어. ¶ *I employed him on the* ~ *of your recommendation.* 나는 너의 추천을 믿고 그를 고용하였다.

up to 〔***below***〕 ***strength,*** having 〔less than〕 the full complement of men. 정원에 달한〔미달된〕.

***strength·en** [stréŋkθən] *vt.* (P6) make (someone or something) strong or stronger. …을 강하게 하다; 강화하다. ¶ ~ *one's conviction* 신념을 강화하다. — *vi.* (P1) become or grow stronger. 강해지다; 튼튼해지다.

stren·u·ous [strénjuəs] *adj.* **1** requiring great effort or energy. 대단한 노력을 요하는. ¶ ~ *work.* **2** very eager; zealous; full of energy. 열심인; 열렬한; 정력적인. ¶ *a* ~ *worker* 정력적인 근로자 / *make* ~ *efforts* 힘껏 노력하다; 분발하다. [L.]

stren·u·ous·ly [strénjuəsli] *adv.* in a strenuous manner. 열심히; 정력적으로.

strep·to·coc·ci [strèptəkáksai / -kɔ́k-] *n.* pl. of **streptococcus.**

strep·to·coc·cus [strèptəkákəs / -kɔ́k-] *n.* (*pl.* **strep·to·coc·ci**) 연쇄상 구균(連鎖狀球菌). [Gk. *streptos* twisted, *kókkos* berry]

strep·to·my·cin [strèptoumáisən] *n.* Ⓤ a drug obtained from a certain soil and used against various diseases, esp. tuberculosis. 스트렙토마이신《항생제의 일종》. [Gk. *mykēs* fungus]

·stress [stres] *n.* **1** Ⓤ tension; pressure; strain. 강제; 압박. ¶ *be subjected to great* ~ 큰 압박을 받다 / *Under the* ~ *of bad weather the ship had to return.* 험악한 날씨 때문에 배는 되돌아오지 않을 수 없었다. **2** Ⓤ pressing condition; urgency. 긴장; 긴급; 긴박. ¶ *in times of* ~ 긴박한 때에; 상황(商況)이 분망한 때에. **3** ⓊⒸ accent given to a speech sound or to a music note. 강세; 악센트. ¶ *In 'hero', the* ~ *is* 〔*falls*〕 *on the first syllable.* 'hero'의 악센트는 첫 음절에 있다. **4** ⓊⒸ emphasis; importance. 강조; 중점. **5** 《phys.》 a force, esp. one causing change of shape or volume. 응력(應力).

lay 〔***place, put***〕 (***a***) ~ ***on*** 〔***upon***〕 ***....*** …에 중점을 두다; …을 강조〔역설〕하다. ¶ *That school lays* ~ *on foreign languages.* 그 학교에서는 외국어에 중점을 두고 있다.

— *vt.* (P6) **1** put stress, pressure, tension, etc. on (something). …을 강제하다; …에 압력을 가하다. **2** give stress or accent to (something). …을 강하게 발음하다; …에 강세를 두다. ¶ *stressed syllables* 강세를 둔 음절 / *Stress the important words of a sentence.* 문장의 중요 낱말에 강세를 두어 발음해라. **3** emphasize. …을 강조하다. ¶ ~ *the importance of health* 건강의 중요성을 강조하다. [→strain[1]]

:stretch [stretʃ] *vt.* **1** (P6,7,18) draw (something) out to a greater length or width; draw (something) tight; expand. …을 잡아당기다; 팽팽하게 하다; …을 펴다; 깔다. ¶ ~ *a rope tight* 로프를 팽팽히 잡아당기다 / ~ *trousers* 바지의 구김살을 펴다 / ~ *a rubber band* 고무줄을 당기다 / ~ *the violin string* 바이올린의 현을 조이다 / ~ *a pair of gloves to make them fit* (처음 낄 때) 잘 맞게 장갑을 잡아당겨 펴다. **2** (P6) extend (oneself, the body, limbs, wings, etc.) to the full length; straighten out. (몸·손발·날개 따위를) 한껏 쭉 펴다. ¶ ~ *one's arms* 팔을 쭉 펴다 / ~ *one's neck in order to see over the heads of a crowd* 군중의 머리 너머를 보기 위해 목을 길게 빼다 / *The bird stretched its wings.* 새는 날개를 한껏 폈다 / *He stretched himself into wakefulness.* 그는 기지개를 켜며 잠을 깼다 / *He stretched himself out on the lawn.* 그는 잔디 위에 몸을 쭉 뻗고 누웠다. **3** (P6) extend (the law, the truth, etc.) beyond its proper limits; exaggerate. (법률·진리 따위를) 확대 해석하다; 곡해하다; 억지로 갖다 붙이다. ¶ ~ *the law* 〔*a rule, a clause*〕 법률〔규칙, 조항〕을 무리하게 확대 해석하다〔남용하다〕 / ~ *the facts* 〔*the truth*〕 사실〔진실〕을 왜곡하여 침소 봉대하다〔거짓말하다〕 / ~ *the law to suit one's purpose* 자기 목적에 알맞도록 법을 악용〔확대 해석〕하다. **4** (P6) strain (a muscle, etc.) to the utmost. (근육·신경 따위를) 극도로 긴장시키다. ¶ ~ *every nerve* 전신경을 긴장시키다 / ~ *one's powers* 젖 먹은 힘을 다 내어 노력

〔분투〕하다.

— *vi.* (P1,2A,2B) **1** extend one's limbs fully. 몸을 펴다; 기지개를 켜다; (팔 다리를) 뻗다. ¶ ~ *out on the sofa* 소파 위에 길게〔팔다리를 뻗고〕 눕다 / *He stretched and yawned.* 그는 기지개를 켜며 하품을 했다 / ~ (*out*) *for a book* 책을 집으려고 팔을 뻗다. **2** (of rubber, etc.) become longer or wider under use, pressure, etc. (고무 따위가) 늘어나다. ¶ *Rubber stretches.* 고무는 신축성이 있다 / *It stretched like elastic.* 그것은 고무줄처럼 늘어났다. **3** extend; spread; last. 퍼지다; 뻗다; 계속되다. ¶ *The road stretches away.* 도로가 멀리까지 뻗어 있다 / *The war stretched over three years.* 전쟁은 3년이 넘게 계속되었다 / *The forest stretches for miles.* 숲은 여러 마일에 걸쳐 펼쳐 있다.

— *n.* Ⓒ **1** the act of stretching; the state of being stretched. 뻗기; 펴기; 펼침. ¶ *make a ~ of the arm* 팔을 뻗다 / *get up with a ~ and a yawn* 기지개를 켜고 하품을 하며 일어나다 / *I cannot understand by any ~ of my imagination.* 아무리 상상을 해도 이해할 수가 없다. **2** Ⓤ elasticity. 신축성. ¶ *There's not much ~ in this girdle.* 이 거들은 별로 신축성이 없다. **3** a continuous line, surface, or period. 범위; 퍼짐; 한 연속의 시간. ¶ *a ~ of flat land* 넓디넓은 평지 / *at the utmost ~ of one's voice* 목청껏. **4** tension; exaggeration; abuse. 긴장; 과장; 남용. ¶ *nerves on the ~* 긴장된 신경 / *keep the spirit on the ~* 정신을 긴장시켜 두다. **5** the straight section of the race course, esp. before the goal. (경기장의) 직선 코스; (경주·선거 따위의) 최종 단계. **6** a short walk. 산보; 산책. [E.]

at a stretch, at a time; without stopping to rest. 한 번에; (쉬지 않고) 계속적으로. ¶ *How long do you work at a ~?* 너는 한 번에 몇 시간 일하느냐.

bring to the stretch, strain. 긴장시키다.

by a stretch of authority, use one's authority to the utmost; abuse one's authority. 권력을 최대로 남용하여.

on 〔***upon***〕 ***the stretch,*** strained to attention or exertion. 긴장하여.

put 〔***set***〕 ***upon the*** (***full***) ***stretch,*** make someone do his best. 최선을 다하게 하다.

stretch·er [strétʃər] *n.* Ⓒ **1** a person or thing that stretches. 뻗는〔펴는, 펼치는〕 사람〔것〕; 신장구(伸張具). ¶ *a hat* 〔*boot*〕 ~ 모자〔구두〕의 골. **2** a frame with canvas for carrying the sick, wounded or dead; a litter. 들것. **3** a board in a boat against which a rower presses his feet. (노잡이가 발을 뻗딛는) 판자.

strew [struː] *vt.* (**strewed, strewed** or **strewn**) (P6,13) **1** scatter; sprinkle. …을 (흩)뿌리다. ¶ ~ *seed on* 〔*over*〕 *a garden bed* 화단에 씨를 뿌리다. **2** cover the surface of (something) with anything scattered or sprinkled. …에 흩뿌리다; (뿌려서 표면을) 온통 뒤덮다. ¶ ~ *the road with sand* 도로 표면에 모래를 뿌리다 / *The ground was strewn with leaves.* 지면은 잎들로 온통 뒤덮여 있었다. [L. *sterno* spread out]

strewn [struːn] *v.* pp. of **strew.**

stri·at·ed [stráieitid] *adj.* striped; variegated. 평행의 줄이〔줄무늬가〕 있는; 얼룩덜룩한. [L.]

:strick·en [stríkən] *v.* 《*arch.*》 pp. of **strike.**

— *adj.* **1** struck; wounded. (수렵 따위에서 탄환에) 맞은; 다친; 상처 입은. ¶ *a ~ deer* 총에 맞은 사슴. **2** hit or attacked by diseases, sorrow, etc. 병에 걸린; 슬픔에 잠긴; 고통받는. ¶ *the drought-stricken region* 한해(旱害) 지역 / ~ *with disease* 병에 걸린 / *terror-stricken* 공포에 휩싸인 / *a ~ heart* 슬픔에 잠긴 마음. [→strike]

stricken in years, very old. 몹시 늙은.

·strict [strikt] *adj.* **1** not allowing to turn away from standards or rules; severe; stern. 엄한; 엄중한; 엄격한. ¶ ~ *orders* 〔*rules*〕 엄중한 명령〔규칙〕 / *a ~ observer of rules* 규칙을 엄수하는 사람 / *keep ~ watch* 엄중히 감시하다 / *a ~ teacher* 엄격한 선생님 / *He is very ~ with his pupils.* 그는 학생들에게 매우 엄격하다. **2** accurate; precise. 정밀한; 정확한. ¶ *a ~ interpretation* 정확한 해석 / *a ~ statement of facts* 사실의 정확한 진술 / *the ~ truth* 엄정한 사실 / *a ~ search* 면밀한 조사 / *in the ~ sense* (*of the word*) (그 낱말의) 엄밀한 뜻으로는. **3** perfect; absolute. 완전한; 순전한; 절대의. ¶ ~ *neutrality* 엄정 중립 / *tell a secret in ~ confidence* 극비로 비밀을 이야기하다 / *live in ~ seclusion* 완전히 세상을 등지고 살다.

● **strict·ness** [´nis] *n.* [→strain[1]]

·strict·ly [stríktli] *adv.* in a strict manner; exactly; precisely. 엄격히; 정확히. ¶ *be ~ prohibited* 엄금되어 있다 / *Smoking is ~ forbidden.* 흡연은 엄격히 금지되어 있다.

strictly speaking, if the words are to be used in their strict sense. 엄밀히 말하자면. ¶ *Strictly speaking, you ought not to leave.* 엄밀히 말하자면, 너는 떠나서는 안 된다 / *It's not, ~ speaking, true.* 엄밀히 말해서 그것은 진실이 아니다.

stric·ture [stríktʃər] *n.* Ⓒ **1** 《usu. *pl.*》 a harsh or severe criticism. 비난; 혹평. ¶ *Strictures were passed on his conduct.* 그의 행동에 비난들이 쏟아졌다. **2** 《med.》 the narrowing of a duct, etc. so that liquid cannot pass. (요도 따위의) 협착(狹窄). [*strict*]

·strid·den [strídn] *v.* pp. of **stride.**

·stride [straid] *v.* (**strode, strid·den**) *vi.* **1** (P1,2A) walk with long steps. 큰 걸음으로 걷다; 활보하다. ¶ ~ *to the door* 문쪽으로 성큼성큼 걸어가다 / ~ *away* 성큼성큼 가 버리다 / *The tall man strode rapidly down the street.* 그 키 큰 사람은 거리를 성큼성큼 서둘러 내려갔다. **2** (P3) 《*across, over*》 pass over in one long step. (성큼) 넘어서다.

¶ ~ *over a fence* 울타리를 성큼 넘어서다 / ~ *across* 〔*over*〕 *a brook* 시내를 건너뛰다. —*vt.* (P6) **1** pass over (a ditch, etc.) in one step. …을 훌쩍 넘어가다. ¶ ~ *a ditch.* **2** sit or stand across (a fence, etc.) with the legs widely separated. …에 걸터앉다〔서다〕. ¶ ~ *a horse* 말에 걸터앉다.
—*n.* Ⓒ **1** a long step. 큰 걸음; 활보. ¶ *walk with big* 〔*rapid*〕 *strides* 성큼성큼 〔아주 서둘러〕 걷다 / *The child could not keep up with his father's* ~. 아이는 아버지의 걸음을 따라갈 수 없었다. **2** the length of one long step. 한 걸음의 폭. [E.]
at a stride, with one long step. 한 걸음으로.
《U.S.》 ***hit*** 〔《Brit.》 ***get into***〕 ***one's stride,*** reach one's normal speed or rate of activity. (일·운동 등이) 본궤도에 오르다; 제가락이 나다.
make great 〔***rapid***〕 ***strides,*** 《*in*》 make great progress. (…에) 장족의 진보를 이루다.
take something in one's stride, do something easily; not be affected by bad news, etc. …을 쉽게〔무난히〕 해결해 내다; …에 동요하지 않다.

stri·dent [stráidənt] *adj.* (of a sound) loud and rough; creaking. (소리 따위가) 삐걱거리는; 귀에 거슬리는. ¶ *a* ~ *voice* 귀에 거슬리는 목소리. ● **stri·dent·ly** [-li] *adv.* [L.]

***strife** [straif] *n.* ⓊⒸ a conflict; a fight; a struggle. 다툼; 싸움; 불화. ¶ *domestic* ~ 가정 불화 / *an internal* ~ 내분 / *be at* ~ (*with*) (…와) 다투고 있다; 불화하다 / *make* ~ 불화를〔반목을〕 일으키다. [L.]

⁝**strike** [straik] *v.* (**struck, struck** or 《*arch.*》 **strick·en**) *vt.* **1** (P6,13,14) give a blow to (someone or something); deliver (a blow); hit. …에 타격을 주다; (타격)을 가하다; 치다; 때리다. ¶ ~ *someone in the face* 아무의 얼굴을 때리다 / *He struck the ball with his racket.* 그는 라켓으로 공을 쳤다 / *He struck me on the head.* 그는 나의 머리를 쳤다 / *The speaker struck the table with his fist.* 연사는 주먹으로 책상을 쳤다 / *Lightning struck the barn.* 창고에 낙뢰하였다 / *Who struck the first blow?* 누가 싸움을 시작했느냐. **2** (P6,13) 《*into*》 thrust; stab; pierce. …을 찌르다; 꿰뚫다. ¶ ~ *someone to the heart with a dagger* = ~ *a dagger into someone's heart* 아무의 가슴에 단검을 찌르다 / *He struck the spurs in the horse.* 그는 말에 박차를 가했다. **3** (P6,13) bring (one thing) into contact with another; come into contact with (something) suddenly. …을 부딪치다; …에 충돌하다〔부딪다〕. ¶ ~ *one's head against the door* (*in the dark*) (어둠 속에서) 머리를 문에 부딪다 / *He struck his foot against a stone.* 그는 발을 돌에 부딪쳤다 / *We struck our heads together.* 우리는 서로 머리를 부딪쳤다 / *A car struck the wall.* 자동차가 벽을 들이받았다 / *The ball struck him in the eye.* 공이 그의 눈에 맞았다. **4** (P6) find or come upon; discover luckily. …와 마주치다; …을 (우연히) 발견하다. ¶ ~ *gold* 〔*oil*〕 금맥〔유맥〕을 발견하다 / ~ *a bad hotel* 안 좋은 호텔을 만나다 / ~ *a shortcut* 우연히 지름길을 발견하다 / *We struck the main road after a short drive.* 잠시 차를 달리니까 큰 도로가 나왔다. **5** (P6,7) (of an idea or a thought) occur suddenly; come to the mind of; occur to. (생각 따위가) …의 마음에 떠오르다. ¶ *A bright idea struck him.* 멋진 생각이 그의 머리에 떠올랐다. **6** (P6) affect the feelings of (someone); impress; influence. (아무)의 마음을 때리다〔끌다〕; (아무)에게 감명을 주다; 인상지우다. ¶ *He was struck with her beauty.* 그는 그녀의 아름다움에 마음이 끌렸다 / *How does the news* ~ *you?* 그 뉴스를 어떻게 생각하느냐 / *We were struck by the city's rapid modernization.* 우리는 그 도시의 급속한 근대화에 감명을 받았다 / *Something in his tone struck her disagreeably.* 그의 말투에는 그녀에게 불쾌한 인상을 주는 무언가가 있었다 / *The idea strikes me as being very practical.* 그 착상은 매우 실용적이라는 인상이 들게 했다. **7** (P13,18) put (terror, etc.) into someone's heart, etc.; fill or inspire with (fear, terror, etc.); put (someone) into a certain condition suddenly. (공포 따위)를 마음에 불어넣다〔주다〕; (아무)를 갑자기 …로 만들다. ¶ ~ *fear into someone* 아무에게 공포심을 불어넣다 / ~ *terror into someone's heart* 아무를 공포로 오싹하게 하다 / *The horrible scene struck a chill into my heart.* 그 무시무시한 광경으로 심장이 얼어붙는 것 같았다 / ~ *someone blind* 아무를 갑자기 장님으로 만들다 / *A stray bullet struck the soldier dead.* 유탄에 맞아 그 병사는 죽었다 / 《*fig.*》 *He was struck dumb with terror.* 그는 공포로 말을 잃었다. **8** (P6) (of illness, disaster, etc.) attack suddenly and violently. (질병 따위)가 갑자기 …을 엄습하다. ¶ *The plague struck the small town.* =*The small town was struck by the plague.* 전염병이 그 작은 마을을 휩쓸었다 / *He was struck with fever* 〔*consumption*〕. 그는 열병〔결핵〕에 걸렸다. **9** (P6) set (a match) on fire by rubbing it. (성냥)을 긋다. ¶ *He struck a match.* 그는 성냥을 그었다 / *The man struck a match and lit his cigar.* 그 사내는 성냥을 그어 여송연에 불을 붙였다. **10** (P6) make (a coin, a medal, etc.) by stamping. (화폐·메달 따위)를 주조〔자작〕하다; 찍어내다. ¶ ~ *a coin* 〔*medal*〕 / *A medal was struck to commemorate the world exposition.* 만국 박람회를 기념하기 위하여 메달이 제작되었다. **11** (P6) (of a clock) sound (the time). (시계가 시간)을 알리다; 치다. ¶ *The clock struck ten.* 시계가 열 시를 쳤다 / *a clock that strikes the quarters,* 15 분마다 울리는 시계 / *It has just struck four.* 이제 막 4 시를 쳤다. **12** (P6) lower; take down (a sail, a flag, a tent, etc.) (돛·기 따위)를 내리다; (천막)을 접다. ¶ ~ *one's flag* 기를 내려 항복하다 / ~ *camp*

〔*tents*〕 천막을 걷다; 캠프를 철수하다. **13** (P6,13) remove; cancel. …을 말소하다; 삭제하다. ¶ *You had better ~ the passage from the minutes.* 그 1절은 의사록에서 삭제하는 것이 좋겠다. **14** (P6) assume (an attitude or a pose); take up (an attitude). (포즈·태도)를 취하다. ¶ *~ an attitude* 거드름 피우다; 젠체하다 / *He likes to ~ a noble pose.* 그는 고상한 체하기를 좋아한다. **15** (P6) touch (keys, etc.) so as to produce a musical sound. (악기의 건반·현)을 쳐서 울리다; 연주하다. ¶ *~ a chord* 화음을 연주하다. **16** (P6) balance; calculate. …을 결산하다; 산출하다. ¶ *~ an average* 〔*a mean*〕 평균을 내다 / *He struck a balance.* 그는 수지(收支) 계정을 맞췄다〔결산했다〕. **17** (P6) agree on or conclude (a bargain, etc.). (계약 따위)를 체결〔타결〕하다; 확정짓다. ¶ *~ a bargain* 계약을 체결하다 / *~ a compromise* 타협점에 도달하다 / *We have struck an agreement.* 우리는 계약을 맺었다. **18** (P6) cause to penetrate the ground. 뿌리내리게 하다. ¶ *The plant has not struck root yet.* 그 식물은 아직 뿌리를 내리지 않았다.

— *vi.* (P1,2A,3) **1** give a blow; aim a blow. 치다; 때리다. ¶ *I struck at the ball, but missed.* 공을 쳤지만 빗맞았다 / 《*prov.*》 *Strike while the iron is hot.* 쇠는 달았을 때 쳐라. **2** be in contact with something; hit; collide. 부딪다; 충돌하다. ¶ *The two steamers struck in mid channel.* 두 척의 기선이 수로 중앙에서 충돌했다 / *The ship struck against* 〔*on*〕 *a rock.* 그 배는 바위에 부딪쳤다〔좌초했다〕. **3** attack. 공격하다. ¶ *The enemy struck at daybreak.* 적은 새벽에 공격을 개시했다 / *The rattlesnake stood ready to ~.* 방울뱀이 머리를 곧추세우고 공격 태세를 취했다. **4** (of a match) be set on fire by rubbing. (성냥이) 켜지다. ¶ *These matches won't ~.* 이 성냥은 불이 잘 켜지지 않는다. **5** (of a clock) sound the time. (시계 따위가 시간을) 울리다; 치다. ¶ *The clock strikes twelve times at noon.* 괘종 시계는 정오에 열두 번 친다 / *One o'clock has struck.* 한 시를 쳤다 / 《*fig.*》 *The hour has struck for him.* 그의 명줄이 끝날 때가 왔다. **6** cease from work until certain demands are met. 스트라이크를 하다; 파업하다. ¶ *~ for higher pay* 임금 인상을 요구하여 파업하다 / *The workers struck against the bad working condition.* 근로자들은 열악한 노동 환경에 항의하여 파업을 일으켰다. **7** direct one's course; proceed; advance. 나아가다; 향하다. ¶ *He struck northward.* 그는 북쪽을 향하여 나아갔다 / *~ through the wood* 숲속을 나아가다 / *We struck off on a new course.* 우리는 새 진로를 향해 출발했다 / *There the road struck to the east.* 거기서 길은 동쪽으로 꺾였다. **8** thrust through; penetrate. 꿰뚫다; 스며들다. ¶ *The cold was striking into his marrow.* 추위가 뼈 속에까지 스며들고 있었다 / *The light struck through the cloud.* 빛이 구름을 뚫고 지나갔다. **9** take down a flag, esp. as a sign of surrender or respect. (항복이나 경의의 뜻으로) 기를 내리다. **10** (of plants) send out roots. 뿌리를 내리다. **11** (of fish) grab at the bait. (고기가) 미끼를 물다; 입질하다.

It strikes me that .... I have just thought that .... …이라는 생각이 든다〔떠오른다〕.

strike a blow for, do one's best to win or protect. …을 위해 전력을 다하다.

strike a line 〔***path***〕, march; shape one's course. 진로를 잡다.

strike *someone* ***all of a heap,*** 《*colloq.*》 dumbfound. …을 어리둥절하게 만들다.

strike aside, turn aside (a weapon, a blow, etc.). …을 받아넘기다; 피하다.

strike at, aim at; aim a blow or attack at. …에게 덤벼들다; …을 공격하다. ¶ *He struck at me, but did not hit me.* 그는 내게 덤벼들었으나 때리지는 못했다.

strike at the root 〔***foundation***〕 ***of,*** attempt to destroy completely. …을 근절시키려고 하다; 뿌리째 뽑으려 하다.

strike down, knock down; kill. …을 때려 눕히다; 죽이다.

strike home, give an effective blow. 급소를 찌르다.

strike in, interrupt. …에 말참견하다. ¶ *Here someone struck in with a question.* 여기서 누군가가 질문을 하며 끼어들었다.

strike into, start suddenly. 갑자기 …하기 시작하다. ¶ *~ into a gallop* 갑자기 전속력으로 달리기 시작하다.

strike it rich, 《U.S.》 **a**) discover rich oil by boring. 석유를 찾아 내다. **b**) become rich suddenly. 뜻밖의 큰 성공을 거두다.

strike off, **a**) cut off (the head, etc.). (목 따위)를 베어 버리다〔내다〕. ¶ *~ off a chop* 고깃점을 베어 내다 / *~ off someone's head* 아무의 목을 자르다. **b**) remove (an item, a name, etc.) from a record. …을 빼 버리다. ¶ *I struck his name off the register.* 나는 등록부에서 그의 이름을 빼 버렸다. **c**) print (copies). …을 인쇄하다. ¶ *They struck off 500 copies of the book.* 그 책을 500부 인쇄했다. **d**) go in another way. 옆길로 빠지다〔가다〕.

strike on 〔***upon***〕, come upon suddenly and unexpectedly to. (생각 따위가) 갑자기 떠오르다. ¶ *strike on* 〔*upon*〕 *a good solution* 좋은 해결책이 떠오르다.

strike out, **a**) invent or contrive (a plan, a theory, etc.). …을 안출하다. ¶ *~ out a new idea* 〔*plan*〕 새 아이디어를〔계획을〕 생각해 내다. **b**) remove (something) from a record. …을 삭제하다. ¶ *Strike out any expressions that do not apply.* 해당되지 않는 표현에는 모두 삭제하시오. **c**) start in the direction of a certain place. …을 향해 나아가기 시작하다. ¶ *~ out for the shore* 해변을 향해 헤엄치기 시작하다 / *He is striking out left and right.* 그는 동분서주하고 있다. **d**) (in baseball) be put out or put (a batter)

out by pitching three strikes. 삼진하다; (타자)를 삼진시키다.
***strike out for oneself* [*on one's own*],** begin to work without aid; set up one's own business. 독력으로 일하기 시작하다; 자영 사업을 시작하다.
strike through, **a**) erase (a word) by drawing a line through it. 말소[삭제]하다. **b**) penetrate. 꿰뚫다. ¶ *a chill that struck even through the thick-layered suit* 두꺼운 천의 옷도 뚫고 스며든 추위.
strike up, **a**) begin playing, singing, etc. …을 연주[노래]하기 시작하다. ¶ *The brass band struck up.* 취주 악단이 연주를 시작했다 / *Then the band struck up a tune.* 그 다음에 악대가 곡을 연주하기 시작했다. **b**) begin (a friendship, etc.). (교제 따위)를 시작하다; 맺다. ¶ *~ up a friendship.*
—*n.* Ⓒ **1** a blow; the act of striking. 치기; 때리기; 타격. ¶ *the ~ of the clock* 시계 치는 소리 / *a lightning ~* 낙뢰; 천둥의 일격. **2** a new or unexpected discovery of rich oil, gold, etc.; great success. (석유·금 따위의) 발견; 대성공. ¶ *make a lucky ~* 생각잖은 행운을 만나다 / *an oil ~* 유맥[석유]의 발견. **3** ⒸⓊ a general refusal of workmen to work. 파업; 스트라이크. ¶ *go on ~* 파업에 들어가다 / *The workers are on ~.* 근로자들은 파업중이다 / *call* [*call off*] *a ~* 파업 개시[중지]를 선언하다. **4** 《baseball》 a nice pitched ball which a batter misses or hits foul. 스트라이크. **5** 《bowling》 the act of knocking down all the pins with one ball. 스트라이크《일구(一球)로 핀 전체를 쓰러뜨리는 일》. [E. =go]
break up a strike, take the places of strikers. 파업을 깨다.
strike of day, dawn. 새벽.
strike-bound [stráikbàund] *adj.* closed down by a strike. 파업으로 문을 닫은. ¶ *a ~ factory.*
strike-break·er [stráikbrèikər] *n.* a person who takes part in breaking up a strike of workers, either by working himself or by supplying workers for the employer. 파업을 깨는 사람[근로자](cf. *blackleg*).
:strike-out [stráikàut] *n.* Ⓒ 《baseball》 an out made by a batter to whom three strikes have been piched. 삼진(三振).
strik·er [stráikər] *n.* Ⓒ **1** a person or thing that strikes. 치는 사람[것]; 타자. **2** a worker on strike. 파업 참가자. **3** 《U.S. Army》 a soldier acting as an officer's servant. (장교 등의) 당번병.
:strik·ing [stráikiŋ] *adj.* **1** hitting. 치는; 공격하는. ¶ *a ~ clock* 자명종[괘종] 시계. **2** attracting attention; attractive; remarkable. 두드러진; 매력 있는; 주의를 끄는. ¶ *a ~ example* [*change*] 두드러진 예[변화] / *a ~ scene* 인상적인 광경 / *She is a lady of ~ beauty.* 그녀는 남의 이목을 끄는 미인이다. **3** being on strike. 파업중의. ¶ *~ workers.*
strik·ing·ly [stráikiŋli] *adv.* attractively; remarkably. 눈에 띄게; 두드러지게; 현저히. ¶ *a ~ beautiful woman* 절세의 미인.
:string [striŋ] *n.* Ⓒ **1** ⓊⒸ a thick thread; a fine cord; a very thin rope. 끈; 줄; 실. 參考 cord보다 가늘고 thread보다 굵은 것. ¶ *a piece of ~* 한 가닥의 끈 / *The package is tied with red ~.* 소포는 붉은 끈으로 묶여 있다. **2** ⓊⒸ anything used for tying or binding. (묶는) 끈; 노끈. ¶ *a shoe ~* 구두끈. **3** a set of things arranged on a cord. 실로 꿴 것; 한 꿰미. ¶ *a ~ of beads* [*dried fish*] 한 꿰미의 구슬[건어물] / *She wore a ~ of pearls around her neck.* 그녀는 목에 진주 목걸이를 하고 있었다. **4** a slender cord for musical instruments, etc. (악기·활 따위의) 현(弦). ¶ *the strings of a guitar* 기타의 현[줄] / *the A ~* (현악기의) A선. **5** a number of things in a line; a row; a series. 일련(一連); 일렬; 연속. ¶ *a ~ of lies* [*questions*] 거짓말[질문]의 연속 / *a ~ of successes* 잇따른 성공 / *a ~ of people* 일렬로 늘어선 사람들 / *in a long ~* 기다란 줄을 이루고 / *A ~ of cars sped by.* 자동차의 행렬이 질주해 지나갔다. **6** 《*the ~s*》 ⓐ musical instruments such as violins, cellos, etc. 현악기. ¶ *touch the strings* 현악기를 연주하다[타다]. ⓑ the players of such instruments. 현악기 연주자들. **7** a fiber of a plant. (식물의) 섬유. **8** 《*pl.*》 《U.S. *colloq.*》 a condition attached to an offer, etc. (제공 등을 할 때의) 부대 조건; 단서(但書). ¶ *an offer without strings* 부대 조건이 없는 제공 / *accept an offer with a ~ attached to it* 조건부의 제안을 수락하다 / *There were no strings attached to his offer.* 그의 제안에는 부대 조건이 없었다.
a second string to one's bow, what one relies upon alternatively. 다른 수단; 제2의 방법.
harp on one* [*the same*] *string, dwell on the same subject, idea, etc. 같은 것을 되풀이하다.
have someone on a string, have someone under one's control. …을 조종[지배]하다.
have two strings to one's bow, have an alternative way of doing or getting something. 제2의 방책이 있다; 만일의 대비가 있다.
pull* (*the*) *strings, use one's personal influence with someone secretly to gain advantage. 배후에서 조종하다; 막후 조종자가 되다.
the first string, a person or thing that main reliance is placed upon. 가장 신뢰하는 사람[것]; 제1의 방책[수단].
touch a string in someone's heart, excite a particular feeling in someone's heart. …의 심금을 울리다; …을 감동시키다.
—*v.* (**strung**) *vt.* **1** (P6) put or thread (something) on a string. …을 실에 꿰다; (염주 모양으로) 연이어 꿰다. ¶ *~ pearls on a thread* 진주를 실에 꿰다 / *beads strung on*

wire 철사에 꿴 구슬 / *The child is stringing beads.* 아이는 구슬을 실에 꿰고 있다. **2** (P6) provide (something) with strings. (현악기)에 줄[현]을 매다; (활)에 시위를 얹다[메우다]; (라켓)에 줄을 매다. ¶ ~ *a tennis racket* / *He strung his bow.* 그는 활에 시위를 메웠다. **3** (P6) tune the strings of (a musical instrument) by tightening, etc. (악기)의 현을 죄다; 조율하다. **4** (P7) 《often in *passive*》 make (someone) tense or excited. (아무를) 긴장시키다; 흥분케 하다. ¶ *a highly strung person* 매우 민감한 사람 / *be highly strung* 크게 흥분하고 있다 / ~ *oneself up to a high pitch of expectancy* 큰 기대로 긴장하다 / *They were all strung up before the examination.* 그들은 시험을 앞두고 매우 긴장되어 있었다. **5** (P6) remove the strings or fibers from (beans, etc.). (콩 따위)의 줄기[덩굴손, 섬유]를 없애다[따다]. ¶ *She strung the beans.* 그녀는 콩의 줄기를 땄다. **6** (P6) arrange (something) in a row. …을 줄지어 늘어놓다; 배열하다. ¶ ~ *out scouts along the road* 정찰병을 연도에 배치하다. **7** (P6) stretch; extend. (밧줄 따위)를 치다; 펴다; (끈 따위)로 묶다. ¶ ~ *a cable* 케이블을 팽팽히 치다. **8** (P6,7,13) tie or hang with a string or rope. (끈·밧줄 따위로) 묶다; 매달다. ¶ *string pictures on a wall* 벽에 그림을 걸다 / *Lamps were strung up across the street.* 길을 가로질러 등들이 걸려 있었다. —*vi.* (P1) **1** form into a string; (of glue) become stringy. 실이 되다; 실처럼 되다. **2** move along in a line. 줄지어 나아가다. [E.]

string** someone **along, 《*colloq.*》 fool; deceive. …을 놀리다; 속이다.

***string along with** someone,* follow faithfully; go along with. 아무를 충실히 따르다.

string out, 《U.S. *colloq.*》 prolong; extend. …을 잡아늘이다; 연장하다. ¶ *The parade strung out for miles.* 행렬은 수 마일 뻗쳤다.

string up, 《*colloq.*》 kill (someone) by hanging. …을 교살하다.

string-bean [stríŋbìːn] *n.* 《U.S.》 the unripe pod of a bean plant; the plant itself. 꼬투리째 먹는 콩《덜 익은 깍지 강낭콩 따위》.

stringed [striŋd] *adj.* **1** (of musical instruments) having strings. 현(絃)이 있는. ¶ *a ~ instruments* 현악기 / *four-stringed,* 4현(絃)의. **2** produced by strings. 현악기에 의한. ¶ ~ *music* 현악.

strin·gen·cy [stríndʒənsi] *n.* Ⓤ **1** strictness; severity. 엄중; 엄격. ¶ *the ~ of the rules* 규칙의 엄격함. **2** scarcity, esp. of money. (금융 따위의) 경색(梗塞). ¶ *monetary ~.* **3** convincing force of reasoning. (학설 따위의) 설득력; 박력. [↓]

strin·gent [stríndʒənt] *adj.* **1** strict; rigid. 엄중한; 엄격한. ¶ ~ *rules* 엄격한 규칙 / ~ *laws against speeding* 과속에 대한 엄격한 법률. **2** short in loan or investment money; tight. (금융 따위가) 경색된; 핍박한. ¶ *a ~ stock market* 경색된 주식 시장 / ~ *economic conditions* 경색된 경제 사정. **3** convincing. 설득력 있는. ¶ *a ~ argument.* [→strict]

strin·gent·ly [stríndʒəntli] *adv.* in a stringent manner. 엄중히; 절박하여.

string·er [stríŋər] *n.* **1** one who or that which strings. (활)시위를 메우는 장색; (악기의) 현을 매는 기술자. **2** 《archit.》 a long timber; a tie-beam. 세로보. **3** 《railway》 a longitudinal sleeper. 세로로 깐 침목. **4** 《U.S.》 a part-time newspaper correspondent. 지방 통신원. [*string*]

string·y [stríŋi] *adj.* (**string·i·er, string·i·est**) **1** like a string or strings. 실[끈] 같은. ¶ ~ *weeds* 실 같은 잡초 / ~ *hair* 실같이 굵은 머리칼. **2** full of strings; having hard fibers; tough. 섬유질의; 힘줄이 많은. ¶ *a ~ piece of meat* 힘줄이 많은 고깃점. **3** having good muscular development. 근골(筋骨)이 건장한; 힘줄이 툭툭 불거진. ¶ *a ~ youth* 체격이 건장한 청년. **4** forming strings. 실처럼 되는; 끈적끈적한. ● **string·i·ness** [-nis] *n.*

:strip[1] [strip] *v.* (**stripped** or *rarely* **stript, strip·ping**) *vt.* (P6,7,13) **1** 《*from, of*》 take off the covering of (something); undress. (껍질 따위)를 벗기다; …을 벌거벗기다. ¶ ~ *the bark from the oak* =~ *the oak of its bark* 떡갈나무의 껍질을 벗기다 / ~ *off one's shirt* 셔츠를 벗다 / ~ *the paint from a wall* 벽에서 페인트를 벗겨 내다 / ~ *someone maked* [*to the skin*] 아무를 벌거벗기다 / *He stripped to the waist.* 그는 웃통을 벗어제쳤다. **2** ⓐ take away or clear out (furniture, etc.) from a house, etc. (가구 따위를) 없애다; 제거하다; 떼어내다. ¶ ~ *a room of its furniture* (비우기 위해) 방에서 가구를 끄집어 내다 / ~ *a house of its contents* 집에서 세간 등을 모두 들어내다. ⓑ take away (fruit, offshoots, etc.). (과일 등)을 모두 따다. ¶ *We stripped the fruit from a trees.* 우리는 나무에서 과일을 모두 땄다. **3** 《*of*》 rob; take away honors, titles, possessions, etc. away from (someone or something). …에서 빼앗다; 강탈하다; …에게서 명예[직함] 따위를 박탈하다. ¶ ~ *someone of all his honors* 아무에게서 온갖 명예를 박탈하다 / *He stripped me of all my belongings.* 그는 나의 모든 재산을 강탈했다. **4** break the thread of (a gear, bolt, etc.). (나사산)을 닳게 하다. **5** draw the last milk from (a cow). (젖소의 젖)을 다 짜내다. —*vi.* (P1) **1** take off one's clothes; undress. 옷을 벗다; 벌거벗다. ¶ ~ *off* 옷을 벗어 던지다 / ~ *for a bath* 목욕하려고 옷을 벗다. **2** separate; come off. (껍질이) 벗겨지다. ¶ *Bananas ~ easily.* 바나나는 껍질이 잘 벗겨진다. **3** lose the thread of a screw, etc. (나사산 등이) 닳다; 마모되다. [E.]

:strip[2] [strip] *n.* Ⓒ **1** a long, narrow, flat piece of cloth, land, tape, etc. (헝겊·판자·토지 등의) 길고 가느다란 조각. ¶ *a comic ~* (신문 따위의) 연속 만화 / *a ~ of wood* 기다

란 나뭇조각 / *in strips* 길고 가느다란 조각이 되어 / *use a ~ of paper as a bookmark* 좁다란 종이를서표(書標)로 사용하다 / *He bought a ~ of land along the coast.* 그는 해변에 연해 있는 길고 가느다란 땅을 매입했다. **2** a place for airplanes to take off and land; an airstrip. 활주로. [E.]

***stripe** [straip] *n.* Ⓒ **1** a long, narrow band. 줄무늬; 줄. ¶ *stripes on a soldier's trousers* 군인의 바지에 있는 세로 줄 / *The material is blue with yellow stripes.* 그 천은 하늘색 바탕에 노랑 줄무늬가 있다 / *A zebra has stripes.* 얼룩말은 줄무늬가 있다. **2** 《*pl.*》 a number of pieces of braid sewn on a uniform showing rank, length of service, etc. 수장(袖章); 견장(肩章). ¶ *The stripes on a sergeant's sleeve show his rank.* 하사관의 수장은 그의 계급을 나타낸다. **3** 《*arch.*》 a blow with a whip; a welt. 채찍질; 채찍 자국. **4** kind; type. 형(型); 종류. ¶ *a diplomat of that ~* 그러한 형의 외교관 / *He is a scholar of quite a different ~.* 그는 아주 별난 학자다 / *They are people of the same ~.* 그들은 같은 형의 사람들이다.

***get* 〔*lose*〕 *one's* stripes,** be promoted from 〔degraded to〕 the ranks. 승진하다〔강등되다〕.

— *vt.* (P6) mark (something) with stripes. …에 줄을 붙이다〔달다〕; 줄무늬를 넣다. [Du.]

striped [straipt] *adj.* having stripes. 줄무늬가〔줄이〕 있는.

strip·ling [stríplıŋ] *n.* Ⓒ a youth just passing from boyhood to manhood. 애송이; 풋내기; 젊은이. [*stripe*]

***strive** [straiv] *vi.* (**strove, striv·en**) **1** (P1,3,4) make great efforts; try hard. 노력하다; 애쓰다. ¶ *~ to understand* 이해하려고 노력하다 / *He strives for success.* 그는 성공하려고 노력한다 / *I ~ to convince him.* 그를 납득시키려고 애쓴다. **2** (P1,3) struggle; fight. 싸우다; 다투다. ¶ *~ together =~ with each other* 서로 겨루다 / *They strove against tyranny.* 그들은 폭정에 대항하여 싸웠다. [G. *streben* endeavor]

striv·en [strívən] *v.* pp. of **strive.**

strode [stroud] *v.* p. of **stride.**

:stroke[1] [strouk] *n.* Ⓒ **1** the act of striking with a hammer, a weapon, etc.; a blow. 치기; 타격; 일격. ¶ *a finishing ~* 최후의 일격 / *a ~ of lightning* 낙뢰(落雷) / *receive 20 strokes of the lash* 스무 대의 채찍을 맞다 / *He drove in the nail with one ~ of the hammer.* 그는 망치로 못을 단번에 때려 박았다 / 《*prov.*》 *Little strokes fell great oaks.* 열 번 찍어 안 넘어가는 나무 없다. **2** the sound of a striking clock. 시계〔종〕 치는 소리. ¶ *on the ~ of two* 두 시를 치면 / *They arrived there at the ~ of seven.* 그들은 시계가 7시를 칠 때 거기에 도착했다 / *The bell hammered out 108 strokes.* 종은 108번 울렸다. **3** a beat of the heart. 심장의 고동. ¶ *the ~ of the pulse.* 맥박. **4** a mark or movement made by a pen, a brush, etc. (펜·붓 따위의) 일필; 한 획; 필체. ¶ *a fine* 〔*thick*〕 *~* 가느다란〔굵다란〕 획필 / *a character of three strokes,* 3획의 글자 / *dash off a picture with a few strokes* 두서너 번 붓을 놀려 그림을 완성하다 / *He painted with bold strokes.* 그는 힘찬 필치로 그림을 그렸다 / *He writes with a thick ~.* 그는 굵은 필체로 글씨를 쓴다. **5** a vigorous effort or attempt to accomplish something. 목적 달성을 위한 노력〔시도〕. ¶ *a bold ~ for freedom* 자유를 얻으려는 대담한 시도〔노력〕 / *He refused to do a ~ of work.* 그는 아무 일도 하려들지 않았다. **6** any particularly successful, brilliant effort or its achievement. 솜씨; 공훈. ¶ *a ~ of genius* 천재적 솜씨 / *a fine ~ of business* 멋진 거래 솜씨 / *a great ~ of diplomacy* 훌륭한 외교 수완. **7** a way of swimming; a single movement of the arms, hands, oars, etc. 수영법; (팔·손 따위의) 한번 놀리기; (노를) 한 번 젓기. ¶ *He swims the breast ~.* 그는 평영으로 헤엄친다 / *The boat is gaining at every ~.* 보트는 한 번 저을 때마다 전진한다. **8** a sudden action or event. 갑작스런 행위; 뜻밖의 일. ¶ *a ~ of misfortune* 불행 / *He made a fortune by a ~ of good luck.* 그는 뜻밖의 행운으로 재산을 모았다. **9** a sudden attack of disease. 발작. ¶ *a ~ of apoplexy* 뇌일혈; 뇌졸중 / *He had a ~ of paralysis.* 그는 중풍에 걸렸다. **10** the rower who leads the rate of rowing. 보트의 정조수(整調手).

a fine stroke, a great success. 큰 성공.

a stroke above, 《*colloq.*》 the upper hand. (…보다) 한 수 위인. ¶ *be a ~ above someone* 아무보다 한 수 위이다.

at a stroke, at a blow; at one time; by an effort. 일격으로; 즉각; 일거에.

keep stroke, make strokes or row in rhythm. 박자에 맞춰 노를 젓다.

stroke and strife, riot. 난동; 소란.

with a stroke of the pen, by merely signing a document. 일필 휘지로.

— *vt.* (P6) act as a stroke for (a boat). (보트의) 정조수 노릇을 하다. ¶ *Who stroked the Cambridge crew?* 누가 케임브리지 팀의 정조수 역할을 했느냐. ● **strok·er** [⌐ər] *n.* [→strike]

:stroke[2] [strouk] *vt.* (P7) rub (something) gently with the hand. …을 쓰다듬다; 어루만지다. ¶ *~ one's kitten* 새끼고양이를 쓰다듬다 / *~ down one's hair* 머리를 쓰다듬어 내리다 / *She likes to ~ her dog.* 그녀는 자기 개 쓰다듬기를 좋아한다.

stroke** someone **down, soothe his anger. 아무를 달래다.

stroke** someone **the wrong way, make him angry. 아무를 성나게 하다.

— *n.* Ⓒ a soft, repeated movement of the hand, etc. in one direction. 쓰다듬기; 어루만지기. [↑]

***stroll** [stroul] *vi.* (P1,2A) walk about in a leisurely manner; wander from place to place. 산책〔소요〕하다; 여기저기 슬슬 거닐다. ¶ *Let's ~ up toward the cabin.* 오두막을 향해 천천히 거닐기로 하자. — *vt.* (P6) walk leisurely along or through (a place). …을 한가로이 거닐다; …을 산책〔소요〕하다. ¶ *We strolled the broad avenue.* 우리는 큰길을 한가로이 거닐었다. — *n.* Ⓒ a leisurely walk. 한가로이 거닐기; 산책. ¶ *go for* 〔*take*〕 *a ~* 산책하다. [? G.]

stroll·er [stróulər] *n.* Ⓒ **1** a wanderer. 방랑자. **2** a strolling actor or performer. 순회 공연자〔연예인〕. **3** a light carriage in which very small children sit. 유모차.

:strong [strɔ(:)ŋ, strɑŋ] *adj.* **1** having physical power; tough; in good health; soud. 힘센; 기운이 있는; 건강한; 튼튼한. ¶ *a ~ boxer* 힘센 권투 선수 / *a ~ man* 튼튼한 사람 / *~ arms* 힘센 팔 / *~ eyes* 시력이 좋은 눈 / *~ in body* 신체가 튼튼하여 / *I feel stronger today.* 오늘은 기운이 더 나는 것 같다 / *A ~ man can lift heavy things.* 힘센 사람은 무거운 물건을 들어 올릴 수 있다 / *He is as ~ as a horse* 〔*bull*〕. 그는 대단히 튼튼하다. **2** having great mental or moral power; intellectually powerful; firm. (정신력·신념 따위가) 강한; 강력한; (지력(知力)이) 강한. ¶ *~ nerves* 강인한 신경 / *a ~ faith* 강한 신념 / *a ~ brain* 강한 지력 / *a ~ imagination* 강한 상상력 / *~ affection* 강한 애정 / *~ in faith* 신앙심이 강한 / *be ~ under temptation* 유혹을 당해도 끄떡도 하지 않다 / *He is a man of ~ will.* 그는 의지가 강한 사람이다. **3** ⓐ not easily broken or damaged; tough; firm. 쉽게 깨지지〔부서지지, 줄지〕 않는; 강인한; 견고한. ¶ *~ cloth* 질긴〔잘 해지지 않는〕 천 / *a ~ foundation* 견고한 기초 / *~ chains* 〔*cords*〕 잘 끊어지지 않는〔튼튼한〕 체인 〔코드〕 / *~ china* 잘 깨지지 않는 도자기 / *Is the branch ~ enough to hold you?* 그 나뭇가지는 네가 매달려도 괜찮겠느냐. ⓑ difficult to take; well protected. 점령하기 어려운; 튼튼히 방어된. ¶ *a ~ castle* 〔*fortress, town*〕 튼튼히 방어된 성곽〔요새, 도시〕. **4** producing a great effect; able or tending to persuade or convince. (의론·증거 따위가) 유력한; 힘찬; (수단 따위가) 강경한. ¶ *~ evidence* 유력한 증거 / *a ~ expression* 〔*literary style*〕 힘찬 표현〔문체〕 / *~ words* 격렬한 언사; 독설 / *He made a ~ speech.* 그는 힘이 담긴 연설을 했다 / *~ remedies* 〔*opinions*〕 강경한 대책〔의견〕 / *He took ~ measures.* 그는 강경 수단을 취했다. **5** great in numbers and wealth; having influence; sufficient. 다수의; 유력한; 세력이 있는; 병력 …의. ¶ *the ~ force of the enemy* 막강한 적군 / *a ~ nation* 〔*state*〕 강국 / *~ national economy* 강력한 국가 경제 / *a ~ bank* 〔*candidate*〕 유력한 은행〔후보자〕 / *~ in number* 인원수가 많은 / *an army 200,000 ~* 병력 20만의 군대 / *How many ~ are they? —They are 50 ~.* "그들은 인원수가 몇 명이나 되느냐". — "50 명이다." **6** having a large amount or proportion of the essential quality. (성분 따위가) 강한; 강도의. ¶ *a ~ color* 〔*shadow*〕 짙은 색깔〔그림자〕 / *~ perfume* 강한 향수 / *a ~ voice* 굵고 큰 목소리 / *~ black coffee* 진한 블랙 커피 / *~ beer* 독한〔강한〕 맥주 / *a ~ adhesive* 〔*detergent*〕 강력 접착제〔세제〕 / *a ~ taste of salt* 지독히 짠 맛. **7** affecting one of the senses powerfully; intense. (감각에 대한 자극이) 강한. ¶ *a ~ light* 강렬한 빛 / *a ~ odor* 지독한 냄새 / *a ~ flavor* 아주 진한 맛 / *~ onions* 〔*butter*〕 냄새가 독한 양파〔버터〕. **8** deeply earnest; passionate. 열심인; 열렬한. ¶ *a man of ~ affections and ~ dislikes* 기호(嗜好)가 매우 까다로운 사람 / *a ~ advocate* 열성적인 옹호자 / *be ~ against compromise* 타협에 강렬히 반대하다 / *I gave ~ support to him.* 그에게 큰〔열렬한〕 지원을 해 주었다. **9** (of the wind, the tide, etc.) blowing or moving forcefully. (바람 따위가) 세찬; 강한. ¶ *a ~ wind* 세찬 바람 / *~ tide* 거센 (조수의) 물결. **10** 《*colloq.*》《*in*》 having special ability. (자신 있게) 잘 하는; 유능한. ¶ *one's ~ point* 장점 / *He is ~ in physics.* 그는 물리를 잘 한다 / *He is not ~ on literature.* 그는 문학을 잘 못한다. **11** 《comm.》 rising to higher prices. 오름세〔강세〕의; 등귀하는. ¶ *a ~ market* 강세의 시장 / *Prices are ~.* 시세는 오름세다 / *The silk market is very ~.* 비단의 시세는 강한 오름세를 나타내고 있다. **12** 《gram.》 (of verbs) forming the variation of tense by a change of vowel within the root of the word; irregular. 강변화의; 불규칙 변화의. 參考 give, gave, given 따위.

a strong situation, a conjuncture in a play or story calculated to move an audience deeply. 감격적인 장면.

by the strong arm 〔***hand***〕, by force. 힘으로; 우격다짐으로.

strong breath, ill-smelling breath. 구린내 나는 입김.

take strong root, become rooted strongly. 든든히 뿌리 박다.

the strong, those who have might on their side. 강자(強者)들.

the strong(er) sex, the male sex. 남성.

— *adv.* powerfully; strongly. 강하게; 강력하게. ¶ *Suspicions have run ~.* 의심이 지금도 강하게 남아 있다. [E.]

come 〔***go***〕 ***it strong,*** 《*colloq.*》 go to great lengths in something. 정도가 지나치다; 극단으로 흐르다. ¶ *That's coming it a bit ~.* 그것은 좀 지나친데 그래.

going strong, 《*colloq.*》 **a**) continuing race or other occupation vigorously. 기운차게〔활발히〕 하고 있는. ¶ *The book is going ~.* 그 책은 지금 인기가 한창이다. **b**) of good health or trim. 건강한; 튼튼한. ¶ *He is still going ~.* 그는 아직 건강하다.

strong·box [strɔ́(:)ŋbɑ̀ks, strɑ́ŋ- / -bɔ̀ks]

n. Ⓒ a strongly made box to hold money, jewels, etc. 금고; 귀중품 보관 상자.

strong·hold [strɔ́(:)ŋhòuld, strɑ́ŋ-] *n.* Ⓒ **1** a place or building which is built to stand against the attack of enemies; a fortress; a safe place of refuge. 성채; 요새; 안전한 장소. ¶ *a robbers' ~ in the mountains* 산적의 성채. **2** a central place of support for a certain idea or cause. 중심점; 거점. ¶ *the ~ of superstition* 미신의 거점.

strong language [ˊ ˊ-] *n.* forcible expressions of abuse. 심한 말; 욕설.

:strong·ly [strɔ́(:)ŋli, strɑ́ŋ-] *adv.* in a strong manner; severely; with force. 강하게. ¶ *be ~ against it* 그것에 강경히 반대하다 / *This bridge is ~ built.* 이 다리는 견고하게 건설되었다 / *I ~ advise you to meet him.* 그를 꼭 만나도록 해라.

strong·man [strɔ́(:)ŋmæ̀n] *n.* (*pl.* **-men** [-mèn]) a political leader who controls by force; dictator. (힘으로 지배하는) 정치적 지도자; 독재자.

strong meat [ˊ ˊ] *n.* doctrine acceptable only to persons of developed intelligence. 어려운 교의(敎義).

strong-mind·ed [strɔ́(:)ŋmáindid, strɑ́ŋ-] *adj.* having a strong mind; determined. 단호한; 결단력이 있는. ¶ *I need a ~ boy.* 나는 심지가 굳은 소년이 필요하다.

strong waters [ˊ ˊ-] *n.* 《*arch.*》 alcoholic spirit. 술.

stron·ti·um [strɑ́nʃiəm, -tiəm / strɔ́n-] *n.* Ⓤ a hard chemical element resembling calcium, found only in combination. 스트론튬《칼슘 비슷한 금속 원소의 하나》. [Place]

strop [strɑp / strɔp] *n.* Ⓒ a leather strip used for sharpening razors. 혁지(革砥). — *vt.* (**stropped, strop·ping**) (P6) sharpen (a razor) on a strop. …을 혁지로 날을 세우다(갈다). [→strap]

***strove** [strouv] *v.* p. of **strive.**

:struck [strʌk] *v.* p. and pp. of **strike.** — *adj.* closed or affected by a labor strike. 파업으로(스트라이크로) 폐쇄된. ¶ *a ~ factory* 파업 중인 공장. [→strike]

struc·tur·al [strʌ́ktʃərəl] *adj.* **1** of or relating to structure. 구조상의; 건축 구조상의. ¶ *the ~ beauty of a building* 건물의 구조상의 아름다움 / *Structural changes were made to the city hall.* 시청 건물에 대한 구조상의 변경이 행해졌다. **2** used in building. 건축용의. ¶ *~ steel* (*iron*) 건축용 철강(철재). ● **struc·tur·al·ly** [-i] *adv.* [↓]

:struc·ture [strʌ́ktʃər] *n.* **1** Ⓤ the manner of building; construction. 건조(建造); 구축(술). **2** Ⓤ the form or arrangement of all the parts or elements. 구조; 조립; 구성. ¶ *the ~ of a house* (*a machine, an organ, an poem*) 가옥(기계, 기관(器官), 시)의 구조 / *the existing ~ of society* 사회의 현존 기구 / *the ~ of an English sentence* 영어의 문장 구조 / *a pyramidal ~* 피라미드형 구조 / *Today the class ~ of the nation is changing.* 오늘날 국가의 계급 구성은 변해가고 있다. **3** Ⓒ something built; a building; any complex whole. 건조(건축)물; 조직물. ¶ *the oldest wooden ~* 가장 오래된 목조 건축물 / *The human body is a complex ~.* 인간의 신체는 복합적 조직물이다. [L. *struo* build, construct]

:strug·gle [strʌ́gəl] *vi.* (P1,2A,3,4) **1** 《*against, with*》 make great efforts to escape from a grasp, danger, etc.; contend. 싸우다; 맞붙어 대결하다(대적하다); 발버둥이치다; 버둥거리다. ¶ *~ against the superior numbers* 대군과 싸우다 / *~ against the desire for sleep* 졸음과 싸우다 / *~ with mathematical problems* 수학 문제와 씨름하다 / *Animals ~ to survive.* 동물은 생존을 위해 싸운다 / *The small boat struggled against the violent current of the river.* 조그마한 보트가 강의 격류와 싸우고 있었다. **2** fight eagerly against difficulties; strive; labor. 열심히 노력하다; 분투하다; 애쓰다. ¶ *~ to get a position in society* 출세하려고 노력하다 / *~ for breath* 호흡을 하려고 헐떡이다 / *~ for existence* 생활(생존)을 위해 애쓰다 / *He struggled to overcome his bad habits.* 그는 악습을 극복하기 위해 무진 애썼다. **3** make one's way with great efforts. 헤치고(애쓰며) 나아가다. ¶ *~ through a crowd* 군중 속을 헤치고 나아가다 / *~ on in life* 힘겹게 살아나가다.
— *n.* Ⓒ **1** a great effort; a hard piece of work. 굉장한 노력; 힘든 일; 중노동. ¶ *the ~ for existence* 생존 경쟁 / *He had a hard ~ to get his work done in time.* 일을 제때에 마치려고 굉장한 노력을 했다. **2** a fight; a strong effort with the body. 싸움; 몸싸움. ¶ *a violent ~ to escape* 도망치려는 처절한 몸부림 / *a sharp ~ with the police* 경찰과의 격렬한 몸싸움 / *a ~ over power* 권력 투쟁 / *His life was a hard ~ against poverty.* 그의 일생은 빈곤과의 싸움이었다. [E.]

strug·gler [strʌ́glər] *n.* Ⓒ a person who struggles. 몸부림치는 사람; 노력가.

strug·gling [strʌ́gliŋ] *adj.* **1** engaged in a struggle. 분투(고투)하는. **2** working hard to overcome poverty. 생활고와 싸우는. ¶ *a ~ painter* 생활고와 싸우는 화가.

strum [strʌm] *vt., vi.* (**strummed, strum·ming**) (P6; 1,2A,3) play on (a guitar, etc.) unskillfully or carelessly. (현악기를) 서투르게(아무렇게나) 치다(켜다, 타다). ¶ *~ on the piano* 피아노를 서투르게(아무렇게나) 치다 / *He used to ~ a banjo.* 그는 밴조를 내키는 대로 습관적으로 통탕거리고는 하였다. — *n.* Ⓒ 《*sing.* only》 an act or a sound of strumming. (현악기를) 서투르게 켜기; 그 소리. [→thrum]

strum·pet [strʌ́mpit] *n.* Ⓒ a prostitute. 매춘부. [E.]

***strung** [strʌŋ] *v.* p. and pp. of **string.**

strut[1] [strʌt] *vi.* (**strut·ted, strut·ting**) (P1,2A) walk in a vain, proud or self-satisfied manner. 뽐내며〔으스대며〕 걷다. ¶ ~ *upon the stage* 무대 위를 뽐내며 걷다 / *The bully strutted around the room.* 골목대장은 으스대며 방 안을 걸어다녔다. — *n.* Ⓒ a strutting walk. 뽐낸 걸음걸이. [E.]

strut² [strʌt] *n.* Ⓒ a piece of wood or metal used in a framework for resisting pressure. 지주(支柱); 버팀목. — *vt.* (**strut·ted, strut·ting**) (P6) support (something) with struts. …을 지주로 받치다. [E.]

strych·nine [stríkni(:)n, -nain] *n.* Ⓤ 《chem.》 a powerful poison obtained from certain plants, used in medicine, esp. as a stimulant for the nerves and the heart. 스트리키닌《신경 흥분제》. [Gk. = night-shade]

stub [stʌb] *n.* Ⓒ **1** the short remaining part of a tree after it has been cut down; a stock. (나무의) 그루터기. **2** (of a cigarette, a pencil, etc.) any short remaining piece. 쓰다 남은 토막《연필의 동강, 담배의 꽁초 따위》. **3** the part of a check, bill, ticket, etc. kept as a record. (수표책 따위의) 떼어 주고 남은 쪽; 부본(副本). **4** a pen with a short and not sharp point. 뭉툭해진 펜촉.
— *vt.* (**stubbed, stub·bing**) **1** (P6) clear (land) of stumps, roots, etc. 그루터기·뿌리 따위를 제거하다. **2** (P6,13) strike (one's toe or foot) against something hard. (발부리를) 그루터기〔돌〕 따위에 부딪치다. [E.]
stub out, put out (a cigarette) by pressing its lighted end against something. (피우던 궐련을) 비벼 끄다.

stub·ble [stʌ́bəl] *n.* Ⓒ **1** the short remaining piece of grain left standing after the harvest. 벼〔밀〕 따위의 그루터기. **2** any short rough growth; a short growth of beard. 그루터기 모양의 것; 짧은 턱수염; 다박나룻. ¶ *He had three days' ~ on his chin.* 그는 3일간이나 자란 짧은 턱수염이 나 있었다. [L. *stipula*]

***stub·born** [stʌ́bərn] *adj.* **1** fixed in an opinion, etc.; determined; persistent; (unreasonably) obstinate; firm. 단호한; 불굴의; 완강한; 완고한. ¶ ~ *courage* 불굴의 용기 / *a ~ refusal* 단호한 거절 / ~ *resistance* 완강한 저항 / *a ~ child* 말을 안 듣는 (고집 센) 아이 / *a ~ face* 고집이 센 (성격을 나타내는) 얼굴 / *a ~ opponent of foreign aid* 해외 원조에 단호히 반대하는 사람 / *He is as ~ as a mule.* 그 녀석은 정말로 고집이 세다. **2** hard to treat, manage or handle. 다루기 어려운〔힘든〕. ¶ ~ *problems* 난제 / *a ~ horse* 다루기 어려운〔힘든〕 말 / *a ~ pain* 좀처럼 가시지 않는 아픔 / *Facts are ~ things.* 사실이란 왜곡될 수 없는 것; 사실이란 이론대로 이루어지는 것이 아니다. [*stub*]

stub·born·ly [stʌ́bərnli] *adv.* in a stubborn manner. 완고히; 완고하게.

stub·born·ness [stʌ́bərnnis] *n.* Ⓤ the state or quality of being stubborn. 고집; 불굴(不屈); 완고함.

stub·by [stʌ́bi] *adj.* (**-bi·er, -bi·est**) **1** short, thick, and stiff. 땅딸막한; 짧고 굵은. ¶ *a ~ bit of pencil* 짧은 몽당연필 / *The old man has ~ fingers.* 그 노인은 손가락이 짧고 굵다 / *He wears a ~ beard.* 그는 턱수염이 짧고 억세다. **2** covered with stubble(s). 그루터기 투성이의. [*stub*]

stuc·co [stʌ́kou] *n.* ⓊⒸ (*pl.* **-cos** or **-coes**) a kind of plaster used for covering walls, etc. 치장 벽토. — *vt.* (P6) cover (something) with stucco. …에 치장 벽토를 바르다. [Teut.]

***stuck** [stʌk] *v.* p. and pp. of **stick.**

stuck-up [stʌ́kʌ́p] *adj.* 《colloq.》 very pleased with oneself; conceited. 거만한; 건방진. [→stick]

stud¹ [stʌd] *n.* Ⓒ **1** a large-headed nail, knob, etc. projecting from a surface. 장식못; 장식용 징. ¶ *He wears a belt with silver studs.* 그는 장식용 은색 못을 박은 벨트를 차고 있다. **2** a kind of small button used as a fastener. 장식 단추. **3** an upright piece in walls to which other pieces of wood are nailed. 샛기둥.
— *vt.* (**stud·ded, stud·ding**) (P13) **1** decorate or set (something) with studs. …을 못〔징〕으로 장식하다. **2** set thickly. …을 점점이 박다; 산재시키다. ¶ *a box studded with gems* 보석이 점점이 박힌 상자 / *an iron-studded door* 장식용 못이 점점이 박힌 문. **3** be scattered over (a place, etc.). …에 흩어지다; 점재해 있다. ¶ *a plain studded with farms* 여기저기 농장이 점재해 있는 평야 / *a sea studded with islands* 섬이 산재해 있는 바다. [E. = post]

stud² [stʌd] *n.* Ⓒ **1** a group of horses kept for breeding, racing, etc. 말 떼. **2** the place where such horses are kept. 말의 사육장. **3** 《U.S.》 a studhorse. 종마(種馬). [E.]

stud·book [stʌ́dbùk] *n.* Ⓒ the register of horses' pedigrees. (말의) 혈통 대장; 마적부(馬籍簿). [↑]

:stu·dent [stjúːdənt] *n.* Ⓒ **1** a person who studies. 연구가; 학자. ¶ *a ~ of folklore* 민화(民話) 연구가 / *a ~ of life* 인생의 탐구자 / *an earnest ~ of history* 〔*nature*〕 역사〔자연〕에 대한 성실한 연구자. **2** a person who studies at a school, a college, etc. 학생; 생도. ¶ *a college ~* 대학생 / *a medical* 〔*law*〕 ~ 의학〔법학〕생 / *a ~ teacher* 교육 실습생 / *a ~ at Harvard* 하버드 대학생 / *one's ~ days* 〔*life*〕 학창 시절〔생활〕. [L. *studium* zeal]
a student of life, a holder of fellowship or scholarship. 급비생(給費生).

student interpreter [ˊ-- -ˊ--] *n.* a grade of civil servant in consular employ. (영사관의) 수습 통역관.

stud·horse [stʌ́dhɔ̀ːrs] *n.* Ⓒ a male horse kept for breeding purposes; a stallion. 종마(種馬). [→stud²]

•stud·ied [stʌ́did] *adj.* **1** carefully considered or planned. 신중히 고려된; 숙려된. ¶ *one's ~ lecture* 용의 주도한 강의 / *one's ~ acceptance* 깊이 생각한 후의 수락 / *It's a well-studied plot.* 그것은 잘 짜여진 음모이다. **2** done on purpose; calculated. 일부러의; 고의의. ¶ *a ~ insult* 계획적인 모욕 / *a ~ indifference* 일부러 꾸민 무관심. [→student]

•stu·di·o [stjúːdiòu] *n.* Ⓒ (*pl.* **-di·os**) **1** the workroom of an artist. (예술가의) 작업장. **2** a place where motion pictures are made. 촬영소. **3** a place where a radio or television program is broadcast or recorded. 방송실; 녹음〔녹화〕실. [L. *studium*]

stu·di·ous [stjúːdiəs] *adj.* **1** fond of study. 학문을 좋아하는; 학구적인. ¶ *a ~ life* 학구 생활 / *~ tastes* 학구적 취미 / *He is a ~ boy and likes school.* 그는 공부하기 좋아하고 학교를 좋아하는 소년이다. **2** thoughtful; zealous. 신중한; 공을 들인; 열심인. ¶ *make a ~ effort to please the guests* 손님들을 즐겁게 하려고 열심히 노력하다 / *a child ~ to catch insects* 곤충 채집에 열심인 아이 / *~ attention to detail* 세부 사항에 대한 세심한 주의 / *a ~ program to maintain peace* 평화 유지를 위해 공들여 짜여진 계획.

stu·di·ous·ly [stjúːdiəsli] *adv.* in a studious manner; thoughtfully. 일부러; 열심히.

:stud·y [stʌ́di] *n.* (*pl.* **stud·ies**) **1** Ⓤ effort to learn by reading, thinking, etc. 공부; 면학; 학습. ¶ *the hours of ~* 공부 시간 / *the ~ of history* 역사 공부 / *He is fond of ~.* 그는 공부를 좋아한다 / *He likes sport more than ~.* 그는 공부보다 운동을 좋아한다 / *After an hour's hard ~ he knew his lesson.* 한 시간의 정력적인 공부를 하고 나서 그는 그의 학과를 알게 되었다. **2** Ⓒ《often *pl.*》 the act or process of pursuing some branch of knowledge; a careful examination. 연구; 학문; 조사; 검토. ¶ *the ~ of modern languages* 현대어의 연구 / *take up the ~ of...* …의 연구를 시작하다 / *make a ~ of English usage* 영어 관용법을 연구하다 / *devote one's life to ~* 생애를 학문〔연구〕에 바치다 / *the ~ of a document* 문서의 조사〔검토〕 / *a close ~ of the situation* 사태에 대한 면밀한 조사 / *He made a ~ of certain plants.* 그는 어떤 식물의 연구를 했다 / *The document is under ~.* 그 문서는 현재 검토 중이다. **3** Ⓒ a branch or department of learning; a subject that is studied. 학과; 학문; 연구 제목〔과목〕. ¶ *the ~ of medicine* 의학과 / *humane studies* 인문학과 / *Of all my studies I like English best.* 나의 모든 학과 중에서 나는 영어를 가장 좋아한다 / *Archeology is a comparatively modern ~.* 고고학은 비교적 근대의 학문이다 / *History is an interesting ~.* 역사는 재미있는 학과이다. **4** Ⓒ《*sing.* only》 something deserving to be examined. 연구 가치가 있는 것; 구경거리. ¶ *His character is a perfect ~.* 그의 성격은 정말로 연구해 볼 만하다 / *His face was a perfect ~.* 그의 얼굴은 정말 볼 만하였다. **5** Ⓒ a room used for reading and writing. 서재; 공부방. ¶ *He is reading in his ~.* 그는 서재에서 책을 읽고 있다. **6**《often *pl.*》 education. 학업. ¶ *pursue* 〔*attend*〕 *to one's studies* 학업에 열심히 종사하다 / *be tired of one's studies* 학업〔연구〕에 싫증이 나다 / *Don't stop your studies.* 학업을 중단하지 마라. **7** Ⓒ ⓐ an earnest effort. 노력; 수고. ¶ *Her constant ~ is to do her duty well.* 그녀는 의무를 다하는 일에 끊임없는 노력을 하고 있다 / *He made a ~ of my health.* 그는 끊임없이 나의 건강에 유의해 주었다. ⓑ《*arch.*》 an object of endeavor. 노력의 대상. ¶ *Your comfort shall be my ~.* 너를 안락하게 해주는 일을 나의 임무로 하겠다. **8** Ⓒ a sketch for a picture, a story, etc.; a piece of music for practice; étude. 습작(習作); 연습곡. ¶ *a ~ of a flower* 꽃의 스케치 / *A painter's method is best revealed in his studies.* 화가의 수법은 습작 중에 가장 잘 나타난다. **9** Ⓒ《*sing.* only》 deep thought; meditation. 깊은 생각; 궁리. ¶ *be in a deep ~* 깊은 생각에 잠기다 / *lost in a ~* 명상에 잠겨.

in a brown study, deep in thought and not noticing what is happening around one. 망연히. ¶ *He is in a brown ~.* 그는 망연히 생각에 잠겨 있다.

make a study of, try to secure; examine carefully. …을 연구하다.

— *v.* (**stud·ied**) *vt.* (P6,7) **1** seek knowledge of (a subject) by study; make an effort to learn; learn in a systematic way. …을 공부하다; 연구하다. ¶ *~ one's lesson* 학과를 공부하다 / *~ typing* 타자를 배우다 / *He studies history of America.* 그는 미국 역사에 대해 연구한다. **2** consider or examine carefully; look at (something) carefully. …을 주의해서 보다〔살피다〕; …을 조사하다. ¶ *~ a menu* 메뉴를 잘 보다 / *~ the situation* 정세를 조사하다 / *He is studying the map to find the shortest road home.* 그는 집으로 가는 가장 가까운 길을 찾기 위해 지도를 조사해 보고 있다 / *I'll ~ this problem.* 이 문제를 충분히 조사하겠다 / *He studied her face.* 그는 그녀의 얼굴을 주시했다. **3** think out; plan. …을 생각해내다; 궁리하다; …을 꾀하다. ¶ *~ out a good way to...* …하는 좋은 방법을 생각해내다 / *I was studying how I should please her.* 어떻게 하면 그녀를 기쁘게 할까 궁리하고 있었다 / *He studied ways to escape from the island.* 그는 섬으로부터 탈출하는 방법들을 궁리했다. **4** learn (something) by heart. …을 외다; 암기하다. ¶ *~ one's part* 자기의 대사를 외다. **5** try hard; think about (something) carefully. …을 위해 애쓰다; …에 마음을 쓰다; …을 고려하다. ¶ *~ one's own interest* 자신의 이익을 도모하다 / *~ the next move* 다음의 수를〔수단을〕 고려하다 / *~ other's convenience* 남의 편의를 도모하다〔애쓰다〕. — *vi.* (P1,3,4) **1** seek knowledge. 공부하다; 배우다. ¶ *~ hard* 열심

히 공부하다 / ~ *to become a lawyer* 변호사가 되기 위해 공부하다 / ~ *at a university* 대학에서 공부하다 / ~ *at home* 〔*school*〕 집〔학교〕에서 공부하다 / ~ *under someone* 아무에게서 배우다 / *He is studying to be a scientist.* 그는 과학자가 되기 위해 공부하고 있다 / ~ *for the church* 〔*bar*〕 목사〔변호사〕가 되려고 공부하다. **2** be a student. 제자가 되다. **3** ⓐ think deeply; meditate. 생각에 잠기다; 숙고하다. ⓑ try constantly to do. …하려고 (늘) 노력하다. ¶ *He studied to avoid disagreeable topics.* 그는 불유쾌한 화제를 피하려고 노력했다 / *We must ~ to do right.* 옳은 일을 하도록 애써야 한다. [L. *studium*]

study out, **a**) puzzle out; solve. (수수께끼 따위를) 풀다. **b**) think out; plan. 생각〔궁리〕해 내다.

:stuff [stʌf] *n.* **1** ⓊⒸ the material out of which something is made; any material. 재료; 원료; 자료. ¶ *wood, steel, and other ~ for building* 목재, 철강재, 기타의 건축용 자재 / *a house built of poor ~* 허술한 재료로 지은 집 / *collect the ~ for a book* 책을 쓰기 위한 자료를 모으다. **2** Ⓤ the quality or character of a person, a matter, etc.; basic elements. 소질; 요소; 본질. ¶ *the ~ of democracy* 〔*tradition*〕 민주주의〔전통〕의 본질 / *He has plenty of good ~ in him.* 그에게는 좋은 소질이 많이 있다. **3** Ⓤ personal belongings; goods; a thing. 소지품; 물건; 물(物). ¶ *sweet ~* 과자 / *sleeping ~* 수면제 / *household ~* 가구 / *some ~ they call petrol* 가솔린이라 불리는 것 / *food ~* 식료품 / *real ~* 진짜 / *He left his ~ in the room.* 그는 방 안에 소지품을 두고 왔다. **4** Ⓤ cloth, esp. woolen cloth. 직물; (특히) 모직물. ¶ *silk ~* 견직물 / *woolen ~* 모직물 / *a dress made of grey ~* 회색 모직물로 지은 정장. **5** Ⓤ a worthless collection; worthless ideas, writings, etc. 잡동사니; 허튼〔실없는〕 소리; 졸작. ¶ *a lot of ~ and nonsense* 쓸데없이 많은 허튼 소리 / *Take that ~ away.* 저 잡동사니를 저리 치워라 / *What ~ he writes!* 이런 졸작을 쓰다니.

do one's stuff, 《*colloq.*》 do what one is expected to do or good at doing. 자기가 해야 할 일을 하다; 솜씨〔장기〕를 보이다.

hot stuff, 《*sl.*》 having high skill; very skillful. 매우 숙련된〔능숙한〕. ¶ *He's hot ~ on the saxophone.* 그는 색소폰에 매우 능숙하다.

know one's stuff, have a thorough knowledge of the field in which one is concerned. (자기 분야에) 능수 능란하다.

That's the stuff (***to give 'em***). 《*sl.*》 That is the right way to treat, or the right thing to say to, them. 그게 당연한 조치다; 그래야 마땅하다.

— *vt.* **1** 《*into, with*》 (P6,7,13) fill or pack closely; fill up. …을 채워 넣다; 채우다. ¶ ~ *potatoes into a bag* = ~ *a bag with potatoes* 자루에 감자를 채워 넣다 / *a cushion stuffed with feathers* 새털을 채워 넣은 방석 / *She stuffed the pillow with feathers.* 그녀는 베개 속에 새털을 채워 넣었다 / *The train is stuffed with passengers.* 열차는 승객들로 대만원이다〔콩나물 시루 같다〕. **2** (P6) fill the skin of (a dead animal, bird, etc.) so as to keep its natural form and appearance. …을 박제로 하다. ¶ *a stuffed lion* 〔*bird*〕 박제한 사자〔새〕. **3** (P6) fill (a chicken, a turkey, etc.) with seasoned bread crumbs, etc. (요리하는 새 따위에) 소를 넣다〔채우다〕. ¶ ~ *a chicken* (요리할) 닭의 배에 소를 넣다 / *The turkey is stuffed with forcemeat and onions.* 칠면조의 배는 다진 고기와 양파의 소로 채워졌다. **4** (P6,13) fill (one's stomach) with food. (배에 음식을) 채워 넣다; …의 배를 채우다. ¶ ~ *a child* (*with food*) 아이를 배불리 먹이다. **5** (P6,7,13) stop up (a crack, a hole, etc.); block. (구멍 따위를) 메우다; 틀어막다. ¶ ~ (*up*) *one's ears with cotton-wool* =~ *cotton-wool into one's ears* 솜으로 귀를 틀어막다 / *My nose is stuffed up.* 코가 막혀 있다. — *vi.* (P1) eat too much. 배불리〔게걸스레〕 먹다. [Rom. =web, cloth]

stuff someone, tell someone what is untrue. …를 속이다.

stuff oneself, eat too much. 과식하다.

stuff·ing [stʌ́fiŋ] *n.* **1** Ⓤ the material with which a mat, a cushion, a pillow, etc. is packed. (방석·베개·매트 따위를 채우는) 속《솜·깃털·짚 따위》; 충전물. ¶ *the ~ of a pillow* 베갯속. **2** ⓊⒸ a seasoned mixture of bread, chopped meat, etc. put into a chicken, a turkey, etc. before cooking. (요리용 새의 뱃속에 채워 넣는) 소.

stuff·y [stʌ́fi] *adj.* (**stuff·i·er, stuff·i·est**) **1** lacking fresh air; close. 통풍이 잘 안 되는. ¶ *a ~ room* 통풍이 잘 안 되는 방. **2** causing difficult breathing. 숨이 막힐 듯한. ¶ *I feel ~ in this room.* 이 방은 숨이 막힐 것 같다. **3** dull; not interesting. 재미 없는; 싫증나는. ¶ *a ~ conversation* 따분한 대화. **4** 《*colloq.*》 opposed to change; conservative; not open to new ideas. 케케묵은; 보수적인. **5** 《*colloq.*》 easily offended; angry. 성난; 화를 낸. ● **stuff·i·ness** [-nis] *n.*

stul·ti·fy [stʌ́ltəfài] *vt.* (**-fied**) (P6) **1** cause (someone) to appear foolish. …을 바보로〔어리석어〕 보이게 하다. ¶ ~ *oneself by silly conduct* 어리석은 행위로 창피를 당하다 / *He stultified his action in the eyes of the people.* 그의 행동은 사람들 눈에 바보스러워 보였다. **2** make (something) worthless or useless. …을 쓸모없게 하다; 무효로 하다. ¶ *the stultifying atmosphere* 기분을 상하게 하는 분위기 / ~ *oneself* 망신하다. [L. *stultus* foolish]

·stum·ble [stʌ́mbəl] *vi.* (P1,2A,3) **1** trip by striking the foot against something; fall or trip in walking, running, etc. 발이 걸려 넘어지다; 비틀거리다. ¶ ~ *over a stub* 그루터기에 걸려 넘어지다 / ~ *and fall* 비틀거리다가 넘어지다 / *He stumbled to his knees.* 그는 비틀거리다가 무릎을 꿇었다. **2** walk unsteadily. 비틀거리며 걷다. ¶ *The old man stumbled along the road.* 그 노인은 길을 비틀거리며 걸어갔다 / *The key stumbled into the lock.* 열쇠가 자물쇠 안으로 근근히 들어갔다. **3** hesitate; speak or act in a hesitating manner. 망설이다; 말을더듬다. ¶ ~ *over one's words* 말이 막히다 / *He stumbled through a speech.* 그는 연설을 더듬거리며 마쳤다. **4** do wrong; make a mistake. 실패하다; 잘못하다. ¶ ~ *and learn* 실패하는 것에 의해 배우다 / ~ *in carrying out a plan* 계획을 실행하는 단계에서 실패하다. **5** 《*on, upon*》 find or happen on something by chance. 우연히 발견하다; 마주치다. ¶ ~ *on the truth* 우연히 진상을 알게 되다 / ~ *upon a rare book* 진귀한 책을 우연히 발견하다.

stumble across =***stumble on*** 〔***upon***〕, come upon or discover by chance. 우연히 만나다〔마주치다〕.

stumble at, hesitate over. 망설이다.

— *n.* Ⓒ **1** an act of tripping. 걸려 넘어짐; 비틀거림. **2** a mistake; an error. 실패; 실수. [E.]

stumbling block [ㅅㅡ ㅅ] *n.* **1** an obstacle. 방해물. ¶ *a* ~ *to progress* 진보에 방해가 되는 것. **2** anything causing difficulty. 장애(물). ¶ *a* ~ *to faith* 신앙의 장애.

•**stump** [stʌmp] *n.* Ⓒ **1** the part of a tree or plant left after it has been cut down. (나무의) 그루터기. ¶ *We sat on the top of a* ~. 우리는 (나무의) 그루터기 위에 앉았다. **2** the part of an arm, a leg, a tooth, etc. left after the rest has been removed. 부러진 이의 뿌리; 손·발의 잘리고 남은 부분; (물건의) 쓰다 남은 몽당이〔것〕. ¶ *the* ~ *of a cigar* 〔*pencil*〕 꽁초〔몽당연필〕 / *The dog wagged his* ~ *of a tail from side to side.* 개는 잘리고 남은 짧은 꼬리의 끝을 좌우로 흔들었다. **3** a wooden leg. 의족. ¶ *wear a wooden* ~ 목제 의족을 착용하고 있다. **4** a platform from which a political speech is made. 정견 발표 연단. ¶ *go on the* ~ 선거 연설을 하고 다니다. **5** a heavy step; the sound of such a step. 무거운 발걸음; 그런 발소리. **6** (in cricket) one of the sticks which are put upright in the ground. (크리켓의) 기둥.

on the stump, carrying on political agitation. 정치 운동을 하여.

stir one's stumps, 《*colloq.*》 moves one's legs; walk; hurry. (빨리) 걷다; 서두르다.

up a stump, **a**) unable to act, answer, etc.; impotent. 무능한. **b**) baffled. 당황하여.

— *vt.* (P6) **1** remove stumps from (land). 그루터기를 없애다〔제거하다〕. ¶ ~ *land* 땅에서 그루터기를 없애다. **2** puzzle; confuse. (아무를) 난처하게 하다; 당황〔혼란〕하게 하다. ¶ *be stumped by an examinatin* 시험이 어려워서 애를 먹다 / *Your question certainly stumps me.* 너의 질문은 정말로 나를 당황하게 한다 / *I am stumped.* 야단났군; 어찌할 바를 모르겠다 / *Everybody was stumped by this riddle.* 이 수수께끼 때문에 모두 쩔쩔맸다. **3** travel over (a district) making political speeches. (어떤 지방을) 유세하다; 선거 연설을 하다. ¶ *The candidates will* ~ *the country.* 그 후보자들은 지방을 유세할 것이다.

— *vi.* (P2A) **1** walk heavily with noisy steps. 뚜벅뚜벅〔쿵쿵거리며〕 걷다. ¶ ~ *across the room* 방 안을 뚜벅뚜벅 걸어가다 / *The injured man stumped along the corridor.* 부상자는 복도를 따라 쿵쿵거리며 걸어갔다. **2** go about making political speeches. 유세하다. [E.]

stump·er [stʌ́mpər] *n.* Ⓒ **1** a person or thing that stumps. 당혹스럽게 하는 사람〔것〕. **2** an extremely difficult problem, task, etc. 난문; 난제. **3** a person who goes about making political speeches. 선거 유세자; 정견 발표자. [Teut.]

stump orator [ㅅ ㅅㅡㅡ] *n.* an agitator. 가두 정치 연설자; 민중 선동자.

stump speech [ㅅㅅ] *n.* a political campaign speech, esp. one made on a campaign tour. (유세중에 행하는) 정치〔선거〕 연설.

stump·y [stʌ́mpi] *adj.* (**stump·i·er, stump·i·est**) **1** short and thick. 땅딸막한. **2** having many stumps. 그루터기투성이의. ¶ *a* ~ *field* 그루터기투성이의 들판. [*stump*]

stun [stʌn] *vt.* (**stunned, stun·ning**) (P6) **1** make (someone) unconscious, as by a blow; knock senseless. (때려서) …를 기절시키다. ¶ *I was stunned by the blow.* = *The blow stunned me.* 그 일격으로 나는 기절하였다. **2** daze; shock. …을 멍하게 만들다; 간담을 서늘하게 하다. ¶ *The news stunned him.* 그 소식에 그는 망연자실했다 / *He was completely stunned by the disaster into silence.* 그는 재난으로 인해 멍하니 말을 하지 못하게 됐다. [→stonish]

•**stung** [stʌŋ] *v.* p. and pp. of **sting.**

stunk [stʌŋk] *v.* p. and pp. of **stink.**

stun·ning [stʌ́niŋ] *adj.* **1** that stuns; shocking. 기절시키는; 간담을 서늘하게 하는. ¶ *deliver a* ~ *blow* 기절할 정도의 일격을 가하다. **2** 《*colloq.*》 very attractive; good-looking; remarkable. 아주 매력적인; 아름다운; 멋진. ¶ *She is a* ~ *beauty.* 그녀는 아주 매력적인 미인이다. ●**stun·ning·ly** [-li] *adv.* [*stun*]

stunt[1] [stʌnt] *vt.* check (someone or something) in growth. …의 발육〔성장〕을 방해하다. ¶ ~ *the growth of a nation's power* 국력의 발전을 저지하다 / *Lack of water stunted these potted plants.* 물의 부족은 이들 화분에 있는 화초들의 성장을 저해했다. — *n.* ⓊⒸ the act of stunting. 발육 저해〔저지〕. [E.]

stunt[2] [stʌnt] *n.* Ⓒ 《*colloq.*》 something done to show skill or boldness; a striking performance or feat. 묘기; 아슬아슬한 재주; 곡예. ¶ ~ *flying* 곡예 비행 / *The members of the circus performed all sorts of riding stunts.* 서커스 단원들은 온갖 종류의 승마 곡예를 공연했다 / *That's a good stunt.* 그것 참 묘안이다 / *pull a* ~ (때로 어리석은) 책략

을 쓰다. —— *vt., vi.* (P6;1) perform a stunt with (something). (…으로) 묘기를 부리다. [?]

stu·pe·fac·tion [stjù:pəfǽkʃən] *n.* Ⓤ the act of stupefying; the state of being stupefied; a dazed or senseless condition; amazement. 마비(시키기); 의식 불명(의 상태); 깜짝 놀람. [↓]

stu·pe·fy [stjú:pəfài] *vt.* (**-fied**) (P6) **1** make (someone) stupid or senseless. …을 마비시키다; 멍하게 하다. ¶ *be stupefied with drink* 〔*grief*〕 술로〔슬픔으로〕 머리가 멍해지다. **2** astonish. …을 깜짝 놀라게 하다. ¶ *They were stupefied by the accident.* 그들은 그 사고로 깜짝 놀랐다. ● **stu·pe·fi·er** [-ər] *n.* [→stupid, -fy]

stu·pen·dous [stju:péndəs] *adj.* amazing, esp. because of great size; marvelous. 놀랄만한; 터무니없는; 거대한; 멋들어진. ¶ *a ~ achievement* 놀랄 만한 업적 / *a ~ error* 〔*folly*〕 터무니없는 잘못〔어리석은 행위〕. ● **stu·pen·dous·ly** [-li] *adv.* **stu·pen·dous·ness** [-nis] *n.* [↓]

•**stu·pid** [stjú:pid] *adj.* **1** dull; foolish; not intelligent. 머리가 둔한; 어리석은; 바보의(opp. wise). ¶ *a ~ boy* 머리가 둔한 소년 / *a ~ mistake* 어리석은 잘못 / *It is ~ of you to believe him.* 그의 말을 믿다니 너도 어리석군. **2** not interesting; dull. 재미 없는; 시시한. ¶ *a ~ joke* 시시한 농담 / *What a ~ book!* 참 재미없는 책이군. **3** senseless. 무감각의; 마비된. ¶ *~ from* 〔*with*〕 *drink* 〔*sleep*〕 취해서 제정신을 잃은〔졸려서 앞뒤를 못 가리는〕. [L. *stupeo* be torpid]

stu·pid·i·ty [stju:pídəti] *n.* (*pl.* **-ties**) **1** Ⓤ foolishness. 어리석음; 우둔함. **2** Ⓒ 《*pl.*》 a foolish act, idea, etc. 어리석은 짓〔생각〕.

stu·pid·ly [stjú:pidli] *adv.* in a stupid manner. 어리석게.

stu·por [stjú:pər] *n.* ⒸⓊ **1** a condition in which someone is nearly unconscious; a loss of the power to feel. 실신; 무감각; 인사불성. ¶ *fall into a heavy ~* 인사 불성이 되다. **2** the state of being amazed. 아연실색; 몹시 놀람. [*stupid*]

stur·di·ness [stə́:rdinis] *n.* Ⓤ the state or quality of being sturdy. 튼튼함; 억셈; 건장함. [↓]

•**stur·dy** [stə́:rdi] *adj.* (**-di·er, -di·est**) **1** strong; stout. 억센; 튼튼한. ¶ *a ~ youngster* 체격이 늠름한 젊은이 / *a ~ house* 튼튼한 구조의 집 / *~ legs* 튼튼한 다리. **2** firm; not yielding. 불굴의. ¶ *a ~ resistance* 완강한 저항 / *~ courage* 〔*patriotism*〕 불굴의 용기〔애국심〕 / *~ common sense* 건전한 상식. [F. *estourdi* amazed]

stur·geon [stə́:rdʒən] *n.* Ⓒ (*pl.* **-geons** or *collectively* **-geon**) a large edible fish. 철갑상어. [Teut.]

stut·ter [stʌ́tər] *vi.* (P1) repeat the same sound because one has difficulty in speaking; stammer. 말을 더듬다. —— *vt.* (P6,7) repeat (a sound) with difficulty. …을 더듬거리며 말하다. —— *n.* Ⓒ the act of stuttering. 말더듬기. [E.]

St. Vi·tus's dance [sèint váitəsiz ⌐] *n.* 《med.》 chorea. 무도병.

sty[1] [stai] *n.* Ⓒ (*pl.* **sties**) **1** a place where pigs are kept. 돼지우리. **2** a dirty place. 더러운〔불결한〕 장소. [E.]

sty[2], **stye** [stai] *n.* Ⓒ (*pl.* **styes** or **sties**) 《med.》 a swelling on the edge of the eyelid. 다래끼. ¶ *have a ~ in one's eye* 눈에 다래끼가 나다. [E.]

Styg·i·an [stídʒiən] *adj.* **1** 《Gk. myth.》 of the river Styx or the lower world. 삼도천(三途川)의; 지옥의. **2** like hell; dark; murky; gloomy. 지옥 같은; 어두운; 음울한. ¶ *~ gloom* 〔*darkness*〕 (지옥 같은) 캄캄한 어둠. [→styx]

:**style** [stail] *n.* **1** ⓊⒸ fashion (in dresses, etc.). 유행; 스타일. ¶ *in* 〔*out of*〕 *~* 유행하는〔유행에 뒤진〕 / *the latest styles from Paris* 파리에서 직수입한 최신 스타일 / *dress in good ~* 품위 있는〔스마트한〕 복장을 하다 / *the latest ~ in coats* 최신 유행의 코트. **2** Ⓤ manner or method of doing or making something. (사물의) 행하는 방법; 양식. ¶ *in fine ~* 훌륭하게; 화려하게 / *the modern ~ of living* 현대식 생활 양식 / *cooking in purely Korean ~* 순한국식 요리 / *This is the way to knock in American ~.* 이것은 미국식 노크의 방법이다. **3** ⒸⓊ a distinctive manner of writing or speaking. 문체; 말투. ¶ *a concise ~* 간결한 문체 / *an easy ~* 쉬운 문체 / *a ~ of one's own* 독자적인 문체 / *a writer without ~* 독자적인 문체를 갖지 않은 작가 / *take a lofty ~ with us* 우리에게 잘난 체하는 말투를 쓰다 / *Books for children should have a clear, easy ~.* 아동용 책은 뜻이 명료하고 쉬운 문체이어야 한다 / *The ~ is better than the matter.* 문장 쪽이 내용보다 우수하다. **4** ⒸⓊ a characteristic manner of expression. (예술 작품의) 유파; 양식; …식〔풍〕. ¶ *the Gothic ~ of architecture* 고딕식 건축 / *in the Elizabethan ~* 엘리자베스조 풍으로 / *the epic* 〔*lyric*〕 *~* 서사〔서정〕시체(詩體) / *sing in the Italian ~* 이탈리아식으로 노래하다. **5** Ⓤ an elegant or distinguished manner of living or way of acting. 기품; 품위; 고상함. ¶ *live in* (*grand*) *~* 호화로운 생활을 하다 / *a woman of ~* 품위있는 여인 / *There is no ~ about her.* =*She has no ~.* 그녀는 기품이 없다〔평범하다〕. **6** Ⓤ kind; sort; a form or design. 종류; …류(類); 형(型); 모양. ¶ *a gentleman of the old ~* 옛날형의 신사 / *different styles of writing* 여러 종류의 서식 / *hats in all sizes and styles* 각종 크기와 여러 가지 모양의 모자 / *What ~ of house do you require?* 어떤 형의 집을 구하십니까 / *What is the proper ~ for addressing a king?* —*Your Majesty.* 왕을 부르는 알맞은 칭호는 무엇이냐 —폐하이다 / *What ~ man is he?* 그는 어떤 형의 사람이냐. **7** Ⓒ someone's

full title; a trade name. (아무의 정식) 칭호; (상사 따위의) 상호. ¶ *a firm under the ~ of...* …이라는 상호〔이름〕의 상회. **8** Ⓒ a pointed instrument used in ancient times for writing on wax; a stylus. (고대인이 사용하던) 첨필(尖筆). **9** Ⓒ 《bot.》 the stem-like part of the pistil of a flower. 암술대; 화주(花柱). **10** Ⓒ a mode of reckoning time or dates. 역법(曆法). ¶ *the New* 〔*Old*〕 *Style* 신〔구〕력(曆).
— *vt.* (P6) **1** give a title to (someone); name; call. (…을) 부르다; 칭하다. ¶ *~ oneself a count* 백작이라고 자칭하다 / *Jesus Christ is styled the Savior.* 예수 그리스도는 구세주라고 지칭된다. **2** design. (일정한 양식에 따라) 디자인하다. ¶ *~ an evening dress* 이브닝 드레스를 유행에 따라 디자인하다 / *clothes styled for young men* 젊은이에 맞게 디자인된 옷. [L. *stilus*]

style·book [stáilbùk] *n.* Ⓒ **1** a book on various fashions in dress. (복장의) 스타일북. **2** a book for printers, in which rules of punctuation, capitalization, etc. are shown. (인쇄업자의) 구두점·활자 따위의 견본책; 인쇄 편람.

sty·li [stáilai] *n.* pl. of **stylus**.

styl·ish [stáiliʃ] *adj.* very modern; fashionable. (초)현대식의; 유행의; 멋진. ¶ *She wears ~ clothes.* 그녀는 멋진〔유행에 따른〕 옷을 입고 있다.

styl·ist [stáilist] Ⓒ **1** a writer who has a good style. 명문가; 문장가. **2** a designer of interior decorations, clothes, etc. (실내장식·옷의) 디자이너. ¶ *a fashion ~* 패션 디자이너.

sty·lis·tic [stailístik] *adj.* of or about style. 문체(상)의.

sty·lis·ti·cal·ly [stailístikəli] *adv.* with regard to style. 문체상.

sty·lus [stáiləs] *n.* Ⓒ (*pl.* **-li** or **-lus·es**) **1** a pointed instrument for writing on wax. 철필(鐵筆); 첨필(尖筆). **2** a needle used in playing phonograph records. (축음기의) 바늘. [*style*]

sty·mie [stáimi] *n.* Ⓒ **1** 《golf》 obstruction by the opponent's ball lying between the player and the hole. 방해구(妨害球). **2** an obstacle. 방해물. — *vt.* (P6) hinder. …을 방해하다. [E.]

styp·tic [stíptik] *adj.* that checks bleeding. 출혈을 멈추는. — *n.* Ⓒ something that stops bleeding. 지혈제. [Gk.]

Styx [stiks] *n.* 《Gk. myth.》 a river across which the souls of the dead were transported. 삼도내〔천〕; 지옥의 강. [Gk.]
cross the Styx, die. 죽다.

sua·sion [swéiʒən] *n.* Ⓤ persuation. 설득. [L. *suadeo* urge]

suave [swɑːv] *adj.* agreeable; polite. 기분 좋은; 상냥한; 공손한. ¶ *~ manners* 상냥한 태도 / *a ~ smile* 상냥한 미소. [L. *suavis*]

suave·ly [swáːvli] *adv.* agreeably; politely. 기분 좋게; 공손〔상냥〕하게.

sua·vi·ty [swáːvəti] *n.* Ⓤ agreeable quality; politeness. 기분 좋음; 상냥〔공손〕함.

sub [sʌb] *n.* 《*colloq.*》 =substitute; subscription; subaltern; submarine.

sub- [sʌb-] *pref.* **1** under; below. '아래'의 뜻. ¶ *subway* 지하철. **2** again; further. '다시, 더욱이, 게다가'의 뜻. ¶ *sublet* 전대(轉貸). **3** near; nearly. '아(亞)'의 뜻. ¶ *subarctic* 아북극 지대. **4** slightly. '약(弱), 약간'의 뜻. ¶ *subacid* 약간 신. **5** assistant. '부(副)'의 뜻. ¶ *subeditor* 부주필; 편집 차장. [L.]

sub·al·tern [səbɔ́ːltərn / sʌ́bltən] *n.* Ⓒ 《Brit.》 an army officer ranking below a captain. 육군 중위; 소위. — *adj.* **1** subordinate; of less importance; lower in position or rank. 부(副)〔차(次)〕의; 하위의; 부하의. **2** ranking below a captain. 중위〔소위〕의. [sub-]

sub·com·mit·tee [sʌ́bkəmìtiː] *n.* Ⓒ a small committee chosen from a larger committee. 분과 위원회.

sub·con·scious [sʌbkánʃəs / -kɔ́n-] *adj.* existing in the mind but not felt. 잠재 의식의. — *n.* Ⓤ 《*the ~*》 the mental activity of which the individual is not aware. 잠재 의식.

sub·con·scious·ly [sʌbkánʃəsli / -kɔ́n-] *adv.* in a subconscious. 잠재 의식적으로; 희미하게 의식하여.

sub·con·ti·nent [sʌbkántənənt / -kɔ́n-] *n.* Ⓒ a large land mass, smaller than a continent. 아대륙(亞大陸).

sub·con·tract [sʌbkántrækt / -kɔ́n-] *n.* Ⓒ a contract which is made to supplement a primary or previous contract. 하도급; 하청; 하도급〔하청〕 계약.
— *v.* [sʌ̀bkəntrǽkt] *vt.* (P6) make a subcontract for (something). …의 하도급〔하청〕(계약)을 하다. — *vi.* (P1) make a subcontract. 하도급〔하청〕하다; 하도급〔하청〕을 발주〔수주〕하다.

sub·con·trac·tor [sʌ̀bkántrætər / -kɔntrǽk-] *n.* Ⓒ a person who takes on a subcontract. 하도급〔하청〕 계약자.

sub·cu·ta·ne·ous [sʌ̀bkjuːtéiniəs] *adj.* under the skin. 피하의. ¶ *a ~ injection* 피하 주사 / *~ fat* 피하 지방. [sub-]

sub·dea·con [sʌbdíːkən] *n.* Ⓒ 《Cath.》 a clergyman next below a deacon in rank. 차부제(次副祭).

sub·di·vide [sʌ̀bdiváid] *vt.* (P6) divide (what has already been divided) into even smaller parts. …을 다시 나누다; 세분하다. — *vi.* (P1) become separated into smaller parts. 다시 나뉘다; 세분되다.

sub·di·vi·sion [sʌ́bdivìʒən] *n.* **1** Ⓒ a part subdivided, esp. a piece of land near a city subdivided into many lots for houses. 세분된 것; 건축 부지용으로 구획된 땅. **2** Ⓤ the act of subdividing. 재분할.

sub·du·al [səbdjú:əl] *n.* Ⓤ the act of subduing. 정복.

***sub·due** [səbdjú:] *vt.* (P6) **1** conquer; overcome. …을 정복하다. ¶ ~ *nature* 자연을 정복하다 / ~ *an enemy* 적군을 정복하다 / ~ *feelings* 〔*impulses*〕 감정〔충동〕을 억제하다. **2** soften; tone down. …을 누그러뜨리다; (목소리를) 낮추다. ¶ *subdued light* 잔잔한 빛 / *a subdued voice* 부드럽게 낮춘 목소리. [L. *duco* bring]

sub·head [sʌ́bhèd] *n.* Ⓒ a title or heading of a subdivision. 작은 표제; 부표제. [sub-]

sub·head·ing [sʌ́bhèdiŋ] *n.* =subhead.

⁑**sub·ject** [sʌ́bdʒikt] *n.* Ⓒ **1** a person who is under the power or control of another or of a certain government. (군주제하의) 국민; 신민(臣民); 신하; 부하. ¶ *a British* ~ 영국민; 영국(왕)의 신민 / *rulers and subjects* 통치자와 피통치자 / *the liberty of the* ~ 신민의 자유《입헌정 치하의 여러 특권》/ *a loyal* ~ 충실한 신하 / *a* ~ *of the Crown* 국왕의 한 신민. **2** a topic treated or chosen in conversation, study, writing, painting, etc.; a theme. 주제; 문제; 제목; 화제; (음악의) 주제. ¶ *a* ~ *of conversation* 화제 / *the* ~ *in hand* 당면한 문제 / *Let's change the* ~. 우리 화제를 바꾸자 / *the* ~ *of a story* 〔*play, poem*〕 이야기〔연극, 시〕의 제목 / *wander from the* ~ 주제에서 벗어나다; 탈선하다 / *I could write if I could think of a* ~. 무언가 주제만 생각해 낸다면 써나갈 수 있을 텐데. **3** a course of study taught in a school, a college, etc. 학과; 과목. ¶ *an elective* 〔*a required*〕 ~ 선택〔필수〕 과목 / *take five subjects in one's examination* 시험을 다섯 과목 치르다. **4** 《gram.》 the noun or pronoun governing a verb. 주어; 주부(主部). **5** 《*for, of*》 a cause or motive. 원인; 동기; …의 원인. ¶ *a* ~ *for complaint* 불평의 원인 / *a* ~ *of ridicule* 웃음거리 / *the sole* ~ *of my grief* 나의 슬픔의 유일한 원인 / *a* ~ *of animosity* 원한의 대상 / *a* ~ *for rejoicing* 〔*congratulation*〕 기뻐해야〔축하해야〕 할 일. **6** a person or animal on whom an experiment is performed; a dead body used for experimentation. (의학 따위의) 피실험자; 해부 시체. ¶ *a medical* 〔*surgical*〕 ~ 내과〔외과〕 환자 / *a hypnotic* ~ 최면술의 실험대상자 / *make someone the* ~ *of an experiment* 아무를 실험의 재료로 삼다. **7** 《philos.》 the thinking and feeling mind or ego; substance; the thing itself. 주관; 자아; (행위의) 주체; 실체.

— *adj.* **1** 《*to*》 under the power of another. 복종하는; 종속의; 지배를 받는. ¶ *a* ~ *province* 〔*nation, state*〕 속령〔속국〕 / *a state* ~ *to foreign rule* 외국의 지배를 받는 나라 / *Everything is* ~ *to the laws of nature.* 만물은 자연의 법칙에 지배된다. **2** 《*to*》 apt to suffer frequently; likely to have. (…을) 받기 쉬운; …이 되기 쉬운; (…을) 입는〔받는〕. ¶ *be* ~ *to damage* 손상되기 쉬운 / *a country* ~ *to earthquakes* 지진이 자주 일어나는 나라 / *She is* ~ *to colds.* 그녀는 감기에 잘 걸린다 / *The prices are* ~ *to change without notice.* 가격은 예고 없이 변동되는 경우가 있다 / *Men are* ~ *to temptation.* 인간은 유혹에 빠지기 쉽다 / *Such conduct is* ~ *to criticism.* 그러한 행위는 사람들로부터 비난당하기 쉽다. **3** 《*to*》 dependent on; on the condition of. …이라는 조건이 붙는; (…을) 필요로 하는. ¶ *a plan* ~ *to your approval* 귀하의 승인을 필요로 하는 계획 / *The treaty is* ~ *to ratification.* 이 조약은 비준을 필요로 한다.

— *adv.* depending on; on the condition of. …에 근거하여; …을 조건으로 하여; …을 가정하여. ¶ *Subject to your consent, I will try again.* 하락하신다면 다시 해보겠습니다.

— [səbdʒékt] *vt.* (P6,13) **1** 《*to*》 bring (someone or something) under control. …을 복종〔종속〕시키다; 지배 아래 두다. ¶ ~ *a neighboring country to one's rule* 이웃 나라를 지배하에 두다 / ~ *the mind of the people* 사람들의 마음을 지배하다. **2** 《*to*》 expose; cause (someone) to experience or endure. …당하게 하다; 입히다. ¶ ~ *oneself to insult* 모욕을 당하다 / ~ *a prisoner to torture* 죄수를 고문하다 / *Violations of the law will* ~ *offenders to fines.* 이 법률을 위반하면 위반자는 벌금이 부과된다. **3** 《*to*》 submit. …을 제출하다. ¶ ~ *one's plans to a committee* 자기의 계획을 위원회에 제출하다. [L. *jacio* lay]

be subjected to, undergo; experience. …을 받다; 당하다; …에 처해지다. 「입다〔받다〕.

subject oneself to, suffer; undergo. …을

sub·jec·tion [səbdʒékʃən] *n.* Ⓤ **1** the act of conquering. 정복. ¶ *The* ~ *of the Indians took a long time.* 인디언의 정복에는 오랜 시간이 걸렸다. **2** the state of being under the control of some power. 복종; 종속. ¶ *bring someone under* ~ 아무를 복종시키다 / *They lived in complete* ~ *to the Romans.* 그들은 로마인의 완전한 종속 상태에서 살았다.

sub·jec·tive [səbdʒéktiv, sʌb-] *adj.* **1** existing only in the mind of someone; personal. 주관의; 주관적인; 개인적인(opp. objective). ¶ ~ *impressions* 〔*judgment*〕 주관적 인상〔판단〕 / *a* ~ *evaluation* 개인적인 평가 / *the* ~ *feelings of a patient* 환자의 특유한 감정. **2** 《gram.》 of the subject. ¶ *the* ~ *case* 주격(主格).

sub·jec·tive·ly [səbdʒéktivli, sʌb-] *adv.* in a subjective manner. 주관적으로.

sub·jec·tiv·i·ty [sʌ̀bdʒektívəti] *n.* Ⓤ a subjective quality. 주관성.

subject matter [⌐-⌐-] *n.* **1** something thought about, discussed, etc. 주제(主題); 논제. **2** the meaning of a talk, book, etc. (as distinguished from its form or style). 취지.

sub·join [səbdʒɔ́in] *vt.* (P6) add (something) at the end of something written or said. …을 추가〔첨가〕하다. [sub-]

sub·ju·gate [sʌ́bdʒugèit] *vt.* (P6) conquer; subdue; bring into subjection. …을 정복하다; 복종시키다. [L. *jugum* yoke]
sub·ju·ga·tion [sʌ̀bdʒugéiʃən] *n.* Ⓤ conquest. 정복.
***sub·junc·tive** [səbdʒʌ́ŋktiv] *n.* 《*the* ~》 《gram.》 the mood of a verb which expresses a state or action, not as a fact, but as something imagined. 가정법. — *adj.* of this mood. 가정법의. ¶ *the ~ mood* 가정법. [→junction]
sub·lease [sʌ́blì:s] *n.* Ⓒ a lease granted by one who is already a lessee of a property, as an apartment. 전대(轉貸). — *vt.* (P6) grant or take a sublease of. …을 전대〔전차(轉借)〕하다. [sub-]
sub·let [sʌ̀blét] *vt.* (**-let**) (P6) **1** rent to another (something that has already been rent to oneself). …을 전대(轉貸)하다. **2** give part of (a contract) to another. (일 따위를) 하도급〔하청〕 주다. [sub-]
sub·lieu·ten·ant [sʌ̀blu:ténənt / -lət-] *n.* Ⓒ 《Brit.》 해군 중위.
sub·li·mate [sʌ́bləmèit] *vt.* (P6) **1** 《chem.》 make (a solid substance) pure by converting it into a gas and then condensing the gas back to a solid form. 승화(昇華)시키다. **2** 《psych.》 direct the energy of (desires and impulses) from a lower to a higher level; refine. 승화(昇華)하다《성적·공격적 충동을 문화적인 좋은 방향으로 향하게 하는 일》. ¶ ~ *one's sexual desires* 성적 욕구를 승화하다. **3** make pure; elevate. …을 순수하게 하다; 고상하게 하다. ¶ *To read about great men sublimates ambition.* 위인에 관해서 읽으면 야망은 한층 더 고상한 것이 된다.
— *vi.* (P1) become pure; become elevated. 순화하다; 승화하다.
— [-mit, -mèit] *n.* ⓊⒸ 《chem.》 a sublimated substance. 승화물(昇華物).
— [-mit, -mèit] *adj.* purified; sublimated. 순화된; 승화된. [L.]
sub·li·ma·tion [sʌ̀bləméiʃən] *n.* Ⓤ the act of sublimating. 순화(純化); 승화.
***sub·lime** [səbláim] *adj.* (**-lim·er, -lim·est**) **1** very grand and noble; lofty. 숭고한; 웅대한; 장엄한. ¶ ~ *beauty* 장려한 아름다움 / ~ *scenery* 웅대한 경치 / ~ *self-sacrifice* 숭고한 자기 희생 / *Beethoven's music is often* ~. 베토벤의 음악은 대체로 장엄하다. **2** haughty; proud. 거만한; 건방진. **3** 《*colloq.*》 of the highest degree; very great. 극도의; 터무니없는. ¶ ~ *self-conceit* 〔*ignorance*〕 굉장히 높은 자부심〔형편 없는 무지〕.
— *n.* 《*the* ~》 all that is sublime; sublimity. 숭고(함); 숭고한 것.
— *vt., vi.* (P6;1) **1** 《chem.》 sublimate; be sublimated. 승화시키다〔하다〕. **2** dignify supremely; be ennobled. 고상하게 하다; 고상해지다. [L.]
sub·lime·ly [səbláimli] *adv.* in a sublime manner. 숭고하게; 고상하게.
sub·lim·i·nal [sʌblímənəl] *adj.* subconscious. 잠재의. [L. =below the threshold]
sub·lim·i·ty [səblíməti] *n.* (*pl.* **-ties**) **1** Ⓤ the state of being sublime. 숭고; 웅대. **2** Ⓒ 《often *pl.*》 someone or something sublime. 숭고한 사람〔것〕. [L.]
sub·machine gun [sʌ̀bməʃí:n gʌ̀n] *n.* a light automatic gun, designed to be fired from the shoulder or waist. 경기관총; 기관단총. [sub-]
***sub·ma·rine** [sʌ́bmərì:n, ╲-╱] *n.* Ⓒ a warship that can move under water. 잠수함. — *adj.* living, being or growing under water. 수중의; 해저의. ¶ ~ *plants* 해저 식물 / *a* ~ *cable* 해저 전선 / *a* ~ *terrace* 해저의 단구(段丘). — *vt.* (P6) 《*colloq.*》 attack (the enemy) by means of a submarine. …을 잠수함으로 공격하다. [sub-]
sub·max·il·la·ry [sʌbmǽksəlèri / -ləri] *n., adj.* (of) the lower jaw or lower jawbone. 아래턱(의); 하악골(의). [sub-]
sub·merge [səbmə́:rdʒ] *vt.* (P6) put (something) under water; cover (something) with water. …을 물 속에 가라앉히다; 물에 잠그다. ¶ *submerged houses* 침수 가옥 / *rocks submerged at high tide* 만조 때에는 물에 잠기는 바위들 / *be submerged beneath the sea* 해저에 가라앉혀지다 / *The waves submerged the boat.* 파도는 보트를 삼켜버렸다 / *The river overflowed and submerged the field.* 강이 범람하여 밭이 수몰되었다.
— *vi.* (P1) sink under water; go under water. 가라앉다; 잠수하다. [sub-]
the submerged tenth, the hopelessly poor class. 사회의 최하층 사람들.
sub·mer·gence [səbmə́:rdʒəns] *n.* Ⓤ the act of submerging; the state of being submerged. 침수; 잠수; 침몰.
sub·mer·sion [səbmə́:rʒən, -ʃən] *n.* = submergence.
sub·mis·sion [səbmíʃən] *n.* Ⓤ **1** the act of yielding to the power or authority of another. 굴복; 복종. ¶ *bring someone into* ~ 아무를 굴복시키다 / *offer one's* ~ 귀순을 신청하다 / *starve someone into* ~ 아무를 굶겨서 굴복시키다. **2** obedience; humbleness. 순종; 온화; 겸손. ¶ *in* ~ *to the king's order* 왕명에 순종하여 / *bow with all due* ~ 아주 공손히 절하다. [→mission]
sub·mis·sive [səbmísiv] *adj.* unresisting; obedient. 복종적인; 순종하는.
sub·mis·sive·ly [səbmísivli] *adv.* in a submissive manner; obediently. 유순하게; 순순히.
:sub·mit [səbmít] *v.* (**-mit·ted, -mit·ting**) *vt.* **1** (P6,13) 《*oneself to*》 place (oneself) under the control of another; yield or surrender oneself. …을 복종시키다; …에 따르다. ¶ *We must* ~ *ourselves to God's will.* 우리는 신의 뜻에 따라야 한다 / *I'll not* ~ *myself to insult* 〔*hard treatment*〕. 나는 모욕을〔학대를〕

감수하지는 않을 것이다. **2** (P6,13) offer 〔present〕 (something) for consideration, judgment, etc.; bring forward. …을 제출〔제기〕하다; 부탁하다. ¶ ~ *a case to the court* 법원에 소송을 제기하다 / ~ *a report* 보고서를 제출하다 / *He submitted a question to the meeting.* 그는 회의에 (해결해야 할) 하나의 문제를 제안했다. **3** (P6) offer humbly as an opinion; suggest. 공손히 의견을 말하다〔아뢰다〕. ¶ *I* ~ *that this should be allowed.* 제 생각으론 이것은 허가되어야 한다고 여겨집니다마는 / *That, I* ~ *, is a false inference.* 그것을 나는 잘못된 추측이 아닌가 생각합니다. — *vi.* (P1,3) 《*to*》 yield to authority; give way. 복종〔굴복〕하다. [sub-, L. *mitto* send]

sub·nor·mal [sʌbnɔ́:rməl] *adj.* below normal. 정상 이하의. — *n.* Ⓒ a subnormal person. 저능자(低能者). [sub-]

***sub·or·di·nate** [səbɔ́:rdənit] *adj.* **1** lower in rank, value, importance, etc. 하위의; 다음가는. ¶ *a* ~ *officer* 하급 장교 / *a* ~ *position* 하위 / *Pleasure should be* ~ *to duty.* 쾌락은 의무 다음이어야 한다. **2** under the control of others; dependent. 종속하는; 부수하는. ¶ 《gram.》 *a* ~ *clause* 〔*conjunction*〕 종속절〔종속 접속사〕.
— *n.* Ⓒ a person who is below another in rank. 부하; 아랫사람.
— [-nèit] *vt.* (P6,13) place (something) in a lower rank; make secondary. …을 종속시키다; 하위에 두다. ¶ ~ *the passions to reason* 정욕을 이성에 따르게 하다; 이성으로 정욕을 억누르다 / ~ *one's own interests to the public good* 공익을 앞세우고 사리(私利)를 뒤로 하다. [→order]

sub·or·di·na·tion [səbɔ̀:rdənéiʃən] *n.* Ⓤ **1** the act of subordinating; the state of being subordinated. 하위에 두기〔있음〕; 하위. **2** submission to authority; obedience. 종속; 복종.

sub·or·di·na·tive [səbɔ́:rdənèitiv, -dnə-] *adj.* subordinate; secondary. 종속적인.

sub·orn [sʌbɔ́:rn] *vt.* (P6) induce by bribery to commit perjury or other unlawful act. (뇌물 등을 주어) …에 위증〔거짓 맹세〕시키다. [L. *orno* equip]

sub·p(o)e·na [səbpí:nə] *n.* Ⓒ 《law》 a writ commanding one's attendance in court. 소환장. — *vt.* (P6) summon with such an order. …를 소환하다. [L. =under penalty]

sub·rou·tine [sʌ́bru:tì:n] *n.* Ⓒ 《computer》 a sequence of instructions directing a computer to perform a specific operation in the solution. 서브루틴; 아랫경로《특정 또는 다수의 프로그램 중에서 반복 사용할 수 있는 독립된 명령군(群)》. [sub-]

subs. subscription; subsidiary.

***sub·scribe** [səbskráib] *vt.* (P6) **1** give (money) to some good purpose; contribute. …을 기부하다. ¶ ~ *money to a charity* 자선 사업에 돈을 기부하다 / *He subscribed ₩100,000 to the campaign for a new hospital.* 그는 10만 원을 새 병원을 위한 캠페인에 기부했다. **2** promise to buy (something). …을 예약하다. **3** sign one's name to (a document). …에 서명하다. ¶ ~ *one's name to a petition* 청원서에 자기 이름을 서명하다 / *President subscribed his name to the document.* 대통령은 그 문서에 서명했다.
— *vi.* (P1,3) **1** 《*to*》 give money. 기부하다. ¶ ~ *to a charity hospital* 자선 병원에 기부하다〔기부를 약속하다〕 / *He subscribes every year for the Democratic party.* 그는 매년 민주당에 기부를 한다. **2** arrange to take a newspaper, a magazine, etc.; order in advance and pay (for a book, magazine, etc.). (신문·잡지의) 구독을 예약하다. ¶ ~ *to a newspaper* 〔*magazine*〕 *for a year,* 1년간 신문〔잡지〕의 구독을 예약하다 / *I have subscribed for the dictionary.* 나는 그 사전의 구입을 예약했다. **3** show agreement. 찬성〔찬동〕하다. ¶ *I don't* ~ *to such ideas* 〔*opinions*〕. 나는 그런 생각〔의견〕에 찬성할 수 없다. **4** sign one's name. 서명하다. ¶ ~ *to a document* 서류에 서명하다. [→scribble]

sub·scrib·er [səbskráibər] *n.* Ⓒ **1** a person who contributes a sum of money. 기부자. **2** a person who orders and pays for successive issues of a magazine, etc. (예약) 구독자. ¶ *a* ~ *for a book* 〔*shares*〕 책의 예약자〔주식 응모자〕 / *The magazine made a special offer to new subscribers.* 그 잡지는 새로운 구독자에게 특별 제안을 했다.

sub·script [sʌ́bskript] (opp. superscript) *adj.* written underneath or low on the line. (글자 따위) 바로 밑에 붙인〔쓴〕. ¶ *an iota* ~ 밑에 붙인 이오타《ᾳ의 ι따위》. — *n.* a number, letter, etc., written underneath and to one side of a symbol. (글자) 밑에 붙인 문자〔기호·숫자〕. ¶ *In H_2O the '2' is a* ~. H_2O에서 '2'는 subscript이다.

***sub·scrip·tion** [səbskrípʃən] *n.* Ⓤ **1** the act of subscribing. 기부; 예약. ¶ *by* ~ 예약으로. **2** a sum of money subscribed; a contribution or donation. 기부금; 예약금; 예약 구독금. ¶ *raise a* ~ 기부금을 모집하다 / *We are raising a* ~ *for the families who have suffered from the typhoon.* 태풍으로 고통을 받고 있는 가족들을 위해 기부금을 모집하고 있다 / *Your* ~ *to the newspaper runs out next month.* 너의 예약된 신문 구독 대금은 다음 달에 바닥이 난다.

sub·se·quence [sʌ́bsikwəns] *n.* Ⓤ the state of being subsequent; a subsequent event or occurrence. 뒤〔다음〕임; 뒤이어 일어남; 결과. [↓]

***sub·se·quent** [sʌ́bsikwənt] *adj.* coming later; following. 그 뒤에 일어나는; 뒤의. ¶ *Subsequent events showed that I was right.* 뒤이어 일어나는 사건들은 내가 옳았다는 것을 나타냈다. [→second]

sub·se·quent·ly [sʌ́bsikwəntli] *adv.* afterward; later. 그 후에; 계속해서. ¶ ~ *to the election* 선거 후에.

sub·serve [səbsə́ːrv] *vt.* (P6) be of help or use to (something); assist. …에 도움이 되다; 공헌하다; …을 돕다. [→serf]

sub·ser·vi·ence [səbsə́ːrviəns] *n.* Ⓤ **1** the state of being of use. 도움이 됨; 공헌함. **2** servility. 노예 근성; 비굴.

sub·ser·vi·ent [səbsə́ːrviənt] *adj.* **1** 《*to*》 useful as a means; serving to help a purpose or end. 도움이 되는; 공헌하는. **2** very obedient, like a slave; servile. 예속적인; 비굴한.

sub·side [səbsáid] *vi.* (P1) **1** fall to the bottom; sink gradually; fall〔pass, sink〕 to a lower level. 침하하다; 내려〔가라〕앉다; (물 따위가) 빠지다. ¶ *The flood waters began to* ~. 홍수의 물이 빠지기 시작했다 / *The land over the mine began to* ~. 광산 위의 지면이 내려앉기 시작하였다. **2** become calm; abate. 잠잠해지다; 진정되다. ¶ *The storm subsided.* 폭풍이 잠잠해졌다 / *The wind subsided to a calm.* 바람이 멎고 조용해졌다 / *A startled expression on his face subsided into a smile.* 그의 얼굴에 있던 놀란 표정은 미소로 바뀌었다. **3** sink into sitting. (주저)앉다. ¶ ~ *into a chair* 의자에 앉다. [L. *sido* settle]

sub·sid·ence [səbsáidəns, sʌ́bsəd-] *n.* Ⓤ the act of subsiding; a downward movement of the ground. 진정; 감퇴; (지반의) 침하. ¶ *the* ~ *of a flood* 홍수의 진정 / *the* ~ *of land* 땅의 침하.

sub·sid·i·ar·y [səbsídièri] *adj.* **1** supplementary; useful to assist; serving as a secondary help. 보조의; 보충하는. ¶ *a* ~ *book* 보조부(簿) / ~ *business* 부업 / ~ *to the main business* 부업으로서. **2** subordinate; secondary. 종속적인; 부차적인. ¶ *a* ~ *stream* 지류 / *a* ~ *company* 자회사. **3** being given money by a government or another company. 보조금을 받는. ¶ ~ *payments* 보조금. — *n.* Ⓒ (*pl.* **-ar·ies**) **1** 《usu. *pl.*》 a person or thing that assists. 보조자〔물〕. **2** a company most of whose stock is held by another company. 자회사. [→subsidy, -ary]

sub·si·dize [sʌ́bsidàiz] *vt.* (P6) assist (a company, etc.) by giving money. (회사 따위에) 보조금을 주다. ¶ *a subsidized newspaper* 어용 신문 / *a subsidized line* 보조〔명령〕 항로. [↓]

sub·si·dy [sʌ́bsidi] *n.* Ⓒ (*pl.* **-dies**) a sum of money given by a government to an enterprise, etc. as help. 보조금; 장려금. [L. =reserve troops]

sub·sist [səbsíst] *vi.* (P1) **1** continue to be; remain in existence; exist. 존재하다; 존속하다. ¶ *a country where superstition still subsists* 아직도 미신이 남아 있는 나라 / *Old customs still* ~ *in many countries.* 낡은 관습들은 아직도 많은 나라에 존재한다. **2** 《*on, by*》 maintain life; live. 살아가다; 생존하다. ¶ ~ *on vegetables*〔*rice*〕 채식으로〔쌀로〕 살아가다 / ~ *by begging* 걸식으로 연명하다 / ~ *on one's old-age pension* 노령 연금으로 생활하다 / *We are unable to* ~ *without air and water.* 공기와 물이 없으면 우리는 생존할 수 없다. — *vt.* (P6) feed. …에게 먹을 것을 주다. ¶ ~ *the army* 군대를 양성하다. [L. *sto* stand]

sub·sist·ence [səbsístəns] *n.* Ⓤ **1** existence. 존재. ¶ *His income is at* ~ *level.* 그의 수입은 입에 풀칠할 정도이다. **2** means of living; livelihood. 살림; 호구지책; 생계.

sub·soil [sʌ́bsɔ̀il] *n.* Ⓤ the layer of earth that lies just under the soil. 하층토(下層土); 밑흙; 심토(心土). [sub-]

:sub·stance [sʌ́bstəns] *n.* Ⓤ **1** ⓊⒸ the material of which a thing consists; matter. 물질; 물체; 요소; 재료. ¶ *Wood is a solid* ~. 나무는 고체(固體)이다 / *Ice, snow and water are the same* ~ *in different forms.* 얼음,눈,물은 형태가 다른 동일한 물질이다 / *Soils consist of various chemical substances.* 토양은 다양한 화학적 물질로 구성되어 있다. **2** the real and essential part of a thing; the essence. 실체; 본질. ¶ *The very* ~ *of the ambitions is merely the shadow of a dream.* 야망의 본질은 꿈의 그림자에 지나지 않는다 / *The* ~ *of democracy is equal rights, opportunity and treatment.* 민주주의의 본질은 권리, 기회 및 대우의 평등이다 / *That was but a shadow, this was the* ~. 저것은 그림자에 지나지 않았고 이것이 실체였다. **3** the chief point of a speech or a book. 요지; 대의. ¶ *the* ~ *of his speech* 그의 연설의 요지. **4** wealth. 자산. ¶ *a man of* ~ 자산가 / *waste one's* ~ 재산을 낭비하다. **5** solid quality or character; density; real content. 실질; (직물 따위) 바탕(의 짜임새); 실속. ¶ *This cloth lacks* ~. 이 옷감은 바탕이 얇다 / *There is no* ~ *in his beliefs.* 그의 신념에는 알맹이가 없다. [L. *sto* stand]

in substance, **a**) mainly. 대체적으로. ¶ *I agree with you in* ~. 나는 대체적으로 너에게 동의한다. **b**) really; in fact. 실제로.

sub·stand·ard [sʌbstǽndərd] *adj.* below standard; not adequate or sufficient. 표준 이하의; (법정) 기준에 맞지 않는. [sub-]

·sub·stan·tial [səbstǽnʃəl] *adj.* **1** really existing; actual. 실재(實在)의; 실제의. ¶ *a* ~ *being* 실재하는 것〔사람〕 / *the* ~ *world* 현실의 세계 / *Dreams and ghosts are not* ~. 꿈과 유령은 실체적이 아니다. **2** made of a good substance; solid; strong. 견실한; 튼튼한. ¶ *a* ~ *building* 견고한 건물 / *a man of* ~ *build* 튼튼한 체격을 가진 사람 / *a* ~ *meal* 실속 있는 식사. **3** of real worth; important; considerable. 가치 있는; 중요한; 꽤 많은. ¶ *a* ~ *sum of money* 꽤 많은 금액 / *a* ~ *income*〔*gain*〕 상당한 (액수의) 수입〔이익〕 / *make a* ~ *contribution* 다대(多大)한 공헌을〔기부를〕

하다 / *He has made ~ improvement in English.* 그는 영어가 꽤 많이 향상되었다. **4** deserving the name in essentials, virtual, practical; real or true for the most part; in substance. 본질적인; 실질상의. ¶ *~ performance of contract* 실질상의 계약 이행 / *two stories in ~ agreement* 본질적〔기본적〕으로는 일치하고 있는 두 이야기 / *There is a ~ reason for doubt.* 의심할 만한 충분한 이유가 있다. **5** wealthy. 재산이 있는. ¶ *a ~ firm* 재력이 있는 회사. [→substance]

sub·stan·ti·al·i·ty [səbstæ̀nʃiǽləti] *n.* Ⓤ the state of being substantial; real existence; solidity; real worth. 실재(實在); 실체; 견고; 진가(眞價).

sub·stan·tial·ly [səbstǽnʃəli] *adv.* essentially; really; mainly; strongly. 실질상; 참으로; 대체로; 튼튼히. ¶ *Our ideas are ~ the same.* 우리들의 생각은 대체로 같다.

sub·stan·ti·ate [səbstǽnʃièit] *vt.* **1** (P6) prove (something) to be true by showing evidence. …의 존재를〔정당성을〕 실증〔입증〕하다. ¶ *~ a claim* 〔*statement*〕 요구〔진술〕의 정당성을 실증하다. **2** give substantial existence to (something); make (something) real. …을 실체화하다. ¶ *~ an idea through action* 생각을 행동으로 나타내다.

sub·stan·ti·a·tion [səbstæ̀nʃiéiʃən] *n.* Ⓤ the act of substantiating; the state of being substantiated; proof; embodiment. 입증; 실체화.

sub·stan·tive [sʌ́bstəntiv] *n.* Ⓒ 《gram.》 a noun; a word or a group of words used as a noun. 명사; 명사 상당어(구). ¶ *a ~ adjective* 명사적 형용사. — *adj.* **1** 《gram.》 showing existence; used as a noun. 존재를 나타내는; 명사로서 쓰이는. ¶ *The verb 'to be' is the ~ verb.* 동사 'to be'는 존재를 나타내는 동사이다. **2** independent. 자립의. ¶ *a ~ nation* 독립국. **3** real. 실재의. ¶ *a ~ being* 영속성이 있는 실재물 / *He is temporarily a major but his ~ rank is captain.* 그는 임시 소령이지만 실제 계급은 대위이다. [→substance]

sub·sta·tion [sʌ́bstèiʃən] *n.* Ⓒ a branch station. 지서; 지국. [sub-]

:sub·sti·tute [sʌ́bstitjù:t] *n.* Ⓒ a thing used instead of another; a person taking the place of another. 대리; 대용품. ¶ *substitutes for butter* 버터의 대용품 / *a sugar ~* 설탕의 대용품.

— *vt.* (P13) 《*for*》 use or place (something) in place of another. …으로 바꾸다; …을 대용하다. ¶ *~ nylon for cotton* 면 대신에 나일론을 사용하다 / *erase a word and ~ another* 한 낱말을 지우고 다른 낱말을 대신 넣다 / *They substituted Mr. Smith for him.* 그들은 그 사람 대신 스미스씨를 썼다.

— *vi.* (P3) take the place of another. 대리〔대신〕하다. ¶ *He substituted for his president who was in hospital.* 그는 입원 중인 사장의 대리 노릇을 했다. [L. *statuo* put]

sub·sti·tu·tion [sʌ̀bstətjú:ʃən] *n.* ⓊⒸ the act of substituting; the state of being substituted. 대리; 대용; 대체; 교환.

sub·stra·ta [sʌ́bstrèitə, -rǽtə] *n.* pl. of **substratum.**

sub·stra·tum [sʌ́bstrèitəm, -rǽt-] *n.* Ⓒ (*pl.* **-stra·ta** or **-stra·tums**) **1** the layer lying below another. 하층. **2** a basis; a foundation. 토대; 기초. [sub-, L. *sterno* spread, strew]

sub·struc·ture [sʌ́bstrʌ̀ktʃər] *n.* Ⓒ a structure which forms the foundation of a building; foundation; the supporting part of a structure or building. 기초; 토대; 하부 구조. [sub-]

sub·sume [sʌbsú:m] *vt.* (P6) 《log.》 include in some particular class. 포함하다. [→assume]

sub·teen [sʌ́btí:n] *n.* a person approaching the teens. 13세 이하〔10대 미만〕의 어린이. [sub-]

sub·tend [səbténd, sʌb-] *vt.* (P6) 《math.》 be opposite to. (현(弦)·삼각형의 변이 호(弧)·각(角)에) 대(對)하다.

sub·ter·fuge [sʌ́btərfjù:dʒ] *n.* Ⓒ a trick or an excuse to escape from a difficulty, blame, etc. (곤란·비난을 피하려는) 속임수; 핑계; 구실. [L.]

sub·ter·ra·ne·an [sʌ̀btəréiniən] *adj.* under the earth; underground; hidden. 지하의; 숨은. ¶ *a ~ railway* 〔*railroad*〕 지하철 / *~ water* 지하수 / *a ~ line* (전선 등의) 지하선(線). [→terra]

sub·ter·ra·ne·ous [sʌ̀btəréiniəs] *adj.* =subterranean.

sub·ti·tle [sʌ́btàitl] *n.* Ⓒ **1** an additional title of a book, etc. (책 따위의) 부제(副題). **2** printed explanatory words in motion pictures. (영화 따위의 화면에서) 설명 자막. [sub-]

***sub·tle** [sʌ́tl] *adj.* (**sub·tler, sub·tlest**) **1** delicate; faint; mysterious. 미묘한; 희미한; 신비적인. ¶ *a ~ smile* 엷은 미소 / *a ~ distinction* 미세한 구별 / *~ irony* 미묘한 빈정거림 / *a ~ charm* 〔*power*〕 신비스런 매력〔힘〕 / *The flowers send out a ~ odor.* 꽃들은 희미한 향기를 풍긴다 / *Subtle humor is hard to understand.* 미묘한 유머는 이해하기가 어렵다. **2** clever; keen. 민감한; 예민한. ¶ *~ insight* 〔*intellect*〕 예민한 통찰력〔지성〕 / *a ~ observer* 〔*scholar*〕 치밀한 관찰자〔학자〕. **3** cunning; sly. 교활한. ¶ *a ~ enemy* 방심할 수 없는 적 / *a ~ plan to cheat him* 그를 속이려는 교활한 계획. [L. =finewoven]

sub·tle·ty [sʌ́tlti] *n.* (*pl.* **-ties**) **1** Ⓤ the quality of being subtle. 미묘; 예민; 교묘; 음험. **2** Ⓒ something subtle. 미묘한 것.

sub·tly [sʌ́tli] *adv.* in a subtle manner. 미묘하게; 예민하게; 교활하게.

sub·tract [səbtrǽkt] *vt.* (P6,13) take away; deduct. …을 빼다; 감하다(opp. add). ¶ *Subtract 2 from 5, and have 3.* 5에서

2를 빼면 3이 된다 / *That subtracts nothing from his merit.* 그것으로 인해 그의 공적은 조금도 감소되지 않는다. [→trace]

·**sub·trac·tion** [səbtrǽkʃən] *n.* UC the act of subtracting. 공제; 뺄셈(opp. addition).

sub·trop·i·cal [sʌ̀btrápikəl / -trɔ́p-] *adj.* of the regions bordering on the tropics; nearly tropical. 아열대의. ¶ *a ~ plant* 아열대 식물. [sub-]

:**sub·urb** [sʌ́bəːrb] *n.* C 《usu. *pl.*》 a district on the outskirts of a large city. 교외. ¶ *I live in the suburbs of Seoul.* 나는 서울 교외에 살고 있다. [→urban]

sub·ur·ban [səbə́ːrbən] *adj.* **1** of the suburbs. 교외의. ¶ *a ~ supermarket* 교외에 있는 슈퍼마켓 / *a ~ community* 교외의 공동사회. **2** characteristic of life in the suburbs. 교외 생활 특유의.

sub·ur·bi·a [səbə́ːrbiə] *n.* U 《*collectively*》 **1** suburbs. 교외. **2** people living in the suburbs. 교외 거주자.

sub·ven·tion [səbvénʃən] *n.* C money given by a government to help or support a study, an undertaking, etc.; subsidy. 보조금; 조성금. [L. *venio* come]

sub·ver·sion [səbvə́ːrʒən, -ʃən] *n.* U the act of subverting; the state of being subverted; overthrow; ruin. 전복; 타도; 파괴. [*subvert*]

sub·ver·sive [səbvə́ːrsiv] *adj.* tending to subvert or overthrow; liable to cause ruin; destructive. 전복하는; 타도하는; 파괴하는. ¶ *~ activities* 파괴 활동.

sub·vert [səbvə́ːrt] *vt.* (P6) overthrow; destroy; ruin. …을 전복하다; 타도하다; 파괴하다. ¶ *~ the government* 〔*empire*〕 정부를〔제국을〕 전복하다. [L. *verto* turn]

:**sub·way** [sʌ́bwèi] *n.* C **1** 《U.S.》 an underground railway. 지하철. **2** 《Brit.》 an underground passage. 지하도. [sub-]

:**suc·ceed** [səksíːd] *vi.* **1** (P1,3) 《*in*》 do well; have success; be fortunate in one's career. 성공하다; 출세하다(opp. fail). 參考 명사형은 success. ¶ *~ in the examination* 시험에 합격하다 / *~ as an artist* 〔*a doctor*〕 예술가〔의사〕로서 성공하다 / *~ in life* 입신 출세하다 / *~ beyond all expectations* 예상 이상으로 성공하다 / *I succeeded in finding an empty seat.* 운 좋게 빈 자리를 발견할 수 있었다 / *Half hearted attempts rarely ~.* 뜨뜻미지근한 시도는 좀처럼 성공하지 못한다 / *The business succeeded with him.* 그는 사업에 성공하였다. **2** (P1,3) 《*to*》 be next to take an office, a position, a rank, etc.; follow; become heir. 잇따르다; 뒤를 잇다; 후임이 되다; 상속하다. ¶ *~ to the throne* 〔*office*〕 왕위를 계승하다〔직책의 후임자가 되다〕 / *He succeeded to his father's estate* 〔*property*〕. 그는 아버지의 재산을 상속했다 / *I succeeded to a hard work.* 나는 어려운 일을 물려받았다 / *The storm died down, and a great calm succeeded.* 폭풍이 잠자고 아주 잔잔한 고요가 그 뒤를 이었다 / *On Kennedy's death, Johnson succeeded as President.* 케네디의 사후 존슨이 대통령으로 그 뒤를 이었다. 參考 명사형은 succession. — *vt.* (P6) **1** 《*as, in*》 come after and take the place of (someone). …의 뒤를 잇다; (지위·재산 따위를) 상속하다. ¶ *~ one's father* 아버지의 뒤를 잇다 / *~ someone as Premier* 아무의 후임으로서 수상이 되다 / *Elizabeth succeeded Mary as queen.* 엘리자베스는 여왕으로서 메리의 뒤를 이었다. **2** follow (something) in order or time. …에 잇따르다; …의 뒤에 오다; …에 잇따라 일어나다. ¶ *Night succeeds day.* 낮이 가면 밤이 온다 / *Rumor succeeded rumor.* 소문이 소문을 낳아 점점 퍼져 나갔다 / *The applause was succeeded by a silence.* 박수 갈채가 멎고 조용해졌다. [L. *cedo* go]

succeed in (*doing*), manage to do. …에 성공하다.

succeed in rich, become rich. 부자가 되다.

:**suc·cess** [səksés] *n.* **1** UC the act of succeeding; a favorable result; good fortune; triumph. 성공; 행운; 승리(opp. failure). ¶ *a military ~* 전승 / *one's ~ in business* 사업에서의 성공 / *drink ~ to someone* 아무의 성공을 축하해서 건배하다 / *My efforts were crowned with ~.* 나의 노력은 성공을 거두었다 / *He has had great ~ in life.* 그는 크게 성공〔입신 출세〕했다. **2** C a person or thing that succeeds. 성공자; 성공한 것. ¶ *He is a ~ in business.* 그는 실업계의 성공자이다 / *The circus was a great ~.* 서커스는 대성공이었다 / *I count that book among my successes.* 그 책은 나의 성공작들 중의 하나다. [↑]

make a success of (=*succeed in*) *something.* …을 훌륭하게 해내다.

:**suc·cess·ful** [səksésfəl] *adj.* **1** having a favorable result; having achieved success. 성공한; 좋은 결과의; 잘된. ¶ *a ~ candidate* 당선자; 합격자 / *a ~ war* 이긴 전쟁 / *His attempts were very* 〔*highly*〕 *~.* 그의 시도는 대성공이었다 / *He was ~ in the examination.* 그는 시험에 합격했다 / *I tried to persuade him but was not ~.* 나는 그를 설득하려고 했으나 잘 되지 않았다. **2** favored in one's career; fortunate; prosperous. 행운의; 입신 출세한. ¶ *He is a ~ man in life.* 그는 인생에 있어서 성공자이다.

·**suc·cess·ful·ly** [səksésfəli] *adv.* with success. 성공적으로; 훌륭하게.

·**suc·ces·sion** [səkséʃən] *n.* **1** C the coming of one thing or person after another; a series. 연속; 계속하여〔뒤이어〕 일어남; 연속물. ¶ *in ~* 연속해서 / *a ~ of misfortunes* 불행의 연속 / *win three victories in quick ~* 잇따라서 세 번 승리를 거두다 / *many troubles in ~* 꼬리를 물고 일어나는 말썽거리 / *I had a ~ of colds.* 나는 계속 감기가 들었다 / *A ~ of accidents spoiled our car trip.* 연이어 일어난 사고로 우리의 자동차 여행은 엉망이 되었다. **2** U the act or right of succeeding to a position, property, etc. 계승; 상속(권). ¶ *the ~ to the throne* 왕위 계승 / *the law of ~* 상속법 / *~ duties* 상속세 / *in ~ to...* …의 뒤를 이어; …의 후임으로 / *claim the ~* 상속권을 주장하다 / *settle the ~* 계승자를 결정하다 / *He is not in the ~.* 그에게는 상속권이 없다 / *He is second in the ~.* 그는 상속 순위 제2위이다.

by succession, by heredity. 세습에 의해.

in succession, one after another. 잇따라; 연속해서.

·suc·ces·sive [səksésiv] *adj.* coming one after another. 잇따르는; 연속하는. ¶ *He won three ~ games.* 그는 연속 세 게임을 이겼다.

suc·ces·sive·ly [səksésivli] *adv.* one after another. 잇따라; 차례로.

·suc·ces·sor [səksésər] *n.* Ⓒ **1** a person who succeeds or follows another. 계승자. **2** a thing that comes after another. 뒤에 오는 것; 대신하는 것.

suc·cinct [səksíŋkt] *adj.* (sometimes **-er, -est**) clearly expressed in few words. 문체가 간결한. [→cincture]

suc·cinct·ly [səksíŋktli] *adv.* in a succinct manner. 간결히.

suc·cinct·ness [səksíŋktnis] *n.* Ⓤ the state of being succinct. 간결; 간명.

suc·cor, 《Brit.》 **-cour** [sʌ́kər] *n.* **1** Ⓤ help; aid. 원조; 구원. ¶ *give someone ~* 아무를 구조하다. **2** Ⓒ a person or thing that helps. 구조자〔물〕. — *vt.* (P6) help (someone in difficulty). …을 돕다; 구원하다. [→course]

suc·cu·lence [sʌ́kjələns] *n.* Ⓤ juiciness. 즙이 많음; 다즙(多汁). [↓]

suc·cu·lent [sʌ́kjələnt] *adj.* full of juice. 다즙의; 즙이 많은. ¶ *a ~ fruit* 즙이 많은 과일. [L. *succus* juice]

suc·cumb [səkʌ́m] *vi.* (P1,3) **1** be conquered by a person or thing and obey. 지다; 굴복하다. ¶ *~ to temptation* 유혹에 지다 / *~ to one's enemies* 〔*numbers*〕 적〔다수〕에게 굴복하다. **2** yield to disease; die. 병으로 쓰러지다; 죽다. ¶ *~ to heart disease* 심장병으로 쓰러지다〔죽다〕 / *~ from head injuries* 머리의 부상으로 죽다. [L. *cumbo* lie]

:such [sʌtʃ, sətʃ] *adj.* 《the order with *a* or *an* is *such a,* not *a such*》 **1** 《showing a particular person or thing already or to be mentioned or meant》 of that kind, degree, or quality. 그러한; 이〔그〕와 같은; 그런; 그 같은. ¶ *~ a man* 그러한 사람 / *all ~ men* 그런 사람은 모두 / *food of ~ kind* 그 같은 종류의 식품 / *Such men are dangerous.* 그런 사람들은 위험하다 / *I said no ~ thing.* 그러한 것은 아무 말도 하지 않았다 / 《*prov.*》 *Such master, ~ man.* 그 주인에 그 머슴 / *Such luxury was unfamiliar to her.* 그런 사치는 그녀에게 익숙지 않았다 / *You will never have another ~ chance.* 이와 같은 기회는 두 번 다시 없을 것이다. **2** 《with *as*》 of the same kind, degree, or quality. (…와 같은) 그런; 그러한. ¶ *children ~ as these* 이들과 같은 그런 아이들 / *~ things as iron, silver, and gold* 철, 은, 금과 같은 것들 / *a tradesman, ~ as a baker or a shopkeeper* 빵장수나 소매 상인과 같은 장사꾼 / *Such painters as Picasso are rare.* =*Painters ~ as Picasso are rare.* 피카소와 같은 화가는 드물다 / *He is a great scientist ~ as we all admire.* 그는 우리 모두가 존경하는 위대한 과학자이다. **3** 《with *that*》 of the kind, degree, or quality (that). …(할이)만큼〔정도〕의; 대단히 …한. ¶ *He had ~ a fright that he could not speak.* 그는 너무 놀라서 말을 할 수가 없을 정도였다 / *She had ~ a fever that she fainted.* 그녀는 열이 높아서 졸도하였다 / *His behavior was ~ that everyone disliked him.* 그의 행동은 좋지 않아서 모두가 그를 싫어했다. **4** so great, so much, so good, etc. 그렇게〔이렇게, 저토록〕 (…한); 대단한; 훌륭한; 지독한. ¶ *~ a good* 〔*kind*〕 *man* 그렇게 좋은〔친절한〕 사람 / *~ a wonderful time* 이렇게 멋진 시간 / *I have never seen ~ a large one.* 이렇게 큰 것은 아직껏 본 적이 없다 / *I never dreamed of ~ a kind reception.* 그런 환대는 꿈에도 생각지 못했다 / *He is ~ a liar!* 참 그는 지독한 거짓말쟁이군 / *Did you ever see ~ wealther?* 참, 이런 고약한 날씬 처음 보겠군 그래.

such and such, certain. 이러이러〔여차여차〕한.

such a*(*n*) *one, a certain person. 이런 사람; 모(某)….

such as it is, not of a very good kind or quality. 변변치 못하지만; 대단한 것은 아니지만. ¶ *The food, ~ as it was, was plentiful.* 음식은 변변치 못했으나 많이 있었다 / *You can use my car, ~ as it is.* 좋은 자동차는 아니지만, 내 차를 이용하십시오.

— *pron.* **1** this or that kind of person or thing; such a person 〔persons〕 or thing 〔things〕. 이러한〔그러한〕 사람〔물건·일〕. ¶ *Such is life.* 인생이란 그런 것이다 / *In his pocket were marbles, stones and ~.* 그의 주머니 속에는 공기돌, 돌맹이 따위가 있었다 / *Peace to all ~!* 그런 사람들 모두에게 평화가 있기를 / *Such was his real intention.* 그의 참뜻은 그런 것이었다. **2** 《with *as*》 those people who. 그런 사람들. ¶ *Such as have erred must be punished.* 잘못을 범한 사람은 처벌을 받아야 한다 / *He seemed to be a friend but was not ~.* 그는 보기에는 친구 같았지만 실제는 친구랄 게 없었다. **3** this thing, these circumstances, etc. 이런 일; 사정. ¶ *~ being the case* 이런〔그런〕 사정으로 / *If ~ is the case, I will go.* 사정이 그렇다면 내가 가겠다. [E. =so-like]

as such, **a**) as being what has been mentioned. 그런〔이런〕 것〔자격〕으로서. ¶ *He is a child, and must be treated as ~.* 그는 아이니까 아이로서 취급을 받아야 한다 / *He is a leader, and as ~, must be obeyed.* 그는 지도자이므로 지도자로서 (사람들의) 복종을 받아

야 한다. **b**) in itself. 그 자체로; 그것만으로. *The gift, as ~, was of little worth.* 선물 그 자체로는 별로 가치가 없었다.

such as, for example; like. 예를 들면; …같은. [E. =so like]

such·like [sʌ́tʃlàik] *adj.* 《*colloq.*》 of such a kind. 이와 같은. — *pron.* persons or things of such a kind. 이러한 사람[것].

*__suck__ [sʌk] *vt.* **1** (P6,7,13,18) 《*from, out of, through*》 draw (liquid) into the mouth by the action of the lips and tongue; draw the liquid from (something). …을 빨다; 홀쩍홀쩍[빨아] 마시다. ¶ *~ an orange dry* 오렌지를 즙이 없어질 때까지 빨다 / *~ the milk from the bottle* 병에서 우유를 홀쩍홀쩍 마시다 / *~ the breast* 젖을 빨다 / *~ lemonade through [from] a straw* 빨대로 레몬수를 빨아 마시다 / *Bees ~ honey.* 벌들이 꿀을 빤다 / *The baby was sucking its mother's breast.* 어린애가 엄마의 젖을 빨고 있었다. **2** (P6,7,13) 《*from*》 draw (moisture, air, etc.) by any process resembling this; absorb. …을 빨아들이다; 들이마시다; 흡수하다. ¶ *~ in the morning air* 아침 공기를 들이마시다 / *A sponge sucks in water.* 스펀지는 물을 흡수한다 / *Plants ~ moisture from the earth.* 식물은 땅에서 습기를 흡수한다. **3** (P6) keep (candy, one's thumb, etc.) in the mouth, pushing the tongue against it but not biting. (손가락 따위를) 빨다; 핥다. ¶ *Small children ~ their thumbs.* 어린아이들은 엄지손가락을 빤다 / *He was sucking a piece of candy.* 그는 알사탕을 입 안에 넣고 빨아먹고 있었다. **4** (P6,7,13) gain or take in (knowledge, profit, etc.). (지식 따위를) 흡수[획득]하다; (이익을) 얻다. ¶ *~ advantage out of something* …에서 이익을 보다[얻다] / *~ knowledge into one's mind* 지식을 흡수하다. — *vi.* (P1,2A,3) **1** draw milk from a breast or bottle into the mouth; draw something by sucking. 젖을 빨다; 홀짝홀짝 마시다. **2** make the sound of sucking. (펌프가) 빨아들이는 소리를 내다; 홀짝거리다.

suck in, **a**) absorb. …을 흡수하다. **b**) (of whirlpool) engulf. …을 휘말아들이다.

suck up, draw up as by suction. …을 흡수하다; 빨아올리다.

suck up to, try to win over by flattery. …에 아첨하다.

— *n.* **1** Ⓤ the act of sucking; the sound or force of sucking. 빨기; 젖을 빨기; 빠는[빨아들이는] 소리; 빠는 힘. ¶ *give ~ to a baby* 어린아이에게 젖을 빨리다[먹이다] / *be at ~* 젖을 먹고 있다 / *a child at ~* 젖 먹는 아이. **2** Ⓒ small drink; what is sucked at one time. 한 모금; 한 번 빨기[홀짝하기]. ¶ *take a ~ at something* …을 한 번 빨다 / *She put the cigarette between her lips and took a long ~.* 그녀는 담배를 입에 물고 한 모금 길게 빨았다 / *a ~ of wine* 한 모금의 술. [E.; G. *saugen*]

suck·er [sʌ́kər] *n.* Ⓒ **1** a person or thing that sucks; a baby or young animal. 빠는 사람[것]; 젖먹이. **2** a disc-shaped organ of some animals used for sucking or holding to a surface. (낙지 따위의) 흡반; 빨판. **3** a shoot or young branch of a plant growing from the roots or the lower part of the stem. 흡지(吸枝). **4** 《*colloq.*》 a person who is very easily deceived or fooled. 잘 속는 사람; 봉. ¶ *You're a ~ to believe his stories.* 그 자의 말을 곧이듣는 너도 숫보기다. **5** 《U.S.》 =lollipop.

suck·ing [sʌ́kiŋ] *adj.* being in the state of drinking milk. (아직) 젖이 떨어지지 않은. ¶ *a ~ child.*

suck·ing-pig [sʌ́kiŋpig] *n.* a pig that is being suckled. 돼지의 젖먹이 새끼.

suck·le [sʌ́kəl] *vt.* (P6) feed (a baby) with milk; bring up. …에게 젖을 먹이다; …을 양육하다. — *vi.* (P1) suck at the breast. 젖을 먹다. [↓]

suck·ling [sʌ́kliŋ] *n.* Ⓒ **1** a baby or young animal fed with milk. 젖먹이; 유아; 아직 젖 먹는 짐승 새끼. **2** an inexperienced person 풋내기; 신출내기. [*suck*]

babes and sucklings, innocent children; 《*fig.*》 young, inexperienced persons. 천진한 아이; 풋내기.

suc·tion [sʌ́kʃən] *n.* Ⓤ the act of sucking. 흡수; 흡인. ¶ *a ~ pump* 빨펌프. [L. *sugo* suck]

Su·dan [suːdǽn, -dɑ́ːn] *n.* **1** a vast region in Africa, south of Egypt. 수단. **2** a republic in northeast Africa, south of Egypt. 수단 공화국.

Su·dan·nese [sùːdəníːz] *a.* of Sudan. 수단의. — *n.* a Sudan native. 수단 사람.

:**sud·den** [sʌ́dn] *adj.* happening or done quickly or unexpectedly; unexpected. 돌연한; 갑작스러운; 별안간의. ¶ *his ~ death* 그의 갑작스러운 죽음 / *a ~ turn [bend] in the road* 도로의 급커브 / *be ~ in action* 행동이 느닷없다. — *n.* Ⓤ the state of being sudden. 갑작스러움. [L. *subitus*]

all of a sudden =***on a sudden,*** suddenly; unexpectedly. 갑자기; 불시에.

:**sud·den·ly** [sʌ́dnli] *adv.* in a sudden manner; with suddenness. 갑자기; 불시에.

sud·den·ness [sʌ́dnnis] *n.* Ⓤ the state or quality of being sudden. 갑작스러움.

su·dor·if·ic [sùːdərífik] *adv.* causing one to sweat. 땀나게 하는. — *n.* a sudorific medicine. 발한제(發汗劑). [L. *sūdor*]

suds [sʌdz] *n. pl.* **1** soapy water; small round balls of soapy water. 비눗물; 비누 거품. **2** 《U.S. *sl.*》 beer. 맥주. [? Du.]

Sue [suː / sjuː] *n.* a nickname for Susan or Susanna. Susan, Susanna의 애칭.

sue [suː / sjuː] *vt.* (P6,13) **1** make a claim against (someone) in a court of law. …을 고소하다. ¶ *~ someone [company] for damages* 손해 배상으로 아무[회사]를 고소하다 / *He sued the railway because his trunk* *had been damaged.* 그는 가방이 망가졌기 때문에 철도 회사를 고소했다. **2** 《*for*》 beg or ask for. …을 간청하다.

— *vi.* (P1,3) **1** 《*for*》 make a claim in a court of law. 소송을 제기하다; 고소하다. ¶ ~ *for divorce* 이혼 소송을 제기하다 / ~ *for a breach of promise* 위약(違約)의 소(訴)를 제기하다. **2** 《*for*》 beg; ask. 간청하다; 구〔청〕하다. ¶ ~ *for mercy* 자비를 구하다 / ~ *for a favor* 〔*peace*〕 애고(愛顧)〔평화〕를 구하다. [→second]

suede [sweid] *n.* Ⓤ a kind of soft, tanned leather. 스웨이드 가죽. ¶ ~ *gloves.* [*swede*]

suet [sú:ət] *n.* Ⓤ the hard fat of cattle or sheep. 쇠기름; 양기름. [L. *sebum* tallow]

Su·ez [sú:ez, –´] *n.* the narrow neck of land between Asia and Africa. 수에즈 지협.

Suez Canal [´––´], **the** *n.* the canal across Suez. 수에즈 운하.

:suf·fer [sʌ́fər] *vt.* (P6) **1** have, feel, or experience (pain, hardship, discomfort, grief, etc.). (고통·손해 따위를) 입다; 받다; 당하다. ¶ ~ *loss* 손해를 입다 / ~ *punishment* 벌을 받다 / ~ *wrong* 해를 입다; 학대받다 / ~ *death* 처형되다 / *He suffered a heart attack.* 그는 심장 발작을 일으켰다 / *The company suffered 20% drop in sales.* 회사는 매상이 20% 떨어졌다. **2** 《usu. in *negative*》 allow; permit; endure. …을 참다; 견디다; 허용〔용서〕하다. ¶ *I'll not* ~ *such conduct.* 그런 행위는 용서할 수 없다 / *These trees cannot* ~ *a cold winter.* 이 나무들은 추운 겨울을 견디지 못한다 / *I will* ~ *you to be present.* 나는 네가 참석하는 것을 허용하겠다.

— *vi.* (P1,3) **1** 《*from*》 feel pain, grief, etc. 괴로워하다; 고통을 겪다; 앓다. ¶ ~ *from fever* 열병에 걸리다 / *learn to* ~ *without complaning* 고통을 당해도 불평을 않도록 명심하다 / *She suffers from headaches.* 그녀는 두통을 앓고 있다. / *Korea is suffering from over population.* 한국은 인구 과잉으로 고통을 당하고 있다. **2** 《*from*》 experience harm, damage, loss, etc.; be punished. 해를 입다, 손해를 보다; 벌을 받다. ¶ *Trade is suffering from the depression.* 무역은 경기 침체로 부진하다 / *The engine suffered severely.* 엔진이 심하게 손상됐다 / *You will* ~ *for your foolishness some day.* 너의 미련한 행동 때문에 언젠가는 혼이 날 것이다. [sub-, L. *fero* bear]

not suffer fools gladly, be impatient of fooly in others. 어리석은 짓을 용서치 않다.

suf·fer·a·ble [sʌ́fərəbəl] *adj.* bearable. 참을〔견딜〕 수 있는.

suf·fer·ance [sʌ́fərəns] *n.* Ⓤ tacit or silent consent; the power to bear. 묵인; 허용〔인내〕력. ¶ *be beyond* ~ 참을 수 없다.

on sufferance, allowed, but not really supported. 묵인되어; 눈감아 주어. ¶ *He is here on* ~. 그는 (환영받지는 못하나) 여기 있도록 묵인되고 있다.

suf·fer·er [sʌ́fərər] *n.* Ⓒ a person who suffers. 고통받는 사람; 환자. ¶ *a* ~ *from a fever* 열병 환자 / *sufferers from earthquake* 〔*war*〕 지진〔전쟁〕 이재민.

***suf·fer·ing** [sʌ́fəriŋ] *n.* **1** Ⓤ the experience of pain. 괴로움; 수난; 고통. ¶ *die without much* ~ 큰 고통 없이 죽다. **2** 《often *pl.*》 something that is suffered by someone. 재난; 고생스러움; 고통. ¶ *Their sufferings were beyond description.* 그들의 고생은 이루 형언할 수 없었다.

***suf·fice** [səfáis, -fáiz] *vi.* (P1,3,4) be enough or sufficient. 족하다; 충분하다. ¶ *A hint will* ~. 힌트 하나로 족하다 / *That suffices to prove it.* 그것은 이것을 증명하는 데 충분하다 / *A hundred dollars a month sufficed for his daily needs.* 한 달에 100달러는 그의 일용품을 사는 데 충분했다. — *vt.* (P6) be enough for; satisfy. …을 만족시키다. ¶ *Two meals a day* ~ *an old man.* 노인에겐 하루 두 끼의 식사로 족하다. [L. *facio* make]

suffice it to say…, It is enough if we say. …이라고 말하면 충분하다.

suf·fi·cien·cy [səfíʃənsi] *n.* Ⓤ 《usu. *a* ~》 an amount which is enough. 충분한 양. ¶ *a* ~ *of fuel* 충분한 양의 연료 / *The ship had a* ~ *of provisions for a voyage of two months.* 그 배는 두 달간의 항해를 위한 충분한 양의 식량을 갖고 있었다. [↓]

:suf·fi·cient [səfíʃənt] *adj.* **1** enough; as much as is needed. 충분한. ¶ ~ *proof* 충분한 증거 / *a* ~ *pension for livng expenses* 생활비에 충분한 연금 / *The food was not* ~ *for all of us.* 식량이 우리 모두를 위해서는 충분치 않았다. **2** 《*arch.*》 capable; competent; well-qualified. 기량〔능력, 자격〕이 있는. ¶ *a scholar* ~ *for the work* 그 연구를 해낼 수 있는 학자. [→suffice]

***suf·fi·cient·ly** [səfíʃəntli] *adv.* in a sufficient amount; enough. 충분히.

***suf·fix** [sʌ́fiks] *n.* Ⓒ 《gram.》 an addition placed at the end of a word. 접미사.

— [–´] *vt.* (P6) add (-ly, -ness, etc.) as a suffix. …을 접미사로서 붙이다. [sub-]

suf·fo·cate [sʌ́fəkèit] *vt.* (P6) kill (someone) by stopping the breath; make it difficult for (someone) to breathe. …을 질식(사) 시키다. ¶ *The smoke almost suffocated me.* 그 연기로 나는 질식할 뻔했다 / *The baby was suffocated in bed.* 그 어린아이는 침대에서 질식(사)했다. — *vi.* (P1) be difficult to breathe. 숨이 막히다; 질식하다. ¶ *I was suffocating with anger* 〔*excitement*〕. 노여움〔흥분〕으로 숨이 막힐 지경이었다. [sub-, L. *fauces* throat]

suf·fo·ca·tion [sʌ̀fəkéiʃən] *n.* Ⓤ the act of suffocating. 질식.

suf·fra·gan [sʌ́frəgən] *a.* assisting. 보조의. ¶ *a* ~ *bishop* 부감독. — *n.* a suffragan bishop. 부감독. [↓]

suf·frage [sʌ́fridʒ] *n.* **1** Ⓒ a vote in favor of someone or something. (찬성) 투표. **2** Ⓤ

the right to vote. 투표(선거)권. ¶ *universal ~* 보통 선거권 / *Korea granted the ~ to women in 1945.* 한국은 1945년에 여성에게 선거권(참정권)을 주었다. [L. =vote]

suf·fra·gette [sʌ̀frədʒét] *n.* a woman who agitates for the right of women to vote. 여성 참정권론자.

suf·fra·gist [sʌ́frədʒist] *n.* a person who favors giving the suffrage to more people, esp. to women. (특히) 여성 참정권론자.

suf·fuse [səfjúːz] *vt.* (P6) spread all over; cover. …을 뒤덮다. ¶ *The sky was suffused with sunlight.* 하늘은 햇빛으로 가득했다 / *eyes suffused with tears* 눈물이 글썽거리는 눈. [L. *fundo* pour]

suf·fu·sion [səfjúːʒən] *n.* Ⓤ the act of suffusing; the state of being full. 가득 채움; 충만.

:sug·ar [ʃúgər] *n.* **1** ⓐ Ⓤ a sweet white powder used in cooking. 설탕. ¶ *a lump (spoonful) of ~* 각설탕 한 개(설탕 한 숟가락) / *~ and water* 설탕물. ⓑ Ⓒ a lump of sugar. 각설탕 하나. ¶ *How many sugars in your coffee?* 커피에 설탕을 몇 개나 넣지. **2** 《chem.》 one of many kinds of sweet substances found in plants. 당(糖). ¶ *milk ~* 유당(乳糖) / *grape ~* 포도당. **3** 《*fig.*》 words intended to please. 감언; 달콤한 겉치레 말.
—*vt.* (P6) **1** make (something) sweet by mixing sugar. …을 설탕으로 달게 하다. ¶ *~ a cake* 케이크에 설탕을 치다 / *~ one's coffee* 커피에 설탕을 넣다. **2** make (someone or something) pleasant; speak honeyed words. …을 기분좋게 하다; 아첨하다. [Arab.]

sugar beet [⌐–⌐] *n.* a kind of plant from which sugar is made. 사탕무.

sugar candy [⌐–⌐–] *n.* a kind of candy made by boiling pure sugar. 얼음사탕; 고급 알사탕.

sugar cane [⌐–⌐] *n.* a tall grass from which sugar is obtained. 사탕수수.

sug·ar·y [ʃúgəri] *adj.* **1** sweet like sugar; containing sugar. 설탕처럼 단; 설탕이 든. **2** 《*fig.*》 excessively sweet. 매우 달콤한. ¶ *~ music* 달콤한(감미로운) 음악 / *a ~ voice* 달콤한 목소리 / *~ words* 감언(甘言).

:sug·gest [səgdʒést] *vt.* (P6,11) **1** 《*to*》 recall (an idea) to the mind of a person. …을 연상시키다. ¶ *Winter suggests skating and skiing.* 겨울은 스케이트나 스키 타는 것을 연상시킨다 / *Does the name ~ anything to you?* 그 이름을 듣고 무언가 생각나는 것이 없느냐. **2** offer (a plan) for consideration; lay before; put forward; propose. …을 제안(제의)하다. ¶ *~ a plan (walk)* 계획(산책)을 제안(제의)하다 / *He suggested going to the theater.* 그는 극장에 가지 않겠느냐고 했다 / *I suggested to them that somebody neutral take the chair.* 불편 부당한 인물을 의장으로 삼는 것이 좋겠다고 그들에게 제의했다 / *I'd like to ~ alternative plan.* 나는 다른 안을 제의할까 하오. **3** hint; show (something) in an indirect way. …을 암시하다; 넌지시 비추다(말하다). ¶ *His skill suggests long training.* 그의 솜씨는 오랜 훈련을 암시한다 / *Her appearance suggests that she is living a happy life.* 그녀의 외모는 그녀가 행복하게 살고 있다는 것을 말해 준다. **4** 《*I ~ that…* 의 형태로》 say or state as a possibility. …이라고 생각하는데 정말이지. 參考 변호사가 증인 심문시 사용되는 상투 문구. ¶ *I ~ that you are not speaking the truth.* 네가 진실을 말하고 있지 않다고 생각하는데, 어떤가 / *I ~ that you concluded a secret agreement with him.* 너와 그 사이에 밀약이 있었던 것으로 아는데, 정말이지. [sub-, L. *gero* bring]
suggest itself to (*someone*), occur to (him); come into (his mind). (…의) 마음(머리)에 떠오르다. ¶ *An idea suggested itself to me.* 어떤 생각이 머리에 떠올랐다.

sug·gest·i·ble [səgdʒéstəbəl] *adj.* **1** open to (hypnotic suggestion). (최면술의) 암시에 걸리기 쉬운. ¶ *a ~ girl.* **2** that can be suggested. 암시(제의)할 수 있는.

sug·ges·ti·o fal·si [sədʒéstiou fǽlsai] *n.* 《L.》 a positive misrepresentation not involving a direct lie. (고의가 아닌) 허위의 암시.

·sug·ges·tion [səgdʒéstʃən] *n.* **1** Ⓤ the act of recalling an idea to the mind of a person; Ⓒ an idea brought to the mind by a natural connection. 연상시키기; 연상. ¶ *call up suggestions of…* …을 연상시키다. **2** Ⓤ the act of offering a plan; Ⓒ a plan, an idea, etc. that is offered. 제안(하기); 제안된 것. ¶ *at (on) the ~ of* …의 제안으로(발의로) / *suggestions for improvements* 개선안 / *I made the ~ that the meeting (should) be brought to an end.* 나는 폐회할 것을 제안했다 / *His ~ was approved.* 그의 제안은 승인되었다. **3** Ⓤ the act of showing something in an indirect way; Ⓒ a hint. 넌지시 비춤; 암시. ¶ *a talk full of suggestions* 시사하는 바가 많은 담화. **4** Ⓒ a trace; a very slight amount. 기미(氣味); 매우 적은(희미한) 양. ¶ *blue with a ~ of green* 희미한 녹색을 띤 청색 / *There is no ~ of a foreign accent in his speech.* 그의 말에는 외국 억양이 조금도 없다.

sug·ges·tive [səgdʒéstiv] *adj.* **1** tending to suggest; full of suggestions; suggesting. 암시적인; 암시하는; 연상시키는. ¶ *a ~ article (commentary)* 암시적인 기사(논평) / *weather ~ of autumn* 가을을 연상시키는 날씨 / *The symphony is ~ of a sunrise.* 그 교향곡은 일출을 연상시킨다. **2** tending to suggest something improper or indecent. 외설스러운. ¶ *~ remarks.*

sug·ges·tive·ly [səgdʒéstivli] *adv.* with a suggestion. 암시적으로.

su·i·cid·al [sùːəsáidl] *adj.* of suicide; causing suicide. 자살의; 자살하고 싶은 충동에 사로잡히는. ¶ *with ~ intent* 자살의 목적으

로 / *a* ~ *explosion* 자폭 / *I was feeling positively* ~. 강한 자살 욕구를 느끼고 있었다. [↓]

•**su·i·cide** [sú:əsàid] *n.* **1** ⓊⒸ the act of killing oneself. 자살(행위). ¶ *commit* ~ 자살하다. **2** Ⓒ a person who kills himself. 자살자. **3** 《*fig.*》 destruction of one's own interests. 자멸(적) 행위. ¶ *political* ~ 정치적 자멸 행위. [L. *se* self, *caedo* kill]

⁝**suit** [su:t] *n.* **1** Ⓒ a set of clothes worn together, as a jacket and either trousers or a skirt. (한 벌의) 옷. ¶ *a* ~ *of clothes* 한 벌의 옷 / *A man's* ~ *consists of a jacket, waistcoat, and trousers; a woman's* ~ *of a coat and a skirt.* 남자의 옷 한 벌은 윗도리, 조끼 및 바지로 이루어지며, 여성의 옷 한 벌은 윗도리와 스커트이다. **2** Ⓒ a claim or question to be settled by a court of law; an action taken to a court of law. 고소; 소송. ¶ *start a* ~ *to cover damages* 손해 배상 소송을 제기하다 / *bring* 〔*file, institute, start*〕 *a* ~ *against someone* 아무를 고소하다 / *win* 〔*lose*〕 *a* ~ 승소〔패소〕하다 / *a civil* 〔*criminal*〕 ~ 민사〔형사〕 소송. **3** Ⓒ one of the four sets (spades, hearts, diamonds, and clubs) of playing cards. (트럼프 패의) 짝패 한 벌. ¶ *black suits* 검은 짝패《clubs와 spades》. **4** ⓊⒸ 《*lit.*》 an act of asking or requesting, esp. for marriage made by men. 청원; 탄원; (특히) 구혼. ¶ *make* ~ *to someone* …에게 청원하다 / *press* 〔*push*〕 *one's* ~ 애소하다; 거듭 탄원〔구혼〕하다 / *grant someone's* ~ 아무의 소원을 받아들이다 / *fail* 〔*prosper*〕 *in one's* ~ 구혼에 실패〔성공〕하다.

follow suit, **a**) follow the example of another. 남이 하는 대로 하다. **b**) play a card of the same suit as that led. (카드놀이에서) 처음 내놓은 패와 같은 패를 내다.

in one's birthday suit, naked. 나체로.

make suit, urge humble request. 탄원하다.

— *vt.* (P6) **1** 《*to, for*》 make (someone or something) suitable; fit. …을 적합하게 하다; 일치시키다. ¶ ~ *one's action to one's word* (협박 따위를) 말한 대로 실행하다 / ~ *one's style to one's audience* 말하는 식을 청중에게 맞추다 / *He is not suited for teaching.* = *He is not suited to be a teacher.* 그는 선생으로 적격이 아니다. **2** look well on (someone or something). (옷 따위가) …에 잘 어울리다. ¶ *This necktie does not* ~ *me.* 이 넥타이는 나에게 잘 어울리지 않는다 / *The color suits her* (*complexion*) *admirably.* 그 색은 그녀(의 피부색)에게 참으로 잘 어울린다. **3** be convenient for (someone); satisfy; please. (목적·조건·필요 따위)에 형편이 들어맞다; 알맞다; …의 마음에 들다. ¶ ~ *oneself* 좋을 대로〔마음대로〕 하다 / *The climate suits me.* 기후가 나에게 맞는다 / *That does not* ~ *all tastes.* 그것이 모든 사람의 취향에 맞을 수는 없다 / *Would it* ~ *you to come tomorrow?* 내일 오실 수 있을는지요 / *It's impossible to* ~ *everyone.* 모든 사람의 마음에 들게 할 수는 없다.

— *vi.* (P1) be convenient; be satisfactory. 형편이 들어맞다〔알맞다〕; 만족스럽다. ¶ *Will that time* ~*?* 그 시간에 괜찮겠느냐. [→second]

suit·a·bil·i·ty [sù:təbíləti] *n.* Ⓤ the state of being suitable. 적합; 적당; 적부; 어울림.

•**suit·a·ble** [sú:təbəl] *adj.* 《*for, to*》 proper; well-fitting. 어울리는; 적당한. ¶ *a* ~ *house in a* ~ *place* 알맞은 장소에 있는 적당한 집 / *a* ~ *actress for the play* 그 연극에 딱 들어맞는 여배우 / *A simple dress is* ~ *for school wear.* 간단한 복장이 교복에 적당하다.

suit·a·bly [sú:təbli] *adv.* in a suitable manner. 적당히; 알맞게; 어울리게.

•**suit·case** [sú:tkèis] *n.* Ⓒ a flat traveling case for carrying clothes. 여행 가방.

suite [swi:t] *n.* Ⓒ **1** a number of things making a set or series. 한 벌; 한 세트. **2** a set of furniture for one room. 가구 한 벌. **3** 《mus.》 several instrumental movements or pieces composed as a group. 조곡(組曲); 모음곡. **4** a group of attendants or followers. 수행원; 일행. **5** a set of connected rooms as an appartment or in a hotel. (두 칸 이상이) 달려 있는 한 구획의 방. ¶ *A* ~ *in a hotel consists of a bedroom, a sitting-room, and a bathroom.* 호텔에서 스위트는 침실, 거실 및 화장실로 구성된다. [*suit*]

suit·ing [sú:tiŋ] *n.* cloth for making suits. 양복지.

suit·or [sú:tər] *n.* Ⓒ **1** a man who asks a woman to marry him. 구혼자. **2** a person who brings a case into a law court. 원고(原告). **3** a person who makes a request. 청원자.

sul·fate, 《Brit.》 **-phate** [sʌ́lfeit] *n.* ⓊⒸ 《chem.》 any salt of sulfuric acid. 황산염. [↓]

•**sul·fur,** 《Brit.》 **-phur** [sʌ́lfər] *n.* Ⓤ 《chem.》 a yellow material burning with a blue flame and producing a sharp smell. 황. — *adj.* greenish-yellow. 황색의. [L.]

sul·fu·re·ous, 《Brit.》 **-phu-** [sʌlfjúəriəs] *adj.* of or containing sulfur; like sulfur; sulfurous. 황의; 황을 함유하는; 황 모양의.

sul·fu·ric, 《Brit.》 **-phu-** [sʌlfjúərik] *adj.* containing or of sulfur. 황을 함유한; 황의.

sul·fur·ous, 《Brit.》 **-phur-** [sʌ́lfərəs] *adj.* of or containing sulfur; sulfureous. 황의; 황을 함유한.

sulk [sʌlk] *vi.* (P1) keep silent in an ill-humored state; be sullen. 시무룩해지다; 부루퉁해지다. — *n.* 《usu. *pl.*》 a sulky state. 부루퉁함; 시무룩함. [*sulky*]

sulk·i·ly [sʌ́lkili] *adv.* in a sullen mood. 부루퉁해서; 심술나서; 시무룩해서.

sulk·i·ness [sʌ́lkinis] *n.* Ⓤ the state of being sulky; sullenness; displeasure. 부루퉁함; 찌무룩함.

sulk·y [sʌ́lki] *adj.* (**sulk·i·er, sulk·i·est**)

in a bad humor; sullen. 부루퉁한; 실쭉한. — *n.* Ⓒ (*pl.* **sulk·ies**) a light two-wheeled carriage for one person. 1인승 2륜 마차. [O.E. *solcen-* lazy]

·**sul·len** [sʌ́lən] *adj.* **1** silent; showing bad humor. 부루퉁한; 찌무룩한; 기분이 언짢은. ¶ *a ~ face* 〔*expression*〕 부루퉁한 얼굴〔기분이 언짢은 표정〕 / *He is ~ by nature.* 본디 무뚝뚝한 사람이다 / *It is not agreeable to have to sit at the same table with a ~ person.* 부루퉁한 사람과 같은 식탁에 앉아야 한다는 것은 유쾌한 일이 아니다. **2** gloomy; dismal. 음울한; 음산한. ¶ *a ~ landscape* 음울한 풍경 / *a ~ winter day* 음산한 겨울 날. [L. *solus* alone]

sul·len·ly [sʌ́lənli] *adv.* in a sullen mood. 실쭉하여; 부루퉁해서.

sul·len·ness [sʌ́lənnis] *n.* Ⓤ the state of being sullen. 부루퉁함; 언짢음; 음울함.

sul·ly [sʌ́li] *vt.* (**-lied**) (P6) make (something) dirty; cause the loss of (respect, etc.). …을 더럽히다; (명성 따위를) 훼손하다. ¶ *The accident sullied her record as a driver.* 그 사고로 그녀의 운전 경력에 흠이 났다 / *a reputation sullied by many crimes* 많은 범죄로 더럽혀진 명성. [soil[2]]

sul·phate [sʌ́lfeit] *n.* 《Brit.》 =sulfate.

·**sul·phur** [sʌ́lfər] *n.* 《Brit.》 =sulfur.

sul·phu·re·ous [sʌlfjuərəs] *adj.* 《Brit.》 = sulfureous.

sul·phu·ric [sʌlfjúərik] *adj.* 《Brit.》 =sulfuric.

sul·phur·ous [sʌ́lfərəs] *adj.* 《Brit.》 = sulfurous.

sul·tan [sʌ́ltən] *n.* Ⓒ **1** a Mohammedan ruler. 이슬람 교국 군주; 술탄. **2** 《*the S-*》 the former emperor or Turkey. (옛날의) 오스만 투르크 황제. [Arab.]

sul·tan·a [sʌltǽnə, -tɑ́:nə] *n.* Ⓒ **1** the wife of a sultan. 이슬람 교국 왕비. **2** a kind of small, seedless raisin. 건포도의 일종.

sul·tan·ate [sʌ́ltənit] *n.* Ⓤ the position of a sultan; Ⓒ the territory of a sultan. 술탄의 지위〔영토〕.

sul·tri·ness [sʌ́ltrinis] *n.* the state of being sultry. 무더위; 후덥지근함. [↓]

sul·try [sʌ́ltri] *adj.* (**-tri·er, -tri·est**) **1** (of weather, etc.) hot and moist. 무더운. ¶ *We must expect ~ weather during the rainy season.* 장마철에는 무더운 날씨를 각오해야 한다. **2** showing or suggesting passion. 정열적〔관능적〕인. [*swelter*]

:**sum** [sʌm] *n.* Ⓒ **1** the result of adding two or more numbers or quantities; the total numbers or quantities. (수·수량의) 합; 합계; 총계. ¶ *The ~ of 2 and 3 is 5.* 2와 3의 합(合)은 5다. **2** an amount of money. 금액. ¶ *a large* 〔*small*〕 *~ of money* 다액〔소액〕의 돈 / *a ~ of 15 dollars* 일금 15달러 / *give* 〔*lend*〕 *a small ~ to someone* 아무에게 약간의 돈을 주다〔빌려주다〕 / *The expenses came to an enormous ~.* 비용은 굉장한 금액이 되었다. **3** a problem in arithmetic; 《*pl.*》 calculation. 산술 문제; 계산. ¶ *do sums* 계산하다; 문제를 풀다 / *be good at sums* 산술을 잘 하다 / *He can do easy sums in his head but has to write out hard ones.* 그는 쉬운 산술 문제는 암산으로 할 수 있으나 어려운 문제는 써서 계산해야 했다. **4** 《*the ~*》 the main points; a summary. 대의; 개요. ¶ *the ~ of the whole matter* 전체의 골자 / *the ~ and substance of a book* 〔*theory*〕 책〔학설〕의 요지.

in sum, in short; briefly and comprehensively put. 요컨대; 요약하면; 결국.

the sum (***and substance***) ***of,*** all that is essential of something. …의 요점; 요지.

— *v.* (**summed, sum·ming**) *vt.* (P7) **1** 《*up*》 add together; total. …을 합계〔총계〕하다. ¶ *~ up one's takings* 매상고를 합계하다 / *~ up advantages and disadvantages* 이점과 불리한 점을 모두 계산에 넣다. **2** express the main points of (something); state briefly; summarize. …을 요약하다. ¶ *~ up the facts* 〔*arguments*〕 사실을〔논의를〕 요약하다 / *It can be summed up in two words.* 그것은 요약해서 두 낱말로 말할 수 있다. **3** 《*up*》 form a judgment on. …에 관해 판단〔평가, 파악〕하다. ¶ *He summed up the situation in a minute.* 그는 즉시 상황을 파악했다 / *He summed her up as a spoilt girl.* 그녀가 버릇없는 아이라는 것을 그는 알아차렸다. — *vi.* (P1) **1** make a summary. 요약하다. **2** 《*to*》 reach a sum of; amount to. 합계 …이 되다. ¶ *It sums* (*up*) *to $1000.* 합계 1천 달러가 된다.

to sum up, in short; to speak briefly. 요약하면. [→summit]

sum·ma·rize [sʌ́məràiz] *vt.* (P6) sum up; speak briefly. …을 요약하다. [↓]

·**sum·ma·ry** [sʌ́məri] *n.* Ⓒ (*pl.* **-ries**) a brief statement giving only the main points. 적요; 개요. ¶ *give a ~ of…* …의 개요를 말하다. — *adj.* **1** giving the substance in a few words; brief; concise. 간략한; 간결한. ¶ *~ reports* 개략 보고서 / *a ~ account* 대체적인 이야기; 약술(略述). **2** done without delay. 즉결의. ¶ *~ punishment* 즉결의 형벌 / *~ justice* 즉결 재판 / *~ conviction* 즉결 처분. [*sum*]

:**sum·mer**[1] [sʌ́mər] *n.* ⓊⒸ 《usu. *~* or *the ~*》 **1** the hottest season of the year, between spring and autumn. 여름. ¶ *in* (*the*) *~* 여름에; 여름이 되면. **2** 《usu. *the ~*》 《*fig.*》 a period of the finest development; the prime of life. 장년기; 한창때. ¶ *the ~ of life* 장년기. ¶ *the ~ holidays* 〔*vacation*〕 여름 휴가 / *~ lightning* 마른 번개. **3** 《*pl.*》《*poet.*》 the years of one's age, esp. if young or strong. (젊은이의) 나이; …살(cf. *winter*). ¶ *a girl of ten summers,* 10세의 소녀. — *adj.* of summer. 여름의. — *vi.* (P2A, 3) pass the summer. 여름을 지내다. [E.]

sum·mer[2] [sʌ́mər] *n.* 《archit.》 a large

beam or stone serving as a lintel or base of arch or the like. 대들보; 주춧돌. [Gk. *sagma* packsaddle]

summer time [⌐–⌐] *n.* 《Brit.》 the system of time in summer, when the clocks are advanced one hour; daylight-saving time. 일광 절약 시간; 서머타임.

sum·mer·time [sʌ́mərtàim] *n.* Ⓤ the season of summer. 하계(夏季); 여름철. [*summer*[1]]

***sum·mit** [sʌ́mit] *n.* Ⓒ **1** the top; the highest point. 정상; 정점. ¶ *climb to the* ~ 정상까지 올라가다. **2** the highest state or degree. 절정; 극치; 극도. ¶ *He reached the* ~ *of fame.* 그는 명성의 절정에 이르렀다. **3** (of government, etc.) the highest members of the government, the staff, etc. (정부 따위의) 최고 수뇌부; 수뇌급. ¶ *a meeting at the* ~ = *a* ~ *meeting* 〔*conference*〕 수뇌 회담. **4** a summit meeting. 수뇌 회담. [L. *summus* highest]

:sum·mon [sʌ́mən] *vt.* **1** (P6,7,13) order (someone) to come (to court); call for; send for. …을 소환하다; 부르다; 호출하다. ¶ ~ *a doctor* 의사를 부르다 / *The church bells* ~ *people to worship.* 교회종이 신도들을 예배에 불렀다 / *He was summoned to* 〔*to appear in*〕 *court.* 그는 법정으로 소환되었다. **2** (P6,7) 《often *up*》 stir to action; arouse; gather together. (용기 따위를) 불러 일으키다; 내다. ¶ ~ (*up*) *all one's energy* 〔*strength*〕 있는 기운〔힘〕을 다 내다 / ~ *up one's courage for* 〔*to do*〕 *the work* 그 일을 하려고 있는 용기를 다 내다. **3** (P6) order to meet; call together. …을 소집하다. ¶ *The Queen summoned Parliament.* 여왕은 의회를 소집했다. [↓]

sum·mons [sʌ́mənz] *n.* Ⓒ (*pl.* ~·**es**) **1** the act of ordering (someone) to come (to court). 소환; 소집; 호출. ¶ *answer one's* ~ 소환에 응(應)하다. **2** a message containing such an order. 소환장; 호출장(cf. *subpoena*). ¶ *serve a* ~ *on someone* =*serve someone with a* ~ 아무에게 소환장을 보내다 / *He received a* ~ *to be at the court at 10 a.m., October 6.* 그는 10월 6일 오전 10시, 법정에 출두하라는 소환장을 받았다. — *vt.* (P6) 《*colloq.*》 summon (someone) to court; issue a summons to. …을 소환하다; …에 소환장을 발부하다. [sub-, L. *moneo* warn]

sum·mum bo·num [sʌ́məm bóunəm] *n.* the chief good. 지선(至善). [L.]

sump [sʌmp] *n.* **1** the bottom part of an engine where the oil collects. (엔진의) 기름통. **2** a pit or well for reception of superfluous water. 오수(汚水) 모으는 웅덩이. [Teut.]

sump·ter [sʌ́mptər] *n.* 《*arch.*》 a horse or mule for carrying burdens. 짐 싣는 노새. [→summer[2]]

sump·tu·ar·y [sʌ́mptʃuèri / -əri] *adj.* of or about saving money or expenses. 비용 절감의; 절약의; 사치를 금하는. ¶ ~ *laws* 사치 금지법. [↓]

sump·tu·ous [sʌ́mptʃuəs] *adj.* costly; magnificent. 사치스러운; 화려한; 호화로운. ¶ ~ *clothes* 사치스러운 옷 / *a* ~ *meal* 호화로운〔값진〕 식사. [L. *sumptus* cost]

sump·tu·ous·ly [sʌ́mptjuəsli] *adv.* in a sumptuous manner. 사치스럽게; 화려하게.

sump·tu·ous·ness [sʌ́mptjuəsnis] *n.* the quality of being sumptuous. 사치스러움.

sum total [⌐⌐–] *n.* the emphatic for sum. 총계. [*sum*]

:sun [sʌn] *n.* **1** Ⓒ 《usu. *the* ~》 the brightest heavenly body, around which the earth and the other planets move. 태양; 해. ¶ *The* ~ *rises in the east and sets in the west.* 태양은 동쪽에서 떠서 서쪽으로 진다 / *The* ~ *shines in the sky.* 태양은 하늘에서 빛난다 / *rise with the* ~ 아침 일찍 일어나다. **2** Ⓤ 《often *the* ~》 the light and heat of the sun; sunshine. 일광; 햇빛; 햇볕; 양지. ¶ *lay at full length in the* ~ 양지에 드러눕다 / *take the* ~=*bathe* 〔*bask*〕 *in the* ~ 햇볕을 쬐다; 일광욕을 하다 / *keep… out of the* ~ …을 햇빛이 쬐지 않는〔그늘진〕 곳에 두다 / *open the windows to let in the* ~ 햇빛을 들이기 위해 창문을 열다. **3** Ⓒ a fixed star around which planets move. (위성을 가진) 항성. **4** Ⓒ one's best days; glory. 전성(기); 한창 때. ¶ *hail the rising* ~ 권세 있는 사람에게 아첨하다 / *His* ~ *is set.* 그의 전성기는 지났다.

against the sun, counter-clockwise. 태양의 운행 방향과 반대로; 시계 바늘과 반대의 방향으로.

a place in the sun, an advantageous position; a position of success. 좋은 환경; 유리한 지위〔입장〕.

from sun to sun, 《*arch.*》 from sunrise to sunset. 하루 종일.

hold a candle to the sun, perform a useless action. 쓸데없는 짓을 하다.

see the sun, be alive. 살아 있다.

under the sun, on earth; in the whole world. 이 세상에; 하늘 아래. ¶ *There's nothing new under the* ~. 하늘 아래 새로운 것이란 없다.

with the sun, clockwise. 시계 바늘과 같은 방향으로.

— *v.* (**sunned, sun·ning**) *vt.* (P6) expose (something) to the sun. …을 햇볕에 쬐다. ¶ *She put the mattresses out to* ~ *them.* 그녀는 매트리스를 햇볕에 쬐기 위해 내다 널었다 / ~ *oneself* 일광욕을 하다.

— *vi.* (P1) expose oneself to the sun. 일광욕을 하다. ¶ *We swam and sunned.* 수영과 일광욕을 했다. [E.]

Sun. Sunday.

sun bath [⌐⌐] *n.* an exposure of the body to sunshine. 일광욕.

sun·bathe [sʌ́nbèið] *vi.* (P1) take a sunbath. 일광욕을 하다.

:**sun·beam** [sʌ́nbìːm] *n.* Ⓒ a ray of sunlight. 태양 광선; 일광; 햇살.

sun·bon·net [sʌ́nbɑ̀nit / -bɔ̀n-] *n.* Ⓒ a bonnet with a wide brim to shade the face. (여성·어린이의) 햇빛 가리는 모자.

sun·burn [sʌ́nbə̀ːrn] *n.* ⒸⓊ a reddening the skin, caused by excessive exposure to the sun. 볕에 탐. — *v.* (**-burned** or **-burnt**) *vi.* (P1) become burned by the sun. 햇볕에 타다. ¶ *I ~ very easily.* 나는 햇볕에 잘 탄다. — *vt.* (P6) (of the sun) burn the skin of (someone). …을 햇볕에 태우다. ¶ *An hour in the Florida sun had sunburned me severely.* 플로리다에서 햇볕에 1시간을 쬐었더니 얼얼할 정도로 심하게 그을었다.

sun·burned [sʌ́nbə̀ːrnd] *adj.* made dark by exposure to the sun. 햇볕에 탄[그은].

sun·burnt [sʌ́nbə̀ːrnt] *v.* p. and pp. of **sunburn.** — *adj.* =sunburned.

sun·dae [sʌ́ndei, -di] *n.* Ⓒ ice cream with syrup and fruit, etc. placed on top. 선디《시럽·과일 등을 얹은 아이스크림》. [?]

:**Sun·day** [sʌ́ndi, -dei] *n.* the first day of the week; (among Christians) the day of rest and worship. 일요일; 기독교의 안식일. 參考 Sun.로 생략함. [E. =sun's day]
a week* [*month*] *of Sundays, a long period. 오랫동안.

Sunday best [**clothes**] [⌐–⌐[⌐]] *n.* best clothes kept for Sunday use. 나들이옷.

Sunday school [⌐– ⌐] *n.* a school held on Sunday for studying religion and the Bible. (교회의) 주일 학교.

sun·der [sʌ́ndər] *vt., vi.* (P6;1) 《*arch., poet.*》 divide; separate. …을 (둘로) 가르다; 떼다. ¶ *Time often sunders friends.* 세월은 친구를 갈라놓기 일쑤다. [E.]

sun·dew [sʌ́ndjùː] *n.* Ⓒ a plant with sticky hairs growing in a marsh. 끈끈이주걱《식충 식물》.

sun·di·al [sʌ́ndàiəl] *n.* Ⓒ an instrument that shows the time by position of the shadow thrown by sunlight. 해시계. [*sun*]

sun·down [sʌ́ndàun] *n.* Ⓤ sunset. 일몰.

sun-dried [sʌ́ndràid] *adj.* dried by the sun. 햇볕에 말린. ¶ *~ bricks* 햇볕에 말린 벽돌. [*sun*]

sun·dry [sʌ́ndri] *adj.* various; several. 여러 가지의; 잡다한. ¶ *talk of ~ matters* 잡다한 일에 관해 이야기하다 / *~ goods* 잡화(雜貨). — *n.* Ⓒ (*pl.* **-dries**) 《usu. *pl.*》 various small articles; groceries. 잡화; 잡동사니. ¶ *We spent much money on sundries.* 우리는 많은 돈을 잡동사니에 써버렸다. [E.]
all and sundry, everybody. 각자 모두.

sun·flow·er [sʌ́nflàuər] *n.* Ⓒ a tall plant with large yellow flowers. 해바라기. [*sun*]

:**sung** [sʌŋ] *v.* pp. of **sing.**

sun·glass·es [sʌ́nglæ̀siz / -glɑ̀ːs-] *n. pl.* spectacles with colored glass to protect the eyes from the sun. 색안경; 선글라스. [*sun*]

:**sunk** [sʌŋk] *n.* p. and pp. of **sink.**

·**sunk·en** [sʌ́ŋkən] *v.* pp. of **sink.**
— *adj.* **1** ⓐ sunk; lying under water. 가라앉은. ¶ *a ~ ship* 침몰된 배 / *a ~ rock* 암초. ⓑ below the surrounding level. 내려앉은. ¶ *a ~ garden* 한단 낮은 정원. **2** (of eyes, cheeks, etc.) fallen; hollow. (눈·뺨 따위가) 움푹 들어간[팬]. ¶ *~ cheeks* [*eyes*] 움푹 들어간 뺨[눈]. [*sink*]

sun lamp [⌐⌐] *n.* an electric lamp which gives off ultraviolet rays. (자외선을 방사하는) 태양등《피부병 치료·미용용》. [*sun*]

sun·less [sʌ́nlis] *adj.* without sunlight; dark. 볕이 들지 않는; 어두운. ¶ *Most flowers will not grow in a ~ place.* 대부분의 꽃들은 볕이 들지 않는 곳에서는 자라지 않는다.

·**sun·light** [sʌ́nlàit] *n.* Ⓤ the light of the sun. 일광; 햇빛.

sun·lit [sʌ́nlìt] *adj.* lighted by the sun. 볕이 드는. ¶ *~ meadows* 햇볕이 드는 목초지.

sun·ni·ly [sʌ́nili] *adv.* with much sunlight; merrily. 햇볕이 들어; 명랑하게. [↓]

·**sun·ny** [sʌ́ni] *adj.* (**-ni·er, -ni·est**) **1** having much sunlight. 햇볕이 잘 드는; 양지바른. ¶ *a ~ garden* 양지바른 정원 / *a ~ room* 햇볕이 잘 드는방 / *~ weather* 햇볕이 좋은 날씨. **2** cheerful; bright. 명랑한; 밝은. ¶ *a ~ disposition* 명랑한 기질 / *a ~ smile* 상냥한 미소 / *look on the ~ side of things* 사물을 낙관하다. [*sun*]

sun·proof [sʌ́nprùːf] *adj.* not allowing the rays of the sun to pass through something; not affected by the rays of the sun. 햇빛이 통하지 않는; 내광성의.

·**sun·rise** [sʌ́nràiz] *n.* Ⓤ the rising of the sun; the time when the sun rises. 일출; 해돋이; 일출 시간. ¶ *We started at ~.* 우리는 해가 뜰 때 출발했다 / *an hour before* [*after*] *~* 일출 전[후] 1시간.

sun·room [sʌ́nrù(ː)m] *n.* Ⓒ a room with many windows to let in sunlight; a sun parlor. 일광욕실; 선룸.

·**sun·set** [sʌ́nsèt] *n.* Ⓤ the setting of the sun; the time when the sun sets. 일몰; 해넘이; 일몰 시간(opp. sunrise). ¶ *get home just before ~* 일몰 직전에 귀가하다 / *This flower opens at sunrise and closes at ~.* 이 꽃은 일출시에 피고 일몰시에 오므라든다.

sun·shade [sʌ́nʃèid] *n.* Ⓒ **1** a parasol. 양산. **2** a window covering to shade a room from the rays of the sun. 차양.

:**sun·shine** [sʌ́nʃàin] *n.* Ⓤ **1** the light or rays of the sun. 햇빛; 일광. ¶ *in the ~* 양지에서. **2** fine weather. 맑은 날씨. **3** brightness; cheerfulness. 쾌활; 명랑. ¶ *the ~ of her smile* 밝고 상냥한 그녀의 미소 / *Her smile is always full of ~.* 그녀의 웃음은 언제나 밝고 명랑하다.

sun·shin·y [sʌ́nʃàini] *adj.* of or full of sunshine. 햇볕이 잘 드는; 맑게 갠.

sun·spot [sʌ́nspɑ̀t / -spɔ̀t] *n.* Ⓒ a dark point on the sun. 태양의 흑점.

sun·stroke [sʌ́nstròuk] *n.* Ⓤ a sudden illness caused by exposure of the heat of the sun. 일사병. ¶ *take* 〔*be affected by*〕 ~ 일사병에 걸리다.

sun·ward [sʌ́nwərd] *adv.* toward the sun. 태양 쪽으로. —*adj.* facing the sun. 태양을 향한.

sun·wards [sʌ́nwərdz] *adv., adj.* =sunward.

sup[1] [sʌp] *v.* (**supped, sup·ping**) *vi.* (P1) eat supper. 저녁을 먹다. ¶ ~ *on bread and milk* 저녁으로 빵과 우유를 먹다 / ~ *at home* 집에서 저녁을 먹다. —*vt.* (P6) give a supper to (someone). …에게 저녁을 주다. [→supper]

sup[2] [sʌp] *vt., vi.* (**supped, sup·ping**) (P6;1) take a little (liquid or liquid food) into the mouth at a time. (국물·죽 따위를) 홀짝이다; 홀짝홀짝 마시다. ¶ *He supped his soup with a spoon.* 그는 숟가락으로 국물을 홀짝홀짝 마셨다. —*n.* Ⓒ a little mouthful of liquid; a sip. 한 모금; 한 번 마시기. [E.]

su·per [súːpər] *n.* **1** 《*colloq.*》 a supernumerary actor. 단역(端役). **2** 《comm.》 a superfine cloth or manufacture. 특등품. **3** an expensively produced film designed for exhibition as the principal item in cinema programs. 특작(特作) 영화. —*adj.* **1** (of feet, yards, etc.) superficial or in square measure. 평방의; 면적의. **2** 《comm.》 superfine. 특등품의. [abbr.]

su·per- [súːpər-] *pref.* above; more than. '위…, …이상, 초(超)…, 과(過)…'의 뜻. [L. *super* over, above]

su·per·a·ble [súːpərəbəl] *adj.* that can be overcome or conquered. 이길〔정복할〕 수 있는. [↑]

su·per·a·bun·dance [sùːpərəbʌ́ndəns] *n.* ⓊⒸ an amount more than is usual or needed. 과잉; 여분. ¶ *a* ~ *of rain* 지나치게 많은 비.

su·per·a·bun·dant [sùːpərəbʌ́ndənt] *adj.* more than is usual or needed. 과잉의; 여분의; 과다한.

su·per·add [sùːpərǽd] *vt.* (P6) add (something) further; add besides. …을 덧붙이다; 더 보태다.

su·per·an·nu·ate [sùːpərǽnjuèit] *vt.* (P6) cause (someone) to leave a school or a place of employment because he is too weak or too old. …을 병약(病弱)〔노령〕 때문에 퇴교〔퇴직〕시키다. [→annual]

su·per·an·nu·at·ed [sùːpərǽnjuèitid] *adj.* **1** too old for work or use. 노령으로〔노후로〕 인해 일할〔사용할〕 수 없는. **2** obsolete; out-of-date. 쓸모없이 된; 시대에 뒤떨어진. ¶ ~ *ideas* 시대에 뒤진 생각.

su·per·an·nu·a·tion [sùːpərӕ̀njuéiʃən] *n.* **1** Ⓤ the act of superannuating; the state of being superannuated. 노령 퇴직. **2** Ⓒ money given to someone who leaves his work because of old age. 퇴직금; 연금.

su·perb [supə́ːrb] *adj.* (sometimes **-perb·er, -perb·est**) of the first quality; very grand and beautiful; very fine; excellent. 최고〔최상〕의; 훌륭한; 멋진; 뛰어난. ¶ *a* ~ *binding* 호화로운 장정(裝幀) / ~ *jewels* 고가의 화려한 보석 / *a* ~ *performance* 절묘한 연기 / *a* ~ *beauty* 주변을 압도하는 미인 / *a* ~ *epic poem* 웅장한 서사시. [L. =proud]

su·perb·ly [supə́ːrbli] *adv.* in a superb manner. 당당하게; 훌륭히.

su·per·car·go [súːpərkɑ̀ːrgou] *n.* Ⓒ (*pl.* **-goes** or **-gos**) an officer on a merchant ship who has charge of the goods carried on the ship. 승선(乘船)한 화물 관리인 《상선에 실은 하물(荷物)을 감독하는 하주 대리인》. [super-]

su·per·charge [súːpərtʃɑ̀ːrdʒ] *vt.* (P6) force an extra amount. 과급(過給)하다.

su·per·cil·i·a·ry [sùːpərsílièri / -əri] *adj.* of the brows; over the eye. 눈썹의; 눈 위의. [L. *cilium* eyelid]

su·per·cil·i·ous [sùːpərsíliəs] *adj.* proud; treating others as if they were not so good as oneself. 거만한; 건방진. ¶ *with a* ~ *look* 건방진 모습으로.

su·per·cool [sùːpərkúːl] *vt., vi.* (P6; 1) 《chem.》 cool (a liquid) below its freezing-point without solidification. (액체를) 응결시키지 않고 빙점 이하로 냉각하다. [super-]

su·per·dread·nought [sùːpərdrédnɔ̀ːt] *n.* a warship of greater power than a dreadnought. 초노급(超弩級) 전함.

su·per·e·go [sùːpəríːgou, -égou] *n.* (*pl.* **-gos**) 《psych.》 the part of the psyche which mediates between ego drives and social ideals, acting as a conscience. 초자아(超自我). [super-, *ego*]

su·per·em·i·nent [sùːpərémənənt] *adj.* having higher rank, character, etc. 탁월한; 빼어난. [L. *emineo* project]

su·per·e·rog·a·to·ry [sùːpərərɑ́gətɔ̀ːri / -rərɔ́gətəri] *adj.* doing more than the duty requires; unnecessary. 직무 이상의; 여분의. [L. *erogo* pay]

su·per·ex·cel·lent [sùːpəréksələnt] *adj.* very excellent. 매우 우수한; 무상(無上)의; 탁월한; 절묘한. [super-]

su·per·fat·ted [sùːpərfǽtid] *adj.* (of soaps) with excess of fatty matter over alkali. 지방 함유 과다의.

su·per·fi·cial [sùːpərfíʃəl] *adj.* **1** on the surface only; outward. 표면(상)의; 외면의. ¶ *a* ~ *likeness* 〔*difference*〕 표면상 같음〔다름〕 / ~ *characteristics* 표면에 나타난 특징 / *His cut* 〔*wound*〕 *was only* ~ *and soon get well.* 그의 상처는 찰과상 정도여서 곧 나았다. **2** not deep; shallow. 천박한; 피상적인 (opp. profound). ¶ ~ *knowledge* 천박한 지

식 / *a* ~ *observer* 〔*writer*〕 피상적인 관찰자〔작가〕. [L. *facies* face]

su·per·fi·ci·al·i·ty [sù:pərfìʃiǽləti] *n.* Ⓤ the state or quality of being superficial. 표면적임; 천박; 피상(皮相).

su·per·fi·cial·ly [sù:pərfíʃəli] *adv.* in a superficial manner; not thoroughly. 표면적으로; 천박하게; 피상적으로.

su·per·fine [sù:pərfáin] *adj.* **1** 《comm.》 of the finest quality; very fine. 극상의; 최상의. **2** too subtle. 지나치게 세밀〔미세〕한. ¶ *a* ~ *distinction* 지나치게 세밀한 구별. [super-]

su·per·flu·i·ty [sù:pərflú:əti] *n.* (*pl.* **-ties**) **1** Ⓤ a greater amount than is needed. 여분; 과잉; 과다. **2** 《usu. *pl.*》 something not needed. 여분〔필요 이상〕의 것. [↓]

su·per·flu·ous [su:pə́:rfluəs] *adj.* more than is needed; excessive; needless. 남는; 여분의; 불필요한. ¶ ~ *knowledge* 〔*wealth*〕 필요 이상의 지식〔부〕 / ~ *clothes* 〔*water*〕 여분의 의류〔물〕 / ~ *persistence* 필요 이상의 고집 / *Your acknowledgment is* ~. 인사 따위는 안해도 된다. [→fluent]

su·per·flu·ous·ly [su:pə́:rfluəsli] *adv.* in a superfluous manner; excessively; needlessly. 여분으로; 불필요하게.

su·per·het·e·ro·dyne [sù:pərhétərədàin] *n.* a powerful and highly selective wireless receiving set. 슈퍼헤테로다인《고감도 수신 장치》. [super-]

su·per·hu·man [sù:pərhjú:mən] *adj.* above or beyond what is human; supernatural; divine. 초인적인; 사람의 짓이 아닌; 신의 솜씨인. ¶ *a* ~ *effort* 초인적인 노력.

su·per·im·pose [sù:pərimpóuz] *vt.* (P6) 《*on*》 put on the top of something else. …의 위에 놓다.

su·per·in·cum·bent [sù:pərinkʌ́mbənt] *adj.* lying on the top of something. …의 위에 드러누운〔있는〕.

su·per·in·duce [sù:pərindjú:s] *vt.* (P6) develop or bring in as an addition. 덧붙이다; 첨가하다.

su·per·in·tend [sù:pərinténd] *vt.* (P6) watch, direct, or manage (work, an institution, or workers). …을 감독하다; 관리하다. ¶ ~ *the workmen* 인부들을 관리〔지휘〕하다. [→intend]

su·per·in·tend·ence [sù:pərinténdəns] *n.* Ⓤ guidance and direction; management. 감독; 관리; 지휘. ¶ *under the* ~ *of* ... …의 감독 하에.

su·per·in·tend·en·cy [sù:pərinténdənsi] *n.* the position, office, or work of a superintendent. 감독의 지위〔직무, 업무〕.

***su·per·in·tend·ent** [sù:pərinténdənt] *n.* Ⓒ a person who watches, directs, or manages others. 감독자; 관리자. ¶ *the* ~ *of education* 〔*schools*〕 교육장(長).

:su·pe·ri·or [səpíəriər, su-] *adj.* **1** 《*to*》 higher or better in quality, value; above the average. 뛰어난; 우수〔우월〕한; 우위의 (opp. inferior). ¶ ~ *knowledge* 뛰어난 지식 / ~ *cloth* 〔*leather*〕 고급 천〔가죽〕 / ~ *persons* 우수한 사람들; 《*iron.*》 높은 양반들 / ~ *math students* 수학의 우등생 / ~ *merchandise* 우량 상품 / ~ *grade of coffee* 상질의 커피 / *This car is* ~ *in speed to any other machine.* 이 자동차는 속도면에서 다른 어떤 차보다도 우수하다. **2** higher or above in place, position, rank, or office. 위의; 상위의. ¶ *a* ~ *office* 상급 관청 / *one's* ~ *officer* 상관 / ~ *classes* 상층 계급 / *A captain is* ~ *to a lieutenant.* 대위는 중위보다 상위이다. **3** larger in number or amount. (수·양적으로) 우세한; 다수〔다액〕의. ¶ *fight against* ~ *forces* 다수의 군세(軍勢)와 싸우다 / *The enemy were* ~ *in numbers.* 적은 수적으로 우세했다. **4** showing a feeling of being above others; proud. 거만한; 잘난 체하는. ¶ *with a* ~ *air* 잘난 듯이 / *I don't like her* ~ *manner.* 나는 그녀의 거만한 태도가 싫다. **5** 《*to*》 not giving in to; not influenced by; above yielding to. …에 좌우되지〔굽히지〕 않는; …을 초월한. ¶ *be* ~ *to temptation* 〔*prejudice*〕 유혹에 넘어가지 않다〔편견에 사로잡히지 않다〕 / *rise* ~ *to hardship* 어려움에 굴하지 않고 일어나다 / *A wise man is* ~ *to flatter.* 현명한 사람은 아첨에 영향을 받지 않는다.

— *n.* Ⓒ **1** a person who is superior. 뛰어난 사람; 우월한 사람; 상관; 선배. ¶ *look up to one's superiors* 상관을〔선배를〕 존경하다 / *You are my* ~ *in ability.* 능력 면에서 너는 나보다 한 수 위이다 / *As a pianist, he has no* ~. 피아니스트로서, 그는 첫째 간다. **2** the head of a religious house. 수도원장. ¶ *the Father* 〔*Mother*〕 *Superior* 수도〔수녀〕원장. [L. *superus* upper]

superior court [-ˊ-- ˊ] *n.* a court of higher rank. 상급 법원.

superior figure [-ˊ-- ˊ-] *n.* one placed above the line. 어깨글자.

su·pe·ri·or·i·ty [səpìərió(:)rəti, su-, -ár-] *n.* Ⓤ the state or quality of being superior. 우월; 탁월; 뛰어남(opp. inferiority). ¶ *social* ~ 사회적 우월 / *assume an air of* ~ 잘난 체하다 / *No one doubts the* ~ *of our products to* 〔*over*〕 *those of our competitors.* 우리의 제품이 경쟁자들의 제품보다 우수하다는 것은 아무도 의심하지 않는다.

superior letter [-ˊ-- ˊ-] *n.* =superior figure.

superior numbers [-ˊ-- ˊ-] *n.* more men or their presence. 다수; 우세.

***su·per·la·tive** [səpə́:rlətiv, su:-] *adj.* **1** better than all others. 최상의; 비길 데 없는; 무비(無比)의. ¶ ~ *beauty* 비길 데 없는 아름다움 / *a man of* ~ *wisdom* 비길 데 없는 지혜를 가진 사람. **2** 《gram.》 expressing the highest degree of an adjective and adverb. 최상급의.

— *n.* **1** 《*the* ~》 《gram.》 the form of the highest degree of an adjective or adverb. 최상급. **2** Ⓒ a word or words expressing

this degree. 최상급의 낱말. **3** Ⓒ a very good person or thing. 최상(급)의 사람〔것〕. [L. *lat-* carry]
full of superlatives, overstrongly expressed. 과장투성이의.
speak 〔***talk***〕 ***in superlatives,*** exaggerate. 과장하여 말하다.

su·per·man [sú:pərmæ̀n] *n.* Ⓒ (*pl.* **-men** [-mèn]) a person who is more than human in ability. 초인; 슈퍼맨. [super-]

super·market [sú:pərmὰ:rkit] *n.* Ⓒ a large self-service store. 슈퍼마켓.

su·per·mun·dane [sù:pərmʌ́ndein] *adj.* superior to earthly things. 초현세적(超現世的)인.

su·per·nal [su:pə́:rnl] *adj.* heavenly; divine. 천상에 있는; 신의. [*super-*]

su·per·nat·u·ral [sù:pərnǽtʃərəl] *adj.* above or beyond what is natural; not explained by the laws of nature; heavenly; divine. 초자연의; 불가사의한; 신의 조화의. — *n.* 《*the* ～》 something which is supernatural. 신의 조화; 신비.

su·per·nu·mer·ar·y [sù:pərnjú:mərèri / -əri] *adj.* more than the usual or necessary number. 정원 외의; 여분의. — *n.* Ⓒ (**-ar·ies**) a supernumerary person or thing. 과잉 인원; 여분의 물건. [→numeral]

su·per·pose [sù:pərpóuz] *vt.* (P6;13) place (something) above or on something else. …을 겹쳐 놓다; 포개 놓다. [→pose]

su·per·po·si·tion [sù:pərpəzíʃən] *n.* Ⓤ the act of superposing; the state of being superposed. (물건을) 겹쳐 놓기; 포개기.

su·per·pow·er [sú:pərpàuər] *n.* **1** power, esp. mechanical or electric power, on an extremely large scale secured by the linking together of a number of separate power systems. 초출력(超出力). **2** an extremely powerful nation. 초강대국.

su·per·scribe [sù:pərskráib] *vt.* (P6) write (words, letters, one's name, etc.) above, on, or outside something; address (a letter or parcel). …의 위에 쓰다; (편지)에 수취인 주소를 쓰다. [→scribble]

su·per·script [sú:pərskrìpt] (opp. subscript) *adj.* written above. 위에 쓴. — *n.* a number, letter, etc., written above and to one side of another. 어깨글자〔기호〕; 어깨 숫자. ¶ *In* $a^3 \times b^n$ *the '3' and the 'n' are superscripts.* $a^3 \times b^n$에서 '3'과 'n'은 어깨숫자〔글자〕이다.

su·per·scrip·tion [sù:pərskrípʃən] *n.* Ⓒ **1** the act of writing one's name, etc. on or outside of something. 위에 쓰기. **2** a name, address, etc. written on or outside a letter, a parcel, etc. 표제; (수취인의) 주소 성명.

su·per·sede [sù:pərsí:d] *vt.* (P6) take the place of (someone or something); cause (something) to be set aside. …에 대신하다; …을 바꾸다〔대체하다〕. ¶ ～ *an old car with a new one* 헌 차를 새 차로 바꾸다 / *Mr. A has superseded Mr. B as manager.* A씨는 관리자로 B씨의 뒤를 이었다 / *In our city buses superseded trains last year.* 작년에 우리 시에서는 전차를 버스로 바꾸었다. [L. *sedeo* sit]

su·per·ses·sion [sù:pərséʃən] *n.* Ⓤ the act of superseding; the state of being superseded. 폐기; 대용; 경질.

su·per·son·ic [sù:pərsάnik / -sɔ́n-] *adj.* faster than sound. 초음속의. ¶ *a* ～ *airplane* 초음속기 / ～ *waves* 초음파. [L. *sonus* sound]

supersonic transport [--ˊ-- ˋ-] *n.* a large aircraft moving faster than the speed of sound. 초음속 수송기. 參考 SST로 생략함.

•**su·per·sti·tion** [sù:pərstíʃən] *n.* Ⓤ an unreasoning fear or belief in something unknown or mysterious. 미신; (초자연적인 것·미신 등으로 생기는) 막연한 공포심. [L. *sto* stand]

su·per·sti·tious [sù:pərstíʃəs] *adj.* of or full of superstition; caused by superstition. 미신적인; 미신에 사로잡힌. ¶ ～ *people* 〔*beliefs, customs*〕 미신적인 사람들〔신앙, 관습〕.

su·per·struc·ture [sú:pərstrʌ̀ktʃər] *n.* **1** Ⓤ anything built on something else. 상부 구조〔구축〕(물). **2** Ⓤ the part of a building above the ground 〔foundation〕. (기초 위의) 건축(물); 건(조)물. **3** Ⓒ the part of a ship above the main deck. (배의) 주갑판 위의 부분(opp. substructure). **4** Ⓒ a philosophy or system in relation to its principles. (사상의) 원리 위에 세워진 철학(체계). [super-]

su·per·tax [sú:pərtæ̀ks] *n.* ⓊⒸ a tax in addition to the normal income tax. 부가 소득세; 부가세.

su·per·va·ca·ne·ous [sú:pərvəkéiniəs] *adj.* superfluous. 여분의. [→vacant]

su·per·vene [sù:pərví:n] *vi.* (P1) happen while something else is happening; happen as something additional. 병발(竝發)하다; 부수하여 일어나다. [L. *venio* come]

su·per·ven·tion [sù:pərvénʃən] *n.* **1** Ⓤ the act of supervening. 부가; 추가. **2** Ⓒ a supervening event. 속발(續發); 병발(竝發).

su·per·vise [sú:pərvàiz] *vt.* (P6) watch over (persons, machines, etc.) to see that they work properly. …을 감독〔관리〕하다. [L. *video* see]

•**su·per·vi·sion** [sù:pərvíʒən] *n.* Ⓤ the act of supervising; oversight. 관리; 감독. ¶ *under the* ～ *of...* …의 감독 하에.

su·per·vi·sor [sú:pərvàizər] *n.* Ⓒ a person who supervises; a superintendent. 감독자; 관리인.

su·per·vi·so·ry [sù:pərváizəri] *adj.* of a supervisor or supervision. 감독자〔관리자〕

의; 감독[관리]의. ¶ ~ *duties* [*powers*] 감독의 의무[권한].

su·pine[1] [su:páin] *adj.* **1** lying on the back. 반듯이 누운(opp. prone). **2** lazy; idle. 게으른; 태만한. [L.]

su·pine[2] [su:páin] *n.* a Latin verbal noun used in special constructions. 동사상(動詞狀) 명사. [↑]

:**sup·per** [sʌ́pər] *n.* ⓊⒸ the last meal of the day; the evening meal. 만찬; 저녁 식사. ¶ *at* ~ 저녁 식사 때에 / *have* [*eat, take*] ~ 저녁 식사를 하다. [F. souper]

sup·plant [səplǽnt, -plɑ́:nt] *vt.* (P6) **1** take the place of (something or someone); replace. …에 대신 들어 앉다; 대신하다. ¶ *The computer can never* ~ *the mental faculties of human.* 컴퓨터는 결코 인간의 지능을 대신할 수 없다 / *The use of machinery has largely supplanted men's labor.* 기계의 사용은 사람의 일을 크게 대신하게 되었다. **2** take the place of (another) by unfair methods or force. …을 밀어내다. ¶ *plot to* ~ *the king* 왕을 밀어내려는 음모를 꾸미다. [L. =trip up]

sup·ple [sʌ́pəl] *adj.* (**-pler, -plest**) **1** easily bent; flexible. 나긋나긋한; 유연한. ¶ ~ *leather* 부드러운 가죽 / ~ *movement* 경쾌한 동작 / *a* ~ *dancer* 동작이 유연한 무희 / *Her body was long and* ~. 그녀의 몸매는 늘씬하고 유연했다. **2** adaptable to different ideas, circumstances, etc. 유순한; 순응성이 있는. ¶ *a* ~ *mind* 순한 마음 / *have a keen head and* ~ *mind* 머리가 명민하고 마음은 순응성이 있다. —*vt.* (P6) make (something or someone) supple. …을 유연[나긋나긋]하게 하다. —*vi.* (P1) grow or become supple. 유연해지다; 나긋나긋해지다. [L. *plico* fold]

sup·ple·ment [sʌ́pləmənt] *n.* Ⓒ **1** something added to complete a thing. 보유(補遺); 증보; 추가. **2** an added part of a newspaper, a magazine, or a book. (신문·잡지의) 부록; (책의) 보유(補遺). —[-mènt] *vt.* (P6,13) complete; add to (something). …을 보충하다; 증보하다; 추가하다; 부록을 달다. [L. *pleo* fill]

sup·ple·men·tal [sʌ̀pləméntl] *adj.* added to supply what is lacking; additional. 보족[보충]의; 추가[부록]의.

sup·ple·men·ta·ry [sʌ̀pləméntəri] *adj.* =supplemental.

sup·pli·ant [sʌ́pliənt] *adj.* asking humbly and earnestly. 탄원하는; 간청하는. —*n.* Ⓒ a person who begs for a favor. 탄원자; 간청자. [↓]

sup·pli·cate [sʌ́pləkèit] *vt.* (P6,13,20) 《*for*》 beg or pray to (someone) for something humbly and earnestly. …을 탄원하다; 간청하다. ¶ ~ *one's master for mercy* 주인에게 자비를 간청하다 / ~ *someone to help* 아무에게 원조를[도움을] 간곡히 부탁하다. [→supple]

sup·pli·ca·tion [sʌ̀pləkéiʃən] *n.* Ⓤ the act of supplicating. 탄원; 간청; 기원.

sup·pli·ca·to·ry [sʌ́plikətɔ̀:ri / -təri] *adj.* supplicating. 탄원의; 기원의.

sup·pli·er [səpláiər] *n.* Ⓒ a person who supplies. 공급자; 보충자. [↓]

:**sup·ply** [səplái] *vt.* (**-plied**) (P6,13) **1** 《*with, for*》 give (something needed or wanted); provide (someone) with; fill the needs of (something or someone). (필수품을) 공급하다; …에 (—을) 대주다; 지급하다. ¶ ~ *a city with electricity* = ~ *electricity to a city* 도시에 전기를 공급하다 / ~ *information* [*money*] 정보를 제공[돈을 지급]하다 / ~ *fresh meat for the table* 신선한 고기를 식탁에 내다 / *Cows* ~ *milk for* [*to*] *us.* 젖소는 우리에게 우유를 제공한다 / *Trees* ~ *shade in summer.* 나무는 여름에 그늘을 제공한다 / *We supplied food and clothes for the sufferers.* 이재민들에게 식품과 옷을 공급하였다 / *He supplied me the answer.* 그는 나에게 답을 가르쳐 주었다. **2** furnish (a loss, a lack, a need, etc.); satisfy (a need). (부족 따위를) 보충하다; (필요를) 채우다; 충족시키다. ¶ ~ *a demand* [*need*] 요구[필요]에 응하다 / ~ *a deficiency* [*want*] 결핍[부족]을 채우다 / ~ *a loss* 손실을 보충하다.

supply the place of, fill the place of; serve as a substitute for; replace. …의 대행을[대리를] 하다. ¶ *The book supplies the place of a dictionary.* 그 책은 사전 대용으로 쓰인다 / *No one can* ~ *the place of Mr. Kim.* 김 선생을 대신할 유능한 사람은 없다.

—*n.* (*pl.* **-plies**) **1** Ⓤ the act of supplying. 공급; 보급; 보충. ¶ *The new recruits were supplied with uniforms.* 신병들은 군복을 지급받았다 / *the law of* ~ *and demand* 수요 공급의 법칙 / *a base of* ~ 보급 기지 / *the* ~ *of gas to the town* 도시로의 가스 공급 / *Supply and demand plays an important part in economy.* 수요와 공급의 관계는 경제에서 중요한 역할을 한다. **2** Ⓒ something supplied; an amount wanted. 공급품; 재고품; 공급량. ¶ *relief supplies* 구호 물자 / *send an abundant* ~ *of food* [*water*] 식량[물]을 충분히 공급하다 / *a small* ~ *of provision* 식량의 적은 비축 / *have a good* [*a large*] ~ *of reading matter* (지루하지 않도록) 많은 읽을거리를 준비해 두다 / *Goods are in short* ~. 물품의 재고가 떨어졌다. **3** 《usu. *pl.*》 the amount of daily necessaries required; a store of food used in an army, etc. 생활 필수품; (군대 따위의) 양식; 군량. ¶ *lay in supplies for the winter* 겨울에 대비해서 생필품을 사들이다 / *military* [*war*] *supplies* 군수품[물자]. **4** Ⓒ 《often *pl.*》 money allowed for the expenses of a government. (국회가 인정한) 세출. **5** a person who takes the place of another for a short time, esp. a teacher, servant, or clergyman. (잠정적인) 대리(代理); (특히) 대리 교사[목사]. [L. *pleo* fill]

the Committee of Supply, the committee of the House of Commons discussing details of estimates. (영국 하원의) 예산 위원회.

the line of supply, a commissary line. 병참선.

:sup·port [səpɔ́ːrt] *vt.* (P6) **1** keep (something) from falling, sinking, slipping, etc.; hold up; carry the weight of (something). …을 지탱하다; 받치다; 지지하다; …의 무게에 견디다. ¶ ~ *oneself with a stick* 지팡이에 몸을 의지하다 / *The foundation supports a house.* 기초는 집을 받쳐 준다 / *Will this old ladder* ~ *me?* 이 낡은 사다리가 내 몸무게를 지탱할 수 있을까 / *She supported her chin on her hand.* 그녀는 턱을 손으로 받쳤다. **2** give hope or courage to (someone); comfort; carry on; maintain. (…에게) 힘을 북돋우다; 기운나게 하다; …을 격려하다; (생명 등)을 유지하다. ¶ *be supported by courage* [*hope*] 용기로[희망으로] 기운이 나게 되다 / ~ *life* [*one's strength*] 생명[기운]을 유지하다 / *His wife supported him in time of trouble.* 그의 아내는 어려운 시기에 그를 격려해줬다 / *What supported him was a glass of brandy.* 그에게 힘을 북돋우어 준 것은 한 잔의 브랜디였다 / *Air is necessary to* ~ *life.* 공기는생명을 유지하는 데 필수적이다. **3** supply (someone) with food, clothes, etc.; provide money for (someone or something). (가족 따위)를 부양하다; (재정적으로 사업·시설 등)을 지원[원조·유지]하다. ¶ ~ *oneself* 자활하다 / ~ *a school* 학교를 원조[지원]하다 / *I have a large family to* ~. 나는 부양해야 할 대가족이 있다 / *This hospital is supported by voluntary contributions.* 이 병원은 독지가의 기부에 의해 유지되고 있다. **4** be actively in favor of (a policy, a claim, etc.); back up. (정책 따위)를 지지하다; …을 지원하다. ¶ ~ *a candidate* [*leader*] 입후보자[지도자]를 지지[지원]하다 / ~ *a policy* 정책을 지지하다 / ~ *increasing wages* 임금 인상에 찬성하다. **5** (of facts, etc.) show proof for (a theory, etc.); give proof of; confirm. (사실 따위가) …을 입증하다; 뒷받침[확인]하다. ¶ ~ *a statement* [*claim*] 진술[주장]을 확인하다 / *His theory is supported by facts.* 그의 이론은 사실에 의해 입증되었다 / *Neighbors supported his alibi.* 이웃 사람들이 그의 알리바이를 증명하였다. **6** endure; bear; suffer. …을 참다[견디다]. ¶ *I can't* ~ *your insults any more.* 나는 더 이상 너의 모욕을 참을 수 없다 / *I supported the pain* [*misfortune*] *bravely.* 나는 용감하게 고통[불행]을 견뎌 냈다.

— *n.* **1** Ⓤ the act of supporting; the state of being supported; means of providing; help. 버팀; 지지; 부양; 원조. ¶ *give* ~ *to a roof* 지붕을 받쳐 주다 / *He can stand without* ~. 그는 도움없이도 견딜 수 있다 / *His income was not sufficient for the* ~ *of his family.* 그의 수입은 가족을 부양하기에 충분하지 못하다 / *I need his* ~. 나는 그의 원조가 필요하다. **2** Ⓒ a person or thing that supports; a proof. 지지물; 지지자; 증거. ¶ *Place it on a* ~. 그것을 기둥으로 받쳐라 / *He is the chief* ~ *for the cause.* 그가 그 주의를[운동을] 지지하는 중심 인물이다 / *The neck forms a* ~ *for the head.* 목은 머리의 지지물이라 할 수 있다. **3** Ⓒ an actor who assists others in a play. 조연자. **4** a means of support or living; a livelihood. 생계(비). ¶ *The pension was his only* ~. 연금은 그의 유일한 생계비였다. [L. *porto* carry]

give support to, be behind (someone). …을 지지하다.

in support of, in order to uphold. …의 원조로.

sup·port·a·ble [səpɔ́ːrtəbəl] *adj.* that can be supported; bearable. 지탱할 수 있는; 지지받을 수 있는; 원조[부양]할 수 있는; 참을 수 있는.

·sup·port·er [səpɔ́ːrtər] *n.* Ⓒ a person or thing that supports. 지지자[물]; 부양자. ¶ *He is a firm* ~ *of justice* [*the football team*]. 그는 정의[축구팀]의 확고한 옹호[후원]자이다.

:sup·pose [səpóuz] *vt.* **1** (P6,11,21) take (something) as true for the sake of argument; consider (something) as possible; expect. …이라고 가정하다; …을 기대하다. ¶ *Let's* ~ *that the rumor is true.* 그 소문이 사실이라고 가정하자 / *I* ~ *I'll see you at the meeting.* 모임에서 너를 만날 수 있을 것이다. **2** (P6,11,21) imagine; think; believe. …이라고 상상하다; 추측하다; 생각하다. ¶ *I* ~ *he'll come.* 나는 그가 오리라고 생각한다 / *I* ~ *that's the best way.* 나는 그것이 최선의 방법이라고 생각한다 / *I* ~ *you like Korea.* 나는 네가 한국을 좋아한다고 생각하는데 / *What do you* ~ *he'll do?* 너는 그가 무얼 하리라고 생각하느냐 / *The key is in the bag, I* ~. 그 열쇠는 아마 가방 안에 있을 거야 / *The place was worse than I had supposed.* 그 장소는 내가 상상했던 것보다 더 나빴다. **3** (P11) 《in *imperative* or *participle*》 if; consider (something) as a proposal or suggestion. (만일) …이라면; …이라 하더라도; …이라면 어떨까. ¶ *Suppose you had one million won, what would you do?* 만일 네게 백만 원이 있다고 한다면 어떻게 하겠는가 / *Suppose we go for a walk.* 우리 산책을 하는 것이 어떨까 / *Suppose you tell me the story.* 그 이야기를 내게 말해 주지 않겠느냐 / *Suppose you have an accident!* 사고라도 당하면 어쩔려고. **4** (P6) (of a theory or result) require (something) as a condition. (이론 따위가) …을 전제로[조건으로] 하다. ¶ *Democracy supposes free elections.* 민주주의는 당연히 자유 선거를 전제로 한다 / *This theory supposes life on the planet.* 이 학설은 그 행성 위에 생물의 존재를 상정(想定)하고 있다. [→pose]

be supposed to do, **a**) be imagined to do. …할 것으로 상상[기대]되다. ¶ *Cats are supposed to have nine lives.* 고양이는 목숨이 아홉개나 있다고 한다《좀처럼 죽지 않는 데서》. **b**) be expected to do. …하기로 되어 있다.

¶ *She is supposed to come here.* 그녀는 여기에 오기로 되어 있다. **c**) 《*colloq.*》《in *negative*》 be allowed to do. …하여서는 안 되게 되어 있다. ¶ *We are not supposed to use that door.* 우리는 그 문을 사용해서는 안 되게 되어 있다.

*__sup·posed__ [səpóuzd] *adj.* believed to exist; considered as possible; assumed. 가정상의; 상상상의; 상상된. ¶ *a ~ case* 가정된 경우; 가정 / *the ~ site* (유적 따위의) 추정상의 위치 / *the ~ efficiency* (기계 따위의) 추정 효율(效率) / *The ~ friend turned out to be an enemy.* 친구라고 생각되었던 사람이 적으로 판명되었다.

sup·pos·ed·ly [səpóuzidli] *adv.* according to what is or was supposed. 상상으로; 아마. ¶ *Supposedly, he is a rich man.* 아마, 그는 부자겠지.

sup·pos·ing [səpóuziŋ] *conj.* if; assuming; in the event that. 만일 …이라면. ¶ *Supposing (that) it is true, what would happen?* 만일 그게 정말이라면 어떻게 되느냐 / *Supposing you were in his place, what would you do?* 만일 네가 그의 입장이라면 어떻게 하겠느냐.

sup·po·si·tion [sʌ̀pəzíʃən] *n.* **1** Ⓤ the act of supposing. 상상; 추정; 상정. ¶ *be based on mere ~* 순전한 상상에 근거하다 / *confirm one's ~* 추측을 확인하다. **2** Ⓒ something supposed. 가정; 가설. ¶ *The writer planned his book on the ~ that his readers would be high school students.* 작가는 그의 독자들이 고등 학교 학생들이라고 가정하고 그의 책을 구상하였다.

sup·po·si·tion·al [sʌ̀pəzíʃənəl] *adj.* of or based on supposition. 상상상의; 가정적인; 추측의.

*__sup·press__ [səprés] *vt.* (P6) **1** ⓐ put down (someone or something) by force; put an end to (something). …을 억압하다; 진압하다. ¶ *The soldiers speedily suppressed the rebellion.* 병사들은 신속하게 반란을 진압했다. ⓑ stop or prevent by authority; prohibit. (권력으로 활동을) 금지하다. ¶ *Their meetings were suppressed by the police.* 그들의 집회는 경찰에 의해 금지되었다. **2** hold back; restrain; check; prevent (something) from being known. …을 억제하다; (하품 따위를) 억누르다; 참다; (증거 따위를) 감추다. ¶ *~ one's laughter* 〔*a yawn*〕 웃음〔하품〕을 꾹 참다 / *~ one's feelings* 감정을 억제하다 / *~ the truth* 진실을 감추다 / *They suppressed all news that was not favorable to them.* 그들은 그들에게 호의적이 아닌 모든 뉴스를 은폐하였다. **3** ⓐ stop the publication of (a book, etc.); keep from being published. …의 발행을 금지하다. ¶ *~ a newspaper* 〔*book*〕 신문〔책〕의 발행을 금지하다. ⓑ cut out. (문구 따위를) 삭제하다. ¶ *~ a passage in a book* 책의 한 절을 삭제하다. [sub-]

sup·press·i·ble [səprésəbəl] *adj.* that can be suppressed. 억제〔억압〕할 수 있는.

sup·pres·sion [səpréʃən] *n.* Ⓤ the act of suppressing; the state of being suppressed. 억압; 억제; 은폐; 발매 금지. ¶ *~ of evidence* 증거의 은폐.

sup·pres·si·o ve·ri [səprésiòu vέərai / -víərai] *n.* hiding of truth, tacit misrepresentation. 진실의 은폐.

sup·pu·rate [sʌ́pjərèit] *vi.* (P1) (of a poisoned wound) produce a yellow-white liquid. 곪다; 화농(化膿)하다. ¶ *The wound has suppurated.* 상처가 화농하였다. [→pus]

sup·pu·ra·tion [sʌ̀pjəréiʃən] *n.* Ⓤ **1** the state or condition of suppurating. 화농(化膿). **2** the liquid which comes out of a poisoned wound; pus. 고름.

su·pra [sú:prə] *adv.* 《L.》 above or before (in a book or writing). 위〔앞〕에(opp. infra). [L. *suprā* above]

vide supra [váidi-], see above. 상기 참조.

su·prem·a·cy [səpréməsi, su(:)-] *n.* Ⓤ **1** the state of being supreme. 지고(至高); 최고. **2** the highest rank or power. 주권; 지상권; 패권. ¶ *naval ~* 해상 제패; 제해권 / *a struggle for ~* 패권 다툼. [↓]

:**su·preme** [səprí:m, su(:)-] *adj.* highest in authority or rank; highest in degree or importance; greatest or best possible. (지위·권위 따위가) 최고의; 최상의; (품질·정도·중요성 따위가) 극상의; 지고(至高)의; 더할 나위 없는; 궁극의. ¶ *~ power* 지상권(至上權) / *the ~ commander* 최고 사령관 / *~ devotion* 절대의 신앙 / *~ wisdom* 〔*courage*〕 지고의 영지(英智)〔용기〕 / *at the ~ moment* 가장 중요한 때에 / *the ~ end* 궁극의 목적 / *make the ~ sacrifice* (국가를 위해) 목숨을 바치다. [L. =super-]

Supreme Being [-⌐⌐-], **the** *n.* God. 하느님.

Supreme Court [-⌐⌐], **the** *n.* the highest court in the United States; a similar court in other countries. (미국의) 최고 법원; 대법원(大法院).

su·preme·ly [səprí:mli, su(:)-] *adv.* in or with a supreme manner. 최상으로; 더할 나위 없이.

sur-[1] [sʌr, sər] *pref.* =sub-.

sur-[2] [sʌr, sər] *pref.* =super-.

sur·cease [sə:rsí:s] *n.* 《*arch.*》 an end. 정지; 그침. —*vi.* (P1) come to an end; stop. 그치다; 정지하다. [→supersede]

sur·charge [sə́:rtʃὰ:rdʒ] *n.* **1** Ⓒ money to be paid in addition to what has been paid already; an extra charge; an overcharge. 추가〔부가, 특별〕 요금; 가중 과세(加重課稅). ¶ *an import ~* 수입 부가금. **2** Ⓤ an additional or excessive load. 과중(過重); 과도하게 쌓기.

—[⌐⌐] *vt.* **1** (P6,13,14) charge too much; overcharge; demand additional payment from. …에 부당〔과도〕한 대금을

청구하다. **2** (P6) overload; put too great weight on. …에 과적하다; 지나친 무게를〔부담을〕 싣다〔주다〕. **3** (P6) print additional words on (a postage stamp). (우표에) 가격〔날짜〕 정정인(訂正印)을 찍다. [sur-², → charge]

:sure [ʃuər] *adj.* **1** 《in *predicative*》《*of, that*》 convinced; having a good reason for belief. 확신하는; 자신이 있는. ¶ *I am ~ of his honesty.* =*I am ~ that he is honest.* 나는 그의 정직을〔그가 정직함을〕 확신한다 / *Are you ~ of success?* 너는 성공에 자신이 있느냐〔성공을 확신하느냐〕 / *I'm not ~ about tomorrow.* 내일의 일은 잘 모르겠다 / *Don't be too ~.* (지나치게) 너무 자신하지 마라 / *I'm not ~ if I can do it.* 그것을 할 수 있을런지 자신이 없다 / *I'm not ~ whether he will come or not.* 그가 올지 안 올지 잘 모르겠다. **2** 《in *predicative*》《*of*》 without fail; never missing. 꼭〔반드시〕 …하는. ¶ *He is ~ to succeed.* 그는 반드시 성공한다 / *It's ~ to rain.* 틀림없이 비가 온다 / *Such a day is ~ to come.* 그러한 날은 반드시 온다 / *Be ~ to come early.* 꼭 일찍 오너라 / *Be ~ you finish it.* 반드시 끝내거라 / *Be ~ to write me, won't you?* 꼭 편지를 해다오. **3** certain; reliable; safe. 확실한; 신뢰할 수 있는; 안전한. ¶ *a ~ friend* 신뢰할 수 있는 친구 / *a ~ method* 확실한 방법 / *a surest way to victory* 가장 확실하게 승리하는 법 / *a ~ source* 믿을만한 출처〔소식통〕 / *by a ~ hand* 확실한 사람의 손을 통해서 / *Put a thing in a ~ place.* 안전한 장소에 물건을 놓아라. **4** firm; steady. 튼튼한; 요동치 않는. ¶ *a ~ footing* 튼튼한 발판〔입장〕 / *a ~ foundation* 확고한〔튼튼한〕 기초 / *a ~ faith* 강한 신념 / *stand on ~ ground* 튼튼한〔안정된〕 토대 위에 서다.

feel sure that, be confident that. …임을 확신하다.

for sure, certainly. 확실히.

make sure, get precautions. 확인하다; 다짐하다.

make sure of, **a**) establish the truth of; ensure the happening of. …을 다짐〔확인〕하다. ¶ *make ~ of the time* 시간을 확인하다 / *Make ~ of your facts.* (너의) 사실을 확인하라. **b**) secure possession of. 미리 …을 구하다〔손에 넣다〕. ¶ *I must make ~ of a seat for the play.* 그 연극의 좌석을 확보해 두어야 한다.

Sure thing! Certainly! 그렇고 말고.

To be sure. Indeed. 정말로.

Well, I'm sure! Well, I declare! 원; 이런.

— *adv.* 《U.S. *colloq.*》《expressing *agreement*》 certainly. 확실히; 좋고 말고. ¶ *Are you coming? —Sure!* 너 오겠느냐—그럼, 가고말고 / *That ~ was a good dinner.* 정말로 훌륭한 정찬(正餐)이었습니다. [→secure]

(***as***) ***sure as ...,*** as certainly as .... 확실히; 틀림없이.

sure enough, **a**) as was expected; in fact. 아니나 다를까; 과연; 실제로. ¶ *I said he would come, and, ~ enough, he was there.* 그가 올 것이라고 말했는데, 아니나 다를까 그는 거기에 있었다. **b**) you may be sure; certainly. 반드시; 틀림없이. ¶ *That will happen ~ enough.* 그런 일은 반드시 일어난다 / *He will be there ~ enough.* 그는 틀림없이 거기 있을 것이다.

:sure·ly [ʃúərli] *adv.* in a sure manner; certainly; undoubtedly; without fail. 확실히; 안전하게; 반드시; 꼭; 틀림없이. ¶ *slowly but ~* 천천히 그러나 확실하게 / *plant one's feet ~ on the ground* 땅바닥에 발을 (정신차려) 안전하게 내려 딛다 / *He will ~ accept it.* 그는 꼭 받아들일 것이다 / *Surely we have met before.* 틀림없이 이전에 만난 적이 있다 / *There is no truth in it, ~.* 그것은 설마 사실이 아니겠지 / *Are you willing to try?—Surely.* 해보겠느냐—물론이죠.

sure·ness [ʃúərnis] *n.* Ⓤ the state of being sure. 확실; 정확; 안전.

sure·ty [ʃúərti, ʃúərəti] *n.* Ⓒ (*pl.* **-ties**) **1** Ⓤ the state of being sure; certainty. 확실한 것; 확실성. **2** Ⓒ a thing or promise given to make (someone) safe against loss, damage, etc.; a pledge; guarantee. 보증; 담보. **3** a person who promises to be responsible for another. 보증인. [*sure*]

of a surety, certainly. 틀림없이; 꼭.

stand surety for, become so responsible for another. …의 보증인이 되다.

surf [səːrf] *n.* Ⓤ the breaking waves of the sea. (해안에) 밀려드는 파도. [E.]

:sur·face [sə́ːrfis] *n.* Ⓒ **1** the outer, and esp. the upper, side or part of anything. 표면; 외면; 외부. ¶ *The box has a rough* 〔*smooth*〕 *~.* 상자는 표면이 거칠다〔매끄럽다〕 / *on the ~ of the earth* 〔*ocean*〕 지구〔대양〕의 표면에. **2** 《math.》 that which has length and breadth but no thickness. 면(面). ¶ *a plane* 〔*curve*〕 *~* 평면〔곡면〕 / *a developable ~* 전개 가능한 곡면. **3** the outward appearance. 외관; 외모. ¶ *look only at the ~ of men and things* 사람이나 사물의 외면만을 보다 / *look below* 〔*beneath*〕 *the ~ of things* 사물의 내면을 보다 / *Her gentleness is only on the ~.* 그녀의 온순함은 겉보기에만 그렇다.

— *adj.* of, on, or at the surface. 표면의; 외관〔외모〕의; 피상적인. ¶ *~ transportation* 육상〔해상〕 교통 / *a ~ force* 수상 부대 / *~ mail* 육상〔해상〕 우편(cf. *airmail*) / *~ appearance* 외관 / *~ politeness* 겉으로만의 공손함 / *His information is of the most ~ kind.* 그의 정보는〔지식은〕 극히 피상적인 것이다.

— *vt.* (P6) put a surface on (something); make (something) smooth. …에 표면을 달다; …을 포장(鋪裝)하다; 평탄하게 하다. ¶ *~ a table with paint* 테이블에 페인트를 칠하다 / *The road is surfaced.* 도로는 포장되었다.

— *vi.* (P1) come up to the surface from

below. 부상(浮上)하다. ¶ *The fish surfaced and jumped.* 물고기가 물 위에 떠올라 튀었다. [→superficies]

surf·board [sə́:rfbɔ̀:rd] *n.* Ⓒ a long, narrow board used for riding incoming ocean waves. 파도타기 널; 서프보드. [*surf*]

sur·feit [sə́:rfit] *n.* Ⓤ excess in eating or drinking; the feeling of fullness or sickness resulting from such excess. 과식; 과음; 만복; 식상(食傷). —*vt.* (P6) 《*with*》 overfeed. …에게 과식하게 하다; …을 물리게 하다. ¶ ~ *oneself with fruit* 과일을 지나치게 많이 먹다 / *be surfeited with pleasure* 쾌락에 식상하다. [sur-², L. *facio* do]

surf·rid·ing [sə́:rfràidiŋ] *n.* Ⓤ the act or sport of riding on a surfboard. 파도타기; 서핑. [*surf*]

***surge** [sə:rdʒ] *n.* Ⓒ **1** a large wave. 큰 파도; 놀. **2** a strong and sudden rising motion, feeling, etc. 동요; 파동; 격동; 소용돌이. ¶ *a* ~ *of smoke* 〔*flame*〕 너울거리며 하늘로 치솟는 연기〔불꽃〕 / *Our boat was upset by the* ~. 우리 보트는 큰 파도에 의해 뒤집혔다 / *A* ~ *of anger rushed over him.* 그는 분노가 치밀어 올라왔다.
—*vi.* (P2A,3) move up and down like waves; rush like a large wave. 파도치다; 큰 파도가 일다; (파도처럼) 밀려오다. ¶ *surging crowds* 노도처럼 밀려오는 군중 / *The floods surged over the village.* 홍수가 그 마을을 덮쳤다 / *The demonstrators surged through the streets.* 시위 군중이 파도처럼 거리를 휩쓸고 지나갔다 / *Blood surged to his face.* 그의 얼굴이 벌겋게 달아 올랐다 / *A great wave of emotion surged over us.* 큰 감동의 물결이 우리를 감쌌다. [L. =rise]

***sur·geon** [sə́:rdʒən] *n.* Ⓒ **1** a doctor who performs operations. 외과 의사. **2** a medical officer in the army or navy; a ship's doctor. 군의관; 선의(船醫). [↓]

sur·ger·y [sə́:rdʒəri] *n.* (*pl.* **-ger·ies**) **1** Ⓤ the art and science of medical operations. 외과(학). **2** Ⓒ an office or operating room of a surgeon. 외과 진료실; 수술실. **3** 《Brit.》 Ⓒ a doctor's office. 의원(醫院). [Gk. *kheir* hand, *ergō* work]

sur·gi·cal [sə́:rdʒikəl] *adj.* of surgery or surgeons; used in surgery. 외과의; 외과의 의; 외과 수술(용)의. ¶ *a* ~ *operation* 외과 수술 / ~ *treatment* 외과적 처치〔치료〕 / ~ *instruments* 외과용〔수술용〕 기구.

sur·ly [sə́:rli] *adj.* (sometimes **-li·er, -li·est**) ill-humored; bad-tempered and unfriendly. 성미가 까다로운; 지르퉁한; 무뚝뚝한; 쌀쌀맞은. [→sir, -ly]

sur·mise [sə:rmáiz] *vt., vi.* (P6,11; 1) guess; suppose. …을 추측하다; (…인가 하고) 생각하다. ¶ *I surmised that he had failed in his business.* 나는 그가 사업에 실패했다고 추측했다 / *He surmised that this was the true situation.* 그는 이것이 진짜 상황이 아닌가 하고 생각했다. —[ˊ–, –ˊ] *n.* Ⓤ a guess or thought based on something not evident. 추측; 억측. [sur-², L. *mitto* send]

sur·mount [sərmáunt] *vt.* (P6) **1** get over (a difficulty); overcome. (곤란 등을) 이겨내다; 극복(克服)하다. ¶ *He surmounted many difficulties.* 그는 많은 어려움을 극복했다. **2** climb over (a hill, etc.). (산을) 오르다; 타고 넘다. **3** stand or lie on top of (something). …의 위에 있다〔눕다, 솟다〕. ¶ *A cross surmounts the steeple of a church.* 십자가가 교회의 첨탑 위에 솟아〔설치되어〕 있다 / *peaks surmounted with snow* 눈으로 덮여 있는 산봉우리. [sur-²]

sur·mount·a·ble [sərmáuntəbəl] *adj.* that can be overcome. 이겨낼 수 있는; 타파할 수 있는.

sur·mul·let [sərmʌ́lit] *n.* 《fish》 a red mullet. 노랑촉수. [F.]

sur·name [sə́:rnèim] *n.* Ⓒ **1** a family name; a last name. 성(姓)(opp. Christian name, first name). ¶ *Smith is the* ~ *of John Smith.* 'Smith'는 'John Smith'의 성이다. **2** a name added to the real name. 별명; 이명. —*vt.* (P6) give an added name to (someone); call (someone) by his surname. …에 별명을 붙이다; …을 성〔별명〕으로 부르다. ¶ *Alfred surnamed the Great* '대왕'이라고 호칭되는 알프레드. [sur-²]

***sur·pass** [sərpǽs, sərpɑ́:s] *vt.* (P6) **1** be better or bigger than (someone or something). …보다 낫다〔우수하다〕. ¶ ~ *someone in ability* 능력에서 아무보다 우수하다 / *The result surpassed all our expectations.* 결과는 전혀 예상 이상이었다. **2** go beyond; exceed. (역량·범위 따위를) 초월하다; 능가하다. ¶ ~ *oneself* 자기 능력 이상의 것을 하다 / *beauty surpassing all description* 형언 할 수 없는 아름다움 / *a task that surpasses one's skill* 힘에 부치는 일. [sur-², →pass]

〈surplice〉

sur·plice [sə́:rplis] *n.* Ⓒ a loose white garment with broad sleeves worn by a priest. 중〔소〕백의(中〔小〕白衣). [sur-², L. *pellis* skin]

sur·plus [sə́:rpləs, -plʌ̀s] *n.* ⓊⒸ an amount above what is needed; a remainder; excess. 잉여; 여분; 나머지; 초과액(opp. deficit). ¶ *in* ~ 여분으로. —*adj.* more than is needed. 과잉의; 잉여의. ¶ ~ *population* 과잉 인구 / *the* ~ *food of America* 미국의 잉여 식량 / ~ *funds* 잉여금. [sur-², →plus]

‡sur·prise [sərpráiz] *vt.* **1** (P6) cause (someone) to feel wonder or astonishment; startle; shock. (깜짝) 놀라게 하다; 소스라치게 하다. ¶ *His sudden fury surprised me.* 나는 그의 갑작스런 격노에 깜짝 놀랐다 / *Her behavior surprised us.* 우리들은 그녀의 행동에 깜짝 놀랐다 / *I was surprised at the* *news.* 나는 그 뉴스에 깜짝 놀랐다 / *I'm surprised that you still remain here.* 네가 아직까지 여기 남아있다니 참으로 놀랐다 / *I shouldn't be surprised if it rains* (*rained*). 비가 온다 해도 놀라울 건 없겠어; 아무래도 비가 올 것 같다. **2** (P6,13) catch or attack suddenly and unexpectedly; take by surprise. …을 급습(기습)하다; …을 불시에 덮치다(잡다). ¶ ~ *an enemy* 적을 급습하다 / ~ *a robber breaking into a bank* 은행에 침입한 강도를 덮치다 / ~ *a pickpocket* (*in the act of*) *stealing* 소매치기를 현장(現場)에서 체포하다 / *We surprised the enemy while they were sleeping.* 우리는 잠들어 있는 적을 기습하였다. **3** (P6,13) ⦅*into*⦆ startle and cause (someone) to say or to do something that he has not intended; bring (something) to light by such means. (아무를) 놀라게 하여…하게 하다(시키다); …을 드러나게 하다. ¶ ~ *someone into telling the truth* 아무를 놀라게 해서 진실을 말하게 하다 / *He surprised me into consent.* 그가 느닷없이 다그치는 통에 동의하고 말았다 / *I surprised the secret out of him.* 나는 그의 의표를 찔러서 비밀을 알아냈다.

I shouldn't be surprised if, I rather expect that…. …하여도 당연하다고 생각한다; 필시 …일 것이다.

surprise someone into, hurry him by surprise into. …을 놀라게 해서 —시키다.

— *n.* **1** Ⓤ the feeling caused by something sudden or unexpected. 놀람; 경악. ¶ *with a look of* ~ 놀란 얼굴로 / *exclaim in* ~ 놀라서 소리치다 / *show some* (*much*) ~ (*at*) (…에) 조금(크게) 놀란 모습을 나타내다 / *Did he show any* ~ *at the news?* 소식을 듣고 그는 놀라더냐 / *Listen without* ~. 놀라지 말고 들어다오 / *His* ~ *was visible.* 그의 놀람은 역력했다. **2** Ⓒ something sudden or unexpected. 뜻밖의 일(것); 놀랄 만한 일. ¶ *a pleasing* ~ 뜻밖의 기쁜 일; 유쾌한 놀람 / *Here is a small* ~ *for you.* 여기 너를 놀라게 할 조그마한 선물(기쁜 소식)이 있다 / *His visit was a great* ~ *to me.* 그의 방문은 뜻밖의 일이었다 / *What a* ~*!* 이거 참 놀라운 일인데. **3** Ⓤ the act of attacking or catching suddenly or unexpectedly. 불의의 습격(덮치기); 급습. ¶ *capture a fortress by* ~ 요새를 기습 점령하다 / *resist a* ~ 기습을 저지하다. [sur-², L. *prehendo* take]

catch by surprise, astonish; surprise. 놀라게 하다.

take** someone* or *something* ***by surprise, **a**) catch or attack suddenly. …을 기습하다; 기습하여 붙잡다. ¶ *He took me by* ~. 그는 기습하여 나를 붙잡았다. **b**) surprise. …을 놀라게 하다. ¶ *The news took Washington by* ~. 그 뉴스는 미국 정부를 경악하게 했다.

sur·prised [sərpráizd] *adj.* showing or feeling surprise. 놀란. ¶ *look* ~ 놀란 것처럼 보이다 / *a* ~ *look* 놀란 얼굴 모습.

sur·prised·ly [sərpráizidli] *adv.* in a surprised manner. 놀라서; 깜짝 놀라.

***sur·pris·ing** [sərpráiziŋ] *adj.* causing surprise. 놀랄 만한; 뜻밖의; 이상한. ¶ *make* ~ *progress* 눈부신 발전을(진보를) 이룩하다 / *It is* ~ *that….* …이라는 것은 놀라운 일이다.

sur·pris·ing·ly [sərpráiziŋli] *adv.* in a surprising manner; to a surprising degree. 놀라서; 놀랄 정도로; 뜻밖에. ¶ *Surprisingly enough, everybody was there.* 놀랍게도 모든 사람이 그곳에 있었다.

sur·re·al·ism [sərí:əlizəm] *n.* a movement purporting to express the subconscious mind by images, etc. 초현실주의. [sur-², →realism]

***sur·ren·der** [səréndər] *vt.* (P6,13) give (something) up to someone or something; give (oneself) up to something; yield. …을 내어(넘겨) 주다; 포기하다; (몸을) 맡기다; 항복하다. ¶ ~ *a city to the enemy* 도시를 적에게 내어주다 / ~ *someone to the police* 아무를 경찰에 넘기다 / ~ *a ticket at the exit* 출구에서 표를 넘겨주다 / *We shall never* ~ *our hope* (*liberty*). 우리는 절대로 희망을(자유를) 포기하지 않을 것이다 / ~ *oneself to despair* 절망에 빠지다 / ~ *oneself to justice*(*police*) 자수하다 / *She surrendered herself willingly to his embrace.* 그녀는 기꺼이 그의 포옹에 몸을 맡겼다.

— *vi.* (P1) yield; submit after defeat; give oneself up. 항복하다. ¶ ~ *to the enemy* 적에게 항복하다 / *The murderer surrendered to the police.* 살인범은 경찰에 자수했다.

— *n.* ⓊⒸ the act of surrendering. 인도(引導); 포기; 항복. [sur-², →render]

surrender value [-ˊ-- ˋ--] *n.* an amount payable to an insured person who surrenders his policy. 중도 해약 환급금(還給金).

sur·rep·ti·tious [sə̀:rəptíʃəs / sʌ̀r-] *adj.* done secretly; secret. 비밀의; 내밀한. ¶ *a* ~ *glance* 몰래 훔쳐보기 / ~ *pleasures* (*acts*) 남의 눈을 피해서 몰래 하는 쾌락(행위) / ~ *negotiation* 비밀 교섭. [sur-¹, L. *rapio* snatch]

sur·rep·ti·tious·ly [sə̀:rəptíʃəsli / sʌ̀r-] *adv.* in a surreptitious manner; secretly. 은밀히; 몰래.

sur·rey [sʌ́ri] *n.* a light, four-wheeled carriage having two seats. 2석 4인승 4륜마차(자동차). [Place]

sur·ro·gate [sə́:rəgèit, -git, sʌ́r-] *n.* a deputy of a bishop or of his chancellor. 감독 대리. [L. *rogo* ask]

:sur·round [səráund] *vt.* enclose (someone or something) on all sides. …을 둘러싸다(에워싸다). ¶ *A high wall surrounds the city.* 높은 성벽이 도시를 에워싸고 있다 / *Korea is surrounded with* (*by*) *the sea on three sides.* 한국은 3면이 바다로 둘러싸여 있다 / *A crowd surrounded him.* =*He was surrounded by a crowd.* 그는 군중에 둘러싸였다 / *Troops surrounded the city.* 군대가 그 도시를 포위했다 / ~ *a park with a wall* 공원 주

위에 담을 둘러치다 / *She grew up surrounded by luxury.* 그녀는 사치스런 환경에서 자랐다. [sur-², L. *unda* wave]

sur·round·ing [səráundiŋ] *a.* lying on all sides. 주위의.

·sur·round·ings [səráundiŋz] *n. pl.* all the conditions that surround someone; surrounding things, objects, person, etc. 주위; 환경; 주위의 사물〔사람〕. ¶ *home* ~ 가정 환경 / *live in comfortable* ~ 안락한 환경에서 살다 / *in ugly* ~ (주변) 환경이 나쁜 곳에.

sur·tax [sə́:rtæ̀ks] *n.* Ⓤⓒ 《U.S.》 a tax added to the normal income tax(cf. 《Brit.》 *supertax*). 부가세. — *vt.* (P6) impose an extra tax on. 부가세를 과하다. [sur-²]

sur·veil·lance [sə:rvéiləns] *n.* Ⓤ careful watch; constant watch kept over someone. 감시; 감독. ¶ *work under someone's* ~ 아무의 감독 아래에서 일하다 / *He is under* ~. 그는 감시당하고〔감시 아래에〕 있다. [sur-², vigil]

:sur·vey [sə:rvéi] *vt.* (P6) **1** look at (something) carefully; examine generally. …을 주의 깊게 보다; 조망(眺望)하다; 개관(概觀)하다. ¶ ~ *the scene from the hill* 언덕에서 그 경치를 내려다보다 / ~ *the history of science* 과학의 역사를 조사〔개관〕하다 / ~ *the current situation* 현재의 정세를 개관하다 / *The police surveyed the scene of the crime.* 경찰은 범행현장을 주의 깊게 조사하였다 / *He surveyed me from head to foot.* 그는 나를 머리끝에서 발끝까지 자세히 살펴봤다. **2** measure. …을 측량하다.
— [sə́:rvei, sərvéi] *n.* ⓒ **1** the act of surveying; a general examination. 주의 깊게 살펴보기; 개관. ¶ *make a* ~ *of the situation* 정세를 개관하다 / *make a rapid* ~ *of a house and grounds* 가옥과 대지를 서둘러 조사하다〔살펴보다〕. **2** the act of measuring land carefully. 측량. ¶ *the department of* ~ 측량부. [sur-², →view]

sur·vey·ing [sə:rvéiiŋ] *n.* Ⓤ the act or art of measuring land. 측량(술).

sur·vey·or [sərvéiər] *n.* ⓒ a person who measures land. 측량 기사.

sur·viv·al [sərváivəl] *n.* **1** Ⓤ the act or state of surviving. 살아남음; 생존; 잔존. ¶ *the* ~ *of the fittest* 적자 생존. **2** ⓒ a person, thing, custom, belief, etc., that has lasted from an earlier time. 생존자; 잔존물; 유물; 유풍. ¶ *survivals of medieval customs* 중세의 유풍. [↓]

·sur·vive [sərváiv] *vt.* (P6) live longer than (others); live beyond some dangerous experience. …보다 오래 살다; …의 뒤에도 아직 살아 있다. ¶ ~ *one's children* 자식들보다 오래 살다 / ~ *the storm* 무사히 폭풍을 헤어나다 / *He survived his wife many years.* 그는 아내의 사후 여러 해 동안 살았다 / *Fortunately he survived the traffic accident.* 다행히 그는 교통 사고를 겪고도 살아남았다 / ~ *one's fame* 명성을 잃고도 살아 있다.
— *vi.* (P1) remain alive or in existence. 살아남다; 잔존하다. ¶ ~ *to our times* 오늘날까지 살아남다 / ~ *for two years* 2년 동안 목숨을 부지하다 / *The custom still survives.* 그 풍습은 지금까지 남아 있다 / *Only two survived out of the whole party.* 일행 전체 중 겨우 두 사람만이 살아남았다. [sur-², →vivacious]
survive one's usefulness, become a good-for-nothing. (오래 살아서) 무용지물이 되다.

sur·vi·vor [sərváivər] *n.* ⓒ a person or thing that remains alive. 잔존자〔물〕. ¶ *the survivors of the earthquake* 지진에서 살아남은 사람들.

Su·san [sú:zən], **Su·san·na(h)** [su:zǽnə] *n.* a woman's name. 여자 이름. 參考 애칭은 Sue.

sus·cep·ti·bil·i·ty [səsèptəbíləti] *n.* **1** Ⓤ the quality of being susceptible. 감수성; 다감함; (병에) 감염되기 쉬움. ¶ *have* ~ *to colds* 감기에 걸리기 쉽다 / *one's* ~ *to emotion* 정에 약함. **2** (*pl.*) sensitive feelings. 감정. ¶ *wound* 〔*offend*〕 *national susceptibilities* 국민 감정을 해치다. [↓]

sus·cep·ti·ble [səséptəbəl] *adj.* **1** 《*to*》 easily affected by feelings, emotions, diseases, etc.; very sensitive. 느끼기 쉬운; 민감한. ¶ *be* ~ *to influenza* 독감에 걸리기 쉽다 / *a* ~ *young man* 다감한〔감수성이 예민한〕 젊은이 / *a person* ~ *to female charms* 여성의 매력에 꼼짝 못 하는 사람 / *He is a* ~ *fellow where the ladies are concerned.* 그는 여자에 관한 것이라면 민감한 녀석이다. **2** 《*of*》 allowing; admitting. …을 허용하는; 할 수 있는. ¶ *facts not* ~ *of proof* 증거를 댈 수 없는 사실 / *The passage is* ~ *of a number of interpretations.* 이 구절은 여러 가지로 해석할 수 있다. [L. *capio* take]

:sus·pect [səspékt] *vt.* **1** (P6,13) imagine or believe (something) to exist. (…의 존재를) 느낌으로 알다; …의 낌새를 채다; …을 눈치채다. ¶ ~ *danger* 〔*a plot*〕 위험을〔음모를〕 느끼다〔눈치채다〕 / *I suspected the presence of fire from the odor.* 냄새로 불이 났다는 것을 느꼈다. **2** (P6,11,21) think likely; suppose. …이 아닌가 하고 생각하다; …이라고 생각하다; 상상하다. ¶ *chemicals suspected of causing cancer* 암을 유발할 가능성이 있다고 생각되는 화학 약품 / *I* ~ *him* (*to be*) *mad.* =*I* ~ *that he is mad.* 나는 그가 미치지 않았나 하고 생각한다 / *They suspected that he had been murdered.* 사람들은 그가 이미 살해된 것이 아닌가 하고 생각했다 / *I* ~ *the book to be mine.* 그 책은 내 것이 아닌가 생각한다. **3** (P6) doubt the truth of (something); doubt. (사물이 정말인지 아닌지를) 의심하다; 미심쩍어하다; …을 믿지 않다. ¶ *I* ~ *her motives.* 나는 그녀의 동기를 의심한다 / *I suspected the picture of being a fake.* 나는 그 그림이 가짜라고 의심했다. **4** (P13) 《*of*》 believe (someone) to be guilty, but without proof. …에 혐의를 두다. ¶ *They* ~ *him of* *murder.* 그들은 그에게 살인 혐의를 두고 있다 / *He is suspected of stealing.* 그는 도둑질의 혐의를 받고 있다.

—[sʌ́spekt] *n.* Ⓒ a person suspected, esp. of a crime; a person suspected of having or spreading a disease. 용의자; 혐의자. ¶ *a political* ~ 정치상의 요주의 인물 / *a murder* ~ 살인 용의자 / *the suspects in the high incidence of cancer* 암의 높은 발생률로 의심받는 물질 / *The policeman arrested one* ~ *for the murder.* 경찰은 살인범 용의자를 한 사람 체포했다.

—[sʌ́spekt] *adj.* 《as *predicative*》 suspected; questionable. 의심스러운. ¶ *The man's honesty is* ~. 그 사람의 정직성이 의심스럽다. [L. *specio* look]

*__sus·pend__ [səspénd] *vt.* (P6,13) **1** 《*from*》 hang. …을 매달다; 걸다. ¶ ~ *a lamp from the ceiling* 천장에 등불을 매달다 / ~ *a medal from one's neck* 목에 메달을 걸다. **2** stop (something) for a while. …을 중지하다. ¶ ~ *business* 영업을 중지하다 / ~ *a license* 면허를 정지하다 / ~ *a law* 법률을 일시 정지하다 / ~ *payment* (회사 따위가 파산으로) 지급을 정지하다. **3** 《chiefly in *passive*》 put (a balloon, smoke, etc.) in place, as if hanging. …을 뜨게 하다; (안개·구름 따위를) 자욱이 떠 있게 하다. ¶ *The oil is suspended in the water.* 기름이 물에 떠 있다 / *The smoke was suspended in the air.* 연기가 공중에 자욱이 감돌고 있었다 / *A pall of smog was suspended over the city.* 덮개와 같은 스모그가 도시 상공(上空)을 덮고 있었다. **4** keep (something) undecided. …을 미결로 남겨두다; 보류하다. ¶ *Judgement was suspended till the following Monday.* 판결은 다음 월요일까지 보류되었다. **5** exclude for a while from an office, position, etc. 정직〔정학〕시키다. ¶ ~ *a clergyman* 목사를 정직(停職)시키다 / *He was suspended from school for a month.* 그는 1개월 정학 처분을 받았다. [L. *suspendo*]

sus·pend·ers [səspéndərz] *n. pl.* **1** 《U.S.》 bands worn by men to keep up their trousers. 바지의 멜빵. 參考 영국에서는 braces 라고 한다. **2** 《Brit.》 bands worn to keep up the stockings. 양말대님.

sus·pense [səspéns] *n.* Ⓤ **1** anxiety resulting from an uncertain situation; the state of being uncertain; doubt. 걱정; 불안; (정신적으로) 허공에 떠 있는 불안한 상태; 의혹. ¶ *They waited in great* ~ *for the doctor's arrival.* 그들은 의사의 도착을 매우 근심스러운 불안 상태에서 기다렸다 / *keep someone in* ~ 아무를 불안하게 해두다〔마음 졸이게 하다〕. **2** the state of being undecided. 미결; 미정 상태. ¶ *hold one's judgement in* ~ 판단〔의견〕 따위를 미결 상태로 놔두다 / *The question remains in* ~. 그 문제는 미결로 남아 있다.

sus·pen·sion [səspénʃən] *n.* Ⓤ the act of suspending; the state of being suspended; stop; an undecided state. 매달기; 공중에 매달린 상태; 중지; 미결정.

suspension bridge [⌐–⌐] *n.* a bridge hung from cables supported by towers. 출렁다리; 현수교(懸垂橋), 조교(弔橋).

sus·pen·sive [səspénsiv] *adj.* stopping; undecided. 정지의; 중지의; 결단이 안 서는.

:**sus·pi·cion** [səspíʃən] *n.* **1** ⓊⒸ the act of suspecting; the feeling that something is bad, wrong, etc. 혐의; 의심. ¶ *hold someone in* ~ =*cast* ~ *on someone* 아무에게 혐의를 두다; 아무를 의심하다 / *arose* ~ 의혹을 낳다 / *with* ~ 의심하여 / *I had a* ~ *that I was being followed.* 미행당하고 있는 듯한 느낌이 들었다 / *I have grave suspicions about that man's honesty.* 나는 그 사람의 정직성에 관해서 크게 의심하고 있다 / *There is a strong* ~ *against him.* 그에게 짙은 혐의가 걸려 있다. **2** 《usu. *a* ~》 a very small amount; a slight taste. 극소량; 기미. ¶ *a* ~ *of whisky* 극소량의 위스키 / *without a* ~ *of dissatisfaction* 조금의 불만도 없이 / *He has not a* ~ *of humor.* 그는 유머를 조금도 알아차리지 못한다. [→suspect]

be above suspicion, too obviously good to be suspected. 의심할 바 없다.

have a suspicion of, entertain suspicion. …을 의심하다.

*__sus·pi·cious__ [səspíʃəs] *adj.* **1** 《*of*》 showing doubt; suspecting; likely to think badly of others. 수상쩍은; 의심하는 듯한; 의심 많은. ¶ *a* ~ *glance* 의심쩍어하는 눈초리 / *He is* ~ *of you.* 그는 너를 의심하고 있다 / *a* ~ *nature* 의심 많은 성질 / *The ignorant are* ~. 무지한 사람은 의심이 많다 / *The dog is* ~ *of strangers.* 개는 낯선 사람을 의심한다. **2** causing doubt; questionable. 의심스러운; 의심을 낳게 하는. ¶ ~ *actions* 의심스러운 행위 / *a* ~ *character* 의심스러운 인물 / *under* ~ *circumstance* 의심을 받기 쉬운 사정하에서 / *The matter seemed* ~ *to him.* 그 일은 그에게 수상쩍어 보였다.

sus·pi·cious·ly [səspíʃəsli] *adv.* in a suspicious manner. 의심 많게; 수상쩍게.

sus·pire [səspáiər] *vi.* (P1) 《poet.》 **1** sigh. 한숨짓다. **2** breathe. 호흡하다. [sub-, →spirit]

*__sus·tain__ [səstéin] *vt.* **1** support; hold up. …을 떠받치다〔받쳐주다〕. ¶ *pillars that* ~ *arch* 아치를 떠받치는 기둥 / *Stone arches* ~ *the weight of the dome.* 석조 아치는 돔의 무게를 지탱한다. **2** suffer; experience; undergo. (손해 따위를) 입다; …을 경험하다; 당하다. ¶ ~ *a loss* 손실을 입다 / ~ *severe injuries* 심한 상처를 입다 / *She sustained the loss of two sons in the war.* 그녀는 전쟁으로 두 아들을 잃었다. **3** bear; endure. …에 견디다; 참다. ¶ ~ *a shock* 충격에 견디다. **4** support (oneself, one's family, etc.); keep alive; continue. …을 유지하다; 지속하다. ¶ ~ *a family* 가족의 생계를 유지하다 / ~ *conversa-*

tion for hours 몇 시간 동안 담화를 계속하다 / ~ *an institution* 공공 시설을 유지하다. **5** admit; allow; uphold. …을 인정하다; 지지하다. ¶ *The judge sustained his objection.* 재판관은 그의 이론(異論)을 받아들였다. **6** agree with; confirm; prove. 확인〔확증〕하다; 입증하다. ¶ *His theory has been sustained by the facts.* 그의 이론은 사실에 의해 입증되었다. **7** 《theatr.》 act (a role) in a fitting manner. (맡은 역을) 훌륭히 해내다. ¶ ~ *one's role* 맡은 역을 훌륭히 해내다. [sub-, L. *teneo* hold]

sus·tain·a·ble [səstéinəbəl] *adj.* capable or being sustained. 지탱〔지지, 유지〕할 수 있는; 견딜〔참을〕 수 있는; 확인〔입증〕할 수 있는.

sus·te·nance [sʌ́stənəns] *n.* Ⓤ the act of sustaining; food. 지지; 지속; 생계; 음식. ¶ *How shall we get ~?* 어떻게 생계를 꾸려나가나 / *without any ~ of any kind* 아무 음식물도 없이. [*sustain*]

sut·ler [sʌ́tlər] *n.* a camp-follower selling food, etc. 종군 매점 상인. [Du.]

Su·tra, su·tra [súːtrə] *n.* Ⓒ a holy writing of the Buddhist religion. (불교의) 경전.

sut·tee [sʌ́tiː, sʌtíː] *n.* Ⓒ a Hindu widow who immolates herself on her husband's pyre. 순사(殉死)하는 아내. [Skr.]

su·ture [súːtʃər] *n.* Ⓤ the act of sewing up a wound; Ⓒ a seam formed by such a way. (상처의) 봉합; 상처의 꿰맨 자리. [L. *suo* sew]

su·ze·rain [súːzərèin, -rin] *n.* Ⓒ a ruler; a state controlling another state politically. 영주(領主); 종주(宗主); 종주국. [F.]

su·ze·rain·ty [súːzərèinti, -rin-] *n.* Ⓤ the position or power of a suzerain. 종주권; 영주의 지위〔권력〕.

SW, S.W., s.w. southwest.

swab [swɑb / swɔb] *n.* Ⓒ **1** a mop for cleaning decks, floors, etc. 자루걸레; 몹. **2** a piece of cotton for cleaning some part of the body. 소독면. — *vt.* (**swabbed, swabbing**) (P6,7) clean (something) with a swab. …을 자루걸레로 닦다; 훔치다. ¶ ~ *down the decks* 갑판을 자루걸레로 청소하다. [Du.]

swad·dle [swɑ́dl / swɔ́dl] *vt.* (P6) wrap (a baby) with clothes. (갓난애를) 포대기로 싸다. — *n.* Ⓒ the cloth used for swaddling. 포대기; 강보. [*swathe*]

swad·dling clothes [swɑ́dliŋklòuðz / swɔ́d-] *n. pl.* **1** many clothes wrapped around a newborn baby; baby clothes. (갓난애를 둘둘 감는) 두렁이; 배내옷; (길고 헐렁한) 갓난애의 옷. **2** the period of early childhood; the control of parents. 유년기; (어린이에 대한) 부모의 속박〔감시〕. ¶ *still in* 〔*hardly out of*〕 *one's* ~ 아직 철없는 어린 나이여서 부모가 눈을 뗄 수 없는.

swag [swæg] *n.* Ⓤ 《*sl.*》 things stolen. 약탈물; 훔친 물건. [obs. *swag* to sway]

swag·ger [swǽgər] *vi.* **1** (P1,2A,3) walk in a proud, self-satisfied way. 뽐내며〔으스대며〕 걷다. **2** talk or act in such a way. 으스대다; 뻐기다; 흰소리치다. ¶ ~ *about one's possessions* 자기 재산을 가지고 큰소리치다〔으스대다〕. — *n.* Ⓒ the act of swaggering. 으스대며〔뽐내며〕 걷기; 허풍; 자랑. — *adj.* 《*colloq.*》 smart; fashionable. 멋진; 맵시 있는. [↑]

swain [swein] *n.* Ⓒ 《*arch. poet.*》 a country lad; a male lover. 시골 청년; 애인. [N=lad]

:swal·low[1] [swɑ́lou / swɔ́l-] *vt.* (P6,7) **1** take (food, etc.) down the throat into the stomach. …을 들이켜다; 꿀꺽 삼키다. ¶ ~ *food without chewing* (*it*) 음식을 씹지도 않고 (꿀꺽) 삼키다 / ~ *wine at one gulp* 포도주를 한 입에 꿀꺽 마시다. **2** take (something) in; use up; conceal (something) from sight. …을 흡수하다; 다 써버리다; (보이지 않게) 싸다〔가리다, 덮다〕. ¶ *Expenses ~ up earnings.* 지출이 수입을 다 까먹었다 / *He was swallowed up in the mist.* 그는 안개 속으로 모습을 감췄다 / *The water swallowed them up.* 그들은 물 속으로 휘말려 들어갔다. **3** believe too easily; accept without question. …을 쉽사리 곧이 듣다; 곧이곧대로 받아들이다. ¶ *He swallows everything that is told him.* 그는 그에게 들려 주는 모든 것을 곧이곧대로 다 믿는다 / *Such stories are rather hard to ~.* 그러한 이야기들은 곧이곧대로 받아들일 수 없다. **4** bear quietly. …을 참다; 감내하다; 견뎌내다. ¶ ~ *a yawn* 하품을 꾹 참다 / ~ *a laugh* 웃음을 참다 / *He swallowed the insults without saying anything.* 그는 아무 말도 않고 모욕을 참고 견뎠다 / ~ *one's feelings* 자기의 감정을 누르고 겉으로 나타내지 않다. **5** take back (what one has said); withdraw. …을 취소하다. ¶ ~ *one's words* 자기가 한 말을 취소하다. — *vi.* (P1) swallow food or drink 삼키다; 들이켜다.

swallow the bait, fall into the trap. 함정에 빠지다; 덫에 걸리다.

— *n.* **1** Ⓤ the act of swallowing. 삼키기; 마시기. ¶ *in one ~* 한 입〔모금〕에. **2** Ⓒ the amount swallowed at one time. 한 모금. ¶ *take a ~ of water* 물을 한 모금 마시다. [E.]

·swal·low[2] [swɑ́lou / swɔ́l-] *n.* Ⓒ a bird with long, pointed wings and a forked tail. 제비. [E.]

swal·low·tail [swɑ́loutèil / swɔ́l-] *n.* Ⓒ **1** a swallow's tail. 제비 꼬리. **2** =swallow-tailed coat.

swal·low-tailed coat [swɑ́loutèild kóut / swɔ́l-] *n.* a man's formal coat with a forked tail like a swallow's. 연미복.

:swam [swæm] *v.* p. of **swim.**

:swamp [swɑmp / swɔmp] *n.* ⓊⒸ a piece of soft, very wet land. 늪; 습지.

— *vt.* **1** (P6) fill (something) with water and sink (it). 물에 잠기게 하다; 침몰시키다; 물을 채워 가라앉히다. ¶ *A big wave swamped* the boat. =*The boat was swamped by a big wave.* 큰 파도가 보트를 물에 잠기게 했다 / *The fugitive slaves were swamped in the stream.* 도망치는 노예들은 강물에 잠겨버렸다. **2** (P6,13) 《usu. in *passive*》 cover or swallow up (something or someone) completely; make (someone) helpless; overwhelm. …을 압도하다; 궁지에 빠뜨리다〔몰아넣다〕. ¶ *be swamped with invitations* 초대(招待) 공세를 받다 / *I am swamped with work.* 나는 일에 몰려 정신이 없다 / *He swamped us with ideas and new plans.* 그는 여러 가지 착상과 새로운 계획을 들고 나와서 우리를 압도했다. [Teut. (sump)]

swamp·y [swάmpi / swɔ́mpi] *adj.* (**swamp·i·er, swamp·i·est**) of or like a swamp. 늪지의; 질퍽질퍽한.

***swan** [swɑn / swɔn] *n.* Ⓒ **1** a large, beautiful water bird with a long neck. 백조. **2** a sweet singer; a poet. 가수; 시인. ¶ *the (sweet) Swan of Avon* 에이번의 백조 《Shakespeare 의 별칭》. [E.]

swan dive [⌐⌐] *n.* swallow dive. 제비식 다이빙.

swank[1] [swæŋk] *n.* Ⓤ a proud outward show; proud action; smartness. 허세; 허풍; 멋을 냄. —*vi.* (P1) show off. 과시하다; 허세부리다. [G. =flexible]

swank[2] [swæŋk] *vi.* p. of **swink.**

swank·y [swǽŋki] *adj.* (**swank·i·er, swank·i·est**) stylish; smart. 멋진; 화려한.

swan song [⌐⌐] *n.* **1** (in legends) the song supposed to be sung by a dying swan. (전설에서) 백조가 죽을 때 부른다는 아름다운 노래. **2** someone's last work before death. 최후의 작품; 절필; 마지막 업적. [*swan*]

swap [swɑp / swɔp] *vt., vi.* (**swapped, swap·ping**) (P6;1) 《*colloq.*》 exchange. (물물) 교환하다. ¶ ~ *foreign stamps* 외국 우표를 교환하다 / ~ *a knife for a book* 나이프를 책과 교환하다. —*n.* Ⓒ an exchange. 교환; 바꾸기. [E. =hit]

sward [swɔːrd] *n.* Ⓤ grassy land; lawn. 풀밭; 잔디. [E.=skin]

***swarm**[1] [swɔːrm] *n.* Ⓒ **1** 《*of*》 a large crowd of bees or birds. (새·벌 따위의) 우글거리는 떼; 무리. ¶ *a* ~ *of bees* 우글거리는 벌떼 / *in a* ~ 떼〔무리〕를 지어. **2** 《*of*》 a large crowd of persons; a great number. 떼; 군중; 많은 수. ¶ *swarms of children* 〔*sightseers, refugees*〕 우글거리는 아이들〔구경꾼, 피난민〕(의 떼) / *a* ~ *of letters* 많은 편지.
—*vi.* **1** (P1) (of bees) fly off together from a hive to start a new colony. (벌이) 분봉(分蜂)하다. **2** (P1,2A,3) move or come together in great numbers. 떼지어 이동하다〔모이다〕. ¶ *A crowd of people swarmed to the spot.* 군중이 현장에 떼지어 모여들었다 / *Flies* ~ *about food.* 음식 주위에 파리떼가 모여든다. **3** 《*with*》 (of places) be crowded with. …으로 가득 차다; 우글거리다. ¶ *The road was swarming with people.* 도로는 사람들로 꽉 메워지고 있었다 / *The beach is swarming with bathers.* 해변은 수영하는 사람들로 가득 차 있다. [E.]

swarm[2] [swɔːrm] *vt., vi.* (P6;3) 《*up*》 climb. (나무 따위에) 기어 오르다. ¶ ~ (*up*) *a rope* 밧줄을 타고 오르다. [?]

swarth·y [swɔ́ːrði, -θi] *adj.* (**swarth·i·er, swarth·i·est**) dark-skinned; dark. (얼굴·피부가) 거무스레한. [E.]

swash [swɑʃ / swɔʃ] *vi., vt.* (P1;6) dash (water, etc.) with a splashing sound; splash. (물 따위가) 철썩 튀기는 소리를 내다; (파도 따위가) 철썩 부딪치다. ¶ ~ *against the cliff* 벼랑에 (밀려오는 파도가) 철썩 부딪치다. —*n.* ⓊⒸ a swashing sound or action. 철썩하고 부딪치기〔부딪치는 소리〕. ¶ *the* ~ *of waves against a pier* 방파제에 부딪치는 파도 소리. [Imit.]

a swashing blow, a hard blow. 강타; 통격.

swash·buck·ler [swάʃbʌ̀klər / swɔ́ʃ-] *n.* Ⓒ a person, esp. a soldier, who speaks proudly and noisily. 허세 부리는 사람.

swash·buck·ling [swάʃbʌ̀kliŋ / swɔ́ʃ-] *adj.* speaking in a proud, noisy, self-satisfied manner. 허세 부리는.

swas·ti·ka [swάstikə / swɔ́s-] *n.* Ⓒ **1** a symbol supposed to bring good fortune. 만자(卍; 십자가의 변형). **2** the symbol of the followers of Hitler in Germany. 옛 독일의 나치스의 기장(記章). [Skr.]

swat [swɑt / swɔt] *vt.* (**swat·ted, swat·ting**) (P6) hit or strike (a fly, etc.) with a sharp, quick blow. …을 찰싹 때리다〔치다〕. ¶ ~ *a fly* 파리를 찰싹 하고 치다 / ~ *a ball into the outfield* 공을 외야로 장타하다. —*n.* ⓊⒸ 《*colloq.*》 a sharp or quick blow. 찰싹 때림. [→sweat]

swatch [swɑtʃ / swɔtʃ] *n.* a sample of cloth or other material. (직물 따위의) 견본(조각). [?]

swath [swɑθ, swɔːθ / swɔːθ] *n.* Ⓒ (*pl.* **swaths** [-θz, -ðz]) a line of cut grass in a field. 한 번 낫질한 넓이〔자취〕. [E.]

swathe [sweið, swɑð] *vt.* (P6,13) bind (a wound, etc.) with a long piece of cloth; wrap; enclose. …을 붕대로 감다; 감다; 싸다. ¶ *His arm was swathed in bandage.* 그의 팔은 붕대로 감겨져 있었다 / *The fog swathed the whole city.* 안개가 시 전체를 감싸고 있었다. —*n.* Ⓒ a bandage. 붕대; 감는〔싸는〕 천. [O.E. *swaþum* bandages]

:sway [swei] *vt.* (P6) **1** swing (something) back and forth; move (something) from side to side. (…을) 전후〔좌우〕로 움직이다; 흔들다. ¶ ~ *oneself* 몸을 흔들다 / ~ *one's head* 머리를 흔들다 / *The wind sways the branches.* 바람으로 나뭇가지가 흔들린다. **2** make (someone's mind) lean to one side; move; influence. (마음 따위를) 한쪽으로 기울게 하다; 동요시키다; 좌우하다. ¶ ~ *many votes* 많은 표를 좌우하다 / ~ *someone's deci-*

sion 아무의 결심을 동요시키다 / *The high salary swayed him to accept the job.* 높은 급료는 그 일을 맡도록 그의 마음을 움직였다. **3** 《*arch.*》 rule or govern (a nation or a country); rule by authority; control. …을 지배〔통치〕하다.
— *vi.* (P1,2A) move or swing from side to side. 흔들리다; 동요하다. ¶ *Branches swayed in the wind.* 가지들이 바람에 흔들렸다. **2** lean to one side. 한쪽으로 기울다.
— *n.* **1** Ⓤ Ⓒ the act of swaying. 동요; 진동. **2** Ⓤ control. 지배; 통치. [Teut.]
hold sway over, rule. …을 지배하다.
under the sway of, influenced by. …의 지배를 받아.

***swear**[swɛər] *v.* (**swore, sworn**) *vi.* (P1,2A,3) **1** 《*to*》 make a serious statement, with an appeal to God as witness. 맹세하다; 선서하다; 증언하다. ¶ ~ *by* 〔*on*〕 *the Bible* 성서에 손을 얹고 선서하다 / ~ *to one's identity* 본인임에 틀림없다고 선서하고 증언하다 / ~ *against someone* 아무에게 불리한 증언을 하다 / *I will* ~ *to it.* 나는 그것을 맹세한다 / *I wouldn't* ~ *to it* 〔*having seen him there*〕. 나는 그렇다고〔거기서 그를 목격했다고〕 단언할 자신은 없다. **2** 《*at*》 use bad language against someone; utter curses. 욕설하다; 악담하다. ¶ *He swore at his friend.* 그는 친구에게 욕을 퍼부었다. — *vt.* **1** (P6,8,11, 13,21) say (something) seriously in the name of God. …을 신에게 맹세하다; 선서하다. ¶ ~ *eternal friendship* 영원한 우정을 맹세하다 / *I* ~ *to love her as long as I live.* 내 목숨이 살아 있는 한 그녀를 사랑할 것을 맹세한다 / *He swears that he is innocent.* 그는 자기가 무죄임을 맹세했다. **2** declare. …을 단언하다. **3** cause (someone) to make a promise. …에게 맹세케 하다; 선서시키다. [E.]
enough to swear by, a very small amount. 극히 조금.
swear an oath, make a solemn vow. 선서하다.
swear at, use profane oaths at. …을 욕하다.
swear before 〔***to***〕***,*** appeal to as witness and guarantee of oath. …을 걸고 맹세하다.
swear by, **a**) name (someone or something) as a witness. …을 걸고 맹세하다. ¶ *I* ~ *by God that….* 신을 걸고 …을 맹세하다. **b**) have great faith in (someone or some thing). …을 깊이 신뢰하다. ¶ *He swears by his doctor* 〔*the medicine*〕. 그는 담당 의사를〔그 약을〕 신뢰하고 있다.
swear in, induct (someone) into an office by oath. …을 (선서한 다음) 취임시키다.
swear off, declare or take an oath to give up. 맹세하고 …을 끊다. ¶ ~ *off drinking* 술을 딱 끊다 / *Father swore off smoking.* 아버지는 맹세하고 금연했다.
swear to, say (something) with an oath; guarantee. …을 증언하다. ¶ ~ *to his faithfullness* 그의 성실성을 증언하다.

***sweat** [swet] *n.* **1** Ⓤ the liquid coming through the skin when it is hot; sweat-like drops forming on the surface of a thing. 땀; 물방울. ¶ *nightly sweats* 도한(盜汗) / ~ *on a pipe* 파이프에 서린 물방울 / *wipe the* ~ *off one's brow* 이마의 땀을 닦다 / *Sweat ran from her face.* 그녀의 얼굴에서 땀이 흘렀다. **2** Ⓒ the act of sweating; the condition of sweating. 땀을 내기; 땀 흘리기; 발한 (상태). ¶ *A* ~ *will do you good.* 한바탕 땀을 흘리면 몸에 좋다 / *A good* ~ *often cures a cold.* 땀을 많이 흘리면 감기가 잘 낫는다. **3** Ⓒ 《usu. *sing.*》《*colloq.*》 a piece of hard work; heavy labor. 힘드는 일. ¶ *Making a dictionary is an awful* ~. 사전을 만드는 일은 굉장히 힘든 일이다 / *a horrible* ~ 매우 힘든 일 / *I cannot stand the* ~ *of it.* 그 힘든 일에는 도저히 견딜 수가 없다.
all of a sweat, dripping with sweat. 땀투성이가 되어.
by the sweat of** one's **brow, by hard work. (정직하게) 열심히 일하여.
in a cold sweat, greatly frightened and having a chilly feeling; in a state of acute fear or anxiety. 식은땀을 흘리고; 식은땀이 날 정도로 근심하여; 두려워서. ¶ *He was in a cold* ~ *from fear.* 그는 두려움으로 식은땀을 흘리고 있었다.
in a sweat, in a state of anxiety. 근심 걱정하여.
in 〔***by***〕 ***the sweat of** one's **brow,*** by dint of toil. 고생하여; 이마에 땀을 흘려.
— *v.* (**sweat** or **sweat·ed**) *vi.* (P1,2A,3) **1** give off sweat. 땀을 흘리다. ¶ ~ *with fear* 무서워서 식은땀을 흘리다. **2** come out in drops; become damp on the outside of a thing. 물방울이 되어 나오다; (표면에) 물기가 서리다〔맺히다〕. ¶ *A glass of cold water sweats.* 냉수가 담긴 컵에 물방울이 서린다 / *The walls are sweating.* 벽에 물기가 맺히고 있다. **3** 《*colloq.*》 work very hard. 열심히 일하다. ¶ *He is always sweating at his job.* 그는 언제나 열심히 일을 한다 / ~ (*away*) *at one's job* 땀을 흘리며 일을 하다.
— *vt.* (P6,7) **1** cause (someone or something) to sweat. …에게 땀을 흘리게 하다. ¶ ~ *a horse* 말이 땀을 흘리게 하다 / *Doctors sometimes* ~ *their patients.* 의사들은 때때로 환자들에게 땀을 흘리게 한다. **2** 《U.S.》 make (something) wet with sweat. …을 땀에 흠뻑 젖게 하다. ¶ ~ *one's shirt* 셔츠를 땀투성이로 만들다. **3** cause (someone) to work hard for very low wages. …을 싼 임금으로 혹사하다. ¶ *sweated labor* 착취당하는 노동 / *sweated goods* 저임금 노동으로 만든 제품. [E.]
sweat out 〔***off, away***〕***,*** get rid of (a cold, etc.) by sweating. 땀을 흘리게 해서 …을 없애다〔제거하다〕. ¶ ~ *away a fever* 〔*cold*〕 땀을 흘려 열을〔감기를〕 제거하다 / ~ *off ten kilograms in the steam room* 증기욕실에서 10킬로그램의 체중을 땀으로 빼다.

sweat·er [swétər] *n.* Ⓒ **1** a person who

sweats. 땀을 흘리는 사람. **2** a woollen garment for the upper part of the body. 스웨터. **3** an employer who underpays his workers. 싼 임금으로 근로자를 혹사하는 고용주; 노동 착취자.

sweat·shop [swétʃàp / -ʃɔ̀p] *n.* Ⓒ a workshop or factory where workers are employed at low wages under bad working conditions. 착취 공장《저임금으로 악조건 아래에서 일을 하게 하는 공장》.

sweat·y [swéti] *adj.* (**sweat·i·er, sweat·i·est**) **1** convered with sweat; causing sweat; sweating. 땀투성이의; 땀에 젖은; 땀이 나게 하는. ¶ ~ *underwear* 땀에 젖은 속내의. **2** laborious. 힘이 드는. ¶ ~ *work* 힘든 일.

Swede [swi:d] *n.* Ⓒ a person of Sweden. 스웨덴 사람. [Teut.]

Swe·den [swí:dn] *n.* a country in northern Europe on the Scandinavian peninsula. 스웨덴. 參考 수도는 Stockholm.

Swe·dish [swí:diʃ] *adj.* of Sweden, its people or their language. 스웨덴의; 스웨덴 사람〔말〕의. —*n.* **1** Ⓤ the language of Sweden. 스웨덴 어. **2** 《*the* ~》 the people of Sweden. 스웨덴 사람.

:sweep [swi:p] *v.* (**swept**) *vt.* **1** (P6,7) clean (a floor, a room, etc.) with a broom, a brush, etc.; clean off (dust, etc.) by using a broom, etc. (빗자루로) …을 쓸다〔청소하다〕; (먼지 따위를) 털다. ¶ ~ *a room* 방을 청소하다 / ~ *the dust off a coat* 코트에 묻은 먼지를 털다 / ~ *the room clean* 방을 깨끗이 쓸다 / ~ *a chimney* 굴뚝을 청소하다. **2** (P6,7) drive or carry (something) away, off or down with a violent force; clean away. …을 일소하다; 밀어〔씻어〕 내리다; 불어 날리다. ¶ ~ *off the snow* 눈을 불어 날리다 / ~ *the seas* 소해(掃海)하다; 해상의 적을 일소하다 / ~ *all obstacles from the path* 통로에서 모든 장애물을 제거하다 / *The flood swept away the bridge.* 홍수로 다리가 떠내려 갔다 / *A gust swept his hat off.* 일진 돌풍으로 그의 모자가 날아갔다 / ~ *the country of crime* 국내로부터 범죄를 일소하다. **3** (P6) pass over or through (a region, etc.) quickly. (장소를) 휙 지나가다. ¶ *An epidemic swept the country.* 전염병이 전국을 휩쓸고 지나갔다 / *a searchlight sweeping the sky* 하늘을 휙 비치고 지나가는 탐조등 빛. **4** pass over or across (something) with a swift and steady movement; search quickly or thoroghly. …을 전망하다; 한눈에 바라보다. ¶ ~ *the faces of an audience with a glance* 한눈에 청중의 얼굴을 바라보다 / *He swept the horizon with a telescope.* 그는 망원경으로 지평선을 바라보았다 / *Her eyes swept the faces in the hall.* 그녀는 홀 안에 있는 사람들의 얼굴을 휙 둘러 보았다. **5** touch lightly in passing over. 가볍고 날렵하게 어루만지다; (현악기를) 켜다〔타다〕. ¶ *Her fingers swept the strings of the harp.* 그녀의 손가락들은 하프의 현을 어루만지듯 날렵하게 켰다. **6** trail upon (something). (옷자락 따위가) …의 위에 끌리다. ¶ ~ *the ground* 지면에 끌리다 / *Her dress swept the floor.* 그녀는 옷자락을 질질 끌면서 마루 위를 지나갔다.

—*vi.* **1** (P1) clean with a broom, etc. (빗자루로) 청소하다. ¶ 《*prov.*》 *A new broom sweeps clean.* 새 비는 잘 쓸린다《새로 부임한 사람은 일을 잘 하게 마련이다》. **2** (of news, disease, etc.) pass with speed and force. 휙 지나가다; 휩쓸다; 습격하다. ¶ *A strong wind swept along the street.* 강풍이 거리를 거칠게 휩쓸며 지나갔다 / *The cavalry swept down on the enemy.* 기병대는 적군을 급습하였다 / *A hurricane swept over the whole region.* 허리케인이 온 지역을 휩쓸고 지나갔다 / *The car swept past.* 자동차가 휙 지나갔다. **3** (P2A,3) move in a swift, proud, stately manner. 의젓이〔당당하게〕 나아가다〔걷다〕. ¶ ~ *into a room* 당당히 방 안으로 들어오다 / *She swept out of the room with her chin held high.* 그녀는 턱을 치켜들고 당당히 방을 걸어 나갔다. **4** (P2A,3) move or extend in a long, curving course. 널리 퍼지다〔미치다〕; 길게〔굽이굽이〕 이어지다〔뻗어 있다〕. ¶ *The plain sweeps away to the sea.* 평야는 멀리 바다까지 펼쳐져 있다 / *The shore sweeps to the north for miles.* 해변은 북쪽으로 몇 마일이나 길게 뻗어 있다 / *His eyes* 〔*glance*〕 *swept slowly round the room.* 그는 천천히 방을 한 바퀴 휙 둘러 보았다.

—*n.* Ⓒ **1** an act of sweeping. 쓸기; 청소. ¶ *give a room a good* ~ 방을 깨끗이 청소하다. **2** a long sweeping motion; a stroke or blow. 한 번 흔들기〔휘두르기, 젓기〕. ¶ *a* ~ *of the oars* 노를 한 번 젓기 / *at one* 〔*a*〕 ~ 일격으로; 일거에 / *with the* ~ *of one's hand* 손을 한 번 휘둘러. **3** a steady, driving motion; a smooth, flowing motion. (바람·물 따위의) 빠르고 강한 흐름; 휘몰아침; 매끄러운 움직임. ¶ *the* ~ *of the wind* 바람의 휘몰아침 / *the* ~ *of verse* 시(詩)의 유창한 흐름. **4** Ⓤ a wide expanse; extent. 범위; (땅의) 퍼짐; 뻗침. ¶ *the great* ~ *of the meadow* 광활한 목장 / *within* 〔*beyond*〕 *the* ~ *of the eye* 눈이〔시계가〕 미치는〔미치지 않는〕 곳에 / *The subject is stupendous in its* ~. 이 문제는 그 미치는 범위가 말할 수 없이 넓다. **5** a curve; a curving line; a great curve of a road, etc. 만곡(彎曲); 곡선; 꾸불꾸불한 길. **6** a long pole, attached to a post, used to raise or lower a bucket in a well. (방아두레박의) 기다란 대. **7** a big victory. 대승리. **8** a person who sweeps chimneys, streets, etc. 굴뚝 청소부; 청소부. [*swoop*]

beyond the sweep of, out of the range of something that has sweeping motion. …이 미치지 않는 곳에.

make a clean sweep of, get rid of (something) completely and thoroughly; liquidate. …을 (깨끗이) 일소하다; 청산하다.

sweep·er [swí:pər] *n.* Ⓒ a person or device that sweeps. 청소부〔기〕. ¶ *a car-*

pet-sweeper 융단 청소기.

·sweep·ing [swíːpiŋ] *adj.* of a wide range or extent; complete; thorough-going. 광범위한; 전반에 걸친; 완전〔철저〕한. ¶ *a ~ glance* 한번 대충 훑어) 봄 / *a ~ victory* 압승 / *~ changes* 전면적인 개혁. ―*n.* 《*pl.*》 dust; scraps; rubbish. 먼지; 쓰레기. ¶ *the sweepings of the gutter* 최하층민.

sweep·ing·ly [swíːpiŋli] *adv.* in a sweeping manner. 일소하여; 대충.

sweep·stake [swíːpstèik] *n.* =sweepstakes.

sweep·stakes [swíːpstèiks] *n. pl.* 《used as *sing.* or *pl.*》 **1** a form of gambling on horse-races, etc. 내깃돈 독점 경마(獨占競馬)《내기 경마에서 혼자 또는 몇 사람이 휩쓰는》. **2** a prize in such gambling. 내기에 건 돈.

:sweet [swiːt] *adj.* **1** having a taste like sugar or honey. 단; 달콤한(opp. bitter, sour). ¶ *Sugar is ~.* 설탕은 달다 / *~ cakes* 〔*apples*〕 달콤한 케이크〔사과〕 / *She likes her tea ~.* 그녀는 차를 달게 해서 마시는 것을 좋아한다. **2** having a pleasant smell; (of sounds) pleasant. (냄새가) 향기로운; (소리가) 감미로운; 듣기 좋은. ¶ *~ herbs* 향기로운 풀 / *a ~ smell* 향기로운 냄새 / *~ sounds of music* 감미로운 음악 소리 / *a ~ sound* 감미로운 소리 / *It smells ~.* 향기로운 냄새가 난다 / *The garden is ~ with roses.* 정원은 장미의 향기로운 냄새로 가득하다 / *Her voice sounds ~.* 그녀 목소리는 듣기에 좋다. **3** fresh; not sour or salted. 신선한; 신맛〔짠맛〕이 없는. ¶ *~ air* 〔*milk*〕 신선한 공기〔우유〕 / *~ water* (신선한) 담수; 음료수 / *~ butter* 짠맛이 없는 버터. **4** gentle; kind; mild. 온화〔다정〕한; 친절한; 상냥한. ¶ *a ~ temper* 다정한 기질; 고운 마음씨 / *That is very ~ of you.* 참으로 친절도 하시군요 / *She was very ~ to me.* 그녀는 나에게 매우 친절하게 대해 줬다. **5** pleasant; delightful. 기분이 좋은; 유쾌한. ¶ *a ~ sleep* 기분 좋은 수면 / *~ love* 달콤한 사랑 / *It is ~ to hear oneself praised.* 남에게 칭찬을 듣는 것은 기분 좋은 일이다 / *Life is ~.* 인생은 즐겁다. **6** 《*colloq.*》 charming; lovely. 애교가 있는; 귀여운. ¶ *a ~ little girl* 귀여운 소녀 / *a ~ smile* 애교 있는 웃음.

at one's own sweet will, just as or when one pleases; arbitrarily; at random. 좋을 대로; 마음대로.

be sweet on 〔***upon***〕***,*** in love with. …에게 반하다; …을 사랑하다.

have a sweet tooth, like sweet things. 단것을 무척 좋아하다.

sweet one! darling! (사랑하는) 당신.

―*n.* Ⓒ **1** Ⓤ a sweet taste or smell; something sweet. 감미; 단맛; 단것. ¶ *a palate for ~ and sour* 단맛과 신맛의 미각. **2** 《chiefly Brit.》 a candy. 사탕 과자; 캔디. **3** 《Brit.》 《*pl.*》 the dessert course of a meal, such as puddings, ice cream or jellies. 식후에 나오는 달콤한 요리. **4** 《*pl.*》 pleasures; delights. 즐거움; 유쾌; 기쁨. ¶ *the sweets of victory* 승리의 기쁨. [E.]

sweet·bread [swíːtbrèd] *n.* Ⓒ an inner part of the body of a calf, a lamb, etc., used as food. 송아지·새끼양의 췌장.

sweet·bri·er, -bri·ar [swíːtbràiər] *n.* a rose with a tall stem and pink flowers. 해당화《들장미의 일종》.

sweet corn [ㅅㅅ] *n.* a kind of Indian corn with a sweetish flavor, eaten in its unripe state; green corn. 사탕옥수수.

sweet·en [swíːtn] *vt.* (P6) **1** make (something) sweet. (…을) 달게 하다. ¶ *He sweetened his coffee with three lumps of sugar.* 그는 커피에 각사탕 세 개를 넣어 달게 했다. **2** make (something or someone) agreeable or pleasant; make more bearable; soften. …을 기분 좋게〔유쾌하게, 즐겁게〕 하다; 누그러지게 하다. ¶ *~ life* 인생을 즐겁게 하다 / *~ suffering* 〔*his temper*〕 고통〔그의 기질〕을 누그러뜨리다. ―*vi.* (P1) become sweet. 달게 되다; 달아지다.

sweet·en·ing [swíːtniŋ] *n.* **1** Ⓤ the process of making something sweet. 달게 함. **2** Ⓒ something that sweetens. 감미료.

·sweet·heart [swíːthὰːrt] *n.* Ⓒ a lover, esp. a girl or woman who is in love. 연인; 애인.

sweet·ish [swíːtiʃ] *adj.* rather sweet. (약간) 달콤한; 귀여운.

·sweet·ly [swíːtli] *adv.* **1** in a sweet manner; agreeably; comfortably; pleasantly. 달게; 귀엽게; 기분 좋게; 즐겁게. ¶ *speak* 〔*reply*〕 *~* 상냥하게〔친절하게〕 이야기〔대답〕하다. **2** smoothly; easily. 부드럽게; 용이(容易)하게. ¶ *The car runs ~.* 자동차가 미끄러지듯 매끄럽게 달린다.

sweet·meats [swíːtmìːts] *n. pl.* candy; bonbons. 사탕 과자; 캔디; 봉봉 과자.

·sweet·ness [swíːtnis] *n.* Ⓤ the quality or state of being sweet. 달콤함; 단맛; 유쾌; 부드러움; 귀여움.

sweet oil [ㅅㅅ] *n.* an oil obtained from olives; olive oil. 올리브 기름.

sweet pea [ㅅㅅ] *n.* a kind of plant with sweet-smelling flowers; the flower of this plant. 스위트피《콩과의 원예 식물》.

sweet pepper [ㅅㅅ–] *n.* a kind of pepper plant bearing a mild fruit; its fruit; the green pepper. 피망.

sweet potato [ㅅ–ㅅ–] *n.* a plant that produces edible, sweet, thick yellow or reddish roots. 고구마.

sweet·scent·ed [swíːtsèntid] *adj.* having a pleasant smell. 향기가 좋은; 향기로운; 방향(芳香)이 있는.

sweet shop [ㅅㅅ] *n.* 《Brit.》 a shop which sells candies, etc. 과자 가게. 參考 미국에서는 candy store 라고 함.

sweet-sul·tan [swíːtsʌ́ltən] *n.* a garden flower. 수레국화의 일종《국화과(科)의 풀》.

sweet-tem·pered [swíːttémpərd] *adj.* having a gentle nature; good-natured. 마음씨가 고운; 상냥한.

sweet-wil·liam [swíːtwíljəm] *n.* 《bot.》 a plant with small flowers in groups. 수염패랭이꽃.

:swell [swel] *v.* (**swelled, swelled** or **swol·len**) *vi.* (P1,2A) **1** increase in size, volume, or force; grow bigger. 부풀다; 커지다; 부어오르다; 증수(增水)하다. ¶ *Buds* ~. 꽃봉오리가 부푼다 / *A balloon began to* ~. 풍선이 부풀어 올랐다 / *The river has swollen with melted snow.* 녹은 눈으로 강물이 불어났다 / *His injured leg began to* ~ *(up).* 그의 다친 다리가 부어오르기 시작했다 / *The book has swelled to monstrous size.* 그 책은 (페이지가 늘어서) 방대한 크기가 되었다. **2** increase in number, degree, or quantity. (수량이) 증대하다; 증가하다. ¶ *Her savings swelled as she continued to work hard.* 그녀의 저금은 일을 열심히 계속하는 만큼 (그에 비례해서) 불어났다 / *The membership swelled to 100.* 회원이 증가하여 100명이 되었다. **3** become rough with waves; be higher or thicker in a particular place; stick out. 파도가 거칠어지다; 불쑥 튀어나오다; (땅이) 융기하다. ¶ *The cask swells in the middle.* 통은 배가 불쑥 튀어나와 있다 / *The sea is swelling.* 바다는 파도가 거칠어지고 있다 / *The ground swells into an eminence.* 땅이 융기하여 언덕이 되어 있다. **4** (of a sound) become louder. (소리가) 높아지다. ¶ *The music swelled to a climax.* 음악은 높아져서 클라이맥스에 이르렀다 / *The murmur swelled into a roar.* 작은 속삭임 소리가 높아져서 고함 소리가 되었다. **5** become filled with pride, grief, or some other strong feelings. 자랑하다; 뽐내다; (감정으로) 가슴이 벅차지다. ¶ *His heart swelled with pride and happiness.* 그의 가슴은 자랑스러움과 행복감으로 벅차올랐다 / *He swelled with grief.* 그는 슬픔으로 가슴이 메는 것 같았다. — *vt.* (6,7) **1** cause (something) to increase in size, volume, force, etc. …을 부풀게 하다; 크게 하다; 증대하다; 증가하다. ¶ *Wind swells the sail.* 바람은 돛을 부풀게 한다 / *The rain will* ~ *the river.* 비는 강물을 불어나게 할 것이다 / *Her eyes were swollen with tears.* 그녀의 두 눈은 울어서 퉁퉁 부어 있었다. **2** fill (someone) with pride or some other strong feelings. …한 감정으로 가슴 벅차게 만들다. ¶ *be swollen with pride* 자만하고 있다; 의기 양양해 있다.

have* 〔*suffer from*〕 *a swelled* 〔*swollen*〕 *head, 《*colloq.*》 have too high an opinion of oneself; be conceited. 자신을 과대 평가하다; 자만해지다.

swelled head, conceit. 자만.

***swell the chorus* (*of admiration*),** join one's voice or add one's opinion to those of others. 찬성〔부화 뇌동〕하다.

— *n.* **1** Ⓤⓒ the act of swelling; the state of being swollen. (형태·수량·정도 따위의) 증대; 증가; 팽창; 늘어남. ¶ *a rapid* ~ *in the population* 인구의 급속한 팽창〔증가〕. **2** Ⓒ a part that swells out; a bulge. 부푼〔불룩한〕 부분. ¶ *the* ~ *of a belly* 배의 불룩하게 튀어나온 부분 / *the* ~ *of her breasts* 그녀 가슴의 불룩한 부분. **3** Ⓒ a gradual rise in the height of the ground; a large, unbroken wave. (토지의) 융기; 큰 파도; (파도의) 굽이침. ¶ *a heavy* ~ *after the storm* 폭풍 후의 거센 파도 / *rock in the* ~ (배가) 큰 파도에 흔들리다. **4** Ⓤ a swelling tone or sound. (음·목소리의) 높아짐. ¶ *the* ~ *of the violin's tone* 바이올린 음의 고조(高調). **5** Ⓒ 《*colloq.*》 ⓐ a well-dressed or socially important person. 명사; 멋쟁이. ¶ *a* ~ *in politics* 정계의 명사 / *The President and other swells sat on the platform.* 대통령과 명사들이 연단(演壇)에 앉아 있었다. ⓑ a person who is far better than others in something. 명수; 대가. ¶ *He is a* ~ *at tennis.* 그는 테니스의 대가이다.

— *adj.* 《*colloq.*》 first-rate; well-dressed. 일류의; 멋쟁이의. ¶ ~ *clothes* 멋있는 복장 / *a* ~ *hotel* 일류〔특급〕 호텔 / *I feel* ~. 아주 최상의 기분이다 / *You look* ~. 아주 멋지게 보이는데. [E.]

swell·dom [swéldəm] *n.* 《*colloq.*》 high society; smart society. 상류 사회; 유행 사회.

swell·ing [swéliŋ] *n.* **1** Ⓤ increase; growth. 팽창; 증대. **2** Ⓒ a swollen part of the body. 종기; 부스럼.

swel·ter [swéltər] *vi.* (P1) suffer from the heat; feel very hot; sweat. 무더위에 지치다; 더위먹다; 땀투성이가 되다. ¶ *under the sweltering sky* 염천 아래에서. — *vt.* (P6) cause (someone) to swelter. …을 더위먹게 하다. — *n.* Ⓤ the condition of being very hot. 폭서; 무더위. [E.]

:swept [swept] *v.* p. and pp. of **sweep.**

swerve [swəːrv] *vi., vt.* (P1,2A,3,4; 6) curve or cause (something) to turn aside from a straight line. 빗나가다; 벗어나다; …을 벗어나게 하다. ¶ *The car swerved from the road.* 자동차는 도로에서 벗어났다 / *One ought not to* ~ *from the path of duty.* 사람은 자기 본분에서 벗어난 일을 해서는 안 된다. — *n.* Ⓒ the act of swerving; something that swerves. 벗어남; 빗나감; 벗어난 것. [E.]

Swift [swift], **Jonathan** *n.* (1667-1745) a British writer. 스위프트《영국의 작가》. 參考 Gulliver's Travels의 저자.

:swift [swift] *adj.* 《*to do*》 able to move very fast; rapid in acting; quick; speedy; prompt. 빠른; 곧 …하는; 신속한; 즉석의 (opp. slow). ¶ ~ *to act* 곧〔즉각〕 행동하는 / *a* ~ *response* 〔*decision*〕 즉답〔즉결〕 / *a* ~ *ship* 쾌속선 / ~ *years* 화살처럼 빨리 지나는 세월 / *He is not* ~ *but sure.* 그는 빠르지는 않으나 확실하다. — *adv.* quickly; rapidly. 빨리; 신속히(=swiftly). — *n.* Ⓒ a small bird somewhat like a swallow. 칼새. [E.]

:**swift·ly** [swíftli] *adv.* in a swift manner; quickly; rapidly. 재빨리; 신속하게.

swift·ness [swíftnis] *n.* Ⓤ speed; rapid motion; quickness. 속도; 빠른 동작; 빠름. ¶ *He escaped with surprising* ~. 그는 놀라울 정도로 재빠르게 도망쳤다.

swig [swig] *n.* Ⓒ 《*colloq.*》 a big drink drunk without breathing. 벌컥벌컥 마심; 통음(痛飮). ¶ *take a quick ~ of beer* 맥주를 벌컥벌컥 마시다. — *vt., vi.* (**swigged, swigging**) (P6;1) drink heartily; gulp. …을 벌컥벌컥 마시다; 통음하다. [?]

swill [swil] *n.* **1** Ⓤ kitchen rubbish; pigs' food. (부엌의) 음식 찌끼《돼지 사료》. **2** Ⓒ a deep drink. 통음(痛飮). — *vt., vi.* (P6,7;1) **1** drink too much. …을 통음하다. ¶ ~ *beer* 맥주를 들이켜다. **2** wash out (something); rinse. …을 헹구다. ¶ ~ *a dirty bucket* 더러운 양동이를 헹구다. [E.]

:**swim** [swim] *v.* (**swam, swum, swim·ming**) *vi.* **1** (P1,2A,2B,3,4) move in the water by moving the arms and legs; cross a river, etc. by swimming. 헤엄치다; 수영하다; 헤엄쳐서 건너다. ¶ ~ *about* 헤엄쳐 다니다 / ~ *across a river* 강을 헤엄쳐 건너다 / ~ *on one's back* 드러누워서 헤엄치다 / ~ *against the current* 물결을 거슬러 헤엄치다 / *go to* ~ =*go swimming* 수영하러 가다 / ~ *hand over hand* 크롤(crawl)로 헤엄치다. **2** (P2A,3) float on water or in the air. (물·공중에서) 뜨다. ¶ *a leaf swimming down the river* 강물에 떠내려가는 나뭇잎 / *Oil swims on water.* 기름은 물에 뜬다 / *specks of dust that ~ in the sunbeams* 태양광선 속에 떠다니는 먼지의 작은 알갱이들. **3** (P1,2A,3) go smoothly; glide. 미끄러지듯이 가다〔움직이다〕. ¶ *She swam into the room.* 그녀는 미끄러지듯 방안으로 들어왔다 / *The swans are swimming over the lake.* 백조가 호수 위에서 유영(遊泳)하고 있다. **4** be dizzy. 현기증이 나다; 어지럽다. ¶ *My head swims.* 머리가 어지럽다. — *vt.* (P6) **1** move in or across (a river, etc.) by swimming. …을 헤엄치다; 헤엄쳐서 건너다. ¶ *He swam the river.* 그는 강을 헤엄쳐 건넜다. **2** cause (someone) to swim or float. …을 헤엄치게 하다; 뜨게 하다. ¶ *He swam his horse across the river.* 그는 말에게 강을 헤엄쳐 건너게 했다.

swim like a stone =***swim to the bottom,*** cannot swim; sink. 헤엄칠 줄 모르다; '맥주병'이다.

swim with the tide 〔***stream***〕, follow popular custom. 관습〔대세〕에 따르다.

— *n.* **1** Ⓒ the act of swimming. 수영; 유영(遊泳). **2** 《*the* ~》 the current of affairs. (사건·사물)의 주된 흐름; 대세. ¶ *be in* 〔*out of*〕 *the* ~ (*of things*) 실정(實情)에 밝다〔어둡다〕. [E.]

swim·mer [swímər] *n.* a person who swims. 헤엄치는 사람. ¶ *a good* 〔*poor*〕 ~ 헤엄을 잘〔못〕 치는 사람.

swimming bath [∠-∸] *n.* a pool for swimming in, usu. indoors. (보통 실내의) 수영장.

swim·ming·ly [swímiŋli] *adv.* with great ease; smoothly; easily. 아주 쉽게; 막힘없이; 무난히. ¶ *Everything* 〔*Things*〕 *went* ~. 모든 것〔일들〕이 순조롭게 되었다.

swimming pool [∠-∸] *n.* an artificial pool for swimming in. 수영 풀.

swim·suit [swímsùːt] *n.* a garment worn while swimming; a bathing suit. 수영복.

swin·dle [swíndl] *vt., vi.* (P6,13;1) get (something) by deceiving; cheat. …을 속여 빼앗다; 사취하다; 속이다. ¶ ~ *someone out of his money* =~ *money out of someone* 아무에게서 돈을 사취하다 / *He is not so easily swindled.* 그는 그리 호락호락 사기를 당하지 않는다. — *n.* Ⓒ an act of swindling; a cheat. 사취; 협잡; 사기. [E.]

swin·dler [swíndlər] *n.* Ⓒ a person who swindles. 사기꾼.

swine [swain] *n.* Ⓒ (*pl.* **swine**) **1** a pig. 돼지. **2** a very greedy, dishonest or immoral person. 탐욕스런 사람; 비열한 녀석. [E.]

swine·herd [swáinhə̀ːrd] *n.* Ⓒ a person who looks after pigs. 양돈가; 돼지 기르는 사람.

:**swing** [swiŋ] *v.* (**swung**) *vi.* **1** (P1,2A) move forward and back, esp. with a regular motion, like a thing hanging from a string. 흔들리다; 진동하다. ¶ *The lamp hanging overhead swung in the wind.* 머리 위에 매달려 있는 등불은 바람에 흔들렸다. **2** (P1,2A) move in a curve; turn. 회전하다; 빙그르르 돌다. ¶ ~ *round on one's heel* 뒤꿈치로 빙그르르 돌다 / ~ *round the bend in the road* 도로에서 빙그르르 커브를 돌다 / *The door swung open* 〔*shut*〕. 문이 획 열렸다〔닫혔다〕 / *The car swung right and stopped.* 자동차는 오른쪽으로 커브를 돌더니 정지했다. **3** (P2A,3) walk quickly and rhythmically, moving the arms to and fro. (팔 따위를 흔들면서) 기운차게 걷다. ¶ *The boys went swinging down the road.* 소년들은 기운차게 길을 걸어갔다. **4** (P3) hang down; 《*colloq.*》 be executed by hanging. 매달리다; 교수형을 받다. ¶ ~ *from a branch* 나뭇가지에 매달리다 / *You will ~ for this!* 넌 이런 짓을 했으니 교수형을 받을 거다. **5** (P1,3) go back and forth in a swing. 그네 뛰다.

— *vt.* (P6,7,18) **1** cause (something) to sway back and forth, esp. with a regular motion. …을 흔들다; 흔들어 움직이다. ¶ *She swung her arms as she walked.* 그녀는 걸을 때 양팔을 흔들었다 / ~ *one's legs* 다리를 흔들거리다. **2** cause (something grasped) to move in a circle or a part of a circle. (잡고 있는 것을) 휘두르다. ¶ ~ *a bat* 〔*an ax*〕 배트를 〔도끼를〕 휘두르다 / *The batter swung the bat at the ball.* 그 타자는 공을 향하여 배

트를 휘둘렀다. **3** cause (someone) to go back and forth in a swing. (그네 따위에 태워서) …를 흔들다. ¶ ~ *a child* 아이를 그네에 태워 흔들다. **4** cause (something) to hang. …을 매달다; 걸다. ¶ ~ *a hammock* 해먹을 매달다〔걸다〕/ ~ *a bag from one's arm* 팔에 가방을 걸어 늘어뜨리다. **5** cause (something) to turn around. (빙그르르) …의 방향을 바꾸다. ¶ ~ *a car* 차의 방향을 휙 돌리다 / *He swung his car into a byroad.* 그의 차는 커브를 휙 돌더니 옆길로 쑥 들어갔다. **6** 《U.S. *colloq.*》 manage or handle (something) successfully. …을 잘 처리하다; 마음대로 움직이다. ¶ ~ *a job* 〔*sale*〕 일을〔판매를〕 잘 해내다 / ~ *the voting in an election* 선거에서 투표를 마음대로 조작〔좌우〕하다 / *Will she be able to ~ it ?* 그녀가 그것을 잘 처리할 수 있을까 / *He won't be able to ~ a car on his income.* 그의 수입으로는 자동차를 몰고 다니기가 무리일 것이다. **7** play (music) in the style of swing. (노래·곡을) 스윙 풍으로 연주〔노래〕하다.

no room to swing a cat in, very little space. 매우 비좁은.

swing for it, be hanged. 교수형에 처해지다.

swing the lead, 《mil. *sl.*》 malinger. 꾀병을 부리다.

swing to, close; be shut. 쾅하고 닫히다. ¶ *The door swung to.* 문이 쾅하고 닫혔다.

— *n.* **1** Ⓤⓒ the act or manner of swinging; the amount of swinging. 진동; 동요; 휘두르기; 흔드는〔휘두르는〕 법; 진폭(振幅). ¶ *the ~ of the pendulum* 시계추의 진동; 《비유적으로》(여론 따위의) 흔들리는 경향; 세력의 부침(浮沈) / *a ~ of 3 inches* = *a 3 inch ~*, 3인치의 진폭 / *be on the ~* 흔들리고 있다 / *a batter with a powerful ~* 스윙이 강력한 타자. **2** ⓒ a free, easy motion, esp. in marching or walking. 기운찬〔활달한〕 걸음걸이〔움직임〕. ¶ *walk with a ~* (몸을 흔들며) 활기차게 걷다. **3** ⓒ a seat hung from ropes in which one may sit and swing; the act of moving thus. 그네; 그네 타기. ¶ *my turn for a ~* 그네를 탈 나의 차례 / *go on a ~* =*sit* 〔*ride*〕 *in* 〔*on*〕 *a ~* 그네를 타다. **4** Ⓤ freedom of action. 자유 활동; 활동의 자유. ¶ *give full* 〔*free*〕 *~ to him* 그를 자유롭게〔제멋대로〕 활동케 하다 / *have one's full* 〔*free*〕 *~ in the matter* 일을 자기 뜻대로 자유롭게 처리하다. **5** Ⓤⓒ a jazz music in which the players improvise freely on the original melody; the rhythmic beat of music or poetry. 스윙 음악; (시나 음악의) 그 리듬; 가락《1935-1945년대의 세련되고 홍취 있는 재즈 음악》. [E.]

in full swing, fully operating or proceeding. 한창 진행중인; 한창 신이 나서. ¶ *The party was in full ~*. 파티는 한창 진행중이었다.

swinge [swindʒ] *vt.* (P6) strike hard. 세게 치다〔때리다〕. [→swing]

swinge·ing [swíndʒiŋ] *adj.* 《*colloq.*》 very forcible or powerful; very huge; very good. (타격이)강한; 센; 거대한; 굉장한. ¶ *a ~ blow* 강타; 강한 일격 / *a ~ lie* 터무니 없는 거짓말 / *~ damages* 막대한 손해 배상(금).

swing·ing [swíŋiŋ] *adj.* **1** moving from side to side. 흔들리는. **2** vigorous; lively. 활기 있는; 기운찬. **3** 《*colloq.*》 excellent. 훌륭한; 뛰어난. [*swing*]

swin·gle [swíŋgəl] *n.* a swinging bar of flail; flax-beating implement. 도리깨열; 타마기(打麻器). — *vt.* (P6) beat (flax). 타마기로 치다. [→swinge]

swin·ish [swáiniʃ] *adj.* like a pig; disgusting; mean. 돼지 같은; 탐욕스러운; 상스러운. [→swine]

swink [swiŋk] 《*arch.*》 *vi.* (**swank** or **swonk, swonk·en**) (P1) toil. 애쓰다; 땀흘려 일하다. — *n.* Ⓤ toil; labor. 노고; 수고; 노동. [E.]

swipe [swaip] *n.* ⓒ 《*colloq.*》 (in cricket, etc.) a hard blow. 강타. — *vi., vt.* (P1;6,7,13) **1** 《*colloq.*》 hit hard. (…을) 강타하다. **2** 《*colloq.*》 snatch away; steal. 날치기하다; 훔치다. [=sweep]

swirl [swəːrl] *n.* ⓒ **1** a circular motion of water or the like. 소용돌이. **2** a twist; a curl. 소용돌이 꼴; 고수머리. ¶ *a ~ of hair* 고수머리. — *vi.* (P1) move quickly with a circular motion; feel dizzy. 소용돌이치다; (머리가) 어지럽다. ¶ *dust swirling in the air* 공중에서 소용돌이치는 먼지. [Teut.]

swish [swiʃ] *vi.* (P1,2A,3) (of a whip, wings, etc.) make a light, hissing sound by cutting through the air. 휙 소리를 내다; 휙하고 바람을 가르다. ¶ *~ out of the room* 방에서 휙 뛰어나가다 / *A car swished by.* 자동차가 휙 지나갔다. — *vt.* (P6) **1** beat (something) with a whip; whip. …을 채찍으로 때리다. **2** cause (something) to swish. …을 휙 소리 나게 하다. — *n.* ⓒ a swishing movement or sound. 채찍을 한번 휘두르기; 휙하는 소리. [Imit.]

***Swiss** [swis] *n.* ⓒ (*pl.* **Swiss**) a person of Switzerland; 《*the ~, collectively*》 the people of Switzerland. 스위스 사람. — *adj.* of Switzerland, its people, or its culture. 스위스의; 스위스 사람의; 스위스 문화의. [G. *Switz.*]

Swiss guards [ˊ-ˊ] *n.* Swiss mercenaries formerly employed in France, etc. and still at the Vatican. 스위스인 (호)위병.

Swiss roll [ˊ-ˊ] *n.* a kind of jam sandwich baked and rolled up. 롤빵.

***switch** [switʃ] *n.* ⓒ **1** a long, thin, slender shoot or branch. 휘청휘청한 나뭇가지. **2** a very thin stick used in whipping; a blow with a whip. 채찍; 회초리; (회초리의) 한 번 휘두르기. **3** a device for turning an electric current on and off. (전기의) 스위치; 개폐기. **4** 《U.S.》 a set of movable rails for turning a train from one track to another. (철도의) 전철기. 參考 영국에서는 points라고 함. **5** a bunch of dead hair used in hair dressing.

(여성이 머리에 드리는) 다리 꼭지. **6** a sudden or complete change. 전환; 변경. ¶ *a ~ of the conversation to another topic* 대화를 다른 화제로 바꾸기 / *a sudden policy ~* 급격한 정책 전환 / *His sudden death caused a ~ in the program.* 그의 급사로 계획이 변경됐다. — *vt.* **1** (P6,13) beat (someone or something) with a switch. …을 채찍으로 때리다; 채찍질하다. ¶ *He switched the dog with a small stick.* 그는 작은 작대기로 개를 때렸다. **2** (P6) swing or move (something) back and forth or up and down like a whip. (채찍·꼬리 따위를) 흔들다; 휘두르다. ¶ *~ a cane* 〔*fishing line*〕 지팡이를〔낚싯줄을〕 휘두르다 / *The horse switched her tail.* 말은 꼬리를 흔들었다. **3** (P6,7,13) turn (a train) from one track to another. (열차 따위를) 전철하다; (다른 선로에) 바꾸어 넣다. ¶ *~ a train from one track to another* 열차를 전철하다 / *The train was switched into the siding.* 열차는 측선(側線)으로 전철되었다. **4** (P7,13) 《chiefly U.S.》 direct (thoughts, talk, etc.) to some other subject; change. (화제 따위를) 바꾸다; …을 변경하다. ¶ *~ conversation from a painful subject to another* 대화를 마음 아픈 화제로부터 다른 화제로 돌리다. **5** 《U.S. *colloq.*》 exchange. 교환하다; 서로 바꾸다. ¶ *~ seats at the movie* 영화관에서 좌석을 서로 바꾸다. **6** turn on or off (an electric light or current). (전기의) 스위치를 움직이다〔작동하다〕. ¶ *~ the radio on* 〔*off*〕 라디오의 스위치를 켜다〔끄다〕 / *~ off a current* 전류의 스위치를 끄다 / *He switched out the light and got into bed.* 그는 전등의 스위치를 끄고 잠자리에 들었다. — *vi.* (P1,2A) change; turn aside; shift. 바뀌다; (방향 따위를) 바꾸다. ¶ *The wind switched to the south.* 바람의 방향이 남쪽으로 바뀌었다 / *He suddenly switched* (*off*) *to another topic.* 그는 갑자기 다른 화제로 이야기를 바꿨다. [Teut.]

switch on 〔***off***〕, turn on 〔off〕 (an electric light or an electric current, etc.) using a switch; turn on 〔off〕 a radio, a television set, etc. …의 스위치를 넣다〔끄다〕; (라디오·TV 따위를) 켜다〔끄다〕. ¶ *~ on* 〔*off*〕 *the radio* 라디오를 켜다〔끄다〕.

switch·back [swítʃbæ̀k] *n.* Ⓒ a railroad which runs up and down steep slopes; a railroad which runs in a zigzag manner. 전향선(轉向線)《급한 언덕을 지그재그로 오르게 한 철도선》.

switch·blade (knife) [swítʃblèid (ㅅ)] *n.* a pocket-knife with its long blade released by spring. (스프링에 의해) 날이 튀어 나오게 된 나이프.

switch·board [swítʃbɔ̀ːrd] *n.* Ⓒ a board or panel with switches and plugs for connecting electric lines, esp. telephone lines. (전력·전등 따위의) 배전반; (전화의) 교환대. ¶ *a telephone ~* 전화 교환기.

switch·man [swítʃmən] *n.* Ⓒ (*pl.* **-men** [-mən]) a man who operates railroad switches. (철도의) 전철수(轉轍手).

·Switz·er·land [swítsərlənd] *n.* a small country in central Europe. 스위스. 參考 수도는 Bern.

swiv·el [swívəl] *n.* Ⓒ a coupling device which allows two parts to turn freely. 회전 (이음) 고리. — *vt., vi.* (P6,7;1,2A) (**-eled, -el·ing** or 《Brit.》 **-elled, -el·ling**) turn (something) around freely; revolve. …을 선회시키다〔선회(旋回)하다〕; 회전시키다〔회전하다〕. ¶ *He swiveled his chair round to see me.* 그는 나를 보기 위해 의자를 빙그르르 돌렸다. [E.]

swivel chair [ㅅ-ㅅ] *n.* a chair which turns around on its base. 회전 의자.

swob [swɑb / swɔb] *n., vt.* =swab.

·swol·len [swóulən] *v.* pp. of **swell.** — *adj.* increased in size or volume; puffed up. 부푼; 늘어난; 부어오른.

swonk [swʌŋk] *vi.* p. of **swink.**

swonk·en [swʌ́ŋkən] *vi.* pp. of **swink.**

swoon [swuːn] *n.* Ⓒ a sudden loss of all feeling caused by illness or shock; a faint. 기절; 졸도. ¶ *fall into* 〔*be in*〕 *a ~* 기절하다. — *vi.* (P1) fall senseless; faint. 기절하다; 졸도하다. ¶ *~ for joy* 〔*with pain*〕 너무 기뻐서 정신이 멍해지다〔고통으로 기절하다〕 / *She swooned at the dreadful sight.* 그녀는 무시무시한 광경에 그만 기절했다. [E.]

swoop [swuːp] *vi.* (P1,2A) 《*down, upon*》 suddenly descend through the air, esp. to attack something. 하늘에서 내리 덮치다; 습격하다. ¶ *The eagle swooped down on* 〔*upon*〕 *the hare.* 독수리는 그 토끼를 겨냥하여 하늘에서 내리 덮쳤다 / *The airplanes swooped down upon the enemy positions.* 비행기들은 급강하하여 적의 진지를 습격하였다. — *vt.* (P7,13) 《*up*》 carry (something) off suddenly; snatch. 갑자기 …을 잡아 채다. ¶ *He swooped her up in his arms.* 그는 그녀를 와락 끌어안았다. — *n.* Ⓒ the act of swooping; a sudden attack. 급습; 불의의 습격. [E.]

at one swoop, at a stroke; at one single blow. 단번에; 일거에.

with a swoop, suddenly. 갑자기.

swop [swɑp / swɔp] *v.* (**swopped, swop·ping**), *n.* =swap.

:sword [sɔːrd] *n.* **1** Ⓒ a long, cutting weapon used by a soldier. 검(劍); 칼. ¶ *put up a ~* 칼을 칼집에 넣다. **2** 《*the ~*》 military power; war. 무력; 전쟁. ¶ *appeal to the ~* 무력에 호소하다 / 《*prov.*》 *The pen is mightier than the ~.* 문(文)은 무(武)보다 강하다. [E.]

at sword's points (*with each other*), very unfriendly; ready to quarrel. 불화(不和)하여; 적대하여.

at the point of sword, under threat of death. 총검을 들이대어; 무력으로.

cross 〔***measure***〕 ***swords with,*** **a**) fight with; begin struggle with. …와 싸우다. **b**) 《*fig.*》

argue violently; quarrel with. 격론하다; 논쟁하다.

draw* 〔*sheathe*〕 *the sword, begin 〔cease from〕 war. 칼을 빼다〔칼집에 꽂다〕; 전단(戰端)을 열다〔화해하다〕.

fire and sword, killing and burning; destruction by war. 살인과 방화; 전쟁에 의한 파괴.

put* (*someone*) *to the sword, kill (someone) with a sword. (아무를) 베어 죽이다.

the sword of justice, the power of the law. 사법권.

sword belt [ˊ-ˋ] *n.* a belt from which a sword is hung. 검대(劍帶).

sword dance [ˊ-ˋ] *n.* a dance using swords. 칼춤; 검무(劍舞).

sword·fish [sɔ́ːrdfìʃ] *n.* Ⓒ (*pl.* **-fish·es** or *collectively* **-fish**) a very large salt-water edible fish with a swordlike point. 황새치.

sword·play [sɔ́ːrdplèi] *n.* Ⓤ the act or art of using a sword; fencing. 검술(의 묘기); 펜싱.

swords·man [sɔ́ːrdzmən] *n.* Ⓒ (*pl.* **-men** [-mən]) **1** a person skilled in the use of a sword. 검객; 검사(劍士). **2** a person who uses a sword. 군인; 무사.

***swore** [swɔːr] *v.* p. of **swear.**

***sworn** [swɔːrn] *v.* pp. of **swear.** — *adj.* declared; promised in the name of God. 맹세한. ¶ ~ *brothers* 의형제 / ~ *enemies* 불구대천의 원수〔적〕. [*swear*]

swot [swɑt / swɔt] *vt., vi.* (P7; 1) work hard on books; 《*up*》 learn with pains. 책과 씨름하다; 열심히 공부하다. — *n.* hard study; effort or task requiring it. 기를 쓰고 하는 공부; 힘드는 일. [*sweat*]

swum [swʌm] *v.* pp. of **swim.**

***swung** [swʌŋ] *v.* p. and pp. of **swing.**

syb·a·rite [síbəràit] *n.* Ⓒ a person who loves pleasure and luxury. 사치와 향락에 탐닉하는 자. [*Sybaris* in ancient Italy]

syc·a·mine [síkəmàin, -min] *n.* 《Bible, bot.》 a black-mulberry tree. (검은 오디가 열리는) 뽕나무의 일종《누가 복음(福音)에서》. [Heb.]

syc·a·more [síkəmɔ̀ːr] *n.* Ⓒ **1** a kind of fig tree. 무화과나무의 일종. **2** a kind of maple tree; the sycamore maple. 큰단풍나무. [↑]

syc·o·phant [síkəfənt] *n.* Ⓒ a person who tries to win favor by flattering. 알랑쇠; 아첨꾼. [Gk. =informer]

Syd·ney [sídni] *n.* the largest city and most important seaport in Australia. 시드니.

syl·la·ba·ry [síləbèri / -bəri] *n.* Ⓒ a set of characters representing syllables in some languages as alphabet represents simple sounds in others. 자음표(字音表); 음절 문자표. ¶ *the Korean* ~ 한글의 가나다 음표. [→syllable]

syl·la·bi [síləbài] *n.* pl. of **syllabus.**

syl·lab·ic [silǽbik] *adj.* **1** of or in syllables. 음절의; 음절을 이루는; 철자의. ¶ *a* ~ *character* 〔*symbol*〕 음절 문자〔부호〕 / *a* ~ *poem* 음절시 / *a* ~ *consonant* 음절 자음. **2** pronounced syllable by syllable. 음절마다 발음하는; 발음이 똑똑한. ¶ *one's* ~ *style of speaking* 음절의 발음을 명확히 하는 말투. [→syllable]

syl·lab·i·cate [silǽbəkèit] *vt.* (P6) divide (a word, etc.) into syllables. (단어를) 음절로 나누다.

syl·lab·i·ca·tion [silæ̀bəkéiʃən] *n.* Ⓤ the division of words into syllables. 음절로 나누기; 분철법.

syl·lab·i·fy [silǽbəfài] *vt.* =syllabicate.

***syl·la·ble** [síləbəl] *n.* Ⓒ **1** a part of a word pronounced as a unit. 음절. ¶ *'sym-' is the first* ~ *of 'symbol'.* 'sym-'은 'symbol'의 첫 음절이다. **2** the smallest unit of speech. 한 마디. ¶ *I never uttered a* ~. 나는 한 마디도 말하지 않았다. [Gk. *sul-* syn-, *lambanō* take]

syl·la·bus [síləbəs] *n.* Ⓒ (*pl.* **-bus·es** or **-bi**) **1** a brief statement of a course of study. (강의의) 개요; 대요(大要). **2** a written list of subjects to be studied. 교수 세목(細目); 강의 요목(要目). [corrupt. of Gk. *sittuba* label]

syl·lep·ses [silépsiːz] *n.* pl. of **syllepsis.**

syl·lep·sis [silépsis] *n.* (*pl.* **-ses**) application of a word to two others in different senses, or to two of which it grammatically suits one only. 겸용법(兼用法). ● **syl·lep·tic** [-tik] *adj.* [→syllable]

syl·lo·gism [sílədʒìzəm] *n.* ⓊⒸ a form of reasoning consisting of two statements and a conclusion. 삼단 논법. ● **syl·lo·gis·tic** [sìlədʒístik] *adj.* [→logos]

syl·lo·gize [sílədʒàiz] *vt., vi.* (P6;1) argue or reason by syllogisms; use syllogisms. 삼단 논법으로 추론하다〔논하다〕. [↑]

sylph [silf] *n.* Ⓒ **1** a fairy of the air. 공기〔대기〕의 요정. **2** a slender, graceful girl. 날씬한 미녀. [L.]

syl·van, sil·van [sílvən] *adj.* of or consisting of the woods or trees; wooded. 숲의; 수목이 우거진. ¶ *a* ~ *retreat* 숲 속에 있는 오두막 / *lead a* ~ *life* 숲 속에서 살다. [L.]

Syl·vi·a [sílviə] *n.* a woman's name. 여자 이름.

***sym·bol** [símbəl] *n.* Ⓒ a sign; something that represents or stands for something else. 부호; 기호; 상징; 표상(表象). ¶ *White is the* ~ *of purity.* 백(白)은 순결의 상징이다 / *the* ~ *of the State* 국가의 상징 / *a chemical* ~ 화학 기호 / *a phonetic* ~ 음성〔발음〕 기호 / *The sign '÷' is the* ~ *of division.* '÷'의 기호는 나눗셈의 부호이다. [Gk. *ballō* throw]

sym·bol·ic [simbɑ́lik / -bɔ́l-], **-i·cal** [-əl] *adj.* **1** used as a symbol; of a symbol. 부호〔기호〕의; 상징적인. ¶ ~ *meaning* 상징적 의

미 / *The dove is ~ of peace.* 비둘기는 평화의 상징이다. **2** expressed by a symbol. 부호〔기호〕로 나타낸.

sym·bol·ism [símbəlìzəm] *n.* Ⓤ **1** the use of symbols to express ideas. 부호〔기호〕 사용; 부호〔기호〕로 나타냄. **2** an artistic or literary movement in which symbols are emphasized; the theory or practice of using symbols. 상징주의. **3** symbolic meaning. 상징적 의미.

sym·bol·ize [símbəlàiz] *vt.* (P6) be a symbol of (something); represent (something) by a symbol. …의 상징이다; …을 상징하다; 부호〔기호〕로 나타내다. — *vi.* (P1) use symbols. 부호〔기호〕를 쓰다. [→symbol, -ize]

***sym·met·ric** [simétrik], **-ri·cal** [-əl] *adj.* having symmetry; well-proportioned. 대칭적인; 균형이 잡힌. [→metre]

sym·met·ri·cal·ly [simétrikəli] *adv.* in a symmetrical manner. 대칭적으로; 균형 있게.

sym·me·trize [símətràiz] *vt.* (P6) make (something) symmetrical. …을 대칭적으로 하다; …의 균형을 잡히게 하다.

***sym·me·try** [símətri] *n.* Ⓤ **1** similarity of form or arrangement on the opposite sides of a line or plane. (좌우) 상칭; 대칭(對稱). **2** well-balanced form or arrangement of parts. 균형; 균정(均整); 조화.

***sym·pa·thet·ic** [sìmpəθétik] *adj.* **1** sharing the feelings of another; agreeable; showing kind feelings toward others. 공감〔공명〕하는; 찬성하는; 호의적인; 동정하는; 인정있는. ¶ *We are ~ to your plan.* 우리는 너의 계획에 찬성한다 / *They were not ~ toward young people.* 그들은 젊은이들에 대하여 호의적이 아니다 / *~ tears* 동정의 눈물 / *~ words* 동정적인 말 / *a ~ person* 동정적인 사람. **2** well-suited. 꼭 맞는; 성미에 맞는. ¶ *~ friends* 마음 맞는 친구들 / *live in ~ surroundings* 자기 성미에 맞는 환경에서 살다. [→sympathy]

sym·pa·thet·i·cal·ly [sìmpəθétikəli] *adv.* in a sympathetic manner. 동정하여; 인정 있게.

***sym·pa·thize** [símpəθàiz] *vi.* (P3) 《*with*》 **1** share the feelings of another. 공감하다; 동의하다; 공명〔찬성〕하다. ¶ *~ with someone in his view* 아무의 의견에 찬성하다 / *My father never sympathized with my desire to become an actor.* 부친께서는 배우가 되고 싶다는 내 생각에 결코 동의해 주시지 않았다. **2** feel or show sympathy toward others. 동정하다. ¶ *~ with someone in his grief* 아무와 슬픔을 함께 하다 / *I ~ heartily with you.* 진심으로 너에게 동정을 전한다 / *I ~ with you in your grief.* 너의 슬픔을 가슴 아프게 생각한다.

sym·pa·thiz·er [símpəθàizər] *n.* Ⓒ a person who sympathizes. 동정자; 지지자; 공감〔공명〕자.

:**sym·pa·thy** [símpəθi] *n.* **1** Ⓤ sameness of feeling; the state of sharing another's feeling. 동감; 공감; 공명. ¶ *a man of broad sympathies* 이해의 폭이 넓은 사람 / *be in* 〔*out of*〕 *~ with a plan* 계획에 찬성하다〔찬성하지 않다〕 / *I have every ~ with you in your love of country life.* 나는 전원 생활에 대한 너의 애착에 전적으로 공감하는 바이다. **2** ⓊⒸ the ability to share sorrow or trouble with another person. 동정; 인정. ¶ *an understanding ~* 이해심 있는 동정 / *You have my ~.* =*Accept my sympathies.* 참으로 마음 아프게 생각합니다《화를 당한 사람에 대한 인사말》. **3** Ⓤ the feeling of pity. 연민. [syn-, L. *pathos* feeling]

sym·phon·ic [simfánik / -fɔ́n-] *adj.* 《mus.》 of or having the nature of a symphony. 교향악의; 교향악적인. [→phonetic]

sym·pho·ny [símfəni] *n.* Ⓒ (*pl.* **-nies**) **1** 《mus.》 a piece of music for an orchestra. 교향곡; 심포니. ¶ *a ~ orchestra* 교향악단. **2** a pleasant harmony of sounds. 조화; 화음(和音). [↑]

sym·po·si·a [simpóuziə] *n.* pl. of **symposium.**

sym·po·si·um [simpóuziəm] *n.* Ⓒ (*pl.* **-ums** or **-si·a**) **1** a collection of writing by different writers on one subject. (하나의 문제에 관한) 논문집. **2** a meeting for the discussion of one subject. 심포지엄; 토론회. [Gk. *posis* drinking]

***symp·tom** [símptəm] *n.* Ⓒ **1** 《med.》 a manifestation in the body or its functions that indicates disease. 증상(症狀); 증후(症候). ¶ *a ~ of cancer* 암의 증상 / *an objective* 〔*a subjective*〕 *~* 타각〔자각〕 증상 / *Fever is a ~ of illness.* 발열은 발병의 증후이다. **2** a sign or indication of the existence or happening of something. 징후; 징조. ¶ *symptoms of an earthquake* 지진이 일어날 징조 / *We have not yet a reassuring ~ of peace.* 고무적인 평화의 징후는 아직 보이지 않는다. [Gk. *piptōn* fall]

symp·to·mat·ic [sìmptəmǽtik] *adj.* of symptoms; signifying; indicative. 징후적〔증후적〕인; 징후〔증후〕의; …을 나타내는. ¶ *a condition ~ of cholera* 콜레라의 증상 / *a ~ classification of disease* 증상에 의한 질병의 분류. [↑]

syn- [sin-] *pref.* together. '더불어, 함께'의 뜻. [Gk. *sun* with]

syn·a·gogue [sínəgàg / -gɔ̀g] *n.* Ⓒ **1** an assembly of Jews for religious purposes. 유대인 집회. **2** a building for Jewish worship. 유대교 회당. [Gk. *ago* bring]

syn·chro·nism [síŋkrənìzəm] *n.* Ⓤ **1** the state of being synchronous. 동시적임; 동시 발생; 동시성. **2** the arrangement of historical events or persons in order of time. (역사적 사건·인물의) 연대별 배열. [→chronicle]

syn·chro·nize [síŋkrənàiz] *vi.* (P1) **1** happen at the same time. 동시에 일어나다. **2** (of clocks, etc.) keep the same time. (둘 이상의 시계가) 같은 시간을 나타내다. — *vt.* (P6,13) **1** cause (something) to happen at the same time. …을 동시에 하다〔진행시키다〕; …에 동시성을 갖게 하다. **2** arrange (historical events or persons) according to dates. …을 발생 연대순으로 배열하다. **3** make (something) agree in time. …의 시간을 일치시키다. ¶ ~ *all the clocks in a building* 빌딩 안에 있는 모든 시계의 시간을 일치(一致)시키다. **4** 《cinema》 add sound effects or dialogue timing them to accompany the action. 동시(同時)녹음하다. ¶ *The sound track of a film should be synchronized with the movement of the actors' lips.* 영화 필름의 사운드 트랙은 배우들의 입놀림과 함께 동시 녹음되어야 한다. [↑]

synchronized swimming [–́–– –́–] *n.* a sport growing out of water ballet in which swimmers, in solo, duet, and team efforts, complete various required figures by performing motions. 수중 발레; 싱크로나이즈드 스위밍.

syn·chro·nous [síŋkrənəs] *adj.* happening at the same time. 동시의; 동기(同期)의.

syn·co·pate [síŋkəpèit] *vt.* **1** 《gram.》 shorten (a word) by taking letters or sounds from the middle. (낱말)의 중간 음절을 생략하다; 중략(中略)하다. 參考 over를 o'er로, never를 ne'er로 하는 따위. **2** 《mus.》 begin (a tone) from the unaccented beat and hold it into an accented one. …을 절분(切分)하다. [Gk. *koptō* cut]

syn·co·pa·tion [sìŋkəpéiʃən] *n.* Ⓤ the act of syncopating; the state of being syncopated. (낱말의) 생략; 중략(中略); (음(音)의) 절분(切分); 싱코페이션.

syn·di·cate [síndikit] *n.* Ⓒ **1** persons or companies united in carrying out some plan, usu. needing a large amount of money. 신디케이트; 기업 연합. **2** an organization which supplies special articles, pictures, etc. to newspapers, etc. 신문 잡지용(用) 기사 공급자 기업. —[-kèit] *vt.* (P6) **1** combine (companies) into a syndicate. …을 신디케이트 조직으로 하다. **2** publish (articles, etc.) through a syndicate. …을 신디케이트를 통해 발표하다. [Gk. *sundikos* counsel or advocate]

syn·drome [síndroum, -drəm] *n.* a group of signs and symptoms that collectively indicate or characterize a disease, psychological disorder, etc. 증후군(症候群). [syn-, Gk. *dramein* run]

syne [sain] *adv.* 《Sc.》 since; ago. 이전에; 전에. [E.]

syn·ec·do·che [sinékdəki] *n.* 《rhet.》 a figure of speech in which a part is used to express the whole. 제유(提喩)(법)《일부로써 전체를, 특수로써 일반을 나타내는 표현법; e.g. *blade* for *sword*; *sail* for *ship*》. [Gk.]

syn·od [sínəd] *n.* Ⓒ a meeting of officers of a church; an assembly; a council. 종교 회의(宗敎會議); 회의; 집회. [Gk. *hodos* road]

syn·o·nym [sínənim] *n.* Ⓒ a word having the same or almost the same meaning as another word. 동의어; 유의어(類義語) (opp. antonym). [Gk. *onoma* name]

syn·on·y·mous [sinánəməs / -nɔ́n-] *adj.* having the same or almost the same meaning. 같은 뜻의; 유사한.

syn·op·ses [sinápsiːz / -nɔ́p-] *n.* pl. of **synopsis.**

syn·op·sis [sinápsis / -nɔ́p-] *n.* Ⓒ (*pl.* **-ses**) a short statement outlining a subject, a book, etc. 대강; 개요; (대충의) 줄거리. [Gk. *opsis* seeing]

syn·op·tic [sináptik / -nɔ́p-] *adj.* giving a general view or outline. 개요(槪要)의; 개괄적인.

syn·op·ti·cal·ly [sináptikəli / -nɔ́p-] *adv.* in a synoptical manner; in outline; as a summary. 개괄적으로.

Synoptic Gospels [–́–– –́–], **the** *n.* the first three books of the New Testament (i.e. Matthew, Mark, and Luke). 공관(共觀) 복음서.

syn·tac·tic [sintǽktik], **-ti·cal** [-əl] *adj.* of syntax. 구문론의. [→tactics]

syn·tac·ti·cal·ly [sintǽktikəli] *adv.* according to the rules of syntax. 문장론적으로; 문장 구성상(上).

syn·tax [síntæks] *n.* Ⓤ **1** sentence structure. 문장 구조; 구문. **2** the arrangement of words. 어구 배열. **3** the branch of grammar dealing with this. 구문론〔법〕; 통어(統語)론〔법〕; 문장론. [→taxis]

syn·the·ses [sínθəsiːz] *n.* pl. of **synthesis.**

syn·the·sis [sínθəsis] *n.* (*pl.* **-ses**) **1** Ⓤ the combination of parts or elements so as to form a whole. 종합; 합성(opp. analysis). **2** Ⓒ a whole formed by combining parts. 종합체. **3** Ⓤ the formation of a chemical compound substance. 합성. [→thesis]

syn·thet·ic [sinθétik], **-i·cal** [-əl] *adj.* **1** of synthesis. 종합의; 합성적인(opp. analytic). **2** 《chem.》 produced artificially, chiefly by chemical reactions. 합성의; 인조(人造)의. ¶ ~ *rubber* 인조 고무 / *a* ~ *drug* 〔*detergent*〕 합성 약제〔세제〕/ ~ *fruit juice* 합성 과즙. [↑]

syn·the·ti·cal·ly [sinθétikəli] *adv.* in a synthetic manner; through synthesis. 종합적으로; 합성적으로.

syph·i·lis [sífəlis] *n.* Ⓤ a dangerous disease which finally affects the brain. 매독. [Person]

sy·phon [sáifən] *n.* =siphon.

Syr·i·a [síriə] *n.* a country in western Asia. 시리아. 參考 수도는 Damascus.

Syr·i·an [síriən] *n.* Ⓒ the people of Syria; Ⓤ the language of Syria. 시리아 사람; 시리아어. — *adj.* of Syria or Syrians. 시리아(사람)의; 시리아(어)의.

sy·ringe [sərínd3, sírind3] *n.* Ⓒ a device for injecting medical liquid, etc. into a body. 주사기; 세척기; 관장기(灌腸器). — *vt.* (P6,13) clean or inject (something) by using a syringe. …을 주사기로 주사하다; 세척기로 세척하다. [Gk. =pipe]

syr·up, sir- [sírəp, sə́ː-] *n.* Ⓤ very sweet liquid made from sugar or fruit juices. 시럽; 당밀. [Arab. →sherbet]

:sys·tem [sístəm] *n.* Ⓒ **1** a group of things, ideas, etc. forming a whole which operates or moves in harmony. 조직; 계통. ¶ *a supply* ~ 공급 계통 / *the social* ~ 사회 조직 / *a railway* ~철도망 / *the solar* ~ 태양계. **2** a classified and arranged group of facts, principles, rules, etc. in a certain field of study. (학문적) 체계. ¶ *a* ~ *of philosophy* [*grammar*] 철학[문법] 체계. **3** 《*the* ~ or *one's* ~》 the human body as a whole. 신체. ¶ *the* ~ 인체 / *have one's* ~ *out of order* 몸을[건강을] 해치다 / *Too much coffee is bad for the* ~. 커피의 과음은 몸에 나쁘다. **4** a group of bodily organs having the same function. (신체기관의) 계통. ¶ *the digestive* ~ 소화기 계통. **5** 《*this* [*the*] ~》 the universe. 우주. ¶ *this* [*the great*] ~ 우주. **6** a plan or method of putting things into classes or groups. 분류법. ¶ *the Linnean* ~ 린네의 (식물) 분류법. **7** an orderly way of getting things done; a plan; a method. 체계적[조직적]인 방식; 순서. ¶ *a sales* ~ 판매방식 / *the decimal* ~ 십진법 / *arrangement without* ~ 불규칙한 배열 / *He has no* ~ *in his work.* 그의 일에는 체계적인 순서가[방식이] 없다. [syn-, Gk. *histēmi* put]

·sys·tem·at·ic [sìstəmǽtik], **-i·cal** [-əl] *adj.* **1** according to a system; orderly; methodical. 조직[계통·체계]적인; 질서 있는. ¶ *a* ~ *method* 조직적 방법 / *a* ~ *course of study* 조직적인 학습 과정 / ~ *efforts* 일관된 노력. **2** having a plan. 계획적인; 고의의. ¶ *a* ~ *liar* 일부러 거짓말을 하는 사람. **3** of putting things into classes; classifying. 분류적인; 분류상의. ¶ *the* ~ *names of plants* 식물의 분류학적 명칭《학명》.

sys·tem·at·i·cal·ly [sìstəmǽtikəli] *adv.* according to a system; in a systematic manner. 계통을 세워서; 조직적으로; 정연히; 계획적으로; 분류적으로.

sys·tem·a·ti·za·tion [sìstəmətizéiʃən] *n.* Ⓤ the act of systematizing; the state of being systematized. 계통화; 조직화; 분류.

sys·tem·a·tize [sístəmətàiz] *vt.* put (something) into a system; arrange (something) according to a system. …을 조직화하다; 계통을 세우다; 체계화하다; 분류하다.

sys·tem·ic [sistémik] *adj.* **1** of a system. 계통의; 조직의. **2** of or affecting the body as a whole. 온 몸의; 전신에 영향을 주는. ¶ *a* ~ *disease* 전신병(全身病) / *the* ~ *arteries* 전신 동맥.

sys·to·le [sístəli] *n.* contraction of heart or other organ alternating with diastole. 심장 수축. ● **sys·tol·ic** [sistálik / -tɔ́l-] *adj.* [syn-, Gk. *stellō* send]

t T

T, t [tiː] *n.* Ⓒ (*pl.* **T's, t's, Ts, ts** [-z]) **1** the 20th letter of the English alphabet. 영어 알파벳의 제20번째 글자. **2** an object shaped like T. T자 모양의 것.

cross the t's, pay careful attention to very minute points. 세세한 데까지 주의하다.

to a T, exactly; perfectly. 정확히; 완전히. ¶ *It suits me to a T.* 내게 딱 들어맞는다.

T. Territory; Testament; Tuesday.

t. teaspoon; tense; territory; time; ton(s); town; township; transitive.

Ta 《chem.》 tantalum.

ta [tɑː] *interj.* 《Brit. *colloq., child's word*》 thank you. 고맙습니다.

tab [tæb] *n.* Ⓒ **1** a small piece of cloth or paper attached to a coat, etc. used for hanging it up, etc. (옷을 거는) 짓끈; (옷·리본 따위의) 드림 (장식). **2** a tag; a label. 꼬리표; 부전. **3** 《*colloq.*》 an account; a check. 계산서; 전표. [*tablet*]

keep a tab 〔***tabs***〕 ***on,*** 《*colloq.*》 **a**) keep an account of (income, outgo, etc.). …을 기장(記帳)하다. **b**) keep (someone or something) under observation. …을 감시〔감독〕하다. ¶ *As he is a dangerous criminal, the police are keeping tabs on him.* 그는 위험한 범인이므로 경찰이 감시하고 있다.

tab·by [tǽbi] *n.* (*pl.* **-bies**) **1** Ⓒ a brown or gray cat with black stripes; a female cat. 얼룩〔범무늬〕 고양이; 암고양이. **2** Ⓒ ⓐ a gossiping and spiteful woman. 심술궂고 수다스러운 여자. ⓑ an old maid. 노처녀. [Arab.]

tab·er·nac·le [tǽbərnækəl] *n.* Ⓒ **1** a tent or hut used as a house for a while. 임시로 묵을 오두막〔천막〕. **2** 《*fig.*》 the human body considered as the place where the soul exists. (영혼이 일시 머무는) 육체. **3** 《*the T-*》 a Jewish temple; a place of worship. 유대 신전; 예배당. [L. *taberna* shop]

:ta·ble [téibəl] *n.* Ⓒ **1** a piece of furniture having a smooth, flat top and legs. 탁자; 식탁; 테이블. ¶ *lay* 〔*set, spread*〕 *the* ~ 식탁〔밥상〕을 차리다 / *a billiard* ~ 당구대 / *a writing* ~ 책상. **2** 《used as *sing.*》 the food served at table. 식탁에 내는 요리; 음식. ¶ *She sets* 〔*keeps*〕 *a good* 〔*bad*〕 ~. 그녀는 늘 성찬〔소찬〕을 차린다 / *pleasures of the* ~ 먹는 재미; 식도락. **3** 《*collectively*》 the people seated at a table to eat, talk, etc. 식탁에 앉은 사람들; 한 자리에 모인 사람들. ¶ *amuse the whole* ~ 좌중을 즐겁게 하다. **4** a flat surface; a high area of flat land. 평면; 대지(臺地). **5** a thin, flat piece of wood, stone, metal, etc.; a tablet. (나무·돌·금속 등의) 평판; 명판(銘板). **6** a list; an orderly arrangement of facts, information, figures, etc. (각종의) 표; 일람표; 목록. ¶ *a* ~ *of contents* (책의) 목차 / *a* ~ *of interest* 이자표 / *a* ~ *of weights and measures* 도량형표 / *a statistical* ~ 통계표 / *a multiplication* ~ 구구표(九九表).

at table, having a meal; at meals. 식사 중. ¶ *He was at* ~ *when I called.* 찾아 갔더니 그는 식사 중이었다.

lay 〔***put***〕 ***on*** 〔***upon***〕 ***the table,*** expose (papers, etc.) for inspection; submit for discussion; (in Parliament) leave (a report, bill, etc.) for the present; postpone indefinitely. 공개하다; 토의에 부치다; (의안 따위를) 보류〔연기〕하다.

lie on 〔***upon***〕 ***the table,*** (in Parliament) be postponed indefinitely. (의안 심의가) 무기 연기되다.

turn the tables (***on someone***), bring (someone) to the position of disadvantage lately held by oneself; change the situation to the contrary. 형세를 역전시키다; 주객이 전도되다.

under the table, 《*colloq.*》 **a**) very drunk (after dinner). 몹시 취하여. **b**) secretly, and often illegally. 몰래; 은밀히.

— *vt.* (P6) **1** put on a table. …을 탁자에 (펴) 놓다. **2** ⓐ 《Brit.》 put forward (a proposal, etc.) for consideration by an assembly. (의안)을 상정하다. ⓑ 《U.S.》 postpone a decision on (a proposal, etc.) indefinitely. (의안 심의 등)을 무기 연기시키다; 묵살하다. **3** make a list of (something). …의 표를 만들다. [L. *tabula* board]

tab·leau [tǽblou, -́] *n.* Ⓒ (*pl.* **-leaus** or **-leaux**) **1** a representation of a well-known picture, statue, scene, etc. by living persons posing and dressed in costume. 활인화(活人畫). **2** a picture. 그림; 회화. **3** a striking scene. 극적인 장면. [F.]

tab·leaux [tǽblouz, -́] *n.* pl. of **tableau.**

ta·ble·cloth [téibəlklɔ̀(ː)θ, -klɑ̀θ] *n.* Ⓒ a cloth for covering a table, esp. for use at meals. 테이블보; 식탁보.

ta·ble d'hôte [tɑ́ːbəl dóut, tǽb-] *n.* 《F.》 Ⓒ (*pl.* **ta·bles d'hôte** [tɑ́ːbəlz dóut / tǽbəlz -]) **1** a meal served at a fixed time and price at a hotel or restaurant. 정식(定食)(opp. à la carte). **2** a public table for guests at a hotel, etc. (호텔 등의) 공동 식탁.

ta·ble-hop [téibəlhɑ̀p / -hɔ̀p] *vi.* (P1) 《*colloq.*》 move from table to table greeting people in a restaurant, night club, etc. (레스토랑 등에서) 테이블 사이를 돌아다니며

T

이야기하다.

ta·ble·land [téibəllæ̀nd] *n.* Ⓒ a high plain; a plateau. 고원; 대지(臺地).

∗**ta·ble·spoon** [téibəlspù:n] *n.* Ⓒ **1** a large spoon used to prepare and serve food. (식탁 용의) 큰 스푼; 테이블 스푼. **2** = tablespoonful

ta·ble·spoon·ful [téibəlspù:nful] *n.* (*pl.* **-fuls**) Ⓒ the amount a tablespoon will hold. 테이블 스푼 하나의 분량.

∗**tab·let** [tǽblit] *n.* Ⓒ **1** a small flat sheet of stone, wood, etc., used to write on; a stone or metal plate with letters carved on it. 명판(銘板); 각판(刻板); 패(牌). ¶ *an ancestral* ~ 위패 / *a memorial* ~ 기념패. **2** a number of sheets of writing paper fixed together at one end; a writing pad. (떼서 쓰게 된) 메모지; 편지지. **3** a small, flat piece of medicine. 타블렛; 정제(錠劑). [→table]

table talk [ㄹ–ㄹ] *n.* informal conversation at meals. 식사 때의 잡담.

table tennis [ㄹ– ㄹ–] *n.* an indoor sport played on a table with small bats and a celluloid ball; ping-pong. 탁구; 핑퐁.

ta·ble·ware [téibəlwɛ̀ər] *n.* Ⓤ dishes, knives, spoons, forks, etc., used to set a table or to serve food and drink. (식탁 용의) 식기류.

tab·loid [tǽblɔid] *n.* Ⓒ **1** 《*T-*》《trademark》 a tablet of medicine. 알약; 정제. **2** a small daily newspaper with many photographs. 타블로이드판 신문. ¶ *I never read the tabloids* 〔*the* ~ *press*〕. 난 타블로이드판 신문은 안 읽는다. [L. *tabula* board]

in tabloid form, in condensed, compressed form. 요약된; 간추린.

ta·boo [təbú:, tæ-] *n.* ⒸⓊ (*pl.* **-boos**) (esp. among primitive races) the state of being prohibited to use, to speak of, etc. by social force or custom. 터부; 금기(禁忌); 금제(禁制). — *adj.* forbidden or prohibited by social force. 금기〔금지〕된. ¶ ~ *words* 금기어 / *Don't talk to her about her divorce. It's a* ~ *subject.* 그녀에게 이혼 이야기를 하지 마라. 그건 꺼리는 화제야. — *vt.* (P6) forbid to do (something) by taboo. …을 금지하다. ¶ *The subject is tabooed.* 그 화제는 금물이다. [Native]

〈tabor〉

ta·bor, 《Brit.》 **-bour** [téibər] *n.* Ⓒ a small drum formerly used to accompany oneself on a pipe or fife. (피리 반주용의) 작은 북. [F.]

ta·bu [təbú:, tæ-] *n., adj., vt.* = taboo.

tab·u·lar [tǽbjələr] *adj.* **1** having a flat, tablelike surface. 평판(모양)의. ¶ *a* ~ *crystal* 판상(板狀) 수정 / *a* ~ *rock* 판상암(板狀岩). **2** arranged in a list. 표(表)의; 표로 한. ¶ *The report was in* ~ *form.* 보고서는 표로 되어 있었다. [L. *tabula* board]

tab·u·la ra·sa [tǽbjələ rá:zə, -rá:sə] *n.* 《L.》 Ⓒ (*pl.* **tab·u·lae ra·sae** [-rá:zí:, -si:]) the surface ready to be written on. 글자를 쓰지 않은 서판(書板).

tab·u·late [tǽbjəlèit] *vt.* (P6) arrange (facts, numbers, etc.) in lists. …을 표로 하다. — *adj.* [tǽbjəlit, -lèit] having a flat surface. 평면의; 평판 모양의. [→tabular]

tab·u·la·tion [tæ̀bjəléiʃən] *n.* Ⓤ arrangement in lists. 표로 만들기; 표의 작성.

tab·u·la·tor [tǽbjəlèitər] *n.* Ⓒ **1** a person who tabulates. 도표 작성자. **2** a machine for this purpose, esp. one which is attached to a typewriter. (타자기의) 도표 작성 장치.

ta·chom·e·ter [tækámitər / tækɔ́m-] *n.* an instrument for measuring engine speed in airplanes, motorboats, etc. 태코미터; (항공기 엔진 따위의) 회전 속도계. [Gk. *tachos* speed, →meter]

tac·it [tǽsit] *adj.* silent; not spoken; understood without being said. 무언의; 암묵(暗默)의. ¶ *a* ~ *agreement* 묵약 / ~ *consent* 무언의 승낙 / *a* ~ *understanding* 무언의 양해; 묵계(默契). [L. *taceo* be silent]

tac·it·ly [tǽsitli] *adv.* in a tacit manner. 말없이; 암암리에; 잠자코.

tac·i·turn [tǽsətə̀:rn] *adj.* speaking very little; not liking to talk. 말 없는; 말수가 적은(opp. talkative). ¶ *a* ~ *person* 말수가 적은 사람. [→tacit]

tac·i·tur·ni·ty [tæ̀sətə́:rnəti] *n.* Ⓤ the state or quality of being taciturn. 말이 없음; 무언; 과묵.

tack [tæk] *n.* Ⓒ **1** a short nail with a broad, flat head. 압정(押釘). **2** 《*pl.*》 a long, loose stitch used as a temporary fastening in sewing. 시침질; 가봉. **3** 《*fig.*》 a course of action. (행동) 방침. ¶ *change one's* ~ 방침을 고치다 / *He took a new* ~. 새로운 방침을 택했다 / *The speaker suddenly started off on a different* ~ *and left us all rather confused.* 연사가 갑자기 다른 말을 시작해 우리 모두는 적잖이 어리둥절해졌다. **4** 《naut.》 the action of sailing a zigzag course against the wind. 맞바람을 비스듬히 받고 지그재그 항법으로 나아가기.

be on the wrong 〔***right***〕 ***tack,*** be in the wrong 〔right〕 course. 방침이〔침로가〕 그르다〔옳다〕.

come 〔***get***〕 ***down to*** (***brass***) ***tacks,*** deal with the most important facts. 요점을 말하다; 핵심을 찌르다.

on the port 〔***starboard***〕 ***tack,*** with the wind on the port 〔starboard〕 side. 좌현〔우현〕에 바람을 받고.

— *vt.* **1** (P6,7,13) fasten (something) with tacks. …을 압정으로 고정시키다. ¶ ~ *the* *carpet down* 압정으로 카펫을 고정시키다 / ~ *a notice* (*on*) *to the wall* 압정으로 벽에 게시문을 붙이다. **2** (P6,13) stitch (something) loosely together. …을 시침질하다; 가봉하다. ¶ ~ *two pieces of silk together* 비단 두 쪽을 시쳐 붙이다. **3** (P6,7,13) append. …을 부가하다; 덧붙이다.

— *vi.* (P1) **1** 《naut.》 sail in a zigzag course against the wind. (배가) 지그재그로 〔갈짓자형으로〕 나가다. ¶ *The ship was tacking.* **2** 《*fig.*》 change one's course, one's opinions, etc. 방침〔의견〕을 바꾸다. [F. *tache* nail]

·tack·le [tǽkəl] *n.* **1** ⒸⓊ a set of ropes and wheels for moving heavy weights, sails, etc. 고패〔도르래〕 장치. **2** Ⓤ all the things needed for a play or task; gear. 연장; 도구. ¶ *fishing* ~ 낚시 도구 / *writing* ~ 필기구. **3** Ⓒ 《football》 the act of tackling. 태클. ¶ *a strong* 〔*hard*〕 ~ 심한 태클.

— *vt.* (P6) **1** try to solve (a problem); try to do (a piece of work, etc.). (일·문제 따위)에 달라붙다; 달려들다. ¶ *Everyone has his own problems to* ~. 모두 해결해야 할 자신의 문제가 있다 / *new measures aimed at tackling unemployment* 실업 문제 해결을 위한 새 조치들. **2** ⓐ 《football》 seize and stop (an opponent ball-carrier). …에 태클하다. ⓑ to seize suddenly, esp. in order to stop. …을 붙잡다. ¶ *The robber tried to get away but the man ran and tackled him.* 도둑이 달아나려고 했으나 그 사람이 달려가 붙잡았다. **3** harness. …에 마구를 달다.

— *vi.* (P1) 《football》 seize and pull down or stop an opponent ball-carrier. 태클하다. [Teut.]

tack·y[1] [tǽki] *adj.* (**tack·i·er, tack·i·est**) feeling sticky when touched. 끈적끈적한. ¶ *The paint on the door is still* ~. 문의 페인트칠이 아직 끈적거린다. [*tack*]

tack·y[2] [tǽki] *adj.* (**tack·i·er, tack·i·est**) 《U.S. *colloq.*》 shabby; of poor quality. 초라한. ¶ *a small* ~ *house* 초라한 오두막. [G.]

tact [tækt] *n.* **1** Ⓤ ability to deal wisely with others, esp. in a difficult situation. 재치; 기지; 요령. **2** Ⓒ 《mus.》 a stroke in beating time. 박자; 택트. [L. *tango* touch]

tact·ful [tǽktfəl] *adj.* having or showing tact. 재치 있는; 약삭빠른.

tac·ti·cal [tǽktikəl] *adj.* **1** of or belonging to tactics. 전술의; 전술적인. ¶ *a* ~ *point* 전략상의 요점 / ~ *nuclear weapons* 전술 핵무기. **2** (of a person or his actions) skillful in making a plan. (사람이) 책략이〔술수가〕 능한. ● **tac·ti·cal·ly** [-i] *adv.* [Gk. *tassō* arrange]

tac·ti·cian [tæktíʃən] *n.* Ⓒ an expert in tactics. 전술가; 책략가.

tac·tics [tǽktiks] *n. pl.* **1** 《usu. used as *sing.*》 the art or science of arranging and using military and naval forces during a battle. 전술; 병법(cf. *strategy*). ¶ *An army commander must be skilled in* ~. 군사령관은 병법에 밝아야 한다. **2** 《used as *pl.*》 any skillful methods used to gain an end. 책략; 방책; 술책. ¶ *These* ~ *will help him.* 이러한 방책이 그에게 도움이 될 것이다.

tac·tile [tǽktil, -tail] *adj.* of or having the sense of touch; that can be felt by touch. 촉각의; 촉각이 있는; 만져서 알 수 있는. ¶ *a* ~ *organ* 촉각 기관. [→tact]

tact·less [tǽktlis] *adj.* not having or showing tact. 재치가〔요령이〕 없는.

tad·pole [tǽdpòul] *n.* Ⓒ a young frog when it first comes out of its egg. 올챙이. [*toad, poll*]

tael [teil] *n.* a former Chinese unit of money. 테일; 냥(兩)《중국의 옛 화폐 단위》. [Malay]

taf·fer·el [tǽfərəl, -rèl] *n.* =taffrail.

taf·fe·ta [tǽfitə] *n.* Ⓤ a kind of silk fabric. 태피터; 호박단(緞). [Pers.]

taff·rail [tǽfrèil] *n.* Ⓒ a rail around the ship's stern. 선미의 난간; 고물 난간. [→table; *-rail*]

taf·fy [tǽfi] *n.* ⓊⒸ (*pl.* **-fies**) 《U.S.》 a candy made of sugar, butter and nuts; toffee. 태피. [? F. *tafia*]

tag[1] [tæg] *n.* Ⓒ **1** ⓐ a piece of cardboard, paper, etc. attached to something to show what it is or where it is to be sent. (화물의) 꼬리표; 물표; 태그. ⓑ a card fixed on to something. 표; 표지. ¶ *A price* ~ *is one with the price marked on it.* 가격표는 그 물건의 값을 적은 것이다. **2** a metal point at the end of a string. 끈 끝의 쇠붙이. ¶ *a shoelace* ~. **3** a phrase or sentence often quoted. 판에 박은 인용어; 상투어구. ¶ *His writing is always full of Latin tags.* 그의 글에는 늘 라틴어 인용구투성이다.

— *v.* (**tagged, tag·ging**) *vt.* (P6) **1** fix or furnish with a tag. …에 꼬리표를 달다. ¶ *All his trunks are tagged with his name and address.* 그의 모든 트렁크에는 이름과 주소를 적은 꼬리표가 붙어 있다. **2** 《*colloq.*》 follow closely. …을 바짝 붙어다니다; 따라다니다.

— *vi.* (P1,2A,3) 《*colloq.*》 《*along, after*》 follow closely. 바짝 붙어다니다. ¶ *The child is always tagging after his mother.* 그 아이는 늘 어머니를 따라 다닌다. [E.]

tag[2] [tæg] *n.* Ⓤ a children's game in which one runs after and tries to touch another. 술래잡기. — *vt.* (P6) (**tagged, tag·ging**) touch or tap (someone) with the hand. (술래가) …을 붙잡다. [E.]

:tail [teil] *n.* Ⓒ **1** the movable part at the end of the body of an animal, bird, or fish. (짐승·새·물고기 등의) 꼬리. **2** something like a tail in its shape; a long braid of hair. 꼬리 모양의 것; 땋아 늘인 머리. ¶ *the* ~ *of a comet* 혜성의 꼬리 / *the* ~ *of a kite* 연꼬리. **3** the end or last part of anything; back or rear. 후부; 끄트머리; 말미. ¶ *the ~ of a procession* 행렬의 후미 / *the ~ of one's eye* 눈초리 / *the ~ of a storm* 폭풍의 흔적〔자취〕/ *The boys fastened their sleds to the ~ of the cart.* 아이들은 자기들 썰매를 수레 뒤에다 매었다. 4 《*pl.*》 the reverse side of a coin. (동전 던지기에서) 주화의 뒷면(opp. heads). 5 《*pl.*》 《*colloq.*》 a tail coat 연미복.

keep tails up, be in good spirits. 원기 왕성하다.

turn tail, run away from danger, difficulty, trouble, etc. 달아나다; 꽁무니를 빼다.

twist someone's tail, cause someone to feel pain; torment. …을 괴롭히다.

with the 〔*one's*〕 ***tail between the*** 〔*one's*〕 ***legs,*** utterly defeated and frightened. 기가 죽어; 겁에 질려; 주눅 들어.

— *vt.* (P6) 1 provide (a coat, etc.) with a tail. …에 꼬리를 달다. 2 connect (something) at the end. …을 (뒤에) 붙이다. 3 remove a tail from (something). …의 꼬리를 자르다. ¶ *~ a lamb* 새끼양의 꼬리를 자르다. 4 《*colloq.*》 follow (someone) closely and secretly. …을 미행하다. ¶ *~ a thief* 도둑을 미행하다 / *The police have been tailing me — they know I am here.* 경찰이 내 뒤를 밟아 왔다. 그들은 내가 여기 있는 것을 안다. — *vi.* (P1,2A,3) 1 《*along, behind*》 follow as a tail; form a tail. 꼬리처럼 되다; 꼬리를 이루다. 2 grow less. 점점 작아지다〔희미해지다〕. 3 《*colloq.*》 《*after*》 follow closely behind. 뒤따라가다. [E.]

tail away 〔***off***〕, fall away or behind in a scattered line; gradually decrease; die away. 뒤져서 흩어진 줄이 되다; 점점 작아〔적어〕지다; 소멸되다. ¶ *Her voice tailed off.* 그녀의 목소리가 점점 작아졌다.

tail on, join on as an addition. 부가하다; 덧붙이다.

T

tail·coat [ˊ-ˋ] *n.* a man's coat with long tails in the back, usu. worn on formal occasions. 연미복.

tail·less [téillis] *adj.* without a tail. 꼬리가 없는.

tail·light [téillàit] *n.* Ⓒ a light at the back end of a vehicle. (차의) 미등(尾燈).

:tai·lor [téilər] *n.* Ⓒ a person whose business is to make or repair clothes. 재봉사 (cf. *dressmaker*). ¶ *sit ~ fashion* 책상 다리를 하고 앉다 / *The ~ makes the man.* 옷이 날개. — *vt., vi.* (P6,13;1) 1 make (clothes) by a tailor's work. (양복을) 짓다. ¶ *The suit was well tailored.* 옷이 잘 만들어졌다. 2 《chiefly in *pp.*》 make clothes for. …의 옷을 만들다. ¶ *He is well tailored.* 그의 옷은 잘 만들어졌다. 3 make, alter or adapt for a particular purpose. (어떤 목적에) 맞게 만들다〔고치다〕. ¶ *a study program tailored to the needs of foreign students* 외국인 학생들의 필요에 알맞도록 짜여진 학습계획 / *Her novel is tailored to popular tastes.* 그녀의 소설은 대중의 기호에 맞도록 쓰여져 있다. [→tally]

tai·lored [téilərd] *adj.* (usu. of a woman's dress) simple and well-fitting. (흔히 여성 옷이) 몸에 꼭 맞는.

tai·lor-made [téilərméid] *adj.* 1 tailored. 몸에 꼭 맞는. 2 custom-made; made-to-order. 맞춤 양복의; 주문에 따라 만든.

tail·piece [téilpì:s] *n.* 1 a piece of anything forming its tail or end. 꼬리 부분의 부속물. 2 《print.》 a small ornamental drawing at the end of a chapter. 책의 장(章) 끝의 여백에 넣는 장식 커트(cf. *headpiece*). [→tail]

tail·race [téilrèis] *n.* the part of a millstream below the water-wheel. (물방아의) 배수로.

tail-skid [téilskìd] *n.* a runner at the rear of an airplane to keep the tail off the ground. (항공기 꼬리의) 활재(滑材).

tail·spin [téilspìn] *n.* 1 a circling, downward motion of an airplane. (항공기의) 나선식 강하. 2 《*fig.*》 a panic. 공황; 심한 불경기.

taint [teint] *n.* 1 Ⓒ a spot or stain. 더럼; 얼룩. 2 a trace of something bad, impure, or corrupt. (좋지 않은 것의) 기미; 흔적. ¶ *a ~ of insanity.* 광기(狂氣). 3 Ⓤ infection; corruption; moral degeneration. 감염; 부패; 타락. — *vt.* (P6) give a taint to (something); spoil. …을 더럽히다; 오염시키다; 부패시키다. ¶ *Smog has tainted the air.* 스모그가 공기를 오염시켰다. — *vi.* (P1) become tainted; decay. 더러워지다; 부패하다. [L. *tingo* dye]

:take [teik] *v.* (**took, tak·en**) *vt.* 1 (P6,7,13) grasp; hold; embrace. …을 (손에) 쥐다; 잡다; 껴안다. ¶ *She took me by the hand.* 그녀가 내 손을 잡았다 / *~ a card and read* 카드를 들고 읽다 / *~ someone's arm* 아무의 팔을 잡아주다; 부축하다 / *He took her in his arms.* 그는 그녀를 껴안았다. 2 (P6,7,13,19) get possession of (something); catch; seize; capture; catch by force. …을 손에 넣다; 붙잡다; 빼앗다. ¶ *~ the enemy's fort* 적진을 빼앗다 / *The police took him.* 경찰이 그를 붙잡았다 / *~ someone prisoner* 아무를 포로로 하다 / *~ fish* 고기를 잡다. 3 (P6) gain; obtain; win; earn. …을 얻다; 획득하다; 벌다. ¶ *~ a degree* 학위를 취득하다 / *~ first place* 1등을 차지하다 / *~ a high salary* 급료를 많이 받다 / *~ the first prize in a contest* 경연에서 1등상을 타다 / *~ 200 dollars a week,* 1주에 200불을 벌다. 4 (P6) rent; hire. …을 빌리다; 세내다. ¶ *~ a house at the seaside* 해변에 집 한 채를 세내다 / *~ a cottage for the summer* 여름 동안 시골 집을 빌리다. 5 (P6,7,13) ⓐ buy or receive (a newspaper, etc.) regularly by paying for it; subscribe to. …을 구독하다; (정기적으로) 구매하다. ¶ *She takes two pints of milk daily.* 그녀는 매일 2파인트의 우유를 받는다 / *~ a newspaper* 〔*magazine*〕 신문을〔잡지를〕 구독하다. ⓑ

get with payment of money; buy. …을 사다. ¶ *I'll ~ this hat.* 이 모자를 사겠소. **6** (P6,7,13) ⓐ receive or accept willingly. …을 받다; 받아들이다. ¶ *~ a present from someone* 아무에게서 선물을 받다 / *~ money* 〔*a bribe*〕 돈〔뇌물〕을 받다. ⓑ receive into body; eat, drink, or breathe in; have. …을 (체내에) 섭취하다; 먹다; 마시다; 흡수하다. ¶ *~ a meal* 식사를 하다 / *I don't ~ sugar in my coffee.* 나는 커피에 설탕은 넣지 않는다 / *~ one's medicine* 〔*a sleeping pill*〕 약을〔수면제를〕 먹다 / *The swimmer came to the shore and took a deep breath.* 수영자는 해변에 와서 심호흡을 했다. **7** (P6,7,13) remove; subtract; take out; steal; put an end to. …을 제거하다; 꺼내다; 가지고 가다; 훔치다; 죽이다. ¶ *~ 7 from 12,* 12에서 7을 빼다 / *Cancer took her husband.* 암이 그녀의 남편을 앗아갔다 / *~ a key from one's pocket* 주머니에서 열쇠를 꺼내다 / *He was taken from us in his youth.* 그는 젊어서 우리 곁을 떠났다 / *~ someone's money from a drawer* 서랍에서 아무의 돈을 꺼내가다. **8** (P6) catch; affect; suffer an attack of (a disease, etc.) (병)에 걸리다. ¶ *~ cold* 감기에 걸리다 / *be taken with a violent pain* 심한 통증이 오다 / *He was taken ill.* 그는 병이 났다. **9** (P6,13,21) receive (someone) into some relation; adopt. …을 맞아들이다; 채용하다. ¶ *~ a new member into a club* 클럽에 새 회원을 맞다 / *She decided to ~ him for* 〔*to be*〕 *her husband.* 그녀는 그를 남편으로 맞을 결심을 하였다. **10** (P6,13) make use of (something). …을 이용하다. ¶ *You should ~ every opportunity.* 모든 기회를 이용해야 한다. **11** (P6,7,13) ⓐ pick up out of a number; choose; select. …에서 골라 가지다; 선택하다. ¶ *You can ~ whatever you want.* 원하는 것은 무엇이든 가져라 / *He took a large one.* 그 중에서 큰 것을 골랐다 / *I'll ~ another one.* 다른 걸 고르겠소. ⓑ adopt (a road); follow. (길)을 가다; 취하다. ¶ *Which way shall I ~?* 어느 길로 갈까요 / *~ a short cut* 지름길을 택하다 / *~ the shortest way home* 가장 가까운 길로 집에 가다. **12** (P6,7,13) 《*to*》 lead; conduct (someone) to a place; go leading. …을 데리고 가다; 안내〔인도〕하다. ¶ *This road takes you to the park.* 이 길로 가면 공원에 닿는다 / *Take me with you.* 나를 데리고 가 주십시오 / *I'll ~ you home* 〔*there*〕. 집에〔거기에〕 데려가 주마 / *~ a dog out for a walk* 개를 산책에 데리고 나가다. **13** (P6,7,13,14) carry; go carrying. …을 가져 가다. ¶ *~ letters to the post office* 편지를 우체국에 가져 가다 / *She took him some flowers.* 그녀는 그에게 꽃을 좀 갖고 갔다 / *Take your umbrella with you.* 우산을 갖고 가거라. **14** (P6,14) require; need; spend. …을 요하다. 語法 종종 it을 주어로 씀. ¶ *The baggage takes much room.* 이 짐은 자리를 많이 차지한다 / *It took them many years to make this.* 이것을 만드는 데 그들은 여러 해를 소요했다 / *It will ~ me a long time to get the data.* 그 자료를 얻는 데 시간이 걸리겠다 / *It takes two men to move this.* 이것을 옮기는 데는 두 사람이 있어야 한다 / *Take your time.* 서두를 건 없다. **15** (P6) please; attract; charm; seize the interest of. (마음)을 끌다; 기쁘게 하다; 흥미를 끌다. ¶ *~ someone's fancy* 아무의 마음에 들다〔환심을 사다〕 / *She was taken with the painting on sight.* 그 그림을 보자 그녀는 마음이 끌렸다 / *~ someone's eye* 〔*attention*〕 아무의 시선을〔주의를〕 끌다. **16** (P6) travel by (a bus, train, etc.). …을 타고 가다. ¶ *~ a plane to Jeju* 비행기로 제주에 가다 / *~ a train* 〔*bus*〕 기차〔버스〕를 타다 / *~ one's car* 차를 타다. **17** (P6) undergo; endure; deal with; accept in a passive manner. …을 받아 들이다; 대처하다; 감수하다. ¶ *~ punishment* 처벌을 받다 / *~ an examination* 시험을 치르다 / *~ the blame* 비난을 받다 / *She took the bad news calmly.* 그녀는 그 흉보를 조용히 받아들였다 / *~ a dare* 도전에 응하다. **18** (P6,13) get or make by drawing, photographing, etc.; make a copy or likeness of. (초상)을 그리다; (사진)을 찍다; 베끼다. ¶ *She takes a good picture.* 그녀는 사진을 잘 찍는다 / *~ someone's fingerprints* 아무의 지문을 채취하다 / *~ a speech on* 〔*in*〕 *tape* 연설을 녹음하다. **19** (P6,13) have (something) in mind; feel; experience. …을 느끼다; 경험하다. ¶ *~ pride in one's work* 자기 일에 긍지를 느끼다 / *~ pleasure in painting* 그림을 그리는 데서 즐거움을 찾다 / *She took no interest in him.* 그녀는 그에게 아무 관심도 없었다 / *He took a fancy to the stranger.* 그는 그 낯선 사람에게 호감을 느꼈다. **20** (P6) do; perform; execute. (어떤 동작)을 하다; 행하다; 취하다. ¶ *~ a leap* 뛰다; 도약하다 / *~ care* 주의를 하다 / *~ exercise* 운동하다 / *~ definite action* 확실한 행동을 취하다 / *~ no notice of a fact* 사실에 유의하지 않다 / *~* (*a*) *rest* 휴식하다. **21** (P6,7) write down; make a record of; put down. …을 적(어 두)다; 기록하다. ¶ *The students took notes on the lecture.* 학생들은 강의를 필기하였다 / *~ a conversation in writing* 〔*shorthand*〕 대화를 적다〔속기하다〕 / *~ an inventory* 재고 목록을 작성하다. **22** (P6) find out (something) by inquiry, measurement, etc.; make certain. …을 재다; 조사하다; 확인하다. ¶ *~ one's measure for a new dress* 새 옷을 맞추려고 치수를 재다 / *~ someone's temperature* 〔*pulse*〕 아무의 열〔맥박〕을 재다. **23** (P6,13,21) regard; consider; assume as a fact; understand. …라고 생각하다; 여기다; 이해하다. ¶ *~ something easy* …을 쉽게 생각하다 / *~ something ill* 〔*well*〕 …을 나쁘게〔좋게〕 보다 / *~ people as they are* 사람들을 있는 그대로 보다 / *How do you ~ his remarks?* 그의 말을 어떻게 생각하나 / *Do you ~ me?* 내 말 알겠느냐 / *~ life as a big adventure* 인생을 큰 모험으로 생각하다 / *~ a matter seri-*

T

ously 일을 심각하게 보다 / *I ~ him to be an honest man.* 나는 그가 성실하다고 본다 / *I ~ it* (*that*) *you'll accompany me.* 난 네가 같이 갈 줄 알았는데. **24** (P6,13) surprise or attack esp. suddenly; strike. …을 놀래다; 덮치다; 기습하다; 치다. ¶ *~ the enemy in the rear* 적의 배후를 치다 / *The blow took him on the nose.* 그 일격은 그의 코를 갈겼다. **25** (P6) enjoy; indulge in (a nap, etc.) (휴식 등)을 취하다; 즐기다. ¶ *~ one's ease* 쉬다 / *~ a holiday* 휴가를 얻다. **26** (P6,13) get from some source; borrow; quote. …에서 인용하다; 빌리다. ¶ *The word is taken from French.* 그건 프랑스어에서 온 말이다 / *~ a line from Milton* 밀턴에서 한 구절 인용하다.

— *vi.* **1** (P1) get possession; catch. 얻다; 획득하다. ¶ *~ as heir* 재산을 상속하다. **2** (P1) have effect; prove effective; act. (우두 따위가) 잘 되다; (약이) 듣다. ¶ *The vaccination took.* 예방접종이 잘 됐다. **3** (P1,2A) (of a plant) take root. (식물이) 뿌리 내리다. **4** (P1,2A) become popular; gain favor. 인기를 얻다; 호평받다. ¶ *That book took well.* 그 책은 평이 좋았다 / *The play did not ~.* 그 극은 인기가 없었다. **5** (P5) 《U.S. *colloq.*》 become ill or sick. (병에) 걸리다. ¶ *He took sick.* 그는 병에 걸렸다. **6** (P2A) be photographed in a specified way. (사진이) 찍히다. ¶ *She always takes well.* 그녀는 사진이 늘 잘 받는다. **7** (P2A,3) 《*from*》 take away; detract. 감(減)하다; 손상하다. ¶ *That foolish indiscretion took away from his public image.* 그 어리석은 무분별로 그의 사회적 이미지가 구겨졌다. **8** (P3) (of a part of a machine) become engaged; catch. (기계가) 걸리다; 물리다. **9** (P1) (of a fish) bite the hook. (물고기가 미끼를) 물다; 낚이다. ¶ *The fish don't seem to be taking today.* 오늘은 고기가 안 잡힐 모양이다.

take after, **a**) resemble; look like. …와 비슷하다; 닮다. ¶ *She takes after her mother.* 그녀는 어머니를 닮았다. **b**) run after; pursue. …을 뒤쫓다; 추적하다.

take back, **a**) regain possession. 되찾다. ¶ *Shopkeepers will not usually ~ back goods after they have been paid for.* 상인들은 흔히 한번 판 물건은 물러 주지 않으려 든다. **b**) withdraw. 철회하다. ¶ *If you do not ~ back what you said, I shall not speak to you again.* 네가 한 말을 철회하지 않는다면 너와 다시는 말을 하지 않겠다.

take down, **a**) write down; make a record of. …을 쓰다; 기록하다. ¶ *~ down every word that is said* 말한 것을 빠짐없이 적다. **b**) lower (someone) in power, pride, etc. …에게 망신을 주다; …의 기를 꺾다. ¶ *I'd like to ~ him down a little.* 그 자의 기를 좀 꺾어줄까 보다 / *~ someone down a peg* (*or two*) ⇨peg. **c**) remove from a high place; lower. …을 내리다; 낮추다. ¶ *~ down a flag* 기를 내리다. **d**) pull down (something) piece by piece. …을 허물다. ¶ *~ down a building* 건물을 헐다 / *~ down a tent* 천막을 걷다 / *~ down a machine* 기계를 해체하다. **e**) swallow (food) with difficulty. …을 억지로 삼키다.

take for, **a**) consider or believe to be; regard as. …이라고 생각하다. ¶ *I ~ it for a fact.* 그것은 사실이라고 생각한다 / *What do you ~ me for?* 너는 나를 어떻게 보나 / *~* (*it*) *for granted* (*that*...) ⇨grant. **b**) consider falsely to be ; mistake for. …로 잘못 알다. ¶ *They often ~ me for my brother.* 그들은 가끔 나를 내 동생으로 잘못 본다.

take in, **a**) receive into one's home for pay; admit. …을 받아들이다; 수용하다. ¶ *~ in boarders* 하숙인을 받다 / *~ in travelers* 길손을 받다. **b**) receive in one's hand; accept. …을 받다. ¶ *~ in money* 돈을 받다. **c**) receive (some work) to do at home. …을 내직으로 맡다〔받다〕. ¶ *She was poor and took in washing.* 그녀는 가난했기 때문에 내직으로 빨래를 했다. **d**) visit; attend. …을 방문하다. **e**) include. …을 포함〔포괄〕하다. **f**) receive or buy regularly; subscribe to. …을 정기 구독〔구매〕하다. ¶ *~ in a newspaper.* **g**) 《*colloq.*》 cheat; deceive. …을 속이다(cf. *take-in*). ¶ *I am not to be taken in by your lies.* 네 거짓말에 속을 내가 아니다. **h**) understand; comprehend. …을 이해〔납득〕하다. ¶ *~ in the situation* 사태를 파악하다. **i**) conduct (someone) into the dining room. …을 식당으로 안내하다. **j**) make narrower or smaller. …을 줄이다; 작게 하다. ¶ *~ in a dress at the waist* 드레스의 허리를 줄이다 / *~ in sail* 돛을 줄이다; 야심〔욕망〕을 억누르다.

take it out of, 《*colloq.*》 **a**) exhaust; tire (someone) greatly. …을 피곤하게 만들다; 지치게 하다. **b**) get one's revenge upon. …에게 분풀이하다.

take it that, assume or believe that. …라고 생각하다.

take off, **a**) remove (clothes) from the body; draw or pull off. (옷)을 벗다; 벗기다; 떼다. ¶ *~ off one's coat* 〔*hat, shoes*〕 코트〔모자, 구두〕를 벗다. **b**) remove; unfasten. …을 제거하다; 벗기다; 풀다. ¶ *~ one's hat off the hook* 모자걸이에서 모자를 벗기다 / *~ the cover off a box* 상자 뚜껑을 벗기다 / *Take your hands off me.* 내 몸에서 손을 떼라 / *What a load you have taken off my shoulders!* 내 어깨의 짐을 덜어주었구나. **c**) lead or conduct away. 데리고〔끌고〕 가다; 연행하다. ¶ *Take the prisoner off to jail.* 저 죄수를 감옥에 처넣어라. **d**) remove from a post, office, etc.; withdraw. (직위 등)에서 물러나게 하다; 철수시키다. ¶ *Take the guard off the place.* 보초를 그만 세워도 좋다. **e**) draw off (an amount); subtract. (양)을 줄이다; 빼다. ¶ *~ 10 percent off the price* 값을 10퍼센트 할인하다 / *~ off weight* 체중을 줄이다. **f**) get or have as time of rest. (휴식으로서) 일

을 쉬다. ¶ ~ *an hour off from work* 일을 한 시간 쉬다 / ~ *a day off every week* 매주 하루를 쉬다 / *Take a few days off.* 며칠 쉬어라. **g**) rise from the ground or water. 이륙〔이수〕하다(cf. *take-off*). ¶ *Three airplanes took off at the same time.* 비행기 세 대가 동시에 이륙했다. **h**) 《*colloq.*》 go away; depart 가버리다; 떠나가다. ¶ ~ *off for a city* 도시로 떠나다 / ~ *off by plane* 비행기로 가버리다. **i**) give a funny imitation of; mimic. 흉내내다 (cf. *take-off*).

take on, **a**) take on board. …을 싣다; 태우다. ¶ *A boat takes on water and food supplies.* 배에 물과 식료품을 싣는다 / ~ *on passengers* 승객을 태우다. **b**) employ; hire; engage. …을 고용하다. ¶ ~ *on workers* 노동자를 고용하다. **c**) accept a fight or contest with. (경기 따위에서) …와 대전〔대결〕하다. ¶ ~ *someone on at tennis* 아무와 테니스 대전을 하다. **d**) accept (a work, duty) on oneself; undertake. (일 따위)를 떠맡다. ¶ ~ *on extra work* 여분의 일을 맡다 / ~ *on the responsibility* 책임을 떠맡다. **e**) show (an appearance or character); put on; acquire. (외관·성질 따위)를 띠다; 지니다; 시늉을 하다. ¶ *His face took on a worried expression.* 그의 얼굴은 걱정스러운 표정이었다 / ~ *on the appearance of honesty* 정직한 체하다. **f**) 《*colloq.*》 show great emotion. 흥분하다. ¶ *Keep calm, don't* ~ *on so.* 조용히 해. 그렇게 열낼 건 없어.

take out, **a**) remove. …을 꺼내다. **b**) 《*colloq.*》 accompany; escort. …와 같이 가다; 안내하다. ¶ *He keeps asking if he can* ~ *me out.* 그는 자꾸 나와 같이 갈 수 있겠느냐고 묻는다. **c**) obtain (a license, etc.). (면허 등)을 얻다. ¶ ~ *out a driving license* 운전 면허를 따다.

take over, **a**) take the place of another in doing (work or duty); take control of (by force); succeed to. …을 인계받다; 접수하다; 점거하다. ¶ ~ *over the business (from one's father)* (부친에게서) 사업을 인계받다 / *The rebel army took over the whole country.* 반란군이 온 나라를 점거해 버렸다. **b**) carry across. (건너편으로) 운반해 가다. ¶ *The boat will* ~ *you over.* 이 배가 너를 건네줄 것이다.

take to, **a**) fall into the habit of. …의 습관이 붙다; 습관에 빠지다. ¶ ~ *to drink* 술 먹는 버릇이 들다. **b**) become fond of; begin to like. …을 좋아하게 되다. ¶ *They took to each other at once.* 그들은 곧 서로 좋아하게 됐다 / *I'm not sure if he'll* ~ *to the idea.* 그 생각을 그가 좋아할지는 모르겠다 / *He took to this country life.* 그는 이 시골 생활이 마음에 들었다 / ~ *kindly to* …을 좋아하다. **c**) go to for hiding, rest, etc. (숨거나 쉬는 데)에 가다. ¶ *The cat took to the woods and became wild.* 그 고양이는 숲에 들어가더니 사나워졌다 / *Father's ill, so he has taken to his bed.* 아버지는 편찮으셔서 잠자리에 드셨다 / *The criminals took to the hills.* 범인들은 산으로 달아났다. **d**) adopt (some measure); resort to. …에 의지하다; 호소하다. ¶ ~ *to flight* = ~ *to one's heels* 도망치다.

take to pieces, separate into parts. …을 분해〔해체〕하다. ¶ *He took the clock to pieces.* 그는 시계를 분해했다.

take up, **a**) 《*arch.*》 lift; raise; pick up. …을 집어들다; 올리다; 태우다. ¶ ~ *up a book* 〔*pen*〕 책〔펜〕을 집어들다 / *The lift will* ~ *you up to any floor.* 이 승강기를 타면 어느 층이든 갈 수 있다. **b**) suck up (liquid); absorb. …을 흡수하다; 빨아 올리다. ¶ *The blotting-paper takes up ink.* 압지는 잉크를 빨아들인다. **c**) turn one's attention to; attend to; deal with. …에 주의를 돌리다; …을 다루다. ¶ *No one took up my suggestion.* 아무도 내 제안에 관심이 없었다 / *I'll* ~ *this matter up with my lawyers.* 이 문제는 변호사들과 상의해 보겠다. **d**) begin again; return to and continue. (끊겼던 얘기 등)을 시작하다. ¶ ~ *up one's story* 하던 얘기를 다시 계속하다 / ~ *up the thread of the conversation* 대화의 실마리를 풀다. **e**) arrest. …을 체포〔연행〕하다. ¶ ~ *up someone for inquiry* 심문하려고 아무를 연행하다. **f**) fill (a place or time); occupy. (자리 등)을 차지하다. ¶ *The desk takes up a lot of room.* 책상이 자리를 많이 차지한다 / *I will not* ~ *up much of your time.* 내가 많은 시간을 빼앗지는 않겠다. **g**) make shorter. …을 줄이다. ¶ ~ *up a dress* 〔*the hem*〕 드레스〔가두리〕를 줄이다.

take up with, 《*colloq.*》 become friendly with; associate with. …와 친해지다; 사귀다.

— *n.* Ⓒ **1** the quantity of fish. 어획량. ¶ *a large* ~ *of fish* 많은 어획량. **2** the act or process of taking. 취득; 거두어들임. **3** 《U.S.》 an amount taken or received in payment. 매상고; 이득. ¶ *The farmer made a large* ~. 농부는 추수를 많이 했다 / *carry away one's* ~ 자기 몫을 가져가다. **4** a process of making a photograph or scene in a motion picture; a portion of a scene photographed. (영화에서 연속된) 한 신〔장면〕의 촬영; 촬영한 그 장면〔신〕. [E.]

take-home pay 〔**wages**〕 [téikhòum pèi〔wèidʒiz〕] *n.* 《*colloq.*》 wages or salary remaining after taxes, insurance fees, etc. have been deducted. (세금 등을 공제한) 실제 급료.

take-in [téikìn] *n.* Ⓒ 《*colloq.*》 cheating; trickery. 협잡; 사기.

:tak·en [téikən] *v.* pp. of **take.**

take-off [téikɔ̀(:)f, -àf] *n.* Ⓒ **1** 《*colloq.*》 an amusing imitation; a caricature. (익살맞은) 흉내; 풍자 만화; 캐리커처. ¶ *a funny* ~ *of leading politicians* 거물 정치인들의 익살스러운 풍자 만화. **2** the place at which the feet leave the ground in jumping; the place where an airplane leaves the ground. 도약 지점; 이륙 지점. **3** the act or process of taking off. 도약; 이륙.

tak·er [téikər] *n.* a person or thing that takes; a person who accepts a bet. 잡는 사람〔물건〕; 포획자; 내기에 응하는 사람.

take-up [téikʌ̀p] *n.* an instrument for tightening a band in a machine. (기계의) 죄는 기구.

tak·ing [téikiŋ] *adj.* **1** attractive; pleasing. 매력〔애교〕 있는. ¶ *a ~ manner* 애교〔매력〕 있는 태도. **2** infectious. 전염하는. ¶ *a ~ disease* 전염성 질병. — *n.* Ⓒ **1** something taken. 포획물. **2** 《*pl.*》 earnings; receipts. 소득; 매상고. **3** 《*colloq.*》 perplexity; a state of agitation. 당혹; 동요; 흥분; 번민. ¶ *in a great ~* 몹시 고민하여 / *She was in a terrible ~.* 그녀는 심한 번민에 빠져 있었다.

talc [tælk] *n.* Ⓤ a soft, smooth mineral, used to make face powder, etc. 활석(滑石); 탤크. [↓]

tal·cum [tǽlkəm] *n.* Ⓤ **1** =talc. **2** powder for the body and face made from talc; talcum powder. (화장용(化粧用)) 탤컴 파우더. [Arab.]

:tale [teil] *n.* Ⓒ **1** a story. 이야기. ¶ *a fairy ~* 옛날 이야기 / *tell one's ~* 자기 일신상의 이야기를 하다 / *His ~ is told.* 그는 이제 글렀다《운이 다했다》. **2** 《*pl.*》 a piece of gossip or scandal; a falsehood; a lie. (남의) 소문 이야기; 고자질; 험담; 낭설; 거짓말. ¶ *old wives' tales* (노파들의) 실없는〔허튼〕 이야기〔소리〕 / *if all tales be true* 그 모든 낭설이 사실이라면. [E.]

tell its own tale, explain itself. 자명한 일이다; 설명이 필요 없을 정도로 명백하다.

tell tales **(*out of school*),** tell someone else's secrets; gossip. 고자질하다.

tale·bear·er [téilbὲərər] *n.* Ⓒ a person who gossips or tells secrets. 고자질하는 사람; 밀고자.

T

·tal·ent [tǽlənt] *n.* **1** ⒸⓊ ability to do something well. 재주; 재능; 기량. ¶ *a man of ~* 재사(才士) / *He has a ~ for writing.* 글재주가 있다 / *develop one's talents* 재능을 기르다 / *She has a ~ for music.* 음악에 재능이 있다. **2** ⓐ《*collectively*》 people who have talent. 재주 있는 사람들; 인재. ¶ *all the ~ of the country* 한 나라의 인재들 / *look out for local ~* 지방의 인재를 찾다. ⓑ a talented person. 재능 있는 사람; 예능인; 탤런트. ¶ *younger talents* 재능 있는 젊은이들 / *one of Hollywood's most luminous talents* 할리우드의 가장 빛나는 탤런트의 한 사람. [Gk. *talanton*]

hide one's talents in a napkin, allow one's gifts and abilities to lie idle. (자기의) 재능을 썩이다.

tal·ent·ed [tǽləntid] *adj.* having talent; gifted. 재능 있는; 유능한.

tal·ent·less [tǽləntlis] *adj.* without talent. 재주가 없는; 무능한.

tale·tell·er [téiltèlər] *n.* Ⓒ a storyteller; a talebearer. 이야기꾼; 고자쟁이. [*tale*]

tal·is·man [tǽlismən, -liz-] *n.* Ⓒ (*pl.* **-mans**) a stone, ring, etc. engraved with figures, supposed to have magic power and to bring good luck; a charm. 호부(護符); 부적. [Gk. *teleo* consecrate]

:talk [tɔːk] *vi.* **1** (P1,2,3) express ideas by spoken words; communicate. 말하다; 지껄이다; 이야기하다. ¶ *~ sensible* 〔*big, tall*〕 분별있는 말을 하다〔허풍을 떨다〕 / *~ by signs* 몸짓으로 말하다 / *Her baby can't ~ yet.* 그녀의 갓난아기는 아직 말을 못한다 / *~ during* 〔*in one's*〕 *sleep* 잠꼬대하다 / *He talks too much.* 그는 말이 너무 많다〔수다스럽다〕. **2** (P1,3) have a conversation; consult; speak together. 대화〔이야기〕를 나누다; 의논하다; 상담하다. ¶ *What are you talking about?* 자네 무슨 이야기를 하고 있는가 / *Have you talked together yet?* 벌써 상의를 했느냐 / *He wants someone to ~ to.* 그는 의논할 상대를 원하고 있다 / *My father and I talked in detail on* 〔*over*〕 *the matter.* 아버지와 나는 그 일에 관해 상세히 의논했다 / *I have been talking with* 〔*to*〕 *someone.* 아무와 이야기를 나누고 있던 중이다. **3** (P1) chatter; gossip; spread rumor. 수다떨다; 남의 이야기를〔험담을〕 하다; 소문을 퍼뜨리다. ¶ *~ behind one's back.* 뒤에서 남의 말을 하다 / *People will ~.* 사람들의 입을 막을 수는 없다; 물의를 일으킬 것이다 / *I don't want to be talked about.* 남의 입에 오르내리는 게 싫다. **4** (P1) make sounds that suggest speech. 지껄이는 듯한 소리를 내다. ¶ *The kettle is talking on the stove.* 주전자가 난로 위에서 부글부글 소리를 내며 끓고 있다 / *The birds are talking loudly.* 새들이 짹짹거리고 있다. **5** (P1,2) spread ideas by other means than speech. (신호·몸짓 따위로) 뜻을 전하다; 알리다; 신호를 보내다. ¶ *~ by signs* 〔*looks*〕 손짓〔눈짓〕으로 말하다 / *People who cannot speak or hear can ~ by using signs.* 말하지도 듣지도 못하는 사람은 손짓으로 말할 수 있다.

— *vt.* **1** (P6,7) express (something) in speech; discuss. …을 말하다; 의논〔상의〕하다. ¶ *~ nonsense* 바보같은 소리를 하다 / *~ business* 장사 얘기를 하다. **2** use (a certain language) in speaking. (외국어 따위)를 말하다. ¶ *~ French* 프랑스어를 하다 / *Do you ~ Chinese?* 중국어를 할 줄 아느냐. **3** (P7,13,18) 《*into, out of*》 bring (someone) into a certain state or condition by talking; persuade. 이야기해서 …에게 —시키다; 설득하다. ¶ *~ oneself hoarse* 너무 지껄여 목이 쉬다 / *~ a child to sleep* 이야길 해주어 아기를 재우다 / *~ one's head off* = *~ someone's leg off* 장광설을 늘어놓아 남을 진저리나게 하다 / *He talked me into telling the truth.* 그는 나를 설득하여 진실을 말하게 했다 / *She talked him out of the habit.* = *She talked him into giving up the habit.* 그녀는 그를 설득하여 그 버릇을 고치게〔버리게〕 했다.

talk someone around [《Brit.》 ***round***], persuade; cause to agree. …을 설득하다.

talk at, 《U.S.》 say something critical of

(someone) in his presence but to a third person; speak indirectly to. (상대방에게) 들으란 듯이 …에게 말하다; …에게 빗대어 말하다.
talk back, answer in an impolite manner. 말대꾸하다.
talk down, **a**) make (someone) silent by talking loudly and effectively. (큰 목소리·조리 있는 이야기 등으로) 아무를 꼼짝 못하게 하다. **b**) give (an aircraft) instructions for landing. (항공기의) 착륙을 유도하다.
talk down to, talk to (someone) in a rude manner as if he were inferior. (아무)에게 반말지거리하다; 무례한 말을 쓰다. ¶ *The manager always talks down to the clerks.* 지배인은 직원들에게 늘 반말지거리다.
talk of, **a**) take (something) as a topic of conversation; discuss. …을 화제로 삼다. ¶ *Talk of the devil, and he is sure to appear.* 호랑이도 제 말 하면 온다. **b**) express one's intention of (doing something); mention as a possibility. …을 할 의향〔생각〕이라고 말하다. ¶ *He is talking of going abroad.* 그는 해외에 나갈 생각이라고 말하고 있다.
talk on, **a**) ⇨*vi.* 2 **b**) give a lecture or speech about. …을 강의하다; 이야기 해주다. ¶ ~ *on English literature* 영문학을 강의하다.
talk out, **a**) talk until conversation is exhausted. 기탄 없이 다 이야기하다; 철저히 논하다. **b**) 《Brit.》 prevent the passage of (a bill) by prolonging the discussion. 토의를 지연시켜 (의안의) 통과를 방해하다.
talk over, **a**) persuade. …을 설득하다. **b**) discuss. …을 의논하다.
talk up, **a**) speak clearly and openly. 큰 소리로 똑똑히 말하다. **b**) praise. …을 칭찬하다. **c**) speak to (someone) to promote his interest. …을 흥미가 가도록 이야기하다.
— *n.* **1** UC the act of talking; conversation; idle chatter; spoken words. 이야기; 담화; 좌담. ¶ *big* ~ 호언 장담; 허풍 / *end in* ~ 말만으로 끝나다 / *have a heart-to-heart* ~ *with someone* 아무와 흉금을 털어놓고 이야기하다. **2** C an informal speech; an address. (약식의) 짧은 강연〔강화(講話)〕; 연설. ¶ *give a* ~ *to the students on a problem* 어떤 문제에 대하여 학생들에게 강연하다 / *give a* ~ *on art* 예술에 대해 얘기하다. **3** U rumor; gossip; the subject of gossip or conversation. 풍문; 소문; 화젯거리. ¶ *the* ~ *of the town* 마을의 화젯거리 / *He* 〔*His new work*〕 *is the* ~ *of the whole country.* 그는〔그의 새 작품은〕 온 나라의 화제다 / *There is a wide* ~ *about her scandal.* 그녀의 스캔들에 대해 여러가지 말들이 많다. **4** a meeting for discussion; a conference. 회담; 회의. ¶ *preliminary talks* 예비 회담. **5** U the way of talking. 말투; 어조. ¶ *a slick* 〔*halting*〕 ~ 매끄러운〔떠듬거리는〕 말씨. **6** idle, worthless talk. 실없는 말; 객담. ¶ *He is all* ~. 그는 말뿐인 사람이다 / *His threats are just* ~. *Don't worry.* 그의 협박은 그저 말뿐이다. 걱정할 것 없다. [*tale*]

talk·a·tive [tɔ́:kətiv] *adj.* fond of talking. 수다스러운(opp. taciturn).

talk·er [tɔ́:kər] *n.* C **1** a person who talks. 이야기하는 사람. ¶ *a good* ~ 화술이 좋은 사람; 이야기꾼. **2** a talkative person. 수다스러운 사람; 말뿐인 사람.

:talk·ie [tɔ́:ki] *n.* 《often *pl.*》 《*colloq.*》 **1** a talking picture. 토키; 발성영화(opp. silent film). **2** 《*the* ~*s*》 the sound-picture industry. 영화 산업.

talk·ing [tɔ́:kiŋ] *adj.* **1** that talks; talkative. 말을 하는; 수다스러운. **2** expressive. 표정이 있는. ¶ ~ *eyes* (입처럼) 말하는 눈. — *n.* U discussion; conversation. 담화; 수다.

talk·ing-to [tɔ́:kiŋtù:] *n.* C (**-tos**) 《*colloq.*》 a severe rebuke. 잔소리; 꾸지람. ¶ *I'll give him a good* ~. 좀 따끔하게 야단쳐야겠다.

:tall [tɔ:l] *adj.* **1** high; higher than the average. 키가 큰; 높은(opp. short). ¶ *a* ~ *man* 키 큰 사람 / *How* ~ *are you?* 키가 얼마나 되느냐 / *a* ~ *building* 〔*tree, chimney*〕 높은 건물〔나무, 굴뚝〕. **2** of a certain height. 키〔높이〕가 …인. ¶ *The man is 5 feet 8 inches* ~. 저 사람은 키가 5피트 8인치다. 參考 지금은 대개 tall 대신 high를 씀. **3** 《*colloq.*》 impossible or almost impossible to believe; excessive. 터무니 없는; 과장된. ¶ *a* ~ *price* 터무니 없는 값 / *a* ~ *order* 되지도 않을 얘기 / *a* ~ *tale* 허풍; 흰소리.
— *adv.* 《*sl.*》 boastfully. 터무니없이; 과장해서. ¶ *talk* ~ 허풍 떨다 / *walk* ~ 으스대다; 기고 만장하다. [E. =swift]

tal·low [tǽlou] *n.* U the fat from animals, such as sheep, cows, etc. used to make candles and soap. 수지(獸脂). — *adj.* made of tallow. 수지로 만든. ¶ *a* ~ *candle* 수지 양초. [E.]

tal·low-faced [tǽloufèist] *adj.* having a pale, unhealthy color in the face. 창백한 안색의.

tal·ly [tǽli] *n.* C (*pl.* **-lies**) **1** a stick on which scores are recorded to show the amount of a payment. 부절(符節); 부신(符信). **2** anything used as a record for an account. 계산서. **3** a cut mark made on a tally. 부신에 새긴 눈금; 계인(契印). **4** an account; the score. 계산; 득점. ¶ *a* ~ *of a game* 경기의 득점. **5** a mark made to register a certain number of items. 계수 표시.

〈tally 5〉

— *vt.* (P6) **1** mark (a score) on a tally; record; count up. (부신에) …을 새기다; 기록하다. **2** make (two things) agree or correspond. …을 부합〔일치〕시키다.
— *vi.* (P1,3) 《*with*》 agree; correspond. 부합〔일치〕되다. ¶ *His statement does not* ~ *with the facts.* 그의 말은 사실과는 다르다. [L.

T

talea rod]

tal·ly-ho [tæ̀lihóu] *n.* (*pl.* **-hos**) **1** a hunter's cry to his hounds. 쉿쉿《사냥개를 부추기는 소리》. **2** 《U.S.》 a carriage drawn by four horses. 말 네 필이 끄는 마차. [F.]

tal·ly-sheet [tǽliʃìːt] *n.* a sheet on which a record or score is kept. (계산·득점) 기입표. [→tally]

Tal·mud [tɑ́ːlmud, tǽl-] *n.* the whole body of Jewish law. 탈무드《유대교 율법서》. [Heb. =instruction]

tal·on [tǽlən] *n.* Ⓒ 《usu. *pl.*》 a claw of a bird such as eagle or an hawk. (독수리 따위의 맹금의) 발톱. [L. *talus* ankle]

tam·a·ble [téiməbəl] *adj.* that can be tamed. 길들일 수 있는. [E.]

tam·a·risk [tǽmərisk] *n.* Ⓒ 《bot.》 a small evergreen tree with slender, feathery branches. 위성류(渭城柳). [L.]

tam·bou·rine [tæ̀mbəríːn] *n.* Ⓒ a small drum with several pairs of metal disks used in some dances. 탬버린. [→tabor]

***tame** [teim] *adj.* **1** (of animal) changed from a wild state to a harmless and gentle state; gentle; harmless. 길들여진; 길이 든; 유순한. ¶ *a ~ bird* 길든 새 / *~ cats* 집고양이 / *The birds are so ~ that they will eat from our hands.* 새들은 길이 들어 우리 손의 것도 받아 먹는다. **2** without spirit; dull; not interesting. 무기력한; 지루한; 재미가 없는. ¶ *a ~ debate* 생기 없는 토론 / *a ~ fight* 무기력한 싸움 / *Life in the country was too tame for him.* 시골 생활이 그는 너무나 따분했다.

— *vt.* (P6) **1** make (an animal) gentle and harmless; domesticate. (짐승)을 길들이다. ¶ *~ a bird* [*an animal*] / *The lion was tamed for circus.* 사자는 서커스를 하도록 길들어져 있었다. **2** make gentle or obedient; make softer. …을 유순하게 만들다; 복종시키다; 누이다. ¶ *~ someone's spirit* 아무의 기를 죽이다.

— *vi.* (P1) become gentle and harmless. (짐승이) 길들다. [E.]

tame·a·ble [téiməbəl] *adj.* =tamable.

tame·ly [téimli] *adv.* in a tame manner. 길이 들어; 순하게.

tame·ness [téimnis] *n.* Ⓤ the state or quality of being tame. 길듦; 유순.

tam-o'-shan·ter [tǽməʃæ̀ntər, ⌐-⌐-] *n.* Ⓒ a Scotch cap with a loose, round top like a beret. 베레형(型)의 모자. 參考 그냥 tam이라고도 함. [Person] 〈tam-o'-shanter〉

tamp [tæmp] *vt.* (P6,7) **1** pack down (the earth) by a series of blows or taps. (땅)을 다져 굳히다. **2** fill (a hole) with mud, etc. so that it may not explode outwards. (남폿구멍)을 진흙 등으로 틀어 막다. [→stamp]

tam·per [tǽmpər] *vi.* (P3) 《*with*》 **1** change dishonestly or harmfully; change in a wrong way so as to cause damage. 부정하게[함부로] 변경을 가하다[고치다, 손질하다]; (망가뜨리려고) 만지작거리다. ¶ *~ with a written paper* 서류의 글자를 함부로 고치다 / *~ with a machine* 기계를 만지작거려 못쓰게 만들다. **2** bribe. 뇌물을 주다. ¶ *~ with a witness* 증인에게 뇌물을 주다. [→temper]

***tan** [tæn] *v.* (**tanned, tan·ning**) *vt.* (P6) **1** turn (the skin of an animal) into leather with a special liquid. (가죽)을 무두질하다. **2** (of the sun) make (a person's skin) brown. (피부)를 볕에 태우다. ¶ *a complexion tanned by the sun* 볕에 탄 피부의 빛깔 / *He is deeply tanned by* [*with*] *the sun.* 그는 볕에 아주 많이 그을렸다. **3** 《*sl.*》 beat; punish with a stick. …을 매질하다. ¶ *~ someone's hide* 아무를 후려갈기다. — *vi.* (P1) **1** be made into leather. (무두질한) 부드러운 가죽이 되다. **2** become brown by the sun. 살갗이 볕에 타다. — *n.* Ⓤ a yellowish-brown color; a brown color given to a person's skin by the sun. 황갈색; 볕에 탄 살빛. — *adj.* yellowish-brown. 황갈색의. [F.]

tan·dem [tǽndəm] *adv.* (of two horses) one behind another. (말 두 필을) 앞뒤 한 줄로 매고. ¶ *drive horses ~* 마차에 말 두 필을 앞뒤 한 줄로 매고 달리다. — *n.* Ⓒ **1** a pair of horses which pull a carriage arranged one behind the other; such a carriage. 앞뒤 한 줄로 맨 두 필의 말; 그 마차. **2** a bicycle with two seats, one behind the other. 2인승 자전거. — *adj.* arranged tandem. 말 두 필을 세로로 맨; 2인승의. [L. =at length]

tang[1] [tæŋ] *n.* Ⓒ **1** the part of a knife, etc. that is connected with the handle. (칼 따위의) 슴베. **2** a strong taste; a sharp smell. 강하게 톡 쏘는 맛[냄새]. [N. *tange* point]

tang[2] [tæŋ] *n.* Ⓒ a sharp ringing sound. 강하게[쨍하고] 울리는 소리. [Imit.]

tang[3] [tæŋ] *n.* 《bot.》 a tangle. 다시마류(類). [Icel.]

tan·gent [tǽndʒənt] *adj.* touching; 《geom.》 touching a curve at one point only. 접하는; 접선(接線)의. ¶ *a straight line ~ to a curve* 곡선에 접하는 직선. — *n.* Ⓒ 《geom.》 a tangent line. 접선. [L. *tango* touch]

fly* [*go*] *off at a* [*on*] *tangent, change suddenly from one line of thought or action to another. (이야기·생각 따위가) 갑자기 옆길로 새다.

tan·ge·rine [tæ̀ndʒəríːn] *n.* Ⓒ a small orange with a thick, loose skin. 탄제린《귤의 일종》. [*Tangier Place*]

tan·gi·bil·i·ty [tæ̀ndʒəbíləti] *n.* Ⓤ the

quality or state that can be touched; clearness. 만질 수 있음; 명백. [↓]

tan·gi·ble [tǽndʒəbəl] *adj.* **1** touchable. 만질 수 있는; 만져서 알 수 있는. **2** real; clear; actual. 명백한; 현실적〔실체적〕인. ¶ *a ~ ground of complaint* 불평할 만한 분명한 근거. —*n.* 《*pl.*》 material assets. 유형 재산. [→tangent]

tan·gle[1] [tǽŋgəl] *vt.* (P6) **1** twist (threads, etc.) in a confused mass. …을 엉키게〔얽히게〕 하다. ¶ *tangled threads* 얽힌 실. **2** 《*fig.*》 confuse; make (something) difficult to understand. …을 혼란시키다; 복잡하게 만들다. —*vi.* (P1) become tangled. 얽히〔엉키〕다; 혼란〔복잡〕해지다. —*n.* **1** Ⓒ a tangled mass. 엉킨 것; 엉킴; 얽힘. ¶ *a ~ of wool* 엉킨 양털 뭉치 하나 / *get one's hair in a ~* 머리가 엉클어지다. **2** 《*fig.*》 a confused state. 혼란; 혼잡; 분규. ¶ *the mideast ~* 중동 분쟁 / *traffic ~* 교통 혼잡 / *His affairs were in a ~.* 그의 일들은 혼란스럽게 뒤엉켜 있었다. [Scand.]

tan·gle[2] [tǽŋgəl] *n.* =tang[3].

tan·go [tǽŋgou] *n.* Ⓒ (*pl.* **-gos**) a slow dance for two persons originally from South America; music for this dance. 탱고춤; 그 곡. [Sp.]

***tank** [tæŋk] *n.* Ⓒ **1** a large metal container for holding a liquid or gas. (물·기름·가스 등의) 탱크. ¶ *a ~ ship* 탱커 / *a gasoline ~* 가솔린 탱크 / *an oil ~* 유조 탱크. **2** a heavy fighting motor-car carrying guns, used in battle. 전차; 탱크. **3** 《U.S.》 a pool or pond. 물 웅덩이; 연못. **4** (in India, Pakistan, etc.) an artificial reservoir for water. (인공) 저수지. —*vt.* (P6) put or store in a tank. …을 탱크에 넣다〔저장하다〕. [L. *stagnum* pond]

tank·ard [tǽŋkərd] *n.* Ⓒ a large cup with one handle used for drinking beer. 큰 맥주 조끼. [E.]

〈tankard〉

tank car [∠∠] *n.* a railway car with a tank for carrying liquids. 탱크차《액체·가스 등을 수송하는 화차》. [→tank]

tank·er [tǽŋkər] *n.* Ⓒ a ship with tanks for carrying oil. 유조선. [→tank]

tan·ner [tǽnər] *n.* Ⓒ 《Brit. *sl.*》 a person whose business is to make leather by tanning the skins of animals. 무두장이; 제혁업자. [*tan*]

tan·ner·y [tǽnəri] *n.* Ⓒ (*pl.* **-ner·ies**) a place where the skin of animals are tanned. 무두질 공장. [*tan*]

tan·nic [tǽnik] *adj.* of or found in tannic acid. 타닌의. [↑]

tannic acid [∠-∠-] *n.* a strong acid found in tea, etc. 타닌산.

tan·nin [tǽnin] *n.* =tannic acid.

tan·ta·lize [tǽntəlàiz] *vt.* trouble or tease (someone) by exciting hopes or fears which will not be realized. …을 애타게 만들다; 감질나게 하다. ¶ *A tantalizing smell came out of the restaurant as we passed.* 우리가 지나갈 때 식당에서는 우리를 감질나게 하는 냄새가 풍겨 나왔다. [Gk. *Tantalos*]

Tan·ta·lus [tǽntələs] *n.* 《Gk. myth.》 a Greek king, who was punished in the lower world with eternal hunger and thirst: he had to stand up to his chin in water which disappeared when he tried to drink, and under branches laden with fruit which constantly withdrew from his reach. 탄탈로스《그리스 신화에 나오는 왕. 제우스의 아들. 신들의 비밀을 인간에게 누설한 죄로 영원히 허기와 갈증을 느끼는 벌을 받았다고 함》. [↑]

tan·ta·mount [tǽntəmàunt] *adj.* equal to; of equal effect to. 같은; 동등한. ¶ *an invitation which is ~ to a command* 명령이나 다름없는 초대. [L. *tantus* so great, →amount]

tan·ta·ra [tǽntərə, tæntǽrə] *n.* flourish on trumpet. 딴따라따《나팔 소리》. [Imit.]

tan·tiv·y [tæntívi] *n.* a rapid gallop. 질주; 돌진. —*adv.* at such a pace. 질주하여; 쏜살같이. [↑]

tan·trum [tǽntrəm] *n.* Ⓒ 《*sl.*》 a sudden burst of ill temper. 불끈하기. ¶ *fly*〔*go*〕 *into a ~* 벌컥 성내다. [Imit.]

Ta·o·ism [tá:ouìzəm, dáu-] *n.* the religious doctrines of Lao-tse. 도교(道敎). [Chin.]

***tap**[1] [tæp] *v.* (**tapped, tap·ping**) *vt.* (P6,13) **1** strike or touch lightly. …을 가볍게 치다; 똑똑 두드리다. ¶ *~ someone on the shoulder* 아무의 어깨를 툭 치다 / *~ one's stick against the window* 지팡이로 창문을 톡톡 두드리다. **2** strike lightly again and again. …을 계속 가볍게 두드리다. ¶ *A woodpecker tapped a hole in the tree.* 딱따구리가 부리로 딱딱 나무를 쪼아 구멍을 냈다. **3** 《U.S.》 fix a piece of leather on to, in repairing. 구두창을 (갈아) 대다. ¶ *~ the heel of a shoe* 구두(의) 뒤축을 갈아대다. —*vi.* (P1,3) strike light blows. 가볍게 두드리다.

—*n.* Ⓒ **1** a light blow; the sound made by such a blow. 가볍게 두드림; 그 소리. ¶ *I heard a ~ at the door.* 문 두드리는 소리를 들었다. **2** 《U.S.》 a small piece of leather used to repair the sole or heel of a shoe. 구두의 창갈이용 가죽. **3** 《*pl., sing.* in use》 《U.S. mil.》 a signal on a bugle or drum to put out lights at night. 소등 나팔 또는 북. [Imit.]

tap[2] [tæp] *n.* Ⓒ **1** a pipe or hole of a cask through which liquor is drawn; a cock. (술통의) 주둥이; 꼭지; 마개. ¶ *turn on*〔*off*〕 *a ~* 꼭지를 틀어 열다〔잠그다〕. **2** a tool for cutting screw threads on an

T

inner surface. 암나사의 이를 내는 공구. **3** 《electr.》 a point where connection is made. 탭; 콘센트.

on tap, **a**) (of liquor) kept in a cask with a tap and ready to be drawn off. 마개가 있어 언제든지 따라낼 수 있는. **b**) 《*colloq.*》 ready for use. 준비가 되어.

— *vt.* (**tapped, tap·ping**) (P6,13) **1** fit a tap to; make a hole in to let out liquid. …에 꼭지를 달다; (흘러 나오도록) …에 구멍을 내다. ¶ *Sugar-maples are tapped when the sap begins to flow.* 수액이 흐르기 시작하면 사탕단풍에 칼 자국을 낸다. **2** listen secretly or illegally to (someone, telephone conversation, etc.) by making a connection to (the telephone, etc.). (전화기 따위에 전선을 접속하여) …을 도청하다. ¶ *The secret agent suspects that his phone is being tapped.* 첩보원은 그의 전화가 도청되고 있다는 낌새를 챘다. [E.]

tap-dance [tǽpdæ̀ns, -dɑ̀ːns] *n.* Ⓒ a dance in which the steps are accented by loud taps of the foot, toe, or heel. 탭댄스. — *vi.* (P1) dance a tap-dance. 탭댄스를 추다. [tap[1]]

·**tape** [teip] *n.* **1** ⓊⒸ a long, narrow strip of cloth, paper or metal used to tie something; material in the form of a narrow strip. 납작한 끈; 테이프. ¶ *a package tied with* ~ 테이프로 묶은 짐. **2** ⓊⒸ tape of paper on which telegraph messages are recorded. 전신 수신용 테이프. **3** Ⓒ a tape measure. 줄자. — *vt.* (P6) **1** fasten or bind with a tape. …을 테이프로 매다[묶다]. **2** taperecord. …을 녹음[녹화]하다. [E.]

breast the tape, reach the finishing line in a race. 테이프를 끊다; 경주에서 일등을 하다.

tape·line [téiplàin] *n.* =tape measure.

tape measure [⌐ ⌐-] *n.* a long narrow strip of cloth, paper, metal, etc. used for measuring length. 줄자.

·**ta·per** [téipər] *n.* Ⓒ a long wick coated with wax, used to light candles. 초 먹인 가는 심지《점화용》.

— *adj.* 《chiefly *poet.*》 becoming smaller toward one end. 끝이 가늘어지는. ¶ *She has* ~ *fingers.* 그녀는 손가락 끝이 갸름하다.

— *vi.* (P1,2A) **1** become gradually smaller toward one end. 끝이 가늘어지다; 뾰족해지다. ¶ *The sword tapers (off) to a point.* 칼은 끝이 뾰족하다. **2** slow down or decrease gradually. 점점 줄다. ¶ *Interest in the scandal seems to be tapering off.* 그 스캔들에 대한 호기심은 시들해지는 모양이다.

— *vt.* (P6,7) make (something) gradually smaller toward one end. …의 끝을 가늘게[뾰족하게] 하다. [L.]

·**tape recorder** [⌐ -⌐-] *n.* an electrical machine for recording and playing back sound on magnetic tape. 테이프 리코더; 녹음기. [*tape*]

tap·es·try [tǽpistri] *n.* ⓊⒸ (*pl.* **-tries**) cloth with pictures or designs woven in it, used to decorate a room. 태피스트리《색실로 무늬를 짠 실내 장식용 천》. [Gk. *tapēs*]

tape·worm [téipwə̀ːrm] *n.* Ⓒ a long, flat worm that lives in the bowels of man and other animals. 촌충. [*tape*]

tap·i·o·ca [tæ̀pióukə] *n.* Ⓤ a starchy food obtained from the root of the cassava plant and used for puddings, etc. 타피오카《식용 녹말》. [Brazil]

ta·pir [téipər] *n.* Ⓒ a large piglike animal with a long nose in Central and South America. 맥(貘). [Brazil]

tap·room [tǽprù(ː)m] *n.* Ⓒ 《Brit.》 a room in an inn where alcoholic drinks are served; a barroom. (여관 등의) 바. [tap[2]]

tap·root [tǽprùːt, -rùt] *n.* Ⓒ the main root of a plant. 주근(主根); 원뿌리. [tap[2]]

·**tar** [tɑːr] *n.* Ⓤ **1** a thick, black, oily substance obtained from wood, coal, etc. 타르. ¶ *coal* ~ 콜타르. **2** 《*sl.*》 a sailor. 선원; 뱃사람.

— *vt.* (**tarred, tar·ring**) (P6) cover (something) with tar. …에 타르칠을 하다. [E.]

be tarred with the same brush [***stick***], have the same faults as someone else. 같은 결점을 가지고 있다.

tar and feather, cover (someone) with heated tar and feathers as a punishment. 몸에 뜨거운 타르를 칠하고 새털을 씌우다《옛날 아메리카 흑인의 린치의 하나》.

tar·an·tel·la [tæ̀rəntélə] *n.* Ⓒ a dance of southern Italy in which two persons turn round quickly; music for this dance. 타란텔라《남이탈리아에서 추는 발랄한 춤》; 그 곡. [L.]

tar·ant·ism [tǽrəntìzəm] *n.* 《med.》 hysterical impulse to dance. 무도병(舞蹈病). [↑]

tar·di·ly [tɑ́ːrdili] *adv.* slowly; late. 느릿느릿; 천천히. [*tardy*]

tar·di·ness [tɑ́ːrdinis] *n.* Ⓤ the quality or condition of being tardy. 느림; 늦음; 지각.

tar·dy [tɑ́ːrdi] *adj.* (**-di·er, -di·est**) **1** slow in action. 느린; 더딘. **2** late; behind time. 늦은; 지각한. ¶ *make a* ~ *appearance* 지각하다 / *We apologize for our* ~ *response to your letter.* 귀하의 서신에 대한 회신이 늦어진 것을 사과드립니다. [L. *tardus* slow]

tare[1] [tɛər] *n.* **1** Ⓒ 《bot.》 noxious weeds among corn; vetch. 살갈퀴. **2** 《*pl.*》 《Bible》 a weed which is poisonous; evil influence. 독초; 해독. [E.]

tare[2] [tɛər] *n.* Ⓤ the weight of the container, wrapper, truck, etc. 포장[용기] 중량; 차체(車體) 중량. — *vt.* mark the tare of (a container, etc.). …의 용기[포장] 중량을 재다. [Arab.]

targe [tɑːrdʒ] *n.* 《*arch.*》 a small round

shield. 작고 둥근 방패. [N.]

·**tar·get** [tά:rgit] *n.* Ⓒ **1** a mark to shoot at. 과녁; 표적. ¶ *a ~ area* (폭격의) 표적 지구 / *The enemy's main ~ is our oil refinery.* 적의 주요 표적은 우리의 정유 시설이다. **2** a person, action, etc. that is the object of scorn, criticism, attack, etc. 대상. ¶ *The poor boy was made the ~ of their scorn.* 그 불쌍한 소년은 그들의 조롱의 대상이 되었다. [↑]

·**tar·iff** [tǽrif, -rəf] *n.* Ⓒ **1** a list or system of taxes on exports or imports; a tax of this kind, or its rate. 관세; 세율표; 관세율. ¶ *There is a very high ~ on jewelry.* 보석류에 대한 관세율은 매우 높다. **2** any list or scale of prices. (철도·여관 등의) 요금표. [Arab. =notification]

tar·iff-wall [tǽrifwɔ̀:l] *n.* a trade barrier in the form of a tariff. 관세 장벽.

tarn [tɑ:rn] *n.* Ⓒ a small lake in the mountains. 산 속의 작은 호수. [N.]

tar·nish [tά:rniʃ] *vt.* (P6) make (something) lose its shine or brightness; stain; 《*fig.*》 disgrace. …을 흐리게 만들다; 녹슬게 하다; (명예 등)을 더럽히다. ¶ *Salt will ~ silver.* 염분은 은을 변색시킨다 / *~ someone's name* 〔*honor*〕 아무의 이름을〔명예를〕 더럽히다. — *vi.* (P1) lose shine or brightness. 흐려지다; 녹슬다. ¶ *Brass will ~.* 놋쇠는 녹이 슨다. — *n.* **1** Ⓤ the loss of luster or brightness. 흐림; 녹슮; 변색. **2** ⒸⓊ a stain. 녹; 더럼; 오점. [F. *terne* dull]

ta·ro [tά:rou] *n.* Ⓒ (*pl.* **-ros**) 《bot.》 a tropical plant with a starchy root, grown for food; the root of this plant. 타로토란. [Tahitian]

tar·pau·lin [tɑ:rpɔ́:lin] *n.* **1** Ⓤ strong waterproof canvas. 타르 입힌 방수천. **2** Ⓒ a sailor's hat or coat made of this cloth. (선원의) 방수모; 방수 외투. **3** Ⓒ a sailor. 선원; 뱃사람. [*tar, pall*]

tar·ra·did·dle [tǽrədìdl] *n.* 《*colloq.*》 a lie. 거짓말. [*diddle*]

tar·ry[1] [tǽri] *vt., vi.* (P6;1,2A,3) 《*lit.*》 **1** remain; stay; wait. 머무르다; 체재하다; 기다리다. ¶ *He tarried in London longer than he originally intended.* 그는 처음의 의도보다 오래 런던에 머물렀다 / *He tarried* (*behind*) *for his wife.* 그는 (뒤에 남아) 아내를 기다렸다. **2** be late; be slow in acting or starting; delay. 늦어지다; 늦추다. ¶ *Why do you ~ so long?* 왜 그렇게 늦나. [E.]

tar·ry[2] [tά:ri] *adj.* (**-ri·er, -ri·est**) of or like tar; covered with tar. 타르의; 타르 같은; 타르를 바른. [*tar*]

tar·sal [tά:rsəl] *adj.* of or pertaining to the tarsus. 부골(跗骨)의. [↑]

tar·si [tά:rsai] *n.* pl. of **tarsus.**

tar·sus [tά:rsəs] *n.* (*pl.* **-si**) 《anat.》 the seven small bones of the ankle; a bird's shank. 부골(跗骨); (새의) 부척골(跗蹠骨). [Gk.]

tart[1] [tɑ:rt] *adj.* **1** sharp to the taste; sour. 신; 시큼한. ¶ *Some apples are ~.* 어떤 사과는 시다. **2** 《*fig.*》 (of the temper, etc.) sharp. 신랄한; 매서운. ¶ *Her reply was too ~ to be polite.* 그녀 대답은 공손하기는커녕 아주 매서웠다. ●**tart·ly** [-li] *adv.* **tart·ness** [-nis] *n.* [E.]

tart[2] [tɑ:rt] *n.* Ⓒ **1** 《Brit.》 a fruit pie. 과일 파이. **2** 《U.S.》 a pie filled with fruit or jam and open at the top. (속이 보이는) 작은 파이. [F.]

tart[3] [tɑ:rt] *n.* 《*sl.*》 a loose woman; a prostitute. 매춘부. [↑]

tar·tan [tά:rtn] *n.* **1** Ⓤ checked woolen cloth worn esp. in the Scotch Highlands. 타탄《격자 무늬의 모직물》. **2** Ⓒ any tartan pattern or design. 격자 무늬. — *adj.* of or like tartan. 타탄의; 격자 무늬의. [? Tartar]

Tar·tar [tά:rtər] *n.* **1** Ⓒ a member of a group of peoples including Truks, Cossacks, etc. (터키 등지의) 타타르 사람. **2** Ⓤ any of their languages. 타타르말. **3** Ⓒ 《usu. *t-*》 a savage or bad-tempered person. 사나운 사람.

catch a Tartar 〔***tartar***〕, attack a very strong person; have to deal with a very difficult person. 만만찮은〔골치 아픈〕 상대를 만나다.

— *adj.* of a Tartar or Tartans. 타타르 사람의. [Native]

tar·tar [tά:rtər] *n.* Ⓤ **1** an acid substance found on the inside of wine casks while the wine is being made. 주석(酒石)《포도주의 앙금》. ¶ *cream of ~* 주석영(酒石英). **2** a hard substance found on the teeth. 치석(齒石); 이똥. [F.]

tar·tar·ic [tɑ:rtǽrik, -tά:r-] *adj.* of tartar. 주석(酒石)의. ¶ *~ acid* 타르타르〔주석〕산.

Tar·ta·rus [tά:rtərəs] *n.* 《Gk. myth.》 a place of punishment below Hades; Hell. 타르타루스; 지옥; 나락(奈落).

Tar·ta·ry [tά:rtəri] *n.* a vast region of central and western Siberia and southern Russia. 타타르 지방.

:**task** [tæsk, tɑ:sk] *n.* Ⓒ a piece of work to be done. 일(거리); 직무; 과업. ¶ *home ~* 숙제 / *be at one's ~* 일하고 있다 / *set someone to a ~* 아무에게 일을 맡기다 / *daily tasks* 일과 / *take a ~ upon oneself* 일을 떠맡다 / *Her ~ is to set the table.* 상 차리는 것이 그녀의 일이다.

take 〔***call, bring***〕 ***someone to task for,*** blame someone for. …의 이유로 —을 야단치다; 꾸짖다. ¶ *The teacher took the boy to ~ for not studying hard.* 선생님은 공부를 열심히 하지 않는다고 소년을 야단쳤다.

— *vt.* (P6) **1** give a task to (someone). …에게 일거리를 주다. **2** burden; strain; force to work. …에게 무거운 짐을 지우다; 혹사하다. ¶ *The master tasked his slaves beyond their strength.* 주인은 노예들에게 그들이 감당 못 할 일을 시켰다 / *It tasks my powers.*

그것은 내게 힘겹다. [→tax]

task force [ˊ ˋ] *n.* 《U.S. mil.》 a military unit organized for a special purpose. 기동부대; 특수 임무 부대.

task·mas·ter [tǽskmæ̀stər, tɑ́:skmɑ̀:stər] *n.* Ⓒ a person who gives tasks to others. 감독; 작업반장.

tas·sel [tǽsəl] *n.* Ⓒ **1** a hanging ornament made of a tuft of threads or cords of silk, wool, etc.; 《bot.》 the hanging flower or head of certain plants. 술; 장식술; 총상 화서(總狀花序). **2** something resembling a tassel. 술 비슷한 것. ¶ *Indian corn has tassels.* 옥수수에는 (술 같은) 수염이 달려 있다. — *v.* (**-seled, -sel·ing,** 《Brit.》 **-selled, -sel·ling**) *vt.* (P6) **1** put tassels on (something). …에 (장식)술을 달다. **2** take tassels from (corn, etc.). (옥수수의) 수염을 따다. — *vi.* (P1,2A) grow tassels. (옥수수에) 수염이 나다; 술이 되다. [F.]

tas·seled, 《Brit.》 **-selled** [tǽsəld] *adj.* having a tassel or tassels. 술이 달린(있는).

:taste [teist] *vt.* (P6) **1** ⓐ test the flavor of (something) by the tongue. …을 맛보다. ¶ *Just ~ this and you'll see how nice it is.* 이거 맛 좀 보렴. 아주 맛있을 게다 / *I want to ~ that wine; it is so tempting.* 그 포도주 맛을 보고 싶군. 구미가 당긴다. ⓑ 《in *negative*》 eat or drink a little. 조금 먹다; 마시다. ¶ *I have tasted no food today.* 오늘은 아무것도 먹지 않았다 / *I've never tasted such delicious beef!* 이렇게 맛있는 고기는 먹어 본 적이 없다. **2** experience. …을 경험하다; 겪다. ¶ *~ great sorrow* 큰 슬픔을 맛보다 / *~ the sweets and bitters of life* 인생의 단맛 쓴맛을 보다 / *~ the fear of death* 죽음의 공포를 맛보다.

— *vi.* **1** (P3,5) have a certain flavor. (어떤) 맛이 나다. ¶ *This orange tastes sour.* 이 오렌지는 시다 / *This soup tastes of chicken.* 이 수프는 닭고기 맛이 난다 / *Good medicine tastes bitter to the mouth.* 좋은 약은 입에 쓰다. **2** (P1) have the sense of taste. 맛을 알다. ¶ *I have a cold; I cannot ~.* 감기가 걸려 맛을 알 수 없다. **3** (P3) experience. 경험하다; 맛보다. ¶ *~ of danger* 위험을 겪다.

— *n.* Ⓒ **1** 《*the* ~》 the feeling which is gotten by the tongue; flavor. 미각; 맛. ¶ *be sour to the ~* 맛이 시다 / *A cold dulls one's ~.* 감기는 미각을 둔하게 한다. **2** 《*sing.* only》 ⓐ a small amount put into the mouth; a mouthful. 한 입; 한 모금. ¶ *Give me just a ~ of the cake.* 그 케이크 한 입만 먹어 보자 / *have a ~ of wine* 포도주 한 모금을 마시다. ⓑ a slight experience. 약간의 경험. ¶ *a ~ of adventure* 잠시 맛본 모험. ⓒ a slight suggestion; a touch; a trace. 낌새; 기미; 흔적. ¶ *There was a ~ of sadness in his remark.* 그의 말에는 슬픈 기미가 있었다. **3** ⓊⒸ ⓐ the ability to judge what is beautiful and excellent; the manner or style that shows such ability. 심미안(審美眼); 감식력; (말씨·태도 등의) 멋; 정취. ¶ *show ~ in fine arts* 미술에 대한 안목이 있다 / *a man of good ~* (예술 등에 대한) 취향이 세련된 사람 / *a fine* (*cultivated*) *~ in art* 예술에 대한 세련된 감상력. ⓑ the sense of what is fitting or proper in social life. (사회생활에 대한) 양식; 분별. ¶ *His conduct was not in good ~.* 그의 처신은 온당하지 못했다. **4** ⓊⒸ 《*for*》 a particular liking; fondness. 취향; 기호. ¶ *have a ~ for traveling* 여행을 좋아하다 / 《*prov.*》 *There is no accounting for tastes.* 오이를 거꾸로 먹어도 제 멋 / 《*prov.*》 *Everyone to his tastes.* 취미도 가지가지 / *have a ~ for sweets* 단것을 좋아하다. [Rom. →tax]

in good* (*excellent*) *taste, showing a sense of beauty, excellence, etc. 취미가 고상해; 멋을 알아.

leave a bad taste in the mouth, cause a bad impression or a feeling. 뒷맛이 쓰다; 나쁜 인상을 남기다.

to taste, to the amount desired. 기호에 따라.

to one's taste, agreeable or pleasing to one. 마음에 들어.

taste·ful [téistfəl] *adj.* having or showing good taste. 취미가 좋은; 풍류를 아는; 안목이 있는. ●**taste·ful·ly** [-fuli] *adv.*

taste·less [téistlis] *adv.* **1** without taste or flavor. 맛 없는. **2** lacking good taste; in poor taste. 품위가 없는; 멋이 없는. ¶ *a ~ hat* 볼품 없는 모자.

taste·less·ly [téistlisli] *adv.* in a tasteless manner. 맛(멋) 없이; 무미 건조하게.

tast·y [téisti] *adj.* (**tast·i·er, tast·i·est**) 《*colloq.*》 **1** tasting good. 맛이 좋은. **2** having or showing good taste. 품위 있는; 멋진; 고상한. ●**tast·i·ly** [-li] *adv.* **tast·i·ness** [-nis] *n.*

tat [tæt] *vi., vt.* (**tat·ted, tat·ting**) (P1;6) make tatting; make by tatting. 가볍게 치다; 똑똑 두드리다. [Imit.]

ta·ta [tǽtɑ́] *interj.* 《*child's word*》 goodbye. 안녕; 빠이빠이. [?]

Ta·tar [tɑ́:tər] *n., adj.* =Tartar.

Ta·ta·ry [tɑ́:təri] *n.* =Tartary.

tat·ter [tǽtər] *n.* Ⓒ **1** a torn piece. 넝마. **2** 《usu. *pl.*》 torn or ragged clothes. 누더기. ¶ *in ~* 누더기를 걸치고 / *tear to tatters* 갈기갈기 찢다 / *His coat was* (*hanging*) *in tatters.* 그의 옷은 너덜너덜 해져 있었다. — *vt.* (P6) tear or wear (something) to pieces; make ragged. …을 너덜너덜 해뜨리다. — *vi.* (P1) become ragged. 너덜너덜 해어지다. [Scand.]

tat·ter·de·mal·ion [tæ̀tərdiméiljən] *n.* Ⓒ a person in tattered clothes. 누더기를 입은 사람. [↑]

tat·tered [tǽtərd] *adj.* **1** ragged. 누덕누덕한. **2** wearing ragged clothes. 누더기를

결친.

tat·tle [tǽtl] *vi.* (P1) talk idly; tell tales; gossip. 객담을 늘어놓다; 남의 일을 수군거리다. — *vt.* (P6) reveal (a secret). (비밀)을 누설하다. — *n.* Ⓤ idle talk; gossip. 객담; 수다; 남의 말 하기. [Imit.]

tat·tler [tǽtlər] *n.* Ⓒ a person who tattles. 수다스러운 사람; 수다쟁이.

tat·too[1] [tætúː] *n.* Ⓒ (*pl.* **-toos**) **1** 《*sing.* only》 a signal on a bugle, drum, etc. calling soldiers, etc. back to their quarters at night. 귀영 나팔〔북〕. **2** a public show given by a large number of soldiers, usu. at night. (야간) 군악 행진. **3** a continuous beating or tapping. 탕탕〔둥둥〕 두드리기. [Du. =tap toe !]

tat·too[2] [tætúː] *n.* Ⓒ (*pl.* **-toos**) a design marked on the skin by pricking and then rubbing in dye. 문신(文身). — *vt.* (P6) mark (the skin) with tattoos. …에 문신하다. [Polynesian]

:taught [tɔːt] *v.* p. and pp. of **teach.**

taunt [tɔːnt, tɑːnt] *vt.* (P6,13) **1** mock or reproach (someone) with words or conduct. …을 조롱하다; 힐난하다. ¶ ~ *someone with cowardice* 아무를 겁이 많다고 조롱하다. **2** drive (someone) by taunting. …을 조롱해서 —하게 하다. ¶ ~ *someone into losing his temper* 아무를 조롱해서 화나게 만들다. — *n.* Ⓒ **1** a scornful remark; gibe. 조롱; 냉소. **2** an object of taunts. 조롱거리. [F. *tant pour tant* tit for tat]

taut [tɔːt] *adj.* **1** (of a rope, etc.) tightly stretched. (밧줄 따위가) 켕긴; 팽팽한. ¶ *a ~ rope / ~ nerves* 〔*muscles*〕 긴장한 신경〔근육〕. **2** in good condition; tidy. 정리〔정돈〕된. [E.]

tau·to·log·i·cal [tɔːtəlɑ́dʒikəl / -lɔ́dʒ-] *adj.* of or using tautology. 같은〔비슷한〕 말을 중복하는; 용어(冗語)의. [↓]

tau·tol·o·gy [tɔːtɑ́lədʒi / -tɔ́l-] *n.* Ⓤ the act of saying the same thing over again in different words; useless repetition. 동의어〔유의어〕 반복(*e.g.* most supreme; widow woman); 중복(어); 쓸데없는 반복. [Gk.]

·tav·ern [tǽvərn] Ⓒ *n.* **1** a place where alcoholic drinks are sold and drunk. 술집. **2** an inn. 여인숙. [L. *taberna* shop]

taw·dry [tɔ́ːdri] *adj.* (**-dri·er, -dri·est**) showy and cheap; gaudy; looking nice but of bad quality. 값싸고 뻔드레한. [*St. Audry*]

taw·ny [tɔ́ːni] *adj.* (**-ni·er, -ni·est**) brownish yellow. 황갈색의. ¶ *a ~ lion.* [→tan]

:tax [tæks] *n.* **1** ⓊⒸ money paid by people to the government for public purposes. 세; 세금. ¶ *free of ~* 면세의 / *lay* 〔*levy*〕 *a ~ on* 〔*upon*〕 *something* …에 세금을 부과하다 / *an additional ~* 부가세 / *business* 〔*income*〕 *~* 영업〔소득〕세 / *national* 〔*local*〕 *taxes* 국세〔지방세〕 / *a succession ~* 상속세(税). **2** 《*fig.*》 《*sing.* only》 a serious burden; a heavy demand. 무거운 짐; 부담. ¶ *a ~ on one's strength* 〔*endurance, resourses*〕 힘에 부치는〔참기 어려운; 자력이 못 미치는〕 부담. — *vt.* **1** (P6) put a tax on (income, property, etc.). …에 세금을 과하다. ¶ *They were taxed heavily.* 그들에게 무거운 세금이 매겨졌다. **2** (P6) 《*fig.*》 lay a heavy burden on (someone). …에 무거운 짐을 지우다; 큰 부담을 주다. **3** (P13) reprove; accuse. …을 책하다; 비난하다. ¶ ~ *someone with a fault* 아무의 과실을 책(責)하다 / *The teacher taxed the boy with laziness* 〔*having been lazy all day*〕. 선생님은 게으르다고〔종일 빈둥거린다고〕 그 소년을 꾸짖었다. [L. *taxo* censure]

tax·a·ble [tǽksəbəl] *adj.* that can be taxed. 과세할 수 있는; 유세(有税)의.

·tax·a·tion [tækséiʃən] *n.* Ⓤ **1** the act or system of taxing. 과세; 세제; 징세. ¶ *progressive ~* 누진세 / *the ~ office* 세무서 / *be subject to ~* 과세되다. **2** the amount of money imposed as a tax. 세액.

·tax·i [tǽksi] *n.* Ⓒ a motorcar for hire with a taximeter. 택시. — *vi., vt.* (**taxied, tax·i·ing** or **tax·y·ing**) **1** ride in a taxi. 택시로 가다. **2** (of an airplane) run along the ground or on the surface of the water just before rising or after landing. 활주하다. [*taxicab*]

tax·i·cab [tǽksikæ̀b] *n.* =taxi.

tax·i·der·my [tǽksidə̀ːrmi] *n.* the art of preparing and stuffing the skins of dead birds or animals and setting them up to look like live ones. 박제법(剝製法). [Gk. *tassō* arrange, *derma* skin]

tax·i·me·ter [tǽksimìːtər] *n.* Ⓒ a small machine fitted to a taxicab that shows the fare to be paid. 택시미터. [*taxi*]

tax·pay·er [tǽkspèiər] *n.* Ⓒ a person who pays a tax. 납세자. [*tax*]

:tea [tiː] *n.* **1** Ⓒ a low tree of eastern Asia, cultivated for its leaves. 차나무. **2** Ⓤ the dried leaves of this plant; the drink made by pouring boiling water on the leaves. 찻잎; 차; 홍차. ¶ *black ~* 홍차 / *green ~* 녹차 / *make ~* 차를 끓이다. **3** Ⓤ any of the drinks resembling tea. (홍차 비슷한) 음료. **4** ⓊⒸ 《chiefly Brit.》 a light meal in the late afternoon at which tea is served. 오후의 차. **5** ⓊⒸ an afternoon reception at which tea is served. 오후의 (다과회) 초대. [Chin.]

:teach [tiːtʃ] *v.* (**taught**) *vt.* (P6,13,14,15, 16,17,20) **1** give knowledge or lessons to (someone); instruct; guide the study of. …을 가르치다; 교수〔교육〕하다. ¶ ~ *English* 영어를 가르치다 / ~ *a girl English* = ~ *English to a girl* 소녀에게 영어를 가르치다 / 《U.S.》 ~ *school* 교편을 잡다 / *I was taught in a good school.* 나는 좋은 학교에서 공부하였다 / *Experience taught me what poverty was.* 가난이 무엇인지 겪어 봐서 알고

T

있다. **2** show how to do (something); help to learn; train; accustom; make understand. …에게 (방법을) 가르치다; 훈육하다; 익히도록 하다; 훈련시키다; 알게 하다. ¶ *~ a dog to beg* 개에게 뒷발로 서는 것을 가르치다 / *~ a boy how to swim* 소년에게 수영을 가르치다 / *~ the ear to distinguish sounds* 소리를 분간하도록 귀를 훈련하다 / *~ a child to read* 아이에게 읽는 법을 가르치다 / *~ one's children* 자식들을 훈육하다 / *~ a boy to obey* 소년에게 순종하도록 가르치다 / *I will ~ him* (*that*) *he can't play such a trick again.* 그에게 다시는 그런 농간을 못 부리게 하겠다 / *~ someone not to tell a lie* 아무에게 거짓말을 못하게 일러 주다.
— *vi.* (P1) **1** give lessons or instruction. 가르치다. **2** be a teacher. 선생 노릇을 하다. ¶ *The widow teaches for a living.* 그 미망인은 생활을 위해 선생 노릇을 한다. [E.]

teach·a·ble [tíːtʃəbl] *adj.* **1** that can be taught. 교육받을 수 있는; 배울 수 있는. ¶ *a ~ boy* 가르침을 잘 받는 소년; 온순한 소년. **2** that can be used for teaching. (교재 등이) 학습에 좋은.

:teach·er [tíːtʃər] *n.* Ⓒ a person who teaches; one who does this as a profession. 선생. ¶ *a ~ of English* 영어 선생 / *a ~ of drawing* 그림 선생 / *be one's own ~* 독학하다 / *A child's first ~ is usually his mother.* 아이의 최초의 선생은 흔히 그의 어머니다.

teach-in [tíːtʃìn] *n.* an exchange of opinions about a subject of social interest, held e.g. in a college by students, teachers, guest speakers, etc. 티치인《대학 같은 데서 갖는 사회적 관심사에 관한 토론회》.

:teach·ing [tíːtʃiŋ] *n.* Ⓤ **1** the act or profession of a teacher. 가르치기; 교육; 수업(授業). ¶ *She went into ~.* 그녀는 수업에 들어갔다. **2** 《usu. *pl.*》 something that is taught. 가르침; 교훈.

tea·cup [tíːkʌ̀p] *n.* Ⓒ a cup for tea. 찻잔. ¶ *a storm* 〔*tempest*〕 *in a ~* 집안 싸움. [*tea*]

tea garden [∸ ⌒] *n.* **1** a garden where tea and other light refreshments are served. 다과점이 있는 공원. **2** a tea plantation. 다원(茶園).

tea·house [tíːhàus] *n.* Ⓒ (**-hous·es** [-hàuziz]) a restaurant in China, etc. where tea is served. (동양의) 찻집; 다방.

teak [tiːk] *n.* **1** Ⓒ a large East Indian tree with very hard wood. 티크 나무. **2** Ⓤ the wood of this tree, used for ship-building, making fine furniture, etc. 티크재(材). [Native]

tea·ket·tle [tíːkètl] *n.* Ⓒ a kettle for boiling water to make tea. 차 끓이는 솥; 차탕관. [*tea*]

:team [tiːm] *n.* Ⓒ **1** a group of people who work, act, esp. play together. 팀; 조; 작업조. ¶ *a baseball ~* 야구 팀 / *a ~ race* 단체 경주 / *~ spirit* 단체 정신 / *a ~ of researchers* 연구진(陣). **2** two or more horses, oxen, etc. harnessed together to pull a cart. 수레에 맨 한 떼의 가축. ¶ *a ~ of horses.*
— *vt.* (P6) **1** join (someone or something) together in a team. …을 한동아리로 만들다. **2** transport (animals, etc.) with a team. (가축)을 한 무리로 해서 운반하다. — *vi.* (P1) drive a team. 가축을 한 무리로 해서 몰다. [E.]
team up (= *work together*) **with** *others.* 《*colloq.*》 …와 협동〔협력〕하다. ¶ *I teamed up with Jane to do the job.* 나는 그 일을 제인과 어울려 했다.

team·mate [tíːmmèit] *n.* Ⓒ a fellow member of a team. 팀 동료.

team·ster [tíːmstər] *n.* Ⓒ **1** a driver of a team of horses or other animals. 가축 떼를 모는 사람. **2** 《U.S.》 a driver of a truck. 트럭 운전사. [→team]

team·work [tíːmwə̀ːrk] *n.* Ⓤ the activity of a number of people working together in a team. 공동 작업; 팀워크.

tea party [∸ ⌒] *n.* a social gathering at an afternoon tea. (오후의) 다과회. [*tea*]

tea·pot [tíːpɑ̀t / -pɔ̀t] *n.* Ⓒ a vessel with a spout and handle for making and serving tea. 찻주전자; 찻병.

:tear[1] [tɛər] *v.* (**tore, torn**) *vt.* **1** (P6,7,18) break (paper, cloth, etc.) by pulling it apart; rip. …을 찢다; 째다. ¶ *~ up a letter* 편지를 찢다 / *~ open an envelope* 봉투를 찢어 열다 / *She has torn her dress in pieces.* 그녀는 자기 옷을 갈기갈기 찢었다. **2** (P6,7,13) 《*from*》 pull violently away; drag off. …을 잡아뜯다; 우격으로 떼 놓다. ¶ *~ off a leaf from the calendar* 달력의 낱장을 뜯어내다 / *She tore the baby from its mother's breast.* 그녀는 어머니 품에서 아이를 낚아챘다 / *The roof was torn off by the hurricane.* 태풍에 지붕이 날아갔다 / *He tore down the notice from the wall.* 그는 벽에서 벽보를 뜯어냈다. **3** (P6) wound (something) by tearing; make (a cut, hole, etc.) by tearing. …을 찢어 상처를〔구멍을〕 내다. ¶ *He tore his hand on a nail.* 그는 못에 손을 다쳤다 / *~ a hole in one's dress* 옷이 찢겨 구멍이 나다. **4** (P6) 《*fig.*》 cause deep sorrow or pain in (someone's heart); 《usu. in *passive*》 ruin the peace of (something); make division in. (마음)을 찢어 놓다; 괴롭히다; …의 평화를 어지럽히다; 분열시키다. ¶ *It tore his heart to leave his home.* 집을 떠나게 되어 그의 가슴은 찢어지는 듯했다 / *My heart was torn by grief.* 가슴이 찢어지는 것처럼 슬펐다 / *a country torn by a civil war* 내란으로 분열된 나라. — *vi.* **1** (P1) become torn. 찢어지다; 찢기다. ¶ *This paper tears easily.* 이 종이는 잘 찢어진다. **2** (P3) 《*at*》 pull violently; attempt to tear. 잡아찢다; 찢으려 하다. ¶ *He tore at the covering of the parcel.* 그는 소포 포장지를 잡아뜯었다. **3** (P2A,3) ⓐ 《*colloq.*》 move violently or hurriedly; rush. 질주〔돌진〕하다. ¶ *A car came tearing along* *the street.* 차 한 대가 거리를 질주해 왔다 / *He tore off without saying good-bye.* 그는 인사도 없이 황급히 가 버렸다. ⓑ move with great force or haste. 날뛰다. ¶ *They were tearing about* [(*a*)*round*] *in excitement.* 그들은 흥분해서 날뛰었다.

be torn between, be painfully unable to choose between (two alternatives). …의 사이에 끼여 (선택에) 고심하다.

tear oneself away, make up one's mind to go away. 떠나기로 마음먹다. ¶ *He could not ~ himself away from the scene.* 그는 그 자리를 뿌리치고 떠날 수가 없었다.

tear one's hair, pull one's hair violently; 《*fig.*》 show signs of despair, anger, etc. 머리를 쥐어뜯다; 절망에 빠지다; 분개하다.

— *n.* Ⓒ **1** an act of tearing. 찢기; 잡아뜯기. **2** a cut or hole made by tearing. 째진 데. ¶ *She had a big ~ in her dress.* 그녀의 옷이 크게 찢겨 있었다. **3** rush; rage. 돌진; 격분. [E.]

:tear² [tiər] *n.* Ⓒ **1** 《often *pl.*》 a drop of salty water coming from the eye; teardrop. 눈물; 눈물 방울. ¶ *in tears* 울면서; 눈물을 흘리며 / *shed tears* 눈물을 흘리다 / *burst into tears* 울음을 터뜨리다 / *Tears stood in her eyes.* 그녀 눈에 눈물이 고였다 / *wipe away one's tears* 눈물을 닦다 / *Few of us shed any tears when he left.* 그가 떠나도 우린 별로 슬프지 않았다. **2** something like a tear; a drop of liquid. 눈물 비슷한 것; 물방울. **3** 《*pl.*》 grief; sorrow. 비애; 비탄. [E.]

draw tears from someone, move someone to tears. …의 눈물을 자아내다.

tear·drop [tíərdràp / -drɔ̀p] *n.* Ⓒ a tear. 눈물 (방울). [*tear²*]

tear·ful [tíərfəl] *adj.* **1** full of tears. 눈물어린; 눈물이 헤픈. **2** causing tears; sad. 눈물나게 하는; 슬픈.

tear·ful·ly [tíərfəli] *adv.* in a tearful manner. 눈물을 흘리며; 눈물을 머금고.

tear gas [⁓⁓] *n.* a gas that causes tears and blindness. 최루 가스.

tear·ing [tɛ́əriŋ] *adj.* 《*colloq.*》 violent; raging. 맹렬한; 격렬한. ¶ *a ~ rage* 격분 / *in a ~ hurry* 황급히; 부랴부랴. [*tear¹*]

tear·less [tíərlis] *adj.* without tears; not weeping. 눈물이 없는; 울지 않는. [*tear²*]

tea·room [tí:rù(:)m] *n.* Ⓒ a room or shop where tea, coffee, light lunches, etc. are served. 다방; 다실. [*tea*]

tear shell [⁓⁓] *n.* a bomb causing the shedding of tears. 최루탄. [*tear²*]

***tease** [ti:z] *vt.* **1** (P6,13) trouble playfully. …을 지분거리다; 놀리다. ¶ *Don't take it seriously — he was only teasing.* 정색할 것 까진 없다. 그는 그저 농지거리를 했을 뿐이다 / *Stop teasing the cat!* 그 고양이를 지분거리지 마라. **2** (P6,11,13,20) ⓐ 《*for*》 beg. …을 조르다. ¶ *~ someone for* [*to do*] *something* 아무에게 어떤 것을 달라고[해 달라고] 조르다 / *The little boy teased his father to tell an interesting story.* 아이는 재미있는 얘기를 해 달라고 아버지를 졸랐다. ⓑ trouble with questions, requests, etc. (질문 등으로) 귀찮게 굴다; 괴롭히다. **3** (P6,7) comb (wool, etc.); roughen the surface of (cloth). (양털 따위)를 빗다; 소모(梳毛)하다; (모직물의) 보풀을 세우다. ¶ *~ flax* 삼을 빗다.

— *n.* **1** Ⓒ a person who teases. (짓궂게) 지분거리는 사람. **2** Ⓤ teasing or being teased. 지분거리기; 괴롭힘을 당함. [E.]

tea·sel [tí:zəl] *n.* Ⓒ a plant with stiff flower heads; one of these dried flower heads. 산토끼꽃의 일종; 그 열매《모직물의 보풀을 세우는 데 씀》. — *vt.* (**-seled, -sel·ing,** 《Brit.》 **-selled, -sel·ling**) (P6) roughen the surface of (cloth) with teasels. (모직물의) 겉면에 보풀을 세우다. [↑]

teas·er [tí:zər] *n.* Ⓒ **1** a person who teases. 짓궂게 구는 사람; 놀리는 사람. **2** 《*colloq.*》 a puzzling question or task. 어려운 질문[일]. [*tease*]

tea-service [tí:sə̀:rvis] *n.* Ⓒ a set of cups, plates, etc. for use at tea. 차제구(茶諸具) 일습; 티세트. [*tea*]

tea-set [tí:sèt] *n.* = tea-service.

tea shop [⁓⁓] *n.* = tearoom.

:tea·spoon [tí:spù:n] *n.* Ⓒ a small spoon used to stir tea or coffee. 찻숟가락. [*tea*]

tea·spoon·ful [tí:spu:nfùl] *n.* Ⓒ a quantity as much as a teaspoon will hold. 찻숟가락 하나(의 분량).

teat [ti:t] *n.* Ⓒ the part of a breast through which milk is drawn. 젖꼭지. [E.]

tea table [⁓⁓–] *n.* a small table used in serving tea for several people. 차탁자; 찻상. [*tea*]

tea-things [tí:θìŋz] *n. pl.* a tea-set. 차제구(茶諸具); 다구(茶具).

tea·time [tí:tàim] *n.* Ⓤ the time at which tea is taken in the afternoon. 오후의 차 마시는 시간.

tea tray [⁓⁓] *n.* a tray on which tea-things are placed. 찻쟁반.

tea wagon [⁓⁓–] *n.* a small tea table on wheels. 티왜건《바퀴 달린 차도구 운반대》.

〈tea wagon〉

tea·zel [tí:zəl] *n., vt.* = teasel.

tech·nic [téknik] *n.* **1** = technique. **2** 《usu. *pl.*》 the science dealing with mechanical or industrial arts. 공예(학). **3** 《*pl.*》 technical terms. 술어; 전문어. [Gk. *takhnē* art]

***tech·ni·cal** [téknikəl] *adj.* **1** of a particular science or technique. 전문의; 전문적인; 학술(상)의. ¶ *a ~ book* 전문 서적 / *~ terms* 전문어; 술어 / *~ knowledge* 전문 지식. **2** of mechanical or industrial arts. 공예의; 공업의. ¶ *a ~ school* 공업 학교.

tech·ni·cal·i·ty [tèknəkǽləti] *n.* **1** Ⓤ the state or quality of being technical. 전문적

임. **2** Ⓒ 《often *pl.*》 a technical detail, expression, term, etc. 전문적 사항〔표현〕; 전문어.

tech·ni·cal·ly [téknikəli] *adv.* in a technical manner; in technical terms. 전문적〔기술적〕으로; 전문 용어로.

tech·ni·cian [tekníʃən] *n.* Ⓒ a person skilled in the technicalities of a subject. 전문가; 기술자.

Tech·ni·col·or [téknikʌ̀lər] *n.* Ⓤ 《trademark》 a special process by which many three-color photographs are combined in one film. 테크니컬러; 컬러〔천연색〕 영화〔사진〕. [*techni*(cal), *color*]

∗**tech·nique** [tekní:k] *n.* Ⓤ technical skill in art, music, etc.; Ⓒ a special method or system used to complete something. 기교; 기술; 수법; 기법; 예풍(藝風); 연주법.

tech·no·log·i·cal [tèknəlɑ́dʒikəl / -lɔ́dʒ-] *adj.* of technology. 과학 기술의; 공예(학)상의. ● **tech·no·log·i·cal·ly** [-i] *adv.*

tech·nol·o·gy [teknɑ́lədʒi / -nɔ́l-] *n.* Ⓤ **1** the science of industrial arts. 과학 기술; 공예(학). **2** technical terms used in an art, science, etc. (과학·예술 등의) 전문어; 술어.

Ted [ted] *n.* a nickname for Edward or Theodore. Edward, Theodore 의 애칭.

ted·der [tédər] *n.* a machine that spreads out hay for drying. 건초기. [Norse.]

Ted·dy [tédi] *n.* =Ted.

teddy bear [∸‐ ∸] *n.* a child's toy bear. 장난감 곰. [=*Theodore* (*Roosevelt*)]

Ted·dy-boy [tédibɔ̀i] *n.* 《Brit. *colloq.*》 a type of young English hooligan with fastidious taste in clothes. 테디보이《Edward 7세 때의 까다로운 복장을 한 1950-60년대 초의 불량 소년들》.

∗**te·di·ous** [tí:diəs, -dʒəs] *adj.* tiresome. 지루한; 따분한. ¶ ~ *work* 따분한 일 / *a* ~ *talk* 지루한 얘기 / *a* ~ *lecture* 따분한 강의. ● **te·di·ous·ly** [-li] *adv.* [L. *taedet* it bores]

te·di·ous·ness [tí:diəsnis, -dʒəs-] *n.* Ⓤ the quality of being tedious. 따분함; 권태.

te·di·um [tí:diəm] *n.* Ⓤ tediousness; tiresomeness. 따분함; 지루함. [*tedious*]

tee [ti:] *n.* Ⓒ **1** the mark aimed at in some games (such as quoits). (고리던지기 따위의) 목표. **2** 《golf》 the place where a player starts in playing each hole; a small wooden, plastic, metal, or rubber peg from which the ball is driven, as in teeing off. 티; 구좌(球座). — *vt., vi.* (P6; 1) put (a golf ball) on a tee. (공을) 구좌〔티〕 위에 놓다. [?]

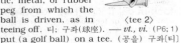

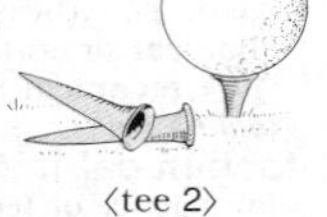
〈tee 2〉

tee off, **a**) make a first stroke in golf. 티에서 제1구(球)를 치다; 티오프하다. **b**) commence operations. (경기 따위를) 시작하다; 행동을 개시하다.

teem [ti:m] *vi.* **1** (P3) 《*in, with*》 be full; be abundant; swarm. 충만하다; 풍부하다; 시글시글하다. ¶ *a river teeming with fish* 물고기가 시글시글한 강 / *His brain teems with ideas.* 그의 머리에는 아이디어가 꽉 차 있다 / *Wild life teems in the forest.* 그 숲에는 야생 동식물이 지천으로 많이 있다. **2** 《*arch.*》 (P1) bring forth young. 아이를 낳다. [*team*]

teem·ing [tí:miŋ] *adj.* full; abundant. (넘치도록) 많은; 풍부한.

teen-age [tí:nèidʒ] *adj.* in one's teens. 10 대의. [→teens]

∗**teen-ag·er** [tí:nèidʒər] *n.* Ⓒ a teen-age person. 10 대의 소년·소녀.

∗**teens** [ti:nz] *n. pl.* the years of one's life from 13 to 19. 10 대. ¶ *in his late* ~ 그의 열아홉 살 때에/ *a girl in* 〔*just out of*〕 *her* ~, 10 대의〔막 10 대를 지난〕 소녀. [*ten*]

tee·pee [tí:pi:] *n.* =tepee.

tee·ter [tí:tər] *n., v.* 《U.S.》 =seesaw.

:**teeth** [ti:θ] *n.* pl. of **tooth.**

teethe [ti:ð] *vi.* (P1) (of a baby) grow teeth. 이〔젖니〕가 나다. ¶ *Baby is teething.* 애기가 이가 나고 있다. [*tooth*]

teeth·ing [tí:ðiŋ] *n.* Ⓤ the process or period of growing teeth. 이가 남; 그 시기.

tee·to·tal [ti:tóutl] *adj.* **1** drinking no alcoholic drinks. 절대 금주의. ¶ ~ *society* 금주회(禁酒會). **2** 《*colloq.*》 complete; absolute. 완전한; 절대적인. [*total*]

tee·to·tal·er [ti:tóutlər] *n.* Ⓒ a person who drinks no alcoholic drinks. 절대 금주자(禁酒者).

tee·to·tum [tì:toutʌ́m, ti:tóutəm] *n.* a small, four-sided top, spun with the fingers, with letters on each side to indicate the player's score. 네모팽이《승부내기용; 손가락으로 돌리며, 네 측면에 끗수가 적혀 있음》. [L. *totus* whole]

like a teetotum, whirling. 빙빙 돌아서.

teg·u·ment [tégjəmənt] *n.* 《more usu. *integument*》 the natural covering of an animal body or of any part of it. (생물의) 외피; 포피(包皮). ¶ *A skin, hide, or shell is a* ~. 피부, 짐승 가죽, 조개 껍질 등을 외피라고 한다. [L.]

Te·he·ran, Te·hran [tì:ərɑ́:n, -rǽn, tèhə-] *n.* the capital of Iran. 테헤란《이란의 수도》.

tel. **1** telephone. **2** telegram. **3** telegraph.

tele- [télə- / -li-] *pref.* at or to a distance. '원거리의〔로〕, 전신, 전송'의 뜻. ¶ *television* / *telescope.* [Gk. *tēle* far off]

tel·e·cast [téləkæ̀st, -kɑ̀:st] *vt., vi.* (P6; 1) broadcast (a program) by television. 텔레비전으로 방송하다. — *n.* Ⓒ a television broadcast. 텔레비전 방송. [tele-]

:**tel·e·gram** [téləgræ̀m] *n.* Ⓒ a message sent by telegraph. 전보. ¶ *a* ~ *form* 전보용지 / *by* ~ 전보로 / *send a* ~ *to* (*someone*) …에게 전보를 치다. [↑]

:tel·e·graph [téləgræ̀f, -grɑ̀:f] *n.* Ⓒ an apparatus or a method for sending messages by electricity; a telegram. 전신기; 전신; 전보. ¶ *a ~ office* 〔*station*〕 전신국 / *a ~ slip* 전보 용지 / *by ~* 전신으로; 전보로. — *vt.* (P6,11,13,14,15) **1** send (a message) by telegraph; send a telegram to (someone). (메시지)를 타전하다; …에게 전보를 치다. ¶ *~ news* 뉴스를 전송하다. **2** 《*fig.*》 convey (one's wishes, etc.) to someone by signs. (신호·눈짓 등으로) 알리다; 전하다. — *vi.* (P1,3) send a telegram. 타전하다. ¶ *~ off for money* 돈 보내라고 전보를 치다.

te·leg·ra·pher [təlégrəfər] *n.* Ⓒ a person who sends and receives telegraphic messages. 전신 기사.

tel·e·graph·ic [tèləgræ̀fik] *adj.* of or by the telegraph. 전신기의; 전신〔전보〕의. ¶ *a ~ message* 전문 / *~ address* (전보의) 수신인 약호 / *~ instruments* 전신기.

te·leg·ra·phy [tilégrəfi] *n.* Ⓤ the process or art of sending messages by telegraph. 전신(술). ¶ *electric wave ~* 무선 전신술.

te·lep·a·thy [təlépəθi] *n.* Ⓤ the power of passing thought from one mind to another without the use of words or signs. 텔레파시; 정신 감응; 이심 전심. [→pathos]

:tel·e·phone [téləfòun] *n.* ⒸⓊ an instrument or method for sending sound or speech over a distance by electricity. 전화; 전화기. ¶ *a public ~* 공중 전화 / *a ~ directory* 〔*book*〕 전화 번호부 / *a ~ set* 전화기 / *by ~* 전화로 / *call someone on the ~* 아무를 전화통에 불러내다 / *a ~ receiver* (전화) 수화기 / *You are wanted on the ~.* 네게 전화가 와 있다 / *speak to someone over* 〔*on*〕 *the ~* 아무와 전화로 이야기하다.
— *vi.* (P3) use a telephone. 전화를 걸다; 전화로 이야기하다. ¶ *~ to say that …* 전화를 걸어 …라고 이야기하다 / *He telephoned for a doctor* 〔*taxi*〕. 전화로 의사〔택시〕를 불렀다.
— *vt.* (P6) **1** send (a message) by telephone. 전화로 …을 전하다: …을 전화로 이야기하다. ¶ *~ someone for advice* 아무에게 전화로 충고를 구하다 / *He telephoned the police to come at once.* 경찰에 빨리 오라고 전화하였다 / *I've been telephoned all morning, but I haven't been able to speak to the doctor.* 아침 내내 전화했으나 의사와 통화를 할 수 없었다. **2** talk through a telephone. …에게 전화를 걸다; …에게 전화로 이야기하다. ¶ *Telephone me tomorrow.* 내일 내게 전화해라. [tele-, →phonetic]

tel·e·phon·ic [tèləfɑ́nik / -lifɔ́n-] *adj.* of or sent by telephone. 전화의; 전화에 의한; 전화로 전한. ¶ *~ communication* 전화에 의한 통신; 통화.

tel·e·phon·i·cal·ly [tèləfɑ́nikəli / -lifɔ́n-] *adv.* by means of a telephone. 전화로.

te·leph·o·nist [təléfənist] *n.* Ⓒ a person who operates a telephone. 전화 교환원〔기사〕.

te·leph·o·ny [təléfəni] *n.* Ⓤ the art of sending and receiving sounds by telephone. 전화술. ¶ *wireless ~* 무선 전화.

tel·e·pho·to [téləfòutou] *adj.* of or for a telephotograph. 망원 사진의; 전송 사진의. ¶ *a ~ lens* 망원 렌즈. — *n.* Ⓒ a telephotograph. 망원〔전송〕 사진. [tele-]

tel·e·pho·to·graph [tèləfóutəgræ̀f / -grɑ̀:f] *n.* Ⓒ a photograph taken with a telephoto lens which makes far objects seem close; a photograph sent by telegraphy. 망원 사진; 전송 사진. — *vt., vi.* (P6; 1) take (photographs) with a telephoto lens; send (photographs) by telegraphy. 망원 렌즈로 촬영하다; (사진을) 전송하다. [tele-]

·tel·e·scope [téləskòup] *n.* Ⓒ an instrument with lenses which makes distant objects appear nearer and larger. 망원경. ¶ *an astronomical ~* 천체 망원경.
— *vi.* (P1) slide into one another like telescope tubes. (망원경의 통처럼) 끼워 넣어지다; 포개지다. ¶ *This instrument will ~ small enough to fit into this box.* 이 기구는 이 상자 속에 들어갈 정도로 작게 포개진다.
— *vt.* (P6) **1** make (two things) slide into one another; cause to become shorter in length or time; shorten. …을 끼워 넣다; …을 단축하다; 줄이다. ¶ *For the purposes of the film, three months' action telescoped into two hours.* 영화의 목적하는 바에 따라 석 달의 활동을 두 시간으로 단축했다. **2** force (two things) into one another. …을 서로 들어박히게 하다. ¶ *The crashed cars were telescoped.* 충돌한 차들은 서로 들어박혀 포개졌다. [→scope]

tel·e·scop·ic [tèləskɑ́pik / -skɔ́p-] *adj.* **1** of a telescope; seen by means of a telescope; visible only through a telescope. 망원경의; 망원경으로 본; 망원경으로만 보이는. ¶ *a ~ view of the moon* 망원경으로 보는 달의 관측 / *~ stars* 망원경으로만 보이는 별들. **2** consisting of sections which slide one inside another. 끼워〔접어〕 넣을 수 있는; 신축 자재의. ¶ *The tripod has ~ legs.* 삼각대의 다리는 접어 넣게 되어 있다.

T

tel·e·type [télətàip] *n.* Ⓒ a telegraphic device that sends and receives signals like a typewriter; 《*T-*》 the trademark for this. 텔레타이프; 전신 인자기(電信印字機); 그 상표명. — *vt.* (P6) send (a message) by teletype. (메시지)를 텔레타이프로 보내다. [tele-]

tel·e·vise [téləvàiz] *vt.* (P6) send or receive (a program, etc.) by television. …을 텔레비전으로 방송〔수상(受像)〕하다. ¶ *The President's news conference was televised.* 대통령의 기자 회견이 TV로 방송됐다. [tele-]

:tel·e·vi·sion [téləvìʒən] *n.* Ⓤ the process of sending and receiving images by electric waves to a distant place; Ⓒ a television receiving set. 텔레비전; 텔레비전 수상기.

參考 TV, T.V.로 생략함. ¶ *watch* ~ 텔레비전을 보다 / *a ~ set* 텔레비전 수상기 / *watch boxing on* (*the*) ~ 텔레비전으로 권투를 보다 / *appear on* ~ 텔레비전에 나오다 / *She looks young on* ~. 그녀는 TV에 나오면 젊게 보인다 / *What's on* (*the*) ~ *tonight?* 오늘 밤 TV 프로에는 어떤 것들이 있느냐.

tel·e·vi·sor [téləvàizər] *n.* a television apparatus. 텔레비전 송신〔수신〕 장치.

:tell [tel] *v.* (**told**) *vt.* **1** (P6,13,14,15,16,17) express (something) in words; make (something) known; say; narrate. …을 말하다; 이야기하다; 알리다; 고(告)하다; 전하다. ¶ ~ *a lie* 〔*the truth*〕 거짓말을 하다〔진실을 말하다〕 / ~ *someone a secret* 아무에게 비밀을 이야기하다 / ~ *the news* 〔*fact*〕 뉴스를〔사실을〕 전하다 / *I can't ~ how happy I am.* 나는 말할 수 없을 정도로 행복하다 / *Tell me all you know.* 네가 아는 바를 전부 말해라 / *I told her that he had been ill in bed.* 난 그녀에게 그가 앓고 있었다고 알렸다 / *I will ~ you what.* 저어, 얘기할 것이 있는데 / *I will ~ you.* 내 얘기해 줄 테니 들어 보게나 / *I will ~ you what to do.* 무엇을 해야 하는지 말해 주마 / ~ *someone good-bye* 아무에게 작별 인사를 하다 / *He told me that he had good news for me.* 그는 내게 좋은 소식이 있다고 말했다 / *Tell me, was I wrong?* 내가 틀렸는지 말해 봐라. **2** (P6,7,12,13,14) reveal; show; disclose; point out. …을 보이다; 나타내다; 지적하다. ¶ *His face told his joy.* 그의 얼굴에 기쁨이 나타나 있었다 / *The red lamp tells you* (*that*) *the machine is working.* 빨간 불은 기계가 작동하고 있음을 나타낸다 / *The clock tells time.* 시계는 시각을 알린다. **3** (P20) order; command. …을 명하다; 지시하다. ¶ *I ~ her to come at once.* 나는 그녀에게 곧 오라고 했다 / *Do what I ~ you.* 내가 이른 대로 해라 / *I was told to keep my mouth shut.* 발설하지 말라는 명을 받았다 / *He told me to wait.* 그는 내게 기다리라고 했다. **4** (P6,10,12,13) 《with *can* or *be able to*》 distinguish; recognize; know. …을 식별〔분간〕하다; 알다. ¶ *I can't ~ George from his twin brother.* 나는 조지와 그의 쌍둥이 동생을 분간 못 하겠다 / *I couldn't ~ what to do.* 무엇을 해야 할지 몰랐다 / *Tell the difference between them.* 그것들 사이의 다른 점을 말해 보라 / *There is no telling what may happen.* 무슨 일이 일어날지 예상할 수 없다 / *How do things go? —I can't ~ yet.* 일이 어떻게 되어 가고 있는가 — 아직 모르겠다 / *I can ~ it from your eyes.* 나는 그것을 너의 눈을 보고 알겠다. **5** (P6,7) 《*arch.*》 count. …을 세다. ¶ ~ *sheep* 양의 마릿수를 세다 / ~ *one's beads* 염주를 돌리며 기도하다.

— *vi.* **1** (P3) 《*about, of*》 give a story or report. 이야기하다; 보고하다. ¶ *He told about his trip.* 그의 여행담을 이야기했다 / ~ *of the bygone days* 지난날을 이야기하다 / ~ *of an accident* 사고를 보고하다 / *Tell me about yourself.* 너 자신에 대해서 말해 봐라. **2** (P3) give evidence. 증명하다; 나타내다. ¶ *ruins telling of an ancient city* 고대 도시의 존재를 말하고 있는 폐허(廢墟) / *His ragged clothes ~ of his poverty.* 해진 옷을 입은 걸 보니 가난한 모양이다. **3** (P1,3) make secrets known. 비밀을 누설하다; 고자질하다; 밀고하다. ¶ *He promised not to ~.* 아무에게도 말하지 않겠다고 약속했다. **4** (P1,3) 《*on, upon, about, against*》 produce a result; be effective; influence. 효과를 나타내다; 효력이 있다; 영향을 주다. ¶ *Every shot told.* 탄환은 모두 명중했다《백발 백중이었다》 / *The hard work is telling on him.* 중노동은 그의 몸에 영향을 주고 있다 / *His efforts are beginning to ~.* 그의 노력이 효과를 나타내기 시작하고 있다 / *This fact will ~ him in his favor.* 이 사실은 그에게 유리하게 작용할 것이다. [E.]

all told, in all; counting all. 전부; 합쳐서. ¶ *There were 70 all told.* 모두 70 명이 있었다.

tell a tale 무슨 까닭이 있다.

tell off, **a**) 《Brit. *colloq.*》 scold. …을 야단치다; 잔소리하다. ¶ *Mother told him off for not doing his homework.* 어머니는 숙제를 안 한다고 그를 야단치셨다. **b**) number; pick out (a specified number of persons). 세어서 가르다〔나누다〕; 일을 할당하다. ¶ *Ten soldiers were told off to dig ditches.* 군인 10 명이 호명되어 호를 파는 임무가 주어졌다〔할당되었다〕.

tell on, **a**) 《*colloq.*》 tell something secret about (someone); inform against. …에 관한 비밀을 누설하다; …를 고자질하다. ¶ *John told on Bill.* 존은 빌의 일을 고자질했다 / *Don't ~ on me.* 나에 대한 고자질을 하지 마라. **b**) ⇨4.

tell the world, 《*colloq.*》 announce openly. 공언하다.

tell·er [télər] *n.* Ⓒ **1** a person who tells a story; a narrator. 이야기하는 사람. ¶ *He is a good ~ of stories* 이야기를 재미있게 하는 사람이다. **2** a person who counts, pays out, and receives money; a clerk in a bank. 계산하는 사람; (은행의) 금전 출납원. ¶ *a deposit ~* 예금계 / *a paying* 〔*receiving*〕 ~ 지출〔수납〕계. **3** a person who counts votes (e.g. in the House of Commons). (하원의) 계표원(計票員).

tell·ing [téliŋ] *adj.* having effect or force; striking. 효과가 있는; 잘 듣는; 현저한. ¶ *His word had a ~ effect.* 그의 말은 잘 먹혀들었다 / *a ~ blow* 강타; 매서운 일격 / *a ~ evidence* 유력한 증거.

tell·ing·ly [téliŋli] *adv.* in a telling manner. 유효하게; 힘있게.

tell·tale [téltèil] *n.* Ⓒ **1** a person who tells tales; a person who reveals secrets. 고자질하는 사람; 남의 말을 잘 하는 사람. **2** an outward look that reveals a secret; evidence. (내막 따위를) 폭로하는 것; 증거. **3** an indicator. 자동 표시기. — *adj.* revealing secrets, hidden feelings, etc. 비밀·속내를 드러내는. ¶ *a ~ blush* (감추려 해도) 저절로

T

붉어지는 얼굴. [→tell]

tel·ly [téli] *n.* 《Brit. *colloq.*》 television. 텔레비전.

tem·blor [témblɔːr, -blər] *n.* 《U.S.》 = earthquake.

tem·er·ar·i·ous [tèmərέəriəs] *adj.* 《*lit.*》 foolishly bold. 무모한. [L. *temere* at random]

te·mer·i·ty [timérəti] *n.* foolish boldness. 무모한 짓; 만행. ¶ *The clerk had the ~ to criticize the firm before the manager's son.* 그 점원은 겁도 없이 지배인 아들한테 회사의 험담을 했다. [↑]

:tem·per [témpər] *n.* ⓊⒸ **1** one's natural way of feeling; disposition; mood. 기질; 천성; 성질; 기분. ¶ *a sweet* 〔*hot, quick, short*〕 *~* 상냥한〔성마른〕 성미 / *a stubborn ~* 완고한 성질. **2** anger; irritation; passion. 화; 노기(怒氣); 울화. ¶ *be in a ~* 화가 나 있다 / *get into* 〔*in*〕 *a ~* (버럭) 화를 내다 / *get out of ~ =lose one's ~* 울화통을 터뜨리다; 버럭 화를 내다 / *He was behaving so stupidly that I found it hard to keep my ~.* 그자가 어찌나 몰상식하게 구는지 화가 나서 참을 수 없었다. **3** the hardness (of steel, clay, etc.) obtained by tempering. (점토 따위) 반죽의 정도; (강철의) 불림; 경도(硬度). ¶ *the ~ of steel* 강철의 불림〔경도〕.

— *vt.* **1** (P6,13) make (something) less extreme; soften; moderate. …을 부드럽게 하다; 누이다; 조절〔조합, 완화〕하다; 누르다. ¶ *~ one's grief* 슬픔을 삭이다 / *~ strong drink with water* 독한 술에 물을 타다 / *~ justice with mercy* 정의에 자비를 가미하다; 정상 참작을 하다. **2** (P6) change the quality of (iron, etc.). (강철)을 불리다. ¶ *He tempered the steel by heating and sudden cooling.* 그는 강철을 달궜다 급히 식혔다 하며 불렸다. **3** (P6) mix to the proper degree of softness. …을 이기다. ¶ *~ clay* 진흙을 반죽하다. **4** (P6) 《mus.》 tune or moderate (a piano, violin, etc.). (피아노 등)을 조율하다.

— *vi.* (P1) become soft and tempered. 유연해지다; 부드러워지다; (쇠 따위가) 단련되다; 불려지다. [L. *tempero* proportion duly]

tem·per·a [témpərə] *n.* **1** Ⓤ a technique of painting in which the whites of egg are used instead of oil. 템페라 화법. **2** Ⓒ a painting made by this technique. 템페라화(畫). [↑]

·tem·per·a·ment [témpərəmənt] *n.* ⓊⒸ one's nature or disposition. 기질; 성미. ¶ *a melancholic ~* 우울한 성질 / *an artistic ~* 예술가적 기질 / *She has a nervous ~.* 그녀는 신경질이 있다.

tem·per·a·men·tal [tèmpərəméntl] *adj.* **1** of or caused by temperament. 기질상의; 기분의. ¶ *Some boys have a ~ dislike for study.* 어떤 아이들은 기질상으로 공부를 싫어한다. **2** easily excited; liable to sudden changes of mood; moody. 걸핏하면 화내는; 변덕이 심한. ¶ *The actress was so ~ that many people refused to work with her.* 그 여배우는 너무 신경질적이어서 많은 사람들이 그녀와 함께 일하기를 거부했다.

tem·per·a·men·tal·ly [tèmpərəméntəli] *adv.* excitedly; moodily. 기질상; 흥분하기 쉽게; 변덕스럽게.

·tem·per·ance [témpərəns] *n.* Ⓤ **1** the state of being not extreme in action, speech, etc. 절제; 중용(中庸). **2** the state of using alcoholic drinks not at all or not too much. 절주(節酒); 금주. ¶ *a ~ hotel* (술을 일체 내지 않는) 금주 호텔 / *a ~ movement* 〔*league, society*〕 금주 운동〔동맹, 회〕. [→temper]

·tem·per·ate [témpərət] *adj.* **1** self-controlled; moderate. 절제하는; 삼가는; 온건한. **2** using alcoholic drinks not at all or not too much. 절주〔금주〕의. ¶ *He is a ~ man, and never drinks too much.* 그는 술을 삼가는 사람이라서 절대로 과음하지 않는다. **3** (of climate, or parts of the earth) neither hot nor cold. 온난한. ¶ *the Temperate Zones* 온대.

:tem·per·a·ture [témpərətʃər] *n.* ⓊⒸ **1** the degree or amount of heat or cold measured by a thermometer. 온도. **2** the degree of heat of the human body. 체온. ¶ *take one's ~* 체온을 재다 / *a ~ chart* 체온표. **3** an excess of this heat above normal; fever. 고열. ¶ *have a ~* (높은) 열이 있다.

tem·pered [témpərd] *adj.* **1** softened; moderated. 부드러워진; 완화된; 조절된. **2** 《in *compounds*》 having a specified state of mind. …한 기질의. ¶ *a good-tempered person* 기질이 고운 사람. **3** treated so as to become hard but not too brittle. (쇠가) 불린. ¶ *~ steel* 단강(鍛鋼). [→temper]

·tem·pest [témpist] *n.* Ⓒ **1** a violent storm. 폭풍우. ¶ *The ~ drove the ship on the rocks.* 폭풍우로 배가 좌초했다. **2** 《*fig.*》 a violent disturbance. 야단 법석; 대혼란. ¶ *a ~ of weeping* 울고불고하는 소란 / *cause a political ~* 정치적 대혼란을 가져오다 / *She burst into a ~ of anger.* 그녀는 화가 나서 길길이 뛰었다. [L. *tempestas*]

tem·pes·tu·ous [tempéstʃuəs] *adj.* **1** stormy. 폭풍우의. ¶ *It was a ~ night.* 그 날은 폭풍우가 치는 밤이었다 / 《*fig.*》 *a ~ meeting of the city council* 난장판을 이룬 시의회. **2** violent. 격렬한.

tem·pi [témpi] *n.* pl. of **tempo.**

tem·plate [témplit] *n.* =templet.

tem·ple[1] [témpəl] *n.* Ⓒ **1** a building used for the worship of a god or gods. 신전; 사원; 절. ¶ *the Temple of Apollo* 아폴로 신전 / *the Temple* (예루살렘의) 성전. **2** a building for Christian public worship. 교회; 성당. **3** 《*fig.*》 any place where some special activity is carried on or something of value resides. 전당(殿堂). ¶ *a ~ of learning* 〔*art*〕 학문〔예술〕의 전당 / *a ~ of music* 음악의 전당 / *The body is the ~ of the* *soul.* 신체는 영혼이 깃들이는 전당이다. [L. *templum*]

:**tem·ple**[2] [témpəl] *n.* Ⓒ 《usu. *pl.*》 the flat part on either side of the forehead. 관자놀이. [L. *tempus*]

tem·plet [témplit] *n.* a thin plate used as a pattern in cutting wood or stone. (나무나 돌을 뜰 때의) 형판(型板); 본뜨는 공구. [L.]

tem·po [témpou] *n.* Ⓒ (*pl.* **-pos** or **-pi**) 《It.》 **1** 《mus.》 the time or rate at which music is played. 템포; 박자. **2** the rate or pattern of activity. 속도; 빠르기. ¶ *the fast ~ of modern life* 현대 생활의 빠른 템포. [L. *tempum* time]

tem·po·ral[1] [témpərəl] *adj.* **1** of this world; of this life. 이승의; 속세의. **2** of time. 시간의(opp. spatial). **3** lasting for a short time; temporary. 일시적인(opp. eternal). **4** 《gram.》 expressing time; of verbal tense. 때를 나타내는; 시제의. [→temper, -al]

tem·po·ral[2] [témpərəl] *adj.* of, near, forming a part of, the temples. 관자놀이의. — *n.* a temporal bone. 관자놀이뼈; 측두골(側頭骨). [→temple[2]]

tem·po·rar·i·ly [témpərèrili / -rəri-] *adv.* for a short time. 일시적으로; 잠시. ¶ *The work is postponed ~.* 일은 잠시 연기됐다.

*__tem·po·rar·y__ [témpərèri / -rəri] *adj.* **1** lasting for a short time only. 일시적인; 덧없는(opp. permanent). ¶ *~ pleasures* 일시적인 쾌락 / *We apologize for the ~ inconvenience caused by these building works.* 건축 공사로 당분간 불편을 드려 죄송합니다. **2** held during a limited time only. 임시의. ¶ *a ~ job* 임시의 일; 임시직 / *~ account* 가(假)계정. [L. *tempus* period of time]

tem·po·rize [témpəràiz] *vi.* (P1) **1** adjust oneself to the time or occasion. 시국에 영합하다; 세속에 따르다. **2** delay a decision or action so as to gain time or to avoid argument. 사태를 관망하다; 우물쭈물하다; 미봉책을 쓰다. [↑]

*__tempt__ [tempt] *vt.* (P6,7,13,20) **1** persuade; try to persuade. …할 마음이 생기게 하다; 꾀다; 부추기다. ¶ *~ someone to sin* 아무를 부추겨 죄짓게 하다 / *Hunger tempted him to steal* 〔*into stealing*〕. 배가 고파 그는 그만 도둑질을 했다. **2** appeal strongly to; attract. …의 마음을 끌다; 유혹하다. ¶ *The cake tempts me.* 그 과자를 보니 회가 동한다 / *Your offer doesn't ~ me at all.* 네 제안에 난 통 흥미가 없다. **3** 《*arch.*》 test. …을 시험하다. ¶ *God did tempt Abraham.* 하느님이 아브라함을 시험하셨다. [L. *tento* try]

tempt Providence, take a great risk. 대모험을 하다.

*__temp·ta·tion__ [temptéiʃən] *n.* **1** Ⓤ the act of tempting; the state of being tempted. 유혹. ¶ *fall into ~* 유혹에 빠지다 / *lead someone into ~* 아무를 유혹에 빠뜨리다 / *No ~ could make him false to a friend.* 어떤 유혹에도 그는 친구를 배신하지 않았다. **2** Ⓒ something that tempts. 유혹하는 것; 유혹물. ¶ *Money left carelessly about is a ~ to some people.* 돈을 아무렇게나 방치하면 흑심을 갖게 되는 사람도 있다 / *Many temptations beset the young.* 젊은이들 주변에는 많은 유혹이 도사리고 있다.

tempt·er [témptər] *n.* **1** Ⓒ a person who tempts. 유혹하는 사람. **2** 《*the T-*》 Satan; the Devil. 악마; 사탄.

tempt·ing·ly [témptiŋli] *adv.* alluringly; attractively. 유혹하듯이.

:**ten** [ten] *n.* **1** the number between nine and eleven; 10. 열; 10. ¶ *~ to one* 십중 팔구. **2** a group or set of ten persons or things. 10인 1조(組); 열 개 한 벌의 물건. — *adj.* of ten. 10의. ¶ *I'd ~ times rather stay here.* 여기 있는 것이 훨씬 좋다 / *He is ~ times the man you are.* 그는 너보다 열 곱이나 나은 사람이다. [E.]

ten·a·ble [ténəbəl] *adj.* **1** that can be defended or maintained. 방어〔유지〕할 수 있는. **2** (of an opinion, etc.) reasonable; logical. 이치에 닿는; 조리 있는. [L. *teneo* hold]

te·na·cious [tənéiʃəs] *adj.* **1** holding fast; persistent. 꽉 잡은; 집요한; 끈질긴. ¶ *~ efforts* 끈질긴 노력 / *He held on to my arm with a ~ grip.* 그는 내 팔을 꽉 잡고 놓지 않았다 / *be ~ of one's rights* 자기 권리를 고집하다. **2** that can remember. 기억력이 좋은. ¶ *a ~ memory* 확실한 기억력. **3** sticky as glue. 끈끈한; 차진. ¶ *~ clay.* **4** tough as steel. 강한. ¶ *a hard and ~ alloy* 단단하고 강한 합금. [↑]

te·na·cious·ly [tənéiʃəsli] *adv.* in a tenacious manner. 끈질지게; 집요하게.

te·nac·i·ty [tənǽsəti] *n.* Ⓤ the state of being tenacious. 완강; 고집; 끈질김; 끈기. [→tenable]

ten·an·cy [ténənsi] *n.* (*pl.* **-cies**) **1** Ⓤ the act of renting land, a house, etc.; the condition of being a tenant. (토지·가옥 등의) 차용. **2** Ⓒ a property occupied by a tenant. 차지(借地); 차가(借家); 셋집. **3** 《*a ~*》 the length of time a tenant occupies a property. 차용 기간. [↑]

*__ten·ant__ [ténənt] *n.* Ⓒ **1** a person who pays rent for the use of land, a building, etc. 차지인(借地人); 차가인(借家人). ¶ *a ~ farmer* 소작인 / *a ~ right* 차지권. **2** an occupant; a dweller. 거주인. ¶ *tenants of the woods* 〔*trees*〕 새《숲의 거주자》 / *Eskimos are the only tenants of this icy waste.* 에스키모만이 이 얼음 벌판의 거주민이다 / *the ~ of grave* 묘의 거주인; 사자(死者). — *vt.* occupy (land, a house, etc.) as a tenant. (땅·집)을 빌리다; 차용하다; 거주하다. [L. *teneo* hold]

ten·ant·less [ténəntlis] *adj.* without a tenant; unoccupied. 빌려 쓰는 사람이 없는; 거주자가 없는; 빈 터〔집〕의.

ten·ant·ry [ténəntri] *n.* **1** 《*collectively*》 all the tenants on an estate. 차지인(借地人);

차가인(借家人); 소작인. **2** Ⓤ tenancy. (토지·가옥의) 차용.

Ten Commandments [⌐–⌐–], **the** *n.* 《Bible》 the ten rules of living and worship given to Moses by God on Mount Sinai. 모세의 십계(十戒).

:tend[1] [tend] *vi.* (P3,4) **1** 《*to, toward*》 be apt, liable; have a tendency to do something. …하기 쉽다; 경향이 있다. ¶ *He tends to follow the opinions of others.* 그는 남의 의견을 좇는 편이다 / *He tends toward conservatism.* 그는 보수주의적 경향이 있다 / *It tends to become very cold at night now.* 이제 밤이면 아주 추워지기 쉽다 / *He tends to cruelty* 〔*to be cruelty*〕. 성격이 잔인한 편이다. **2** 《*to, toward* 》 proceed; go; be directed. 향하다; 향해 가다. ¶ *This road tends north.* 이 길은 북쪽으로 나 있다. **3** 《*to*》 lead or conduce to a certain result. (어떤 결과로) 이끌다; 이바지하다; 도움이 되다. ¶ *Too much smoking tends to cancer.* 담배를 너무 피우면 암을 유발한다. [L. *tendo* stretch]

:tend[2] [tend] *vt.* (P6) look after; attend to; watch over (something). …을 보살피다; (가축 따위)를 지키다. ¶ ~ *the sick* 환자를 돌보다 / ~ *a store* 가게를 지키다 / *The shepherd tends his flock.* 목동이 양들을 지킨다.
— *vi.* (P3) **1** 《*on*》 wait on. 시중들다; 돌보다. **2** 《*colloq.*》 《*to*》 pay attention. 주의하다; 배려하다. ¶ ~ *to one's own affairs* 자기 일에 신경 쓰다. [*attend*]

·tend·en·cy [téndənsi] *n.* Ⓒ (*pl.* **-cies**) an inclination; a trend. 경향; 풍조; 성향(性向); 취향. ¶ *a* ~ *to drink too much* 과음하는 경향 / *a* ~ *to improvement* 개선되는 경향 / *The* ~ *of events is toward war.* 사태의 추세는 전쟁으로 가고 있다 / *a* ~ *to corpulence* 비만 체질 / *She has a* ~ *to talk too much.* 그녀는 말이 너무 많은 경향이 있다. [→tend[1]]

ten·den·tious [tendénʃəs] *adj.* (of a speech, piece of writing, etc.) having a special effect or aim. (발언·문서 등이) 특별한 의도가 있는. [↑]

:ten·der[1] [téndər] *adj.* (**-der·er, -der·est**) **1** soft; not hard. 부드러운; 연한. ¶ ~ *meat* 연한 고기. **2** easily hurt; weak; feeble. 상하기 쉬운; 무른; 약한. ¶ *a* ~ *skin* 상하기 쉬운 피부 / *the* ~ *shoots of a plant* 식물의 여린 애가지. **3** too young to be strong enough; immature. 아직 어린; 미숙한. ¶ *of* ~ *age* 〔*years*〕 나이 어린 / ~ *buds* 어린 싹. **4** sensitive; delicate; easily moved; kind. 민감한; 예민한; 친절한. ¶ *the* ~ *passion* 애정 / *a* ~ *glance* 〔*smile*〕 다정한 시선〔미소〕. **5** feeling pain quickly; sore. 닿으면 아픈〔쓰린〕. ¶ ~ *teeth* 아픈 이 / *a* ~ *spot* 아픈 데 / *My bruise is still* ~. 멍든 데가 아직도 건드리면 아프다. **6** mild; light. (색깔·빛이) 연한; 약한. ¶ ~ *colors* 부드러운 색 / ~ *green* 신록(新綠). **7** gentle. 온화한; 부드러운. ¶ *a* ~ *touch of her hand* 그녀 손의 부드러운 감촉. **8** requiring careful handling. 신중을 요하는. ¶ ~ *questions* 신중을 요하는 문제 / *a* ~ *situation* 미묘한 입장. [L. *tener*]

·ten·der[2] [téndər] *vt.* (P6,13,14) **1** present; offer. …을 제공하다; 제출하다; 신청하다. ¶ ~ *someone a reception* 아무의 환영회를 베풀다 / ~ *one's services* 봉사를 자청하다 / ~ *thanks for something* …에 대한 사의를 표하다 / *He tendered his apology.* 그는 사과했다. **2** offer (money, goods, etc.) to pay a debt, etc. …을 지불하다; 갚다.
— *vi.* (P1,3) offer to carry out work at a specified price. 입찰하다.
— *n.* **1** Ⓒ something offered; an offer; a bid. 제출; 신청; 제공물; 입찰. **2** Ⓤ anything that one cannot refuse to receive when offered in payment for a debt. (수령 거부 불능의) 변제 물건. ¶ *legal* ~ 법화; 법정 화폐. [→tend[1]]

ten·der[3] [téndər] *n.* Ⓒ **1** a person who takes care of someone. 돌보는 사람; 간호인; 감시인. **2** a small boat used for carrying goods and passengers between a large ship and the land. 거룻배. **3** a small railroad car containing coal and water, attached behind a locomotive. (증기 기관차의) 탄수차(炭水車). [tend[2]]

ten·der·foot [téndərfùt] *n.* (*pl.* **-foots** or **-feet** [-fìːt]) 《*sl.*; orig. U.S.》 a newcomer (to a hard life); a beginner; an inexperienced person. 풋내기; 신참자; 신출내기. [→tender[1]]

:ten·der-heart·ed [téndərhάːrtid] *adj.* having a tender heart; sympathetic; kindly. 마음씨 고운; 착한; 정에 무른. ¶ *She was too* ~ *to refuse.* 그녀는 너무 착해서 거절을 못 했다.

ten·der·loin [téndərlɔ̀in] *n.* ⓊⒸ the tenderest part of a loin of beef, pork, etc. (소·돼지 따위의) 연한 옆구리살(cf. *sirloin*).

·ten·der·ly [téndərli] *adv.* in a tender manner; with tenderness; gently. 부드럽게; 친절하게. [*tender*[1]]

·ten·der·ness [téndərnis] *n.* Ⓤ the state of being tender. 부드러움; 착함; 친절; 민감.

ten·don [téndən] *n.* Ⓒ a tough, thick cord that attaches a muscle to a bone; a sinew. 힘줄; 건(腱). [Gk. *tenōs*]
tendon of Achilles, the tendon attaching the calf to the heel. 아킬레스건.

ten·dril [téndril] *n.* Ⓒ a thin curling part of a climbing plant that attaches itself to something and makes the plant able to climb; something like this. 덩굴손; 그런 모양의 것. [F.]

ten·e·ment [ténəmənt] *n.* Ⓒ **1** a house or part of a house rented by a tenant; a dwelling house. 셋집; 가옥. **2** 《law》 any kind of permanent property rented from another. 보유 재산; 차지(借地); 차가(借家). **3** =tenement house. [L. *teneo* hold]

tenement of clay = ***the soul's tenement,*** 《*poet.*》 body. 영혼이 머무는 데《육체》.

tenement house [⸗—⸗] *n.* a building divided into cheap apartments, esp. such a building in the poorer sections of large cities. (대도시 영세 지역의) 아파트; 공동 주택.

ten·et [ténət, tíː-] *n.* Ⓒ a firm belief; a principle; a doctrine. 주의; 교의(教義); 신조. [→tenement]

ten·fold [ténfòuld] *adj., adv.* ten times as many or as much. 10 배[곱]의; 10 배로[곱으로]. [*ten*]

Tenn. Tennessee.

Ten·nes·se·an [tènəsíːən] *n.* Ⓒ a person of Tennessee. 테네시 주(州)의 사람. —*adj.* of Tennessee. 테네시 주(州)의.

Ten·nes·see [tènəsíː] *n.* a south central state of the United States. 테네시 주. 參考 Tenn.으로 생략함. 주도는 Nashville.

:ten·nis [ténis] *n.* Ⓤ a game for two or two pairs of persons played by hitting a ball back and forth over a net with a racket. 테니스; 정구. ¶ *a* ~ *ball* / *a* ~ *court* 테니스 코트 / ~ *sets* 테니스 용구. [F. *tenez* take (as server's call)]

ten·on [ténən] *n.* Ⓒ 《archit.》 the end of a board shaped to be inserted into a hole in another so as to hold the two together. 장부(cf. *mortise*). —*vt.* (P6) joint (two boards) by tenon and hole; make a tenon in (a board). …을 장부촉 이음하다; 장부를 만들다. [L. *teneo* hold]

ten·or[1] [ténər] *n.* Ⓒ **1** the general tendency or course. 진로; 방침. ¶ *the quiet* ~ *of his life* 그의 조용한 인생 행로. **2** the general meaning; the drift. 취지; 대의(大意). ¶ *I could not get the* ~ *of his speech.* 그의 연설의 요지가 뭔지 모르겠다. [↑]

ten·or[2] [ténər] *n.* 《mus.》 **1** Ⓤ the highest men's voice; 《*the* ~》 the part in a song taken by this voice. 테너; 차중음(次中音). **2** Ⓒ a man who sings such a part; Ⓒ an instrument which plays it. 테너 가수; 테너 악기. [↑]

ten·pins [ténpìnz] *n. pl.* 《U.S.》 《as *sing.*》 a bowling game played with ten pins and a ball; Ⓒ the pins used for this game. 십주희(十柱戲); 그 경기용의 핀. 參考 영국의 ninepins 에 해당함. 그 핀 하나는 a tenpin. [*ten*]

:tense[1] [tens] *adj.* tightly stretched; strained. 바짝 당긴; 팽팽한; 긴장한(opp. lax, loose). ¶ *a* ~ *cord* 팽팽한 줄 / ~ *nerves* 긴장한 신경 / *a* ~ *situation* [*atmosphere*] 긴장 상태[긴장된 분위기] / *Everybody was* ~ *with expectation.* 모두가 잔뜩 기대하고 있었다. [→tend[1]]

tense[2] [tens] *n.* Ⓒ 《usu. *the* ~》 《gram.》 the form of a verb showing the time of an action or state. (동사의) 시제(時制); 시칭. ¶ *the past* [*present, future*] ~ 과거[현재, 미래] 시제. [L. *tempus* time]

tense·ly [ténsli] *adv.* in a tense manner. 팽팽하게; 긴장해서. [*tense*[1]]

tense·ness [ténsnis] *n.* Ⓤ the state of being tense. 긴장 (상태).

ten·sile [ténsəl / ténsail] *adj.* **1** that can be stretched without breaking. 잡아늘일 수 있는. **2** of or relating to tension. 장력(張力)의. ¶ ~ *force* 인장력(引張力). [tend[1]]

tensile strength [⸗—⸗] *n.* 《phys.》 the load necessary to rupture a given material when pulled in the direction of length. 항장력(抗張力); 인장(引張) 강도. ¶ *the* ~ *of wire* 철사의 항장력[인장 강도].

·ten·sion [ténʃən] *n.* Ⓤ **1** the act of stretching or straining; the state of being tightly stretched or strained. 긴장; 팽팽함. ¶ *the* ~ *of the muscles* 근육의 켕김 / *The guitar string was snapped under the* ~. 기타 줄이 켕겨 끊어졌다. **2** mental strain. (정신적인) 긴장. ¶ ~ *of feeling* 긴장감 / *We feel some* ~ *before we take an exam.* 우리는 시험을 앞두고 약간 긴장한다. **3** a state of strained relation; friction. (관계 등의) 긴장 상태; 알력. ¶ *There is* ~ *between the two rivals.* 두 경쟁자 간에 갈등이 있다. **4** 《electr.》 voltage. 전압. ¶ *a high-tension current* 고압 전류 / *"Danger. High* ~ *wires. Keep clear !"* "위험. 고압선. 접근 금지!"《게시》. [*tense*[1]]

:tent [tent] *n.* Ⓒ a cloth shelter for camping supported by poles and ropes. 텐트; 천막. ¶ *pitch* [*strike*] *a* ~ 천막을 치다[걷다] / *a* ~ *peg* 천막 말뚝. —*vt., vi.* (P6; 1) **1** live in a tent. 천막에서 지내다. ¶ *We are tenting tonight.* 오늘 밤엔 천막에서 지낸다. **2** cover with or as with a tent. 천막 (같은 것)으로 덮다. [L. *tendo* stretch]

ten·ta·cle [téntəkəl] *n.* Ⓒ a long, slender organ growing around the mouth of a certain animal, used to touch and feel; a sensitive, hairlike growth on the head of an insect or the leaves of a certain plant. (하등 동물의) 촉수; (곤충의) 촉각; (식물의) 촉모(觸毛); 섬모(纖毛). [L. *tento* try]

ten·tac·u·lar [tentǽkjələr] *adj.* like or of the nature of a tentacle. 촉수[촉모(觸毛)] (모양)의.

ten·ta·tive [téntətiv] *adj.* made or done as a trial. 임시의; 시험적인. ¶ *a* ~ *theory* 가설(假說) / *a* ~ *plan* 시안(試案) / *a* ~ *opinion* 가정적인 의견《상대방의 의향을 듣기 위한》.

● **ten·ta·tive·ness** [-nis] *n.* [L. *tento* try]

ten·ter [téntər] *n.* a frame for stretching cloth so that it may dry without shrinking. 텐터; 재양틀. [L. *tentus*]

ten·ter·hook [téntərhùk] *n.* one of the hooks that hold cloth on a tenter. 재양틀 갈고리.

on tenterhooks, in a state of suspense, anxiety, etc. 조바심하여; 안달하여.

:tenth [tenθ] *n.* **1** 《usu. *the* ~》 number 10; 10th. 제10; 10 번째. **2** Ⓒ one of 10 equal parts of anything. 10분의 1. — *adj.* of 10th. 제10의; 10분의 1의. [*ten*]

ten·u·ous [ténjuəs] *adj.* **1** thin; slender; not dense. 엷은; 가는; 희박한. ¶ *a ~ thread* 가는 실 / *The air high above the earth is ~.* 지구 고공(高空)의 공기는 희박하다. **2** of little important. 대단찮은; 하찮은. ¶ *a ~ distinction* 미미한 차이 / *~ evidence* 미약한 증거. ● **ten·u·ous·ly** [-li] *adv.* **ten·u·ous·ness** [-nis] *n.* [L. *tenuis*]

ten·ure [ténjuər] *n.* **1** Ⓤ the act or right of holding land, buildings, etc.; the condition on which something is held. (부동산의) 보유; 보유권; 보유 조건. ¶ *One of the conditions of ~ is that you must keep the land under cultivation.* 보유 조건의 하나는 그 땅을 경작해야 한다는 것이다. **2** Ⓒ the period during which something is held. 보유 기간. ¶ *Changes took place during his ~ of office.* 그의 임기 중에 변화가 있었다. **3** 《U.S.》 Ⓤ permanent appointment (as a teacher, etc.). (교직 등의) 종신제(終身制). [L. *teneo* hold]

tep·id [tépid] *adj.* **1** a little warm. 미지근한. ¶ *Bring me a glass of ~ water.* 미지근한 물 한 컵 다오. **2** 《*fig.*》 not showing strong feeling. 열의가 없는. ¶ *a ~ reception* 시들한 접대 / *a rather ~ welcome* 별로 내키지 않는 환대. ● **tep·id·ness** [-nis] *n.* [L.]

te·pid·i·ty [tepídəti] *n.* Ⓤ the state or quality of being tepid. 미지근함; 미온; 열의가 없음.

ter·cen·te·nar·y [tə̀ːrsenténəri / tə̀ːrsentíːnəri] *adj.* of a period of 300 years. 300년(간)의. — *n.* Ⓒ (*pl.* **-nar·ies**) a period of 300 years; a 300th anniversary. 300년; 300년제(祭). [→centenary]

ter·cet [tə́ːrsit] *n.* **1** 《*poet.*》 a group of three lines rhyming together. 3행 연구(聯句). **2** 《mus.》 triplet. 셋잇단음표. [L. *tertium* third]

ter·gi·ver·sate [tə́ːrdʒivəːrsèit] *vi.* (P1) keep changing one's opinions or plans. 핑계대다; 변절하다. [L. *tergum* back, *verto* turn]

ter·gi·ver·sa·tion [tə̀ːrdʒivəːrséiʃən] *n.* evasion; apostasy. 핑계; 둘러대기; 변절.

:**term** [təːrm] *n.* Ⓒ **1** a fixed or limited period of time. 기간. ¶ *a ~ of office* 임기 / *a ~ of imprisonment* 형기(刑期) / *When does his term expire?* 그의 임기는 언제까지냐. **2** a date for payment. 지급 기일. ¶ *~ day* 지급일. **3** a part of a school year. 학기. ¶ *keep a ~* 한 학기 동안 출석하다 / *the first ~*, 1학기. **4** a word or phrase, esp. one expressing a special meaning or idea in some science, art, etc. 말; 용어; 전문어. ¶ *medical terms* 의학 용어 / *legal* 〔*technical*〕 *terms* 법률〔전문〕 용어 / *terms about radio* 라디오 전문어 / *Hero is hardly the ~ to apply to him.* 영웅이란 말은 그에게는 가당찮은 말이다. **5** 《*pl.*》 a way of speaking; mode of expression. 말씨; 말투. ¶ *in plain terms* 쉬운 말로 / *in high terms* 극구 칭찬하여 / (*speak*) *in set terms* 딱 잘라 (말하다) / *He spoke in terms of approval* 〔*in flattering terms*〕. 그의 말은 찬성〔아첨〕하는 투였다 / *a contradiction in terms* 자기 모순적인 말. **6** 《*pl.*》 mutual relationships among or between persons; friendly relations. 관계; 친한 사이. ¶ *on good terms with someone* 아무와 친한 사이로 / *be on speaking terms with someone* 아무와 서로 말하는〔만나는〕 사이다 / *They are not on terms.* 그들은 좋은 사이가 아니다. **7** 《*pl.*》 conditions (with regard to payment). (지급·요금 따위의) 조건. ¶ *on even terms* 대등한 조건으로 / *set terms* 조건을 붙이다 / *the terms of an agreement* 협정 조건 / *The terms asked for such lodgings are too high.* 이런 하숙에서 요구하는 하숙비가 너무 비싸다 / *sell furniture at reasonable terms* 가구를 괜찮은 값으로 팔다.

bring someone to terms, force someone to surrender; cause someone to accept conditions. …을 항복시키다; 납득시키다.

come to terms with (=*reach an agreement with; yield to*) *someone*. …와 타협하다; …에 양보하다; 굴복하다.

In terms of, **a**) in the language of. …한 말(투)로. **b**) by means of. …으로; …에 의하여. **c**) from the standpoint of. …의 견지에서. **d**) concerning. …에 관하여.

not on any terms, not for anything. 결코 … 않다.

on bad terms with, in discord with. …와 사이가 나빠.

— *vt.* (P7,18,19) call (something) by a term; give a name to (something). …라고 부르다; 칭하다; …을 —라고 이름짓다. ¶ *Her life may be termed happy.* 그녀의 생애가 행복하다고 말할 수도 있다 / *The chairman of this parliament is termed 'the speaker'.* 이 의회의 사회자를 이름하여 '의장'이라 한다. [→terminus]

ter·ma·gant [tə́ːrməgənt] *n.* Ⓒ a noisy, scolding woman. 잔소리 심한 여자. — *adj.* quarrelsome; scolding. 잔소리하는; 시끄러운. [name of a heathen deity]

ter·mi·na·ble [tə́ːrmənəbəl] *adj.* that can be ended (after a certain time). 유한의; 기한이 있는. ¶ *a ~ contract* 기한부 계약 / *~ 10 years from now* 향후 10년내 끝나는. ● **ter·mi·na·bly** [-i] *adv.* [↓]

ter·mi·nal [tə́ːrmənəl] *adj.* **1** forming the end. 끝의; 종점의. ¶ *the ~ station* 종착역. **2** coming at the end of a school term. 학기(말)의; 매학기의; 정기의. ¶ *a ~ examination* 학기말 시험. — *n.* Ⓒ **1** an end; a limit. 끝; 종말. **2** 《electr.》 a device attached to the end of an electric wire. 단자(端子). **3** 《U.S.》 the end of a railroad line; the last station. 종점; 종착역 (cf. 《Brit.》 *terminus*). [L. *terminus* boundary]

ter·mi·nal·ly [tə́ːrminəli] *adv.* at the end;

every term. 종말에; 말단에; 정기적으로.

ter·mi·nate [tə́ːrmənèit] *vt.* (P6) **1** bring (something) to an end; finish. …을 끝내다. ¶ *The two countries terminated friendly relations.* 두 나라의 우호 관계는 종식되었다. **2** limit; bound. (장소 등)을 제한하다. — *vi.* (P1,3) 《*at, in, with*》 come to an end; end. 끝나다. ¶ *The contract terminates in June.* 계약은 6월에 끝난다. ● **ter·mi·na·tor** [-ər] *n.*

ter·mi·na·tion [tə̀ːrmənéiʃən] *n.* UC the state of being terminated; the end; the conclusion. 종료; 종결; 결말. ¶ *bring something to a* ~ …을 종결시키다 / *put a* ~ *to something* …을 끝내다 / *the* ~ *of a journey* [*one's life, game*] 여행[인생, 경기]의 끝 / *the* ~ *of an agreement* 협정의 만료.

ter·mi·ni [tə́ːrmənài] *n.* pl. of **terminus.**

ter·mi·nol·o·gy [tə̀ːrmənálədʒi / -nɔ́l-] *n.* U 《*collectively*》 the special or technical words used in science, art, etc. 술어; 전문 용어. [*terminal*]

ter·mi·nus [tə́ːrmənəs] *n.* C (*pl.* **-mi·ni** or **-nus·es**) **1** a limit; an end; a goal. 종점; 끝; 목적지. **2** 《Brit.》 a station or town at the end of a railway or bus line, etc. 종착역; 종점 도시(cf. 《U.S.》 *terminal*). [L. *terminus*]

ter·mite [tə́ːrmait] *n.* C a white ant. 흰개미. [L.]

tern [təːrn] *n.* C a sea-bird like a gull, but more slender, smaller, and faster. 제비갈매기. [N.]

ter·ra [térə] *n.* 《L.》 the earth. 지구; 대지(大地).

ter·race [térəs] *n.* C **1** an outdoor space touching a house like a balcony. 테라스. **2** a flat, raised piece of land made in the side of a hill. 단지(段地); 단구(段丘). **3** a row of houses on a raised level. 고지대에 늘어선 집들. [*terra*]

ter·ra cot·ta [térə kátə / -kɔ́tə] *n.* 《L.》 **1** hard baked earth of a brownish-red color, used for making vases, ornamental figures, etc. 테라코타. **2** a brownish-red color. 적갈색. [*terra*]

ter·ra fir·ma [térə fə́ːrmə] *n.* 《L.》 solid earth; dry land (as contrasted with water). 육지; 뭍.

ter·rain [təréin] *n.* C a stretch of land, esp. when considered from a military point of view. (군사상 관점에서의) 지형(地形); 지세(地勢). [L. *terra* earth]

ter·ra in·cog·ni·ta [térə inkagníːtə / -kɔg-] *n.* 《L.》 an unknown country; 《*fig.*》 an unfamiliar region of thought or knowledge. 미지의 땅; (학문 등의) 미지의 영역.

ter·ra·pin [térəpin] *n.* C a turtle used for food, found in fresh water of North America. (북아메리카산의) 식용 거북. [Amer-Ind.]

ter·res·tri·al [təréstriəl] *adj.* **1** of or belonging to the earth. 지구(상)의(opp. celestial). ¶ ~ *magnetism* 지자기(地磁氣) / *a* ~ *being* 지상의 생물 / ~ *heat* 지열(地熱) / *a* ~ *globe* 지구의(儀). **2** worldly; earthly. 현세의. **3** living on or growing in the ground. 뭍에 사는[자라는]. ¶ ~ *animals* 육서(陸棲) 동물. [*terra*]

:ter·ri·ble [térəbəl] *adj.* **1** dreadful; causing terror. 무서운. ¶ *a* ~ *look* [*sight*] 무서운 표정[광경] / *a* ~ *fire* 무서운 불 / *be* ~ *in anger* 화나면 무섭다. **2** 《*colloq.*》 severe; hard to bear; causing extreme discomfort. 지독한; 아주 불쾌한. ¶ *a* ~ *heat* 혹서 / *a* ~ *winter* 엄동 / *a* ~ *accident* 끔찍한 사고 / *a* ~ *man for drink* 술고래. **3** 《*colloq.*》 very bad. 아주 나쁜. ¶ *My English is* ~. 내 영어는 형편 없다. ● **ter·ri·ble·ness** [-nis] *n.* [L. *terreo* frighten]

:ter·ri·bly [térəbli] *adv.* **1** in a terrible manner. 무섭게. **2** 《*colloq.*》 extremely; very. 몹시; 굉장히. ¶ *I am* ~ *hungry.* 배고파 죽겠다 / *We were* ~ *lucky to find you here.* 너를 여기서 만나 꿈만 같았다. **3** 《*colloq.*》 very badly. 아주 서투르게[형편없이]. ¶ *He played that piece of music* ~. 그의 그 악곡 연주는 아주 형편없었다.

ter·ri·er [tériər] *n.* C an active, intelligent, courageous dog, usu. of a small size, such as a Scotch terrier or a fox-terrier. 테리어개《몸집이 작고 영리한 애완견》. [→terra]

·ter·rif·ic [tərífik] *adj.* **1** causing terror; terrible; dreadful. 무서운; 무시무시한. ¶ *a* ~ *earthquake* 무서운 지진. **2** 《*colloq.*》 extreme; very great in size or degree. 지독한; 맹렬한; 엄청난. ¶ *She drove at a* ~ *speed.* 그녀는 맹렬한 속도로 차를 몰았다. **3** 《*colloq.*》 amazing; amazingly good; excellent. 굉장한; 아주 멋있는. ¶ *What a* ~ *party!* 야아, 굉장한 파티다. [→terrible]

·ter·ri·fy [térəfài] *vt.* (**-fied**) (P6) 《*at, with, into*》 fill (someone) with great fear; frighten very much. …을 크게 겁주다; 매우 놀라게 하다. ¶ *be terrified at* [*with*] … …에 크게 놀라다; …에 간담이 서늘해지다 / *be terrified out of one's senses* 놀라서 혼비 백산하다 / ~ *someone into compliance* 아무를 겁주어 승낙하게 하다 / *You* ~ *me.* 아이구, 깜짝이야 / *Terrified by the sight of the lion, he quickly ran for a tree.* 사자를 보고 놀란 그는 황급히 나무 있는 데로 뛰어갔다. [↑]

ter·ri·to·ri·al [tèrətɔ́ːriəl] *adj.* **1** of territory; of land. 영토의; 토지의. ¶ ~ *rights* 영토권 / ~ *expansion* 영토 확장 / ~ *air* 영공 / ~ *waters* 영해 / ~ *property* 토지 재산. **2** local; of a particular district. 지방의; 특정 지방의. [L.]

:ter·ri·to·ry [térətɔ̀ːri / -təri] *n.* (*pl.* **-ries**) **1** UC the land and waters which a state or government controls. 영토. ¶ *Once India was British* ~. 인도는 한때 영국의 영토였다. **2** UC a large area of land; a part of a country. 지역; 지방. ¶ *Much* ~ *in northwest*

China is desert. 중국 서북 지역의 대부분은 사막이다. **3** Ⓒ the facts belonging to science or learning. (과학·학문 등의) 영역; 분야. ¶ *Esoteric religions are a bit of outside my* ～. 비교(祕敎)는 나의 분야 밖이라 잘 모른다. **4** ⓐ Ⓒ the area where a salesman sells. (외판원 등의) 담당 구역. ¶ *As the company's northern sales manager, I'm responsible for quite a large* ～. 회사의 북부 지역 판매책으로서 나는 꽤 넓은 구역을 책임맡고 있다. ⓑ 《zool.》 the area which is defended by a male bird or mammal as breeding and feeding ground. (동물의) 세력권; 테리터리《동물의 활동·서식 범위》. **5** 《*T-*》 《U.S.》 a district of the country not admitted as a State. (미국의) 준주(準州). [L.]

:ter·ror [térər] *n.* **1** ⓊⒸ great fear; a thing or person that causes great fear. (심한) 공포; 공포의 대상(원인); 무서운 사람(것). ¶ *a novel of* ～ 공포(괴기) 소설 / *have a holy* ～ *of* …을 몹시 무서워하다 / *strike* ～ *into someone's heart* 아무를 공포로 떨게 하다 / *He was a* ～ *to all.* 그는 우리 모두에게 두려운 대상이었다 / *I have a* ～ *of insect.* 난 벌레가 무섭다. **2** Ⓒ 《*colloq.*》 a thing or person that causes much trouble and unpleasantness. 성가신 사람(것); 골칫거리. ¶ *a perfect* (*holy*) ～ 정말로 골치 아픈 녀석 / *Your son is a real* ～ *! Can't you control him ?* 당신 아들은 정말 말썽꾸러기이군, 어떻게 다스릴 수 없겠소. **3** Ⓤ violent action for political purposes; terrorism. (정치적 목적의) 폭력 행위; 테러리즘. ¶ *rule by* ～ 공포 정치를 행하다 / *a* ～ *campaign against the colonial rulers* 식민지 통치자에 저항하는 테러. [L. *terreo* frighten]

ter·ror·ism [térərìzəm] *n.* Ⓤ **1** the state of terror; politics that governs by the use of terror; the use of terror and violence (to achieve an end). 공포 상태; 공포 정치; 테러 행위. ¶ *The government is determined to combat international* ～. 정부는 국제 테러리즘에 대항할 것을 결정했다. **2** a condition of terror produced by such a method. 전율(戰慄).

ter·ror·ist [térərist] *n.* Ⓒ a person who uses terrorism. 공포 정치가; 폭력주의자; 테러리스트.

ter·ror·ize [térəràiz] *vt.* (P6) fill (someone) with terror; rule or dominate (a nation, etc.) by means of terror. …을 무서워하게 하다; 공포 정책으로 지배하다. ¶ *Bandits have been terrorizing the border regions.* 산적들은 변경 지방을 공포에 떨게 하고 있다.

ter·ror·strick·en [térərstrìkən] *adj.* stricken or overwhelmed by terror; terrified. 공포에 휩싸인; 공포에 질린.

ter·ror·struck [térərstrʌ̀k] *adj.* struck with great fear. 공포에 질린.

terse [təːrs] *adj.* (of speech style, or speakers) elegantly brief and to the point. 간명(간결)한; 요령 있는. ¶ *a* ～ *letter* (*style*) 간결한 편지(문체). ● **terse·ness** [ˊnis] *n.* [L. *tergo* wipe]

terse·ly [tə́ːrsli] *adv.* in a terse manner. 간결하게.

ter·tian [tə́ːrʃən] *adj.* (of a fever or disease) occurring every other day. (열 등이) 하루 걸러 일어나는. —*n.* Ⓤ such a fever or disease, esp. malaria. 격일열(隔日熱); 말라리아. [L. *tertius* third]

ter·ti·ar·y [tə́ːrʃièri, -ʃəri] *adj.* **1** of the third rank or order; third. 제3(위)의. **2** 《*T-*》 《geol.》 of the Tertiary. 제3기(紀)의. —*n.* 《*the T-*》 《geol.》 the third period in the formation of rocks. 제3기(紀). [↑]

tes·sel·late [tésəlèit] *vt.* pave (floors, pavements, etc.) with small blocks in a mosaic pattern. …을 모자이크(바둑판) 무늬로 짜다; (길)을 모자이크식으로 포장하다. [Gk. *tessares* four]

tes·sel·la·ted [tésəlèitid] *adj.* made up of many small blocks of stone forming a pattern. 바둑판 무늬의; 모자이크식의. ¶ ～ *pavement* 모자이크식 포장.

:test [test] *n.* Ⓒ **1** an examination; trial. 시험; 검사; 테스트. ¶ *a* ～ *pilot* 시험 비행사 / *a* ～ *for color blindness* 색맹 검사 / *put to the* ～ 시험하다 / *an intelligence* (*aptitude*) ～ 지능(적성) 검사 / *give a* ～ *in English* 영어 시험을 치르다 / *stand* (*bear*) *the* ～ 시험에 합격하다(시련에 견디다). **2** means of trial; touchstone. 시험의 수단; 시금석. ¶ *Poverty is a* ～ *of character.* 가난은 인격의 시금석이다. **3** 《chem.》 an analysis; the substance used in the analysis. 분석; 시약(試藥).

—*vt.* (P6) **1** examine; try. …을 검사(시험)하다. ¶ ～ *a wall for cracks* 벽의 균열을 검사하다 / ～ *someone's character* 아무의 인격을 시험하다. **2** analyze; examine the quality of (something). …을 분석(감식)하다. ¶ ～ *ore for gold* 광석을 분석하여 금의 함량을 알아보다 / ～ *a solution by litmus paper* 용액을 리트머스 시험지로 감식하다. [L. *testum* pot]

·tes·ta·ment [téstəmənt] *n.* Ⓒ **1** 《law》 a written document in which a person declares what to do with his property after his death; a will. 유언; 유서. 參考 흔히 one's last will and testament 라고 함. **2** 《*the T-*》 ⓐ either of the two main parts of the Bible. 신약(구약) 성서. ⓑ 《*colloq.*》 the New Testament. 신약 성서. ¶ *the Old* (*New*) *Testament* 구약(신약) 성서. [L. *testis* witness]

tes·tate [tésteit] *adj.* having made and left a will at death. 유언을 남기고 죽은. —*n.* Ⓒ a person who has died leaving a will. 유언하고 죽은 사람. [↑]

tes·ta·tor [tésteitər, ―ˊ―] *n.* a person who has made a will; a person who has died leaving a will. 유언자.

tes·ta·tri·ces [testéitrəsìːz] *n.* pl. of **tes-**

tatrix.

tes·ta·trix [testéitriks] *n.* (*pl.* **-tri·ces**) a woman who makes a will. 여성 유언자.

test·er [téstər] *n.* Ⓒ a person or thing that tests. 시험자; 시험 기구. [→test]

***tes·ti·fy** [téstəfài] *v.* (**-fied**) *vi.* (P1,3) 《*to*》 bear witness; give evidence. 입증하다; 증언〔증명〕하다. ¶ *This fact testifies to his innocence.* 이 사실이 그의 무죄를 증명한다 / *~ on behalf of someone* 아무에게 유리한 증언을 하다 / *~ against someone* 아무에게 불리하게 증언하다. ── *vt.* (P6,11) bear witness to; prove; give evidence of (something); profess. …을 증명〔입증〕하다; 증언하다; 확언〔언명〕하다. ¶ *This fact testifies that he is innocent.* 이 사실이 그의 결백을 증명한다 / *He testified that he had seen the man.* 그는 그 남자를 보았다고 증언했다. [→testament]

tes·ti·ly [téstili] *adv.* in a testy manner. 화난 듯이; 퉁명스럽게. [→testy]

tes·ti·mo·ni·al [tèstəmóuniəl] *n.* Ⓒ **1** a letter telling the character, ability, etc., of a person, or the value of a thing. (인격·능력·가치 등에 대한) 증명서; 추천장. ¶ *The boy looking for a job should have testimonials from his teachers and a former employer.* 일자리를 찾고 있는 그 아이는 선생님과 전(前)고용주의 추천장이 있어야만 했다. **2** a gift showing esteem, thankfulness, etc. 감사장; 기념품. [→testimony]

***tes·ti·mo·ny** [téstəmòuni / -mə-] *n.* (*pl.* **-nies**) **1** Ⓤ the statement by a witness on oath; attestation. 증언; 증명. ¶ *I can bear ~ to his good character.* 나는 그가 훌륭한 인물임을 증명〔입증〕할 수 있다 / *call someone in ~* 아무를 증인으로 세우다 / *A witness gave ~ that Mr. A was at home 9 to 12 p.m.* 한 증인은 A씨가 오후 9시에서 12시까지 집에 있었다고 증언했다. **2** ⓊⒸ anything that shows or make clear; outward proof; evidence. 증명이 되는 것; 증거. ¶ *produce ~ of* 〔*to*〕 *the fact* 그 사실에 대한 증거를 제출하다 / *Fossil-bearing rocks give ~ of life in former ages.* 화석(化石)을 지닌 암석은 먼 옛날에 생물의 존재를 증명하고 있다. [L. *testis* witness]

bear testimony to, affirm. 입증하다.

in testimony of, as evidence or proof of. …의 증거로서.

test pilot [←―] *n.* a pilot who tests new or experimental airplanes. 테스트파일럿; 시험 비행사. [→test]

test tube [←―] *n.* a thin glass tube, closed at one end, used in chemical tests. 시험관.

tes·ty [tésti] *adj.* (**-ti·er, -ti·est**) quick-tempered; irritable; impatient. 화를 잘내는; 성마른. [→test]

tet·a·nus [tétənəs] *n.* Ⓤ a serious nerve disease causing stiffness of the muscles and even death. 파상풍(破傷風). [Gk. *teinō* stretch]

teth·er [téðər] *n.* **1** Ⓒ a rope or chain to tie cattle. (마소를) 잡아매는 밧줄〔사슬〕. ¶ *The cow had broken her ~ and was in the cornfield.* 소는 잡아맨 밧줄을 끊고 옥수수 밭에 들어가 있었다. **2** Ⓤ the range of one's ability, endurance, resources, etc. (능력 등의) 한계; 범위.

at the end of one's tether, having no more money, strength, power to act, etc. 백계(百計)가 다하여; 한계에 이르러. ¶ *I'm at the end of my ~.* 나는 이제 더는 어쩔 수가 없다.

beyond one's tether, beyond one's scope. 힘이 못미쳐; 힘에 부쳐.

── *vt.* (P6,7,13) fasten (cattle, etc.) with a tether. …을 밧줄로 (잡아)매다. [N.]

tet·ra- [tétrə-] *pref.* four. '넷'의 뜻. 語法 모음 앞에서는 보통 tetr- 가 됨. [Gk.]

tet·ra·gon [tétrəgàn / -gən] *n.* 《geom.》 a four-sided figure. 4각〔변〕형. [tetra-]

tet·ra·he·dra [tètrəhí:drə / -hé-] *n.* pl. of **tetrahedron.**

tet·ra·he·dron [tètrəhí:drən / -hé-] *n.* (*pl.* **-drons** or **-dra**) a solid four-sided figure. 사면체(四面體).

Teu·ton [tjú:tən] *n.* Ⓒ **1** a member of the group of people including the Germans, Dutch, Anglo-Saxons and Scandinavians. 튜턴 사람. **2** a German. 독일인. [L.]

Teu·ton·ic [tju:tánik / -tɔ́n-] *adj.* **1** of the Teutons or their languages. 튜턴 사람〔민족, 언어〕의. **2** German. 독일인의; 독일어의. ¶ *~ thoroughness* 독일인의 철저성. ── *n.* Ⓤ the Teutonic languages; Germanic. 튜턴〔게르만〕어.

Tex·as [téksəs] *n.* a southern State of the United States, on the gulf of Mexico. 텍사스. 參考 Tex.로 생략함. 주도는 Austin.

:text [tekst] *n.* **1** Ⓤ the main body of a book or printed page. 본문. ¶ *This book contains 300 pages of ~, and 50 pages of notes.* 이 책은 본문이 300 페이지에 주석이 50 페이지이다 / *Children's books often have more pictures than ~.* 아이들 책은 흔히 본문보다 그림이 더 많다. **2** Ⓒ the original words of a writer. 원문. ¶ *The newspaper published the whole ~ of the speech.* 신문은 그 연설의 원문 전체를 게재했다. **3** Ⓒ a short passage in the Bible used as the subject of a sermon, etc. (설교 등에서 인용한) 성경 구절. **4** Ⓒ a subject of a discussion; a theme. 화제; 논제. ¶ *stick* 〔*strike*〕 *to one's ~* (이야기 따위가) 탈선하지 않다. **5** Ⓒ 《U.S.》 a textbook esp. used in schools. 교과서. ●**text·less** [⌐lis] *adj.* [L. *texo* weave]

:text·book [tékstbùk] *n.* Ⓒ a book used in schools and colleges. 교과서.

tex·tile [tékstail, -til] *adj.* **1** of weaving. 직물〔피륙〕의. ¶ *~ industry* 직물〔섬유〕 산업. **2** woven. 짠; 방직된. ¶ *~ fabrics* 직물; 피륙. **3** that can be woven. 방직할 수 있는. ── *n.* Ⓒ 《usu. *pl.*》 **1** woven fabric. 천; 피륙; 직

물. **2** textile material. 직물의 원료. [*text*]

tex·tu·al [tékstʃuəl] *adj.* of the text; based on the text. 본문의; 원문대로의. ¶ *a ~ error* 원문의 오류 / *~ criticism* (특히 성서의)원문 대조 비평. [→textile]

tex·ture [tékstʃər] *n.* ⒸⓊ **1** the character of the woven fabrics resulting from the quality or arrangement of the thread. (피륙의) 짜임새; 바탕. ¶ *cloth of a loose* 〔*fine*〕 *~* 발이 성긴〔고운〕 천. **2** the arrangement of the parts; structure. 조직; 구조. ¶ *the compact ~ of clay* 점토의 치밀한 구조. **3** the quality of the surface. (피부·목재·암석 등의) 결; 감촉. ¶ *Her skin has a fine ~.* 그녀의 살결은 곱다 / *the smooth ~ of silk* 비단의 보드라운 감촉. [→textile]

Th. Thursday.

Thai [tai, tá:i] *n.* **1** Ⓤ a branch of the Indo-Chinese languages; the language of Thailand. 타이〔샴〕어(語). **2** Ⓒ a member of a group of Thai-speaking people; the people of Thailand. 타이 사람. —*adj.* of Thailand. 타이 사람의; 타이 어의.

Thai·land [táilæ̀nd, tá:i-] *n.* a country in southeastern Asia, between Myanmar and Malaya. 타이; 태국. 參考 구칭은 Siam, 수도는 Bankok.

Thai·land·er [táilæ̀ndər, tá:i-] *n.* Ⓒ a person of Thailand. 타이 사람; 태국인.

thal·a·mi [θǽləmài] *n.* pl. of **thalamus.**

thal·a·mus [θǽləməs] *n.* (*pl.* **-mi**) 《anat.》 a part of the brain where an optic nerve emerges. 시상(視床). [Gk. *thálamos* inner chamber]

thal·li [θǽlai] *n.* pl. of **thallus.**

thal·lus [θǽləs] *n.* (*pl.* **-lus·es** or **thal·li**) 《bot.》 a plant not divided into leaves, stem, and root. 엽상체(葉狀體). [Gk.]

·**Thames** [temz], **the** *n.* a river in southern England. 템스 강.

:**than** [ðæn, ðən] *conj.* **1** 《used after *comparative adjectives, adverbs,* and such other word, as *other, otherwise* and *else*》 in comparison with (or that...). …보다는; …에 비하여. ¶ *I know you better ~* (*I know*) *him.* 나는 그보다도〔그를 아는 이상으로〕 당신을 더 잘 알고 있소 / *I love her more ~ he* (*loves her* 〔*does*〕). 나는 그가 그녀를 사랑하는 이상으로 그녀를 사랑한다 / *It's less cold in March ~ in February.* 3월은 2월만큼 춥지 않다. **2** 《used after *soon, rather,* etc.》 if ... at all; if one should have to.... …하느니보다는 차라리; …할 바에는 오히려. ¶ *I would rather* 〔*sooner*〕 *starve to death ~ steal.* 도둑질을 하느니 차라리 굶어 죽겠다 / *I'd rather play football ~ go swimming.* 수영하러 가느니 축구를 하겠다 / *She said she'd rather leave her job ~ be forced to work for such an unpleasant man.* 그녀는 그 따위 꼴보기 싫은 자를 위해 일해야 할 바에는 직장을 그만 두겠다고 했다. **3** 《used after some *adverbs* and *adjectives,* such as *else, other,* and *otherwise, anywhere,* 《U.S.》 *different,* etc.》 except; besides. … 이외에 (는); …밖에는. ¶ *We had no choice other ~ this.* 이렇게 할 도리밖에 없었다 / *No other ~ his parents can help him.* 부모 이외에는 그를 도울 사람이 없다 / *She did nothing else ~ sob.* 그녀는 그저 흐느껴 울 뿐이었다 / *She is otherwise ~ he thought.* 그녀는 그가 생각했던 그런 여자가 아니다 / *I have no other friend ~ you.* 나는 친구라고는 너 밖에 없다 / *It was no* 〔*none*〕 *other ~ the king.* 그것은 다른 사람이 아닌 바로 왕 자신이었다.

—*prep.* **1** 《usu. in the phrase *than whom*》 in relation to; compared to. …보다도; … 이상으로. ¶ *She is a girl ~ whom I can imagine no one prettier.* 그녀보다 더 예쁜 소녀는 상상이 안 된다 / *Here is my son ~ whom a better does not exist.* 이놈이 내 아들인데 내게는 이보다 더 좋은 녀석은 없다. **2** 《used after the *comparative degree*》 in comparison with. …에 비하여. ¶ *They arrived earlier ~ usual.* 그들은 평시보다 일찍 도착했다 / *They favor gradual rather ~ radical change.* 그들은 급격한 변동보다는 점진적인 것을 선호한다 / *Offenders are liable to a fine of not more ~ $100.* 위반자들에게는 최고 100달러의 벌과금을 부과하도록 되어 있다. [*then*]

:**thank** [θæŋk] *n.* Ⓒ 《*pl.*》 gratitude; a grateful feeling; an expression of gratitude. 감사; 감사의 말; 치사. ¶ *express one's thanks* 사의를 표하다 / *give* 〔*return*〕 *thanks to someone* 아무에게 감사(해)하다; (건배에 대하여) 답사하다; (식사 전후에) 감사 기도를 드리다 / *She smiled her thanks.* 그녀는 미소로서 사의를 표했다 / *I owe you thanks.* 자네에게 감사해야 되겠다《신세 따위를 졌을 때 인사말》/ *Many* 〔*A thousand, My best*〕 *thanks.* 참으로 고맙습니다 / *No, thanks.* 아니 괜찮습니다(=No, thank you.) / *No thanks!* 별로 달갑지 않다(=Thank you for nothing.) / *Please accept my best thanks.* 정말 대단히 고맙습니다 / *No thanks to him though.* 그래도 그 사람에겐 아무 신세진 것 없다.

small 〔***no***〕 ***thanks to,*** no need to say thanks to; without any help from. …의 덕분〔덕택〕이 아니라. ¶ *We succeeded, small thanks to him.* 우리가 그 사람 덕에 성공한 건 아니다.

thanks to, owing to; on account of. …의 덕분에; …이 원인으로. ¶ *Thanks to your help, I was able to do it.* 자네 덕분에 그 일을 할 수 있었다.

—*vt.* **1** (P6,13) 《*for*》 express gratitude to (someone). …에게 감사하다; 사례하다; 사의를 표하다. ¶ *Thank you for the beautiful pearl necklace.* 아름다운 진주 목걸이를 주셔서 감사합니다 / *Thank you for nothing.* 하나도 고맙지 않다《별로 달갑지 않다》/ *No, ~ you.* 아니, 괜찮습니다 / *She thanked me with a smile.* 웃으면서 내게 고마워했다 / *Thank Heaven* 〔*goodness*〕*!* 아이구 고맙기도 해

라 / *Thanking you in anticipation.* 여불비례(餘不備禮). **2** (P13,20,21) ask; demand. …에게 ―을 부탁하다. ¶ *I will ~ you to open the door.* 문을 좀 열어 주십시오 / *I will ~ you to be a little more polite.* 좀더 정중했으면 좋겠습니다 / *I will ~ you not to interfere with my affairs.* 내 일에 참견 말아 주게나 / *You will ~ yourself for it.* = *You have yourself to ~ for it.* 그건 네 자업자득이다. [E.]

·thank·ful [θǽŋkfəl] *adj.* feeling or expressing thanks; grateful. 감사한; 고마운; 매우 기쁜. ¶ *I am ~ to you for your favors.* 배려해 주셔서 감사합니다 / *I am ~ that I saw him before he died.* 그의 임종을 보게 되어 감사하고 있다 / *with a ~ heart* 감사하는 마음으로 / *I am ~ to know that he is safe.* 그가 무사하다니 매우 기쁘다.

thank·ful·ly [θǽŋkfəli] *adv.* with thanks; gratefully. 감사하여.

thank·ful·ness [θǽŋkfəlnis] *n.* Ⓤ the state of being thankful; gratitude. 감사; 사의(謝意).

thank·less [θǽŋklis] *adj.* **1** not feeling or expressing thanks; not grateful. 감사하지 않는; 고마운 줄 모르는; 배은 망덕한. **2** not leading to be rewarded with thanks; unprofitable. 감사받지 못하는; 달가워하지 않는; 수지 맞지 않는. ¶ *a ~ task* 〔*job*〕 수지 안 맞는 일 / *Giving advice is usually a ~ job* 〔*task*〕. 충고를 준다는 것은 흔히 달가운 일이 못된다.
● **thank·less·ness** [-nis] *n.*

thank·less·ly [θǽŋklisli] *adv.* in a thankless manner. 고마운 줄〔은혜를〕 모르고; 배은 망덕하게도.

·thanks·giv·ing [θæ̀ŋksgíviŋ / ⌐⌐‒] *n.* **1** Ⓤ the expression of gratitude, esp. to God. 신에 대한 감사. **2** Ⓒ a prayer expressing thanks to God. 감사의 기도. **3** 《*T-*》 = Thanksgiving Day.

Thanksgiving Day [⌐‒‒ ⌐] *n.* 《U.S.》 a national holiday for giving thanks to God, on the fourth Thursday in November. (추수) 감사절.

:that [ðæt, ðət, ðt] *adj.* (*pl.* **those** [ðouz]) **1** already told or pointed out; the. 저; 그; 예의. ¶ *The wind blew ~ night.* 그날 밤엔 바람이 불었다 / *What's ~ loud noise ?* 저 시끄러운 소리는 뭣이냐 / *In those days they worked very hard.* 그 시절에 그들은 열심히 일했다 / *Oh, I've heard ~ story before.* 아, 전에 나는 그 얘기를 들었다 / *From ~ moment he was completely changed.* 그 때부터 그는 완전히 달라졌다 / *Those complaints of his make me sick.* 늘 하는 그자의 우는 소리엔 신물이 난다. **2** 《indicating a person or thing more or less distant》 which is at a distance. 저쪽의; 저…(cf. *this*). ¶ *You see ~ tower.* 저 탑이 보이지 / *What is ~ noise ?* 저 소리가 무슨 소리냐 / *~ house across the street* 길 건너 저 집 / *Who are those people over there ?* 저기 있는 저 사람들은 누구냐. **3** 《in contrast with *this*》 the other; another; farther of two or more. 다른 한쪽의; 저편〔쪽〕의. ¶ *This car is mine and ~ one is hers.* 이건 내 차고 저건 그녀의 것이다 / *This room is a lot warmer than ~ one* (*across the passage*). 이 방이 (통로 건너의) 저 방보다 훨씬 따스하다.

― *adv.* to that extent; to such a degree; so. 그 정도로; 그렇게. ¶ *The little girl can't walk ~ far.* 그 어린 소녀는 그렇게 멀리까지 못 걷는다 / *He has done only ~ much.* 그는 그 정도 밖에 하지 않았다 / *It's not all ~ hot.* 그렇게까지 덥지는 않다 / 《*vulg.*》 *I was ~ angry I struck him on the head.* 난 얼마나 화가 났던지 그놈의 머리를 쥐어박았다.

― *pron.* (*pl.* **those**) **1** the person or thing already known or understood. 그것; 그 일. ¶ *After ~ his attitude changed.* 그 일이 있고 나서 그의 태도가 달라졌다 / *That will do.* 그것으로 좋다〔됐다〕 / *Her manner was ~ of a lady.* 그녀의 태도는 숙녀의 그것이었다 / *That's what he said.* 그가 말한 것이 바로 그거다 / *The climate is like ~ of America.* 기후는 미국의 기후와 같다 / *Is ~ the man you mean ?* 저이가 네가 말하는 그분이냐. **2** 《in contrast with *this*》 the farther of two or more things; one of two or more persons or things. 다른 쪽; 또 한쪽. ¶ *Which do you like better, this or ~ ?* 어느 것이 더 좋으냐, 이것이냐 저것이냐. **3** a person or thing which is at a distance. 저것; 저쪽의 것. ¶ *Can you see ~ ?* 저것이 보이느냐 / *This is cheaper than ~.* 이것이 저것보다 값이 싸다 / *This is Mary and ~ is Bety.* 이 애가 메리고 저 애가 베티다. **4** 《in contrast with *this*》 the former. 전자. ¶ *Virtue and vice before you; this leads to misery, and ~ to peace.* 덕과 악덕이 너의 앞에 있다. 후자는 불행으로, 전자는 평화로 인도한다 / *Work and play are both necessary to health; this gives us rest, and ~ gives us energy.* 일과 유희는 모두 건강에 필요하다. 후자는 휴식을 주고 전자는 활력을 준다. **5** [ðæt, ðət] 《as an *antecedent* to a *relative pronoun*》 (…하는 바의) 일〔것〕. ¶ *What was ~ he said ?* 그가 말한 것이 무엇이었더냐 / 《*prov.*》 *Heaven helps those who help themselves.* 하늘은 스스로 돕는 자를 돕는다 / *That which you told me to do I did.* 분부하신 일을 했습니다.

and all that, and what not; etc. …따위; 등등.

at that, 《*colloq.*》 besides; further more; even so. 게다가; 더구나; 그 위에; 그렇다 하더라도. ¶ *He lost an arm, and the right arm at ~.* 그는 한쪽 팔을 잃었다. 그것도 오른 팔을.

for all that, in spite of that. 그럼에도 불구하고.

in that, because. …한 이유로.

that is (***to say***), namely. 이를테면; 즉. 參考 i.e.라고 생략.

That's right. 《Brit.》 Yes, just so.; 《U.S.》

Hear, hear. 그래 좋다〔됐다, 맞다〕; 찬성이오; 옳소.
That's that. 《*colloq.*》 That is finished or decided. 그것으로 끝났다〔결정됐다〕.
with that, after that; thereupon. 그렇게 말하고; 그리하여. ¶ *With ~ he shut the door.* 그렇게 말하고 그는 문을 닫았다.
— *rel. pron.* **1** who; whom; which. …하는 바의. 語法 목적절을 이끄는 경우, 특히 구어에서는 일반적으로 생략함. ¶ *the greatest writer ~ has ever lived* 불세출의 대(大)문호 / *the girl ~ you met yesterday* 네가 어제 만났던 그 소녀 / *the man ~ I want to see* 내가 만나기를 원하는 그 사람 / *the boy that spoke to me* 내게 말을 걸었던 그 소년. **2** 《in place of a *relative adverb*》 when; where. …라는 바의 (날, 시간, 장소). ¶ *the last time ~ I saw her* 내가 그녀를 마지막으로 보았을 때 / *This is the place ~ I was born.* 여기가 내 출생지다. **3** 《*It is…that…*》 …하는 것은. ¶ *It is Sakespeare ~ I like best.* 내가 가장 좋아하는 사람은 셰익스피어다 / *It is you ~ are in the wrong.* 틀린 것은 바로 너다 / *It is you ~ are to blame.* 잘못〔책임〕은 바로 네게 있다 / *It was peace ~ they fought for.* 그들이 싸운 것은 평화를 위해서였다.
— *conj.* [ðːet, ðət] **1** 《used to introduce a *noun clause*》 …이라는 것; …한다는 것. ¶ *That you would fail was certain.* 네가 실패할 것은 자명했다 / *It is certain ~ our team will win.* 우리 팀이 이길 것은 분명하다 / *I have no doubt ~ he will succeed.* 그가 성공하리라는 것은 의심할 여지가 없다 / *It is hoped ~ all will go well.* 만사가 잘 되기를 바라고 있다 / *The trouble is ~ he is ill in bed.* 문제는 그가 앓아 누웠다는 것이다. **2** 《used to introduce an *adverb clause*》 ⓐ 《expressing *purpose*》 with a purpose. …하도록; …하기 위해. ¶ *I hurried ~* 〔*so ~ =in order ~*〕 *I might be in time.* 시간에 대기 위해 나는 서둘렀다 / *Work ~ you may succeed.* 성공을 위해 열심히 공부해라 / *We eat so ~ we may live.* 우린 살기 위해 먹는다. ⓑ 《expressing *result*》 with the result. 그러므로; 따라서. ¶ *I was so tired ~ I could not go on any further.* 너무 피곤해서 더는 갈 수 없었다 / *The news gave her such a shock ~ her face turned white.* 그 소식이 얼마나 충격을 주었던지 그녀 얼굴은 새하얘졌다 / *She is such a good girl ~ everyone loves her.* 그녀는 얼마나 착한 소녀인지 누구나 그녀를 사랑한다. ⓒ 《expressing *cause* or *reason*》 because. …때문에; …이므로. ¶ *I am sorry ~ I cannot help you.* 도와 주지 못해 미안하다 / *If I scold you, it is ~ I want you to be a good boy.* 내가 너를 야단치더라도 그것은 네가 착한 아이가 되기를 바라기 때문이다 / *I am surprised that he did such a thing.* 그가 그런 일을 저질렀다니 놀랍기만 하다. **3** 《used to introduce a sentence expressing *desire, surprise,* or other *strong emotion*》 …이라면; …면 좋을 텐데; …하다니. ¶ *That he should do such a thing!* 그가 그런 일을 하다니 / *O ~ I were in Rome now!* 아아, 내가 지금 로마에 있다면 (좋을 텐데) / *Now ~ he has got well, he ought to come and see us.* 회복되었으면 우릴 만나러 오면 좋으련만. **4** 《emphasizing *an adverb* (*phrase*)》 …한〔하는, 이라는〕 것은. ¶ *It was yesterday ~ I met him.* 내가 그를 만난 것은 어제였다 / *It's much to be regretted ~ he died.* 그가 죽었다니 너무너무 안됐다〔가엾다〕. [E.]
now that, since; because. …이므로; …한 이상.
seeing that, since; because. …한 것을 보면; …이므로.

thatch [θætʃ] *n.* **1** Ⓒ a roof or covering made of straw, reeds, palm-leaves, etc. 초가 지붕. **2** Ⓤ the material used as a roof or covering. 지붕 이는 재료; 이엉; 짚; 억새. **3** Ⓤ 《*colloq.*》 the hair of the head. 머리털《더부룩한》. — *vt.* (P6) cover or roof (a house, etc.) with thatch. (지붕)을 짚으로 이다. [E.]

***that's** [ðǽts] that is.

***thaw** [θɔː] *vi.* (P1) **1** (of ice, snow or anything frozen) melt; become water. (얼음 등이) 녹다. ¶ *It is thawing.* (눈 등이) 녹고 있다. **2** ⓐ(of the weather) grow warm enough to melt ice and snow. 얼음·눈이 녹는 철이 되다; 따뜻해지다. ⓑ 《*fig.*》 (of a person) become warm. 몸이 녹다〔풀리다〕. ¶ *I was half frozen after my drive, but I'm gradually thawing.* 드라이브 후에 몸이 얼다시피했는데 이제 차차 풀려온다. **3** 《*fig.*》 become friendly. (감정 따위가) 누그러지다. ¶ *After their third meeting she began to ~.* 세 번 만나고 난 후로 그녀의 태도는 누그러지기 시작했다.
— *vt.* (P6,7) cause (the ice) to melt; cause (someone) to be friendly. …을 녹이다; (마음 따위가) 풀리게〔누그러지게〕 하다. ¶ *The sun at noon thaws the ice on the streets.* 한낮의 태양이 거리의 얼음을 녹인다 / *Come and ~ out in front of fire.* 이리 불 앞에 와서 몸을 녹이시오.
— *n.* Ⓒ 《usu. *sing.*》 the state of the weather when ice or snow is melting. 눈석임; 해동; 해빙(기); 눈녹는 따뜻한 날씨. [E.]

:the [ðiː, ðə, *before vowels* ði] *def. art.* **1** already known or understood; obvious without relating; that. 그; 이; 예(例)의. ¶ *Please open ~ window.* 그 창문 좀 열어 다오 / *The girl I met yesterday was my niece.* 내가 어제 만난 소녀는 내 조카딸이다 / *I have a black dog and a white dog; ~ black one is called Rover.* 나에겐 검은 개 한마리와 흰 개 한마리가 있는데 검은 놈의 이름은 로버다 / *~ man I loved* 내가 사랑하던 그 사람. **2** unique; only one; sole. 단 하나의; 독특한; 유일의. ¶ *~ sun* 태양 / *~ world* 세계 / *~ Bible* 성경 / *~ winter* / *~ south* / *~ Devil* 마왕 / *~ earth* 지구. **3** (of a part of the body) one's. 사람의; 아무의. ¶ *take someone by* ~ *hand* 아무의 손을 잡다. **4** 《in names of diseases》 《병명에 붙여》. ¶ ~ *blues* 우울증 / *have* ~ *measles* 홍역을 앓다. **5** whole of class or species of; every; any. (종류의 전체를 가리켜) 모든; …라는 것. ¶ *The dog is a faithful animal.* 개는 충실한 동물이다 / *The pen is mightier than* ~ *sword.* 문(文)은 무(武)보다 강하다. **6** such; so; enough. …하는 그러한. ¶ *He was not* ~ *man to betray her.* 그는 그녀를 배반할 그런 사람이 아니었다 / *He had* ~ *kindness to show me the way.* 그는 친절하게도 나에게 길을 가르쳐 주었다. **7** typical; real; true. 전형적인; 진정한; 진짜의. ¶ *He is* ~ *man.* 그 사람이야말로 진짜 사나이다 / *This is* ~ *life.* 인생이란 이런 것이다. **8** best. 가장 좋은; 최고의. ¶ *Beer is* ~ *drink for hot weather.* 맥주가 더운 계절에는 최고의 음료이다 / *This is* ~ *hotel in this town.* 이것이 이 읍내에서는 가장 좋은 호텔이다 / *He is* ~ *poet of* ~ *day.* 그는 당대 제일의 시인이다. **9** per; a. …에 대하여; …마다. ¶ *5 dollars* ~ *pound* 파운드당 5달러 / *so much* ~ *hour* 한 시간에〔시간당〕 그만큼. **10** 《used before *proper nouns*》 《고유명사에 붙여》. ¶ ~ *United States* (*of America*) (아메리카) 합중국 / ~ *Himalayas* 히말라야 산맥 / ~ *Mississippi* 미시시피 강 / ~ *Pacific Ocean* 태평양 / ~ *Suez Canal* 수에즈 운하 / ~ *Bay of Asan* 아산만 / ~ *White House* 백악관 / ~ *Bank of Korea* 한국 은행 / *The New York Times* 뉴욕 타임스 지(紙). **11** 《used before a *title* and *family name*》 《칭호·가명에 붙여》. ¶ *Alfred* ~ *Great* 알프렛 대왕 / ~ *Duke of Wellington* 웰링턴 공작. **12** 《before the name of a ship》 《선명에 붙여》. ¶ ~ *Queen Elizabeth* 퀸 엘리자베스호. **13** 《before certain institution》 《공공시설·건조물 앞에 붙여》. ¶ ~ *Savoy* 사보이 호텔 / ~ *British Museum* 대영 박물관 / *We went to* ~ *theater last night.* 어젯밤 연극 구경을 갔었다. **14** 《used before *adjective* to make *nouns*》 《형용사에 붙여》. ¶ ~ *young* 젊은이들 / ~ *living and* ~ *dead* 산 자와 죽은 자 / ~ *beautiful* 미(美) / ~ *poor* 가난한 사람들.

— *adv.* 《used with the *comparative degree*》 by so much; that much; to that extent. 더욱 (더); 도리어; 오히려; …하면 할수록; 그만큼…. ¶ *The higher we go up in the air,* ~ *colder it becomes.* 공중에 오르면 오를수록 공기는 더 차가워진다 / *I take a walk every morning and feel* ~ *better for it.* 매일 아침 산책을 하는데 할수록 더 느낌이 좋아진다 / *I like him all* ~ *better for his faults.* 그가 결점이 있으므로 해서 (그만큼) 더 그를 좋아한다 / *The sooner,* ~ *better.* 빠르면 빠를수록 좋다. [E.]

:the·a·ter, 《Brit.》 **-tre** [θí(:)ətər] *n.* Ⓒ **1** a place where plays are acted; a place where motion pictures are shown. 극장; 영화관. 參考 미국에서도 극장명으로는 theatre를 흔히 씀. **2** 《*the* ~》 the drama; the dramatic art. 극; 연극. ¶ *the modern* ~ 현대극 / *go to the* ~ 연극 구경 가다. **3** a hall or room with seats like a theater, used for lectures in a university, etc. (대학 따위의) 계단식 강당〔교실〕. **4** a place of important action; the scene of some important event. 활동의 장소〔무대〕; 사건의 현장. ¶ *the* ~ *of public life* 공적 생활의 무대 / *The* ~ *of war was in Spain.* 전쟁의 무대는 스페인이었다. **5** the dramatic writings of a particular writer or period. (특정 작가·시대의) 극작품. ¶ *Geothe's* ~ 괴테의 극작〔희곡(戲曲)〕 / *the Elizabethan* ~ 엘리자베스조(朝)의 극문학〔연극〕. [Gk. *thea* spectacle]

the·at·ri·cal [θiǽtrikəl] *adj.* of a theater; of the drama; (of words or action) better for the theater than for real life; not natural. 극장의; 연극의; 연극조의; 부자연한. ¶ ~ *costumes* 연극 의상 / ~ *performance* 연극; 연기 / ~ *effect* 극적 효과 / *with* ~ *gestures* 과장된〔연극조의〕 몸짓으로. — *n.* 《*pl.*》 dramatic performances, esp. by amateurs. 소인극(素人劇).

the·at·ri·cal·ly [θiǽtrikəli] *adv.* in a theatrical manner. 연극조로; 과장되게.

·thee [ðiː, ði] *pron.* 《*arch.*》 objective case of **thou.**

theft [θeft] *n.* Ⓤ **1** 《sometimes *a* ~》 the act of stealing. 절도; 도둑질. ¶ *commit a* ~ 도둑질하다 / *be guilty of* ~ 절도죄를 범하다 / *be insured against* ~ 도난 보험에 들다. **2** Ⓒ 《*obs.*》 the property stolen. 도둑맞은 물건; 장물. [*thief*]

:their [ðεər, *before vowels* ðər] *pron.* the possessive case of **they.**

:theirs [ðεərz] *pron.* (possessive form of **they**) the one or ones belonging to them. 그들의 것. ¶ *a favorite picture of* ~ 그들이 좋아하는 영화 / *The land is* ~. 이 땅은 그들의 것이다 / *Our car is older than* ~. 우리 차는 그들의 것보다 오래됐다 / *Those books are* ~, *not mine.* 이들 책은 그들의 것이지 내 것이 아니다. [N.]

the·ism [θíːizəm] *n.* Ⓤ belief in a god or gods; belief in one God, the creator and ruler of the universe. 유신론(有神論); 일신교(cf. *atheism, deism*). [Gk. *theos* God]

the·ist [θíːist] *n.* Ⓒ a beliver in theism. 유신론자(cf. *atheist*).

:them [ðem, ðəm] *pron.* **1** the objective case of **they.** 그들을〔에게〕; 그것들을〔에게〕. ¶ *I like* ~. / *I gave* ~ *the apples.* 그들에게 사과를 주었다. **2** 《*sl., dial., joc.*》 =those. ¶ *some of* ~ *books* 그 책 몇 권 / *Them are the women I meant.* 저들이 내가 말하던 여인들이다. **3** 《used as the predicate》 ¶ *It's* ~. 그들이다. [*they*]

·theme [θiːm] *n.* Ⓒ **1** the topic or subject of a speech, essay, etc. 화제; 논제. **2** 《esp. U.S.》 a short essay on a certain subject. (과제) 작문. **3** 《mus.》 the chief melody in a piece of music; a theme song. 주제(主題); 주선율(主旋律); 주제〔테마〕 음악; 테마송. [→thesis]

:them·selves [ðəmsélvz, ðém-] *pron.* the emphatic or reflexive form of **they** or **them.** 그들 자신(이, 을, 에게). ¶ *They hid* ~. 그들은 숨었다 / *They did it* ~. 그들 스스로가 그걸 했다 / *The teachers* ~ *said the test was too hard.* 선생들 자신도 시험은 너무 어려웠다고 말했다 / *The boys hurt* ~ *sliding down hill.* 아이들이 언덕을 미끄러져 내려오다가 다쳤다 / *They were ashamed of* ~. 그들은 스스로가 부끄러웠다. [*they, self*]

:then [ðen] *adv.* **1** at that time in the future or in the past. 그때(에); 당시. ¶ *She was a little girl* ~. 그 당시 그녀는 소녀였다 / *Things will be different* ~. 그때가 되면 사태는 달라질 것이다 / *We were still young* ~. 그 당시 우리는 아직 젊었었다 / *We lived in the country* ~. 그 시절 우리는 시골에 살았다. **2** soon afterward; after that. 그 다음에 (곧); 다음에는. ¶ *She shut the door and* ~ *burst into tears.* 그녀는 문을 닫고 나서 울음을 터뜨렸다 / *First comes spring,* ~ *summer.* 처음에 봄이 오고 다음에 여름이 온다 / *The noise stopped and* ~ *began again.* 소리가 그치더니 이내 또 나기 시작했다. **3** besides; and also. 게다가; 그 밖에 (또). ¶ *I like to walk, and* ~ *it's good for the health.* 나는 걷기를 좋아한다. 그리고 그것이 건강에 좋고 / *The dress seems too good to throw away, and* ~ *it is so becoming.* 그 옷은 버리기엔 너무 좋은 것 같다. 게다가 입으면 아주 어울리기도 하고. **4** in that case; therefore. 그렇다면; 그러면. ¶ *He isn't here. Where is he,* ~*?* 그는 여기 없다. 그럼 어디 있지 / *If you are tired,* ~ *you had better stay at home.* 피곤하면 집에 있는 것이 좋다 / *Oh, all right* ~, *do what you like.* 음 알겠다. 그렇다면 네 좋을 대로 해라 / *You don't want to go after all,* ~. 그렇다면 넌 끝내 안 가겠단 말이지 / *What* ~*?* 그럼 어떻게 되는 거냐.

— *adj.* of that time; existing at that time. 그때의; 당시의. ¶ *The* ~ *governor was a man of honor.* 당시의 통치자는 신의를 중히 여기는 분이었다.

— *n.* Ⓤ that time. 당시; 그때. ¶ *before* 〔*by, since*〕 ~ 그 이전에〔그때까지(는), 그 이후〕 / *from* ~ *on* 그 이후부터 / *up to* 〔*till*〕 ~ 그때까지. [E.]

but then, but on the other hand; but at the same time. 그러나 한편〔동시에〕. ¶ *He lost the race, but* ~ *he never really expected to win.* 그는 경주에 졌고, 또 정말 이기리라는 기대도 하지 않았다.

every now and then, sometimes. 때때로; 이따금. ¶ *She meets her old boyfriend for a drink every now and* ~. 그녀는 이따금 예전 남자 친구와 술 한잔 하기 위해 만난다.

now then, I say; listen to me; at any rate. 이봐이봐; 자아 (그런데, 그래서).

then and there =***there and then,*** at once; at that time and place. 즉시; 즉석에서; 그때 그 자리에서. ¶ *He decided on it* ~ *and there.* 그는 당장 결정을 내렸다.

·thence [ðens] *adv.* 《*arch.*》 **1** from that place. 거기서부터. ¶ *She departed* ~. 그녀는 거기서 떠났다 / *He went to Italy,* ~ *to France.* 그는 이탈리아로 가 거기서 프랑스에 갔다. **2** for that reason or source; therefore. 그렇기 때문에. ¶ *You are young, and* ~ *romantic.* 너는 젊고, 그래서 로맨틱하다. **3** from then. 그때부터. ¶ *a week* ~ 그때부터 1주일. [E.]

thence·forth [ðènsfɔ́ːrθ] *adv.* from that time on; thereafter. 그때부터; 거기서부터.

thence·for·ward [ðènsfɔ́ːrwərd] *adv.* = thenceforth.

theo- [θiːə-] *pref.* God. '신'의 뜻. ¶ *theology* / *theologian.* [Gk. *theos* god]

the·oc·ra·cy [θiːɑ́krəsi / -ɔ́k-] *n.* (*pl.* **-cies**) Ⓤ a form of polity in which people claim to be governed by a God.; Ⓤ government by priests; Ⓒ a country governed in this way. 신정(神政); 신권 정치; 신정국(神政國). [theo-]

the·o·crat·ic [θìːəkrǽtik] *adj.* of theocracy; having a theocracy. 신정(神政)의.

the·od·o·lite [θiːɑ́dəlàit / -ɔ́d-] *n.* Ⓒ an instrument for measuring angles. (측량용) 경위의(經緯儀). [?]

the·o·lo·gian [θìːəlóudʒiən] *n.* Ⓒ a person who is skilled in theology. 신학자. [theo-]

the·o·log·i·cal [θìːəlɑ́dʒikəl / -lɔ́dʒi-] *adj.* of theology. 신학(상)의; 신학적인.

the·ol·o·gy [θiːɑ́lədʒi / -ɔ́l-] *n.* Ⓤ the systematic study of God and His relations to man and the universe; the science of religion. 신학. [theo-]

the·o·rem [θíːərəm] *n.* Ⓒ a statement, proposition, or rule that can be proved to be true by logical reasoning. 법칙; 정리(定理). [Gk. *theōría* spectacle]

the·o·ret·ic [θìːərétik], **-i·cal** [-ikəl] *adj.* based on theory, not practical or based on experience. 이론(상)의(opp. empirical). [↑]

the·o·ret·i·cal·ly [θìːərétikəli] *adv.* in a theoretical manner; according to theory. 이론상; 이론적으로.

the·o·rist [θíːərist] *n.* Ⓒ a person who forms theories. 이론가; 공론가(空論家).

the·o·rize [θíːəràiz] *vi.* (P1,3) form theories. 이론을 세우다.

:the·o·ry [θíːəri] *n.* (*pl.* **-ries**) Ⓒ **1** the general and fundamental principles of an art, science, etc. (실제에 대한) 이론(opp. practice). ¶ *the* ~ *of music* 음악 이론 / *We have two chemistry exam, one on* ~ *and one practical.* 화학 시험이 둘인데, 하나는 이론이고 또 하나는 실기 시험이다 / *It is not so easy in practice as in* ~. 실제로는 이론처럼 그렇게 쉽지는 않다. **2** a reasoned supposition put forward to explain facts or events. 학설; 논(論). ¶ *the ~ of evolution* 진화론 / *disprove a ~* 학설을 논박하다. **3** a peculiar opinion; an idea. 의견; 견해; 생각. ¶ *My ~ is that it is not true.* 내 생각으로는 그건 사실이 아니다 / *I have a ~ that hot bath at night makes one sleepless.* 밤에 더운 물로 목욕하면 잠이 오지 않는다는 것이 내 지론(持論)이다. [→theorem]

ther·a·peu·tics [θèrəpjú:tiks] *n. pl.* 《used as *sing.*》 the branch of medicine that deals with the treatment and cure of diseases. 치료학(治療學). [↓]

ther·a·py [θérəpi] *n.* Ⓤ the treatment aimed at curing diseases. 치료; 요법. [Gk. *therapeuō* tend]

:there [ðɛər] *adv.* **1** in that place; to or toward that place. 거기〔저기〕에서; 거기에 (opp. here). ¶ *here and ~* 여기저기 / *go ~* 거기에 가다 / *He was not ~.* 그는 거기에 없었다 / *We will stay ~ all summer.* 우린 거기서 여름을 날 것이다 / *The boy ~ is my nephew.* 저기 있는 소년은 내 조카다 / *Put it ~.* 그걸 거기 두어라 / *Does he work ~?* 그가 거기서 일하나 / *Hand me that book ~, please.* 거기 있는 책 좀 집어다오. **2** at that point. 그 점에서; 거기서. ¶ *There we can't agree with him.* 그 점에서 그와 뜻이 안 맞는다 / *There I am wrong.* 그 점에서 내가 틀렸다 / *Don't stop ~, go on.* 거기서 멈추지 말고 계속해라 / *There is where the English differ from us.* 그 점에서 영국인이 우리와 다르다. **3** 《used to call *attention*》 Hear!; Listen! 이봐; 저봐; 자자; 자아. ¶ *There she goes!* 저봐; 그녀가 간다 / *There goes the whistle!* 잠깐, 호각 소리가 들린다 / *There it is!* 자; 그렇다; 그게 문제다 / *There it goes!* 저런, 떨어진다〔깨진다, 없어진다〕. **4** 《used in sentences in which the verb comes before the subject》 …이 ―하다; …이 있다. ¶ *There came to the city a stranger.* 어떤 낯선 사람이 이 시에 왔다 / *There is a dictionary on the desk.* 책상 위에 사전이 한 권 있다 / *There remains for you to work hard.* 이제 네가 열심히 공부할 일만 남았다 / *There is no one here.* 여기엔 아무도 없다.

be all there, be alert; be wide-awake; be not mad. 빈틈없다; 제정신이다. ¶ *He is not all ~.* 그는 머리가 좀 돌았다.

get there, 《*sl.*》 succeed. 성공하다.

get there and back, go to that place and come back again. 왕복하다. ¶ *It took me ten hours to get ~ and back.* 왕복 10시간 걸렸다.

have been there (***before***), know all about it. 다 알고 있다.

over there, at a far or farther place. 저쪽에.

then and there =***there and then,*** at that particular time and place. 그때 그 자리에서.

There is no doing…. It is impossible to do…. …할 수 없다; …하기는 불가능하다. ¶ *There is no stopping a woman's tongue.* 여자 입은 막을 수 없다.

there or thereabout, warning that specification of place, amount, etc. is approximately. 그쯤; 그 정도; 그 근처.

There you are! I told you so. 그것 봐라, 내가 뭐랬나.

— *pron.* that place or point. 거기; 저기. ¶ *He lives near ~.* 그는 그 부근에 산다 / *I came from ~.* 나는 거기서 왔다 / *He left there yesterday.* 그는 어제 거기를 떠났다.

— *interj.* 《used to express *satisfaction, comfort,* etc.》 좋아좋아; 이봐; 자자; 자(봐라); 그래. ¶ *There, ~, don't worry about that!* 자자, 걱정할 것 없다 / *There now!* 그것 보라니까《내 말대로지》 / *There now, that's done.* 됐다; 다 지난 일이다. [E.]

there·a·bout [ðέərəbàut], **-bouts** [-bàuts] *adv.* near that place, time, number, etc.; nearly. 그 부근〔근방〕에; 그때쯤; 그 정도; 대략. ¶ *He lives Chongno or ~.* 그는 종로 어디쯤에 살고 있다 / *ten dollars a year or ~,* 1년에 10달러쯤 / *I'll see you at nine o'clock or ~.* 아홉 시쯤에 만나자.

·there·af·ter [ðὲərǽftər, ðɛərɑ́:f-] *adv.* after that; afterward; subsequently. 그 후에; 그 이래; 그로부터. ¶ *Thereafter we had no further communication with them.* 그 이후로 우리는 그들과 더 이상 연락이 없었다.

·there·by [ðὲərbái] *adv.* by that means; in that connection. 그것에 의해; 그것으로; 그에 대해서〔관해서〕. ¶ *She consented and ~ avoided an argument.* 그녀는 동의하고 그것으로 논쟁을 피했다 / *Thereby hangs a tale.* 거기에는 좀 내력이 있다.

:there·fore [ðέərfɔ̀:r] *adv.* for that reason; on that account; accordingly. 그렇기 때문에; 따라서. ¶ *I was ill* (*and*) *~ could not come.* 아팠기 때문에 올 수 없었다 / *These birds are very rare and ~ protected by law.* 이들 새는 아주 희귀하다. 그래서 법으로 보호하고 있다.

there·from [ðὲərfrʌ́m / -frɔ́m] *adv.* from this; from that; from it. 거기서부터; 그〔이〕로부터.

there·in [ðὲərín] *adv.* in that place; in it; in that respect. 그 속에; 거기에; 그 점에서. ¶ *The captain thought all danger was past; ~ he made a mistake.* 선장은 모든 위험은 지났다고 생각했는데 그것이 그의 오판이었다. [E.]

·there·of [ðὲərʌ́v / -ɔ́v] *adv.* **1** of that; of it. 그것을; 그것에 관하여. **2** from that; from it. 그로부터.

:there's [ðɛərz] there is; there has.

there·to [ðὲərtú:] *adv.* to that; to it; in addition to that. 거기에; 거기로; 게다가. ¶ *The castle stands on the hill; the road ~ is steep and rough.* 성은 산 위에 있고, 거기 가는 길은 가파르고 험하다. [*there*]

there·un·der [ðὲərʌ́ndər] *adv.* **1** under that; under it. 그 밑에. ¶ *the land, with some minerals found ~…* 그 밑에서 몇 가지 광물이 발견된 땅…. **2** under the authority of that; according to that. 거기에 따라서; 그

런 조건하에. ¶ *royalties paid* ~ 그에 따라 지불된 인세(印稅).

there·un·to [ðɛ̀ərʌ́ntu(:)] *adv.* 《*arch.*》= thereto.

***there·upon** [ðɛ̀ərəpɔ́n] *adv.* **1** 《*arch.*》 upon that; upon it. 그 위에. **2** as a result of that. 그 결과로. **3** at that point (of time); just after that. 그 때; 그러자 곧. ¶ *The speaker sat down,* ~ *the people clapped.* 연사는 자리에 앉았다. 그러자 청중은 박수를 쳤다.

there·with·al [ðɛ̀ərwiðɔ́:l] *adv.* besides; moreover; in addition to that. 게다가; 더욱이; 거기에 더해.

therm [θə:rm] *n.* Ⓒ 《phys.》 a unit of heat, fit in reckoning gas supply. 섬《열량 단위》. [Gk. *thermos* hot, warm]

ther·mal [θə́:rməl] *adj.* having to do with heat; hot. 열의; 열량의; 뜨거운. ¶ ~ *waters* 〔*springs*〕 온천.

ther·mite [θə́:rmait] *n.* 《chem.》 a mixture of aluminium in fine grains with an oxide of iron. 테르밋. [thermo-]

ther·mo- [θə́:rmou] *pref.* heat. '열'의 뜻. 語法 모음 앞에서는 보통 therm-이 됨. [Gk. *thermós* hot]

ther·mo·dy·nam·ics [θə̀:rmoudainǽmiks] *n.* Ⓤ the science of the relations between heat and mechanical energy. 열역학(熱力學). [thermo-]

***ther·mom·e·ter** [θərmɑ́mitər / -mɔ́m-] *n.* Ⓒ an instrument for measuring temperature. 온도계; 한란계; 체온계. ¶ *a Centigrade* ~ 섭씨 온도계 / *a Fahrenheit* ~ 화씨 온도계.

ther·mos bottle [θə́:rməs bɑ̀tl / θə́:rmɔs bɔ́tl] *n.* a bottle for keeping water or other liquid hot or cold. 보온병.

ther·mo·stat [θə́:rməstæ̀t] *n.* Ⓒ a device which controls the temperature automatically. 서머스탯; 온도 조절 장치. [thermo-]

the·sau·ri [θisɔ́:rai] *n.* pl. of **thesaurus.**

the·sau·rus [θisɔ́:rəs] *n.* Ⓒ (*pl.* **-sau·ri** or **-es**) **1** a place where treasures are kept. 보물 창고; 보고. **2** a collection of much information and knowledge, such as a dictionary, encyclopedia, etc. 지식의 보고《사전·백과 사전 등》. [Gk. =treasure]

⁑**these** [ði:z] *adj., pron.* pl. of **this.**

the·ses [θí:si:z] *n.* pl. of **thesis.**

the·sis [θí:sis] *n.* ⓊⒸ (*pl.* **the·ses**) **1** a written essay written in order to get a university degree. (학위·졸업의) 논문. **2** a statement of an idea to be proved. 명제(命題). [Gk. *tithēmi* place]

thews [θju:z] *n. pl.* muscles; strength of a body. 근육; 체력. [E. =habit]

⁑**they** [ðei, ðe] *pron.* **1** pl. of **he, she,** or **it. 2** people in general. (세상) 사람들(cf. *one*). ¶ *They grow rice in this part of the country.* 이 지역에서 사람들은 쌀을 재배한다 / *They say that she will marry.* 그녀가 결혼한다고들 말한다 / *They say prices are going to increase again.* 물가가 또 오른다는 소문이다. **3** 《*colloq.*》《people of either sex》 he or she. ¶ *If anyone has any questions, will* ~ *please speak to me afterward?* 누구든 무슨 문제가 있거든 나중에 내게 말해 주시겠습니까. [N.]

***they'd** [ðeid] they had; they would.

***they'll** [ðeil] they will; they shall.

***they're** [ðéiər] they are.

***they've** [ðeiv] they have.

⁑**thick** [θik] *adj.* **1** having much space from one surface to another; not thin. 두꺼운(opp. thin). ¶ ~ *cloth* 두꺼운 천 / *a* ~ *board* 〔*book, wall*〕 두꺼운 널판〔책, 벽〕/ *How* ~ *is it?* 두께가 얼마냐. **2** from one surface to another. 두께가 …인. ¶ *a board 4 inches* ~, 4인치 두께의 널판. **3** having a large diameter in relation to length; of great circumference relatively to length. 굵은. ¶ *a* ~ *pipe* 〔*finger, neck, trunk*〕 굵은 파이프〔손가락, 목, 줄기〕. **4** compact; closely crowded together. 밀생한; 우거진. ¶ ~ *hair* 숱 많은 머리 / *a* ~ *wood* 〔*forest*〕 울창한 숲 / ~ *foliage* 빽빽한 나뭇잎 / *The garden is* ~ *with weeds.* 정원엔 잡초가 무성하다. **5** full; abundant; crowded. 꽉 찬; 가득한; 붐비는. ¶ *a bus* ~ *with children* 아이들이 꽉 찬 버스 / *the air* ~ *with mist* 습기가 많은 공기. **6** dense; heavy; muddy. 진한; 걸쭉한. ¶ *a* ~ *fog* 짙은 안개 / *a* ~ *syrup* 진한 시럽 / ~ *clouds of smoke coming out of the factory chimneys* 공장 굴뚝에서 뭉게뭉게 솟는 짙은 연기. **7** not clear. 흐린; 탁한. ¶ *The air was* ~ *with dust.* 공기는 먼지로 자욱했다 / *The river looked* ~ *after the rain.* 비 온 뒤의 강물은 탁했다 / *The weather was* ~. 날씨는 흐려 있었다. **8** (of voice) husky; hoarse. 목쉰 소리의; 허스키한. ¶ *a* ~ *voice* 쉰 목소리. **9** slow in understanding; stupid; dull. 우둔한; 어리석은. ¶ *He has a* ~ *head.* 그는 머리가 둔하다. **10** 《*colloq.*》《as *predicative*》 intimate; very friendly. 친한. ¶ *He and I are very* ~. 나는 그 사람과 아주 친하다 / *I have been* ~ *with his family for years.* 그 집 식구와는 여러 해 동안 친밀하게 지내오고 있다.

— *adv.* =thickly.

— *n.* Ⓤ **1** 《*the* ~》 the thickest part; the most active part. 가장 두꺼운〔굵은, 무성한, 밀집된〕 부분. ¶ *the* ~ *of the town* 도시의 가장 번화한 데. **2** 《*the* ~》 the most intense moment; the center of action. 한창 때; (활동이) 가장 심한 곳. ¶ *the* ~ *of the battle* 전투의 절정. **3** 《*colloq.*》 =thickhead. [E.]

a bit* 〔*rather, a little too*〕 *thick, 《Brit. *sl.*》 (of conduct, demands, etc.) too much to put up with; hard to bear. (참고) 견딜 수 없는. ¶ *It's a bit* ~ *to expect me to work untill midnight!* 내게 오밤중까지 일하라니 그건 너무 지나치다.

(**as**) ***thick as thieves,*** 《*colloq.*》 very friendly. 아주 친한.

give someone a thick ear, 《Brit. *sl.*》 make someone's ear swollen by giving him a blow. …을 귀싸대기가 붓도록 갈기다.

in the thick of, in the midst of. …의 한가운데에; 절정에.

lay it on thick, 《*colloq.*》 exaggerate. 과장하다; 허풍 떨다.

through thick and thin, through all kinds of difficulties. 만난을 무릅쓰고; 끝까지 변함없이. ¶ *She stuck by her husband through ~ and thin.* 그녀는 어떤 역경에서도 남편에게 충실했다.

thick·en [θíkən] *vt., vi.* (P6; 1) make or become thick or thicker. 두껍게 하다〔되다〕. ¶ *The clouds ~.* 구름이 짙어진다 / *I always ~ my coffee by adding its powder.* 나는 늘 커피 가루를 더 넣어 커피를 진하게 한다. [*thick*]

thick·et [θíkit] *n.* Ⓒ a thick growth of small trees. (관목의) 숲; 덤불. [→thick]

thick·head [θíkhèd] *n.* a stupid person. 멍텅구리; 바보.

thick-head·ed [θíkhédid] *adj.* a little foolish; slow in understanding or learning. 머리가 둔한. ● **thick-head·ed·ness** [-nis] *n.*

thick·ly [θíkli] *adv.* **1** in a thick manner. 두껍게; 짙게; 빽빽하게. ¶ *~ covered with snow* 눈이 두껍게 덮인. **2** in great numbers; very often; heavily. 숱하게; 자주; 빈번히; 심하게. ¶ *Snow falls ~ and fast.* 줄기차게 눈이 온다. **3** indistictly; not clearly. 불분명하게. ¶ *speak ~* 중얼거리다.

•**thick·ness** [θíknis] *n.* **1** Ⓤ the state or quality of being thick. 두꺼움; 굵음; 짙음; 밀도; 밀집; 빈번. ¶ *The ~ of the walls shuts out all sounds.* 두꺼운 벽은 모든 소리를 차단한다 / *The ~ of his arms shows great muscular development.* 굵은 그의 팔이 대단한 근육 발달을 말해주고 있다. **2** ⓊⒸ the distance between the opposite outside parts of a book, tree, etc. 두께; 굵기. ¶ *The large dictionary is three inches in ~.* 그 대사전의 두께는 3인치다 / *The beam has a ~ of 4 inches.* 도리의 굵기가 4인치다. **3** Ⓒ a layer. 층. ¶ *two thicknesses of cloth* 두 겹 천.

thick-set [θíksét] *adj.* **1** closely planted; thickly set. 무성한; 조밀한. ¶ *a ~ hedge* 촘촘한 산울타리. **2** having a short, stout body. 땅딸막한. ¶ *a ~ man.*

thick-skinned [θíkskínd] *adj.* **1** having a thick skin. 가죽이 두꺼운. **2** not sensitive to other people's bad opinion of oneself. 둔감한.

:**thief** [θi:f] *n.* Ⓒ (*pl.* **thieves**) a person who steals or robs, esp. secretly and without violence. 도둑; 좀도둑. [E.]

thieve [θi:v] *vt., vi.* (P6; 1) steal; rob. 훔치다; 도둑질하다. [↑]

thiev·ery [θí:vəri] *n.* ⓊⒸ the act or habit of stealing; theft. 절도; 도벽. [→thief]

thieves [θi:vz] *n.* pl. of **thief.**

thiev·ish [θí:viʃ] *adj.* having the habit of stealing; like a thief. 도벽이 있는; 도둑 같은.

•**thigh** [θai] *n.* Ⓒ the thick part of the leg between the hip and the knee. 넓적다리. [E.]

thigh·bone [θáibòun] *n.* Ⓒ the bone of the thigh. 대퇴골.

thill [θil] *n.* either of the shafts between which a horse is placed for drawing a vehicle. (수레의) 채. [E.]

thim·ble [θímbəl] *n.* Ⓒ a small cap of metal, celluloid, etc. to protect the finger when pushing the needle in sewing. 골무. [*thumb*]

:**thin** [θin] *adj.* (**thin·ner, thin·nest**) **1** having little space from one surface to another. 얇은. ¶ *~ paper*〔*clothes*〕/ *The ice on the pond is too ~ for skating.* 스케이트 타기에는 못의 얼음이 너무 얇다. **2** having a small diameter in relation to length. 가는. ¶ *a ~ thread* / *~ fingers.* **3** having little flesh; slender; slim. 홀쭉한; 마른. ¶ *~ in face* 얼굴이 마른 / *She is ~.* 그녀는 날씬하다 / *He looks ~ after his illness.* 그는 앓고 나더니 야윈 듯하다. **4** not close together; scattered; scanty. 드문드문한; 성긴. ¶ *a ~ meeting* 참석자가 적은 회합 / *a ~ population* 희박한 인구 / *He has ~ hair.* 그는 머리 숱이 적다 / *The actors played to a ~ audience.* 배우들은 많지 않은 관중을 놓고 연기를 했다. **5** not dense; watery. 묽은. ¶ *~ beer* 싱거운 맥주 / *~ milk*〔*soup*〕 멀건 우유〔수프〕. **6** weak; faint. 약한; 희미한. ¶ *the ~ sunlight* 약한 햇빛 / *the ~ twilight* 희미한 땅거미. **7** 《*fig.*》 easily seen through; slight; shallow. 뻔한; 속보이는. ¶ *It was a ~ excuse that satisfied no one.* 아무도 납득 못할 얕은 변명이었다 / 《*colloq.*》 *That's too ~.* 속셈이 빤히 들여다보인다. **8** 《*fig.*》 scanty; meager. 빈약한. ¶ *The style of the book is fine, but the matter is rather ~.* 책이 모양은 좋은데 내용이 좀 빈약하다 / *a ~ story* 알맹이 없는 이야기. **9** 《*sl.*》 uncomfortable. 싫은; 언짢은. ¶ *have a ~ time* 거북한 시간을 보내다.

— *v.* (**thinned, thin·ning**) *vt.* (P6,7) make (something) thin. …을 얇게〔엷게, 가늘게〕 하다. ¶ *The war thinned* (*down*) *the population.* 전쟁으로 인구가 희박해졌다 / *~* (*out*) *the branches of a tree* 나뭇 가지를 치다 / *~* (*out*) *flowers* 꽃을 솎다.

— *vi.* (P1,2A) become thin. 야위다; 가늘어지다; 희박해지다; 성기어지다. ¶ *My hair is thinning.* 머리 숱이 적어진다 / *The crowd began to ~ out.* 군중은 하나 둘씩 흩어지기 시작했다 / *The smoke thinned as it rose.* 연기는 위로 올라감에 따라 희미해졌다. [E.]

•**thine** [ðain] *pron.* 《*arch.*》 **1** =yours. **2** 《before *a vowel*》 =your.

:thing [θiŋ] *n.* Ⓒ **1** all that exist; any material object. 물건; 물체. ¶ *a living* ~ 생물 / *Put these things in the bags.* 이것들을 가방에 넣어라 / *all things* 만물 / *All things in the house were burned.* 집안에 있는 물건은 모조리 타 버렸다. **2** all that can be thought or imagined, such as a fact, an idea, an opinion, and an act. (생각할 수 있는) 것; 사물. ¶ *It is a good ~ to think so.* 그런 생각도 좋다 / *What a nasty ~ to say to your sister!* 동생한테 그 무슨 잡된 소리냐 / *One ~ is certain—I'm not lending him any money again.* 한 가지 일은 분명하다. 다시는 그자에게 돈을 빌려주지 않겠다. **3** ⓐ an event; an affair; a matter. 사건; 사항. ¶ *A strange ~ has happened.* 이상한 일이 생겼다 / *This is the ~ in question.* 이것이 문제거리다 / *He spoke of many interesting things.* 그는 많은 재미있는 얘기를 했다 / *things of the mind and not of the body* 육체적인 것이 아니라 정신적인 일. ⓑ an action; a task. 행위; 일. ¶ *do great things* 큰 일을 하다 / *I've got a lot of things to do.* 할 일이 많다. **4** a fellow; a person. 녀석; 사람. ¶ *a little ~* 꼬마 / *Oh, poor ~!* 아, 불쌍한 놈 / *He's rather stupid old ~.* 좀 멍청한 친구다. **5** 《often *pl.*》 the state of affairs; circumstances. 형세; 사정; 사태. ¶ *Things are going well.* 사정이 좋아지고 있다 / *I have many things to trouble me.* 골치아픈 일이 많다 / *I fear things are going wrong.* 사태가 악화될까봐 걱정이다 / *How are things going on?* 사정이 어떻게 돼가고 있나. **6** 《*pl.*》 things that belong to someone; someone's belongings. 소지품; 재산. ¶ *I have left my things in the car.* 내 물건을 차에 놓고 왔다 / *Take your things and go away.* 네것들 챙겨서 꺼져버려. **7** 《*pl.*》 clothes; outdoor clothes. 옷; 외출복. ¶ *take off one's things* 옷을 벗다 / *Put on your things.* 옷을 입어라 / *I haven't got a ~ to wear.* 입을 것이라고는 없다. **8** 《*pl.*》 instruments; tools. 도구; 연장; 용구. ¶ *kitchen things* 부엌세간 / *tea things* 차도구 / *swimming things* 수영 용품. **9** 《*the* ~》 what is fitting or what one wants. 적당〔필요, 중요〕한 일 또는 물건. ¶ *It is not the ~ to stare at women.* 여자를 빤히 보는 건 좋지 않다 / *It is just the ~.* 그것 제격〔안성맞춤〕이다. **10** 《*pl.* with *adj.* following》 all that can be so described. 풍물; 문물(文物). ¶ *things Korean* 〔*foreign*〕 한국〔외국〕의 문물. [E.]

above all things, more than anything else; above all. 다른 것은 차치하고; 무엇보다도; 특히.

... and things, 《*colloq.*》 and the like. …등등.

for one thing, as one reason. 한 가지 이유로서. ¶ *For one ~, I am busy.* 우선 나는 바쁘다.

know a thing or two, be experienced or wise. 물정에 밝다; 빈틈이 없다.

make a good thing of (= *profit by*) *something.* …으로 이익을 보다.

not look 〔***feel***〕 ***quite the thing,*** 《*colloq.*》 not look 〔feel〕 in good health. (건강이) 안 좋아 보이다.

of all things, an exclamation of surprise, anger, etc. 놀랍게도; 하필이면.

see things, 《*colloq.*》 have the illusion. 헛보다; 허깨비를 보다.

(***the***) ***first thing,*** before anything else. 우선 첫째(로).

the thing is, the main point, problem, etc. is. 문제는; 요는. ¶ *The thing is, will he join us or not?* 요는 그가 우리와 함께 한다는 거냐 싫다는 거냐.

thing·a·my, thing·um·my [θíŋəmi] *n.* 《*colloq.*》 a thing or person whose name one cannot remember. 그 뭐라던가 하는 것〔사람〕. [↑]

:think [θiŋk] *v.* (**thought**) *vt.* **1** (P6) form or have (an idea, an opinion, etc.) in mind; conceive. …을 생각하다; 마음에 품다. ¶ ~ *happy* 〔*noble*〕 *thoughts* 행복〔고상〕한 생각을 하다 / ~ *evil things* 못된 생각을 하다 / *What makes you ~ that?* 어째서 그런 생각을 하게 됐니. **2** (P10,12) imagine. …을 상상하다. ¶ *I can't ~ how you do it.* 네가 어떻게 그것을 하는지 상상이 안 된다 / *I can't ~ when she will come.* 그녀가 언제 올지 알 수 없다. **3** (P11,21) judge; regard. …라고 생각하다; 간주하다. ¶ *I ~* (*that*) *she will come.* 나는 그녀가 오리라 생각한다 / *They thought him* (*to be*) *mad.* 그들은 그가 미쳤다고 생각했다 / *He'd thought* (*that*) *life was meant to be enjoyed.* 그는 인생이란 즐기는 것이라고 생각했다 / *I never thought that you would be here.* 나는 네가 여기 있으리라고는 꿈에도 생각 못했다. **4** (P8,11) intend; expect. (…할) 생각으로 있다; …라고 예상하다. ¶ *I ~ I'll start tomorrow.* 내일 떠날 생각이다 / *He did not ~ to meet her at such a place.* 그는 그런 데서 그녀를 만나리라고는 예상 못했다 / *They didn't ~ he'd be this late.* 그가 이렇게 늦으리라고 그들은 생각하지 못 했다. **5** (P6,7,10,12) call (something) to mind; remember. …을 생각해 내다; 기억하다. ¶ *He was thinking what to do next.* 그는 다음에 무엇을 할 것인지를 생각하고 있었다 / *I cannot ~ what he said.* 그가 한 말을 기억 못하겠다. **6** (P12) understand. …을 이해하다. ¶ *I can't ~ why she wept yesterday.* 그녀가 어제 왜 울었는지 모르겠다. **7** (P12) feel (something) in one's mind. …을 마음으로 느끼다. ¶ *The boy was thinking how strange the man was.* 소년은 그 사람이 참 이상하다는 생각을 하고 있었다. **8** (P7,13,18) bring to a certain condition by thinking. 생각해서 …(으로) 하다. ¶ ~ *oneself out of a difficulty* 생각해서 어려움을 헤쳐 나가다 / ~ *oneself stupid* 너무 생각해서 멍해지다 / *You can't ~ away your troubles.* 아무리 걱정거리를 잊으려해도 소용없다. — *vi.* **1** (P1) have an opinion. 생각하다. ¶ ~ *ahead* 앞일을 생각하

다 / *Are animals able to* ~ *?* 짐승은 생각을 할 수 있을까. **2** (P1,3) use one's mind hard to understand something; reflect; meditate. 숙고하다. ¶ ~ *in English* 영어로 생각하다; 생각이 영어로 떠오르다 / *Think before you speak.* 말하기 전에 잘 생각해라. [E.]

think about, **a**) consider. 숙고하다. ¶ *His proposal needs to be thought about very carefully.* 그의 제의는 신중히 생각해 볼 필요가 있다. **b**) have an opinion about (something). …에 대해 의견을 가지다. ¶ *Tell me what you ~ about this novel.* 이 소설에 대한 소견을 말해 봐라. **c**) be interested in; give one's mind to (something). …에 관심을 가지다; 마음을 쓰다. ¶ *She thinks about nothing but clothes.* 그녀는 옷에만 관심이 있다.

think aloud, speak one's thoughts as they come into one's mind. 무심결에 혼잣말하다.

think better of, **a**) consider again and change one's mind or decide more wisely about. 다시 생각하다; 재고하다. ¶ *He started to say something, but he thought better of it.* 그는 무슨 말을 하려다가 다시 생각했다. **b**) have a more favorable opinion of. …을 더 좋게 보다; 재인식하다. ¶ *I had thought better of him than to suppose that he could be so cruel.* 그리도 잔인할 수 있을까라고 생각하기보다는 그에 대한 인식을 고쳐보기로 했다.

think of, **a**) call (something) to mind. …을 생각해내다. ¶ *I cannot ~ of his name.* 그의 이름이 생각나지 않는다. **b**) have (an idea) in mind. …을 상상하다. ¶ *In those days space travel had not been thought of.* 당시엔 우주 여행은 상상도 못 했다. **c**) intend; plan. …할 생각이다. ¶ ~ *of going to Hawaii* 하와이에 갈 생각이다. **d**) have an opinion of (something). …에 대한 의견을 가지다. **e**) consider. …을 숙고하다.

think out, think about (something) to the end. …을 깊이 생각하다; 생각해내다.

think over, reflect; consider. …을 다시 생각하다; 숙고하다. ¶ *He thought it over for a moment.* 그는 그 일을 잠시 숙고했다 / ~ *something over* (*and over*) …을 곰곰이 생각하다.

think through, think about (something) until one gets a conclusion. 끝까지[충분히] 생각하다; …의 결론을 내다.

***think to** oneself,* speak to oneself; consider secretly in one's mind. 마음속으로 생각하다; 혼잣말하다.

think twice, think again before acting; hesitate. 다시 생각하다; 망설이다.

think up, 《*colloq.*》 make up by thinking; invent. …을 생각해내다; 발명하다. ¶ ~ *up a lie* 거짓말을 생각해내다.

think·a·ble [θíŋkəbəl] *adj.* that can be thought. 생각할 수 있는; 상상이 되는.

think·er [θíŋkər] *n.* Ⓒ a person who thinks. 생각하는 사람; 사색가; 사상가.

·think·ing [θíŋkiŋ] *adj.* that thinks; that can think; thoughtful. 생각하는; 사고력이 있는. — *n.* Ⓤ thought; way of thought. 생각; 사고. ¶ *to my* ~ 내 생각으로는.

put on** one's **thinking cap, 《*colloq.*》 think about a problem, etc. …을 숙고하다; 깊이 생각하다.

thin·ly [θínli] *adv.* in a thin manner; in small numbers. 얇게; 가늘게; 성기게. [*thin*]

thin·ness [θínnis] *n.* Ⓤ the state of being thin. 얇음; 희박; 성김.

:third [θəːrd] *n.* **1** 《usu. *the* ~》 number 3; 3rd. 제3; 세 번째. ¶ *Henry the Third* 헨리 3세 / *the ~ floor* 《영》 4층; 《미》 3층 / *He married for the ~ time.* 세 번째로 결혼했다. **2** Ⓒ one of 3 equal parts of anything. 3분의 1. ¶ *the ~ part of a ton,* 1톤의 1/3 / *one-third,* 3분의 1 / *two-thirds,* 3분의 2. — *adj.* of 3rd. 제 3의; 3번째의; 3분의 1의. [E.]

third-class [θə́ːrdklǽs, -kláːs] *adj.* of the third class; less good than the first and second class. 3등[급]의; 하등의; 열등한. — *adv.* by third class. 3등으로.

third degree [⌐ –⌐], **the** *n.* the use of torture by the police to force a person to give information or a confession. 고문.

third estate [⌐ –⌐], **the** *n.* common people. 평민; 중산층《프랑스 혁명 이전의》.

third·ly [θə́ːrdli] *adv.* in the third place. 세 번째로; 셋째로.

third party [⌐ ⌐–], **the** *n.* another party other than the two principals. 제3당; 제삼자.

third person [⌐ ⌐–], **the** *n.* any one present at interview or concerned in negotiations, etc. besides the principals; 《gram.》 a form of pronouns. 제삼자; 3인칭.

·third-rate [θə́ːrdréit] *adj.* of the third rate; inferior. 3류의; 하등의; 열등한. ¶ *a ~ hotel* 삼류 호텔.

:thirst [θəːrst] *n.* Ⓤ 《often *a* ~》 **1** a painful feeling caused by need of something to drink; a desire for drink. 목마름; 갈증. ¶ *Running five miles gave him a ~.* 그는 5마일을 뛰었더니 갈증이 났다. **2** 《*for, after, of*》 a strong desire for anything. 열망; 갈망. ¶ *a ~ for knowledge* 지식욕 / *the ~ for power* 권력욕. — *vi.* (P3) **1** 《*arch.*》 feel thirst. 목이 마르다; 갈증을 느끼다. **2** 《*after, for*》 have a strong desire. 열망하다; 갈망하다. ¶ ~ *for fame* 명성을 갈망하다 / ~ *after new experiences* 새로운 경험을 열망하다. [E.]

thirst·i·ly [θə́ːrstili] *adv.* **1** with thirst. 목이 말라. **2** eagerly. 열망하여.

:thirst·y [θə́ːrsti] *adj.* (**thirst·i·er, thirst·i·est**) **1** feeling thirst. 목이 마른. ¶ *I am ~.* 목이 마르다. **2** (of the soil, etc.) dry; without water. 건조한. ¶ *The country was dry and*

～. 그 지역은 아주 건조했다. **3** having a strong desire. 열망하는. ¶ *He was ～ for riches.* 그는 부(富)를 갈망했다. **4** fond of drink. 술을 좋아하는. ¶ *He is a ～ soul.* 그는 술꾼이다. **5** 《*colloq.*》 causing thirst. 갈증이 나게 하는. ¶ *Haymaking is ～ work.* 건초 만드는 일은 목이 타는 일이다.

:thir·teen [θə́ːrtíːn] *n.* Ⓒ the number between twelve and fourteen; 13. 열셋; 13.
the thirteen superstition, the superstition that 13 is an unlucky number, esp. as that of a company at table. 13이 불길하다는 미신. — *adj.* of 13. 13의. [*three*]

:thir·teenth [θə́ːrtíːnθ] *n.* **1** 《usu. *the* ～》 the number 13; 13th. 제13. **2** Ⓒ one of 13 equal parts of anything. 13분의 1. — *adj.* of the 13th. 13번째의; 13분의 1의.

:thir·ti·eth [θə́ːrtiiθ] *n.* **1** 《usu. *the* ～》 the number 30; 30th. 제30. **2** Ⓒ one of 30 equal parts of anything. 30분의 1. — *adj.* of the 30th. 제30의; 30분의 1의.

:thir·ty [θə́ːrti] *n.* Ⓤ three times 10; 30. 30. — *adj.* of 30. 30의.

:this [ðis] *adj.* (*pl.* **these**) **1** which is near in time or space, or which has just been mentioned. 이; 지금의; 현재의; 방금 말한. ¶ ～ *month* 〔*year*〕 이 달〔이 해, 금년〕/ ～ *day week* 내주〔지난 주〕의 오늘 / *This house is mine.* 이 집은 내 집이다 / *Come ～ way please.* 이리로 오세요 / ～ *very moment* 바로 이 순간 / *Who are these people in the next room?* 옆 방의 이 사람들은 누구냐 / ～ *morning* 오늘 아침. **2** 《in contrast with *that*》 which is here; nearer of two or more. (that와 상관적으로 쓰여) 이; 이쪽의. ¶ *This car is better than that one.* 이 차가 저 차보다 좋다.
— *pron.* (*pl.* **these**) **1** the thing or person near in time or space. 이; 이 사람〔것〕. ¶ ～ *time* (지금) 이 시간 / *Who is ～?* 이 분 누구냐 / *This is Sunday.* 오늘은 일요일이다 / *This is our new teacher.* 이분이 새로 오신 우리 선생님이다 / *Will you send these to Mr. Brown and those to Mr. Smith?* 이것들은 브라운씨, 저것들은 스미스씨에게 보내주겠나. **2** the fact or idea about to be mentioned or which has just been mentioned. 방금 말한 것; 다음 말하는 것. ¶ *Do it like ～.* 이렇게〔이제부터 이르는 대로〕 해라 / *Answer me ～.* 이걸 내게 대답해라 / *I have heard ～ before.* 이 말은 전에 들었다 / *This is what I think.* 이게 내 생각이다 / *You mustn't behave like ～.* 이래서는 안 된다. **3** 《in contrast with *that*》 the thing or person here; the nearer of two or more things. 이것; 이 사람; 이 일. ¶ *This is newer than that.* 이게 저것보다 새롭다. **4** 《in contrast with *that*》 the latter. 후자(後者). ¶ *Health is above wealth, for ～ can not give so much happiness as that.* 건강이 부(富)보다 낫다. 왜냐하면 후자는 전자만큼 행복을 가져다 주지 못하니까.
— *adv.* 《*colloq.*》 to this extent; so. 이만큼; 이 정도로. ¶ ～ *big* 〔*early, much, far*〕 이렇게 크게〔일찍, 많이, 멀리〕/ *I've never been out ～ late before.* 전엔 이렇게까지 늦은 외출이 없었다 / *Cut off about ～ much thread.* 실을 이 정도로 잘라라. [E.]
for all this, in spite of this. 이에도 불구하고.
this and that, various things; one thing and another. 이것저것; 여러 가지.
this, that and the other, all kinds of things. 이것저것 잡다한 것; 가지각색의 것. ¶ *They sat up late into the night, talking about ～, that and the other.* 그들은 이것저것 이야기하면서 늦도록 자지 않았다.

this·tle [θísl] *n.* Ⓒ 《bot.》 a plant with a prickly stalk and leaves, and usu. with purple flowers. 엉겅퀴(cf. *rose*[1], *shamrock*). [E.]
grasp the thistle firmly, face, and deal with, difficulties boldly. 감연히 난관에 대처하다.

this·tle·down [θísldàun] *n.* Ⓒ a soft, feathery substance part on thistle seeds. 엉겅퀴씨의 관모(冠毛).

·thith·er [θíðər, ðíðər] *adv.* 《*arch.*》 to that place; in that direction. 저기에; 저쪽에 (opp. hither).
hither and thither ⇨hither.
— *adj.* on that side; farther. 저쪽의; 저편의. ¶ *on the ～ side of the river* 강 저편에. [E.]

·tho, 《Brit.》 **tho'** [ðou] *conj., adv.* =though.

thong [θɔ(ː)ŋ, θɑŋ] *n.* Ⓒ a narrow strip of leather; the lash of a whip. 가죽끈; 가죽 채찍. [E.]

tho·ra·ces [θɔ́ːrəsìːz] *n.* pl. of **thorax.**

tho·rac·ic [θɔːrǽsik] *adj.* of or belonging to the thorax. 가슴의; 흉부의. ¶ *the ～ cavity* 흉강(胸腔). [Gk.]

tho·rax [θɔ́ːræks] *n.* Ⓒ (*pl.* **-rax·es** or **-ra·ces**) **1** (of the human body) the chest. 가슴; 흉부; 흉곽. **2** (of insects) the middle of the three main sections of the body. (곤충의) 흉부. [↑]

·thorn [θɔːrn] *n.* Ⓒ **1** a sharp point on the stem of a plant; a prickle. 가시. ¶ 《*prov.*》 *No rose without a ～.* 가시 없는 장미는 없다. **2** a plant that has thorns on it. 가시나무. [E.]
a thorn in one's flesh 〔***side***〕, a cause of constant trouble. 고통〔걱정〕거리. ¶ *His laziness is a ～ in her side.* 그의 나태가 그녀의 골칫거리다.
be 〔***sit, stand, walk***〕 ***on*** 〔***upon***〕 ***thorns,*** be in a painful state of anxiety. 늘 불안에 시달리다.

thorn·y [θɔ́ːrni] *adj.* (**thorn·i·er, thorn·i·est**) **1** with thorns; full of thorns. 가시가 있는; 가시투성이의. **2** 《*fig.*》 difficult; full of obstacles, etc. 곤란한; 장애가 많은. ¶ *a ～ problem* 곤란한 문제 / *tread a ～ path* 가시밭길을 가다. [↑]

·thor·ough [θə́:rou, θʌ́r-] *adj.* complete; absolute; accurate; careful. 완전한; 절대적인; 정확한; 조심스러운. ¶ *It wants a ~ change.* 철저한 변화가 필요하다 / *~ knowlege* 완벽한 지식 / *a ~ blackguard* 철저한 악당 / *a ~ rest* 완전한 휴식 / *a ~ gentleman* 완벽한 신사. [*through*]

thor·ough·bred [θə́:roubrèd, θʌ́r-] *adj.* **1** (of an animal) pure-bred. 순종(純種)의. **2** (of persons) noble; of good birth and breeding. 출신이 좋은; 기품〔교양〕 있는. — *n.* Ⓒ **1** a thoroughbred animal, esp. a horse. 순종의 동물; (특히) 서러브레드. **2** a well-bred person. 기품〔교양〕 있는 사람.

thor·ough·fare [θə́:roufɛ̀ər, θʌ́r-] *n.* Ⓒ a street, road, or passage open at both ends. 통로; 길.

No thoroughfare, people are forbidden to go through (this street). 통행 금지《게시》.

thor·ough·go·ing [θə́:rougòuiŋ, θʌ́r-] *adj.* thorough; complete. 철저한; 완전한. ¶ *~ reforms* 철저한 개혁.

:thor·ough·ly [θə́:rouli, θʌ́r-] *adv.* fully; completely. 철저하게; 완전히. ¶ *a ~ bad man* 철저한 악인 / *do a thing ~* 일을 완벽하게 하다.

thor·ough·ness [θə́:rounis, θʌ́r-] *n.* Ⓤ completeness. 완전; 철저.

thor·ough·paced [θə́:roupèist, θʌ́rə-] *adj.* thorough; out-and-out. 철저한; 완전한. ¶ *a ~ villain* 철저한 악인.

:those [ðouz] *adj., pron.* pl. of **that.**

·thou [ðau] *pron.* (*pl.* **ye** or **you**) 《*arch., poet.*》 you. 너; 그대; 당신. [E.]

:though [ðou] *conj.* **1** in spite of the fact that; although. …이지만; …이긴 하지만. ¶ *Though (he is) rich, he works very hard.* 그는 부자지만 아주 열심히 일한다 / *He is still active ~ (he is) very old.* 그는 아주 나이가 많지만 아직 활동적이다 / *Though it was raining, he went there.* 비가 오는데도 그는 거기에 갔다. **2** yet; still; nevertheless; however. 비록 …하더라도〔할지라도〕. ¶ *She is better, ~ not yet cured.* 그녀는 아직 낫지는 않았을지라도 차도는 있다 / *Though I fail, I shall try again.* 비록 실패하더라도 또 해볼 테다.

— *adv.* 《placed at the end of a sentence》 however; all the same. 역시; 그래도. ¶ *It was quite true, ~.* 역시 그건 정말 사실이었다 / *The grapes, ~, may be sour.* 포도는 역시 시다. [E.]

as though, as if. 마치 …처럼. ¶ *You look as ~ you were tired.* 너 피곤해 보이는구나 / *I felt as ~ I should die of hunger.* 배가 고파 죽을 것만 같았다.

even though, even if. 비록 …일지라도. ¶ *I shall go even ~ it snows.* 눈이 오더라도 나는 가겠다 / *It is better to ask him even ~ he (should) refuse.* 그가 비록 거절할지라도 부탁을 해보는 게 좋다.

what though, what does it matter if. …이더라도 어떻단 말이야. ¶ *What ~ he should die.* 그가 죽는다 한들 그게 무슨 상관이냐.

:thought [θɔ:t] *v.* p. and pp. of **think.**

— *n.* Ⓤ **1** the act or process of thinking; the working of the mind. 생각하기; 사고. ¶ *He spent whole hours in ~.* 생각하며 시간을 다 보냈다. **2** the power of thinking, imagining, reasoning, etc. 사고력; 상상력. **3** Ⓒ 《usu. *pl.*》 that which a person thinks; a product of thinking, such as an idea, or an opinion. 의견; 안(案); 생각. ¶ *Let me have your thoughts on the subject.* 그 문제에 대한 당신 생각을 말해보시오 / *What are your thoughts of that man?* 저 사람을 어떻게 생각하나 / *I have very few thoughts on the subject.* 나는 그 문제에 대해 생각한 바가 거의 없다. **4** care; consideration; concern. 사려; 배려; 관심. ¶ *Many thanks for your kind ~ of me in sending back my umbrella.* 친절한 배려로 우산을 돌려주시니 정말 고맙습니다. **5** a way of thinking characteristic of a period, nation, etc. 사상; 사조(思潮). ¶ *modern ~* 현대 사상 / *the scientific ~ in 20th century,* 20 세기의 과학 사조 / *ancient Greek ~* 고대 그리스 사상. **6** 《*a ~*》 a little; somewhat. 조금; 어느 정도. ¶ *He was a ~ more kindly.* 그가 좀 더 친절했다 / *She is a ~ too cool for my liking.* 그녀는 좀 너무 냉정해서 내 비위에 안 맞는다. [*think*]

have no thought (=*have no intention*) ***of doing.*** …할 생각이 없다.

on second thoughts 〔《U.S.》 ***thought***〕, after thinking again. 다시 생각하여; 숙고하여.

take thought for (=*worry about*) something. …을 걱정하다. ¶ *take no ~ for the morrow* 내일을 걱정하지 않다.

·thought·ful [θɔ́:tfəl] *adj.* **1** full of thought; serious. 사려 깊은; 신중한. ¶ *~ looks* 신중한 표정. **2** 《*of*》 kind; careful of others. 친절한; 동정심이 있는; 정이 많은. ¶ *He is ~ of his friends.* 그는 친구들에게 친절하다 / *She is always ~ of her mother.* 그녀는 항상 어머니에게 자상하다.

·thought·ful·ly [θɔ́:tfəli] *adv.* **1** in a thoughtful manner. 사려 깊게. **2** kindly. 친절히.

thought·ful·ness [θɔ́:tfəlnis] *n.* Ⓤ **1** the state of being thoughtful. 사려 깊음. **2** kindness. 친절함; 동정심이 있음.

thought·less [θɔ́:tlis] *adj.* **1** without thought; careless. 생각이 없는; 신중하지 못한. ¶ *He is a ~ boy and is always making mistakes.* 그는 지각 없는 아이라서 늘 실수만 한다. **2** unkind. 인정이 없는. ¶ *It is ~ of her to keep us waiting so long.* 우리를 이렇게 오래 기다리게 하다니 그녀도 인정머리가 없다.

:thou·sand [θáuzənd] *n.* Ⓒ **1** ten hundred; 1,000. 천; 1000. **2** 《*pl.*》 《*of*》 a large number. 다수; 무수. ¶ *thousands of books* 무수한 책 / *A ~ thanks!* 대단히 고맙소 / *People died in thousands.* 무수한〔수 천명의〕 사람이

죽었다 / *thousands of people* 무수한 사람.
(a) thousand and one, too many to count. 무수한. ¶ *I have a ~ and one things to ask you.* 네게 물어 볼 말이 너무나도 많다.
one in a thousand, an extremely good person or thing. 천에 하나《절세의 영웅·미인 등》.
— *adj.* **1** of 1,000. 천의; 1000의. **2** indefinitely many. 다수의; 무수한. [E.]

thou·sand·fold [θàuzəndfòuld] *adj.* a thousand times as much or as many. 천 배의. — *adv.* a thousand times. 천 배로.

·**thou·sandth** [θáuzəndθ] *n.* **1** 《usu. *the* ~》 number 1,000; 1,000th. 천 번째. **2** Ⓒ one of the 1,000 equal parts of anything. 천분의 1. — *adj.* of a thousandth. 천 번째의; 천분의 1의. ¶ *I told him for the ~ time.* 그에게 수없이 말했다.

thrall [θrɔːl] *n.* **1** a slave. 노예. **2** Ⓤ bondage. 속박. **3** =thralldom. [N.]
in thrall, in bondage. 노예의 몸으로.
in thrall to, in bondage to. …에 속박되어.

thrall·dom, thral- [θrɔ́ːldəm] *n.* Ⓤ the state of being a slave. 노예 신분. [↑]

thrash [θræʃ] *vt.* (P6) **1** separate (grain) from its straw, husks, etc.; thresh. …을 탈곡하다; 도리깨질하다. **2** beat (someone) in punishment. …을 때리다; 매질하다. ¶ *The man thrashed the boy for stealing apples.* 그 남자는 아이가 사과를 훔쳤다고 때렸다. **3** 《*colloq.*》 defeat (someone) completely or mercilessly. …을 철저히 패배시키다. — *vi.* (P1,2A,3) **1** move violently; toss about. 심하게 움직이다; 몸부림치다. ¶ *The fishes thrashed in the net.* 고기들은 그물 속에서 펄떡거렸다 / *The patient with a high fever thrashed about in bed.* 고열의 환자는 침대에서 딩굴었다. **2** separate grain from its straw, husks, etc.; thresh. 탈곡하다. **3** sail against a strong wind. 바람을 거슬러 항해하다. [E.]
thrash out, settle by thorough discussion. 논의하여 해결하다. ¶ *~ out the solution to a problem* 논의하여 문제 해결책을 세우다.
thrash over, go over again and again either in thought or discussion. (생각·논의)를 거듭하다.

thrash·er [θrǽʃər] *n.* Ⓒ **1** a person or thing that thrashes. 탈곡하는 사람; 탈곡기; 매질하는 사람. **2** a large shark. 환도상어. [E.]

:**thread** [θred] *n.* Ⓒ **1** ⓊⒸ the fine, twisted fiber of cotton, flax, wool, silk, etc. 실; 섬유. ¶ *(a piece of) cotton* 〔*nylon*〕 *~* (한 올의) 무명〔나일론〕실 / *sew with ~* 실로 꿰매다. **2** something like a thread. 실처럼 가는 것. ¶ *a ~ of smoke* 〔*light*〕 한줄기의 연기〔빛〕. **3** the course of life. 인간의 수명. ¶ *the ~* (*course*) *of life* 수명; 명줄. **4** something that connects the parts of anything. (이야기 등의) 줄거리; 맥락. ¶ *the ~ of argument* 〔*narrative*〕 논의〔이야기〕의 줄거리 / *There is a consistent ~ running through all these policies.* 이들 모든 정책에는 일관된 맥락이 흐르고 있다. **5** the spiral ridge of a screw. 나삿니. ¶ *The ~ is gone.* 나삿니가 닳았다.
hang by a thread, be in a dangerous state. 위험한 상태에 있다.
have not a dry thread, be wet through. 흠뻑 젖다.
— *vt.* (P6,13) **1** pass a thread through (a needle, beads, etc.). …에 실을 꿰다. ¶ *She threaded her needle.* / *The child threaded the beads.* 아이는 구슬을 실에 꿰었다. **2** make (one's way) through. …을 누비듯이 나아가다. ¶ *He threaded the path of the forest.* 그는 숲속의 길을 따라 나아갔다. **3** form a thread on (a screw). …에 나삿니를 내다.
— *vi.* (P1) move in a thread-like course. 누비듯이 나아가다〔지나가다〕. ¶ *The cat threaded its way among the dishes on the shelf.* 고양이는 선반의 접시 사이를 요리조리 빠져 나갔다.
●**thread·like** [⌐làik] *adj.* [→throw]

thread·bare [θrédbɛ̀ər] *adj.* **1** (of clothes) so much worn out that threads are seen; shabby. (옷이) 해져 실이 드러나 보이는; 닳아 해진. ¶ *a ~ coat.* **2** (of persons) wearing threadbare clothes. 해진 옷을 입은. ¶ *a ~ beggar* 누더기를 걸친 거지. **3** 《*fig.*》 worn-out; old. 진부한; 케케묵은. ¶ *~ jokes* 진부한 농담.

·**threat** [θret] *n.* Ⓒ **1** a sign or warning of evil or trouble to come. …의 조짐; 징조. ¶ *There's a ~ of rain.* 비가 올 모양이다. **2** a saying that someone will be hurt or punished; a menace. 위협; 협박. ¶ *They used the ~ of strike action to enforce their demands.* 그들은 자기들 요구를 강요하기 위해 파업하겠다고 을렀다 / *Some people see computers as a ~ to their jobs.* 컴퓨터를 자기들 일자리에 대한 위협으로 보는 사람도 있다 / *He confessed under the ~ of imprisonment.* 그는 투옥한다고 위협하는 바람에 자백했다. [E.]

:**threat·en** [θrétn] *vt.* **1** (P6,8,11,13) make a threat against (someone). …을 위협〔협박〕하다; 으르다. ¶ *~ someone with punishment* 벌 주겠다고 아무를 으르다 / *~ to kill someone* 아무를 죽이겠다고 협박하다 / *He threatened that he would make it public.* 그는 그것을 공개하겠다고 위협했다. **2** (P6) give a sign of (evil or trouble to come). …의 조짐을〔징조를〕 보이다. ¶ *The clouds ~ a storm.* 저 구름은 폭풍우를 몰고 오겠다 / *Danger threatens us on every side.* 사방에서 위험이 우리를 위협하고 있다. **3** be a cause of danger to (something). …을 위태롭게 하다. ¶ *The fever threatens the city.* 열병 때문에 도시가 위험하다.
— *vi.* **1** (P1) make a threat. 위협〔협박〕하다. **2** (P1,4) be likely to occur. …할 것 같

다. ¶ *It threatens to rain.* 금방이라도 비가 올 것 같다. [*threat*]

threat·en·ing [θrétniŋ] *adj.* **1** making a threat. 위협하는. ¶ *a ~ letter* 협박장. **2** showing a sign of possible evil or trouble. 험악한. ¶ *a ~ sky* 찌푸린 하늘.

:three [θriː] *n.* Ⓒ the number between two and four. 셋; 3. — *adj.* of three. 셋〔세 개〕의. [E.]

give someone three times, give three cheers for someone. …을 위하여 만세 삼창을 하다.

three-cor·nered [θrìːkɔ́ːrnərd] *adj.* **1** having three corners or angles. 세모〔삼각〕의. ¶ *a ~ hat* 삼각모. **2** having three competitors, parties, etc. 삼파전의; 삼각관계의. ¶ *The election was a ~ fight.* 선거는 삼파전이었다.

three·fold [θríːfòuld] *adj.* having three times as much or as many. 세 배의; 세 겹의. — *adv.* three times as much or as many. 세 배로; 세 겹으로.

three-mile limit [θríːmàil límit] *n.* 《*the* ~》 the distance from the shore that is included within the power of the state possessing the coast. (해안에서 3해리 이내의) 영해폭.

three·pence [θrépəns, θríp-] *n.* Ⓤ three pence; Ⓒ a coin of this value. 3펜스; 3펜스 동전.

three·pen·ny [θrépəni, θríp-] *adj.* **1** of three pence. 3펜스의. **2** of little worth; cheap. 보잘것 없는; 싸구려의.

three·per·cent [θríːpərsént] *n.* 《*the ~ s*》 public securities at 3%. 이자 3프로의 공채(公債).

three·score [θríːskɔ́ːr] *adj.* three times twenty; sixty. 20의 3배의; 60의. ¶ (*a man of*) ~ *years,* 60세(의 사람) / 《Bible》 ~ (*years*) *and ten,* 70세《인간의 수명》.

thresh [θreʃ] *v.* =thrash.

thresh·er [θréʃər] *n.* =thrasher.

·thresh·old [θréʃhould] *n.* Ⓒ **1** the piece of stone or wood under a door; a doorway. 문지방; 문간; 입구. **2** 《*fig.*》 a beginning point. 출발점; 발단. ¶ *He was on the ~ of an important discovery.* 그는 중요한 발견의 실마리〔단서〕를 잡았다. [*thrash*]

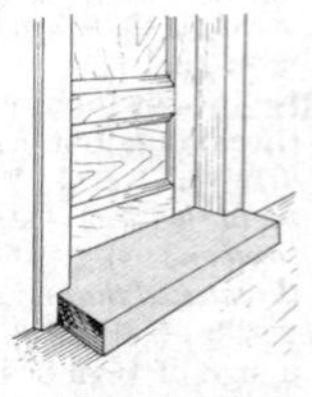
〈threshold 1〉

:threw [θruː] *v.* p. of **throw.**

·thrice [θrais] *adv.* 《*arch., lit.*》 three times; very much. 3회; 세 번; 대단히; 매우. ¶ *be ~ happy* 대단히 기쁘다. [*three*]

thrift [θrift] *n.* Ⓤ the act of saving money; economy. 검약; 검소; 경제. [*thrive*]

thrift·i·ly [θríftili] *adv.* in a thrifty manner; economically. 검약〔절약〕해서.

thrift·less [θríftlis] *adj.* without thrift; wasteful. 아끼지 않는; 낭비하는.

thrift·y [θrífti] *adj.* (**thrift·i·er, thrift·i·est**) **1** careful about spending money or resources; saving; economical. 검소한; 알뜰한. ¶ *a ~ housewife* 알뜰한 주부. **2** growing thickly; prosperous. 번영하는.
● **thrift·i·ness** [-nis] *n.*

·thrill [θril] *n.* Ⓒ an example of intense excitement or emotion; Ⓤ the act of trembling or shaking. 스릴; 가슴 설레는 생각; 떨림; 전율. ¶ *a ~ of joy* 가슴 설레는 기쁨 / *I felt a ~ of terror as the door began to creak open.* 문이 삐거덕하고 열리자 나는 무서워서 소름이 끼쳤다.
— *vt.* (P6) cause intense excitement to (someone); cause (someone) to tremble. …을 가슴 설레게 하다; 감격시키다; 떨게 하다. ¶ *The story of adventure thrilled him.* 모험담은 그를 가슴 설레게 했다.
— *vi.* (P1,3) **1** be deeply excited; feel a strong wave of emotion. 오싹하다; 감격하다. ¶ *Our hearts thrilled with joy at the sight of the Christmas-tree.* 크리스마스트리에 우리들은 가슴이 설레었다. **2** tremble with emotion. (감격으로) 떨리다. ¶ *Her voice thrilled with emotion.* 그녀는 감격하여 음성이 떨렸다. [*through*]

thrill·er [θrílər] *n.* Ⓒ something that arouses intense excitement; a mystery story, play or film, etc. 가슴 설레게 하는 것; (소설·극·영화 등의) 스릴물(物).

thril·ling [θríliŋ] *adj.* **1** causing a thrill; exciting. 오싹하게 하는; 감격적인. ¶ ~ *news* 감격적인 뉴스. **2** trembling. 떨리는. ¶ *a ~ voice* 떨리는 목소리.

·thrive [θraiv] *vi.* (**throve** or **thrived, thrived** or **thriv·en**) (P1,3) grow rich or well; prosper; succeed. 번영하다; 무성하다; 성공하다. ¶ *Children ~ in the country air.* 아이들은 시골 공기를 마시며 잘 자란다 / *Few plants or animals ~ in the desert.* 식물이고 동물이고 사막에서는 거의 자라지 못한다. [N.]

thriv·en [θrívən] *v.* pp. of **thrive.**

thro', thro [θruː] *adv., prep.* =through.

:throat [θrout] *n.* Ⓒ **1** the front part of the neck; the passage through it. 목(구멍); 기관; 숨통. ¶ *cut someone's ~* 아무의 목을 따다; 아무를 파멸시키다 / *take* 〔*seize*〕 *someone by the ~* 아무의 멱살을 잡다 / *A bone stuck in his ~.* 그는 목에 가시가 걸렸다. **2** a narrow passage. 좁은 통로. ¶ *The ~ of the valley was blocked by fallen rocks.* 계곡의 좁은 길은 낙석으로 막혀 있었다. [E.]

at the top of one's throat, as loudly as possible. 목청껏.

clear one's throat, hem; cough. (말하기 전에) 헛기침하다.

cut one's own throat, destroy or hurt oneself. 자멸하다; 화를 자초하다.

full to the throat, gorged. 배가 꽉 차서.

give someone the lie in his throat, accuse

someone of his gross lying. …의 거짓말을 나무라다; 거짓의 가면을 벗기다.
jump down** someone's **throat, attack or criticize someone with sudden verbal violence. …에게 욕설을 퍼붓다.
ram* [*thrust*] *down** someone's **throat, force someone to accept against his will. …에게 자기 주장을 강요하다.
stick in** one's **throat, be hard or unpleasant to say; be difficult to accept (a proposal, etc.). (말 따위가) 여간해서 안 나오다; (제안 등을) 받아들이기 어렵다.

throat·y [θróuti] *adj.* (**throat·i·er, throat·i·est**) **1** (of the voice) sounding as though produced in the back of the throat. 후음(喉音)의; 목쉰 소리의. **2** (of a person) having a throaty voice. 목소리가 쉰.

throb [θrɑb / θrɔb] *vi.* (**throbbed, throb·bing**) (P1,2A,3) **1** (of the heart and pulse) beat rapidly or strongly. (가슴이) 두근거리다; 고동[맥박]치다. ¶ *His heart had ceased to* ~ [*stopped throbbing*]. 그의 심장이 멎었다《죽었다》. **2** tremble; quiver; vibrate. 떨리다; 진동하다. — *n.* Ⓒ (of the heart and pulse) a rapid or strong beating; a regular beating. 동계; 고동; 맥박. [E.]

throe [θrou] *n.* 《usu. *pl.*》 **1** sharp pain. 격통. **2** the pains of childbirth; a violent or desperate struggle; anguish. 산고(産苦); 진통; 고투(苦鬪). ¶ *the throes of child* 출산의 진통. [E.]
in the throes of, struggling desperately with. …으로 몹시 괴로워. ¶ *He is in the throes of stomachache.* 그는 복통으로 몹시 괴로워하고 있다.

•**throne** [θroun] *n.* Ⓒ the seat, power, or authority of a king, queen, bishop, etc. 왕좌; 왕위; 왕권. ¶ *come to* [*mount*] *the* ~ 왕위에 오르다. — *vt.* (P6) place (someone) on a throne. …을 왕위에 앉히다. — *vi.* (P1) occupy a throne. 왕위에 오르다; 즉위하다. [Gk.]

•**throng** [θrɔ(ː)ŋ, θrɑŋ] *n.* Ⓒ a great number of people gathered at a place; a crowd. 군중. ¶ *Throngs of visitors crowded through art gallery.* 많은 관객들이 미술관에 밀어닥쳤다. — *vt.* (P6,13) fill (a place) with a crowd. …에 떼지어 모이다. ¶ *People thronged the theater to see the new play.* 새 연극을 보기 위해 사람들이 극장에 몰려들었다. — *vi.* (P2A,3,4) come together in a crowd; go or press in large number. 모여들다; 북적거리다. ¶ *People thronged to the big cities in search of jobs.* 사람들은 일자리를 찾아 대도시로 모여들었다 / *streets thronged with Christmas shoppers* 크리스마스 상품을 사려는 사람들로 북적거리는 거리들. [E.]

thros·tle [θrɑ́sl / θrɔ́sl] *n.* 《Brit.》 Ⓒ a kind of thrush; the song thrush. 노래지빠귀. [E.]

throt·tle [θrɑ́tl / θrɔ́tl] *n.* Ⓒ **1** 《mech.》 a valve controlling the flow of steam, gas, etc. to an engine. (가스·증기 등의) 조절판; 절기판(節氣瓣). **2** 《*rare*》 a throat. 목구멍. — *vt.* **1** (P6) make (someone) unable to breathe by pressing the throat; choke. …의 목을 조르다; 질식시키다. **2** (P6,7) 《mech.》 control the flow of steam, gas, etc. to an engine by means of a throttle valve. (가스·증기 등의 흐름)을 절기판으로 조절하다. ¶ ~ *a steam-engine.* [*throat*]

⁝**through** [θruː] *prep.* **1** from one end to the other end of; from one side to the other side of. …을 지나서; 관통하여; …의 끝에서 끝까지. ¶ *The road runs* ~ *the village.* 그 길은 마을을 관통하고 있다 / *I threw it* ~ *the window.* 난 그것을 창문밖으로 집어 던졌다 / *The train passed* ~ *the tunnel.* 기차는 터널을 빠져나갔다. **2** (of time) from the beginning to the end of. …동안 내내; 줄곧. ¶ ~ *the day* 온종일 / ~ (*one's*) *life* 평생토록 / *stay* ~ *the summer* 여름내 머물다 / *all* ~ *the night* 밤새도록 / *He won't last* ~ *the night.* 그는 오늘 밤을 넘기지 못할 것이다《죽을 것이다》. **3** (of place) among; over the whole surface of; all over; here and there in. 여기저기에[를]; 도처에. ¶ *The rumor spread* ~ *the town.* 온 마을에 소문이 퍼졌다. **4** by way of; by means of. …을 지나서; …에 의하여. ¶ *go out* ~ *the window* 창문으로 밖에 나가다 / *I heard of you* ~ *your sister.* 네 누이에게서 네 소식 들었다 / *He became rich* ~ *hard work.* 열심히 일해서 부자가 됐다 / *The man went* ~ *the doorway.* 그 남자는 출입구를 지나갔다. **5** on account of; by reason of. …때문에; …한 나머지. ¶ *run away* ~ *fear* 무서운 나머지 도망치다 / *I succeeded chiefly* ~ *your help.* 나는 오로지 네 덕으로 성공했다 / *How many working days were lost* ~ *sickness?* 아파서 며칠이나 일을 못 했지. **6** finished with; past. 끝나서; 지나서. ¶ *go* ~ *the work* 일을 끝내다 / *We are* ~ *our work at five.* 일은 다섯 시에 끝난다 / *Did you get* ~ *your exams?* 시험을 잘 치렀니. **7** 《U.S.》 to the end of; up to and including. (…에서) …까지 내내. ¶ *from A* ~ *B,* A부터 B까지 / *from 1990* ~ *1995,* 1990년에서 1995년까지. **8** against and in spite of (a noise). (소음 따위) 속에서도. ¶ *The politician struggled to speak* ~ *the shouts of the crowd.* 그 정치가는 군중들의 고함 소리 속에서도 연설을 계속하려고 애썼다.
— *adv.* **1** from end to end; from side to side. 통과하여; 꿰뚫어. ¶ *shoot a wall* ~ (총알이) 벽을 관통하다 / *May we go* ~*?* (문 따위를) 지나가도 괜찮습니까 / *The guard at the entrance wouldn't let us* ~. 입구의 수위는 우리를 들여보내지 않았다. **2** from the beginning to the end; to a conclusion. 처음부터 끝까지; 완성까지. ¶ *read a book* ~ 책을 통독하다 / *sing a song* ~ 노래를 끝까지 다 부르다 / *see it* ~ 그것의 완성을 지켜보다 / *Have you read the letter* ~*?* 편지를 다 읽었느냐. **3** all the way. 줄곧; 내내. ¶ *We*

talked the whole night ~. 우리는 밤새도록 이야기했다. **4** finished. 끝내서; 마쳐. ¶ *I'm almost* ~. 나는 거의 끝났다. **5** completely; thoroughly. 완전히; 철저히. ¶ *She was wet* ~. 그녀는 함빡 젖어 있었다.

be through with, **a**) have finished with; have completed. …을 끝내다; 마치다. ¶ *be* ~ *with the book* 책을 다 읽다 / *I am* ~ *with that fellow.* 나는 저 녀석과는 이제 손을 끊었다. **b**) 《*colloq.*》 have had enough of; be tired of. (…에) 물리다; 신물(싫증)이 나다. ¶ *I'm* ~ *with this job.* 나는 이 일에는 이제 싫증이 났다.

through and through, completely; thoroughly. 완전히; 철저히. ¶ *an honest man* ~ *and* ~ 아주 정직한 사람 / *We were wet* ~ *and* ~. 우리는 흠뻑 젖어 있었다.

— *adj.* **1** passing from one end to the other. 통과할(빠져 나갈) 수 있는. ¶ *a* ~ *street* 통과할 수 있는 거리 / *No* ~ *road.* 통과 못함《게시》. **2** traveling to the destination without stops; going all the way without change of line. 직행의; 직통의. ¶ *a* ~ *ticket* 직행표 / *a* ~ *train* 직행 열차. [E.]

·through·out [θru:áut] *prep.* **1** in every part of. …의 도처에; …에 널리. ¶ *It is easily found* ~ *this country.* 그건 이 지방 어디서나 쉽게 발견된다 / *His name is famous* ~ *the world.* 그의 명성은 세계적이다. **2** for the whole time of; during. …동안 내내; 죽. ¶ ~ *one's life* 전 생애를 통해. — *adv.* **1** in every part; everywhere. 모든 점에서; 구석구석이. ¶ *The house is well built* ~. 이 집은 어느 모로나 잘 지은 집이다. **2** from beginning to end; during the whole time. 처음부터 끝까지; 시종. ¶ *sit still* ~ 끝까지 잠자코 앉아 있다.

throve [θrouv] *v.* p. of **thrive.**

:throw [θrou] *v.* (**threw, thrown**) *vt.* **1** (P6,7,13,14) 《*at, to*》 ⓐ cause (something) to move through the air with force, esp. with a motion of the arm; cast; hurl. (공·돌 따위)를 냅다 던지다. ¶ ~ *stones at a dog* 개한테 돌을 던지다 / *I threw the ball to him.* =*I threw him the ball.* 그에게 공을 던졌다 / ~ *a stone into a pool* 물웅덩이에 돌을 던지다 / *Don't* ~ *anything out of the windows.* 창 밖으로 어떤 것도 내던지지 마라. ⓑ cast by a mechanical means; project. …을 발사하다. ¶ *A big gun throws a heavy shell.* 대포가 무거운 포탄을 발사하다 / ~ *a missile* 미사일을 발사하다. ⓒ cast; direct; send forth. (시선 등)을 던지다(보내다, 돌리다). ¶ ~ *an angry look at someone* 아무를 노려보다 / *He threw me a glance of contempt.* 그는 내게 경멸의 시선을 보냈다 / *A tree* ~ *a shadow on the wall.* 나무가 벽에 그림자를 드리우고 있다. **2** (P13) cause (something or someone) to fall to the ground or floor. …을 내동댕이치다; 넘어뜨리다. ¶ ~ *someone to the floor* 아무를 마룻바닥에 동댕이치다 / ~ *one's opponent* 상대를 쓰러뜨리다 / *The horse threw the rider.* 말이 기수를 내동댕이쳤다 / *He threw himself on the grass.* 그는 풀 위에 덜렁 드러누웠다. **3** (P6) move or send rapidly. …을 급히 움직이다(보내다). ¶ ~ *troops into battle* 부대를 전투에 투입하다 / ~ *a troop across the river* 일단의 군인들을 강 건너쪽으로 이동시키다. **4** (P6) 《*on, over, off*》 put hurriedly or carelessly; cast off. (옷 따위)를 급히 입다; 벗어던지다. ¶ ~ *a cloak over one's shoulders* 망토를 어깨에 걸치다 / ~ *hat on* 모자를 아무렇게나 쓰다 / ~ *off one's coat* (*gloves*) 코트를(장갑을) 벗어 던지다 / ~ *off one's mask* 가면을 벗다. **5** (P6) 《*into, out of*》 put (something or someone) in a certain state or position. (어떤 상태·위치로) …을 던지다; 확 만들다; 빠뜨리다. ¶ ~ *oneself into the arms of* …의 팔안에 몸을 던지다 《애인이 되다》 / ~ *someone out of work* 아무를 해고하다 / ~ *someone into prison* 아무를 투옥하다 / *The fire threw the people into confusion.* 화재는 사람들을 혼란에 빠뜨렸다. **6** 《U.S. *colloq.*》 let an opponent win (a race, game, etc.), often in return money. (미리 짜고) …에게 일부러 져주다. ¶ ~ *a contest, game, etc.* 경쟁·게임 등에서 일부러 져주다. **7** cast (dice); make (a specified cast) of dice. (주사위)를 던지다; (주사위)를 던져서 …끗이 나오게 하다. **8** (P6) (of animals) give birth to; bring forth. (새끼)를 낳다. ¶ *The cow threw its young.* 암소가 새끼를 낳았다. **9** (P6) give or have (a party); hold. (파티)를 열다. ¶ ~ *a cocktail party* 칵테일 파티를 열다. **10** (P6) twist (silk, etc.) into thread. (생사(生絲))를 꼬다.

— *vi.* (P2A,2B,3) cast, fling, or hurl something. 던지다; 투구(投球)하다.

throw about, **a**) wave violently. …을 휘두르다. **b**) waste; scatter. …을 낭비하다.

throw** oneself **at (=*try very hard to get the friendship or love of*) *someone.* 아무의 우정(사랑)을 얻고자 애쓰다.

throw away, **a**) waste. …을 낭비하다. ¶ ~ *money away* 돈을 낭비하다. **b**) get rid of (something). …을 버리다.

throw back, **a**) delay. …을 늦추다. **b**) reflect (light, etc.). …을 반사하다. **c**) show characteristics inherited from a remote ancestor. (동식물 따위가) 먼 조상의 성질로 되돌아가다; 귀선유전(歸先遺傳)하다.

throw cold water on (=*discourage*) *one's idea, etc.* (계획 등)에 찬물을 끼얹다.

throw in, **a**) interject (a remark). …을 삽입하다(끼워넣다). **b**) add extra. …을 덤으로 추가하다.

throw** oneself **into (=*work very hard at*) *something.* …에 열중(몰두)하다; 정력을 쏟다.

throw off, **a**) cast off (clothes). (옷)을 벗어던지다. **b**) recover from; get rid of. …에서 회복하다; …을 벗어나다. ¶ ~ *off a cold* 감기를 고치다(낫게 하다). **c**) write or speak quickly; improvise (verses, etc.). (시 따위)

를 즉석에서 짓다.

throw on, put on (a garment) carelessly or hastily. (옷)을 급히 입다; 걸치다.

***throw** oneself* (=*be dependent*) ***on** someone,* rely on for support; trust oneself entirely to. 아무를 의지하다; …에게 매달리다.

throw open, **a**) open suddenly or completely. …을 확〔활짝〕 열다〔열어제치다〕. **b**) allow everyone to enter into or take part in. …을 개방하다. ¶ *The garden was thrown open to the public.* 그 공원은 누구에게나 개방되어 있었다.

throw out, **a**) cast out; turn out. …을 버리다; 쫓아내다. ¶ ~ *someone out* (*of a room*) 아무를 (방에서) 쫓아내다. **b**) refuse to pass; reject. 부결하다. ¶ ~ *out a bill in parliament* 의회에서 의안을 부결하다. **c**) utter; drop (a hint). 말하다; 암시하다. ¶ ~ *out little hints* 약간의 힌트를 말하다.

throw over, desert; abandon. …을 저버리다; 파기하다. ¶ ~ *over a plan* 계획을 포기하다 / ~ *over a friend* 친구를 저버리다.

throw together, **a**) make or construct carelessly or hastily. …을 서둘러〔어설프게〕 만들어내다; 그러 모으다. ¶ *I just threw the meal together so I hope it's all right.* 이것저것 그러모아 만든 식사인데 괜찮았으면 한다. **b**) introduce someone to another by chance. 우연히 만나게 하다.

throw up, **a**) abandon (a job). …을 사직하다. **b**) construct rapidly. …을 급조하다. **c**) lift up. …을 밀어올리다. ¶ ~ *up a window* 창문을 밀어올려서 열다. **d**) 《*colloq.*》 vomit. …을 토하다.

— *n.* Ⓒ **1** the action or an instance of throwing. 던지기; 던짐. ¶ *a straight* ~ 직구 / *a* ~ *of hammer* 투해머. **2** the distance a thing is or can be thrown. 던져서 닿는 거리. ¶ *at a stone's* ~ 돌을 던지면 닿는 거리에; 지척에. **3** a cast of dice or the number cast. 주사위를 던지기; 던져서 나온 끗수. **4** 《*colloq.*》 a venture; risk; a chance. 모험; 운; 기회. ¶ *It was his last* ~. 그건 그의 마지막 기회였다. **5** 《U.S.》 a light blanket for a bed, etc. 얇은 담요; 홑이불 (따위). [E. =twist]

throw·back [θróubæ̀k] *n.* **1** a throwing back. 되던지기. **2** set back; check. 좌절; 저지. **3** the reversion to an ancestral character. (생물의) 귀선유전(歸先遺傳)하기.

***thrown** [θroun] *v.* pp. of **throw.**

throw-out [θróuàut] *n.* an article thrown aside. 불량품.

thru [θruː] *prep., adv.* 《chiefly U.S. *colloq.*》 =through.

thrum [θrʌm] *v.* (**thrummed, thrum·ming**) *vi.* (P1,3) play on a guitar, banjo, etc. carelessly or idly. 현악기를 아무렇게나 타다〔퉁기다〕. — *vt.* (P6) **1** play carelessly or idly. (현악기)를 아무렇게나 타다〔퉁기다〕. **2** tap (a table) with the fingers. (탁자)를 똑똑 두드리다. ¶ ~ *on a table.* — *n.* Ⓒ the sound made by thrumming. (현악기 따위를) 퉁겨 울리는 소리. [Imit.]

thrush [θrʌʃ] *n.* Ⓒ a bird which sings in a very sweet voice. 개똥지빠귀. [E.]

:**thrust** [θrʌst] *v.* (**thrust**) *vt.* (P6,7,13) **1** push (something or someone) with force; shove. …을 냅다 밀다; 밀어내다〔넣다〕. ¶ ~ *a paper into one's pocket* 종이를 주머니에 찔러넣다 / *He* ~ *me into the car.* 그는 나를 차에 밀어넣었다. **2** 《*into, through*》 pierce; stab. …을 찌르다; 꿰뚫다. ¶ ~ *a sword into his back* 그의 등을 칼로 찌르다 / *Their swords* ~ *him through.* 그들의 칼은 그의 몸을 여러 군데 꿰뚫었다. **3** 《*into*》 force (someone) into some condition. …을 억지로 어떤 상태에 두다. ¶ *He* ~ *himself into danger.* 그는 일부러 몸을 위험에 내맡겼다. **4** 《*on, upon*》 impose. …을 강제로 떠맡기다; 강제하다. ¶ ~ *a dollar into the waiter's hand,* 1 달러를 웨이터 손에 억지로 쥐어주다 / ~ *extra work* 〔*full responsibility*〕 *on someone* 과외의 일〔전책임〕을 아무에게 억지로 떠맡기다. **5** force (a way) by pushing. …을 밀치고 나아가다. ¶ *He* ~ *his way through the crowd.* 그는 군중 속을 헤치고 나아갔다. **6** put in (a question, etc.) while another person is speaking. 남의 말에 끼어들다. ¶ ~ (*in*) *a question* 질문에 끼어들다. **7** extend (a branch, etc.) into some place. (가지 따위)를 뻗다. ¶ ~ *its branches high* 가지를 높이 뻗다.

— *vi.* (P1,2A) **1** push against something. 밀다. ¶ ~ *aside* 옆으로 밀어내다. **2** make a stab. 찌르다; 찌르려고 달려들다. ¶ *She* ~ *at him with a dagger.* 그녀는 단검으로 그를 찌르려고 덤벼들었다. **3** 《*through, into*》 force one's way. 밀어젖히고 나아가다. **4** extend. (가지 따위를) 뻗다.

thrust** oneself **forward, draw attention to oneself. 주제넘게 나서다.

thrust** one's **nose into (= *interfere in*) *someone else's affairs.* …에 간섭하다; 남의 일에 참견하다〔끼어들다〕.

— *n.* Ⓒ **1** a sudden push; a stab. 갑자기 밀기; 찌르기. ¶ *a* ~ *with a knife* 칼로 한번 쿡 찌르기. **2** a driving force, one esp. one produced by a jet engine, a propeller, or a rocket. (프로펠러·제트엔진 등의) 추진력. **3** the force of one thing pushing on another. 압력. [N.]

thud [θʌd] *n.* Ⓒ a heavy sound made by something falling. 쿵〔털썩〕 떨어지는 소리. — *v.* (**thud·ded, thud·ding**) *vi.* (P3) **1** make a heavy sound. 쿵 소리를 내다. **2** fall with a thud. 쿵하고 떨어지다. — *vt.* (P6) beat (something) with a heavy sound. …을 쿵하고 치다. [Imit.]

thug [θʌg] *n.* Ⓒ **1** 《*hist.*》 an Indian professional robber and murderer. (인도의) 직업적 살인 강도단의 일원. **2** a murderer. 살인자; 자객. [Hind.]

·**thumb** [θʌm] *n.* Ⓒ the shortest and

thickest finger of the hand; the part of a glove covering the thumb. 엄지손가락; 장갑의 엄지손가락.

all thumbs, very unskillful in work. 손재주가 없어. ¶ *His fingers are all thumbs.* 그는 도무지 손재주가 없다.

a rule of thumb, a rough way of doing things found out by experience. 눈〔손〕대중; 경험에 의한 방법.

thumbs down up, 《*colloq.*》 a sign of no. 거부(의 손짓).

under the thumb of =***under*** *someone's* ***thumb,*** in the power of. 아무가 시키는 대로 하여. ¶ *I have him under my* ~. 그는 내가 시키는 대로 한다.

— *vt.* (P6) **1** turn over (a book) with the thumb. 엄지손가락으로 (책장)을 넘기다. **2** soil or wear (the pages of a book) with the thumb or by handling. (책상 따위)를 엄지손가락으로 만져 더럽히다〔닳게 하다〕. ¶ *a much thumbed book* 책장이 많이 닳은〔더럽혀진〕 책. **3** (of a hitchhiker) ask for (a ride) by signaling with the thumb. 엄지손가락으로 태워달라는 신호를 하다. [E.]

thumb index [∠ ∠–] *n.* 《print.》 a series of rounded indentations in the front edge of a book, each labeled, as with a letter, to indicate a section of the book. 반달색인.

thumb·nail [θʌ́mnèil] *n.* Ⓒ **1** the nail of the thumb. 엄지 손톱. **2** something very short or small. 아주 짧은〔작은〕 것. — *adj.* of the size of a thumbnail; very short or small. (크기가) 엄지손가락만한; 아주 짧은〔작은〕.

thumb nut [∠∠] *n.* a nut that has a head that can be turned easily by a thumb and a finger. (나비 모양의) 암나사.

thumb·screw [θʌ́mskrùː] *n.* Ⓒ a nail-shaped piece of metal that has a head that can be turned easily by a thumb and a finger. (대가리가 나비 모양의) 수나사.

thumb·tack [θʌ́mtæ̀k] *n.* Ⓒ a pin used to fasten paper, cloth, etc. on a wall with the thumb. 압핀; 압정(押釘).

***thump** [θʌmp] *vt.* (P6,18) strike (something) with a heavy thing. …을 쿵 치다. ¶ ~ *the desk with fist* 주먹으로 책상을 쿵 치다. — *vi.* (P1,2A,3) **1** strike heavily. 쿵하고 치다. **2** walk with heavy steps. 쿵쿵거리며 걷다. **3** (of the heart) beat violently. (가슴이) 두근거리다. ¶ ~ *with excitement* 흥분으로 가슴이 두근거리다. — *n.* Ⓒ a heavy knock; a sound made by a thump. 쿵하고 때리기; 그 소리. ¶ *He hit him a* ~ *on the back.* 그는 그의 등을 탁 쳤다 / *The man fell with a* ~. 그 남자는 쿵하고 넘어졌다. ● **thump·er** [∠ər] *n.* [Imit.]

:thun·der [θʌ́ndər] *n.* **1** Ⓤ the loud noise which is heard in the sky as a result of the passage of lightning. 우레. **2** 《usu. *pl.*》 a loud noise like thunder. 우레 같은 소리. ¶ *the* ~ *of the Niagara Falls* 나이아가라 폭포의 우레 같은 소리 / *a* ~ *of applause* 우레 같은 박수 갈채. **3** threat; denunciation. 위협; (공연한) 비난.

steal *someone's* ***thunder,*** use another's idea without his permission; prevent someone from appearing at his best by using his idea, etc. first. 남의 생각을 가로채다; (그렇게 해서) …의 기선(機先)을 제(制)하다.

— *vi.* (P1,2A) **1** 《using *it* as the subject》 give forth thunder. 천둥치다. ¶ *It thundered, but no rain fell.* 천둥은 쳤지만 비는 오지 않았다. **2** make a loud noise like thunder. 우레와 같은 소리를 내다. ¶ *The guns thundered.* 대포가 우레와 같은 소리를 냈다 / ~ *at the door* 문을 요란하게 두드리다 / *The waves* ~ *upon the shore.* 파도가 우레 같은 소리를 내며 해안을 친다. **3** shout out; roar. 고함치다; 소리소리지르다. ¶ *Preachers* ~ *weekly from a thousand pulpits.* 수많은 설교단(說敎壇)에서는 매주 전도사들이 고래고래 소리를 지른다.

— *vt.* (P6,7,13) shout out at (someone). …에게 소리지르다. [E.]

thun·der·bolt [θʌ́ndərbòult] *n.* Ⓒ **1** a flash of lightning with the noise of thunder. 천둥 번개. ¶ *It came upon me like a* ~. =*It was a regular* ~ *to me.* 그것은 내게 실로 청천 벽력이었다. **2** something terrible that happens suddenly. 생각지 않은 변고; 예기치 못한 재난. ¶ *The news of the bank's failure was a* ~. 그 은행의 파산 소식은 충격이었다.

thun·der·clap [θʌ́ndərklæ̀p] *n.* Ⓒ **1** a loud noise of thunder. 천둥 소리. **2** something unexpected. 예기치 못한 일; 돌발 사고.

thun·der·cloud [θʌ́ndərklàud] *n.* Ⓒ a dark cloud that brings thunder and lightning. 뇌운(雷雲).

thun·der·head [θʌ́ndərhèd] *n.* Ⓒ one of the white masses of cloud which often develop into thunderclouds. 소나기구름; 적란운; 쌘비구름.

thun·der·ous [θʌ́ndərəs] *adj.* of thunder; like thunder. 천둥의; 우레 같은. ¶ ~ *applause* 우레 같은 박수 갈채.

thun·der·storm [θʌ́ndərstɔ̀ːrm] *n.* Ⓒ a storm with thunder and lightning. 뇌우(雷雨).

thun·der·struck [θʌ́ndərstrʌ̀k] *adj.* **1** struck by a thunderbolt. 벼락을 맞은. **2** very surprised. 대경 실색한.

Thurs., Thur. Thursday.

:Thurs·day [θə́ːrzdi, -dei] *n.* the fifth day of the week. 목요일. 參考 Thurs. 또는 Thur.로 생략함. [→thunder]

:thus [ðʌs] *adv.* **1** in this way. 이렇게; 이와 같이. ¶ *He spoke* ~. 그가 이렇게 말했다. **2** to this degree or extent. 이 정도로; 이만큼. ¶ *Why* ~ *sad ?* 어찌 이토록 슬픈가.

3 accordingly; therefore; so. 따라서; 그러므로. ¶ *Thus we see that plants need light.* 그런 까닭에 식물에는 빛이 필요한 것이다. [E.]

thus and thus, in such and such a way. 여차여차하게.

thus far, so far. 지금까지는; 여기까지는. ¶ *Thus far may you go and no farther.* 여기까지만 가고 더는 가지 마라.

thus much, this much. 이만큼은.

thwack [θwæk] *vt.* (P6,7) strike (something) sharply with something flat. (납작한 것으로) …을 철썩 때리다. —*n.* Ⓒ a sharp blow with something flat. (납작한 것으로) 철썩 때리기. [Imit.]

thwart [θwɔːrt] *vt.* (P6) 《*from*》 do not agree with (someone); oppose; prevent. …에 반대하다; …을 방해하다. ¶ *His family thwarted his plan.* 가족은 그의 계획을 반대했다 / *Our plans for picnic were thwarted by rain.* 비 때문에 우리의 소풍 계획은 좌절되었다. —*n.* Ⓒ a rower's seat across a boat. (노젓는 사람이 앉는 배의) 가로장. —*adj.* lying across. 가로누운; 가로지른. —*adv.* across. 가로누워; 가로질러. [N.=across]

***thy** [ðai] *pron.* 《*arch., poet.*》 =your. [*thou*]

thyme [taim] *n.* Ⓒ a small plant with leaves which are used to give a good taste to food. (꿀풀과의) 백리향속(白里香屬) 식물의 하나《잎은 향료》. [Gk.]

thy·mol [θáimoul, -mɔ(ː)l, -mɑl] *n.* 《chem.》 a strong disinfectant. 티몰《방부제》. [Gk.]

thy·roid [θáirɔid] *n.* Ⓒ a small gland in the neck which produces a liquid to control the growth of the body. 갑상선(甲狀腺). —*adj.* of the thyroid. 갑상선의. [Gk.=shield-shaped]

thy·rox·in, -ine [θairɑ́ksiːn / -rɔ́k-] *n.* Ⓤ the principal secretion of the thyroid gland. 티록신《갑상선 호르몬의 일종》. [↑]

***thy·self** [ðaisélf] *pron.* 《*arch.*》 =yourself. [*thou*]

ti [tiː] *n.* 《mus.》 the seventh tone of the scale. 시; 나음《장음계의 제7음》.

Ti. 《chem.》 titanium.

ti·ar·a [tiέərə, -ɑ́ːrə] *n.* Ⓒ **1** a jewelled crown worn by ladies. (여자의 머리 장식용) 보석 박은 관. **2** the crown of the Pope. (로마 교황의) 삼중관(三重冠). **3** a head dress worn by ancient Persians. (옛 페르시아 사람들의) 두건; 관. [Gk.]

〈tiara 1〉

Ti·bet [tibét] *n.* a country in central Asia, now a part of China. 티베트. 參考 Thibet라고도 씀.

Ti·bet·an [tibétən] *adj.* of or belonging to Tibet. 티베트(사람·어)의. —*n.* **1** Ⓒ a person of Tibet. 티베트 사람. **2** Ⓤ the language of Tibet. 티베트어.

tib·i·a [tíbiə] *n.* (*pl.* **-i·ae** or **-i·as**) the larger of the two bones of the lower leg. 정강이뼈. [L.]

tib·i·ae [tíbiiː] *n.* pl. of **tibia.**

tic [tik] *n.* a twitching of the muscles of the face. 안면 근육 경련; 안면 신경통. [F.]

***tick**[1] [tik] *n.* Ⓒ **1** a sound made by a clock, watch, etc. (시계 등의) 똑딱똑딱 소리. **2** 《Brit. *colloq.*》 a moment. 순간; 찰나. **3** a check mark indicating that something is approved of, correct, or noted; a dot. (점검·대조필 등의) 체크표 《✓》.

to the tick, very correctly; very punctual. 아주 정확히; 꼭.

—*vi.* (P1,2A) make a tick. (시계가) 똑딱거리다. ¶ *A watch ticks.*

—*vt.* (P6,7) **1** announce (time) by ticking sounds. (시간)을 알리다. **2** 《*off*》 mark (something) with a tick. …에 표시를 하다; 체크하다. ¶ *He ticked off the items one by one.* 그는 물품을 하나씩 체크했다. [Imit.]

tick off, 《*colloq.*》 scold. …을 꾸짖다. ¶ *I got well ticked off for my mistake.* 잘못 탓으로 욕깨나 먹었다.

tick[2] [tik] *n.* Ⓒ a small insect that sucks the blood of man and other animals. 진드기. [E.]

tick[3] [tik] *n.* Ⓒ a covering of a mattress or pillow. 이불잇; 베갯잇. [→thesis]

tick[4] [tik] *n.* Ⓤ 《*colloq.*》 credit. 신용; 외상거래. [*ticket*]

give tick, sell on credit. 외상으로 팔다.

go* (*on*) *tick, buy on credit. 외상으로 사다.

on tick, on credit. 외상으로.

tick·er [tíkər] *n.* Ⓒ **1** a person or thing that ticks. 기장(記帳)하는 사람; 똑딱거리는 물건. **2** a telegraphic instrument that automatically prints the changes in market prices on a paper tape. 주식 시세 자동 표시기. **3** 《*colloq.*》 a clock; the heart. 시계; 심장. [*tick*[1]]

:tick·et [tíkit] *n.* Ⓒ **1** a small piece of paper that gives its owner a certain right, as to ride on a train. 차표; (극장 따위의) 입장권. ¶ *a one-way* ~ 편도표 / *a round-trip* ~ 왕복표 / *a commutation* ~ 정기권 / *buy a* ~ *for the opera* 오페라 입장권을 사다 / *buy one's* ~ *to Oxford* 옥스퍼드행 차표를 사다. **2** a small card showing the price of goods in a shop. 정가표; 정찰(正札). ¶ *a price* ~ 가격표. **3** 《U.S.》 a list of candidates for election, belonging to a particular party. 공천 후보자 명단. **4** 《*the* ~》 《*colloq.*》 the proper 〔correct〕 thing. 적당한〔알맞은〕 것; 정당〔당연〕한 일. ¶ *That's the* ~. 그것은 안성맞춤이다; 바로 그거다 / *That's not quite the* ~. 그것은 합당하지는 않다. **5** a summons to appear at court for traffic violation. (교통 법규 위반에 대한) 호출장; 딱지.

— *vt.* (P6) put a ticket on (something). …에 표를 달다; (주차 위반) 딱지를 붙이다. ¶ *She was ticketed for illegal parking.* 그녀는 주차 위반 딱지를 받았다. [Teut. (→stick)]

tick·et-of-leave [tíkitəvlíːv] *n.* 《Brit.》 permission given to a prisoner to go out of prison before the end of the fixed term. 가석방 허가. ¶ *a ~ man.*

tick·ing [tíkiŋ] *n.* Ⓤ a strong cloth for covering a mattress or pillow. (질긴) 이불잇; 베갯잇. [*tick*[3]]

·tick·le [tíkəl] *vt.* (P6) **1** touch (someone) lightly to cause a thrill, laughter, etc. …을 간질이다. **2** please; amuse. …을 기쁘게 하다. ¶ *I was tickled by his good stories.* 그의 구수한 얘기가 재미있었다. — *vi.* (P1) have a tingling feeling. 간지럽다. ¶ *My throat* 〔*nose*〕 *tickles.* 목이〔코가〕 근질거린다. — *n.* Ⓒ a tickling feeling. 간지러움; 근질거림. [E.]

tick·lish [tíkliʃ] *adj.* **1** of a nature to be easily moved by tickling. 간지럼 타는. **2** (of a person) difficult to deal with; delicate; apt to get angry. 까다로운; 성마른. ¶ *He is ~ on that matter.* 그 문제에 그는 깐깐하다. **3** (of an affair) difficult; requiring skillful handling. (일이) 신중을 요하는. ¶ *a ~ problem* 까다로운 문제. **4** easily upset; unstable. 불안정한. ● **tick·lish·ly** [-li] *adv.* [E.]

tick·tack [tíktæ̀k] *n.* Ⓒ a light sound repeating regularly; the sound of the heart or a clock. 규칙적인 똑딱 소리; (심장의) 고동; 시계 소리. [*tick*[1]]

tick·tock [tíktɑ̀k/-tɔ̀k] *n.* Ⓒ the sound made by a clock. (시계의) 똑딱똑딱(하는 소리). [↑]

tid·al [táidl] *adj.* of tides; affected by tides. 조수(潮水)의; 조수의 작용을 받는. [→tide]

tidal wave [⌐-⌐] *n.* **1** a very large ocean wave caused by an earthquake or a heavy wind. 해일(海溢). **2** 《*fig.*》 a great movement; overwhelming outburst of general emotion. 큰 변동〔파란〕; (민심의) 큰 동요.

tid·bit [tídbìt] *n.* Ⓒ 《U.S.》 **1** a delicious bit of food. 한입거리의 맛있는 음식; 한입의 진미(珍味). **2** a pleasing bit of news. 재미있는 토막 뉴스. ¶ *a few tidbits of gossip* 재미있는 가십 몇 가지. [E.]

:tide [taid] *n.* **1** ⒸⓊ the regular rise and fall of the ocean caused by the pull of the moon and the sun. 조수; 조수의 간만(干滿); 조류. **2** 《*fig.*》 Ⓒ ⓐ anything that rises and falls like the tide. 성쇠; 영고(榮枯). ¶ *the high* 〔*ebb*〕 *~ of fortune* 행운의 절정〔운세의 내리막〕 / *the full ~ of pleasure* 쾌락의 절정 / *There is a ~ in the affairs of men.* 인간사(人間事)에는 부침(浮沈)이 있다. ⓑ a current. 풍조; 경향. ¶ *the ~ of social conservation* 사회의 보수적 풍조. **3** Ⓤ 《*arch.*》 a season; a period. 계절; 철; 때. ¶ 《*prov.*》 *Time and ~ wait for no man.* 세월은 사람을 기다려 주지 않는다 / *Christmas ~* 크리스마스 계절.

go with the tide, 《*fig.*》 do what others do. 시류에 따르다.

the turn of the tide, the reversal of fortune. 운수의 역전; 형세의 일변.

turn the tide, change from one condition to the opposite. 형세를 역전〔일변〕시키다.

work double tides, work day and night. 밤낮으로 일하다.

— *vi.* flow as the tide does; flow with the tide. 조수처럼 흐르다; 조수를 타다. — *vt.* (P6) carry (something) along as the tide does; carry by the tide. …을 조수처럼 조류에 실어 나르다. [E. =time]

tide over, get over; manage to overcome. …을 극복하다. ¶ *~ over difficulties* 〔*hard times*〕 곤란을〔불경기를〕 이겨내다.

tide-wa·ter [táidwɔ̀ːtər, -wɑ̀t-] *n.* 《U.S.》 **1** water on the seacoast having tides. 조수의 영향을 받는 강의 물《만조 때 해안을 덮음》. **2** a seacoast. 해안; 연안. ¶ *a ~ country* 연안 지방.

ti·di·ly [táidili] *adv.* in a tidy manner; with tidiness. 말끔하게; 깨끗이. [*tidy*]

ti·di·ness [táidinis] *n.* Ⓤ the state of being tidy. 정연함; 깨끗함.

·ti·dings [táidiŋz] *n. pl.* 《used as *sing.* or *pl.*》 《chiefly *lit.*》 news; information. 소식; 통지; 기별. ¶ *good* 〔*evil*〕 *~* 희소식〔비보〕 / *The messenger brought ~ from the battle-front.* 전선에서 전령이 소식을 가지고 왔다. [N.]

ti·dy [táidi] *adj.* (**-di·er, -di·est**) **1** neat and in good order. 말끔한; 잘 정돈된. ¶ *a ~ room* 말끔히 잘 정돈된 방 / *the tidiest woman in the world* 세상에서 가장 깔끔한 여자. **2** 《*colloq.*》 fairly good; considerable. 꽤 좋은; 상당한. ¶ *a ~ income* 괜찮은 수입 / *a ~ sum of money* 상당한 금액.

— *vt.* (**-died, -dy·ing**) (P6,7) 《*up*》 make tidy; put (something) in order. …을 깨끗이 정돈〔정리〕하다. ¶ *~ up the table* 〔*room*〕 식탁〔방〕을 깨끗이 정돈하다 / *She tidied the room* 〔*garden*〕. 그녀는 방〔정원〕을 말끔히 정리했다 / *~ oneself* 몸단장을 하다 / *I must just ~ up a bit.* 정리를 좀 해야겠다.

— *n.* Ⓒ (*pl.* **-dies**) **1** a cover for the arm or back of a chair. etc. (의자 따위의) 커버. **2** a box-like container for keeping things tidy. 자질구레한 물건을 챙겨 두는 상자. [*tide* (orig. sense *seasonable*)]

:tie [tai] *v.* (ppr. **ty·ing**) *vt.* **1** (P6,7,13) bind, fasten, or attach (something) with a string, rope, etc. (끈 따위로) …을 매다; 묶다. ¶ *~ a package* 소포를 묶다 / *~ back one's hair* 머리를 뒤에서 묶다 / *~ a dog to a tree* 개를 나무에 매놓다 / *~ flowers in a bunch* 꽃을 다발로 묶다 / *~ a ship to a*

landing stage 배를 부잔교(浮棧橋)에 매두다 / *a box tied with red ribbon* 붉은 리본으로 묶은 상자. **2** (P6) make (a knot or bow) in a cord, etc.; secure (a cord, etc.) by a knot or bow. (끈)을 매다; (매듭)을 짓다. ¶ ~ *a knot* 매듭을 짓다 / ~ *one's shoelaces* 구두끈을 매다 / *Tie in* 〔*into*〕 *a bow.* 나비 넥타이를 매라 / ~ *one's necktie* 넥타이를 매다. **3** (P6,7,13) fasten or connect firmly. (일반적으로) …을 단단히 매다〔묶다, 잇다〕. ¶ *They were tied by common interests.* 그들은 공통의 이해로 묶여져 있었다 / *Deep affection tied them.* 깊은 애정이 그들을 단단히 묶어 놓았다. **4** (P6,7,13) 《*to*》 restrict; limit; bind by duty, promise, etc. …을 (책임 등으로) 구속〔속박〕하다. ¶ ~ *someone to a bad condition* 아무를 악조건 아래 묶어두다 / *I am tied to my work.* =*My work ties me.* 나는 일에서 헤어날 수 없다 / *I am much tied.* 눈코 뜰 사이도 없다 / *I am tied to* 〔*for*〕 *time.* 마감 시간에 몹시 쫓기고 있다. **5** (P6) ⓐ equal (the score of an opponent) in a contest; equal the score of (an opponent). (경기에서) …와 타이를 이루다; 동점이 되다. ¶ ~ *one's competitor* 경쟁자와 비기다 / *His team tied mine.* 그의 팀은 우리 팀과 동점이다. ⓑ bind (someone, the hands, etc.) with rope, cord, etc. …을 (밧줄 등으로) 묶다; 결박하다. ¶ *His hands were tied behind his back.* 그는 등 뒤로 양 손이 묶였다 / ~ *the hands of* …의 양 손을 묶다 / *be tied hand and foot* 손발이 묶이다; 행동의 자유를 잃다.
— *vi.* **1** (P1) form a bow or knot. 매이다; 묶이다. ¶ *That rope doesn't* ~ *well.* 그 새끼는 잘 매지지 않는다 / *My dress ties at the back.* 내 드레스는 뒤에서 매게 되어 있다. **2** (P1,3) be equal in a contest. (경기에서) 동점이 되다. ¶ *The two teams tied.* 두 팀은 비겼다 / *Our team tied with his.* 우리 팀은 그의 팀과 동점이다.

tie down, **a**) bind by duty, conditions, etc.; limit the activities of; restrict. …을 제한〔구속〕하다. **b**) tie or fasten so as to keep from rising or moving. (몸을) 옴쭉 못하게 묶어 두다.

tie in, **a**) connect or be connected. 접합(接合)하다. **b**) be in agreement. 꼭 일치하다. ¶ *The police found a fact that might* ~ 〔*be tied*〕 *in with the murder case.* 경찰은 그 살인 사건과 일치하는 한 가지 사실을 발견했다.

tie up, **a**) fasten (someone or something) with a rope, string, etc. …을 단단히 묶다. **b**) delay; stop. (교통)을 방해하다; 정체시키다. ¶ *The railway was tied up by the accident.* 그 사고로 철도가 막혔다〔정체되었다〕. **c**) cause to be busy; engage; occupy. 바빠 꼼짝 못 하게 하다; 구속하다. ¶ *All the nurses are tied up.* 한가한 간호사는 하나도 없다.

— *n.* Ⓒ **1** a rope, cord, or string that is used to tie; a necktie; a shoelace. (매는 데 쓰이는) 끈; 밧줄; 넥타이; 구두끈. **2** a knot; an ornamental knot. (장식) 매듭. **3** something that unites; a link; a bond; 《often *pl.*》 obligation; burden. (일반적으로) 매는〔묶는〕 것; 연분; 인연; 기반; 거치적거리는 것〔짐〕. ¶ *political ties* 정치적 제휴 / *Her children were a great* ~ *to the widow.* 그녀의 자식들은 과부인 그녀에게 거치적거리는 매우 큰 짐이었다 / *the ties of blood* 혈연 관계. **4** 《mus.》 a curved line joining two notes of the same pitch. 붙임줄; 타이(⁀,‿). **5** a state of equality in a contest. (경기의) 동점; 타이. ¶ *The game ended in a* ~. 시합을 비겼다. **6** 《archit.》 a beam holding together a structure; 《U.S.》 one of the beams to which the rails of a railroad are fastened. 이음목; (철도의) 침목(枕木). [E.]

play off the tie, have a deciding match. 결승 시합을 하다.

tie·pin [táipìn] *n.* Ⓒ a pin for fastening the necktie. 넥타이 핀.

tier[1] [tiər] *n.* Ⓒ one of a series of rows arranged one above and behind another. (관람석 등의) 단(段); 줄; 층. — *vi.* raise in tiers. 층층으로 되어 있다. — *vt.* arrange (something) in tiers. …을 층층으로 쌓다. [F.]

tier[2] [táiər] *n.* Ⓒ a person or thing that ties. 매는 사람〔것〕. [*tie*]

tie-up [táiʌ̀p] *n.* Ⓒ **1** a stopping of work or action caused by a strike of the employees or an accident. (파업 등으로 인한) 정지; 휴업. **2** 《*colloq.*》 connection; relation. 관계; 제휴; 타이업. [*tie*]

tiff [tif] *n.* Ⓒ **1** a little quarrel. 승강이; 사소한 언쟁. ¶ *have a* ~ *with one's wife* 아내와 사소한 언쟁을 벌이다. **2** ill temper. 기분이 언짢음. [?]

tif·fin [tífin] *n.* Ⓒ 《Brit.》 lunch. 점심. — *vi.* (P1) eat lunch. 점심을 먹다. [obs. *tiff* liquor]

:ti·ger [táigər] *n.* Ⓒ **1** a large, fierce animal of the cat family. 범; 호랑이. **2** 《*fig.*》 a violent, cruel, merciless man. 잔인한 사람. **3** 《U.S. *sl.*》 a loud cry after the three excited cheers. (만세 삼창 후에) 덧부르는 함성《Tiger ! 라고 외침》. ¶ *three cheers and a* ~ *for someone* 아무에 대한 만세 삼창과 환호성. ● **ti·ger·like** [-làik] *adj.* [Gk. *tigris*]

tiger lily [⌐-⌐-] *n.* 《bot.》 a lily with orange flowers spotted with black. 참나리.

ti·ger's-eye [táigərzài] *n.* a golden-brown semiprecious stone. 호안석(虎眼石).

:tight [tait] *adj.* **1** stretched; tense. 팽팽한; 켕긴(opp. slack, loose). ¶ *a* ~ *rope* 팽팽히 켕긴 줄 / *Pull the thread* ~. 실을 팽팽하게 당겨라. **2** firm; knotted; closed; firmly or closely fixed in place. 단단히 맨; 단단한; 꽉 들어찬; 단단히 고정된. ¶ *a* ~ *knot* 단단히 맨 매듭; 옭매듭 / *a* ~ *little bud* 아직 단단한 작은 꽃망울 / *This drawer is so* ~ *I can't open it.* 이 서랍은 너무 빡빡해서 나는 열 수가 없다. **3** close; fitting (too) closely. (옷 따위가) 너무〔꼭〕 끼는. ¶ ~ *shoes* 꼭 끼는 신 / *a ~ coat* 꼭 끼는 외투 / *feel ~ around the waist* 허리가 너무 꼭 낀다. **4** 《esp. in *compounds*》 not letting water, air or gas in or out. 빈틈이 없는; (물·공기 따위가) 새지 않는; 방(防)…. ¶ *a ~ ship* 〔*roof*〕 물이 스미지 않는 배〔지붕〕/ *watertight shoes* 방수화. **5** (of a situation) difficult or dangerous to deal with; severe; strict. (입장 따위가) 난처한; 대처하기 어려운; 엄격한. ¶ *a ~ situation* 난처한〔어려운〕 입장 / *be in a ~ place* 〔*corner, spot*〕 진퇴 양난이다; 궁지에 몰려 있다 / *He kept ~ control over his pupils.* 그는 학생들을 엄격하게 다루었다. **6** (of a commodity) difficult to obtain; (of money) scarce. (상품 등이) 구하기 힘든; 돈에 쪼들리는(cf. *easy*). ¶ *Money will be ~ next year.* 내년에는 돈 사정이 나빠질 것이다 / *During a depression, money is ~.* 불경기에는 돈〔자금〕이 딸린다. **7** 《*colloq.*》 stingy. 쩨쩨한; 인색한. **8** 《*colloq.*》 drunk. 술에 취한.

keep a tight rein 〔***hand***〕 ***on,*** train severely; keep under one's strict control. …을 엄격히 다루다; 다잡다.

— *adv.* tightly; firmly. 단단히; 굳게. ¶ *She kept her mouth ~ shut.* 그녀는 입을 굳게 다물고 열지 않았다 / *a coat made to fit ~* 몸에 꼭 끼게 만든 상의.

hold tight, grasp firmly; hold strongly to (something). …을 꽉 잡다; 단단히 쥐다.

sit tight, **a**) stay where one is. …에 꼼짝 않고 앉아 있다. **b**) 《*colloq.*》 stick to one's position, rights, opinions, etc. 자기 입장〔주장〕을 고수하다.

— *n.* 《*pl.*》 a tightly-fitting garment worn by acrobats, dancers, etc. (곡예사, 댄서 등이 입는) 타이츠. [N.]

***tight·en** [táitn] *vi.* (P1,2A) become tight. 꽉 죄이다; 팽팽해지다. ¶ *A tent-rope tightens when it gets wet.* 천막 끈은 젖으면 팽팽해진다. — *vt.* (P6,7) make (something) tight. …을 꽉 죄다. ¶ *~ one's grip* 더 꽉 움켜쥐다 / *~ the reins* 고삐를 바싹 당기다 / *~ a screw* 나사를 죄다. [↑]

tighten one's belt, 《*joc.*》 go without food; cut down expenditure. 허리띠를 졸라매다; 내핍 생활을 하다.

tight-fist·ed [táitfístid] *adj.* stingy. 쩨쩨한; 인색한.

tight-lipped [táitlípt] *adj.* **1** keeping the lips firmly together. 입을 꽉 다문. **2** saying little or nothing. 말수가 적은; 입이 무거운.

***tight·ly** [táitli] *adv.* in a tight manner; firmly. 단단히; 꽉; 굳게.

tight·ness [táitnis] *n.* Ⓤ the state of being tight. 꽉 죄임.

tight·rope [táitròup] *n.* Ⓒ a tightly-stretched rope or wire on which acrobats walk or move. (줄타기용으로) 팽팽하게 맨 줄. ¶ *a ~ dancer* 줄타기 곡예사.

tight·wad [táitwɑ̀d / -wɔ̀d] *n.* 《U.S. *sl.*》 a stingy person. 인색한 사람; 노랭이.

***ti·gress** [táigris] *n.* Ⓒ **1** a female tiger. 암범. **2** a fierce, cruel, violent woman. 암범 같은 여자; 잔인한 여자. [*tiger*]

Ti·gris [táigris], **the** *n.* a river in southwestern Asia. 티그리스 강.

tike, tyke [taik] *n.* 《*colloq.*》 **1** a rough dog; a cur. 들개; 똥개. **2** a mischievous child; a child. 개구쟁이. **3** a rough, ill-bred fellow. 배우지 못한 인간; 망나니. [N.]

til·de [tíldə] *n.* Ⓒ a mark used on some letters to show a nasal sound, such as ñ and ã. 비음(鼻音)을 나타내는 기호《*ñ, ã* 등의 ~》. [Sp.]

***tile** [tail] *n.* Ⓒ **1** a thin piece of baked clay for covering roofs, floors, etc. 타일; 기와. **2** 《*colloq.*》 a high silk hat. 실크해트. — *vt.* (P6) cover (roofs, floors, etc.) with tiles. …에 타일을 붙이다; 기와를 이다. [L. *tego* cover]

have a tile loose, 《*sl.*》 be not quite right in the head. 머리가 좀 돌다.

til·ing [táiliŋ] *n.* **1** 《*collectively*》 tiles. 타일류(類); 기와. **2** the work of covering with tiles. 타일 붙이기; 기와 이기. **3** a covering or structure of tiles. 타일을 입힌 것. [↑]

:till[1] [til] *prep.* up to the time of. …까지. ¶ *I waited for him ~ seven.* 그를 일곱 시까지 기다렸다 / *~ tomorrow* 〔*next week*〕 내일〔다음 주〕까지 / *~ now* 지금까지. — *conj.* **1** up to the time when. (…때)까지. ¶ *Wait ~ he comes back.* 그가 돌아올 때까지 기다려라. **2** 《in *negative constructions*》 before; unless. …하기 전에; …하지 않으면. ¶ *She won't come ~ you call her.* 네가 부르지 않는 한 그녀가 올 리 없다. [N.]

till[2] [til] *vt.* (P6) prepare (land) for growing crops; cultivate. (땅)을 갈다; 경작하다. [E. =strive]

till[3] [til] *n.* Ⓒ a money drawer in a shop. (가게의) 돈궤; 돈 서랍. [E.]

till·age [tílidʒ] *n.* Ⓤ **1** the act of tilling; cultivation. 경작. **2** tilled land. 경작지. [*till*[2]]

till·er [tílər] *n.* Ⓒ a handle or bar for turning the rudder of a boat. 키의 손잡이. [L. *tela* web]

***tilt** [tilt] *vi.* **1** (P1,2A,3) lean; slope. 기울다; 경사지다. ¶ *be apt to ~ over* 걸핏하면 기울어진다 / *The boat tilted.* 보트가 상하로 기우뚱거렸다. **2** (P1) fight with a spear on horseback. 마상 창시합하다. **3** (P1,3) 《*at*》 make an attack. 공격하다. — *vt.* (P6,7) **1** cause (something) to lean; raise (something) at one end. …을 기울게 하다; …의 한쪽 끝을 들어올리다. ¶ *~ a stone* 돌의 한쪽을 들어올리다. **2** attack (someone) with a spear. …을 창으로 공격하다.

tilt at a windmill, make a useless attack at an unreal enemy. 가상의 적과 싸우다.

— *n.* Ⓒ **1** a slope; a sloping position. 기

울기; 경사. ¶ *give a ~ to a barrel* 통을 기울이다. **2** a fight on horseback with a lance. 마상 창시합. **3** a quarrel. 언쟁; 논전(論戰). [E. =unsteady]

(*at*) *full tilt,* at full speed; with great force. 전속력으로; 전력을 다해.

on the tilt, inclining. 기울어.

tilth [tilθ] *n.* **1** Ⓤ the act of tilling. 경작. **2** tilled land. 경(작)지. [*till*[2]]

:tim·ber [tímbər] *n.* Ⓤ **1** wood before it is ready for building and making things. 재목; 목재. **2** Ⓒ a large piece of wood used for house-building or ship. (건물의) 들보〔대들보〕용 재목; (배의) 늑재(肋材); 선재(船材). **3** Ⓒ woodland from which timber is taken. (재목을 내는) 삼림지. **4** Ⓤ《U.S.》personality; quality. 성격. — *vt.* (P6) support (something) with timber. …을 목재로 받치다. [E.=edifice]

tim·bered [tímbərd] *adj.* **1** made of timber. 목재를 쓴. **2** covered with growing trees. 수목으로 덮인; 나무가 울창한. ¶ *well-timbered land* 수목이 많은 지대.

timber hitch [ˊ-ˋ] *n.* 《naut.》 a knot used to fasten a rope around a spear, post, etc. 옭매듭《원재(圓材) 따위에 밧줄을 매는 방식의 하나》.

tim·bre [tǽmbər, tím-] *n.* Ⓤ 《F.》 the special quality of the sound of a voice or musical instrument that makes it different from others. 음색(音色).

tim·brel [tímbrəl] *n.* a small drum played with the hand; a tambourine. 작은 북의 일종; 탬버린. [Gk. =drum]

:time [taim] *n.* Ⓤ **1** 《without *an article*》 the concept of past, present, and future, taken separately or as a whole. 때; 시간; 세월. ¶ *~ and space* 시간과 공간 / 《*prov.*》 *Time flies like an arrow.* 세월은 화살과 같다 / 《*prov.*》 *Time and tide wait for no man.* 세월은 사람을 기다리지 않는다. **2** Ⓒ 《usu. *a ~*》 a length of time; a period. 기간 ¶ *a short ~* 단기간 / *for a ~* 잠시; 한동안 / *in a short ~* 이윽고 / *The play continued for two hours' ~.* 연극은 두 시간 동안 계속되었다 / *That will take a long ~.* 그건 시간이 오래 걸리겠다. **3** ⓊⒸ an appointed, fit, or proper time for something to happen. (…하기에 알맞은 또는 어떤 정해진) 시간; 시기; 때. ¶ *It is ~ to go home.* 집에 갈 시간이다 / *There is a ~ for everything.* 무슨 일에나 때라는 것이 있다 / *This is no ~ for trifling.* 우물쭈물하고 있을 때가 아니다 / *It's ~ for lunch.* (이제) 점심 시간이다 / *Have I ~ to catch train?* 기차 시간에 댈 수 있을까 / *This is the first ~ I've been here.* 이곳에 온 것은 이번이 처음이다. **4** Ⓒ an occasion; a portion of time in which an action or event is repeated; the point when something occurs. …할〔한〕 때; 시기. …한 적; 기회; …(때)마다; …번〔회〕. ¶ *next ~* 다음 번〔기회〕/ *many and many a ~* 몇 번이고 몇 번이고 / *at all times* 언제나; 늘 / *three times a day* 하루에 세 번 / *At that ~ she was away from home.* 그때 그녀는 외출하고 집에 없었다 / *He's in a good temper, so now is the ~ to tell him you've crashed his car.* 그는 지금 기분이 좋은 상태이니, 지금이야 말로 네가 그의 차를 받았다고 말할 좋은 기회이다 / *Each ~ I see him I like him more and more.* 나는 그를 만날 때마다 그가 더욱 더 좋아진다. **5** some particular hour in the day; a system of measuring the passage of time. 시각; 표준시. ¶ *by this ~* 이 시각까지 / *keep good ~* (시계가) 정확히 잘 간다 / *Greenwich ~* 그리니치 표준시 / *standard ~* 표준시 / *What ~ is it?* 지금 몇 시냐 / *Will you kindly fix a ~ to call?* 방문 시각을 정해 주시겠습니까. **6** leisure or spare time. 여가; 틈. ¶ *I have little ~ to play.* =*I have little ~ for playing.* 한가한 시간이 거의 없다. **7** 《usu. *pl.*》 a particular period; age; epoch; era; 《*the ~*》 the present time. 시대; 연대; 현대. ¶ *in modern* 〔*ancient*〕 *times* 현대〔고대〕에 / *in the ~ of Julius Caesar* 카이사르 시대에 / *with the change of the times* 시대의 추이에 따라 / *He was no longer a professor at that college in my ~.* 나의 재학 시절에 그는 이미 그 대학의 교수가 아니었다 / *the good old times* 좋았던 옛 시절. **8** 《often *pl.*》 one's experience during a certain time; conditions of life at present or a certain period. (어떤 시기의) 경험; 경기; 시세. ¶ *hard times* 불경기 / *have an easy* 〔*a bad*〕 *~* (*of it*) 편하게 지내다〔혼이 나다〕/ *pass through a terrible ~* 끔찍한 경험을 하다. **9** a particular part of a year, day, etc.; season. 계절; 시절; (특정한) 시간〔때〕. ¶ *Christmas ~* 크리스마스 계절 / *dinner ~* 식사 때 / *It is very cold for this ~ of year.* 지금의 계절로 치면 매우 춥다. **10** Ⓒ the state of being multiplied by a number. (몇) 번; …회; 곱. ¶ *She has three times as many books as I have.* 그녀에겐 내 세곱의 책이 있다 / *Four times six is twenty-four.* 4 곱하기 6은 24이다. **11** lifetime; time of death. 생애; 일생; 죽을 때. ¶ *near one's ~* 임종이 가까운 / *His ~ has come.* 죽을 때가 됐다 / *Such things never happened in his ~.* 그의 생애 중 그런 일은 한번도 없었다. **12** the rate of speed in marching, driving, etc. 행진 속도; 운전 속도. **13** 《mus.》 tempo or rhythm; the length of a note or rest. 박자; 속도; 리듬. ¶ *beat ~* 박자를 맞추다 / *keep ~ with something* …와 장단을 맞추다 / *two-four ~,* 4분의 2박자. **14** the period occupied by one's work; rate of pay, esp. reckoned by the hour. 근무 시간; 시간급(時間給). **15** a signal for the end or suspension of play in a game; the period in which a game is played. (경기의 시작·종료) 신호; (경기의) 소요 시간. **16**

《*sl.*》 a period of imprisonment. 형기(刑期). ¶ *He's served ~ for burglary.* 절도죄로 형을 살았다.

against time, trying to finish in a given time; as fast as possible. 시간을 다투어; 전속력으로.

all in good time, soon enough; no need for haste. 때를 기다리노라면; 때가 되면.

all the time, continuously; throughout a specified period. 그 동안 줄곧; 시종; 언제든. ¶ *Why must you keep complaining all the ~?* 너 뭣 때문에 노상 불평이냐.

at no time, never. 결코〔한 번도〕…없다〔않다〕.

at one time, **a**) formerly. 한 때; 일찍이. **b**) at the same time. 동시에.

at the same time, **a**) however; nevertheless; on the other hand. 하지만; 그래도. ¶ *She didn't like to spend any more money. At the same ~, she wanted to go on the trip.* 그녀는 더는 돈을 쓰기 싫었다. 그렇지만 여행은 하고 싶었다. **b**) in the same period. 동시에. ¶ *Can you watch television and do your homework at the ~ time?* 텔레비전 시청과 숙제를 동시에 할 수 있느냐.

at times, now and then; sometimes. 때때로; 이따금. ¶ *At times I wonder if it's all worth while.* 이따금 나는 그것이 그만한 가치가 있는 것인지 생각해 본다.

behind the 〔*one's*〕 ***times,*** old-fashioned. 구식의; 시대에 뒤진.

be pressed for time =have no time to spare.

for the time being, for the present time. 당분간.

from time to time, now and then; occasionally. 때때로; 이따금. ¶ *They come to see me from ~ to ~.* 그들은 이따금 나를 만나러 온다.

gain time, **a**) (of a watch) go too fast. (시계가) 너무 빠르다. **b**) save time. 시간을 벌다.

have a good time (***of it***)***,*** enjoy oneself. 재미있게〔즐겁게〕 지내다.

have no time to spare, have no leisure; be very busy. 여가가 없다; 바쁘다.

in good time, **a**) at the proper time. 딱 좋은 때에. **b**) quickly. 즉시; 곧.

in no time, almost at once; very quickly. 곧(바로); 즉시. ¶ *We'll have that leak fixed in no ~.* 그 누수(漏水)는 즉시 막아야 한다.

in one's own good time, when one chooses. 형편 닿는 대로; 마음 내킬 때에.

in time, **a**) early enough; in the future; eventually. 조만간; 결국. **b**) in the correct tempo. 가락을 맞춰.

lose time, go at too slow a rate. 꾸물거리다; 늑장부리다.

make time, go fast to recover lost time. 서두르다; 지체된 시간을 만회하다.

many a time, many times; again and again. 종종; 여러번.

near her time, (of a woman) shortly to give birth. 해산이 임박한.

on time, at the appointed time; punctual(ly). 제시각에; 정각에.

out of time, **a**) not at the usual time. 제철이 아닌. **b**) not in the proper rhythm. 박자가 틀리는.

pass the time of day, exchange brief words of greeting. (아침·저녁의) 인사를 나누다.

serve one's time, **a**) serve the agreed period of apprenticeship. 도제(徒弟)살이를 마치다. **b**) go through one's time. 형기를 치르다.

take one's time, be slow in doing something. 서두르지 않다. ¶ *Take your ~* (*over it*). 천천히 하세요.

time after time, again and again; repeatedly; continually. 몇 번이고; 재삼 재사.

time of life, (a person's) age. (사람의) 나이.

time out of mind, from time immemorial; since long long ago. 먼 옛날부터.

— *vt.* **1** (P6,7) choose the moment or occasion for (something). …의 기회를 노리다; 때를 맞추다. ¶ *~ one's punches* (권투 선수가) 기회를 놓치지 않고 타격을 가하다 / *We timed our visit to suit her convenience.* 그녀의 형편에 맞추어 방문하기로 했다 / *His remark was well timed.* 그의 말은 시의(時宜) 적절했다. **2** (P6,7) arrange or set the time of (something); adjust (a watch). …의 시간을 정하다; 시계를 맞추다. ¶ *Time your watch with mine.* 네 시계를 내 것에 맞춰라. **3** (P6) record the time of (something). (경기 등의) 시간을 재다. ¶ *~ a race* 경주의 시간을 재다. **4** (P6) regulate; cause (something) to agree in rhythm. …을 조절하다; …을 박자에 맞추다. ¶ *~ one's steps to the music* 음악에 스텝을 맞추다 / *~ the speed of a machine* 기계의 속도를 조절하다.

— *vi.* keep or beat time. 박자를 맞추다.

— *adj.* **1** of time. 시간의; 시간에 관한. **2** designed to explode, open, etc. at a fixed time. 시한 장치가 된. **3** based on installment payments. 월부의. [E.]

time bomb [⌐⌐] *n.* **1** a bomb designed to explode at a particular time. 시한 폭탄. **2** a situation resembling such a bomb. (시한 폭탄 같은) 위험을 내포한 상황. ¶ *The high level of youth unemployment is a ~ that could one day have disastrous social consequence.* 젊은 층의 높은 실업률은 언제고 사회적으로 비극적인 결과를 낳게 되는 시한 폭탄이다.

time capsule [⌐⌐–] *n.* a container that is filled with objects representative of its time and then buried, so that it can be dug up and examined in a future age. 타임캡슐.

time·card [táimkɑ̀ːrd] *n.* Ⓒ 《U.S.》 a card for recording one's working time. 근무 시간 기록표; 타임카드.

time clock [ㅅㅅ] *n.* 《U.S.》 a clock with a device to record the time when workers arrive and leave. 근무 시간 기록계(計); 타임 리코더.

time-con·sum·ing [táimkənsù:miŋ] *adj.* using or taking a long time or too much time. 오랜 시간이 걸리는; 시간 낭비의. ¶ *Keeping the house clean can be a very ~ job.* 집안을 깨끗이 유지하는 것은 시간을 여간 많이 잡아 먹는 일이 아니다.

time-hon·ored, 《Brit.》 **-hon·oured** [táimɑ̀nərd / -ɔ̀n-] *adj.* old; continued over a long period; respected because of age or long usage. 예로부터의; 전통 있는; 유서 깊은. ¶ *a ~ custom* 오랜 전통 있는 관습.

time·keep·er [táimkì:pər] *n.* Ⓒ **1** a watch; a clock. 시계. ¶ *This old watch of mine's a good ~.* 내 이 시계는 오래 됐지만 시간은 잘 맞는다. **2** a person or thing that records the period when workmen work. 작업〔근로〕 시간 기록기〔기록원〕.

time-lapse [táimlæ̀ps] *adj.* technical of or being a method of filming very slow actions (such as flowers growing) using many single pictures, which when run at the ordinary speed of a film show the action much faster. 저속도 촬영의《식물의 성장 따위를 보이는 기록 영화를 만들 때 쓰이는 기법에서》.

time·less [táimlis] *adj.* **1** never ending; eternal. 영원한; 영구의. ¶ *the ~ universe* 무한한 우주. **2** restricted to no special time. 부정기(不定期)의.

time·ly [táimli] *adj.* (**-li·er, -li·est**) at the right time; occuring at a suitable time. 적시(適時)의; 때 맞춘. ¶ *~ help* 적시의 도움.
●**time·li·ness** [-nis] *n.*

time·piece [táimpì:s] *n.* Ⓒ anything that records the time; a watch; a clock. 계시기(計時器); 시계.

tim·er [táimər] *n.* Ⓒ **1** a person who records time. (경기 등의) 시간 기록원. **2** a device for recording time; a stop watch. 스톱 워치. **3** an instrument for controlling machinery at a fixed time. 일정 시간에 자동으로 작동하는 스위치; 타임 스위치. ¶ *Don't forget to set the ~ on the oven.* 오븐에 타이머를 맞춰 두는 것을 잊지 마라.

time·sav·ing [táimsèiviŋ] *adj.* reducing the time needed to do something. 시간 절약의.

time·serv·er [táimsə̀:rvər] *n.* Ⓒ a person who easily varies his opinions for his own selfish purposes. 기회주의자.

time switch [ㅅㅅ] *n.* an electrical switch that can be set to start a machine or operation at a particular time. 타임 스위치.

time·ta·ble [táimtèibl] *n.* Ⓒ a list of times at which trains, buses, ships, etc. are due to arrive and leave. (열차 등의) 시각표.

time·work [táimwə̀:rk] *n.* Ⓤ work paid for by the hour. 시간급(給) 작업(cf. *piecework*).

time·worn [táimwɔ̀:rn] *adj.* worn-out by long use or existence. 낡아빠진; 노후한. ¶ *~ steps* 노후한 층계 / 《*fig.*》 *~ clichés* 진부한 표현.

time zone [ㅅㅅ] *n.* an area where the standard time is the same. 표준 시간대.

***tim·id** [tímid] *adj.* (**-id·er, -id·est**) lacking in courage; easily frightened; shy. 겁이 많은; 수줍음을 잘 타는. ¶ (*as*) *~ as a hare* 아주 겁이 많은. [L. *timeo* fear]

ti·mid·i·ty [timídəti] *n.* Ⓤ the state of being timid; shyness. 겁; 소심함; 수줍음.

tim·id·ly [tímidli] *adv.* in a timid manner. 겁에 질려; 소심하게.

tim·or·ous [tímərəs] *adj.* very timid; easily frightened; fearful. 아주 겁이 많은.
●**tim·or·ous·ly** [-li] *adv.* [→timid]

tim·o·thy [tíməθi] *n.* 《bot.》 《U.S.》 a kind of grass used for hay. 큰조아재비《목초》. [Person]

tim·pa·ni [tímpəni] *n. pl.* (*sing.* **-no**) a set of two or more kettledrums played by one man in an orchestra or band. 팀파니. [It.]

tim·pa·no [tímpənòu] *n.* sing. of **timpani.**

:tin [tin] *n.* Ⓤ **1** a soft, silvery-white, metallic element. 주석. **2** thin plate of iron or steel covered with tin. 양철; 함석. **3** Ⓒ ⓐ 《Brit.》 any can, box, etc. made of tin. 양철 그릇; 깡통(cf. 《U.S.》 *can*[2]). ⓑ the contents of a tin box. 깡통에 든 것. ¶ *eat a whole ~ of biscuits* 〔*sardines*〕 비스킷〔정어리〕 한 깡통을 다 먹다. **4** 《*sl.*》 money. 돈.
— *adj.* made of tin. 양철로 만든. ¶ *a ~ box.*
— *vt.* (P6) **1** cover (something) with tin. …에 주석을 입히다. **2** keep (something) in a tin can. …을 통조림으로 하다. [E.]

tinct [tíŋkt] 《*arch.*, poet.》 *adj.* colored. 물들인. — *n.* a color; a shade of color. 색; 색조. [L. *tingo* dye]

tinc·ture [tíŋktʃər] *n.* **1** Ⓤ a medicinal solution in alcohol. 팅크; 정기(丁幾). ¶ *~ of iodine* 요오드팅크; 옥도 정기. **2** Ⓒ a color. 색(조). **3** Ⓒ 《*of*》 a slight trace or flavor. 기미; 티; 냄새. ¶ *a ~ of garlic* 마늘 냄새 / *a ~ of hope* 다소의 희망 / *some ~ of education* 좀 배운 티. — *vt.* (P6,13) **1** color; tinge. 착색하다; 물들이다. **2** 《*with*》 give a trace to (something). …에 —의 색채〔기미〕를 띠게 하다. ¶ *be tinctured with humanity* 인간미가 있다. [↑]

tin·der [tíndər] *n.* Ⓤ very inflammable material that catches fire easily from a spark. 부싯깃. [E. =kindle]

tin·der·box [tíndərbɑ̀ks / -bɔ̀ks] *n.* Ⓒ **1** a box for keeping tinder, flint and steel. 부시통. **2** a very dangerous uncontrollable place or situation. (분쟁 등의) 불씨; 화약고. ¶ *Racial tension is a real ~.* 종족간의 긴장 상태는 정말 일촉 즉발이다.

tine [tain] *n.* Ⓒ a sharp projecting point.

(사슴 뿔·포크 등의) 가지. ¶ *the tines of a fork.* [E.]

tin foil [⌐⌐] *n.* a very thin sheet of tin for wrapping goods. 은종이; 은박지. [*tin*]

ting [tiŋ] *n.* a clear, ringing sound, as of a small bell. 땡그랑〔딸랑〕하는 소리. — *vi., vt.* (P1; 6) make such a sound; ring (a bell). 딸랑〔땡그랑〕소리가 나다〔를 내다〕. [Imit.]

tinge [tindʒ] *vt.* (P6,13) **1** 《*with*》 color slightly. …을 엷게 물들이다. ¶ *The sunrise tinged the clouds with pink.* 해가 솟으며 구름은 연분홍색으로 물들었다 / *Her cheeks are tinged with red.* 그녀의 볼이 살짝 붉어졌다. **2** 《*fig.*》 《*with*》 give a flavor to (something); affect slightly. …한 기미를 띠게 하다. ¶ *Melancholy tinged his words.* 그의 어조에는 우울한 데가 있었다.
— *n.* Ⓒ **1** a slight color; a tint. 엷은 색조. **2** a small amount; a trace; a touch. 기미; …한 티. ¶ *There was a ~ of sadness in her voice.* 그녀 음성은 어딘가 슬프게 들렸다 / *There was a ~ of sarcasm in his remarks.* 그의 말은 비꼬는 투였다. [L. *tingo* dye]

tin·gle [tíŋɡəl] *vi.* (P1,3) **1** have a pricking feeling. 따끔거리다; 쑤시다; 얼얼하다. ¶ *My ears were tingling with cold.* 추위로 귀가 얼얼했다. **2** feel stirred with excitement or emotion. 흥분하다; (가슴이) 설레다. ¶ *I felt a ~ of excitement.* 나는 흥분을 느꼈다 / *We were all tingling with eagerness.* 우리 모두는 열의에 들떠 있었다. — *n.* Ⓤ a tingling condition; a pricking feeling; an excited emotion. 따끔거림; 욱신거림; 흥분. [*tinkle*]

tin god [⌐⌐] *n.* an undeservedly idolized person or thing. 우상(偶像). [*tin*]

tin hat [⌐⌐] *n.* 《U.S. *sl.*》 a steel helmet. 철모.

tink·er [tíŋkər] *n.* Ⓒ **1** a person who repairs kettles, pans, etc. 땜장이. **2** an unskilled worker; a person who makes unskilled repairs. 서툰 장색(匠色). **3** a person who does all kinds of small reparing. 만물 수선인.

***not care a tinker's damn* 〔*curse*〕,** not care at all. 전혀 개의치 않다.

— *vi., vt.* (P1,2A,3; 6,7) **1** work as a tinker. 땜장이 노릇하다. **2** repair roughly or clumsily. (…을) 어설프게 고치다. ¶ *~ up a broken-down car* 고장난 차를 임시로 수리하다. [E.]

tin·kle [tíŋkəl] *vi., vt.* (P1,2A; 6) **1** make sounds like a little bell. 딸랑거리다. **2** cause to tinkle. 딸랑거리게 하다. — *n.* such a sound. 딸랑딸랑〔따르릉〕하는 소리. [Imit.]

tin liz·zie [tín lízi] *n.* 《U.S. *sl.*》 a small, cheap automobile. 소형 싸구려 자동차《본디, Ford의 Model T의 애칭》. [*tin*]

tinned [tind] *adj.* **1** covered with tin. 주석을 입힌; 주석으로 도금한. **2** 《Brit.》 (of food, etc.) kept in a can. 통조림한. ¶ *~ fruit* 〔*beans, beef*〕. [*tin*]

tin·ner [tínər] *n.* **1** a person who works in a tin mine. 주석 광부. **2** a person who works with tin; 《Brit.》 a canner. 양철장이; 양철공; 통조림 제조 업자. [*tin*]

tin·ny [tíni] *adj.* (**-ni·er, -ni·est**) of or containing tin; (of sound or looks) like tin; (of food) having the taste of tin. 주석의; 주석을 함유한; 주석 같은 음색의; (음식이) 양철 냄새가 나는.

tin opener [⌐⌐–] *n.* 《Brit.》 a device for opening a tin. 깡통따개(cf. 《U.S.》 *can-opener*).

tin plate [⌐⌐] *n.* a thin sheet of iron or steel covered with tin. 양철; 함석.

tin·sel [tínsəl] *n.* Ⓤ **1** a thin piece of glittering metal used for decoration. (장식용의) 번쩍거리는 쇳조각. **2** something showy but of little value. 번드레한 싸구려 물건. — *vt.* (**-seled, -sel·ing** or 《Brit.》 **-selled, -sel·ling**) (P6) decorate (something) with tinsel. …을 금〔은〕박(箔)으로 장식하다. — *adj.* of or like tinsel; showy but of little value. 뻔쩍거리는; 번드레한 싸구려의. [→scintillate]

tin·smith [tínsmìθ] *n.* Ⓒ a person who works with tin. 양철공. [*tin*]

·tint [tint] *n.* Ⓒ **1** a variety of color or hue. 색조; 배색. ¶ *several tints of yellow* 다양한 노랑 색조. **2** a faint color. 엷은 빛깔; 담색. — *vt.* (P6,18) color slightly. …을 엷게 착색하다. [→tinge]

tin·ware [tínwὲər] *n.* Ⓤ articles made of tin plate. 양철 제품. [*tin*]

:ti·ny [táini] *adj.* (**-ni·er, -ni·est**) very small; minute. 작은; 조그마한. ¶ *a ~ bit* 아주 조금 / *a ~ little* 〔*little ~*〕 *girl* 아주 작은 소녀. [E.]

:tip[1] [tip] *n.* Ⓒ **1** the pointed or thinner end of anything. 끝; 첨단. ¶ *walk on the tips of one's toes* 발 끝으로 걷다 / *the ~ of an animal's tail* 〔*wing*〕 짐승의 꼬리〔날개〕 끝 / *the tips of the fingers* 손가락 끝 / *the ~ of a spear* 창 끝. **2** a small piece put on the end of something; cap. 끝〔끄트머리〕에 대는〔씌우는〕 것; 두겁. ¶ *the ~ of a cane* 단장 끝의 쇠두겁.

at* 〔*on*〕 *the tip of one's tongue, **a**) just about to say. 하마터면 말할 뻔하여. ¶ *I had it on the ~ of my tongue.* 하마터면 그것을 말할 뻔했다. **b**) not quite able to be remembered. 말이 혀끝에서 돌 뿐 생각이 잘 안 나. ¶ *Now what's her name ? It's on the ~ of my tongue.* 그녀 이름이 뭐더라. 입에서 뱅뱅 돌기는 하는데.

from tip to toe, through and through; completely. 철두 철미.

have at the tips of one's fingers **=*have at one's fingertips,*** have (knowledge, material, etc.) readily available; have a thorough knowledge of. …을 훤히 알고 있다; 정통하다.

to the tips of one's fingers **=*to one's finger***

tips, completely. 철저히.
— *vt.* (**tipped, tip·ping**) **1** (P6) furnish (something) with a point. …에 끝을 대다[붙이다]. **2** (P13) 《*with*》 cover the point of (something). …의 끄트머리를 장식하다. ¶ *a staff tipped with gold* 끝에 금을 입힌 지팡이. [E.]

·tip² [tip] *v.* (**tipped, tip·ping**) *vt.* (P6,7,13) **1** cause (something) to incline. …을 기울이다. ¶ *~ a table* [*chair*] 탁자[의자]를 기울이다. **2** take off (one's hat) in salutation. (모자)를 조금 들어 인사하다. ¶ *He tipped his hat to me.* 그는 모자를 살짝 들어 나에게 인사했다. **3** 《Brit.》 empty (the contents) by tipping. (그릇을 엎어) 내용물을 비우다. ¶ *She tipped all the money in her purse on to the table.* 그녀는 지갑의 돈을 모조리 탁자 위에 쏟아 비웠다. — *vi.* (P1,2A) become inclined. 기울다. ¶ *The car tipped up.* 차가 전복될 뻔했다.
tip over, cause (something) to overturn; become overturned; upset. …을 뒤집어엎다; 뒤집히다. ¶ *~ over a glass of water* 물컵을 뒤엎다 / *~ a vase over* 꽃병을 뒤집어엎다.
— *n.* 《Brit.》 a place where waste matter is tipped from carts. 쓰레기 버리는 데. ¶ *a rubbish ~*. [E.]

·tip³ [tip] *n.* Ⓒ **1** a small present of money given to a waiter, porter, etc. for services done. 팁; 행하(行下). ¶ *give the waiter a ~* 웨이터에게 팁을 주다 / *Shall I leave a ~ for the waiter?* 웨이터에게 팁을 줄까 / *a ~ of 10%,* 10 퍼센트의 팁. **2** a friendly hint or suggestion; a piece of secret or private information about horse-racing, money-market, etc. 조언; 충고; (경마 등의) 비밀 정보; 예상. ¶ *Take my ~ and keep well away from that place.* 내 말대로 그 곳에 범접(犯接)을 않도록 해라 / *the straight ~* 확실한 조언[정보].
— *v.* (**tipped, tip·ping**) *vt.* (P6,13,14) **1** give a small present of money to (someone). …에게 팁을 주다. ¶ *~ a waitress five cents.* 여급에게 팁 5센트를 주다. **2** give secret information to (someone). …에게 비밀 정보를 알리다[흘리다]. ¶ *~ a winner* 우승 예상 말을 알려 주다. — *vi.* give a tip. 팁을 주다. [E.]
tip someone off, 《*colloq.*》 give secret information to someone; warn. …에게 정보를 주다; 경고하다.

tip⁴ [tip] *vt.* (**tipped, tip·ping**) (P6,14) **1** strike lightly. …을 가볍게 치다. **2** 《baseball, cricket》 strike (a ball) a glancing blow. (공)을 팁하다. ¶ *His bat just tipped the ball.* 그의 배트에 공이 가볍게 스쳤다.
— *n.* Ⓒ a light, glancing stroke; a tap. 팁; 가볍게 침. [E.]

tip-off [típɔ̀ːf / -ɔ̀f] *n.* Ⓒ 《U.S. *colloq.*》 a piece of secret information; a warning. 비밀 정보; 경고. [*tip³, off* →tipster]

tip·per [típər] *n.* Ⓒ a person that tips. 팁 주는 사람. ¶ *She is not a very good ~.* 그녀는 팁을 그리 잘 주는 편은 아니다. [*tip³*]

tip·ple [típəl] *vi., vt.* (P1; 6) drink (strong liquor) little by little but repeatedly or to excess. (독한 술을) 노상 찔끔찔끔 마시다; 술에 젖어 살다. ¶ *He sits tippling all day long.* 그는 종일 앉아서 술을 찔끔 마신다.
— *n.* Ⓤ (a kind of) strong liquor. 독한 술. ¶ *What's your favorite ~?* 독한 술로 뭘 좋아하나. [*tip²*]

tip·ster [típstər] *n.* Ⓒ a person who obtains money by giving advice as to which horses will probably win races. (경마 따위의) 정보 제공자. [E.]

tip·sy [típsi] *adj.* (**-si·er, -si·est**) slightly drunk; unsteady; tilted. 얼근히 취한; 거나한; 갈짓자 걸음의. [*tip²*]

tip·toe [típtòu] *n.* Ⓒ the end of a toe. 발끝.
***on tiptoe*(*s*),** **a**) on one's toes. 발끝으로. ¶ *She stood on ~ and tried to see over the wall.* 그는 발끝으로 서서 담너머를 보려고 했다. **b**) eagerly. 열심히. **c**) stealthily; secretly. 몰래.
— *vi.* (P1,2A,3) walk on the toes. 발끝으로 걷다. ¶ *The nurse tiptoed down the hall so as not to wake the patient up.* 간호사는 환자가 깰까봐 발끝으로 걸어 홀을 지나갔다.
— *adv.* on the toes; stealthily. 발끝으로; 몰래; 살짝. [E.]

tip·top [típtɑ̀p / -tɔ̀p] *n.* Ⓒ the highest point. 절정. — *adj.* of the very best; very fine; first-rate. 최고의; 극상(極上)의. ¶ *in the ~ condition* 최고의 컨디션에 / *a ~ dinner* 진수 성찬. — *adv.* 《*colloq.*》 quite satisfactorily. 나무랄 데 없이; 더할 나위 없이. [*tip¹, top*]

ti·rade [táireid, tiréid] *n.* Ⓒ a long, scolding speech. (비난·공격 등의) 장광설. [F. *tirer* shoot]

:tire¹ [taiər] *vt.* (P6,7,13) **1** make (someone) weary. …을 피곤하게 만들다. ¶ *Walking soon tires me.* 걸으면 쉬 피곤해진다 / *a very tiring day looking after children* 아이들 시중으로 매우 고단한 날. **2** make (someone) lose interest or patience. …을 싫증[넌더리]나게 하다. ¶ *He always tires me with his old stories.* 그는 항상 옛날 얘기로 나를 싫증나게 한다. — *vi.* (P1,3) **1** 《*with*》 become weary. 피곤해지다. ¶ *The old woman soon tires with walking.* 그 노부인은 조금만 걸어도 피곤해진다. **2** 《*of*》 lose interest or patience. 물리다; 싫증나다. ¶ *She'll ~ of the work.* 그녀는 그 일에 싫증을 낼 게다 / *Jane never tires of talking about her work.* 제인은 자기의 일 얘기라면 지칠 줄 모른다. [E.]
tire out [***to death***], make (someone) very tired. …을 몹시 지치게 하다. ¶ *He is tired out.* 그는 기진 맥진했다. [E.]

:tire², 《Brit.》 **tyre** [taiər] *n.* Ⓒ a hoop of rubber or iron around the rim of a wheel. 타이어; 바퀴. — *vt.* (P6) furnish (something) with a tire. …에 타이어를 끼우다. [*attire*]

:tired [taiərd] *adj.* (sometimes **tired·er, tired·est**) **1** 《*with*》 physically weary; weakened by effort. 피곤한. ¶ *He was ~ with the long walk.* 그는 오래 걸어서 피곤했다 / *I am too ~ to stand.* 너무 피곤해서 서 있지 못하겠다 / *I'm so ~ I could sleep for a week.* 어찌나 피곤한지 1주일이라도 잘 것 같다. **2** 《*of*》 mentally weary. 넌더리나는; 물린. ¶ *I am ~ of reading.* 독서에는 물렸다 / *I'm ~ of your lame excuse.* 네 말같잖은 핑계에 신물이 난다. [*tire*¹]

tired·ness [táiərdnis] *n.* Ⓤ the state of being tired. 피로; 권태.

tire·less [táiərlis] *adj.* that does not grow tired; that does not stop. 지칠 줄 모르는; 꾸준한. ¶ *a ~ worker* / *~ efforts* 부단한 노력.

tire·less·ly [táiərlisli] *adv.* without growing tired. 지치지 않고; 부단히.

tire·less·ness [táiərlisnis] *n.* Ⓤ the state or quality of being tireless. 피곤을 모름; 물리지 않음.

·tire·some [táiərsəm] *adj.* **1** irritating; troublesome. 성가신; 귀찮은. ¶ *a ~ child* 성가신 아이 / *It's very ~, but it can't be helped.* 골치 아픈 일이지만 어쩔 수가 없다. **2** boring; dull. 지루한; 따분한. ¶ *a ~ speech* 지루한 연설. ● **tire·some·ly** [-li] *adv.* **tire·some·ness** [-nis] *n.*

tir·ing [táiəriŋ] *adj.* tending to make tired; causing fatigue. 지루한; 지치게 하는. ¶ *a very ~ job* 몹시 힘든 일.

ti·ro [táirou] *n.* Ⓒ (*pl.* **-ros**) a beginner. 풋내기; 초심자. [L.=recruit]

·'tis [tiz] 《poet.》 it is.

·tis·sue [tíʃuː] *n.* **1** ⓊⒸ 《biol.》 the groups of cells forming the parts of animals or plants. (생물의) 조직. ¶ *the nervous ~* 신경조직. **2** ⓊⒸ a thin woven cloth. 얇은 직물; 사(紗). **3** Ⓒ a connected series or mass. 연속. ¶ *a ~ of lies* 거짓말의 연속; 거짓말투성이. **4** Ⓤ =tissue paper. [→textile]

tissue paper [⌐–⌐–] *n.* very thin, soft paper for wrapping fine articles or for toilet use, etc. 티슈 페이퍼; 박엽지(薄葉紙).

tit¹ [tit] *n.* =titmouse.

tit² [tit] *n.* Ⓒ 《*colloq.*》 the part of the breast from which milk is given; a teat. 젖꼭지. [O.E. *titt*]

***give* 〔*pay*〕 *someone* tit for tat,** return someone blow for blow; do to others as they have. 앙갚음하다; 맞받아 쏘아붙이다.

Ti·tan [táitən] *n.* **1** 《Gk. myth.》 one of the giants who ruled the world before the Olympian gods. 타이탄. **2** 《*t-*》 a person of great strength. 장사(壯士). [Gk.]

Ti·tan·ic [taitǽnik] *adj.* **1** of or like the Titans. 타이탄의〔같은〕. **2** 《often *t-*》 very large; having great power. 거대한; 힘이 장사인.

tit·bit [títbìt] *n.* =tidbit.

tithe [taið] *n.* **1** one-tenth of a crop or income given to the church. 십일조. **2** a tenth part; a small part of anything. 조금. ¶ *I cannot remember a ~ of it.* 그건 도무지 기억에 없다. — *vt.* (P6) put a tithe on. …에 십일조를 물리다. [→ten]

tit·il·late [títəlèit] *vt.* (P6) **1** touch (someone) lightly to cause him to laugh. …을 간질이다. **2** excite (someone) pleasantly or agreeably. …의 흥을 돋우다. [L.]

tit·il·la·tion [tìtəléiʃən] *n.* Ⓤ the act of titillating; the state of being titillated. 간질임; 흥을 돋움.

tit·i·vate, tit·ti- [títəvèit] *vt., vi.* (P6; 1) 《*colloq.*》 make (oneself) clean and neat in appearance. (외출 전에) 몸치장하다; 맵시내다. [*tidy*]

tit·lark [títlàːrk] *n.* a small bird like a lark. 논종다리류(類). [*tit*]

:ti·tle [táitl] *n.* Ⓒ **1** the name of a book, picture, poem, film, etc. 책이름; 제목; 표제; (영화의) 자막. ¶ *the ~ of a chapter* 〔*poem*〕 장〔시〕의 제목 / *publish a book under the ~ of* …라는 제목의 책을 내다. **2** the signification of a person's rank or profession, such as Doctor or Lady, usu. placed before a person's name. 직함; 칭호. ¶ *the man of ~* 직함이 있는 사람; 귀족. **3** 《*to, in, of*》 a claim or right. (요구할 수 있는 정당한) 권리; (권리 등을 주장할) 자격. ¶ *I don't have the ~ to expect obedience.* 내겐 복종을 기대할 자격이 없다. **4** Ⓤ the legal right of ownership; Ⓒ the paper giving such right. 소유권; 권리 증서. ¶ *~ to property* 재산 소유권 / *a ~ to land* 토지 권리증. **5** 《sports》 championship. 선수권; 타이틀. ¶ *defend the ~* 타이틀을 방어하다 / *lose the ~* 타이틀을 잃다 / *play for the ~* 타이틀 매치를 하다. — *vt.* (P6) give a title to (someone or something). …에 칭호를 주다; (책 따위)에 이름을 붙이다. [L. *titulus*]

ti·tled [táitld] *adj.* having a title. 칭호가〔직함이〕 있는. ¶ *a ~ gentleman.*

title deed [⌐–⌐] *n.* a document showing a person's ownership of land. 토지 권리증.

title page [⌐–⌐] *n.* the front page of a book containing the title, the author's name, the publisher, etc. of the book. (책의) 속표지.

title role [⌐–⌐] *n.* the character in a play from whom the name of the play is taken. 주제역(主題役).

tit·mice [títmàis] *n.* pl. of **titmouse.**

tit·mouse [títmàus] *n.* Ⓒ (*pl.* **-mice**) any one of a number of small song-birds with dull-colored feathers. 박샛과의 작은 새. [Obs. *tit mose* small bird]

tit·ter [títər] *vi.* (P1) laugh in partly suppressed way; laugh quietly. 킥킥거리다. [Imit.]

tit·tle [títl] *n.* **1** 《*a ~*, in *negative*》 a very

small amount. 아주 조금. ¶ *There is not a ~ of truth in his words.* 그의 말에는 진실성이 조금도 없다 / *not a ~ of evidence against him* 그에게 불리한 증거는 조금도 없다. **2** a small mark over a letter in writing or printing. 글자 위의 작은 점. ¶ *The dot over an 'i' is a ~.* [→title]

to a tittle, precisely. 정확히; 틀림없이.

tit·tle-tat·tle [títltæ̀tl] *n.* Ⓤ gossip; chatter. 객적은 이야기; 잡담. — *vi.* (P1) gossip. 잡담하다; 수다 떨다. [*tattle*]

tit·u·lar [títʃulər] *adj.* **1** having a title. 칭호가〔직함이〕 있는. **2** of a title. 표제의. **3** existing in name only. 유명 무실한. ¶ *a ~ leader* 이름뿐인 지도자 / *The king is only the ~ head of government.* 왕은 이름뿐인 정부 수반이다. [L. *titulus*]

:to [(before consonants) tə, (before vowels) tu, (in a final position) tuː] *prep.* **1** 《expressing movement》 toward; in the direction of. …(쪽)으로. ¶ *from east ~ west* 동쪽에서 서쪽으로 / *He went ~ the left.* 그는 왼쪽으로 갔다 / *The station is ~ the south of the park.* 역은 공원의 남쪽에 있다 / *turn ~ the right* 오른쪽으로 돌다 / *walk ~ the house* 집으로 걸어가다 / *on the way ~ the station* 역으로 가는 도중에. **2** 《implying arrival》 as far as. …까지; …로. ¶ *go ~ New York* 뉴욕으로 가다 / *fall ~ the ground* 땅에 떨어지다 / *I am going ~ London tomorrow.* 내일 영국으로 갈 생각이다 / *He came ~ my office today.* 그는 오늘 내 사무실에 왔다. **3** 《expressing a final point in time》 before; until. …때〔시점〕까지; (…분) 전(前). ¶ *~ this day* 오늘까지 / *from Saturday ~ Monday* 토요일에서 월요일까지 / *I shall stay ~ the end of June.* 6월말까지 머무르겠다 / *a quarter ~ five* 다섯 시 15분 전 / *It is ten minutes ~* (《U.S.》 *of*) *five.* 다섯시 10분 전이다. **4** 《expressing purpose》 for the purpose of; for. …을 위하여; …의 목적으로. ¶ *They came ~ our rescue.* 그들은 우리를 도우러 왔다 / *drink ~ the health of* …의 건강을 위해 건배하다 / *We sat down ~ dinner.* 우리는 저녁을 먹기 위해 앉았다. **5** 《expressing some point reached or extent》 until it becomes the state of; causing or resulting in. …이 되기까지; …하게도; …한 것은. ¶ *The house was burnt ~ ashes.* 집은 타서 잿더미가 됐다 / *~ one's surprise* 〔*sorrow*〕 놀랍게도〔슬프게도〕 / *To my disappointment, my son failed in the entrance examination.* 유감스럽게도 아들이 시험에 떨어졌다 / *be sick ~ death* 앓다가 죽다 / *He tore it ~ pieces.* 그는 그것을 발기발기 찢었다 / *freeze ~ marrow* 뼛속까지 시리다 / *This apple is rotten ~ the core.* 이 사과는 속까지 썩었다. **6** in agreement 〔harmony〕 with; fitting. …에 맞아. ¶ *This job is not ~ my taste.* 이 일은 내 기호에 맞지 않는다 / *a boot made ~ my foot* 발에 맞게 지은 신발. **7** accompanied by; along with. …에 맞추어〔따라서〕. ¶ *They danced ~ the music.* 그들은 음악에 맞추어 춤추었다. **8** 《expressing comparison》 compared with. …에 비교하여; 대응시켜서. ¶ *three shillings ~ the pound* 파운드당 3실링 / *prefer beer ~ whisky* 위스키보다 맥주를 즐기다 / *We often compare life ~ a voyage.* 흔히들 인생을 항해에 비유한다 / *He is quite rich ~ what he once was.* 그는 예전에 비하면 아주 부자다. **9** of; belonging to 〔with〕. …의; …에 속하는. ¶ *a daughter ~ the Queen* 여왕의 딸 / *a key ~ the room* 방 열쇠 / *He got a job as secretary ~ a doctor.* 그는 의사의 비서로 취직했다 / *She wants a room ~ herself.* 그녀는 자기 방을 갖고 싶어한다. **10** on; against. …에; …에 대해서. ¶ *She is deeply attached ~ her friend's brother.* 그녀는 친구 오빠에게 깊은 관심이 있다 / *stick ~ one's opinion* 자기 견해를 고집하다 / *Fasten it ~ the wall.* 그걸 벽에 붙여라 / *apply soap ~ a towel* 수건에 비누를 칠하다. **11** 《expressing progress, a change of condition》 …으로; …하게. ¶ *go from bad ~ worse* 점점 나빠지다 / *She went ~ sleep.* 그녀는 잠이 들었다 / *He was brought ~ poverty.* 그는 가난해졌다. **12** within the scope of. …의 범위까지(는); …의 정도로는. ¶ *To my knowledge he has not come.* 내가 알기로 그는 오지 않았다. **13** 《used with the infinitive form of verbs》 …하는 것; …하기 위한; …하기 위하여. ¶ *I want ~ do it.* 그것을 하고 싶다 / *It is necessary for him ~ do it at once.* 그는 그것을 당장 해야 한다 / *To err is human, ~ forgive is divine.* 잘못은 인지상사요, 용서는 신의 일이다 / *I warned him not ~ be late.* 늦지 말라고 그에게 주의를 주었다 / *I've nothing ~ eat.* 먹을 것이라고는 없다 / *I studied ~ pass the exam.* 시험에 붙으려고 공부했다 / *These oranges are fit ~ eat.* 이 오렌지들은 먹기 알맞다 / *I am very happy ~ meet you.* 널 만나서 아주 기쁘다 / *She grew up ~ be an actress.* 그녀는 자라서 여배우가 됐다 / *~ speak frankly* 솔직히 말하면.

— [tuː] *adv.* forward; in the usual position, esp. a still or close one. 앞쪽에〔으로〕; 본디 상태에. ¶ *Is the door ~?* 문은 닫혀 있느냐 / *Your hat is on the wrong side ~.* 모자를 거꾸로 썼구나 / *I can't get the lid of my trunk quite ~.* 트렁크의 뚜껑이 제대로 닫히지 않는다 / *come ~ = come ~ oneself* 제 정신이 들다 / *He doesn't seem so young when you see him close ~.* 그는 가까이서 보면 그다지 젊어 보이지 않는다. [E.]

to and fro, back and forth; up and down; from place to place. 이리저리; 왔다갔다; 여기저기.

***toad** [toud] *n.* Ⓒ **1** a small frog-like animal with a rough skin, living on land rather than in water. 두꺼비. **2** a disgusting person. 징그러운〔꼴보기 싫은〕 사람〔녀석〕. [E.]

a toad under the harrow, a person who is always subjected to oppression. 늘 눌려지

내는 사람.

eat someone's toad, flatter someone. …에게 아첨하다; 빌붙다.

toad·eat·er [tóudìːtər] *n.* =toady.

toad·stool [tóudstùːl] *n.* a poisonous, umbrella-shaped fungus, as distinguished from an edible mushroom. 독버섯의 일종.

toad·y [tóudi] *n.* Ⓒ (*pl.* **toad·ies**) a person who flatters a rich or powerful person. 아첨꾼; 알랑쇠; 빌붙어 지내는 사람. [E.]

·**toast**[1] [toust] *n.* Ⓤ a slice of bread made brown on both sides by heat. 토스트. — *vt.* (P6) **1** make (bread, etc.) brown by heating it. (빵 따위)를 노르스름하게 굽다. ¶ *~ bread.* **2** 《*colloq.*》 warm (oneself) thoroughly before the fire. 불을 쬐다. ¶ *He was toasting his feet by the fire.* 불에 발을 쬐고 있었다. — *vi.* (P1) (of bread, etc.) become brown by heat. (빵 따위가) 노랗게 구워지다. [L. *torreo* parch, scorch]

toast[2] [toust] *n.* Ⓒ **1** the act of drinking in honor of someone or something. 축배. ¶ *drink a ~* 축배를 들다 / *Ladies and gentlemen, I'd like to propose a ~ to the bride and groom.* 여러분, 신랑 신부를 위해 축배를 듭시다. **2** a person whose health is drunk. 축배를 받는 사람. **3** a woman whose beauty and charm are frequently honored in toasts. 자주 축배를 받는 인기 있는 미인. ¶ *She was the ~ of the evening.* 그녀는 그날밤 축배의 대상이었다. — *vt.* (P6) drink to the health of. …의 건강을 위해 축배를 들다. ¶ *The men toasted the general.* 그 남자는 장군을 위해 축배를 들었다. [↑]

toast·er [tóustər] *n.* Ⓒ **1** a person who toasts bread, etc. 빵 굽는 사람. **2** an instrument for toasting bread. 토스터; 빵 굽는 기구.

toast·mas·ter [tóustmæ̀stər, -màːs-] *n.* Ⓒ **1** a person who proposes drinking to someone's health or success. 축배를 제창하는 사람. **2** a person who acts as the chairman at a dinner. (연회의) 사회자.

:**to·bac·co** [təbǽkou] *n.* (*pl.* **-cos** or **-coes**) **1** ⓊⒸ a plant with large leaves which are dried and used for smoking. 담배. **2** Ⓤ the dried leaves of this plant. 담배; 살담배. ¶ *a ~ pipe* 파이프; 담뱃대. [Carib]

to·bac·co·nist [təbǽkənist] *n.* Ⓒ a person who sells tobacco and other smoking supplies. 담배 장수.

to·bac·co-pouch [təbǽkoupàutʃ] *n.* Ⓒ a bag or case in which tobacco is carried in the pocket. 담배 쌈지.

-to-be [-təbíː] *suf.* in the future. '미래의'의 뜻. ¶ *a minister-to-be* 장관 예정자 / *a bride-to-be* 신붓감. [*to,be*]

to·bog·gan [təbágən / -bɔ́g-] *n.* Ⓒ a long, narrow, flat sled made of thin board which carries four or more persons, used for sliding down a snow-covered hill. 터보건. — *vi.* (P1) **1** slide down a snow-covered hill on a toboggan. 터보건으로 언덕을 활강하다. **2** 《U.S. *colloq.*》 fall sharply and rapidly in price, value, etc. (가격 등이) 폭락하다. [Amer-Ind.]

〈toboggan〉

toc·ca·ta [təkáːtə] *n.* 《mus.》 a kind of rapid brilliant composition for piano, organ, etc. 토카타. [It. (touch)]

toc·sin [táksin / tɔ́k-] *n.* Ⓒ 《chiefly *fig.*》 an alarm bell; the sound of an alarm bell. 경종; 경종 소리. [→touch, sign]

:**to·day, to-day** [tədéi, tu-] *n.* Ⓤ **1** this day. 오늘. ¶ *in the course of ~* 오늘 중에 / *Bring me today's paper.* 오늘 신문을 가져오너라. **2** the present time. 현재; 오늘날; 현대. ¶ *the writers of ~* 오늘날의 작가 / *The fashions of ~ change fast.* 요즘의 유행은 변화가 빠르다. — *adv.* **1** on this day. 오늘. ¶ *It is Monday ~.* 오늘은 월요일이다 / *I've met him twice ~.* 오늘 그를 두 번 만났다. **2** at the present time. 현재〔오늘날〕에는. ¶ *Many girls wear their hair short ~.* 오늘날에는 많은 소녀들이 머리를 짧게 한다. [*to, day*]

tod·dle [tádl / tɔ́dl] *vi.* (P1,2A,3) **1** walk with short, unsteady steps like a baby. 아장아장 걷다. **2** saunter. 어정거리다; 산책하다. ¶ *I'm just toddling over to Mary's. Why don't you come?* 메리네 집에 슬슬 가는 길일세. 함께 가지 않겠나. — *n.* **1** a toddling walk. 아장아장 걷기. **2** 《*colloq.*》 a toddling child. 아장아장 걷는 아기. **3** a stroll. 산책. [→dodder]

tod·dler [tádlər / tɔ́dl-] *n.* Ⓒ a child that has just learnt to walk. 걸음발 타는 아기.

tod·dy [tádi / tɔ́di] *n.* ⓊⒸ (*pl.* **-dies**) a drink made of whisky, brandy, etc. plus hot water, sugar, and spices. 토디《위스키 따위에 뜨거운 물을 붓고 설탕·레몬 따위를 넣은 음료》. [Hind.=palm]

to-do [tədúː, tu-] *n.* Ⓒ (*pl.* **-dos**) 《*colloq.*》 an ado; a fuss. 소동; 야단. ¶ *make a terrible ~ about losing one's luggage* 보따리를 잃고 온통 법석을 떨다 / *What a ~!* 정말 소란스럽기도 하다. [*to, do*]

:**toe** [tou] *n.* Ⓒ **1** one of the five separate parts at the end of a foot. 발가락(cf. *finger*). ¶ *a big* 〔*great*〕 *~* 엄지발가락 / *a little ~* 새끼발가락. **2** the front part of any foot covering, such as of a shoe or stocking. (신이나 양말의) 앞부분. **3** anything like a toe. 발가락 비슷한 것. **4** 《*colloq.*》 the foot of a man as a whole. (사람의) 발.

from top to toe, from head to foot. 머리끝에서 발끝까지.

on one's toe, ready to act; alert. 대기하고 있

는; 긴장해 있는.

***toast** one's **toes**,* warm one's feet. 발을 따뜻이 하다.

***tread** 〔**step**〕 **on** someone's **toe**,* hurt someone's feelings. …의 감정을 해치다.

***turn up** one's **toes**,* 《*sl.*》 die. 죽다; 뻗다.

— *v.* (**toed, toe·ing**) *vt.* (P6) **1** furnish with a toe; mend the toe of. (…의) 앞 부리를 대다〔수선하다〕. **2** touch or kick with the toes. 발끝으로 건드리다〔차다〕. **3** 《golf》 strike (the ball) with the toe (of the club). 토로 (공을) 치다. — *vi.* (P1,2A) **1** stand, walk, etc., with the toes in a specified position. 발끝으로 서다〔걷다〕. **2** 《dance》 tap with the toes. 발끝으로 가볍게 디디다. [E.]

toe in 〔***out***〕*,* turn toes in 〔out〕 in walking. 안짱〔밭장〕 다리로 걷다.

toe the line 〔***mark***〕*,* **a**) stand on the starting line of a race with the toes touching it. (경기 등에서) 출발선에 발끝을 대고 서다. **b**) 《*colloq.*》 obey orders, rules, etc. exactly. 명령〔규칙〕대로 하다.

toe·cap [tóukæ̀p] *n.* a leather or metal covering for the toe of a shoe or boot. (신발의) 앞닫이.

toff [tɔ(:)f, tɑf] *n.* 《*colloq.*》 a gentleman; a well-dressed person. 신사; 멋쟁이. [*tuft*]

tof·fee, -fy [tɔ́:fi, tɑ́fi] *n.* ⓊⒸ 《usu. Brit.》 a hard candy made of boiled sugar and butter. 태피《당과(糖菓)의 일종》. [E.]

tog [tɑg / tɔg] *n.* **1** 《usu. *pl.*》 《*colloq.*》 clothes. (한 벌로 된) 옷. ¶ *golf togs* 골프복. **2** an outer garment. 외투. — *vt.* (**togged, tog·ging**) (P6,7) 《*out, up*》 dress (someone) carefully and smartly. …에 옷을 입히다. [↓]

〈toga〉

to·ga [tóugə] *n.* Ⓒ (*pl.* **-gas** or **-gae**) **1** a loose outer dress worn by ancient Romans. 토가《옛 로마의 헐렁한 겉옷》. **2** a robe of office. 제복. [L.]

to·gae [tóudʒi:] *n.* pl. of **toga.**

:to·geth·er [təgéðər] *adv.* **1** with each other; in company. 함께; 같이; 더불어. ¶ *We went out* 〔*about*〕 ~. 우리는 함께 외출했다〔돌아다녔다〕 / *The strings and brass weren't quite ~ in that passage.* 현악기부와 금관악기부는 그 악절에서 조화를 이루지 못했다. **2** into one body or place; so as to unite. 함께 되어〔만나〕; 합쳐져; 이어져. ¶ *call the people ~* 사람들을 불러모으다 / *sew pieces ~* 조각들을 한데 꿰매다 / *Tie the ends ~.* 끝을 한데 묶어라 / *Add these numbers ~.* 이 숫자들을 합산해라. **3** at the same time. 동시에. ¶ *shout ~* 일제히 소리치다 / *All my troubles seem to come ~.* 모든 재난이 한꺼번에 닥치는 것 같다 / *Don't speak all ~.* 동시에 말하지 말고 따로따로 말해라. **4** (of time) in succession; without a break. 계속해서; 중단없이. ¶ *study for hours ~* 여러 시간을 내리 공부하다 / *He was moody for days ~.* 그는 계속 며칠을 저기압이었다. [*gather*]

together with, along with; as well as; and also. …와 같이〔함께〕. ¶ *I am sending you some stamps, ~ with the postcards.* 우표 몇 장을 엽서 몇 장과 함께 보낸다.

tog·gery [tɑ́gəri / tɔ́g-] *n.* 《*colloq.*》 clothes, esp. some special kind of dress, uniform, etc. (특수한) 의상; 제복. ¶ *an actor's ~* 배우 의상 / *a general's ~* 장군의 제복. [→toga]

tog·gle [tɑ́gəl / tɔ́gəl] *n.* Ⓒ a metal pin, bolt, or rod for putting through a loop of rope or the link of a chain to prevent slipping. 비녀장. [var. of *tackle*]

:toil[1] [tɔil] *n.* Ⓤ hard work. 힘든 일; 노역; 고역. ¶ *with ~ and moil* 뼈빠지게 일해서. — *vi.* (P1,2A,3) **1** 《*at*》 work hard. 수고하다; 애쓰다. ¶ *~ at the knitting* 뜨개질에 힘쓰다 / *~ all day* 종일토록 수고하다. **2** move with difficulty and effort. 힘들게 움직이다〔나아가다〕. ¶ *~ up a steep hill* 가파른 언덕을 힘들여 오르다 / *~ along the road* 길을 터벅터벅 걸어가다. [F.=stir up]

toil[2] [tɔil] *n.* 《usu. *pl.*》 《*arch.*》 a snare; a net. 덫; 올가미. [→toilet]

in the toils, **a**) caught in the net. 올가미에 걸려. **b**) 《*fig.*》 in the toils of crime. 범죄의 늪에 빠져.

toil·er [tɔ́ilər] *n.* a hard worker; a laborer. 임금 노동자. [*toil*[1]]

·toi·let [tɔ́ilit] *n.* Ⓒ **1** the act or process of dressing, bathing, washing, arranging the hair or clothes, etc. 화장; 몸단장《목욕·머리 손질 따위》. ¶ *a brief ~* 간단한 화장 / *~ articles* 화장품 / *perform one's ~* 몸단장하다. **2** 《U.S. *colloq.*》 a bathroom; a water closet. 화장실. ¶ *~ paper* 화장지. **3** = toilette. **4** 《med.》 cleansing of a part after operation. (수술 후의) 세정(洗淨). — *adj.* of or for toilet. 화장(용)의; 변기용의. ¶ *a ~ brush* 변기 세척솔. [L. *tela* web]

toi·lette [twɑ:lét, tɔilét] *n.* 《F.》 the process or style of dressing; elaborate costume. 화장; 몸단장; (특정한) 의상.

toil·some [tɔ́ilsəm] *adj.* requiring toil; laborious. 힘든; 고된. [toil[1]]

toil·worn [tɔ́ilwɔ̀:rn] *adj.* worn out by toil. 지친; 힘든 일로 수척해진.

·to·ken [tóukən] *n.* **1** Ⓒ a sign or symbol of some fact, feeling, etc.; a mark that proves some fact. 표; 상징; 증거. ¶ *A four-leaf clover is a ~ of good luck.* 네잎 클로버는 행운의 상징이다 / *They wave a white flag in ~ of surrender.* 그들은 항복의 표시로 백기를 흔든다. **2** something kept as a reminder; a memorial thing. 기념품. ¶ *My husband gave me a ring as a ~ of our first* *meeting.* 남편은 우리들 첫 만남의 기념으로 반지를 주었다. **3** a piece of metal used instead of money. 대용 경화(硬貨); 토큰. ¶ *a bus* ～. **4** a sort of special ticket, usu. fixed to a greeting card, which one can exchange for the stated thing in a shop. 상품 교환권. ¶ *a £10 record* ～, 10 파운드 레코드 교환권 / *a book* ～ 서적 구입권 / *a gift* ～ 선물 교환권.

by the same token =***by that token,*** 《*arch., joc.*》 **a**) more; furthermore. 게다가; 그 위에. **b**) for the same reason; in the same way; similarly. 같은 이유로; 마찬가지로.

more by token, 《*arch., joc.*》 still more; the more so. 한층 더; 하물며; 더군다나.

— *adj.* serving as a token; slight and not real. 보증이 되는; 이름뿐인. ¶ *a* ～ *resistance* 형식적인 반항. [E.]

:told [tould] *v.* p. and pp. of **tell.**

tol·er·a·ble [tɑ́lərəbəl / tɔ́l-] *adj.* **1** that can be endured or suffered. 참을 수 있는. ¶ *The pain was bad, but it was* ～. 고통이 심했으나 참을 만했다. **2** fairly good; not bad. 꽤 좋은; 그만한. ¶ *His drawing was* ～. 그의 그림은 쓸 만했다 / *a* ～ *attempt* 괜찮은 계획 / *a* ～ *health* 꽤 좋은 건강. ●**tol·er·a·ble·ness** [-nis] *n.* [L. *tolero*]

tol·er·a·bly [tɑ́lərəbli / tɔ́l-] *adv.* to a tolerable degree; fairly. 상당히; 꽤. ¶ *I feel* ～ *well today.* 오늘은 기분이 꽤 좋다.

tol·er·ance [tɑ́lərəns / tɔ́l-] *n.* Ⓤ **1** state of being, or hope to be, tolerant of other's opinions or customs; the act of tolerating. 관용; 포용력; 아량. ¶ *Try and show some* ～. 좀 아량을 베풀도록 해라 / *the government's* ～ *to political dissent* 정치적 이견에 대한 정부의 포용력. **2** the power of resisting the action of a medicine, poison, etc. 내성(耐性); 저항력. [↓]

tol·er·ant [tɑ́lərənt / tɔ́l-] *adj.* **1** 《*of*》 willing to allow other people's beliefs, opinions or actions which are different from one's own. 관대한. ¶ *a* ～ *father* 너그러운 아버지 / *The government is* ～ *toward all religious beliefs.* 정부는 모든 종교에 대해 관대하다 / *be* ～ *of criticism* 비판을 용인하다. **2** able to resist the action of a medicine or poison. 내성(耐性)이 있는. ●**tol·er·ant·ly** [-li] *adv.* [L. *tolero* bear, endure]

tol·er·ate [tɑ́lərèit / tɔ́l-] *vt.* (P6,9) **1** allow (something) to exist against one's own liking; bear; endure; allow; permit. …을 관대히 다루다; 참다; 묵인하다. ¶ *We must* ～ *other people's ideas.* 우리는 다른 사람의 의견도 잘 들어줘야 한다 / *I won't* ～ *your bad manner any longer.* 네 못된 태도를 더는 용납하지 않겠다 / *He never could* ～ *bores.* 그는 따분하여 도저히 참을 수 없었다. **2** bear or resist the action of (a medicine, poison, etc.). …에 대한 내성(耐性)이 있다. [↑]

tol·er·a·tion [tɑ̀ləréiʃən / tɔ̀l-] *n.* Ⓤ **1** tolerance. 관용. **2** allowance of religions which are different from the officially recognized religion. 종교의 자유. ¶ *religious* ～. 신앙의 자유

•toll[1] [toul] *vt.* (P6) ring (a bell) slowly and with a single stroke at regular intervals. (종)을 천천히 치다. ¶ *Bells were tolled all over the country at his death.* 전국의 종들이 그의 죽음을 애도하여 천천히 울렸다. — *vi.* (P1) ring or sound in this way. 천천히 울리다. ¶ *The bell tolled three.* 종은 천천히 세 번 울렸다. — *n.* 《as *sing.*》 the sound or the stroke of a tolling bell. 종소리; 종을 울리기. [E.=pull]

toll[2] [toul] *n.* Ⓒ **1** the fee paid for using something or passing through some place. 사용료; 통행료. ¶ *pay a* ～ 통행료를 내다. **2** a charge for a long-distance telephone call. 장거리 전화료. ¶ *a* ～ *call* 장거리 전화. **3** 《hist.》 grain retained by a miller as compensation for grinding. 방앗간의 빻는 삯《곡물로 냄》. — *vi.* collect tolls. 통행료를 징수하다. [Gk. *telos*]

toll bar [⁄ ⁄] *n.* a bar or gate across a road where toll is taken. (통행료를 받기 위해 있는) 차단봉. [*toll*[2]]

toll bridge [⁄ ⁄] *n.* a bridge at which toll is paid for passage. 유료(有料) 다리.

toll·gate [tóulgèit] *n.* Ⓒ a gate on a road or bridge where toll is taken. (도로의) 통행료 징수소; 톨게이트.

toll·house [tóulhàus] *n.* Ⓒ (*pl.* **-hous·es** [-hauziz]) a house at a tollgate where the tollkeepers live. 통행료 징수소; 징수인 대기소.

toll·keep·er [tóulkìːpər] *n.* Ⓒ a person who collects tolls. 통행료 징수인.

tom [tɑm / tɔm] *n.* **1** 《*T-*》 a nickname for Thomas. 토마스의 애칭. **2** the male of various animals; a male animal, esp. tomcat. 짐승의 수컷; (특히) 수고양이. [*Thomas*]

long tom, a long gun. 대포; 장거리포.

Old Tom, a strong kind of gin. (독한) 진의 일종.

Tom, Dick, and Harry, 《*sl.*》 persons taken at random. 어중이떠중이.

tom·a·hawk [tɑ́məhɔ̀ːk / tɔ́m-] *n.* Ⓒ a kind of light ax or hatchet used by North American Indians as a weapon and a tool. 전부(戰斧).

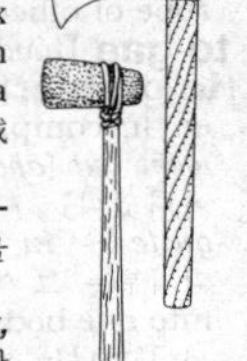
〈tomahawk〉

bury 〔***lay aside***〕 ***the tomahawk,*** stop fighting. 싸움을 그만두다; 화친하다.

take 〔***dig***〕 ***up the tomahawk,*** begin fighting. 싸움을 시작하다.

— *vt.* (P6) **1** strike, kill, or cut (something) with a tomahawk. …을 도끼로 찍다〔죽이다, 자르다〕. **2** criticize savagely. 혹평하다; 내리깎다. [Native]

:to·ma·to [təméitou / -mɑ́:-] *n.* (*pl.* **-toes**) Ⓒ **1** a plant with yellow flowers, hairy leaves and red, juicy fruit which are eaten. 토마토. **2** a fruit of this plant. 토마토《열매로서의》. [Mex.]

·tomb [tu:m] *n.* **1** Ⓒ a grave for a dead body. 무덤; 묘(墓). **2** 《*the* ~》 death. 죽음. — *vt.* bury (a dead body). …을 묻다; 매장하다. [Gk. *tumbos*]

tom·boy [támbɔ̀i / tɔ́m-] *n.* Ⓒ a girl who behaves like a boy. 말괄량이.

tomb·stone [tú:mstòun] *n.* Ⓒ a stone or monument over a grave, usu. bearing at least the name and dates of birth and death of the dead person. 묘석; 묘비. [*tomb*]

tom·cat [támkæ̀t / tɔ́m-] *n.* Ⓒ a male cat. 수고양이. [*tom*]

tome [toum] *n.* Ⓒ 《*lit., joc.*》 a book; a large, heavy book. 큰 책. [Gk. *temnō* cut]

tom·fool [támfú:l / tɔ́m-] *n.* Ⓒ a silly, stupid person; a buffoon. 멍텅구리; 바보; 어릿광대. — *vi.* (P1) play the fool; act in trifling manner. 바보같은 짓을 하다. [*tom*]

tom·fool·er·y [tàmfú:ləri / tɔ̀m-] *n.* (*pl.* **-er·ies**) ⓊⒸ silly and stupid behavior; nonsense. 바보 같은 짓; 허튼 짓.

Tom·my [támi / tɔ́mi] *n.* a nickname for Thomas. Thomas 의 애칭.

tom·my [támi / tɔ́mi] *n.* **1** 《usu. *T*-》 《Brit. *colloq.*》 a private soldier. 사병; 졸병 (=Tommy Atkins). **2** bread, esp. as given to a workman instead of wages; this system of payment. 임금 대신에 주는 흑빵; 그 제도. **3** 《mech.》 a kind of wrench or turnscrew. 스패너; 나사돌리개. [*Thomas*]

tommy gun [´-´] *n.* 《U.S. *colloq.*》 《sometimes *T- g-*》 a Thompson submachinegun. 톰슨식 기관총; 경기관총.

tom·my·rot [támiràt / tɔ́mirɔ̀t] *n.* 《*colloq.*》 nonsense. 허튼 소리; 난센스. [↑]

tom-nod·dy [támnàdi / tɔ́mnɔ̀di] *n.* a block-head; fool. 돌대가리; 바보. [*tom*]

:to·mor·row [təmɔ́:rou, -már-, tu- / -mɔ́r-] *n.* Ⓤ **1** the day after today. 내일. ¶ *the day after* ~ 모레 / *Tomorrow never comes.* 내일은 결코 오지 않는다《오늘 일은 오늘 해라》/ *I hope it will be sunny* ~. 내일 날씨가 좋았으면 한다 / *Don't put it off till* ~. 그 일을 내일로 미루지 마라. **2** the near future. 가까운 장래. ¶ *a brighter* ~ 보다 밝은 내일〔미래〕/ *What will the young people of* ~ *think of us?* 내일의 젊은이들이 우리를 어떻게 생각할 것인가. — *adv.* **1** on the day after today. 내일. ¶ *I'm going there* ~. 내일 거기에 가겠다 / *Tomorrow I shall be very busy.* 내일 나는 몹시 바쁘다. **2** at some future time. 장차; 가까운 장래(에). ¶ *People* ~ *will have different ideas.* 장차 사람들은 다른 생각을 하게 될 것이다. [*to, morrow*]

tomorrow week, 《chiefly Brit.》 eight days from or before tomorrow. 다음〔지난〕 주의 내일.

tom-tom [támtàm / tɔ́mtɔ̀m] *n.* Ⓒ an Indian drum, usu. beaten with the hands. 톰톰《인도 등지에서 사용하는 손으로 치는 북》. — *vi.* (P1) beat this drum. 톰톰 북을 치다. [Hind.]

:ton [tʌn] *n.* Ⓒ **1** a unit of weight. 중량 단위; 톤. ¶ *the long* 〔*gross*〕 ~ 롱 톤; 영(英)톤 《2,240 pounds》/ *the short* 〔*American*〕 ~ 미(美)톤《2,000 pounds》/ *a metric* ~ 미터톤; 불(佛)톤《1,000 kilograms》. **2** a unit of the internal capacity of ships. 선박의 용적 단위; 군함의 배수톤. ¶ *capacity* ~ 화물 적재톤 / *shipping* ~ 적재톤. **3** a unit of volume of freight. 화물의 체적의 단위; 적재톤. **4** 《*pl.*》 《*colloq.*》 a great deal; large quantities. 대량. ¶ *tons of money* 〔*books*〕 엄청난 돈〔서적〕/ *with tons of love* 극진한 사랑으로 / 《as *adv.*》 *This is tons better than that.* 이것이 저것보다 훨씬 좋다 / *I bought tons of fruit while it was cheap.* 과일이 쌀 때 왕창 사두었다. **5** 《*the* ~》 《*colloq.*》 speed of 100 mph attained by car or motorcycle. (자동차 등의) 매시 100 마일의 속도. [→tun]

ton·al [tóunəl] *adj.* of tone. 음조〔음색〕의; 색조의. [*tone*]

·tone [toun] *n.* **1** Ⓒ a sound; the quality of sound; intonation. 음질; 음색; 억양. ¶ *sweet tones of a harp* 하프의 아름다운 가락 / *the tones of the voice* 어조. **2** the manner of speaking or writing. 어조; 말씨. ¶ *speak in an angry* ~ 화난 어조로 말하다 / *She spoke in an imploring* ~. 그녀는 애원조로 말했다 / *I don't like your* ~ (*of voice*). 난 네 말투가 싫단 말이다 / *Don't take that* ~ *with me.* 그런 투로 말하지 말게나. **3** the general character; mental attitude; spirit; style. 경향; 기색; 기풍; 기품. ¶ *the* ~ *of the school* 교풍 / *A* ~ *of refinement prevails in her room.* 그녀의 방에선 고상한 분위기가 풍긴다 / *the optimistic* ~ *of the report* 보고의 낙관적인 흐름. **4** the general effect of color or light; tint; hue; shade. 색채 효과; 색조; 명암. ¶ *a light* ~ *of blue* 밝은〔선명한〕 남빛 / *a vivid* 〔*dull, cool*〕 ~ 선명한〔칙칙한, 차가운〕 색조 / *The room was decorated in several tones of green.* 방은 몇 가지 초록의 색조로 꾸며져 있었다. **5** Ⓤ 《med.》 normal healthy condition. (신체·정신의) 컨디션; 건강 상태. ¶ *keep one's body in* ~ 몸의 상태를 좋게 해두다 / *Exercise improves muscle* ~. 운동은 근육을 튼튼하게 한다. **6** 《mus.》 Ⓒ a note of definite pitch; an interval of the larger kind between successive tones. 온음(정)(音(程)).

— *vi.* **1** (P2A,3) 《*in, with*》 harmonize. 조화하다. ¶ *The hat tones* (*in*) *well with her coat.* 그 모자는 그녀의 코트와 잘 어울린다. **2** (P2A) attune. 조율하다. — *vt.* (P6,7) give a tone to; change the tone of (a sound). …에 가락을 붙이다; 색조를 띠게 하다; …의 가락을〔색조를〕 바꾸다. ¶ *Sorrow toned her voice.* 슬픔으로 인해서 그녀 음성이 달라졌다.

[Gk. *teinō* stretch]

tone down, make or become less intense; soften. 가락을 낮추다〔누그러뜨리다〕; 가락이 부드러워지다.

tone in with, agree with each other. …와 조화하다. ¶ *The wallpaper tones in with the curtains.* 벽지가 커튼과 잘 어울린다.

tone up, give more sound, color, strength to; become more intense. (소리·색깔·강도를) 높이다; 높아지다; 강하게 하다; 강해지다. ¶ *Swimming is the best way to ~ up your body.* 수영이 네 체력을 높이는 데 가장 좋다.

tong [tɔ(:)ŋ, tɑŋ] *n.* a Chinese association or secret club. 중국인 비밀 결사. [Chin.]

tongs [tɔ(:)ŋz, tɑŋz] *n. pl.* a tool with two arms, joined by a hinge, used for holding things. 집게; 부젓가락 (등). ¶ *a pair of ~* 부젓가락 하나 / *sugar* 〔*ice*〕 *~* 설탕〔얼음〕 집게 / *I won't touch him with a pair of ~.* 그 자와는 닿기도 싫다. [E.]

⟨tongs⟩

:tongue [tʌŋ] *n.* Ⓒ **1** the movable organ in the mouth used for licking, tasting, and talking. 혀. **2** the manner or faculty of speaking. 말씨; 언어 능력. ¶ *an eloquent ~* 능변; 달변 / *a flattering ~* 아첨 / *a slip of the ~* 실언 / *a gentle ~* 점잖은 말씨 / *She has rather a sharp ~.* 그녀는 입정이 좀 사납다. **3** a language. 언어. ¶ *the Greek* 〔*English*〕 *~* 그리스어〔영어〕 / *one's mother ~* 모국어. **4** anything like a tongue in shape, movement, or use. 혀 모양의 것. ¶ *Tongues of flame leaped from the burning hut.* 불타는 오두막에서 널름거리는 불길이 솟았다 / *a ~ of land* 갑(岬); 곶. **5** a vibrating reed in a musical instrument. (관악기의) 혀. [E.]

give 〔***throw***〕 ***tongue,*** (of people) shout with a loud voice; (of hounds) begin to bark, esp. on finding the scent. (사람이) 큰 소리로 말하다; (사냥개가 냄새를 맡고) 짖어대다.

have a ready tongue, speak fluently. 말이 유창하다; 입담이 좋다.

have 〔***put***〕 ***one's tongue in one's cheek,*** speak ironically or insincerely. 비꼬듯 말하다; 함부로〔불성실하게〕 말하다.

hold one's tongue, keep silent. 말하지 않다; 잠자코 있다.

lose one's tongue, cannot speak for a moment. (부끄럽거나 해서) 말을 못하다.

on the tip of one's tongue, almost spoken; ready to be spoken. 말이 목구멍까지 나와.

on the tongues of men, talked of. 사람들의 입에 올라; 소문이 나서.

tongue·less [tʌ́ŋlis] *adj.* **1** having no tongue. 혀가 없는. **2** not speaking. 말을 하지 않는; 잠자코 있는.

tongue-tied [tʌ́ŋtàid] *adj.* **1** not able to speak clearly because of some defect of the tongue. 혀짤배기의. **2** not able to speak because of amazement, embarrassment, shyness, fear, etc. (놀라거나 해서) 말이 나오지 않는. ¶ *Fear kept them all ~.* 무서워서 그들 모두 말을 못했다.

ton·ic [tɑ́nik / tɔ́nik] *n.* Ⓒ **1** a medicine that gives strength and energy. 강장제. ¶ *a hair ~* / *Cod-liver oil is a ~.* 간유는 강장제다 / *When I was depressed I found her advice a real ~.* 내가 실의에 빠졌을 때 그녀의 충고가 참 힘이 되었다. **2** 《mus.》 the keynote of scale. 으뜸음; 바탕음. — *adj.* **1** giving vigor and strength. 원기를 돋우는. ¶ *a ~ medicine* 강장제. **2** 《mus.》 of a keynote or tone. 으뜸음의. [→tone]

:to·night, to-night [tənáit, tu-] *n.* Ⓤ the night of today. 오늘 밤. — *adv.* on or during this night. 오늘 밤(은, 에). ¶ *I go ~.* 오늘 밤 간다 / *Tonight I shall be quite free.* 오늘 밤은 아주 한가하다. [*to, night*]

tonk [tɑŋk / tɔŋk] *vt.* 《*sl.*》 (P6) hit hard; defeat easily. 세게 갈기다; 강타하다; 쉽게 이기다; 낙승하다. [?]

ton·nage [tʌ́nidʒ] *n.* Ⓤ **1** the carrying capacity of a ship, measured in tons. (선박의) 용적 톤수(cf. *burden*[1]). ¶ *The ship's ~ is 21,000 tons.* 그 배의 용적 톤수는 2만 천 톤이다. **2** all the ships of a country reckoned in tons. (한 나라 선박의) 총 톤수. **3** duty or tax laid on ships according to the cargo carried. (배·뱃짐에 과하는) 톤세(稅). [→ton]

ton·neau [tʌnóu / tɔ́nou] *n.* (*pl.* **-neaus** or **-neaux**) the rear part of an automobile body, with seats for passengers. 자동차의 뒷좌석. [F.]

ton·neaux [tʌnóuz / tɔ́nouz] *n.* pl. of **tonneau.**

ton·sil [tɑ́nsil / tɔ́n-] *n.* Ⓒ 《anat.》 one of a pair of oval-shaped masses of tissue on the sides of the throat. 편도선. [L.]

ton·sil·lar [tɑ́nsilər / tɔ́n-] *adj.* of the tonsils. 편도선의.

ton·sil·li·tis [tɑ̀nsəláitis / tɔ̀n-] *n.* inflammation of the tonsils. 편도선염.

ton·so·ri·al [tɑnsɔ́:riəl / tɔn-] *adj.* 《*joc.*》 having to do with hairdressing. 이발(사)의. [↓]

ton·sure [tɑ́nʃər / tɔ́n-] *n.* **1** Ⓤ the act of shaving the crown of the head to become a priest; the state of being shaven in this way. 삭발; 출가(出家). **2** Ⓒ the part of the head shaved in this way. 머리를 민 데. — *vt.* (P6) shave the head of (someone). …의 머리를 밀다. ¶ *~ a monk.* [L. *tondeo* shave]

⟨tonsure 2⟩

ton-up [tʌ́nʌ̀p / tɔ́n-] *adj.* fond of traveling at 100 mph by motorcycle. (시속 100 마일로 달리는) 폭주족의. [→ton]

:too [tuː] *adv.* **1** also; moreover; besides. 또한; 게다가. ¶ *She is kind, and pretty ~.* 그녀는 친절하고 게다가 예쁘다 / *He can speak English and German, ~.* 그는 영어를 아는 데 독일어도 할 줄 안다 / *Won't you come(,) ~?* 너도 오지 않으련 / *We, ~, are going away.* 우리 또한 떠나려 한다. **2** excessive; more than enough. 지나치게; 너무나 …해서. ¶ *It is ~ beautiful for words.* 너무 아름다워 형언하기 어렵다 / *We cannot be ~ careful.* 아무리 조심해도 지나치다는 법이 없다 / *The problem is ~ difficult for me to solve.* 내가 풀기에는 문제가 너무 어렵다 / *It is never ~ late to mend.* 고치는 데 너무 늦다는 법은 없다 / *My dress is ~ long for you.* 내 옷이 네게는 너무 길다 / *She is ~ fat to be beautiful.* 그녀는 미인이기에는 너무 뚱뚱하다. **3** 《*colloq.*》 very; so. 대단히; 매우. ¶ *She is ~ happy.* 그녀는 매우 행복하다 / *He is not ~ well today.* 오늘 그는 별로 기분이 안 좋다 / *You are really ~ kind.* 정말 친절하십니다. [*to*]

but 〔***only***〕 ***too,*** **a**) to be regretted that .... 유감이지만. ¶ *It is but ~ true.* 섭섭하겠지만 그건 사실이다. **b**) extremely; very. 매우; 대단히. ¶ *I shall be only ~ glad to help you.* 기꺼이 도와 드리겠습니다.

none too, not at all. 조금도 … 않은. ¶ *The trip was none ~ pleasant.* 여행은 조금도 즐겁지 않았다 / *The service in this restaurant is none ~ fast and the food is none ~ good, either.* 이 식당은 서비스가 굼뜬 데다가 음식 또한 엉망이다.

too much for, more than a match for; too difficult for. …에게는 벅찬〔힘겨운〕. ¶ *This task is ~ much for me.* 이 일은 내게 힘겹다.

too much (***of a good thing***), unbearable. 너무 심한〔지독한〕; 견딜 수 없는. ¶ *This is really ~ much (of a good thing).* 이건 정말 너무 심하다.

:took [tuk] *v.* p. of **take.**

:tool [tuːl] *n.* Ⓒ **1** an instrument used with the hands in doing work. 연장; 도구; 공구. ¶ *a machine ~* 기계 공구 / *a set of carpenter's tools* 목수 연장 한 벌 / *gardener's tools* 정원사의 연장. **2** anything that serves in the manner of a tool; a means. 수단; 방편. ¶ *Words are the tools of his trade.* 말이 그의 장사 밑천이다. **3** 《*fig.*》 a person used by another to work, esp. dishonestly. 앞잡이; 끄나풀. ¶ *He used him as a ~.* 그는 그를 앞잡이로 내세웠다 / *He is a ~ of the party boss.* 그는 당수의 손발이다.

— *vt., vi.* (P6;1) **1** shape or form (something) with a tool; use a tool on; work with a tool. (…을) 도구로 만들다; 연장을 쓰다. ¶ *hand-tooled leather boots* 수제(手製) 가죽 구두. **2** 《*colloq.*》 drive or ride. (마차·차 따위)를 몰다; 탈것으로 가다. ¶ *~ along the road* 차로 도로를 달리다. [E.]

toot [tuːt] *vt.* (P6) cause (a horn, whistle, etc.) to sound. (피리·나팔 따위)를 뚜우뚜우 불다. ¶ *The drivers were tooting their horns.* 운전사들이 경적을 울리고 있었다. — *vi.* (P1) give a short, sharp sound on a horn. 뚜우뚜우 울리다. — *n.* Ⓒ an act or sound of tooting. (피리 등을) 불기; 그 소리.
● **toot·er** [túːtər] *n.* [Imit.]

:tooth [tuːθ] *n.* (*pl.* **teeth**) Ⓒ **1** one of the hard, bony growths in the jaws, used for biting and chewing. 치아; 이. ¶ *a decayed ~* 충치 / *a false* 〔*an artificial*〕 *~* 의치〔틀니〕 / *have a ~ out* 이를 뽑다〔빼다〕 / *Brush your teeth twice a day.* 하루 두 번씩 양치질해라. **2** something like a tooth, as of comb, saw or rake. 이 모양의 것《빗살·톱니·갈퀴발 따위》. ¶ *the teeth on a wheel* 〔*saw, comb*〕. [E.]

cast *something* ***in*** *someone's* ***teeth,*** reproach someone for something. (과실 따위를 구실로) …을 야단치다; 꾸짖다.

draw *someone's* ***teeth,*** deprive someone of the cause of his complaints; render someone harmless. …의 불평의 원인을 제거하다.

escape by the skin of *one's* ***teeth,*** escape narrowly. 간신히 도망치다.

get 〔***sink***〕 *one's* ***teeth into,*** **a**) go to work on seriously. …에 열중하다〔파묻히다〕. **b**) have a firm understanding of. …을 철저하게 익히다〔이해하다〕.

have a sweet tooth ⇨sweet.

in the teeth of, straight against; in spite of. …을 무릅쓰고; …에도 불구하고. ¶ *In the teeth of great obstacles, he won.* 많은 큰 장애에도 불구하고 그는 승리했다.

lie in *one's* ***teeth,*** tell a black lie. 새빨간 거짓말을 하다.

long in the teeth, old. 늙어서.

put teeth into (*a law, regulation, etc.*), make (it) effective. (법률 따위)의 효과를 높이다〔강화하다〕.

set *one's* ***teeth,*** **a**) clench the jaws tightly. 이를 악물다. **b**) 《*fig.*》 make up one's mind. 결심을 굳히다.

set *someone's* ***teeth on edge*** ⇨edge.

show *one's* ***teeth,*** show anger or hostility. (이를 드러내고) 화내다; 덤벼들다.

tooth and nail, with all one's force. 전력을 다해; 필사적으로. ¶ *We fought ~ and nail to get our plans accepted.* 계획을 받아들이게 하려고 우리는 갖은 노력을 했다.

to the teeth, fully. 완전히. ¶ *armed to the teeth* 완전 무장하고.

:tooth·ache [túːθèik] *n.* ⒸⓊ a continuous ache in a tooth. 치통.

:tooth·brush [túːθbrʌ̀ʃ] *n.* Ⓒ a small brush for cleaning the teeth. 칫솔.

toothed [tuːθt, tuːðd] *adj.* **1** having teeth. 이가 있는. **2** having a V-shaped cut. 톱니 모양의. ¶ *a ~ wheel* 톱니바퀴.

tooth·ful [tú:θfùl] *n.* 《*sl.*》 a drop of brandy, etc. (술 따위의) 한 모금.

tooth·less [tú:θlis] *adj.* having no teeth. 이가 없는.

tooth·paste [tú:θpèist] *n.* Ⓤ a paste for cleaning the teeth. 크림 치약.

tooth·pick [tú:θpìk] *n.* Ⓒ a small, pointed piece of wood used for removing bits of food from the teeth. 이쑤시개.

tooth powder [⌐−−] *n.* Ⓤ powder for cleaning the teeth. 가루 치약.

tooth·some [tú:θsəm] *adj.* (of food) pleasing to the taste; delicious. 맛있는; 맛좋은. ¶ *a ~ bit of food* 맛좋은 약간의 음식.

too·tle [tú:tl] *v., n.* =toot.

:top[1] [tɑp / tɔp] *n.* Ⓒ **1** the highest point or part; the upper end or surface. 꼭대기; 정상. ¶ *the ~ of a hill* 〔*mountain, tree*〕 언덕 〔산, 나무〕 꼭대기 / *the ~ of the page* 페이지 맨 위 / *Her name was at the ~ of the list.* 그녀 이름이 명단의 맨 위에 있었다. **2** the highest rank or place. 최고위; 수석. ¶ *sit at the ~ of the table* 식탁의 상석에 앉다 / *He is* (*at*) *the ~ of his class.* 그가 학급에서 일등이다 / *the ~ of one's profession* (그 방면의) 제일인자. **3** the highest degree or extent; the utmost; height. 절정; 극한(極限). ¶ *run at the ~ of one's speed* 전속력으로 달리다 / *cry* 〔*shout*〕 *at the ~ of one's voice* 목청껏 소리치다 / *He has reached the ~ of his condition.* 그의 컨디션이 절정에 이르렀다. **4** 《usu. *pl.*》 the part of a plant that grows above ground, esp. of an edible root. (무 등의) 지상(地上) 부분; (근채의) 잎. ¶ *radish* 〔*carrot*〕 *tops.* **5** a covering; a lid. 뚜껑. ¶ *the bottle ~* 병뚜껑. **6** the upper part of a shoe or foot. (구두나 발의) 윗부분. **7** the head; the top of the head. 머리; 정수리. **8** a bunch of hair, fibers, etc. (투구 등의 앞에 꽂는) 털술; 섬유 등의 다발. **9** 《naut.》 a platform around the upper part of a lower mast on a ship. 장루(檣樓). **10** the cover of a car, carriage, etc. (자동차 등의) 지붕. **11** 《*pl.*》 metal buttons plated, etc. only on face. 겉만 도금한 단추.

blow one's top, 《*colloq.*》 become violently angry. 벌컥 성내다; 분통을 터뜨리다.

come out on top, beat others in a fight; be successful in life. 상대를 이기다; 출세〔성공〕하다.

from top to bottom 〔***toe, tail***〕***,*** completely; from head to foot. 완전히; 머리 끝에서 발 끝까지.

on top, successful; above. 성공하여; (상대보다) 위에. ¶ *The company will have to expand if it wants to stay on ~.* 회사가 계속 우위에 머무른다면 사업의 확장이 불가피할 것이다.

on (***the***) ***top of,*** in addition to; following immediately after. …의 위에; …에 더하여; 곧이어; …을 뒤쫓아. ¶ *On ~ of everything else, I've caught a cold.* 게다가 또 나는 감기까지 들었다.

the top of the tree 〔***ladder***〕***,*** 《*fig.*》 the highest position in a profession. 최고의 지위; 제일인자.

top and tail, the whole; completely. 전체; 완전히.

top or tail, at all. 전혀; 조금도. ¶ *I cannot make ~ or tail of it.* 그것을 전혀 짐작도 못하겠다.

to the top of one's bent, as best as one may. 바랄 수 있는 한의; 마음껏; 한껏.

— *adj.* **1** at the top; highest. 최상의; 맨 위의. ¶ *the ~ shelf* 〔*step*〕 선반〔계단〕의 맨 위 / *the ~ right-hand corner* (*of a page*) (페이지의) 우측 상단 / *the ~ rung of a ladder* 사다리 맨 위 가로장 / 《*fig.*》 *the ~ rung* 성공의 절정; 최고 지위. **2** highest in degree; greatest. 최고의; 최대의. ¶ *The runners set off at ~ speed.* 주자들은 전속력으로 달리기 시작했다 / *~ prices* 최고가 / *~ secret* 극비. **3** chief; highest in rank, etc. 수위의. ¶ *the ~ place in a class* 반의 수석 / *the ~ boy* 수석인 소년.

— *v.* (**topped, top·ping**) *vt.* (P6) **1** put a top on; be the top of (something); cover the top of. …에 씌우다; …의 꼭대기를 덮다. ¶ *a church topped with* 〔*by*〕 *a spire* 뾰족탑이 있는 교회 / *the mountain topped with snow* 꼭대기에 눈이 덮인 산 / *A church tops the hill.* 교회는 언덕 맨 위에 있다. **2** be better, larger, taller, stronger, etc. than (someone); surpass; outdo. …을 능가하다; …보다 낫다. ¶ *He tops us all at chess.* 그는 우리들 중에서 체스가 최고다 / *He tops his father by four inches* 〔*half a head*〕. 그는 아버지보다 키가 4인치 더 〔머리 반만큼〕 크다 / *His composition topped all the rest.* 그의 작문이 그 중 제일 나았다. **3** reach the top of (a hill, etc.). …의 정상에 이르다. ¶ *We topped the mountain toward noon.* 정오 무렵 우리는 산꼭대기에 이르렀다. **4** rise above (something). …의 위에 오르다. ¶ *The moon topped the horizon.* 달이 지평선 위에 떴다. **5** 《naut.》 raise one end of (a yard, etc.) above the other. (활대 등)의 한쪽 끝을 올리다. **6** cut off the top of (a plant). (나무)의 순을 치다; 전정(剪定)하다. ¶ *~ a tree* 나무를 전정하다. **7** 《golf》 hit (a ball) at the top. (공)의 상단을 치다; 톱스핀하다. [E.]

top off, complete; end. 완성하다; 끝내다.

top up, fill up (a partly empty container). (액체 등으로 용기)를 가득 채우다.

·top[2] [tɑp / tɔp] *n.* Ⓒ a child's toy shaped like a cone with a point on which it spins. 팽이. [E.]

sleep like a top ⇨sleep.

to·paz [tóupæz] *n.* ⓊⒸ a mineral, usu. yellow in color but sometimes blue or green, used as a gem. 토파즈; 황옥(黃玉). [Gk.]

top boots [⌐⌐] *n. pl.* a kind of riding

boot reaching almost up to the knee. 승마용 장화《무릎까지 오는》. [top¹]

top·coat [tápkòut / tɔ́p-] *n.* Ⓒ a lightweight over coat. 톱코트; 가벼운 외투.

to·pee [toupíː, ⌐—] *n.* =topi.

top·er [tóupər] *n.* Ⓒ a person who drinks alcoholic liquor in large amounts; a drunkard. 술고래. [*top*¹]

top·flight [tápflàit / tɔ́p-] *adj.* 《*colloq.*》 of highest rank or quality. 최고의; 일류의. ¶ ~ *scientists* 〔*executives*〕 일류 과학자들〔최고 경영진〕. [*top*¹]

top·gal·lant [tàpgǽlənt / tɔ́p-] *n.* 《naut.》 the mast or sail next above the topmast. (횡범선(橫帆船)의 밑에서 세 번째 돛대. — *adj.* of the topgallant. 밑에서 세 번째 돛대의. ¶ *the* ~ *sails.* [↑]

〈top hat〉

top hat [⌐ ⌐] *n.* a man's tall silk hat. 실크해트.

top-heav·y [táphèvi / tɔ́p-] *adj.* having the top much heavier than the base and therefore unsteady and likely to fall over. 머리〔상부〕가 무거운; 불안정한. ¶ 《*fig.*》 *With so many high-ranking executives, this organization is getting* ~. 이 조직은 고급 간부들이 너무 많아서 균형을 잃고 있다.

to·pi [toupíː, ⌐—] *n.* a hat worn to protect the head from the sun. 토피《차양이 넓은 헬멧 모자》. [Hind.]

to·pi·ar·y [tóupièri / -əri] *adj.* of the clipping of trees into decorative shapes. (기하학적인) 장식 무늬로 전정(剪定)한. ¶ ~ *art* 장식적 전정술(術). [↓]

:top·ic [tápik / tɔ́p-] *n.* Ⓒ a subject for conversation, discussion, writing, etc. 토픽; 화제; 논제(論題); 제목. ¶ *topics of the day* 시사 문제 / *Politics or religion are always interesting topics of conversation.* 정치나 종교는 늘 흥미 있는 이야깃거리다 / *the topics of government* 정부에 대한 화제. [Gk. *topos* place]

top·i·cal [tápikəl / tɔ́p-] *adj.* **1** about something having local or current interest. 화제의; 시사 문제의. ¶ *articles on* ~ *subjects* 시사 문제에 대한 기사. **2** of or belonging to a topic. 논제의; 제목의; 총론적〔개괄적〕인. ¶ *Some books have* ~ *outlines before each chapter.* 어떤 책은 각 장의 앞에 개요를 싣고 있다.

top·knot [tápnàt / tɔ́pnɔ̀t] *n.* a knot of hair on the top of the head; tuft; crest. (머리의) 상투; 볏; 도가머리. [*top*¹]

top·less [táplis / tɔ́p-] *adj.* **1** lacking an upper part; bare-breasted. 윗부분이 없는; 토플리스의. ¶ *a* ~ *bathing suit* 토플리스 수영복. **2** extremely high. 까마득하게 높은. ¶ *the* ~ *Alps.*

top·mast [tápmæ̀st, 《naut.》 -məst / tɔ́pmàːst, 《naut.》 -məst] *n.* Ⓒ 《naut.》 the second section of a mast above the deck of a ship. 톱마스트; 중간 돛대.

top·most [tápmòust / tɔ́p-, -məst] *adj.* highest; at the very top. 최고〔최상〕의.

top·notch [tápnátʃ / tɔ́pnɔ́tʃ] *adj.* 《*colloq.*》 first-rate; best possible. 일류의; 최고급의. [?]

to·pog·ra·pher [toupágrəfər / -pɔ́g-] *n.* Ⓒ **1** a person who is skilled in topography. 지형학자(地形學者). **2** a person who accurately describes a place or area. 지지학자(地誌學者). [*topography*]

top·o·graph·ic [tàpəgrǽfik / tɔ̀p-], **-i·cal** [-əl] *adj.* of or belonging to topography. 지형학의; 지세(地勢)의.

to·pog·ra·phy [toupágrəfi / -pɔ́g-] *n.* Ⓤ **1** the science of making a map or showing the surface features of a place or region. 지형학. **2** the surface of a place or region. 지세(地勢). [→topic]

to·pol·o·gy [təpálədʒi / -pɔ́l-] *n.* 《math.》 the study of the properties of a geometrical figure that are unaffected when subjected to any continuous transformation. 위상(位相) 수학. [Gk. *topos* place]

top·per [tápər / tɔ́p-] *n.* Ⓒ **1** 《*colloq.*》 a person or thing that is first-rate. 뛰어난 인물; 우량품. **2** a woman's short topcoat. (여성용) 토퍼. **3** 《comm.》 fine fruit, etc. put at the top of a stock for show. 과일 따위를 잘 보이게 하려고 맨 위에 얹어 놓은 것. [→topple]

top·ping [tápiŋ / tɔ́p-] *adj.* **1** that is at the top in degree, rank, height, etc. 높이 치솟은; 발군(拔群)의. **2** 《Brit. *colloq.*》 excellent; very good. 훌륭한; 아주 좋은. ¶ *We had a* ~ *dinner.* 훌륭한 만찬이었다. [↓]

top·ple [tápəl / tɔ́pəl] *vi., vt.* (P1,2A;7,13) **1** become unsteady; cause (something) to be unsteady. 흔들리다; 뒤뚱거리(게 하)다. **2** 《*down, over*》 turn over; cause (something) to turn over. 쓰러지다; 넘어뜨리다. ¶ *The chimney toppled over on the roof.* 굴뚝이 지붕에 넘어졌다 / *This scandal could* ~ *the government.* 이 스캔들로 정부가 쓰러질 수도 있었다. [→top¹, obs. *terve* topple]

top·rank·ing [tápræ̀ŋkiŋ / tɔ́p-] *adj.* 《U.S. *colloq.*》 highest in rank, quality, etc. 일류〔최고〕의. [→top¹]

tops [taps / tɔps] *adj.* 《U.S. *colloq.*》 first-rate. 최고〔일류〕의. ¶ *She is the* ~ *at tennis.* 테니스에선 그녀가 일급이다. [*top*¹]

top·sail [tápsèil, 《naut.》-səl / tɔ́psəl, -seil] *n.* Ⓒ 《naut.》 the second sail above the lowermost sail on a mast. 톱세일《중간 돛대의 돛》. [*top*¹]

top·side [tápsàid / tɔ́p-] *n.* the upper part of a ship's side, esp. the part above the water line. 건현(乾舷)《흘수선 위의 현측(舷側)》.

top·soil [tápsɔ̀il / tɔ́p-] *n.* the upper part of

the soil. 표토(表土); 상층토.

top·sy-tur·vy [tápsitə́:rvi / tɔ́p-] *adv., adj.* **1** in a confused condition or in disorder. 뒤죽박죽으로; 엉망이 된. ¶ *He left his room all ~.* 방을 엉망으로 해놨다 / *The whole world's going ~.* 온 세상이 뒤죽박죽이 돼 간다. **2** upside down. 거꾸로; 거꾸로 된. — *n.* Ⓤ the state of confusion or disorder. 뒤죽박죽; 혼란. — *vt.* (P6) turn topsy-turvy. …을 거꾸로 하다; 엉망으로 만들다. [*toppie*]

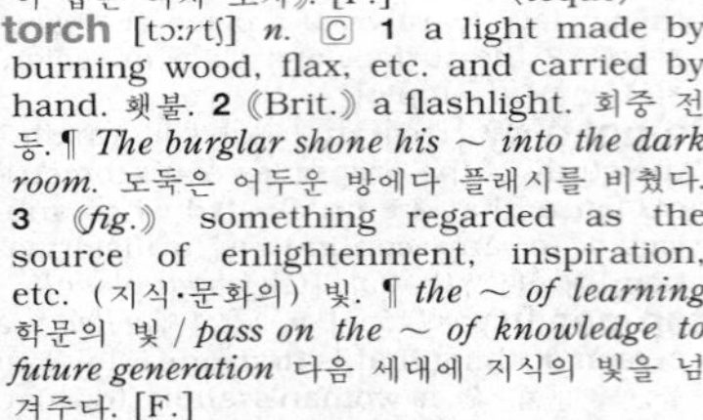
〈toque〉

toque [touk] *n.* Ⓒ a woman's small hat without a brim. 토크《작고 챙이 좁은 여자 모자》. [F.]

·torch [tɔ:rtʃ] *n.* Ⓒ **1** a light made by burning wood, flax, etc. and carried by hand. 횃불. **2** 《Brit.》 a flashlight. 회중 전등. ¶ *The burglar shone his ~ into the dark room.* 도둑은 어두운 방에다 플래시를 비췄다. **3** 《*fig.*》 something regarded as the source of enlightenment, inspiration, etc. (지식·문화의) 빛. ¶ *the ~ of learning* 학문의 빛 / *pass on the ~ of knowledge to future generation* 다음 세대에 지식의 빛을 넘겨주다. [F.]

carry a* [*the*] *torch for, be in love with, esp. someone who doesn't return one's love. …을 사랑하다《특히 짝사랑》.

the torch of Hymen, the passion of love. 사랑의 불길.

torch·bear·er [tɔ́:rtʃbɛ̀ərər] *n.* Ⓒ **1** a person who carries a torch. 횃불 드는 사람. **2** a person who is a leader in a movement, a campaign, a crusade, etc. (개혁 운동 등의) 선구자; 계몽가.

torch·light [tɔ́:rtʃlàit] *n.* Ⓤ the light which a torch gives off. 횃불의 빛. [*torch*]

:tore [tɔ:r] *v.* p. of **tear**[1].

tor·e·a·dor [tɔ́:riədɔ̀:r, tár- / tɔ́r-] *n.* Ⓒ a bullfighter on horseback in Spain. 토레아도르《스페인의 기마 투우사》(cf. *matador*). [L. *taurus* bull]

·tor·ment[tɔ́:rment] *n.* **1** ⓊⒸ great mental or physical pain. (정신적·육체적) 고통; 고민. ¶ *He suffered torment(s) from his aching teeth.* 그는 이가 아파 고통을 받았다. **2** Ⓒ a cause of suffering, anxiety, or pain. 고민거리; 골칫거리. ¶ *His undutiful sons are the ~ of his life.* 불충한 자식들이 그의 평생 두통거리다. —[-ˊ] *vt.* (P6,13) cause pain to (someone) mentally or physically. …을 괴롭히다. ¶ *The knowledge of his guilt tormented him.* 그는 자신의 죄를 알고 괴로워했다 / *He tormented the nurse with complaints.* 그는 칭얼거리며 유모를 들볶았다. [L. *torqueo* twist]

tor·men·tor, -ment·er [tɔ:rméntər] *n.* Ⓒ a person or thing that torments others. 괴롭히는 사람〔것〕.

:torn [tɔ:rn] *v.* pp. of **tear**[1].

tor·na·do [tɔ:rnéidou] *n.* Ⓒ (*pl.* **-does** or **-dos**) a violent, whirling wind that destroys everything in its course. 토네이도; 회오리바람; 맹렬한 선풍. [Sp. *tronada* thunderstorm]

·tor·pe·do [tɔ:rpí:dou] *n.* Ⓒ (*pl.* **-does**) **1** a large, cigar-shaped missile which goes underwater by its own power, used for blowing up enemy ships; a similar explosive weapon discharged by aircraft. 어뢰; 수뢰; 공중 어뢰. **2** a small firework which explodes when thrown against a hard object. 딱총. **3** 《railway》 an explosive put on a railway track which makes a loud noise for a signal when a wheel of the engine runs over it. (선로 위에 설치한) 정지(停止) 신호 뇌관. — *vt.* (P6) **1** attack or destroy with a torpedo. 어뢰로 공격〔파괴〕하다. **2** 《*fig.*》 destroy by a surprise attack. …을 기습 파괴하다. [→torpid]

torpedo boat [-ˊ-- ˋ] *n.* Ⓒ a small, fast, maneuverable warship discharging torpedoes. 어뢰〔수뢰〕정. ¶ *a ~ destroyer* 대(對) 어뢰정용 구축함.

tor·pe·do-net [tɔ:rpí:dounèt] *n.* a steel-wire crinoline keeping torpedoes from reaching a ship. 어뢰 방어망.

tor·pid [tɔ́:rpid] *adj.* **1** (of animals) not moving or feeling; dormant. 움직이지 않는; 동면하는. ¶ *A snake is ~ in winter.* 뱀은 겨울에는 동면한다. **2** dull; inactive. 둔한; 활기 없는. ¶ *The heat and humidity made us (feel) ~.* 우리는 무더위로 나른해졌다. [L. *torpeo* be numb]

tor·por [tɔ́:rpər] *n.* Ⓤ torpid condition; dullness; numbness. 동면; 무감각; 활기가 없음. [↑]

·tor·rent [tɔ́:rənt, tár- / tɔ́r-] *n.* Ⓒ **1** a violent, rapid stream. 급류; 분류(奔流); 격류. ¶ *The mountain ~ dashed over the rocks.* 계곡의 세찬 물이 바위를 치고 내려갔다. **2** 《*pl.*》 a violent flow of rain, words, etc. 억수; (질문 등의) 연발. ¶ *a ~ of abuse* 퍼부어 대는 욕설 / *torrents of rain* 억수 / *in torrents* 빗발치듯. [L. *torreo* scorch]

tor·ren·tial [tɔ:rénʃəl, tɑr- / tɔr-] *adj.* of or like a torrent; violent. 급류〔분류〕 같은; 세찬. ¶ *a ~ downpour* 억수로 내리는 비.

tor·rid [tɔ́:rid, tár- / tɔ́r-] *adj.* dried by the scorching heat of the sun; extremely hot. (볕으로) 바싹 마른; 뙤약볕의. ¶ *a ~ desert* 불타듯 뜨거운 사막 / *the ~ zone* 열대 / *~ weather* 건조하고 뜨거운 날씨. [→torrent]

tor·si [tɔ́:rsi:] *n.* pl. of **torso.**

tor·sion [tɔ́:rʃən] *n.* Ⓤ the act of twisting; the state of being twisted. 비틂; 비틀림. ¶ *a ~ balance* 비틀림 저울《비틀림을 이용해서 미소한 힘을 잼》. [→torment]

tor·so [tɔ́:rsou] *n.* Ⓒ (*pl.* **-sos** or **-si**) **1** the upper part of the human body without the head or the limbs. (인체(人體)의) 몸통.

2 a headless and limbless statue of the human trunk. 토르소《머리·손발이 없는 나체 조상(彫像)》. **3** an unfinished work. 미완성품. [→thyrsus]

***tor·toise** [tɔ́:rtəs] *n.* Ⓒ (*pl.* **-tois·es** or **-toise**) a turtle, esp. one that lives on land. (뭍에 사는) 거북. [L. *tortuca*]

tortoise shell [ㅅ-ㅅ] *n.* the hard shell, with yellow and brown spots, of a turtle or tortoise, used for combs and ornaments. (거북의) 등딱지; 별갑.

tor·tu·ous [tɔ́:rtʃuəs] *adj.* **1** twisting; winding. 뒤틀린; 꼬부라진. ¶ *a ~ path* 꼬불꼬불한 길. **2** crooked in mind. (마음이) 비꼬인. **3** 《*fig.*》 (of a policy, etc.) not direct or simple. 에두르는; 솔직하지 못한. ¶ *~ policies.* [↓]

***tor·ture** [tɔ́:rtʃər] *n.* **1** Ⓤ the act of causing severe pain to someone in order to make him do something, usu. confess. 고문. ¶ *put someone to* (*the*) *~* 아무를 고문하다. **2** ⓊⒸ extreme pain. 심한 고통; 격통. ¶ *She suffered tortures from rheumatism.* 그녀는 류머티즘을 몹시 앓았다 / *It was sheer ~ to hear him play the violin so badly.* 그가 긁어대는 바이올린 소리는 정말 지겨웠다. — *vt.* (P6,13) **1** 《*with, by*》 cause extreme pain or agony to (someone). …을 고문하다. **2** twist or distort (another's words, etc.). (남의 말 등)을 곱새기다; 곡해하다. ● **tor·tur·er** [-tʃərər] *n.* [L. *tortus* a twist]

To·ry [tɔ́:ri] *n.* Ⓒ (*pl.* **-ries**) **1** 《Brit. hist.》 a member of the political party that supported the royal power. 왕당원(王黨員). 參考 지금은 없어졌으나 보수당(Conservative Party)원을 지칭하기도 함. **2** 《U.S. hist.》 an American who favored the British during the American Revolution. (독립 전쟁 당시, 영국에 가담한) 영국파. **3** 《*t-*》 a conservative person. 보수주의자. [Ir. =pursuer (applied to Irish outlaws including papists and royalists)]

To·ry·ism [tɔ́:riìzəm] *n.* Ⓤ the doctrines or beliefs of a Tory. 토리주의; 왕당〔보수〕주의.

tosh [tɑʃ / tɔʃ] *n.* Ⓤ 《Brit. *sl.*》 nonsense; foolish talk. 실없는 소리; 난센스. [E.]

:toss [tɔ:s, tɑs / tɔs] *vt.* **1** (P6,7,13,14) 《*to, into, aside*》 throw (something) up lightly into the air; fling; pitch. …을 가볍게 던지다; (공을) 토스하다. ¶ *~ a coin to a beggar = ~ a beggar a coin* 거지에게 동전을 던져주다 / *The horse tossed its rider.* 말은 기수를 내동댕이쳤다 / *She tossed the ball to the baby.* 그녀는 아기한테 공을 던져주었다 / *They tossed their hats in the air.* 그들은 모자를 공중으로 던졌다. **2** (P6,7) raise or throw up suddenly. (머리 따위)를 뒤로 젖히다; 쳐들다《경멸·항의 등의 몸짓》. ¶ *The girl tossed her head scornfully.* 소녀는 비웃듯이 머리를 뒤로 젖혔다. **3** (P6,7) cause (something or someone) to move up and down or from side to side continuously or fitfully. …을 뒤흔들다; (몸)을 뒤척이다. ¶ *The boat was tossed by waves.* 배는 파도에 이리저리 흔들렸다 / *The trees tossed their branches in the wind.* 나뭇가지가 바람에 뒤흔들렸다 / *He was tossing about all night. He couldn't get to sleep.* 그는 밤새껏 몸을 뒤척이고 있었다. 잠을 잘 수 없었다. **4** (P6,7,13) throw (a coin, etc.) into the air to decide something by the way it falls. 동전을 던져 …을 결정하다. ¶ *I'll ~ you for who goes first.* 누가 먼저 갈건지 동전을 던져보자 / *The two captains tossed* (*up*) *a coin before the match.* 두 주장은 경기에 앞서 동전을 던졌다 / *There's only one cake left. I'll ~ you for it.* 과자가 한 개 남았다. 누가 먹을지 동전던지기를 하자. **5** (P6,7) disturb; agitate. (마음)을 어지럽히다; 안절부절 못하게 하다. ¶ *She was tossed by jealousy.* 그녀는 샘이 나서 안절부절 못 했다. — *vi.* (P1,2A) **1** throw oneself from side to side. 몸을 뒤치락거리다. ¶ *~* (*about*) *in one's bed all night* 밤새도록 잠자리에서 뒤치락거렸다. **2** move restlessly or violently. 몹시 흔들리다. **3** throw a coin. 동전던지기하다.

toss off, **a**) do or make quickly and easily. 쉽게 해치우다. ¶ *The painter tossed off a couple of sketches before lunch.* 화가는 점심전에 힘들이지 않고 스케치를 몇 개 해치웠다. **b**) drink all at once. (술)을 단숨에 들이켜다. ¶ *Jack tossed off several pints of beer in quick succession.* 잭은 여러 잔의 맥주를 거푸 들이켰다.

toss up, throw a coin to decide between two alternatives. 동전던지기로 …을 정하다. ¶ *Let's ~ up who is to pay.* 계산을 누가 할지 동전을 던져보자.

— *n.* Ⓒ **1** the act of tossing; a throw. 던져올리기. ¶ *a ~ of the ball.* **2** the act of tossing a coin to decide something. 동전던지기. ¶ *win* 〔*lose*〕 *the ~* 동전던지기에서 이기다〔지다〕. **3** the distance to which something is or can be tossed. 던져서 닿는 거리. ¶ *within the ~ of a ball* 공을 던지면 닿을 거리에. [N.]

take a toss, 《Brit.》 **a**) be thrown by a horse. 낙마하다. **b**) 《*fig.*》 suffer a defeat. 지다; 패배하다.

toss-up [tɔ́:sʌ̀p, tɑ́s- / tɔ́s-] *n.* Ⓒ **1** the act of tossing a coin to decide something. 동전 던지기. **2** 《*colloq.*》 an even chance. 반반의 기회. ¶ *It is a ~ whether he succeeds or not.* 그가 성공할지 못 할지는 가능성이 반반이다.

tot[1] [tɑt / tɔt] *n.* Ⓒ **1** a small child. 어린아이; 꼬마. ¶ *a tiny ~* **2** 《Brit.》 a small glass of alcoholic liquor. 작은 술잔. **3** a small amount of a strong alcoholic drink. (독한 술) 한 모금. ¶ *a ~ of rum* 럼주 한 모금. [N.]

tot[2] [tɑt / tɔt] *n.* Ⓒ a total. 합계. — *vt., vi.* (**tot·ted, tot·ting**) (P6,7;1,2A,3) add up. (…을) 합계하다. [↓]

tot up to, amount to. 합계 …가 되다.

:to·tal [tóutl] *adj.* **1** whole; entire. 전체의; 총계의. ¶ *the sum* ~ 총액 / *the* ~ *amount* 총량 / *the* ~ *number of cars produced this month* 이 달 제작된 차량의 총수. **2** complete; absolute. 완전한; 절대적인. ¶ *a* ~ *eclipse* 개기식(皆旣蝕) / *a* ~ *loss* 전손(全損) / ~ *abstinence* 절대 금주 / *a* ~ *war* 총력전 / *We sat in* ~ *silence.* 우린 아무 말도 없이 앉아 있었다 / *He stayed away, in* ~ *disregard of my instructions.* 그는 내 지시를 전적으로 무시하고 결석했다.

— *n.* Ⓒ the whole sum or amount. 총액; 합계; 총계. ¶ *grand* ~ 총계 / *The* ~ *of his gains amounted to millions.* 그의 총수익은 수백만 달러에 달했다.

— *vt., vi.* (**-taled, -tal·ing** or esp. 《Brit.》 **-talled, -tal·ling**) (P6;1) **1** add up; find the total of. …을 합계하다. ¶ ~ *a column of figures* 한 단의 숫자를 합하다. **2** 《*to, up to*》 reach an amount of; amount to. 총계가 …이 되다. ¶ *My expenses totaled 50,000 won.* 나의 총비용은 5만 원이었다 / *They have debts totaling $100,000.* 그들이 진 빚은 합해서 10만 달러다 / *The visitors totaled* (*up*) *to 250.* 방문객은 모두 250명이 됐다. [L. *totus* whole]

to·tal·i·tar·i·an [toutæ̀lətɛ́əriən] *adj.* of totalitarianism. 전체주의의. ¶ *a* ~ *state* 전체주의 국가. — *n.* Ⓒ a person who believes in and supports totalitarianism. 전체주의자. [↑]

to·tal·i·tar·i·an·ism [toutæ̀lətɛ́əriənìzəm] *n.* Ⓤ the doctrine that everything should be used just for the good of a country under a government controlled by one political party as in Fascist Italy or in Germany under the Nazi regime. 전체주의.

to·tal·i·ty [toutǽləti] *n.* (*pl.* **-ties**) **1** Ⓤ the state or quality of being total. 전체. **2** ⓊⒸ the total amount or number. 총계; 총액.

to·tal·ize [tóutəlàiz] *vt., vi.* (P6;1) add (accounts, etc.) together; make a total of (bills, etc.). (…을) 합계[합산]하다.

·to·tal·ly [tóutəli] *adv.* completely; entirely. 완전히; 전적으로. ¶ *The man is* ~ *blind.* 저 사람은 전혀 보지를 못한다.

tote [tout] *vt.* (P6) 《U.S. *colloq.*》 **1** carry, esp. with difficulty. (특히) 힘들게 나르다. **2** have and use (esp. a gun) habitually; bear. (늘) 지니다; 휴대하다. ¶ *a gun-toting cowboy* 늘 총을 지니고 다니는 카우보이. [O.F. *tauter*]

to·tem [tóutəm] *n.* Ⓒ **1** an animal or object believed by primitive American Indians to be closely related by blood to their tribe and family. 토템《미개인, 특히 북아메리카 토인 사이에서 세습적으로 씨족의 상징으로 숭배하는 자연물 또는 동물》. **2** a carved or painted image of a totem. 토템상(像). [Native]

totem pole [⌐-⌐] *n.* a post carved and painted with totems, erected in front of their houses by several tribes of American Indians. 토템폴; 토템 기둥.

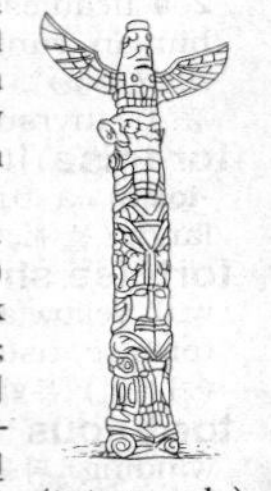
〈totem pole〉

tot·ter [tátər / tɔ́tər] *vi.* (P1,2A) **1** (of persons) stand unsteadily; walk with weak, unsteady steps; stagger. 비트적거리다; 비실비실 걷다. ¶ *The old lady tottered down the stairs.* 노부인은 뒤뚝거리며 계단을 내려갔다. **2** (of buildings, etc.) shake as if about to fall down. (쓰러질 듯이) 기우뚱거리다; 근들거리다. ¶ *The pile of books tottered then fell.* 책더미가 근들거리더니 무너졌다 / 《*fig.*》 *The empire was tottering to its fall.* 제국은 당장이라도 쓰러질 듯했다. [E.]

tou·can [tú:kæn, -kɑ:n, -⌐] *n.* Ⓒ a noisy, bright-colored bird with a very large bill, found in tropical America. (열대 아메리카산의) 큰부리새. [Braz.]

:touch [tʌtʃ] *vt.* **1** (P6,13) 《*to, on, with*》 put the hand or some other part of the body in contact with (something) to feel it; come into contact with and perceive (something). (손·손가락 따위를) …에 대다; …을 만지다[건드리다]. ¶ ~ *someone on the head* 아무의 머리에 손을 대다《주의를 끌려고》 / ~ *it with a stick* 지팡이로 그것을 건드리다 / *Don't* ~ *the wet paint.* 칠 주의《게시》 / *Please don't* ~ *me.* 내게 손대지 마시오 / ~ *one's hat to someone* 모자에 손을 대 아무에게 인사하다. **2** (P6,13) be in or come into contact with (something). (물건이) …에 닿다; (서로) 접촉하다. ¶ *The sun touched the horizon.* 해가 지평선에 닿았다 / *Your sleeve is touching the butter.* 너의 옷소매에 버터가 묻는다 / *They stood close together with their shoulders touching.* 그들은 서로 어깨를 맞대고서 있었다 / *The branches hung down and touched the water.* 나뭇가지가 늘어져 수면에 닿았다 / *She touched a lipstick to her lips.* 그녀는 입술에 루주를 발랐다. **3** (P6,13) play on (a musical instrument); strike lightly or gently; tap. (현악기)를 연주하다[타다, 켜다]; …을 가볍게 두드리다[누르다]. ¶ ~ *the keys of the piano* 피아노의 건반을 가볍게 두드리다 / ~ *a bell* 벨을 누르다 / ~ *a horse with a whip* 채찍으로 말을 찰싹 때리다 / ~ *the strings of a harp* 하프를 타다 / *I haven't touched the piano for months.* 나는 여러 달 피아노를 치지 못했다. **4** (P6) attain; come up to; reach. …에 이르다[달하다]; 닿다. ¶ ~ *the ceiling* 천장에 닿다 / *The temperature touched 65 degrees.* 온도가 65도에 이르렀다 / *His head nearly touches the ceiling.* 그의 머리는 천장에 거의 닿는다 / *The speedometer needle touched 90 mph.* 속도계의 바늘이 시속 90마일에 달했다. **5** (P6,13) 《used in *negative*》《*in, for*》 compare with; equal. …와 비견하다〔겨루다〕; …에 필적하다. ¶ *My skill at tennis doesn't ~ yours.* 테니스에서 내 기술은 너를 못 따른다 / *Nobody can ~ her in English conversation.* 영어 회화에서 그녀와 겨룰만한 사람이 없다 / *When it comes to making speeches, there's no one to ~ him.* 연설이라 하면 그를 따를 사람이 없다 / *His work could not ~ his teacher's.* 그의 작품이 그의 선생의 것에는 미치지 못했다. **6** (P6) adjoin; border on (something). …에 인접하다; …와 경계를 접하다. ¶ *The state touches the lake.* 그 주는 호수에 접해 있다. **7** (P6) 《usu. used in *negative* or *interrogative*》 eat; drink; taste. 먹다; 마시다; (음식에) 입을 대다. ¶ *He never touches alcohol.* 그는 술을 입에도 대지 않는다 / *He did not ~ his lunch.* 그는 점심을 먹지 않았다 / *~ another drink* 한 잔 더하다. **8** (P6,13) concern; relate to; mention, esp. in a casual way. …에 관계하다; 언급하다. ¶ *~ various topics during the conversation* 이야기를 나누는 동안 여러 가지 문제들이 화제에 올랐다 / *The problem touches you.* 그 문제는 너와 관계가 있다 / *Anything touching the problem interested him.* 그 문제에 관계되는 것이면 무엇이건 다 그의 흥미를 끌었다. **9** (P6) 《usu. in *negative*》 handle; move or disturb by handling. (함부로) …에 손을 대다; 다루다. ¶ *Don't ~ anything before the police come.* 경찰이 올 때까지 아무 것에도 손대지 마라 / *"Who's broken my camera ?" —"Not me. I never touched it."* 누가 내 카메라를 망가뜨렸나. —난 아니다. 난 손도 대지 않았다. **10** (P6) injure, wound, or affect slightly. …을 손상하다; 해치다; …에 작용하다. ¶ *The heavy rain touched the flowers.* 폭우로 꽃이 못쓰게 됐다 / *The child was hardly touched by the fall.* 아이는 떨어졌는데도 다치지 않았다 / *Water won't ~ that stain.* 물로는 그 얼룩이 빠지지 않을 것이다 / *The books were not touched by the fire.* 책들은 그 화재에 손상되지 않았다 / *He is slightly touched in the mind.* 그는 머리가 좀 돌았다. **11** (P6) move; affect emotionally; arouse an emotion of sympathy, gratitude, etc. in (someone); make (someone) angry or pain. …을 감동시키다; …의 마음을 움직이다; 동정〔감사〕하는 마음이 되게 하다; …을 화나게 하다. ¶ *The scene touched him to the heart.* 그 광경은 그를 크게 감동시켰다 / *His story touched her to tears.* 그의 이야기에 감동되어 그녀는 눈물을 흘렸다 / *He is touched with joy.* 그는 마음이 즐거워졌다 / *He was touched with pity for the poor girl.* 그는 그 불쌍한 소녀가 측은해졌다. **12** (P6,7) modify or improve by a stroke here and there. …을 수정하다; 가필(加筆)하다. **13** (P6,13) 《*colloq.*》《*sl.*》 borrow money from; ask for money. …에서 돈을 꾸다; …에게 돈을 요구하다. ¶ *He touched me for fifty dollars.* 그는 내게서 50달러를 우려 냈다. **14** (P6,13) 《*sl.*》 make use of unlawfully; steal. …을 착복하다; 훔치다. ¶ *Somebody touched her for her purse.* 그녀는 누군가에게 지갑을 도둑 맞았다. **15** (P6) stop at; call at, as a ship. …에 들르다; 배가 기항하다. ¶ *~ port* 〔*shore*〕 (배가) 기항하다.

— *vi.* **1** (P1) be in contact. 접촉하다; 닿다; 만지다. ¶ *The two hands touched.* 서로의 손이 닿았다. **2** (P3) make a stop or call at. (배가) 기항(寄港)하다.

touch at, (of a ship) call at (a harbor). (배가) …에 기항하다.

touch bottom, **a**) reach the bottom of water with toes. 발끝이 물의 바닥에 닿다. ¶ *My feet can't ~ bottom.* 발이 바닥에 닿지 않는다. **b**) reach the lowest point. 최하위점에 이르다. ¶ *The prices have now touched bottom.* 물가는 지금 바닥 시세다.

touch down, **a**) (of an airplane) land usu. briefly; reach the ground. (비행기가) 착륙하다. **b**) 《football》 score a try by touching the ground with the ball behind the opponent's goal-line. 볼을 터치다운하다.

touch off, **a**) set off; cause (something) to explode; ignite. …을 발사하다; 폭발시키다. **b**) represent exactly. …을 정확히 나타내다〔표현하다〕. **c**) cause to happen; start (an argument, quarrel, discussion, etc.). (논쟁·싸움 등)을 시작하다. ¶ *~ off a heated discussion* 열띤 토론을 벌이다.

touch on 〔***upon***〕***,*** **a**) come near to (something). …에 접근하다. **b**) mention (a subject) briefly. (문제)에 관해 간단히 언급하다. **c**) relate to (something). …에 관계하다.

touch (*someone*) ***to the quick,*** injure deeply the feelings of (someone). …의 감정을 해치다; …의 아픈 데를 건드리다. ¶ *The remark touched him to the quick.* 그 말은 그의 아픈 데를 건드렸다.

touch up, **a**) modify; improve or finish (a painting, etc.) by making slight changes. …을 수정하다; 마무르다. ¶ *~ up a painting* 〔*photograph*〕 그림〔사진〕을 수정하다 / *~ up a literary work* 작품을 완성하다. **b**) strike lightly; remind; excite. (말 따위에) 가볍게 채찍을 대다; (기억 따위를) 환기하다; 흥분시키다.

— *n.* **1** Ⓒ the act of touching; the state or fact of being touched; a contact; a gentle stroke, tap, etc. 만지기; 닿기; 접촉; 가볍게 두드리기〔치기〕. ¶ *give someone a ~* 아무를 건드리다〔만지다〕 / *I felt a ~ on my left shoulder.* 왼쪽 어깨에 무엇인가 닿는 것을 느꼈다 / *strike the keys of a typewriter with a uniform ~* 타자기의 키를 고른 터치로 두드리다 / *A soap-bubble bursts at a ~.* 비눗방울은 닿기만 해도 터진다. **2** ⓊⒸ the sense by which things are felt; the sense of feeling. 촉감; 감촉. ¶ *the sense of ~* 촉각; 촉감 / *soft to the ~* 감촉이 부드럽다 / *have a* keen ~ 촉감이 예민하다 / *the silky ~ of a fabric* 직물의 비단 같은 매끄러운 감촉 / *It is soft* 〔*rough*〕 *to the ~*. 감촉〔촉감〕이 부드럽다〔거칠거칠하다〕. **3** Ⓤ a close relation of communication, agreement, sympathy, etc.; harmony. (정신적) 접촉; 교제; 연락; 공감(共感); 동정(同情); 조화. ¶ *lose ~ with the world* 세상과 인연이 끊기다 / *I've been trying to get in ~ with you all afternoon.* 나는 오후 내내 너와 연락을 취하려 했었다 / *She was out of ~ with reality.* 그녀는 현실을 인식하지 못하고 있었다. **4** Ⓒ a very small amount, degree, etc.; a trace. 소량; 조금; 낌새; 기미. ¶ *a ~ of red* 좀 붉은기 / *a ~ of winter in the air* 대기 중에서 느껴지는 겨울의 기미 / *The soup wants a ~ of salt.* 수프에 소금기가 좀 모자란다 / *a ~ of humor* 좀 유머러스한 데 / *You have a ~ of genius.* 네게는 천재다운 데가 있다. **5** Ⓒ a slight attack of illness. (가벼운) 병〔탈, 이상〕. ¶ *My son is in bed with a ~ of a cold.* 아들놈이 감기 기운이 있어 누워 있다 / *a ~ of fever* 가벼운 신열 / *a ~ of the sun* 가벼운 일사병. **6** ⓐ Ⓒ a delicate stroke with a brush in painting; a slight change in or addition to a painting, story, or other work. (그림 따위의) 일필(一筆); 가필; 필치; 마무리; 솜씨. ¶ *finishing touches* 마무리의 가필 / *a happy ~* 교묘한 필치 / *a sculpture with a bold ~* 끌을 사용한 대담한 솜씨의 조각 / *He finished his picture with a few touches.* 약간의 화필을 가해 그림을 완성했다 / *Mother was giving a last ~ to the flowers.* 어머니께서는 꽃꽂이에 마무리 손질을 하고 계셨다. ⓑ ⓊⒸ a characteristic handling in art, literary work, etc. (작품 등의) 특징; 특성; 특색. ¶ *give literary ~ to one's writing* 글을 문학적인 특성을 살려 쓰다 / *There are some individual touches in the furnishings of the room.* 실내의 가구에는 약간의 개인적인 특색〔취향〕들이 있다. **7** Ⓒ 《mus.》 the manner of playing. 탄주법(彈奏法). ¶ *The pianist has an excellent ~.* 그 피아니스트는 타건법(打鍵法)이 훌륭하다 / *She plays with a light* 〔*firm*〕 *~.* 그녀는 악기의 탄주법이 부드럽다〔안정돼 있다〕. **8** Ⓒ 《*arch.*》 a test or trial. 시험. **9** Ⓤ 《football》 the area just outside the side-lines. 터치 라인의 외측 부분. [Rom.]

a near touch, a narrow escape. 구사일생(九死一生).

an easy 〔***a soft***〕 ***touch,*** 《*sl.*》 a person from whom one can beg or borrow easily. (남의 청을 거절하지 못하는) 마음이 약한〔너그러운, 무던한〕 사람.

a touch of nature, human feeling. 인정(人情).

get in touch (=*communicate*) ***with*** *someone.* 아무와 접촉〔연락〕이 있다. ¶ *I'm trying to get in ~ with my brother in Australia.* 오스트레일리아에 있는 동생과 연락할 길을 찾고 있다.

keep in touch (=*remain in communication*) ***with*** *someone.* 아무와 접촉〔연락〕을 유지하다. ¶ *keep in ~ with one's family* 가족과의 연락을 유지하고 있다.

lose touch (=*fail to maintain communication*) ***with*** *someone.* 아무와의 접촉이 끊기다. ¶ *I've lost ~ with her.* 그녀와의 연락이 끊겼다.

out of touch (=*not in communication*) ***with*** *someone.* 아무와 접촉하지 않고.

touch-and-go [tʌ́tʃəngóu] *adj.* involving risk; extremely uncertain. 위태로운; 아슬아슬한. ¶ *a ~ business* 〔*situation*〕 위험한 사업〔상황〕 / *It was ~ with him.* 그에게 있어서는 죽느냐 사느냐의 아슬아슬한 순간이었다 / *It was ~ whether the doctor would get there in time.* 의사가 제시간에 거기에 도착할지 못할지 조마조마했다.

touch·down [tʌ́tʃdàun] *n.* 《football》 the act of a player in putting the ball on the ground behind the opponent's goal-line. 터치다운.

touched [tʌtʃt] *adj.* 《*colloq.*》 **1** slightly crazed; stirring emotionally. 정신이 좀 이상해진. **2** feeling grateful. 고마운; 감사하는. ¶ *I was deeply ~ by their present.* 그들의 선물이 정말 고마웠다.

touch·ing [tʌ́tʃiŋ] *adj.* arousing the emotions or feelings of sympathy. 감동적인; 애처로운. ¶ *a ~ story* 감동적인〔애처로운〕 이야기 / *The two lovers parting at the station — what a ~ scene it made.* 정거장에서 이별을 나누는 두 연인, 아 얼마나 감동적인 장면이었던고. — *prep.* in regard to; concerning. …에 관하여. ¶ *give one's opinion ~ the subject under discussion* 토의 중인 안건에 대한 자기 의견을 말하다.

touch-line [tʌ́tʃlàin] *n.* 《Rugby football》 either of the two side-lines marking the playing field. 터치라인.

touch·stone [tʌ́tʃstòun] *n.* Ⓒ **1** a kind of black stone used to test the purity of gold or silver. 시금석. **2** a test for deciding the qualities or value of a thing; a standard. 사물의 진가를 알아내는 시험〔방법〕; 표준. ¶ *Time is the ~ of literary merit.* 시간이야말로 문학의 진가를 알아내는 방법이다.

touch·y [tʌ́tʃi] *adj.* (**touch·i·er, touch·i·est**) **1** easily offended; irritable; too sensitive. 걸핏하면 화내는; 성마른; 신경 과민의. ¶ *She's in a very ~ mood today.* 그녀는 오늘 매우 신경이 과민〔예민〕한 상태이다. **2** needing skillful or delicate handling. 다루기 힘든〔까다로운〕. ¶ *a ~ situation in Northern Ireland* 다루기 까다로운 북아일랜드 상황. ● **touch·i·ly** [-li] *adv.*

*__tough__ [tʌf] *adj.* **1** hard to break, cut or bend; sticky. 단단한; 부러지지 않는; 질긴; 끈기 있는. ¶ *~ leather* 〔*wood*〕 단단한 가죽〔나무〕 / *~ meat* 질긴 고기 / *~ clay* 찰흙. **2** ⓐ (of a person) able to endure hardship or suffering; strong; stubborn. 불굴의; 끈질긴; 튼튼한; 완고한. ¶ *a ~ customer* 만만찮은 상대 / *a ~ soldier* 불굴의 용사. **3** difficult; 《*colloq.*》 unpleasant. 어려운; 불쾌한. ¶ *a ~ job* 어려운 일 / *~ luck* 악운 / *a ~ question to* *answer* 대답하기 어려운 질문〔문제〕/ *Dragging the load uphill was ~ work for the horses.* 치받이로 무거운 짐을 끄는 일은 말들에게 힘든 일이었다. **4** 《*colloq.*》 violent. 난폭한.

—*n.* Ⓒ 《U.S. *colloq.*》 a violent, brutal person; a ruffian. 불량배; 깡패. [E.]

tough·en [tʌ́fn] *vi., vt.* (P1;6) become or make tough. 단단해지다〔하게 하다〕.

tough·ness [tʌ́fnis] *n.* Ⓤ the quality of being tough. 굳셈; 완강; 완고.

***tour** [tuər] *n.* Ⓒ **1** a long journey for sightseeing or inspection or on business. 관광 여행; 만유. ¶ *go on a ~* 관광 여행을 가다 / *a ~ of observation* 시찰 여행 / *a foreign ~* 해외 관광 / *cycling*〔*motoring*〕 *~* 자전거〔자동차〕 여행. **2** a short journey; an excursion. 짧은 여행; 소풍. ¶ *an educational ~* 수학 여행 / *He has gone on a walking ~.* 그는 도보 여행을 떠났다. **3** 《mil.》 a period of duty at one place. (한 곳에서의) 근무 기간. **4** a journey of a theatrical company. (극단의) 지방 (순회) 공연.

on tour, touring, said esp. of theatrical companies and traveling entertainers. 순회 공연하여.

—*vi.* (P1,2A,3) 《*about, through*》 go on a tour. 유람〔관광〕 여행하다; 여행하다. ¶ *~ through Europe* 유럽을 관광 여행하다.

—*vt.* (P6) go on a tour through (a place). …을 여행하다. ¶ *~ Canada* 캐나다를 여행하다 / *Last year they toured Europe.* 지난해 그들은 유럽을 여행했다. [→turn]

tour·ism [túərizəm] *n.* **1** traveling for pleasure. 관광 여행. **2** the business of providing services for tourists. 관광 사업. ¶ *The country depends on ~ for much of its income.* 그 나라는 대부분의 재원을 관광 사업에 의지하고 있다.

tour·ist** [túərist] *n.* Ⓒ a person who travels in many places just for pleasure. 관광객. ¶ ***a ~ bureau 여행 협회 / ***a ~ party*** 관광단 / ***~ spots*** 관광지.

tour·na·ment** [túərnəmənt, tə́ːr-] *n.* Ⓒ **1** a series of contests to determine a championship. 선수권 대회; 승자 진출전; 토너먼트. ¶ ***a tennis ~. **2** (in the Middle Ages) a contest between armed knights with blunt weapons and on horseback. (중세의) 마상 무술 시합. [→turn]

tour·ney [túərni, tə́ːr-] *n.* Ⓒ =tournament 2. —*vi.* (P1) take part in a tournament. 시합에 나가다. [↑]

tour·ni·quet [túərnikit, tə́ːr-] *n.* Ⓒ a bandage or other device for tightly pressing a blood vessel to stop a flow of blood. 지혈기(止血器); 압박 붕대. [↑]

tou·sle [táuzəl] *vt.* (P6) put (the hair) into disorder; make (the hair) untidy. (머리)를 엉클다; 헝클어뜨리다. —*n.* Ⓤ an untidy mass of hair; ⓊⒸ a disordered condition. 헝클어진 머리; 난잡; 무질서. ¶ *tousled hair* 헝클어진 머리. [E.]

tout [taut] *vi.* (P1,2A) **1** ask people in a persistent and annoying manner to buy goods or agree to some request or to give support or help. (물건을) 강매(强賣)하다; 끈질기게 조르다〔권유하다〕. ¶ *Our company does not ~ its wares on television.* 우리 회사는 제품을 집요하게 텔레비전에 선전하지 않는다. **2** obtain and deal in horse-racing information. 경마에 대한 정보를 획득〔매매〕하다. —*n.* a person who touts (in both senses). tout 하는 사람. [E. =peep]

tout ensemble [tuː tɑːŋ sɑ́ːŋbəl] *n.* 《F.》 the general effect; the whole taken together. (작품 등의) 전체적 효과; 전체; 전부.

tow[1] [tou] *vt.* (P6,7) **1** pull or drag (a boat, etc.) by a rope or line. (배)를 밧줄로 끌다〔당기다〕; 견인하다. ¶ *The tug is towing three barges.* 예인선이 바지선 세 척을 견인하고 있다. **2** pull or drag (something) behind. …을 끌고 가다.

—*n.* **1** Ⓤ the act of towing; the state of being towed. 밧줄로 끌기〔끌려가기〕. ¶ *The ship arrived in the ~ of a tug.* 그 배는 예인선에 끌리어 도착했다 / *My car's broken down; will you give me a ~?* 내 차가 고장났는데 좀 끌어 주겠나. **2** Ⓒ something pulled by a rope or line. 밧줄에 끌리는 것. **3** Ⓒ the rope or line used in towing. 끄는 밧줄. [E.]

have 〔***take***〕 *someone* (*something*) ***in tow,*** **a**) pull (a boat) by a rope. …를〔을〕 밧줄로 끌다. ¶ *We took the boat in ~.* 우리는 배를 끌고 갔다. **b**) have (someone) under one's charge; take charge of him. …을 보살피다〔보호하다〕. ¶ *take a child in ~* 아이들을 보호하다〔보살피다〕.

tow[2] [tou] *n.* Ⓤ **1** the short, rough, broken fibers of flax or hemp. 삼부스러기; 조마(粗麻). **2** the material of which ropes are made. 밧줄 재료. —*adj.* made from tow. 삼부스러기로 만든. [E.]

tow·age [tóuidʒ] *n.* Ⓤ **1** the act of towing; the state of being towed. (배 따위를) 끌기; 견인. **2** the charge for towing. 견인료. [*tow*[1]]

:**to·ward** [tɔːrd, təwɔ́ːrd] *prep.* **1** in the direction of. (운동이) …쪽으로; …을 향해서. ¶ *go ~ the beach* 해안 쪽으로 가다 / *make efforts ~ peaceful settlement* 평화적인 해결 방향으로 노력하다 / *We have made great strides ~ sexual equality.* 우리는 남녀 평등을 향해 장족의 진전을 이루었다. **2** facing. (위치가) …을 향해. ¶ *My house looks ~ the sea.* 우리 집은 바다를 향해 있다 / *She wept with her back ~ me.* 그녀는 내게 등을 돌리고 울었다 / *The house faces ~ south.* 그 집은 남향이다 / *Your road lies* 〔*is*〕 *~ the north.* 네가 가는 길은 북쪽으로 향해 있다. **3** (of time) near; just before. (시간이) …가까이; …무렵. ¶ *He came back ~ midnight* 〔*morning*〕. 그는

자정〔아침〕 무렵에 귀가했다 / *It must be ~ six o'clock.* 지금 여섯 시쯤 됐으리라. **4** as regards; concerning. (관계가) …에 관해서는; …에 대하여. ¶ *one's attitude ~ the question* 그 문제에 대한 태도 / *What is your attitude ~ marriage?* 네 결혼관은 뭐냐 / *feel kindly ~ someone* 아무에게 호감을 가지다 / *What is their policy ~ America?* 그들의 대미 정책은 무엇인가. **5** for the purpose of. (목적이) …을 위해. ¶ *She is saving ~ her old age.* 그녀는 자신의 노후에 대비해 저축하고 있다 / *Will you give something ~ our new hospital? Here is a dollar ~ it.* 우리 새 병원을 위해 뭐 좀 보태 줄 수 있겠나. 자, 1 달러 기부하겠네. **6** about; nearly as much (many) as. (수량이) …만큼. ¶ *She was ~ thirty.* 그녀는 30세 전후였다 / *There were ~ a thousand of them.* 천 명 정도의 사람이 있었다. —[tɔːrd, tóuəd] *adj.* 《*pred.* only》 about to happen; impending; in progress. 막 일어나려고 하는; 절박한; 진행중인. ¶ *There is a wedding ~.* 곧 결혼식이 있다 / *Then I saw what was ~.* 그 때 나는 무슨 일이 일어나고 있는지 알고 있었다. [*to, -ward*]

:to·wards [tɔːrdz, təwɔ́ːrdz] *prep.* =toward.

tow·boat [tóubòut] *n.* Ⓒ a boat for towing; a tugboat. 예인선. [*tow*[1]]

:tow·el [táuəl] *n.* Ⓒ a piece of cloth or paper used for wiping and drying something wet. 타월; 수건. ¶ *a bath ~* 목욕 수건 / *wring a ~* 수건을 짜다 / *dry oneself with a ~* 타월로 몸을 닦다. [Teut.]

throw in the towel, admit defeat or failure. 패배〔실패〕를 인정하다.

—*vt., vi.* (**-eled, -el·ing** or 《Brit.》 **-elled, -el·ling**) (P6;1) wipe or dry with a towel. (…을) 수건으로 닦다〔훔치다〕.

towel-horse [táuəlhɔ̀ːrs], **-rack** [-ræ̀k] *n.* a wooden frame to hang towels on. 수건걸이.

tow·el·ing, 《Brit.》 **-el·ling** [táuəliŋ] *n.* **1** Ⓤ material for making towels. 타월천; 수건감. **2** 《*colloq.*》 whipping. 매질.

:tow·er [táuər] *n.* Ⓒ **1** a high structure standing alone or forming a part of another building. 탑. ¶ *a bell ~* 종탑 / *the* 〔*a*〕 *~ of ivory* 상아탑 / *the Eiffel Tower* 에펠탑 / *an air traffic control ~* 관제탑. **2** 《*the T~*》 the Tower of London. 런던 타워. **3** a fortress; a protector. 성채; 옹호자.

a tower of strength, a reliable person. 의지가 되는 사람; 옹호자.

—*vi.* (P2A,3) **1** rise high up. 높이〔우뚝〕 솟다. ¶ *~ against the sky* 하늘 높이 솟다 / *The mountains seemed to ~ to the clouds.* 산들은 구름에까지 닿을 듯 우뚝 솟아 있었다. **2** 《*above*》 ⓐ be much taller or higher than. …보다 더 크다〔높다〕. ¶ *He towered above the crowd.* 그는 모인 군중들보다 키가 컸다. ⓑ be greater than in ability, power of mind, character, etc. (능력 등이) 월등하다; 더 우수하다. ¶ *~ above one's fellow-workers in intellect* 지성이 동료 일꾼들보다 한 수 위다. [L. *turris*]

tow·ered [táuərd] *adj.* having a tower. 탑이 있는.

tow·er·ing [táuəriŋ] *adj.* **1** rising very high; lofty. 높이 솟은. ¶ *a ~ tree* 높이 솟은 나무. **2** very great. (아주) 큰. ¶ *a man of ~ ambition* 큰 야망을 가진 사람 / *~ debt* 거액의 빚. **3** very violent. 맹렬한. ¶ *in a ~ rage* 불같이 노하여. **4** of great importance; outstanding. 아주 중요한; 발군(拔群)의. ¶ *one of the ~ intellects of our time* 우리 시대의 뛰어난 지성인의 한 사람.

tow·ery [táuəri] *adj.* **1** having towers. 탑이 있는. **2** towering; very high. 높이 솟은.

tow·head [tóuhèd] *n.* Ⓒ (a person having) a head of very light blond hair. 머리칼이 담황색인 사람. [*tow*[2]]

towing line [⌐-⌐] *n.* =towline.

towing path [⌐-⌐] *n.* =towpath.

tow·line [tóulàin] *n.* Ⓒ a rope, chain, etc. used in towing a boat or car. (배·차 따위를) 끄는 밧줄. [*tow*[1]]

:town [taun] *n.* Ⓒ **1** a group of houses and buildings larger than a village and smaller than a city. 읍; 도회지; 크지 않은 도시(cf. *country*). ¶ (*one's*) *home* 〔*native*〕 *~* 고향(마을) / *live in a small ~* 작은 도회지에서 살다. **2** 《*the ~*》 the people of a town. 읍내 사람; 도회지 사람. ¶ *The whole ~ knows of it.* 그걸 모르는 읍내 사람은 없다 / *the talk of the ~* 읍내의 소문〔평판〕. **3** the business or shopping center; a market town. 도심; 시장〔저자〕 거리; 상업 지구. ¶ *have one's office in ~* 도심지에 사무실이 있다 / *the old ~* 구시가 / *the Korea* 〔*China*〕 *~* 한국인〔중국인〕 거리. **4** the city as opposed to the country. (시골에 대한) 도회; 읍내. ¶ *~ life* 읍내의 생활. **5** 《without *article*》 the chief city or town nearest to where one lives; the capital city, esp. in England London. 살고 있는 근처의 도시; (특히) 런던. ¶ *come* 〔*go*〕 (*up*) *to ~* 상경하다; 런던에 가다 / *live out of ~* 교외〔시골〕에서 살다. [E.]

a man about town, a fashionable, gay man of leisure, esp. in London. (특히 런던의) 건달; 한량(閑良)

on the town, **a**) 《U.S.》 dependent on the town for support. 읍의 보조를 받고. ¶ *go on the ~* 생활 보조를 받다. **b**) enjoying oneself wildly, esp. at night, in places of entertainment. (도시의 유흥가에서) 환락을 좇아; 흥청거리며.

out of town, in the country. 도시를 떠나; 시골에서.

paint the town red, go on a racket. 유흥가를 흥청거리며 다니다.

woman of the town, a prostitute. 매춘부.

town hall [⌐⌐] *n.* a building in a town which contains the public offices and often, a hall for public meetings. 읍사무소; 시(市) 공회당(公會堂); 시의회 의사당.

town house [⌐⌐] *n.* a house in town owned by a person who has another house in the country. (시골에 저택이 있는 사람의) 도회지 저택.

town·i·fied [táunəfàid] *adj.* of a town; of town life. 도회의; 도회지풍(風)의 (opp. countrified).

towns·folk [táunzfòuk] *n. pl.* people living in a town. 도시 사람; 읍민(邑民).

towns·man [táunzmən] *n.* Ⓒ (*pl.* **-men** [-mən]) **1** a person living in a town. 도시〔읍내〕 사람. **2** a person living in his own town; people in the same town. 같은 읍내 사람.

towns·peo·ple [táunzpì:pl] *n. pl.* = townsfolk.

tow·path [tóupæ̀θ, -pɑ̀:θ] *n.* Ⓒ a path along a canal or river used for towing boats by men, horses, etc. (운하·강 연변의) 배 끄는 길. [*tow*[1]]

tow-rope [tóuròup] *n.* =towline.

tox·ic [tɑ́ksik / tɔ́k-] *adj.* poisonous; of a poison. 독의. ¶ ~ *symptoms* 중독 증상 / ~ *smoke* 독가스 / *The factory had been sending out* ~ *waste*〔*fumes*〕. 그 공장은 유독 폐기물을〔가스를〕 배출해 왔다. [Gk. *toxa* bow and arrows (with reference to poisoning of arrows)]

tox·i·col·o·gy [tɑ̀ksikɑ́lədʒi / tɔ̀ksikɔ́l-] *n.* Ⓤ the study of the nature or effects of poisons. 독물학(毒物學).

tox·in [tɑ́ksin / tɔ́k-] *n.* Ⓒ any poison naturally produced in a plant or animal. 독소.

:toy [tɔi] *n.* Ⓒ **1** a plaything for a child. 장난감. ¶ *a* ~ *dog* 작은 애완견 / *play with toys* 장난감을 가지고 놀다 / *He is as pleased with it as a child with a new* ~. 그는 어린 아이가 새 장난감을 갖고 기뻐하듯이 그것을 갖게 된 것을 기뻐했다 / *Don't play with that gun; it's not a* ~*!* 그 총 만지지 마라. 그건 장난감이 아니다. **2** something of little value. 보잘것 없는 것. **3** a small ornament; a trinket. 자질구레한 장신구.

make a toy of (=*amuse oneself by* =*play with*) *something.* …을 가지고 놀다; 장난하다.

— *vi.* (P3) 《*with*》 handle or treat something in a half-hearted way; play; trifle. 가지고 놀다; 장난치다; 우습게 보다. ¶ ~ *with dolls* 인형을 가지고 놀다 / ~ *with a pencil* 연필을 가지고 장난치다 / *He toyed with the idea of becoming an actor.* 그는 배우나 되어 볼까 하는 막연한 생각을 가지기도 했다. [E.]

toy·shop [tɔ́iʃɑ̀p / -ʃɔ̀p] *n.* Ⓒ a store where toys are sold. 장난감 가게.

:trace[1] [treis] *n.* Ⓒ **1** 《often *pl.*》 a visible mark, sign, piece of evidence, etc., left by a person, thing or event. 자취; 흔적; 증거. ¶ *the traces of an ancient civilization* 고대 문명의 유적 / *Sorrow had left its traces on her face.* 그녀 얼굴에는 슬픈 자국이 남아 있었다 / *War had left its traces on the countryside.* 시골에는 전쟁의 흔적들이 남아 있었다 / *Every* ~ *of the crime had been removed.* 범행의 증거가 될 만한 것은 모두 제거되어 있었다. **2** a footprint or beaten path left by people, animals or vehicles. 자국; 발자국. ¶ *follow up a* ~ 발자국을 더듬어 가다 / *find the traces of big game* 큰 사냥감의 자취를 발견하다. **3** a very small amount or quantity. 조금; 소량. ¶ *a* ~ *of fear* 약간의 공포의 빛 / *A* ~ *of poison was found in the food.* 음식에서 약간의 독물이 발견되었다 / *There is no* ~ *of color in her cheeks.* 그녀의 양볼에는 핏기라곤 전혀 없었다 / *without a* ~ *of sympathy* 동정의 기미라곤 조금도 없이. **4** a drawing or sketch of something. 선; 도형(圖形).

— *vt.* **1** (P6,7,13) follow a trail or footprint of (something). …의 자국을 좇아가다〔밟다〕; 추적하다 ¶ *A policeman traced a thief.* 경찰은 도둑을 추적했다 / ~ *someone's footsteps in the snow* 눈 위의 아무의 발자국을 뒤쫓아가다 / *The dog traced the fox to its den.* 개는 여우를 소굴까지 추적했다. **2** (P6) find out; follow the course of (something) by going backward. …을 찾아내다; …의 과거로 더듬어 올라가다. ¶ *We cannot* ~ *any letter of that date.* 그 날짜의 편지를 찾을 수 없다 / ~ *the history*〔*origin*〕 *of a family* 한 가문의 연혁〔혈통〕을 밝혀 내다 / *I am unable to* ~ *the document to which you refer.* 나는 당신이 문의한 그 서류를 찾을 도리가 없습니다. **3** (P6,7) copy (a drawing, etc.) by following the lines; copy (a drawing, etc.) on thin, transparent paper. …을 선으로 그리다; …을 복사〔투사〕하다. ¶ *He traced the map.* 그 지도를 복사했다 / ~ *out the plan of a house* 집의 도면을 그리다. **4** (P6,7) make a plan. …을 계획〔정〕하다. ¶ ~ (*out*) *a line of conduct* 행동 방침을 정하다. **5** (P6) follow the course of; move or walk along. (길)을 따라가다〔걷다〕. ¶ *We traced the winding path of the wood.* 우리는 숲의 고불고불한 길을 따라갔다.

— *vi.* (P1) go back to (the past). (옛날로) 거슬러 올라가다. [E.]

trace[2] [treis] *n.* Ⓒ one of the two straps, ropes by which an animal (esp. a horse) pulls a wagon or carriage. (말의 수레를 끄는) 봇줄; 가죽끈. [L. *traho* drag]

kick over the traces, get out of control or restraint; act independently. (말이) 봇줄을 차 버리다《속박을 벗어나다》; (사람이) 제멋대로 행동하다.

trac·er [tréisər] *n.* Ⓒ **1** a person who traces or searches for something lost. 추적자; 분실물 수색계원. **2** an instrument for tracing drawings, designs, etc. 철필; (재봉용) 트레이서. **3** 《U.S.》 an inquiry for a missing letter, package, etc. 분실 우편물 수색 조회서. **4** 《mil.》 a bullet that is shot up in the air leaving behind a trail of smoke or fire. 예광탄(曳光彈). [*trace*[1]]

〈tracery〉

trac·er·y [tréisəri] *n.* ⓊⒸ (*pl.* **-er·ies**) an ornament or design based on lines, as in a Gothic window. 트레이서리 《고딕식 창의 장식 격자(格子)》. [*trace*[1]]

tra·che·a [tréikiə / trəkí:ə] *n.* Ⓒ (*pl.* **-as** or **-ae**) 《anat.》 an air tube at the back of the mouth, leading to the lungs. 기관(氣管). [Gk.]

tra·che·ae [tréikiì: / trəkí:i] *n.* pl. of **trachea.**

tra·cho·ma [trəkóumə] *n.* Ⓤ 《med.》 a disease of the inner eyelids. 트라코마; 과립성 결막염. [Gk. *trachus* rough]

trac·ing [tréisiŋ] *n.* Ⓤ **1** the act of a person who traces. 투사(透寫); 복사; 추적(追跡). **2** a copy of a picture, map, design, etc. made by tracing the lines on thin, transparent paper. 투사; 투사도; 복사; 투사〔복사〕물. ¶ ~ *cloth* 투사포(布); 트레이싱 클로스 / ~ *paper* 투사지; 트레이싱 페이퍼. **3** the record traced by a self-recording instrument. 자동 기록기의 기록. [*trace*[1]]

:track [træk] *n.* Ⓒ **1** the mark left by something which has passed along. 지나간 자국. ¶ *follow up a* ~ 자국을 따라가다 / *the* ~ *of a wagon* 수레가 지나간 자국 / *a* ~ *of wheel* 바퀴 자국. **2** 《*pl.*》 footprints or other marks, left by an animal, car, etc. 발자국; 흔적. ¶ *find the tracks of a bear* 곰 발자국을 발견하다 / *There were not any car tracks.* 차의 흔적은 없었다. **3** ⓐ a path; a trodden path or trail taken by persons, animals or vehicles. 밟고 다녀서 생긴 작은 길; 통로. ¶ *a mountain* ~ 산중의 등산길. ⓑ the course which something takes. 진로. ¶ *the* ~ *of a bird* 새가 날아가는 길 / *the* ~ *of a storm* 폭풍의 진로. **4** a course for races; 《U.S.》 running or hurdling events performed on a track. 트랙; 경주로; 트랙 경기. ¶ *a* ~ *meet* 육상 경기 대회. **5** metal rails on which trains or streetcars run. 궤도; 선로. **6** an endless belt used for the wheels of some very heavy vehicles to make movement over rough ground. 무한 궤도. ¶ *tank tracks.*

***cover one's track*(*s*),** keep one's movements or plans secret; abscond. 행동〔계획〕을 비밀로 하다; 종적을 감추다.

keep track of 《U.S.》 (=*follow the course of; keep in touch with*) *something.* …을 따라가다; 놓치지 않다.

leave the track, 《U.S.》 (of a train, etc.) run off the rails. 탈선하다.

lose track of 《U.S.》 (=*lose sight or knowledge of*) *something.* …을 놓쳐 버리다; …의 소식이 끊어지다.

make tracks, 《*colloq.*》 go very fast; go off in a hurry. 급하게〔황급히〕 가다.

off the track, away from the subject, objective, etc. 탈선하여; 정도(正道)를 벗어나.

on the track, 《*fig.*》 following the right course; keeping to the subject. 정도(正道)를 따라; 주제를 벗어나지 않아.

on the track of (=*in search of*) *something.* …을 추적하여.

the beaten track, the ordinary routine of action. 상도(常道); 관례.

throw off the track, give (someone) the slip. …을 따돌리다.

— *vt.* (P6,7) **1** follow (someone or something) by means of footprints, marks, etc. left on the ground. …을 추적하다. ¶ *The hunters tracked the bear and killed it.* 사냥꾼들은 곰을 추적해서 죽였다 / *They tracked the criminal to his hiding place.* 그들은 범인을 은신처까지 추적했다. **2** draw or pull (a ship) from a shore. (배)를 끌다; 예인하다. **3** find out by means of traces. (흔적으로) …을 찾아내다. [F.]

track down, follow after and catch; search and find out; run down. 추적하여 잡다; 수색하여 찾아내다; 따라잡다. ¶ ~ *down an escaped prisoner* 달아난 죄수를 추적 체포하다.

track·less [trǽklis] *adj.* **1** without a track, path, etc. 발자국이 없는; 인적 미답의. ¶ *a* ~ *waste* 인적 없는 황야. **2** having no rails; not running on rails. 궤도가 없는. ¶ ~ *trolleys* 트롤리 버스.

·tract [trækt] *n.* Ⓒ **1** an expanse of land, water, sky, etc. (땅·바다·하늘 등의) 넓이; 넓은 지면; 지역. ¶ *a* ~ *of country* 한 지역 / *an immense* ~ *of land* 광대한 땅 / *a wild mountain* ~ 황량한 산간 지역. **2** 《*poet., arch.*》 a period of time. 기간(期間). **3** 《anat.》 a system of bodily organs serving a particular function. 관(管); 도(道); 계통. ¶ *the digestive* ~ 소화관. **4** a little book or paper on a religious topic. (종교 관계의) 소책자. [L. *tractus* drawing, extent]

trac·ta·ble [trǽktəbəl] *adj.* **1** easily controlled or trained. 다루기 쉬운. ¶ *a* ~ *child*〔*horse*〕 다루기 쉬운 아이〔말〕. **2** easily made into various shapes. 세공하기 쉬운. ¶ *Copper is a* ~ *metal.* 구리는 세공하기 좋은 금속이다.

trac·tile [trǽktil, -tail] *adj.* that can be drawn out to a greater length. 신축성이 있는; 늘어나기 잘 하는. [*tract*]

trac·tion [trǽkʃən] *n.* Ⓤ **1** the act of pulling or drawing along a surface, road, railroad, etc.; the state of being pulled. 끌기; 견인; 끌림. **2** the power used for pulling. 견인력. ¶ *steam*〔*electric*〕 ~ 증기〔전기〕 견인력. **3** friction. 정지(靜止) 마찰. ¶ *Wheels slip on ice because there is too little* ~. 마찰이 너무 적기 때문에 바퀴는 얼음에서 미끌어진다. [*tract*]

traction engine [⌐– ⌐–] *n.* a steam

engine used for pulling heavy trucks along roads or ploughs. 견인차(牽引車).

*__trac·tor__ [trǽktər] *n.* Ⓒ **1** a traction-engine; a heavy vehicle for pulling wagons, plows, etc. 트랙터; 견인차. **2** something used for pulling. 견인자〔물〕. **3** an airplane with engine in front. 견인식 비행기. [*tract*]

:**trade** [treid] *n.* **1** Ⓤ the act of buying, selling or exchanging goods; commerce. 상거래; 장사; 매매; 무역. ¶ *foreign* ~ 해외 무역 / *free* ~ 자유 무역 / *be engaged in* ~ 장사를 하다 / *home* 〔*domestic*〕 ~ 국내 거래 / *The fall in the value of the pound may help to stimulate international* ~. 파운드화의 가치 하락이 국제 무역의 자극제가 될 것이다. **2** Ⓒ an occupation by which a person earns his living, esp. skilled work; a calling. 직업; 가업(家業); 생업. ¶ *Jack of all trades* 무엇이든 좀 아는〔하는〕 사람 / *He is a barber by* ~. 그는 직업이 이발사다 / 《*prov.*》 *Everyone to his* ~. 사람은 저마다 장기가 있는 법 / *He is learning the carpenter's* ~. 그는 목수일을 배우고 있다 / *What is his* ~*?* 그 사람 직업이 뭐냐. **3** Ⓤ 《*collectively*》 all the people engaged in the same kind of work or business. 동업자; (동종)업계. ¶ *the publishing* ~ 출판업자 / *a* ~ *association* 동업(자) 조합 / 《cinema》 *a* ~ *show* 시사(試寫). **4** Ⓤ retail business; shopkeeping. 소매상; 소매업. ¶ *His father was in* ~. 그의 부친은 소매상이었다. **5** Ⓤ customers. 단골; 고객. **6** 《*pl.*》 trade winds. 무역풍.

— *vi., vt.* **1** (P1,3) buy and sell. 매매하다; 거래〔교역〕하다. ¶ ~ *in cotton* 〔*furs*〕 면직물〔모피〕 장사를 하다 / ~ *with America* 미국과 거래하다. **2** (P13) 《*for, with*》 barter; exchange. 교환하다. ¶ *They traded knives with the savages for skins.* 그들은 날붙이를 미개인의 피혁과 교환했다. **3** (P3) 《*to*》 go on trading voyages. (배가) 상품〔화물〕을 나르다. [Teut. (tread)]

trade in, give (one's used automobile, etc.) as part payment for something. …을 웃돈을 주고 신품을 사다. ¶ ~ *in an old car for a new car* 중고차를 얹어 주고 새 차를 사다.

trade on 〔***upon***〕***,*** make use of for one's own ends; take advantage of. …을 이용하다; …에 편승하다. ¶ *He trades on his father's reputation.* 그는 아버지의 명성을 이용한다 / ~ *upon someone's tender heart* 아무의 사람 좋음을 이용하다.

trade·mark [tréidmὰːrk] *n.* Ⓒ a mark, picture, name, or design used by a manufacturer to distinguish his goods from the goods of others. 상표. ¶ *a registered* ~ 등록 상표.

trade name [⌐⌐] *n.* **1** a name given by a manufacturer or dealer to articles that he sells. 상품명. **2** the business name of a company. 상호; 옥호(屋號).

*__trad·er__ [tréidər] *n.* Ⓒ **1** a person engaged in trade. 상인; 무역업자. ¶ *an African* ~ 아프리카 상인. **2** a ship used in trade. 무역선; 상선.

trades·man [tréidzmən] *n.* Ⓒ (*pl.* **-men** [-mən]) **1** a shopkeeper. 소매상(인). **2** a person skilled in a certain craft; a craftsman. 장인(匠人); 장색(匠色).

trades·peo·ple [tréidzpìːpl] *n. pl.* storekeepers; tradesman as a class. 상인; 소매상.

trades union [⌐⌐–] *n.* 《Brit.》 = trade union.

trade union [⌐⌐–] *n.* an association of workers in a particular trade for mutual aid and for the protection of their rights; a labor union. 노동 조합(=《U.S.》 labor union).

trade unionism [⌐⌐––] *n.* the principles, system, or theory of trade unions. 노동 조합의 주의〔조직, 이론〕.

trade wind [⌐⌐] *n.* a wind which blows continuously toward the equator from the northeast on the north and from the southeast on the south. 무역풍.

trading stamp [⌐– ⌐] *n.* a type of stamp given by a shop to a customer each time the customer spends a certain amount, for sticking in a book and later exchanging for goods or money. 경품(景品) 교환권; 경품 스탬프.

:**tra·di·tion** [trədíʃən] *n.* ⓊⒸ **1** the act of handing down beliefs, customs, tales, rules, etc. from generation to generation; things handed down in this way. 구전(口傳); 전승(傳承); 전설; 관습; 인습; 전통. ¶ *The old tales have come down to us by* ~. 옛 설화들이 우리들에게 전승되어 왔다 / *He intends to continue the family* ~ *and seek a career in politics.* 그는 가문의 전통을 이어 정계에 들어갈 생각이다. **2** any time-honored set of practices. 관행. ¶ *cast off old traditions* 묵은 인습을 버리다. [L. *trado* hand over]

tra·di·tion·al [trədíʃənəl] *adj.* of, based on, or handed down by tradition; customary. 전설의; 전통적인. ¶ *The* ~ *English breakfast includes bacon and eggs.* 영국인의 전통적인 아침 식사는 베이컨에 달걀 반숙을 얹은 요리를 먹는다.

tra·di·tion·ar·y [trədíʃənèri / -nəri] *adj.* = traditional.

tra·duce [trədjúːs] *vt.* (P6) speak evil of (someone) falsely; blacken the character of. (남)을 비방하다; 헐뜯다. [L. =lead past (i.e. as a spectacle)]

:**traf·fic** [trǽfik] *n.* Ⓤ **1** trade; the act of buying and selling goods. 매매; 상거래; 교역. **2** the movement of people, cars, ships, etc. from place to place. (사람·차 따위의) 통행; 교통. ¶ *heavy* ~ 격심한 통행〔왕래〕 / *a* ~ *constable* 교통 경찰 / ~ *volume* 교

통량 / ~ *jam* 교통 체증 / *The police control the ~ in large cities.* 대도시에서는 경찰이 교통을 관리한다 / *one-way ~* 일방 통행 / *slow ~ of cars* 차량의 느린 통행 / *a ~ (control) signal* 교통 신호(기). **3** ⓐ business done by a railway line, steamship line, airline, etc. 운송. ⓑ the number of passengers or amount of goods carried. 수송량.

— *vi.* (**-ficked, -fick·ing**) (P3) **1** 《*in, with*》 buy and sell goods; deal in goods. 장사하다; 거래하다. ¶ ~ *in cotton* 무명 장사를 하다 / *They trafficked with the natives for bear skins.* 그들은 원주민과 곰가죽 거래를 했다. **2** 《*for*》 sacrifice. 희생하다. [Rom.]

be opened to traffic, be opened for traffic. 개통하다.

traf·fi·ca·tor [trǽfəkèitər] *n.* Ⓒ a light or other device on a motorcar to show which way it is going to turn. (차량의) 방향 지시기. [↑] 「traffic.

traf·ficked [trǽfikt] *v.* p. and pp. of

traf·fick·er [trǽfikər] *n.* Ⓒ (usu. in a bad sense) a person who buys and sells; a person who carries on an illegal trade; a trader. (부정한) 무역상; 상인. ¶ *a ~ in slaves* 노예 상인 / *drug traffickers* 마약 밀매인.

traf·fick·ing [trǽfikiŋ] *v.* ppr. of **traffic.**

tra·ge·di·an [trədʒíːdiən] *n.* Ⓒ **1** an actor in tragedy. 비극 배우. **2** a writer of tragedies. 비극 작가. [*tragedy*]

***trag·e·dy** [trǽdʒədi] *n.* (*pl.* **-dies**) **1** Ⓤ a drama which has an unhappy ending. (극의) 비극(opp. comedy). **2** Ⓒ a play of this kind of drama. (하나의) 비극 작품. ¶ *'Hamlet' is one of Shakespeare's best known tragedies.* 햄릿은 셰익스피어의 가장 잘 알려진 비극의 하나이다. **3** Ⓤ the act of writing this kind of drama. 비극의 창작. **4** Ⓒ a very sad or dreadful event in real life. 비극적인 사건. ¶ *The father's sudden death was a great ~ to his family.* 아버지의 갑작스러운 사망은 그의 가족에게 큰 비극이었다. [Gk.]

***trag·ic** [trǽdʒik] *adj.* **1** of or like tragedy. 비극의; 비극적인. ¶ *a ~ actor* 〔*poet*〕 비극 배우〔시인〕. **2** very sad; feeling or showing great unhappiness. 비참한; 참혹한; 애처로운. ¶ *a ~ death* 비참한 죽음 / *a ~ accident* 끔찍한 사고 / *a ~ face* 〔*voice*〕 애처로운 표정〔음성〕. [Gk.]

trag·i·cal [trǽdʒikəl] *adj.* =tragic.

trag·i·cal·ly [trǽdʒikəli] *adv.* in a tragic manner. 비극적으로; 비참하게.

trag·i·com·e·dy [træ̀dʒəkɑ́mədi / -dʒi-kɔ́m-] *n.* ⓊⒸ (*pl.* **-dies**) a play or story containing both tragic and comic elements; a real event or situation like this. 희비극(喜悲劇). [*tragic*]

trag·i·com·ic [træ̀dʒəkɑ́mik / -dʒikɔ́m-] *adj.* of tragicomedy. 희비극적인. [↑]

:**trail** [treil] *n.* Ⓒ **1** a mark, footprint, etc. left by a person or animal; a smell left by an animal on the ground. 지나간 자국; 발자국; (짐승의) 냄새 자국. ¶ *a ~ of blood* 핏자국 / *His ~ stops just there.* 그의 발자국은 바로 거기서 그쳤다 / *He followed their trails carefully.* 그들이 남긴 흔적을 주의깊게 따라갔다. **2** a path or track made by treading through woods or wilderness. (산 속·들판에 난) 길. ¶ *follow a ~ through the woods* 숲 속의 길을 따라가다. **3** a stream of dust, smoke, light, etc. that is made behind something that has passed. (연기 등이) 길게 뻗친; (유성(流星) 등의) 꼬리; (차량 등의) 줄; 열. ¶ *The car left a ~ of dust behind it.* 차가 한 줄기 먼지를 남기고 지나갔다.

off the trail, **a**) out of the right course. 정도를 벗어나. ¶ *throw someone off the ~* 아무를 그릇 인도하다. **b**) off the track. (사냥개가) 냄새 자국을 잃어; 길을 잃어.

on the trail (***of***)***,*** pursuing on the right course. …을 추적(追跡)하여. ¶ *The police are on the ~ of the criminal.* 경찰이 범인을 추적하고 있다 / *hot on the ~* 맹렬히 추적하여.

— *vt.* **1** (P6,7) pull (something) behind oneself along the ground, floor, etc. …을 (질질) 끌다. ¶ *The woman trailed her dress through the mud.* 부인은 진창에 옷자락을 질질 끌며 갔다 / *He sat on the side of the boat and trailed his feet in the water.* 그는 뱃전에 앉아 양 발을 물 속에 담그고 갔다. **2** (P6) follow the track left by (something); hunt by smell, evidence, etc. …의 뒤를 좇다; 추적하다. ¶ *The cat trailed the mouse.* 고양이는 쥐를 좇아갔다 / *~ someone to his hiding place* 아무를 은신처까지 뒤밟다. **3** (P6) 《U.S.》 make (a path, track) by treading down grass, plants, etc. 밟아서 (길)을 내다. ¶ *~ a path.*

— *vi.* (P1,2A,3) **1** fall or hang down so as to sweep along the ground. 끌리다. ¶ *Her dress trailed.* 그녀의 옷이 질질 끌렸다. **2** (of a plant) grow along the ground or over a surface. (덩굴이) 붙어서 뻗어 가다. ¶ *The ivies ~ over the walls.* 담쟁이가 온 벽면에 뻗어 있다. **3** (of a person) walk slowly and wearily. 발을 질질 끌며 가다. **4** ⓐ float or drift in a stream. 구름 따위가 흐르듯이 길게 뻗치다. ¶ *Smoke trails in the air.* 연기가 공중으로 피어오르고 있다. ⓑ become gradually weak or faint. 점점 약해지다. ¶ *His voice trailed off.* 그의 음성은 점점 작아졌다. [→tract]

trail·er [tréilər] *n.* Ⓒ **1** a person or animal that follows another secretly. 추적자. **2** a vine or plant creeping along the ground or over walls. 덩굴 식물; 만초(蔓草). **3** a wagon, cart, etc. pulled along behind by another automobile, truck, etc. 트레일러.

:**train** [trein] *vt.* **1** (P6,7,13,20) teach; bring up; instruct; rear. …을 가르치다; 교육하다. ¶ *~ a boy to obey* 〔*to obedience*〕 소년을 말을 잘 듣도록 가르치다 / *She is training her daughter as a doctor.* 그녀는 딸을 의사가 되도

록 가르치고 있다. **2** (P6,7,13,20) make (someone) do often so as to be skillful; practice; drill. …을 훈련시키다; 길들이다. ¶ ~ *dancers* 댄서들을 가르치다 / ~ *a boy to play the piano* 아이에게 피아노를 가르치다 / ~ *dogs to catch rabbits* 개에게 토끼를 잡도록 훈련시키다 / ~ *girls to read music at sight* 소녀들을 악보를 보고 읽도록 훈련시키다 / *These dogs are trained to detect explosive.* 이 개들은 폭발물을 발견하도록 훈련되어 있다. **3** (P6,13) 《*on, upon*》 aim; direct. …을 목표로 향하게 하다; 조준하다. ¶ ~ *a camera on the scene* 카메라를 장면 쪽으로 돌리다 / ~ *guns upon enemy ships* 대포를 적의 함대 쪽으로 조준하다. **4** (P6,13) cause (plants) to grow in a certain way. …을 취향에 맞는 모양으로 가꾸다. ¶ ~ *vines around a post* 덩굴이 기둥을 감아 오르게 하다 / ~ *roses against the wall* 장미가 담장을 타고 뻗게 하다. — *vi.* **1** (P1,3) 《*for, on*》 prepare for something by practice. 훈련〔연습〕하다. ¶ ~ *for a race.* **2** (P1,2A,2B) go by train. 기차로 가다.

train down, get oneself into condition. 단련하여 체중을 줄이다.

train off, go wildly. (탄알이) 빗나가다.

— *n.* Ⓒ **1** a line of railroad cars. 열차. ¶ *a passenger* ~ 여객 열차 / *an express* ~ 급행 열차 / *a through* ~ 직행 열차 / *take the 8:30 (a.m.)* ~ *to the city* 시로 가는 오전 여덟 시 반 기차를 타다. **2** a group of followers; a procession. (일단의) 수행원; 행렬. ¶ *the princess and her* ~ 공주와 그 수행원들 / *a funeral* ~ 장례 행렬 / *a long* ~ *of camels* 긴 낙타의 행렬. **3** a group of things happening one after another. (사건의) 연속. ¶ *a* ~ *of events* 〔*thought*〕 일련의 사건〔사고(思考)〕 / *a long* ~ *of misfortunes* 긴 불행의 연속. **4** something that trails. (끌리는) 옷자락; (길게 끌리는) 꼬리. ¶ *the* ~ *of her gown* 끌리는 그녀의 드레스 / *the* ~ *of a comet* 혜성의 꼬리 / *the* ~ *of a peacock* 공작의 긴 꼬리. **5** a line of gunpowder that act as a fuse. 도화선. **6** a course of action; a process of movement, development, etc. 순서; 절차. [L. *traho* drag, draw]

by train, by the railway. 열차로(cf. *by sea*). ¶ *go by* ~ 열차로 가다.

in (***good***) ***train,*** ready to operate. 만반의 준비가 되어.

in the train of, following. …에 잇따라. ¶ *in the* ~ *of peace* 평화의 뒤를 이어.

⁎**train·er** [tréinər] *n.* Ⓒ a person who trains people for sports contests, animals for races, etc. 훈련시키는 사람; 코치; 조련사(調練師).

train ferry [⌐⌐] *n.* a ferryboat to carry a railway train (usu. loaded). 열차 연락선.

:**train·ing** [tréiniŋ] *n.* Ⓤ **1** the act of instructing or exercising. 훈련; 연습. ¶ *go into* ~ 훈련에 들어가다 / ~ *for teachers* 교사 양성 / *a school for the* ~ *of nurses* 간호사 양성 학교; 간호 학교 / *a* ~ *program* 훈련 계획. **2** good condition kept by such instruction or exercise. (연습에 의한 좋은) 컨디션. ¶ *be in* 〔*out of*〕 ~ *for a race* 경기하기에 컨디션이 좋다〔나쁘다〕. **3** the act of controlling plants to grow them in a desirable shape. (정원수 등의) 다듬기; 가꾸기; 정지(整枝). [*train*]

training college [⌐⌐⌐] *n.* a college for training school-teachers. 교육 대학 (《U.S.》 a teachers college).

train·man [tréinmən] *n.* Ⓒ (*pl.* **-men** [-mən]) 《U.S.》 a person employed to work on a train, esp. a brakeman. 열차 승무원 (제동수(制動手) 등).

train-oil [tréinɔ̀il] *n.* Ⓤ whale-blubber oil. 고래 기름. [Du. *traan* train oil]

traipse, trapes [treips] *vi.* (P1,2A) walk about idly, aimlessly, or wearily. 어슬렁거리다. ¶ ~ *up and down a street* 공연히 거리를 왔다갔다하다. [? *tramp*]

trait [treit] *n.* Ⓒ **1** a characteristic; a distinguishing mark. 특성; 특징. ¶ *English traits* 영국의 국민성 / *a* ~ *of humor* 익살기 / *Honesty and diligence are the chief traits of his character.* 정직과 근면이 그의 성격의 주된 특징이다. **2** 《*arch.*》 a stroke in a drawing. 휘호(揮毫). [→trace]

⁎**trai·tor** [tréitər] *n.* Ⓒ 《*to*》 a person who betrays his country, friends, etc. 반역자. ¶ *turn* 〔*become*〕 ~ *to* …에 반역하다; 배신하다 / *He was hanged as a* ~. 그는 반역자로서 교수형을 당했다. [→tradition]

trai·tor·ous [tréitərəs] *adj.* of a traitor; unfaithful. 반역의; 불충한.

trai·tor·ous·ly [tréitərəsli] *adv.* in a traitorous way. 반역하여.

trai·tress [tréitris] *n.* Ⓒ a woman traitor. 여성 반역자.

tra·jec·to·ry [trədʒéktəri] *n.* Ⓒ (*pl.* **-ries**) the curved path of something shot through space, such as a rocket or comet. 탄도(彈道); 궤도. [trans-, L. *jacio* throw]

⁎**tram** [træm] *n.* Ⓒ **1** 《Brit.》 a car on an electric railway running in the street; a tramcar. (시내) 전차. ¶ *go by* ~ 전차로 가다. **2** a tramline. 전차 선로. **3** a truck or car on which loads are carried in coal-mines. 광차(鑛車); 석탄 운반차. — *vt., vi.* (**trammed, tram·ming**) (P6;1,3) travel or carry by tram. 전차로 가다; …을 전차〔광차〕로 나르다. [Teut. =beam]

tram·car [trǽmkɑ̀ːr] *n.* Ⓒ 《Brit.》 a streetcar. 시내 전차.

tram·line [trǽmlàin] *n.* Ⓒ 《Brit.》 a streetcar line. 전차 선로; 전찻길.

tram·mel [trǽməl] *n.* Ⓒ **1** 《*pl.*》 anything that checks and stops free action, movement, etc. 방해; 속박; 장애물. ¶ *the trammels of etiquette* 〔*custom*〕 예절〔관습〕 속박; 번거로운〔귀찮은〕 예절〔관습〕. **2** a net for catching fish or birds. (물고기·새 잡는) 그물. **3** a hook for holding pots, kettles, etc. over a fire. (화덕 위에 냄비를 매다는)

자재(自在) 갈고리. —— *vt.* (**-meled, -mel·ing,** 《Brit.》 **-melled, mel·ling**) (P6) prevent the free movement of (someone); hinder. …을 방해하다. [tri-, L. *macula* mesh]

·**tramp** [træmp] *vt., vi.* **1** (P1,2A,3) walk with a firm, heavy step. (힘있게) 쿵쿵 걷다. ¶ *We heard soldiers tramping by.* 군인들이 저벅저벅 (군화 소리를 내며) 지나가는 소리를 들었다. **2** (P6; 2A,2B,3) travel about on foot; go on foot. 걸어서 가다; 도보 여행을 하다. ¶ ~ *it* 터벅터벅 걷다 / ~ *up and down* 여기저기 걸어다니다 / *We tramped a hundred miles.* 우리는 백 마일을 걸었다 / *They tramped the streets all night.* 그들은 밤새도록 거리를 돌아다녔다. **3** (P2A) step heavily; tread. …을 짓밟다. ¶ ~ *the snow down* 눈을 꽉꽉 밟(아 다지)다 / ~ *on a snail* 달팽이를 짓밟다.

—— *n.* Ⓒ **1** the act of tramping. 밟음; 짓밟음. **2** the sound of heavy steps. 저벅거리는 발소리. ¶ *the ~ of marching feet* 행진하는 발소리. **3** a person who travels about on foot doing odd jobs or begging; a wanderer. 도보 여행자; 떠돌이; 방랑자. ¶ *look like a* ~ 차림새가 추레하다 / *on* (*the*) ~ 방랑하여; 떠돌아다녀. **4** a ship which takes goods when and where it can. 부정기 화물선.

●**tramp·er** [-ər] *n.* [Teut.]

·**tram·ple** [trǽmpəl] *vi., vt.* (P2A,3; 6,7) **1** walk over and press down with the feet. 짓밟다; 밟아 뭉개다. ¶ ~ *grapes* 포도를 밟아 으깨다 / ~ *grass down* 풀을 밟아 눕히다 / *Don't ~ on the flowers.* 꽃을 밟지 마라 / ~ *on someone's right* 〔*liberty*〕 아무의 권리〔자유〕를 짓밟다 / ~ *down someone's feeling* 아무의 감정을 해치다. **2** walk with heavy steps. 쿵쿵거리며 걷다. ¶ ~ *about* 쿵쾅거리며 돌아다니다. —— *n.* Ⓤ the act or sound of trampling. 쿵쿵거리며 걸음; 짓밟음; 그 소리. [↑]

tram·po·line [trǽmpəlìːn, ⌐-⌐] *n.* 《sports》 a large canvas sheet stretched in a frame by springs for exercising on. 트램폴린. [Sp.]

tram·way [trǽmwèi] *n.* 《Brit.》 the track for trams. 시내 전차 궤도. [*tram*]

trance [træns, trɑːns] *n.* Ⓒ **1** an unconscious state like sleep; a deep sleep produced by illness. 인사 불성; 혼수 상태. ¶ *fall into a* ~ 실신하다. **2** a dreamy state; ecstasy. 황홀(경); 몽환(夢幻)(의 상태). ●**trance·like** [-làik] *adj.* [trans-, L. *eo* go]

·**tran·quil** [trǽŋkwil] *adj.* (**-quil·er, -quil·est,** 《Brit.》 **-quil·ler, -quil·lest**) calm; peaceful; quiet. 조용한; 평온한; 차분한; 고요한. ¶ *live a ~ life* 조용하게 살다 / *a ~ face* 평화로운 얼굴 / *a ~ lake* 고요한 호수. [L.]

tran·quil·ize, -quil·lize [trǽŋkwəlàiz] *vt., vi.* (P6;1,2A) make (something) or become calm and peaceful. 잠잠하게 하다〔되다〕; 진정시키다〔되다〕; 조용해지다; (마음을〔이〕) 차분하게 하다〔되다〕.

tran·quil·iz·er, -quil·liz- [trǽŋkwəlàizər] *n.* Ⓒ **1** a person or thing that tranquilizes. 진정시키는 사람〔것〕. **2** a medicine that controls a person's anxiety, fear, etc. 진정제; 신경 안정제.

tran·quil·li·ty, -quil·i- [træŋkwíləti] *n.* Ⓤ the state of being tranquil; calmness. 평온; 침착; 고요.

trans- [træns-, trænz-] *pref.* **1** across. '횡단하여'의 뜻. ¶ *transcontinental.* **2** beyond. '초월하여'의 뜻. ¶ *transcend.* **3** on the other side of. '다른 쪽으로'의 뜻. ¶ *transatlantic.* **4** into a different state, quality, etc. '다른 상태〔장소〕로'의 뜻. ¶ *transform.* [L.]

trans·act [trænsǽkt, trænz-] *vt.* (P6) conduct; manage; perform (business). (업무·교섭 등)을 행하다; (사무 등)을 처리〔집행〕하다. ¶ *He transacts business with several stores in Seoul.* 그는 서울의 몇 상점과 거래하고 있다. —— *vi.* (P3) 《*with*》 do business. 거래하다. [→act]

trans·ac·tion [trænsǽkʃən, trænz-] *n.* **1** Ⓤ the act of transacting; the state of being transacted. (사무) 처리. **2** Ⓒ something transacted; a business deal; a piece of business. 상거래; 매매; 업무. ¶ *be engaged in various transactions* 여러 가지 일을 하고 있다. **3** 《*pl.*》 the published records of what was done at the meetings of a society, a club, etc. 의사〔회의〕록; 회보; 보고서.

trans·al·pine [trænsǽlpain, trænz-] *adj.* beyond the Alps as seen from Italy; passing through the Alps. 알프스 저편의; 알프스 횡단의. [→Alpine]

trans·at·lan·tic [trænsətlǽntik, trænz-] *adj.* **1** crossing the Atlantic. 대서양 횡단의. ¶ *a ~ liner* 대서양 항로 정기선(定期船). **2** on the other side of the Atlantic. 대서양 건너편의. [→atlas]

trans·ceiv·er [trænssíːvər] *n.* 《radio》 a small, portable receiving and transmitting radio set. 트랜스시버(cf. *walkie-talkie*). [*trans*mitter, re*ceiver*]

tran·scend [trænsénd] *vt.* (P6) **1** go or rise beyond the limits of. (한계·범위)를 넘다. ¶ ~ *words* 말로 표현할 길이 없다 / ~ *the limits of human power* 인간의 힘의 한계를 넘다 / ~ *understanding* 이해할 길이 없다. **2** be superior to; surpass; exceed. …보다 뛰어나다; …을 능가하다. ¶ *His latest symphony transcends anything he has ever written before.* 그의 최근의 교향곡은 이전에 지은 어떤 것보다도 뛰어나다. [L. *scando* climb]

tran·scend·ence [trænséndəns] *n.* Ⓤ the state or quality of being transcendent. 초월; 탁월. ⌈transcendence.

tran·scend·en·cy [trænséndənsi] *n.* =

tran·scend·ent [trænséndənt] *adj.* **1** much

more excellent than others in quality or extent. 탁월한; 뛰어난. ¶ *the ~ beauty of a sunset* 해질녘 하늘의 비길 데 없는 아름다움 / *the ~ genius of Mozart* 모차르트의 탁월한 천재성. **2** 《theol.》 outside of the universe. 초월적인. —*n.* Ⓒ a person or thing that is transcendent. 탁월한 사람〔물건〕. ● **tran·scend·ent·ly** [-li] *adv.*

tran·scen·den·tal [trӕnsendéntl] *adj.* **1** =transcendent. **2** 《philos.》 beyond human knowledge, experience, or thought. (인간의 경험·지식을) 초월한; 선험적(先驗的)인. **3** supernatural. 초자연적인.

trans·con·ti·nen·tal [trӕnskɑntənéntl / -kɔnt-] *adj.* **1** crossing a continent. 대륙 횡단의. ¶ *a ~ railway* 〔*railroad*〕 대륙 횡단 철도. **2** on the other side of a continent. 대륙 저쪽의. [*continent*]

tran·scribe [trӕnskráib] *vt.* (P6) **1** copy (something) by writing or typewriting. …을 베끼다; 복사하다. ¶ *~ a document* 문서를 복사하다 / *~ a conversation from a tape-recording* 녹음 테이프의 대화를 필기하다. **2** arrange (music) for an instrument, voice, etc. …을 편곡하다. **3** make a recording of (something) for broadcasting. …을 녹음하다. **4** represent in another language, alphabet, or other form. …을 번역하다; 다른 글자로 옮겨 쓰다. ¶ *~ a sentence into English* 〔*phonetic signs*〕 어떤 문장을 영어〔음표 문자〕로 옮기다. ● **tran·scrib·er** [-ər] *n.* [→scribble]

tran·script [trǽnskript] *n.* Ⓒ a written, printed, or typewritten copy; a reproduction of another document. 베낀 것; 사본. ¶ *A ~ of the tape was presented as evidence in court.* 테이프의 사본 하나가 법원에 증거로 제출되었다.

tran·scrip·tion [trӕnskrípʃən] *n.* **1** Ⓤ the act of transcribing. 전사(轉寫). **2** Ⓒ a copy. 사본. **3** ⒸⓊ the act of recording or broadcasting a phonograph record, a play, etc. (라디오의) 녹음 (방송).

:trans·fer [trӕnsfə́ːr] *v.* (**-ferred, -fer·ring**) *vt.* (P6,13) **1** carry or remove (something) from one place or person to another. …을 옮기다; 이동하다. ¶ *~ a book from a table to a shelf* 탁자의 책을 선반에 옮기다 / *~ a boy to another school* 아이를 다른 학교로 전학시키다 / *That football player is hoping to ~ to another team soon.* 저 축구 선수는 빨리 다른 팀으로 이적했으면 한다 / *~ one's affection to another object* 애정을 다른 대상으로 옮기다. **2** 《*to*》 give over the possession of (something). (재산 등)을 양도하다. ¶ *This farm has been transferred to him.* 이 농장은 그에게 양도되었다. **3** copy or imprint (a drawing, design, etc.) on one surface from another. (그림 등)을 전사하다. ¶ *Callas's original recording has been transferred to compact disc.* 칼라스의 본디의 녹음이 콤팩트 디스크로 복제(複製)되었다.

—*vi.* (P1,3) **1** change from one train, bus, etc. to another. 갈아타다. ¶ *~ from a train to a bus* 기차에서 버스로 갈아타다. **2** change from one place or position to another. 이동하다; 전근〔전학〕하다.

—[trǽnsfər] *n.* **1** ⓊⒸ the act of transferring; the state of being transferred. 이전; 이동. ¶ *She wants for a ~ to another part of the company.* 그녀는 회사의 다른 부서로 옮기고 싶어한다. **2** Ⓒ 《U.S.》 a place for changing trains, buses, etc. 갈아타는 곳. **3** Ⓒ 《U.S.》 a ticket allowing someone to change a train, bus, etc. 갈아타는 표. **4** ⓐ Ⓤ the act of giving over a right or possession from one person to another. (재산·권리의) 양도. ⓑ Ⓒ 《law》 (a document effecting) a conveyance of property. 양도 증서. **5** Ⓒ a picture, design, pattern, etc. that is imprinted from a surface to another. 전사한 그림〔무늬〕. [L. *fero* carry]

trans·fer·a·ble [trӕnsfə́ːrəbəl] *adj.* that can be transferred. 옮길 수 있는; 양도 가능한; 전사할 수 있는.

trans·fer·ence [trӕnsfə́ːrəns, trǽnsfər-] *n.* Ⓤ the act of transferring; the state of being transferred. 이전; 양도.

trans·fig·u·ra·tion [trӕnsfigjəréiʃən] *n.* **1** ⓊⒸ the act of transfiguring; the state of being transfigured. 변모. **2** 《*the T-*》 the supernatural change in appearance of Christ recorded in the New Testament. (예수의) 현성용(顯聖容). [↓]

trans·fig·ure [trӕnsfígjər, -fígər] *vt.* (P6) **1** change (something) in appearance or form of. …의 모습을 바꾸다. **2** make (something) bright and beautiful; make more glorious. (얼굴 등)을 (기쁨으로) 밝게〔환하게〕하다. ¶ *Hope transfigured his face.* 희망으로 그의 얼굴은 밝아졌다 / *a face transfigured with happiness* 행복으로 환해진 얼굴. [→figure]

trans·fix [trӕnsfíks] *vt.* (P6,13) **1** 《*with*》 make a hole through (something) with a sharp-pointed tool. …을 꿰뚫다. ¶ *~ a bird with an arrow* 새를 화살로 꿰뚫다 / *an animal transfixed with a spear* 창에 찔린 짐승. **2** make (someone) motionless with surprise, terror, etc. …을 꼼짝 못 하게 하다. ¶ *be transfixed with terror* 무서워서 움직이지 못하다. [→fix]

***trans·form** [trӕnsfɔ́ːrm] *vt.* (P6,13) **1** change (something or someone) in form or appearance. …의 외형을 바꾸다; …을 변형시키다. ¶ *A caterpillar is transformed into a butterfly.* 풀쐐기가 나비로 탈바꿈하다 / *~ a barn into a garage* 헛간을 차고로 고치다. **2** change (something or someone) in nature; change (something) from one form of energy to another; change into one of higher or lower voltage; change into a difference substance. …의 성질〔기능〕을 바꾸다; 에너지를 변환하다; 변압(變壓)하다;

…을 다른 물질로 바꾸다. ¶ *Heat transforms ice into water.* 열은 얼음을 물로 바꾼다 / *A steam engine transforms heat into power.* 증기 기관은 열을 동력으로 변환한다. **3** change (someone) in character or personality. …을 다른 사람이 되게 하다. ¶ ~ *a criminal into a good and honest man* 범죄자를 착하고 정직한 사람으로 만들다 / *Getting that new job has completely transformed her!* 새 일자리를 얻자 그녀는 완전히 다른 사람이 됐다. [→form]

trans·for·ma·tion [trӕ̀nsfərméiʃən] *n.* UC the act of transforming; the state, condition of being transformed. 변형; 변질; 변태(變態). ¶ *the* ~ *of a silkworm into a cocoon* 누에의 고치로의 변태.

trans·form·er [trӕnsfɔ́:rmər] *n.* C **1** a person or thing that transforms something. 변화시키는 사람(것). **2** 《electr.》 a device for changing the current of electrical voltage. 트랜스; 변압기.

trans·fuse [trӕnsfjú:z] *vt.* (P6) **1** transfer (water, etc.) from one glass into another. (액체 등을) 옮겨 따르다(붓다). **2** transfer (blood) from one person into another. 수혈하다. [→fuse]

trans·fu·sion [trӕnsfjú:ʒən] *n.* UC the act of transfusing. 옮겨붓기; 수혈. ¶ *receive a blood* ~ 수혈을 받다.

trans·gress [trӕnsgrés, trӕnz-] *vt., vi.* (P6; 1) **1** break a law or rule; break moral or religious principles. (법규 등을) 어기다; (도덕적인 죄를) 범하다. ¶ ~ *the law* (*the divine commands*) 법(신의 율법)을 어기다. **2** go without control; go beyond (any limit). (한계를) 넘다. ¶ ~ *the bounds of good manners* 바른 예의 범절의 한계를 벗어나다. [L. *gradior* walk]

trans·gres·sion [trӕnsgréʃən, trӕnz-] *n.* UC the act of transgressing; breaking a law, rule, etc. 위반; (종교·도덕상의) 죄.

trans·gres·sor [trӕnsgrésər, trӕnz-] *n.* C a person who transgresses; a sinner. 위반자; (종교·도덕상의) 죄인.

tran·sient [trǽnʃənt, -ziənt] *adj.* not lasting; temporary; lasting but a short time. 일시적인; 짧은; 덧없는. ¶ *the* ~ *affairs of this life* 덧없는 인생 / *a* ~ *smile* 잠깐 보인 미소 / ~ *joys* (*pleasure*) 일시적인 기쁨(쾌락). — *n.* C 《U.S.》 a visitor who stays for a short time. 단기 체류객. ¶ *a motel for transients* 단기 체류객을 위한 모텔. [→trance]

tran·sient·ly [trǽnʃəntli, -ziənt-] *adv.* for a moment; for a short time; briefly. 일시적으로; 덧없이.

tran·sis·tor [trӕnzístər, -sís-] *n.* C **1** a small electronic device for controlling the current, used in portable radios, etc. 트랜지스터. **2** 《*colloq.*》 a radio with transistors in it. 트랜지스터 라디오. [*trans*fer, re*sister*]

trans·it [trǽnsit, -zit] *n.* U **1** the act of passing or carrying across or through; the state of being passed or carried across or through. 통과; 수송. ¶ *allow two days for the* ~ *of the lake* 호수 통과에 이틀이 걸리다 / ~ *duty* 통행세 / *overland* ~ 육상 수송로 / *the* ~ *of goods* 물자 수송 / *The goods were damaged in* ~. 물건들이 수송 중에 손상됐다. **2** 《astron.》 the passing of a heavenly body across the disc of a larger one or across the meridian. (천체의) 다른 천체면 통과; (천체의) 자오선(子午線) 통과. **3** = transit compass. [→trance]

transit compass [´– ⌣–] *n.* an instrument with a telescope for measuring horizontal angles. (토지 측량용) 트랜싯.

tran·si·tion [trӕnzíʃən, -síʃən] *n.* UC **1** the change or movement from one place, period, state, etc., to another. 변이(變移); 변천; 과도기. ¶ *the* ~ *from boyhood to manhood* 소년기에서 장년기로의 이행 / *a* ~ *period* 과도기 / *a rapid* ~ *from poverty to wealth* 가난에서 부(富)로의 빠른 변천. **2** 《mus.》 a sudden change from one key to another. 일시적 조(調)바꿈; 이행부; 추이.

tran·si·tion·al [trӕnzíʃənəl, -síʃ-] *adj.* of transition. 과도기의. ¶ *The tadpole is a* ~ *form between egg and frog.* 올챙이는 알에서 개구리로의 중간 단계다.

•**tran·si·tive** [trǽnsətiv, -zə-] *adj.* 《gram.》 taking a direct object to complete the meaning. 타동(他動)의(cf. *intransitive*). ¶ *a* ~ *verb* 타동사. — *n.* C a transitive verb. 타동사.

tran·si·to·ry [trǽnsətɔ̀:ri / -təri] *adj.* passing or changing quickly; lasting only a short time. 일시적인; 순간의; 덧없는. ¶ *this* ~ *life* 덧없는 인생.

•**trans·late** [trӕnsléit, trӕnz-] *vt.* **1** (P6,13) change (a language) into another language. …을 번역하다. ¶ ~ *English into Korean* 영어를 한국어로 번역하다 / ~ *word for word* 축어역(逐語譯)을 하다 / ~ *a story from France into English* 프랑스어로 된 이야기를 영어로 번역하다. **2** (P6,13) change into another words. 다른 말로 바꾸다; 환언하다. ¶ ~ *scientific language for the laymen* 과학 용어를 문외한도 알 수 있게 바꾸다. **3** (P6,13) change the state, position, or form of (something). …을 옮기다; 변형시키다. ¶ ~ *promises* (*emotion*) *into action* 약속을 실행에 옮기다(감정을 행동으로 나타내다) / ~ *an invention into money* 발명품을 팔다 / *She was translated to fairy palace in a second.* 그녀는 순식간에 요정의 궁전으로 옮겨졌다. **4** (P6,7) explain the meaning of (something); interpret. …을 해석하다. **5** (P6,13) 《Bible》 convey to heaven without death. …을 산 채로 승천시키다.

— *vi.* (P1) **1** put something written or spoken from one language into another. 번역하다. **2** be able to be translated. 번역할 수 있다. ¶ *This novel translates well.* 이 소설

은 번역하기 쉽다 / *Poetry does not* ~ *easily.* 시는 번역이 쉽지 않다.

● **trans·lat·a·ble** [-əbəl] *adj.* [→transfer]

***trans·la·tion** [trænsléiʃən, trænz-] *n.* **1** Ⓤ the act of translating; the state of being translated. 번역; 변형. ¶ *literal* ~ 직역. **2** Ⓒ something translated, esp. of a literary work. 번역된 것; 번역물. ¶ *I've only read Tolstoy in* ~. 나는 톨스토이 작품을 번역판으로만 읽었다.

trans·la·tor [trænsléitər, trænz-] *n.* Ⓒ a person who translates books, speeches, etc. 번역자; 통역인.

trans·lit·er·ate [trænslítərèit, trænz-] *vt.* (P6,13) change (words, letters, etc.) into symbols of another alphabet or language that represent the same sounds. …을 음역하다; (다른 나라의 해당 문자)로 고쳐쓰다; 자역(字譯)하다. ¶ ~ *Korean into Roman letters* 한국어를 로마자로 표기하다. [→letter]

trans·lu·cence [trænslú:səns, trænz-] *n.* Ⓤ the state or quality of being translucent. 반투명(半透明). [↓]

trans·lu·cent [trænslú:sənt, trænz-] *adj.* letting the light pass through, but not transparent. 반투명의. ¶ *Frosted glass is* ~. 젖빛 유리는 반투명이다. [→lucid]

trans·mi·grant [trænsmáigrənt, trænz-] *n.* an alien passing through a country on his way to another. 이주(移住)자. [↓]

trans·mi·gra·tion [træ̀nsmaigréiʃən, træ̀nz-] *n.* Ⓤ **1** the act of moving from one place or country to another. 이주(移住). **2** the passage of a soul at death into a new body or a new life. 전생(轉生); 윤회(輪廻). [*migrate*]

trans·mis·si·ble [trænsmísəbəl, trænz-] *adj.* that can be transmitted. 전할 수 있는; 유전성(전염성)의. ¶ *a* ~ *disease* 전염병. [↓]

trans·mis·sion [trænsmíʃən, trænz-] *n.* Ⓤ **1** the act of transmitting; the state of being transmitted. 전달; 전염; 양도. ¶ *the* ~ *of news* 뉴스 전달 / *the* ~ *of disease* 질병의 전염. **2** the broadcasting of radio waves from a transmitting station to a receiving station. 송신(送信). ¶ *We interrupt our normal transmissions to bring you a special news flash.* 뉴스 속보(速報)를 전해 드리기 위해 우리의 정규 방송은 중단합니다. **3** Ⓒ the part of an automobile which transmits power from the engine to the driving wheels. 트랜스미션; 전동(傳動)장치. [→transmit]

trans·mit [trænsmít, trænz-] *vt.* (**-mit·ted, -mit·ting**) (P6,13) **1** send. …을 보내다; 발송하다. ¶ ~ *the parcel by train* 소포를 철도편으로 보내다 / ~ *a letter by hand* 편지를 사람을 시켜 보내다. **2** hand down (something) from parents to children. (자손)에게 전하다. ¶ ~ *the title from father to son* 아버지가 아들에게 소유권을 물려주다. **3** spread (disease) to others. (질병 등)을 전염시키다. ¶ *Rats* ~ *disease.* 쥐는 질병을 전염시킨다. **4** pass on (news, information, etc.). …을 전하다. **5** cause or allow (light, heat, electricity, etc.) to pass through. (열·전기 따위)를 전도하다; 투과시키다. ¶ *Glass transmits light but not sound.* 유리는 빛을 투과시키지만 소리는 투과시키지 못한다. **6** send out (signals, a voice, etc.) by radio. (전파·신호 등)을 보내다. ¶ *The survivors of the shipwreck transmitted a distress signal every hour.* 난파선의 생존자들은 매시간 조난 신호를 보냈다 / ~ *news by wire* 뉴스를 전보(전화)로 알리다. [L. *mitto* send]

trans·mit·ter [trænsmítər, trænz-] *n.* Ⓒ **1** a person or thing that transmits. 송달(전달)자; 양도자; 전도물(傳導物). **2** a device for sending out signals, messages, a voice, etc., such as the mouthpiece of a telephone or a radio set. 송신기.

trans·mu·ta·tion [træ̀nsmju:téiʃən, træ̀nz-] *n.* Ⓤ the act of transmuting; the state of being transmuted; a change from one nature, substance, or form into another. 변형; 변질. [↓]

trans·mute [trænsmjú:t, trænz-] *vt.* (P6,13) change (something) into another form, nature or substance; transform. …을 변화시키다; 변형(변질)시키다. ¶ ~ *water power into electric power* 수력을 전력으로 바꾸다 / *Medieval alchemists attempted to* ~ *base metals into gold.* 중세의 연금술사(師)들은 비(卑)금속을 황금으로 변화시키려고 했다. [L. *muto* change]

trans·o·ce·an·ic [træ̀nsouʃiǽnik, træ̀nz-] *adj.* **1** crossing the ocean. 대양 횡단의. **2** located on the other side of the ocean. 대양 저쪽의. [→ocean]

tran·som [trǽnsəm] *n.* Ⓒ **1** a small hinged window above a door or other window; a transom window. (문 위쪽의) 채광창(採光窓). **2** a horizontal crossbar across the top of a window or door. 교창(交窓) 아래의 상인방(上引枋). [L. *transtrum*] 〈transom 1〉

trans·pa·cif·ic [træ̀nspəsífik] *adj.* **1** crossing the Pacific. 태평양 횡단의. **2** located on the other side of the Pacific. 태평양 저쪽의. [→pacific]

trans·par·en·cy [trænspέərənsi] *n.* **1** Ⓤ the state or quality of being transparent. 투명(성). **2** Ⓒ something transparent; a picture, design, etc. on glass made visible when light shines through. 투명한 것; 투명화(무늬) (등). [↓]

***trans·par·ent** [trænspέərənt] *adj.* **1** so clear or thin that objects on the other side can be seen. 투명한(opp. opaque). ¶ ~ *colors* 투명 그림물감 / *Window glass is* ~. 창유리는 투명하다 / (*as*) ~ *as air* 공기처

럼 투명한. **2** frank. 솔직한. **3** easy to recognize or find out. 명백한; 평이한. ¶ *The meaning of this passage seems quite* ~. 이 구절의 뜻은 아주 명료해 보인다. **4** ill adapted to deceive; obvious. 빤히 들여다보이는. ¶ *a* ~ *lie* 뻔한 거짓말. [L. *pareo* appear]

trans·par·ent·ly [trænspέərəntli] *adv.* in a transparent manner. 투명하게; 명백히.

tran·spi·ra·tion [træ̀nspəréiʃən] *n.* Ⓤ the act or process of transpiring. 증발. [↓]

tran·spire [trænspáiər] *vi.* (P1) **1** send out vapor, moisture, etc. through the surface or the pores of the skin, etc. 수증기〔냄새〕를 발산하다. **2** pass through the surface, pores, etc. 발산하다; 증발하다. **3** become known. (비밀 등이) 새다; 드러나다. ¶ *It later transpired that he hadn't been telling truth.* 그가 거짓말을 하고 있었다는 것이 나중에 드러났다 / *Nothing transpired of all that happened.* 일어났던 일은 아무 것도 밝혀지지 않았다. **4** 《*colloq.*》 happen; occur; take place. 일어나다; 생기다. ¶ *Let's wait and see what transpires.* 무슨 일이 있을지 기다려 봅시다.
— *vt.* (P6) send out (vapor, moisture, etc.) through the surface. (수증기·냄새 등)을 발산하다; 배출하다. [L. *spiro* breathe]

trans·plant [trænsplǽnt, -plɑ́ːnt] *vt.* (P6,13) **1** take (a plant) from one place and plant it in another place. …을 이식하다. **2** move (people) from one place to another. …을 이주시키다. ¶ *Under the Tudors many English people were transplanted to Ireland.* 튜더 왕조 때 많은 영국인이 아일랜드에 이주했다. **3** 《surg.》 transfer (an organ or tissue) from one part of the body to another or from one body to another. (기관·조직)을 이식하다. ¶ ~ *a heart* 심장을 이식하다. [*plant*]

trans·plan·ta·tion [træ̀nsplæntéiʃən, -plɑːn-] *n.* ⓊⒸ **1** the act of transplanting; the state of being transplanted. 이식. **2** a transplanted plant, person, etc. 이식한 식물; 이민; 식민(植民).

trans·pon·tine [trænspɑ́ntin / -pɔ́ntain] *adj.* beyond the bridge. 다리 저편의. [L. *pons* bridge]

:**trans·port** [trænspɔ́ːrt] *vt.* **1** (P6,13) carry or move (something) from one place to another. …을 수송하다; 운반하다. ¶ *Wheat is transported from the farms to the mill.* 밀은 밭에서 제분소로 운반된다. **2** (P6,13) 《hist.》 send (a criminal) away to another country or to a remote place; exile. (죄인)을 해외로 추방하다; 귀양 보내다. **3** (P6) 《usu. in *passive*》 carry away (someone) by strong emotion or feeling. …을 도취〔열중〕시키다. ¶ *She was transported with joy by the good news.* 좋은 소식에 그녀는 기뻐서 어찌할 바를 몰랐다.
— [trǽnspɔːrt] *n.* **1** Ⓤ ⓐ the act of transporting. 수송; 운반. ¶ *The* ~ *of goods by air is expensive.* 물자의 항공 수송은 비용이 많이 든다 / *Trucks are used much for* ~. 트럭이 수송에 많이 쓰인다. ⓑ a method of being transported. 수송 수단. ¶ *I'd like to go to the concert, but I don't have any* ~. 콘서트에 가고 싶으나 타고갈 것이 없다. **2** Ⓒ a ship or plane for carrying troops, passengers, military stores, etc. 수송선; 수송기. **3** Ⓒ an exiled criminal. 유형수(流刑囚). **4** Ⓤ a strong feeling or emotion. 열중; 도취; 격정. ¶ *He cried out in a* ~ *of rage.* 그는 부아가 나서 고래고래 소리쳤다 / *be in a* ~ *of joy* 기뻐서 어쩔 바를 모르다. ● **trans·port·er** [-ər] *n.* [L. *porto* carry]

*__trans·por·ta·tion__ [træ̀nspərtéiʃən / -pɔːr-] *n.* Ⓤ **1** the act of transporting; the state of being transported. 수송. ¶ *the railway* ~ 철도 수송. **2** 《Brit.》 the act of sending away a criminal. 유형; 귀양; 추방. ¶ *be sentenced to* ~ 유형 선고를 받다. **3** 《U.S.》 means or cost of transporting. 수송기관; 수송료; 운임. **4** Ⓒ 《U.S.》 tickets for travel or transport. 차표; 운송 허가증.

trans·pose [trænspóuz] *vt.* (P6,13) **1** change the place or order of (something). (…의 위치·순서)를 바꾸다. **2** 《math.》 bring (a term) from one side of an equation to the other. …을 이항하다. **3** 《mus.》 perform or write (a musical composition) in a different key. …을 조옮김하다. **4** change the usual or right order of (letters or words). (문자·낱말)을 바꾸어 쓰다〔말하다〕. ¶ *If you* ~ *the letters of 'at' it reads 'ta'.* 'at'의 글자를 거꾸로 쓰면 'ta'라 읽는다 / *dial a wrong number by transposing the figures in one's mind* 전화 번호 숫자를 바꾸어 생각하고 다이얼을 잘못 돌리다. [→pose]

trans·po·si·tion [træ̀nspəzíʃən] *n.* ⓊⒸ the act of transposing; the state of being transposed. (위치 등의) 전환; 전위(轉位).

trans·ship [trænsʃíp] *vt.* (**-shipped, -shipping**) (P6) move (passengers, things, etc.) from one ship, train, etc. to another. (승객·화물)을 다른 배〔열차 등〕에 옮겨 태우다〔싣다〕. [*ship*]

trans·ship·ment [trænsʃípmənt] *n.* Ⓤ the act of transshipping. 옮겨 태우기〔싣기〕.

tran(s)·son·ic [træn(s)sɑ́nik / -sɔ́n-] *adj.* moving at a speed close to the speed of sound, 700-780 miles per hour. 음속에 가까운; 천음속(遷音速)의. [→sonic]

tran·sub·stan·ti·a·tion [træ̀nsəbstæ̀nʃiéiʃən] *n.* Ⓤ 《religion》 the conversion of the eucharistic elements into the body and blood of Christ. 성변화(聖變化). [→substance]

trans·ver·sal [trænsvə́ːrsəl, trænz-] *adj.* = transverse. — *n.* 《geom.》 a line cutting two or more other lines. 횡단선(線). [↓]

trans·verse [trænsvə́ːrs, trænz- / ⌐–] *adj.* placed across or in a cross direction;

crosswise. 가로의; 가로지르는; 횡단한. ¶ *a ~ section* 횡단면 / *a ~ wave* (전파의) 횡파(橫派). —— *n.* Ⓒ something transverse. 가로지르는 것; 횡단 도로. [L. *verto* turn]

:trap[1] [træp] *n.* Ⓒ **1** an instrument for catching animals; a snare; a trick for deceiving a person. 올가미; 덫; 계략; 함정. ¶ *lay* 〔*set*〕 *a ~ for a fox* 여우덫을 놓다 / *walk* 〔*fall*〕 *into a ~* 덫에 걸리다; 함정에 빠지다 / *The police set traps to make him confess.* 경찰은 그가 자백하도록 책략을 썼다. **2** a machine to throw clay disks into the air as rifle targets. (클레이 사격의) 표적 사출기. **3** an S- or U- shaped pipe for preventing the escape of gas or bad smells. (방취용) U자관; 트랩. **4** =trap door. **5** 《Brit.》 a light two-wheeled carriage. 이륜경마차. **6** 《*sl.*》 a mouth. 입. ¶ *Shut your ~!* 입 닥쳐.

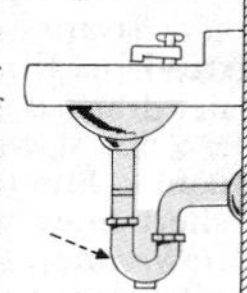
〈trap[1] 3〉

—— *v.* (**trapped, trap·ping**) *vt.* (P6) **1** catch (an animal) in a trap; set with traps. …을 덫으로 잡다; …에 덫을 놓다. ¶ *~ a rabbit* 토끼를 덫으로 잡다 / *~ the wood* 숲에 덫을 놓다 / *The bear was trapped.* 곰이 덫에 걸렸다. **2** cheat; deceive. …을 계략에 빠뜨리다; 속이다. ¶ *By clever questioning they trapped him into (making) a confession.* 계략적으로 교묘한 심문을 하여 그들은 그를 자백케 했다. **3** hold back; block. …을 막다; 저지하다. ¶ *Sand and leaves trapped the water in the stream.* 모래와 나뭇잎들이 시냇물을 막았다. —— *vi.* (P1,3) **1** 《*for*》 set traps. 덫을 놓다. ¶ *~ for rabbits* 토끼덫을 놓다. **2** follow the occupation of a trapper. 덫사냥을 하다. [E.]

trap[2] [træp] *n.* Ⓒ 《usu. *pl.*》 《*colloq.*》 personal belongings; baggage. 휴대품; 세간; 짐. —— *vt.* (P6) furnish with trappings. (말)에 장식을 하다; …을 성장(盛裝)시키다. [F. *drap* cloth]

trap door [ˊ-ˋ] *n.* a hinged or sliding door in a floor, roof, etc. (마루·지붕 등의) 뚜껑문; 들창. [*trap*[1]]

tra·peze [træpíːz / trə-] *n.* Ⓒ a swinging horizontal bar hung by two ropes, used in gymnastics, circus performances, etc. 트래피즈《체조·곡예용 그네》. [Gk. *trapeza* table]

tra·pe·zia [trəpíːzjə] *n.* pl. of **trapezium.**

tra·pe·zi·um [trəpíːziəm] *n.* (*pl.* **-zi·ums** or **-zia**) **1** 《Brit.》 a quadrilateral having only two sides parallel. 사다리꼴. **2** 《U.S.》 = trapezoid 1. [*trapeze*]

trap·e·zoid [trǽpəzɔ̀id] *n.* **1** 《Brit.》 a quadrilateral having no parallel sides. 부등변 사각형. **2** 《U.S.》 =trapezium 1. [↑]

trap·per [trǽpər] *n.* Ⓒ a person who traps animals, esp. for their furs, skins. (특히 모피가 목적인) 덫사냥꾼. [*trap*[1]]

trap·pings [trǽpiŋz] *n. pl.* **1** ornamental harness or covering for a horse. (의식용) 마구; 말장식. **2** ceremonial dress of an ornamental character. 예복. ¶ *the ~ of a king and his court* 왕과 그 조신(朝臣)들의 예복. [*trap*[2]]

trash [træʃ] *n.* **1** Ⓤ broken or torn parts. 부스러기; 지저깨비. **2** Ⓤ worthless things; rubbish. 쓰레기. ¶ *a ~ can* 쓰레기통(cf. 《Brit.》 *dust bin*). **3** Ⓤ worthless or foolish talk, ideas, or writing. 하찮은 이야기〔생각, 글〕. ¶ *What you're saying is a absolute ~.* 네가 하고 있는 말은 아무 쓸데 없는 소리야. **4** Ⓤ poor literature, art, or music. (문학·미술·음악 등의) 졸작(拙作). **5** 《*collectively*》 worthless people. 건달. [N. =lumber]

trash·y [trǽʃi] *adj.* (**trash·i·er, trash·i·est**) of or like trash; having no value; useless. 쓰레기의〔같은〕; 쓸모 없는.

trav·ail [trəvéil, trǽveil] *n.* 《*arch.*》 Ⓤ **1** the pains endured in childbirth. (출산의) 진통(陣痛). **2** severe agony. 고통.

be in travail, suffer the pains of childbirth. 산고(産苦)를 겪다.

—— *vi.* (P1) **1** suffer the pains of childbirth. 진통하다. **2** work hard; toil. 고생하다. [Rom. =put on the *trepalium* (L. *tres* three, *palus* stake)]

:trav·el [trǽvəl] *v.* (**-eled, -el·ing** or 《Brit.》 **-elled, -el·ling**) *vi.* **1** (P1,2A,3) go from one place to another over a long distance; make a trip. 여행하다. ¶ *~ abroad* 해외 여행을 하다 / *~ round the world* 세계 일주 여행을 하다 / *~ second-class to London by air* 항공편으로 런던까지 이등석으로 가다 / *~ for one's health* 건강〔보양〕을 위해 여행하다 / *~ for one's pleasure* 유람하다 / *~ (for) six months,* 6개월 동안 여행하다 / *He has traveled widely.* 그는 두루 여행을 했다. **2** (P1,3) go from place to place to sell goods or obtain business order. 장사하러〔주문받으러〕 다니다. ¶ *~ for a company* 회사의 외판원 노릇을 하다 / *~ in jewelry* 보석을 팔러 다니다. **3** (P3) 《over》 move or pass from one point to another. (기억·시선 따위가) 연해 옮겨지다. ¶ *Her mind traveled over her past happy days.* 그녀는 지난 날의 행복했던 시절을 이것저것 회상했다 / *His eyes traveled over the scene.* 그는 경치를 죽 둘러보았다. **4** (P1,2B) move; run; walk; go; proceed. 이동하다; 달리다; 가다; 나아가다. ¶ *The moon travels round the earth.* 달은 지구 주위를 돈다 / *A bullet travels in a straight line.* 총알은 직선으로 나아간다 / *The motor car traveled 100 miles an hour.* 그 차는 시속 100마일로 달렸다 / *Light travels much faster than sound.* 빛은 소리보다 훨씬 빨리 진행한다. **5** (P1) 《U.S. *colloq.*》 move or advance with speed. 빨리 움직이다〔나아가다〕. ¶ *That motorbike was really traveling. It must have been doing 100 miles an hour.* 모터바이크는 무척 빨리 달리더군. 분명

히 시속 100마일은 됐을 거야.
— *vt.* (P6) make a journey through (a place); pass across (a place). …을 여행하다. ¶ ~ *England from end to end* 영국을 끝에서 끝까지 여행하다.
— *n.* **1** Ⓤ the act of traveling; 《*pl.*》 journeys abroad. 여행; 해외 여행. ¶ *a* ~ *agency* 〔*bureau*〕 여행사 / *She loves* ~. 그녀는 여행을 좋아한다 / *He came home after years of foreign travels.* 그는 여러 해 동안의 해외 여행에서 돌아왔다 / *They say* ~ *broadens the mind.* 여행은 마음〔견문〕을 넓힌다고 한다. **2** 《usu. *pl.*》 a book about travels and experiences. 여행기; 기행(紀行). ¶ *'Gulliver's Travels'* 걸리버 여행기 / *I am fond of reading travels.* 나는 여행기를 읽기 좋아한다. [→travail]

trav·eled, 《Brit.》 **-elled** [trǽvld] *adj.* **1** having experienced many journeys; having visited many lands. 여행에 익숙한; 각지를 돌아다닌. ¶ *a* ~ *man* 견문이 넓은 사람. **2** (of roads, etc.) used frequently by travelers. (길 따위가) 여행자가 많은. ¶ *a* ~ *road* / *a* ~ *district* 여행객이 많은 지역.

:**trav·el·er,** 《Brit.》 **-el·ler** [trǽvlər] *n.* Ⓒ **1** a person who travels. 여행자; 나그네. **2** a traveling salesman; a commercial traveler. 외판〔외무〕원; 행상인.

trav·el·ing, 《Brit.》 **-el·ling** [trǽvliŋ] *adj.* **1** that travels. 여행하는. ¶ *a* ~ *salesman* 외판원. **2** connected with travel; used for travel. 여행(용)의. ¶ *a* ~ *bag* / *a* ~ *theater company* 순회〔유랑〕 극단 / *When she returned to England, she claimed her* ~ *expenses from her company.* 영국에 돌아와 그녀는 회사에 여비를 청구했다. — *n.* the action of traveling. 여행.

trav·e·log, 《Brit.》 **-logue** [trǽvəlɔ̀(:)g, -lɑ̀g] *n.* Ⓒ a lecture or talk on travel with the aid of pictures, a motion picture, etc. (슬라이드·영화를 이용한) 여행담. [→travel, *-logue*]

*__trav·erse__ [trǽvəːrs, trəvə́ːrs] *vt.* (P6) **1** pass across, over, on, or through (a place); travel across. …을 가로지르다; 횡단 여행하다. ¶ *The ship traversed the Pacific Ocean in nine days.* 배는 9일 동안에 태평양을 횡단했다 / *The railway line traverses the road at this point.* 철길은 여기서 길을 가로지른다 / ~ *the desert* 사막을 가로지르다. **2** extend across or over (a place). …의 위에 뻗다〔걸리다〕. ¶ *A bridge traverses the river.* 다리가 강 위에 뻗어 있다. **3** discuss thoroughly; survey carefully. …을 전반적으로〔상세히〕 논하다; 주의 깊게 고찰하다. ¶ ~ *a subject in a lecture* 강의에서 한 주제를 상설(詳說)하다. **4** oppose; deny; call in question. …에 반대하다; 거부하다; 문제 삼다. ¶ ~ *someone's opinion* 〔*statement*〕 아무의 의견〔말〕에 반대하다. **5** move or turn from side to side in aiming. (겨냥하기 위해 총구)를 좌우로 선회하다. ¶ ~ *a gun* 총구를 좌우로 움직이다.
— *vi.* pass along or go across something. 가로질러 가다; 횡단하다.
— *n.* Ⓒ **1** the act of crossing. 횡단. **2** anything that lies between two things; an obstacle; opposition. 가로질러 있는 것; 방해(물); 반대. [→transverse]

trav·es·ty [trǽvəsti] *n.* Ⓒ (*pl.* **-ties**) any treatment that makes a serious work seem ridiculous; a ridiculous imitation or translation of a serious work. (진지한 작품을) 우습게 바꿔놓음; 우습게 만든 작품. — *vt.* (**-tied**) (P6) make (a serious work) ridiculous. (진지한 작품)을 우습게 만들다. [trans-, L. *vestis* garment]

trawl [trɔːl] *n.* Ⓒ **1** a strong bag-shaped net dragged along the bottom of the sea. 트롤망; 저인망(底引網). **2** 《U.S.》 a long fishing line to which are attached many short lines with baited hooks. 주낙(=trawl line). — *vt.*, *vi.* (P6; 1) fish or catch (fish) with a trawl. 트롤 어업을 하다. [? E.]

trawl·er [trɔ́ːlər] *n.* Ⓒ **1** a boat used for trawling. 저인망 어선; 트롤선. **2** a person who works on such a boat. 트롤선 어부. [↑]

*__trawl·net__ [trɔ́ːlnèt] *n.* =trawl 1.

*__tray__ [trei] *n.* Ⓒ a flat piece of wood, glass, etc., with a raised rim, used for carrying or holding things. 쟁반; 쟁반; 접시. [E.]

*__treach·er·ous__ [trétʃərəs] *adj.* **1** deceiving; disloyal; not faithful. 배신하는; 불충한; 믿을 수 없는. ¶ *a* ~ *smile* 〔*move*〕 속일 것 같은 웃음〔행동〕 / *The* ~ *soldier carried reports to the enemy.* 그 반역병은 보고서를 적에게 넘겨줬다 / *a* ~ *plot to poison the king* 왕을 독살하려는 모반 음모. **2** not reliable in spite of appearance. (보기와는 달리) 방심할 수 없는; 위험한. ¶ ~ *weather* 변덕스러운 날씨 / *a* ~ *floor* (견고한 것 같으면서) 위험한 마루. [F. (→trick)]

*__treach·er·y__ [trétʃəri] *n.* (*pl.* **-er·ies**) ⓊⒸ the act of treason; the state of being treacherous; deceit. (국가에 대한) 배반; 모반.

trea·cle [tríːkəl] *n.* Ⓤ 《U.S.》 dark, thick syrup produced in refining sugar; molasses. 당밀(糖密). [Gk. *thēr* wild beast]

*__tread__ [tred] *v.* (**trod, trod·den** or **trod**) *vi.* (P1,2A,3) **1** walk; go; proceed. 걷다; 가다; 진행하다. ¶ ~ *cautiously* 조심스럽게 나아가다: 신중하게 일을 진행하다 / ~ *lightly* 조용조용히 걷다; 신중하게 하다 / *He trod quietly across the room.* 그는 조용히 방 안을 걸어서 갔다. **2** 《*on, upon*》 set one's foot; crush or injure by stepping. 밟다; 짓밟다; 밟아 뭉개다. ¶ ~ *on someone's foot* 아무의 발을 밟다 / ~ *on a cigarette butt* 담배 꽁초를 짓밟아 뭉개다 / *Don't* ~ *on the flower beds.* 화단을 밟지 마라.
— *vt.* (P6,7) **1** step or walk on or along (a

place). (어떤 장소)를 걷다; 가다; 지나다. ¶ ~ *the ground* 산책하다; 거닐다 / ~ *this world* 〔*earth*〕 살아 있다 / 《*fig.*》 ~ *a safe path* 안전한 길을 가다. **2** press (something) under the feet; step on (something) to crush it. …을 짓밟다; 밟아 뭉개다; 밟아서 …하다. ¶ ~ *clothes* 옷을 밟아서 세탁하다 / ~ *grapes* (포도주를 만들기 위해) 포도를 밟아 뭉개다 / *be trod to death* 짓밟혀 죽다 / ~ *grain* 밟아 곡물을 탈곡하다 / ~ *the flame out* 화염을 밟아서 끄다. **3** win a victory over (something); conquer; oppress; treat harshly. …을 정복하다; 억압〔유린〕하다. ¶ ~ *someone's rights under foot* 아무의 권리를 유린하다 / ~ *down a sad feeling* 슬픈 감정을 억누르다.

tread in the steps of, follow the example of. …을 따라〔본받아〕 하다.

tread on air, feel very happy and gay. 좋아 어쩔 줄 모르다.

tread on** someone's **toes 〔***corns***〕, make someone angry. …을 화나게 하다.

tread the deck, become a sailor. 선원이 되다.

— *n.* Ⓒ **1** the act, sound, or way of treading. 걷기; 밟기; 발소리; 걸음새. ¶ *walk with an airy* ~ 경쾌한 걸음새로 걷다 / *the* ~ *of the soldiers* 군인들의 발자국 소리 / *We heard our father's heavy* ~ *on the staircase.* 계단을 밟는 아버지의 무거운 발소리를 들었다. **2** the flat upper surface of a stair. 계단의 디딤판. **3** the part of a boat or shoe which touches the ground; the part of a tire of a wheel that touches the ground. (배의) 바닥; 신발창; 지면에 닿는 부분; (바퀴·타이어 등의) 접지면. [E.]

trea·dle [trédl] *n.* Ⓒ a level or pedal on which the foot presses to operate a machine. (자전거·재봉틀 따위의) 발판; 디딤판; 페달. — *vi.* (P1) operate a treadle. 페달을 밟다. [*tread*]

tread·mill [trédmil] *n.* Ⓒ **1** a wheel that is turned round by a person or animal treading on a moving, endless belt. 밟아서 돌리는 바퀴《옛 감옥에서 죄수에게 징벌로 밟게 했음》. **2** a monotonous and tiresome routine of work or activity. 단조롭고 힘든 일. [E.]

***trea·son** [trí:zən] *n.* Ⓤ an attempt to overthrow a government in some illegal way. 반역(죄). ¶ *commit* ~ 반역하다; 반역죄를 저지르다 / *high* ~ 대역죄(大逆罪). [→tradition]

trea·son·a·ble [trí:znəbəl] *adj.* of treason; treacherous. 반역의.

trea·son·ous [trí:znəs] *adj.* treasonable. 반역의.

:**treas·ure** [tréʒər] *n.* **1** ⓊⒸ valuable things, as money, jewels or precious metals, etc. (돈·금은·보석 따위의) 재보(財寶); 보물; 재화. ¶ *a store of hidden* ~ 미발견의 많은 보물 / *The war cost the country great sacrifices in blood and* ~. 전쟁은 그 나라로 하여금 막대한 인명과 재산의 희생을 치르게 했다. **2** Ⓒ a person or thing highly valued. 애지중지하는 사람〔것〕; 귀중품. ¶ *My* ~*!* 내 사랑하는 이여 / *He is a* ~ *to our country.* 그는 나라의 보배이다 / *treasures of art in the museum* 박물관의 귀중한 미술품들.

— *vt.* **1** (P6,7) ⓐ store or save up (something) for future use. …을 비축〔저장〕하다. ¶ ~ *up money and jewels* 돈과 보석을 비축하다. ⓑ retain 〔keep〕 carefully in the mind. …을 마음에 소중히 간직하다〔새겨두다〕. ¶ ~ *the memory of one's old days* 지난 날의 추억을 마음에 간직하다. **2** value (something) highly; cherish; prize. …을 소중히 하다. ¶ *She treasures his letters.* 그녀는 그의 편지들을 소중히 한다 / *a treasured book* 소중한 책 / *This is the child she treasured.* 이 애가 그녀가 아끼던 아이입니다. [Gk. *thēsauros*]

treasure house [⌐-⌐] *n.* **1** a building or room where treasure is stored. 보물 창고. **2** a place where many valuable things can be found. 보고(寶庫). ¶ *a* ~ *of knowledge* 지식의 보고.

***treas·ur·er** [tréʒərər] *n.* Ⓒ a person in charge of receiving and paying out money. 회계원; 출납원.

treas·ure-trove [tréʒərtròuv] *n.* Ⓤ 《law》 treasure found hidden, the owner of which is unknown. 소유자 불명의 발굴물(發掘物).

***treas·ur·y** [tréʒəri] *n.* (*pl.* **-ur·ies**) Ⓒ **1** a place where treasure or money is kept; a treasure house. 보고(寶庫). **2** 《often *the T-*》 a place where public funds are kept. 국고(國庫); 공고(公庫). **3** the funds of an organization. 자금; 기금(基金). **4** 《*the T-*》 the department of the government that manages a nation's money. (미국·영국의) 재무부.

:**treat** [tri:t] *vt.* **1** (P7) act or behave toward (someone). …을 다루다; 대우하다. ¶ ~ *one's friends with respect* 친구들을 존중히 다루다 / *He treats his children well.* 그는 아이들에게 잘해 준다 / *He treats me as a child.* 그는 나를 어린애 취급한다 / *Treat him kindly.* 그를 친절하게 대해라 / *This firm has always treated its workers well.* 이 회사는 근로자들을 늘 잘 대우해 왔다. **2** (P7) regard; consider. …으로 간주하다; 생각하다. ¶ *Don't* ~ *it too seriously.* 그거 너무 심각하게 생각하지 마라 / *I treated his words as a joke.* 그의 말을 농담으로 받아들였다 / ~ *one's position as a means of securing one's own ends* 자기 지위를 자신의 목표를 이루는 수단으로 생각하다 / *Our employer treated our suggestions as a complaint.* 고용주는 우리 제안들을 무슨 불평쯤으로 간주했다. **3** (P6,13) give medical care to (someone). …을 치료하다. ¶ ~ *him for his illness* 그의 병을 치료하다 / ~ *a wound* 상처를 치료하다 / *My sister is being treated for a heart condition.* 누이는 심장의

이상을 치료 받고 있다. **4** (P6,13) 《*to*》 entertain (someone) with food, drink, or amusement. …에게 음식을 대접하다; 한턱 내다; 환대하다. ¶ ~ *her to a box at the opera house* 그녀를 오페라 극장의 특등석으로 정중히 모시다 / *No, no, put your money away, let me ~ you.* 아니다, 아냐, 그 돈 치워라, 내가 한턱 내겠다 / *She treated herself to a dinner at a Chinese restaurant.* 그녀는 큰맘 먹고 정찬으로 중국 요리를 먹었다. **5** (P7) deal with (something) as the subject of art or literature; discuss; express. …을 논하다; (주제〔테마〕로) 다루다. ¶ *The writer treated his subject realistically.* 저자는 그의 테마를 리얼하게 다루었다. **6** (P6,13) give a certain effect to (something) in order to get a certain result. …을 처리하다; …에 작용시키다. ¶ ~ *a metal with acid* 금속을 산으로 처리하다.

— *vi.* (P1,3) **1** 《*of*》 deal with a subject in speech or writing. 논하다; (주제로) 다루다. ¶ *His lecture treated of life and youth.* 그는 강의에서 인생과 청춘 문제를 다루었다 / *This book treats of the progress of medicine.* 이 책은 의학의 발달을 취급하고 있다. **2** discuss; negotiate. 논의하다; 교섭하다. ¶ ~ *with them for peace* 그들과 화평을 교섭하다. **3** pay the expense of food, entertainment, etc. for others. 한턱 내다; 대접하다. ¶ *It is your turn to ~ now.* 이번에는 네가 한턱 낼 차례다 / *Whose turn is it to ~ next?* 다음은 누가 한턱 낼 차례냐.

— *n.* Ⓒ **1** the act of entertaining; a gift of food, drink, or entertainment. 한턱 내기; 대접; 접대. ¶ *This is my ~.* 이건 내가 한턱 내는 거다. **2** a delight; anything that gives great pleasure. 큰 기쁨; 대단한 즐거움. ¶ *It was a ~ to hear his good lecture.* 그의 훌륭한 강의를 듣는 것은 참다운 즐거움이었다 / *a children's Sunday school ~* 주일 학교의 어린이 잔치《운동회·소풍 따위》. [L. *tracto* handle]

trea·tise [tríːtis, -tiz] *n.* Ⓒ 《*on*》 a formal and systematic book or essay written on a particular subject. 논문. [↑]

:treat·ment [tríːtmənt] *n.* ⓊⒸ **1** the act or way of treating. 취급; 대우. ¶ *receive bad* 〔*kind*〕 ~ 푸대접〔친절한 대접〕을 받다 / *the newspapers' sensational ~ of the story* 그 이야기에 대한 언론들의 대대적인 취급 / *These minority groups were given preferential ~.* 이 소수 집단들은 차별적인 대우를 받았다. **2** a kind of medical or surgical care. 치료(법). ¶ *surgical ~* 외과적 치료(법) / *emergency ~* 응급 처치 / *a new ~ for polio* 소아마비의 새 치료법 / *undergo medical ~* 치료를 받다 / *Her illness is not responding to ~.* 그녀의 병은 치료해도 효험을 보이지 않고 있다. [*treat*]

***trea·ty** [tríːti] *n.* (*pl.* **-ties**) Ⓒ **1** a formal agreement between nations about peace, trade, etc. 조약. ¶ *conclude* 〔*enter into*〕 *a ~* 조약을 체결하다 / *denounce a ~* 조약을 파기하다 / *The peace ~ was signed in Paris.* 평화 조약이 파리에서 서명〔체결〕되었다. **2** Ⓤ the act of bargaining; technical agreement between people. 교섭; (개인간의) 약속; 약정. ¶ *be in ~ with…* …와 교섭중이다 / *We sold the house by private ~.* 우리는 개인간의 합의로 집을 팔았다. [→treat]

tre·ble [trébəl] *adj.* **1** three times. 3배의; 세 곱의. ¶ *They sold the house for ~ the amount they paid for it.* 그들은 산 값의 세 곱을 받고 그 집을 팔았다. **2** 《mus.》 of the highest instrumental or vocal part. 최고음부(最高音部)의. **3** high-pitched; shrill. (음성이) 날카로운; 새된.

— *n.* Ⓒ **1** ⓐ 《mus.》 the highest part in music. 최고음(부). ⓑ a singer or player that performs this part. 최고음부의 가수〔연주자〕. **2** a voice or an instrument taking the highest part; soprano. 고음부의 소리〔악기〕; 소프라노. **3** a shrill voice. 날카로운 음성.

— *vt., vi.* (P6; 1) make (something) or become three times as many or much. 세 곱으로〔3배로〕 하다〔되다〕. ¶ *This year he trebled his income.* 금년 그의 수입은 3배가 됐다 / *Their profits have trebled in the last two years.* 지난 2년 동안에 그들의 수익은 3배가 됐다. [→L. *triplus* triple]

:tree [triː] *n.* Ⓒ **1** a large plant with a woody trunk, branches, and leaves. 나무; 교목(喬木). 參考 낮은 것은 bush, shrub 이라 함. **2** a piece of wood used for a certain purpose. 재목; 목재. ¶ *a boot* 〔*shoe*〕 ~ 구두골 / *an axle-tree* 굴대 / *a saddle-tree* 안장틀. **3** something like a tree. 나무처럼 가지를 뻗는 것; 계도(系圖). ¶ *a family ~* 가계도(家系圖).

at the top of a tree, at the top of one's profession. 최고 지위에; 우두머리 자리에.

up a tree, in a difficult situation; at a loss. 진퇴양난이 되어; 궁지에 몰려.

— *vt.* (P6) **1** drive (something) up a tree. …을 나무 위로 몰아 올리다. ¶ *The dog treed the cat.* 개가 고양이를 나무 위로 쫓아올렸다. **2** 《*colloq.*》 put (someone) into a difficult situation. …을 궁지에 몰아넣다. [E.]

tree fern [⌐⌐] *n.* 《*bot.*》 a large fern with a stem like a trunk. 목생(木生) 양치류.

tree·less [tríːlis] *adj.* having no trees. 나무가〔수목이〕 없는.

tree trunk [⌐⌐] *n.* the main stem of a tree. (나무의) 줄기.

tref·oil [tríːfɔil, tré-] *n.* =clover. [tri-, → foil]

trek [trek] *vi.* (**trekked, trek·king**) (P1,2A,3) **1** go on a long journey by ox wagon; migrate. 달구지로 먼 길을 여행하다; 이주(移住)하다. **2** travel slowly or with difficulty, esp. on foot. 느릿느릿〔고난을 겪으며〕 도보 여행하다. — *n.* Ⓒ **1** a long journey, esp. by ox wagon. (장거리) 달구지 여행. **2** migration. 이주. [Du. =draw]

trel·lis [trélis] *n.* Ⓒ a light frame of wood or metal used for supporting growing vines or as a garden screen. (포도 등 덩굴 식물을 올리는) 격자 시렁〔지주, 울타리〕. —*vt.* (P6) **1** support (vines) on a trellis. (덩굴)을 시렁으로 떠받치다. ¶ ~ *a climbing rose* 장미덩굴을 시렁으로 떠받쳐 주다. **2** provide (a window) with a trellis. (창)에 격자(格子)를 달다. [tri-, L. *licium* warp-thread]

〈trellis〉

:trem·ble [trémbəl] *vi.* **1** (P1,2A,3) shake with fear, cold, etc. (두려움, 추위 따위로) 떨다; 벌벌〔와들와들〕 떨다. ¶ ~ *in the snow* 눈 속에서 와들와들 떨다 / *Her voice trembled with anger.* 화가 나서 그녀의 목소리는 부들부들 떨렸다 / *He trembled at his father's voice.* 그는 아버지의 음성을 듣고 벌벌 떨었다 / *His hands ~ from oversmoking.* 과도한 흡연으로 인해 그의 두 손은 부들부들 떨린다. **2** (P1,3,4) move gently; quake; be shaken. 가볍게 흔들리다; 살랑거리다. ¶ *The leaves were trembling in the breeze.* 나뭇잎들이 미풍에 살랑거리고 있었다 / *Flags ~ in the wind.* 깃발이 바람에 나부낀다 / 《*fig.*》 *His life is trembling in the balance.* 그는 아슬아슬한 순간에 처해 있다. **3** (P1,3,4) 《*for*》 feel great fear or anxiety. 조바심하다; 안절부절 못하다. ¶ *I trembled to think what had become of her.* 그녀가 어찌되었나 생각하곤 안절부절 못 했다 / *I ~ for your safety.* 네 안위가 크게 걱정이다.

—*n.* Ⓒ the act or state of trembling. 몸을 떪; 전율; 떨림. [L. *tremo*]

be all of a tremble, 《*colloq.*》 tremble all over. 전신을 와들와들〔부들부들〕 떨다.

trem·bling [trémbliŋ] *n.* Ⓤ the state of trembling. 떪; 전율. —*adj.* that trembles; shaking or shivering. 떠는; 전율하는. ● **trem·bling·ly** [-li] *adv.*

:tre·men·dous [triméndəs] *adj.* **1** terrible; very important. 무서운; 중대한. ¶ *a ~ catastrophe* 무서운 천재 지변 / *a ~ responsibility* 중대한 책임 / *The army suffered a ~ defeat.* 군은 참담하게 패배했다. **2** 《*colloq.*》 very great; amazing; enormous. 거대한; 굉장한; 엄청난. ¶ *a ~ difference* 엄청난 차이 / *with a ~ effort* 대단한 노력으로 / *This rocket travels at a ~ speed.* 이 로켓의 속력은 엄청나다 / 《*fig.*》 *She's a ~ talker.* 그녀는 수다스럽기 이를 데가 없다 / *His performance was ~.* 그의 연주는 정말 훌륭했다. ● **tre·men·dous·ly** [-li] *adv.* **tre·men·dous·ness** [-nis] *n.* [L. *tremo*]

trem·o·lo [tréməlòu] *n.* (*pl.* **-los**) Ⓒ 《mus., It.》 a trembling tone produced by the rapid repetition of the same tone in singing or playing an instrument. 트레몰로; 전음(顫音); 떤꾸밈음. [L. *tremo*]

trem·or [trémər] *n.* Ⓒ **1** a shivering or trembling of the voice, leaves, etc. (음성·나뭇잎 등의) 떨림. ¶ *have ~ of the hands* 수전증(手顫症)이 있다 / *a slight ~ in the voice* 목소리의 가벼운 떨림 / *an earth ~* 미진(微震). **2** a shrinking of courage; the state of being excited; a thrill of emotion. 겁; 불안; 전율. ¶ *He faced death without a ~.* 그는 조금도 겁내지 않고 죽음에 직면했다 / *The story was so frightning that it sent tremors down my spine.* 그 이야기가 얼마나 무서웠던지 나는 등골이 오싹하는 전율을 느꼈다. [↑]

trem·u·lous [trémjələs] *adj.* **1** trembling or quivering. 떨리는. ¶ *a voice ~ with fear* 공포로 떨리는 음성. **2** cowardly; nervous. 겁 많은; 소심한. [↑]

trem·u·lous·ly [trémjələsli] *adv.* tremblingly; timidly. 떨며; 주뼛거리며.

***trench** [trentʃ] *n.* Ⓒ **1** ⓐ a long, narrow ditch dug in the earth to protect soldiers in a battle field. 참호; 트렌치. ¶ ~ *warfare* 참호전 / *a ~ mortar* 박격포. ⓑ 《*pl.*》《*fig.*》 the front line of battle. 일선; 최전방. **2** a deep ditch. (깊은) 도랑. ¶ *dig a ~ and fill it with manure* 도랑을 파고 거름을 채우다.

—*vt.* (P6) **1** surround (something) with a trench. …을 참호로 두르다. **2** dig a trench in (some place). …에 참호를〔도랑을〕 파다. **3** cultivate. 땅을 갈다. —*vi.* (P1) dig a trench. 참호를〔도랑을〕 파다. [F. =cut]

trench on 〔***upon***〕***,*** **a**) encroach or trespass on. …을 침해〔침입〕하다. ¶ ~ *upon someone's time* 아무의 시간을 빼앗다. **b**) come close to. …에 접근하다.

trench·ant [tréntʃənt] *adj.* **1** biting; keen. 통렬한; 날카로운. ¶ *a ~ criticism* 신랄한 비평 / ~ *wit* 날카로운 위트. **2** clear; distinct. 간결한; 명확한. [*trench*]

trench·er[1] [tréntʃər] *n.* Ⓒ a person who digs trenches. 참호〔도랑〕 파는 사람.

trench·er[2] [tréntʃər] *n.* Ⓒ a wooden plate for serving meat. 나무 접시; 목판.

trench·er·man [tréntʃərmən] *n.* (*pl.* **-men** [-mən]) a person who eats; an eater. 먹는 사람. ¶ *a good* 〔*poor*〕 ~ 대식가(大食家)〔소식가〕. [F. =cut]

***trend** [trend] *n.* Ⓒ **1** the general tendency; a drift. 경향; 추세. ¶ *the ~ of public opinion* 여론의 경향 / *the ~ of time* 시대의 추세 / *The rise in violent crime is a disturbing new ~.* 폭력 범죄의 증가는 하나의 골치 아픈 새로운 경향이다. **2** the direction of a road, river, mountains, etc. (도로·하천 따위의) 방향. ¶ *The hills have a western ~.* 이 산맥은 서향이다. —*vi.* (P2A,3) 《*toward*》 **1** turn, bend, or run in a certain direction. (…으로) 향하다; 기울다. ¶ *The road trends to the north.* 그 길은 북쪽으로 나 있다. **2** have a general tendency. (…한) 경향이

있다. ¶ *Prices are trending upward.* 물가는 등귀 추세이다. [E.] 「=trephine.

tre·pan [tripǽn] *vt.* (**-panned, -pan·ning**)

tre·pang [tripǽŋ] *n.* ⟪zool.⟫ a sea cucumber. 해삼. [Malay]

tre·phine [trifáin, -fíːn] ⟪surg.⟫ *n.* a cylindrical saw used in cutting a portion of bone from the skull. 트레핀⟪천두용(穿頭用)의 관상(冠狀) 톱⟫. — *vt.* (P6) operate on with this instrument. 트레핀으로 수술하다. [L. *tres* three, *fines* ends]

trep·i·da·tion [trèpədéiʃən] *n.* fear and excitement; trembling. 공포; 전율. [L. *trepidus* flurried]

tres·pass [tréspəs, -pæ̀s] *vi.* **1** (P1,3) ⟪*on, upon*⟫ go on someone's land without permission. (남의 땅에) 침입하다; 침범하다. ¶ ~ *on someone's land* 아무의 땅에 함부로 들어 가다; 불법 침입하다 / *No trespassing.* 들어오지 마시오⟪게시⟫ / *Trespassers will be prosecuted.* 무단 침입자는 고발됨⟪게시⟫. **2** (P1,3) ⟪*against*⟫ commit an offense; do wrong; sin. (죄를) 범하다; 범법하다. ¶ ~ *against the law* 법을 어기다. **3** (P3) take too much of someone's time, privacy, attention, etc.; encroach on 〔upon〕. (타인의 권리를) 침해하다; (남의 시간·사생활을) 방해하다. ¶ ~ *on someone's right* 〔*privacy*〕 남의 권리를〔사생활을〕 침해하다.

— [tréspəs] *n.* ⓊⒸ **1** the act of going on someone's land or property unlawfully. 불법 침입. **2** ⟪*arch.*⟫ a wrong; sin. 악; 죄과; (종교적) 죄. [trans-, →pass]

tres·pass·er [tréspəsər, -pæ̀-] *n.* Ⓒ a person who trespasses. 침입자; 침해자.

tress [tres] *n.* Ⓒ ⟪usu. *pl.*⟫ a curl or lock of hair. (여자의) 머릿단; 삼단 같은 머릿다발; 치렁치렁하게 땋은 머리. ¶ *golden tresses* 치렁치렁한 금발의 머릿단. [F.]

tres·tle [trésəl] *n.* Ⓒ **1** a movable frame with two pairs of spreading legs used to support a platform, table tap, etc. 가대(架臺); 버팀다리; 트레슬. **2** a rigid framework for supporting a bridge across a gap. 교각(橋脚); 구각(構脚). [→transom]

trestle bridge [∸∸ ∸] *n.* a bridge supported by trestles. 구각교(構脚橋).

tri- [trai-] *pref.* **1** having three. '셋의, 세 개의'의 뜻. ¶ *tricycle* 삼륜차. **2** three times; into three parts. '세 곱의, 3등분의'의 뜻. ¶ *trisect* 삼등분하다. **3** once in three; every third. '3…마다'의 뜻. ¶ *triweekly,* 3주마다. [L. & Gk.]

tri·ad [tráiəd, -æd] *n.* Ⓒ a group of three persons or things. 3인조; 세 개 한 벌. [Gk. =three]

:tri·al [tráiəl] *n.* Ⓒ **1** the act of trying or testing; a test. 시도; 시험. ¶ *the ~ of a new car* 새 차의 테스트 / *by way of* ~ 시험적으로; 시험삼아 / *run a* ~ 시운전하다 / *He gave the machine another ~ to see if it would work.* 그는 기계가 작동되는지를 알려고 또 다른 테스트를 해 봤다 / *The ~ of the new airplane proved it unsatisfactory.* 신형 비행기의 시험은 만족스럽지 못했다. **2** the state of being tested. 시험〔테스트〕 받기. **3** ⓐ a hardship or trouble that tries one's endurance; suffering. 시련; 고난. ¶ *stand the* ~ 시련에 견디다. ⓑ a source of annoyance; a nuisance. 골칫거리. ¶ *That child is a ~ to his parents.* 저 아이는 제 부모의 골칫거리다. **4** the inquiry into or decision on a case in a court of law. 심리; 재판. ¶ *bring someone to ~ = put someone on* ~ 아무를 재판에 회부하다 / *stand one's ~ = take* 〔*undergo*〕 *one's* ~ 재판을 받다 / *the ~ of a murder case* 살인 사건의 재판 / *a criminal* ~ 형사 재판 / *a ~ of a man for theft* 절도범의 재판.

on trial, in order to test; when tested; under judicial examination or inquiry. 시험적으로; 시험 중인; 재판 중에. ¶ *take* 〔*have, employ*〕 *someone on* ~ 아무를 시험적으로 채용하다 / *He was on ~ for swindling.* 그는 사기죄로 재판받고 있었다.

trial and error, a method of finding a solution by learning from failures. 시행 착오.

— *adj.* of a trial or test. 시험의; 시험적인. ¶ *a ~ flight* 시험 비행 / *a ~ cruise* (선박의) 시운전 / *a ~ run* 〔*trip*〕 시운전 / *a ~ match* 예선 경기 / ~ *boring* 시굴(試掘). [→try]

tri·an·gle [tráiæ̀ŋgəl] *n.* Ⓒ **1** a figure with three sides and angles; a triangular instrument used in drawing figures. 삼각형; 삼각자. **2** ⟪mus.⟫ a triangular musical instrument made of steel and played by being struck with a metal rod. 트라이앵글. [→angle]

the eternal triangle, a situation involving three persons, esp. one in which two of them are in love with the third. 삼각 관계.

tri·an·gu·lar [traiǽŋgjələr] *adj.* **1** having the shape of a triangle. 삼각형의. **2** of three persons, parties, parts, etc. 삼자〔당,파〕간의. ¶ *a ~ treaty,* 3국 조약.

trib·al [tráibəl] *adj.* of a tribe. 종족〔부족〕의. ¶ ~ *customs* 〔*legends*〕 종족 관습〔전설〕. [↓]

:tribe [traib] *n.* Ⓒ **1** a group of primitive people living under one chief. 종족; 부족. ¶ *a ~ of Indians* 인디언의 한 종족 / *a cannibal* ~ 식인종 / *a member of the Zulu* ~ 줄루족의 한 사람. **2** ⟪usu. *contempt.*⟫ a group of people who have the same habits, interests, occupation, etc. 한동아리; 패; (같은 직업의) 동료. ¶ *a ~ of politicians* 정상배의 한 족속 / *the ~ of artists* 예술가들 / *lawyers and all their* ~ 변호사와 그 모든 패거리들. **3** ⟪biol.⟫ a group, class or kind of animals or plants. (동식물의) 족(族); 유(類). ¶ *the dog* ~ 견족(犬族). [L.]

tribes·man [tráibzmən] *n.* Ⓒ (*pl.* **-men** [-mən]) a member of a tribe. 같은종족의 일원.

trib·u·la·tion [trìbjəléiʃən] *n.* ⓊⒸ **1** great

suffering or trouble; distress. 고난; 재난; 고통. ¶ *in great* ~ 심한 고난 속에 / *After many trials on tribulations, we finally reached our destination.* 갖은 간난 신고 끝에 마침내 우리는 목적지에 도착했다. **2** anything that causes suffering. 고난의 씨; 화근. [L. *tribulum* threshing-sledge]

tri·bu·nal [traibjú:nl, tri-] *n.* Ⓒ **1** a court of justice. 법원(法院); 법정(cf. *bar*). ¶ *He was brought before the* ~ *for trial.* 그는 재판을 받으러 법정에 끌려 나갔다. **2** the seat in the court where the judge sits. 판사석 (cf. *bar*). **3** anything that has the power to judge or decide. (여론 등의) 심판. ¶ *the* ~ *of conscience* 양심의 심판 / *by the* ~ *of public opinion* 여론의 심판에 의해. [↓]

trib·une[1] [tríbju:n, ─ˊ] *n.* Ⓒ **1** 《Rom. hist.》 an ancient Roman official elected by the people to protect their rights and liberties. (고대 로마의) 호민관(護民官). **2** a defender of the rights and liberties of the people. 민중의 권리 옹호자. 參考 신문 이름에 쓰이는 일이 많음. [L. *tribunus*]

trib·une[2] [tríbju:n, ─ˊ] *n.* a raised platform for public speakers. 연단(演壇). [L. *tribuna*]

***trib·u·tar·y** [tríbjətèri / -təri] *n.* Ⓒ (*pl.* **-tar·ies**) **1** a ruler or nation that pays tribute to a superior, more powerful one. 속국(屬國)(의 왕). **2** a stream flowing into a larger one. 지류(支流). ¶ *the tributaries of the Rhine.* — *adj.* **1** paying tribute to another nation. 조공을 바치는; 종속하는. ¶ *a* ~ *state* 속국. **2** flowing into a larger stream. 지류의. ¶ *a* ~ *stream* 지류. [↓]

***trib·ute** [tríbju:t] *n.* ⓊⒸ **1** money paid by a nation to a superior, more powerful nation in return for peace or safety. 공물(貢物). **2** a gift, words, etc. given to show respect, praise, honor, etc. (존경·감사를 나타내는) 선물〔말〕; 찬사. ¶ *a* ~ *of praise* 찬사 / *pay (a)* ~ *to the memory of the founder* 창립자를 기려 경의를 표하다 / *a* ~ *to the bravery of the dead* 고인의 용감한 행위에 대한 헌사〔조사〕/ *a floral* ~ *for someone's funeral* 조화(弔花). [L. *tribuo* give]

trice[1] [trais] *n.* Ⓒ an instant; a moment. 순간. [Du.]

in a trice, in a moment; in an instant. 즉시.

trice[2] [trais] *vt.* (P7) 《naut.》 pull up and tie with a rope. …을 끌어올려 묶다. ¶ ~ *up a sail* 돛을 올리고 고정시키다. [↑]

tri·chi·na [trikáinə] *n.* (*pl.* **-nae**) a small, slender worm that lives in the intestines or muscles of man and animals. 선모충(旋毛蟲)《사람·돼지 따위에 기생》. [Gk.]

tri·chi·nae [trikáini:] *n.* pl. of **trichina.**

trich·i·no·sis [trìkənóusis] *n.* 《med.》 disease due to the presence of trichinae in the intestines or muscular tissues. 선모충병(病). [↑]

:trick [trik] *n.* Ⓒ **1** ⓐ an act done in order to deceive or cheat. 계략; 속임수. ¶ *His illness proved a* ~ *to avoid school.* 그가 아프다는 것은 학교에 안 가려는 속임수였다 / *try all sorts of tricks to gain one's end* 목적 달성을 위해 온갖 계략을 다 쓰다 / *That's a dirty* ~. 그건 치사한 속임수다. ⓑ a deceiving appearance; an illusion. 착각. ¶ *a* ~ *of eyesight* 환각 / *a* ~ *of the senses* 의식의 착각 / *tricks of memory* 기억의 착각〔혼돈〕. **2** a mischievous action; a playful act. (악의의) 장난. ¶ *play a* ~ *upon someone* 아무에게 장난치다 / *the tricks of fortune* 운명의 장난. **3** (a peculiar) habit; a characteristic. 버릇; 특징. ¶ *He has a* ~ *of stroking his nose when he speaks.* 그는 말할 때 코를 비비는 버릇이 있다 / *tricks of style* 문체의 특징. **4** the best way of doing something; a knack. 비결; 요령. ¶ *the tricks of the trade* 장사의 비결 / *the* ~ *of making good soup* 맛있는 수프를 만드는 비결 / *get* 〔*learn*〕 *the* ~ *of it* 요령을 익히다〔터득하다〕/ *There's a* ~ *to opening this lock.* 이 자물쇠를 여는 데는 요령이 필요하다. **5** ⓐ a kind of magic; a piece of jugglery. 요술. ⓑ a clever act designed to amuse. 재주; 곡예. ¶ *teach an animal clever tricks* 짐승에게 재주를 가르치다. **6** 《cards》 the cards played in one round. 한판에 돌리는 패. **7** 《naut.》 a turn or round of duty at steering a ship. (배의 키를 잡는) 1회 교대 근무 시간.

do 〔***turn***〕 ***the trick,*** 《*colloq.*》 get the desired result or effect. 잘 해내다; 소기의 성과를 거두다.

take 〔***win***〕 ***a trick,*** win one round of a card game. 카드놀이에서 한판 이기다.

— *vt.* **1** (P6,7) 《*into, out of*》 cheat; deceive. …을 속이다. ¶ ~ *someone out of his money* 아무를 속여서 돈을 우려내다 / *We were tricked into buying a poor car.* 속아서 고물 같은 차를 샀다. **2** (P7) 《*out, up*》 adorn; dress up. 장식하다; 치장하다. ¶ *She is tricked out in jewels.* 그녀는 보석으로 온통 치장하고 있다. [F.]

trick·er·y [tríkəri] *n.* Ⓤ the act of cheating; the practice of playing tricks. 속임수; 계교; 간계(奸計). [↑]

trick·le [tríkəl] *vi.* (P1,2A,3) **1** 《*down*》 flow slowly in a small or thin stream or fall in drops. 졸졸 흐르다; 뚝뚝 떨어지다. ¶ *Tears trickled down her cheeks.* 그녀 볼에 눈물이 뚝뚝 떨어졌다 / *Rain trickles from the trees.* 나무에서 빗방울이 뚝뚝 떨어진다. **2** come or go slowly and irregularly. 드문드문 오다〔가다〕. ¶ *Subscriptions are trickling in.* 기부 청약이 띄엄띄엄 들어오고 있다 / *Summer visitors are trickling home.* 피서객들은 하나 둘씩 귀가하고 있다.

— *vt.* (P7) cause (liquid) to flow in a small, thin stream. …을 뚝뚝 듣게 하다; 졸졸 흘리다.

— *n.* Ⓒ a small stream or drop. 뚝뚝 떨어짐; 실개천. [E.]

trick·ster [tríkstər] *n.* Ⓒ a person who cheats or deceives. 사기꾼. [*trick*]

trick·sy [tríksi] *adj.* capricious. 변덕스러운.

trick·y [tríki] *adj.* (**trick·i·er, trick·i·est**) **1** (of persons) apt to play tricks; unreliable. 교활한; 방심할 수 없는. ¶ *a ~ politician* 교활한 정치가 / *Be careful to deal with him, he's a ~ customer.* 그자와 상대할 때는 조심하게, 교활한 녀석이니까. **2** difficult to handle or understand. 까다로운; 다루기 힘든. ¶ *a ~ problem* 까다로운 문제 / *I am in a rather ~ position, can you help me out?* 내 입장이 지금 좀 난처한데, 빠져 나오도록 도와 줄 수 없겠나. **3** (of work, etc.) skilled; complicated; intricate. (일 등이) 손이 많이 가는; 정교한; 복잡한. ¶ *a ~ lamp* 정교하게 만든 램프. [*trick*]

tri·col·or [tráikʌ̀lər / tríkələr] *adj.* having three colors. 3색의. — *n.* Ⓒ a flag of three colors, esp. the flag of France. 3색기; 프랑스 국기. [*color*]

***tri·cy·cle** [tráisikəl] *n.* Ⓒ **1** a child's vehicle with three wheels moved by pedals. 세발 자전거. **2** a motorcycle with three wheels. 3륜 오토바이. [→cycle]

tri·dent [tráidənt] *n.* Ⓒ 《myth.》 a three-pointed spear used by the sea god Neptune. 삼지창(三枝槍)《해신(海神) Neptune이 가진 제해권의 표장(標章)》. [L. *dens* tooth]

:tried [traid] *v.* p., pp. of **try**.
— *adj.* tested and proved; reliable. 시험필의; 확실한. ¶ *~ and true* 절대로 확실한 / *a ~ friend* 믿을 수 있는 친구. [*try*]

tri·en·ni·al [traiéniəl] *adj.* **1** lasting three years. 3년간 계속되는. **2** occurring every three years. 3년마다의. ¶ *a ~ meeting,* 3년마다 있는 회합. — *n.* an event that takes place once in three years. 3년마다의 행사. [tri-, L. *annus* year]

tri·er [tráiər] *n.* a person who tries or tests; a person who persistently attempts. try 하는 사람; 시험자〔관〕; (…하려고) 노력하는 사람. [*try*]

***tri·fle** [tráifəl] *n.* Ⓒ **1** 《often *pl.*》 something of little value or importance. 보잘것 없는 것; 하찮은 것. ¶ *Don't worry over such trifles.* 그런 하찮은 일에 걱정할 것 없다 / *be angry at a ~* 사소한 일에 화내다 / *be interested in trifles* 하찮은 일들에 흥미를 가지다 / *I don't know why you waste your money* 〔*time*〕 *on such a trifles.* 나는 네가 왜 그런 하찮은 일에 돈〔시간〕을 낭비하는지 모르겠다. **2** 《*a ~*》 ⓐ a small amount of money. 소액의 돈. ¶ *The house was sold for a ~.* 그 집은 얼마 안 되는 소액에 팔렸다 / *The repairs cost only a ~.* 수리비는 거저나 다름없었다. ⓑ a small amount of anything; a little bit. 소량; 조금. ¶ *Just a ~ of sugar in my tea.* 내 차에는 설탕을 조금만 넣으시오. ⓒ 《as *adv.*》 slighty; somewhat. 조금; 약간. ¶ *a ~ sad* 좀 슬픈 / *a ~ too old* 좀 너무 늙은 / *The room was a ~ dark.* 방은 좀 어두웠다.
— *vi.* (P1,2A,3) **1** 《*with*》 talk, act, or handle insincerely or lightly; play with something. 희롱거리다; 우습게 보다; 만지작거리다. ¶ *a man not to be trifled with* 만만히〔우습게〕 볼 수 없는 사람 / *~ with one's moustache* 콧수염을 만지작거리다 / *I'm in no mood for trifling.* 농담할 기분이 아니다 / *~ with someone's feelings* 〔*affections*〕 아무의 감정〔애정〕을 농락하다. **2** spend one's time idly or wastefully. 헛되이 시간을 보내다; 빈둥거리다. ¶ *~ through the best years of one's life* 인생의 한창 때를 허송 세월하다.
— *vt.* (P7) 《*away*》 waste; spend. 낭비하다. ¶ *He trifled away the whole afternoon by the lake.* 그는 오후 내내 호숫가에서 빈둥빈둥 지냈다. [F.]

tri·fler [tráiflər] *n.* Ⓒ a person who talks and acts insincerely, esp. one who wastes away time. 희롱거리는〔실없이 구는〕 사람; 게으름뱅이.

***tri·fling** [tráifliŋ] *adj.* **1** of little importance or value; small in amount. 보잘것 없는; 하찮은; 약간의. ¶ *a ~ error* 사소한 잘못 / *a ~ character* 하찮은 사람 / *It may cost a ~ sum.* 돈이 몇 푼 안 들 거다. **2** not serious. 경박한; 진지하지 못한. ¶ *a ~ talk* 농담.

trig [trig] *adj.* 《Brit., *arch.*》 trim; smart. 말쑥한; 멋진. ¶ *a ~ co-ed* 멋진 (남녀 공학의) 여대생. — *vt., vi.* (**trigged, trig·ging**) (P6;1) **1** smarten; deck. 멋을 내다; 꾸미다. **2** wedge; check motion of. 쐐기를 박다; 멈추게 하다; 멈추다. — *n.* **1** a wedge used to trig a wheel. 바퀴 멈추개. **2** trigonometry. 삼각법. [N. (→true)]

trig·ger [trígər] *n.* Ⓒ **1** a small lever to fire a gun by pulling it back with the finger. 방아쇠. ¶ *pull the ~.* **2** an act, impulse, etc. that initiates an action, etc. (사건·행동의) 동기; 계기; 자극. — *vt.* (P6, 7) **1** fire or activate by pulling a trigger. 방아쇠를 당기다; 발사하다. **2** start or cause (esp. a number of events, often of an undesirable kind). …을 일으키다; 유발하다. ¶ *Large price increases could ~ demands for even larger wage increases.* 대폭적인 물가 인상은 그보다 더 많은 임금 상승을 유발하게 된다. [→treck]

trig·o·nom·e·try [trìgənámətri / -nɔ́m-] *n.* Ⓤ a branch of mathematics dealing with the relations between the sides and angles of triangles. 삼각법. [Gk. *gōnia* angle]

tri·hed·ra [traihí:drə / -héd-] *n.* pl. of **trihedron.**

tri·hed·ron [traihí:drən / -héd-] *n.* (*pl.* **-rons** or **-ra**) 《geom.》 a figure formed by three planes meeting at a point. 삼면체(三面體). [tri-, Gk. *hedra* base]

tri·lat·er·al [trailǽtərəl] *adj.* having three sides. 세 변(邊)이 있는. [tri-]

trill [tril] *vt., vi.* **1** sing or speak in a shaking voice. (목소리를) 떨다; 떨리는 소리

로 노래하다〔말하다〕. ¶ *The birds are trilling in the treetops.* 나무 꼭대기에서 새들이 지저귄다. **2** pronounce (a sound or word) with a trill. 혀를 말아〔전동음으로〕 발음하다. —*n.* Ⓒ **1** a shaking sound or voice. 떨리는 목소리〔소리〕. **2** a pronunciation made by a rapid vibration of the tongue. 전동음(顫動音)《R 따위》; (새의) 지저귐. [It.]

tril·lion [tríljən] *n.* Ⓒ **1** 《U.S.》 a thousand billions. 1조(兆)《10^{12}》; 100만의 제곱. **2** 《Brit., F.》 a million million million. 1경(京)《10^{18}》; 100만의 세제곱. —*adj.* amounting to a trillion. 1조의; 1경(京)의. [→million]

tri·lo·bite [tráiləbàit] *n.* a kind of fossil crustacean. 삼엽충(三葉蟲). [→lobe]

tril·o·gy [tríləd3i] *n.* Ⓒ (*pl.* **-gies**) a set of three plays, novels, musical compositions, etc. that makes a completely related series though each part has its own unity. 3부작(部作); 3부곡(曲). [→logos]

:trim [trim] *v.* (**trimmed, trim·ming**) *vt.* **1** (P6,13,18) cut off the edge of (something) neatly; make tidy, esp. by cutting into a desired shape and size. …을 가지런히 다듬다〔깎다, 치다〕. ¶ ~ *one's nails* 손·발톱을 깎다 / ~ *a hedge* 산울타리의 가지를 치다 / *a neatly trimmed beard* 잘 다듬은 수염 / *I'm having my hair trimmed tomorrow.* 내일 이발을 해야겠다. **2** (P6,13,18) put (something) into shape; make (something) ready for use. (깎거나 대패로 밀어서) …의 모양을 만들다; …을 쓸 수 있도록 준비하다. ¶ ~ *the lumber* 재목을 마르다. **3** (P6,7) 《*reflexively*》 decorate; dress. …을 장식하다; 꾸미다. ¶ ~ *the dress with lace* 드레스에 레이스 장식을 달다 / *The girl trimmed herself up.* 소녀는 몸치장을 했다 / *a jacket trimmed with fur* (소매 등) 가장자리를 모피로 장식한 재킷 / ~ *up Christmas trees* 크리스마스 트리를 장식하다. **4** (P6,13,18) ⓐ cut off; cut down. …을 삭감하다; 줄이다. ¶ ~ *the cost* 〔*one's expenses*〕 비용을 줄이다 / ~ *a budget by 5%,* 예산을 5% 삭감하다 / ~ *an additional 400 employees* 추가로 400명의 종업원을 줄이다. ⓑ clip; cut. …을 잘라내다. ¶ ~ *dead branches off the tree* 나무에서 삭정이를 잘라내다. **5** (P6) change (one's opinions, etc.) to suit circumstances. (의견 따위를) 형편에 따라 바꾸다; (사정에 따라) 조정하다. **6** scold; 《U.S. *colloq.*》 beat; defeat. …을 꾸짖다; …을 매질하다; 패배시키다.

—*vi.* (P1) **1** perform the act of trimming. 다듬다; 손질하다; 치다. **2** maintain a middle course; try to please both sides or parties at the same time. 중립적〔기회주의적〕 태도를 취하다. ¶ ~ *between two parties* 양쪽에 다 좋은〔나쁘지 않은〕 입장을 취하다.

—*n.* Ⓤ **1** good order or condition. 정돈; 좋은 컨디션. ¶ *in good* 〔*proper*〕 ~ 잘 정돈되어; 상태가 괜찮아 / *put a home* 〔*garden*〕 *in good* 〔*proper*〕 ~ 집〔정원〕을 정돈하다. **2** decoration. 장식. **3** preparation. 준비. ¶ *in figting* ~ 전투 준비를 하고 / *in hunting* ~ 사냥의 복장으로.

—*adj.* (**trim·mer, trim·mest**) orderly; neat; in good condition. 말쑥한; 정돈된; 손질이 잘된. ¶ *A* ~ *maid appeared.* 말쑥하게 차린 하녀가 나타났다 / ~ *lawns* 손질이 잘된 잔디밭. [E. =firm]

trim·e·ter [trímətər] *n.* Ⓒ a poetry having three metrical feet in each line. (시(詩)의) 삼보격(三步格). —*adj.* having three metrical feet. 삼보격의. [tri-]

trim·ly [trímli] *adv.* in a trim manner. 말쑥하게; 깔끔하게. [*trim*]

trim·mer [trímər] *n.* **1** a person or thing that trims. trim하는 사람〔기구〕. **2** a person who has no firm belief, policy, etc., esp. in politics. 기회주의자《특히 정치에서》.

trim·ming [trímiŋ] *n.* Ⓤ **1** the act of a person who trims. 정돈; 손질. **2** 《*pl.*》 decoration, esp. of clothes. (의복 등의) 장식. ¶ *the trimmings on a hat* 모자 장식. **3** 《*pl.*》 additions to a meal. (주된 요리에) 곁들여 나오는 음식; (요리의) 고명. ¶ *We had roasted duck with all the* ~. 우리는 구운 오리 고기와 이에 곁들인 음식들을 먹었다. **4** parts removed by trimming. 깎아 다듬어낸 것〔찌꺼기〕; 가윗밥. **5** 《*colloq.*》 scolding; beating. 꾸지람; 매질.

tri·ni·tro·tol·u·ene [trainàitroutáljuì:n / -tɔ́l-], **tri·ni·tro·tol·u·ol** [trainàitroutálјuòul / -tɔ́l-] *n.* a substance used as an explosive. 트리니트로톨루엔; 티엔티. 參考 TNT 로 생략함. [*nitre,* →toluene]

Trin·i·ty [tríniti] *n.* **1** 《*the* ~》 the union of Father, Son, and Holy Ghost in one God. 삼위 일체. **2** 《*t-*》 Ⓒ a group of three persons or things. 3인조; 3개 한 벌의 것. [L. *tres* three]

trin·ket [tríŋkit] *n.* Ⓒ **1** a small ornament, jewel, etc. (자질구레한) 장신구. **2** something of little value. 하찮은〔시시한〕 것. [F.]

tri·o [trí:ou] *n.* Ⓒ **1** 《mus.》 a composition for three players; a group of three singers or players. 3중주(곡); 3중주단; 트리오. **2** a group of three persons or things. 3인조; 3개 한 벌의 것. [→Trinity]

tri·ode [tráioud] *adj.* having three electrodes. 삼극 진공관의. [tri-, (electr)ode]

:trip [trip] *n.* Ⓒ **1** a journey or voyage usu. short and esp. for pleasure. (짧은) 여행; 항해. ¶ *take a* ~ *to Kyŏngju* 경주로 여행가다 / *a round* ~ 왕복 여행 / *a car* 〔*yachting*〕 ~ 자동차〔요트〕 여행. **2** a light, quick step. 경쾌한 발걸음. ¶ *I know her by her* ~. 경쾌한 발걸음으로 그녀임을 안다. **3** stumble; slip; mistake. 곱드러짐; 실족; 실수. ¶ *a* ~ *of the tongue* 실언 / *make a* ~ 곱드러지다; 실족하다.

— *v.* (**tripped, trip·ping**) *vi.* **1** (P1,2A) run with short steps; skip. 가벼운 발걸음으로 걷다; (깡충깡충) 뛰다. ¶ *The boy came tripping down.* 아이가 깡충깡충 뛰어내려 왔다. **2** (P1,2A,3) 《*on, over*》 stumble; slip. (발이) 걸려 넘어지다; 미끄러져 넘어지다. ¶ *The little boy tripped over the stone.* 어린 소년이 돌에 걸려 넘어졌다. **3** commit an error; make a mistake in a statement, speaking, etc. 잘못을 저지르다; 실수하다; 말을 더듬다; 잘못 말하다. ¶ ~ *on a difficult problem* 어려운 문제에서 실수하다 / *catch someone tripping* 아무의 실수를 잡아내다.

— *vt.* (P6,7) **1** cause (someone) to stumble and fall; overthrow. …을 걸려 넘어지게 하다; 뒤집어 엎다. ¶ *The frozen road tripped him.* 그는 언 길에서 넘어졌다 / *The boy put his foot out to ~ him.* 소년은 그를 넘어뜨리려고 발을 걸었다. **2** cause (someone) to make a mistake. …을 실수하게 하다. ¶ *I was tripped by the artful question.* 나는 그 교묘한 질문에 걸려 실수하고 말았다. **3** perform (a dance) lightly. (춤을) 경쾌하게 추다. [Teut.]

tri·par·tite [traipɑ́ːrtait] *adj.* of or divided into three parts; made or shared between three parties. 3조의; 3부로 나뉜; 3자간의. ¶ *a ~ treaty* 삼국 조약. [tri-, *part*]

tripe [traip] *n.* **1** a part of the stomach of an ox, etc. used for food. (반추 동물의) 위(胃)《식용》. **2** 《*sl.*》 anything of no value; rubbish; nonsense; foolish talk or writing. 쓸모 없는 것; 폐물; 허튼 소리. ¶ *Why do you read such ~?* 그 따위 쓸모 없는 것을 뭣하러 읽나. [F.]

tri·ple [trípəl] *adj.* **1** three times as much or as many. 세 곱의; 세 겹의. ¶ *a ~ window mirror* 삼면경. **2** consisting of three parts. 세 부분으로 이루어진. ¶ ~ *alliance* 삼국 동맹.

— *n.* **1** an amount three times as much or as many. 세 배의 수(양). **2** a group of three; triad. 세 개 한 벌(조). **3** 《baseball》 a three-base hit. 3루타.

— *vi., vt.* (P1;6) **1** become or make (something) three times as much or as many. 3배로 되다(하다). ¶ *The firm tripled its profits last year.* 회사는 지난해 세 곱의 수익을 올렸다 / *He tripled his efforts.* 그는 세 배로 애썼다. **2** 《baseball》 make a three-base hit. 3루타를 치다. [→Trinity]

tri·plet [tríplit] *n.* Ⓒ **1** a set of three things. 세 개 한벌의 것. **2** one of three children born at a single birth. 세 쌍둥이 중의 하나. [↑]

triple time [∠–∠] *n.* 《mus.》 time or rhythm which has three beats to the measure. 3박자.

tri·plex [trípleks] *adj.* triple; threefold. 3중(3배)의; 3부로 되는. ¶ ~ *glass* 3중 유리. — *n.* Ⓒ 《mus.》 triple time. 3박자.

trip·li·cate [tríplәkit] *adj.* threefold; made in three copies. 3중의; 세 통의. — *n.* Ⓒ one of the same three copies. 세 통 중의 하나. ¶ *a ~ of a letter* 세 통 작성한 서신의 하나. — [tríplikèit] *vt.* (P6) **1** make (something) threefold. …을 3배로(3중으로) 하다. **2** make three copies of (something). …을 세 통 작성하다. [→triple]

tri·pod [tráipɑd / -pɔd] *n.* Ⓒ a stand, support, table, etc. with three legs. 삼각대. ¶ *a photographic ~* 사진기의 삼각대. — *adj.* having three legs. 3각의. ¶ *a ~ race,* 2인 3각 (경기). [Gk. =threefooted]

trip·per [trípər] *n.* Ⓒ 《Brit.》 a person who goes out on a short journey for pleasure. (행락을 위한) 여행자. [*trip*]

trip·ping [trípiŋ] *adj.* walking with light and quick steps. 발걸음이 가벼운.

trite [trait] *adj.* (**trit·er, trit·est**) worn out by too much use; commonplace. 진부한; 흔해빠진. [L. *tero* rub]

trit·i·um [trítiәm] *n.* 《chem.》 an isotope of hydrogen, the explosive used in a hydrogen bomb. 트리튬; 삼중 수소《폭발성 물질》. [L.]

Tri·ton [tráitn, -tɑn] *n.* 《Gk. myth.》 a sea-god having the head and body of a man and the tail of a fish. 트리톤《반인반어(半人半魚)의 해신(海神)》. [Gk.]

a Triton among* (*of*) *the minnows, a person who seems great because those around him are small. 군계일학(群鷄一鶴).

trit·u·rate [trítʃurèit] *vt.* (P6) rub or grind to powder. 가루로 만들다. [→trite]

:tri·umph [tráiәmf] *n.* **1** ⓊⒸ the state of being victorious; a victory; a success. 승리; 성공. ¶ *shouts of ~* 승리의 함성 / *win* (*achieve*) *a ~* 승리하다; 성공을 거두다. **2** Ⓤ joy over victory or success. 승리(성공)의 기쁨; 득의 양양. ¶ *be full of ~* 득의 양양하다 / *with a note of ~ in one's voice* 기쁨에 찬 목소리로. **3** Ⓒ a parade in celebration of a victory in ancient Rome. (고대 로마의) 개선 퍼레이드.

in triumph, triumphantly. 의기 양양해서.

— *vi.* (P1,3) **1** gain the victory; win success. 승리를 거두다; 성공하다. ¶ ~ *over an enemy* 적에게 승리하다 / *Right will ~ over wrong.* 정의는 불의를 이긴다. **2** rejoice because of victory or success. 개가를 올리다; 의기 양양해 하다. ¶ ~ *in one's success* 성공하여 우쭐해 하다. [L.]

tri·um·phal [traiʌ́mfәl] *adj.* of a triumph; celebrating a triumph or victory. 개선의; 승리를 축하하는. ¶ *a ~ arch* 개선문 / *a ~ feast* 승리의 향연.

·tri·um·phant [traiʌ́mfәnt] *adj.* **1** having gained a victory or success; victorious. 승리한; 성공을 거둔. ¶ *the ~ progress of knowledge* 눈부신 지식의 진보 / *a ~ army* 승리의 군대. **2** showing joy over victory or success. 의기 양양한. ¶ ~ *cries* 승리의 함성.

tri·um·phant·ly [traiʌ́mfəntli] *adv.* in a triumphant manner; victoriously; rejoicingly. 의기 양양하여; (승리로) 우쭐해서. ¶ *"I've done it !" he exclaimed* ~. 그는 "나는 해냈다"라고 의기 양양하게 외쳤다.

•**triv·i·al** [tríviəl] *adj.* not important; of little value; ordinary. 사소한; 하찮은; 평범한. ¶ ~ *matters* 〔*mistakes*〕 하찮은 일들〔실수들〕/ *a* ~ *sum* 〔*loss*〕 대단찮은 금액〔손실〕/ ~ *round of daily life* 평범한 일상 생활. ● **triv·i·al·ly** [-i] *adv.* [L. *trivium* street-corner]

triv·i·al·i·ty [trìviǽləti] *n.* (*pl.* **-ties**) **1** Ⓤ the state of being trivial. 하찮음. **2** Ⓒ something that has little importance and value. 하찮은 것〔일〕. [↑]

tro·cha·ic [troukéiik] *adj.* 《prosody》 of trochees. 강약격(強弱格)의; 장단격(長短格)의. — *n.* a trochaic verse or line. 강약격〔장단격〕의 시. [Gk. *trekhō* run]

tro·chee [tróuki:] *n.* 《prosody》 a foot of two syllables, the first long or accented and the second short or unaccented. 강약격(⏑×); 장단격(–⏑). [↑]

•**trod** [trɑd / trɔd] *v.* p. and pp. of **tread.**

trod·den [trádn / trɔ́dn] *v.* pp. of **tread.**

trog·lo·dyte [trágləddàit / trɔ́g-] *n.* Ⓒ **1** an ancient man who lived in a cave. 혈거인(穴居人). **2** a person living alone. 은자(隱者). [Gk.]

troi·ka [trɔ́ikə] *n.* **1** a Russian wagon drawn by a team of three horses abreast. 트로이카; (러시아의) 삼두마차. **2** a team of three horses driven abreast. 옆으로 나란히 맨 세 마리 말. **3** any group of three persons, nations, etc. 3인조; 3자 연합. ¶ *a* ~ *conference* 트로이카 방식의 회의. [Russ.]

〈troika 2〉

Tro·jan [tróudʒən] *n.* Ⓒ a person of Troy. 트로이 사람. — *adj.* of Troy or Trojan. 트로이 (사람)의. [Gk.]

troll[1] [troul] *vt., vi.* (P6;1) **1** sing the different parts of the same melody in succession. 돌림노래하다. **2** sing merrily. 즐겁게 노래하다. **3** fish with a moving line. 견지낚시를 하다. — *n.* **1** a song having parts sung in succession. 윤창; 돌림노래. **2** the act of trolling for fish. 견지낚시질. ● **troll·er** [-ər] *n.* [F.]

troll[2] [troul] *n.* 《Scand. myth.》 a giant or dwarf living in caves or underground. (동굴·지하에 산다는) 난쟁이〔거인〕. [N.]

trol·ley [tráli / trɔ́li] *n.* (*pl.* **-leys**) Ⓒ **1** 《U.S.》 a trolley bus. 트롤리 버스. **2** 《Brit.》 a handcart. 손수레. **3** a small wheel at the end of a pole on a trolley bus, streetcar, etc. (트롤리 버스·전차 등의 폴 끝의) 촉륜(觸輪). **4** 《Brit.》 a low four-wheeled car running on railway lines, esp. one operated by hand lever. 광차(鑛車). [*troll*[1]]

trolley bus [⌐– ⌐] *n.* a bus driven by electric current taken from overhead wires. 트롤리 버스; 무궤도 전차(無軌道電車).

trolley car [⌐– ⌐] *n.* 《U.S.》 an electric streetcar. (시내) 전차.

trom·bone [trámboun, –⌐ / trɔmbóun] *n.* Ⓒ a long brass musical instrument with a U-shaped tube. 트롬본. [→trump]

:**troop** [tru:p] *n.* Ⓒ **1** a large group of persons or animals. (사람·짐승의) 떼; 무리. ¶ *a* ~ *of boys* 〔*cattle*〕 한 무리의 소년들〔소〕. **2** 《*pl.*》 a body of soldiers or police officer. 군대; 경관대. ¶ *send troops to the front* 전선에 군대를 보내다.

— *vi., vt.* (P2A,3;6) **1** 《*up, together*》 gather or move in a crowd. 떼지어 모이다〔움직이다〕. ¶ *Children trooped together around the pretty dog.* 아이들이 예쁜 개 둘레에 모여들었다. **2** move in or out in large numbers. 무리지어 들어가다〔나가다〕. ¶ *People came trooping out of the theater.* 사람들이 극장에서 무리지어 쏟아져 나왔다 / *We all trooped into the dining-room.* 우리는 모두 식당으로 우르르 몰려 들어갔다. [F.]

trooping the colours, 《Brit.》 a military ceremony showing respect to their special flag by soldiers. 군기 분열식.

troop·er [trú:pər] *n.* Ⓒ **1** a soldier or a policeman on a horse. 기병(騎兵); 기마 경관. **2** 《Brit.》 =troopship.

like a trooper, very much; hard; extremely. 엄청나게; 몹시. ¶ *swear like a* ~ 마구〔호되게〕 욕설을 퍼붓다.

troop·ship [trú:pʃìp] *n.* Ⓒ a ship for carrying military troops. (군대) 수송선.

trope [troup] *n.* Ⓒ deviation from the normal way of saying something. 전의(轉義). [Gk. *trepō* turn]

•**tro·phy** [tróufi] *n.* Ⓒ (*pl.* **-phies**) **1** a prize given to a winner in a contest, such as a silver cup. 우승의 상품; 우승배; 트로피. ¶ *She presented* 〔*awarded*〕 *the* ~ *to the winning team.* 그녀는 우승팀에게 트로피를 수여했다 / *a tennis* ~ 테니스 우승배. **2** ⓐ something taken from the enemy in war as a memorial of victory. 전리품. ¶ *a* ~ *of war* 전리품. ⓑ anything kept in memory of victory, success, etc. 기념품〔물〕. ¶ *He hung the lion's head on the wall as a* ~. 그는 사냥의 기념물로 사자 머리를 벽에 걸었다. [↑]

trop·ic [trápik / trɔ́p-] *n.* Ⓒ **1** either of two imaginary circles around the earth parallel to the equator. 회귀선(回歸線). ¶ *the Tropic of Cancer* 북회귀선 / *the Tropic of Capricorn* 남(南)회귀선. **2** 《*the* ~*s*》 the hottest region on the earth, between the Tropic of Cancer and the Tropic of Capricorn. 열대 (지방). — *adj.* of the tropic; tropical. 열대(지방)의. [↑]

·trop·i·cal [trάpikəl / trɔ́p-] *adj.* **1** of the tropics. 열대의. ¶ ~ *plants* 〔*fruit*〕 열대 식물〔과일〕 / ~ *fish* 열대어. **2** very hot. 몹시 더운.

trop·o·sphere [trάpəsfìər / trɔ́p-] *n.* 《meteor.》 that part of the atmosphere extending about seven miles upwards from the earth's surface. 대류권(對流圈) (cf. *stratosphere*). [→trope]

·trot [trɑt / trɔt] *v.* (**trot·ted, trot·ting**) *vi.* (P1,2A) **1** (of a horse) go at a pace faster than a walk. (말이) 속보로 걷다. **2** go at a quick pace; hurry; run with short steps. (사람이) 속보로 걷다; 종종걸음 치다. ¶ *We must be trotting off home.* 이젠 서둘러 집에 가야 한다 / *The child trotted along after his mother.* 아이는 종종걸음으로 엄마 뒤를 따라갔다.

— *vt.* **1** (P6,7) cause (a horse) to trot. (말)을 속보로 가게 하다. ¶ ~ *a horse.* **2** (P6,7) go along (a road, etc.) by trotting. …을 빠른 걸음으로 가다. ¶ ~ *a winding path* 꼬불꼬불한 작은 길을 빠른 걸음으로 가다. **3** (P7) bring out something for others to see. …을 꺼내서 보이다. ¶ ~ *out one's best wines* 최고급의 포도주를 꺼내 보이며 자랑하다.

— *n.* Ⓒ **1** 《used as *sing.*》 the motion of a trotting horse. (말의) 속보. ¶ *go at a* ~ 속보로 가다〔달리다〕. **2** the quick walk or run of a person. (사람의) 빠른 걸음; 종종걸음. ¶ *proceed at a* ~ 빠른 걸음으로 나아가다. **3** busy, quick movement. 분주함; 분주한 일. [F.]

on the trot, busy. 바쁜. ¶ *They kept me on the* ~. 그들은 나에게 조금도 쉴 틈을 주지 않았다.

troth [trɔːθ, trouθ] *n.* Ⓤ 《*arch.*》 faith; truth to one's word. 성실. [*true*]

plight one's troth, pledge oneself in betrothal. 부부의 약속을 하다.

trot·ter [trάtər / trɔ́tər] *n.* **1** a horse trained for trotting. 속보를 익힌 말. **2** the foot of a sheep or pig, used as food. 양〔돼지〕다리《식용의》. **3** 《*colloq.*》 《*pl.*》 the foot of a person, esp. of a child or young girl. (어린이나 소녀의) 발. [*trot*]

trou·ba·dour [trúːbədɔ̀ːr, -dùər] *n.* Ⓒ 《F.》 one of the poets or singers who were popular in France, Spain, and Italy from the 11th to the 13th centuries. 음유 서정 시인(吟遊敍情詩人).

:trou·ble [trʌ́bəl] *n.* **1** ⓊⒸ anxiety; worry; difficulty. 걱정; 근심(거리); 고민; 곤란. ¶ *be in financial* ~ 재정난에 처해 있다 / *unfold one's troubles* 근심거리〔고뇌〕를 털어놓다 / *That will get him into* ~. 그 일로 그는 곤란해질 것이다 / *give someone so much* ~ 아무에게 큰 걱정을〔폐를〕 끼치다 / *a heart full of* ~ 고민에 가득 찬 마음 / *One could read* ~ *on his face.* 그의 얼굴엔 근심이 드러나 보였다 / *Paying the rent is the least of my troubles at present.* 내게 지금 집세를 내는 건 문젯거리도 안 되는 작은 일이다 / *Life is full of troubles.* 삶에는 뜻대로 안 되는 어려운 일들이 많다. **2** 《often *pl.*》 disturbance; social or political unrest. 분쟁; 분규; 쟁의. ¶ *domestic troubles* 국내〔가정〕 문제 / *labor troubles* 노동 쟁의 / *political troubles* 정쟁(政爭). **3** ⓊⒸ disease; illness. 병. ¶ *suffer from mental* ~ 정신 질환을 앓다 / *heart* ~ 심장병 / *gastric* ~ 위의 장애; 위장병 / *children's troubles* 어린이들의 병. **4** Ⓤ inconvenience; effort; labor; pain. 불편; 폐; 수고; 노고; 고심. ¶ *put someone to* ~ 아무에게 수고〔폐〕를 끼치다 / *have much* ~ *to keep out of debt* 빚을 지지 않으려고 무척 고심하다 / *I have some* ~ *in reading his handwriting.* 그의 필적은 읽기가 좀 힘이 든다 / *He opened the heavy door without any* ~. 그는 전혀 힘들이지 않고 그 무거운 문을 열었다 / *"I hope we haven't put you to any* ~*." "No* ~ *(at all)."* 불편〔번거로움〕이나 끼치지 않았는지 모르겠네요. 아니 괜찮습니다. **5** Ⓒ a person or thing that causes trouble. 골칫거리; 고통거리. ¶ *I always find it a great* ~ *to get up early in the morning.* 아침 일찍 일어나는 것이 늘 고통거리다 / *He is a great* ~ *to his mother.* 그는 제 어미에게 큰 골칫덩어리이다.

ask 〔***look***〕 ***for trouble,*** 《*colloq.*》 show lack of caution. 경솔한 짓을 하다.

get into trouble, **a**) do something that will bring trouble. 문제를〔말썽을〕 일으키다. **b**) (of an unmarried woman) become pregnant. (미혼 여성이) 임신하다.

— *vt.* **1** (P6) cause trouble to (someone); make anxious; disturb; worry. …을 괴롭히다; 걱정시키다. ¶ *What troubles me most is that I am weak.* 가장 걱정되는 것은 내가 몸이 약하다는 것이다 / *I'm troubled with a bad cold.* 독감으로 고생하고 있다 / *He is troubled about his only daughter.* 그는 외동딸 일로 고민하고 있다 / *Don't let it* ~ *you.* 그 일로 걱정하지 말게나. **2** (P6,13, 20) give trouble to (someone); cause inconvenience; cause difficulty to. …에게 폐를 끼치다; …에게 번거로움을 주다. ¶ *I'm sorry to* ~ *you so much, but ….* 폐를 끼치게 되어 대단히 죄송하지만… / *May I* ~ *you for some money?* 돈 좀 빌려 줄 수 있겠나 / *I fear I must* ~ *you to come upstairs.* 미안하지만 이층으로 좀 올라와 주겠나 / *I do not* ~ *myself about* 〔*with*〕 *such things.* 나는 그런 일로 속을 썩이지〔고민하지〕 않는다. **3** (P6) cause pain or discomfort. …을 괴롭히다. ¶ *His wound troubles him a great deal.* 상처가 그를 몹시 괴롭히고 있다 / *He is always troubling me about his private affairs.* 그는 그의 개인 문제로 나를 노상 귀찮게 한다.

— *vi.* **1** (P1,4) 《esp. *negative* and *interrogative*》 cause oneself inconvenience; make an effort. 수고하다; 노력하다. ¶ *Don't* ~ *to come to the door.* 문까지 나올 것 없다 / *Why should I* ~ *to apologize?* 뭣 때문에 내가 사과까지 해야 하느냐. **2** (P1,3) feel anxious; worry. 근심〔걱정, 염려〕하다.

¶ *Don't ~ about small things.* 사소한 일로 걱정할 것 없다. [→turbid]

trou·bled [trʌ́bld] *adj.* **1** stormy; disturbed. 거친; 어수선한. ¶ *a ~ sea* 〔*waters*〕 거친 바다; 혼란 상태. **2** worried; annoyed. 걱정스러운; 불안한. ¶ *a ~ look* 걱정스러운 얼굴 / *look ~* 불안스러운 모습을 하고 있다.

fish in troubled waters, gain an advantage in the midst of confusion. 혼란을 틈타 한몫 보다.

trou·ble·mak·er [trʌ́blmèikər] *n.* Ⓒ a person who causes trouble or difficulties for others. 말썽꾸러기.

trou·ble-shoot·er [trʌ́blʃùːtər] *n.* 《U.S.》 a person who eliminates causes of trouble. (분쟁) 해결사.

*__trou·ble·some__ [trʌ́blsəm] *adj.* causing trouble or difficulties. 골치 아픈; 성가신. ¶ *this ~ world* 이 골치 아픈 세상 / *a ~ job* 힘든 일 / *a ~ child* 성가신 아이.

trou·blous [trʌ́bləs] *adj.* 《*arch.*》 troubled; troublesome. 거친; 어지러운. ¶ *~ times* 어지러운 시대.

trough [trɔ(ː)f, trɑf] *n.* Ⓒ **1** a wooden container used to keep water or food for horses or cattle. 구유; 여물통. ¶ *a pig's ~.* **2** something shaped like this, used by bakers. 구유 모양의 것; 반죽 그릇. **3** a channel for carrying away rain water. 홈통; 물받이. **4** the hollow between two waves. (놀과 놀 사이의) 골. [E.(→tray, tree)]

trounce [trauns] *vt.* (P6) **1** beat (someone) severely; inflict severe punishment. …을 호되게 패다〔때리다, 치다〕; 엄벌에 처하다. **2** 《*colloq.*》 defeat completely. 참패시키다. ¶ *We were thoroughly trounced by the opposing team.* 상대팀에게 참패했다. [→truncheon]

troupe [truːp] *n.* Ⓒ a group of performers such as actors, singers, or acrobats. (배우·곡예사 등의) 일단; 한 패. [*troop*]

*__trou·sers__ [tráuzərz] *n. pl.* two-legged outer clothing covering the body from the waist to the ankles or knees. (남자의) 바지. ¶ *a pair of ~* 바지 한 벌. [Celt. *triubhas*]

wear the trousers, (of a wife) domineer over a husband; be master in the house. 남편을 깔고 뭉개다; 내주장하다.

trous·seau [trúːsou, ─́] *n.* Ⓒ (*pl.* **-seaux** or **-seaus**) the clothes, jewelry, personal things, etc. of a bride. 혼숫감. [F.]

trous·seaux [trúːsouz, ─́] *n.* pl. of **trousseau.**

*__trout__ [traut] *n.* ⓊⒸ (*pl.* **trouts** or *collectively* **trout**) **1** a food fish living in clear freshwater, belonging to the salmon family. 송어. **2** 《*contempt.*》 《*old ~*》 an unattractive or annoying old person. 추한〔지겨운〕 노인. [Gk. *trōgō* nibble]

trow·el [tráuəl] *n.* Ⓒ **1** a tool with a thin, flat blade of wood or metal used for spreading or smoothing mortar. (미장이 등의) 흙손. **2** a tool used to take small plants from one place to another. 모종삽.

lay it on with a trowel, praise or flatter too much. 너무 입발린 말을 하다; 아첨하다 (cf. *lay*[1]).

— *vt.* (**-eled,** 《Brit.》 **-elled**) (P6,7) **1** apply or smooth with a trowel. …을 흙손으로 바르다〔고르다〕. **2** dig up or loosen with a trowel. 모종삽으로 파다〔흙덩이를 깨다〕. [L. *trua* ladle]

Troy [trɔi] *n.* an ancient city in northwestern Asia Minor. 트로이.

troy [trɔi] *n.* =troy weight.

troy weight [╴╴] *n.* a system of weight used for precious metals, gems, etc. 트로이형(衡); 금형(金衡)《금·은·보석의 무게를 다는 형량; 12온스가 1파운드》. [Place *Troyes*]

tru·an·cy [trúːənsi] *n.* ⓊⒸ (*pl.* **-cies**) the act of being absent from school without any proper reason. (학교의) 무단 결석; 농땡이짓. [*truant*]

tru·ant [trúːənt] *n.* Ⓒ **1** a child who stays away from school without any proper reason or without permission. 무단히 학교를 빼먹는 학생; 무단 결석 학생. ¶ *play ~* 학교를 무단 결석하다. **2** a person who neglects his duty. 임무 태만자; 게으름뱅이. — *adj.* being absent from school without any proper reason or without permission; lazy; wandering. 학교를 무단 결석하는; 빈들거리는; 게으름 피우는. [Celt. = wretched]

truce [truːs] *n.* ⒸⓊ **1** a temporary peace in a war made possible by mutual agreement; an armistice. 휴전. ¶ *a ~ talk* 휴전 회담 / *make a ~* 휴전하다 / *a flag of ~* 휴전의 백기 / *declare the ~* 휴전을 발표하다. **2** a pause or rest from trouble, pain, etc. (고난·고통 등의) 중단; 휴지. [→true]

:**truck**[1] [trʌk] *n.* Ⓒ **1** 《U.S.》 a large, strong vehicle for carrying heavy loads. 트럭; 화물 자동차. **2** a small cart with two wheels used for carrying luggage. 손수레. **3** 《Brit.》 an open railroad freight car. 무개 화차(無蓋貨車). — *vt.* (P6) carry goods on a truck; carry on a truck. (물건을) 트럭에 싣다; 트럭으로 나르다. [Gk. *trekhō* run]

truck[2] [trʌk] *n.* Ⓤ **1** exchange; barter; changing goods for goods. 물물 교환. ¶ *~ system* (임금의) 현물 지급제. **2** 《*colloq.*》 business; dealings. 거래; 교제. ¶ *have no ~ with* …와 아무 관계〔거래〕가 없다. **3** 《U.S.》 vegetables cultivated for sale in a market. 시장에 낼 야채류; 상품 작물《특히 야채류》. **4** 《*colloq.*》 objects of small value; rubbish. 하찮은 물건; 잡동사니. ¶ *The old house is full of ~.* 그 헌집은 허섭스레기로 가득하다. — *vt., vi.* (P6,13;1,3) exchange (goods) for other goods. 물물 교환하다;

교역하다. ¶ ～ *a thing with someone* =～ *for a thing with someone* 아무와 물건을 교환하다. [F.]

truck·er [trʌ́kər] *n.* Ⓒ **1** a person who drives a truck. 트럭 운전사. **2** a person or company engaged in carrying goods, etc. by trucks. 트럭 운송업자. [*truck*[1]]

truck farm [ˊ ˋ] *n.* ⟪U.S.⟫ a farm where vegetables are grown to be sold in a market. 시판용 채소 재배 농장(cf. ⟪Brit.⟫ *market garden*). [*truck*[2]]

truck·le [trʌ́kəl] *vi.* (P1,3) ⟪*to*⟫ submit or yield weakly to; be servile or submissive to. 굽실거리다; 굴종하다. ¶ ～ *to unreasonable demands* 당찮은 요구에 굴종하다. [→truck[1]]

truckle-bed [trʌ́kəlbèd] *n.* a small, low bed on wheels that can be pushed beneath another bed when not in use; a trundle-bed. 바퀴 달린 낮은(작은) 침대(낮에는 큰 침대 밑에 밀어넣어 둠). [↑]

truck·man [trʌ́kmən] *n.* (*pl.* **-men** [-mən]) =trucker.

truc·u·lence [trʌ́kjələns, trú:-] *n.* Ⓤ the state or quality of being truculent. 사나움; 잔인. [↓]

truc·u·lent [trʌ́kjələnt, trú:-] *adj.* very fierce and cruel; ready to fight. 사나운; 영악한; 잔인한. [L. *trux* fierce]

trudge [trʌdʒ] *vt., vi.* (P6;1,2A,2B) walk wearily and laboriously. 터벅터벅(무거운 걸음으로) 걷다. ¶ *An old man trudged home through the deep snow.* 한 노인이 깊은 눈 속을 터벅터벅 걸어 집으로 갔다. —*n.* Ⓒ a long, wearying walk. 무거운 걸음; 터벅터벅 걷기. ¶ *It was a hard* ～ *up the hill.* 그 산을 오르기는 힘든 일이었다. [Teut.]

:true [tru:] *adj.* **1** according to fact; correct; not false. 진실한; 참된; 정말의; 사실대로의 (opp. false). ¶ *the* ～ *meaning* 참뜻 / *a* ～ *story* 실화 / *What you say sounds not* ～. 네 말은 거짓말 같다 / *Is it* ～ *that she refused?* 그녀가 거절한 건 정말이냐 / *That is only too* ～. 섭섭하지만 그것은 사실이다 / *His story is too good to be* ～. 그의 이야기는 너무나 그럴듯해서 믿어지지가 않는다. **2** real; genuine. 진짜의; 순수한; 진정한. ¶ ～ *kindness* 순수한 친절 / ～ *gold* 순금 / ～ *love* (*friendship*) 진정한 사랑(우정) / *the* ～ *heir to the property* 재산의 진짜 상속인. **3** ⟪*to*⟫ exact; accurate; right. 확실한; 정확한; 틀림없는. ¶ ～ *to life* 실물(현실) 그대로의 / ～ *to time* 시간대로; 정시에 / ～ *to nature* 진짜에 가까운 / *hold* ～ 들어맞다; (규칙 등이) 유효하다 / *Weights and measures ought to be strictly* ～. 무게와 치수는 아주 정확해야 한다. **4** ⟪*to*⟫ faithful; loyal; sincere. 성실한; 충실한. ¶ ～ *to one's principles* 자기 신념(주의)에 충실한 / *a translation* ～ *to the original* 원문에 충실한 번역 / *True to his words, he came to see me.* 그는 말했던 대로 나를 만나러 왔다 / *A man should remain* ～ *to his wife.* 남자는 자기 아내에게 성실하지 않으면 안 된다. **5** (of a voice) in perfect tune; (of a tool, wheel, etc.) in correct position. (소리가) 음조에 맞는; (기구 등이) 제 위치에 있는. ¶ *His voice is* ～. 그의 목소리는 음조가 맞는다 / *This wheel isn't* ～. 이 바퀴가 제대로 끼워지지 않는다.

come true, become real; happen as expected. 실현되다; (예언이) 적중하다. ¶ *His dream came* ～. 그의 꿈은 실현되었다.

true as steel, very faithful; most reliable. 아주 충실한; 믿을 수 있는.

true to oneself, not going out of one's character. 자기 분수를 지키는.

true to type, typical. 전형적인.

—*adv.* truly; exactly; accurately. 정말로; 정확히. ¶ *aim* ～ 똑바로 겨누다 / *Please tell me* ～. 정직하게 말해 주시오 / *speak* ～ 사실을 말하다 / *ring* ～ 정말처럼 들리다 / *These sheep will breed* ～. 이 양들은 변종을 낳지 않을 것이다. [E.]

true blue [ˊ ˊ] *n.* **1** a fast blue color. 바래지 않는 남빛. **2** a person faithful to a party or principle. (자기 신념·주의에) 충실한 사람.

true-blue [trú:blú:] *adj.* very loyal; faithful. (주의 따위에) 충실한.

true·bred [trú:bréd] *adj.* **1** thoroughbred. 순종의. **2** wellbred. 올바르게(교양 있게) 자란; 예절 바른.

true·heart·ed [trú:há:rtid] *adj.* true and faithful; honest. 성실한.

tru·ism [trú:izəm] *n.* Ⓒ a statement that is clearly true and well-known. 자명한 이치. [*true*]

:tru·ly [trú:li] *adv.* **1** indeed. 정말로; 참으로. ¶ *a* ～ *surprising report* 참으로 놀라운 보고 / *I can* ～ *say.* 정말로 그렇다 / *Truly, I am sorry.* 정말 미안합니다 / *Truly, that was a disaster!* 참으로 대단한 재해였다. **2** sincerely; faithfully. 진정으로; 성실히. ¶ *serve* ～ 성실히 섬기다 / *speak* ～ 정직하게 말하다. **3** correctly; really. 바르게; 진실하게. ¶ *It is* ～ *said that time is money.* 시간이 돈이란 말은 옳은 말이다 / *Tell me* ～ *what you think.* 네 생각을 사실대로 말해라. [*true*]

Yours truly =***Truly yours,*** words concluding a letter. 총총; 여불비(례)(餘不備(禮)).

trump [trʌmp] *n.* Ⓒ **1** any playing card of a suit that is temporarily ranked higher than any other suit. (트럼프 놀이의) 으뜸패. ¶ *play a* ～ 으뜸패를 내놓다; 비장의 수를 쓰다. **2** ⟪*colloq.*⟫ a good, reliable person. 미더운 사람.

turn up trumps, unexpectedly prove to be helpful, friendly, etc.; do much more than was expected. (어려울 때) 뜻밖의 도움이 되다; 예상 외로 일이 잘 돼 가다.

—*vt., vi.* (P6;1) take (a card) with a trump; play a trump card. 으뜸패로 따다; 으뜸패를 내놓다. [→triumph]

trump up, invent (a false accusation,

statement, etc.) to deceive someone. (남을 속이려고 없는 것을) 날조하다; 조작하다. ¶ ~ *up a charge against someone* 아무에게 누명을 씌우다.

trump card [∠∠] *n.* a trump. 으뜸패.

trump·er·y [trʌ́mpəri] *n.* UC (*pl.* **-er·ies**) something showy but worthless. 겉만 뻔드레한 것; 굴퉁이. —— *adj.* good in appearance but without value. 겉만 번드르르한. ¶ *This clothing is very* ~. 이 옷은 정말로 겉만 번드르르하다. [F. *tromperie* deceit]

·**trum·pet** [trʌ́mpit] *n.* C **1** a musical instrument with a curved brass tube, keys, a bell-shaped mouth, etc. producing a powerful tone. 트럼펫. **2** something like a trumpet in shape or sound. 트럼펫 모양의 것; 트럼펫 비슷한 소리. ¶ *an ear* ~ 보청기.

blow one's own trumpet, boast of oneself. 제자랑하다; 큰소리치다.

—— *vi.* (P1) **1** blow a trumpet. 트럼펫을 불다. **2** make a sound like a trumpet. 트럼펫 같은 소리를 내다. ¶ *The elephant trumpeted.* 코끼리가 트럼펫 같은 소리를 냈다.

—— *vt.* (P6,7) 《often *contempt.*》 announce (something) in a loud voice; make known widely and loudly. …을 큰 소리로 알리다; 널리 퍼뜨리다. ¶ ~ *someone's fame abroad* 아무의 명성을 해외에 널리 알리다 / *She is always trumpeting the cleverness of her son.* 그녀는 노상 제 아들이 영리하다고 떠벌리고 다닌다. [L. *trompe*]

trum·pet·er [trʌ́mpitər] *n.* C a person who blows a trumpet; a soldier who blows a trumpet as a signal. 트럼펫 주자; 나팔수.

trumpet lily [∠-∠-] *n.* a lily that has long trumpetlike flowers. 나팔나리; 백향나리.

trun·cate [trʌ́ŋkeit] *vt.* (P6) **1** cut off the top of (something). (나무 따위의) 꼭대기를[끝을] 자르다. **2** shorten (a sentence) by cutting off some parts of it. (문장 등)을 잘라 줄이다. ●**trun·ca·tion** [trʌŋkéiʃən] *n.* [→trunk]

trun·cheon [trʌ́ntʃən] *n.* C **1** 《chiefly Brit.》 a short, thick stick or club. 곤봉(cf. *baton*). ¶ *a policeman's* ~ 경찰봉. **2** a staff or club carried as a symbol of office or authority. (권위의 상징으로 들고 다니는) 직장(職杖); 지휘봉. [↑]

trun·dle [trʌ́ndl] *vt.* (P6,7) cause (something heavy) to roll along. (무거운 것)을 드르르 굴리다; 굴려가다. ¶ ~ *a wheelbarrow* 외바퀴 손수레를 드르르 밀고 가다 / *The man trundled his heavy trunk along the street.* 그 사람은 그의 무거운 트렁크를 드르르 굴리며 거리를 지나갔다. —— *vi.* (P2A) roll along. (드르르) 구르다. —— *n.* C **1** the act or state of rolling. 구르기; 굴러감. **2** a small, strong wheel for supporting or carrying something heavy. (침대·피아노 등의) 각륜(脚輪); 작은 다리바퀴. **3** a low bed on wheels; a trundle bed; a truckle bed. 바퀴 달린 낮은 침대. [E.]

:**trunk** [trʌŋk] *n.* C **1** the main stem of a tree. (나무의) 줄기. **2** the body of a man or an animal, apart from the head and limbs. (사람·짐승의) 몸통. **3** the main part of anything; a trunk line. 본체; 주요부; 간선(幹線); 본선. ¶ *the* ~ *of a column* 기둥의 주요부. **4** a large box or chest to hold or carry clothes or personal belongings. 트렁크. **5** the large nose of an elephant. 코끼리 코. **6** 《*pl.*》 very short trousers worn by athletes, swimmers, etc. (운동용) 팬츠. **7** 《U.S. *colloq.*》 the compartment of an automobile for holding baggage, etc. 트렁크《자동차 뒤의 짐 싣는 칸》.

—— *adj.* main; chief. 주된; 주요한(cf. 《Brit.》 *boot*). [L. *truncus* cut short]

trunk-call [trʌ́ŋkkɔ̀ːl] *n.* 《Brit.》 a long-distance telephone call. 장거리 전화.

trunk line [∠∠] *n.* the main line of a railroad, canal, long distance telephone exchange, etc. (철도·운하·장거리 전신 등의) 간선(幹線); 본선.

trunk road [∠∠] *n.* a main road. 간선 도로.

truss [trʌs] *vt.* **1** (P6,7) tie (something) into a bundle. …을 다발로 하다[묶다]. **2** (P6) bind the wings of (a fowl) to the body before cooking. (요리 전에 닭의 날개와 몸통)을 묶다. **3** (P6) bind (a person's arms) to the body. (사람의 양팔)을 몸통에 묶다[동이다]. **4** (P6) 《archit.》 support (a roof, bridge, etc.) with a framework. (지붕·교량)을 트러스로 받치다[지지하다].

—— *n.* C **1** a bundle of hay or straw. (건초 등의) 다발. ¶ *a* ~ *of straw* 짚단. **2** a cluster of flowers. 꽃송이. **3** 《archit.》 a framework of wood or metal supporting a roof or bridge. 트러스《지붕이나 교량 등에서 하중을 지탱하는 목재 또는 철골의 구조물》. **4** a bandage used in case of rupture. 탈장대(脫腸帶). [F.]

trust [trʌst] *n.* **1** U firm belief in other's honesty, ability, etc. 신용; 신뢰. ¶ *have* [*put, place, repose*] ~ *in someone* 아무를 신용[신뢰]하다 / *an agreement made on a basis of mutual* ~ 서로의 신용을 바탕으로 이루어진 협약 / *I don't place any* ~ *in the government promises.* 나는 정부의 약속들은 믿지를 않는다. **2** C a person or thing firmly believed in. 믿을 수 있는 사람[물건]. ¶ *She is our sole* ~. 그녀만이 우리가 믿는 사람이다 / *Our* ~ *is in God.* 우리들의 믿음은 신(神)에게 있다. **3** U charge; duty; responsibility. 위탁; 책임; 의무. ¶ *hold something in* ~ …을 보관하다 / *leave something in* ~ …을 위탁하다 / *be in a position of* ~ 책임있는 지위에 있다 / *I regard it as a sa-*

cred ~ to fulfill my father's last wishes. 아버지의 유언을 성취하는 것은 내 신성한 의무라 생각한다. **4** Ⓤ business credit. 신용 대출; 외상 (판매). ¶ *buy things on* 〔*upon*〕 ~ …을 외상으로 사다. **5** something trusted to one's charge and care. 위탁물. **6** the act of holding property for the owner's benefit. 신탁 재산. **7** a union of several business houses so as to have complete control of the buying or selling of certain goods. 트러스트; 기업 합동(cf. *cartel*).

in trust, given to the care of someone. 위탁받고.

on* 〔*upon*〕 *trust, **a**) without cash payment; on credit. 외상으로. ¶ *sell* 〔*buy*〕 *goods on ~* 물건을 외상으로 팔다〔사다〕. **b**) without proof or examination. 증거 따위도 없이; 그냥 믿고. ¶ *"How do I know you're telling the truth?" — "You'll just to take it on ~."* "네가 사실대로 말하는지 내가 어떻게 아느냐" —"내 말을 그냥 믿어 줘."

— *vt.* **1** (P6) rely on; have faith in (someone or something). …을 믿다; 신용〔신뢰〕하다. ¶ *I cannot ~ your account.* 네 이야기는 믿지 못하겠다 / *I don't ~ his judgment.* 나는 그의 판단을 믿지 않는다 / *He is not a man to be trusted.* 그는 믿을 사람이 못 된다. **2** (P6) 《*for*》 sell things to (someone) on the condition of future payment; give credit to (someone). …에게 외상으로 팔다. ¶ *Will you ~ me till next Friday?* 다음 주 금요일까지 외상으로 주겠느냐 / *He trusted me for the camera.* 그는 카메라를 외상으로 줬다 / *The butcher will ~ us with the meat.* 고깃간 주인은 우리에게 고기를 외상으로 줄 것이다. **3** (P13) 《*to, with*》 put (something) into another's care; entrust. …에 맡기다; 위탁하다. ¶ *~ my typewriter to him* 내 타자기를 그에게 맡기다 / *~ him with my watch* 그에게 내 시계를 맡기다 / *I should not like to ~ him with large sums of money.* 그에게 큰 돈을 맡기고 싶지는 않다. **4** (P13) tell a secret to (someone); confide. 비밀 등을 …에게 털어놓다. ¶ *~ someone with secrets* 아무에게 비밀을 털어 놓다. **5** (P20) allow without fear. 안심하고 …하게 하다. ¶ *She didn't ~ her little boy out of her sight.* 그녀는 어린 아들에게서 눈을 떼면 무슨 짓을 할지 마음이 안 놓였다 / *He could ~ the man to do the work.* 그는 그 사람이 그 일을 하는 것이 미더웠다. **6** (P8,11,13) hope; expect; believe. 기대〔희망〕하다; 믿다; 확신하다. ¶ *I ~ that she will soon feel better.* 그녀의 기분은 곧 좋아질 것이라 생각한다 / *I ~ that nothing will prevent our meeting.* 아무것도 우리가 만나는 것을 막지 못할 것이다 / *I ~ to be able to help you.* 당신을 꼭 도울 수 있으리라 확신한다. — *vi.* (P3) 《*in, on, to*》 have faith. 믿다; 신뢰하다. ¶ *I ~ in God.* 나는 신을 믿는다. [N.]

trust for, expect; earnestly hope. 기대하다; 간절히 바라다.

trust in, believe. …을 믿다.

trust on, rely on. 의지하다.

trust to, leave to. …에 맡기다. ¶ *~ to chance* 운에 맡기다.

trust company [∠ ∠–] *n.* a company that takes charge of the money or property of others. 신탁 회사〔은행〕.

trust deed [∠ ∠] *n.* a deed that transfers property in trust. (담보) 신탁 증서.

trus·tee [trʌstíː] *n.* Ⓒ a person or firm who is responsible for the property or affairs of another person or company. 피(被)신탁인; 보관자; 수탁인. [*trust*]

trus·tee·ship [trʌstíːʃip] *n.* Ⓤ **1** the position or function of a trustee. 수탁인의 권능. **2** the administrative control of some region, colony, etc. granted to another country by the United Nations. (유엔의) 신탁 통치.

trust·ful [trʌ́stfəl] *adj.* ready to believe; full of confidence; trusting. (굳게) 믿는; 신뢰하는. ● **trust·ful·ly** [-fəli] *adv.* **trust·ful·ness** [-nis] *n.*

trust·ing [trʌ́stiŋ] *adj.* that trusts; apt to believe in other people; trustful. 믿는; 신용하는; 잘 믿는. [*trust*]

trust·wor·thy [trʌ́stwə̀ːrði] *adj.* that can be relied on; worthy of trust; reliable. 믿을 수 있는; 믿을 만한. ¶ *a ~ young man* 신뢰할 수 있는 청년.

trust·y [trʌ́sti] *adj.* (**trust·i·er, trust·i·est**) reliable; trustworthy. 믿을 수 있는; 신뢰할 수 있는. ¶ *a ~ servant* 신뢰할 수 있는 하인.
— *n.* Ⓒ (*pl.* **trust·i·es**) **1** a trusty person. 믿을 수 있는 사람. **2** 《orig. U.S.》 a prisoner considered to be trustworthy and so given special privileges. 모범수. ● **trust·i·ly** [-li] *adv.* **trust·i·ness** [-nis] *n.*

:truth [truːθ] *n.* (*pl.* **truths** [truːðz, -θs]) **1** Ⓤ the quality or state of being real or according to fact. 진리; 진실; 진짜. ¶ *There is some ~ in what he says.* 그의 말에도 다소의 진실이 있다 / *~ to nature* 〔*life*〕 진짜〔실물〕 그대로임 / *There wasn't a grain of ~ to this rumor.* 이 소문은 완전히 허구였다. **2** Ⓒ an established fact or principle; that which is true. 사실; 진상. ¶ *Tell me the whole ~.* 모든 사실을 내게 말해라 / *To tell the ~, he is not honest.* 사실을 말하면 그는 정직하지 않다 / *scientific truths* 과학적 사실. **3** sincerity. 성실. ¶ *doubt someone's ~* 아무의 성실을 의심하다. [*true*]

in truth, 《*lit.*》 truly; really; in fact. 참으로; 실제는.

out of truth, not correct; not in exact position. 정확하지 않은.

truth·ful [trúːθfəl] *adj.* **1** (of a person) telling the truth habitually. 정직한; 거짓말을 않는. **2** (of a statement) according to the fact; true. 사실대로의; 참말의. ¶ *a ~ account of what happen* 사건에 대한 사실대로의 보고.

truth·ful·ly [trú:θfəli] *adv.* with truth or honesty; in a truthful manner. 성실하게; 올바르게.

truth·ful·ness [trú:θfəlnis] *n.* Ⓤ the state or quality of being truthful. 정직; 성실; 진실.

:try [trai] *v.* (**tried**) *vt.* **1** (P6,8) attempt; endeavor. …을 해보다; …을 하려고 노력하다. ¶ ~ *one's best* 최선을 다하다 / *Try to get it finished by tomorrow.* 내일까지 그것을 마치도록 해라 / *She tried hard to keep back her tears.* 그녀는 눈물을 안 보이려고 무진 애를 썼다 / *Don't criticize him so much; he is trying his hardest.* 제딴에는 힘껏 하고 있으니, 그를 너무 나무라지 마라 / *Try not to think about it.* 그건 생각 않도록 해라. **2** (P6,7, 12,13) test; put to test. …을 시험하다; 시험해 보다. ¶ ~ *a new suit on* 새옷이 맞나 안 맞나 입어보다 / *Please ~ me for the job.* 시험적으로 내게 그 일을 시켜보시오 / *I tried the door to find out whether it was locked.* 문이 잠겼는지 알아보려고 손잡이를 돌려봤다 / ~ *one's skill* 〔*strength*〕 자기의 기량〔힘〕을 시험해 보다 / ~ *one's luck* 행운이 있는지 없는지 시험해 보다 / *Try how far you can jump.* 얼마나 멀리 뛰는지 해봐라 / ~ *a door* 열리는지 문을 열어보다. **3** (P6) afflict; put (something) to a severe test; strain. …을 괴롭히다; 시련을 겪게 하다. ¶ *His patience* 〔*courage*〕 *was severely tried.* 그에겐 대단한 인내〔용기〕가 필요했다 / *Reading tries my eyes.* 독서가 눈에 부담을 준다 / *The waitress tries my patience.* 그 웨이트리스는 나를 화나게 한다 / *The pain tries me a great deal.* 이 통증은 참아내기가 여간 힘들지 않다 / *He is sorely tried by his failure.* 그는 실패한 것이 못 견디게 괴로웠다. **4** (P6,13) 《law》 《*for*》 examine and judge (something or someone) in a law court. …을 심리〔재판〕하다. ¶ ~ *a case* 사건을 심리하다 / ~ *someone for election law violation* 아무의 선거법 위반을 심리하다 / *The prisoner was tried for murder.* 그 피고는 살인죄로 재판에 회부됐다 / *His case will be tried in the High Court.* 그의 사건은 고등 법원에서 심리될 것이다. **5** (P7) 《*obs.*》 《*out*》 make pure; refine. …을 제련〔정련〕하다.
— *vi.* **1** (P1,4) make an effort; attempt; endeavor. 해보다; 시도하다; 노력하다. ¶ ~ *for a prize* 〔*job*〕 상을 타려고〔일자리를 얻으려고〕 노력하다 / ~ *for a prison break* 탈옥을 시도하다 / *I don't think I can do it, but I'll* ~. 내가 그것을 할 수 있을지 모르겠지만, 노력해 보겠다. **2** (P3) take pains. 애쓰다; 수고하다. **3** (P3) apply or compete for. 지원하다. ¶ ~ *for the post* 그 자리를 지원하다.

try for, apply for. …을 지원하다. ¶ ~ *for the post* 직장을 구하다.

try it on, attempt something bold to see how far one will be allowed to go; take chance. (상대가 어떻게 나올지) 대담하게 시도해 보다; 운에 맡기고 해보다.

try on, put on (an article of clothing) to see if it will fit. (옷을) 입어 보다. ¶ ~ *a coat on* 코트를 입어 보다 / *She tried on her new dress.* 그녀는 새로 맞춘 드레스를 입어 봤다.

try out, test thoroughly the quality or ability of. (질·능력 등)을 철저히〔엄밀히〕 테스트하다.

— *n.* Ⓒ (*pl.* **tries**) **1** an attempt; an effort. 시도; 노력. ¶ *Let me have a* ~ (*at it*). 내가 한번 해보리다 / *This may not work, but it is worth a* ~. 이건 작동되지 않을수도 있지만 한 번 시도해 볼 만하다. **2** 《Rugby》 the act of putting the ball on the ground beyond the opponent's goal line. 트라이. [F. *trier* sift]

·try·ing [tráiiŋ] *adj.* very annoying and difficult; painful; hard to bear. 괴로운; 견디기 어려운. ¶ *a* ~ *bit of work* 좀 힘든 일 / *a* ~ *journey* 고된 여행.

tryp·sin [trípsin] *n.* a digestive ferment formed in the pancreas. 트립신《췌액(膵液) 중의 소화 효소》. [Gk. *tripsis*]

tryst [trist, traist] *n.* 《*arch.*》 ⒸⓊ **1** an agreement to meet. 만날 약속. ¶ *a lovers'* ~ 애인과의 밀회 / *keep* 〔*hold*〕 ~ *with* …와 만날 약속을 지키다. **2** an appointed meeting or meeting-place. 약속한 회합; 회합의 장소; 밀회 장소. [F.]

tsar [zɑːr, tsɑːr] *n.* Ⓒ the title of the emperor of Russia; czar. 러시아 황제의 칭호. [Russ. (→czar)]

tset·se(-fly) [tsétsi(flài)] *n.* Ⓒ a fly in South Africa which carries sleeping sickness. 체체 파리《수면병을 매개하는 파리》. [Native]

T-shirt [tíːʃəːrt] *n.* Ⓒ an undershirt for a man or boy with short sleeves and a round collarless neckline. T셔츠.

T-square [tískwεər] *n.* Ⓒ a T-shaped ruler, used in drawing. T자.

Tu. Tuesday.

·tub [tʌb] *n.* Ⓒ **1** a large open container of wood or metal, used to hold water for washing, etc. (큰) 물통; 함지; 큰 대야. **2** a bathtub. 목욕통; 욕조. **3** a small cask for holding butter or lard. (버터·라드 등을 넣는) 통. **4** the amount contained in a tub. 물통〔통〕 하나의 분량. ¶ *a* ~ *of water.* **5** 《Brit. *colloq.*》 a bath. 목욕. ¶ *take hot* ~ *every night* 매일 밤 뜨거운 물에 목욕하다. **6** 《*colloq.*》 a slow boat or ship used in practicing rowing. (연습용의 작은) 배; 보트.
— *vt., vi.* (**tubbed, tub·bing**) (P6;1) wash or bathe in a tub; put or keep in a tub. 통속에서 씻다〔목욕하다〕; 통에 넣다〔저장하다〕. [E.]

tu·ba [tjúːbə] *n.* Ⓒ a large brass wind instrument that produces deep tones. 튜바《최저음의 금관 악기》. [L.]

tub·by [tʌ́bi] *adj.* (**tub·bi·er, tub·bi·est**) like a tub; fat and round. 통 모양의; 땅딸막한; 똥똥한. [*tub*]

:tube [tju:b] *n.* Ⓒ **1** ⓐ a long pipe of metal, glass, rubber, etc. 튜브; 관(管). ¶ *a test* ~ 시험관. ⓑ an organ of the body in the form of a tube. 관 모양의 기관(器官). ¶ *the bronchial* ~ 기관지. **2** an enclosed hollow container made of thin metal, with a screw cap at the end, used for holding toothpaste, paint, etc. (치약·그림 물감 따위의) 튜브. ¶ *a* ~ *of toothpast* 〔*paint*〕. **3** 《Brit.》 an underground railway. 지하철 (=《U.S.》 subway). ¶ *a* ~ *train* 지하철의 전동차 / *go by* ~ 지하철로 가다 / *I took a* ~ *to Broadway.* 브로드웨이까지 전철을 탔다. **4** 《U.S.》 a bulb containing a vacuum and used in X-rays, radios, etc.; an electron tube. 진공관. [L.]

tu·ber [tjúːbər] *n.* Ⓒ 《bot.》 a thick round part of an underground stem bearing buds or eyes from which new plants grow. 덩이줄기; 괴경(塊莖). ¶ *The potato is a* ~. 감자는 덩이줄기 식물이다. [L. =bump, truffle]

tu·ber·cle [tjúːbərkəl] *n.* **1** 《anat.》 a small rounded swelling. 소류(小瘤); 작은 결절(結節). **2** a swelling caused by tuberculosis. 결절(結節); 결핵 결절. [↑]

tu·ber·cu·lar [tjubə́ːrkjələr] *adj.* of tuberculosis. 결핵성(結核性)의.

tu·ber·cu·lin [tjubə́ːrkjəlin] *n.* Ⓤ a liquid made from the germ causing tuberculosis, used as a test of the presence of tuberculosis by being injected under the skin. 투베르쿨린《결핵 검사용 주사액》. [→tuber]

tu·ber·cu·lo·sis [tjubə̀ːrkjəlóusis] *n.* Ⓤ a disease affecting various parts of the body, esp. the lungs. 결핵(cf. *consumption*).

tu·ber·cu·lous [tjubə́ːrkjələs] *adj.* of tuberculosis; tubercular. 결핵(성)의.

·tuck [tʌk] *vt.* **1** (P7,13) push the edge of (something) into a narrow space. …을 끼워〔쑤셔, 찔러〕 넣다. ¶ *The bird tucks its head under its wings when it sleeps.* 새는 잘 때 머리를 날개 밑에 파묻고 잔다 / *She tucked her bag under her arm.* 핸드백을 겨드랑이 밑에 끼워넣었다 / ~ *a letter in one's pocket* 편지를 주머니에 찔러 넣다 / *Tuck the money into the top of your sock for safekeeping.* 안전을 위해 돈을 발목의 양말 속에 찔러 넣어 두어라 / ~ *a napkin in one's collar* 칼라에 냅킨을 끼워 넣다. **2** (P6,7,13) gather up (a dress) into a fold; draw together so as to make shorter. (옷에) 주름〔단〕을 만들다; (옷)을 접어 넣어 줄이다; 호아 올려 짧게 하다. ¶ *The baby's dress was beautifully tucked.* 아기 옷을 맵시있게 접어 넣어 줄였다. **3** fold (sleeves, etc.) tightly. (소매 따위)를 걷어올리다. ¶ ~ *up one's sleeves* 소매를 걷어 올리다. — *vi.* (P1) **1** draw together into folds. 주름〔단〕을 잡다. **2** sew an end of dress so as to make it shorter. 호아 올리다; 시쳐 넣다.

tuck away, **a**) store in a safe place. (안전한 곳에) 챙겨넣다. ¶ *She's got a lot of money tucked away.* 그녀는 상당한 돈을 잘 챙겨두었다. **b**) eat (a lot of food). (많이) 먹다.

tuck in 〔***into***〕, 《*colloq.*》 eat or drink heartily. …을 배불리 먹다〔마시다〕. ¶ *I was just tucking into my dinner when the phone rang.* 전화가 울렸을 때 나는 한창 저녁을 먹고 있었다.

tuck (*a child*) ***up in bed,*** pull the sheets over; cover comfortable in bed. (아이에게) 이불을 잘 덮어주다.

— *n.* **1** Ⓒ cloth folded for ornament or to make a dress shorter. (옷의) 단; 주름 겹단; 접어올린 단. **2** Ⓤ 《Brit. *sl.*》 food, esp. cakes, sweets, etc. 음식《특히 과자류》. [E.]

Tu·dor [tjúːdər] *n.* the name of a royal family in England from 1485 to 1603. 튜더 왕가.

Tues. Tuesday.

:Tues·day [tjúːzdi, -dei] *n.* the third day of the week. 화요일. 參考 Tues., Tue., Tu. 로 생략함. [M.E. *tewesday*]

tuft [tʌft] *n.* Ⓒ **1** a small bunch of feathers, grass, hair, threads, etc. held together at the base. (풀·깃털 따위의) 술; 타래. ¶ *a* ~ *of feathers.* **2** a group of plants or trees. (풀·나무의) 수풀; 덤불. ¶ *a* ~ *of grass* 풀숲. **3** a small chin-beard. (한 줌의) 턱수염. ¶ *A goat has a* ~ *of hair on its chin.* 염소의 턱엔 작은 수염이 있다. — *vt.* (P6) put tufts on; furnish with tufts. …에 술을 달다〔장식하다〕. — *vi.* (P1) grow in tufts. 총생(叢生)하다. [L. *tufa* helmet-crest]

tuft·ed [tʌ́ftid] *adj.* **1** decorated with a tuft. 술을 단. **2** forming a tuft. 술 모양의.

·tug [tʌg] *vt., vi.* (**tugged, tug·ging**) (P6,7,13; 1,3) **1** pull with force; pull hard. (…을) 힘껏 당기다. ¶ *The child tugged at his mother's hand.* 아이는 제 엄마의 손을 힘껏 당겼다 / ~ *the cart out of the mire* 진창에 빠진 달구지를 힘껏 당겨 끌어내다 / *We tugged the boat on to shore.* 우리는 배를 기슭으로 끌어올렸다. **2** pull by a tugboat. 예인선으로 끌다.

— *n.* Ⓒ **1** the act of pulling hard. 세게 당김〔끎〕. ¶ *The baby gave a* ~ *at Mary's hair.* 아기가 메리의 머리카락을 확 잡아당겼다. **2** =tugboat. **3** one of a pair of long leather straps by which a horse pulls a wagon, cart, etc. (마구의) 끄는 가죽 끈〔줄〕. [E.]

tug·boat [tʌ́gbòut] *n.* Ⓒ a small, powerful boat used to pull large ships. 예인선.

tug of war [∠-∠] *n.* Ⓒ **1** a test of strength in which two teams pull against each other on a rope, each trying to pull the other over the winning line. 줄다리기. **2** a decisive fight. 결전(決戰).

tu·i·tion [tjuːíʃən] *n.* Ⓤ **1** 《now rare》

teaching; lessons. 교수; 수업. ¶ *give* 〔*have*〕 *private* ~ *on the violin* 바이올린의 개인지도를 하다〔받다〕. **2** the payment for teaching. 교수〔수업〕료. ¶ *increase in* ~ 수업료를 인상하다 / *He's already paid a year's* ~. 그는 일 년치 수업료를 이미 냈다. [→tutor]

:tu·lip [tjú:lip] *n.* Ⓒ a plant that has a brilliant-colored flower shaped like a cup; its flower or bulb. 튤립; 그 꽃〔구근〕. [→turban]

tulip tree [∠-∠] *n.* a tall tree in North America which has tuliplike flowers and wood which is used in making furniture. (북아메리카산) 목련과의 교목.

:tum·ble [tʌ́mbəl] *vi.* **1** (P1,2A,3) fall down suddenly and violently by losing one's footing or support. 굴러떨어지다; 넘어지다; 엎드러지다. ¶ ~ *down the stairs* 계단에서 굴러떨어지다 / ~ *from* 〔*off*〕 *a horse* 말에서 굴러 떨어지다 / ~ *over a chair* 의자에 걸려 넘어지다. **2** (P2A,3) roll about; roll from side to side. 뒹굴다; 굴러다니다; 몸부림치다. ¶ *He tumbled restlessly in his bed.* 침대에서 자꾸 몸을 뒤치락거렸다. **3** (P1,2A) turn in an acrobatic way. 공중제비하다; 재주넘다. **4** (P1,2A) move in a hurried way. 서두르다; 허둥거리다. ¶ ~ *into the room* 방으로 허둥지둥 들어가다 / *He tumbled out of bed.* 침대에서 뛰쳐나왔다 / ~ *into one's clothes* 허둥지둥 옷을 입다 / *The children tumbled off the bus into the park.* 아이들이 우르르 버스에서 뛰어내려 공원으로 달려갔다. **5** (P1,2A,3) drop in price; fall from power; decline. 값이 떨어지다; (권세가) 쇠락〔몰락〕하다. **6** (P3) 《*colloq.*》《*to*》 understand suddenly; realize. 갑자기 깨닫다; 이해하게 되다. **7** (P3) 《*into, on*》 come across; meet with. 우연히 만나다; 부닥뜨리다.

— *vt.* **1** (P7,13) cause (something or someone) to fall down; overthrow. …을 (내리) 굴리다; 쓰러뜨리다; 뒤집어 엎다. ¶ ~ *over a barrel* 통을 굴리다 / ~ *someone in wrestling* 레슬링에서 아무를 쓰러뜨리다. **2** (P6) put into confusion; disturb. …을 어지럽히다; 엉클어뜨리다. ¶ ~ *one's clothes* 〔*hair*〕 옷〔머리칼〕을 헝클어뜨리다. **3** (P7,13) throw down. …을 내팽개치다; 내던지다. ¶ ~ *passengers out of a bus* 버스 밖으로 승객들을 내몰다.

— *n.* Ⓒ **1** an act of falling down suddenly. 엎드러짐; 전도(顚倒). **2** a skillful acrobatic act. 공중제비. **3** a confused heap of things. 뒤범벅; 어지럽게 쌓인 것. ¶ *Things are all in a* ~. 모든 게 뒤범벅이다. [E.]

tum·ble-down [tʌ́mbəldàun] *adj.* ready to fall down; in a state of ruin; ruinous. 곧 무너질 것 같은; 황폐한. ¶ *a* ~ *old house* 곧 허물어질 것 같은 고옥(古屋).

tum·bler [tʌ́mblər] *n.* Ⓒ **1** a person who performs tricks of jumping and falling; an acrobat. 곡예사; 공중제비를 하는 사람. **2** a drinking glass without foot or stem; the amount it holds. 굽이나 손잡이가 없는 컵; 텀블러(cf. *goblet*); 그 한 잔의 양. **3** that part of a lock which must be put into a certain position by a key in order to open the lock. (자물쇠의) 날름쇠; 자물쇠청.

tum·brel [tʌ́mbrəl], **-bril** [-bril] *n.* **1** a heavy two-wheeled covered cart. 덮개 있는 2륜 짐수레. **2** 《hist.》 a cart used during the French Revolution to carry prisoners to the guillotine. (프랑스 혁명 때의) 사형수 호송차. [Teut. (→tumble)]

tu·mid [tjú:mid] *adj.* **1** swollen. 부어 오른. **2** using many fine words but little meaning; pompous. 미사 여구를 늘어놓은; 과장된. [L. *tumeo* swell]

tum·my [tʌ́mi] *n.* (*pl.* **-mies**) 《*baby talk, colloq.*》 stomach; belly. 배. [Abbr.]

tu·mor, 《Brit.》 **-mour** [tjú:mər] *n.* Ⓒ a swelling part of the body. 종기; 종창. [*tumid*]

tu·mu·li [tjú:mjəlài] *n.* pl. of **tumulus.**

·tu·mult [tjú:mʌlt, -məlt] *n.* ⓊⒸ **1** noise and confusion caused by great excitement; disturbance. 소동; 소란; 혼란. ¶ *a great* ~ 대소동; 야단법석 / *make a* ~ 소동을 벌리다; 법석을 떨다 / *the* ~ *of business centers* 번화가의 혼잡 / *His announcement was drowned in the* ~. 그의 발표는 북새통에 들리지 않았다. **2** excitement; agitation of mind and emotion. 흥분; (마음의) 격동; 격정. ¶ *in a* ~ *of feeling* 감정이 어지러워 / *She had a severe mental* ~. 그녀는 심한 정신적 혼란을 느꼈다. [L. *tumeo* swell]

tu·mul·tu·ous [tju:mʌ́ltʃuəs] *adj.* full of tumult; excited; confused; stormy. 소란스러운; 흥분된; 혼란한. ¶ *a* ~ *meeting* 소란스러운 회합 / ~ *passion* 격정. ● **tu·mul·tu·ous·ness** [-nis] *n.*

tu·mul·tu·ous·ly [tju:mʌ́ltʃuəsli] *adv.* in a tumultuous way; noisily; with agitation. 소란스럽게; 흥분해; 마음이 어지러워.

tu·mu·lus [tjú:mjələs] *n.* Ⓒ (*pl.* **-lus·es** or **-li**) an ancient mound of earth over a grave. 봉분; 고분(古墳). [*tumult*]

tun [tʌn] *n.* **1** a large barrel for holding wine or beer. 큰 술통. **2** formerly, a measure for wine, etc., equal to 252 gallons. (술 따위의) 용량 단위. [E.]

tu·na [tjú:nə] *n.* Ⓒ (*pl.* **-nas** or *collectively* **-na**) 《U.S.》 a very large fish caught for food in warm seas. 다랑어; 참치(cf. 《Brit.》 *tunny*). [Amer-Sp.]

tun·dra [tʌ́ndrə, tún-] *n.* Ⓒ a vast, frozen plain in the northern part of Canada, Russia, etc. 툰드라(지대); 동토대(凍土帶). [Russ.]

:tune [tju:n] *n.* **1** Ⓒ a piece of music; an air or melody. 곡; 곡조; 가락. ¶ *sing a merry* ~ 명랑한 노래를 부르다 / *dance to a* ~ 곡에 맞추어 춤추다 / *play a gay* ~ *on the organ* 풍금으로 경쾌한 곡을 치다 / *whistle a favorite*

〔*popular*〕 ~ 휘파람으로 좋아하는 곡을〔유행가를〕 부르다 / *He strolled along humming a* ~. 그는 콧노래를 흥얼거리며 걸었다. **2** Ⓤ the state of having the correct musical pitch. 올바른 가락; 장단. ¶ *sing in* ~ 가락에 맞게 노래하다 / *This piano is out of* ~. 이 피아노는 음률이 안 맞는다 / *The piano and the violin are in* ~. 피아노와 바이올린은 가락이 잘 맞는다 / *He can't sing in* ~. 그는 가락이 맞게 노래하지 못한다. **3** Ⓤ the state of harmonious adjustment. 조화. ¶ *He is in* ~ *with his friends.* 그는 친구들과 잘 어울려 지낸다 / *in* 〔*out of*〕 ~ *with the present time* 현 시류에 조화되어〔되지 않아〕.

***change** one's* **tune** =**sing another** 〔**a different**〕 **tune,** change one's way of talking, behavior, etc. (as from scorn to respect). 말〔태도 등〕을 바꾸다. ¶ *When I met him next time, he sang a different* ~. 다음에 그를 만났더니 그는 태도가 달라졌었다.

to the tune of, to the sum or amount of; at the heavy cost of. 금액 …; …라는 거금에. ¶ *We were robbed to the* ~ *of £5,000.* 우린 자그마치 5천 파운드나 털렸다.

— *vt.* **1** (P6,7) put in tune. …을 조율하다. ¶ ~ *a piano* 피아노를 조율하다. **2** (P13) bring into harmony or agreement; bring to a desired condition. …을 일치〔조화〕시키다; 적합하게 하다. ¶ ~ *one's views to the prevailing opinion* 일반적인 의견에 자기 견해를 맞추다. **3** (P6,7) 《*up*》 put into good working order. (기계 등)을 조정하다. **4** (P7,13) 《*to, in*》 adjust to a certain wave length or frequency. …에 파장을 맞추다; 동조시키다. **5** 《*arch.*》 sing; play. …을 연주〔취주〕하다.

— *vi.* **1** (P2A) adjust a receiving set so as to bring in a given sound. (수신기의) 파장을 맞추다; 동조시키다. **2** (P2A) 《*up*》 start tuning; begin to play or sing. 악음(樂音)을 내다; 연주〔취주〕를 시작하다. [→tone]

tune in 〔***out***〕, adjust a receiving set so as to bring in 〔shut out〕 a given sound. (라디오·TV 등의 다이얼을 조정하여) 파장을 …에 맞추다〔소리가 안 들리게 하다〕. ¶ *Will you please* ~ *in to a music program?* 다이얼을 음악 프로에 맞춰 주겠나 / ~ *in the radio.*

tune up, **a**) put (musical instruments) in the same pitch, as in an orchestra. (관현악단 같은 데서) 악기를 같은 음으로 맞추다. **b**) ⇨*vt.* 3. **c**) ⇨*vi.* 2.

tune·ful [tjúːnfəl] *adj.* full of melody; musical. 가락이 좋은; 선율이 아름다운; 음악적인. ¶ *The robin has a* ~ *note.* 울새는 소리가 곱다.

tune·less [tjúːnlis] *adj.* not melodious; not musical. 가락이 맞지 않는.

tun·er [tjúːnər] *n.* Ⓒ **1** a person who adjusts musical instruments to some standard state of harmony. 조율사. ¶ *a piano* ~. **2** a device for tuning. 튜너; 동조기(同調器). [→tone]

tung·sten [tʌ́ŋstən] *n.* Ⓤ 《chem.》 a hard, heavy, metallic element used in making steel and for electric-lamp filaments. 텅스텐. [Sw. =heavy stone]

tu·nic [tjúːnik] *n.* Ⓒ **1** a shirt-like garment worn by the ancient Greeks and Romans. (고대 그리스인·로마인의) 셔츠 비슷한 옷. **2** 《Brit.》 a short coat worn by soldiers or policemen. (군인·경찰 등의) 웃옷의 일종. **3** a woman's long jacket, usu. reaching below the hips. (여성의) 긴 상의; 튜닉. [L.]

tuning fork [⌐-⌐] *n.* 《mus.》 a small steel instrument which gives a fixed tone when struck. 소리굽쇠; 음차(音叉). [*tune*]

:tun·nel [tʌ́nl] *n.* Ⓒ an underground passageway for a railroad, etc. 터널; 굴. ¶ *The train went through a* ~. 기차가 터널을 지나갔다. — *vt., vi.* (**-neled, -nel·ing** or 《Brit.》 **-nelled, -nel·ling**) (P6;3) make a tunnel. 굴을 파다. ¶ ~ (*through*) *a hill* 산에 터널을 파다. [→tun]

tun·ny [tʌ́ni] *n.* Ⓒ (*pl.* **-nies** or *collectively* **-ny**) 《Brit.》 the tuna; a large sea fish caught for food and sport. 참치(cf. 《U.S.》 *tuna*). [Gk.]

tup·pence [tʌ́pəns] *n.* 《Brit. *colloq.*》 = twopence.

tur·ban [tə́ːrbən] *n.* Ⓒ **1** a scarf to wind about the head, chiefly worn by men in India or in Mohammedan countries. 터번. **2** a woman's hat shaped like this turban with little or no brim. 터번 비슷한 모자. [Pers.]

tur·baned [tə́ːrbənd] *adj.* wearing a turban. 터번을 쓴.

tur·bid [tə́ːrbid] *adj.* **1** (of water, etc.) muddy; (of clouds, smoke, etc.) thick. (물·구름이) 흐린; 혼탁한; 짙은. ¶ *a* ~ *river* 흐린 강 / ~ *smog* 짙은 스모그. **2** confused; not clear. 어지러운; 혼란된. ¶ ~ *thought* 혼란된 생각. [L. *turba* tumult]

tur·bine [tə́ːrbin, -bain] *n.* Ⓒ a kind of engine or motor operated by the force of water, steam, or air falling on the rim of a wheel. 터빈. [L. *turbo* wheel]

tur·bo·jet [tə́ːrboudʒèt] *n.* Ⓒ a jet propulsion engine that has a turbine-driven air compressor. 터보제트 엔진. [↑]

tur·bu·lence [tə́ːrbjələns] *n.* Ⓤ the state of being turbulent; disorder; confusion. 어지러움; 혼란. ¶ *political* ~ 정치적 혼란. [↓]

tur·bu·lent [tə́ːrbjələnt] *adj.* violently agitated or disturbed; not easy to control; disorderly. 사나운; 거친; 난폭한. ¶ *a* ~ *mob* 난폭한 군중 / ~ *winds* 사나운 바람 / ~ *weather* 험악한 날씨. [→turbid]

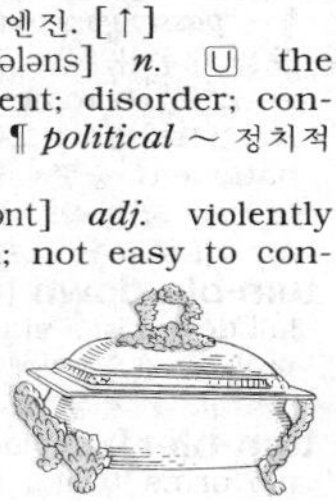

〈tureen〉

tu·reen [tjuríːn] *n.*

Ⓒ a large, deep dish with a lid for holding soup, etc. on a table. (수프 따위를 담는) 뚜껑 있는 움푹한 그릇. [→terra]

***turf** [təːrf] *n.* (*pl.* **turfs** or **turves**) **1** Ⓤ《*collectively*》 short and thick grass with the earth under it; Ⓒ a piece of this; sod. 떼; 뗏장(cf. *lawn, sward*). **2** ⓊⒸ a solid mass of partly rotted plants and moss found in a marsh, used as fuel; peat. 이탄(泥炭). **3** 《*the* ~》 a track for horse racing; horse racing. 경마장; 경마. — *vt.* (P6,7) cover with turf. 떼로 덮다. [E.]

turf out, 《Brit. *colloq.*》 throw out: dismiss. 집어던지다; 내쫓다. ¶ *He's been turfed out of the club.* 그는 그 클럽에서 추방되었다.

tur·gid [tə́ːrdʒid] *adj.* **1** swollen. 부어오른. **2** (of language, etc.) full of fine but unimportant words or expressions. 미사 여구를 늘어 놓은; 과장된. [L. *turgeo* swell]

tur·gid·i·ty [təːrdʒídəti] *n.* Ⓤ the state or quality of being turgid. 부어오름; 과장.

Turk [təːrk] *n.* Ⓒ **1** a native of Turkey. 터키 사람. **2** a Mohammedan who lives in Turkey. (터키의) 이슬람교도. **3** an unmanageable child. 다루기 힘든 아이.

Tur·key [tə́ːrki] *n.* a country in Asia Minor. 터키. 參考 수도는 Ankara임.

:**tur·key** [tə́ːrki] *n.* Ⓒ a large domestic bird, the flesh of which is used for food; Ⓤ its flesh. 칠면조; 칠면조 고기. [*Turkey*]

talk turkey, 《U.S. *sl.*》 talk frankly or directly; discuss a serious matter. 솔직히(대놓고) 말하다; 진지한 일을 논의하다.

Turk·ish [tə́ːrkiʃ] *adj.* of Turkey; of the Turks or their language. 터키(사람, 어)의. — *n.* Ⓤ the language of the Turks. 터키어.

tur·moil [tə́ːrmɔil] *n.* ⓊⒸ confusion; disturbance. 소란; 혼란. ¶ *in the ~ of war* 전쟁의 와중에 / *She couldn't think; her mind was in* (*a*) *complete ~.* 그녀는 어떤 생각도 할 수 없었다. 정신이 완전히 혼란에 빠져 있었기 때문에. [? F.]

:**turn** [təːrn] *vt.* **1** (P6,7,13) cause (something) to move round a point; rotate. …을 회전시키다; 돌리다. ¶ *~ the handle* (*knob*) *of the door* 문의 손잡이를 돌리다 / *~ a key in a lock* 자물통 열쇠를 돌리다 / *I turned the screw a few more times to tighten it.* 단단히 조이게 나사를 몇 번 더 돌렸다. **2** (P6,7) change the position or sides of (something); cause (something) to become upside down; reverse; roll; upset. …을 뒤집다; 거꾸로 하다; (책장)을 넘기다; 굴리다. ¶ *~* (*over*) *the pages of a book* 책장을 넘기다 / *She turned her collar up.* 그녀는 옷깃을 세웠다 / *~ a suit inside out* 옷을 뒤집다 / 《*fig.*》 *~ one's coat* 생각을 바꾸다; 변절하다 / *~ a bottle upside down* 병을 거꾸로 하다 / *Be careful not to ~ over the lamp.* 남포를 둘러엎지 않도록 조심해라 / *~ a log over* 통나무를 굴리다. **3** (P6,7,13) 《*to, toward, on*》 change the direction of (one's eyes, face, etc.); direct; aim. …을 (어떤 방향으로) 바꾸게 하다. ¶ *~ one's attention to someone* 아무에게로 관심을 돌리다 / *~ one's eyes around* 주위를 둘러다 보다 / *~ one's course to the west* 진로를 서쪽으로 돌리다 / *~ one's head* 고개를 돌리다 / *~ one's back on* …을 저버리다 / *She turned the car toward downtown.* 그녀는 차를 중심가 쪽으로 돌렸다. **4** (P6,7,13,18) change the nature or state of (something); make; translate. (…의 모양·성질·마음)을 바꾸다; 번역하다. ¶ *~ love to hate* 사랑을 증오로 바꾸다 / *The sound turned him pale.* 그 소리에 그는 얼굴이 창백해졌다 / *Turn this passage into Korean.* 이 구절을 한국어로 번역하라 / *~ water into ice* 물을 얼리다 / *~ goods into money* 물건을 현금화하다 / *Blood turned his shirt to a red color.* 피가 그의 셔츠를 붉게 물들였다 / *The heat has turned the milk* (*sour*). 더워서 우유가 상했다. **5** (P6,7) cause (someone) to go away; send; drive. …을 쫓아버리다; 돌려보내다. ¶ *She always turns* (*away*) *beggars from her door.* 그녀는 늘 거지를 문전에서 쫓아버린다 / *~ him adrift in the world* 그를 세상에 내팽개치다 / *~ someone away from his position* 아무를 면직시키다. **6** (P6) go beyond; reach and pass. …을 지나다; 넘다. ¶ *~* (*the age of*) *eighty* 나이가 80을 넘다 / *It has just turned two.* 시계가 막 두 시를 지났다. **7** (P6) go around (a corner). (모퉁이)를 돌다. ¶ *~ a street corner* 길 모퉁이를 돌다 / *The ship turned a cape.* 배가 곶을 돌았다. **8** (P7) 《*over*》 think about (something) carefully; consider. …을 곰곰이 생각하다; 숙고하다. ¶ *Turn that over in your mind.* 그 일을 잘 생각해 보아라 / *We have turned this problem over and over.* 우리는 이 문제를 곰곰이 생각해 보았다. **9** (P13) put to some use or purpose. (어떤 목적·용도에) 충당하다; 돌리다. ¶ *~ one's hand to useful work* 유익한 일을 시작하다 / *~ one's opportunity to good account* 기회를 잘 활용하다. **10** (P6) shape, cut out, on a lathe. …을 녹로로(선반으로) 만들다(깎다). ¶ *~ a candlestick out of brass* 놋쇠로 촛대를 만들다. **11** (P6) disturb the mind of; put out of order. (머리)를 돌게 만들다; 혼란시키다. ¶ *Sorrow has turned her brain.* 비탄한 나머지 그녀는 머리가 이상해졌다 / *Too much praise turned his head.* 너무 칭찬을 받아 그는 머리가 얼떨떨해졌다.

— *vi.* **1** (P1,2A,3) move in a circle. 돌다; 회전하다. ¶ *The moon turns round the earth.* 달은 지구 주위를 돈다 / *Wheels ~ round and round.* 바퀴들이 빙빙 돈다 / *The knob won't ~ easily.* 손잡이가 잘 안 돈다. **2** (P1,2A,3) change a course or direction of movement. 방향을 바꾸다. ¶ *~ around the corner to the left* 모퉁이를 왼쪽으로 돌다 / *This road turns at that points.* 이 길은

그 지점에서 꼬부라진다 / *He turned when she called (to) him.* 그녀가 불렀더니 그는 돌아 봤다. **3** (P3) 《*on, to*》 depend; be determined by. 의지[의거]하다; (…의 여하에) 달리다. ¶ *Everything turns upon the result of the battle.* 모든것은 전쟁의 결과에 달렸다 / *Success of the meeting turns on the weather.* 회합의 성과는 날씨 여하에 있다 / *She has no one but you to ~ to.* 그녀에게는 너밖에 의지할 사람이 없다. **4** (P3,5) 《*into*》 become changed in nature or condition. …으로 되다; 변하다. ¶ ~ *red* 붉어지다 / *Milk turns sour.* 우유가 시어진다 / *Water turns into ice.* 물이 언다 / *The rain has turned to snow.* 비가 눈으로 바뀌었다 / *Caterpillars ~ into butterflies.* 풀쐐기가 나비로 된다 / *He turned pale.* 그는 얼굴이 창백해졌다. **5** (P1) (of leaves) change the color. (나뭇잎이) 변색하다; 단풍들다. ¶ *The leaves are turning.* 나뭇잎이 물들고 있다 / *Poplars began to ~.* 포플러잎이 물들기 시작했다. **6** (P3) 《*against*》 change one's feelings, attitude, etc. 태도 등을 바꾸다; 변절하다. ¶ *He turned against his sweetheart.* 그는 애인에게 변심했다. **7** (P1) become disturbed; become sick. 어지러워지다; 구역질 나다. ¶ *My stomach turns at the sight.* 그걸 보니 속이 메스꺼워진다. **8** (P5) change one's opinion, profession, etc. (의견·직업 등을 바꾸어) …이 되다; …으로 전직[개종]하다. 語法 관사 없는 명사를 보어로 취함. ¶ ~ *soldier* [*Christian*] 군인[기독교인]이 되다. **9** (P1) use a lathe. 선반(旋盤)을 돌리다.

turn about, look back; face to the back. 뒤돌아보다; 뼁 돌다[돌리다]. ¶ ~ *one's head about* (고개를 돌려) 뒤돌아보다.

turn and rend, scold; abuse. 꾸짖다; 비난하다.

turn around [***round***]***,*** turn or move so as to face the opposite direction. (반대쪽으로) 방향(方向)을 바꾸(게 하)다; 뒤돌아 보다. ¶ *He turned around and went to his house.* 그는 뒤돌아서 집으로 가버렸다.

turn aside, put on a different course; pursue a new course; step aside. 길을 잘못 들다; 다른 길로 들어서다; 옆으로 비키다.

turn away, **a**) dismiss; reject. …을 해고하다; 거절하다. **b**) avert one's face; refuse to look. 외면하다.

turn back, **a**) go or come back; return. 되돌아가다[오다]. **b**) force to go away; send back. …을 쫓아버리다. **c**) fold back (a sheet of paper, etc.). (종이 등)을 접다.

turn down, **a**) 《*colloq.*》 reject. 거절하다. ¶ ~ *down the scheme* 계획을 퇴짜 놓다. **b**) make less; reduce; lessen the flow, volume, etc. of. 작게 하다; 줄이다; (소리 등)을 약하게 하다. ¶ ~ *down the light* [*gas*] 빛을[가스를] 약하게 하다. **c**) fold or bend down. 접다; 구부리다. ¶ ~ *down one's collar* 옷깃을 접다.

turn in, **a**) 《*colloq.*》 go to bed. 잠자리에 들다. **b**) 《chiefly U.S.》 hand over. 건네다; 제출하다. ¶ ~ *in the report to the committee* 위원회에 보고서를 제출하다 / ~ *in weapons* 무기를 넘겨주다. **c**) return. 돌려주다. **d**) exchange. 교환하다. ¶ ~ *in an old car for a new one* 헌차를 새차로 바꾸다. **e**) pay a casual or short visit; drop in. 잠깐 들르다. ¶ ~ *in at a restaurant* 식당에 들르다. **f**) (cause to) point inwards. 안쪽으로 굽(히)다. ¶ ~ *in one's toes* 발가락을 안으로 굽히다.

turn loose, set free. 해방하다; 놓아주다.

turn off, **a**) stop the flow of (liquid or gas). (수도·가스)의 마개를 틀어 잠그다. ¶ ~ *off the flow of water* [*gas*] 수도[가스]를 잠그다. **b**) put out; extinguish. (불 따위)를 끄다. ¶ ~ *off the lights* [*fire in a stove*] 불[난롯불]을 끄다. **c**) 《Brit.》 send away; dismiss. 내보내다; 해고하다. **d**) leave the road and enter a side road; branch off. 샛길로 들어서다; 분기(分岐)하다. ¶ ~ *off at a corner* 모퉁이에서 샛길로 들다. **e**) divert attention from. …에서 관심을 딴 데로 돌리다. **f**) 《*colloq.*》 hang (a criminal). (범인)을 처형하다.

turn on, **a**) start the flow of (liquid or gas); start; open. (수도·가스)의 마개를 틀어 나오게 하다; (불 따위)를 켜다. ¶ ~ *on an electric current* 전류가 흐르게 하다 / ~ *on a lamp* [*light*] 남포를[불을] 켜다 / ~ *on a radio* 라디오를 켜다. **b**) attack (without warning); become hostile to. (불시에) 공격하다; …를 적대하다. ¶ ~ *on one's friend* 친구를 적대하다.

turn out, **a**) send away; drive out; dismiss. …을 내쫓다; 해고하다. ¶ ~ *someone out* (*of a room*) 아무를 (방에서) 내쫓다 / ~ *someone out of his office* 아무를 해고하다. **b**) empty (a pocket, room, etc.) of its contents. (속의 것)을 비우다. ¶ *The policeman told him to ~ out his pockets.* 경찰은 그에게 호주머니에 있는 것을 모두 꺼내라고 말했다. **c**) make; manufacture; produce. …을 생산하다. ¶ *The factory turns out 100 cars in a day.* 그 공장은 차를 하루에 백 대 만들어낸다. **d**) fit out; dress. …을 성장(盛裝)시키다. ¶ *a woman turned out beautifully* [*in full dress*] 아름답게 차려입은[성장한] 부인. **e**) =turn off a), b). **f**) be found; prove to be. …임이 밝혀지다; 판명되다. ¶ *His story turned out* (*to be*) *true.* 그의 말은 사실이었다 / *It turned out that she had not known.* 그녀는 모르고 있었음이 밝혀졌다. **g**) come to be; end up; result. 결국 …이 되다. ¶ *How did the meeting turn out ? —It turned out a success.* 모임은 어떻게 됐나 — 성공적이었습니다 / *Everything turned out well.* 만사가 잘 됐다. **h**) come or go out for duty or service; assemble. 출동하다; 집합하다. ¶ *Fireengines turned out as soon as the fire broke out.* 불이 나자마자 소방차가 달려왔다. **i**) 《*colloq.*》 get out of bed. 잠자리에서 일어나다.

turn over, **a**) move so that the other side is up; cause to roll over. 뒤집다; 굴리다. **b**) hand or pass over; deliver. …을 건네주다; 제출하다. ¶ ～ *money* [*a letter*] *over to someone* 아무에게 돈을[편지를] 건네주다 / ～ *one's business over to one's son* 아들에게 사업을 넘겨주다. **c**) buy and then sell; do business to the amount of. 거래하다; …만큼의 매상을 올리다. ¶ ～ *over £5,000 a week* 1 주일에 5000 파운드의 거래를 하다 / *Our firm turned over a million dollars last year.* 우리 회사의 작년 거래액은 100만 달러였다. **d**) ⇨ *vt.* 8.

turn to, **a**) set to work; begin. (일)에 착수하다. ¶ *The committee turned to and soon produced a plan.* 위원회는 작업에 착수해 이내 한 가지 안(案)을 제시했다. **b**) go to for help, advice, etc.; apply to. …에 의지하다; 호소하다. ¶ *Don't hesitate to* ～ *to me if you are in difficulty.* 어려울 때는 망설이지 말고 내게 말하시오.

turn up, **a**) bend or be bent up; fold back. 위로 구부리다[구부러지다]; 접어올리다; 접어꺾다. ¶ ～ *up one's collar* 칼라를 세우다 / ～ *up the ends of one's trousers* 바지 가랑이 끝을 접어올리다 / *The branches* ～ *up at the end.* 나뭇가지는 끝에서 위로 구부러진다. **b**) (cause to) face upward; lift or be lifted up. 위를 향하(게 하)다; 쳐들다. ¶ ～ *up one's face* 얼굴을 들다 / *Her nose turns up.* 그녀 코는 들창코다. **c**) bring to the surface by digging. 파 뒤집다; 발굴하다. ¶ ～ *up ancient coins* 옛 화폐를 발굴하다. **d**) be found. 발견되다. ¶ *The book I lost has turned up.* 잃어버린 책이 나왔다. **e**) increase the flow, volume, etc. of. (유량·음량 등)을 올리다; 늘리다. ¶ ～ *up the volume* 음량을 높이다 / ～ *up the gas* 가스를 세게 나오게 하다 / ～ *up the radio* 라디오 소리를 크게 하다. **f**) cause to vomit. (먹은 것)을 토하게 하다. **g**) 《*colloq.*》 make an appearance; arrive. 모습을 나타내다; 도착하다. ¶ *My brother has turned up from India.* 형이 인도에서 돌아왔다. **h**) 《Brit.》 come about; happen. (일이) 일어나다; 발생하다. ¶ *You can call me if anything turns up.* 무슨 일이 생기거든 내게 전화해라 / *wait for something to* ～ *up* 무슨 일이 일어날까 하고 기다리다; 추이를 살피다.

turn up one's nose at ⇨nose.

— *n.* Ⓒ **1** the act of moving around; rotation. 회전. ¶ *the* ～ *of a wheel* 바퀴의 회전 / *give a handle a* ～ 핸들을 한 바퀴 돌리다 / *a* ～ *of the wrist* 팔목을 비틀기. **2** a change of state or movement. 변화; 전기(轉機); 일변(一變). ¶ *take a* ～ 변하다 / *at the* ～ *of the century* 세기의 전환기에 / *Matters took a bad* ～. 일이 악화되었다 / *The sick girl took a* ～ *for the better* [*worse*]. 소녀의 병세가 좋아졌다[나빠졌다] / *There has been an unusual* ～ *of events.* 예사롭지 않은 사태 전환이 있었다. **3** a curve; a bend. 모퉁이; 커브; 구부러진 곳. ¶ *a* ～ *in the path* 길의 커브[도는 데] / *Take the third* ～ *to the right.* 세 번째 모퉁이를 오른쪽으로 돌아라. **4** a change in direction. 방향 전환. ¶ *a* ～ *to the left* 좌회전 / *Make a left* ～ *after the bank.* 둑을 지나서 좌회전해라. **5** a characteristic; a talent. 성격; 재능. ¶ *be of a humorous* ～ 유머러스한 성격이다 / *have a special* ～ *for music* 음악에 특별한 재능이 있다 / *He has a gloomy* ～ *of mind.* 그는 좀 우울한 성격이다 / *She has a witty* ～ *of phrase.* 그녀는 말을 재치있게 한다. **6** one's time or chance for doing something. 순번; 차례. ¶ *It is your* ～ *to sing.* 네가 노래할 차례다 / *wait one's* ～ 자기 차례를 기다리다. **7** 《*a* ～》 an act; a spell of work. 행위; 한 차례의 일. ¶ *a good* ～ 좋은 행위 / *take a* ～ *of work* 한 바탕 일하다. **8** a short walk for exercise or pleasure. 산책. ¶ *take a* ～ *in the garden* 정원을 거닐다. **9** form; style. 형; (문장·말의) 표현(법). ¶ *I like the* ～ *of his sentences.* 나는 그의 문체가 좋다 / *a happy* ～ *of expression* 적절한 표현. **10** 《*colloq.*》 a shock of terror. 충격; 쇼크. ¶ *It gave him a* ～. 그것은 그에게 충격을 주었다. **11** use; purpose. (특정한) 용도; 목적. ¶ *The tool will serve my* ～. 그 연장은 요긴하게 쓰겠다. [Gk. *tornos* lathe]

at every turn, very often; every time; without exception. 노상; 언제나; 예외 없이.

by turns, one after another; in succession. 교대로; 번갈아. ¶ *They work by turns.* 그들은 교대로 일한다 / *She cried and laughed by turns.* 그녀는 울다가 웃다가 했다.

in turn, in proper order. 차례로; 차례차례. ¶ *She shook hands with each of them in* ～. 그녀는 그들과 차례로 악수했다.

on the turn, about to turn or change. 바뀌려고 하여; 바뀌는 고비에. ¶ *The tide is now on the* ～. 물때가 되었다.

out of turn, not in proper order; at the wrong time. 순서 없이; 나쁜 계제에. ¶ *speak out of* ～ 두서 없이 얘기하다.

take turns, do one after another in order; rotate. …을 교대로 하다. ¶ *take turns in driving* 교대로 운전하다.

to a turn, just to the right degree; perfectly. 적당히; 충분히. ¶ *food cooked to a* ～ 알맞게 요리된 음식.

turn and turn about =by turns.

turn·coat [tə́ːrnkòut] *n.* Ⓒ a person who gives up his former party or principles. 배신자; 변절자.

turn·down [tə́ːrndàun] *adj.* having the upper part folded or doubled down. 접은 깃의. ¶ *a* ～ *collar.*

turn·er [tə́ːrnər] *n.* Ⓒ a person or thing that turns, esp. a person who operates a machine to shape articles of wood, metal, etc. 돌리는 사람[물건]; 회전하는 사람[물건]; 선반공(旋盤工).

turn·er·y [tə́ːrnəri] *n.* **1** Ⓒ a place where

a turner works. 선반 공장. **2** Ⓤ Ⓒ the art or product of a turner. 선반 세공〔제품〕.

***turn·ing** [tə́ːrniŋ] *n.* **1** Ⓤ the act of a person or thing that turns. 회전. **2** Ⓒ a place where a road turns or branches off. 모퉁이; 분기점. ¶ *Take the second ~ to the right.* 두 번째 모퉁이에서 우회전하시오.

turning point [⌐─⌐] *n.* **1** a place where something moving changes its direction. 전환〔회전〕 지점. **2** a time when a big change happens; a decisive moment. 전환기; 전기(轉機); 고비; 위기. ¶ *the ~ of someone's life* 생의 전환기 / *the ~ of an illness* 병의 고비.

tur·nip [tə́ːrnip] *n.* Ⓒ 《bot.》 a plant with a large, edible, round root. 순무. [*turn,* L. *napus* rape]

turn·key [tə́ːrnkìː] *n.* Ⓒ a person who keeps keys of prison doors; a jailer. 옥지기; 교도관. [*turn*]

turn·out [tə́ːrnàut] *n.* Ⓒ **1** a group of people gathered for a special purpose; attendance. (집회 등의) 출석자. ¶ *There was quite a good ~ at the lecture.* 그 강연엔 꽤 많은 사람이 있었다. **2** the amount produced; output. 산출〔생산〕고. **3** a carriage with its horses and attendants. (말과 말구종을 포함한) 마차. **4** 《Brit.》 a labor strike. 파업. **5** 《U.S.》 the way in which a person is dressed and equipped. 옷맵시; 몸차림. ¶ *a colorful ~* 화려한 차림.

turn·o·ver [tə́ːrnòuvər] *n.* Ⓤ **1** the act of turning over; an upset. (마차 등의) 전복. **2** ⓐ the total amount of money handled in a business during a given period. (일정 기간의) 총매상고. ⓑ the total amount of business done in a given time. (일정 기간의) 거래액. ¶ *These new products have had a quick ~.* 이 신제품은 날개 돋힌 듯 팔렸다. **3** 《Brit.》 an article in a newspaper extending from one page to another. 다음 면에 이어지는 기사(記事).

turn·pike [tə́ːrnpàik] *n.* Ⓒ **1** a gate where tolls are paid. 통행료 징수소. **2** a toll road. 유료 고속 도로. [*turn*]

turn·spit [tə́ːrnspìt] *n.* **1** a device for turning a roast of meat on a spit. 꼬치구이 틀. **2** a kind of small dog. 턴스피트《꼬치구이 틀을 돌리는 데 쓰던 작은 개》.

turn·stile [tə́ːrnstàil] *n.* a post with horizontal cross bars that turn, used at entrances for making persons pass one by one; a similar mechanical device, as at a subway entrance. 턴스타일《지하철역 따위에 설치되어 있는 한 사람씩 드나들게 되어 있는 회전식 장치》. [*turn*]

〈turnstile〉

turn·ta·ble [tə́ːrntèibəl] *n.* **1** Ⓒ a round platform that turns, used for turning locomotives or cars around. (철도의) 전차대(轉車臺). **2** a similar platform for turning phonograph records. (레코드의) 회전반; 턴테이블.

tur·pen·tine [tə́ːrpəntàin] *n.* Ⓤ a sticky, light-colored oil obtained from pine trees, used in paint and varnish. 테레빈. [Gk.]

tur·pi·tude [tə́ːrpitjùːd] *n.* Ⓤ wickedness; baseness. 사악(邪惡); 비열(한 행위). ¶ *moral ~* 부도덕한 행위; 타락. [L. *turpis* base]

tur·quoise [tə́ːrkwɔiz] *n.* Ⓤ Ⓒ **1** a blue or greenish-blue precious stone. 터키석(石). **2** the color of this stone. 청록색. [→Turk.]

tur·ret [tə́ːrit, tʌ́rit] *n.* Ⓒ **1** a small tower added to the corner of a building or large tower. 작은 탑. **2** a low, round, turning structure on a warship, tank, fort, etc. from which guns are fired. (군함·전차·요새 등의) 회전식 포탑(砲塔). [→tower]

〈turret 1〉

tur·ret·ed [tə́ːritid, tʌ́r-] *adj.* having a turret or turrets. 소탑〔포탑〕이 있는.

tur·tle [tə́ːrtl] *n.* Ⓒ a sea animal with a hard shell around its soft body. 바다거북. [→tortoise]

turn turtle, (of a car, boat, etc.) turn upside down. (배 따위가) 전복하다.

tur·tle·dove [tə́ːrtldʌ̀v] *n.* Ⓒ 《bird》 a kind of small European dove with a long tail, noted for its affection toward its mate. 호도애《암수가 사이 좋음》. [L. *turtur*]

a pair of turtledoves, 《*fig.*》 lovers. 연인.

turtle shell [⌐─⌐] *n.* tortoise shell. 별갑(鱉甲).

tusk [tʌsk] *n.* Ⓒ a long, pointed tooth projecting from the mouths of some animals, such as elephants and wild boars. (코끼리·멧돼지 등의) 송곳니; 엄니. 參考 독사·맹수의 그것은 fang. [E.]

tus·sle [tʌ́səl] *n.* Ⓒ a rough struggle. 드잡이; 난투. — *vi.* (P1,3) 《*with*》 struggle roughly. 심하게 싸우다. [→tousle]

tus·sock [tʌ́sək] *n.* Ⓒ a thick tuft or bunch of growing grass, twigs, etc. 덤불; 풀숲. [↑]

tut [tʌt, ɿ] *interj.* a sound made to express impatience, rebuke, annoyance, or contempt. 체; 젠장; 피《초조·경멸 등을 나타냄》. ¶ *Tut ! I've got some chalk on my coat.* 제기랄. 외투에 분필이 묻었잖아. [Imit.]

tu·te·lage [tjúːtəlidʒ] *n.* Ⓤ **1** protection. 보호; 후견(後見). **2** the state of being under a tutor or guardian. 보호됨. **3** teaching; instruction. 지도; 교육. ¶ *He made good progress under her ~.* 그는 그녀의 지도 아래

장족의 발전을 했다. [→tutor]

tu·te·lar·y [tjú:təlèri / -ləri] *adj.* **1** serving as a protector or guardian. 수호하는. ¶ *a ~ angel* 수호 천사. **2** of a protector or guardian. 수호의; 후견의.

·**tu·tor** [tjú:tər] *n.* Ⓒ **1** a private teacher. 가정 교사. **2** 《Brit.》 an officer in charge of the studies of undergraduates in universities or colleges, esp. at Oxford and Cambridge. (대학에서 개인적으로 연구를 지도하는) 지도 교수. **3** 《U.S.》 a teacher ranked lower than an instructor in some universities and colleges. 대학 강사. — *vt.* (P6) teach privately. …에게 개인적으로 가르치다[지도하다]. — *vi.* (P1) act as a tutor. 가정 교사 노릇하다. [L. *tueo* protect]

tu·to·ri·al [tju:tɔ́:riəl] *adj.* of a tutor. 가정 교사의; 개인 지도의. ¶ *~ classes* 개별 지도반 / *the ~ system* (대학의) 개인 지도제.

tux·e·do, Tux·e·do [tʌksí:dou] *n.* Ⓒ (*pl.* **-dos** or **-does**) 《U.S.》 a man's black coat for evening wear with no tails. 턱시도(=《Brit.》 a dinner-jacket). [Place]

〈tuxedo〉

TV television.

TVA 《U.S.》 Tennessee Valley Authority.

TWA Trans World Airlines.

twad·dle [twɑ́dəl / twɔ́dəl] *n.* Ⓤ silly, tiresome talk or writing. 실없는[되잖은] 소리. — *vi.* (P1) talk or write in a silly or tiresome way. 실없이 지껄이다; 객담을 늘어놓다. [→tattle]

twain [twein] *n., adj.* 《*arch., poet.*》 =two.

twang [twæŋ] *n.* Ⓒ **1** a sharp, quick, ringing sound of the string of a musical instrument, etc. 탕; 윙《현(絃) 따위를 튕겼을 때의 소리》. ¶ *The bow made a ~ when I shot the arrow.* 내가 활시위를 놓았을 때 활은 윙 소리를 내었다. **2** a nasal tone of voice. 콧소리; 비음(鼻音). ¶ *He spoke with a nasal ~.* 그는 코맹맹이 소리로 말했다. — *vt.* (P6) cause (something) to make a sharp, ringing sound. …을 탕하고 울리다. — *vi.* (P1) **1** make a sharp, ringing sound. 탕 울리다. **2** utter a nasal sound. 콧소리를 내다. [Imit.]

·**'twas** [twɑz, twəz / twɔz] 《*poet.*》 =it was.

tweak [twi:k] *vt.* (P6) pinch and twist (the nose, ears, etc.) suddenly and sharply with the fingers. …을 꼬집다; 비틀다. ¶ *~ someone's nose.* — *n.* Ⓒ a sudden and sharp pinch and twist. 꼬집기; 비틀기. ¶ *He gave her ear a friendly little ~.* 그는 그녀의 귀를 장난으로 좀 꼬집었다. [E. (→twitch)]

tweed [twi:d] *n.* Ⓤ **1** a soft woolen cloth with a rough surface, usu. made from two or more colors of yarn. 트위드. **2** 《*pl.*》 clothes made of tweed. 트위드 옷. ¶ *a ~ suit.* [=*twilled*]

'tween [twi:n] *prep.* 《*poet.*》 =between.

tweet [twi:t] *n.* Ⓒ the chirping sound of a young bird. 새가 지저귀는 소리; 짹짹. — *vi.* (P1) utter a tweet. (새가) 짹짹거리다. [Imit.]

tweez·ers [twí:zərz] *n. pl.* a small instrument for pulling out hairs or picking up very small things. 족집게. ¶ *pluck one's eyebrows with ~* 눈썹을 족집게로 뽑다. [F. *étue*]

:**twelfth** [twelfθ] *n.* **1** 《usu. *the ~*》 number 12; 12th. 제12. **2** Ⓒ one of 12 equal parts of anything. 12분의 1; 1/12. — *adj.* of the 12th. 제12의; 12분의 1의. [↓]

:**twelve** [twelv] *n.* **1** Ⓤ the number between eleven and thirteen; 12. 12. **2** Ⓒ any group or set of twelve persons or things. 12개; 12인. **3** Ⓤ twelve o'clock. 12시.

the Twelve Apostles, twelve persons chosen by Christ to preach the gospel to all the world. 예수의 12사도.

— *adj.* of 12. 12의; 12개의; 12인의. [E.]

twelve·fold [twélvfòuld] *adj.* **1** twelve times as much or as many. 12배의. **2** having twelve parts. 12부분으로 이루어진. — *adv.* twelve times as much or as many. 12배로.

twelve·month [twélvmʌ̀nθ] *n.* Ⓒ 《chiefly Brit.》 twelve months; a year. 12개월; 1년. ¶ *this day ~* 1년 후의 오늘.

:**twen·ti·eth** [twéntiiθ] *n.* **1** 《usu. *the ~*》 number 20; 20th; a person or thing coming next after the nineteenth. 제20; 스무번째의 사람[물건]. **2** Ⓒ one of 20 equal parts of anything. 20분의 1. — *adj.* of the 20th. 제20의; 20분의 1의. [↓]

:**twen·ty** [twénti] *n.* Ⓤ two times ten; 20. 20. — *adj.* of 20. 20의. [E.]

'twere [twə:r, twər] =it were.

:**twice** [twais] *adv.* **1** two times; on two occasions. 두 번; 2회. ¶ *wash one's face ~ a day* 세수를 하루 두 번 하다 / *Take the medicine ~ a day.* 이 약을 하루 2회 복용하시오. **2** doubly. 2배; 두 곱. ¶ *Twice two is four.* 2를 두 곱하면 4다 / *I want ~ as much.* 나는 두 곱을 주시오 / *I work ~ as hard as you.* 나는 너보다 곱이나 힘들게 일한다 / *Since his holiday he's been ~ the man he was.* 휴가 이후 그는 갑절이나 튼튼해졌다. [→two]

not think twice about, not think of again; forget; do something without hesitation. …을 다시 생각하지 않다; 잊다; 망설이지 않다. ¶ *I should not think ~ about refusing his offer.* 나 같으면 그의 제의를 당장에 거절하겠다.

think twice, think well before acting; hesitate. 재고하다; 주저하다.

twice-told [twáistóuld] *adj.* **1** told twice. 두 번 이야기한. **2** told many times before; common and not fresh. 여러 번 말한; 진부

한. ¶ ~ *tales* 진부한 이야기.

twid·dle [twídl] *vt.* (P6) turn (something) around idly; twirl. …을 만지작거리다. — *vi.* (P1,3) 《*with*》 play idly. 만지작거리다; 가지고 놀다. [Imit.]

twiddle one's thumbs, sit idly doing nothing; spend one's time idly. 아무 것도 하지 않고 있다; 빈둥거리며 시간을 보내다.

***twig** [twig] *n.* Ⓒ a small, slender branch of a tree or shrub. 잔 가지. [E.]

:twi·light [twáilàit] *n.* Ⓤ **1** the faint light from the sky before sunrise or after sunset. (해뜨기 전·해진 뒤의) 박명(薄明); 땅거미; 황혼. ¶ *morning* ~ 여명 / *evening* ~ 땅거미 / *work in the* ~ 해질녘에 일하다. **2** any faint light. 희미한 빛. **3** the period after or before full development. (전성기 전후의) 여명〔쇠퇴〕기. ¶ 《*fig.*》 *old ladies in the* ~ *of their lives* 인생의 황혼기에 있는 노부인들. — *adj.* **1** of twilight. 여명의; 해질녘의. **2** done during twilight. 어둑어둑할 때 행해지는. ¶ *a* ~ *baseball game* 해질녘의 야구 경기. [*two, light*]

twill [twil] *n.* Ⓤ a strong cloth that shows parallel diagonal lines on the surface. 능직(綾織). — *vt.* (P6) weave in the manner of a twill. …을 능직으로 짜다. [E. =two-thread]

'twill [twil] 《*arch., poet.*》 =it will.

twilled [twild] *adj.* woven in diagonal lines. 능직으로 짠; 능직의. [*twill*]

***twin** [twin] *n.* Ⓒ **1** one of two children or animals born at a single birth. 쌍둥이의 한 쪽(cf. *triplet*). ¶ *My brother and I look so alike that people often think we are twins.* 동생과 나는 너무 닮아서 사람들은 흔히 우리가 쌍둥이인 줄 안다. **2** one of two persons or things looking exactly like each other in appearance, shape, etc. 꼭 닮은 사람〔물건〕의 한 쪽; 쌍이 된 한 쪽.
— *adj.* **1** born at a single birth. 쌍둥이의. ¶ ~ *brothers* 쌍둥이 형제. **2** of two things separated but similar. 쌍으로 된. ¶ ~ *beds* 트윈베드 / *a* ~ *engine plane* 쌍발기.
— *vt., vi.* (**twinned, twin·ning**) **1** give birth to twins. 쌍둥이를 낳다. **2** join or connect closely; pair or couple. 밀접하게 결합시키다; 쌍으로 하다. [E. =double]

***twine** [twain] *n.* ⓊⒸ **1** a strong, twisted thread or string of two or more strands. 꼰 실〔끈〕. **2** the act of twisting; the state of being twisted. 꼼; 엉클어짐. — *vt.* (P6,7,13) twist. …을 꼬다; 짜다; 엮다. ¶ ~ *garlands* 화환을 만들다 / ~ *a pole with ribbons* 막대기에 띠를 감다 / *She twined her arms around his neck.* 그녀는 두 팔로 그의 목을 껴안았다. — *vi.* (P1,3) 《*about, round*》 wind round. 감기다. ¶ *The snake twined around an apple tree.* 뱀은 사과나무를 둘둘 감았다 / *The vine twines round the tree.* 덩굴은 나무를 감는다. [E.]

twinge [twindʒ] *n.* Ⓒ a sudden, sharp pain in body or mind. (찌르는 듯한 육체·정신적) 아픔; 고통; 가책. ¶ *a* ~ *of rheumatism* / *a* ~ *of conscience* 양심의 가책 / *a* ~ *of toothache* 심한 치통 / *twinges of sorrow* 뼈아픈 설움. — *vi.* (P1) feel a sudden sharp pain. 격통〔가책〕을 느끼다. — *vt.* (P6) cause such pain in (something). …을 아프게 하다. [E.]

***twin·kle** [twíŋkəl] *vi.* (P1) **1** shine with a flickering light. 반짝이다. ¶ *Stars* ~. 별들이 반짝인다. **2** (of eyes) become bright. (눈이) 반짝 빛나다. ¶ *His eyes twinkled.* 그의 눈이 반짝 빛났다. **3** move quickly and lightly. 경쾌하게 움직이다. ¶ *The dancer's feet twinkled.* 무용수들의 발놀림이 경쾌했다. — *vt.* light flickeringly. …을 반짝거리게 하다.
— *n.* ⓊⒸ **1** a flickering light from cheerfulness, pleasure, amusement, etc. 반짝임; 번득임. ¶ *A* ~ *appeared in her eyes.* 그녀의 눈이 반짝 빛났다. **2** a wink of the eye. 깜박임. ¶ *in a* ~ 눈 깜짝할 사이에; 순식간에. [E.]

twin·kling [twíŋkliŋ] *n.* ⓊⒸ **1** 《*sing.* only》 an instant; without delay. 순간. ¶ *in a* ~ =*in the* ~ *of an eye* 눈 깜짝할 사이에; 순식간에 / *I'll be back in a* ~. 곧 돌아오마. **2** a rapid flash or sparkle. 반짝임. ¶ *the* ~ *of the stars.*

twirl [twəːrl] *vt.* (P6,7) **1** turn (something) around rapidly. …을 빙빙 돌리다; 휘두르다. ¶ ~ *a cane* 지팡이를 휘두르다 / *twirling round the dance floor* 무도장을 빙글빙글 돌며. **2** twiddle. …을 비비 틀다. ¶ ~ *one's mustache* 콧수염을 비비 꼬다. — *vi.* (P1,2A) revolve rapidly. 빙빙 돌다. — *n.* Ⓒ the act of twirling; the state of being twirled. 빙빙 돎; 회전; 비비 틂. [Imit.]

:twist [twist] *vt.* **1** (P6,7,13) join (two or more threads, etc.) by winding one around another; make (a rope, etc.) in this way; intertwine; wind together. (새끼 따위)를 꼬다; 엮다; 꼬아서 (…으로) 만들다. ¶ ~ *together threads into a rope* 실을 꼬아서 끈을 만들다 / ~ *a rope* 줄을 꼬다 / *She twisted flowers into a wreath.* 그녀는 꽃을 엮어 화환을 만들었다. **2** (P6,7,13) coil (something) about something else; wind; encircle. …을 감다; 휘감다. ¶ ~ *a tape around a stick* 단장에 테이프를 감다 / *She twisted her arms about her mother.* 그녀는 양팔로 어머니를 껴안았다 / ~ *wreaths round a column* 화환을 기둥에 휘감다. **3** (P6,7,13) turn two ends of (something) in opposite directions. …을 비틀다. ¶ ~ *a wet towel* 젖은 수건을 비틀어 짜다 / ~ *off a piece of wire* 철사를 비틀어 끊다 / ~ *a stick out of someone's hand* 아무의 손에서 단장을 비틀어 빼앗다 / ~ *a wrist* 손목을 비틀다. **4** (P13) make (one's way) often changing from one direction to another. …을 누비며 나아가다. ¶ ~ *one's way through the crowd* 군중 속을 헤치고 나아가다. **5** (P6) injure the muscle of (a part of the body) by twisting; wrench. …을 접질리다; 삐다. ¶ ~ *one's ankle* 발목을 삐다. **6** (P6,13) make (one's face) out of shape; give an ugly expression to (one's face); distort. (얼굴)을 찡그리다. ¶ *Her face was twisted with pain.* 그녀의 얼굴은 고통으로 일그러졌다 / *He twisted his face into a grin.* 그는 이를 드러내고 씩 웃었다. **7** (P7,13) pull suddenly. …을 홱 당기다. ¶ *The man twisted the letter out of her hand.* 그 남자는 그녀 손에서 편지를 잡아챘다. **8** (P6,13) change the original meaning of (something); represent wrongly. (뜻)을 왜곡하다; 곡해하다. ¶ *They twisted her words into a hundred meanings.* 그들은 그녀의 말을 여러 가지 뜻으로 곡해하였다. **9** 《chiefly Brit. *colloq.*》 cheat. …을 속이다; 기만하다.

— *vi.* (P1,2A,3) **1** be joined by winding one around another; be intertwined. 꼬이다; 얽히다. ¶ *a twisted thread* 꼬인 실. **2** wind or coil around something. 휘감기다; 감겨붙다. **3** (of a road, etc.) curve; wind. (길이) 꼬불꼬불 구부러지다. ¶ *a twisting mountain road* 꼬불꼬불한 산길 / *The path twists up the hillside.* 길은 언덕 중턱 위로 구불구불 나 있다 / *The path twists in and out among the rocks.* 길이 바위 사이로 구불구불 나 있다. **4** go or move by often changing from one direction to another. 누비고 나아가다. ¶ *They twisted through the crowd.* 그들은 군중속을 누비며 나아갔다. **5** be injured in the muscle by twisting. 접질리다; 삐다. ¶ *My ankle twisted.* 발목을 삐었다. **6** become twisted; writhe. 뒤틀리다; 몸부림치다. ¶ *Her mouth twisted into a smile.* 그녀는 입가에 미소를 띠었다 / *She twisted with pain.* 그녀는 고통스러워 몸부림쳤다. **7** 《*colloq.*》 dance twist. 트위스트를 추다. **8** 《*sl.*》 act dishonestly. 부정 행위를 하다.

— *n.* Ⓒ **1** the act of twisting; the state of being twisted. 꼬임; 비틀림. ¶ *a ~ in a rope* 밧줄의 꼬임 / *give a ~* 꼬다; 비틀다 / *give a ~ to someone's arm* 아무의 팔을 비틀다 / *throw a ball with a ~* 곡구를 던지다. **2** something made by twisting. 꼰 것. ¶ *a ~ of bread* 꼬인 빵. **3** a sharp turn. 심한 굴곡. ¶ *a road with many twists* 굴곡이 많은 길. **4** an eccentric characteristic. 괴벽; 변덕. ¶ *His behavior shows his mental ~.* 그의 행위는 비뚤어진 정신 상태를 보여준다 / *a ~ in one's nature* 비뚤어진 성격. **5** the twisting of the true meaning. (뜻의) 곡해; 왜곡. **6** an unexpected change or development. (사태 등의) 뜻밖의 변화〔전개〕. ¶ *There's an unusual ~ at the end of the book — the detective is murdered.* 그 책은 끝에서 특이하게 전개된다 —탐정이 살해된다. **7** 《*colloq.*》 a kind of lively dance. 트위스트(춤). [E.]

twist·er [twístər] *n.* **1** a person or thing that twists. (새끼 따위를) 꼬는 사람〔기계〕. **2** 《chiefly Brit. *colloq.*》 a dishonest person. 부정직한 사람. **3** 《U.S. *colloq.*》 a tornado or cyclone. 돌개바람; 선풍. **4** 《baseball》 a curved pitched ball. 곡구(曲球).

twitch [twitʃ] *vt.* (P6,7,13) **1** pull (something) with a quick, sharp movement. …을 홱 당기다. ¶ ~ *the tablecloth from the table* 식탁에서 테이블보를 홱잡아당기다 / ~ *the curtain aside* 커튼을 확 열어젖히다. **2** move (a part of the body) with a sudden movement. (몸의 일부)를 씰룩거리다; 경련시키다. ¶ ~ *one's fingers* 손가락을 떨다 / *The horse twitched its ears.* 말이 양 귀를 쫑긋거렸다.

— *vi.* (P1) **1** pull suddenly. 홱 당기다. **2** move suddenly in a quick manner. 경련하다; 씰룩거리다. ¶ *His face twitched with pain.* 그의 얼굴은 고통으로 씰룩거렸다.

— *n.* Ⓒ **1** a sudden pull. 홱 당김. **2** a quick, sudden movement of a muscle. (근육의) 경련. [E.]

twit·ter [twítər] *n.* Ⓒ **1** a sharp sound made by a bird. (새의) 지저귐. **2** an act of laughing voicelessly; a giggle. 킥킥 웃음. **3** an excited and restless condition. 흥분; 떨림. ¶ *in a ~* 몹시 흥분하여. — *vt., vi.* (P6; 1,2A) **1** (of a bird) sing. (새가) 지저귀다. **2** giggle; laugh voicelessly. 킥킥거리다; 킥킥 웃다. **3** tremble from excitement. 흥분해서 몸을 떨다. [Imit.]

'twixt [twikst] *prep.* 《*poet.*》 =between.

:two [tuː] *n.* **1** Ⓤ the number between one and three; 2. 둘; 2. ¶ *a day or ~* 하루 이틀 / *cut in ~* 양분하다 / *one or ~* 한둘; 조금. **2** Ⓒ any set of two persons or things. 두 사람; 두 개. ¶ *by twos and threes* 삼삼 오오; 두 세사람씩 / ~ *by* 〔*and*〕 ~ 두 사람〔개〕씩. **3** Ⓒ anything shaped like 2. 2자 모양의 것. **4** 《*colloq.*》 Ⓤ two o'clock. 두시.

put two and two together, draw an obvious conclusion; get a correct answer, by considering several facts together. (이것저것 종합해서) 명백한〔바른〕 결론을 내다.

— *adj.* one more than one; of two. 2의; 두 개〔사람〕의. [E.]

two-edged [túːédʒd] *adj.* **1** (of a sword, etc.) having two cutting edges. 양날의. **2** 《*fig.*》 having two different meanings; capable of two opposite uses or effects. 두 가지 뜻이 있는; 상반된 두 가지 효과가 있는; 애매한. ¶ *a ~ remark* 칭찬도 비난도 아닌 말.

two-faced [túːfèist] *adj.* **1** having two faces. 양면이 있는. **2** 《*fig.*》 ready to deceive others; dishonest. 위선적인.

two·fold [túːfòuld] *adj.* double; made of two parts. 두 곱의; 두 겹의. — *adv.* doubly. 두 곱〔겹〕으로.

two-hand·ed [túːhǽndid] *adj.* **1** having two hands. 양손이 있는. **2** for use by two persons. 2인용의. ¶ *a ~ saw* (인거(引鋸)하는) 큰톱. **3** needing two persons to operate. 둘이서 하는. ¶ *a ~ game* (트럼프 등) 둘이서 하는 놀이. **4** using both hands equally well. 양손잡이의. **5** requiring both hands to wield or manage. 양손으로 쓰는《칼 따위》. ¶ *a heavy ~ sword.*

two-mast·ed [tú:mæstid/-má:stid] *adj.* having two masts. (돛대가) 둘 있는.

two·pence [tʌ́pəns] *n.* Ⓤ 《Brit.》 the sum of two pennies. 2펜스.

two·pen·ny [tʌ́pəni] *adj.* **1** worth twopence. 2펜스의. **2** 《*colloq.*》 of little value; worthless; insignificant. 보잘것 없는; 시시한.

two-seat·er [tú:sí:tər] *n.* Ⓒ a car or an airplane furnished with two seats. 2인승 자동차〔비행기〕.

two·some [tú:səm] *n.* Ⓒ **1** two people together; a pair or couple. 2인조; 한 쌍. ¶ *John and Helen make a nice ~, don't you think?* 존과 헬렌은 좋은 한 쌍이야, 안 그래. **2** a game played by two people. 두 사람이 하는 경기.

two-step [tú:stèp] *n.* Ⓒ a kind of dance in 2/4 time; music for this dance. 투스텝《사교 댄스의 일종》; 그 곡.

two-storied [tú:stɔ́:rid] *adj.* having two stories or floors. 2층의; 2층으로 된.

'twould [twud, twəd] 《*arch., poet.*》 =it would.

ty·coon [taikú:n] *n.* Ⓒ 《U.S. *colloq.*》 a wealthy, powerful businessman. (실업계의) 거물. [Jap.]

:ty·ing [táiiŋ] *v.* ppr. of **tie.**

tyke [taik] *n.* =tike.

tym·pa·na [tímpənə] *n.* pl. of **tympanum.**

tym·pa·num [tímpənəm] *n.* Ⓒ (*pl.* **-nums** or **-na**) **1** the middle ear. 중이(中耳). **2** the eardrum; thin skin in the ear which helps in hearing sounds. 고막(鼓膜). [Gk. =drum]

:type [taip] *n.* Ⓒ **1** a class, kind, or group having common characteristics. 형(型); 타입. ¶ *different types of hats* 다른 모양의 모자들 / *He is of a poetic ~.* 그는 시인 타입이다. **2** a person or thing representing the characteristics, qualities, etc. of a kind, class, group, etc. 전형(典型); 표본. ¶ *a perfect ~ of English country gentleman* 완벽한 영국 시골 신사의 전형 / *He is the ~ of the modern athlete.* 그는 현대 경기자의 표본이다. **3** 《print.》 ⓐ a piece of metal or wood with a letter on its surface; 《*collectively*》 a set of such pieces. 활자. ⓑ Ⓤ the style, shape, or kind of type. 자체(字體). ¶ *The book is printed in small but clear ~.* 그 책은 작지만 깨끗한 자체로 인쇄돼 있다 / *in italic ~* 이탤릭체로. **4** a printed letter, figure, design, etc. on either side of a coin or medal. (화폐·메달 등 앞뒤의) 문자; 도형(圖形). **5** something that represents or symbolizes another; a sign; a symbol. 상징; 표상. ¶ *The king's scepter is a ~ of royal authority.* 왕의 홀은 왕권의 상징이다.

in type, set up in the press. 활자로 짜여져.

true to type ⇨true.

— *vt., vi.* (P6,7;1,2A) **1** write or print (something) with a typewriter. 타자기로 치다. ¶ *Would you ~ the letter out for me?* 내 편지를 타자 쳐 주시겠습니까. **2** become a model for (something). …의 전형이 되다. **3** find out the type of. …의 형을 알아내다. ¶ *~ one's blood* 자기 혈액형을 알아내다. [Gk. *tuptō* strike]

type·script [táipskrìpt] *n.* Ⓒ a typewritten copy. 타자기로 친 원고.

type·set·ter [táipsètər] *n.* Ⓒ a person or machine that sets type. 식자공(植字工); (자동) 식자기(機).

type·set·ting [táipsètiŋ] *n.* Ⓤ the act of setting type. 식자. ¶ *a ~ machine* 자동 식자기.

type·write [táipràit] *vt., vi.* (**-wrote, -written**) (P6;1) write or print with a typewriter. 타자기로 치다.

***type·writ·er** [táipràitər] *n.* Ⓒ **1** a machine for printing letters on paper by means of keys which are operated by the fingers. 타자기; 타이프라이터. ¶ *a portable ~ / write a letter on a ~* 편지를 타자기로 치다. **2** a typist. 타자수; 타이피스트.

type·writ·ing [táipràitiŋ] *n.* Ⓤ the act or art of using a typewriter; work done by such an act. 타자 치기; 타자술(術); 타자 친 것. ¶ *His ~ is very clear.* 그가 타자한 것은 아주 깨끗하다.

type·writ·ten [táiprìtn] *v.* pp. of **typewrite.** — *adj.* printed by a typewriter; typed. 타자기로 친.

type·wrote [táipròut] *v.* p. of **typewrite.**

ty·phoid [táifɔid] *n.* Ⓤ a serious illness carried by dirty water or food, common in hot countries. 장티푸스. — *adj.* of typhoid. 장티푸스의. ¶ *~ fever* 장티푸스. [→typhus]

***ty·phoon** [taifú:n] *n.* Ⓒ a violent storm occurring in the western Pacific area. 태풍 (cf. *hurricane*). [Chin. =great wind]

ty·phus [táifəs] *n.* Ⓤ a serious disease which is carried to man by lice and other insects and which causes red spots on the skin. 발진(發疹) 티푸스. [Gk. =stupor]

***typ·i·cal** [típikəl] *adj.* representing the characteristics, qualities, etc., of a kind, group, class, etc. 전형적인; 대표적인. ¶ *a ~ example* 대표적인 예 / *a man ~ of his class* 그 계급을 대표하는 사람 / *It was ~ of him to be so rude.* 뻔뻔한 게 그 사람의 특징이다. [→type]

typ·i·cal·ly [típikəli] *adv.* in a typical way; to a typical degree. 전형적으로.

typ·i·fi·ca·tion [tìpəfikéiʃən] *n.* ⓊⒸ the act of typifying; the state of being typified. 전형; 상징.

typ·i·fy [típəfài] *vt.* (P6) represent (the characteristics, qualities, etc.) of a kind, class, etc. …의 전형이 되다; …을 대표하다.

¶ *He typifies the pioneer.* 그는 전형적인 개척자다.

typ·ing [táipiŋ] *n.* Ⓤ the act of printing by a typewriter; the art of using a typewriter. 타자를 침; 타자기 사용법.

***typ·ist** [táipist] *n.* Ⓒ a person who works with a typewriter, esp. one who does it as an occupation. 타자수; 타이피스트.

ty·pog·ra·pher [taipágrəfər / -pɔ́g-] *n.* a printer. 인쇄(식자)공.

ty·po·graph·ic [tàipəgrǽfik], **-i·cal** [-ikəl] *adj.* of typography or printing. (활판) 인쇄(술)의. [*type*]

ty·pog·ra·phy [taipágrəfi / -pɔ́g-] *n.* Ⓤ **1** the art of printing. 인쇄술. **2** the style or arrangement of printing. 활자 조판의 체재.

ty·ran·ni·cal [tirǽnikəl, tai-], **-nic** [-nik] *adj.* of or like a tyrant; cruel; oppressive. 폭군의; 횡포한; 압제적인. ¶ *a ~ master* 폭군 같은 주인 / *her ~ father* 그녀의 포악한 아버지. [→tyrant]

ty·ran·ni·cal·ly [tirǽnikəli, tai-] *adv.* in a tyrannical manner; cruelly. 압제적으로; 포악하게.

tyr·an·nize [tírənàiz] *vt., vi.* (P6; 3) 《*over*》 rule as a tyrant with power and cruelty; oppress. 포악한 정치를 하다; 학대하다.

tyr·an·nous [tírənəs] *adj.* =tyrannical.

***tyr·an·ny** [tírəni] *n.* (*pl.* **-nies**) ⓊⒸ **1** the cruel and oppressive exercise of power. 압제(壓制); 폭정. **2** Ⓒ a tyrannical act. 포악한 짓. **3** government by a cruel, absolute ruler. 전제 정치.

***ty·rant** [táiərənt] *n.* Ⓒ **1** a cruel, oppressive, and unjust ruler or person. 폭군. **2** 《Gk. hist.》 an absolute ruler. 참주(僭主). [Gk. *turannos*]

***tyre** [táiər] *n.* 《Brit.》 =tire.

ty·ro [táirou] *n.* (*pl.* **-ros**) =tiro.

Ty·rol [táiroul, tairóul, tiróul] *n.* a region in the Alps partly in western Austria and partly in Italy and Germany. 티롤(지방).

tzar [zɑːr, tsɑːr] *n.* =czar. [*Caesar*]

tzar·i·na [zɑːríːnə, tsɑː-] *n.* =czarina.

u U

U, u [ju:] *n.* Ⓒ (*pl.* **U's, Us, u's, us** [ju:z]) **1** the 21st letter of the English alphabet. 영어 알파벳의 스물한째 글자. **2** something shaped like the letter U. U자 모양의 것. ¶ *a U tube* U자관 / *U turn* 유턴.

u·biq·ui·tous [ju:bíkwətəs] *adj.* existing or appearing everywhere at the same time. 동시에 어디에나 있는; 편재(遍在)하는(cf. *omnipresent*). [L. *ubique* everywhere]

u·biq·ui·ty [ju:bíkwəti] *n.* Ⓤ the state of being ubiquitous. 편재(遍在)(cf. *omnipresence*). [↑]

U-boat [jú:bòut] *n.* a German submarine. U 보트《제1·2차 세계 대전 때 활약한 독일 잠수함》. [G. *Unterseeboot*]

U bolt [ㅗ ㅗ] *n.* a U-shaped bolt with threads and a nut at each end. U자 볼트.

ud·der [ʌ́dər] *n.* Ⓒ (of a cow, a goat, etc.) the part of the body from which the milk comes. (소·염소 등의) 젖통이; 유방. [E.]

UFO [jù:èfóu, jú:fou] *n.* (*pl.* **UFOs, UFO's** [-z]) unidentified flying object. 미확인 비행 물체(cf. *flying saucer*).

ugh [u:x, ʌx, ʌ, u, ʌg] *interj.* an exclamation expressing horror, disgust, etc. 아; 우. [Imit.]

ug·li·ness [ʌ́glinis] *n.* Ⓤ the state of being ugly. 추함; 못생김; 추악. [↓]

:ug·ly [ʌ́gli] *adj.* (**-li·er, -li·est**) **1** not pleasant to look at. 못생긴; 추한(opp. beautiful). ¶ *an ~ face* 추한 얼굴 / *~ clothes* 보기 흉한 옷 / *She is as ~ as sin.* 그녀는 추악하다 / *~ houses* 보기 흉한 집들. **2** bad; disagreeable; unpleasant. 나쁜; 불쾌한; 싫은. ¶ *~ news* 흉보 / *an ~ rumor* 나쁜 소문 / *an ~ task* 싫은 일 / *~ language* 욕설 / *an ~ smell* 고약한 냄새. **3** threatening; dangerous. 험악한; 위험한. ¶ *an ~ wound* 중상 / *The sky has an ~ look.* 하늘이 잔뜩 찌푸리고 있다 / *The situation becomes more ~ every day.* 사태는 날마다 더 악화된다 / *an ~ sea* 험한 바다. **4** 《U.S. *colloq.*》 ill-natured; bad-tempered. 심술궂은; 성미가 고약한. ¶ *He turned upon her with his ugliest look.* 그는 무서운 형상을 하고 그녀에게 대들었다 / *He has an ~ pen, an ~ tongue, and an ~ temper.* 그는 독필(毒筆)에다, 독설에다 게다가 성미마저 고약하다. [N.]

cut up ugly, 《*colloq.*》 become very angry. 격분하다.

ugly customer [ㅗ ㅗ-] *n.* 《*colloq.*》 a dangerous, rough person. 위험 인물; 난폭한 사람.

ugly duckling [ㅗ- ㅗ-] *n.* a dull or plain child who becomes a clever or attractive adult. 미운 오리 새끼.

UHF, uhf ultrahigh frequency.

U.K. United Kingdom.

ukase [jú:keis, -keiz, -ㅗ] *n.* **1** an order of the ruler or government in Tsarist Russia. (제정(帝政) 러시아의) 칙령(勅令). **2** any official proclamation or order. 공고; 포고(布告). [Russ. *ukaz* order]

u·ku·le·le [jù:kəléili] *n.* Ⓒ a four-stringed guitar-shaped instrument of Hawaiian origin. 우쿨렐레. [Native]

ul·cer [ʌ́lsər] *n.* Ⓒ **1** an open sore that discharges pus. 궤양(潰瘍). **2** 《*fig.*》 a morally bad influence. 병폐; 폐해. [L.]

ul·cer·ate [ʌ́lsərèit] *vt., vi.* (P6; 1) **1** 《usu. in *pp.* as *adj.*》 cause (the stomach, etc.) to have an ulcer; have or form an ulcer. …에 궤양이 생기(게 하)다. ¶ *an ulcerated sore* 짓무른 헌데 / *an ulcerated stomach* 궤양이 생긴 위 / *Worry ulcerated his stomach.* 근심 걱정으로 위가 헐었다. **2** 《*fig.*》 morally corrupt. 도덕적으로 부패하게 만들다. [↑]

ul·cer·a·tion [ʌ̀lsəréiʃən] *n.* Ⓤ the act of ulcerating; the state of being ulcerated; an ulcer or group of ulcers. 궤양 상태; 궤양(형성).

ul·cer·ous [ʌ́lsərəs] *adj.* of ulcers; having ulcers. 궤양성의; 궤양에 걸린.

ulna [ʌ́lnə] *n.* (*pl.* **-nae**) 《anat.》 the inner larger bone of the lower part of the arm. 척골(尺骨). [L.]

ulnae [ʌ́lni:] *n.* pl. of **ulna.**

ul·ster [ʌ́lstər] *n.* a long heavy overcoat, often with a belt. 얼스터코트. [Place]

ult. ultimate(ly); ultimo.

ul·te·ri·or [ʌltíəriər] *adj.* **1** (of position) on the farther side; lying beyond. 저쪽의. ¶ *on the ~ side of the river* 강 저쪽에. **2** beyond what is expressed; hidden. 말 못할; 숨겨진; 이면의. ¶ *for the sake of an ~ end* 생각〔꿍꿍이속〕이 있어 / *I suspect he may have had an ~ motive for being so generous.* 그가 저렇게 너그러울 때는 뭔가 저의가 있는 모양이다. **3** (of time) later; future. 앞으로의; 장차의. ¶ *Ulterior steps will be taken to secure this object.* 이 목적을 달성하기 위해 앞으로 조치가 있을 것이다. [L.=further]

ul·ti·ma·ta [ʌ̀ltəméitə] *n.* pl. of **ultimatum.**

·ul·ti·mate [ʌ́ltəmit] *adj.* **1** coming at the end; final. 최후의; 궁극의. ¶ *man's ~ end* 인간의 궁극의 목적 / *look forward to an ~ peace* 궁극적인 평화를 기대하다. **2** fundamental; basic. 근본적인; 기본의. ¶ ~ *principles* 근본 원리 / *the ~ facts of nature* 자연계의 구극적(究極的) 사실. **3** farthest. 가장 먼. ¶ *the ~ end of the globe* 세계의 끝. [L. *ultimus* last]

ul·ti·mate·ly [ʌ́ltəmitli] *adv.* finally; in the end. 최후로; 궁극적으로.

ul·ti·ma·tum [ʌ̀ltəméitəm] *n.* Ⓒ (*pl.* **-tums,** or **-ma·ta**) a final word or terms offered with threats. 최후 통첩. ¶ *deliver* 〔*issue*〕 *an ~* 최후 통첩을 내다.

ul·ti·mo [ʌ́ltəmòu] *adj.* 《L.》 in the last month. 지난달의 (cf. *instant, proximo*). 參考 ult.로 생략함. 주로 상용문(商用文)에 쓰임. ¶ *your letter received on the 10th ult.* 귀하의 지난달 10일자 편지. [→ultimate]

ul·tra [ʌ́ltrə] *adj.* extreme in views, opinions, etc. 극단적인; 과격한. ¶ *an ~ nationalist* 국수주의자. — *n.* Ⓒ a person who has extreme opinions or who urges extreme measures. 과격론자; 급진론자. ¶ *He equally welcomed ultras and liberals.* 그는 과격론자든 자유주의자든 똑같이 환영했다 / *She is an ~ in dress.* 그녀는 의상에 있어서는 유행의 최첨단을 걷는다. [↓]

ul·tra- [ʌ́ltrə-] *pref.* a word element meaning 'beyond what is usual'. '극단으로, 초(超)…, 과(過)…' 등의 뜻. [L.=beyond]

ul·tra·ma·rine [ʌ̀ltrəmərí:n] *n.* Ⓤ a bright, pure blue color. 감청색(紺靑色). — *adj.* **1** of a bright pure, blue color. 감청색의. **2** beyond the sea; from overseas. 바다 저쪽의; 해외의. ¶ *~ provinces* 〔*dominions*〕 해외 영토. [ultra-]

ul·tra·mi·cro·scope [ʌ̀ltrəmáikrəskòup] *n.* a highly powered microscope used to study very small objects. 한외(限外)현미경. [ultra-]

ul·tra·mi·cro·scop·ic [ʌ̀ltrəmaikrəskápik / -skɔ́p-] *adj.* too small to be seen by a microscope. 한외 현미경적인.

ul·tra·short [ʌ̀ltrəʃɔ́:rt] *adj.* 《phys.》 having a wave-length below 10 meters. 초단파의.

ul·tra·son·ic [ʌ̀ltrəsánik / -sɔ́n-] *adj.* of sound waves beyond the limit of human audibility; supersonic. 초음파의.

ul·tra·vi·o·let [ʌ̀ltrəváiəlit] *adj.* of the invisible part of the spectrum just beyond the violet. 자외(선)의. ¶ *~ rays* 자외선.

ultra vires [ʌ́ltrə váiəri:z] *adj., adv.* 《L.》 《Law》 beyond one's power or authority. 자기 권한을 넘어; 월권의. ¶ *act ~* 월권 행위를 하다.

U·lys·ses [ju:lísi:z, jú:ləsì:z] *n.* 《Gk. myth.》 the hero of Homer's 'Odyssey'. 율리시스.

um·bel [ʌ́mbəl] *n.* 《bot.》 an inflorescence in which flower-stalks spring like umbrella-ribs. 산형(繖形) 꽃차례〔화서(花序)〕. [→umbra]

um·ber [ʌ́mbər] *n.* Ⓤ a brown earth used as coloring matter; a brown or dark brown. 엄버《황갈색의 천연 안료(顔料)》; 황갈색. — *adj.* of brown or dark brown. 황갈색의. [↓]

um·bra [ʌ́mbrə] *n.* (*pl.* **-brae**) **1** 《astron.》 a shadow of the earth or moon that hides the sun. 본(本)그늘; 본그림자. **2** a shade; shadow. 그림자. [L.=shadow]

um·brae [ʌ́mbri:] *n.* pl. of **umbra.**

um·brage [ʌ́mbridʒ] *n.* Ⓤ **1** feeling of offence; displeasure. 불쾌감; 불만; 화남. ¶ *give ~ to someone* 아무를 화나게 하다 / *take ~ at someone's rudeness.* 아무의 무례함에 불쾌감을 느끼다〔화를 내다〕. **2** all the leaves of a tree. (무성한) 나뭇잎. **3** 《*arch., poet.*》 shade; shadow. 그늘; 그림자. ¶ *an evening without any cloudy ~* 구름 한점 없이 맑은 저녁. [↑]

:um·brel·la [ʌmbrélə] *n.* Ⓒ **1** a light, folding frame covered with cloth, used as a protection against rain or sun. 우산; 양산. **2** something that covers from above, as military aircraft, ballistic missile, atom bomb, etc. (지상 작전을 돕는) 공중 엄호(掩護). **3** any kind of protection. 보호하는 것. [→umbra]

um·pire [ʌ́mpaiər] *n.* Ⓒ **1** 《law》 a person chosen to settle disputes. 중재자; 재정인(裁定人). **2** a person who rules on the plays in a game; a judge. 심판원. ¶ *The ~ called the ball a foul.* 심판은 파울볼을 선언했다. — *vi.* (P1) act as umpire (in a game, dispute, etc.). 심판하다; 중재하다. ¶ *Will you ~ for our side ?* 우리측의 중재역을 해주시겠소 / *He umpired in the last tennis match.* 그가 테니스 최종 경기의 심판을 했다. — *vt.* (P6) act as umpire in. …을 심판〔중재〕하다. ¶ *~ a championship game* 결승전〔선수권 대회〕 심판을 보다. [→non, par; i.e., nonrival]

UN, U.N. United Nations.

un, 'un [ən] *pron.* Ⓒ 《*colloq.*》 one. 놈; 녀석. ¶ *He's a good ~.* 좋은 놈이다 / *He's a tough ~.* 그 녀석 여간내기가 아니다. [E.]

un- [ʌn-] *pref.* **1** 《before *adjectives* and *adverbs*》 not. '부정'의 뜻. ¶ *uninteresting.* **2** 《before *nouns*》 lack of. '결여, 반대'의 뜻. ¶ *unhappiness.* **3** 《before *verbs*》 do the opposite of. '반대되는 행위'의 뜻. ¶ *unfold.* [E., of two origins, expressing (1) negation, (2) reversal]

un·a·bashed [ʌ̀nəbǽʃt] *adj.* not ashamed. 부끄러움을 모르는; 태연한. ¶ *Found in the act, he is ~.* 현장을 들키고도 그는 태연하다 / *His trousers fell down but he appeared quite ~.* 바지가 흘러내렸는데도 전혀 부끄럽지 않은 모양이었다. [un-]

un·a·bat·ed [ʌ̀nəbéitid] *adj.* in full force; as violent as before. 줄지 않는; 약해지지 않는. ¶ *The storm continued with ~ violence.* 폭풍우는 여전하게 맹위를 떨쳤다. [un-]

:un·a·ble [ʌnéibəl] *adj.* not able; incapable. …을 할 수 없는. ¶ *The baby was ~ to walk yet.* 애기는 아직 걷지 못했다 / *I'd like to* go, but I'm ~ to. 가고 싶지만 그럴 수 없다.

un·a·bridged [ʌ̀nəbrídʒd] *adj.* not shortened; complete. 생략하지 않은; 완전한. ¶ *an ~ edition of a book* 어떤 책의 무삭제판(版). [un-]

un·ac·com·pa·nied [ʌ̀nəkʌ́mpənid] *adj.* **1** not accompanied. 동행이 없는. ¶ *children ~ by an adult* 어른이 동행하지 않은 아이들 / *Unaccompanied children will not be admitted.* 아이들만의 입장은 불가《게시》. **2** (in music) without any instrument to support the main music. 무반주(無伴奏)의. ¶ *an ~ song* 반주 없는 노래.

un·ac·count·a·ble [ʌ̀nəkáuntəbəl] *adj.* **1** that can not be accounted for; strange. 설명할 수 없는; 기묘한. ¶ *for some ~ reason* 어떤 말 못 할 이유로 해서 / *His disappearance was quite ~.* 그의 실종은 참으로 수수께끼였다. **2** not responsible. 책임이 없는. ¶ *The king is absolute and ~.* 왕은 절대자이며 책임이 없다.

un·ac·cus·tomed [ʌ̀nəkʌ́stəmd] *adj.* **1** 《*to*》 not accustomed; not used to. 익숙지 않은. ¶ *~ to public speaking* 대중 연설에 익숙지 못한 / *She is ~ to the work.* 그 일에는 서툴다. **2** not familiar; strange. 눈에 선; 관례가 아닌. ¶ *with ~ rudeness* 전에 없이 무례하게 / *his ~ absence* 전에 없던 그의 결석.

un·a·dorned [ʌ̀nədɔ́ːrnd] *adj.* not adorned; simple. 장식이 없는; 간소한; 소박한.

un·ad·vised [ʌ̀nədváizd] *adj.* **1** done without due consideration; unwise. 무분별한; 경솔한. **2** not advised. 충고를 받지 않은.

un·ad·vis·ed·ly [ʌ̀nədváizidli] *adv.* in an unadvised manner. 분별 없이; 경솔하게.

un·af·fect·ed [ʌ̀nəféktid] *adj.* **1** without pretense; simple; sincere; natural. 꾸밈없는; 소박〔성실〕한; 자연스러운. ¶ *He stared at me in ~ astonishment.* 솔직히 놀랐다는 듯이 눈을 크게 뜨고 나를 보았다 / *He expressed ~ delight.* 그는 기쁨을 감추지 않았다. **2** 《*by*》 not affected; not influenced. 영향을 받지 않은. ¶ *He was quite ~ by the appeal.* 그는 간청을 듣고〔받고〕도 끄떡도 하지 않았다.

un·aid·ed [ʌnéidid] *adj.* not aided; without help. 도움이 없는. ¶ *He did it ~.* 그는 혼자 힘으로 그 일을 했다 / *with the ~ eyes* 육안으로.

u·na·nim·i·ty [jùːnənímǝti] *n.* Ⓤ complete agreement or unity. 만장 일치; 전원 동의. ¶ *the ~ of the applause* 만장의 박수 갈채 / *the ~ of the cabinet* 전각료의 의견 일치. [L. *ūnus* one, *animus* mind]

u·nan·i·mous [juːnǽnəməs] *adj.* being of one opinion or mind; showing complete agreement. 만장 일치의; 이구 동성의. ¶ *a ~ agreement* 전원 동의 / *We were ~ in our decision.* 우리의 결정에 전원이 찬성했다 / *a ~ vote* 전원 일치의 표결. [↑]

***u·nan·i·mous·ly** [juːnǽnəməsli] *adv.* in a unanimous manner; with complete agreement. 만장 일치로; 이의 없이.

un·an·swered [ʌ̀nǽnsərd, -ɑ́ːn-] *adj.* **1** not replied to. 대답〔답변〕이 없는. ¶ *an ~ letter* 〔*question*〕 회답〔답변〕이 없는 편지〔질문〕. **2** not proved wrong or mistaken. 반박되지 않는. ¶ *an ~ argument* 반론이 없는 논의. **3** not returned. 보답이 없는. ¶ *~ love* 짝사랑. [un-]

un·ap·proach·a·ble [ʌ̀nəproutʃəbəl] *adj.* that can not be approached; very hard to approach; without an equal. 근접하기 어려운; 무적(無敵)의. ¶ *a cold, aloof, ~ man* 차갑고 도도하고 접근하기 어려운 남자.

un·arm [ʌnɑ́ːrm] *vt., vi.* (P6; 1) take away weapons or means of attack. 무장을 해제하다. ¶ *~ someone of his weapon* 아무의 무기를 빼앗다 / *The soldiers unarmed their prisoners.* 병사들은 포로들의 무기를 거둬들였다 / *The soldiers were unarming.* 병사들은 무장을 풀고 있었다.

un·armed [ʌnɑ́ːrmd] *adj.* not armed; without weapons; disarmed. 무장하지 않은; 비무장의.

un·asked [ʌnǽskt / -ɑ́ːskt] *adj.* not asked for. 부탁〔요구〕받지 않은.

un·as·sail·a·ble [ʌ̀nəséiləbəl] *adj.* that can not be attacked. 공격할 수 없는; 난공불락의.

un·as·sum·ing [ʌ̀nəsjúːmiŋ] *adj.* unaffected; modest; not putting on airs. 젠체하지 않는; 겸손한. ¶ *an ~ manner* 겸손한 태도. ● **un·as·sum·ing·ly** [-li] *adv.*

un·a·vail·a·ble [ʌ̀nəvéiləbəl] *adj.* not available. 쓸모 없는; 입수할 수 없는.

un·a·vail·ing [ʌ̀nəvéiliŋ] *adj.* without effect; useless. 무효의; 무익한. ¶ *~ efforts to rescue a person from drowning.* 물에 빠진 사람을 구하려는 헛된 노력. ● **un·a·vail·ing·ly** [-li] *adv.*

un·a·void·a·ble [ʌ̀nəvɔ́idəbəl] *adj.* that can not be escaped. 피할 수 없는; 부득이한. ¶ *The latest consignment was subject to ~ delays.* 최근의 탁송 수화물의 적송 지연은 불가피했다.

***un·a·ware** [ʌ̀nəwέər] *adj.* 《as *predicative*》 not aware; not knowing; ignorant. 알지 못하는. ¶ *He was ~ of the danger.* 그는 위험을 모르고 있었다 / *I was ~ that war was near.* 전쟁이 임박했으리라고는 생각지도 못했다 / *I was ~ of what was going on.* 무엇이 어떻게 돼 가는지 나는 몰랐다. [un-]

un·a·wares [ʌ̀nəwέərz] *adv.* without being aware; by surprise; unintentionally. 모르고; 불시에; 무심코. ¶ *do something ~* …을 저도 모르게 하다 / *be taken ~* 기습당하다 / *The police caught the burglar ~.* 경찰은 도둑을 기습 체포했다.

un·bal·anced [ʌnbǽlənst] *adj.* **1** not balanced. 균형을 잃은; 불안정한. ¶ *an ~ seat* 불안정한 좌석 / *The scales were ~.* 저울은 균형이 잡혀 있지 않았다 / *an ~ style of writing* 균형이 안 잡힌 필체 / *an ~ budget* 불균형 예산. **2** slightly mad. 머리가 좀 이상

U

해진. ¶ *an ~ mind* 제정신이 아닌 사람.

un·bar [ʌnbɑ́:r] *vt.* (**-barred, -bar·ring**) (P6) **1** remove the bars from (something); unlock. 가로장을 떼다; 빗장을 빼다. ¶ *~ a gate* 〔*door*〕 / 《*fig.*》 *The path to knowledge is unbarred.* 학문에의 대도는 열려 있다. **2** make open. …을 개방하다. ¶ *These concessions could ~ the way to peace.* 이들 양보가 평화에로의 길을 열어줄 것이다. [un-]

un·bear·a·ble [ʌnbɛ́ərəbəl] *adj.* not bearable; impossible to endure. 견딜 수 없는. ¶ *~ pains* 참을 수 없는 고통. ● **un·bear·a·ble·ness** [-nis] *n.*

un·bear·a·bly [ʌnbɛ́ərəbəli] *adv.* in an unbearable manner. 견딜 수 없게. ¶ *It was an ~ hot day.* 무섭게 더운 날이었다.

un·beat·en [ʌ̀nbí:tn] *adj.* **1** not struck. (매)맞지 않은. **2** not defeated. 져본 일이 없는; 불패의. **3** not trodden. 밟지 않은; 미답의. ¶ *an ~ track* 사람이 안 다닌 길; 전인 미답의 땅. [un-]

un·be·com·ing [ʌ̀nbikʌ́miŋ] *adj.* **1** not suitable. 어울리지 않는. ¶ *conduct ~ to a gentleman* 신사답지 않은 행동 / *This house is ~ in a person of his class.* 이 집은 그 계층의 사람에게는 어울리지 않는다. **2** improper; indecent. 버릇 없는; 점잖지 못한. ¶ *~ language* 상말. **3** not suited (to the wearer). (옷이) 어울리지 않는; 모양이 나지 않는. ¶ *an ~ style of dress* 맵시가 나지 않는 옷 / *a pretty face spoiled by an ~ hat* 어울리지 않은 모자로 인해 망친 미모.

un·be·lief [ʌ̀nbilí:f] *n.* Ⓤ lack of belief; lack of belief in God. 의혹; 불신; 불신앙(不信仰). ¶ *I received the news with ~.* 그 소식을 나는 반신 반의했다 / *Unbelief is blind.* 믿음이 없으면 봉사나 다름없다.

un·be·liev·a·ble [ʌ̀nbilí:vəbəl] *adj.* not believable; that can not be believed or trusted. 믿기지 않는; 거짓말 같은.

un·be·liev·er [ʌ̀nbilí:vər] *n.* Ⓒ a person who does not believe; a person who does not believe in God. 회의자(懷疑者); 신앙이 없는 사람; 불신자.

un·bend [ʌnbénd] *v.* (**-bent** or **-bend·ed**) *vt.* (P6) **1** make (something bent) straight. …을 곧게 펴다. ¶ *~ a bow* (시위를 벗겨) 활을 펴다. **2** 《*fig.*》 relax; relieve. (긴장)을 누그러뜨리다; (몸 등)을 쉬게 하다. ¶ *~ the mind* 마음을 놓다 / *~ oneself in familiar company* 다정한 사람들과 더불어 쉬다. **3** 《naut.》 unfasten (a rope, sail, etc.). (밧줄·돛 따위)를 풀다. —*vi.* (P1) **1** become straight. 펴지다. **2** become relaxed. 누그러지다; 마음 놓다. ¶ *He only unbends in the family circle.* 그는 집안 사람들과 있을 때에만 마음이 편해진다. [un-]

un·bend·ing [ʌnbéndiŋ] *adj.* **1** not bending; stiff. 굽지 않는; 굳은; 빳빳한. **2** 《*fig.*》 (of character, purpose, etc.) firm; not easily moved. (성격 등이) 완고한; 꺾이지 않는; 불굴의. ¶ *~ determination* 단호한 결심. —*n.* Ⓤ relaxation. 긴장을 풂.

un·bent [ʌnbént] *v.* p. and pp. of **unbend.**

un·bi·ased, -assed [ʌnbáiəst] *adj.* not prejudiced; fair. 편견이 없는; 공평한. ¶ *an ~ view* 〔*judge*〕 편견이 없는 견해〔법관〕.

un·bid·den [ʌ̀nbídn] *adj.* **1** not commanded. 명령받지 않은. **2** not invited. 초대받지 않은. ¶ *an ~ guest* 불청객.

un·bind [ʌnbáind] *vt.* (**-bound** [-báund]) (P6) **1** untie; unfasten; let loose. …을 풀다; 끄르다. ¶ *~ a bandage* 붕대를 풀다. **2** set free from bonds. …을 해방〔석방〕하다.

un·blem·ished [ʌnblémiʃt] *adj.* **1** not marked with stains. 때묻지 않은; 깨끗한. **2** spotless; faultless. 오점이 없는. ¶ *an ~ reputation* 〔*character, life*〕 흠이 없는 명성〔인격, 생활〕. [un-]

un·blessed, -blest [ʌnblést] *adj.* not blessed; unhappy; miserable; not holy. 축복받지 못한; 불행한; 신성하지 않은.

un·blush·ing [ʌnblʌ́ʃiŋ] *adj.* not blushing; shameless. 얼굴을 붉힐 줄 모르는; 파렴치한.

un·bod·ied [ʌnbɑ́did / -bɔ́d-] *adj.* having no body; formless. 육체를 떠난; 실체가 없는; 무형의.

un·born [ʌnbɔ́:rn] *adj.* not yet born; of the future; still to come. 아직 태어나지 않은; 미래〔장차〕의. ¶ *an ~ child* 태어나지 않은〔태내에 있는〕 아이 / *the ~ generations* 다음 세대; 후세.

un·bos·om [ʌnbúzəm] *vt.* (P6) reveal; confess. …을 털어놓다; 고백하다. ¶ *~ oneself* 심정을 털어놓다 / *~ one's feelings* 〔*secrets*〕 자기의 생각〔비밀〕을 밝히다.

un·bound [ʌnbáund] *v.* p. and pp. of **unbind.**
—*adj.* **1** not bound. 묶이지 않은. ¶ *Unbound sheets of music were scattered about the room.* 묶이지〔철하지〕 않은 악보들이 온 방안에 흐트러져 있었다. **2** free from bonds. (속박에서) 풀린; 해방된. ¶ *The prisoner was left ~.* 죄수는 결박되어 있지 않았다.

un·bound·ed [ʌnbáundid] *adj.* **1** without limits. 무한한. ¶ *~ space* 무한한 공간. **2** not kept within limits; not controlled; boundless. 무제한의; 제약이 없는. ¶ *~ pride* 〔*joy, ambition*〕 억제할 수 없는 자만심〔기쁨, 야망〕.

un·bri·dled [ʌnbráidld] *adj.* not having a bridle on; 《*fig.*》 not controlled. 재갈이 물려 있지 않은; 구속되지 않은. ¶ *an ~ horse* 고삐 풀린 말 / *an ~ tongue* 요설; 수다 / *~ anger* 참을 수 없는 분노. [un-]

un·bro·ken [ʌnbróukən] *adj.* **1** not broken; whole. 깨지지 않은; 온전한. ¶ *an ~ window* 깨지지 않은 창문. **2** not interrupted; continuous. 방해되지 않는; 연이은. ¶ *She had seven hours of ~ sleep.* 그녀는 내리 일곱 시간을 잤다 / *~ fine weather* 연이은 쾌청한 날씨 / *~ peace* 항구적 평화. **3** not beaten. 파손되지 않은. ¶ *an ~ record.* **4**

U

(of a horse) not tamed. 길들여지지 않은. ¶ *manage an ~ horse* 길이 안 든 말을 다루다. **5** not opened up by the plough. 개간이 안 된. ¶ *~ soil*〔*land*〕 미개간의 땅〔토지〕. **6** not violated; kept. 위반되지 않은; 지켜진. ¶ *~ promises* 지켜진 약속.

un·buck·le [ʌnbʌ́kəl] *vt.* (P6) unfasten the buckle or buckles of (something). …의 죔쇠를〔버클을〕 풀다. ¶ *~ a shoe* 구두의 죔쇠를 끄르다 / *~ a sword from its belt* 칼을 혁대에서 풀다. [un-]

un·bur·den [ʌnbə́ːrdn] *vt.* (P6,13) remove a load from (something); relieve (one's mind or heart) by talking. …에서 짐을 부리다; (마음의) 무거운 짐을 덜다. ¶ *A servant hurried to ~ him of his bag.* 한 하인이 그에게서 가방을 받아들려고 서둘렀다 / *She unburdened herself of her terrible secret.* 그녀는 자기의 끔찍한 비밀을 털어놓고 속이 후련해졌다. [un-]

un·but·ton [ʌnbʌ́tn] *vt.* (P6) unfasten the button or buttons or (something). …의 단추를 끄르다.

un·called-for [ʌnkɔ́ːldfɔ̀ːr] *adj.* not required or desired; not necessary; out of place. 달갑잖은; 지나친; 불필요한; 부당한. ¶ *an ~ remark*〔*insult*〕 부당한 비평〔모욕〕/ *an ~ intrusion* 지나친 간섭.

un·can·ny [ʌnkǽni] *adj.* (**-ni·er, -ni·est**) strange; mysterious. 기묘한; 불가사의한.

un·cared-for [ʌnkɛ́ərdfɔ̀ːr] *adj.* not looked after; neglected. 돌보는 이 없는; 방치된. ¶ *The boy left ~ then.* 그때 소년을 돌보는 사람은 없었다.

un·ceas·ing [ʌnsíːsiŋ] *adj.* without stop; continuous. 끊임없는; 부단한. ¶ *~ joy* 끊임없는 기쁨 / *make ~ efforts* 꾸준한 노력을 하다. ●**un·ceas·ing·ly** [-li] *adv.*

un·cer·e·mo·ni·ous [ʌ̀nserəmóuniəs] *adj.* informal; lacking in polite behavior. 격식을 차리지 않는; 터놓은; 예의 없는. ¶ *He made an ~ exit.* 무례하게 그는 퇴장했다.

un·cer·e·mo·ni·ous·ly [ʌ̀nserəmóuniəsli] *adv.* in an unceremonious manner. 격식 차리지 않고; 버릇없이.

•**un·cer·tain** [ʌnsə́ːrtn] *adj.* **1** (*of*) doubtful; not sure; undecided; unsteady. 의심스러운; 불확실한; 부정(不定)의. ¶ *I am ~ of success.* 내가 성공할지는 잘 모르겠다 / *It is ~ how long I shall stay.* 내가 얼마 동안 머무를 지는 확실하지 않다 / *Our holiday plans are still ~.* 우리 휴가 계획은 아직 미정이다 / *The danger is plain, success is ~.* 위험한 건 분명하고 성공은 불확실하다 / *a person of ~ character* 성격이 분명치 않은 사람 / *His aim was somewhat ~.* 그의 의도는 좀 불안정했다. **2** often changing; not reliable. 잘 변하는; 미덥지 못한. ¶ *~ weather* 변덕스러운 날씨 / *a man with an ~ temper* 변덕스러운 사람 / *I told him in no ~ terms what I thought of him.* 그에 대한 내 생각을 분명하게 말해줬다. [un-]

un·cer·tain·ty [ʌnsə́ːrtnti] *n.* (*pl.* **-ties**) **1** Ⓤ ⓐ lack of certainty; doubt. 불확실; 미정; 의심스러움. ¶ *be in a state of ~* 불확실한 상태다 / *There was some ~ about his guilt.* 그의 유죄는 좀 의심스러웠다 / *the ~ of life* 인생의 무상. ⓑ being changeable; tendency to change. 변덕스러움. ¶ *~ of temper* 변덕. **2** Ⓒ something uncertain. 불확실한 것〔일〕.

un·chain [ʌntʃéin] *vt.* (P6) set free (from a chain or chains); let loose. …을 사슬에서 풀다; 놓아주다. ¶ *~ a dog* 개를 풀어주다 / *~ the door* 문을 잠그지 않고 두다.

un·change·a·ble [ʌntʃéindʒəbəl] *adj.* impossible or unlikely to be changed. 변하지 않는; 불변의. [un-]

un·changed [ʌntʃéindʒd] *adj.* not changed. 변화가 없는.

un·char·i·ta·ble [ʌntʃǽrətəbəl] *adj.* **1** (of an action, feeling, etc.) not kind in dealing with others; harsh in judging others. (행동·감정 등이) 무자비한; 가차 없는. ¶ *~ criticism* 가차 없는 비평. **2** 《rare》 (of a person, etc.) not generous; not charitable. (사람이) 인색한; 인정머리 없는.

un·chart·ed [ʌntʃɑ́ːrtid] *adj.* not mapped; not marked or described on a chart. 해도(海圖)〔지도〕에 없는; 해도〔지도〕에 표시가 없는. ¶ *Many ~ islands were discovered.* 해도에 없는 많은 고도들이 발견되었다.

un·chris·tian [ʌnkrístʃən] *adj.* **1** not Christian; unworthy of Christians. 기독교도가 아닌; 기독교도답지 못한. ¶ *~ behavior*〔*conduct*〕 기독교인답지 못한 행동〔처신〕. **2** 《*colloq.*》 dreadful. 끔찍한; 무서운.

un·church [ʌntʃə́ːrtʃ] *vt.* (P6) expel from a church; deprive of church rights and privileges. …을 파문하다; 교회의 특권을 빼앗다.

un·civ·il [ʌnsívəl] *adj.* **1** not civil; impolite. 예의를 모르는; 버릇 없는. ¶ *an ~ remark*〔*letter*〕 무례한 언사〔편지〕. **2** not civilized. 야만적인.

un·civ·i·lized [ʌnsívəlàizd] *adj.* not civilized; savage; barbarous. 미개한; 야만적인. ¶ *~ manners* 야만적인 풍습.

un·clasp [ʌnklǽsp, -klɑ́ːsp] *vt.* (P6) unfasten; release (something) from a clasp or grasp. …의 죔쇠를 벗기다; (쥐었던 것)을 놓다. ¶ *~ a brooch* 브로치를 끄르다 / *~ one's hand* 쥔 것을 놓다. — *vi.* (P1) become unfastened; open. 벗겨지다; 풀리다. [un-]

:**un·cle** [ʌ́ŋkəl] *n.* Ⓒ **1** the brother of one's father or mother. 숙부; 백부. **2** the husband of one's aunt. 고모부; 이모부. **3** 《U.S. *colloq.*》 a term of respectful or familiar address to an older man. 아저씨. ¶ *'Uncle Tom's Cabin'.* **4** 《*sl.*》 a pawnbroker. 전당포 주인. [L. *avunculus*]

come the uncle over someone, 《*colloq.*》 treat someone in a patronizing manner. …에게 아저씨나 되는 것처럼 굴다. ¶ *Don't* *come the ~ over me.* 내게 이래라 저래라 마라. **say uncle,** admit defeat. 항복하다. **talk** *to someone* **like a Dutch uncle** ⇨*Dutch.*

un·clean [ʌnklíːn] *adj.* **1** dirty; not clean. 더러운; 지저분한. ¶ *an ~ clothes* 〔*hair*〕 지저분한 옷〔머리〕. **2** not pure morally; evil. 부정(不貞)한; 사악한. ¶ *an ~ scene* 부정한 장면. [un-]

Uncle Sam [⌐— ⌐] *n.* the government or people of the United States. 미국 정부; (전형적인) 미국 사람.

un·cloak [ʌnklóuk] *vt.* (P6) **1** remove the coat or cover from. 외투〔덮개〕를 벗기다. **2** 《*fig.*》 expose; reveal. 폭로하다; (가면을) 벗기다. [un-]

un·close [ʌnklóuz] *vt., vi.* (P6; 1) open; disclose. (…을) 열다; 폭로하다.

un·clothe [ʌnklóuð] *vt.* (P6) **1** strip of clothes; undress. …에서 옷을 벗기다. **2** lay bare; uncover. …을 폭로하다.

un·coil [ʌnkɔ́il] *vt.* (P6) unwind; unfasten the coil of. …을 풀다. ¶ *~ a rope* 밧줄을 풀다 / *The snake slowly uncoiled.* 뱀은 천천히 사리를 풀었다.

·**un·com·fort·a·ble** [ʌ̀nkʌ́mfərtəbəl] *adj.* not comfortable; uneasy; disagreeable. 편치않은; 불안한; 불쾌한. ¶ *be ~ in tight boots* 구두가 작아 불편하다 / *feel ~ with strangers* 낯선 사람이 있어 거북하다 / *an ~ chair* 〔*hat*〕 편치 않은 의자〔모자〕. [un-]

·**un·com·mon** [ʌnkámən / -kɔ́m-] *adj.* unusual; rare; strange; remarkable. 흔하지 않은; 보기 드문; 진귀한; 대단한. ¶ *an ~ bird* 희귀조 / *an ~ act of courage* 비범하고 용감한 행위. — *adv.* 《*colloq.*》 = uncommonly. ¶ *I feel ~ queer.* 몹시 기분이 좋지 않다 / *~ good beer* 아주 좋은 맥주. ●**un·com·mon·ness** [-nis] *n.*

un·com·mon·ly [ʌnkámənli / -kɔ́m-] *adv.* not common; unusually; remarkably. 드물게; 진귀하게; 대단히. ¶ *a bird ~ found in here* 여기선 드물게 보는 새 / *an ~ tall man* 키가 무척 큰 사람 / *Traffic accidents occur not ~.* 교통 사고란 흔히 있다.

un·com·pro·mis·ing [ʌ̀nkámprəmàiziŋ / -kɔ́m-] *adj.* firm; determined. 타협하지 않는; 강경한; 완고한. ¶ *an ~ patriot* 강경한 애국자 / *an ~ attitude* 완강한 태도. [un-]

un·con·cern [ʌnkənsə́ːrn] *n.* Ⓤ lack of concern or interest. 무관심; 냉담. ¶ *He regarded such matters with complete ~.* 그는 그런 일들을 철저히 무시해버렸다.

un·con·cerned [ʌ̀nkənsə́ːrnd] *adj.* **1** not concerned; not interested. 무관심한; 태연한; 신경을 쓰지 않는. ¶ *I am ~ about the future.* 나는 미래에 대해서 관심이 없다 / *He is ~ with politics.* 그는 정치에 대해선 무관심하다. **2** not taking part in. 관계가 없는; 관여하지 않은. ¶ *He was ~ in the conspiracy.* 그 음모에 관련이 없었다.

un·con·cern·ed·ly [ʌ̀nkənsə́ːrnidli] *adv.* in an unconcerned manner; indifferently. 무관심하게; 태연히.

un·con·di·tion·al [ʌ̀nkəndíʃənəl] *adj.* without conditions; absolute. 무조건의; 절대적인. ¶ *demand ~ agreement* 조건 없는 동의를 요구하다 / *give an ~ refusal* 단호히 거절하다 / *~ reflex* 무조건 반사. [un-]

un·con·form·i·ty [ʌ̀nkənfɔ́ːrməti] *n.* lack of agreement; being inconsistent. 불일치(不一致); 모순.

un·con·quer·a·ble [ʌnkáŋkərəbəl / -kɔ́ŋ-] *adj.* that can not be conquered. 정복할 수 없는.

un·con·scion·a·ble [ʌ̀nkánʃənəbəl / -kɔ́n-] *adj.* **1** (of a person) not guided or restrained by conscience; having no conscience. 양심이 없는. ¶ *What an ~ man he is!* 정말 양심도 없는 사람이군. **2** (of an action, etc.) showing no regard for conscience. (행동이) 비양심적인; 부당한. ¶ *I cannot stand his ~ behavior.* 그 자의 비양심적인 행실은 참을 수 없다. **3** unreasonably excessive; outrageous. 지나친; 터무니 없는. ¶ *an ~ price* 터무니 없는 값. [un-]

***un·con·scious** [ʌ̀nkánʃəs / -kɔ́n-] *adj.* **1** not conscious; not clearly perceived to exist. 무의식의; 의식 불명의. ¶ *After the accident he was ~ for several days.* 그 사고로 그는 여러 날 동안 의식 불명이었다 / *remain in an ~ condition* 의식이 깨어나지 않고 있다. **2** 《*of*》 not aware. 모르는; 깨닫지 못하는. ¶ *He was ~ of his guilt.* 그는 자기 죄를 모르고 있었다 / *I am ~ of having said so.* 나는 그런 말을 한 기억이 없다 / *They were ~ of any danger.* 그들은 위험을 전혀 깨닫지 못하고 있었다. **3** not deliberate; not intended. 고의가 아닌; 부지중(不知中)의. ¶ *an ~ omission* 〔*mistake*〕 부지중의 탈락〔잘못〕 / *an ~ smile* 저도 모르게 나온 미소.
— *n.* 《*the ~*》 《psych.》 the unconscious state of mind. 무의식. [un-, *conscious*]

un·con·scious·ly [ʌ̀nkánʃəsli / -kɔ́n-] *adv.* in an unconscious manner. 무의식적으로; 부지중에.

un·con·sti·tu·tion·al [ʌ̀nkanstətjúːʃənəl / -kɔn-] *adj.* contrary to the constitution. 위헌의. [un-]

un·con·ven·tion·al [ʌ̀nkənvénʃənəl] *a.* not bound by or conforming to convention, rule, or precedent. 관례에 따르지 〔매이지〕 않는.

un·cork [ʌ̀nkɔ́ːrk] *vt.* (P6) **1** pull a cork from (something). …의 코르크 마개를 뽑다. ¶ *~ a bottle of wine.* **2** 《*colloq.*》 set loose what is bottled up. (맺힌 감정 등)을 토로하다. ¶ *~ one's feelings* 감정을 토로하다 / *Their courage was uncorked at the news.* 그 소식에 그들은 용기가 솟았다.

un·cou·ple [ʌ̀nkʌ́pəl] *vt.* (P6) **1** loose (dogs, etc.) from a leash or couple; unfasten. (개 따위)를 가죽끈에서 풀어놓다; …을 풀다. ¶ *The dogs were uncoupled.* 개들이 풀렸다. **2** disconnect; separate. 분리하

다; 떼어놓다. ¶ ~ *railway-cars* 객차를 분리하다. [un-]

un·couth [ʌnkúːθ] *adj.* **1** not skillful; lacking in polish and grace. 솜씨가 서툰; 멋이 없는. ¶ *an ~ young man* 촌스러운 젊은이. **2** strange; unusual and unpleasant. 이상한; 기괴한. ¶ *The poor idiot made ~ noises.* 그 가엾은 백치는 야릇한 소리를 냈다. [E. = unknown]

***un·cov·er** [ʌ̀nkʌ́vər] *vt.* (P6) **1** remove the top or cover from (something); take the hat or cap from (one's head). …의 뚜껑을[덮개를] 벗기다; …에서 모자를 벗기다. ¶ ~ *a dish of food* 음식 그릇의 뚜껑을 열다 / ~ *one's head* 모자를 벗다. **2** 《*fig.*》 expose; reveal; lay bare; make known. …을 폭로하다; 밝히다; 털어놓다. ¶ *The plot was uncovered.* 음모가 드러났다 / ~ *one's position* 자기 입장을 밝히다 / ~ *one's heart to* …에게 심중을 털어놓다. — *vi.* (P1) 《*arch.*》 take off the hat or cap out of respect; bow. (경의를 표해) 모자를 벗다. ¶ *Everyone uncovered when the signal sounded.* 신호가 울리자 모두 모자를 벗었다. [un-]

uncover oneself, remove one's hat or cap as a sign of respect or salutation. (경의를 표해) 모자를 벗다.

unc·tion [ʌ́ŋkʃən] *n.* Ⓤ **1** the act of rubbing with oil at a religious ceremony; the oil used for this. (축성식(祝聖式)의) 도유(塗油); 그 성유(聖油). **2** the oil used to heal wounds. (의료용(用)의) 바르는 기름; 연고. **3** 《*fig.*》 soothing words or comforting thought. (말 따위의) 마음을 달래는 것. ¶ *the ~ of flattery* 발림말. **4** a sympathetic and persuasive quality in speaking. 감동적인 어조. ¶ *The sermons of today lack ~.* 오늘의 설교는 감동을 주지 못했다. [L. *ungo* anoint]

un·cul·ti·vat·ed [ʌ̀nkʌ́ltəvèitid] *adj.* **1** not cultivated. 미(未)개간의. ¶ ~ *land.* **2** 《*fig.*》 not developed; not practised. 연마되지 않은. ¶ *an ~ art* 미숙한 기술. **3** uncivilized; rude. 교양이 없는. ¶ ~ *races* 미개 종족. **4** not improved by study, care, etc. 학습[교육]에 의하지 않은; 타고난. ¶ *an ~ genius* 타고난 천재. [un-]

un·curl [ʌ̀nkə́ːrl] *vt.* (P6) straighten out. (고수머리 따위)를 펴다. ¶ ~ *feathers* 고불고불한 깃털을 펴다. — *vi.* (P1) become straight. 펴지다; 똑바로 되다.

un·cut [ʌ̀nkʌ́t] *adj.* **1** not cut. 자르지 않은. **2** 《of books》 with edges of pages still joined; with margins not cut down. (책을) 도련하지 않은. **3** (of a film or story) not made shorter. (영화 등이) 무(無)삭제의. ¶ *the ~ version of "Lady Chatterly's Lover"* "Lady Chatterly's Lover"의 무삭제판.

un·daunt·ed [ʌ̀ndɔ́ːntid] *adj.* not afraid; bold; courageous. 겁없는; 대담한; 용감한. [un-]

un·de·ceive [ʌ̀ndisíːv] *vt.* free (someone) from deception, mistake, or a belief for which there is no foundation. …의 미망(迷妄)[잘못]을 깨우쳐 주다. ¶ *He believes that he is certain to win, and I have not the heart to ~ him.* 그는 반드시 자기가 이길 거라고 확신하는 터라 나로선 그 환상을 깨우쳐 줄 마음이 안든다.

un·de·cid·ed [ʌ̀ndisáidid] *adj.* **1** not decided; not having made up one's mind. 미정의; 미결의. ¶ *an ~ question* 현안의 문제 / *I'm ~ whether to go or not.* 갈지 말지 망설이고 있다. **2** (of weather) not settled. (날씨가) 어떻게 될지 모르는. **3** lacking decision of character. 우유 부단한. ¶ *an ~ character* 우유 부단한 사람. **4** not clearly marked. (모습이) 뚜렷하지 않은.

un·de·fined [ʌ̀ndifáind] *adj.* **1** not described or explained exactly; indefinite. 정의가 내려져 있지 않은; 막연한. ¶ *an ~ word.* **2** not clearly marked; indefinite. (경계가) 확실하지 않은. ¶ ~ *boundaries* 애매한 경계선.

un·de·ni·a·ble [ʌ̀ndináiəbəl] *adj.* **1** that can not be denied; unquestionable; excellent. 부정할 수 없는; 나무랄 데 없는. ¶ *an ~ truth* 부인 못할 진실 / *an ~ evidence* 확실한 증거 / ~ *quality* 우수한 자질. **2** unmistakable. 틀림없는. ¶ *an ~ politician* 틀림이 없는 정치가. [un-]

un·de·ni·a·bly [ʌ̀ndináiəbəli] *adv.* beyond denial; certainly. 틀림없이; 명백히.

⁑**un·der** [ʌ́ndər] *prep.* **1** situated below; beneath. …의 아래에; 밑에; 기슭에. ¶ *Tired, they rested ~ a tree.* 피곤하여 그들은 나무 밑에서 쉬었다 / *They sang in the open air ~ the moon.* 그들은 야외 달빛 아래서 노래하였다 / *a river flowing ~ a bridge* 다리 아래 흐르는 강 / *The cat was ~ the table.* 그 고양이는 탁자 밑에 있었다 / *a village lying ~ a hill* 산기슭에 있는 마을. **2** in a position lower than the surface of; covered by; sheltered by. …의 표면 밑에; …에 덮여. ¶ *the water ~ the ground* 지하수 / ~ *heavy blankets* 무거운 담요 밑에 / ~ *cover of darkness* 어둠을 틈타 / *hide one's face ~ the bedclothes* 침대 시트에 얼굴을 묻다. **3** less or below in number, amount, quality, etc. than. (수·양 따위가) …미만의. ¶ *He looks to be ~ forty.* 그는 마흔 살이 안돼 보인다 / *I bought this hat for ~ £2.* 이 모자를 2파운드 미만으로 샀다 / *Children ~ 18 years old are not admitted.* 18세 미만의 아이들은 입장할 수 없다 / *Under 20 people were there.* 20명이 채 안되는 사람이 거기 있었다. **4** subject to the control, influence, instruction, etc. of. …의 지배 아래; 영향 아래; 지시를 받고. ¶ ~ *the leadership of two statesmen* 두 정치인의 지휘 아래 / *He studied ~ a noted scientist.* 그는 저명한 과학자의 지도를 받았다 / *He was an officer ~ Napoleon.* 그는 나폴레옹 치하의 장교였다 / ~ *(the reign of) Queen Victoria* 빅토리아 여왕 통치하에 / *He*

U

has six men ~ *him.* 그에겐 부하가 여섯 명 있다 / ~ *the sentence of death* 사형 선고를 받고. **5** during the time or rule of. …의 동안; …시대에(의). ¶ *Under this sovereign, the country became the theater of a long war.* 그의 치세 중 그 나라는 오랜 전쟁의 무대가 되었다. **6** subjected to the effort or action of; in the process of. …을 받고; 진행 중인(의). ¶ *a building* ~ *construction* 건축 중인 건물 / *a question* ~ *discussion* 논의되고 있는 문제 / *be* ~ *medical treatment* 치료를 받고 있다 / *a road* ~ *repair* 보수 중인 도로. **7** according to; bound by. …에 따라; 얽매여. ¶ ~ *oath* 선서하고 / ~ *the terms of the contract* 계약 조건에 따라 / ~ *a vow of secrecy* 비밀 엄수를 서약하고 / ~ *such conditions* 그러한 조건에서. **8** suffering the effect of. (약효 등이) 나타나; 들어. ¶ ~ *an anesthetic* 마취되어. **9** because of. …때문에. ¶ ~ *the circumstances* 환경 때문에. **10** represented by. (위장·구실) 아래; …라는 이름으로. ¶ ~ *a false name* 가명으로 / ~ *the mask of friendship* 우정이라는 탈을 쓰고. **11** beneath in classification. (분류 따위에서) …에 속하는. ¶ ~ *this subject* 이 주제 안에 / *That book is classified* ~ *"Fiction".* 그 책은 소설로 분류된다.

— *adv.* in or to a lower position or state; below. 아래에; 밑에; 종속되어; 이하로. ¶ *A cork floated, but a stone went* ~. 코르크는 떴지만 돌은 가라앉았다 / *He's* ~. 그는 의식이 없다 / *Go over the fence, not* ~. 울타리를 넘어 가거라, 밑으로 가지 말고.

— *adj.* lower in position, rank, amount, or degree. 아래의; 하부의. ¶ *the* ~ *lip* 아랫입술 / *the* ~ *surface of a leaf* 잎의 아래면 / *an* ~ *cook* 요리사의 조수. [E.]

under- [ʌ́ndər-] *pref.* **1** below in position; below a surface or covering. '아래(밑)에(의)'의 뜻. ¶ *undershirt* 내의. **2** inferior. '…보다 못한, 하위의, 열등한'의 뜻. **3** insufficiently. '불충분한(하게)'의 뜻. ¶ *underestimate* 싸게 어림잡다; 과소 평가하다 / *undervalue* 싸게 견적하다; 얕보다. [E.]

un·der·act [ʌ̀ndərǽkt] *vt., vi.* (P6;1) act with too little spirit. 연기력이 부족하다; 소극적으로 연기하다. [under-]

un·der·age [ʌ̀ndəréidʒ] *a.* not of full age. 미성년의.

un·der·bid [ʌ̀ndərbíd] *vt.* (**-bid, -den** [-bídn] or **-bid, -ding**) make a lower bid than (another). …보다 싸게 입찰하다; 더 싼 값으로 부르다. ¶ *Our commercial rivals can* ~ *us in foreign markets.* 우리 라이벌 회사는 해외 시장에서 우리보다 싸게 입찰할 수도 있다(opp. overbid).

un·der·brush [ʌ́ndərbrʌ̀ʃ] *n.* Ⓤ 《U.S.》 bushes or small trees growing beneath large trees in a forest. (큰 나무 밑에 자라는) 관목(灌木); 덤불.

un·der·car·riage [ʌ́ndərkæ̀ridʒ] *n.* **1** the supporting framework, as of a motorcar. (자동차의) 차대. **2** 《chiefly Brit.》 the landing gear of an aircraft. (항공기의) 착륙장치. [under-]

un·der·clothes [ʌ́ndərklòuðz] *n. pl.* underwear; clothes worn under a suit or dress. 속옷; 내의.

un·der·cloth·ing [ʌ́ndərklòuðiŋ] *n.* Ⓤ =underclothes.

un·der·cov·er [ʌ́ndərkʌ̀vər, ⌐–⌐–] *adj.* working or done in secret. 몰래 한; 비밀의. ¶ *an* ~ *agent* 첩보원; 공작원.

un·der·cur·rent [ʌ́ndərkə̀ːrənt / -kʌ̀-] *n.* Ⓒ **1** a current of water flowing beneath the surface. 저류(底流); 암류(暗流). **2** 《*fig.*》 a hidden or underlying tendency of feeling or opinion. 내면적 의향; 저의(底意). ¶ *There was an* ~ *of melancholy beneath his jokes.* 그의 농담엔 어딘가 우울한 데가 있었다.

un·der·cut [ʌ́ndərkʌ̀t] *vt.* (**-cut, -cutting**) (P6) **1** cut away (something) from below or beneath. …의 하부를 잘라 버리다. **2** offer (goods, etc.) at a lower price than one's competitors. …을 싼 값으로 팔다. **3** (in games) hit (a golf ball, etc.) so that it rises high and comes to rest without rolling far. (공)을 쳐올리다. — *n.* [⌐–⌐] **1** Ⓒ a cut made underneath. 하부를 잘라냄. **2** Ⓤ the tenderloin or fillet of beef. (소의) 허릿살. — *adj.* cut away underneath. 아래를 잘라낸.

un·der·de·vel·oped [ʌ̀ndərdivéləpt] *adj.* not yet fully developed. 발육 부전(不全)의; (사진의) 현상(現像) 부족의.

un·der·dog [ʌ́ndərdɔ̀(ː)g, -dɑ̀g] *n.* Ⓒ **1** the losing dog in a dogfight. 싸움에 진 개. **2** 《*fig.*》 《usu. *the* ~》 a loser or probable loser in a contest or struggle. (경쟁·투쟁에서의) 패배자; 낙오자.

un·der·done [ʌ̀ndərdʌ́n] *adj.* not cooked enough. 설구운(cf. *welldone, overdone*). ¶ ~ *meat* (*beef*) 설구운 고기.

un·der·es·ti·mate [ʌ̀ndəréstəmèit] *vt.* (P6) estimate (something) below the actual value, amount, etc. …을 싸게 어림잡다(견적하다); 과소 평가하다(opp. overestimate). ¶ ~ *someone's abilities* …의 능력을 얕잡다 / *We underestimated the cost of materials, and ended up making a loss.* 우리는 재료값을 싸게 잡았고 끝내는 손해를 보고 말았다. — [-mit] *n.* Ⓒ an estimate that is too low. 싼 견적; 과소 평가. [under-]

un·der·ex·po·sure [ʌ̀ndərekspóuʒər] *n.* ⓊⒸ exposure to the light for too short a time; an underexposed film or plate. (필름 등의) 노출 부족; 노출 부족이 된 필름.

un·der·fed [ʌ̀ndərféd] *v.* p. and pp. of **underfeed.** — *adj.* given insufficient food; not properly nourished. 식량 부족의; 영양 실조의.

un·der·feed [ʌ̀ndərfíːd] *v.* (**-fed**) *vt.* (P6) supply with too little food. …에게

충분한 음식을 주지 않다. ¶ *Never ~ children.* 아이들을 잘〔충분히〕 먹여라. —*vi.* (P1) eat less than the normal amount of food. 감식(減食)하다. [under-]

un·der·foot [ʌ̀ndərfút] *adv.* **1** beneath the feet; under one's foot or feet. 발 밑에. ¶ *The ground is damp ~.* 발 밑의 땅이 질척거린다. **2** under the foot, esp. against the ground. 짓밟아서. ¶ *Some of the children got trampled ~ as the crowd fled in panic.* 군중들이 황망히 달아나면서 몇 명의 어린애들이 발밑에 깔렸다. **3** 《*fig.*》 in a subordinate position. 굴종시켜; 설설 기게. ¶ *The king kept his subjects ~.* 왕은 백성들을 굴종케 했다. **4** 《U.S.》 in the way. 방해가 되어. ¶ *The children are always getting ~.* 아이들은 늘 거치적거린다.

un·der·gar·ment [ʌ́ndərgɑ̀ːrmənt] *n.* Ⓒ an article of underwear. 속옷.

•**un·der·go** [ʌ̀ndərgóu] *vt.* (**-went, -gone**) (P6) experience; be subjected to; endure; suffer. …을 경험하다; 당하다; 겪다; 받다. ¶ *~ an operation* 수술을 받다 / *The town has undergone a great change during the last five years.* 그 시는 지난 5년 동안에 괄목할 변화를 했다 / *The soldiers underwent many hardships.* 병사들은 수많은 고초를 겪었다. [under-]

un·der·gone [ʌ̀ndərgɔ́ːn / -gɔ́n] *v.* pp. of **undergo.**

un·der·grad·u·ate [ʌ̀ndərgrǽdʒuit, -èit] *n.* Ⓒ a university student who has not yet received a degree. (재학중인) 대학생(opp. postgraduate). —*adj.* of or for undergraduates. (재학중인) 대학생의.

•**un·der·ground** [ʌ́ndərgràund] *adj.* **1** beneath the surface of the earth. 지하의. **2** 《*fig.*》 secret. 비밀의. ¶ *Spying is an ~ activity.* 첩보는 비밀 활동이다 / *~ newspapers* 지하 신문 / *an ~ group of anti-government guerrillas* 반정부 게릴라의 비밀 집단.
—*n.* Ⓒ 《usu. *the ~*》 《Brit.》 an underground railway. 지하철(=《U.S.》 subway, cf. *tube*). ¶ *travel by the ~* 지하철로 가다.
—[ʌ̀ndərgráund] *adv.* **1** beneath the surface of the ground. 지하에(서). ¶ *Miners work ~.* 광부들은 지하에서 작업한다 / *The nuclear waste was buried deep ~.* 핵폐기물은 땅속 깊이 묻혔다. **2** 《*fig.*》 secretly; in or into a secret place. 비밀히; 비밀 장소에〔로〕. ¶ *make a plan ~* 비밀리에 계획을 세우다 / *The terrorists have had to go ~.* 테러리스트들은 지하로 잠입할 수 밖에 없었다.

un·der·grown [ʌ́ndərgròun] *adj.* not fully grown or developed. 발육이 불충분한.

un·der·growth [ʌ́ndərgròuθ] *n.* bushes, small trees, etc., growing under large trees in woods or forests; underbrush. (큰나무 밑의) 관목(灌木); 덤불.

un·der·hand [ʌ́ndərhæ̀nd] *adj.* **1** (of a ball) thrown with the hand kept below the level of the shoulder. 치던지는. ¶ *~ bowling* 〔*service*〕. **2** 《*fig.*》 not open; secret; dishonest; sly. 비밀의; 음험한. ¶ *~ intrigues* 음모 / *He acquired the money in a most ~ manner.* 그는 아주 음험한 방법으로 그 돈을 취득했다. [under-]

un·der·hand·ed [ʌ́ndərhǽndid] *adj.* secret; lacking the required number of workers, etc. 비밀의; 일손이 모자라는.

un·der·laid [ʌ̀ndərléid] *v.* p. and pp. of **underlay.**

un·der·lain [ʌ̀ndərléin] *v.* pp. of **underlie.**

un·der·lay [ʌ̀ndərléi] *vt.* (**-laid**) (P6) lay (something) under something else. …을 (…의) 밑에 놓다〔깔다〕.

un·der·lie [ʌ̀ndərlái] *vt.* (**-lay, -lain, -lying**) (P6) **1** lie or be beneath. …의 밑에 있다. ¶ *the coal seams which ~ the English Channel.* 영국 해협 밑에 있는 탄층(炭層). **2** be at the basis of (something). …의 기초가 되다. ¶ *the principles which ~ our foreign policy* 우리 외교 정책의 기조를 이루는 기본 방침 / *What motives ~ his acts?* 그의 행동의 동기는 무엇일까.

un·der·line [ʌ̀ndərláin] *vt.* (P6) **1** draw a line beneath (a word, words, etc.). …에 밑줄을 치다. ¶ *~ a word* 단어에 밑줄을 긋다. **2** emphasize. …을 강조하다. ¶ *The sudden summoning of the cabinet underlines the seriousness of the situation.* 돌연한 각의(閣議) 소집은 사태의 심각성을 강조하고 있다.
—[´-`] *n.* Ⓒ a line underneath; an underscore. 밑줄.

un·der·ling [ʌ́ndərliŋ] *n.* Ⓒ a person of a lower rank or position; a subordinate. 아랫사람; 부하; 졸개.

un·der·men·tioned [ʌ̀ndərménʃənd] *a.* mentioned below or later. 하기(下記)의; 아래에 적은. ¶ *Please supply me with the ~ goods.* 아래에 적은 물품을 배달해 주십시오. [under-]

un·der·mine [ʌ̀ndərmáin] *vt.* (P6) **1** dig beneath; make a tunnel under (a wall, etc.). …의 밑을 파다; 아래에 갱도를 파다. ¶ *The soldiers undermined the wall.* 병사들은 성벽 밑을 팠다. **2** 《*fig.*》 work against (something) secretly. …을 몰래 훼손〔손상〕하다. ¶ *~ someone's reputation* 〔*influence*〕 아무의 명성〔영향력〕을 음해질하다. **3** weaken gradually. …을 서서히 약화시키다. ¶ *Many severe colds had undermined his health.* 여러 번의 심한 감기가 그의 건강을 서서히 좀먹었다. **4** wear away the foundations of. …의 기초를 침식하다. ¶ *The cliff was undermined by the waves.* 암벽은 파도에 의해 깎여 나갔다.

un·der·most [ʌ́ndərmòust] *adj.* lowest in place, position, or rank. (자리·지위 등이) 맨 아래의; 최하위의.

•**un·der·neath** [ʌ̀ndərníːθ] *adv., prep.* beneath; below (something). …의 아래에; 낮게. ¶ *the river flowing ~ the bridge* 다리 밑을 흐르는 강 / *It sounds as if there is a rat ~*

U

the floor. 마루 밑에 쥐가 한 마리 있는 모양이다. [under-, →beneath]

un·der·nour·ished [ʌ̀ndərnə́:riʃt / -nʌ́riʃt] *adj.* not sufficiently nourished. 영양 부족의. ¶ *This child is seriously* ～. 이 아이는 지나치게 영양 불량이다. [under-]

un·der·pass [ʌ́ndərpæ̀s] *n.* ⟪U.S.⟫ a path underneath; a road under railway tracks or under another road. (철도나 다른 도로 밑을 지나가는) 지하도.

un·der·pay [ʌ̀ndərpéi] *vt.* (**-paid**) (P6) pay insufficiently or too little. …에게 불충분한 임금을 주다; 저임금을 주다. ¶ *We're overworked and underpaid.* 우리는 일은 너무 많이 하고 임금은 적게 받는다.

un·der·pin [ʌ̀ndərpín] *vt.* (P6) support or strengthen (something) from beneath. …을 받쳐주다; 떠받치다.

un·der·pop·u·lat·ed [ʌ̀ndərpápjəlèitid / -pɔ́p-] *a.* (of a country) having a small population compared with its size. 인구가 적은; 희소 인구의.

un·der·priv·i·leged [ʌ́ndərprívəlidʒd] *a.* having less privilege than others; poor. 남보다 특권이 적은; 가난한.

un·der·pro·duc·tion [ʌ̀ndərprədʌ́kʃən] *n.* Ⓤ shortage of production. 생산 부족; 저(低)생산.

un·der·proof [ʌ̀ndərprú:f] *a.* containing less alcohol than proof spirit. (알코올)이 표준 도수 이하의. [under-]

un·der·rate [ʌ̀ndəréit] *vt.* (P6) place too low a value or estimate upon (something); underestimate. …을 낮게 평가하다; 경시하다. ¶ *One should not* ～ *the abilities of one's opponent.* 상대의 능력을 얕보아서는 안된다.

un·der·score [ʌ̀ndərskɔ́:r] *vt.* underline. …에 밑줄을 긋다. ── [⌐─⌐] *n.* Ⓒ an underscored line. 밑줄.

un·der·sea [ʌ́ndərsì] *adj.* beneath the surface of the sea. 해저의. ¶ ～ *plants* 해저 식물. ── [⌐─⌐] *adv.* =underseas.

un·der·seas [ʌ̀ndərsí:z] *adv.* beneath the surface of the sea. 바다 밑에(서); 해저에(서).

un·der·sec·re·tar·y [ʌ̀ndərsékrətèri / -təri] *n.* Ⓒ (*pl.* **-tar·ies**) an assistant secretary, esp. of a government department. 차관(次官).

un·der·sell [ʌ̀ndərsél] *vt.* (**-sold**) (P6) sell goods at a lower price than (a competitors'). …을 (남)보다 싸게 팔다. ¶ *This store can* ～ *other stores because it sells for cash.* 이 가게는 물건을 현금으로 팔기 때문에 다른 가게들보다 싸다.

un·der·shirt [ʌ́ndərʃə̀:rt] *n.* Ⓒ a shirt worn next to the skin under other clothing. 내의; 속옷.

un·der·shot [ʌ̀ndərʃát / -ʃɔ́t] *adj.* **1** (of a water wheel) driven by water passing beneath. (물레방아가) 하사식(下射式)의. **2** having the lower jaw projecting beyond the upper. 아래턱이 쑥 내민. [under-]

un·der·side [ʌ́ndərsàid] *n.* Ⓒ an under or lower side. 하면; 아래쪽. ¶ *The* ～ *of the rock was covered with seaweed.* 그 바위의 밑바닥은 해초로 덮여 있었다.

un·der·sign [ʌ̀ndərsáin] *vt.* (P6) sign one's name at the end of (a letter, a document, etc.). (편지 등)의 끝에 서명하다.

un·der·signed [ʌ̀ndərsáind] *adj.* signed at the end of a letter or document. (편지 따위)의 끝에 서명한. ¶ *the* ～ *members* 서명자. ── *n.* ⟪*the* ～⟫ the person or persons signing a document. (문서의)서명자. ¶ *I, the* ～ 소생, 서명자(는).

un·der·sized [ʌ́ndərsáizd] *adj.* smaller than the usual size. 보통 것보다 작은; 소형의. [under-]

:un·der·stand [ʌ̀ndərstǽnd] *v.* (**-stood**) *vt.* **1** (P6,9,10,12) get the meaning of (something). …(의 뜻)을 알다; 이해하다. ¶ *Do you* ～ *me?* =*Do you* ～ *what I say?* 내 말(뜻)을 알겠느냐 / *I can't* ～ *your doing that.* =*I can't* ～ *why you did* 〔*do*〕 *that.* 네가 왜 그랬는지〔그러는지〕 난 모르겠다 / *Do you* ～ *this notice?* 이 공고의 뜻을 알겠는가 / *He does not* ～ *the question.* 그는 질문의 뜻을 모르고 있다. **2** (P6,11) have knowledge of (something); know well. …에 대한 지식이 있다; 정통하다. ¶ *I* ～ *a good deal of what is going on around me.* 내 주변에 무슨 일이 벌어지고 있는지 잘 알고 있다 / *I* ～ *you are not satisfied.* 네가 불만스러워 하는 것을 알고 있다 / *A good teacher should* ～ *children.* 훌륭한 선생이란 아이들에 대해서 잘 알아야 한다 / *We do not* ～ *the nature of electricity.* 우리는 전기의 본질에 대해 잘 모르고 있다. **3** (P11,20) accept (something) as a fact; interpret; assume; believe. …을 해석하다; 미루어 알다; 믿다. ¶ *I* ～ *her to be happy.* = *I* ～ *that she is happy.* 나는 그녀가 행복하다고 생각한다 / *I understood him to say that.* 나는 그가 그렇게 말한 것으로 생각했다. **4** (P6,11) get (something) as information; hear or learn. …을 들어서 알고 있다. ¶ *I* ～ *that you are going to marry Mary.* 네가 메리와 결혼하는 걸로 알고 있다 / *I* ～ *that you have been ill.* 네가 앓고 있다는 것을 알고 있다. **5** (P6) ⟪in *passive*⟫ supply (a word, idea, etc.) in the mind. (어구 등)을 보충해서 생각하다; 생략하다. ¶ *In the sentence "Come here," the subject "you" is understood.* "Come here."라는 문장에서는 주어 "you"가 생략되어 있다. ── *vi.* (P1) **1** be able to get the meaning; comprehend. 알다; 이해하다. ¶ *She is slow to* ～. 그녀는 이해가 더디다. **2** hear; be informed. 들어서 알고 있다. ¶ *The situation is better, so I* ～. 사태는 호전되었다고 듣고 있다. [under-]

give someone to understand, tell or inform someone. …에게 알리다〔말하다〕. ¶ *He gave me to* ～ *that he would not be re-*

U

turning. 그는 나에게 돌아오지 않겠다고 알려왔다.

make** oneself **understood, make one's meaning clear. 자기 말을 알아듣게 하다. ¶ *I failed to make myself understood in English.* 영어로 내 말을 알아듣게 할 수 없었다.

understand one another, be clear as to each other's aims and opinions; come to an agreement with one another; be on good terms through sympathizing with each other's aims. 서로 의사가 소통하다; 서로 이해하다; 기맥을 통하다.

un·der·stand·a·ble [ʌ̀ndərstǽndəbəl] *adj.* that can be understood. 이해할 수 있는. ¶ *The loudspeaker announcement was barely* ~. 확성기의 말을 겨우 알아들었다.

un·der·stand·a·bly [ʌ̀ndərstǽndəbəli] *adv.* so as to be understandable; in an understandable manner; naturally. 알아듣게; 이해할 수 있게.

:un·der·stand·ing [ʌ̀ndərstǽndiŋ] *n.* **1** Ⓤ knowledge; comprehension. 지식; 이해; 납득. ¶ *have a clear* ~ *of the problem* 문제를 명확히 알고 있다 / *He tried to get some* ~ *of the question.* 그는 그 문제를 좀 알아보려고 했다. **2** Ⓤ the power to think and learn; intelligence. 이해력; 지력(知力). ¶ *a man of* ~ 이해력이 있는 사람. **3** Ⓒ 《*sing.* only》 mutual agreement. 서로의 이해; (의견 따위의) 일치. ¶ *come to an* ~ *with* …와 양해가 성립되다 / *have* 〔*keep*〕 *an* ~ *with* …와 의견이 상통하다 / *You must reach* 〔*come to*〕 *an* ~ *with him.* 너는 그와 의견의 일치를 봐야 한다.

on the understanding that, on condition that. …이라는 조건으로.

on* 〔*with*〕 *this understanding, on this condition. 이 조건으로. ¶ *On this* ~, *I am willing to accept your offer.* 이 조건으로 당신의 제의를 받아들이겠소.

— *adj.* able to understand; intelligent. 이해가 빠른; 분별 있는.

un·der·state [ʌ̀ndərstéit] *vt.* (P6) state too weakly; tell less than the truth about (something). …을 삼가서〔안틀어〕 말하다. ¶ *In an understated speech he made clear his views.* 조심스럽게 말하면서도 그는 자기 견해를 분명히 밝혔다. [under-]

un·der·state·ment [ʌ̀ndərstéitmənt] *n.* **1** Ⓤ the act of understating. 삼가서 말하기. **2** Ⓒ a statement that is too weak or moderate. 삼가서 하는 말.

:un·der·stood [ʌ̀ndərstúd] *v.* p. and pp. of **understand.**

un·der·strap·per [ʌ́ndərstræ̀pər] *n.* 《*contempt.*》 an officer, official, employee, etc. of low rank and little importance. 아랫사람; 하위직; 졸개.

un·der·study [ʌ́ndərstʌ̀di] *n.* a person who learns the part of an actor so as to act if he is ill or absent. (배우의) 대역(代役). [under-]

·un·der·take [ʌ̀ndərtéik] *v.* (**-took, -ta·ken**) *vt.* **1** (P6) take (something) upon oneself; take steps to perform; set about. …을 떠맡다; 착수하다; 시작하다. ¶ ~ *a new enterprise* 새로운 사업을 시작하다 / ~ *a responsible post* 책임 있는 자리를 맡다 / ~ *a journey* 여행을 떠나다. **2** (P6,8) contract to do (something); promise. …을 약속하다. ¶ *She undertook to be back home by six o'clock.* 그녀는 여섯시까지 집에 돌아오겠다고 약속했다. **3** (P11) affirm; guarantee. …을 보증하다. — *vi.* (P1) 《*colloq.*》 carry on the business of an undertaker. 장의사를 경영하다. [under-]

un·der·tak·er [ʌ̀ndərtéikər] *n.* **1** Ⓒ a person who undertakes something. 떠맡는 사람; 인수자; 도급인(都給人); 기업가. **2** [ˊ-ˋ-] a person who makes a business of preparing the dead for burial and of taking charge of funerals. 장의사 업자.

·un·der·tak·ing [ʌ̀ndərtéikiŋ] *n.* **1** Ⓒ something undertaken; a task; an enterprise. (일·책임 따위의) 인수; 도급; (떠맡은) 일〔사업〕; 기업. ¶ *a difficult* 〔*dangerous*〕 ~. **2** Ⓒ a promise; a guarantee. 약속; 보증. ¶ *an* ~ *to pay the debt within six months,* 6개월 안에 빚을 갚는다는 약속. **3** [ˊ-ˋ-] Ⓤ the business of preparing the dead for burial and taking charge of funerals. 장의사업(業).

un·der·tone [ʌ́ndərtòun] *n.* Ⓒ **1** a low or very quiet tone. 낮은〔작은〕 소리. ¶ *talk in* ~ 작은 소리로 말하다. **2** a subdued color. 엷은〔부드러운〕 색깔. **3** 《*fig.*》 an underlying quality. 잠재적 성질; 저류(底流). ¶ *an* ~ *of sadness in her gaiety* 그녀의 명랑함 속에 깔려 있는 애수 / *a strong* ~ *of the romantic in his work* 그의 작품의 밑바닥에 흐르고 있는 강한 낭만주의.

·un·der·took [ʌ̀ndərtúk] *v.* p. of **undertake.**

un·der·tow [ʌ́ndərtòu] *n.* **1** any strong current below the surface, moving in a direction different from that of the surface current. 표면의 흐름과는 역방향의 강한 저류(底流). **2** the backward flow from waves breaking on a beach. (해안에 밀려왔다가) 물러가는 물결. [under-]

un·der·val·ue [ʌ̀ndərvǽlju:] *vt.* (P6) value too low; regard (something) too lightly. …을 과소 평가하다; 경시하다. ¶ *She felt that the company undervalued her work.* 그녀는 회사가 그녀의 일을 과소 평가한다고 느꼈다.

un·der·vest [ʌ́ndərvèst] *n.* Ⓤ 《Brit.》 an undershirt. 내의.

un·der·wa·ter [ʌ́ndərwɔ́:tər, -wɑ́t-] *adj.* below the surface of the water; made for use under the water. 물속의; 수중의; 수중용의. ¶ *an* ~ *boat* 잠수함 / *an* ~ *gun* 수중총 / ~ *cameras* 수중 카메라 / *They swam* ~. 그들은 물 밑에서 헤엄쳤다.

un·der·wear [ʌ́ndərwɛ̀ər] *n.* Ⓤ underclothing. 내의; 속옷.

un·der·went [ʌ̀ndərwént] *v.* p. of **undergo.**

un·der·world [ʌ̀ndərwə̀ːrld] *n.* Ⓒ 《usu. *the* ～》 **1** the earth. 지구. **2** the world of the dead; Hades. 저승; 하계. **3** the lower, degraded, or criminal part of society. 사회의 최하층(민); 범죄 사회. ¶ *a woman of the* ～ 윤락 여성 / *the kings of the* ～ 암흑가의 왕. **4** the opposite side of the earth. 지구의 뒤쪽. [under-]

un·der·write [ʌ̀ndərráit, ⌐–⌐] *v.* (**-wrote, -writ·ten**) *vt.* (P6) **1** 《usu. in *passive*》 write (something) under other written matter; sign one's name to (a document, etc.). …을 (…의) 밑에 쓰다; 서명하다. ¶ *The government has agreed to* ～ *the new project with a grant of ten million dollars.* 정부는 1천만 달러의 보조금이 부대(附帶)되는 신규 사업에의 서명에 동의했다. **2** insure (property) against loss. …을 보험에 들다; 보증하다. **3** agree to buy (an issue of stocks, bonds, etc.). (사채(社債) 등)의 구입을 승인하다. — *vi.* (P1) act as an underwriter. 보험업을 경영하다.

un·der·writ·er [ʌ́ndəràitər] *n.* Ⓒ **1** a person who underwrites insurance, esp. ships and cargoes against loss and damage. (해상) 보험업자. **2** a person who underwrites issues of stocks, bonds, etc. (주식·공채 등의) 인수인.

un·der·writ·ten [ʌ̀ndərítn, ⌐–⌐–] *v.* pp. of **underwrite.**

un·der·wrote [ʌ̀ndəróut, ⌐–⌐] *v.* p. of **underwrite.**

un·de·sir·a·ble [ʌ̀ndizáiərəbəl] *adj.* not desirable; disagreeable. 바람직하지 않은; 달갑지 않은; 불쾌한. ¶ *an* ～ *person* 바람직하지 않은 사람 / ～ *manners* 〔*language*〕 탐탁하지 않은 태도〔언사〕 / *make an* ～ *marriage* 바라지도 않은 결혼을 하다 / *He called at a most* ～ *moment.* 그는 가장 달갑지 않은 때에 찾아 왔다. — *n.* Ⓒ an undesirable person or thing. 바람직하지 못한 사람〔것〕. [un-]

un·de·vel·oped [ʌ̀ndivéləpt] *adj.* **1** (of a person) not fully grown. (심신이) 충분히 발달하지 않은; 미발육의. ¶ *an* ～ *child* 〔*body*〕 발육이 덜된 아이〔신체〕 / *an* ～ *mind* 〔*character*〕 성숙하지 못한 정신〔인격〕. **2** (of land) not put to full use. (땅이) 미개발의; 미발달의. ¶ *an* ～ *area* 미개발 지역 / *The land is* ～. 그 땅은 개발이 안 돼 있다.

***un·did** [ʌndíd] *v.* p. of **undo.**

un·dies [ʌ́ndiz] *n. pl.* 《*colloq.*》 women's underclothes. 여성의 속옷류(類). [abbr.]

un·dis·ci·plined [ʌndísəplind] *adj.* not disciplined; untrained. 훈련이 안 된; 미숙한. [un-]

un·dis·guised [ʌ̀ndisgáizd] *adj.* **1** not disguised; not covered under a mask. 변장하지 않은; 가면을 쓰지 않은. **2** unconcealed; open; plain. 숨김 없는; 공공연한. ¶ *with* ～ *pleasure* 사뭇 기쁜 듯이 / *He made an* ～ *attack on me.* 공공연하게 나를 공격했다.

un·dis·put·ed [ʌ̀ndispjúːtid] *adj.* not disputed; not doubted. 다툼 나위 없는; 이의 없는; 의심할 것 없는. [un-]

un·dis·turbed [ʌ̀ndistə́ːrbd] *adj.* not disturbed; calm. 방해받지 않은; 조용한.

un·di·vid·ed [ʌ̀ndiváidid] *adj.* not divided; whole; continuous. 나뉘지 않은; 완전한; 연속된. ¶ ～ *attention* 전념(專念) / ～ *affection* 한결같은 애정.

***un·do** [ʌndúː] *vt.* (**-did, -done**) (P6) **1** do away with; cause (something) to be as if it had never been done. …을 취소하다; 원상태로 되돌리다. ¶ ～ *a match* 혼약을 취소하다 / 《*prov.*》 *What's done cannot be undone.* 엎지른 물은 도로 담을 수 없다 / *attempt to* ～ *the past* 과거를 되돌리려고 하다. **2** unfasten; loosen. (매듭·묶은 것 따위)를 풀다; 늦추다; 끄르다. ¶ ～ *a parcel* 짐을 풀다 / ～ *the string* 끈을 풀다. **3** bring (something or someone) to ruin; spoil. …을 파멸시키다; 망쳐놓다. ¶ *His laziness will* ～ *him sooner or later.* 그는 게을러서 언제고 신세를 망칠 것이다 / *I am undone! My secret has been discovered!* 나는 망했다. 나의 비밀이 드러났단 말이다. [un-]

un·do·ing [ʌndúːiŋ] *n.* **1** the act of untying, opening, etc. 풀기; 끄르기. ¶ *the* ～ *of a parcel.* **2** the act of reversing, doing away with, or spoiling what has been done. 되돌리기; 취소; 만회(挽回). ¶ *There can be no* ～ *of the injury done to him.* 그에게 입힌 해를 없었던 것으로 할 수는 없다. **3** destruction; ruin. 파멸. **4** a cause of destruction or ruin. 파멸의 원인. ¶ *Pride was her* ～. 자만심이 그녀의 파멸의 원인이었다.

un·done [ʌndʌ́n] *v.* pp. of **undo.**
— *adj.* **1** not done; not finished. 하지 않은; 끝내지 않은; 미완성의. ¶ *leave a thing* ～ 일을 하지 않고 내버려〔방치해〕 두다 / *remain* ～ 미완성인 채로 있다. **2** brought to ruin; destroyed. 파멸한; 망쳐진. ¶ *We are* ～*!* 우린 끝장이다 / *I am* ～*!* 나는 망했다 / *A soul without justice is a soul* ～. 정의를 모르는 정신은 썩은 정신이다. **3** unfastened; untied. 풀어진.

un·doubt·ed [ʌndáutid] *adj.* not to be doubted; certain. 의심의 여지가 없는; 확실한. ¶ ～ *evidence* 확증 / *an* ～ *masterpiece* 의심할 여지가 없는 걸작.

***un·doubt·ed·ly** [ʌndáutidli] *adv.* beyond doubt; certainly. 의심할 여지없이; 확실히. ¶ *You are* ～ *right.* 의심할 여지없이 네가 옳다.

un·draw [ʌndrɔ́ː] *vt.* (**-drew, -drawn**) (P6) draw back or away. (커튼 따위)를 당겨서 열다. ¶ *She undrew the curtain.* [un-]

un·dreamed-of [ʌndríːmdɑ̀v / -ɔ̀v], **un·dreamt-of** [ʌndrémtɑ̀v / -ɔ̀v] *adj.* unimagined; not thought of. 꿈에도 생각 못한; 뜻밖의. ¶ *These technical advances were* ～ *even 20 years ago.* 이들 기술적 진보는 20년전

U

만 해도 꿈에도 생각 못한 것이었다.

un·dress [ʌndrés] *vt.* (P6) take off the clothing of (someone); strip. …의 옷을 벗기다. ¶ ~ *oneself* 옷을 벗다 / *Undress the baby and put him in the bath.* 아기옷을 벗기고 목욕을 시켜라. — *vi.* (P1) take off one's clothes. 옷을 벗다. — *n.* Ⓤ loose, informal dress; ordinary clothes. (헐렁한) 약복(略服); 평상복. — *adj.* of informal or ordinary clothes. 약복의; 평상복의. [un-]

un·due [ʌndjúː / -djúː] *adj.* **1** excessive; not proper. 과도한; 지나친. ¶ *an ~ fondness for liquor* 술에 대한 지나친 기호(嗜好) / *It would be wise not to give ~ importance to his criticism.* 그의 비평에 너무 신경쓰지 않는 게 좋을 거다 / *treat the matter with ~ haste* 문제를 너무 서둘러 처리하다. **2** not right; not fitting; improper. 부당한; 부적당한. ¶ *an ~ claim* 부당한 요구 / ~ *influence* 부당한 압박〔위압(威壓)〕. [un-, →due]

un·du·late [ʌ́ndʒəlèit / -djə-] *vi.* (P1) **1** move in waves. 파동치다; 물결치다. ¶ *undulating water* 파동치는 물결. **2** have a wavy form or surface. 굽이치다; 기복하다. ¶ *undulating hair* 굽이치듯 곱슬곱슬한 머리 / *The land undulates as far as the eye can see.* 땅은 눈길 닿는 데까지 아득히 굽이치듯 기복이 이어져 있다. — *vt.* (P6) **1** cause (something) to move in waves. …을 굽이치게 하다. **2** give a wavy form or surface to (something). …을 물결 모양으로 하다. — *adj.* [ʌ́ndʒəlìt] wavy. 물결 모양의; 파상의. [L. *unda* wave]

un·du·la·tion [ʌ̀ndʒəléiʃən, -djə-] *n.* **1** Ⓤ wave-like motion or form. 파동; 물결 모양; 기복(起伏). **2** Ⓒ one of a number of wave-like curves or slopes. 굽이침; 물결침.

un·du·ly [ʌndjúːli] *adv.* **1** excessively; unnecessarily. 과도하게; 공연히. ¶ *We're not ~ worried.* 우리가 공연히 걱정하는 건 아니다. **2** improperly. 부(적)당하게. ¶ ~ *confident* 걸맞지 않게 자신하는. [un-]

un·dy·ing [ʌndáiiŋ] *adj.* immortal; eternal. 불사의; 불멸의; 영원한. ¶ ~ *fame* 불멸의 명성 / *my ~ gratitude* 나의 영원한 감사.

un·earned [ʌnə́ːrnd] *adj.* **1** not earned by work. 노력하지 않고 얻은. ¶ *an ~ income* 불로 소득. **2** not deserved. 어울리지 않는; 부당한. ¶ ~ *praise* 과찬.

un·earth [ʌnə́ːrθ] *vt.* (P6) **1** dig up. …을 파내다; 발굴하다. ¶ ~ *a buried city* 매몰된 (옛)도시를 발굴하다. **2** 《*fig.*》 bring (something) to light; discover. …을 밝혀내다. ¶ ~ *a plot* 〔*secret, truth*〕 음모를 〔비밀을, 진실을〕 밝혀내다.

un·earth·ly [ʌnə́ːrθli] *adj.* **1** not of this world; supernatural. 이 세상의 것 같지 않은; 초자연적인. ¶ ~ *beauty* 이 세상 것이라고 생각할 수 없는 아름다움. **2** strange; mysterious; ghostly. 기묘한; 불가사의한; 섬뜩한. ¶ *I felt an ~ presence in the room.* 방안에서 섬뜩한 어떤 요기(妖氣)를 느꼈다 / *an ~ cry* 섬뜩한 비명소리. **3** 《*colloq.*》 unnatural; absurdly early or inconvenient. 보통이 아닌; (시간 따위가) 터무니 없이 이른〔불편한〕. ¶ *What an ~ time of night to call!* 이 한밤중에 무슨 전화야.

un·eas·i·ly [ʌníːzili] *adv.* in an uneasy manner; anxiously; uncomfortably; awkwardly. 불안〔불쾌, 불편〕하게; 걱정스레; 어색〔거북〕한 듯이. [un-]

un·eas·i·ness [ʌníːzinis] *n.* Ⓤ the quality or state of being uneasy. 불안; 불편; 근심; 거북함.

***un·eas·y** [ʌníːzi] *adj.* (**-eas·i·er, -eas·i·est**) **1** anxious; restless; worried. 걱정되는; 불안한. ¶ *I feel ~ about my health.* 내 건강이 걱정이다 / *feel ~ about the future* 〔*weather*〕 미래〔날씨〕에 불안을 느끼다 / *I'm ~ about this decision.* 이 결정에 마음이 안 놓인다 / 《*fig.*》 *The young king was ~ on the throne.* 젊은 왕은 왕위에 있는 것이 불안했다. **2** not comfortable. 불편한; 거북한. ¶ *I feel ~ in tight clothes.* 옷이 꼭 끼어 불편하다. **3** not easy in manner; awkward. 딱딱한; 어색한. ¶ ~ *manners* 어색한 태도.

un·em·ployed [ʌ̀nemplɔ́id] *adj.* **1** not employed; not in use. 놀고 있는; 쓰이지 않는. ¶ ~ *energy* 무위하게 놀리고 있는 정력 / ~ *capital* 유휴 자본. **2** not occupied. 한가한; 여가가 있는. ¶ *have a few hours ~* 몇 시간의 여가가 있다. **3** out of work. 실직한. ¶ *an ~ laborer* 실직한 노동자 / *He's ~ at present.* 그는 지금 실직 상태이다. — *n.* 《*the ~, collectively*》 all the people out of work. 실업자. ¶ *My friend is one of the ~.* 내 친구도 실업자 중의 한 사람이다. [un-]

·un·em·ploy·ment [ʌ̀nemplɔ́imənt] *n.* Ⓤ the state of being out of work. 실업; 실직; 실직 상태. ¶ *an ~ benefit* 〔*pay*〕 실업 수당 / ~ *insurance* 실업 보험 / *an ~ problem* 실업 문제 / *statistics of ~* 실업 통계 / *These closures will mean ~ for about 500 workers.* 이번의 휴업으로 약 5백 명의 실업 근로자가 생기게 될 것이다.

***un·e·qual** [ʌníːkwəl] *adj.* **1** not of the same size, strength, amount, etc. 같지〔동등하지〕 않은. ¶ ~ *amounts.* **2** not balanced or fair; not equally matched. 균형이 맞지 않는; 불균형의. ¶ *an ~ contest* (균형이 맞지 않는) 불공평한 시합 / *an ~ marriage* 서로 어울리지 않는 결혼. **3** not even; not regular. 고르지〔한결같지〕 않은. ¶ *Her steps are not only slow, but ~.* 그녀의 걸음걸이는 느릴 뿐만 아니라 고르지도 않다. **4** not enough; not adequate. 불충분한; 부적당한. ¶ *be ~ to the task* 그 일을 감당 못하다. [un-]

un·e·quiv·o·cal [ʌ̀nikwívəkəl] *adj.* not equivocal; plain; clear. 애매하지 않은; 분명한. ¶ ~ *evidence* 명백한 증거 / *an ~ refusal* 단호한 거절.

un·err·ing [ʌnə́ːriŋ] *adj.* making no mistakes; without error; accurate. 잘못이 없는; 정확한; 틀림없는. ¶ *an ~ aim* 정확한 조

준 / *an ~ judgment* (*insight*) 잘못이 없는 판단(통찰력). [un-]

UNESCO [ju:néskou] *n.* the United Nations Educational Scientific, and Cultural Organization. 유네스코《국제 연합 교육 과학 문화 기구》.

un·e·ven [ʌní:vən] *adj.* **1** not level; not smooth or flat; rough. 고르지 못한; 울퉁불퉁한. ¶ *~ ground* 고르지 못한 땅 / *an ~ surface* (*road*) 울퉁불퉁한 표면(길). **2** not uniform; not equal. 한결같지 않은; 균일하지 않은. ¶ *a man of ~ temper* 변덕스런 남자 / *an ~ performance* 고르지 못한 연기. **3** (of a number) that cannot be divided by 2 without a remainder; odd. 홀수의 (opp. even[1]). ¶ *27 and 9 are ~ numbers.* [un-]

un·e·vent·ful [ʌ̀nivéntfəl] *adj.* without important or striking occurrences. 평온 무사한. ¶ *an ~ life* (*journey*) 평온 무사한 일생(여행). [↑]

un·ex·am·pled [ʌ̀nigzǽmpld, -zá:m-] *adj.* having no parallel or similar case; without precedent. 유례(전례) 없는. ¶ *His run of 100 meters in 10 seconds is ~.* 백 미터를 10초에 달린 그의 주력은 전례 없는 기록이다.

un·ex·cep·tion·a·ble [ʌ̀niksépʃənəbəl] *adj.* beyond criticism; wholly admirable; excellent. 나무랄 데 없는; 더할 나위 없는. ¶ *an ~ person* (*character*) 나무랄 데 없는 사람(인격) / *~ taste* 더할 나위 없는 취미(맛) / *~ style* 훌륭한 문체.

un·ex·cep·tion·al [ʌ̀niksépʃənəl] *adj.* **1** ordinary; usual; not remarkable. 보통의; 대단찮은. ¶ *His performance is ~.* 그의 연기는 보통이다. **2** not admitting of exceptions. 예외를 인정하지 않는. ¶ *This regulation is ~.* 이 규칙은 예외가 없다.

***un·ex·pect·ed** [ʌ̀nikspéktid] *adj.* not expected; sudden. 예기치 못한; 뜻밖의. ¶ *an ~ accident* 불의의 사고 / 《*prov.*》 *The ~ always happens.* 예상 외의 일은 항용 있는 법. [un-]

***un·ex·pect·ed·ly** [ʌ̀nikspéktidli] *adv.* in a way that is not expected; suddenly. 뜻밖에; 갑자기.

un·fail·ing [ʌnféiliŋ] *adj.* **1** not failing. 틀림이 없는. ¶ *an ~ remedy* 확실한 치료법. **2** never running short; always present. 끊임없는; 다함이 없는. ¶ *an ~ water supply* 끊임없는 물의 공급 / *with ~ interest* 무한한 흥미를 가지고 / *~ courage* 불굴의 용기. **3** reliable; certain. 믿을 수 있는; 확실한. ¶ *an ~ friend* 의지가 되는 벗.

un·fair [ʌnfɛ́ər] *adj.* not fair; unjust; not honest. 불공평한; 옳지 못한; 부정직한. ¶ *an ~ judge* (*judgment*) 불공정한 재판관(심판) / *an ~ player* 부정 선수 / *an ~ means* 부정한 수단. ● **un·fair·ly** [-li] *adv.* **un·fair·ness** [-nis] *n.*

un·faith·ful [ʌnféiθfəl] *adj.* **1** not faithful; untrue. 불성실한; 부정(不貞)한. ¶ *an ~ servant* (*friend*) 성실하지 못한 하인(친구) / *an ~ wife* 부정한 아내. **2** not accurate or exact; not true to fact. 부정확한. ¶ *an ~ transcript* (*version*) 부정확한 사본(번역판).

un·fal·ter·ing [ʌnfɔ́:ltəriŋ] *adj.* **1** not wavering; firm; steady; intent. 흔들림이 없는; 확고한; 열중해 있는. ¶ *~ steps* 확고한 보조 / *an ~ voice* (*tone*) (떨리지 않는) 차분한 목소리(음성) / *an ~ gaze* 뚫어져라 보는 시선; 응시. **2** not hesitating; resolute. 망설이지 않는; 단호한. ¶ *~ courage* 단호한 용기.

un·fa·mil·iar [ʌ̀nfəmíljər] *adj.* not familiar; not acquainted; strange; not accustomed to. 친하지 않은; 낯선; 생소한; 익숙하지 않은. ¶ *I am ~ with this job.* = *This job is ~ to me.* 나는 이런 일에 서툴다 / *~ faces* 낯선 얼굴들 / *The subject is ~ to me.* 그 문제는 나에겐 생소하다 / *He is quite ~ with the habits of the upper class.* 그는 상류 계급의 풍습에는 전혀 익숙지 않다. [un-]

un·fas·ten [ʌnfǽsn, -fá:sn] *vt.* untie; loosen; open. …을 풀다; 늦추다; 벗기다.

un·fath·om·a·ble [ʌnfǽðəməbəl] *adj.* too deep to measure; 《*fig.*》 impossible to understand. 깊이를 헤아릴 수 없는; 이해할 수 없는; 불가해한. ¶ *an ~ sea* (*lake*) 깊이를 헤아릴 수 없는 바다(호수) / *an ~ mystery* 불가해한 신비.

un·fath·omed [ʌnfǽðəmd] *adj.* not measured; 《*fig.*》 not understood or not solved; immense. 측량할 수 없는; 미해결의; 무한정의; 광대한. ¶ *the ~ might of man* 인간이 가진 무한한 힘.

un·fa·vor·a·ble, 《Brit.》 **-vour-** [ʌnféivərəbəl] *adj.* not favorable; disadvantageous; harmful. 형편이(계제가) 나쁜; 불리한. ¶ *an ~ wind* 역풍 / *an ~ reply* (*opinion*) 부정적인 대답(의견) / *work under the ~ condition* 좋지 않은 조건에서 일하다.

un·feel·ing [ʌnfí:liŋ] *adj.* not able to feel; not sensible; hard-hearted; cruel. 감각(감정)이 없는; 무정한; 냉혹한. ¶ *an ~ statue* 감각이 없는 상(像) / *They appeared so cheerful and ~ of their own wrongs.* 그들은 무척 즐거워했지만, 자기들의 잘못은 모르는 모양이었다 / *He is an ~ beggar.* 인정머리 없는 놈이다.

un·feigned [ʌnféind] *adj.* real; sincere; without pretence. 성실한; 진실한; 꾸밈없는. ¶ *~ joy* 참된 기쁨. [un-]

un·fet·tered [ʌnfétərd] *adj.* without chains; free; without restraint. 차꼬가 풀린; 자유로운; 속박(구속)을 받지 않는.

un·fin·ished [ʌnfíniʃt] *adj.* **1** not finished; not complete. 미완성의; 미완결의. ¶ *an ~ letter* 쓰다 만 편지 / *an ~ house* (아직 짓고 있는) 미완성의 집. **2** not polished; rough. 세련되지 않은; 거친. ¶ *an ~ style* 세련되지 않은 문체.

un·fit [ʌnfít] *adj.* (**-fit·ter, -fit·test**) **1** not suitable; not fit; not qualified. 부적당한; 적임이 아닌. ¶ *~ for work* 일에 부적격인 / *a house ~ to live in* 거주하기에 적당치 않은

집 / *She is ~ for motherhood.* 그녀는 어머니 구실을 제대로 할 사람이 못된다. **2** not sound; diseased in body or mind. 건강하지 못한; (심신이) 불건전한. ¶ *She was ~ and couldn't play in the big match.* 그녀는 몸이 약해서 그런 큰 경기에는 무리였다.

— *vt.* (**-fit·ted, -fit·ting**) (P6,13) 《*for*》 make (someone or something) unfit. …을 부적당하게 만들다; 자격을 잃게 하다. ¶ *His age unfits him for such work.* 그 나이에는 그 일이 부적당하다 / *Drink unfits a man for work.* 술을 마시면 사람은 일을 할 수 없게 된다.

un·flinch·ing [ʌnflíntʃiŋ] *adj.* not flinching, yielding or shrinking; firm. 굽히지 않는; 위축되지 않는; 확고한. ¶ *~ courage* 불굴의 용기. [un-]

***un·fold** [ʌnfóuld] *vt.* **1** (P6) open the folds of; open and spread out (something). …을 펴다; 펼치다. ¶ *~ a napkin* 냅킨을 펴다 / *Unfold your arms.* 양팔을 벌려라 / *She unfolded the map and spread it on the table.* 그녀는 지도를 펴서 탁자 위에 펼쳐 놓았다. **2** (P6) reveal; show; explain. …을 나타내다; 보이다; 설명하다. ¶ *~ the details of one's plans* 자기 계획의 내용을 설명하다 / *It was a strange tale he unfolded.* 그가 한 이야기는 이상했다.

— *vi.* (P1) (of leaves, buds) become unfolded. 열리다; 펴지다. ¶ *Buds ~ in the sunshine.* 양지에서 꽃봉오리들이 벌어진다.

un·fore·seen [ʌ̀nfɔːrsíːn] *adj.* not known beforehand; unexpected. 예기치 못한; 뜻밖의. ¶ *~ events* 불의의 사고.

***un·for·tu·nate** [ʌnfɔ́ːrtʃənit] *adj.* **1** not fortunate; not lucky. 불행한; 불운한(opp. fortunate). ¶ *an ~ day* 불행한 날; 재수 없는 날 / *an ~ accident* 불행한 사고. **2** not suitable. 부적당한. ¶ *He has a rather ~ manner.* 그는 매너가 좀 안 좋다. — *n.* Ⓒ an unfortunate person. 불행한 사람.

***un·for·tu·nate·ly** [ʌnfɔ́ːrtʃənitli] *adv.* in an unfortunate manner. 불행하게(도); 운 나쁘게(도).

U

un·found·ed [ʌnfáundid] *adj.* not founded on fact; without reason; untrue. 근거가 없는; 사실 무근의. ¶ *an ~ rumor* 헛소문 / *an ~ hope* 허망한 기대; 헛기대.

un·fre·quent·ed [ʌnfríːkwəntid, ʌ̀nfri(ː)kwént-] *adj.* seldom visited; lonely. 인적이 드문; 좀처럼 사람이 오지 않는. ¶ *an ~ spot* 인적이 드문 곳.

un·friend·ly [ʌnfréndli] *adj.* **1** not friendly; unkind. 우정이 없는; 불친절한. ¶ *an ~ act* 불친절한 행동. **2** not favorable; not pleasant. 불리한; (날씨·형편 등이) 나쁜. ¶ *an ~ climate* 좋지 않은 날씨. ●**un·friend·li·ness** [-nis] *n.*

un·frock [ʌnfrák / -frɔ́k] *vt.* (P6) deprive (a priest) of his religious rank or function. …의 성직(권)을 박탈하다. [un-]

un·fruit·ful [ʌnfrúːtfəl] *adj.* **1** not fruitful; not productive. 열매를 맺지 않는; 불모의. ¶ *an ~ tree* 열매를 맺지 않는 나무 / *an ~ land* 불모의 땅. **2** 《*fig.*》 not producing wanted results; fruitless. 효과가〔보람이〕 없는; 헛된. ¶ *Our efforts at reform were at first ~.* 우리의 개혁 노력이 처음엔 신통치 않았다.

un·furl [ʌnfə́ːrl] *vt., vi.* (P6; 1) spread out; unfold. (…을) 펴다; 펴지다. [un-]

un·gain·ly [ʌngéinli] *adj.* (**-li·er, -li·est**) clumsy; awkward. 볼품 없는; 몰골스러운; 어색한. ¶ *~ manners* 어색한 태도 / *a tall ~ youth* 멀대 같은 청년.

un·god·ly [ʌngádli / -gɔ́d-] *adj.* (**-li·er, -li·est**) **1** not religious; wicked; sinful. 신앙심이 없는; 사악한; 죄 많은. ¶ *the ~* 사악한 사람. **2** 《*colloq.*》 shocking; dreadful; unreasonable. 심한; 지독한; 당치 않은. ¶ *an ~ noise* 지독한 소음 / *I had to get up at an ~ hour this morning.* 나는 오늘 아침엔 꼭두새벽에 일어나야 했다.

un·gov·ern·a·ble [ʌngʌ́vərnəbəl] *adj.* impossible to control; wild. 제어할 수 없는; 어쩔 도리가 없는; 난폭한. ¶ *~ anger* 참을 수 없는 분노 / *an ~ temper* 불같은 성미.

un·gra·cious [ʌngréiʃəs] *adj.* **1** rude; not polite. 무례한; 공손치 않은. ¶ *There is nothing ~ in him.* 그에게 전혀 불손한 데가 없다. **2** unpleasant; disagreeable. 불쾌한; 탐탁지 않은.

***un·grate·ful** [ʌngréitfəl] *adj.* **1** not grateful. 은혜를 모르는. ¶ *an ~ person.* **2** (of a task etc.) unpleasant. 불쾌한; 싫은. ¶ *an ~ task* 하기 싫은 일.

un·ground·ed [ʌngráundid] *adj.* without foundation or reason; baseless; unfounded. 근거 없는; 사실 무근의. ¶ *an ~ fancy* 터무니 없는 공상.

un·guard·ed [ʌngáːrdid] *adj.* **1** not guarded; not protected. 무방비의. ¶ *an ~ city* 무방비 도시 / *an ~ gate* 수위가 없는 문. **2** careless. 부주의한; 경솔한. ¶ *in an ~ moment* 방심한 순간에 / *an ~ remark* 경솔한 말. [un-]

un·hal·lowed [ʌnhǽloud] *adj.* **1** not made holy; not sacred. 축성(祝聖)되지 않은; 부정(不淨)한. **2** wicked. 사악한. ¶ *~ pleasure* 사악한 쾌락.

un·hand [ʌnhǽnd] *vt.* (P6) take the hands from (something); let (something) go. …을 손에서 놓다; …에서 손을 떼다. ¶ *Unhand me, or I will cry for help.* 내게서 손을 떼시오, 아니면 소리칠테요.

un·hand·some [ʌnhǽnsəm] *adj.* **1** not good-looking; plain or ugly. 볼품없는; 추한. ¶ *a large and ~ house* 덩그렇게 크기만 한 집. **2** not courteous; rude. 무례한; 예절 없는. ¶ *~ treatment*〔*conduct*〕 무례한 대우〔행동〕. **3** not generous; stingy. 인색한; 쩨쩨한. ¶ *an ~ offer* 인색한 기부(寄附).

un·hand·y [ʌnhǽndi] *adj.* **1** not convenient. 불편한. **2** awkward; clumsy. 서투른; 솜씨없는.

un·hap·pi·ly [ʌnhǽpili] *adv.* **1** not happily; unfortunately. 불행〔불운〕하게. **2** unsuitably. 부적당하게. [un-]

:un·hap·py [ʌnhǽpi] *adj.* (**-pi·er, -pi·est**) **1** unfortunate; unlucky. 불운한; 재수없는; 공교로운. ¶ *an ~ meeting* 공교로운 조우〔해후(邂逅)〕. **2** sad; sorrowful; miserable. 불행한; 비참한. ¶ *an ~ life* 불행한 인생. **3** not suitable. 적절하지 못한. ¶ *an ~ remark* 〔*choice*〕 부적절한 말〔선택〕.

un·har·ness [ʌnhá:rnis] *vt.* (P6) **1** take harness or gear off from (a horse, etc.). (말)에서 마구를 벗기다. **2** take off armor from (a knight, etc.); disarm. …의 갑옷을 벗기다; …에게 무장을 풀게 하다.

un·health·ful [ʌnhélθfəl] *adj.* bad for the health. 건강에 나쁜; 몸에 해로운.

un·health·y [ʌnhélθi] *adj.* (**-health·i·er, -health·i·est**) **1** not in good health; sickly. 건강이 안 좋은; 병약한. ¶ *~ children who don't get good food and fresh air* 잘먹지 못하고 신선한 공기도 접하지 못하는 건강이 나쁜 아이들. **2** not good for the health; harmful to the health. 건강에 해로운; 비위생적인. ¶ *~ living conditions* 건강에 나쁜 생활 조건 / *an ~ environment* 불결한 환경. **3** indicating poor health. 건강이 좋지 않은 듯한. ¶ *an ~ complexion.*

un·heard [ʌnhə́:rd] *adj.* **1** not perceived by the ear; not heard. 들리지 않는. ¶ *The cry went ~.* 울음소리는 안 들렸다. **2** not given a hearing or audience. 변명을 들어주지 않는; 경청해 주지 않는. ¶ *be condemned ~* 변명이 허락되지 않은 채 단죄(斷罪)되다. **3** not heard of before. 들어보지 못한. ¶ *an ~ name* 〔*secret*〕 처음 듣는 이름〔비밀〕.

un·heard-of [ʌnhə́:rdɑ̀v / -ɔ̀v] *adj.* not heard of before; unknown. 전대 미문의; 전례가 없는. ¶ *an ~ event* 전대 미문의 사건 / *It's ~ for anyone to pass the exam so young.* 그 시험에 그렇게 젊은 나이로 합격한 전례는 없다.

un·heed·ed [ʌnhí:did] *adj.* not paid attention; not heeded; disregarded. 주의를 끌지 못하는; 돌보는 이 없는; 무시된.

un·hinge [ʌnhíndʒ] *vt.* (P6) **1** remove (something) from the hinges; remove the hinges from (something). …의 돌쩌귀를 벗기다. **2** throw (the mind, etc.) into confusion. …을 혼란에 빠뜨리다; 곤혹스럽게 하다. ¶ *The terrible experience has unhinged his mind.* 그 끔찍한 경험으로 그는 정신적 혼란에 빠졌다. **3** detach. …을 떼어놓다. [un-]

un·ho·ly [ʌnhóuli] *adj.* (**-li·er, -li·est**) **1** not holy; godless; wicked. 신성하지 않은; 신앙심이 없는; 사악한. **2** 《*colloq.*》 dreadful; fearful. 지독한; 무서운. ¶ *They made an ~ din.* 그들은 요란한 소란을 피웠다.

un·horse [ʌnhɔ́:rs] *vt.* (P6) throw (a rider) from a horse's back. (기수)를 말에서 떨어뜨리다.

un·hurt [ʌnhə́:rt] *adj.* not hurt; not injured. 부상하지 않은; 상처가 없는. [un-]

u·ni- [jú:ni-] *pref.* one. '단(單)'의 뜻. [L. *unus* one]

u·ni·cam·er·al [jù:nəkǽmərəl] *adj.* (of a law-making body) composed of only one group. 단원(單院)(제의). [↑]

UNICEF [jú:nəsèf] *n.* UN (International) Children's (Emergency) Fund. 국제 연합 아동 기금; 유니세프.

u·ni·corn [jú:nəkɔ̀:rn] *n.* Ⓒ an imaginary horselike animal with a horn on its forehead. 일각수(一角獸). [L. *cornus* horn]

〈unicorn〉

un·i·den·ti·fied [ʌ̀naidéntəfàid] *adj.* not identified. 미확인의; 신원 미상의. [un-]

u·ni·fi·ca·tion [jù:nəfikéiʃən] *n.* Ⓤ the act of unifying; the state of being unified. 통일; 단일화. ¶ *the ~ of many states into one nation* 일국으로의 다수 국가의 통합. [*unify*]

:u·ni·form [jú:nəfɔ̀:rm] *adj.* **1** (of a single object etc.) always the same; not changing. 불변의; 일정한. ¶ *The earth turns round at a ~ rate.* 지구는 일정 불변의 속도로 돌고 있다 / *keep the room at a ~ temperature* 실내를 일정한 온도로 유지하다. **2** (of various things) all alike; like one another. 동일한; 한결같은. ¶ *be ~ in shape* 모양이 일정하다 / *be ~ with* …와 동일하다 / *things of ~ weight* 같은 무게의 것들 / *All the bricks have a ~ size.* 모든 벽돌은 크기가 다 같다.
— *n.* ⓊⒸ a special kind of clothing worn by a member of a group. 제복; 군복; 유니폼(cf. *mufti*). ¶ *in* (*full*) *~* 제복으로 / *out of ~* 평복으로 / *Soldiers, policemen, and nurses wear uniforms.* 군인·경관·간호사는 제복을 입는다 / *He was in ~ for three years.* 그는 삼년간 군에 복무했다.
— *vt.* (P6) **1** clothe (someone) in or supply (someone) with a uniform. …에게 제복을 입히다. **2** make (things) uniform. …을 한결같이 하다. [→form]

u·ni·formed [jú:nəfɔ̀:rmd] *adj.* wearing a uniform. 제복을 입은.

u·ni·form·i·ty [jù:nəfɔ́:rməti] *n.* Ⓤ the state of being uniform; sameness. 동일; 한결같음; 일정(불변성); 일률(성); 불변; 균일성. ¶ *~ of style* 문체의 일양성(一様性) / *the weariness ~ of TV commercials* 텔레비전 광고 방송의 싫증나는 획일성 / *the drab ~ of the houses in the area* 이 지역 가옥들의 한결같은 단조로움.

u·ni·form·ly [jú:nəfɔ̀:rmli] *adv.* in a uniform manner. 한결같이; 균등하게; 일률적으로. ¶ *These cakes are ~ disgusting.* 이 케이

U

크들은 하나같이 넌더리나는 것들이다.

u·ni·fy [jú:nəfài] *vt.* (**-fied**) make (things) into one; unite. …을 하나로 하다; 통일하다; 통합하다. ¶ *Spain was unified in the 16th century.* 스페인은 16세기에 통일됐다. [uni-, L. *facio* make]

u·ni·lat·er·al [jù:nəlǽtərəl] *adj.* **1** one-sided; of, occurring, on or affecting one side only. 한쪽의; 한쪽만의. **2** 《law》 done by or obligating one side only. 편무(片務)의; 일방적인. ¶ *an ~ contract* 편무 계약. [uni-]

un·im·peach·a·ble [ʌ̀nimpí:tʃəbəl] *adj.* not impeachable; blameless. 나무랄 데 없는; 더할 나위 없는. ¶ *~ honesty* 더할 나위 없는 성실성. [un-]

un·im·proved [ʌ̀nimprú:vd] *adj.* **1** not improved. 개량되지 않은. **2** not made use of. 이용되지 않은.

un·in·tend·ed [ʌ̀ninténdid] *adj.* not intended. 고의가 아닌.

un·in·ter·est·ed [ʌníntərəstid] *adj.* **1** not having interests. 이해 관계가 없는. **2** not interested; paying no attention. 흥미를 느끼지 않는; 무관심한.

un·in·ter·est·ing [ʌníntərəstiŋ] *adj.* not interesting; dull. 흥미 없는; 지루한; 따분한. ¶ *an ~ story* 흥미없는 이야기.

:un·ion [jú:njən] *n.* Ⓒ **1** Ⓤ ⓐ the act of uniting two or more things into one whole; the state of being united. 결합; 연합; 합동; 합병; 화합. ¶ *Union is strength.* 단결은 힘이다 / *in ~* 화합하여; 공동으로 / *effect the ~ between two countries* 두 나라 사이의 연합을 달성하다 / *the ~ of soul and body* 혼과 육체의 합일(合一) / *a ~ between two families* [*states*] 두 가족〔국가〕간의 화합 / *We worked together in perfect ~.* 우리는 혼연일체가 되어 일했다. ⓑ a marriage. 결혼. ¶ *a happy ~* 행복한 결혼 / *an illicit ~* 불륜의 관계 / *Their ~ was blessed by children.* 그들은 결혼해서 아이를 낳았다. **2** a league or an association formed to protect and promote a common interest. 동맹; 조합. ¶ *a trade ~* 동업자 조합 / *a labor ~* 노동 조합 / *Do you belong to a ~?* 노조에 가입했느냐 / *craft ~* 직업별〔직능별〕 조합. **3** a group of people, states, etc. united for some purpose. 연합 국가; 연방. ¶ *The American colonies formed a ~ against England.* 미국의 여러 식민지들은 영국에 대항해 연방을 만들었다. **4** 《*the U-*》 the United States of America; the United Kingdom. 아메리카 합중국; (영국) 연합 왕국. **5** a device for joining together parts of a machine, etc. 접합 장치. [uni-]

Union Flag [⸗⸗], **the** *n.* =union jack.

un·ion·ism [jú:njənìzəm] *n.* Ⓤ **1** the principle of union. 연합주의; 조합주의. **2** the system or principles of labor unions. 노동 조합 주의.

un·ion·ist [jú:njənist] *n.* Ⓒ **1** a person who believes in unionism. 연합주의자 (opp. separatist). **2** a member of a labor union. 노동 조합원. **3** 《*U-*》 a supporter of the Federal government of the United States during the Civil War. (남북 전쟁 시의) 연방주의자; 연합 합동주의자《남북 분리를 반대한》. **4** a member of a party which opposed self-government for territories of the British Empire, esp. Ireland. 연합론자; 통일당원《아일랜드 자치안에 반대한》.

un·ion·i·za·tion [jù:njənizéiʃən / -naiz-] *n.* 노동 조합화; 노동 조합에 가입함〔시킴〕.

un·ion·ize [jú:njənàiz] *vt., vi.* (P6; 1) form into a (labor) union; join in a labor union. 노동 조합화하다; 노동 조합에 가입하다.

union jack [⸗⸗], **the** *n.* 《sometimes *U- J-*》 the British national flag. 영국 국기.

·u·nique [ju:ní:k] *adj.* **1** having no like or equal; different from all others. 유일한; 비길 데 없는; 독특한. 語法 원칙적으로 비교급·최상급은 없음. ¶ *Each person's fingerprints are ~.* 사람마다의 지문은 모두 다르다. **2** 《*colloq.*》 rare; unusual; wonderful. 드문; 진기한; 굉장히 좋은. ¶ *We had rather a ~ experience.* 우리는 좀 희한한 경험을 했다. [L. *unus* one]

u·ni·son [jú:nəsən, -zən] *n.* Ⓤ **1** agreement; harmony. 조화; 일치. ¶ *The feet of marching soldiers move in ~.* 행진하는 군인들의 발은 하나가 되어 움직인다 / *The governments acted in ~ to combat terrorism.* 정부들은 테러리즘과 싸우기 위해 일치하여 행동했다. **2** 《mus.》 a passage of music in which all performers sing or play the same part. 제창(齊唱); 제주(齊奏). ¶ *sing in ~* 제창하다. [L. *sonus* sound]

·u·nit [jú:nit] *n.* Ⓒ **1** a single thing or person. 한 개; 한 사람; 개체(個體). **2** a group of things or persons considered as one part of a whole. 구성 단위; 일단(一團); (한) 부대. ¶ *The family is the ~ of society.* 가족은 사회의 한 구성 단위다 / *A division is now regarded as the ~ of an army.* 사단은 지금 군의 한 편제 단위로 간주되고 있다 / *a mechanized ~* 기계화 부대 / *a tactical ~* 전술 단위. **3** 《math.》 the smallest whole number; one. 최소 완전수; 1. **4** a fixed amount or quantity taken as a standard of measurement. 단위. ¶ *The meter is a ~ of length.* 미터는 길이의 한 단위이다 / *A pound is a ~ of weigh.* 파운드는 무게의 한 단위이다. [abbr. *unity*]

:u·nite [ju:náit] *vt.* (P6,13) **1** join together; combine (two or more) so as to make one. …을 하나로 하다; 결합하다. ¶ *~ two families by marriage* 결혼에 의해 양가를 하나로 맺다 / 《*prov.*》 *United we stand, divided we fall.* 뭉치면 살고 흩어지면 죽는다 / *~ states into a nation* 여러 주를 결합해서 한 국가를 만들다 / *The two companies plan to ~.* 그 두 회사는 합병하려 한다. **2** have or show (qualities, etc.) in combination.

(성질 등)을 겸비하다. ¶ *She unites beauty and intelligence.* 그녀는 재색(才色)을 겸비하고 있다.
— *vi.* **1** (P1,3,4) become joined or combined together; become one. 결합하다; 하나가 되다. ¶ *Smoke unites with fog to form smog.* 연기는 안개와 결합하여 스모그를 생기게 한다 / *Oil and water will not* ~. 기름과 물은 하나가 되지 않는다 / *Several firms united to form one company.* 몇 개 상사가 합쳐서 한 회사가 되었다. **2** (P1) act together, as for a purpose. (목적 등을 위해) 행동을 같이하다; 협력하다. ¶ *People or societies who* ~ *for some purpose form a union.* 어떤 목적을 위해 행동을 같이 하는 사람들이나 모임은 조합을 만든다 / *Let us* ~ *to make this a success.* 이 일의 성사를 위해 우리 힘을 합치자. [uni-]

:u·nit·ed [juːnáitid] *adj.* joined together; joined in spirit; in harmony. 결합〔연합〕한; 화합한. ¶ *a* ~ *family* 화목한 가족 / *break into a* ~ *laugh* 일제히 웃음을 터뜨리다 / *We are united in our determination to eradicate famine.* 가난을 근절시키자는 결의로 우리는 뭉쳐져 있다.

United Kingdom [–⊥– ⊥–], **the** *n.* (the Kingdom of) Great Britain and Northern Ireland. 연합 왕국.

United Nations [–⊥– ⊥–], **the** *n.* an international organization formed to promote international peace, security, and cooperation. 국제 연합; 유엔.

:United States (of America) [–⊥– ⊥ (– –⊥––)], **the** *n.* a country in North America made up of 50 States and the District of Columbia. 아메리카 합중국.

·u·ni·ty [júːnəti] *n.* (*pl.* **-ties**) Ⓤ **1** the state of being united; oneness. 단일(체); 통일(체); 개체. ¶ *A Nation has more* ~ *than a group of tribes.* 한 나라에는 부족들의 집단보다 더 많은 단일체가 있다 / *national* ~ 거국일치 / *the* ~ *of national opinion* 국론의 통일 / *a nation as a* ~ 통일체로서의 국가. **2** harmony; agreement. 일치; 화합; 조화. ¶ *live in* ~ *with all neighbors* 모든 이웃들과 화합하여 생활하다 / *family* ~ 일가 화합 / *Brothers and sisters should live together in* ~. 형제자매들은 서로 화목하게 지내야 한다 / *These pictures lack* ~. 이들 그림에는 조화가 결여돼 있다. **3** Ⓒ《math.》the numeral one. (수량의 단위로서의) 1. [uni-]

Univ. University.

:u·ni·ver·sal [jùːnəvə́ːrsəl] *adj.* **1** belonging to or done by everyone; of or for all; of the universe. 만인의; 우주의; 전세계의. ¶ *the* ~ *law of gravitation* 만유 인력 / *a* ~ *peace* 세계 평화. **2** existing everywhere; general. 보편적인; 일반적인(opp. particular). ¶ ~ *rules* 〔*practice*〕 일반적 법칙〔관습〕 / *There was* ~ *agreement as to who should become chairman.* 누가 의장이 되는가에는 대체적인 합의가 있었다 / *Food, fire, and shelter are* ~ *needs.* 불, 음식 및 주거는 보편적인 필수품이다. **3** adaptable to any use. 만능의. ¶ *Leonardo da Vinci was a* ~ *genius.* 레오나르도 다빈치는 만능 천재였다.
— *n.* Ⓒ **1**《log.》a universal proposition. 전칭 명제(全稱命題). **2**《philos.》a general concept. 일반 개념. [→versatile]

u·ni·ver·sal·i·ty [jùːnəvəːrsǽləti] *n.* Ⓤ the state of being universal. 일반성; 보편성.

·u·ni·ver·sal·ly [jùːnəvə́ːrsəli] *adv.* without exception; everywhere. 일반적으로; 예외없이; 도처에. ¶ *a* ~ *accepted fact* 일반적으로 널리 받아들여지고 있는 사실.

·u·ni·verse [júːnəvə̀ːrs] *n.* Ⓒ《*the* ~》**1** the whole system of suns, planets, etc. existing in their places; the cosmos. 우주. ¶ *Our world is but a small part of the* ~. 지구는 우주의 작은한 부분이다. **2** the whole system of created things viewed as a whole. 만물(萬物). **3** the world. 세계. ¶ *He behaves as though he owned the* ~. 그는 마치 온 세상이 제것인 양 처신한다. [uni-, L. *verto* turn]

u·ni·ver·si·ade [jùːnəvə́ːrsiæ̀d] *n.* an international contest held by university students only. 유니버시아드《국제 대학생 경기 대회》.

:u·ni·ver·si·ty [jùːnəvə́ːrsəti] *n.* (*pl.* **-ties**) **1** Ⓒ an institution for learning of the highest grade, usu. divided into schools. 종합 대학(교)(cf. *college*). ¶ *He goes to the* ~. 그는 대학교에 다닌다 / *Where do you go to* ~? 어느 대학의 학생이냐. **2** the members of a university. 대학생; 대학 당국(자). ¶ *the opinion of the* ~ 대학 당국의 견해. **3** Ⓒ a team or crew representing a university. 대학 선수단; 대학팀. [*universe, -ity*]

·un·just [ʌndʒʌ́st] *adj.* not just; unfair. 부정(不正)한; 불공평한. ¶ *an* ~ *judge* 〔*sentence*〕 불공평한 판사〔부당한 판결〕 / *the* ~ 부정직한 사람. ●**un·just·ly** [-li] *adv.* **un·just·ness** [-nis] *n.* [un-]

un·kempt [ʌnkémpt] *adj.* **1** untidy; neglected. 단정치 못한; 너저분한. ¶ *a* ~ *appearance* 단정치 못한 외양. **2** not combed. 빗질을 안한; 텁수룩한. ¶ ~ *hair* 텁수룩한 머리. [=uncombed]

un·kind [ʌnkáind] *adj.* not kind; cruel. 불친절한; 박정한. ¶ ~ *words.* [un-]

un·kind·ness [ʌnkáindnis] *n.* **1** Ⓤ the state of being unkind. 불친절; 몰인정. **2** Ⓒ an unkind action. 불친절〔박정〕한 행동.

:un·known [ʌnnóun] *adj.* not known; not familiar; not discovered. 미지의; 알려지지 않은; 무명의; 미발견의. ¶ *address* ~ 주소 불명 / *an* ~ *country* 미지의 나라 / *experience* ~ *delights* 말할 수 없이 즐거운 경험 / *a thing of* ~ *origin* 기원이 불명한 것 / *a man* ~ *to fame* 이름이 알려지지 않은 사람 / ~ *of any* 아무도 모르게; 몰래 / *I did it* ~ *to him.* 나는 그가 모르게 그것을 했다. — *n.*《*the* ~》**1** an unknown person. 미지의 사람. ¶ *the*

U

unfortunate unknowns 미지의 불행한 사람들. **2** that which is unknown. 미지의 것. ¶ *venture into the* ~ 미지의 세계에 도전하다 / *The spaces voyagers set off on their journey into the* ~. 우주 항해사들은 미지로의 길을 떠났다. [un-]

unknown quantity [⌐— ⌐——] *n.* **1** a number represented by the letter x. 미지수. **2**) 《*fig.*》 a person or thing whose influence, power, etc. is not known. (세력·힘 따위가) 미지수인 사람〔것〕.

un·lace [ʌnléis] *vt.* (P6) undo the laces of (something). …의 끈을 풀다. ¶ ~ *a shoe* 구두끈을 풀다. [un-]

***un·law·ful** [ʌnlɔ́:fəl] *adj.* against the law; illegal. 불법의; 위법의. ¶ *an* ~ *act* 위법행위.

un·law·ful·ly [ʌnlɔ́:fəli] *adv.* in an unlawful manner; illegally. 불법으로; 부정〔부당〕하게. ¶ ~ *killed* 암살된.

un·learn [ʌnlə́:rn] *vt.* (**-learned** or **-learnt**) forget (something learned). (배운 것)을 잊다.

un·learn·ed [ʌnlə́:rnid] *adj.* **1** not educated; ignorant. 배우지 못한; 무학의. ¶ *a man not* ~ *in English literature* 영문학에 정통한 사람. **2** [ʌnlə́:rnt] not learned; known without being learned. 배우지 않은; 배우지 않고 아는. ¶ *an* ~ *lesson* 배우지 않은 학과.

un·learnt [ʌnlə́:rnt] *v.* p. and pp. of **unlearn.** — *adj.* =unlearned.

un·leash [ʌnlí:ʃ] *vt.* free (something) from a leash; release (something) from control. …의 가죽끈을 풀다; …을 해방하다. ¶ *All his anger was unleashed upon us.* 그는 우리에게 모든 분풀이를 했다. [un-]

un·leav·ened [ʌnlévənd] *adj.* **1** (of bread) made without yeast. (빵에) 이스트를 넣지 않은. ¶ *Unleavened bread is made without yeast.* 무교병(無酵餠)은 이스트없이 만든다. **2** not modified or influenced in any way. 변화되지 않은; 영향을 받지 않은. ¶ ~ *hatred in one's heart* 변함없는 증오심.

:un·less [ənlés] *conj.* if not; except that. 만일 …이 아니면; (만일) …하지 않으면. ¶ *We shall go* ~ *it rains.* 비가 안 오면 우리는 간다 / *Unless you work harder you will fail.* 더 열심히 공부하지 않으면 넌 시험에 떨어질 거다. [=*onless* on a lower condition (than)]

unless and until, until. …까지.

un·let·tered [ʌnlétərd] *adj.* not educated; not able to read or write. 무학의; 글을 모르는. [un-]

***un·like** [ʌnláik] *adj.* not like; different. 같지〔닮지〕 않은; 다른. ¶ *The two cases are quite* ~. 그 두 경우는 판이하게 다르다 / *No two people could be more* ~ *in appearance or character.* 두 사람의 외양이나 성격이 이렇게 다를 수는 없다.

— *prep.* **1** different from. …와 달라서; 닮지 않고. ¶ *This picture is quite* ~ *her.* 이 사진은 조금도 그녀 같지 않다 / *Unlike their commercial rivals, the company has made big profit this year.* 그들의 경쟁 회사들과는 달리 그 회사는 올해 크게 흑자를 냈다. **2** not becoming; not typical of. …답지 않게. ¶ *It's* ~ *him to be late, he's usually on time.* 그사람답지 않게 늦는구나, 언제나 시간을 잘 지키는데 / *behavior* ~ *a soldier* 군인답지 못한 행동. [un-]

un·like·ly [ʌnláikli] *adj.* **1** not likely to happen; not probable. 있음직하지 않은. ¶ *It is* ~ *to rain.* 비가 올 것 같지는 않다 / *A victory is* ~ *but not impossible.* 승리할 것 같지는 않으나 불가능하지도 않다 / *He is* ~ *to come.* 그는 올것 같지 않다 / *It's* ~ *that he will succeed.* 그 사람 성공하기가 어려울 것 같다 / *in the* ~ *event of* ... (있음직하지는 않으나) 만일 …한 경우에는. **2** not likely to succeed. 성공할 가망 없는; 성산이 없는. ¶ *an* ~ *plan* 성산이 없는 계획 / *be engaged in an* ~ *adventure* 성공할 가망이 없는 모험을 하다.

***un·lim·it·ed** [ʌnlímitid] *adj.* **1** without limits. 무한한; 한없는. ¶ *the* ~ *expanse of the sky* 〔*the ocean*〕 광대 무변의 하늘〔대양〕 / ~ *power* 무한한 힘 / ~ *liability* 무한 책임 / *the* ~ *surrender of the enemy* 적의 무조건 항복. **2** very great; excessive. 대단한; 과도의. ¶ *He has* ~ *assurance.* 그는 자신만만하다 / ~ *impudance* 후안 무치.

un·load [ʌnlóud] *vt.* (P6) **1** remove (a load, a cargo, etc.); take the load from (a car, a ship, etc.). (짐)을 부리다〔내리다, 풀다〕; …에서 짐을 내리다. ¶ ~ *a truck* 트럭의 짐을 내리다 / ~ *the cargo from a ship* 배에서 짐을 부리다. **2** remove power, shot, etc. from (a gun, etc.). (총 따위)에서 탄환을 빼다. ¶ ~ *a gun.* **3** relieve (someone or something) from care or trouble. (터놓고 말하여) 마음의 짐을 덜다. ¶ ~ *one's mind* / *He had no one to whom he could* ~ *his anxieties.* 그에게는 그의 근심을 터놓고 말할 만한 사람이 아무도 없었다. **4** (of stocks, etc.) get rid of one's holding; sell out. (주식 등)을 처분하다.

— *vi.* (P1) discharge a cargo. 짐을 부리다. ¶ *The ship will* ~ *tomorrow.* 그 배는 내일 짐을 부린다.

***un·lock** [ʌnlák / -lɔ́k] *vt.* (P6) **1** open the lock of (a door, a box, etc.); open (anything firmly closed). …의 자물쇠를 열다; …을 열다. ¶ ~ *the door* 〔*box*〕 / *Scientists have unlocked the secrets of atom.* 과학자들은 원자의 비밀을 벗겼다. **2** 《*fig.*》 make (something) clear; reveal; let loose. …을 털어놓다; 밝히다. ¶ ~ *one's heart* 〔*secrets*〕 심중〔비밀〕을 밝히다. — *vi.* (P1) become unlocked. (자물쇠가) 열리다.

un·looked-for [ʌnlúktfɔ̀:r] *adj.* unexpected. 뜻밖의; 예기치 않은.

un·loose [ʌnlú:s] *vt.* (P6) let loose; release; set free. …을 풀다; 늦추다; 해방하다;

놓아 주다. ¶ *He unloosed the stream of abuse.* 그는 마구 욕을 퍼부어댔다.

·**un·luck·y** [ʌnlʌ́ki] *adj.* (**-luck·i·er, -luck·i·est**) **1** not lucky; unfortunate; unsuccessful. 불운한; 불행한; 잘 되지 않은. ¶ *be ~ at cards* 카드놀이에 지다 / *be ~ in love* 실연하다. **2** bringing, indicating, or forecasting bad luck. 불길한. ¶ *Friday is believed to be an ~ day.* 금요일은 불길한 날로 여겨지고 있다. **3** not happily chosen; badly timed. 공교로운; 때〔계제〕가 나쁜. ¶ *an ~ moment for their meeting* 그들이 만나기에 안 좋은 때 / *in an ~ hour* 공교롭게도. ● **un·luck·i·ly** [-li] *adv.*

un·man [ʌnmǽn] *vt.* (**-manned, -man·ning**) deprive (someone) of the qualities of a man; weaken or break down the spirit of. …의 남성다움을 잃게 하다; …의 기를 죽이다. ¶ *be quite unmanned by the terrible news* 〔*sight*〕 그 끔찍한 소식〔광경〕에 기가 질리다. [un-]

un·man·ly [ʌnmǽnli] *adj.* not manly; weak; cowardly. 남자답지 못한; 연약한; 소심한. ¶ *~ manners* 나약한 태도 / *an ~ way of speaking* 소심한 말씨.

un·manned [ʌnmǽnd] *adj.* without a crew; designed to operate without a crew. 승무원이 타지 않는; 무인의; 무인 조종의. ¶ *an ~ spacecraft* 무인 우주선 / *an ~ mission to Mars* 화성으로의 무인 비행 임무 / *an ~ level crossing* 철도의 무인 건널목.

un·man·ner·ly [ʌnmǽnərli] *adj.* having bad manners; rude. 버릇없는; 건방진; 거친. — *adv.* in an unmannerly way; rudely. 버릇없이. ¶ *behave ~* 버릇없이 굴다.

un·mask [ʌnmǽsk, -mɑ́ːsk] *vt.* (P6) **1** remove a mask or disguise from (someone). …의 가면을 벗기다. **2** show the true nature of (someone or something). …의 정체를 밝히다〔폭로하다〕. ¶ *~ a traitor* 배신자의 정체를 밝히다 / *The thief was unmasked.* 도둑의 정체가 드러나다. — *vi.* (P1) **1** take off a mask or disguise. 가면을 벗기다. **2** appear in one's true character. 정체를 드러내다.

un·matched [ʌnmǽtʃt] *adj.* not matched or equaled. 상대가 없는; 대항할 수 없는. ¶ *~ courage* 무쌍의 용기 / *He remains ~ as a writer of satire.* 그는 여전히 풍자 작가로서의 일인자다.

un·mean·ing [ʌnmíːniŋ] *adj.* without meaning or sense; senseless. 무의미한; 하찮은; 시시한.

un·meas·ured [ʌnméʒərd] *adj.* **1** not measured or limited. 측정할 수 없는; 무한한. ¶ *~ depths* 측정할 수 없는 깊이 / *~ liberty* 무한한 자유. **2** excessive. 지나친; 과도한. ¶ *~ abuse* 지나친 남용〔욕설〕 / *in ~ terms* 자제를 잃은 몰상식한 말로.

un·men·tion·a·ble [ʌnménʃənəbəl] *adj.* not fit to be spoken about. 말해서 안 되는; 말할 수 없는. [un-]

un·mind·ful [ʌnmáindfəl] *adj.* regardless; careless. 부주의한; 무관심한. ¶ *~ of one's duties* 〔*others*〕 자기 의무에〔남에게〕 무관심한 / *Unmindful of the consequences, she allowed them to do as they wished.* 나중 결과는 생각지 않고 그녀는 그들에게 마음대로 하라고 했다.

un·mis·tak·a·ble [ʌ̀nmistéikəbəl] *adj.* that can not be mistaken; clear; evident. 틀릴 여지가 없는; 명백한. ¶ *the ~ sound of breaking glass* 틀림없이 컵 깨지는 소리 / *That must be Jim—his walk's ~.* 틀림없이 짐이야 —그의 걸음걸이가 틀림이 없어. [un-]

un·mit·i·gat·ed [ʌnmítəgèitid] *adj.* not softened or lessened; absolute. 누그러지지 않은; 줄어들지 않는; 순전한; 절대의. ¶ *~ suffering* 누그러지지 않는 고통 / *an expression of ~ severity* 한결같은 격렬한 표현 / *an ~ liar* 순 거짓말쟁이.

un·mor·al [ʌnmɔ́(ː)rəl, -mɑ́r-] *a.* neither moral nor immoral, not concerned with right and wrong. 초(超)도덕적인.

un·moved [ʌnmúːvd] *adj.* **1** not moved; firm. 부동의; 확고한. ¶ *We found everything ~.* 모든 것이 요지부동하다는 것을 알았다. **2** not disturbed; indifferent; showing no pity or sympathy. 태연한; 냉정한. ¶ *He heard the bad news ~.* 그는 그 흉보에도 흐트러짐이 없었다 / *He remained ~ by her appeals.* 그녀의 호소에도 그는 냉담했다.

un·named [ʌnnéimd] *adj.* **1** without a name; nameless. 이름 없는; 무명의. **2** not indicated or mentioned by name. 이름이 밝혀지지 않은; 지명되지 않은.

·**un·nat·u·ral** [ʌnnǽtʃərəl] *adj.* **1** not natural. 부자연한; 자연스럽지 않은. ¶ *die an ~ death* 횡사(橫死)하다 / *an ~ laugh* 억지 웃음 / *an ~ gesture* 부자연스런 몸짓. **2** lacking human emotion; cruel. 몰인정한; 잔혹한. ¶ *an ~ crime* 극악 무도한 범죄 / *It is ~ not to love one's children.* 자기 자식들을 사랑하지 않는 것은 몰인정한 처사다.

un·nat·u·ral·ly [ʌnnǽtʃərəli] *adv.* in an unnatural manner. 부자연하게; 몰인정하게; 잔혹하게. ¶ *an ~ large head* 이상하게 큰 머리.

·**un·nec·es·sar·y** [ʌnnésəsèri / -səri] *adj.* not necessary; needless. 불필요한; 무용의. ¶ *Don't bring any ~ luggage.* 여행에 불필요한 짐을 가져오지 마라 / *That was an ~ remark; it would have been not to mention her ex-husband.* 그건 쓸데없는 말이었다. 그녀의 전남편 이야기는 하지 않는 것이었는데. ● **un·nec·es·sar·i·ly** [-li] *adv.* [un-]

un·nerve [ʌnnə́ːrv] *vt.* (P6) deprive (someone) of courage or self-control. …의 용기를 잃게 하다; …을 당황하게 하다. ¶ *The experience completely unnerved me.* 그 경험으로 나는 아주 주눅이 들었다 / *The terrible sight unnerved me.* 그 무서운 광경에 나는 기가 죽었다.

·**un·no·ticed** [ʌnnóutist] *adj.* not noticed; not observed. 남의 눈에 띄지 않는; 주목되지

않는. ¶ *pass* ~ 간과되다 / *His death passed quite* ~. 그의 죽음은 아무도 몰랐다.

un·num·bered [ʌnnʌ́mbərd] *adj.* **1** not counted. 세지 않은. **2** too many to be counted. 무수한. [un-]

un·oc·cu·pied [ʌnákjəpàid / -ɔ́k-] *adj.* **1** (of a house, etc.) not occupied; vacant. 점유되지 않은; 비어 있는. **2** (of persons) not engaged in any job; idle. 할 일이 없는; 한가한; 놀고 있는.

un·or·gan·ized [ʌnɔ́ːrgənàizd] *adj.* **1** not formed into an organized whole; 《U.S.》 not organized into labor unions. 조직되어 있지 않은; 미조직의; 노동 조합이 조직되지 않은. **2** 《chem.》 not being a living organism. 무기(無機)의.

un·pack [ʌnpǽk] *vt.* (P6) **1** take (something) out of a package, a trunk, etc.; open and take out the contents of (a package, etc.). (짐을 풀어) …을 꺼내다; (짐을) 풀다. ¶ ~ *one's clothes* (짐에서) 옷을 꺼내다 / *Have you unpacked your suitcase yet?* 벌써 여행 가방을 풀어 옷을 꺼냈느냐. **2** change (information stored in a computer) into a form that takes up more space but is easier to understand. (컴퓨터에 압축되어 있는 데이터)를 이해하기 쉽도록 원래의 형태로 바꾸다. —*vi.* (P1) take out the contents of a package, a trunk, etc. 짐을 풀다. ¶ *I shan't* ~ *until tomorrow morning.* 짐은 내일 아침에나 풀겠다.

un·paid [ʌnpéid] *adj.* not paid. 미불(미납)의; 무급(無給)의. ¶ *letters posted* ~ 우표를 안 붙이고 보낸 편지 / *an* ~ *secretary* 무급 비서 / *an* ~ *bill* 미불의 청구서.

un·par·al·leled [ʌnpǽrəlèld] *adj.* having no equal; unrivaled. 무비(無比)의; 비길 데 없는. ¶ *an* ~ *success* 공전의 성공 / *a period of* ~ *economic prosperity* 전대 미문(前代未聞)의 경제적 번영 기간. [un-]

***un·pleas·ant** [ʌnpléznt] *adj.* not pleasant; disagreeable. 불쾌한; 싫은. ¶ *an* ~ *person* 보기 싫은 사람 / *an* ~ *smell* 불쾌한(역겨운) 냄새 / *an* ~ *voice* 듣기 싫은 목소리 / ~ *manners* 기분 나쁜 태도.

un·pleas·ant·ness [ʌnplézəntnis] *n.* **1** the quality of being unpleasant. 불쾌. ¶ *the* ~ *of a neighborhood* (*of someone's manners*) 이웃(아무의 태도)에 대한 불쾌감. **2** something unpleasant. 싫은(불쾌한) 것. ¶ *the late* (*recent*) ~ 최근의 불쾌했던 일. **3** a quarrel; a disagreeable incident. 싸움; 불화. ¶ *We have had a slight* ~ *with our neighbor.* 이웃과 가벼운 다툼이 있었다.

un·pop·u·lar [ʌnpápjələr / -pɔ́p-] *adj.* not generally liked or approved; not popular. 인기 없는; 평판이 나쁜.

un·pop·u·lar·i·ty [ʌ̀npɑpjəlǽrəti] *n.* Ⓤ the state of being unpopular. 인망이(인기가) 없음; 좋지 않은 평판.

un·prac·ticed, 《Brit.》 **-tised** [ʌnprǽktist] *adj.* **1** not practiced; not used. 실행이(실시가) 안 된; 실용되지 않은. **2** not skilled; not experienced. 서툰; 경험이 없는.

un·prec·e·dent·ed [ʌnprésədèntid] *adj.* having no precedent; never known before. 전례가 없는; 미증유의. ¶ ~ *rainfall* (*price increase*) 전례 없는 호우(물가 상승).

un·prej·u·diced [ʌnprédʒədist] *adj.* without prejudice; fair; impartial. 편견이 없는; 공정한. [un-]

un·pre·med·i·tat·ed [ʌ̀nprimédətèitid] *adj.* not planned or thought in advance. 미리 계획(준비)되지 않은; 고의가 아닌; 우연한. ¶ ~ *homicide* 과실 치사(죄).

un·pre·pared [ʌ̀npripέərd] *adj.* not ready; done without preparation. 준비가 없는; 즉석의; 불의의. ¶ *an* ~ *report* 즉석 보고 / *You caught me* ~. 네게 당했구나.

un·pre·tend·ing [ʌ̀npriténdiŋ] *adj.* unassuming; modest. 젠체하지 않는; 겸손한.

un·prin·ci·pled [ʌnprínsəpəld] *adj.* **1** lacking good moral principles. 부도덕한; 절조가 없는. ¶ ~ *conduct* 절조 없는 행위. **2** bad; unscrupulous. 나쁜; 악랄한. ¶ *an* ~ *rogue* 악당.

un·pro·fes·sion·al [ʌ̀nprəféʃənəl] *adj.* not professional; not belonging to any profession. 전문가가 아닌; 아마추어의; 본업이 아닌. ¶ ~ *conduct* 전문가답지 않은 행위 / *a very* ~ *piece of work* 아주 선부른 하나의 작품.

un·prof·it·a·ble [ʌnprɔ́fitəbəl] *adj.* producing no gain or advantage. 이익이 없는; 수지가 맞지 않는. ¶ *abandon an enterprise as* ~ 이익이 없으면 그만두다.

un·prom·is·ing [ʌnprámәsiŋ / -prɔ́m-] *adj.* not promising; not showing signs of future excellence; not likely to be successful. 가망(장래성)이 없는; 성공할 것 같지 않은.

un·pro·voked [ʌ̀nprəvóukt] *adj.* without provocation. 자극되지 않은; 까닭이 없는.

un·qual·i·fied [ʌnkwáləfàid / -kwɔ́l-] *adj.* **1** lacking the proper qualifications; not competent. 자격이 없는; 부적당한. ¶ *Translators are many, but most of them are* ~. 번역자들은 많으나, 그들 대부분이 시원찮다 / *He is* ~ *to teach others.* 그는 남을 가르칠 자격이 없다. **2** not limited or modified. 무제한의. ¶ ~ *praise* 아낌없는 찬사. **3** complete; absolute. 전적인; 절대적인. ¶ *an* ~ *failure* 완전한 실패 / *He is an* ~ *liar.* 그는 순 거짓말쟁이다. [un-]

un·quench·a·ble [ʌnkwéntʃəbəl] *adj.* that cannot be quenched. 누를(끌, 풀) 수 없는. ¶ *an* ~ *thirst* 참을 수 없는 갈증 / ~ *enthusiasm* 왕성한 의욕.

un·ques·tion·a·ble [ʌnkwéstʃənəbəl] *adj.* beyond question or doubt; certain. 의심할 여지 없는, 확실한. ¶ *His keenness is* ~, *but he may not be experienced enough.* 그가 빈틈없는 사람임에는 의론에 여지가 없으나, 충분한 경험이 있는지는 모르겠다. [un-]

un·ques·tioned [ʌnkwéstʃənd] *adj.* not

questioned; not disputed; undoubted. 조사되지〔질문당하지〕 않은; 의론의 여지가 없는; 확실한. [un-]

un·qui·et [ʌnkwáiət] *adj.* disturbed; not at peace. 불안한; 어수선한; 불온한. ¶ ~ *minds* 어수선한 마음 / *an ~ age* 불온한 시대.

un·rav·el [ʌnrǽvəl] *v.* (**-eled, -el·ing** or 《Brit.》 **-elled, -el·ling**) *vt.* **1** undo (something woven, tangled, etc.); separate the threads of. (엉킨 실)을 풀다. ¶ ~ *a knitted scarf* 뜨개질한 스카프를 풀다. **2** 《*fig.*》 solve; clear up. …을 해명〔해결〕하다. ¶ ~ *the plot of a story* 이야기의 줄거리를 풀어 나가다 / ~ *a mystery* 비밀을 밝히다. — *vi.* become unraveled. 해명되다; 풀리다.

un·re·al [ʌnríːəl] *adj.* not real; imaginary; fanciful. 실재하지 않는; 비현실적인; 가공의.

un·rea·son·a·ble [ʌnríːzənəbəl] *adj.* **1** not reasonable. 이성이 없는; 이치에 안 닿는; 무분별한. ¶ *a ~ man* 무분별한〔분수 없는〕 사람 / ~ *conduct* 분별 없는 행위. **2** not moderate; excessive. 터무니없는; 지나친. ¶ *an ~ price* 터무니없는 가격 / *I think she is making quite ~ demands on us.* 그녀가 우리한테 지나친 요구를 하고 있다.

un·rea·son·a·bly [ʌnríːzənəbəli] *adv.* in an unreasonable manner. 무분별하게; 지나치게; 터무니없이.

un·rea·son·ing [ʌnríːzəniŋ] *adj.* not reasoning. 비이성적인; 이치를 모르는.

un·re·flect·ing [ʌ̀nrifléktiŋ] *adj.* **1** not reflecting the light. 빛을 반사하지 않는. **2** unthinking; thoughtless. 지각 없는; 분수 없는.

un·re·gard·ed [ʌ̀nrigáːrdid] *adj.* disregarded; neglected. 이목을 못 끄는; 무시된.

un·re·lent·ing [ʌ̀nriléntiŋ] *adj.* **1** showing no mercy; cruel. 가차없는; 냉혹한. **2** continuous; without decreasing in power or effort. 꾸준한. ¶ *a week of ~ activity* 활동을 멈추지 않은 한 주일. ● **un·re·lent·ing·ly** [-li] *adv.*

un·re·mit·ting [ʌ̀nrimítiŋ] *adj.* without stopping; not slackening; persistent. 간단없는; 꾸준한; 끈질긴. ¶ ~ *toil* 부단한 수고 / ~ *work* 쉴 틈이 없는 일.

un·re·quit·ed [ʌ̀nrikwáitid] *adj.* not returned or rewarded. 보람이 없는; 보수를 안 받는. ¶ *an ~ labor* 무료 봉사 / ~ *love* 짝사랑. [un-]

un·rest [ʌnrést] *n.* Ⓤ uneasiness; restlessness. 불온; 불안; 근심. ¶ *political ~* 정치적 불안 / *a period of industrial ~ with continual strike* 연이은 파업으로 인한 산업상 불안기.

un·rid·dle [ʌnrídl] *vt.* solve (a riddle, etc.). …의 수수께끼를 풀다.

un·ri·valed, 《Brit.》 **-valled** [ʌnráivəld] *adj.* having no rival; matchless. 경쟁 상대가 없는; 비길 데 없는; 무비(無比)의. ¶ ~ *powers of argument* 이론면에서의 막강한 실력 / *an ~ knowledge of Chinese art* 중국 미술에 대한 다시 없는 지식.

un·roll [ʌnróul] *vt.* (P6) **1** open or spread out (something rolled). (말린 것)을 펴다. ¶ *She unrolled the map* 〔*the carpet*〕. 그녀는 두루마리 지도〔양탄자〕를 폈다. **2** lay open; display. …을 펼쳐 보이다; 전개하다. [un-]

un·ruf·fled [ʌnrʌ́fəld] *adj.* **1** smooth; not rough. 매끈한; 거칠지 않은. ¶ *an ~ summer-sea surface* 잔잔한 여름 바다의 수면 / ~ *snow.* **2** 《*fig.*》 calm; not disturbed. 조용한; 침착한. ¶ *an ~ mind* 침착한 마음.

un·ru·ly [ʌnrúːli] *adj.* (**-rul·i·er, -rul·i·est**) hard to control; lawless; disobedient. 멋대로 노는; 막된. ¶ *an ~ person* 〔*animal*〕 다루기 어려운 사람〔짐승〕.

un·sad·dle [ʌnsǽdl] *vt.* (P6) **1** take the saddle off (a horse, etc.). (말)의 안장을 떼다. **2** cause (someone) to fall from a horse. …을 말에서 떨어뜨리다. — *vi.* (P1) take the saddle off a horse, etc. 말 안장을 떼다.

un·said [ʌnséd] *v.* p. and pp. of **unsay.** — *adj.* not said or spoken. 말하지 않는; 입 밖에 내지 않는. ¶ *a tactless remark that would have been better left ~* 안 하느니만 못한 요령 없는 말.

un·sat·is·fac·to·ry [ʌ̀nsætisfǽktəri] *adj.* not satisfactory. 만족스럽지 못한; 불충분한. ¶ *The answer was ~.* 대답이 마음에 들지 않았다.

un·sat·is·fied [ʌnsǽtisfàid] *adj.* not satisfied. 불만족의.

un·sa·vor·y, 《Brit.》 **-vour-** [ʌ̀nséivəri] *adj.* **1** without flavor; tasteless. 맛없는. **2** unpleasant in taste or smell. 맛이〔냄새가〕 좋지 않은. **3** morally bad; disgusting. (도덕적으로) 좋지 않은. ¶ *an ~ character* 못된 인간 / *his ~ business activities* 그의 부도덕한 상행위. [un-]

un·say [ʌnséi] *vt.* (**-said**) (P6) take back (something said); recall. (먼저 한 말)을 취소하다.

un·scathed [ʌnskéiðd] *adj.* not harmed. 다치지 않은. ¶ *He walked away from the accident completely ~.* 그 사고에 그는 상처 하나 없이 살아났다.

un·sci·en·tif·ic [ʌ̀nsaiəntífik] *adj.* not scientific. 비과학적인.

un·screw [ʌnskrúː] *vt.* (P6) **1** remove a screw or screws from (something). …의 나사를 빼다. ¶ ~ *the lid of a coffin* 관 뚜껑의 나사를 뽑다 / ~ *the hinges to take down the door* 문을 떼기 위해 돌쩌귀의 나사를 빼다. **2** take out or loosen (something) by turning it. …을 돌려 빼다〔늦추다〕. ¶ ~ *a nut* 너트를 돌려서 빼다 / *I can't ~ the top of this bottle.* 이 병마개를 돌려 뺄 수 없다. — *vi.* (P1) become unscrewed. 나사가 빠지다. ¶ *The nut won't ~.* 나사가 안 빠진다.

un·scru·pu·lous [ʌnskrúːpjələs] *adj.* without moral principles; without conscience. 부도덕한; 무도한; 비양심적인. ¶ ~ *business method* 부도덕한 상술. [un-]

un·seal [ʌnsíːl] *vt.* **1** break or remove the seal of (a letter, etc.). …의 봉함을 뜯다; …을 개봉하다. **2** open (something tightly shut or sealed). …을 열다.

un·sea·son·a·ble [ʌnsíːzənəbəl] *adj.* **1** not suitable to the season. 철 아닌; 계절에 맞지 않는. ¶ ~ *weather* 〔*heat*〕 때아닌 날씨〔더위〕. **2** coming at the wrong time; untimely. 계제〔때〕가 나쁜. ¶ *an* ~ *request* 계제 나쁜 요구 / ~ *humor* 어울리지 않는 유머.

un·seat [ʌnsíːt] *vt.* (P6) **1** throw (a rider) from a saddle. …을 낙마(落馬)시키다. **2** remove (someone) from an official position, e.g. a seat in a parliament. …을 퇴직시키다; …의 의석을 빼앗다.

un·seem·ly [ʌnsíːmli] *adj.* not seemly; not proper. 볼썽 나쁜〔사나운〕; 부적당한. ¶ *They left with* ~ *haste.* 그들은 허둥지둥 떠났다. — *adv.* in an unsuitable manner; improperly. 볼썽 사납게; 보기 흉하게.

un·seen [ʌnsíːn] *adj.* not seen; not visible; unobserved. 보이지 않는. ¶ ~ *danger.* — *n.* **1** 《*the* ~》 the invisible world. 영계(靈界). **2** 《*an* ~》 an unprepared passage set for translation in an examination. 즉석 번역 문제. ¶ *a French* ~ 프랑스어 즉석 번역 문제. [un-]

•**un·self·ish** [ʌnsélfiʃ] *adj.* not selfish; generous. 이기적이 아닌; 사심이 없는.

un·set·tle [ʌnsétl] *vt.* (P6) **1** make (something) unstable. …을 흔들리게 하다; 동요시키다. ¶ ~ *someone's opinion* 아무의 소신을 흔들리게 하다. **2** make (someone) uneasy; disturb. …을 불안하게 하다; 어지럽히다. ¶ *The sudden changes unsettled her.* 갑작스런 변화로 그녀는 불안해졌다. — *vi.* (P1) become unstable. 불안해지다; 동요하다; 평정을 잃다.

un·set·tled [ʌnsétld] *adj.* **1** not determined or decided. 결심이 안 된; 미정의. ¶ *a* ~ *question* 미해결의 문제 / *The date of our school-excursion is* ~. 우리의 수학 여행 날짜는 미정이다. **2** changeable; uncertain. 일정치 않은; 잘 변하는. ¶ *The weather is* ~. 날씨는 변하기 쉽다. **3** not inhabited by settlers. 거주자(居住者)가 없는. ¶ *Some parts of the world are still* ~. 지구의 어떤 지역에는 아직도 사람이 살지 않는다. **4** not in proper condition; disturbed; disordered. 무질서한; 어지러운. ¶ *Our house is still* ~. 우리 집은 아직 정리가 안 돼 어지럽다. **5** not fixed or stable. 불안정한. ¶ ~ *political condition* 불안한 정치 상황. **6** unpaid. 지불이 안 된. ¶ ~ *debts* 갚지 않은 부채.

un·shak·en [ʌnʃéikən] *adj.* not shaken; firm. 흔들리지 않는; 단호한.

un·sheathe [ʌnʃíːð] *vt.* (P6) draw (a sword, a knife, etc.) from a sheath. (칼 따위)를 칼집에서 뽑다.

un·ship [ʌnʃíp] *vt.* (P6) take off from a ship. …을 배에서 부리다; 양륙(揚陸)하다.

un·shod [ʌnʃád / -ʃɔ́d] *adj.* without shoes; barefoot. 신을 신지 않은; 맨발의. [un-]

un·sight·ly [ʌnsáitli] *adj.* (**-li·er, -li·est**) not pleasant to look at; ugly. 보기 흉한; 추한. ¶ *an* ~ *spot on his nose* 그의 콧등의 보기 싫은 반점 / *an* ~ *modern office block* 보기 흉한 현대의 사무실용 빌딩.

un·skilled [ʌnskíld] *adj.* **1** not skilled. 미숙한(cf. *unskillful*). ¶ *an* ~ *worker* 서투른 직공. **2** not requiring or using skill. 숙련이 필요치 않은. ¶ ~ *labor* 〔*job*〕 (숙련이 필요하지 않은) 단순한 일〔직업〕.

un·skill·ful, 《Brit.》 **-skil-** [ʌnskílfəl] *adj.* without skill; awkward; clumsy. 서툰; 재주가 무딘(cf. *unskilled*).

un·so·phis·ti·cat·ed [ʌ̀nsəfístəkèitid] *adj.* **1** not sophisticated; simple; genuine. 순진〔순박〕한; 천진한; 순수한. ¶ *a* ~ *young woman* 순박한 젊은 여성. **2** without complexity or refinement. 복잡하지 않은; 단순한. ¶ ~ *machinery* 복잡하지 않은〔단순한〕 기계 장치.

un·sought [ʌnsɔ́ːt] *adj.* not looked for; not sought. 찾지 않는; 원하지 않는.

un·sound [ʌnsáund] *adj.* **1** not in good or healthy condition. 건전〔건강〕하지 못한. ¶ *An* ~ *mind or body is diseased.* 건전하지 못한 마음이나 몸은 병든다 / *His heart is* ~. 그의 심장은 건강하지 않다. **2** rotten. 부패한; 상한. ¶ ~ *fruit* 〔*fish*〕 상한 과일〔생선〕 / ~ *timber* 썩은 목재. **3** not based on sound reasoning. 근거가 박약한. ¶ ~ *arguments* 애매한 논거.

un·spar·ing [ʌnspέəriŋ] *adj.* **1** very generous. 후한; 손이 큰. ¶ ~ *kindness* 아낌없는 친절 / *He is* ~ *in his offers of help.* 그는 서슴없이 도와 주겠다고 제의했다. **2** not merciful; severe. 무자비한; 가차없는. ¶ *an* ~ *master* 몰인정한 주인.

un·speak·a·ble [ʌnspíːkəbəl] *adj.* **1** that cannot be expressed in words. 이루 말할 수 없는. ¶ ~ *joy* 말할 수 없는 기쁨 / *a* ~ *loss* 말 못 할 손실. **2** too bad to be mentioned. 입에 담지 못할; 몹시 나쁜. ¶ *His manners are* ~. 그의 태도는 말도 못 할 정도로 나쁘다 / ~ *pain* 지독한 통증.

un·spot·ted [ʌnspátid / -spɔ́t-] *adj.* 《usu. *fig.*》 without spot; guiltless; pure. 흠이 없는; 결백한. ¶ ~ *from the world* 세속에 물들지 않은 / ~ *honor* 순수한 명예.

un·sta·ble [ʌnstéibəl] *adj.* not stable, fixed, or constant; unsteady. 불안정한; 흔들거리는; 변하기 쉬운.

un·stead·y [ʌnstédi] *adj.* (**-stead·i·er, -stead·i·est**) not steady; likely to change. 불안정한; 변하기 쉬운. ¶ ~ *on one's feet* 발이 휘청거려 / *an* ~ *post* 근들거리는 기둥 / *be* ~ *of purpose* 목적이 확고하지 못하다.

un·string [ʌnstríŋ] *vt.* (**-strung**) (P6) **1** remove or loosen the string or strings of (something). …의 현(絃)을 풀다〔늦추다〕.

2 remove (beads, etc.) from a string. (구슬 등)을 끈에서 빼다. 3 make (someone) weak or nervous. …을 약하게 만들다; 신경질이 되게 하다.

un·strung [ʌnstrʌ́ŋ] *v.* p. and pp. of **unstring.** — *adj.* 1 having the strings loosened. 현이 느슨한. 2 nervous; no longer subject to the will. 신경이 약해진; 자제력을 잃은. ¶ *His nerves are all* ~. 그는 신경이 몹시 쇠약하다. [un-]

un·stud·ied [ʌnstʌ́did] *adj.* 1 not got by study; natural. 배우지 않고 알게 된; 자연스러운. 2 not having knowledge; unlearned. 배우지 않은; 모르는.

un·suc·cess·ful [ʌ̀nsəksésfəl] *adj.* not successful. 성공하지 못한; 실패한. ¶ *an* ~ *effort* 무위로 끝난 노력.

un·suit·a·ble [ʌnsú:təbəl] *adj.* not suitable; inappropriate. 부적당한; 어울리지 않는. ¶ *an* ~ *marriage.*

un·sul·lied [ʌnsʌ́lid] *adj.* 《usu. *fig.*》 without spot or stain; pure. 오점이 없는; 순수한. ¶ ~ *glory* 〔*reputation, honor*〕 나무랄 데 없는 영광〔명성, 명예〕.

un·sung [ʌnsʌ́ŋ] *adj.* not sung; not honored in song or poetry; uncelebrated. 시가(詩歌)로 읊어지지 않는; 시가로 찬미되지 않는.

un·sus·pect·ed [ʌ̀nsəspéktid] *adj.* 1 not suspected. 의심받지 않는. 2 not imagined to be existent. 있을 성싶지 않은. ¶ *an* ~ *danger* 생각지도 못한 위험.

un·taught [ʌntɔ́:t] *v.* p. and pp. of **unteach.** — *adj.* 1 not thought or educated; ignorant. 배우지 못한; 무학(無學)의. 2 (of knowledge) got without being taught. 배우지 않고 알고 있는.

un·teach [ʌntí:tʃ] *vt.* (**-taught**) (P6) 1 cause to forget (something learned). (배운 것)을 잊게 하다. 2 teach the opposite of (something previously taught). (배운 것)의 반대의 것을 가르치다.

un·ten·a·ble [ʌnténəbəl] *adj.* that cannot be defended or maintained. 지키기 어려운; 유지하기 어려운. ¶ *The Prime Minister is now a completely* ~ *position, and must resign.* 수상은 완전히 궁지에 몰려 사직이 불가피하다. [un-]

un·think·a·ble [ʌnθíŋkəbəl] *adj.* 1 that cannot be thought of or imagined. 생각〔상상〕도 못할. ¶ *Defeat is* ~. 패배는 생각할 수 없다. 2 《*colloq.*》 extremely unlikely; unbelievable. 있을 법하지도 않은; 믿을 수 없는. ¶ *It is* ~ *that he would do such a mean trick.* 그가 그런 치사한 짓을 할 리가 없다.

un·think·ing [ʌnθíŋkiŋ] *adj.* thoughtless; careless. 사려 없는; 부주의한. ¶ *an* ~ *remark* 분수 없는 말.

un·thought-of [ʌnθɔ́:tʌ̀v / -ɔ̀v] *adj.* not previously imagined or considered. 생각도 못한; 뜻밖의.

un·ti·dy [ʌntáidi] *adj.* (**-di·er, -di·est**) not in good order; not neat. 단정치 못한; 흐리터분한.

un·tie [ʌntái] *vt.* (P6) 1 unfasten or loosen (something knotted or tied). …을 풀다; 끄르다. ¶ *Untie the string.* 그 끈을 풀어라. 2 free (someone) from fastening or restraint. …을 자유롭게 하다; 해방하다. ¶ ~ *a horse from the post* 말을 기둥에서 풀어 주다. 3 resolve. …을 해결하다. ¶ ~ *a question.* — *vi.* (P1) become unfastened. 풀어지다; 풀리다. [un-]

:un·til [əntíl] *prep.* up to the time of; before. …까지. ¶ *He will stay here* ~ *next Sunday.* 그는 다음 일요일까지 여기 체재할 것이다 / *Wait* ~ *four o'clock* 네 시까지 기다려라 / *It will be cold from Christmas* ~ *April.* 크리스마스부터 4월까지 추울 것이다 / *The problem has never really arisen* ~ *now.* 지금까지는 문제가 전혀 발생하지 않았다 / *He did not go* ~ *night.* 그는 밤까지 가지 않았다. — *conj.* up to the time when; before; to the point that. …하기까지; …할 만큼. 語法 till 보다 문어적임. 주문(主文) 앞에 있는 구, 절을 이끌 때가 많음. ¶ *Until he came back, none of them went out.* 그가 돌아올 때까지 아무도 나가지 않았다 / *Wait here* ~ *I come back.* 내가 돌아올 때까지 여기서 기다려라 / *He waited* ~ *the sun had set.* 그는 해질 때까지 기다렸다 / *He worked* ~ *he was too tired to do any more.* 그는 지쳐서 더 이상 하지 못할 때까지 일했다. [*unto*]

un·time·ly [ʌntáimli] *adj.* 1 not at the right moment. 때아닌; 철이 아닌. ¶ *Snow in May is* ~. 5월의 눈은 제철이 아니다. 2 happening too soon or before the usual time. 너무 이른; 시기 상조의. ¶ *die an* ~ *death* 요절하다. — *adv.* 1 inopportunely. 시기〔계제〕가 나쁜. 2 too soon; prematurely. 너무 일찍. ¶ *He came* ~. 그는 너무 일찍 왔다. [un-]

un·tir·ing [ʌntáiəriŋ] *adj.* not growing tired; tireless. 지칠 줄 모르는; 꾸준한. ¶ *with* ~ *energy* 불굴의 정력으로.

un·ti·tled [ʌntáitld] *adj.* having no title. 칭호가〔직함이〕 없는; 표제(表題)가 없는.

·un·to [ʌ́ntu:, *before consonants often* ʌ́ntə] *prep.* 《*arch., poet.*》 to. …에. ¶ *Come* ~ *me, all ye that labor.* 수고하는 자들은 다 내게로 오라《Matt. 11:28》. [E.]

un·told [ʌntóuld] *adj.* 1 not told; not expressed. 말해지지〔이야기되지〕 않은. ¶ *He left the story* ~. 그는 그 이야기를 안 했다. 2 countless; very great. 무수한; 막대한. ¶ ~ *wealth* 막대한 부 / *She has done* ~ *damage to our chances.* 그녀는 우리의 승기(乘機)를 깡그리 망쳐 버렸다. [un-]

un·touch·a·ble [ʌntʌ́tʃəbəl] *adj.* 1 that can not or should not to be touched. 만질 수 없는; 손대서는 안 되는. 2 out of reach. 손이 닿지 않는. — *n.* Ⓒ a person of the lowest caste in India. (인도의) 불촉 천민(不觸賤民).

un·touched [ʌntʌ́tʃt] *adj.* not touched or affected. 손대지 않은; 감동되지 않은.

un·to·ward [ʌntɔ́ːrd, -tóuərd] *adj.* 《*arch.*》 **1** hard to manage or deal with; willful. 고집 센; 다루기 힘든. **2** inconvenient; unfortunate. 성가신; 운이 나쁜; 재수없는. ¶ ~ *circumstances* 역경 / *an* ~ *wind* 역풍 / *We completed our journey without anything* ~ *happening.* 우리는 이렇다 할 사고 없이 여행을 마쳤다. [un-]

un·trained [ʌntréind] *adj.* without training or education. 훈련을 받지 않은; 미숙한.

un·tried [ʌntráid] *adj.* not tried; not tested. 시험을 거치지 않은.

un·trod [ʌntrɑ́d / -trɔ́d], **-trod·den** [-trɑ́dn / -trɔ́dn] *adj.* never been stepped on by human beings. 인적 미답(人跡未踏)의.

un·true [ʌntrúː] *adj.* **1** not true; false. 진실이 아닌. **2** not faithful. 충실하지 않은; 불성실한. **3** not agreeing with a standard or rule. 표준〔규격〕에 맞지 않는. ¶ ~ *to type* 전형적이 아닌 / *The angles are* ~ *and out of the square.* 각도가 틀려서 정사각형이 아니다.

un·truth [ʌntrúːθ] *n.* **1** Ⓤ lack of truth; falsity. 허위. ¶ *quick to find the* ~ *in rumors* 소문의 허위를 알아 내는 데 신속한. **2** Ⓒ an untrue statement; a lie. 거짓말. ¶ *He never told an* ~ *in his life.* 그는 평생 거짓말을 하지 않았다. [un-]

un·truth·ful [ʌntrúːθfəl] *adj.* **1** not truthful. 거짓의. **2** likely to tell lies. 거짓말하는; 거짓말의. ¶ *an* ~ *account* 허위 계정.

un·tu·tored [ʌntjúːtərd] *adj.* **1** not taught. 배우지 못한; 정식 교육을 받지 않은. **2** unsophisticated; simple. 소박한.

un·used [ʌnjúːzd] *adj.* **1** not used. 쓰이지〔쓰지〕 않는; 쓰인 적이 없는. ¶ *an* ~ *room* 빈 방. **2** [ʌnjúːst, *with the following 'to'* -júːstə] not accustomed. 익숙하지 못한; 서툰. ¶ *be* ~ *to labor* 일에 서툴다 / *I'm* ~ *to having so much responsibility.* 나는 그런 중책에 익숙지 못합니다.

:**un·u·su·al** [ʌnjúːʒuəl] *adj.* not usual; not common; rare; strange. 보통이 아닌; 이상한; 진기한. ¶ *Heavy rain is* ~ *in this part of the world.* 지구의 이 지역에 호우는 좀처럼 없다 / *I like that painting; it is most* ~. 나는 저 그림이 좋다; 아주 독특하다.

***un·u·su·al·ly** [ʌnjúːʒuəli, -ʒwəli] *adv.* in an unusual manner; uncommonly; rarely; extremely. 이상하게; 드물게; 대단히. ¶ *It is* ~ *hot today.* 오늘은 유별나게 덥다.

un·ut·ter·a·ble [ʌnʌ́tərəbəl] *adj.* that cannot be put into words; indescribable. 말로는 못 할; 이루 말할 수 없는. ¶ ~ *despair* 이루 말할 수 없는 실망 / *in* ~ *confusion* 대혼란에 빠져 / *an* ~ *scoundrel* 순 악당 / *an* ~ *fool* 천치 바보.

un·var·nished [ʌnvɑ́ːrniʃt] *adj.* **1** not varnished. 니스 칠을 안 한. **2** unadorned; plain; simple. 꾸밈〔가식〕이 없는. ¶ *Just give me the plain* ~ *truth.* 제발 내게 숨김없는 사실을 말해 다오.

un·veil [ʌnvéil] *vt.* (P6) remove a veil or covering from (something); disclose; reveal. …의 베일을〔덮개를〕 벗기다; …을 털어놓다; 밝히다. ¶ ~ *one's face* 얼굴의 베일을 벗다 / ~ *a monument* 기념비의 막을 걷어내다 / ~ *a secret plan* 비밀 계획을 밝히다 / ~ *oneself* 정체를 드러내다. — *vi.* (P1) take off a veil or covering; reveal oneself. 베일을 벗다; 정체를 드러내다. [un-]

un·vexed [ʌnvékst] *adj.* not troubled; not disturbed; not annoyed; not irritated. 냉정한; 침착한.

un·war·rant·ed [ʌnwɔ́(ː)rəntid, -wɑ́r-] *adj.* unwelcome and done without good reason. 부당한. ¶ *an* ~ *intrusion into our private affairs* 개인적인 일에 대한 부당한 간섭.

un·war·y [ʌnwɛ́əri] *adj.* not cautious; not guarded; not careful. 부주의한; 경솔한.

un·wa·ver·ing [ʌnwéivəriŋ] *adj.* fixed; steadfast. 흔들리지 않는; 확고한.

un·wea·ried [ʌnwíərid] *adj.* **1** not weary; not tired. 지치지 않는. **2** never growing weary; tireless. 지칠 줄 모르는; 꾸준한.

***un·wel·come** [ʌnwélkəm] *adj.* not welcome; not pleasing. 반갑지 않은; 좋아하지 않는. ¶ *an* ~ *guest* 불청객.

un·well [ʌnwél] *adj.* not well; sick, esp. for a short time. (몸의) 컨디션이 좋지 않은; 기분이 좋지 않은; 찌뿌드드한.

un·whole·some [ʌnhóulsəm] *adj.* **1** unhealthy; bad for the body. 건강〔몸〕에 해로운. **2** bad for the mind. 불건전한. ¶ *an* ~ *book* 외설책.

un·wield·y [ʌnwíːldi] *adj.* (**-wield·i·er, -wield·i·est**) difficult to move or manage; hard to handle because of its size. (크거나 무거워) 다루기〔움직이기〕 곤란한. ¶ *an* ~ *piece of furniture* 다루기 어려운 덩치 큰 가구 / *a large* ~ *bureaucracy* 비대(肥大)한 관료 제도. [un-]

***un·will·ing** [ʌnwíliŋ] *adj.* not willing; reluctant. 마음 내키지 않는; 마지못해 하는. ¶ *willing or* ~ 싫든 좋든(간에) / *She is* ~ *to come.* 그녀는 올 생각이 없다 / *an* ~ *helper* 마지못해 돕는 사람.

un·wind [ʌnwáind] *vt.* (**-wound**) (P6) wind off (something wound); uncoil. (감은 것)을 풀다. ¶ *She unwound the wool from the ball.* 그녀는 실꾸리에서 털실을 풀었다. — *vi.* (P1) become unwound; relax. 풀리다; 긴장이 풀리다.

un·wise [ʌnwáiz] *adj.* lacking good judgment; foolish. 슬기롭지 못한; 어리석은.

un·wit·ting [ʌnwítiŋ] *adj.* not knowing; unconscious. 모르는; 무의식의. ¶ *She was their* ~ *accomplice.* 그녀는 자기도 모르게 그들의 공범이 돼 있었다.

un·wit·ting·ly [ʌnwítiŋli] *adv.* unconsciously; not intentionally. 부지중에.

un·wont·ed [ʌnwóuntid, -wɔ́ːnt-] *adj.*

unusual; rare; not accustomed. 이례적인; 드문; 익숙지 않은. ¶ *He arrived with ~ punctuality.* 그는 이례적으로 정시에 도착했다. [un-]

·**un·wor·thy** [ʌnwə́ːrði] *adj.* (**-thi·er, -thi·est**) **1** not worthy; worthless; not having or deserving respect. (도덕적으로) 가치가 없는; 존경할 가치가 없는. ¶ *an ~ man* 가치 없는 사람 / *He is ~ to be regarded as a friend.* 그는 친구로 여길 가치가 없다. **2** not deserving of; not suitable for. …할 가치가 없는; …에 어울리지 않는. ¶ *He is ~ of confidence.* 그는 미덥지 않다 / *a story ~ of belief* 믿기 어려운 이야기 / *conduct ~ of a gentleman* 신사답지 못한 행위. **3** 《often in self-depreciation》 not deserving some special position or reward; shameful. 알맞지 않은; 부끄러운. ¶ *an ~ pupil of a great teacher* 훌륭한 선생님의 이름을 부끄럽게 하는 학생. [un-]

un·wound [ʌnwáund] *v.* p. and pp. of **unwind.**

un·writ·ten [ʌnrítn] *adj.* **1** not expressed or recorded in writing. 쓰거나 기록해 두지 않은. ¶ *an ~ law* 불문법; 관습법 / *~ legends* 구전 전설. **2** without writing; blank. 백지의; 공란의. ¶ *an ~ page.* [un-]

:**up** [ʌp] *adv.* (opp. down) **1** from a lower to a higher place; in the direction opposite to down. 위에; 위쪽으로; 올라가. ¶ *~ in the sky* 하늘에; 공중에 / *She has pulled ~ her stockings.* 그녀는 스타킹을 끌어올렸다 / *The bird flew ~.* 새가 날아올랐다 / *Can you lift that box ~ on to the shelf for me?* 저 상자를 시렁에 얹어 주겠나 / *He lives two floors ~.* 그는 두 층 위에 산다. **2** in or into a standing or upright position; on one's feet; out of bed. 똑바로; 일어나. ¶ *Stand straight ~.* 똑바로 서라 / *She gets ~ early in the morning.* 그녀는 아침 일찍 일어난다 / *Stand ~.* 일어서라; 기립 / *I helped him ~.* 그를 도와 일어나게 했다 / *The patient will be ~ tomorrow.* 환자는 내일은 일어날 것이다 / *He is not ~ yet.* 아직 자고 있다. **3** above the horizon, ground, or level. 지평선 위에; 지상에. ¶ *The sun is ~.* 해가 떴다 / *The corn is ~.* 강냉이가 자랐다. **4** to a higher rank or social condition. (사회적 지위 등이) 올라가; 높아져. ¶ *go ~ in the world* 출세하다 / *come ~ from porverty to high rank* 가난에서 입신 출세하다 / *He went ~ two places in class.* 그는 반에서 석차가 두 자리 올라갔다. **5** to a higher amount, value, price, volume, etc. (가치·값이) 올라가; (양이) 불어. ¶ *Prices have gone ~.* 물가가 올랐다 / *Speak ~, so that I can hear you.* 알아듣게 크게 말해라 / *He has gone ~ considerably in my opinion.* 그에게 대한 내 평가는 아주 높아졌다《그를 다시 보게 되었다》/ *A plant grows ~ from a seed.* 식물은 씨에서 성장한다. **6** into view, notice, or consideration; well informed. (주목·화제·고려 등의 대상)에 올라(들어). ¶ *The question came ~ for discussion.* 그 문제는 토의에 부쳐졌다 / *Your name's ~ in the village.* 네 이름은 마을에 잘 알려져 있다 / *Is anything ~?* 무슨 일이 일어났느냐; 무슨 일이냐 / *What is ~ over there?* 저쪽에 무슨 일이 났지. **7** into activity; into an excited state. 활동적으로; 세차져; 흥분하여. ¶ *be ~ in arms* 무기를 들고 일어나다 / *Her temper is ~.* 그녀는 화가 치밀었다 / *speak ~* 언성을 높이다 / *His blood is ~.* 그는 화가 났다 / *Blow the fire ~.* 풀무질해서 불을 세게 해라 / *play ~* 분투하다 / *He worked ~ the mob.* 그가 폭도를 선동했다. **8** completely. 완전히; 모두; 다 (…하다). 語法 동사와 함께 쓰임. 아무 뜻이 없이 쓰이기도 함. ¶ *light ~ one's pipe* 파이프에 불을 당기다 / *He drank it ~.* 그는 그것을 다 마셨다 / *I am completely used ~.* 아주 지쳐 버렸다 / *eat ~ everything on the table* 식탁의 것을 모조리 먹어치우다 / *The house was burned ~.* 집은 깡그리 탔다 / *The game is ~.* 이젠 끝장이다 / *Your chance is ~.* 넌 볼장 다 봤다. **9** over; at an end. …이 끝나. ¶ *Your time is ~.* 시간이 다 됐다 / *The rain is letting ~.* 비가 멎고 있다 / *He finished it all ~.* 그는 그것을 깨끗이 끝냈다 / *Pack it ~ neatly.* 단정하게 싸거라. **10** to a place or in the direction that is looked on as more important; near. (도시 따위의 중심지·말하는 사람)을 향해; …의 쪽으로. ¶ *come ~ from the country* 시골서 올라오다 / *go ~ to Seoul* 상경하다 / *A lady came ~ to me and asked the time.* 어떤 부인이 내게로 와서 시간을 물었다. **11** from an earlier to a later period. 성장하여; 자라서. ¶ *grow ~ to youth* 자라서 청년이 되다 / *bring ~ a child* 아이를 길러내다. **12** so as to be even with in time, degree, condition, space, etc.; not behind. …에 따라붙어; …을 유지하여; 뒤지지 않게. ¶ *keep ~ with the times* 시대에 뒤지지 않다 / *catch ~ with a friend* 친구를 따라잡다. **13** in a safe place; aside; in reserve. 보관해; 치워 둬; 남겨 둬. ¶ *lay ~ money* 돈을 여축하다 / *put ~ fruit* 과일을 (절임으로) 저장하다 / *Our hay has been ~.* 건초를 치워 뒀다. **14** 《sports, games》 ahead of an opponent with regard to points, etc. …점 이겨; 리드하여. ¶ *We are two games ~.* 우리는 두 게임 앞섰다. **15** (in tennis, etc.) each. 각기; 각각. ¶ *The score is three ~.* 스코어는 각기 3점이다《3대 3이다》. **16** 《baseball》 at bat. 타석에 올라. ¶ *He come ~ twice in the same inning.* 그는 같은 이닝에 두 번 타석에 섰다.

be up against, be faced with. …에 당면해 있다. ¶ *be ~ against serious trouble* 심한 고난에 처해 있다.

be up against it, be in difficulty. 곤경에 빠져 있다. ¶ *We are really ~ against it now.* 우리는 지금 아주 어려운 처지에 있다.

It's all up with …, There is no more hope for…. …은 끝장이다. ¶ *It's all ~ with me now.* 이제 나는 끝장이다.

up and about [***around***], recovered (from sickness) and able to walk about. (환자가) 병석을 털고 일어나.
up and doing, active; busy. 분주하게 움직여; 바빠. ¶ *If you really want to find work, you must be ~ and doing.* 정말 일자리를 찾고 싶으면 바쁘게 돌아다녀 봐야 한다.
up for, being considered for an elective office, etc. (선거 등에) 입후보하여.
up in [***on***], informed about; expert in. …에 정통해; 밝아; 능숙해. ¶ *be (well) ~ in history* 역사에 밝다 / *I am not ~ on speech.* 나는 연설이 서툴다.
up to, **a**) doing; engage in; in process of doing. …에 종사해. ¶ *He is ~ to no good.* 그는 뭔가 좋지 않은 일을 하고 있다 / *What have you been ~ to ?* 무엇을 하고 있었느냐. **b**) dependent upon the decision of; resting on as a duty. …의 결정 여하에; …의 책임[의무]인. ¶ *That's ~ to you.* 그건 네 결정 나름이다 / *It's ~ to me to do so.* 그렇게 하는 것이 내 책임이다. **c**) equal to; able to do. (일 따위)를 (감당)할 수 있어. ¶ *He is not ~ to the job.* 그는 그 일을 할 수 없다; 그 일에 맞지 않는다. **d**) until; as far as; as much as. …까지; …에 이르러. ¶ *~ to date* 오늘(날)까지 / *count ~ to ten* 열까지 세다 / *~ to this time* 이제까지 / *stand ~ to one's knees in the water* 서면 무릎까지 물이 차다.
Up with...! Raise! 일어서라. ¶ *Up with you!* 일어서라; 분발해라 / *Up with it!* 그것을 올려라.
well up in [***on***] =up in [on].
What's up ? What's the matter ?; What's happening ? 무슨 일이냐; 왜 그러냐.
— *prep.* (opp. down) **1** to or at a higher place on or along. …의 위쪽에[으로]. ¶ *climb ~ a tree* 나무 위로 오르다 / *walk ~ a mountain* 등산하다 / *walk one's way ~ a school* 상급 학교에 진학하다 / *He went steadily ~ the social scale.* 그는 꾸준히 사회적으로 지위를 높였다. **2** farther along. …을 따라. ¶ *walk ~ a street* 거리를 따라 걷다. **3** toward the beginning of a river, etc.; toward or in the inner or upper part of a country, etc. (강)의 상류로; (해안에서) 오지(奧地)로; 내륙으로. ¶ *sail ~ the Hudson* 배를 타고 허드슨 강 상류로 가다 / *travel ~ (the) country* 내륙을 여행하다 / *row ~ a stream* 노저어 시내를 올라가다. **4** at or near the top of. …의 정상 쪽에. ¶ *Her house is ~ the hill.* 그녀의 집은 언덕 위에 있다 / *He went ~ garret.* 그는 다락에 올라갔다.
— *adj.* going or directed up. 위로 향하는; 올라가는. ¶ *an ~ train* 상행 열차.
— *n.* Ⓒ an upward movement; 《usu. *pl.*》 a rise in fortune. 상승; 치받이; 번영; 성공.
on the up and up, 《U.S. *colloq.*》 **a**) getting better and better; becoming more and more successful. (사업 등이) 잘 돼 가는; 성공적인. **b**) honest. (사람이) 정직한.
ups and downs, 《*fig.*》 rises and falls; the times of good fortune and bad fortune. (길 등의) 오르내림; 기복(起伏); (운명 등의) 부침(浮沈). ¶ *a road full of ups and downs* 기복이 심한 길 / *the ups and downs of life* 인생의 부침.
— *v.* (**upped** or **up, up·ping**) 《*colloq., joc.*》 *vt.* (P6) **1** raise; increase. …을 늘리다; 올리다. ¶ *~ prices* 값을 올리다 / *~ output* 생산고를 늘리다. **2** put or take up. …을 들어[집어]올리다. ¶ *~ one's stick to beat someone* 아무를 치려고 지팡이를 쳐들다. — *vi.* (P1) get up; jump up. 일어서다; 일어나다. ¶ *He upped and struck me.* 그는 일어나서 는 나를 쳤다. [E.]
up with, 《*colloq.*》 raise; pick up 쳐들다; 집어들다. ¶ *He upped with his fist* [*stick*]. 그는 주먹[단장]을 쳐들었다.
up- [ʌp-] *pref.* upward. '위로[위쪽으로] 향「한'의 뜻.
up-and-com·ing [ʌ́pəndkʌ́miŋ] *adj.* 《U.S.》 **1** showing signs of likely future success or prosperity. 전도 유망한. ¶ *an ~ young opera singer* 장래가 촉망되는 젊은 오페라 가수. **2** alert. 빈틈없는. [E.]
up-and-down [ʌ́pəndáun] *adj.* alternately rising and falling; varying. 오르내리는; 변동하는.
up-and-up [ʌ́pəndʌ́p] *n.* 《U.S. *colloq.*》 **1** improving. 진보하는. **2** honest. 정직한.
on the up-and-up, improving. 진보[향상]하는.
up·borne [ʌ̀pbɔ́:rn] *adj.* borne up; supported. 들어올려진; 받쳐진. [up-]
up·braid [ʌpbréid] *vt.* (P6) scold severely; blame; criticise. …을 나무라다; 책망하다. ¶ *She upbraided him for his rudeness.* 그녀는 그의 무례함을 크게 책했다. — *vi.* (P1) speak with reproach. 나무라다. [*braid*]
up·bring·ing [ʌ́pbrìŋiŋ] *n.* Ⓤ the training and education received during childhood; bringing-up. 양육; 교육; 가정 교육. [up-]
up·coun·try [ʌ́pkʌ̀ntri] *n.* 《*the* ~》 the interior of a country. 내륙; 오지. — *adj.* interior; inland. 내륙[오지]의. — *adv.* toward or in the interior of a country. 내륙으로; 오지로.
up·end [ʌpénd] *vt., vi.* (P6; 1) **1** set on end; stand on end. 곧추세우다[서다]. **2** knock down. 쓰러뜨리다; 때려눕히다. ¶ *He upended his opponent with a single punch.* 그는 한 주먹으로 상대를 눕혔다.
up·grade [ʌ́pgréid] *adj., adv.* uphill. 오르막의[에]. ¶ *go ~* 비탈을 오르다. — [⌐⌐] *vt.* (P6) raise (something) to a higher grade. …을 승진[격상, 승격]시키다. ¶ *He is hoping to be upgraded.* 그는 승진을 기대하고 있다. — [⌐⌐] *n.* Ⓒ an upward slope or incline. 오르막; 치받이. ¶ *on the ~* 오르막에.
up·heav·al [ʌphí:vəl] *n.* **1** Ⓒ a movement or an act of rising up from below; the state of being raised up, esp. in earth-

quake. 밀어올림; 들어올림; (지진에 의한) 융기. **2** Ⓤⓒ a sudden great and violent change in ideas, habits, social conditions, etc. (갑작스러운) 대변동; 격변; 동란. ¶ *the ~ of the French Revolution* 프랑스 혁명이라는 대변동 / *What an ~ it was when we had to change offices!* 사무실을 옮겨야 했을 때는 정말 난리였다. [up-]

up·heave [ʌphíːv] *v.* (**-heaved, -hove**) *vt.* (P6) raise (something) from beneath; lift up; heave up. …을 들어〔밀어〕올리다. — *vi.* (P1) rise. 들리다; 융기하다.

up·held [ʌphéld] *v.* p and pp. of **uphold.**

up·hill [ʌ́phìl] *adj.* **1** up the slope of a hill; rising; ascending. 치받이의; 오르막의. ¶ *an ~ road* 오르막길 / *The road is ~ all the way.* 이 길은 내내 오르막이다. **2** difficult. 힘든; 어려운. ¶ *It's an ~ task teaching them mathematics.* 그들에게 수학을 가르치는 것은 고역이다. — *adv.* upward. 고개 위로. ¶ *the road ~* 치받잇길 / *We walked a mile ~.* 고갯길을 1 마일이나 걸었다.

***up·hold** [ʌphóuld] *vt.* (**-held**) (P6) **1** keep (something) from falling; support. …을 들어올리다; 받치다. ¶ *Stout columns ~ the roof.* 튼튼한 기둥들이 지붕을 받치고 있다. **2** give moral or spiritual support or encouragement to (someone); encourage or aid. …을 지지하다; 격려하다. ¶ *He upheld my opinion.* / *Your praise and sympathy have upheld me greatly.* 네 칭찬과 동정이 내게 큰 힘이 되었다. **3** approve; confirm. …에 찬성하다; …을 확인하다. ¶ *I cannot ~ such conduct.* 그런 행위는 시인할 수 없다 / *The judge upheld the lower court's decision.* 재판관은 하급 법원의 판결을 확인했다.

up·hold·er [ʌphóuldər] *n.* ⓒ a person who upholds; a supporter. 지지자; 후원자. [up-]

up·hol·ster [ʌphóulstər] *vt.* (P6) **1** furnish (a room, etc.) with curtains, carpets, etc. (방 따위)를 장식하다; 꾸미다. ¶ *~ a house* 〔*room*〕 집〔방〕을 꾸미다. **2** provide (furniture, etc.) with cushions, springs, coverings, etc. (의자·침대 따위)에 천〔쿠션·스프링 등〕을 대다〔붙이다〕. ¶ *~ a sofa* 〔*chair*〕. [Obs. *upholdster* =upholder]

up·hol·ster·y [ʌphóulstəri] *n.* Ⓤ **1** 《*collectively*》 the material used in upholstering. 가구류; 실내 장식품. **2** the business of upholstering. 실내 장식업; 가구업.

up·hove [ʌphóuv] *v.* p. and pp. of **upheave.**

up·keep [ʌ́pkìːp] *n.* Ⓤ **1** the act of keeping something in good order; maintenance. 유지. **2** the cost of maintenance. 유지비. ¶ *The ~ of a big car is expensive.* 큰 차는 유지비가 많이 든다. [up-]

up·land [ʌ́plənd, -lǽnd] *n.* ⓒ a high area. 고지; 고원; 대지(臺地). ¶ *broad sunlit uplands* 볕이 내리쬐는 광활한 고원. — *adj.* of or in high land. 고지의.

up·lift [ʌplíft] *vt.* (P6) **1** lift up; raise. …을 들다; 올리다; 높이다. ¶ *with uplifted hands* 손을 들고. **2** raise socially or morally. …을 향상〔앙양〕시키다. ¶ *His spirit was uplifted by the news.* 그 소식에 그는 사기가 올랐다. — [∠∸] *n.* **1** ⓒ the act of lifting up. 들어올림. ¶ *an ~ of strata* 지층 융기. **2** 《U.S.》 Ⓤ social or moral improvement. 향상; 앙양. [up-]

:up·on [əpɑ́n, əpən / əpɔ́n] *prep.* 《*upon* is preferred in some phrases》 =on. ¶ *~ my word* 맹세코 / *depend ~ it* 꼭; 반드시 / *once ~ a time* 옛날에. [*up, on*]

:up·per [ʌ́pər] *adj.* 《as *attributive*》 **1** higher. 상부의; 위쪽의. ¶ *the ~ deck* 상갑판 / *the ~ lip* 윗입술 / *the ~ notes of a singer's voice* 가수 목소리의 높은 음역 / *the ~ story* 〔*floor*〕 위층. **2** farther from the sea. 오지〔내륙〕의. ¶ *the ~ course of a river* 강의 상류 / *the ~ reaches of the Nile* 나일 강의 상류 지역. **3** higher in rank, office, etc. 상위의; 상류의. ¶ *the ~ classes* 상류 계급.

get the upper hand of ⇨hand.

— *n.* 《usu. *pl.*》 the part of a shoe or boot above the sole. 구두의 갑피. [*up*]

upper case [∠-∠] *n.* 《print.》 the upper one of a pair of type cases containing capital letters. 대문자 활자용 상자(abbr. U.C., cf. *lower case*).

***on one's* uppers,** 《*colloq.*》 wearing worn-out shoes; very poor. 구두창이 닳아; 궁핍한; 몹시 가난한.

up·per-class [ʌ́pərklǽs, -klɑ́ːs] *adj.* **1** of the upper class. 상류 계급의. **2** of the junior and senior classes in a high school, college, etc. 상급반의.

up·per·cut [ʌ́pərkʌ̀t] *n.* ⓒ 《boxing》 a swinging blow directed upward. 어퍼컷. — *vt.* (**-cut, -cut·ting**) hit (someone) with an uppercut. …에 어퍼컷을 먹이다.

Upper House [∠-∠], **the** *n.* the smaller and less representative branch of a legislature; 《Brit.》 the House of Lords; 《U.S.》 the Senate. 상원(上院)(opp. Lower House).

up·per·most [ʌ́pərmòust / -məst] *adj.* highest in position, rank, influence, etc.; topmost. 최고의; 최상의. — *adv.* in the highest place; first. 최상에; 최고로; 최초에. ¶ *the question that comes ~ in our minds* 우리 마음에 맨 먼저 떠오르는 문제.

upper story [∠-∠] *n.* 《*colloq.*》 the head; brains. 머리; 두뇌. ¶ *There's something wrong in his ~.* 그 사람 머리가 좀 이상하다.

upper ten (**thousand**) [∠-∠(∠-)], **the** *n.* 《Brit.》 the highest social class. 상류 사회; 귀족 계급.

up·pish [ʌ́piʃ] *adj.* 《*colloq.*》 somewhat arrogant or conceited. 우쭐대는; 건방진. [*up, -ish*]

up·raise [ʌ̀préiz] *vt.* (P6) 《*arch.*》 《usu. in

pp.》 raise up; lift. …을 (들어)올리다. ¶ *with hands upraised to heaven* 손을 높이 들고 / *with voice upraised in anger* 화가 나서 언성을 높여. [E.]

up·rear [ʌpríər] *vt.* (P6) **1** rear up; bring up. …을 일으키다; 기르다. **2** lift up; raise. …을 들다; 올리다. ¶ ~ *one's head* 고개를 들다.

:up·right [ʌ́pràit, –ˊ] *adj.* **1** standing erect; vertical. 직립한; 곧추선. ¶ *an* ~ *tree* 곧추선 나무 / *take an* ~ *position* 곧추서다; 자세를 바로하다 / *have an* ~ *figure* 자세가 바르다 / *She sat bolt* ~. 그녀는 빳빳이 앉아 있었다. **2** just; honest; honorable. 옳은; 정직한; 훌륭한. ¶ *an* ~ *man* 〔*citizen*〕. —*adv.* in an erect position. 똑바로. ¶ *set a pole* ~ 장대를 바로 세우다. —*n.* **1** Ⓤ the state of being upright. 똑바른 상태. ¶ *be out of* ~ 기울어 있다. **2** Ⓒ something upright. 직립한 것. **3** Ⓒ an upright piano. 수형(豎型) 피아노. [*up, right*]

up·right·ness [ʌ́praitnis] *n.* Ⓤ **1** justness; honesty. 결백; 정직. **2** an upright position. 직립.

upright piano [ˊ– –ˊ–] *n.* a piano with vertical strings. 수형(豎型) 피아노.

up·rise [ʌpráiz] *vi.* (**-rose, -ris·en**) (P1) **1** 《*poet.*》 get up; rise. 일어나다; 올라가다. **2** increase in volume, size, etc. (양이) 늘다; 커지다. **3** rise into view. 나타나다; 출현하다. **4** rise in revolt. 폭동을 일으키다. —*n.* Ⓒ **1** the act of rising up. 상승. **2** an upward slope. 오르막. [*up*]

up·ris·en [ʌprízən] *v.* pp. of **uprise.**

up·ris·ing [ʌ́praiziŋ, –ˊ–] *n.* Ⓒ **1** an upward slope; an ascent. 오르막; 치받이. **2** a revolt. 반란; 폭동. ¶ *an* ~ *of the savage tribes* 미개족들의 반란.

up·roar [ʌ́prɔ̀ːr] *n.* Ⓤ 《sometimes *an* ~》 **1** a noisy disturbance. 대소동; 소란. ¶ *The city was in* (*an*) ~. 시는 온통 야단법석이었다. **2** a loud noise. 소음. ¶ *an* ~ *of shot and shell* 요란한 총포 소리. [Du.=commotion]

up·roar·i·ous [ʌprɔ́ːriəs] *adj.* **1** noisy and disorderly. 시끄러운; 소란스러운. ¶ *an* ~ *crowd* 소란스러운 군중. **2** loud, noisy and cheerful. 시끄럽고 즐거운. ¶ ~ *laughter* 와자한 웃음 소리.

up·root [ʌprúːt] *vt.* (P6) **1** tear up (a plant, etc.) by the roots; 《*fig.*》 put an end to (something). …을 뿌리째 뽑다; 근절하다. ¶ *The storm uprooted many trees.* 폭풍우로 많은 나무들이 뿌리째 뽑혔다 / *Long-established customs and habits are hard to* ~. 오랫동안 형성된 관습이나 습관은 근절하기 어렵다. **2** remove (someone) from a place of residence. …을 몰아내다; 이동시키다. ¶ *To take the new job she had to* ~ *her whole family and settle abroad.* 그녀는 새 일자리를 구하기 위해 가족을 거느리고 해외에 정주해야 했다. [up-]

up·rose [ʌpróuz] *v.* p. of **uprise.**

***up·set** [ʌpsét] *v.* (**up·set, -set·ting**) *vt.* (P6) **1** trun over; tip over. …을 뒤집어엎다; 뒤엎다. ¶ *A child has* ~ *his glass of milk.* 아기가 우유잔을 엎었다 / ~ *a boat* 〔*motorcar*〕 배〔자동차〕를 뒤엎다 / *He* ~ *the cup and the coffee went all over the floor.* 그가 컵을 엎질러 온 마루에 커피가 쏟아졌다. **2** overthrow; bring to ruin. …을 전복시키다. ¶ ~ *the government* 정부를 전복시키다. **3** 《U.S.》 defeat unexpectedly. 예상 밖으로 …을 이기다. **4** throw (something) out of order; disturb greatly. …을 혼란에 빠뜨리다; 망쳐 놓다. ¶ *Don't* ~ *his plans now.* 지금 그의 계획을 망치지 마라 / *The rain* ~ *our plan.* 비 때문에 우리 계획이 틀어졌다. **5** disturb mentally. …을 정신적으로 혼란에 빠뜨리다; 당황하게 하다. ¶ *My mother was very much* ~ *when my brother failed in the examination.* 동생이 시험에 떨어졌을 때 어머니는 크게 당황했다. **6** make (someone) sick. …에 병이 생기게 하다; 기분 나쁘게 하다. ¶ ~ *someone's stomach* …의 위를 버리게 만들다 / *The raw fish I had last night* ~ *me.* 어젯밤 먹은 생선회 때문에 속이 안 좋다. —*vi.* (P1) be disturbed or turned over; be distressed. 뒤집히다; 전복하다; 기분이 나빠지다. ¶ *The car* ~. / *If you don't sit still, the boat will* ~. 가만히 앉아 있지 않으면 배가 뒤집힌다.
—[ˊ–] *n.* Ⓒ **1** an act of upsetting; a fall. 전복; 전도. ¶ *He had a bad* ~ *from a bicycle.* 그는 자전거에서 냅다 굴러 떨어졌다. **2** a state of disorder and confusion. 혼란; 고장. ¶ *The sudden death of our servant caused rather an* ~. 우리 하인의 돌연사로 적지 않은 혼란이 생겼다 / *a complete* ~ *of our plans* 우리 계획의 대혼란. **3** a disagreement; a quarrel. 불화; 싸움. ¶ *a bit of an* ~ *with one's father* 부친과의 약간의 불화. —[–ˊ] *adj.* **1** mentally or physically disturbed. 당황한; 낭패한; (몸이) 탈이 난. **2** overturned. 뒤집힌; 전복한. [up-]

upset price [ˊ– –] *n.* the lowest selling price at an auction. 경매의 최저가.

up·shot [ʌ́pʃɑ̀t / -ʃɔ̀t] *n.* Ⓒ 《*the* ~》 the conclusion; the result. 결론; 결과. ¶ *the* ~ *of the whole trouble* 모든 분쟁의 결과 / *What was the* ~ *of all that talk?* 그 모든 이야기는 결론이 어떻게 났나.

***up·side** [ʌ́psàid] *n.* 《*the* ~》 the upper side or part. 위쪽; 상부. [*up*]

up·side-down [ʌ́psàiddáun] *adv.* **1** having what should be on the top at the bottom. 거꾸로; 뒤집혀. ¶ *Turn the box* ~. 상자를 덮어 놔라 / *The slice of bread and butter fell* ~ *on the floor.* 버터에 구운 빵 조각이 마루에 떨어져 뒤집혔다. **2** 《*fig.*》 in complete confusion or disorder. 엉망이 되어; 어지럽혀져. ¶ *The children turned the house* ~. 아이들이 집 안을 엉망으로 만들었다. —*adj.* in total disorder. 엉망이 된. ¶ *an* ~ *arrange-*

ment 뒤죽박죽의 배열.

up·stage [ʌ́pstéidʒ] *adj.* **1** at the back of the stage. 무대 안쪽의. **2** 《*colloq.*》 aloof; stand-offish; haughty. 초연한; 냉담한; 도도한. — *adv.* toward or at the back of the stage. 무대 안쪽에〔으로〕. [*up*]

:up·stairs [ʌ́pstέərz] *adv.* **1** up the stairs; on an upper floor. 위층에(서); 2층에(서) (opp. downstairs). ¶ *Go ~ and look at the view.* 위층에 가서 경치를 내다봐라 / *He is ~ in bed.* 그는 2층 침대에 누워 있다. **2** 《*colloq.*》 (of aircraft) at a high altitude. 고공에. — *adj.* on an upper floor. 위층〔2층〕의. ¶ *an ~ room* / *an ~ lavatory* 2층 화장실. — *n. pl.* 《usu. used as *sing.*》 an upper story or stories. 위층; 2층. ¶ *The ~ of this house is entirely rented.* 이 집 2층은 모두 세를 줬다.

up·stand·ing [ʌ̀pstǽndiŋ] *adj.* standing upright; honorable. 똑바로 선; 훌륭한.

up·start [ʌ́pstɑ́ːrt] *n.* Ⓒ 《*contempt.*》 a person who has suddenly risen to wealth or power; a conceited person. 벼락 출세한 사람; 벼락 부자; 건방진 놈. ¶ *A crowd of upstarts pushed themselves into high place after the war.* 벼락 출세한 무리들이 전쟁이 끝나자 고위직에 들어앉았다. — *adj.* suddenly risen to wealth or power; conceited. 벼락 출세한; 벼락 부자의; 오만한. ¶ *these ~ pushers into society* 사회에 진출한 이들 벼락 출세자들. — *vt., vi.* (P6; 1) start up. 갑자기 일어서(게 하)다. [up-]

up·stream [ʌ́pstríːm] *adv., adj.* against the current of a stream. 상류에〔의〕; 흐름을 거슬러 올라가(는)(opp. downstream).

·up-to-date [ʌ́ptədéit] *adj.* **1** extending to or including the present time. 최근〔현대〕까지의. **2** of the present time; of the newest sort. 최근의; 최신의; 현대의(cf. *out-of-date*). ¶ *an ~ hair style* 최신의 헤어스타일 / *This factory uses the most ~ methods.* 이 공장은 최신식 방법을 쓰고 있다. [*up*]

up-to-the-min·ute [ʌ́ptəðəmínit] *adj.* modern; latest; very modern. 최근의; 최신의.

up·town [ʌ́ptáun] *adv.* (opp. downtown) **1** in or to the upper part of a town or city. 높은 지대에〔로〕. **2** 《U.S.》 in or to the residential portion of a town or city. 주택 지구에〔로〕. ¶ *He went ~.* — *adj.* of or in the upper part of a town or city. 높은 지대의. — *n.* ⓊⒸ the upper part of a town or city. 높은 지대.

up·turn [ʌptə́ːrn] *vt.* (P6) turn up; throw up. …을 위로 향하게 하다; 파헤치다; 뒤집다. ¶ *~ one's face* 얼굴을 쳐들다. — [ʌ́ptəːrn] *n.* Ⓒ an upward turn; a change for the better. 상향; 호전. ¶ *an ~ in business activity* 상황(商況)의 호전 / *an ~ in prices* 물가 상승.

:up·ward [ʌ́pwərd] *adj.* moving toward a higher place; in a higher position. 위로 향한; 상승의; 위쪽의(opp. downward). ¶ *cast an ~ glance* 치떠보다 / *an ~ tendency* 상승 경향 / *the constant ~ movement of prices* 물가의 꾸준한 상승세 / *an ~ trend in social customs and manners* 사회 풍습의 향상 추세. — *adv.* toward a higher place; toward a higher rank, amount, etc.; above; more. 위쪽으로; 위를 향해; …이상; 이후. ¶ *from his youth ~* 그의 소싯적부터 / *children of six years and ~,* 6세 이상의 아이들 / *The boy climbed ~ till he reached the apple.* 소년은 사과가 손에 닿는 데까지 올라갔다 / *The explorers followed the river ~.* 탐험대는 내륙쪽으로 강을 거슬러 올라갔다 / *He looked ~ at the sky.* 하늘을 쳐다보았다. [up-]

upward of, more than. …보다 많이; …이상.

up·wards [ʌ́pwərdz] *adv.* =upward.

U·ral-Al·ta·ic [júərəlæltéiik] *adj.* **1** of the Urals and Altai. 우랄알타이(지역)의. **2** pertaining to a great family of agglutinative languages or the people whose mother tongues are combined in it. 우랄알타이 어족의.

U·rals [júərəlz] *n. pl.* 《*the U-*》 a range or chain of mountains in Russia, between Europe and Asia. 우랄 산맥. [Place]

u·ra·ni·um [juəréiniəm] *n.* Ⓤ a heavy, white, radioactive metallic element. 우라늄. [Gk. *ouranos* heaven]

ur·ban [ə́ːrbən] *adj.* **1** of or belonging to cities or towns. 도시〔도회〕의. ¶ *an ~ district* 도시 지역 / *~ life* 도시 생활. **2** living in cities. 도시에 사는. ¶ *the ~ population* 도시 인구. **3** characteristic of cities. 도시풍의; 도시 특유의. **4** accustomed to cities. 도시(생활)에 익숙한. [L. *urbs* town]

urban renewal, a renewal of a town or city. 도시 재개발.

ur·bane [əːrbéin] *adj.* polite; refined; elegant. 예의바른; 점잖은; 우아한. [↑]

ur·ban·i·ty [əːrbǽnəti] *n.* (*pl.* **-ties**) **1** Ⓤ the state of being urbane; politeness; refinement. 우아; 정중; 품위. **2** 《*pl.*》 polite manners. 예의.

ur·ban·i·za·tion [ə̀ːrbənizéiʃən / -nai-] *n.* Ⓤ the act of urbanizing; the state of being urbanized. 도시〔도회〕화.

ur·ban·ize, 《Brit.》 **-ise** [ə́ːrbənàiz] *vt.* (P6) change (the character of a rural district) into an urban one. …을 도시화하다.

ur·chin [ə́ːrtʃin] *n.* Ⓒ **1** a mischievous small boy. 개구쟁이. **2** a poor, ragged child. 부랑아. **3** =sea urchin. [L. *ericius* hedgehog]

Ur·du [úərduː, –́, ə́ːr-] *n.* Ⓤ Hindustani. 우르두어(語). [Hind.]

u·re·a [júəriə] *n.* Ⓤ a substance found in urine. 요소(尿素). [Gk. *ouron* urine]

u·re·mi·a [juəríːmiə] *n.* a poisoned condition resulting from the accumulation in the blood of waste products. 요독증(尿毒症). [↑]

u·re·thra [juərí:θrə] *n.* 《anat.》 the duct by which urine is discharged. 요도(尿道) ● **u·re·thral** [-θrəl] *adj.* [↑]

:**urge** [ə:rdʒ] *vt.* **1** (P6,7,13) drive (something) with force; push forward. …을 몰다; 몰아대다; 다그치다. ¶ ~ *a horse on* 말을 몰아대다 / *I urged the people into another room.* 사람들을 다그쳐 다른 방으로 들어가게 하였다 / ~ *one's way* 길을 재촉하다. **2** (P6,7,13,20) try to influence (someone) by arguments; try hard to persuade; ask earnestly. …을 강력히 권하다; (동기·필요 따위가) …을 하도록 강제하다; 격려하다. ¶ *Please don't* ~ *me to eat more.* 더 먹으라고 너무 권하지 마시오 / *I did it, urged by necessity.* 필요에 쫓겨 어쩔 수 없이 그것을 했다 / *She urged him to accept the offer.* 그녀는 그에게 강권하여 그 제안을 받아들이도록 했다 / ~ *(on) the crew to greater action* 선원을 격려하여 더욱 활약케 하다. **3** (P6,13) 《*upon*》 speak one's opinion about (something) strongly and earnestly; argue earnestly. …을 주장하다; 역설하다; 강요하다. ¶ ~ *a petition* 집요하게 탄원하다 / ~ *the difficulty of the situation* 시국의 어려움을 역설하다 / *The speaker urged immediate action against the illegal regime.* 연사는 비합법 정권에 대항하는 즉각적인 행동을 역설했다 / *Let me* ~ *upon you the importance of this measure.* 당신에게 이 조치의 중요성을 강조하는 바이오.
—*n.* CU a driving force or impulse; a strong motive. 충동; 자극; 강한 동기. ¶ *the sex* ~ 성적 충동 / *have an* ~ *to go* 가고 싶은 강한 충동을 느끼다 / *I had a sudden* ~ *to tell the boss what I thought of him.* 갑자기 나는 사장에게 그에 대한 내 생각을 말해 주고 싶은 충동을 느꼈다. [L. *urgeo*]

ur·gen·cy [ə́:rdʒənsi] *n.* U **1** the quality or state of being urgent; need for action. 절박; 화급; 긴급. ¶ *a matter of great* ~ 긴급을 요하는 문제. **2** the act of urging. 강요; 역설. [↓]

·**ur·gent** [ə́:rdʒənt] *adj.* **1** calling for immediate action or attention; pressing. 긴급한; 절박한. ¶ *an* ~ *question* 긴급 문제 / *on* ~ *business* 급한 일로 / *be in* ~ *need of help* 신속한 도움이 필요하다 / *It's not* ~. *It can wait untill tomorrow.* 그 일은 급하지 않다. 내일까지 기다려도 된다. **2** insistent; persistent. 끈덕진; 귀찮게 조르는. ¶ *an* ~ *suitor* 귀찮게 조르는 구혼자 / *He was* ~ *in his demands.* 그는 자기 요구에 집요했다. [→urge]

ur·gent·ly [ə́:rdʒəntli] *adv.* **1** in an urgent manner 〔degree〕. 긴급히. **2** insistently. 집요하게.

u·ri·nal [júərənəl] *n.* **1** a container for urine. 요강. **2** a place for passing urine. 소변소(小便所); 오줌 누는 곳. [→urine]

u·ri·nar·y [júərənèri] *adj.* of urine. 오줌의; 비뇨의. ¶ *the* ~ *organs* 비뇨기.

u·ri·nate [júərənèit] *vi.* (P1) pass urine. 오줌 누다.

u·rine [júərin] *n.* U the fluid formed in the kidneys and eliminated from the body as waste. 오줌; 소변. [L. ūrīna]

urn [ə:rn] *n.* C **1** a vase with a foot or pedestal, esp. a large one for holding the ashes of the dead. 항아리; 단지; (특히) 뼈단지; 골호(骨壺). ¶ *Urns were used in Greece and Rome to hold the ashes of the dead.* 그리스, 로마 시대엔 죽은이의 재를 담는 뼈단지를 썼다. **2** a large metal container in which tea or coffee is made and kept hot. 커피〔차〕 끓이는 기구〔포트〕. [L.]

u·ros·co·py [juərάskəpi / -rɔ́s-] *n.* 《med.》 an examination of the urine. 요(尿)검사; 소변 검사. [→urine, -scope]

Ur·sa [ə́:rsə] *n.* =Ursa Major 〔Minor〕.

Ursa Major [ㅗ- ㅗ-] *n.* 《astron.》 the Great Bear, the most prominent northern constellation, containing the seven stars that form the Big Dipper. 큰곰자리. [L. =bear]

Ursa Minor [ㅗ- ㅗ-] *n.* 《astron.》 the Little or Lesser Bear, the northernmost constellation, containing the stars that form the Little Dipper, the outermost of which, at the end of the handle, is Polaris. 작은곰자리. [↑]

U·ru·guay [júərəgwài, -wèi] *n.* a country in the southeastern part of South America. 우루과이.

:**us** [əs, ʌs] *pron.* **1** (*obj.* case of **we**) 우리들을; 우리들에게. ¶ *Father took* ~ *to the zoo.* 아버지께서는 우리들에게 동물원 구경을 시켜 주셨다 / *He gave* ~ *a lecture.* 그는 우리들에게 훈계〔잔소리〕를 했다. **2** 《used by a king, an editor, etc.》 =me. **3** 《as *predicative*》 《*colloq.*》 =we. 우리(는). ¶ *It's* ~. 그건 우리다. [E.]

:**U.S.A.** the United States of America.

us·a·ble [jú:zəbl] *adj.* able or fit to be used. 쓸 수 있는; 편리한. [→use]

us·age [jú:sidʒ, -zidʒ] *n.* **1** U the act or way of using; treatment. 사용(법); 대우. ¶ *annual* ~ 연간 사용량 / *ill-usage* 학대; 혹사 / *suffer ill* ~ 학대를 받다 / *be damaged by rough* ~ 마구 써서 망가지다 / *Such delicate instruments will not stand rough* ~. 이런 정교한 기계(器械)들은 난폭하게 사용하면 곧 망가진다. **2** UC the customary way of using words. 어법; (언어의) 관용법. ¶ *modern English* ~ 현대 영어 관용법 / *Expressions used by good writers are mostly good usages.* 훌륭한 작가들이 쓴 표현법이 대개는 옳은 어법이다. **3** UC a long-continued practice; habit; custom. 습관; 관습; 관례. ¶ *social* ~ 사교상의 관례 / *according to* ~ 관례에 따라 / *the usages of the last twenty years* 과거 20년간에 걸친 관습 / *keep old usages alive* 옛 관습을 지키다 / *Strangers living in a country should learn its usages.* 낯선 고장에서 사는 사람은 그 곳의 관습을 익혀야

한다. [→use]

us·ance [jú:zəns] *n.* ⟪comm.⟫ the length of time allowed by custom or usage for the payment of foreign bills or exchange. 유전스⟪환어음의 지급 기한⟫. ¶ *bills drawn at* ~ (관습) 기한부 어음. [→use]

:use [ju:z] *vt.* **1** (P6) put (something) into action or service; employ. …을 쓰다; 사용〔이용〕하다. ¶ ~ *tools* 연장을 쓰다 / *The spinning-wheel was used by early American settlers.* 물레는 초기 미국 이주민들에 의해 사용됐다 / *We* ~ *a knife to cut meat.* 고기를 자를 때 칼을 쓴다 / *May I* ~ *your telephone?* 전화 좀 쓸까요 / *During the war the castle was used for keeping prisoners in.* 전쟁 중 그 성은 포로들을 수용하는 데 썼다. **2** (P6) exercise; practice. …을 행사하다; 활용하다. ¶ ~ *care* 주의하다 / ~ *one's brains* 머리를 쓰다; 잘 생각하다 / ~ *one's common sense* 상식을 활용하다 / ~ *all one's skill* 가진 모든 솜씨를 동원하다 / ~ *ears* 듣다 / ~ *force* 폭력에 호소하다 / ~ *one's utmost endeavors* 최선의 노력을 다하다. **3** (P7) conduct or behave oneself toward (someone); treat. …을 다루다; 대우하다. ¶ ~ *someone well*〔*ill*〕 아무를 친절히 대하다〔학대하다〕 / *He has used me like a dog.* 그는 나를 개 취급했다 / *Use others as you would have them* ~ *you.* 남들이 너를 대해 주기를 바라듯 그들을 대접해라 / *He considered that he had been ill used.* 그는 자기가 푸대접을 받아왔다고 생각했다. **4** (P6,7) expend; consume. …을 소비하다. ¶ *We* ~ *much coal every day.* 매일 석탄을 많이 쓴다 / *We used lots of money to buy a new car.* 새 차를 사는 데 적지 않은 돈을 썼다 / *Do you* ~ *sugar in your coffee?* 커피에 설탕을 넣을까요. **5** (P6) employ (something) habitually. …을 습관적으로 쓰다. ¶ *She often used anodyne for a headache.* 그녀는 두통에 종종 진통제를 썼다 / *I think he's using drugs.* 그 사람이 마약을 사용하는 모양이다. **6** (P6) use (someone) selfishly for one's own purpose; exploit. (아무를) 이기적인 목적으로 이용하다. ¶ *He was always using his younger sister.* 그는 늘 제 누이동생을 이용해 먹더군 / *He's just using you for his own ends.* 그는 너를 단지 자기 목적에 이용하고 있다.

— *vi.* (P1) ⟪~ *to do*⟫ be accustomed. ⇨used[2].

use up, consume completely. 다 써버리다; 지치게 하다. ¶ *All the gasoline is used up.* 가솔린이 한 방울도 안 남았다 / *feel used up* 몹시 피곤하다 / *Try not to* ~ *up all the flour.* 밀가루를 다 쓰지 않도록 해라.

— [ju:s] *n.* Ⓤ **1** the act of using or employing; the way of using. 사용; 이용; 용법. ¶ *He made frequent* ~ *of quotations from the Bible.* 그는 성경 구절을 자주 이용했다 / *It can be enriched or spoiled by its* ~. 사용법에 따라 좋게도 나쁘게도 된다 / *The* ~ *of the telephone is growing very rapidly.* 전화 이용이 급속히 증가하고 있다 / *teach the* ~ *of tools* 연장 쓰는 법을 가르치다 / *a wasteful* ~ *of valuable resources* 귀중한 자원의 낭비 / *She put her knowledge of German to good* ~. 그녀는 독일어 지식을 유용하게 사용했다. **2** the right or permission to use. 사용권; 사용 허가. ¶ *the* ~ *of the estate for life* (한) 토지에 대한 평생 사용권 / *He gave us the* ~ *of his name.* 그는 우리에게 자기 이름을 써도 좋다고 허락했다 / *He put the* ~ *of his house at my disposal.* 그는 자기 집을 내 마음대로 쓰도록 허락했다. **3** the power, ability, or opportunity to use. 사용할 힘〔능력〕. ¶ *She lost the* ~ *of her left eye.* 그녀는 왼쪽 눈의 시력을 잃었다 / *regain the* ~ *of one's injured arm* 부상당한 팔의 힘을 회복하다. **4** ⒸⓊ the need, purpose, or reason to use; practical worth; usefulness. 사용할 필요; 용도; 사용 목적; 유용; 효용. ¶ *Will there be any further* ~ *for big battleships in war?* 전쟁에서 대형 전함을 더 이상 쓸 필요가 있을까 / *What* ~ *does this tool have*〔*serve*〕? 이 연장은 무엇에 쓰이나 / *a machine with many uses* 용도가 많은 기계 / *It's no* ~ *crying.* 울어도 소용없다. **5** ⓊⒸ custom; habit; practice. 습관; 관습. ¶ *according to an ancient* ~ 고대 관습에 따라 / *It was his* ~ *to walk ten miles everyday.* 매일 10마일을 걷는 것이 그의 습관이었다. **6** ⟪religion⟫ Ⓤ a special ritual. (교회마다의) 특유한 의식. **7** Ⓤ the profit from lands held in trust for another. (신탁 토지의) 수익. [L. *ūsus, ūti*]

bring into use, begin to use (something). …을 쓰기 시작하다. ¶ *Atomic energy should be brought into greater* ~ *for peaceful purposes.* 원자력은 평화적 목적에 더욱 크게 쓰여져야 한다.

come into use, begin to be used. 쓰이게 되다. ¶ *This word has lately come into common* ~. 이 낱말은 최근에 와서 흔히 쓰이게 됐다.

have no use for, ⟪*colloq.*⟫ see no merits in; dislike strongly. …의 필요가 없다; …은 아주 싫다. ¶ *I have no* ~ *for his services.* 그의 도움을 받을 필요가 없다 / *I have no* ~ *for flatterers.* 난 아첨꾼들은 딱 질색이다.

in use, being used. 쓰여져. ¶ *The compass was already in* ~. 나침반은 이미 쓰이고 있었다.

make use of, use. …을 사용〔이용〕하다. ¶ *She makes good* ~ *of her times.* 그녀는 시간을 잘 이용하고 있다.

of use, useful. 유용한; 쓸모 있는. ¶ *It is of great* ~. 그것은 대단히 쓸모가 있다.

out of use, no longer used. 쓰이지 않게 되어. ¶ *The custom is*〔*has fallen*〕 *out of* ~. 그 관례는 이젠 안 쓰인다.

put to use =make use of.

with use, by using constantly. 계속〔오래〕 사용하여. ¶ *This carpet has got worn with* ~. 이 융단은 오래 써서 해졌다.

:used[1] [ju:zd] *adj.* **1** that has been used; secondhand; no longer new. 써서 낡은; 중고의. ¶ ~ *tickets* 쓰고 난 헌 차표〔입장권 따

위] / *He bought a ~ car.* 중고차를 샀다. **2** [ju:st] 《*~ to doing*》 accustomed. …에 익숙한. ¶ *You'll soon get ~ to getting up early.* 일찍 일어나는 데 곧 익숙해질 것이다 / *I am ~ to his scolding.* 그의 잔소리엔 이골이 났다 / *I'm not ~ to spicy food.* 나는 향신료를 넣은 음식에 익숙지 않다.

:used² [ju:st] *vi.* (P4) 《*~ to do*》 was accustomed. 늘 …하곤 했다; …하는 것이 예사였다. ¶ *I ~ to drive a Ford.* 나는 늘 포드차를 몰았다 / *There ~ to be a tall tree here.* 전에는 여기에 큰 나무가 한 그루 있었다 / *We ~ to walk to school.* 우린 학교에 걸어다니는 것이 예사였다 / *She use(d)n't* [《*colloq.* or U.S.》 *didn't use*] *to like chocolate.* 그녀는 초콜릿을 좋아하지 않았다 / *He doesn't work here now, but he ~ to.* 그는 지금 여기서 일하지 않으나, 전에는 했었다.

:use·ful [júːsfəl] *adj.* **1** of use; helpful; serviceable. 유용[유익]한; 쓸모 있는(opp. useless). ¶ *~ books for young students* 학생들에게 유익한 책들 / *make oneself generally ~* 여러 모로 도움을 주다 / *give ~ advice* 유익한 충고를 하다. **2** 《*sl.*》 very capable; effective. 아주 유능한; 효과적인. ¶ *She is pretty ~ at cooking.* 그녀는 요리를 썩 잘한다.

use·ful·ly [júːsfəli] *adv.* in a useful manner. 유용[유익]하게.

use·ful·ness [júːsfəlnis] *n.* Ⓤ the state of being useful. 유용; 유익. ¶ *This old radio has outlived its ~.* 이 오래된 라디오가 이제는 제구실을 못 하게 되었다.

:use·less [júːslis] *adj.* **1** of no use; worthless. 쓸모 없는; 무익한. ¶ *It's ~ to complain.* =*It's ~ complaining.* 우는소리해야 소용 없다 / *It is ~ to ask him.* 그에게 부탁해도 소용 없다 / *Resistance is ~.* 반항해야 소용없다. **2** 《*colloq.*》 unfit for anything; not able to do anything properly. 아무 일도 제대로 못하는; 아무 짝에도 못쓸. ¶ *You're ~! You've done it wrong again!* 이 병신아, 또 틀렸구나.

use·less·ly [júːslisli] *adv.* in a useless manner. 쓸데없이; 무익하게.

use·less·ness [júːslisnis] *n.* Ⓤ the state of being useless. 무익; 무용; 쓸모 없음.

us·er [júːzər] *n.* **1** Ⓒ a person who uses. 쓰는 사람; 사용자. ¶ *The users of this pencil will probably be disappointed.* 이 연필을 쓰는 사람은 아마 실망할 것이다. **2** Ⓤ 《law》 use or enjoyment of a right. 권리 향수(享受). [→use]

U-shaped [júːʃèipt] *adj.* having the shape of the letter U. U자형(形)의.

ush·er [ʌ́ʃər] *n.* Ⓒ **1** a person who shows people to their seats in a church, a theater, etc. (교회·극장 등의) 안내인. **2** 《Brit. *arch.*》 an assistant teacher in a school. (학교의) 조교사(助教師).
— *vt.* (P7,13) walk before and guide; escort; conduct. …을 안내하다; 호위[선도]하다. ¶ *I ushered him to a seat.* 그를 자리에 안내했다 / *I was at length ushered to his presence.* 가까스로 그의 면전에 안내되었다. [L. *ostium* door]

usher in, **a**) lead into a room. 방 안으로 안내하다. **b**) 《*poet.*》 herald. …을 미리 알리다; 선도하다. ¶ *the song of birds that ushers in the dawn* 새벽을 알리는 새 소리 / *The bombing of Hiroshima ushered in the nuclear age.* 히로시마의 폭격으로 원자 시대가 열렸다.

USIS United States Information Service.

U.S.M. United States Mail; United States Marine.

U.S.M.A. United States Military Academy.

USMC United States Marine Corps [Commission].

U.S.N. United States Navy.

U.S.N.A United States Naval Academy.

U.S.N.G. United States National Guard.

USO United Service Organization.

U.S.S. United States Senate; United States Ship [Steamer].

:u·su·al [júːʒuəl] *adj.* common; ordinary; customary. 보통의; 일상의; 통례의. ¶ *as is ~ with him* 그에게는 언제나 있는 일이지만; 그는 언제나 그렇지만 / *He got up earlier than ~.* 그는 평소보다 일찍 일어났다 / *He asked the ~ questions.* 그는 늘 하는 질문을 했다 / *It is ~ for him to sit up late at night.* 그가 밤늦도록 안 자는 것은 예사로운 일이다 / *This work isn't up to your ~ standard.* 이 작품은 네 평소의 것만 못하다. [→use]

as usual, in the usual manner. 평소와 같이; 여느 때처럼. ¶ *She was late, as ~.* 여느 때처럼 그녀는 늦었다.

the usual (***thing***)***,*** that which is usu. done, said, received, etc. 늘 하는 일[말 따위]. ¶ *He says the ~ things.* 그는 늘 똑같은 말을 한다.

:u·su·al·ly [júːʒuəli] *adv.* according to what is usual; customarily. 보통; 흔히; 평소(대로). ¶ *We are ~ in bed by ten.* 우리는 늘 열시까지는 잠자리에 든다 / *It's more than ~ crowded today.* 오늘은 평소보다 붐빈다.

u·su·rer [júːʒərər] *n.* Ⓒ a person who lends money at an excessively high rate of interest. 고리(高利) 대금업자. [→usury]

u·su·ri·ous [juːzjúəriəs] *adj.* **1** taking extremely high interest for the use of money. 고리의; 고리를 받아먹는. **2** of usury. 고리 대금(貸金)의.

u·surp [juːzə́ːrp] *vt.* (P6) take possession of (power, position, authority, etc.) by force or unjust means. (권력·지위 등)을 빼앗다; 강탈[찬탈]하다. ¶ *Henry IV usurped the throne of England.* 헨리 4세가 영국의 왕위를 찬탈하였다. — *vi.* (P1) 《*upon, on*》 commit usurption. 침해하다. [L. *usurpo*]

u·sur·pa·tion [jùːzərpéiʃən] *n.* ⓊⒸ the act of usurping. 강탈; 찬탈; 횡령. [↑]

u·su·ry [júːʒəri] *n.* Ⓤ **1** the act of lending money at an excessively high rate of interest. 고리로 돈을 빌려줌. **2** a very high rate of interest. 고리. [L. *ūsus* use]

u·ten·sil [ju:ténsəl] *n.* Ⓒ an instrument or tool used in cooking, housework, etc. 가정 용품; 부엌 세간; 기구; 도구. ¶ *farming* ~ 농기구 / *Pens and pencils are writing utensils.* 펜, 연필은 필기구이다 / *Pots, pans, and kettles are kitchen utensils.* 단지, 프라이팬, 주전자 등은 부엌 세간이다. [→use]

u·ter·i [jú:tərài] *n.* pl. of **uterus.**

u·ter·us [jú:tərəs] *n.* Ⓒ (*pl.* **-ter·i**) the womb. 자궁. [L.]

u·til·i·tar·i·an [ju:tìlətέəriən] *adj.* **1** of utility. 공리적(功利的)인. **2** of utilitarians or their ideas. 공리주의(자)의. **3** aiming at usefulness rather than beauty, style, etc. 실리적인; 실용의. — *n.* Ⓒ a person who believes in utilitarianism. 공리주의자. [→use]

u·til·i·tar·i·an·ism [ju:tìlətέəriənìzəm] *n.* Ⓤ **1** the doctrine or belief that the purpose of all action should be to bring about the greatest happiness of the greatest number of people. 공리설; 공리주의. **2** the doctrine or belief that anything is good when it is useful. 실용주의.

***u·til·i·ty** [ju:tíləti] *n.* (*pl.* **-ties**) **1** Ⓤ the quality or state of being suitable for use; usefulness. 쓸모가 있음; 유익; 효용. **2** 《usu. *pl.*》 a useful thing. 유용물. **3** Ⓒ 《U.S.》 an organization that performs public service to a community; a public service. 공익 사업. ¶ *Railways, tram-cars' and bus lines, and gas and electric companies are public utilities.* 철도, 전철 및 버스 회사들과 가스 및 전력 회사들을 공익 사업체라 한다. — *adj.* (of clothes, furniture, etc.) severely practical, made in standard styles. (옷 따위가) 실용적인; 실용 본위의. [→use]

utility man [–ˊ––ˋ] *n.* **1** an actor of the smallest parts in plays. 단역. **2** 《baseball》 a player expected to serve in any capacity. 만능(보결) 선수.

u·ti·li·za·tion [jù:təlizéiʃən] *n.* Ⓤ the act of utilizing; the state of being utilized. 이용(상태). [↓]

***u·ti·lize** [jú:təlàiz] *vt.* (P6) use (something) for a practical purpose; make use of (something). …을 이용하다; 활용하다. ¶ *Surgery now utilizes X-rays.* 오늘날 외과에서는 엑스선이 활용되고 있다. [→use]

***ut·most** [ʌ́tmòust] *adj.* **1** most distant; farthest. 가장 먼. ¶ *to the ~ ends of the earth* 땅 끝까지 / *He walked to the ~ edge of the cliff.* 그는 벼랑의 맨 끝까지 걸어갔다. **2** of the highest degree; greatest. 최대(최고)의; 극도의. ¶ *with the ~ pleasure* 무한히 기뻐서 / *Sunshine is of the ~ importance to health.* 햇빛은 건강에 더할 나위 없이 중요한 것이다 / *a matter of the ~ concern* 최대의 관심사. — *n.* 《*the* ~ or *one's* ~》 the most that is possible; extreme limit or degree. 최대한; 최고도. ¶ *at the ~* 기껏해야 / *I did my ~ to prevent it.* 그걸 막으려고 나는 전력(최선)을 다했다 / *to the ~* 극도로; 극력 / *That is the ~ I can do.* 그게 내가 할 수 있는 한계다 / *get the ~ out of* …을 최대로 활용하다. [=*outmost*]

***U·to·pi·a** [ju:tóupiə] *n.* **1** an imaginary island described in 'Utopia' by Sir Thomas More. 유토피아. **2** Ⓒ 《often *u-*》 an ideal place or state. 이상향. [Gk. =no-place]

***U·to·pi·an** [ju:tóupiən] *adj.* **1** of or like Utopia. 유토피아의(같은). **2** 《often *u-*》 idealistic; visionary. 이상적인; 몽상적인. — *n.* Ⓒ **1** a person of Utopia 유토피아의 주민. **2** 《often *u-*》 an idealist; an eager but impractical reformer. 몽상가; 공상적인 사회 개량가.

***ut·ter**[1] [ʌ́tər] *adj.* 《as *attributive*》 complete; entire; absolute. 완전한; 전적인; 철저한. ¶ ~ *darkness* 칠흑 같은 어둠 / ~ *surprise* 대경 실색 / *an ~ stranger* 생판 모르는 사람 / *What ~ rubbish he talks!* 무슨 당찮은 개소리야. [*out*]

***ut·ter**[2] [ʌ́tər] *vt.* (P6) **1** speak; express. …을 말하다; 이야기하다; 표현하다. ¶ ~ *one's feelings* 자기 느낌을 말하다 / ~ *the truth* (*a lie*) 진실을 말하다(거짓말을 하다). **2** give out; produce (a cry, groan, sigh). (신음·한숨 소리 등)을 내다. ¶ ~ *a sigh* 한숨을 쉬다 / *He uttered a cry of pain.* 아파서 소리를 질렀다 / *The wounded man uttered a groan.* 부상자는 신음 소리를 냈다 / *She didn't ~ a word all night.* 그녀는 밤새도록 말 한 마디 안 했다. **3** put (bad checks or money) into circulation. (위조 지폐 따위)를 사용하다. ¶ ~ *false coin* 가짜 동전을 사용하다. [*out*]

***ut·ter·ance** [ʌ́tərəns] *n.* **1** Ⓤ the act of uttering; expression in words. 입 밖에 냄; 발언. ¶ *She has not yet given ~ her opinion.* 그녀는 아직 자기 소견을 말하지 않았다. **2** Ⓤ 《sometimes *an* ~》 a way of speaking. 말씨; 어조. ¶ *defective ~* 불완전한 발음; 눌변(訥辯) / *a clear ~* 똑똑한 말씨. **3** Ⓒ something uttered; a spoken word. (입 밖에 낸) 말; 언설. ¶ *someone's public ~* 아무의 공적인 말.

***ut·ter·ly** [ʌ́tərli] *adv.* completely; absolutely. 전적으로; 아주. ¶ ~ *useless* 전혀 쓸모 없는 / *You are ~ crazy.* 너 아주 미쳤구나 / *He was ~ charmed by her.* 그는 그녀에게 홀딱 반했다.

ut·ter·most [ʌ́tərmòust] *adj., n.* Ⓤ 《*the* ~》 utmost. 최대한(의); 최고(의). ¶ *to the ~ of one's power* 힘껏; 극력 / *to the ~ ends of the earth* 땅 끝까지. [*utter*[1]]

u·vu·la [jú:vjələ] *n.* Ⓒ (*pl.* **-las** or **-lae**) 《anat.》 a small piece of flesh hanging at the back of the throat. 목젖; 현옹(수)(懸壅(垂)). [L. *uva* grapecluster]

u·vu·lae [jú:vjəlì:] *n.* pl. of **uvula.**

u·vu·lar [jú:vjələr] *adj.* 《phon.》 pronounced with vibration of the uvula. 연구개음(軟口蓋音)의. [↑]

ux·o·ri·ous [ʌksɔ́:riəs] *adj.* too fond of one's wife. 아내에게 무른. [L. *uxor* wife]

v V

V, v [vi:] *n.* Ⓒ (*pl.* **V's, Vs, v's, vs** [vi:z]) **1** the 22nd letter of the English alphabet. 영어 알파벳의 스물두째 글자. **2** something shaped like the letter V. V자 모양(의 것). ¶ *the V sign.* **3** the Roman number for five. (로마 숫자의) 5.
V 《chem.》 vanadium; vector; velocity.
V, v volt; volume.
V. Venerable; Viscount.
v. valve; ventral; verse; version; versus (L. =against); vide (L. =see); village; violin; vocative; voice; voltage; von (G. =of); verb; very.
V.A. Veterans Administration; Vicar Apostolic; Vice-Admiral; Victoria and Albert.
vac [væk] *n.* **1** 《Brit. *colloq.*》 vacation. 방학. **2** a vacuum cleaner. 진공 청소기.
vac. vacuum.
va·can·cy [véikənsi] *n.* **1** Ⓤ the state or condition of being vacant; emptiness. 빔; 공허. ¶ *look on the ~ of the fields* 빈 들판을 바라다보다. **2** Ⓒ an unoccupied space or position. 빈 자리; 공석; 결원. ¶ *His death made a ~ in the business.* 그가 죽어서 사업장에 결원이 생겼다 / *when a ~ occurs* 결원이 생길 때. **3** Ⓒ a room, space, or apartment for rent. 빈 방; 빈 집; 공터. ¶ *There is still a ~ for another house in the new road.* 새로 난 도로에는 집 한 채를 더 지을 공터가 있다. **4** Ⓤ idleness; emptiness of mind. 허탈; 방심. ¶ *a look of ~ on his face* 그의 허탈한 표정. **5** Ⓒ a gap; a blank or break. 간극(間隙); 틈. ¶ *It will fill a ~ in our knowledge.* 그것은 우리 지식의 공백을 메워 줄 것이다. [*vacant*]
***va·cant** [véikənt] *adj.* **1** ⓐ empty; not filled; not lived in by anyone. 비어 있는; 사는 사람이 없는. ¶ *~ space* 빈 공간 / *There are not many situations ~.* 빈 자리가 많지 않다 / *a ~ house* 빈 집 / *the ~ regions of the country* 그 나라의 무인 지대 / *a ~ room* 빈 방. ⓑ not engaged or let. 쓰고 있지 않은. ¶ *not a room ~ in the hotel* 그 호텔에 빈 방이 없다 / *Is this seat ~?* 이 자리 비었소 / *many ~ seats in the theater* 극장의 많은 빈자리. **2** not occupied by work or business; not engaged. 한가한; 틈이 있는. ¶ *Keep a day next week ~ if you can.* 된다면 다음 주에 하루 시간을 내주게 / *~ hours* 한가한 시간 / *The job was advertised in the "Situations Vacant" column in the newspaper.* 그 일자리가 신문의 구인란에 났었다. **3** empty of thought or intelligence; idle; thoughtless. 멍청한; 얼빠진. ¶ *His mind seems ~.* 그는 얼빠진 것 같다 / *~ life* 무위한 생활 / *a ~ smile* [*look*] 맥빠진 미소[표정] / *look with ~ eyes* 멍청하게 바라보다. [L. *vaco* be empty]
be vacant of (=*be wanting in*) *something.* …이 비어 있다; …이 없다.
fall vacant, become unoccupied. (방·자리가) 비다; 공석이 되다.
va·cant·ly [véikəntli] *adv.* in a vacant manner; absent-mindedly. 멍하니; 멍청하게. ¶ *laugh ~* 바보처럼 웃다.
va·cate [véikeit / vəkéit] *vt.* (P6) leave (a room, a post, etc.) empty or unoccupied. (방·자리 등)을 비우다; 떠나가다; (직위 등)을 사퇴하다. ¶ *~ a house* / *The enemy vacated the town.* 적군이 마을에서 철수했다 / *He is expected to ~ his job soon.* 그는 머지 않아 직장을 그만 둘 모양이다 / *~ the throne* 왕위를 물러나다. — *vi.* give up a house, an office, a position, etc. 물러나다; 철수하다; 사직하다. [*vacant*]
:va·ca·tion [veikéiʃən, vək-] *n.* **1** ⒸⓊ a period of time for recreation and rest from work. 휴가. ¶ *the summer ~* 여름 휴가. **2** Ⓤ the act of vacating; resignation. (집·지위 등을) 비우기; 물러나기; 퇴직; 사직. ¶ *the ~ of his position.* — *vi.* (P1) 《U.S.》 take or spend a vacation. 휴가를 얻다[보내다].
va·ca·tion·ist [veikéiʃənist, vək-] *n.* Ⓒ 《U.S.》 a person who is taking a vacation. 휴가를 얻은 사람(=《Brit.》 holidayer).
vac·ci·nate [vǽksənèit] *vt.* (P6) give (someone) vaccine or some other preventive injection to protect him from smallpox or from a severe attack of any other disease. …에게 종두(種痘)하다; 예방[백신] 주사를 놓다. ¶ *be vaccinated against typhus* 발진 티푸스 예방 주사를 맞다. [→vaccine]
vac·ci·na·tion [vǽksənéiʃən] *n.* ⒸⓊ the act of vaccinating. 백신 주사; 종두. ¶ *take* [*undergo*] *~* 백신 주사를 맞다 / *Vaccination has made smallpox a very rare disease.* 종두로 천연두는 아주 희귀한 질병이 됐다.
vac·cine [vǽksi(:)n, -⌐] *n.* ⓊⒸ **1** the germs obtained from cowpox, used to protect a person from smallpox. 우두종(牛痘種). **2** any preparation of disease germs used in vaccination. 백신. [L. *vacca* cow]
vac·il·late [vǽsəlèit] *vi.* (P1,2) **1** swing to and fro; move to and fro. 흔들거리다; 흔들흔들하다. **2** be undecided in opinion or purpose. (마음)이 흔들리다. ¶ *~ between two courses* 두 노선을 방황하다. [L. *vacillo*]
vac·il·la·tion [vǽsəléiʃən] *n.* ⓊⒸ **1** the

V

act of vacillating. 흔들림; 동요. **2** unsteadiness of mind or opinion. (마음의) 동요; 우유 부단.

vac·u·a [vǽkjuə] *n.* pl. of **vacuum.**

va·cu·i·ty [vækjúːəti, və-] *n.* (*pl.* **-ties**) **1** Ⓤ emptiness of mind. (마음의) 공허. **2** Ⓒ an empty space. 빈 곳. **3** 《usu. *pl.*》 something foolish or absurd. 하찮은 일. [→vacant]

vac·u·ous [vǽkjuəs] *adj.* **1** containing nothing; empty. 빈; 공허한. **2** vacant in mind; without purpose; idle. 마음이 공허한; 얼빠진; 무위(無爲)의. ¶ *a ~ stare* 멍청한 시선 / *a selfish, ~ life* 이기적이고 무위한 생활. **3** unintelligent; foolish. 우둔한; 어리석은. ¶ *an idle and ~ fellow* 게으르고 우둔한 친구. [↑]

vac·u·um [vǽkjuəm, -kjəm] *n.* Ⓒ (*pl.* **-ums** or **vac·u·a**) **1** a space completely empty, without even air. 진공. **2** a machine used for cleaning; a vacuum cleaner. 진공 청소기. [↑]

vacuum bottle [⌐-- ⌐-] *n.* a glass container with a double wall to keep liquids hot or cold. 보온병.

vacuum cleaner [⌐-- ⌐-] *n.* a machine used for cleaning carpets, etc. by the act of sucking. 진공 청소기.

vacuum tube [⌐-- ⌐] *n.* 《electr.》 a tube from which all the air has been removed, used in radio sets to control the flow of electric currents. 진공관.

va·de me·cum [véidi míːkəm, váː-] *n.* **1** a useful thing which a person carries about with him. 필수 휴대품. **2** a guide book; a handbook. 편람; 안내서. [L.]

vag·a·bond [vǽgəbὰnd / -bɔ̀nd] *n.* Ⓒ **1** a person who wanders from place to place without purpose. 부랑인; 방랑자. **2** a bad, dishonest person. 건달; 불량배. ¶ *She called her husband a lazy old ~.* 그녀는 남편을 게으른 늙은 건달이라고 비난했다. — *adj.* **1** moving about without purpose; wandering from place to place. 방랑하는. ¶ *a ~ singer* 유랑 가객(歌客) / *lead a ~ life* 방랑 생활을 하다 / *~ habits* 방랑벽. **2** valueless; useless. 아무 쓸모 없는. ¶ *a ~ kind of fellow.* [L. *vagus* wandering]

vag·a·bond·age [vǽgəbὰndidʒ / -bɔ̀nd-] *n.* **1** the state or character of a vagabond; a vagabond life or habit. 방랑; 방랑 생활; 방랑벽. ¶ *the charm of ~ which some people feel* 어떤 사람들이 가지는 방랑 생활에 대한 유혹 / *take to ~* 방랑벽에 빠지다. **2** 《*collectively*》 vagabonds. 방랑자.

va·gar·i·ous [vəgέəriəs] *adj.* capricious; fanciful. 변덕스러운; 엉뚱한. [↓]

va·gar·y [véigəri, vəgέəri] *n.* Ⓒ (*pl.* **-garies**) a strange and fanciful act or thought; a passing fancy; a sudden fancy. 기발하고 엉뚱한 짓[생각]; 변덕스럽고 일시적인 생각. ¶ *the vagaries of a dream* 꿈의 허황됨. [→vague]

va·gran·cy [véigrənsi] *n.* Ⓤ **1** the act or state of wandering from place to place without purpose. 부랑(浮浪); 방랑. **2** 《*collectively*》 vagrants. 부랑인; 방랑객. ¶ *Vagrancy has increased since the war.* 전후에 부랑자가 늘었다. [↓]

va·grant [véigrənt] *n.* Ⓒ a person who wanders about, having no home; a wanderer. 부랑인; 방랑자[객]. — *adj.* **1** wandering about; unsettled. 방랑하는; 정처 없는. ¶ *a band of ~ beggars* 한떼의 떠돌이 걸인들 / *a ~ life* 유랑 생활 / *~ habits* 방랑벽. **2** of a vagrant. 유랑자[방랑자]의. **3** 《*fig.*》 random; wayward. 일정치 않은; 종잡을 수 없는; 변하기 쉬운. [→vague]

·vague [veig] *adj.* **1** not clearly seen. 희미한. ¶ *a ~ outline* 희미한 윤곽 / *In the fog everything looks ~.* 안개 속에서는 무엇이나 어렴풋이 보인다 / *the ~ shapes of sheep coming through the mist* 안개 속에서 다가오는 희미한 양들의 모습. **2** not clearly understood by the mind. 막연한. ¶ *~ hopes* [*ideas*] 막연한 희망[생각] / *His knowledge is rather ~.* 그 사람의 지식은 좀 막연하다 / *I don't have the vaguest idea who she is.* 그녀가 누군지 난 통 모른다. **3** not clearly expressed. 애매한; 모호한. ¶ *~ answers* [*statements, promises*]. **4** (of a person) absent-minded; not giving clear statements. (사람이) 얼빠진; 말이 분명치 않은. ¶ *He is very ~ as to what he really wants.* 그가 정말로 원하는 것이 뭔지 도무지 모르겠다. [L. *vagus* wandering]

vague·ly [véigli] *adv.* in a vague way. 희미하게; 막연히; 애매하게.

:vain [vein] *adj.* **1** having a high opinion or admiration of oneself; boastful; self-satisfied. 허영심이 강한; 자만하는. ¶ *She is a nice girl, but inclined to be ~.* 괜찮은 아가씨지만 잘난 체하는 데가 있다 / *a very ~ man* 허영심이 강한 사람 / *She is ~ of her beauty.* 그녀는 자기의 미를 자만하고 있다. **2** useless; without success. 쓸데 없는; 보람 없는. ¶ *They made a ~ search for him.* 그들이 그를 찾았으나 허사였다 / *in the ~ hope of success* 성공하리라는 헛된 희망에 / *I made ~ attempts.* 내 시도는 헛수고였다 / *It's ~ to try to escape.* 도망가려 해도 소용 없다. **3** empty; valueless. 헛된; 실질적 가치가 없는. ¶ *~ delights* 헛된 기쁨 / *~ words* 쓸데 없는 말 / *~ promises* 허황된 약속. [L. *vanus*]

in vain, without success; to no purpose. 헛되이; 보람없이. ¶ *All my efforts were in ~.* 내 노력은 모조리 허사였다 / *We tried in ~ to make him change his mind.* 그의 마음을 돌리려 했지만 무위로 끝났다.

vain·glo·ri·ous [vèinglɔ́ːriəs] *adj.* extremely proud; vain. 자부심[허영심]이 강한. [↓]

vain·glo·ry [vèinglɔ́ːri] *n.* Ⓤ **1** excessive or boastful vanity. 허영; 자만. **2** unworthy or empty show. 허세; 과시(誇示). [*vain, glory*]

vain·ly [véinli] *adv.* **1** without success; in vain; uselessly. 헛되이; 무익하게. ¶ *He ~ tried to speak.* 말하려고 했지만 허사였다. **2** conceitedly. 젠체하여. ¶ *He is ~ proud of his appearance.* 그는 잘났다고 자만한다. [*vain*]

val·ance [vǽləns, véil-] *n.* Ⓒ **1** a short curtain hanging over the top of a window. (창문 위의) 짧은 장식 커튼. **2** a short curtain around a bedstead. (침대 가두리의) 드리운 짧은 휘장. [Place]

〈valance 2〉

•**vale**[1] [veil] *n.* Ⓒ 《*poet.*》 a valley. 골짜기. ¶ 《*fig.*》 *the ~ of tears* =*the earthly ~* 눈물의 골짜기《현세》. [→valley]

va·le[2] [vá:lei, véili] *interj.* farewell. (그럼) 안녕. [L. *valeo* be well]

val·e·dic·tion [vælədíkʃən] *n.* Ⓒ **1** the act of saying farewell. 작별; 고별. **2** the words uttered in parting. 고별사. [↑]

val·e·dic·to·ry [vælədíktəri] *n.* Ⓒ (*pl.* **-ries**) 《chiefly U.S.》 an address of farewell, esp. at the ceremony of graduation from school. (특히, 졸업식의) 고별사 (cf. *salutatory*). —*adj.* said or done at farewell. 고별(이별)의. ¶ *a ~ speech* (*letter*) 고별사(문).

val·en·tine [vǽləntàin] *n.* Ⓒ **1** a card or gift sent on Saint Valentine's Day, February 14. 발렌타인 축일에 보내는 사랑의 카드나 선물. **2** a sweetheart chosen on this day. 이 날에 택한 연인. [Person]

va·le·ri·an [vəlíəriən] *n.* **1** Ⓒ 《bot.》 a strong smelling plant with white or pink flowers. 쥐오줌풀. **2** Ⓤ a drug made from the root of the valerian plant. 그 뿌리에서 만든 진정제. [F.]

val·et [vǽlit] *n.* Ⓒ **1** a manservant who takes care of clothes, rooms, etc. 시종; 근시(近侍). **2** a servant who cleans and presses clothes, shines shoes, etc. in a hotel. (호텔의) 보이. —*vt.* (P6) serve (someone) as a valet. …을 시종으로서 섬기다. ¶ *He valets me very well.* 그는 내 시중을 아주 잘 든다. [→varlet]

V

val·e·tu·di·nar·i·an [vælətjù:dənέəriən] *adj.* **1** in poor health; sickly. 병약한. **2** worrying or thinking too much about one's health. 건강에 너무 신경을 쓰는. —*n.* Ⓒ a valetudinarian person. 병약한 사람; 너무 건강에 신경쓰는 사람. [→vale[2]]

•**val·iant** [vǽljənt] *adj.* without fear; full of courage; brave. 겁 없는; 용감한. ¶ *~ deeds* / *~ soldiers.* [→vale[2]]

val·id [vǽlid] *adj.* (opp. invalid[2]) **1** based on or supported by fact; sound; true. 사실에 근거한; 근거가 확실한. ¶ *Have you any ~ reason against the proposal?* 그 제안에 반대하는 그럴만한 이유라도 있나. **2** having legal effect. 법적으로 유효한. ¶ *a ~ marriage* (*contract*) 법적으로 유효한 결혼(계약) / *The railway ticket is ~ for a week.* 이 기차표는 유효기간이 1주일이다. [L. *valeo* be well]

val·i·date [vǽlədèit] *vt.* (P6) **1** give (something) legal power. …에 법적 효력을 주다. ¶ *~ an election* 선거가 적법하다고 인정하다. **2** make (something) certain by verifying facts; confirm. …을 확인하다. ¶ *In order to ~ the agreement, both parties sign it.* 조약의 확인을 위해 양 당사자는 서명한다. [↑]

va·lid·i·ty [vəlídəti] *n.* Ⓤ **1** the state of being valid. 정당; 확인. **2** effectiveness; force. 법적인 효력; 유효. ¶ *the ~ of a pledge* (*mariiage*) 서약(결혼)의 법률적 효력. [↑]

va·lise [vəlí:s / -lí:z] *n.* Ⓒ a traveling bag; a soldier's kit-bag. 여행 가방; (군인의) 배낭; 잡낭. [It.]

:**val·ley** [vǽli] *n.* Ⓒ **1** a narrow, low strip of land between hills, etc. 골짜기. **2** a wide district along a river. (큰 강의) 유역. ¶ *the ~ of the Nile* 나일강 유역. [L. *vallis*]

the valley of the shadow of death, 《Bible》 the fearful hour when death comes near. 죽음의 골짜기.

•**val·or,** 《Brit.》 **-our** [vǽlər] *n.* Ⓤ the state of being brave; fearlessness. 용기; 용맹. [→vale[2]]

val·or·ous [vǽlərəs] *adj.* courageous; brave. 용감한.

valse [vɑ(:)ls] *n.* 《F.》 =waltz.

:**val·u·a·ble** [vǽlju:əbəl, -ljəbəl] *adj.* **1** having value; of great value. 값진; 가치 있는; 귀중한. ¶ *a ~ ring* / *~ papers* 유가 증권 / *~ information* 귀중한 정보 / *a ~ friend* 소중한 벗. **2** costing much. 고가의; 비싼. ¶ *a collection of ~ pictures* 고가 미술품의 수집. —*n.* 《usu. *pl.*》 something of great value. 비싼 물건; 귀중품. ¶ *She keeps her jewelry and other valuables in a safe.* 보석류와 기타 귀중품은 금고에 보관한다. [→value]

val·u·a·bly [vǽlju:əbəli] *adv.* in a valuable manner; usefully. 값있게; 유용하게. ¶ *His support has helped the cause most ~.* 그의 지지가 그 운동의 가장 큰 도움이 되었다.

val·u·a·tion [væljuéiʃən] *n.* **1** Ⓤ the act of judging the value of something. 평가; 값을 매기기. **2** Ⓒ the estimated value or price. 평가액. ¶ *The ~ of her jewels was very high.* 그녀 보석의 평가액은 아주 높게 나왔다 / *take someone at* (*on*) *his own ~* 아무의 능력을 본인이 평가하는 대로 받아들이다.

:**val·ue** [vǽlju:] *n.* ⓊⒸ **1** Ⓤ worth; usefulness; relative worth; real worth. 가치; 유용성; 상대적 가치; 진가. ¶ *anything of real ~* 진정 가치 있는 것 / *one's sense of values* 가치관 / *the values of classical learning* 고전 학문의 가치 / *the question of the ~ of fresh air* 신선한 공기에 대한 가치 문제 / *It has ~ if used regularly.* 제대로만 사용한다면 유용하다 / *The government sets a higer ~ on de-*

fense than on education. 정부는 교육보다 방위에 더 상대적인 가치를 둔다. **2** amount of money or other goods for which a thing may be exchanged; price; fair return. (금전적) 가치; 값; 대가. ¶ *nominal* [*face*] ~ 명목[액면] 가격 / *the market ~ of a house* 가옥의 시장 가격[시세] / *get full ~ for one's money* 치른 돈에 대해서 충분한 값어치가 있는 것을 받다 / *She bought the jewel for less than its ~.* 그녀는 그 보석을 값어치 이하의 값을 치르고 샀다 / *The thieves took some clothes and a few books, but nothing of any ~.* 도둑은 옷가지 몇 벌, 책 몇 권을 훔쳐 갔으나 값나가는 것은 하나도 없었다. **3** esteem; regard; importance. 높은 평가; 존중. ¶ *His opinion was of ~ to us.* 그의 의견이 우리에겐 귀중했다 / *I set a high ~ on my time.* 나는 시간을 소중히 생각한다. **4** exact meaning. (어구 등의) 정확한 뜻. ¶ *the true ~ of a word* 낱말의 정확한 뜻. **5** power to buy. 구매력. ¶ *the ~ of money* / *Because of continual price increases, the ~ of the pound has fallen in recent years.* 물가가 자꾸 올라 최근 몇 년 사이 파운드의 구매력이 떨어졌다. **6** degree of lightness and darkness in painting. (그림의) 명암도(明暗度). ¶ *out of ~* 명암의 균형이 좋지 않아. **7** 《math.》 the amount of which a sign is representative. (기호 등이 나타내는) 수치(數値); 값.
— *vt.* (P6,13) **1** estimate the worth of (something); put a price on (something). …을 평가하다; …의 값을 매기다. ¶ *The insurer valued the insured items.* 보험 회사가 보험물을 평가했다 / *The land is valued at 5,000,000 won.* 그 땅값은 5백만 원이다. **2** think highly of (something); esteem. …을 존중하다; 높이 평가하다. ¶ *~ his judgment highly* 그의 판단을 존중하다 / *I always ~ your friendship.* 나는 네 우정을 늘 존중한다. [L. *valeo* be strong [worth]]

value oneself on, take pride in. …을 우쭐해하다; 자만하다.

val·ued [vǽljuːd] *adj.* **1** highly estimated or determined. 높이 평가된. **2** highly esteemed or considered. 존중되는; 귀중한. ¶ *a ~ friend.*

·val·ue·less [vǽljuːlis] *adj.* of no worth; worthless. 무가치한; 하찮은(cf. *invaluable*). ¶ *~ pictures* 시원찮은 그림 / *a book ~ for its purpose* 내용이 빈약한 책 / *~ advice* 쓸모 없는 충고.

·valve [vælv] *n.* Ⓒ **1** a part of a blood vessel or other device which prevents a backward flow. 판; 판막(瓣膜). ¶ *The valves of the heart control the flow of blood.* 심장 판막은 피의 흐름을 조절한다. **2** a part of a device which shuts and opens the passage. 개폐판(開閉瓣); 밸브. **3** either of the shells of a shellfish. 조개 껍질; 조가비. **4** 《chiefly Brit.》 a vacuum tube used in radio, etc. 진공관(=《U.S.》 tube). ¶ *a ~ detector* 진공관 검파기. — *vi.* (P1) control the flow of (a liquid, gas, etc.) by a valve. 밸브로 조절하다.
— *vt.* (P6) furnish with a valve or valves. …에 밸브를 달다. [L. *valva* leaf of double door]

vamp[1] [væmp] *n.* Ⓒ **1** the upper front part of a shoe or boot. (구두의) 앞닫이. **2** anything added to an old thing to make it look new. 낡은 것을 새것처럼 보이게 덧대는 것. — *vt.* **1** (P6) repair (a shoe) with a vamp. (구두)에 새 앞닫이를 대다. **2** (P7) 《*up*》 make (an old thing) look new; repair. (낡은 것)을 새것처럼 보이게 하다; 고치다. ¶ *~ up some old furniture.* **3** (P6) 《mus.》 improvise an accompaniment. (반주)를 즉석에서 하다. [→van[1], pedal]

vamp[2] [væmp] *vi.* make love just to get money or please one's vanity. 남자를 호리다. — *n.* Ⓒ 《U.S. *colloq.*》 a woman who vamps; a vampire. 요부. [↓]

vam·pire [vǽmpaiər] *n.* Ⓒ **1** a ghost supposed to leave its grave and suck the blood of sleeping people. 흡혈귀. **2** a person who preys on others. 남을 등쳐먹는 자. **3** a woman who ruins the man she tempts; a vamp. 요부. **4** one of various South American bats that suck blood. (남아메리카의) 흡혈박쥐. [Magyar]

:van[1] [væn] *n.* Ⓒ 《often *the ~*》 **1** the front part of an army, fleet or marching group; a vanguard. 전위; 선도(先導); 선진(先陣). ¶ *the ~ of a procession* 행렬의 선두. **2** 《*fig.*》 those who lead any movement. 선두; 선구(先驅). ¶ *lead the ~ of* …의 선구 역할을 하다; 주도하다 / *in the ~ of* …진두[선두]에 서서. [→advance]

van[2] [væn] *n.* Ⓒ **1** a large covered truck or wagon for transporting goods. (대형) 유개(有蓋) 트럭[마차]. **2** 《Brit.》 a closed railroad baggage car. 유개 화차. ¶ *a luggage* [*goods*] *~* 유개 수하물차. **3** a closed carriage for conveying prisoners by road. 죄수 호송차. — *vt.* (**-nned**) (P6) place (goods) in a van; convey (goods) by a van. (짐)을 van 에 싣다; van 으로 나르다. [*caravan*]

〈van[2] 1〉

van[3] [væn] *n.* 《*poet.*》 the wing of a bird. 날개. [→fan]

van·dal [vǽndəl] *n.* Ⓒ **1** a person who destroys a work of art or another beautiful

V

thing. 예술품·자연미 등을 파괴하는 자. **2** 《*V-*》 a member of a Germanic tribe which invaded Spain and North Africa and captured Rome in 455 A.D. 반달인(人). [→wander]

van·dal·ism [vǽndəlìzəm] *n.* Ⓤ the act of damaging beautiful or valuable things. 예술·문화의 파괴.

vane [vein] *n.* Ⓒ **1** a device to show the direction of the wind; a weathercock. 바람개비; 풍향계(風向計). **2** a flat leaf of a windmill; a propeller of a ship. (풍차의) 날개; (선박의) 프로펠러. [E.=flag]

van·guard [vǽngɑ̀:rd] *n.* Ⓒ **1** the front part of an army or marching group. 선두; 전위; 선봉(opp. rear guard). ¶ *The ~ is* 〔*are*〕 *under attack.* 전위 (부대)가 공격을 받고 있다. **2** 《*collectively*》 《*fig.*》 the leaders of a political movement, an artistic movement, etc. 선도〔주도〕자. ¶ *In the 19th century Britain was in the ~ of industrial progress.* 19세기에 영국이 산업 발달을 선도했다. [→van¹]

va·nil·la [vənílə] *n.* Ⓒ **1** Ⓤ a flavoring essence used in candy, etc. 바닐라 향료. **2** the tropical plant, the beans of which are used in making this flavoring. 바닐라. **3** the bean itself. 바닐라 열매. [L. *vaina* sheath]

:van·ish [vǽniʃ] *vi.* (P1) **1** go out of sight; disappear; pass out of sight. 사라지다. ¶ *The sun vanished behind a cloud.* 해가 구름 뒤로 사라졌다 / *The ship vanished beyond the horizon.* 배가 수평선 저쪽으로 사라졌다. **2** fade away; decay and disappear. (빛·색 따위가) 희미해지다; 소멸하다. ¶ *All the color has vanished from the picture.* 그림의 색깔이 모두 바래 버렸다. **3** cease to exist. 없어지다. ¶ *Their fears vanished when the storm ended.* 폭풍우가 멎자 그들의 공포도 없어졌다 / *Many species of animal have now vanished* (*from the face of the earth*). 많은 종류의 동물이 오늘날 (지상에서) 절멸되었다. **4** 《math.》 become zero. 영이 되다. [→vain]

van·ish·ing cream [vǽniʃiŋ krì:m] *n.* a kind of cream which is absorbed quickly, used to apply to the face. 배니싱 크림.

V

vanishing point [⌐−−⌐] *n.* 《paint.》 the point where receding parallel lines seem to meet each other. (투시 화법의) 소점(消點).

•van·i·ty [vǽnəti] *n.* (*pl.* **-ties**) **1** Ⓤ too much pride in one's looks, ability, etc. 허영(심); 자부; 자만; 겉치레. ¶ *Her ~ made her look in the mirror often.* 허영심으로 해서 그녀는 자주 거울을 들여다본다. **2** Ⓤ the state or quality of being valueless; emptiness. 무익; 헛됨; 허무; 공허. ¶ *the ~ of human wishes* 인간의 소망의 덧없음. **3** Ⓒ anything of no real worth. 헛된〔부질 없는〕 것. ¶ 《Bible》 *All is ~.* 모든 것이 헛되고 헛되도다《전도서 Ⅰ : 2》. [L. *vānus*]

vanity case [⌐−−⌐] *n.* a case containing various kinds of cosmetics. 화장품통.

Vanity Fair [⌐−−⌐] *n.* the fashionable world of society. 허영의 도시《Bunyan작 Pilgrim's Progress 속의 시장 이름》. [→vanish]

van·quish [vǽŋkwiʃ] *vt.* (P6) defeat thoroughly; conquer. …에게 이기다; 정복하다. ¶ *~ the enemy in battle* 싸움에서 적을 정복하다 / 《*fig.*》 *~ the temptations of the flesh* 육욕(肉慾)을 이겨내다. [L. *vinco* conquer]

van·tage [vǽntidʒ, vɑ́:n-] *n.* Ⓤ **1** a better position or condition; advantage. 유리한 입장〔상태〕. ¶ *gain a point of ~ in a battle* 전투에서 유리한 위치를 차지하다. **2** 《chiefly Brit. tennis》 the first point scored after deuce. 밴티지. [→advantage]

vantage ground [⌐−⌐] *n.* a favorable position. 유리한 지위; 지리(地利).

vantage point [⌐−⌐] *n.* **1** a good position from which to attack, defend, or see something. 유리한 위치; 지리(地利). ¶ *Security police took up vantage points overlooking the route of the procession.* 비밀 경찰들은 행렬의 향로가 내려다보이는 지점을 차지했다. **2** a point of view; perspective. 견해. ¶ *I quite agree that from your ~ his action must have seemed unwise.* 그의 행동이 슬기롭지 않다는 견해에 나는 전적으로 동감이다.

vap·id [vǽpid] *adj.* without flavor; not interesting; not active. 김빠진; 흥미 없는; 시들한. ¶ *~ beer* / *a ~ speech* 맥빠진 연설 / *run ~* 맥빠지다. [L.]

•va·por, 《Brit.》 **-pour** [véipər] *n.* **1** Ⓤ steam coming from boiling water; moisture in the air that can be seen. 김; 수증기. **2** Ⓒ a gas formed from a substance which is usu. in a liquid or a solid form. 증기; 기화(氣化) 물질. **3** Ⓒ 《*fig.*》 an idle fancy; something imaged. 망상; 공상. ¶ *His brain was clouded by vapors and dreams.* 그의 머리는 공상과 꿈으로 흐리멍덩해 있었다. **4** 《*the ~s*》 《*pl.*》 hypochondria or hysteria. 우울증; 히스테리. ¶ *a fit of vapors* 히스테리의 발작.
— *vt.* (P6) **1** 《rare》 pass off as vapor. 증발시키다; 발산케 하다. **2** 《*colloq.*》 boast. 허풍떨다. [L. *vapōrem* steam]

va·por·ing [véipəriŋ] *n.* 《often *pl.*》 idle boasting; meaningless talk. 허풍.

va·por·ish [véipəriʃ] *adj.* **1** like vapor. 증기 같은. **2** full of vapor. 증기로 꽉 찬. **3** in low spirits. 기운 없는; 맥빠진.

va·por·i·za·tion [vèipərizéiʃən] *n.* Ⓤ the act of vaporizing; the state of being vaporized. 증발; 기화(氣化).

va·por·ize [véipəràiz] *vt.* (P6) change (liquid, etc.) into vapor. …을 기화〔증발〕시키다. — *vi.* (P1) be changed into vapor. 증기가 되다; 증발하다. ¶ *Water vaporizes when it boils.* 물은 끓이면 증발한다.

va·por·iz·er [véipəràizər] *n.* Ⓒ a device for vaporizing; an atomizer. 기화기(氣化

器); 분무기(噴霧器).

va·por·ous [véipərəs] *adj.* **1** covered or hidden by mist; filled with vapor. 안개낀; 김이 서린. ¶ *a ~ evening* 안개낀 저녁. **2** like vapor. 수증기 같은. **3** lacking real worth; useless. 실속이 없는; 쓸모없는. ¶ *~ dreams* 헛된 꿈.

vapor trail [⊂-⊃] *n.* a cloud formed from the vapor of an airplane. 비행운; 비행기 구름.

va·por·y [véipəri] *adj.* =vaporous.

var·i·a·bil·i·ty [vὲəriəbíləti] *n.* Ⓤ the state of being variable. 변하기 쉬움; 가변성.

var·i·a·ble [vέəriəbəl] *adj.* **1** changeable; likely to change; not certain. 변하기 쉬운; 일정하지 않은. ¶ *~ weather* 변덕스러운 날씨 / *a man of ~ temper* 변덕이 심한 사람. **2** that can be changed. 변경할 수 있는. ¶ *a ~ condenser* 가변 콘덴서 / *Prices are ~ according to the exchanges.* 물가는 환시세에 따라 변한다 / *a rod of ~ length* 신축 자재봉(自在棒); 여의봉(如意棒). **3** 《biol.》 varying from the strict biological type. 변이(變異)하는. ¶ *a ~ species* 변이종. **4** 《astron.》 changing a brightness. (별이) 변광(變光)하는. ¶ *a ~ star.* **5** 《math.》 increasing or decreasing. 가변의. ¶ *~ quantities* 변수. — *n.* Ⓒ a thing or quantity that varies. 변하는 것; 변수(變數). [→various]

var·i·ance [vέəriəns] *n.* Ⓤ **1** difference in opinion, etc.; disagreement. 불일치; 상위. **2** variation; change. 변화; 변동. ¶ *Some ~ of temperature is to be expected.* 어느 정도의 기온의 변화는 예상되게 마련이다. [→vary]
at variance, not in agreement; in conflict. 일치하지 않아; 모순되어; 불화하여. ¶ *His acts are at ~ with his words.* 그의 행동과 말에 모순이 있다 / *old friends now at ~* 지금은 틀어진 옛 친구들. [↑]

var·i·ant [vέəriənt] *adj.* **1** different; varying. 다른; 여러 가지의. ¶ *forty ~ types of pigeon* 비둘기의 40가지 변종 / *'Rhyme' is a ~ spelling of 'rime'.* Rhyme 은 rime 의 다른 철자다. **2** changeable. 변하기 쉬운. — *n.* Ⓒ **1** a varying form. 변형. **2** a different form of pronouncing or spelling a certain word. (발음·철자의) 이형(異形); 전화(轉化). [↑]

***var·i·a·tion** [vὲəriéiʃən] *n.* **1** ⓊⒸ a change in condition, degree, etc. 변화; 변동; 변경. ¶ *Prices are subject to ~.* 가격은 변동하기 쉽다 / *according to the ~ of temperature* 기온 변화에 따라. **2** ⓊⒸ the amount of change. 변화량. ¶ *marked* 〔*slight*〕 *variations in speed* 속도에서의 두드러진〔약간의〕 변화. **3** Ⓒ a changed form. 변화형; 변형. **4** Ⓒ 《mus.》 the act of repeating a single tune or theme with changes; a series of such repetition. 변주(變奏); 변주곡. **5** 《biol.》 deviation from type. 변이; 변종. **6** 《gram.》 inflexion. 어형 변화. **7** 《astron.》 any deviation from the mean orbit of a heavenly body. 편차(偏差). [L. *vario,* →vary]

var·i·col·ored, 《Brit.》 **-oured** [vέərikʌ̀lərd] *adj.* **1** of or having many different colors. 잡색의; 가지 각색의. **2** =varied.

***var·ied** [vέərid] *adj.* **1** of different kinds; various. 다양한; 가지 각색의. ¶ *~ scenes* 여러 가지 장면 / *birds of the most ~ kinds* 가장 품종이 다양한 새 / *~ pleasures* 여러 가지의 즐거움 / *a singer with a very ~ repertoire* 레퍼토리가 아주 다양한 가수. **2** changing from time to time; having variety. 자주 변하는; 다채로운. ¶ *live a ~ life* 다채로운 삶을 살다 / *delightfully ~ scenery* 변화가 풍부하고 재미있는 경치. [→various]

var·ie·gat·ed [vέəriəgèitid] *adj.* **1** different in appearance; marked with various colors. 다채로운; 잡색의. ¶ *Pansies are usually ~.* 팬지는 색깔이 다양하다. **2** showing different qualities together. (성질이) 잡다한. ¶ *a character strangely ~ with good and evil* 이상하게 선악이 뒤섞인 성격. [↑]

:va·ri·e·ty [vəráiəti] *n.* (*pl.* **-ties**) **1** Ⓤ the state of being different; lack of sameness; change. 변화가 많음; 다양성. ¶ *the ~ of town life* 도시 생활의 다양성 / *the extraordinary ~ of his character* 유난히 자주 바뀌는 그의 성격. **2** Ⓒ a collection of many different things. 잡다한 것; 그러모은 것; 잡동사니. ¶ *This shop has a ~ of magazines.* 이 가게에는 가지가지의 잡지가 있다 / *for a ~ of reasons* 여러 가지 이유로. **3** Ⓒ a kind; a sort. 종류. ¶ *a rare ~ of old English glass* 희귀한 종류의 옛 영국 유리 제품. **4** Ⓤ 《chiefly Brit.》 a performance consisting of several different kinds of acts. 버라이어티. ¶ *a ~ show* 버라이어티 쇼. [→various]

var·i·o·rum [vὲərió:rəm] *n.* Ⓒ a book with the comments and notes of many editors or critics. 여러 전문가들의 주(註)가 있는 책; 집주본(集註本). — *adj.* of a variorum. 여러 전문가들의 주(註)가 있는; 집주(集註)의. [↑]

:var·i·ous [vέəriəs] *adj.* **1** different; differing from one another; several; many. 여러 가지의; 가지 각색의; 다양한; 각종의. ¶ *The effects of this disease are ~ in different cases.* 이 병의 영향은 각 증상에 따라 여러 가지다 / *the ~ colors of autumn leaves* 가을 나뭇잎들의 다양한 색깔 / *~ occupations* 〔*experiences*〕 다양한 직업〔경험〕 / *for ~ reasons* 여러 가지 이유로 / *I came across ~ people.* 나는 별의별 사람을 만났다. **2** 《rare》 many-sided. 여러 방면의; 다재다능한. ¶ *a ~ man* 재주가 많은 사람. **3** 《*sl.*》 《as *pron.* or *n.*》 several; many. 몇 사람; 몇 개. ¶ *Various of the speakers were inaudible.* 몇 연사들의 말은 들리지 않았다 / *I spoke with ~ of them.* 그들 몇 사람과 이야기를 했다. [L. *varius* changing, varied]

var·i·ous·ly [vέəriəsli] *adv.* in many ways; in various manners. 여러 가지로; 다양하게.

var·let [vá:rlit] *n.* **1** 《hist.》 a personal servant of a knight or squire. (기사 등의) 종복

V

(從僕); 시종(cf. *valet*). **2** 《*arch.*》 rascal. 악한; 깡패. [→vassal]

var·mint [vá:rmint] *n.* 《*sl.*》 a naughty child; a fox. 악동; 여우. [*vermin*]

var·nish [vá:rniʃ] *n.* Ⓤ Ⓒ **1** a liquid used to give a smooth surface to wood, cloth, etc. 니스; 와니스. **2** 《*fig.*》 false appearance; outside show; outward polish. 겉치레; 허세. ¶ *a ~ of good manners* 겉만 훌륭한 태도 / *put a ~ on* …을 꾸미다; 분식(粉飾)하다. — *vt.* (P6) **1** put varnish on the surface of (something). …에 니스칠을 하다; …의 겉을 꾸미다. **2** 《*fig.*》 hide (something) under a false appearance. …을 꾸미다; 분식하다. ¶ *~ errors* 실수를 얼버무리다. [F.]

var·si·ty [vá:rsəti] *n.* Ⓒ (*pl.* **-ties**) **1** 《U.S.》 the most important team playing a sport in a university or college. (대학교의) 대표팀. **2** 《chiefly Brit. *colloq.*》 a university. 대학교. [*university*]

:var·y [vέəri] *v.* (**var·ied**) *vt.* (P6) make (something) different; give variety to (something); change. …을 바꾸다; …에 변화를 주다. ¶ *~ the idea* 생각을 바꾸다 / *The price varies according to the season.* 값은 계절에 따라 변한다 / *She varied the appearance of the room by rearranging the furniture.* 그녀는 가구 배치를 다시 하여 방의 외양에 변화를 주었다. — *vi.* (P1) become different; differ; change. 바뀌다; 달라지다. ¶ *Customs ~ with the times.* 관습은 시대에 따라 바뀐다 / *Opinions ~ on this point.* 이 점에서 의견이 다르다 / *The weather varies from hour to hour.* 날씨는 시시각각으로 변한다. [L. *vario,* →various]

vary* (*directly*) *as, 《math.》 increase correspondingly to the increase of. …에 정비례(正比例)해서 변하다.

vary inversely as, decrease correspondingly to the increase of. …에 반비례해서 변하다.

vas·cu·lar [vǽskjələr] *adj.* 《biol.》 of vessels for conveying blood or sap. 도관(導管)의; 물관(管)의. [↓]

:vase [veis, veiz, vɑ:z] *n.* Ⓒ an ornamental vessel used for holding flowers. 꽃병. [L. *vas* vessel]

Vas·e·line, vas- [vǽsəli:n, ∸-∸] *n.* Ⓤ (a trade name for) a kind of grease. 바셀린. [Gk. =water-oil]

vas·sal [vǽsəl] *n.* Ⓒ **1** 《hist.》 a person who receives land and protection in return for doing certain duties. (봉건 시대의) 가신(家臣). **2** a servant; a bondman. 노복; 하인. — *adj.* of or like a vassal; subject. 가신의 (같은); 예속하는. ¶ *a ~ state* 속국. [Celt.]

vas·sal·age [vǽsəlidʒ] *n.* Ⓤ **1** the state of being a vassal. 가신임; 종속적 지위. **2** feudal homage; loyalty. 충순(忠順). **3** the ruled land controlled by a vassal. 봉토(封土). [↑]

:vast [væst, vɑ:st] *adj.* **1** extremely large in breadth, size; huge. 광대한; 거대한. ¶ *a ~ desert in Africa* 아프리카의 광대한 사막 / *the ~ mountains of the Andes* 거대한 안데스 산맥 / *a ~ iceberg* 거대한 빙산 / *~ plans of development* 웅대한 개발 계획. **2** very great in number, amount, or quantity. (수·양이) 엄청난; 막대한. ¶ *~ sums of money* 막대한 돈 / *~ quantities of wine* 엄청난 양의 포도주 / *a ~ crowd of people* 엄청난 인파. **3** 《*colloq.*》 very great. 대단한. ¶ *There is a ~ difference between this and that.* 이것과 저것 사이에는 엄청난 차이가 있다 / *of ~ importance* 매우 중요한 / *~ improvements* 굉장한 향상.
— *n.* 《*a ~* or *the ~*》 《*arch., poet.*》 a vast space. 광막함; 넓디 넓음. ¶ *a* 〔*the*〕 *~ of ocean* 〔*water*〕 광막한 대양(大洋) / *~ heaven* 광대한 하늘. [L. *vastus*]

vast·ly [vǽstli, vá:st-] *adv.* very greatly; to a vast extent or degree. 광대〔광막〕하게; 엄청나게.

vast·ness [vǽstnis, vá:st-] *n.* Ⓤ the state of being vast. 광대; 막대; 거대.

vat [væt] *n.* Ⓒ a large container for liquid, esp. in the process of formantation etc. (양조 등에 쓰이는) 큰 통. — *vt.* (**-ted**) (P6) place, store or mix in a vat. …을 통에 넣(어 섞)다. ¶ *old vatted whiskies* 오래 저장된 위스키. [E.]

Vat·i·can [vǽtikən], **the** *n.* **1** the palace of the Pope in Rome. 바티칸 궁전; 교황청. **2** the authority of Pope; the papal government. 교황권; 교황 정부. [Place]

Vatican City [∸-∸ ∸-], **the** *n.* an independent state in Rome ruled by the Pope. 바티칸 시국(市國).

vaude·ville [vɔ́:dəvil, vóud-] *n.* Ⓤ **1** 《Brit.》 a light musical comedy. 경희가극(輕喜歌劇). **2** 《U.S.》 a performance consisting of different kinds of acts, i.e. songs, dances, acrobatic feats. (노래, 춤 따위가 있는) 흥행; 보드빌(cf. *variety*). [F.]

·vault¹ [vɔ:lt] *n.* Ⓒ **1** an arched roof or ceiling. (아치형의) 둥근 천장. **2** an underground storehouse. 지하 저장실. ¶ *a wine ~* 포도주 지하 저장고. **3** an underground place for burial. 지하 납골소. ¶ *a family ~*. **4** a room in a bank for keeping valuable things. 귀중품 저장실; 금고실. **5** an arched cave. 굴; 동굴.

〈vault¹ 1〉

— *vt.* (P6) **1** cover (something) with a vault. …에 둥근 천장을 하다. **2** make in the form of a vault. 둥근 천장 모양으로 만들다. [L. *volvo* roll]

vault² [vɔ:lt] *vi., vt.* (P1,2A; 6) leap or jump over (something) with the aid of hands or a pole. 도약하다; (…을) 뛰어 넘다. ¶ ~ *over a ditch* 도랑을 뛰어 넘다 / ~ *on* 〔*from*〕 *a horse* 말에 뛰어 올라 타다〔내리다〕/ *The thief vaulted* (*over*) *the wall and ran away.* 도둑은 담을 뛰어 넘어 달아났다 / ~ *a gate* 문을 뛰어 넘다. — *n.* Ⓒ a jump or leap made in this way. 뜀; 도약. [↑]

vault·ing [vɔ́:ltiŋ] *n.* Ⓤ **1** a vaulted building. 둥근 천장의 건축물. **2** 《*collectively*》 an arched roof or ceiling. 둥근 천장.

vaulting horse [ˊ-- ˋ] *n.* a wooden horse used for jumping over in gymnastics. 뜀틀.

vaunt [vɔ:nt, vɑ:nt] *vi.* (P1,2A,3) show off; boast of (something); speak boastfully and triumphantly. 자랑하다; 뽐내다; 허풍떨다. ¶ ~ *of one's skill* 솜씨를 자랑하다 / ~ *over* …을 자랑하다; 뽐내다; 허풍떨다 / ~ *over another's failure* 남의 실수를 떠벌리다. — *vt.* (P6) **1** boast about. …을 자랑하다; 뽐내다. ¶ *his vaunted courage* 그가 자랑하는 용기. **2** praise highly. …을 크게 칭찬하다. ¶ ~ *the beauties of the Scottish lochs* 스코틀랜드 호수들의 아름다움을 격찬하다. [→vain]

v.aux. auxiliary verb.

vb. verb.

vb.n. verbal noun.

V.C. Vice-Chairman; Vice-Chancellor; Vice-Consul; Victoria Cross.

VD venereal disease.

Vd vanadium.

v.d. vapor density; various dates.

veal [vi:l] *n.* Ⓤ the meat of a calf used for food. 송아지 고기. [L. *vitulus* calf]

vec·tor [véktər] *n.* **1** 《math.》 a quantity involving direction as well as magnitude. 벡터. **2** 《biol.》 an insect, such as a fly or mosquito, which can carry a disease from one living thing to another. 병균 매개 곤충. **3** the course of an aircraft, missile or the like. (항공기·미사일 등의) 진로; 궤적. [L. *vector* carrier]

Veep [vi:p] *n.* 《U.S. *colloq.*》 the Vice-President. (미국의) 부통령. [abbr.]

veer[1] [viər] *vi.* (P1,2A) **1** change direction. 방향이 바뀌다. ¶ *The wind veered to the east.* 풍향이 동쪽으로 바뀌었다. **2** 《*fig.*》 change from one opinion, belief etc. to another. (의견·신념 등이) 바뀌다; 전향하다. ¶ ~ *round to the opposite party* 반대당 쪽으로 전향하다. — *vt.* (P6) change the direction of (a ship, etc.). …의 방향을 바꾸다. [E. *virer* turn]

veer[2] [viər] *vt.* (P6) 《naut.》 pay out (a rope or cable). (밧줄 따위)를 풀어내다. [Du. *vieren* slacken]

veer and haul, slacken and tighten (a rope or chain) alternately. (밧줄 따위)를 늦췄다 당겼다 하다.

veer out, pay out (a rope or chain). (밧줄)을 풀어내다.

Ve·ga [ví:gə, véigə] *n.* 《astron.》 a star of the first magnitude in the Lyra constellation; the weaving girl star. 베가; 직녀성. [L.]

:veg·e·ta·ble [védʒətəbəl] *n.* Ⓒ **1** a plant or a part of a plant used for food. 야채. **2** a plant. 식물. **3** Ⓒ a human being who has little or no power of thought or sometimes also movement. 식물 인간. ¶ *Since she suffered brain damage in the accident she's just been a* ~. 그 사고로 머리를 다친 그녀는 식물 인간이 되었다.

become a mere vegetable, become thoroughly inactive in mind and body. 심신의 생기가 죽어버리다; 식물 인간이 되다.

— *adj.* **1** of or like a plant. 식물의〔같은〕. ¶ *the* ~ *kingdom* 식물계 / ~ *life* 식물의 생명. **2** made of vegetables. 식물에서 낸〔만든〕; 식물성의. ¶ ~ *oils* 식물성 기름 / *a* ~ *diet* 채식 / *a* ~ *dish* 야채 요리. [L. *vegeo* quicken]

veg·e·tar·i·an [vèdʒətέəriən] *n.* a person who eats vegetables but no meat. 채식주의자. — *adj.* **1** eating vegetables but no meat; having to do with vegetarians. 채식주의의; 채식만 하는. ¶ ~ *principles* 채식주의 / *a* ~ *restaurant* 채식만 내는 식당. **2** containing no meat. 야채뿐인. ¶ ~ *dishes* 야채 요리 / *a* ~ *meal* 채식. [↑]

veg·e·tar·i·an·ism [vèdʒətέəriənìzəm] *n.* Ⓤ the principle of eating vegetables only. 채식주의.

veg·e·tate [védʒətèit] *vi.* (P1) **1** grow like plants. 식물처럼 자라다. **2** live in an idle or monotonous way. 무위 도식하다. ¶ *Since he lost his job he's just been vegitating at home.* 실직하고는 집에서 죽치고 지낸다.

·veg·e·ta·tion [vèdʒətéiʃən] *n.* Ⓤ **1** 《*collectively*》 plants. 식물. ¶ *The* ~ *is sparse.* 식물이 드문드문 나있다 / *There is not much* ~ *in desert.* 사막엔 식물이 별로 없다 / *tropical* ~ 열대 식물. **2** the act of vegetating; the growth of plants. 식물의 생장〔발육〕. ¶ *Vegetation is at its height in spring.* 식물은 봄에 가장 발육이 왕성하다.

veg·e·ta·tive [védʒətèitiv / -tətiv] *adj.* **1** growing like plants. 식물처럼 자라는. **2** of plants. 식물의. **3** able to grow plants. 식물을 자라게 하는. ¶ ~ *soil* 비옥한 땅; 옥토. **4** 《*fig.*》 not moving; quiet; inactive. 비활동적인; 정적인. ¶ *a* ~ *life* 무위 도식.

ve·he·mence [ví:əməns] *n.* Ⓤ the state of being vehement; rough force; violence. 열렬; 격렬; 맹렬. ¶ *the* ~ *of the storm* 폭풍우의 맹위 / *with* ~ 맹렬하게 / *speak with* ~ 격한 어조로 말하다. [↓]

ve·he·ment [ví:əmənt] *adj.* **1** having passion; having strong feelings; passionate. 열렬한; 열성적인. ¶ *a* ~ *desire* 뜨거운 욕망 / *a man of* ~ *character* 격정적인 사람 / *a* ~ *denial* 단호한 거부. **2** full of force; very forceful; violent. 맹렬한. ¶ ~ *heat* 〔*opposition*〕 맹렬한 더위〔반대〕. [L.]

ve·he·ment·ly [ví:əməntli] *adv.* in a vehement manner; passionately; violently. 열렬하게; 맹렬히.

·ve·hi·cle [ví:ikəl, ví:hi-] *n.* Ⓒ **1** anything used for carrying passengers or goods, esp. on land. 탈것; 수레; 차. ¶ *"Is this your ~, sir?" asked the policeman.* "이게 당신 차요?" 하고 경찰이 물었다 / *motor vehicles* 자동차 / *a space ~* 우주선. **2** a means of conveying ideas, information, etc. 전달 수단; 매개물. ¶ *Air is the ~ of sound.* 공기는 소리의 매질(媒質)이다 / *Milk is often a ~ of infection.* 우유는 종종 전염병을 옮긴다 / *Language is the ~ of thought.* 언어는 생각의 전달〔매개〕 수단이다. [L. *veho* carry]

:veil [veil] *n.* Ⓒ **1** a piece of thin material worn over the head, the face or the shoulders. 베일. ¶ *drop* 〔*raise*〕 *a ~* 베일을 내리다〔올리다〕. **2** anything that covers; curtain. 덮개; 씌우개; 장막. ¶ *a ~ of mist* 안개의 장막 / *A ~ of cloud hid the sun.* 한조각 구름이 해를 가렸다. **3** 《*fig.*》 anything that screens or hides; disguise; pretense. 구실; 가면; 핑계. ¶ *under the ~ of friendship* 〔*religion*〕 우정이란〔종교란〕 미명 아래.

beyond the veil, beyond this world. 저승에.

draw a 〔***the***〕 ***veil over,*** cover; conceal. …을 덮어 가리다; 숨기다.

take the veil, become a nun. 수녀가 되다.

— *vt.* (P6) **1** cover with or as with a veil. …에 베일을 씌우다; 베일로 가리다. ¶ *~ one's face* 〔*head*〕 얼굴을〔머리를〕 베일로 가리다. **2** cover; hide. …을 감추다; 숨기다. ¶ *Clouds veiled the sun.* 구름이 해를 가렸다 / *~ one's dislike* 〔*suspicion*〕 싫어하는〔의심하는〕 내색을 않다. [L. *velum*]

veiled [veild] *adj.* **1** wearing a veil; covered with a veil. 베일을 쓴; 베일로 가린. ¶ *a ~ nun* 수녀 / *with ~ eyes* 눈을 가리고. **2** hidden; not openly expressed. 숨겨진; 감춰진. ¶ *~ hatred* 드러내지 않은 증오심 / *a ~ threat* 은근한 협박.

veil·ing [véiliŋ] *n.* Ⓤ cloth used for making veils. 베일 감.

:vein [vein] *n.* Ⓒ **1** one of the blood vessels which carries the blood to the heart. 정맥 (opp. artery). **2** one of the branching lines on a leaf or the wing of an insect. 엽맥(葉脈); 시맥(翅脈). **3** a crack or seam in rock filled with other material. 광맥; 암맥. ¶ *a ~ of coal* 탄맥. **4** a long thin mark of a different color in wood or marble. (나무·대리석 등의) 결; 나뭇결; 돌결. **5** 《*sing.* only》 a state of mind or feeling; a mood. 마음; 기분. ¶ *be in the ~ for writing* 글이 쓰고 싶어지다 / *He spoke in a light playful ~.* 그는 가볍게 농을 섞어가며 이야기했다 / *I'm not in* (*the*) *~ for sing.* 노래할 생각이 안 난다. **6** a particular character or tendency. 기질; 성격; 특질. ¶ *a joking ~* 익살스러운 기질 / *He has a strong ~ of humor* 〔*cruelty*〕. 그의 성격은 아주 유머러스〔잔인〕한 데가 있다.

V

— *vt.* (P6) mark (something) with lines like veins. …에 맥 같은 줄을 넣다. [L. *vena*]

vel. vellum.

vela [ví:lə] *n.* pl. of **velum.**

ve·lar [ví:lər] *adj.* **1** of a velum. 연구개의. **2** 《phon.》 produced with the back of the tongue near or touching the soft palate. 연구개음의. — *n.* a velar sound. 연구개음. [→velum]

veld, veldt [velt, felt] *n.* Ⓒ an open large grassland in South Africa. (남아프리카의) 대초원(大草原). [Du. (→field)]

vel·lum [véləm] *n.* Ⓤ **1** fine parchment for writing or for binding books, usu. made of calfskin. (송아지 가죽으로 된) 고급 피지(皮紙). **2** a kind of writing paper made in imitation of this. 모조 피지. [→veal]

ve·loc·i·pede [vəlɑ́səpì:d / -lɔ́s-] *n.* Ⓒ **1** a small vehicle with three wheels for children. 세발 자전거. **2** an early kind of bicycle or tricycle. (구식의) 2륜〔3륜〕차. [↓, →pedal]

ve·loc·i·ty [vəlɑ́səti / -lɔ́s-] *n.* ⓊⒸ (*pl.* **-ties**) **1** the quickness of motion; speed. 빠르기; 속력. ¶ *What limit is there to an aeroplane's ~?* 비행기의 한계 속력은 얼마냐 / *The world was rushed into war with unexpected ~.* 세계는 예상 밖의 속도로 전쟁에 돌입했다. **2** the rate of motion. 속도. ¶ *at a ~ of 2 miles a minute* 분속 2 마일로 / *the ~ of light* 빛의 속도; 광속. [L. *velox* swift]

ve·lour, -lours [vəlúər] *n.* **1** Ⓤ cloth made of silk, wool or cotten woven like velvet. 벨루어《벨벳의 일종》. **2** Ⓒ a hat of this material. 벨루어 모자. [F.]

ve·lum [ví:ləm] *n.* (*pl.* **-la**) **1** 《biol.》 a membranous covering. 막(膜). **2** 《anat.》 the soft palate. 연구개(軟口蓋). [L.=sail, covering]

:vel·vet [vélvit] *n.* Ⓤ **1** cloth with a thick, soft pile made of silk. 벨벳; 비로드; 우단. **2** something made like velvet. 벨벳 비슷한 것.

be on velvet, be in an advantageous position in money matters. 유복(裕福)하다.

— *adj.* **1** made of velvet. 벨벳제의. ¶ *a ~ coat.* **2** like velvet. 벨벳 같은. ¶ *~ lawns* 비로드 같은 잔디. [L. *villus* hair]

vel·vet·een [vèlvətí:n] *n.* Ⓤ cotton cloth like velvet. 모조 벨벳; 면비로드.

vel·vet·y [vélviti] *adj.* soft and smooth like velvet. 벨벳 같은.

ve·nal [ví:nl] *adj.* **1** (of a person) willing to work only for money; willing to get money unfairly. 뇌물에 움직이는; 돈에 좌우되는. ¶ *a ~ politician* 〔*policeman*〕 돈에 움직이는 정치가〔경찰관〕. **2** (of actions) influenced by unfair money; corrupt. 매수된; 부패한. ¶ *~ conduct* 타산적 행위 / *~ practices* 수회 행위. [L. *venum* sale]

ve·nal·i·ty [vi(:)nǽləti] *n.* Ⓤ the state of being venal. 수회(收賄); 돈에 좌우됨.

ve·na·tion [venéiʃən] *n.* Ⓤ **1** a pattern of veins in a leaf or in an insect's wing. 잎맥·시맥(翅脈)의 분포 상태. **2** 《*collectively*》 the veins of such a pattern. 잎맥; 시맥. [L. *vēna* vein]

vend [vend] *vt.* (P6) sell; peddle. …을 팔다; 행상하다; 도부 치다. [→vendor]

vend·er, -or [véndər] *n.* Ⓒ **1** a person who sells something. 파는 사람; 행상인. ¶ *a peanut* ~ 땅콩 장수. **2** 《law》 a seller of real property. 부동산 매각인. **3** = vending machine. [→venal, L. *do* give]

ven·det·ta [vendétə] *n.* a feud for revenge by bloodshed usu. carried on by the relatives of a murdered man. (두 가족 사이의) 유혈 복수. [→vindicate]

vend·i·ble [véndəbəl] *adj.* capable of being sold. 팔 수 있는; 팔리는. —*n.* a salable thing. 매물. [→vend]

vending machine [⌐–⌐] *n.* a machine from which a person gets something by putting in a coin or coins. 자동판매기.

ve·neer [vəníər] *n.* **1** ⓊⒸ a thin layer of fine wood or other material used to surface a substance of poorer quality. 베니어 단판(單板)(cf. *plywood*). **2** Ⓒ 《*fig.*》 the outside appearance; pretence. 겉치레; 허식. ¶ *Beneath that* ~ *of respectability there lurked a cunning and unscrupulous criminal.* 저렇게 겉으로는 사회적 신망을 얻고 있지만 그 이면에는 교활하고 악랄한 범죄가 숨어 있었다 / *a thin* ~ *of education* 얄팍한 겉치레뿐인 피상적 교육.

—*vt.* (P6) **1** cover (something) with a veneer. …에 베니어 판을 붙이다. **2** 《*fig.*》 make (something cheap or mean) look bright and beautiful. …의 겉치레를 하다. [→furnish]

ven·er·a·ble [vénərəbəl] *adj.* **1** deserving and receiving respect because of age, character, etc. (나이·인격 등으로) 존경할 만한. ¶ *a* ~ *oak* 훌륭한 떡갈나무 노목 / *a* ~ *priest* [*commander*] 존경받는 성직자[사령관]. **2** honored because of historical, religious associations. (역사적·종교적 연관성으로) 신성한; 거룩한. ¶ ~ *ruins* 성지(聖趾). **3** 《Church of England》 a title for an archdeacon. 부주교; …사(師). **4** 《*colloq.*》 old; aged. 오래된; 고령의. [L.]

ven·er·ate [vénərèit] *vt.* (P6) look upon (someone) with respect. …을 존경[숭배]하다. ¶ *He venerates his father's memory.* 아버지의 유물을 소중히 간직하고 있다. [↑]

ven·er·a·tion [vènəréiʃən] *n.* Ⓤ deep respect; worship. 존경; 숭배.

Ve·ne·tian [viníːʃən] *adj.* of Venice. 베니스의. —*n.* a native or an inhabitant of Venice. 베니스 사람[주민]. [*Venice*]

Venetian blind [–⌐–⌐] *n.* a window blind made of many horizontal slats of wood, etc. that can be opened or closed to regulate the light, air, etc. 베니션 블라인드 《끈을 당겨 오르내리는 많은 수평의 오리로 된》.

venge·ance [véndʒəns] *n.* ⓊⒸ punishment in return for a wrong; the return of evil for evil. 복수; 보복. ¶ *take* [*inflict*] ~ *upon* …을 복수하다 / *a terrible* ~ 끔찍한 보복 / 《*prov.*》 *Heaven's* ~ *is slow but sure.* 천벌은 더디지만 반드시 온다. [→vindicate]

exact a vengeance from** (someone)* ***for, take revenge on someone, esp. for murder. …에게 —의 복수를 하다.

with a vengeance, 《*colloq.*》 **a**) with great force and energy; violently. 거칠게; 심하게. ¶ *It rains with a* ~. 비가 억수로 쏟아진다 / *strike with a* ~ 후려갈기다. **b**) much more than wanted; very. 극도로; 대단히.

venge·ful [véndʒfəl] *adj.* full of a strong wish for revenge; revengeful. 복수심에 불타는; 복수의. [↑]

ve·ni·al [víːniəl] *adj.* **1** that can be excused; deserving pardon; that can be pardoned. 용서할 수 있는; 크게 나무랄 바 못되는. ¶ *a* ~ *error* 사소한 잘못 / *childish,* ~ *faults* 철없이 저지른 가벼운 과실. **2** 《theol.》 that may be pardoned. 소죄(小罪)의. [L. *venia* pardon]

Ven·ice [vénis] *n.* a city on the northeastern coast of Italy. 베니스《베네치아의 영어명》.

ven·i·son [vénəzən, -sən] *n.* Ⓤ the meat of deer. 사슴 고기. [L. *venor* hunt]

ven·om [vénəm] *n.* Ⓤ **1** the poisonous liquid of snakes, etc. (독사 등의) 독; 독액. **2** 《*fig.*》 strong desire to do harm to others; ill will. 악의. ¶ *She cast a look of* ~ *at him.* 날카롭게 그를 쏘아보았다. [L. *venenum* poison]

ven·om·ous [vénəməs] *adj.* **1** containing poison. 독이 있는. ¶ *a* ~ *serpent* 독사. **2** desiring to do harm to others. 악의에 찬. ¶ *a* ~ *look* 악의에 찬 시선 / ~ *criticism* 혹평 / *She had a* ~ *tongue.* 입정이 사납다.

vent [vent] *n.* Ⓒ **1** a small hole or opening for the passage of air, smoke, etc. (공기·액체 등이 드나드는) 구멍; 통기구; 누수구. ¶ *the* ~ *of a chimney* 굴뚝 아가리 / *the* ~ *of a cask* 통의 주둥이 / *a* ~ *in the crater of a volcano* 화산의 분화구 / *an air* ~ 통기구. **2** the act of letting out, esp. in speech; expression. (감정 등의) 발로; 표출. ¶ *His passion found* ~ *in writing.* 그는 저작에 정열을 쏟았다 / *Her sorrow found* (*a*) ~ *in tears.* 슬퍼서 눈물이 쏟아졌다 / *He found some* ~ *for his anger in bad language.* 그는 욕설을 퍼부어 화풀이를 했다. **3** a finger hole in a musical instrument. (관악기의) 지공(指孔).

give vent to, give a means of escape to; express freely. …에 (분 따위)를 터뜨리다. ¶ *He at last gave* ~ *to his anger.* 그는 끝내 분통을 터뜨렸다.

V

— *vt.* **1** (P6,13) express (one's feelings) freely in words or actions; utter. (감정 등)을 터뜨리다; 드러내다; 토로하다. ¶ *She vented her anger on her friends.* 그녀는 친구들에게 화풀이했다. **2** (P6) make (smoke, etc.) escape through a hole; make a vent in (something). (연기 따위)를 내보내다; …에 구멍을 만들다. ¶ *The chimney vented the smoke.* 굴뚝에서 연기가 나왔다 / *~ a cask* 통에 구멍을 내다. [L. *ventus* wind]

*__ven·ti·late__ [véntəlèit] *vt.* (P6) **1** bring fresh air in and drive stale air out of (a room, etc.). …의 환기를 하다. ¶ *We ventilated a room by opening windows.* 창문들을 열어 방을 환기시켰다 / *a well-ventilated room* 환기가 잘 되는 방. **2** make (blood, etc.) pure by supplying fresh air. …을 신선한 공기로 깨끗이 하다. ¶ *The lungs ~ the blood.* 폐는 피를 깨끗이 한다. **3** 《*fig.*》 make (something) known openly; discuss openly. …을 공표하다; 자유롭게 토의하다. ¶ *The new policy has now been freely ventilated.* 새 정책은 요즘 자유롭게 토의되어 왔다. **4** supply (a room, etc.) with a vent. …에 환기구를 만들다. [↑]

*__ven·ti·la·tion__ [vèntəléiʃən] *n.* Ⓤ **1** the act of ventilating; the state of being ventilated. 환기; 환기 상태. **2** the means of ventilating. 환기 장치. ¶ *The ~ of the mine broke down.* 광산의 환기 장치가 고장났다. **3** free discussion; public examination and discussion. 자유 토의; 공개 토의.

*__ven·ti·la·tor__ [véntəlèitər] *n.* Ⓒ a device for changing or supplying air; a contrivance for changing or improving the air. 환기〔통풍〕 장치.

ven·tral [véntrəl] *adj.* **1** of the belly of an animal. (짐승의) 배의; 복부의. **2** of or on the surface of the belly of an animal. 배 거죽에 있는; 복면(腹面)에 있는. ¶ *a ~ scale of a snake* 뱀의 복면 비늘. [L. *venter* belly]

ven·tri·cle [véntrikəl] *n.* 《anat.》 one of the two lower cavities of the heart which receive blood and force it into the arteries. 심실(心室). [↑]

ven·tril·o·quism [ventríləkwìzəm] *n.* Ⓤ the art of speaking in which the voice seems to come from some other person than the speaker. 복화술(腹話術). [↑]

ven·tril·o·quist [ventríləkwist] *n.* Ⓒ a person who is skilled in the art of ventriloquism. 복화술사(腹話術師).

:**ven·ture** [véntʃər] *n.* **1** ⓊⒸ a risky course of action; a risky piece of business; risk; chance; luck. 모험; 위험한 일. ¶ *be ready for any ~* 어떤 위험에도 대처하다 / *A bold ~ is often successful.* 대담한 모험이 종종 성공한다. **2** Ⓒ a business enterprise. 투기(投機); 투기 사업. ¶ *a profitable ~* 유리한 투기 / *a business ~* 투기 사업 / *take a ~ in stocks* 투기 사업으로 주(株)에 손을 대다 / *He lost his first ~ in oil stock.* 석유주(株) 투기에서 그는 최초의 실패를 했다 / *A lucky ~ in oil stock made his fortune.* 석유주의 투기가 잘 들어맞아 그는 한 재산 모았다.

at a venture, by chance; at random; at a guess; without any fixed idea. 운에 맡기고; 무턱대고.

— *vt.* **1** (P6,7,13) expose (something) to danger, risk, or chance; risk. …을 위험에 내맡기다; (돈·목숨 따위를) …에 걸다. ¶ *~ money in speculations* 투기에 돈을 걸다 / *~ one's life on a doubtful enterprise* 불확실한 사업에 생(生)을 걸다 / 《*prov.*》 *Nothing ~, nothing have* 〔*win*〕. 호랑이 굴에 들어가야 호랑이를 잡는다 / *~ a fortune on a single chance* 단 한번의 기회에 전 재산을 걸다. **2** (P6,8) dare to say or do. …을 과감히 말하다; 감행하다. ¶ *~ a guess* 과감히 추측해 보다 / *~ an opinion* 과감히 의견을 말하다 / *He ventured a critical comment.* 그는 과감하게 비판적인 평을 했다 / *He ventures to say what he believes.* 과감하게 그는 소신을 피력한다 / *No one ventured to interrupt the speaker.* 어느 누구도 감히 연사의 말을 가로막지 못했다.

— *vi.* (P1,3,4) take a risk; dare to do or go something dangerous. 위험을 무릅쓰다; 위험을 무릅쓰고 가다〔행하다〕. ¶ *He ventured from his hiding place.* 그는 은신처에서 위험을무릅쓰고나왔다 / *I should not ~ too near the edge if I were you.* 내가 너라면 너무 가장자리로는 안 가겠다 / *Will you ~ on another glass of wine ?* 포도주 한 잔 더 하지 않겠느냐. [→adventure]

ven·ture·some [véntʃərsəm] *adj.* **1** willing to take risks; daring. 모험을 좋아하는; 대담한; 무모한. **2** dangerous; risky. 위험한.

ven·ue [vénjuː] *n.* **1** 《law》 the place in which a case must be tried and the jury gathered. 재판지(裁判地). **2** 《*colloq.*》 a meeting place. 회합 장소. [L. *venio* come]

Ve·nus [víːnəs] *n.* **1** 《Rom. myth.》 the goddess of love and beauty. 비너스. **2** a very beautiful woman. 미인. **3** the most brilliant planet, second in order from the sun. 금성. [L.]

ve·ra·cious [vəréiʃəs] *adj.* **1** always telling the truth; truthful; trustworthy. 성실한; 믿을 만한. ¶ *a ~ witness* 정직한 증인. **2** founded on the truth; true. 바른; 진실의. ¶ *a ~ story.* [→very]

ve·rac·i·ty [vərǽsəti] *n.* Ⓤ **1** the state of being truthful. 성실; 정직. **2** something which is true. 진실. ¶ *Some doubt the ~ of his statements.* 그의 말의 진실성을 의심하는 사람들도 있다. **3** exactness; the state of having no mistakes. 정확; 확실. [↑]

ve·ran·da, -dah [vərǽndə] *n.* Ⓒ a long, open porch with a roof. 베란다. [Port.]

:**verb** [vəːrb] *n.* Ⓒ 《gram.》 a word that expresses an action, a state of being, or a condition. 동사. [L. *verbum* word]

ver·bal [vɔ́ːrbəl] *adj.* **1** of or consisting of words. 말의; 어구의. ¶ ~ *expression* 언어 표현 / ~ *mistakes* 어구〔말〕의 잘못 / *A description is a ~ picture.* 서술은 언어에 의한 묘사이다. **2** expressed by spoken words; not written; by word of mouth. 말로 하는; 구두의. ¶ *a ~ message* 〔*communication*〕 구두 보고; 전언(傳言) / *a ~ agreement* 〔*contract*〕 구두 약속〔계약〕. **3** word for word; literal. 글자대로의; 축어적(逐語的)인. ¶ *a ~ translation* 축어역(譯); 직역. **4** concerned with the words only; not with the substance. (사상·내용 등에 관계 없이) 말〔어구〕만의; (내용보다) 어구〔자구〕상의. ¶ *a ~ criticism* 어구의 비평 / *a ~ difference* 어구상의 차이 / *a ~ promise* 말뿐인 약속; 언약. **5** 《gram.》 of or derived from a verb. 동사의; 동사에서 나온. ¶ ~ *adjectives* 동사적 형용사.
— *n.* Ⓒ 《gram.》 an infinitive, gerund or participle. 준(準)동사. [*verb*]

ver·bal·ly [vɔ́ːrbəli] *adv.* **1** in words. 말로. **2** by spoken words. 구두(口頭)로. **3** word for word. 축어적(逐語的)으로. **4** in words only. 말뿐으로; 말만으로. **5** as a verb. 동사로서.

verbal noun [⌐–⌐] *n.* a noun derived from a verb, formed by adding *-ing* at the end of a verb or *to* before a verb; a gerund or infinitive. 동사적 명사; 동명사; 명사 용법 부정사.

ver·ba·tim [vəːrbéitim] *adv., adj.* word for word; literal(ly); in exactly the same words. 축어적(逐語的)으로〔인〕; 글자대로(의); 똑같은 말로. ¶ *translate a book ~* 책을 축어적으로 번역하다 / *She repeated his remarks ~.* 그녀는 그의 말을 말한 그대로 반복했다. [*verb*]

ver·be·na [vərbíːnə] *n.* Ⓒ 《bot.》 a garden plant with a mass of small flowers in various colors and with various smells. 마편초속(屬)의 식물; 버베나. [L.]

ver·bi·age [vɔ́ːrbiidʒ] *n.* Ⓤ the use of too many words. (군)말이 많음. [→verb]

ver·bose [vəːrbóus] *adj.* expressed in or using too many words; wordy. 말이 많은; 장황한. ¶ *a ~ sermon* 〔*explanation*〕 장황한 설교〔설명〕. [↑]

ver·bos·i·ty [vəːrbásəti / -bɔ́s-] *n.* Ⓤ the state of being verbose. 말이 많음; 수다스러움.

ver·dant [vɔ́ːrdənt] *adj.* **1** covered with grass or leaves; fresh and green. 온통 푸른; 푸릇푸릇한; 신록의. ¶ *the ~ grass* 〔*trees, leaves*〕 / *a ~ landscape* 푸르른 전망. **2** 《*fig.*》 fresh and not experienced. 미숙한; 풋내기의. ¶ *in one's ~ youth* 순진한 청년 시절에. [L. *viridis* green]

ver·dict [vɔ́ːrdikt] *n.* Ⓒ **1** the judgment made by a jury in a law court. (배심원의) 평결; 답신(答申)(cf. *sentence*). ¶ *The jury returned a ~ of 'Not Guilty.'* 배심원은 '무죄'평결을 답신했다. **2** the act of making up one's mind. 결의; 결단. ¶ *My ~ differs from yours in this matter.* 이 문제에서 내 결단은 너와 다르다. [→very, diction]

ver·di·gris [vɔ́ːrdəgriːs] *n.* Ⓤ the green, poisonous compound formed on brass, bronze or copper which has been kept for a long time without being cleaned. 녹청(綠靑). [F. =green of Greece]

ver·dure [vɔ́ːrdʒər] *n.* Ⓤ **1** greenness; freshness. 푸르름; 신록. **2** fresh green grass or growing plants. 푸른 초목. **3** 《*fig.*》 freshness, as of youth. 생기(生氣); 활력. [→verdant]

ver·dur·ous [vɔ́ːrdʒərəs] *adj.* fresh and green. 푸릇푸릇한. ¶ ~ *meadows* 푸르디푸른 풀밭〔목초지〕.

verge [vəːrdʒ] *n.* Ⓒ **1** an edge; a brink. 가장자리; 가. ¶ *on the ~ of the lake* 호수가에. **2** a limit; a border. 경계; 한계. ¶ *beyond the ~ of possibility* 가능성의 한계를 넘어 / *within the ~ of one's ability* 능력의 범위 안에서 / *to the ~ of extinction* 절멸 지경에 이르기까지.
be on the verge of, be approaching closely. …하기 직전에 있다; 당장에라도 …할 것 같다. ¶ *be on the ~ of tears* 곧 울음이 터질 것 같다 / *be on the ~ of ruin* 〔*war*〕 파멸〔전쟁〕 직전에 있다.
— *vi.* **1** (P3) 《*on*》 become near to something; approach. 다가가다; 접근하다. ¶ *the path verging on a cliff* 벼랑으로 다가가는 작은 길. **2** (P2A,3) 《*to, toward*》 tend; incline. 향하다; 기울다. ¶ *The sun is now verging toward the horizon.* 해는 지금 지평선에 기울고 있다. [mixture of L. *verga* wand and L. *virgo* incline]

ver·ger [vɔ́ːrdʒər] *n.* Ⓒ **1** a person who takes charge of a church; a sexton. 교회〔성당〕지기. **2** a person who carries the rod symbolic of his position or rank before a bishop, etc. (주교 등의 앞에서) 권표(權標) 받드는 사람. [↑]

ver·i·fi·ca·tion [vèrəfikéiʃən] *n.* Ⓤ **1** the act of proving the truth of a fact. 입증; 증명. **2** a statement made in order to prove something. 증언. [↓]

ver·i·fy [vérəfài] *vt.* (**-fied**) (P6) **1** prove the truth of (something); confirm. …을 실증〔확인〕하다. ¶ *The report of the accident was verified by an eyewitness.* 사고 보고는 한 목격자에 의해 확인됐다 / *Events have verified the prophecy.* 사건들은 그 예언이 진실이었음을 입증했다. **2** test the exactness of (something). …을 확실히 하다; 대조 확인하다. ¶ ~ *a list of prices* 가격표를 대조 확인하다. **3** carry out. …을 실행하다. ¶ ~ *a promise* 약속을 이행하다. **4** 《law》 prove the authenticity of, by proofs, affidavits. (증거·선서 등에 의해) 입증하다. [→very]

ver·i·ly [vérəli] *adv.* 《*arch.*》 in truth; truly; really. 진실로; 참으로; 사실로.

ver·i·si·mil·i·tude [vèrəsimílətjùːd] *n.* Ⓤ **1** the state of being likely or probable;

V

likelihood. 있음직함; 정말 같음. **2** something which seems to be true. 사실같이 보이는 일. [→very, similar]

ver·i·ta·ble [vérətəbəl] *adj.* actual; real; genuine. 사실의; 진정한; 진짜의. ¶ *The rain was a ~ godsend.* 그 비는 진정 하늘의 선물이었다. [→very]

ver·i·ty [vérəti] *n.* **1** Ⓤ the state or quality of being true; reality. 진실(성). ¶ *I doubt the ~ of the statement.* 나는 그 말의 진실성을 의심한다. **2** Ⓒ something taken as fundamentally and essentially true. 진리. ¶ *one of the eternal verities* 하나의 영원한 진리. [↑]

in all verity, 《*arch.*》 surely. 참으로; 진실로.

of a verity, 《*arch.*》 in truth; surely. 참으로; 실로.

ver·meil [vɔ́:rmil, -meil] *n., adj.* **1** 《*poet.*》 =vermilion. **2** gilded silver, bronze, etc. 금도금한 은·청동 등. [→vermilion]

ver·mi·cel·li [və̀:rmi:tʃéli, -séli] *n.* Ⓤ food like macaroni and spaghetti, but thinner and longer. 버미첼리. [L. *vermis* worm]

ver·mi·cide [vɔ́:rməsàid] *n.* Ⓒ any drug that kills worms, esp. those that live in the bowels. 살충제; (특히) 회충약.

ver·mi·form [vɔ́:rməfɔ̀:rm] *adj.* shaped like a worm. 연충(蠕蟲) 모양의. ¶ *the ~ appendix* 충양 돌기.

ver·mil·ion [vərmíljən] *n.* Ⓤ **1** a bright red color. 주홍색. **2** a material making a bright-red color. 주(朱); 진사(辰砂). — *adj.* bright red. 주홍색의. — *vt.* (P6) make bright red. …을 주홍으로 물들이다. [L. *vermis* worm (named from confusion with cochineal)]

ver·min [vɔ́:rmin] *n.* Ⓤ 《*collectively*, usu. used as *pl.*》 **1** harmful and unpleasant insects, small creature such as fleas, lice, bed-bugs, rats, mice, owls, etc. 해충; 유해한 작은 동물. **2** 《*fig.*》 people who are very unpleasant and troublesome like vermin. 사회적 해충; 인간 쓰레기; 망나니; 악당; 건달. [L. *vermis*]

ver·min·ous [vɔ́:rmənəs] *adj.* **1** troubled by harmful insects or animals. 해충이 꾄〔생긴〕. ¶ *the tramp's ~ old coat* 방랑자의 이가 들끓는 남루한 코트. **2** caused by vermin. 해충에 의한. ¶ *~ disease* 기생충병. **3** 《*fig.*》 (of a person) like vermin in character; base; harmful. (사람이) 해충 같은; 비열〔치사〕한; 해를 끼치는. [↑]

Ver·mont [vərmánt / -mɔ́nt] *n.* a State of the northeastern United States; a part of New England. 버몬트 주. 參考 Vt.라 생략함. 주도는 Montpelier.

ver·mouth [vərmú:θ] *n.* Ⓤ a kind of white wine flavored with various strong-smelling plants. 베르무트 술. [G. (→wormwood)]

ver·nac·u·lar [vərnǽkjələr] *n.* Ⓒ **1** a native language; the language used by the people of a certain country, district. 제 나라 말; 지방어; 사투리; 방언. ¶ *His speech was given in his own ~.* 그가 한 연설은 그의 지방 고유의 말이었다. **2** informal language spoken every day. (평이한) 일상어. **3** the language of a class or a profession. 전문〔직업〕어; 은어. ¶ *There are many strange words in the ~ of sailors.* 뱃사람들의 은어에는 생소한 것들이 많다.
— *adj.* **1** (of language) used by the people in a certain place. 모국〔자국〕의; 지방의《말·어법 따위》. ¶ *the ~ languages of India* 인도의 토어(土語) / *a ~ idiom* 한 지방의 관용어. **2** native. 토착(土着)의. ¶ *a ~ disease* 풍토병. **3** of the native language. 지방어(地方語)의. [L. *verna* homeborn slave]

ver·nal [vɔ́:rnl] *adj.* **1** of or like spring. 봄의; 봄 같은. ¶ *the ~ bloom* 봄의 꽃 / *~ weather* 봄날씨 / *the ~ aspect of the woods and fields* 숲과 들의 봄빛 모습. **2** 《*fig.*》 having the looks of youth; fresh. 청춘의; 생기 넘치는. ¶ *the ~ spirits of youth* 젊음의 발랄한 생기 / *There was a ~ freshness about her.* 그녀에게는 생기 발랄한 데가 있었다. [L. *ver* spring]

ver·ni·er [vɔ́:rniər] *n.* Ⓒ a small, movable scale attached to a larger, fixed scale and used for measuring fractional parts or divisions. 아들자; 부척(副尺); 버니어. [Person]

ve·ron·i·ca [viránikə / -rɔ́n-] *n.* Ⓒ **1** 《bot.》 a shrub with blue, pink or white flowers. 현삼과의 식물. **2** a cloth on which Christ's face is drawn. 예수의 얼굴을 그린 헝겊; 베로니카의 성백(聖帛). [L.]

ver·sa [vɔ́:rsə] *adv.* ⇨vice versa.

Ver·sailles [vərsái, vɛər-] *n.* **1** a city near Paris. 베르사유. **2** a large palace in this city. 베르사유 궁전.

ver·sa·tile [vɔ́:rsətl / -tàil] *adj.* **1** that can do many things well. 다재 다능한. ¶ *a very ~ performer* 다재 다능한 연기자. **2** having many different uses. 용도가 많은; 다목적의. ¶ *Nylon is a ~ material.* 나일론은 쓰이는 데가 많은 재료이다. **3** changeable. 잘 변하는; 변덕스러운. ¶ *a ~ disposition* 변덕. **4** able to turn freely. 자유롭게 돌아가는. ¶ *a ~ spindle* (가전성(可轉性)의) 회전축. [L. *verto* turn]

:verse [və:rs] *n.* Ⓒ **1** a single line of poetry. 시의 한 행. **2** a group of lines of poetry; a stanza. (시의) 한 절(節); 연(聯). **3** Ⓤ a literary composition with rhythm; poetry. 운문(韻文); 시(cf. *prose*). **4** a short, numbered division of a chapter in the Bible. (성경의) 절. [↑]

·versed [və:rst] *adj.* having experience; well practiced; skillful. 경험 있는; 숙달〔정통〕한. ¶ *She is well ~ in speaking.* 그녀는 언변이 아주 능하다 / *a doctor well ~ in medicine* 명의(名醫) / *be well ~ in the arts of diplomacy* 외교술에 능하다.

ver·si·fi·ca·tion [və̀ːrsəfikéiʃən] *n.* Ⓤ **1** the act of making verses. 작시(作詩). **2** the art or method of making verses. 작시법. **3** the form or pattern of poetry. 시형(詩形). [→versify]

ver·si·fi·er [və́ːrsəfàiər] *n.* Ⓒ a person who makes verse; a poet. 시인; 작시가.

ver·si·fy [və́ːrsəfài] *vt.* (**-fied**) (P6) **1** write poetry about (something). …의 시를 쓰다. **2** translate (prose) into poetry. (산문)을 시로 고치다. — *vi.* (P1) tell in poetry. 시로 말하다[짓다]. [→verse, -fy]

·**ver·sion** [və́ːrʒən, -ʃən] *n.* Ⓒ **1** a translation from one language to another. 번역(서); 번역문. ¶ *the Authorized Version* 흠정역(欽定譯) 성서 / *the Revised Version* 개역(改譯) 성서. **2** a particular remark; a statement from a personal point of view. (개인적 또는 특정 입장에서 행해지는) 설명; 이야기; 의견. ¶ *my ~ of the affair* 그 사건에 대한 내 의견 / *Each of the three boys gave his own ~ of the quarrel.* 세 아이들은 제각기 그 말다툼에 관하여 설명했다 / *Let me hear your own ~ of it.* 네 입장에서의 그것에 관한 이야기를 들려 다오. [*verse*]

vers li·bre [vɛ̀ər líːbrə] *n.* (*pl.* **-li·bres** [-z]) 《F.》 verse not following a fixed metrical form. 자유시(=free verse).

ver·so [və́ːrsou] *n.* (*pl.* **-sos**) **1** any left-hand or reverse page of a book. (책의) 왼쪽 페이지; 뒤 페이지(opp. recto). **2** the reverse of a coin, medal, etc. (동전 등의) 이면. [*verse*]

ver·sus [və́ːrsəs] *prep.* against. … 대(對)《abbr. v., vs.》. ¶ *Oxford ~ Cambridge* 옥스퍼드 대 케임브리지 / *plaintiff ~ defendant* 원고(原告) 대 피고. [→versatile]

ver·te·bra [və́ːrtəbrə] *n.* (*pl.* **-brae** or **-bras**) one of the joints of the backbone. 추골(椎骨); 등뼈. [L. *verto* turn]

ver·te·brae [və́ːrtəbrìː] *n.* pl. of **vertebra.**

ver·te·bral [və́ːrtəbrəl] *adj.* of a vertebra or the vertebrae. 척추골의. ¶ *the ~ column* 척주(脊柱).

ver·te·brate [və́ːrtəbrèit, -brit] *n.* Ⓒ an animal having a backbone, such as fishes, birds, and mammals. 척추 동물. — *adj.* having a backbone. 척추가 있는. ¶ *a ~ animal* 척추 동물. [→vertebra]

ver·tex [və́ːrteks] *n.* (*pl.* **-ti·ces** or **-tex·es**) **1** the highest point; the top; the crown of the head. 정점(頂點); 절정. ¶ *the ~ of an arch* 아치의 정점. **2** 《geom.》 the point or angle of a figure opposite to the base. 꼭지점; 정점. **3** 《astron.》 the zenith. 천정(天頂). [L. *verto* turn]

·**ver·ti·cal** [və́ːrtikəl] *adj.* straight up and down; upright; erect. 직립한; 곧추 선; 수직의; 세로의(opp. horizontal). ¶ *a ~ line* 수직[연직(鉛直)]선 / *a ~ motion* 상하 운동; 상하동(上下動) / *a ~ turn* 수직 선회 / *a ~ rudder* (*of an airplane*) (비행기의) 방향타(方向舵) / *The northern face of the mountain is almost ~.* 산의 북쪽 면은 거의 수직이다 / *a ~ takeoff* (항공기의) 수직 상승. — *n.* 《*the ~*》 a vertical line, plane, position, etc. 수직선[면]; 수직의 위치. [L. *vertic-*, ↑]

ver·ti·cal·ly [və́ːrtikəli] *adv.* in a vertical position; at right angles; uprightly. 수직으로; 직립하여.

ver·ti·ces [və́ːrtəsiːz] *n.* pl. of **vertex.**

ver·tig·i·nes [vəːrtídʒəniːz] *n.* pl. of **vertigo.**

ver·tig·i·nous [vəːrtídʒənəs] *adj.* **1** turning round and round; rotating. 빙글빙글 도는; 선회하는. **2** of vertigo; dizzy. 어지러운; 눈이 빙빙 도는. ¶ *~ heights* 눈이 어찔해지는 고도. **3** changeable; unstable. 변화가 심한; 불안정한. [↓]

ver·ti·go [və́ːrtigòu] *n.* (*pl.* **-tig·i·nes** or **-goes**) Ⓤ the feeling as if one's head were turning around; dizziness. 현기(증). ¶ *He suffers from ~.* 그는 현기증이 있다. [L. *verto* turn]

verve [vəːrv] *n.* Ⓤ a strong feeling of animation; active strength or energy; force; spirit. 열정; 활기; 힘; 기력; 열의. ¶ *He's a poor singer but we had to admire the sheer ~ of his performance.* 그는 노래를 잘 못 하지만 노래를 부르는 태도에 보이는 진지한 열의는 인정해야 했다. [F.]

⁑**ver·y** [véri] *adv.* **1** 《with *adv., adj.* and *participial adj.*》 in a high degree; greatly; extremely. 대단히; 몹시; 매우. ¶ *~ wet* 몹시 젖은 / *a ~ wet day* 몹시 비오는 날 / *~ thoughtfully planned* 대단히 치밀하게 계획된 / *a ~ interesting book* 아주 재미있는 책 / *~ much troubled* 아주 골치 아픈 / *a play ~ well received* 아주 평판이 좋은 극 / *a ~ worried look* 몹시 근심스러운 표정 / *~ well stated* 표현이 썩 잘된 / *a ~ good cake* 아주 맛있는 과자 / *I feel ~ much better today.* 오늘은 아주 기분이 좋다 / *~ respectfully yours* 경백(敬白) / *a ~ pleasing voice* 매우 듣기 좋은 음성 / *~ much annoyed* 몹시 난처한. 語法 감정을 나타내는 수동태에는 원칙으로 much 가 많이 쓰이나 구어에서는 very 를 쓰는 경향이 많아지고 있음. **2** 《with *negative*》 rather. 그다지; 그리[별로] (…아니다); 조금도 …않다. ¶ *It is not ~ warm today.* 오늘은 그다지 따뜻하지 않다 / *This is not a ~ good book.* 이건 별로 좋은 책이 아니다 / *Are you busy ?—No, not ~.* 지금 바쁘냐—아니 (뭐) 별로. **3** 《with *a superlative, my, your, his, own,* etc.》 absolutely; really. 실로; 정말; 바로. ¶ *my ~ own* 바로 내 것 / *He drank it to the ~ last drop.* 그는 마지막 한 방울까지 마셔 버렸다 / *This is the ~ last time I offer to help you.* 이번이 내가 너에게 도움을 제안하는 마지막 기회이다 / *two accidents in the ~ same place* 바로 똑같은 장소에서 일어난 두 건의 사고.

— *adj.* (**ver·i·er, ver·i·est**) **1** 《*arch.*》 real;

V

true. 참된; 정말의; 진짜의. ¶ *in ~ truth* 진실로 / *her ~ son* 그녀의 친아들 / *the ~ God of peace* 진실된 평화의 신 / *A verier rogue would be hard to meet.* 이런 악당은 천하에 없을 게다 / *The veriest simpleton knows it.* 아무리 바보라도 그건 알고 있다. **2** 《as an *intensive,* placed after *the, this, that, my, your, his*》 same; precise; actual; absolute. 바로 그; 다름 아닌; 아주 꼭 …한; 틀림없는. ¶ *at the ~ moment* 바로 그 순간(때) / *On the ~ day she was married, she had an accident.* 결혼한 바로 그날 그녀는 사고를 당했다 / *this ~ day* 바로 이날 / *He did it under my ~ eyes.* 바로 내 눈 앞에서 그 짓을 했다 / *They say he died in that ~ bed.* 그는 바로 저 침대에서 임종했다고 한다 / *He is the ~ picture of his father.* 그는 그의 아버지를 빼쏘았다. **3** 《as an *intensive*》 even; mere. …조차; …까지도. ¶ *The ~ thought of war makes me shudder.* 전쟁은 생각만 해도 몸서리난다 / *His ~ children despise him.* 자식들조차 그를 멸시한다. [L. *verus* true]

ves·per [véspər] *n.* Ⓤ **1** 《*V-*》 the evening star; Hesperus. 개밥바라기; 금성. **2** 《usu. *pl.*》 an evening prayer or church service. 저녁 기도; 만과(晩課). — *adj.* **1** of evening; appearing in the evening. 저녁의; 저녁에 보이는. **2** of vespers. 만과의. [L. =evening]

***ves·sel** [vésəl] *n.* Ⓒ **1** a hollow container for liquids. 그릇; 용기(容器). ¶ *Cups, bowls, pitchers, bottles, etc. are vessels.* 컵, 사발, 주전자, 병 등은 그릇이라 한다. **2** a tube in a body carrying blood or other liquids. 관; 도관(導管). ¶ *a blood ~* 혈관. **3** a large boat; ship. 배. ¶ *a war ~* 전함 / *a merchant ~* 상선. [L. *vas*]

***vest** [vest] *n.* Ⓒ **1** 《U.S., comm.》 a short, sleeveless garment worn by men under the coat. 조끼. **2** 《U.S.》 a similar garment worn by women. 베스트《조끼 비슷한 여성용 윗도리》. **3** 《Brit.》 an undershirt. 속옷; 내의.
— *vt.* (P6,13) **1** 《*arch.*》 put clothes on (someone). …에게 옷을 입히다. ¶ *They vested the choir in white robes.* 그들은 합창단에게 흰 가운을 입혔다. **2** give power, rights, authority, etc. to (someone). …에게 권력 등을 주다. ¶ *Congress is vested with the power to declare war.* 의회에 전쟁 선포의 권한이 주어져 있다. **3** put (power, authority, etc.) into the care or possession of someone. (권력 등)을 …에게 주다; (아무)의 관리하에 두다. ¶ *The power to pardon is vested in the governor.* 사면권은 통치자에게 주어져 있다 / *The houses were vested in the trustees.* 집들은 관재인의 관리하에 있었다.
— *vi.* **1** (P1) clothe oneself, esp. in ceremonial garments. 제복(祭服)을 입다. **2** (of a right, etc.) become fixed or vested in someone. (권리 따위가) 아무에게 귀속하다. [L. *vestis* garment]

Ves·ta [véstə] *n.* **1** 《Rom. myth.》 the goddess of the hearth. 베스타《난로의 여신》. **2** Ⓒ 《*v-*》 a kind of short wax match. 짤막한 성냥의 일종; 밀랍 성냥. [L. =goddess of the hearth and home]

ves·tal [véstl] *n.* Ⓒ **1** 《Rom. myth.》 a girl serving Vesta; a vestal virgin. 베스타 여신의 시중을 든 처녀. **2** an unmarried woman; a virgin. 처녀. **3** a nun. 수녀; 수도녀. — *adj.* **1** of Vesta. 베스타 여신의. **2** pure; virgin. 순결한; 처녀의. [↑]

vest·ed [véstid] *adj.* **1** 《law》 fixed; settled. 기득(既得)의; 기정(旣定)의. ¶ *~ right* (*interest*) 기득권(이권). **2** dressed in robes, esp. in church garments. 제복(祭服)을 입은. [*vest*]

ves·ti·bule [véstəbjù:l] *n.* Ⓒ **1** a passage or hall between the outer door and the inside of a building; an entrance hall. 현관; 현관의 홀. **2** 《U.S.》 the enclosed space at the end of a railway passenger car. 객차 입구에 있는 작은 공간. [L.]

ves·tige [véstidʒ] *n.* Ⓒ **1** a mark made by something which has passed; a trace. 자취; 흔적. ¶ *vestiges of an earlier civilization* 초기 문명의 자취 / *I found no ~ of his presence.* 그의 존재의 형적을 찾을 수 없었다. **2** 《biol.》 a part or an organ that is no longer useful. 퇴화한 기관; 흔적 기관. ¶ *the ~ of a tail in the human body* 인체의 꼬리 흔적. **3** 《*poet.*》 the mark of a foot left on the ground; the track of man or animal. 사람(짐승)의 발자국. **4** 《usu. with a *negative*》 a bit. 조금. ¶ *No ~ of a change appeared.* 변한 데라고는 없다 / *My parents had no ~ of humor.* 나의 양친에게는 유머 감각이 털끝만치도 없었다. [L. =footstep]

ves·tig·i·al [vestídʒiəl] *adj.* of a vestige. 흔적의; 자취로 남은; 퇴화한. [↑]

vest·ment [vés*t*mənt] *n.* Ⓒ **1** any article of dress or clothing. 의복. **2** a robe or garment worn by a clergyman in a ceremony. (성직자의) 가운; 제복(祭服). [→vest]

vest-pock·et [véstpɑ̀kit / -pɔ̀k-] *adj.* that can be put into a pocket of a vest; very tiny; small-sized. (조끼 주머니에 들어갈 정도로) 작은; 소형의. [→vest]

ves·try [véstri] *n.* Ⓒ (*pl.* **-tries**) **1** a room in a church where vestments are kept. (교회의) 제복실(祭服室). **2** a room in a church used for Sunday School, prayer meetings, etc. (기도회·주일 학교 등에 쓰이는) 교회 부속실. **3** a meeting of the people of a parish on church business. 교구회(敎區會). [→vest]

ves·ture [véstʃər] *n.* ⓊⒸ 《*poet.*》 **1** garments; clothes. 의복; 옷. **2** anything that covers or protects. 덮개; 가리개. ¶ *a ~ of mist* 안개의 장막. [↑]

vet [vet] *n.* Ⓒ 《*colloq.*》 =veterinarian.
— *vt.* (**vet·ted, vet·ting**) (P6) **1** treat (an animal) medically. (짐승)을 치료하다. **2** 《*joc.*》 give (a person) medical or surgical

treatment. (사람)을 치료하다. **3** examine carefully for correctness, past record, etc. (상세하게) 조사〔검사〕하다. [→veterinary]

vetch [vetʃ] *n.* Ⓒ 《bot.》 a plant of the pea family grown as food for cattle. 살갈퀴《누에콩속(屬)의 식물; 사료용》. [L. *vicia*]

•**vet·er·an** [vétərən] *n.* Ⓒ **1** a person who has had much experience in war. 고참병; 노병(老兵). **2** 《U.S.》 a person who has done military service. 퇴역 군인. **3** a person who has had much experience in some profession or position. 노련한 사람; 베테랑. — *adj.* **1** having much experience in war. 전쟁 경험이 많은. **2** experienced; long-trained. 노련한. ¶ *a ~ statesman* 노련한 정치가. [L. *vetus* old]

Veterans Day [ˊ-- ˋ] *n.* 《U.S.》 November 11, observed as a legal holiday in commemoration of the end of World War I in 1918 and World War II in 1945. 재향 군인의 날《11월 11일》.

vet·er·i·nar·i·an [vètərənέəriən] *n.* Ⓒ a doctor who treats animals. 수의(사). [↓]

vet·er·i·nar·y [vétərənèri / -nəri] *adj.* concerning the medical or surgical treatment of animals. 수의의. ¶ *a ~ hospital* 가축〔동물〕 병원 / *a ~ surgeon* 수의(사) / *~ science* 수의학. — *n.* Ⓒ (*pl.* **-nar·ies**) a veterinarian. 수의(사). [L. *veterinae* cattle]

ve·to [víːtou] *n.* Ⓒ (*pl.* **-toes**) **1** the right of a president, etc. to refuse bills and so prevent them from becoming law. 거부권. ¶ *The president has the power of ~ over most bills passed in Congress.* 대통령은 의회를 통과한 거의 모든 법안에 대하여 거부권을 가진다 / *The ~ of the Crown has not been exercised since the reign of Queen Anne.* 영국 국왕의 거부권은 앤 여왕의 치세 이래 행사된 적이 없다. **2** the use of this right. 거부권의 행사; 거부. ¶ *put* 〔*set*〕 *a ~ on a proposal* 제안에 거부권을 행사하다; 제안을 거부하다. **3** refusal of consent or agreement; prohibition. 금지. ¶ *I'll put a ~ on football in the garden in case the children break any more windows.* 아이들이 유리창을 더 깰 경우 정원에서 축구하는 것을 금지시키겠다.

— *adj.* of a veto. 거부(권)의; 부인의.

— *vt.* (P6) **1** refuse (bills) by a veto. …을 거부하다. ¶ *The president last week vetoed a cereal price cut.* 지난 주 대통령은 곡물가 인하안을 거부했다. **2** forbid someone to consent to (something); prohibit. …을 금하다. ¶ *In public schools smoking by the boys is vetoed.* 공립 학교에서 학생들의 흡연은 금지되어 있다. [L.=forbid]

•**vex** [veks] *vt.* (P6) **1** make (someone) angry, esp. by a worthless idea; annoy; irritate. …을 화나게 하다; 애타게〔짜증나게〕 하다; 초조하게 하다. ¶ *It is vexing to have to wait for anyone* 남을 기다려야 한다는 것은 짜증나는 일이다 / *His conduct vexed me very much.* 그의 행동에 나는 몹시 화가 났다 / *I was vexed with him.* 나는 그 사람 때문에 애를 먹었다. **2** disturb; trouble. …을 어지럽히다; 괴롭히다. ¶ *Angry winds vexed the sea.* 사나운 바람이 바다를 거칠게 만들었다 / *I am vexed to hear such bad news.* 그런 나쁜 소식에 나는 매우 괴로웠다. [L. *vexo* afflict]

vex·a·tion [vekséiʃən] *n.* **1** Ⓤ the act of vexing; the state of being vexed. 화〔짜증〕나게 함; 애태움; 짜증. ¶ *His face showed his ~ at the delay.* 그의 얼굴에는 늦어짐에 따라 짜증스러움이 역력했다 / *Much to my ~, I missed a good chance to see him.* 분하게도 그를 만날 절호의 기회를 놓쳤다. **2** Ⓒ a thing which annoys. 고민〔두통〕 거리. ¶ *One must put up with all the trifling vexations.* 사소한 골칫거리 따위는 모름지기 다 참아야 한다. [↑]

vex·a·tious [vekséiʃəs] *adj.* **1** causing vexation; worrying. 화나는; 골치 아픈; 성가신. ¶ *Moving house is a ~ business.* 이사한다는 것은 골치 아픈 일이다. **2** 《law》 done for the purpose of annoyance. (소송 목적이) 남을 괴롭히기 위한. ¶ *a ~ suit* 〔*action*〕 남소(濫訴).

v.i., vi. intransitive verb.

vi·a [váiə, víːə] *prep.* 《L.》 by way of; passing through; 《U.S.》 by means of. …경유로; …을 거쳐; …에 의하여. ¶ *He returned home ~ America.* 그는 미국을 경유해 귀국했다 / *~ airmail* 항공편으로. — *n.* **1** a way; a road. 길; 도로. **2** 《anat.》 a tube. 관(管). [L. =a way, road]

vi·a·duct [váiədʌ̀kt] *n.* Ⓒ a bridge built to carry a road or railway over a valley. (골짜기를 가로지르는 도로나 철로의) 고가교(高架橋); 육교. [via, L. *duco* lead]

vi·al [váiəl] *n.* Ⓒ a small glass bottle for holding medicines; a bottle. (작은) 약병; 병. [→phial]

pour out the vials of one's wrath upon 〔***on***〕, **a**) 《Bible》 take vengeance on. …에게 복수하다. **b**) 《*colloq.*》 express anger at. …에게 화풀이하다.

Vi·a Lac·te·a [váiə lǽktiə, víːə-] *n.* 《L.》 the Milky Way. 은하.

vi·and [váiənd] *n.* Ⓒ **1** an article of food. 식품. **2** 《*pl.*》 food, esp. articles of choice food; provisions. 음식; (특히) 요리; 식량. [→victual]

vi·brant [váibrənt] *adj.* **1** moving rapidly to and fro; vibrating. 진동하는; 떨리는. **2** continuing to sound; ringing. 울리는; 울려 퍼지는. ¶ *the ~ tones of a violin* 울려퍼지는 바이올린 소리. **3** alive; forceful; powerful and exciting. 힘찬; 활력 있는; 스릴 있는. ¶ *a city ~ with life* 활기가 넘치는 도시 / *a youthful ~ voice* 젊고 활기찬 목소리. [↓]

•**vi·brate** [váibreit / -ˊ] *vi.* (P1) **1** move quickly back and forth; tremble; shake. 진

V

동하다; 떨리다; 흔들리다. **2** 《*fig.*》 have an exciting feeling; thrill; throb. 흥분하다; 떨다; 전율하다; 두근거리다. ¶ *The heart vibrates with excitement.* 흥분해서 가슴이 두근거린다. **3** hesitate between two opinions, two courses of action. (마음이) 흔들리다; 갈피를 못 잡다; 망설이다.

— *vt.* (P6) **1** cause to vibrate; make (something or someone) swing. …을 진동시키다; 흔들다. ¶ *The hammers strike the piano strings and ~ them.* 해머가 현을 쳐서 진동시킨다. **2** give an exciting feeling to (someone). …을 흥분〔감동〕시키다; (가늘게) 떨게 하다. [L. *vibro* shake, swing]

vi·bra·tion [vaibréiʃən] *n.* UC a quick movement to and fro. 떨림; 진동.

vic·ar [víkər] *n.* C **1** a person performing the service in a church of an English parish. (영국 국교의) 교구 목사. **2** a clergyman in a parish of the Protestant Episcopal Church. (감독 교회의) 회당(會堂) 목사. **3** a clergyman representing the Pope or a bishop of a Roman Catholic church. 교황 대리; 대목(代牧). **4** 《rare》 a person who acts in place of another. 대리인. [L. *vicem* turn]

vic·ar·age [víkəridʒ] *n.* C the house of a vicar. vicar의 주택; 목사관.

vi·car·i·ous [vaikέəriəs, vi-] *adj.* **1** acting for another. 대리의; 대신하는. ¶ *a ~ agent* 대리인. **2** done or suffered for another. 대신해서 받는〔겪는〕. ¶ *~ punishment* 대신해서 받는 형벌. **3** felt by sympathizing with another's experience. 동감하는; 남의 입장이 되어 느끼는. [↑]

:vice[1] [vais] *n.* UC **1** a bad habit or tendency. 악습; 악폐. ¶ *the vices of modern civilization* 〔*of a political party*〕 현대 문명〔정당〕의 악폐 / *He has the ~ of gluttony.* 그는 과식하는 나쁜 버릇이 있다. **2** evil conduct; wickedness. 비행; 악덕; 사악. ¶ *Vice of all kinds exists in all big cities.* 모든 대도시에는 가지가지의 죄악이 존재한다 / *The police have smashed a ~ ring in Chicago.* 경찰은 시카고의 범죄 집단을 소탕해버렸다. **3** a bad habit or fault of a horse, a dog, etc. (말이나 개의) 나쁜 버릇. **4** a physical defect. 신체적 결함. **5** a fault in expression. (문체 등의) 결함. ¶ *a ~ of literary style* 문체상의 결함. [L. *vitium*]

vice[2] [vais] *n.* 《Brit.》 =vise.

vice[3] [vais] *n.* 《*colloq.*》 vice-chancellor, vice-president, etc. 부총장〔회장〕; 대리. [↓]

vi·ce[4] [váisi] *prep.* 《L.》 in place of; instead of. …대신으로; …의 대리로. ¶ *be Brigade Major ~ Captain A promoted* 승진한 A 대위를 대신해 여단(旅團) 부관이 되다. [L. *vicem* turn, →vicar]

vice- [vais-] *pref.* acting in the place of; next in rank to. (관직 등의 명사에 붙어) '부(副); 차(次)' 의 뜻. ¶ *a vice-agent* 부대리인 / *a vice-chancellor* 대학 부총장; 장관대리 / *a vice-consul* 부영사. [↑]

vice admiral [ˊ-ˊ--] *n.* a naval officer next below an admiral in rank. 해군 중장.

vice·ge·rent [vaisdʒí(:)ərənt] *n.* C a person appointed by a ruler, etc. to exercise his power and authority. 대리인. ¶ *God's ~* 교황. — *adj.* acting in another's place; exercising the power or authority of another. 대리의; 대리 권한을 행사하는. [vice-, L. *gero* carry]

vice-gov·er·nor [váisgʌ́vənər] *n.* C an officer next below a governor in rank. 부총독; 부지사. [vice-]

vice-pres·i·dent [váisprézədənt] *n.* C an officer ranked next below a president. 부통령; 부회장; 부사장; 부교장; 교감.

vice·roy [váisrɔi] *n.* C a person who rules a country, province or colony as representative of a king or queen. 태수(太守); 총독. ¶ *the ~ of India* 인도 총독. [vice-, F. *roi* King; →rex]

vi·ce ver·sa [váisi vǝ́:rsə] *adv.* 《L.》 the other way round; conversely; just the opposite. 반대로; 거꾸로; 역(逆) 또한 같음. 參考 v.v.로 생략함. ¶ *He distrusts her, and ~.* 그는 그녀를 불신하고 그녀 또한 그를 불신한다 / *The cat stole the dog's dinner, and ~.* 고양이가 개밥을 훔치고 개는 고양이 밥을 훔쳤다 / *The man blames his wife, and ~.* 남자는 아내를 비난하고 아내는 남편을 비난한다 / *He is afraid of horses, and ~.* 그는 말을 무서워하고 말은 그를 무서워한다.

·vi·cin·i·ty [visínəti] *n.* U **1** the state of being near; nearness. 가까움; 근접. ¶ *towns in close ~* 근접 도시. **2** the surrounding area; the neighborhood. 근처; 부근; 이웃. ¶ *There are no houses to let in this ~.* 이 근처에는 셋집이 없다 / *the village in the ~* 이웃 마을. [L. *vicus* district]

in the vicinity of, close to. …의 부근에. ¶ *He is in the ~ of fifty.* 그는 50세 전후다 / *He is in the ~ of death's door.* 그는 지금 죽어가고 있다.

·vi·cious [víʃəs] *adj.* **1** evil; wicked. 나쁜; 악덕한; 타락한; 사악한. ¶ *a ~ companion* 나쁜 벗 / *lead a ~ life* 타락한 생활을 하다 / *a ~ book* 음란 서적. **2** full of faults; not correct. 결점이 있는; 틀린. ¶ *a ~ pronunciation* 틀린 발음 / *~ reasoning* 잘못된 추리. **3** full of malice or ill will; spiteful. 악의에 찬; 심술궂은. ¶ *~ remarks* 악담 / *a ~ look* 심술궂은 표정 / *He gave the dog a ~ blow with his stick.* 개를 지팡이로 후려갈겼다. **4** 《*colloq.*》 extremely unpleasant; ill-tempered. 지독한; 고약한; 성마른. ¶ *a ~ headache* 심한 두통 / *a ~ dog* 〔*horse*〕 성질이 고약한 개〔말〕. ●**vi·cious·ly** [-li] *adv.* **vi·cious·ness** [-nis] *n.* [*vice*[1]]

vicious circle [ˊ-ˊ-] *n.* **1** a situation in which the attempt to solve one problem leads to a new problem and increases the difficulty of solving the original problem. 악순환(惡循環). 2 《log.》 the use of one proposition to establish a second, when the second is in turn used to define the first. 순환 논법.

vi·cis·si·tude [visísətjùːd] *n.* 1 Ⓒ 《usu. *pl.*》 continual changes, esp. from good to bad, in one's nature, condition of life, etc. 변화; 변천; (인생·운명 등의) 영고 성쇠; 부침(浮沈). ¶ *The vicissitudes of life may suddenly make a rich man very poor.* 인생의 부침은 부자를 갑자기 빈곤의 나락으로 몰기도 한다 / *the vicissitudes of war* 〔*fate*〕 전쟁〔운명〕의 추이(推移). 2 Ⓤ 《*poet.*》 a regular change. 규칙적인 변화. [→vice⁴]

•**vic·tim** [víktim] *n.* Ⓒ 1 a living being killed as a sacrifice to some god. 산 제물. 2 a person or an animal injured or killed in some accident, misfortune, etc. 희생자; 피해자. ¶ *victims of the war* 전쟁의 피해자 / *the victims of his pitiless ambition* 그의 냉혹한 야망에 희생된 사람들 / *He fell a ~ to his own avarice.* 그는 자기 자신의 탐욕의 희생물이 됐다. [L. *victima*]

vic·tim·ize [víktimàiz] *vt.* (P6) 1 make (someone) a victim of someone or something else. …을 희생시키다; 산 제물로 바치다. 2 cause (someone) to suffer. …을 괴롭히다. 3 cheat. …을 속이다.

Vic·tor [víktər] *n.* a man's name. 남자 이름.

•**vic·tor** [víktər] *n.* Ⓒ a winner; a conqueror. 승리자; 정복자. — *adj.* of a victor; victorious. 승리(자)의. ¶ ~ *troops* 승리〔전승〕군. [L. *vinco* conquer]

Vic·to·ri·a [viktɔ́ːriə] *n.* 1 a woman's name. 여자 이름. 2 the queen of England from 1837 to 1901. 빅토리아 여왕. [Person]

Vic·to·ri·an [viktɔ́ːriən] *adj.* 1 of the time of Queen Victoria. 빅토리아 여왕 시대의. 2 showing characteristics of the people who lived in the Victorian period. 빅토리아 왕조풍(風)의. — *n.* Ⓒ any of the writers of the Victorian age. 빅토리아 여왕 시대의 작가.

•**vic·to·ri·ous** [viktɔ́ːriəs] *adj.* having won a victory in battle or contest; of victory. 승리를 거둔; 이긴; 승리의. ¶ *a ~ army* 승리군 / *the ~ football team* 축구 우승팀 / *a ~ battle* 승리의 싸움 / *a ~ day* 승리의 날 / *come out ~* 승리를 얻다; 전승하다. ● **vic·to·ri·ous·ly** [-li] *adv.* [↓]

:**vic·to·ry** [víktəri] *n.* ⓊⒸ (*pl.* **-ries**) the defeat of an enemy; success in any contest. 승리; 전승; 우승(opp. defeat). ¶ *The game ended in a ~ for our school.* 게임은 우리 학교의 승리로 끝났다 / *win the ~ over the enemy* 적군에게 이기다 / *He gained the* 〔*a*〕 *~ over his passions.* 그는 격정(激情)을 이겨냈다〔극복했다〕. [→victor]

vict·ual [vítl] *n.* 《usu. *pl.*》 《*colloq.*》 food; provisions. 음식; 식량. — *v.* (**-ualed, -ual·ing** or 《Brit.》 **-ualled, -ual·ling**) *vt.* (P6) provide (someone) with food. …에 식량을 공급하다. ¶ *The captain victualed his ship for the voyage.* 선장은 항해에 필요한 식량을 배에 실었다. — *vi.* (P1) 1 take on a supply of food. 식량을 공급하다. 2 《*arch.*》 get one's meals. 음식을 먹다. [L. *vivo* live]

vict·ual·er, 《Brit.》 **-ual·ler** [vítlər] *n.* Ⓒ 1 a person who supplies food to a ship, an army, etc. (선박·군대 등에의) 식료품 공급자. 2 《Brit.》 an innkeeper licensed to sell alcohol. (주류(酒類) 판매 면허가 있는) 여관〔음식점〕 주인. 3 a ship employed to carry stores for other ships. 식량 수송선.

vid. vide.

vi·de [váidiː] *v.* 《L.》 see; refer to. (…을) 보라; 참조하라.

vide in·fra [váidiː ínfrə] *v.* 《L.》 see below. 아래를 보라.

vi·de·li·cet [vidéləsèt] *adv.* 《L.》 that is to say; namely. 즉; 바꿔 말하면. 參考 흔히 viz. 라고 써서 namely 라고 읽음. [L. *video* see, *licet* is allowed]

vid·e·o [vídiòu] *adj.* 《U.S.》 of or used in the transmission or reception of a televised image. 텔레비전 영상(映像) 수송(受送)(용)의(opp. audio). — *n.* Ⓤ television. 텔레비전. [L. *video* see]

vide su·pra [váidiː súːprə] *v.* 《L.》 see above. 위를 보라.

vie [vai] *vi.* (**vied, vy·ing**) (P3) 《*with*》 enter into rivalry; compete. (우열을) 다투다; …와 경쟁하다; 겨루다. ¶ ~ *with another for power* 권력을 차지하기 위해 남과 서로 겨루다 / *In my opinion few fruits can ~ with the apple.* 내 생각에는 사과만한 과일은 별로 없다. [→invite]

Vi·en·na [viénə] *n.* the capital of Austria, on the Danube. 빈; 비엔나. 參考 독일명은 Wien.

Vi·en·nese [vìəníːz, -níːs] *n.* (*pl.* **-nese**) a person of Vienna. 빈 사람. — *adj.* of Vienna or the Viennese people. 빈 (사람)의.

Vi·et·nam, Vi·et Nam [vìètnáːm, vjèt-, -nǽm] *n.* a country in southeastern Asia, formerly a part of French Indo-China. 베트남. 參考 정식명은 The Socialist Republic of Vietnam. 수도는 Hanoi.

:**view** [vjuː] *n.* Ⓒ 1 the act of seeing; a look. 보기; 봄; 구경. ¶ *This lake is well worth our ~.* 이 호수는 볼 만하다〔한 가치가 있다〕. 2 Ⓤ the power of seeing; the range of the eye. 시력; 시계(視界); 시야. ¶ *The ship soon came into ~.* 배는 곧 시야에 들어왔다 / *The top of the hill is beyond our ~.* 산 꼭대기는 우리 눈에 보이지 않는다〔우리 시계 밖에 있다〕 / *The castle gradually passed from our ~.* 성은 서서히 시야에서 사라졌다. 3 that which is seen; a scene. 보이는 것; 전망; 경치. ¶ *From the road I had a good ~ of the sea.* 도로에서 바다가 잘 보였다 / *The ~ from our house is very beautiful.* 우리 집에서 보이는 전망은 아주 아름답다. 4 a picture of some scene, esp. of a landscape. 풍경화; 풍경 사진. ¶ *Various views of the castle hung on the walls.* 그 성의 가지각색 사진〔그림〕이 벽마다 걸려 있었다 / *take some views of the lake* 호수 사진을 몇 장 찍다. **5** the way of looking at a matter; an opinion; a thought; a judgment; mental examination. 사물을 보는 방식; 견해; 의견; 판단; 고찰. ¶ *He spoke his views on the election.* 그는 선거에 대한 자기 의견을 말했다 / *What is your ~ of life after death?* 사후 생명에 대한 너의 견해는 어떠한가 / *quite a new ~ of the affair* 사태에 대한 아주 새로운 견해 / *hold extreme views* 과격한 의견을 갖다. **6** ⓊⒸ a purpose; an intention; a prospect; an expectation. 목적; 의도; 기대; 가망. ¶ *a definite plan in ~* 의도하는 확정안 / *He is obliged to work on with no ~ of success.* 그는 성공할 가망도 없이 계속 일 해야 한다 / *I have views on a meal in the next town.* 다음 마을에서 할 식사에 기대를 가지고 있다. **7** a mental picture; an idea. (심적(心的)인) 인상; (대략적인) 개념. ¶ *This book will give you a general ~ of the World War.* 이 책을 읽으면 세계 대전에 대한 대략적인 개념을 얻게 될 것이다.

in view, **a**) in sight. 보여. **b**) under consideration. 생각 중인. **c**) as a purpose; as an expectation. 의도하여; 기대하여.

in view of, **a**) in sight of. 보이는 곳에. ¶ *stand in full ~ of the scene* 전경을 볼 수 있는 곳에 서다. **b**) considering; because of. …을 고려하여; …때문에. ¶ *in ~ of the grave situation* 대국적인 견지에서.

on view, open for people to see; on display. 전시〔진열〕되어.

take a view of, observe; examine; notice. …을 관찰하다; …을 검사〔주의〕하다.

with a view to =***with the view of*** (*doing*), for the purpose of. …할 목적으로. ¶ *He works hard with a ~ to winning a scholarship.* 장학금을 얻으려고 열심히 공부하고 있다 / *with a ~ to cutting down expenses* 비용을 줄일 목적으로.

— *vt.* (P6,7,13) **1** look at (something) carefully; see; examine. …을 (유의해서) 보다; 조사〔검사〕하다. ¶ *Columbus first viewed the land on October 12.* 콜럼버스는 10월 12일에 최초로 그 땅을 보았다 / *~ the body* 검시(檢屍)하다 / *Several possible buyers have come to ~ the house.* 몇몇 원매자(願買者)들이 집을 살피러 왔다. **2** consider; regard; form an opinion about (something). …라고 간주하다; …을 생각하다; …한 견해를 가지다. ¶ *The proposal was viewed favorably by the authorities.* 그 제안은 당국에서 호의적으로 고려되었다 / *I ~ his conduct in the gravest light.* 나는 그의 행동을 매우 중대시하고 있다. **3** 《*colloq.*》 watch (television). (텔레비전)을 보다. ¶ *The viewing figures for this program have been poor.* 이 프로그램의 시청률은 시원찮았다. [L. *video* see]

view·find·er [vjú:fàindər] *n.* Ⓒ a device attached to a camera for selecting view to photograph. (카메라의) 파인더.

view·less [vjú:lis] *adj.* **1** not able to be seen; invisible. 보이지 않는. ¶ *Ghosts are ~.* 유령은 눈에 보이지 않는다. **2** 《U.S.》 having no view or opinion. 의견〔주견〕이 없는. **3** offering no view. 전망이 좋지 않은. **4** blind. 장님의.

·**view·point** [vjú:pɔ̀int] *n.* Ⓒ **1** a place from which someone looks at something. (사물이) 보이는 지점. ¶ *sketch a river from the ~ of a bluff* 단애(斷崖)에서 강(江)을 스케치하다. **2** a way of looking at something; a point of view. 견지; 견해; 관점. ¶ *Consider it from another ~.* 다른 입장에서 생각해라 / *a person of very narrow ~* 아주 소견이 좁은 사람 / *from the ~ of history* 역사의 관점에서.

vig·il [vídʒil] *n.* **1** Ⓤ the act of staying awake all night for some purpose. 밤샘; 철야; 불침번. ¶ *keep ~* 불침번을 서다; (간병·조상(弔喪) 따위로) 밤샘하다 / *keep ~ over a sick person* 밤새워 간병하다. **2** 《usu. *pl.*》 a religious service, prayers, etc. on the night before a festival. 축일 전야의 철야 기도. [L. *vigil* awake]

vig·i·lance [vídʒələns] *n.* Ⓤ **1** the state of being vigilant; watchfulness. 밤새워 지킴; 경계; 조심. ¶ *keep a strict ~ over ...* …에 엄중한 경계를 계속하다 / *The cat watched the mouse-hole with ~.* 고양이는 쥐구멍을 지켰다. **2** 《med.》 insomnia. 불면증.

vig·i·lant [vídʒələnt] *adj.* watchful to prevent or avoid possible danger; keenly watchful; attentive. 조심하는; 경계하는; 주의 깊은. ¶ *keep a ~ guard* 주의 깊게 경계〔감시〕하다 / *The police said the public should remain ~.* 경찰은 주민들에게 경계를 게을리하지 말 것을 일렀다. ● **vig·i·lant·ly** [-li] *adv.*

vi·gnette [vinjét] *n.* Ⓒ **1** a decorative design on the title page of a book. (책 속표지의) 장식 무늬. **2** a literary description in words. 소품문(小品文)《간결하고 짧은 인물 묘사의 글 따위》. **3** a drawing, etc. in which figures shade off gradually at the edge. 비네트《윤곽을 바림한 그림》. [F. *vigne* vine]

·**vig·or,** 《Brit.》 **-our** [vígər] *n.* Ⓤ mental or physical strength; energy or force. 원기; 정력; 활기; 힘. ¶ *He is full of ~.* 원기 왕성하다 / *a man of great ~* 정력이 대단한 사람 / *For a man of seventy he still has surprising ~.* 나이 일흔에도 그는 아직 놀랍도록 정정하다. [L. *vigeo* be lively]

·**vig·or·ous** [vígərəs] *adj.* full of vigor or strength; energetic; lively; showing intellectual vigor and strength of character. 왕성한; 힘찬; 정력적인; 활발한. ¶ *a ~ style* 힘찬 문체 / *a ~ young man* 원기 왕성한 청년 / *a ~ plant* 쑥쑥 잘 자라는 식물 / *a ~ attack* 맹렬한 공격 / *He keeps himself ~ by taking exercise.* 그는 운동으로 활력을 유지하고 있다 / *a ~ thinker* 〔*writer*〕 정력적인 사색

가[작가]. [↑]

vig·or·ous·ly [vígərəsli] *adv.* in a vigorous manner; actively; powerfully. 힘있게; 활발하게; 씩씩하게; 정력적으로.

Vi·king [váikiŋ] *n.* 《also *v-*》 one of the Scandinavian pirates who made raids upon the coasts of Europe from the 8th to the 10th centuries. 바이킹; 북유럽 해적. [E.＝campman]

•**vile** [vail] *adj.* **1** wicked; morally base; evil; disgraceful. 사악한; 비열한; 나쁜; 혐오감을 주는; 천박한. ¶ *the vilest of mankind* 극악인(極惡人) / *The criminal was guilty of ~ behavior.* 범인은 파렴치범이었다 / *a ~ practice* 비열한 짓 / *use ~ language* 천박한 말을 쓰다. **2** 《*colloq.*》 extremely bad. 아주 못된; 고약한. ¶ *What a ~ pen !* 이 무슨 악필이람 / *~ weather* 악천후 / *a ~ smell* 〔*odor*〕 악취 / *She has a ~ temper.* 그녀는 성미가 아주 고약하다. **3** 《*arch.*》 mean; worthless. 하잘것 없는; 무가치한. ¶ *Silver was thought a ~ thing in the days of Solomon.* 솔로몬 시대에 은은 대단한 물건이 아니었다 / *a poor man in ~ clothes* 허름한 옷을 입은 가난한 사람 / *the ~ tasks of the kitchen* 부엌의 허드렛일. ● **vile·ly** [-li] *adv.* **vile·ness** [-nis] *n.* [L. *vilis* worthless]

vil·i·fy [víləfài] *vt.* (**-fied**) (P6) speak evil of (someone). …을 욕하다; 헐뜯다. ● **vil·i·fi·er** [-ər] *n.* [↑]

vil·la [vílə] *n.* Ⓒ a large elegant house in the country or the suburbs. (교외의) 별장; 저택; 빌라. ¶ *rent a ~ in the winter* 겨울에 별장을 빌리다. [L.＝farm]

:**vil·lage** [vílidʒ] *n.* Ⓒ **1** a group of houses in the country, smaller than a town. 마을; 촌락. ¶ *a fishing ~* 어촌. **2** 《*the ~, collectively*》 the people of a village. 마을 사람; 촌민. ¶ *The whole ~ turned out to the baker's funeral.* 온마을 사람들이 빵집 장례식에 모였다. [↑]

vil·lag·er [vílidʒər] *n.* Ⓒ a person who lives in a village, esp. one of the poorer inhabitants of a village. 마을[시골] 사람.

vil·lain [vílən] *n.* Ⓒ **1** a wicked person; a scoundrel. 악인; 악당. ¶ *The ~ stole the money and cast the blame on his friend.* 그 나쁜 놈은 돈을 훔치고는 그 책임을 친구에게 씌웠다. **2** the enemy of the hero in a play. (극에서의) 악역(惡役). **3** 《*joc.*》 a fellow. 놈; 자식. ¶ *You little ~!* 요놈아. **4** 《hist.》＝villein. [→villa]

vil·lain·ous [vílənəs] *adj.* **1** very wicked; evil. 극악한; 악독한. ¶ *~ conduct* 악독한 행위 / *He was brandishing a villainous-looking knife.* 그는 무시무시한 칼을 들이대고 있었다. **2** 《*colloq.*》 extremely bad or unpleasant. 아주 나쁜; 형편 없는; 고약한. ¶ *a ~ hotel* 형편 없는 호텔 / *~ weather* 고약한 날씨 / *~ tea* 맛이 형편 없는 차. [↑]

vil·lain·y [víləni] *n.* (*pl.* **-lain·ies**) **1** Ⓤ the state of being villainous. 흉악; 사악; 비도(非道). **2** Ⓒ 《*pl.*》 a very wicked act; a crime. 악행; 못된[나쁜] 짓.

vil·lein [vílən] *n.* Ⓒ 《hist.》 a class of half-free peasants under the feudal system in the Middle Ages. 농노(農奴).

vim [vim] *n.* Ⓤ 《*colloq.*》 force; energy; spirit. 힘; 정력; 활력. [→vis]

v. imp. verb impersonal. 「이름.

Vin·cent [vínsənt] *n.* a man's name. 남자

Vin·ci [víntʃi], **Leonardo da** *n.* (1452-1519) an Italian painter, sculptor, architect and scientist. 레오나르도 다 빈치《이탈리아의 화가·조각가·건축가·과학자》.

vin·di·cate [víndəkèit] *vt.* (P6) **1** defend (a right, cause, course of conduct, etc.) against opposition; defend the cause of (a person, religion, etc.) successfully. …을 옹호[변호]하다; …을 지키다. ¶ *~ one's honor* 명예를 지키다 / *~ the glory of his name against all competition* 온갖 경쟁에서 그의 이름의 영예를 지키다 / *The report of the committee of inquiry completely vindicates him.* 조사 위원회의 보고는 전적으로 그를 옹호하고 있다. **2** prove the existence or justice of (one's truth, courage, etc.); prove. (진실·용기 등)을 입증[증명]하다. ¶ *~ one's claim* 〔*rights*〕 요구[권리]를 입증[주장]하다. [L. *vindico* claim]

vin·di·ca·tion [vìndəkéiʃən] *n.* ⓊⒸ **1** proof and establishment of right or innocence. 입증; 증명; 확립. **2** a successful defense against unjust criticism, opposition, etc. 변호. ¶ *in ~ of* …을 변호하여.

vin·dic·tive [vindíktiv] *adj.* full of a desire for revenge; bearing a feeling to revenge. 복수심에 찬; 앙심을 품은. ¶ *a ~ person.* [→vindicate]

:**vine** [vain] *n.* Ⓒ **1** a grape plant; a grapevine. 포도나무. **2** a plant with a long stem that climbs on a wall, a tree, or another support. 덩굴. [L. *vinum* wine]

•**vin·e·gar** [vínigər] *n.* Ⓤ a sour liquid used in flavoring or pickling food. (식)초. [↑]

vine·yard [vínjərd] *n.* Ⓒ a place where grapevines are grown. 포도원[밭].

vi·nous [váinəs] *adj.* **1** of or like wine. 포도주의[같은]. ¶ *of ~ taste* 포도주 맛의 / *~ spirits* 포도 증류주. **2** affected by wine. 포도주에 취한. ¶ *in a ~ condition* 포도주에 취해. [*vine*]

vin·tage [víntidʒ] *n.* **1** Ⓒ an year's production of grapes. 포도의 수확고. ¶ *We have had a poor ~ this year.* 금년 포도는 흉작이다 / *The ~ is abundant.* 포도는 대풍작이다. **2** Ⓒ the act of gathering grapes for wine. 포도 수확. **3** Ⓒ the season for gathering grapes. 포도 수확기. **4** ⓊⒸ a specially good wine made from a certain crop of grapes. (특정 연도의 포도로 빚은) 고급 포도주. ¶ *the ~ of 1870,* 1870년 포도주 / *~ wine* (상표·연호가 붙은) 고급 포도주.

5 Ⓒ the type or model of a particular year or period. (특정 연도·시기에 생산된) 제품; 형(型). ¶ *a car of prewar* ~ 전쟁 이전 형(型)의 자동차. [*vine*]

vint·ner [víntnər] *n.* Ⓒ 《Brit.》 a wine dealer. 포도주 상인. [L. *vinum* wine]

vi·nyl [váinəl, vín-] *n.* Ⓤ 《chem.》 a radical which is obtained from ethylene and which is used to form resins and plastics. 비닐(기(基)). [↑]

vi·ol [váiəl] *n.* Ⓒ a musical instrument of the Middle Ages, with six strings and played with a bow. 비올《중세의 현악기》. [F.]

vi·o·la [vióulə] *n.* Ⓒ a musical instrument like a violin but a little larger and deeper in tone. 비올라. [↑]

***vi·o·late** [váiəlèit] *vt.* (P6) **1** break (an agreement, a law, a rule, etc.). (규칙 등)을 어기다; 위반하다. **2** treat (something holy) with lack of respect. (신성한 것)을 더럽히다; 모독하다. ¶ ~ *the church* 교회를 모독하다. **3** disturb; interrupt; break in upon. …을 방해[침해]하다. ¶ ~ *another's privacy* 남의 사생활을 침해하다 / *The sound of guns violated the usual calm of Sunday morning.* 몇 발의 총성이 평소의 조용한 일요일 아침의 정적을 깼다 / ~ *someone's sleep* 아무의 수면을 방해하다. [L. *violo* treat with violence]

vi·o·la·tion [vàiəléiʃən] *n.* ⓊⒸ **1** the act of breaking (an agreement, a law, a rule, etc.). 위반. **2** treatment with lack of respect. (신성) 모독. **3** interruption; disturbance. 방해; 침해. **4** rape. (부녀자에 대한) 폭행.

vi·o·la·tor [váiəlèitər] *n.* Ⓒ a person who violates. 위반자; 방해자; 폭행자.

:**vi·o·lence** [váiələns] *n.* Ⓤ **1** violent conduct or treatment of physical force; great strength in action; intensity. 폭력; 폭행; 난폭[격렬, 맹렬]함. ¶ *Tom slammed the door with* ~. 톰은 쾅하고 난폭하게 문을 닫았다 / *handle a prisoner with* ~ 포로를 난폭하게 다루다 / *resort to* ~ 폭력에 호소하다 / *use* ~ 폭력을 사용하다 / *attack an enemy with* ~ 맹렬하게 적을 공격하다. **2** intensity in natural phenomena. (자연의) 맹위. ¶ *the* ~ *of a tempest* 사나운 폭풍의 맹위. **3** 《law》 unlawful exercise of physical force or intimidation by a display of this. (불법의) 폭력 행위. **4** vehemence of feeling, expression, or passion. (감정 등의) 격렬함; 격정. ¶ *the* ~ *of his passion* 그의 격정. **5** injury; insult. 해(害); 모욕. ¶ *do* ~ *to someone's feeling* 아무의 감정을 손상시키다 / *It would do* ~ *to her principles to work on Sundays.* 일요일에 일을 계속하는 것은 그녀의 원칙에 반하는 것이 된다. [↓]

:**vi·o·lent** [váiələnt] *adj.* **1** severe; forceful; acting with great physical force. 맹렬한; 격렬한; 심한. ¶ *a* ~ *dislike* 심한 혐오 / *a* ~ *storm* 맹렬한 폭풍(우) / *a* ~ *wind* [*earthquake*] 심한 바람[지진] / *a* ~ *blow* [*attack*] 맹렬한 일격[공격] / *a* ~ *pain* 심한 통증 / *a* ~ *change* 격변. **2** resulting from the use of force, strong feeling, action, etc. 난폭한; 폭력에 의한. ¶ ~ *deeds* 폭행 / *a* ~ *death* 횡사. [→violate]

***vi·o·lent·ly** [váiələntli] *adv.* in a violent manner. 세차게; 맹렬하게; 심하게.

:**vi·o·let** [váiəlit] *n.* **1** Ⓒ a small, low plant with purple, blue or white flowers; its flower. 바이올렛. **2** Ⓤ the color of the common violet. 보라색. — *adj.* of the violet color. 보라색의. [L.]

violet rays [⌐–– ⌐] *n.* 《phys.》 **1** the shortest rays of the spectrum. 자선(紫線)《스펙트럼 중 파장이 가장 짧은 광선》. **2** ultraviolet rays. 자외선.

:**vi·o·lin** [vàiəlín] *n.* Ⓒ **1** a musical instrument with four strings and played with a bow. 바이올린. **2** =violinist. [→viol]

vi·o·lin·ist [vàiəlínist] *n.* Ⓒ a person who plays the violin. 바이올린 연주자.

vi·o·lon·cel·list [vàiələntʃélist, vì:ələn-] *n.* Ⓒ a person who plays the violoncello; a cellist. 첼로 연주자; 첼리스트.

vi·o·lon·cel·lo [vàiələntʃélou, vì:ələn-] *n.* Ⓒ (*pl.* **-los**) a musical instrument with four strings, larger than and tuned below the viola; a cello. 첼로. 參考 cello로 생략함.

VIP, V.I.P. [ví:áipí:, vip] *n.* Ⓒ (*pl.* **VIPs, V.I.P.'s** [-pí:z, vips]) 《U.S. *colloq.*》 a very important person. 주요 인물; 요인; 거물.

vi·per [váipər] *n.* Ⓒ **1** any of several kinds of poisonous snakes. 독사; 살무사류(類). **2** an evil and treacherous person. 독사 같은 사람; 악인. [L.]

vi·ra·go [viréigou, -rá:-] *n.* Ⓒ (*pl.* **-goes** or **-gos**) a bad-tempered woman who always shouts and scolds. 입정사나운[잔소리 심한] 여자. [L.=heroine]

***vir·gin** [və́:rdʒin] *n.* **1** Ⓒ a pure and unmarried woman or girl; a maiden. 처녀. **2** 《*the V-*》 the Virgin Mary. 성모마리아. — *adj.* **1** of or suited to a virgin; chaste and pure. 처녀의; 처녀다운. ¶ ~ *modesty* 처녀처럼 얌전함 / *the Virgin Queen* 엘리자베스 1세. **2** fresh; new; untouched. 처음인; 더럽혀지지 않은; 손대지 않은. ¶ *a* ~ *forest* 처녀림 / *a* ~ *voyage* 처녀 항해 / ~ *soil* 처녀지; 미개간지. **3** pure; spotless. (광물 등이) 순수한; 깨끗한. ¶ ~ *gold* 순금 / ~ *snow* 초설; 첫눈. [L. *virgo*]

vir·gin·al [və́:rdʒənl] *adj.* of or like a virgin; pure and chaste. 처녀의[같은]; 순결한. ¶ ~ *bloom* 처녀의 한창때.

Vir·gin·ia [və:rdʒínjə] *n.* **1** a woman's name. 여자 이름. **2** a State in the southeastern part of the United States. 버지니아주. 參考 Va., Virg.로 생략함. 주도는 Richmond.

Virginia creeper [–⌐– ⌐–] *n.* 《bot.》 a woody vine with large leaves, greenish flowers and blue-black berries, also called the American ivy. 양담쟁이.

vir·gin·i·ty [vərdʒínəti] *n.* Ⓤ the state of being a virgin; maidenhood. 처녀임; 처녀성; 순결. [→virgin]

Virgin Mary [ˊ- ˊ-], **the** *n.* the mother of Christ. 성모 마리아.

vir·ile [vírəl, -rail] *adj.* **1** of a man; manly. 남성의; 남자다운; 남성적인(opp. feminine, womanly). ¶ ~ *strength* 〔*courage*〕 남성다운 힘〔용기〕 / *a* ~ *voice* 남성 같은 음성. **2** strong; forceful. 힘찬. ¶ *a* ~ *government* 강력한 정부 / *a* ~ *mind* 〔*literary style*〕 강한 마음〔문체〕. [L. *vir* man]

vi·ril·i·ty [viríləti] *n.* Ⓤ the state or quality of being virile. 남자다움; 남성적임; 힘참. [↑]

vir·tu·al [vəːrtʃuəl] *adj.* really so in effect, though not so in name. 사실상의; 실질적인. ¶ *That was their ~ defeat.* 그건 사실상 그들의 패배다 / *Mr. Smith is the ~ president, though his title is secretary.* 직함은 비서이지만, 스미스 씨가 실질적인 사장이다. [→virtue]

vir·tu·al·ly [vəːrtʃuəli] *adv.* almost; actually; really. 사실상. ¶ *He is ~ dead.* 사실, 그는 죽은 거나 다름 없다 / *Virtually all the members were in agreement with the proposal.* 사실상 전 회원이 그 제안에 동의했다.

:vir·tue [vəːrtʃuː] *n.* (opp. vice) **1** Ⓤ moral excellence in general; goodness. 도덕적인 탁월; 덕(德); 선(善). ¶ ~ *and vice* 덕과 악 / *a man of* ~ 덕망가. **2** Ⓒ a particular moral excellence. 구체적인 덕; 미덕. ¶ *the ~ of charity* 자선의 미덕 / *Patience is a* ~. 인내는 미덕이다 / *Faith, hope and charity are three Christian virtues.* 신앙, 희망, 사랑은 기독교의 세 가지 미덕이다. **3** Ⓒ a good quality; a merit; a value. 미점; 장점; 가치. ¶ *Taciturnity is sometimes a* ~. 침묵이 때론 미점이기도 하다 / *Jack counted the virtues of his car.* 잭은 자기 차의 장점들을 열거하였다 / *This room has the ~ of being cool in summer.* 이 방은 여름에 시원하다는 장점이 있다. **4** Ⓤ (of a medicine, etc.) power to produce an effect. 효력; 효능. ¶ *a medicine without* ~ 효력 없는 약 / *There is little ~ in that remedy.* 그 치료법은 효과가 별로 없다 / *The magnet has lost its* ~. 그 자석은 자력(磁力)이 다했다. **5** Ⓤ the state of being chaste or pure. 정절(貞節); 순결. ¶ *a woman of* ~ 정숙한 부인 / *a lady of easy* ~ 몸가짐이 헤픈 여자.

by* 〔*in*〕 *virtue (=*by the authority, force, or fact*) ***of something.*** …의 힘으로; …에 의하여. [L. *virtus* manliness, excellence]

vir·tu·o·si [vəːrtʃuóusiː, -ziː] *n.* pl. of **virtuoso.**

vir·tu·o·so [vəːrtʃuóusou, -zou] *n.* Ⓒ (*pl.* **-sos** or **-si**) **1** a person with great interest or skill in art; a collector of art objects or curios. 미술 애호가; 골동품 전문가. **2** a person with great skill in some fine art, esp. in playing a musical instrument. (예술의) 대가; (특히) 음악의 거장. [→virtue]

***vir·tu·ous** [vəːrtʃuəs] *adj.* **1** having or showing moral excellence. 덕망이 높은; 고결한. **2** chaste; pure. 정숙한; 절개 있는. ● **vir·tu·ous·ly** [-li] *adv.* **vir·tu·ous·ness** [-nis] *n.* [↑]

vir·u·lence [vírjuləns] *n.* Ⓤ **1** the state or quality of being virulent. 독성; 유독. ¶ *the ~ of a rattlesnake's bite* 방울뱀에 물린 상처의 독. **2** hostility; violent bitterness. 적의; 증오; 신랄함. [↓]

vir·u·lent [vírjulənt] *adj.* **1** very poisonous; deadly. 독성의; 유독한; 치명적인. ¶ ~ *serpents* 독사. **2** bitterly hostile; malicious 악의에 찬. ¶ ~ *abuse* 악의에 찬 욕설. ● **vir·u·lent·ly** [-li] *adv.* [→virus]

vi·rus [váiərəs] *n.* Ⓒ **1** any of a group of living things, smaller than bacteria, which cause various diseases. 바이러스. **2** a poison produced in the body by a disease. 병독. **3** something which poisons the mind or the character. (정신상의) 해독. ¶ *the ~ of revolution* 혁명의 해독. [L. *virus* poison]

vis [vis] *n.* 《L.》 force; strength. 힘. ¶ ~ *animi* [ǽnimi] 용기 / ~ *major* 《law》 불가항력 / ~ *inertiae* [inəːrʃiìː] 타성 / ~ *viva* [váivə] 활력. [L. =force]

vi·sa [víːzə] *n.* Ⓒ a signature on a passport by a representative of a country showing that it has been examined and approved so that a person can enter that country. (여권 따위의) 비자; 사증(査證). — *vt.* (P6) **1** put a visa on (a passport). (여권)에 배서(背書)하다. **2** give a visa to (someone). …에 비자를 내주다. [→view]

vis·age [vízidʒ] *n.* Ⓒ 《lit.》 the face (of a person); a countenance. 얼굴; 용모. [↑]

vis·a·vis [vìːzəvíː] *adv., adj.* face to face. 마주보고(있는). ¶ *sit ~ in a train.* — *prep.* **1** face to face with. …와 마주보는. **2** in relation to. …에 관하여. — *n.* Ⓒ a person who is face to face with another. 마주하고 있는 사람. [F.]

vis·cer·a [vísərə] *n. pl.* (*sing.* **vis·cus**) the inside organs of the body, esp. the heart, lungs, bowels, liver, etc. 내장. [L.]

vis·cid [vísid] *adj.* thick and sticky like a syrup or glue; viscous. 끈적거리는; 끈끈한. [→viscous]

vis·cose [vískous] *n.* Ⓤ a kind of cellulose used in making rayon thread, fabrics and cellophane. 비스코스. [↑]

vis·cos·i·ty [viskɑ́səti / -kɔ́s-] *n.* Ⓤ the state or quality of being viscous. 점질(粘質); 점성(粘性).

vis·count [váikàunt] *n.* Ⓒ a nobleman next below an earl in rank. 자작(子爵). [*vice, count*]

vis·count·ess [váikàuntis] *n.* Ⓒ the wife of a viscount. 자작 부인.

vis·cous [vískəs] *adj.* thick and sticky like syrup. 끈적거리는; 점성의. [L. *viscum* mistletoe]

vis·cus [vískəs] *n.* sing. of **viscera.**

vise [vais] *n.* Ⓒ 《U.S.》 a tool with two jaws to hold objects firmly while work is being done on them. 바이스(cf. esp. 《Brit.》 *vice*). [L. *vitis* vine]

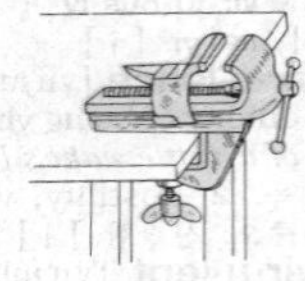
〈vise〉

as firm as a vice, very firm. (바이스처럼) 확고 부동한; 단단한. ***grip something like a vice,*** grip something very firm. …을 꽉 쥐다.

vi·sé [víːzei, ─╯] *n., v.* (**vi·séed, vi·sé·ing**) =visa.

vis·i·bil·i·ty [vìzəbíləti] *n.* Ⓤ **1** the state or quality of being visible. 눈에 보임. **2** 《meteor.》 the degree of things being able to be seen at a given distance, with a certain atmosphere, etc. 시계(視界); 시도(視度). ¶ *The fog is heavy, and* ~ *is down to 20 meters.* 안개가 짙고 시계는 20 미터로 떨어졌다. [↓]

∙vis·i·ble [vízəbəl] *adj.* **1** able to be seen. 눈에 보이는(opp. invisible). ¶ *the* ~ 물질 / *a dark, cloudy night with no stars* ~ 별이 하나도 보이지 않는 어둡고 흐린 밤 / *The shore was scarcely* ~ *through the fog.* 안개로 해변이 거의 보이지 않았다 / *Nothing was* ~. 아무것도 보이지 않았다. **2** apparent; obvious. 명백한; 분명한. ¶ *with* ~ *impatience* 초조감을 역력히 드러내고 / *without any* ~ *cause* 뚜렷한 이유 없이. **3** prepared to receive callers. 면회인을 만날 뜻이 있는. ¶ *Is she* ~*?* 그녀를 만날 수 있겠소. [→view]

vis·i·bly [vízəbəli] *adv.* to a visible extent; plainly. 눈에 보여; 명백히.

:vi·sion [víʒən] *n.* **1** Ⓤ power of seeing; the sense of sight. 시력; 시각. ¶ *poor* ~ 약한 시력 / *the field of* ~ 시야; 시계 / *beyond our* ~ 우리 눈에 안 보이는. **2** Ⓒ something which can be seen; sight. 눈에 보이는 것. ¶ *a lovely* ~ *of the bride* 신부의 사랑스러운 자태 / *the beautiful* ~ 아름다운 광경 / *She was a* ~ *of delight.* 그녀는 아주 명랑해 보였다. **3** Ⓒ something seen in imagination, a dream, etc. 공상; 몽상; 환상. ¶ *romantic visions of youth* 청년 시대의 낭만적인 공상 / *a* ~ *of wealth* 부자가 되는 꿈 / *visions of the future* 미래에 대한 꿈. **4** Ⓤ foresight; imagination; the power of perceiving. 선견(先見); 통찰〔관찰〕력. ¶ *a man of* ~ 선견지명이 있는 사람 / *the* ~ *of a prophet* 예언자의 통찰력.

— *vt.* (P6) see (something) in a vision. …을 환상으로 보다. [L. *video* see]

vi·sion·ar·y [víʒənèri / -nəri] *adj.* **1** of or seen in a vision; not real; imaginary. 환상의; 비현실적인. ¶ *a* ~ *castle* 환상의 성 / *a* ~ *plan* 비현실적인 계획. **2** having a tendency to see visions; dreamy. 환상에 잠기는; 공상적인. ¶ *her* ~ *eyes* 꿈꾸는 듯한 그녀의 눈 / *a* ~ *boy* 공상에 잠기는 소년. — *n.* Ⓒ an impractical person; an idealist. 공상〔몽상〕가.

:vis·it [vízit] *vt.* (P6) **1** go or come to see (someone) socially for a short time; call on (someone). (사교적으로) …을 방문하다. ¶ *A friend of mine visited me.* 한 친구가 나를 만나러 왔다 / *Father visited my uncle in (the) hospital.* 아버지가 입원해 있는 삼촌을 문병했다 / ~ *a new neighbor* 새로 이사온 이웃을 방문하다 / *go to* ~ *someone at his house* 아무를 그의 집으로 방문하다. **2** be a guest of (someone); stay with as a guest. …의 손님으로 머물다. ¶ *He is visiting his aunt in the country for a week.* 그는 시골의 숙모 집에 일 주일 동안 머물고 있다. **3** go to see (a place). …을 구경하러 가다. ¶ *He visited Songnisan for the first time.* 그는 속리산을 처음 구경했다 / ~ *a museum* 〔*an exhibition*〕 박물관〔전시회〕 구경을 가다 / *When we were in London we visited the Tower twice.* 런던 있을 때 런던 타워를 두 번 구경했다. **4** inspect; call on (a sick person) officially. (직무상) …을 시찰하다; 왕진하다. ¶ ~ *a factory* 공장을 견학하다 / ~ *the sick* 환자를 왕진하다 / *An inspector visits schools.* 장학사가 학교를 순시한다. **5** cause great pain or trouble to (someone); attack; come upon (someone). (재해 등이) …을 덮치다; 엄습하다. ¶ *She was visited by a series of misfortunes.* 그녀는 연거푸 불행을 당했다 / *She was visited by a strange notion.* 그녀는 이상한 생각에 사로잡혔다 / *Plague and famine visited the country.* 역병과 기근이 그 나라를 덮쳤다. **6** 《*arch.*》 ⓐ bring punishment on (someone) or for (a sin). (사람·죄)를 벌하다; (고통·벌)을 주다. ¶ 《Prayer Book》 *The sins of the fathers are visited upon the children.* 그 아비의 죄업이 자식들에게 닥친다. ⓑ come upon with blessing. (신이) …에 축복을 내리다. ¶ *God hath visited his people.* 하느님이 자기 백성을 돌보셨도다.

— *vi.* (P2A,3) **1** make a visit; be a guest. 방문하다; 머물다. ¶ *"Do you live in this town?" "No we're only visiting."* "이 마을에 사시오." "아니 그저 다니러 왔소." / ~ *at a house* 집을 방문하다 / ~ *in the country* 시골에 머물다. **2** 《*with*》 ⓐ visit and be visited; associate with. 서로 내왕하다〔사귀다〕. ⓑ 《U.S. *colloq.*》 talk with; converse with. 이야기〔잡담〕하다. ¶ ~ *with someone on the telephone* 아무와 통화하다 / *Just stay and* ~ *with me for a minute.* 좀 있으면서 나와 잠시 얘기나 하세.

— *n.* Ⓒ **1** a social or business call; a short stay. 방문; 문병; 잠시의 체재. ¶ *I* *made* 〔*paid*〕 *him a short* ~. 잠시 그를 방문했다 / *I had* 〔*received*〕 *a* ~ *from a friend.* 친구가 찾아왔었다 / *He came here for a two-day* ~. 그는 여기 이틀 동안 머물려고 왔다 / *return a* ~ 답례로 방문을 하다. **2** an official or professional call for inspection or examination. (직무·직업상의) 순시; 시찰; 왕진. ¶ *receive a* ~ *from a policeman* 경찰의 방문〔임검〕을 받다 / *a doctor's* ~ *to his patient* 의사의 환자 왕진. **3** 《U.S. *colloq.*》 a friendly talk; a chat. 이야기; 회담; 잡담. [→vision]

vis·it·ant [vízətənt] *n.* Ⓒ **1** 《*poet.*》 a temporary guest; a visitor. 방문객. **2** a migratory bird. 철새. — *adj.* 《*arch.*》 visiting. 방문하는. [↑]

vis·it·a·tion [vìzətéiʃən] *n.* Ⓒ **1** the act of visiting. 방문. **2** an official visit for inspection or examination. 순시; 시찰; 임검. **3** a reward or punishment by God. 하늘의 응보; 천벌. ¶ *The plague was formerly regarded as a* ~ *of God for the people's sins.* 예전에는 역병을 사람들이 지은 죄에 대한 천벌이라고 생각했다. **4** 《international law》 an official inspection of foreign ship to learn her character and purpose. (외국 선박에 대한) 임검(臨檢). ¶ *the right of* ~ 임검권. **5** 《*colloq.*》 a long visit. 장기 체류.

visiting card [⌐-- ⌐] *n.* 《Brit.》 a calling card. 명함. [↑]

:vis·i·tor [vízitər] *n.* Ⓒ a person who makes a visit. 방문객; 시찰자(opp. resident). ¶ 《Brit.》 *a visitor's book* 숙박부; (박물관 등의) 방명록. [*visit*]

vi·sor, -zor [váizər] *n.* Ⓒ **1** 《hist.》 the movable front part of a helmet that protects the face. (투구의) 면갑(面甲). **2** 《U.S.》 the brim of a cap. (모자의) 챙. [F. *vis* face]

vis·ta [vístə] *n.* Ⓒ **1** a view through a long, narrow opening; a passage with trees framing such a view. (가로수·건물 등 사이로) 멀리 내다본 경치. ¶ *The opening between the two rows of trees afforded a* ~ *of the lake.* 두 줄로 늘어선 가로수 사이로 멀리 호수가 보였다. **2** such an opening or passage itself. (가로수 등 사이의) 길게 뻗은 공간〔길〕. **3** a mental view of a series of events in the past or future. 추억; (미래에의) 예상. ¶ *the vistas of one's future* 미래의 전망 / *a dim* ~ *of the past* 과거의 희미한 추억 / *The news opened up a long* ~ *of hope.* 그 소식으로 멀리 희망을 바라보게 되었다. [L. *visus;* →vision]

vis·u·al [víʒuəl] *adj.* **1** of sight. 시각의. ¶ *the* ~ *nerve* 시신경 / *the* ~ *sense* 시각 / *the* ~ *organ* 시각 기관. **2** that can be seen; visible. 보이는. ¶ *a* ~ *field* 시야 / *a* ~ *angle* 시각(視角). [→vision]

visual aids [⌐-- ⌐] *n. pl.* something used in helping learning through the sense of sight, such as motion pictures and charts. 시각 교육 기재.

vis·u·al·ize [víʒuəlàiz] *vt.* (P6) **1** make (something) visible; render visual. …을 보이게 하다. ¶ *Bacteria are visible only when they are visualized by means of microscope.* 박테리아는 현미경에 의해서만 보인다. **2** form a mental picture of (something). …을 마음에 그리다. ¶ *If I shut my eyes, I can* ~ *the scene and actors as I actually saw them.* 눈을 감으면 그 장면과 연기자들을 실제로 본 것처럼 마음에 그려볼 수 있다. — *vi.* (P1) form a clear mental image of something. 생생하게 마음에 그리다.

Vi·ta·glass [váitəglæ̀s, -glɑ̀:s] *n.* 《trademark》 a special kind of glass which allows ultraviolet rays to pass through. 바이타 글라스《자외선 투과 유리》. [→visual]

***vi·tal** [váitl] *adj.* **1** of life. 생명의. ¶ ~ *energies* 생명력. **2** necessary to life. 생명에 필요한. ¶ *The heart is one of* ~ *organs of the body.* 심장은 생명에 필요한 신체 기관의 하나다. **3** very important; essential. 극히 중요한; 긴요한. ¶ ~ *to one's purpose* 목적에 불가결한 / *a* ~ *question* =*a question of* ~ *importance* 중대〔사활의〕 문제 / *Your support is* ~ *to* 〔*for*〕 *the success of my plan.* 내 계획의 성공에는 네 협조가 반드시 있어야 한다. **4** causing death or ruin; affecting life; fatal. 사활에 관한; 치명적인. ¶ *a* ~ *wound* 치명상 / *a* ~ *spot* 〔*part*〕 급소(急所). **5** full of life or energy; vivid. 활력이 넘치는; 생기 있는. ¶ *Their leader's* ~ *and cheerful manner filled his men with courage.* 그들 리더의 활기차고 명랑한 태도가 그들에게 용기를 심어줬다. [L. *vita* life]

vital capacity [⌐- -⌐--] *n.* the breathing capacity of the lungs; lung capacity. 폐활량.

vi·tal·i·ty [vaitǽləti] *n.* Ⓤ **1** power to keep on living; vital force. 생명력. **2** strength or liveliness of mind. 생기; 활기. ¶ *Her* ~ *was lessened by illness.* 병으로 해서 기운이 줄었다. **3** strength to endure. 지속〔존속〕력.

vi·tal·ize [váitəlàiz] *vt.* (P6) give life or vigor to (something); give spirit to. …에 생명〔활력〕을 주다; 원기를 돋우다. ¶ *Good food vitalizes the blood.* 좋은 음식은 피에 생기를 준다. ●**vi·tal·i·za·tion** [vàitəlizéiʃən, -lai-] *n.*

vi·tal·ly [váitəli] *adv.* to a vital degree. 치명적으로.

vi·tals [váitls] *n. pl.* **1** the organs of the body necessary to life. 생명 유지에 필요한 기관. ¶ *The brain, heart, lungs and stomach are vitals.* 뇌, 심장, 폐 및 위는 생명 유지의 필요 기관이다. **2** the essential parts of anything. 급소; 핵심. ¶ *the* ~ *of the matter* 문제의 핵심. [*vital*]

vital statistics [⌐- -⌐-] *n. pl.* statistics dealing with births, marriages, and deaths in a certain area. 인구 동태 통계.

***vi·ta·min** [váitəmin / vít-] *n.* Ⓒ any of certain substances contained in natural food and necessary for health and the growth of the body. 비타민. [L. *vita* life, Am(monia)]

vi·ti·ate [víʃièit] *vt.* (P6) **1** make (something) impure and faulty; spoil. …을 더럽히다; 나쁘게 하다. ¶ *vitiated air* 오염된 공기 / *Exaggeration vitiated his style.* 과장이 그의 문체를 망쳤다 / *a vitiated judgment* 그릇된 판단. **2** weaken morally. …을 타락시키다. **3** render ineffective; destroy the legal force of. …을 무효화하다. ¶ *Omission of even a single word may* ~ *a contract.* 한 단어만 빠져도 계약은 무효가 될 수 있다. ● **vi·ti·a·tion** [vìʃiéiʃən] *n.* [vice[1]]

vit·i·cul·ture [vítəkʌ̀ltʃər] *n.* Ⓤ the cultivation of grapes. 포도 재배. [L. *vitis* vine → culture]

vit·re·ous [vítriəs] *adj.* **1** of or like glass. 유리의[같은]. ¶ *the* ~ *body* [*humor*] (눈알의) 유리체[유리체액]. **2** made of glass. 유리로 만든. [L. *vitrum* glass]

vit·ri·ol [vítriəl] *n.* Ⓤ **1** 《chem.》 any salt of sulfuric acid. 황산염. ¶ *blue* ~ 황산구리 / *throw* ~ *over* [*at*] …의 (얼굴)에 황산을 끼얹다 / *green* ~ 황산 제일철. **2** sulfuric acid. 황산. **3** 《*fig.*》 sharp, severe speech or criticism. 신랄한 말[비평]. ¶ *put plenty of* ~ *in a speech* 연설에 신랄한 어구를 많이 쓰다. [↑]

vi·tu·per·ate [vaitjú:pərèit, vi-] *vt.* (P6) scold severely; blame (someone) in abusive words. …을 몹시 꾸짖다; 욕하다. [L.]

vi·tu·per·a·tion [vaitjù:pəréiʃən, vi-] *n.* Ⓤ the act of vituperating; bitter and severe words. 욕(설); 질책.

vi·tu·per·a·tive [vaitjú:pərèitiv, vi-] *adj.* having the nature of vituperation; abusive. 욕을 하는; 욕질하는.

vi·va[1] [ví:və] *interj.* long live (someone)! 만세. [It.=let-live]

vi·va[2] [váivə] *n.* Ⓒ a viva voce examination. 구두 시험. [→viva voice]

vi·va·ce [vivá:tʃei] *adv.* 《mus.》 with spirit and liveliness. 비바체《활발하게》. [It.]

vi·va·cious [vivéiʃəs, vai-] *adj.* lively; high spirited. 활기찬. ¶ *a* ~ *girl* 발랄한 처녀. ● **vi·va·cious·ly** [-li] *adv.* **vi·va·cious·ness** [-nis] *n.* [L. *vivo* live]

vi·vac·i·ty [vivǽsəti, vai-] *n.* Ⓤ high spirits; liveliness. 쾌활; 활기. [↑]

vi·va vo·ce [váivə vóusi] *adv., adj.* by the mouth; oral(ly). 구두로[의]. — *n.* an oral examination. 구두 시험. [L.=by living voice]

·**viv·id** [vívid] *adj.* **1** full of life; active. 활기찬; 생기있는; 발랄한. ¶ *a man of* ~ *imagination* 상상력이 왕성한 사람 / *a* ~ *face* 생기 있는 얼굴 / *a* ~ *personality* 활달한 성격. **2** realistic; life-like. 실감이 나는; 박진감 있는; 사실 그대로의. ¶ *a* ~ *description* 생생한 묘사 / *a* ~ *picture of life in the fields* 들에서의 생활의 실감나는 그림. **3** (of color) bright; brilliant. (색깔이) 선명한(opp. dull). ¶ ~ *green* 선녹색 / *a* ~ *reflection in the water* 물에 뚜렷이 비친 그림자 / *the* ~ *colors of a rainbow* 무지개의 선명한 색깔들. [L. *vivo* live, →vivacious]

viv·id·ly [vívidli] *adv.* **1** actively; in a lively manner. 활발[발랄]하게. **2** brilliantly; distinctly. 선명하게; 뚜렷이.

viv·id·ness [vívidnis] *n.* Ⓤ the state or quality of being vivid. 발랄; 선명.

viv·i·fy [vívəfài] *vt.* (**-fied**) (P6) give life to (someone); make (something) vivid. …을 생기띠게 하다; …에 활기를 주다. ● **viv·i·fi·ca·tion** [vìvəfikéiʃən] *n.* [L. *vivus* alive, → -fy]

vi·vip·a·rous [vaivípərəs, 《Brit.》 viv-] *adj.* bringing forth living young instead of laying eggs. 태생의(opp. oviparous). [↑, L. *pareo* bear, produce]

viv·i·sect [vívəsèkt, ⌐–⌐] *vt.* (P6) cut up the living body of (an animal, etc.) for scientific study. …을 생체 해부하다. — *vi.* (P1) practice vivisection. 생체 해부하다. [↑, L. *seco* cut]

viv·i·sec·tion [vìvəsékʃən] *n.* ⓊⒸ an operation done on living animals for scientific study. 생체 해부.

vix·en [víksən] *n.* Ⓒ **1** a female fox. 암여우. **2** 《*fig.*》 a bad-tempered, quarrelsome woman. 심술궂은 여자. [→fox]

viz. [néimli] =videlicet.

viz·ard [vízərd] *n.* =visor.

vi·zier [vizíər, vízjər] *n.* Ⓒ a high official in a Moslem country, esp. a state minister. (회교국의) 고관; 장관. [Arab.]

vi·zor [váizər, víz-] *n.* =visor.

vo. 《print.》 verso.

voc. vocational; vocative.

vocab. vocabulary.

·**vo·cab·u·lar·y** [voukǽbjəlèri / -ləri] *n.* (*pl.* **-lar·ies**) **1** Ⓤ a list of words arranged in alphabetical order and with their meanings. 어휘표; 어구[단어]집; 사전. ¶ *There is a* ~ *of technical words at the end of the book.* 책의 끝머리에 전문 용어표가 있다. **2** ⓊⒸ 《*collectively*》 all the words used by a class, a group, a person, etc. (어떤 계층의 사람이나 개인이 쓰는) 용어; 어휘(수); 용어 범위. ¶ *Shakespear's rich* ~ 세익스피어의 풍부한 어휘 / *the ever-increasing scientific* ~ 계속 늘어나는 과학 용어 / *have a limited* ~ 어휘가 제한되어 있다; 용어 범위가 좁다 / *Reading will increase your* ~. 독서를 하면 어휘를 많이 알게 된다. [→voice]

vo·cal [vóukəl] *adj.* **1** of the voice. 소리의. ¶ ~ *music* 성악 / *the* ~ *organs* 발성 기관. **2** uttered with the voice. 구두의. ¶ *a* ~ *message* 구두 전갈. **3** full of sound; inclined to speak freely. 시끄러운; 의견을 자유로이 말하는. ¶ *Public opinion has at last become* ~. 여론이 마침내 시끄러워졌다. **4** 《phon.》 voiced. 유성음의. — *n.* Ⓒ a vocal sound; a vowel. 유성음; 모음. [→voice]

vocal cords [ㅗ-ㅗ] *n. pl.* two pairs of thin, skinlike objects in the throat which vibrate to produce sound. 성대(聲帶).

vo·cal·ist [vóukəlist] *n.* Ⓒ a singer. 성악가; (유행가) 가수.

vo·ca·tion [voukéiʃən] *n.* **1** Ⓤ a call or summons by a god. 신의 부름. ¶ *He felt no ~ for the ministry.* 그는 목사가 되라는 소명이 느껴지지 않았다. **2** Ⓤ special fitness or natural ability for a particular kind of work. 적성; 소질; 천직; 사명. ¶ *~ for literature* 문학의 재능 / *She chose teaching as her ~.* 그녀는 교사를 천직으로 택했다. **3** Ⓒ a profession; an occupation. 직업. ¶ *change one's ~* 직업을 바꾸다 / *mistake one's ~* 직업을 잘못 택하다. [→voice]

vo·ca·tion·al [voukéiʃənəl] *adj.* of a vocation. 직업의. ¶ *a ~ bureau* 직업 상담소 / *a ~ test* 직업 적성 검사 / *~ training* 직업 훈련 / *~ guidance* 직업 지도 / *a ~ aptitude* 직업 적성.

voc·a·tive [vákətiv / vɔ́k-] *adj.* 《gram.》 showing a person or thing addressed. 호격(呼格)의. ¶ *the ~ case* 호격.

vo·cif·er·ate [vousífərèit] *vi., vt.* (P1;6) cry out with a loud voice; shout. (고래고래) 소리지르다. ¶ *The crowd vociferated, "Sit down!"* "앉아라" 하고 군중들이 소리를 질렀다. [→voice, L. *fero* bear]

vo·cif·er·a·tion [vousìfəréiʃən] *n.* Ⓤ the act of vociferating; a loud cry. 고함치기; 소리 지름.

vo·cif·er·ous [vousífərəs] *adj.* speaking out noisily; loud and noisy. 소리지르는. ¶ *a ~ person* / *~ cheers* 요란한 만세 소리. ●**vo·cif·er·ous·ly** [-li] *adv.* **vo·cif·er·ous·ness** [-nis] *n.*

vod·ka [vádkə / vɔ́d-] *n.* Ⓤ a Russian alcoholic drink made from rye, potatoes, etc. 보드카. [Russ.]

vogue [voug] *n.* Ⓒ **1** the fashion of the time. 유행. ¶ *out of ~* 유행이 지나 / *This kind of shirt is in ~ now.* 이런 셔츠가 요즘 유행이다 / *the ~ of mini-skirts* 미니스커트의 유행 / *a mere passing ~* 그저 한때의 유행. **2** popularity. 인기. ¶ *His lectures have a great ~.* 그의 강의는 대단한 인기다. [It. *vogare* to row]

all the vogue, the latest thing. 최신 유행품. ¶ *Long skirts were then (all) the ~.* 당시 롱스커트가 대 유행이었다.

come into vogue, become fashionable. 유행되다.

have a vogue, be in vogue. 유행하다. ¶ *have a short ~* 잠시 유행하다.

:voice [vɔis] *n.* **1** ⓊⒸ the sound coming from the mouth, esp. from the human mouth, in speaking, etc. 목소리; 음성. ¶ *in low voices* 낮은 목소리로 / *a soft ~* 부드러운 음성 / *recognize someone's ~* 아무의 목소리임을 알다 / *the ~ of a bird* 새소리 / *a veiled ~* 탁한 목소리 / *the human ~* 사람 목소리 / *the breaking of ~* 변성(기). **2** Ⓒ a sound suggesting, resembling a human voice or speech. (사람 음성에 비유한) 소리. ¶ *the voices of the wind* 〔*waves*〕 바람〔파도〕 소리 / *He loved to listen to the voices of nature.* 그는 자연의 소리를 듣기 좋아하였다 / *The people's ~ is the ~ of God.* 민중의 소리가 신의 소리다; 민심은 천심 / *still small ~* 양심의 소리. **3** Ⓤ an expressed opinion, choice, or wish. (표명된) 의견; 선택; 희망. ¶ *the ~ of the majority* 다수의 의견 / *His ~ was for* 〔*against*〕 *the plan.* 그의 의견은 그 계획에 찬성이었다〔반대였다〕 / *general* 〔*public*〕 *~* 민중의 소리. **4** Ⓤ the right to express an opinion or choice; a vote. 발언권; 투표권. ¶ *He has no ~ in this matter.* 그는 이 문제에 발언권〔투표권〕이 없다 / *The feminists have found their political ~ at last.* 여성 해방론자들이 마침내 정치적 자기 발언을 할 수 있게 됐다. **5** Ⓤ the power to make sounds through the mouth. 발성력. ¶ *lose* 〔*recover*〕 *one's ~* 목소리가 안〔다시〕 나오게 되다. **6** Ⓒ a part of a piece of music produced by one kind of singer or instrument. (성악의) 소리; 성부(聲部). ¶ *a mixed ~* 혼성 / *The song is sung by several voices.* 그 노래는 몇 가지 (다른 음계의) 소리로 불린다. **7** Ⓒ a singer. 가수. **8** Ⓒ 《gram.》 《usu. *the ~*》 a form of the verb indicating whether the subject is passive or active. (동사의) 태(態). ¶ *the active* 〔*passive*〕 *~* 능동〔수동〕태. **9** Ⓤ 《phon.》 a sound produced by the vocal organs, not with mere breath. 유성음(有聲音).

find one's voice, utter; dare to express. 음성이 나오다; 용단을 내서 말〔발언〕하다.

give voice to, express in words. …을 입 밖에 내다; 표명하다. ¶ *They gave ~ to their misgivings.* 그들은 자신들의 불안을 토로했다.

in voice, in good condition for singing or talking. 목소리가 잘 나오는.

lift up one's voice, **a**) sing; speak. 노래하다; 말하다. **b**) shout; protest; complain. 외치다; 항의하다; 불평하다.

raise one's voice, speak loudly. 언성을 높이다. ¶ *raise one's ~ in anger* 화가 나서 언성을 높이다.

with one voice, unanimously. 이구동성으로; 한 목소리로; 만장 일치로. ¶ *She was chosen with one ~.* 만장 일치로 선출됐다.

— *vt.* (P6) **1** give expression to (something); speak; report. …을 말로 나타내다; 표명하다. ¶ *~ the feelings of the meeting* 회중(會衆)의 기분을 말하다 / *They voiced their approval of the plan.* 그들은 그 안을 찬성한다고 했다. **2** 《phon.》 make (sound) with the vocal cords, not with the breath. …을 유성음으로 하다. **3** regulate the tones of (an organ, etc.). (풍금 등)을 조율하다. [L. *vox*]

voiced [vɔist] *adj.* **1** having a voice; having a special kind of or tone of voice. 유성의;

소리가 …한. ¶ *a sweet-voiced girl* 목소리가 아름다운 소녀. **2** expressed by the voice. 소리로 나타낸. **3** 《phon.》 spoken with the aid of the vocal cords. 성대(聲帶)를 쓴; 유성음의(opp. voiceless).

voice·less [vɔ́islis] *adj.* **1** having no voice; unable to utter words; silent. 소리 없는; 무언의; 말을 못 하는; 조용한. ¶ *The old castle was dark and* ~. 그 고성은 어둡고 조용했다. **2** 《phon.》 spoken without the aid of the vocal cords. 무성(음)의. ¶ *The consonant 'p', 't', 'k' are* ~. 자음 p, t, k는 무성음이다.

•**void** [vɔid] *adj.* **1** empty; vacant. 빈. ¶ *a* ~ *house* 빈 집 / *a* ~ *space* 공간. **2** lacking; wanting. …이 결여된; 없는. ¶ *He is* ~ *of learning.* 그는 학식이 없다 / *a scene* ~ *of all beauty* 아름다움이라고는 없는 경치 / *a man quite* ~ *of common sense* 몰상식한 사람 / *a gentleman* ~ *of all bad habits* 나쁜 버릇이 하나도 없는 신사. **3** 《law》 without legal force or effect; of no effect. (법적으로) 무효의 (opp. valid). ¶ *A contract made by a madman is* ~. 미친 사람이 한 계약은 무효다.

null and void ⇨null.

—*n.* **1** Ⓒ an empty space. 빈 데; 공간. ¶ *The bird vanished into the* ~. 새는 허공으로 사라졌다 / *the* ~ *of heaven* 천공(天空). **2** Ⓤ a feeling of loss or emptiness. 공허감. ¶ *His death has left a* ~ *in our lives which can never be filled.* 그의 죽음은 우리들 생활에 결코 채워질 수 없는 공허감을 남겼다 / *an aching* ~ (*in one's heart*) 견딜 수 없는 허전함.

—*vt.* (P6) **1** make (something) of no effect. …을 무효화하다. **2** discharge. …을 배설하다. [F.]

voile [vɔil] *n.* Ⓤ a very thin material used for women's dresses. 보일《사(紗)의 일종》. [F.]

vol. volcano; volume; volunteer.

vol·a·tile [válətil / vɔ́lətàil] *adj.* **1** changing into gaseous form quickly and easily. 휘발성의. ¶ ~ *oils* 휘발성 기름. **2** 《*fig.*》 ⓐ changeable in mood or interest. 변덕스러운. ¶ *a* ~ *disposition* 변덕. ⓑ full of life; gay and light. 활발[쾌활]한. [L. *volo* fly]

vol·a·til·i·ty [vὰlətíləti / vɔ̀l-] *n.* Ⓤ volatile quality; an example of being volatile. 휘발성; 변덕.

vol·a·til·ize [válətəlàiz / vɔ́l-] *vt.* (P6) cause (some liquid) to become vapor. …을 휘발시키다. —*vi.* (P1) change into vapor. 휘발하다.

vol·can·ic [vαlkǽnik / vɔl-] *adj.* **1** of a volcano; produced by a volcano. 화산의; 화산 활동으로 생긴. ¶ ~ *activity* 화산 활동 / ~ *ashes* 화산재. **2** 《*fig.*》 violent like a volcano. 격렬한. ¶ *a* ~ *character* 불 같은 성격. [→Vulcan]

•**vol·ca·no** [vαlkéinou / vɔl-] *n.* Ⓒ (*pl.* **-noes** or **-nos**) a mountain with an opening or some openings through which steam, ashes, and liquid rock are forced out. 화산. ¶ *an active* 〔*a dormant, an extinct*〕 ~ 활〔휴, 사〕화산.

vole [voul] *n.* Ⓒ a small ratlike animal with a short tail, living in the fields. 들쥐류. [Norw.]

vo·li·tion [voulíʃən] *n.* Ⓤ **1** the act of exercising one's will. 결단; 의지 작용. ¶ *by one's own* ~ 자기 의지로; 자의로 / *I didn't tell her to go; she went of her own* ~. 나는 가라고 하지 않았다. 그녀가 자의로 간 것이다. **2** the power of willing. 결단〔의지〕력. ¶ *The use of drugs has weakened his* ~. 마약 복용으로 해서 그는 의지가 약해졌다. [L. *volo* wish]

vo·li·tion·al [voulíʃənəl] *adj.* of volition. 의지의. ¶ ~*power* 의지력.

vol·ley [váli / vɔ́li] *n.* Ⓒ **1** the act of throwing many bullets, arrows, etc. at one time. 일제 사격. ¶ *a* ~ *of arrows* / *The soldiers fired a* ~ *into the air as a warning to the rioters.* 군인들은 폭도들에 대한 경고로 일제히 공중에다 발포했다. **2** 《*fig.*》 a rapid, continuous, noisy speaking of oaths, abuse, etc. (욕설 등의) 퍼부음; (질문 등의) 연발. ¶ *a* ~ *of curses.* **3** (in sports) the act of striking the ball back before it touches the ground. 발리. —*vt., vi.* (P6;1) **1** discharge many things at one time. 일제 사격을 하다. **2** speak (in) a volley. (욕설 등을) 퍼붓다. **3** (in sports) strike a ball before it touches the ground. 발리를 하다. [L. *volo* fly]

vol·ley·ball [válibɔ̀ːl / vɔ́li-] *n.* **1** Ⓤ a game in which two teams try to hit a large ball back and forth over a high net with the hands, without letting the ball touch the ground. 배구. **2** Ⓒ a ball used in this game. 배구공.

vol·plane [válplèin / vɔ́l-] *vi.* (P1) glide toward the earth in an airplane without using motor power. (엔진을 끄고) 활공(滑空)하다. [F.]

vols. volumes.

volt [voult] *n.* Ⓒ 《electr.》 the unit of electromotive force. 볼트. [Person *Volta*]

volt·age [vóultidʒ] *n.* Ⓤ electromotive force as measured in volts. 볼트수; 전압.

vol·ta·ic [vαltéiik / vɔl-] *adj.* producing an electric current by chemical action; of an electric current. 기전력(起電力)이 있는; 전류의.

volte-face [vαltəfáːs, vɔ(ː)lt-] *n.* Ⓒ a reversal of opinion or policy. 방향 전환. [F.]

volt·me·ter [vóultmìːtər] *n.* Ⓒ an instrument for measuring electromotive force. 전압계. [*volt, meter*]

vol·u·bil·i·ty [vὰljəbíləti / vɔ̀l-] *n.* Ⓤ the state or quality of being voluble. 다변(多辯). [↓]

vol·u·ble [váljəbəl / vɔ́l-] *adj.* **1** talking

too much; having the habit of talking much. 다변의; 수다스러운. **2** talking with a rapid flow of words; fluent. 말이 유창한. ¶ ~ *excuse* 구변 좋은 변명. [L. *volvo* roll]

:vol·ume [válju:m / vɔ́l-] *n.* **1** Ⓒ a number of printed sheets bound together; a book. 책; 서적. ¶ *We have a library of 3,000 volumes.* 우리 서재에는 책이 3천 권 있다. **2** Ⓒ one of the books in a set or series. (책의) 권《vol. 로 생략, 복수는 vols.》. ¶ *a novel in three volumes,* 3권으로 된 소설 / *Volume Two of the novel* 소설의 제 2권 / *Vol.I. has just appeared.* 제1권이 막 출판됐다. **3** Ⓒ a large amount. 대량; 많음. ¶ *a ~ of smoke* 자욱한 연기 / *a great ~ of water* 다량의 물 / *Letters had poured in large ~.* 편지가 쇄도했다. **4** Ⓤ the amount of space occupied by a liquid, a gas, etc. 분량; 용적. ¶ *the ~ of water in a tank* 탱크 하나의 수량 / *The storeroom has a ~ of 40 cubic meters.* 광의 용적은 40입방미터다. **5** Ⓤ the amount of sound; (degree of) loudness of sound. 음량; 볼륨. ¶ *a voice of great ~* 풍부한 성량 / *a voice lacking in ~* 성량이 부족한 음성 / *turn down* 〔*raise*〕 *the ~ of the radio* 라디오의 소리를 낮추다〔높이다〕. [↑]

speak volumes for, afford strong or favorable testimony in favor of. …을 증명하고도 남음이 있다. ¶ *That fact speaks volumes for his honesty.* 그 사실이 그가 정직하다는 명백한 증거다.

vo·lu·mi·nous [vəlú:mənəs] *adj.* **1** consisting of many volumes; forming, filling, or writing a large or many books. 권수가 많은; 저서가 많은. ¶ *a ~ library* 많은 장서 / *Shakespeare is one of the most ~ writers.* 셰익스피어는 가장 다작(多作)한 작가의 한 사람이다. **2** large in quantity or size. 부피가 큰; 다량의. ¶ ~ *correspondence* 방대한 양의 통신 / *a ~ skirt* 큰 치마.

vol·un·tar·i·ly [válәntèrili / vɔ́l-] *adv.* by one's own free will; without compulsion; freely. 자유 의지로. [↓]

***vol·un·tar·y** [válәntèri / vɔ́lәntәri] *adj.* (opp. involuntary) **1** acting of one's own free will or by one's own desire; not forced; done or made freely. 자발적인; 임의의; 강제가 아닌; 자유 의지로 한. ¶ *a ~ worker* 자원해서 일하는 사람 / *a ~ choice* 자의 선택 / ~ *service* 자원 봉사 / *The thief's confession was quite ~.* 도둑의 자백은 강제된 것이 아니었다 / *a ~ appearance* 임의 출두 / *a ~ army* 지원병; 의용군. **2** intended; intentional; done on purpose; deliberate. 고의적인(opp. accidental). ¶ ~ *manslaughter* 모살(謀殺). **3** acting or done without payment; controlled or supported by voluntary contributions. 무상(無償)의; (독지가의) 기부로 운영〔유지〕되는. ¶ *a ~ hospital* / *Many social services are still provided by ~ societies.* 많은 사회 사업들이 아직도 무보수로 일하는 단체들에 의해 꾸려지고 있다. **4** 《physiol.》 controlled by the will. 수의(隨意)의. ¶ ~ *muscles* 수의근(筋).

— *n.* Ⓒ **1** anything done of one's own will. 자발적으로 한 일. **2** an organ solo played at a church service. (교회 예배 때의) 오르간 독주(獨奏). [→volition]

***vol·un·teer** [vὰlәntíәr / vɔ̀l-] *n.* Ⓒ a person who enters into any service, esp. a military service or one in some other way dangerous, of his own free will. 지원자; 지원병. ¶ *This work costs us nothing. It's all done by volunteers.* 이 일에 우리는 아무 것도 든 것이 없다. 모두 자원한 사람들에 의해 행해졌다.

— *vt.* (P6,8) offer (one's service, etc.) willingly. 자진해서 제공하다〔말다〕; 자발적으로 나서다. ¶ ~ *one's service* 자진해서 봉사하다 / ~ *to do the work* 그 일을 하겠다고 나서다 / ~ *one's opinion* 자진해서 의견을 제시하다 / *Jenny volunteered to clear up afterward.* 제니는 나중에 자기가 치우겠다고 했다.

— *vi.* (P1,3) **1** work as a volunteer. 자진해서 하다; 지원하다. ¶ *She volunteered as a nurse.* 그녀는 간호사를 자원했다. **2** become a volunteer soldier. 지원병이 되다. ¶ *As soon as the war was declared, many men volunteered.* 전쟁이 선포되자마자 많은 사람이 군대에 지원했다 / *He volunteered for military service.* 그는 지원 입대했다.

— *adj.* **1** of a volunteer or volunteers. 지원자〔병〕의. **2** made up of volunteers. 지원자에 의해 구성된. ¶ *a ~ corps* 의용군. [↑]

vo·lup·tu·ar·y [vәlʌ́ptʃuèri / -әri] *n.* Ⓒ (*pl.* **-ar·ies**) a person devoted to luxurious or sensual pleasures. 주색에 빠진 사람. [↓]

vo·lup·tu·ous [vәlʌ́ptʃuәs] *adj.* **1** devoted to the pleasures of the senses. 주색에 빠진. ¶ *a ~ person* / *the ~ life of the Romans in ancient times* 고대 로마인들의 주색에 탐닉한 생활. **2** full of or suggesting sensual delights and pleasures. 육감적인. ¶ *The dancer's movements were slow and ~.* 그 무희의 동작은 느리면서도 관능적이었다 / *her ~ curves* 그녀의 관능적인 곡선미 / *a ~ picture* 춘화. [L. *voluptas* pleasure]

vo·lute [vәlú:t] *n.* Ⓒ **1** a spiral ornament in architecture used in Ionic and Corinthian capitals. 소용돌이 장식. **2** 《shell》 a turn of a spiral shell. (고둥의) 소용돌이. [L. *volvo* roll]

vom·it [vámit / vɔ́m-] *vi.* **1** (P1) throw up the contents of the stomach through the mouth. 토하다; 게우다. ¶ *The unpleasant smell made her feel so sick that she began to ~.* 그녀는 악취에 속이 메스꺼워져 토하기 시작했다. **2** (P1,3) (of a volcano) discharge lava, ashes, etc. (화산이) 뿜어내다; 분출하다.

— *vt.* (P6,7) **1** throw up (something eaten) from the stomach. …을 토하다. ¶ ~ *one's dinner* 저녁 먹은 것을 토해내다. **2** throw out (something) with force. …을 뿜

어내다. ¶ *The chimney is vomiting (forth) smoke.* 굴뚝이 연기를 뿜어내고 있다 / *The volcano vomited out great black clouds of smoke.* 화산에서 엄청난 검은 연기가 솟아올랐다. **3** 《*arch.*》 cause to vomit. …을 토하게 하다《토제(吐劑)로》. **4** 《*fig.*》 put forth violently in speech. (욕설 따위)를 퍼붓다. ¶ ~ *insult* 〔*abuse*〕.

— *n.* Ⓤ **1** the act of vomiting. 토하기; 구토. **2** something vomited from the stomach. 토한 것. **3** rough or cruel words in speech or writing. 입정 사나운 말〔글〕. ¶ 《*fig.*》 *the foul ~ of lampoonists* 풍자 작가들의 구역질나는 언사〔작품〕. **4** a medicine which causes vomiting. 토제(吐劑). [L.]

voo·doo [vúːduː] *n.* (*pl.* **-doos**) **1** Ⓤ a religion of African origin, characterized by belief in magic, the use of charms, etc., prevailing in the West Indies and southern U.S. 부두교(敎). **2** Ⓒ a person who practices such magic. 무술사(巫術師). [Afr.]

vo·ra·cious [vouréiʃəs] *adj.* **1** greedy in eating; eager to eat much. 게걸스럽게 먹는. ¶ *The wolf is a ~ animal.* 이리는 폭식하는 짐승이다 / *a ~ appetite* 왕성한 식욕 / 《*fig.*》 *a ~ reader* 왕성한 독서가; 책벌레. **2** very eager to do something. 탐욕스러운. [L. *voro* devour]

vo·ra·cious·ly [vouréiʃəsli] *adv.* in a voracious manner. 게걸스럽게; 탐욕스럽게.

vo·rac·i·ty [vɔːrǽsəti, və-] *n.* Ⓤ the state or quality of being voracious. 대식(大食); 탐욕.

vor·tex [vɔ́ːrteks] *n.* Ⓒ (*pl.* **-tex·es** or **-ti·ces**) **1** a whirling liquid or gas that sucks in everything near it; a whirlpool; a whirlwind. 소용돌이; 회오리 바람. **2** 《*fig.*》 anything that seems to swallow up everything into it. (전쟁·논쟁 따위의) 소용돌이; 혼란. ¶ *be driven into the ~ of war* 전쟁의 와중에 말려들다 / *the ~ of revolution* 혁명의 소용돌이. **3** 《phys.》 a portion of fluid whose particles rotate. 소용돌이. [→versatile]

vor·ti·ces [vɔ́ːrtəsìːz] *n.* pl. of **vortex.**

vo·ta·ress [vóutəris] *n.* Ⓒ a woman votary. votary 의 여성형. [↓]

vo·ta·ry [vóutəri] *n.* Ⓒ (*pl.* **-ries**) **1** a person bound by vows to a religious life, as a monk or a nun. 신에 봉사하는 사람. **2** a person devoted to something; a devotee. (열렬한) 애호가. ¶ *a ~ of music* 〔*golf*〕 음악〔골프〕 애호가. [→vow]

:vote [vout] *n.* Ⓒ **1** a formal expression of will or opinion in regard to some question. (의안 등에 대한) 찬부의 의사 표시. ¶ *an open* 〔*a secret*〕 ~ 공개〔비밀〕 투표 / *put a bill* 〔*a question*〕 *to the ~* 법안을〔문제를〕 표결에 부치다 / *come* 〔*go, proceed*〕 *to the ~* 표결에 부쳐지다 / *It was decided by ~.* 그것은 표결에 의해 결정됐다 / *The person receiving the most votes is elected.* 가장 많은 표를 얻은 사람이 선출된다. **2** the method by which such a choice is expressed, such as by written ballot, by voice, or by a show of hands; a ballot. 투표(의 한 표). ¶ *cast a ~ for* 〔*against*〕... …에 찬성표〔반대표〕를 던지다 / *one man one ~*, 1인 1표 / *give one's ~ to* 〔*for*〕... …에 투표하다 / *The ~ yesterday went in his favor.* 어제의 투표는 그에게 유리했다. **3** the right to express such a choice or wish. 투표〔의결〕권. ¶ *I have no ~ in this matter.* 나는 이 문제에 대해서 투표권이 없다 / *Not everybody has the ~.* 누구에게나 투표권이 있는 것은 아니다. **4** something expressed by a majority. (표결된) 결의 사항. ¶ *a ~ of censure* 불신임 결의 / *a ~ of thanks* 감사 결의. **5** 《*collectively*》 the entire number of such expressions. 총투표수; 득표. ¶ *a large ~* 다수의 투표.

— *vi.* (P1,3) express one's wish or choice by a vote; cast a vote. 투표하다. ¶ ~ *for* 〔*against*〕 *a measure* 의안에 찬성〔반대〕 투표를 하다. — *vt.* **1** (P7,11) decide, or establish (something) by a vote. …을 투표로 정하다; 가결하다. ¶ ~ *a reform* 개혁안을 가결하다 / ~ *someone into* 〔*out of*〕 *office* 아무를 직위에 선출하다〔투표로 직위에서 쫓아내다〕 / *The government is afraid it will be voted out of office at the next election.* 정부는 다음 선거의 투표 결과 정권을 잡지 못할까봐 우려하고 있다. **2** (P21) 《*colloq.*》 declare (something) by general consent. (세간에서) …라고 인정〔간주〕하다. ¶ *They voted the new play a success.* 새 연극은 성공적이란 평이었다. **3** (P11) 《*colloq.*》 suggest or propose. …을 제안하다. ¶ *I ~ (that) we go to the movie tonight.* 오늘 밤 영화 구경을 가자. **4** (P6,13) grant; approve. …을 찬성하다. [→vow]

vote down, vote against; defeat (something) by a vote. …을 부결하다.

vote for, **a**) propose; favor; approve. 찬성하다. **b**) announce a proposal. 제의하다.

vote in, elect by votes. 선거〔선출〕하다.

vote through, get (a measure) passed by voting. (법안)을 통과시키다.

·vot·er [vóutər] *n.* Ⓒ a person who votes or who has a legal right to vote; an elector. 투표자. ¶ *a casting ~* 결정 투표자.

vot·ing [vóutiŋ] *n.* Ⓤ the act of casting a vote. 투표.

vo·tive [vóutiv] *adj.* given in accordance with a vow or promise. 기원을 드린; 봉헌(奉獻)한. ¶ *a ~ offering* 봉헌물; 공물(供物).

vouch [vautʃ] *vi.* (P3) 《*for*》 guarantee; be responsible. 보증하다; (보)증인이 되다. ¶ ~ *for the truth of the story* 이야기가 사실임을 보증하다 / *I will ~ for his honesty.* 그가 정직하다는 것을 보장한다. [→voice, *safe*]

vouch·er [váutʃər] *n.* Ⓒ **1** a person who gives a guarantee for something. 보증인. **2** a written paper showing that a sum of money has been paid, etc. 영수증. **3** a kind of ticket that maybe used instead of money for a particular purpose. (현금 대용의) 상환권; 상품권. ¶ *Some firms give their workers luncheon vouchers.* 어떤 회사에서는 직원들에게 점심 식권을 주고 있다.

vouch·safe [vautʃséif] *vt.* (P6,8,13,14) **1** give something in a gracious manner or out of pity. …을 주다. ¶ *Can you ~ me a visit?* 찾아가 뵈어도 좋겠습니까 / *Tom vouchsafed no reply.* 톰은 대답해 주지 않았다. **2** do something in a kind or polite way. 친절하게도 …하다. ¶ *She vouchsafed to listen to us.* 고맙게도 그녀는 우리 말을 들어 주었다.

:vow [vau] *n.* Ⓒ **1** an earnest promise to God; a pledge of love and faithfulness. 맹세; 서약. ¶ *a ~ of secrecy* 비밀 엄수의 서약 / *marriage vows* 결혼 서약. **2** the content of a vow. 맹세〔서약〕의 내용.

be under a vow, bind oneself by a vow. 맹세하고 있다. ¶ *be under a ~ to drink no wine* 금주를 맹세하고 있다.

make 〔***take***〕 ***a vow,*** bind oneself by a vow; vow. …을 맹세하다.

— *vt.* **1** (P6,8,11,13) make a vow to do or make. …을 맹세하다. ¶ *~ that one will be loyal to the king* 왕에게 충성할 것을 맹세하다 / *When Bob was caught stealing he vowed he'd never do it again.* 도둑질하다 들켰을 때 보브는 다시는 안 그러겠다고 서약했다 / *~ oneself to a life of self-sacrifice* 자기 희생의 생애를 보내겠다고 맹세하다. **2** (P8,11) declare earnestly and firmly. …을 단언하다. ¶ *She vowed never to leave home again.* 다시는 가출을 않겠다고 다짐했다. [L. *voveo*]

vow·el [váuəl] *n.* Ⓒ **1** 《phon.》 a simple vocal sound with the mouth and lips partly open. 모음(opp. consonant). **2** a letter representing such a sound, such as a, e, i, o and u. 모음자. [→voice]

vox [vɑks / vɔks] *n.* 《L.》 a voice.

vox De·i [vɑ́ks dí:ai] *n.* 《L.》 the voice of God. 하느님의 소리.

vox po·pu·li [vɑ́ks pɑ́pjəlài / vɔ́ks pɔ́p-] *n.* 민중의 (목)소리.

:voy·age [vɔ́iidʒ] *n.* Ⓒ a journey by sea or by air. 항해; 항공 여행. ¶ *a ~ around the world* 세계 일주 항해 / *Bon ~* [bɔ̀n vwɑ:jɑ́:ʒ / bɔ̀n-] 여행길 무사하시기를 / *on the ~* 항해중인. — *vt., vi.* (P6; 1,2A) travel by sea or by air. 배〔비행기〕로 여행하다. [L. *via* way]

voy·ag·er [vɔ́iidʒər, vɔ́iədʒ-] *n.* Ⓒ a person who makes a voyage. 항해〔항공〕 여행자.

V. P. Vice-President.

V. Rev. Very Reverend.

vs. versus.

V. S. Veterinary Surgeon.

v.s. vide supra.

vss versions.

VSTOL [ví:stɔ̀(:)l, ví:stòul] *n.* 《aeron.》 vertical short take-off and landing. 수직 단거리 이착륙(방식).

v.t. transitive verb.

VT fuze [vì:tí:fjù:z] *n.* variable timing fuze. 근접 (자동·전파) 신관.

VTO 《aeron.》 vertical take-off.

VTOL [ví:tòul] *n.* 《aeron.》 vertical take-off and landing. 수직 이착륙(기).

Vul·can [vʌ́lkən] *n.* 《Rom. myth.》 the god of fire and metalworking. 불과 대장간 일의 신(=Gk. myth. *Hephaestus*). [L.]

vul·can·ite [vʌ́lkənàit] *n.* Ⓤ a hard, black substance, also called ebonite, used for making combs, etc. 에보나이트 《경질(硬質) 고무》.

vul·can·ize [vʌ́lkənàiz] *vt.* (P6) treat (rubber) with sulfur to make it more elastic and harder. (고무)를 경화시키다; 가황(加黃)하다.

***vul·gar** [vʌ́lgər] *adj.* **1** belonging to the common people; common. 일반 민중의; 대중의. ¶ *~ life* 서민 생활 / *the ~ circle* 서민 사회 / *the ~* 서민. **2** showing a lack of culture, refinement, taste, etc. 저속한; 속된 (opp. refined). ¶ *~ manners* 저속한 태도 / *a ~ way of speaking* 저속한 말씨 / *the ~ display of wealth* 부의 야비한 과시. [L. *vulgus* the people]

vul·gar·ism [vʌ́lgərìzəm] *n.* **1** Ⓒ a word or an expression used only in coarse speech. 상말. **2** Ⓤ vulgarity. 속악.

vul·gar·i·ty [vʌlgǽrəti] *n.* (*pl.* **-ties**) **1** Ⓤ the state or quality of being vulgar. 속악; 비속. ¶ *Talking loudly in a public place is a sign of ~.* 남들 앞에서 떠드는 것은 상스러운 탓이다. **2** 《*pl.*》 vulgar actions, habits, speech, writing, etc. 저속한 언행.

vul·gar·ize [vʌ́lgəràiz] *vt.* (P6) **1** make (something) vulgar. …을 속되게 만들다. **2** 《rare》 make popular. 통속화하다.

Vul·gate [vʌ́lgeit, -git], **the** *n.* the Latin translation of the Bible made in the 4th century A.D., long used by the Roman Catholic Church. 불가타 성서《카톨릭 교회 공인의 라틴어역 성서》.

vul·ner·a·bil·i·ty [vʌ̀lnərəbíləti] *n.* Ⓤ the state or quality of being vulnerable. 비난받기 쉬움; 약점. [↓]

vul·ner·a·ble [vʌ́lnərəbəl] *adj.* **1** that can be injured or wounded; open to attack. 상처받기 쉬운; (요새 따위가) 공격받기 쉬운. ¶ *a ~ part of the body* 몸의 상처입기 쉬운 곳 / *They were in a ~ position, with the enemy on the hill above them.* 적이 그들보다 위쪽 언덕 위에 있었기 때문에 그들은 공격을 받기 쉬운 위치에 있었다. **2** open to injury or criticism. 비난받기 쉬운. ¶ *a ~ point* 약점 / *be ~ to ridicule* 조롱당하기 쉽다 / *Your arguments are rather ~ to criticism.* 네 논거는 비판의 대상이 되기 쉽다. ● **vul·ner·a·bly** [-i] *adv.* [L. *vulmus* wound]

vul·ture [vʌ́ltʃər] *n.* Ⓒ **1** a large bird of prey with a bald head that eats the flesh of dead animals. 독수리. **2** 《*fig.*》 a greedy, cruel person. 탐욕하고 잔인한 사람. [L.]

vy·ing [váiiŋ] *v.* ppr. of **vie**.

W w

W, w [dʌ́blju̇(:)] *n.* Ⓒ (*pl.* **W's, Ws, w's, ws** [dʌ́blju(:)z]) **1** the 23rd letter of the English alphabet. 영어 알파벳의 스물셋째 글자. **2** something having the form of W. W자 모양의 것.

W 《chem.》 wolfram; 《electr.》 watt; west; western.

W. Wales; Warden; Wednesday; Welsh; Western.

w. watt; week; west; western; wide; width; wife; with.

wab·ble [wɑ́bəl / wɔ́bəl] *vi., n.* =wobble.

wad [wɑd / wɔd] *n.* Ⓒ **1** a small mass of soft material, used to stop up an opening or to keep things in place. (솜·종이 등의) 작은 뭉치. ¶ *She stuffed wads of cotton in her ears to keep out the noise.* 그녀는 시끄러워서 솜 뭉치로 귀를 막았다. **2** 《colloq.》 a pile of paper money. 지폐 뭉치. ¶ *a ~ of bills* 지폐 뭉치. **3** a plug to hold powder and shot in place in a gun. (탄환의) 화약 마개.
— *vt.* (**wad·ded, wad·ding**) (P6) **1** make (something) into a small mass. …을 작은 뭉치로 만들다. **2** stuff (something) with a wad; stop up (a hole) with a wad. (충전물로) …에 채워넣다; …을 틀어막다. **3** line (clothes) with wadding. …에 안감을 대다. [Sw.]

wad·ding [wɑ́diŋ / wɔ́d-] *n.* Ⓤ a soft material for packing, stuffing, lining, etc. 채워 넣는[틀어 막는] 것; 충전물; 안감.

wad·dle [wɑ́dl / wɔ́dl] *vi.* (P1,2A) walk with short steps and a swaying motion as a duck. 아장아장[뒤뚱거리며] 걷다. ¶ *The fat man waddled up to her.* 그 뚱뚱한 사람은 뒤뚱거리며 그녀에게로 갔다. — *n.* Ⓒ 《sing. only》 the act of waddling. 뒤뚱거리며 걷기. [↓]

***wade** [weid] *vi.* (P1,2A,3) **1** walk through water, mud, sand, etc. that hinders progress. (강·진창길 등을) 걸어 건너다; 도섭(徒涉)하다. ¶ *~ across a stream* / *~ through the mud* 진창을 걸어가다. **2** 《fig.》 pass or proceed with effort or difficulty. 힘들게 나아가다. ¶ *~ through an uninteresting book* 재미 없는 책을 억지로 읽어가다 / *~ through a tedious lesson* 지루한 훈시를 참고 듣다. **3** 《fig.》 《in, into》 began with energy; attack strongly. 힘차게 달려들다[공격하다]. ¶ *He waded into his work.* 그는 힘차게 일을 시작했다.
— *vt.* (P6) cross or pass through (a stream, etc.) by wading. …을 걸어서 건너다; 힘들게 지나가다.
— *n.* Ⓤ the act of wading. 걸어서 건넘; 도섭. [E.]

wad·er [wéidər] *n.* **1** Ⓒ a person who wades. 걸어서 건너는 사람. **2** Ⓒ a long-legged bird that wades about in water in search of food. 섭금류(涉禽類). ¶ *Herons and curlews are waders.* 왜가리와 마도요는 섭금류다. **3** 《pl.》 《Brit.》 high waterproof boots. (낚시할 때 신는) 긴 장화. [↑]

〈wader 3〉

wa·fer [wéifər] *n.* Ⓤ **1** a thin, flat biscuit or cake. 웨이퍼. **2** 《arch.》 a small piece of colored paper for fastening or sealing. 봉함지(封緘紙); 풀종이. **3** 《med.》 a sheet of dry paste. 오블라토. **4** the thin round piece of bread used in Catholic Mass and the communion service. 성체(聖體); 제병(祭餠). [Teut.]

waf·fle[1] [wɑ́fəl / wɔ́fəl] *n.* Ⓒ a flat cake baked between two hinged metal plates. 와플. [Du. *wafel*]

waf·fle[2] [wɑ́fəl / wɔ́fəl] *vi.* (P1) 《chiefly Brit. colloq.》 talk or write too vaguely. 실없이 지껄이다; 되잖은 글을 쓰다. — *n.* nonsense. 난센스; 허무 맹랑. [Obs. *waff*]

waft [wɑ:ft, wæft] *vt.* (P6,7) carry (something) lightly over water or through air. …을 부동(浮動)시키다; 가볍게 띄워 보내다. ¶ *The breeze wafted the scent of roses.* 장미 향기가 미풍에 날려 왔다 / *The waves wafted the boat to shore.* 파도가 배를 기슭으로 밀어 보냈다 / *A distant song was wafted to our ears.* 멀리서 노랫소리가 들려왔다.
— *vi.* (P1) float smoothly on the water or through the air. 부동하다; 떠돌다. ¶ *Cooking smells wafted along the hall.* 요리하는 냄새가 복도를 따라 퍼졌다.
— *n.* Ⓒ **1** the act of wafting; the state of being wafted. 떠다님; 부동(浮動). **2** a breath of air, wind or fragrance. 풍기는 향기; 한 차례 부는 바람. **3** a waving movement. (새의) 날개짓. [Obs. *wafter* convoy, →watch]

***wag**[1] [wæg] *v.* (**wagged, wag·ging**) *vt.* (P6,7) cause (something) to move from side to side or up and down rapidly. …을 상하[좌우]로 흔들다. ¶ *The dog wagged its tail.* 개가 꼬리를 흔들었다 / *~ one's finger at someone* 아무를 향해 (코끝에서) 손가락을 까닥거리다《경멸·경고·비난의 동작》/ *The tail wags the dog.* 하극상(下剋上).
— *vi.* (P1,2A) move from side to side or up and down rapidly. 흔들리다《상하좌우로》. ¶ *Your tongue wags too freely.* 너는 너

W

무 수다스럽다〔입이 싸다〕.

set tongues 〔***chins, jaws, beards***〕 ***wagging,*** cause people to talk, esp. mild scandal. 사람들의 입에 오르내리게 하다. ¶ *Her behavior set local tongues wagging.* 그녀의 행동 거지는 마을의 회자(膾炙)거리가 됐다.

So the world wags. 《*arch.*》 Thus human affairs go on. 세상이란 그런 거다.

wag the tongue, talk too much. 수다 떨다.

— *n.* Ⓒ the act of wagging. 흔듦. ¶ *show disagreement by a* ~ *of the head* 고개를 가로 저어 동의하지 않음을 나타내다 / *a* ~ *of tail.* [E.]

wag² [wæg] *n.* Ⓒ a person who is fond of making jokes. 익살꾼. [↑]

:wage [weidʒ] *n.* 《usu. *pl.*》 **1** 《sometimes used as *sing.*》 money paid for work, now chiefly of manual labor. 임금; 품삯 (cf. *salary, stipend*). ¶ *a living* ~ 생활급(生活給) / *a* ~ *increase* 임금 인상 / *a weekly* ~ 주급(週給) / *A good workman gets good wages.* 일 잘 하는 사람이 좋은 삯을 받는다. **2** 《*arch.*》 《used as *sing.*》 something given as a reward. (죄 따위의) 응보. ¶ 《Bible》 *The wages of sin is death.* 죄의 값은 죽음이니라.

— *vt.* (P6) **1** carry on, engage in (a war, struggle, campaign, etc.). (전쟁 등)을 벌이다; (수행)하다. ¶ *He waged a long war against poverty.* 그는 가난과의 오랜 싸움을 했다. **2** stake; wager. (내기 등)에 걸다.

● **wage·less** [´lis] *adj.* [Teut. →gage]

wage earner [´ ``] *n.* a person who works for wages. 임금 노동자.

wa·ger [wéidʒər] *n.* a bet. 내기; 노름.

— *vt., vi.* (P6,11,13;1) **1** bet; stake; make a bet. (내기 등에) 걸다. ¶ *I'll* ~ *10 dollars on it.* 난 거기에 10달러 걸겠다. **2** pledge. …을 보증하다.

wag·ger·y [wǽgəri] *n.* (*pl.* **-ger·ies**) **1** Ⓤ the action or spirit of a humorous person. 익살. **2** Ⓒ a joke. 농(담). [*wag*]

wag·gish [wǽgiʃ] *adj.* **1** fond of playing jokes. 익살을 좋아하는. ¶ *a* ~ *fellow.* **2** humorous or comical. 익살스러운. ¶ *a* ~ *speech* 익살 / *He gave me a* ~ *look.* 내게 익살스러운 시선을 보냈다. [*wag*]

wag·gle [wǽgəl] *vt., vi.* (P6;1) **1** 《*colloq.*》 move quickly and repeatedly from side to side; wag. (이리저리) 흔들다; 흔들리다. ¶ *The hula-dancer waggled her hips.* / *The car's broken aerial waggled in the breeze.* 차의 부러진 안테나가 미풍에 흔들렸다. **2** walk with a rolling move. 엉덩이〔허리〕를 흔들며 걷다. [*wag*]

:wag·on, 《Brit.》 **wag·gon** [wǽgən] *n.* Ⓒ **1** a four-wheeled vehicle drawn by horses and used to carry loads. 4륜 짐마차; 왜건. **2** an open railroad freight car. 무개 화차. **3** =teawagon. [Du. (→wain)]

on the wagon, 《*sl.*》 not drinking alcohol. 술을 끊고; 금주하여.

wag·on·er, 《Brit.》 **wag·gon·er** [wǽgənər] *n.* Ⓒ a person who drives a wagon. 짐마차꾼.

wag·on·ette, 《Brit.》 **wag·gon·ette** [wæ̀gənét] *n.* Ⓒ a light, open carriage with side-seats facing each other. (마주 앉게 된) 유람 마차.

wa·gon-lit [vɑgɔ̃li] *n.* 《F.》 a railway sleeping-car in Europe. (철도의) 침대차.

waif [weif] *n.* Ⓒ (*pl.* **waifs**) **1** a person without a home; a homeless wandering person. 방랑객; 유랑인. **2** a lost animal; a lost child. 임자 없는 동물〔가축〕; 미아(迷兒). **3** an object without an owner, esp. something carried along by wind or water. (소유주 불명의) 표류물. [N. *veifa* wave]

waifs and strays, homeless children; junk. 부랑아들; 잡동사니.

***wail** [weil] *vi.* (P1,2A) **1** cry loud in grief or pain. (슬픔·고통 등으로) 소리쳐 울다; 울부짖다. ¶ *The baby wailed for hours.* 아기는 몇 시간이고 울어댔다 / *Indians* ~ *at funerals.* 인디언들은 장례식 때에 울부짖는다 / *Stop weeping and wailing and do something about it!* 울부짖지만 말고 뭔가 손을 써라. **2** express sorrow. 한탄하다. ¶ ~ *over one's misfortunes* 〔*fate*〕 불행〔운명〕을 한탄하다. **3** 《*fig.*》 make a sound like a cry. 우는 것 같은 소리를 내다. ¶ *The wind wailed in the woods all night.* 바람이 밤새도록 숲에서 윙윙거렸다.

— *n.* Ⓒ **1** a long, loud cry of pain or grief. 울부짖는 소리. **2** a sound like a cry. 우는 것 같은 소리. [N. (→woe)]

wain [wein] *n.* **1** 《*arch., poet.*》 a farm wagon or cart. 농업용 짐마차. **2** 《astron.》 《*the W-*》 the seven bright stars in the constellation of the Great Bear. 북두 칠성. [E.]

wain·scot [wéinskət, -skòut] *n.* Ⓤ 《archit.》 a wooden lining on the walls of a room. (방안의) 징두리널; 벽판. — *vt., vi.* (**-scot·ed, -scot·ing** or 《Brit.》 **-scot·ted, -scot·ting**) (P6;1) line (a wall) with wood. (벽에) 징두리널을 대다. ¶ *a wainscoted room.* [Teut. (→wake)]

wain·scot·ing, 《Brit.》 **-scot·ting** [wéinskətiŋ, -skòut-] *n.* **1** =wainscot. **2** material used for wainscots. 징두리널 재료.

:waist [weist] *n.* Ⓒ **1** the part of the body between the ribs and the hips. 허리. ¶ *She has large* 〔*small*〕 ~. / *She has no* ~. 그녀는 허리가 없다〔절구통이다〕. **2** 《U.S.》 a garment or the part of a garment covering the waist. 옷의 허리 부분; 동의(胴衣). **3** 《naut.》 the middle part of a ship. (선박의) 중앙부 상갑판. **4** = waistline. **5** well-marked narrowness of the figure at the waist. (옷 따위의) 가는〔좁은〕 허리. ¶ *A sack-dress has no* ~. 색드레스는 허리가 없다. [Teut.]

waist·band [wéistbæ̀nd] *n.* Ⓒ a band

around the waist on trousers or a skirt. 허리띠; 허리끈.

waist·coat [wéistkòut, wéskət] *n.* Ⓒ 《Brit.》 a man's vest; a short coat reaching to the waist. 조끼(=《U.S.》 vest).

waist·line [wéistlàin] *n.* Ⓒ **1** (the length of) the line around the waist. 허리 둘레. **2** the narrow part of a woman's dress. (여자 옷의) 웨이스트; 허리통. **3** the line where the waist and skirt of a dress meet. (여자 옷의) 웨이스트라인.

:wait [weit] *vi.* (P1,2B,3,4) **1** 《*for*》 stay or remain until someone comes or something happens. 기다리다. ¶ ~ *and see* 사태를 관망하다 / ~ *around* 〔《Brit.》 *about*〕 (부근을) 어정거리며 기다리다 / *I'm sorry to have kept you waiting.* 기다리게 해서 미안하다 / *I have been waiting to hear from you.* 네 소식을 기다리고 있다 / 《*prov.*》 *Time and tide ~ for no man.* 세월은 사람을 기다리지 않는다 / *She is waiting outside* 〔*in the car*〕. 그녀가 밖〔차 안〕에서 기다리고 있다 / ~ *for someone's return* 〔*answer*〕 아무가 돌아오기를〔아무의 대답을〕 기다리다 / ~ *for train* 〔*lift*〕 기차〔승강기〕를 기다리다 / ~ *for the clock to strike* 시계가 치기를 기다리다 / *Wait for me!* (그렇게 빨리 걷지 말고) 좀 기다려라 / ~ *for someone to stop talking* 아무의 말 끝나기를 기다리다. **2** be in readiness; be ready. 준비되어 있다; 기다리고 있다. ¶ *Boys, dinner's waiting for you.* 얘들아, 저녁 준비가 됐다 / *have a car* 〔*a table*〕 ~ 차를 대기시키다〔식탁을 차리게 하다〕 / *We waited and waited but no one came.* 우린 기다리고 또 기다렸으나 아무도 오지 않았다. **3** remain neglected for a time; be delayed or postponed. 그대로 내버려 두다; 미루다. ¶ *He says it cannot ~.* 그는 그것을 미룰 수 없다고 합니다 / *The business discussions can ~ until after dinner.* 사업 얘기는 식후에 해도 늦지 않다 / *I want to talk to you.* —*Can't it ~ till later?* 너와 얘기 할게 있는데. —나중에 하면 안 되나. **4** 《*on, upon*》 be or act as a waiter or waitress, esp. at table. (식사의) 시중을 들다. ¶ ~ *on* 〔《Brit.》 *at*〕 *table*(*s*) 식사 시중을 들다. —*vt.* (P6,13) **1** 《chiefly *lit.*》 wait for (something); await. …을 기다리다. ¶ ~ *one's chance* 기회〔때〕를 기다리다 / *You can't have it yet. You will have to ~ your turn.* 넌 아직 받을 수 없다. 차례를 기다려야지 / *He was just waiting his chance to get his revenge.* 그는 복수할 기회만을 기다리고 있었다. **2** 《*colloq.*》 delay or put off (a meal). (식사)를 늦추다. ¶ *Don't ~ supper for me; I shall be late.* 저녁을 먼저 먹어라, 난 늦을 터이니.

wait on 〔***upon***〕, **a**) ⇨ *vi.* 4. **b**) work as an attendant or servant; serve; attend upon. …을 모시다; …의 시중을 들다. ¶ *She has no one to ~ upon her.* 그녀는 자기를 돌봐줄 사람이 아무도 없다 / *Shopmen ~ on customers.* 점원들이 고객의 시중을 든다 / *Are you waited on?* (점원이 손님에게) 무얼 도와 드릴까요. **c**) 《*arch.*》 pay a visit to; call on. …을 방문하다; 문안드리다. **d**) follow as a result; attend. (결과로서) …이 수반하다. ¶ *Success waits on diligence.* 부지런하면 성공한다 / *May good luck ~ upon you.* 행운을 빕니다.

wait up (=*put off going to bed*) ***for*** *someone or something.* 자지 않고 …을 기다리다.

—*n.* **1** Ⓒ the act or time of waiting. 기다리기; 기다리는 시간. ¶ *It was a long ~ before we found a taxi.* 택시 잡는 데 오랜 시간이 걸렸다. **2** 《esp. Brit.》 《*the ~s*》 persons going from door to door at Christmas singing songs. 성탄절에 집집을 돌아다니는 성가대. [Teut.=watch]

lie in wait (=*hide and wait*) ***for*** *someone or something.* …을 숨어 기다리다. ¶ *The robber was lying in ~ for his victim.* 도둑은 숨어서 털 사람을 기다렸다.

·wait·er [wéitər] *n.* Ⓒ **1** a person who serves at table in a hotel or restaurant. 사환; 웨이터(cf. *waitress*). **2** a tray for carrying dishes. (요리 운반용) 쟁반.

·wait·ing [wéitiŋ] *adj.* serving 시중 드는. ¶ *a ~ man* 시종; 하인 / *a ~ maid* 시녀. —*n.* Ⓤ the act of serving someone. 시중 들기. ¶ *in ~* 모시고.

waiting game [∠-∠] *n.* delaying to see what happens before taking action. 대기 전술. ¶ *The government is playing ~ with the unions that are on strike.* 정부는 파업 중인 노조에 대기 전술을 쓰고 있다.

waiting room [∠-∠] *n.* a room at a railroad station, etc. where people wait for trains, etc. 대합실.

wait·ress [wéitris] *n.* Ⓒ a woman who serves at table in a hotel or restaurant. 웨이트리스(cf. *waiter*).

waive [weiv] *vt.* (P6) **1** give up (a right, a chance, rule, etc.). (권리 등)을 버리다; 포기하다. ¶ *We cannot ~ this rule except in case of illness.* 아픈 경우를 제외하고 이 규칙은 유효하다. **2** put (something) off until later. …을 보류하다; 연기하다. [→waif]

waiv·er [wéivər] *n.* **1** Ⓤ the act of waiving. (권리 등의) 포기. **2** Ⓒ 《law》 a written statement of this. 기권〔권리 포기〕 증서. ¶ *Please sign this ~.* 이 기권 증서에 서명하십시오.

:wake[1] [weik] *v.* (**waked** or **woke, waked**) *vi.* (P1,2A) **1** 《*arch.* except *ppr.*》 stay awake; not sleep. 깨어 있다; 자지 않고 있다. ¶ *in one's waking hours* 깨어 있는 시간에 / *Waking or sleeping, I think of you.* 자나 깨나 너를 생각한다. **2** stop sleeping. 잠을 깨다; 일어나다. ¶ *I usually ~ up at six.* 나는 보통 여섯 시에 일어난다 / ~ (*up*) *from a sound sleep* 깊은 잠〔단잠〕을 깨다 / ~ *up with a start* 놀라서 깨다. **3** become active or alive; become conscious of. 활기 띠다;

W

깨닫다; 눈뜨다; 각성하다. ¶ ~ *from one's daydreams* 백일몽〔공상〕에서 깨어나다 / *She began to ~ up to the situation.* 그녀는 사태를 인식하기 시작했다.

— *vt.* (P6,7) **1** cause (someone) to stop sleeping. …을 깨우다. ¶ *Please ~ me at seven.* 일곱 시에 깨워 주십시오 / *The noise woke the guests up.* 그 소리에 손님들은 잠을 깼다. **2** make (someone or something) alive or active; make (someone) aware of. …을 활기 띠게 하다; 깨닫게 하다. ¶ *This failure will ~ him up a little.* 이번 실패로 그는 정신 좀 차릴 것이다 / *be woken up to the danger* 위험을 깨닫다. **3** stir up; rouse; excite. (기억·노염 따위)를 불러일으키다; 야기시키다. ¶ ~ *sad memories* 슬픈 기억을 되살리다 / *The name woke furies in him.* 그 이름을 듣자 그는 분이 치밀었다. **4** keep watch by a dead person. (초상집에서) 밤샘하다.

— *n.* Ⓒ an all-night watch over a dead body before burial. (초상집에서의) 철야; 밤샘. [E. (→wait, watch)]

wake[2] [weik] *n.* Ⓒ the trail left behind a moving ship. 배 지나간 자국. [O.N. *vǫk*]

in the wake of, **a**) (of a ship) following in the track of. …의 자국을 좇아서. **b**) 《*fig.*》 following close behind; immediately after. …을 뒤따라. ¶ *In the ~ of the explorers came merchants.* 탐험대를 뒤좇아 장사꾼들이 왔다 / *Miseries follow in the ~ of a war.* 전쟁 뒤끝은 비참하다.

wake·ful [wéikfəl] *adj.* **1** free from sleepiness; unable to sleep. 잠이 오지 않는. ¶ *a ~ night* 잠 못 이루는 밤 / *pass a ~ night* 뜬눈으로 밤을 새우다. **2** wide-awake; watching carefully. 자지 않는; 방심하지 않는. ¶ *a ~ watch* 불침번. [*wake*[1]]

:wak·en [wéikən] *v.* =wake[1].

wale [weil] *n.* Ⓒ **1** a streak made on the skin by a stick or whip. 채찍 자국 (cf. *welt*). **2** a raised line made in the weave of cloth. (피륙의) 골. — *vt.* (P6) **1** mark (the skin) with wales. …에 채찍 자국을 내다. **2** make (cloth) with wales. (천)을 골지게 짜다. [E.]

Wales [weilz] *n.* a division of Great Britain west of England; the land of the Welsh. 웨일스 지방. ¶ *the Prince of ~* 영국 황태자.

:walk [wɔːk] *vi.* (P1,2A,2B) **1** ⓐ go or travel on foot at a moderate pace; go about on foot for the purpose of exercise or pleasure. 걷다; 걸어가다; 산책하다. ¶ ~ *about* 돌아다니다 / ~ *up and down* 여기저기 거닐다 / *I would rather ~ than ride.* 타고 가느니 차라리 걸어가겠다 / *He came walking with a firm step.* 그는 힘찬 걸음으로 걸어왔다 / ~ *across* 〔*over*〕 *the lawn* 잔디밭을 가로질러 가다 / *He was walking in the park this morning.* 그는 오늘 아침 공원을 산책하고 있었다 / ~ *out into the street* 한길로 걸어나가다. ⓑ (of a horse) move go along with two feet at least touching the ground; go at the slowest pace. (말이) 보통 걸음으로 걷다; 천천히 가다. **2** (of a ghost) go about on the earth. (유령이) 나타나다; 나다니다. ¶ *The ghost walks on such a dark night.* 유령은 그런 어두운 밤에 나다닌다. **3** 《*lit.*》 live in a particular manner; conduct oneself; behave. 처신하다; 처세하다. ¶ ~ *in the darkness* 그늘진 생활을 하다 / ~ *in the path of fair* 떳떳하게 살다. **4** 《baseball》 advance to first base after four balls have been pitched. 포 볼〔4구〕로 1루에 나가다

— *vt.* (P6,7) **1** go over (some place) on foot; go (a certain distance) on foot. …을 걷다; 걸어가다. ¶ ~ *the streets at night* 밤길을 걷다 / *They walked the deck, talking.* 그들은 이야기를 하면서 갑판을 걸어다녔다 / ~ *the whole way home* 집까지 내내 걸어가다. **2** cause (a person or an animal) to walk. …을 걸리다. ¶ ~ *the horse* / *The policeman walked him away* 〔*off*〕. 경찰이 그를 끌고 갔다 / ~ *someone off his legs* = ~ *someone to exhaustion* 아무를 지치도록 걸리다 / ~ *a dog on a lead* 개를 끈에 매어 걸리다. **3** accompany or lead (someone) on foot. (아무)와 동행하다; (아무)를 데리고 가다. ¶ *I'll ~ you to the station.* 역까지 동행하겠다 / ~ *a friend around the village* 벗을 데리고 마을을 돌아다니다 / *I'll ~ you home.* 집까지 바래다 주마. **4** 《baseball》 advance (a batter) to first base by pitching four balls. (타자)를 포 볼〔4구〕로 1루에 내보내다.

walk away from, **a**) go far ahead; beat (one's enemy, etc.) easily in a contest. …을 훨씬 앞지르다; …을 쉽게 이기다. ¶ *My horse just walked away from all the others in the race.* 내 말이 경주에서 다른 말들을 훨씬 앞질러 나갔다. **b**) come out of (accident) unhurt or almost unhurt. (사고)를 상처〔별탈〕 없이 넘기다.

walk away* 〔*off*〕 *with, **a**) steal; carry away. …을 훔치다; 가져가 버리다. ¶ ~ *away with all the money* 돈을 몽땅 가져가 버리다. **b**) win or gain. (상품 등)을 획득하다; 따다.

walk in, enter; come; go in. 들어가다. ¶ *Walk in, please.* 들어 오세요.

walk into, **a**) 《*sl.*》 eat heartily of. …을 잔뜩 먹다. ¶ ~ *into a pie.* **b**) 《*sl.*》 scold; abuse. …을 꾸짖다. ¶ *His father walked into him for staying out so late.* 아버지는 너무 늦도록 나다닌다고 그를 꾸짖었다. **c**) 《*colloq.*》 fall a prey to easily. (함정 등)에 빠지다; 걸려들다. ¶ *He walked into the trap.* 그는 계략에 빠졌다.

walk off, **a**) leave, esp. without saying good-bye. (아무 말도 없이) 가 버리다. **b**) get rid of (something) by walking. 걸어서 (두통 등)을 없애다. ¶ *I usually ~ off my sleepiness.* 나는 보통 걸어서 졸음을 쫓는다.

walk out, **a**) depart suddenly; go out (of a

meeting, etc.) angrily. 불쑥 나가 버리다; 분연히 퇴장하다. **b**) 《*colloq.*》 refuse to work; go on strike. 파업하다. **c**) be lovers. 사랑에 빠지다. ¶ *John and Mary are walking out.* 존과 메리는 사랑하는 사이다.

walk out on, 《U.S. *colloq.*》 leave (someone); abandon; forsake. …을 저버리다; 포기하다.

walk over, win easily. …에 쉽게 이기다; 낙승하다.

— *n.* Ⓒ **1** the act of walking, esp. a little journey on foot for exercise or pleasure. 걷기; 산책; 도보 여행. ¶ *take* 〔*go for*〕 *a* ~ 산책 나가다 / *take someone for a* ~ 아무를 산책에 데리고 가다 / *I've been for a little* ~. 산책을 좀 하고 왔다. **2** a distance walked. 보행 거리. ¶ *It is a ten-minutes* ~ *to the station.* 역까지 걸어서 10 분이면 간다 / *It is a long* ~ *from here.* 여기서 걸어가면 한참 걸린다. **3** a manner of walking; a gait. 걸음걸이. ¶ *He has a* ~ *like a duck.* 그는 뒤뚱거리며 걷는다 / *a hurried* 〔*vigorous*〕 ~ 분주한〔힘찬〕 걸음걸이 / *know someone by his* ~ 걸음걸이로 아무를 알아보다. **4** a path for walking; a route taken in walking. 산책길. ¶ *This is my favorite* ~. 이 길이 내 좋아하는 산책길이다 / *a cement* ~ 시멘트로 된 산책길. **5** (of a horse) a slow pace. (말의) 보통 걸음걸이. ¶ *go at a* ~. **6** 《baseball》 an advance to first base as a result of four balls. 포 볼〔4구〕로 타자를 1 루로 내보내기〔나가기〕. [E.]

walk of 〔***in***〕 ***life,*** an occupation; a rank in society. 직업; 지위; 계급. ¶ *people in every* ~ *of life* 각계 각층의 사람들 / *persons in the humbler walks of life* 미천한 신분의 사람들.

walk·a·way [wɔ́:kəwèi] *n.* 《*colloq.*》 an easy victory. 낙승(樂勝). ¶ *That race was just a* ~ *for my horse.* 그 경마가 내 말에게는 식은 죽 먹기였다.

walk·er [wɔ́:kər] *n.* a person who walks, esp. one who is fond of walking. 보행자; (특히) 산책을 즐기는 사람. ¶ *a good* 〔*poor*〕 ~ 다리 힘이 좋은〔약한〕 사람. [E.]

walk·ie-talk·ie [wɔ́:kitɔ́:ki] *n.* (*pl.* **-s**) a small, portable receiving and transmitting radio set. 워키토키(cf. *transceiver*).

walk·ing [wɔ́:kiŋ] *n.* Ⓤ the act or motion of a person who walks, esp. for exercise. 걷기. ¶ *Walking is a good form of exercise.* 걷는 것은 좋은 운동이다 / *I am fond of* ~. 나는 걷기를 좋아한다.

W

walking papers [⁓-⁓-] *n.* 《*colloq.*》 a notice of dismissal (from employment). 해고 통지.

walking stick [⁓-⁓] *n.* 《Brit.》 a stick carried when a person takes a walk; a cane. 단장; 지팡이.

walk·out [wɔ́:kàut] *n.* Ⓒ 《U.S. *colloq.*》 a strike of workmen. 파업; 스트라이크.

walk·o·ver [wɔ́:kòuvər] *n.* Ⓒ 《*colloq.*》 an easy victory. 낙승.

:wall [wɔ:l] *n.* Ⓒ **1** the side of a building; a fence built of wood, brick, etc. 벽; 담. ¶ *a blank* ~ (출입구·창·장식 따위가 없는) 민벽 / *a wooden* ~ 판자벽 / *within four walls* 방안에서; 은밀히 / *lean against the* ~ 벽에 기대다 / *be at bay against the* ~ 궁지〔막다른 골〕에 몰리다 / *There is a map on the* ~. 벽에 지도가 한 장 걸려 있다 / 《*prov.*》 *Walls have ears.* 벽에도 귀가 있다《말조심하라》 / *a partition* 〔*party*〕 ~ 격벽; 내벽 / *build the walls of a house* 집을 담장으로 두르다. **2** 《usu. *pl.*》 a defensive wall of a town, a city, etc. 성벽. ¶ *town walls* 도시의 성벽 / *the Great Wall of China* 만리 장성 / *the walls of a castle* 성벽. **3** something like a wall. 벽 같은 것. ¶ *a* ~ *of bayonets* 총검의 벽《총검을 가지고 늘어선 병사의 열》 / *A* ~ *of fire advanced through the dry forest.* 벽처럼 타오르는 불길이 마른 숲을 태워 나갔다 / *Our inquiries were met by a* ~ *of silence.* 우리의 문의에 묵묵 부답이었다 / *a* ~ *of suspicion* 의혹의 장벽. **4** 《often *pl.*》 the inside surface of a vessel, etc. (기관(器官) 등의) 내벽. ¶ *the walls of the heart* 심장벽 / *the walls of a vessel* 그릇의 내면.

drive 〔***push***〕 *someone* ***to the wall,*** force someone into a difficult situation. …를 궁지에 몰다.

give *someone* ***the wall,*** 《*arch.*》 allow someone to pass. …에게 길을 내주다〔터주다〕.

go to the wall, **a**) suffer defeat; be pushed aside in competition. 지다; 패배하다. **b**) fail in business. 사업에 실패하다.

run *one's* ***head against a wall,*** try to do something impossible. 불가능한 일을 하려들다.

see through 〔***into***〕 ***a brick wall,*** have a wonderful insight. 예리한 통찰력이 있다.

take the wall of *someone,* 《*arch.*》 refuse to allow someone to pass on the inside. …에게 길을 내주지 않다.

with *one's* ***back to the wall,*** in a position where escape is impossible. 궁지에 빠져.

— *vt.* (P6,7) **1** divide, enclose, or protect (something) with a wall. …을 벽으로 가르다〔두르다〕; …을 성벽으로 지키다. ¶ *The city was walled before the war.* 전쟁 전에 도시를 성벽으로 둘러막았다 / *The headmaster's house is walled off from the school.* 교장의 사택은 학교와 담으로 구획돼 있다 / *walled towns* 성벽을 두른 도시. **2** close up (an opening) with a wall. …을 벽으로 막다. ¶ ~ *up a window* 창을 벽으로 막다. [L. *vallum* rampart]

***wal·let** [wálit / wɔ́l-] *n.* Ⓒ **1** a leather case for holding paper money, cards, etc. in one's pocket. 지갑. **2** 《*arch.*》 a bag for food and light articles for a journey. (나그네의) 바랑; 전대. **3** a small leather bag or case for tools, etc. (연장 따위를 넣는) 작은 가죽 주머니〔통〕. [E.]

wall·eye [wɔ́:lài] *n.* any various fishes

with large staring eyes. 눈알이 큰 물고기. [N.=film-eye]

wall·eyed [wɔ́:làid] *adj.* **1** having eyes that show much white and little color. (눈의) 각막이 부옇게 된. **2** having large staring eyes. 눈알이 큰; 퉁방울눈의.

wall·flow·er [wɔ́:lflàuər] *n.* Ⓒ **1** 《*colloq.*》 a woman who sits by the wall at a dance because she has no partner. 무도회에서 춤 상대가 없는 여인. **2** 《bot.》 a plant with yellow or red flowers that have a sweet smell. 계란풀. [*wall*]

wal·lop [wáləp / wɔ́l-] *vt.* (P6) 《*colloq.*》 **1** hit very hard; thrash. 후려갈기다. **2** defeat completely. 완패시키다. —*n.* 《*colloq.*》 a very hard blow. 강타; 강펀치. ¶ *He landed him a ~ on the jaw.* 턱에다가 강펀치를 먹였다. [→gallop]

wal·low [wálou / wɔ́l-] *vi.* (P1,2A) **1** roll about (in mud, a dirty water, etc.). (진구렁 등에서) 뒹굴다. ¶ *Pigs like wallowing in the mud.* 돼지는 진흙탕에서 뒹구는 것을 좋아한다. **2** 《*fig.*》 indulge oneself with pleasures or enjoyment. (쾌락 등에) 탐닉하다. ¶ *~ in sensuality* 색에 빠지다 / *~ in luxury* 사치에 빠지다 / *Don't just ~ in self-pity; do something about your problem.* 자기 연민에만 빠져 있지 말고 네 문제를 어떻게 좀 해봐. —*n.* Ⓒ **1** the act of wallowing. 뒹굴기. **2** a muddy place where animals wallow. (소 따위가 뒹구는) 수렁. [E.]

wall·pa·per [wɔ́:lpèipər] *n.* Ⓤ paper used for pasting on walls. 벽지. —*vt.* (P6) cover (something) with wallpaper. …에 도배하다. [*wall*]

Wall Street [⌐ ⌐] *n.* **1** a street in New York which is the location of the chief American financial center. 월스트리트; 월가(街). **2** the money market of the United States. 미국 금융 시장[금융계].

***wal·nut** [wɔ́:lnʌ̀t, -nət] *n.* Ⓒ a hard-shelled nut that may be eaten; its tree; Ⓤ the wood of this tree. 호두; 호두나무; 호두나무 목재. [E. =foreign nut]

wal·rus [wɔ́(:)lrəs, wál-] *n.* Ⓒ (*pl.* **-rus·es** or *collectively* **-rus**) a large sea animal of the Arctic regions which is valued for its tusks and skin. 해마. [N=whale-horse]

waltz [wɔ:lts] *n.* Ⓒ a smooth, graceful dance in triple rhythm for couples; the music for it. 왈츠(곡). —*vi., vt.* (P1,2A, 3;7,13) **1** dance a waltz. 왈츠를 추다[추게 하다]. **2** 《*in, out, round*》 dance with joy. 신나게 춤추다. **3** 《*colloq.*》 go easily, successfully, or confidently. 잘 돼가다; 쉽게 진행하다. ¶ *We can't just ~ up to a complete stranger and introduce ourselves.* 생판 모르는 사람에게 다가가서 통성명할 수는 없다 / *He waltzed through the exam.* 그는 시험에 쉽게 합격했다. [G.=revolve]

wam·pum [wámpəm, wɔ́:m-] *n.* Ⓤ **1** beads made from shells used formerly by American Indians for money or ornament. (옛 북아메리카 인디언들의) 조가비 염주《화폐나 장식으로 썼음》. **2** 《*colloq.*》 money. 돈. [Native]

wan [wan / wɔn] *adj.* (**wan·ner, wan·nest**) **1** pale. 창백한. ¶ *a ~ complexion* 창백한 안색 / *His face was worn and ~.* 그의 얼굴은 초췌하고 창백했다. **2** looking tired and weak. 피곤해 보이는; 힘없는. ¶ *with a ~ smile* 힘없는 미소로. **3** 《*arch.*》 (of the sky etc.) dark; black. (하늘이) 흐린; 어두운. ● **wan·ly** [-li] *adv.* **wan·ness** [-nis] *n.* [E.=dark]

***wand** [wand / wɔnd] *n.* Ⓒ **1** a slender stick or a rod for a magician. (마법의) 지팡이. **2** a staff of authority. (그것을 지닌 사람의 신분·권위를 나타내는) 권표; 관장(官杖). **3** 《mus.》 a conductor's baton. 지휘봉. [N. (→wind)]

:**wan·der** [wándər / wɔ́n-] *vi.* (P1,2A,2B) **1** move aimlessly here and there. (정처 없이) 돌아다니다; 헤매다(cf. *ramble, roam, rove*). ¶ *~ about the world* 세상을 떠돌아다니다 / *Johnny's wandered off somewhere.* 조니는 어디론가 훌쩍 가 버렸다 / *~ through the woods* 숲을 헤매다. **2** lose one's way; stray away. 길을 잃다; 옆길로 빗나가다. ¶ *The dog wandered off and got lost.* 개는 길을 잘못 들어 실종됐다. **3** go astray in thought and speech; go out of one's sense; go aside from a subject. 생각이 헷갈리다; (정신이) 이상해지다; (이야기가) 옆으로 새다. ¶ *He is wandering in his head.* 그는 머리가 이상해졌다 / *The speaker began to ~ from the subject.* 연사는 본제와 상관없는 말을 하기 시작했다 / *His mind wanders at times.* 그는 때때로 정신이 오락가락한다. **4** (of the eyes) shift from point to point. (눈이) 두리번거리다; 시선을 자꾸 옮기다. ¶ *I saw his eyes ~ away from the picture.* 그림에서 그의 시선이 떠나는 것을 봤다.
—*vt.* (P6) 《*poet.*》 roam through (a place, etc.) without any particular purpose. …을 방랑[방황]하다. [E. *wendan* wend]

wan·der·er [wándərər / wɔ́n-] *n.* Ⓒ **1** a person or animal that wanders. 방랑자; 길잃은 짐승. **2** a person who is in the habit of wandering. 방랑벽이 있는 사람.

wan·der·ing [wándəriŋ / wɔ́n-] *n.* 《usu. *pl.*》 **1** the act of moving about without purpose. 방랑; 유랑. **2** a journey from place to place. 만유(漫遊). ¶ *return from one's wanderings* 유랑길에서 돌아오다. **3** confused speech, esp. during a high fever. 종잡을 수 없는 말; (특히 고열로 인한) 헛소리. —*adj.* moving about without purpose. 방랑[유랑]하는.

Wandering Jew [⌐–– ⌐], **the** *n.* persons always on the move, with reference to the legend of Christ's condemning an insulting Jew to wander on earth till His second coming. 방랑하는 유대인《예수를 모욕한 탓으로 그의 재림 때까지 방랑한다는》.

wan·der·lust [wándərlʌ̀st / wɔ́n-] *n.* Ⓤ 《G.》 eager desire for traveling or wandering. 방랑벽; 여행열(熱).

wane [wein] *vi.* (P1) **1** (of the moon) become smaller. (달이) 기울다; 이지러지다(opp. wax). ¶ *The moon waxes and wanes every month.* 달은 매월 기울었다 찼다 한다 / *The moon wanes after it has become full.* 달은 만월이 됐다가 기운다. **2** decline in strength, importance, influence, etc. (힘·세력 등이) 약해지다. ¶ *the waning power of Roman Empire in the 5th century,* 5세기의 로마 제국의 쇠퇴. **3** approach the end. 끝나가다. ¶ *The day is waning.* 날이 저물고 있다.
— *n.* 《*the* ~》 Ⓤ **1** a gradual decrease in strength, importance, influence, etc. 쇠퇴; 쇠미. **2** the decrease in the size of the visible face of the moon. (달의) 기욺; 이지러짐. [E.]

wan·gle [wǽŋgəl] *vt.* (P6,13) 《*colloq.*》 obtain, persuade, etc., by trick or cleverness. 책략으로 손에 넣다; 구슬려 …시키다. ¶ *I wangled George into giving me an invitation.* 조지를 구슬려 나를 초대하게 만들었다 / ~ *10 dollars out of someone* 아무에게서 10달러를 우려내다. [?]

wan·nish [wániʃ / wɔ́n-] *adj.* somewhat wan. 좀 창백한. [*wan*]

:want [wɔ(:)nt, wɑnt] *vt.* **1** (P8,17,20,24) wish; desire. …을 원하다; 바라다. ¶ *I ~ to go there.* / *I ~ you to try it.* 네가 그것을 해보기 바란다 / *I don't ~ you making a fool of me.* 나를 바보 취급하지 않았으면 좋겠다 / *I ~ this work finished promptly.* 이 일을 빨리 마쳐 주면 좋겠다 / *Ask him what he wants.* 그에게 뭘 원하는지 물어봐라 / *Do you ~ to go now?* 지금 가고 싶니 / *I ~ you to be happy.* 네가 행복하기를 바란다. **2** (P6,8,9) 《esp. Brit.》 require; need; ought. …을 필요로 하다; …할 필요가 있다; …해야 하다. 語法 이 용법에서는 흔히 be wanting in을 씀. ¶ *I ~ more money.* 돈이 좀 더 필요하다 / *You don't ~ to be rude.* 버릇 없이 굴면 안 된다 / *The trousers ~ pressing.* 바지를 다림질해야겠다 / *Do you ~ him?* 네게 그 사람이 필요하니 / *Children ~ plenty of sleep.* 아이들은 잠을 충분히 자야 한다 / *You ~ to see a doctor at once.* 자넨 즉시 의사한테 진찰을 받아야 하네. **3** (P6) lack; be short of; fall short of. …이 없다; …이 모자라다; 빠져 있다. ¶ *The book wants a page.* 이 책은 한 페이지가 빠져 있다 / *He wants judgment* 〔*intelligence*〕. 그는 판단〔지능〕이 모자란다 / *The statue wants the head.* 그 상(像)에는 머리가 없다 / *It wants five minutes to* 〔*of*〕 *nine.* 아홉 시 5분 전이다. **4** (P6) wish to see or speak to (someone). …에게 볼일이 있다; …을 만나고 싶다. ¶ *Father wants you.* 아버지가 널 보자고 하신다 / *He is wanted by the police.* 경찰이 그를 찾고 있다《수배되었다》/ *You won't be wanted this afternoon.* 오늘 오후에는 네게 볼일이 없다 / *Will you be wanting me tomorrow?* 내일 내가 할 일이 있습니까.
— *vi.* (P1,3) **1** 《*for*》 have a need; be lacking; be in a state of poverty. 필요로 하다; 부족하다; 모자라다. ¶ *He shall ~ for nothing.* 그에겐 무엇 하나 부족하지 않게 하겠소. **2** lack the necessities of life; be very poor. 생활이 군색하다; 옹색하다.
— *n.* Ⓤ **1** lack; shortage. 결핍; 부족. ¶ *for ~ of* …이 부족해서 / *suffer from ~ of food* 식량이 모자라 고생하다 / *The plants died from ~ of water.* 초목들이 물이 모자라 죽었다 / *I feel the ~ of a good friend.* 좋은 친구가 아쉽다 / *The plan failed for ~ of money.* 자금이 모자라 계획은 실패했다. **2** poverty. 궁핍; 가난. ¶ *the bitterness of ~* 가난의 괴로움 / *He is in extreme ~.* 그는 몹시 궁핍하다 / *live in ~* 가난하게 살다. **3** need. 필요. ¶ *Are you in ~ of money?* 돈이 필요하냐 / *The house is in ~ of repair.* 그 집은 수리할 필요가 있다. **4** Ⓒ 《use. *pl.*》 something needed or desired. 필요한 것; 탐나는 것. ¶ *a man of few wants* 욕심이 적은 사람 / *a man of various wants* 욕심이 많은 사람. [N.]

***want·ing** [wɔ́(:)ntiŋ, wánt-] *adj.* **1** 《*in*》 lacking or absent. …이 없는; 모자라는. ¶ *He is a bit ~ in politeness.* 그는 예의가 좀 없다 / *There is a volume ~ to complete the set.* 질(帙)에서 한 권이 모자란다 / *~ in courage* 용기가 부족한. **2** not up to standard; not adequate. 기준에 못 미치는; 불충분한. ¶ *He was tried and found ~.* 그를 시험해 본즉 부적격이었다. **3** 《*colloq.*》 foolish; half-witted; slightly mad. 어리석은; 저능한; 정신이 좀 돈. ¶ *He is a little ~.* 그는 사람이 좀 모자란다.
— *prep.* without. …이 없는; 모자라는. ¶ *a month ~ two days* 이틀이 모자라는 한 달 / *Wanting a leader, nothing could be done.* 지도자가 없으면 아무 것도 안 된다.

wan·ton [wɔ́(:)ntən, wán-] *adj.* **1** playful; frolicsome. 장난이 심한. ¶ *a ~ child.* **2** (esp. of a woman) not moral; unchaste. 부정(不貞)한; 바람난. ¶ *a ~ woman* / *~ glances* 음탕한 시선. **3** heartless; cruel. 무자비한; 잔인한. **4** not controlled; unrestrained; capricious. 무절제한; 멋대로의; 변덕스러운. ¶ *a ~ wind* 멋대로 부는 바람 / *a ~ waste of money* 무절제한 돈의 낭비. **5** having no just cause or motive. 이렇다할 이유〔동기〕가 없는. ¶ *a ~ murder* 이유 없는 살인 / *~ destruction* 맹목적인 파괴. — *n.* Ⓒ a wanton person. 바람둥이; 음탕한 여자; 장난꾸러기. [E.=untrained]

:war [wɔːr] *n.* **1** Ⓒ a fight with armed force between nations or between parties within a nation; Ⓤ the state created by such a fight. 전쟁; 전쟁 상태. ¶ *a civil ~* 내란 / *World War II* 제2차 세계대전 參考 world war two로 읽음 / *in times*

of ~ 전시에 / *declare* ~ *against* 〔*on*〕 …에 선전 포고하다 / *make* 〔*wage*〕 ~ *on* 〔*upon*〕 *a country* 어떤 나라에 싸움을 걸다 / *go to* ~ 전쟁하다; 출전하다 / *a holy* ~ 성전(聖戰). **2** Ⓒ a conflict; fighting. 싸움; 투쟁. ¶ *a* ~ *of nerves* 신경전 / *a* ~ *of words* 언쟁 / *the* ~ *against disease* 〔*a crime*〕 질병과의〔범죄와의〕 싸움. **3** Ⓤ the art or science of fighting. 전술. ¶ *Soldiers are trained for* ~. 군인은 전술을 익힌다. **4** Ⓤ unfriendly feelings; bitterness of spirit. 적의; 반목; 불화. ¶ *have* ~ *in one's heart* 적의를 품다.

***be at war* (with),** be engaged in a war (with). (…와) 전쟁〔교전〕 중이다. ¶ *The two nations were at* ~ *with each other.* 그 두 나라는 전쟁 상태에 있었다.

go to the wars, go as a soldier. 출정하다.

have been in the wars, show signs of physical injury. 상처투성이이다; 부상한 흔적이 있다.

sinews of war, 《*fig.*》 money necessary for carrying on a war. 군자금.

— *vi.* (**warred, war·ring**) (P1,2A,3) make war; fight or struggle. 싸우다; 전쟁하다. ¶ ~ *with* 〔*against*〕 *evil* 악과 싸우다. [Teut.]

war·ble [wɔ́ːrbəl] *vi.* (P1,2A) (of birds) sing in a trembling way. (새가) 지저귀다. — *vt.* (P6,7) sing like a bird with a trembling of the voice. 목소리를 떨며 노래하다. — *n.* Ⓒ the act, sound, of warbling. 지저귐; 지저귀는 소리; 떨리는 목소리. [Teut.(→whirl)]

war·bler [wɔ́ːrblər] *n.* Ⓒ **1** a person or bird that warbles. 목청을 떨며 노래하는 사람; 지저귀는 새. **2** any one of several small, brightly-colored singing birds. 개개비《휘파람샛과의 작은 새》.

war cry [⌐ ⌐] *n.* **1** a word or cry shouted in battle to create or sustain spirit. (전투에서 공격·돌격시의) 함성. **2** the slogan of a political party. (정당의) 슬로건; 구호.

***ward** [wɔːrd] *n.* Ⓒ **1** Ⓤ 《now only in *watch and ward*》 the act of guarding; protection. 보호. ¶ *The soldiers kept watch and* ~ *over the castle.* 군인들이 성을 감시하고 있었다. **2** a young person under the care of a court or guardian. 피후견인; 피보호자. **3** a division of a city. 구(區)《도시의 행정 구역》. **4** a division of a hospital or prison. 병실; 병동; 감방. ¶ *an isolation* ~ 격리 병동 / *a maternity* ~ 산과 병동; 분만실. **5** Ⓤ 《*arch.*》 the state of being under the control of a guardian. (미성년자가) 후견인의 보호에 있는 상태.

be in ward to, be protected by a guardian. …의 후견(後見)을 받고 있다.

be under ward, be confined in a room. 감금되어 있다.

put someone in ward, confine someone in a room; imprison. …을 감금하다.

— *vt.* **1** (P6) 《*arch.*》 guard; defend; protect. …을 지키다. **2** (P7) 《*off*》 turn aside; keep off. …을 격퇴하다. ¶ *Brushing your teeth regularly helps to* ~ *off tooth decay.* 늘 양치질을 하면 충치를 예방하는 데 좋다 / *He shook his head as if to* ~ *off sleep.* 그는 잠을 쫓으려는 듯 머리를 흔들었다 / *a necklace to* ~ *off evil spirits* 악귀를 쫓는 목걸이. [E.=watching]

war dance [⌐ ⌐] *n.* 《U.S.》 a dance of primitive tribes before going to war or to celebrate victory. (원시인의) 출전〔전승〕의 춤.

ward·en [wɔ́ːrdn] *n.* Ⓒ **1** 《*arch.*》 a person in charge of something; a guardian. 관리인; 감시인. **2** 《U.S.》 the head keeper of a prison. 교도소장. **3** 《Brit.》 the head of certain colleges, schools, etc. 학장; 학교장. **4** a man who patrols to see that cars are not wrongly parked. 주차 위반 단속인. [→ward]

ward·er [wɔ́ːrdər] *n.* Ⓒ **1** 《Brit. *arch.*》 a keeper; a guard. 감시인. ¶ *the Tower Warders* 런던탑 감시인. **2** 《Brit.》 a gaoler; a prison keeper. 교도관. **3** 《hist.》 a staff as a sign of authority carried by a sovereign, commander, etc. 권장(權杖); 지휘봉. [↑]

ward heeler [⌐ ⌐–] *n.* 《U.S. *colloq.*》 a minor hanger-on of a political machine. 하급 당원.

ward·robe [wɔ́ːrdròub] *n.* **1** Ⓒ a piece of furniture for storing clothes. 옷장; 양복장. **2** 《*collectively*》 all of one's clothes; a stock of clothes. 옷(가지); 의류. ¶ *She has a limited* ~. 옷이 별로 없다 / *a* ~ *dealer* 헌옷 장수. [*ward*]

ward·room [wɔ́ːrdrù(ː)m] *n.* Ⓒ 《naut.》 a room in a warship used by all the commissioned officers. 사관실(士官室).

***ware**[1] [wɛər] *n.* **1** 《usu. *pl.*》 articles for sale. 판매품; 상품. ¶ *praise one's own wares* 자화 자찬하다 / *He sold his wares cheap.* 그는 (가게) 물건을 싸게 팔았다 / *peddler and his wares* 행상인과 그의 상품. **2** Ⓤ 《in *compounds*》 manufactured articles. 제품. ¶ *iron* 〔*hard*〕 ~ 철기; 철물 / *table* ~ 식기. **3** Ⓤ pottery. 도기; 도자기. [E (→ward)]

ware[2] [wɛər] *adj.* 《as *predicative*》《*poet.*》 = aware. — *vt.* (P6) 《only in *imperative*》 **1** (esp. in hunting) look out for. …을 조심하다. ¶ *Ware wire!* 철사에 조심해라. **2** 《*colloq.*》 guard against; avoid. …을 경계하다; 삼가다. ¶ *Ware women!* 여자를 경계하라. [↑]

ware·house [wɛ́ərhàus] *n.* Ⓒ **1** a building where goods are kept. 창고. **2** a wholesale store; a large retail store. 도매상점; 큰 가게. — [-hàuz, -hàus] *vt.* (P6) store in a warehouse. 창고에 넣다. [*ware*[1]]

***war·fare** [wɔ́ːrfɛ̀ər] *n.* Ⓤ the act or process of making war; the state of being at war. 전투; 교전 (상태). ¶ *air*

〔*chemical*〕 ~ 공중〔화학〕전 / *economic* ~ 경제 전쟁. [*war*]

war·head [wɔ́ːrhèd] *n.* Ⓒ the front part of a missile, torpedo, bomb, etc. that contains the explosive charge. 탄두(彈頭). ¶ *nuclear warheads* 핵탄두.

war-horse [wɔ́ːrhɔ̀ːrs] *n.* Ⓒ **1** a horse used in battle. 군마(軍馬). **2** a veteran soldier or politician. 노병(老兵); (노련한) 정치가.

war·i·ly [wέərili] *adv.* cautiously; in a wary manner. 조심스럽게; 신중하게. [*wary*]

war·i·ness [wέərinis] *n.* Ⓤ the state of being cautious. 경계. ¶ *The cat and dog eyed each other with* ~. 고양이와 개는 경계하며 노려보았다. [*wary*]

war·like [wɔ́ːrlàik] *adj.* **1** of war; having to do with war. 전쟁의; 전쟁에 관한. ¶ ~ *preparations* 전비(戰備); 군비(軍備). **2** fond of war; quick to fight. 호전적〔도전적〕인. ¶ ~ *tribes* 호전족(好戰族). [*war*]

:warm [wɔːrm] *adj.* **1** having or giving out a moderate degree of heat; serving to maintain heat esp. to a satisfactory degree. 알맞은 더위의; 따뜻한; 따스한(opp. cool). ¶ *It's* ~ *today.* / *She wears* ~ *clothing.* 그녀는 옷을 따뜻하게 입었다 / ~ *water* 따뜻한 물 / *Come and get* ~ *by the fire.* 와서 불을 쬐어라 / ~ *milk* 따끈한 우유 / *a* ~ *bath* 온욕(溫浴). **2** having bodily heat. (몸이) 화끈거리는; 더워지는. ¶ *I am* ~ *from exercise.* 운동을 했더니 덥다 / *I got* ~ *playing in the sun.* 볕에서 놀았더니 몸이 화끈거렸다. **3** hearty; sincere. 다정스러운; 마음에서 우러나는. ¶ *a* ~ *friend* 다정한 친구 / ~ *thanks* 충심에서의 감사 / *receive a* ~ *welcome* 따뜻한 환영을 받다. **4** enthusiastic; lively; excited. 열의 있는; 활발한; 흥분한. ¶ *a* ~ *temperament* 격하기 쉬운 성질 / *a* ~ *argument* 열띤 논의 / *The dispute got* 〔*grew*〕 ~. 토론은 열을 더해 갔다 / *in* ~ *blood* 성나서; 흥분해서. **5** (of colors) suggesting warmth. (색이) 따뜻한(opp. cool). ¶ *Red, yellow, and orange are called* ~ *colors.* 빨강, 노랑 및 오렌지색은 따뜻한 색깔이다. **6** (of the scent in hunting) fresh; strong. (냄새가) 생생한; 강한. ¶ *The scent was still* ~. 사냥감의 냄새가 아직 생생했다. **7** 《Brit. *colloq.*》 wealthy; rich. 부유한. ¶ *a* ~ *man* 부자. **8** (in children's games) being near find or guessing. (숨바꼭질·알아맞히기 따위의 놀이에서) 거의 찾게〔알아맞히게〕 된. ¶ *You're getting* ~. 거의 찾게 됐다; 거의 맞아 간다. **9** uncomfortable; unpleasant. 불쾌한. **10** (of fighting) fierce. (싸움에서) 격렬한. ¶ ~ *resistance* 격렬한 저항 / *a* ~ *corner* 격전지.

keep a seat 〔***place***〕 ***warm,*** occupy a seat 〔place〕 temporarily for another who is not yet qualified to hold it. (아무가 자격을 얻을 때까지) 잠시 그 자리에 있어 주다.

make it warm for, make it too hot for. …을 그 자리에 배겨나지 못하게 하다.

— *vt.* (P6,7) **1** make (someone or something) warm; heat again. …을 데우다; 덥게 하다. ¶ ~ *oneself at the fire* 불을 쬐다 / *The sun has warmed the air.* 해가 나서 공기가 더워졌다 / *A glass of rum will* ~ *you up.* 럼 한 잔 마시면 몸이 더워질 것이다 / *We'll* ~ *up yesterday's mutton.* 어제의 양고기를 데우겠다. **2** inspire or fill (someone) with kindly emotions. …의 마음을 따뜻하게 하다. ¶ *The sight of the baby warmed the killer.* 아기를 보자 살인자의 마음은 부드러워졌다. **3** make (someone or something) enthusiastic, lively, excited, etc. …을 열중하게 하다; 기운나게 하다; 흥분시키다. — *vi.* (P1,2A) **1** 《often *up*》 become warm. 더워지다. ¶ *The milk is warming on the stove.* 난로 위의 우유가 데워지고 있다 / *The room will soon* ~ *up.* 방이 곧 따뜻해질 것이다. **2** 《*to, toward*》 become kindly. 동정〔호감〕을 가지다. ¶ *My heart warms to him.* 그가 좋아진다. **3** become enthusiastic, lively, excited, etc. 열중하다; 흥분하다. ¶ *The speaker began to* ~ (*up*). 연사는 흥분하기 시작했다. **4** 《*up*》 practice or exercise for a few minutes before entering a game, contest, etc. (경기 전에) 준비 운동을 하다; 워밍업하다.

get a warming, receive a hard blow. 얻어터지다.

warm *someone's* ***jacket,*** 《*colloq.*》 deal someone a lick. …를 후려갈기다.

— *n.* 《usu. *a* ~》 the act of warming. 데우기; 따뜻해지기; 따뜻하게 하기. ¶ *have* 〔*get, take*〕 *a* ~ 더워지다. [E.]

warm-blood·ed [wɔ́ːrmblʌ́did] *adj.* **1** having warm blood. 온혈의(opp. cold-blooded). ¶ ~ *animals* 온혈 동물. **2** eager; having strong feeling. 격하기 쉬운; 열정적인.

warm·er [wɔ́ːrmər] *n.* Ⓒ a device for making something warm. 온열기; 온열〔가열〕 장치.

warm·heart·ed [wɔ́ːrmhɑ́ːrtid] *adj.* having a warm heart; sympathetic; friendly. 마음이 따뜻한; 친절한. ¶ *a* ~ *offer of help* 도와주겠다는 따뜻한 제안.

·warm·ly [wɔ́ːrmli] *adv.* in a warm manner. 따뜻하게; 친절히; 열심히.

:warmth [wɔːrmθ] *n.* Ⓤ **1** the state of being warm; moderate heat. 따뜻함; 온난. ¶ *the* ~ *of climate* 기후의 온난. **2** enthusiasm; eagerness; friendness. 열심; 친절; 우정. ¶ *the* ~ *of welcome* 환영의 따뜻함. **3** warm feeling. 동정; 배려. **4** emotional excitement; anger. 흥분; 노여움. ¶ *reply with some* ~ 다소 흥분해서 대답하다. [→warm]

warm-up [wɔ́ːrmʌ̀p] *n.* ⓊⒸ the act of practicing before going into a game, race, etc. 워밍업; (경기 전의) 가벼운 예비 운동.

warm work [∠∠] *n.* an arduous task; a hard fight. 힘든 일; 격전(激戰).

W

:warn [wɔːrn] *vt.* (P6,7,13,15,20) **1** make (someone) aware of possible danger; advise (someone) to be careful. …에게 조심하게 하다; 경고하다. ¶ ~ *someone of danger* 아무에게 위험하다고 주의 주다 / *We warned him not to go out in the storm.* 우리는 그에게 폭풍우 속에 밖으로 나가지 말라고 일렀다 / *I ~ you that you will be punished.* 경고하건데 넌 처벌될 것이다. **2** give a notice to (someone); inform. …에게 예고[통고]하다. ¶ *The siren warned us that a police car was chasing us.* 사이렌 소리를 듣고 경찰차가 우리를 쫓고 있다는 것을 알았다 / *~ a tenant out of* [*from*] *a house* 세든 사람에게 집을 비우라고 통고하다. [E.]

∗warn·ing [wɔ́ːrniŋ] *n.* **1** Ⓒ something that warns. 경보; 교훈. ¶ *Let this be a ~ to you.* 이것이 네게 교훈이 됐으면 한다. **2** Ⓤ a notice given in advance; announcement that employment is to end. 예고; 해고의 예고. ¶ *I've given the cook ~.* 요리사에게 해고를 예고했다 / *a month's ~* 한 달 전의 해고 통지. **3** Ⓤ the action of warning. 경고; 주의. ¶ *The branch fell without the slightest ~.* 느닷없이 가지가 부러졌다.

∗warp [wɔːrp] *n.* Ⓒ **1** the lengthwise thread in a piece of cloth. 날실 (opp. woof). ¶ *The ~ is crossed by the woof.* 날실은 씨실과 교차된다. **2** a bend or twist. 휨; 비틀림. ¶ *Dampness gave the board a bad ~.* 습기로 인해 판자가 뒤틀렸다. **3** a mental twist. 마음의 비꼬임. **4** 《naut.》 a rope used in moving a ship. (배를 끄는) 밧줄.

— *vt.* (P6) **1** turn or twist out of shape; bend. …을 휘게[뒤틀리게] 하다. ¶ *The sun has warped the boards.* 볕에 판자들이 휘었다 / 《*fig.*》 *~ the mind* 마음을 비뚤어지게 하다 / *His whole character was warped.* 그의 성격이 온통 비꼬였다 / *Prejudice warps our judgment.* 편견이 판단을 그르치게 만든다 / *If you really enjoy such unpleasant jokes you must have a warped mind.* 그런 온당치 못한 농담을 좋아하다니 그건 네 마음이 비뚤어진 탓이다. **2** move (a ship, etc.) by ropes fastened to something fixed. (배 따위)를 밧줄로 끌어 이동시키다.

— *vi.* (P1) **1** become bent or twisted. 꼬이다; 뒤틀리다. **2** be moved by means of warps. (배가) 밧줄에 끌려 이동하다. [E.]

war-paint [wɔ́ːrpèint] *n.* **1** paint applied to the face and body, as by American Indian tribes, preparing to make war. 출진 화장(出陣化粧). **2** 《*colloq.*》 a woman's make-up. 여성의 화장(품). [*war*]

war·path [wɔ́ːrpæ̀θ, -pɑ̀ːθ] *n.* the path or course taken by North American Indians on the way to battle. 출진로(出陣路).

on the warpath, **a)** ready for or engaged in a conflict. 출전(出戰)의 채비로. **b)** ready to make trouble; angry. 시비조로; 불끈하여.

war·plane [wɔ́ːrplèin] *n.* a military or naval aeroplane. 군용기; 전투기.

∙war·rant [wɔ́(ː)rənt, wɑ́r-] *n.* **1** Ⓤ a good and sufficient reason for belief; a guarantee. 정당한 이유; 보증; 근거. ¶ *without ~* 까닭 없이 / *What ~ do you have to say such a thing?* 무슨 근거로 그런 소리를 하느냐 / *He has no ~ for his action.* 그의 행동은 근거가 없다 / *I will be your ~.* 내가 네 보증을 서지. **2** Ⓒ a document giving someone a legal right to do something. 위임장; 영장. ¶ *a search ~* 수색 영장 / *The magistrate issued a ~ for his arrest.* 치안 판사는 그의 체포 영장을 발부했다. **3** Ⓒ something which gives a right; authority; justification. 권한; (행위의) 정당성.

— *vt.* **1** (P6) justify; give a right to. …을 정당화하다; 권한을 부여하다. ¶ *The crime warranted severe punishment.* 그 죄는 엄벌에 처해 마땅하다 / *The facts ~ the conclusion.* 그 결론이 옳다는 것을 그 사실이 증명하고 있다. **2** guarantee; affirm as certain. …을 보증하다. ¶ *I'll ~ him a perfectly honest man.* 그가 진짜 정직한 사람임을 내가 보증한다. [Teut.]

war·ran·tee [wɔ̀(ː)rəntíː, wɑ̀r-] *n.* Ⓒ a person to whom a warranty is made. 피보증인.

war·ran·ter, -tor [wɔ́(ː)rəntər, wɑ́r-] *n.* Ⓒ a person who warrants. 보증인.

war·ran·ty [wɔ́(ː)rənti, wɑ́r-] *n.* Ⓒ (*pl.* **-ties**) **1** a reasonable ground. 정당한 이유. **2** 《law.》 a guarantee, usu. in written or printed form. 보증; 담보. **3** a writ. 영장.

war·ren [wɔ́(ː)rən, wɑ́r-] *n.* Ⓒ **1** a place for raising rabbits. 토끼 사육장. **2** a crowded district. 사람이 북적대는 데; 과밀 지역. [G. *warinne* game park]

:war·ri·or [wɔ́(ː)riər, wɑ́r-] *n.* Ⓒ 《chiefly *poet.*》 a soldier; a fighter, esp. a veteran fighting-man. 전사(戰士); 무인; 역전의 용사. ¶ *the Unknown Warrior* 무명 용사. [→ war]

war·ship [wɔ́ːrʃip] *n.* Ⓒ a ship armed for war. 군함; 전함. [*war*]

wart [wɔːrt] *n.* Ⓒ a small hard lump on the skin or on a plant stem. 사마귀; (나무줄기의) 옹두리. [E.]

with one's warts, without concealment. 있는 그대로; 숨김 없이.

war·time [wɔ́ːrtàim] *n.* Ⓤ the period during which a war continues. 전시(opp. peacetime). [*war*]

war·y [wέəri] *adj.* (**war·i·er, war·i·est**) habitually on guard; careful. 조심성 있는; 방심치 않는; 신중한. ¶ *The old farmer was ~ of city folk.* 그 늙은 농부는 도시 사람들에게 방심치 않았다 / *a ~ eye* 경계하는 눈 / *a ~ observation* 신중한 관찰 / *~ answers* 신중한 대답 / *Be ~ of strangers.* 낯선 사람을 조심해라. [*ware*[2]]

W

:was [wɑz, wəz / wɔz] *v.* p. of **is** or **am.**

:wash [wɑʃ, wɔ(ː)ʃ] *vt.* **1** (P6,7,18) clean (one's body, clothes, etc.), usu. with water. (몸 따위)를 씻다; (옷 따위)를 빨다; 세탁하다. ¶ ~ *one's hands* 손을 씻다 / ~ *oneself* 세수하다; 몸을 씻다 / *Wash your hands clean before eating.* 식사 전에 손을 깨끗이 닦아라 / *Wash your mouth out.* 입 안을 깨끗이 헹구어라 / *Mother washed a lot of clothes yesterday.* 어머니는 어제 많은 옷을 세탁하셨다 / *Tom washed his car clean.* 톰은 자기 차를 깨끗이 세차했다. **2** (P6,7) 《*away, off, out*》 remove (spots, stains, etc.) by washing. (얼룩·더럼 등)을 씻어 내다. ¶ ~ *off stains from a coat* 코트의 얼룩을 씻어 빼다 / *Wash the ink off* 〔*from*〕 *your hands.* 손에 묻은 잉크를 닦아 내라. **3** (P6,7) 《*away*》 free from (sin, guilt, etc.); purify (the soul). (죄 따위)를 면하다〔씻다〕; (종교적 의미에서) 깨끗이 하다. ¶ ~ *away one's sin* 죄를 씻다 / ~ *someone's brain* (설득하고 깨우치게 해서) 아무의 옳지 못한 생각을 바꾸게 하다. **4** (P6,7,13) (of the sea, a river, waves, etc.) flow through, over, or against (something). (바닷물 등이) …을 씻다; (파도 따위가) …에 밀려 오다. ¶ *The waves washed the shore.* 파도가 해안을 철썩이고 있었다 / *The cliffs are washed by the sea.* 벼랑은 바닷물에 의해 철썩철썩 씻겼다. **5** (P6,13) make (something) wet. …을 적시다. ¶ *The flowers were washed with dew.* 꽃들은 이슬로 축축히 젖어 있었다. **6** (P6,7) 《*away*》 remove or carry away (something) by the action of water, etc. …을 떠내려 보내다; 밀려가게 하다; (물이) …을 운반하다. ¶ *The bridge was washed away by the flood.* 홍수로 다리가 떠내려갔다 / *The boat was washed ashore* 〔*out to sea*〕. 보트가 해안으로 밀려 올라왔다〔바다로 떠내려갔다〕. **7** (P6) wear (something) by flowing over it; make or form (a channel, etc.). …을 파다〔에다〕; …을 침식하다; (물이 해협 따위)를 만들다. ¶ *The rain washed a channel in the ground.* 비로 인해 지면에 도랑이 생겼다 / *The road was washed out by the rain.* 비로 인해 도로가 패여 나갔다. **8** (P6,7,13) cover (something) with a thin coat of metal or of paint. …을 도금하다; (그림 물감)을 엷게 칠하다. ¶ ~ *walls with blue* 벽을 파랗게 칠하다 / *copper washed over with gold* 금도금을 한 구리. **9** (P6,7) 《mine》 separate valuable ore from (earth, sand, etc.) by the action of water; separate (ore) in this way. 세광(洗鑛)하다.

— *vi.* **1** (P1) wash one's hands, face, etc.; wash oneself. 손을 씻다; 세수하다; 목욕하다. ¶ *You must ~ before dinner.* 저녁 식사 전에 손을 씻어야 한다 / ~ *in cold water* 찬물에 세수하다 / *You haven't washed behind your ears.* 귀 뒤는 씻지 않았구나. **2** (P1) wash clothes. 옷을 빨다; 세탁하다. ¶ ~ *once a week* 한 주에 한 번 빨래하다. **3** (P1,2A) be able to stand washing without damage. 세탁이 잘 되다; (천이 상하지 않고) 때가 잘 지다. ¶ *This cloth won't* ~. 이 천은 세탁이 잘 안 된다 / *Will this material ~?* 이 옷감은 세탁이 잘 됩니까. **4** (P1,2A) 《*against, over, along*》 beat or flow with a lapping sound. (파도가) 철썩철썩 밀려오다; 기슭을 씻다. ¶ ~ *ashore* 해안을 철썩철썩 씻다 / *hear the waves washing against the cliff* 벼랑에 철썩철썩 부딪는 파도 소리를 듣다. **5** (P1,2A) 《*away, out*》 be removed or carried by the action of water. (물에) 밀려〔떠〕내려가다; 침식되다. ¶ *The bank has washed away.* 둑이 떠내려갔다. **6** 《as *negative*》 《*colloq.*》 bear or stand testing; be found to be true. (시험·조사 따위)에 견디다; 입증되다. ¶ *The story won't* ~. 그 이야기는 미심쩍다.

wash down, **a**) clean by washing; clean completely. …을 씻어 내다; 말끔히 씻다. ¶ ~ *down the walls* 벽을 말끔히 씻어 내다/ ~ *down one's car* 세차하다. **b**) help the chewing or swallowing of (a food) by drinking water, etc. (물 따위로 입 안의) 음식을 넘기다. ¶ ~ *food down with beer* 맥주와 함께 음식을 넘기다.

washed out, **a**) lacking color; faded in color, esp. from washing. (빨아서) 빛이 바랜. **b**) tired or worn out; exhausted. 몹시 지친〔피곤한〕. ¶ *He looks washed out.* 피곤한 모양이다 / *feel washed out* 피곤을 느끼다.

wash for a living, be a laundryman by profession. 세탁업을 하다.

wash one's hands of, **a**) withdraw from. …에서 손을 떼다. ¶ *I ~ my hands of you.* 너와는 결별이다. **b**) decline responsibility for. 책임지기를 거부하다.

wash up, **a**) 《U.S.》 wash one's face and hands. 세수하다. **b**) 《Brit.》 wash (dishes, etc.) after meals. 설거지하다.

— *n.* **1** Ⓒ Ⓤ 《usu. *a* ~》 the act of washing. 세탁; 씻기. ¶ *have* 〔*get*〕 *a* ~ 세탁하다 / *give something a good* ~ 어떤 것을 잘 세탁하다 / *give a car a good* ~ 깨끗이 세차하다 / *at* 〔*in*〕 *the* ~ 세탁 중이다; 세탁소에 보냈다 / *send clothes to the* ~ 옷을 세탁소에 보내다. **2** 《*collectively*》 《*the* ~》 clothes, etc. to be washed or being washed; 《Brit.》 the process of washing at a laundry. 세탁물; 빨랫감; 세탁소에서의 세탁. ¶ *She is hanging out the* ~. 세탁물을 널고 있다 / *He sends clothes to the ~ once a week.* 1주일에 한 번 옷가지를 세탁소에 보낸다 / *have a heavy* ~ 빨랫감이 많다. **3** Ⓒ 《*the* ~》 the movement or flow of water; the sound of this. 파도의 밀어닥침; 그 파도 소리. ¶ *hear* 〔*listen to*〕 *the ~ of the waves* 철썩거리는 파도 소리를 듣다. **4** Ⓒ a liquid for washing eyes, hair, etc. 세(척)제; 화장수. ¶ *a ~ for the eyes* 세안수(洗眼水) / *a ~ for the hair* 세발제; 샴푸. **5** Ⓤ weak liquid or food. 물기 있는 음

W

식; 유동식. ¶ *This soup is mere* ~. 이 수프는 너무 멀겋다. **6** Ⓤ waste liquid containing waste food from the kitchen. (설거지한) 구정물; 그 찌끼. **7** Ⓤ 《*the* ~》 the disturbed water left behind a moving ship, etc.; disturbed air behind a moving airplane. (배 지난 뒤의) 물결의 굽이침; (비행기 지난 뒤의) 기류의 소용돌이. **8** Ⓤ a thin coat of gold, silver, etc. laid on something. (금속 따위의) 엷게 입힌 도금. **9** Ⓤ 《usu. *the* ~》 the matter that is carried and deposited by flowing water. (유수에 의해 운반되어 온) 토사(土砂); 개흙; 침전물.
— *adj.* 《U.S.》 washable. 세탁이 잘 되는; 빨아도 되는. ¶ *a ~ dress.* [E.]

wash·a·ble [wάʃəbəl, wɔ́(:)ʃ-] *adj.* **1** that can be washed. 세탁이 잘 되는; 빨아도 되는. ¶ ~ *cloth* 빨아도 변하지 않는 천 / *a* ~ *ink spot* 빨면 지는 잉크 얼룩. **2** soluble in water. 물에 용해되는; 수용성의.

wash-and-wear [wάʃənwέər, wɔ́(:)ʃ-] *adj.* of a garment that can be washed, that dries quickly, and that needs little or no ironing. 빨아서 다리지 않고 바로 입을 수 있는.

wash·ba·sin [wάʃbèisn, wɔ́(:)ʃ-] *n.* Ⓒ 《Brit.》 =washbowl.

wash·board [wάʃbɔ̀:rd, wɔ́(:)ʃ-] *n.* Ⓒ a board with ridges used for rubbing the dirt out of clothes. 빨래판.

wash·bowl [wάʃbòul, wɔ́(:)ʃ-] *n.* Ⓒ 《U.S.》 a bowl or basin for washing one's hands and face, etc. 세면기; 대야.

wash·cloth [wάʃklɔ̀(:)θ, wɔ́(:)ʃ-, -klὰθ] *n.* Ⓒ **1** 《U.S.》 a small cloth for washing the face and body. (세수) 수건. **2** 《Brit.》 a cloth for washing dishes. 행주.

wash-day [wάʃdèi, wɔ́(:)ʃ-] *n.* 《U.S.》 a day when clothes are washed (at home). (가정의) 세탁일.

washed-out [wάʃtáut, wɔ́(:)ʃt-] *adj.* **1** faded during washing. (빨아서) 색이 바랜. **2** 《*colloq.*》 quite tired; tiredlooking. 지친; 기운 없는.

washed-up [wάʃtʌ́p, wɔ́(:)ʃt-] *adj.* 《*colloq.*》 defeated; having failed. 좌절된; 실패한.

wash·er [wάʃər, wɔ́(:)ʃ-] *n.* Ⓒ **1** a person who washes. 빨래하는〔씻는〕 사람. **2** a washing machine. 세탁기. **3** a flat ring of metal, leather, rubber, etc. used to give tightness to a joint. 똬리쇠; (볼트의) 워셔.

wash·er·man [wάʃərmən, wɔ́(:)ʃ-] *n.* Ⓒ (*pl.* **-men** [-mən]) a person who washes for money; a launderer. 세탁인; 세탁업자.

wash·er·wom·an [wάʃərwùmən, wɔ́(:)ʃ-] *n.* Ⓒ (*pl.* **-wom·en**) a woman who washes for money; a laundress. (직업적인) 세탁부.

wash·er·wom·en [wάʃərwìmin] *n.* pl. of **washerwoman.**

·**wash·ing** [wάʃiŋ, wɔ́(:)ʃ-] *n.* Ⓤ **1** the work of washing cloth or clothes; cleaning with water; the process of being washed. 세탁; 씻기; 빨기. ¶ *She is engaged in* ~. 그녀는 세탁일을 하고 있다 / *I gave myself a good* ~. 나는 몸을 깨끗이 씻었다 / *Children dislike* ~. 아이들은 몸을 씻기를 질색한다. **2** 《*collectively*》 articles that have been or are to be washed. 세탁물; 빨랫감. ¶ *hang out the* ~ *to dry* 말리기 위해 빨래를 널다. **3** 《usu. *pl.*》 waste liquid or matter. 세탁〔세척〕에 사용된 구정물. ¶ *the washings of plates and dishes* 설거지한 물. [*wash*]

washing machine [∠-∸] *n.* a machine for washing clothes, etc. 세탁기.

washing stand [∠-∸] *n.* =washstand.

:**Wash·ing·ton** [wάʃiŋtən, wɔ́(:)ʃ-] *n.* **1** the capital of the United States. 워싱턴(시). 參考 주(州)와 구별하기 위해 보통 D.C.를 붙임. **2** a State in the northwestern part of the United States. 워싱턴 주. 參考 Wash.로 생략함. **3 George** (1732-99) the first President of the United States. 조지 워싱턴.

wash-leath·er [wάʃlèðər, wɔ́(:)ʃ-] *n.* 《Brit.》 a piece of leather, usu. sheepskin, used for cleaning windows, cars, etc. (영양 가죽의) 유피(柔皮)《먼지·때 따위를 닦아내는 세척용》. [*wash*]

wash·out [wάʃàut, wɔ́(:)ʃ-] *n.* Ⓤ **1** ⓐ the washing out or away of earth, etc. by a flood, etc. (폭우 따위로 인한 토사의) 유실. ⓑ a place where earth, rocks, etc., have been so carried away. (폭우 따위로) 유실된 곳. **2** 《*sl.*》 an unsuccessful person or enterprise; a complete failure. 실패한 사람〔기업〕; 대실패. ¶ *He was a* ~ *as a teacher.* 그는 선생으로서 실패한 사람이었다 / *The undertaking was a complete* ~. 그 사업은 쫄딱 망했다.

wash·stand [wάʃstæ̀nd, wɔ́(:)ʃ-] *n.* Ⓒ a stand for supporting a basin, pitcher, etc. for washing the hands and face. 세면대.

wash·tub [wάʃtʌ̀b, wɔ́(:)ʃ-] *n.* Ⓒ a large wooden tub for washing clothes. 빨래통.

wash·wom·an [wάʃwùmən, wɔ́(:)ʃ-] *n.* (*pl.* **-wom·en**) =washerwoman.

wash·y [wάʃi, wɔ́(:)ʃi] *adj.* (**wash·i·er, wash·i·est**) watery; weak. 물기 많은; 묽은.

:**was·n't** [wάznt, wʌ́z- / wɔ́z-] =was not.

wasp [wɑsp, wɔ(:)sp] *n.* Ⓒ a flying insect with a powerful sting and a slender body of black and yellow stripes. 장수말벌; 나나니벌. [E.]

wasp·ish [wάspiʃ, wɔ́(:)sp-] *adj.* **1** like a wasp. 장수말벌 같은. **2** easily angered; bad-tempered; irritable. 걸핏하면 성내는. **3** full of ill-will. 심보가 나쁜; 심술궂은. [↑]

was·sail [wάsəl, -seil / wɔ́seil] *n.* Ⓒ 《*arch.*》 **1** a drinking party. 주연; 술자리. **2** the liquor drunk at such a party. 주연에서 마시는 술; 잔칫술. — *vi.* (P1) **1** take part in a wassail. 주연에 나가다〔참석하다〕. **2**

drink to the health of someone. 건배하다. — *interj.* Your health! (건강을 위하여) 건배. [E. =be whole]

wast [wɑst, wəst / wɔst] *vi.* 《*arch., poet.*》 p. of **art**². ¶ *Thou* ~.

wast·age [wéistidʒ] *n.* Ⓤ **1** loss by use; decay; waste. 손실; 소모. ¶ *We expect to lose over 50 people from our work force every year by natural* ~. 자연적인 소모로 해마다 50명의 인력이 손실되리라 예상한다. **2** the amount wasted. 소모액(량). [→waste]

⁑waste [weist] *adj.* **1** not cultivated; not inhabited; wild; barren; desolate. 미개간의; 사람이 살지 않는; 황폐한; 불모의. ¶ ~ *land* 황무지 / *The land still lies* ~. 그 땅은 아직도 황무지 그대로다. **2** of no value; useless; thrown aside as worthless. 무가치한; 쓸모 없는; 남아 도는; 내버려진. ¶ ~ *paper* 휴지 / ~ *energy* 쓰이지 않는 에너지 / ~ *materials* 폐품.

lay waste, destroy completely; make (something) desolate. …을 황폐케 하다. ¶ *The building was laid* ~ *by war.* 그 건물은 전쟁으로 폐허가 됐다.

— *vt.* **1** (P6,13) spend uselessly or carelessly; throw away. …을 낭비하다; 헛되이 쓰다. ¶ *Don't* ~ *your time and money.* 돈과 시간을 헛되이 쓰지 마라 / *You are wasting your breath.* 쓸데없는 말을 하는군; 말해야 소용 없다 / *Kind words are wasted upon him.* 친절한 말도 그에겐 소용 없다. **2** (P6) destroy; ruin. …을 황폐하게 하다. ¶ *World War III will* ~ *the whole world.* 제3차 세계대전은 전세계를 쑥밭으로 만들 것이다. **3** (P6) wear away gradually; make (something or someone) weak or feeble. …을 서서히 소모시키다; 쇠약하게 하다. ¶ *His body was wasted by a long illness.* 오랜 병으로 그는 몸이 쇠약해졌다.

— *vi.* **1** (P1,2A) become weak; lose strength. 쇠약해지다; 약화되다. ¶ ~ *from disease* 병으로 쇠약해지다 / ~ *away for lack of food* 음식물의 결핍으로 쇠약해지다 / *She wasted away with grief.* 슬픔으로 그녀는 쇠약해졌다. **2** be used up gradually; be used badly. 점점 소모되다(줄다); 낭비되다(하다). ¶ *The resources of the country are rapidly wasting.* 나라의 자원은 급속히 소모되고 있다 / 《*prov.*》 *Waste not, want not.* 낭비하지 않으면 모자라는 것이 없다. **3** (P1) 《*arch.*》 (of time) pass gradually. (때가) 지나다.

— *n.* **1** ⓊⒸ the act of wasting; the state of being wasted. 낭비; 허비. ¶ *It's a* ~ *of time to argue further.* 이 이상 논의하는 것은 시간 낭비일 뿐이다 / *I think betting is a complete* ~ *of money.* 돈내기는 순전히 돈의 낭비다. **2** Ⓒ a piece of waste land; an unbroken expanse (of land, water, etc.). 황무지; 불모지; 광막한 지역(바다). ¶ *a* ~ *of waters* 망망 대해 / *There are many wastes in this country.* 이 나라에는 황무지가 많다 / *No crops will grow on these stony wastes.* 이런 돌투성이 황무지에서는 작물이 자랄 수가 없다. **3** Ⓤ gradual destruction or decay. 소모; 쇠약. **4** Ⓤ waste material. 폐(기)물; 쓰레기. ¶ *kitchen* ~ 부엌 쓰레기 / *A lot of poisonous* ~ *from chemical works goes into the river.* 화학 공장에서 나오는 많은 유독성 폐기물이 하천으로 버려지고있다. **5** Ⓒ 《law》 damage of property, etc. through neglect. (고의·태만으로 인한 자산의) 훼손. [L. *vastus* empty, desolate]

run* (*go*) *to waste, be wasted; become useless or spoiled. 낭비되다; 폐물이(못 쓰게) 되다.

waste·bas·ket [wéistbæ̀skit, -bɑ̀ːs-] *n.* Ⓒ a basket for wastepaper; a wastepaper basket. 휴지통.

waste·ful [wéistfəl] *adj.* using or spending more than is necessary. 낭비하는; 비경제적인; 헛된. ¶ *He is* ~ *of his parents' money.* 부모 돈을 마구 쓰고 있다 / *a* ~ *man* 낭비가.

waste·ful·ly [wéistfəli] *adv.* in a wasteful manner. 헛되이; 비경제적으로.

waste·ful·ness [wéistfəlnis] *n.* Ⓤ the act of causing waste; the state of being wasteful. 낭비; 불경제.

waste·pa·per [wéistpèipər] *n.* Ⓤ paper thrown away as useless. 휴지; 파지.

waste pipe [ㄹㄴ] *n.* a pipe to carry off waste water. (오수) 배수관.

wast·ing [wéistiŋ] *adj.* **1** laying waste; devastating. 황폐화시키는; 파괴적인. **2** gradually destructive to the body. 서서히 쇠약하게 만드는; 소모성의. ¶ *a* ~ *disease* (*fever*) 소모성 질환(열병).

wast·rel [wéistrəl] *n.* a wasteful person; a person who wastes his life. 낭비가 심한 사람; 부랑자; 건달.

⁑watch [wɑtʃ, wɔːtʃ] *n.* **1** Ⓒ a small timepiece for the pocket or the wrist. 회중(손목) 시계(cf. *clock*). ¶ *a* ~ *and chain* 쇠줄이 달린 회중 시계 / *look at one's* ~ 시계를 보다 / *He wound up his* ~. 시계의 태엽을 감았다. **2** Ⓤ the act of keeping the eyes on something; guard; a look-out. 경계; 망보기. ¶ *be on the* ~ *for* …을 경계하다 / *keep* ~ 망을 보다 / *keep a close* ~ *on someone* (*a place*) 아무(어떤 장소)를 예의 감시하다 / *keep* ~ *against danger* 위험을 경계하다. **3** Ⓒ an act of keeping awake for some special purpose. 불침번; 밤샘. ¶ *a mother's* ~ *over a sick baby* 아픈 아기를 밤새워 돌보는 어머니. **4** 《hist.》 Ⓒ a person or a group of persons on guard, esp. at night. (한 사람 또는 조(組)로 된) 야간 경비원; 야경꾼; 파수꾼. ¶ *place a* ~ (야간) 경비원을 두다. **5** Ⓒ 《naut.》 a period (usu. four hours) of duty of a ship's crew; a part of a crew on duty during such a period. (배에서, 4시간 교대의) 당직 시간; 당직원. ¶ *be on* (*off*) ~ 당직(비번)이다.

in the watches of the night, while one lies awake. 밤에 자지 않고 있을 때에.
pass as a watch in the night, be soon forgotten. 곧 잊혀져 버리다.
watch and ward, guard by night and day. 밤낮 없는 감시; 엄한 경계.
— *vi.* (P1,2A,3,4) **1** 《*for*》 look carefully; observe; be careful; wait carefully. 지켜보다; 주목〔주시〕하다; (준비를 다 하고) 기다리다〔대기하다〕. ¶ *He watched to see what would happen.* 무엇이 일어나는가를 (가만히) 지켜보았다 / *I watched for the chance to kill him.* 나는 그를 살해할 기회를 기다렸다 / *He watched for the bus.* 그는 버스를 기다렸다. **2** keep awake; look at someone or something carefully, without sleeping. 잠자지 않고 깨어 있다; 철야하다; 잠자지 않고 간병하다〔지키다〕. ¶ ~ *with a sick person* 잠자지 않고 환자를 돌보다〔간호하다〕/ *My guardian angel will ~ over me.* 수호 천사가 나를 지켜 주실 것이다. **3** keep guard. 망보다; 감시하다. ¶ *I asked him to ~.* 나는 그에게 망을 보라고 했다 / *There is a policeman watching outside the house.* 집 밖에서 경찰이 감시하고 있다. — *vt.* (P6,7,10,12,22,23) **1** look at; observe; direct the attention upon (someone or something). …을 (지켜)보다; 주시〔관찰〕하다; …에 주의하다. ¶ ~ *television* 텔레비전을 보다 / ~ *a game* 경기를 구경하다 / ~ *the house burning* 불타고 있는 집을 보다 / ~ *someone's face closely* 아무의 얼굴을 찬찬히 응시하다 / ~ *the development of a case* 사건의 진전을 지켜보다 / *He watched how the flower opened.* 그는 어떻게 꽃이 피는지를 지켜보았다 / *I watched him do* 〔*doing*〕 *it.* 나는 그가 그걸 하는〔하고 있는〕 것을 지켜보았다. **2** guard; tend; keep a watchful eye on. …을 망보다〔지키다〕; …을 간호〔감시〕하다. ¶ *She watched the poor old man.* 그 불쌍한 노인을 돌봤다 / *Dogs ~ over a flock of sheep.* 개들이 양떼를 지키고 있다 / *I knew I was watched.* 내가 감시당하고 있음을 알고 있었다. **3** wait carefully for (someone or something). …을 기다리다. ¶ ~ *one's time* 〔*opportunity*〕 시기〔기회〕를 기다리다〔엿보다〕. [*wake*[1]]
watch out, be careful; look out. …을 조심하다; 경계하다. ¶ *Watch out! There is a car coming.* 조심해, 차가 온다 / *Watch out for a tall man in a black hat.* 검은 모자를 쓴 키 큰 남자를 경계해라.
watch over, guard; tend. …을 돌보다; 간호하다.
***watch one's step*(*s*),** **a**) be careful in walking. 발밑을 조심하다. ¶ *Now ~ your step on the dark stairs.* 얘야, 어두운 계단에서 발밑을 조심해라. **b**) be careful in one's conduct; be on one's guard. 신중히 행동하다; 조심하다.

watch·dog [wɑ́tʃdɔ̀(:)g, wɔ́:tʃ-, -dɑ̀g] *n.* Ⓒ a dog for guarding a building, property, etc. 경비견.

watch·er [wɑ́tʃər, wɔ́:tʃ-] *n.* Ⓒ a person who watches. 감시인; 당직자; 간병인.

watch·fire [wɑ́tʃfàiər, wɔ́:tʃ-] *n.* a fire kept burning at night as a signal or for the use of those staying awake to watch or guard. 횃불; (야경·신호용의) 모닥불.

watch·ful [wɑ́tʃfəl, wɔ́:tʃ-] *adj.* watching carefully; alert; wide-awake. 주의 깊은; 조심스러운; 경계하는. ¶ *a ~ guard* 주의 깊은 경비원 / *She was ~ for any signs of activity in the empty house.* 그녀는 빈 집에 어떤 움직임이 있는지 예의 주시했다.

watch glass [⌐⌐] *n.* 《Brit.》 a cover of glass for a watch. (회중〔손목〕 시계의) 유리 뚜껑(cf. 《U.S.》 *crystal*).

watch guard [⌐⌐] *n.* a chain, a cord, etc. attached to a watch. 회중 시계의 쇠줄〔끈〕.

watch·mak·er [wɑ́tʃmèikər, wɔ́:tʃ-] *n.* Ⓒ a person who makes or repairs watches. 시계 제조인〔수리인〕.

watch·man [wɑ́tʃmən, wɔ́:tʃ-] *n.* Ⓒ (*pl.* **-men** [-mən]) a guard. 경비원; 야경꾼.

watch night [⌐⌐] *n.* the last night of the year. 섣달 그믐날 밤.

watch·tow·er [wɑ́tʃtàuər, wɔ́:tʃ-] *n.* Ⓒ a tower from which a guard keeps watch. 망루; 감시탑.

watch·word [wɑ́tʃwə̀:rd, wɔ́:tʃ-] *n.* Ⓒ **1** a secret word known only among a limited number of people; a password. 암호; 군호(軍號). **2** a motto; a slogan. 표어; 슬로건.

:wa·ter [wɔ́:tər, wɑ́t-] *n.* **1** Ⓤ the commonest liquid; the liquid which fills rivers, seas, etc. 물. ¶ *hot* ~ 더운 물 / *hard* 〔*soft*〕 ~ 센물〔단물〕/ *sea* ~ 바닷물 / *No living things can live without ~.* 물 없이는 아무 것도 살지 못한다 / *This reservoir supplies the whole city with ~.* 이 저수지가 시 전체에 물을 공급하고 있다. **2** Ⓒ 《often *pl.*》 a body of water, such as a river, lake, sea, etc. 강; 호수; 바다; (강·호수·바다 등의) 물. ¶ *the Korean waters* 한국 근해 / *on the waters* 해상에(서) / *across the waters* 강〔호수·바다〕 저쪽에 / *Fish live in water.* 물고기는 물에 산다 / *Still waters run deep.* 잔잔한 물이 깊다 / *The goods came by ~, not by air.* 상품은 항공편 아닌 배편으로 왔다. **3** Ⓤ the state of the tide. 조수. ¶ *high* 〔*low*〕 ~ 만조〔간조〕. **4** Ⓤ the water used for drinking. 음료수; 먹는 물. ¶ *I want a glass of ~.* 물 한 잔이 마시고 싶다. **5** 《*pl.*》 the water which contains minerals. 광천수; 온천. ¶ *table waters* 식탁용 광천수 / *drink* 〔*take*〕 *the waters* 광천수를 마시다〔탕치(湯治)하다〕. **6** Ⓤ 《often *pl.*》 waves. 파도. **7** Ⓤ a liquid that contains water. 용액. ¶ *rose* ~ 장미 향수 / *soda* ~ 소다수. **8** Ⓤ the liquid like water which comes out from the body of animals. 분비액《눈물·땀·오줌 등》. ¶ *make* 〔*pass*〕 ~ 오줌 누다 / *Water runs from her eyes.* 그녀 눈

에서 눈물이 흐른다.
above water, out of difficulty; free from debt. 어려움을[재정적 위기를] 벗어나; 빚지지 않고. ¶ *The company has managed to keep its head above* ~ . 그 회사는 그럭저럭 재정적 위기를 넘겼다.
by water, by boat or ship. 수로로; 배편으로.
cast** one's **bread upon the waters, do good without looking for gratitude or immediate or definite return. 음덕을 베풀다; 보수를 바라지 않고 선행하다.
get into [***be in***] ***hot water,*** get into trouble. 곤경에 빠지다.
go through fire and water ⇨fire.
hold water, **a**) contain water safely. 물이 새지 않다. **b**) be logical; be sound. 이치에 맞다; 견실하다. ¶ *The theory does not hold* ~. 그 이론은 이치에 어긋난다.
***in deep water*(s),** in great difficulty. 큰 어려움에 처해.
in low water, in depressed condition, esp. badly off for money. 돈에 궁색해; 불경기로.
***in smooth water*(s),** in the state of no longer having difficulties; having an easy progress. 어려운 고비를 넘겨; 순조롭게.
keep** one's **head above water ⇨head.
like a fish out of water, uncomfortable or ill at ease because of strange surroundings. 주위 환경에 익숙하지 않아 불안을 느끼는.
like water, freely; generously; wastefully. 아낌없는; 헛되이; 마구. ¶ *She spends her money like* ~ . 돈을 물쓰듯 한다.
make water, **a**) (of a ship) admit water to come in; leak. (배에) 물이 새다. **b**) (of a person) urinate. 오줌누다.
of the first water, of the finest quality. 일류의; 최고급품의. ¶ *an artist of the first* ~ 일류 화가.
on the water, in a boat or ship; on the surface of the sea. 물 위에; 해상에.
red water, bloody urine. 혈뇨(血尿).
take the water, be launched. (배가) 진수(進水)하다.
take to the water, 《aeron.》 alight on the water. 착수(着水)하다.
take water, 《U.S. *colloq.*》 yield; give way. 항복하다; 손들다.
throw cold water on, discourage; try to prevent. …에 찬물을 끼얹다; 흥을 깨뜨리다; 탈을 잡다.

written in water, (of a name, achievements, etc.) soon forgotten. (명성·업적 등이) 곧 잊혀지는; 덧없는.
— *vt.* (P6) **1** give water to or sprinkle with water on (something); make (something) wet with water. …에 물을 주다[뿌리다]; …을 적시다. ¶ ~ *flowers* [*the plants*] 꽃[식물]에 물을 주다 / ~ *the road* 길에 물을 뿌리다. **2** supply (something) with water; give water to a horse, etc. to drink. …에 급수하다; …에 물을 먹이다. ¶ *Have the horses been fed and watered?* 말들에게 먹이와 물을 주었느냐 / *The city was not well watered last summer.* 그 도시는 지난 해 여름 물사정이 좋지 않았다 / *Egypt is watered by the Nile.* 이집트는 나일강에서 물을 얻고 있다. **3** 《*down*》 add water to and so weaken (something). …에 물을 타서 묽게 하다. ¶ ~ *milk* 우유에 물을 타다. / ~ *one's wine* 자기 포도주에 물을 타다. **4** 《chiefly in *pp.*》 make a wavy marking on. …에 물결 무늬를 넣다. ¶ *watered silk* 물결 무늬의 비단. — *vi.* (P1) **1** (of an animal) drink water; go to a watering-place. (동물이) 물을 마시다; 물 있는 데로 가다. **2** (of a ship or an engine) take in a supply of water. 급수되다. ¶ *a ship watered before sailing* 항해 전에 급수된 선박. **3** fill with tears. 눈물이 가득 괴다. ¶ *His eyes watered in the smoke.* 연기로 눈물이 철철 흘렀다 / *Onions make one's eyes* ~ . 양파는 눈물을 나게 한다. [E.(→wet)]
make** someone's **mouth water, stir desire or envy. 아무를 군침이 흐르게 하다; 몹시 탐나게 하다. ¶ *The sight made his mouth* ~. 그것을 보고 그는 입에 군침이 돌았다.
water down, **a**) weaken (milk, etc.) by adding water. …에 물을 타서 묽게 하다. **b**) 《*fig.*》 weaken the force of (a statement, etc.). (성명 등)의 강도[효력 따위]를 약하게 하다[누그러뜨리다]; 적당히 조절하여 말하다. ¶ *I've watered down the report's conclusions so as not to alarm the director.* 감독이 놀라지 않도록 보고서의 결론을 적당히 누그러뜨려 말했다.

water bird [⌐– ⌐] *n.* a bird that swims in or lives near water, such as a duck or a swan. 물새.

wa·ter·borne [wɔ́ːtərbɔ̀ːrn, wɑ́t-] *adj.* **1** supported by water; floating. 물에 뜨는. **2** conveyed by a boat, etc.; carried by on water. 수상 운송[수송]의; (전염병 등이) 수인성(水因性)의. ¶ ~ *trade* 수상 무역 / ~ *diseases* 수인성 전염병.

water bottle [⌐– ⌐–] *n.* a bottle for holding water. 물병; 수통.

water buffalo [⌐– ⌐––] *n.* (*pl.* **w- buffaloes, w- buffalos** or *collectively* **w- b-**) a buffalo of Asia and the Philippines. 물소.

water cart [⌐– ⌐] *n.* a cart carrying water for sprinkling on dusty road, etc. 살수차(撒水車); 물 운반차.

water clock [⌐– ⌐] *n.* an instrument to measure time by the fall or flow of water. 물시계.

water closet [⌐– ⌐–] *n.* a toilet flushed by water. (수세식) 변소.

wa·ter·col·or [wɔ́ːtərkʌ̀lər, wɑ́t-] *n.* **1** 《usu. *pl.*》 a paint which is mixed with water instead of oil. 그림 물감. **2** Ⓒ a picture made with watercolors. 수채화. **3** the art of painting in such colors. 수채화법(水彩畫法).

wa·ter·course [wɔ́ːtərkɔ̀ːrs, wɑ́t-] *n.* Ⓒ **1**

a stream of water; a river; a brook. 수류(水流); 하천; 개울. **2** a channel for water. 물길; 수로; 운하.

wa·ter·craft [wɔ́:tərkræ̀ft, -krɑ̀:ft, wɑ́t-] *n.* **1** skill in water sports, as boating, swimming, etc. 수상 기술《운동·경조(競漕)·수영 등》. **2** 《*collectively*》 a ship, boat, etc. 선박.

wa·ter·cress [wɔ́:tərkrès, wɑ́t-] *n.* 《bot.》 a plant that grows in water, used for salads. (샐러드용의) 양갓냉이.

wa·ter-di·vin·er [wɔ́:tərdivàinər, wɑ́t-] *n.* =dowser.

***wa·ter·fall** [wɔ́:tərfɔ̀:l, wɑ́tərfɔ̀:l] *n.* Ⓒ a stream of water falling from a high place; a cataract. 폭포.

wa·ter·fowl [wɔ́:tərfàul, wɑ́t-] *n.* Ⓒ (*pl.* **-fowls** or *collectively* **-fowl**) a water bird; 《*collectively*》 water birds. 물새.

wa·ter·front [wɔ́:tərfrʌ̀nt, wɑ́t-] *n.* 《U.S.》 the land at the water's edge, esp., the part of a city beside a river, lake, or harbor. 강[호수·바다]에 접한 땅; 호숫가의 거리; 해안 거리; 부두; 선창.

water gauge [⌐–⌐] *n.* a device for showing the height of water in a tank, boiler, etc. 수면계(水面計)《탱크 안의 수면 높이를 표시함》.

water glass [⌐–⌐] *n.* **1** a drinking glass; a tumbler. 큰 물컵. **2** an instrument with a glass bottom for looking at things in water. 물안경. **3** =water gauge. **4** sodium silicate, used for keeping eggs from spoiling. (달걀 보존용) 물유리.

wa·ter·hole [wɔ́:tərhòul, wɑ́t-] *n.* a small area of water in dry country, where wild animals go to drink. (건조지의) 물웅덩이.

wa·ter·ing place [⌐–––⌐] *n.* 《U.S.》 **1** = waterhole. **2** a seaside or lakeside place for recreation. (해안·호반(湖畔)의) 휴양[행락]지. **3** a place with springs for recreation. 온천장.

water lily [⌐–⌐–] *n.* 《bot.》 a water plant with broad, flat, floating leaves and beautiful, sweet-smelling flowers. 수련(水蓮).

water line [⌐–⌐] *n.* 《naut.》 the line along which the surface of the water touches the side of a ship. 흘수선(吃水線).

wa·ter-logged [wɔ́:tərlɔ̀(:)gd, -lɑ̀gd, wɑ́t-] *adj.* **1** (of wood) completely soaked with water. (재목이) 물이 밴. **2** (of a ship) so filled with water as to be unable or almost unable to float. (배가) 물이 차서 조종 불능이 된. **3** (of the ground) so filled with water that it remains swampy. (땅에) 물이 질퍽한.

Wa·ter·loo [wɔ́:tərlù:, wɑ́t-, ⌐–⌐] *n.* the village in Belgium where Napoleon was defeated. 워털루《벨기에에 있는 나폴레옹의 패전지》. [Place]

water main [⌐–⌐] *n.* a main pipe for carrying water. 수도 본관(本管). [*water*]

wa·ter·man [wɔ́:tərmən, wɑ́t-] *n.* Ⓒ (*pl.* **-men** [-mən]) a boatman; an oarsman. 뱃사공; 노 젓는 사람.

wa·ter·mark [wɔ́:tərmɑ̀:rk, wɑ́t-] *n.* Ⓒ **1** a faintly visible design made in some kinds of paper. (종이의) 내비치는 무늬. ¶ *The ~ on* [*in*] *the banknote is to prevent forgery.* 지폐의 내비치는 무늬는 위조를 방지하기 위함이다. **2** a mark which shows the height of the rise of water. 수위표(水位標).

wa·ter·mel·on [wɔ́:tərmèlən, wɑ́t-] *n.* Ⓒ a large melon with a juicy, pink, or red pulp; the plant on which this melon grows. 수박.

water mill [⌐–⌐] *n.* a mill whose machinery is driven by water. 물방아.

water plant [⌐–⌐] *n.* any plant which grows in water; an aquatic plant. 수초(水草).

water polo [⌐–⌐–] *n.* a ball game played in a swimming pool by two teams of seven swimmers each. 수구(水球); 워터폴로.

water power [⌐–⌐–] *n.* power produced by flowing or falling water; hydraulic power. 수력(水力).

wa·ter·proof [wɔ́:tərprù:f, wɑ́t-] *adj.* not allowing water to pass through. 방수의. — *n.* (*pl.* **-proofs**) Ⓤ waterproof cloth; Ⓒ a raincoat. 방수포; 방수복; 레인코트. — *vt.* (P6) make (cloth) waterproof. (천)에 방수처리를 하다.

wa·ter·shed [wɔ́:tərʃèd, wɑ́t-] *n.* Ⓒ **1** a dividing line between areas drained by different river systems. 분수계(分水界); 분수령. **2** a region drained by a single river system. 유역(流域).

wa·ter·side [wɔ́:tərsàid, wɑ́t-] *n.* Ⓒ the land along a river, a lake, the sea, etc. 물가《강변, 바닷가, 호숫가 따위》.

water ski [⌐–⌐] *n.* a kind of ski used to glide over water. 수상 스키.

water·skin [wɔ́:tərskin, wɑ́t-] *n.* Ⓒ a skin bag for carrying water. 물을 담는 가죽 부대.

wa·ter·spout [wɔ́:tərspàut, wɑ́t-] *n.* Ⓒ **1** 《meteor.》 a wind condition over the sea which carries water in a tall pipeshaped turning mass; a whirlwind over the sea. 용오름; 물기둥. **2** a pipe for carrying away rain water. 배수관; 물받이 홈통.

water supply [⌐– –⌐] *n.* **1** a system of getting and storing water from rivers, lakes, etc. to supply a house, town, etc. (급수) 시설; 상수도. **2** the water used or supplied by such a system. 수돗물; 상수(上水).

water table [⌐–⌐–] *n.* the level below

which the ground is saturated with water. 지하 수면.

wa·ter-tight [wɔ́:tərtàit, wɑ́t-] *adj.* **1** so closely made that water cannot pass in. 물이 새지 않는; 방수의. ¶ *a ~ box* 물이 새지[새어 들어오지] 않는 상자. **2** 《*fig.*》 (of a plan, an argument, etc.) so clear that there cannot be any misunderstanding. (계획·논의 등이) 전연 빈틈없는; 완벽한. ¶ *a ~ argument* 빈틈없는 의론.

water tower [⌐–⌐–] *n.* a tower for holding water; an apparatus for extinguishing a fire in a tall building by throwing water. 급수[저수]탑; (고층 건물의 소화용) 방수 장치.

water vapor [⌐–⌐–] *n.* water in a gaseous state. 수증기.

water wagon [⌐–⌐–] *n.* a wagon for carrying water; a water cart. 급수차(給水車).

off the water wagon, 《*colloq.*》 again drinking alcoholic beverages after a period of abstinence. 다시 술을 마시기 시작하여; 금주를 그만두고.

on the water wagon, 《*colloq.*》 not drinking alcohol. 술을 끊고; 금주하여.

wa·ter·way [wɔ́:tərwèi, wɑ́t-] *n.* Ⓒ **1** a river, a canal, etc. where a ship can go. 수로; 항로. **2** a channel for water. 운하.

water wheel [⌐–⌐] *n.* a wheel turned by water. 물레바퀴; 수차.

wa·ter·works [wɔ́:tərwə̀:rks, wɑ́t-] *n. pl.* 《often used as *sing.*》 a system for supplying a city or town with water. 급수 시설; 상수도.

turn on the waterworks, 《*sl.*》 shed tears; weep. 울다.

wa·ter·worn [wɔ́:tərwɔ̀:rn, wɑ́t-] *adj.* made smooth or worn by the action of water. (돌 따위가) 물의 작용으로 마멸되어 둥글게 된.

wa·ter·y [wɔ́:təri, wɑ́t-] *adj.* **1** of or like water. 물의; 물 같은. **2** (of boiled food) containing too much water; overboiled. 물기가 너무 많은; (맛이) 싱거운; 너무 삶은. ¶ *~ tea* 싱거운 차 / *~ soup* 멀건 수프 / *~ cabbage* 너무 삶은 양배추. **3** tearful. 눈물어린. ¶ *~ eyes* 눈물이 글썽한 눈. **4** (of a color) weak; pale. (빛이) 엷은; 연한. ¶ *a ~ green* 연둣빛. **5** 《*fig.*》 like water; without force; uninteresting. 맹물 같은; 맥없는; 재미가 없는. ¶ *~ humor* 싱거운 익살. **6** (of the weather) likely to rain. 비가 올 것 같은. ¶ *a ~ sky* 비 올 듯한 하늘. [*water*]

watt [wɑt / wɔt] *n.* Ⓒ a unit of electric power. 와트. [Person]

wat·tage [wɑ́tidʒ / wɔ́t-] *n.* electric power expressed in watts. 와트수(數).

watt·hour [wɑ́tàuər / wɔ́t-] *n.* Ⓒ the unit of electric energy, equal to one watt maintained for one hour. 와트시(時).

wat·tle [wɑ́tl / wɔ́tl] *n.* Ⓒ **1** a framework of twigs and sticks woven together. 욋가지(세공물). **2** a fence made of interwoven twigs and sticks. 욋가지로 엮은 울타리. **3** the folds of loose red flesh hanging from the throat of a bird such as a turkey. (칠면조 등의) 늘어진 붉은 목살. **4** the acacia in Australia. (오스트레일리아산) 아카시아. — *vt.* (P6) make (a fence, framework, etc.) by interweaving twigs and sticks. 욋가지로 (울타리·세공물 등)을 만들다. [E.]

:wave [weiv] *n.* Ⓒ **1** an up and down and rolling movement on the surface of water. 파도; 물결. ¶ *The waves will run high.* 파도가 높아지겠다 / *The waves beat upon the shore.* 파도가 기슭에 철썩대고 있다 / *The boat was tossed by the waves.* 보트는 파도에 몹시 흔들렸다. **2** 《*the ~*》 《*poet.*》 the sea. 바다. **3** a movement like a wave. 파도와 같은 움직임; 너울거림. ¶ *attack in waves* 파도처럼 밀어닥치다; 파상 공격을 하다 / *waves of people* 인파 / *a cold ~* 한파(寒波) / *a ~ of prosperity* 호경기의 물결 / *waves of wheat in the wind* 바람에 물결치는 밀. **4** a sudden increase or a rush of feelings, excitement, etc. (감정 등의 급격한) 고조; 격발. ¶ *a ~ of enthusiasm* 열광의 고조 / *I felt a ~ of anger* [*nausea*]. 나는 울컥하는 분노[욕지기]를 느꼈다. **5** a curve like a wave in the hair, in cloth, etc.; a curl. (머리·천 등의) 웨이브. ¶ *She has a beautiful ~ in her hair.* 그녀의 머리 웨이브는 아름답다 / *a permanent* [*natural*] *~* 파마[자연] 머리의 웨이브. **6** a wave-like movement of electric current, sound, heat, etc. 파동; 음파; 전파. ¶ *short* [*long, medium*] *waves* 단[장, 중]파 / *sound waves* 음파. **7** an act of moving up and down, etc.; a sign made with a wave of the hand, a flag, etc. 흔들기; 수신호(手信號).

— *vi.* (P1,2A) **1** move up and down and roll; swing. 파도치다; 흔들리다. ¶ *her beautiful hair waving in the breeze* 산들바람에 나부끼는 그녀의 아름다운 머리 / *A flag was waving in the breeze.* 깃발이 미풍에 나부끼고 있었다. **2** have curves or waves. 파도[물결]치다; 기복(起伏)하다. ¶ *The road waves along the valley.* 길은 계곡을 따라 꾸불어진다 / *His hair waves naturally.* 그의 머리는 자연스럽게 물결치고 있다. **3** make a signal by waving a hand, etc. 손을 흔들어 신호하다. ¶ *~ in farewell* 손을 흔들어 작별 인사하다 / *She waved toward a chair.* 그녀는 손을 내밀어 의자를 권했다 / *He waved to them to be silent.* 그는 손을 흔들어 그들에게 조용히 하라고 신호했다.

— *vt.* (P6,7,13) **1** cause (something) to move like a wave; swing. …을 흔들어 움직이다; …을 흔들다. ¶ *~ a flag* 깃발을 흔들다 / *~ a handkerchief* 손수건을 흔들다 / *~ one's hand in greeting* 인사로 손을 흔들다 / *The cat is waving its tail.* 고양이가 꼬리

를 흔들고 있다. **2** make a signal to (someone) by waving a hand, etc.; express (something) by waving a hand, etc. 손 따위를 흔들어 …에게 신호하다; …을 손짓해 알리다. ¶ ~ *someone on* 〔*away, off*〕 아무에게 손을 흔들어 전진하게 하다〔쫓아 버리다〕 / ~ *a goodbye to someone* 아무에게 작별 인사하다. **3** give a curving form to (something). …을 물결 모양으로 하다; …에 웨이브를 하다. ¶ *I have my hair waved.* 나는 머리를 웨이브했다. [E.]

wave aside, set aside (objections, etc.). …을 거절하다. ¶ ~ *aside the money* 〔*proposal*〕 돈〔제안〕을 거절하다.

wave length [∸∸] *n.* 《phys.》 the distance from a point on one wave to the corresponding point of the next. 파장.

·**wa·ver** [wéivər] *vi.* (P1,3) **1** tremble; flicker. 흔들리다; 너울거리다. ¶ *The flame wavered and then went out.* 불길은 너울거리더니 꺼졌다 / *a wavering shadow* 흔들리는 그림자. **2** begin to give way; fail. 들뜨다; 무너지기〔흐트러지기〕 시작하다; 굴복하다. ¶ *The line of troops wavered.* 군인들의 대오(隊伍)는 흐트러지기 시작했다 / *She never wavered in her loyalty to us.* 그녀는 우리에게 신의를 저버리는 일이 없었다. **3** hesitate; be undecided. 망설이다; 결심이 흔들리다. ¶ *He wavered between accepting and refusing.* 그는 수락과 거절 사이에서 망설였다. — *n.* Ⓤ hesitation. 망설임. [*wave*]

wav·y [wéivi] *adj.* (**wav·i·er, wav·i·est**) **1** moving like waves.; waving as grass in the wind. 흔들리는; 물결치는; 파동하는. **2** having waves. 물결 모양의; 기복이 있는. ¶ ~ *hair* 물결 모양의 머리 / *a* ~ *line* 파선(波線). [*wave*]

:**wax**[1] [wæks] *n.* Ⓤ **1** a sticky, yellowish substance of a honeycomb. 밀랍. ¶ *a* ~ *candle* 양초. **2** any mineral or vegetable substance like this. 밀(랍) 비슷한 것《파라핀 등》.

like wax (***in one's hands***), easily influenced. 쉽게 …의 뜻대로 되는.

— *vt.* (P6) cover or polish (floors, furniture, etc.) with wax. …에 밀랍을 칠하다; …을 밀로 광내다〔닦다〕.

— *adj.* made of wax. 밀랍으로 만든. [E.]

wax[2] [wæks] *vi.* (**waxed, waxed** or 《*poet.*》 **wax·en, wax·ing**) **1** (P1) (esp. of the moon) grow bigger or greater; increase in number or size. (달 따위가) 차다; 커지다; 증대하다 (opp. wane). ¶ *The moon waxes till it becomes full, and then wanes.* 달은 만월이 될 때까지 커지다가 이후는 이지러진다. **2** (P5) 《*arch.*》 gradually become. 서서히 …이 되다. ¶ *The party waxed gay.* 파티는 점점 흥겨워졌다 / ~ *fat* 살이 오르다 / ~ *angry* 화가 나다 / *He waxed eloquent as he described his plans.* 계획을 설명하면서 그는 달변이 되어 갔다. [E.]

wax and wane, (esp. of the moon) grow bigger and then smaller. (달이) 찼다 이울었다 하다.

wax[3] [wæks] *n.* 《*colloq.*》 a fit of anger. 불끈함. [?]

get into a wax, get angry. 불끈 성내다.

waxed [wækst] *adj.* covered or polished by wax. 밀랍을 바른; 밀랍으로 닦은〔윤을 낸〕. [*wax*[1]]

wax·en [wǽksən] *adj.* **1** 《*arch.*》 of wax; made of wax. 밀랍의; 밀랍으로 만든. **2** like wax; smooth, pale or soft like wax. 밀랍 같은; 매끄러운; 창백한. ¶ *Her complexion was* ~. 그녀의 안색이 창백했다.

wax·work [wǽkswə̀ːrk] *n.* Ⓤ **1** statues made of wax. 납세공(細工); 납인형. **2** 《*pl.*, used as *sing.*》 an exhibition of such statues. 납세공〔인형〕 진열장. [↑] [*wax*[1]]

wax·y [wǽksi] *adj.* (**wax·i·er, wax·i·est**) (made) of wax; like wax. 납의; 납으로 된; 밀랍 같은.

:**way**[1] [wei] *n.* Ⓒ **1** a means used to go from one place to another; a path; a street. 길; 도로. ¶ *a rough* ~ 험한 길 / *lead the* ~ (앞장 서서) 길을 안내하다 / *make one's* ~ (애써) 나아가다; 가다 / *lose the* 〔*one's*〕 ~ 길을 잃다 / *keep* 〔*hold*〕 *one's* ~ 길을 잃지 않고 바로 가다 / *the other side* (*of*) *the* ~ 길 저쪽 / *point out the* ~ 길을 가리키다 / 《*prov.*》 *The longest* ~ *round is the shortest* ~ *home.* 급할수록 돌아가라 / *This is the way home.* 이것이 집으로 가는 길이다 / *Which is the* ~ *out ?* 어느 것이 나가는 길이요. **2** travel or movement along a route. 가는 길〔도중〕; 노정(路程). ¶ *on the* 〔*one's*〕 ~ *home* 귀가 길에 / *go on one's* ~ (길을) 계속 가다; 여행을 계속하다 / *go separate ways* 각기 다른 길을 가다. **3** a space for passing or go ahead. 진로; 통로. ¶ *Get it out of the* ~. 길을 비켜라 / *This table is in the* ~. 이 탁자가 진로를 막고 있다 / *Make* ~ *for the king !* 예라, 게 들어섰거라《벽제(辟除) 소리》. **4** distance. 거리. ¶ *a long* ~ *off* 아주 멀리 / *He has come quite a* ~. 그는 먼 곳을 일부러 찾아왔다 / *walk all the* ~ *back* 줄곧 걸어서 돌아가다 / *It is only a little* ~ *to the station.* 정거장까지는 아주 가까운 거리다 / *It's a long* ~ *from here.* 여기서는 멀다. **5** direction. 방향. ¶ *this* ~ *and that* 이쪽 저쪽에 / *Step this* ~, *please.* 이리로 오세요 / *He went that* ~. 그는 저쪽으로 갔다 / *Which* ~ *is he going ?* 그는 어느 쪽으로 가고 있나 / *Look this* ~. 이쪽을 봐라. **6** a method; a manner; a style; a means. 방법; 방식; 수단. ¶ *in this* ~ 이렇게; 이런 방식으로 / *to one's* ~ *of thinking* …의 생각으로는 / *In what* ~ *did you find the secret ?* 어떻게 그 비밀을 알아 냈나 / *I don't like your* ~ *of speaking.* 네 말투가 마음에 들지 않는다 / *She is wearing her hair in a new* ~. 그녀의 머리 모양이 새로운 형식으로 달라졌다 / *Try new ways of working.* 일을 다른 식으로

해 봐라 / *This is the* ~ *of doing* 〔*to do*〕 *it.* 이것이 그걸 하는 방식이다 / *There is no two ways about it.* 그것에 관해서는 달리 생각할 필요가 없다《'그것은 틀림없다'의 뜻》. **7** a habit or custom. 버릇; 습관; 관행. ¶ *the* ~ *of the world* 세상의 일반적인 관례 / *the good old ways* 옛날부터의 풍습 / *He has a* ~ *of thinking things over.* 그는 너무 철저하게 생각하는 버릇이 있다 / *It's not his* ~ *to be generous.* 관용이란 걸 모르는 사람이다. **8** Ⓤ progress; advance. 진행; 진보. ¶ *make one's* (*own*) ~ 나아가다; 번영하다 / *make one's* ~ *home* 귀로에 오르다 / *fight* 〔*push*〕 *one's* ~ 싸워〔밀고〕 나아가다 / *force one's* ~ 억지로 밀고 나아가다. **9** respect; point. (…할) 점. ¶ *in a* 〔*one*〕 ~ 어느 점에서는; 다소; 얼마간 / *The plan is bad in several ways.* 그 계획은 몇 가지 점에서 좋지가 않다 / *This is no* ~ *inferior to that.* 이건 전혀 그것에 못지않다. **10** 《*colloq.*》 a state; a condition. 상태; 형편. ¶ *be in a bad* ~ 형편이 좋지 않다 / *live in a small* ~ 조촐하게 살다. **11** Ⓤ one's wish or will. 희망; 뜻; 의지. ¶ *want one's* ~ 자기 고집대로 하려 들다 / *have* 〔*get*〕 *one's* ~ 제멋대로 하다. **12** range or scope of experience; occupation. (경험의) 범위; 영역; 직업. ¶ *be in the bakery* ~ 제과점을 하다 / *Such things have never come in my* ~. 그런 일은 겪은 적이 없다 / *Hunting is not* 〔*does not lie*〕 *in my* ~. 사냥에 대해서는 생소하다. [E.]

be in a (***great***) ***way,*** 《Brit. *colloq.*》 (greatly) excited. (몹시) 흥분하다. ¶ *He was in a* (*great*) ~ *about it.* 그 일에 대해 크게 흥분해 있었다.

be under way, **a**) (esp. of a ship) be moving forward. (배가) 나아가고 있다. **b**) 《*fig.*》 be in progress. 진행중이다. ¶ *Preparations are now under* ~. 지금 준비가 진행되고 있다.

by the way, **a**) on the way. 도중에. **b**) 《*fig.*》 in passing; incidentally. (말이 난) 김에; 그런데 ….

by way of, **a**) through; via. …을 지나서; …경유로. ¶ *He came by* ~ *of Taiwan.* 대만을 거쳐서 왔다. **b**) for the purpose of; as a kind of. …을 할 목적으로; …로서; …의 대용으로. ¶ *Let me say a few words by* ~ *of introduction.* 서두로서 몇 말씀 드릴까 합니다.

feel** one's **way, proceed with great caution. (길을) 조심조심 나아가다.

gather way, (of a ship) gain speed. (배가) 속력을 내다.

get 〔***have***〕 *one's* 〔***own***〕 ***way,*** get or do what one wants. 원하는 것을 얻다; 마음대로 하다.

give way, **a**) break down. 무너지다; 꺾이다. **b**) withdraw; yield. 물러가다; 양보하다.

go out of the 〔*one's*〕 ***way,*** **a**) make a special effort. 일부러〔고의로〕 …하다. ¶ *He went out of his* ~ *to be rude to us.* 그는 일부러 우리를 무례하게 대했다. **b**) lose one's way. 길을 잃다.

go** one's **own way, act independently or as one wishes. 개별적으로 행동하다; 제멋대로 행동하다.

go the way of all the earth 〔***of all flesh, of nature***〕, die. 죽다.

go (*one's*) ***way,*** start; leave. 출발하다; 떠나다.

***have a way with** someone,* be charmingly persuasive. 설득을 잘 하다; (아무를) 잘 다루는 요령을 알고 있다.

have it both ways, benefit by each of two contrary possibilities. 양다리 걸치다.

have way on =be under way.

in a 〔***one***〕 ***way,*** in some respects; to some extent. 어느 점에서는; 어느 정도.

in the family way, 《Brit. *colloq.*》 pregnant. 임신하여.

lose way, (of a ship) lose speed; slow down. (배가) 속력을 잃다〔낮추다〕.

make the best of** one's **way, go as fast as possible. 전속력으로 가다; 길을 재촉하다.

make way (=*clear or prepare the way*) ***for** someone,* **a**) …을 위해 길을 비키다. ¶ *Motocars must make* ~ *for fire-engine.* 일반 자동차들은 소방차에게 길을 양보해야 한다. **b**) go ahead; progress; advance. 나아가다; 진보〔전진〕하다.

make** one's **way, advance; prosper. 발전하다; 성공하다. ¶ *He made his* ~ *in business.* 그는 사업에 성공했다.

once in a way, every now and then. 때때로.

one way or another, in some way. 그럭저럭.

on the way, traveling or approaching. 도중에(서).

out of the way, **a**) in a position so as not to hinder. 방해가 되지 않는 곳에. **b**) not on the right or usual route. 길을 잘못 들어. **c**) unusual; unfamiliar. 상궤(常軌)를 벗어난; 이상한. ¶ *He has done nothing out of the* ~. 그는 하나도 이상한 일을 하지 않았다.

pave the way (=*prepare*) ***for** something.* …의 준비를 하다.

put** someone **in the way of, give someone an opportunity to. 아무에게 기회를 주다.

put** oneself **out of the way, take trouble. 수고하다; 애쓰다. ¶ *He put himself out of the* ~ *for the poor.* 가난한 사람을 위해 수고를 아끼지 않았다.

put** someone **out of the way, confine or secretly kill someone. 아무를 죽이다〔감금하다〕.

see** one's **way (***clear***) ***to,*** find (something) to be possible. …을 할 수 있다고 생각하다. ¶ *Can you see your* ~ *to paying more?* 더 지불할 수 있다고 생각하느냐.

stand in the way of (=*be an obstacle to*) *something.* …의 방해를 하다.

take** one's **way to, go to. …에 가다.

the other way about 〔(***a***)***round***〕, the opposite way; conversely. 반대로; 거꾸로.

the parting of the ways, branching out of two roads. 갈림길.

the right of way ⇨right-of-way.
under way, a) (of a ship) moving. (배가) 항행중인. ¶ *The ship is under* ~. 그 배는 항해중이다. b) making progress. 진행중인. ¶ *Our project is now well under* ~. 우리 사업은 지금 잘 진행되고 있다.
ways and means, a) devices and resources for doing something. 방법과 재원(財源). b) legislation and means of raising revenue. 세입 재원.

way² [wei] *adv.* 《U.S. *colloq.*》 away; far; much. 멀리; 훨씬. ¶ ~ *down the road* 그 길을 한참 가면 거기에. [*away*]

way·bill [wéibìl] *n.* a list of passengers or goods carried. 승객 명단; 화물 송장(送狀). [*way¹*, *bill*]

way·far·er [wéifɛ̀ərər] *n.* Ⓒ a traveler, esp. on foot. 나그네《특히 걸어다니는》. [*way¹*]

way·far·ing [wéifɛ̀əriŋ] *adj.* of a wayfarer; traveling. 나그네의; 도보 여행의. — *n.* Ⓤ the act of traveling, esp. on foot. 도보 여행.

way·laid [wèiléid] *v.* p. and pp. of **waylay.**

way·lay [wèiléi] *vt.* (**-laid**) (P6) lie in wait for (someone) to rob, kill, etc. him; attack (someone) on a street, etc. …을 매복해 기다리다; 요격(邀擊)하다. ¶ *Robin Hood waylaid travelers and robbed them.* 로빈후드는 나그네들을 숨어 기다렸다가 그들을 털었다. [*way¹*, *lay*]

way·side [wéisàid] *n.* Ⓒ the edge of a road or path. 노변; 길가. ¶ *a* ~ *inn* 노변의 여인숙. — *adj.* on or along the side of a road. 노변〔길가〕의. [*way¹*]

way·ward [wéiwərd] *adj.* **1** disobedient. 제멋대로 구는; 고집스러운. ¶ *a* ~ *son* 골치 아픈 아들. **2** not steady; irregular; capricious. 변덕스러운. ¶ ~ *behavior* 변덕스러운 행동. [*away*]

way·ward·ness [wéiwərdnis] *n.* Ⓤ the quality or state of being wayward. (외)고집; 변덕.

way·worn [wéiwɔ̀ːrn] *adj.* tired with traveling. 여로에 지친 ¶ ~ *travelers* 여로에 지친 나그네들. [*way¹*]

W.C., w.c. water closet.

:we [wi(ː)] *pron.* 《sing. **I**》 **1** the first person plural of the personal pronoun; the group of people including the speaker or writer. 우리(들); 저희(들); 우리는〔가〕. ¶ *We are students.* 우리들은 학생이다 / *Shall* ~ *sit together, Mary?* 메리, 우리 같이 앉을까. **2** the pronoun used by an author, editor, king, etc. instead of I. 우리들(은)《신문·잡지의 논설 등에서, 필자의 자칭》; 짐(朕)(은)《군주 등의 자칭》. 參考 신문의 논설 등에서는 editorial 'we', 왕은 royal 'we'라 함. [E.]

:weak [wiːk] *adj.* **1** not strong; lacking in bodily strength; easily broken under pressure or strain. 약한; 연약한; 허약한; (압력·긴장 따위에) 잘 견디지 못하는. ¶ *a* ~ *old woman* 허약한 늙은 여인 / *a* ~ *bridge* 구조가 약한 다리 / *a* ~ *point* 〔*side*〕 약점 / *a* ~ *heart* 약한 심장 / ~ *supports* 〔*foundations*〕 (취)약한 지지물〔기반〕 / *the weaker vessel* 〔*sex*〕 여성 / *a* ~ *hand* (카드놀이의) 약수(惡手) / ~ *sunlight* 약한 햇빛 / *answer in a* ~ *voice* 힘 없는 목소리로 대답하다 / *be too* ~ *to walk* 몸이 약해 걷지 못하다. **2** lacking in mental power, judgment, etc.; foolish. 결단력이 없는; 우둔한. ¶ ~ *compliance* 마지못해 하는 승낙 / *a* ~ *mind* 저능(한 사람) / *a* ~ *will* 무기력한 의지 / *a boy of* ~ *intellect* 지능이 모자라는 아이. **3** in bad health; not functioning normally or well. 몸이 약한; 제대로 기능을 하지 못하는. ¶ *be* ~ *in judgment* 〔*faith, decision*〕 판단력〔신앙심, 결심〕이 약하다 / ~ *eyes* 시력이 약한 눈 / *a* ~ *stomach* 〔*chest, heart*〕 기능이 약한 위〔폐, 심장〕. **4** not good at; lacking skill. 서투른; 기술〔능력〕이 부족한. ¶ *be* ~ *in English* 〔*spelling*〕 영어가〔철자법이〕 서투르다. **5** not containing the usual amount of the main element; watery. 묽은; 멀건; 물기가 많은. ¶ ~ *tea* 싱거운 차. **6** not convincing. 설득력이 없는. ¶ *a* ~ *evidence* 불충분한 증거 / *a* ~ *argument* 설득력이 없는 의론. **7** (of literary work) showing little ability. (문체가) 힘〔기량〕이 모자라는. ¶ *a very* ~ *book* 힘〔기량〕이 빈약한 내용의 책 / *a* ~ *sentence* 장황한 문장. **8** lacking in power, force, etc.; not able to rule well. 무력한; 지배력이 없는. ¶ *a* ~ *king* 무력한 왕 / *a* ~ *law* 구속력이 없는 법률. **9** 《comm.》 not firm; slack. 부진한; 저조한(opp. strong). ¶ *The market was* ~. 시황(市況)은 저조했다. **10** 《gram.》 (of verbs) regular; forming the past and past participle by adding -ed. 규칙 변화의; 약변화의(opp. strong). [N.]

***weak·en** [wíːkən] *vt.* (P6) make (someone or something) weak or less strong. …을 약하게 하다; …의 힘을 빼다. ¶ *The illness weakened her heart.* 병으로 그녀의 심장이 나빠졌다 / *These internal disputes have weakened the government's position.* 이들 국내 논쟁이 정부의 입장을 약화시켰다. — *vi.* (P1) become weak or less strong. 약해지다. [*weak*]

weak-kneed [wíːkníːd] *adj.* **1** having weak knees. 무릎이 약한. **2** of a weak will; yielding easily. 우유 부단한; 나약한.

weak·ling [wíːkliŋ] *n.* Ⓒ a weak person. 나약한 사람; 겁쟁이.

weak·ly [wíːkli] *adj.* (**-li·er, -li·est**) weak; sickly. 약한; 병약한. — *adv.* in a weak manner. 약하게; 가냘프게.

weak-mind·ed [wíːkmáindid] *adj.* **1** of or showing a weak mind; feeble-minded. 저능한. **2** lacking firmness of mind. 마음이 약한.

:weak·ness [wíːknis] *n.* **1** Ⓤ the quality or state of being weak; lack of power or force. 약함; 허약함. ¶ *Weakness kept him in bed.* 허약해서 그는 누워서 지냈다 / *the ~ and helplessness of old age* 노년의 허약함과 무력감. **2** Ⓒ a weak point in the character, etc.; a slight fault. 약점; 결함. ¶ *There is a ~ in your plan.* 네 안(案)에는 결함이 하나 있다 / *Drinking is his ~.* 술이 그의 약점이다. **3** Ⓒ 《*a ~*》 a special liking. 못 견디게〔매우, 특별히〕 좋아하는 것; 기호; 편애. ¶ *have a ~ for the bottle* 〔*tobacco*〕 술을〔담배를〕 무척 좋아하다 / *Girls have a ~ for sweets.* 소녀들은 단것을 너무 좋아한다 / *Strawberries* 〔*Detective stories*〕 *are my ~.* 딸기라면〔탐정 소설이라면〕 나는 사족을 못 쓴다. [*weak*]

weal[1] [wi:l] *n.* Ⓤ well-being; happiness. 복리; 행복. ¶ *in ~ and woe* 행복하든 불행하든 / *for the public ~* 공공 복리를 위하여. [E.]

weal[2] [wi:l] *n.* =wale.

:wealth [welθ] *n.* **1** Ⓤ a large amount of money or property; being rich; riches. 부(富); (많은) 재산. ¶ *a man of ~* 부자 / *To possess ~ is not always to be happy.* 재산이 많다고 반드시 행복해지는 것은 아니다. **2** rich people. 부자(들); 부유 계급. **3** Ⓒ 《usu. *sing*》 abundance of anything. (물질의) 풍부; 다량; 막대함. ¶ *a ~ of experience* 〔*imagination, wit*〕 풍부한 경험〔상상력, 기지〕 / *Wealth of words is not eloquence.* 다변은 웅변이 아니다. [E.]

:wealth·y [wélθi] *adj.* (**wealth·i·er, wealth·i·est**) rich; abundant. 부유한; 풍부한. ¶ *a ~ spinster* 돈 많은 노처녀.

wean [wi:n] *vt.* **1** (P6,13) accustom (a child or young animal) to take food different from its mother's milk. (아기를) 젖을 떼다; 이유(離乳)시키다. ¶ *~ a baby from the mother* 〔*breast*〕 아기를 젖떼다 / *~ a baby on baby food* 아기에게 이유식을 주어 젖을 떼다. **2** (P7) 《*away, from*》 cause (someone) to turn away from a habit or an interest. (나쁜 습관·취미 따위)를 서서히 버리게 하다. ¶ *~ someone from drinking and smoking* 아무로 하여금 술·담배를 서서히 끊게 하다 / *He was sent away to school to ~ him from bad companions.* 나쁜 친구들과 떨어지게 하기 위해 그는 기숙 학교에 보내졌다 / *She tried to ~ him* (*away*) *from* (*taking*) *drugs.* 그녀는 그가 마약을 끊게 하려고 애썼다. —*n.* 《Sc.》 a child. 아이. [E.=accustom]

:weap·on [wépən] *n.* Ⓒ **1** anything used in fighting, such as swords, arrows, guns, teeth, horns, etc. 무기; 흉기. ¶ *They used anything that came to hand—stones, pieces of wood, bottles—as weapons.* 그들은 돌멩이, 막대기, 빈병 등 손에 잡히는 것이면 무엇이나 다 무기로 사용했다. **2** any means of attack or defence. 공격〔방어〕 수단. ¶ *the strike as a political ~* 정치적 무기로서의 파업. [E.]

weap·on·ry [wépənri] *n.* Ⓤ **1** weapons collectively. 무기류. **2** the invention and production of weapons. 무기의 발명〔설계·제조〕.

:wear [wɛər] *v.* (**wore, worn**) *vt.* **1** (P6,7,18) have or put (something) on the body; be dressed in; be clothed with. …을 몸에 걸치고〔입고, 쓰고, 신고〕 있다(cf. *put on*). ¶ *~ a hat* 모자를 쓰고 있다 / *~ a pair of glasses* 안경을 쓰고 있다 / *She always wears green.* 그녀는 늘 초록색 차림이다 / *~ a diamond ring* 다이아몬드 반지를 끼고 있다 / *She wore a green jacket and a skirt to match.* 초록의 재킷과 그에 어울리는 치마를 입고 있었다. **2** arrange (hair, etc.) in a special way. (머리·수염 등)을 …모양으로 하다〔기르다〕. ¶ *~ one's hair waved* 머리를 곱슬거리게 하다 / *~ a mustache* 콧수염을 기르다. **3** (P6) (of looks) have or show; bear or show in expression or appearance. (어떤 표정·태도·모습)을 하다〔나타내다, 짓다, 띠다〕. ¶ *~ a smile* 미소를 띠다 / *~ a discontented look* 불만을 나타내다 / *She wore a troubled look.* 그녀는 난처한 표정을 지었다 / *~ a careless manner* 무관심한 태도를 보이다 / *The house wore an air of sadness.* 그 집엔 슬픈 분위기가 감돌았다. **4** (P6,7) bear. …을 마음에 지니다. ¶ *~ one's honors* 긍지를 지니다. **5** (P6,7) damage or waste (something) by constant or hard use; bring (something) to a certain state by using it. …을 닳게 하다; 써서 낡게 하다. ¶ *I wore my coat to rags.* 코트가 너덜너덜 해지도록 입었다 / *The gloves are worn at the fingertips.* 장갑의 손가락 끝이 해어졌다. **6** (P6,13) make (a hole, etc.) by rubbing, flowing, etc. (마찰(摩擦) 등으로 구멍)을 뚫다. ¶ 《*prov.*》 *Constant dropping wears the stone.* 낙숫물이 댓돌을 뚫는다 / *Water has worn a channel down the slope.* 물이 흘러 경사면에 홈이 패었다 / *Walking wore a hole in my shoes.* 걸어서 신에 구멍이 났다. **7** (P7) tire or exhaust; make the body or mind tired. (심신)을 지치게〔수척하게〕 하다. ¶ *The labor wore him.* 그 힘든 일로 그는 지쳤다 / *He was worn with care and anxiety.* 근심 걱정으로 그는 수척해졌다. —*vi.* **1** (P2A) become damaged or wasted by constant use; become exhausted. 닳아 해지다〔없어지다〕; 마멸〔마모〕되다; 지치다. ¶ *The cloth has worn thin.* 그 천은 닳아서 얄팍해졌다 / *His shoes have begun to ~.* 그의 구두는 해져서 떨어지기 시작했다 / *I like this shirt, but the collar has worn.* 나는 이 셔츠를 좋아하지만 깃이 해어졌다. **2** (P1,2A) endure continued use; last. (물건 따위가) 계속된 사용에 견디다; 오래 가다. ¶ *This jacket wears for years.* 이 재킷은 여러 해 입어도 괜찮다 / *~ well* 〔*badly*〕 오래 가다〔못가다〕 / *This color won't ~.* 이 색깔은 오래 못 가겠다 / *This coat has worn wonderfully.* 이

코트는 놀랍도록 오래 입었다. **3** (P2A) come to a certain state. (서서히) …한 상태가 되다; …이 되다. ¶ *My hope wore thin.* 내 희망은 점점 희박해졌다 / *Coins ~ thinner with use.* 동전은 쓸수록 닳아서 얇아진다 / *My patience is wearing thin.* 내 인내도 이젠 한계에 이르고 있다. **4** (P2A) (of time) pass away gradually. (시간이) 서서히 지나가다; 경과하다. ¶ *The day wears toward its close.* 날이 점점 저물어 간다 / *Time wore away.* 시간이 경과했다.

wear away, **a**) waste or become thin by use; rub out or be rubbed out. …을 마멸시키다; 마멸되다. ¶ *Time has worn away the inscription.* 세월은 비문을 판독할 수 없도록 마멸시켰다 / *The inscription has worn away.* 비문은 마멸되어 판독할 수 없다. **b**) (of time) pass, spend. (시간이) 지나다; (시간)을 보내다. ¶ *The long winter night wore away.* 긴긴 겨울 밤이 지나갔다.

wear down, **a**) waste or become thin by use. …을 마멸시키다[되다]; …을 닳게 하다[닳아서 낮아지게 하다]. ¶ *The heels of my shoes are worn down.* 구두 뒤축이 닳아서 낮아졌다 / *The constant rubbing worn down the surface of the stone.* 끊임없는 마찰이 돌의 표면을 닳게 했다. **b**) break down by constant attack; overcome by persistent effort. 이겨내다; 부단한 노력으로 극복하다. ¶ *We wore down their opposition after hours of persuasion.* 몇 시간의 설득으로 그들의 반대를 잠재웠다.

wear off, **a**) waste or become thin by use. …을 닳아 없애다[없어지다]. **b**) pass away gradually. …이 점차로 없어지다; 서서히 사라지다. ¶ *Her toothache wore off at last.* 마침내 그녀의 치통이 멎었다 / *The strangeness will ~ off in time.* 이상한 느낌도 조만간 스러질 것이다.

wear on, (of time) pass slowly and gradually. (때가) 서서히 지나다. ¶ *The meeting worn on all afternoon.* 회합은 오후 내내 질질 끌었다 / *The time wore on toward midnight.* 시간은 서서히 지나 한밤중이 다 되었다.

wear out, **a**) make or become useless by use. …을 닳아 떨어지게 하다; …이 닳아 떨어지다; 마모되게 하다; 마모되다. ¶ *Your clothes will soon ~ out.* 네 옷은 얼마 안 가서 해질 것이다 / *The machine is quickly wearing out.* 그 기계는 마모가 빠르다. **b**) tire out. …을 지치게 하다. ¶ *I'm worn out with this work.* 나는 이 일로 피곤해서 녹초가 되었다 / *These children are wearing me out.* 이 아이들이 나를 녹초가 되게 하는군. **c**) waste gradually. …을 서서히 소모시키다. ¶ *~ one's strength* 체력을 소모시키다.

wear the trousers, be master in the house. 내주장하다; 남편을 깔아 뭉개다.

wear one's years well, look younger than one is. 나이보다 젊게 보이다.

— *n.* Ⓤ **1** the act of putting clothes on. 옷입기; 착용. ¶ *cloth for summer ~* 여름 옷감 / *My coat has been many years in ~.* 내 코트는 여러 해 입은 거다 / *clothes for everyday ~* 평상복. **2** things worn on body; clothing. 옷; 의복. ¶ *children's* [*men's*] *~* 아동[남성]복 / *beach ~* 해변복; 비치웨어. **3** the fashion of dress. (옷의) 유행. ¶ *in general ~* 유행하여. **4** the ability to endure. 오래 견딤; 질김; 내구력. ¶ *There is plenty of ~ in your hat yet.* 네 모자는 아직 꽤 오래 쓸 수 있다 / *The shoes give excellent ~.* 그 구두는 아주 질기다. **5** damage from use. 닳아 해짐; 마멸. ¶ *~ and tear* 마멸; 소모 / *The coat shows* (*signs of*) *~.* 그 코트는 해질 때가 됐다. [E.]

be in wear, be fashionable. 유행되고 있다.

be the worse for wear, be damaged by use. 오래 입어서 낡았다.

have in wear, be regularly wearing. (늘) 입고 있다.

*__wea·ri·ly__ [wíərili] *adv.* in a weary manner. 지쳐서; 피곤해서; 싫증이 나서. [E.]

wea·ri·ness [wíərinis] *n.* Ⓤ the weary state or feeling. 피곤; 권태; 싫증.

wea·ri·some [wíərisəm] *adj.* causing fatigue; tedious. 피곤하게 하는; 넌더리나게[물리게] 하는. ¶ *~ work* 신물나는 일 / *~ child* 사람을 지치게 하는 아이.

:**wea·ry** [wíəri] *adj.* (**-ri·er, -ri·est**) **1** tired. 피곤한. ¶ *be ~ after hard work* 힘든 일을 하고 지치다 / *~ feet* 피곤한 발 / *a ~ brain* 피곤해진 머리 / *~ in body and mind* 심신이 피곤한. **2** causing tiredness. 진저리나는; 따분한. ¶ *a ~ journey* 지루한 여행 / *a ~ wait* 넌더리나는 기다림 / *this ~ world* [*life*] 이 따분한 세상[생활] / *a ~ lecture* 따분한 강의 / *I'm ~ of all his grumble.* 그의 투덜대는 소리에 진저리난다.

— *vt.* (P6,7,13) make (someone) weary or bored. …을 피곤하게 하다; 진저리나게 하다. ¶ *~ someone with idle talk* 쓸데없는 얘기로 아무를 피곤하게 하다 / *You are wearing me with all these silly questions.* 넌 하나같이 어리석은 질문으로 사람을 애먹이는구나.

— *vi.* (P1,3) become weary; be bored. 피곤해지다; 따분해지다. ¶ *He began to ~ of the work.* 그는 그 일이 싫증나기 시작했다. [E.]

wea·sel [wíːzəl] *n.* Ⓒ a small, active animal which feeds on birds, eggs, mice, etc. 족제비. [E.]

:**weath·er** [wéðər] *n.* Ⓤ **1** the general condition of a place at a certain time with respect to sun, wind, temperature, cloudiness, etc. 일기; 날씨; 기후(cf. *climate*). ¶ *good* [*bad, fine, wet, hot, windy*] *~* 좋은[나쁜, 화창한, 비 오는, 더운, 바람 부는] 날씨 / *in all weathers* 어떤 날씨든 / *~ permitting* 날씨가 좋으면 / *How is the ~?* 날씨는 어떤가요 / *What will the ~ be like tomorrow?* 내일 날씨는 어떻게 될까. **2**

windy, rainy, or stormy weather. 비바람; 폭풍우; 악천후. ¶ *under stress of* ~ 험악한 날씨 때문에 / *for protection against the* ~ 풍우에 대비해서 / *We were exposed to the* ~. 우리는 비바람에 시달렸다.

have the weather gauge of, **a**) be to the windward of. …의 바람 불어 오는 쪽에 있다. **b**) 《*fig.*》 gain an advantage over. …보다 유리한 위치에 서다.

keep one's weather eye open, be alert; be on one's guard. …에 경계(警戒)를 게을리하지 않다.

make fair weather, reconcile; cajole. 타협하다; 구워삶다.

make good* 〔*bad*〕 *weather, 《naut.》 meet with good 〔bad〕 weather. (배가) 좋은 날씨 〔폭풍우〕를 만나다.

make heavy weather of, find (something) difficult. 어려움을 당하다. ¶ *He made heavy* ~ *of his homework.* 그는 숙제하느라고 큰 고생을 했다.

under the weather, 《*colloq.*》 **a**) slightly ill; not feeling well. 몸이 좀 나빠; 기분이 언짢아. ¶ *I am just feeling a bit under the* ~. 지금 컨디션이 좀 안 좋다. **b**) somewhat drunk. 좀 얼큰해서.

— *vt.* (P6) **1** expose (something) to the weather. …을 비바람을 맞히다; 볕에 쬐다. ¶ ~ *timber* 재목을 햇볕에 말리다 / *Wood turns grey if weathered for a long time.* 나무를 오랫동안 볕에 두면 회색으로 변한다. **2** wear away, discolor, etc. (something) by such exposure. …을 풍화시키다. ¶ *Wind and water* ~ *rocks.* 바람과 물이 바위를 풍화시킨다. **3** slope (a roof, etc.) in order to throw off rain, etc. (빗물 등이 잘 흘러내리도록 지붕 등)을 경사지게 하다. **4** come through (a storm or something difficult) successfully. (폭풍우·역경 등)을 뚫고 나가다; 넘기다. ¶ ~ *a storm* 〔*a crisis*〕 폭풍우〔위기〕를 헤쳐 나가다 / ~ *financial difficulties* 재정적 곤란을 이겨 내다.

— *vi.* (P1) be affected or discolored by exposure to the weather. 풍화하다.

— *adj.* 《naut.》 facing or toward the wind; windward. 바람 불어 오는 쪽의(opp. lee). [E.]

weath·er-beat·en [wéðərbìːtn] *adj.* **1** worn by the sun, wind, and rain. 풍우에 시달린〔손상된〕. ¶ *an old,* ~ *castle* 풍우에 시달린 옛 성. **2** (of skin) bearing marks which are due to exposure to the sun. 볕에 탄. ¶ *a wrinkled* ~ *face* 볕에 탄 주름투성이의 얼굴.

weath·er·board [wéðərbɔ̀ːrd] *n.* a clapboard. 미늘 판자. — *vt.* (P6) cover with clapboards. 미늘 판자를 대다.

weath·er·board·ing [wéðərbɔ̀ːrdiŋ] *n.* overlapping boards forming an outer covering for part of a building, used to throw off rain from it; a clapboard. 미늘 판자.

weath·er-bound [wéðərbàund] *adj.* delayed by bad weather. 풍우로 출항이 지연된. ¶ *a* ~ *ship.*

Weather Bureau [⌐–⌐–] *n.* the bureau of the United States Department of Commerce responsible for recording and forecasting the weather. 기상국(氣象局).

weath·er·cock [wéðərkɑ̀k / -kɔ̀k] *n.* Ⓒ **1** a device, esp. in the shape of a cock, to show the direction of the wind. 바람개비; 풍향계. **2** 《*fig.*》 a person who changes easily or often. 변덕이 심한 사람.

weather forecast [⌐– ⌐–] *n.* a statement about the weather for the future. 일기 예보.

weath·er·glass [wéðərglæ̀s, -glɑ̀ːs] *n.* Ⓤ an instrument for showing changes in the weather; a barometer. 청우계; 기압계.

weath·er·ing [wéðəriŋ] *n.* Ⓤ destructive force of air, frost, snow, water, etc. esp. on rock. 풍화 (작용).

weath·er·man [wéðərmæ̀n] *n.* Ⓒ (*pl.* **-men** [-mèn]) 《*colloq.*》 a person who records and forecasts the weather. 일기 예보자; 기상대원.

weather map [⌐– ⌐] *n.* a map in which various weather conditions at a particular time are shown. 기상도; 일기도.

weather vane [⌐– ⌐] *n.* = weathercock.

:weave [wiːv] *v.* (**wove, wov·en** or **wove**) *vt.* (P6,7,13) **1** form (threads or strips) into a fabric, etc.; make (cloth) out of threads. …을 짜다; 엮다; 트다. ¶ ~ *thread into cloth* 실로 천을 짜다 / ~ *straw into hats* 짚을 엮어 모자를 만들다 / *A spider weaves its web.* 거미가 거미집을 친다 / ~ *a basket* 바구니를 엮다. **2** unite or entwine (details, incidents, etc.) into a story, poem, etc.; combine into a whole. (부분을) 종합하다; (전체를) 만들어 내다. ¶ *He wove a fascinating story from a few forgotten incidents.* 그는 잊혀진 몇 가지 사건들을 엮어서 근사한 이야기를 만들어 냈다.

— *vi.* (P1) **1** make something by interlacing; practice weaving. 피륙을 짜다. **2** move from side to side or in and out. 누비듯이 나아가다. ¶ *The road weaves through the valley.* 길은 골짜기를 누비듯이 나 있다.

— *n.* Ⓒ a method, manner, or pattern of weaving. 짜는〔뜨는〕 방식. ¶ *cloth with a plain* ~ 평직(平織)의 천. [E.]

weav·er [wíːvər] *n.* Ⓒ a person who weaves. 짜는 사람; 직공(織工).

·web [web] *n.* Ⓒ **1** a network of threads made by a spider. 거미집. **2** a whole piece of cloth woven at one time. 한 베틀분의 천. **3** the skin joining the toes of ducks, beavers, etc. 물갈퀴. **4** something woven. 피륙; 천; 직물. **5** anything like a web. 거미집 모양의 것; 망상(網狀) 조직. [*weave*]

webbed [webd] *adj.* **1** having a web; formed like a web. 거미집을 친; 거미집 모양의. **2** having fingers or toes joined by webs. 물갈퀴가 있는. ¶ *Ducks have ~ feet.* 오리발은 물갈퀴발이다.

web·foot [wébfùt] *n.* Ⓒ (*pl.* **-feet**) **1** a foot whose toes are joined by a web. 물갈퀴가 있는 발. **2** a bird or animal with webfeet. 물갈퀴가 있는 새〔짐승〕.

wed [wed] *vt.* (**wed·ded, wed·ded** or **wed, wed·ding**) 《rare》 **1** (P6,13) marry. …와 결혼하다. **2** (P13) join; unite. 맺다; 결합시키다. — *vi.* (P1) marry. 결혼하다. [E.=pledge]

be wedded to** one's **work, be extremely devoted to one's work. 일에 전념하다.

we'd [wi:d, wid] 《*colloq.*》 =we would; we had; we should.

Wed. Wednesday.

wed·ded [wédid] *adj.* **1** married. 결혼한. ¶ *a newly ~ pair* 신혼 부부. **2** devoted. 전념하는. ¶ *He is ~ to his work.* 그는 일에 열심이다. [*wed*]

:**wed·ding** [wédiŋ] *n.* Ⓒ **1** a marriage ceremony. 결혼식. **2** a marriage anniversary. 결혼 기념일. ¶ *the golden ~* 금혼식 / *the diamond ~* 다이아몬드 혼식 / *A silver ~ is the twenty-fifth anniversary of a marriage.* 은혼식은 결혼 25주년 기념식이다. [*wed*]

wedding cake [⌐-⌐] *n.* a large cake for a wedding ceremony. 웨딩 케이크.

wedding march [⌐-⌐] *n.* march played during a wedding ceremony. 결혼 행진곡.

wedding ring [⌐-⌐] *n.* a ring which is put on a bride's finger at a wedding ceremony. 결혼 반지.

***wedge** [wedʒ] *n.* Ⓒ **1** a piece of wood or metal, thick at one side and thin at the other, used for splitting a log, a rock, etc. 쐐기. **2** anything like a wedge. 쐐기 모양의 것.

the thin end of the wedge, a small change that is likely to lead to a further, serious change. 사소하지만 장차 중대한 결과를 가져올 실마리.

— *vt.* (P6,7,18) **1** split (something) by the use of a wedge. 쐐기로 쪼개다. ¶ *~ open a log* 통나무를 쐐기로 쪼개다. **2** use a wedge for fastening (something); 《*fig.*》 fix firmly. …을 쐐기로 고정시키다; …에 쐐기를 박다. ¶ *~ the door open* 문을 쐐기로 고정시켜 열어 두다. **3** ⓐ force (something) in like a wedge. …을 끼어들게 하다; 밀어넣다. ¶ *~ oneself in* …에 끼어들다 / *He was wedged between two fat ladies.* 뚱뚱한 두 여자 틈에 끼였다. ⓑ force one's way by pressing through. 밀어 헤치고 나아가다. ¶ *He wedged his way through the crowd.* 그는 군중을 헤치고 나아갔다. [E.]

wed·lock [wédlɑk / -lɔk] *n.* Ⓤ the state of being married; marriage; married life. 혼인; 결혼 생활. [E.=pledge-work]

born in 〔***out of***〕 ***wedlock,*** born of married 〔unmarried〕 parents. 적출(嫡出)〔서출〕의.

:**Wednes·day** [wénzdi, -dei] *n.* the fourth day of the week. 수요일. W., Wed.로 생략함. [E. *Woden* =Mercury]

***wee** [wi:] *adj.* (**we·er, we·est**) very small; tiny. 아주 작은; 조그마한. ¶ *a ~ bit* 아주 조금. [obs. *we* a bit]

:**weed** [wi:d] *n.* Ⓒ **1** 《usu. *pl.*》 a wild, useless plant which grows without cultivation. 잡초. ¶ *grow like a ~* 잡초처럼 마구 자라다. **2** 《*the ~*》 《*colloq.*》 tobacco; a cigar; a cigarette. 담배; 여송연; 궐련. **3** a thin, ungainly person or animal. 말라 빠진 볼품 없는 사람〔짐승〕. — *vt.* **1** (P6) remove weeds out of (a garden, etc.). …의 잡초를 뽑다. ¶ *~ a garden.* **2** (P7) take out (something useless or harmful). …을 제거하다; 일소하다. ¶ *~ out useless books from one's library* 서재의 쓸데없는 책들을 치워 버리다. — *vi.* (P1) remove weeds. 잡초를 뽑다. [E.]

weed·er [wí:dər] *n.* Ⓒ a person who weeds; a tool for weeding. 풀 뽑는 사람; 제초기.

weeds [wi:dz] *n.* clothes worn by a widow as a sign of mourning. 과부의 상복(喪服). [E.=garment]

weed·y [wí:di] *adj.* (**weed·i·er, weed·i·est**) **1** full of weeds. 잡초가 무성한. **2** growing quickly like weeds. 잡초같이 빨리 자라는. **3** (of persons and animals) thin and tall like weeds. 마르고 껑충한. [*weed*]

:**week** [wi:k] *n.* Ⓒ **1** a period of seven days, usu. counted from Sunday to Saturday. 주. ¶ *this* 〔*next*〕 *~* 이번〔다음〕 주 / *What day of the ~ is it ?* 오늘이 무슨 요일이냐. **2** 《*colloq.*》 the six working days of the week. (일요일을 뺀) 6일간; 취업일; 평일. ¶ *He is away all the ~ but comes home for Sundays.* 그는 주 내내 나가 있다가 일요일에 귀가한다 / *The museum is open during the ~.* 박물관은 평일에는 개관한다. **3** any period of seven days. 7일간; 1주일 《요일에 관계 없이》. ¶ *He stayed for a ~.* 그는 1주일간 머물렀다 / *in a ~ or so,* 1주일간이나 그 정도에 / *last Saturday* 〔*yesterday*〕 *~* 지난 주의 토요일〔어제〕 / *I did it weeks ago.* 몇 주 전에 그것을 했다 / *the ~ of April 1,* 4월 1일부터 1주일간 / *a ~ ago today* 지난 주 오늘 / *a ~ from now* 내주의 오늘. [E.]

a week of Sundays 〔***weeks***〕, seven weeks. 7주간; (넌더리나게) 긴 동안.

knock 〔***send***〕 *someone* ***into the middle of next week,*** hit someone very hard; send him flying. 후려갈기다; 쫓아 버리다.

this day 〔***today***〕 ***week,*** **a**) 《chiefly Brit.》 a week from today; on the day one week after today. 다음 주 오늘. ¶ *The wedding is today* ～. 결혼식은 다음 주 오늘이다. **b**) 《rare》 a week ago today; on the day one week before today. 지난 주 오늘. ¶ *He left today* ～. 그는 지난 주 오늘 떠났다.

week after week, each week. 매주.

week in, week out = week after week.

week·day [wíːkdèi] *n.* Ⓒ any day of the week except Sunday. 평일; 위크데이. ¶ *I only work on weekdays, not at weekends.* 나는 평일에만 일하고 주말에는 안 한다.

·**week·end** [wíːkènd] *n.* Ⓒ the time from Friday night or Saturday afternoon to Monday morning. 주말. ¶ *a long* ～ 주말 전후에 하루 이틀을 더 보탠 휴가 / *have one's weekends free* 주말을 자유롭게 지내다 / *a* ～ *trip* 주말 여행. — *adj.* of a weekend. 주말의. — *vi.* (P1,2A) spend a weekend. 주말을 보내다.

:**week·ly** [wíːkli] *adj.* **1** of a week; every week; lasting a week. 1주일의; 매주의; 1주일 치의. ¶ *one's* ～ *wages* 주급 / *a* ～ *magazine* 주간지. **2** done once a week. 주 1회의. — *adv.* every week; once a week. 매주; 주마다; 1주 1회. ¶ *be published* ～ 매주 출간되다. — *n.* Ⓒ (*pl.* **-lies**) 《usu. *pl.*》 a newspaper or magazine published once a week. 주간 신문; 주간지(誌).

ween [wiːn] *vt.* (P11) 《*poet., arch*》 think; believe. 생각하다; 믿다. [E.]

:**weep** [wiːp] *v.* (**wept**) *vi.* (P1,2A,3) **1** express grief, sorrow or other strong emotion by shedding tears; shed tears; cry. 울다; 눈물을 흘리다. ¶ *She wept for her son.* 그녀는 아들 때문에 울었다 / ～ *with pain* 〔*for joy*〕 아파서〔기뻐서〕 울다 / *He wept over his sad fate.* 그는 자신의 서글픈 운명을 한탄하며 울었다. **2** let fall drops of water or another liquid; drip. 물방울을 떨어뜨리다. **3** send forth water or another liquid. 물이 (스며)나오게 하다. — *vt.* (P6,7,13) **1** weep for (someone or something). …을 울며 슬퍼하다. **2** shed (tears). (눈물)을 흘리다. **3** send forth (water or another liquid). (물 따위)를 스며 나오게 하다. **4** bring (someone or something) to a desired condition by weeping. 울어서 …하게 하다. ¶ *The baby wept itself to sleep.* 아기는 울다가 잠들었다. [E.]

weep away, spend (time) in weeping. 울며 지내다.

weep oneself out, weep as much as one wants to. 실컷 울다.

weep out, talk while crying. 울면서 말하다.

wee·vil [wíːvəl] *n.* Ⓒ a small beetle with a hard shell which destroys cotton, grain, fruit, etc. 바구밋과의 곤충. [E.]

weft [weft] *n.* Ⓒ the threads that cross from side across the warp in a piece of cloth, etc. (피륙의) 씨실(cf. *warp*). [*weave*]

:**weigh** [wei] *vt.* **1** (P6) 《*in, on*》 determine the weight of (something) by means of a scale or balance; balance (something) in the hand in order to estimate its weight. …을 저울에 달다; …의 무게를 달다; 손으로 …의 무게를 가늠하다. ¶ ～ *oneself on the scales* 저울에 체중을 재다 / *I weighed the stone in my hands.* 손으로 그 돌의 무게를 가늠해 봤다 / ～ *eggs on a scale* 달걀을 저울에 달다 / *Have you weighed yourself lately?* 요즘 체중을 재 보았느냐. **2** (P6,13) consider carefully; consider (something) in order to make a choice. …을 숙고하다; 비교 고찰하다. ¶ ～ *one's words* 잘 생각하고 말하다 / ～ *one plan against* 〔*with*〕 *another* 두 가지 계획을 비교 고찰하다 / ～ *the consequence* 〔*pros and cons*〕 결과〔찬부〕를 신중히 생각하다 / *He weighed the ideas in his mind.* 그는 의견들을 곰곰이 생각해 보았다. **3** (P7) 《*down*》 press down; burden. …을 내리누르다; (마음)을 무겁게 하다. **4** 《naut.》 lift (an anchor). (닻)을 올리다. ¶ ～ *anchor.* — *vi.* **1** (P2B) have a certain weight. 무게가 …하다. ¶ *He weighs 60 pounds.* 그는 체중이 60 파운드 나간다 / *How much do you* ～? 체중이 얼마냐. **2** (P2A,3) 《*with*》 have importance. 중요시되다. **3** 《*on, upon*》 be a burden. 부담이 되다; 압박하다. ¶ *Many troubles weighed on* 〔*upon*〕 *his mind.* 여러 가지 골치 아픈 일이 그의 마음을 무겁게 했다. [E.=carry ⌐→wain)]

weigh down, **a**) cause (something) to bend under a load. …을 무게로 처지게 하다. ¶ *The branches of the trees were* ～ *down by snow.* 나뭇가지들이 눈 무게 때문에 처졌다. **b**) bring (someone) under emotional stress. …을 우울하게 만들다. ¶ *weighed down by grief* 슬픔으로 침울해진 / *He is weighed down with cares.* 그는 걱정거리로 마음이 무겁다.

weigh in, weigh (a boxer) before a fight. (권투 선수 등)의 체중을 경기 전에 검사하다.

weigh out, measure out (something) by weighing; serve out by weight. …을 달아서 나누다. ¶ ～ *out five pounds of butter* 버터 5 파운드를 달아 가르다.

weigh the thumb, 《U.S.》 give short weight. 저울눈을 속이다.

weigh up, raise by counter-weight or by leverage, etc. 한쪽 무게로 다른 쪽이 튀어오르다.

weigh with, have specified importance to. …에게 중요한 관계가 있다. ¶ *His opinion doesn't* ～ *with me.* 그의 의견 따윈 내게 중요하지 않다 / *Her evidence weighed quite strongly with the judge.* 그녀의 증언은 판사에게는 대단히 중요했다.

:**weight** [weit] *n.* **1** Ⓤ the amount of heaviness; the amount something or someone weighs. 무게; 중량; 체중. ¶ *sell by* ～ 달아서 팔다 / *under the* ～ *of* …의 무게 때문에 / *gain* 〔*lose*〕 ～ 체중이 늘다〔줄다〕 / *give short* ～ 저울눈을 속이다 / *The* *poor horse sank beneath the ~ of its load.* 그 불쌍한 말은 짐 무게로 인해 주저앉았다 / *What is your ~?* 체중이 얼마요 / *She's put on ~ since I last saw her.* 그녀는 지난 번 만난 이후 체중이 늘었다. **2** Ⓤ the force with which a body is pulled toward the center of the earth; gravity. 중력(重力). ¶ *Astronauts in space have no ~.* 우주에서 우주 비행사는 중력이 없다. **3** Ⓒ 《often *a ~* or *the ~*》 a burden; a load. 무거운 짐; 부담. ¶ *a ~ of care* 근심의 중압 / *a ~ on one's mind* 마음의 부담 / *That is a great ~ off my mind.* 그것으로 마음의 짐이 덜어졌다. **4** Ⓤ influence; importance. 영향력; 중요성. ¶ *a man of ~* 유력한 사람 / *His opinion carries ~ in the government.* 그의 의견은 정부내에서 영향력이 있다 / *an opinion of no ~* 중요하지 않은 의견 / *give ~ to* …을 중요시하다 / *I don't attach any ~ to these rumors.* 이런 소문들을 중요시하지 않는다 / *have ~ with* …에 있어서 중요하다. **5** Ⓒ a heavy object; a piece of metal used on a balance or scale in weighing. 무거운 것; 분동(分銅); 추. ¶ *keep papers down with a ~* 서류를 문진(文鎭)으로 눌러 놓다 / *You must not lift weights.* 무거운 걸 들어서는 안 된다 / *a pound ~,* 1 파운드의 분동. **6** ⓊⒸ a system of units for expressing weight; a unit of mass or weight. 중량 단위; 형량(衡量). ¶ *a table of weights and measures* 도량형표.

pull one's weight, do one's part or share of work. 자기 몫〔역할〕을 다하다.

put on weight, grow fat; become heavier. 체중이 늘다; 살찌다.

throw one's weight about 〔***around***〕, 《*colloq.*》 use one's position, power, etc. more than is necessary. 권력을 휘두르다; 지위를 이용하다.

— *vt.* **1** (P6,7,13) 《*with*》 add weight to (something); make (something) heavy or heavier. …에 무게를 가하다; …을 무겁게 만들다. ¶ *The elevator is weighted too heavily.* 승강기에 너무 무겁게 실었다. **2** (P6,13) burden. …에 무거운 짐을 지우다; …을 괴롭히다. ¶ *He weights himself with care.* 그는 마음 고생을 한다. [*weigh*]

weight down, fasten down with a weight. …을 (무거운 것으로) 누르다. ¶ 《*fig.*》 *He's weighted down with cares.* 그는 걱정거리로 마음이 무겁다.

weight·less [wéitlis] *adj.* having no weight; of the condition of experiencing no apparent gravitational pull. 무게가 없는; 무중력(상태)의.

weight·y [wéiti] *adj.* (**weight·i·er, weight·i·est**) **1** heavy. 무거운. ¶ *a ~ load* / *a package too ~ for the post* 우편물로는 과중한 소포. **2** important; influential; convincing. 중요한; 유력한; 설득력 있는. ¶ *a ~ argument* / *~ matters of state* 중대한 정무(政務). **3** burdensome. 견디기 어려운; 벅찬; 짐스러운. ¶ *~ responsibility* 벅찬 책임 / *after a ~ pause* 무거운 침묵 끝에.

weir [wiər] *n.* Ⓒ **1** a dam in a river to hold back water. 둑. **2** a fence set in a river to catch fish. 어살. [E.]

weird [wiərd] *adj.* **1** of destiny or fate. 운명〔숙명〕의. **2** strange; mysterious; unearthly. 불가사의한; 이 세상의 것이 아닌. ¶ *It was a ~ old house full of soot and webs.* 그 집은 온통 그을음과 거미집의 기분 나쁜 고옥이었다. **3** 《*colloq.*》 curious; funny; odd. 기묘한; 이상한. ¶ *She has some ~ ideas.* 그녀는 생각이 좀 이상하다 / *He had a rather ~ appearance.* 그의 생김새는 좀 특이했다. — *n.* destiny. 운명. [O.E. *wyrd* fate, destiny]

:wel·come [wélkəm] *adj.* **1** (of a person) gladly received; received with pleasure on arrival. 환영받는. ¶ *a ~ guest* 반가운 손님 / *make someone ~* 아무를 환대하다 / *You are ~.* 어서 오십시오. 參考 미국에서는 "Thank you."에 대한 대답으로 '천만의 말씀'이란 뜻. **2** 《*to*》 permitted gladly to use or enjoy. 마음대로 써도〔해도〕 좋은. ¶ *You are ~ to any book in my library.* 내 서재의 어느 책이든 마음대로 봐라 / *You are ~ to pick the flowers.* 꽃을 꺾어도 좋다 / *You are quite ~ to come and go as you please.* 가든 오든 전적으로 네 자유다 / 《*iron.*》 *You are ~ to your own opinion.* 네멋대로 지껄여라 / *He didn't make his guests, very ~.* 그는 손님들을 건성으로 맞았다. **3** (of events, circumstances, etc.) greeted with satisfaction. (일·사정 등이) 좋은; 만족스러운. ¶ *A holiday is very ~ after a long spell of work.* 오랫동안 일만 하다가 쉬는 날은 매우 좋다 / *a ~ rest* 흡족한 휴식.

— *n.* Ⓒ a kindly greeting or reception. 환영; 환대; 환영 인사. ¶ *a hearty ~* 충심에서의 환영 / *bid someone ~ = say ~ to someone* 아무를 환대하다 / *wear out* 〔*outstay*〕 *one's ~* 너무 자주 와서〔오래 머물러〕 눈총받다 / *He received a cold ~.* 그는 푸대접을 받았다.

— *vt.* (6,7,13) say welcome to (someone); receive (someone or something) with pleasure. …을 환영하다; …을 기꺼이 받아들이다. ¶ *~ one's criticism* 비판을 기꺼이 받아들이다 / *He was warmly welcomed.* 그는 따뜻한 환영을 받았다 / *I ~ your help.* 도와 주면 고맙겠다.

— *interj.* an expression of kind greeting. 어서 오십시오. ¶ *Welcome to Korea!* / *Welcome home!* 잘 다녀왔니. [*will, come;* orig. sense *come for another's pleasure*]

weld [weld] *vt.* (P6,7,13) **1** join (two pieces of metal) by heating their edges to the melting point and then pressing them together. (금속)을 용접하다. ¶ *He welded the broken rod.* **2** unite closely. …을 밀착시키다; 결합하다. ¶ *~ (together) the different elements of a party* 당의 이질 분자

들을 융합시키다. — *vi.* (P1) be welded; be able to be welded. 용접하다; 용접이 되다. ¶ *Iron welds easily.* 철은 용접이 잘 된다. — *n.* **1** Ⓤ the act of welding; the state of being welded. 용접. **2** Ⓒ a welded joint. 용접점. [Scand. (→well[1])]

·**wel·fare** [wélfɛ̀ər] *n.* Ⓤ the state of having good health, happiness, prosperity, etc. 복리; 복지; 후생. [*well*[2], *fare*]

welfare state [⌐–⌐] *n.* a state in which the government aims to insure the welfare of its people through National Insurance, free medical treatment, old-age pensions, etc. 복지 국가.

welfare work [⌐–⌐] *n.* an organized effort made for the welfare of a community or group. 복지(후생) 사업.

:**well**[1] [wel] *n.* Ⓒ **1** a deep hole made in the ground to get oil, water, etc. 우물. ¶ *an oil* ~ 유정(油井). **2** a natural spring or fountain of water. 샘. **3** a source of much knowledge, etc. (지식 등의) 원천; 근원. ¶ *My father is a ~ of information.* 나의 아버지는 지식의 샘이다. **4** something like a well in shape or use; a stairwell. 우물 모양의 것; 층계의 뚫린 공간. — *vi.* (P2A,3) come forth; spring. 솟아오르다; 분출하다. ¶ *Tears welled* (*up*) *from* (*in*) *her eyes.* 그녀의 눈에서 눈물이 솟았다 / *Blood welled* (*out*) *from the cut.* 베인 데에서 피가 솟았다 / *Water wells from a spring beneath the rock.* 바위 밑 샘에서 물이 솟아오른다. [E.]

:**well**[2] [wel] *adv.* (**bet·ter, best**) **1** in a desirable, satisfactory manner. 잘; 만족하게(opp. badly). ¶ *Things are going* ~. 만사 잘 되고 있다 / *dine* ~ 잘 먹다 / *sleep* ~ 푹 자다 / *Well done!* 잘 했다 / *Well met!* 잘 만났다 / *He's always done his job extremely* ~. 그는 일을 언제나 완벽하게 잘 한다. **2** in a good, proper, or friendly manner. 정당하게; 적절히; 친절하게. ¶ *He spoke ~ of you.* 그는 너에 대해서 좋게 말했다 / *You did ~ to refuse.* 거절하기를 잘했다 / *That's ~ said.* 그 말이 맞습니다. **3** skillfully; excellently. 능숙하게; 익숙하게. ¶ *speak English* ~ 영어를 잘 하다 / *Well played!* 잘 연주했다 / *do a thing* ~ 일을 능숙하게 하다 / *The work is ~ done.* 일은 잘 되었다. **4** 《*may* ~》 with reason; in justice; probably. 당연하게; 아마도. ¶ *You may ~ say so.* 네가 그렇게 말하는 것도 당연하다 / *It may ~ be true.* 그건 아마 사실일 거다 / *We might ~ ask him to do it.* 그에게 해 달라고 부탁하는 것이 좋겠다. **5** fully; thoroughly; clearly. 충분히; 확실히. ¶ *shake ~ before opening* 열기 전에 잘 흔들다 / *Think ~ before you act.* 행동 전에 충분히 생각해라 / *You know ~ what I mean.* 내 말을 잘 알겠지 / *You ought to be ~ beaten.* 너 좀 맞아야 하겠다 / *Our team was ~ and truly beaten.* 우리 팀은 보기 좋게 패배했다. **6** to a considerable degree or extent; much. 꽤; 상당히; 훨씬. ¶ *That man is ~ past sixty.* 저 사람은 족히 예순은 넘었다 / *My study is ~ advanced.* 내 연구는 상당히 진척됐다 / ~ *over a hundred years* 백 년은 훨씬 넘어 / *Profits were ~ above our original forecast.* 소득은 우리의 당초 예상보다 훨씬 많았다. **7** closely; personally. 친히; 개인적으로. ¶ *I know him* ~. 나는 그를 잘 알고 있다. **8** in a successful manner; richly. 유복하게. ¶ *do oneself* ~ 유복하게 지내다 / *They lived ~ here.* 그들은 여기서 잘 살았었다. **9** easily. 쉽게. ¶ *I can't ~ decline her offer.* 그녀의 제의를 쉽게 거절할 수 없다 / *I can't very ~ manage to come tomorrow.* 내일 가기가 어려울 것 같다 / *I can't ~ tell you.* 네게 말하기가 어렵다.

as well, **a**) in addition; besides. 또한; 게다가. ¶ *Take this book as* ~. 이 책도 가져가거라. **b**) equally. 마찬가지로.

as well as, **a**) in addition to. …도 또한; …뿐만 아니라 —도. ¶ *He gave me clothes as ~ as money.* 그는 내게 돈뿐만 아니라 옷도 주었다. **b**) equally as. …와 마찬가지로. ¶ *I know him as ~ as I know myself.* 내가 나를 아는 만큼 그를 알고 있다.

be well out of, be lucky to be free from. …을 용케 면하다. ¶ *He was ~ out of the trouble.* 그는 용케 분쟁에 말려들지 않았다.

come off well, have good luck; succeed. 운이 좋다; 성공하다.

do oneself well, provide oneself with good things, esp. comforts and luxuries. 호화롭게 살다; 잘 지내다.

***do well by** someone,* treat someone well. …을 잘 해 주다; 우대하다.

do well (=*be wise*) ***to*** *do.* …하는 것이 좋다. ¶ *You would do ~ to be quiet.* 조용히 하는 것이 좋겠다.

live well =do oneself well.

may as well (=*had better*) *do.* …하는 편이 낫다. ¶ *We may as ~ go at once.* 곧 가는 것이 낫다 / *You might as ~ throw your money into the sea as lend it to him.* 그에게 돈을 꾸어 주느니 바다에 버리는 편이 낫겠다 / *You might as ~ talk to him.* 그에게 말해 주는 것이 좋겠다.

pretty well, almost. 거의; 대체로. ¶ *You are pretty ~ the only person who is willing to help.* 기꺼이 도와 줄 사람은 너뿐인 것 같다.

speak well for, be favorable evidence of. …의 유리한 증거가 되다. ¶ *It speaks ~ for him that ....* …라는 것이 그에게 유리하다는 증거다.

speak well of, praise. …을 칭찬하다. ¶ *He is ~ spoken of by everybody.* 모든 사람이 그를 칭찬한다.

***stand well with** someone,* be in someone's favor. …의 마음에 들다. ¶ *He stands ~ with his employer.* 그는 고용주의 호감을 사고 있다.

think well of, have a high opinion of. …을 좋게 여기다.

— *adj.* (**bet·ter, best**) 《as *predicative*》 **1** in good health; sound in body and mind. 건강한(opp. ill). ¶ *look* ~ 건강해 보이다 / 《U.S.》 *a* ~ *man* 건강한 사람 / *I am not feeling very* ~ *today.* 오늘 몸의 컨디션이 별로 안 좋다 / *How are you ? — Quite* ~ , *thank you.* 건강은 어떻습니까 —썩 좋소. 고맙소. **2** in a good condition. (형편이) 좋은; 나무랄 데 없는. ¶ *All's* ~ (*with us*). 저희들은 잘 있습니다 / *It is all very* ~ , *but ....* 그것이 과연 좋기는 하다만…. **3** proper; suitable; fortunate. 적당〔타당〕한; 바람직한. ¶ *He is* ~ *enough as a teacher.* 그는 선생으로는 적격이다 / *It is just as* ~ *to be careful.* 조심하는 게 좋겠다 / *It is* ~ *that you came.* 네가 와서 잘 됐다 / *It would be* ~ *to inquire.* 문의하는 게 좋을 것이다 / *It is just as* ~ *we didn't plan our picnic for yesterday, as it rained all day.* 어제는 종일 비가 왔으니 우리가 소풍 안 가기로 한 건 잘한 일이다.

— *interj.* **1** 《expressing *surprise, relief, expectation,* etc.》 저런; 어; 맙소사; 글쎄. ¶ *Well, to be sure !* 어휴, 놀라라 / *Well, then ?* 그래, 그렇다면 (어떻게 되는 거지) / *Well, come if you like.* 그래, 올 테면 와 봐라 / *Well, you may be right.* 글쎄, 네 말이 맞겠지. **2** used to continue one's speech. 그런데. ¶ *Well, as I was saying, ...* 그래서, 내가 말했듯이… / *Well, who was it ?* 그런데, 그게 누구였을까. [E.]

***we'll** [wiːl] we shall 〔will〕.

well-ad·vised [wélədváizd] *adj.* thoughtful; careful; wise. 사려 깊은; 신중한; 현명한. ¶ *a* ~ *step* 〔*action*〕 현명한 조치〔행동〕 / *a sound and* ~ *judgment* 건전하고 신중한 판단 / *You would be* ~ *to see the doctor about that case.* 그 증상은 의사의 진찰을 받는 게 좋을 겁니다. [*well*²]

well-ap·point·ed [wéləpɔ́intid] *adj.* with very good equipment or furnishings. 준비가 갖춰진; 설비가 잘 된. ¶ *a* ~ *hotel* 시설이 좋은 호텔 / *a* ~ *dinner* 성찬.

well-bal·anced [wélbǽlənst] *adj.* **1** properly balanced. 균형이 (잘) 잡힌. ¶ *a* ~ *diet* 균형식(食). **2** with common sense; sensible. 분별 있는; 상식 있는. ¶ *a* ~ *young man* 분별이 있는 청년.

well-be·haved [wélbihéivd] *adj.* having or showing good manners; behaving well. 행실이 좋은.

well-be·ing [wélbíːiŋ] *n.* Ⓤ health and happiness; welfare. 행복; 복지. ¶ *The warm sunny weather always gives me a sense of* ~ . 따뜻한 볕이 나는 날에 나는 늘 행복감을 느낀다.

well·born [wélbɔ́ːrn] *adj.* born of a good family. 가문이 좋은.

well-bred [wélbréd] *adj.* **1** showing good breeding in manners; polite. 본데있게 자란; 소양이 좋은; 점잖은. **2** (of animals) of good stock or birth. (동물이) 혈통이 좋은; 순종의. [*well*²]

well-con·duct·ed [wélkəndʌ́ktid] *adj.* having good manners. 품행이 좋은.

well-con·nect·ed [wélkənéktid] *adj.* having good or important relatives. 문벌이 좋은; 훌륭한 친척이 있는.

well-de·fined [wéldifáind] *adj.* **1** clearly stated or described. 명확히 정의된. ¶ ~ *policies* 분명한 정책 / *a* ~ *boundary* 명확한 경계. **2** clear in form or nature; easily recognizable. (윤곽이) 뚜렷한. ¶ *The trees are* ~ *in the picture.* 그림에서 나무들은 윤곽이 뚜렷하게 그려져 있다.

well-dis·posed [wéldispóuzd] *adj.* **1** rightly or suitably placed. 적정 배치의. **2** having a favorable or kind nature. 마음씨가 좋은. ¶ *a* ~ *nature* 착한 천성.

well-done [wéldʌ́n] *adj.* (of meat) thoroughly cooked. (고기가) 잘 조리된〔구워진〕 (cf. *underdone, rare*²).

well-earned [wélə́ːrnd] *adj.* well deserved. 제 힘으로 얻은; 당연한 보상의. ¶ *a* ~ *rest after so much hard work* 힘든 일을 한 뒤에 얻은 휴식.

well-fa·vored [wélféivərd] *adj.* having good looks; attractive; beautiful. 미모의.

well-fed [wélféd] *adj.* showing the result of good feeding. 영양이 충분한.

well-found·ed [wélfáundid] *adj.* based on facts or good reasons; not imaginative. 근거가 충분한. ¶ *Our suspicions were* ~ . *—She turned out to be a thief.* 우리의 의심은 틀림없었다—그녀가 도둑으로 판명됐으니까. [*well*²]

well-groomed [wélgrúːmd] *adj.* **1** (of a person) neat in dress and appearance. 차림·생김새가 깔끔한. ¶ *a* ~ *woman.* **2** (of a horse, etc.) well cared. (말 따위가) 손질이 잘 된. ¶ *a* ~ *horse* 손질이 잘 된 말 / *a* ~ *lawn* 잘 다듬어진 잔디.

well-ground·ed [wélgráundid] *adj.* **1** with a good knowledge of the basic principles of a subject. 기본 교육〔훈련〕을 받은. ¶ *The soldiers were* ~ *in the skills needed to survive in the desert.* 군인들은 사막에서 살아남을 수 있는 여러 가지 기술을 익혔다. **2** = well-founded.

well·head [wélhèd] *n.* Ⓒ a source of water; a fountainhead; 《*fig.*》 a source. 수원(水源); 근원; 원천. [*well*¹]

well-in·formed [wélinfɔ́ːrmd] *adj.* **1** with wide knowledge and information about various subjects. 견문이 넓은; 박식한. **2** having reliable or full information on a subject. (어떤 일에) 정통한; 잘 알고 있는. [*well*²]

well-in·ten·tioned [wélintén∫ənd] *adj.* coming from a good will or good intentions. 선의의; 선의로 행한. ¶ *a* ~ *effort to help* 도와 주려는 선의의 노력.

well-kept [wélképt] *adj.* kept with good

care. 잘 손질된. [*well*²]

well-knit [wélnít] *adj.* **1** (of the body) firmly or strongly made. 근골(筋骨)이 억센; 튼튼한. **2** carefully or closely joined or related. 잘 짜여진; (조직 등이) 정연한.

:well-known [wélnóun] *adj.* **1** widely known; famous. 유명한. ¶ *a ~ author.* **2** familiar. 잘 알고 있는; 친밀한. ¶ *a ~ fact* 〔*face*〕 잘 알려진 사실〔얼굴〕.

well-man·nered [wélmǽnərd] *adj.* having good manners; polite. 예의바른; 점잖은; 공손한.

well-mean·ing [wélmí:niŋ] *adj.* having good intentions; well intentioned. 선의의. ¶ *a ~ person* 호인 / *a ~ effort* 잘 하려고 하는 노력.

well-meant [wélmént] *adj.* said or done with good intentions. 선의로 한. ¶ *Her help was ~, but it just made the job take longer.* 그녀가 선의로 도운 것이지만 일만 더디게 만들었다.

well-nigh [wélnái] *adv.* 《*arch.*》 very nearly; almost. 거의. ¶ *~ exhausted* 거의 지쳐 버린 / *be ~ perfect* 거의 완전하다.

well-off [wélɔ́(:)f, -ɑ́f] *adj.* in good or favorable conditions; rich; wealthy. 순탄한; 유복한(opp. badly-off). 語法 주로 서술적으로 쓰임.

well-read [wélréd] *adj.* having wide knowledge through reading. 박식한; 책을 많이 본.

well-reg·u·lat·ed [wélrégjəlèitid] *adj.* in good order. 정돈이 잘된; 규칙이 잘된.

well-round·ed [wélráundid] *adj.* well-balanced. 균형이 잘 잡힌. ¶ *a ~ education* 균형 잡힌 교육.

well-spo·ken [wélspóukən] *adj.* **1** speaking fittingly and pleasingly in a refined manner. 말을 잘하는; 말씨가 고운. **2** properly or aptly spoken. 용어가 적절한.

well·spring [wélspriŋ] *n.* Ⓒ **1** the source of a stream; a fountainhead. 수원(水源); 샘. **2** the source of an abundant supply of anything; a source. (풍부한) 자원. [*well*¹]

well-timed [wéltáimd] *adj.* timely. 시의(時宜) 적절한. ¶ *~ advice.* [*well*²]

well-to-do [wéltədú:] *adj.* fairly rich; prosperous. 넉넉한; 부유한. ¶ *the ~* 부유층.

well-turned [wéltə́:rnd] *adj.* (of a phrase, etc.) expressed to the point; graceful. 잘 표현한. ¶ *a ~ compliment* 적절한 치하(致賀).

well-wish·er [wélwíʃər] *n.* Ⓒ a person who wishes the happiness of another person or persons. 남의 행복을 비는 사람.

well-worn [wélwɔ́:rn] *adj.* **1** much used. 써서 낡은. **2** stale; hackneyed. 진부한. ¶ *a ~ cliché* 진부한 표현〔문구〕.

Welsh [welʃ, weltʃ] *n.* **1** the people of Wales. 웨일스 사람. **2** the language spoken in Wales. 웨일스어. — *adj.* of Wales or Welsh. 웨일스 사람〔말〕의. [E.=foreign]

Welsh·man [wélʃmən, wéltʃ-] *n.* Ⓒ (*pl.* **-men** [-mən]) a person of Wales. 웨일스 사람.

welt [welt] *n.* **1** a strip of leather between the upper part and the sole of a shoe. 대다리《구두창과 갑피를 맞꿰매는 가죽 테》. **2** a red, swollen mark raised on the skin by a whip or a blow. 채찍 자국; 맷자국. — *vt.* (P6) **1** furnish (a shoe) with a welt. (구두에) 대다리를 대다. **2** 《*colloq.*》 beat severely. 후려갈기다. [E.]

wel·ter [wéltər] *vi.* (P2A,3) roll about. 구르다; 뒹굴다. — *n.* Ⓤ **1** (of waves) the act of rolling. (파도의) 굽이침. **2** confusion. 혼란. [Teut. (→wallow)]

wel·ter·weight [wéltərwèit] *n.* Ⓒ 《box-ing》 a boxer or wrestler having a weight between that of a lightweight and a middleweight. 웰터급 선수.

wen [wen] *n.* Ⓒ a harmless growth on the skin. (머리 등의) 종기; 혹. [E.]

wench [wentʃ] *n.* Ⓒ 《*arch., joc.*》 a girl or a young woman; a country girl; a woman servant. 계집아이; 촌색시; 하녀. — *vi.* (P1) 《*arch.*》 consort harlots. 매춘부와 관계하다. [E.=child]

wend [wend] *v.* (**wended** or 《*arch.*》 **went**) *vi.* go; travel. 가다; 전진하다. — *vt.* direct; continue. (진로)를 향하다; 계속하다. [E.]

:went [went] *v.* p. of **go.**

:wept [wept] *v.* p. and pp. of **weep.**

:were [wə:r, wər] *v., auxil. v.* p. of **are.**

as it were, so to speak. 이를테면.

if it were not for =***were it not for,*** without. 만일 …이 없다면.

were to, if… should. 만일 …이라면.

:we're [wiər] =we are.

:were·n't [wə:rnt] =were not.

wer(e)·wolf [wíərwùlf, wə́:r-] *n.* (*pl.* **-wolves** [-wùlvz]) 《legend》 a person who has been changed into a wolf; a person who can change himself into a wolf. 이리가 된 사람; 인간 늑대. [E.=man-wolf]

wert [wə:rt, wərt] *v.* 《*arch.*》 《used with *thou*》 =were. ¶ *Thou ~* (=you were).

:west [west] *n.* 《usu. *the ~* 》 **1** one of the main points of the compass; the direction of the sunset. 서(西); 서쪽(opp. east). ¶ *The sun sets in the ~.* 해는 서쪽으로 진다 / *I'm lost — which direction is ~?* 길을 잃었다—서쪽이 어느 쪽이지. **2** the area or section to the west; the part of any country in the west. 서부 (지방). ¶ *He lives in the ~ of England.* 그는 영국의 서부에 살고 있다 / *The rain will spread to the ~ later.* 비는 나중에 서부로 확산될 것이다. **3** 《*the W-*》 the western part of the United States. (미국의) 서부. **4** 《*the W-*》 Western Europe; the Occident. 서양; 서구(西歐).

to the west of, farther west than. …의 서쪽

에. ¶ *The island lies to the ~ of Korea.* 그 섬은 한국의 서쪽에 있다.
— *adj.* situated in the west; coming from the west; toward the west. 서쪽에 있는; 서쪽에서 오는; 서향(西向)의. ¶ *a ~ room* 〔*window*〕.
— *adv.* toward, in or from the west. 서쪽에; 서쪽으로〔에서〕. ¶ *sail* 〔*travel*〕 *~* 서쪽으로 항해〔여행〕하다. [E.]
go west, 《*colloq.*》 **a**) die. 죽다. **b**) be destroyed; be damaged or ruined. 결딴나다; 망하다.

west·er·ly [wéstərli] *adj., adv.* of, toward, in or from the west. 서(쪽)의; 서쪽으로부터(의); 서쪽으로(의). ¶ *a ~ wind* 서풍 / *The wind blows ~.* 바람이 서쪽으로 분다 / *a light ~ breeze* 서쪽에서 부는 남실바람 / *We set off in a ~ direction.* 우리는 서쪽을 향해 길을 떠났다.

:west·ern [wéstərn] *adj.* of, toward, from or in the west. 서(쪽)의; 서쪽으로부터의. ¶ *the ~ front* 서부 전선 / *The Russian ballet is making a tour of ~ Europe.* 러시아 발레단이 서유럽을 순회 공연하고 있다.
— *n.* **1** =westerner. **2** a story or film dealing with cowboy or frontier life in the American West. (개척 시대의 미국 서부 생활을 묘사한) 서부 이야기〔영화〕; 웨스턴. ¶ *an Italian ~* 이탈리아 제작의 서부극 영화.

west·ern·er [wéstərnər] *n.* a native of the west, esp. of the western United States. (미국의) 서부(지방) 사람.

west·ern·i·za·tion [wèstərnizéiʃən] *n.* Ⓤ the act of westernizing. 서구화(西歐化).

west·ern·ize [wéstərnàiz] *vt.* (P6) introduce (the idea, habits or things) of Western civilization. (생각·습관)을 서구화하다.

west·ern·most [wéstərnmòust / -məst] *adj.* farthest west. 가장 서쪽의; 극서의.

West·min·ster [wéstmìnstər] *n.* **1** the part of London where Westminster Abbey and the Houses of Parliament are located. 웨스트민스터 지구. **2** the Houses of Parliament. 영국 국회 의사당.
at Westminster, at the Diet. 의회에서.

West Virginia [´-´--] *n.* the eastern state of the United States. 웨스트 버지니아. 參考 W.Va.로 생략. 주도는 Charleston.

***west·ward** [wéstwərd] *adj., adv.* toward the west. 서향(西向)의; 서쪽에.

west·wards [wéstwərdz] *adv.* =westward.

:wet [wet] *adj.* (**wet·ter, wet·test**) **1** covered with water or another liquid; damp. 젖은; 습한; 축축한. ¶ *The grass is ~ with dew.* 잔디가 이슬에 젖어 있다 / *It is dangerous to drive on ~ roads.* 젖은 도로에서의 운전은 위험하다 / *Take off your ~ clothes.* 젖은 옷을 벗어라 / *Her eyes were ~ with tears.* 그녀의 눈은 눈물에 젖어 있었다. **2** (of paint, ink, etc.) not yet dry. (페인트 등이) 덜 마른. ¶ *Wet Paint.* 칠 주의《게시》. **3** rainy. 비의; 비 내리는. ¶ *a ~ day* / *~ or fine* 비가 오건 개건 / *a ~ season* 장마철. **4** 《U.S. *colloq.*》 not forbidding the sale of alcoholic drinks. 주류 판매를 허락하는 (opp. dry). ¶ *a ~ town* 〔*state*〕 비(非)금주 도시〔주〕.
be all wet, 《U.S.》 be quite wrong. 전적으로 틀리다.
wet behind the ears ⇨*ear*[1].
wet through =***wet to the skin,*** with one's clothes soaked. 흠뻑 젖어.
— *v.* (**wet** or **wet·ted, wet·ting**) *vt.* (P6) make (something) wet; cover with any liquid. …을 적시다. ¶ *~ the bed* 자면서 오줌 싸다. — *vi.* become wet. 젖다.
wet a bargain, close a bargain with drink. 한잔하고 계약을 맺다.
wet one's whistle, 《*colloq.*》 drink. 술 마시다; 한잔하다.
— *n.* **1** Ⓤ 《often *the ~* 》 liquid which wets something; water; wetness. 수분; 물; 습기; 물기. **2** 《usu. *the ~*》 rain or rainy weather. 비; 비내림; 강우; 우천(雨天). ¶ *He walked in the ~ with her.* 그는 그녀와 함께 빗속을 걸었다 / *Come in out of ~.* 비 맞지 말고 들어오시오. **3** Ⓒ 《*sl.*》 drink. 술. ¶ *have a ~* 한잔하다. **4** Ⓒ 《U.S. *colloq.*》 an anti-Prohibitionist. 금주 반대론자(opp. dry). [E. (→water)]

wet blanket [´ ´-] *n.* a person who makes others feel sad or hopeless, or who spoils the pleasure of a party, etc. 낙심시키는〔흥을 깨는〕 사람.

wet goods [´ ´] *n.* alcoholic liquor. 주류; 술.

weth·er [wéðər] *n.* Ⓒ a male sheep. (거세한) 수양. [E.]

wet nurse [´ ´] *n.* a woman who suckles another's child. 유모(乳母)(cf. *dry nurse*). [*wet*]

***we've** [wiːv, wiv] =we have.

whack [*h*wæk] *n.* Ⓒ **1** 《*colloq.*》 a sharp, noisy blow. 철썩 때리기; 세게 치기. **2** 《*colloq.*》 a share; portion. 분배; 몫. ¶ *Have you all had your ~?* 다들 몫은 받았나. **3** 《U.S.》 trial; attempt. 시도; 기도.
have a whack at, 《*colloq.*》 try one's hand at. …을 시도하다; 해 보다.
have one's whack of, 《*colloq.*》 have as much as one wants. …을 실컷 맛보다.
— *vt.* (P6,13) strike (someone or something) with a sharp blow. …을 냅다 갈기다. [Imit.]

whale [*h*weil] *n.* Ⓒ **1** a huge animal which lives in the sea. 고래. **2** a person or thing that is very large. 거대한 사람〔물건〕.
a whale of, 《*colloq.*》 exceedingly much of; no end of. 굉장한; 대단한. ¶ *We had a ~ of a (good) time.* 아주 재미있게 지냈다 / *a ~ of a scholar* 〔*wrestler*〕 대단한 학자〔씨름꾼〕.

***be a whale on* [*at, for*],** be very good at or keen on (something). …에 뛰어나다; 매우 열심이다.

very like a whale, an ironical assent to an absurd statement. 아무렴 그렇고 말고요《모순된 상대방의 말을 비꼬는 투》.

— *vi.* (P1) hunt whales. 고래잡이하다. [E.]

whale·boat [*h*wéilbòut] *n.* Ⓒ a long and narrow ship's lifeboat formerly used in catching whales. (앞뒤가 뾰족한) 구명용 보트《원래 포경용》.

whale·bone [*h*wéilbòun] *n.* **1** Ⓤ an elastic, horny substance in the upper jaw of certain whales. 고래수염. **2** Ⓒ a thing made of whalebone, e.g. a corset stay. (고래수염) 세공품.

whal·er [*h*wéilər] *n.* Ⓒ **1** a person who hunts whales. 고래잡이《사람》. **2** a ship used in hunting whales. 포경선.

whang [*h*wæŋ] *vt.* (P6,13) strike (something) with a heavy blow. …을 강타하다[세게 치다]. — *n.* Ⓒ a sharp, heavy blow. 강타. [M.E. *thwang*]

***wharf** [*h*wɔːrf] *n.* (*pl.* **wharves** or **wharfs**) a platform built on the shore where a ship can load or unload; a pier; a quay. 부두; 선창. [E.=dam]

wharf·age [*h*wɔ́ːrfidʒ] *n.* Ⓤ **1** the use of a wharf. 부두 사용. **2** the charge made for the use of a wharf. 부두 사용료. [↑]

⁑**what** [*h*wɑt, *h*wʌt, *h*wət] *adj.* **1** 《*interrogative adjective*》 ⓐ which; which kind of, etc. 어떤; 무슨; 어느. ¶ *What news?* 뭐 별난 소식이 있나 / *What ship is that?* 저건 무슨 배냐 / *I know ~ books you will need.* 어떤 책이 너에게 필요한지를 안다 / *What kind of person is he?* 그는 어떤 사람이냐 / *I don't know ~ plans he has made.* 그의 계획이 무엇인지 모른다. ⓑ how much. 얼마나; 얼마만큼. ¶ *What money have you got?* 돈을 얼마나 갖고 있지. **2** 《in *exclamations*》 how greatly, etc. 얼마나; 참(으로). ¶ *What an idea!* 거참 멋있는 생각이군 / *What a fine day* (*it is*)*!* 정말 좋은 날씨군 / *What splendid ships* (*they are*)*!* 기막히게 좋은 배들이군 / *What fools they are!* 저런 멍텅구리를 봤나 / *What a pity* (*it is*)*!* 저런; 가엾기도 해라 / *What a strange thing to say!* 거참; 이상한 말도 하는군. **3** 《*relative adjective*》 the … that; as much [many] as; any … that. (…하는) 바의 그; (…하는) 만큼의; (…하는) 어떤. ¶ *I will give you ~ help I can.* 내가 도울 수 있는 한 도와 주겠다 / *He has sold ~ books he had.* 그는 가지고 있던 책들을 팔았다 / *Wear ~ clothes you please.* 어떤 옷이든 좋을 대로 입으십시오 / *Lend me ~ money you can.* 빌려줄 수 있는 대로 돈을 빌려다오.

— *pron.* **1** 《*interrogative pronoun*》 what thing; what things. 무엇; 어떤 것[일]. ¶ *What has happened?* 무슨 일이 생겼나 / *What is the matter with you?* 무슨 일인가 / *What is his name?* 그의 이름이 뭐냐 / *What is he?* 무엇하는 사람이냐 / *What are those things on the table?* 탁자 위에 있는 그것들은 뭐냐 / *What are you talking about?* 무슨 얘기를 하고 있는 거냐 / *What is the price?* 값은 얼마냐 / *What about it?* 그걸 어떻게 생각하나 / *I was at a loss ~ to do.* 어찌해야 좋을지 난감했다 / *What do you say to …?* …하면 어떨까; …하지 않겠나 / *What next?* 다음은 어떻게 되나 / *Do you know ~ it is?* 그게 뭔지 아니 / *Who did ~?* 누가 무엇을 했다고 / *Because ~?* 원인이 뭔데 / *What followed is doubtful.* 그 다음은 어찌되었는지 잘 모르겠다 / *What would I not give to see her!* 그녀를 만날 수만 있다면 무엇을 못 주겠어. **2** 《in *exclamations*》 how much; what a large amount. 얼마; 무엇. ¶ *What, do you really mean it?* 뭐라고, 진정으로 하는 말이냐 / *What these ancient walls could tell us!* 이 옛 성벽은 얼마나 많은 사연을 우리에게 말해 주는가 / *What rubbish you talk!* 그게 무슨 되지 않은 소리냐. **3** 《*relative pronoun*》 that which; those which. (…하는) 바의 것[일]. ¶ *I don't understand ~ he says.* 그가 말하는 것을 알아듣지 못하겠다 / *What I say is true.* 내가 말하는 것은 사실이다 / *He lost his money and, ~ was worse, his life.* 그는 돈을 잃었고 게다가 더 안된 것은 목숨까지 잃은 것이다 / *What followed was unpleasant.* 다음에 일어난 일은 불쾌했다. **4** anything that; whatever. (…하는) 무엇이건. ¶ *Do ~ you please.* 너 좋을 대로 해라. **5** the kind of thing or person that; such. … 같은 물건[사람]. ¶ *She is not ~ she was.* 그녀는 과거의 그녀가 아니다.

and what not, and other things of all sorts; and so forth. …등등; …따위.

I know what. I have an idea. 좋은 생각이 있다.

I will tell you what. Here is a suggestion. 실은 이렇다; 그럼 이렇게 하지.

know what's what, have common sense. 상식이 있다; 요령[실정]을 알고 있다.

no matter what …, in spite of anything that … (비록) 무엇이 …한다 해도.

So what? 《*colloq.*》 =What of it?

What about …? ⇨about.

what for, why; for what reason or purpose. 무엇 때문에; 어째서.

What if …? What is[will be] the result if …? …라면 어찌 될까. ¶ *What if we were to try?* 우리가 해본다면 어떻게 될까 / *What if she can't come after all?* 어쨌건 그녀가 못 온다면 어떻게 되지.

What is that to you? What business or concern is that of yours? 그것이 네게 무슨 상관이 있나; 그것을 알아 무엇 하는가.

What … like? 《asking for *an explanation*》 어떤 …인가. ¶ *What's the weather like this morning?* 오늘 아침 날씨는 어떠냐 / *What is* *he like ?* 그는 어떤 사람이냐.

What of it ? What does it matter? 그게 어떻단 말이냐. ¶ *Well, ~ of it ?* 그래, 그게 어쨌다는 거냐.

what's what, 《*colloq.*》 the true state of affairs. 사실; 진상. ¶ *He knows what's ~ in wives.* 그는 아내란 무엇인지 안다.

What though ... ? It doesn't matter if ... ? (설사 …이더라도) 무슨 상관이냐. ¶ *What though* 〔*if*〕 *we are poor ?* 우리가 가난한들 무슨 상관이냐 / *What though the sky is cloudy today ?* 오늘 날씨가 흐리다고 무슨 상관이냐.

— *adv.* 《in *questions*》 how much; in what way. 얼마나; 어떻게. ¶ *What does it profit you ?* 그게 네게 얼마만큼 이익이 되나 / *What is he the better for it ?* 그것으로 그가 어느 정도 이득을 얻나 / *What does it matter ?* 그것이 어쨌다는 건가; 아무래도 상관없지 않은가.

what with... and (***what with***), owing partly to (one thing) and partly to (another). …이다 …이다 하여. ¶ *What with the wind and* (*~ with*) *the rain our trip was spoiled.* 바람이니 비니 하여 우리 여행은 엉망이 됐다 / *What with money and* (*~ with*) *promises, I bribed him.* 돈이랑 약속으로 그를 매수했다.

— *conj.* 《*colloq.*》 as much as; as many as. …만큼; …대로. ¶ *I helped him ~ I could.* 내가 할 수 있는 만큼 그를 도왔다.

but what, 《*colloq.*》 that ... not. …하지 않는. ¶ *There was not a day but ~ it rained.* 비 오지 않는 날이 없었다.

— *interj.* 《as *an exclamation* to show *surprise, anger, liking, etc.*》 뭐; 뭣이라고. ¶ *What! rain again ?* 뭐라고, 또 비냐 / *What ! no dinner !* 뭐, 식사가 없다고. [E.]

what·e'er [*h*wɑtέər, *h*wʌt- / *h*wɔt-] *pron., adj.* 《*poet.*》 =whatever.

:what·ev·er [*h*wɑtévər, *h*wʌt- / *h*wɔt-] *pron.* **1** anything that. 무엇이건. ¶ *You shall have ~ you like.* 네가 좋아하는 거라면 뭐든 주겠다 / *Do ~ you think fit.* 온당하다 생각하면 무엇이든 해라 / *Whatever I have is yours.* 내가 가진 것은 무엇이든 네 것이다. **2** no matter what. 무엇이 …이더라도. ¶ *Do it ~ happens.* 무슨 일이 있어도 그것을 해라 / *Whatever it is, it is all right with me.* 그게 무엇이든 내게는 지장이 없소 / *I am right ~ you may think.* 네가 어떻게 생각하든 내가 옳다 / *Whatever happens, I will go.* 무슨 일이 생기든 나는 가겠다. **3** 《*colloq.*》《in *interrogative,* a strong form of *what*》 what in the world. 도대체 무엇이〔을〕. ¶ *Whatever has happened ?* 도대체 무슨 일이 일어났는가 / *Whatever are you doing ?* 도대체 뭘하고 있니 / *Look at that strange animal ! Whatever is it ?* 저 괴상한 짐승 좀 봐. 도대체 뭘까.

— *adj.* **1** of no matter what type, degree, etc. 어떤 …이라도. ¶ *Whatever orders he gives are obeyed.* 그가 무슨 명령을 하더라도 잘 지켜진다 / *Whatever he says, do it.* 그가 뭐라건 그것은 해라 / *You may have ~ help you want.* 네가 원한다면 무엇이든 도와 주마 / *Whatever excuses he may make, we will not believe him.* 그가 무슨 변명을 하든 우리는 믿지 않을 거다 / *Whatever result follow, I will consent.* 결과가 어떻든 나는 동의하겠다. **2** being what or who it may be. 비록 …일지라도. ¶ *Whatever task it may be, you should not slight it.* 무슨 일이든 소홀해서는 안 된다. **3** 《in *negative* or *interrogative,* used after *no* or *any*》 of any kind; at all. 어떤 …도; 조금의 …도. ¶ *There is no doubt ~ .* 추호의 의혹도 없다 / *Is there any chance ~ ?* 조금이라도 가망은 있소 / *I can see nothing ~ .* 아무것도 보이지 않는다 / *No one ~ would accept.* 아무도 수락하지 않을 것이다. [E.]

what·not [*h*wátnàt, *h*wʌ́t- / *h*wɔ́tnɔ̀t] *n.* Ⓒ a set of shelves for books, small ornaments, etc. 장식 선반. [*what, not*]

〈whatnot〉

·what's [*h*wʌts, *h*wɑts, *h*wəts / *h*wɔts] 《*colloq.*》 =what is; what has; what does.

what·so·e'er [*h*wʌ̀tsouέər, *h*wɑ̀t- / *h*wɔ̀t-] *pron., adj.* 《*poet.*》 =whatsoever. [*what*]

what·so·ev·er [*h*wʌ̀tsouévər, *h*wɑ̀t- / *h*wɔ̀t-] *adj., pron.* 《*arch., emph.*》 =whatever.

:wheat [*h*wi:t] *n.* Ⓤ the grain from which flour is made; the plant on which this grain grows. 밀(cf. *barley, rye, oats*). [E.]

wheat·en [*h*wí:tn] *adj.* 《*lit.*》 made of wheat or wheat flour. 밀(가루)로 만든. [↑]

whee·dle [*h*wí:dl] *vt.* (P6,13) **1** 《*into*》 influence (someone) by flattery; coax. …을 감언으로 유혹하다. ¶ *The children wheedled their mother into letting them go on the picnic.* 아이들은 어머니를 구슬러 소풍을 갔다 / *She wheedled him into taking her with him.* 그녀는 같이 데리고 가달라고 그를 구워삶았다. **2** 《*out of*》 get (something) by flattery. 감언이설로 속이다〔우려내다〕. ¶ *He wheedled me out of the money.* 그는 갖은 말을 다해 내게서 돈을 알겨냈다. [E.]

:wheel [*h*wi:l] *n.* Ⓒ **1** a round frame turning on a central axis or axle. (수레)바퀴. ¶ *Most cars have four wheels, but this one has only three.* 모든 차는 바퀴가 넷인데 이 차는 셋뿐이다. **2** a vehicle or machine with a wheel or wheels as an essential part; 《*colloq.*》 a bicycle. 바퀴 달린 것; 자전거. ¶ *a steering ~* (선박의) 타륜(舵輪) / *a spinning ~* 물레 (바퀴) / *I'm rather tired; will you take the ~ ?* 나 좀 피곤한데, 네가 운전해라. **3** a round, movable part of a machine. (기계의) 회전 부분. **4** a movement like the turning of a wheel. 회전; 선회 운동. ¶ *Platoon, right ~!* 소대, 줄줄이 우로가 / *the wheels and somersaults of gulls* 갈매기들의 선회와 공중제비. **5** 《usu. *pl.*》 the propelling or driving force. 원동력; 추진〔지배〕력.

be at the wheel, **a**) drive or steer a car or ship, etc. 타륜(舵輪)〔핸들〕을 잡다. **b**) be in control. 지배권을 잡다.

break a butterfly upon a wheel, use a powerful means to gain a small object. 아무것도 아닌 일에 크게 애쓰다; 우도할계(牛刀割鷄).

go on wheels, go on smoothly. 순조롭게 진행되다.

put a spoke in** someone's **wheel, hinder someone; prevent someone from making progress. 아무를 훼방하다.

put 〔***set***〕 *one's* ***shoulder to the wheel*** ⇨ shoulder.

the man at the wheel, a steersman; a person on whom responsibility rests. 키잡이; 타수; 책임자.

wheel of fortune, Fortune's wheel; the ups and downs of life; fate. 운명(의 수레바퀴); 영고 성쇠.

wheels within wheels, complicated circumstances. 얽히고 설킨 사정.

— *vt.* (P6,7) **1** carry or move (something) on wheels. …을 수레로 나르다. **2** cause to turn; cause (a line of soldiers) to turn around like a wheel. …을 선회시키다; (대열)의 방향을 바꾸게 하다. ¶ *The rider wheeled his horse about.* 기수는 말머리를 돌렸다. **3** provide (something) with wheels. …에 바퀴를 달다.

— *vi.* (P1,2A) **1** turn; (of a line of soldiers or a bird) turn around like a wheel. 선회하다; (대열이) 방향을 바꾸다. ¶ *She wheeled round to face her accusers.* 그녀는 뒤돌아서서 자기를 비난하는 사람들을 노려봤다 / *The vultures were wheeling over head.* 독수리가 머리 위를 빙빙 돌고 있었다. **2** 《*colloq.*》 ride a bicycle. 자전거를 타다. [E.]

wheel·bar·row [*h*wíːlbæ̀rou] *n.* Ⓒ a vehicle with one wheel and two handles pushed by hand. (외바퀴) 손수레. [↑]

wheel chair [⌐⌐] *n.* a chair with wheels used by a person who can't walk. (환자용) 휠체어.

wheeled [*h*wiːld] *adj.* with wheels. 바퀴 달린. ¶ *a two-wheeled cart* 이륜 달구지.

wheel·wright [*h*wíːlràit] *n.* Ⓒ a person who makes or repairs vehicles. 수레(바퀴) 만드는〔수리하는〕 사람.

wheeze [*h*wiːz] *vi.* (P1) **1** breathe hard and noisily. 숨을 씨근거리다. ¶ *Reaching the top of the stairs he was panting and wheezing.* 계단 꼭대기에 닿자 그는 숨이 차서 씨근거리고 있었다. **2** make a sound like this. 씨근거리다. — *vt.* (P7) say (something) with a wheezing sound. …을 씨근〔식식〕거리며 말하다. — *n.* Ⓒ **1** noisy breathing; the sound of this. 식식하는 숨소리. **2** 《*sl.*》 an old and funny saying or story. 진부한 농담; 우스갯소리. [N.=hiss]

wheez·y [*h*wíːzi] *adj.* (**wheez·i·er, wheez·i·est**) making noises in breathing. 씨근거리는; 헐떡거리는.

whelk [*h*welk] *n.* Ⓒ a small sea animal with a spiral shell, used for food in Europe. 쇠고둥. [E.]

whelm [*h*welm] *vt.* (P6) 《*poet.*》 **1** cover with water; engulf. 물에 잠기다; 파도에 휩쓸리다. **2** crush or ruin completely. …을 부수다; 결딴내다. [E.]

whelp [*h*welp] *n.* Ⓒ **1** the young of a dog, lion, fox, etc. (개·사자 따위의) 새끼. **2** 《*contempt.*》 an unpleasant, worthless young man or boy. 건달; 개구쟁이. — *vt., vi.* (P6; 1) (of animals) give birth (to young). (새끼를) 낳다. [E.]

:when [*h*wen] *adv.* **1** 《*interrogative adverb*》 at what time. 언제. ¶ *When did you see her last?* 마지막으로 그녀를 만난 것이 언제지 / *Tell me ~ to start.* 언제 떠나야 좋을지 말해 다오 / *When will you come?* 언제 오지 / *I don't know ~ it was* 〔*to arrive*〕. 그게 언제였는지〔언제 도착하는지〕 모르겠다. **2** 《*relative adverb*》 at or on which; and then; just then. …하는 (때); 그리고〔그러자〕 그 때. ¶ *I don't know the time ~ he will arrive.* 그가 도착하는 시간을 모른다 / *We were about to start, ~ it began to rain.* 마침 나가려는데 그 때부터 비가 오기 시작했다 / *It was a time ~ motorcars were rare.* 자동차가 드문 때였다 / *You always come on the days ~ I am busy.* 넌 늘 내가 바쁠 때 오는구나 / *Wait till six, ~ he will be back.* 여섯 시까지 기다려라, 그땐 그가 돌아올 것이다 / *I was about to reply, ~ Jones cut.* 내가 대답을 하려던 참에 존스가 끼어들었다.

Say when. (in pouring drinks, etc.) Tell me when to stop. 됐을 때 말해라《술·차 따위를 따를 때 적당한 분량이 되면 그만 따르라고 하라는 말》. 參考 이에 대한 대답은 "When."(됐다).

— *conj.* **1** at, during, or after the time that. (…하는) 때에. ¶ *~ due* 만기에는 / *~ speaking* 말할 때 / *~ ready* 준비가 되면 / *You may leave ~ you have finished your task.* 일이 끝나면 가도 좋다 / *I always see him at the restaurant ~ I'm having lunch.* 식당에서 점심을 먹을 때는 늘 그를 만난다 / *It was raining ~ we started.* 우리가 출발했을 땐 비가 내리고 있었다. **2** every time that. (…하는) 때는 언제나. ¶ *She cries ~ you criticize her.* 네가 그녀를 비난하면 그녀는 늘 운다 / *When he goes out, he takes his dog with him.* 외출할 때 그는항상 개를 데리고 다닌다 / *A dog wags his tail ~ pleased.* 개는 기분이 좋으면 늘 꼬리를 흔든다 / *It is cold ~ it snows.* 눈만 오면 춥다. **3** in spite of the fact that; although; though. …임에도 불구하고; …인데도. ¶ *We have only three books ~ we need five.* 책이 다섯 권 필요한데 세 권뿐이다 / *He walks ~ he might ride.* 차를 타도 될 텐데 그는 걷는다. **4** if; in the event that. …하면; …이면. ¶ *I'll give it to you ~ you say, 'Please'.* '아무쪼록'이라고 하면 그걸 네게 주겠다. **5** being what time it may be. 언제 …하더라도. ¶ *Die ~ you will, I will be with you.* 네가 언제 죽든 나는 너와 함께 있겠다. **6** considering the fact that. …을 생각〔고려〕하면. ¶ *How can I refuse ~ refusal means death?* 거절하면 죽일 터인데 어떻게 거절할 수 있나.

— *pron.* what time; which time. 언제. ¶ *Since ~ has she been ill?* 그녀가 언제부터 앓고 있나 / *Till ~ can you stay?* 언제까지 머물 수 있겠나 / *Since ~ have you been here?* 언제부터 여기 와 있나.

— *n.* 《rare》《*the* ~》 the time or moment. 때. ¶ (*the*) *~ and* (*the*) *where* 때와 장소 / *He told me the ~ and the why of it.* 그는 내게 그 시기와 이유에 대해서 말했다. [E.]

:whence [*h*wens] *adv.* 《*poet., arch.*》 **1** 《*interrogative adverb*》 from what place; from where. 어디서(opp. whither). ¶ *Whence did you come?* 당신은 어디서 왔소 / *Tell me ~ you came.* 출신지가 어딘지 말해봐라 / *Whence comes it that …?* 어째서 …이냐. **2** 《*relative adverb*》 ⓐ from which. …하는. ¶ *Let him return to the place ~ he came.* 그가 온 데로 돌아가게 해라. ⓑ to the place from which. …하는 그 곳에. ¶ *Return ~ you came.* 네가 있던 곳으로 돌아가라.

— *pron.* **1** 《*interrogative pronoun*》 what starting place. 어디《기원을 물음》. ¶ *From ~ is he?* 그는 어디 출신이냐. **2** 《*relative pronoun*》 which source. …하는 그 곳. ¶ *the source from ~ these evils spring* 이런 악이 생기는 근원. [*when*]

whene'er [*h*wenέər] *adv.* 《*poet.*》 = whenever.

:when·ev·er [*h*wenévər] *conj., adv.* **1** at any time; at whatever time. 언제든; …할 때마다. ¶ *I will see him ~ he likes to come.* 그가 찾아오면 언제든 만나겠다 / *Whenever I come here it rains!* 여기 올 때마다 비가 온단 말이야. **2** 《*emph.*》 when in the world. 도대체 언제. ¶ *Whenever did you buy that?* 대체 그것은 언제 샀어 / *Whenever did I say so?* 대관절 언제 내가 그런 말을 했지. [↑]

:where [*h*wεər] *adv.* **1** 《*interrogative adverb*》 at or in what place; to or toward what place; in what respect; from what place or source. 어디에; 어디로; 어떤 점에서; 어디서부터. ¶ *Where are you going?* 어디로 가는 거냐 / *Where do I come into the matter?* 어떤 점에서 그 사건을 다룰까요 / *Where do you live?* 너는 어디에 사니 / *Where did you get your information?* 어디서 정보를 얻었느냐 / *Where are you getting off?* (버스 등에서) 어디서 내리느냐 / *Where are you going to stay?* 어디서 머물거니 / *Where shall we be if the price falls?* 값이 떨어지면 우린 어떻게 됩니까 / *Where is everybody?* 다 어디 있나. **2** 《*relative adverb*》 in or to which; and there. …하는 바의 (장소); 그리고 거기서. ¶ *This is the house ~ I was born.* 이 집에서 내가 태어났다 / *He went to Paris, ~ he stayed for a week.* 그는 파리로 가서, (거기서) 1주일 동안 체류했다 / *This is a situation ~ great care is needed.* 이건 대단한 신경을 써야 하는 사태다.

— *conj.* at, in, or to the place or situation in which. …하는 곳에〔에서, 으로〕. ¶ *You may go ~ you like.* 가고 싶은 데로 가거라 / *Leave the book ~ he can get it.* 그가 집을 수 있는 데에 책을 둬라 / 《*prov.*》 *Where there's a will, there's a way.* 뜻이 있는 곳에 길이 있다 / *We must camp ~ we can get water.* 물이 있는 곳에서 야영해야 한다.

— *pron.* **1** 《*interrogative pronoun*》 what place. 어디. ¶ *Where are you going to?* 어딜 가는 거냐 / *Where do you come from?* 어디서 왔나요; 출신지는 어딥니까 / *Where from?* 어디서 왔지 / *Where is he at?* 그는 어디 있나. **2** 《*relative pronoun*》 the place at, in or to which. (…하는) 장소. ¶ *This is the place ~ he comes from.* 여기가 그의 출신지다 / *This is ~ I live.* 여기가 내가 사는 곳이다 / *He came up to ~ we were.* 그는 우리가 있는 곳으로 왔다 / *We stayed a day in Athens, from ~ we proceeded to Cairo.* 아테네에서 하룻밤 자고, 거기서 카이로로 계속 갔다.

— *n.* Ⓤ 《*the* ~》 the place. 장소. ¶ *the wheres and the whens* 장소와 일시 / *The ~ and when are not known.* 장소와 시간은 미상이다. [E.]

where·a·bouts [*h*wέərəbàuts] *adv.* at or near what place; where. 어디쯤에(서); …하는 곳. ¶ *Whereabouts did you put it?* 그걸 어디쯤에 두었나 / *Whereabouts in Seoul do you live?* 서울 어디쯤에 살고 있소. — *n.* 《*one's* or *the* ~, used as *sing.* or *pl.*》 the place where a person or thing is. 있는 곳; 소재; 행방. ¶ *Her ~ is* 〔*are*〕 *still unknown.* 그의 행방은 아직 불명이다 / *Do you know his present ~?* 지금 그가 있는 곳을 알고 있나.

***where·as** [*h*wεərǽz] *conj.* **1** 《*lit.*》 considering that; since. …인 까닭에; 때문에. **2** on the contrary; while; but. …임에도; …에 반하여. ¶ *He is fat, ~ his wife is thin.* 그는 뚱뚱한데 그의 아내는 말랐다 / *I thought you were wrong, ~ actually you were right.* 나는 네가 틀렸다고 생각을 했었는데 사실은 네가 옳았다.

where·at [*h*wεərǽt] *adv.* 《*arch.*》 at which. 그것에 대하여. ¶ *the things ~ you are displeased.* 네 마음에 들지 않는 것들.

***where·by** [*h*wεərbái] *adv.* **1** by what; why; how. 무엇에; 무엇에 의해; 어째서.

¶ *Whereby did he escape ?* 무엇 때문에 도망갔지 / *Whereby will he do it ?* 그가 어떻게 그것을 할까 / *Whereby shall we know him ?* 무엇으로 우리가 그를 알아볼 수 있을까. **2** by which. 그것에 의해. ¶ *This is the only way ~ we live.* 이것이 우리의 유일한 생활 방편이다.

:where·fore [*h*wέərfɔ̀ːr] *adv.* 《*arch.*》 **1** for what reason; why. 왜; 무엇 때문에. ¶ *Wherefore does she cry ?* 그 여자가 왜 울지 / *Wherefore art thou Romeo ?* 어째서 그대는 로미오인가. **2** for which reason. 그러므로; 그 때문에. ¶ *He was angry, ~ I was afraid.* 그는 화가 나 있었다. 그래서 나는 두려웠다. — *n.* 《*the ~s*》 the reason. 이유. ¶ *the why(s) and wherefore(s) of it* 그 까닭.

where·in [*h*wɛərín] *adv.* 《*lit.*》 **1** in what; in what point. 무엇이; 어디가; 어느 점이. ¶ *Wherein am I wrong ?* 나의 어디가 나쁘단 말인가 / *Wherein lies the difficulty ?* 어떤 점이 어려우냐 / *Wherein is it wrong ?* 어느 점이 틀렸나. **2** in which. 그 안에(서). ¶ *the room ~ she was murdered* 그녀가 살해된 방.

where·of [*h*wɛərάv / -ɔ́v] *adv.* 《*arch.*》 **1** of what. 무엇으로; 무엇의; 무엇에 관하여. ¶ *Whereof does he talk ?* 그가 무엇에 관해 얘기하느냐. **2** of which; of whom. 그것에 관하여; 그것의; 그 사람의. ¶ *the matter ~ he talks* 그가 말하고 있는 화제.

where·on [*h*wɛərάn / -rɔ́n] *adv.* 《*arch.*》 **1** on what; to whom. 무엇에 (관해); 누구에게. ¶ *Whereon do you rely ?* 너는 무엇에 의지하나. **2** on which. 그 위에; 그것에. ¶ *a person ~ we depend* 우리가 의지하고 있는 사람 / *the table ~ lay the food* 음식이 차려진 식탁.

where·so·ev·er [*h*wὲərsouévər] *adv.* 《*arch., emph.*》 =wherever.

where·to [*h*wɛərtúː] *adv.* 《*arch.*》 **1** to what place; where; for what. 어디로; 무엇 때문에. ¶ *Whereto did you go yesterday ?* 어제 어디로 갔었나 / *Whereto are we to work ?* 우리가 무엇 때문에 일을 하는 거지. **2** to which. 그것에; 거기로. ¶ *the address ~ the letter is to be sent* 서신의 수신처 / *the point ~ they hasten* 그들이 서둘러 가는 지점.

where·un·to [*h*wɛərʌ́ntuː, ⌐-⌐] *adv.* 《*arch.*》 =whereto.

where·up·on [*h*wὲərəpάn / -pɔ́n] *adv.* 《*lit.*》 **1** upon what; whereon. 무엇에; 누구에게. **2** upon or at which; as the result of which; after which. 그래서; 그 후에. ¶ *Whereupon he rose to speak.* 그래서 그는 발언하려고 일어섰다 / *..., ~ we ate lunch.* 그리고 우리는 점심을 먹었다.

:wher·ev·er [*h*wɛərévər] *adv.* **1** in whatever place; to any place. 어디든지; 어디로든지. ¶ *Wherever you go, I go too.* 네가 어디로 가든 나도 가겠다. **2** 《*colloq.*》 where. 어디에; 어디로; 어디서. ¶ *Wherever did you get that idea ?* 어디서 그걸 알았나. **3** 《*colloq., emph.*》 where in the world. 도대체 어디에 〔서, 로〕. ¶ *Wherever are you going ?* 대체 어디로 간다는 거냐.

where·with [*h*wɛərwíð, -wíθ] *adv.* 《*arch.*》 **1** with what. 무엇을 가지고; 무엇으로. ¶ *Wherewith did you make this ?* 무엇으로 이걸 만들었나. **2** with which. 그것을 가지고; 그것으로. ¶ *without even a shirt ~ to cover one's body.* 몸을 가릴 셔츠조차 없이.

where·with·al [*h*wέərwiðɔ̀ːl, -wiθ-] *adv.* 《*arch.*》 =wherewith. — [*h*wέəwiðɔ̀ːl] *n.* 《*the ~*》 the money, etc. needed. 필요한 돈(따위). ¶ *Has she the ~ to pay for the trip ?* 그녀에게 여비는 있나.

whet [*h*wet] *vt.* (**whet·ted, whet·ting**) (P6) **1** sharpen. …을 갈다. ¶ *~ a knife* 칼을 갈다. **2** cause (one's appetite, etc.) to increase. (식욕 따위)를 돋우다; 자극하다. ¶ *The smell of food whetted my appetite.* 그 음식 냄새가 식욕을 자극했다. — *n.* **1** Ⓤ the act of whetting. 갊; 연마(硏磨); 자극. **2** Ⓒ an appetizer, like wine. 식욕을 돋우는 것; 반주. [F. *hwæt* sharp]

:wheth·er [*h*wéðər] *conj.* **1** 《introducing *an indirect question*》 if it be the case or fact that ... …인지 어떤지. 參考 whether ~ or…의 형식이 될 경우가 많음. ¶ *I don't know ~ it is true or not.* 그것이 정말인지 아닌지 모르겠다 / *I asked him ~ he would come.* 그에게 올지 어떨지를 물었다 / *I don't know ~ to laugh or to cry.* 웃어야 할지 울어야 할지 모르겠다 / *I wonder ~ he will go himself.* 그가 갈는지 모르겠다 / *I don't know ~ he is ill.* 그가 아픈지 알 수 없다 / *The question is ~ he is fit to travel.* 문제는 그가 여행에 견딜지 어떨지다. **2** in either case that ...; no matter if ... or. …이든 아니든. ¶ *You must do it ~ you like it or not.* 네가 좋아하든 싫어하든 그걸 하지 않으면 안 된다 / *Whether sick or well she was always cheerful.* 그녀는 아프건 안 아프건 늘 명랑했다 / *Whether we help him or not, he will fail.* 우리가 도와 주건 아니건 그는 실패한다. [E.]

whether or no, in either case. 하여튼; 어느 쪽이든. ¶ *We must keep our promise(,) ~ or no.* 가부간 우린 약속을 지켜야 한다.

whet·stone [*h*wétstòun] *n.* Ⓒ a stone for sharpening knives or blades. 숫돌. [*whet*]

whew [*h*wjuː, hjuː] *interj.* an exclamation of surprise, disgust, etc. 아이구; 어휴; 허. [Imit.]

whey [*h*wei] *n.* Ⓤ the thin, watery part of milk that is separated from the curds in making cheese. 유장(乳漿). [E.]

:which [*h*witʃ] *adj.* **1** 《*interrogative adjective*》 being what one or ones out of a group. 어느 쪽의; 어느. ¶ *Which book is yours ?* 어느 게 네 책이냐 / *Which one do you mean ?* 어느 것을 말하느냐 / *Which subject do you like best ?* 어느 과목을 제일

좋아하는가 / *Which boy won the prize ?* 어느 소년이 상을 탔나 / *Say ~ book you prefer.* 어느 책을 더 좋아하는지 말해라 / *Which way shall we go ?* 어느 길로 가야 하나. **2** 《*relative adjective*》 whatever. 어떤…이든. ¶ *Run ~ way you will, you won't escape.* 어느 길로 가든 너는 도망치지 못할 것이다 / *Try ~ method he pleased, he could not succeed.* 어느 방법을 써도 그는 성공하지 못했다. **3** 《*relative adjective*》 that. 그리고 그. ¶ *We went to Rome, at ~ place we parted.* 우리는 로마까지 가서 그곳에서 헤어졌다.

— *pron.* **1** 《*interrogative pronoun*》 what one or ones. 어느 쪽(의 물건·사람). ¶ *Which do you like better, an apple or an orange ?* 사과와 오렌지 중 어느 쪽을 더 좋아하나 / *Which do you like best ?* 어느 것이 제일 좋으냐 / *Which of these umbrellas is yours ?* 이 우산들 중에 어느 것이 네 것이냐 / *Can you tell ~ is ~ ?* 어느 것이 어느 것인지 알겠나 / *Which is the right road ?* 어느 쪽이 바른 길이냐 / *Say ~ you take.* 어느 걸 집을지 말해봐라 / *Which of you has done it ?* 너희들 중 누가 그 일을 했나. **2** 《*relative pronoun*》 that; and this or these. …하는; 그리고 그것은〔을〕. 參考 지금은 선행사가 사람인 경우는 쓰지 않음. ¶ *This is the house ~ my father lived in.* 이게 아버지가 사셨던 집이오 / *He is rich, ~ no other people know.* 그는 부자인데, 남들은 모른다 / *He said he had no brother, ~ was a lie.* 그는 형제가 없다고 했는데, 그것은 거짓말이었다 / *My parents intended me for a doctor, ~ I did not like.* 부모님은 내가 의사가 되길 바라셨지만 나는 싫었다 / *That book of yours, ~ I finished reading last night, was exciting.* 너의 그 책을 어제 밤에 다 읽었는데 아주 재미있었다 / *We visited a beautiful place, the name of ~ I have forgotten.* 아름다운 곳을 가봤는데 그 이름을 잊었다. **3** 《*relative pronoun*》 any that; whichever. …하는 것은 어느 것이든. ¶ *You may take ~ you like.* 네가 좋아하는 것은 어느 것이든 가져가거라. [*who, like*]

·**which·ev·er** [*h*witʃévər] *pron., adj.* **1** anything that. 어느 것이든. ¶ *You may have ~ you want.* 원하는 건 어느 것이든 가져라. **2** no matter which. 어느 것을〔이〕 …하든. ¶ *Whichever road you take, it will lead you to town.* 어느 길을 택하든 읍내에 이를 것이오.

whiff [*h*wif] *n.* Ⓒ **1** a slight breath, wind, or smoke; a puff. (바람 등의) 한 번 붊; 한 번 내뿜는 담배 연기. **2** a faint smell. 냄새. — *vt., vi.* (P6; 1) **1** blow lightly; puff. 가볍게 불다. **2** smell faintly. 냄새가 풍기다. [Imit.]

Whig [*h*wig] *n.* Ⓒ **1** 《hist.》 a member of the Whig Party, a former political party of Great Britain. 휘그 당원(cf. *Tory*). ¶ *The 'Whig party' is now called the 'Liberal party'.* '휘그당'은 지금 '자유당'이라고 불린다. **2** 《U.S. hist.》 an American who supported the War of Independence against England. 독립당원. **3** 《U.S. hist.》 a member of a political party that opposed the policies of the Democrats and was succeeded in 1856 by the Republican party. 휘그당원. [*whiggamor* nickname of Sc. covenanters]

:**while** [*h*wail] *n.* Ⓒ a space of time; a period. 동안. ¶ *after a ~* 잠시 후 / *all the* 〔*that, this*〕 *~* 그〔그, 이〕 동안 내내 / *at whiles* 때때로; 이따금 / *between whiles* 틈틈이 / *Don't keep me waiting a long ~.* 오래 기다리지 않게 해라 / *What have you been doing all this ~ ?* 여태까지 내내 뭘 하고 있었나.

be worth** someone's **while, repay someone for time and trouble taken. 수고한 보람이 있다. ¶ *It is worth your ~ to see the museum.* 그 박물관은 가볼 만한 가치가 있다.

for a while, for a (short) time. 잠시 동안. ¶ *We rested for a ~.* 우리는 잠시 쉬었다.

in a little while, soon. 곧. ¶ *I'll be back in a little ~.* 나는 이내 돌아올 것이다.

once in a while, occasionally. 이따금; 때때로.

the while, during that time; at the same time. 그 동안; 동시에. ¶ *He went about his work and sang the ~.* 그는 열심히 일하면서 노래를 불렀다.

— *conj.* **1** during or in the time that. …하는 동안. ¶ *While* (*I am*) *in New York, I often visit my aunt.* (내가) 뉴욕에 있는 동안에는 자주 고모를 찾아뵌다 / 《*prov.*》 *Make hay ~ the sun shines.* 쇠뿔도 단김에 빼라 / *While I was speaking, he said nothing.* 내가 말하는 동안 그는 한 마디도 하지 않았다 / *They got married ~ still at the university.* 그들은 대학 재학 중에 결혼했다. **2** at the same time that; although. …하면서도; …하지만. ¶ *While they don't agree, they continue to be friends.* 그들은 마음이 안 맞으면서도 교우 관계는 계속했다 / *While he loves his students, he is very strict with them.* 그는 제자들을 사랑하면서도 몹시 엄격하다. **3** 《*colloq.*》 whereas; and. 그런데 한편; 그리고. ¶ *Wise men seek after truth, ~ fools despise it.* 현자는 진리를 추구하는데 어리석은 자는 이를 경멸한다 / *His father is a doctor, and his mother is a doctress, ~ he is a medical student.* 아버지와 어머니는 의사이고 그는 의학도이다 / *Some people like coffee, ~ others like tea.* 커피를 즐기는 사람도 있고 홍차를 즐기는 사람도 있다.

— *vt.* (P6,7) spend or pass (time) idly; cause to pass pleasantly and smoothly. (시간을) 빈둥거리며 보내다; 즐겁게〔한가히〕 지내다. ¶ *~ away the time fishing* 낚시로 세월을 보내다 / *She whiled away the hours of waiting by looking at the shops.* 그녀는 기다리는 동안 가게들을 구경하며 시간을 보냈다. [E.]

whiles [*h*wailz] *conj.* 《*arch.*》 =while.

whilst [*h*wailst] *conj.* 《chiefly Brit.》 = while.

whim [*h*wim] *n.* Ⓒ a sudden fancy; a sudden turn of mind. 일시적인 생각; 변덕. ¶ *She bought a new hat on a* ～. 충동적으로 그녀는 새 모자를 하나 샀다. [E.]

whim·per [*h*wímpər] *vi.* (P1) **1** cry with low, broken sounds, in the way that a sick child or dog does. (어린애가) 훌쩍훌쩍 울다; 개가 깽깽거리다. ¶ *The little dog whimpered when I try to bathe its wounds.* 상처를 씻어주려 하자 개는 깽깽거렸다. **2** complain in a weak way. 투덜거리다. ― *vt.* (P6) say (something) with a whimper. …을 우는 소리로 말하다. ¶ *"Don't hurt me !" he whimpered.* "날 해치지 말아요" 그는 우는 소리로 말했다. ― *n.* Ⓒ a low, feeble cry or sound. 훌쩍거리기; 깽깽〔낑낑〕거리는 소리. [Imit.]

whim·si·cal [*h*wímzikəl] *adj.* **1** full of whims. 마음이 잘 변하는; 변덕스러운. **2** fanciful; odd. (기)묘한. ¶ ～ *poem* 〔*smile*〕 별난 시〔묘한 미소〕. [*whim*]

whim·sy [*h*wímzi] *n.* Ⓒ (*pl.* **-sies**) a whim; an odd fancy. 변덕; 별난 생각.

whine [*h*wain] *vi.* (P1,3) **1** make a low, complaining cry. 애처로운 소리로 울다; 흐느껴 울다; (개 따위가) 깽깽거리다. ¶ *The dog whined at the door, asking to be let out.* 개가 밖으로 내보내달라고 문앞에서 깽깽거렸다. **2** complain in a childish or weak way. 우는 소리를 하다; 종알거리다; 투덜거리다. ¶ *I wish you'd stop whining.* 그만 보채라 / *She is always whining about something.* 그녀는 늘 무언가 투덜거린다. ― *vt.* (P6,7) say (something) with a whine. …을 투덜투덜하다. ― *n.* Ⓒ **1** a low, complaining cry or sound. 우는 소리; 깽깽거리는 소리. **2** a childish complaint. 칭얼거림; 보챔. [E.]

whin·ny [*h*wíni] *n.* Ⓒ (*pl.* **-nies**) the sound which a horse makes; a neigh. 히힝 《말의 울음 소리》. ― *vi.* (P1) (**-nied**) (of a horse) make such sound. (말이) 히힝 울다. [*whine*]

:whip [*h*wip] *v.* (**whipped** or 《U.S.》 **whipt, whip·ping**) *vt.* **1** (P6) strike (a person or an animal) with a lash, rod, etc. …을 때리다; 채찍질하다. ¶ ～ *a cow* 소를 채찍질하다. **2** (P6,7,13,20) force or urge by whipping. …을 때려 가르치다〔시키다〕. ¶ ～ *a slave to work* 노예를 매질하며 일을 시키다 / ～ *manners into a child* 아이를 때려서 예절을 가르치다 / ～ *a fault out of a child* 아이를 때려서 잘못을 고치게 하다 / ～ *up one's horse* 말을 채찍질해서 몰아대다. **3** (P6) 《*colloq.*》 defeat. …을 패배시키다; 이기다. ¶ *Their team really whipped ours at basketball.* 그쪽 농구팀이 우리를 두말 못하게 이겼다. **4** (P6) beat (something) in a manner like whipping. …을 채찍질하듯 때리다. ¶ *The rain whipped our tin roof.* 비가 양철 지붕을 세차게 때렸다. **5** (P7,13) move, pull or seize (something) quickly and suddenly. …을 갑자기 움직이다〔잡아당기다; 움켜잡다〕. ¶ ～ *off one's coat* 코트를 훌렁 벗어던지다 / ～ *out a knife* 칼을 쑥 뽑다 / *He whipped out his gun.* 그가 권총을 잽싸게 뽑아들었다. **6** (P6) beat (eggs, cream, etc.) with a beater, a mixer, etc. (달걀 등)을 휘저어 거품일게 하다. ¶ *whipped cream* 거품 낸 크림 / ～ *eggs* 달걀을 휘저어 거품을 내다. **7** (P6) fish (a stream) with a rod and line. …에서 던질낚시를 하다. ¶ ～ *a stream* 시내에서 던질낚시를 하다. **8** (P6,13) bind (a rope, etc.) with a cord, etc.; wind round. …을 끈으로 칭칭 감다; (밧줄 따위)를 휘감다. ¶ ～ *the rope twice round the pole* 기둥에 밧줄을 두 번 감다. **9** (P6) sew over (a seam). (솔기를) 감치다. ― *vi.* (P1,2A,3) **1** use a whip. 채찍질하다; 매질하다. **2** move, go or pass quickly and suddenly. 급히 움직이다; 돌진하다. ¶ *The fox whipped out of sight.* 여우는 재빨리 시야에서 사라졌다. **3** wave up and down. 펄럭이다. ¶ *The flags whipped in the wind.* 깃발이 바람에 펄럭였다.

whip (***all***) ***creation,*** 《*colloq.*》 surpass all rivals. 무엇보다 뛰어나다〔뒤지지 않다〕.

whip in, a) call up; gather. (사람·당 등)을 불러모으다. b) direct. 지휘〔통솔〕하다.

whip off, a) seize suddenly away. 홱 잡아채다. ¶ ～ *the cloth off the table* 식탁보를 홱 벗기다. b) carry away; drive away by whipping. 갑자기 데리고 가다; 채찍으로 쫓아버리다. c) go off hastily or suddenly. 급히〔갑자기〕 출발하다. d) take off quickly. 홱 벗어버리다. ¶ *He whipped off his coat.* 그는 외투를 홱 벗었다.

whip out, a) draw or pull out with a sudden quick action. 갑자기 뽑다. b) speak suddenly and violently. 불쑥 퉁명스럽게 말하다. ¶ ～ *out a reply* 퉁명스레 대답하다. c) go out hastily. 서둘러 나가다. ¶ ～ *out of the door* 문 밖으로 휙 나가다.

whip round, turn round suddenly and swiftly. 휙 돌아보다.

whip up, a) make (a horse) run faster by whipping. 채찍질을 하여 …을 빨리 몰다. b) prepare quickly. …을 급히 준비하다. ¶ *She whipped up a lunch for picnic.* 그녀는 서둘러 소풍 갈 도시락을 마련했다. c) rouse; excite. …을 자극하다.

― *n.* Ⓒ **1** an instrument for striking or beating, such as a rod with a lash. 채찍. **2** a person who uses a whip; a driver. 채찍을 쓰는 사람; 마부. ¶ *I am no* ～. 나는 마부가 아니다 / *a good* ～ 유능한 마부. **3** =whipper-in. **4** a dessert made of fruit, sugar, and whipped cream or the whipped whites of eggs. 디저트의 일종《크림·달걀 등을 휘저어 거품을 내어 만듦》. **5** a manager of a political party. (정당의) 원내 총무. [E.]

whip·hand [*h*wíphæ̀nd] *n.* the hand that holds the whip in driving, i.e. the

right hand. 채찍 잡은 손; 오른손.
have the whiphand of, have control of; have advantage over. …을 좌우하다.

whip·lash [*h*wíplæ̀ʃ] *n.* **1** Ⓒ the lash for a whip. 채찍 끝의 가죽끈. **2** Ⓤ a neck injury caused by a sudden stopping of a car. 차량의 급정거로 목이 꺾이는 일; 편타증(鞭打症).

whip·per-in [*h*wípərín] *n.* (*pl.* **-pers-in**) **1** a person who keeps the dogs from wandering while hunting. 사냥개 담당. **2** 《in Brit. Parliament》 (국회의) 원내 총무. [E.]

whip·per-snap·per [*h*wípərsnæ̀pər] *n.* an insignificant person who thinks he is smart and important. (제딴은 잘났다고 생각하는) 시건방진 사람. [E.]

whip·pet [*h*wípit] *n.* **1** a dog somewhat like a greyhound but smaller, used for racing. 경주용 개의 일종. **2** a small fast tank. 경전차(輕戰車). 參考 제1차 세계 대전 때 연합군의. [↑]

whip·ping-boy [*h*wípiŋbɔ̀i] *n.* **1** 《hist.》 a boy who was educated with a prince and was punished in place of the prince. (왕자의 학우로) 왕자를 대신해 매맞던 소년. **2** a person punished for the faults of another; a scapegoat. 남을 대신해 벌받는 사람; 희생자. [*whip*]

whip·poor·will [*h*wípərwìl] *n.* 《zool.》 an American night-bird having a cry that sounds like its name. (미국산) 쏙독새. [Imit.]

whir, whirr [*h*wəːr] *vi.* (P1,2A) (**whirred, whir·ring**) move quickly with a humming sound. 휙 날다; 윙윙 돌다. ¶ *The motor whirs.* 모터가 윙윙 돈다. — *n.* Ⓒ 《usu. used as *sing.*》 the sound made by moving things rapidly. 휙하고 나는 소리; 윙윙하고 도는 소리. ¶ *the ~ of an airplane propeller* 비행기 프로펠러의 윙윙 소리. [Scand.]

:**whirl** [*h*wəːrl] *vi.* (P1,2A,3) **1** turn around and around; spin quickly. 빙글빙글[빙빙] 돌다; 회전하다. ¶ *The earth whirls on its axis.* 지구는 지축을 중심으로 회전한다 / *a whirling top* 빙글빙글 도는 팽이 / *The leaves whirled in the wind.* 나뭇잎이 바람에 휘날렸다 / *The dancers whirled around the floor.* 무용수들은 무대를 뱅글뱅글 돌았다. **2** move swiftly. 휙 움직이다; 질주하다. ¶ *The carriage whirled out of sight.* 마차는 쏜살같이 달려 시야에서 사라졌다. **3** ⓐ feel dizzy; seem to spin round. 현기증이 나다; (머리가) 핑 돌다. ¶ *My brain whirled.* 머리가 핑 돌았다[어찔했다]. ⓑ (of thoughts, etc.) be in confusion. (생각 등이) 헷갈리다.
— *vt.* (P6,7,13) **1** cause (something) to turn around and around. …을 빙글빙글 돌리다; 선회시키다. ¶ *~ a hat on one's finger* 모자를 손끝으로 돌리다 / *He whirled his stick about his head.* 머리께에서 지팡이를 빙빙 돌렸다. **2** carry (something) quickly. …을 빠르게 나르다. ¶ *The cart whirled him down the hill.* 그를 태운 달구지는 빠르게 언덕을 내려갔다.
— *n.* Ⓒ **1** 《often *a* ~》 a circular motion. 회전; 선회. ¶ *a ~ of dust* 먼지의 소용돌이 / *the ~ of a top.* **2** (of water) a quick act of spinning around. 소용돌이. **3** 《*fig.*》 a confusion of mind. (정신의) 혼란; 어지러움. ¶ *My head's in a ~ ; I must sit down and think.* 머리가 복잡하구나. 앉아서 생각해 봐야겠다. [N.]

whirl·i·gig [*h*wə́ːrligìg] *n.* a toy that spins; a merry-go-round; anything that spins round rapidly. 빙글빙글 도는 장난감 《팽이·팔랑개비 등》; 회전 목마; 도는 것. ¶ 《*fig.*》 *the ~ of time* 시운(時運)의 변전(變轉). [↑]

whirl·pool [*h*wə́ːrlpùːl] *n.* Ⓒ (of water) the act of spinning rapidly and violently. 소용돌이.

whirl·wind [*h*wə́ːrlwìnd] *n.* Ⓒ **1** a current of air circling violently with a spiral motion. 선풍; 회오리 바람. **2** anything like a whirlwind, as in destructiveness. 격정; 급격한 행동.
sow the wind and reap the whirlwind, suffer bad results because of bad actions. 나쁜 짓을 하여 몇 곱으로 호되게 벌을 받다; 되로 주고 말로 받다.

whisk [*h*wisk] *n.* Ⓒ **1** a small brush or broom. 작은 솔[비]. **2** a sudden, quick motion. 신속한 동작. **3** a quick motion of brushing. 휙 텀. ¶ *The cow brushed away the flies with a ~ of its tail.* 소는 꼬리를 휘둘러 파리를 쫓았다. **4** an instrument for whipping eggs, cream, etc. (달걀·크림 따위의) 거품 내는 기구.
— *vt.* **1** (P7,13) remove with a light, quick motion; drive away quickly. (먼지 따위를) 털다; (파리 따위)를 쫓아버리다. ¶ *~ flies away* 파리를 휙 쫓다 / *The wind whisked away the scraps of paper.* 바람이 종잇조각을 날려 버렸다. **2** (P7,13) take or carry off suddenly. …을 급히 가져가다[데려가다]. ¶ *The waiter whisked my plate away.* 웨이터가 내 접시를 잽싸게 치웠다. **3** (P6) wave lightly and quickly through the air. 흔들다; 휘두르다. ¶ *The cow whisked her tail.* 암소가 꼬리를 흔들었다. **4** (P6) beat (eggs, creams, etc.) into a froth. (달걀·크림 따위를) 휘젓다; 거품 내다.
— *vi.* (P2A,3) move rapidly and quickly. 휙 움직이다. ¶ *The squirrel whisked up the tree.* 다람쥐는 날쌔게 나무 위로 올라갔다. [Scand.]

whisk·er [*h*wískər] *n.* Ⓒ 《usu. *pl.*》 **1** hair growing on the side of a man's face. 구레나룻(cf. *beard, mustache*). **2** long hair growing near the mouth of a cat, a rat, etc. (고양이·쥐 따위의) 수염. [↑]

***whis·key, -ky** [*h*wíski] *n.* **1** Ⓤ a strong alcoholic drink made from various grains, esp. rye and barley. 위스키. ¶ *Scotch ~.* **2** Ⓒ a drink of whisky. 위스

키 한 잔. ¶ *Three whiskys, please.* 위스키 석 잔 주시오. [Ir. *uisce breatha* water of life]

·whis·per [*h*wíspər] *vi.* (P1,13) **1** speak in a very soft and low voice. 속삭이다. ¶ *The children were whispering in the corner.* 아이들이 구석에서 속삭이고 있었다 / *"Listen !" she whispered.* "내 말 들어라"하고 그녀는 작은 소리로 일렀다. **2** talk secretly or privately. 내밀한 이야기를 하다; 수군거리다. ¶ ~ *against* 〔*about*〕 *someone* 아무의 험담을 수군거리다. **3** make a soft, rustling sound like a whisper. (나뭇잎 등이) 살랑살랑 소리내다. ¶ *The leaves whispered in the breeze.* 나뭇잎이 미풍에 살랑거렸다.
— *vt.* (P6,7,11) **1** say (something or someone) very softly. …을〔에게〕 작은 소리로 말하다. **2** 《often in *passive*》 to suggest (something) or pass (information) secretly. 살그머니 (정보 따위를) 퍼뜨리다. ¶ *It's whispered that he may resign.* 그가 사임할 것이라는 소문이 있다.
— *n.* Ⓒ **1** a very soft and low voice. 속삭임; 귀엣말. ¶ *speak in a* ~ 귀엣말하다; 소곤거리다 / *She said it in a* ~*, so I couldn't hear.* 그녀가 작은 소리로 말해서 나는 알아들을 수 없었다. **2** a soft, faint, rustling sound. 속삭이는 듯한 소리. ¶ *the* ~ *of the leaves* 나뭇잎의 살랑대는 소리. **3** a hint; a rumor. 암시; 시사. ¶ *I've heard a* ~ *that he was put to death without trial.* 그가 재판 없이 처형됐다는 소문을 들었다. [E.]

whist[1] [*h*wist] *interj.* 《Brit. rare》 Hush ! Silence. 쉿, 조용히. [E.]

whist[2] [*h*wist] *n.* Ⓤ a card game for four players. 휘스트《카드놀이의 일종》(cf. *bridge*[2]). [*whisk* (cards being whisked up)]

:whis·tle [*h*wísəl] *vi.* (P1,2A,3) **1** make a shrill sound by forcing the breath between the teeth or rounded lips or with a whistle. 휘파람을 불다; 호각을 불다. ¶ *The policeman whistled for the motorcar to stop.* 경관은 정차하라고 호각을 불었다 / *He whistled as he walked down the street.* 그는 거리를 내려가면서 휘파람을 불었다. **2** make any similar sound. 휘파람 비슷한 소리를 내다. ¶ *The wind whistles.* 바람이 씽씽 분다 / *Arrows whistled past him.* 화살이 씽 소리를 내며 그를 지나갔다. **3** make a sharp, clear sound. 날카로운 소리를 내다. — *vt.* (P6,7) **1** call or signal (something) by a whistling. 휘파람으로 부르다〔알리다〕. ¶ ~ *a dog back* 휘파람으로 개를 되돌아오게 하다. **2** produce (a tune) by whistling. …을 휘파람으로 불다. ¶ ~ *a tune* 휘파람으로 노래하다. [E.]
whistle for, **a**) call (someone or something) by a whistle. …을 휘파람으로 부르다. **b**) 《*colloq.*》 fail to get (something); vainly seek. …을 구해도 헛일이다; 헛되이 구하다.
— *n.* Ⓒ **1** a shrill sound made by whistling. 휘파람 (소리). **2** an instrument for producing such a sound. 피리; 호각; 기적. [E.]
not worth the whistle, valueless. 아무 쓸모 없는.
pay for one's whistle, pay too much money for something worthless. 쓸데없는 것을 비싸게 사다.
wet one's whistle ⇨ wet.

whit [*h*wit] *n.* 《*a* ~ 》 a very small bit. 아주 조금; 미소(微小). [*wiht*=wight]
not 〔***never***〕 ***a whit,*** not at all; not in the least. 조금도 …아니다〔않다〕. ¶ *The sick man is not a* ~ *better.* 그 환자는 차도가 조금도 없다 / *There is not a* ~ *of truth in the rumor.* 그건 터무니 없는 헛소문이다. [M.E. *wiht* =wight]

:white [*h*wait] *adj.* **1** of the color of snow or pure milk; of no color. 흰(opp. black); 무색의. ¶ ~ *clouds* 흰구름 / *as* ~ *as milk* 〔*chalk*〕 새하얀; 순백의 / ~ *hands* (노동을 않은) 흰 손; 결백 / ~ *light* 백색광; 편견 없는 판단 / *as* ~ *as snow* 눈처럼 흰 / ~ *hair* 백발. **2** of a light or pale color. 색깔이 엷은; 창백한. ¶ *She turned* ~ *at the news.* 그 소식을 듣고 그녀는 창백해졌다 / *be in* ~ *terror* 무서워 얼굴이 새하얘지다 / *Her face went* ~. 그녀의 얼굴에서 핏기가 가셨다 / ~ *wine* 백포도주. **3** of a silver color; gray; covered with snow; blank. 은빛의; 눈으로 덮인; 백지의; 씌어 있지 않은. ¶ *a* ~ *metal* 가짜 은 / *a* ~ *Christmas* 눈이 있는 크리스마스 / *a* ~ *page* 공백의 페이지. **4** without a stain; pure; innocent; harmless. 결백한; 순진한; 순진무구한; 무해한. ¶ *a* ~ *lie* 선의의 거짓말 / *My father made his name* ~ *again.* 아버지는 오명을 씻었다. **5** having a light-colored skin. 백색 인종의. ¶ *the* ~ *race* 백인종 / ~ *culture* 〔*civilization*〕 백인 문화〔문명〕. **6** (of wine) light yellow. 호박색의.
bleed someone white, drain away all of someone's money or energy. 아무를 짜낼 수 있는 데까지 짜내다. ¶ *The blackmailer bled him* ~. 그 갈취자는 그를 빈털터리로 만들었다.
— *n.* **1** Ⓤ white color. 백색(opp. black). **2** Ⓤ the state of being white; innocence. 순진; 결백; 무해. **3** ⒸⓊ white coloring material. 흰 그림물감. ¶ *A grain or two of* ~ *fell on the surface of the desk.* 한두 방울의 흰색 물감이 책상 위에 떨어졌다. **4** Ⓤ white cloth; 《usu. *pl.*》 white garments. 흰 천; 흰옷; 백의. ¶ *a woman in* ~ 흰옷을 입은 부인. **5** 《often *W-*》 Ⓒ a white person. 백인. ¶ *White only.* 백인 전용. **6** the white part of something, such as an eye or an egg. (눈·달걀의) 흰자위. [E.]

white·cap [*h*wáitkæ̀p] *n.* Ⓒ 《usu. *pl.*》 the ridge of a wave as it breaks into foam. 흰 물마루.

white clover [⌐ ⌐–] *n.* 《bot.》 a kind of

clover with white flowers. 흰토끼풀.

white coffee [ˊ ˊ–] *n.* 《Brit.》 coffee mixed with milk or cream. 밀크 커피.

white-col·lar [*h*wáitkálər / -kɔ́lər] *adj.* of a person who is engaged in business or professional work. 두뇌 노동자의; 사무직의(cf. *blue-collar*). ¶ *a ~ worker.* 「물건.

white crow [ˊ ˊ] *n.* a rare thing. 진귀한

white elephant [ˊ ˊ––] *n.* something costly but troublesome and useless to its owner. 흰코끼리《비용·수고만 드는 성가신 물건》; 무용지물.

white feather [ˊ ˊ–] *n.* a symbol of cowardice. 겁먹은 증거. ¶ *show the ~* 겁을 먹다.

white flag [ˊ ˊ] *n.* a flag of truce or surrender. 휴전기; 백기(白旗).

white gold [ˊ ˊ] *n.* gold alloyed variously with nickel, zinc, etc. to give it a white, platinumlike appearance, for use in jewelry. 화이트 골드.

White·hall [*h*wáithɔ̀:l] *n.* **1** a street in London where there are many important government offices. 런던의 관청가. **2** the British government. 영국 정부.

white heat [ˊ ˊ] *n.* **1** the temperature at which metals become white. 백열. **2** 《*fig.*》 (of passion) great intensity. 격정.

white-hot [*h*wáithát / -hɔ́t] *adj.* **1** very hot; white with heat. 백열의. **2** very excited; angry. 흥분한; 격노한.

White House [ˊ ˋ], **the** *n.* the official residence of the President of the United States, in Washington, D.C. 화이트 하우스; 백악관.

white lie [ˊ ˊ] *n.* a lie told without intention of malice. 선의의 거짓말.

white-liv·ered [*h*wáitlívərd] *adj.* **1** cowardly. 겁이 많은. **2** pale; unhealthy looking. 창백한; 파리한.

white meat [ˊ ˋ] *n.* any light-colored meat, as veal, pork, the breast of poultry, etc. (송아지·돼지·닭 따위의) 흰 살코기.

whit·en [*h*wáitn] *vt.* (P6) make (something) white. …을 희게 하다[칠하다]; 표백하다. — *vi.* (P1) become white. 희게 되다.

white·ness [*h*wáitnis] *n.* Ⓤ **1** the state of being white. 흼; 순백; 창백. **2** cleanliness; purity. 결백.

white paper [ˊ ˊ–] *n.* a report issued by the British Government to give information; a similar report issued by any government. (영국 정부의) 백서; (일반적으로) 백서.

white scourge [ˊ ˊ], **the** *n.* epidemic consumption. (풍토병으로서의) 폐병.

white·wash [*h*wáitwàʃ, -wɔ̀(:)ʃ] *n.* Ⓤ a substance for whitening walls, fences, etc. 백색 도료; 회반죽. — *vt.* (P6) **1** whiten (walls, fences, etc.) with whitewash. (벽·울타리 따위)를 흰 도료로 칠하다. **2** (P8) 《*fig.*》 cover up or hide the mistakes of (someone). …을 감싸다; …의 실수를 숨기다. ¶ *The report attempts to ~ recent events.* 보고서는 저간의 사건들을 호도(糊塗)하려고 한다. **3** 《U.S. *colloq.*》 defeat without a score for the loser. …을 영패시키다.

·**whith·er** [*h*wíðər] *adv.* 《*poet., arch.*》 **1** to what place. 어디에; 어느 쪽으로(opp. whence). ¶ *Whither are you going ?* 어디로 가는 거냐. **2** to the place which; where. (…하는) 그곳에. ¶ *the shore ~ we landed* 우리가 상륙한 해안 / *the place ~ he went* 그가 갔던 곳. **3** to whatever place, point, etc.; wherever. 어디든. ¶ *Go ~ you will.* 어디든 가고 싶은 데로 가게. — *n.* the place to which one goes or is going. 행선지; 목적지. [E.]

whit·ing [*h*wáitiŋ] *n.* **1** Ⓤ white chalk. 백악(白堊). **2** Ⓒ (*pl.* **-ings** or *collectively* **-ing**) a small sea fish for food. 대구과의 물고기.

whit·ish [*h*wáitiʃ] *adj.* somewhat white. 희끄무레한. [*white*]

Whit·sun [*h*wítsən] *adj.* of Whitsunday. 성신 강림 축일(聖神降臨祝日)[강림절]의. [↓]

Whit·sun·day [*h*wítsʌ́ndi, -səndèi] *n.* the seventh Sunday after Easter. 성신 강림 축일《부활절 후의 제 7 일요일》. [*white* (w. ref. to white robes of Whitsunday baptisms)]

Whit·sun·tide [*h*wítsəntàid] *n.* the week that begins with Whitsunday, esp. the first three days of that week. 성신 강림절. [↑]

whit·tle [*h*wítl] *vt.* **1** (P6,13) cut (a piece of wood) with a knife; cut away. 칼로 …을 깎다[깎아내다]. ¶ *He whittled the wood into a figure.* 그는 나무를 깎아서 조상(彫像)을 만들었다. **2** (P6,7) 《*down, away*》 reduce (something) little by little. …을 조금씩 줄이다; 삭감하다. ¶ *Bad financial management has whittled away the company's profits.* 재정 관리의 부실이 회사의 수익을 좀먹었다. — *vi.* (P1,3) cut (wood) with a knife for fun. 재미로 나무를 깎다. [E.]

whiz, whizz [*h*wiz] *n.* Ⓒ **1** a hissing sound made by something which moves quickly through the air. 윙; 핑; 쉭《화살·총알 따위가 공중을 나는 소리》. **2** 《U.S. *colloq.*》 a specialist. 전문가. — *vi.* (P2A,3) (**whizzed, whizz·ing**) make a hissing sound; move with a hissing sound. 윙[핑, 쉭]하는 소리를 내다; 휙하고 날다. ¶ *An arrow whizzed over his head.* 화살 한 대가 핑하며 그의 머리 위를 날았다 / *The car whizzed past us.* 차가 윙하고 우리 곁을 지나갔다. [Imit.]

WHO World Health Organization.

:**who** [hu(:)] *pron.* **1** 《*interrogative pronoun*》 what or which person(s). 누구; 어떤 사람. ¶ *Who says so ?* 누가 그런 말을 하니 / "*Who is he ?*" "*He is Mr. Smith.*" "그 사람은 누구냐", "스미스씨다" / *He may be the best source of information as to ~ was* *where at what time.* 누가 어느 때 어디 있었는가에 관해서는 그가 가장 밝은 정보통이다 / *It was a question of* ~ *had taken the money.* 누가 돈을 받았느냐 하는 것이 문제였다 / *I don't know* ~ *to give it to.* 그것을 누구에게 줘야 할지 모르겠다 / *Who is this letter from? =From whom is this letter?* 이 편지는 누구에게서 왔느냐 / *Who else was there with you?* 그 밖에 누가 너와 같이 거기 있었나 / *Who is coming to the party?* 누가 파티에 오기로 되어 있니 / *Who helped you?* 누가 도와 주더냐. **2** [hu(:), u(:)] 《*relative pronoun*》 that; and he; any person that. …하는 (사람); 그리고 그 사람은; …하는 사람은 누구나. ¶ *the man* ~ *came here yesterday* 어제 여기 왔던 사람 / *There is somebody at the door* (~) *wants to see you.* 문간에 너를 만나자는 어떤 사람이 있다 / 《*prov.*》 *Who steals my purse steals trash.* 내 지갑을 훔치는 자는 쓰레기를 훔치는 자다; 돈은 도둑맞아도 아깝지 않다 / *I lived with Mr. A,* ~ *taught me English.* 나는 A씨와 살았는데 그가 내게 영어를 가르쳐 주었다 / *I sent it to Jones,* ~ *passed it to Smith.* 내가 그것을 존스에게 보냈는데 존스는 그것을 스미스에게 보냈다 / *My cousin,* ~ *is a painter, is in France.* 내 사촌은 화가인데 프랑스에 있다 / *Who is not for us is against us.* 우리에게 찬성 않는 자는 우리를 반대하는 것이다. [E.]

whoa [*h*wou / wou] *interj.* (to a horse, etc.) Stop! 워《말을 멈추게 할 때》. [Obs. *who*, →ho]

who·dun·it [hu:dʌ́nit] *n.* Ⓒ 《*colloq.*》 a story, motion picture or drama that deals with crime and its detection. 추리소설〔영화, 극〕; 서스펜스물(物); 스릴러. [who done it?]

who·e'er [hu(:)ɛ́ər] *pron.* 《*poet.*》 =whoever.

·**who·ev·er** [hu:évər] *pron.* **1** any person that. …하는 (자는) 누구든지. ¶ *Whoever wants the treasure shall have it.* 재물을 원하는 사람은 누구든 그것을 얻게 될 것이다 / *Whoever comes will be welcome.* 오는 자는 누구든 환영한다. **2** no matter who. 누가 …하더라도. ¶ *Whoever tries it, he will never succeed.* 누가 하든지 결코 성공 못 한다 / *Whoever may say so, it is not true.* 누가 그렇게 말하든 그건 사실이 아니다. **3** 《*colloq., emph.*》 (in question) who in the world. 도대체 누가. ¶ *Whoever said so?* 도대체 누가 그런 말을 하든 / *Whoever could have dreamed of such a thing?* 도대체 누가 그런 일을 꿈꾸었을까. [*who*]

⁝**whole** [houl] *adj.* **1** 《*the* 〔*one's*〕 ~》 containing all parts; full; entire. 전체의; 모든(opp. partial). ¶ *the* ~ *country* 전국 / *the* ~ *world* 전세계 / *the* ~ *truth* 모든 〔있는 그대로의〕 사실 / *with one's* ~ *heart* 진심으로 / *put one's* ~ *heart and soul into something* …에 온 심혈을 기울이다 / *Whole cities were destroyed.* 모든 도시들이 파괴되었다 / *the* ~ *priesthood* 전체 성직자. **2** complete; not divided. 온…; 만(滿)…. ¶ *a* ~ *day* 하루 종일 / *for five* ~ *days* 꼬박 닷새 동안 / *It lasted three* ~ *days.* 그것은 꼬박 사흘을 끌었다. **3** not broken; not injured; sound. 완전〔온전〕한; 상처 없는. ¶ *with a* ~ *skin* 아무 상처 없이 / *They roasted a pig* ~. 그들은 돼지를 통째로 구웠다 / *There is not a single* ~ *cup in the house.* 집안에는 컵 하나 성한 것이 없다. **4** 《math.》 integral. 정수(整數)의. ¶ *a* ~ *number* 정수. **5** 《*arch.*》 well; healthy. 건강〔건전〕한.

a whole lot of, 《*colloq.*》 much; a great amount of. 많은; 다량의. ¶ *He talked a* ~ *lot of nonsense.* 그는 말같잖은 소리만 잔뜩 늘어놓았다.

go the whole hog ⇨hog.

— *n.* Ⓒ **1** 《*the* ~》 the entire amount, extent, or sum. 전체(opp. part). ¶ *the* ~ *of one's property* 전 재산 / *the* ~ *and the parts* 전체와 부분 / *The* ~ *is greater than its parts.* 전체는 부분보다 크다 / *The golden rule contains the* ~ *of morality.* 황금률은 도덕률의 모든 것을 포함한다. **2** a thing complete in itself; a unity. 완전체; 통일체; 완전한 모습. ¶ *Nature is a* ~. 자연은 통일체다 / *Two halves make a* ~. 절반이 둘이면 완전체가 된다. [E.]

as a whole, as a complete unit. 전체로서. ¶ *There are some areas of poverty, but the country as a* ~ *is fairly prosperous.* 가난한 지역도 있지만 나라 전체로서는 꽤 부유하다.

on 〔***upon***〕 ***the whole,*** in general. 전체로 보아; 대체로. ¶ *On the* ~, *I'm satisfied with her progress.* 그녀의 진척에 그런 대로 나는 만족하고 있다.

whole-heart·ed [hóulhá:rtid] *adj.* full of sincerity; hearty and cordial; single-hearted. 진심에서의; 성심 성의의. ¶ ~ *cooperation* 진정한 협동 / ~ *sympathy* 진심에서 우러나오는 동정.

whole·sale [hóulsèil] *adj.* **1** selling in large quantities. 도매의(opp. retail). ¶ *a* ~ *dealer* 도매상 / *They cost $50 in the stores, but the* ~ *price is $35.* 그것들은 가게에서는 값이 50달러이나 도매가는 35달러이다. **2** having a large scale. 대규모의. ¶ ~ *slaughter* 대량 무차별 학살 / *a* ~ *arrest* 일제 검거. — *adv.* in large quantities. 도매로; 대규모로. — *n.* Ⓤ the sale of goods in large quantities. 도매(opp. retail). — *vt.* (P6) sell (goods) in large quantities. (물건)을 도매하다.

·**whole·some** [hóulsəm] *adj.* **1** good for the health; healthful. 건강에 좋은; 건강한. ¶ *Milk is a* ~ *food.* 우유는 건강 식품이다. **2** good for the mind; sound. 건전한. ¶ *a clean,* ~ *story* 외설스럽지 않은 건전한 이야기. [*whole, some*]

who'll [hu:l] =who will; who shall.

·**whol·ly** [hóu*l*li] *adv.* entirely; completely;

altogether. 전적으로; 완전히; 전부. ¶ *Few men are ~ bad.* 전적으로 나쁜 사람은 거의 없다 / *You were not ~ to blame for the accident.* 그 사고가 전적으로 네 잘못은 아니었다 / *I don't ~ agree.* 내가 전적으로 동의하는 것은 아니다. [*whole*]

:whom [hu(:)m] *pron.* the objective case of **who.** **1** 《*interrogative pronoun*》 what person. 누구를; 누구에게. ¶ *Whom are you looking for?* 누구를 찾고 있니 / *To ~ did you give it?* 그것을 누구한테 주었나. **2** 《*relative pronoun*》 that person. 그 사람을. ¶ *I visited my uncle ~ I had not seen for years.* 나는 여러 해 뵙지 못한 숙부를 방문했다 / *a man ~ you can trust* 네가 믿을 수 있는 사람. [*who*]

whom·ev·er [hu:mévər] *pron.* the objective case of **whoever.**

whom·so·ev·er [hù:msouévər] *pron.* the objective case of **whosoever.**

whoop [hu(:)p, *h*wu(:)p] *n.* Ⓒ **1** a loud cry. 야아〔우아〕하는 외침. **2** the cry of an owl, a crane, etc. (올빼미 따위의) 후우후우 우는 소리. **3** a gasping cough. (백일해로) 그렁그렁거리는 소리.

not care a whoop, not care at all. 조금도 개의치 않다.

— *vi.* (P1) **1** shout loudly. 고함치다. **2** make a whooping noise like an owl, a crane, etc. (올빼미 따위가) 후우후우 울다. [Imit.]

whoop it up, 《*colloq.*》 make much noise, usu. joyfully. 야단 법석을 떨다.

whoop·ing-cough [hú:piŋkɔ̀:f, -kɑ̀f / -kɔ̀f] *n.* an infectious disease of children characterized by fits of coughing. 백일해.

whop [*h*wɑp / *h*wɔp] *vt.* (**whopped**) (P6) **1** beat, esp. with a stick or whip. …을 매질하다; 채찍질하다. **2** 《*fig.*》 defeat. …을 완패시키다. [E.]

whop·per [*h*wɑ́pər / *h*wɔ́pər] *n.* Ⓒ 《*colloq.*》 **1** something very large. 엄청나게 큰 것〔물건〕. ¶ *Did you catch that fish? What a ~!* 네가 그 고기를 낚았나. 되게 큰 놈이구나. **2** a big lie. 터무니없는 거짓말〔허풍〕. ¶ *He told a real ~ to excuse his lateness.* 늦어진 데 대해 터무니없는 거짓말을 꾸며댔다. [E.]

whop·ping [*h*wɑ́piŋ / *h*wɔ́p-] *n.* ⓊⒸ 《*colloq.*》 **1** the act of beating with a stick. 매질; 채찍질. **2** defeat. 패배(敗北). — *adj.* 《*colloq.*》 very or unusually large. 엄청나게 큰. — *adv.* very; extraordinarily. 대단히; 터무니없이.

whore [hɔ:r] *n.* a woman who sells herself for money. 매춘부(cf. *prostitute*). [N.]

whore·dom [hɔ́:rdəm] *n.* prostitution. 매음; 매춘.

whorl [*h*wə:rl] *n.* Ⓒ **1** one turn of a spiral shell. (소라의) 나선; 나선의 한 감김. **2** 《bot.》 a circle of leaves, petals, flowers, etc. around a part on a stem. 윤생체(輪生體). [E. (→whirl)]

who's [hu:z] =who is; who has.

:whose [hu:z] *pron.* the possessive case of **who** and **which.** **1** 《*interrogative pronoun*》 ⓐ of whom. 누구의. ¶ *Whose pencil is this?* 이건 누구 연필이냐 / *Whose shoes are these?* 이것은 누구의 신발인가. ⓑ the one possessed by someone. 누구의 것. ¶ *Whose is this pencil?* 이 연필은 누구 것이냐. **2** 《*relative pronoun*》 of which. (그 사람〔물건〕의 —이) …하는. ¶ *An orphan is a child ~ parents are dead.* 고아란 그 양친이 죽은 아이이다 / *a mountain ~ top is covered with snow* 꼭대기에 눈이 덮인 산. [*who*]

who·so·ev·er [hù:souévər] *pron.* =whoever.

:why [*h*wai] *adv.* **1** 《*interrogative adverb*》 for what reason or purpose; on what grounds. 어째서; 왜. ¶ *Why did you do it?* 왜 그걸 했나 / *Why so?* 왜냐 / *Why are you here?* 왜 여기 있나 / *Why don't you try?* 해 보는 게 어떻겠나 / *Why not stop here?* 여기 멈추는 게 어때. **2** 《*relative adverb*》 because of or on account of which; for which. …하는 이유. ¶ *That is (the reason) ~ I cannot go.* 그것이 내가 못 가는 이유다 / *Do you know ~ he was absent?* 그가 어째서 결석했는지 아니 / *I know ~ you were scolded.* 네가 꾸중들은 까닭을 나는 안다 / *Tell us the reason ~ you came here.* 여기 오게 된 사연을 우리한테 말해라 [語法] 선행사 the reason은 흔히 생략됨.

— *n.* Ⓒ (*pl.* **whys**) the reason; the cause; the purpose. 이유; 까닭. ¶ *the why(s) and wherefore(s)* 이유와 사정 / *None of your whys!* 왜냐왜냐하고 그렇게 꼬치꼬치 묻지 마라.

— *interj.* 《expressing surprise, protest, etc., or introducing a new idea》 아니; 저런; 어머; 뭐라고; 에; 저어. ¶ *Why, it is surely Tom.* 아니, 너 정말 톰이구나 / *Why, of course I know.* 그럼, 난 물론 알지 / *Why, yes, I think so.* 뭐라고, 그래, 난 그렇게 생각한다 / *Why, it's nearly five o'clock.* 저어, 다섯 시가 다 돼 가네. [E.]

wick [wik] *n.* ⓊⒸ a cord of woven or twisted fibers in a candle or oil lamp that draws up melted fat or oil. (양초·램프의) 심지. [E.]

wick·ed [wíkid] *adj.* **1** bad; evil; sinful. 부정한; 사악한. ¶ *a ~ thought* 못된 생각. **2** mischievous. 장난기 있는. ¶ *He had a ~ twinkle in his eye.* 그의 반짝이는 눈에는 장난기가 서려 있었다. **3** harmful; dangerous. 해로운; 위험한. ¶ *a ~ blow* 심한 타격. [E.]

wick·ed·ness [wíkidnis] *n.* Ⓤ **1** the state of being wicked. 사악; 부정. ¶ *the ~ of our hearts* 우리들 마음의 사악함. **2** Ⓒ a wicked act. 사악한 짓. **3** wicked thoughts or actions. 악의; 심술. ¶ *practise ~* 심술을 부리다.

wick·er [wíkər] *n.* Ⓒ **1** an easily bent

twig or branch; a slender twig. 작은 가지; 고리버들. ¶ *Wicker is used in making baskets and furniture.* 고리버들은 바구니와 가구를 만드는 데 쓰인다. **2** baskets, furniture, etc. made of such twigs woven together. 고리버들 세공《바구니·가구 등》. — *adj.* made of wicker. 가는 가지를 엮어 만든; 고리버들 세공의. [E.=twig]

wick·et [wíkit] *n.* Ⓒ **1** a small gate or door. 작은 문. ¶ *The big door has a ~ in it.* 큰 문에는 쪽문이 있다. **2** a small window or opening, such as in a bank or a ticket office. 매표구; (은행 등의) 창구. ¶ *Buy your ticket at this ~.* 표는 이쪽 매표구에서 사세요. **3** 《cricket》 a set of three sticks between which one side tries to bowl the ball. 위킷; 삼주문(三柱門). [F. *guichet*]

wick·et·keep·er [wíkitkìːpər] *n.* Ⓒ 《cricket》 the player who stands just behind the wicket. 삼주문(三柱門) 수비자.

:wide [waid] *adj.* **1** extending over a large area; broad. 폭이 넓은. ¶ *a ~ cloth* 폭이 넓은 천 / *at ~ intervals* 넓은 간격으로 / *a ~ road* 〔*river, ribbon, ditch, skirt*〕 폭이 넓은 길〔강, 리본, 도랑, 치마〕 / *The gate isn't ~ enough to get the car through.* 문은 차가 통과하기에는 폭이 충분치 못하다. **2** having a certain distance from side to side. 폭이 …인. ¶ *How ~ is it?* 폭이 얼마냐 / *It is 5 feet ~.* 폭이 5피트다. **3** vast; extensive; spacious; far open. 넓은; 광대한; 탁 트인. ¶ *Suddenly there opened a ~ field.* 갑자기 넓은 들이 (눈앞에) 펼쳐졌다 / *the ~ sea* 넓디넓은 바다 / *the ~ world* 이 넓은 세상 / *a ~ domain* 광대한 영지. **4** open to the full; loose. 활짝 열린; (옷 등이) 헐거운; 낙낙한. ¶ *with one's eyes ~ with terror* 공포로 눈을 휘둥그래 뜨고 / *~ knickerbockers* 헐렁한 반바지 / *This vest is too ~ for me.* 이 조끼는 내게 너무 헐렁하다. **5** of great scope or range; extensive; of wide range. 범위가 넓은; 광범위한; 해박한; 다방면의. ¶ *his ~ experience as a teacher* 교사로서의 그의 폭넓은 경험 / *~ knowledge* 광범위한 지식 / *a ~ circle of readers* 넓은 독서층 / *a man ~ fame* 널리 알려진 사람 / *~ reading* 다방면의 독서; 다독. **6** far from a certain point. (목표 따위에서) 먼; (견해 등이) 동떨어진; 엉뚱한. ¶ *be ~ of the truth* 진리와는 거리가 멀다 / *There is a ~ difference between two.* 양자간의 견해 차이는 현격하다 / *an answer quite ~ of the mark* 아주 엉뚱한 대답. **7** 《*sl.*》 crafty; cunning. 약은; 교활한. ¶ *a ~ boy* 약아빠진 아이. **8** 《phon.》 uttered with a relatively wide opening of the vocal organs. 개구음(開口音)의.

— *adv.* **1** to a great distance from side to side. 넓게. ¶ *search* 〔*wander*〕 *far and ~* 널리 수색하다〔돌아다니다〕. **2** to the full extent; fully. 크게〔충분히〕 열어. ¶ *with eyes ~ open* 두 눈을 크게 뜨고. **3** far from the point aimed at. (목표에서) 멀리 빗나가서; 엉뚱하게. ¶ *speak ~ of the mark* 동떨어진 얘기를 하다 / *He is shooting ~.* 그는 과녁에서 멀리 빗나가게 쏘고 있다 / *His blow went ~.* 그의 주먹이 빗나갔다. [E.]

wide-a·wake [wáidəwéik] *adj.* **1** awake and with eyes open wide; thoroughly awake. 완전히 잠이 깬. **2** watchful; prudent. 방심 않는; 빈틈없는; 신중한.

wide-eyed [wáidàid] *adj.* with the eyes open wide. 눈을 크게 뜬.

:wide·ly [wáidli] *adv.* to a great extent. 널리; 멀리; 크게. ¶ *He is ~ known.* 그는 널리 알려진 사람이다 / *~ scattered over Europe* 유럽 전역에 널리 흩어진 / *the most ~ read papers* 가장 널리 읽히는 신문 / *a ~ inaccurate estimate* 크게 부정확한 견적 / *differ ~* 크게 다르다.

·wid·en [wáidn] *vt.* (P6) make (something) wider. …을 넓게 하다; 넓히다. ¶ *~ a ditch* 도랑을 넓히다 / *~ one's outlook* 견해를 넓히다. — *vi.* (P1) become wider. 넓어지다. ¶ *Here the river widens.* 여기서 강은 넓어진다. [*wide*]

·wide-open [wáidóupən] *adj.* opening widely; opened as much as possible. 크게 벌린; 활짝 열린.

·wide·spread [wáidspréd] *adj.* **1** opened or spread to full extent. (날개 따위를) 한껏〔넓게〕 펼친〔편〕. ¶ *a bird's ~ wings* 활짝 펼친 새의 날개. **2** spread over a large area; very common. 널리 퍼진〔보급된〕. ¶ *a ~ superstition* 널리 퍼진 미신 / *English is a ~ language.* 영어는 널리 보급된 언어다 / *a ~ flood* 넓은 지역의 홍수.

:wid·ow [wídou] *n.* Ⓒ a woman whose husband is dead. 미망인; 과부(cf. *widower*). ¶ 《Bible》 *a widow's mite* 과부의 정성어린 소액의 헌금; 빈자(貧者)의 일등(一燈). — *vt.* (P6) **1** make (a woman) a widow. …을 과부로 만들다. ¶ *She has been widowed three times.* 그녀는 세 번이나 과부가 되었다. **2** 《*fig.*, chiefly *poet.*》 strip (someone) of anything greatly loved or needed, esp. by death or disaster. (죽음 등으로) …을 빼앗다. [E.]

wid·ow·er [wídouər] *n.* Ⓒ a man whose wife is dead. 홀아비(cf. *widow*).

wid·ow·hood [wídouhùd] *n.* Ⓤ the state of being a widow. 과부 신세〔살이〕.

widow's cruse [⌐-⌐] *n.* an inexhaustible supply. 무진장; 화수분.

:width [widθ, witθ] *n.* Ⓤ **1** the size of something from side to side. 폭; 너비; 넓이. ¶ *a river of considerable ~* 폭이 상당히 넓은 강 / *have a ~ of 6 feet* 너비가 6피트이다 / *What is its ~?* 폭이 얼마냐. **2** the state or quality of being wide. (지식 등의) 넓이; 해박함. ¶ *the ~ of knowledge* 〔*mind*〕 지식〔마음〕의 넓이〔넓음〕. **3** Ⓒ something of a certain width. 일정한 폭이 있는 것〔나비의 직물〕. ¶ *join two widths* *of paper* 같은 폭의 종이 두 장을 이어 붙이다. [*wide*]

wield [wi:ld] *vt.* (P6) **1** use (a tool, etc.) with the hands; handle; use with full power. (도구 따위)를 쓰다; 다루다; 휘두르다. ¶ ~ *a sword* 〔*an ax*〕 칼을〔도끼를〕 휘두르다 / ~ *a facile pen* 줄줄 써 내리다. **2** rule over; have control or power over. …을 지배하다. ¶ ~ *a kingdom* 왕국을 지배하다. **3** have at one's command. (권력)을 휘두르다; 장악하다. ¶ ~ *power* 권력을 휘두르다 / ~ *influence* 영향력을 행사하다. [E. =rule]

wie·ner [wí:nər] *n.* Ⓤ Ⓒ sausage made of pork and beef mixed together. 비엔나 소시지. [abbr.]

:wife [waif] *n.* Ⓒ (*pl.* **wives**) **1** a married woman. 아내; 처. ¶ *one's ex-wife* 전처 / *a good ~ and mother* 현모 양처 / *husband and ~* 부부. **2** 《*arch.*》 a woman. 여자; 여인. ¶ *an old ~* 노파. [E.]

all the world and his wife ⇨world.

old wives' tale, a foolish story or superstitious belief. 어리석은〔허황된 미신 같은〕 이야기.

take a woman to wife, marry. (여자를) 아내로 맞다.

wife·like [wáiflàik] *adj.* like or suitable to a wife. 아내다운; 아내로서 어울리는. ¶ ~ *concern* 아내다운 염려.

wife·ly [wáifli] *adj.* (**-li·er, -li·est**) of or like a wife. 아내의; 아내다운.

wig [wig] *n.* Ⓒ a covering of hair for the head. 가발. ¶ *wear a ~* 가발을 쓰다. [→periwig]

wigs on the green, a rough, hand-to-hand fight. 거친 주먹다짐; 드잡이; 난투.

wigged [wigd] *adj.* wearing a wig. 가발을 쓴.

wig·gle [wígəl] *vi., vt.* (P1;6) move with short, quick movements. (꼬리 따위를) 흔들다; (방정맞게) 간댕거리다〔까불다〕. ¶ *Stop wiggling your feet.* 발을 방정맞게 흔들지 마라 / *He wiggled his toes.* 그는 발끝을 방정맞게 까딱거렸다. [E.]

Get a wiggle on (***you***)***!*** 《U.S. *colloq.*》 hurry. 서둘러라.

wig·wag [wígwæ̀g] *vi., vt.* (**-wagged, -wag·ging**) (P1;6) **1** move back and forth or to and fro. 흔들(리)다; 기를 흔들다. **2** signal by moving flags or flashing lights. (수기 등으로) 신호하다. —*n.* Ⓤ the act of signaling by flags or lights. (수기·등화 등에 의한) 신호. [*wiggle*]

〈wigwam〉

wig·wam [wígwɑm / -wɔm] *n.* Ⓒ a hut used by North American Indians. (북아메리카 원주민의) 오두막집. [Native]

:wild [waild] *adj.* **1** (of animals or plants) not trained or produced by man; living or growing in a natural state; not cultivated〔tamed〕. 사람의 손으로 기르지〔가꾸지〕 않은; 야생의; 길들여지지 않은. ¶ ~ *plants* 야생 식물 / *grow ~* 들에서 자라다; 자생(自生)하다 / *The lion is a ~ animal.* 사자는 야생 동물이다 / *Some ~ flowers are growing in a corner of the garden.* 정원한 구석에 야생화가 몇 그루 자라고 있다. **2** not civilized; savage; (of land) waste; with few or no inhabitants. 미개한; 야만의; 황량한. ¶ *a ~ tribe* 미개족 / *a ~ land* 황무지 / *the ~ state* 미개 상태. **3** violent; stormy; rough. 격렬한; 거친; 사나운. ¶ *a ~ sea* 거친 바다 / ~ *weather* 거친 날씨 / *a ~ night* 폭풍우의 밤 / ~ *times* 난세. **4** not obeying; lawless; not controlled. 난폭한; 제멋대로의; 방종한. ¶ *a ~ fellow* 난폭자 / *a ~ temper* 난폭한 성미 / ~ *mobs* 무법의 폭도들 / *He spent a ~ youth.* 그는 방종한 젊은 시절을 보냈다. **5** not orderly; disturbed. 난잡한; 흐트러진. ¶ ~ *hair* 흐트러진 머리; 쑥대머리 / *The room was in ~ disorder.* 방은 몹시 어지러웠다. **6** crazy; greatly excited; very eager; 《*colloq.*》 very angry. 미친 것 같은; 광기의; 몹시 흥분한; 열중한; 격노한. ¶ ~ *rage* 격노 / ~ *eyes* 광기어린 눈 / *be ~ about* …에 열중해〔빠져〕 있다 / *be ~ with excitement* 미친 듯이 흥분해 있다 / *be ~ to go* 가고 싶어 안달하다 / *be ~ for revenge* 복수심에 불타 있다 / *drive someone ~* 아무를 열중〔발광〕케 하다 / ~ *with joy* 펄 듯이 기뻐하는 / *She is ~ about me.* 그녀는 나에게 홀딱 빠져 있다 / *His speech was greeted with ~ applause.* 그의 연설은 열광적인 박수를 받았다. **7** reckless; missing the aim. 무모한; 엉뚱한; 허튼. ¶ *a ~ plan* 무모한 계획 / *a ~ pitch* 폭투(暴投) / *a ~ shot* 난사 / *I'll make a ~ guess.* 내 추측은 엉뚱할 게다《사실을 모르니》 / *a ~ talk* 허튼 이야기; 농담.

run wild, be without control or limitation. 난폭해지다. ¶ *They let their children run ~.* 그들은 아이들이 멋대로 굴게 내버려 두었다.

— *adv.* in a wild manner; without aim. 난폭하게; 되는 대로. ¶ *shoot ~* 무작정 쏘다; 난사하다 / *talk ~* 마구 지껄이다.

— *n.* Ⓒ (*pl.* or *the ~*) an area far from the dwellings of men; a desert. 황야; 황무지. ¶ *He lives somewhere out in the wilds of Scotland.* 그는 스코틀랜드의 어느 황야에서 살고 있다. [E.]

wild boar [ㅅㅅ] *n.* a wild hog. 멧돼지.

wild·cat [wáildkæ̀t] *n.* Ⓒ **1** a savage and wild animal like a cat. 살쾡이. **2** an ill-natured person. (살쾡이처럼) 심사가 고약한 사람. **3** a reckless or unsafe business.

무모한 사업. — *adj.* **1** wild; reckless. 무모한. ¶ ~ *schemes* 무모한 계획. **2** illegal; not authorized. 비합법적인. ¶ *a* ~ *strike* (본부의 승인없이 행하는) 비합법적인 쟁의.

wild-duck [wáilddʌ̀k] *n.* a mallard; a wild swimming bird. 들오리.

Wilde [waild], **Oscar** *n.* (1856-1900) a British writer of poems, novels and plays. 오스카 와일드.

:wil·der·ness [wíldərnis] *n.* Ⓒ 《*sing.* only》 a place without people living in it; a wild place. 황야; 황무지. [*wild*]

wild-eyed [wáildàid] *adj.* having wild eyes; staring wildly or angrily. 눈에 광기가 어린; 눈이 노여움으로 이글거리는.

wild·fire [wáildfàiər] *n.* Ⓤ **1** a substance which catches fire easily and is hard to put out. 소이제(燒夷劑) 《옛날 적의 배에 불지를 때 쓴》. **2** anything which spreads rapidly. 삽시간에 번지는 일〔것〕; 들불; 도깨비불.

spread like wildfire, (of a report, rumor, etc.) spread very rapidly. (소문 등이) 삽시간에 번지다〔퍼지다〕.

wild·fowl [wáildfàul] *n.* Ⓒ hunting birds, such as ducks and pheasants. 엽조《들오리·꿩 따위》.

wild goose [⌐⌐] *n.* any goose that is not cultivated. 기러기.

wild-goose chase [⌐⌐⌐] *n.* a fruitless search or pursuit. 헛된 수색〔추구〕.

***wild·ly** [wáildli] *adv.* **1** with a wild nature; violently. 야성적으로; 난폭하게. **2** recklessly; not thoughtfully. 무모하게; 함부로. ¶ *I was* ~ *in love with her.* 물불을 가리지 않고 그녀를 사랑했다.

wild·ness [wáildnis] *n.* Ⓤ the state or quality of being wild. 야성; 야생; 난폭; 방종.

wile [wail] *n.* Ⓒ 《usu. *pl.*》 a cunning trick. 간계(奸計); 농간; 책략(策略). — *vt.* (P7,13) 《*from, into*》 get (someone) to do something in a cunning way. …을 속이다; 속여서 …하게 하다. ¶ *She wiled the secret from him.* 그녀는 그를 속여서 비밀을 알아냈다. [→guile]

wile away, while away. (시간 따위를) 그럭저럭 보내다. ¶ ~ *away the time* 이럭저럭 시간을 보내다.

Wil·fred [wílfrid] *n.* a man's name. 남자 이름.

wil·ful [wílfəl] *adj.* 《Brit.》 =willful.

wil·ful·ly [wílfəli] *adv.* 《Brit.》 =willfully.

:will [wil] *auxil. v.* (**would**) (P25) **1** be going to; be about to. …일〔할〕 것이다(cf. *shall*). 語法 평서문에서는 2·3인칭에 쓰이며, 1인칭은 shall. 그러나 미국에서는 I〔we〕 will이 단순 미래에 쓰임. 의문문에서는 3인칭에 쓰임. ¶ *You* ~ *succeed.* 너는 성공할 것이다 / *It'll be fine tomorrow.* 내일은 날씨가 좋을 것이다 / *Will he be at home tomorrow ?* 그가 내일 집에 있을까 / *When* ~ *this train get to Seoul ?* 이 기차는 서울에 몇 시에 도착하느냐 / *You* 〔*He*〕 ~ *be punished.* 너〔그〕는 처벌될 것이다 / *I hope the weather* ~ *be fine and you* ~ *have a good time.* 날씨가 좋아져 너희들이 즐거운 시간을 보냈으면 한다 / *Will you be back early this evening ?* 오늘 저녁 일찍 돌아오겠느냐. **2** be determined to. …하겠다; …할 작정이다. ¶ *I* ~ *write to him at once.* 곧 그에게 편지를 쓰겠다 / *Will you come for a walk this evening ?* 오늘 저녁 산책 가겠느냐 / *I shall be glad* 〔*pleased*〕 *to go, if you* ~ *accompany me.* 네가 함께 가준다면 기꺼이 가겠다 / *I* ~ *not tolerate such behavior.* 나는 그 따위 행동을 그냥 놔두지 않을 테다 / *He won't do as he is told.* 그는 시킨 대로 하지 않을 것이다. **3** 《expressing a firm resolution》 기어코〔반드시, 꼭〕 …하다. ¶ *You* ~ *have your own way, whatever I say.* 내가 뭐라 하든, 너는 기어이 네 고집대로 하려 드는구나 / *I* ~ *be obeyed.* 하라는 대로 말을 들어 주어야 한다 / *I* ~ *have it so.* 꼭 그렇게 하고 말겠다 / *I won't make that mistake again.* 다시는 그런 실수를 않겠다. **4** do usu. or often; be accustomed to. 곧잘 …하곤 하다; …하는 것이 예사이다. ¶ *He* ~ *sit there for hours.* 몇 시간이고 거기에 앉아 있곤 했다 / *He* ~ *often sit up reading all night.* 밤새도록 독서하기 일쑤다 / *She* ~ *cry for hours at a time.* 울었다 하면 몇 시간이고 운다. **5** be willing to; wish to. 기꺼이 …하다; …을 원하다. ¶ *This door* ~ *not open.* 이 문은 여간해서 열리지 않는다 / *If you* ~ *kindly sign here, we can complete the contract.* 당신이 여기에 서명해 주신다면, 계약을 체결하게 됩니다 / *The party* ~ *go very well if everyone* ~ *only cooperate.* 모두가 협조만 해준다면 파티는 아주 순조롭게 진행될 것이다 / *Ask him if he* ~ *have some money.* 그에게 돈을 좀 원하는지 물어 보아라. **6** be apt or inclined to. …하기(가) 쉽다; …하는 경향이 있다. ¶ *Boys* ~ *be boys.* 애들은 역시 애들이다《어쩔 수 없다》/ *Accidents* ~ *happen.* 사고는 일어나게 마련이다 / *Murder* ~ *out.* 나쁜 일은 드러나게 되어 있다. **7** 《expressing probability, expectation, etc.》 아마도 …일 것이다. ¶ *This'll be our train, I fancy.* (내 생각에) 이번 기차가 우리가 탈 기차일 것 같다 / *I suppose this* ~ *be the Tower of London.* 아마 이게 런던탑일 것이다 / *This* ~ *be the house he was speaking of.* 이것이 그가 말하던 집인 것 같다 / *This coat* ~ *last you a lifetime, sir.* 선생님, 이 코트는 평생 입으실 수 있을 겁니다. **8** be required to. …이 필요할 것이다; …이 요구되다. ¶ *You* ~ *do it at once.* 너는 그것을 즉시 해야 한다 / *You* ~ *report here at 7:30 in the morning.* 아침 7시 30분에 여기로 출두하라. **9** can; be able to. …할 수 있다. ¶ *The flower* ~ *live without water for two weeks.* 그 꽃은 물 없이도 2주일동안은 살 수 있다.

— *n.* 《*sing.* only》 **1** Ⓒ 《*the* ~ 》 the mental power by which a person can decide how to act. 의지; 의사(cf. *volition*). ¶ *the freedom of the* ~ 의사의 자유 / *free* ~ 자유 의지. **2** [U][C] the mental power by which a person can control himself; strong intention. 의지력; 결의; 의욕; 의도. ¶ *have a strong* 〔*a weak*〕 ~ 의지가 강〔약〕하다 / *He has no* ~ *of his own.* 그는 독자적 의지가 없다 / *have the* ~ *to succeed* 성공하겠다는 의욕을 가지다 / 《*prov.*》 *The* ~ *is as good as the deed.* 무슨 일에나 의지력이 중요하다 / 《*prov.*》 *Where there's a* ~, *there's a way.* 뜻이 있는 곳에 길이 있다 / *The* ~ *to live helps a patient to recover.* 살려는 의욕이 환자의 회복을 빠르게 한다. **3** [C] enthusiasm. 열의; 열성. ¶ *He works with a* ~. 그는 열의를 가지고 일을 한다. **4** [C] a wish; a desire; a pleasure. 소망(所望); 바람; 욕망. ¶ *against one's* ~ 본의 아니게 / *have one's* ~ 제 뜻대로 하다 / *the* ~ *to fight* 싸우려는 생각. **5** [U] manner or feeling towards others. (남에게 대해 갖는) 마음; 기분; 태도. ¶ *good* 〔*ill*〕 ~ 호의〔악의〕 / *show good* ~ 호의를 보이다. **6** [C] a written statement showing what is to be done with a person's money and goods after his death. 유언; 유서. ¶ *make one's* ~ 유언서를 작성하다 / *leave something by* ~ 유언으로 어떤 것을 남기다.

at will =***at*** *one's* (***own sweet***) ***will,*** at one's pleasure. 마음 내키는 대로; 임의로. ¶ *He comes and goes at* ~. 그는 제 마음대로 오고 가고 한다.

do the will (=*obey the wish or command*) ***of*** *someone.* …의 희망〔명령〕에 따르다.

of *one's* ***own free will,*** willingly; voluntarily. 자발적으로.

— *vt.* **1** (P6,8,11) determine; decide; wish. …을 의지로 결정하다; 결의하다. ¶ *The girl willed to be honest.* 소녀는 정직해지려고 마음먹었다 / *Whatever he wills he can accomplish.* 그는 의도하는 것은 무엇이고 다 이룰 수 있다 / *Many wish, but few* ~, *to be good.* 착해지고 싶다고 바라는 사람은 많으나 그렇게 되려고 애를 쓰는 사람은 적다. **2** (P13,20) influence or control (someone) by exercising the will. (남)에게 의지의 힘으로 …시키다. ¶ *He willed himself into contentment.* 그는 스스로를 만족시켰다 / *She willed the man to turn round.* 그녀는 그 사람을 뒤돌아보게 했다. **3** (P7,13) leave (money, etc.) by means of a will. …을 유언에 의해 주다. ¶ *He willed his money to a school.* 그는 유언으로 자기 재산을 학교에 기증했다.

— *vi.* (P1) **1** exercise the will. 의지를 작용시키다. ¶ *To* ~ *is not enough; one must act.* 하려는 생각만으론 충분치 않다. 실행해야만 한다. **2** wish; desire. 원하다; 바라다. ¶ *They wandered as they willed.* 그들은 자기들 가고 싶은 대로 돌아다녔다. [E.]

will·ful, 《Brit.》 **wil-** [wílfəl] *adj.* **1** done on purpose. 고의의; 계획적인. ¶ ~ *neglect* 〔*murder*〕 고의적인 태만〔살인〕. **2** determined to have one's own way; stubborn. 제멋대로의; 외고집의. ¶ *a* ~ *child* 고집센 아이.

will·ful·ly, 《Brit.》 **wil-** [wílfəli] *adv.* in a willful manner. 고의로; 제멋대로.

will·ful·ness, 《Brit.》 **wil-** [wílfəlnis] *n.* [U] the state or quality of being willful. 고의; 외고집.

:will·ing [wíliŋ] *adj.* **1** 《*to do*》 cheerful; ready. 기꺼이 …하는. ¶ *She is* ~ *to join us.* 그녀는 기꺼이 우리와 합세하려고 한다 / *I am quite* ~ *to do anything for you.* 당신을 위해서라면 무엇이든 기꺼이 하겠다 / *If the management is* ~, *the talks can be held today.* 경영진이 마음만 있다면 회담은 오늘도 가질 수 있다. **2** given or done readily or gladly. 자발적인; 자유 의지의. ¶ ~ *assistance* 자발적인 조력.

***will·ing·ly** [wíliŋli] *adv.* in a willing manner. 기꺼이; 쾌히; 자발적으로.

will·ing·ness [wíliŋnis] *n.* [U] the state or quality of being willing. 기꺼이〔자진해서〕 행함; 자발성.

will-o'-the-wisp [wíləðəwísp] *n.* [C] **1** a light seen moving at night over wet or marshy places. 도깨비불. **2** a thing that misleads or deceives. 사람을 호리는 것. [=William of the torch]

***wil·low** [wílou] *n.* [C] a tree with easily bent branches. 버드나무; 버들. [E.]

wil·low·y [wíloui] *adj.* **1** like a willow; easily bent; graceful. 버들 같은; 유연한. **2** full of willows. 버들이 무성한.

wil·ly-nil·ly [wílinílі] *adv.* willingly or not; with or against one's wishes. 싫든 좋든; 좋아하든 말든. ¶ *The new law will be passed* ~ *so we will have to consider how it affects us.* 싫든 좋든 새 법률은 가결될 것이니, 그것이 우리에게 어떤 영향을 미칠 것인지 생각해 봐야 할 것이다. [=*will be, nill*(=will not) *be*]

***wilt**[1] [wilt] *vi.* (P1) **1** (of a plant) become dry and lifeless; lose freshness; wither. (초목이) 시들다; 생기를 잃다. ¶ *The flowers are wilting from lack of water.* 물이 없어 꽃들이 시들고 있다. **2** (of a person) become weak or faint. (사람이) 기운이 없어지다; 약해지다. ¶ *I am wilting in this heat.* (날씨가) 더워 힘이 빠진다. — *vt.* (P6) cause (a plant, a person, etc.) to wilt. …을 시들게〔약해지게〕 하다. [var. of *welk*]

wilt[2] [wilt] *auxil. v.* 《*arch.*》 =will. 參考 주어는 thou.

wil·y [wáili] *adj.* (**wil·i·er, wil·i·est**) full of tricks; cunning. 교활한. [*wile*]

wim·ble [wímbəl] *n.* a tool with a cross handle for boring. 송곳. [E.]

wim·ple [wímpəl] *n.* [C] a linen headdress worn by nuns. (수녀가 쓰는) 두건의 일종; 베일. — *vt.* (P6) cover or muffle (something) with a wimple. …을 베일로 덮다〔싸다〕. — *vi.* (P1) ripple. 잔물결이 일다. [E.]

:win [win] *v.* (**won, win·ning**) *vt.* (P6,7,13, 20) **1** be successful in (a game, a battle, etc.). (경기·전쟁 등)에 이기다〔승리하다, 우승하다〕(opp. lose). ¶ ~ *a game* 〔*an election*〕 경기에〔선거에〕 이기다 / *She won a beauty contest.* 그녀는 미인 대회에서 우승했다 / *The winning team was given a silver cup.* 승리한 팀에게 은컵이 수여됐다 / ~ *victory in a war* 싸움에 승리를 획득하다. **2** gain (a prize, fame, love, etc.); achieve; earn. (상·명성·사랑 등)을 얻다; 획득하다; 벌어들이다. ¶ ~ *one's bread* 생활비를 벌다 / ~ *a prize in a contest* 경쟁에 이겨 상품을 타다 / ~ *someone's heart* 아무의 마음을 사로잡다 / *The book won him fame.* 그 책으로 그는 유명해졌다 / *Her graciousness won all hearts.* 그녀의 우아함은 모든 사람을 매혹했다 / ~ *a lady* = ~ *a lady's hand* 한 여성에게서 결혼 승낙을 받다 / *Do you think he will* ~ *the party's nomination?* 그가 당의 공천을 받을 것 같으냐. **3** succeed in reaching (a place, etc.) by great effort. (곤란을 물리치고) …에 도달하다. ¶ ~ *the summit* 정상에 이르다 / ~ *repose* 안식의 경지에 이르다 / *The ship won the harbor.* (마침내) 배는 항구에 다다랐다. **4** persuade; convince. …을 설득하다; 납득시키다. ¶ *We won him to consent.* 그를 설득해 승낙하도록 했다 / *He won her over to his side.* 그는 그녀를 설득하여 자기 편으로 끌어들였다 / *You've won me.* 네 말에 내가 졌다《더이상 반대하지 않겠다》.

— *vi.* (P1,2A) **1** gain a victory. 이기다; 승리하다. ¶ ~ *by a boat's length* 배 하나 길이의 차로 이기다 / ~ *against someone* 아무와 경쟁에서 이기다 / 《U.S.》 ~ *over an opposing team* 상대팀을 제압하다 / *Our team won with a score of 3:0.* 우리 팀은 3대 0으로 이겼다. **2** succeed, after a struggle, in reaching a certain state or place. 도달〔도착〕하다; 이르다. ¶ ~ *home* 집에 도착하다 / ~ *to shore* (드디어) 해변〔강(江)가〕에 다다르다.

win free 〔***clear, loose***〕, make one's way through; escape by successful effort. 뚫고 나아가다; 자유롭게 되다.

win out 〔***through***〕, **a**) make one's way through. 헤쳐나가다. ¶~ *through difficulties* 어려움을 헤치고 나아가다. **b**) succeed. 성공하다.

win the day 〔***the field***〕, gain a victory. 싸움에 이기다; 승리하다.

win one's way, **a**) go with great effort. 힘들여〔애써〕 나아가다. **b**) succeed in life by effort. 노력해서 성공하다. ¶ ~ *one's way in the world* 노력해서 출세하다.

— *n.* **1** the act of winning; a victory. 승리. ¶ *four wins and three defeats,* 4승 3패 / *I have three wins against him.* 나는 그에게 세 판 이겼다. **2** a profit; a gain; winnings. 이득; 이익; 상금; 상품. ¶ *She had a big* ~ *in the lottery.* 그녀는 복권에서 크게 한몫 봤다. [E.=fight, toil]

wince [wins] *vi.* (P1,3) draw back suddenly because of fear, pain, etc. 주춤하다; 움츠리다. ¶ *She winced as she touched the cold body.* 그녀는 차가운 시체에 닿자 움찔했다 / *He winced mentally at her angry words.* 그는 그녀의 성난 말에 기가 죽었다〔위축되었다〕 / *bear pain without wincing* 태연하게 고통을 견디내다. — *n.* Ⓒ an act of suddenly drawing back; flinching. 움츠림; 움찔하기; 위축. [Teut.]

winch [wintʃ] *n.* Ⓒ a machine for lifting or pulling by means of a rope or chain wound on a roller. 윈치. [E.]

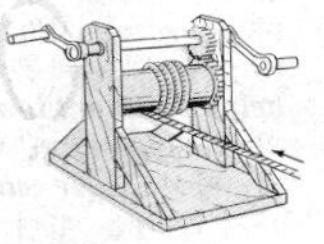
〈winch〉

:wind[1] [wind, 《*poet.*》 waind] *n.* **1** ⒸⓊ a current of air; air moved by a fan, etc.; a strong wind; a storm. 바람; (인위적인) 바람; 강풍; 폭풍. ¶ *a gentle* ~ 미풍 / *a strong* ~ 강풍 / *a wet* ~ 비를 머금은 바람 / *a fair* 〔*contrary*〕 ~ 순풍〔역풍〕 / ~ *from a bellows* 풀무바람 / *the* ~ *of the passing train* 지나가는 기차에서 나는 바람 / ~ *and rain* 풍우; 비바람 / *a gust of* ~ 일진의 바람 / *with the* ~ 바람 부는 대로; 바람과 함께 / *The* ~ *rises* 〔*falls*〕. 바람이 일다〔자다〕 / *There is a high* ~. 바람이 세게 불고 있다 / *into the* ~ 바람 불어오는 쪽으로 / *off the* ~ 바람을 등지고 / *to the* ~ 바람 불어오는 쪽을 향하여 / 《*prov.*》 *It is an ill* ~ *that blows nobody good.* 누구에게도 득이 안되는 바람이란 불지 않는 법이다; 갑의 손해가 을에게는 득(得) / *High* 〔*Strong*〕 *winds made driving conditions dangerous.* 강풍으로 인해서 자동차 운전 조건이 위험해졌다. **2** Ⓤ a smell carried by the wind; a hint; a rumor. (바람에 실려오는) 향기; 냄새; 예감; 소문. ¶ *keep the* ~ 냄새의 자취를 잃지 않도록 하다 / *get* 〔*take*〕 ~ 소문으로 전해지다 / *get* 〔*have*〕 ~ *of* (…라는 소문)을 알아내다; 눈치채다 / *The hounds got* ~ *of the fox.* 사냥개는 여우의 냄새를 맡아냈다 / *I got* ~ *of where she was.* 그녀가 어디에 있는지 알아냈다. **3** Ⓤ breath; the power of breathing. 숨; 호흡(력). ¶ *broken* ~ 헐떡임; 가쁜 숨 / *second* ~ (숨찬 상태에서 회복된) 정상적인 호흡 / *get* 〔*recover*〕 *one's* ~ 숨을 돌리다 / *I have lost my wind.* 숨이 차다 / *catch one's* ~ 숨을 죽이다 / *knock the* ~ *out of someone* 아무를 때려 숨도 제대로 못 쉬게 만들다. **4** Ⓤ gas or air produced in the stomach. 위(胃) 속의 가스. ¶ *suffer from* ~ 헛배가 불러 고생하다 / *break* ~ 방귀 뀌다. **5** Ⓤ empty talk; nonsense. 빈말; 허튼소리; 흰소리. ¶ *His speech is always only* ~. 그의 연설은 늘 알맹이가 없는 빈말 뿐이다. **6** 《*the* ~, *collectively*》 the wind instruments; 《*the* ~*s*》 the members of an orchestra who play the wind instruments. 관악기; 그 연주자들(cf. *strings*).

against* 〔*into*〕 *the wind towards the direction from which the wind is blowing; to the windward. 바람을 정면으로 안고; 바람을 거슬러.
between wind and water, **a**) close to the water line of a ship. (배의) 흘수선부(吃水線部)에. **b**) in dangerous spot. 급소에.
cast* 〔*fling*〕** (fears, modesty, etc.) ***to the winds, neglect; take no thought of. …을 무시하다; 저버리다; 내버려두다.
down the wind =***before the wind,*** in the direction of the wind; carried along by the wind. 바람을 등지고; 바람에 실려.
get* 〔*have*〕 *the wind of, have an advantage over; be in a more favorable position than. …보다 유리한 위치에 있다.
in the teeth of the wind =against 〔into〕 the wind.
in the wind, **a**) to the windward. 바람 불어오는 쪽으로. **b**) happening or about to happen secretly. 몰래 행해져; (일이) 일어날 듯한. ¶ *What's in the* ~*?* 무슨 일이 행해지고 있느냐 / *There's something unusual in the* ~. 무언가 비정상적인 일이 일어날 것 같다.
***know* 〔*find out, see*〕 *how the wind blows* 〔*lies*〕,** know what the state of affairs, public opinion, etc. is. 세상의 동향을〔여론의 추이를〕 알다.
like the wind, very fast. (바람처럼) 아주 빨리. ¶ *run like the* ~ 쏜살같이 달리다.
***put the wind up** someone,* 《*sl.*》 frighten someone. …을 깜짝 놀라게 하다. ¶ *The news put the* ~ *up him.* 그 소식에 그는 깜짝 놀랐다.
raise the wind, 《*colloq.*》 get money somehow or other. 이럭저럭 돈을 마련하다; 자금을 조달하다.
sail close to the wind, **a**) sail nearly against the wind. 옆바람을 받으며 나아가다. **b**) do something that is almost dishonest, indecent, etc. (법률·도덕 따위에 저촉될까 말까의) 아슬아슬한 위태로운 처세를 하다.
take the wind out of** someone's **sails, do or say what someone else was going to do or say; interrupt someone in his conversation, usu. while boasting. (남)을 꼭뒤지르다; (남)의 말을 가로막고 나서다.
take* 〔*get*〕 *wind, be rumored. 남들의 소문거리가 되다.
the four winds, all sides; all directions. 사면 팔방.
up the wind, in a direction opposite or nearly opposite the wind. 바람을 거슬러; 바람을 향해서.
— *vt.* (P6) **1** expose (something) to the wind. …을 바람에 쐬다. **2** follow the smell of (something). …을 낌새채다; 알아내다. ¶ ~ *a plot* 음모를 탐지해내다 / *The hound winded the fox.* 사냥개는 여우의 냄새를 맡아냈다. **3** cause (someone) to be out of breath. (아무)를 숨차게 하다; 헐떡이게 하다. ¶ *I was quite winded by the climb.* 나는 산에 오르느라 몹시 숨이 찼다 / *be winded by running* 달리기에 숨이 차다. **4** rest (a horse, etc.) to allow recovery of breath. (말 따위에게) 숨을 돌리게 하다. ¶ *stop in order to* ~ *a horse* 말이 숨을 돌리게 멈춰 서다. [E.]

wind[2] [waind, wind] *vt.* (**wound**) (P6) blow (a horn, bugle, etc.). (뿔피리·나팔 등)을 불다. ¶ *The hunter winds his horn.* 사냥꾼이 뿔피리를 분다. [↑]

:wind[3] [waind] *v.* (**wound**) *vt.* (P6,7,13) **1** form (a thread, cord, etc.) into a ball by rolling; coil (something) around something else; twist together. …을 감다; 휘감다. ¶ ~ *string into a ball* 끈을 감아 둥글게 뭉치다 / ~ *a bandage around one's finger* 손가락에 붕대를 감다. **2** tighten the spring of (a watch, etc.) by turning some part of it. (시계의 태엽 등)을 감다. ¶ ~ *up one's watch* 시계(의) 태엽을 감다 / *The clock's stopped, you'd better* ~ *it* (*up*). 시계가 섰구나. 태엽을 감아 줘야겠다. **3** turn. …을 돌리다. ¶ ~ *a handle* 핸들을 돌리다 / *I wound down the car window.* 손잡이를 돌려 차의 문을 내렸다. **4** raise (something) by winding. …을 감아〔자아〕 올리다. ¶ ~ *water from a well* 우물에서 물을 길어올리다. **5** wrap closely. …을 단단히 싸다〔감다〕. ¶ ~ *a shawl around a baby* 아기를 숄로 감싸다 / *The boy wound his arms round his mother's neck.* 그 애는 양팔로 어머니의 목을 껴안았다. **6** make (one's way) in a frequent bending course. (길 따위)를 굽이쳐 나아가다. ¶ *Our bus wound its way.* 버스는 길을 따라 구불구불 따라갔다. **7** follow cautiously. 조심스럽게 뒤를 밟다. — *vi.* (P1,2A,3) **1** (of a road, stream, etc.) go or move in a curving or zigzagging manner. 구불구불 나아가다; 꼬불꼬불 구부러지다. ¶ *The road winds among the hills.* 도로는 언덕 사이로 구불구불 나 있다 / *A path* 〔*brook*〕 *winds through the woods.* 작은 길〔시냇물〕이 숲속으로 구불구불 나 있다〔흐른다〕. **2** 《*about, around*》 (of a snake, climbing plants, etc.) twist or turn around something. 감기다; 휘감기다. ¶ *The flag winds around the flagpole.* 깃발이 깃대에 감겨 있다 / *the tendrils that* ~ *round the poles* 장대에 휘감긴 덩굴손. **3** undergo winding. (시계가) 감기다. ¶ *a clock which winds with a key* 열쇠 같은 것으로 태엽을 감는 시계.
wind off, unwind. (감은 것)을 풀다.
wind** someone **round** one's **fingers, make someone do what one pleases. (아무)를 제마음대로 농락하다〔부려먹다〕.
wind up, **a**) form into a ball. …을 감아서 둥글게 뭉치다. ¶ ~ *up wool* 〔*string*〕 양털〔끈〕을 둥글게 감아 뭉치다. **b**) 《*fig.*》 increase the tension of ; excite. …을 긴장〔흥분〕시키다. ¶ *He wound himself up into a rage.* 그는 벌컥 화를 내고야 말았다. **c**) bring to an end; finish. …을 끝내다. ¶ *He wound up his*

speech by a quotation from the Bible. 그는 성경에서의 인용구 한 마디를 끝으로 연설을 마쳤다 / *The company has been wound up.* 회사는 문을 닫았다. **d**) 《baseball》 give a preparatory swing to the arm before pitching a ball. (야구에서) 투수가 와인드업하다.

— *n.* Ⓒ **1** a turn; a curve; a bend. 굽음; 굽이(짐); 굴곡; 커브. ¶ *out of* ~ 굽지 않은 / *the winds of* 〔*in*〕 *a path* 오솔길의 꾸불꾸불한 커브. **2** a single turn of something wound. 한번 돌기〔돌리기〕; 한번 감기. ¶ *Give the handle a few more winds.* 핸들을 몇 번 더 돌려라. [E.]

wind·bag [wíndbæ̀g] *n.* Ⓒ 《*colloq.*》 a person who talks much but does not say anything of importance. 수다쟁이; 풍이 심한 사람; 떠버리. [*wind*[1]]

wind-blown [wíndblòun] *adj.* **1** blown by the wind. 바람에 날린. **2** with the hair cut short and brushed forward. (여자 머리를) 짧게 잘라 앞으로 매만져 붙인.

wind-borne [wíndbɔ̀ːrn] *adj.* (of seed, pollen, etc.) carried by the wind. (씨앗·꽃가루·모래 등이) 바람에 옮겨진〔운반된〕; 풍매(風媒)의. ¶ ~ *sand.*

wind-break [wíndbrèik] *n.* Ⓒ a shelter or protection from the wind, such as a row of trees or a walls. 바람막이; 방풍림; 방풍벽(壁).

wind·break·er [wíndbrèikər] *n.* Ⓒ a jacket for outdoor wear, made of wool, leather, etc. (스포츠용) 잠바.

wind·fall [wíndfɔ̀ːl] *n.* Ⓒ **1** a piece of fruit fallen from the tree because of the wind. 바람으로 떨어진 과일. ¶ *These apples are windfalls, but they're good.* 이 사과들은 바람에 떨어진 것들이지만 괜찮다. **2** good luck; a gain, esp. of money, etc., that is unexpected. 행운; 횡재.

wind gauge [ㅊㅅ] *n.* an instrument for measuring the speed and force of the wind. 풍력계.

wind·ing sheet [wáindiŋ ʃìːt] *n.* a cloth for wrapping a dead person. 시체를 싸는 천; 수의. [*wind*[3]]

wind instrument [ㅊ ㅅ-–] *n.* a musical instrument played by blowing air into it. 관악기. [*wind*[1]]

wind·lass [wíndləs] *n.* Ⓒ a machine for lifting or pulling; a winch. 자아틀; 윈치. [*wind*[3]]

wind·less [wíndlis] *adj.* **1** without wind. 바람이 없는; 고요한. **2** out of breath. 숨찬. [*wind*[1]]

•**wind·mill** [wíndmìl] *n.* Ⓒ **1** a mill or machine for grinding operated by wind. 풍차. **2** a child's toy with naves which revolve in the wind. 팔랑개비.

fight 〔***tilt at***〕 ***windmills,*** expend energy in overcoming imaginary obstacles or opponents. 가상의 적과 싸우다《Don Quixote가 풍차에 도전한 이야기에서》. [*wind*[1]]

⁝**win·dow** [wíndou] *n.* Ⓒ **1** an opening in a wall, roof, etc. in order to let in air or light, usu. covered with glass. 창문. ¶ *look out of the* ~ 창 밖을 내다보다 / *It's cold in here; shut the* ~. 여긴 춥구나, 창문을 닫아라. **2** the framework, panes of glass, etc. filling such an opening. 창유리; 창틀. **3** =window envelope. [N.= wind-eye]

have all one's goods in the front window, be merely superficial. 겉치레〔허울〕뿐이다; 피상적이다; 천박하다.

window box [ㅊ- ㅅ] *n.* a box for growing plants put under a window. 창가에 두는 화초 가꾸는 상자.

window dressing [ㅊ- ㅅ-] *n.* **1** the decoration or display of a store window. (상점의) 진열창〔쇼윈도〕 장식(법). **2** the act of intending to give a misleadingly favorable impression. (호감을 주기 위한) 겉치레; 보기 좋게 꾸미기.

window envelope [ㅊ- ㅊ--] *n.* an envelope which has paraffin paper or a similar transparent section on its front so that we can read the address on the letter inside. (수신인의 주소·성명이 비쳐보이는 파라핀지(紙)) 창 봉투(cf. *window* 3).

win·dow·pane [wíndoupèin] *n.* Ⓒ a panel of glass in a window. (끼워놓은) 창유리.

window seat [ㅊ- ㅅ] *n.* a bench which is built into the wall of a room, beneath a window. 창 밑에 붙박이한 걸상.

window-shop [wíndouʃɑ̀p / -ʃɔ̀p] *vi.* (**-shopped, -shop·ping**) (P1) look at the displays of goods in store windows without buying. (물건을 사지는 않고) 가게의 진열창을 들여다보며 다니다.

wind·pipe [wíndpàip] *n.* 《med.》 the passage from the throat to the lungs. 기관(氣管); 숨통. [*wind*[1]]

wind·screen [wíndskrìːn] *n.* Ⓒ 《Brit.》 = windshield.

wind·shield [wíndʃìːld] *n.* Ⓒ 《U.S.》 a sheet of glass at the front of a car, etc. to protect people from wind, rain, etc. (자동차의) 방풍(防風) 유리(cf. 《Brit.》 *windscreen*). [*wind*[1]]

wind·storm [wíndstɔ̀ːrm] *n.* Ⓒ a storm, a hurricane, etc. often without rain. (흔히, 비를 수반하지 않는) 폭풍.

wind·swept [wíndswèpt] *adj.* exposed to the wind. 바람받이의; 바람에 노출된. ¶ *a* ~ *plain* 바람에 내맡겨진 들판.

wind-up [wáindʌ̀p] *n.* Ⓒ **1** end; conclusion. 종결. **2** 《baseball》 preparatory arm movements of a pitcher before pitching. (투수의) 와인드업. [*wind*[3]]

wind·ward [wíndwərd] *adj.* on the side from which the wind blows. 바람맞이 쪽의.

— *adv.* toward the direction from which

the wind blows. 바람맞이로; 바람을 안고. ¶ *We steered* ~. 우리는 바람을 안고 항해했다. — *n.* Ⓤ the side from which the wind blows. 바람맞이. [*wind*[1]]

to the windward of, toward the place which is in a better position than. …보다 유리한 쪽으로.

wind·y [wíndi] *adj.* (**wind·i·er, wind·i·est**) **1** having much wind. 바람이 많이 부는. ¶ *a ~ season* 바람이 심한 계절. **2** exposed to the wind. 바람을 세게 받는. ¶ *the ~ side of the building* 건물의 바람받이쪽 / *a ~ hillside* 바람이 심한 언덕의 중턱. **3** talking too much or emptily. 수다스러운; 말뿐인. ¶ *a ~ speech* 알맹이 없는 연설〔담화〕. **4** producing gas in the stomach, etc. 헛배가 부른; 배에 가스가 차는. **5** 《*sl.*》 frightened. 깜짝 놀란. [*wind*[1]]

:wine [wain] *n.* Ⓤ **1** alcoholic drink made from the juice of grapes. 포도주. ¶ 《*prov.*》 *Good ~ needs no bush.* 좋은 술에는 간판이 필요 없다. **2** a similar drink made from other fruits or plants. 과실주. **3** the color of red wine; a dark-red color. 포도주 빛; 검붉은 색. **4** 《Brit. univ.》 a friendly evening party at which wine is drunk. (만찬 후의) 포도주 파티.

be in wine, be drunk. 취하다.

new wine in old bottles, something new which is expressed in old forms. 헌 가죽 부대에 채운 새 술《낡은 형식으로는 다루지 못하는 새로운 주의》.

take wine with *someone,* drink to each other's health. …와 건배하다.

— *vt., vi.* (P6; 1) entertain with wine; drink wine. 포도주를 대접하다; 포도주를 마시다. ¶ *~ and dine a friend* 친구를 포도주와 음식으로 대접하다. [O.E., M.E. *win*]

wine·glass [wáinglæ̀s, -glɑ̀ːs] *n.* Ⓒ a glass used for drinking wine. 포도주 잔; 와인 글라스.

wine press [ˊ ˋ] *n.* a machine used for pressing the juice from grapes. 포도 짜는 기구.

wine·skin [wáinskìn] *n.* Ⓒ a container made of the skin of a goat, hog, etc., used for holding wine. 포도주 담는 가죽 부대《염소 따위의 가죽을 통째로 씀》.

:wing [wiŋ] *n.* Ⓒ **1** the part of a bird, insect, etc. by which it flies. 날개. **2** one of the main supporting surfaces of an airplane. 비행기(의) 날개. **3** the vane of a windwill. 풍차의 날개. **4** 《*iron.*》 a person's arm. (사람의) 팔. **5** a part of a building projecting from the main part. 건물의 물림; 퇴(退). ¶ *The house is square with a ~ at each side.* 그 집은 양옆에 퇴를 낸 네모 반듯한 집이다 / *He built a new ~.* 물림을 새로 붙였다. **6** the stage platform in a theater. 무대의 좌우 공간. ¶ *The spaces to the right or left of the stage in a theater are called the wings.* 극장 무대의 좌우 공간을 윙이라 한다. **7** ⓐ (in the army or navy) the extreme right or left of the main force. 군대의 좌·우익(翼). ⓑ 《U.S.》 an administral and technical unit of the Air Force. 비행 대대. ⓒ 《U.S.》 an aviation badge. 항공 배지; 공군 기장. **8** a part of a political party. 당파《정당의 주의(主義) 상의 좌익·우익》.

add 〔***give***〕 ***wings to,*** promote; increase the speed of. …을 촉진하다; …을 가속화하다.

on the wing, **a**) in flight; flying. 날아서; 비행 중에. ¶ *catch butterflies on the ~* 날고 있는 나비를 잡다. **b**) moving; traveling; in the act or process of starting. 활동 중에; 여행〔이동〕 중에; 출발 과정에.

on the wings of the wind, very swiftly. 아주 빨리; 나는 듯이; 신속히.

take wing, fly away; go away. 날아가다; 도망치다.

under the wing of, under the protection of. …의 비호〔보호〕 아래.

— *vt.* **1** (P6) supply (something) with wings; furnish (an arrow, etc.) with wings. …에 날개를 달다; (화살)에 깃을 붙이다. **2** (P6) cause (an arrow, etc.) to fly. …을 날리다. ¶ *~ an arrow at the mark* 과녁을 향해 화살을 쏘다. **3** (P6,7) fly across, over or through (something). …을 날다. ¶ *~ the air* 하늘을 날다 / *~ its way* 〔*flight*〕 (새가) 날아가다. **4** (P6,7) increase the speed of. …의 속도를 늘리다〔빠르게 하다〕. ¶ *Terror winged his steps as the bear drew nearer.* 곰이 다가오자 공포로 인해 그의 걸음은 더 빨라졌다. **5** (P6) hurt (a bird or person) in the wings or arms. …의 날개를〔팔을〕 다치게 하다. ¶ *The poor bird was badly winged.* 그 가엾은 새는 날개를 몹시 다쳤다.

— *vi.* (P1) fly. 날다. ¶ *The birds winged across the lake.* 새들은 호수를 가로질러 날아갔다 / *The plane came winging down toward the coast.* 비행기는 해안 쪽으로 내려가고 있었다. [N.]

winged [wiŋd, 《*poet.*》 wíŋid] *adj.* **1** having wings. 날개가 있는. **2** swift; flying like an arrow. 고속의; 살처럼 빠른. **3** having the wings damaged or hurt. 날개를 다친.

wing·less [wíŋlis] *adj.* without wings; unable to fly. 날개가 없는; 날 수가 없는.

wing·span [wíŋspæ̀n] *n.* Ⓒ **1** the distance between the wing tips of an airplane. 날개 길이; 익폭(翼幅). ¶ *an aircraft with a ~ of 50 meters* 날개가 50미터 길이의 항공기. **2** =wingspread.

wing·spread [wíŋsprèd] *n.* Ⓒ the distance between the tips of a pair of fully spread wings. (새·곤충의) 날개폭; 익폭(翼幅). ¶ *the eagle's huge ~* 독수리의 굉장한 날개 길이.

·wink [wiŋk] *vt.* (P6,7) **1** close and open (one or both eyes) quickly. (눈)을 깜박이다. **2** move or remove (something) by winking. …을 눈을 깜박여 제거하다. ¶ ~

away one's tears 눈을 깜박여 눈물을 떨구다〔지우다〕.
— *vi.* **1** (P1,3) 《*at*》 close and open one or both eyes quickly. 눈을 깜박이다(cf. *blink*). **2** (P1,3) 《*at*》 give a hint or signal by doing so. 눈짓하다. ¶ *Father winked at Dick as a sign for him to keep still and Dick winked back.* 아버지는 딕에게 잠자코 있으라는 눈짓을 하자 딕은 알았다는 눈짓을 보냈다. **3** (P1,3) 《*at*》 pretend not to see. 보고도 못본 체하다; 눈감아 주다. ¶ ~ *at someone's mistake* 아무의 실수를 보고도 못본 체하다 / ~ *at slight errors* 사소한 실수는 눈감아 주다. **4** (P1) (of the stars or lights, etc.) twinkle; flash on and off. (별 따위가) 반짝이다; (플래시가) 점멸(點滅)하다. ¶ *the winking lights on a Christmas tree* 크리스마스 트리의 깜박이는 불빛.
— *n.* Ⓒ **1** the act of winking. 눈을 깜박임; 눈짓. ¶ *I gave him a ~ to follow.* 그에게 따라오라는 눈짓을 했다. **2** a very short time; an instant. 일순간. ¶ *in a ~* 순식간에 / *do not get a ~ of sleep* 한잠도 못 자다. [E. (→ wince)]
get the winks, receive a signal by winking. 눈짓을 받다.
tip someone the wink, give someone a secret signal or hint; wink at someone. 아무에게 신호를 보내다〔힌트를 주다〕; 눈짓하다.

·win·ner [wínər] *n.* Ⓒ a person or thing that wins. 승리자; 우승마(馬); 수상자〔작품〕. [*win*]

·win·ning [wíniŋ] *adj.* **1** victorious; successful. 이긴; 승리의. ¶ *the ~ team* 〔*horse*〕 우승팀〔마〕. **2** attractive; charming. 애교 있는; 매력적인. ¶ *a ~ personality* 〔*smile*〕 매력 있는 개성〔미소〕/ ~ *manners* 호감이 가는 태도. — *n.* **1** ⓊⒸ victory; the act of gaining. 승리; 성공; 획득. **2** 《*pl.*》 money which one has won, esp. won in gambling. (도박의) 소득; 상금. [*win*]

winning post [ㅅ-ㅅ] *n.* the goal of a race; the post at the end of racecourse. (경마장의) 결승점(의 푯대).

win·now [wínou] *vt.* (P6,7,13) 《*away, from*》 **1** blow off or drive away the strawlike bits from (grain) by a current of air. …을 까부르다; 키질하다. **2** 《*fig.*》 sort out; separate. …을 가려내다. ¶ ~ *truth from falsehood* 진위(眞僞)를 가려내다. — *vi.* (P1) blow off the strawlike bits from grain. 곡물의 겨를 키질하여〔까불러서〕 날려보내다. [*wind*]

win·now·er [wínouər] *n.* Ⓒ **1** a person who winnows. 까부르는 사람. **2** a machine for winnowing grain, etc. 까부르는 기구; 키; 풍구.

win·some [wínsəm] *adj.* sweet and charming; attractive; cheerful. 매력 있는; 쾌활한. [E. =joyous]

:win·ter [wíntər] *n.* **1** ⓊⒸ the coldest season of the year; the last of the four seasons. 겨울. ¶ *a hard ~* 엄동 / *a ~ sleep* 동면 / *the ~ solstice* 동지(冬至) / *in depths of ~* 한겨울에 / *It seldom snows here in ~.* 여기는 겨울에 눈이 별로 안 온다. **2** Ⓒ 《*poet.*》 the last period of a man's life; a period suggesting decline, gloom, etc. 만년(晩年); 늘그막; 쇠퇴기. ¶ *a man of eighty winters* 나이 여든의 노인 / *in the ~ of old age* 노령의 쇠퇴기에.
— *adj.* **1** of winter; used in winter. 겨울의; 겨울에 쓰는. ¶ ~ *clothing* 동복. **2** (of fruit and vegetables) of a kind that may be kept for use during the winter. 겨울에 저장이 가능한〔되는〕. ¶ ~ *apples* 겨울 사과.
— *vi.* (P1,3) 《*in, at*》 pass the winter. 겨울을 나다; 월동하다. ¶ *Frogs ~ in the ground.* 개구리는 땅 속에서 겨울을 난다 / *Some birds ~ in south.* 어떤 새들은 남쪽에서 겨울을 난다.
— *vt.* (P6) 《*in, at*》 keep (cattle, etc.) during the cold season. (가축)을 겨울 동안 사육하다. ¶ *We wintered our cattle in the warm valley.* 우리는 가축을 겨울 동안 따스한 골짜기에서 기른다. [E.]

win·ter·tide [wíntərtàid] *n.* 《*poet.*》 = wintertime. 「울.

win·ter·time [wíntərtàim] *n.* Ⓤ winter. 겨

win·ter·y [wíntəri] *adj.* =wintry.

win·try [wíntri] *adj.* (**-tri·er, -tri·est**) **1** of or like winter; characteristic of winter. 겨울의; 겨울 같은; 추운; 쓸쓸한. ¶ *a ~ sky* 〔*day*〕 겨울 같은 하늘〔날〕/ ~ *scenes* 쓸쓸한 풍경. **2** 《*fig.*》 cold and not friendly. 쌀쌀한; 냉담한. ¶ *a ~ greeting* 쌀쌀한 인사 / *a ~ smile* 차가운 미소. [*winter*]

win·y [wáini] *adj.* (**win·i·er, win·i·est**) **1** tasting, smelling, or looking like wine. (맛·냄새 등이) 포도주 같은. **2** affected by wine. 포도주에 취한. [*wine*]

:wipe [waip] *vt.* (P6,7,13,18) **1** 《*away, off, out, up*》 rub (something) with a cloth or some soft material in order to clean or dry; remove (something) by wiping. …을 닦다; 훔치다; 닦아 없애다. ¶ ~ *one's eyes* = ~ *one's tears away* 눈물을 닦다 / ~ *dishes clean* 접시를 깨끗이 닦다 / *Wipe your shoes clean* (*on the mat*). (매트에) 신발을 깨끗이 닦아라 / ~ *a floor clean* 마루를 깨끗이 닦다 / ~ *one's hands on a towel* 수건에 손을 닦다 / ~ *the mud with a cloth* 걸레로 진흙을 닦아내다 / ~ *the ink off one's hands* 손에 묻은 잉크를 닦아 없애다 / ~ *up spilt milk* 엎지른 우유를 훔치다 / ~ *out a mark* 〔*stain*〕 자국〔얼룩〕을 닦아내다. **2** rub (a cloth, etc.) over something. (천 따위로) …을 문지르다. ¶ ~ *a cloth over a table* 테이블을 걸레로 문지르다. **3** 《*fig.*》 remove as if by rubbing; get ride of. (치욕·모욕 따위)를 씻다; (빚 따위)를 청산하다; (적·범죄)를 일소하다. ¶ ~ *away an insult* 모욕을 씻다 / ~ *out debts* 〔*losses*〕 부채를〔손실을〕 청산해 버리다 / ~ *the enemy out of existance*

적을 섬멸하다. **4** (P6) aim a sweeping blow at. …을 후려갈기다.
wipe** someone's **eye, outdo someone. …을 앞지르다; 허를 찌르다.
wipe** one's **hands of, wash one's hands of. …와의 관계를 끊다; 손을 떼다.
wipe out, **a**) remove (something) by wiping. …을 닦아내다. **b**) wipe the inside of. …의 속을 닦다. ¶ ~ *out a bath* 욕조를 닦다. **c**) 《*colloq.*》 kill; murder. 죽이다. ¶ ~ *out an opponent* 상대를 처치해 버리다.
***wipe the floor with** someone,* defeat someone completely. …을 철저히 때려눕히다.
wipe up, take up by rubbing with a cloth, paper, etc. (헝겊·종이 따위로) …을 닦아 없애다; 닦아내다. ¶ ~ *up the oil* 기름을 닦아 없애다 / *She wiped up the milk she had spilled.* 그녀는 엎지른 우유를 닦아냈다.
— *n.* Ⓒ **1** the act of wiping; a rub. 닦음; 훔침. ¶ *give the floor a* ~ 마루를 닦다; 걸레질하다. **2** 《*sl.*》 a sweeping blow or stroke. 후려 침; 갈김. **3** 《*sl.*》 a handkerchief. 손수건. [E.]

wip·er [wáipər] *n.* Ⓒ **1** a person who wipes. 닦는 사람. **2** a thing used for wiping. 닦는 물건; 걸레; 와이퍼. ¶ *a windshield* ~ *on a car* 자동차 앞유리의 와이퍼.

⁝**wire** [waiər] *n.* **1** Ⓤ metal drawn out into a very long, thin thread; Ⓒ a piece of this. 철사; 전선; (악기의) 현. ¶ *barbed* ~ 가시 철사; 유자(有刺) 철선 / *telephone wires* 전화선 / *a live* ~ 전기가 통하고 있는 전선; 활동가 / ~ *entanglement* 철조망 / ~ *netting* 철망 / *a lead-in* ~ 도입선; 접속선 / *an open* ~ 나선(裸線) / *an under-ground* ~ 지하선. **2** ⓐ Ⓤ telegraph. 전신. ¶ *by* ~ 전신으로. ⓑ 《*colloq.*》 Ⓒ a telegram. 전보. ¶ *send a* ~ *home* 집에 전보를 치다 / *receive a* ~ 전보를 받다.
be on the wire, be irritated. 안절부절 못하고 있다.
get under the wire, 《U.S. *colloq.*》 manage to enter or achieve barely on time. 가까스로 시간에 대다[해내다].
pull* (*the*) *wires, **a**) move puppets by means of wires, etc. (인형극에서) 인형을 실로 다루다. **b**) 《*fig.*》 control affairs through secret influence. 뒤[막후]에서 조종하다.
— *vt.* **1** (P6,7,13) fasten, connect, bind, or string (something) with a wire or wires. …을 철사로 고정시키다[매다, 잇다]. ¶ *He wired firewood together.* 장작을 한데 묶었다 / ~ *the stems of flowers* (약한) 꽃자루를 철사로 묶어 든든하게 하다 / ~ *a broken chair together* 부서진 의자를 철사로 묶어 제대로 해놓다. **2** (P6) supply (a house, etc.) with a system of wires for electricity. (옥내)에 전선을 끌다. ¶ ~ *a house for electric light* 집에 전등선을 끌다[가설하다] / *Is the house wired up yet?* 집에 이미 전선을 끌었느냐. **3** (P6) catch (birds, etc.) with wire. (새 따위)를 쇠그물로 잡다. **4** (P6,13,15,20) 《*to*》 《*colloq.*》 telegraph; send (a message, etc.); send a message to. …에 타전하다; 전보를 치다. ¶ *He wired us to get it ready by next Monday.* 그는 다음 월요일까지 그것을 해놓으라고 우리에게 전보를 보내왔다 / *Wire him to come.* 그에게 오라고 전보를 쳐라.
— *vi.* (P1) 《*colloq.*》 send a telegram. 전보를 치다. ¶ *He wired for me to come.* 그는 내게 와 달라는 전보를 보냈다 / ~ *back to someone* 아무에게 답전을 보내다 / *Please* ~ *me as soon as you hear.* 듣는 대로 전보를 쳐 주시오. [E.]

wire cutter [ˊ ˋ–] *n.* 《usu. *pl.*》 a tool for cutting wire. 철사 끊는 기구[가위]. ¶ *a pair of wire cutters.*

wire·haired [wáiərhὲərd] *adj.* (of a dog) with coarse, stiff hair. (개 따위가) 털이 뻣뻣한.

***wire·less** [wáiərlis] *adj.* **1** without wires; having no wire(s). 무선의; 무선 전신의. ¶ ~ *telegraphy* 무선 전신(술) / *a* ~ *apparatus* 무전기 / ~ *telephone* 무선 전화. **2** 《Brit.》 of or by radio. 라디오의; 라디오 방송에 의한.
— *n.* Ⓤ **1** ⓐ wireless telegraph or telephone. 무선 전신[전화]. ⓑ a telegram. 전보. **2** 《*the* ~》 《Brit.》 radio. 라디오 (방송). ¶ *listen to the news over the* ~ 라디오로 뉴스를 듣다.
— *vt.* (P6) **1** 《Brit.》 send (messages) by radio. …을 라디오로 방송하다. **2** send a message to (someone), by wireless. …을 무선으로 알리다; 타전하다. ¶ *They wirelessed the news of the discovery.* 그들은 발견했다는 소식을 타전했다.

wire·pull·er [wáiərpùlər] *n.* Ⓒ **1** a person who pulls wires, as in moving dolls, etc. (인형극의) 인형[꼭두각시] 놀리는 사람. **2** a person who uses secret means to control others or gain his own ends. 막후에서 책동[조종]하는 사람; 막후 인물.

wire rope [ˊ ˊ] *n.* a rope made of twisted wires. 강철 밧줄; 와이어로프.

wire·tap [wáiərtæ̀p] *n.* ⓊⒸ an act of wiretapping or an electrical connection for wiretapping. (전신·전화의) 도청 (장치). ¶ ~ *evidence* 도청으로 얻은 증거. — *vt.* (**-tapped, -tap·ping**) (P6) obtain (information, evidence, etc.) by tapping telephone or telegraph wires. …을 도청하다; …을 도청하여 증거[정보]를 모으다. ¶ *The police wiretapped his house.* 경찰은 그의 집을[집 전화를] 도청했다. [*wire, tap*]

wire·tap·ping [wáiərtæ̀piŋ] *n.* Ⓤ listening secretly to other people's telephone conversations by an unofficial or illegal connection. (전신·전화의) 도청 (행위). ¶ *a* ~ *device* 도청 장치.

wire wool [ˊ ˊ] *n.* very fine wire woven together and arranged in a round fairly solid piece, e.g. used for cleaning pans. 쇠수세미(cf. *steel wool*).

wir·ing [wáiəriŋ] *n.* Ⓤ a system of wires for electric currents, etc. 배선 (조직). ¶ *We're having this old* ~ *replace.* 이 낡은 배선을 교체하고 있다 / *faulty* ~ 잘못된 배선.

wir·y [wáiəri] *adj.* (**wir·i·er, wir·i·est**) **1** of shape like wire; stiff. 철사 모양의; 빳빳한. ¶ ~ *hair.* **2** made of wire. 철사로 만든. **3** (of a person. etc.) thin, but with strong muscles. (말랐으나) 근육이 탄탄한; 강단 있는. ¶ *his* ~ *athletic body* 운동으로 단련된 그의 강인한 신체. [*wire*]

Wis·con·sin [wiskánsin / -kɔ́n-] *n.* a north central State of the United States. 위스콘신 주. 參考 Wis(c).로 생략함. 주도는 Madison.

Wis·con·sin·ite [wiskánsinàit / -kɔ́n-] *n.* Ⓒ a person of Wisconsin. 위스콘신 주 주민.

:wis·dom [wízdəm] *n.* Ⓤ **1** the quality of being wise; good judgment and common sense. 지혜; 분별; 현명함. ¶ *the* ~ *of the ancients* 옛 사람들의 지혜. **2** learning; knowledge gained by study. 학식; 학문; 지식. ¶ *a man of great* ~ 학문이 매우 뛰어난 사람. **3** wise words; a maxim. 금언. [*wise*[1]]

wisdom tooth [ㅅ- ㅅ] *n.* the back tooth on either side of the human jaw, usu. appearing at the age of about 20. 사랑니.

:wise[1] [waiz] *adj.* **1** having or showing good judgment. 현명한; 슬기로운(opp. foolish). ¶ *a* ~ *man* / *a* ~ *saw* 〔*saying*〕 금언 / *He is wiser than he looks.* 그는 보기보다 현명한 사람이다 / *It was* ~ *of you to refuse his offer.* 그의 제의를 거절한 것은 잘한 일이다 / *You will understand when you're older and wiser.* 나이를 더 먹고 더 현명해지면 이해가 될 것이다. **2** learned. 박식한. ¶ *be* ~ *in the law* 법률에 조예가 깊다. **3** 《usu. *the wiser*》 having knowledge or information. 알고 있는. ¶ *Nobody will be the wiser.* 아무도 알지〔알아차리지〕 못할 것이다 / *Who will be the wiser?* 누군들 알겠는가 / *We were none the wiser for his explanation.* 그의 설명을 들어도 모르기는 마찬가지였다. **4** suggestive of wisdom. 현명한 것 같은; 박식한 체하는. ¶ *look* ~ 박식한 체 거드름 피우다 / *So he answered, with a* ~ *shake of the head.* 아는 체 고개를 끄덕이며 그렇게 대답했다. **5** 《Brit. *arch.*》 having knowledge of supernatural things. 마법〔비법〕에 통달한. ¶ *a* ~ *man* 마법사 / *a* ~ *woman* 여자 마법사〔점쟁이〕; 조산원. [E. (→wit)]

be* 〔*get*〕 *wise to, 《U.S. *colloq.*》 be 〔become〕 aware of (something). …을 알고 있다〔알게 되다〕; 알다.

none the wiser* =*no wiser than befor* =*as wise as before, knowing no more than before. 여전히 모르는 (채로). ¶ *He explained it all to me, but I was none the wiser.* 그가 내게 그 모든 것을 설명했지만 나는 여전히 모르는 상태였다.

put someone wise to* 〔*on*〕*, 《U.S. *colloq.*》 inform someone about (something). (아무)에게 …을 알리다.

wise[2] [waiz] *n.* Ⓒ 《*sing.* only》 《*arch.*》 manner; way; fashion. 방식; 방법; (…)식(式). ¶ *in some* ~ 이럭저럭 / *in this* ~ 이와 같이; 이렇게 / *in any* ~ 아무리 해도. [E.]

in no wise, by no means. 조금도 … 않는. ¶ *They are in no* ~ *to blame.* 그들은 조금도 나무랄 바 못된다《잘못이 없다》.

-wise [-waiz] *suf.* after the fashion of; arranged like; in conformity with. '…을 따라서, …와 같이, …방향으로'의 뜻. ¶ *crabwise* 옆으로; 비스듬히 / *crosswise* 옆으로; 가로질러 / *budgetwise* 예산으로서는 / *be superior qualitywise* 질적인 면에서는 뛰어나다. [↑]

wise·a·cre [wáizèikər] *n.* Ⓒ a person who thinks he knows everything. 무엇이든 아는 체하는 사람. [E.]

wise·crack [wáizkræ̀k] *n.* Ⓒ **1** a witticism. 재담(才談); 경구(警句). **2** one who makes such remarks. 경구·재담을 말하는 사람. — *vi.* (P1) make such remarks. 경구·재담을 말하다. [E.]

wise·ly [wáizli] *adv.* in a wise manner. 현명하게; 빈틈없이. [*wise*[1]]

:wish [wiʃ] *vt.* (P6,7,8,11,13,14,18,20) **1** want; desire. …을 원하다; …하고 싶어하다. ¶ *I* ~ *to read Aesop's Fables.* 이솝 이야기를 읽고 싶다 / *I wished to have come.* 오고 싶었으나 오지 못했다 / *I* ~ *you to go at once.* 나는 자네가 지금 곧 갔으면 싶다 / *I* ~ *the promise kept.* 약속이 지켜졌으면 한다 / *Do you* ~ *wine with your meal, sir?* 손님, 포도주를 반주로 드시겠습니까 / *Do you* ~ *my help?* 내가 도와 줄까 / *You may have whichever you* ~. 어느 것이든 원하는 것을 가져도 좋다. **2** have or express a desire that …; be anxious that …. (실현이 어려운 일)을 바라다; …이면〔이었으면〕 좋겠다고 생각하다. 語法 that은 흔히 생략됨. ¶ *I* ~ *I were a bird.* 내가 새라면 좋겠는데 / *I* ~ *I were there.* 내가 거기에 있다면 좋겠는데 / *I* ~ *I had been there.* 내가 거기에 있었으면 좋겠는데 / *I* ~ *(that) it would rain.* 비가 왔으면 좋겠다 / *I* ~ *I could see him.* 그를 만났으면 좋겠는데 / *How did this happen?* —*I* ~ *I knew.* 어떻게 이 일이 일어났을까. —그것을 알고 싶다 / *I* ~ *(that) you would get a good job.* 네가 좋은 일자리를 구했으면 좋으리라 생각한다 / *I* ~ *you would keep secret.* 비밀을 지켜 주었으면 좋겠다 / *We* ~ *this house were a little larger.* 이 집이 좀더 컸으면 좋겠구나. **3** express a desire to or for (someone). (아무)가 …이었으면〔…이면〕 좋겠다고 여기다〔생각하다〕; (아무가) …이기를 바라다. ¶ ~ *someone away* 아무가 가버리면 좋겠다고 생각하다 / ~ *oneself dead* 죽어 있으면 좋을 것을 하고 생각하다 / *I* ~ *myself at home.* 내가 집에 있었으면 하고 생각한다 / ~ *someone well*

〔ill〕 아무의 행복〔불행〕을 바라다 / *He wishes nobody ill.* 그는 아무도 불행해지기를 바라고 있지 않다. **4** express a desire with respect to the fortune, etc. of (someone); give a certain greeting to (someone). (아무)에게 …이기를 빌다; 기원하다 ¶ *I ~ you joy.* 축하합니다 / *I ~ you a Happy New Year.* 새해 복 많이 받으세요 / *She wished him good night.* 그에게 안녕히 주무세요라고 인사했다. **5** request or order. …을 요구하다; …하기를 바라다. ¶ *I ~ you to do it.* 네가 그 일을 해 주었으면 좋겠다 / *~ someone to go out* 아무가 나가 주기를 요구하다 / *I ~ you to answer.* 대답해 주길 바란다 / *What does he ~ me to do?* 그가 내게 바라는 게 뭐냐 / *I ~ it to be finished.* 그걸 끝내 주었으면 좋겠다.

— *vi.* (P1,3) 《*for*》 have a desire; hope. 원하다; 바라다. ¶ *I would not ~ for anything better.* 이 이상의 것은 바라지 않는다 / *We are apt to ~ for what we can't have.* 사람이란 얻을 수 없는 것을 바라는 법이다 / *I will send you the book you wished for.* 네가 원하던 책을 보내주마 / *You'll have everything you could ~ for.* 네가 원하는 무엇이든 주겠다.

— *n.* **1** ⓒⓤ a desire to do or to gain something; a longing. 바람; 소원; 희망. ¶ *with every good ~* 충심으로 / *with best wishes* 행복〔성공〕을 빌며《편지 등의 끝맺음말》/ *Please send your parents my best wihes.* 부모님께 안부 전해 주십시오 / *We obtained results to our wishes.* 결과는 우리가 바라던 대로 됐다 / *attain* 〔*carry out*〕 *one's wish* 소원을 이루다 / *He has a great ~ to go abroad.* 그에게는 해외로 나가려는 큰 꿈이 있다 / *His last ~ was that he could see his grandchildren.* 생전에 손자들을 보는 것이 그의 소원이었다. **2** ⓒ something wished for. 바라는 것. ¶ *He has got his ~.* 바라던 것을 얻었다 / *You shall have your all wishes.* 네가 원하는 것을 다 주겠다. **3** ⓒ 《*pl.*》 any expression of desire for another's health, success, etc. 행복을 비는 말. ¶ *Please accept my best wishes for your health.* 건강하시길 빕니다 / *send* 〔*give*〕 *one's wishes for someone's success* 아무의 성공을 바라는 말을 전하다. **4** ⓒ a desire implying an order. 요청; 의뢰. ¶ *carry out someone's ~* 아무가 바라는 대로 해주다 / *The prisoners were released in accordance with the king's wishes.* 포로들은 국왕의 희망에 따라 석방되었다. [E. →win, ween]

wish·ful [wíʃfəl] *adj.* **1** having or showing a wish. 원하는; 바라는. ¶ *be ~ for happier days* 보다 행복한 날을 바라다 / *be ~ to do something* …을 하고 싶어하다. **2** desirous. 열망하는; 탐내는. ¶ *~ eyes* 탐내는 듯한 눈빛.

wishful thinking [⌐-⌐-] *n.* believing something to be true that one wishes. 희망적 관측〔사고〕.

wish·bone [wíʃbòun], **wish·ing bone** [wíʃiŋ bòun] *n.* the forked bone in front of the breast of a bird (when this is pulled apart by two persons, the one holding the longer part is supposed to be able to get what he wishes). (새의) 창사골(暢思骨)《이 뼈의 양끝을 당겨, 긴 쪽을 가진 사람은 소원이 성취된다고 함》.

wish·y-wash·y [wíʃiwɑ̀ʃi / -wɔ̀ʃi] *adj.* **1** thin and weak. 묽은(cf. *washy*). ¶ *~ soup* 멀건 수프. **2** lacking in spirit or vigor; poor. 박력이 없는; 하찮은; 시시한. ¶ *a ~ story* 싱거운 얘기 / *He is a ~ liberal.* 그는 그저 그런 자유주의자다 / *~ ideas* 하찮은 생각. [*wash*]

wisp [wisp] *n.* ⓒ **1** (of grass, etc.) a small bundle; a handful; (of hair, etc.) a small amount. (풀 따위의) 작은 단; 한 단; (머리 카락 따위의) 한 줌. **2** will-o'-the-wisp. 도깨비불. **3** a whisk-broom. 작은 비. [E.]

wist [wist] *v.* p. and pp. of **wit.**

wis·tar·i·a [wistíːriə, -tέər-], **-te·ri·a** [-tíəriə] *n.* ⓒ 《bot.》 a climbing tree with purple flowers. 등나무. [Person]

wist·ful [wístfəl] *adj.* **1** longing; full of desire. 동경하는; 탐내는. ¶ *a ~ look* 탐내는 듯한 표정 / *cast a ~ glance at something* …에 부러운 시선을 보내다. **2** thoughtful and sad. 사색에 잠긴. ¶ *in a ~ mood* 생각에 잠겨 / *He grew silent and ~.* 그는 묵묵히 생각에 잠겼다. [Obs. *wisthy* intently]

:wit [wit] *n.* **1** ⓤ the ability to say clever and amusing things. 기지; 재치. ¶ *a man of ~* 재치 있는 사람 / *His ~ made even troubles seem amusing.* 그의 위트는 골칫거리도 재미 있는 것처럼 만들었다 / *conversation sparkling with ~* 재치가 넘치는 대화. **2** ⓒ a person with such power. 재치 있는 사람. ¶ *Oscar Wilde was a famous ~.* 오스카 와일드는 유명한 재사였다. **3** ⓒ 《often *pl.*》 intelligence; understanding; the power to know. 지혜; 이해력; 분별. ¶ *have quick wits* 이해가 빠르다 / *in one's wits* 제정신으로 / *People with quick wits learn easily.* 이해력이 빠른 사람은 쉽게 익힌다〔배운다〕.

***at one's* wit's end,** at a loss; not knowing what to do or say. 어찌할 바를 몰라; 난감해져. ¶ *I'm at my wits end for money.* 돈을 마련할 방도가 없어 난감하다.

have 〔**keep**〕 ***one's* wits about** *one,* be observant and careful. 빈틈 없다.

***live by one's* wits,** live by cunning rather than by hard work. 꾀바르게 처세하다; 약게 굴다.

out of *one's* **wits,** mad. 제정신을 잃고. ¶ *His persistent questions nearly drove me out of my wits.* 그의 집요한 질문에 나는 거의 미칠 지경이었다.

— *vt., vi.* (**wist, wit·ting**) 《*arch.*》 know. 알다. 語法 현재는 다음 성구로만 쓰임. [E.=knowledge]

to wit, that is to say. 이를테면.

•**witch** [witʃ] *n.* Ⓒ a woman who has magic power; an ugly old woman; 《*colloq.*》 a charming young woman. 마녀 (cf. *wizard*); 간악한〔추한〕 노파; 매혹적인 여자. ¶ *a white* ~ 좋은 일을 하는 마녀. ― *vt.* (P6) exert magic power toward (someone); charm. …에 마법을 걸다; …을 매혹하다. [E. →wicked]

witch·craft [wítʃkræ̀ft / -krɑ̀ːft] *n.* Ⓤ magic; the power and practices of a witch. 마법; 마술; 마력.

witch doctor [ㅗ ㅗ] *n.* (in some less developed societies) a person who is believed to have magical powers and be able to cure people. (미개 사회의) 주술사(呪術師).

witch·er·y [wítʃəri] *n.* Ⓤ magic; charm. 마법; 매력.

witch·ing [wítʃiŋ] *adj.* magical; charming. 마력이 있는; 매혹적인.

:with [wið, wiθ] *prep.* **1** accompanied by; in the company of. …와 함께; 더불어; …을 데리고. ¶ *walk* ~ *one's friend* 친구와 같이 걷다 / *In the Great War they fought* ~ *the French against the Germans.* 세계 대전에서 그들은 프랑스와 더불어 독일에 대항해 싸웠다 / *Come* ~ *me.* 나와 함께 가자 / *Who was that man you were* ~ *last night ?* 어젯밤 함께 있던 사람은 누구냐 / *I stayed* ~ *an uncle of mine.* 아저씨 한 분과 함께 머물렀다 / *The president arrived* ~ *his secretary.* 사장은 비서와 함께 도착했다. **2** in some particular relation to; concerning; in regard to. …와(의); …에 대〔관〕하여; …에 관해서는. ¶ *have dealings* ~ …와 거래하다 / *I have nothing to do* ~ *that affair.* 그 일과 나는 아무 관계가 없다 / *have done* ~ …을 끝내다; …와 관계를 끊다 / *negotiate* ~ …와 교섭하다 / *What do you want* ~ *me ?* 내게 무슨 볼일 있니 / *What is the matter* ~ *you ?* 어찌 된 일이냐; 무슨 일이냐 / *It is usual* ~ *him.* 그에겐 그게 보통이다 / *We are pleased* ~ *the house.* 우린 이 집에 만족한다 / *It has nothing to do* ~ *you.* 그것은 너와 아무 상관 없다 / *I can do nothing* ~ *him.* 그와는 아무 일도 못 하겠다. **3** of the same opinion, belief, etc. as; in support of. …와 같은 의견으로; …에 찬성하여; …을 지지하여. ¶ *in harmony* ~ …와 조화되어 / *I am entirely* ~ *you in this.* 이 점에서는 전적으로 너와 동감이다 / *Blue goes* ~ *white.* 파랑과 흰색은 조화가 된다 / *I feel* ~ *you.* 너와 동감이다 / *I disagree* ~ *you there.* 그 점에서는 너와 생각이 다르다. **4** in proportion to. …에 따라서; …에 비례하여. ¶ *A man grows wiser* ~ *age.* 사람은 나이가 듦에 따라 현명해진다. **5** ⓐ having as a possession; wearing. …을 가지고; …이 있는 (opp. without). ¶ *a lady* ~ *golden hair* 금발의 여인 / *a man* ~ *ten thousand dollars a year* 연수입이 1만 달러인 사람 / *an old man* ~ *gray hair* 머리가 희끗희끗한 사람 / *a telegram* ~ *bad news* 나쁜 소식의 전보 / *He entered the house* ~ *his hat on.* 모자를 쓴 채 집에 들어왔다. ⓑ bringing also with one. 몸에 지니고. ¶ *Take an umbrella* ~ *you.* 우산을 가지고 가거라. **6** in keeping or in care of. …을 보관하여; …의 손에 맡겨. ¶ *I will leave the children* ~ *my grandmother.* 아이들은 할머니에게 맡기겠다 / *Leave the luggage* ~ *the porter.* 짐꾼에게 짐을 맡겨라 / *Leave it* ~ *me.* 그건 내게 맡겨라. **7** because of; as a result of. …으로 인해; …의 때문에. ¶ *bent* ~ *age* 늙어서 허리가 굽다 / *eyes dim* ~ *tears* 눈물로 침침해진 눈 / *I am dying* ~ *hunger.* 배가 고파 죽겠다 / *He is shaking* ~ *cold.* 그는 추위에 떨고 있다. **8** not withstanding; in spite of. …임에도 불구하고. ¶ *With the best of intentions, he made a mess of the job.* 성심성의껏 했는데도 그는 그 일을 망쳤다. **9** by means of; by the use of. …으로; …을 써서. ¶ *cut* ~ *a knife* 칼로 자르다 / *I have not a pen to write* ~. 쓸 펜이 없다 / *I've got no money to buy it* ~. 그걸 살 돈이 없다 / *I filled the glass* ~ *water.* 컵에다 물을 채웠다 / *The garden is enclosed* ~ *a fence.* 정원은 울타리로 둘러싸여 있다 / *amuse oneself* ~ *a book* 독서를 즐기다 / *The streets are paved* ~ *stone.* 길은 자갈로 포장돼 있다. **10** (of manner) using or showing. (모양·태도가) …하여. ¶ ~ *ease* 쉽게 / ~ *care* 조심스럽게 / ~ *courage* 용감하게 / ~ *an ugly smile on his face* 징그럽게 웃으며. **11** at the same time as; during. …와 동시에. ¶ *contemporary* ~ …와 동시대의 / *rise* ~ *the sun* 해돋이와 함께 일어나다 / *With this battle the war ended.* 이 싸움과 동시에 전쟁은 끝났다 / *He gave a little wave, and* ~ *that he was gone.* 그는 손을 좀 흔들고는 가버렸다. **12** (of separation) from. …와 떨어져. ¶ *part* ~ *a friend* 친구와 헤어지다 / *He differed* ~ *me.* 그는 나와 (의견이) 다르다 / *I parted* ~ *him at the door.* 그와 문간에서 헤어졌다 / *He broke* ~ *his family and left home.* 그는 가족과 헤어져서 집을 떠났다. **13** in opposition to; against. …을 상대로; 반대하여; …와. ¶ *fight* ~ *the enemy* 적과 싸우다 / *He argued* ~ *his wife.* 아내와 다퉜다 / *quarrel* ~ *a friend* 친구와 싸우다 / *cope* 〔*compete*〕 ~ *so much work* 산더미처럼 쌓인 일과 씨름하다 / *fight* ~ *the English* 영어와 씨름하다. [E.]

be with it, be up-to-date; understand new ideas, etc. (복장·사상·행동 등이) 시대〔유행〕의 최첨단을 걷다; 최신식이다. ¶ *He is not* ~ *it.* 그는 구식이다.

what with ... and (***what with***) ⇨what.

with all, in spite of. …에도 불구하고. ¶ *With all his efforts, he failed.* 온갖 노력에도 불구하고 그는 실패했다 / *With all his faults, I like him.* 결점이 많은데도 난 그를 좋아한다.

with·al [wiðɔ́ːl, wiθ-] *adv.* 《*arch.*》 besides; still; at the same time; nevertheless. 게다가; 한편으로는; 그렇지만. ¶ *He was wise and handsome, and rich* ~. 그는 현명하고 잘 생긴데다가 부자다 / *The lady is fair and wise* ~. 부인은 예쁘고 게다가 현명하다. — *prep.* with. …으로(써). 語法 항상 문말에 둔다. ¶ *He has nothing to fill his belly* ~. 그는 먹을 것이 하나도 없다. [*with, all*]

***with·draw** [wiðdrɔ́:, wiθ-] *v.* (**-drew, -drawn**) *vt.* **1** (P6,13) pull back; draw (money, etc.) back. (손 따위를) 움츠리다; (돈 따위를) 도로 찾다; 회수하다. ¶ *She quickly withdrew her hand from the hot iron.* 그녀는 뜨거운 쇠에서 얼른 손을 뗐다 / *She withdrew $50 from her bank account.* 그녀는 당좌 예금에서 50 달러를 인출했다. **2** (P6,13) remove. …을 거두다; 물러나게 하다; 철수하다. ¶ *Bill's parents withdrew him from school.* 빌의 아버지는 그에게 학교를 그만두게 했다 / ~ *soldiers from a country* 군인들을 나라에서 철수시키다. **3** (P6) take back. …을 철회하다; 취소하다. ¶ ~ *a statement* 〔*promise, allegation*〕 성명〔약속·주장〕을 철회〔취소〕하다. — *vi.* **1** (P1,3) move back; go away; retreat. 물러나다; 가버리다; 철수하다. ¶ ~ *from someone's presence* 아무의 면전에서 물러나다 / *He withdrew from the room.* 그는 방에서 나갔다 / *The troops withdrew.* 군대는 철수했다. **2** (P3) remove oneself (from an organization, society, etc.). (기구나 단체 따위로부터) 탈퇴〔탈회〕하다. ¶ ~ *from a society* 협회를 탈회하다. [*with, draw*]

with·draw·al [wiðdrɔ́:əl, wiθ-] *n.* UC the act of withdrawing; the state of being withdrawn. 움츠림; 물러남; (예금 등의) 인출; 철회; 철수. ¶ *a* ~ *from a room* 방에서 물러남 / *a* ~ *of money from the bank* 은행에서의 예금 인출 / *the* ~ *of a promise* 약속의 취소 / ~ *of financial support for his scheme* 그의 계획에 대한 재정적 지원의 철회 / *a gradual* ~ *of troops from the war zone* 전투 지역에서의 단계적인 병력 철수.

with·drawn [wiðdrɔ́:n, wiθ-] *v.* pp. of **withdraw.**

with·drew [wiðdrú:, wiθ-] *v.* p. of **withdraw.**

withe [wiθ, wið, waið] *n.* C a willow twig; any tough, easily bent twig suitable for binding things together. 가는 버들가지; (나뭇단 등을 묶기에 좋은) 실가지. [E.]

***with·er** [wíðər] *vi.* (P1,2A) **1** (of plants and flowers) dry up and fade. 시들다; 말라 죽다. ¶ *The grass withered in the hot sun.* 뙤약볕에 풀이 시들었다 / *Flowers* ~ *unless they have water.* 물이 없으면 꽃은 말라 죽는다. **2** (of affection, hopes, etc.) grow weaker; die away. (애정·희망 따위가) 희박해지다; 쇠퇴하다. ¶ *Her affections withered.* 그녀의 애정은 식었다. — *vt.* (P6,7) **1** cause (something) to dry up and fade. …을 시들게 하다; 말라 죽게 하다. **2** cause (someone) to feel ashamed or to lose vigor. …을 움츠러들게 하다; 기죽게 하다. ¶ ~ *someone with an angry glance* 노려서 아무의 기를 죽이다. [→weather]

with·held [wiðhéld, wiθ-] *v.* p. and pp. of **withhold.**

with·hold [wiðhóuld, wiθ-] *vt.* (P6,13) (**-held**) **1** keep or hold (something) back; keep (someone) from action. …을 보류하다; (아무를) 제지하다. ¶ ~ *oneself* 자제하다 / *The captain withheld his men from the attack.* 대장은 공격을 못 하게 부하들을 제지했다 / *I withheld payment until they had fulfilled the contract.* 그들이 계약을 이행할 때까지 지불을 미뤘다. **2** refuse to grant or give. …을 허락하지 않다; 주지 않다. ¶ *There was no school play because the principal withheld his consent.* 교장이 허락을 유보한 탓으로 학교 연극을 상연하지 못했다. [*with, hold*]

⁝**with·in** [wiðín, wiθ-] *adv.* **1** in the inner part; inside. 안에; 내부에(opp. without). ¶ *It is green without, but yellow* ~. 바깥쪽은 초록이지만 안쪽은 노랑이다. **2** at home; indoors. 집 안에; 옥내에. ¶ *He is* ~. 집에 있다 / *go* ~ 집에 들어가다 / *"This house to be sold. Inquire* ~*."* "집을 팖. 안에 들어와 문의하시오"《게시》. **3** in the mind or conscience. 마음 속으로; 심중에. ¶ *be pure* ~ 마음이 깨끗하다.

— *prep.* **1** in the inner part of; inside of; in. …의 안에; …의 내부에(opp. without). ¶ ~ *the room* 방 안에 / ~ *doors* 집 안에 / ~ *and without the town* 도시 안팎에 / *By X-rays, doctors can see* ~ *the body.* 엑스선으로 의사는 인체의 내부를 볼 수 있다 / *Hope sprang up* ~ *him.* 그의 마음 속에 희망이 솟아 올랐다. **2** in the limits, range, or scope of; not beyond. …의 범위 안에; …을 넘지 않고. ¶ ~ *hearing* 들리는 곳에 / ~ *ten minutes* 10분 안에 / ~ *a stone's throw* 돌을 던지면 닿는 곳에 / *Live* ~ *your income.* 수입 한도 내에서 생활해라 / *They live* ~ *a few miles of Paris.* 그들은 파리에서 수 마일 떨어진 곳에 살고 있다 / *Is the shelf* ~ *your reach ?* 선반이 손에 닿나 / ~ *the laws of the land* 나라 법의 테두리 안에서 / *a task well* ~ *his power* 그의 역량으로 능히 할 수 있는 일 / *remain* ~ *call* 〔*reach*〕 부르면 들리는〔손 닿는〕 곳에.

— *n.* U the inside. 내부; 안(opp. without). ¶ *Their actions are seen from* ~. 그들의 행동은 안에서 보인다 / *The door opened from* ~. 문은 안쪽에서 열렸다. [*with, in*]

⁝**with·out** [wiðáut, wiθ-] *prep.* **1** 《*arch.*》 outside of; beyond. …의 밖에; 밖으로 (opp. within). ¶ ~ *doors* 집 밖에서 / ~ *the gate* 〔*house*〕 문〔집〕밖에. **2** not having; lacking in; with no. …이 없이; …을 갖지 않고(opp. with). ¶ ~ *leave* 무단히 / ~ *number* 무수한 / ~ *reserve* 거침〔기탄〕 없

이 / ~ *a single word spoken* 말 한 마디 없이 / *A cat is walking ~ noise.* 고양이 한 마리가 소리 없이 걷고 있다 / *Without health, life is difficult.* 건강하지 않고는 생활하기가 힘들다 / ~ *fail* 틀림없이. **3** 《~ *doing*》 with avoidance or neglect of. …(하지) 않고; …(당하는) 일 없이; …을 면해. ¶ *He went away ~ saying good-bye.* 그는 작별 인사도 하지 않고 가버렸다 / *He offered to do it ~ being paid.* 그는 그 일을 무보수로 하겠다고 했다 / *How can you do it ~ anybody knowing it?* 아무도 모르게 어떻게 그걸 할 수 있다는 거냐.

do without ⇨do.

go without ⇨go.

It goes without saying that .... ⇨go.

not* 〔*never*〕 *... without doing, never fail to do when .... …하면 반드시 …하다. ¶ *They never meet ~ quarreling.* 그들은 만나면 반드시 싸운다.

— *adv.* 《*arch.*》 outside; out of doors. 밖에; 옥외에(opp. within). ¶ *within and ~* 안팎에 / *He is waiting ~.* 그는 밖에서 기다리고 있다 / *fair ~ and foul within* 겉은 멀쩡하고 속은 더러운 / *a door locked ~* 밖에서 채워진 문.

— *conj.* 《*arch., sl.*》 unless. …이 아니면; …하지 않고는.

— *n.* 《*arch.*》 the outside. 외부; 밖(opp. within). ¶ *A strange sound came from ~.* 밖에서 이상한 소리가 들려 왔다. [*with, out*]

·**with·stand** [wiðstǽnd, wiθ-] *vt.* (P6) (**-stood**) stand against; oppose; resist; endure. …에 반항〔대항〕하다; 잘 견디다; 버티다. ¶ *The soldiers withstood the enemy's attack for hours.* 병사들은 몇 시간 동안 적의 공격에 버텼다 / *This coat will ~ hard wear.* 이 코트는 마구 입어도 괜찮다. [*with, stand*]

with·stood [wiðstúd, wiθ-] *v.* p. and pp. of **withstand.**

with·y [wíði] *n.* (*pl.* **with·ies**) =withe.

wit·less [wítlis] *adj.* without sense; stupid; foolish. 지혜〔재치〕 없는; 어리석은. ¶ *a ~ remark* 바보 같은 소리. [*wit*]

:**wit·ness** [wítnis] *n.* **1** Ⓤ evidence; proof. 증거. ¶ *in ~ of ...* …의 증거로 / *give ~ on behalf of...* …을 위해 증언하다 / *call* 〔*take*〕 *someone to ~* 아무를 증인으로 세우다. **2** Ⓒ a person who actually saw an event; a person or thing furnishing proof. 목격자; 증거가 되는 사람〔물건〕; 증거물. ¶ *a ~ of the accident* 그 사건의 목격자 / *Police have appealed for ~ to come forward.* 경찰은 목격자는 앞으로 나서 달라고 간청했다 / *A receipt is ~ that a bill has been paid.* 영수증은 계산이 끝났다는 증거물이다 / *a ~ to the will* 유언장의 입회인. **3** Ⓒ a person who swears to tell the truth in court. 증인. ¶ *the chief ~ for the prosecution* 검찰측의 중요한 증인. **4** Ⓒ a person attesting another's signature to a document. 연서인(連署人); 입회인.

bear witness to* 〔*of*〕*, give evidence about (something). …을 입증하다. ¶ *The man's fingerprints bore ~ to his guilt.* 그 남자의 지문이 그가 유죄임을 입증했다.

with a witness, without a doubt. 명백히.

— *vt.* **1** (P6) be present and see (an event, etc.); see personally; observe. …을 목격하다. ¶ *Many people witnessed the accident.* 많은 사람들이 그 사건을 목격했다 / ~ *a beautiful sight* 아름다운 경치를 보다. **2** (P6,11) give evidence of (an event, etc.). …을 입증하다; 증언하다. ¶ *He witnessed that it was the driver's fault.* 그는 그것이 운전자의 과실이라고 증언했다 / *Her blush witnessed her confusion.* 얼굴이 붉어진 것으로 보아 그녀가 당황했음이 분명했다. **3** (P6) sign (a paper) as a witness. (증인으로서) …에 서명하다. ¶ *The two servants witnessed his will.* 하인 둘이 그의 유언장에 서명했다.

— *vi.* (P1,3) 《*for, against, to*》 give or serve as evidence; bear witness. 증언〔증명·입증〕하다. ¶ ~ *to someone's reputation* …의 명성을 증명하다 / ~ *against someone* 아무에게 불리한 증언을 하다 / ~ *to someone's innocence* 아무의 무죄를 증언하다. [*wit*]

wit·ness-box [wítnisbɑ̀ks / -bɔ̀ks] *n.* 《Brit.》 the stand from which a witness gives evidence in a court of law. 증인석.

witness stand [∠-∠] *n.* 《U.S.》 =witness-box.

wit·ti·cism [wítəsìzəm] *n.* Ⓒ a witty remark. 재치있는 말; 재담; 경구(警句). [*wit*]

wit·ti·ly [wítili] *adv.* in a witty manner. 재치 있게.

wit·ting·ly [wítiŋli] *adv.* intentionally; knowingly. 일부러; 알면서. ¶ *I would not ~ hurt your feelings.* 일부러 네 기분을 해칠 생각은 없다.

wit·ty [wíti] *adj.* (**-ti·er, -ti·est**) clever and amusing in speech. 재치 있는. ¶ *a ~ speaker* 재담가 / *a ~ remark* 재치 있는 말.

:**wives** [waivz] *n.* pl. of **wife.**

wiz·ard [wízərd] *n.* Ⓒ **1** a man who has magic power. (남자) 마법사(cf. *witch*). **2** a conjurer. 마술사. **3** 《*colloq.*》 a very clever or skillful person. 재주꾼; 천재; 명인.

— *adj.* 《*sl.*》 marvelous; excellent. 굉장한; 훌륭한. [*wise*]

wiz·ened [wízənd] *adj.* dried up; faded; wrinkled. 시든; 여윈; 주름진. ¶ ~ *apples* 시든 사과 / *a ~ old woman* 얼굴이 쭈글쭈글한 노파. [E.]

wk. week; work.

wks. weeks; works.

w.l. wave length.

W.N.W. west-northwest.

W.O. War Office.

wo[1], **whoa** [wou] *interj.* (to a horse) stop! (말에게) 워《서라》.

wo[2] [wou] *n.* =woe.

woad [woud] *n.* **1** 《bot.》 a European

plant of the mustard family. 대청(大靑) 《유럽산 겨잣과의 식물》. **2** the dye extracted from this plant. (이 나무의 잎에서 얻은) 청색 물감. [E.]

wob·ble [wábəl / wɔ́bəl] *vi.* (P1,2A,3) **1** move unsteadily from side to side; shake; tremble. (이리저리) 흔들리다; 건들거리다; 떨리다. ¶ *The bridge does not feel safe, it wobbles.* 다리가 불안정하다; 흔들거린다. **2** 《*fig.*》 be undecided in opinions or actions. (생각·행동이) 자주 바뀌다. — *n.* Ⓒ the act of wobbling; Ⓤ the state of being wobbly. 흔들림; 동요. [E.]

wob·bly [wábli / wɔ́b-] *adj.* (**-bli·er, -bli·est**) unsteady; shaky. 불안정한; 흔들리는. ¶ ~ *handwriting* 불안정한 필적. [↑]

·woe [wou] *n.* Ⓤ 《*poet.*》 deep grief. 비애; 비통. ¶ *in weal and* ~ 행복하든 불행하든 / *a tale of* ~ 슬픈 신세 타령 / *Woe is me!* 아아 슬프도다 / *Woe (be) to* 〔*unto*〕 *him.* 놈에게 재앙이 있으라. [E.]

woe·be·gone [wóubigɔ̀(:)n, -gàn] *adj.* looking very sad. 슬픔〔수심〕에 잠긴. ¶ ~ *eyes.* [E. *wo begon*]

woe·ful [wóufəl] *adj.* sorrowful; pitiful. 슬픈; 비참한. ●**woe·ful·ly** [-fəli] *adv.* [*woe*]

:woke [wouk] *v.* p. and pp. of **wake.**

wold [would] *n.* ⓊⒸ a gently sloping, treeless region; an open, uncultivated region. (불모의) 황야; 벌판. [E.]

:wolf [wulf] *n.* Ⓒ (*pl.* **wolves**) **1** a wild animal like a dog. 이리. **2** a cruel, greedy person. 잔인한〔탐욕스런〕 사람. ¶ 《Bible》 *a* ~ *in sheep's clothing* =*a* ~ *in a lamb's skin* 위선자 / *have a* ~ *in the stomach* 몹시 시장기를 느끼다. **3** 《*sl.*》 a man who flirts with women. 여자를 지분거리는 남자.

cry wolf, raise a false alarm. 거짓을 전하다; 거짓 경고를 발하다.

keep the wolf from the door, get just enough food or money to live on. 가까스로 굶주림을 면하다.

— *vt.* (P6,7) eat (food) quickly and greedily. …을 게걸스럽게 먹다. ¶ *He wolfed his meal down.* 그는 게걸스럽게 음식을 먹어치웠다. [E.]

wolf·hound [wúlfhàund] *n.* Ⓒ a large dog formerly used for hunting wolves. 울프하운드《옛날 이리 사냥에 쓰던》.

wolf·ish [wúlfiʃ] *adj.* like a wolf; cruel; greedy. 이리 같은; 잔인한; 탐욕스러운.

·wolves [wulvz] *n.* pl. of **wolf.**

:wom·an [wúmən] *n.* Ⓒ (*pl.* **wom·en**) **1** a grown-up human female. (성인이 된) 여성. ¶ *a married* ~ 부인(婦人) / *My daughter will soon be a* ~. 딸은 곧 성인이 된다. **2** Ⓤ 《*collectively,* without article》 the female sex. (일반적인) 여성. ¶ *Frailty, thy name is* ~. 약한 자여 그대의 이름은 여자니라 / *Woman lives longer than man in most countries.* 대개의 나라에서 남자보다 여자가 오래 산다. **3** 《*the* ~》 womanly qualities. 여성다움. ¶ *There is little of the* ~ *in her.* 그녀에겐 여자다운 데가 거의 없다. **4** a womanish man. 여자 같은 남자. ¶ *all the women of both sexes* 남녀를 불문하고 연약한 사람. **5** a lady-in-waiting. 여관(女官); 시녀. [E. *wif* female, *mann* person]

a woman of the world, a woman experienced in society. 세상 물정에 밝은 여자.

a woman with a past, a woman with some scandal attaching to her past life. 과거가 있는 여자.

born of woman, human. 인간으로 태어난; 인간으로서의.

make an honest woman of, 《often *joc.*》 marry after seducing. (관계한 여자와) 정식으로 결혼하다.

play the woman, weep or show fear. 여자처럼 굴다.

wom·an·hood [wúmənhùd] *n.* Ⓤ **1** the condition of being a woman. 여자다움(cf. *manhood*). ¶ *She has grown to* ~. 그녀는 성숙한 여성이 되었다. **2** 《*collectively*》 women in general. 여성.

wom·an·ish [wúməniʃ] *adj.* (of a man or his feelings, conduct, etc.) like a woman; weak. (남자가) 여자 같은; 유약한. ¶ *a* ~ *walk* 여자 같은 걸음걸이.

wam·an·kind [wúmənkàind] *n.* Ⓤ 《*collectively*》 women; the female sex. 여성; 부인. ¶ *one's* ~ 집안의 여자들.

wom·an·like [wúmənlàik] *adj.* womanly; like a woman. 여성다운; 여자 같은.

wom·an·ly [wúmənli] *adj.* (**-li·er, -li·est**) like a woman; suitable for a woman; having the good qualities of a woman; tender; kind. 여성다운; 여성에 어울리는; 부드러운; 친절한. ¶ ~ *feelings* 〔*modesty*〕 여성다운 감정〔수줍음〕 / *She showed a* ~ *concern for their health.* 그녀는 그들에게 여성다운 자상한 관심을 보였다.

woman suffrage [ㄹ-ㅡ ㅅ-] *n.* extension or possession of political suffrage to or by women. 여성 참정권.

woman's wit [ㄹ-ㅅ] *n.* instinctive insight or resource of a woman. 여성 특유〔본능〕의 통찰력.

womb [wu:m] *n.* Ⓒ the organ in the female body in which the young are grown till birth. 자궁. [E.]

fruit of the womb, children. 아이들.

in the womb of time, 《*fig.*》 in the unknown future. 미래에; 장차 (일어날).

:wom·en [wímin] *n.* pl. of **woman.**

wom·en·folk [wíminfòuk] *n. pl.* women as a group. (가족·단체의) 여성들. ¶ *the* 〔*one's*〕 ~ 집안의 여자들.

:won[1] [wʌn] *v.* p. and pp. of **win.**

won[2] [wɑn / wɔn] *n.* Ⓒ (*pl.* **won**) the unit of money in Korea. 원. 參考 기호는 ₩, ₩.

:won·der [wʌ́ndər] *n.* **1** Ⓤ an emotion or feeling of surprise, awe, admiration, etc. excited by something strange or unexpected. 경탄; 경이; 놀라움. ¶ *be filled with* ~ 몹시 경탄하다 / *be lost in* ~ 경탄해 마지않다 / *He looked at her in* ~. 그는 놀라서 그녀를 바라보았다. **2** Ⓒ a person, thing or event that excites surprise and admiration; a miracle. 경이로운 사람〔물건, 일〕; 불가사의한 것; 기적. ¶ *the seven wonders of the world* 세계의 7대 불가사의 / *a nine day's* ~ 일시적 평판 / *to a* ~ 놀랄 만큼 / *do* 〔*work*〕 *wonders* 기적을 행하다 / *He failed, and no* ~. 그는 실패했으나 이상할 것도 없다 / *It is a* ~ (*that*) *he is alive.* 그가 살아 있다는 것은 기적이다 / *It is no* ~ (*that*) *he didn't want to go.* 그가 가기 싫어한 것은 당연한 일이다 / *What* ~ (*that*) *he didn't come?* 그가 오지 않았다고 해서 무엇이 이상하단 말이냐 / *The* ~ *is that he was alive.* 놀랍게도 그는 살아 있었다.

for a wonder, as a strange and surprising thing. 이상하게도. ¶ *He was punctual for a* ~. 신기하게도 그는 시간을 지켰다 / *For a* ~ *she was in time.* 놀랍게도 그녀는 지각을 하지 않았다.

— *vi.* (P1,3,4) 《*at*》 be filled with wonder; marvel. 이상하게 생각하다; 놀라다. ¶ *I* ~ *at you.* 네게 손들었다 / *I* ~ *to see you here.* 널 여기서 만나다니 놀랍다 / *I shouldn't* ~ *if it rained soon.* 곧 비가 온다해도 이상할 것은 없다 / *Can you* ~ *at it?* 그런 것은 이상하게 생각할 것 없잖나 / *I don't* ~ *at her anxiety.* 그녀가 근심하는 것은 당연하다.

— *vt.* **1** (P11) be surprised. …을 이상하게 여기다; …에 놀라다. ¶ *I* ~ *that he did not ask you about it.* 그가 그 일에 대해 네게 묻지 않았다는 것은 이상하다 / *He wondered you had done it.* 네가 그런 일을 했다는 데에 그는 놀랐다 / *I* ~ (*that*) *you were able to escape.* 네가 달아날 수 있었다니 놀랍다. **2** (P10,12) want to know. …일까〔아닐까〕 생각하다. ¶ *I* ~ *whether* 〔*if*〕 *I might ask you to help me.* 좀 도와주실 수 있는지요 / *I* ~ *who he is.* 그가 누구일까 / *I* ~ *what time it is.* 지금 몇 시일까 / *He wondered how to get there.* 어떻게 하면 거기에 갈 수 있나 생각했다 / *I* ~ *if* 〔*whether*〕 *he is ready.* 그가 준비는 했을까 / *I* ~ *why he refused.* 어째서 그가 거절했을까. [E.=portent]

:won·der·ful [wʌ́ndərfəl] *adj.* **1** astonishing; surprising; marvelous. 놀라운; 불가사의한. ¶ ~ *courage* 놀라운 용기 / *a* ~ *sight* 신기한 광경 / *a man of* ~ *patience* 참을성이 비상한 사람. **2** 《*colloq.*》 very good; splendid. 훌륭한; 굉장한. ¶ *a* ~ *dinner* / *have a* ~ *time* 멋진 시간을 보내다 / ~ *news* 굉장한 뉴스. ● **won·der·ful·ly** [-fəli] *adv.*

won·der·land [wʌ́ndərlæ̀nd] *n.* Ⓒ a land full of wonders; a fairyland. 이상한 나라; 동화의 나라.

won·der·ment [wʌ́ndərmənt] *n.* Ⓤ a feeling or state of wonder; surprise. 경탄; 경이.

won·der·struck [wʌ́ndərstrʌ̀k] *adj.* struck with wonder; feeling surprise. 몹시 놀란; 경탄한; 아연 실색한.

***won·drous** [wʌ́ndrəs] *adj.* wonderful. 놀라운. — *adv.* wonderfully. 놀랍도록. ¶ ~ *kind* 놀랍도록 친절한 / ~ *beautiful* 아름답기 이를데 없는.

***wont** [wɔːnt, wount, wʌnt] 《*lit.*》 *adj.* 《*to do*》 accustomed. 버릇처럼〔늘〕 …하는. ¶ *as he was* ~ *to say* 그가 늘 말하듯이 / *He was* ~ *to read the paper before breakfast.* 그는 늘 조반 전에 신문을 읽었다. — *n.* Ⓤ custom; habit. 습관; 버릇. ¶ *according to his* ~ 그의 버릇대로 / *He rose early, as is his* ~. 언제나처럼 그는 일찍 일어났다. [E.]

:won't [wount, wʌnt] will not.

wont·ed [wɔ́ːntid, wóunt-, wʌ́nt-] *adj.* 《as *attributive*》 accustomed; usual. 버릇이 된; 평소의. ¶ *He won every game with his* ~ *ease.* 평소처럼 침착하게 그는 모든 경기에서 이겼다 / *return at one's* ~ *hour* 평소의 시간에 돌아오다. [*wont*]

***woo** [wuː] *vt.* 《*lit.*》 **1** (P6) try to gain the love of (someone). …에게 구혼하다. **2** (P6) 《*fig.*》 try to get; attempt to obtain. …을 추구하다. ¶ ~ *fame* 〔*wealth*〕 명예〔부〕를 추구하다 / ~ *one's own destruction* 파멸을 자초하다. **3** (P13,20) entreat. …을 간청하다. ¶ *The beggar wooed every passer-by for a handout.* 그 거지는 지나가는 사람에게마다 적선을 빌었다. [E.]

:wood [wud] *n.* **1** Ⓒ 《often *pl.*》 a land covered with trees, etc.; a small forest. 숲. ¶ *ride through the wood*(*s*) 말을 타고 숲속을 지나다. **2** Ⓤ trees cut up for making something; timber; lumber. 목재; 목질(木質); 재목. ¶ *a polished* ~ *floor* 반질반질한 나무 마루 / *The box is made of* ~. 그 상자는 목제(木製)이다. **3** Ⓤ firewood. 땔나무. ¶ *Put some more* ~ *on the fire.* 불에다 장작을 더 지펴라. **4** 《*the* ~》 the woodwind instruments of an orchestra. 목관 악기. **5** 《*the* ~》 a cask or barrel (of wine, etc.). 술통. ¶ *sherry from the* ~ 술통에서 낸 셰리주. **6** Ⓒ 《golf》 a club with a wooden head. 우든 클럽.

cannot see the wood*(*s*) *for the tree, cannot see the whole because of too many details. 나무는 보고 숲은 못 보다; 작은 일에 구애되어 대국(大局)을 놓치다.

out of the woods, 〔《Brit.》 ***wood***〕, out of danger; clear of difficulties. 위기를〔난국을〕 벗어나. ¶ *Don't halloo till you are out of the wood*(*s*). 지레 좋아하지 마라.

— *vt.* (P6) **1** plant with wood. …에 나무를 심다. **2** supply with wood. …에 땔나무를 공급하다.

— *vi.* (P1) get supplies of wood. 땔나무를 공급받다.

— *adj.* made of wood. 목제(木製)의; 목재로 만든. ¶ *a* ~ *ceiling.*

wood alcohol [´ ´––] *n.* methyl alcohol. 메틸 알코올.
wood·bine [wúdbàin] *n.* Ⓤ 《bot.》 honeysuckle. 인동덩굴속(屬)의 식물.
wood block [´ ´] *n.* **1** a block of wood. (포장용(鋪裝用)) 나무 벽돌. **2** a piece of wood on which figures are carved. 목판(木版).
wood carving [´ ´–] *n.* the art of carving objects by hand from wood. 목각(木刻)(술).
wood·chuck [wúdtʃʌ̀k] *n.* Ⓒ a brown animal of the rat family; a North American marmot. (북아메리카산) 마못류(類).
wood·cock [wúdkɑ̀k / -kɔ̀k] *n.* Ⓒ (*pl.* **-cocks** or *collectively* **-cock**) 《bird》 a small brown game bird. 누른도요.
wood·craft [wúdkræ̀ft, -krɑ̀:ft] *n.* Ⓤ the skill or knowledge of living in or finding one's way through woods and forests. 산림학; 숲〔산림〕에 대한 지식.
wood·cut [wúdkʌ̀t] *n.* Ⓒ a piece of wood cut so as to print a picture; a picture printed from such a block. 목판(木版); 목판화.
wood·cut·ter [wúdkʌ̀tər] *n.* Ⓒ a person who cuts down trees; a person who makes woodcuts. 나무꾼; 초부(樵夫); 목판 조각사.
wood·ed [wúdid] *adj.* covered with trees. 나무가 우거진. ¶ *a densely ~ hill* 수목이 우거진 언덕.
:wood·en [wúdn] *adj.* **1** made of wood. 나무로 만든; 목조의. **2** lifeless; stiff as wood; awkward. 활기 없는; 딱딱한; 어색한. ¶ *~ manners* 어색한 태도 / *a ~ expression* 굳은 표정. **3** not skillful. 서투른. ¶ *The actress gave a rather ~ performance.* 그 여배우는 연기가 좀 서툴렀다.
wood engraver [´ –´–] *n.* a person who cuts a design on wood for printing. 목각사(木刻師); 목판사(木版師).
wood engraving [´ –´–] *n.* the art or process of cutting designs on wood for printing. 목판(술); 목각(술).
wood·en-head·ed [wúdnhèdid] *adj.* dull; foolish. 멍청한; 우둔한.
wood·land [wúdlənd, -læ̀nd] *n.* Ⓤ a piece of land covered with trees; forest. 산림 지대. —*adj.* of woods. 산림 (지대)의. ¶ *~ scenery* 산림의 경치.
wood louse [´ ´] *n.* 《zool.》 a very small insect-like animal with 14 legs which lives under wood, stones, etc. 쥐며느리.
wood·man [wúdmən] *n.* Ⓒ (*pl.* **-men** [-mən]) 《Brit.》 **1** a wood-cutter. 나무꾼; 초부. **2** a person who lives in the woods. 숲에서 사는 사람. **3** a person who takes care of forests. 산림 간수.
wood·peck·er [wúdpèkər] *n.* 《bird》 Ⓒ a brightly-colored bird which makes holes in trees in order to get insects to eat. 딱따구리.
wood pulp [´ ´] *n.* pulp made from wood and from which paper is made. 목재 펄프.
woods·man [wúdzmən] *n.* (*pl.* **-men** [-mən]) **1** a person accustomed to life in the woods and skilled in hunting, trapping, etc. 숲에 밝은 사람《사냥꾼·나무꾼 따위》. **2** 《U.S.》 =woodman.
wood·wind [wúdwìnd] *n.* Ⓒ **1** 《*pl.*》 the wind instruments of an orchestra, esp. those made of wood. 목관 악기류〔부〕. **2** any of these wind instruments. 목관 악기. ¶ *a ~ instrument.*
wood·work [wúdwə̀:rk] *n.* Ⓤ the wooden parts of a house, e.g. doors, stairs, etc.; work done in or with wood. (문 따위) 목제부(木製部); 목제 공예; 나무 세공.
wood·y [wúdi] *adj.* (**wood·i·er, wood·i·est**) **1** having many trees; covered with trees. 수목이 많은〔우거진〕. ¶ *a ~ valley* 수목이 울창한 계곡. **2** like or of the nature of wood. 나무의; 나무 비슷한; 목질의. ¶ *a ~ smell* 나무 비슷한 냄새 / *a ~ plant* 목본(木本). [*wood*]
woo·er [wú:ər] *n.* Ⓒ a person who woos. 구애자; 구혼자. [*woo*]
woof [wu:f] *n.* Ⓤ **1** the cross threads in cloth. (피륙의) 씨줄(opp. warp). **2** woven material; cloth. 피륙; 천. [→web]
:wool [wul] *n.* Ⓤ **1** the soft hair of sheep, etc. 양털; 양모(羊毛); 모사(毛絲). **2** cloth, thread made of wool. 털실; 모직물. ¶ *He wears ~ in winter.* 그는 겨울에는 모직물을 입는다. **3** anything like wool. 양털 같은 것. ¶ *cotton ~* 목화; 솜. **4** short, thick, curly hair. 고수머리. [E.]
all wool and a yard wide, genuine; admirable. 진짜의; 순수한; 훌륭한.
dyed in the wool, **a**) dyed before spinning or weaving. (짜기 전에) 실에 물들인. **b**) 《*fig.*》 thoroughgoing; out-and-out. (사상 등을) 철저히 침투시킨.
go for wool and come home shorn, have tables turned on one. 혹 떼러 갔다가 혹 붙이고 오다; 도리어 당하다.
lose one's wool, 《*colloq.*》 get angry. 성내다.
much cry and little wool, disappointing result; fiasco. 태산 명동(泰山鳴動)에 서일필(鼠一匹)《크게 떠벌리되, 실제의 결과는 미미한 것의 비유》; 헛소동.
pull the wool over someone's eyes, 《*colloq.*》 cast 〔throw〕 a mist before someone's eyes; deceive. …을 속이다.
·wool·en, 《Brit.》 **wool·len** [wúlən] *adj.* made of wool; of wool. 모직의; 양모(제)의. ¶ *~ cloth* 모직물; 나사. —*n.* ⓊⒸ **1** material made from wool. 모직물; 나사. ¶ *He is dressed in ~.* 그는 모직물을 입고 있다. **2** 《*pl.*》 woolen clothes. 모직의 옷. ¶ *Woolens must be washed carefully.* 모직 옷은 주의해서 빨아야 한다.

wool·gath·er·ing [wúlgæ̀ðəriŋ] *n.* Ⓤ absent-mindedness. 방심. — *adj.* absent-minded. 멍청한.

wool·ly, wool·y [wúli] *adj.* (**wool·(l)i·er, wool·(l)i·est**) **1** like wool; covered with wool, etc. 양털 같은; 털이 많은. ¶ *~ hair* 텁수룩한 머리 / *~ clouds* 뭉게 구름. **2** 《*fig.*》 lacking clearness. 선명치 못한; 흐릿한; 흐리멍덩한. ¶ *a ~ voice* 쉰 목소리 / *His ideas are a bit ~.* 그의 생각에는 다소 엉성한 데가 있다. — *n.* Ⓒ a sweater; something made from wool. 스웨터; 모직 제품.

:word [wəːrd] *n.* **1** Ⓒ a sound or series of sounds, or a letter or group of letters, used as a unit of language. 말; 낱말; 단어. ¶ *words and phrases* 단어와 어구 / *I can't hear a ~ (of what) you say.* 네 말을 알아듣지 못하겠다 / *He can't read a ~ of it.* 그는 그것을 한 마디도 읽지 못한다 / *an English ~* 영어 단어 / *a deep ~* 뜻이 깊은 말. **2** Ⓒ 《usu. *pl.*》 a speech; a thing said; a remark. 이야기; 한 마디 말. ¶ *a man of few* 〔*many*〕 *words* 말이 적은〔많은〕 사람 / *big words* 큰 소리 / *a ~ in* 〔*out of*〕 *season* 시의(時宜)에 적절한〔적절하지 못한〕 말 / *I want to have a ~ with you.* 너와 이야기 좀 하고 싶다 / *He is honest in ~ and deed.* 그는 언행(言行)이 성실하다 / *He is brave in ~ only.* 그는 말만 앞선다. **3** Ⓒ 《usu. *pl.*》 a quarrel; dispute. 말다툼; 언쟁. ¶ *hot words* 논쟁 / *have words with* …와 언쟁하다 / *come to* (*high*) *words* 언성이 높아〔커〕지다 / *They had words.* 그들은 말다툼을 했다. **4** Ⓤ 《usu. without *an article*》 news; information; a message. 소식; 기별; 전갈. ¶ *bring ~* 소식을 전하다 / *get ~ from* …에게서 소식을 듣다 / *send ~* 소식을 알리다 / *leave ~* 전갈을 남기다 / *I received ~ of his coming.* 그가 온다는 소식을 들었다 / *I have had no ~ from him since he left.* 그가 떠난 후로는 그의 소식을 못 들었다. **5** Ⓤ 《*one's ~*》 a promise; an assurance. 약속. ¶ *a man of his ~* 약속을 지키는 사람 / *give* 〔*pass*〕 *one's ~* 약속하다 / *keep* 〔*break*〕 *one's ~* 약속을 지키다〔어기다〕 / *On my ~ of honor, I'll get it.* 명예를 걸고 그것을 손에 넣겠다 / *I give you my ~ for it.* 그건 내가 보증한다 / *His ~ is as good as his bond.* 그의 말〔약속〕은 증서나 마찬가지이다. **6** Ⓒ 《*one's ~, the ~*》 an order or a command; a password; a watchword. 명령; 지시; 암호. ¶ *give the ~ to fire* 발포 명령을 내리다 / *give the ~* 암호를 말하다 / *Mum's the ~!* 잠자코 있어라; 남에게 말하지 마라 / *You must give the ~ before you can pass.* 통과하려면 암호를 말하시오. **7** 《*the W-*》 《theol.》 the Holy Bible; the teaching about God. 성서; 복음.

at a 〔***one***〕 ***word,*** immediately. 일언지하에; 즉시; 당장에.

a word in someone's ear, a private or secret remark, hint, etc. 귓엣말; 내밀한 이야기.

A word to the wise. A wise man doesn't need a long explanation. 현자에게는 말 한 마디로 족하다.

be as good as one's word, hold to one's promise. 약속을 지키다.

by word of mouth, by speech; orally. 구두로 (opp. in writing).

eat one's words, take back one's statement; admit that one was wrong. 앞에서 한 말을 취소〔철회〕하다.

give someone one's good word, recommend someone for a post. …에게 일자리를 추천하다.

hang on someone's words, listen eagerly to someone. …의 말을 열심히 듣다.

have not a word to throw at a dog, seldom or never speak. 말수가 적다; 입을 열지 않다.

have no words for, be unable to describe. …을 표현할 길이 없다.

have the last word, make the final remark in an argument; win an argument. (토론 등에서) 결정적인 말로 상대방의 입을 봉하다. ¶ *The headmistress always has the last ~ on matters of school policy.* 학교 방침에 관한 문제는 늘 여교장의 말로 결론이 난다.

in a 〔***one***〕 ***word,*** in short; briefly. 한 마디로 말하면; 요컨대.

in so many words, precisely; literally. 분명히; 정확히. ¶ *"Did she say she liked him ?" "Not in so many words, but…."* "그녀가 그를 사랑한다든" "분명하지는 않으나…"

my word upon it, on my honor. 확실히; 맹세코.

on 〔***with***〕 ***the word,*** as soon as something is said. 그렇게 말하자마자; 일언지하에.

say 〔***put in***〕 ***a good word for,*** speak favorably of (something); commend. …을 좋게 말하다; 칭찬하다.

suit the action to the word, carry out the action mentioned. 말대로 실행하다.

take someone at his word, take someone's statement to be literally true. …의 말을 곧이듣다; 말하는 대로 믿다.

take the words out of someone's mouth, say something that someone else was going to say. …가 말하려는 것을 앞질러 말하다.

upon my word, **a**) on my honor. 맹세코. ¶ *Upon my ~, I never heard of such a thing.* 맹세코 나는 그런 말을 들은 일이 없다. **b**) 《an exclamation of surprise, irritation, etc.》 indeed ! 이거 참 (놀랍군).

word for word, literally. 한 마디 한 마디; 말 그대로. ¶ *Tell me what she said, ~ for ~.* 그녀가 한 말을 그대로 내게 말해라 / *translate ~ for ~.*

— *vt.* (P6) express (something) in words. …을 말로 나타내다. ¶ *~ one's ideas clearly* 자기 생각을 분명하게 말하다 / *a beautifully worded address* 아름다운 말을 쓴 연설 / *She worded the explanation well.* 그녀는 설명을 훌륭하게 했다. [E.]

word·book [wə́ːrdbùk] *n.* Ⓒ a dictionary; a list of words. 사전; 단어집. ¶ *The exact ~ of a legal contract should be extremely important.* 법적 효력을 갖는 계약서엔 정확한 어구 선택이 참으로 중요하다.

word·ing [wə́ːrdiŋ] *n.* Ⓤ a way of expressing a thought; choice of words. 표현법; 말씨.

word·less [wə́ːrdlis] *adj.* speechless; without words; having nothing to say. 무언의; 말이 없는.

word·y [wə́ːrdi] *adj.* (**word·i·er, word·i·est**) of words; using too many words. 말의; 말이 많은. ¶ *~ warfare* 설전(舌戰) / *a ~ speech* 장황한 연설 / *a ~ person* 수다스러운 사람.

:wore [wɔːr] *v.* p. of **wear.**

:work [wəːrk] *n.* **1** Ⓤ bodily or mental effort to do something; labor; toil. 일; 작업; 노동. ¶ *a good day's ~* 꼬박 하루의 일 / *hard ~* 힘든〔어려운〕 일 / *~ of time* 시간이 걸리는 일 / 《*prov.*》 *All ~ and no play makes Jack a dull boy.* 공부만 시키고 놀리지 않으면 아이가 바보가 된다 / *He hasn't done a stroke of ~ all day.* 그는 하루 종일 일을 한 번도 하지 않았다 / *He does the ~ of two men.* 그는 두 사람 몫의 일을 한다 / *set someone to ~* 아무에게 일을 시작하게 하다. **2** ⓐ Ⓤ something to be done or made; a task. (해야 할) 일; 업무; 과업. ¶ *I have a lot of ~ to do.* 해야 할 일이 많다 / *begin* 〔*finish*〕 *the day's ~* 그날의 일을 시작하다〔마치다〕. ⓑ things needed in a task. 일에 필요한 것. ¶ *Bring your ~ to your room.* 일거리를 네 방으로 가져 가거라. **3** Ⓤ employment; occupation; trade. 직업; 일자리; 장사. ¶ *look for ~* 일자리를 찾다 / *It is my ~ to write books.* 책 쓰는 것이 내 직업이다 / *Selling is his ~.* 판매가 그의 일이다 / *go to ~* 일하러〔일터에〕 가다. **4** Ⓤ 《*collectively*》 that which is produced by effort or activity. 세공〔공작〕품; 가공물. ¶ *This mat is my own ~.* 이 돗자리는 내 손으로 만든 것이다 / *a beautiful piece of ~* 아름다운 세공품. **5** Ⓒ a product of the intellect or the imagination. 작품; 저작. ¶ *the ~ of Rodin* 로댕의 작품 / *a ~ of art* 미술품 / *literary works* 문학 작품 / *the complete works of Shakespeare* 셰익스피어 전집. **6** 《usu. *pl.*, often used as *sing.*》 a place where work is done; a factory. 제작소; 공장. ¶ *a glass works* 유리 공장 / *a brick works* 벽돌 공장. **7** Ⓒ 《usu. *pl.*》 the working parts of a watch, etc. (시계 등의) 장치; 구조; 기계. ¶ *the works of a clock* / *Something must be wrong with the works.* 기계의 어딘가가 고장난게 틀림없다. **8** Ⓒ 《often. *pl.*》 an act; a deed. 행위; 짓. ¶ *This is the ~ of the enemy.* 이건 적군의 짓이다 / *the works of the devil* 악마의 소행. **9** Ⓤ manner of working; workmanship. 일하는 품; 솜씨. ¶ *unskillful ~* 서툰 솜씨 / *make sad ~ of it* 어설프게 하다 / *That's quick ~.* 날랜 솜씨다. **10** 《phys.》 force in action. 일; 작업량. ¶ *change heat into ~* 열을 일로 바꾸다.

all in the* 〔*a*〕 *day's work, normal; what is usual. 당연한 (일).

at work, working. 일하고. ¶ *She is hard at ~.* 그녀는 열심히 일하고 있다 / *"Danger; men at ~!"* 위험, 작업중《게시》.

fall* 〔*get, set, go*〕 *to work, start doing something; begin to work. 일에 착수하다.

give someone the works, 《U.S. *sl.*》 treat someone harshly or cruelly. …을 푸대접하다; 학대하다.

have one's work cut out for one, have as much a task as one can do; have very much to do; have a hard task. 할 일이 꽉 차다; 몹시 바쁘다; 힘든 일감을 갖고 있다.

in* 〔*out of*〕 *work, having 〔not having〕 a job. 일자리가 있어〔실직해서〕.

make short* 〔*quick*〕 *work of, finish or get rid of quickly. …을 재빨리 해치우다.

— *v.* (**worked** or 《*arch.*》 **wrought**) *vi.* **1** (P1,2A,3,4) do work; labor. 일하다. ¶ *~ hard* / *~ at a desk* 사무원으로 일하다 / *~ for the public good* 공익을 위해 일하다 / *I have to ~ to earn a living.* 생계를 위해 일해야 한다 / *~ late at night* 밤늦게까지 일하다 / *They are working hand in glove.* 그들은 협심해서 일하고 있다. **2** (P3) be employed. 근무〔종사〕하고 있다. ¶ *~ in a factory* 공장에서 일하다 / *He works at* 〔*in*〕 *a bank.* 그는 은행에 근무하고 있다 / *~ in a shop* 점원 일을 하다 / *He is working in film.* 그는 영화의 일을 하고 있다. **3** (P1,2A) (of a machine, a bodily organ, etc.) operate; act. (기계·기관(器官) 등이) 움직이다; 작용하다. ¶ *The electric bell won't ~.* 벨이 울리지 않는다 / *His heart is working badly.* 그는 심장이 좋지 않다 / *The machine will not ~.* 기계가 작동하지 않는다 / *I know well how his mind works.* 그의 심중이 어떤지 나는 잘 안다. **4** (P1,2A) (of a plan, etc.) be successful or effective; achieve the desired result. (계획 등이) 잘 돼 가다; (약 등이) 듣다. ¶ *The medicine works like magic.* 그 약은 신기하게 잘 듣는다 / *The plan worked well.* 계획은 제대로 돼 갔다 / *Everything worked fair.* 만사가 순조로웠다. **5** (P2A,3,5) move slowly and with difficulty; gradually become. (힘들여) 나아가다; 서서히 …되다. ¶ *Her elbow had worked through the sleeve.* 가까스로 팔꿈치가 소매에 들어갔다 / *The wind has worked around.* 풍향이 바뀌었다 / *The nail has worked off.* 못이 빠져 버렸다 / *The window catch has worked loose.* 창문 고리가 헐거워졌다. **6** (P1,3) move in agitation. (얼굴·마음 등이) 경련을 일으키다; 동요하다. ¶ *His face worked violently.* 그의 얼굴이 격렬하게 실룩거렸다. **7** (P1,2A,3) (of yeast or a liquid) undergo a slow chemical change. 발효하

다. ¶ *Yeast makes beer* ~. 이스트가 맥주를 발효시킨다. **8** (P1,3) have an effect or influence. 영향을 주다. **9** (P1) do needlework; embroider. 바느질하다; 수를 놓다. —*vt.* **1** (P6,7) cause (a machine, etc.) to operate; cause (a person, horse, etc.) to labor. …을 움직이게 하다; 일 시키다. ¶ ~ *a pump* 펌프를 조작하다 / ~ *one's servants unmercifully* 하인들을 혹사하다 / ~ *one's jaws* 턱을 움직이다 / *The boss* ~ *us nearly to death.* 사장은 우리를 너무 부려먹는다 / ~ *a machine* 기계를 운전하다. **2** (P6) operate; manage. …을 경영하다. ¶ ~ *a farm* 농장을 경영하다 / *The fisherman works the stream.* 어부는 그 시내에서 고기잡이를 한다 / ~ *gold-mines* 금광업을 경영하다. **3** (P6,7) solve (a sum, problem). …을 풀다; 해결하다; 산출(算出)하다. ¶ ~ *calculation in one's head* 암산하다 / *You have worked your sum wrong.* 네 계산은 틀렸다. **4** (P6, 7,13) form; shape; knit. …을 만들다; (어떤 모양으로) 하다; 뜨다; 짜다. ¶ *He worked the clay into a pretty vase.* 그는 진흙을 빚어 예쁜 꽃병을 만들었다 / ~ *a shawl* 〔*sweater*〕 숄을〔스웨터를〕 뜨다 / ~ *a design on cloth* 천에 무늬를 수놓다 / *The wood is easily worked.* 그 나무는 세공〔목각〕하기가 좋다. **5** (P6) bring about; accomplish. …을 가져오다; …을 이루다. ¶ ~ *one's will* 뜻을 이루다 / *Time works many changes.* 시간은 많은 변화를 가져온다. **6** (P6,13) achieve (something) by effort or work; cause to move slowly in a certain direction. 노력해서 …을 얻다; (천천히) 애써 나아가다. ¶ ~ *one's way through a crowd* 군중 속을 비집고 나가다 / ~ *a car to the left side* 서서히 차를 왼쪽으로 틀다 / ~ *one's way through college* 고학으로 대학을 졸업하다 / ~ *one's way along in darkness* 어둠 속을 더듬더듬 나아가다. **7** (P6,13) excite, move, or stir (someone's feelings). …을 흥분시키다; 자극하다. ¶ ~ *someone into rage* 아무를 화나게 하다 / ~ *oneself into a temper* 벌컥 화를 내다. **8** (P6) cause to ferment. …을 발효시키다. **9** (P6) prepare or treat by kneading, hammering. …을 반죽하다; (쇠)를 불리다. ¶ ~ *dough* 반죽을 하다 / ~ *iron* 쇠를 제련하다. **10** (P6) carry on one's occupation in, through, or along (a region, etc.). (어떤 지역)을 일터로 하다. ¶ *The salesman works the western states.* 그 판매원은 서부의 주들을 맡고 있다 / *The beggar works this town.* 그 거지는 이 마을에서 구걸한다. [E.]

work against time, work hard so as to finish something within a limited time. 시간을 다투어 일하다. ¶ *We worked against time to get out the newspaper.* 신문을 내려고 우리는 시간을 다투며 일했다.

work at, apply oneself to (something); study. …에 종사하다; …을 공부하다.

work away 〔***on***〕, continue to work. 계속〔꾸준히〕 일하다. ¶ ~ *away at one's homework* 열심히 숙제를 하다.

work for, make effort to gain or earn; strive for. …을 위해〔얻으려고〕 노력하다. ¶ ~ *for a prize* 〔*one's living*〕 상을 타려고〔생계를 위해〕 힘쓰다 / ~ *for peace* 평화를 위해 노력하다.

work in, **a**) bring or put in; insert; introduce. …을 삽입하다. ¶ ~ *in some jokes* 몇 마디의 농담을 곁들이다. **b**) fit in with; match with; combine with. 알맞다; 조화되다. ¶ *His plan will not* ~ *in with ours.* 그의 계획은 우리 것과 맞지 않는다.

work off, get rid of; dispose of (something); sell. …을 제거〔처분〕하다; 매각하다. ¶ *I have three years to* ~ *off the debt.* 빚을 청산하는 데 3년이 걸린다.

work on 〔***upon***〕, **a**) try to persuade. 설득하다. **b**) influence. …을 감화시키다; …에 영향을 주다.

work out, **a**) calculate. 산출하다; 계산해내다. ¶ ~ *out the expenditure* 비용을 계산해내다. **b**) solve. 해결하다; 풀다. ¶ ~ *out a difficult problem* 어려운 문제를 해결하다 / *The puzzle won't* ~ *out.* 그 수수께끼가 풀리지 않는다. **c**) bring about by work. 노력해서 해내다. ¶ ~ *out one's own salvation* 스스로 자구책을 강구하다. **d**) exhaust through working. (…을) 다 파내다. ¶ *The mine was worked out long ago.* 그 광산은 오래 전에 바닥이 났다. **e**) plan out; develop. 안출해내다; 입안하다. ¶ ~ *out a plan* 〔*new method*〕 계획〔새로운 방법〕을 입안하다. **f**) be calculated. 산정되다. ¶ *The expenses worked out at £5 each.* 비용은 각기 5파운드로 나왔다. **g**) accomplish; get the result. …을 이루다; …이 되다; 끝나다. ¶ *Everything is working out well.* 매사가 잘 돼 가고 있다 / *Our plans didn't* ~ *out.* 우리 계획은 좌절됐다.

work up, **a**) build up (something) gradually by effort. (노력해서) 천천히 만들어내다. ¶ ~ *up business* 사업을 일으켜 세우다 / ~ *up reputation* 점차로 명성을 올리다. **b**) excite; stir or arouse. …을 흥분시키다; 자극하다. ¶ ~ *up enthusiasm* 분발시키다 / ~ *up an appetite* 식욕을 돋우다 / ~ *up one's nervous feeling* 신경을 자극하다. **c**) elaborate. 공들여 만들다. ¶ ~ *up a picture.* **d**) advance; rise. …으로 나아가다. **e**) develop; prepare. …을 발전시키다; 준비하다. ¶ *I want to* ~ *up these notes into a book.* 이 메모들을 정리해서 책을 만들고 싶다.

work·a·ble [wə́ːrkəbəl] *adj.* **1** that can be worked; can be used for a particular purpose. 일할 수 있는; 사용할 수 있는. ¶ *The ground is too wet to be* ~. 그 운동장은 사용하기엔 너무 질다. **2** that can be carried out; able to succeed; able to be put into practice. 실행 가능한. ¶ *a* ~ *plan* 실행할 수 있는 계획.

work·a·day [wə́ːrkədèi] *adj.* **1** of working days. 일하는 날의; 평일의. **2** ordinary; practical; dull. 평범한; 실제적인; 무미 건조

한. ¶ *this ~ world* 무미 건조한 이 세상.

work-bas·ket [wə́ːrkbæ̀skit / -bɑ̀s-] *n.* a small basket for holding sewing materials. 반짇고리. [*work*]

work·bench [wə́ːrkbèntʃ] *n.* Ⓒ a table at which work is done. 작업대.

work·book [wə́ːrkbùk] *n.* Ⓒ **1** 《esp. U.S.》 a book with questions and answers which students use to study. 연습 문제집; 워크북. **2** a book that contains the rules for doing certain work. (일 따위의) 규정서〔집〕.

work·day [wə́ːrkdèi] *n.* Ⓒ a day for work; a day on which work is done. 근무일; 작업일; 평일(cf. *Sunday, holiday*).

:work·er [wə́ːrkər] *n.* Ⓒ **1** a person who works; a person who works for wages; a laborer. 일하는 사람; 노동자. **2** 《zool.》 ants, bees, etc. that work for their colony. 일벌; 일개미.

work·house [wə́ːrkhàus] *n.* Ⓒ **1** 《U.S.》 a kind of prison where criminal boys and girls are confined and made to work in order to reform them. 소년원. **2** 《Brit. hist.》 a place for homeless poor people. 구빈원(救貧院).

:work·ing [wə́ːrkiŋ] *n.* **1** ⓊⒸ operation; action. 작업; 운전; 작용; 활동. ¶ *the ~ of an engine* 엔진의 작동 / *the workings of his conscience* 그의 양심의 작용. **2** 《usu. *pl.*》 parts of a mine, quarry, etc. where work is done. (광산의) 채굴장. — *adj.* **1** of, used for, or including work. 일하는; 노동의; 운전의. ¶ *a ~ committee* 운영 위원회 / *~ expenses* 운영비; 경영비 / *~ hours* 노동 시간 / *a ~ plan* 작업 계획 / *~ knowledge* 실용적 지식. **2** engaged actively in work, esp. with hands. (실제) 노동에 종사하는. ¶ *~ population* 노동 인구 / *the ~ class* 노동 계급.

working day [⊿– ⊿] *n.* a day on which work is done; the part of a day during which work is done. 작업일; 일일 근무 시간.

work·ing-day [wə́ːrkiŋdèi] *adj.* =workaday.

working drawing [⊿– ⊿–] *n.* **1** a drawing for guiding workmen in making a machine, etc. 시공도(施工圖); 공작도. **2** a plan serving as guide for construction. 설계도.

work·ing·man [wə́ːrkiŋmæ̀n] *n.* Ⓒ (*pl.* **-men** [-mèn]) a person who works, esp. with his hands; a laborer. 근로자; 직공; 육체 노동자.

:work·man [wə́ːrkmən] *n.* Ⓒ (*pl.* **-men** [-mən]) a worker; a laborer; a person who is skilled in his trade; a craftsman. 직공; 공원; 기능공. ¶ *a good ~* 숙련공 / *a workman's train* (근로자용) 조조 할인 열차 / 《*prov.*》 *A bad ~ blames his tools.* 서툰 직공이 연장만 탓한다.

work·man·like [wə́ːrkmənlàik] *adj.* like a good workman; skillful; well made. 숙련공다운; 능숙한; 잘 만든.

work·man·ship [wə́ːrkmənʃìp] *n.* Ⓤ the art or skill of a worker; skill; the quality of something made; the work which is done. 솜씨; 기량; 만듦새; 세공; 제작물.

work·out [wə́ːrkàut] *n.* Ⓒ 《U.S. *colloq.*》 an exercise e.g. when training for a sport; a trial; a test. (예비) 연습; 시험.

work·peo·ple [wə́ːrkpìːpl] *n. pl.* 《chiefly Brit.》 people who work, esp. with their hands or machines. (남녀)노동자들; (특히) 공원들.

work·room [wə́ːrkrù(ː)m] *n.* Ⓒ a room where work is done. 작업실.

work·shop [wə́ːrkʃɑ̀p / -ʃɔ̀p] *n.* Ⓒ **1** a shop or building where work is done. 작업장; 공장; 일터. **2** 《U.S.》 an occasion when a group of people meet for special study, work, etc. 연수회(研修會); 연구 발표회; 워크숍. ¶ *a drama* 〔*theater*〕 *~* 연극 연수〔연구〕회 / *a two-day ~ on management techniques,* 2일 코스의 경영 기술 연수회.

work·shy [wə́ːrkʃài] *adj.* not liking work and habitually try to avoid it. 일하기 싫어하는; 게을러 빠진.

:world [wəːrld] *n.* Ⓒ **1** 《usu. *the ~*, used as *sing.*》 the earth; the universe; all created things; a star or planet. 세계; 지구; 천지; 우주; 만물; 별. ¶ *the whole* 〔*all the*〕 *~* 전세계 / *go round the ~* 세계를 일주하다 / *the world's fastest airplane* 세계에서 가장 빠른 항공기 / *sail around the ~* 세계를 주항(周航)하다 / *the external ~* 외계 / *A satellite goes round the ~.* 한 위성이 지구를 선회하고 있다. **2** 《*the ~*》 human life on earth; this present life. 현세; 이 세상. ¶ *another ~* =*a better ~* 내세 / *this ~ and the next ~* 현세와 내세 / *the ~ to come* 저 세상; 저승 / *in this ~* 이 세상에서 / *depart out of this ~* 세상을 뜨다; 죽다 / *be weary of the ~* 세상이 싫어지다. **3** 《*the ~*》 human life and experience; human society in general. (살아가는) 세상; 세간(世間); 세상사(事); 인간 세상〔사회〕. ¶ *a man of the ~* 세상 물정을 아는 사람 / *be out of touch with the ~* 세상사〔속세〕와 관계를 끊고 있다 / *All the ~ admired him.* 온 세상이 그를 칭찬했다 / *How is the ~ using you?* 어떻게 지내고 계십니까 / *The ~ goes very well with me.* 탈없이 (잘)지내고 있다 / *know the ~* 세상 (물정)을 알고 있다 / *go out into the ~* (실)사회에 나가다 / *take the ~ as it is* =*take the ~ as one finds it* 세상 돌아가는 대로 따르다; 시세〔세상 형편〕에 순응하다. **4** 《usu. *the ~*, used as *sing.*》 the earth and its people; mankind; the public; worldly people; everybody. 세계 속의 사람들; 인류; 세인(世人); 세상〔세간〕 사람들; 속인. ¶ *The whole ~ knows it.* 온 세상 사람들이 다 알고 있다 / *What will the ~ say?* 세상 사람들이 뭐라고 하겠느냐 / *He showed* *the ~ that he was not a fool.* 그는 자기가 바보가 아니었다는 것을 세상에 보여주었다 / *The whole ~ suffered in the World War.* 전 인류가 세계 대전 중 고통을 당했다 / *The ~ waited anxiously for the results of the peace talks.* 온 세상 사람들이 그 평화 회담의 결과를 애타게 기다렸다. **5** 《usu. *the* ~》 any sphere of interest or activity. (특정 인종·직업·집단 따위의) …계(界); …사회. ¶ *the fashionable ~* 유행계 / *the movie ~* 영화계 / *the great ~* 상류 사회 / *the literary ~* = *the ~ of letters* 문단. **6** 《usu. *the* ~》 a division of things belonging to the earth. (자연계의) …계. ¶ *the animal* 〔*vegetable, mineral*〕 *~* 동물〔식물, 광물〕계. **7** 《often *W-*》 some part of the earth. (지구의) 어떤 지방; 지역; 세계. ¶ *the New* 〔*Old*〕 *World* 신〔구〕세계 / *the civilized ~* 문명 세계 / *the ancient ~* 고대의 세계; 고대. **8** 《often *pl.*, *a ~ of*》 a large number or amount. 다량; 다수. ¶ *a ~ of waters* 대양 / *a ~ of difference* 굉장히 큰 차이 / *Sunshine does children a ~ of good.* 햇볕은 아이들에게 크게 유익하다 / *a ~ of trouble(s)* 끝도 없이 많은 두통거리 / *His explanation gave me a ~ of confidence.* 그의 설명은 내게 큰 자신감을 주었다. [E.]

all the world and his wife, everybody, esp. all the fashionable people. (남녀 가리지 않고) 누구나 다; (유행을 좇는) 어중이떠중이 모두. ¶ *All the ~ and his wife were present.* 누구 할 것없이 다 나와 있었다.

all the world over = ***all over the world,*** in all the world. 온 세계에.

as the world goes, speaking generally. 일반적으로〔통례대로〕 말하면.

at the world's end, at the farthest attainable distance. 땅끝까지.

a world too, far too; by far. 너무나 …한. ¶ *It's a ~ too wide.* 그것은 너무나 넓다.

be all the world to, be everything to (someone); be very important to (someone). …에게 있어 더없이 중요하다. ¶ *My family is* 〔*means*〕 *all the ~ to me.* 내 가족이란 나에게 더없이 중요한 존재이다.

begin the world, start one's career. 실사회에 나가다.

bring** a child **into the world, give birth to a child. (자식)을 낳다.

***carry the world before** one,* have quick and complete success. 순식간에 크게 성공하다.

come into the world, be born. 태어나다.

dead to the world, 《*colloq.*》 fast asleep; as if dead; unconscious. 깊이 잠들어; 의식이 없어.

for all the world, **a**) exactly. 틀림없이; 확실히. ¶ *He is for all the ~ like a monkey.* 그는 아무리 봐도 꼭 원숭이 같다. **b**) for any consideration at all. 무슨 일이 있더라도; 결코; 절대로. ¶ *Don't kill yourself for all the ~.* 절대로〔무슨 일이 있어도〕 자살은 하지 마라.

in the world, **a**) on earth. 도대체. ¶ *What in the ~ does he mean?* 도대체 그는 어쩔 작정인가. **b**) at all. 전혀.

not for the world, not on any account; not for any reason. 결코 …않다〔아니다〕. ¶ *I wouldn't marry her for the ~.* 나는 그 여자하고는 절대로 결혼하지 않겠다.

on top of the world, 《*colloq.*》 very happy or successful. 하늘에 오를 듯이 기뻐; 크게 성공하여. ¶ *I was on top of the ~.* 나는 하늘에라도 오를 듯한 기분이었다.

out of this 〔***the***〕 ***world,*** 《*colloq.*》 exceptionally fine; splendid. 아주 훌륭한; 굉장히 좋은. ¶ *Her beauty was out of the ~.* 그녀는 굉장한 미인이었다.

(***the***) ***world without end,*** forever. 영원히.

think the world of, esteem very highly. …을 높이 평가하다. ¶ *He may get angry sometimes, but really he thinks the ~ of you.* 그는 때때로 화를 낼는지 모르지만 실은 너를 끔찍이 생각한다.

to the world, 《*sl.*》 utterly. 완전히; 철저히. ¶ *He was tired to the ~.* 그는 기진맥진해 있었다.

world-beat·er [wə́:rldbì:tər] *n.* Ⓒ a person or thing that is thought to be able to compete successfully in the world. (동류의 모든 것을) 능가하는 사람〔물건〕; 기록 보유자; 제일인자. ¶ *This runner* 〔*new invention*〕 *is a ~.* 이 주자는〔새 발명품은〕 단연 최고다.

world-class [wə́:rldklǽs, -klɑ̀:s] *adj.* among the best in the world. 세계적인; 세계 일류의. ¶ *That cricketer is ~.* 저 크리켓 선수는 세계 정상급이다.

world-fa·mous [wə́:rldféiməs] *adj.* famous all over the world. 세계적으로 유명한.

world language [⌐─] *n.* a language that is spoken in various parts of the world. 세계어; 국제어.

world·li·ness [wə́:rldlinis] *n.* worldly ideas, ways, conduct, etc. (생각·행동 등이) 세속적임.

world·ling [wə́:rldliŋ] *n.* Ⓒ a worldly person. 속물; 속인.

***world·ly** [wə́:rldli] *adj.* (**-li·er, -li·est**) **1** of this world; not of heaven. 이 세상의; 현세의; 속세의. ¶ *~ affairs* 세상 일 / *~ goods* 〔*property*〕 (속세의) 재화; 재산 / *~ pleasure* 현세의 즐거움. **2** caring much for the material things of life. 명리를 추구하는; 세속적인; 물욕이 많은. ¶ *a ~ person* 속인(俗人) / *~ life* 세속적인 생활 / *~ wisdom* (특히 이기적인) 세재(世才).

world·ly-mind·ed [wə́:rldlimáindid] *adj.* caring much for worldly pleasures, interests, etc. 명리를 좇는; 세속적인.

world-wide [wə́:rldwáid] *adj.* spread all over the world. 세계적으로 알려진. ¶ *~ fame* 세계적인 명성 / *cars with a ~ reputation for reliability* 신뢰성에서 세계적인 평이 나 있는 차량들 / *a ~ movement* 세계적인 운동 / *the ~ recession* 세계적인 불황 / *of ~*

importance 세계적으로 중요한.

:worm [wəːrm] *n.* Ⓒ **1** any small creeping animal without legs or with very short ones. 벌레《지렁이·구더기 따위》. ¶ *become food for worms* 죽다 / 《*prov.*》 *A* ～ 〔*Even a* ～〕 *will turns.* =*Tread on a* ～ *and it will turn.* 지렁이도 밟으면 꿈틀한다 / *Many birds eat worms.* 많은 새들은 벌레를 잡아 먹는다 / *I accidently cut a* ～ *in half with my spade.* 나는 우연히 삽으로 지렁이를 두 동강 냈다 / *This dog has worms.* 이 개는 기생충이 있다. **2** a person who is useless, mean, etc. like a worm. 벌레 같은 인간; 쓸모 없는〔비열한〕 사람. ¶ *You* ～*!* 이 벌레 같은 놈 / *He is a little* ～. 벌레 같은 비열한 놈이다. **3** something that injures someone slowly. (마음을 좀먹는) 고통; 고뇌; 회한(悔恨). ¶ *the* ～ *of conscience* 양심의 가책. **4** a screw; the spiral of a screw. 나사; (나사의) 나선(螺線); 웜.
—*vt.* (P7,13) **1** move (one's way, etc.) like a worm. …을 천천히 나아가게 하다. ¶ ～ *one's way out of a crowd* 군중 속에서 겨우 빠져 나오다 / ～ *one's way* 〔*oneself*〕 *through the bushes* 덤불 속을 느리게〔기듯이〕 지나가다 / ～ *oneself into someone's favor* 교묘히 슬금슬금 아무의 환심을 사다 / *The soldiers wormed their way toward the enemy.* 병사들은 살금살금 적에게로 다가갔다. **2** obtain (information, etc.) by slow and indirect means. (정보 등)을 알아내다; 빼내다. ¶ ～ *a secret out of someone* 아무에게서 비밀을 빼내다. **3** remove worms from. …에게서 기생충을 없애다. ¶ ～ *a dog.*
—*vi.* (P1) move like a worm. 기듯이 나아가다. [E.]

worm-eat·en [wə́ːrmìːtən] *adj.* **1** full of holes caused by worms. 벌레〔좀〕 먹은. ¶ ～ *wood* 〔*fruit*〕 벌레 먹은 재목〔과일〕. **2** out-of-date; worn-out. 구식의; 진부한. ¶ ～ *regulations* 〔*customs*〕 진부한〔낡은〕 규칙〔관습〕.

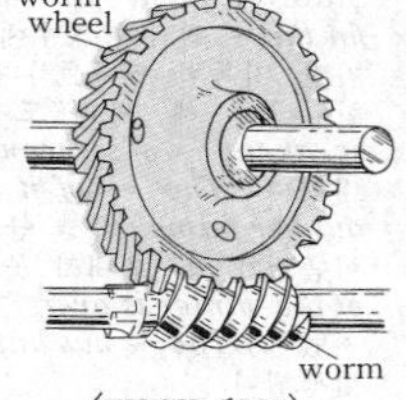

〈worm gear〉

worm gear [∸ ∸] *n.* a wheel with teeth on its edges to enable it to move with a worm; a worm wheel. 웜 기어; 웜 기어 장치《동력 전달 기어 장치》.

worm wheel [∸ ∸] *n.* =worm gear.

worm·wood [wə́ːrmwùd] *n.* Ⓤ **1** a kind of very bitter plant used in medicine, etc. 쑥의 일종《국화과 식물》. **2** 《*fig.*》 something bitter or extremely unpleasant. 고민거리; 고뇌.

worm·y [wə́ːrmi] *adj.* (**worm·i·er, worm·i·est**) **1** eaten or damaged by worms. 벌레 먹은; 벌레먹어 못쓰게 된. **2** full of worms; like a worm. 벌레투성이의; 벌레 같은. **3** mean-spirited. 비굴한; 치사한.

:worn [wɔːrn] *v.* pp. of **wear.**
—*adj.* **1** damaged by long wear, etc. 닳아빠진; 입어서〔써서〕 해진〔닳은〕. ¶ ～ *clothes* 헌 옷 / *a* ～ *inscription* 닳아서 판독이 어려운 묘비명(銘). **2** tired. 지친; 피곤한. ¶ *a* ～ *face* 피곤한 얼굴. [*wear*]

worn-out [wɔ́ːrnáut] *adj.* **1** used until no longer serviceable. 닳아빠진. ¶ ～ *shoes.* **2** thoroughly tired; tired out. 기진맥진한; 지친. ¶ *I was* ～ *after the long hike.* 먼 길을 걸어 나는 지쳐 있었다 / *You look* ～. 너는 지쳐 보인다.

:wor·ry [wə́ːri, wʌ́ri] *v.* (**-ried**) *vt.* **1** (P6, 13,20) bother; trouble; make (someone) anxious. …을 괴롭히다; 성가시게 굴다; 걱정시키다; (…의) 속을 태우다. ¶ ～ *oneself* 혼자 끙끙 속을 앓다 / *get* 〔*be*〕 *worried* 고민하다〔하고 있다〕 / *look worried* 근심스런 얼굴이다 / ～ *someone with perpetual questions* 집요한 질문으로 아무를 성가시게 하다〔괴롭히다〕 / *There's really nothing to be worried about.* 정말이지 걱정할 것 하나도 없다 / *It worries me that he doesn't say anything.* 그가 도무지 말이 없어 걱정이다 / *You cannot be worried by such a thing.* 그런 일로 신경을 쓰다간 한이 없다 / ～ *over trifling things* 하찮은 일들로 고민하다 / *The noise of the traffic worried her.* 시끄러운 차 소리가 그녀를 괴롭혔다. **2** (P6) (of a dog, etc.) seize and shake (something) with the teeth; bite at. (개 따위가) …을 물어뜯다; 물고 흔들다. ¶ *The dog worried a rat.* 개가 쥐를 물고 흔들었다. **3** (P15) 《*out*》 attack (a problem, etc.) again and again till it is solved. (문제 따위)를 애써 해결하다; 풀다. ¶ ～ *out the meaning of the passage* 그 구절의 뜻을 마침내 풀어내다.
—*vi.* (P1,2A,3) 《*about*》 be troubled, anxious, or uneasy. 괴로워하다; 걱정하다. ¶ *Don't* ～ *about it.* 그것은 걱정하지 마라 / 《U.S. *colloq.*》 *I should* ～*!* 아무 상관도 없다; 내 알 바 아니다 / *You have no cause to* ～. 너는 뭣 때문에 고민하는 거냐 / *What's the use of worring?* 근심해서 무슨 소용이 있나.
worry along 〔***through***〕, manage to get on in spite of difficulties. 고생하면서 헤쳐나가다. ¶ *He managed to* ～ *through the obstacle.* 그는 그럭저럭 장애물을 뚫고 나갔다 / *She tried to* ～ *along without him.* 그녀는 그 없이 그럭저럭 꾸려나가보려고 했다.
—*n.* (*pl.* **-ries**) **1** Ⓤ the act of worrying; anxiety; uneasiness. 근심; 걱정; 고뇌. ¶ *Her voice showed her* ～. 그녀의 목소리는 근심스러워 보였다. **2** Ⓒ 《usu. *pl.*》 a cause of anxiety; a trouble. 걱정〔골칫〕거리. ¶ *We have many worries in life.* 사노라면 여러 가지 걱정거리가 있게 마련이다 / *It's a* ～ *to me having to leave the children alone in the house.* 아이들만 집에 남겨두는 것이 걱정이 된다. [E.]

:worse [wəːrs] *adj.* (compar. of **bad** or **ill**) **1** bad in a greater degree; less good. 더욱 나쁜; 훨씬 더 나쁜. ¶ *so much the* ~ 그 만큼 더 나쁜 / *be* ~ *than useless* 유해무익하다 / *It got* ~ *and* ~. 그것은 악화일로였다 / *You are only making things* ~. 너는 일을 더 나쁘게만 만들고 있다 / *The situation grew* ~ *and* ~. 사태는 계속 나빠져 갔다 / *He's a* ~ *player than his brother.* 그는 동생보다 못한 선수다 / *It might have been* ~. (결과 따위가) 어쩌면 더 나빴을지도 모른다 《이만 하기가 다행이다》. **2** 《as *predicative*》 in a less good state of health; more ill. 건강이 전보다 더 나쁜. ¶ *He grew rapidly* ~. 그의 병세는 급속히 악화되었다 / *The patient is* ~ *this morning.* 환자는 오늘 아침 상태가 더 나쁘다. **3** 《as *predicative*》 in a less good condition. (사정이) 더 나빠져 〔어렵게 된〕. ¶ *He will not be the* ~ *for the change.* 그는 달라져봐야 더 나빠질 것도 없다 / *It is the* ~ *for the change.* 변화로 인해 더욱 나빠졌다.

be the worse for drink 〔***liquor***〕, be drunk. 「술에 취하다.

be the worse for wear, badly worn as the result of long wear. 오래 입어서 낡다.

none the worse for, not harmed by. 아무렇지도 않은; …에도 불구하고 같은 상태인. ¶ *He was none the* ~ *for the accident.* 사고를 당하고도 아무렇지 않았다.

to make matters worse = (***and***) ***what is worse,*** to mention a fact which is worse. 더욱 더 곤란한 것은; 설상가상으로. ¶ *The car broke down when I was driving home from work, and to make matters* ~ *it was pouring with rain.* 차를 몰고 집으로 퇴근하는 길에서 차가 고장났다. 설상가상으로 비까지 억수로 쏟아지고 있었다.

— *adv.* (compar. of **badly** or **ill**) **1** more badly. 더 나쁘게. ¶ *sing* ~ *than before* 전보다 더 노래를 못하다 / *They said they had fixed the car, but it's now running even* ~ *than before.* 그들이 차를 고쳤다고 했으나 주행 상태는 더 나쁘다. **2** to a worse degree. 더 심하게. ¶ *It is blowing* ~ *than before.* 바람은 더 세차게 불고 있다.

be worse off, be more badly situated. 살기가 더 어렵다.

none the worse, no less; all the better. 여전히; 그럼에도 불구하고. ¶ *I like him none the* ~ *for his rudeness.* 그가 건방지긴 해도 나는 여전히 그가 좋다.

— *n.* Ⓤ that which is worse; 《*the* ~》 a worse state. 더욱 나쁜 것; 불리; 패배. ¶ *a change for the* ~ 악화 / *for better or* ~ 좋건 나쁘건 / *do* ~ 더 나쁜〔어리석은〕 짓을 하다 / *have the* ~ 패배하다 / *put someone to the* ~ 아무를 패배시키다 / *I have* ~ *to tell.* = *Worse remains to tell.* (그뿐 아니라) 더 나쁜 일이 있다 / *The patient took a turn for* ~. 환자는 병세가 악화됐다. [E.]

go from bad to worse ⇨bad.

worsen [wə́ːrsən] *vt., vi.* (P6;1) make or become worse. 더 나빠지(게 하)다. ¶ *The rain has worsened our difficulties.* 비 때문에 우리는 더 어려워졌다 / *the worsening economic crisis* 악화 일로의 경제 위기.

:wor·ship [wə́ːrʃip] *n.* Ⓤ **1** respect, honor, etc. paid to God or another religious object. 신을 섬기기; 예배; 참배. **2** ceremonies in honor of God. 예배식. ¶ *public* ~ (교회의) 예배식 / *a house* 〔*place*〕 *of* ~ 교회; 예배당. **3** great or excessive admiration. 숭배. **4** 《Brit.》 《*your W-, his W-*》 a title of respect of a mayor or magistrate. (시장 등에 대한 경칭으로) 각하.

— *v.* (**-shiped, -ship·ing** or 《Brit.》 **-shipped, -ship·ping**) *vt.* (P6) **1** pay great honor or respect to (God, etc.). (신)을 참배〔예배〕하다. ¶ *People go to church to* ~ *God.* 사람들은 신을 예배하기 위해 교회에 간다. **2** consider (someone or something) very precious; adore. …을 숭배하다; …을 중히 여기다. ¶ ~ *money* 돈을 중히 여기다.

— *vi.* (P1) take part in worship; attend church service. 예배하다; 예배하러 가다. ¶ *Many people have worshipped in this church.* 많은 사람들이 이 교회에서 예배를 보았다. [→worth]

:worst [wəːrst] *adj.* (superl. of **bad** or **ill**) bad to the highest degree; least good. 가장 나쁜; 최악의. ¶ *the* ~ *frost for fifty years,* 50년 만의 심한 서리 / *This is the* ~ *fever I've ever had.* 이 같은 열은 내 생전 처음이다 / *a criminal of the* ~ *kind* 가장 흉악한 범인.

— *adv.* (superl. of **badly** or **ill**) most badly. 가장 나쁘게. ¶ ~ *of all* 무엇보다 나쁜 것은 / *There were many who played badly, but he played* ~. 경기를 잘 못한 사람들이 많이 있었지만 그가 가장 못했다 / *the worst-dressed man in the office* 사무실에서 가장 옷맵시가 없는 남자.

— *n.* Ⓤ that which is worst; the worst state or part. 최악의 것〔사태〕. ¶ *prepare for the* ~ 최악의 경우에 대비하다 / *do one's* ~ 가장 지독한 짓을 하다 / *Do your* ~ *!* 어디 할 테면 해 봐라《도전적으로 하는 말》/ *speak the* ~ *of someone* 아무를 헐뜯다; 깎아내리다 / *The* ~ *of it is, I didn't even find out her name.* 가장 난처한 것은 내가 그녀의 이름조차 생각해내지 못했다는 것이다 / *The* ~ *of the winter is over.* 겨울의 가장 추운 때는 지났다 / *The* ~ *has happened.* 최악의 사태가 발생했다.

at (***the***) ***worst,*** under the most unfavorable circumstances; (even) in the worst case. 최악의 경우에〔는〕(opp. at (the) best). ¶ *He is a fool at* (*the*) *best, and at* (*the*) ~ *he's a criminal.* 그는 아주 잘봐 줘서 바보고, 아주 나쁘게 말하면 범죄인이다.

get the worst of it, be defeated. 지다; 패배하다.

give *someone* ***the worst of it,*** defeat. 아무를 지우다〔패배시키다〕.

if (***the***) ***worst comes to*** (***the***) ***worst,*** if the worst happens. 최악〔만일〕의 경우에는. ¶ *If the ~ comes to the ~, we can always go by bus tomorrow.* 만일의 경우에는 우린 내일 언제라도 버스로 가면 된다.

make the worst (=*consider only the least favorable aspects*) **of** *something.* …을 최악의 경우로 생각하다.

***put someone* to the worst,** defeat. 아무를 지우다; 패배시키다.

— *vt.* (P6) defeat; beat. …을 지우다. ¶ *The enemy were worsted.* 적은 패배했다. [*worse*]

wor·sted [wústid, wə́:r-] *n.* Ⓤ **1** fine, twisted woolen thread. 소모사(梳毛絲); 우스티드. **2** cloth made from worsted. 모직물. — *adj.* made of worsted. 소모사로 만든; 모직물의. [Place]

:worth [wəːrθ] *adj.* 《as *predicative*》 **1** having a certain value or price; equal in value to. …의 가치가 있는; …한 값어치의. ¶ *It is not ~ a penny.* 그건 한푼의 가치도 없다 / *You can have it for £400, but it is ~ more.* 그걸 400파운드에 팔겠소. 하지만 그것은 그 이상의 값어치가 있는 것이오 / *be ~ little* 〔*much*〕 거의 무가치하다〔아주 값지다〕 / 《*prov.*》 *A bird in the hand is ~ two in the bush.* ⇨bird. **2** deserving or worthy of. …할 만한 가치가 있는; …하기에 족한. ¶ *a task ~ the trouble* 애써 해 볼 만한 일 / *We may not succeed, but it's ~ of try.* 성공을 못 할지도 모르지만 그것은 해 볼 만한 일이다 / *It is ~ reading.* 읽을 가치가 있다 / *It is ~ seeing.* 그것은 볼 만하다 / *This book is well ~ reading.* 이 책은 읽을 만한 가치가 충분히 있다 / *I hope you will be ~ your fee.* 받는 사례만큼의 일을 해 주었으면 좋겠다. **3** having property amounting to. 재산이 …의; …만큼의 재산이 있는. ¶ *He is ~ a million.* 그 사람 백만 장자다 / *He died ~ a million pounds.* 그는 백만 파운드를 남기고 죽었다 / *What is he ~? — He is ~ several millions.* 그 사람 재산이 얼마나 되느냐— 수백만 달러가 된다.

for all *one* **is worth,** 《*colloq.*》 to the extent of one's power. 전력을 다해서. ¶ *He ran for all he was ~.* 그는 힘을 다해 달렸다.

not 〔**hardly**〕 **worth** *one's* **salt** ⇨salt.

take ... for what it is worth, accept ... as it is worth; do not overvalue. 값어치〔사실〕 그대로 받아들이다.

worth while =《*colloq.*》 **worth it,** worth the time or trouble spent on it. (시간·노고 등을 들일 만한) 가치가 있는. ¶ *It is not ~ while reading* 〔*to read*〕 *the book.* 그것은 읽을 만한 가치가 없는 책이다 / *Is it ~ it?* 고생할 가치가 있느냐.

— *n.* Ⓤ **1** value; merit; virtue; excellence. 가치; 진가. ¶ *of* (*great*) *~* 아주〔크게〕 가치 있는 / *a man of ~* 훌륭한 인물 / *a jewel of great ~* 아주 귀중한 보석 / *a thing of little* 〔*no*〕 *~* 거의〔전혀〕 가치가 없는 것 / *Few knew his true ~.* 그의 진가를 아는 사람은 거의 없었다 / *He appreciates me at my true ~.* 그는 나의 진가를 알아주고 있다. **2** the amount of somthing that may be had for a given sum. …의 값만큼의 분량; …어치. ¶ *a shilling's ~ of fruit,* 1실링어치의 과일 / *twenty dollars' ~ of halves,* 20 달러 분량의 50 센트 은화. [E.=valuable]

put 〔**get**〕 **in** *one's* **two cents worth,** give one's own opinion. (토론 등에서) 자기 의견을 말하다.

·worth·less [wə́:rθlis] *adj.* 《as *attributive*》 without worth; useless; valueless. 무가치한; 하찮은; 쓸모 없는. ¶ *Don't read ~ books.* 쓸모 없는 책은 읽지 마라 / *The jewels he sold us turned out to be completely ~.* 그가 우리에게 판 보석은 전혀 가치가 없는 것들임이 드러났다.

worth·while [wə́:rθhwáil] *adj.* of true value, importance, etc.; worth time and trouble. …할 보람이〔가치가〕 있는; (시간·노력을) 들일 만한. ¶ *a ~ attempt* 해 볼 만한 시도 / *It is ~ to try.* 그것은 해 볼 만한 가치가 있다 / *We had a long wait, but it was ~ because we got the tickets.* 우리는 오래 기다렸지만 표를 구했으니 그 보람은 있었다.

:wor·thy [wə́:rði] *adj.* (**-thi·er, -thi·est**) **1** having worth or excellence; respectable. 가치있는; 훌륭한. ¶ *a ~ man* 훌륭한 사람 / *live a ~ life* 훌륭한 생애를 보내다 / *a ~ cause* 훌륭한 목적〔동기〕. **2** deserving; praiseworthy. …하기에 족한; …에 상응한; (칭찬)할 만한. ¶ *a ~ reward* 상응한 보수 / *find a ~ adversary* 상대하기에 족한 적수를 발견하다 / *a man of ~ of confidence* 신뢰할 만한 사람 / *a poet ~ of the name* 시인다운 시인. **3** appropriate to. …에 알맞은〔적절한, 어울리는〕. ¶ *I can find no word ~ of this occasion.* 이 경우에 어울리는 적절한 말이 없다.

— *n.* Ⓒ (*pl.* **-thies**) **1** an excellent or admirable person. 훌륭한 사람; 명사. **2** 《*iron.*》 a person. 양반. ¶ *Who is the ~ over there?* 저기 저 양반은 누구냐.

:would [wud, wəd, əd] *auxil. v.* p. of **will.** **1** 《expressing the future in *indirect narration*》 …일〔할〕 것이다. ¶ *I said he ~ succeed.* 나는 그가 성공할 것이라고 말했다 / *He said that he ~ never come there again.* 그는 결코 거기에 다시 가는 일이 없을것이라 말했다. **2** 《expressing condition》 (만약 …이라면) …할 것이다; …할 텐데. ¶ *If I had a chance, I ~ try.* 기회가 주어진다면 나는 해 볼 것이다 / *You ~ do so if you could.* 너는 할 수 있다면 그렇게 할 것이다 / *If he had been there, he ~ have seen it.* 그가 거기 있었다면 그것을 보았을 것인데 / *I ~ have gone there if I'd known.* 내가 알았다면 거기에 갔을 텐데. **3** 《expressing past habitual action》 used to. 곧잘 …하곤 했다. ¶ *When I was young, I ~ often go there.* 내가 젊었을 때는 거기에 자주 가곤 했다 / *He ~ come to see us every day.* 그는

매일 우리를 만나러 오곤 했다 / *He ~ sit for hours doing nothing.* 그는 몇 시간이고 하는 일 없이 앉아 있고는 했다. 語法 과거의 불규칙 습관에는 흔히 would 를, 규칙적 습관에는 used to 를 씀. **4** 《*arch.*》《expressing a wish》 …이면 좋으련만. ¶ *Would to God that ....* …이라면 좋겠는데 / *Would that I were young again.* 다시 한 번 젊어진다면 좋겠는데. 語法 종종 I 를 생략함. **5** 《expressing a polite request》 …해줄 수 있겠나. ¶ *Would you kindly show me the way?* 내게 길을 좀 가르쳐 주시겠습니까 / *Would you open the window, please?* 창문을 좀 열어 주시겠습니까. **6** 《expressing intention or determination》 wished to; be willing to; be determined to. …할 작정이(었)다. ¶ *I ~ rather not accept your offer.* 나는 네 제의를 수락할 생각이 없다 / *I ~ fain do it.* 나는 기꺼이 그것을 하고 싶다. [*will*]

would-be [wúdbìː] *adj.* 《as *attributive*》 wishing or aiming to be; intended to be. …이 되고 싶어하는; …연(然)하는; 자칭의. ¶ *a ~ poet* 〔*gentleman*〕 자칭 시인〔신사〕 / *She intended to avoid her ~ husband.* 그녀는 그녀의 남편이 되고 싶어하는 남자를 피할 생각이었다.

·would·n't [wúdnt] would not.

:wound[1] [wuːnd, 《*arch., poet.*》 waund] *n.* **1** Ⓒ a cut, hurt or an injury to the body. 상처; 부상. ¶ *a mortal* 〔*fatal*〕 *~* 치명상 / *He had a bullet ~ in his head.* 머리에 총상을 입었다 / *It's only a flesh ~.* 가벼운 상처일 뿐이다 / *He received a serious stomach ~.* 복부에 중상을 입었다. **2** 《*fig.*》 Ⓒ a hurt or an injury to someone's feelings or reputation. (정신적인) 타격; 고통; 모욕. ¶ *a ~ to someone's pride* 아무의 자존심을 해치는 것 / *get deep psychological wounds* 정신적으로 깊은 상처를 입다.

— *vt.* (P6,7,13) **1** injure (someone) by force. …에게 상처를 입히다. ¶ *be wounded in the arm* 팔에 상처를 입다 / *Is he seriously* 〔*badly*〕 *wounded?* 그는 중상이냐. **2** hurt the feelings of (someone). …의 감정을 해치다. ¶ *willing to ~* 악의 있는 / *wounded feeling* 〔*pride*〕 상처입은 감정〔자존심〕 / *be wounded at ...* …에 감정을 상하다. [E.]

wound[2] [waund] *v.* p. and pp. of **wind**[2,3].

wove [wouv] *v.* p. and pp. of **weave.**

wo·ven [wóuvən] *v.* pp. of **weave.**

wow [wau] *interj.* an expression of surprise, pleasure, etc. 야아, 와, 우《놀람·기쁨 등의 소리》. ¶ *Wow! What a fantastic dress!* 와아, 멋진 옷이다. — *n.* 《U.S. *colloq.*》 a sensational success. 대성공. [?]

wrack [ræk] *n.* Ⓤ **1** 《*arch., poet.*》 ruin; destruction. 파멸; 파괴(cf. *rack*[3]). ¶ *Everything is gone to ~.* 모든 것이 결딴났다 / *go to (w)rack and ruin* ⇨rack[3]. **2** wreckage. 난파. **3** seaweed thrown up on the shore. 바닷가에 밀려 올라온 해초. [*wreck*]

wraith [reiθ] *n.* Ⓒ the spirit of a person supposed to appear just before or after his death. (임종 전후에 나타난다는) 생령(生靈); 사령(死靈); 유령. [N.]

wran·gle [rǽŋgəl] *vt., vi.* (P6;1,2A,3) argue or quarrel noisily. 말다툼하다; 논쟁하다; 다투다. — *n.* Ⓒ a noisy or angry argument or quarrel. 말다툼; 언쟁; 논쟁. ¶ *We were involved in another ~ with the management over our pay.* 우리는 경영자측과 임금 문제로 또 다른 언쟁에 말려들었다. [E.]

wran·gler [rǽŋgələr] *n.* Ⓒ **1** a person who wrangles. 논쟁자. **2** 《Brit.》 a student in the highest class in mathematics at Cambridge University. 케임브리지 대학의 수학 학위 시험 우등생.

:wrap [ræp] *vt.* (**wrapped** or **wrapt, wrapping**) (P6,7,13) **1** 《*up, in*》 cover or envelop (something) by winding or folding something else around it. …을 싸다; 감싸다; 꾸리다. ¶ *~ oneself up in a cloak* 외투로 몸을 감싸다 / *~ (up) a package in paper* 포장지로 짐을 꾸리다 / *The river is wrapped in mist.* 강은 안개에 싸여 있다 / 《*fig.*》 *be wrapped in mystery* 신비에 싸여 있다. **2** wind or fold (something) as a covering. …을 두르다; 감다; 걸치다. ¶ *She wrapped her shawl around her neck.* 그녀는 목에다 숄을 감았다 / *~ one's gown round one* 가운을 몸에 걸치다. **3** cover; hide. …을 덮다; 감추다. — *vi* (P2A) 《*up*》 put on warm clothes. (몸을 옷 따위로) 휘감다; 감싸다.

be wrapped up in, be devoted to; be deeply absorbed in; be deeply interested in. …에 열중해 있다; 몰두하고 있다. ¶ *He is wrapped up in his work.* 그는 자기 일에 여념이 없다 / *She's so wrapped up in him she can't see his faults.* 그녀는 그에게 너무 빠져 있어 그의 결점이 눈에 안 보인다.

— *n.* Ⓒ 《often *pl.*》 an outer covering. 싸개; 덮개; 목도리; 외투. [E.]

wrap·per [rǽpər] *n.* Ⓒ **1** a person or thing that wraps; a covering; a cover. 싸는 사람〔물건〕; 포장지; (잡지 따위의) 커버. ¶ *a book's ~* 책커버. **2** a woman's loose gown worn indoors. (여성용) 실내복.

wrap·ping [rǽpiŋ] *n.* 《usu. *pl.*》 paper, cloth, etc. in which something is wrapped. 포장지; 보자기.

·wrath [ræθ, rɑːθ / rɔːθ] *n.* Ⓤ 《*lit.*》 very great anger. 격노; 분노. ¶ *the grapes of ~* 분노의 포도《신의 노여움의 상징으로서》 / *Management incurred the ~ of the union by breaking the agreement.* 경영자측은 협약을 위반함으로써 노조측의 격분을 샀다. [→wroth]

wrath·ful [rǽθfəl, rɑ́ːθ- / rɔ́ːθ-] *adj.* 《*lit.*》 very angry; full of wrath. 격노한.

wreak [riːk] *vt.* (P6,13) **1** bring (one's idea, one's anger, etc.) into effect; inflict (punishment, vengeance, etc.). …을 실행에 옮기다; (처벌·복수 따위)를 가하다; (원수)를 갚다. ¶ *They wreaked vengeance to* *him.* 그들은 그에게 원수를 갚았다. **2** give expression to (one's feelings, etc.). (감정 등)을 드러내다. ¶ *He wreaked his anger on his servants.* 그는 하인들에게 화풀이를 했다. [E.=avenge]

*__wreath__ [ri:θ] *n.* Ⓒ (*pl.* **wreaths** [rí:ðz, -θs]) **1** a circle of leaves and flowers. 화환. ¶ *place* 〔*lay*〕 *a ~ on the grave* 묘에 화환을 바치다. **2** something like a ring or a curl. 동그라미; 둥근 고리; 소용돌이. ¶ *a ~ of smoke* 소용돌이치는 연기. **3** 《*poet.*》 a circle (of dancers, spectators). (무용수·구경꾼들의) 원을 이룬 한 무리. [E.=bandage]

wreathe [ri:ð] *vt.* (P6,13) **1** make (something) into a circle. …을 둥글게 하다; …을 화환으로 만들다. ¶ *~ daisies into a garland* 데이지를 엮어 화환을 만들다. **2** decorate (something) with, or as, a wreath. …을 화환으로〔처럼〕 장식하다. ¶ *a poet's brow wreathed with laurel* 월계관을 쓴 시인의 이마. **3** envelop. (감)싸다. **4** make a ring around (something or someone); wind. …을 친친 휘감다; 감다. ¶ *The snake wreathed itself around the branch.* 뱀이 나뭇가지를 친친 휘감았다 / *~ one's arms about someone* 아무를 양 팔로 껴안다. — *vi.* (P2A) **1** (of branches, etc.) get twisted. 휘감기다; 뒤얽히다. **2** (of smoke, etc.) take the form of a wreath; move in coils. 원을〔둥근 고리를〕 이루다; 감돌다. [↑]

:**wreck** [rek] *n.* **1** Ⓤ damage or the breaking up of a ship caused by wind, a storm, etc. 난파(難破). **2** Ⓒ a ship so broken up; remains of anything, esp. of a ship, that has been destroyed or much injured. 난파선(의 잔해). ¶ *Divers have found a hoard of gold in the ~.* 잠수부들이 난파선에서 사장된 금을 찾아냈다. **3** Ⓤ the destruction of a building, train, motorcar, etc. (건물, 열차, 자동차 따위의) 파괴; 파괴된 잔해. **4** Ⓒ a person whose health or spirits have been destroyed. (병으로) 몰골이 참혹하게 된 사람; 기백이 쇠잔한 사람. ¶ *He's been a complete ~ since his illness.* 병이 든 이래 그의 몰골은 말이 아니다.

— *vt.* (P6) **1** cause the wreck of (something). …을 난파시키다; …을 파괴하다. ¶ *The ship was wrecked on the rocks.* 배는 좌초하여 난파되었다. **2** bring ruin upon (plans, hopes). …을 파멸시키다; 결딴내다. ¶ *The accident wrecked his health.* 그 사고로 그의 건강은 결딴이 났다 / *The weather has completely wrecked our plans.* 날씨로 해서 우리의 계획은 엉망이 됐다.

— *vi.* (P1) be wrecked; suffer damage, ruin, etc. 난파〔파멸〕하다; 파괴되다. [Anglo-F. *wrec*]

wreck·age [rékidʒ] *n.* Ⓤ **1** the act of wrecking; the state of being wrecked. 난파; 파괴. **2** the remains of anything that has been wrecked. (난파선 따위의) 잔해.

wreck·er [rékər] *n.* Ⓒ **1** a person or thing that wrecks; a person who steals cargo, etc. from wrecked ships. 난파〔파괴〕시키는 사람〔것〕; 난파선 약탈자. **2** a person, ship, etc. that is employed to recover cargo from wrecked ships, etc. 난파선 구조자〔선〕. **3** 《U.S.》 a person, car, boat, etc. that removes wrecks. 구난 작업자〔차, 선〕; 레커차(=《Brit.》 breakdown van).

wrench [rentʃ] *n.* Ⓒ **1** a sudden, violent twist or pull. (확) 비틀기; 뒤틀기. ¶ *give a ~ of the door handle* 문의 손잡이를 비틀다. **2** an injury caused by such a pull. 접질림; 삠. ¶ *give a ~ to one's ankle* 발목을 삐다. **3** 《*fig.*》 the pain or grief of parting. 이별의 고통〔슬픔〕. ¶ *the ~ of parting with one's children* 아이들과의 쓰라린 이별. **4** 《chiefly U.S.》 a tool for turning nuts, bolts, etc. 렌치; 스패너(=《Brit.》 spanner).

— *vt.* (P6,7,13,18) **1** twist or pull (something) suddenly and with force. …을 비틀다; 비틀어 떼다. ¶ *~ fruit off a branch* 가지에서 열매를 비틀어 따다 / *~ the door open* 문을 비틀어 열다 / *~ one's enemy's sword from him* 적의 칼을 비틀어 빼앗다. **2** injure (an ankle, etc.) in this way. …을 삐다; 접질리다. ¶ *I fell and wrenched my ankle.* 넘어져서 발목을 삐었다. **3** give a twist to (a meaning, statement, fact, etc.). (뜻·말·사실 등)을 왜곡하다. [E.=guile]

wrest [rest] *vt.* (P6,7,13) **1** twist or turn (something) by force; pull or take (something) away violently. …을 비틀다; 뒤틀다; 비틀어〔잡아〕 떼다. ¶ *~ a gun from a gangster* 갱으로부터 총을 강제로 잡아 빼앗다 / *He wrested the football from my arms.* 그는 내 팔에서 축구공을 잡아 뺏었다. **2** turn away from its true meaning. (사실 따위)를 왜곡하다. ¶ *~ the facts* / *~ someone's meaning* 아무의 말뜻을 곡해하다 / *~ a citation to a different sense* 인용문을 왜곡해 딴 뜻으로 파악하다 / *You ~ my words out of their real meaning.* 넌 내 말의 참뜻을 왜곡하고 있다. — *n.* Ⓒ the act of wresting; a twist. 비틂. [E.]

wres·tle [résəl] *vi.* (P1,2A,3) **1** struggle with one's opponent to throw him to the ground; try to throw each other in a contest. 씨름하다; 레슬링하다. ¶ *~ together* (둘이서) 맞붙어 싸우다. **2** 《*with, against*》 ⓐ struggle against. (유혹·재난 따위와) 싸우다. ¶ *~ with temptation* 유혹과 싸우다. ⓑ try hard; try to solve. 전력을 다하다; 해결에 노력하다. ¶ *wrestling with a difficult examination paper* 어려운 시험지와 씨름하는 / *~ with a problem* 문제 해결에 전력을 다하다.

— *vt.* (P6) try to throw down. …와 맞붙어 싸우다.

— *n.* **1** Ⓒ a wrestling match. 레슬링 시합. **2** Ⓤ a hard struggle. 분투. [E.]

wres·tler [réslər] *n.* Ⓒ a person who wrestles, esp. in regular matches. 레슬링 선수; 씨름꾼.

wres·tling [résliŋ] *n.* Ⓤ a sport in which

opponents struggle and try to throw each other to the ground. 레슬링; 씨름.

wretch [retʃ] *n.* Ⓒ **1** a very unfortunate or miserable person. 불행한〔가엾은〕 사람. ¶ *Poor ~!* 가엾은〔불쌍한〕 사람이군. **2** a bad, shameless person. 못되고 비열한 사람; 철면피. **3**《often *joc.*》a mischievous fellow. 녀석; 놈. ¶ *You little ~!* 요 개구쟁이야. [E. =outcast]

***wretch·ed** [rétʃid] *adj.* **1** very unfortunate or unhappy. 아주 불행한; 비참한. **2** very unsatisfactory; miserable. 형편없는; 고약한. ¶ *a ~ hat* 형편없는 모자 / *~ weather* 고약한 날씨. **3** very bad. 매우 나쁜. ¶ *The food at this hotel is ~.* 이 호텔의 음식은 매우 나쁘다. **4** tiresome; troublesome. 따분한; 성가신.

wrig·gle [rígəl] *vi.* (P1,2A,3) **1** twist and turn; move like a snake. 꿈틀거리다; 꿈틀거리며 나아가다. ¶ *Keep still, and don't ~.* 가만 있어, 꼼짝 말고. **2** proceed by tricks or shifty means. 그럭저럭 헤어나다. — *vt.* (P6,7,18) cause (something) to wriggle. …을 꿈틀거리게 하다. ¶ *~ oneself free from a rope* 몸을 꿈지럭거려 묶인 밧줄에서 벗어나다 / *~ oneself out at a small hole* 작은 구멍에서 몸을 꿈틀거려 빠져 나오다.

wriggle along, move along with wriggling motions. 꿈틀거리며 나아가다.

wriggle out of, manage to escape by wriggling; 《*fig.*》 escape from (an awkward situation) by cunning. 꿈틀거려서 헤어나오다; …에서 교묘히 벗어나다. ¶ *You know you're to blame, so don't try to ~ out of it.* 네 잘못을 알겠지, 그러니 발뺌하려들지 마라.

wriggle one's way, make one's way by wriggling. 꿈틀거리며 나아가다.

— *n.* Ⓒ the act or motion of twisting. 꿈틀거림. [E.]

wright [rait] *n.* Ⓒ 《usu. in *combinations*》 a person who makes something. 장인(匠人); 제조인; 제작자. ¶ *a cartwright* 수레 만드는 목수 / *a playwright* 극작가 / *a shipwright* 배목수. [E.]

***wring** [riŋ] *vt.* (**wrung**) **1** (P6,7,13) squeeze or twist hard. …을 비틀다; (비틀어) 짜다. ¶ *~ the washing dry* 빨래를 짜서 말리다 / *Wring out your wet clothes.* 젖은 옷을 짜거라 / *~ a chicken's neck* 닭의 목을 비틀다. **2** (P6,7) force (something) out by twisting or by force. …을 짜내다; 우려내다; 착취하다. ¶ *~ money out of someone* 아무에게서 돈을 우려내다 / *That man could ~ sympathy from anyone by his sad story.* 저 사내는 그 청승맞은 이야기로 아무에게서나 동정을 자아낼 수 있었다 / *They wrung a confession from the prisoner.* 그들은 형사 피고인으로부터 자백을 받아냈다. **3** (P6) give pain to (someone). …을 괴롭히다.

wring someone's hand, press someone's hand warmly. (아무)의 손을 정답게 꽉 쥐다.

wring one's hands, squeeze one's hands together in sorrow and despair. (슬픔과 절망으로) 두 손을 쥐어 틀다.

wring out, get forcibly (from). (…에게서) 짜내다; 우려내다.

— *n.* Ⓒ the act of wringing. 비틀기; 쥐어짜기. [E.]

wring·er [ríŋər] *n.* Ⓒ a person or thing that wrings; a machine for squeezing wet clothes. 쥐어짜는 사람〔기계〕; 탈수기 《세탁물용》.

***wrin·kle**[1] [ríŋkəl] *n.* Ⓒ a small fold on a surface. 주름(살). ¶ *wrinkles in the face or skin* / *take the wrinkles out of one's belly* 뱃가죽의 주름이 팽팽해질 때까지 먹다 / *It needs iron out of the wrinkles in this dress.* 이 드레스를 다림질해서 주름을 펴야겠다. — *vt.* (P6,7) make wrinkles in (something). …에 주름을 잡다〔짓다〕. ¶ *The rain wrinkled his suit.* 비를 맞아 그의 옷이 구겨졌다 / *~ (up) one's forehead* 이마를 찌푸리다. — *vi.* (P1,2A) become wrinkled. 주름이 지다〔잡히다〕. ¶ *My dress wrinkles easily.* 내 옷은 쉬이 구겨진다 / *The skin round her eyes wrinkled when she smiled.* 그녀가 웃을 때 눈가에 주름이 잡혔다. [E.]

wrin·kle[2] [ríŋkəl] *n.* 《*colloq.*》 a clever trick; a useful idea or suggestion. 묘안; 유용한 조언. ¶ *Give me a ~ or two.* 좋은 수〔묘안〕 좀 가르쳐 주게나 / *Ask him; he knows all the wrinkles.* 그에게 묻지 그래, 그는 묘계백출(妙計百出)하는 사람이야 / *I can give you a ~.* 내게 좋은 생각이 하나 있다. [E.]

:wrist [rist] *n.* Ⓒ the joint connecting the arm and the hand. 손목. [→writhe]

wrist·band [rístbæ̀nd] *n.* Ⓒ the part of a sleeve fitting around the wrist. 소맷동; 소맷부리.

wrist·watch [rístwɑ̀tʃ / -wɔ̀tʃ] *n.* a watch worn on the wrist. 손목시계.

writ [rit] *n.* Ⓒ **1** 《*arch.*》 something written. 문서; 서면. ¶ *the Holy* 〔*Sacred*〕 *Writ* 성경. **2** 《law》 a written order from a law court. 영장. ¶ *serve a ~ on someone* 아무에게 영장을 발부하다 / *a ~ of attachment* 압류 영장. [↓]

:write [rait] *v.* (**wrote, writ·ten**) *vi.* **1** (P1, 2A,3) form words or letters with a pen or pencil. 글씨를 쓰다. ¶ *He cannot read or ~.* 그는 글씨를 읽거나 쓰지 못한다 / *She writes well.* 그녀는 달필이다 / *I always ~ in ink* 〔*with a pencil*〕. 늘 잉크〔연필〕로 글씨를 쓴다 / *~ (in) a clear hand* 똑똑하게 글씨를 쓰다 / *~ in block letters* 블록 글자체로 쓰다. **2** (P1) 《*on, about, of*》 compose books or other literary matter; do the work of a writer. 글〔책〕을 쓰다; 저술〔저작, 집필〕하다. ¶ *~ for a living* 문필을 업으로 하다 / *He is writing for 'Life'.* 그는 라이프지에 기고하고 있다 / *~ against the regime* 체제 비판의 글을 쓰다 / *~ to The Times* 타임스지에 투고하다 / *He writes.* 그는 저술〔저작, 집필〕이 업이다. **3** (P1) write a letter or letters. 편지를 쓰다. ¶ ~ *home* / *He wrote to me for money.* 그는 나에게 돈을 빌려달라는 편지를 했다.

— *vt.* **1** (P6,7) form (words, etc.) on a surface. (글씨 등)을 쓰다. ¶ ~ *Chinese characters* 한자를 쓰다 / ~ *a letter in ink* 잉크로 글씨를 쓰다 / *He writes himself 'Colonel'.* 그는 스스로를 '대령'이라고 쓴다 / *Have you finished writing that report yet?* 그 보고서를 이제는 다 썼는가. **2** (P6) express; put down in writing. …라고 기술〔기록〕하다; 적다. ¶ *It is written that….* …라고 기술되어〔적혀〕 있다. **3** (P6) produce (a literary or musical composition). (책 따위)를 쓰다; 작곡하다. ¶ *He wrote many books.* 그는 많은 책을 썼다 / *Beethoven wrote nine symphonies.* 베토벤은 아홉 편의 교향곡을 작곡했다 / *He writes articles for local papers.* 지방 신문에 기사를 쓰고 있다. **4** (P6,7,13,14,15,17,20) send a letter to (someone). (…에게) 편지를 쓰다. ¶ *He wrote me the news.* 그는 그 소식을 편지로 내게 알려왔다 / *He wrote his mother to come up to Seoul.* 그는 어머니에게 상경하시라고 편지를 썼다. **5** (P6) 《usu. in *passive*》 show clear signs of (something). …을 분명히〔역력히〕 나타내다. ¶ *Honesty is written on his face.* 정직하다는 것이 그의 얼굴에 역력히 나타나 있다 / *His fear is written all over his face.* 그의 온 얼굴에는 두려움이 역력히 나타나 있다 / *The tendencies of the times are written in current events.* 이즈음의 사건들에서 시대의 추세를 분명히 알 수 있다. [E.]

write down, **a**) make a note of (something); record. …을 적어두다; 기록하다. ¶ *Write it down before you forget it.* 잊기 전에 그걸 적어 두어라 / ~ *down a telephone number* 전화 번호를 적어두다. **b**) put a lower value on (something); make little of or show badly in writing as; describe as. …을 지상(紙上)에서 깎아내리다; …이라고 쓰다〔평하다〕. ¶ ~ *down someone* 〔*his work*〕 아무를〔그의 작품을〕 지상에서 내리깎다 / ~ *someone down* (*as*) *a fool* 아무를 바보라고 쓰다. **c**) (of stock, goods) reduce the nominal value. (주식·상품 따위) 장부 가격을 내리다.

write off, **a**) compose quickly and easily. …을 쉽게〔술술〕 쓰다. **b**) cancel; remove from account. (부채 따위를) 장부에서 지워버리다; 삭제하다. ¶ ~ *off old debts* 묵은 빚을 장부에서 지워버리다.

write out, write (something) in full; make a fair copy of. …을 (빠뜨리지 않고) 다 쓰다; 정서(淨書)하다. ¶ ~ *out a memo* 〔*statement*〕 메모〔성명서〕를 정서하다 / *In French it is polite to* ~ *out 'Monsieur' in full.* 프랑스어에서는 'Monsieur'를 생략하지 않고 그대로 다 쓰는 것이 예의이다.

write up, **a**) praise (something or someone) in writing. …을 칭찬해서 쓰다. ¶ *The critics wrote the new play up.* 평론가들은 그 신극을 칭찬해서 썼다. **b**) write (something) in detail. …을 상세히 쓰다. ¶ ~ *up a report* 〔*one's diary*〕 보고서〔일기〕를 자세히 쓰다.

:writ·er [ráitər] *n.* Ⓒ **1** a person who writes. 쓰는 사람; 필자. ¶ *The* ~ *of this letter is known to me.* 이 편지의 필자를 나는 안다. **2** a person whose occupation is writing; an author. 저술가; 작가; 저자. ¶ *a* ~ *of children's books* 동화 작가 / *He is a* ~ *but doesn't make enough money to live from his books.* 작가이긴 하지만 그것으로는 생활이 넉넉하지 못하다. **3** a clerk, esp. in a government office. (관청 등의) 서기.

writhe [raið] *vi.* (P1,2A) **1** twist and turn about in pain. (고통으로) 몸부림치다〔뒹굴다〕. ¶ ~ *with a toothache* 치통으로 몸부림치다. **2** 《*fig.*》 suffer from mental distress. 몸부림치며 괴로워하다; 번민하다. ¶ ~ *at* 〔*under*〕 *an insult* 모욕을 당하고 몹시 괴로워하다. [E.]

:writ·ing [ráitiŋ] *n.* Ⓤ **1** anything that is written. 쓴 것; 문서; 서류. **2** handwriting; penmanship. 필적; 서법(書法). ¶ *Your* ~ *is almost illegible.* 네 글씨는 거의 알아보지 못하겠다. **3** the profession of a writer. 문필〔저술〕업. **4** Ⓒ 《*pl.*》 literary works. 저작; 작품. ¶ *His writings include poetry and prose.* 그의 저작에는 시와 산문이 있다. **5** literary style. 문체. **6** the act of literary composition. 저술. ¶ *busy with one's* ~ 저술에 바쁘다. [*write*]

writing desk [⌐–⌐] *n.* a desk for writing at. 글 쓰는 책상.

writing ink [⌐–⌐] *n.* ink for writing. 필기용 잉크.

writing paper [⌐– ⌐–] *n.* paper for writing on. 필기〔원고〕 용지; 편지지.

:writ·ten [rítn] *v.* pp. of **write.**

:wrong [rɔːŋ, rɑŋ] *adj.* (opp. right) **1** not morally right; sinful; wicked. (도덕적으로) 나쁜; 그릇된; 옳지 않은; 부정한. ¶ *It is* ~ *to steal.* 도둑질은 나쁘다 / *It was very* ~ *of you to go there.* 네가 거기 간 것은 큰 잘못이었다. **2** not correct or true; not proper or suitable. 틀린; 잘못된; 부적당한. ¶ *the* ~ *answer* 틀린 대답; 오답 / *take the* ~ *way* 〔*direction*〕 길〔방향〕을 잘못 잡다 / *Sorry,* ~ *number.* (전화에서) 잘못 거셨습니다 / *No, you're* ~ *; She didn't say that.* 아니, 네가 잘못이야. 그녀는 그런 말을 하지 않았어 / *His clothes were* ~ *for the occasion.* 그의 옷은 그러한 경우에 입을 만한 알맞은 것이 못 되었다 / *This is the* ~ *time to make a visit.* 지금은 방문하기에 좋은 시간이 아니다 / *We must be on the* ~ *road.* 우리는 길을 잘못 든 게 분명하다. **3** 《in *predicative*》 out of order. 상태가 나쁜; 고장난. ¶ *My watch is* ~. 시계가 고장이다 / *Something is* ~ *with the engine.* 엔진이 어딘가 고장이다 / 《*colloq.*》 *What's* ~ *with it?* 그게 어쨌

다는 거냐《괜찮은 것 같은데》 / *Something is ~ with him in the head.* 그 사람 머리가 좀 이상하다. **4** (of cloth) not meant to be seen; back. 안 쪽의; 뒷면의. ¶ *the ~ side of cloth* 천의 안 쪽.

get hold of the wrong end of the stick, misunderstand; confuse one thing with another. 오해하다; 잘못 알다; 착각하다.

in the wrong box, in an awkward position. 난처〔어색〕한 입장에; 틀려.

on the wrong side of, **a**) older than. (나이가) …을 초과한〔넘은〕. **b**) shut out from. …에서 내쫓겨.

wrong side out, with the inner side outside. 뒤집어서. ¶ *He put his gloves on ~ side out.* 그는 장갑을 뒤집어 꼈다.

— *adv.* **1** in a wrong manner; incorrectly. 나쁘게; 잘못되게; 틀리게. ¶ *answer ~* 잘못 대답하다 / *do a thing ~* 일을 잘못하다 / *guess ~* 잘못 짐작하다 / *do a sum ~* 계산을 잘못하다〔틀리다〕. **2** in a mistaken direction. 잘못된 방향으로; 반대로; 거꾸로. ¶ *lead someone ~* 아무를 잘못 인도하다. **3** unjustly; unfairly; not rightly. 부정(不正)하게; 불공정하게; 부당하게. ¶ *We ought not to act ~.* 우리는 부정하게 행동해서는 안 된다.

get someone in wrong, 《U.S. *colloq.*》 bring someone into disfavor. …를 눈밖에 나게〔미움 받게〕 하다.

get someone wrong, misunderstand. …를 오해하다. ¶ *Don't get me ~; I'm not really criticizing you.* 나를 오해하지 마라. 너를 정말로 비난하는 것은 아니다.

get something wrong, **a**) miscalculate. 잘못 계산하다. **b**) misunderstand. 오해하다.

go wrong, **a**) take the wrong path; go astray. 길을 잘못 들다; 길을 잃다. **b**) (of a girl) fall from virtue. 타락하다; 몸을 망치다. **c**) (of events, etc.) fail. 실패하다. **d**) (of a watch, etc.) fail to keep correct time. (시계가) 고장나다.

— *n.* **1** Ⓤ that which is wrong; Ⓒ a wrong action. 부정(不正); 악; 죄; 나쁜 짓. ¶ *do ~* 나쁜 짓을 하다 / *distinguish* 〔*know*〕 *between right and ~* 옳고 그름을 판별하다. **2** Ⓤ injustice; harm; ill-treatment; Ⓒ an instance of this. 부당 (행위); 학대; 해(害); 비행(非行). ¶ *suffer ~* 학대를 받다 / *do someone ~ =do ~ to someone* 아무에게 부당한 행위를 하다; 아무를 학대하다〔오해하다〕 / *You do me ~.* 너는 나를 오해하고 있다 / *He has done me a great ~.* 그는 내게 아주 못된 짓을 했다.

get in wrong with *someone,* 《U.S. *colloq.*》 be disliked by someone. …의 미움을 사다.

in the wrong, wrong; to be blamed. 잘못되어 (있는); 나쁜; 부정으로. ¶ *I was quite in the ~.* 내가 크게 잘못했다 / *Which of the two drivers was in the ~?* 그 두 운전자 중 누가 잘못했나 / *You are both in the ~.* 너희 둘 다 나쁘다.

put *someone* ***in the wrong,*** make someone appear responsible for a mistake, etc. 잘못을 …의 탓으로 돌리다. ¶ *put oneself in the ~* 자기에게 잘못이 있음을 인정하다.

— *vt.* (P6) **1** do wrong to (someone); injure. …을 학대하다; …에게 해를 끼치다. ¶ *a wronged orphan* 학대를 받은 고아 / *He had deeply wronged his wife.* 그는 아내를 학대했다; 아내에게 아주 심하게 굴었다 **2** dishonor; judge unfairly. …의 명예를 손상시키다; 오해하다. ¶ *I wronged him by thinking he took your book.* 네 책을 그가 가져갔다고 생각한 것은 내 오해였다 / *I thought he had done it, but I see I wronged him.* 그가 그짓을 했다고 생각했는데 그건 내 오해였다. [E.]

wrong·do·er [rɔ́:ŋdú:ər, rɑ́ŋ-] *n.* Ⓒ a person who does wrong. 나쁜 짓을 하는 사람; 비행인(非行人); 가해자.

wrong·do·ing [rɔ́:ŋdú:iŋ, rɑ́ŋ-] *n.* Ⓤ the act of doing wrong; evil actions; sin. 나쁜 짓 하기; 비행(非行); 악행; 죄. ¶ *They found no evidence of ~.* 그들은 범죄의 증거를 전혀 찾아내지 못했다.

wrong·ful [rɔ́:ŋfəl, rɑ́ŋ-] *adj.* wrong; evil; unjust; unlawful. 부정한; 유해한; 불법의; 부당한. ¶ *~ dismissal* / *~ imprisonment* 불법 감금 / *~ taking of property* 재산 횡령.

wrong-head·ed [rɔ́:ŋhédid, rɑ́ŋ-] *adj.* hard to change in opinions, esp. in wrong opinions. 완고한; 고집 불통의; 생각이 그릇된〔비뚤어진〕. ¶ *the most ~ opinions* 아주 완고한 의견 / *~ students who think they can cure the world's evils by destroying society* 사회를 파괴함으로써 세상의 악을 치유할 수 있다는 그릇된 생각을 가진 학생들.

wrong·ly [rɔ́:ŋli, rɑ́ŋ-] *adv.* unjustly; unlawfully. 그릇되게; 부정〔불법〕하게.

:wrote [rout] *v.* p. of **write.**

wroth [rɔ:θ, rɑθ / rouθ] *adj.* 《*arch., poet.*》 very angry. 격노한. [E.]

·wrought [rɔ:t] *v.* p. and pp. of **work.**
— *adj.* 《*arch., poet.*》 worked; fashioned; did; done. 세공(細工)한; 만든; 가공된. ¶ *a highly* 〔*an elaborately*〕 *~ article* 공들인 세공품 / *~ goods* (마감 손질이 된) 가공 제품 / *carefully ~ works of literature* 정성들여 다듬어진 문학 작품. [*work*]

wrought iron [∠ ∠–] *n.* a kind of iron that is hard and yet soft enough to be hammered into shape. 단철(鍛鐵).

wrought-up [rɔ́:tʌ́p] *adj.* greatly excited and nervous. 몹시 흥분한.

wrung [rʌŋ] *v.* p. and pp. of **wring.**

wry [rai] *adj.* (**wri·er, wri·est** or **wry·er, wry·est**) twisted. 뒤틀린; 찌푸린. ¶ *make a ~ face* 〔*mouth*〕 얼굴을 찌푸리다. [E.]

WTO World Trade Organization. 세계 무역 기구.

Wy., Wyo. Wyoming.

Wy·o·ming [waióumiŋ] *n.* a northwestern State of the United States. 와이오밍주. 參考 Wy., Wyo.라 생략함. 주도는 Cheyenne.

x X

X, x [eks] *n.* Ⓒ (*pl.* **X's, Xs, x's, xs** [éksiz]) **1** the twenty-fourth letter of the English alphabet. 영어 알파벳의 스물넷째 자. **2** 《math.》 the Roman number 10. 로마 숫자의 10. **3** a term for an unknown quantity, etc. 미지수의 기호; 미지의 것. **4** anything shaped like an X. X 자 모양의 것.

X.C., x.c., x-cp. 《L.》 *ex coupon*(=without coupon).

X.D., x-div. 《L.》 *ex dividend*(=without dividend).

X chromosome [⌐ ⌐–⌐] *n.* 《biol.》 chromosome related to femaleness—an egg containing two X chromosomes, one from each parent, develops into a female. X 염색체.

Xe 《chem.》 xenon.

xe·bec [zí:bek] *n.* 《naut.》 a small, three-masted vessel of the Mediterranean. (지중해의) 세대박이 작은 돛배. [F *chebec*]

xen·on [zénɔn] *n.* Ⓤ 《chem.》 a heavy, colorless gas, Xe, that is chemically inactive. 크세논. [Gk.]

xen·o·pho·bi·a [zènəfóubiə, zìnə-] *n.* hatred or fear of foreigners. 외국인 기피증. [Gk. *xenos*, stranger, *phobos* fear]

xer(o)- [zíər(ou)-] *pref.* dryness; dry. '건조(한)'의 뜻. [Gk. *xērós*]

xe·rog·ra·phy [zirágrəfi / zirɔ́g-] *n.* a dry photographic or photocopying process. 제로그래피; 전자 사진(술). [xero-]

xe·ro·phyte [zíərəfàit] *n.* 《bot.》 a plant that loses very little water and can grow in deserts or very dry ground, as cacti, sage-brush, etc. 건생(乾生) 식물《선인장 등》. [Gk.]

Xer·ox [ziərɑks / -rɔks] *n.* a photocopying process or machine using xerography. 제록스 복사법[기]. — *vt., vi.* (P6;1) reproduce by Xerox. (제록스로) 복사하다. [Trademark]

Xmas [krísməs] *n.* =Christmas.

***X ray** [⌐ ⌐] *n.* **1** 《usu. *pl.*》 a Roentgen ray. 엑스선; 뢴트겐선. **2** a photograph made by means of X rays. 엑스선 사진.

***X-ray** [éksrèi] *vt.* (P6) use X rays to examine (something); examine or treat (someone) with X rays. 엑스선으로 …을 조사[치료]하다. — *adj.* of X rays. 엑스선의. ¶ *an ~ examination* 엑스선 검사.

xy·lem [záiləm, -lem] *n.* 《bot.》 the woody tissue of plants. 목질부(木質部). [Gk. *xylon* wood]

xy·lo·graph [záiləgræf, -grɑ̀:f] *n.* engraving on wood; a wood-cut. 목판(木版). [↑]

xy·lo·nite, Xy- [záilənàit] *n.* 《orig. trademark》 Ⓤ celluloid. 자일로나이트《합성수지》. [↑]

xy·lo·phone [záiləfòun, zílə-] *n.* Ⓒ a musical instrument made of pieces of wood, each giving a different note when struck. 실로폰; 목금(木琴). [↑]

y Y

Y, y [wai] *n.* Ⓒ (*pl.* **Y's, Ys, y's, ys** [waiz]) **1** the twentyfifth letter of the English alphabet. 영어 알파벳의 스물다섯째 자. **2** 《math.》 the usual symbol for a second unknown quantity (x being the first). 제2 미지수. **3** something shaped like the letter Y; a Y-shaped structure. Y 자 모양의 것.

Y 《chem.》 yttrium.

:yacht [jɑt / jɔt] *n.* Ⓒ a boat for pleasure or racing. 요트. — *vi.* (P1) sail or race in a yacht. 요트를 타다; 요트를 조종하다. [Du.]

yacht·ing [jɑ́tiŋ / jɔ́t-] *n.* Ⓤ the art or practice of sailing or racing in a yacht. 요트 조정(술).

yachts·man [jɑ́tsmən / jɔ́ts-] *n.* Ⓒ (*pl.* **-men** [-mən]) a person who sails or owns a yacht. 요트 조종자[소유자].

yah [jɑ:] *interj.* **1** exclamation of derision. 흥; 어럽쇼. **2** =yes. [Imit.]

Ya·hoo [jɑ́:hu:, jéi-, jɑhú:] *n.* **1** an imaginary disgusting creature, having the forms of man but the habits of the lower animals. 야후《사람 모습을 한 가상의 짐승》. **2** (*y-*) a coarse, rude person. 거칠고 막된 사람. [*Gulliver's Travels* Pt. IV]

yak [jæk] *n.* Ⓒ an animal like a cow, but with longer hair. 야크. 參考 티벳산(產)의 털이 긴 소. [Native]

yam [jæm] *n.* Ⓒ **1** a root grown for food in warm countries. 마속(屬) 식물의 뿌리. **2** 《U.S.》 a kind of sweet potato. 고구마의 일종. [Sp.]

yank [jæŋk] *vt.* (P6,7) 《*colloq.*》 give a sharp pull to; pull suddenly. 확 잡아당기다. [?]

·**Yan·kee** [jǽŋki] *n.* Ⓒ **1** a person of New England. 뉴잉글랜드 사람. **2** 《chiefly Brit. *colloq.*》 a person of the United States. 미국인; 양키. — *adj.* of or like Yankees. 양키의; 양키식의. [?]

Yan·kee·ism [jǽŋkiìzəm] *n.* Ⓤ **1** a Yankee's nature and special quality. 양키풍; 양키 기질. **2** a particular Yankee word or expression. 미국〔양키〕 사투리; 미국어.

Yankee notions [∠-∠-] *n.* American appliances. 미국식 고안물.

yap [jæp] *n.* Ⓒ **1** a short, sharp noise which a dog makes when very excited. 시끄러운 개 짖는 소리. **2** 《*sl.*》 noisy or foolish talk. 시끄러운 수다. **3** 《*colloq.*》 a peevish or noisy person. 수다스러운 사람. — *vi.* (**yapped, yap·ping**) (P1) **1** make a yap; yelp. 요란하게 짖다. **2** 《*colloq.*》 talk snappishly, noisily, or foolishly. 수다떨다. [Imit.]

:yard[1] [jɑːrd] *n.* Ⓒ **1** a small piece of ground near or round a house. 안마당; 안뜰; 구내. ¶ *a front* ~ 앞마당 / *farmyard* 농가의 마당. **2** a space of open ground with fences round it in which some particular business is carried on. 일터; 작업장. ¶ *a builder's* ~ 목수의 일터 / *a railway* ~ 조차장(操車場) / *a navy* ~ 해군 조선소 / *a brickyard* 벽돌 공장. 參考 흔히 합성어를 만듦. **3** 《Brit.》 《*the Y-*》 =Scotland Yard. — *vt.* (P6) put (animals, etc.) into a yard. …을 울 안에 넣다. [E. →garden]

:yard[2] [jɑːrd] *n.* Ⓒ **1** a unit of length equal to three feet. 야드. 參考 yd.로 생략함. **2** 《naut.》 a pole to which a sail is fixed on a ship. 활대. [E.=stick]

yard·age [jɑ́ːrdidʒ] *n.* **1** length in yards. 야드로 잰 길이. **2** amount measured in yards. 야드로 잰 양.

yard-arm [jɑ́ːrdɑ̀ːrm] *n.* 《naut.》 either half of a sailyard. (가로돛의) 활대 양끝.

yard·mas·ter [jɑ́ːrdmæ̀stər, -mɑ̀ːs-] *n.* a man in charge of a railway yard. 조차장장(操車場長). [*yard*[1]]

yard measure [∠∠-] *n.* a stick, tape, etc. used for measuring. 야드 자.

yard·stick [jɑ́ːrdstìk] *n.* Ⓒ **1** a wooden or metal stick one yard long, used for measuring. (목제·금속제) 야드 자. **2** 《*fig.*》 a standard of comparison. (비교의) 기준. ¶ *Is profit the only ~ of success ?* 이윤만이 성공의 척도인가.

·**yarn** [jɑːrn] *n.* **1** Ⓤ a spun thread used for weaving, knitting and rope-making. (자은) 실; 피륙 짜는 실; 방적사. ¶ *knit stockings from* ~ 실로 양말을 뜨다. **2** Ⓒ 《*colloq.*》 a tale or story of adventures, travels, etc. which is hard to believe. (별로 미덥지 못한) 이야기; 모험〔여행〕담.

spin a yarn, tell a story; make a false or doubtful statement. 이야기하다; 미덥지 못한 이야기를 늘어놓다.

— *vi.* (P1,2A) 《*colloq.*》 tell a yarn; hold a long conversation. 이야기를 하다; 길게 떠벌리다. [E.]

yar·row [jǽrou] *n.* Ⓒ a plant with small pink or white flowers with a strong smell and with finely-divided leaves. 서양톱풀. [E.]

yaw [jɔː] *vi.* (P1) (of a ship or an airplane) go unsteadily and leave the right course. 침로를 벗어나다. — *n.* Ⓒ the act of yawing. 침로를 벗어남. [Du.]

·**yawn** [jɔːn] *vi.* (P1,2A,3) **1** open the mouth wide because one is tired or sleepy. 하품하다. ¶ *make someone* ~ 아무를 지루하게 만들다. **2** open wide; gape. (입·구멍 등이) 크게 벌어지다. ¶ *The hole yawned before him.* 큰 구멍이 그의 앞에 입을 벌리고 있었다 / 《*fig.*》 *yawning gaps in the law* 법망에 나 있는 큰 구멍들.

— *vt.* (P6) say (something) with a yawn. 하품하면서 …을 말하다. ¶ ~ *someone good night* 하품하면서 잘 자라고 인사하다.

— *n.* Ⓒ **1** the act of yawning. 하품. ¶ *give a* ~ 하품하다. **2** 《*colloq.*》 a dull uninteresting person or thing. 따분한 사람〔것〕. ¶ *The party was a big* ~. 아주 재미없는 파티였다. [E.]

Yb 《chem.》 ytterbium.

yd. yard.

yds. yards.

·**ye** [ji(ː)] *pron. pl.* **1** 《*arch.*》 you. 너희들은〔이〕. ¶ *Oh, ~ gods!* 아아, 신들이여 / *If ~ are thirsty, drink.* 너희들 목마르거든 물을 마셔라. **2** 《*poet., joc.*》 《as a form of address》 you. ¶ *Ye fools !* 이 바보들. 參考 단수형은 thou. [Indo-European *yu-*]

·**yea** [jei] *adv.* 《*arch.*》 **1** yes; indeed. 그렇지; 그렇고말고(opp. nay). **2** moreover. 게다가. — *n.* Ⓒ an expression of agreement. 긍정; 찬성(cf. *aye*[2]). ¶ ~*s and nays* 찬반(투표). [E.]

:year [jiər / jəːr] *n.* Ⓒ **1** the period from January 1 to December 31; twelve moths. 연(年); 해. ¶ *this* 〔*last, next*〕 ~ 금년〔작년, 내년〕 / *a common* 〔*leap*〕 ~ 평년〔윤년〕 / *for years* 여러 해 동안 / *It has been years since he left his country.* 그가 고국을 떠난 지 오래다 / *I bought this hat the ~ I was in Paris.* 이 모자는 내가 파리에 있던 해에 샀다 / *It is just a ~ since I saw him.* 그를 본 지 꼭 1년이 됐다 / *It's been a good ~ for films.* 이 해에는 좋은 영화가 많이 나왔다. **2** the part of a year given to a certain kind of activity. 연도; 학년. ¶ *the school* ~ 학년 / *the fiscal* ~ 회계 연도 / *second ~ students,* 2학년생. **3** 《usu. *pl.*》 age; time of life. 나이; 연령. ¶ *a man of years* 노인 / *She is seventy years old.* 그녀는 일흔 살이다 / *You look young for your years.* 당신은 나이보다 젊어 보입니

다 / *a man of my years* 내 나이 또래의 남자 / *the years of discretion* 분별 연령 / 《*prov.*》 *Years bring wisdom.* 나이가 들면 지혜로워진다. [E.]

all the year round =《U.S.》 ***the year round,*** throughout the year. 1년 내내.

from year to year = ***year after*** 〔***by***〕 ***year,*** every year; each year. 매년; 해마다.

in the year one 〔***1***〕***,*** very long ago; a long, long time ago. 옛날 옛적에; 아득한 옛날에.

year in, year out, every year; going on year after year. 세세연년; 오는 해도 가는 해도; 끊임없이.

year·ling [jíərliŋ / jə́ːr-] *n.* Ⓒ an animal between one and two years old. (짐승의) 한두 살짜리; 일년생. — *adj.* one year old. 당년생의; 한 살의.

year·long [jíərlɔ̀(ː)ŋ, -lɑ̀ŋ] *adj.* lasting for a year. 1년에 걸친; 1년 계속의. ¶ *She came back after a ~ absence.* 그녀는 1년 만에 돌아왔다.

***year·ly** [jíərli / jə́ːr-] *adj.* happening each or every year; done once a year. 해마다의; 연 1회의. ¶ *a ~ event* 연례 행사 / *a five-yearly medical examination,* 5년마다의 건강진단 / *a ~ pay award* 연봉 / *a ~ income* 연수(年收). — *adv.* every year; once a year; annually. 매년; 1년에 한 번.

***yearn** [jəːrn] *vi.* **1** (P3) 《*for, after*》 desire greatly. 그리워하다. ¶ *~ for* 〔*after*〕 *home* 고향을 그리워하다. **2** (P3) 《*over, for*》 feel pity. 동정하다. ¶ *~ over the orphan* 고아를 불쌍해 하다. **3** (P4) desire to do. …하기를 열망하다; 간절히 …하고 싶어하다. ¶ *He yearned for her to return.* 그녀가 돌아오기를 간절히 바랐다. [E.]

yearn·ing [jə́ːrniŋ] *n.* Ⓤ strong desire; deep longing. 동경; 그리움; 사모; 열망. — *adj.* that yearns. 그리워〔동경〕하는.

yeast [jiːst] *n.* **1** Ⓤ the yellow material used to make beer and bread. 이스트; 효모; 누룩. **2** Ⓒ small round balls of liquid filled with air, etc.; foam. 거품. [E.]

yeast·y [jíːsti] *adj.* (**yeast·i·er, yeast·i·est**) **1** of, like, or containing yeast. 효모의〔같은〕. **2** of or forming yeast; foamy. 발효하는; 거품이 있는. **3** empty and swelling. 실질이 없는; 건성인.

***yell** [jel] *vi.* (P1,2A,3) cry out loudly. 소리지르다; 외치다. ¶ *~ with pain* 고통스러워 소리지르다 / *~ with laughter* 웃음을 터뜨리다 / *Don't ~ at me like this!* 내게 이렇게 고함지르지 마라. — *vt.* (P6,7) say (something) by yelling. 소리치며 …이라 하다. ¶ *~ (out) an order* 큰 소리로 명령하다. — *n.* Ⓒ **1** a loud voice; a loud sharp cry. (크고 날카로운) 외침 소리. ¶ *a ~ of pain* 〔*fear*〕. **2** 《U.S. univ.》 a special shout given by students at a football game, etc. 옐《대학에서 응원할 때 쓰는 특정한 외침 소리》. [E.]

:**yel·low** [jélou] *adj.* (**-low·er, -low·est**) **1** of the color like that of gold, butter or a ripe lemon. 노란. ¶ *a ~ ribbon* / *the ~ race* 황색 인종 / *~ fever* 황열병 / *turn* 〔*go*〕 *~* 노래지다. **2** 《*colloq.*》 cowardly; untrustworthy. 겁이 많은; 비겁한. ¶ *He is ~.* 그는 겁이 많다. **3** jealous; envious. 시기심〔질투심〕이 많은. ¶ *~ looks* 질투하는 눈매. **4** (of a newspaper, etc.) sensational. 선정적인. ¶ *~ journals* 선정적인 신문; 황색 신문.
— *n.* **1** Ⓤ the color yellow. 황색; 노랑. **2** Ⓤ yellow paint or dye. 노란 그림물감; 황색 안료. **3** Ⓒ something having a yellow color; the yellow part of an egg. 노란 것; (달걀) 노른자위. **4** Ⓤ 《*colloq.*》 cowardice. 겁. **5** 《*pl.*》 plant disease. 위황병(萎黃病).
— *vi.* (P1) become yellow. 노래지다.
— *vt.* (P6) make (something) yellow. …을 노랗게 하다. ¶ *The curtain has been yellowed.* 커튼이 노랗게 바랬다. [E.]

yellow dirt [⌐-⌐] *n.* gold. 황금; 돈.

yel·low·ish [jélouiʃ] *adj.* rather yellow. 누르스름한; 노란색을 띤.

yel·low·y [jéloui] *adj.* rather yellow. 누르스름한; 노릇한.

yelp [jelp] *n.* Ⓒ a sudden sharp cry of a dog when hurt. (개가 다쳐서) 캥캥 짖는 소리. — *vi.* (P1) give such a cry; utter a yelp. 캥캥 짖다; 소리 지르다. [E. =boast]

yen [jen] *n.* Ⓒ (*pl.* **yen**) the unit of money in Japan. 엔《일본의 화폐 단위》. 參考 기호는 ¥. [Chin.]

yeo·man [jóumən] *n.* Ⓒ (*pl.* **-men** [-mən]) **1** 《Brit.》 (in olden days) a small landowner; (nowadays) a farmer who owns his farm. 자작농; 소지주. **2** 《U.S. nav.》 a petty officer with clerical duties. 서무계 하사관. [E.]

a yeoman of the Guard, a member of a royal bodyguard. 영국왕 근위병.

yeo·man·ry [jóumənri] *n.* **1** 《*collectively*》 yeomen. 자작농; 소지주들. **2** 《Brit.》 special soldiers who fight on horseback and who are normally farmers. 의용 기마병〔대〕.

yeoman('s) service [⌐-⌐-] *n.* real help in need. 유사시의 도움; 다급할 때의 원조. ¶ *He did us ~ then.* 그 때 그는 다급한 우리를 도와 주었다.

:**yes** [jes] *adv.* (opp. no) **1** 《expressing agreement, consent or affirmation》 just so; it is so; as you say. 네; 그래; 그렇습니다. ¶ *"Can you swim?" "Yes, I can."* "수영할 줄 아나" "그래, 안다" / *"Isn't it snowing?" "Yes, it is."* "눈이 안 오나" "아니, 오고 있다" / *"Are you ready?" "Yes."* "준비됐나" "응, 됐다" / *"Don't you like it?" "Yes, I do like it."* "그거 싫은가" "아니, 아주 좋아한다". 語法 질문의 형식이 어떻든 대답이 긍정이면 Yes로 대답함. **2** and what is more; in addition; moreover. 아니 (그뿐인가); 게다가. ¶ *His lecture was good, ~, very good.* 그의 강의는 좋았다, 좋다뿐인가 아주 훌륭했다 / *I could do it, ~ and well too.* 난 그거 할 수 있

없어, 해도 잘 했을 거란 말이야. **3** 《used in a rising tone and expressing doubt, interest, etc.》 ⓐ Is it so?; Indeed? 그러냐; 정말이냐. ¶ *"He made a large profit." "Yes?"* "그 사람 돈 많이 벌었어" "그래, 정말인가" / *"I was always good at reading faces." "Yes?"* "내가 늘 남의 관상을 잘 봤지" "정말인가". ⓑ Do you understand?; Do you agree? 알겠나. ¶ *We first go two miles west, then bear to the north and continue in a straight line for several miles—yes?* 처음 우리는 서쪽으로 2 마일 가서 그리고 방향을 북쪽으로 틀어 곧장 수 마일을 가는거야, 알겠지. **4** 《in answer to a call》 I am here. I am attending to you. 네. ¶ *"Waiter!" "Yes, sir."* "웨이터!" "예 (갑니다)."

—n. Ⓒ (*pl.* **yes·es**) an answer that agrees or consents; an affirmative reply or vote. 긍정[승낙]의 말; 찬성(투표). ¶ *2 yeses and 3 noes* 찬성 2, 반대 3 / *He said* ～. 그는 승낙했다 / *Did you answer* ～ *or no.* 수락했나 반대했나 / *Confine yourself to yes(es) and no(es).* '네', '아니오' 라고만 대답하시오. [= *wea, be it*]

yes man [´ ´] *n.* 《*sl.*》 a person who always agrees with his superior, officer, etc. 윗사람에게 맹목적으로 복종하는 사람; 예스맨(opp. no man).

:yes·ter·day [jéstərdi, -dèi] *n.* Ⓤ **1** the day before today. 어제. ¶ *yesterday's paper* 어제 신문 / *the day before* ～ 그저께 / *a week (from)* ～ 지난 주의 어제 / *Where was he* ～ *morning [night]?* 어제 아침[저녁] 그는 어디 있었나 / *He left* ～ *afternoon.* 그는 어제 오후 떠났다. **2** ⓐ the recent past. 작금; 최근. ¶ *The thing is but of* ～. 그 일은 아주 최근의 일이다. ⓑ 《*pl.*》 former times. 과거. ¶ *in the dim yesterdays* 어렴풋한 지난 날에. **—adv.** on the day before today; recently. 어제; 최근. ¶ *He went away* ～. 그는 어제 갔다 / *I was not born* ～. 나는 애송이가 아니야. [E.]

:yet [jet] *adv.* **1** 《in *negative*》 up to the present time; so far. 아직 (…않다). ¶ *The work is not* ～ *done.* 일이 아직 끝나지 않았다 / *It was not* ～ *dark.* 아직 어둡지 않다 / *"Have you seen it?" "Not* ～*."* "그거 보았나" "아니, 아직" / *Don't start* ～. 아직 떠나지 마라 / *He has not come* ～. 그는 아직 오지 않았다 / *I know nothing* ～. 아직 아는 게 없다 / *It will not happen just* ～. 그건 지금 당장은 일어나지 않을 게다. **2** 《in *affirmative*》 still; even now. 아직; 여전히. ¶ *She is sick* ～. 아직 앓고 있다 / *There is* ～ *a chance for success.* 아직 성공할 가망은 있다 / *He is* ～ *alive.* 그는 아직 살아 있다 / *There is* ～ *time.* 아직 시간은 있다 / *There is one* ～ *missing.* 아직 하나가 모자란다. **3** 《often with *compar.*》 in addition; still; moreover. 더 한층; 더욱; 그 위에. ¶ *more and* ～ *more* 더욱 더 / *You must study* ～ *harder.* 너는 더욱 열심히 배워야 한다 / *a* ～ *harder work* 더욱 힘든 일. **4** 《in *interrogative*》 by this time; now. 벌써; 이미. ¶ *Has she gone* ～? 그녀가 벌써 갔나 / *Has he returned* ～? 그가 이미 돌아왔나 / *Need you go* ～? 벌써 가야 하나. [語法] yet 대신에 already를 쓰면 놀람이나 뜻밖이란 뜻을 나타냄. **5** some future day; sometime; eventually. 언젠가는; 조만간. ¶ *He will win the championship* ～. 그가 언젠가는 우승할 것이다 / *I shall catch him* ～. 언젠가는 그를 잡고 말겠다 / *The plan could* ～ *succeed.* 계획이 언젠가는 성공할 것이다. **6** nevertheless; for all that. 그러나; …이긴 하나. ¶ *She is pretty,* ～ *unwise.* 그녀는 예쁘긴 하나 아둔하다 / *poor,* ～ *honest* 가난하지만 정직한.

and yet, but. 그러나. ¶ *I am tired, and* ～ *I must work hard.* 피곤하지만 열심히 일해야만 한다.

as yet, until now; up to now. 아직(은). ¶ *Nothing has been done as* ～. 아직 아무 것도 된 게 없다.

nor yet, even as much as; either. …도 또한 —않다. ¶ *He can't read nor* ～ *write.* 그는 읽지도 쓰지도 못한다 / *The work is not finished, nor* ～ *started.* 일이 끝나기는커녕 시작하지도 않았다.

—*conj.* but still; nevertheless; however. 그런데도; 그럼에도 불구하고. ¶ *She is not rich* ～ *she looks happy.* 그녀는 부유하지는 않으나 행복해 보인다 / *He has done bad things,* ～ *I love him.* 나쁜 짓을 했지만 나는 그가 좋다 / *It is strange, and* ～ *(it is) true.* 이상하긴 하지만 그게 사실이다. [E.]

yet·i [jéti] *n.* the native name for an animal supposed to inhabit the Himalaya mountains, known as the Abominable Snowman. (히말라야 산맥의) 설인. [Tibetan]

yew [ju:] *n.* Ⓒ 《bot.》 a large, cone-bearing, evergreen tree with dark green leaves. 주목(朱木). [E.]

:yield [ji:ld] *vt.* **1** (P6) produce; bring forth. …을 생기게 하다; 산출하다. ¶ *The farms* ～ *rice and wheat.* 농장에서는 쌀과 밀이 산출된다 / *The investment yielded rich profits.* 그 투자는 많은 이익을 가져왔다 / *Cows* ～ *milk.* 젖소에서 우유가 난다 / *My labor yielded but poor results.* 일했지만 성과가 시원찮았다 / *Their long search failed to* ～ *any clues.* 오래 조사했어도 단서 하나 못 잡았다. **2** (P6,7,13) give away (something) to force; give up; surrender. (강제되어) …을 양도[포기]하다; 양보하다; 명도하다; 굴복하다. ¶ ～ *a town to the enemy* 적에게 마을을 내주다 / *She yielded herself (up) to temptation.* 그녀는 유혹에 졌다 / ～ *one's place* 지위를 내놓다. **3** give consent; grant; permit. …을 동의하다; 허락하다. ¶ ～ *consent* 승낙하다 / ～ *possession* 소유권을 내주다 / ～ *precedence to someone* 아무에게 차례를 양보하다 / ～ *the point in an argument* 논점을 양보하다. **—vi.** **1** (P1) produce. (작물·땅이) 내다; 산출하다. ¶ *This apple tree yields well.* 이 사과나무는 결실이 좋다 / *The land*

yields abundantly. 그 땅에서는 소출이 많다. **2** (P1,3) 《*to*》 give away; surrender. 굴복하다; 양보하다; 지다. ¶ ~ *to none* 누구에게도 뒤지지 않다 / ~ *to pleasure* 향락에 빠지다 / *They yielded to enemy.* 그들은 적에게 굴복했다 / *The door yielded to a strong push.* 힘껏 밀었더니 문이 열렸다 / ~ *to temptation* 유혹에 지다.

yield consent, accept. 승낙하다.

yield the palm to (=*be exceeded by*) *someone.* …에게 지다; 굴복하다.

***yield up the life* 〔*ghost, soul, breath, spirit*〕,** die. 죽다.

— *n.* Ⓒ the amount yielded; something yielded; products. 산출고; 수확(량). ¶ *The yields of the farm have increased recently.* 최근 농장의 수확(량)이 늘었다 / *yields on bonds* 〔*securities*〕 채권〔증권〕의 수익. [E. = pay]

yield·ing [jíːldiŋ] *adj.* soft; easily bent. 유연한; 잘 구부러지는. ¶ *a* ~ *disposition* 유연한 기질.

Y.M.C.A., YMCA Young Men's Christian Association.

yo·del, -dle [jóudl] *n.* Ⓒ a song sung by quickly changing from a high to a low note, as the Swiss in the mountains do. 요들. [G.]

yo·ga [jóugə] *n.* Ⓤ a system of Hindu religious philosopy. 요가《인도의 신비 철학》. [Hind.]

yo·g(h)urt [jóugəːrt / jɔ́-] *n.* a food made from fermented milk. 요구르트. [Turk.]

yo·gi [jóugi] *n.* a person who practices or follows yoga. 요가 수도자. [→yoga]

yo-heave-ho [jóuhìːvhóu], **yo-ho** [jouhóu] *interj.* an exclamation used by sailors in pulling or lifting together. 어기여차《본디 뱃사람들이 닻을 올릴 때의 소리》. [*heave*]

***yoke** [jouk] *n.* Ⓒ **1** a wooden frame to fasten a pair of oxen together. 멍에. **2** 《used as *sing.* and *pl.*》 a pair of oxen working together under a yoke. 멍에에 맨 한 쌍의 소. ¶ *a* 〔*five*〕 ~ *of oxen* 두〔열〕 마리의 소 / 《Brit. *arch.*》 *a* ~ *of land* (멍에에 맨) 한 쌍의 소가 하루에 갈 수 있는 면적의 땅. **3** something like a yoke in shape or use; a frame fitting over the shoulders for carrying pairs of pails. 멍에 모양의 것; 멜대. **4** something that connects or unites; a bond; a tie. 기반(羈絆); 유대. ¶ *the* ~ *of love* 〔*brotherhood*〕 애정〔형제〕의 유대 / *the* ~ *of marriage* 결혼이라는 굴레. **5** 《usu. *the* ~》 《*fig.*》 rule; power; the state of being a slave. 지배; 권력; 굴종(屈從). ¶ *endure the* ~ 남의 지배를 받다 / *cast* 〔*shake, throw*〕 *off the* ~ 굴레〔멍에〕를 벗다 / *submit to someone's* ~ 아무의 지배에 복종하다.

〈yoke 1〉

pass* 〔*come*〕 *under the yoke, yield; surrender; be conquered. 굴복하다.

send* someone *under the yoke, make someone give in; defeat. …을 굴복시키다.

— *vt.* (P6,7,13) put a yoke on (someone or something); join or link together; unite. …에 멍에를 씌우다; …을 연결하다; 매다. ¶ *yoked in marriage* 결혼으로 맺어진.

— *vi.* (P2A) be joined together. 결합하다; 매어지다. [E.]

yoke·fel·low [jóukfèlou] *n.* Ⓒ a person who joins or associates with another in marriage or work. 배우자; (함께 일하는) 동료; 협동자.

yo·kel [jóukəl] *n.* Ⓒ a country fellow. 시골 사람; 촌사람. [?]

yoke·mate [jóukmèit] *n.* =yokefellow.

yolk [jou*l*k] *n.* ⓊⒸ the yellow part of an egg. (계란) 노른자위. ¶ *Separate the white from the* ~. 흰자나 노른자를 따로 분리해라. [*yellow*]

***yon** [jɑn / jɔn] *adj., adv.* 《*arch., dial.*》 =yonder.

:yon·der [jɑ́ndər / jɔ́n-] *adj.* situated at a distance, but in sight. 저쪽의; 저기의. ¶ ~ *group of trees* 저쪽의 나무 숲 / ~ *hills* 저쪽 언덕 / *the* ~ *side of the valley* 골짜기의 저쪽 편. — *adv.* over there. 저쪽〔저기〕에. ¶ *Yonder stands an old tree.* 저쪽에 고목 나무가 하나 서 있다. [E.]

yore [jɔːr] *n.* Ⓤ 《*arch.*》 a time long ago. 옛날 옛적. ¶ *in days of* ~ 아주 옛날에. [E. = long ago]

:you [ju(ː), jə] *pron.* (*pl.* **you**) **1** the person or persons spoken to. 당신(들)은〔이〕; 당신(들)을〔에게〕. ¶ ~ *and I* 너와 나 / *The dog will do* ~ *no harm.* 개는 당신을 해치지 않아요 / *You are a good boy.* 넌 착한 아이다 / *You are all fools.* 너희들은 모두 바보야 / *Can I pour* ~ *a cup of tea?* 차 한 잔 따라 드릴까요. **2** one; anyone; people in general. (사람) 누구나. ¶ *You never can tell it.* 아무도 모른다 / *You never know what may happen.* 무슨 일이 일어날지 아무도 모른다 / *You have to be careful with people* ~ *don't know.* 모르는 사람한테는 신중해야 한다. **3** 《*arch.*》 yourself. 당신 자신. ¶ *Rest* ~ *there.* 저기서 쉬어라 / *You must choose* ~ *a wife.* 아내는 네 스스로 골라야지. [E.]

***you'd** [juːd, jəd] you had; you would.

***you'll** [ju(ː)l, jəl] you will; you shall.

:young [jʌŋ] *adj.* (opp. old) **1** in the early period of life or growth; not middle-aged or old. 젊은; 어린. ¶ *the* ~ 젊은이들 語法 형용사에 the를 붙인 명사적 용법 / *a* ~ *girl* 소녀 / *in one's young(er) days* 젊었을 때 / *When* ~, *he learned how to fly.* 젊어서 그는 비행기 조종술을 익혔다. **2** having the looks or qualities of youth; youthful; vigorous; fresh. 한창 젊은; 기운찬; 발랄한. ¶ ~ *passion* 〔*ambitions*〕 젊은이다운 정열〔야망〕 / *He is* ~ *in heart.* 그는 마음이 젊다 /

Y

She is ~ for her age. 그녀는 나이에 비해 젊다. **3** (of a period, time, etc.) in an early state; not far advanced. (시일 등이) 아직 얼마 안 된; 일천한. ¶ *a ~ wine* 덜 익은 포도주 / *a ~ moon* 초승달 / *The night was still ~ when they parted.* 그들이 헤어졌을 때는 아직 초저녁이었다. **4** (of countries) recently established; newly born; new. (나라가) 역사가 짧은; 신흥의. ¶ *a ~ nation in Africa* 아프리카의 신생국. **5** the younger of two persons in a family having the same name; junior. (부모 자식·형제간의) 나이가 아래인. ¶ *the young(er) Sam* 아들 샘 / *(the) ~ Mrs. Johnson* 젊은〔손아래〕 존슨씨 부인. **6** without much experience or practice; inexperienced. 경험이 없는; 미숙한. ¶ *He is still ~ at〔in〕this work.* 그는 아직 이 일에 서툴다 / *~ in crime* 초범의. **7** (in the name of progressive political parties) having new ideas, tendency, etc. 진보적인.

a young man in a hurry, an impatient and ardent reformer. 급진적 개혁자.

young and old, (all) the young people and old people. 남녀 노소.

one's ***young man*** 〔***woman***〕 《*colloq.*》 one's sweet heart. 연인; 애인.

— *n.* Ⓤ 《*collectively*》 the offspring of an animal. (짐승의) 새끼. ¶ *The lion fought to protect her ~.* 사자는 새끼를 지키기 위해 싸웠다 / *the ~ of the elephant* 코끼리 새끼 / *a fox and her ~* 여우와 그 새끼. [E.]

with young, (of a female animal) pregnant. 새끼를 밴.

young blood [⌐⌐] *n.* **1** youthful strength, energy, etc. 젊은 혈기. **2** 《*collectively*》 young energetic youth. 혈기 왕성한 청년.

young·ish [jʌ́ŋiʃ] *adj.* rather young. 좀〔다소〕 젊은.

***young·ster** [jʌ́ŋstər] *n.* Ⓒ **1** a young person; a lad. 젊은이. **2** a child. 아이. **3** a young animal. 어린 짐승.

youn·ker [jʌ́ŋkər] *n.* Ⓒ 《*arch., colloq.*》 a young man. 청년; 젊은이. [E.]

:your [juər, jɔːr, jər] *pron.* (the possessive form of **you**) **1** of you; belonging to you; 당신(들)의; 너(희들)의. ¶ *What's ~ name?* 네 이름이 뭐냐 / *Thank you for ~ kindness.* 친절에 감사합니다 / *You must all come and bring ~ husbands.* 여러분은 남편을 동반하시고 모두 오셔야 합니다. **2** one's; of people in general. (사람) 누구나의. ¶ *The church is on ~ right.* 교회는 오른쪽에 있습니다. **3** 《*arch., colloq.,* usu. *contempt.*》 that you know of. (흔히들 말하는) 이른바; 소위. ¶ *This is ~ fair play.* 이것이 이른바 페어 플레이라는거다 / *He was ~ typical English gentleman.* 그는 이른바 전형적 영국 신사였다. **4** 《as a form of address to the holder of the title》 ¶ *Your Excellency〔Highness, Majesty〕.* 각하〔전하, 폐하〕. [→ye]

***you're** [juər, jər] you are.

:yours [juərz, jɔːrz] *pron.* (the possessive form of **you**) the one or ones belonging to you. 당신(들)의 것. ¶ *This book is ~.* 이건 네 책이다 / *my mother and ~* 내 어머니와 네 어머니 / *Yours is better than mine.* 네 것이 내 것보다 더 좋다. [*your*]

of yours, belonging to you. 네게 속하는; 네 것의. ¶ *I saw a friend of ~.* 네 친구를 한 사람 만났다.

Yours truly 〔***sincerely, faithfully, affectionately,*** *etc.*〕 = ***Sincerely*** 〔***Faithfully***〕 ***yours,*** forms used at the end of letters before one's signature. (편지 끝맺음 말로서) 경구(敬具); 여불비례(餘不備禮).

:your·self [juərsélf, jər-, jɔːr-] *pron.* (*pl.* **-selves**) **1** a reflexive and emphatic form of **you.** 당신 자신. ¶ *You told me so ~!* 네 입으로 그렇게 말하지 않았나 / *Do it ~.* 네 스스로 해라 / *Did you hurt ~?* 다쳤느냐. **2** your normal physical or mental condition. 당신의 (심신의) 정상 상태. ¶ *You don't seem ~ today.* 너 오늘 좀 이상해 보인다. [*your*]

(***all***) ***by yourself,*** **a**) alone; without company. 혼자서. ¶ *Have you been all by ~ all day?* 온 종일 너 혼자 있었나. **b**) without help from others. 혼자 힘으로. ¶ *Did you make this by ~?* 네가 이걸 혼자 힘으로 만들었나.

:your·selves [juərsélvz, jər-, jɔːr-] *pron.* pl. of **yourself.**

:youth [juːθ] *n.* (*pl.* **youths** [juːðz, -θs]) **1** Ⓤ the state of being young. 젊음. ¶ *the secret of keeping one's ~* 젊음을 유지하는 비결 / *She keeps her ~.* 그녀는 여전히 젊다 / *He lost his ~ a long time ago.* 그는 젊음을 오래 전에 잃었다. **2** Ⓤ the early part of life. 청춘; 청년 시대. ¶ *in the days of his ~* 그의 청년 시절에 / *After thirty we feel that ~ is slipping away.* 서른이 지나면 청춘이 스러져가는 것을 느낀다 / *In (his) ~ he had shown great promise.* 청년 시절 그는 장래가 크게 촉망됐었다. **3** Ⓒ a young man. 청년. ¶ *a promising ~* 전도 유망한 청년. **4** Ⓤ 《*collectively*》 young men and women; young people of both sexes. 청춘 남녀; 젊은이들. ¶ *the ~ of a nation* 한 나라의 젊은이들 / *a ~ hostel* 유스 호스텔. **5** Ⓤ an early or first stage of development. 초기. ¶ *during the ~ of this country* 이 나라의 발전 초기 동안 / *the ~ of the world* 태고; 고대. [*young*]

***youth·ful** [júːθfəl] *adj.* young; of or suitable for youth. 젊은; 젊은이의; 청년다운. ¶ *a ~ appearance* 젊은이다운 풍모 / *She is over 50 but has a ~ complexion.* 그녀는 쉰을 넘었지만 얼굴 모습이 젊다.

***you've** [ju(ː)v, jəv] you have.

yowl [jaul] *n.* Ⓒ a long, sad cry; a loud, prolonged cry, as of a dog or a cat. 신음 소리; (개나 고양이 따위가) 길고 슬프게 짖는〔우는〕 소리. — *vi.* (P1) make such a cry. 길고 슬프게 짖다〔울다〕. [Imit.]

yr(.) year; your; younger.

yrs(.) years; yours.
Yt 《chem.》 yttrium《지금은 Y》.
yt·ter·bi·um [itə́ːrbiəm] *n.* Ⓤ 《chem.》 a rare metallic element, Yb, belonging to the yttrium group. 이테르븀. [Swed.]
yt·tri·um [ítriəm] *n.* Ⓤ 《chem.》 a rare metallic element. 이트륨. [Swed.]
yu·an [juːάːn] *n.* Ⓒ (*pl.* **yuan**) the monetary unit of China. 원(元)(=juan dollar). [Chin.]
yuc·ca [jʌ́kə] *n.* Ⓒ a plant of the agave family. 유카속(屬)의 목본(木本) 식물. [Amer-Ind.]
yule, Yule [juːl] *n.* Ⓤ the Christmas season or festival. 크리스마스 계절(축제). [E.]
yule log [ㄹㄹ] *n.* a huge log burned on Christmas Eve. 크리스마스 전야에 태우는 큰 통나무 장작.
yule·tide [júːltàid] *n.* Ⓤ the Christmas season. 크리스마스 계절.
Y.W.C.A., YWCA Young Women's Christian Association.

z Z

Z, z [ziː / zed] *n.* Ⓒ (*pl.* **Z's, Zs, z's, zs** [ziːz / zedz]) **1** the twenty-sixth and last letter of the English alphabet. 영어 알파벳의 스물여섯째 자. ¶ *from A to Z* 처음부터 끝까지. **2** something shaped like the letter Z. Z자 모양의 것. [Gk. *zēta*]
Z 《chem.》 atomic number; zenith.
Z. zero; zone.
za·ny [zéini] *n.* Ⓒ (*pl.* **-nies**) **1** a foolish person. 바보. **2** 《hist.》 an attendant clown in the 16th century Italian drama. 어릿광대. [It.]
zap [zæp] *vt., vi.* (P6;1) **1** attack or destroy. 공격하다; 파멸시키다. **2** (cause to) move quickly or forcefully. 갑자기 움직이(게 하)다. ¶ *She zapped the car from a standstill to 70 miles per hour in 10 seconds.* 그녀는 정지 상태에서 차를 10초 안에 시속 70마일로 내달았다 / 《*fig.*》 *I'll have to ~ through the work to make the deadline.* 마감 시간에 대자면 일을 서둘러 해야겠다. [? *zip, slap*]
Za·ra·thus·tri·an [zæ̀rəθúːstriən] *adj.* = Zoroastrian.
***zeal** [ziːl] *n.* Ⓤ eager desire or effort for a person, cause, work, etc. 정열; 열의. ¶ *with ~* 열심히; 열의를 갖고 / *He worked for the cause with great ~.* 그는 대단한 열의를 가지고 대의를 위해 일했다 / *religious ~* 종교적 열의. [Gk. *zēlos*]
zeal·ot [zélət] *n.* Ⓤ a person who is too eager and fixed in his beliefs. 열중하는 사람; 열광자. ¶ *religious zealots* 광신자.
zeal·ot·ry [zélətri] *n.* Ⓤ the actions or emotions of a zealot; too great zeal. 열광; 광적인 행동.
***zeal·ous** [zéləs] *adj.* 《*for*》 eager; earnest. 열성적인; 열심인; 열정적인. ¶ *a ~ patriot* 열렬한 애국자 / *be ~ for liberty* 자유를 열망하다 / *He is ~ to please his wife.* 아내를 기쁘게 하려고 열심이다. [*zeal, -ous*]
zeal·ous·ly [zéləsli] *adv.* in a zealous manner. 열심히; 열중해서.
ze·bra [zíːbrə] *n.* Ⓒ an African animal like a horse but with black and white lines on the body. 얼룩말. [W-Afr.]
zebra crossing [ㄹ-ㄹ-] *n.* 《Brit.》 a crossing for walkers on foot, painted with broad white stripes. 횡단 보도《도로에 흰 줄 무늬를 친》.
ze·bu [zíːbjuː] *n.* Ⓒ an animal like an ox with a large hump, kept in India and China. 제부《등에 큰 혹이 있는 소의 일종》. [F.]
Zeit·geist [tsáitgàist] *n.* 《G.》 Ⓤ the spirit of the age; the general opinions and tendencies of a particular period. 시대정신(사조). [G. =time-spirit]
Zend-A·ves·ta [zèndəvéstə] *n.* the sacred writings of the Zoroastrians in ancient Persia. 젠드아베스타《조로아스터교의 경전》. [Zend]
ze·nith [zíːniθ / zén-] *n.* Ⓒ 《usu. *the ~* or *one's ~*, used as *sing.*》 **1** the part of the sky just above one's head. 천정(天頂); 제니스(opp. nadir). **2** 《*fig.*》 the highest point; the top. 절정; 정점. ¶ *be at the ~ of one's powers* (*fame*) 권력(명성)의 절정에 있다 / *pass its ~* 그 정점을 지나다. [Arab.]
zeph·yr [zéfər] *n.* **1** Ⓤ 《Z-》 the west wind regarded as a person. (의인화(擬人化)한) 서풍(西風). **2** Ⓒ 《*poet.*》 a gentle wind; a breeze. 산들바람. **3** Ⓤ a kind of fine woolen material. 얇은 캐시미어 천. [Gk.]
Zep·pe·lin [zépəlin], **Zep(p)** [zep] *n.* Ⓒ 《*colloq.*》 a large airship. 체펠린 비행선. [Person]
:**ze·ro** [zíərou] *n.* (*pl.* **-ros** or **-roes**) **1** Ⓒ 0; nothing. 제로; 영(cf. *naught*). **2** Ⓤ the point marked 0 on a scale, from which readings begin in either direction. 영점(零點); (온도계의) 영도; 어는점. ¶ *three degrees below ~* 영하 3도. **3** Ⓤ 《*fig.*》 the lowest point; nothingness. 최하점; 밑바닥. ¶ *His courage was at ~.* 그는 의기 소침해

있었다 / *Our hopes were reduced to* ~. 우리의 희망은 사라졌다. [→cipher]

zero hour [∸–∸] *n.* **1** 《mil.》 the time set for beginning an attack, etc. 행동〔공격〕 개시 시각. ¶ *Zero hour is fixed for midnight.* 작전 개시 시각은 밤 12시다. **2** a critical or decisive moment. 결정적 순간; 위기.

zest [zest] *n.* Ⓤ **1** something added to give a sharp and pleasant taste. 향미(香味); 풍미를 더하는 것. ¶ *give* 〔*add*〕 ~ *to something* …에 풍미〔풍취〕를 더하다. **2** keenness; eagerness. 열의; 열정. ¶ *enter into a game* 〔*a piece of work*〕 *with* ~ 열의를 가지고 경기를〔일을〕 시작하다. [F. =walnut skin]

ze·ta [zéitə, zí:-] *n.* ⓊⒸ the sixth letter of the Greek alphabet(Z, ζ). 그리스어 알파벳의 여섯째 자; 제타.

Zeus [zju:s] *n.* 《Gk. myth.》 the chief god; the ruler of gods and men. 제우스 (=《Rom. myth.》 Jupiter).

zig·zag [zígzæ̀g] *adj.* (of a line) shaped like the letter Z; having short, sharp turns. Z자 모양의; 지그재그(모양)의. ¶ *a* ~ *path.* — *n.* Ⓒ one of such turns; a zigzag line. 지그재그; 갈짓자 모양. — *vi.* (**-zagged, -zag·ging**) (P1,2A) follow a zigzag course. 지그재그(꼴)로 나아가다. ¶ *The path zigzags up the hill.* 길은 언덕 위로 꾸불꾸불 나 있다. — *adv.* so as to follow a zigzag line. 지그재그로; 갈짓자 모양으로. ¶ *The road ran* ~ *across the hill.* 길은 지그재그로 언덕을 가로질러 났다. [F.]

zinc [ziŋk] *n.* Ⓤ a white metal used to protect iron from the wet. 아연(亞鉛). — *vt.* (**zincked** or **zinced, zinck·ing** or **zinc·ing**) (P6) coat or cover (something) with zinc. 아연을 입히다. [G.]

zincked [ziŋkt] *v.* p. and pp. of **zinc.**

zinck·ing [zíŋkiŋ] *v.* ppr. of **zinc.**

zing [ziŋ] *n., interj.* a sharp humming sound. 핑〔쌩〕하는 소리. — *vi.* (P1) make such a sound in going rapidly. 핑핑〔쌩쌩〕 소리나다. [Imit.]

zin·ni·a [zíniə, -njə] *n.* Ⓒ 《bot.》 a garden plant with large, showy flowers. 백일초(百日草). [Person *zinn*]

Zi·on [záiən] *n.* **1** a hill in Jerusalem. 시온산. **2** 《*collectively*》 the Jewish people. 유대인. **3** heaven. 천국. **4** the Christian church. 그리스도 교회. [Heb.]

Zi·on·ism [záiənìzəm] *n.* Ⓤ a plan or movement to establish a national home for the Jews in Palestine. 시온주의; 시오니즘.

Zi·on·ist [záiənist] *n.* Ⓒ a person who approves of Zionism. 시온주의자; 시오니스트.

zip [zip] *n.* **1** Ⓒ the sound made by an object passing quickly through the air. 핑《총알 등이 나는 소리》. ¶ *We heard the* ~ *of a bullet.* 쌩하는 총 소리가 들렸다. **2** Ⓤ 《*colloq.*》 energy. 정력; 활기. **3** =zipper. — *vi.* (**zipped, zip·ping**) (P1,3) **1** make a zip. 핑 소리가 나다. **2** 《*colloq.*》 act quickly. 신속히〔힘차게〕 하다. ¶ *We zipped through the customs.* 우리는 빠르게 세관을 통과했다. [Imit.]

zip code [∸∸] *n.* 《U.S.》 a system of numbers added to addresses to speed and simplify the delivery of post. 우편 번호 (cf. 《Brit.》 *post-code*).

zip-fasten·er [zípfæ̀snər, -fɑ̀:s-] *n.* = zipper.

zip·per [zípər] *n.* Ⓒ a sliding fastener. 지퍼. [→zip]

zip·py [zípi] *adj.* (**-pi·er, -pi·est**) 《*colloq.*》 lively; bright. 활발한; 기운 찬.

zith·er [zíθər, zíð-] *n.* Ⓒ a musical instrument having 30 to 40 strings, played with the fingers. 치터《현악기의 일종》. [→cithern]

zo·di·ac [zóudiæ̀k] *n.* Ⓒ 《*the* ~》 《astron.》 an imaginary belt of sky, followed by the sun, the moon, and planets; a plan of part of the sky divided into twelve equal parts showing the places of certain stars. 황도대(黃道帶); 십이궁(十二宮). [Gk. *zōon* animal; L. for *ram*]

the signs of the zodiac, Ram, Bull, Twins, Crab, Lion, Virgin, Balance, Scorpion, Archer, Goat, Watercarrier, and Fishes. 황도 십이궁.

zom·bi, -bie [zɑ́mbi / zɔ́m-] *n.* 《U.S.》 **1** Ⓒ a corpse brought back to life by supernatural agency. (마법으로) 되살아난 시체. **2** Ⓒ 《*colloq.*》 a very unintelligent and morbid appearing person. (송장처럼) 도무지 생기 없는 사람; 멍청이. **3** Ⓤ a strong alcoholic drink. 좀비 술. [Congo *zumbi* devil]

zon·al [zóunəl] *adj.* **1** of or having to do with a zone or zones. 띠의; 대상(帶狀)의. ¶ *a* ~ *structure* 대상 구조(帶狀構造). **2** divided into zones. 지역으로 갈린. [↓]

·zone [zoun] *n.* Ⓒ **1** 《*arch., poet.*》 a belt. 띠. **2** an area that is set off or differentiated from other areas in some respect. 지대(地帶); 지구. ¶ *a safety* ~ 안전 지대 / *a residence* ~ 주택 지구 / *the wheat* ~ 소맥(小麥) 지대 / *a demilitarized* ~ 비무장 지대 / *the Torrid Zone* 열대 / *the Frizid Zone* 한대 / *the Temperate Zone* 온대. **2** 《U.S.》 a particular area of a country or a city in which certain postal and telephone rates are charged. (우편·전화 등의) 동일 요금 지대. — *vt.* (P6) divide or separate (a place, etc.) into zones. …을 지대〔지구〕로 나누다; (동일 우편 요금의) 우편구로 나누다. [Gk.]

:zoo [zu:] *n.* Ⓒ a place where living animals are kept for the public to see; a zoological garden. 동물원. [Gk. *zōon* animal]

zo·o·log·i·cal [zòuəlɑ́dʒikəl / -lɔ́dʒ-] *adj.* of (the study of) animal life. 동물(학상)의.

zoological garden [∸–∸–– ∸–] *n.* a zoo. 동물원.

zo·ol·o·gist [zouɑ́lədʒist / -ɔ́l-] *n.* Ⓒ a student or a specialist who is skilled in

Z

zoology. 동물학자.

zo·ol·o·gy [zouálədʒi / -ɔ́l-] *n.* Ⓤ the study of animlas, as their ways of living, etc. 동물학.

zoom [zu:m] *n.* Ⓤ **1** 《aeron.》 a sudden vertical upward flight. (항공기의) 급상승. **2** a deep, low sound of a vehicles. (차량·항공기 등의) 붕하는 소리. —*vi.* (P1,2A) **1** (of an airplane) climb for a short time at a very steep angle. (항공기가) 급각도(急角度)로 상승〔급상승〕하다. **2** make a deep, low sound. 붕 소리를 내다. **3** 《photog.》 focus a camera by using a zoom lens. 줌 렌즈로 촬영하다. [Imit.]

zoom lens [⌐⌐] *n.* 《photog.》 a system of lenses in a camera that can change the size of an image continuously while keeping the image in focus. 줌 렌즈.

Zo·ro·as·ter [zɔ́:rouæ̀stər, ⌐—⌐—] *n.* a founder of the ancient Persian religion. 조로아스터. [Person]

Zo·ro·as·tri·an [zɔ̀:rouǽstriən] *adj.* of or belonging to Zoroaster and his religion. 조로아스터의. —*n.* Ⓒ a worshipper of Zoroaster. 조로아스터교도.

Zu·rich, Zü- [zúrik / zjúə-] *n.* a city in northern Switzerland. 취리히.

zy·gote [záigout, zíg-] *n.* Ⓒ 《biol.》 any cell formed by the union of two gametes. 접합자(接合子). [Gk. =yoked]

zy·mase [záimeis] *n.* Ⓤ 《chem.》 an enzyme in yeast that changes sugar into alcohol and carbon dioxide. 치마아제. [Gk. *zūme* fermentation]

zy·mur·gy [záimə:rdʒi] *n.* Ⓤ applied chemistry dealing with the process of fermentation. 양조학(釀造學). [↑, Gk. *urgy* technology]

SUPPLEMENTS (부록)

1 VERB PATTERNS (동사의 문형)

동사의 문형은 크게 조동사와 본동사의 문형으로 나뉘며, 본동사는 다시 기본 5 문형으로 나뉜다.

Ⅰ. S+V의 문형에서 동사는 완전 자동사(complete intransitive verb)이며, 동사만으로 완전한 뜻을 나타낸다.

Ⅱ. S+V+C의 문형에서 동사는 불완전 자동사(incomplete intransitive verb)이며, 보어가 있어야 완전한 뜻을 나타낼 수 있다.

Ⅲ. S+V+O의 문형에서 동사는 완전 타동사(complete transitive verb)이며, 목적어가 따른다.

Ⅳ. S+V+I.O.+D.O.의 문형에서 동사는 수여 동사(dative verb)이며, 「…에게」에 해당하는 간접 목적어(indirect object)와 「…을」에 해당하는 직접 목적어(direct object)가 따른다.

Ⅴ. S+V+O+C의 문형에서 동사는 불완전 타동사(incomplete transitive verb)이며, 목적어뿐만 아니라 보어가 있어야 비로소 완전한 뜻을 나타낼 수 있다.

이 사전에서는 본동사의 문형 25개, 조동사의 문형 5개, 도합 30개의 문형으로 세분하였다.

P1 **S+V** (주어+동사)

자동사만으로 문장의 뜻이 완전히 성립되는 가장 간단한 문형이다. 이 문형에는 진주어가 절로 되어 길기 때문에 형식상 It를 가주어로 내세운 It+V+S(명사절)의 문형도 포함된다.

보기 : Flowers *bloom.* 꽃이 핀다.
It *rains.* 비가 온다.
Who *came?* 누가 왔느냐.
What he says does not *matter.* 그가 말하는 것은 문제가 안 된다.
It *seems* that he is honest. 그는 정직해 보인다.
It does not *matter* whether he will join us. 그가 우리와 같이 가든 안 가든 상관 없다.

P2A **S+V+Adverb** (주어+동사+부사)

자동사에 부사가 따르는 문형이다. There+V+S의 문형도 이에 포함되는데, 이 경우 There는 단순히 문장을 유도하기 위한 것이므로 「거기에」라는 뜻은 없다.

보기 : He *got up.* 그는 일어났다.
Who *came in?* 누가 들어왔느냐.
It will *clear up.* 날씨가 갤 것이다.
There is a cat on the sofa. 소파 위에 고양이가 있다.
There is no hope of his recovery. 그가 회복할 가망은 없다.
There runs a river through this city. 이 도시에는 강이 흐르고 있다.

P2B **S+V+(for) Adverb** (주어+동사+(for) 부사)

자동사에 전치사가 생략된 부사구가 따르는 문형이다. 일반적으로 명사가 부사 구실을 하려면 앞에 전치사가 있어야 하나, 때·거리·기간·정도·모양·나이 따위를 나타내는 부사구는 전치사를 생략하는 경우가 많다.

보기 : He *walked (for) five miles.* 그는 5 마일 걸었다.
I'll *start next Sunday.* 나는 다음 일요일에 떠난다.
He *fell a hundred feet.* 그는 100 피트나 추락했다.
We *waited (for) two hours.* 우리는 두 시간 동안 기다렸다.

The desk *measures four feet by two feet.* 책상은 세로 4 피트, 가로 2 피트이다.

P3 **S+V+Preposition+O** (주어+동사+전치사+목적어)

자동사 뒤에 전치사와 그 목적어가 따르는 문형이다. 어떤 자동사는 뜻에 따라 특정한 전치사를 뒤에 취하는 경우가 많다. 이 때 전치사와 그 목적어는 형식상으로는 부사구이나, look at, listen to와 같이 자동사와 전치사가 동사구(phrasal verb)를 이루는 것이 많다는 점에 유의할 필요가 있다.

보기 : He *failed in* business. 그는 사업에 실패했다.
He *shouted for* help. 그는 도와 달라고 소리쳤다.
Can you *count on* his help? 그의 도움을 기대할 수 있느냐.
Listen to the radio. 라디오를 들어봐라.
In his business he cannot *do without* a car. 그는 자동차 없이는 사업을 할 수 없다.
We *thought of* living in the country. 우리는 시골에서 살려고 생각했다.

P4 **S+V+Infinitive** (주어+동사+부정사)

자동사 뒤에 부사적 용법의 부정사가 따르는 문형이다. He appeared to be happy. (그는 행복한 것처럼 보였다)와 같이 부정사가 부사 용법인가 형용사 용법인가 결정하기 어려운 경우도 있으나 편의상 이런 것도 이 문형에 포함시켰다.

보기 : He *stopped to smoke.* 그는 담배를 피우기 위해 섰다.
He *ran to help her.* 그는 그녀를 돕기 위해 달려갔다.
Don't *hesitate to speak English.* 영어로 말하기를 주저하지 마라.
He *lived to be eighty.* 그는 80세까지 살았다.
I *rejoiced to hear of your success.* 너의 성공 소식을 듣고 기뻤다.
He *seemed not to notice it.* 그는 그것을 알아차리지 못하는 것처럼 보였다.
We *are to be get married in April.* 우리는 4월에 결혼하기로 되어 있다.
They *happened to be there.* 그들은 우연히 거기 있었다.

P5 **S+V+C** (주어+동사+보어)

자동사 뒤에 보어가 따르는 문형이다. 이 경우 보어는 주어를 설명하는 주격 보어로서, 명사·대명사·형용사·부정사·동명사·명사절이다. 이 문형에서는 보어로 쓰인 형용사 뒤에 부정사, 전치사구, 절 따위가 올 때 특히 주의할 필요가 있다.

보기 : He *is a student.* 그는 학생이다.
It *is she.* 그것은 그녀이다.
He *looks angry.* 그는 화난 것처럼 보인다.
To see *is to believe.* 보는 것이 믿는 것이다.
My hobby *is collecting stamps.* 내 취미는 우표 수집이다.
Is this *what you are looking for?* 이것이 네가 찾고 있는 것이냐.
I *was impatient* for the bus to come. 나는 버스가 오기를 안타깝게 기다렸다.
It *is* very *kind* of you to say so. 그렇게 말해 주니 참 친절하구나.
I *am sure* of his success. 나는 그의 성공을 확신한다.
I *am afraid* that I don't know. 죄송하지만 모르겠는데요.
I *am doubtful* (about) when I should start. 나는 언제 떠나야 할지 모르겠다.
It's *no use* trying to excuse yourself. 변명하려 해도 소용 없다.
It's *a pity* that he should give up his studies. 그가 연구를 그만두어야 하다니 유감이다.

P6 **S+V+O** (주어+동사+목적어)

타동사에 동작의 대상이나 그 결과를 나타내는 명사·대명사가 목적어로 따르는 문형이다. attend(…에 출석하다), resemble(…와 닮다), mention(…에 언급하다)과 같은 동사는 전치사를 수반하지 않으며, cost, take 따위와 같이 수동태를 취하지 않는 동사도 있음에 유의해야 한다.

보기 : I *know* his name. 나는 그의 이름을 알고 있다.
He *resembles* me. 그는 나와 닮았다.
This book *cost* ten dollars. 이 책은 10달러 들었다.
She *laughed* a merry laugh. 그녀는 유쾌하게 웃었다.
She *smiled* her thanks. 그녀는 웃음으로 감사함을 표시했다.
I *am surprised.* 나는 놀랐다.
He *said* "Good morning." 그는 "안녕하세요"라고 말했다.

P7 **S+V+O+Adverb** (주어+동사+목적어+부사)

「타동사+부사」가 술어 동사로 되는 문형이다. 이 문형에서는 목적어가 명사이면 부사는 목적어 앞에, 목적어가 대명사이면 부사가 목적어 뒤에 오는 것이 일반적이지만, 동사에 따라서는 목적어가 명사든 대명사이든 동사와 부사 사이에 오는 것도 있음에 유의해야 한다.

보기 : What *brought about* the quarrel? 무엇 때문에 싸움이 일어났느냐.
What *brought* it *about?* 무엇 때문에 그런 일이 생겼느냐.
It is difficult to *carry* plans *out.* 계획을 실행하기는 어렵다.
He *carried* it *out.* 그는 그것을 실행했다.
Let's *get* the job *over* quickly. 일을 빨리 해치우자.
He will *back* me *up.* 그는 나를 후원해줄 것이다.
Put your hat *on.* 모자를 쓰십시오.

P8 **S+V+Infinitive** (주어+동사+부정사)

타동사가 목적어로 부정사를 취하는 문형이다. 동사에 따라서는 목적어로서 부정사만을 취하는 것, 동명사만을 취하는 것, 양쪽 다 취하는 것이 있음에 유의해야 한다. 이 문형에 자주 쓰이는 동사는 attempt, *begin,* care, *cease, continue,* dare, decide, expect, *fear, forget,* hope, *like, need, prefer,* pretend, promise, refuse, *start, try, want,* wish 따위이다(이탤릭체로 된 것은 동명사도 목적어로 취하는 동사임).

보기 : I *like to swim.* 나는 수영하기를 좋아한다.
It has *begun to rain.* 비가 내리기 시작했다.
I *forgot to post* the letter. 나는 편지 부치는 것을 잊었다.
He *pretended not to see* me. 그는 나를 못 본 척했다.

P9 **S+V+Gerund** (주어+동사+동명사)

타동사가 목적어로 동명사를 취하는 문형이다. 이 문형에 자주 쓰이는 동사는 admit, avoid, consider, deny, enjoy, finish, mind, miss, practice, stop, suggest 따위이다. remember가 목적어로 부정사를 취하면 「(이제부터) …할 것을 잊지 않고 있다」, 동명사를 취하면 「(과거에) …한 것을 기억하고 있다」란 뜻이 되듯이, 동사에 따라서 의미상의 차이가 생기는 것도 있다.

보기 : You should *stop smoking.* 너는 담배를 끊어야 한다.
I *admit having cut* down the tree. 나는 그 나무를 벤 것을 시인한다.
I *remember seeing* him in London. 나는 그를 런던에서 본 기억이 있다.
Do you *mind* my *smoking* here? 여기서 담배 피워도 괜찮겠느냐.

P10 **S+V+what+Infinitive** (주어+동사+what+부정사)

「의문사+부정사」가 타동사의 목적어로 쓰인 문형이다.

보기 : I *wonder what to do* next. 다음에는 무엇을 해야 할지 모르겠다.
Do you *know how to drive* a car? 자동차를 운전하는 법을 아느냐.
We *decided when to start.* 우리는 출발할 시기를 정했다.
Have you *decided where to go?* 어디로 갈지 정했느냐.

P11 **S+V+that Clause** (주어+동사+that절)

타동사가 목적어로 that절을 취하는 문형이다. 이 경우 that절의 접속사 that은 구어체에서는 흔히 생략한다. suggest나 insist 따위의 목적어로 쓰이는 that절에는 should가 관용적으로 쓰인다.

보기 : I *think* (*that*) he knows it. 나는 그가 그것을 알고 있다고 생각한다.
I *hope* you will soon get well. 네가 곧 회복하기를 바란다.
He *insisted that* we should start early. 그는 우리가 일찍 출발해야 한다고 주장했다.
He *commanded that* we should do it. 그는 우리에게 그것을 하라고 명령했다.

P12 **S+V+what Clause** (주어+동사+what절)

타동사가 목적어로 의문사 who, what, why, how 따위와 접속사 if, whether가 이끄는 절을 취하는 문형이다. 이 문형에 쓰이는 주요 동사는 know, wonder, believe, say, imagine, decide, suggest, ask, discover, show, tell 따위이다.

보기 : Nobody *knows what* will happen in future. 장래 무슨 일이 일어날지 아무도 모른다.
I'll *find out who* has done it. 누가 그것을 했는지 찾아내겠다.
I couldn't *imagine why* he was so angry. 그가 왜 그렇게 화가 났는지 알 수가 없었다.
Ask him *if* it is true. 그것이 사실인지 그에게 물어봐라.
I don't *know whether* he is at home (or not). 그가 집에 있는지 (없는지) 모르겠다.

P13 **S+V+O+Preposition+O** (주어+동사+목적어+전치사+목적어)

타동사의 목적어 뒤에 전치사와 그 목적어가 따르는 문형이다. congratulate, prevent 따위와 같은 동사는 이 문형으로만 쓰이고, 전치사도 동사에 따라 정해져 있으므로 동사구로서 기억해 둘 필요가 있는 것이 많다. 또, 간접 목적어가 직접 목적어 뒤로 올 때도 이 문형을 취한다.

보기 : I *congratulate* you *on* your success. 너의 성공을 축하한다.
He *spends* a lot of money *on* books. 그는 책에 많은 돈을 쓴다.
They *took* me *for* a physician. 그들은 나를 의사로 잘못 알았다.
I *sold* my car *to* a friend of mine. 차를 친구한테 팔았다.
She *made* coffee *for* all of us. 그녀는 우리 모두에게 커피를 끓여 주었다.
I *asked* a question *of* my teacher. 선생님에게 질문을 했다.

P14 **S+V+I.O.+D.O.** (주어+동사+간접 목적어+직접 목적어)

타동사가 간접 목적어와 직접 목적어를 취하는 문형이다. give, send, tell, pay 따위의 동사는 보통 이 문형을 취하는데, 이들 동사를 특히 수여 동사라 한다. 간접 목적어가 인칭 대명사처럼 짧을 때에는 이를 직접 목적어 앞에 두지만, 긴 말일 때에는 전치사를 써서 위 문형(P13)을 쓰는 것이 보통이다.

보기 : He *gave* me some money. 그는 나에게 돈을 좀 주었다.

Did it *cause* you trouble? 폐가 되었나요.
Will you *do* me a favor? 부탁할 일이 있는데요.
Please *tell* us some stories. 이야기 좀 해주세요.

P15 **S+V+O+that Clause** (주어+동사+목적어+that절)

타동사가 간접 목적어 뒤에 직접 목적어로서 that절을 취하는 문형이다.

보기 : He *told* me *that* the news was true. 그는 그 뉴스가 사실이라고 나에게 말했다.
He *assured* me *that* they were alive. 그는 그들이 살아 있다고 나에게 확언했다.
Remind him *that* the meeting is on Monday. 회의가 월요일에 있다고 그에게 상기시켜 주시오.
They *satisfied* themselves *that* all the doors were closed. 그들은 문이 모두 잠겨 있는 것을 확인했다.

P16 **S+V+O(+what)+Infinitive** (주어+동사+목적어(+what)+부정사)

타동사가 간접 목적어 뒤에 직접 목적어로서 부정사 또는 「의문사+부정사」를 취하는 문형이다. 의문사 없이 쓴 부정사의 경우에는 형식상 P20과 같지만 부정사의 의미상의 주어가 P20에서는 목적어인 데 비해 이 문형에서는 주어인 점이 다르다.

보기 : He *promised* me *to give* the book. 그는 나에게 그 책을 주겠다고 약속했다.
He *showed* me *how to swim.* 그는 나에게 수영하는 법을 가르쳐 주었다.
Will you *advise* me *which to buy?* 내가 어느 것을 사야할지 가르쳐 주겠니.
Ask the man *where to get* tickets. 그 사람에게 차표를 어디서 사는지 물어보아라.

P17 **S+V+O+what Clause** (주어+동사+목적어+what절)

타동사가 간접 목적어 뒤에 직접 목적어로 의문사 who, what, why, how 따위와 접속사 if, whether 가 이끄는 절을 취하는 문형이다.

보기 : I *asked* him *what* he is. 나는 그에게 직업을 물어보았다.
Tell me *who* told you that. 누가 너에게 그것을 말했는지 내게 말해다오.
He *showed* me *how* the machine worked. 그는 나에게 기계가 어떻게 작동하는지 가르쳐 주었다.
Ask him *if* it is true. 그에게 그것이 사실인지 물어봐라.
Can you *inform* me *whether* this train stops at Nonsan? 이 열차는 논산에서 정차합니까.

P18 **S+V+O+Adjective** (주어+동사+목적어+형용사)

타동사가 목적어 뒤에 보어로 형용사를 취하는 문형이다. 이 경우 형용사는 목적어를 설명하는 목적격 보어이다. 목적어인 명사·대명사가 보어인 형용사의 의미상의 주어가 된다.

보기 : I *found* the cage *empty.* 나는 새장이 비어 있는 것을 알았다.
I *like* coffee *strong.* 나는 커피가 진한 것이 좋다.
He *pushed* the door *open.* 그는 문을 밀어 열었다.
He *set* the prisoner *free.* 그는 죄수를 석방하였다.
The cat *licked* the saucer *clean.* 고양이는 접시를 깨끗이 핥았다.
They *beat* him *black and blue.* 그들은 그를 시퍼렇게 멍이 들도록 때렸다.

P19 **S+V+O+Noun** (주어+동사+목적어+명사)

타동사가 목적어 뒤에 보어로서 명사를 취하는 문형이다. 이 경우 보어로 쓰인 명사는 목적어와 대등한 관계를 나타내는 목적격 보어이다.

보기 : They *elected* him chairman. 그들은 그를 의장으로 선출하였다.

I *named* my eldest son George. 나는 장남의 이름을 조지라고 지었다.
They *crowned* Caesar king. 그들은 카이사르를 왕위에 오르게 했다.
They *left* the city a ruin. 그들은 그 도시를 폐허로 만들어 놓았다.

P20 S+V+O+Infinitive (주어+동사+목적어+부정사)

타동사가 목적격 보어로서 부정사를 취하는 문형이다. 이 때 목적어로 쓰인 명사·대명사가 보어인 부정사의 의미상의 주어가 된다.

보기 : He *expected* his son *to succeed.* 그는 아들이 성공하기를 기대했다.
The prisoner *begged* the judge *not to send* him to prison. 죄수는 판사에게 교도소로 보내지 말아달라고 간청했다.
Did he *mean* us *to know?* 그는 우리에게 알릴 작정이었느냐.
He was *ordered to go* to Italy. 그는 이탈리아로 가라는 명령을 받았다.

P21 S+V+O+(to be) C (주어+동사+목적어+(to be) 보어)

타동사가 목적어 뒤에 보어로「to be+형용사 또는 명사」를 취하는 문형이다. 아래 보기에서처럼 to be는 생략되는 경우가 있다. 다만, 완료 부정사(to have been)는 생략되지 않는다.

보기 : We *considered* him (*to be*) innocent. 우리는 그가 결백하다고 믿었다.
I *believe* it *to have been* a mistake. 나는 그것이 과오였다고 믿는다.
I *like* coffee (*to be*) strong. 나는 커피가 진한 것이 좋다.
I should *guess* him *to be* about sixty. 나는 그가 60살쯤 된다고 생각한다.
He *declared* himself (*to be*) the leader of the organization. 그는 자기가 그 조직의 지도자라고 선언했다.

P22 S+V+O+Bare Infinitive (주어+동사+목적어+원형 부정사)

타동사가 목적격 보어로서 원형 부정사를 취하는 문형이다. 이 문형을 취하는 동사는 지각 동사와 사역 동사이며, 목적어로 쓰인 명사·대명사가 원형 부정사의 의미상의 주어가 된다.

보기 : I *saw* him *dance.* 나는 그가 춤추는 것을 보았다.
I *heard* her *call* out for help. 그녀가 도와달라고 외치는 소리가 들렸다.
We *looked* at the boy *jump.* 우리는 그 소년이 뛰는 것을 보았다.
Did you *notice* anyone *come* in? 누가 들어오는 것을 알아차렸느냐.
He *made* me *work* too hard. 그는 나에게 지나치게 일을 시켰다.
He *bade* me *sit* down. 그는 나에게 앉으라고 했다.
Let me *go.* 가게 해 다오.

P23 S+V+O+Present Participle (주어+동사+목적어+현재 분사)

타동사가 목적격 보어로서 현재 분사를 취하는 문형이다. 부정사를 보어로 쓴 경우와 달리 현재 분사는 동작이 진행되고 있음을 나타낸다.

보기 : I *saw* him *dancing.* 나는 그가 춤추고 있는 것을 보았다.
Can you *smell* something *burning?* 뭔가 타고 있는 냄새가 나느냐.
I *caught* him *stealing* apples from my garden. 나는 그가 내 정원에서 사과를 훔치고 있는 것을 붙잡았다.
I can't *have* my son *doing* that. 나는 내 아들이 그런 짓을 하고 있는 걸 놔둘 수 없다.
Can you *imagine* it *happening?* 그것이 일어나고 있는 것을 상상할 수 있느냐.

P24 S+V+O+Past Participle (주어+동사+목적어+과거 분사)

타동사가 목적격 보어로서 과거 분사를 취하는 문형이다. 목적어로 쓰인 명사·대명사는 보어로 쓰인 과거 분사에 대해 의미상 수동의 주어로 되는 점에 유의해야 한다.

보기 : He *heard* his name *called*. 그는 자기 이름을 부르는 소리를 들었다.
I *want* this work *finished* quickly. 나는 이 일이 빨리 끝나기를 바란다.
I must *get* my hair *cut*. 나는 머리를 깎아야겠다.
He *had* his house *burnt* down in the great fire. 그의 집이 큰 불로 소실되었다.
I *prefer* meat well *done*. 고기는 잘 익힌 것이 좋다.

P25 **S+V.Aux.+Bare Infinitive** (주어+조동사+원형 동사)

조동사 뒤에 동사의 원형이 오는 문형이다. do, will, shall, can, may, must, dare, need가 이 문형을 취하는 조동사이다. 다만, dare나 need는 부정문·의문문에서 조동사로 쓰이나, 본동사로서 긍정·부정·의문에 두루 쓰여 뒤에 to 부정사를 취하기도 한다는 점에 유의해야 한다.

보기 : I *will go* there. 나는 거기에 가겠다.
It *may* 〔*must*〕 *be* true. 그것은 사실일지도 모른다〔임에 틀림없다〕.
We *should obey* the law. 우리는 법에 따라야 한다.
He *dared* not *come*. 그는 감히 오지 못했다.
Need he *go* with us? 그가 우리와 갈 필요가 있느냐.

P26 **S+V.Aux.+Infinitive** (주어+조동사+부정사)

조동사 뒤에 to 부정사가 오는 문형이다. 이 문형을 취하는 조동사는 ought와 be이며, ought to는 의무·당연·추측 따위의 뜻을, be to는 의무·예정·가능·운명 따위의 뜻을 나타낸다. 흔히 조동사와 관련하여 have (got) to와 used to가 다루어지기도 하는데, 이 경우 have와 used는 본동사이다.

보기 : We *ought to obey* the law. 우리는 법에 따라야 한다.
It *ought to be* fine tomorrow. 내일은 틀림없이 날씨가 좋을 것이다.
You *ought to have bought* the book. 너는 그 책을 샀어야 했는데 (사지 않았구나).
You *are* not *to speak* in this room. 이 방에서는 말을 해서는 안 된다.
You *are to go*. 너는 가기로 되어 있다.
Nothing *was to be seen*. 아무것도 볼 수 없었다.

P27 **S+V.Aux.+Present Participle** (주어+조동사+현재 분사)

조동사 be가 현재 분사와 함께 진행형을 이루는 문형이다.
보기 : He *is writing* a letter. 그는 편지를 쓰고 있다.
He *was writing* a letter. 그는 편지를 쓰고 있었다.
He *has been writing* a letter. 그는 편지를 계속 쓰고 있다.

P28A **S+V.Aux.+Past Participle** (주어+조동사+과거 분사)

조동사 have가 과거 분사와 함께 완료형을 이루는 문형이다.
보기 : He *has written* a letter. 그는 편지를 썼다.
He *had written* a letter. 그는 편지를 썼었다.
A letter *has been written*. 편지가 써졌다.

P28B **S+V.Aux.+Past Participle** (주어+조동사+과거 분사)

조동사 be가 과거 분사와 함께 수동태를 이루는 문형이다.
보기 : A house *is built*. 집이 지어진다.
A house *was built*. 집이 지어졌다.
A house *has been built*. 집이 지어졌다.

2 NUMBERS (수)

	cardinal numbers(기수)		ordinal numbers(서수)
0	naught, zero	–	zeroth [zíərouθ]
1	one	1st	first
2	two	2nd, 2d	second
3	three	3rd, 3d	third
4	four	4th	fourth
5	five	5th	fifth [fifθ]
6	six	6th	sixth
7	seven	7th	seventh
8	eight	8th	eighth [eitθ]
9	nine	9th	ninth [nainθ]
10	ten	10th	tenth
11	eleven	11th	eleventh
12	twelve	12th	twelfth [twelfθ]
13	thirteen	13th	thirteenth
14	fourteen	14th	fourteenth
15	fifteen	15th	fifteenth
16	sixteen	16th	sixteenth
17	seventeen	17th	seventeenth
18	eighteen	18th	eighteenth
19	nineteen	19th	nineteenth
20	twenty	20th	twentieth [twéntiiθ]
21	twenty-one	21st	twenty-first
…		…	
30	thirty	30th	thirtieth [θə́ːrtiiθ]
40	forty	40th	fortieth
50	fifty	50th	fiftieth
60	sixty	60th	sixtieth
70	seventy	70th	seventieth
80	eighty	80th	eightieth
90	ninety	90th	ninetieth
100	a [one] hundred	100th	a [one] hundredth[3]
101	a [one] hundred (and) one[1]	101st	a [one] hundred and first[3]
1,000	a [one] thousand	1,000th	a [one] thousandth[3]
10,000	ten thousand	10,000th	ten thousandth
100,000	a [one] hundred thousand	100,000th	a [one] hundred thousandth[3]
1,000,000	a [one] million	1,000,000th	a [one] millionth[3]
10,000,000	ten million(s)[2]	10,000,000th	ten millionth
100,000,000	a [one] hundred million(s)[2]	100,000,000th	a [one] hundred millionth[3]

주 1) 미국에서는 hundred 다음의 and를 종종 생략한다.
2) 수로서 독립하여 쓰일 때에는, hundred, thousand의 경우와는 달리 two millions, three millions와 같이 끝에 s가 붙는다. 다만, two million people과 같이 뒤에 명사가 올 때는 s가 붙지 않는다.
3) the hundredth와 같이 앞에 the가 붙으면 a나 one이 생략된다.

3 SIGNS and SYMBOLS (기호와 약호)

.	period, full stop
,	comma
;	semicolon
:	colon
’	apostrophe
?	question mark
!	exclamation mark
—	dash
-	hyphen
=(⸗)	double hyphen
“ ”	double quotation marks
‘ ’	single quotation marks
“ (″, ″)	ditto marks
/	virgule, slant
… (•••, --)	ellipsis
…	suspension points
~	swung dash
•	dot
´	acute accent: employé
`	grave accent: première
^	circumflex: château
~	tilde: *señora*
¯	macron: bācon
˘	breve: băckt
¨	dieresis: coöperation
¸	cedilla: façade
( )	parentheses
[ ]	brackets
〈 〉	angle brackets
{ }	braces
*	asterisk
†	dagger
‡	double dagger
§	section: §12
¶ (⁋)	paragraph
☞	index, fist
∵, ∴	asterism
©	copyright(ed)
®	registered trademark
@	at: 300 @ $700 each
%	percent
‰	per thousand
&	ampersand: Brown & Co.
&c.	and so on, and the rest
c/o	care of: Mr. F. Morris c/o

	Dr. H.L. Jones
¢	cent(s)
$, $	dollar(s)
£	pound(s)
₩, ₩	won
#	number: a #6 bolt
	pounds: 53#
♂ (♂)	male
♀	female
○	individual (female)
□	individual (male)
×	crossed with (of a hybrid)
+	plus
−	minus
×	multiplied by, times
÷	divided by
=	equals
<	is less than
>	is greater than
∞	infinity
∥	parallel: AB ∥ CD
∠	angle: ∠DEF
∟	right angle
⊥	perpendicular: EF ⊥ MN
$\frac{1}{2}$	a half
$\frac{2}{3}$	two thirds
$\frac{1}{4}$	a quarter
$7\frac{2}{5}$	seven and two fifths
$\frac{215}{329}$	two hundred (and) fifteen over three hundred (and) twenty-nine
0.314	zero point three one four
$\sqrt{9}$	the square root of 9
$\sqrt[3]{9}$	the cube root of 9
x^2	x squared
x^3	x cubed
x^n	x to the power of n, x to the *n*th power
3′	three feet, three minutes
3″	three inches, three seconds
50° C	fifty degrees centigrade
90° F	ninety degrees Fahrenheit

4 WEIGHTS and MEASURES (도량형)

Linear Measure (길이)

	1 inch	=	2.54 cm	(1 cm = 0.3937 in.)
12 inches	= 1 foot	=	0.3048 m	(1 m = 3.2808 ft.)
3 feet	= 1 yard	=	0.9144 m	(1 m = 1.0936 yd.)
5.5 yards	= 1 rod	=	5.029 m	(1 m = 0.1988 rd.)
320 rods	= 1 mile	=	1.6093 km	(1 km = 0.6214 mi.)

Square Measure (넓이)

	1 square inch	=	6.452 cm^2	(1 cm^2 = 0.1550 sq. in.)
144 square inches	= 1 square foot	=	929.0 cm^2	(1 cm^2 = 0.0011 sq. ft.)
9 square feet	= 1 square yard	=	0.8361 m^2	(1 m^2 = 1.1960 sq. yd.)
30.25 square yards	= 1 square rod	=	25.29 m^2	(1 m^2 = 0.0395 sq. rd.)
160 square rods	= 1 acre	=	0.4047 ha	(1 ha = 2.4711 acres)
640 acres	= 1 square mile	=	2.590 km^2	(1 km^2 = 0.3861 sq. mi.)

Cubic Measure (부피)

	1 cubic inch	=	16.387 cm^3	(1 cm^3 = 0.0610 cu. in.)
1728 cubic inches	= 1 cubic foot	=	0.0283 m^3	(1 m^3 = 35.3148 cu. ft.)
27 cubic feet	= 1 cubic yard	=	0.7646 m^3	(1 m^3 = 1.3080 cu. yd.)

Liquid Measure (액량) USA [Great Britain]

	1 gill	=	0.1183 [0.142] *l*	(1 lit. = 8.4531 [7.0423] gi.)
4 gills	= 1 pint	=	0.4732 [0.568] *l*	(1 lit. = 2.1133 [1.7606] pt.)
2 pints	= 1 quart	=	0.9464 [1.136] *l*	(1 lit. = 1.0566 [0.8803] qt.)
4 quarts	= 1 gallon	=	3.7853 [4.546] *l*	(1 lit. = 0.2642 [0.2200] gal.)

Dry Measure (건량) USA [Great Britain]

	1 pint	=	0.5506 [0.568] *l*	(1 lit. = 1.8162 [1.7606] pt.)
2 pints	= 1 quart	=	1.1012 [1.136] *l*	(1 lit. = 0.9081 [0.8803] qt.)
8 quarts	= 1 peck	=	8.8096 [9.092] *l*	(1 lit. = 0.1135 [0.1100] pk.)
4 pecks	= 1 bushel	=	35.2383 [36.368] *l*	(1 lit. = 0.0284 [0.0275] bu.)

Avoirdupois Weight (무게)

	1 dram	=	1.772 g	(1 g = 0.5643 dr. av.)
16 drams	= 1 ounce	=	28.35 g	(1 g = 0.0353 oz. av.)
16 ounces	= 1 pound	=	453.59 g	(1 kg = 2.2046 lb. av.)
2000 pounds	= 1 (short) ton	=	907.185 kg	(1 kg = 0.0011 s. t.)
2240 pounds	= 1 (long) ton	=	1016.05 kg	(1 kg = 0.0010 l. t.)

Troy Weight (금·은·보석 무게)

	1 grain	=	0.0648 g	(1 g = 15.4321 gr.)
24 grains	= 1 pennyweight	=	1.5552 g	(1 g = 0.6430 pwt.)
20 pennyweights	= 1 ounce	=	31.1035 g	(1 g = 0.0322 oz. t.)
12 ounces	= 1 pound	=	373.24 g	(1 kg = 2.6792 lb. t.)

Apothecaries' Weight (약제용 무게)

	1 grain	=	0.0648 g	(1 g = 15.4321 gr.)
20 grains	= 1 scruple	=	1.296 g	(1 g = 0.7716 s. ap.)
3 scruples	= 1 dram	=	3.8879 g	(1 g = 0.2572 dr. ap.)
8 drams	= 1 ounce	=	31.1035 g	(1 g = 0.0322 oz. ap.)
12 ounces	= 1 pound	=	373.24 g	(1 kg = 2.6792 lb. ap.)

5 MONETARY UNITS (화폐 단위)

(본위 화폐와 보조 화폐 단위의 비율은 별도 표시가 없으면 1:100.
*표는 ( ) 안에 표시된 국가의 화폐를 법화로 하는 경우임.)

country	monetary units *basic: fractional*
Afghanistan	afghani: pul
Albania	lek: qintar
Algeria	dinar: centime
Andorra	*(*Fr.*) franc: centime *(*Sp.*) peseta: centimo
Angola	kwanza: lwei
Antigua and Barbuda	dollar: cent
Argentina	peso: centavo
Armenia	ruble: kopeck
Australia	dollar: cent
Austria	schilling: groschen
Azerbaijan	ruble: kopeck
Bahamas	dollar: cent
Bahrain	dinar: fils(1:1000)
Bangladesh	taka: paisa
Barbados	dollar: cent
Belarus	ruble: kopeck
Belgium	franc: centime
Belize	dollar: cent
Benin	franc: centime
Bhutan	ngultrum: chetrum
Bolivia	boliviano: peso boliviano, *also* peso (1:1000)
Bosnia and Herzegovina	dinar: para
Botswana	pula: thebe
Brazil	cruzeiro: centavo
Brunei	dollar: cent
Bulgaria	lev: stotinka
Burkina Faso	franc: centime
Burundi	franc: centime
Cambodia	riel: sen
Cameroon	franc: centime
Canada	dollar: cent
Cape Verde	escudo: centavo
Central African Republic	franc: centime
Chad	franc: centime
Chile	peso: centesimo
China	yuan: fen
Colombia	peso: centavo
Comoros	franc: centime
Congo	franc: centime
Costa Rica	colon: centimo
Croatia	dinar: para
Cuba	peso: centavo
Cyprus	pound: cent
Czech Republic	koruna: haler
Denmark	krone: øre
Djibouti	franc: centime
Dominica	dollar: cent
Dominican Republic	peso: centavo
Ecuador	sucre: centavo
Egypt	pound: piaster
El Salvador	colon: centavo
Equatorial Guinea	franc: centime
Estonia	ruble: kopeck
Ethiopia	birr: cent
Fiji	dollar: cent
Finland	markka: penni
France	franc: centime
Gabon	franc: centime
Gambia	dalasi: butut
Georgia	ruble: kopeck
Germany	deutsche mark: pfennig
Ghana	cedi: pesewa
Greece	drachma: lepton
Grenada	dollar: cent
Guatemala	quetzal: centavo
Guinea	franc: centime
Guinea-Bissau	peso: centavo
Guyana	dollar: cent
Haiti	gourde: centime
Honduras	lempira: centavo
Hungary	forint: fillér
Iceland	króna: eyrir
India	rupee: paisa
Indonesia	rupiah: sen
Iran	rial: dinar
Iraq	dinar: fils (1:1000)
Ireland	pound: penny
Israel	shekel: agora
Italy	lira: centesimo
Ivory Coast	franc: centime
Jamaica	dollar: cent
Japan	yen: sen
Jordan	dinar: fils (1:1000)
Kazakhstan	ruble: kopeck
Kenya	shilling: cent

Country	Unit
Kiribati	*(*Austral.*) dollar: cent
Korea	won: jeon *or* jun
Kuwait	dinar: fils (1:1000)
Kyrgyzstan	som: —
Laos	kip: at
Latvia	ruble: kopeck
Lebanon	pound: piaster
Lesotho	loti: lisente
Liberia	dollar: cent
Libya	dinar: dirham (1:1000)
Liechtenstein	*(*Swiss*) franc: centime
Lithuania	litas: —
Luxembourg	franc: centime
Macedonia	denar: —
Madagascar	franc: centime
Malawi	kwacha: tambala
Malaysia	ringgit: sen
Maldives	rufiyaa: lari
Mali	franc: centime
Malta	lira: cent
Mauritania	ouguiya: khoums (1:5)
Mauritius	rupee: cent
Mexico	peso: centavo
Moldova	ruble: kopeck
Monaco	*(*Fr.*) franc: centime
Mongolia	tugrik: mongo
Morocco	dirham: centime
Mozambique	metical: centavo
Myanmar	kyat: pya
Namibia	dollar: cent
Nauru	*(*Austral.*) dollar: cent
Nepal	rupee: pice
Netherlands	guilder: cent
New Zealand	dollar: cent
Nicaragua	cordoba: centavo
Niger	franc: centime
Nigeria	naira: kobo
Norway	krone: øre
Oman	rial: baiza (1:1000)
Pakistan	rupee: paisa
Panama	balboa: cent
Papua New Guinea	kina: toea
Paraguay	guaraní: centimo
Peru	sol: centimo
Philippines	peso:centavo
Poland	zloty: grosz
Portugal	escudo: centavo
Qatar	riyal: dirham
Romania	leu: ban
Russia	ruble: kopeck
Rwanda	franc: centime
San Marino	*(*It.*) lira: centesimo
São Tomé and Príncipe	dobra: centavo
Saudi Arabia	riyal: halala
Senegal	franc: centime
Seychelles	rupee: cent
Sierra Leone	leone: cent
Singapore	dollar: cent
Slovakia	koruna: haler
Slovenia	tolar: —
Solomon Islands	dollar: cent
Somalia	shilling: cent
South Africa	rand: cent
Spain	peseta: centimo
Sri Lanka	rupee: cent
St. Kitts and Nevis	dollar: cent
St. Lucia	dollar: cent
St. Vincent and the Grenadines	dollar: cent
Sudan	pound: piaster
Suriname	guilder: cent
Swaziland	lilangeni: cent
Sweden	krona: öre
Switzerland	franc: centime
Syria	pound: piaster
Taiwan	dollar: cent
Tajikistan	ruble: kopeck
Tanzania	shilling: cent
Thailand	baht: satang
Togo	franc: centime
Tonga	pa'anga: seniti
Trinidad and Tobago	dollar: cent
Tunisia	dinar: millime (1:1000)
Turkey	lira: kurus
Turkmenistan	ruble: kopeck
Tuvalu	*(*Austral.*) dollar: cent
Uganda	shilling: cent
Ukraine	ruble: kopeck
United Arab Emirates	dirham: fils
United Kingdom	pound: penny
United States	dollar: cent
Uruguay	peso: centesimo
Uzbekistan	ruble: kopeck
Vanuatu	vatu: —
Vatican City	*(*Ital.*)lira: centesimo
Venezuela	bolívar: centimo
Vietnam	dong: —
Western Samoa	tala: sene
Yemen	riyal: fils (1:1000)
Yugoslavia	dinar: para
Zaire	zaire: likuta
Zambia	kwacha: ngwee
Zimbabwe	dollar: cent

6 IRREGULAR VERBS (불규칙 동사)

(고딕체는 주요어, 이탤릭체는 고어체)

verb	past tense	past participle
abide	abode, abided	abode, abided
arise	**arose**	**arisen**
awake	**awaked, awoke**	**awaked, awoken**
backbite	backbit	backbitten, backbit
backslide	backslid	backslidden, backslid
be (**am, is, are**)	**was, were**	**been**
bear	**bore**	**borne, born**
beat	**beat**	**beaten, beat**
become	**became**	**become**
befall	befell	befallen
beget	begot, *begat*	begotten, begot
begin	**began**	**begun**
begird	begirt	begirt
behold	beheld	beheld
bend	**bent**	**bent**
bereave	bereaved, bereft	bereaved, bereft
beseech	besought	besought
beset	beset	beset
bespeak	bespoke	bespoken, bespoke
bestrew	bestrewed	bestrewed, bestrewn
bestride	bestrode, bestrid	bestridden, bestrid
bet	bet, betted	bet, betted
betake	betook	betaken
bethink	bethought	bethought
bid	**bade, bid**	**bidden, bid**
bide	bode, bided	bided
bind	**bound**	**bound**
bite	**bit**	**bitten, bit**
bleed	bled	bled
bless	**blessed, blest**	**blessed, blest**
blow	**blew**	**blown**
break	**broke**	**broken**

verb	past tense	past participle
breed	bred	bred
bring	**brought**	**brought**
broadcast	broadcast, broadcasted	broadcast, broadcasted
browbeat	browbeat	browbeaten
build	**built**	**built**
burn	**burned, burnt**	**burned, burnt**
burst	**burst**	**burst**
buy	**bought**	**bought**
can	**could**	—
cast	**cast**	**cast**
catch	**caught**	**caught**
chide	chid, chided	chidden, chid, chided
choose	**chose**	**chosen**
cleave	clove, cleft	cloven, cleft
cling	clung	clung
clothe	**clothed,** *clad*	**clothed,** *clad*
come	**came**	**come**
cost	**cost**	**cost**
countersink	countersank	countersunk
creep	**crept**	**crept**
crow	crowed, crew	crowed
curse	cursed, *curst*	cursed, *curst*
cut	**cut**	**cut**
dare	**dared,** *durst*	**dared**
deal	dealt	dealt
dig	**dug**	**dug**
do	**did**	**done**
draw	**drew**	**drawn**
dream	**dreamed, dreamt**	**dreamed, dreamt**
drink	**drank**	**drunk**
drive	**drove**	**driven**
drop	**dropped, dropt**	**dropped, dropt**
dwell	dwelt, dwelled	dwelt, dwelled
eat	**ate**	**eaten**
fall	**fell**	**fallen**
feed	**fed**	**fed**

verb	past tense	past participle
feel	**felt**	**felt**
fight	**fought**	**fought**
find	**found**	**found**
flee	fled	fled
fling	flung	flung
fly	**flew**	**flown**
forbear	forbore	forborne
forbid	**forbade, forbad**	**forbidden**
forecast	forecast, forecasted	forecast, forecasted
forego	forewent	foregone
foreknow	foreknew	foreknown
foresee	foresaw	foreseen
foreshow	foreshowed	foreshown
foretell	foretold	foretold
forget	**forgot**	**forgotten, forgot**
forgive	forgave	forgiven
forgo	forwent	forgone
forsake	forsook	forsaken
forswear	forswore	forsworn
freeze	froze	frozen
gainsay	gainsaid	gainsaid
get	**got**	**got,** 《U.S.》 **gotten**
gild	gilded, gilt	gilded, gilt
gird	girded, girt	girded, girt
give	**gave**	**given**
gnaw	gnawed	gnawed, gnawn
go	**went**	**gone**
grave	graved	graved, graven
grind	**ground**	**ground**
grow	**grew**	**grown**
hang	**hung, hanged**	**hung, hanged**
have (has)	**had**	**had**
hear	**heard**	**heard**
heave	heaved, hove	heaved, hove
hew	hewed	hewed, hewn
hide	**hid**	**hidden, hid**
hit	**hit**	**hit**
hold	**held**	**held**
hurt	**hurt**	**hurt**
inlay	inlaid	inlaid
inset	inset	inset
interbreed	interbred	interbred

verb	past tense	past participle
interweave	interwove, interweaved	interwoven, interweaved
keep	**kept**	**kept**
kneel	knelt	knelt
knit	knitted	knitted
know	**knew**	**known**
lade	laded	laded, laden
lay	**laid**	**laid**
lead	**led**	**led**
lean	《Brit.》 **leant, leaned**	《Brit.》 **leant, leaned**
leap	**leapt, leaped**	**leapt, leaped**
learn	**learnt, learned**	**learnt, learned**
leave	**left**	**left**
lend	**lent**	**lent**
let	**let**	**let**
lie	**lay**	**lain**
light	**lighted, lit**	**lighted, lit**
lose	**lost**	**lost**
make	**made**	**made**
may	**might**	—
mean	**meant**	**meant**
meet	**met**	**met**
melt	**melted**	**melted, molten**
methinks	methought	—
miscast	miscast	miscast
misgive	misgave	misgiven
mislay	mislaid	mislaid
mislead	misled	misled
misread	misread	misread
misspell	misspelled, misspelt	misspelled, misspelt
misspend	misspent	misspent
mistake	**mistook**	**mistaken**
misunderstand	misunderstood	misunderstood
mow	mowed	mown
must	**must**	—
offset	offset	offset
outbid	outbid, outbade	outbid, outbidden
outdo	outdid	outdone
outgrow	outgrew	outgrown
outlay	outlaid	outlaid
outride	outrode	outridden
outrun	outran	outrun

verb	past tense	past participle
outshine	outshone	outshone
outspread	outspread	outspread
outwear	outwore	outworn
overbear	overbore	overborne
overcast	overcast	overcast
overcome	overcame	overcome
overdo	overdid	overdone
overdraw	overdrew	overdrawn
overeat	overate	overeaten
overfeed	overfed	overfed
overgrow	overgrew	overgrown
overhang	overhung	overhung
overhear	overheard	overheard
overlay	overlaid	overlaid
overleap	overleaped, overlept	overleaped, overlept
overlie	overlay	overlain
override	overrode	overridden
overrun	overran	overrun
oversee	oversaw	overseen
overset	overset	overset
overshoot	overshot	overshot
oversleep	overslept	overslept
overspread	overspread	overspread
overtake	overtook	overtaken
overthrow	overthrew	overthrown
overwork	overworked, overwrought	overworked, overwrought
partake	partook	partaken
pay	**paid**	**paid**
prepay	prepaid	prepaid
put	**put**	**put**
quit	quitted, quit	quitted, quit
read	**read**	**read**
rebuild	rebuilt	rebuilt
recast	recast	recast
relay	relaid	relaid
remake	remade	remade
rend	rent	rent
repay	repaid	repaid
reread	reread	reread
resell	resold	resold
reset	reset	reset
retake	retook	retaken
retell	retold	retold
rewrite	rewrote	rewritten
rid	rid, ridded	rid, ridded
ride	**rode**	**ridden**

verb	past tense	past participle
ring	**rang**	**rung**
rise	**rose**	**risen**
rive	rived	riven, rived
run	**ran**	**run**
saw	sawed	sawn, sawed
say	**said**	**said**
see	**saw**	**seen**
seek	**sought**	**sought**
sell	**sold**	**sold**
send	**sent**	**sent**
set	**set**	**set**
sew	**sewed**	**sewn, sewed**
shake	**shook**	**shaken**
shall	**should**	—
shave	shaved	shaved, shaven
shear	sheared	shorn, sheared
shed	**shed**	**shed**
shew	shewed	shewn
shine	**shone, shined**	**shone, shined**
shoe	shod	shod
shoot	**shot**	**shot**
show	**showed**	**shown, showed**
shrink	shrank, shrunk	shrunk, shrunken
shrive	shrove, shrived	shriven, shrived
shut	**shut**	**shut**
sing	**sang**	**sung**
sink	**sank, sunk**	**sunk, sunken**
sit	**sat**	**sat**
slay	slew	slain
sleep	**slept**	**slept**
slide	slid	slid, *slidden*
sling	slung	slung
slink	slunk	slunk
slit	slit	slit
smell	**smelt, smelled**	**smelt, smelled**
smite	smote	smitten
sow	**sowed**	**sown, sowed**
speak	**spoke**	**spoken**
speed	**sped, speeded**	**sped, speeded**
spell	**spelt, spelled**	**spelt, spelled**
spend	**spent**	**spent**

verb	past tense	past participle
spill	spilt, spilled	spilt, spilled
spin	spun, span	spun
spit	spat	spat
split	split	split
spoil	**spoilt, spoiled**	**spoilt, spoiled**
spread	**spread**	**spread**
spring	**sprang, sprung**	**sprung**
squat	squatted, squat	squatted, squat
stand	**stood**	**stood**
stave	staved, stove	staved, stove
steal	**stole**	**stolen**
stick	stuck	stuck
sting	stung	stung
stink	stank, stunk	stunk
strew	strewed	strewn, strewed
stride	strode	stridden
strike	**struck**	**struck, stricken**
string	strung	strung
strive	strove	striven
sublet	sublet	sublet
sunburn	sunburned, sunburnt	sunburned, sunburnt
swear	**swore**	**sworn**
sweat	sweated, sweat	sweated, sweat
sweep	**swept**	**swept**
swell	**swelled**	**swollen, swelled**
swim	**swam**	**swum**
swing	**swung**	**swung**
take	**took**	**taken**
teach	**taught**	**taught**
tear	**tore**	**torn**
telecast	telecast, telecasted	telecast, telecasted
tell	**told**	**told**
think	**thought**	**thought**
thrive	throve, thrived	thriven, thrived
throw	**threw**	**thrown**
thrust	thrust	thrust

verb	past tense	past participle
tread	trod	trodden, trod
typewrite	typewrote	typewritten
unbend	unbent	unbent
unbind	unbound	unbound
underbid	underbid	underbid
undercut	undercut	undercut
underfeed	underfed	underfed
undergo	underwent	undergone
underlie	underlay	underlain
underpay	underpaid	underpaid
undersell	undersold	undersold
undershoot	undershot	undershot
understand	**understood**	**understood**
undertake	undertook	undertaken
underwrite	underwrote	underwritten
undo	undid	undone
undraw	undrew	undrawn
unsay	unsaid	unsaid
unwind	unwound	unwound
uphold	upheld	upheld
uprise	uprose	uprisen
upset	upset	upset
wake	**woke, waked**	**waked, woken**
waylay	waylaid	waylaid
wear	**wore**	**worn**
weave	**wove**	**woven, wove**
wed	wedded, 《rare》 wed	wedded, 《rare》 wed
weep	**wept**	**wept**
wet	wetted, 《U.S.》 wet	wetted, 《U.S.》 wet
will	**would**	—
win	**won**	**won**
wind	**wound**	**wound**
wit	wist	wist
withdraw	withdrew	withdrawn
withhold	withheld	withheld
withstand	withstood	withstood
work	**worked,** *wrought*	**worked,** *wrought*
wrap	wrapped, wrapt	wrapped, wrapt
wring	wrung	wrung
write	**wrote**	**written**

MINJUNG'S
Essence
ENGLISH-ENGLISH
KOREAN DICTIONARY

엣센스 영영한사전

1995년 3월 20일 초 판 발행
2025년 1월 10일 제 32쇄 발행

편 자 민중서림편집국
발행인 김 철 환

발행처 사전전문 民衆書林

10881 경기도 파주시 회동길 37-29
(파주출판문화정보산업단지)
전화 (영업) 031) 955-6500~6 (편집) 031) 955-6507
Fax (영업) 031) 955-6525 (편집) 031) 955-6527
E-mail editmin@minjungdic.co.kr (편집)
홈페이지 http: // www.minjungdic.co.kr
등록 1979. 7. 23. 제2-61호

ISBN 978-89-387-0420-7

정가 44,000원

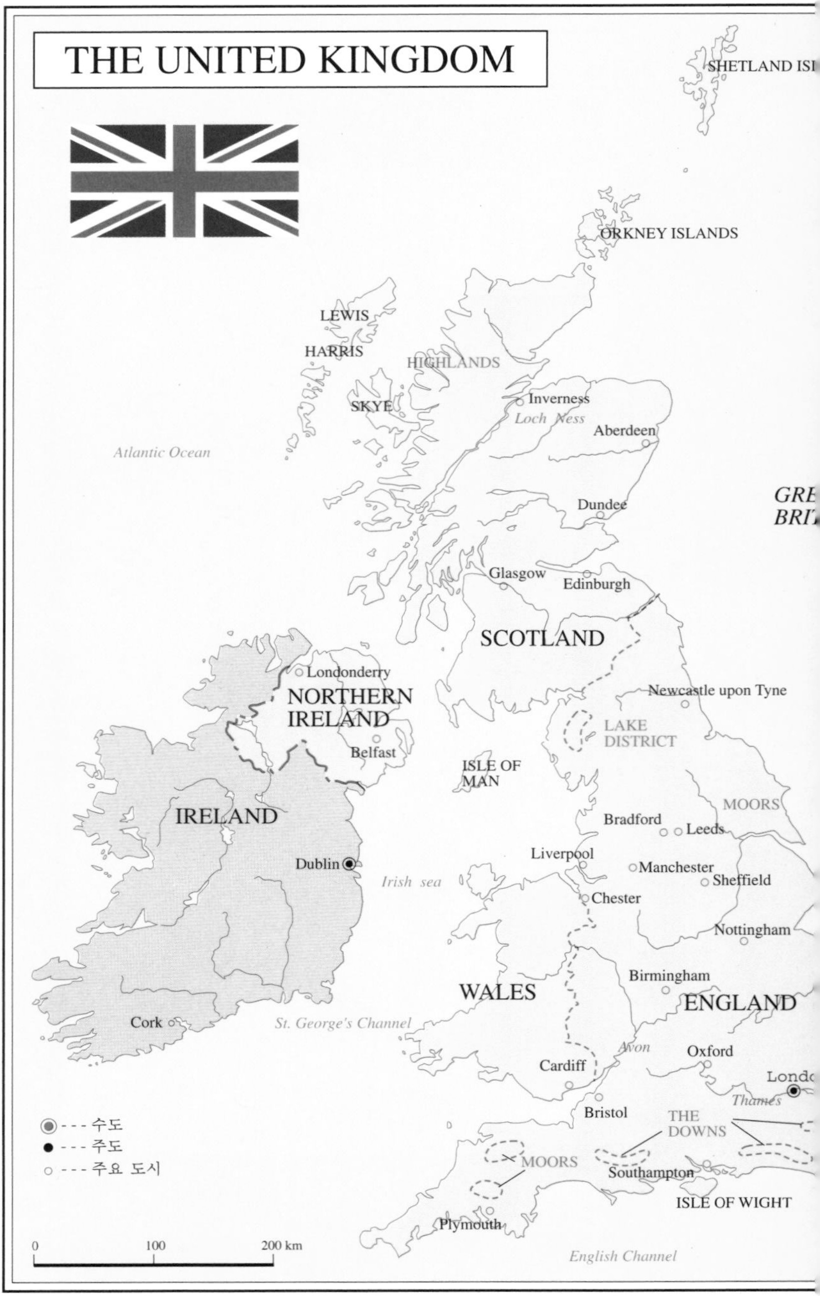

THE UNITED KINGDOM

SHETLAND ISL
ORKNEY ISLANDS
LEWIS
HARRIS
HIGHLANDS
SKYE
Inverness
Loch Ness
Aberdeen
Atlantic Ocean
Dundee
GRE
BRIT
Glasgow
Edinburgh
SCOTLAND
Londonderry
NORTHERN IRELAND
Newcastle upon Tyne
LAKE DISTRICT
Belfast
ISLE OF MAN
MOORS
IRELAND
Bradford
Leeds
Liverpool
Dublin
Manchester
Irish sea
Sheffield
Chester
Nottingham
Birmingham
WALES
ENGLAND
Cork
St. George's Channel
Avon
Oxford
Cardiff
Lond
Thames
Bristol
THE DOWNS
MOORS
Southampton
ISLE OF WIGHT
Plymouth
English Channel

◉ - - - 수도
● - - - 주도
○ - - - 주요 도시

0 100 200 km